THE BEST OF TIMES . . . JUST GOT BETT

We're very proud of the huge success of our Nichols' Chilton Labor Guide 2000, but we're not stopping there. The fact that the 2000 edition is praised by technicians, beat projected sales goals, expanded into new markets, and is widely accepted by warranty companies, might be enough for some publishers—but that's just not enough for us.

So, to make the Nichols' Chilton Labor Guide better than ever, we've come out with a brand new 2001 Labor Guide, providing 21 years of coverage, 1981-2001. The all new labor times developed by Nichols' editors take into account vehicle age and parts wear and tear, and we've included domestic car factory times for the past 6 years.

Now you can get the most accurate, easy-to-use, and complete Labor Guide available, in your choice of print or CD-ROM formats. Keep up with the times with Nichols' Chilton Labor Guide 2001.

Contact your Nichols Distributor, or Call Nichols' Customer Service Toll-Free 877-424-4586

NICHOLS PUBLISHING

1025 Andrew Drive, West Chester, PA 19380
(610) 738-9280 • Fax (610) 738-9370
www.labortime.com

Chilton is a registered trademark of Cahners Business Information, A Division of Reed Elsevier, Inc., and has been licensed to W.G. Nichols, Inc.

CHILTON'S
AUTO
SERVICE MANUAL
2001

C.E.O.
Rick Van Dalen

President
Dean F. Morgantini, S.A.E.

Vice President—Sales
Glenn D. Potere

Vice President—Finance
Barry L. Beck

Vice President—Electronic Product Sales
Charles J. McGroarty

Executive Editor
Kevin M. G. Maher, A.S.E.

Manager—Professional Service Information
Richard J. Rivele

Manger—Consumer Service information
Richard Schwartz, A.S.E.

Manager—Marine/Recreation
James R. Marotta, A.S.E.

Project Managers
Thomas A. Mellon, A.S.E., S.A.E., Eric Michael Mihalyi, A.S.E., S.T.S., S.A.E.,
Christine Sheeky, S.A.E., Richard T. Smith, Ron Webb

Editors—Professional Service Information
Tim Crain, A.S.E., Michael Magliano, Richard E. Rathman

Editorial Staff
David R. Back, A.S.E., Paul DeSanto, A.S.E., Jim Keating, Robert McAnally,
Norman D. Norville, A.S.E., Joe Pellicciotti, Keith Reynolds

Production Specialists
Brian Hollingsworth, Melinda Possinger

Schematics Editors
Christopher G. Ritchie, A.S.E., S.A.E., S.T.S., Stephanie Spunt

CHILTON *AUTOMOTIVE INFORMATION*

PUBLISHED BY **W. G. NICHOLS, INC.**

Manufactured in USA, © 2000 W. G. Nichols, Inc., 1025 Andrew Drive, West Chester, PA 19380
ISBN 0-8019-9306-7
Library of Congress Catalog Card No. 00-132206
0123456789 9876543210

Table of Contents

Table of Contents

Car Sections

Model Index

HOW TO USE THIS MANUAL

Specifications

Specifications charts for all models covered in this book are located in Chapter 1. They include: Vehicle and Engine Identification, General Engine Specifications, Engine Tune-Up Specifications, Capacities, Valve Specifications, Crankshaft & Connecting Rod Specifications, Piston & Ring Specifications, Engine Fastener Torque Specifications, Brake Specifications, Maintenance Interval Specifications, Ball Joint Specifications and Wheel & Tire Specifications.

Unit Repair Sections

The Unit Repair Sections (URS's) are written to cover all applicable 1997-01 models for the specific URS system or component, unless specifically noted otherwise. The procedures covered in the URS's are not repeated in the model specific sections; therefore, refer to the URS's for the service procedures for the applicable systems or components. Refer to the Table of Contents for URS coverage.

Model Specific Sections

The model specific sections are grouped by manufacturer and arranged in alphabetical order. The text and illustrations that comprise the service procedures in each model specific section are arranged in the following order of systems and components: Engine Repair (Gasoline, then Diesel if applicable), Fuel System (Gasoline, then Diesel if applicable), Drive Train, Steering and Suspension.

All illustrations are located as close as possible to the applicable procedure. Procedures are for all models in the particular section unless specifically noted otherwise.

Locating Information

The Table of Contents, located at the front of the book, lists each Unit Repair Section (URS) and model specific section in this manual.

To find where a particular model specific section is located in the book, you need only look in the Table of Contents. Once you have found the proper section, you may wish to find where specific procedures located in that section. Turn to the Index at the front of the model specific section. At the upper left-hand side is a listing of the main topics within that section and the page number on which they may be found. Following the main topics is an alphabetical listing of all of the procedures within the section and their page numbers.

The Model Index, located just after the Table of Contents in the beginning of this manual, may also be used to locate the specific section for any vehicle model covered in this manual.

Safety Notice

Proper service and repair procedures are vital to the safe, reliable operation of all motor vehicles, as well as the personal safety of those performing the repairs. This manual outlines procedures for servicing and repairing vehicles using safe effective methods. The procedures contain many NOTES, WARNINGS and CAUTIONS which should be followed along with standard safety procedures to eliminate the possibility of personal injury or improper service which could damage the vehicle or compromise its safety.

It is important to note that repair procedures and techniques, tools and parts for servicing vehicles, as well as the skill and experience of the individual performing the work vary widely. It is not possible to anticipate all of the conceivable ways or conditions under which vehicles may be serviced, or to provide cautions as to all of the possible hazards that may result. Standard and accepted safety precautions and equipment should be used when handling toxic or flammable fluids, and safety goggles or other protection should be used during cutting, grinding, chiseling, prying, or any other process that can cause material removal or projectiles.

Some procedures require the use of tools specially designed for a specific purpose. Before substituting another tool or procedure, you must be completely satisfied that neither your personal safety, nor the performance of the vehicle will be endangered.

Although information in this manual is based on industry sources and is as complete as possible at the time of publication, the possibility exists that some vehicle manufacturers made later changes which could not be included here. Information on very late models may not be available in some circumstances. While striving for total accuracy, Nichols Publishing cannot assume responsibility for any errors, changes, or omissions that may occur in the compilation of this data.

Part Numbers

Part numbers listed in this book are not recommendations by Nichols Publishing for any product by brand name. They are references that can be used with interchanges manuals and aftermarket supplier catalogs to locate each brand supplier's discrete part number.

Special Tools

Special tools are recommended by the vehicle manufacturer to perform their specific job. Use has been kept to a minimum, but where absolutely necessary, they are referred to in the text by the part number of the tool manufacturer. These tools may be purchased, under the appropriate part number, from your local dealer or regional distributor, or an equivalent tool can be purchased locally from a tool supplier or parts outlet. Before substituting any tool for the one recommended, read the previous Safety Notice.

Acknowledgements

This publication contains material that is reproduced and distributed under a license from Ford Motor Company. No further reproduction or distribution of the Ford Motor Company material is allowed without the expressed written permission from Ford Motor Company.

Portions of the material contained herein have been reprinted with permission of General Motors Corporation, Service Technology Group.

Nichols Publishing would like to express thanks to all of the fine companies who participate in the production of our books:
• Hand tools supplied by Craftsman are used during all phases of our vehicle teardown and photography.
• Many of the fine specialty tools used in our procedures were provided courtesy of Lisle Corporation.
• Lincoln Automotive Products (1 Lincoln Way, St. Louis, MO 63120) has provided their industrial shop equipment, including jacks (engine, transmission and floor), engine stands, fluid and lubrication tools, as well as shop presses.
• Rotary Lifts (1-800-640-5438 or www.Rotary-Lift.com), the largest automobile lift manufacturer in the world, offering the biggest variety of surface and in-ground lifts available, has fulfilled our shop's lift needs.
• Much of our shop's electronic testing equipment was supplied by Universal Enterprises Inc. (UEI).
• Safety-Kleen Systems Inc. has provided parts cleaning stations and assistance with environmentally sound disposal of residual wastes.
• United Gilsonite Laboratories (UGL), manufacturer of Drylok® concrete floor paint, has provided materials and expertise for the coating and protection of our shop floor.

SPECIFICATIONS

1

CHRYSLER CORP.
Chrysler Sebring Coupe • Dodge Avenger

ENGINE AND VEHICLE IDENTIFICATION

Engine							Model Year	
Code ①	Liters (cc)	Cu. In.	Cyl.	Fuel Sys.	Engine Type	Eng. Mfg.	Code ②	Year
N	2.5 (2497)	152	V6	MFI	SOHC	Mitsubishi	V	1997
Y	2.0 (1996)	122	I4	MFI	DOHC	Chrysler	W	1998
							X	1999
							Y	2000
							1	2001

MFI: Multi-port Fuel Injection

DOHC: Double Overhead Camshaft

SOHC: Single Overhead Camshaft

① 8th position of the Vehicle Identification Number (VIN).

② 10th position of VIN.

93061C01

GENERAL ENGINE SPECIFICATIONS
All measurements are given in inches.

Year	Model	Engine Displacement Liters (cc)	Engine Series (ID/VIN)	Fuel System	Net Horsepower @ rpm	Net Torque @ rpm (ft. lbs.)	Bore x Stroke (in.)	Compression Ratio	Oil Pressure @ rpm
1997	Avenger	2.5 (2497)	N	MFI	155@5500	161@4400	3.29 x 2.99	9.5:1	35-75@3000
		2.0 (1996)	Y	MFI	140@6000	130@4800	3.44 x 3.27	9.6:1	25-80@3000
	Sebring Coupe	2.5 (2497)	N	MFI	155@5500	161@4400	3.29 x 2.99	9.5:1	35-75@3000
		2.0 (1996)	Y	MFI	140@6000	130@4800	3.44 x 3.27	9.6:1	25-80@3000
1998	Avenger	2.5 (2497)	N	MFI	155@5500	161@4400	3.29 x 2.99	9.4:1 ①	35-75@3000
		2.0 (1996)	Y	MFI	140@6000	130@4800	3.44 x 3.27	9.6:1	25-80@3000
	Sebring Coupe	2.5 (2497)	N	MFI	155@5500	161@4400	3.29 x 2.99	9.4:1 ①	35-75@3000
		2.0 (1996)	Y	MFI	140@6000	130@4800	3.44 x 3.27	9.6:1	25-80@3000
1999	Avenger	2.5 (2497)	N	MFI	155@5500	161@4400	3.29 x 2.99	9.4:1 ①	35-75@3000
		2.0 (1996)	Y	MFI	140@6000	130@4800	3.44 x 3.27	9.6:1	25-80@3000
	Sebring Coupe	2.5 (2497)	N	MFI	155@5500	161@4400	3.29 x 2.99	9.4:1 ①	35-75@3000
		2.0 (1996)	Y	MFI	140@6000	130@4800	3.44 x 3.27	9.6:1	25-80@3000
2000-01	Avenger	2.5 (2497)	N	MFI	155@5500	161@4400	3.29 x 2.99	9.4:1 ①	35-75@3000
	Sebring Coupe	2.5 (2497)	N	MFI	155@5500	161@4400	3.29 x 2.99	9.4:1 ①	35-75@3000

MFI: Multi-port Fuel Injection

① California - 9.0:1

93061C02

ENGINE TUNE-UP SPECIFICATIONS

Year	Engine Displacement Liters (cc)	Engine ID/VIN	Spark Plug Gap (in.)	Ignition Timing (deg.)	Fuel Pump (psi)	Idle Speed (rpm)		Valve Clearance	
						MT	AT	In.	Ex.
1997	2.0 (1996)	Y	0.033-0.038	①	47-50	800	800	HYD	HYD
	2.5 (2497)	N	0.039-0.043	①	47-50	—	750	HYD	HYD
1998	2.0 (1996)	Y	0.033-0.038	①	47-50	800	800	HYD	HYD
	2.5 (2497)	N	0.039-0.043	①	47-50	—	750	HYD	HYD
1999	2.0 (1996)	Y	0.033-0.038	①	47-50	800	800	HYD	HYD
	2.5 (2497)	N	0.039-0.043	①	47-50	—	750	HYD	HYD
2000-01	2.5 (2497)	N	0.039-0.043	①	47-50	—	750	HYD	HYD

NOTE: The Vehicle Emission Control Information label often reflects specification changes made during production. The label figures must be used if they differ from those in this chart.

HYD: Hydraulic

① Basic ignition timing is not adjustable.

93061C03

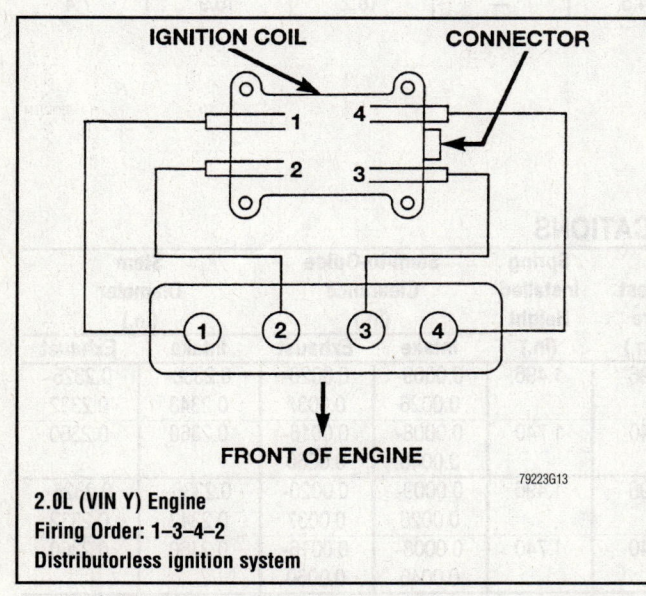

2.0L (VIN Y) Engine
Firing Order: 1–3–4–2
Distributorless ignition system

79223G13

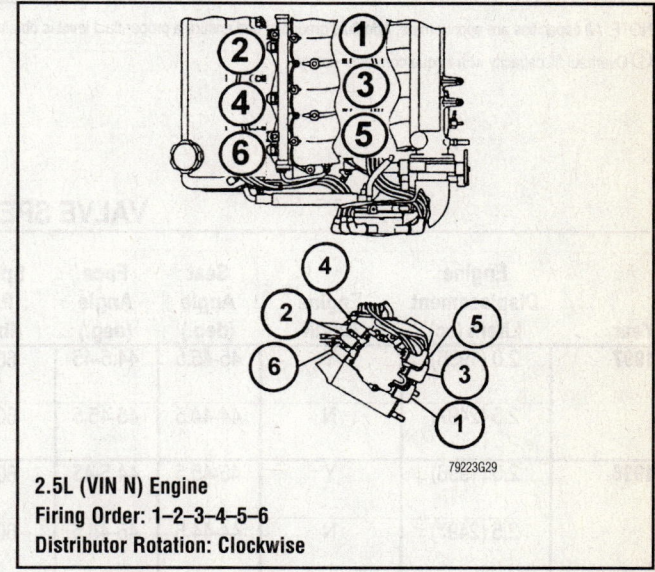

2.5L (VIN N) Engine
Firing Order: 1–2–3–4–5–6
Distributor Rotation: Clockwise

79223G29

CAPACITIES

Year	Model	Engine Displacement Liters (cc)	Engine ID/VIN	Engine Oil with Filter (qts.)	Transmission (pts.) Manual	Transmission (pts.) Auto.①	Fuel Tank (gal.)	Cooling System (qts.)
1997	Avenger	2.0 (1996)	Y	4.5	4.2	18.2	16.9	7.4
		2.5 (2497)	N	4.5	—	18.2	16.9	7.4
	Sebring Coupe	2.0 (1996)	Y	4.5	4.2	18.2	16.9	7.4
		2.5 (2497)	N	4.5	—	18.2	16.9	7.4
1998	Avenger	2.0 (1996)	Y	4.5	4.2	18.2	16.9	7.4
		2.5 (2497)	N	4.5	—	18.2	16.9	7.4
	Sebring Coupe	2.0 (1996)	Y	4.5	4.2	18.2	16.9	7.4
		2.5 (2497)	N	4.5	—	18.2	16.9	7.4
1999	Avenger	2.0 (1996)	Y	4.5	4.2	18.2	16.9	7.4
		2.5 (2497)	N	4.5	—	18.2	16.9	7.4
	Sebring Coupe	2.0 (1996)	Y	4.5	4.2	18.2	16.9	7.4
		2.5 (2497)	N	4.5	—	18.2	16.9	7.4
2000-01	Avenger	2.5 (2497)	N	4.5	—	18.2	16.9	7.4
	Sebring Coupe	2.5 (2497)	N	4.5	—	18.2	16.9	7.4

NOTE: All capacities are approximate. Add fluid gradually and ensure a proper fluid level is obtained.

① Overhaul fill capacity with torque converter empty

93061C04

VALVE SPECIFICATIONS

Year	Engine Displacement Liters (cc)	Engine ID/VIN	Seat Angle (deg.)	Face Angle (deg.)	Spring Test Pressure (lbs. @ in.)	Spring Installed Height (in.)	Stem-to-Guide Clearance (in.) Intake	Stem-to-Guide Clearance (in.) Exhaust	Stem Diameter (in.) Intake	Stem Diameter (in.) Exhaust
1997	2.0 (1996)	Y	45-45.5	44.5-45	60@1.496	1.496	0.0009-0.0026	0.0020-0.0037	0.2336-0.2343	0.2325-0.2332
	2.5 (2497)	N	44-44.5	45-45.5	60@1.740	1.740	0.0008-0.0040	0.0016-0.0060	0.2360	0.2360
1998	2.0 (1996)	Y	45-45.5	44.5-45	60@1.496	1.496	0.0009-0.0026	0.0020-0.0037	0.2336-0.2343	0.2325-0.2332
	2.5 (2497)	N	44-44.5	45-45.5	60@1.740	1.740	0.0008-0.0040	0.0016-0.0060	0.2360	0.2360
1999	2.0 (1996)	Y	45-45.5	44.5-45	60@1.496	1.496	0.0009-0.0026	0.0020-0.0037	0.2336-0.2343	0.2325-0.2332
	2.5 (2497)	N	44-44.5	45-45.5	60@1.740	1.740	0.0008-0.0040	0.0016-0.0060	0.2360	0.2360
2000-01	2.5 (2497)	N	44-44.5	45-45.5	60@1.740	1.740	0.0008-0.0040	0.0016-0.0060	0.2360	0.2360

93061C05

CRANKSHAFT AND CONNECTING ROD SPECIFICATIONS

All measurements are given in inches.

Year	Engine Displacement Liters (cc)	Engine ID/VIN	Crankshaft				Connecting Rod		
			Main Brg. Journal Dia.	Main Brg. Oil Clearance	Shaft End-play	Thrust on No.	Journal Diameter	Oil Clearance	Side Clearance
1997	2.0 (1996)	Y	2.0469-2.0475	0.0009-0.0024	0.0035-0.0094	3	1.8894-1.8900	0.0010-0.0023	0.0051-0.0150
	2.5 (2497)	N	2.3600	0.0008-0.0016	0.0020-0.0098	3	1.9700	0.0008-0.0020	0.0039-0.0098
1998	2.0 (1996)	Y	2.0469-2.0475	0.0009-0.0024	0.0035-0.0094	3	1.8894-1.8900	0.0010-0.0023	0.0051-0.0150
	2.5 (2497)	N	2.3600	0.0008-0.0016	0.0020-0.0098	3	1.9700	0.0008-0.0020	0.0039-0.0098
1999	2.0 (1996)	Y	2.0469-2.0475	0.0009-0.0024	0.0035-0.0094	3	1.8894-1.8900	0.0010-0.0023	0.0051-0.0150
	2.5 (2497)	N	2.3600	0.0008-0.0016	0.0020-0.0098	3	1.9700	0.0008-0.0020	0.0039-0.0098
2000-01	2.5 (2497)	N	2.3600	0.0008-0.0016	0.0020-0.0098	3	1.9700	0.0008-0.0020	0.0039-0.0098

93061C06

PISTON AND RING SPECIFICATIONS

All measurements are given in inches.

Year	Engine Displacement Liters (cc)	Engine ID/VIN	Piston Clearance	Ring Gap			Ring Side Clearance		
				Top Compression	Bottom Compression	Oil Control	Top Compression	Bottom Compression	Oil Control
1997	2.0 (1996)	Y	0.0005-① 0.0017	0.009-0.020	0.019-0.031	0.009-0.026	0.0010-0.0026	0.0010-0.0026	0.0002-0.0070
	2.5 (2497)	N	0.0008-0.0016	0.010-0.016	0.016-0.022	0.006-0.019	0.0012-0.0028	0.0008-0.0024	NA
1998	2.0 (1996)	Y	0.0005-① 0.0017	0.009-0.020	0.019-0.031	0.009-0.026	0.0010-0.0026	0.0010-0.0026	0.0002-0.0070
	2.5 (2497)	N	0.0008-0.0016	0.010-0.016	0.016-0.022	0.006-0.019	0.0012-0.0028	0.0008-0.0024	NA
1999	2.0 (1996)	Y	0.0005-① 0.0017	0.009-0.020	0.019-0.031	0.009-0.026	0.0010-0.0026	0.0010-0.0026	0.0002-0.0070
	2.5 (2497)	N	0.0008-0.0016	0.010-0.016	0.016-0.022	0.006-0.019	0.0012-0.0028	0.0008-0.0024	NA
2000-01	2.5 (2497)	N	0.0008-0.0016	0.010-0.016	0.016-0.022	0.006-0.019	0.0012-0.0028	0.0008-0.0024	NA

NA: Not Available

① Clearance at 11/16 inch from the bottom of the skirt

93061C07

Timing chain and gear service is covered in the model specific sections of this manual

TORQUE SPECIFICATIONS
All readings in ft. lbs.

Year	Engine Displacement Liters (cc)	Engine ID/VIN	Cylinder Head Bolts	Main Bearing Bolts	Rod Bearing Bolts	Crankshaft Damper Bolts	Flywheel Bolts	Manifold		Spark Plugs	Lug Nuts
								Intake	Exhaust		
1997	2.0 (1996)	Y	①	55 ②	③	105	70	17	17	20	88-103
	2.5 (2497)	N	80	69	37	134	68	16	22	18	88-103
1998	2.0 (1996)	Y	①	55 ②	③	105	70	17	17	20	88-103
	2.5 (2497)	N	80	69	37	134	68	16	22	18	88-103
1999	2.0 (1996)	Y	①	55 ②	③	105	70	17	17	20	88-103
	2.5 (2497)	N	80	69	37	134	68	16	22	18	88-103
2000-01	2.5 (2497)	N	80	69	37	134	68	16	22	18	88-103

① Step 1: Fasteners 1 through 6 to 24 ft. lbs.
  Fasteners 7 through 10 to 20 ft. lbs.
  Step 2: Fasteners 1 through 6 to 48 ft. lbs.
  Fasteners 7 through 10 to 20 ft. lbs.
  Step 3: Fasteners 1 through 6 to 48 ft. lbs.
  Fasteners 7 throught 10 to 20 ft. lbs.
  Step 4: Tighten all fasteners 1/4 turn
② Tighten side bolts to 21 ft. lbs.
③ Step 1: 20 ft. lbs.
  Step 2: 1/4 turn

93061C08

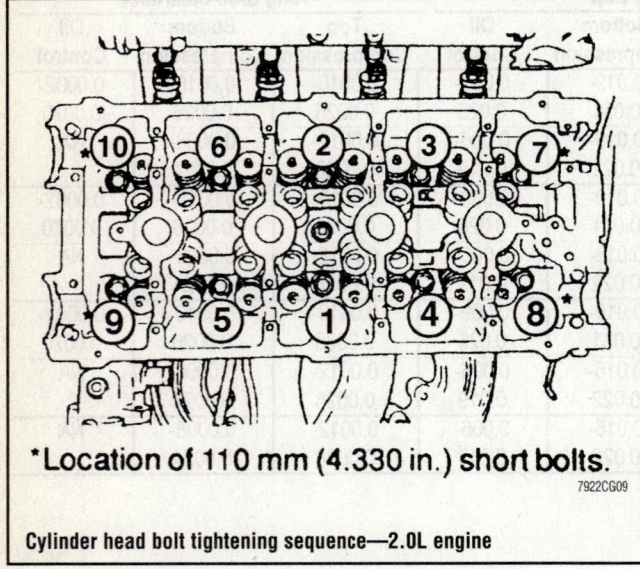

*Location of 110 mm (4.330 in.) short bolts.

7922CG09

Cylinder head bolt tightening sequence—2.0L engine

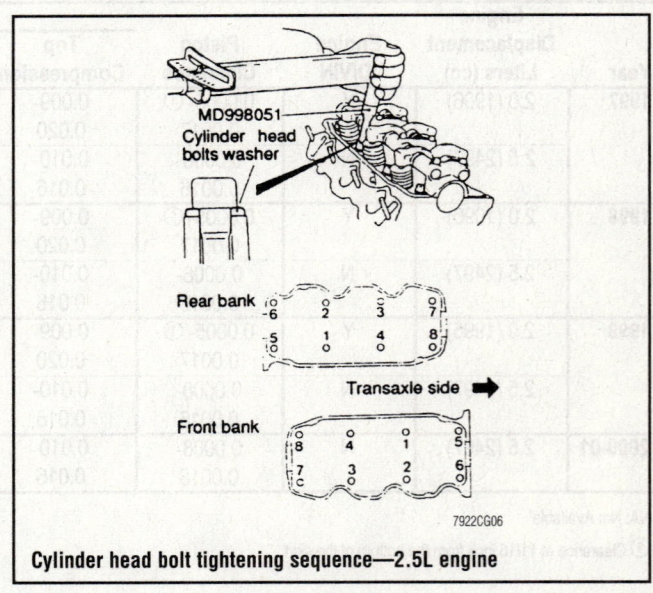

7922CG06

Cylinder head bolt tightening sequence—2.5L engine

BRAKE SPECIFICATIONS
CHRYSLER SEBRING COUPE, DODGE AVENGER
All measurements in inches unless noted

| Year | Model | | Brake Disc | | | Brake Drum Diameter | | | Min. Lining Thickness | Brake Caliper | |
			Original Thickness	Minimum Thickness	Maximum Run-out	Original Inside Diameter	Max. Wear Limit	Maximum Machine Diameter		Bracket Bolts (ft. lbs.)	Mounting Bolts (ft. lbs.)
1997	Avenger	F	0.940	0.880	0.003	—	—	—	0.080	65	54
		R	0.390	0.330	0.003	①	②	②	0.039	—	38
	Sebring	F	0.940	0.880	0.003	—	—	—	0.080	65	54
	Coupe	R	0.390 ③	0.330 ④	0.003	①	②	②	0.039	—	38
1998	Avenger	F	0.940	0.880	0.003	—	—	—	0.080	65	54
		R	0.390	0.330	0.003	①	②	②	0.039	—	38
	Sebring	F	0.940	0.880	0.003	—	—	—	0.080	65	54
	Coupe	R	0.390 ③	0.330 ④	0.003	①	②	②	0.039	—	38
1999	Avenger	F	0.940	0.880	0.003	—	—	—	0.080	65	54
		R	0.390	0.330	0.003	①	②	②	0.039	—	38
	Sebring	F	0.940	0.880	0.003	—	—	—	0.080	66	54
	Coupe	R	0.390 ③	0.330 ④	0.003	①	②	②	0.039	—	38
2000-01	Avenger	F	0.940	0.880	0.003	—	—	—	0.080	65	54
		R	0.390	0.330	0.003	—	—	—	0.039	—	38
	Sebring	F	0.940	0.880	0.003	—	—	—	0.080	66	54
	Coupe	R	0.390 ③	0.330 ④	0.003	—	—	—	0.039	—	38

F: Front

R: Rear

① Minimum diameter: 9.00 in.

② Maximum diameter is stamped on drum

③ Vented rear disc: 0.790

④ Vented rear disc: 0.720

93061C09

Ignition system service is covered in the model specific sections of this manual

SCHEDULED MAINTENANCE INTERVALS
(CHRYSLER SEBRING & DODGE AVENGER)

TO BE SERVICED	TYPE OF SERVICE	VEHICLE MILEAGE INTERVAL (x1000)												
		7.5	15	22.5	30	37.5	45	52.5	60	67.5	75	82.5	90	97.5
Engine oil & filter	R	✓	✓	✓	✓	✓	✓	✓	✓	✓	✓	✓	✓	✓
Coolant level, hoses & clamps	S/I	✓	✓	✓	✓	✓	✓	✓	✓	✓	✓	✓	✓	✓
Rotate tires	S/I	✓	✓	✓	✓	✓	✓	✓	✓	✓	✓	✓	✓	✓
Automatic transaxle fluid level	S/I		✓		✓		✓		✓		✓		✓	
Brake hoses & disc brake pads	S/I		✓		✓		✓		✓		✓		✓	
Drive shaft boots & front suspension components	S/I		✓		✓		✓		✓		✓			
Air filter element	R				✓				✓				✓	
Engine coolant	R				✓				✓				✓	
Spark plugs (DOHC)	R				✓				✓				✓	
Spark plugs (SOHC) ①	R				✓				✓				✓	
Accessory drive belts	S/I				✓				✓				✓	
Ball joints & steering linkage seals	S/I				✓				✓				✓	
Exhaust system	S/I				✓				✓				✓	
Fuel hoses	S/I				✓				✓				✓	
Manual transaxle oil	S/I				✓				✓				✓	
PCV valve	S/I				✓				✓				✓	
Rear drum brake lining & rear wheel cylinders	S/I				✓				✓				✓	
Camshaft timing belt	R								✓					
Ignition cables	R								✓					
Distributor cap & rotor	S/I								✓					
EVAP system	S/I								✓					
Fuel system	S/I								✓					

R: Replace   S/I: Service or Inspect

① Spark plugs: replace every 100,000 miles.

FREQUENT OPERATION MAINTENANCE (SEVERE SERVICE)

If a vehicle is operated under any of the following conditions it is considered severe service:

- Extremely dusty areas.

- 50% or more of the vehicle operation is in 32°C (90°F) or higher temperatures, or constant operation in temperatures below 0°C (32°F).

- Prolonged idling (vehicle operation in stop and go traffic).

- Frequent short running periods (engine does not warm to normal operating temperatures).

- Police, taxi, delivery usage or trailer towing usage.

Oil & oil filter change: change every 3000 miles.

Disc brake pads: check every 6000 miles.

Air filter element: change every 15,000 miles.

Automatic transaxle fluid: change every 15,000 miles.

Rear drum brake linings & rear wheel cylinders: check every 15,000 miles.

Spark plugs: change every 15,000 miles.

93061C10

SCHEDULED MAINTENANCE INTERVALS
DAIMLERCHRYSLER CORPORATION
CHRYSLER SEBRING
DODGE AVENGER

The following should be used as a guide when determining the amount of work required for a particular service.
In estimating how long a particular Scheduled Maintenance Service should take, please observe the following:

- Labor Time is time based on field research and data supplied by the vehicle manufacturer.
- Labor time operations are given in hours and tenths of an hour.
- All labor operations are to be used as a guide.

Mechanic Skill Level Codes:
(A) PRECISION: Highly skilled with multiple certification.
(B) GENERAL: Normally skilled with certification.
(C) MAINTENANCE: Semi-skilled working on certification.

	LABOR TIME
7500 Mile Service (C)	
All Models	1.3
15000 Mile Service (C)	
All Models	1.6
22500 Mile Service (C)	
All Models	1.3
30000 Mile Service (B)	
All Models	3.3

	LABOR TIME
37500 Mile Service (C)	
All Models	1.3
45000 Mile Service (C)	
All Models	1.7
52500 Mile Service (C)	
All Models	1.3
60000 Mile Service (B)	
All Models	6.1
67500 Mile Service (C)	
All Models	1.3

	LABOR TIME
75000 Mile Service (C)	
All Models	1.7
82500 Mile Service (C)	
All Models	1.3
90000 Mile Service (B)	
All Models	3.3
97500 Mile Service (C)	
All Models	1.3

93061C11

CHRYSLER CORP.
Chrysler Cirrus • Sebring Convertible • Dodge Stratus • Plymouth Breeze

ENGINE AND VEHICLE IDENTIFICATION

Code ①	Liters (cc)	Cu. In.	Cyl.	Fuel Sys.	Engine Type	Eng. Mfg.	Code ②	Year
				Engine				Model Year
C	2.0 (1996)	122	I4	MFI	SOHC	Chrysler	V	1997
H	2.5 (2497)	152	V6	MFI	SOHC	Mitsubishi	W	1998
X	2.4 (2429)	148	I4	MFI	DOHC	Chrysler	X	1999
							Y	2000
							1	2001

MFI: Multi-point Fuel Injection
SOHC: Single Overhead Camshaft
DOHC: Double Overhead Camshaft

① 8th position of VIN
② 10th position of VIN

93061C12

GENERAL ENGINE SPECIFICATIONS
All measurements are given in inches.

Year	Model	Engine Displacement Liters (cc)	Engine Series (ID/VIN)	Fuel System	Net Horsepower @ rpm	Net Torque @ rpm (ft. lbs.)	Bore x Stroke (in.)	Com-pression Ratio	Oil Pressure @ rpm
1997	Breeze	2.0 (1996)	C	MFI	132@6000	129@5000	3.44x3.26	9.8:1	25-80@3000
	Cirrus	2.4 (2429)	X	MFI	150@5200	167@4000	3.44x3.98	9.4:1	25-80@3000
	Cirrus	2.5 (2497)	H	MFI	168@5800	170@4350	3.29x2.99	9.4:1	25-80@3000
	Sebring Convertible	2.4 (2429)	X	MFI	150@5200	167@4000	3.44x3.98	9.4:1	25-80@3000
	Sebring Convertible	2.5 (2497)	H	MFI	168@5800	170@4350	3.29x2.99	9.4:1	25-80@3000
	Stratus	2.0 (1996)	C	MFI	132@6000	129@5000	3.44x3.26	9.8:1	25-80@3000
	Stratus	2.4 (2429)	X	MFI	150@5200	167@4000	3.44x3.98	9.4:1	25-80@3000
	Stratus	2.5 (2497)	H	MFI	168@5800	170@4350	3.29x2.99	9.4:1	25-80@3000
1998	Breeze	2.0 (1996)	C	MFI	132@6000	129@5000	3.44x3.26	9.8:1	25-80@3000
	Cirrus	2.4 (2429)	X	MFI	150@5200	167@4000	3.44x3.98	9.4:1	25-80@3000
	Cirrus	2.5 (2497)	H	MFI	168@5800	170@4350	3.29x2.99	9.4:1	25-80@3000
	Sebring Convertible	2.4 (2429)	X	MFI	150@5200	167@4000	3.44x3.98	9.4:1	25-80@3000
	Sebring Convertible	2.5 (2497)	H	MFI	168@5800	170@4350	3.29x2.99	9.4:1	25-80@3000
	Stratus	2.0 (1996)	C	MFI	132@6000	129@5000	3.44x3.26	9.8:1	25-80@3000
	Stratus	2.4 (2429)	X	MFI	150@5200	167@4000	3.44x3.98	9.4:1	25-80@3000
	Stratus	2.5 (2497)	H	MFI	168@5800	170@4350	3.29x2.99	9.4:1	25-80@3000
1999	Breeze	2.0 (1996)	C	MFI	132@6000	129@5000	3.44x3.26	9.8:1	25-80@3000
	Cirrus	2.4 (2429)	X	MFI	150@5200	167@4000	3.44x3.98	9.4:1	25-80@3000
	Cirrus	2.5 (2497)	H	MFI	168@5800	170@4350	3.29x2.99	9.4:1	25-80@3000
	Sebring Convertible	2.4 (2429)	X	MFI	150@5200	167@4000	3.44x3.98	9.4:1	25-80@3000
	Sebring Convertible	2.5 (2497)	H	MFI	168@5800	170@4350	3.29x2.99	9.4:1	25-80@3000
	Stratus	2.0 (1996)	C	MFI	132@6000	129@5000	3.44x3.26	9.8:1	25-80@3000
	Stratus	2.4 (2429)	X	MFI	150@5200	167@4000	3.44x3.98	9.4:1	25-80@3000
	Stratus	2.5 (2497)	H	MFI	168@5800	170@4350	3.29x2.99	9.4:1	25-80@3000
2000-01	Breeze	2.4 (2429)	X	MFI	150@5200	167@4000	3.44x3.98	9.4:1	25-80@3000
	Cirrus	2.4 (2429)	X	MFI	150@5200	167@4000	3.44x3.98	9.4:1	25-80@3000
	Cirrus	2.5 (2497)	H	MFI	168@5800	170@4350	3.29x2.99	9.4:1 ①	25-80@3000
	Sebring Convertible	2.5 (2497)	H	MFI	168@5800	170@4350	3.29x2.99	9.4:1 ①	25-80@3000
	Stratus	2.4 (2429)	X	MFI	150@5200	167@4000	3.44x3.98	9.4:1	25-80@3000
	Stratus	2.5 (2497)	H	MFI	168@5800	170@4350	3.29x2.99	9.4:1 ①	25-80@3000

MFI: Multi-point Fuel Injectiom

① California: 9.0:1

93061C13

GASOLINE ENGINE TUNE-UP SPECIFICATIONS

Year	Engine Displacement Liters (cc)	Engine ID/VIN	Spark Plug Gap (in.)	Ignition Timing (deg.)		Fuel Pump (psi) ①	Idle Speed (rpm)		Valve Clearance	
				MT	AT		MT	AT	In.	Ex.
1997	2.0 (1996)	C	0.035	②	②	48	③	③	HYD	HYD
	2.4 (2429)	X	0.050	—	②	49	—	③	HYD	HYD
	2.5 (2497)	H	0.038-0.043	—	②	49	—	③	HYD	HYD
1998	2.0 (1996)	C	0.035	②	②	48	③	③	HYD	HYD
	2.4 (2429)	X	0.050	—	②	49	—	③	HYD	HYD
	2.5 (2497)	H	0.038-0.043	—	②	49	—	③	HYD	HYD
1999	2.0 (1996)	C	0.035	②	②	48	③	③	HYD	HYD
	2.4 (2429)	X	0.050	—	②	49	—	③	HYD	HYD
	2.5 (2497)	H	0.038-0.043	—	②	49	—	③	HYD	HYD
2000-01	2.4 (2429)	X	0.050	—	②	49	③	③	HYD	HYD
	2.5 (2497)	H	0.038-0.043	—	②	49	—	③	HYD	HYD

NOTE: The Vehicle Emission Control Information label often reflects specification changes made during production. The label figures must be used if they differ from those in this chart.

HYD: Hydraulic

① This reading measured with vacuum hose disconnected from fuel pressure regulator.

② Ignition timing cannot be adjusted. Base engine timing is set at TDC during assembly.

③ Refer to the Vehicle Emission Control Information label for correct specifications.

93061C14

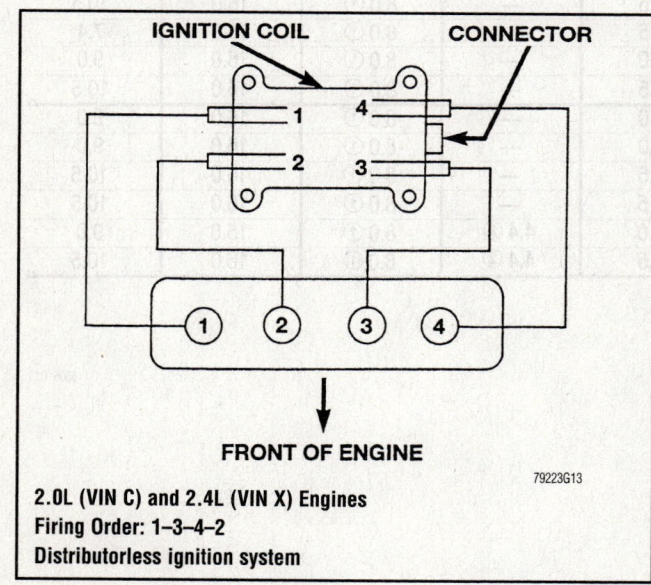

2.0L (VIN C) and 2.4L (VIN X) Engines
Firing Order: 1–3–4–2
Distributorless ignition system

79223G13

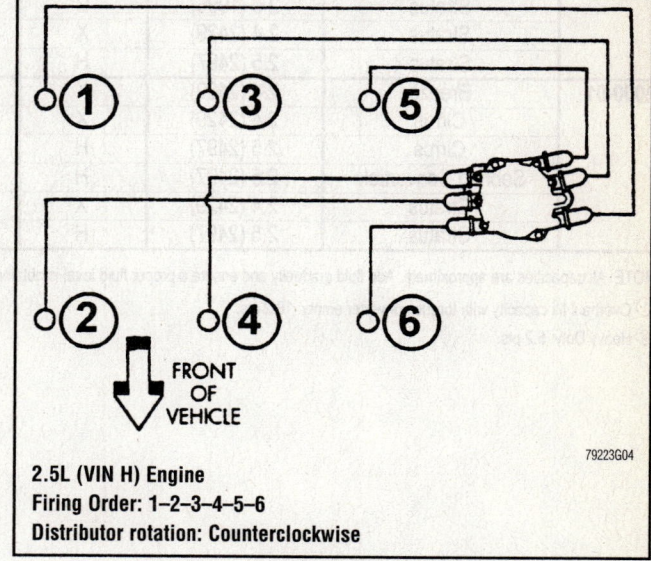

2.5L (VIN H) Engine
Firing Order: 1–2–3–4–5–6
Distributor rotation: Counterclockwise

79223G04

CAPACITIES

Year	Model	Engine Displacement Liters (cc)	Engine ID/VIN	Engine Oil with Filter (qts.)	Transmission (pts.) 5-Spd	Transmission (pts.) Auto.	Fuel Tank (gal.)	Cooling System (qts.)
1997	Breeze	2.0 (1996)	C	4.5	4.4	8.0 ①	16.0	7.4
	Cirrus	2.4 (2429)	X	5.0	—	8.0 ①	16.0	9.0
	Cirrus	2.5 (2497)	H	4.5	—	8.0 ①	16.0	10.5
	Sebring Convertible	2.4 (2429)	X	5.0	—	8.0 ①	16.0	9.0
	Sebring Convertible	2.5 (2497)	H	4.5	—	8.0 ①	16.0	10.5
	Stratus	2.0 (1996)	C	4.5	4.4	8.0 ①	16.0	7.4
	Stratus	2.4 (2429)	X	5.0	—	8.0 ①	16.0	9.0
	Stratus	2.5 (2497)	H	4.5	—	8.0 ①	16.0	10.5
1998	Breeze	2.0 (1996)	C	4.5	4.4	8.0 ①	16.0	7.4
	Cirrus	2.4 (2429)	X	5.0	—	8.0 ①	16.0	9.0
	Cirrus	2.5 (2497)	H	4.5	—	8.0 ①	16.0	10.5
	Sebring Convertible	2.4 (2429)	X	5.0	—	8.0 ①	16.0	9.0
	Sebring Convertible	2.5 (2497)	H	4.5	—	8.0 ①	16.0	10.5
	Stratus	2.0 (1996)	C	4.5	4.4	8.0 ①	16.0	7.4
	Stratus	2.4 (2429)	X	5.0	—	8.0 ①	16.0	9.0
	Stratus	2.5 (2497)	H	4.5	—	8.0 ①	16.0	10.5
1999	Breeze	2.0 (1996)	C	4.5	4.4	8.0 ①	16.0	7.4
	Cirrus	2.4 (2429)	X	5.0	—	8.0 ①	16.0	9.0
	Cirrus	2.5 (2497)	H	4.5	—	8.0 ①	16.0	10.5
	Sebring Convertible	2.4 (2429)	X	5.0	—	8.0 ①	16.0	9.0
	Sebring Convertible	2.5 (2497)	H	4.5	—	8.0 ①	16.0	10.5
	Stratus	2.0 (1996)	C	4.5	4.4	8.0 ①	16.0	7.4
	Stratus	2.4 (2429)	X	5.0	—	8.0 ①	16.0	9.0
	Stratus	2.5 (2497)	H	4.5	—	8.0 ①	16.0	10.5
2000-01	Breeze	2.4 (2429)	X	5.0	—	8.0 ①	16.0	9.0
	Cirrus	2.4 (2429)	X	5.0	—	8.0 ①	16.0	9.0
	Cirrus	2.5 (2497)	H	4.5	—	8.0 ①	16.0	10.5
	Sebring Convertible	2.5 (2497)	H	4.5	—	8.0 ①	16.0	10.5
	Stratus	2.4 (2429)	X	5.0	4.4 ②	8.0 ①	16.0	9.0
	Stratus	2.5 (2497)	H	4.5	4.4 ②	8.0 ①	16.0	10.5

NOTE: All capacities are approximate. Add fluid gradually and ensure a proper fluid level is obtained.

① Overhaul fill capacity with torque converter empty: 18.2 pts.

② Heavy Duty: 5.2 pts.

93061C15

VALVE SPECIFICATIONS

Year	Engine Displacement Liters (cc)	Engine ID/VIN	Seat Angle (deg.)	Face Angle (deg.)	Spring Test Pressure (lbs. @ in.)	Spring Installed Height (in.)	Stem-to-Guide Clearance (in.)		Stem Diameter (in.)	
							Intake	Exhaust	Intake	Exhaust
1997	2.0 (1996)	C	44.5-45	45-45.5	75@1.54	1.540	0.0018-0.0025	0.0029-0.0037	0.2340	0.2330
	2.4 (2429)	X	45-44.5	45-45.5	76@1.50	1.496	0.0018-0.0025	0.0029-0.0037	0.2340	0.2330
	2.5 (2497)	H	45-44.5	45-45.5	60@1.74	1.740	0.0008-0.0020	0.0016-0.0028	0.2360	0.2360
1998	2.0 (1996)	C	44.5-45	45-45.5	75@1.54	1.540	0.0018-0.0025	0.0029-0.0037	0.2340	0.2330
	2.4 (2429)	X	45	44.5-45	76@1.50	1.496	0.0018-0.0025	0.0029-0.0037	0.2340	0.2330
	2.5 (2497)	H	45-44.5	45-45.5	60@1.74	1.740	0.0008-0.0020	0.0016-0.0028	0.2360	0.2360
1999	2.0 (1996)	C	44.5-45	45-45.5	75@1.54	1.540	0.0018-0.0025	0.0029-0.0037	0.2340	0.2330
	2.4 (2429)	X	45	44.5-45	76@1.50	1.496	0.0018-0.0025	0.0029-0.0037	0.2340	0.2330
	2.5 (2497)	H	45-44.5	45-45.5	60@1.74	1.740	0.0008-0.0020	0.0016-0.0028	0.2360	0.2360
2000-01	2.4 (2429)	X	45	44.5-45	76@1.50	1.496	0.0018-0.0025	0.0029-0.0037	0.2340	0.2330
	2.5 (2497)	H	45-44.5	45-45.5	60@1.74	1.740	0.0008-0.0020	0.0016-0.0028	0.2360	0.2360

93061C16

Refer to the model specific sections for fuel system service procedures

CRANKSHAFT AND CONNECTING ROD SPECIFICATIONS

All measurements are given in inches.

Year	Engine Displacement Liters (cc)	Engine ID/VIN	Crankshaft				Connecting Rod		
			Main Brg. Journal Dia.	Main Brg. Oil Clearance	Shaft End-play	Thrust on No.	Journal Diameter	Oil Clearance	Side Clearance
1997	2.0 (1996)	C	2.0469-2.0475	0.0008-0.0024	0.0035-0.0094	3	1.8894-1.8900	0.0010-0.0023	0.0050-0.0150
	2.4 (2429)	X	2.3610-2.3625	0.0007-0.0023	0.0035-0.0095	3	1.9670-1.9685	0.0009-0.0027	0.0051-0.0150
	2.5 (2497)	H	2.3620	0.0008-0.0016	0.0020-0.0160	3	1.9690	0.0008-0.0016	0.0040-0.0160
1998	2.0 (1996)	C	2.0469-2.0475	0.0008-0.0024	0.0035-0.0094	3	1.8894-1.8900	0.0010-0.0023	0.0050-0.0150
	2.4 (2429)	X	2.3610-2.3625	0.0007-0.0023	0.0035-0.0095	3	1.9670-1.9685	0.0009-0.0027	0.0051-0.0150
	2.5 (2497)	H	2.3620	0.0008-0.0016	0.0020-0.0160	3	1.9690	0.0008-0.0016	0.0040-0.0160
1999	2.0 (1996)	C	2.0469-2.0475	0.0008-0.0024	0.0035-0.0094	3	1.8894-1.8900	0.0010-0.0023	0.0050-0.0150
	2.4 (2429)	X	2.3610-2.3625	0.0007-0.0023	0.0035-0.0095	3	1.9670-1.9685	0.0009-0.0027	0.0051-0.0150
	2.5 (2497)	H	2.3620	0.0008-0.0016	0.0020-0.0160	3	1.9690	0.0008-0.0016	0.0040-0.0160
2000-01	2.4 (2429)	X	2.3610-2.3625	0.0007-0.0023	0.0035-0.0095	3	1.9670-1.9685	0.0009-0.0027	0.0051-0.0150
	2.5 (2497)	H	2.3620	0.0008-0.0016	0.0020-0.0120	3	1.9690	0.0008-0.0016	0.0040-0.0160

93061C17

PISTON AND RING SPECIFICATIONS
All measurements are given in inches.

Year	Engine Displacement Liters (cc)	Engine ID/VIN	Piston Clearance	Ring Gap			Ring Side Clearance		
				Top Compression	Bottom Compression	Oil Control	Top Compression	Bottom Compression	Oil Control
1997	2.0 (1996)	C	0.0004- ① 0.0017	0.009- 0.020	0.019- 0.031	0.009- 0.026	0.0010- 0.0026	0.0010- 0.0026	0.0002- 0.007
	2.4 (2429)	X	0.0009- ② 0.0022	0.010- 0.020	0.009- 0.018	0.010- 0.025	0.0011- 0.0031	0.0011- 0.0031	0.0004- 0.0070
	2.5 (2497)	H	0.0008- 0.0016	0.010- 0.015	0.005- 0.021	0.006- 0.020	0.0012- 0.0028	0.0008- 0.0024	NA
1998	2.0 (1996)	C	0.0004- ① 0.0017	0.009- 0.020	0.019- 0.031	0.009- 0.026	0.0010- 0.0026	0.0010- 0.0026	0.0002- 0.007
	2.4 (2429)	X	0.0009- ② 0.0022	0.010- 0.020	0.009- 0.018	0.010- 0.025	0.0011- 0.0031	0.0011- 0.0031	0.0004- 0.0070
	2.5 (2497)	H	0.0008- 0.0016	0.010- 0.015	0.005- 0.021	0.006- 0.020	0.0012- 0.0028	0.0008- 0.0024	NA
1999	2.0 (1996)	C	0.0004- ① 0.0017	0.009- 0.020	0.019- 0.031	0.009- 0.026	0.0010- 0.0026	0.0010- 0.0026	0.0002- 0.007
	2.4 (2429)	X	0.0009- ② 0.0022	0.010- 0.020	0.009- 0.018	0.010- 0.025	0.0011- 0.0031	0.0011- 0.0031	0.0004- 0.0070
	2.5 (2497)	H	0.0008- 0.0016	0.010- 0.015	0.005- 0.021	0.006- 0.020	0.0012- 0.0028	0.0008- 0.0024	NA
2000-01	2.4 (2429)	X	0.0009- ② 0.0022	0.010- 0.020	0.009- 0.018	0.010- 0.025	0.0011- 0.0031	0.0011- 0.0031	0.0004- 0.0070
	2.5 (2497)	H	0.0008- 0.0016	0.010- 0.015	0.005- 0.021	0.006- 0.020	0.0012- 0.0028	0.0008- 0.0024	NA

NA: Not Available

① Clearance at 11/16 inch from bottom of skirt

② Clearance at 9/16 inch from bottom of skirt

93061C18

Refer to the model specific sections for engine electrical system service procedures

TORQUE SPECIFICATIONS
All readings in ft. lbs.

Year	Engine Displacement Liters (cc)	Engine ID/VIN	Cylinder Head Bolts	Main Bearing Bolts	Rod Bearing Bolts	Crankshaft Damper Bolts	Flywheel Bolts	Manifold Intake	Manifold Exhaust	Spark Plug	Lug Nut
1997	2.0 (1996)	C	①	②	③	105	70	17	17	20	95
	2.4 (2429)	X	①	②	③	100	70	17	17	20	95
	2.5 (2497)	H	80	69	37	134	70	16	33	18	95
1998	2.0 (1996)	C	①	②	③	105	70	17	17	20	95
	2.4 (2429)	X	①	②	③	100	70	17	17	20	95
	2.5 (2497)	H	80	69	37	134	70	16	33	18	95
1999	2.0 (1996)	C	①	②	③	105	70	17	17	20	95
	2.4 (2429)	X	①	②	③	100	70	17	17	20	95
	2.5 (2497)	H	80	69	37	134	70	16	33	18	95
2000-01	2.4 (2429)	X	①	②	③	100	70	17	17	20	95
	2.5 (2497)	H	80	69	37	134	70	16	33	18	95

① Step 1: 25 ft. lbs.
Step 2: 50 ft. lbs.
Step 3: 50 ft. lbs.
Step 4: Plus 1/4 turn

② Step 1: 30 ft. lbs
Step 2: Plus 1/4 turn

③ Step 1: 20 ft. lbs.
Step 2: Plus 1/4 turn

93061C19

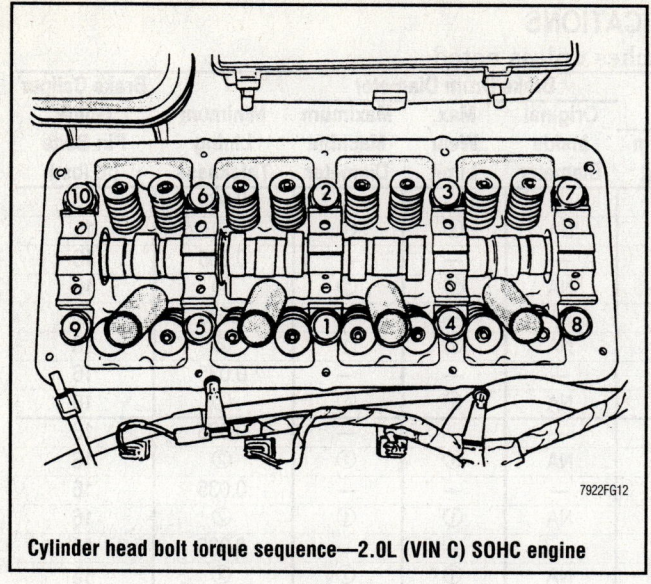

Cylinder head bolt torque sequence—2.0L (VIN C) SOHC engine

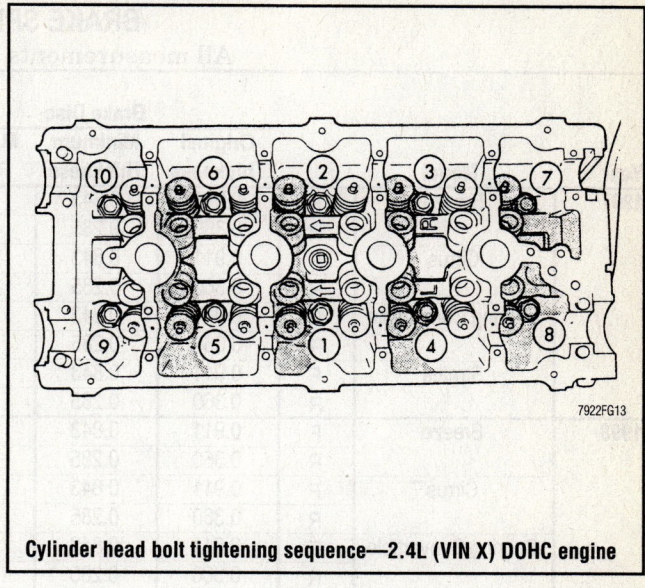

Cylinder head bolt tightening sequence—2.4L (VIN X) DOHC engine

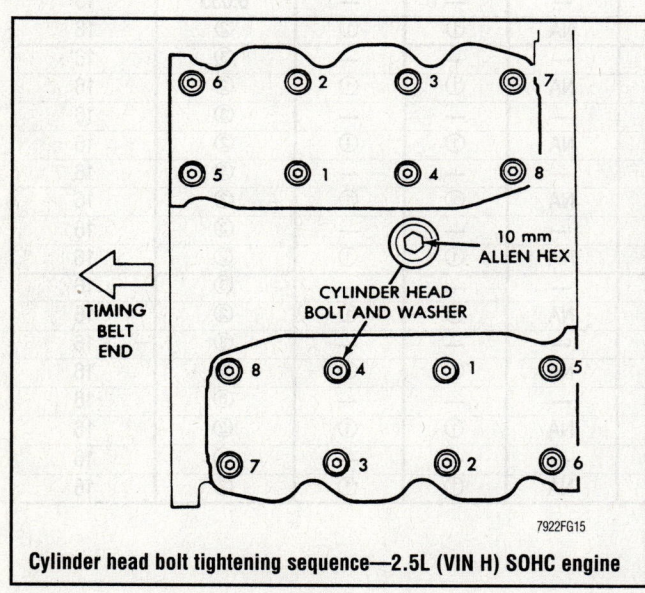

Cylinder head bolt tightening sequence—2.5L (VIN H) SOHC engine

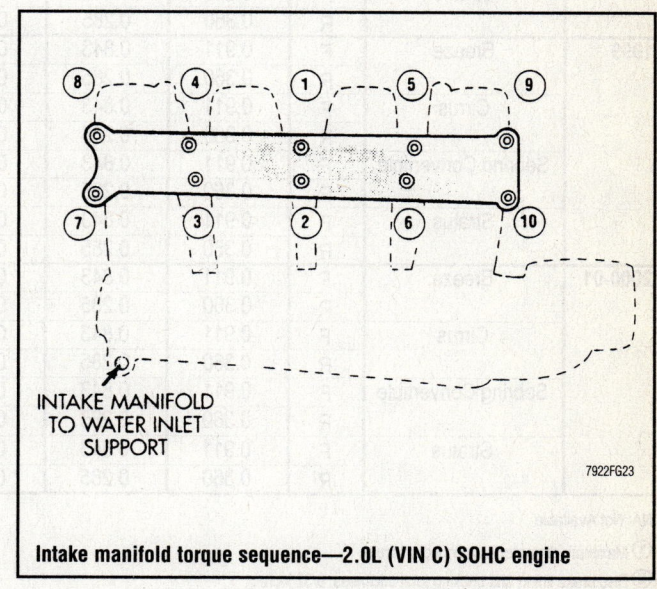

Intake manifold torque sequence—2.0L (VIN C) SOHC engine

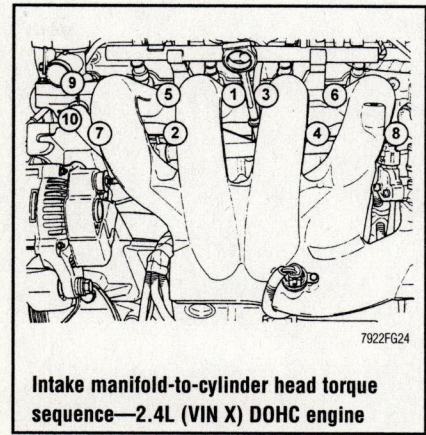

Intake manifold-to-cylinder head torque sequence—2.4L (VIN X) DOHC engine

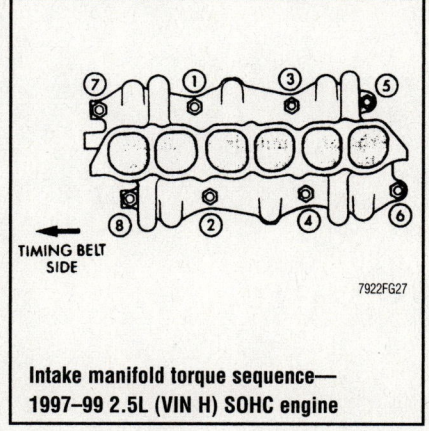

Intake manifold torque sequence—1997–99 2.5L (VIN H) SOHC engine

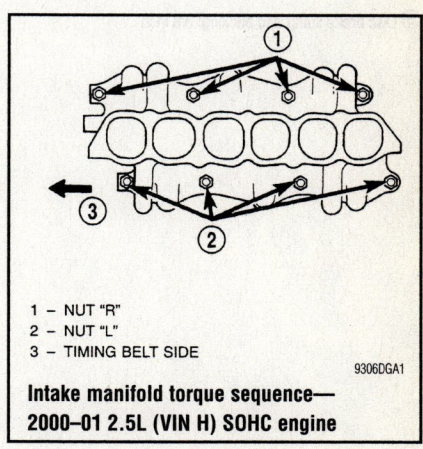

Intake manifold torque sequence—2000–01 2.5L (VIN H) SOHC engine

For accessory drive belt replacement procedures see the model specific sections of this manual

BRAKE SPECIFICATIONS
All measurements in inches unless noted

Year	Model		Original Thickness	Brake Disc Minimum Thickness	Maximum Run-out	Brake Drum Diameter Original Inside Diameter	Max. Wear Limit	Maximum Machine Diameter	Minimum Lining Thickness	Brake Caliper Guide Pin Bolts (ft. lbs.)
1997	Breeze	F	0.911	0.843	0.003	—	—	—	0.035	16
		R	0.360	0.285	0.005	NA	①	①	②	16
	Cirrus	F	0.911	0.843	0.005	—	—	—	0.035	16
		R	0.360	0.285	0.005	NA	①	①	②	16
	Sebring Convertible	F	0.911	0.843	0.005	—	—	—	0.035	16
		R	0.360	0.285	0.005	NA	①	①	②	16
	Stratus	F	0.911	0.843	0.003	—	—	—	0.035	16
		R	0.360	0.285	0.005	NA	①	①	②	16
1998	Breeze	F	0.911	0.843	0.003	—	—	—	0.035	16
		R	0.360	0.285	0.005	NA	①	①	②	16
	Cirrus	F	0.911	0.843	0.005	—	—	—	0.035	16
		R	0.360	0.285	0.005	NA	①	①	②	16
	Sebring Convertible	F	0.911	0.843	0.005	—	—	—	0.035	16
		R	0.360	0.285	0.005	NA	①	①	②	16
	Stratus	F	0.911	0.843	0.003	—	—	—	0.035	16
		R	0.360	0.285	0.005	NA	①	①	②	16
1999	Breeze	F	0.911	0.843	0.003	—	—	—	③	16
		R	0.360	0.285	0.005	NA	①	①	②	16
	Cirrus	F	0.911	0.843	0.005	—	—	—	③	16
		R	0.360	0.285	0.005	NA	①	①	②	16
	Sebring Convertible	F	0.911	0.843	0.005	—	—	—	③	16
		R	0.360	0.285	0.005	NA	①	①	②	16
	Stratus	F	0.911	0.843	0.003	—	—	—	③	16
		R	0.360	0.285	0.005	NA	①	①	②	16
2000-01	Breeze	F	0.911	0.843	0.003	—	—	—	③	16
		R	0.360	0.285	0.005	NA	①	①	②	16
	Cirrus	F	0.911	0.843	0.005	—	—	—	③	16
		R	0.360	0.285	0.005	NA	①	①	②	16
	Sebring Convertible	F	0.911	0.843	0.005	—	—	—	③	16
		R	0.360	0.285	0.005	NA	①	①	②	16
	Stratus	F	0.911	0.843	0.003	—	—	—	③	16
		R	0.360	0.285	0.005	NA	①	①	②	16

NA: Not Available

① Maximum diameter is stamped on drum

② Disc brake lining and backing total thickness: 9/32 inch

   Drum brake shoe lining and backing total thickness: 1/8 inch

③ Disc brake lining and backing: 3/8 inch

93061C20

SCHEDULED MAINTENANCE INTERVALS
(CHRYSLER CIRRUS & SEBRING CONVERTIBLE, DODGE STRATUS & PLYMOUTH BREEZE)

TO BE SERVICED	TYPE OF SERVICE	VEHICLE MILEAGE INTERVAL (x1000)												
		7.5	15	22.5	30	37.5	45	52.5	60	67.5	75	82.5	90	97.5
Engine oil & filter	R	✓	✓	✓	✓	✓	✓	✓	✓	✓	✓	✓	✓	✓
Brake hoses	S/I	✓	✓	✓	✓	✓	✓	✓	✓	✓	✓	✓	✓	✓
Coolant level, hoses & clamps	S/I	✓	✓	✓	✓	✓	✓	✓	✓	✓	✓	✓	✓	✓
CV joints & front suspension components	S/I	✓	✓	✓	✓	✓	✓	✓	✓	✓	✓	✓	✓	✓
Exhaust system	S/I	✓	✓	✓	✓	✓	✓	✓	✓	✓	✓	✓	✓	✓
Rotate tires	S/I	✓	✓	✓	✓	✓	✓	✓	✓	✓	✓	✓	✓	✓
Accessory drive belts	S/I		✓			✓			✓		✓		✓		
Brake linings	S/I			✓			✓			✓			✓		
Air filter element	R					✓			✓				✓		
Spark plugs ①②	R														
Lubricate front & rear ball joints	S/I				✓				✓				✓		
Engine coolant	R						✓				✓				
PCV valve	S/I								✓				✓		
Ignition cables ②③	R														
Camshaft timing belt ④	R														

R: Replace   S/I: Service or Inspect

① 4-cylinder: every 30,000 miles.

② 6-cylinder: 100,000 miles.

③ 4-cylinder: 60,000 miles.

④ Replace at 105,000 miles for normal service; replace at 102,000 miles for severe service

FREQUENT OPERATION MAINTENANCE (SEVERE SERVICE)

If a vehicle is operated under any of the following conditions it is considered severe service:

- Extremely dusty areas.

- 50% or more of the vehicle operation is in 32°C (90°F) or higher temperatures, or constant operation in temperatures below 0°C (32°F).

- Prolonged idling (vehicle operation in stop and go traffic).

- Frequent short running periods (engine does not warm to normal operating temperatures).

- Police, taxi, delivery usage or trailer towing usage.

Oil & oil filter change: change every 3000 miles.

Rotate tires every 6000 miles.

Brake linings: check every 12,000 miles.

Air filter element: change every 15,000 miles.

Automatic transaxle fluid: service or inspect every 15,000 miles.

PCV valve: check every 30,000 miles.

Engine coolant, replace at 36,000, 51,000 & 81,000 miles.

93061C21

For brake related suspension and axle service, refer to the model specific sections of this manual

SCHEDULED MAINTENANCE INTERVALS
DAIMLERCHRYSLER CORPORATION
CHRYSLER CIRRUS, SEBRING CONVERTIBLE
DODGE STRATUS, PLYMOUTH BREEZE

The following should be used as a guide when determining the amount of work required for a particular service.
In estimating how long a particular Scheduled Maintenance Service should take, please observe the following:

- Labor Time is time based on field research and data supplied by the vehicle manufacturer.
- Labor time operations are given in hours and tenths of an hour.
- All labor operations are to be used as a guide.

Mechanic Skill Level Codes:
(A) PRECISION: Highly skilled with multiple certification.
(B) GENERAL: Normally skilled with certification.
(C) MAINTENANCE: Semi-skilled working on certification.

	LABOR TIME		LABOR TIME		LABOR TIME
7500 Mile Service (C)		**37500 Mile Service (C)**		**75000 Mile Service (C)**	
All Models	1.3	All Models	1.3	All Models	1.9
15000 Mile Service (C)		**45000 Mile Service (B)**		**82500 Mile Service (C)**	
All Models	1.4	All Models	2.1	All Models	1.3
22500 Mile Service (C)		**52500 Mile Service (C)**		**90000 Mile Service (B)**	
All Models	1.6	All Models	1.3	All Models	3.1
30000 Mile Service (B)		**60000 Mile Service (B)**		**97500 Mile Service (C)**	
All Models	2.6	All Models	3.6	All Models	1.3
		67500 Mile Service (C)			
		All Models	1.6		

93061C22

CHRYSLER CORP.
Chrysler 300M • Concorde • LHS • Dodge Intrepid • Eagle Vision

ENGINE AND VEHICLE IDENTIFICATION

		Engine						Model Year	
Code ①	Liters (cc)	Cu. In.	Cyl.	Fuel Sys.	Engine Type	Eng. Mfg.		Code ②	Year
F	3.5 (3518)	215	V6	MFI	SOHC	Chrysler		V	1997
G	3.5 (3518)	215	V6	MFI	SOHC	Chrysler		W	1998
J	3.2 (3231)	195	V6	MFI	SOHC	Chrysler		X	1999
R	2.7 (2736)	167	V6	MFI	DOHC	Chrysler		Y	2000
T	3.3 (3301)	201	V6	MFI	OHV	Chrysler		1	2001
U	2.7 (2736) ③	167	V6	MFI	DOHC	Chrysler			
V	3.5 (3518) ④	215	V6	MFI	DOHC	Chrysler			

MFI: Multi-point Fuel Injection
DOHC: Double Overhead Camshafts
SOHC: Single Overhead Camshaft
OHV: Overhead Valve

① 8th position of the Vehicle Identification Number (VIN)
② 10th position of VIN
③ 120 amp alternator
④ Magnum

93061C23

GENERAL ENGINE SPECIFICATIONS
All measurements are given in inches.

Year	Model	Engine Displacement Liters (cc)	Engine Series (ID/VIN)	Fuel System	Net Horsepower @ rpm	Net Torque @ rpm (ft. lbs.)	Bore x Stroke (in.)	Compression Ratio	Oil Pressure @ rpm
1997	Concorde	3.3 (3300)	T	MFI	161@5300	181@3200	3.66x3.19	8.9:1	30-80@3000
		3.5 (3518)	F	MFI	214@5800	221@3100	3.78x3.19	9.6:1	25-80@3000
	Intrepid	3.3 (3300)	T	MFI	161@5300	181@3200	3.66x3.19	8.9:1	30-80@3000
		3.5 (3518)	F	MFI	214@5800	221@3100	3.78x3.19	9.6:1	25-80@3000
	LHS	3.5 (3518)	F	MFI	214@5800	221@3100	3.78x3.19	9.6:1	25-80@3000
	Vision	3.3 (3300)	T	MFI	161@5300	181@3200	3.66x3.19	8.9:1	30-80@3000
		3.5 (3518)	F	MFI	214@5800	221@3100	3.78x3.19	9.6:1	25-80@3000
1998	Concorde	2.7 (2736)	R	MFI	200@5800	190@4850	3.39x3.09	9.6:1	25-105@3000
		3.2 (3231)	J	MFI	225@6300	225@3800	3.62x3.19	9.5:1	25-105@3000
	Intrepid	2.7 (2736)	R	MFI	200@5800	190@4850	3.39x3.09	9.6:1	25-105@3000
		3.2 (3231)	J	MFI	225@6300	225@3800	3.62x3.19	9.5:1	25-105@3000
1999	300M	3.5 (3518)	G	MFI	253@6400	255@3950	3.78x3.19	9.6:1	25-105@3000
	Concorde	2.7 (2736)	R	MFI	200@5800	190@4850	3.39x3.09	9.6:1	25-105@3000
		3.2 (3231)	J	MFI	225@6300	225@3800	3.62x3.19	9.5:1	25-105@3000
	Intrepid	2.7 (2736)	R	MFI	200@5800	190@4850	3.39x3.09	9.6:1	25-105@3000
		3.2 (3231)	J	MFI	225@6300	225@3800	3.62x3.19	9.5:1	25-105@3000
	LHS	3.5 (3518)	G	MFI	253@6400	255@3950	3.78x3.19	9.6:1	25-105@3000
2000-01	300M	3.5 (3518)	G	MFI	253@6400	255@3950	3.78x3.19	9.6:1	25-105@3000
	Concorde	2.7 (2736)	R	MFI	200@5800	190@4850	3.39x3.09	9.6:1	25-105@3000
		2.7 (2736)	U	MFI	200@5800	190@4850	3.39x3.09	9.6:1	25-105@3000
		3.5 (3518)	V	MFI	253@6400	255@3950	3.78x3.19	9.6:1	25-105@3000
		3.2 (3231)	J	MFI	225@6300	225@3800	3.62x3.19	9.5:1	25-105@3000
	Intrepid	2.7 (2736)	R	MFI	200@5800	190@4850	3.39x3.09	9.6:1	25-105@3000
		2.7 (2736)	U	MFI	200@5800	190@4850	3.39x3.09	9.6:1	25-105@3000
		3.5 (3518)	V	MFI	253@6400	255@3950	3.78x3.19	9.6:1	25-105@3000
		3.2 (3231)	J	MFI	225@6300	225@3800	3.62x3.19	9.5:1	25-105@3000
	LHS	3.5 (3518)	G	MFI	253@6400	255@3950	3.78x3.19	9.6:1	25-105@3000

MFI: Multi-point Fuel Injection

93061C24

Refer to the model specific sections for driveline service procedures

ENGINE TUNE-UP SPECIFICATIONS

Year	Engine Displacement Liters (cc)	Engine ID/VIN	Spark Plug Gap (in.)	Ignition Timing (deg.)	Fuel Pump (psi)	Idle Speed (rpm)	Valve Clearance Intake	Valve Clearance Exhaust
1997	3.3 (3301)	T	0.048-0.053	①	55 ②	①	HYD	HYD
	3.5 (3518)	F	0.033-0.038	①	48 ②	①	HYD	HYD
1998	2.7 (2736)	R	0.048-0.053	①	49	①	HYD	HYD
	3.2 (3231)	J	0.048-0.053	①	49	①	HYD	HYD
1999	2.7 (2736)	R	0.048-0.053	①	49	①	HYD	HYD
	3.2 (3231)	J	0.048-0.053	①	49	①	HYD	HYD
	3.5 (3518)	G	0.048-0.053	①	49	①	HYD	HYD
2000-01	2.7 (2736)	R	0.048-0.053	①	58	①	HYD	HYD
	2.7 (2736)	U	0.048-0.053	①	58	①	HYD	HYD
	3.5 (3518)	V	0.048-0.053	①	58	①	HYD	HYD
	3.2 (3231)	J	0.048-0.053	①	58	①	HYD	HYD
	3.5 (3518)	G	0.048-0.053	①	58	①	HYD	HYD

NOTE: The Vehicle Emission Control Information label often reflects specification changes made during production. The label figures must be used if they differ from those in this chart.

HYD: Hydraulic

① Controlled by the Powertrain Control Module (PCM)

② This reading measured with vacuum hose disconnected from fuel pressure regulator

93061C25

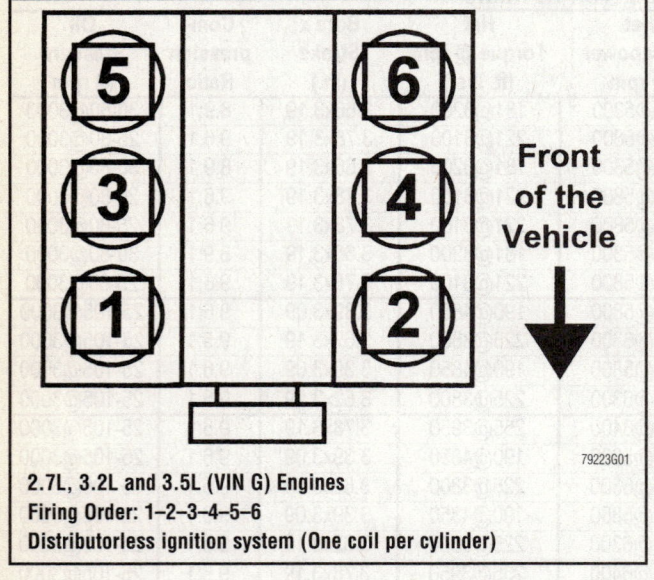

2.7L, 3.2L and 3.5L (VIN G) Engines
Firing Order: 1–2–3–4–5–6
Distributorless ignition system (One coil per cylinder)

79223G01

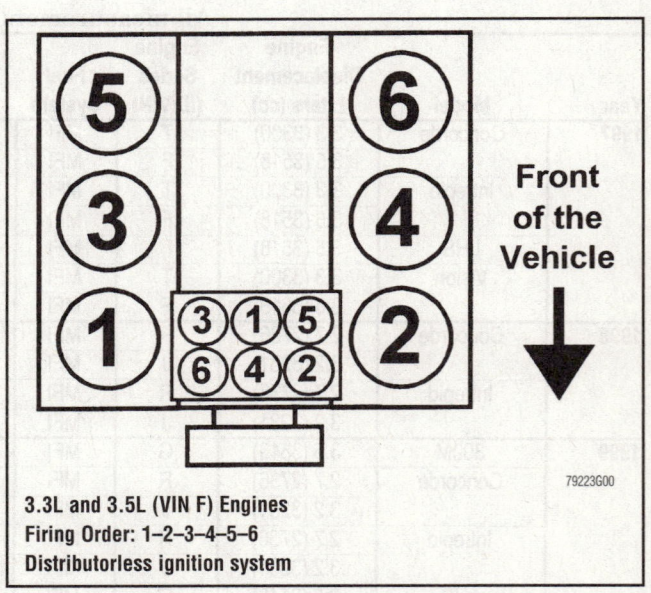

3.3L and 3.5L (VIN F) Engines
Firing Order: 1–2–3–4–5–6
Distributorless ignition system

79223G00

CAPACITIES

Year	Model	Engine Displacement Liters (cc)	Engine ID/VIN	Engine Oil with Filter (qts.)	Auto. Transmission (pts.) ①	Front Drive Axle (pts.)	Fuel Tank (gal.)	Cooling System (qts.)
1997	Concorde	3.5 (3518)	F	5.5	19.7	2.0	18.0	11.8
	Intrepid	3.3 (3300)	T	5.0	19.8	2.0	18.0	10.2
		3.5 (3518)	F	5.5	19.8	2.0	18.0	11.8
	LHS	3.5 (3518)	F	5.5	19.8	2.0	18.0	11.8
	Vision	3.3 (3301)	T	5.0	19.8	2.0	18.0	10.2
1998	Concorde	2.7 (2736)	R	5.0	19.8	2.0	18.0	8.0
		3.2 (3231)	J	5.0	19.8	2.0	18.0	8.0
	Intrepid	2.7 (2736)	R	5.0	19.8	2.0	18.0	8.0
		3.2 (3231)	J	5.0	19.8	2.0	18.0	8.0
1999	300M	3.5 (3518)	G	5.0	19.8	2.0	18.0	9.4
	Concorde	2.7 (2736)	R	5.0	19.8	2.0	18.0	9.4
		3.2 (3231)	J	5.0	19.8	2.0	18.0	9.4
	Intrepid	2.7 (2736)	R	5.0	19.8	2.0	18.0	9.4
		3.2 (3231)	J	5.0	19.8	2.0	18.0	9.4
	LHS	3.5 (3518)	G	5.0	19.8	2.0	18.0	9.4
2000-01	300M	3.5 (3518)	G	5.0	19.8	2.0	18.0	9.4
	Concorde	2.7 (2736)	R	5.0	19.8	2.0	18.0	9.4
		2.7 (2736)	U	5.0	19.8	2.0	18.0	9.4
		3.5 (3518)	V	5.0	19.8	2.0	18.0	9.4
		3.2 (3231)	J	5.0	19.8	2.0	18.0	9.4
	Intrepid	2.7 (2736)	R	5.0	19.8	2.0	18.0	9.4
		2.7 (2736)	U	5.0	19.8	2.0	18.0	9.4
		3.5 (3518)	V	5.0	19.8	2.0	18.0	9.4
		3.2 (3231)	J	5.0	19.8	2.0	18.0	9.4
	LHS	3.5 (3518)	G	5.0	19.8	2.0	18.0	9.4

NOTE: All capacities are approximate. Add fluid gradually and ensure a proper fluid level is obtained.

① Overhaul fill capacity with torque converter empty
  Estimated service fill: 9 pts.

93061C26

For exhaust manifold replacement procedures, see the model specific sections of this manual

VALVE SPECIFICATIONS

Year	Engine Displacement Liters (cc)	Engine ID/VIN	Seat Angle (deg.)	Face Angle (deg.)	Spring Test Pressure (lbs. @ in.)	Spring Installed Height (in.)	Stem-to-Guide Clearance (in.)		Stem Diameter (in.)	
							Intake	Exhaust	Intake	Exhaust
1997	3.5 (3518)	F	45-45.5	44.5-45	①	1.496	0.0009-0.0026	0.0020-0.0037	0.2730-0.2737	0.2719-0.2726
	3.3 (3301)	T	45-45.5	44.5-45	②	1.622-1.681	0.0010-0.0100	0.0020-0.0060	0.3120-0.3130	0.3112-0.3119
1998	3.2 (3231)	J	45-45.5	44.5-45	③	1.496	0.0009-0.0026	0.0020-0.0037	0.2730-0.2737	0.2719-0.2726
	2.7 (2736)	R	44.5-45	45-45.5	④	1.496	0.0009-0.0026	0.0020-0.0033	0.2337-0.2344	0.2326-0.2333
1999	3.5 (3518)	G	45-45.5	44.5-45	③	1.496	0.0009-0.0026	0.0020-0.0037	0.2730-0.2737	0.2719-0.2726
	3.2 (3231)	J	45-45.5	44.5-45	③	1.496	0.0009-0.0026	0.0020-0.0037	0.2730-0.2737	0.2719-0.2726
	2.7 (2736)	R	44.5-45	45-45.5	④	1.496	0.0009-0.0026	0.0020-0.0033	0.2337-0.2344	0.2326-0.2333
2000-01	3.5 (3518)	G	45-45.5	44.5-45	⑤	1.496	0.0009-0.0026	0.0020-0.0037	0.2730-0.2737	0.2719-0.2726
	3.2 (3231)	J	45-45.5	44.5-45	⑤	1.496	0.0009-0.0026	0.0020-0.0037	0.2730-0.2737	0.2719-0.2726
	2.7 (2736)	R	44.5-45	45-45.5	④	1.496	0.0009-0.0026	0.0020-0.0033	0.2337-0.2344	0.2326-0.2333
	2.7 (2736)	U	44.5-45	45-45.5	④	1.496	0.0009-0.0026	0.0020-0.0033	0.2337-0.2344	0.2326-0.2333
	3.5 (3518)	V	45-45.5	44.5-45	⑤	1.496	0.0009-0.0026	0.0020-0.0037	0.2730-0.2737	0.2719-0.2726

① Intake: 201.7-218.3 lbs.@1.1752 in.
Exhaust: 158.5-171.5 lbs.@1.239 in.

② Intake: 95-100 lbs.@1.570 in. valve closed
Exhaust: 207-229 lbs.@1.169 in. valve closed

③ Intake: 69.5-80.5 lbs.@1.496 in. valve closed
Intake: 188.0-204.0 lbs.@1.1594 in. valve opened
Exhaust: 56-64 lbs.@1.4961 in. valve closed
Exhaust: 124-136 lbs.@1.239 in. valve opened

④ 56-64 lbs.@ 1.496 in. valve closed
Intake: 147.9-162.1 lbs.@1.1417 in. valve opened
Exhaust: 138.0-150.8 lbs.@1.811 in. valve opened

⑤ Intake: 69.5-80.5 lbs.@1.496 in. valve closed
Intake: 188.0-204.0 lbs.@1.1594 in. valve opened
Exhaust: 71-79 lbs.@1.4961 in. valve closed
Exhaust: 130-144 lbs.@1.239 in. valve opened

93061C27

CRANKSHAFT AND CONNECTING ROD SPECIFICATIONS
All measurements are given in inches.

Year	Engine Displacement Liters (cc)	Engine ID/VIN	Crankshaft				Connecting Rod		
			Main Brg. Journal Dia.	Main Brg. Oil Clearance	Shaft End-play	Thrust on No.	Journal Diameter	Oil Clearance	Side Clearance
1997	3.3 (3300)	T	2.5190-2.5200	0.0007-0.0028	0.0040-0.0090	2	2.2830-2.2840	0.0008-0.0034	0.0050-0.0150
	3.5 (3518)	F	2.5185-2.5195	0.0007-0.0022	0.0040-0.0120	2	2.2830-2.2840	0.0008-0.0030	0.0050-0.0150
1998	2.7 (2736)	R	2.4997-2.5004	0.0014-0.0021	0.017 max.	3	2.1067-2.1060	0.0010-0.0026	0.0052-0.0150
	3.5 (3518)	J	2.5190-2.5200	0.0007-0.0028	0.0040-0.0120	2	2.2820-2.2830	0.0008-0.0034	0.0050-0.0157
1999	2.7 (2736)	R	2.4997-2.5004	0.0014-0.0021	0.017 max.	3	2.1067-2.1060	0.0010-0.0026	0.0052-0.0150
	3.2 (3231)	J	2.5190-2.5200	0.0007-0.0034	0.0040-0.0120	2	2.2830-2.2840	0.0008-0.0034	0.0050-0.0150
	3.5 (3518)	G	2.5190-2.5200	0.0004-0.0022	0.0040-0.0120	2	2.2830-2.2840	0.0008-0.0034	0.0050-0.0150
2000-01	2.7 (2736)	R	2.4997-2.5004	0.0014-0.0021	0.017 max.	3	2.1067-2.1060	0.0010-0.0026	0.0052-0.0150
	2.7 (2736)	U	2.4997-2.5004	0.0014-0.0021	0.017 max.	3	2.1067-2.1060	0.0010-0.0026	0.0052-0.0150
	3.5 (3518)	V	2.5190-2.5200	0.0004-0.0022	0.0040-0.0120	2	2.2830-2.2840	0.0008-0.0034	0.0050-0.0150
	3.2 (3231)	J	2.5190-2.5200	0.0007-0.0034	0.0040-0.0120	2	2.2830-2.2840	0.0008-0.0034	0.0050-0.0150
	3.5 (3518)	G	2.5190-2.5200	0.0004-0.0022	0.0040-0.0120	2	2.2830-2.2840	0.0008-0.0034	0.0050-0.0150

93061C28

Refer to the model specific sections for cooling system service procedures

PISTON AND RING SPECIFICATIONS
All measurements are given in inches.

Year	Engine Displacement Liters (cc)	Engine ID/VIN	Piston Clearance	Ring Gap			Ring Side Clearance		
				Top Compression	Bottom Compression	Oil Control	Top Compression	Bottom Compression	Oil Control
1997	3.3 (3300)	T	0.0009-0.0022	0.012-0.022	0.012-0.022	0.010-0.040	0.0012-0.0037	0.0012-0.0037	0.0005-0.0089
	3.5 (3518)	F	0.0003-0.0018	0.008-0.014	0.012-0.022	0.010-0.030	0.0012-0.0031	0.0012-0.0031	0.0019-0.0077
1998	2.7 (2736)	R	0.0001-0.0016	0.008-0.014	0.0146-0.0249	0.010-0.030	0.0016-0.0031	0.0016-0.0031	0.0025-0.0082
	3.5 (3518)	J	0.0003-0.0018	0.008-0.014	0.0087-0.0193	0.010-0.030	0.0016-0.0031	0.0016-0.0031	0.0015-0.0073
1999	2.7 (2736)	R	0.0001-0.0016	0.008-0.014	0.0146-0.0249	0.010-0.030	0.0016-0.0031	0.0016-0.0031	0.0025-0.0082
	3.2 (3231)	J	0.0003-0.0018	0.008-0.014	0.0087-0.0193	0.010-0.030	0.0016-0.0031	0.0016-0.0031	0.0015-0.0073
	3.5 (3518)	G	0.0003-0.0018	0.008-0.014	0.0087-0.0193	0.010-0.030	0.0016-0.0031	0.0016-0.0031	0.0015-0.0073
2000-01	2.7 (2736)	R	0.0001-0.0016	0.008-0.014	0.0146-0.0249	0.010-0.030	0.0016-0.0031	0.0016-0.0031	0.0025-0.0082
	2.7 (2736)	U	0.0003-0.0018	0.008-0.014	0.0146-0.0249	0.010-0.030	0.0016-0.0031	0.0016-0.0031	0.0025-0.0082
	3.5 (3518)	V	0.0003-0.0018	0.008-0.014	0.0087-0.0193	0.010-0.030	0.0016-0.0031	0.0016-0.0031	0.0015-0.0073
	3.2 (3231)	J	0.0003-0.0018	0.008-0.014	0.0087-0.0193	0.010-0.030	0.0016-0.0031	0.0016-0.0031	0.0015-0.0073
	3.5 (3518)	G	0.0003-0.0018	0.008-0.014	0.0087-0.0193	0.010-0.030	0.0016-0.0031	0.0016-0.0031	0.0015-0.0073

93061C29

TORQUE SPECIFICATIONS
All readings in ft. lbs.

Year	Engine Displacement Liters (cc)	Engine ID/VIN	Cylinder Head Bolts	Main Bearing Bolts	Rod Bearing Bolts	Crankshaft Damper Bolts	Flywheel Bolts	Manifold Intake	Manifold Exhaust	Spark Plugs	Lug Nuts
1997	3.5 (3518)	F	①	②	③	85	75	21	17	20	100
	3.3 (3301)	T	④	⑤	③	40	75	17	17	20	100
1998	3.2 (3231)	J	①	⑥	③	75	75	⑦	200 ⑧	20	100
	2.7 (2736)	R	⑨	⑥	⑩	125	75	105 ⑧	200 ⑧	15	100
1999	3.5 (3518)	G	①	⑥	③	70	75	⑦	200 ⑧	20	100
	3.2 (3231)	J	①	⑥	③	70	75	⑦	200 ⑧	20	100
	2.7 (2736)	R	⑨	⑥	⑩	125	75	105 ⑧	200 ⑧	15	100
2000-01	3.5 (3518)	G	①	⑥	③	70	70	⑦	200 ⑧	20	100
	3.2 (3231)	J	①	⑥	③	70	70	⑦	200 ⑧	20	100
	2.7 (2736)	R	⑨	⑥	⑩	125	70	105 ⑧	200 ⑧	15	100
	2.7 (2736)	U	⑨	⑥	⑩	125	70	105 ⑧	200 ⑧	15	100
	3.5 (3518)	V	①	⑥	③	70	70	⑦	200 ⑧	20	100

① Step 1: 45 ft. lbs.
　Step 2: 65 ft. lbs.
　Step 3: 65 ft. lbs.
　Step 4: Plus 1/4 turn
　Final torque should be over 90 ft. lbs.

② Main cap bolts: 30 ft. lbs. plus 1/4 turn
　Main cap tie bolts: 40 ft. lbs.

③ Step 1: 40 ft. lbs.
　Step 2: Plus 1/4 turn

④ Step 1: 45 ft. lbs.
　Step 2: 65 ft. lbs.
　Step 3: 65 ft. lbs.
　Step 4: Plus 1/4 turn
　Torque small bolt in rear of cylinder head to 25 ft. lbs.

⑤ Step 1: 30 ft. lbs.
　Step 2: Plus 1/4 turn

⑥ Main cap inside bolts: 15 ft. lbs. plus 1/4 turn
　Main cap outside bolts: 20 ft. lbs. plus 1/4 turn
　Main cap tie bolts: 250 inch lbs.

⑦ M8 bolts: 250 inch lbs.
　M6 bolts: 105 inch lbs.

⑧ Inch lbs.

⑨ Step 1: 35 ft. lbs.
　Step 2: 55 ft. lbs.
　Step 3: 55 ft. lbs.
　Step 4: Plus 90 degrees
　Step 5: M8 bolts (3 front) 250 inch lbs.

⑩ Step 1: 20 ft. lbs.
　Step 2: Plus 1/4 turn

93061C30

For complete service labor times order Nichols' Chilton Labor Guide Manual

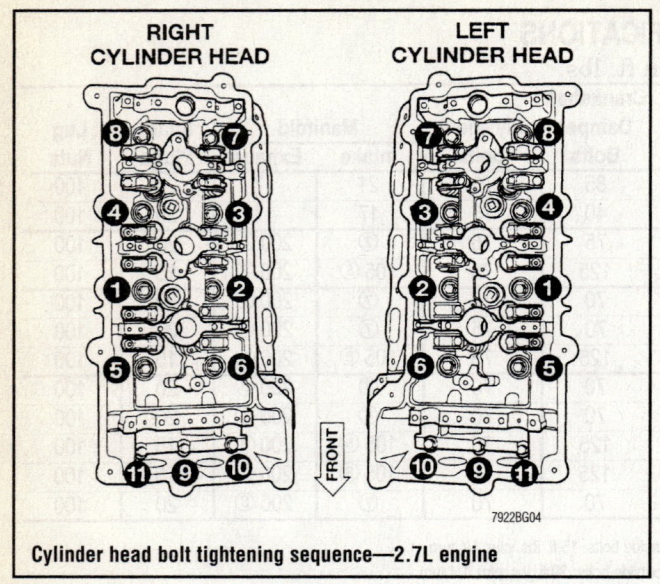

Cylinder head bolt tightening sequence—2.7L engine

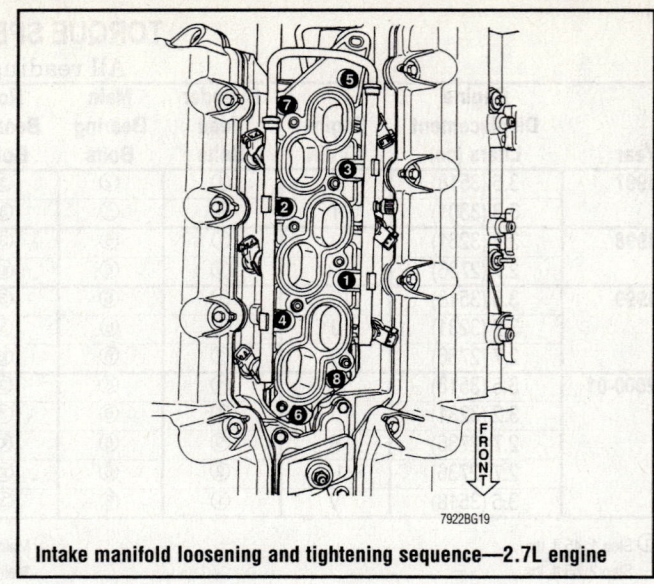

Intake manifold loosening and tightening sequence—2.7L engine

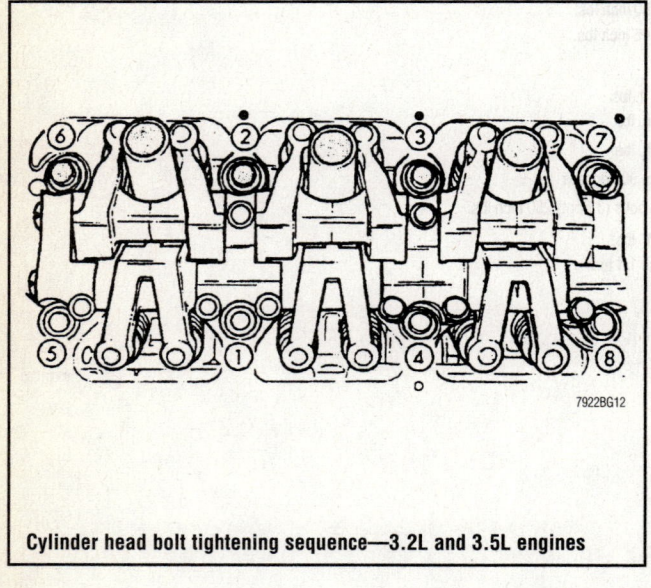

Cylinder head bolt tightening sequence—3.2L and 3.5L engines

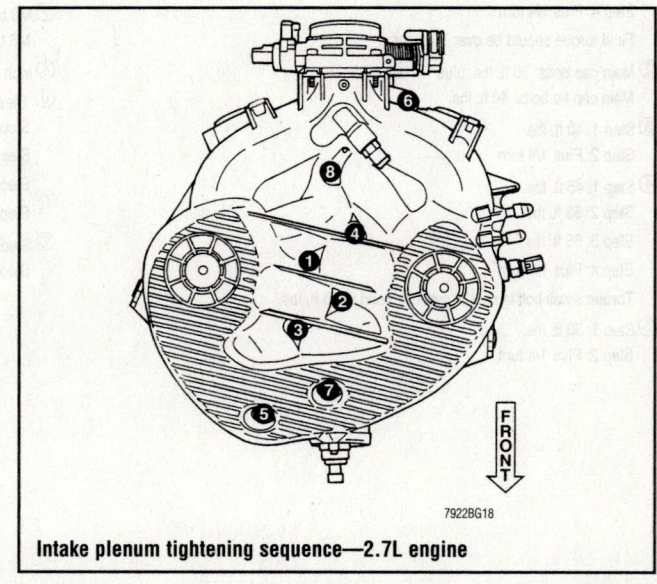

Intake plenum tightening sequence—2.7L engine

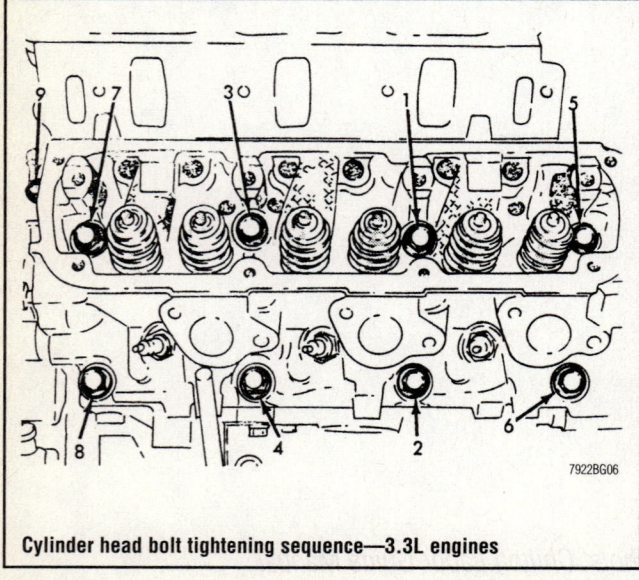

Cylinder head bolt tightening sequence—3.3L engines

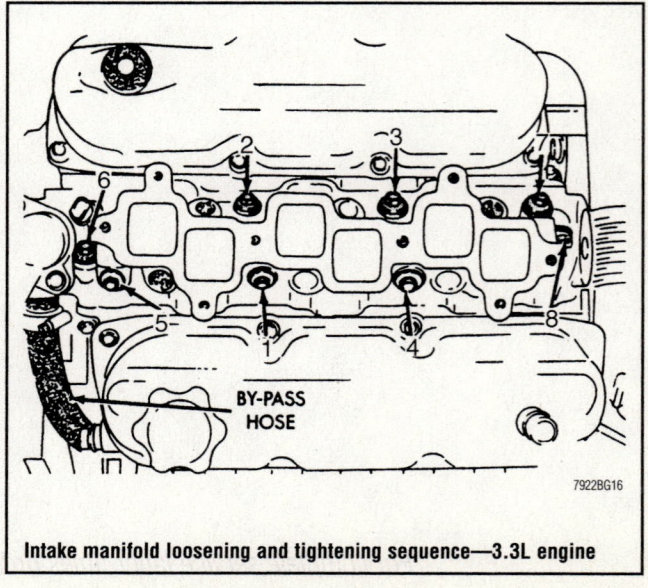

Intake manifold loosening and tightening sequence—3.3L engine

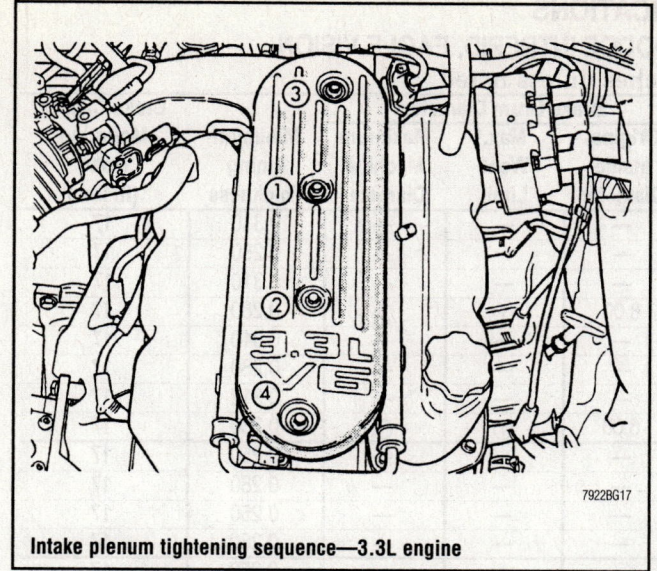

Intake plenum tightening sequence—3.3L engine

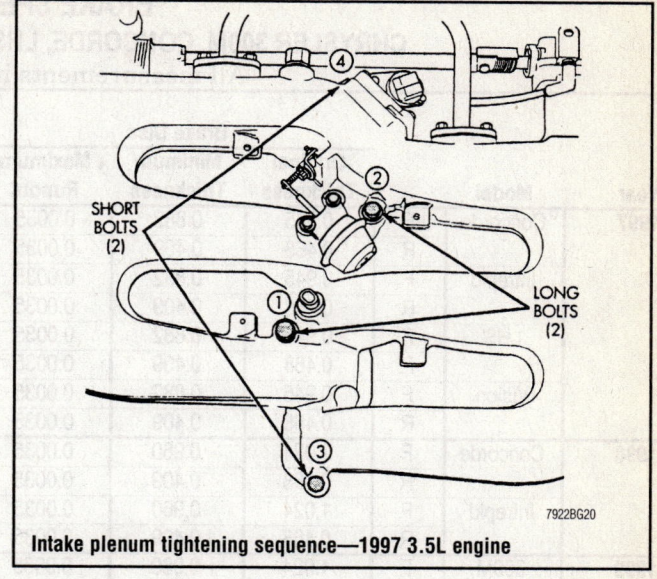

Intake plenum tightening sequence—1997 3.5L engine

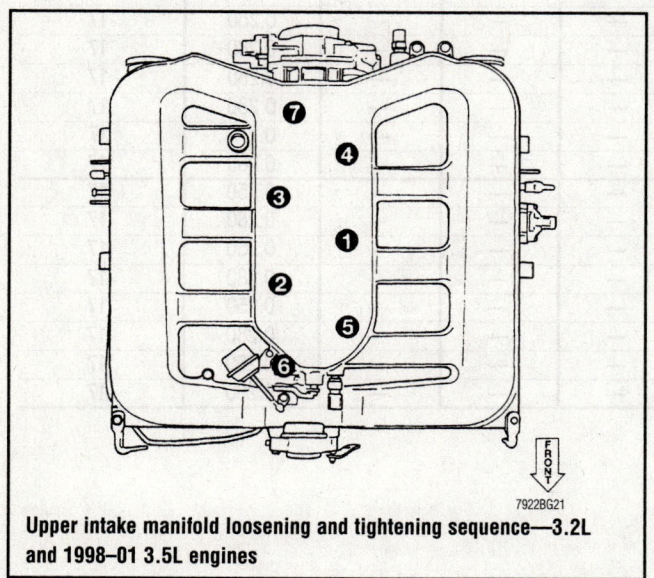

Upper intake manifold loosening and tightening sequence—3.2L and 1998–01 3.5L engines

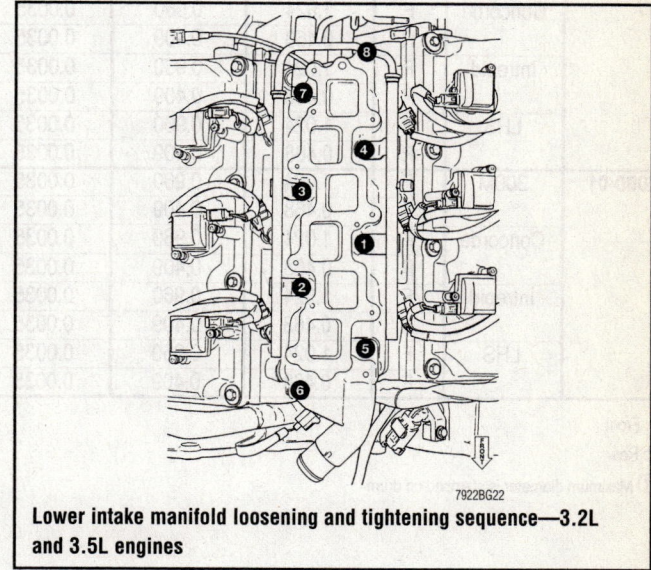

Lower intake manifold loosening and tightening sequence—3.2L and 3.5L engines

Timing chain and gear service is covered in the model specific sections of this manual

BRAKE SPECIFICATIONS
CHRYSLER 300M, CONCORDE, LHS, DODGE INTREPID, EAGLE VISION
All measurements in inches unless noted

| Year | Model | | Brake Disc | | | Brake Drum Diameter | | | Minimum Lining Thickness | Brake Caliper Mounting Bolts (ft. lbs.) |
			Original Thickness	Minimum Thickness	Maximum Runout	Original Inside Diameter	Max. Wear Limit	Maximum Machine Diameter		
1997	Concorde	F	0.945	0.882	0.0035	—	—	—	0.310	17
		R	0.468	0.409	0.0035	—	—	—	0.280	17
	Intrepid	F	0.945	0.882	0.0035	—	—	—	0.310	17
		R	0.468	0.409	0.0035	8.00	①	①	0.280	17
	LHS	F	0.945	0.882	0.0035	—	—	—	0.310	17
		R	0.468	0.409	0.0035	—	—	—	0.280	17
	Vision	F	0.945	0.882	0.0035	—	—	—	0.312	17
		R	0.468	0.409	0.0035	8.00	①	①	0.280	17
1998	Concorde	F	1.024	0.960	0.0035	—	—	—	0.250	17
		R	0.468	0.409	0.0035	—	—	—	0.280	17
	Intrepid	F	1.024	0.960	0.0035	—	—	—	0.250	17
		R	0.468	0.409	0.0035	—	—	—	0.280	17
1999	300M	F	1.024	0.960	0.0035	—	—	—	0.250	17
		R	0.468	0.409	0.0035	—	—	—	0.280	17
	Concorde	F	1.024	0.960	0.0035	—	—	—	0.250	17
		R	0.468	0.409	0.0035	—	—	—	0.280	17
	Intrepid	F	1.024	0.960	0.0035	—	—	—	0.250	17
		R	0.468	0.409	0.0035	—	—	—	0.280	17
	LHS	F	1.024	0.960	0.0035	—	—	—	0.250	17
		R	0.468	0.409	0.0035	—	—	—	0.280	17
2000-01	300M	F	1.024	0.960	0.0035	—	—	—	0.250	17
		R	0.468	0.409	0.0035	—	—	—	0.280	17
	Concorde	F	1.024	0.960	0.0035	—	—	—	0.250	17
		R	0.468	0.409	0.0035	—	—	—	0.280	17
	Intrepid	F	1.024	0.960	0.0035	—	—	—	0.250	17
		R	0.468	0.409	0.0035	—	—	—	0.280	17
	LHS	F	1.024	0.960	0.0035	—	—	—	0.250	17
		R	0.468	0.409	0.0035	—	—	—	0.280	17

F: Front

R: Rear

① Maximum diameter is stamped on drum

93061C31

SCHEDULED MAINTENANCE INTERVALS
(CHRYSLER 300M, CONCORDE, LHS, DODGE INTREPID & EAGLE VISION)

TO BE SERVICED	TYPE OF SERVICE	VEHICLE MILEAGE INTERVAL (x1000)											
		7.5	15	22.5	30	37.5	45	52.5	60	67.5	75	82.5	90	97.5
Engine oil & filter	R	✓	✓	✓	✓	✓	✓	✓	✓	✓	✓	✓	✓	✓
Exhaust system	S/I	✓	✓	✓	✓	✓	✓	✓	✓	✓	✓	✓	✓	✓
Brake hoses	S/I	✓	✓	✓	✓	✓	✓	✓	✓	✓	✓	✓	✓	✓
CV joints & front suspension components	S/I	✓	✓	✓	✓	✓	✓	✓	✓	✓	✓	✓	✓	✓
Rotate tires	S/I	✓	✓	✓	✓	✓	✓	✓	✓	✓	✓	✓	✓	✓
Coolant level, hoses & clamps	S/I	✓	✓	✓	✓	✓	✓	✓	✓	✓	✓	✓	✓	✓
Accessory drive belts	S/I		✓				✓		✓		✓		✓	
Brake linings	S/I		✓	✓				✓	✓				✓	
Spark plugs	R				✓				✓				✓	
Air filter element	R				✓				✓				✓	
Lubricate steering linkage & tie rod ends	S/I				✓				✓				✓	
Engine coolant	R						✓				✓			
PCV valve	S/I								✓				✓	
Ignition cables	R								✓					
Camshaft timing belt	R								✓					

R: Replace   S/I: Service or Inspect

FREQUENT OPERATION MAINTENANCE (SEVERE SERVICE)

If a vehicle is operated under any of the following conditions it is considered severe service:

- Extremely dusty areas.
- 50% or more of the vehicle operation is in 32°C (90°F) or higher temperatures, or constant operation in temperatures below 0°C (32°F).
- Prolonged idling (vehicle operation in stop and go traffic).
- Frequent short running periods (engine does not warm to normal operating temperatures).
- Police, taxi, delivery usage or trailer towing usage.

CV joints & front suspension components: check every 3000 miles.

Oil & oil filter change: change every 3000 miles.

Rotate tires every 3000 miles.

Brake linings: check every 9000 miles.

Air filter element: change every 15,000 miles.

Automatic transaxle fluid: change every 15,000 miles.

Differential fluid: change every 15,000 miles.

Tie rod ends & steering linkage: lubricate every 15,000 miles.

PCV valve: check every 30,000 miles.

93061C32

Ignition system service is covered in the model specific sections of this manual

SCHEDULED MAINTENANCE INTERVALS
DAIMLERCHRYSLER CORPORATION
CHRYSLER 300M, CONCORDE, LHS
DODGE INTREPID, EAGLE VISION

The following should be used as a guide when determining the amount of work required for a particular service.
In estimating how long a particular Scheduled Maintenance Service should take, please observe the following:

- Labor Time is time based on field research and data supplied by the vehicle manufacturer.
- Labor time operations are given in hours and tenths of an hour.
- All labor operations are to be used as a guide.

Mechanic Skill Level Codes:
(A) PRECISION: Highly skilled with multiple certification.
(B) GENERAL: Normally skilled with certification.
(C) MAINTENANCE: Semi-skilled working on certification.

	LABOR TIME		LABOR TIME		LABOR TIME
7500 Mile Service (C)		**45000 Mile Service (B)**		**75000 Mile Service (C)**	
All Models	1.3	All Models	2.4	All Models	1.9
15000 Mile Service (C)		**52500 Mile Service (C)**		**82500 Mile Service (C)**	
All Models	1.9	All Models	1.3	All Models	1.3
22500 Mile Service (C)		**60000 Mile Service (B)**		**90000 Mile Service (B)**	
All Models	1.8	All Models	3.7	All Models	3.5
30000 Mile Service (B)		*Replace timing belt add*	3.6	**97500 Mile Service (B)**	
All Models	2.8	**67500 Mile Service (C)**		All Models	1.3
37500 Mile Service (C)		All Models	1.8		
All Models	1.3				

93061C33

CHRYSLER CORP.
Dodge/Plymouth Neon

ENGINE AND VEHICLE IDENTIFICATION

				Engine					
Code ①	Liters	Cu. In. (cc)	Cyl.	Fuel Sys.	Engine Type	Eng. Mfg.		Code ②	Year
C	2.0	122 (1996)	4	MFI	SOHC	Chrysler		V	1997
Y	2.0	122 (1996)	4	MFI	DOHC	Chrysler		W	1998

Model Year	
Code ②	Year
V	1997
W	1998
X	1999
Y	2000
1	2001

MFI: Multi-point Fuel Injection

SOHC: Single Overhead Camshaft

DOHC: Double Overhead Camshaft

① 8th position of VIN

② 10th position of VIN

93061C34

GENERAL ENGINE SPECIFICATIONS
All measurements are given in inches.

Year	Model	Engine Displacement Liters (cc)	Engine Series (ID/VIN)	Fuel System	Net Horsepower @ rpm	Net Torque @ rpm (ft. lbs.)	Bore x Stroke (in.)	Compression Ratio	Oil Pressure @ rpm
1997	Neon	2.0 (1996)	C	MFI	132@6000	129@5000	3.44x3.26	9.8:1	25-80@3000
	Neon	2.0 (1996)	Y	MFI	150@4400	NA	3.44x3.26	9.6:1	25-80@3000
1998	Neon	2.0 (1996)	C	MFI	132@6000	129@5000	3.44x3.26	9.8:1	25-80@3000
	Neon	2.0 (1996)	Y	MFI	150@4400	NA	3.44x3.26	9.6:1	25-80@3000
1999	Neon	2.0 (1996)	C	MFI	132@6000	129@5000	3.44x3.26	9.8:1	25-80@3000
	Neon	2.0 (1996)	Y	MFI	150@4400	NA	3.44x3.26	9.6:1	25-80@3000
2000-01	Neon	2.0 (1996)	C	MFI	132@6000	129@5000	3.44x3.26	9.8:1	25-80@3000

NA: Not available

MFI: Multi-point Fuel Injection

SOHC: Single Overhead Camshaft

DOHC: Double Overhead Camshaft

93061C35

ENGINE TUNE-UP SPECIFICATIONS

Year	Engine Displacement Liters (cc)	Engine ID/VIN	Spark Plugs Gap (in.)	Ignition Timing (deg.)		Fuel Pump (psi)	Idle Speed (rpm)		Valve Clearance	
				MT	AT		MT	AT	In.	Ex.
1997	2.0 (1996)	C	0.035	①	①	48	②	②	HYD	HYD
	2.0 (1996)	Y	0.035	①	①	48	②	②	HYD	HYD
1998	2.0 (1996)	C	0.035	①	①	48	②	②	HYD	HYD
	2.0 (1996)	Y	0.035	①	①	48	②	②	HYD	HYD
1999	2.0 (1996)	C	0.035	①	①	48	②	②	HYD	HYD
	2.0 (1996)	Y	0.035	①	①	48	②	②	HYD	HYD
2000-01	2.0 (1996)	C	0.035	①	①	48	②	②	HYD	HYD

NOTE: The Vehicle Emission Control Information label often reflects specification changes made during production. The label figures must be used if they differ from those in this chart.

HYD : Hydraulic

① Refer to the Vehicle Emission Control Information label for correct timing specifications with a range of +/- 2 degrees
   Ignition timing cannot be adjusted. Base engine timing is set at TDC during assembly.

② Refer to Vehicle Emissions Control Information label for proper specification

93061C36

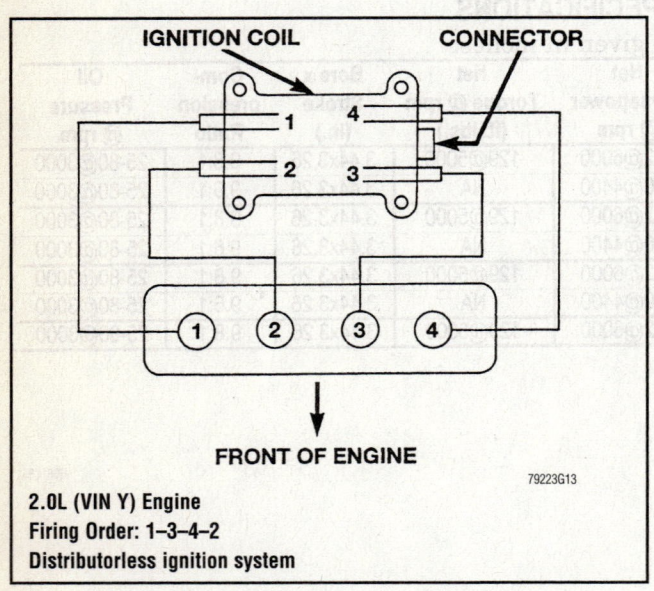

2.0L (VIN Y) Engine
Firing Order: 1–3–4–2
Distributorless ignition system

79223G13

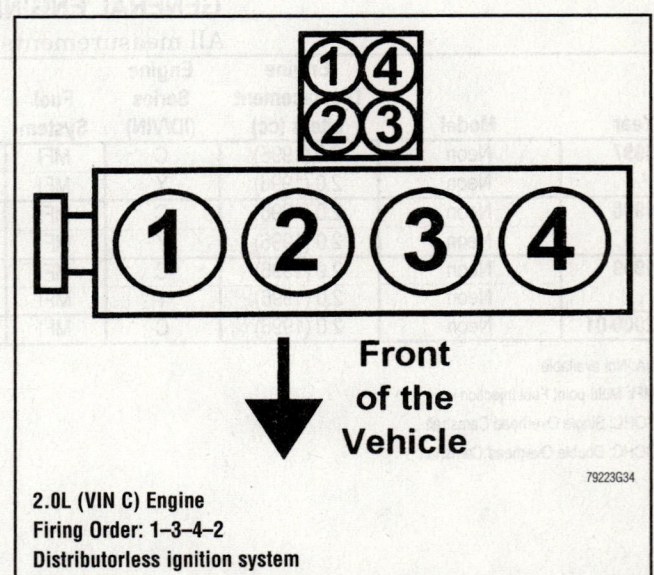

2.0L (VIN C) Engine
Firing Order: 1–3–4–2
Distributorless ignition system

79223G34

CAPACITIES

Year	Model	Engine Displacement Liters (cc)	Engine ID/VIN	Engine Oil with Filter (qts.)	Transmission (pts.)		Fuel Tank (gal.)	Cooling System (qts.)
					5-Spd	Auto.		
1997	Neon	2.0 (1996)	C	4.5	4.0-4.6	8.0	12.5	7.4
	Neon	2.0 (1996)	Y	4.5	4.0-4.6	8.0	12.5	7.4
1998	Neon	2.0 (1996)	C	4.5	4.0-4.6	8.0	12.5	7.4
	Neon	2.0 (1996)	Y	4.5	4.0-4.6	8.0	12.5	7.4
1999	Neon	2.0 (1996)	C	4.5	4.0-4.6	8.0	12.5	7.4
	Neon	2.0 (1996)	Y	4.5	4.0-4.6	8.0	12.5	7.4
2000-01	Neon	2.0 (1996)	C	4.5	4.0-4.6	8.0	12.5	6.5

NOTE: All capacities are approximate. Add fluid gradually and ensure a proper fluid level is obtained.

① Fill to bottom of fill hole

93061C37

VALVE SPECIFICATIONS

Year	Engine Displacement Liters (cc)	Engine ID/VIN	Seat Angle (deg.)	Face Angle (deg.)	Spring Test Pressure (lbs. @ in.)	Spring Installed Height (in.)	Stem-to-Guide Clearance (in.)		Stem Diameter (in.)	
							Intake	Exhaust	Intake	Exhaust
1997	2.0 (1996)	C	45	45-45.5	70@1.57	1.580	0.0018-0.0025	0.0029-0.0037	0.2340	0.2330
	2.0 (1996)	Y	44.5-45	45-45.5	55-60@1.49	1.490	0.0018-0.0025	0.0029-0.0037	0.2340	0.2330
1998	2.0 (1996)	C	45	45-45.5	70@1.57	1.580	0.0018-0.0025	0.0029-0.0037	0.2340	0.2330
	2.0 (1996)	Y	44.5-45	45-45.5	55-60@1.49	1.490	0.0018-0.0025	0.0029-0.0037	0.2340	0.2330
1999	2.0 (1996)	C	45	45-45.5	70@1.57	1.580	0.0018-0.0025	0.0029-0.0037	0.2340	0.2330
	2.0 (1996)	Y	44.5-45	45-45.5	55-60@1.49	1.490	0.0018-0.0025	0.0029-0.0037	0.2340	0.2330
2000-01	2.0 (1996)	C	45	45-45.5	70@1.57	1.580	0.0018-0.0025	0.0029-0.0037	0.2340	0.2330

93061C38

CRANKSHAFT AND CONNECTING ROD SPECIFICATIONS
All measurements are given in inches.

Year	Engine Displacement Liters (cc)	Engine ID/VIN	Crankshaft				Connecting Rod		
			Main Brg. Journal Dia.	Main Brg. Oil Clearance	Shaft End-play	Thrust on No.	Journal Diameter	Oil Clearance	Side Clearance
1997	2.0 (1996)	C	2.0469-2.0475	0.0008-0.0024	0.0035-0.0094	3	1.8894-1.8900	0.0010-0.0023	0.0050-0.0150
	2.0 (1996)	Y	2.0469-2.0475	0.0009-0.0024	0.0035-0.0094	3	1.8894-1.8900	0.0010-0.0023	0.0051-0.0150
1998	2.0 (1996)	C	2.0469-2.0475	0.0008-0.0024	0.0035-0.0094	3	1.8894-1.8900	0.0010-0.0023	0.0050-0.0150
	2.0 (1996)	Y	2.0469-2.0475	0.0009-0.0024	0.0035-0.0094	3	1.8894-1.8900	0.0010-0.0023	0.0051-0.0150
1999	2.0 (1996)	C	2.0469-2.0475	0.0008-0.0024	0.0035-0.0094	3	1.8894-1.8900	0.0010-0.0023	0.0050-0.0150
	2.0 (1996)	Y	2.0469-2.0475	0.0009-0.0024	0.0035-0.0094	3	1.8894-1.8900	0.0010-0.0023	0.0051-0.0150
2000-01	2.0 (1996)	C	2.0469-2.0475	0.0008-0.0024	0.0035-0.0094	3	1.8894-1.8900	0.0010-0.0023	0.0050-0.0150

93061C39

Refer to the model specific sections for fuel system service procedures

PISTON AND RING SPECIFICATIONS
All measurements are given in inches.

Year	Engine Displacement Liters (cc)	Engine ID/VIN	Piston Clearance	Ring Gap			Ring Side Clearance		
				Top Compression	Bottom Compression	Oil Control	Top Compression	Bottom Compression	Oil Control
1997	2.0 (1996)	C	0.0004-0.0017	0.0090-0.0200	0.0190-0.0310	0.009-0.026	0.0010-0.0026	0.0010-0.0026	0.0002-0.0070
	2.0 (1996)	Y	0.0007-0.0020	0.0090-0.0200	0.0190-0.0310	0.009-0.026	0.0010-0.0026	0.0010-0.0026	0.0002-0.0070
1998	2.0 (1996)	C	0.0004-0.0017	0.0090-0.0200	0.0190-0.0310	0.009-0.026	0.0010-0.0026	0.0010-0.0026	0.0002-0.0070
	2.0 (1996)	Y	0.0007-0.0020	0.0090-0.0200	0.0190-0.0310	0.009-0.026	0.0010-0.0026	0.0010-0.0026	0.0002-0.0070
1999	2.0 (1996)	C	0.0004-0.0017	0.0090-0.0200	0.0190-0.0310	0.009-0.026	0.0010-0.0026	0.0010-0.0026	0.0002-0.0070
	2.0 (1996)	Y	0.0007-0.0020	0.0090-0.0200	0.0190-0.0310	0.009-0.026	0.0010-0.0026	0.0010-0.0026	0.0002-0.0070
2000-01	2.0 (1996)	C	0.0003-0.0006	0.0090-0.0200	0.0190-0.0310	0.009-0.026	0.0010-0.0026	0.0010-0.0026	0.0002-0.0070

93061C41

TORQUE SPECIFICATIONS
All readings in ft. lbs.

Year	Engine Displacement Liters (cc)	Engine ID/VIN	Cylinder Head Bolts	Main Bearing Bolts	Rod Bearing Bolts	Crankshaft Damper Bolts	Flywheel Bolts	Manifold		Spark Plugs	Lug Nut
								Intake	Exhaust		
1997	2.0 (1996)	C	①	②	③	105	70	8.5	17	20	100
	2.0 (1996)	Y	④	②	③	105	70	21	17	20	100
1998	2.0 (1996)	C	①	②	③	105	70	8.5	17	20	100
	2.0 (1996)	Y	④	②	③	105	70	21	17	20	100
1999	2.0 (1996)	C	①	②	③	105	70	8.5	17	20	100
	2.0 (1996)	Y	④	②	③	105	70	21	17	20	100
2000-01	2.0 (1996)	C	①	②	③	100	70	8.5	17	20	95

① Step 1: 25 ft. lbs.
   Step 2: 50 ft. lbs.
   Step 3: 50 ft. lbs.
   Step 4: plus 90 degrees

② M8: 22 ft. lbs.
   M11: 60 ft. lbs.

③ Step 1: 20 ft. lbs.
   Step 2: plus 90 degrees

④ Step 1:
   Bolts 1-6: 25 ft. lbs.
   Bolts 7-10: 20 ft. lbs.
   Step 2:
   Bolts 1-6: 50 ft. lbs.
   Bolts 7-10: 20 ft. lbs.
   Step 3:
   Bolts 1-6: 50 ft. lbs.
   Bolts 7-10: 20 ft. lbs.
   Step 4: plus 90 degrees

93061C40

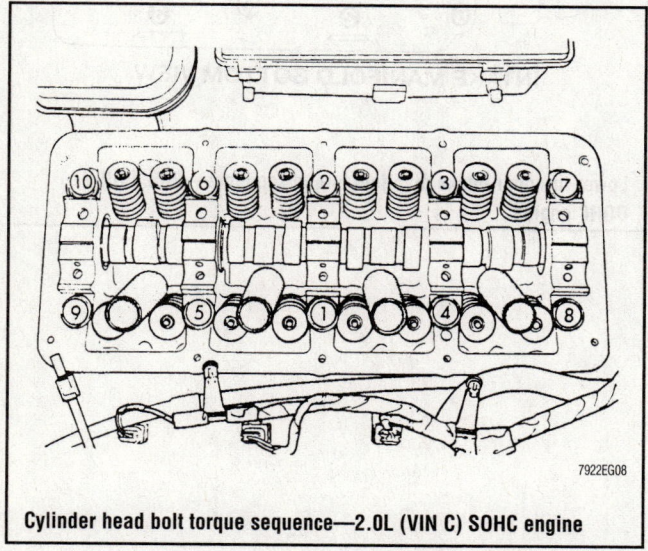

Cylinder head bolt torque sequence—2.0L (VIN C) SOHC engine

7922EG08

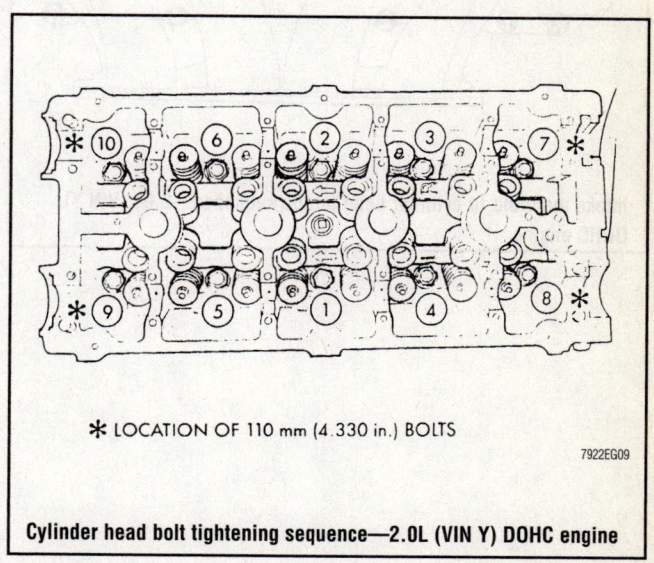

✳ LOCATION OF 110 mm (4.330 in.) BOLTS

7922EG09

Cylinder head bolt tightening sequence—2.0L (VIN Y) DOHC engine

Refer to the model specific sections for engine electrical system service procedures

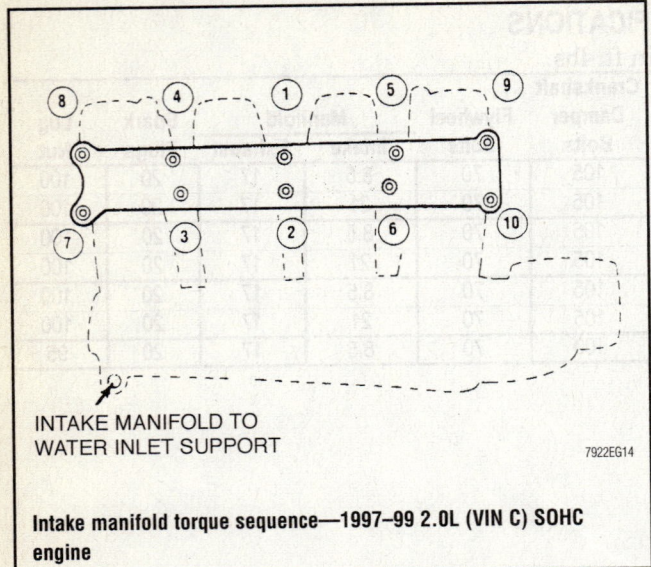

INTAKE MANIFOLD TO
WATER INLET SUPPORT

7922EG14

Intake manifold torque sequence—1997–99 2.0L (VIN C) SOHC
engine

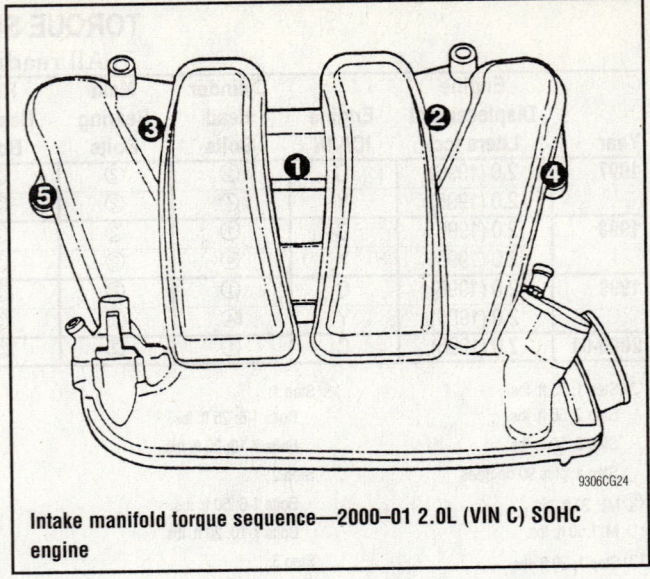

9306CG24

Intake manifold torque sequence—2000–01 2.0L (VIN C) SOHC
engine

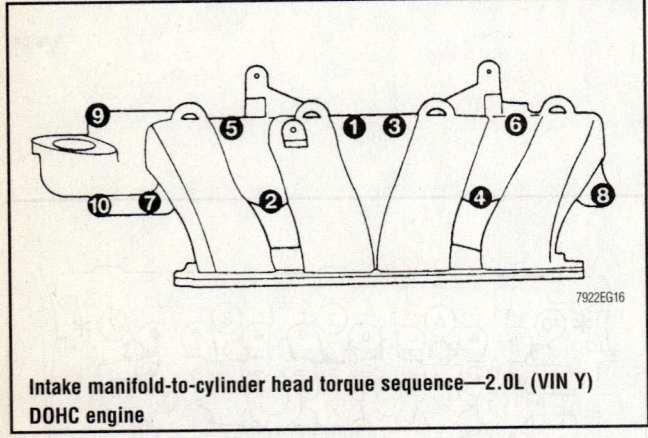

7922EG16

Intake manifold-to-cylinder head torque sequence—2.0L (VIN Y)
DOHC engine

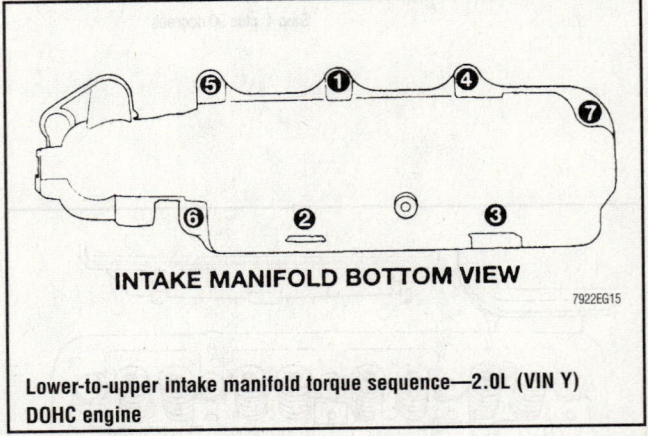

INTAKE MANIFOLD BOTTOM VIEW

7922EG15

Lower-to-upper intake manifold torque sequence—2.0L (VIN Y)
DOHC engine

BRAKE SPECIFICATIONS
All measurements in inches unless noted

Year	Model		Brake Disc Original Thickness	Brake Disc Minimum Thickness	Brake Disc Maximum Runout	Brake Drum Diameter Original Inside Diameter	Brake Drum Diameter Max. Wear Limit	Brake Drum Diameter Maximum Machine Diameter	Minimum Lining Thickness	Brake Caliper Bracket Bolts (ft. lbs.)	Brake Caliper Mounting Bolts (ft. lbs.)
1997	Neon	F	0.792	0.724	0.005	—	—	—	0.300 ①	55	16
		R	0.364	0.285	0.005	7.88	NA	②	③	55	16
1998	Neon	F	0.792	0.724	0.005	—	—	—	0.300 ①	55	16
		R	0.364	0.285	0.005	7.88	NA	②	③	55	16
1999	Neon	F	0.792	0.724	0.005	—	—	—	0.300 ①	55	16
		R	0.364	0.285	0.005	7.88	NA	②	③	55	16
2000-01	Neon	F	0.866	0.803	0.003	—	—	—	0.300 ①	55	16
		R	0.364	0.285	0.003	7.88	NA	②	③	55	16

NA: Not Available

① If equipped with rear drum brakes: 0.827
   If equipped with rear disc brakes: 0.875

② Stamped on the outer edge of drum

③ Disc brake pad total thickness - 0.281
   Brake shoe lining thickness - 0.0625

93061C42

For accessory drive belt replacement procedures see the model specific sections of this manual

SCHEDULED MAINTENANCE INTERVALS
(DODGE NEON & PLYMOUTH NEON)

TO BE SERVICED	TYPE OF SERVICE	VEHICLE MILEAGE INTERVAL (x1000)												
		7.5	15	22.5	30	37.5	45	52.5	60	67.5	75	82.5	90	97.5
Engine oil & filter	R	✓	✓	✓	✓	✓	✓	✓	✓	✓	✓	✓	✓	✓
Brake hoses	S/I	✓	✓	✓	✓	✓	✓	✓	✓	✓	✓	✓	✓	✓
Coolant level, hoses & clamps	S/I	✓	✓	✓	✓	✓	✓	✓	✓	✓	✓	✓	✓	✓
CV joints & front suspension components	S/I	✓	✓	✓	✓	✓	✓	✓	✓	✓	✓	✓	✓	✓
Exhaust system	S/I	✓	✓	✓	✓	✓	✓	✓	✓	✓	✓	✓	✓	✓
Manual transaxle oil	S/I	✓	✓	✓	✓	✓	✓	✓	✓	✓	✓	✓	✓	✓
Rotate tires	S/I	✓	✓	✓	✓	✓	✓	✓	✓	✓	✓	✓	✓	✓
Accessory drive belts	S/I		✓		✓		✓		✓		✓		✓	
Brake linings	S/I			✓			✓			✓			✓	
Air filter element	R				✓				✓				✓	
Spark plugs	R				✓				✓				✓	
Lubricate ball joints	S/I				✓				✓				✓	
Engine coolant	R						✓				✓			
PCV valve	S/I								✓				✓	
Ignition cables	R								✓					
Camshaft timing belt ①	R													

R: Replace   S/I: Service or Inspect

① Camshaft timing belt: replace at 105,000 miles.

FREQUENT OPERATION MAINTENANCE (SEVERE SERVICE)

If a vehicle is operated under any of the following conditions it is considered severe service:

- Extremely dusty areas.

- 50% or more of the vehicle operation is in 32°C (90°F) or higher temperatures, or constant operation in temperatures below 0°C (32°F).

- Prolonged idling (vehicle operation in stop and go traffic).

- Frequent short running periods (engine does not warm to normal operating temperatures).

- Police, taxi, delivery usage or trailer towing usage.

Oil & oil filter change: change every 3000 miles.

Rotate tires every 6000 miles.

Brake linings: inspect every 12,000 miles.

Air filter element: service or inspect every 15,000 miles.

Automatic transaxle: change fluid & adjust bands every 15,000 miles.

Manual transaxle fluid: replace every 15,000 miles.

Engine coolant: replace at 36,000 miles and every 30,000 miles thereafter.

93061C43

SCHEDULED MAINTENANCE INTERVALS
DAIMLERCHRYSLER CORPORATION
DODGE NEON
PLYMOUTH NEON

The following should be used as a guide when determining the amount of work required for a particular service. In estimating how long a particular Scheduled Maintenance Service should take, please observe the following:

● Labor Time is time based on field research and data supplied by the vehicle manufacturer.
● Labor time operations are given in hours and tenths of an hour.
● All labor operations are to be used as a guide.

Mechanic Skill Level Codes:
(A) PRECISION: Highly skilled with multiple certification.
(B) GENERAL: Normally skilled with certification.
(C) MAINTENANCE: Semi-skilled working on certification.

	LABOR TIME		LABOR TIME		LABOR TIME
7500 Mile Service (C)		**37500 Mile Service (C)**		**75000 Mile Service (C)**	
All Models	1.4	All Models	1.4	All Models	2.0
15000 Mile Service (C)		**45000 Mile Service (B)**		**82500 Mile Service (C)**	
All Models	1.5	All Models	2.3	All Models	1.4
22500 Mile Service (C)		**52500 Mile Service (C)**		**90000 Mile Service (B)**	
All Models	1.7	All Models	1.4	All Models	2.8
30000 Mile Service (B)		**60000 Mile Service (B)**		**97500 Mile Service (C)**	
All Models	2.3	All Models	2.9	All Models	1.4
		67500 Mile Service (C)			
		All Models	1.7		

93061C44

For brake related suspension and axle service, refer to the model specific sections of this manual

CHRYSLER CORP.
Chrysler PT Cruiser

ENGINE AND VEHICLE IDENTIFICATION

	Engine						Model Year	
Code ①	Liters (cc)	Cu. In.	Cyl.	Fuel Sys.	Engine Type	Eng. Mfg.	Code ②	Year
B	2.4 (2429)	148	I4	SMFI	DOHC	Chrysler	1	2001

DOHC: Double Overhead Camshaft

① 8th position of VIN

② 10th position of VIN

93061C45

GENERAL ENGINE SPECIFICATIONS

Year	Model	Engine Displacement Liters (cc)	Engine Series (ID/VIN)	Fuel System	Net Horsepower @ rpm	Net Torque @ rpm (ft. lbs.)	Bore x Stroke (in.)	Compression Ratio	Oil Pressure @ rpm
2001	PT Cruiser	2.4 (2429)	B	SMFI	150@5200	167@4000	3.44x3.98	9.4:1	25-80@3000

SMFI: Sequential Multi-port Fuel Injection

93061C46

ENGINE TUNE-UP SPECIFICATIONS

Year	Engine Displacement Liters (cc)	Engine ID/VIN	Spark Plug Gap (in.)	Ignition Timing (deg.)	Fuel Pump (psi)	Idle Speed (rpm)	Valve Clearance	
							In.	Ex.
2001	2.4 (2429)	B	0.048-0.053	①	49	②	HYD	HYD

NOTE: The Vehicle Emission Control Information label often reflects specification changes made during production. The label figures must be used if they differ from those in this chart.

HYD: Hydraulic

① Ignition timing is regulated by the Powertrain Control Module (PCM), and cannot be adjusted.

② Idle speed is controled by the Powertrain Control Module (PCM), and cannot be adjusted.

93061C47

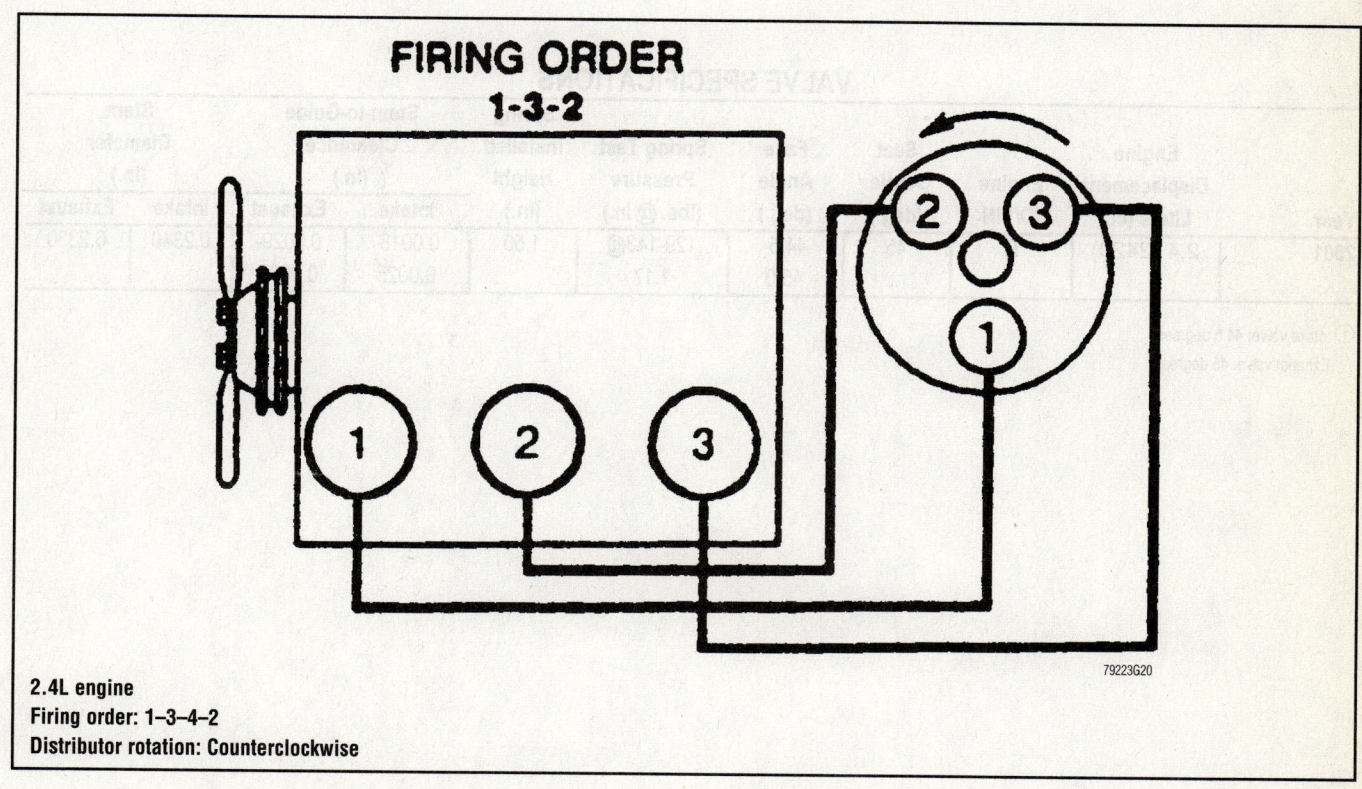

FIRING ORDER
1-3-2

2.4L engine
Firing order: 1–3–4–2
Distributor rotation: Counterclockwise

79223G20

CAPACITIES

Year	Model	Engine Displacement Liters (cc)	Engine ID/VIN	Engine Oil with Filter (qts.)	Automatic Transaxle (qts.)	Power Transfer Unit (qts.)	Rear Drive Axle (pts.)		Fuel Tank (gal.)	Cooling System (qts.)
2001	PT Cruiser	2.4 (2429)	B	4.5	①	1.22	4.0	②	20.0	9.5

NOTE: All capacities are approximate. Add fluid gradually and check to be sure a proper fluid level is obtained.

① 31TH overhaul fill capacity with torque converter empty: 8.5 qts.

31TE overhaul fill capacity with torque converter empty: 9.1 qts.

② Overrunning clutch: 0.75 pts.

93061C48

VALVE SPECIFICATIONS

Year	Engine Displacement Liters (cc)	Engine ID/VIN	Seat Angle (deg.)	Face Angle (deg.)	Spring Test Pressure (lbs. @ in.)	Spring Installed Height (in.)	Stem-to-Guide Clearance (in.)		Stem Diameter (in.)	
							Intake	Exhaust	Intake	Exhaust
2001	2.4 (2429)	B	45	44.5-45.0	129-143@1.17	1.50	0.0018-0.0025	0.0029-0.0037	0.2340	0.2330

① Intake valve: 44.5 degrees

Exhaust valve: 45 degrees

93061C49

CRANKSHAFT AND CONNECTING ROD SPECIFICATIONS

All measurements are given in inches.

Year	Engine Displacement Liters (cc)	Engine ID/VIN	Crankshaft				Connecting Rod		
			Main Brg. Journal Dia.	Main Brg. Oil Clearance	Shaft End-play	Thrust on No.	Journal Diameter	Oil Clearance	Side Clearance
2001	2.4 (2429)	B	2.3610-2.3625	0.0007-0.0023	0.0035-0.0094	2	1.9670-1.9685	0.0009-0.0027	0.0051-0.0150

93061C50

PISTON AND RING SPECIFICATIONS

All measurements are given in inches.

Year	Engine Displacement Liters (cc)	Engine ID/VIN	Piston Clearance	Ring Gap			Ring Side Clearance		
				Top Compression	Bottom Compression	Oil Control	Top Compression	Bottom Compression	Oil Control
2001	2.4 (2429)	B	0.0009-0.0022	0.0098-0.0200	0.0090-0.0180	0.0098-0.0250	0.0011-0.0031	0.0011-0.0031	0.0004-0.0070

① Oil control ring side rails must be free to rotate after assembly

93061C51

For exhaust manifold replacement procedures, see the model specific sections of this manual

TORQUE SPECIFICATIONS
All readings in ft. lbs.

Year	Engine Displacement Liters (cc)	Engine ID/VIN	Cylinder Head Bolts	Main Bearing Bolts	Rod Bearing Bolts	Crankshaft Damper Bolts	Flywheel Bolts	Manifold Intake	Manifold Exhaust	Spark Plugs	Lug Nuts
2001	2.4 (2429)	B	①	②	③	100	70	20	17	20	100

① Step 1: 25 ft. lbs.
　Step 2: 50 ft. lbs.
　Step 3: 50 ft. lbs.
　Step 4: Plus 1/4 turn

② M8 bolts: 20 ft. lbs.
　M11 bolts: 30 ft. lbs. plus 1/4 turn

③ Step 1: 20 ft. lbs.
　Step 2: Plus 1/4 turn

93061C52

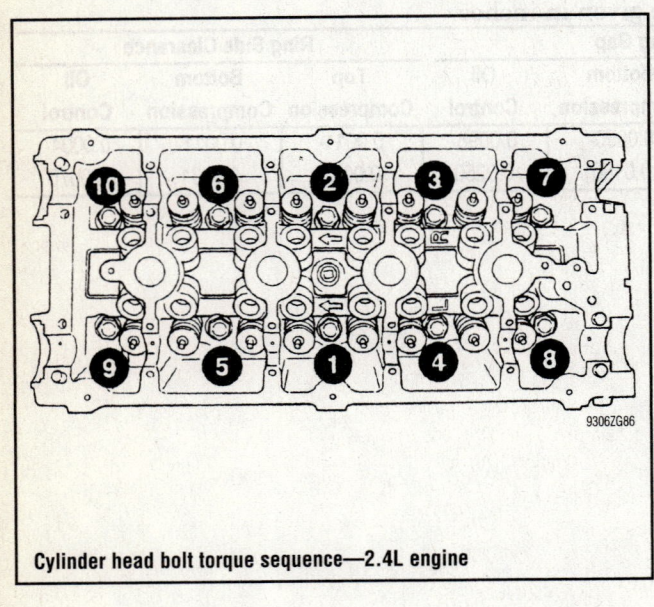

Cylinder head bolt torque sequence—2.4L engine

93062G86

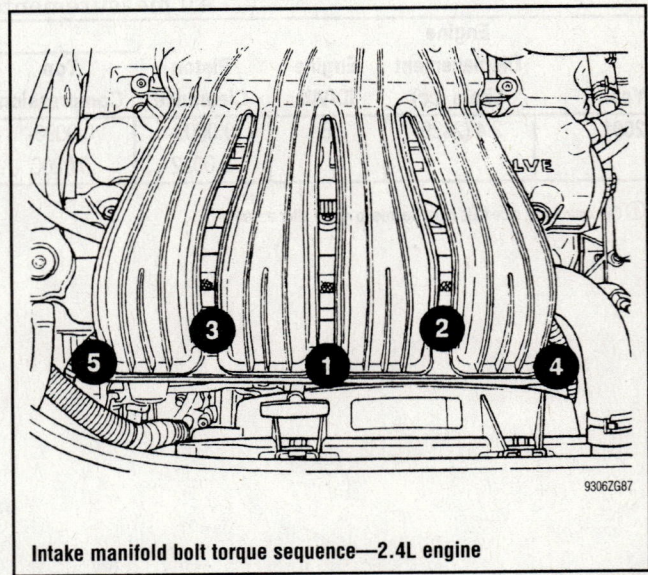

Intake manifold bolt torque sequence—2.4L engine

93062G87

BRAKE SPECIFICATIONS
CHRYSLER PT CRUISER
All measurements in inches unless noted

| Year | Model | | Brake Disc | | | Brake Drum Diameter | | | Min. Lining Thickness | Caliper Guide Pin Bolts (ft. lbs.) |
			Original Thickness	Minimum Thickness	Maximum Run-out	Original Inside Diameter	Max. Wear Limit	Maximum Machine Diameter		
2001	PT Cruiser	F	0.902-0.909	0.803	0.005	—	—	—	0.313	26①
		R	0.344-0.364	0.285	0.005	8.63-8.65	NA	NA	②	16①

NA: Not Available
F: Front
R: Rear
① Lbs. lbs.

② Rear Disc: 0.350 in.
  Rear Bonded Shoes: 0.062 in.
  Rear Riveted Shoes: 0.031 in.

93061C53

Refer to the model specific sections for cooling system service procedures

SCHEDULED MAINTENANCE INTERVALS
(CHRYSLER PT CRUISER)

TO BE SERVICED	TYPE OF SERVICE	VEHICLE MILEAGE INTERVAL (x1000)												
		7.5	15	22.5	30	37.5	45	52.5	60	67.5	75	82.5	90	97.5
Engine oil & filter	R	✔	✔	✔	✔	✔	✔	✔	✔	✔	✔	✔	✔	✔
Brake hoses	S/I	✔	✔	✔	✔	✔	✔	✔	✔	✔	✔	✔	✔	✔
Coolant level, hoses & clamps	S/I	✔	✔	✔	✔	✔	✔	✔	✔	✔	✔	✔	✔	✔
CV joints & front suspension components	S/I	✔	✔	✔	✔	✔	✔	✔	✔	✔	✔	✔	✔	✔
Exhaust system	S/I	✔	✔	✔	✔	✔	✔	✔	✔	✔	✔	✔	✔	✔
Manual transaxle oil	S/I	✔	✔	✔	✔	✔	✔	✔	✔	✔	✔	✔	✔	✔
Rotate tires	S/I	✔	✔	✔	✔	✔	✔	✔	✔	✔	✔	✔	✔	✔
Accessory drive belts	S/I		✔		✔		✔		✔		✔		✔	
Brake linings	S/I			✔			✔			✔			✔	
Air filter element	R				✔				✔				✔	
Spark plugs	R				✔				✔				✔	
Lubricate ball joints	S/I				✔				✔				✔	
Engine coolant ①	R													
PCV valve	S/I								✔				✔	
Ignition cables	R								✔					
Camshaft timing belt ②	R													

R: Replace   S/I: Service or Inspect

① Engine coolant: flush and replace at 100,000 miles.

② Camshaft timing belt: replace at 120,000 miles.

FREQUENT OPERATION MAINTENANCE (SEVERE SERVICE)

If a vehicle is operated under any of the following conditions it is considered severe service:

- Extremely dusty areas.

- 50% or more of the vehicle operation is in 32°C (90°F) or higher temperatures, or constant operation in temperatures below 0°C (32°F).

- Prolonged idling (vehicle operation in stop and go traffic).

- Frequent short running periods (engine does not warm to normal operating temperatures).

- Police, taxi, delivery usage or trailer towing usage.

Oil & oil filter change: change every 3000 miles.

Rotate tires every 6000 miles.

Brake linings: inspect every 12,000 miles.

Air filter element: service or inspect every 15,000 miles.

Automatic transaxle: change fluid & adjust bands every 15,000 miles.

Manual transaxle fluid: replace every 15,000 miles.

Engine coolant: replace at 36,000 miles and every 30,000 miles thereafter.

93061C54

SCHEDULED MAINTENANCE INTERVALS
DAMILERCHRYSLER CORPORATION
CHRYSLER PT CRUISER

The following should be used as a guide when determining the amount of work required for a particular service.
In estimating how long a particular Scheduled Maintenance Service should take, please observe the following:

- Labor Time is time based on field research and data supplied by the vehicle manufacturer.
- Labor time operations are given in hours and tenths of an hour.
- All labor operations are to be used as a guide.

Mechanic Skill Level Codes:
(A) PRECISION: Highly skilled with multiple certification.
(B) GENERAL: Normally skilled with certification.
(C) MAINTENANCE: Semi-skilled working on certification.

	LABOR TIME		LABOR TIME		LABOR TIME
7500 Mile Service (C)		**37500 Mile Service (C)**		**75000 Mile Service (C)**	
All Models	1.4	All Models	1.4	All Models	2.0
15000 Mile Service (C)		**45000 Mile Service (B)**		**82500 Mile Service (C)**	
All Models	1.5	All Models	2.3	All Models	1.4
22500 Mile Service (C)		**52500 Mile Service (C)**		**90000 Mile Service (B)**	
All Models	1.7	All Models	1.4	All Models	2.8
30000 Mile Service (B)		**60000 Mile Service (B)**		**97500 Mile Service (C)**	
All Models	2.3	All Models	2.9	All Models	1.4
		67500 Mile Service (C)			
		All Models	1.7		

93061C55

CHRYSLER CORP.
Eagle Talon

ENGINE AND VEHICLE IDENTIFICATION

Engine							Model Year	
Code ①	Liters (cc)	Cu. In.	Cyl.	Fuel Sys.	Engine Type	Eng. Mfg.	Code ②	Year
F	2.0 (1997)	122	4	MFI Turbo	DOHC	Mitsubsihi	V	1997
Y	2.0 (1996)	122	4	MFI	DOHC	Chrysler	W	1998

MFI: Multi-port Fuel Injection

DOHC: Double Overhead Camshaft

① 8th digit of the Vehicle Identification Number (VIN)

② 10th digit of the VIN

93061C56

GENERAL ENGINE SPECIFICATIONS
All measurements are given in inches.

Year	Engine Displacement Liters (cc)	Engine Series (ID/VIN)	Fuel System	Net Horsepower @ rpm	Net Torque @ rpm (ft. lbs.)	Bore x Stroke (in.)	Compression Ratio	Oil Pressure @ rpm
1997	2.0 (1997)	F	MFI-Turbo	①	②	3.35x3.46	8.5:1	③
	2.0 (1996)	Y	MFI	140@6000	131@4800	3.44x3.27	9.6:1	④
1998	2.0 (1997)	F	MFI-Turbo	①	②	3.35x3.46	8.5:1	③
	2.0 (1996)	Y	MFI	140@6000	131@4800	3.44x3.27	9.6:1	④

MFI: Multi-port Fuel Injection

MFI: Multi-port Fuel Injection

① Automatic: 205@6000
   Manual: 210@6000

② Automatic: 220@3000
   Manual: 214@3000

③ 11.4 psi or more at curb idle speed

④ 4 psi or more at curb idle speed

93061C57

ENGINE TUNE-UP SPECIFICATIONS

Year	Engine Displacement Liters (cc)	Engine ID/VIN	Spark Plug Gap (in.)	Ignition Timing (deg.)		Fuel Pump (psi) ①	Idle Speed (rpm)		Valve Clearance	
				MT	AT		MT	AT	In.	Ex.
1997	2.0 (1997)	F	0.028-0.030	5B	5B	33	750	750	HYD	HYD
	2.0 (1996)	Y	0.033-0.038	②	②	38	800	800	HYD	HYD
1998	2.0 (1997)	F	0.028-0.030	5B	5B	33	750	750	HYD	HYD
	2.0 (1996)	Y	0.033-0.038	②	②	38	800	800	HYD	HYD

NOTE: The Vehicle Emission Control Information label often reflects specification changes made during production. The label figures must be used if they differ from those in this chart.

HYD: Hydraulic

① Pressure at idle with vacuum applied to fuel pressure regulator

② Basic ignition timing is not adjustable

93061C58

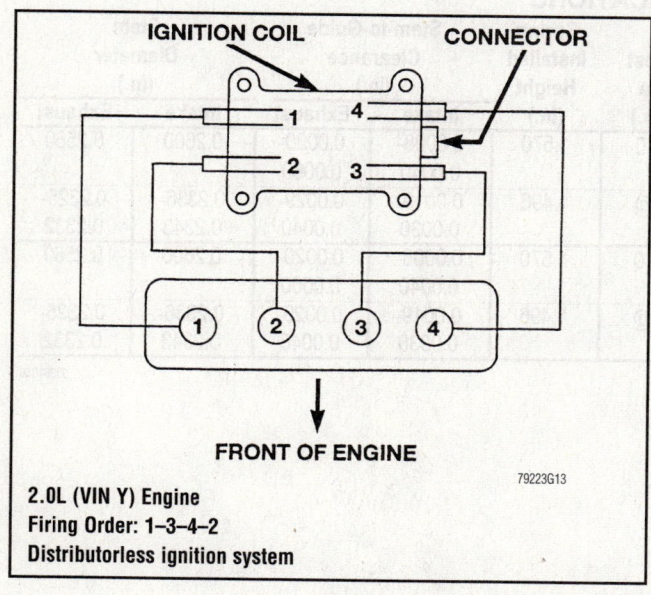

2.0L (VIN Y) Engine
Firing Order: 1–3–4–2
Distributorless ignition system

79223G13

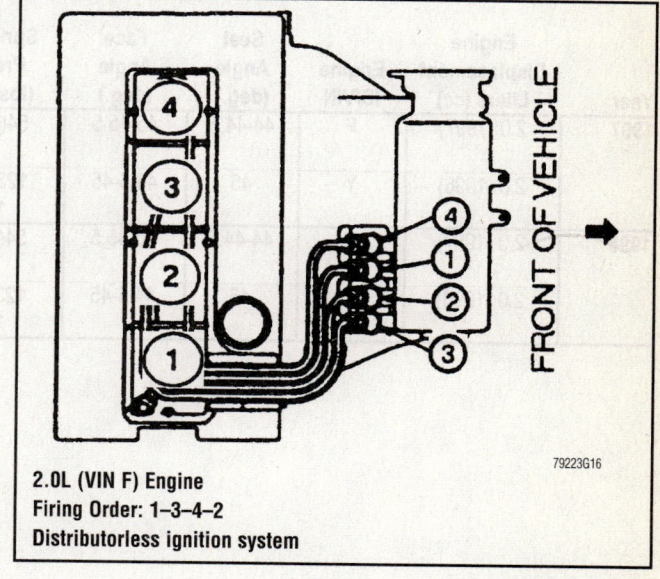

2.0L (VIN F) Engine
Firing Order: 1–3–4–2
Distributorless ignition system

79223G16

Timing chain and gear service is covered in the model specific sections of this manual

CAPACITIES

Year	Engine Displacement Liters (cc)	Engine ID/VIN	Engine Oil with Filter (qts.)	Transmission (pts.)		Drive Axle (qts.)	Fuel Tank	Cooling System
				5-Spd	Auto.			
1997	2.0 (1997)	F	4.6	①	14.2	1.8	16.0	7.4
	2.0 (1996)	Y	4.5	4.2	18.2	—	16.0	7.4
1998	2.0 (1997)	F	4.6	①	14.2	1.8	16.0	7.4
	2.0 (1996)	Y	4.5	4.2	18.2	—	16.0	7.4

NOTE: All capacities are approximate. Add fluid gradually and ensure a proper fluid level is obtained.

① 2WD: 4.6
   4WD: 4.8

93061C59

VALVE SPECIFICATIONS

Year	Engine Displacement Liters (cc)	Engine ID/VIN	Seat Angle (deg.)	Face Angle (deg.)	Spring Test Pressure (lbs. @ in.)	Spring Installed Height (in.)	Stem-to-Guide Clearance (in.)		Stem Diameter (in.)	
							Intake	Exhaust	Intake	Exhaust
1997	2.0 (1997)	F	44-44.5	45-45.5	54@1.570	1.570	0.0008-0.0040	0.0020-0.0060	0.2600	0.2560
	2.0 (1996)	Y	45	44.5-45	123-137@1.153	1.496	0.0019-0.0030	0.0029-0.0040	0.2336-0.2343	0.2325-0.2332
1998	2.0 (1997)	F	44-44.5	45-45.5	54@1.570	1.570	0.0008-0.0040	0.0020-0.0060	0.2600	0.2560
	2.0 (1996)	Y	45	44.5-45	123-137@1.153	1.496	0.0019-0.0030	0.0029-0.0040	0.2336-0.2343	0.2325-0.2332

93061C60

CRANKSHAFT AND CONNECTING ROD SPECIFICATIONS
All measurements are given in inches.

Year	Engine Displacement Liters (cc)	Engine ID/VIN	Crankshaft				Connecting Rods		
			Main Brg. Journal Dia.	Main Brg. Oil Clearance	Shaft End-play	Thrust on No.	Journal Diameter	Oil Clearance	Side Clearance
1997	2.0 (1997)	F	2.2400	0.0008-0.0016	0.0020-0.0071	3	1.7700	0.0008-0.0020	0.0039-0.0098
	2.0 (1996)	Y	2.0469-2.0475	0.0009-0.0024	0.0035-0.0094	3	1.8894-1.8900	0.0010-0.0023	0.0051-0.0150
1998	2.0 (1997)	F	2.2400	0.0008-0.0016	0.0020-0.0071	3	1.7700	0.0008-0.0020	0.0039-0.0098
	2.0 (1996)	Y	2.0469-2.0475	0.0009-0.0024	0.0035-0.0094	3	1.8894-1.8900	0.0010-0.0023	0.0051-0.0150

93061C61

PISTON AND RING SPECIFICATIONS
All measurements are given in inches.

Year	Engine Displacement Liters (cc)	Engine ID/VIN	Piston Clearance	Ring Gap			Ring Side Clearance		
				Top Compression	Bottom Compression	Oil Control	Top Compression	Bottom Compression	Oil Control
1997	2.0 (1997)	F	0.0012-0.0020	0.0098-0.0138	0.0157-0.0217	0.0039-0.0157	0.0016-0.0031	0.0008-0.0024	0.0005-0.0089
	2.0 (1996)	Y	0.0005-0.0017	0.0090-0.0200	0.0190-0.0310	0.0090-0.0260	0.0010-0.0026	0.0010-0.0026	0.0002-0.0070
1998	2.0 (1997)	F	0.0012-0.0020	0.0098-0.0138	0.0157-0.0217	0.0039-0.0157	0.0016-0.0031	0.0008-0.0024	0.0005-0.0089
	2.0 (1996)	Y	0.0005-0.0017	0.0090-0.0200	0.0190-0.0310	0.0090-0.0260	0.0010-0.0026	0.0010-0.0026	0.0002-0.0070

93061C62

Ignition system service is covered in the model specific sections of this manual

TORQUE SPECIFICATIONS
All readings in ft. lbs.

Year	Engine Displacement Liters (cc)	Engine ID/VIN	Cylinder Head Bolts	Main Bearing Bolts	Rod Bearing Bolts	Crankshaft Damper Bolts	Flywheel Bolts	Manifold Intake	Manifold Exhaust	Spark Plugs	Lug Nuts
1997	2.0 (1997)	F	①	②	③	94	94-101	14	18-22	18	65-80
	2.0 (1996)	Y	④	55	⑤	105	—	17	17	20	65-80
1998	2.0 (1997)	F	①	②	③	94	94-101	14	18-22	18	65-80
	2.0 (1996)	Y	④	55	⑤	105	—	17	17	20	65-80

① Step 1: 58 ft. lbs.
   Step 2: Fully loosen
   Step 3: 15 ft. lbs.
   Step 4: Plus 90 degrees
   Step 5: Repeat Step 4

② Step 1: 18 ft. lbs.
   Step 2: Plus 90 degrees

③ 14.5 ft. lbs. plus 90 degrees

④ Step 1:
   Bolts 1-6: 24 ft. lbs.
   Bolts 7-10: 20 ft. lbs.
  Step 2:
   Bolts 1-6: 49 ft. lbs.
   Bolts 7-10: 20 ft. lbs.
  Step 3: Plus 90 degrees

⑤ 20 ft. lbs. plus 90 degrees

93061C63

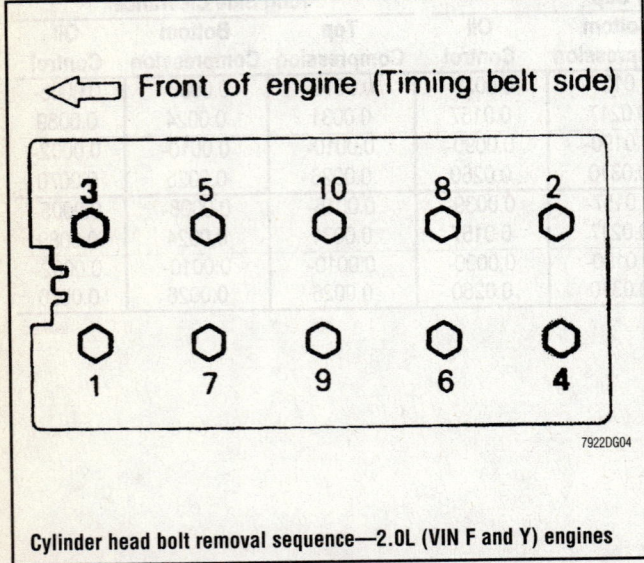

Cylinder head bolt removal sequence—2.0L (VIN F and Y) engines

7922DG04

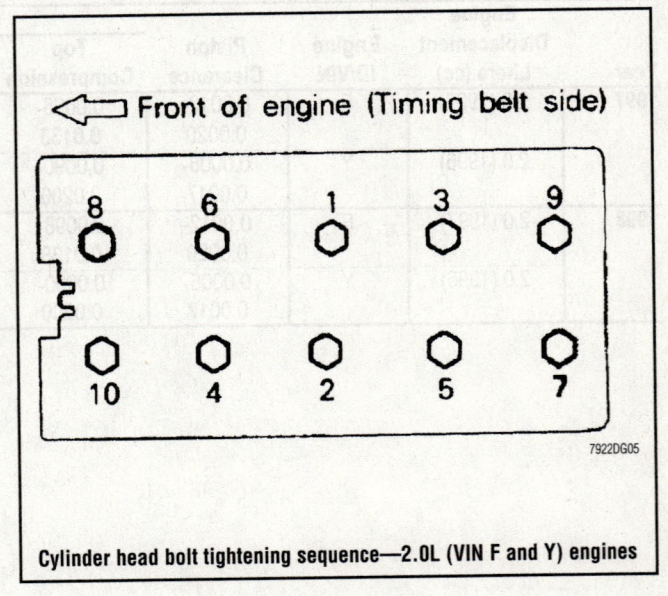

Cylinder head bolt tightening sequence—2.0L (VIN F and Y) engines

7922DG05

BRAKE SPECIFICATIONS
EAGLE TALON
All measurements in inches unless noted

| Year | Model | | Brake Disc | | | Minimum Lining Thickness | Bake Caliper | |
			Original Thickness	Minimum Thickness	Maximum Runout		Bracket Bolts (ft.bs.)	Mounting Bolts (ft.bs.)
1997	Talon	F	0.940	0.882	0.003	0.080	65	54
		R	0.390	0.331	0.003	0.080	—	38
1998	Talon	F	0.940	0.882	0.003	0.080	65	54
		R	0.390	0.331	0.003	0.080	—	38

93061C64

SCHEDULED MAINTENANCE INTERVALS
(EAGLE TALON)

TO BE SERVICED	TYPE OF SERVICE	VEHICLE MILEAGE INTERVAL (x1000)												
		7.5	15	22.5	30	37.5	45	52.5	60	67.5	75	82.5	90	97.5
Engine oil & filter (Non-turbo) ①	R	✓	✓	✓	✓	✓	✓	✓	✓	✓	✓	✓	✓	✓
Coolant level, hoses & clamps	S/I	✓	✓	✓	✓	✓	✓	✓	✓	✓	✓	✓	✓	✓
Rotate tires	S/I	✓	✓	✓	✓	✓	✓	✓	✓	✓	✓	✓	✓	✓
Automatic transaxle fluid level	S/I		✓		✓		✓		✓		✓		✓	
Brake hoses & disc brake pads	S/I		✓		✓		✓		✓		✓		✓	
Driveshaft boots & front suspension components	S/I		✓		✓		✓		✓		✓		✓	
Air filter element	R				✓				✓				✓	
Automatic transaxle fluid & filter ②	R				✓				✓				✓	
Engine coolant	R				✓				✓				✓	
Spark plugs	R				✓				✓				✓	
Accessory drive belts	S/I				✓				✓				✓	
Ball joints & steering linkage seals	S/I				✓				✓				✓	
Exhaust system	S/I				✓				✓				✓	
Fuel hoses	S/I				✓				✓				✓	
Manual transaxle oil (including transfer)	S/I				✓				✓				✓	
Rear axle oil (AWD)	S/I				✓				✓				✓	
Camshaft timing belt	R								✓					
Ignition cables	R								✓					
EVAP & fuel system	S/I								✓					

R: Replace   S/I: Service or Inspect

① Engine oil & filter (Turbo): change every 5000 miles.

② Turbo w/ A/T only.

FREQUENT OPERATION MAINTENANCE (SEVERE SERVICE)

If a vehicle is operated under any of the following conditions it is considered severe service:

- Extremely dusty areas.

- 50% or more of the vehicle operation is in 32°C (90°F) or higher temperatures, or constant operation in temperatures below 0°C (32°F).

- Prolonged idling (vehicle operation in stop and go traffic).

- Frequent short running periods (engine does not warm to normal operating temperatures).

- Police, taxi, delivery usage or trailer towing usage.

Oil & filter change: change every 3000 miles.

Air filter element: service or inspect every 7500 miles.

Automatic transaxle fluid: change every 15,000 miles.

Spark plugs: change every 15,000 miles.

Disc brake pads: check more frequently than every 7500 miles.

93061C65

SCHEDULED MAINTENANCE INTERVALS
DAIMLERCHRYSLER CORPORATION
EAGLE TALON

The following should be used as a guide when determining the amount of work required for a particular service.
In estimating how long a particular Scheduled Maintenance Service should take, please observe the following:

- Labor Time is time based on field research and data supplied by the vehicle manufacturer.
- Labor time operations are given in hours and tenths of an hour.
- All labor operations are to be used as a guide.

Mechanic Skill Level Codes:
(A) PRECISION: Highly skilled with multiple certification.
(B) GENERAL: Normally skilled with certification.
(C) MAINTENANCE: Semi-skilled working on certification.

	LABOR TIME		LABOR TIME		LABOR TIME
7500 Mile Service (C)		**37500 Mile Service (C)**		**75000 Mile Service (C)**	
All models	1.0	All models	1.0	All models	1.3
15000 Mile Service (B)		**45000 Mile Service (B)**		**82500 Mile Service (C)**	
All models	1.3	All models	1.3	All models	1.0
22500 Mile Service (C)		**52500 Mile Service (C)**		**90000 Mile Service (B)**	
All models	1.0	All models	1.0	All models	4.0
30000 Mile Service (B)		**60000 Mile Service (B)**		**97500 Mile Service (C)**	
All models	4.0	All models	7.5	All models	1.0
		67500 Mile Service (C)			
		All models	1.0		

93061C66

Refer to the model specific sections for engine mechanical service procedures

TIRE, WHEEL AND BALL JOINT SPECIFICATIONS
Chrysler

Year	Model	OEM Tires		Tire Pressures (psi)		Wheel Size	Ball Joint Inspection
		Standard	Optional	Front	Rear		
1997	Cirrus	P195/70R14	P195/65HR15	31	31	6-J	①
	Concorde	P225/60R16	None	35	35	7-JJ	①
	LHS	P225/60R16	None	32	32	7-JJ	①
	New Yorker	P225/60R16	None	32	32	7-JJ	①
	Sebring JX	P205/65R15	P215/55R16	32	32	6-JJ	②
	Sebring Jxi	P215/55R16	None	30	30	6-JJ	②
	Sebring LX	P195/70R14	None	32	29	5.5-J	②
	Sebring Lxi	P205/55R16	None	32	29	6-JJ	②
1998	Cirrus	P195/65R15	None	30	30	6-J	①
	Concorde	P225/60R16	None	30	31	7-JJ	①
	LHS	P225/60R16	None	32	32	7-JJ	①
	New Yorker	P225/60R16	None	30	30	7-JJ	①
	Sebring JX	P205/65R15	P215/55R16	32	32	6-JJ	②
	Sebring Jxi	P215/55R16	None	30	30	6-JJ	②
	Sebring LX	P195/70R14	None	30	30	5.5-J	②
	Sebring Lxi	P205/55R16	None	32	29	6-JJ	②
	Sebring Conv.	P195/65R15	None	32	29	6-JJ	②
1999	300M	P225/55/R17	None	30	30	7-JJ	①
	Cirrus	P195/65R15	None	30	31	6-J	①
	Concorde	P205/70R15	P225/60R16	32	32	6-JJ	①
	LHS	P225/55/R17	None	30	30	7-JJ	①
	New Yorker	P225/55/R17	None	32	32	7-JJ	①
	Sebring Conv.	P205/65R15	P215/55R16	32	32	6-JJ	②
	Sebring JX	P205/65R15	P215/55R16	30	30	6-JJ	②
	Sebring Jxi	P215/55R16	None	30	30	6-JJ	②
	Sebring LX	P195/70R14	P205/55HR16	32	29	5.5-J	②
	Sebring Lxi	P215/50R17	None	32	29	6.5-JJ	②
2000-01	300M	P225/55/R17	None	30	30	7-JJ	①
	Cirrus	P195/65R15	None	30	31	6-J	①
	Concorde	P205/70R15	P225/60R16	32	32	6-JJ	①
	LHS	P225/55/R17	None	30	30	7-JJ	①
	Sebring Conv.	P205/65R15	P215/55R16	32	32	6-JJ	②
	Sebring JX	P205/65R15	P215/55R16	30	30	6-JJ	②
	Sebring Jxi	P215/55R16	None	30	30	6-JJ	②
	Sebring LX	P195/70R14	P205/55HR16	32	29	5.5-J	②
	Sebring Lxi	P215/50R17	None	32	29	6.5-JJ	②
	PT Cruser	P205/55R16	None	32	32	5.5-J	②

OEM: Original Equipment Manufacturer

PSI: Pounds Per Square Inch

STD: Standard

OPT: Optional

L: Lower

U: Upper

① Do not lift car. Grasp the grease fitting and attempt to move or rotate. Replace if any movement is found.

② Replace if any measurable movement is found

93061C67

TIRE, WHEEL AND BALL JOINT SPECIFICATIONS
Dodge

| Year | Model | OEM Tires | | Tire Pressures (psi) | | Wheel Size | Ball Joint Inspection |
		Standard	Optional	Front	Rear		
1997	Intrepid	P225/60R16	None	35	35	7-JJ	①
	Avenger, base	P195/70HR14	None	32	29	5.5-J	①
	Avenger ES	P205/55HR16	None	32	29	6-JJ	①
	Neon, base	P175/70R14	None	30	30	6-JJ	①
	Neon, Highline	P185/65R14	None	32	32	5.5-J	①
	Stratus	P195/70R14	P195/65HR15	31	31	6-JJ	①
	Viper	Fr :P275/40ZR17	None	35	35	10 inch	①
		Rr: P335/35ZR17	None			13 inch	
1998	Intrepid	P225/60R16	None	35	35	7-JJ	①
	Avenger, base	P195/70HR14	P205/55HR16	32	29	5.5-J	①
	Avenger ES	P215/50HR17	None	32	29	6.5-JJ	①
	Neon, base	P175/70R14	None	30	30	6-JJ	①
	Neon, Highline	P185/65R14	None	32	32	5.5-J	①
	Stratus	P195/70R14	P195/65HR15	31	31	6-JJ	①
	Viper	Fr :P275/40ZR17	None	35	35	10 inch	①
		Rr: P335/35ZR17	None			13 inch	
1999	Intrepid, base	P205/70HR15	P225/60R16	35	35	Std: 6-JJ	①
	Avenger, base	P195/70HR14	P205/55HR16	32	29	5.5-J	①
	Avenger ES	P215/50HR17	None	32	29	6.5-JJ	①
	Neon, base	P185/65R14	None	30	30	5.5-JJ	①
	Neon, Competition	P175/65HR14	None	32	32	6-JJ	①
	Stratus	P195/70R14	P195/65HR15	31	31	6-JJ	①
	Viper	Fr: P275/35ZR18	None	35	35	Fr: 10 inch	①
		Rr: P335/30ZR18				Rr: 13 inch	
2000-01	Intrepid, base	P205/70HR15	P225/60R16	35	35	Std: 6-JJ	①
	Avenger, base	P195/70HR14	P205/55HR16	32	29	5.5-J	①
	Avenger ES	P215/50HR17	None	32	29	6.5-JJ	①
	Neon, base	P185/65R14	None	30	30	5.5-JJ	①
	Neon, Competition	P175/65HR14	None	32	32	6-JJ	①
	Stratus	P195/70R14	P195/65HR15	31	31	6-JJ	①
	Viper	Fr: P275/35ZR18	None	35	35	Fr: 10 inch	①
		Rr: P335/30ZR18				Rr: 13 inch	

OEM: Original Equipment Manufacturer

PSI: Pounds Per Square Inch

STD: Standard

OPT: Optional

L: Lower

U: Upper

Fr: Front

Rr: Rear

① Replace if any measurable movement is found.

93061C68

Refer to the model specific sections for fuel system service procedures

TIRE, WHEEL AND BALL JOINT SPECIFICATIONS
Eagle

| Year | Model | OEM Tires | | Tire Pressures (psi) | | Wheel Size | Ball Joint Inspection |
		Standard	Optional	Front	Rear		
1997	Talon ESi	P195/70HR14	None	32	29	5.5-JJ	①
	Talon Tsi	P205/55VR16	None	32	29	6-JJ	①
1998	Talon ESi	P195/70HR14	None	32	29	5.5-JJ	①
	Talon TSi 2wd	P205/55VR16	None	32	29	6-JJ	①
	Talon TSi 4wd	P215/50VR17	None	32	29	6.5-JJ	①

OEM: Original Equipment Manufacturer

PSI: Pounds Per Square Inch

STD: Standard

OPT: Optional

L: Lower

U: Upper

① Torque required in inch lbs. to rotate ball joint when removed from the knuckle

93061C69

TIRE, WHEEL AND BALL JOINT SPECIFICATIONS
Plymouth

| Year | Model | OEM Tires | | Tire Pressures (psi) | | Wheel Size | Ball Joint Inspection |
		Standard	Optional	Front	Rear		
1997	Breeze	P195/70R14	P195/65R15	31	31	6-J	①
	Neon	P175/70R14	P185/65R14	32	32	5.5-J	①
1998	Breeze	P195/70R14	None	31	31	6-J	①
	Neon	P185/65R14	P175/65HR14	32	32	5.5-J	①
			P185/65HR14			6-J	
	Prowler	Fr: P225/40HR17	None	32	32	7.5-J	①
		Rr: P295/40HR20	None			10-J	
1999	Breeze	P195/70R14	None	31	31	6-J	①
	Neon	P185/65R14	P175/65HR14	32	32	5.5-J	①
			P185/65HR14			6-J	
	Prowler	Fr: P225/40HR17	None	32	32	7.5-J	①
		Rr: P295/40HR20	None			10-J	
2000-01	Breeze	P195/70R14	None	31	31	6-J	①
	Neon	P185/65R14	P175/65HR14	32	32	5.5-J	①
			P185/65HR14			6-J	
	Prowler	Fr: P225/40HR17	None	32	32	7.5-J	①
		Rr: P295/40HR20	None			10-J	

OEM: Original Equipment Manufacturer

PSI: Pounds Per Square Inch

STD: Standard

OPT: Optional

① Do not lift car. Grasp the grease fitting and attempt to move or rotate. Replace if any movement is found

93061C70

FORD MOTOR CO.
Ford Aspire

ENGINE AND VEHICLE IDENTIFICATION

			Engine				Model Year	
Code ①	Liters (cc)	Cu. In.	Cyl.	Fuel Sys.	Engine Type	Eng. Mfg.	Code ②	Year
H	1.3 (1319)	81	4	SFI	SOHC	Kia Motors	V	1997

SFI: Sequential Fuel Injection

SOHC: Single Overhead Camshaft

① 8th digit of the Vehicle Identification Number (VIN)

② 10th digit of VIN

93061C71

GENERAL ENGINE SPECIFICATIONS
All measurements are given in inches.

Year	Model	Engine Displacement Liters (cc)	Engine Series (ID/VIN)	Fuel System	Net Horsepower @ rpm	Net Torque @ rpm (ft. lbs.)	Bore x Stroke (in.)	Com-pression Ratio	Oil Pressure @ rpm
1997	Aspire	1.3 (1319)	H	SFI	63@5000	73@3000	2.79x3.29	9.7:1	50-64@3000

SFI: Sequential Fuel Injection

93061C72

ENGINE TUNE-UP SPECIFICATIONS

Year	Engine Displacement Liters (cc)	Engine ID/VIN	Spark Plug Gap (in.)	Ignition Timing (deg.)		Fuel Pump (psi)	Idle Speed (rpm)		Valve Clearance	
				MT	AT		MT	AT	Intake	Exhaust
1997	1.3 (1319)	H	0.040	10B	10B	30-38 ①	700	750	HYD	HYD

NOTE: The Vehicle Emission Control Information label often reflects specification changes made during production. The label figures must be used if they differ from those in this chart.

HYD: Hydraulic

① Fuel pressure with engine running, pressure regulator vacuum hose connected.

93061C73

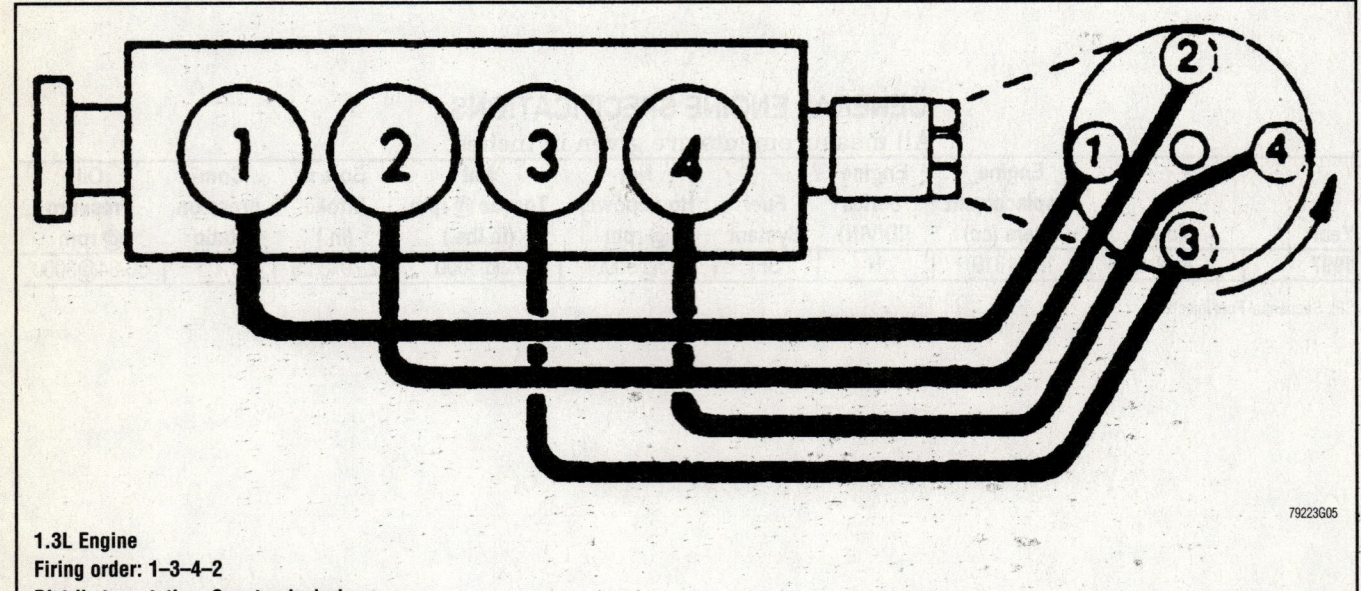

1.3L Engine
Firing order: 1–3–4–2
Distributor rotation: Counterclockwise

79223G05

CAPACITIES

Year	Model	Engine Displacement Liters (cc)	Engine ID/VIN	Engine Oil with Filter (qts.)	Transmission (pts.)		Front Drive Axle (pts.)	Fuel Tank (gal.)	Cooling System (qts.)
					Manual	Auto. ①			
1997	Aspire	1.3 (1319)	H	3.6	5.2	12.0	②	10.0	6.3

NOTE: All capacities are approximate. Add fluid gradually and ensure a proper fluid level is obtained.

① Includes torque converter

② Included in transaxle capacity

93061C74

VALVE SPECIFICATIONS

Year	Engine Displacement Liters (cc)	Engine ID/VIN	Seat Angle (deg.)	Face Angle (deg.)	Spring Test Pressure (lbs. @ in.)	Spring Free-Length (in.)	Stem-to-Guide Clearance (in.)		Stem Diameter (in.)	
							Intake	Exhaust	Intake	Exhaust
1997	1.3 (1319)	H	45	45	NA	1.717	0.0010-0.0024	0.0012-0.0026	0.2744-0.2750	0.2742-0.2748

NA: Not Avaliable

93061C75

For accessory drive belt replacement procedures see the model specific sections of this manual

CRANKSHAFT AND CONNECTING ROD SPECIFICATIONS
All measurements are given in inches.

Year	Engine Displacement Liters (cc)	Engine ID/VIN	Crankshaft				Connecting Rod		
			Main Brg. Journal Dia.	Main Brg. Oil Clearance	Shaft End-play	Thrust on No.	Journal Diameter	Oil Clearance	Side Clearance
1997	1.3 (1319)	H	1.9661-1.9688	0.0007-0.0014	0.0031-0.0111	4	1.5724-1.5731	0.0009-0.0017	0.0120

93061C76

PISTON AND RING SPECIFICATIONS
All measurements are given in inches.

Year	Engine ID/VIN	Engine Displacement Liters (cc)	Piston Clearance	Ring Gap			Ring Side Clearance		
				Top Compression	Bottom Compression	Oil Control	Top Compression	Bottom Compression	Oil Control
1997	H	1.3 (1319)	0.0060	0.006-0.012	0.006-0.012	0.008-0.028	0.001-0.003	0.001-0.003	Snug

93061C77

TORQUE SPECIFICATIONS
All readings in ft. lbs.

Year	Engine Displacement Liters (cc)	Engine ID/VIN	Cylinder Head Bolts	Main Bearing Bolts	Rod Bearing Bolts	Crankshaft Damper Bolts	Flywheel Bolts	Manifold		Spark Plugs	Lug Nuts
								Intake	Exhaust		
1997	1.3 (1319)	H	①	40-43	②	③	71-76	14-20	12-17	15-22	76

Note: Always follow proper torque patterns, and stretch bolts are used in all procedures that require rotating the fastener a certain number of degrees.

The bolts stretch and cannot be reused. For reassembly, replace with new fastners.

① Step 1: 35-40 ft. lbs.
　Step 2: 56-60 ft. lbs.

② Step 1: 11-13 ft. lbs.
　Step 2: 22-25 ft. lbs.

③ Pulley bolts: 9-13 ft. lbs.
　Sprocket bolt: 80-87 ft. lbs.

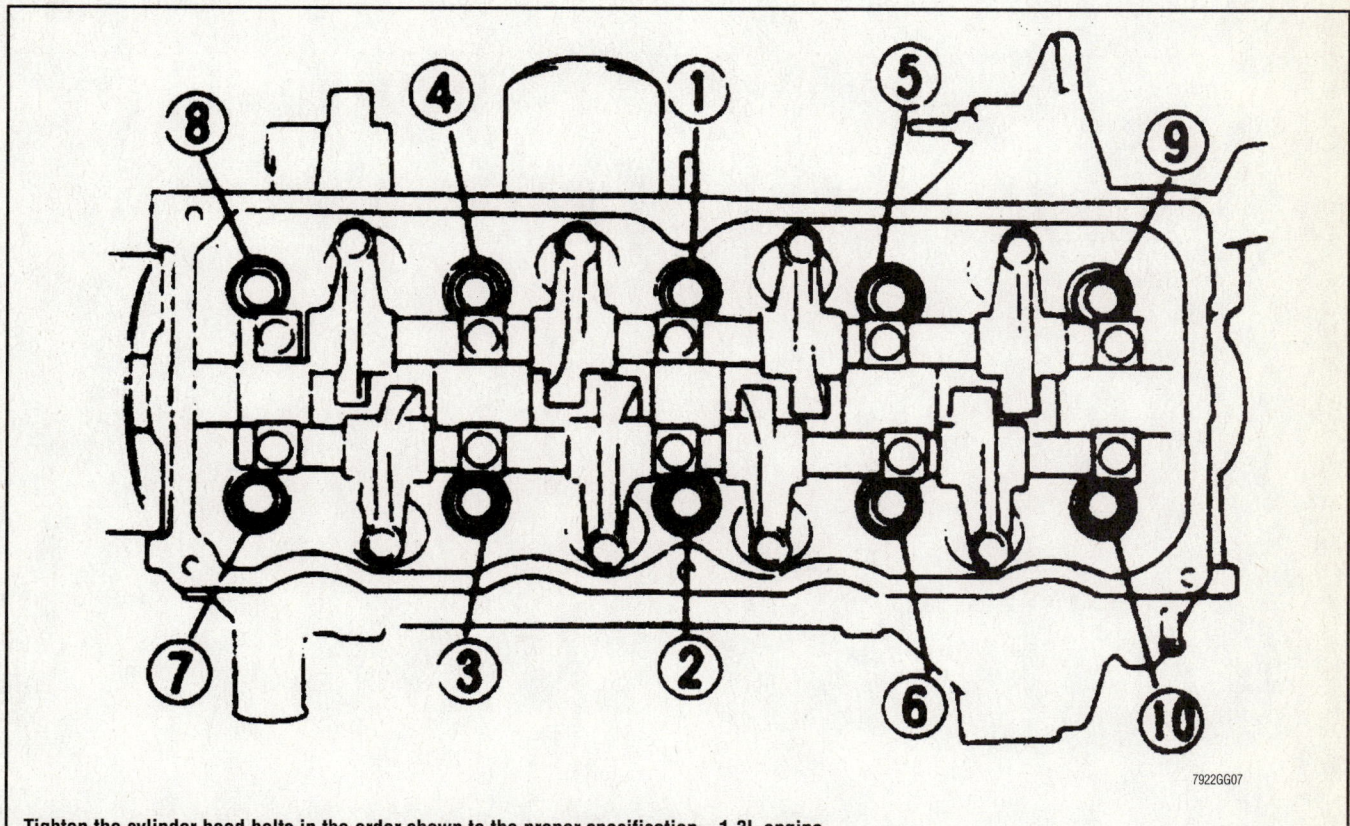

Tighten the cylinder head bolts in the order shown to the proper specification—1.3L engine

For brake related suspension and axle service, refer to the model specific sections of this manual

BRAKE SPECIFICATIONS
FORD ASPIRE
All measurements in inches unless noted

| Year | Model | Master Cylinder Bore | Brake Disc | | | Brake Drum Diameter | | | Minimum Lining Thickness | | Brake Caliper Mounting Bolts (ft. lbs.) |
			Original Thickness	Minimum Thickness	Maximum Run-out	Original Inside Diameter	Max. Wear Limit	Maximum Machine Diameter	Front	Rear	
1997	Aspire ①	②	0.710	0.630	0.004	7.87	7.93	NA	0.080	0.040	29-36
	③	②	0.860	0.780	0.004	7.87	7.93	NA	0.080	0.040	29-36

NOTE: Follow specifications stamped on rotor or drum if figures differ from those in this chart.

NA: Not Available

F: Front

R: Rear

① Manual transaxle

② Without ABS: 0.810
   With ABS: 0.870

③ Automatic transaxle

93061C79

SCHEDULED MAINTENANCE INTERVALS
(FORD ASPIRE)

TO BE SERVICED	TYPE OF SERVICE	VEHICLE MILEAGE INTERVAL (x1000)												
		5	10	15	20	25	30	35	40	45	50	55	60	65
Engine oil & filter	R	✓	✓	✓	✓	✓	✓	✓	✓	✓	✓	✓	✓	✓
Rotate tires	S/I	✓		✓		✓		✓		✓		✓		✓
Air cleaner element & engine coolant	R						✓						✓	
Spark plugs	R						✓						✓	
Automatic transaxle fluid & filter	R													
Exhaust heat shields	S/I						✓							
Disc brake pads & rotors, brake linings, drum, brake lines, hoses & connections	S/I						✓						✓	
Accessory drive belt(s)	S/I						✓						✓	
Fuel lines, hoses & idle speed	S/I						✓						✓	
Cooling system, hoses, clamps & coolant strength	S/I						✓						✓	
Clutch pedal operation	S/I						✓						✓	
Front wheel driveshaft joint boots	S/I						✓						✓	
Front suspension ball joints, steering operation & linkage	S/I						✓						✓	
Timing belt/chain & fuel filter	R												✓	

93061C80

Refer to the model specific sections for driveline service procedures

SCHEDULED MAINTENANCE INTERVALS
(FORD ASPIRE) (Cont.)

TO BE SERVICED	TYPE OF SERVICE	VEHICLE MILEAGE INTERVAL (x1000)												
		5	10	15	20	25	30	35	40	45	50	55	60	65
Fuel lines & tubes (emission)	S/I												✓	
Ignition timing	S/I												✓	
Repack front & rear wheel bearing	S/I												✓	

R: Replace   S/I: Service or Inspect

FREQUENT OPERATION MAINTENANCE (SEVERE SERVICE)
If a vehicle is operated under any of the following conditions it is considered severe service:
- Extremely dusty areas.
- 50% or more of the vehicle operation is in 32°C (90°F) or higher temperatures, or constant operation in temperatures below 0°C (32°F).
- Prolonged idling (vehicle operation in stop and go traffic).
- Frequent short running periods (engine does not warm to normal operating temperatures).
- Police, taxi, delivery usage or trailer towing usage.

Oil & filter change: change every 3000 miles.
Rotate tires at 6000 miles & every 9000 miles thereafter.
Air cleaner element: service or inspect every 15,000 miles.
Automatic transmission fluid & filter: change every 21,000 miles.

93061C81

SCHEDULED MAINTENANCE INTERVALS
FORD MOTOR COMPANY
FORD ASPIRE

The following should be used as a guide when determining the amount of work required for a particular service. In estimating how long a particular Scheduled Maintenance Service should take, please observe the following:

- Labor Time is time based on field research and data supplied by the vehicle manufacturer.
- Labor time operations are given in hours and tenths of an hour.
- All labor operations are to be used as a guide.

Mechanic Skill Level Codes:
(A) PRECISION: Highly skilled with multiple certification.
(B) GENERAL: Normally skilled with certification.
(C) MAINTENANCE: Semi-skilled working on certification.

	LABOR TIME		LABOR TIME		LABOR TIME
5000 Mile Service (C)		**25000 Mile Service (C)**		**50000 Mile Service (C)**	
All Models	.9	All Models	.9	All Models	.4
10000 Mile Service (C)		**30000 Mile Service (B)**		**55000 Mile Service (C)**	
All Models	.4	All Models	3.0	All Models	.9
15000 Mile Service (C)		**35000 Mile Service (C)**		**60000 Mile Service (B)**	
All Models	.9	All Models	.9	All Models	6.1
20000 Mile Service (C)		**40000 Mile Service (C)**		**65000 Mile Service (C)**	
All Models	.4	All Models	.4	All Models	.9
		45000 Mile Service (C)			
		All Models	.9		

93061C82

For exhaust manifold replacement procedures, see the model specific sections of this manual

FORD MOTOR CO.
Lincoln Continental

ENGINE AND VEHICLE IDENTIFICATION

Engine								Model Year	
Code ①	Liters (cc)	Cu. In.	Cyl.	Fuel Sys.	Engine Type	Eng. Mfg.		Code ②	Year
V	4.6 (4593)	281	8	SFI	DOHC	Ford		V	1997
								W	1998
OHV: Overhead Valves								X	1999
DOHC: Double Overhead Camshafts								Y	2000
SFI: Sequential Fuel Injection								1	2001

① 8th digit of the Vehicle Identification Number (VIN)

② 10th digit of the Vehicle Identification Number (VIN)

93061C83

GENERAL ENGINE SPECIFICATIONS

Year	Model	Engine Displacement Liters (cc)	Engine ID/VIN	Fuel System Type	Net Horsepower @ rpm	Net Torque @ rpm (ft. lbs.)	Bore x Stroke (in.)	Com-pression Ratio	Oil Pressure @ rpm
1997	Continental	4.6 (4593)	V	SFI	Auto. ①	265@4750	3.55x3.54	9.8:1	33@1500
1998	Continental	4.6 (4593)	V	SFI	260@5750	270@3000	3.55x3.54	9.8:1	33@1500
1999	Continental	4.6 (4593)	V	SFI	260@5750	270@3000	3.55x3.54	9.8:1	33@1500
2000-01	Continental	4.6 (4593)	V	SFI	260@5750	270@3000	3.55x3.54	9.8:1	33@1500

SFI: Sequential Fuel Injection

93061C84

ENGINE TUNE-UP SPECIFICATIONS

Year	Engine Displacement Liters (cc)	Engine ID/VIN	Spark Plug Gap (in.)	Ignition Timing (deg.)	Fuel Pump (psi) ①	Idle Speed (rpm)	Valve Clearance	
							Intake	Exhaust
1997	4.6 (4593)	V	0.052-0.056	10B	Auto. ①	②	HYD	HYD
1998	4.6 (4593)	V	0.052-0.056	10B	30-45	②	HYD	HYD
1999	4.6 (4593)	V	0.052-0.056	10B	30-45	②	HYD	HYD
2000-01	4.6 (4593)	V	0.052-0.056	10B	30-45	②	HYD	HYD

NOTE: The Vehicle Emission Control Information label often reflects specification changes made during production. The label figures must be used if they differ from those in this chart.

B: Before Top Dead Center

HYD: Hydraulic

NA: Not Adjustable

① Fuel pressure with engine running, pressure regulator vacuum hose connected

② Refer to Vehicle Emission Control Information label

93061C85

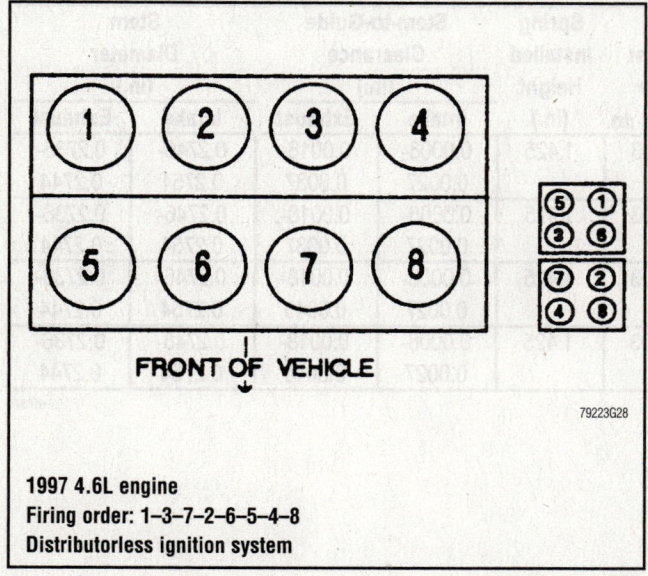

1997 4.6L engine
Firing order: 1–3–7–2–6–5–4–8
Distributorless ignition system

79223G28

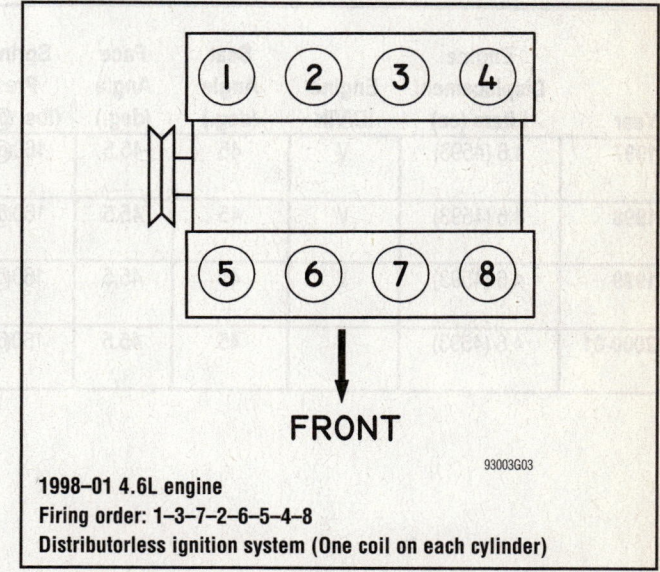

1998–01 4.6L engine
Firing order: 1–3–7–2–6–5–4–8
Distributorless ignition system (One coil on each cylinder)

93003G03

Refer to the model specific sections for cooling system service procedures

CAPACITIES

Year	Model	Engine Displacement Liters (cc)	Engine ID/VIN	Engine Oil with Filter (qts.)	Transaxle (pts.) Auto. ①	Drive Axle (pts.)	Fuel Tank (gal.)	Cooling System (qts.)
1997	Continental	4.6 (4593)	V	6.0	27.4	②	20.0	14.3
1998	Continental	4.6 (4593)	V	6.0	27.4	②	20.0	14.3
1999	Continental	4.6 (4593)	V	6.0	27.4	②	20.0	14.3
2000-01	Continental	4.6 (4593)	V	6.0	27.4	②	20.0	14.3

NOTE: All capacities are approximate. Add fluid gradually and ensure a proper fluid level is obtained.

① Includes torque converter

② Included in transaxle capacity

93061C86

VALVE SPECIFICATIONS

Year	Engine Displacement Liters (cc)	Engine ID/VIN	Seat Angle (deg.)	Face Angle (deg.)	Spring Test Pressure (lbs. @ in.)	Spring Installed Height (in.)	Stem-to-Guide Clearance (in.) Intake	Stem-to-Guide Clearance (in.) Exhaust	Stem Diameter (in.) Intake	Stem Diameter (in.) Exhaust
1997	4.6 (4593)	V	45	45.5	160@1.103	1.425	0.0008-0.0027	0.0018-0.0037	0.2746-0.2754	0.2736-0.2744
1998	4.6 (4593)	V	45	45.5	160@1.103	1.425	0.0008-0.0027	0.0018-0.0037	0.2746-0.2754	0.2736-0.2744
1999	4.6 (4593)	V	45	45.5	160@1.103	1.425	0.0008-0.0027	0.0018-0.0045	0.2746-0.2754	0.2736-0.2744
2000-01	4.6 (4593)	V	45	45.5	160@1.103	1.425	0.0008-0.0027	0.0018-0.0045	0.2746-0.2754	0.2736-0.2744

93061C87

CRANKSHAFT AND CONNECTING ROD SPECIFICATIONS

All measurements are given in inches.

Year	Engine Displacement Liters (cc)	Engine ID/VIN	Crankshaft				Connecting Rod		
			Main Brg. Journal Dia.	Main Brg. Oil Clearance	Shaft Auto. ①	Thrust on No.	Journal Diameter	Oil Clearance	Side Clearance
1997	4.6 (4593)	V	2.6580-2.6576	0.0010-0.0018	0.0051-0.0119	5	2.0859-2.0867	0.0011-0.0027	0.0059-0.0177
1998	4.6 (4593)	V	2.6580-2.6576	0.0010-0.0018	0.0051-0.0119	5	2.0859-2.0867	0.0011-0.0027	0.0059-0.0177
1999	4.6 (4593)	V	2.6580-2.6576	0.0010-0.0018	0.0051-0.0119	5	2.0859-2.0867	0.0011-0.0027	0.0059-0.0177
2000-01	4.6 (4593)	V	2.6580-2.6576	0.0010-0.0018	0.0051-0.0119	5	2.0859-2.0867	0.0011-0.0027	0.0059-0.0177

93061C88

PISTON AND RING SPECIFICATIONS

All measurements are given in inches.

Year	Engine Displacement Liters (cc)	Engine ID/VIN	Piston Clearance	Ring Gap			Ring Side Clearance		
				Top Compression	Bottom Auto. ①	Oil Control	Top Compression	Bottom Compression	Oil Control
1997	4.6 (4593)	V	0.0007-0.0018	0.010-0.020	0.010-0.020	0.006-0.026	0.0004-0.0009	0.0012-0.0032	SNUG
1998	4.6 (4593)	V	0.0007-0.0018	0.010-0.020	0.010-0.020	0.006-0.026	0.0004-0.0009	0.0012-0.0032	SNUG
1999	4.6 (4593)	V	0.0007-0.0018	0.010-0.020	0.010-0.020	0.006-0.026	0.0004-0.0009	0.0012-0.0032	SNUG
2000-01	4.6 (4593)	V	0.0007-0.0018	0.010-0.020	0.010-0.020	0.006-0.026	0.0004-0.0009	0.0012-0.0032	SNUG

93061C89

TORQUE SPECIFICATIONS
All readings in ft. lbs.

Year	Engine Displacement Liters (cc)	Engine ID/VIN	Cylinder Head Bolts	Main Bearing Bolts	Rod Bearing Auto. ①	Crankshaft Damper Bolts	Flywheel Bolts	Manifold Intake	Manifold Exhaust	Spark Plugs	Lug Nuts
1997	4.6 (4593)	V	①	②	③	④	54-64	⑤	⑥	7-15	95
1998	4.6 (4593)	V	⑦	②	③	④	54-64	⑤	⑧	7-15	95
1999	4.6 (4593)	V	⑦	②	③	④	54-64	⑤	⑧	7-15	95
2000-01	4.6 (4593)	V	⑦	②	③	④	54-64	⑤	⑧	7-15	95

① Step 1: 27-32 ft. lbs.
Step 2: Plus 85-95 degrees
Step 3: Plus 85-95 degrees

② Step 1: Main bearing cap bolts: 6-9 ft. lbs.
Step 2: Main bearing cap bolts, outer: 16-21 ft. lbs.
Step 3: Main bearing cap bolts, inner: 27-32 ft. lbs.
Step 4: Rotate main bearing cap bolts 85-95 degrees
Step 5: Main cap adjusting screws 4 ft. lbs. then 7.5 ft. lbs.
Step 6: Main cap side bolts: 7 ft. lbs. then 14-17 ft. lbs.

③ Step 1: 5 ft. lbs.
Step 2: 10 ft. lbs.
Step 3: 18-25 ft. lbs.
Step 4: Plus 85-95 degrees

④ Step 1: 77-99 ft. lbs.
Step 2: Loosen 360 degrees
Step 3: 35-39 ft. lbs.
Step 4: Plus 85-95 degrees

⑤ Step 1: Four inside short bolts: 9-11 ft. lbs.
Step 2: All other bolts: 13-16 ft. lbs.
Step 3: All bolts plus 85-95 degrees

⑥ Studs: 15-22 ft. lbs.
Nuts: 14-16 ft .lbs.

⑦ Step 1: 28-31 ft. lbs.
Step 2: Plus 85-95 degrees
Step 3: Loosen all bolts 360 degrees
Step 4: 28-31 ft. lbs.
Step 5: Plus 85-95 degrees
Step 6: Plus 85-95 degrees

⑧ Studs: 8-9 ft. lbs.
Nuts: 14-16 ft. lbs.

93061C90

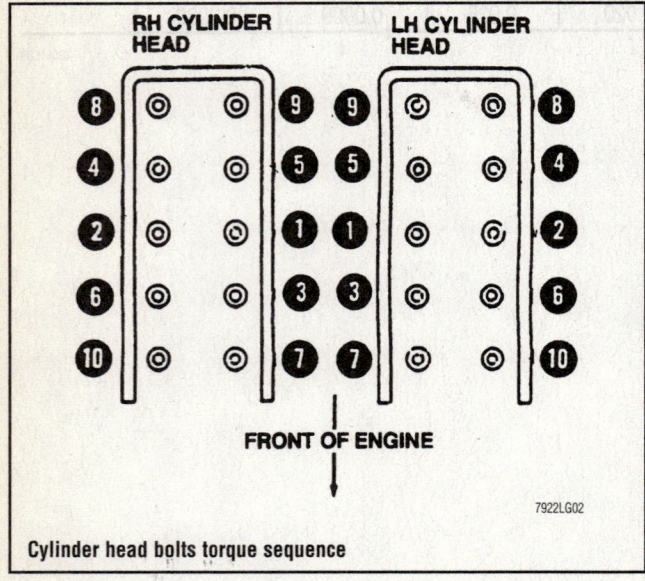

Cylinder head bolts torque sequence

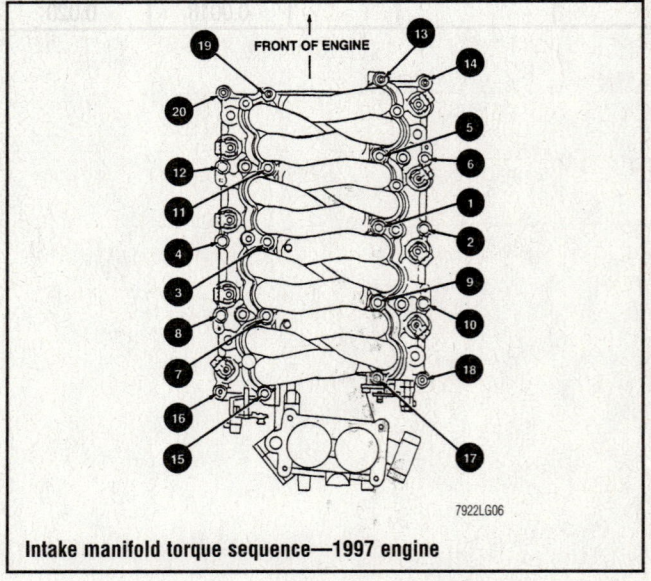

Intake manifold torque sequence—1997 engine

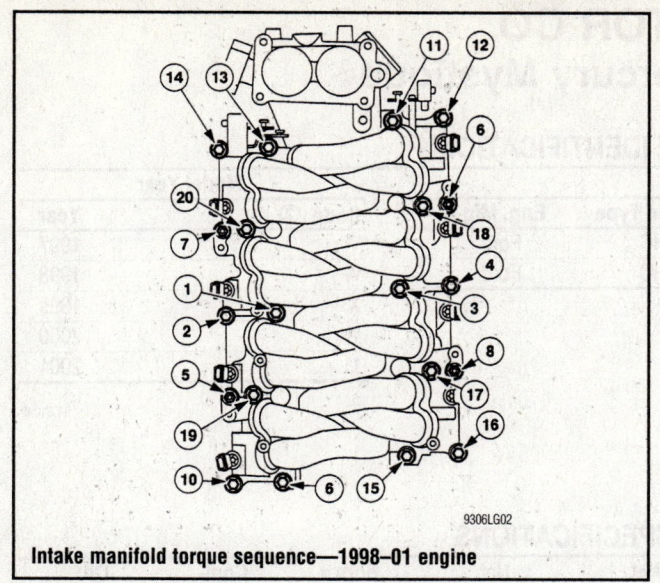

Intake manifold torque sequence—1998–01 engine

9306LG02

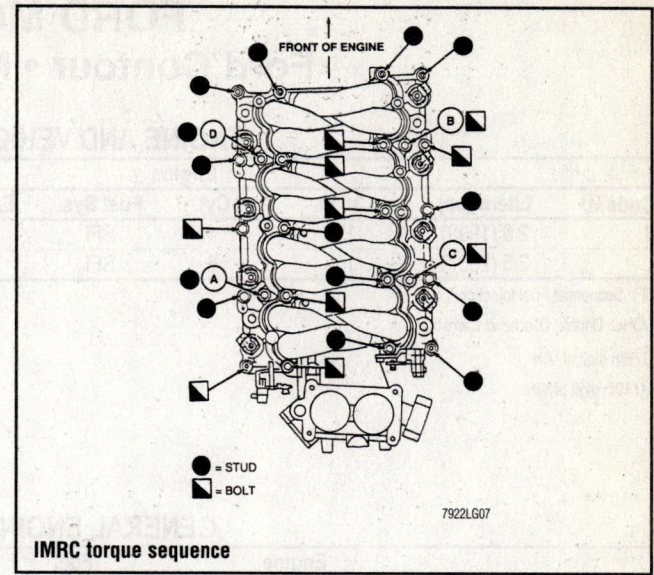

● = STUD

■ = BOLT

IMRC torque sequence

7922LG07

BRAKE SPECIFICATIONS
LINCOLN CONTINENTAL
All measurements in inches unless noted

Year	Model		Brake Disc			Brake Drum			Minimum Lining Thickness	Brake Caliper	
			Original Thickness	Minimum Thickness	Maximum Run-out	Original Inside Diameter	Max. Wear Limit	Maximum Machine Diameter		Bracket Bolts (ft. lbs.)	Mounting Bolts (ft. lbs.)
1997	Continental	F	1.020	0.974	0.003	—	—	—	0.039	65-87	25
		R	0.550	0.502	0.001	—	—	—	0.039	—	25
1998	Continental	F	1.020	0.974	0.003	—	—	—	0.039	65-87	25
		R	0.550	0.502	0.001	—	—	—	0.039	—	25
1999	Continental	F	1.020	0.974	0.003	—	—	—	0.039	65-87	25
		R	0.550	0.502	0.001	—	—	—	0.039	—	25
2000-01	Continental	F	1.020	0.974	0.003	—	—	—	0.039	65-87	25
		R	0.550	0.502	0.001	—	—	—	0.039	—	25

NOTE: Follow specifications stamped on the rotor if figures differ from those in this chart.

F: Front

R: Rear

93061C91

Timing chain and gear service is covered in the model specific sections of this manual

FORD MOTOR CO.
Ford Contour • Mercury Mystique

ENGINE AND VEHICLE IDENTIFICATION

		Engine							Model Year	
Code ①	Liters (cc)	Cu. In.	Cyl.	Fuel Sys.	Engine Type	Eng. Mfg.		Code ②		Year
3	2.0 (1999)	122	4	SFI	DOHC	Ford		V		1997
L	2.5 (2507)	153	6	SFI	DOHC	Ford		W		1998
								X		1999
								Y		2000
								1		2001

SFI: Sequential Fuel Injection

DOHC: Double Overhead Camshaft

① 8th digit of VIN

② 10th digit of VIN

93061C92

GENERAL ENGINE SPECIFICATIONS

Year	Model	Engine Displacement Liters (cc)	Engine ID/VIN	Fuel System Type	Net Horsepower @ rpm	Net Torque @ rpm (ft. lbs.)	Bore x Stroke (in.)	Compression Ratio	Oil Pressure @ rpm
1997	Contour	2.0 (1999)	3	SFI	125@6000	130@4500	3.39x3.46	9.6:1	20-45@1500
		2.5 (2507)	L	SFI	170@6200	165@4200	3.25x3.13	9.7:1	25-45@1500
	Mystique	2.0 (1999)	3	SFI	125@5500	130@4000	3.39x3.46	9.6:1	20-45@1500
		2.5 (2507)	L	SFI	170@6200	165@4200	3.25x3.13	9.7:1	20-45@1500
1998	Contour	2.0 (1999)	3	SFI	125@6000	130@4500	3.39x3.46	9.6:1	20-45@1500
		2.5 (2507)	L	SFI	170@6200	165@4200	3.25x3.13	9.7:1	25-45@1500
	Mystique	2.0 (1999)	3	SFI	125@5500	130@4000	3.39x3.46	9.6:1	20-45@1500
		2.5 (2507)	L	SFI	170@6200	165@4200	3.25x3.13	9.7:1	20-45@1500
1999	Contour	2.0 (1999)	3	SFI	125@6000	130@4500	3.39x3.46	9.6:1	20-45@1500
		2.5 (2507)	L	SFI	170@6200	165@4200	3.25x3.13	9.7:1	25-45@1500
	Cougar	2.0 (1999)	3	SFI	125@6000	130@4500	3.39x3.46	9.6:1	20-45@1500
		2.5 (2507)	L	SFI	170@6200	165@4200	3.25x3.13	9.7:1	25-45@1500
	Mystique	2.0 (1999)	3	SFI	125@5500	130@4000	3.39x3.46	9.6:1	20-45@1500
		2.5 (2507)	L	SFI	170@6200	165@4200	3.25x3.13	9.7:1	20-45@1500
2000-01	Contour	2.5 (2507)	L	SFI	170@6200	165@4200	3.25x3.13	9.7:1	25-45@1500
	Cougar	2.0 (1999)	3	SFI	125@6000	130@4500	3.39x3.46	9.6:1	20-45@1500
		2.5 (2507)	L	SFI	170@6200	165@4200	3.25x3.13	9.7:1	25-45@1500
	Mystique	2.0 (1999)	3	SFI	125@5500	130@4000	3.39x3.46	9.6:1	20-45@1500
		2.5 (2507)	L	SFI	170@6200	165@4200	3.25x3.13	9.7:1	20-45@1500

SFI: Sequential Fuel Injection

93061C93

ENGINE TUNE-UP SPECIFICATIONS

Year	Engine Displacement Liters (cc)	Engine ID/VIN	Spark Plug Gap (in.)	Ignition Timing (deg.)		Fuel Pump (psi) ①	Idle Speed (rpm)		Valve Clearance	
				MT	AT		MT	AT	Intake	Exhaust
1997	2.0 (1999)	3	0.050	10B	10B	37–41	②	②	HYD	HYD
	2.5 (2507)	L	0.054	10B	10B	37–41	②	②	HYD	HYD
1998	2.0 (1999)	3	0.050	10B	10B	37–41	②	②	HYD	HYD
	2.5 (2507)	L	0.054	10B	10B	37–41	②	②	HYD	HYD
1999	2.0 (1999)	3	0.050	10B	10B	37–41	②	②	HYD	HYD
	2.5 (2507)	L	0.054	10B	10B	37–41	②	②	HYD	HYD
2000-01	2.0 (1999)	3	0.050	10B	10B	37–41	②	②	HYD	HYD
	2.5 (2507)	L	0.054	10B	10B	37–41	②	②	HYD	HYD

NOTE: The Vehicle Emission Control Information label often reflects specification changes made during production. The label figures must be used if they differ from those in this chart.

B: Before Top Dead Center

HYD: Hydraulic

① Fuel pressure with engine running, pressure regulator vacuum hose connected

② Refer to Vehicle Emission Control Information (VECI) label

93061C94

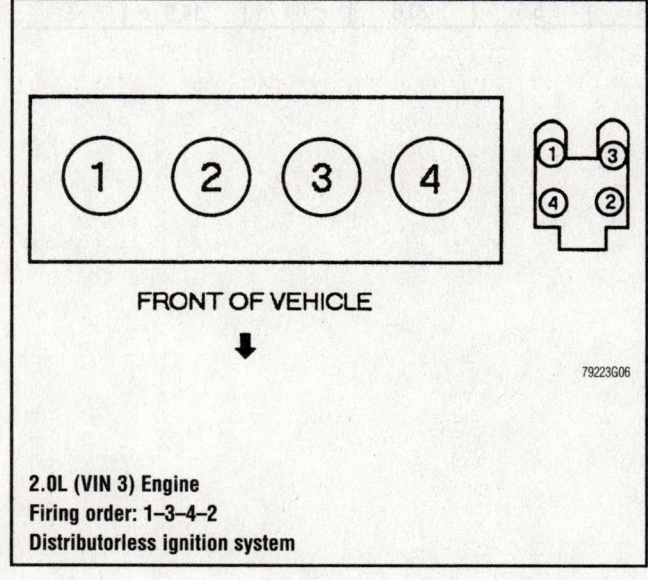

2.0L (VIN 3) Engine
Firing order: 1–3–4–2
Distributorless ignition system

79223G06

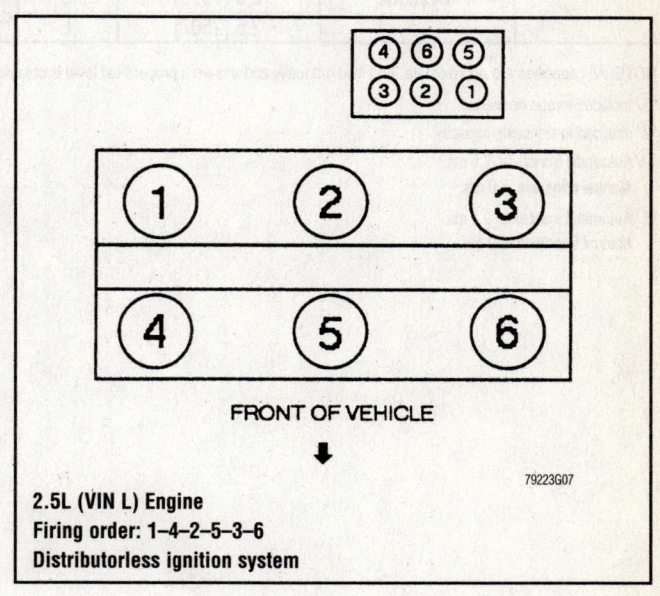

2.5L (VIN L) Engine
Firing order: 1–4–2–5–3–6
Distributorless ignition system

79223G07

Ignition system service is covered in the model specific sections of this manual

CAPACITIES

Year	Model	Engine Displacement Liters (cc)	Engine ID/VIN	Engine Oil with Filter (qts.)	Transaxle (pts.) Manual	Transaxle (pts.) Auto. ①	Front Drive Axle (pts.)	Fuel Tank (gal.)	Cooling System (qts.)
1997	Contour	2.0 (1999)	3	4.5	5.5	18.0	②	14.5	③
		2.5 (2507)	L	5.8	5.5	20.6	②	14.5	④
	Mystique	2.0 (1999)	3	4.5	5.5	18.0	②	14.5	③
		2.5 (2507)	L	5.8	5.5	20.6	②	14.5	④
1998	Contour	2.0 (1999)	3	4.5	5.5	18.0	②	14.5	③
		2.5 (2507)	L	5.8	5.5	20.6	②	14.5	④
	Mystique	2.0 (1999)	3	4.5	5.5	18.0	②	14.5	③
		2.5 (2507)	L	5.8	5.5	20.6	②	14.5	④
1999	Contour	2.0 (1999)	3	4.5	5.5	18.0	②	14.5	③
		2.5 (2507)	L	5.8	5.5	20.6	②	14.5	④
	Cougar	2.0 (1999)	3	4.5	5.5	18.0	②	14.5	④
		2.5 (2507)	L	5.8	5.5	20.6	②	14.5	④
	Mystique	2.0 (1999)	3	4.5	5.5	18.0	②	14.5	③
		2.5 (2507)	L	5.8	5.5	20.6	②	14.5	④
2000-01	Contour	2.5 (2507)	L	5.8	5.5	20.6	②	14.5	④
	Cougar	2.0 (1999)	3	4.5	5.5	18.0	②	14.5	④
		2.5 (2507)	L	5.8	5.5	20.6	②	14.5	④
	Mystique	2.0 (1999)	3	4.5	5.5	18.0	②	14.5	③
		2.5 (2507)	L	5.8	5.5	20.6	②	14.5	④

NOTE: All capacities are approximate. Add fluid gradually and ensure a proper fluid level is obtained.

① Includes torque converter

② Included in transaxle capacity

③ Automatic transaxle: 7.5 qts.
Manual transaxle: 7.0 qts.

④ Automatic transaxle: 9.1 qts.
Manual transaxle: 8.9 qts.

93061C95

VALVE SPECIFICATIONS

Year	Engine Displacement Liters (cc)	Engine ID/VIN	Seat Angle (deg.)	Face Angle (deg.)	Spring Test Pressure (lbs. @ in.)	Spring Installed Height (in.)	Stem-to-Guide Clearance (in.)		Stem Diameter (in.)	
							Intake	Exhaust	Intake	Exhaust
1997	2.0 (1999)	3	45	45	NA	1.346	0.0007-0.0025	0.0014-0.0032	0.2373-0.2379	0.2366-0.2372
	2.5 (2507)	L	44.75	45.5	153@1.18	1.570	0.0007-0.0027	0.0017-0.0037	0.2350-0.2358	0.2343-0.2350
1998	2.0 (1999)	3	45	45	NA	1.346	0.0007-0.0025	0.0014-0.0032	0.2373-0.2379	0.2366-0.2372
	2.5 (2507)	L	44.75	45.5	153@1.18	1.570	0.0007-0.0027	0.0017-0.0037	0.2350-0.2358	0.2343-0.2350
1999	2.0 (1999)	3	45	45	NA	1.346	0.0007-0.0025	0.0014-0.0032	0.2373-0.2379	0.2366-0.2372
	2.5 (2507)	L	44.75	45.5	153@1.18	1.570	0.0007-0.0027	0.0017-0.0037	0.2350-0.2358	0.2343-0.2350
2000-01	2.0 (1999)	3	45	45	NA	1.346	0.0007-0.0025	0.0014-0.0032	0.2373-0.2379	0.2366-0.2372
	2.5 (2507)	L	44.75	45.5	153@1.18	1.570	0.0007-0.0027	0.0017-0.0037	0.2350-0.2358	0.2343-0.2350

93061C96

CRANKSHAFT AND CONNECTING ROD SPECIFICATIONS

All measurements are given in inches.

Year	Engine Displacement Liters (cc)	Engine ID/VIN	Crankshaft				Connecting Rod		
			Main Brg. Journal Dia.	Main Brg. Oil Clearance	Shaft End-play	Thrust on No.	Journal Diameter	Oil Clearance	Side Clearance
1997	2.0 (1999)	3	2.2827-2.2835	0.0008-0.0017	0.0035-0.0100	3	1.8425-1.8504	0.0006-0.0028	0.0035-0.0126
	2.5 (2507)	L	2.4670-2.4790	0.0009-0.0019	0.0040-0.0090	4	1.9670-1.9680	0.0010-0.0025	0.0039-0.0118
1998	2.0 (1999)	3	2.2827-2.2835	0.0008-0.0017	0.0035-0.0100	3	1.8425-1.8504	0.0006-0.0028	0.0035-0.0126
	2.5 (2507)	L	2.4670-2.4790	0.0009-0.0019	0.0040-0.0090	4	1.9670-1.9680	0.0010-0.0025	0.0039-0.0118
1999	2.0 (1999)	3	2.2827-2.2835	0.0008-0.0017	0.0035-0.0100	3	1.8425-1.8504	0.0006-0.0028	0.0035-0.0126
	2.5 (2507)	L	2.4670-2.4790	0.0009-0.0019	0.0040-0.0090	4	1.9670-1.9680	0.0010-0.0025	0.0039-0.0118
2000-01	2.0 (1999)	3	2.2827-2.2835	0.0008-0.0017	0.0035-0.0100	3	1.8425-1.8504	0.0006-0.0028	0.0035-0.0126
	2.5 (2507)	L	2.4670-2.4790	0.0009-0.0019	0.0040-0.0090	4	1.9670-1.9680	0.0010-0.0025	0.0039-0.0118

93061C97

PISTON AND RING SPECIFICATIONS
All measurements are given in inches.

Year	Engine Displacement Liters (cc)	Engine ID/VIN	Piston Clearance	Ring Gap			Ring Side Clearance		
				Top Compression	Bottom Compression	Oil Control	Top Compression	Bottom Compression	Oil Control
1997	2.0 (1999)	3	0.0008-0.0016	0.008-0.010	0.012-0.020	0.016-0.055	0.0016-0.0028	0.0008-0.0021	Snug
	2.5 (2507)	L	0.0005-0.0009	0.004-0.010	0.011-0.017	0.006-0.026	0.0015-0.0029	0.0015-0.0033	Snug
1998	2.0 (1999)	3	0.0008-0.0016	0.008-0.010	0.012-0.020	0.016-0.055	0.0016-0.0028	0.0008-0.0021	Snug
	2.5 (2507)	L	0.0005-0.0009	0.004-0.010	0.011-0.017	0.006-0.026	0.0015-0.0029	0.0015-0.0033	Snug
1999	2.0 (1999)	3	0.0008-0.0016	0.008-0.010	0.012-0.020	0.016-0.055	0.0016-0.0028	0.0008-0.0021	Snug
	2.5 (2507)	L	0.0005-0.0009	0.004-0.010	0.011-0.017	0.006-0.026	0.0015-0.0029	0.0015-0.0033	Snug
2000-01	2.0 (1999)	3	0.0008-0.0016	0.008-0.010	0.012-0.020	0.016-0.055	0.0016-0.0028	0.0008-0.0021	Snug
	2.5 (2507)	L	0.0005-0.0009	0.004-0.010	0.011-0.017	0.006-0.026	0.0015-0.0029	0.0015-0.0033	Snug

93061C98

Refer to the model specific sections for engine mechanical service procedures

TORQUE SPECIFICATIONS
All readings in ft. lbs.

Year	Engine Displacement Liters (cc)	Engine ID/VIN	Cylinder Head Bolts	Main Bearing Bolts	Rod Bearing Bolts	Crankshaft Damper Bolts	Flywheel Bolts	Manifold Intake	Manifold Exhaust	Spark Plugs	Lug Nuts
1997	2.0 (1999)	3	①	55-66	②	81-89	80-87	12-15	13-16	9-13	63
	2.5 (2507)	L	③	④	⑤	⑥	54-64	6-9	13-16	7-15	63
1998	2.0 (1999)	3	①	55-66	②	81-89	80-87	12-15	13-16	9-13	63
	2.5 (2507)	L	③	④	⑤	⑥	54-64	6-9	13-16	7-15	63
1999	2.0 (1999)	3	①	55-66	②	81-89	80-87	12-15	13-16	9-13	63
	2.5 (2507)	L	③	④	⑤	⑥	54-64	6-9	13-16	7-15	63
2000-01	2.0 (1999)	3	①	55-66	②	81-89	80-87	12-15	13-16	9-13	63
	2.5 (2507)	L	③	④	⑤	⑥	54-64	6-9	13-16	7-15	63

NOTE: Always follow proper torque patterns. Stretch bolts are used in all procedures that require rotating the fastener a certain number of degrees.

The bolts stretch and cannot be reused. For reassembly, replace with new fastners.

① Step 1: 15-22 ft. lbs.
Step 2: 30-37 ft. lbs.
Step 3: Tighten 90-120 degrees

② Step 1: 22-25 ft. lbs.
Step 2: Tighten each bolt 85-95 degrees

③ Step 1: 27-32 ft. lbs.
Step 2: Tighten 85-95 degrees
Step 3: Loosen bolts then repeat Step 1
Step 4: Tighten 85-95 degrees
Step 5: Repeat Step 4

④ Step 1: 2.0-3.6 ft. lbs.
Step 2: Push crankshaft rearward.
Lightly seat crankshaft washer forward
Step 3: Outer cap bolts: 16-21 ft. lbs.
Step 4: Inner cap bolts: 27-32 ft. lbs.
Step 5: Tighten inner and outer cap bolts 85-95 degrees
Step 6: Remaining bolts: 15-22 ft. lbs.

⑤ 26-33 ft. lbs. plus 90-120 degrees

⑥ Step 1: 89 ft. lbs.
Step 2: Loosen bolt
Step 3: 35-39 ft. lbs.

93061C99

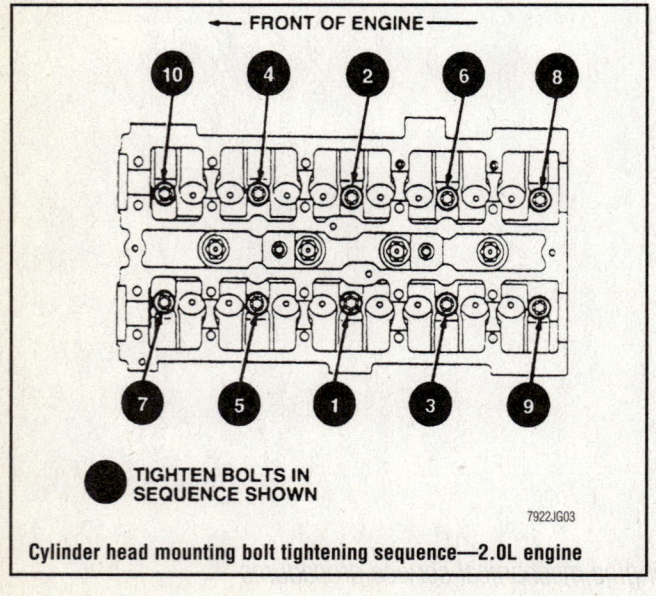

Cylinder head mounting bolt tightening sequence—2.0L engine

7922JG03

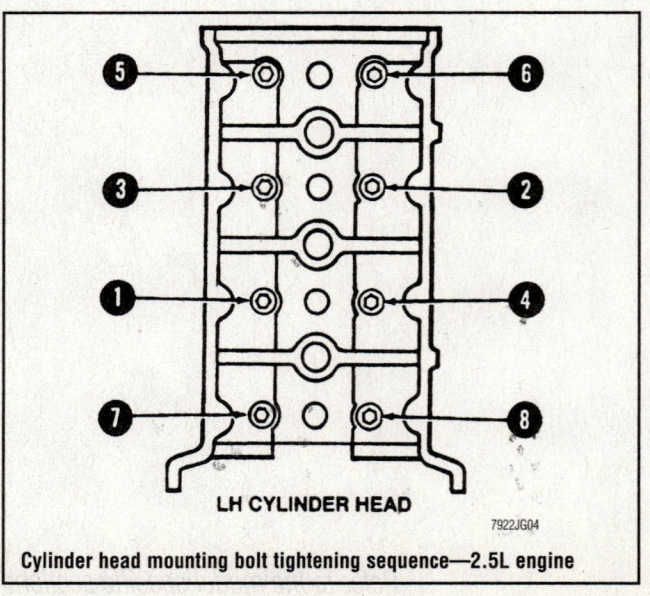

Cylinder head mounting bolt tightening sequence—2.5L engine

7922JG04

Installation Sequence

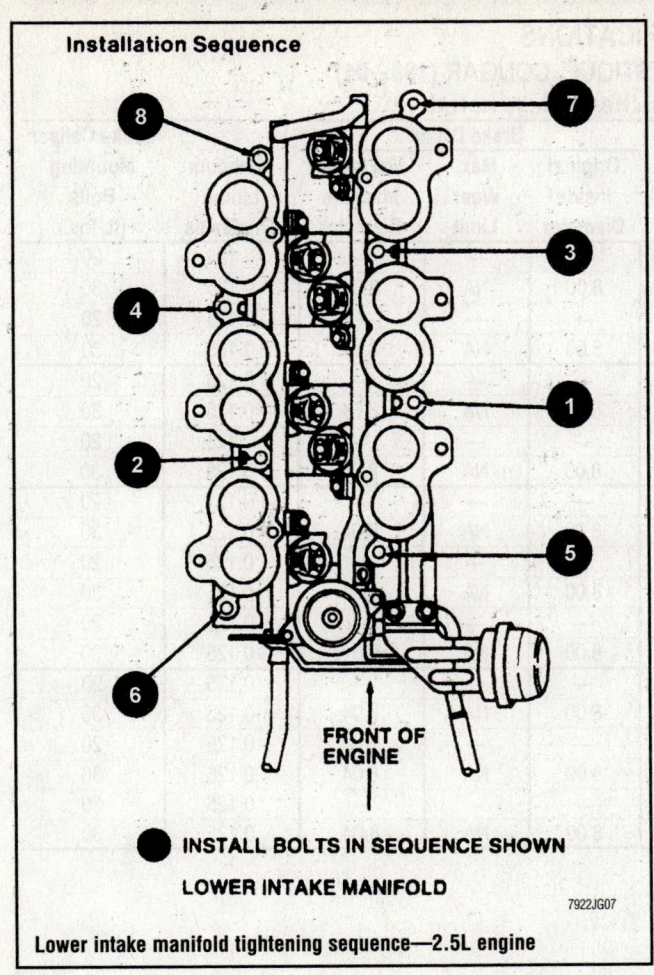

FRONT OF ENGINE

INSTALL BOLTS IN SEQUENCE SHOWN

LOWER INTAKE MANIFOLD

7922JG07

Lower intake manifold tightening sequence—2.5L engine

Installation Sequence

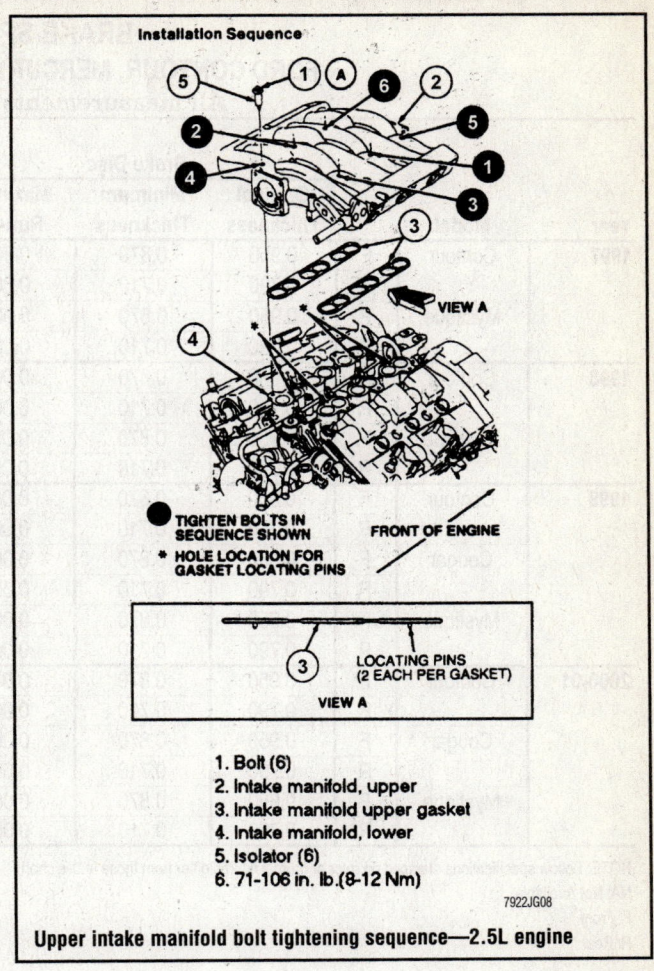

VIEW A

● **TIGHTEN BOLTS IN SEQUENCE SHOWN**

FRONT OF ENGINE

✳ **HOLE LOCATION FOR GASKET LOCATING PINS**

③ **LOCATING PINS (2 EACH PER GASKET)**

VIEW A

1. Bolt (6)
2. Intake manifold, upper
3. Intake manifold upper gasket
4. Intake manifold, lower
5. Isolator (6)
6. 71-106 in. lb.(8-12 Nm)

7922JG08

Upper intake manifold bolt tightening sequence—2.5L engine

Refer to the model specific sections for fuel system service procedures

BRAKE SPECIFICATIONS
FORD CONTOUR, MERCURY MYSTIQUE, COUGAR (1999-01)
All measurements in inches unless noted

Year	Model		Brake Disc Original Thickness	Brake Disc Minimum Thickness	Brake Disc Maximum Run-out	Brake Drum Original Inside Diameter	Brake Drum Max. Wear Limit	Brake Drum Maximum Machine Diameter	Minimum Lining Thickness	Brake Caliper Mounting Bolts (ft. lbs.)
1997	Contour	F	0.950	0.870	0.006	—	—	—	0.125	20
		R	0.790	0.710	0.006	8.00	NA	8.04	0.125	30
	Mystique	F	0.950	0.870	0.006	—	—	—	0.125	20
		R	0.790	0.710	0.006	8.00	NA	8.04	0.125	30
1998	Contour	F	0.950	0.870	0.006	—	—	—	0.125	20
		R	0.790	0.710	0.006	8.00	NA	8.04	0.125	30
	Mystique	F	0.950	0.870	0.006	—	—	—	0.125	20
		R	0.790	0.710	0.006	8.00	NA	8.04	0.125	30
1999	Contour	F	0.950	0.870	0.006	—	—	—	0.125	20
		R	0.790	0.710	0.006	8.00	NA	8.04	0.125	30
	Cougar	F	0.950	0.870	0.006	—	—	—	0.125	20
		R	0.790	0.710	0.006	8.00	NA	8.04	0.125	30
	Mystique	F	0.950	0.870	0.006	—	—	—	0.125	20
		R	0.790	0.710	0.006	8.00	NA	8.04	0.125	30
2000-01	Contour	F	0.950	0.870	0.006	—	—	—	0.125	20
		R	0.790	0.710	0.006	8.00	NA	8.04	0.125	30
	Cougar	F	0.950	0.870	0.006	—	—	—	0.125	20
		R	0.790	0.710	0.006	8.00	NA	8.04	0.125	30
	Mystique	F	0.950	0.870	0.006	—	—	—	0.125	20
		R	0.790	0.710	0.006	8.00	NA	8.04	0.125	30

NOTE: Follow specifications stamped on rotor or drum if figures differ from those in this chart.
NA: Not Available
F: Front
R: Rear

93061CA1

SCHEDULED MAINTENANCE INTERVALS
(FORD CONTOUR, MERCURY MYSTIQUE & 1999-01 COUGAR)

TO BE SERVICED	TYPE OF SERVICE	VEHICLE MILEAGE INTERVAL (x1000)												
		5	10	15	20	25	30	35	40	45	50	55	60	65
Engine oil & filter	R	✓	✓	✓	✓	✓	✓	✓	✓	✓	✓	✓	✓	✓
Rotate tires	S/I	✓		✓		✓		✓		✓		✓		✓
Front & rear brakes	S/I		✓		✓		✓		✓		✓		✓	
Cooling system, hoses, clamps & coolant strength	S/I			✓			✓			✓			✓	
Passenger compartment air filter	R				✓				✓				✓	
Air cleaner element	R						✓						✓	
Automatic transaxle fluid & filter	S/I												✓	
Exhaust heat shields	S/I						✓						✓	
Accessory drive belt(s)	S/I						✓						✓	
Fuel lines & hoses	S/I						✓						✓	
Crankcase emission filter (2.0L)	R						✓							
Engine coolant ①	R										✓			
Spark plugs ②③	R												✓	
PCV valve	R												✓	

R: Replace   S/I: Service or Inspect

① Change initially at 50,000 miles & every 30,000 miles thereafter.

② 2.0L: replace every 60,000 miles.

③ 2.5L: replace every 100,000 miles.

FREQUENT OPERATION MAINTENANCE (SEVERE SERVICE)

If a vehicle is operated under any of the following conditions it is considered severe service:

- Extremely dusty areas.

- 50% or more of the vehicle operation is in 32°C (90°F) or higher temperatures, or constant operation in temperatures below 0°C (32°F).

- Prolonged idling (vehicle operation in stop and go traffic).

- Frequent short running periods (engine does not warm to normal operating temperatures).

- Police, taxi, delivery usage or trailer towing usage.

Oil & filter change: change every 3000 miles.

Front & rear brakes: check every 9000 miles.

Rotate tires at 6000 miles & every 9000 miles thereafter.

Air cleaner element: check every 15,000 miles.

Passenger compartment air filter: change every 18,000 miles.

Automatic transaxle fluid & filter: change every 30,000 miles.

Spark plugs: replace every 60,000 miles.

93061CA2

Refer to the model specific sections for engine electrical system service procedures

SCHEDULED MAINTENANCE INTERVALS
FORD MOTOR COMPANY
FORD CONTOUR, MERCURY MYSTIQUE
MERCURY COUGAR (1999-01)

The following should be used as a guide when determining the amount of work required for a particular service.
In estimating how long a particular Scheduled Maintenance Service should take, please observe the following:

- Labor Time is time based on field research and data supplied by the vehicle manufacturer.
- Labor time operations are given in hours and tenths of an hour.
- All labor operations are to be used as a guide.

Mechanic Skill Level Codes:
(A) PRECISION: Highly skilled with multiple certification.
(B) GENERAL: Normally skilled with certification.
(C) MAINTENANCE: Semi-skilled working on certification.

	LABOR TIME		LABOR TIME		LABOR TIME
5000 Mile Service (C)		**25000 Mile Service (C)**		**50000 Mile Service (B)**	
All Models	.9	All Models	.9	All Models	1.2
10000 Mile Service (C)		**30000 Mile Service (B)**		**55000 Mile Service (C)**	
All Models	.7	All Models	1.7	All Models	.7
15000 Mile Service (C)		**35000 Mile Service (C)**		**60000 Mile Service (B)**	
All Models	1.0	All Models	.9	All Models	3.4
20000 Mile Service (C)		**40000 Mile Service (C)**		*Replace A.T. fluid & filter add* . .	.6
All Models	1.0	All Models	1.0	**65000 Mile Service (C)**	
		45000 Mile Service (C)		All Models	.9
		All Models	1.0		

93061CA3

FORD MOTOR CO.
Ford Thunderbird • Mercury Cougar (1999–01)

ENGINE AND VEHICLE IDENTIFICATION

		Engine						Model Year	
Code ①	Liters (cc)	Cu. In.	Cyl.	Fuel Sys.	Engine Type	Eng. Mfg.		Code ②	Year
4	3.8 (3801)	232	6	MFI	OHV	Ford		V	1997
W	4.6 (4593)	281	8	SFI	SOHC	Ford			

OHV: Overhead Valves

MFI: Multiport Fuel Injection

SFI: Sequential Fuel Injection

SOHC: Single Overhead Camshaft

① 8th digit of the VIN

② 10th digit of the VIN

93061CA4

GENERAL ENGINE SPECIFICATIONS
All measurements are given in inches.

Year	Model	Engine Displacement Liters (cc)	Engine Series (ID/VIN)	Fuel System	Net Horsepower @ rpm	Net Torque @ rpm (ft. lbs.)	Bore x Stroke (in.)	Compression Ratio	Oil Pressure @ rpm
1997	Cougar	3.8 (3802)	4	SFI	145@4000	215@2750	3.81x3.39	9.0:1	40-60@2500
	Cougar	4.6 (4593)	W	SFI	205@4250	280@3000	3.55x3.54	9.0:1	20-45@1500
	Thunderbird	3.8 (3802)	4	SFI	145@4000	215@2750	3.81x3.39	9.0:1	40-60@2500
	Thunderbird	4.6 (4593)	W	SFI	205@4250	280@3000	3.55x3.54	9.0:1	20-45@1500

SFI: Sequential Fuel Injection

93061CA5

For accessory drive belt replacement procedures see the model specific sections of this manual

ENGINE TUNE-UP SPECIFICATIONS

Year	Engine Displacement Liters (cc)	Engine ID/VIN	Spark Plug Gap (in.)	Ignition Timing (deg.)		Fuel Pump (psi) ①	Idle Speed (rpm)		Valve Clearance	
				MT	AT		MT	AT	Intake	Exhaust
1997	3.8 (3802)	4	0.054	①	①	28-54	①	①	HYD	HYD
	4.6 (4593)	W	0.054	10B	10B	35-45	①	①	HYD	HYD

NOTE: The Vehicle Emission Control Information label often reflects specification changes made during production. The label figures must be used if they differ from those in this chart.

B: Before Top Dead Center

HYD: Hydraulic

① Refer to Vehicle Emission Control Information label

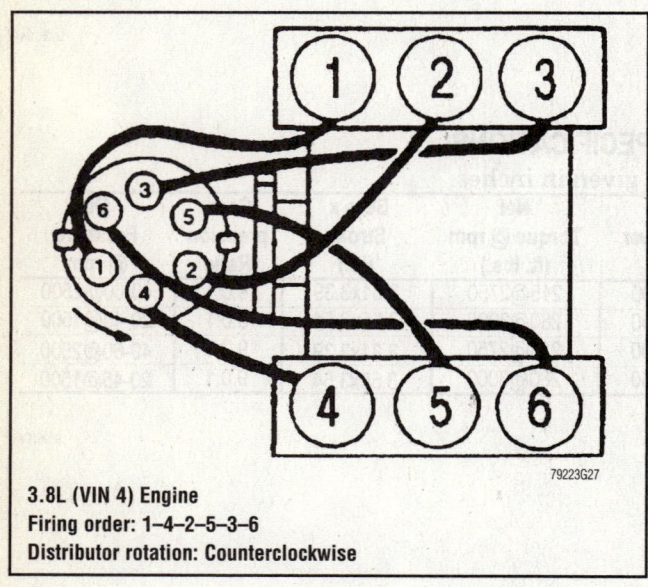

3.8L (VIN 4) Engine
Firing order: 1–4–2–5–3–6
Distributor rotation: Counterclockwise

79223G27

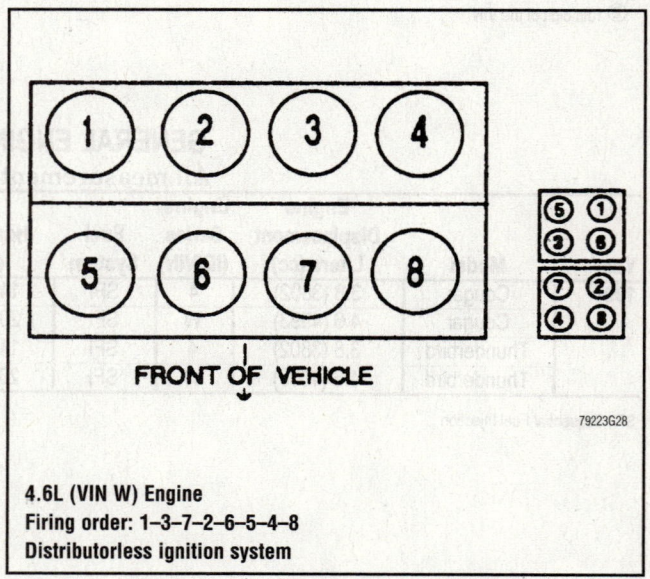

FRONT OF VEHICLE

4.6L (VIN W) Engine
Firing order: 1–3–7–2–6–5–4–8
Distributorless ignition system

79223G28

CAPACITIES

Year	Model	Engine Displacement Liters (cc)	Engine ID/VIN	Engine Oil with Filter (qts.)	Transmission (pts)		Drive Axle Rear (pts.)	Fuel Tank (gal.)	Cooling System (qts.)
					Manual	Auto. ①			
1997	Cougar	3.8 (3802)	4	5.0	—	27.8	②	18.0	12.6
	Cougar	4.6 (4593)	W	5.3	—	27.8	②	18.0	14.1
	Thunderbird	3.8 (3802)	4	5.0	—	27.8	②	18.0	12.6
	Thunderbird	4.6 (4593)	W	5.3	—	27.8	②	18.0	14.1

NOTE: All capacities are approximate. Add fluid gradually and ensure a proper fluid level is obtained.

① Includes torque converter

② 7.50 in. axle: 3.5 pts.
   8.80 in. axle: 3.75 pts.

93061CA7

VALVE SPECIFICATIONS

Year	Engine Displacement Liters (cc)	Engine ID/VIN	Seat Angle (deg.)	Face Angle (deg.)	Spring Test Pressure (lbs. @ in.)	Spring Installed Height (in.)	Stem-to-Guide Clearance (in.)		Stem Diameter (in.)	
							Intake	Exhaust	Intake	Exhaust
1997	3.8 (3802)	4	44.5	45.8	220@1.18	1.650	0.0010-0.0027	0.0015-0.0032	0.3415-0.3423	0.3410-0.3418
	4.6 (4593)	W	45	45.5	132@1.10	1.570	0.0008-0.0027	0.0018-0.0037	0.2746-0.2754	0.2736-0.2744

93061CA8

For brake related suspension and axle service, refer to the model specific sections of this manual

CRANKSHAFT AND CONNECTING ROD SPECIFICATIONS
All measurements are given in inches.

Year	Engine Displacement Liters (cc)	Engine ID/VIN	Crankshaft				Connecting Rod		
			Main Brg. Journal Dia.	Main Brg. Oil Clearance	Shaft End-play	Thrust on No.	Journal Diameter	Oil Clearance	Side Clearance
1997	3.8(3802)	4	①	0.0010-0.0014	0.0040-0.0080	3	2.3103-2.3111	0.0010-0.0014	0.0047-0.0144
	4.6(4593)	W	2.6569-2.6576	0.0011-0.0026	0.0051-0.0119	5	2.0861-2.0867	0.0011-0.0027	0.0006-0.0177

① Journals 1, 2, 3: 2.5194-2.5186 in.
   Journal 4: 2.5100-2.5092 in.

93061CA9

PISTON AND RING SPECIFICATIONS
All measurements are given in inches.

Year	Engine Displacement Liters (cc)	Engine ID/VIN	Piston Clearance	Ring Gap			Ring Side Clearance		
				Top Compression	Bottom Compression	Oil Control	Top Compression	Bottom Compression	Oil Control
1997	3.8 (3802)	4	0.0014-0.0022	0.011-0.012	0.009-0.020	0.015-0.058	0.0016-0.0034	0.0016-0.0034	SNUG
	4.6 (4593)	W	0.0005-0.0010	0.009-0.019	0.009-0.019	0.006-0.026	0.0016-0.0035	0.0018-0.0031	SNUG

93061CA0

TORQUE SPECIFICATIONS
All readings in ft. lbs.

Year	Engine Displacement Liters (cc)	Engine ID/VIN	Cylinder Head Bolts	Main Bearing Bolts	Rod Bearing Bolts	Crankshaft Damper Bolts	Flywheel Bolts	Manifold		Spark Plugs	Lug Nuts
								Intake	Exhaust		
1997	3.8 (3802)	4	①	65-81	31-36	103-132	54-64	②	15-22	7-15	95
	4.6 (4593)	W	③	④	⑤	114-121	54-64	15-22	15-22	7-15	95

① Do not reuse cylinder head bolts.
Step 1: 15 ft. lbs.
Step 2: 29 ft. lbs.
Step 3: 37 ft. lbs.
Step 4: Loosen bolts one at a time and retorque as follows:
Long bolts: 11-18 ft. lbs.
Short bolts: 7-15 ft. lbs.
Step 5: Tighten 85-95 degrees

② Upper intake manifold bolts:
Step 1: 8 ft. lbs.
Step 2: 15 ft. lbs.
Step 3: 24 ft lbs
Lower intake manifold bolts:
Step 1: 13 ft. lbs.
Step 2: 16 ft. lbs.

③ Do not reuse cylinder head bolts.
Step 1: 27-32 ft. lbs.
Step 2: Tighten each bolt 85-95 degrees

④ Do not reuse main cap bolts.
Step 1: Main bearing cap bolts: 22-25 ft. lbs.
Step 2: Tighten each bolt 85-95 degrees
Step 3: Main bearing cap adjust screws: 4 ft. lbs. then 6-8 ft. lbs.
Step 4: Main bearing cap side bolts: 7 ft. lbs. then 14-17 ft. lbs.

⑤ Do not reuse rod bolts.
Step 1: 12 ft. lbs.
Step 2: Tighten 85-95 degrees
Step 6: Tighten an additional 90 degrees

93061CB1

Refer to the model specific sections for driveline service procedures

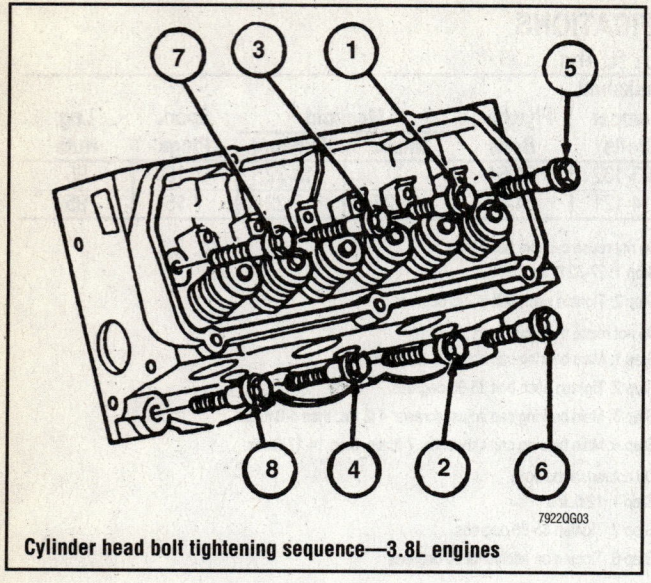

Cylinder head bolt tightening sequence—3.8L engines

7922QG03

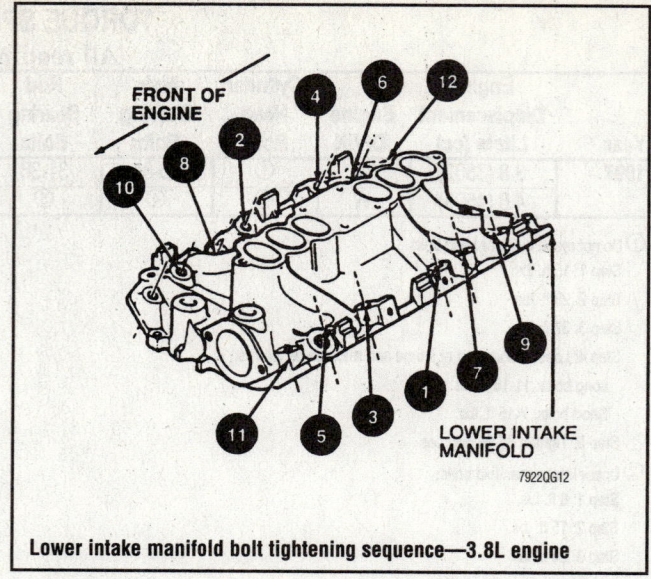

FRONT OF ENGINE

LOWER INTAKE MANIFOLD

Lower intake manifold bolt tightening sequence—3.8L engine

7922QG12

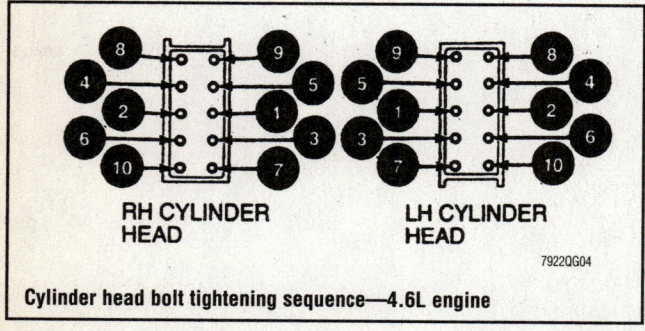

RH CYLINDER HEAD

LH CYLINDER HEAD

Cylinder head bolt tightening sequence—4.6L engine

7922QG04

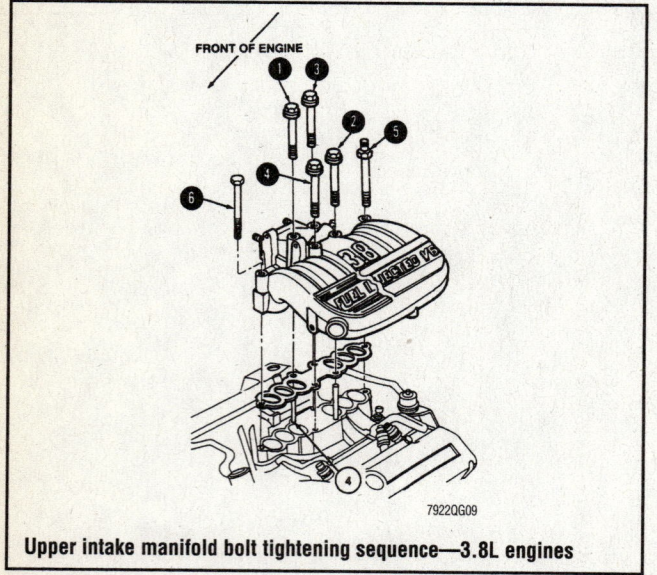

FRONT OF ENGINE

Upper intake manifold bolt tightening sequence—3.8L engines

7922QG09

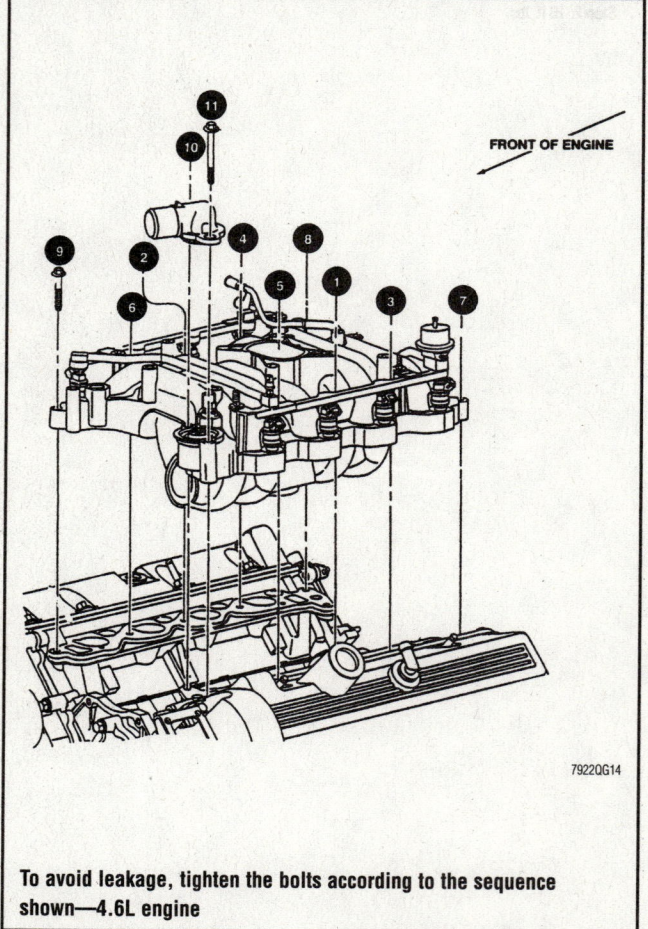

FRONT OF ENGINE

To avoid leakage, tighten the bolts according to the sequence shown—4.6L engine

7922QG14

BRAKE SPECIFICATIONS
FORD THUNDERBIRD & MERCURY COUGAR (1997)
All measurements in inches unless noted

| Year | Model | | Brake Disc | | | Brake Drum Diameter | | | Minimum Lining Thickness | | Brake Caliper Mounting Bolts (ft. lbs.) |
			Original Thickness	Minimum Thickness	Maximum Run-out	Original Inside Diameter	Max. Wear Limit	Maximum Machine Diameter	Front	Rear	
1997	Cougar	F	1.025	0.974	0.002	9.80	NA	9.90	0.125	0.125	60
		R	0.710	0.657	—	—	—	—	—	0.125	26
	Thunderbird	F	1.025	0.974	0.002	9.80	NA	9.90	0.125	0.125	60
		R	0.710	0.657	—	—	—	—	—	0.125	26

NOTE: Follow specifications stamped on rotor or drum if figures differ from those in this chart.

NA: Not Available

F: Front

R: Rear

93061CB2

For exhaust manifold replacement procedures, see the model specific sections of this manual

FORD MOTOR CO.
Ford Crown Victoria • Lincoln Town Car • Mercury Grand Marquis

ENGINE AND VEHICLE IDENTIFICATION

Engine							Model Year	
Code ①	Liters (cc)	Cu. In.	Cyl.	Fuel Sys.	Type	Eng. Mfg.	Code ②	Year
W	4.6 (4593)	281	8	SFI	SOHC	Ford	V	1997
							W	1998
							X	1999
							Y	2000
							1	2001

SFI: Sequential Fuel Injection

SOHC: Single Overhead Camshaft

① 8th digit of the Vehicle Identification Number (VIN)

② 10th digit fo the Vehicle Identification Number (VIN)

93061CB3

GENERAL ENGINE SPECIFICATIONS

Year	Model	Engine Displacement Liters (cc)	Engine ID/VIN	Fuel System Type	Net Horsepower @ rpm	Net Torque @ rpm (ft. lbs.)	Bore x Stroke (in.)	Com-pression Ratio	Oil Pressure @ rpm
1997	Crown Victoria	4.6 (4593)	W	SFI	①	②	3.55x3.54	③	20-45@1500
	Grand Marquis	4.6 (4593)	W	SFI	①	②	3.55x3.54	9.0:1	20-45@1500
	Town Car	4.6 (4593)	W	SFI	210@4250	275@3250	3.55x3.54	9.0:1	20-45@1500
1998	Crown Victoria	4.6 (4593)	W	SFI	①	②	3.55x3.54	③	20-45@1500
	Grand Marquis	4.6 (4593)	W	SFI	①	②	3.55x3.54	9.0:1	20-45@1500
	Town Car	4.6 (4593)	W	SFI	210@4250	275@3250	3.55x3.54	9.0:1	20-45@1500
1999	Crown Victoria	4.6 (4593)	W	SFI	①	②	3.55x3.54	③	20-45@1500
	Grand Marquis	4.6 (4593)	W	SFI	①	②	3.55x3.54	9.0:1	20-45@1500
	Town Car	4.6 (4593)	W	SFI	210@4250	275@3250	3.55x3.54	9.0:1	20-45@1500
2000-01	Crown Victoria	4.6 (4593)	W	SFI	①	②	3.55x3.54	③	20-45@1500
	Grand Marquis	4.6 (4593)	W	SFI	①	②	3.55x3.54	9.0:1	20-45@1500
	Town Car	4.6 (4593)	W	SFI	210@4250	275@3250	3.55x3.54	9.0:1	20-45@1500

SFI: Sequential Fuel Injection

① Single exhaust: 190@4250

Dual exhaust: 210@4250

Crown Victoria with natural gas: 178@4500

② Single exhaust: 265@3250

Dual exhaust: 275@3250

Crown Victoria with natural gas: 237@3500

③ Base engine: 9.0:1

Crown Victoria with natural gas: 10.0:1

93061CB4

ENGINE TUNE-UP SPECIFICATIONS

Year	Engine Displacement Liters (cc)	Engine ID/VIN	Spark Plug Gap (in.)	Ignition Timing (deg.)	Fuel Pump (psi) ①	Idle Speed (rpm)	Valve Clearance Intake	Valve Clearance Exhaust
1997	4.6 (4593)	W	0.054	10B	35-45	②	HYD	HYD
1998	4.6 (4593)	W	0.054	10B	35-45	②	HYD	HYD
1999	4.6 (4593)	W	0.054	10B	35-45	②	HYD	HYD
2000-01	4.6 (4593)	W	0.054	10B	35-45	②	HYD	HYD

NOTE: The Vehicle Emission Control Information label often reflects specification changes made during production. The label figures must be used if they differ from those in this chart.

B: Before Top Dead Center

HYD: Hydraulic

① Fuel pressure with engine running, pressure regulator vacuum hose connected

② Refer to Vehicle Emission Control Information label

93061CB5

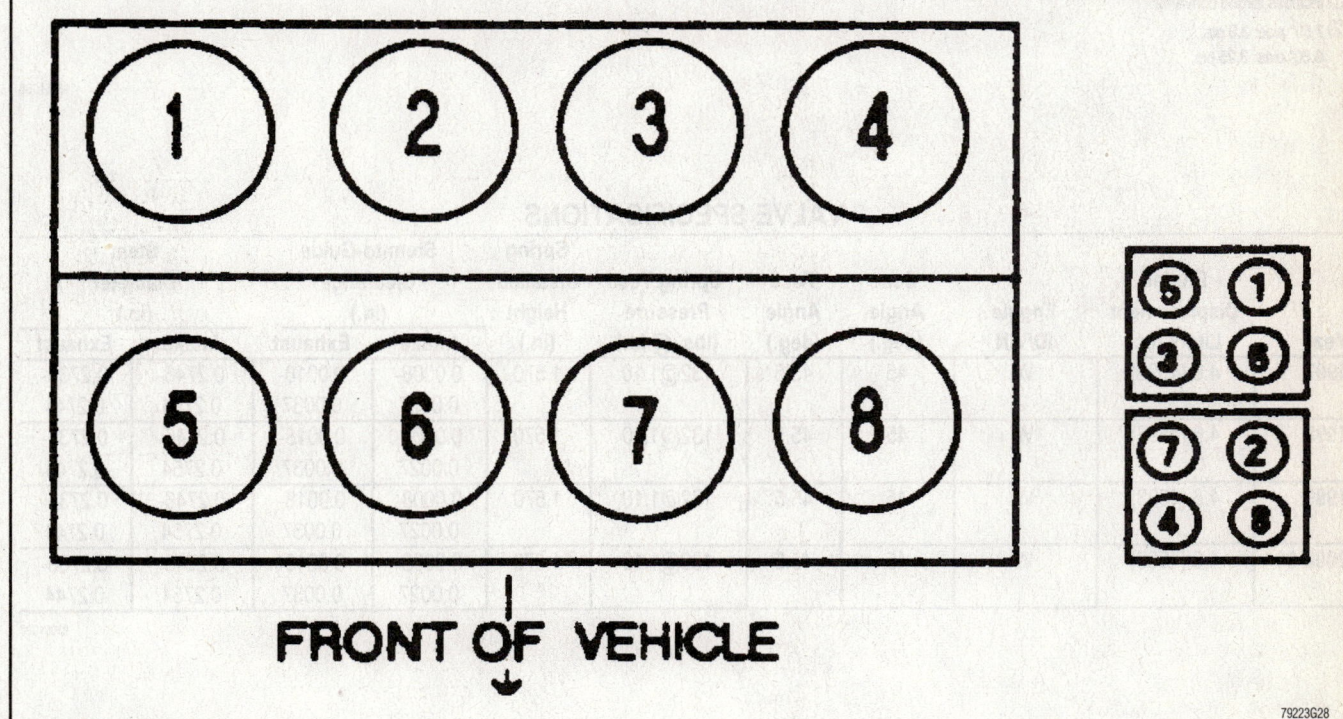

FRONT OF VEHICLE

4.6L (VIN W) Engine
Firing order: 1–3–7–2–6–5–4–8
Distributorless ignition system

79223G28

CAPACITIES

Year	Model	Engine Displacement Liters (cc)	Engine ID/VIN	Engine Oil with Filter (qts.)	Automatic Transmission (pts.) ①	Rear Drive Axle (pts.) ②	Fuel Tank (gal.)	Cooling System (qts.)
1997	Crown Victoria	4.6 (4593)	W	5.0	27.2	3.75	20.0	14.1
	Grand Marquis	4.6 (4593)	W	5.0	28.2	3.75	20.0	15.1
	Town Car	4.6 (4593)	W	5.0	28.2	3.75	20.0	15.1
1998	Crown Victoria	4.6 (4593)	W	5.0	27.2	3.75	20.0	14.1
	Grand Marquis	4.6 (4593)	W	5.0	28.2	3.75	20.0	15.1
	Town Car	4.6 (4593)	W	5.0	28.2	3.75	20.0	15.1
1999	Crown Victoria	4.6 (4593)	W	5.0	27.2	3.75	20.0	14.1
	Grand Marquis	4.6 (4593)	W	5.0	28.2	3.75	20.0	15.1
	Town Car	4.6 (4593)	W	5.0	28.2	3.75	20.0	15.1
2000-01	Crown Victoria	4.6 (4593)	W	5.0	27.2	3.75	20.0	14.1
	Grand Marquis	4.6 (4593)	W	5.0	28.2	3.75	20.0	15.1
	Town Car	4.6 (4593)	W	5.0	28.2	3.75	20.0	15.1

NOTE: All capacities are approximate. Add fluid gradually and ensure a proper fluid level is obtained.

① Includes torque converter
② 7.50" axle: 3.0 pts.
   8.80" axle: 3.25 pts.

93061CB6

VALVE SPECIFICATIONS

Year	Engine Displacement Liters (cc)	Engine ID/VIN	Seat Angle (deg.)	Face Angle (deg.)	Spring Test Pressure (lbs. @ in.)	Spring Installed Height (in.)	Stem-to-Guide Clearance (in.) Intake	Stem-to-Guide Clearance (in.) Exhaust	Stem Diameter (in.) Intake	Stem Diameter (in.) Exhaust
1997	4.6 (4593)	W	45	45.5	132@1.10	1.570	0.0008-0.0027	0.0018-0.0037	0.2746-0.2754	0.2736-0.2744
1998	4.6 (4593)	W	45	45.5	132@1.10	1.570	0.0008-0.0027	0.0018-0.0037	0.2746-0.2754	0.2736-0.2744
1999	4.6 (4593)	W	45	45.5	132@1.10	1.570	0.0008-0.0027	0.0018-0.0037	0.2746-0.2754	0.2736-0.2744
2000-01	4.6 (4593)	W	45	45.5	132@1.10	1.570	0.0008-0.0027	0.0018-0.0037	0.2746-0.2754	0.2736-0.2744

93061CB7

CRANKSHAFT AND CONNECTING ROD SPECIFICATIONS
All measurements are given in inches.

Year	Engine Displacement Liters (cc)	Engine ID/VIN	Crankshaft				Connecting Rod		
			Main Brg. Journal Dia.	Main Brg. Oil Clearance	Shaft End-play	Thrust on No.	Journal Diameter	Oil Clearance	Side Clearance
1997	4.6 (4593)	W	2.6500-2.6570	0.0009-0.0026	0.0051-0.0119	5	2.0870-2.8670	0.0009-0.0026	0.0006-0.0177
1998	4.6 (4593)	W	2.6500-2.6570	0.0009-0.0026	0.0051-0.0119	5	2.0870-2.8670	0.0009-0.0026	0.0006-0.0177
1999	4.6 (4593)	W	2.6500-2.6570	0.0009-0.0026	0.0051-0.0119	5	2.0870-2.8670	0.0009-0.0026	0.0006-0.0177
2000-01	4.6 (4593)	W	2.6500-2.6570	0.0009-0.0026	0.0051-0.0119	5	2.0870-2.8670	0.0009-0.0026	0.0006-0.0177

93061CB8

PISTON AND RING SPECIFICATIONS
All measurements are given in inches.

Year	Engine Displacement Liters (cc)	Engine ID/VIN	Piston Clearance ①	Ring Gap			Ring Side Clearance		
				Top Compression	Bottom Compression	Oil Control	Top Compression	Bottom Compression	Oil Control
1997	4.6 (4593)	W	0.0002-0.0010	0.005-0.012	0.012-0.022	0.006-0.026	②	0.008-0.0024	0.0010-0.0077
1998	4.6 (4593)	W	0.0002-0.0010	0.005-0.012	0.012-0.022	0.006-0.026	②	0.008-0.0024	0.0010-0.0077
1999	4.6 (4593)	W	0.0002-0.0010	0.005-0.012	0.012-0.022	0.006-0.026	②	0.008-0.0024	0.0010-0.0077
2000-01	4.6 (4593)	W	0.0002-0.0010	0.005-0.012	0.012-0.022	0.006-0.026	②	0.008-0.0024	0.0010-0.0077

① Measured 1.96 in. (43mm) from the top
② On 10:1 engines: 0.0012 - 0.0028 in.
   On 9:1 engines: 0.0008 - 0.0024 in.

93061CB9

TORQUE SPECIFICATIONS
All readings in ft. lbs.

Year	Engine Displacement Liters (cc)	Engine ID/VIN	Cylinder Head Bolts	Main Bearing Bolts	Rod Bearing Bolts	Crankshaft Damper Bolts	Flywheel Bolts	Manifold Intake	Manifold Exhaust	Spark Plugs	Lug Nuts
1997	4.6 (4593)	W	①	②	③	114-121	54-64	15-22	13-16	7-15	95
1998	4.6 (4593)	W	①	②	③	114-121	54-64	15-22	13-16	7-15	95
1999	4.6 (4593)	W	①	②	③	114-121	54-64	15-22	13-16	7-15	95
2000-01	4.6 (4593)	W	①	②	③	114-121	54-64	15-22	13-16	7-15	95

NOTE: Stretch bolts are used in all procedures that require rotating the fastener a certain number of degrees. The bolts stretch and cannot be reused. For reassembly, replace with new fasteners.

① Step 1: 22-30 ft. lbs.

    Step 2: Rotate each bolt 85-95 degrees

    Step 3: Repeat Step 2

② Step 1: Main bearing cap bolts: 22-25 ft. lbs.

    Step 2: Rotate each bolt 85-95 degrees

    Step 3: Main bearing cap adjusting screws: 44 inch lbs. then 80-90 inch lbs.

    Step 4: Main bearing cap side bolts: 7 ft. lbs. then 14-17 ft. lbs.

③ Step 1: 8 ft. lbs.

    Step 2: 12 ft. lbs.

    Step 3: 25-34 ft. lbs.

    Step 4: Rotate 85-95 degrees

93061CB0

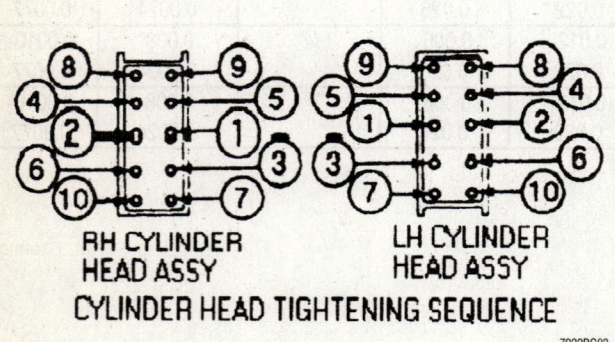

RH CYLINDER HEAD ASSY   LH CYLINDER HEAD ASSY

CYLINDER HEAD TIGHTENING SEQUENCE

7922RG03

Tighten the cylinder head bolts in the proper sequence to prevent damage to the head and possible leaks

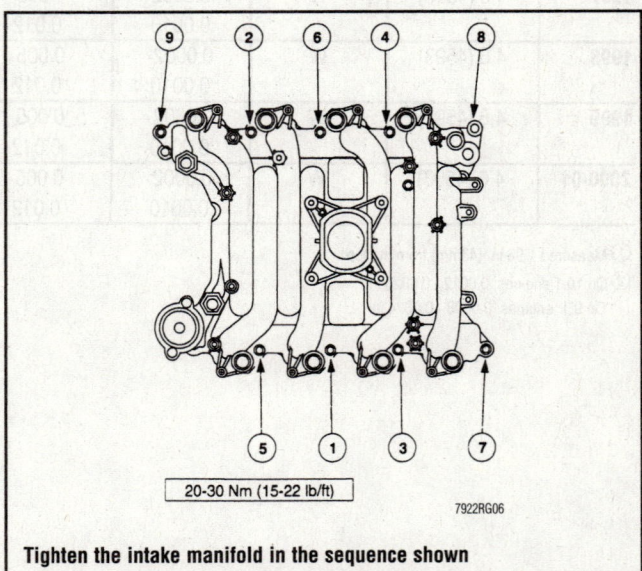

20-30 Nm (15-22 lb/ft)

7922RG06

Tighten the intake manifold in the sequence shown

BRAKE SPECIFICATIONS
FORD CROWN VICTORIA, LINCOLN TOWN CAR, MERCURY GRAND MARQUIS
All measurements in inches unless noted

| Year | Model | Master Cylinder Bore | Front Brake Disc | | | Rear Brake Disc | | | Minimum Lining Thickness | Brake Caliper | |
			Original Thickness	Minimum Thickness	Maximum Run-out	Original Thickness	Minimum Thickness	Maximum Run-out		Bracket Bolts (ft. lbs.)	Mounting Bolts (ft. lbs.)
1997	Crown Victoria	1.000	1.024	0.974	0.002	0.550	0.510	0.002	0.125	125-169	21-26
	Grand Marquis	1.000	1.024	0.974	0.002	0.550	0.510	0.002	0.125	125-169	21-26
	Town Car	1.000	1.024	0.974	0.002	0.550	0.510	0.002	0.125	125-169	21-26
1998	Crown Victoria	1.000	1.024	0.974	0.002	0.550	0.510	0.002	0.125	125-169	21-26
	Grand Marquis	1.000	1.024	0.974	0.002	0.550	0.510	0.002	0.125	125-169	21-26
	Town Car	1.000	1.024	0.974	0.002	0.550	0.510	0.002	0.125	125-169	21-26
1999	Crown Victoria	1.000	1.024	0.974	0.002	0.550	0.510	0.002	0.125	125-169	21-26
	Grand Marquis	1.000	1.024	0.974	0.002	0.550	0.510	0.002	0.125	125-169	21-26
	Town Car	1.000	1.024	0.974	0.002	0.550	0.510	0.002	0.125	125-169	21-26
2000-01	Crown Victoria	1.000	1.024	0.974	0.002	0.550	0.510	0.002	0.125	125-169	21-26
	Grand Marquis	1.000	1.024	0.974	0.002	0.550	0.510	0.002	0.125	125-169	21-26
	Town Car	1.000	1.024	0.974	0.002	0.550	0.510	0.002	0.125	125-169	21-26

NOTE: Follow specifications stamped on rotor or drum if figures differ from those in this chart.

93061CC1

Timing chain and gear service is covered in the model specific sections of this manual

SCHEDULED MAINTENANCE INTERVALS
(FORD CROWN VICTORIA, LINCOLN TOWN CAR & MERCURY GRAND MARQUIS)

TO BE SERVICED	TYPE OF SERVICE	VEHICLE MILEAGE INTERVAL (x1000)												
		5	10	15	20	25	30	35	40	45	50	55	60	65
Engine oil & filter	R	✓	✓	✓	✓	✓	✓	✓	✓	✓	✓	✓	✓	✓
Rotate tires	S/I	✓		✓		✓		✓		✓		✓		✓
Cooling system, hoses, clamps & coolant strength	S/I			✓			✓			✓			✓	
Lubricate steering linkage (Crown Victoria, Grand Marquis)	S/I			✓			✓			✓			✓	
Air cleaner element	R						✓						✓	
Automatic transaxle fluid & filter	R						✓						✓	
Spark plugs ①	R													
Exhaust heat shields	S/I						✓						✓	
Fuel filter (NGV Crown Victoria) ②	R					✓					✓			
Lubricate steering linkage (Town Car)	S/I						✓						✓	
Front & rear brakes	S/I						✓						✓	
Lubricate suspension (Town Car)	S/I						✓						✓	
Engine coolant ③	R										✓			
PCV valve	R												✓	
Accessory drive belt(s)	S/I												✓	

R: Replace   S/I: Service or Inspect

① Replace every 100,000 miles.

② Also drain coalescer assembly. Perform every 24,000 miles for severe service.

③ Change initially at 50,000 miles & thereafter every 30,000 miles.

FREQUENT OPERATION MAINTENANCE (SEVERE SERVICE)

If a vehicle is operated under any of the following conditions it is considered severe service:

- Extremely dusty areas.

- 50% or more of the vehicle operation is in 32°C (90°F) or higher temperatures, or constant operation in temperatures below 0°C (32°F).

- Prolonged idling (vehicle operation in stop and go traffic).

- Frequent short running periods (engine does not warm to normal operating temperatures).

- Police, taxi, delivery usage or trailer towing usage.

Oil & filter change: change every 3000 miles.

Rotate tires at 6000 miles & every 9000 miles thereafter.

Automatic transmission fluid & filter: change every 21,000 miles.

93061CC2

SCHEDULED MAINTENANCE INTERVALS
FORD MOTOR COMPANY
FORD CROWN VICTORIA, LINCOLN TOWN CAR
MERCURY GRAND MARQUIS

The following should be used as a guide when determining the amount of work required for a particular service.
In estimating how long a particular Scheduled Maintenance Service should take, please observe the following:

- Labor Time is time based on field research and data supplied by the vehicle manufacturer.
- Labor time operations are given in hours and tenths of an hour.
- All labor operations are to be used as a guide.

Mechanic Skill Level Codes:
(A) PRECISION: Highly skilled with multiple certification.
(B) GENERAL: Normally skilled with certification.
(C) MAINTENANCE: Semi-skilled working on certification.

	LABOR TIME			LABOR TIME			LABOR TIME
5000 Mile Service			**30000 Mile Service (B)**			**50000 Mile Service (B)**	
All Models	.8		All Models	1.9		All Models	1.7
10000 Mile Service			*Replace auto. trans. fluid*			*Replace engine coolant add*	.5
All Models	.3		*filter add*	.5		**55000 Mile Service**	
15000 Mile Service			**35000 Mile Service**			All Models	.8
All Models	.9		All Models	.8		**60000 Mile Service (B)**	
20000 Mile Service			**40000 Mile Service**			All Models	2.1
All Models	.3		All Models	.3		*Replace auto. trans. fluid*	
25000 Mile Service			**45000 Mile Service**			*filter add*	.5
All Models	.8		All Models	.9		**65000 Mile Service**	
						All Models	.8

93061CC3

Ignition system service is covered in the model specific sections of this manual

FORD MOTOR CO.
Ford Escort • Escort ZX2 • Mercury Tracer

ENGINE AND VEHICLE IDENTIFICATION

	Engine							Model Year	
Code ①	Liters (cc)	Cu. In.	Cyl.	Fuel Sys.	Type	Eng. Mfg.		Code ②	Year
3	2.0 (1990)	121	4	SFI	DOHC	Ford		V	1997
P	2.0 (1999)	121	4	SFI	SOHC	Ford		W	1998
								X	1999
								Y	2000
								1	2001

SFI: Sequential Fuel Injection

DOHC: Double Overhead Camshafts

SOHC: Single Overhead Camshaft

① 8th digit of the VIN

② 10th digit of the VIN

93061CC4

GENERAL ENGINE SPECIFICATIONS

Year	Model	Engine Displacement Liters (cc)	Engine ID/VIN	Fuel System Type	Net Horsepower @ rpm	Net Torque @ rpm (ft. lbs.)	Bore x Stroke (in.)	Com-pression Ratio	Oil Pressure @ rpm
1997	Escort	2.0 (1999)	P	SFI	110@5000	125@3750	3.34x3.46	9.2:1	35-65@2000
	Tracer	2.0 (1999)	P	SFI	110@5000	125@3750	3.34x3.46	9.2:1	35-65@2000
1998	Escort	2.0 (1999)	P	SFI	110@5000	125@3750	3.34x3.46	9.2:1	35-65@2000
	Escort ZX2	2.0 (1999)	3	SFI	125@5500	130@4000	3.34x3.46	10.0:1	35-65@2000
	Tracer	2.0 (1999)	P	SFI	110@5000	125@3750	3.34x3.46	9.2:1	35-65@2000
1999	Escort	2.0 (1999)	P	SFI	110@5000	125@3750	3.34x3.46	9.2:1	35-65@2000
	Escort ZX2	2.0 (1999)	3	SFI	125@5500	130@4000	3.34x3.46	10.0:1	35-65@2000
	Tracer	2.0 (1999)	P	SFI	110@5000	125@3750	3.34x3.46	9.2:1	35-65@2000
2000-01	Escort	2.0 (1999)	P	SFI	110@5000	125@3750	3.34x3.46	9.2:1	35-65@2000
	Escort ZX2	2.0 (1999)	3	SFI	125@5500	130@4000	3.34x3.46	10.0:1	35-65@2000
	Tracer	2.0 (1999)	P	SFI	110@5000	125@3750	3.34x3.46	9.2:1	35-65@2000

SFI: Sequential Fuel Injection

93061CC5

ENGINE TUNE-UP SPECIFICATIONS

Year	Engine Displacement Liters (cc)	Engine ID/VIN	Spark Plug Gap (in.)	Ignition Timing (deg.)		Fuel Pump (psi)	Idle Speed (rpm)		Valve Clearance	
				MT	AT		MT	AT	In.	Ex.
1997	2.0 (1999)	P	0.052-0.056	10B	10B	38-45 ①	②	②	HYD	HYD
1998	2.0 (1999)	3	0.052-0.056	10B	10B	31-38 ①	②	②	HYD	HYD
	2.0 (1999)	P	0.052-0.056	10B	10B	38-45 ①	②	②	HYD	HYD
19990	2.0 (1999)	3	0.052-0.056	10B	10B	31-38 ①	②	②	HYD	HYD
	2.0 (1999)	P	0.052-0.056	10B	10B	38-45 ①	②	②	HYD	HYD
2000-01	2.0 (1999)	3	0.052-0.056	10B	10B	31-38 ①	②	②	HYD	HYD
	2.0 (1999)	P	0.052-0.056	10B	10B	38-45 ①	②	②	HYD	HYD

NOTE: The Vehicle Emission Control Information label often reflects specification changes made during production. The label figures must be used if they differ from those in this chart.

B: Before Top Dead Center

HYD: Hydraulic

① Fuel pressure with engine running, pressure regulator vacuum hose connected

② Refer to Vehicle Emission Control Information label

93061CC6

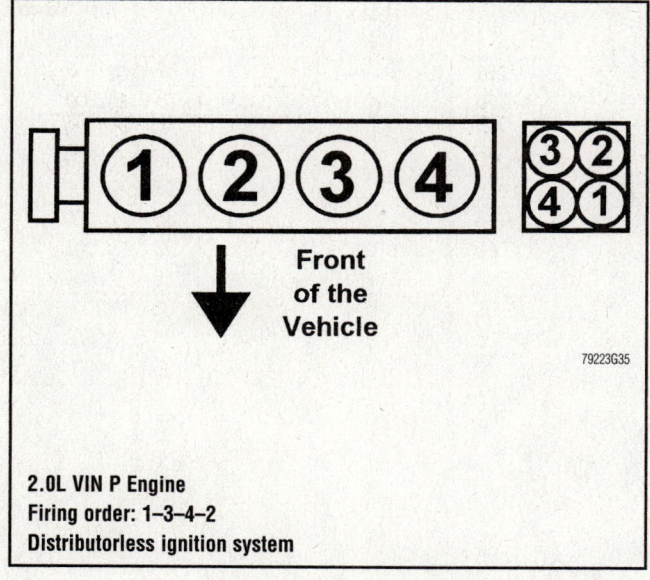

Front of the Vehicle

79223G35

2.0L VIN P Engine
Firing order: 1–3–4–2
Distributorless ignition system

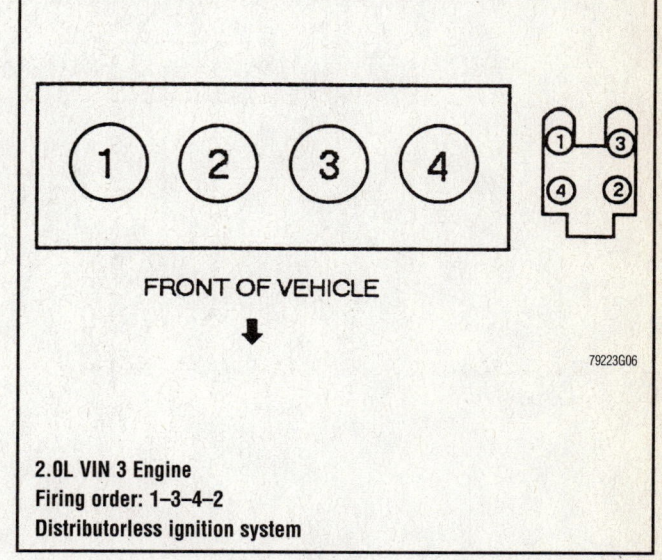

FRONT OF VEHICLE

79223G06

2.0L VIN 3 Engine
Firing order: 1–3–4–2
Distributorless ignition system

CAPACITIES

Year	Model	Engine Displacement Liters (cc)	Engine ID/VIN	Oil with Filter (qts.)	Transmission (pts.) Manual	Transmission (pts.) Auto. ①	Front Axle (pts.)	Fuel Tank (gal.)	Cooling System (qts.)
1997	Escort	2.0 (1999)	P	4.0	6.7	13.4	②	13.2	③
	Tracer	2.0 (1999)	P	4.0	5.7	13.4	②	11.9	③
1998	Escort	2.0 (1999)	P	4.0	5.7	13.4	②	11.9	③
	Escort ZX2	2.0 (1999)	3	4.0	6.7	13.4	②	13.2	④
	Tracer	2.0 (1999)	P	4.0	5.7	13.4	②	11.9	③
1999	Escort	2.0 (1999)	P	4.0	5.7	13.4	②	11.9	③
	Escort ZX2	2.0 (1999)	3	4.0	6.7	13.4	②	13.2	④
	Tracer	2.0 (1999)	P	4.0	5.7	13.4	②	11.9	③
2000-01	Escort	2.0 (1999)	P	4.0	5.7	13.4	②	11.9	③
	Escort ZX2	2.0 (1999)	3	4.0	6.7	13.4	②	13.2	④
	Tracer	2.0 (1999)	P	4.0	5.7	13.4	②	11.9	③

Note: All capacities are approximates. Add fluid gradually and ensure a proper fluid level is obtained.

① Includes torque converter

② Included in transaxle capacity

③ Manual transaxle 7.9
   Automatic transaxle 5.8

④ Manual transaxle 7.0
   Automatic transaxle 7.5

93061CC7

VALVE SPECIFICATIONS

Year	Engine Displacement Liters (cc)	Engine ID/VIN	Seat Angle (deg.)	Face Angle (deg.)	Spring Test Pressure (lbs. @ in.)	Spring Installed Height (in.)	Stem-to-Guide Clearance (in.)		Stem Diameter (in.)	
							Intake	Exhaust	Intake	Exhaust
1997	2.0 (1999)	P	45	45.6	200@1.09	1.420-1.540	0.0008-0.0027	0.0018-0.0037	0.3159-0.3167	0.3149-0.3156
1998	2.0 (1999)	3	45	45	NA	1.346	0.0007-0.0025	0.0014-0.0032	0.2373-0.2379	0.2366-0.2372
	2.0 (1999)	P	45	45.6	200@1.09	1.420-1.540	0.0008-0.0027	0.0018-0.0037	0.3159-0.3167	0.3149-0.3156
1999	2.0 (1999)	3	45	45	NA	1.346	0.0007-0.0025	0.0014-0.0032	0.2373-0.2379	0.2366-0.2372
	2.0 (1999)	P	45	45.6	200@1.09	1.420-1.540	0.0008-0.0027	0.0018-0.0037	0.3159-0.3167	0.3149-0.3156
2000-01	2.0 (1999)	3	45	45	NA	1.346	0.0007-0.0025	0.0014-0.0032	0.2373-0.2379	0.2366-0.2372
	2.0 (1999)	P	45	45.6	200@1.09	1.420-1.540	0.0008-0.0027	0.0018-0.0037	0.3159-0.3167	0.3149-0.3156

93061CC8

Refer to the model specific sections for engine mechanical service procedures

CRANKSHAFT AND CONNECTING ROD SPECIFICATIONS
All measurements are given in inches.

Year	Engine Displacement Liters (cc)	Engine ID/VIN	Crankshaft				Connecting Rod		
			Main Brg. Journal Dia.	Main Brg. Oil Clearance	Shaft End-play	Thrust on No.	Journal Diameter	Oil Clearance	Side Clearance
1997	2.0 (1999)	P	2.2827-2.2835	0.0008-0.0026	0.0040-0.0120	3	1.7279-1.7287	0.0008-0.0026	0.0040-0.0110
1998	2.0 (1999)	3	2.2827-2.2835	0.0008-0.0026	0.0040-0.0120	3	1.8461-1.8500	0.0006-0.0028	0.0040-0.0110
	2.0 (1999)	P	2.2827-2.2835	0.0008-0.0026	0.0040-0.0120	3	1.7279-1.7287	0.0008-0.0026	0.0040-0.0110
1999	2.0 (1999)	3	2.2827-2.2835	0.0008-0.0026	0.0040-0.0120	3	1.8461-1.8500	0.0006-0.0028	0.0040-0.0110
	2.0 (1999)	P	2.2827-2.2835	0.0008-0.0026	0.0040-0.0120	3	1.7279-1.7287	0.0008-0.0026	0.0040-0.0110
2000-01	2.0 (1999)	3	2.2827-2.2835	0.0008-0.0026	0.0040-0.0120	3	1.8461-1.8500	0.0006-0.0028	0.0040-0.0110
	2.0 (1999)	P	2.2827-2.2835	0.0008-0.0026	0.0040-0.0120	3	1.7279-1.7287	0.0008-0.0026	0.0040-0.0110

93061CC9

PISTON AND RING SPECIFICATIONS
All measurements are given in inches.

| Year | Engine Displacement Liters (cc) | Engine ID/VIN | Piston Clearance | Ring Gap | | | Ring Side Clearance | | |
				Top Compression	Bottom Compression	Oil Control	Top Compression	Bottom Compression	Oil Control
1997	2.0 (1999)	P	0.0008-0.0027	0.010-0.030	0.010-0.030	0.016-0.066	0.0015-0.0032	0.0015-0.0035	—
1998	2.0 (1999)	3	0.0004-0.0012	0.0118-0.0197	0.0118-0.0197	0.0158-0.0551	0.0015-0.0032	0.0015-0.0035	—
	2.0 (1999)	P	0.0008-0.0027	0.010-0.030	0.010-0.030	0.016-0.066	0.0015-0.0032	0.0015-0.0035	—
1999	2.0 (1999)	3	0.0010-0.0022	0.012-0.022	0.012-0.022	0.010-0.039	0.0015-0.0032	0.0015-0.0035	—
	2.0 (1999)	P	0.0008-0.0027	0.010-0.030	0.010-0.030	0.016-0.066	0.0015-0.0032	0.0015-0.0035	—
2000-01	2.0 (1999)	3	0.0010-0.0022	0.012-0.022	0.012-0.022	0.010-0.039	0.0015-0.0032	0.0015-0.0035	—
	2.0 (1999)	P	0.0008-0.0027	0.010-0.030	0.010-0.030	0.016-0.066	0.0015-0.0032	0.0015-0.0035	—

93061CC0

Refer to the model specific sections for fuel system service procedures

TORQUE SPECIFICATIONS
All readings in ft. lbs.

Year	Engine Displacement Liters (cc)	Engine ID/VIN	Cylinder Head Bolts	Main Bearing Bolts	Rod Bearing Bolts	Crankshaft Damper Bolts	Flywheel Bolts	Manifold		Spark Plugs	Lug Nut
								Intake	Exhaust		
1997	2.0 (1999)	P	①	66-79	26-30	80-87	71-76	15-22	15-17	12-15	76
1998	2.0 (1999)	3	②	55-65	③	80-87	71-76	11-12	10-12	10-12	76
	2.0 (1999)	P	①	66-79	26-30	80-87	71-76	15-22	15-17	12-15	76
1999	2.0 (1999)	3	②	55-65	③	80-87	71-76	11-12	10-12	10-12	76
	2.0 (1999)	P	①	66-79	26-30	80-87	71-76	15-22	15-17	12-15	76
2000-01	2.0 (1999)	3	②	55-65	③	80-87	71-76	11-12	10-12	10-12	76
	2.0 (1999)	P	①	66-79	26-30	80-87	71-76	15-22	15-17	12-15	76

NOTE: Always follow proper torque patterns

NOTE: Stretch bolts are used in all procedures that require rotating the fastener a certain number of degrees. The bolts stretch and cannot be reused. For reassembly, replace with new fastners.

① Do not reuse cylinder head bolts.
 Step 1: Tighten bolts, in sequence, to 44 ft. lbs.
 Step 2: Loosen bolts approx. two turns, then retighten in sequence to 44 ft. lbs.
 Step 3: Turn all bolts, in sequence, plus an additional 90 degrees
 Step 4: Repeat Step 3

② Step 1: 15-22 ft. lbs.
 Step 2: 30-37 ft. lbs.
 Step 3: Rotate 90-120 degrees

③ Step 1: 22-25 ft. lbs.
 Step 2: Rotate each bolt 85-95 degrees

93061CD1

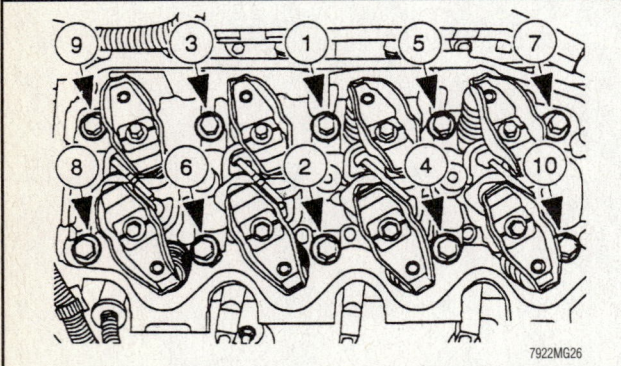

Tighten the cylinder head bolts in the proper sequence in the order specified—2.0L SOHC engines

7922MG26

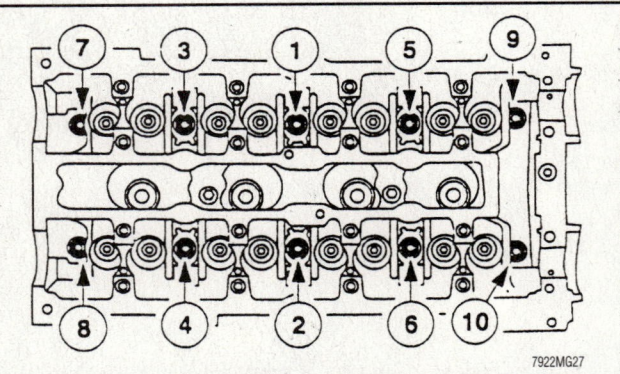

Tighten the cylinder head bolts in the order specified—2.0L Zetec engines

7922MG27

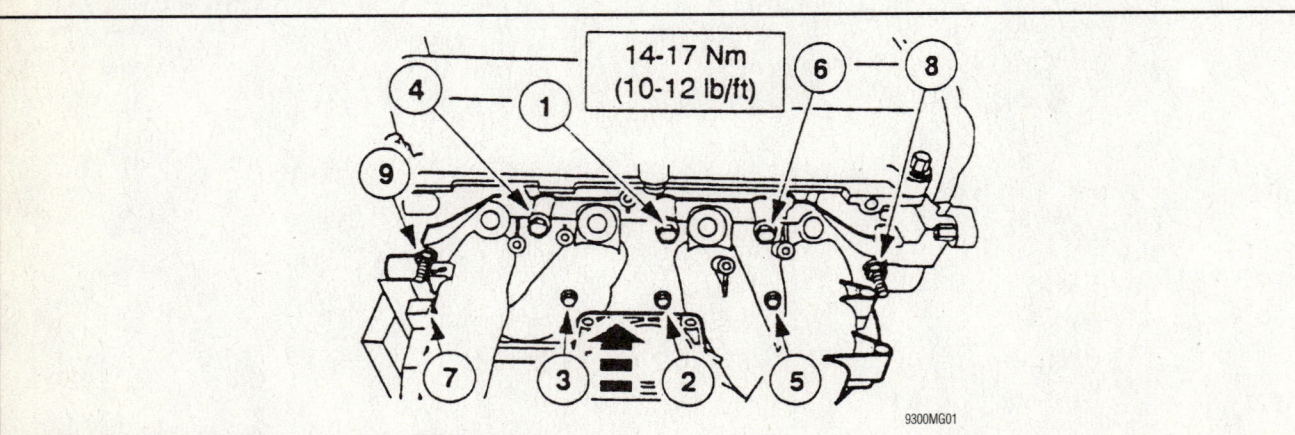

Tighten the manifold bolts and nuts in this sequence—2.0L Zetec

9300MG01

BRAKE SPECIFICATIONS
FORD ESCORT, ESCORT ZX2, MERCURY TRACER
All measurements in inches unless noted

Year	Model		Brake Disc Original Thickness	Brake Disc Minimum Thickness	Brake Disc Maximum Runout	Brake Drum Diameter Original Inside Diameter	Brake Drum Diameter Max. Wear Limit	Brake Drum Diameter Maximum Machine Diameter	Minimum Lining Thickness	Brake Caliper Mounting Bolts (ft. lbs.)
1997	Escort	F	0.870	0.790	0.004	—	—	—	0.080	36–43
		R	0.350	0.280	0.004	7.87	7.95	7.91	0.040	—
	Tracer	F	0.870	0.790	0.004	—	—	—	0.080	36–43
		R	0.350	0.280	0.004	7.87	7.95	7.91	0.040	—
1998	Escort	F	0.870	0.790	0.004	—	—	—	0.080	36–43
		R	0.350	0.280	0.004	7.87	7.95	7.91	0.040	—
	Escort ZX2	F	0.870	0.790	0.004	—	—	—	0.080	36–43
		R	0.350	0.280	0.004	7.87	7.95	7.91	0.040	—
	Tracer	F	0.870	0.790	0.004	—	—	—	0.080	36–43
		R	0.350	0.280	0.004	7.87	7.95	7.91	0.040	—
1999	Escort	F	0.870	0.790	0.004	—	—	—	0.080	36–43
		R	0.350	0.280	0.004	7.87	7.95	7.91	0.040	—
	Escort ZX2	F	0.870	0.790	0.004	—	—	—	0.080	36–43
		R	0.350	0.280	0.004	7.87	7.95	7.91	0.040	—
	Tracer	F	0.870	0.790	0.004	—	—	—	0.080	36–43
		R	0.350	0.280	0.004	7.87	7.95	7.91	0.040	—
2000-01	Escort	F	0.870	0.790	0.004	—	—	—	0.080	36–43
		R	0.350	0.280	0.004	7.87	7.95	7.91	0.040	—
	Escort ZX2	F	0.870	0.790	0.004	—	—	—	0.080	36–43
		R	0.350	0.280	0.004	7.87	7.95	7.91	0.040	—
	Tracer	F	0.870	0.790	0.004	—	—	—	0.080	36–43
		R	0.350	0.280	0.004	7.87	7.95	7.91	0.040	—

NOTE: Follow specifications stamped on rotor or drum if figures differ from those in this chart.
NA: Not Available
F: Front
R: Rear

93061CD2

Refer to the model specific sections for engine electrical system service procedures

SCHEDULED MAINTENANCE INTERVALS
(FORD ESCORT & MERCURY TRACER)

TO BE SERVICED	TYPE OF SERVICE	VEHICLE MILEAGE INTERVAL (x1000)																			
		5	10	15	20	25	30	35	40	45	50	55	60	65	70	75	80	85	90	95	100
Engine oil & filter	R	✓	✓	✓	✓	✓	✓	✓	✓	✓	✓	✓	✓	✓	✓	✓	✓	✓	✓	✓	✓
Tires ①	S/I	✓		✓		✓		✓		✓		✓		✓		✓		✓		✓	
Air Cleaner	S/I						✓						✓						✓		
	R						✓						✓						✓		
Spark Plugs	S/I								Every 100,000 miles												
Drive Belts	S/I												✓								
Cooling system	S/I			✓			✓			✓			✓			✓			✓		
Engine coolant	R										✓						✓				
PCV valve	R												✓								
Exhaust heat shields	S/I						✓						✓						✓		
Brake linings & drums	S/I						✓						✓						✓		
Brake line hoses & connections	S/I						✓						✓						✓		
Front ball joints	S/I						✓						✓						✓		
Bolts & nuts on chassis body	S/I						✓						✓						✓		
Steering linkage operation	S/I						✓						✓						✓		
Brake pads & rotor	S/I						✓						✓						✓		
Clutch pedal operation	S/I						✓						✓						✓		
Halfshaft dust boots	S/I						✓						✓						✓		

R: Replace   S/I: Inspect and service, if needed

① Rotate, inspect the tire tread for wear, and adjust air pressure.

FREQUENT OPERATION MAINTENANCE (SEVERE SERVICE)

If a vehicle is operated under any of the following conditions it is considered severe service:

- Extremely dusty areas.

- 50% or more of the vehicle operation is in 32°C (90°F) or higher temperatures, or constant operation in temperatures below 0°C (32°F).

- Prolonged idling (vehicle operation in stop and go traffic).

- Frequent short running periods (engine does not warm to normal operating temperatures).

- Police, taxi, delivery usage or trailer towing usage.

Oil & filter change: change every 3000 miles.

Rotate tires at 6000 miles & every 9000 miles thereafter.

Automatic transmission fluid & filter: change every 21,000 miles.

93061CD3

SCHEDULED MAINTENANCE INTERVALS
FORD MOTOR COMPANY
FORD ESCORT
MERCURY TRACER

The following should be used as a guide when determining the amount of work required for a particular service. In estimating how long a particular Scheduled Maintenance Service should take, please observe the following:

- Labor Time is time based on field research and data supplied by the vehicle manufacturer.
- Labor time operations are given in hours and tenths of an hour.
- All labor operations are to be used as a guide.

Mechanic Skill Level Codes:
(A) PRECISION: Highly skilled with multiple certification.
(B) GENERAL: Normally skilled with certification.
(C) MAINTENANCE: Semi-skilled working on certification.

	LABOR TIME		LABOR TIME		LABOR TIME
5000 Mile Service (C)		**35000 Mile Service (C)**		**65000 Mile Service (C)**	
All Models	.9	All Models	.9	All Models	.9
10000 Mile Service (C)		**40000 Mile Service (C)**		**70000 Mile Service (C)**	
All Models	.5	All Models	.5	1997-00	.5
15000 Mile Service (C)		**45000 Mile Service (C)**		**75000 Mile Service (C)**	
All Models		All Models		1997-00	1.3
1.8L	.9	1.8L	.9	**80000 Mile Service (C)**	
1.9L	1.3	1.9L	1.1	1997-00	.7
2.0L	1.4	2.0L	1.2	**85000 Mile Service (C)**	
20000 Mile Service (C)		**50000 Mile Service (C)**		1997-00	.8
All Models	.5	All Models		**90000 Mile Service (C)**	
25000 Mile Service (C)		1.8L	.5	1997-00	1.6
All Models	.9	1.9L	.9	**95000 Mile Service (C)**	
30000 Mile Service (B)		2.0L	.7	1997-00	.9
All Models		**55000 Mile Service (C)**		**100000 Mile Service (C)**	
1.8L	2.4	All Models	.9	All Models	.5
1.9L	2.8	**60000 Mile Service (B)**			
2.0L	1.6	All Models			
		1.8L	6.2		
		1.9L	3.1		
		2.0L	1.7		

93061CD4

For accessory drive belt replacement procedures see the model specific sections of this manual

FORD MOTOR CO.
Ford Focus

ENGINE AND VEHICLE IDENTIFICATION

Engine							Model Year	
Code ①	Liters (cc)	Cu. In.	Cyl.	Fuel Sys.	Type	Eng. Mfg.	Code ②	Year
3	2.0 (1999)	121	4	SFI	DOHC	Ford	Y	2000
P	2.0 (1999)	121	4	SFI	SOHC	Ford	1	2001

SFI: Sequential Fuel Injection

DOHC: Double Overhead Camshafts

SOHC: Single Overhead Camshaft

① 8th digit of the VIN

② 10th digit of the VIN

93061CD5

GENERAL ENGINE SPECIFICATIONS

Year	Model	Engine Displacement Liters (cc)	Engine ID/VIN	Fuel System Type	Net Horsepower @ rpm	Net Torque @ rpm (ft. lbs.)	Bore x Stroke (in.)	Compression Ratio	Oil Pressure @ rpm
2000-01	Focus LX	2.0 (1999)	P	SFI	110@5000	125@3750	3.34x3.46	9.2:1	35-65@2000
	Focus SE	2.0 (1999)	P	SFI	110@5000	125@3750	3.34x3.46	9.2:1	35-65@2000
	Focus ZTS	2.0 (1999)	3	SFI	130@5500	130@4000	3.34x3.46	10.0:1	35-65@2000
	Focus ZX3	2.0 (1999)	3	SFI	130@5500	130@4000	3.34x3.46	10.0:1	35-65@2000

SFI: Sequential Fuel Injection

93061CD6

ENGINE TUNE-UP SPECIFICATIONS

Year	Engine Displacement Liters (cc)	Engine ID/VIN	Spark Plug Gap (in.)	Ignition Timing (deg.)		Fuel Pump (psi)	Idle Speed (rpm)		Valve Clearance (in.)	
				MT	AT		MT	AT	In.	Ex.
2000-01	2.0 (1999)	3	0.052-0.056	10B	10B	31-38 ①	②	②	0.004-0.007	0.010-0.013
	2.0 (1999)	P	0.052-0.056	10B	10B	38-45 ①	②	②	HYD	HYD

NOTE: The Vehicle Emission Control Information label often reflects specification changes made during production. The label figures must be used if they differ from those in this chart.

B: Before Top Dead Center

HYD: Hydraulic

① Fuel pressure with engine running, pressure regulator vacuum hose connected

② Refer to Vehicle Emission Control Information label

93061CD7

Front of the Vehicle

2.0L (VIN 3 and P) engines
Firing order: 1–3–4–2
Distributorless ignition system

79223G35

For brake related suspension and axle service, refer to the model specific sections of this manual

CAPACITIES

Year	Model	Engine Displacement Liters (cc)	Engine ID/VIN	Engine Oil with Filter (qts.)	Transmission (pts.)		Drive Front Axle (pts.)	Fuel Tank (gal.)	Cooling System (qts.)
					Manual	Auto.			
2000-01	Focus LX	2.0 (1999)	P	4.0	4.8	14.0	—	13.2	①
	Focus SE	2.0 (1999)	P	4.0	4.8	14.0	—	13.2	①
	Focus ZTS	2.0 (1999)	3	4.5	4.0	14.0	—	13.2	②
	Focus ZX3	2.0 (1999)	3	4.5	4.0	14.0	—	13.2	②

Note: All capacities are approximates. Add fluid gradually and ensure a proper fluid level is obtained.

① Manual transaxle: 7.9
   Automatic transaxle: 5.8

② Manual transaxle: 7.0
   Automatic transaxle: 7.5

93061CD8

VALVE SPECIFICATIONS

Year	Engine Displacement Liters (cc)	Engine ID/VIN	Seat Angle (deg.)	Face Angle (deg.)	Spring Test Pressure (lbs. @ in.)	Spring Installed Height (in.)	Stem-to-Guide Clearance (in.)		Stem Diameter (in.)	
							Intake	Exhaust	Intake	Exhaust
2000-01	2.0 (1999)	3	45	45	NA	1.346	0.0007-0.0025	0.0014-0.0032	0.2373-0.2379	0.2366-0.2372
	2.0 (1999)	P	45	45.6	200@1.09	1.420-1.540	0.0008-0.0027	0.0018-0.0037	0.3159-0.3167	0.3149-0.3156

NA: Not Available

93061CD9

CRANKSHAFT AND CONNECTING ROD SPECIFICATIONS
All measurements are given in inches.

Year	Engine Displacement Liters (cc)	Engine ID/VIN	Crankshaft				Connecting Rod		
			Main Brg. Journal Dia.	Main Brg. Oil Clearance	Shaft End-play	Thrust on No.	Journal Diameter	Oil Clearance	Side Clearance
2000-01	2.0 (1999)	3	2.2827-2.2835	0.0008-0.0026	0.0040-0.0120	3	1.8461-1.8500	0.0006-0.0028	0.0040-0.0110
	2.0 (1999)	P	2.2827-2.2835	0.0008-0.0026	0.0040-0.0120	3	1.7279-1.7287	0.0008-0.0026	0.0040-0.0110

93061CD0

PISTON AND RING SPECIFICATIONS
All measurements are given in inches.

Year	Engine Displacement Liters (cc)	Engine ID/VIN	Piston Clearance	Ring Gap			Ring Side Clearance		
				Top Compression	Bottom Compression	Oil Control	Top Compression	Bottom Compression	Oil Control
2000-01	2.0 (1999)	3	0.0010-0.0022	0.012-0.022	0.012-0.022	0.010-0.039	0.0015-0.0032	0.0015-0.0035	—
	2.0 (1999)	P	0.0008-0.0027	0.010-0.030	0.010-0.030	0.016-0.066	0.0015-0.0032	0.0015-0.0035	—

93061CE1

Refer to the model specific sections for driveline service procedures

TORQUE SPECIFICATIONS
All readings in ft. lbs.

Year	Engine Displacement Liters (cc)	Engine ID/VIN	Cylinder Head Bolts	Main Bearing Bolts	Rod Bearing Bolts	Crankshaft Damper Bolts	Flywheel Bolts	Manifold Intake	Manifold Exhaust	Spark Plugs	Lug Nut
2000-01	2.0 (1999)	P	①	66-79	26-30	80-87	71-76	15-22	15-17	12-15	76
	2.0 (1999)	3	②	55-65	③	80-87	71-76	11-12	10-12	10-12	76

① Step 1: 37 ft. lbs.
Step 2: Loosen bolts 1/2 turn
Step 3: 37 ft. lbs.
Step 4: Plus 90 degrees
Step 5: Plus 90 degrees

② Step 1: 15 ft. lbs.
Step 2: 30 ft. lbs.
Step 3: Plus 90 degrees

③ Step 1: 22-25 ft. lbs.
Step 2: Plus 90 degrees

93061CE2

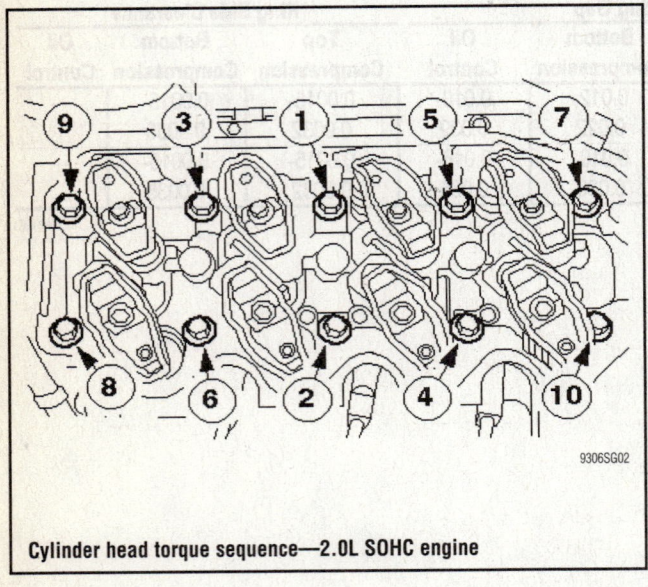

Cylinder head torque sequence—2.0L SOHC engine

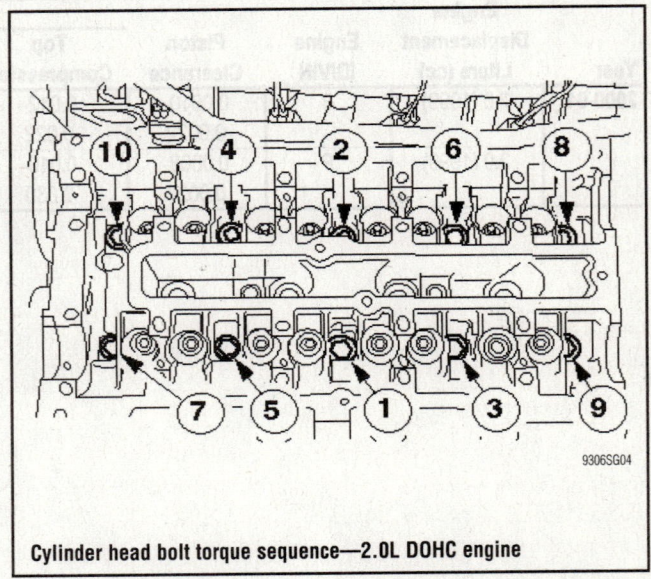

Cylinder head bolt torque sequence—2.0L DOHC engine

BRAKE SPECIFICATIONS
FORD FOCUS
All measurements in inches unless noted

Year	Model	Brake Disc Original Thickness	Brake Disc Minimum Thickness	Brake Disc Maximum Runout	Brake Drum Diameter Original Inside Diameter	Brake Drum Diameter Max. Wear Limit	Brake Drum Diameter Maximum Machine Diameter	Minimum Lining Thickness Front	Minimum Lining Thickness Rear	Brake Caliper Mounting Bolts (ft. lbs.)
2000-01	Focus LX	0.870	0.790	0.002	7.99	8.03	—	0.080	0.040	21
	Focus SE	0.870	0.790	0.002	7.99	8.03	—	0.080	0.040	21
	Focus ZTS	0.870	0.790	0.002	7.99	8.03	—	0.080	0.040	21
	Focus ZX3	0.870	0.790	0.002	7.99	8.03	—	0.080	0.040	21

93061CE3

SCHEDULED MAINTENANCE INTERVALS
(FORD FOCUS)

TO BE SERVICED	TYPE OF SERVICE	VEHICLE MILEAGE INTERVAL (x1000)												
		5	10	15	20	25	30	35	40	45	50	55	60	65
Air cleaner filter	R						✓						✓	
Accessory drive belt	S/I												✓	
Brake system ①	S/I			✓			✓			✓			✓	
Clutch pedal operation	S/I						✓						✓	
Cooling fan operation	S/I		✓		✓		✓		✓		✓		✓	
Cooling system hoses and clamps	S/I			✓			✓			✓			✓	
CV-joint boots & axle seals	S/I						✓						✓	
Engine coolant	R	Ten years or 150,000 miles												
Engine oil & filter	R	✓	✓	✓	✓	✓	✓	✓	✓	✓	✓	✓	✓	✓
Exterior Lights	S/I	Check monthly												
PCV valve	S/I												✓	
Exhaust system & heat shields	S/I						✓						✓	
Parking brake system	S/I	Every 6 months												
Power steering fluid	S/I	Every 6 months												
Rotate tires	S/I	✓		✓		✓		✓		✓		✓		✓
Steering linkage	S/I						✓						✓	
Spark plugs	R	Change at 100,000 miles												
Suspension components	S/I						✓						✓	

R: Replace   S/I: Inspect and service, if necessary   L: Lubricate   A: Adjust   C: Clean

① Inspect the reservoir fluid level, rotor and or drum, brake lines, hoses, calipers and or wheel cylinders

FREQUENT OPERATION MAINTENANCE (SEVERE SERVICE)

If a vehicle is operated under any of the following conditions it is considered severe service:
- Extremely dusty areas.
- 50% or more of the vehicle operation is in 32°C (90°F) or higher temperatures, or constant operation in temperatures below 0°C (32°F).
- Prolonged idling (vehicle operation in stop and go traffic).
- Frequent short running periods (engine does not warm to normal operating temperatures).
- Police, taxi, delivery usage or trailer towing usage.

Oil & oil filter change: change every 3000 miles.
Air filter element: change every 15,000 miles.

93061CE4

For exhaust manifold replacement procedures, see the model specific sections of this manual

SCHEDULED MAINTENANCE INTERVALS
FORD MOTOR COMPANY
FORD FOCUS

The following should be used as a guide when determining the amount of work required for a particular service.
In estimating how long a particular Scheduled Maintenance Service should take, please observe the following:

- Labor Time is time based on field research and data supplied by the vehicle manufacturer.
- Labor time operations are given in hours and tenths of an hour.
- All labor operations are to be used as a guide.

Mechanic Skill Level Codes:
(A) PRECISION: Highly skilled with multiple certification.
(B) GENERAL: Normally skilled with certification.
(C) MAINTENANCE: Semi-skilled working on certification.

	LABOR TIME		LABOR TIME		LABOR TIME
5000 Mile Service (C)		**25000 Mile Service (C)**		**50000 Mile Service (C)**	
All Models	.9	All Models	.9	All Models	.7
10000 Mile Service (C)		**30000 Mile Service (B)**		**55000 Mile Service (C)**	
All Models	.5	All Models	1.6	All Models	.9
15000 Mile Service (C)		**35000 Mile Service (C)**		**60000 Mile Service (B)**	
All Models	1.2	All Models	.9	All Models	1.7
20000 Mile Service (C)		**40000 Mile Service (C)**		**65000 Mile Service (C)**	
All Models	.5	All Models	.5	All Models	.9
		45000 Mile Service (C)			
		All Models	1.2		

93061CE5

FORD MOTOR CO.
Lincoln LS

ENGINE AND VEHICLE IDENTIFICATION

		Engine						Model Year	
Code ①	Liters (cc)	Cu. In.	Cyl.	Fuel Sys.	Type	Eng. Mfg.		Code ②	Year
S	3.0 (3049)	182	6	MFI	DOHC	Ford		Y	2000
A	3.9 (3947)	243	8	MFI	DOHC	Ford		1	2001

MFI: Multi-Port Fuel Injection

DOHC: Double Overhead Camshaft

① 8th digit of the VIN

② 10th digit of the VIN

93061CE6

GENERAL ENGINE SPECIFICATIONS

Year	Model	Engine Displacement Liters (cc)	Engine ID/VIN	Fuel System Type	Net Horsepower @ rpm	Net Torque @ rpm (ft. lbs.)	Bore x Stroke (in.)	Com- pression Ratio	Oil Pressure @ rpm
2000-01	LS6	3.0 (3049)	S	SFI	210@6500	205@4750	3.50x3.13	10.5:1	20-45@1500
	LS8	3.9 (3947)	A	SFI	252@6100	267@4300	NA	10.6:1	NA

NA: Not Available

SFI: Sequential Fuel Injection

93061CE7

Refer to the model specific sections for cooling system service procedures

ENGINE TUNE-UP SPECIFICATIONS

Year	Engine Displacement Liters (cc)	Engine ID/VIN	Spark Plugs Gap (in.)	Ignition Timing (deg.) ①		Fuel Pump (psi)	Idle Speed (rpm) ①		Valve Clearance	
				MT	AT		MT	AT	In.	Ex.
2000-01	3.0 (3049)	S	0.051-0.057	12-17B	12-17B	26-45	650-750	650-750	0.007-0.009	0.013-0.015
	3.9 (3947)	A	0.039-0.043	—	10-20B	43	—	650-750	0.007-0.009	0.009-0.011

The underhood specifications sticker often reflects tune-up specification changes in production. Sticker figures must be used if they disagree with those in this chart.

① Controlled by the engine computer

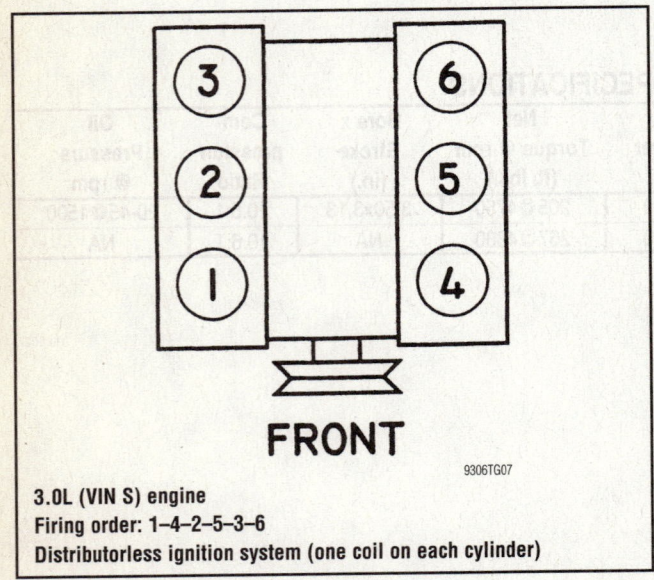

3.0L (VIN S) engine
Firing order: 1–4–2–5–3–6
Distributorless ignition system (one coil on each cylinder)

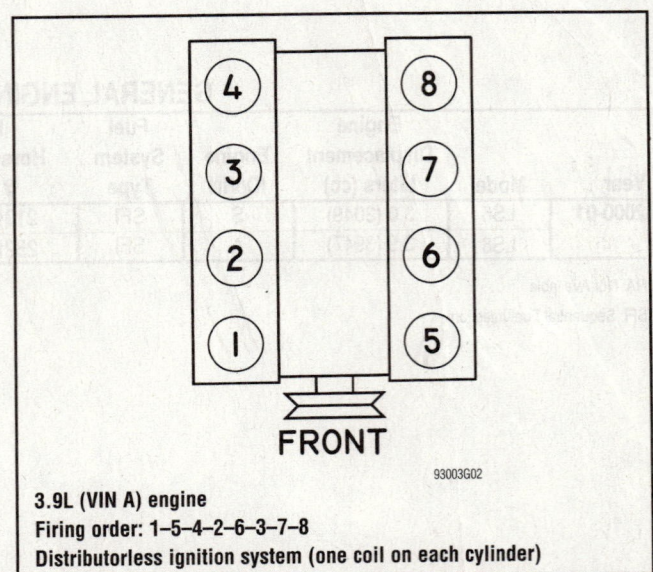

3.9L (VIN A) engine
Firing order: 1–5–4–2–6–3–7–8
Distributorless ignition system (one coil on each cylinder)

CAPACITIES

Year	Model	Engine Displacement Liters (cc)	Engine ID/VIN	Engine Oil with Filter (qts.)	Transmission (pts.)		Drive Axle Rear (pts.)	Fuel Tank (gal.)	Cooling System (qts.)
					Manual	Auto.			
2000-01	LS6	3.0 (3049)	S	6.9	NA	23.8	3.0	18.0	10.6
	LS8	3.9 (3947)	A	NA	—	23.8	3.0	18.0	11.3

N/A: Not Available

93061CE9

VALVE SPECIFICATIONS

Year	Engine Displacement Liters (cc)	Engine ID/VIN	Seat Angle (deg.)	Face Angle (deg.)	Spring Test Pressure (lbs. @ in.)	Spring Free Length (in.)	Stem-to-Guide Clearance (in.)		Stem Diameter (in.)	
							Intake	Exhaust	Intake	Exhaust
2000-01	3.0 (3049)	S	44.75	45.5	153@1.18	1.570	0.0007-0.0027	0.0017-0.0037	0.2350-0.2358	0.2343-0.2350
	3.9 (3947)	A	NA	NA	NA	NA	NA	NA	NA	NA

NA: Not Available

93061CE0

CRANKSHAFT AND CONNECTING ROD SPECIFICATIONS
All measurements are given in inches.

Year	Engine Displacement Liters (cc)	Engine ID/VIN	Crankshaft				Connecting Rod		
			Main Brg. Journal Dia.	Main Brg. Oil Clearance	Shaft End-play	Thrust on No.	Journal Diameter	Oil Clearance	Side Clearance
2000-01	3.0 (3049)	S	2.4670-2.4790	0.0009-0.0018	0.0040-0.0090	4	1.9670-1.9680	0.0010-0.0025	0.0039-0.0118
	3.9 (3947)	A	NA	NA	NA	NA	NA	NA	NA

NA: Not Available

93061CF1

PISTON AND RING SPECIFICATIONS
All measurements are given in inches.

Year	Engine Displacement Liters (cc)	Engine ID/VIN	Piston Clearance	Ring Gap			Ring Side Clearance		
				Top Compression	Bottom Compression	Oil Control	Top Compression	Bottom Compression	Oil Control
2000-01	3.0 (3049)	S	0.0005-0.0009	0.004-0.010	0.011-0.017	0.005-0.026	0.0015-0.0029	0.0015-0.0033	SNUG
	3.9 (3947)	A	NA	NA	NA	NA	NA	NA	NA

NA: Not Available

93061CF2

TORQUE SPECIFICATIONS
All readings in ft. lbs.

Year	Engine Displacement Liters (cc)	Engine ID/VIN	Cylinder Head Bolts	Main Bearing Bolts	Rod Bearing Bolts	Crankshaft Damper Bolts	Flywheel Bolts	Manifold		Spark Plugs	Lug Nut
								Intake	Exhaust		
2000-01	3.0 (3049)	S	①	②	③	④	54-64	⑤	13-16	7-15	100
	3.9 (3947)	A	⑥	NA	NA	⑦	⑧	NA	NA	NA	100

NA: Not Available

① Step 1: 28-31 ft. lbs.
   Step 2: Rotate 85-95 degrees
   Step 3: Loosen one turn
   Step 4: 28-31 ft. lbs.
   Step 5: Rotate 85-95 degrees
   Step 6: Repeat Step 5

② Step 1: Cap bolts 1-8 (outer) 17-20 ft. lbs.
   Step 2: Cap bolts 9-16 (inner) 28-31 ft. lbs.
   Step 3: Rotate bolts 1-16, 85-95 degrees
   Step 4: Bolts 17-22; 15-22 ft. lbs.

③ Step 1: 30-33 ft. lbs.
   Step 2: Rotate 90-120 degrees

④ Step 1: 77-99 ft. lbs.
   Step 2: Loosen 360 degrees
   Step 3: Tighten to 35-39 ft. lbs.
   Step 4: Rotate 85-95 degrees

⑤ 71-106 inch lbs.

⑥ Step 1: Tighten M10 bolts to 15 ft. lbs.
   Step 2: Tighten M10 bolts to 26 ft. lbs.
   Step 3: Tighten M10 bolts to 33 ft. lbs.
   Step 4: Tighten M10 bolts plus 90 degrees
   Step 5: Tighten M10 bolts plus 90 degrees
   Step 6: Tighten M8 bolts to 15 ft. lbs.
   Step 7: Tighten M8 bolts plus 90 degrees

⑦ Step 1: 59 ft. lbs.
   Step 2: Rotate 80 degrees

⑧ Step 1: 11 ft. lbs.
   Step 2: 81 ft. lbs.

93061CF3

Timing chain and gear service is covered in the model specific sections of this manual

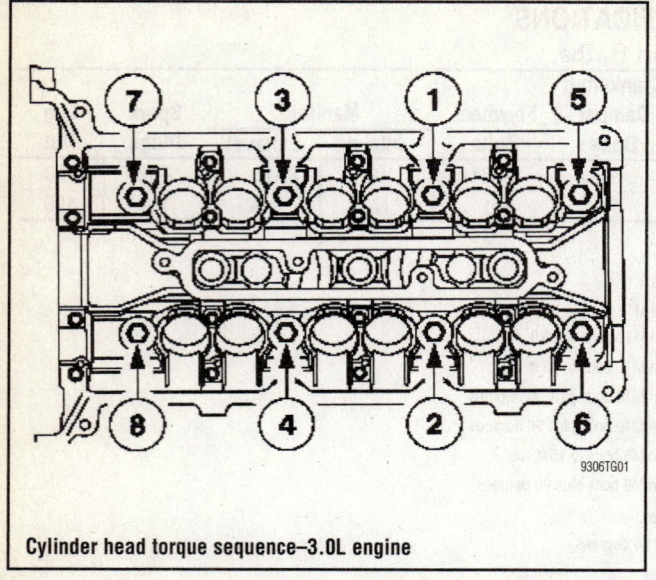

Cylinder head torque sequence–3.0L engine

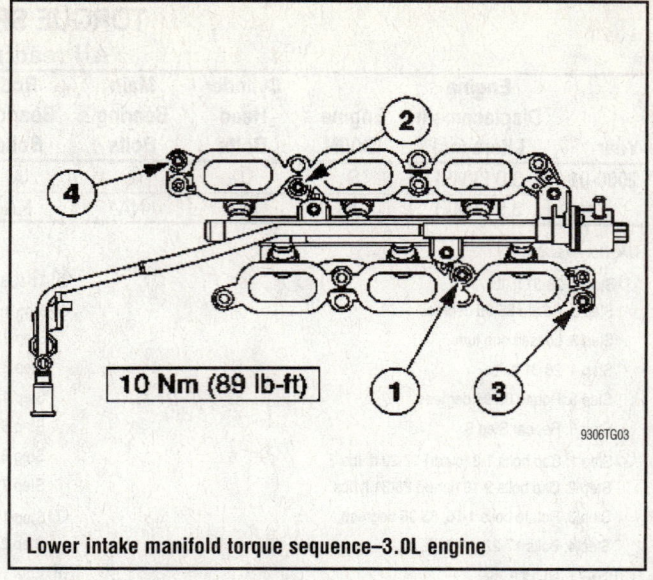

10 Nm (89 lb-ft)

Lower intake manifold torque sequence–3.0L engine

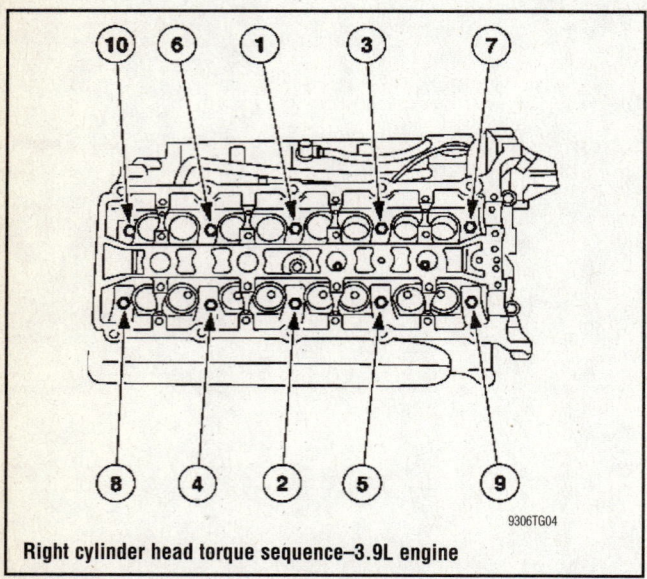

Right cylinder head torque sequence–3.9L engine

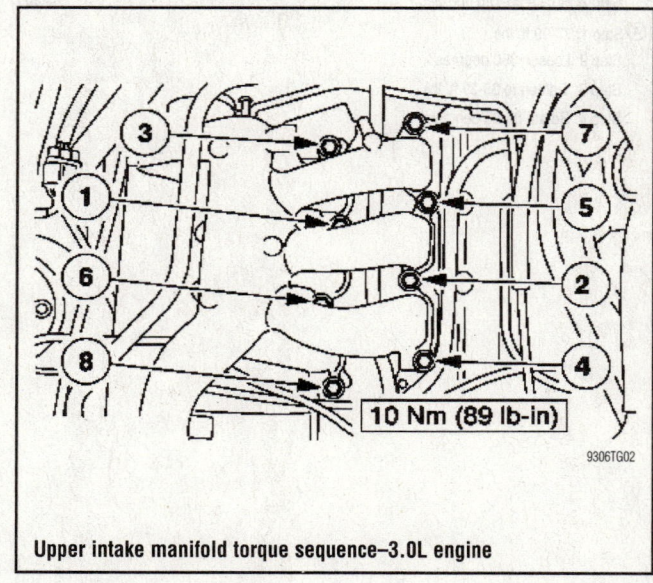

10 Nm (89 lb-in)

Upper intake manifold torque sequence–3.0L engine

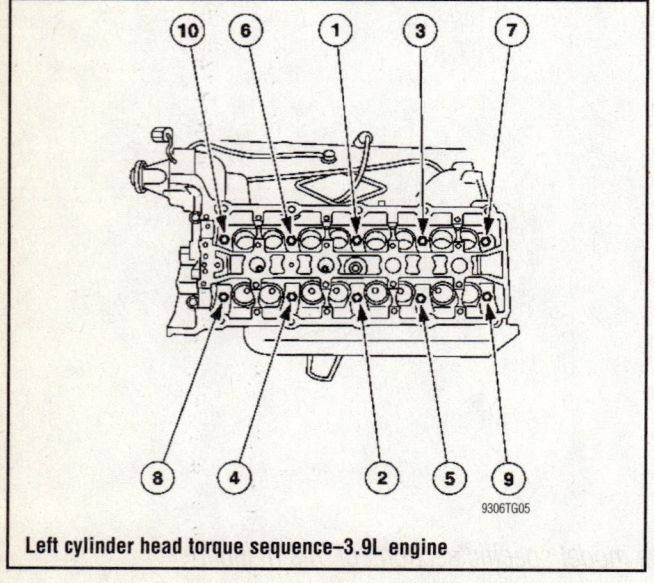

Left cylinder head torque sequence–3.9L engine

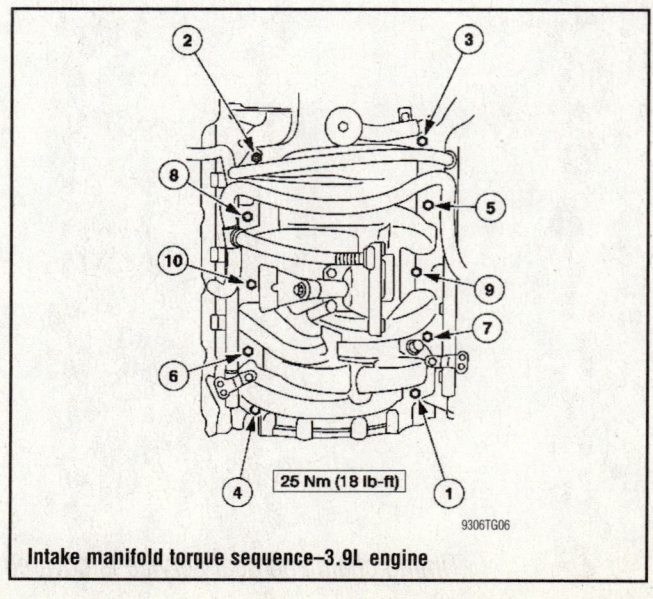

25 Nm (18 lb-ft)

Intake manifold torque sequence–3.9L engine

BRAKE SPECIFICATIONS
Lincoln LS6, LS8
All measurements in inches unless noted

| Year | Model | | Brake Disc | | | Minimum Lining Thickness | Brake Caliper | |
			Original Thickness	Minimum Thickness	Maximum Runout		Bracket Bolts (ft. lbs.)	Mounting Bolts (ft. lbs.)
2000-01	LS6	F	1.180	1.120	0.004	0.079	76	26
		R	0.810	0.740	0.004	0.039	76	25
	LS8	F	1.180	1.120	0.004	0.079	76	26
		R	0.810	0.740	0.004	0.039	76	25

93061CF4

Ignition system service is covered in the model specific sections of this manual

SCHEDULED MAINTENANCE INTERVALS
(LINCOLN LS)

TO BE SERVICED	TYPE OF SERVICE	VEHICLE MILEAGE INTERVAL (x1000)												
		5	10	15	20	25	30	35	40	45	50	55	60	65
Air cleaner filter	R						✓						✓	
Accessory drive belt	S/I												✓	
Brake system ①	S/I			✓			✓			✓			✓	
Clutch pedal operation	S/I						✓						✓	
Cooling system hoses and clamps	S/I			✓			✓			✓			✓	
CV-joint boots & axle seals	S/I						✓						✓	
Engine coolant	R	Ten years or 150,000 miles												
Engine oil & filter	R	✓	✓	✓	✓	✓	✓	✓	✓	✓	✓	✓	✓	✓
Exterior Lights	S/I	Check monthly												
PCV valve	S/I												✓	
Exhaust system & heat shields	S/I						✓						✓	
Parking brake system	S/I	Every 6 months												
Power steering fluid	S/I	Every 6 months												
Rotate tires	S/I	✓		✓		✓		✓		✓		✓		✓
Steering linkage	S/I						✓						✓	
Spark plugs	R	Change at 100,000 miles												
Suspension components	S/I						✓						✓	

R: Replace   S/I: Inspect and service, if necessary   L: Lubricate   A: Adjust   C: Clean

① Inspect the reservoir fluid level, rotor and or drum, brake lines, hoses, calipers and or wheel cylinders

FREQUENT OPERATION MAINTENANCE (SEVERE SERVICE)

If a vehicle is operated under any of the following conditions it is considered severe service:
- Extremely dusty areas.
- 50% or more of the vehicle operation is in 32°C (90°F) or higher temperatures, or constant operation in temperatures below 0°C (32°F)
- Prolonged idling (vehicle operation in stop and go traffic).
- Frequent short running periods (engine does not warm to normal operating temperatures).
- Police, taxi, delivery usage or trailer towing usage.

Oil & oil filter change: change every 3000 miles.

Air filter element: change every 15,000 miles.

93061CF5

SCHEDULED MAINTENANCE INTERVALS
FORD MOTOR COMPANY
LINCOLN LS

The following should be used as a guide when determining the amount of work required for a particular service. In estimating how long a particular Scheduled Maintenance Service should take, please observe the following:

- Labor Time is time based on field research and data supplied by the vehicle manufacturer.
- Labor time operations are given in hours and tenths of an hour.
- All labor operations are to be used as a guide.

Mechanic Skill Level Codes:
(A) PRECISION: Highly skilled with multiple certification.
(B) GENERAL: Normally skilled with certification.
(C) MAINTENANCE: Semi-skilled working on certification.

	LABOR TIME		LABOR TIME		LABOR TIME
5000 Mile Service (C)		**25000 Mile Service (C)**		**50000 Mile Service (C)**	
All Models	.9	All Models	.9	All Models	.7
10000 Mile Service (C)		**30000 Mile Service (B)**		**55000 Mile Service (C)**	
All Models	.5	All Models	1.9	All Models	.9
15000 Mile Service (C)		**35000 Mile Service (C)**		**60000 Mile Service (B)**	
All Models	1.6	All Models	.9	All Models	1.9
20000 Mile Service (C)		**40000 Mile Service (C)**		**65000 Mile Service (C)**	
All Models	.5	All Models	.5	All Models	.9
		45000 Mile Service (C)			
		All Models	1.6		

93061CF6

FORD MOTOR CO.
Ford Mustang • Thunderbird • Lincoln Mark VIII • Mercury Cougar (1997)

ENGINE AND VEHICLE IDENTIFICATION

Engine							Model Year	
Code ①	Liters (cc)	Cu. In.	Cyl.	Fuel Sys.	Engine Type	Eng. Mfg.	Code ②	Year
4	3.8 (3802)	232	6	SFI	OHV	Ford	V	1997
V	4.6 (4593)	281	8	SFI	DOHC	Ford	W	1998
W	4.6 (4593)	281	8	SFI	SOHC	Ford	X	1999
X	4.6 (4593)	281	8	SFI	SOHC	Ford	Y	2000
							1	2001

OHV: Overhead Valve

SOHC: Single Overhead Camshaft

DOHC: Double Overhead Camshaft

SFI: Sequential Fuel Injection

① 8th position of VIN

② 10th position of VIN

93061CF7

GENERAL ENGINE SPECIFICATIONS
All measurements are given in inches.

Year	Model	Engine Displacement Liters (cc)	Engine Series (ID/VIN)	Fuel System	Net Horsepower @ rpm	Net Torque @ rpm (ft. lbs.)	Bore x Stroke (in.)	Com-pression Ratio	Oil Pressure @ rpm
1997	Cougar	3.8 (3802)	4	SFI	145@4000	215@2750	3.81x3.39	9.0:1	40-60@2500
		4.6 (4593)	W	SFI	205@4250	280@3000	3.55x3.54	9.0:1	20-45@1500
	Mark VIII	4.6 (4593)	V	SFI	①	②	3.55x3.54	9.85:1	20-45@1500
	Mustang	3.8 (3802)	4	SFI	150@4000	215@2750	3.81x3.39	9.0:1	40-60@2500
		4.6 (4593)	V	SFI	305@5800	300@4800	3.55x3.54	9.5:1	20-45@1500
		4.6 (4593)	W	SFI	215@4400	285@3500	3.55x3.54	9.0:1	20-45@1500
	Thunderbird	3.8 (3802)	4	SFI	145@4000	215@2750	3.81x3.39	9.0:1	40-60@2500
		4.6 (4593)	W	SFI	205@4250	280@3000	3.55x3.54	9.0:1	20-45@1500
1998	Mark VIII	4.6 (4593)	V	SFI	①	②	3.55x3.54	9.85:1	20-45@1500
	Mustang	3.8 (3802)	4	SFI	150@4000	215@2750	3.81x3.39	9.0:1	40-60@2500
		4.6 (4593)	V	SFI	305@5800	300@4800	3.55x3.54	9.5:1	20-45@1500
		4.6 (4593)	X	SFI	215@4400	285@3500	3.55x3.54	9.0:1	20-45@1500
1999	Mustang	3.8 (3802)	4	SFI	190@5250	220@3000	3.81x3.39	9.0:1	40-60@2500
		4.6 (4593)	V	SFI	320@6000	317@4750	3.55x3.54	9.5:1	20-45@1500
		4.6 (4593)	X	SFI	260@5000	302@4000	3.55x3.54	9.0:1	20-45@1500
2000-01	Mustang	3.8 (3802)	4	SFI	190@5250	220@3000	3.81x3.39	9.0:1	40-60@2500
		4.6 (4593)	V	SFI	320@6000	317@4750	3.55x3.54	9.5:1	20-45@1500
		4.6 (4593)	X	SFI	260@5000	302@4000	3.55x3.54	9.0:1	20-45@1500

SFI: Sequential Fuel Injection

① Mark VIII without LSC package: 280@5500
Mark VIII with LSC package: 290@5750

② Mark VIII without LSC package: 285@4500
Mark VIII with LSC package: 292@4500

93061CF8

ENGINE TUNE-UP SPECIFICATIONS

Year	Engine Displacement Liters (cc)	Engine ID/VIN	Spark Plug Gap (in.)	Ignition Timing (deg.) MT	Ignition Timing (deg.) AT	Fuel Pump (psi) ①	Idle Speed (rpm) MT	Idle Speed (rpm) AT	Valve Clearance Intake	Valve Clearance Exhaust
1997	3.8 (3802)	4	0.054	②	②	28-54	②	②	HYD	HYD
	4.6 (4593)	V	0.054	10B	—	35-45	②	—	HYD	HYD
	4.6 (4593)	W	0.054	10B	10B	35-45	②	②	HYD	HYD
1998	3.8 (3802)	4	0.054	②	②	28-54	②	②	HYD	HYD
	4.6 (4593)	V	0.054	10B	—	35-45	②	—	HYD	HYD
	4.6 (4593)	X	0.054	10B	10B	35-45	②	②	HYD	HYD
1999	3.8 (3802)	4	0.054	②	②	28-54	②	②	HYD	HYD
	4.6 (4593)	V	0.054	10B	—	35-45	②	—	HYD	HYD
	4.6 (4593)	X	0.054	10B	10B	35-45	②	②	HYD	HYD
2000-01	3.8 (3802)	4	0.054	②	②	28-54	②	②	HYD	HYD
	4.6 (4593)	V	0.054	10B	—	35-45	②	—	HYD	HYD
	4.6 (4593)	X	0.054	10B	10B	35-45	②	②	HYD	HYD

NOTE: The Vehicle Emission Control Information label often reflects specification changes made during production. The label figures must be used if they differ from those in this chart.

B: Before Top Dead Center

HYD: Hydraulic

① Fuel pressure with engine running, pressure regulator vacuum hose connected

② Refer to Vehicle Emission Control Information label

93061CF9

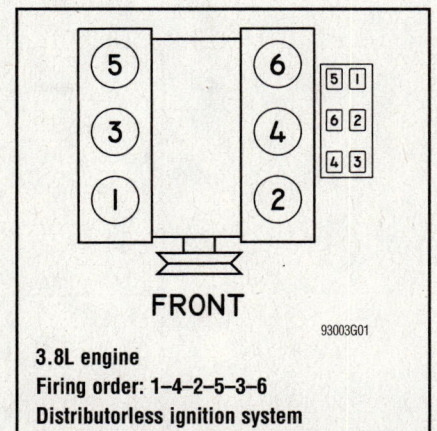

3.8L engine
Firing order: 1–4–2–5–3–6
Distributorless ignition system
93003G01

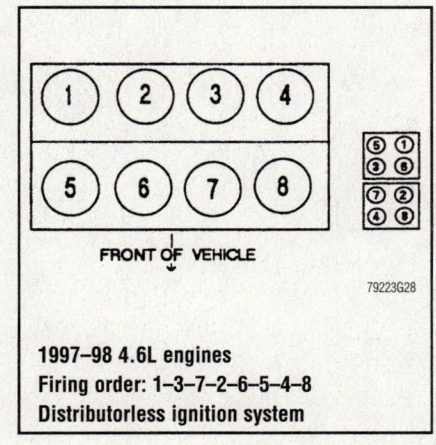

1997–98 4.6L engines
Firing order: 1–3–7–2–6–5–4–8
Distributorless ignition system
79223G28

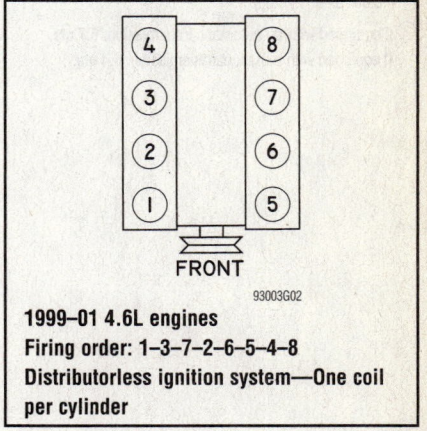

1999–01 4.6L engines
Firing order: 1–3–7–2–6–5–4–8
Distributorless ignition system—One coil per cylinder
93003G02

Refer to the model specific sections for engine mechanical service procedures

CAPACITIES

Year	Model	Engine Displacement Liters (cc)	Engine ID/VIN	Engine Oil with Filter (qts.)	Transmission (pts) Manual	Transmission (pts) Auto. ①	Drive Axle Rear (pts.)	Fuel Tank (gal.)	Cooling System (qts.)
1997	Cougar	3.8 (3802)	4	5.0	—	27.8	②	18.0	12.6
		4.6 (4593)	W	5.3	—	27.8	②	18.0	14.1
	Mark VIII	4.6 (4593)	V	6.0	—	25.6	3.00	18.0	16.0
	Mustang	3.8 (3802)	4	5.0	5.6	27.8	3.50	15.4	11.8
		4.6 (4593)	V	6.0	6.5	27.8	3.75	15.4	14.1
		4.6 (4593)	W	③	6.5	25.6	3.75	15.4	14.1
	Thunderbird	3.8 (3802)	4	5.0	—	27.8	②	18.0	12.6
		4.6 (4593)	W	5.3	—	27.8	②	18.0	14.1
1998	Mark VIII	4.6 (4593)	V	6.0	—	25.6	3.00	18.0	16.0
	Mustang	3.8 (3802)	4	5.0	5.6	27.8	3.50	15.4	11.8
		4.6 (4593)	V	6.0	6.5	27.8	3.75	15.4	14.1
		4.6 (4593)	X	③	6.5	25.6	3.75	15.4	14.1
1999	Mustang	3.8 (3802)	4	5.0	5.6	27.8	3.50	15.7	11.8
		4.6 (4593)	V	6.0	6.5	27.8	3.75	15.7	14.1
		4.6 (4593)	X	③	6.5	25.6	3.75	15.7	14.1
2000-01	Mustang	3.8 (3802)	4	5.0	5.6	27.8	3.50	15.7	11.8
		4.6 (4593)	V	6.0	6.5	27.8	3.75	15.7	14.1
		4.6 (4593)	X	③	6.5	25.6	3.75	15.7	14.1

NOTE: All capacities are approximate. Add fluid gradually and ensure a proper fluid level is obtained.

① Includes torque converter

② 7.50" limited slip axle: 2.75 pts.
7.50" standard axle: 3.0 pts.
8.80" axle: 3.25 pts.

③ If equipped with an automatic transmission: 6.7 qts.
If equipped with a manual transmission: 6.4 qts.

93061CF0

VALVE SPECIFICATIONS

Year	Engine Displacement Liters (cc)	Engine ID/VIN	Seat Angle (deg.)	Face Angle (deg.)	Spring Test Pressure (lbs. @ in.)	Spring Installed Height (in.)	Stem-to-Guide Clearance (in.)		Stem Diameter (in.)	
							Intake	Exhaust	Intake	Exhaust
1997	3.8 (3802)	4	44.5	45.8	220@1.18	1.650	0.0010-0.0027	0.0015-0.0032	0.3415-0.3423	0.3410-0.3418
	4.6 (4593)	V	45	45.5	160@1.10	1.425	0.0008-0.0027	0.0018-0.0037	0.2746-0.2754	0.2736-0.2744
	4.6 (4593)	W	45	45.5	132@1.10	1.570	0.0008-0.0027	0.0018-0.0037	0.2746-0.2754	0.2736-0.2744
1998	3.8 (3802)	4	44.5	45.8	220@1.18	1.650	0.0010-0.0027	0.0015-0.0032	0.3415-0.3423	0.3410-0.3418
	4.6 (4593)	V	45	45.5	160@1.10	1.425	0.0008-0.0027	0.0018-0.0037	0.2746-0.2754	0.2736-0.2744
	4.6 (4593)	X	45	45.5	132@1.10	1.570	0.0008-0.0027	0.0018-0.0037	0.2746-0.2754	0.2736-0.2744
1999	3.8 (3802)	4	44.7	45.7	224@1.16	1.620	0.0450-0.0900	0.0015-0.0033	0.2738-0.2751	0.2728-0.2741
	4.6 (4593)	V	45	45.5	160@1.03	1.660	0.0008-0.0027	0.0018-0.0037	0.2746-0.275	0.2736-0.2744
	4.6 (4593)	X	45	45.5	161@1.03	1.570	0.0008-0.0027	0.0018-0.0037	0.2746-0.2754	0.2736-0.2744
2000-01	3.8 (3802)	4	44.7	45.7	224@1.16	1.620	0.0450-0.0900	0.0015-0.0033	0.2738-0.2751	0.2728-0.2741
	4.6 (4593)	V	45	45.5	160@1.03	1.660	0.0008-0.0027	0.0018-0.0037	0.2746-0.275	0.2736-0.2744
	4.6 (4593)	X	45	45.5	161@1.03	1.570	0.0008-0.0027	0.0018-0.0037	0.2746-0.2754	0.2736-0.2744

93061CG1

Refer to the model specific sections for fuel system service procedures

CRANKSHAFT AND CONNECTING ROD SPECIFICATIONS
All measurements are given in inches.

Year	Engine Displacement Liters (cc)	Engine ID/VIN	Crankshaft				Connecting Rod		
			Main Brg. Journal Dia.	Main Brg. Oil Clearance	Shaft End-play	Thrust on No.	Journal Diameter	Oil Clearance	Side Clearance
1997	3.8 (3802)	4	①	0.0010-0.0014	0.0040-0.0080	3	2.3103-2.3111	0.0010-0.0014	0.0047-0.0144
	4.6 (4593)	V	2.6567-2.6577	0.0001-0.0018	0.0051-0.0119	5	2.0859-2.0867	0.0011-0.0027	0.0006-0.0177
	4.6 (4593)	W	2.6569-2.6576	0.0011-0.0026	0.0051-0.0119	5	2.0861-2.0867	0.0011-0.0027	0.0006-0.0177
1998	3.8 (3802)	4	①	0.0010-0.0014	0.0040-0.0080	3	2.3103-2.3111	0.0010-0.0014	0.0047-0.0144
	4.6 (4593)	V	2.6567-2.6577	0.0001-0.0018	0.0051-0.0119	5	2.0859-2.0867	0.0011-0.0027	0.0006-0.0177
	4.6 (4593)	X	2.6569-2.6576	0.0011-0.0026	0.0051-0.0119	5	2.0861-2.0867	0.0011-0.0027	0.0006-0.0177
1999	3.8 (3802)	4	①	0.0010-0.0014	0.0040-0.0080	3	2.3103-2.3111	0.0010-0.0014	0.0047-0.0144
	4.6 (4593)	V	2.6567-2.6577	0.0001-0.0018	0.0051-0.0119	5	2.0859-2.0867	0.0011-0.0027	0.0006-0.0177
	4.6 (4593)	X	2.6569-2.6576	0.0011-0.0026	0.0051-0.0119	5	2.0861-2.0867	0.0011-0.0027	0.0006-0.0177
2000-01	3.8 (3802)	4	①	0.0010-0.0014	0.0040-0.0080	3	2.3103-2.3111	0.0010-0.0014	0.0047-0.0144
	4.6 (4593)	V	2.6567-2.6577	0.0001-0.0018	0.0051-0.0119	5	2.0859-2.0867	0.0011-0.0027	0.0006-0.0177
	4.6 (4593)	X	2.6569-2.6576	0.0011-0.0026	0.0051-0.0119	5	2.0861-2.0867	0.0011-0.0027	0.0006-0.0177

① Journals 1, 2, 3: 2.5194-2.5186 in.
Journal 4: 2.5100-2.5092 in.

93061CG2

PISTON AND RING SPECIFICATIONS
All measurements are given in inches.

Year	Engine Displacement Liters (cc)	Engine ID/VIN	Piston Clearance	Ring Gap			Ring Side Clearance		
				Top Compression	Bottom Compression	Oil Control	Top Compression	Bottom Compression	Oil Control
1997	3.8 (3802)	4	0.0014-0.0022	0.011-0.012	0.009-0.020	0.015-0.058	0.0016-0.0034	0.0016-0.0034	SNUG
	4.6 (4593)	V	0.0000-0.0010	0.010-0.020	0.009-0.019	0.006-0.026	0.0003-0.0009	0.0012-0.0031	SNUG
	4.6 (4593)	W	0.0005-0.0010	0.009-0.019	0.009-0.019	0.006-0.026	0.0016-0.0035	0.0018-0.0031	SNUG
1998	3.8 (3802)	4	0.0014-0.0022	0.011-0.012	0.009-0.020	0.015-0.058	0.0016-0.0034	0.0016-0.0034	SNUG
	4.6 (4593)	V	0.0000-0.0010	0.010-0.020	0.009-0.019	0.006-0.026	0.0003-0.0009	0.0012-0.0031	SNUG
	4.6 (4593)	X	0.0005-0.0010	0.009-0.019	0.009-0.019	0.006-0.026	0.0016-0.0035	0.0018-0.0031	SNUG
1999	3.8 (3802)	4	0.0007-0.0017	0.011-0.012	0.009-0.020	0.015-0.058	0.0016-0.0034	0.0016-0.0034	SNUG
	4.6 (4593)	V	0.0000-0.0010	0.010-0.020	0.009-0.019	0.006-0.026	0.0003-0.0009	0.0012-0.0031	SNUG
	4.6 (4593)	X	0.0005-0.0010	0.009-0.019	0.009-0.019	0.006-0.026	0.0016-0.0035	0.0018-0.0031	SNUG
2000-01	3.8 (3802)	4	0.0007-0.0017	0.011-0.012	0.009-0.020	0.015-0.058	0.0016-0.0034	0.0016-0.0034	SNUG
	4.6 (4593)	V	0.0000-0.0010	0.010-0.020	0.009-0.019	0.006-0.026	0.0003-0.0009	0.0012-0.0031	SNUG
	4.6 (4593)	X	0.0005-0.0010	0.009-0.019	0.009-0.019	0.006-0.026	0.0016-0.0035	0.0018-0.0031	SNUG

93061CG3

Refer to the model specific sections for engine electrical system service procedures

TORQUE SPECIFICATIONS
All readings in ft. lbs.

Year	Engine Displacement Liters (cc)	Engine ID/VIN	Cylinder Head Bolts	Main Bearing Bolts	Rod Bearing Bolts	Crankshaft Damper Bolts	Flywheel Bolts	Manifold Intake	Manifold Exhaust	Spark Plugs	Lug Nuts
1997	3.8 (3802)	4	①	65-81	31-36	103-132	54-64	②	15-22	7-15	95
	4.6 (4593)	V	③	④	⑤	114-121	54-64	⑥	13-16	7-15	95
	4.6 (4593)	W	③	⑦	⑧	114-121	54-64	15-22	15-22	7-15	95
1998	3.8 (3802)	4	①	65-81	31-36	103-132	54-64	②	15-22	7-15	95
	4.6 (4593)	V	③	④	⑤	114-121	54-64	⑥	13-16	7-15	95
	4.6 (4593)	X	③	⑦	⑧	114-121	54-64	15-22	15-22	7-15	95
1999	3.8 (3802)	4	①	⑨	⑩	118	54-64	②	15-22	7-15	95
	4.6 (4593)	V	⑪	④	⑤	114-121	54-64	⑥	13-16	7-15	95
	4.6 (4593)	X	③	⑦	⑧	114-121	54-64	15-22	15-22	7-15	95
2000-01	3.8 (3802)	4	①	⑨	⑩	118	54-64	②	15-22	7-15	95
	4.6 (4593)	V	⑪	④	⑤	114-121	54-64	⑥	13-16	7-15	95
	4.6 (4593)	X	③	⑦	⑧	114-121	54-64	15-22	15-22	7-15	95

① Do not reuse cylinder head bolts.
Step 1: 15 ft. lbs.
Step 2: 29 ft. lbs.
Step 3: 37 ft. lbs.
Step 4: Loosen bolts one at a time and retorque as follows:
Long bolts: 11-18 ft. lbs.
Short bolts: 7-15 ft. lbs.
Step 5: Tighten 85-95 degrees

② Upper intake manifold bolts:
Step 1: 8 ft. lbs.
Step 2: 15 ft. lbs.
Step 3: 24 ft. lbs
Lower intake manifold bolts:
Step 1: 13 ft. lbs.
Step 2: 16 ft. lbs.

③ Do not reuse cylinder head bolts.
Step 1: 27-32 ft. lbs.
Step 2: Tighten each bolt 85-95 degrees
Step 3: Repeat Step 2

④ Step 1: Main bearing cap bolts: 6-9 ft. lbs.
Step 2: Main bearing cap bolts, outer: 16-21 ft. lbs.
Step 3: Main bearing cap bolts, inner: 27-32 ft. lbs.
Step 4: Tighten main bearing cap bolts 85-95 degrees
Step 5: Main cap adjusting screws: 4 ft. lbs. then 7.5 ft. lbs.
Step 6: Main cap side bolts: 7 ft. lbs. then 14-17 ft. lbs.

⑤ Step 1: 5ft. lbs.
Step 2: 10 ft. lbs.
Step 3: 18-25 ft. lbs.
Step 4: Tighten 85-95 degrees

⑥ Step 1: Four inside short bolts: 9-11 ft. lbs.
Step 2: All other bolts: 13-16 ft. lbs.
Step 3: Tighten 85-95 degrees

⑦ Do not reuse main cap bolts.
Step 1: Main bearing cap bolts: 22-25 ft. lbs.
Step 2: Tighten each bolt 85-95 degrees
Step 3: Main bearing cap adjust screws: 4 ft. lbs. then 6-8 ft. lbs.
Step 4: Main bearing cap side bolts: 7 ft. lbs. then 14-17 ft. lbs.

⑧ Do not reuse rod bolts.
Step 1: 12 ft. lbs.
Step 2: Tighten 85-95 degrees

⑨ Step 1: 37 ft. lbs.
Step 2: Tighten 115-125 degrees

⑩ Step 1: 18 ft. lbs.
Step 2: 33 ft. lbs.
Step 3: Tighten 90-120 degrees

⑪ Step 1: 30 ft. lbs.
Step 2: Tighten 90 degrees
Step 3: Loosen all bolts one (1) turn
Step 4: 30 ft. lbs.
Step 5: Tighten 90 degrees
Step 6: Tighten an additional 90 degrees

93061CG4

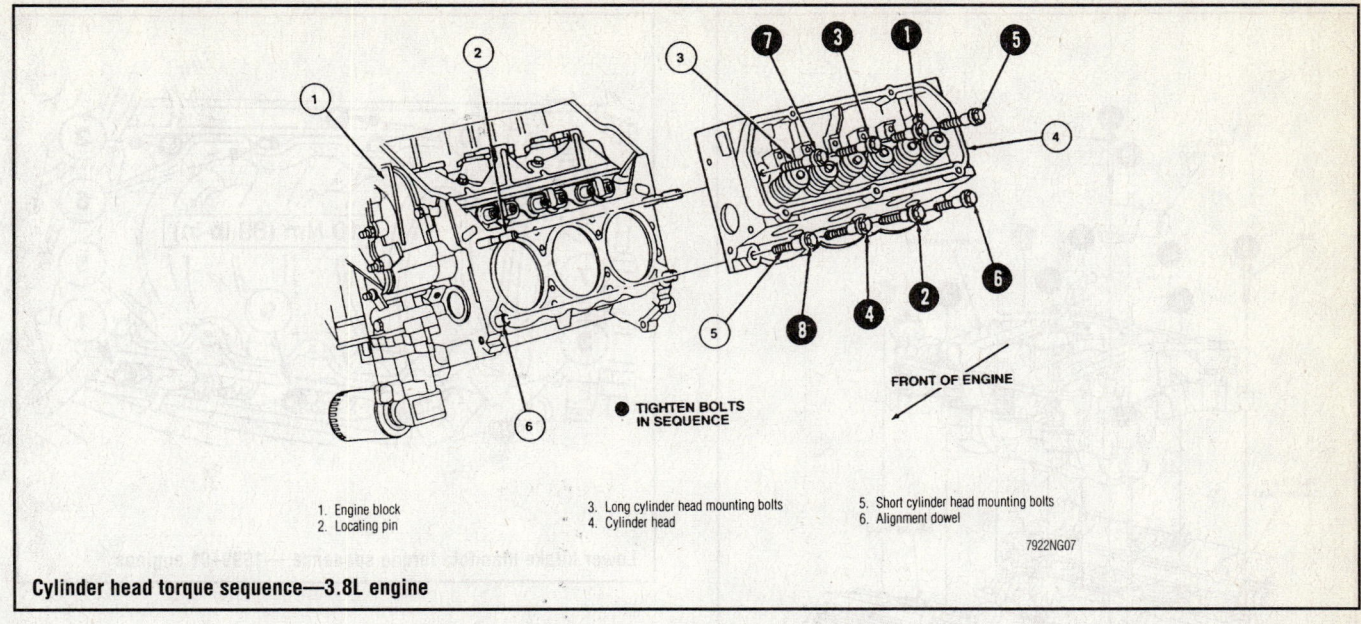

Cylinder head torque sequence—3.8L engine

1. Engine block
2. Locating pin
3. Long cylinder head mounting bolts
4. Cylinder head
5. Short cylinder head mounting bolts
6. Alignment dowel

● TIGHTEN BOLTS IN SEQUENCE

FRONT OF ENGINE

7922NG07

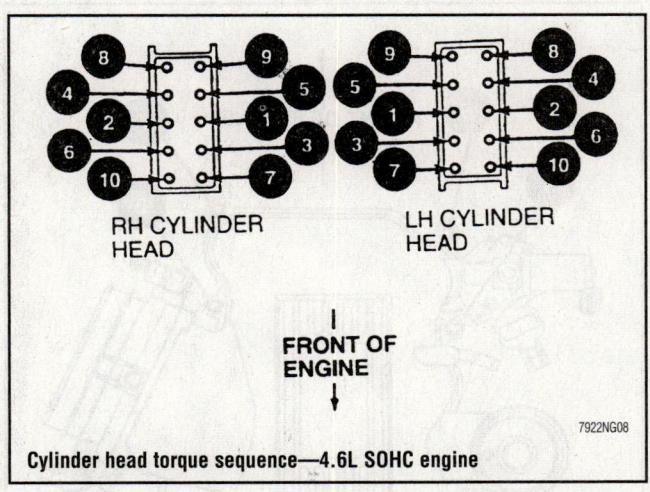

RH CYLINDER HEAD

LH CYLINDER HEAD

FRONT OF ENGINE

7922NG08

Cylinder head torque sequence—4.6L SOHC engine

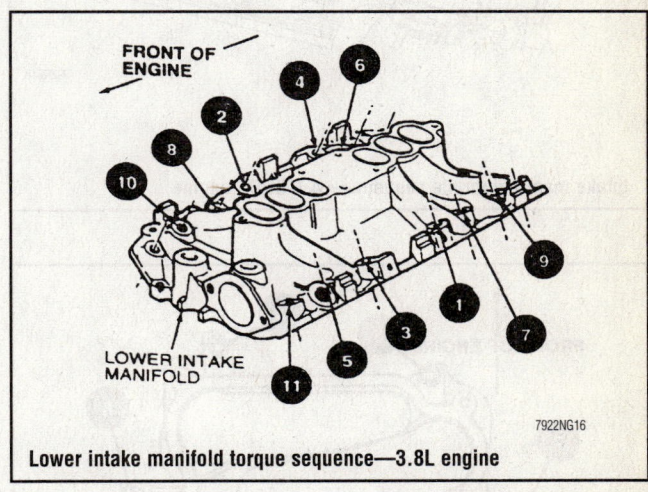

FRONT OF ENGINE

LOWER INTAKE MANIFOLD

7922NG16

Lower intake manifold torque sequence—3.8L engine

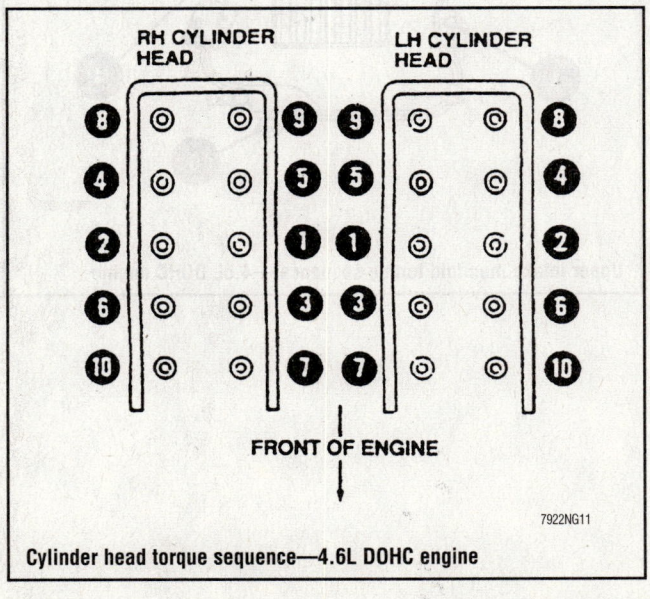

RH CYLINDER HEAD

LH CYLINDER HEAD

FRONT OF ENGINE

7922NG11

Cylinder head torque sequence—4.6L DOHC engine

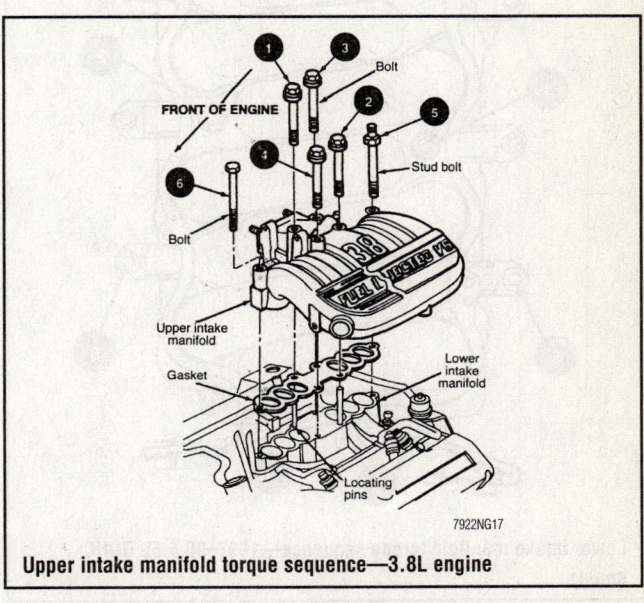

Bolt
Stud bolt
FRONT OF ENGINE
Bolt
Upper intake manifold
Gasket
Lower intake manifold
Locating pins

7922NG17

Upper intake manifold torque sequence—3.8L engine

For accessory drive belt replacement procedures see the model specific sections of this manual

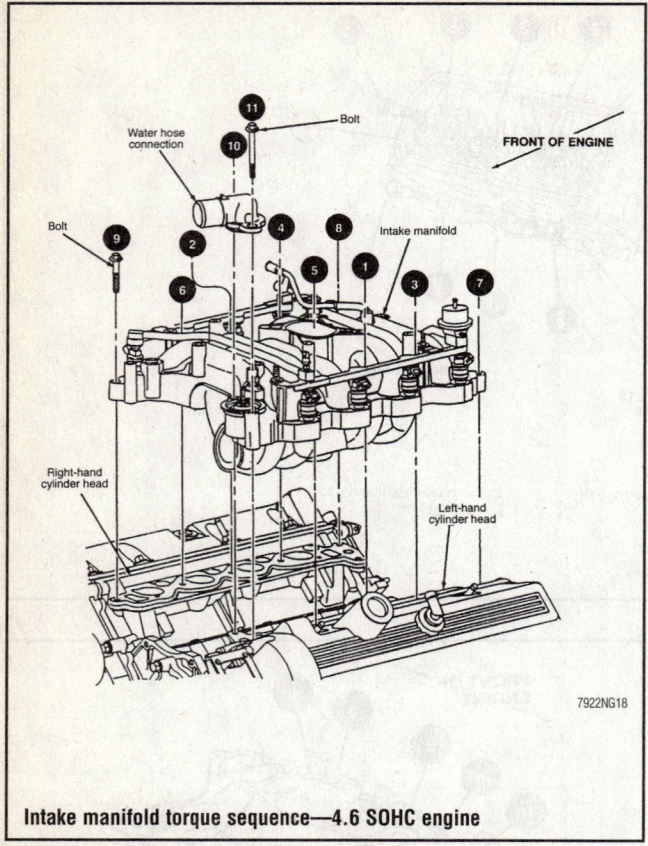

Intake manifold torque sequence—4.6 SOHC engine

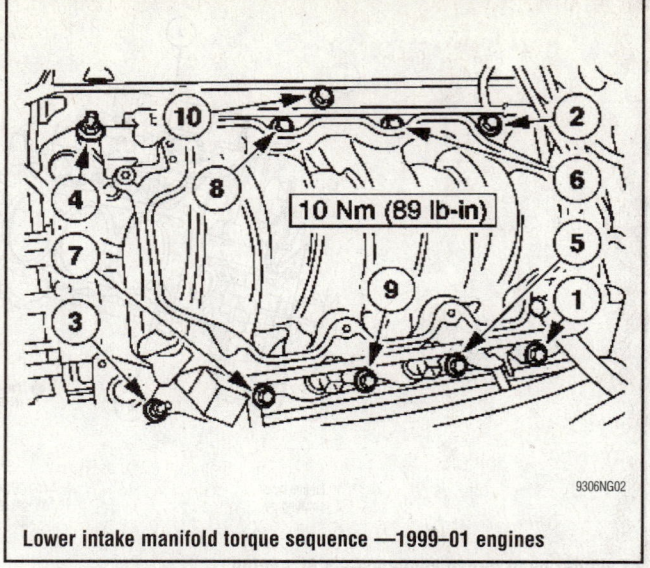

Lower intake manifold torque sequence—1999–01 engines

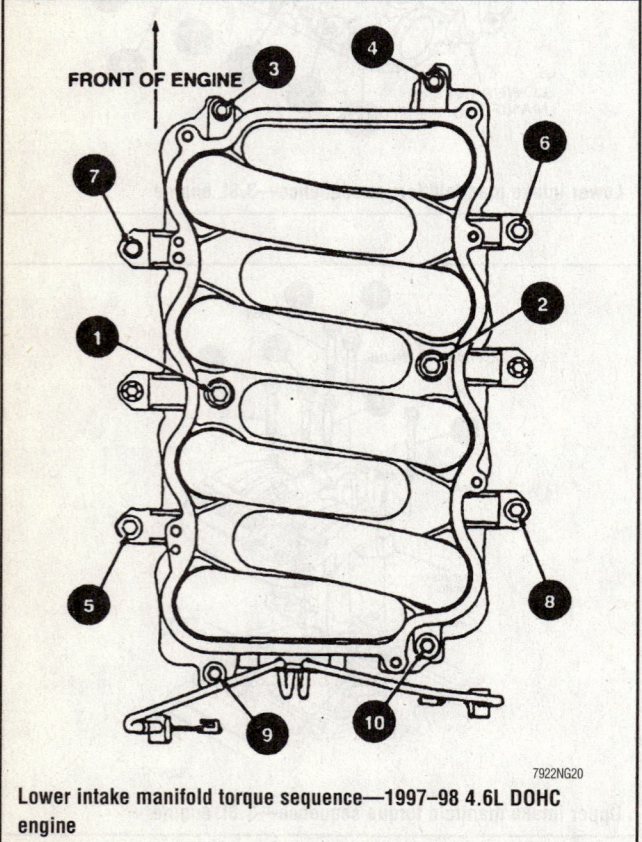

Lower intake manifold torque sequence—1997–98 4.6L DOHC engine

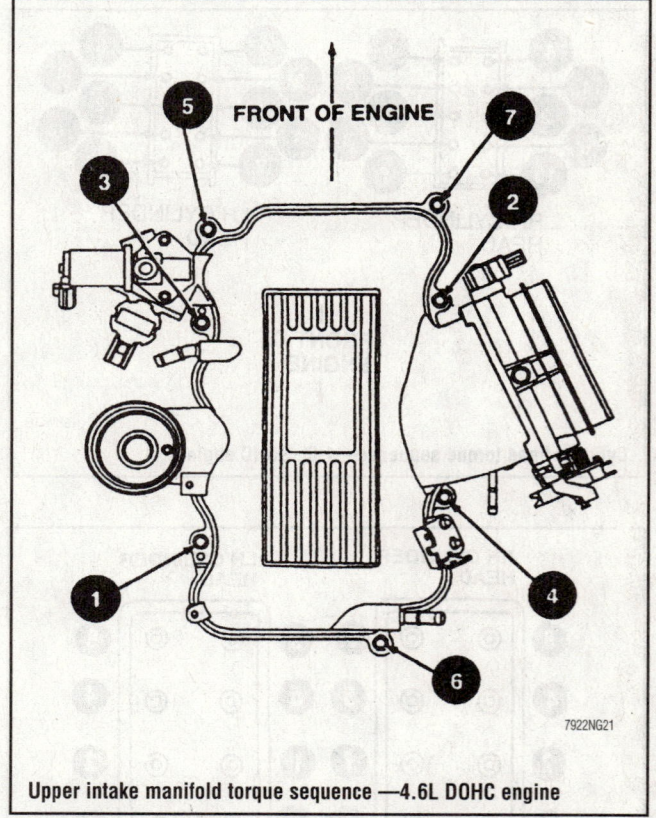

Upper intake manifold torque sequence—4.6L DOHC engine

BRAKE SPECIFICATIONS
FORD MUSTANG, THUNDERBIRD (1997), COUGAR (1997), LINCLON MARK VIII (1997-98)
All measurements in inches unless noted

Year	Model		Brake Disc			Brake Drum Diameter			Minimum Lining Thickness	Brake Caliper Mounting Bolts (ft. lbs.)
			Original Thickness	Minimum Thickness	Maximum Run-out	Original Inside Diameter	Max. Wear Limit	Maximum Machine Diameter		
1997	Cougar	F	1.025	0.974	0.002	—	—	—	0.125	60
		R	0.710	0.657	—	9.80	NA	9.90	0.125	26
	Mark VIII	F	1.024	0.974	0.003	—	—	—	0.125	60
		R	0.709	0.657	0.002	—	—	—	0.125	26
	Mustang	F	1.030	0.970	0.001	—	—	—	0.125	64
		R	0.550	0.500	0.002	—	—	—	0.123	26
	Mustang Cobra	F	1.100	1.040	0.001	—	—	—	0.125	64
		R	0.710	0.660	0.002	—	—	—	0.123	26
	Thunderbird	F	1.025	0.974	0.002	—	—	—	0.125	60
		R	0.710	0.657	—	9.80	NA	9.90	0.125	26
1998	Mark VIII	F	1.024	0.974	0.003	—	—	—	0.125	60
		R	0.709	0.657	0.002	—	—	—	—	26
	Mustang	F	1.030	0.970	0.001	—	—	—	0.125	64
		R	0.550	0.500	0.002	—	—	—	0.123	26
	Mustang Cobra	F	1.100	1.040	0.001	—	—	—	0.125	64
		R	0.710	0.660	0.002	—	—	—	0.123	26
1999	Mustang	F	1.030	0.970	0.001	—	—	—	0.125	64
		R	0.550	0.500	0.002	—	—	—	0.123	26
	Mustang Cobra	F	1.100	1.040	0.001	—	—	—	0.125	64
		R	0.710	0.660	0.002	—	—	—	0.123	26
2000-01	Mustang	F	1.030	0.970	0.001	—	—	—	0.125	64
		R	0.550	0.500	0.002	—	—	—	0.123	26
	Mustang Cobra	F	1.100	1.040	0.001	—	—	—	0.125	64
		R	0.710	0.660	0.002	—	—	—	0.123	26

NOTE: Follow specifications stamped on rotor or drum if figures differ from those in this chart.

NA: Not Available

F: Front

R: Rear

93061CG5

For brake related suspension and axle service, refer to the model specific sections of this manual

SCHEDULED MAINTENANCE INTERVALS
(FORD MUSTANG, THUNDERBIRD, LINCOLN MARK VIII & MERCURY 1997 COUGAR)

TO BE SERVICED	TYPE OF SERVICE	VEHICLE MILEAGE INTERVAL (x1000)												
		5	10	15	20	25	30	35	40	45	50	55	60	65
Engine oil & filter	R	✓	✓	✓	✓	✓	✓	✓	✓	✓	✓	✓	✓	✓
Adjust clutch pedal by lifting pedal	S/I	✓	✓	✓	✓	✓	✓	✓	✓	✓	✓	✓	✓	✓
Rotate tires	S/I	✓		✓		✓		✓		✓		✓		✓
Cooling system, hoses, clamps & coolant strength	S/I			✓			✓			✓			✓	
Lubricate steering linkage (T-Bird/Cougar)	S/I			✓			✓			✓			✓	
Air cleaner element	R						✓						✓	
Automatic transmission fluid & filter	R						✓						✓	
Engine coolant ①	R						✓						✓	
Spark plugs (Mark VIII) ②	R													
Spark plugs (T-Bird & Cougar)	R												✓	
Spark plugs (Mustang)	R													
Accessory drive belt(s)	S/I						✓						✓	
Brake lines, hoses & connections	S/I						✓						✓	
Clutch fluid level (T-Bird)	S/I						✓						✓	
Exhaust heat shields	S/I						✓						✓	
Front & rear brakes	S/I						✓						✓	
PCV valve	R												✓	
Rear axle lubricant ②	R													
Supercharger fluid level	S/I												✓	

R: Replace   S/I: Service or Inspect

① Engine coolant: change engine coolant at 48,000 to 50,000 miles and thereafter every 30,000 miles.

② Replace every 100,000 miles.

FREQUENT OPERATION MAINTENANCE (SEVERE SERVICE)

If a vehicle is operated under any of the following conditions it is considered severe service:

- Extremely dusty areas.

- 50% or more of the vehicle operation is in 32°C (90°F) or higher temperatures, or constant operation in temperatures below 0°C (32°F).

- Prolonged idling (vehicle operation in stop and go traffic).

- Frequent short running periods (engine does not warm to normal operating temperatures).

- Police, taxi, delivery usage or trailer towing usage.

Oil & filter change: change every 3000 miles.

Rotate tires at 6000 miles & every 9000 miles thereafter.

Automatic transmission fluid & filter: change every 21,000 miles.

93061CG6

SCHEDULED MAINTENANCE INTERVALS
FORD MOTOR COMPANY
FORD MUSTANG, THUNDERBIRD
LINCOLN MARK VIII, MERCURY COUGAR (1997)

The following should be used as a guide when determining the amount of work required for a particular service.
In estimating how long a particular Scheduled Maintenance Service should take, please observe the following:

- Labor Time is time based on field research and data supplied by the vehicle manufacturer.
- Labor time operations are given in hours and tenths of an hour.
- All labor operations are to be used as a guide.

Mechanic Skill Level Codes:
(A) PRECISION: Highly skilled with multiple certification.
(B) GENERAL: Normally skilled with certification.
(C) MAINTENANCE: Semi-skilled working on certification.

	LABOR TIME		LABOR TIME		LABOR TIME
5000 Mile Service (C)		All Models	1.0	**50000 Mile Service (C)**	
All Models	1.0	**30000 Mile Service (B)**		All Models	.5
10000 Mile Service (C)		All Models	2.5	**55000 Mile Service (C)**	
All Models	.5	**35000 Mile Service (C)**		All Models	1.0
15000 Mile Service (C)		All Models	1.0	**60000 Mile Service (B)**	
All Models	1.2	**40000 Mile Service (C)**		All Models	3.0
20000 Mile Service (C)		All Models	.5	**65000 Mile Service (C)**	
All Models	.5	**45000 Mile Service (C)**		All Models	1.0
25000 Mile Service (C)		All Models	1.2		

93061CG7

Refer to the model specific sections for driveline service procedures

FORD MOTOR CO.
Probe

ENGINE AND VEHICLE IDENTIFICATION

	Engine Code						Model Year	
Code ①	Liters (cc)	Cu. In.	Cyl.	Fuel Sys.	Engine Type	Eng. Mfg.	Code ②	Year
A	2.0 (1993)	122	4	MFI	DOHC	Mazda	V	1997
B	2.5 (2501)	153	6	MFI	DOHC	Mazda		

MFI: Multi-point Fuel Injection

DOHC: Double Overhead Camshafts

① 8th digit of the VIN

② 10th digit of the VIN

93061CG8

GENERAL ENGINE SPECIFICATIONS
All measurements are given in inches.

Year	Model	Engine Displacement Liters (cc)	Engine (ID/VIN)	Fuel System	Net Horsepower @ rpm	Net Torque @ rpm (ft. lbs.)	Bore x Stroke (in.)	Compression Ratio	Oil Pressure @ rpm
1997	Probe	2.0 (1993)	A	SFI	118@5500	127@4500	3.27x3.62	9.0:1	57-71@2000
	Probe	2.5 (2501)	B	SFI	①	②	3.33x2.92	9.2:1	49-71@3000

SFI: Sequential Fuel Injection

① California: 160@5500
   Except California: 164@5600

② California: 156@5000
   Except California: 160@4800

93061CG9

ENGINE TUNE-UP SPECIFICATIONS

Year	Engine Displacement Liters (cc)	Engine ID/VIN	Spark Plug Gap (in.)	Ignition Timing (deg.)		Fuel Pump (psi) ①	Idle Speed (rpm)		Valve Clearance	
				MT	AT		MT	AT	In.	Ex.
1997	2.0 (1993)	A	0.041	10B	12B	30-38	700	700	HYD	HYD
	2.5 (2501)	B	0.041	10B	10B	30-36	700	700	HYD	HYD

NOTE: The Vehicle Emission Control Information label often reflects specification changes made during production. The label figures must be used if they differ from those in this chart.

HYD: Hydraulic

① Fuel pressure with engine running, pressure regulator vacuum hose connected.

93061CG0

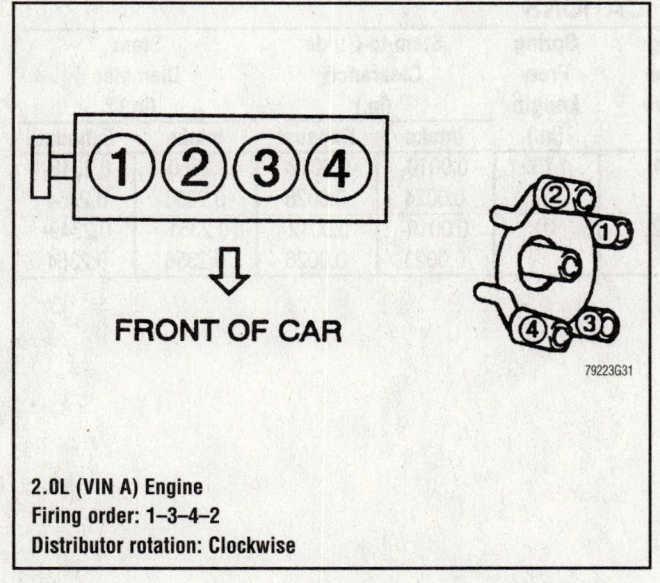

2.0L (VIN A) Engine
Firing order: 1–3–4–2
Distributor rotation: Clockwise

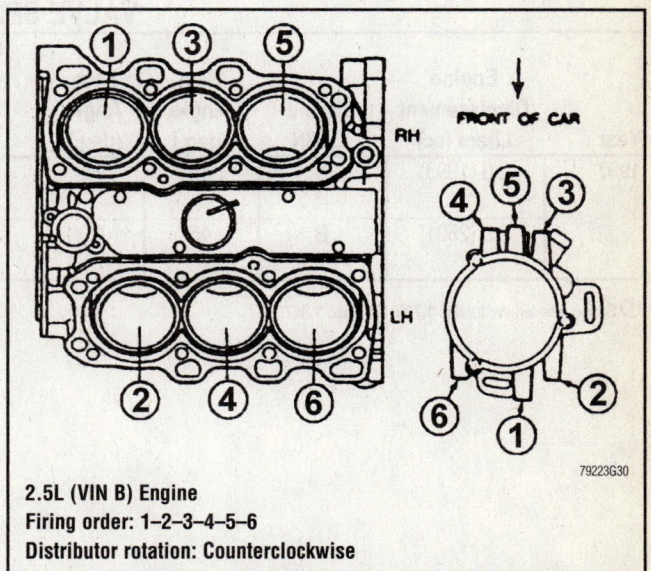

2.5L (VIN B) Engine
Firing order: 1–2–3–4–5–6
Distributor rotation: Counterclockwise

For exhaust manifold replacement procedures, see the model specific sections of this manual

CAPACITIES

Year	Model	Engine Displacement Liters (cc)	Engine ID/VIN	Engine Oil with Filter (qts.)	Transaxle (pts) Manual	Transaxle (pts) Automatic ①	Drive Axle (pts.)	Fuel Tank (gal.)	Cooling System (qts.)
1997	Probe	2.0 (1993)	A	3.7	5.8	17.6	②	15.5	7.4
	Probe	2.5 (2501)	B	4.2	5.8	14.4	②	15.5	7.9

NOTE: All capacities are approximate. Add fluid gradually and ensure a proper fluid level is obtained.

① Includes torque converter

② Included in transaxle capacity

93061CH1

VALVE SPECIFICATIONS

Year	Engine Displacement Liters (cc)	Engine ID/VIN	Seat Angle (deg.)	Face Angle (deg.)	Spring Out-of-Square (in.)	Spring Free-Length (in.)	Stem-to-Guide Clearance (in.) Intake	Stem-to-Guide Clearance (in.) Exhaust	Stem Diameter (in.) Intake	Stem Diameter (in.) Exhaust
1997	2.0 (1993)	A	45	45	0.061	1.732	0.0010-0.0024	0.0012-0.0026	0.2350-0.2356	0.2348-0.2354
	2.5 (2501)	B	45	45	0.642	①	0.0010-0.0023	0.0012-0.0026	0.2351-0.2356	0.2349-0.2354

① Spring-free length: Intake: 1.729, Exhaust: 1.847

93061CH2

CRANKSHAFT AND CONNECTING ROD SPECIFICATIONS
All measurements are given in inches.

Year	Engine Displacement Liters (cc)	Engine ID/VIN	Crankshaft				Connecting Rod		
			Main Brg. Journal Dia.	Main Brg. Oil Clearance	Shaft End-play	Thrust on No.	Journal Diameter	Oil Clearance	Side Clearance
1997	2.0 (1993)	A	2.2022-2.2029	①	0.0031-0.0111	4	1.8874-1.8880	0.0005-0.0015	0.0043-0.0103
	2.5 (2501)	B	2.4385-2.4392	- 0.0015-0.0022	0.0032-0.0111	4	2.0841-2.0848	0.0009-0.0017	0.0070-0.0130

① No. 1, 2, 4 & 5: 0.0009-0.0020 in.
  No. 3: 0.0012-0.0022 in.

93061CH3

PISTON AND RING SPECIFICATIONS
All measurements are given in inches.

Year	Engine Displacement Liters (cc)	Engine ID/VIN	Piston Clearance	Ring Gap			Ring Side Clearance		
				Top Compression	Bottom Compression	Oil Control	Top Compression	Bottom Compression	Oil Control
1997	2.0 (1993)	A	0.0015-0.0020	0.006-0.012	0.006-0.012	0.008-0.028	0.0014-0.0026	0.0014-0.0026	SNUG
	2.5 (2501)	B	0.0012-0.0022	-0.0060-0.0118	0.010-0.015	0.008-0.027	0.0008-0.0026	0.0010-0.0015	SNUG

93061CH4

TORQUE SPECIFICATIONS
All readings in ft. lbs.

Year	Engine Displacement Liters (cc)	Engine ID/VIN	Cylinder Head Bolts	Main Bearing Bolts	Rod Bearing Bolts	Crankshaft Damper Bolts	Flywheel Bolts	Manifold		Spark Plugs	Lug Nut
								Intake	Exhaust		
1997	2.0 (1993)	A	①	②	③	116-123	70-75	14-19	14-21	11-17	85
	2.5 (2501)	B	①	④	③	116-123	45-49	14-18	14-18	11-16	85

NOTE: Always follow proper torque patterns. Stretch bolts are used in all procedures that require rotating the fastener a certain number of degrees.

The bolts stretch and cannot be reused. For reassembly, replace with new fastners.

① Step 1: 8-10 ft. lbs.

Step 2: 13-16 ft. lbs.

Step 3: Tighten 90 degrees

Step 4: Repeat Step 3

② Step 1: 12 ft. lbs.

Step 2: Tighten each bolt 85-95 degrees

③ 16-19 ft. lbs. plus 90 degrees

④ Step 1: Inner main bolts: 10-12 ft. lbs.

Step 2: Inner main bolts: 17-19 ft. lbs.

Step 3: Outer main bolts: 6-8 ft. lbs.

Step 4: Outer main bolts: 13-15 ft. lbs.

Step 5: Tighten inner bolts 75 degrees

Step 6: Tighten outer bolts 60 degrees

Step 7: Repeat Steps 5 and 6

Step 8: Outer cylinder block bolts: 14-15 ft. lbs.

93061CH5

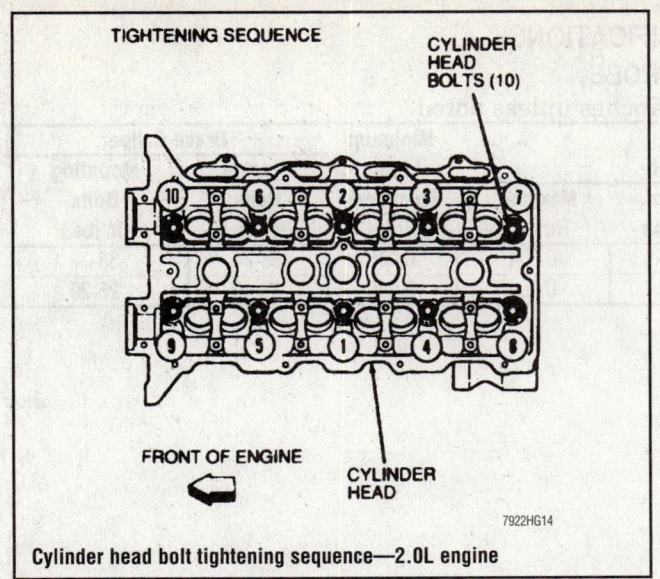

Cylinder head bolt tightening sequence—2.0L engine

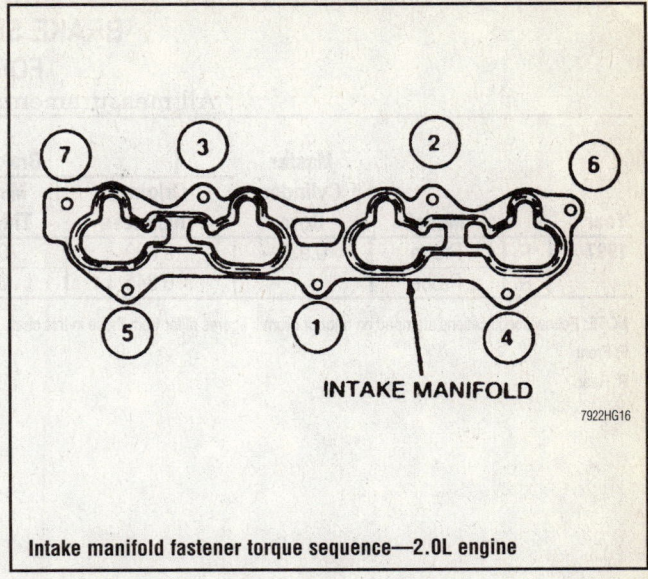

Intake manifold fastener torque sequence—2.0L engine

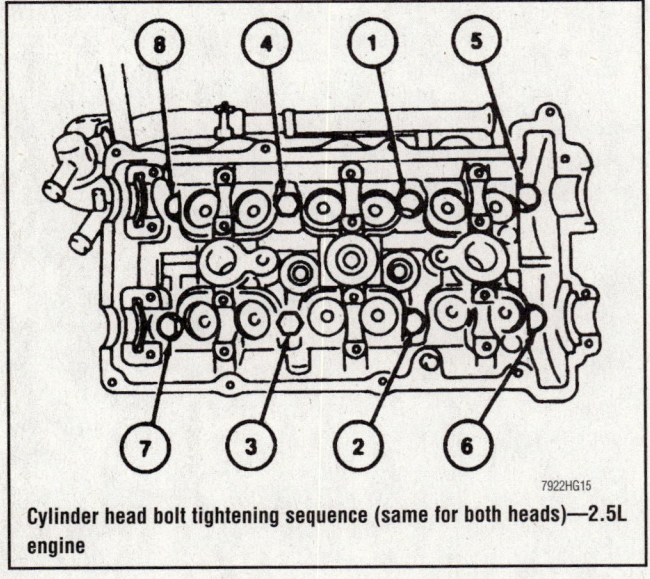

Cylinder head bolt tightening sequence (same for both heads)—2.5L engine

BRAKE SPECIFICATIONS
FORD PROBE
All measurements in inches unless noted

Year		Model	Master Cylinder Bore	Brake Disc			Minimum Lining Thickness Front	Brake Caliper	
				Original Thickness	Minimum Thickness	Maximum Run-out		Bracket Bolts (ft. lbs.)	Mounting Bolts (ft. lbs.)
1997	F	Probe	0.937	0.890 -	0.860	0.004	0.040	58-74	33-36
	R	Probe	—	0.345	0.315	0.004	0.040	33-49	25-29

NOTE: Follow specifications stamped on rotor or drum if figures differ from those in this chart.

F: Front

R: Rear

93061CH6

SCHEDULED MAINTENANCE INTERVALS
(FORD PROBE)

TO BE SERVICED	TYPE OF SERVICE	VEHICLE MILEAGE INTERVAL (x1000)												
		5	10	15	20	25	30	35	40	45	50	55	60	65
Engine oil & filter	R	✓	✓	✓	✓	✓	✓	✓	✓	✓	✓	✓	✓	✓
Rotate tires	S/I	✓		✓		✓		✓		✓		✓		✓
Air cleaner element	R						✓						✓	
Spark plugs	R						✓						✓	
Automatic transmission fluid & filter	R						✓						✓	
Exhaust heart shields	S/I						✓						✓	
Front & rear brakes	S/I						✓						✓	
Accessory drive belt(s)	S/I						✓						✓	
Fuel lines & hoses	S/I						✓						✓	
Cooling system, hoses, clamps & coolant strength	S/I						✓						✓	
Front wheel driveshaft joint boots	S/I						✓						✓	
Brake lines, hoses & connections	S/I						✓						✓	
Front suspension ball joints, steering operation & linkage	S/I						✓						✓	
Idle speed	S/I						✓						✓	
Bolts & nuts on chassis & body	S/I						✓						✓	
Engine coolant	R										✓			
Timing belt/chain & fuel filter	R												✓	
Fuel lines & tubes (emission)	S/I												✓	

R: Replace   S/I: Service or Inspect
① Change initially at 50,000 miles & every 30,000 miles thereafter.

FREQUENT OPERATION MAINTENANCE (SEVERE SERVICE)

If a vehicle is operated under any of the following conditions it is considered severe service:

- Extremely dusty areas.

- 50% or more of the vehicle operation is in 32°C (90°F) or higher temperatures, or constant operation in temperatures below 0°C (32°F).

- Prolonged idling (vehicle operation in stop and go traffic).

- Frequent short running periods (engine does not warm to normal operating temperatures).

- Police, taxi, delivery usage or trailer towing usage.

Oil & oil filter: change every 3000 miles.

Air cleaner element: check every 15,000 miles.

Front & rear brakes: check every 15,000 miles.

Nuts & bolts on chassis & body: check every 15,000 miles.

Automatic transaxle fluid & filter: change every 21,000 miles.

93061CH7

Timing chain and gear service is covered in the model specific sections of this manual

SCHEDULED MAINTENANCE INTERVALS
FORD MOTOR COMPANY
FORD PROBE

The following should be used as a guide when determining the amount of work required for a particular service.
In estimating how long a particular Scheduled Maintenance Service should take, please observe the following:

- Labor Time is time based on field research and data supplied by the vehicle manufacturer.
- Labor time operations are given in hours and tenths of an hour.
- All labor operations are to be used as a guide.

Mechanic Skill Level Codes:
(A) PRECISION: Highly skilled with multiple certification.
(B) GENERAL: Normally skilled with certification.
(C) MAINTENANCE: Semi-skilled working on certification.

	LABOR TIME		LABOR TIME		LABOR TIME
5000 Mile Service (C)		**25000 Mile Service (C)**		**50000 Mile Service (C)**	
All Models	.9	All Models	.9	All Models	1.1
10000 Mile Service (C)		**30000 Mile Service (B)**		**55000 Mile Service (C)**	
All Models	.4	All Models	3.3	All Models	.9
15000 Mile Service (C)		**35000 Mile Service (C)**		**60000 Mile Service (B)**	
All Models	.9	All Models	.9	All Models	5.4
20000 Mile Service (C)		**40000 Mile Service (C)**		**65000 Mile Service (C)**	
All Models	.4	All Models	.4	All Models	.9
		45000 Mile Service (C)			
		All Models	.9		

93061CH8

FORD MOTOR CO.
Ford Taurus • Taurus SHO • Mercury Sable

ENGINE AND VEHICLE IDENTIFICATION

		Engine						Model Year	
Code ①	Liters (cc)	Cu. In.	Cyl.	Fuel Sys.	Engine Type	Eng. Mfg.		Code ②	Year
N	3.4 (3393)	207	8	SFI	DOHC	Yamaha		V	1997
S	3.0 (3049)	182	6	SFI	DOHC	Ford		W	1998
U	3.0 (2982)	181	6	SFI	OHV	Ford		X	1999
								Y	2000
								1	2001

OHV: Overhead Valves

DOHC: Double Overhead Camshafts

SFI: Sequential Fuel Injection

① 8th digit of the Vehicle Identification Number (VIN)

② 10th digit of the Vehicle Identification Number (VIN)

93061CH9

GENERAL ENGINE SPECIFICATIONS

Year	Model	Engine Displacement Liters (cc)	Engine ID/VIN	Fuel System Type	Net Horsepower @ rpm	Net Torque @ rpm (ft. lbs.)	Bore x Stroke (in.)	Compression Ratio	Oil Pressure @ rpm
1997	Sable	3.0 (2982)	U	SFI	145@5250	170@3250	3.50x3.15	9.3:1	40-60@2500
		3.0 (2998)	S	SFI	200@5750	200@4500	3.50x3.13	10.0:1	20-45@1500
	Taurus	3.0 (2982)	U	SFI	145@5250	170@3250	3.50x3.15	9.3:1	40-60@2500
		3.0 (2998)	S	SFI	200@5750	200@4500	3.50x3.13	10.0:1	20-45@1500
	Taurus SHO	3.4 (3393)	N	SFI	235@6100	230@4800	3.25x3.13	10.0:1	20-45@1500
1998	Sable	3.0 (2982)	U	SFI	145@5250	170@3250	3.50x3.15	9.3:1	40-60@2500
		3.0 (2998)	S	SFI	200@5750	200@4500	3.50x3.13	10.0:1	20-45@1500
	Taurus	3.0 (2982)	U	SFI	145@5250	170@3250	3.50x3.15	9.3:1	40-60@2500
		3.0 (2998)	S	SFI	200@5750	200@4500	3.50x3.13	10.0:1	20-45@1500
	Taurus SHO	3.4 (3393)	N	SFI	235@6100	230@4800	3.25x3.13	10.0:1	20-45@1500
1999	Sable	3.0 (2982)	U	SFI	145@5250	170@3250	3.50x3.15	9.3:1	40-60@2500
		3.0 (2998)	S	SFI	200@5750	200@4500	3.50x3.13	10.0:1	20-45@1500
	Taurus	3.0 (2982)	U	SFI	145@5250	170@3250	3.50x3.15	9.3:1	40-60@2500
		3.0 (2998)	S	SFI	200@5750	200@4500	3.50x3.13	10.0:1	20-45@1500
	Taurus SHO	3.4 (3393)	N	SFI	235@6100	230@4800	3.25x3.13	10.0:1	20-45@1500
2000-01	Sable	3.0 (2982)	U	SFI	145@5250	170@3250	3.50x3.15	9.3:1	40-60@2500
		3.0 (2998)	S	SFI	200@5750	200@4500	3.50x3.13	10.0:1	20-45@1500
	Taurus	3.0 (2982)	U	SFI	145@5250	170@3250	3.50x3.15	9.3:1	40-60@2500
		3.0 (2998)	S	SFI	200@5750	200@4500	3.50x3.13	10.0:1	20-45@1500
	Taurus SHO	3.4 (3393)	N	SFI	235@6100	230@4800	3.25x3.13	10.0:1	20-45@1500

SFI: Sequential Fuel Injection

93061CH0

Ignition system service is covered in the model specific sections of this manual

ENGINE TUNE-UP SPECIFICATIONS

Year	Engine Displacement Liters (cc)	Engine ID/VIN	Spark Plug Gap (in.)	Ignition Timing (deg.)	Fuel Pump (psi) ①	Idle Speed (rpm)	Valve Clearance Intake	Valve Clearance Exhaust
1997	3.0 (2982)	U	0.042-0.046	10B	30-45	②	HYD	HYD
	3.0 (2998)	S	0.052-0.056	10B	30-45	②	HYD	HYD
	3.4 (3393)	N	0.042-0.046	10B	35-45	②	0.006-0.010	0.010-0.014
1998	3.0 (2982)	U	0.042-0.046	10B	30-45	②	HYD	HYD
	3.0 (2998)	S	0.052-0.056	10B	30-45	②	HYD	HYD
	3.4 (3393)	N	0.042-0.046	10B	35-45	②	0.006-0.010	0.010-0.014
1999	3.0 (2982)	U	0.042-0.046	10B	26-45	②	HYD	HYD
	3.0 (2998)	S	0.052-0.056	10B	26-45	②	HYD	HYD
	3.4 (3393)	N	0.042-0.046	10B	35-45	②	0.006-0.010	0.010-0.014
2000-01	3.0 (2982)	U	0.042-0.046	10B	26-45	②	HYD	HYD
	3.0 (2998)	S	0.052-0.056	10B	26-45	②	HYD	HYD
	3.4 (3393)	N	0.042-0.046	10B	35-45	②	0.006-0.010	0.010-0.014

NOTE: The Vehicle Emission Control Information label often reflects specification changes made during production. The label figures must be used if they differ from those in this chart.

B: Before Top Dead Center

HYD: Hydraulic

① Fuel pressure with engine running, pressure regulator vacuum hose connected

② Refer to Vehicle Emission Control Information label

93061CI1

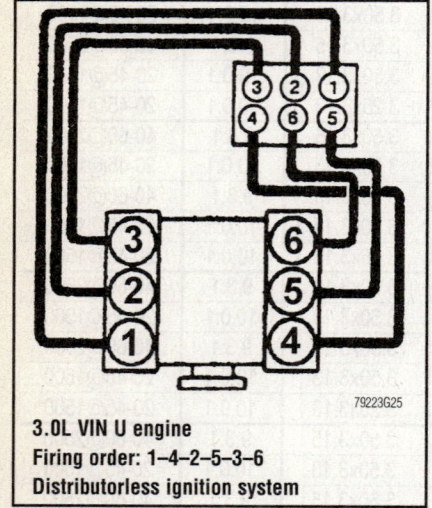

3.0L VIN U engine
Firing order: 1–4–2–5–3–6
Distributorless ignition system

79223G25

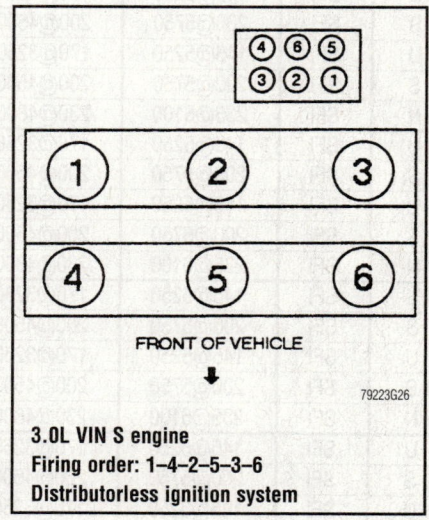

FRONT OF VEHICLE

3.0L VIN S engine
Firing order: 1–4–2–5–3–6
Distributorless ignition system

79223G26

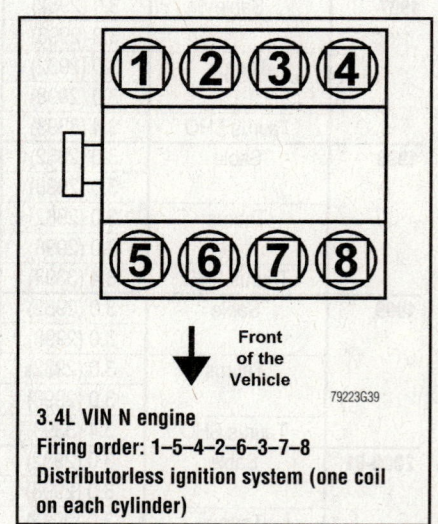

Front of the Vehicle

3.4L VIN N engine
Firing order: 1–5–4–2–6–3–7–8
Distributorless ignition system (one coil on each cylinder)

79223G39

CAPACITIES

Year	Model	Engine Displacement Liters (cc)	Engine ID/VIN	Engine Oil with Filter (qts.)	Transaxle (pts.) Auto. ①	Drive Axle (pts.)	Fuel Tank (gal.)	Cooling System (qts.)
1997	Sable	3.0 (2982)	U	4.5	24.5	②	③	11.6
		3.0 (2998)	S	5.8	27.0	②	③	10.5
	Taurus	3.0 (2982)	U	4.5	24.5	②	③	11.6
		3.0 (2998)	S	5.8	27.0	②	③	10.5
	Taurus SHO	3.4 (3393)	N	5.8	27.0	②	③	10.8
1998	Sable	3.0 (2982)	U	4.5	24.5	②	③	11.6
		3.0 (2998)	S	5.8	27.0	②	③	10.5
	Taurus	3.0 (2982)	U	4.5	24.5	②	③	11.6
		3.0 (2998)	S	5.8	27.0	②	③	10.5
	Taurus SHO	3.4 (3393)	N	5.8	27.0	②	③	10.8
1999	Sable	3.0 (2982)	U	4.5	24.5	②	③	11.6
		3.0 (2998)	S	5.8	27.0	②	③	10.5
	Taurus	3.0 (2982)	U	4.5	24.5	②	③	11.6
		3.0 (2998)	S	5.8	27.0	②	③	10.5
	Taurus SHO	3.4 (3393)	N	6.7	27.0	②	③	10.8
2000-01	Sable	3.0 (2982)	U	4.5	24.5	②	③	11.6
		3.0 (2998)	S	5.8	27.0	②	③	10.5
	Taurus	3.0 (2982)	U	4.5	24.5	②	③	11.6
		3.0 (2998)	S	5.8	27.0	②	③	10.5
	Taurus SHO	3.4 (3393)	N	6.7	27.0	②	③	10.8

NOTE: All capacities are approximate. Add fluid gradually and ensure a proper fluid level is obtained.
① Includes torque converter
② Included in transaxle capacity
③ Standard tank: 16.0 gals.
 Optional extended range tank: 18.6 gals.

93061CI2

VALVE SPECIFICATIONS

Year	Engine Displacement Liters (cc)	Engine ID/VIN	Seat Angle (deg.)	Face Angle (deg.)	Spring Test Pressure (lbs. @ in.)	Spring Installed Height (in.)	Stem-to-Guide Clearance (in.)		Stem Diameter (in.)	
							Intake	Exhaust	Intake	Exhaust
1997	3.0 (2982)	U	45	44	180@1.16	1.580	0.0001-0.0028	0.0015-0.0033	0.3126-0.3134	0.3121-0.3129
	3.0 (2998)	S	44.75	45.5	153@1.18	1.570	0.0007-0.0027	0.0017-0.0037	0.2350-0.2358	0.2343-0.2350
	3.4 (3393)	N	45	45.5	89@1.00	1.360	0.0010-0.0023	0.0012-0.0025	0.2346-0.2352	0.2344-0.2350
1998	3.0 (2982)	U	45	44	180@1.16	1.580	0.0001-0.0027	0.0015-0.0033	0.3126-0.3134	0.3121-0.3129
	3.0 (2998)	S	44.75	45.5	153@1.18	1.570	0.0007-0.0027	0.0017-0.0037	0.2350-0.2358	0.2343-0.2350
	3.4 (3393)	N	45	45.5	89@1.00	1.360	0.0010-0.0023	0.0012-0.0025	0.2346-0.2352	0.2344-0.2350
1999	3.0 (2982)	U	45	44	180@1.16	1.580	0.0010-0.0028	0.0015-0.0033	0.3126-0.3134	0.3121-0.3129
	3.0 (2998)	S	44.75	45.5	153@1.18	1.570	0.0007-0.0027	0.0017-0.0037	0.2350-0.2358	0.2343-0.2350
	3.4 (3393)	N	45	45.5	89@1.00	1.360	0.0010-0.0023	0.0012-0.0025	0.2346-0.2352	0.2344-0.2350
2000-01	3.0 (2982)	U	45	44	180@1.16	1.580	0.0010-0.0028	0.0015-0.0033	0.3126-0.3134	0.3121-0.3129
	3.0 (2998)	S	44.75	45.5	153@1.18	1.570	0.0007-0.0027	0.0017-0.0037	0.2350-0.2358	0.2343-0.2350
	3.4 (3393)	N	45	45.5	89@1.00	1.360	0.0010-0.0023	0.0012-0.0025	0.2346-0.2352	0.2344-0.2350

93061CI3

CRANKSHAFT AND CONNECTING ROD SPECIFICATIONS
All measurements are given in inches.

| Year | Engine Displacement Liters (cc) | Engine ID/VIN | Crankshaft | | | | Connecting Rod | | |
			Main Brg. Journal Dia.	Main Brg. Oil Clearance	Shaft End-play	Thrust on No.	Journal Diameter	Oil Clearance	Side Clearance
1997	3.0 (2982)	U	2.5190-2.5198	0.0009 0.0030	0.0040 0.0080	3	2.1253-2.1261	0.0009 0.0030	0.0060 0.0140
	3.0 (2998)	S	2.4670-2.4790	0.0009-0.0018	0.0040 0.0090	4	1.9670-1.9680	0.0010-0.0025	0.0039-0.0118
	3.4 (3393)	N	2.4794-2.4803	0.0004-0.0012	0.0024-0.0103	3	1.9765-1.9685	0.0009-0.0023	0.0060-0.0120
1998	3.0 (2982)	U	2.5190-2.5198	0.0009 0.0030	0.0040 0.0080	3	2.1253-2.1261	0.0009 0.0030	0.0060 0.0140
	3.0 (2998)	S	2.4670-2.4790	0.0009-0.0018	0.0040-0.0090	4	1.9670-1.9680	0.0010-0.0025	0.0039-0.0118
	3.4 (3393)	N	2.4794-2.4803	0.0004-0.0012	0.0024-0.0103	3	1.9765-1.9685	0.0009-0.0023	0.0060-0.0120
1999	3.0 (2982)	U	2.5190-2.5198	0.0009 0.0027	0.0040 0.0080	3	2.1253-2.1261	0.0009 0.0027	0.0060 0.0140
	3.0 (2998)	S	2.4670-2.4790	0.0009-0.0018	0.0040 0.0090	4	1.9670-1.9680	0.0010 0.0025	0.0039-0.0118
	3.4 (3393)	N	2.4794-2.4803	0.0004-0.0012	0.0024-0.0103	3	1.9675 1.9685	0.0009-0.0023	0.0060 0.0120
2000-01	3.0 (2982)	U	2.5190-2.5198	0.0009 0.0027	0.0040 0.0080	3	2.1253-2.1261	0.0009 0.0027	0.0060 0.0140
	3.0 (2998)	S	2.4670-2.4790	0.0009-0.0018	0.0040 0.0090	4	1.9670-1.9680	0.0010 0.0025	0.0039-0.0118
	3.4 (3393)	N	2.4794-2.4803	0.0004-0.0012	0.0024-0.0103	3	1.9675 1.9685	0.0009-0.0023	0.0060 0.0120

93061CI4

Refer to the model specific sections for engine mechanical service procedures

PISTON AND RING SPECIFICATIONS
All measurements are given in inches.

Year	Engine Displacement Liters (cc)	Engine ID/VIN	Piston Clearance	Ring Gap			Ring Side Clearance		
				Top Compression	Bottom Compression	Oil Control	Top Compression	Bottom Compression	Oil Control
1997	3.0 (2982)	U	0.0014-0.0022	0.010-0.020	0.010-0.020	0.010-0.049	0.0012 0.0031	0.0012 0.0031	SNUG
	3.0 (2998)	S	0.0005-0.0009	-0.004-0.010	0.011-0.017	0.005-0.026	0.0015-0.0029	0.0015-0.0033	SNUG
	3.4 (3393)	N	0.0008-0.0016	0.008-0.014	0.008-0.014	0.008-0.028	0.0018-0.0031	0.0012-0.0028	0.0024-0.0059
1998	3.0 (2982)	U	0.0014-0.0022	0.010-0.020	0.010-0.020	0.010-0.049	0.0012 0.0031	0.0012 0.0031	SNUG
	3.0 (2998)	S	0.0005-0.0009	0.004-0.010	0.011-0.017	0.005-0.026	0.0015-0.0029	0.0015-0.0033	SNUG
	3.4 (3393)	N	0.0008-0.0016	0.008-0.014	0.008-0.014	0.008-0.028	0.0018-0.0031	0.0012-0.0028	0.0024-0.0059
1999	3.0 (2982)	U	0.0014-0.0022	0.010-0.020	0.010-0.020	0.010-0.049	0.0012 0.0031	0.0012 0.0031	SNUG
	3.0 (2998)	S	0.0005-0.0009	0.004-0.010	0.011-0.017	0.006-0.026	0.0015-0.0029	0.0015-0.0033	SNUG
	3.4 (3393)	N	0.0008-0.0016	0.008-0.014	0.008-0.014	0.008-0.028	0.0018-0.0031	0.0012-0.0028	0.0024-0.0059
2000-01	3.0 (2982)	U	0.0014-0.0022	0.010-0.020	0.010-0.020	0.010-0.049	0.0012 0.0031	0.0012 0.0031	SNUG
	3.0 (2998)	S	0.0005-0.0009	0.004-0.010	0.011-0.017	0.006-0.026	0.0015-0.0029	0.0015-0.0033	SNUG
	3.4 (3393)	N	0.0008-0.0016	0.008-0.014	0.008-0.014	0.008-0.028	0.0018-0.0031	0.0012-0.0028	0.0024-0.0059

93061CI5

TORQUE SPECIFICATIONS
All readings in ft. lbs.

Year	Engine Displacement Liters (cc)	Engine ID/VIN	Cylinder Head Bolts	Main Bearing Bolts	Rod Bearing Bolts	Crankshaft Damper Bolts	Flywheel Bolts	Manifold Intake	Manifold Exhaust	Spark Plugs	Lug Nuts
1997	3.0 (2982)	U	①	56-62	23-28	93-121	54-64	15-22	15-18	7-15	95
	3.0 (2998)	S	②	③	④	⑤	54-64	⑥	13-16	7-15	95
	3.4 (3393)	N	⑦	⑧	⑨	⑤	54-64	14-20	11-19	11-15	95
1998	3.0 (2982)	U	①	56-62	23-28	93-121	54-64	⑩	15-18	7-15	95
	3.0 (2998)	S	②	③	④	⑤	54-64	⑥	13-16	7-15	95
	3.4 (3393)	N	⑦	⑧	⑨	⑤	54-64	14-20	11-19	11-15	95
1999	3.0 (2982)	U	⑪	56-62	23-28	93-121	54-64	⑩	15-18	7-15	95
	3.0 (2998)	S	②	③	④	⑤	54-64	⑥	13-16	7-15	95
	3.4 (3393)	N	⑦	⑧	⑨	⑤	55-61	14-20	11-19	11-15	95
2000-01	3.0 (2982)	U	⑪	56-62	23-28	93-121	54-64	⑩	15-18	7-15	95
	3.0 (2998)	S	②	③	④	⑤	54-64	⑥	13-16	7-15	95
	3.4 (3393)	N	⑦	⑧	⑨	⑤	55-61	14-20	11-19	11-15	95

① Step 1: 52-66 ft.lbs
  Step 2: Loosen one turn
  Step 3: 34-40 ft. lbs.
  Step 4: 63-73 ft. lbs.

② Step 1: 28-31 ft. lbs.
  Step 2: Rotate 85-95 degrees
  Step 3: Loosen one turn
  Step 4: 28-31 ft. lbs.
  Step 5: Rotate 85-95 degrees
  Step 6: Repeat Step 5

③ Step 1: Cap bolts 1-8 (outer) 17-20 ft. lbs.
  Step 2: Cap bolts 9-16 (inner) 28-31 ft. lbs.
  Step 3: Rotate bolts 1-16, 85-95 degrees
  Step 4: Bolts 17-22; 15-22 ft. lbs.

④ Step 1: 30-33 ft. lbs.
  Step 2: Rotate 90-120 degrees

⑤ Step 1: 77-99 ft. lbs.
  Step 2: Loosen 360 degrees
  Step 3: Tighten to 35-39 ft. lbs.
  Step 4: Rotate 85-95 degrees

⑥ 71-106 inch lbs.

⑦ Step 1: 20-23 ft. lbs.
  Step 2: Rotate 85-95 degrees

⑧ Step 1: Cap bolts 1-10 (outer) 17-20 ft. lbs.
  Step 2: Cap bolts 11-20 (inner) 28-31 ft. lbs.
  Step 3: Rotate bolts 1-20, 85-95 degrees
  Step 4: Bolts 21-31, 15-22 ft. lbs.

⑨ Step 1: 30-33 ft. lbs.
  Step 2: Rotate 90-120 degrees

⑩ Upper intake: 15-22 ft. lbs.
  Lower Intake:
  Step 1: 15-22 ft. lbs.
  Step 2: 20-23 ft. lbs.

⑪ Step 1: 35-39 ft. lbs.
  Step 2: Loosen one turn
  Step 3: 20-24 ft. lbs.
  Step 4: Rotate 85-95 degrees
  Step 5: Repeat Step 4

93061CI6

Refer to the model specific sections for fuel system service procedures

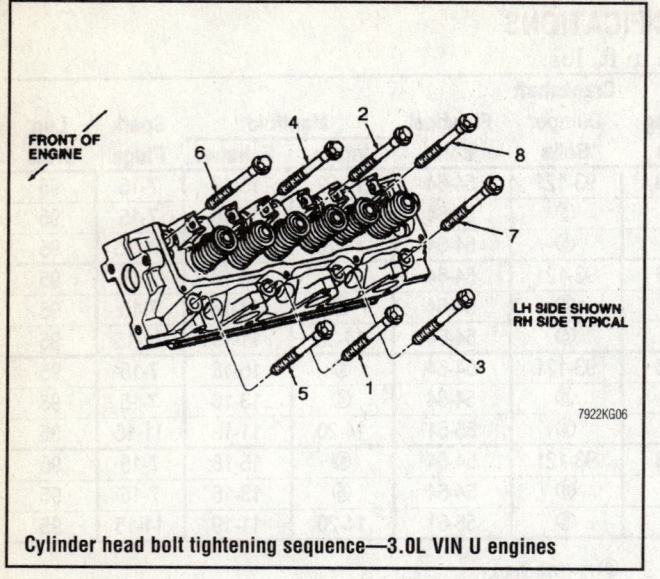

Cylinder head bolt tightening sequence—3.0L VIN U engines

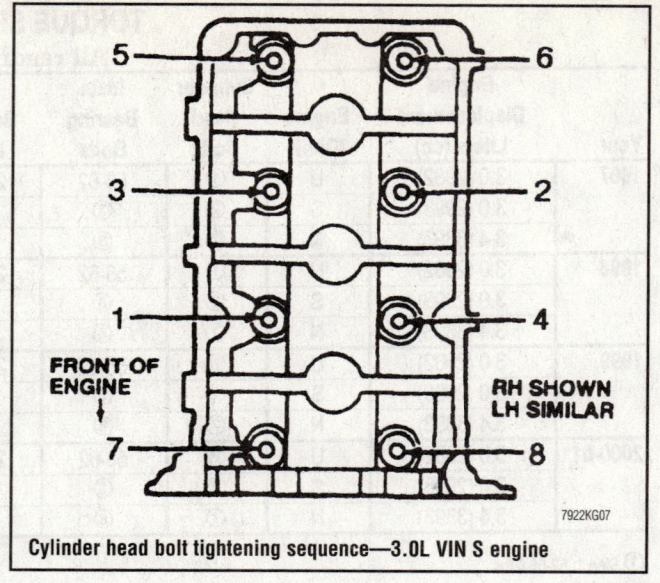

Cylinder head bolt tightening sequence—3.0L VIN S engine

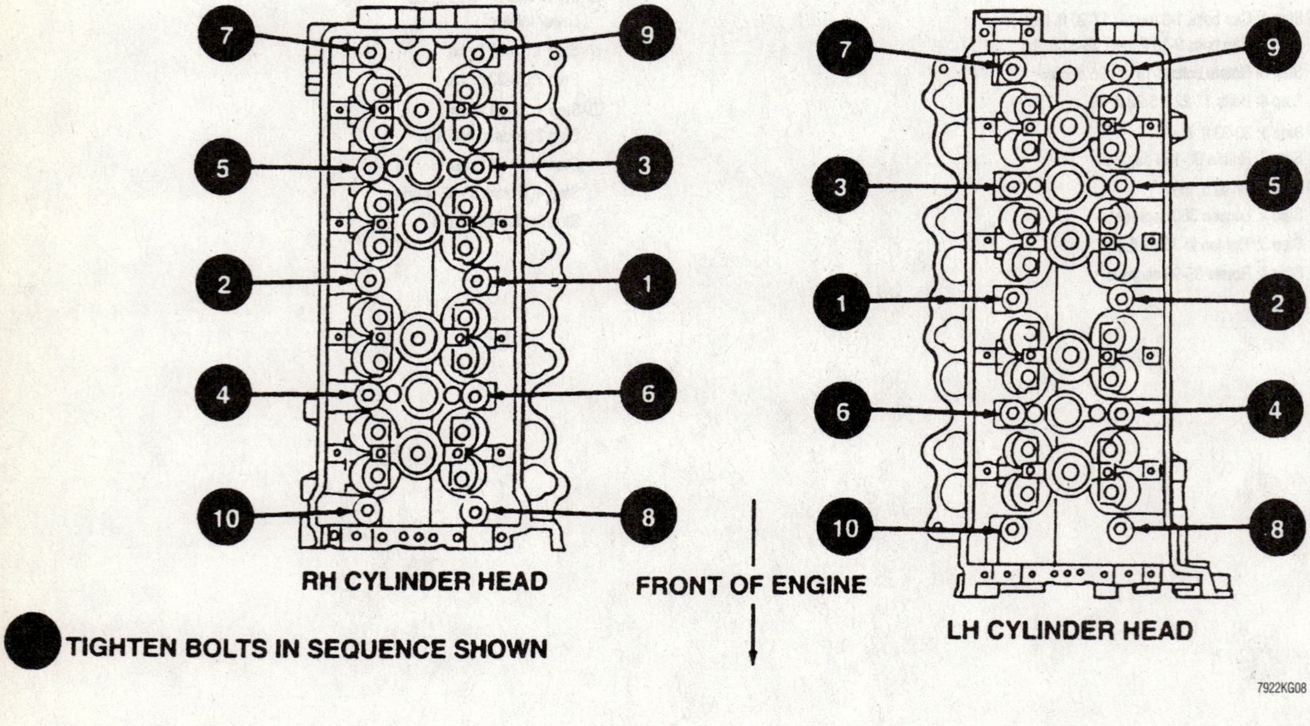

RH CYLINDER HEAD

FRONT OF ENGINE

LH CYLINDER HEAD

● TIGHTEN BOLTS IN SEQUENCE SHOWN

Cylinder head bolt tightening sequence—3.4L VIN N engine

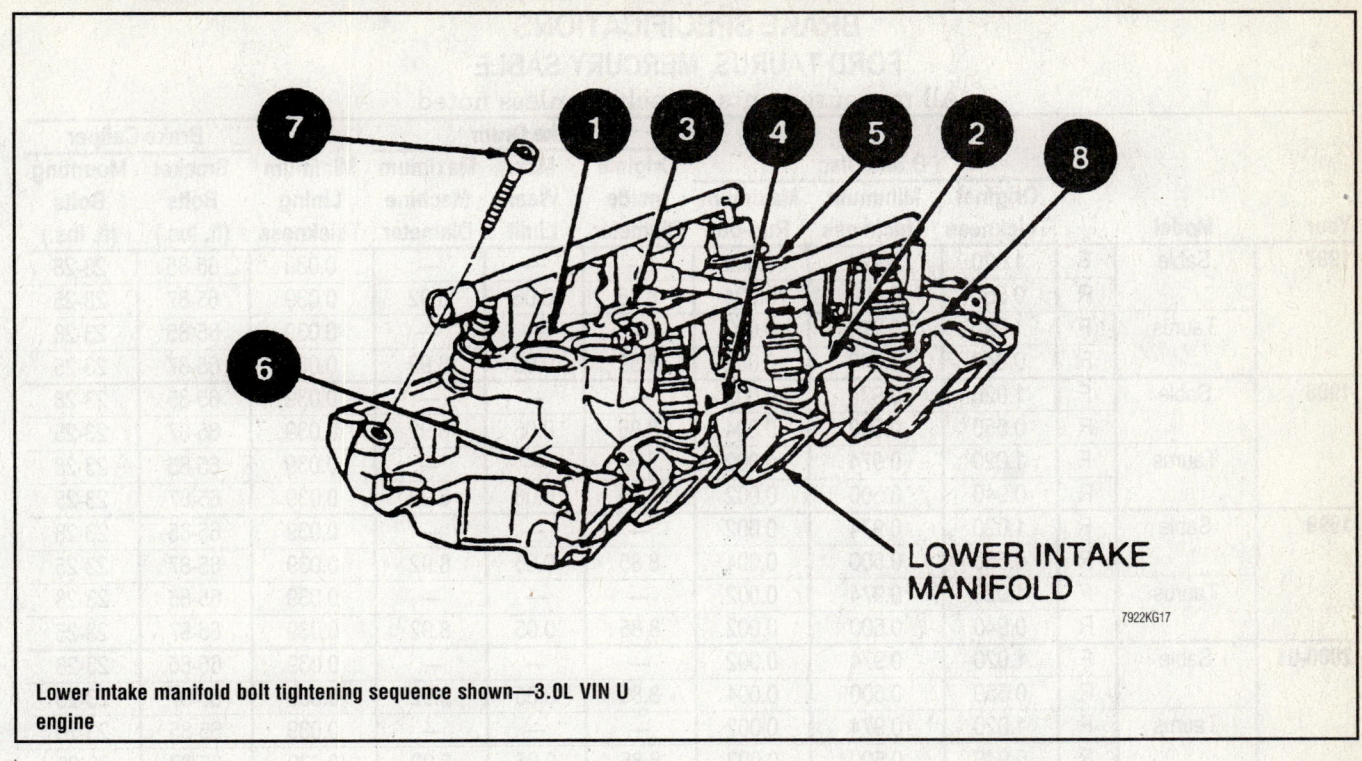

Lower intake manifold bolt tightening sequence shown—3.0L VIN U engine

7922KG17

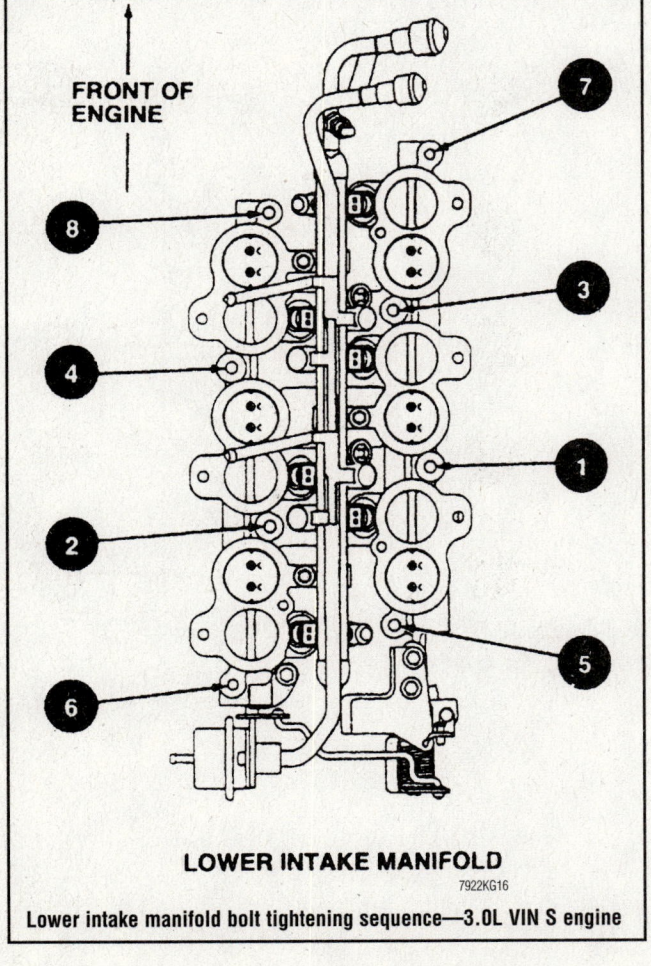

LOWER INTAKE MANIFOLD

7922KG16

Lower intake manifold bolt tightening sequence—3.0L VIN S engine

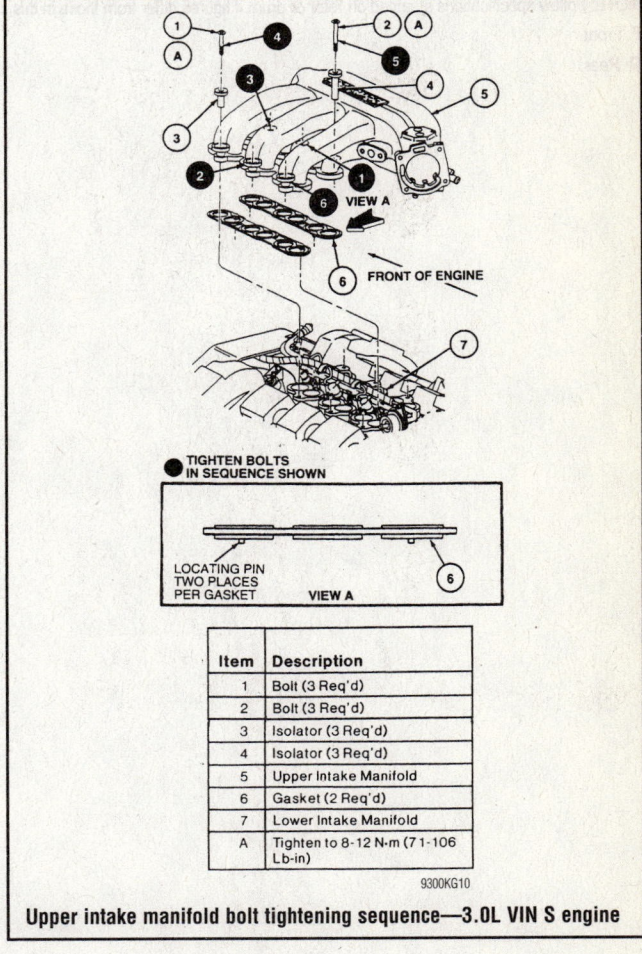

TIGHTEN BOLTS IN SEQUENCE SHOWN

LOCATING PIN TWO PLACES PER GASKET

VIEW A

Item	Description
1	Bolt (3 Req'd)
2	Bolt (3 Req'd)
3	Isolator (3 Req'd)
4	Isolator (3 Req'd)
5	Upper Intake Manifold
6	Gasket (2 Req'd)
7	Lower Intake Manifold
A	Tighten to 8-12 N·m (71-106 Lb-in)

9300KG10

Upper intake manifold bolt tightening sequence—3.0L VIN S engine

Refer to the model specific sections for engine electrical system service procedures

BRAKE SPECIFICATIONS
FORD TAURUS, MERCURY SABLE
All measurements in inches unless noted

Year	Model		Brake Disc Original Thickness	Brake Disc Minimum Thickness	Brake Disc Maximum Run-out	Brake Drum Original Inside Diameter	Brake Drum Max. Wear Limit	Brake Drum Maximum Machine Diameter	Minimum Lining Thickness	Brake Caliper Bracket Bolts (ft. lbs.)	Brake Caliper Mounting Bolts (ft. lbs.)
1997	Sable	F	1.020	0.974	0.002	—	—	—	0.039	65-85	23-28
		R	0.550	0.500	0.004	8.86	0.06	8.92	0.039	65-87	23-25
	Taurus	F	1.020	0.974	0.002	—	—	—	0.039	65-85	23-28
		R	0.940	0.500	0.002	8.86	0.06	8.92	0.039	65-87	23-25
1998	Sable	F	1.020	0.974	0.002	—	—	—	0.039	65-85	23-28
		R	0.550	0.500	0.004	8.86	0.06	8.92	0.039	65-87	23-25
	Taurus	F	1.020	0.974	0.002	—	—	—	0.039	65-85	23-28
		R	0.940	0.500	0.002	8.86	0.06	8.92	0.039	65-87	23-25
1999	Sable	F	1.020	0.974	0.002	—	—	—	0.039	65-85	23-28
		R	0.550	0.500	0.004	8.85	0.05	8.92	0.039	65-87	23-25
	Taurus	F	1.020	0.974	0.002	—	—	—	0.039	65-85	23-28
		R	0.940	0.500	0.002	8.85	0.05	8.92	0.039	65-87	23-25
2000-01	Sable	F	1.020	0.974	0.002	—	—	—	0.039	65-85	23-28
		R	0.550	0.500	0.004	8.85	0.05	8.92	0.039	65-87	23-25
	Taurus	F	1.020	0.974	0.002	—	—	—	0.039	65-85	23-28
		R	0.940	0.500	0.002	8.85	0.05	8.92	0.039	65-87	23-25

NOTE: Follow specifications stamped on rotor or drum if figures differ from those in this chart.

F: Front

R: Rear

93061CI7

SCHEDULED MAINTENANCE INTERVALS
(FORD TAURUS, LINCOLN CONTINENTAL & MERCURY SABLE)

TO BE SERVICED	TYPE OF SERVICE	VEHICLE MILEAGE INTERVAL (x1000)												
		5	10	15	20	25	30	35	40	45	50	55	60	65
Engine oil & filter	R	✓	✓	✓	✓	✓	✓	✓	✓	✓	✓	✓	✓	✓
Rotate tires	S/I	✓		✓		✓		✓		✓		✓		✓
Engine coolant protection, hoses & clamps	S/I			✓			✓			✓			✓	
Pass. compartment air filter (Continental)	R			✓			✓			✓			✓	
Pass. compartment air filter (Taurus & Sable)	R				✓				✓				✓	
Air cleaner filter	R						✓						✓	
Automatic transaxle fluid & filter	R						✓						✓	
Brake lines & connections	S/I						✓						✓	
Exhaust heat shields	S/I						✓						✓	
Front and rear disc brake pads & rotors	S/I						✓						✓	
Accessory drive belt(s)	S/I												✓	
Engine coolant ①	R										✓			
Spark plugs (exc. 3.0L FF) ②	R													
Spark plugs (exc. 3.0L FF)	R						✓						✓	
PCV valve (except 3.0L 4-valve)	R												✓	
PCV valve (except 3.0L 4-valve) ③	R													

R: Replace   S/I: Service or Inspect

① Engine coolant: change initially at 50,000 miles & thereafter every 30,000 miles.

② Platinum tip spark plugs: change every 100,000 miles.

③ Replace every 100,000 miles.

FREQUENT OPERATION MAINTENANCE (SEVERE SERVICE)

- Extremely dusty areas.

- 50% or more of the vehicle operation is in 32°C (90°F) or higher temperatures, or constant operation in temperatures below 0°C (32°F).

- Prolonged idling (vehicle operation in stop and go traffic).

- Frequent short running periods (engine does not warm to normal operating temperatures).

- Police, taxi, delivery usage or trailer towing usage.

Oil & filter change: change every 3000 miles.

Rotate tires at 6000 miles & every 9000 miles thereafter.

Air cleaner element: service or inspect every 15,000 miles.

Automatic transaxle fluid & filter: change every 21,000 miles.

93061CI8

For accessory drive belt replacement procedures see the model specific sections of this manual

SCHEDULED MAINTENANCE INTERVALS
FORD MOTOR COMPANY
FORD TAURUS, LINCOLN CONTINENTAL, MERCURY SABLE

The following should be used as a guide when determining the amount of work required for a particular service.
In estimating how long a particular Scheduled Maintenance Service should take, please observe the following:

- Labor Time is time based on field research and data supplied by the vehicle manufacturer.
- Labor time operations are given in hours and tenths of an hour.
- All labor operations are to be used as a guide.

Mechanic Skill Level Codes:
(A) PRECISION: Highly skilled with multiple certification.
(B) GENERAL: Normally skilled with certification.
(C) MAINTENANCE: Semi-skilled working on certification.

	LABOR TIME		LABOR TIME		LABOR TIME
5000 Mile Service (C)		**30000 Mile Service (B)**		**50000 Mile Service (C)**	
All Models	1.3	All Models	3.6	All Models	1.4
10000 Mile Service (C)		*Replace auto. trans. fluid*		*Replace engine coolant add*	.7
All Models	.5	*filter add*	.7	**55000 Mile Service (C)**	
15000 Mile Service (C)		**35000 Mile Service (C)**		All Models	1.4
All Models	1.8	All Models	1.3	**60000 Mile Service (B)**	
20000 Mile Service (C)		**40000 Mile Service (C)**		All Models	3.7
All Models	.7	All Models	.7	*Replace auto. trans. fluid*	
25000 Mile Service (C)		**45000 Mile Service (C)**		*filter add*	.7
All Models	1.5	All Models	1.3	**65000 Mile Service (C)**	
				All Models	1.5

93061CI9

TIRE, WHEEL AND BALL JOINT SPECIFICATIONS
Ford

| Year | Model | OEM Tires | | Tire Pressures (psi) | | Wheel Size | Ball Joint Inspection |
		Standard	Optional	Front	Rear		
1997	Aspire	P165/70R13	None	32	32	4.5-J	①
	Contour GL, LX	P185/70R14	P195/65R14	34	34	5.5-J	①
	Contour SE	P205/60R15	None	31	34	6-JJ	①
	Crown Victoria	P215/70R15	P225/60R16	31	35	6.5-JJ	①
	Escort	P185/65SR14	P185/60TR15	32	32	5.5-JJ	0.030 in. ②
	Mustang, base	P205/65R15	None	35	35	7-JJ	①
	Mustang GT	P225/55ZR16	P245/45ZT17	30	30	Std: 7.5-JJ Opt: 8-JJ	①
	Mustang Cobra	P245/45ZR17	None	30	30	8-JJ	①
	Probe, base	P195/65R14	P205/55R15	32	36	5.5-JJ	①
	Probe GT	P225/50VR16	None	32	36	7-JJ	①
	Taurus, exc. SHO	P205/65R15	None	35	35	6-JJ	0.030 in. ②
	Taurus SHO	P225/55VR16	P225/55ZR16	30	30	6.5-JJ	0.030 in. ②
	Thunderbird	P205/70R15	P215/70R15	30	30	6-JJ	①
1998	Contour GL, LX	P185/70R14	P195/65R14	34	34	5.5-J	①
	Contour SE	P205/60R15	None	31	34	6-JJ	①
	Crown Victoria	P225/60SR16	P225/60TR16	32	32	7-JJ	①
	Escort	P185/65R14	P185/60R15	32	32	5.5-JJ	0.030 in. ②
	Mustang GT	P225/55ZR16	P245/45ZT17	30	30	Std: 7.5-JJ Opt: 8-JJ	①
	Mustang Cobra	P245/45ZR17	None	30	30	8-JJ	①
	Taurus, exc. SHO	P205/65R15	None	35	35	6-JJ	0.030 in. ②
	Taurus SHO	P225/55VR16	P225/55ZR16	30	30	6.5-JJ	0.030 in. ②
	Thunderbird	P205/70R15	P215/70R15	30	30	6-JJ	①
1999	Contour LX	P185/70R14	P195/65R14	34	34	5.5-J	①
	Contour SE	P205/60R15	None	31	34	6-JJ	①
	Crown Victoria	P225/60SR16	P225/60TR16	32	32	7-JJ	0.030 in. ②
	Escort	P185/65R14	P185/60R15	32	32	5.5-JJ	0.030 in. ②
	Mustang, base	P205/65HR15	None	32	32	7-JJ	①
	Mustang GT	P225/55HR16	P245/45ZR17	30	30	8-JJ	①
	Taurus, exc. SHO	P205/65R15	None	30	30	6-JJ	0.030 in. ②
	Taurus SHO	P225/55ZR16	None	33	33	6.5-JJ	0.030 in. ②
2000-01	Contour LX	P185/70R14	P195/65R14	34	34	5.5-J	①
	Contour SE	P205/60R15	None	31	34	6-JJ	①
	Crown Victoria	P225/60SR16	P225/60TR16	32	32	7-JJ	①
	Escort	P185/65R14	P185/60R15	32	32	5.5-JJ	0.030 in. ②
	Focus	P185/65R14	P195/65R15	32	32	5.5	①
	Mustang, base	P205/65HR15	None	30	30	7-JJ	①
	Mustang GT	P225/55HR16	P245/45ZR17	30	30	8-JJ	①
	Taurus	P225/55ZR16	None	33	33	6.5-JJ	0.030 in. ②

OEM: Original Equipment Manufacturer

PSI: Pounds Per Square Inch

STD: Standard

OPT: Optional

① Replace if any measurable movement is found

② Maximum radial tolerance in inches

93061CI0

For brake related suspension and axle service, refer to the model specific sections of this manual

TIRE, WHEEL AND BALL JOINT SPECIFICATIONS
Lincoln

| Year | Model | OEM Tires | | Tire Pressures (psi) | | Wheel Size | Ball Joint Inspection |
		Standard	Optional	Front	Rear		
1997	Continental	P225/60HR16	P225/60VR16	30	30	7-JJ	①
	Mark VIII	P225/60VR16	None	30	30	7-JJ	①
	Town Car	P215/70R15	P225/60R16	30	30	Std: 6.5-JJ	U ①
						Opt: 7-JJ	L ① ②
1998	Continental	P225/60HR16	P225/60VR16	30	30	7-JJ	①
	Mark VIII	P225/60VR16	None	30	30	7-JJ	①
	Town Car	P215/70R15	P225/60R16	30	30	Std: 6.5-JJ	U ①
						Opt: 7-JJ	L ① ②
1999	Continental	P225/60HR16	P225/60VR16	30	30	7-JJ	①
	Mark VIII	P225/60VR16	None	30	30	7-JJ	①
	Town Car	P215/70R15	P225/60R16	30	30	Std: 6.5-JJ	U ①
						Opt: 7-JJ	L ① ②
2000-01	Continental	P225/60HR16	P225/60VR16	30	30	7-JJ	①
	LS	P215/60R16	None	30	30	7-J	U ①
							L ① ②
	Town Car	P215/70R15	P225/60R16	30	30	Std: 6.5-JJ	U ①
						Opt: 7-JJ	L ① ②

OEM: Original Equipment Manufacturer

PSI: Pounds Per Square Inch

STD: Standard

OPT: Optional

L: Lower

U: Upper

① Replace if any measurable movement is found.

② Do not lift car. Inspect the boss into which the grease fitting is threaded. Replace if the boss is flush or receded below the surface of the ball joint.

93061CJ1

TIRE, WHEEL AND BALL JOINT SPECIFICATIONS
Mercury

Year	Model	OEM Tires Standard	OEM Tires Optional	Tire Pressures (psi) Front	Tire Pressures (psi) Rear	Wheel Size	Ball Joint Inspection
1997	Cougar	P205/70R15	P215/70R15	30	30	Std: 6-JJ Opt: 6.5-JJ	①
	Grand Marquis	P215/70R15	P225/70R15	31	35	6.5-JJ	U ① L ① ②
	Mystique GS	P185/70R14	P195/65R14	34	34	5.5-JJ	①
	Mystique LS	P205/60R15	None	31	34	6-JJ	①
	Sable	P205/65R15	None	35	35	6-JJ	①
	Tracer	P185/65SR14	None	32	32	5-JJ	①
	Villager	P215/70R15	P225/60R16	35	35	6-JJ	①
1998	Grand Marquis	P225/60SR16	P225/60TR16	35	35	6-JJ	U ① L ① ②
	Mystique GS	P185/70R14	P195/65R14	34	34	5.5-JJ	①
	Mystique LS	P205/60R15	None	31	34	6-JJ	①
	Sable	P205/65R15	None	35	35	6-JJ	①
	Tracer	P185/65SR14	P185/60R15	32	32	5.5-JJ	①
	Villager	P215/70R15	P225/60R16	35	35	6-JJ	①
1999	Cougar	P205/60R15	P215/50R16	35	35	6-JJ	①
	Grand Marquis	P225/60SR16	P225/60TR16	35	35	6-JJ	U ① L ① ②
	Mystique GS	P185/70R14	P195/65R14	34	34	5.5-JJ	①
	Mystique LS	P205/60R15	None	31	34	6-JJ	①
	Sable	P205/65R15	P225/55ZR16	35	35	6-JJ	①
	Tracer	P185/65SR14	P185/60R15	32	32	5.5-JJ	①
	Villager	P215/70R15	P225/60R16	35	35	6-JJ	①
2000-01	Cougar	P205/60R15	P215/50R16	35	35	6-JJ	①
	Grand Marquis	P225/60SR16	P225/60TR16	35	35	6-JJ	U ① L ① ②
	Mystique GS	P185/70R14	P195/65R14	34	34	5.5-JJ	①
	Mystique LS	P205/60R15	None	31	34	6-JJ	①
	Sable	P205/65R15	P225/55ZR16	35	35	6-JJ	①
	Tracer	P185/65SR14	P185/60R15	32	32	5.5-JJ	①
	Villager	P215/70R15	P225/60R16	35	35	6-JJ	①

OEM: Original Equipment Manufacturer

PSI: Pounds Per Square Inch

STD: Standard

OPT: Optional

L: Lower

U: Upper

① Replace if any measurable movement is found.

② Do not lift car. Inspect the boss into which the grease fitting is threaded. Replace if the boss is flush or receded below the surface of the ball joint.

93061CJ2

Refer to the model specific sections for driveline service procedures

GENERAL MOTORS C- & H-BODIES
Buick LeSabre • Park Avenue • Oldsmobile Eighty Eight • Ninety Eight • LSS • Regency • Pontiac Bonneville

ENGINE AND VEHICLE IDENTIFICATION

Engine								Model Year	
Code ①	Liters (cc)	Cu. In.	Cyl.	Fuel Sys.	Engine Type	Eng. Mfg.		Code ②	Year
1 ③	3.8 (3785)	231	6	MFI	OHV	BOC		V	1997
K	3.8 (3785)	231	6	MFI	OHV	BOC		W	1998
								X	1999
								Y	2000
								Z	2001

MFI: Multi-point Fuel Injection

BOC: Buick/Oldsmobile/Cadillac

OHV: Overhead Valves

① 8th position of VIN

② 10th position of VIN

③ Supercharged engine

93061CJ3

GENERAL ENGINE SPECIFICATIONS

Year	Model	Engine Displacement Liters (cc)	Engine Series (ID/VIN)	Fuel System	Net Horsepower @ rpm	Net Torque @ rpm (ft. lbs.)	Bore x Stroke (in.)	Compression Ratio	Oil Pressure @ rpm
1997	Bonneville	3.8 (3785)	1 ①	MFI	225@5000	275@3200	3.80x3.40	9.0:1	60@1850
	Bonneville	3.8 (3785)	K	MFI	205@5200	230@4000	3.80x3.40	9.4:1	60@1850
	Eighty-Eight	3.8 (3786)	K	MFI	205@5200	230@4000	3.80x3.40	9.4:1	60@1850
	Eighty-Eight/LSS	3.8 (3785)	1 - ①	MFI	225@5000	275@3200	3.80x3.40	9.0:1	60@1850
	LeSabre	3.8 (3785)	K	MFI	205@5200	230@4000	3.80x3.40	9.4:1	60@1850
	Ninety-Eight	3.8 (3786)	K	MFI	205@5200	230@4000	3.80x3.40	9.4:1	60@1850
	Park Avenue	3.8 (3785)	K	MFI	205@5200	230@4000	3.80x3.40	9.4:1	60@1850
	Park Avenue Ultra	3.8 (3785)	1 ①	MFI	225@5000	275@3200	3.80x3.40	9.0:1	60@1850
1998	Bonneville	3.8 (3785)	1 ①	MFI	225@5000	275@3200	3.80x3.40	9.0:1	60@1850
	Bonneville	3.8 (3785)	K	MFI	205@5200	230@4000	3.80x3.40	9.4:1	60@1850
	Eighty-Eight	3.8 (3786)	K	MFI	205@5200	230@4000	3.80x3.40	9.4:1	60@1850
	LeSabre	3.8 (3785)	K	MFI	205@5200	230@4000	3.80x3.40	9.4:1	60@1850
	LSS	3.8 (3785)	1 ①	MFI	225@5000	275@3200	3.80x3.40	9.0:1	60@1850
	LSS	3.8 (3786)	K	MFI	205@5200	230@4000	3.80x3.40	9.4:1	60@1850
	Park Avenue	3.8 (3785)	1 ①	MFI	225@5000	275@3200	3.80x3.40	9.0:1	60@1850
	Park Avenue	3.8 (3785)	K	MFI	205@5200	230@4000	3.80x3.40	9.4:1	60@1850
	Regency	3.8 (3786)	K	MFI	205@5200	230@4000	3.80x3.40	9.4:1	60@1850
1999	Bonneville	3.8 (3785)	1 ①	MFI	225@5000	275@3200	3.80x3.40	9.0:1	60@1850
	Bonneville	3.8 (3785)	K	MFI	205@5200	230@4000	3.80x3.40	9.4:1	60@1850
	Eighty-Eight	3.8 (3786)	K	MFI	205@5200	230@4000	3.80x3.40	9.4:1	60@1850
	LeSabre	3.8 (3785)	K	MFI	205@5200	230@4000	3.80x3.40	9.4:1	60@1850
	LSS	3.8 (3786)	K	MFI	205@5200	230@4000	3.80x3.40	9.4:1	60@1850
	Park Avenue	3.8 (3785)	1 ①	MFI	225@5000	275@3200	3.80x3.40	9.0:1	60@1850
	Park Avenue	3.8 (3785)	K	MFI	205@5200	230@4000	3.80x3.40	9.4:1	60@1850
	Regency	3.8 (3786)	K	MFI	205@5200	230@4000	3.80x3.40	9.4:1	60@1850
2000-01	Bonneville	3.8 (3785)	1 ①	MFI	225@5000	275@3200	3.80x3.40	9.0:1	60@1850
	Bonneville	3.8 (3785)	K	MFI	205@5200	230@4000	3.80x3.40	9.4:1	60@1850
	Eighty-Eight	3.8 (3786)	K	MFI	205@5200	230@4000	3.80x3.40	9.4:1	60@1850
	LeSabre	3.8 (3785)	K	MFI	200@5200	230@4000	3.80x3.40	9.4:1	60@1850
	Park Avenue	3.8 (3785)	1 ①	MFI	240@5200	280@3600	3.80x3.40	9.0:1	60@1850
	Park Avenue	3.8 (3785)	K	MFI	200@5200	230@4000	3.80x3.40	9.4:1	60@1850

MFI: Multi-point Fuel Injection

① Supercharged engine

93061CJ4

For exhaust manifold replacement procedures, see the model specific sections of this manual

ENGINE TUNE-UP SPECIFICATIONS

Year	Engine Displacement Liters (cc)	Engine ID/VIN	Spark Plug Gap (in.)	Ignition Timing (deg.)	Fuel Pump (psi)	Idle Speed (rpm)	Valve Clearance	
							Intake	Exhaust
1997	3.8 (3786)	1	0.060	①	41-47 ②	③	HYD	HYD
	3.8 (3785)	K	0.060	①	41-47 ②	③	HYD	HYD
1998	3.8 (3786)	1	0.060	①	41-47 ②	③	HYD	HYD
	3.8 (3785)	K	0.060	①	41-47 ②	③	HYD	HYD
1999	3.8 (3786)	1	0.060	①	41-47 ②	③	HYD	HYD
	3.8 (3785)	K	0.060	①	41-47 ②	③	HYD	HYD
2000-01	3.8 (3786)	1	0.060	①	41-47 ②	③	HYD	HYD
	3.8 (3785)	K	0.060	①	41-47 ②	③	HYD	HYD

NOTE: The Vehicle Emission Control Information label often reflects specification changes made during production. The label figures must be used if they differ from those in this chart.

HYD: Hydraulic

① DIS Ignition System timing not adjustable

② Pressure at fuel pump

③ Idle speed maintained by ECM. There is no recommended adjustment procedure

93061CJ5

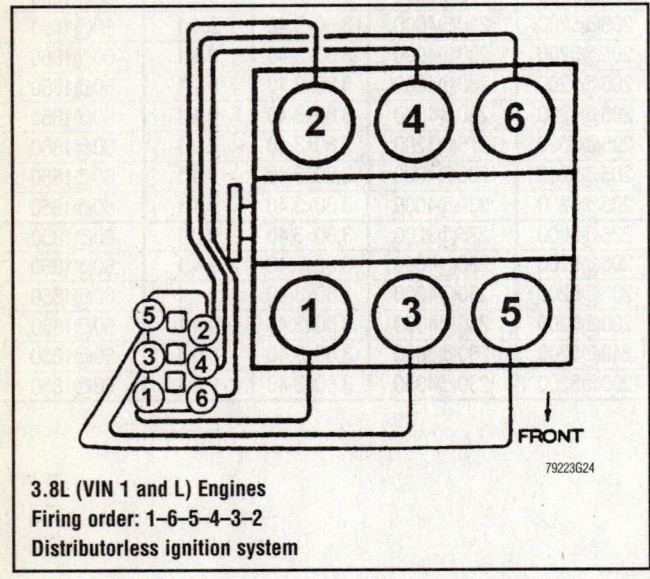

3.8L (VIN 1 and L) Engines
Firing order: 1–6–5–4–3–2
Distributorless ignition system

79223G24

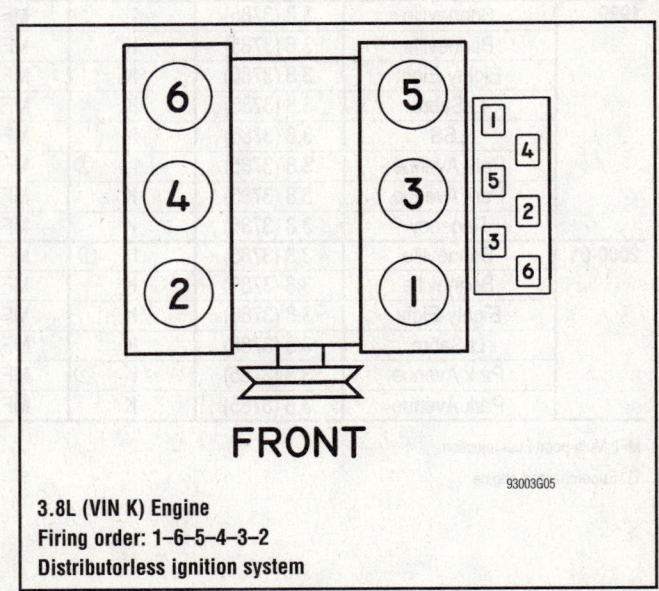

FRONT

3.8L (VIN K) Engine
Firing order: 1–6–5–4–3–2
Distributorless ignition system

93003G05

CAPACITIES

Year	Model	Engine Displacement Liters (cc)	Engine ID/VIN	Engine Oil with Filter (qts.)	Transmission (pts.)	Fuel Tank (gal.)	Cooling System (qts.)
1997	Bonneville	3.8 (3785)	1	4.5	12.0	18.0	13.0
	Bonneville	3.8 (3785)	K	4.5	12.0	18.0	13.0
	Eighty-Eight	3.8 (3785)	K	4.5	12.0	18.0	13.0
	Eighty-Eight/LSS	3.8 (3785)	1	4.5	12.0	18.0	13.0
	LeSabre	3.8 (3785)	K	4.5	12.0	18.0	13.0
	Ninety-Eight	3.8 (3785)	K	4.5	12.0	18.0	13.0
	Park Avenue	3.8 (3785)	K	4.5	12.0	18.0	13.0
	Park Avenue Ultra	3.8 (3785)	1	4.5	12.0	18.0	13.0
1998	Bonneville	3.8 (3785)	1	4.5	12.0	18.0	13.0
	Bonneville	3.8 (3785)	K	4.5	12.0	18.0	13.0
	Eighty-Eight	3.8 (3785)	K	4.5	12.0	18.0	13.0
	LeSabre	3.8 (3785)	K	4.5	12.0	18.0	13.0
	LSS	3.8 (3785)	1	4.5	12.0	18.0	13.0
	LSS	3.8 (3785)	K	4.5	12.0	18.0	13.0
	Park Avenue	3.8 (3785)	1	4.5	12.0	18.0	13.0
	Park Avenue	3.8 (3785)	K	4.5	12.0	18.0	13.0
	Regency	3.8 (3785)	K	4.5	12.0	18.0	13.0
1999	Bonneville	3.8 (3785)	1	4.5	12.0	18.0	13.0
	Bonneville	3.8 (3785)	K	4.5	12.0	18.0	13.0
	Eighty-Eight	3.8 (3785)	K	4.5	12.0	18.0	13.0
	LeSabre	3.8 (3785)	K	4.5	12.0	18.0	13.0
	LSS	3.8 (3785)	K	4.5	12.0	18.0	13.0
	Park Avenue	3.8 (3785)	1	4.5	12.0	18.0	13.0
	Park Avenue	3.8 (3785)	K	4.5	12.0	18.0	13.0
	Regency	3.8 (3785)	K	4.5	12.0	18.0	13.0
2000-01	Bonneville	3.8 (3785)	1	4.5	12.0	18.0	13.0
	Bonneville	3.8 (3785)	K	4.5	12.0	18.0	13.0
	Eighty-Eight	3.8 (3785)	K	4.5	12.0	18.5	13.0
	LeSabre	3.8 (3785)	K	4.5	12.0	18.0	13.0
	Park Avenue	3.8 (3785)	1	4.5	12.0	18.0	13.0
	Park Avenue	3.8 (3785)	K	4.5	12.0	18.0	13.0

NOTE: All capacities are approximate. Add fluid gradually and ensure a proper fluid level is obtained.

93061CJ6

Refer to the model specific sections for cooling system service procedures

CRANKSHAFT AND CONNECTING ROD SPECIFICATIONS

All measurements are given in inches.

Year	Engine Displacement Liters (cc)	Engine ID/VIN	Crankshaft				Connecting Rod		
			Main Brg. Journal Dia.	Main Brg. Oil Clearance	Shaft End-play	Thrust on No.	Journal Diameter	Oil Clearance	Side Clearance
1997	3.8 (3786)	1	2.4988-2.4998	①	0.0030-0.0110	2	2.2487-2.2499	0.0005-0.0026	0.0040-0.0200
	3.8 (3786)	K	2.4988-2.4998	①	0.0030-0.0110	2	2.2487-2.2499	0.0005-0.0026	0.0040-0.0200
1998	3.8 (3786)	1	2.4988-2.4998	①	0.0030-0.0110	2	2.2487-2.2499	0.0005-0.0026	0.0040-0.0200
	3.8 (3786)	K	2.4988-2.4998	①	0.0030-0.0110	2	2.2487-2.2499	0.0005-0.0026	0.0040-0.0200
1999	3.8 (3786)	1	2.4988-2.4998	①	0.0030-0.0110	2	2.2487-2.2499	0.0005-0.0026	0.0040-0.0200
	3.8 (3786)	K	2.4988-2.4998	①	0.0030-0.0110	2	2.2487-2.2499	0.0005-0.0026	0.0040-0.0200
2000-01	3.8 (3786)	1	2.4988-2.4998	①	0.0030-0.0110	2	2.2487-2.2499	0.0005-0.0026	0.0040-0.0200
	3.8 (3786)	K	2.4988-2.4998	①	0.0030-0.0110	2	2.2487-2.2499	0.0005-0.0026	0.0040-0.0200

① Journal 1: 0.0007 - 0.0016
Journals 2 and 3: 0.0010 - 0.0020
Journal 4: 0.0009 - 0.0018

93061CJ7

VALVE SPECIFICATIONS

Year	Engine Displacement Liters (cc)	Engine ID/VIN	Seat Angle (deg.)	Face Angle (deg.)	Spring Test Pressure (lbs. @ in.)	Spring Installed Height (in.)	Stem-to-Guide Clearance (in.)		Stem Diameter (in.)	
							Intake	Exhaust	Intake	Exhaust
1997	3.8 (3785)	1	45	45	80@1.750	1.690-1.720	0.0015-0.0032	0.0015-0.0032	NA	NA
	3.8 (3785)	K	45	45	80@1.750	1.690-1.720	0.0015-0.0032	0.0015-0.0032	NA	NA
1998	3.8 (3785)	1	45	45	80@1.750	1.690-1.720	0.0015-0.0032	0.0015-0.0032	NA	NA
	3.8 (3785)	K	45	45	80@1.750	1.690-1.720	0.0015-0.0032	0.0015-0.0032	NA	NA
1999	3.8 (3785)	1	45	45	80@1.750	1.690-1.720	0.0015-0.0032	0.0015-0.0032	NA	NA
	3.8 (3785)	K	45	45	80@1.750	1.690-1.720	0.0015-0.0032	0.0015-0.0032	NA	NA
2000-01	3.8 (3785)	1	45	45	80@1.750	1.690-1.720	0.0015-0.0032	0.0015-0.0032	NA	NA
	3.8 (3785)	K	45	45	80@1.750	1.690-1.720	0.0015-0.0032	0.0015-0.0032	NA	NA

NA: Not Available

93061CJ8

PISTON AND RING SPECIFICATIONS
All measurements are given in inches.

Year	Engine Displacement Liters (cc)	Engine ID/VIN	Piston Clearance	Ring Gap			Ring Side Clearance		
				Top Compression	Bottom Compression	Oil Control	Top Compression	Bottom Compression	Oil Control
1997	3.8 (3786)	1	0.0004-0.0020	0.012-0.022	0.030-0.040	0.010-0.030-	0.0013-0.0031	0.0013-0.0031	0.0009-0.0079
	3.8 (3786)	K	0.0004-0.0020	0.012-0.022	0.030-0.040	0.010-0.030-	0.0013-0.0031	0.0013-0.0031	0.0009-0.0079
1998	3.8 (3786)	1	0.0004-0.0020	0.012-0.022	0.030-0.040	0.010-0.030-	0.0013-0.0031	0.0013-0.0031	0.0009-0.0079
	3.8 (3786)	K	0.0004-0.0020	0.012-0.022	0.030-0.040	0.010-0.030-	0.0013-0.0031	0.0013-0.0031	0.0009-0.0079
1999	3.8 (3786)	1	0.0004-0.0020	0.012-0.022	0.030-0.040	0.010-0.030-	0.0013-0.0031	0.0013-0.0031	0.0009-0.0079
	3.8 (3786)	K	0.0004-0.0020	0.012-0.022	0.030-0.040	0.010-0.030-	0.0013-0.0031	0.0013-0.0031	0.0009-0.0079
2000-01	3.8 (3786)	1	0.0004-0.0020	0.012-0.022	0.030-0.040	0.010-0.030-	0.0013-0.0031	0.0013-0.0031	0.0009-0.0079
	3.8 (3786)	K	0.0004-0.0020	0.012-0.022	0.030-0.040	0.010-0.030-	0.0013-0.0031	0.0013-0.0031	0.0009-0.0079

93061CJ9

TORQUE SPECIFICATIONS
All readings in ft. lbs.

Year	Engine Displacement Liters (cc)	Engine ID/VIN	Cylinder Head Bolts	Main Bearing Bolts	Rod Bearing Bolts	Crankshaft Damper Bolts	Flywheel Bolts	Manifold		Spark Plugs	Lug Nuts
								Intake	Exhaust		
1997	3.8 (3786)	1	①	②	③	④	⑤	⑥	22	11	100
	3.8 (3786)	K	①	⑦	③	④	⑤	11	38	11	100
1998	3.8 (3786)	1	①	②	③	④	⑤	⑥	22	11	100
	3.8 (3786)	K	①	⑦	③	④	⑤	11	38	11	100
1999	3.8 (3786)	1	①	②	③	④	⑤	⑥	22	11	100
	3.8 (3786)	K	①	⑦	③	④	⑤	11	38	11	100
2000-01	3.8 (3786)	1	①	②	③	④	⑤	⑥	22	11	100
	3.8 (3786)	K	①	⑦	③	④	⑤	11	38	11	100

① Step 1: Tighten all bolts to 35 ft. lbs.
Step 2: Turn all bolts 130 degrees
Step 3: Rotate four center bolts an additional 30 degrees

② Step 1: Tighten caps in equal increments to 52 ft. lbs.
Step 2: Loosen 360 degrees
Step 3: 15 ft. lbs.
Step 4: 54 ft. lbs.
Step 5: Plus three turns of 35 degrees for a total of 105 degrees

③ 20 ft. lbs. plus 50 degrees
④ 111 ft. lbs. plus 76 degrees
⑤ 11 ft. lbs. plus 50 degrees
⑥ Upper manifold: 8 ft. lbs.
Lower manifold: 11 ft. lbs.
⑦ 26 ft. lbs. plus 50 degrees

93061CJ0

Timing chain and gear service is covered in the model specific sections of this manual

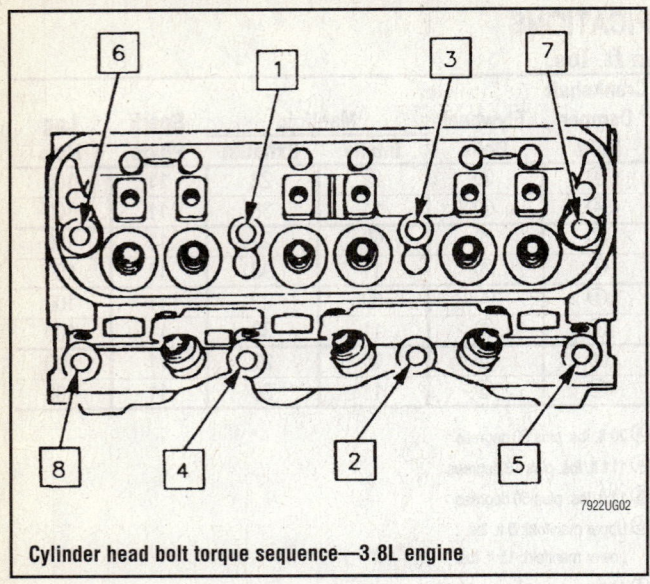

Cylinder head bolt torque sequence—3.8L engine

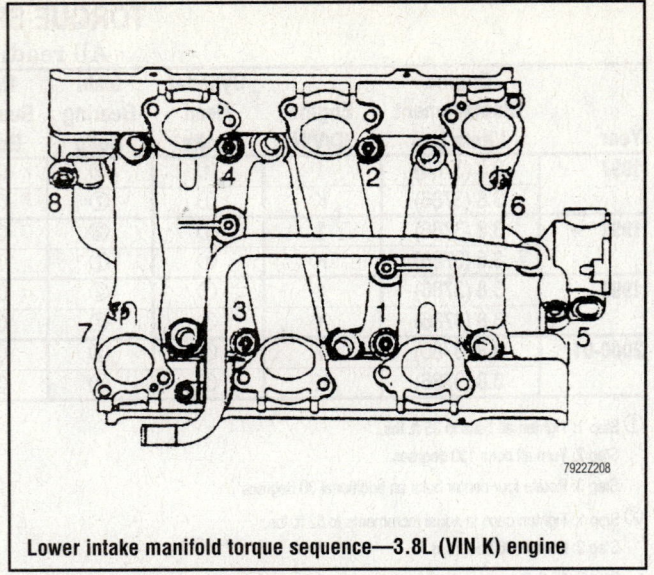

Lower intake manifold torque sequence—3.8L (VIN K) engine

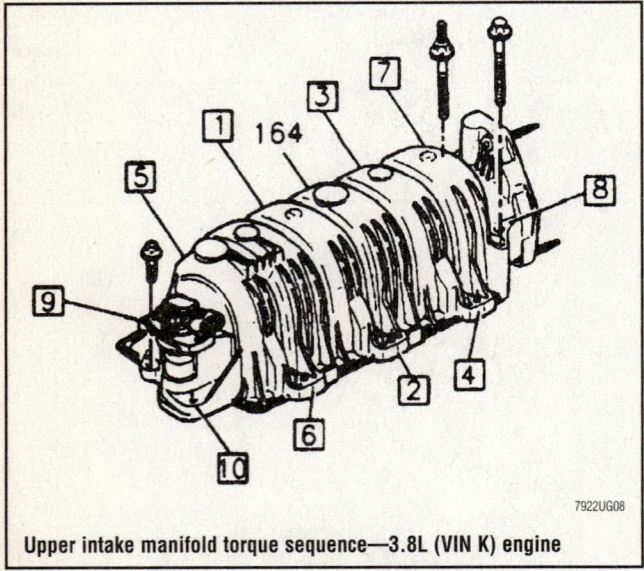

Upper intake manifold torque sequence—3.8L (VIN K) engine

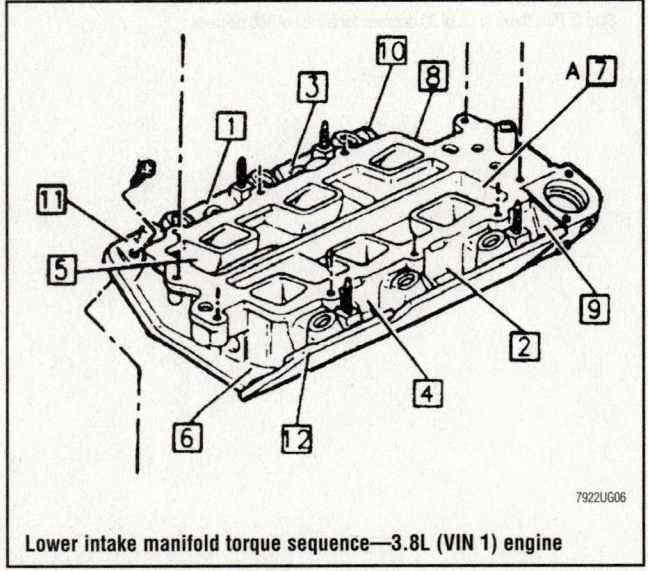

Lower intake manifold torque sequence—3.8L (VIN 1) engine

BRAKE SPECIFICATIONS
All measurements in inches unless noted

| Year | Model | Brake Disc | | | Brake Drum Diameter | | | Minimum Lining Thickness | | Brake Caliper Mounting Bolts |
		Original Thickness	Minimum Thickness	Maximum Runout	Original Inside Diameter	Max. Wear Limit	Maximum Machine Diameter	Front	Rear	(ft. lbs.)
1997	Bonneville	1.260	1.209	0.002	8.860	8.909	8.920	0.030	0.030	38
	Eighty-Eight	1.276	1.209	0.004	8.860	8.909	8.800	0.030	①	38
	LeSabre	1.260	1.209	0.002	8.863	8.909	8.920	0.030	①	38
	Ninety-Eight	1.276	1.209	0.004	8.860	8.909	8.800	0.030	①	38
	Park Avenue	1.260	1.209	0.002	8.863	8.909	8.920	0.030	①	38
1998	Bonneville	1.260	1.209	0.002	8.860	8.909	8.920	0.030	0.030	38
	Eighty-Eight	1.276	1.209	0.004	8.860	8.909	8.800	0.030	①	38
	LeSabre	1.260	1.209	0.002	8.863	8.909	8.920	0.030	①	38
	LSS	1.276	1.209	0.004	8.860	8.909	8.800	0.030	①	38
	Park Avenue	1.260	1.209	0.002	8.863	8.909	8.920	0.030	①	38
	Regency	1.276	1.209	0.004	8.860	8.909	8.800	0.030	①	38
1999	Bonneville	1.260	1.209	0.002	8.860	8.909	8.920	0.030	0.030	38
	Eighty-Eight	1.276	1.209	0.004	8.860	8.909	8.800	0.030	①	38
	LeSabre	1.260	1.209	0.002	8.863	8.909	8.920	0.030	①	38
	LSS	1.276	1.209	0.004	8.860	8.909	8.800	0.030	①	38
	Park Avenue	1.260	1.209	0.002	8.863	8.909	8.920	0.030	①	38
	Regency	1.276	1.209	0.004	8.860	8.909	8.800	0.030	①	38
2000-01	Bonneville	1.260	1.209	0.002	8.860	8.909	8.920	0.030	0.030	38
	Eighty-Eight	1.276	1.209	0.004	8.860	8.909	8.800	0.030	①	38
	LeSabre	1.260	1.209	0.002	8.863	8.909	8.920	0.030	①	38
	Park Avenue	1.260	1.209	0.002	8.863	8.909	8.920	0.030	①	38

① 0.030 over rivet head; If bonded lining, use 0.062 from shoe

93061CK1

Ignition system service is covered in the model specific sections of this manual

SCHEDULED MAINTENANCE INTERVALS
(GM C & H BODIES—BUICK LESABRE, PARK AVENUE, OLDSMOBILE LSS, REGENCY & EIGHTY-EIGHT & PONTIAC BONNEVILLE)

TO BE SERVICED	TYPE OF SERVICE	VEHICLE MILEAGE INTERVAL (x1000)												
		7.5	15	22.5	30	37.5	45	52.5	60	67.5	75	82.5	90	97.5
Engine oil & filter	R	✓	✓	✓	✓	✓	✓	✓	✓	✓	✓	✓	✓	✓
Exhaust system & brake hoses	S/I	✓	✓	✓	✓	✓	✓	✓	✓	✓	✓	✓	✓	✓
Driveshaft boots & front suspension components	S/I	✓	✓	✓	✓	✓	✓	✓	✓	✓	✓	✓	✓	✓
Lubricate chassis, suspension, steering linkage, transaxle shift linkage, parking brake cable guides, underbody contact points & linkage	S/I	✓	✓	✓	✓	✓	✓	✓	✓	✓	✓	✓	✓	✓
Coolant level, hoses & clamps	S/I	✓	✓	✓	✓	✓	✓	✓	✓	✓	✓	✓	✓	✓
Throttle linkage	S/I	✓	✓	✓	✓	✓	✓	✓	✓	✓	✓	✓	✓	✓
Brake linings & rotate tires	S/I			✓			✓		✓		✓		✓		✓
Accessory drive belts supercharger oil	S/I					✓			✓					✓	
Engine coolant ①	R													
Spark plugs ②	R				✓				✓					✓	
Air filter element	R				✓				✓					✓	
PCV filter	R				✓				✓					✓	
Ignition cables	S/I				✓				✓					✓	
EGR & fuel systems	S/I				✓				✓					✓	
Automatic transaxle fluid & filter	R														✓
Throttle body mount bolt torque	S/I	✓													

R: Replace   S/I: Service or Inspect

① Engine coolant: replace every 100,000 miles. Use O.E. specified (DEX-COOL™) coolant only. If any silicate coolant is used, the service interval is every 30,000 miles.

② Platinum tip spark plugs: replace every 100,000 miles.

FREQUENT OPERATION MAINTENANCE (SEVERE SERVICE)

If a vehicle is operated under any of the following conditions it is considered severe service:
- Extremely dusty areas.
- 50% or more of the vehicle operation is in 32°C (90°F) or higher temperatures, or constant operation in temperatures below 0°C (32°F).
- Prolonged idling (vehicle operation in stop and go traffic).
- Frequent short running periods (engine does not warm to normal operating temperatures).
- Police, taxi, delivery usage or trailer towing usage.

CV joints & front suspension components: service or inspect every 3000 miles.
Engine oil & filter change: change every 3000 miles.
Brake linings: check every 6000 miles.
Chassis lubrication: lubricate every 6000 miles.
Suspension, steering linkage, transaxle shift linkage, parking cable guides, underbody contact points: lubricate every 6000 miles.
Throttle body mount bolt torque: tighten at 6000 miles.
Air filter element: service or inspect every 15,000 miles.
Automatic transaxle fluid: change every 50,000 miles (1997).
Inspect throttle body bore & throttle plate for deposits: clean as required every 15,000 miles.
Rotate tires at 6000 miles, then every 15,000 miles.

93061CK2

SCHEDULED MAINTENANCE INTERVALS
GENERAL MOTORS CORPORATION
C & H BODIES
BUICK LESABRE, PARK AVENUE
OLDSMOBILE LSS, REGENCY, EIGHTY EIGHT
PONTIAC BONNEVILLE

The following should be used as a guide when determining the amount of work required for a particular service. In estimating how long a particular Scheduled Maintenance Service should take, please observe the following:

- Labor Time is time based on field research and data supplied by the vehicle manufacturer.
- Labor time operations are given in hours and tenths of an hour.
- All labor operations are to be used as a guide.

Mechanic Skill Level Codes:
(A) PRECISION: Highly skilled with multiple certification.
(B) GENERAL: Normally skilled with certification.
(C) MAINTENANCE: Semi-skilled working on certification.

	LABOR TIME
7500 Mile Service (C)	
All Models	1.8
15000 Mile Service (C)	
All Models	.9
22500 Mile Service (C)	
All Models	1.8
30000 Mile Service (B)	
All Models	4.0

	LABOR TIME
37500 Mile Service (C)	
All Models	1.8
45000 Mile Service (C)	
All Models	.9
52500 Mile Service (C)	
All Models	1.7
60000 Mile Service (B)	
All Models	4.2
67500 Mile Service (C)	
All Models	1.6

	LABOR TIME
75000 Mile Service (C)	
All Models	.9
82500 Mile Service (C)	
All Models	1.6
90000 Mile Service (B)	
All Models	4.0
97500 Mile Service (B)	
All Models	2.2

93061CK3

GENERAL MOTORS E- & K-BODIES
Cadillac DeVille • DeVille Concours • Eldorado • Seville

ENGINE AND VEHICLE IDENTIFICATION

Engine								Model Year	
Code ①	Liters (cc)	Cu. In.	Cyl.	Fuel Sys.	Engine Type	Eng. Mfg.		Code ②	Year
9	4.6 (4565)	279	8	MFI	DOHC	Cadillac		V	1997
Y	4.6 (4565)	279	8	MFI	DOHC	Cadillac		W	1998
								X	1999
								Y	2000
								1	2001

DOHC: Double Overhead Camshafts

MFI: Multi-point Fuel Injection

① 8th position of VIN

② 10th position of VIN

93061CK4

GENERAL ENGINE SPECIFICATIONS

Year	Model	Engine Displacement Liters (cc)	Engine Series (ID/VIN)	Fuel System	Net Horsepower @ rpm	Net Torque @ rpm (ft. lbs.)	Bore x Stroke (in.)	Com- pression Ratio	Oil Pressure @ rpm
1997	DeVille	4.6 (4565)	Y	MFI	275@5600	300@4000	3.66x3.31	10.3:1	35@2000
	DeVille Concours	4.6 (4565)	9	MFI	300@6000	290@4400	3.66x3.31	10.3:1	35@2000
	Eldorado	4.6 (4565)	Y	MFI	275@5600	300@4000	3.66x3.31	10.3:1	35@2000
	Eldorado ETC	4.6 (4565)	9	MFI	300@6000	290@4400	3.66x3.31	10.3:1	35@2000
	Seville SLS	4.6 (4565)	Y	MFI	275@5600	300@4000	3.66x3.31	10.3:1	35@2000
	Seville STS	4.6 (4565)	9	MFI	300@6000	290@4400	3.66x3.31	10.3:1	35@2000
1998	DeVille	4.6 (4565)	Y	MFI	275@5600	300@4000	3.66x3.31	10.3:1	35@2000
	DeVille Concours	4.6 (4565)	9	MFI	300@6000	290@4400	3.66x3.31	10.3:1	35@2000
	Eldorado	4.6 (4565)	Y	MFI	275@5600	300@4000	3.66x3.31	10.3:1	35@2000
	Eldorado ETC	4.6 (4565)	9	MFI	300@6000	290@4400	3.66x3.31	10.3:1	35@2000
	Seville SLS	4.6 (4565)	Y	MFI	275@5600	300@4000	3.66x3.31	10.3:1	35@2000
	Seville STS	4.6 (4565)	9	MFI	300@6000	290@4400	3.66x3.31	10.3:1	35@2000
1999	DeVille	4.6 (4565)	Y	MFI	275@5600	300@4000	3.66x3.31	10.3:1	35@2000
	DeVille Concours	4.6 (4565)	9	MFI	300@6000	290@4400	3.66x3.31	10.3:1	35@2000
	Eldorado	4.6 (4565)	Y	MFI	275@5600	300@4000	3.66x3.31	10.3:1	35@2000
	Eldorado ETC	4.6 (4565)	9	MFI	300@6000	290@4400	3.66x3.31	10.3:1	35@2000
	Seville SLS	4.6 (4565)	Y	MFI	275@5600	300@4000	3.66x3.31	10.3:1	35@2000
	Seville STS	4.6 (4565)	9	MFI	300@6000	290@4400	3.66x3.31	10.3:1	35@2000
2000-01	DeVille	4.6 (4565)	Y	MFI	275@5600	300@4000	3.66x3.31	10.0:1	35@2000
	DeVille DTS	4.6 (4565)	9	MFI	300@6000	295@4400	3.66x3.31	10.0:1	35@2000
	DeVille DHS	4.6 (4565)	Y	MFI	275@5600	300@4000	3.66x3.31	10.0:1	35@2000
	Eldorado	4.6 (4565)	Y	MFI	275@5600	300@4000	3.66x3.31	10.0:1	35@2000
	Eldorado ETC	4.6 (4565)	9	MFI	300@6000	295@4400	3.66x3.31	10.0:1	35@2000
	Seville SLS	4.6 (4565)	Y	MFI	275@5600	300@4000	3.66x3.31	10.0:1	35@2000
	Seville STS	4.6 (4565)	9	MFI	300@6000	295@4400	3.66x3.31	10.0:1	35@2000

MFI: Multi-point Fuel Injection

93061CK5

ENGINE TUNE-UP SPECIFICATIONS

Year	Engine Displacement Liters (cc)	Engine ID/VIN	Spark Plug Gap (in.)	Ignition Timing (deg.)	Fuel Pump (psi)	Idle Speed (rpm)	Valve Clearance	
							Intake	Exhaust
1997	4.6 (4565)	9	0.050	①	40-50	①	HYD	HYD
	4.6 (4565)	Y	0.050	①	40-50	①	HYD	HYD
1998	4.6 (4565)	9	0.050	①	40-50	①	HYD	HYD
	4.6 (4565)	Y	0.050	①	40-50	①	HYD	HYD
1999	4.6 (4565)	9	0.050	①	40-50	①	HYD	HYD
	4.6 (4565)	Y	0.050	①	40-50	①	HYD	HYD
2000-01	4.6 (4565)	9	0.050	①	40-50	①	HYD	HYD
	4.6 (4565)	Y	0.050	①	40-50	①	HYD	HYD

NOTE: The Vehicle Emission Control Information label often reflects specification changes made during production. The label figures must be used if they differ from those in this chart.

HYD: Hydraulic

① Refer to Vehicle Emission Control Information label

93061CK6

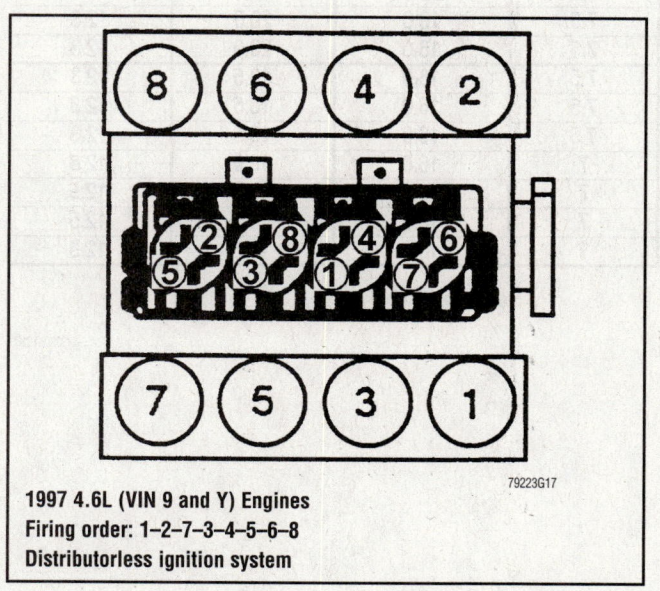

1997 4.6L (VIN 9 and Y) Engines
Firing order: 1–2–7–3–4–5–6–8
Distributorless ignition system

79223G17

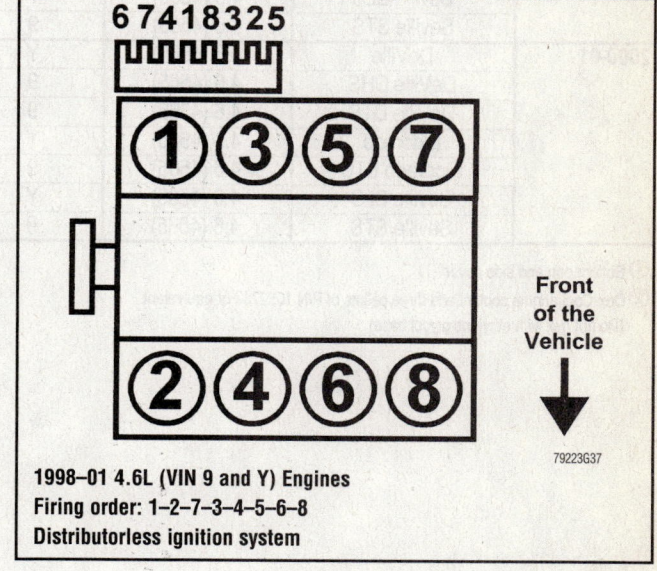

1998–01 4.6L (VIN 9 and Y) Engines
Firing order: 1–2–7–3–4–5–6–8
Distributorless ignition system

79223G37

Front of the Vehicle

Refer to the model specific sections for engine mechanical service procedures

CAPACITIES

Year	Model	Engine Displacement Liters (cc)	Engine ID/VIN	Engine Oil with Filter (qts.)	Transmission (pts.) ①	Fuel Tank (gal.)	Cooling System (qts.) ②
1997	DeVille	4.6 (4565)	Y	7.5	16.0	20.0	12.3
	DeVille Concours	4.6 (4565)	9	7.5	16.0	18.0	12.3
	Eldorado	4.6 (4565)	Y	7.5	16.0	20.0	12.3
	Eldorado ETC	4.6 (4565)	9	7.5	16.0	20.0	12.3
	Seville SLS	4.6 (4565)	Y	7.5	16.0	20.0	12.3
	Seville STS	4.6 (4565)	9	7.5	16.0	20.0	12.3
1998	DeVille	4.6 (4565)	Y	7.5	16.0	20.0	12.3
	DeVille Concours	4.6 (4565)	9	7.5	16.0	18.0	12.3
	Eldorado	4.6 (4565)	Y	7.5	16.0	20.0	12.3
	Eldorado ETC	4.6 (4565)	9	7.5	16.0	20.0	12.3
	Seville SLS	4.6 (4565)	Y	7.5	16.0	20.0	12.3
	Seville STS	4.6 (4565)	9	7.5	16.0	20.0	12.3
1999	DeVille	4.6 (4565)	Y	7.5	16.0	20.0	12.3
	DeVille Concours	4.6 (4565)	9	7.5	16.0	18.0	12.3
	Eldorado	4.6 (4565)	Y	7.5	16.0	20.0	12.3
	Eldorado ETC	4.6 (4565)	9	7.5	16.0	20.0	12.3
	Seville SLS	4.6 (4565)	Y	7.5	16.0	20.0	12.3
	Seville STS	4.6 (4565)	9	7.5	16.0	20.0	12.3
2000-01	DeVille	4.6 (4565)	Y	7.5	16.0	18.5	12.3
	DeVille DHS	4.6 (4565)	9	7.5	16.0	18.5	12.3
	DeVille DTS	4.6 (4565)	9	7.5	16.0	18.5	12.3
	Eldorado	4.6 (4565)	Y	7	16.0	19.0	12.5
	Eldorado ETC	4.6 (4565)	9	7	16.0	19.0	12.5
	Seville SLS	4.6 (4565)	Y	7	16.0	18.5	12.5
	Seville STS	4.6 (4565)	9	7	16.0	18.5	12.5

① Bottom pan and side cover
② Dex-Cool engine coolant and three pellets of P/N 1052753 or equivalent
(Do not mix with ethylene glycol base)

93061CK7

VALVE SPECIFICATIONS

Year	Engine Displacement Liters (cc)	Engine ID/VIN	Seat Angle (deg.)	Face Angle (deg.)	Spring Test Pressure (lbs. @ in.)	Spring Installed Height (in.)	Stem-to-Guide Clearance (in.)		Stem Diameter (in.)	
							Intake	Exhaust	Intake	Exhaust
1997	4.6 (4565)	9	46	45	53@1.190	1.190	0.0010-0.0030	0.0020-0.0040	0.2331-0.2339	0.2331-0.2339
	4.6 (4565)	Y	46	45	46@1.190	1.190	0.0010-0.0030	0.0020-0.0040	0.2331-0.2339	0.2331-0.2339
1998	4.6 (4565)	9	46	45	53@1.190	1.190	0.0010-0.0030	0.0020-0.0040	0.2331-0.2339	0.2331-0.2339
	4.6 (4565)	Y	46	45	46@1.190	1.190	0.0010-0.0030	0.0020-0.0040	0.2331-0.2339	0.2331-0.2339
1999	4.6 (4565)	9	46	45	53@1.190	1.190	0.0010-0.0030	0.0020-0.0040	0.2331-0.2339	0.2331-0.2339
	4.6 (4565)	Y	46	45	46@1.190	1.190	0.0010-0.0030	0.0020-0.0040	0.2331-0.2339	0.2331-0.2339
2000-01	4.6 (4565)	9	46	45	53@1.190	1.190	0.0010-0.0030	0.0020-0.0040	0.2331-0.2339	0.2331-0.2339
	4.6 (4565)	Y	46	45	46@1.190	1.190	0.0010-0.0030	0.0020-0.0040	0.2331-0.2339	0.2331-0.2339

93061CK8

Refer to the model specific sections for fuel system service procedures

CRANKSHAFT AND CONNECTING ROD SPECIFICATIONS
All measurements are given in inches.

Year	Engine Displacement Liters (cc)	Engine ID/VIN	Crankshaft				Connecting Rod		
			Main Brg. Journal Dia.	Main Brg. Oil Clearance	Shaft End-play	Thrust on No.	Journal Diameter	Oil Clearance	Side Clearance
1997	9	4.6 (4565)	2.5335-2.5337	0.0006-0.0025	0.0020-0.0200	3	2.1239-2.1235	0.001-0.003	0.0080-0.0200
	Y	4.6 (4565)	2.5335-2.5337	0.0006-0.0025	0.0020-0.0200	3	2.1239-2.1235	0.001-0.003	0.0080-0.0200
1998	9	4.6 (4565)	2.5335-2.5337	0.0006-0.0025	0.0020-0.0200	3	2.1239-2.1235	0.001-0.003	0.0080-0.0200
	Y	4.6 (4565)	2.5335-2.5337	0.0006-0.0025	0.0020-0.0200	3	2.1239-2.1235	0.001-0.003	0.0080-0.0200
1999	9	4.6 (4565)	2.5335-2.5337	0.0006-0.0025	0.0020-0.0200	3	2.1239-2.1235	0.001-0.003	0.0080-0.0200
	Y	4.6 (4565)	2.5335-2.5337	0.0006-0.0025	0.0020-0.0200	3	2.1239-2.1235	0.001-0.003	0.0080-0.0200
2000-01	9	4.6 (4565)	2.5335-2.5337	0.0006-0.0025	0.0020-0.0200	3	2.1239-2.1235	0.001-0.003	0.0080-0.0200
	Y	4.6 (4565)	2.5335-2.5337	0.0006-0.0025	0.0020-0.0200	3	2.1239-2.1235	0.001-0.003	0.0080-0.0200

93061CK9

PISTON AND RING SPECIFICATIONS
All measurements are given in inches.

Year	Engine Displacement Liters (cc)	Engine ID/VIN	Piston Clearance	Ring Gap			Ring Side Clearance		
				Top Compression	Bottom Compression	Oil Control	Top Compression	Bottom Compression	Oil Control
1997	4.6 (4565)	9	0.0008-0.0020	0.010-0.016	0.014-0.020	0.010-0.030	0.0016-0.0037	0.0016-0.0037	①
	4.6 (4565)	Y	0.0008-0.0020	0.010-0.016	0.014-0.020	0.010-0.030	0.0016-0.0037	0.0016-0.0037	①
1998	4.6 (4565)	9	0.0008-0.0020	0.010-0.016	0.014-0.020	0.010-0.030	0.0016-0.0037	0.0016-0.0037	①
	4.6 (4565)	Y	0.0008-0.0020	0.010-0.016	0.014-0.020	0.010-0.030	0.0016-0.0037	0.0016-0.0037	①
1999	4.6 (4565)	9	0.0008-0.0020	0.010-0.016	0.014-0.020	0.010-0.030	0.0016-0.0037	0.0016-0.0037	①
	4.6 (4565)	Y	0.0008-0.0020	0.010-0.016	0.014-0.020	0.010-0.030	0.0016-0.0037	0.0016-0.0037	①
2000-01	4.6 (4565)	9	0.0008-0.0020	0.010-0.016	0.014-0.020	0.010-0.030	0.0016-0.0037	0.0016-0.0037	①
	4.6 (4565)	Y	0.0008-0.0020	0.010-0.016	0.014-0.020	0.010-0.030	0.0016-0.0037	0.0016-0.0037	①

① Side sealing

93061CK0

Refer to the model specific sections for engine electrical system service procedures

TORQUE SPECIFICATIONS
All readings in ft. lbs.

Year	Engine Displacement Liters (cc)	Engine ID/VIN	Cylinder Head Bolts	Main Bearing Bolts	Rod Bearing Bolts	Crankshaft Damper Bolts	Flywheel Bolts	Manifold		Spark Plugs	Lug Nuts
								Intake	Exhaust		
1997	4.6 (4565)	9	①	②	③	④	⑤	⑥	18	11	100
	4.6 (4565)	Y	①	②	③	④	⑤	⑥	18	11	100
1998	4.6 (4565)	9	①	②	③	④	⑤	⑥	18	11	100
	4.6 (4565)	Y	①	②	③	④	⑤	⑥	18	11	100
1999	4.6 (4565)	9	①	②	③	④	⑤	⑥	18	11	100
	4.6 (4565)	Y	①	②	③	④	⑤	⑥	18	11	100
2000-01	4.6 (4565)	9	①	②	③	④	⑤	⑥	18	11	100
	4.6 (4565)	Y	①	②	③	④	⑤	⑥	18	11	100

① Step 1: 22 ft. lbs.
  Step 2: Plus two turns of 90 degrees

② Step 1: 15 ft. lbs.
  Step 2: Plus 65 degrees

③ Step 1: 18 ft. lbs.
  Step 2: Plus 110 degrees

④ Step 1: 37 ft. lbs.
  Step 2: Plus 120 degrees

⑤ Step 1: 11 ft. lbs.
  Step 2: Plus 50 degrees

⑥ 89 inch lbs.

93061CL1

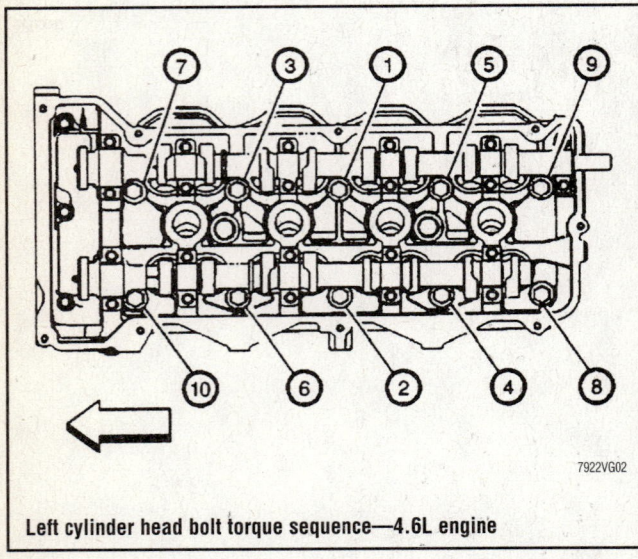

Left cylinder head bolt torque sequence—4.6L engine

7922VG02

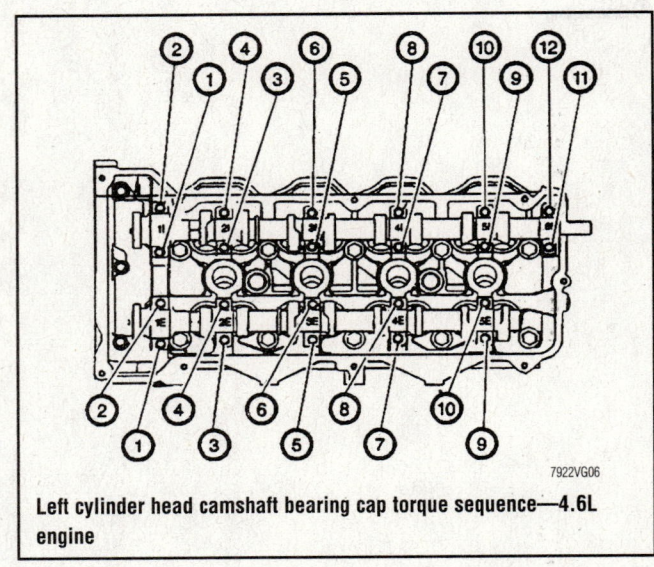

Left cylinder head camshaft bearing cap torque sequence—4.6L engine

7922VG06

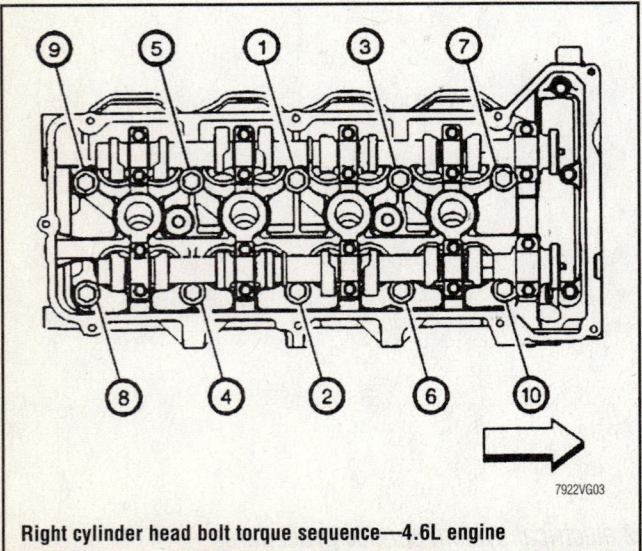

Right cylinder head bolt torque sequence—4.6L engine

7922VG03

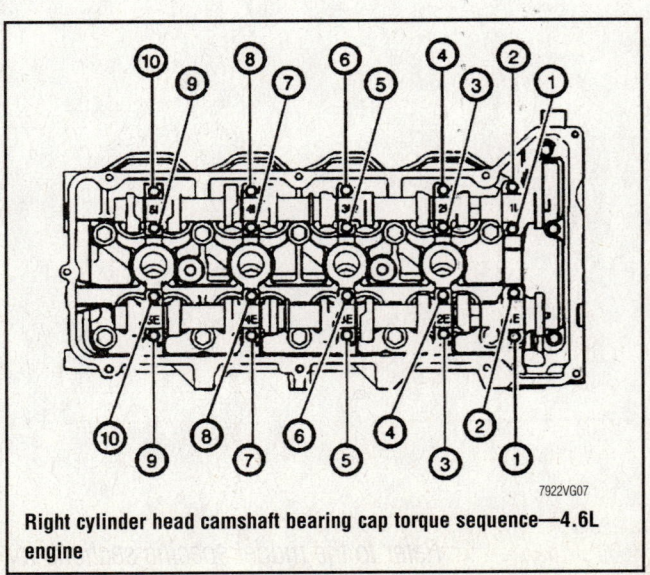

Right cylinder head camshaft bearing cap torque sequence—4.6L engine

7922VG07

BRAKE SPECIFICATIONS
CADILLAC DEVILLE, ELDORADO AND SEVILLE
All measurements in inches unless noted

Year	Model		Brake Disc Original Thickness	Brake Disc Minimum Thickness	Brake Disc Maximum Runout	Minimum Lining Thickness	Brake Caliper Mounting Bolts (ft. lbs.)
1997	DeVille	F	1.268	1.209	0.002	0.030	38
		R	0.433	0.374	0.002	0.030	20
	DeVille Concours	F	1.268	1.209	0.002	0.030	38
		R	0.433	0.374	0.002	0.030	20
	Eldorado	F	1.268	1.209	0.002	0.030	38
		R	0.433	0.374	0.002	0.030	20
	Eldorado ETC	F	1.268	1.209	0.002	0.030	38
		R	0.433	0.374	0.002	0.030	20
	Seville SLS	F	1.268	1.209	0.002	0.030	38
		R	0.433	0.374	0.002	0.030	20
	Seville STS	F	1.268	1.209	0.002	0.030	38
		R	0.433	0.374	0.002	0.030	20
1998	DeVille	F	1.268	1.209	0.002	0.030	38
		R	0.433	0.374	0.002	0.030	20
	DeVille Concours	F	1.268	1.209	0.002	0.030	38
		R	0.433	0.374	0.002	0.030	20
	Eldorado	F	1.268	1.209	0.002	0.030	38
		R	0.433	0.374	0.002	0.030	20
	Eldorado ETC	F	1.268	1.209	0.002	0.030	38
		R	0.433	0.374	0.002	0.030	20
	Seville SLS	F	1.268	1.209	0.002	0.030	38
		R	0.433	0.374	0.002	0.030	20
	Seville STS	F	1.268	1.209	0.002	0.030	38
		R	0.433	0.374	0.002	0.030	20
1999	DeVille	F	1.268	1.209	0.002	0.030	38
		R	0.433	0.374	0.002	0.030	20
	DeVille Concours	F	1.268	1.209	0.002	0.030	38
		R	0.433	0.374	0.002	0.030	20
	Eldorado	F	1.268	1.209	0.002	0.030	38
		R	0.433	0.374	0.002	0.030	20
	Eldorado ETC	F	1.268	1.209	0.002	0.030	38
		R	0.433	0.374	0.002	0.030	20
	Seville SLS	F	1.268	1.209	0.002	0.030	38
		R	0.433	0.374	0.002	0.030	20
	Seville STS	F	1.268	1.209	0.002	0.030	38
		R	0.433	0.374	0.002	0.030	20
2000-01	DeVille	F	1.268	1.209	0.002	0.030	38
		R	0.433	0.374	0.002	0.030	20
	DeVille DHS	F	1.268	1.209	0.002	0.030	38
		R	0.433	0.374	0.002	0.030	20
	DeVille DTS	F	1.268	1.209	0.002	0.030	38
		R	0.433	0.374	0.002	0.030	20
	Eldorado	F	1.268	1.209	0.002	0.030	38
		R	0.433	0.374	0.002	0.030	20
	Eldorado ETC	F	1.268	1.209	0.002	0.030	38
		R	0.433	0.374	0.002	0.030	20
	Seville SLS	F	1.268	1.209	0.002	0.030	38
		R	0.433	0.374	0.002	0.030	20
	Seville STS	F	1.268	1.209	0.002	0.030	38
		R	0.433	0.374	0.002	0.030	20

93061CL2

For accessory drive belt replacement procedures see the model specific sections of this manual

SCHEDULED MAINTENANCE INTERVALS
(GM E & K BODIES—CADILLAC DEVILLE, DEVILLE CONCOURS, ELDORADO & SEVILLE)

TO BE SERVICED	TYPE OF SERVICE	VEHICLE MILEAGE INTERVAL (x1000)												
		7.5	15	22.5	30	37.5	45	52.5	60	67.5	75	82.5	90	97.5
Engine oil & filter	R	✔	✔	✔	✔	✔	✔	✔	✔	✔	✔	✔	✔	✔
Coolant level, hoses & clamps	S/I	✔	✔	✔	✔	✔	✔	✔	✔	✔	✔	✔	✔	✔
Drive shaft boots & front suspension components	S/I	✔	✔	✔	✔	✔	✔	✔	✔	✔	✔	✔	✔	✔
Exhaust system, brake hoses & throttle linkage	S/I	✔	✔	✔	✔	✔	✔	✔	✔	✔	✔	✔	✔	✔
Lubricate chassis, suspension, steering linkage, transaxle shift linkage, parking brake cable guides, underbody contact points & linkage	S/I	✔	✔	✔	✔	✔	✔	✔	✔	✔	✔	✔	✔	✔
Brake linings	S/I	✔		✔		✔		✔		✔		✔		✔
Rotate tires	S/I	✔		✔		✔		✔		✔		✔		✔
Inspect throttle body bore & throttle plate for deposits	S/I		✔				✔				✔		✔	
Air filter element	R				✔				✔				✔	
Engine coolant ①	R													
PCV valve	R				✔				✔				✔	
Spark plugs ②	R				✔				✔				✔	
Accessory drive belt(s)	S/I				✔				✔				✔	
Automatic transaxle fluid & filter	S/I				✔				✔				✔	
EGR & fuel systems	S/I				✔				✔				✔	
Ignition cables	S/I				✔				✔				✔	

R: Replace   S/I: Service or Inspect

① Engine coolant: replace every 100,000 miles. Use O.E. specified (DEX-COOL™) coolant only. If any silicate coolant is used, the service interval is every 30,000 miles.

② Platinum tip spark plugs: replace every 100,000 miles.

FREQUENT OPERATION MAINTENANCE (SEVERE SERVICE)

If a vehicle is operated under any of the following conditions it is considered severe service:

- Extremely dusty areas.

- 50% or more of the vehicle operation is in 32°C (90°F) or higher temperatures, or constant operation in temperatures below 0°C (32°F).

- Prolonged idling (vehicle operation in stop and go traffic).

- Frequent short running periods (engine does not warm to normal operating temperatures).

- Police, taxi, delivery usage or trailer towing usage.

CV joints & front suspension components: service or inspect every 3000 miles.

Engine oil & filter change: change every 3000 miles.

Brake linings: check every 6000 miles.

Chassis lubrication: lubricate every 6000 miles.

Suspension, steering linkage, transaxle shift linkage, parking cable guides, underbody contact points: lubricate every 6000 miles.

Air filter element: service or inspect every 15,000 miles.

Automatic transaxle fluid: change every 50,000 miles (1997 only).

Inspect throttle body bore & throttle plate for deposits: clean as required every 15,000 miles.

Rotate tires at 6000 miles, then every 15,000 miles.

SCHEDULED MAINTENANCE INTERVALS
GENERAL MOTORS CORPORATION
E & K BODIES
CADILLAC DEVILLE, DEVILLE CONCOURS,
ELDORADO, SEVILLE

The following should be used as a guide when determining the amount of work required for a particular service. In estimating how long a particular Scheduled Maintenance Service should take, please observe the following:

- Labor Time is time based on field research and data supplied by the vehicle manufacturer.
- Labor time operations are given in hours and tenths of an hour.
- All labor operations are to be used as a guide.

Mechanic Skill Level Codes:
(A) PRECISION: Highly skilled with multiple certification.
(B) GENERAL: Normally skilled with certification.
(C) MAINTENANCE: Semi-skilled working on certification.

	LABOR TIME		LABOR TIME		LABOR TIME
7500 Mile Service (C)		**37500 Mile Service (C)**		**75000 Mile Service (C)**	
All Models	1.9	All Models	1.6	All Models	1.3
15000 Mile Service (C)		**45000 Mile Service (C)**		**82500 Mile Service (C)**	
All Models	.9	All Models	1.1	All Models	1.8
22500 Mile Service (C)		**52500 Mile Service (C)**		**90000 Mile Service (B)**	
All Models	1.7	All Models	1.7	All Models	4.2
30000 Mile Service (B)		**60000 Mile Service (B)**		**97500 Mile Service (C)**	
All Models	4.2	All Models	4.1	All Models	1.8
		67500 Mile Service (C)			
		All Models	1.7		

93061CL4

For brake related suspension and axle service, refer to the model specific sections of this manual

GENERAL MOTORS F-BODY
Chevrolet Camaro • Pontiac Firebird

ENGINE AND VEHICLE IDENTIFICATION

	Engine							Model Year	
Code ①	Liters (cc)	Cu. In.	Cyl.	Fuel Sys.	Engine Type	Eng. Mfg.		Code ②	Year
G	5.7 (5665)	350	8	SFI	OHV	CPC		V	1997
K	3.8 (3785)	231	6	SFI	OHV	CPC		W	1998
P	5.7 (5737)	350	8	MFI	OHV	CPC		X	1999
								Y	2000
								1	2001

MFI: Multi-point Fuel Injection

SFI: Sequential Fuel Injection

CPC: Chevrolet/Pontiac/Canada

OHV: Overhead Valve

① 8th position of VIN

② 10th position of VIN

93061CL5

GENERAL ENGINE SPECIFICATIONS

Year	Model	Engine Displacement Liters (cc)	Engine Series (ID/VIN)	Fuel System	Net Horsepower @ rpm	Net Torque @ rpm (ft. lbs.)	Bore x Stroke (in.)	Compression Ratio	Oil Pressure @ rpm
1997	Camaro	3.8 (3785)	K	SFI	160@4600	200@3600	3.80x3.40	9.4:1	60@1850
		5.7 (5737)	P	MFI	275@5000	325@2400	4.00x3.48	10.25:1	18@2000
	Firebird	3.8 (3785)	K	SFI	160@4600	200@3600	3.80x3.40	9.4:1	60@1850
		5.7 (5737)	P	MFI	275@5000	325@2400	4.00x3.48	10.25:1	18@2000
1998	Camaro	5.7 (5665)	G	SFI	305@5200	335@4000	3.89x3.62	10.0:1	18@2000
		3.8 (3785)	K	SFI	200@5200	225@4000	3.80x3.40	9.4:1	60@1850
	Firebird	5.7 (5665)	G	SFI	305@5200	335@4000	3.89x3.62	10.0:1	18@2000
		3.8 (3785)	K	SFI	200@5200	225@4000	3.80x3.40	9.4:1	60@1850
1999	Camaro	5.7 (5665)	G	SFI	305@5200	335@4000	3.89x3.62	10.0:1	18@2000
		3.8 (3785)	K	SFI	200@5200	225@4000	3.80x3.40	9.4:1	60@1850
	Firebird	5.7 (5665)	G	SFI	305@5200	335@4000	3.89x3.62	10.0:1	18@2000
		3.8 (3785)	K	SFI	200@5200	225@4000	3.80x3.40	9.4:1	60@1850
2000-01	Camaro	5.7 (5665)	G	SFI	305@5200	335@4000	3.89x3.62	10.0:1	18@2000
		3.8 (3785)	K	SFI	200@5200	225@4000	3.80x3.40	9.4:1	60@1850
	Firebird	5.7 (5665)	G	SFI	305@5200	335@4000	3.89x3.62	10.0:1	18@2000
		3.8 (3785)	K	SFI	200@5200	225@4000	3.80x3.40	9.4:1	60@1850

MFI: Multi-point Fuel Injection

SFI: Sequencial Fuel Injection

93061CL6

ENGINE TUNE-UP SPECIFICATIONS

Year	Engine Displacement Liters (cc)	Engine ID/VIN	Spark Plug Gap (in.)	Ignition Timing (deg.) MT	AT	Fuel Pump (psi)	Idle Speed (rpm) MT	AT	Valve Clearance Intake	Exhaust
1997	3.8 (3785)	K	0.045	①	①	41-47	①	①	HYD	HYD
	5.7 (5737)	P	0.035	—	①	41-47	—	①	HYD	HYD
1998	3.8 (3785)	K	0.045	①	①	41-47	①	①	HYD	HYD
	5.7 (5665)	G	0.060	①	①	48-55	①	①	HYD	HYD
1999	5.7 (5665)	G	0.060	①	①	48-55	①	①	HYD	HYD
	3.8 (3785)	K	0.045	①	①	41-47	①	①	HYD	HYD
2000-01	5.7 (5665)	G	0.060	①	①	48-55	①	①	HYD	HYD
	3.8 (3785)	K	0.045	①	①	41-47	①	①	HYD	HYD

NOTE: The Vehicle Emission Control Information label often reflects specification changes made during production. The label figures must be used if they differ from those in this chart.

HYD: Hydraulic

① Refer to Vehicle Emission Control Information label

93061CL7

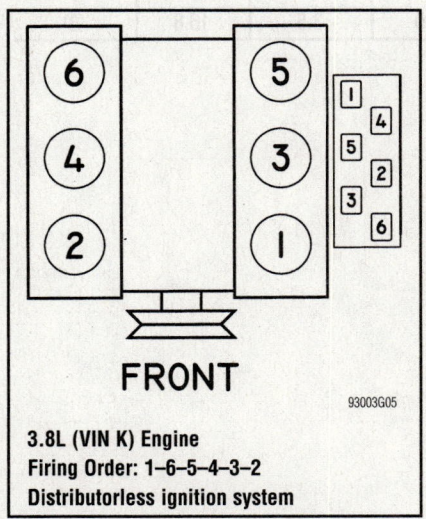

3.8L (VIN K) Engine
Firing Order: 1–6–5–4–3–2
Distributorless ignition system

93003G05

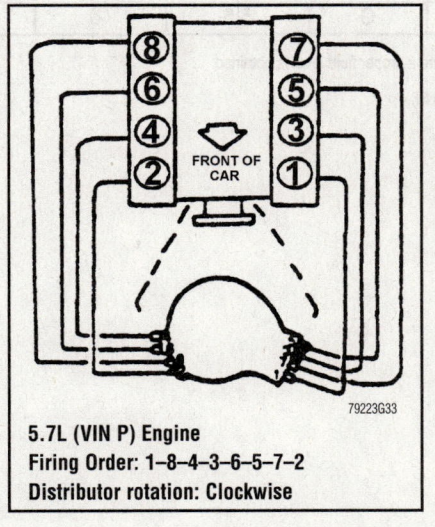

5.7L (VIN P) Engine
Firing Order: 1–8–4–3–6–5–7–2
Distributor rotation: Clockwise

79223G33

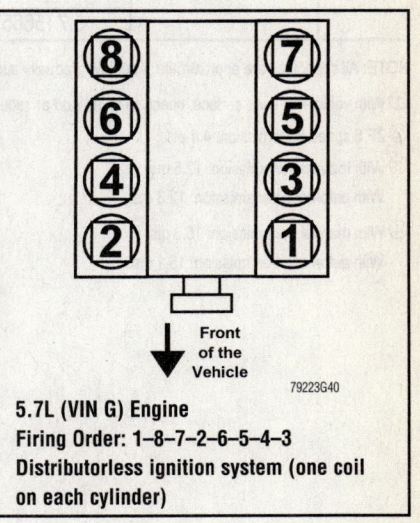

5.7L (VIN G) Engine
Firing Order: 1–8–7–2–6–5–4–3
Distributorless ignition system (one coil on each cylinder)

79223G40

Refer to the model specific sections for driveline service procedures

CAPACITIES

Year	Model	Engine Displacement Liters (cc)	Engine ID/VIN	Engine Oil with Filter (qts.) ①	Transmission (pts.)		Drive Axle (pts.)	Fuel Tank (gal.)	Cooling System (qts.)
					5-Spd	Auto.			
1997	Camaro	3.8 (3785)	K	4.5	5.9	10.0	3.5	15.5	12.5
		5.7 (5737)	P.	4.5	②	10.0	3.5	15.5	15.2
	Firebird	3.8 (3785)	K	4.5	5.9	10.0	3.5	15.5	12.5
		5.7 (5737)	P	4.5	②	10.0	3.5	15.5	15.2
1998	Camaro	3.8 (3785)	K	4.5	5.9	10.0	3.5	15.5	④
		5.7 (5665)	G	5.5	②	10.0	3.5	15.5	③
	Firebird	3.8 (3785)	K	4.5	5.9	10.0	3.5	15.5	④
		5.7 (5665)	G	5.5	②	10.0	3.5	15.5	③
1999	Camaro	3.8 (3785)	K	4.5	5.9	10.0	3.5	15.5	④
		5.7 (5665)	G	5.5	②	10.0	3.5	15.5	③
	Firebird	3.8 (3785)	K	4.5	5.9	10.0	3.5	15.5	④
		5.7 (5665)	G	5.5	②	10.0	3.5	15.5	③
2000-01	Camaro	3.8 (3785)	K	4.5	5.9	10.0	3.5	16.8	④
		5.7 (5665)	G	5.5	②	10.0	3.5	16.8	③
	Firebird	3.8 (3785)	K	4.5	5.9	10.0	3.5	16.8	④
		5.7 (5665)	G	5.5	②	10.0	3.5	16.8	③

NOTE: All capacities are approximate. Add fluid gradually and ensure a proper fluid level is obtained.

① With vehicle on level surface, check oil level. Add as required to fill.

② ZF 6 speed transmission: 4.4 pts.

③ With mauual transmission: 12.5 qts.
   With automatic transmission: 12.3 qts.

④ With manual transmission: 15.3 qts.
   With automatic transmission: 15.1 qts.

93061CL8

VALVE SPECIFICATIONS

Year	Engine Displacement Liters (cc)	Engine ID/VIN	Seat Angle (deg.)	Face Angle (deg.)	Spring Test Pressure (lbs. @ in.) ①	Spring Installed Height (in.)	Stem-to-Guide Clearance (in.)		Stem Diameter (in.)	
							Intake	Exhaust	Intake	Exhaust
1997	3.8 (3785)	K	45	45	210@1.32	1.69-1.72	0.0015-0.0035	0.0015-0.0032	NA	NA
	5.7 (5737)	P	46	45	245-265@1.33	1.78	0.0009-0.0027	0.0009-0.0027	NA	NA
1998	3.8 (3785)	K	45	45	228@1.277	1.69-1.72	0.0015-0.0035	0.0015-0.0032	NA	NA
	5.7 (5665)	G	46	45	220@1.32	1.80	0.0010-0.0026	0.0010-0.0026	0.0313-0.0314	0.0313-0.0314
1999	3.8 (3785)	K	45	45	228@1.277	1.69-1.72	0.0015-0.0035	0.0015-0.0032	NA	NA
	5.7 (5665)	G	46	45	220@1.32	1.80	0.0010-0.0026	0.0010-0.0026	0.0313-0.0314	0.0313-0.0314
2000-01	3.8 (3785)	K	45	45	228@1.277	1.69-1.72	0.0015-0.0035	0.0015-0.0032	NA	NA
	5.7 (5665)	G	46	45	220@1.32	1.80	0.0010-0.0026	0.0010-0.0026	0.0313-0.0314	0.0313-0.0314

NA: Not Available

① With valve open

93061CL9

For exhaust manifold replacement procedures, see the model specific sections of this manual

CRANKSHAFT AND CONNECTING ROD SPECIFICATIONS
All measurements are given in inches.

Year	Engine Displacement Liters (cc)	Engine ID/VIN	Crankshaft				Connecting Rod		
			Main Brg. Journal Dia.	Main Brg. Oil Clearance	Shaft End-play	Thrust on No.	Journal Diameter	Oil Clearance	Side Clearance
1997	3.8 (3786)	K	2.4988-2.4998 -	①	0.0030-0.0110	2	2.2487-2.2499	0.0005-0.0026	0.0040-0.020
	5.7 (5737)	P	②	③	0.002-0.0080	5	2.0978-2.0998	0.0013-0.0035	0.0060-0.0240
1998	3.8 (3786)	K	2.4988-2.4998	①	0.0030-0.0110	2	2.2487-2.2499	0.0005-0.0026	0.0040-0.0200
	5.7 (5665)	G	2.5580-2.5590	0.0007-0.0021	0.0015-0.0078	3	2.0991-2.0999	0.0006-0.0030	0.0043-0.0200
1999	3.8 (3786)	K	2.4988-2.4998	①	0.0030-0.0110	2	2.2487-2.2499	0.0005-0.0026	0.0040-0.020
	5.7 (5665)	G	2.5580-2.5590	0.0007-0.0021	0.0015-0.0078	3	2.0991-2.0999	0.0006-0.0030	0.00433-0.0200
2000-01	3.8 (3786)	K	2.4988-2.4998	①	0.0030-0.0110	2	2.2487-2.2499	0.0005-0.0026	0.0040-0.020
	5.7 (5665)	G	2.5580-2.5590	0.0007-0.0021	0.0015-0.0078	3	2.0991-2.0999	0.0006-0.0030	0.00433-0.0200

① Journal 1: 0.0007 - 0.0016
  Journals 2 and 3: 0.0010 - 0.0020
  Journal 4: 0.0009 - 0.0018

② Journal 1: 2.4484 - 2.4493
  Journals 2, 3 and 4: 2.4481 - 2.4491
  Journal 5: 2.4479 - 2.4491

③ Journal 1: 0.0007 - 0.0021
  Journals 2, 3 and 4: 0.0009 - 0.0024
  Journal 5: 0.0010 - 0.0027

93061CL0

PISTON AND RING SPECIFICATIONS

All measurements are given in inches.

Year	Engine Displacement Liters (cc)	Engine ID/VIN	Piston Clearance	Ring Gap			Ring Side Clearance		
				Top Compression	Bottom Compression	Oil Control	Top Compression	Bottom Compression	Oil Control
1997	3.8 (3786)	K	0.0004-0.0020	0.012-0.022	0.030-0.040	0.010-0.030-	0.0013-0.0031	0.0013-0.0031	0.0009-0.0079
	5.7 (5737)	P	0.0010-0.0027	0.010-0.016	0.018-0.026	0.010-0.030	0.0019-0.0035	0.0019-0.0035	0.0020-0.0070
1998	3.8 (3786)	K	0.0004-0.0020	0.012-0.022	0.030-0.040	0.010-0.030-	0.0013-0.0031	0.0013-0.0031	0.0009-0.0079
	5.7 (5665)	G	0.0007-0.0021	0.009-0.015	0.017-0.025	0.007-0.027	0.0016-0.0034	0.0016-0.0032	0.0004-0.0087
1999	3.8 (3786)	K	0.0004-0.0020	0.012-0.022	0.030-0.040	0.010-0.030-	0.0013-0.0031	0.0013-0.0031	0.0009-0.0079
	5.7 (5665)	G	0.0007-0.0021	0.009-0.015	0.017-0.025	0.007-0.027	0.0016-0.0034	0.0016-0.0032	0.0004-0.0087
2000-01	3.8 (3786)	K	0.0004-0.0020	0.010-0.018	0.023-0.033	0.010-0.030-	0.0013-0.0031	0.0013-0.0031	0.0009-0.0079
	5.7 (5665)	G	0.0007-0.0021	0.009-0.015	0.017-0.025	0.007-0.027	0.0016-0.0034	0.0016-0.0032	0.0004-0.0087

93061CM1

Refer to the model specific sections for cooling system service procedures

TORQUE SPECIFICATIONS
All readings in ft. lbs.

Year	Engine Displacement Liters (cc)	Engine ID/VIN	Cylinder Head Bolts	Main Bearing Bolts	Rod Bearing Bolts	Crankshaft Damper Bolts	Flywheel Bolts	Manifold Intake	Manifold Exhaust	Spark Plugs	Lug Nuts
1997	3.8 (3785)	K	①	②	20	③	④	⑤	18	23	100
	5.7 (5737)	P	65	78	47	60	74	35	22	11	100
1998	3.8 (3785)	K	①	②	20	③	④	⑤	18	23	100
	5.7 (5665)	G	⑥	⑦	⑧	⑨	⑩	⑪	⑫	12	100
1999	3.8 (3785)	K	⑤	②	20	③	④	⑤	18	23	100
	5.7 (5665)	G	⑥	⑦	⑧	⑨	⑩	⑪	⑫	12	100
2000-01	3.8 (3785)	K	⑤	②	20	③	④	⑤	18	23	100
	5.7 (5665)	G	⑥	⑦	⑧	⑨	⑩	⑪	⑫	12	100

NA: Not Available

① Step 1: 37 ft. lbs. plus 130 degrees
   Step 2: Turn center bolts an additional 30 degrees

② Step 1: Tighten to 52 ft. lbs. to fully seat caps
   Step 2: Loosen bearing cap 360 degrees counter-clockwise
   Step 3: Tighten caps 15 ft. lbs., then 30 ft. lbs., then 35 degrees,
   then an additional 35 degrees plus 40 degrees -- for a total of 110 degrees

③ 111 ft. lbs. plus 76 degrees

④ 11 ft. lbs. plus 50 degrees

⑤ Upper manifold: 18 ft. lbs.
   Lower manifold bolt/nut: 22 ft. lbs.
   Upper manifold studs: 89 inch lbs.

⑥ Step 1: 22 ft. lbs.
   Step 2: Rotate 90 degrees
   Step 3: Rotate 90 degrees
   Step 3: Rotate 50 degrees
   Step 4: Tighten inner (M8) bolts to 22 ft. lbs

⑦ Step 1: Inner bolts: 15 ft. lbs.
   Step 2: Inner bolts: Rotate 80 degrees
   Step 3: Outer side studs: 18 ft. lbs.
   Step 4: Outer side studs: Rotate 53 degrees

⑧ Step 1: 15 ft. lbs.
   Step 2: Rotate 60 degrees

⑨ Step 1: Ensure damper is install fully, tighten old bolt 37 ft. lbs.
   Step 2: Ensure damper is install fully, tighten old bolt 240 ft. lbs.
   Step 3: Rotate 140 degrees

⑩ Step 1: 15 ft. lbs.
   Step 2: 37 ft. lbs.
   Step 3: 74 ft. lbs.

⑪ Step 1: 44 inch lbs.
   Step 2: 89 inch lbs

⑫ Step 1: 11 ft. lbs.
   Step 2: 18 ft. lbs

93061CM2

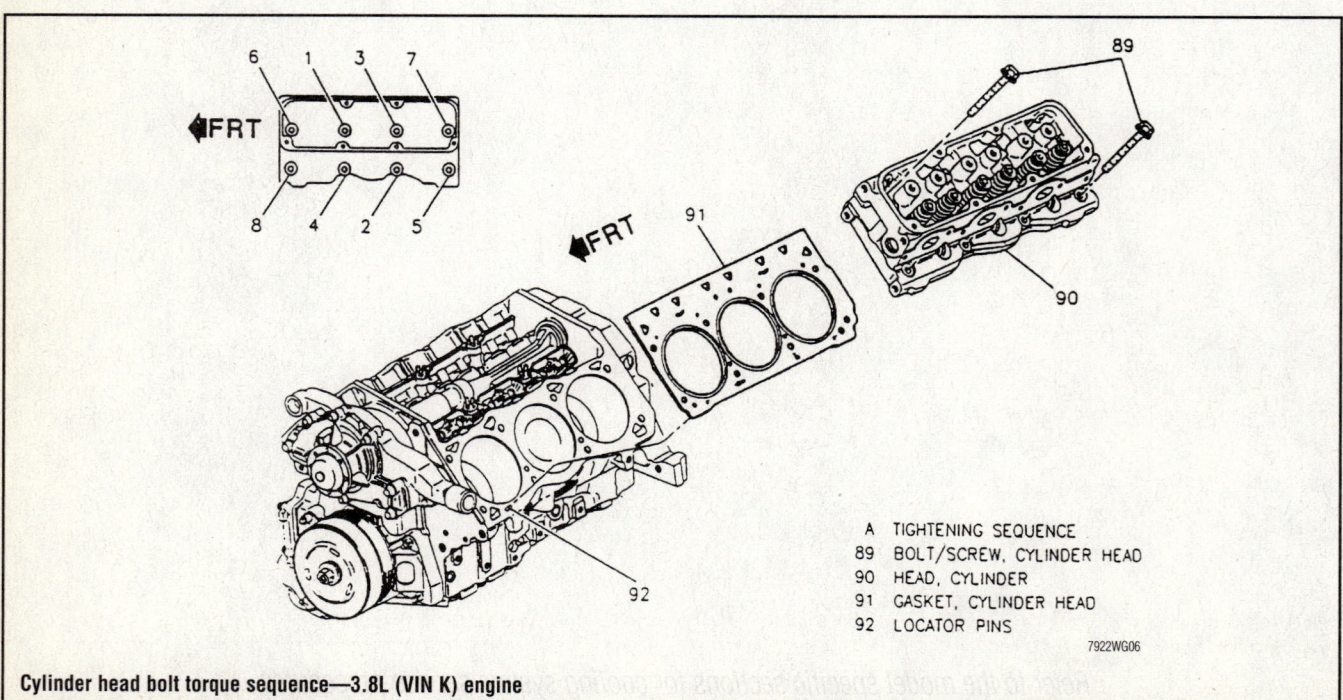

A   TIGHTENING SEQUENCE
89 BOLT/SCREW, CYLINDER HEAD
90 HEAD, CYLINDER
91 GASKET, CYLINDER HEAD
92 LOCATOR PINS

7922WG06

Cylinder head bolt torque sequence—3.8L (VIN K) engine

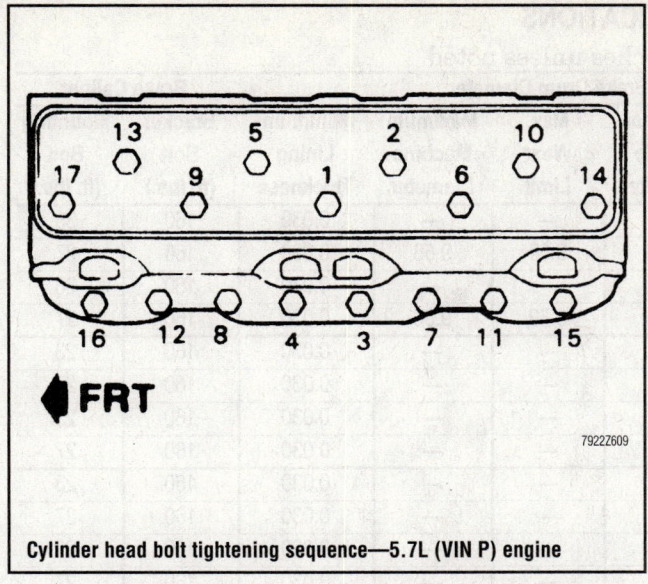

Cylinder head bolt tightening sequence—5.7L (VIN P) engine

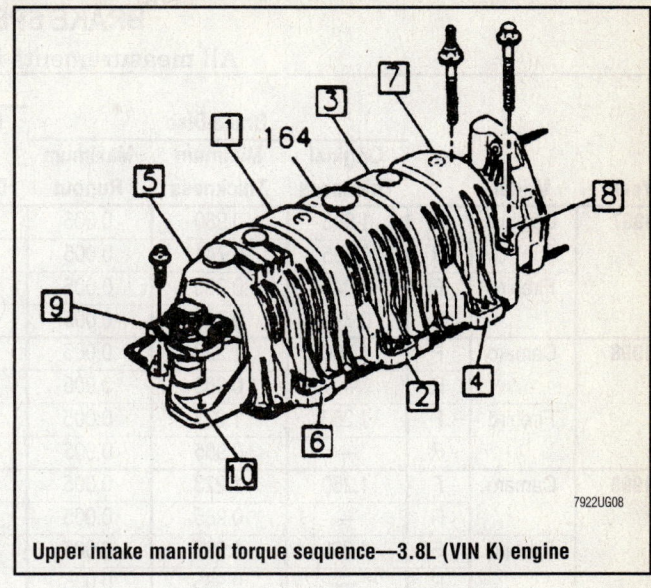

Upper intake manifold torque sequence—3.8L (VIN K) engine

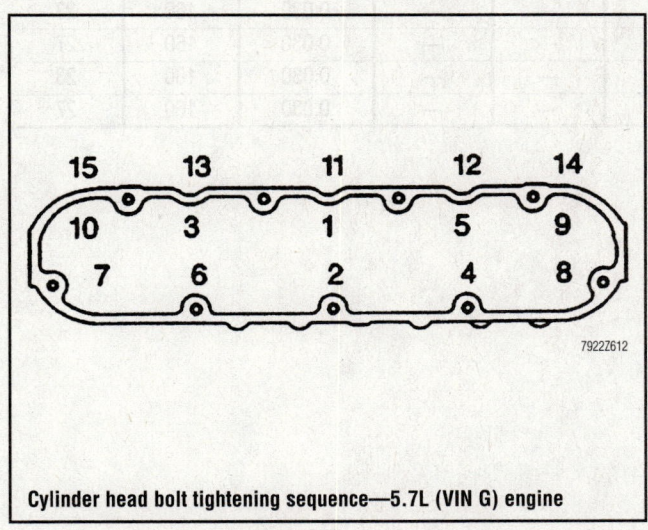

Cylinder head bolt tightening sequence—5.7L (VIN G) engine

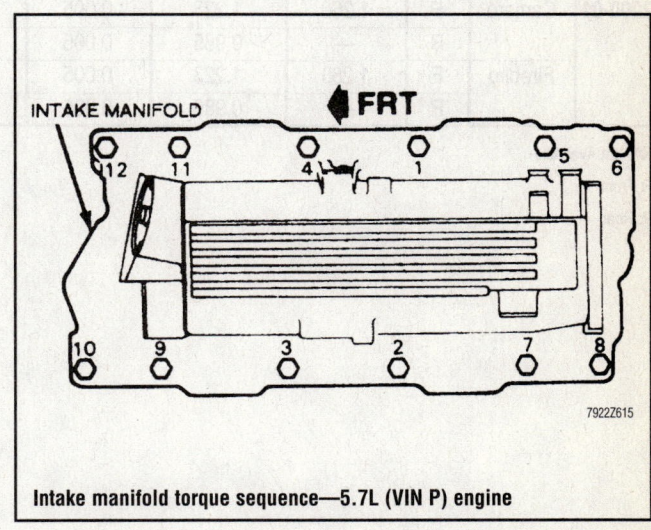

Intake manifold torque sequence—5.7L (VIN P) engine

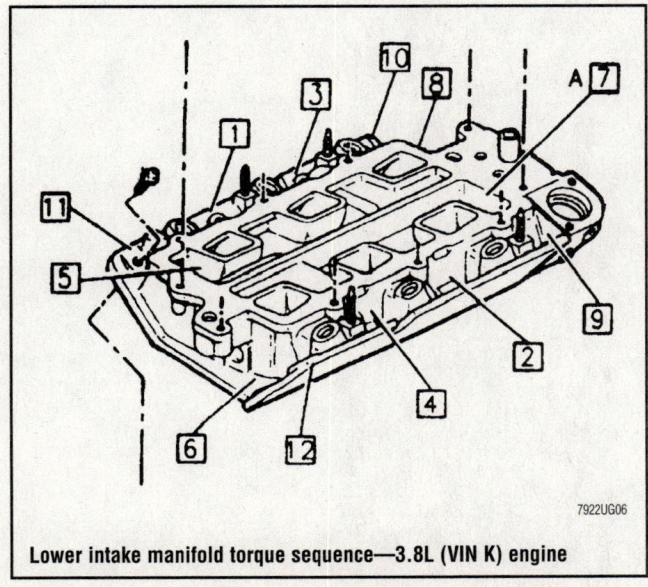

Lower intake manifold torque sequence—3.8L (VIN K) engine

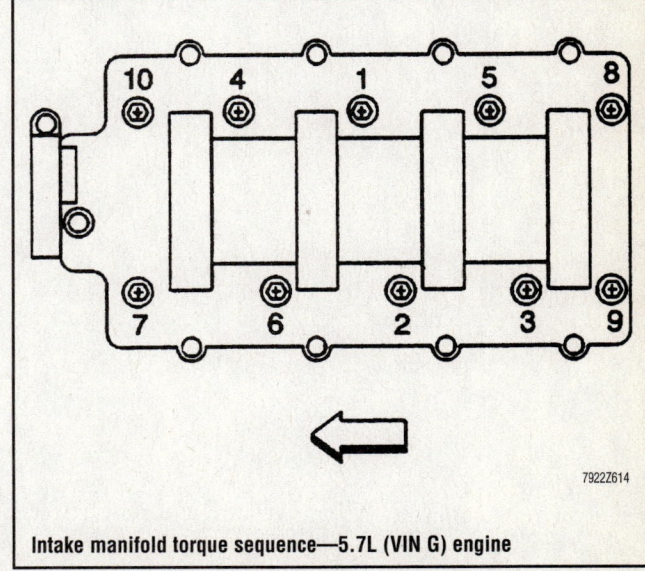

Intake manifold torque sequence—5.7L (VIN G) engine

BRAKE SPECIFICATIONS
All measurements in inches unless noted

Year	Model		Brake Disc Original Thickness	Brake Disc Minimum Thickness	Brake Disc Maximum Runout	Brake Drum Diameter Original Inside Diameter	Brake Drum Diameter Max. Wear Limit	Brake Drum Diameter Maximum Machine Diameter	Minimum Lining Thickness	Brake Caliper Bracket Bolt (ft. lbs.)	Brake Caliper Mounting Bolt (ft. lbs.)
1997	Camaro	F	1.043	0.980	-0.005	—	—	—	0.030	160	38
		R	0.795	0.744	0.005	9.50	9.59	9.56	0.030	160	27
	Firebird	F	1.043	0.980	0.005	—	—	—	0.030	160	38
		R	0.795	0.744	0.005	9.50	9.59	9.56	0.030	160	27
1998	Camaro	F	1.260	1.223	0.005	—	—	—	0.030	160	23
		R	—	0.985	0.005	—	—	—	0.030	160	27
	Firebird	F	1.260	1.223	0.005	—	—	—	0.030	160	23
		R	—	0.985	0.005	—	—	—	0.030	160	27
1999	Camaro	F	1.260	1.223	0.005	—	—	—	0.030	160	23
		R	—	0.985	0.005	—	—	—	0.030	160	27
	Firebird	F	1.260	1.223	0.005	—	—	—	0.030	160	23
		R	—	0.985	0.005	—	—	—	0.030	160	27
2000-01	Camaro	F	1.260	1.223	0.005	—	—	—	0.030	160	23
		R	—	0.985	0.005	—	—	—	0.030	160	27
	Firebird	F	1.260	1.223	0.005	—	—	—	0.030	160	23
		R	—	0.985	0.005	—	—	—	0.030	160	27

NA: Not Available

F: Front

R: Rear

93061CM3

SCHEDULED MAINTENANCE INTERVALS
(GM F BODY—CHEVROLET CAMARO & PONTIAC FIREBIRD)

TO BE SERVICED	TYPE OF SERVICE	VEHICLE MILEAGE INTERVAL (x1000)												
		7.5	15	22.5	30	37.5	45	52.5	60	67.5	75	82.5	90	97.5
Engine oil & filter	R	✓	✓	✓	✓	✓	✓	✓	✓	✓	✓	✓	✓	✓
Coolant level, hoses & clamps	S/I	✓	✓	✓	✓	✓	✓	✓	✓	✓	✓	✓	✓	✓
Exhaust system, brake hoses & throttle linkage	S/I	✓	✓	✓	✓	✓	✓	✓	✓	✓	✓	✓	✓	✓
Lubricate chassis, suspension, steering linkage, transaxle shift linkage, parking brake cable guides, underbody contact points & linkage	S/I	✓	✓	✓	✓	✓	✓	✓	✓	✓	✓	✓	✓	✓
Brake hoses & brake linings	S/I	✓		✓		✓		✓		✓		✓		✓
Rotate tires ①	S/I	✓		✓		✓		✓		✓		✓		✓
Automatic transmission fluid & filter ②	S/I													
Air filter element & PCV filter	R				✓				✓				✓	
Engine coolant ③	R													
Spark plugs ④	R				✓				✓				✓	
Ignition cables, EGR & fuel systems	S/I				✓				✓				✓	
Serpentine drive belt	S/I				✓				✓				✓	
Rear axle oil (Limited slip) ⑤	R	✓												

R: Replace   S/I: Service or Inspect

① For models with P245/50ZR16 tires, rotate front-to-rear only, & be sure that the tires roll in the direction indicated by the arrows on the side walls.

② Automatic transmission fluid & filter: replace every 100,000 miles.

③ Engine coolant: replace every 100,000 miles. Use O.E. specified (DEX-COOL™) coolant only. If any silicate coolant is used, the service interval is every 30,000 miles.

④ Platinum tip spark plugs: replace every 100,000 miles.

③ Engine coolant: replace every 100,000 miles. Use O.E. specified (DEX-COOL™) coolant only. If any silicate coolant is used, the service interval is every 30,000 miles.

⑤ If the vehicle is used to tow a trailer, change the rear axle fluid every 7500 miles in either type of differential.

FREQUENT OPERATION MAINTENANCE (SEVERE SERVICE)

If a vehicle is operated under any of the following conditions it is considered severe service:

- Extremely dusty areas.

- 50% or more of the vehicle operation is in 32°C (90°F) or higher temperatures, or constant operation in temperatures below 0°C (32°F).

- Prolonged idling (vehicle operation in stop and go traffic).

- Frequent short running periods (engine does not warm to normal operating temperatures).

- Police, taxi, delivery usage or trailer towing usage.

Oil & oil filter: change every 3000 miles.

Chassis lubrication: lubricate every 6000 miles.

Automatic transmission fluid & filter: change every 15,000 miles.

Air filter element: service or inspect every 15,000 miles.

Rotate tires at 6000 miles, then every 15,000 miles.

93061CM4

Timing chain and gear service is covered in the model specific sections of this manual

SCHEDULED MAINTENANCE INTERVALS
GENERAL MOTORS CORPORATION
F BODY
CHEVROLET CAMARO, PONTIAC FIREBIRD

The following should be used as a guide when determining the amount of work required for a particular service.
In estimating how long a particular Scheduled Maintenance Service should take, please observe the following:

- Labor Time is time based on field research and data supplied by the vehicle manufacturer.
- Labor time operations are given in hours and tenths of an hour.
- All labor operations are to be used as a guide.

Mechanic Skill Level Codes:
(A) PRECISION: Highly skilled with multiple certification.
(B) GENERAL: Normally skilled with certification.
(C) MAINTENANCE: Semi-skilled working on certification.

	LABOR TIME		LABOR TIME		LABOR TIME
7500 Mile Service (C)		**37500 Mile Service (C)**		**75000 Mile Service (C)**	
All Models	1.8	All Models	1.5	All Models	.9
15000 Mile Service (C)		**45000 Mile Service (C)**		**82500 Mile Service (C)**	
All Models	.9	All Models	.9	All Models	1.5
22500 Mile Service (C)		**52500 Mile Service (C)**		**90000 Mile Service (B)**	
All Models	1.5	All Models	1.5	All Models	2.9
30000 Mile Service (B)		**60000 Mile Service (B)**		**97500 Mile Service (C)**	
All Models	2.9	All Models	2.9	All Models	1.5
		67500 Mile Service (C)			
		All Models	1.5		

93061CM5

GENERAL MOTORS G-BODY
Buick Rivera • Oldsmobile Aurora

ENGINE AND VEHICLE IDENTIFICATION

		Engine						Model Year	
Code ①	Liters (cc)	Cu. In.	Cyl.	Fuel Sys.	Engine Type	Eng. Mfg.		Code ②	Year
H	3.5 (3475)	212	6	SFI	DOHC	BOC		V	1997
1 ③	3.8 (3785)	231	6	MFI	OHV	BOC		W	1998
C	4.0 (3995)	244	8	MFI	DOHC	BOC		X	1999
K	3.8 (3785)	231	6	MFI	OHV	BOC		1	2001

NOTE: Oldsmobile did not market an Aurora for 2000.

DOHC: Double Overhead Camshafts

OHV: Overhead Valves

MFI: Multi-point Fuel Injection

SFI: Sequential Fuel Injection

BOC: Buick/Oldsmobile/Cadillac

① 8th position of VIN

② 10th position of VIN

③ Supercharged Engine

93061CM6

GENERAL ENGINE SPECIFICATIONS

Year	Model	Engine Displacement Liters (cc)	Engine Series (ID/VIN)	Fuel System	Net Horsepower @ rpm	Net Torque @ rpm (ft. lbs.)	Bore x Stroke (in.)	Com-pression Ratio	Oil Pressure @ rpm
1997	Aurora	4.0 (3995)	C	MFI	250@5600	245@4400	3.43x3.31	10.2:1	30@2000
	Riviera	3.8 (3785) ①	1	MFI	225@5000	275@3200	3.80x3.40	9.0:1	60@1850
		3.8 (3785)	K	MFI	205@5200	230@4000	3.80x3.40	9.4:1	60@1850
1998	Aurora	4.0 (3995)	C	MFI	250@5600	245@4400	3.43x3.31	10.2:1	30@2000
	Riviera	3.8 (3785) ①	1	MFI	225@5000	275@3200	3.80x3.40	9.0:1	60@1850
		3.8 (3785)	K	MFI	205@5200	230@4000	3.80x3.40	9.4:1	60@1850
1999	Aurora	4.0 (3995)	C	MFI	250@5600	245@4400	3.43x3.31	10.2:1	30@2000
2001	Aurora	3.5 (3475)	H	SFI	215@5600	230@4400	3.52x3.62	9.3:1	30@2000
		4.0 (3995)	C	SFI	250@5600	260@4000	3.43x3.31	10.2:1	30@2000

MFI: Multi-point Fuel Injection

SFI: Sequential Fuel Injection

① Supercharged Engine

93061CM7

Ignition system service is covered in the model specific sections of this manual

ENGINE TUNE-UP SPECIFICATIONS

Year	Engine Displacement Liters (cc)	Engine ID/VIN	Spark Plug Gap (in.)	Ignition Timing (deg.)	Fuel Pump (psi)	Idle Speed (rpm)	Valve Clearance	
							Intake	Exhaust
1997	3.8 (3785)	1	0.060	①	40–47	②	HYD	HYD
	3.8 (3785)	K	0.060	①	40–47	②	HYD	HYD
	4.0 (3995)	C	0.050	①	41–47	②	HYD	HYD
1998	3.8 (3785)	1	0.060	①	40–47	②	HYD	HYD
	3.8 (3785)	K	0.060	①	40–47	②	HYD	HYD
	4.0 (3995)	C	0.050	①	41–47	②	HYD	HYD
1999	4.0 (3995)	C	0.050	①	41–47	②	HYD	HYD
2001	3.5 (3475)	H	0.050	①	41–47	②	HYD	HYD
	4.0 (3995)	C	0.050	①	41–47	②	HYD	HYD

NOTE: The Vehicle Emission Control Information label often reflects specification changes made during production. The label figures must be used if they differ from those in this chart.

HYD: Hydraulic

① DIS Ignition System timing is not adjustable

② Idle speed is maintained by the ECM. There is no recommended adjustment procedure

93061CM8

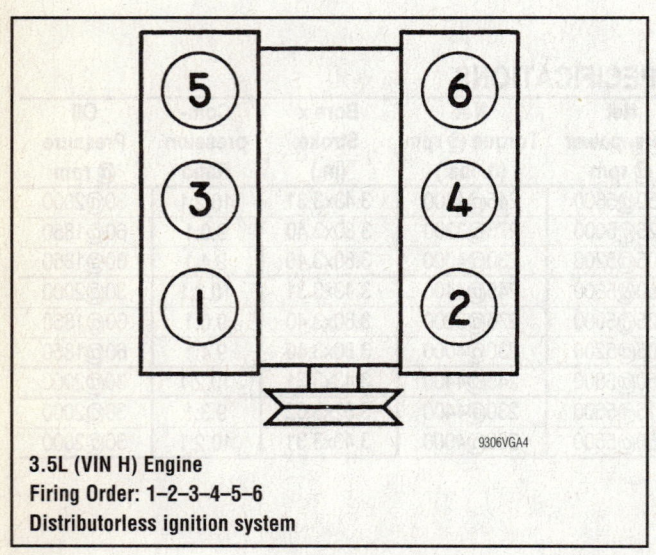

3.5L (VIN H) Engine
Firing Order: 1–2–3–4–5–6
Distributorless ignition system

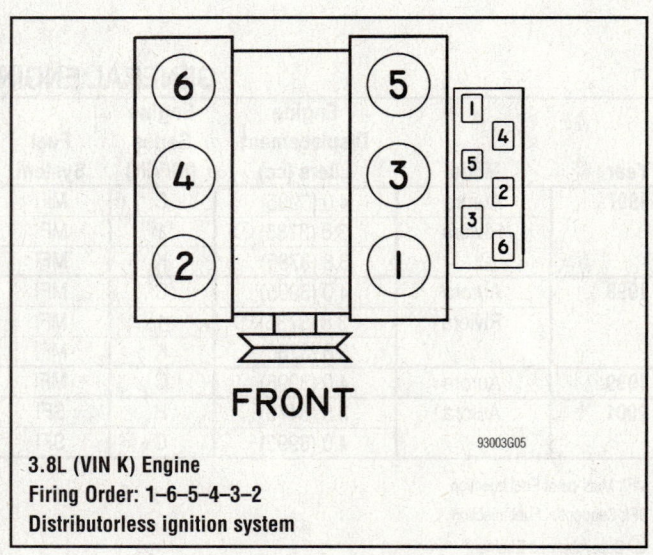

3.8L (VIN K) Engine
Firing Order: 1–6–5–4–3–2
Distributorless ignition system

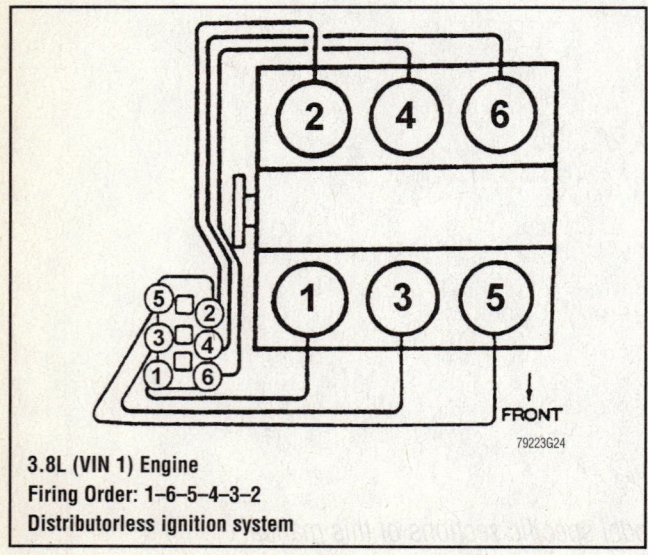

3.8L (VIN 1) Engine
Firing Order: 1–6–5–4–3–2
Distributorless ignition system

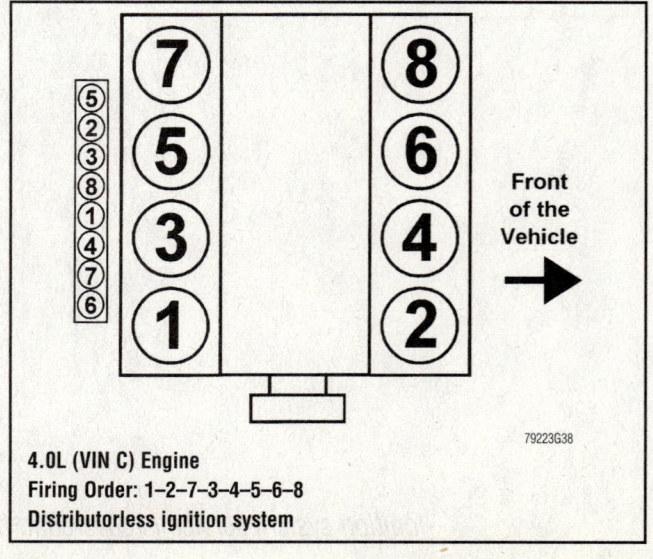

4.0L (VIN C) Engine
Firing Order: 1–2–7–3–4–5–6–8
Distributorless ignition system

CAPACITIES

Year	Model	Engine Displacement Liters (cc)	Engine ID/VIN	Engine Oil with Filter (qts.)	Transmission (pts.)	Fuel Tank (gal.)	Cooling System (qts.)
1997	Aurora	4.0 (3995)	C	7.5	6.5	20.0	13.0
	Riviera	3.8 (3785)	1	5.0	12.0	20.0	13.0
		3.8 (3785)	K	4.5	12.0	20.0	13.0
1998	Aurora	4.0 (3995)	C	7.5	6.5	20.0	13.0
	Riviera	3.8 (3785)	1	5.0	12.0	20.0	13.0
		3.8 (3785)	K	4.5	12.0	20.0	13.0
1999	Aurora	4.0 (3995)	C	7.5	6.5	20.0	13.0
2001	Aurora	3.5 (3475)	H	6.0	12.0	18.5	13.0
		4.0 (3995)	C	7.5	6.5	17.5	13.0

NOTE: All capacities are approximate. Add fluid gradually and ensure a proper fluid level is obtained.

93061CM9

VALVE SPECIFICATIONS

Year	Engine Displacement Liters (cc)	Engine ID/VIN	Seat Angle (deg.)	Face Angle (deg.)	Spring Test Pressure (lbs. @ in.)	Spring Installed Height (in.)	Stem-to-Guide Clearance (in.) Intake	Stem-to-Guide Clearance (in.) Exhaust	Stem Diameter (in.) Intake	Stem Diameter (in.) Exhaust
1997	3.8 (3785)	1	45	45	210@1.315	1.690-1.720	0.0015-0.0035	0.0015-0.0032	NA	NA
	3.8 (3785)	K	45	45	210@1.315	1.690-1.720	0.0015-0.0035	0.0015-0.0032	NA	NA
	4.0 (3995)	C	46	45	92@0.854	1.190	0.0010-0.0030	0.0020-0.0040	NA	NA
1998	3.8 (3785)	1	45	45	210@1.315	1.690-1.720	0.0015-0.0035	0.0015-0.0032	NA	NA
	3.8 (3785)	K	45	45	210@1.315	1.690-1.720	0.0015-0.0035	0.0015-0.0032	NA	NA
	4.0 (3995)	C	46	45	92@0.854	1.190	0.0010-0.0030	0.0020-0.0040	NA	NA
1999	4.0 (3995)	C	46	45	92@0.854	1.190	0.0010-0.0030	0.0020-0.0040	NA	NA
2001	3.5 (3475)	H	45.75	45	136@0.964	1.377	0.0010-0.0030	0.0020-0.0040	0.233-0.234	0.233-0.234
	4.0 (3995)	C	46	45	92@0.854	1.190	0.0010-0.0030	0.0020-0.0040	NA	NA

NA: Not Available

93061CM0

CRANKSHAFT AND CONNECTING ROD SPECIFICATIONS

All measurements are given in inches.

Year	Engine Displacement Liters (cc)	Engine ID/VIN	Crankshaft Main Brg. Journal Dia.	Crankshaft Main Brg. Oil Clearance	Crankshaft Shaft End-play	Crankshaft Thrust on No.	Connecting Rod Journal Diameter ①	Connecting Rod Oil Clearance	Connecting Rod Side Clearance
1997	3.8 (3785)	1	2.4988-2.4998	0.0008-0.0022	0.0030-0.0110	2	2.3738-2.3745	0.0005-0.0026	0.0030-0.0150
	3.8 (3785)	K	2.4988-2.4998	0.0008-0.0022	0.0030-0.0110	2	2.3738-2.3745	0.0005-0.0026	0.0030-0.0150
	4.0 (3995)	C	2.5335-2.5337	0.0006-0.0025	0.0020-0.0200	2	2.2490	0.0010-0.0030	0.0080-0.0200
1998	3.8 (3785)	1	2.4988-2.4998	0.0008-0.0022	0.0030-0.0110	2	2.3738-2.3745	0.0005-0.0026	0.0030-0.0150
	3.8 (3785)	K	2.4988-2.4998	0.0008-0.0022	0.0030-0.0110	2	2.3738-2.3745	0.0005-0.0026	0.0030-0.0150
	4.0 (3995)	C	2.5335-2.5337	0.0006-0.0025	0.0020-0.0200	2	2.2490	0.0010-0.0030	0.0080-0.0200
1999	4.0 (3995)	C	2.5335-2.5337	0.0006-0.0025	0.0020-0.0200	2	2.2490	0.0010-0.0030	0.0080-0.0200
2001	3.5 (3475)	H	2.7550-2.7560	0.0006-0.0021	0.0050-0.0200	3	2.1829-2.1835	0.0009-0.0025	0.0040-0.0130
	4.0 (3995)	C	2.5335-2.5337	0.0006-0.0025	0.0020-0.0200	2	2.2490	0.0010-0.0030	0.0080-0.0200

① Large end of connecting rod ID

93061CN1

PISTON AND RING SPECIFICATIONS
All measurements are given in inches.

Year	Engine ID/VIN	Engine Displacement Liters (cc)	Piston Clearance	Ring Gap			Ring Side Clearance		
				Top Compression	Bottom Compression	Oil Control	Top Compression	Bottom Compression	Oil Control
1997	3.8 (3785)	1	0.0004-0.0020	0.012-0.022	0.030-0.040	0.010-0.030	0.0013-0.0031	0.0013-0.0031	0.0009-0.0079
	3.8 (3785)	K	0.0004-0.0020	0.012-0.022	0.030-0.040	0.010-0.030	0.0013-0.0031	0.0013-0.0031	0.0009-0.0079
	4.0 (3995)	C	0.0008-0.0020	0.010-0.016	0.014-0.020	0.010-0.030	0.0016-0.0037	0.0016-0.0037	side-sealing
1998	3.8 (3785)	1	0.0004-0.0020	0.012-0.022	0.030-0.040	0.010-0.030	0.0013-0.0031	0.0013-0.0031	0.0009-0.0079
	3.8 (3785)	K	0.0004-0.0020	0.012-0.022	0.030-0.040	0.010-0.030	0.0013-0.0031	0.0013-0.0031	0.0009-0.0079
	4.0 (3995)	C	0.0008-0.0020	0.010-0.016	0.014-0.020	0.010-0.030	0.0016-0.0037	0.0016-0.0037	side-sealing
1999	4.0 (3995)	C	0.0008-0.0020	0.010-0.016	0.014-0.020	0.010-0.030	0.0016-0.0037	0.0016-0.0037	side-sealing
2001	3.5 (3475)	H	0.0010-0.0025	0.008-0.018	0.014-0.020	0.010-0.030	0.0016-0.0037	0.0016-0.0037	side-sealing
	4.0 (3995)	C	0.0008-0.0020	0.010-0.016	0.014-0.020	0.010-0.030	0.0016-0.0037	0.0016-0.0037	side-sealing

93061CN2

Refer to the model specific sections for engine mechanical service procedures

TORQUE SPECIFICATIONS
All readings in ft. lbs.

Year	Engine Displacement Liters (cc)	Engine ID/VIN	Cylinder Head Bolts	Main Bearing Bolts	Rod Bearing Bolts	Crankshaft Damper Bolts	Flywheel Bolts	Manifold Intake	Manifold Exhaust	Spark Plugs	Lug Nuts
1997	3.8 (3786)	1	①	②	③	④	⑤	⑥	22	11	100
	3.8 (3786)	K	①	⑦	③	④	⑤	11	38	11	100
	4.0 (3995)	C	⑧	⑨	⑩	⑪	⑤	89	18	⑫	100
1998	3.8 (3786)	1	①	②	③	④	⑤	⑥	22	11	100
	3.8 (3786)	K	①	⑦	③	④	⑤	11	38	11	100
	4.0 (3995)	C	⑧	⑨	⑩	⑪	⑤	89	18	⑫	100
1999	4.0 (3995)	C	⑧	⑨	⑩	⑪	⑤	89	18	⑫	100
2001	3.5 (3475)	H	⑬	⑭	⑮	⑯	⑤	5	18	11	100
	4.0 (3995)	C	⑧	⑨	⑩	⑪	⑤	89	18	⑫	100

① Step 1: 36 ft. lbs.
  Step 2: 130 degrees
  Step 3: Plus 30 degrees additional on four center bolts
  (NOTE: Must use new bolts)

② Step 1: Tighten caps in equil increments to 53 ft. lbs.
  Step 2: Loosen 360 degrees
  Step 3: 15 ft. lbs.
  Step 4: 54 ft. lbs.
  Step 5: Plus 3 turns of 35 degrees-total of 105 degrees

③ Step 1: 20 ft. lbs.
  Step 2: 50 degrees

④ Step 1: 110 ft. lbs.
  Step 2: 76 degrees

⑤ Step 1: 11 ft. lbs.
  Step 2: 50 degrees

⑥ Upper manifold: 8 ft. lbs.
  Lower manifold: 11 ft. lbs.

⑦ Step 1: 26 ft. lbs.
  Step 2: 90 degrees

⑧ Step 1: 22 ft. lbs.
  Step 2: 90 degrees
  Step 3: 75 degrees

⑨ Step 1: 15 ft. lbs.
  Step 2: 65 degrees

⑩ Step 1: 18 ft. lbs.
  Step 2: 90 degrees

⑪ Step 1: 44 ft. lbs.
  Step 2: 120 degrees

⑫ New cylinder head 1st time installation: 20 ft. lbs.
  All others: 11 ft. lbs.

⑬ Step 1: 22 ft. lbs.
  Step 2: 60 degrees
  Step 3: 60 degrees
  Step 4: 80 degrees

⑭ Cap Bolts
  Step 1: 15 ft. lbs.
  Step 2: 70 degrees
  Permiter bolts: 22 ft. lbs.

⑮ Step 1: 22 ft. lbs.
  Step 2: Loosen completely
  Step 3: 18 ft. lbs.
  Step 4: 110 degrees

⑯ Step 1: 37 ft. lbs.
  Step 2: 150 degrees

93061CN3

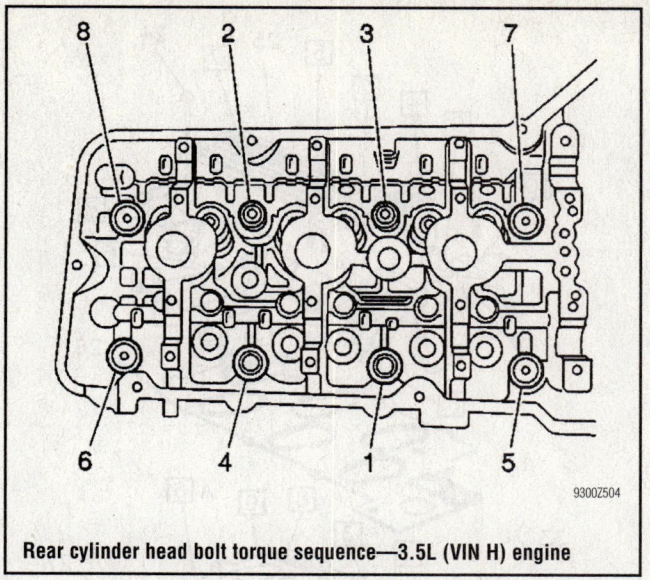

Rear cylinder head bolt torque sequence—3.5L (VIN H) engine

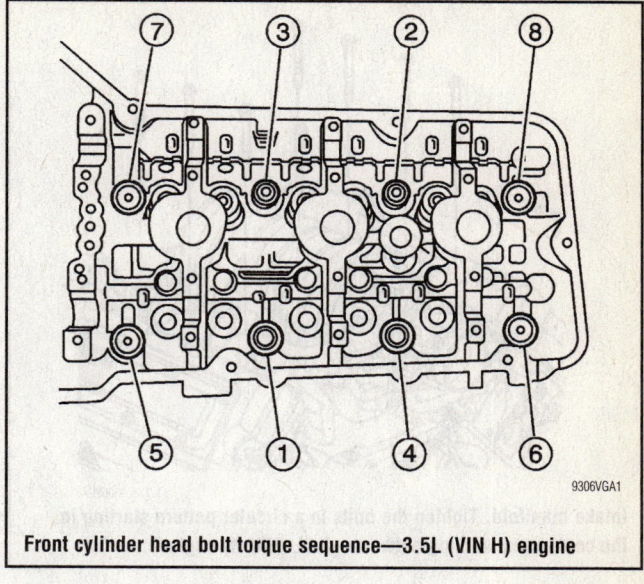

Front cylinder head bolt torque sequence—3.5L (VIN H) engine

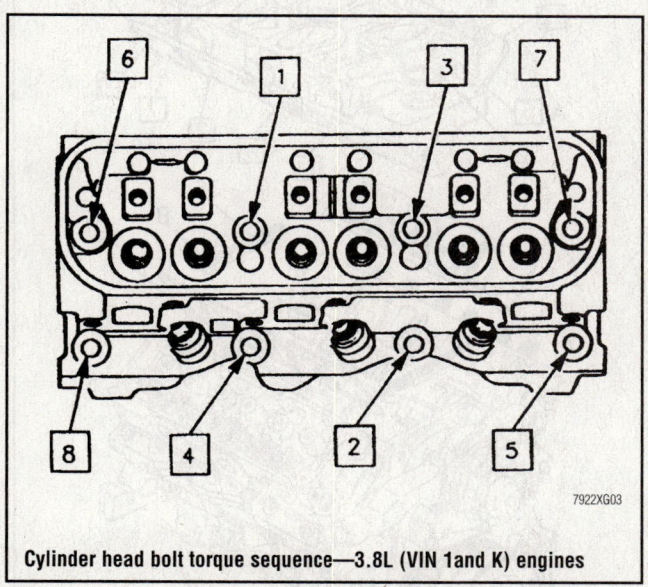

Cylinder head bolt torque sequence—3.8L (VIN 1and K) engines

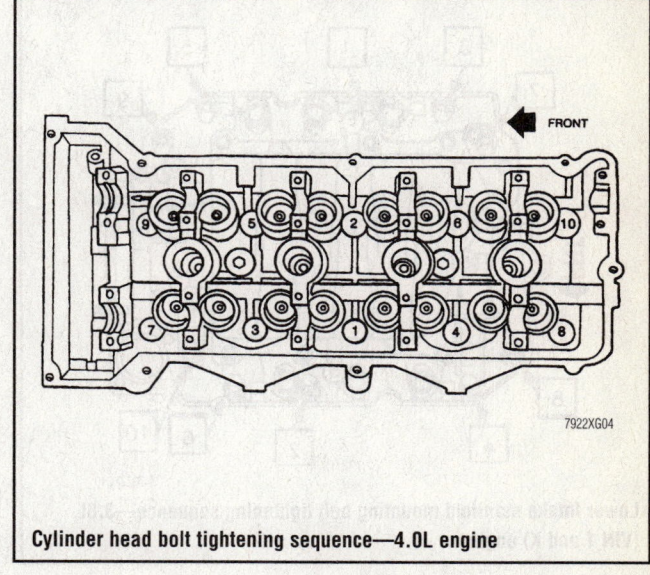

Cylinder head bolt tightening sequence—4.0L engine

Refer to the model specific sections for fuel system service procedures

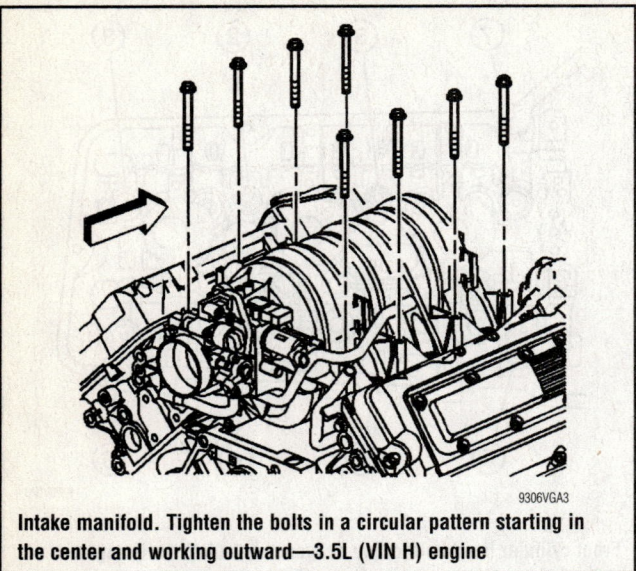

Intake manifold. Tighten the bolts in a circular pattern starting in the center and working outward—3.5L (VIN H) engine

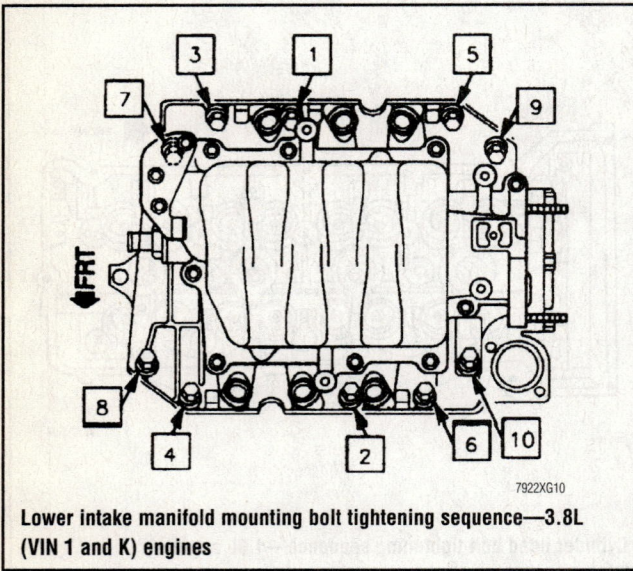

Lower intake manifold mounting bolt tightening sequence—3.8L (VIN 1 and K) engines

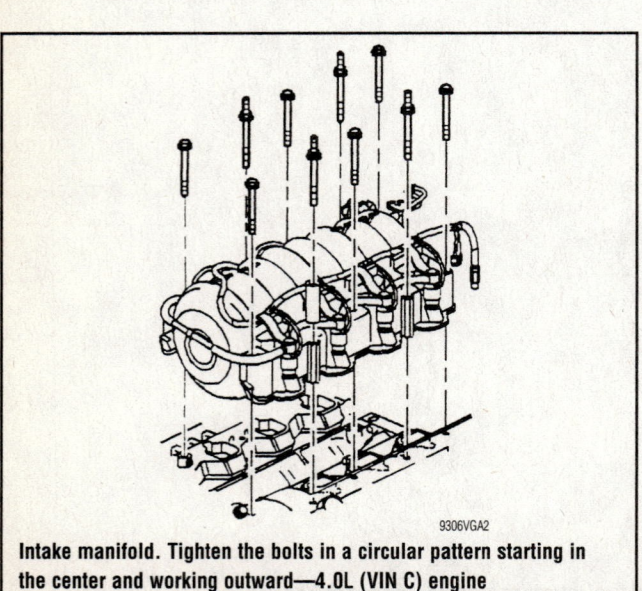

Intake manifold. Tighten the bolts in a circular pattern starting in the center and working outward—4.0L (VIN C) engine

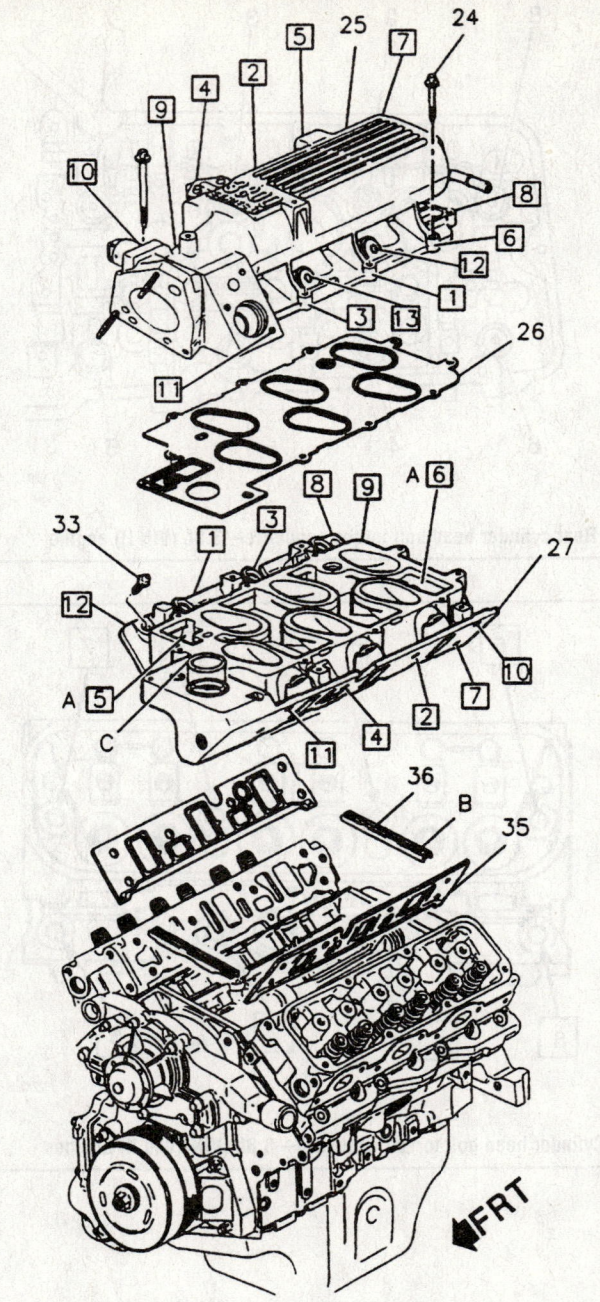

A TWO HIDDEN INTAKE MANIFOLD BOLT/SCREWS
B APPLY GM P/N 9985675 TO BOTH ENDS OF SEAL
C SEAL, LOWER INTAKE MANIFOLD AND GASKET
24 BOLT/SCREW, UPPER INTAKE MANIFOLD
25 MANIFOLD, UPPER INTAKE
26 GASKET, UPPER INTAKE MAINFOLD
27 MANIFOLD, LOWER INTAKE
33 BOLT/SCREW, LOWER INTAKE MANIFOLD
35 GASKET, LOWER INTAKE MANIFOLD GASKET
36 SEAL, INTAKE MANIFOLD
☐ NUMBER IN BOX IDENTIFY TIGHTENING SEQUENCE

Exploded view of the upper intake plenum showing the torque sequence—3.8L (VIN K) engine

BRAKE SPECIFICATIONS
All measurements in inches unless noted

Year	Model		Brake Disc Original Thickness	Brake Disc Minimum Thickness	Brake Disc Maximum Run-out	Minimum Lining Thickness	Brake Caliper Mounting Bolt (ft. lbs.)
1997	Aurora	F	1.260	1.209	0.002	0.030	38
		R	0.433	0.374	0.002	0.030	20
	Riviera	F	1.260	1.209	0.002	0.030	38
		R	0.433	0.374	0.002	0.030	20
1998	Aurora	F	1.260	1.209	0.002	0.030	38
		R	0.433	0.374	0.002	0.030	20
	Riviera	F	1.260	1.209	0.002	0.030	38
		R	0.433	0.374	0.002	0.030	20
1999	Aurora	F	1.260	1.209	0.002	0.030	38
		R	0.433	0.374	0.002	0.030	20
2001	Aurora	F	1.260	1.209	0.002	0.030	38
		R	0.433	0.374	0.002	0.030	20

F: Front

R: Rear

93061CN4

Refer to the model specific sections for engine electrical system service procedures

SCHEDULED MAINTENANCE INTERVALS
(GM G BODY—BUICK RIVIERA & OLDSMOBILE AURORA)

TO BE SERVICED	TYPE OF SERVICE	VEHICLE MILEAGE INTERVAL (x1000)												
		7.5	15	22.5	30	37.5	45	52.5	60	67.5	75	82.5	90	97.5
Engine oil & filter	R	✓	✓	✓	✓	✓	✓	✓	✓	✓	✓	✓	✓	✓
Coolant level, hoses & clamps	S/I	✓	✓	✓	✓	✓	✓	✓	✓	✓	✓	✓	✓	✓
Drive shaft boots & front suspension components	S/I													
Exhaust system & brake hoses	S/I	✓	✓	✓	✓	✓	✓	✓	✓	✓	✓	✓	✓	✓
Lubricate chassis, suspension, steering linkage, transaxle shift linkage, parking brake cable guides, underbody contact points & linkage	S/I	✓	✓	✓	✓	✓	✓	✓	✓	✓	✓	✓	✓	✓
Throttle linkage	S/I	✓	✓	✓	✓	✓	✓	✓	✓	✓	✓	✓	✓	✓
Brake linings	S/I	✓		✓		✓		✓		✓		✓		✓
Rotate tires	S/I	✓		✓		✓		✓		✓		✓		✓
Air filter element	R				✓				✓				✓	
Engine coolant ①	R													
Spark plugs ②	R				✓				✓				✓	
Accessory drive belt(s)	S/I				✓				✓				✓	
Automatic transaxle fluid & filter	S/I				✓				✓				✓	
Fuel system	S/I				✓				✓				✓	
Ignition cables	R				✓				✓				✓	

93061CN5

SCHEDULED MAINTENANCE INTERVALS
(GM G BODY - BUICK RIVIERA & OLDSMOBILE AURORA) (Cont.)

TO BE SERVICED	TYPE OF SERVICE	VEHICLE MILEAGE INTERVAL (x1000)												
		7.5	15	22.5	30	37.5	45	52.5	60	67.5	75	82.5	90	97.5
Inspect throttle body bore & throttle plate for deposits (Oldsmobile)	S/I		✓				✓				✓			
Supercharger oil	S/I				✓				✓				✓	

R: Replace   S/I: Service or Inspect

① Engine coolant: replace every 100,000 miles. Use O.E. specified (DEX-COOL™) coolant only. If any silicate coolant is used, the service interval is every 30,000 miles.

② Platinum tip spark plugs: replace every 100,000 miles.

FREQUENT OPERATION MAINTENANCE (SEVERE SERVICE)

If a vehicle is operated under any of the following conditions it is considered severe service:

- Extremely dusty areas.

- 50% or more of the vehicle operation is in 32°C (90°F) or higher temperatures, or constant operation in temperatures below 0°C (32°F).

- Prolonged idling (vehicle operation in stop and go traffic).

- Frequent short running periods (engine does not warm to normal operating temperatures).

- Police, taxi, delivery usage or trailer towing usage.

CV joints & front suspension components: service or inspect every 3000 miles.

Engine oil & filter change: change every 3000 miles.

Brake linings: check every 6000 miles.

Chassis lubrication: lubricate every 6000 miles.

Suspension, steering linkage, transaxle shift linkage, parking cable guides, underbody contact points: lubricate every 6000 miles.

Throttle body mount bolt torque: tighten at 6000 miles.

Air filter element: service or inspect every 15,000 miles.

Automatic transaxle fluid: change every 50,000 miles (1997).

Inspect throttle body bore & throttle plate for deposits: clean as required every 15,000 miles.

Rotate tires at 6000 miles, then every 15,000 miles.

93061CN6

For accessory drive belt replacement procedures see the model specific sections of this manual

SCHEDULED MAINTENANCE INTERVALS
GENERAL MOTORS CORPORATION
G BODY
BUICK RIVIERA
OLDSMOBILE AURORA

The following should be used as a guide when determining the amount of work required for a particular service. In estimating how long a particular Scheduled Maintenance Service should take, please observe the following:

- Labor Time is time based on field research and data supplied by the vehicle manufacturer.
- Labor time operations are given in hours and tenths of an hour.
- All labor operations are to be used as a guide.

Mechanic Skill Level Codes:
(A) PRECISION: Highly skilled with multiple certification.
(B) GENERAL: Normally skilled with certification.
(C) MAINTENANCE: Semi-skilled working on certification.

	LABOR TIME		LABOR TIME		LABOR TIME
7500 Mile Service (B)		**37500 Mile Service (B)**		**75000 Mile Service (C)**	
All Models	2.0	All Models	1.7	All Models	.9
15000 Mile Service (C)		**45000 Mile Service (C)**		*Inspect throttle body for*	
All Models	.9	All Models	.9	*deposits add*	.1
Inspect throttle body for		*Inspect throttle body for*		**82500 Mile Service (B)**	
deposits add	.1	*deposits add*	.1	All Models	1.7
22500 Mile Service (B)		**52500 Mile Service (B)**		**90000 Mile Service (B)**	
All Models	1.9	All Models	1.9	All Models	3.1
30000 Mile Service (B)		**60000 Mile Service (B)**		**97500 Mile Service (B)**	
All Models	3.1	All Models	3.1	All Models	1.8
		67500 Mile Service (B)			
		All Models	1.8		

93061CN7

GENERAL MOTORS J-BODY
Chevrolet Cavalier • Pontiac Sunfire

ENGINE AND VEHICLE IDENTIFICATION CHART

Code ①	Liters (cc)	Cu. In.	Cyl.	Fuel Sys.	Engine Type	Eng. Mfg.
4	2.2 (2180)	133	4	MFI	OHV	CUS
T	2.4 (2392)	146	4	MFI	DOHC	CUS

Code ②	Year
V	1997
W	1998
X	1999
Y	2000
1	2001

CUS: Chevrolet/United States

MFI: Multi-point Fuel Injection

OHV: Overhead Valves

DOHC: Double Overhead Camshafts

① 8th position of VIN

② 10th position of VIN

93061C09

GENERAL ENGINE SPECIFICATIONS

Year	Model	Engine Displacement Liters (cc)	Engine Series (ID/VIN)	Fuel System	Net Horsepower @ rpm	Net Torque @ rpm (ft. lbs.)	Bore x Stroke (in.)	Compression Ratio	Oil Pressure @ rpm
1997	Cavalier	2.2 (2180)	4	MFI	120@5200	130@3200	3.50x3.46	9.0:1	56@3000
		2.4 (2392)	T	MFI	150@6000	155@4400	3.54x3.70	9.5:1	30@3000
	Sunfire	2.2 (2180)	4	MFI	120@5200	130@3200	3.50x3.46	9.0:1	56@3000
		2.4 (2392)	T	MFI	150@6000	155@4400	3.54x3.70	9.5:1	30@3000
1998	Cavalier	2.2 (2180)	4	MFI	120@5200	130@3200	3.50x3.46	9.0:1	56@3000
		2.4 (2392)	T	MFI	150@6000	155@4400	3.54x3.70	9.5:1	30@3000
	Sunfire	2.2 (2180)	4	MFI	120@5200	130@3200	3.50x3.46	9.0:1	56@3000
		2.4 (2392)	T	MFI	150@6000	155@4400	3.54x3.70	9.5:1	30@3000
1999	Cavalier	2.2 (2180)	4	MFI	120@5200	130@3200	3.50x3.46	9.0:1	56@3000
		2.4 (2392)	T	MFI	150@6000	155@4400	3.54x3.70	9.5:1	30@3000
	Sunfire	2.2 (2180)	4	MFI	120@5200	130@3200	3.50x3.46	9.0:1	56@3000
		2.4 (2392)	T	MFI	150@6000	155@4400	3.54x3.70	9.5:1	30@3000
2000-01	Cavalier	2.2 (2180)	4	MFI	115@5000	136@3600	3.50x3.46	9.0:1	56@3000
		2.4 (2392)	T	MFI	150@5600	155@4400	3.54x3.70	9.5:1	30@3000
	Sunfire	2.2 (2180)	4	MFI	115@5000	136@3600	3.50x3.46	9.0:1	56@3000
		2.4 (2392)	T	MFI	150@5600	155@4400	3.54x3.70	9.5:1	30@3000

MFI: Multi-point Fuel Injection

93061C00

For brake related suspension and axle service, refer to the model specific sections of this manual

ENGINE TUNE-UP SPECIFICATIONS

Year	Engine Displacement Liters (cc)	Engine ID/VIN	Spark Plug Gap (in.)	Ignition Timing (deg.)	Fuel Pump (psi)	Idle Speed (rpm)	Valve Clearance Intake	Valve Clearance Exhaust
1997	2.2 (2180)	4	0.060	①	41-47	①	HYD	HYD
	2.4 (2392)	T	0.060	①	41-47	①	HYD	HYD
1998	2.2 (2180)	4	0.060	①	41-47	①	HYD	HYD
	2.4 (2392)	T	0.060	①	41-47	①	HYD	HYD
1999	2.2 (2180)	4	0.060	①	41-47	①	HYD	HYD
	2.4 (2392)	T	0.060	①	41-47	①	HYD	HYD
2000-01	2.2 (2180)	4	0.060	①	41-47	①	HYD	HYD
	2.4 (2392)	T	0.060	①	41-47	①	HYD	HYD

NOTE: The Vehicle Emission Control Information label often reflects specification changes made during production. The label figures must be used if they differ from those in this chart.

HYD: Hydraulic

① Refer to Vehicle Emission Control Information label

93061CP1

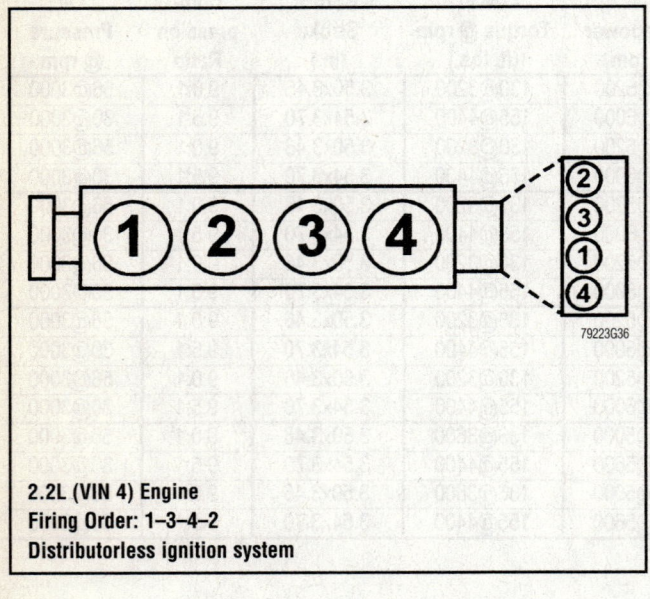

2.2L (VIN 4) Engine
Firing Order: 1–3–4–2
Distributorless ignition system

79223G36

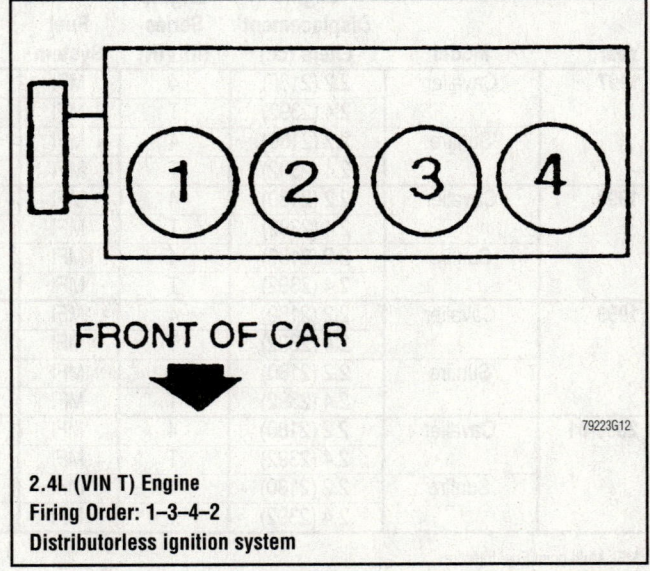

FRONT OF CAR

2.4L (VIN T) Engine
Firing Order: 1–3–4–2
Distributorless ignition system

79223G12

CAPACITIES

Year	Model	Engine Displacement Liters (cc)	Engine ID/VIN	Engine Oil with Filter (qts.)	Transmission (pts.) Manual	Transmission (pts.) Auto.	Fuel Tank (gal.)	Cooling System (qts.)
1997	Cavalier	2.2 (2180)	4	4.0	4.0	①	15.2	10.5
		2.4 (2392)	T	4.5	4.0	①	15.2	10.5
	Sunfire	2.2 (2180)	4	4.0	4.0	①	15.2	10.5
		2.4 (2392)	T	4.5	4.0	①	15.2	10.5
1998	Cavalier	2.2 (2180)	4	4.0	4.0	①	15.2	10.5
		2.4 (2392)	T	4.5	4.0	①	15.2	10.5
	Sunfire	2.2 (2180)	4	4.0	4.0	①	15.2	10.5
		2.4 (2392)	T	4.5	4.0	①	15.2	10.5
1999	Cavalier	2.2 (2180)	4	4.0	4.0	①	15.2	10.5
		2.4 (2392)	T	4.5	4.0	①	15.2	10.5
	Sunfire	2.2 (2180)	4	4.0	4.0	①	15.2	10.5
		2.4 (2392)	T	4.5	4.0	①	15.2	10.5
2000-01	Cavalier	2.2 (2180)	4	4.0	4.0	①	15.2	9.6
		2.4 (2392)	T	4.5	4.0	①	15.2	9.9
	Sunfire	2.2 (2180)	4	4.0	4.0	①	15.2	9.6
		2.4 (2392)	T	4.5	4.0	①	15.2	9.9

NOTE: All capacities are approximate. Add fluid gradually and ensure a proper fluid level is obtained.

① 3 Speed: 8.0 pts.
   4 Speed: 14.8 pts.

93061CP2

Refer to the model specific sections for driveline service procedures

VALVE SPECIFICATIONS

Year	Engine Displacement Liters (cc)	Engine ID/VIN	Seat Angle (deg.)	Face Angle (deg.)	Spring Test Pressure (lbs. @ in.)	Spring Installed Height (in.)	Stem-to-Guide Clearance (in.)		Stem Diameter (in.)	
							Intake	Exhaust	Intake	Exhaust
1997	2.2 (2180)	4	46	45	75-81@1.71	1.710	0.0010-0.0027	0.0014-0.0031	NA	NA
	2.4 (2392)	T	45	46	50-55@1.44	1.437	0.0009-0.0025	0.0016-0.0032	0.2331-0.2339	0.2326-0.2334
1998	2.2 (2180)	4	46	45	72-81@1.60	1.600	0.0007-0.0020	0.0014-0.0029	0.2740-0.2743	0.2731-0.2736
	2.4 (2392)	T	45	46	50-55@1.44	1.437	0.0009-0.0025	0.0016-0.0032	0.2331-0.2339	0.2326-0.2334
1999	2.2 (2180)	4	46	45	72-81@1.60	1.600	0.0007-0.0020	0.0014-0.0029	0.2740-0.2743	0.2731-0.2736
	2.4 (2392)	T	45	46	50-55@1.44	1.437	0.0009-0.0025	0.0016-0.0032	0.2331-0.2339	0.2326-0.2334
2000-01	2.2 (2180)	4	46	45	72-81@1.60	1.600	0.0007-0.0020	0.0014-0.0029	0.2740-0.2743	0.2731-0.2736
	2.4 (2392)	T	45	46	50-55@1.44	1.437	0.0009-0.0025	0.0016-0.0032	0.2331-0.2339	0.2326-0.2334

NA: Not Available

93061CP3

CRANKSHAFT AND CONNECTING ROD SPECIFICATIONS
All measurements are given in inches.

Year	Engine Displacement Liters (cc)	Engine ID/VIN	Crankshaft				Connecting Rod		
			Main Brg. Journal Dia.	Main Brg. Oil Clearance	Shaft End-play	Thrust on No.	Journal Diameter	Oil Clearance	Side Clearance
1997	2.2 (2180)	4	2.4945-2.4954	0.0006-0.0019	0.0020-0.0070	4	1.9983-1.9994	0.0010-0.0030	0.0039-0.0149
	2.4 (2392)	T	2.3634- -2.3636	0.0005-0.0030	0.0034-0.0095	3	1.8887-1.8897	0.0005-0.0020	0.0059-0.0177
1998	2.2 (2180)	4	2.4945-2.4954	0.0006-0.0019	0.0020-0.0070	4	1.9983-1.9994	0.0010-0.0030	0.0039-0.0149
	2.4 (2392)	T	2.3612-2.3631	0.0004-0.0023	0.0034-0.0095	3	1.8887-1.8897	0.0004-0.0026	0.0059-0.0177
1999	2.2 (2180)	4	2.4945-2.4954	0.0006-0.0019	0.0020-0.0070	4	1.9983-1.9994	0.0010-0.0030	0.0039-0.0149
	2.4 (2392)	T	2.3612-2.3631	0.0004-0.0023	0.0034-0.0095	3	1.8887-1.8897	0.0004-0.0026	0.0059-0.0177
2000-01	2.2 (2180)	4	2.4945-2.4954	0.0006-0.0019	0.0020-0.0070	4	1.9983-1.9994	0.0010-0.0030	0.0039-0.0149
	2.4 (2392)	T	2.3612-2.3631	0.0004-0.0023	0.0034-0.0095	3	1.8887-1.8897	0.0004-0.0026	0.0059-0.0177

93061CP4

For exhaust manifold replacement procedures, see the model specific sections of this manual

PISTON AND RING SPECIFICATIONS
All measurements are given in inches.

Year	Engine Displacement Liters (cc)	Engine ID/VIN	Piston Clearance	Ring Gap			Ring Side Clearance		
				Top Compression	Bottom Compression	Oil Control	Top Compression	Bottom Compression	Oil Control
1997	2.2 (2180)	4	0.0007-0.0017	0.0100-0.0200	0.0100-0.0200	0.0100-0.0400	0.0019-0.0027	0.0019-0.0027	0.0019-0.0082
	2.4 (2392)	T	0.0006-0.0018	0.0060-0.0120	0.0120-0.0160	0.0157-0.0551	0.0016-0.0031	0.0012-0.0028	NA
1998	2.2 (2180)	4	0.0006-0.0018	0.0100-0.0200	0.0100-0.0200	0.0100-0.0500	0.0011-0.0019	0.0011-0.0019	0.0019-0.0082
	2.4 (2392)	T	0.0006-0.0015	0.0060-0.0120	0.0098-0.0157	0.0098-0.0299	0.0016-0.0031	0.0012-0.0028	NA
1999	2.2 (2180)	4	0.0006-0.0018	0.0100-0.0200	0.0100-0.0200	0.0100-0.0500	0.0011-0.0019	0.0011-0.0019	0.0019-0.0082
	2.4 (2392)	T	0.0006-0.0015	0.0060-0.0120	0.0098-0.0157	0.0098-0.0299	0.0016-0.0031	0.0012-0.0028	NA
2000-01	2.2 (2180)	4	0.0006-① 0.0018	0.0100-0.0200	0.0120-0.0177	0.0100-0.0300	0.0020-0.0035	0.0016-0.0031	0.0005-0.0087
	2.4 (2392)	T	0.0006-② 0.0009	0.0060-0.0120	0.0098-0.0157	0.0098-0.0299	0.0016-0.0031	0.0012-0.0028	NA

① 42.7mm from top of piston

② 42.7mm from top of piston

93061CP5

TORQUE SPECIFICATIONS
All readings in ft. lbs.

Year	Engine Displacement Liters (cc)	Engine ID/VIN	Cylinder Head Bolts	Main Bearing Bolts	Rod Bearing Bolts	Crankshaft Damper Bolts	Flywheel Bolts	Manifold		Spark Plugs	Lug Nuts
								Intake	Exhaust		
1997	2.2 (2180)	4	①	70	38	77 ②	55	③	18	13	100
	2.4 (2392)	T	④	⑤	⑥	⑦	⑧	⑨	⑩	13	100
1998	2.2 (2180)	4	①	70	38	77 ②	55	⑪	18	13	100
	2.4 (2392)	T	④	⑤	⑥	⑦	⑧	⑨	⑩	13	100
1999	2.2 (2180)	4	①	70	38	77 ②	55	⑪	18	13	100
	2.4 (2392)	T	④	⑤	⑥	⑦	⑧	⑨	⑩	13	100
2000-01	2.2 (2180)	4	①	70	38	77 ②	55	⑪	18	13	100
	2.4 (2392)	T	④	⑤	⑥	⑦	⑧	⑨	⑩	13	100

NA: Not Available

① Step 1: Long bolts: 46 ft. lbs.
  Step 2: Short bolts: 43 ft. lbs.
  Step 3: Long bolts an additional 90 degree turn
  Step 4: Short bolts an additional 90 degree turn

② Center bolt spec shown; Pulley-to-hub bolts: 37 ft. lbs.

③ Lower nuts: 24 ft. lbs.
  Lower studs: 89 inch lbs.
  Upper bolts: 22 ft. lbs.

④ Step 1: bolts 1-8; 40 ft. lbs.
  Step 2: bolts 9-10: 30 ft. lbs.
  Step 3: An additional 90 degree turn

⑤ 15 ft. lbs. plus 90 degrees

⑥ 18 ft. lbs. plus 80 degrees

⑦ 129 ft. lbs. plus 90 degrees

⑧ 22 ft. lbs. plus 45 degrees

⑨ Nuts: 18 ft. lbs.
  Studs: 97 inch lbs.

⑩ Nuts: 31 ft. lbs.
  Studs: 97 inch lbs.

⑪ Bolts: 17 ft. lbs.
  Nuts: 17 ft. lbs.
  Studs: 9 ft. lbs.

93061CP6

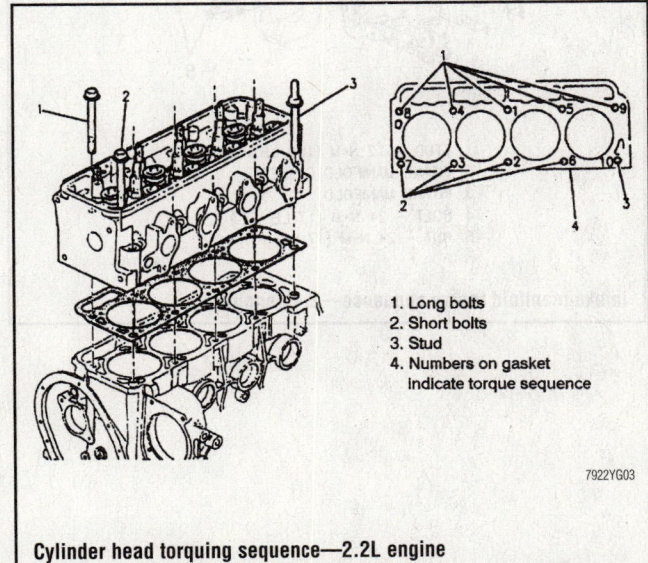

1. Long bolts
2. Short bolts
3. Stud
4. Numbers on gasket indicate torque sequence

7922YG03

Cylinder head torquing sequence—2.2L engine

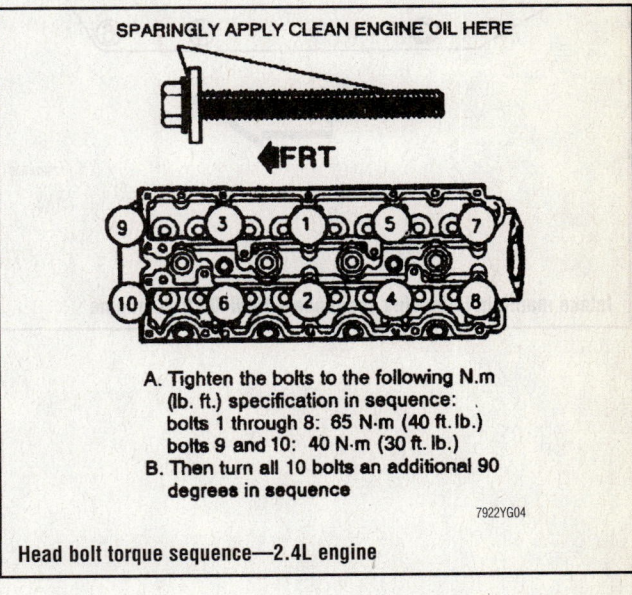

SPARINGLY APPLY CLEAN ENGINE OIL HERE

◄FRT

A. Tighten the bolts to the following N·m (lb. ft.) specification in sequence:
  bolts 1 through 8: 65 N·m (40 ft. lb.)
  bolts 9 and 10: 40 N·m (30 ft. lb.)
B. Then turn all 10 bolts an additional 90 degrees in sequence

7922YG04

Head bolt torque sequence—2.4L engine

Refer to the model specific sections for cooling system service procedures

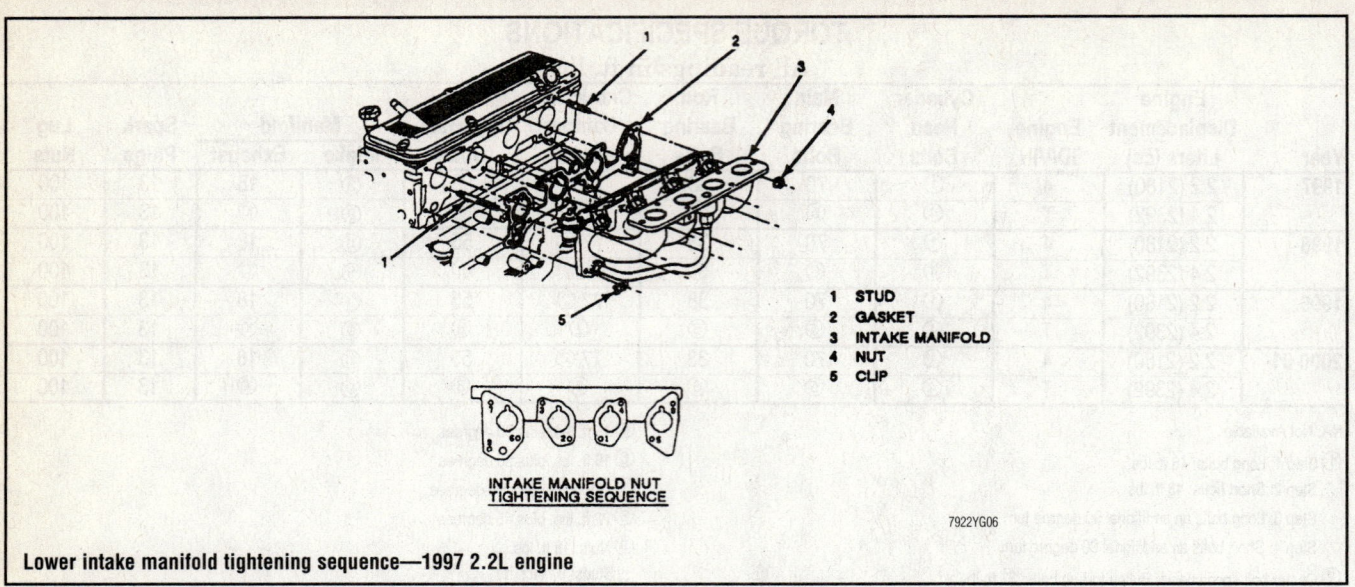

1 STUD
2 GASKET
3 INTAKE MANIFOLD
4 NUT
5 CLIP

INTAKE MANIFOLD NUT
TIGHTENING SEQUENCE

7922YG06

Lower intake manifold tightening sequence—1997 2.2L engine

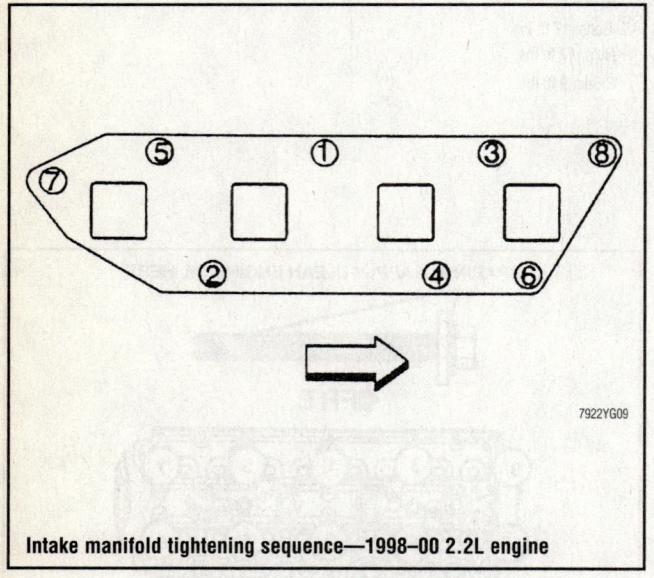

7922YG09

Intake manifold tightening sequence—1998–00 2.2L engine

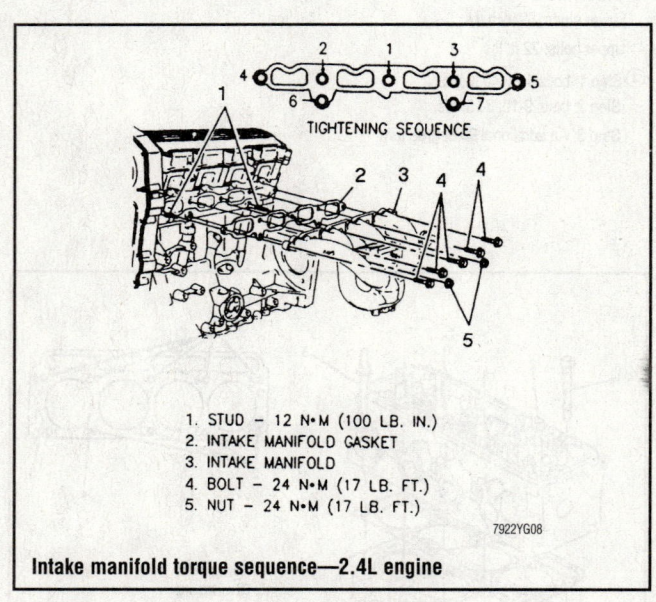

TIGHTENING SEQUENCE

1. STUD – 12 N•M (100 LB. IN.)
2. INTAKE MANIFOLD GASKET
3. INTAKE MANIFOLD
4. BOLT – 24 N•M (17 LB. FT.)
5. NUT – 24 N•M (17 LB. FT.)

7922YG08

Intake manifold torque sequence—2.4L engine

BRAKE SPECIFICATIONS
All measurements in inches unless noted

| Year | Model | Brake Disc | | | Brake Drum | | | Minimum Lining Thickness | | Brake Caliper Mounting Bolts (ft. lbs.) |
		Original Thickness	Minimum Thickness	Maximum Run-out	Original Inside Diameter	Max. Wear Limit	Maximum Machine Diameter	Front	Rear	
1997	Cavalier	0.786	0.736	0.003	7.880	7.930	7.900	0.030	0.030	38
	Sunfire	0.786	0.736	0.003	7.880	7.930	7.900	0.030	0.030	38
1998	Cavalier	0.786	0.736	0.003	7.880	7.930	7.900	0.030	0.030	38
	Sunfire	0.786	0.736	0.003	7.880	7.930	7.900	0.030	0.030	38
1999	Cavalier	0.786	0.736	0.003	7.880	7.930	7.900	0.030	0.030	38
	Sunfire	0.786	0.736	0.003	7.880	7.930	7.900	0.030	0.030	38
2000-01	Cavalier	0.786	0.736	0.003	NA	8.909	8.879	0.030	0.030	38
	Sunfire	0.786	0.736	0.003	NA	8.909	8.879	0.030	0.030	38

NA: Not Available

93061CP7

SCHEDULED MAINTENANCE INTERVALS
(GM J BODY—CHEVROLET CAVALIER & PONTIAC SUNFIRE)

TO BE SERVICED	TYPE OF SERVICE	VEHICLE MILEAGE INTERVAL (x1000)												
		7.5	15	22.5	30	37.5	45	52.5	60	67.5	75	82.5	90	97.5
Engine oil & filter	R	✓	✓	✓	✓	✓	✓	✓	✓	✓	✓	✓	✓	✓
Exhaust system & brake hoses	S/I	✓	✓	✓	✓	✓	✓	✓	✓	✓	✓	✓	✓	✓
Drive shaft boots & front suspension components	S/I	✓	✓	✓	✓	✓	✓	✓	✓	✓	✓	✓	✓	✓
Coolant level, hoses & clamps	S/I	✓	✓	✓	✓	✓	✓	✓	✓	✓	✓	✓	✓	✓
Throttle linkage	S/I	✓	✓	✓	✓	✓	✓	✓	✓	✓	✓	✓	✓	✓
Lubricate chassis, suspension, steering linkage, transaxle shift linkage, parking brake cable guides, underbody contact points & linkage	S/I	✓	✓	✓	✓	✓	✓	✓	✓	✓	✓	✓	✓	✓
Brake linings & rotate tires	S/I	✓		✓		✓		✓		✓		✓		✓
Automatic transmission fluid & filter ①	S/I													
Air filter element & PCV filter	R				✓				✓				✓	
Engine coolant ②	R													
Spark plugs ③	R				✓				✓				✓	
Accessory drive belt(s)	R				✓				✓				✓	
EGR & fuel systems	S/I				✓				✓				✓	
Ignition cables	S/I				✓				✓				✓	

R: Replace   S/I: Service or Inspect

① Automatic transaxle fluid & filter: replace at 100,000 miles (if not changed previously).

② Engine coolant: replace every 100,000 miles. Use O.E. specified (DEX-COOL™) coolant only. If any silicate coolant is used, the service interval is every 30,000 miles.

③ Platinum tip spark plugs: replace every 100,000 miles.

FREQUENT OPERATION MAINTENANCE (SEVERE SERVICE) ADDITIONS

If a vehicle is operated under any of the following conditions it is considered severe service:

- Towing a trailer or using a camper or car-top carrier.

- Extensive idling or low-speed driving for long distances as in heavy commercial use, such as delivery, taxi or police cars.

- Operating on rough, muddy or salt-covered roads.

- Operating on unpaved or dusty roads.

- 50% or more of the vehicle operation is in 32°C (90°F) or higher temperatures, or constant operation in temperatures below 0°C (32°F).

Engine oil and filter: change every 3000 miles or 3 months, whichever occurs first.

Wheels and tires: inspect and rotate every 6000 miles.

Air cleaner element: inspect every 15,000 miles and replace or clean as needed. Replace it at least every 30,000 miles.

Automatic transaxle fluid & filter: replace every 50,000 miles.

93061CP8

SCHEDULED MAINTENANCE INTERVALS
GENERAL MOTORS CORPORATION
J BODY
CHEVROLET CAVALIER
PONTIAC SUNFIRE

The following should be used as a guide when determining the amount of work required for a particular service.
In estimating how long a particular Scheduled Maintenance Service should take, please observe the following:

- Labor Time is time based on field research and data supplied by the vehicle manufacturer.
- Labor time operations are given in hours and tenths of an hour.
- All labor operations are to be used as a guide.

Mechanic Skill Level Codes:
(A) PRECISION: Highly skilled with multiple certification.
(B) GENERAL: Normally skilled with certification.
(C) MAINTENANCE: Semi-skilled working on certification.

	LABOR TIME		LABOR TIME		LABOR TIME
7500 Mile Service (C)		**37500 Mile Service (C)**		**75000 Mile Service (C)**	
All Models	1.6	All Models	1.7	All Models	.9
15000 Mile Service (C)		**45000 Mile Service (C)**		**82500 Mile Service (C)**	
All Models	.9	All Models	.9	All Models	1.6
22500 Mile Service (C)		**52500 Mile Service (C)**		**90000 Mile Service (B)**	
All Models	1.8	All Models	1.8	All Models	4.1
30000 Mile Service (B)		**60000 Mile Service (B)**		**97500 Mile Service (B)**	
All Models	4.1	All Models	4.1	All Models	2.4
		67500 Mile Service (C)			
		All Models	1.8		

93061CP9

Timing chain and gear service is covered in the model specific sections of this manual

GENERAL MOTORS L/N-BODY
Chevrolet Malibu • Oldsmobile Cutlass

ENGINE AND VEHICLE IDENTIFICATION

Engine								Model Year	
Code ①	Liters (cc)	Cu. In.	Cyl.	Fuel Sys.	Engine Type	Eng. Mfg.		Code ②	Year
M	3.1 (3130)	191	6	SFI	OHV	BOC		V	1997
T	2.4 (2392)	146	4	SFI	DOHC	CUS		W	1998
								X	1999
								Y	2000
								1	2001

BOC: Buick/Oldsmobile/Cadillac
CUS: Chevrolet/United States
SF: Sequential Fuel Injection
① 8th position of VIN
② 10th position of VIN

93061CR1

GENERAL ENGINE SPECIFICATIONS

Year	Model	Engine Displacement Liters (cc)	Engine Series (ID/VIN)	Fuel System	Net Horsepower @ rpm	Net Torque @ rpm (ft. lbs.)	Bore x Stroke (in.)	Compression Ratio	Oil Pressure @ rpm
1997	Cutlass	3.1 (3130)	M	SFI	160@5200	185@4000	3.50x3.31	9.5:1	15@1100
	Malibu	3.1 (3130)	M	SFI	160@5200	185@4000	3.50x3.31	9.5:1	15@1100
	Malibu	2.4 (2392)	T	SFI	150@6000	150@5600	3.54x3.70	9.5:1	30@3000
1998	Cutlass	3.1 (3130)	M	SFI	160@5200	185@4000	3.50x3.31	9.5:1	15@1100
	Malibu	3.1 (3130)	M	SFI	160@5200	185@4000	3.50x3.31	9.5:1	15@1100
	Malibu	2.4 (2392)	T	SFI	150@6000	150@5600	3.54x3.70	9.5:1	30@3000
1999	Cutlass	3.1 (3130)	M	SFI	160@5200	185@4000	3.50x3.31	9.5:1	15@1100
	Malibu	3.1 (3130)	M	SFI	160@5200	185@4000	3.50x3.31	9.5:1	15@1100
	Malibu	2.4 (2392)	T	SFI	150@6000	150@5600	3.54x3.70	9.5:1	30@3000
2000-01	Malibu	3.1 (3130)	M	SFI	170@5200	190@4000	3.50x3.31	9.6:1	15@1100

SFI: Multi-point Fuel Injection

93061CR2

ENGINE TUNE-UP SPECIFICATIONS

Year	Engine Displacement Liters (cc)	Engine ID/VIN	Spark Plug Gap (in.)	Ignition Timing (deg.)		Fuel Pump (psi)	Idle Speed (rpm)		Valve Clearance	
				MT	AT		MT	AT	In.	Ex.
1997	2.4 (2392)	T	0.035	①	①	41–47	①	①	HYD	HYD
	3.1 (3130)	M	0.060	①	①	41–47	①	①	HYD	HYD
1998	2.4 (2392)	T	0.035	①	①	41–47	①	①	HYD	HYD
	3.1 (3130)	M	0.060	①	①	41–47	①	①	HYD	HYD
1999	2.4 (2392)	T	0.035	①	①	41–47	①	①	HYD	HYD
	3.1 (3130)	M	0.060	①	①	41–47	①	①	HYD	HYD
2000-01	3.1 (3130)	M	0.060	①	①	41–47	①	①	HYD	HYD

NOTE: The Vehicle Emission Control Information label often reflects specification changes made during production. The label figures must be used if they differ from those in this chart.

HYD: Hydraulic

① Refer to Vehicle Emission Control Information label.

93061CR3

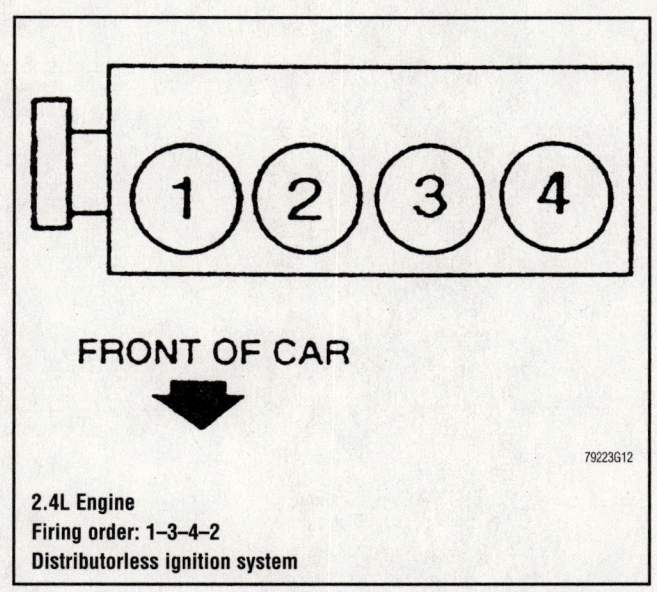

2.4L Engine
Firing order: 1–3–4–2
Distributorless ignition system

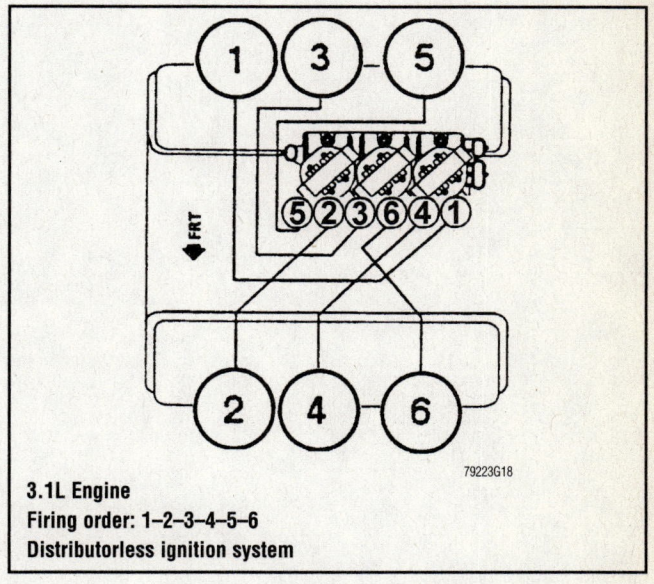

3.1L Engine
Firing order: 1–2–3–4–5–6
Distributorless ignition system

Ignition system service is covered in the model specific sections of this manual

CAPACITIES

Year	Model	Engine Displacement Liters (cc)	Engine ID/VIN	Engine Oil with Filter (qts.)	Transmission (pts.)	Fuel Tank (gal.)	Cooling System (qts.)
1997	Cutlass	3.1 (3130)	M	4.0	14.8	15.2	13.6
	Malibu	3.1 (3130)	M	4.0	14.8	15.2	13.6
	Malibu	2.4 (2392)	T	4.0	14.8	15.2	11.3
1998	Cutlass	3.1 (3130)	M	4.0	14.8	15.2	13.6
	Malibu	3.1 (3130)	M	4.0	14.8	15.2	13.6
	Malibu	2.4 (2392)	T	4.0	14.8	15.2	11.3
1999	Cutlass	3.1 (3130)	M	4.0	14.8	15.2	13.6
	Malibu	3.1 (3130)	M	4.0	14.8	15.2	13.6
	Malibu	2.4 (2392)	T	4.0	14.8	15.2	11.3
2000-01	Malibu	3.1 (3130)	M	4.5	13.8	15.0	13.6

NOTE: All capacities are approximate. Add fluid gradually and ensure a proper fluid level is obtained.

93061CR4

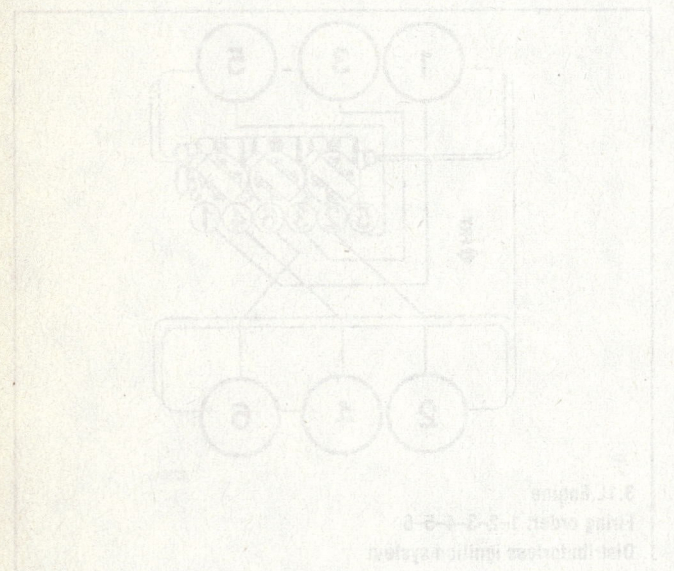

VALVE SPECIFICATIONS

Year	Engine Displacement Liters (cc)	Engine ID/VIN	Seat Angle (deg.)	Face Angle (deg.)	Spring Test Pressure (lbs. @ in.)	Spring Installed Height (in.)	Stem-to-Guide Clearance (in.)		Stem Diameter (in.)	
							Intake	Exhaust	Intake	Exhaust
1997	2.4 (2392)	T	45	46	50-55@ 1.437	1.437	0.0009-0.0025	0.0016-0.0032	0.2331-0.2339	0.2326-0.2334
	3.1 (3130)	M	45	45	230@1.260	1.701	0.0010-0.0027	0.0010-0.0027	NA	NA
1998	2.4 (2392)	T	45	46	50-55@ 1.437	1.437	0.0009-0.0025	0.0016-0.0032	0.2331-0.2339	0.2326-0.2334
	3.1 (3130)	M	45	45	230@1.260	1.701	0.0010-0.0027	0.0010-0.0027	NA	NA
1999	2.4 (2392)	T	45	46	50-55@ 1.437	1.437	0.0009-0.0025	0.0016-0.0032	0.2331-0.2339	0.2326-0.2334
	3.1 (3130)	M	45	45	230@1.260	1.701	0.0010-0.0027	0.0010-0.0027	NA	NA
2000-01	3.1 (3130)	M	45	45	230@1.260	1.701	0.0010-0.0027	0.0010-0.0027	NA	NA

NA: Not Available

93061CR5

CRANKSHAFT AND CONNECTING ROD SPECIFICATIONS
All measurements are given in inches.

| Year | Engine Displacement Liters (cc) | Engine ID/VIN | Crankshaft | | | | Connecting Rod | | |
			Main Brg. Journal Dia.	Main Brg. Oil Clearance	Shaft End-play	Thrust on No.	Journal Diameter	Oil Clearance	Side Clearance
1997	2.4 (2392)	T	2.3622-2.3631	0.0004-0.0023	0.0034-0.0095	3	1.8887-1.8897	0.0004-0.0026	0.0059-0.0177
	3.1 (3130)	M	2.6473-2.6383	0.0008- ① 0.0025	0.0024-0.0083	3	1.9987-1.9994	0.0007-0.0024	0.0070-0.0170
1998	2.4 (2392)	T	2.3622-2.3631	0.0004-0.0023	0.0034-0.0095	3	1.8887-1.8897	0.0004-0.0026	0.0059-0.0177
	3.1 (3130)	M	2.6473-2.6383	0.0008- ① 0.0025	0.0024-0.0083	3	1.9987-1.9994	0.0007-0.0024	0.0070-0.0170
1999	2.4 (2392)	T	2.3622-2.3631	0.0004-0.0023	0.0034-0.0095	3	1.8887-1.8897	0.0004-0.0026	0.0059-0.0177
	3.1 (3130)	M	2.6473-2.6383	0.0008- ① 0.0025	0.0024-0.0083	3	1.9987-1.9994	0.0007-0.0024	0.0070-0.0170
2000-01	3.1 (3130)	M	2.6473-2.6383	0.0008- ① 0.0025	0.0024-0.0083	3	1.9987-1.9994	0.0007-0.0024	0.0070-0.0170

① Thrust bearing: 0.0012 - 0.0030

93061CR6

PISTON AND RING SPECIFICATIONS

All measurements are given in inches.

Year	Engine Displacement Liters (cc)	Engine ID/VIN	Piston Clearance	Ring Gap			Ring Side Clearance		
				Top Compression	Bottom Compression	Oil Control	Top Compression	Bottom Compression	Oil Control
1997	2.4 (2392)	T	0.0006-0.0015	0.006-0.012	0.010-0.016	0.010-0.030	0.0016-0.0031	0.0012-0.0028	0.0005-0.0089
	3.1 (3130)	M	0.0013-0.0027	0.006-0.014	0.020-0.028	0.010-0.050	0.0020-0.0033	0.0020-0.0035	0.0080
1998	2.4 (2392)	T	0.0006-0.0015	0.006-0.012	0.010-0.016	0.010-0.030	0.0016-0.0031	0.0012-0.0028	0.0005-0.0089
	3.1 (3130)	M	0.0013-0.0027	0.006-0.014	0.020-0.028	0.010-0.050	0.0020-0.0033	0.0020-0.0035	0.0080
1999	2.4 (2392)	T	0.0006-0.0015	0.006-0.012	0.010-0.016	0.010-0.030	0.0016-0.0031	0.0012-0.0028	0.0005-0.0089
	3.1 (3130)	M	0.0013-0.0027	0.006-0.014	0.020-0.028	0.010-0.050	0.0020-0.0033	0.0020-0.0035	0.0080
2000-01	3.1 (3130)	M	0.0013-0.0027	0.006-0.014	0.020-0.028	0.010-0.050	0.0020-0.0033	0.0020-0.0035	0.0080

93061CR7

Refer to the model specific sections for engine mechanical service procedures

TORQUE SPECIFICATIONS
All readings in ft. lbs.

Year	Engine Displacement Liters (cc)	Engine ID/VIN	Cylinder Head Bolts	Main Bearing Bolts	Rod Bearing Bolts	Crankshaft Damper Bolts	Flywheel Bolts	Manifold Intake	Manifold Exhaust	Spark Plug	Lug Nut
1997	2.4 (2392)	T	①	②	③	④	⑤	19	31	16	100
	3.1 (3130)	M	⑥	⑦	⑧	76	52	⑨	12	⑩	100
1998	2.4 (2392)	T	①	②	③	④	⑤	19	31	16	100
	3.1 (3130)	M	⑥	⑦	⑧	76	52	⑨	12	⑩	100
1999	2.4 (2392)	T	①	②	③	④	⑤	19	31	16	100
	3.1 (3130)	M	⑥	⑦	⑧	76	52	⑨	12	⑩	100
2000-01	3.1 (3130)	M	⑥	⑦	⑧	76	52	⑨	12	⑩	100

NA: Not Available

① Bolts 1-8: 30 ft. lbs.
  Bolts 9-10: 26 ft. lbs.
  Tighten all bolts an additional 90 degrees
② 15 ft. lbs. plus 90 degrees
③ 18 ft. lbs. plus 80 degrees
④ 129 ft. lbs. plus 90 degrees
⑤ 22 ft. lbs. plus 45 degrees

⑥ Coat threads with sealer and torque to 37 ft. lbs.,
  then turn 1/4 turn (90 degrees)
⑦ 37 ft. lbs. plus 75 degrees
⑧ 15 ft. lbs. plus 75 degrees
⑨ Lower intake manifold bolts: 10 ft. lbs.
  Upper intake manifold bolts: 18 ft. lbs.
⑩ New cylinder first-time installation: 21 ft. lbs.
  All others: 11 ft. lbs.

93061CR8

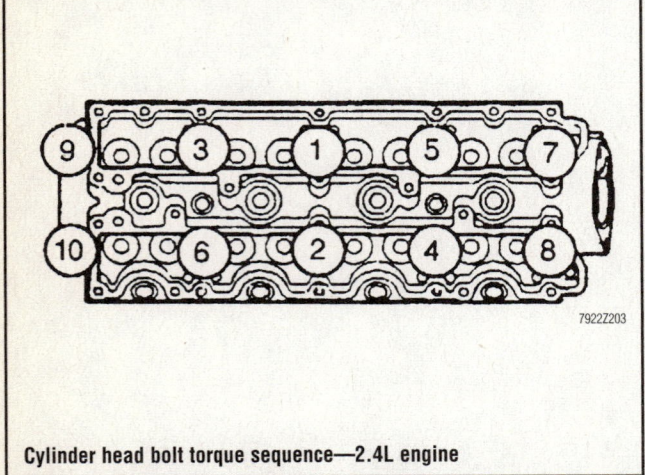

Cylinder head bolt torque sequence—2.4L engine

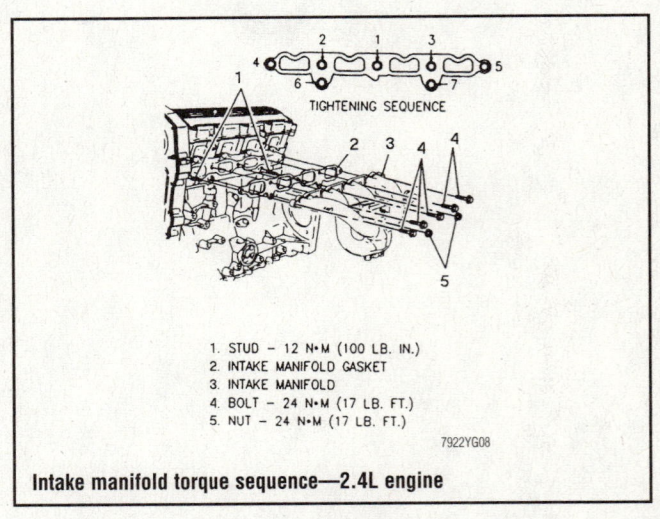

1. STUD – 12 N•M (100 LB. IN.)
2. INTAKE MANIFOLD GASKET
3. INTAKE MANIFOLD
4. BOLT – 24 N•M (17 LB. FT.)
5. NUT – 24 N•M (17 LB. FT.)

Intake manifold torque sequence—2.4L engine

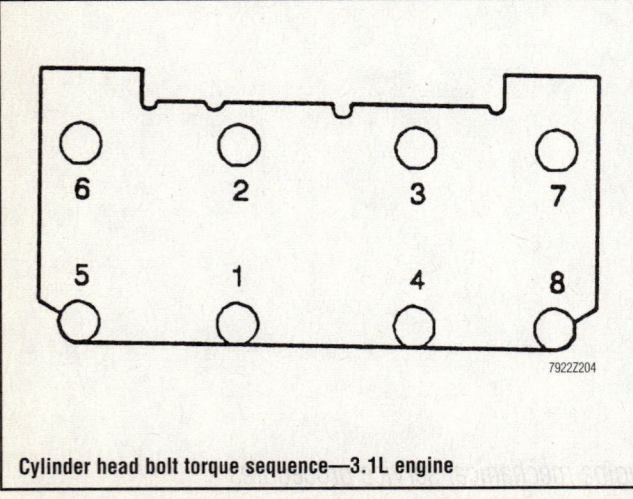

Cylinder head bolt torque sequence—3.1L engine

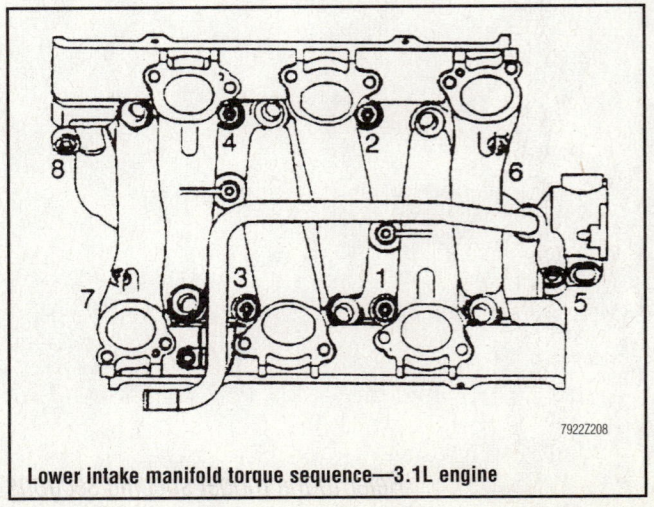

Lower intake manifold torque sequence—3.1L engine

BRAKE SPECIFICATIONS
CHEVROLET MALIBU/OLDSMOBILE CUTLASS
All measurements in inches unless noted

| Year | Model | Brake Disc | | | Brake Drum Diameter | | | Minimum Lining Thickness | | Brake Caliper | |
		Original Thickness	Minimum Thickness	Maximum Runout	Original Inside Diameter	Max. Wear Limit	Maximum Machine Diameter	Front	Rear	Bracket Bolts (ft. lbs.)	Mounting Bolts (ft. lbs.)
1997	Cutlass	1.031	0.987	0.003	8.900-8.909	8.920	8.909	0.030	①	85	23
	Malibu	1.031	0.987	0.003	8.900-8.909	8.920	8.909	0.030	①	85	23
1998	Cutlass	1.031	0.987	0.003	8.900-8.909	8.920	8.909	0.030	①	85	23
	Malibu	1.031	0.987	0.003	8.900-8.909	8.920	8.909	0.030	①	85	23
1999	Cutlass	1.031	0.987	0.003	8.900-8.909	8.920	8.909	0.030	①	85	23
	Malibu	1.031	0.987	0.003	8.900-8.909	8.920	8.909	0.030	①	85	23
2000-01	Malibu	1.031	0.980	0.003	8.900-8.909	8.920	8.909	0.030	①	85	23

① 0.030 over rivet head; If bonded lining, use 0.062 from shoe

93061CR9

Refer to the model specific sections for fuel system service procedures

SCHEDULED MAINTENANCE INTERVALS
(GM L/N BODY—CHEVROLET MALIBU & OLDSMOBILE CUTLASS)

TO BE SERVICED	TYPE OF SERVICE	7.5	15	22.5	30	37.5	45	52.5	60	67.5	75	82.5	90	97.5	100	105	113	120	150
		VEHICLE MILEAGE INTERVAL (x1000)																	
Accessory drive belt(s)	S/I								✓									✓	
Air cleaner element	R				✓				✓				✓					✓	
Cooling system ①	S/I																		✓
Cooling system hoses	S/I																		✓
Engine coolant	R																		✓
Engine oil and filter	R	✓	✓	✓	✓	✓	✓	✓	✓	✓	✓	✓	✓	✓		✓	✓	✓	
Fuel tank, cap & lines	S/I				✓				✓				✓					✓	
Radiator, condenser, pressure cap and neck	C																		✓
Spark plug wires	S/I														✓				
Spark plugs	R														✓				
Tires and wheels ②	S/I	✓	✓	✓	✓	✓	✓	✓	✓	✓	✓	✓	✓	✓		✓	✓	✓	

R: Replace   S/I: Service or Inspect   C: Clean

① Pressure test the cooling system and pressure cap.

② This includes rotating the tires.

FREQUENT OPERATION MAINTENANCE (SEVERE SERVICE) ADDITIONS

If a vehicle is operated under any of the following conditions it is considered severe service:

- Towing a trailer or using a camper or car-top carrier.

- Extensive idling or low-speed driving for long distances as in heavy commercial use, such as delivery, taxi or police cars.

- Operating on rough, muddy or salt-covered roads.

- Operating on unpaved or dusty roads.

- 50% or more of the vehicle operation is in 32°C (90°F) or higher temperatures, or constant operation in temperatures below 0°C (32°F).

Engine oil and filter: change every 3000 miles or 3 months, whichever occurs first.

Wheels and tires: inspect and rotate every 6000 miles.

Air cleaner element: inspect every 15,000 miles and replace or clean as needed. Replace it at least every 30,000 miles.

Automatic transaxle fluid & filter: replace every 50,000 miles.

93061CR0

SCHEDULED MAINTENANCE INTERVALS
GENERAL MOTORS CORPORATION
L/N BODY
CHEVROLET MALIBU
OLDSMOBILE CUTLASS

The following should be used as a guide when determining the amount of work required for a particular service. In estimating how long a particular Scheduled Maintenance Service should take, please observe the following:

- Labor Time is time based on field research and data supplied by the vehicle manufacturer.
- Labor time operations are given in hours and tenths of an hour.
- All labor operations are to be used as a guide.

Mechanic Skill Level Codes:
(A) PRECISION: Highly skilled with multiple certification.
(B) GENERAL: Normally skilled with certification.
(C) MAINTENANCE: Semi-skilled working on certification.

	LABOR TIME		LABOR TIME		LABOR TIME
7500 Mile Service (B)		**52500 Mile Service (C)**		**100000 Mile Service (C)**	
All Models	2.0	All Models	1.8	4 Cyl.	.8
15000 Mile Service (C)		**60000 Mile Service (B)**		V6	1.0
All Models	1.1	All Models	2.8	**105000 Mile Service (C)**	
22500 Mile Service (C)		**67500 Mile Service (C)**		All Models	1.1
All Models	1.8	All Models	1.8	**113000 Mile Service (C)**	
30000 Mile Service (B)		**75000 Mile Service (C)**		All Models	1.1
All Models	2.8	All Models	1.1	**120000 Mile Service (C)**	
37500 Mile Service (C)		**82500 Mile Service (C)**		All Models	2.8
All Models	1.8	All Models	1.8	**150000 Mile Service (C)**	
45000 Mile Service (C)		**90000 Mile Service (B)**		All Models	.8
All Models	1.2	All Models	2.8		
		97500 Mile Service (C)			
		All Models	1.8		

93061CS1

Refer to the model specific sections for engine electrical system service procedures

GENERAL MOTORS N-BODY
Buick Skylark • Oldsmobile Achieva • Alero • Pontiac Grand Am

ENGINE AND VEHICLE IDENTIFICATION

Engine							Model Year	
Code ①	Liters (cc)	Cu. In. (cc)	Cyl.	Fuel Sys.	Engine Type	Eng. Mfg.	Code ②	Year
E	3.4 (3350)	207	4	MFI	OHV	BOC	V	1997
M	3.1 (3130)	191	6	MFI	OHV	BOC	W	1998
T	2.4 (2392)	146	4	MFI	DOHC	CUS	X	1999
							Y	2000
							1	2001

BOC: Buick/Oldsmobile/Cadillac

CUS: Chevrolet/United States

MFI: Multi-point Fuel Injection

① 8th position of VIN

② 10th position of VIN

93061CP0

GENERAL ENGINE IDENTIFICATION

Year	Model	Engine Displacement Liters (cc)	Engine Series (ID/VIN)	Fuel System	Net Horsepower @ rpm	Net Torque @ rpm (ft. lbs.)	Bore x Stroke (in.)	Com-pression Ratio	Oil Pressure @ rpm
1997	Achieva	3.1 (3130)	M	MFI	160@5200	185@4000	3.50x3.31	9.5:1	15@1100
	Achieva	2.4 (2392)	T	MFI	150@6000	150@4400	3.54x3.70	9.5:1	30@3000
	Grand Am	3.1 (3130)	M	MFI	160@5200	185@4000	3.50x3.31	9.5:1	15@1100
	Grand Am	2.4 (2392)	T	MFI	150@6000	150@4400	3.54x3.70	9.5:1	30@3000
	Skylark	3.1 (3130)	M	MFI	160@5200	185@4000	3.50x3.31	9.5:1	15@1100
	Skylark	2.4 (2392)	T	MFI	150@6000	150@4400	3.54x3.70	9.5:1	30@3000
1998	Achieva	3.1 (3130)	M	MFI	160@5200	185@4000	3.50x3.31	9.5:1	15@1100
	Achieva	2.4 (2392)	T	MFI	150@6000	150@4400	3.54x3.70	9.5:1	30@3000
	Grand Am	3.1 (3130)	M	MFI	160@5200	195@4000	3.50x3.31	9.5:1	15@1100
	Grand Am	2.4 (2392)	T	MFI	150@6000	150@4400	3.54x3.70	9.5:1	30@3000
1999	Alero	2.4 (2392)	T	MFI	150@5600	155@4400	3.54x3.70	9.5:1	30@3000
	Alero	3.4 (3934)	E	MFI	170@4800	200@4000	3.62x3.31	9.5:1	15@1100
	Grand Am	2.4 (2392)	T	MFI	150@5600	155@4400	3.54x3.70	9.5:1	30@3000
	Grand Am	3.1 (3130)	M	MFI	160@5200	185@4000	3.50x3.31	9.5:1	15@1100
	Grand Am	3.4 (3934)	E	MFI	170@4800	200@4000	3.62x3.31	9.5:1	15@1100
2000-01	Alero	2.4 (2392)	T	MFI	150@5600	155@4400	3.54x3.70	9.5:1	30@3000
	Alero	3.4 (3934)	E	MFI	170@4800	200@4000	3.62x3.31	9.5:1	15@1100
	Grand Am	2.4 (2392)	T	MFI	150@5600	155@4400	3.54x3.70	9.5:1	30@3000
	Grand Am	3.4 (3934)	E	MFI	170@4800	200@4000	3.62x3.31	9.5:1	15@1100

MFI: Multi-point Fuel Injection

93061CQ1

ENGINE TUNE-UP SPECIFICATIONS

Year	Engine Displacement Liters (cc)	Engine ID/VIN	Spark Plugs Gap (in.)	Ignition Timing (deg.) MT	Ignition Timing (deg.) AT	Fuel Pump (psi)	Idle Speed (rpm) MT	Idle Speed (rpm) AT	Valve Clearance In.	Valve Clearance Ex.
1997	2.4 (2392)	T	0.060	①	①	41-47	①	①	HYD	HYD
	3.1 (3130)	M	0.060	①	①	41-47	①	①	HYD	HYD
1998	2.4 (2392)	T	0.060	①	①	41-47	①	①	HYD	HYD
	3.1 (3130)	M	0.060	①	①	41-47	①	①	HYD	HYD
1999	2.4 (2392)	T	0.060	①	①	41-47	①	①	HYD	HYD
	3.1 (3130)	M	0.060	①	①	41-47	①	①	HYD	HYD
	3.4 (3934)	E	0.060	①	①	41-47	①	①	HYD	HYD
2000-01	2.4 (2392)	T	0.050	①	①	41-47	①	①	HYD	HYD
	3.4 (3934)	E	0.060	①	①	41-47	①	①	HYD	HYD

NOTE: The Vehicle Emission Control Information label often reflects specification changes made during production. The label figures must be used if they differ from those in this chart.

HYD: Hydraulic

① Refer to Vehicle Emission Control Information label

93061CQ2

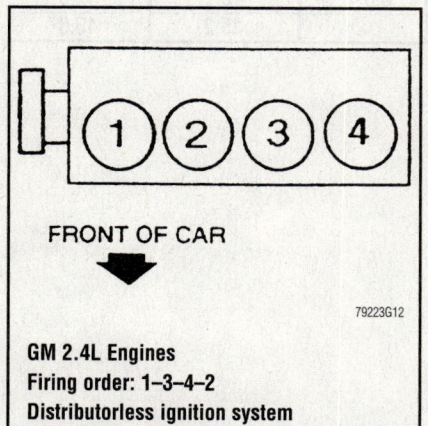

FRONT OF CAR

GM 2.4L Engines
Firing order: 1–3–4–2
Distributorless ignition system

79223G12

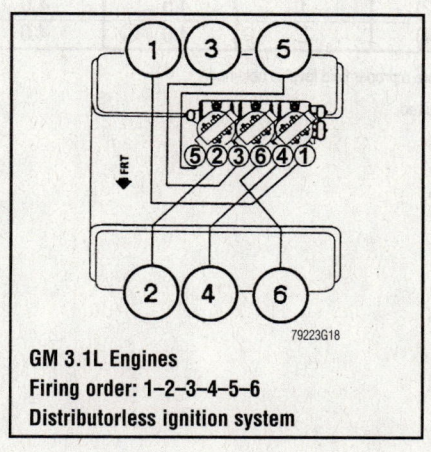

GM 3.1L Engines
Firing order: 1–2–3–4–5–6
Distributorless ignition system

79223G18

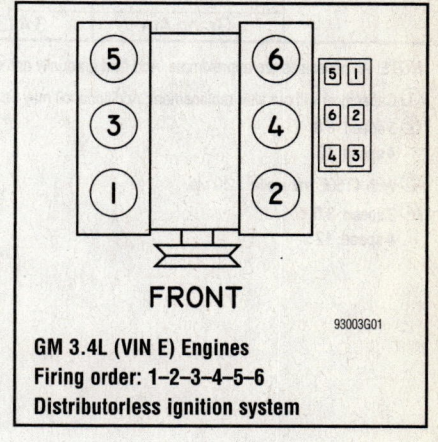

FRONT

GM 3.4L (VIN E) Engines
Firing order: 1–2–3–4–5–6
Distributorless ignition system

93003G01

For accessory drive belt replacement procedures see the model specific sections of this manual

CAPACITIES

Year	Model	Engine Displacement Liters (cc)	Engine ID/VIN	Engine Oil with Filter (qts.)	Transmission (pts.) Manual	Transmission (pts.) Auto.		Fuel Tank (gal.)	Cooling System (qts.)
1997	Achieva	2.4 (2392)	T	4.0 ①	4.0	②		15.2	10.4
	Achieva	3.1 (3130)	M	4.0 ①	4.0	②		15.2	10.8
	Grand Am	2.4 (2392)	- T	4.5	4.0	8.0	③	15.2	10.4
	Grand Am	3.1 (3130)	M	4.5	4.0	8.0	③	15.2	13.1
	Skylark	2.4 (2392)	T	4.0 ①	12.0	8.0	③	15.2	10.4
	Skylark	3.1 (3130)	M	4.0 ①	12.0	8.0	③	15.2	13.1
1998	Achieva	2.4 (2392)	T	4.0 ①	4.0	②		15.2	10.4
	Achieva	3.1 (3130)	M	4.0 ①	4.0	④		15.2	10.8
	Grand Am	2.4 (2392)	T	4.5	4.0	8.0	③	15.2	10.4
	Grand Am	3.1 (3130)	M	4.5	4.0	8.0	③	15.2	13.1
1999	Alero	2.4 (2392)	T	4.0 ①	4.0	②		14.3	11.3
	Alero	3.4 (3934)	E	4.0 ①	4.0	②		14.3	13.6
	Grand Am	2.4 (2392)	T	4.5	4.0	8.0	③	15.2	10.4
	Grand Am	3.1 (3130)	M	4.5	4.0	8.0	③	15.2	11.3
	Grand Am	3.4 (3934)	E	4.0 ①	4.0	②		15.2	13.6
2000-01	Alero	2.4 (2392)	T	4.0 ①	4.0	②		14.3	11.3
	Alero	3.4 (3934)	E	4.0 ①	4.0	②		14.3	13.6
	Grand Am	2.4 (2392)	T	4.5	4.0	8.0	③	15.2	11.3
	Grand Am	3.4 (3934)	E	4.0 ①	4.0	②		15.2	13.6

NOTE: All capacities are approximate. Add fluid gradually and ensure a proper fluid level is obtained.

① Capacity is without filter replacement; Additional oil may be required

② 3 speed: 8.0
   4 speed: 12

③ With 4T60E transaxle: 12.0 pts.

④ 3 speed: 8.0
   4 speed: 12

93061CQ3

VALVE SPECIFICATIONS

Year	Engine Displacement Liters (cc)	Engine ID/VIN	Seat Angle (deg.)	Face Angle (deg.)	Spring Test Pressure (lbs. @ in.)	Spring Installed Height (in.)	Stem-to-Guide Clearance (in.)		Stem Diameter (in.)	
							Intake	Exhaust	Intake	Exhaust
1997	2.4 (2392)	T	45	46	50-55@ 1.437	1.437	0.0009- 0.0025	0.0016- 0.0032	0.2331- 0.2339	0.2326- 0.2334
	3.1 (3130)	M	45	45	250@ 1.239	1.710	0.0010- 0.0027	0.0010- 0.0027	NA	NA
1998	2.4 (2392)	T	45	46	50-55@ 1.437	1.437	0.0009- 0.0025	0.0016- 0.0032	0.2331- 0.2339	0.2326- 0.2334
	3.1 (3130)	M	45	45	250@ 1.239	1.710	0.0010- 0.0027	0.0010- 0.0027	NA	NA
1999	2.4 (2392)	T	45	46	50-55@ 1.437	1.437	0.0009- 0.0025	0.0016- 0.0032	0.2331- 0.2339	0.2326- 0.2334
	3.1 (3130)	M	45	45	250@ 1.239	1.710	0.0010- 0.0027	0.0010- 0.0027	NA	NA
	3.4 (3934)	E	45	45	75@ 1.701	1.701	0.0010- 0.0027	0.0010- 0.0027	NA	NA
2000-01	2.4 (2392)	T	45	46	50-55@ 1.437	1.437	0.0009- 0.0025	0.0016- 0.0032	0.2331- 0.2339	0.2326- 0.2334
	3.4 (3934)	E	45	45	75@ 1.701	1.701	0.0010- 0.0027	0.0010- 0.0027	NA	NA

NA: Not available

93061CQ4

For brake related suspension and axle service, refer to the model specific sections of this manual

CRANKSHAFT AND CONNECTING ROD SPECIFICATIONS
All measurements are given in inches.

Year	Engine Displacement Liters (cc)	Engine ID/VIN	Crankshaft Main Brg. Journal Dia.	Crankshaft Main Brg. Oil Clearance	Crankshaft Shaft End-play	Crankshaft Thrust on No.	Connecting Rod Journal Diameter	Connecting Rod Oil Clearance	Connecting Rod Side Clearance
1997	2.4 (2392)	T	2.3622-2.3631	0.0004-0.0023	0.0034-0.0095	3	1.8887-1.8897	0.0004-0.0026	0.0059-0.0177
	3.1 (3130)	M	2.6473-2.6483	0.0008- ① 0.0025	0.0024-0.0083	3	1.9987-1.9994	0.0007-0.0024	0.0070-0.0170
1998	2.4 (2392)	T	2.3622-2.3631	0.0004-0.0023	0.0034-0.0095	3	1.8887-1.8897	0.0004-0.0026	0.0059-0.0177
	3.1 (3130)	M	2.6473-2.6483	0.0008- ① 0.0025	0.0024-0.0083	3	1.9987-1.9994	0.0007-0.0024	0.0070-0.0170
1999	2.4 (2392)	T	2.3622-2.3631	0.0004-0.0023	0.0034-0.0095	3	1.8887-1.8897	0.0004-0.0026	0.0059-0.0177
	3.1 (3130)	M	2.6473-2.6483	0.0008- ① 0.0025	0.0024-0.0083	3	1.9987-1.9994	0.0007-0.0024	0.0070-0.0170
	3.4 (3934)	E	2.6473-2.6483	0.0008- ① 0.0025	0.0024-0.0083	3	1.9987-1.9994	0.0007-0.0024	0.0070-0.0170
2000-01	2.4 (2392)	T	2.3622-2.3631	0.0004-0.0023	0.0034-0.0095	3	1.8887-1.8897	0.0004-0.0026	0.0059-0.0177
	3.4 (3934)	E	2.6473-2.6483	0.0008- ① 0.0025	0.0024-0.0083	3	1.9987-1.9994	0.0007-0.0024	0.0070-0.0170

① Thrust bearing: 0.0012 - 0.0030

93061CQ5

PISTON AND RING SPECIFICATIONS
All measurements are given in inches.

Year	Engine Displacement Liters (cc)	Engine ID/VIN	Piston Clearance	Ring Gap			Ring Side Clearance		
				Top Compression	Bottom Compression	Oil Control	Top Compression	Bottom Compression	Oil Control
1997	T	2.4 (2392)	0.0006-0.0015	0.006-0.012	0.010-0.016	0.010-0.030	0.0016-0.0031	0.0012-0.0028	0.0005-0.0089
	M	3.1 (3130)	0.0013-0.0027	0.006-0.014	0.0197-0.0280	0.0098-0.0500	0.0020-0.0033	0.0020-0.0035	0.0080
1998	T	2.4 (2392)	0.0006-0.0015	0.006-0.012	0.010-0.016	0.010-0.030	0.0016-0.0031	0.0012-0.0028	0.0005-0.0089
	M	3.1 (3130)	0.0013-0.0027	0.006-0.014	0.0197-0.0280	0.0098-0.0500	0.0020-0.0033	0.0020-0.0035	0.0080
1999	T	2.4 (2392)	0.0006-0.0015	0.006-0.012	0.010-0.016	0.010-0.030	0.0016-0.0031	0.0012-0.0028	0.0005-0.0089
	M	3.1 (3130)	0.0013-0.0027	0.006-0.014	0.0197-0.0280	0.0098-0.0500	0.0020-0.0033	0.0020-0.0035	0.0080
	E	3.4 (3934)	0.0013-0.0027	0.006-0.014	0.0197-0.0280	0.0098-0.0500	0.0020-0.0033	0.0020-0.0035	0.0080
2000-01	T	2.4 (2392)	0.0006-0.0015	0.006-0.012	0.010-0.016	0.010-0.030	0.0016-0.0031	0.0012-0.0028	0.0005-0.0089
	E	3.4 (3934)	0.0013-0.0027	0.006-0.014	0.0197-0.0280	0.0098-0.0500	0.0020-0.0033	0.0020-0.0035	0.0080

93061CQ6

Refer to the model specific sections for driveline service procedures

TORQUE SPECIFICATIONS
All readings in ft. lbs.

Year	Engine Displacement Liters (cc)	Engine ID/VIN	Cylinder Head Bolts	Main Bearing Bolts	Rod Bearing Bolts	Crankshaft Damper Bolts	Flywheel Bolts	Manifold Intake	Manifold Exhaust	Spark Plug	Lug Nut
1997	2.4 (2392)	T	①	②	③	④	⑤	19	31	16	100
	3.1 (3130)	M	⑥	⑦	⑧	76	59	⑨	12	20	100
1998	2.4 (2392)	T	①	②-	③	④	⑤	19	31	16	100
	3.1 (3130)	M	⑥	⑦	⑧	76	59	⑨	12	20	100
1999	2.4 (2392)	T	①	②	③	④	⑤	19	31	16	100
	3.1 (3130)	M	⑥	⑦	⑧	76	59	⑨	12	20	100
	3.4 (3934)	E	⑩	⑪	⑧	76	52	⑫	12	20	100
2000-01	2.4 (2392)	T	①	②	③	④	⑤	⑭	⑬	16	100
	3.4 (3934)	E	⑩	⑪	⑧	76	52	⑫	12	20	100

① Nos. 1-8: 30 ft. lbs.
  Nos. 9-10: 26 ft. lbs.
  Tighten all bolts an additional 90 degrees
② 15 ft. lbs. plus 90 degrees
③ 18 ft. lbs. plus 80 degrees
④ 129 ft. lbs. plus 90 degrees
⑤ 22 ft. lbs. plus 45 degrees
⑥ Coat threads with sealer torque to 37 ft. lbs., then turn 1/4 turn (90 degrees)
⑦ 37 ft. lbs. plus 75 degrees
⑧ 15 ft. lbs. plus 75 degrees

⑨ Torque all bolts to 15 ft. lbs., retorque to 24 ft. lbs.
⑩ 33 ft. lbs. plus 90 degrees
⑪ 37 ft. lbs. plus 77 degrees
⑫ Lower: 115 inch lbs.
  Upper: 18 ft. lbs.
⑬ Nuts: 11 ft. lbs.
  Studs: 97 inch lbs.
⑭ Nuts: 11 ft. lbs.
  Studs: 97 inch lbs.

93061CQ7

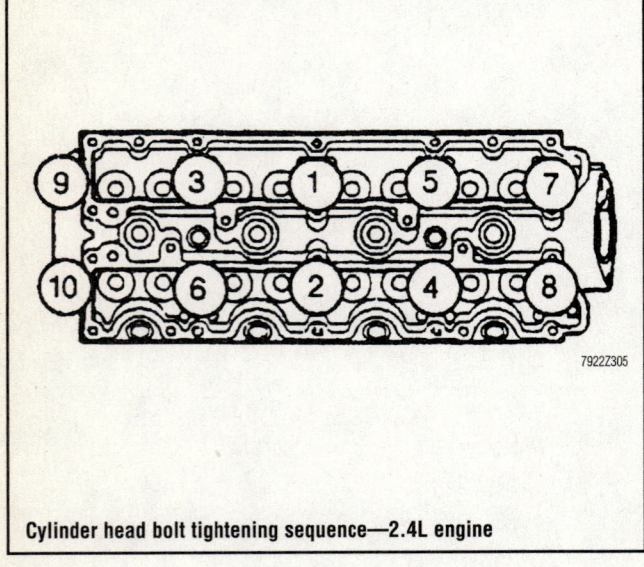

Cylinder head bolt tightening sequence—2.4L engine

7922Z305

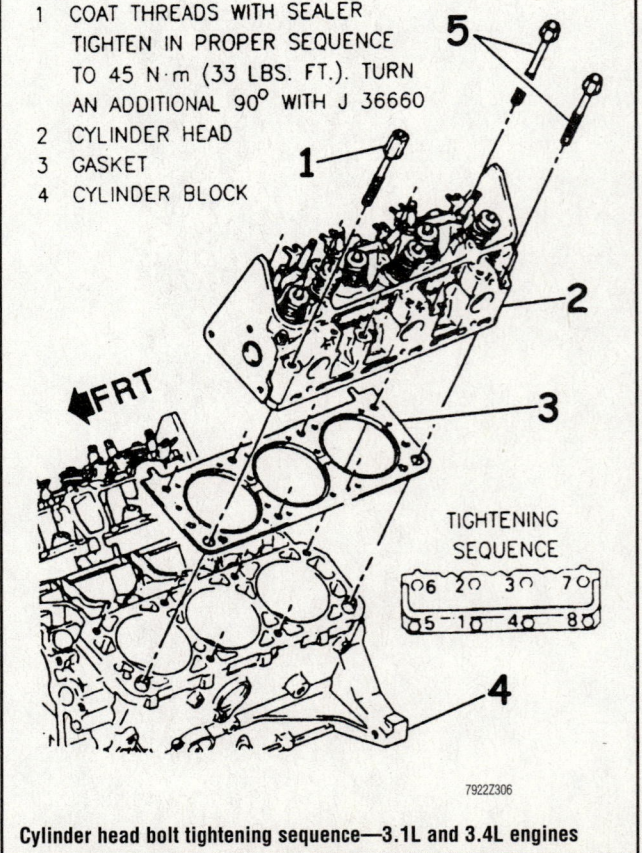

1 COAT THREADS WITH SEALER
  TIGHTEN IN PROPER SEQUENCE
  TO 45 N·m (33 LBS. FT.). TURN
  AN ADDITIONAL 90° WITH J 36660
2 CYLINDER HEAD
3 GASKET
4 CYLINDER BLOCK

TIGHTENING SEQUENCE

Cylinder head bolt tightening sequence—3.1L and 3.4L engines

7922Z306

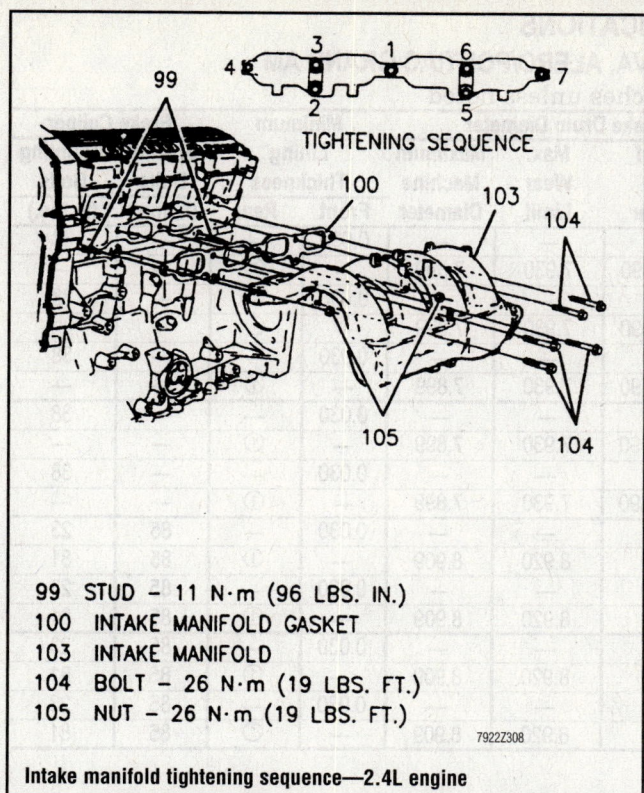

99 STUD – 11 N·m (96 LBS. IN.)
100 INTAKE MANIFOLD GASKET
103 INTAKE MANIFOLD
104 BOLT – 26 N·m (19 LBS. FT.)
105 NUT – 26 N·m (19 LBS. FT.)

Intake manifold tightening sequence—2.4L engine

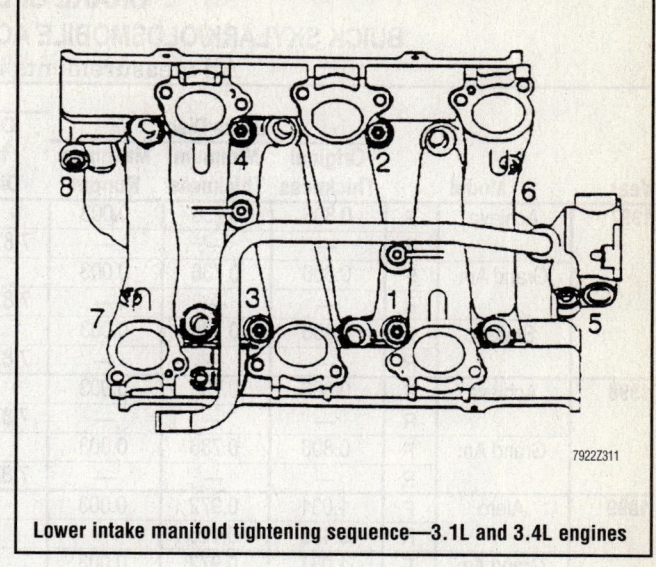

Lower intake manifold tightening sequence—3.1L and 3.4L engines

For exhaust manifold replacement procedures, see the model specific sections of this manual

BRAKE SPECIFICATIONS
BUICK SKYLARK/OLDSMOBILE ACHIEVA, ALERO/PONTIAC GRAND AM
All measurements in inches unless noted

Year	Model		Brake Disc Original Thickness	Brake Disc Minimum Thickness	Brake Disc Maximum Runout	Brake Drum Diameter Original Inside Diameter	Brake Drum Diameter Max. Wear Limit	Brake Drum Diameter Maximum Machine Diameter	Minimum Lining Thickness Front	Minimum Lining Thickness Rear	Brake Caliper Bracket Bolts (ft. lbs.)	Brake Caliper Mounting Bolts (ft. lbs.)
1997	Achieva	F	0.806	0.736	0.003	—	—	—	0.030	—	—	38
		R	—	—	—	7.874-7.890	7.930	7.899	—	①	—	—
	Grand Am	F	0.806	0.736	0.003	—	—	—	0.030	—	—	38
		R	—	—	—	7.874-7.890	7.930	7.899	—	①	—	—
	Skylark	F	0.806	0.736	0.003	—	—	—	0.030	—	—	38
		R	—	—	—	7.874-7.890	7.930	7.899	—	①	—	—
1998	Achieva	F	0.806	0.736	0.003	—	—	—	0.030	—	—	38
		R	—	—	—	7.874-7.890	7.930	7.899	—	①	—	—
	Grand Am	F	0.806	0.736	0.003	—	—	—	0.030	—	—	38
		R	—	—	—	7.874-7.890	7.930	7.899	—	①	—	—
1999	Alero	F	1.031	0.972	0.003	—	—	—	0.030	—	85	23
		R	0.430	0.410	—	8.863	8.920	8.909	—	①	85	81
	Grand Am	F	1.031	0.972	0.003	—	—	—	0.030	—	85	23
		R	0.430	0.410	—	8.863	8.920	8.909	—	①	85	81
2000-01	Alero	F	1.031	0.972	0.003	—	—	—	0.030	—	85	23
		R	0.430	0.410	—	8.863	8.920	8.909	—	①	85	81
	Grand Am	F	1.031	0.972	0.003	—	—	—	0.030	—	85	23
		R	0.430	0.410	—	8.863	8.920	8.909	—	①	85	81

NA: Not available

① 0.030 over rivet head; If bonded lining, use 0.030 from shoe

93061CQ8

SCHEDULED MAINTENANCE INTERVALS
(GM N BODY—BUICK SKYLARK, OLDSMOBILE ACHIEVA, ALERO & PONTIAC GRAND AM)

TO BE SERVICED	TYPE OF SERVICE	VEHICLE MILEAGE INTERVAL (x1000)												
		7.5	15	22.5	30	37.5	45	52.5	60	67.5	75	82.5	90	97.5
Engine oil & filter	R	✓	✓	✓	✓	✓	✓	✓	✓	✓	✓	✓	✓	✓
Automatic transaxle fluid & filter ①	S/I	✓	✓	✓	✓	✓	✓	✓	✓	✓	✓	✓	✓	✓
Brake hoses	S/I	✓	✓	✓	✓	✓	✓	✓	✓	✓	✓	✓	✓	✓
Chassis lubrication	S/I	✓	✓	✓	✓	✓	✓	✓	✓	✓	✓	✓	✓	✓
Coolant level, hoses & clamps	S/I	✓	✓	✓	✓	✓	✓	✓	✓	✓	✓	✓	✓	✓
Driveshaft boots & front suspension components	S/I	✓	✓	✓	✓	✓	✓	✓	✓	✓	✓	✓	✓	✓
Exhaust system	S/I	✓	✓	✓	✓	✓	✓	✓	✓	✓	✓	✓	✓	✓
Lubricate chassis, suspension, steering linkage, transaxle shift linkage, parking brake cable guides, underbody contact points & linkage	S/I	✓	✓	✓	✓	✓	✓	✓	✓	✓	✓	✓	✓	✓
Manual transaxle oil	S/I	✓	✓	✓	✓	✓	✓	✓	✓	✓	✓	✓	✓	✓
Throttle linkage	S/I	✓	✓	✓	✓	✓	✓	✓	✓	✓	✓	✓	✓	✓
Brake linings	S/I	✓		✓			✓			✓		✓		✓	✓
Rotate tires	S/I	✓		✓			✓			✓		✓		✓	✓
Air filter element & PCV filter	R				✓				✓					✓	
Engine coolant ②	R														
Spark plugs ③	R				✓				✓					✓	
Accessory drive belt(s)	S/I				✓				✓					✓	
EGR & fuel systems	S/I				✓				✓					✓	
Ignition cables	S/I				✓				✓					✓	

R: Replace   S/I: Service or Inspect

① Automatic transaxle fluid & filter: replace at 100,000 miles (if not changed previously).

② Engine coolant: replace every 100,000 miles. Use O.E. specified (DEX-COOL™) coolant only. If any silicate coolant is used, the service interval is every 30,000 miles.

③ Platinum tip spark plugs: replace every 100,000 miles.

FREQUENT OPERATION MAINTENANCE (SEVERE SERVICE) ADDITIONS

If a vehicle is operated under any of the following conditions it is considered severe service:
- Towing a trailer or using a camper or car-top carrier.
- Extensive idling or low-speed driving for long distances as in heavy commercial use, such as delivery, taxi or police cars.
- Operating on rough, muddy or salt-covered roads.
- Operating on unpaved or dusty roads.
- 50% or more of the vehicle operation is in 32°C (90°F) or higher temperatures, or constant operation in temperatures below 0°C (32°F).

Engine oil and filter: change every 3000 miles or 3 months, whichever occurs first.

Wheels and tires: inspect and rotate every 6000 miles.

Air cleaner element: inspect every 15,000 miles and replace or clean as needed. Replace it at least every 30,000 miles.

Automatic transaxle fluid & filter: replace every 50,000 miles.

93061CQ9

Refer to the model specific sections for cooling system service procedures

SCHEDULED MAINTENANCE INTERVALS
GENERAL MOTORS CORPORATION
N BODY
BUICK SKYLARK
OLDSMOBILE ACHIEVA, ALERO
PONTIAC GRAND AM

The following should be used as a guide when determining the amount of work required for a particular service.
In estimating how long a particular Scheduled Maintenance Service should take, please observe the following:

● Labor Time is time based on field research and data supplied by the vehicle manufacturer.
● Labor time operations are given in hours and tenths of an hour.
● All labor operations are to be used as a guide.

Mechanic Skill Level Codes:
(A) PRECISION: Highly skilled with multiple certification.
(B) GENERAL: Normally skilled with certification.
(C) MAINTENANCE: Semi-skilled working on certification.

	LABOR TIME		LABOR TIME		LABOR TIME
7500 Mile Service (B)		**37500 Mile Service (C)**		**75000 Mile Service (C)**	
All Models	2.0	All Models	1.8	All Models	1.1
15000 Mile Service (C)		**45000 Mile Service (C)**		**82500 Mile Service (C)**	
All Models	1.1	All Models	1.2	All Models	1.8
22500 Mile Service (C)		**52500 Mile Service (C)**		**90000 Mile Service (B)**	
All Models	1.8	All Models	1.8	All Models	2.8
30000 Mile Service (B)		**60000 Mile Service (B)**		**97500 Mile Service (C)**	
All Models	2.8	All Models	2.8	All Models	1.8
		67500 Mile Service (C)			
		All Models	1.8		

93061CQ00

GENERAL MOTORS V-BODY
Cadillac Catera

ENGINE AND VEHICLE IDENTIFICATION

		Engine						Model Year	
Code ①	Liters (cc)	Cu. In.	Cyl.	Fuel Sys.	Engine Type	Eng. Mfg.		Code ②	Year
R	3.0 (2972)	181	V6	SMFI	DOHC	Opel		V	1997

Code ②	Year
V	1997
W	1998
X	1999
Y	2000
1	2001

SMFI: Sequential Multi-port Fuel Injection

DOHC: Double Overhead Camshaft

① 8th position of VIN

② 10th position of VIN

93061CN8

GENERAL ENGINE SPECIFICATIONS

Year	Model	Engine Displacement Liters (cc)	Engine Series (ID/VIN)	Fuel System	Net Horsepower @ rpm	Net Torque @ rpm (ft. lbs.)	Bore x Stroke (in.)	Com-pression Ratio	Oil Pressure @ rpm
1997	Catera	3.0 (2972)	R	MFI	200@6000	192@3600	3.38x3.34	10.0:1	22@900
1998	Catera	3.0 (2972)	R	MFI	200@6000	192@3600	3.38x3.34	10.0:1	22@900
1999	Catera	3.0 (2972)	R	MFI	200@6000	192@3600	3.38x3.34	10.0:1	22@900
2000-01	Catera	3.0 (2972)	R	MFI	200@6000	192@3600	3.38x3.34	10.0:1	22@900

MFI: Multi-point Fuel Injection

93061CN9

ENGINE TUNE-UP SPECIFICATIONS

Year	Engine Displacement Liters (cc)	Engine ID/VIN	Spark Plug Gap (in.)	Ignition Timing (deg.) AT	Fuel Pump (psi)	Idle Speed (rpm) AT	Valve Clearance In.	Valve Clearance Ex.
1997	3.0 (2972)	R	0.034 - 0.043	①	41-47	①	HYD	HYD
1998	3.0 (2972)	R	0.034 - 0.043	①	41-47	①	HYD	HYD
1999	3.0 (2972)	R	0.034 - 0.043	①	41-47	①	HYD	HYD
2000-01	3.0 (2972)	R	0.034 - 0.043	①	41-47	①	HYD	HYD

NOTE: The Vehicle Emission Control Information label often reflects specification changes made during production. The label figures must be used if they differ from those in this chart.

HYD: Hydraulic

① Refer to Vehicle Emission Control Information label

93061CN0

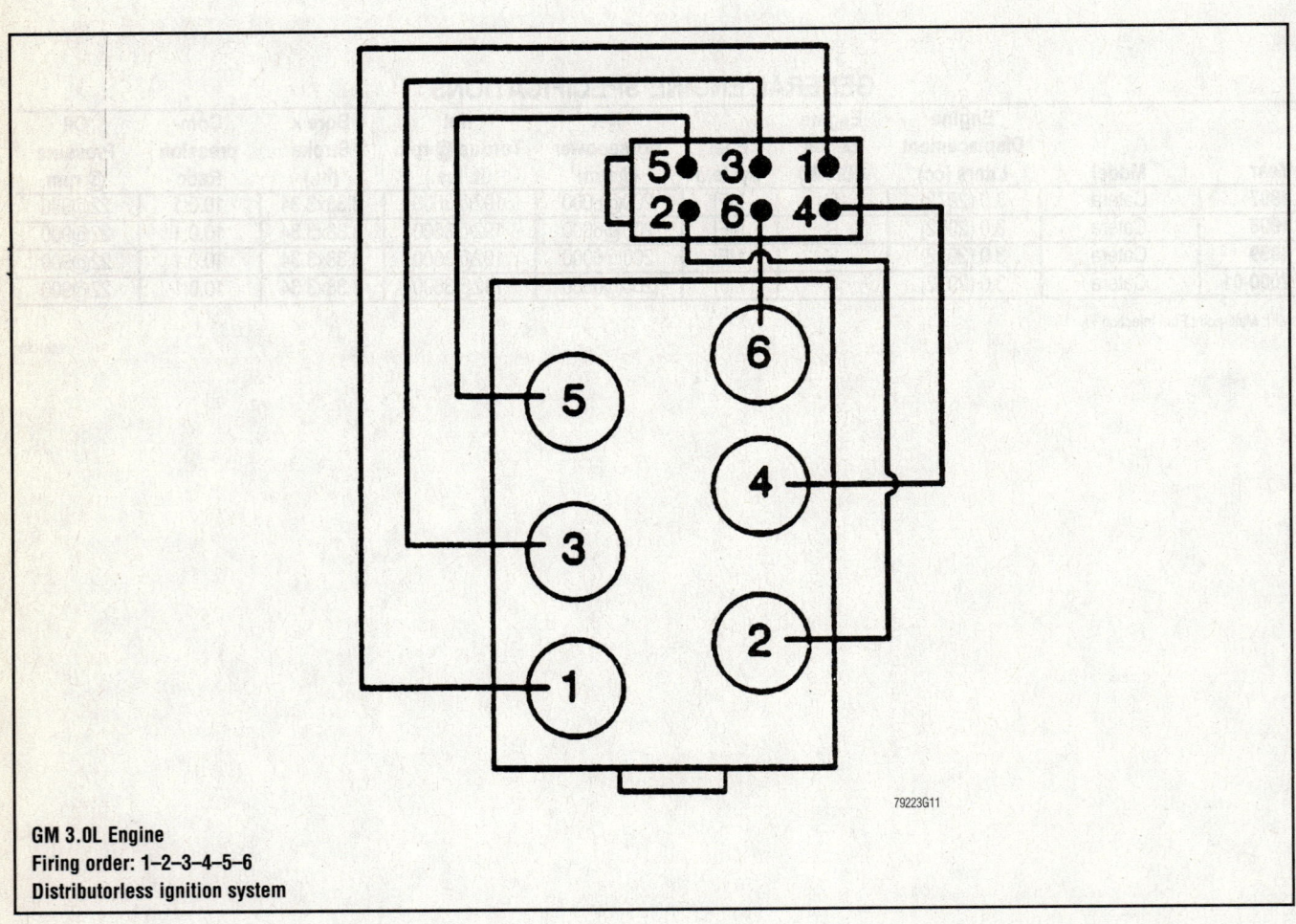

GM 3.0L Engine
Firing order: 1–2–3–4–5–6
Distributorless ignition system

79223G11

CAPACITIES

Year	Model	Engine Displacement Liters (cc)	Engine ID/VIN	Engine Oil with Filter (qts.)	Transmission (pts.)	Drive Axle Rear (pts.)	Fuel Tank (gal.)	Cooling System (qts.)
1997	Catera	3.0 (2972)	R	6.0	14	3.5	18	10
1998	Catera	3.0 (2972)	R	6.0	14	3.5	18	10
1999	Catera	3.0 (2972)	R	6.0	14	3.5	18	10
2000-01	Catera	3.0 (2972)	R	6.0	14	3.5	18	10

NOTE: All capacities are approximate. Add fluid gradually and ensure a proper fluid level is obtained.

93061C01

VALVE SPECIFICATIONS

Year	Engine Displacement Liters (cc)	Engine ID/VIN	Seat Angle (deg.)	Face Angle (deg.)	Spring Test Pressure (lbs. @ in.)	Spring Installed Height (in.)	Stem-to-Guide Clearance (in.) Intake	Stem-to-Guide Clearance (in.) Exhaust	Stem Diameter (in.) Intake	Stem Diameter (in.) Exhaust
1997	3.0 (2972)	R	①	45	56.6@1.338	1.543	0.0012-0.0022	0.0016-0.0026	0.2344-0.2350	0.2341-0.2346
1998	3.0 (2972)	R	①	45	56.6@1.338	1.543	0.0012-0.0022	0.0016-0.0026	0.2344-0.2350	0.2341-0.2346
1999	3.0 (2972)	R	①	45	56.6@1.338	1.543	0.0012-0.0022	0.0016-0.0026	0.2344-0.2350	0.2341-0.2346
2000-01	3.0 (2972)	R	①	45	56.6@1.338	1.543	0.0012-0.0022	0.0016-0.0026	0.2344-0.2350	0.2341-0.2346

① 45 degrees 20 minutes

93061C02

Timing chain and gear service is covered in the model specific sections of this manual

CRANKSHAFT AND CONNECTING ROD SPECIFICATIONS
All measurements are given in inches.

Year	Engine Displacement Liters (cc)	Engine ID/VIN	Crankshaft				Connecting Rod		
			Main Brg. Journal Dia.	Main Brg. Oil Clearance	Shaft End-play	Thrust on No.	Journal Diameter	Oil Clearance	Side Clearance
1997	3.0 (2972)	R	①	0.0006-0.0017	0.0004-0.0300	2	②	0.0005-0.0024	0.0027-0.0110
1998	3.0 (2972)	R	①	0.0006-0.0017	0.0004-0.0300	2	②	0.0005-0.0024	0.0027-0.0110
1999	3.0 (2972)	R	①	0.0006-0.0017	0.0004-0.0300	2	②	0.0005-0.0024	0.0027-0.0110
2000-01	3.0 (2972)	R	①	0.0006-0.0017	0.0004-0.0300	2	②	0.0005-0.0024	0.0027-0.0110

① Green 2.6763 - 2.6766
Brown 26766 - 2.6770
Green/Blue 2.6665 - 2.6668
Brown/Blue 2.6668 - 2.6671
Green/White 2.6566 - 2.6570
Brown/White 2.6570 - 2.6573

② Undersize 0.25; 1.918 - 1.919
Undersize 0.50; 1.908 - 1.909

93061C03

PISTON AND RING SPECIFICATIONS
All measurements are given in inches.

Year	Engine Displacement Liters (cc)	Engine ID/VIN	Piston Clearance	Ring Gap			Ring Side Clearance		
				Top Compression	Bottom Compression	Oil Control	Top Compression	Bottom Compression	Oil Control
1997	3.0 (2972)	R	0.0010-0.0018	0.0118-0.0196	0.0118-0.0196	0.0157-0.0551	0.0008-0.0015	0.0008-0.0015	0.0004-0.0012
1998	3.0 (2972)	R	0.0010-0.0018	0.0118-0.0196	0.0118-0.0196	0.0157-0.0551	0.0008-0.0015	0.0008-0.0015	0.0004-0.0012
1999	3.0 (2972)	R	0.0010-0.0018	0.0118-0.0196	0.0118-0.0196	0.0157-0.0551	0.0008-0.0015	0.0008-0.0015	0.0004-0.0012
2000-01	3.0 (2972)	R	0.0010-0.0018	0.0118-0.0196	0.0118-0.0196	0.0157-0.0551	0.0008-0.0015	0.0008-0.0015	0.0004-0.0012

93061C04

TORQUE SPECIFICATIONS
All readings in ft. lbs.

Year	Engine Displacement Liters (cc)	Engine ID/VIN	Cylinder Head Bolts	Main Bearing Bolts	Rod Bearing Bolts	Crankshaft Damper Bolts	Flywheel Bolts	Manifold		Spark Plugs	Lug Nut
								Intake	Exhaust		
1997	3.0 (2972)	R	①	②	③	④	⑤	15	15	19	100
1998	3.0 (2972)	R	①	②	③	④	⑤	15	15	19	100
1999	3.0 (2972)	R	①	②	③	④	⑤	15	15	19	100
2000-01	3.0 (2972)	R	①	②	③	④	⑤	15	15	19	100

① Step 1: 18 ft. lbs.
Step 2: Rotate 90 degrees
Step 3: Rotate 90 degrees
Step 4: Rotate 90 degrees
Step 5: Rotate 15 degrees

② Step 1: 37 ft. lbs.
Step 2: Rotate 60 degrees
Step 3: Rotate 15 degrees

③ Step 1: 26 ft. lbs.
Step 2: Rotate 45 degrees
Step 3: Rotate 15 degrees

④ Step 1: 184 ft. lbs.
Step 2: Rotate 45 degrees
Step 3: Rotate 15 degrees
Step 4: Harmonic balancer 15 ft. lbs.

⑤ Step 1: 48 ft. lbs.
Step 2: Rotate 30 degrees
Step 3: Rotate 15 degrees

93061C05

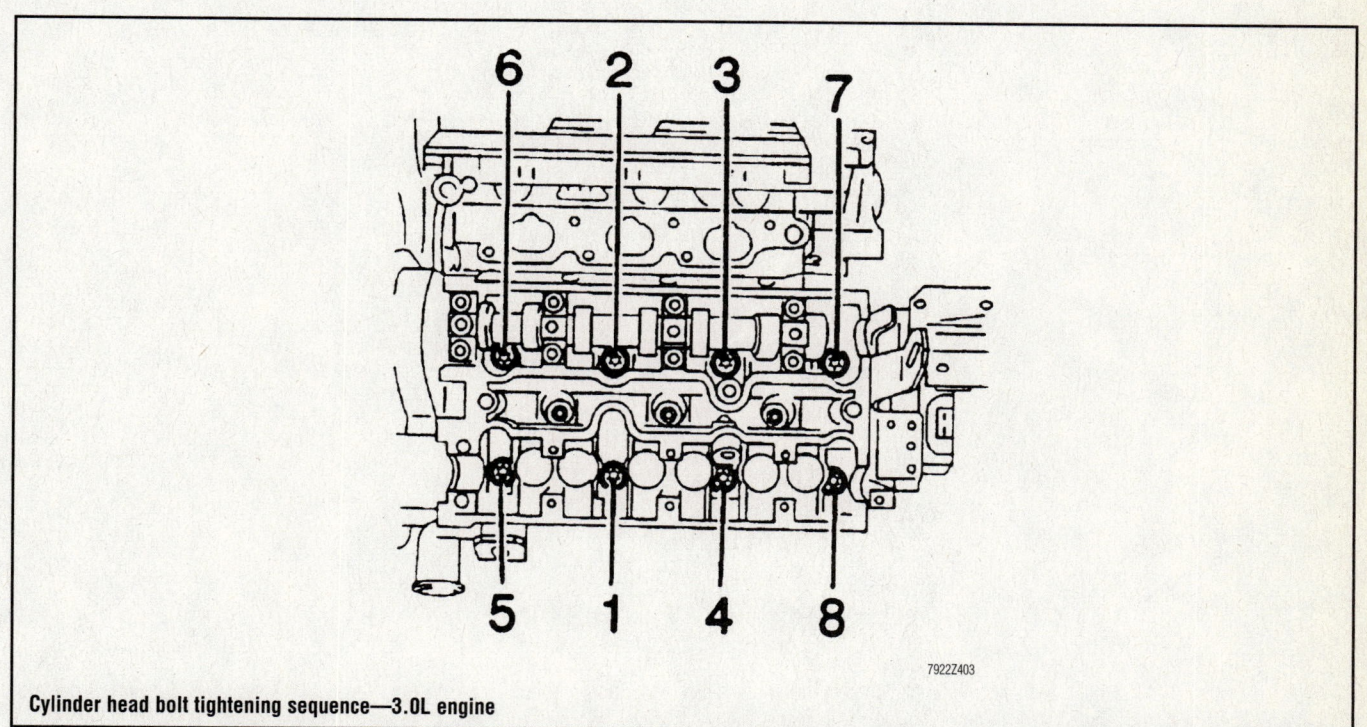

Cylinder head bolt tightening sequence—3.0L engine

7922Z403

Ignition system service is covered in the model specific sections of this manual

BRAKE SPECIFICATIONS
GM V BODY
All measurements in inches unless noted

| Year | Model | | Brake Disc | | | Minimum Lining Thickness | Brake Caliper | |
			Original Thickness	Minimum Thickness	Maximum Runout		Bracket Bolts (ft. lbs.)	Mounting Bolts (ft. lbs.)
1997	Catera	F	1.102	0.984	0.001	0.315 ①	137	63
		R	0.472	0.393	0.004	NA	92	32
1998	Catera	F	1.102	0.984	0.001	0.315 ①	137	63
		R	0.472	0.393	0.004	NA	92	32
1999	Catera	F	1.102	0.984	0.001	0.315 ①	137	63
		R	0.472	0.393	0.004	NA	92	32
2000-01	Catera	F	1.102	0.984	0.001	0.315 ①	137	63
		R	0.472	0.393	0.004	NA	92	32

F: Front

R: Rear

NA: Not available

① Total thickness of lining and backing plate

93061C06

SCHEDULED MAINTENANCE INTERVALS
(GM V BODY—CADILLAC CATERA)

TO BE SERVICED	TYPE OF SERVICE	VEHICLE MILEAGE INTERVAL (x1000)																			
		5	10	15	20	25	30	35	40	45	50	55	60	65	70	75	80	85	90	95	100
Engine oil & filter	R	✓	✓	✓	✓	✓	✓	✓	✓	✓	✓	✓	✓	✓	✓	✓	✓	✓	✓	✓	✓
Rotate tires	S/I	✓		✓		✓		✓		✓		✓		✓		✓		✓		✓	
Brake hoses	S/I	✓		✓		✓		✓		✓		✓		✓		✓		✓		✓	
Passenger Compartment Air Filter (Pollen Filter)	R			✓			✓			✓			✓			✓			✓		
Air filter element	S/I			✓			✓			✓			✓			✓			✓		
	R						✓						✓						✓		
Fuel tank, cap and lines	S/I						✓						✓								
Rear axle fluid level	S/I						✓						✓								
Automatic transaxle fluid & filter ①	R										✓										✓
Accessory drive belt(s)	S/I												✓								
Spark plugs ②	R																				✓
Ignition cables	S/I																				✓
Camshaft timing belt ③	R												✓								✓
Fuel filter	R																				✓
Engine coolant ④	R																				

R: Replace S/I: Service or Inspect

① Automatic transaxle fluid & filter: replace at 50,000 miles (83,000 km) if the vehicle has experienced severe service usage.

② Platinum tip spark plugs: replace every 100,000 miles.

③ Replace at 60,000 miles (96,000 km) if the engine was driven without an engine coolant heater being used and where temperatures fall below -20°F (-28°C).

Otherwise, replace the belt at 100,000 miles (160,000 km).

④ Engine coolant: replace every 150,000 miles. Use O.E. specified (DEX-COOL™) coolant only. If any silicate coolant is used, the service interval is every 30,000 miles.

FREQUENT OPERATION MAINTENANCE (SEVERE SERVICE)

If a vehicle is operated under any of the following conditions it is considered severe service:

- **Extremely dusty areas.**

- **50% or more of the vehicle operation is in 32°C (90°F) or higher temperatures, or constant operation in temperatures below 0°C (32°F).**

- **Prolonged idling (vehicle operation in stop and go traffic).**

- **Frequent short running periods (engine does not warm to normal operating temperatures).**

- **Police, taxi, delivery usage or trailer towing usage.**

Oil & oil filter: change every 5000 miles

Rotate tires at 5000 miles, then every 10,000 miles.

Air filter element: service or inspect every 15,000 miles.

Camshaft timing belt: change every 60,000 miles for severe service.

93061C07

Please visit our web site at www.chiltononline.com

SCHEDULED MAINTENANCE INTERVALS
GENERAL MOTORS CORPORATION
V BODY
CADILLAC CATERA

The following should be used as a guide when determining the amount of work required for a particular service.
In estimating how long a particular Scheduled Maintenance Service should take, please observe the following:

- Labor Time is time based on field research and data supplied by the vehicle manufacturer.
- Labor time operations are given in hours and tenths of an hour.
- All labor operations are to be used as a guide.

Mechanic Skill Level Codes:
(A) PRECISION: Highly skilled with multiple certification.
(B) GENERAL: Normally skilled with certification.
(C) MAINTENANCE: Semi-skilled working on certification.

	LABOR TIME			LABOR TIME			LABOR TIME
5000 Mile Service (C)		**40000 Mile Service (B)**			**75000 Mile Service (C)**		
All Models	.9	All Models		.3	All Models		1.5
10000 Mile Service (C)		**45000 Mile Service (C)**			**80000 Mile Service (B)**		
All Models	.3	All Models		1.5	All Models		.3
15000 Mile Service (C)		**50000 Mile Service (C)**			**85000 Mile Service (C)**		
All Models	1.5	All Models		1.3	All Models		.9
20000 Mile Service (B)		**55000 Mile Service (C)**			**90000 Mile Service (B)**		
All Models	.3	All Models		.9	All Models		.9
25000 Mile Service (C)		**60000 Mile Service (B)**			**95000 Mile Service (C)**		
All Models	.9	All Models		3.9	All Models		.9
30000 Mile Service (C)		**65000 Mile Service (C)**			**100000 Mile Service (B)**		
All Models	1.2	All Models		.9	All Models		4.4
35000 Mile Service (C)		**70000 Mile Service (B)**			*Replace fuel filter add*		
All Models	.9	All Models		.3	*in line*		.5

93061C08

GENERAL MOTORS W-BODY

Buick Regal • 1998–01 Century • Chevrolet Impala • Lumina • Monte Carlo • Oldsmobile Cutlass Supreme • Intrigue • Pontiac Grand Prix

ENGINE AND VEHICLE IDENTIFICATION

Code ①	Liters (cc)	Cu. In.	Cyl.	Fuel Sys.	Engine Type	Eng. Mfg.	Code ②	Year
1	3.8 (3785)	231	6	MFI	OHV	BOC	V	1997
K	3.8 (3785)	231	6	MFI	OHV	CPC	W	1998
H	3.5 (3475)	212	6	MFI	DOHC	BOC	X	1999
M	3.1 (3130)	191	6	MFI	OHV	BOC	Y	2000
X	3.4 (3393)	207	6	MFI	OHV	CPC	1	2001

Header spanning: **Engine Code** over columns Code–Eng. Mfg.; **Model Year** over Code ②–Year.

MFI: Multi-point Fuel Injection
BOC: Buick/Oldsmobile/Cadillac
CPC: Chevrolet/Pontiac/Canada
DOHC: Dual Overhead Camshafts
OHV: Overhead Valves
① 8th position of VIN
② 10th position of VIN

93061CS3

Refer to the model specific sections for engine mechanical service procedures

GENERAL ENGINE SPECIFICATIONS

Year	Model	Engine Displacement Liters (cc)	Engine Series (ID/VIN)	Fuel System	Net Horsepower @ rpm	Net Torque @ rpm (ft. lbs.)	Bore x Stroke (in.)	Compression Ratio	Oil Pressure @ rpm
1997	Cutlass Supreme	3.1 (3130)	M	MFI	160@5200	185@4000	3.50x3.31	9.5:1	15@1100
	Cutlass Supreme	3.4 (3393)	X	MFI	210@5200	215@4000	3.62x3.31	9.25:1	15@1100
	Grand Prix	3.1 (3130)	M	MFI	160@5200	185@4000	3.50x3.31	9.5:1	15@1100
	Grand Prix	3.4 (3393)	X	MFI	210@5200	215@4000	3.62x3.31	9.25:1	15@1100
	Lumina	3.1 (3130)	M	MFI	160@5200	185@4000	3.50x3.31	9.5:1	15@1100
	Lumina	3.4 (3393)	X	MFI	210@5200	215@4000	3.62x3.31	9.25:1	15@1100
	Monte Carlo	3.1 (3130)	M	MFI	160@5200	185@4000	3.50x3.31	9.5:1	15@1100
	Monte Carlo	3.4 (3393)	X	MFI	210@5200	215@4000	3.62x3.31	9.25:1	15@1100
	Regal	3.8 (3785)	K	MFI	205@5200	230@4000	3.80x3.40	9.4:1	60@1850
	Regal	3.8 (3785)	1	MFI	240@5200	280@3200	3.80x3.40	9.0:1	60@1850
	Regal	3.1 (3130)	M	MFI	160@5200	185@4000	3.50x3.31	9.5:1	15@1100
1998	Century	3.1 (3130)	M	MFI	160@5200	185@4000	3.50x3.31	9.5:1	15@1100
	Grand Prix	3.8 (3785)	1	MFI	240@5200	280@3200	3.80x3.40	9.0:1	60@1850
	Grand Prix	3.8 (3785)	K	MFI	205@5200	230@4000	3.80x3.40	9.4:1	60@1850
	Grand Prix	3.1 (3130)	M	MFI	160@5200	185@4000	3.50x3.31	9.5:1	15@1100
	Intrigue	3.8 (3785)	K	MFI	205@5200	230@4000	3.80x3.40	9.4:1	60@1850
	Lumina	3.1 (3130)	M	MFI	160@5200	185@4000	3.50x3.31	9.5:1	15@1100
	Monte Carlo	3.1 (3130)	M	MFI	160@5200	185@4000	3.50x3.31	9.5:1	15@1100
	Regal	3.8 (3785)	1	MFI	240@5200	280@3200	3.80x3.40	9.0:1	60@1850
	Regal	3.8 (3785)	K	MFI	205@5200	230@4000	3.80x3.40	9.4:1	60@1850
	Regal	3.1 (3130)	M	MFI	160@5200	185@4000	3.50x3.31	9.5:1	15@1100
1999	Century	3.1 (3130)	M	MFI	160@5200	185@4000	3.50x3.31	9.5:1	15@1100
	Grand Prix	3.8 (3785)	1	MFI	240@5200	280@3200	3.80x3.40	9.0:1	60@1850
	Grand Prix	3.8 (3785)	K	MFI	205@5200	230@4000	3.80x3.40	9.4:1	60@1850
	Grand Prix	3.1 (3130)	M	MFI	160@5200	185@4000	3.50x3.31	9.5:1	15@1100
	Intrigue	3.8 (3785)	K	MFI	205@5200	230@4000	3.80x3.40	9.4:1	60@1850
	Lumina	3.8 (3785)	K	MFI	205@5200	230@4000	3.80x3.40	9.4:1	60@1850
	Lumina	3.1 (3130)	M	MFI	160@5200	185@4000	3.50x3.31	9.5:1	15@1100
	Monte Carlo	3.8 (3785)	K	MFI	205@5200	230@4000	3.80x3.40	9.4:1	60@1850
	Monte Carlo	3.1 (3130)	M	MFI	160@5200	185@4000	3.50x3.31	9.5:1	15@1100
	Regal	3.8 (3785)	1	MFI	240@5200	280@3200	3.80x3.40	9.0:1	60@1850
	Regal	3.8 (3785)	K	MFI	205@5200	230@4000	3.80x3.40	9.4:1	60@1850
	Regal	3.1 (3130)	M	MFI	160@5200	185@4000	3.50x3.31	9.5:1	15@1100
2000-01	Century	3.1 (3130)	M	MFI	160@5200	185@4000	3.50x3.31	9.5:1	15@1100
	Grand Prix	3.8 (3785)	1	MFI	240@5200	280@3200	3.80x3.40	9.0:1	60@1850
	Grand Prix	3.8 (3785)	K	MFI	205@5200	230@4000	3.80x3.40	9.4:1	60@1850
	Impala	3.4 (3393)	X	MFI	210@5200	215@4000	3.62x3.31	9.25:1	15@1100
	Impala	3.8 (3785)	K	MFI	205@5200	230@4000	3.80x3.40	9.4:1	60@1850
	Intrigue	3.5 (3475)	H	MFI	215@5600	230@4400	3.52x3.62	9.3:1	29@2000
	Lumina	3.8 (3785)	K	MFI	205@5200	230@4000	3.80x3.40	9.4:1	60@1850
	Lumina	3.1 (3130)	M	MFI	160@5200	185@4000	3.50x3.31	9.5:1	15@1100
	Monte Carlo	3.8 (3785)	K	MFI	205@5200	230@4000	3.80x3.40	9.4:1	60@1850
	Monte Carlo	3.1 (3130)	M	MFI	160@5200	185@4000	3.50x3.31	9.5:1	15@1100
	Regal	3.8 (3785)	1	MFI	240@5200	280@3200	3.80x3.40	9.0:1	60@1850
	Regal	3.8 (3785)	K	MFI	205@5200	230@4000	3.80x3.40	9.4:1	60@1850
	Regal	3.1 (3130)	M	MFI	160@5200	185@4000	3.50x3.31	9.5:1	15@1100

MFI: Multi-point Fuel Injection

93061CS4

ENGINE TUNE-UP SPECIFICATIONS

Year	Engine Displacement Liters (cc)	Engine ID/VIN	Spark Plug Gap (in.)	Ignition Timing (deg.)	Fuel Pump (psi)	Idle Speed (rpm)	Valve Clearance In.	Ex.
1997	3.1 (3130)	M	0.060	①	41-47	②	HYD	HYD
	3.4 (3393)	X	0.045	①	41-47	②	HYD	HYD
	3.8 (3785)	1	0.060	①	41-47	②	HYD	HYD
	3.8 (3785)	K	0.060	①	41-47	②	HYD	HYD
1998	3.1 (3130)	M	0.060	①	41-47	②	HYD	HYD
	3.8 (3785)	1	0.060	①	41-47	②	HYD	HYD
	3.8 (3785)	K	0.060	①	41-47	②	HYD	HYD
1999	3.1 (3130)	M	0.060	①	41-47	②	HYD	HYD
	3.5 (3475)	H	0.050	①	41-47	②	HYD	HYD
	3.8 (3785)	1	0.060	①	41-47	②	HYD	HYD
	3.8 (3785)	K	0.060	①	41-47	②	HYD	HYD
2000-01	3.1 (3130)	M	0.060	①	41-47	②	HYD	HYD
	3.4 (3393)	X	0.045	①	41-47	②	HYD	HYD
	3.5 (3475)	H	0.050	①	41-47	②	HYD	HYD
	3.8 (3785)	1	0.060	①	41-47	②	HYD	HYD
	3.8 (3785)	K	0.060	①	41-47	②	HYD	HYD

NOTE: The Vehicle Emission Control Information label often reflects specification changes made during production. The label figures must be used if they differ from those in this chart.

HYD: Hydraulic

① Distributorless Ignition System (DIS) timing is not adjustable

② Idle speed is maintained by the Engine Control Module (ECM). There is no recommended adjustment procedure.

93061CS5

Refer to the model specific sections for fuel system service procedures

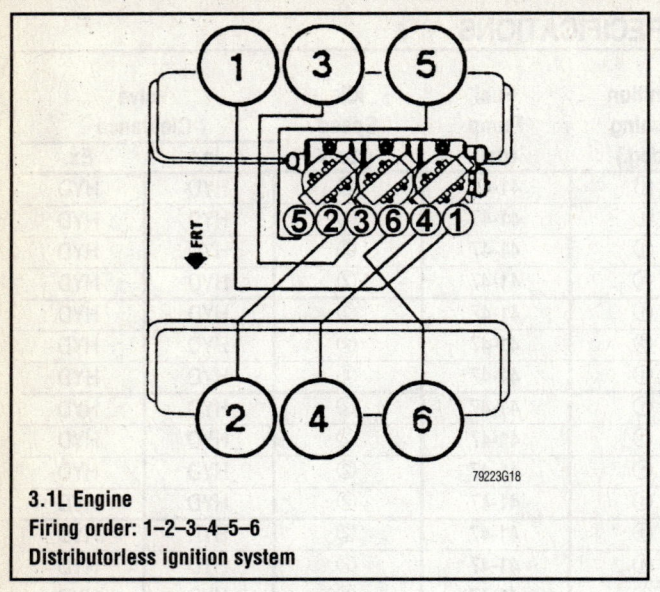

3.1L Engine
Firing order: 1–2–3–4–5–6
Distributorless ignition system

79223G18

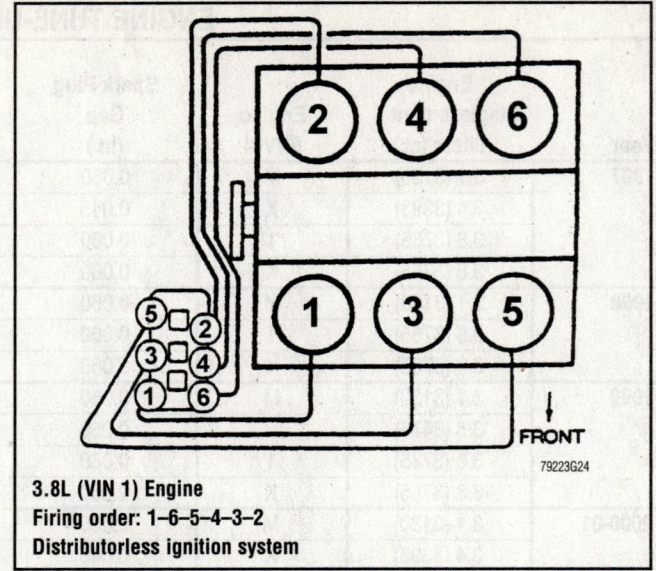

3.8L (VIN 1) Engine
Firing order: 1–6–5–4–3–2
Distributorless ignition system

79223G24

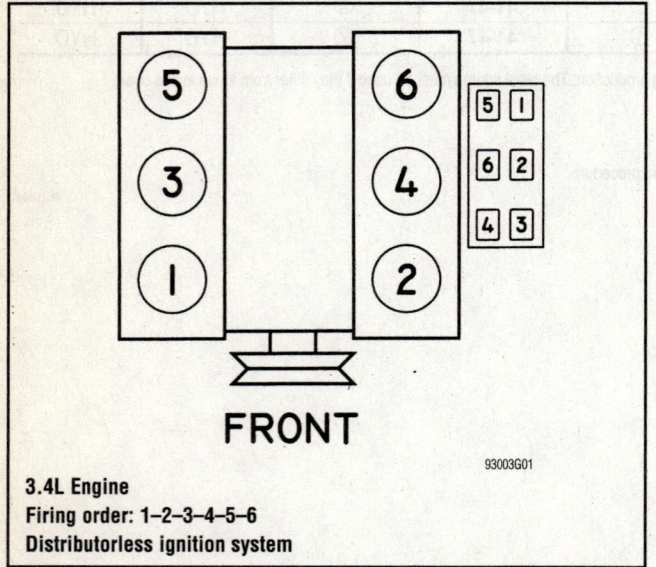

3.4L Engine
Firing order: 1–2–3–4–5–6
Distributorless ignition system

93003G01

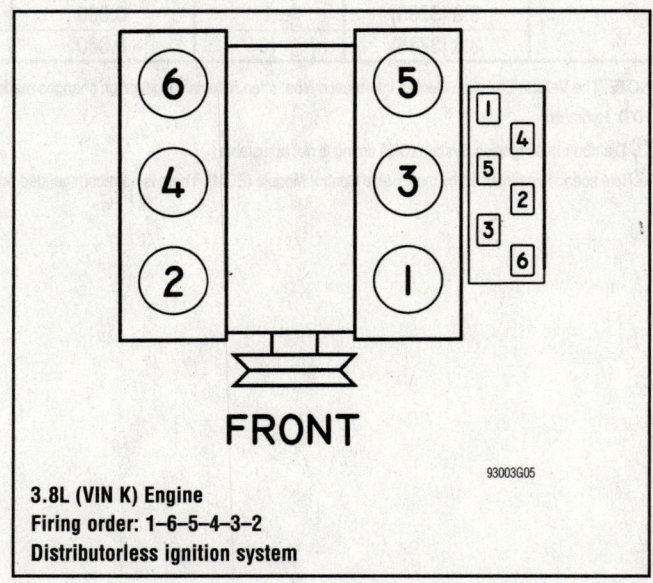

3.8L (VIN K) Engine
Firing order: 1–6–5–4–3–2
Distributorless ignition system

93003G05

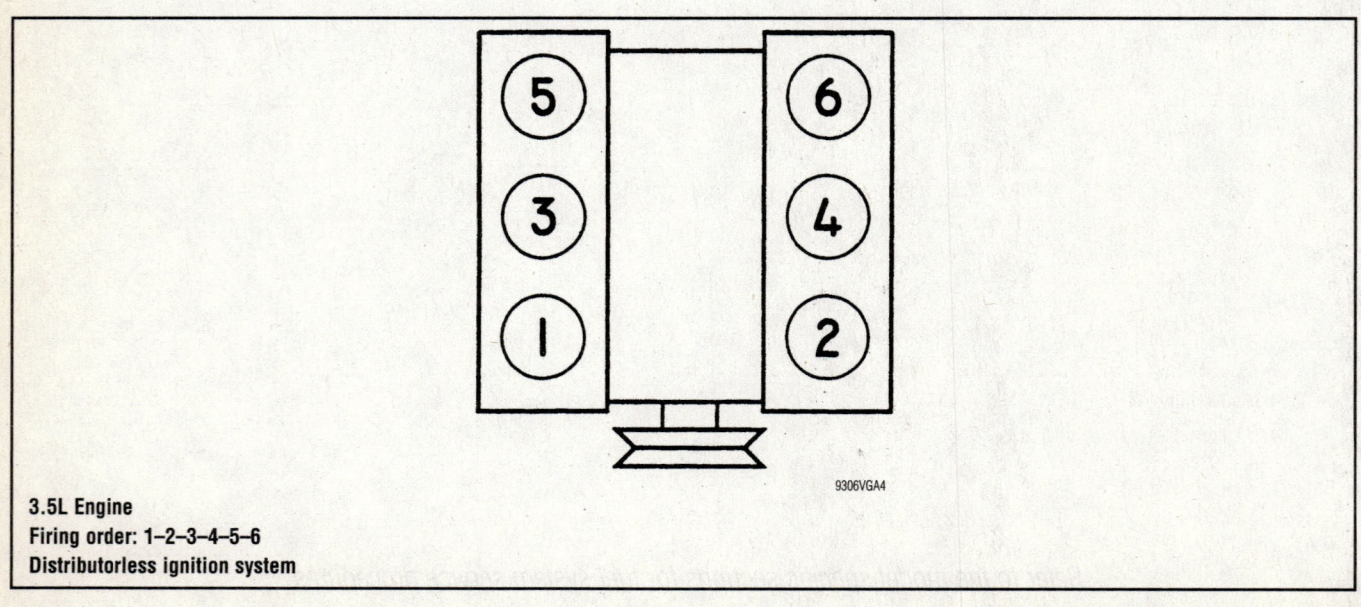

3.5L Engine
Firing order: 1–2–3–4–5–6
Distributorless ignition system

9306VGA4

CAPACITIES

Year	Model	Engine Displacement Liters (cc)	Engine ID/VIN	Engine Oil with Filter (qts.)	Transmission (pts.)	Fuel Tank (gal.)	Cooling System (qts.)
1997	Cutlass Supreme	3.1 (3130)	M	4.5	①	16.0	12.6
	Grand Prix	3.1 (3130)	M	4.5	①	16.0	12.6
	Grand Prix	3.4 (3393)	X	5.0	①	16.5	12.7
	Lumina	3.1 (3130)	M	4.5	①	16.0	12.6
	Lumina	3.4 (3393)	X	5.0	①	16.5	12.7
	Monte Carlo	3.1 (3130)	M	4.5	①	16.5	12.6
	Monte Carlo	3.4 (3393)	X	5.0	①	16.5	12.7
	Regal	3.8 (3785)	K	4.0 ②	①	17.1	11.1
	Regal	3.8 (3785)	1	5.0	①	16.5	12.7
	Regal	3.1 (3130)	M	4.0 ②	①	17.1	12.5
1998	Century	3.1 (3130)	M	4.5	①	16.0	12.6
	Grand Prix	3.8 (3785)	1	5.0	①	16.5	12.7
	Grand Prix	3.8 (3785)	K	5.0	①	16.5	12.7
	Grand Prix	3.1 (3130)	M	4.5	①	16.0	12.6
	Intrigue	3.8 (3785)	K	5.0	①	16.5	12.7
	Lumina	3.1 (3130)	M	4.5	①	16.0	12.6
	Monte Carlo	3.1 (3130)	M	4.5	①	16.5	12.6
	Regal	3.8 (3785)	1	5.0	①	16.5	12.7
	Regal	3.8 (3785)	K	5.0	①	17.1	11.1
	Regal	3.1 (3130)	M	4.5	①	17.1	12.5
1999	Century	3.1 (3130)	M	4.5	①	16.0	12.6
	Grand Prix	3.8 (3785)	1	5.0	①	16.5	12.7
	Grand Prix	3.8 (3785)	K	5.0	①	16.5	12.7
	Grand Prix	3.1 (3130)	M	4.5	①	16.0	12.6
	Intrigue	3.5 (3475)	H	6.0	①	18.0	9.6
	Lumina	3.8 (3785)	K	5.0	①	16.5	12.7
	Lumina	3.1 (3130)	M	4.5	①	16.0	12.6
	Monte Carlo	3.8 (3785)	K	5.0	①	16.5	12.7
	Monte Carlo	3.1 (3130)	M	4.5	①	16.5	12.6
	Regal	3.8 (3785)	1	5.0	①	16.5	12.7
	Regal	3.8 (3785)	K	5.0	①	17.1	11.1
	Regal	3.1 (3130)	M	4.5	①	17.1	12.5
2000-01	Century	3.1 (3130)	M	4.5	①	16.0	12.6
	Grand Prix	3.8 (3785)	1	5.0	①	16.5	12.7
	Grand Prix	3.8 (3785)	K	5.0	①	16.5	12.7
	Grand Prix	3.1 (3130)	M	4.5	①	16.0	12.6
	Impala	3.4 (3393)	X	5.0	①	16.5	12.7
	Impala	3.8 (3785)	K	5.0	①	16.5	12.7
	Intrigue	3.5 (3475)	H	6.0	①	18.0	9.6
	Lumina	3.8 (3785)	K	5.0	①	16.5	12.7
	Lumina	3.1 (3130)	M	4.5	①	16.0	12.6
	Monte Carlo	3.8 (3785)	K	5.0	①	16.5	12.7
	Monte Carlo	3.1 (3130)	M	4.5	①	16.5	12.6
	Regal	3.8 (3785)	1	5.0	①	16.5	12.7
	Regal	3.8 (3785)	K	5.0	①	17.1	11.1
	Regal	3.1 (3130)	M	4.5	①	17.1	12.5

NOTE: All capacities are approximate. Add fluid gradually and ensure a proper fluid is obtained.

① Capacity is without filter replacement; Additional oil may be required

② 4T60 trans.: 12.0 pts.

   4T60E trans.: 14.8 pts.

   4T65E trans.: 14.8 pts.

93061CS6

Refer to the model specific sections for engine electrical system service procedures

VALVE SPECIFICATIONS

Year	Engine Displacement Liters (cc)	Engine ID/VIN	Seat Angle (deg.)	Face Angle (deg.)	Spring Test Pressure (lbs. @ in.)	Spring Installed Height (in.)	Stem-to-Guide Clearance (in.)		Stem Diameter (in.)	
							Intake	Exhaust	Intake	Exhaust
1997	3.1 (3130)	M	45	45	250@1.239	1.710	0.0001-0.0027	0.0010-0.0027	NA	NA
	3.4 (3393)	X	46	45	75@1.40	1.400	0.0011-0.0026	0.0014-0.0031	NA	NA
	3.8 (3785)	1	45	45	80@1.750	1.690-1.720	0.0015-0.0032	0.0015-0.0032	NA	NA
	3.8 (3785)	K	45	45	210@1.32	1.690-1.720	0.0015-0.0035	0.0015-0.0032	NA	NA
1998	3.1 (3130)	M	45	45	250@1.239	1.710	0.0001-0.0027	0.0010-0.0027	NA	NA
	3.8 (3785)	1	45	45	80@1.750	1.690-1.720	0.0015-0.0032	0.0015-0.0032	NA	NA
	3.8 (3785)	K	45	45	210@1.32	1.690-1.720	0.0015-0.0035	0.0015-0.0032	NA	NA
1999	3.1 (3130)	M	45	45	250@1.239	1.710	0.0001-0.0027	0.0010-0.0027	NA	NA
	3.5 (3475)	H	45.75	45	130-142@0.964	1.377	0.0010-0.0030	0.0020-0.0040	0.233-0.234	0.233-0.234
	3.8 (3785)	1	45	45	80@1.750	1.690-1.720	0.0015-0.0032	0.0015-0.0032	NA	NA
	3.8 (3785)	K	45	45	210@1.32	1.690-1.720	0.0015-0.0035	0.0015-0.0032	NA	NA
2000-01	3.1 (3130)	M	45	45	250@1.239	1.710	0.0001-0.0027	0.0010-0.0027	NA	NA
	3.4 (3393)	X	46	45	75@1.40	1.400	0.0011-0.0026	0.0014-0.0031	NA	NA
	3.5 (3475)	H	45.75	45	130-142@0.964	1.377	0.0010-0.0030	0.0020-0.0040	0.233-0.234	0.233-0.234
	3.8 (3785)	1	45	45	80@1.750	1.690-1.720	0.0015-0.0032	0.0015-0.0032	NA	NA
	3.8 (3785)	K	45	45	210@1.32	1.690-1.720	0.0015-0.0035	0.0015-0.0032	NA	NA

NA: Not Available

93061CS7

CRANKSHAFT AND CONNECTING ROD SPECIFICATIONS
All measurements are given in inches.

Year	Engine Displacement Liters (cc)	Engine ID/VIN	Crankshaft				Connecting Rod		
			Main Brg. Journal Dia.	Main Brg. Oil Clearance	Shaft End-play	Thrust on No.	Journal Diameter	Oil Clearance	Side Clearance
1997	3.1 (3130)	M	2.6473-2.6383	0.0008-0.0025 ①	0.0024-0.0083	3	1.9987-1.9994	0.0007-0.0024	0.0070-0.0170
	3.4 (3393)	X	2.6472-2.6479	0.0008-0.0025	0.0024-0.0083	3	1.9987-1.9994	0.0007-0.0024	0.0070-0.0170
	3.8 (3785)	1	2.4988-2.4998	0.0008-0.0022	0.0030-0.0110	2	2.3738-2.3745	0.0005-0.0026	0.0030-0.0150
	3.8 (3785)	K	2.4988-2.4998	0.0008-0.0022	0.0030-0.0110	2	2.3738-2.3745	0.0005-0.0026	0.0030-0.0150
1998	3.1 (3130)	M	2.6473-2.6383	0.0008-0.0025 ①	0.0024-0.0083	3	1.9987-1.9994	0.0007-0.0024	0.0070-0.017
	3.8 (3785)	1	2.4988-2.4998	0.0008-0.0022	0.0030-0.011	2	2.3738-2.3745	0.0005-0.0026	0.0030-0.0150
	3.8 (3785)	K	2.4988-2.4998	0.0008-0.0022	0.0030-0.0110	2	2.3738-2.3745	0.0005-0.0026	0.0030-0.0150
1999	3.1 (3130)	M	2.6473-2.6383	0.0008-0.0025 ①	0.0024-0.0083	3	1.9987-1.9994	0.0007-0.0024	0.0070-0.0170
	3.5 (3475)	H	2.7550-2.7560	0.0006-0.0021	0.0050-0.0200	3	2.1829-2.1835	0.0009-0.0025	0.0040-0.0130
	3.8 (3785)	1	2.4988-2.4998	0.0008-0.0022	0.0030-0.0110	2	2.3738-2.3745	0.0005-0.0026	0.0030-0.0150
	3.8 (3785)	K	2.4988-2.4998	0.0008-0.0022	0.0030-0.0110	2	2.3738-2.3745	0.0005-0.0026	0.0030-0.0150
2000-01	3.1 (3130)	M	2.6473-2.6383	0.0008-0.0025 ①	0.0024-0.0083	3	1.9987-1.9994	0.0007-0.0024	0.0070-0.0170
	3.4 (3393)	X	2.6472-2.6479	0.0008-0.0025	0.0024-0.0083	3	1.9987-1.9994	0.0007-0.0024	0.0070-0.0170
	3.5 (3475)	H	2.7550-2.7560	0.0006-0.0021	0.0050-0.0200	3	2.1829-2.1835	0.0009-0.0025	0.0040-0.0130
	3.8 (3785)	1	2.4988-2.4998	0.0008-0.0022	0.0030-0.0110	2	2.3738-2.3745	0.0005-0.0026	0.0030-0.0150
	3.8 (3785)	K	2.4988-2.4998	0.0008-0.0022	0.0030-0.0110	2	2.3738-2.3745	0.0005-0.0026	0.0030-0.0150

① Thrust bearing: 0.0012 - 0.0030

93061CS8

For accessory drive belt replacement procedures see the model specific sections of this manual

PISTON AND RING SPECIFICATIONS

All measurements are given in inches.

Year	Engine Displacement Liters (cc)	Engine ID/VIN	Piston Clearance	Ring Gap Top Compression	Ring Gap Bottom Compression	Ring Gap Oil Control	Ring Side Clearance Top Compression	Ring Side Clearance Bottom Compression	Ring Side Clearance Oil Control
1997	3.1 (3130)	M	0.0010-0.0018	0.0118-0.0196	0.0118-0.0196	0.0157-0.0551	0.0008-0.0015	0.0008-0.0015	0.0004-0.0012
	3.4 (3393)	X	0.0008-0.0020	0.0080-0.0180	0.0220-0.0320	0.0098-0.0229	0.0013-0.0031	0.0013-0.0031	0.0011-0.0081
	3.8 (3785)	1	0.0004-0.0020	0.0120-0.0220	0.0300-0.0400	0.0100-0.0300	0.0013-0.0031	0.0013-0.0031	0.0009-0.0079
	3.8 (3785)	K	0.0004-0.0020	0.0120-0.0220	0.0300-0.0400	0.0100-0.0300	0.0013-0.0031	0.0013-0.0031	0.0009-0.0079
1998	3.1 (3130)	M	0.0010-0.0018	0.0118-0.0196	0.0118-0.0196	0.0157-0.0551	0.0008-0.0015	0.0008-0.0015	0.0004-0.0012
	3.8 (3785)	1	0.0004-0.0020	0.0120-0.0220	0.0300-0.0400	0.0100-0.0300	0.0013-0.0031	0.0013-0.0031	0.0009-0.0079
	3.8 (3785)	K	0.0004-0.0020	0.0120-0.0220	0.0300-0.0400	0.0100-0.0300	0.0013-0.0031	0.0013-0.0031	0.0009-0.0079
1999	3.1 (3130)	M	0.0010-0.0018	0.0118-0.0196	0.0118-0.0196	0.0157-0.0551	0.0008-0.0015	0.0008-0.0015	0.0004-0.0012
	3.5 (3475)	H	0.0010-0.0025	0.0080-0.0180	0.0140-0.0200	0.0100-0.0300	0.0016-0.0037	0.0016-0.0037	side-sealing
	3.8 (3785)	1	0.0004-0.0020	0.0120-0.0220	0.0300-0.0400	0.0100-0.0300	0.0013-0.0031	0.0013-0.0031	0.0009-0.0079
	3.8 (3785)	K	0.0004-0.0020	0.0120-0.0220	0.0300-0.0400	0.0100-0.0300	0.0013-0.0031	0.0013-0.0031	0.0009-0.0079
2000-01	3.1 (3130)	M	0.0010-0.0018	0.0118-0.0196	0.0118-0.0196	0.0157-0.0551	0.0008-0.0015	0.0008-0.0015	0.0004-0.0012
	3.4 (3393)	X	0.0008-0.0020	0.0080-0.0180	0.0220-0.0320	0.0098-0.0229	0.0013-0.0031	0.0013-0.0031	0.0011-0.0081
	3.5 (3475)	H	0.0010-0.0025	0.0080-0.0180	0.0140-0.0200	0.0100-0.0300	0.0016-0.0037	0.0016-0.0037	side-sealing
	3.8 (3785)	1	0.0004-0.0020	0.0100-0.0160	0.0300-0.0400	0.0100-0.0300	0.0013-0.0031	0.0013-0.0031	0.0009-0.0079
	3.8 (3785)	K	0.0004-0.0020	0.0120-0.0220	0.0300-0.0400	0.0100-0.0300	0.0013-0.0031	0.0013-0.0031	0.0009-0.0079

93061CS9

TORQUE SPECIFICATIONS
All readings in ft. lbs.

Year	Engine Displacement Liters (cc)	Engine ID/VIN	Cylinder Head Bolts	Main Bearing Bolts	Rod Bearing Bolts	Crankshaft Damper Bolts	Flywheel Bolts	Manifold Intake	Manifold Exhaust	Spark Plug	Lug Nut
1997	3.1 (3130)	M	①	②	③	76	61	④	10	⑤	100
	3.4 (3393)	X	⑥	②	39	78	61	18	⑦	11	100
	3.8 (3785)	K	⑧	⑨	20	⑩	⑪	⑫	18	11	100
1998	3.1 (3130)	M	①	②	③	76	61	④	10	⑤	100
	3.8 (3785)	1	⑧	⑨	20	⑩	⑪	⑬	22	11	100
	3.8 (3785)	K	⑧	⑨	20	⑩	⑪	⑫	38	11	100
1999	3.1 (3130)	M	①	②	③	76	61	④	10	⑭	100
	3.5 (3475)	H	⑮	⑯	⑰	⑱	⑲	5	18	15	100
	3.8 (3785)	1	⑧	⑨	⑳	⑩	⑪	⑬	22	11	100
	3.8 (3785)	K	⑧	⑨	⑳	⑩	⑪	⑫	38	11	100
2000-01	3.1 (3130)	M	①	②	③	76	61	④	10	⑭	100
	3.4 (3393)	X	⑥	②	39	78	61	18	⑦	11	100
	3.5 (3475)	H	⑮	⑯	⑰	⑱	⑲	5	18	15	100
	3.8 (3785)	1	⑧	⑨	⑳	⑩	⑪	⑬	22	11	100
	3.8 (3785)	K	⑧	⑨	⑳	⑩	⑪	⑫	38	11	100

① Coat threads with sealer torque to 33 ft. lbs., then turn 1/4 turn (90 degrees)

② 37 ft. lbs. plus 77 degrees

③ 15 ft. lbs. plus 75 degrees

④ Torque all bolts to 15 ft. lbs. Retorque to 24 ft. lbs.

⑤ New cylinder head:
  1st-time installation: 20 ft. lbs.
  All other installations: 11 ft. lbs.

⑥ 37 ft. lbs. plus 90 degrees

⑦ 115 inch lbs.

⑧ Step 1: 35 ft. lbs.
  Step 2: plus 130 degrees
  Step 3: Rotate four center bolts an additional 30 degrees

⑨ 30 ft. lbs. plus 110 degrees
  Side bolts: 11 ft. lbs. plus 45 degrees

⑩ 110 ft. lbs. plus 76 degrees

⑪ 11 ft. lbs. plus 50 degrees

⑫ Upper manifold: 18 ft. lbs.
  Lower manifold bolt/nut: 22 ft. lbs.
  Upper manifold studs: 89 inch lbs.

⑬ Upper manifold: 8 ft. lbs.
  Lower manifold: 11 ft. lbs.

⑭ 20 ft. lbs. plus 50 degrees

⑮ Step 1: 22 ft. lbs.
  Step 2: plus 60 degrees
  Step 3: plus 60 degrees
  Step 4: plus 80 degrees

⑯ Cap bolts
  Step 1: 15 ft. lbs.
  Step 2: plus 70 degrees
  Perimeter bolts: 22 ft. lbs.

⑰ Step 1: 22 ft. lbs.
  Step 2: Loosen completely
  Step 3: 18 ft. lbs.
  Step 4: plus 110 degrees

⑱ Step 1: 37 ft. lbs.
  Step 2: plus 150 degrees

⑲ Step 1: 11 ft. lbs.
  Step 2: plus 50 degrees

⑳ 20 ft. lbs. plus 50 degrees

93061CS0

For brake related suspension and axle service, refer to the model specific sections of this manual

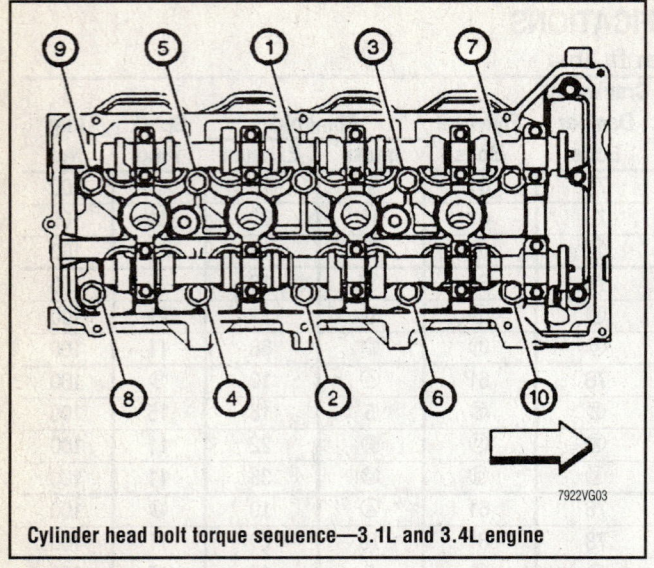

Cylinder head bolt torque sequence—3.1L and 3.4L engine

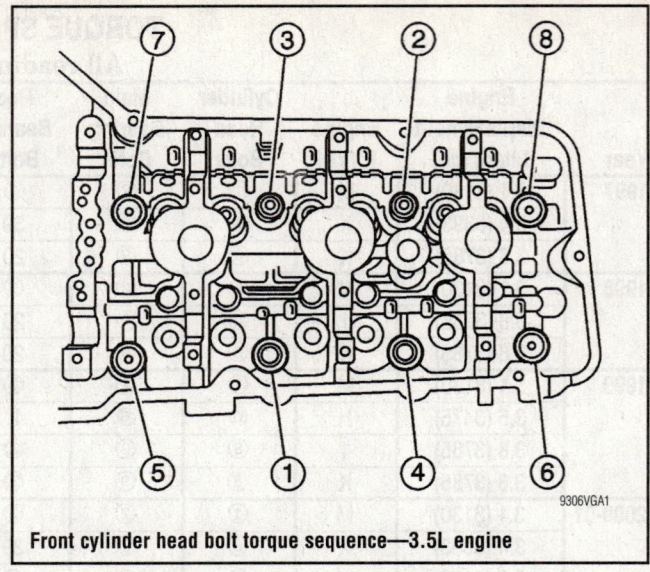

Front cylinder head bolt torque sequence—3.5L engine

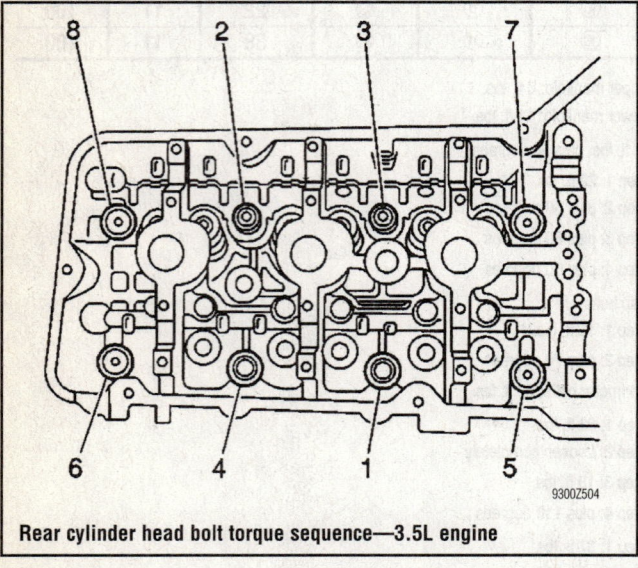

Rear cylinder head bolt torque sequence—3.5L engine

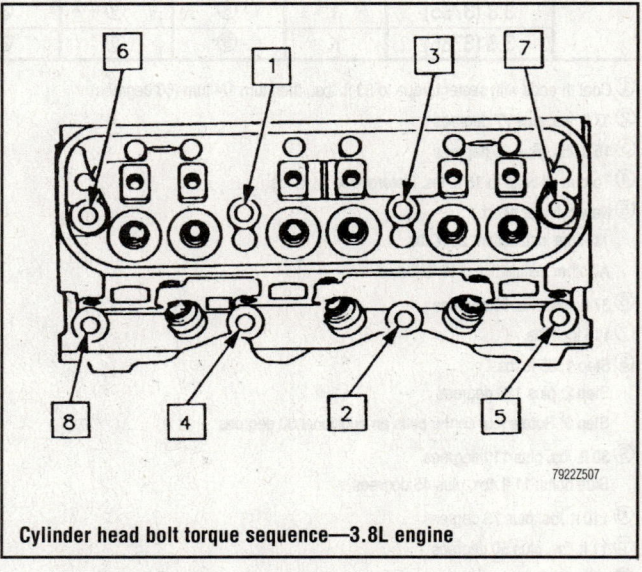

Cylinder head bolt torque sequence—3.8L engine

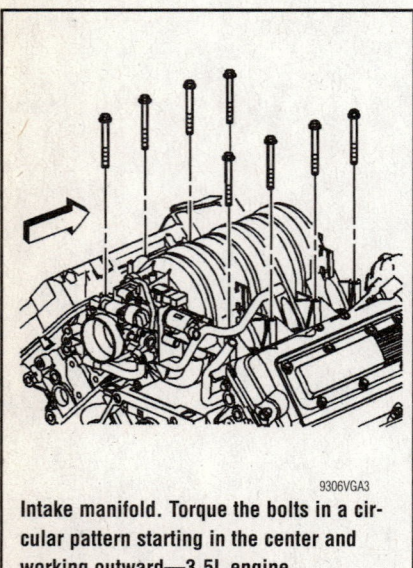

Intake manifold. Torque the bolts in a circular pattern starting in the center and working outward—3.5L engine

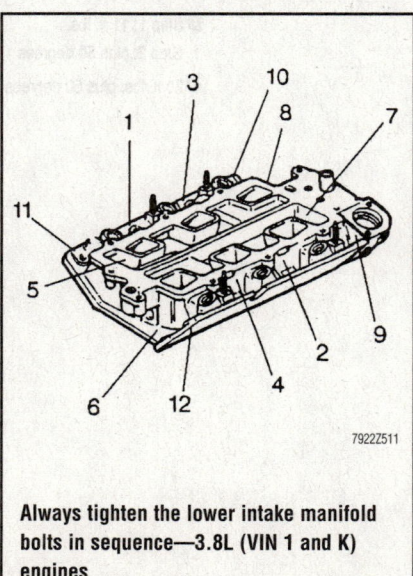

Always tighten the lower intake manifold bolts in sequence—3.8L (VIN 1 and K) engines

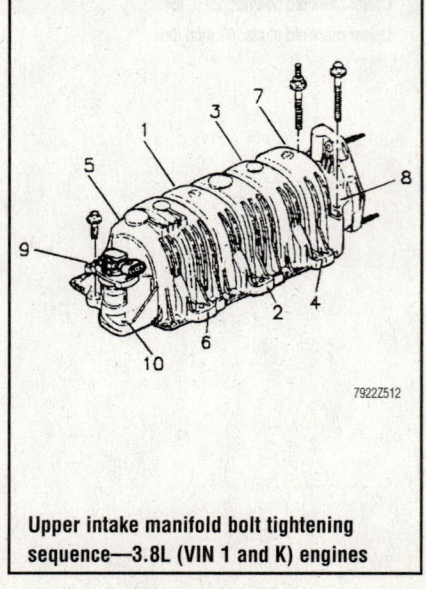

Upper intake manifold bolt tightening sequence—3.8L (VIN 1 and K) engines

BRAKE SPECIFICATIONS
GM W BODY
All measurements in inches unless noted

Year	Model		Brake Disc Original Thickness	Brake Disc Minimum Thickness	Brake Disc Maximum Runout	Brake Drum Diameter Original Inside Diameter	Brake Drum Diameter Max. Wear Limit	Brake Drum Diameter Maximum Machine Diameter	Minimum Lining Thickness Front	Minimum Lining Thickness Rear	Brake Caliper Bracket Bolts (ft. lbs.)	Brake Caliper Mounting Bolts (ft. lbs.)
1997	Cutlass	F	1.039	0.972	0.003	—	—	—	0.030	0.030	148	80
	Supreme	R	0.492	0.429	0.003	8.863	8.920	8.909	0.030	0.030	81	20
	Grand Prix	F	1.039	0.972	0.004	—	—	—	0.030	0.030	148	80
		R	0.492	0.429	0.004	8.863	8.920	8.909	0.030	0.030	81	20
	Lumina	F	1.040	0.972	0.004	—	—	—	0.030	0.030	148	80
		R	0.492	0.429	0.004	8.863	8.920	8.909	0.030	0.030	81	20
	Monte Carlo	F	1.040	0.972	0.004	—	—	—	0.030	0.030	148	80
		R	0.492	0.429	0.004	8.863	8.920	8.909	0.030	0.030	81	20
	Regal	F	1.039	0.972	0.003	—	—	—	0.030	0.030	148	80
		R	0.492	0.429	0.003	8.863	8.920	8.909	0.030	0.030	81	20
1998	Century	F	1.039	0.972	0.003	—	—	—	0.030	0.030	148	80
		R	0.492	0.429	0.003	8.863	8.920	8.909	0.030	0.030	81	20
	Grand Prix	F	1.039	0.972	0.004	—	—	—	0.030	0.030	137	63
		R	0.492	0.429	0.004	8.863	8.920	8.909	0.030	0.030	92	33
	Intrigue	F	1.039	0.972	0.003	—	—	—	0.030	0.030	137	63
		R	0.492	0.429	0.003	—	—	—	0.030	0.030	92	33
	Lumina	F	1.040	0.972	0.004	—	—	—	0.030	0.030	148	80
		R	0.492	0.429	0.004	8.863	8.920	8.909	0.030	0.030	81	20
	Monte Carlo	F	1.040	0.972	0.004	—	—	—	0.030	0.030	148	80
		R	0.492	0.429	0.004	8.863	8.920	8.909	0.030	0.030	81	20
	Regal	F	1.039	0.972	0.003	—	—	—	0.030	0.030	137	63
		R	0.492	0.429	0.003	8.863	8.920	8.909	0.030	0.030	92	33
1999	Century	F	1.039	0.972	0.003	—	—	—	0.030	0.030	137	63
		R	0.492	0.429	0.003	8.863	8.920	8.909	0.030	0.030	92	33
	Grand Prix	F	1.039	0.972	0.003	—	—	—	0.030	0.030	137	63
		R	0.492	0.429	0.003	—	—	—	0.030	0.030	92	33
	Intrigue	F	1.039	0.972	0.003	—	—	—	0.030	0.030	137	63
		R	0.492	0.429	0.003	—	—	—	0.030	0.030	92	33
	Lumina	F	1.040	0.972	0.004	—	—	—	0.030	0.030	148	80
		R	0.492	0.429	0.004	8.863	8.920	8.909	0.030	0.030	81	20
	Monte Carlo	F	1.040	0.972	0.004	—	—	—	0.030	0.030	148	80
		R	0.492	0.429	0.004	8.863	8.920	8.909	0.030	0.030	81	20
	Regal	F	1.039	0.972	0.003	—	—	—	0.030	0.030	137	63
		R	0.492	0.429	0.003	8.863	8.920	8.909	0.030	0.030	92	33
2000-01	Century	F	1.039	0.972	0.003	—	—	—	0.030	0.030	137	63
		R	0.492	0.429	0.003	8.863	8.920	8.909	0.030	0.030	92	33
	Grand Prix	F	1.039	0.972	0.003	—	—	—	0.030	0.030	137	63
		R	0.492	0.429	0.003	8.863	8.920	8.909	0.030	0.030	92	33
	Impala	F	1.040	0.972	0.004	—	—	—	0.030	0.030	148	80
		R	0.492	0.429	0.004	8.863	8.920	8.909	0.030	0.030	81	20
	Intrigue	F	1.039	0.972	0.003	—	—	—	0.030	0.030	137	63
		R	0.492	0.429	0.003	—	—	—	0.030	0.030	92	33
	Lumina	F	1.040	0.972	0.004	—	—	—	0.030	0.030	148	80
		R	0.492	0.429	0.004	8.863	8.920	8.909	0.030	0.030	81	20
	Monte Carlo	F	1.040	0.972	0.004	—	—	—	0.030	0.030	148	80
		R	0.492	0.429	0.004	8.863	8.920	8.909	0.030	0.030	81	20
	Regal	F	1.039	0.972	0.003	—	—	—	0.030	0.030	137	63
		R	0.492	0.429	0.003	8.863	8.920	8.909	0.030	0.030	92	33

F: Front
R: Rear

93061CT1

Refer to the model specific sections for driveline service procedures

SCHEDULED MAINTENANCE INTERVALS
(GM W BODY—BUICK CENTURY, REGAL, CHEVROLET IMPALA, LUMINA, MONTE CARLO, OLDSMOBILE INTRIGUE, CUTLASS SUPREME & PONTIAC GRAND PRIX)

TO BE SERVICED	TYPE OF SERVICE	VEHICLE MILEAGE INTERVAL (x1000)												
		7.5	15	22.5	30	37.5	45	52.5	60	67.5	75	82.5	90	97.5
Engine oil & filter	R	✓	✓	✓	✓	✓	✓	✓	✓	✓	✓	✓	✓	✓
Automatic transaxle fluid & filter ①	S/I	✓	✓	✓	✓	✓	✓	✓	✓	✓	✓	✓	✓	✓
Brake hoses	S/I	✓	✓	✓	✓	✓	✓	✓	✓	✓	✓	✓	✓	✓
Coolant level, hoses & clamps	S/I	✓	✓	✓	✓	✓	✓	✓	✓	✓	✓	✓	✓	✓
Drive shaft boots & front suspension components	S/I	✓	✓	✓	✓	✓	✓	✓	✓	✓	✓	✓	✓	✓
Exhaust system & throttle linkage	S/I	✓	✓	✓	✓	✓	✓	✓	✓	✓	✓	✓	✓	✓
Lubricate chassis, suspension, steering linkage, transaxle shift linkage, parking brake cable guides, underbody contact points & linkage	S/I	✓	✓	✓	✓	✓	✓	✓	✓	✓	✓	✓	✓	✓
Rotate tires	S/I	✓		✓		✓		✓		✓		✓		✓
Air filter element	R				✓				✓				✓	
Engine coolant ②	R				✓				✓				✓	
PCV filter	R				✓				✓				✓	
Spark plugs ③	R				✓				✓				✓	
Accessory drive belt(s)	S/I				✓				✓				✓	
Ignition cables, EGR & fuel systems	S/I				✓				✓				✓	
Camshaft timing belt	R								✓					

R: Replace   S/I: Service or Inspect

① Automatic transaxle fluid & filter: replace at 100,000 miles (if not changed previously).

② Engine coolant: replace every 100,000 miles. Use O.E. specified (DEX-COOL™) coolant only. If any silicate coolant is used, the service interval is every 30,000 miles

③ Platinum tip spark plugs: replace every 100,000 miles.

FREQUENT OPERATION MAINTENANCE (SEVERE SERVICE)

If a vehicle is operated under any of the following conditions it is considered severe service:

- Extremely dusty areas.
- 50% or more of the vehicle operation is in 32°C (90°F) or higher temperatures, or constant operation in temperatures below 0°C (32°F).
- Prolonged idling (vehicle operation in stop and go traffic).
- Frequent short running periods (engine does not warm to normal operating temperatures).
- Police, taxi, delivery usage or trailer towing usage.

Oil & oil filter: change every 3000 miles

Chassis lubrication: lubricate every 6000 miles.

Rotate tires at 6000 miles, then every 12,000 miles.

Air filter element: service or inspect every 15,000 miles.

Camshaft timing belt: change every 60,000 miles.

93061CT2

SCHEDULED MAINTENANCE INTERVALS
GENERAL MOTORS CORPORATION
W BODY
BUICK CENTURY, REGAL
CHEVROLET IMPALA, LUMINA, MONTE CARLO
OLDSMOBILE INTRIGUE, CUTLASS SUPREME
PONTIAC GRAND PRIX

The following should be used as a guide when determining the amount of work required for a particular service.
In estimating how long a particular Scheduled Maintenance Service should take, please observe the following:

● Labor Time is time based on field research and data supplied by the vehicle manufacturer.
● Labor time operations are given in hours and tenths of an hour.
● All labor operations are to be used as a guide.

Mechanic Skill Level Codes:
(A) PRECISION: Highly skilled with multiple certification.
(B) GENERAL: Normally skilled with certification.
(C) MAINTENANCE: Semi-skilled working on certification.

	LABOR TIME		LABOR TIME		LABOR TIME
7500 Mile Service (C)		**37500 Mile Service (C)**		**75000 Mile Service (C)**	
All Models	1.5	All Models	1.3	All Models	.8
15000 Mile Service (C)		**45000 Mile Service (C)**		**82500 Mile Service (C)**	
All Models	.8	All Models	.8	All Models	1.3
22500 Mile Service (C)		**52500 Mile Service (C)**		**90000 Mile Service (B)**	
All Models	1.3	All Models	1.3	All Models	3.1
30000 Mile Service (B)		**60000 Mile Service (B)**		**97500 Mile Service (C)**	
All Models	3.1	All Models	3.1	All Models	1.3
		Add for timing belt R&R.			
		67500 Mile Service (C)			
		All Models	1.3		

93061CT3

For exhaust manifold replacement procedures, see the model specific sections of this manual

GENERAL MOTORS Y-BODY
Chevrolet Corvette

ENGINE AND VEHICLE IDENTIFICATION

			Engine				Model Year	
Code ①	Liters (cc)	Cu. In.	Cyl.	Fuel Sys.	Engine Type	Eng. Mfg.	Code ②	Year
G	5.7 (5665)	350	8	MFI	OHV	CPC	V	1997

Code ②	Year
V	1997
W	1998
X	1999
Y	2000
1	2001

CPC: Chevrolet/Pontiac/Canada
MFI: Multi-point Fuel Injection
OHV: Over Head Valves
① 8th position of VIN
② 10th position of VIN

93061CT4

GENERAL ENGINE SPECIFICATIONS

Year	Model	Engine Displacement Liters (cc)	Engine Series (ID/VIN)	Fuel System	Net Horsepower @ rpm	Net Torque @ rpm (ft. lbs.)	Bore x Stroke (in.)	Compression Ratio	Oil Pressure @ rpm
1997	Corvette	5.7 (5665)	G	MFI	345@5600	350@4400	3.89x3.62	10.1:1	18@2000
1998	Corvette	5.7 (5665)	G	MFI	345@5600	350@4400	3.89x3.62	10.1:1	18@2000
1999	Corvette	5.7 (5665)	G	MFI	345@5600	350@4400	3.89x3.62	10.1:1	18@2000
2000-01	Corvette	5.7 (5665)	G	MFI	345@5600	350@4400	3.89x3.62	10.1:1	18@2000

MFI: Multi-point Fuel Injection

93061CT5

ENGINE TUNE-UP SPECIFICATIONS

Year	Engine Displacement Liters (cc)	Engine ID/VIN	Spark Plug Gap (in.)	Ignition Timing (deg.) MT	AT	Fuel Pump (psi)	Idle Speed (rpm) MT	AT	Valve Clearance In.	Ex.
1997	5.7 (5665)	G	0.060	①	①	48-55	①	①	HYD	HYD
1998	5.7 (5665)	G	0.060	①	①	48-55	①	①	HYD	HYD
1999	5.7 (5665)	G	0.060	①	①	48-55	①	①	HYD	HYD
2000-01	5.7 (5665)	G	0.060	①	①	48-55	①	①	HYD	HYD

NOTE: The Vehicle Emission Control Information label often reflects specification changes made during production. The label figures must be used if they differ from those in this chart.

HYD: Hydraulic

① Refer to Vehicle Emission Control Information label

93061CT6

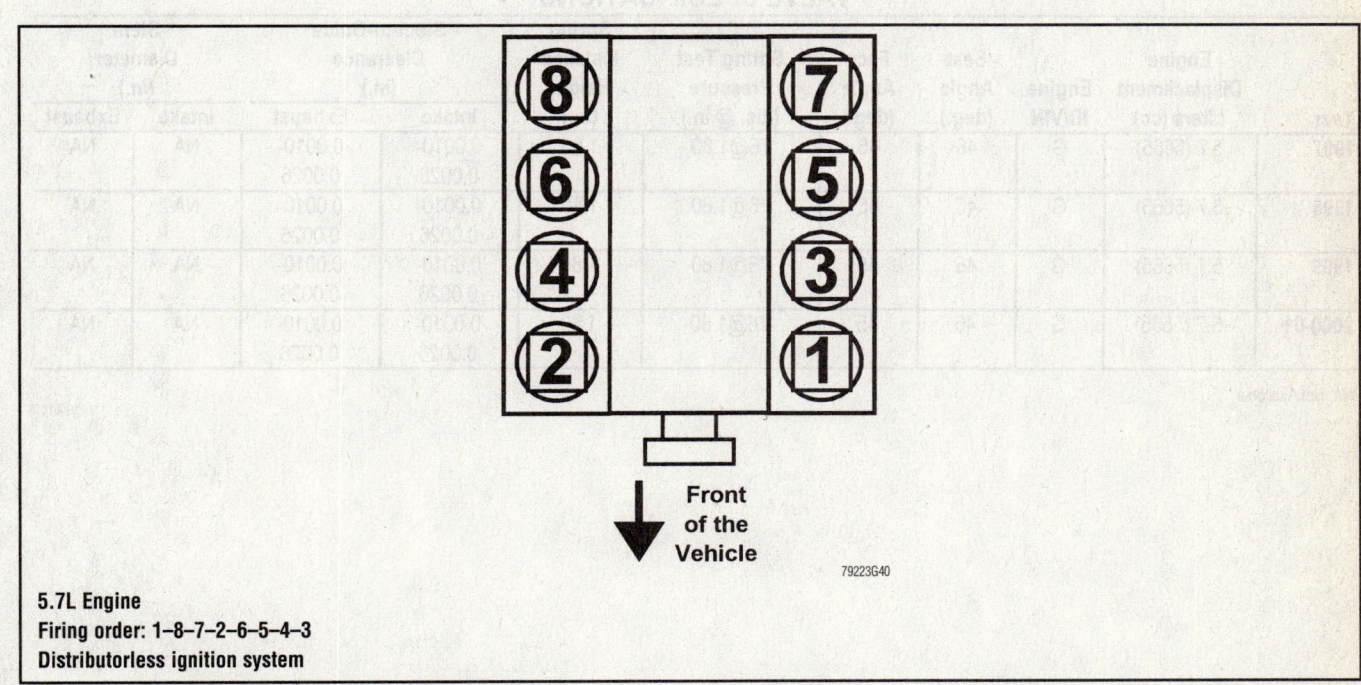

5.7L Engine
Firing order: 1–8–7–2–6–5–4–3
Distributorless ignition system

Refer to the model specific sections for cooling system service procedures

CAPACITIES

Year	Model	Engine Displacement Liters (cc)	Engine ID/VIN	Engine Oil with Filter (qts.)	Transmission (pts.) 6-Spd	Auto.	Drive Axle (pts.)	Fuel Tank (gal.)	Cooling System (qts.)
1997	Corvette	5.7 (5737)	G	6.5	①	②	3.8	20.0	14.7
1998	Corvette	5.7 (5737)	G	6.5	①	②	3.8	20.0	14.7
1999	Corvette	5.7 (5737)	G	6.5	①	②	3.8	20.0	14.7
2000-01	Corvette	5.7 (5737)	G	6.5	①	②	3.8	20.0	14.7

NOTE: All capacities are approximate. Add fluid gradually and ensure a proper fluid level is obtained.

① MM 6 speed trans: 4.1 pts.

② 4L60E trans: 10.0 pts.

93061CT7

VALVE SPECIFICATIONS

Year	Engine Displacement Liters (cc)	Engine ID/VIN	Seat Angle (deg.)	Face Angle (deg.)	Spring Test Pressure (lbs. @ in.)	Spring Installed Height (in.)	Stem-to-Guide Clearance (in.) Intake	Exhaust	Stem Diameter (in.) Intake	Exhaust
1997	5.7 (5665)	G	46	45	76@1.80	1.80	0.0010-0.0026	0.0010-0.0026	NA	NA
1998	5.7 (5665)	G	46	45	76@1.80	1.80	0.0010-0.0026	0.0010-0.0026	NA	NA
1999	5.7 (5665)	G	46	45	76@1.80	1.80	0.0010-0.0026	0.0010-0.0026	NA	NA
2000-01	5.7 (5665)	G	46	45	76@1.80	1.80	0.0010-0.0026	0.0010-0.0026	NA	NA

NA: Not Available

93061CT8

CRANKSHAFT AND CONNECTING ROD SPECIFICATIONS

All measurements are given in inches.

Year	Engine Displacement Liters (cc)	Engine ID/VIN	Crankshaft				Connecting Rod		
			Main Brg. Journal Dia.	Main Brg. Oil Clearance	Shaft End-play	Thrust on No.	Journal Diameter	Oil Clearance	Side Clearance
1997	5.7 (5665)	G	2.558-2.559	0.0007-0.0021	0.0015-0.0078	5	2.0987	0.0006-0.0025	0.0043-0.0200
1998	5.7 (5665)	G	2.558-2.559	0.0007-0.0021	0.0015-0.0078	5	2.0987	0.0006-0.0025	0.0043-0.0200
1999	5.7 (5665)	G	2.558-2.559	0.0007-0.0021	0.0015-0.0078	5	2.0987	0.0006-0.0025	0.0043-0.0200
2000-01	5.7 (5665)	G	2.558-2.559	0.0007-0.0021	0.0015-0.0078	5	2.0987	0.0006-0.0025	0.0043-0.0200

93061CT9

PISTON AND RING SPECIFICATIONS

All measurements are given in inches.

Year	Engine Displacement Liters (cc)	Engine ID/VIN	Piston Clearance	Ring Gap			Ring Side Clearance		
				Top Compression	Bottom Compression	Oil Control	Top Compression	Bottom Compression	Oil Control
1997	5.7 (5665)	G	0.0007-0.0021	0.009-0.015	0.017-0.025	0.007-0.027	0.0016-0.0033	0.0016-0.0031	0.0004-0.0087
1998	5.7 (5665)	G	0.0007-0.0021	0.009-0.015	0.017-0.025	0.007-0.027	0.0016-0.0033	0.0016-0.0031	0.0004-0.0087
1999	5.7 (5665)	G	0.0007-0.0021	0.009-0.015	0.017-0.025	0.007-0.027	0.0016-0.0033	0.0016-0.0031	0.0004-0.0087
2000-01	5.7 (5665)	G	0.0007-0.0021	0.009-0.015	0.017-0.025	0.007-0.027	0.0016-0.0033	0.0016-0.0031	0.0004-0.0087

93061CT0

TORQUE SPECIFICATIONS
All readings in ft. lbs.

Year	Engine Displacement Liters (cc)	Engine ID/VIN	Cylinder Head Bolts	Main Bearing Bolts	Rod Bearing Bolts	Crankshaft Damper Bolts	Flywheel Bolts	Manifold Intake	Manifold Exhaust	Spark Plugs	Lug Nut
1997	5.7 (5665)	G	①	②	③	④	⑤	⑥	⑦	11	100
1998	5.7 (5665)	G	①	②	③	④	⑤	⑥	⑦	11	100
1999	5.7 (5665)	G	①	②	③	④	⑤	⑥	⑦	11	100
2000-01	5.7 (5665)	G	①	②	③	④	⑤	⑥	⑦	11	100

① Step 1: 22 ft. lbs.
Step 2: Rotate 76 degrees
Step 3: Repeat Step 2 except for the medium length bolts at the front and rear.
Step 4: Rotate the medium bolts at the front and rear of each head 34 degrees.

② Step 1: Inner bolts 15 ft. lbs.
Step 2: Inner bolts rotate 80 degrees
Step 3: Side bolts 18 ft. lbs.
Step 4: Outer studs 15 ft. lbs.
Step 5: Outer studs rotate 53 degrees

③ Step 1: 15 ft. lbs.
Step 2: Rotate 60 degrees

④ Step 1: 240 ft. lbs.
Step 2: Loosen bolt and retighten to 37 ft. lbs.
Step 3: Rotate 120 degrees

⑤ Step 1: 15 ft. lbs.
Step 2: 37 ft. lbs.
Step 3: 74 ft. lbs.

⑥ Step 1: 44 inch lbs.
Step 2: 74 inch lbs.

⑦ Step 1: 11 ft. lbs.
Step 2: 18 ft. lbs.

93061CU1

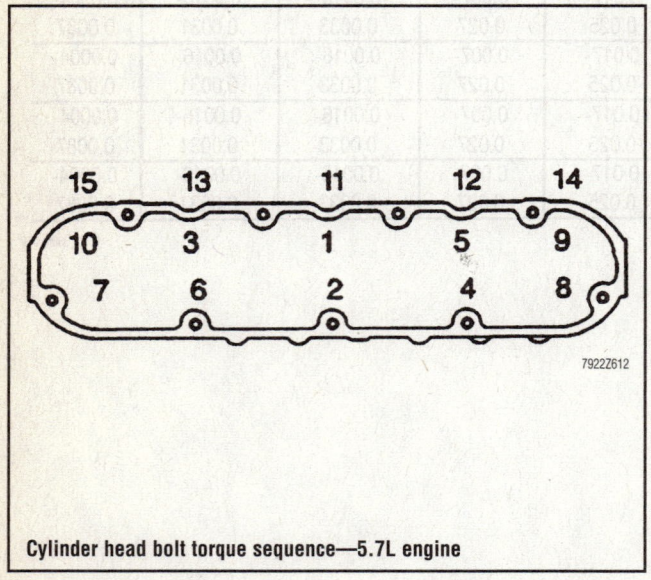

Cylinder head bolt torque sequence—5.7L engine

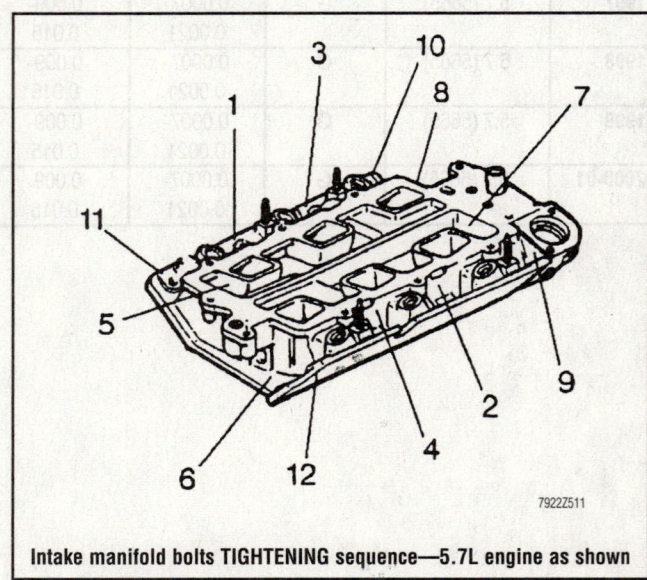

Intake manifold bolts TIGHTENING sequence—5.7L engine as shown

BRAKE SPECIFICATIONS
GM Y BODY
All measurements in inches unless noted

| Year | Model | Brake Disc | | | Minimum Lining Thickness | | Brake Caliper | |
		Original Thickness	Minimum Thickness	Maximum Runout	Front	Rear	Bracket Bolts (ft. lbs.)	Mounting Bolts (ft. lbs.)
1997	Corvette	①	②	0.006	0.030	0.030	—	③
1998	Corvette	①	②	0.006	0.030	0.030	—	③
1999	Corvette	①	②	0.006	0.030	0.030	—	③
2000-01	Corvette	①	②	0.006	0.030	0.030	—	③

① Heavy duty: 1.110; Std.: 0.795
② Heavy duty: 1.059; Std.: 0.744
③ Front: not available, Rear: upper 26 ft. lbs., lower 16 ft. lbs.

93061CU2

Timing chain and gear service is covered in the model specific sections of this manual

SCHEDULED MAINTENANCE INTERVALS
(GM Y BODY—CHEVROLET CORVETTE)

TO BE SERVICED	TYPE OF SERVICE	VEHICLE MILEAGE INTERVAL (x1000)												
		7.5	15	22.5	30	37.5	45	52.5	60	67.5	75	82.5	90	97.5
Engine oil & filter ①	R	✓	✓	✓	✓	✓	✓	✓	✓	✓	✓	✓	✓	✓
Brake hoses & brake lining	S/I	✓	✓	✓	✓	✓	✓	✓	✓	✓	✓	✓	✓	✓
Coolant level, hoses & clamps	S/I	✓	✓	✓	✓	✓	✓	✓	✓	✓	✓	✓	✓	✓
Exhaust system & throttle linkage	S/I	✓	✓	✓	✓	✓	✓	✓	✓	✓	✓	✓	✓	✓
Lubricate chassis, suspension, steering linkage, transaxle shift linkage, parking brake cable guides, underbody contact points & linkage	S/I	✓	✓	✓	✓	✓	✓	✓	✓	✓	✓	✓	✓	✓
Rear axle fluid level	S/I	✓	✓	✓	✓	✓	✓	✓	✓	✓	✓	✓	✓	✓
Automatic transaxle fluid & filter ②	S/I		✓		✓		✓		✓		✓		✓	
Air filter element	R				✓				✓				✓	
Engine coolant ③	R				✓				✓				✓	
Ignition cables, EGR & fuel systems	S/I				✓				✓				✓	
Serpentine drive belt	S/I				✓				✓				✓	
Spark plugs ④	R													

R: Replace   S/I: Service or Inspect

① Corvette engines require a special oil meeting GM Standard 4718M.

② Automatic transaxle fluid & filter: replace at 100,000 miles (if not changed previously).

③ Engine coolant: replace every 100,000 miles. Use O.E. specified (DEX-COOL™) coolant only. If any silicate coolant is used, the service interval is every 30,000 miles.

④ Platinum tip spark plugs: replace every 100,000 miles.

FREQUENT OPERATION MAINTENANCE (SEVERE SERVICE)

If a vehicle is operated under any of the following conditions it is considered severe service:

- Extremely dusty areas.

- 50% or more of the vehicle operation is in 32°C (90°F) or higher temperatures, or constant operation in temperatures below 0°C (32°F).

- Prolonged idling (vehicle operation in stop and go traffic).

- Frequent short running periods (engine does not warm to normal operating temperatures).

- Police, taxi, delivery usage or trailer towing usage.

Engine oil & oil filter: change every 3000 miles

Chassis lubrication: lubricate every 6000 miles.

Lubricate suspension, parking brake cable guides, underbody contact points & linkage: lubricate every 6000 miles.

Air filter element: service or inspect every 15,000 miles.

Automatic transmission fluid & filter: change every 15,000 miles.

93061CU3

SCHEDULED MAINTENANCE INTERVALS
GENERAL MOTORS CORPORATION
Y BODY
CHEVROLET CORVETTE

The following should be used as a guide when determining the amount of work required for a particular service.
In estimating how long a particular Scheduled Maintenance Service should take, please observe the following:

- Labor Time is time based on field research and data supplied by the vehicle manufacturer.
- Labor time operations are given in hours and tenths of an hour.
- All labor operations are to be used as a guide.

Mechanic Skill Level Codes:
(A) PRECISION: Highly skilled with multiple certification.
(B) GENERAL: Normally skilled with certification.
(C) MAINTENANCE: Semi-skilled working on certification.

	LABOR TIME		LABOR TIME		LABOR TIME
7500 Mile Service (C)		**37500 Mile Service (C)**		**75000 Mile Service (C)**	
All Models	1.2	All Models	1.2	All Models	1.3
15000 Mile Service (C)		**45000 Mile Service (C)**		**82500 Mile Service (C)**	
All Models	1.3	All Models	1.3	All Models	1.2
22500 Mile Service (C)		**52500 Mile Service (C)**		**90000 Mile Service (B)**	
All Models	1.2	All Models	1.2	All Models	2.2
30000 Mile Service (B)		**60000 Mile Service (B)**		**97500 Mile Service (C)**	
All Models	2.2	All Models	2.2	All Models	1.2
		67500 Mile Service (C)			
		All Models	1.2		

93061CU4

Ignition system service is covered in the model specific sections of this manual

TIRE, WHEEL AND BALL JOINT SPECIFICATIONS
Buick

Year	Model	OEM Tires Standard	OEM Tires Optional	Tire Pressures (psi) Front	Tire Pressures (psi) Rear	Wheel Size	Ball Joint Inspection
1997	Regal, exc GS	P205/70R15	P215/70R15 P225/60R16	30	30	6-JJ	①
	Regal GS	P225/60R16	None	30	30	6.5-JJ	①
	Century 2dr	P225/60R16	None	30	30	6.5-JJ	①
	Century 4dr	P205/70R15	P225/60R16	30 30	30	Std: 6-JJ Opt: 6.5-JJ	①
	LeSabre	P205/70R15	P215/60R16	30	30	6-JJ	②
	Park Avenue	P225/60R16	None	30	30	6.5-JJ	②
	Riviera	P225/60R16	None	30	30	6.5-JJ	①
	Skylark, exc.GS	P195/70R14	P195/65R15	30	30	6-JJ	①
	Skylark GS	P205/55R16	None	30	30	6.5-JJ	①
1998	Regal, exc GS	P205/70R15	P215/70R15 P225/60R16	30	30	6-JJ	①
	Regal GS	P225/60R16	None	30	30	6.5-JJ	①
	Century 2dr	P225/60R16	None	30	30	6.5-JJ	①
	Century 4dr	P205/70R15	P225/60R16	30	30	Std: 6-JJ Opt: 6.5-JJ	①
	LeSabre	P205/70R15	P215/60R16	30	30	6-JJ	②
	Park Avenue	P225/60R16	None	30	30	6.5-JJ	②
	Riviera	P225/60R16	None	30	30	6.5-JJ	①
	Skylark, exc.GS	P195/70R14	P195/65R15	30	30	6-JJ	①
	Skylark GS	P205/55R16	None	30	30	6.5-JJ	①
1999	Regal, exc GS	P205/70R15	P215/70R15 P225/60R16	30	30	6-JJ	①
	Regal GS	P225/60R16	None	30	30	6.5-JJ	①
	Century 2dr	P225/60R16	None	30	30	6.5-JJ	①
	Century 4dr	P205/70R15	P225/60R16	30	30	Std: 6-JJ Opt: 6.5-JJ	①
	LeSabre	P205/70R15	P215/60R16	30	30	6-JJ	②
	Park Avenue	P225/60R16	None	30	30	6.5-JJ	②
	Riviera	P225/60R16	None	30	30	6.5-JJ	①
	Skylark, exc.GS	P195/70R14	P195/65R15	30	30	6-JJ	①
	Skylark GS	P205/55R16	None	30	30	6.5-JJ	①

93061CU6

Buick

Year	Model	OEM Tires		Tire Pressures (psi)		Wheel Size	Ball Joint Inspection
		Standard	Optional	Front	Rear		
2000-01	Regal, exc GS	P205/70R15	P215/70R15 P225/60R16	30	30	6-JJ	①
	Regal GS	P225/60R16	None	30	30	6.5-JJ	①
	Century 2dr	P225/60R16	None	30	30	6.5-JJ	①
	Century 4dr	P205/70R15	P225/60R16	30	30	Std: 6-JJ Opt: 6.5-JJ	①
	LeSabre	P205/70R15	P215/60R16	30	30	6-JJ	②
	Park Avenue	P225/60R16	None	30	30	6.5-JJ	②
	Riviera	P225/60R16	None	30	30	6.5-JJ	①

OEM: Original Equipment Manufacturer

PSI: Pounds Per Square Inch

STD: Standard

OPT: Optional

L: Lower

U: Upper

① Replace if any measurable movement is found.

② Do not lift car. Inspect the boss into which the grease fitting is threaded. Replace if the boss is flush or receded below the surface of the ball joint.

93061CU7

TIRE, WHEEL AND BALL JOINT SPECIFICATIONS
Cadillac

| Year | Model | OEM Tires | | Tire Pressures (psi) | | Wheel Size | Ball Joint Inspection |
		Standard	Optional	Front	Rear		
1997	Catera	P225/55HR16	None	32	32	7-JJ	0.125 in. ①
	deVille	P225/60R16	None	30	30	7-JJ	①
	Eldorado	P225/60R16	P225/60ZR16	Std: 28 Opt: 29	Std: 26 Opt: 29	7-JJ	①
	Fleetwood	P225/60R16	None	30	30	7-JJ	①
	Seville	P225/60R16	P225/60ZR16	Std: 28 Opt: 29	Std: 26 Opt: 29	7-JJ	①
1998	Catera	P225/55HR16	None	32	32	7-JJ	0.125 in. ①
	deVille	P225/60R16	None	30	30	7-JJ	①
	Eldorado	P225/60R16	P225/60ZR16	Std: 28 Opt: 29	Std: 26 Opt: 29	7-JJ	①
	Fleetwood	P225/60R16	None	30	30	7-JJ	①
	Seville	P225/60R16	P225/60ZR16	Std: 28 Opt: 29	Std: 26 Opt: 29	7-JJ	①
1999	Catera	P225/55HR16	None	32	32	7-JJ	0.125 in. ①
	deVille	P225/60R16	None	30	30	7-JJ	①
	Eldorado	P225/60R16	P225/60ZR16	Std: 28 Opt: 29	Std: 26 Opt: 29	7-JJ	①
	Fleetwood	P225/60R16	None	30	30	7-JJ	①
	Seville	P225/60R16	P235/60ZR16	Std: 28 Opt: 29	Std: 26 Opt: 29	7-JJ	①
2000-01	Catera	P225/55HR16	None	32	32	7-JJ	0.125 in. ①
	deVille	P225/60R16	None	30	30	7-JJ	①
	Eldorado	P225/60R16	P225/60ZR16	Std: 28 Opt: 29	Std: 26 Opt: 29	7-JJ	①
	Fleetwood	P225/60R16	None	30	30	7-JJ	①
	Seville	P225/60R16	P235/60ZR16	Std: 28 Opt: 29	Std: 26 Opt: 29	7-JJ	①

OEM: Original Equipment Manufacturer

PSI: Pounds Per Square Inch

STD: Standard

OPT: Optional

L: Lower

U: Upper

① Replace if any measurable movement is found.

② Do not lift car. Inspect the boss into which the grease fitting is threaded. Replace if the boss is flush or receded below the surface of the ball joint.

93061CU8

TIRE, WHEEL AND BALL JOINT SPECIFICATIONS
Chevrolet

Year	Model	OEM Tires Standard	OEM Tires Optional	Tire Pressures (psi) Front	Tire Pressures (psi) Rear	Wheel Size	Ball Joint Inspection
1997	Camaro base	215/60R16	P235/55R16	30	30	7.5-JJ	U: 0.125 in. L: 0.047 in.
	Camaro RS	P235/55R16	None	30	30	8-J	U: 0.125 in. L: 0.047 in.
	Camaro Z28	P235/55R16	P245/50ZR16	30	30	8-J	U: 0.125 in.
			P275/40ZR17	30	30	9-J	L: 0.047 in.
	Cavalier base	P195/70R14	None	30	30	6-JJ	①
	Cavalier LS, RS	P195/65R15	None	30	30	6-JJ	①
	Cavalier Z24	P205/55R16	None	30	30	6-JJ	①
	Corvette	Fr: P245/45ZR17 Rr: P275/40ZR18	None	30	30	8.5	U: 0.125 in. L: 0.047 in.
	Lumina 3.1L	P205/70R15	P215/65R16	30	30	6-JJ	①
			P225/60R16	30	30	6.5-JJ	
	Lumina 3.4L	P225/60R16	None	30	30	6.5-JJ	①
	Malibu	P215/60R15	None	30	30	6-JJ	①
1998	Camaro base	215/60R16	P235/55R16	30	30	7.5-JJ	
	Camaro RS	P235/55R16	None	30	30	8-J	U: 0.125 in. L: 0.047 in.
	Camaro Z28	P235/55R16	P245/50ZR16	30	30	8-J	U: 0.125 in.
			P275/40ZR17	30	30	9-J	L: 0.047 in.
	Cavalier base	P195/70R14	None	30	30	6-JJ	①
	Cavalier LS, RS	P195/65R15	None	30	30	6-JJ	①
	Cavalier Z24	P205/55R16	None	30	30	6-JJ	①
	Corvette	Fr: P245/45ZR17 Rr: P275/40ZR18	None	30	30	8.5	U: 0.125 in. L: 0.047 in.
	Lumina 3.1L	P205/70R15	P215/65R16	30	30	6-JJ	①
			P225/60R16	30	30	6.5-JJ	
	Lumina 3.4L	P225/60R16	None	30	30	6.5-JJ	①
	Malibu	P215/60R15	None	30	30	6-JJ	①
1999	Camaro RS	P235/55R16	None	30	30	8-J	U: 0.125 in. L: 0.047 in.
	Camaro Z28	P235/55R16	P245/50ZR16	30	30	8-J	U: 0.125 in.
			P275/40ZR17	30	30	9-J	L: 0.047 in.
	Cavalier base	P195/70R14	None	30	30	6-JJ	①
	Cavalier LS, RS	P195/65R15	None	30	30	6-JJ	①
	Cavalier Z24	P205/55R16	None	30	30	6-JJ	①
	Corvette	Fr: P245/45ZR17 Rr: P275/40ZR18	None	30	30	8.5	U: 0.125 in. L: 0.047 in.
	Lumina 3.1L	P205/70R15	P215/65R16	30	30	6-JJ	①
			P225/60R16	30	30	6.5-JJ	
	Lumina 3.4L	P225/60R16	None	30	30	6.5-JJ	①
	Malibu	P215/60R15	None	30	30	6-JJ	①
	Metro	P155/80R13	None	30	30	4.5J	①
	Prizm	P175/65R14	P185/65R14	30	30	5.5J	①

93061CU9

Refer to the model specific sections for engine mechanical service procedures

TIRE, WHEEL AND BALL JOINT SPECIFICATIONS
Chevrolet

Year	Model	OEM Tires		Tire Pressures (psi)		Wheel Size	Ball Joint Inspection
		Standard	Optional	Front	Rear		
2000-01	Camaro RS	P235/55R16	None	30	30	8-J	U: 0.125 in. L: 0.047 in.
	Camaro Z28	P235/55R16	P245/50ZR16	30	30	8-J	U: 0.125 in.
			P275/40ZR17	30	30	9-J	L: 0.047 in.
	Cavalier base	P195/70R14	None	30	30	6-JJ	①
	Cavalier LS, RS	P195/65R15	None	30	30	6-JJ	①
	Cavalier Z24	P205/55R16	None	30	30	6-JJ	①
	Corvette	Fr: P245/45ZR17 Rr: P275/40ZR18	None	30	30	8.5	U: 0.125 in. L: 0.047 in.
	Lumina 3.1L	P205/70R15	P215/65R16	30	30	6-JJ	①
			P225/60R16	30	30	6.5-JJ	
	Lumina 3.4L	P225/60R16	None	30	30	6.5-JJ	①
	Malibu	P215/60R15	None	30	30	6-JJ	①
	Metro	P155/80R13	None	30	30	4.5J	①
	Prizm	P175/65R14	P185/65R14	30	30	5.5J	①

OEM: Original Equipment Manufacturer

PSI: Pounds Per Square Inch

STD: Standard

OPT: Optional

L: Lower

U: Upper

Fr: Front

Rr: Rear

① Replace if any measurable movement is found

93061CU0

TIRE, WHEEL AND BALL JOINT SPECIFICATIONS
Oldsmobile

Year	Model	OEM Tires Standard	OEM Tires Optional	Tire Pressures (psi) Front	Tire Pressures (psi) Rear	Wheel Size	Ball Joint Inspection
1997	Aurora	P235/60R16	P235/60VR16	30	30	7-J	①
	Achieva	P195/70R14	P195/65R15	30	30	6-J	①
	Cutlass Supreme	P215/60R16	None	30	30	6.5-JJ	①
	Eighty-eight	P205/70R15	P215/65R15 P225/60R16	30	30	6-JJ	①
	LSS	P205/70R15	P215/65R15 P225/60R16	30	30	6-JJ	①
	Ninety-eight	P205/70R15	None	30	30	6-JJ	①
	Regency	P205/70R15	None	30	30	6-JJ	①
	Touring Sedan	P205/70R15	None	30	30	6-JJ	①
1998	Aurora	P235/60R16	P235/60VR16	30	30	7-J	①
	Achieva	P195/70R14	P195/65R15	30	30	6-J	①
	Cutlass	P215/60R15	None	30	30	6.5-JJ	①
	Cutlass Supreme	P215/60R16	None	30	30	6.5-JJ	①
	Intrigue	P225/60R16	None	30	30	6.5-JJ	①
	Eighty-eight	P205/70R15	P215/65R15 P225/60R16	30	30	6-JJ	①
	LSS	P205/70R15	P215/65R15 P225/60R16	30	30	6-JJ	①
	Ninety-eight	P205/70R15	None	30	30	6-JJ	①
	Regency	P205/70R15	None	30	30	6-JJ	①
	Touring Sedan	P205/70R15	None	30	30	6-JJ	①
1999	Alero	P215/60R15	P225/50R16	30	30	7-J	①
	Aurora	P235/60R16	P235/60VR16	30	30	7-J	①
	Cutlass	P215/60R15	None	30	30	6.5-JJ	①
	Intrigue	P225/60R16	None	30	30	6.5-JJ	①
	Eighty-eight	P205/70R15	P215/65R15 P225/60R16	30	30	6-JJ	①
	LSS	P205/70R15	P215/65R15 P225/60R16	30	30	6-JJ	①
2000-01	Alero	P215/60R15	P225/50R16	30	30	6-JJ	①
	Aurora	P235/60R16	P235/60VR16	30	30	7-J	①
	Intrigue	P225/60R16	None	30	30	6-JJ	①

OEM: Original Equipment Manufacturer

PSI: Pounds Per Square Inch

STD: Standard

OPT: Optional

① Replace if any measurable movement is found.

93061CV1

Refer to the model specific sections for fuel system service procedures

TIRE, WHEEL AND BALL JOINT SPECIFICATIONS
Pontiac

| Year | Model | OEM Tires | | Tire Pressures (psi) | | Wheel Size | Ball Joint Inspection |
		Standard	Optional	Front	Rear		
1997	Bonneville SE	P215/65R15	P225/60R16	30	30	6-JJ	①
	Bonneville SSE	P225/60R16	None	30	30	7-JJ	①
	Firebird, base	P215/60R16	P235/55R16	30	30	7.5-JJ	0.125 in.
	Firebird Formula	P235/55R16	P245/50ZR16	30	30	8-J	0.125 in.
	Trans Am Coupe	P235/55R16	None	30	30	8-JJ	0.125 in.
	Trans Am Conv.	P245/50ZR16	P275/40ZR17	30	30	8-JJ	0.125 in.
	Grand Prix	P205/70R15	P225/60R16	30	30	7-JJ	0.125 in.
	Grand AM SE	P195/70R14	P195/65R15 P205/55R16	30	30	6-JJ	0.125 in.
	Grand Am GT, GTE	P195/70R14	P195/65R15 P205/55R16	30	30	6-JJ	0.125 in.
	Sunfire SE	P195/70R14	P195/65R15	30	30	6-JJ	0.125 in.
	Sunfire GT	P205/55R16	None	30	30	6-JJ	0.125 in.
1998	Bonneville SE	P215/65R15	P225/60R16	30	30	6-JJ	①
	Bonneville SSE	P225/60R16	None	30	30	7-JJ	①
	Firebird, base	P215/60R16	P235/55R16	30	30	7.5-JJ	0.125 in.
	Firebird Formula	P235/55R16	P245/50ZR16	30	30	8-J	0.125 in.
	Trans Am Coupe	P235/55R16	None	30	30	8-JJ	0.125 in.
	Trans Am Conv.	P245/50ZR16	P275/40ZR17	30	30	8-JJ	0.125 in.
	Grand Prix	P205/70R15	P225/60R16	30	30	7-JJ	0.125 in.
	Grand AM SE	P195/70R14	P195/65R15 P205/55R16	30	30	6-JJ	0.125 in.
	Grand Am GT, GTE	P195/70R14	P195/65R15 P205/55R16	30	30	6-JJ	0.125 in.
	Sunfire SE	P195/70R14	P195/65R15	30	30	6-JJ	0.125 in.
	Sunfire GT	P205/55R16	None	30	30	6-JJ	0.125 in.
1999	Bonneville SE	P215/65R15	P225/60R16	30	30	6-JJ	①
	Bonneville SSE	P225/60R16	None	30	30	7-JJ	①
	Firebird, base	P215/60R16	P235/55R16	30	30	7.5-JJ	0.125 in.
	Firebird Formula	P235/55R16	P245/50ZR16	30	30	8-J	0.125 in.
	Trans Am Coupe	P235/55R16	None	30	30	8-JJ	0.125 in.
	Trans Am Conv.	P245/50ZR16	P275/40ZR17	30	30	8-JJ	0.125 in.
	Grand Prix	P205/70R15	P225/60R16	30	30	7-JJ	0.125 in.
	Grand AM SE	P195/70R14	P195/65R15 P205/55R16	30	30	6-JJ	0.125 in.
	Grand Am GT, GTE	P195/70R14	P195/65R15 P205/55R16	30	30	6-JJ	0.125 in.
	Sunfire SE	P195/70R14	P195/65R15	30	30	6-JJ	0.125 in.
	Sunfire GT	P205/55R16	None	30	30	6-JJ	0.125 in.
2000-01	Bonneville SE	P215/65R15	P225/60R16	30	30	6-JJ	①
	Bonneville SSE	P225/60R16	None	30	30	7-JJ	①
	Firebird, base	P215/60R16	P235/55R16	30	30	7.5-JJ	0.125 in.
	Firebird Formula	P235/55R16	P245/50ZR16	30	30	8-J	0.125 in.
	Trans Am Coupe	P235/55R16	None	30	30	8-JJ	0.125 in.
	Trans Am Conv.	P245/50ZR16	P275/40ZR17	30	30	8-JJ	0.125 in.
	Grand Prix	P205/70R15	P225/60R16	30	30	7-JJ	0.125 in.
	Grand AM SE	P195/70R14	P195/65R15 P205/55R16	30	30	6-JJ	0.125 in.

93061CV2

TIRE, WHEEL AND BALL JOINT SPECIFICATIONS
Pontiac

| Year | Model | OEM Tires | | Tire Pressures (psi) | | Wheel Size | Ball Joint Inspection |
		Standard	Optional	Front	Rear		
2000-01 (Cont.)	Grand Am GT, GTE	P195/70R14	P195/65R15 P205/55R16	30	30	6-JJ	0.125 in.
	Sunfire SE	P195/70R14	P195/65R15	30	30	6-JJ	0.125 in.
	Sunfire GT	P205/55R16	None	30	30	6-JJ	0.125 in.

OEM: Original Equipment Manufacturer

PSI: Pounds Per Square Inch

STD: Standard

OPT: Optional

① Do not lift car. Inspect the boss into which the grease fitting is threaded. Replace if the boss is flush or receded below the surface of the ball joint.

93061CV3

Refer to the model specific sections for engine electrical system service procedures

GEO/CHEVROLET
Metro • Prizm

ENGINE AND VEHICLE IDENTIFICATION

			Engine					Model Year	
Code ①	Liters (cc)	Cu. In.	Cyl.	Fuel Sys.	Engine Type	Eng. Mfg.		Code ②	Year
6	1.0 (993)	(61)	3	TFI	SOHC	Suzuki		V	1997
6	1.6 (1590)	(97)	4	MFI	SOHC	Suzuki		W	1998
8	1.8 (1803)	(110)	4	MFI	DOHC	Toyota		X	1999
9	1.3 (1300)	(79)	4	TFI	DOHC	Suzuki		Y	2000
								1	2001

TFI: Throttle body Fuel Injection

MFI: Multi-point Fuel Injection

DOHC: Dual Overhead Camshaft

SOHC: Single Overhead Camshaft

① 8th position of VIN

② 10th position of VIN

93061CV4

GENERAL ENGINE SPECIFICATIONS

Year	Model	Engine Displacement Liters (cc)	Engine Series (ID/VIN)	Fuel System	Net Horsepower @ rpm	Net Torque @ rpm (ft. lbs.)	Bore x Stroke (in.)	Com-pression Ratio	Oil Pressure @ rpm
1997	Metro	1.0 (993)	6	TFI	55@5700	58@3300	2.91x3.03	9.5:1	54@3000
	Metro	1.3 (1300)	9	TFI	70@5500	74@3500	2.91x3.03	9.5:1	54@3000
	Prism	1.6 (1590)	6	MFI	105@5800	100@4800	3.20x3.00	9.5:1	36-71@3000
	Prizm	1.8 (1803)	8	MFI	115@5200	117@2800	3.20x3.40	9.5:1	36-71@3000
1998	Metro	1.0 (993)	6	TFI	55@5700	58@3300	2.91x3.03	9.5:1	54@3000
	Metro	1.3 (1300)	9	TFI	70@5500	74@3500	2.91x3.03	9.5:1	54@3000
	Prizm	1.8 (1803)	8	MFI	115@5200	117@2800	3.20x3.40	9.5:1	36-71@3000
1999	Metro	1.0 (993)	6	TFI	55@5700	58@3300	2.91x3.03	9.5:1	54@3000
	Metro	1.3 (1300)	9	TFI	70@5500	74@3500	2.91x3.03	9.5:1	54@3000
	Prizm	1.8 (1803)	8	MFI	115@5200	117@2800	3.20x3.40	9.5:1	36-71@3000
2000-01	Metro	1.0 (993)	6	TFI	55@5700	58@3300	2.91x3.03	9.5:1	54@3000
	Metro	1.3 (1300)	9	TFI	70@5500	74@3500	2.91x3.03	9.5:1	54@3000
	Prizm	1.8 (1803)	8	MFI	115@5200	117@2800	3.20x3.40	9.5:1	36-71@3000

TFI: Throttle body Fuel Injection

MFI: Multi-point Fuel Injection

93061CV5

TUNE-UP SPECIFICATIONS

Year	Engine Displacement Liters (cc)	Engine ID/VIN	Spark Plug Gap (in.)	Ignition Timing (deg.) MT	Ignition Timing (deg.) AT	Fuel Pump (psi)	Idle Speed (rpm) MT	Idle Speed (rpm) AT	Valve Clearance Intake	Valve Clearance Exhaust
1997	1.0 (993)	6	0.041	5B ①	5B ①	23-30	800	850	HYD	HYD
	1.3 (1300)	9	0.041	5B ①	5B ①	23-30	800	850	HYD	HYD
	1.6 (1590)	6	0.031	10B ②	10B ②	31-37	700-750	700-750	0.0060-0.0100	0.0100-0.0140
	1.8 (1803)	8	0.031	10B ②	10B ②	31-37	700-750	700-750	0.0060-0.0100	0.0100-0.0140
1998	1.0 (993)	6	0.041	5B ①	5B ①	23-30	800	850	HYD	HYD
	1.3 (1300)	9	0.041	5B ①	5B ①	23-30	800	850	HYD	HYD
	1.8 (1803)	8	0.031	10B ②	10B ②	31-37	700-750	700-750	0.0060-0.0100	0.0100-0.0140
1999	1.0 (993)	6	0.041	5B ①	5B ①	23-30	800	850	HYD	HYD
	1.3 (1300)	9	0.041	5B ①	5B ①	23-30	800	850	HYD	HYD
	1.8 (1803)	8	0.031	10B ②	10B ②	31-37	700-750	700-750	0.0060-0.0100	0.0100-0.0140
2000-01	1.0 (993)	6	0.041	5B ①	5B ①	23-30	800	850	HYD	HYD
	1.3 (1300)	9	0.041	5B ①	5B ①	23-30	800	850	HYD	HYD
	1.8 (1803)	8	0.031	10B ②	10B ②	31-37	700-750	700-750	0.0060-0.0100	0.0100-0.0140

NOTE: The Vehicle Emission Control Information label often reflects specification changes made during production. The label figures must be used if they differ from those in this chart.

B: Before top dead center

HYD: Hydraulic

① Connect a fused jumper from Duty Check cavity 4 to cavity 5 for fixed timing (DLC connector located at left strut tower)

② Insert jumper wire between terminals in DLC connector E1 and TE1

93061CV6

For accessory drive belt replacement procedures see the model specific sections of this manual

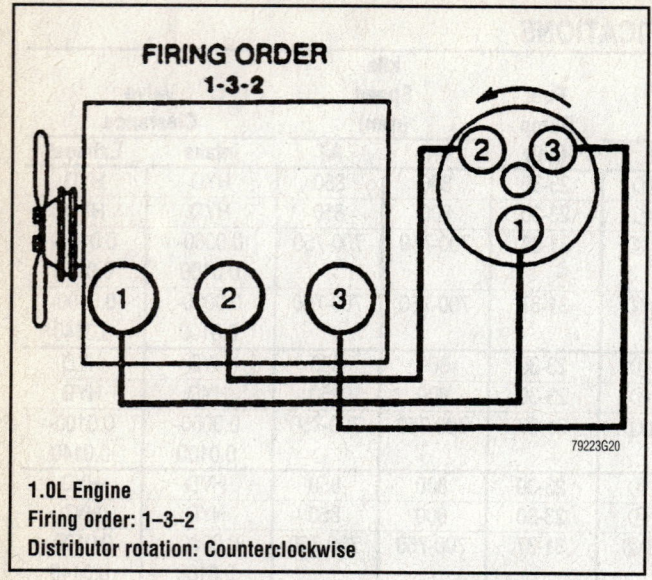

1.0L Engine
Firing order: 1–3–2
Distributor rotation: Counterclockwise

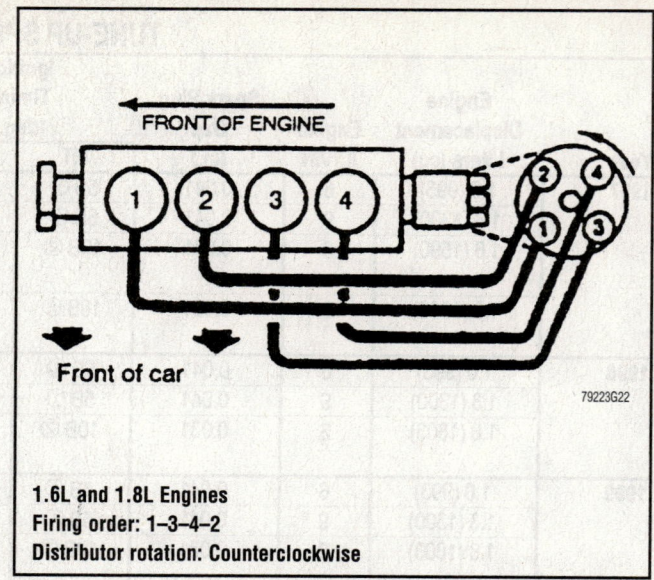

1.6L and 1.8L Engines
Firing order: 1–3–4–2
Distributor rotation: Counterclockwise

FIRING ORDER
1-3-4-2

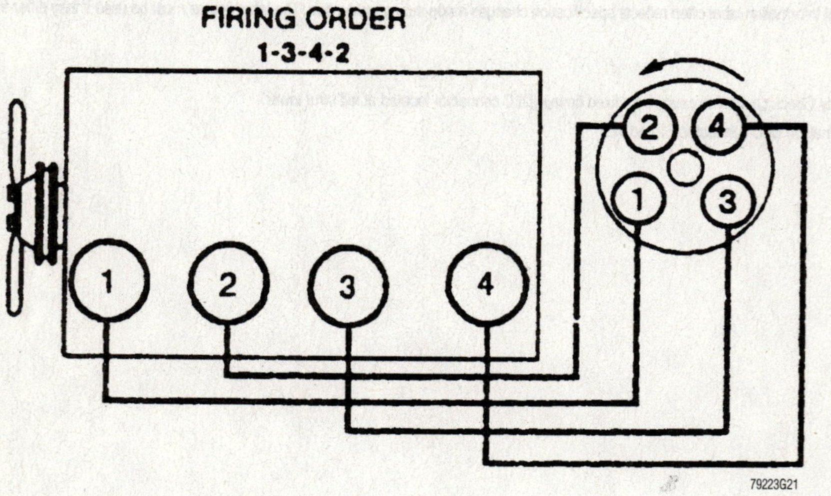

1.3L Engine
Firing order: 1–3–4–2
Distributor rotation: Counterclockwise

CAPACITIES

Year	Model	Engine ID/VIN	Engine Displacement Liters (cc)	Engine Oil with Filter	Transmission (pts.)		Drive Axle (pts.)	Fuel Tank (gal.)	Cooling System (qts.)
					5-Spd	Auto.			
1997	Metro	6	1.0 (993)	3.7	5.0	10.1 ①	—	10.6	4.2
	Metro	9	1.3 (1300)	3.7	5.0	10.1 ①	—	10.6	4.9
	Prizm	6	1.6 (1590)	3.2	4.0	6.6	3.0 ②	13.2	6.7
	Prizm	8	1.8 (1803)	3.9	4.0	6.6	3.0 ②	13.2	6.7
1998	Metro	6	1.0 (993)	3.7	5.0	10.1 ①	—	10.6	4.2
	Metro	9	1.3 (1300)	3.7	5.0	10.1 ①	—	10.6	4.9
	Prizm	8	1.8 (1803)	3.9	4.0	6.6	3.0 ②	13.2	6.7
1999	Metro	6	1.0 (993)	3.7	5.0	10.1 ①	—	10.6	4.2
	Metro	9	1.3 (1300)	3.7	5.0	10.1 ①	—	10.6	4.9
	Prizm	8	1.8 (1803)	3.9	4.0	6.6	3.0 ②	13.2	6.7
2000-01	Metro	6	1.0 (993)	3.7	5.0	10.1 ①	—	10.6	4.2
	Metro	9	1.3 (1300)	3.7	5.0	10.1 ①	—	10.6	4.9
	Prizm	8	1.8 (1803)	3.9	4.0	6.6	3.0 ②	13.2	6.7

NOTE: All capacities are approximate. Add fluid gradually and ensure a proper fluid level is obtained.

① Automatic transmission: Specification is after complete overhaul. Drain and fill will be less

② 3 speed automatic only

93061CV7

For brake related suspension and axle service, refer to the model specific sections of this manual

VALVE SPECIFICATIONS

Year	Engine Displacement Liters (cc)	Engine ID/VIN	Seat Angle (deg.)	Face Angle (deg.)	Spring Test Pressure (lbs. @ in.)	Spring Installed Height (in.)	Stem-to-Guide Clearance (in.)		Stem Diameter (in.)	
							Intake	Exhaust	Intake	Exhaust
1997	1.0 (993)	6	45	45	46.1-51.8@1.28	1.28	0.0008-0.0022	0.0018-0.0028	0.2148-0.2157	0.2142-0.2148
	1.3 (1300)	9	45	45	54.7-64.3@1.63	1.63	0.0008-0.0019	0.0014-0.0025	0.2742-0.2748	0.2737-0.2742
	1.6 (1590)	6	45	45.5	37.3@1.25	1.25	0.0010-0.0024	0.0012-0.0026	0.2350-0.2356	0.2348-0.2354
	1.8 (1803)	8	45	45.5	37.3@1.25	1.25	0.0010-0.0024	0.0012-0.0026	0.2350-0.2356	0.2348-0.2354
1998	1.0 (993)	6	45	45	46.1-51.8@1.28	1.28	0.0008-0.0022	0.0018-0.0028	0.2148-0.2157	0.2142-0.2148
	1.3 (1300)	9	45	45	54.7-64.3@1.63	1.63	0.0008-0.0019	0.0014-0.0025	0.2742-0.2748	0.2737-0.2742
	1.8 (1803)	8	45	45.5	37.3@1.25	1.25	0.0010-0.0024	0.0012-0.0026	0.2350-0.2356	0.2348-0.2354
1999	1.0 (993)	6	45	45	46.1-51.8@1.28	1.28	0.0008-0.0022	0.0018-0.0028	0.2148-0.2157	0.2142-0.2148
	1.3 (1300)	9	45	45	54.7-64.3@1.63	1.63	0.0008-0.0019	0.0014-0.0025	0.2742-0.2748	0.2737-0.2742
	1.8 (1803)	8	45	45.5	37.3@1.25	1.25	0.0010-0.0024	0.0012-0.0026	0.2350-0.2356	0.2348-0.2354
2000-01	1.0 (993)	6	45	45	46.1-51.8@1.28	1.28	0.0008-0.0022	0.0018-0.0028	0.2148-0.2157	0.2142-0.2148
	1.3 (1300)	9	45	45	54.7-64.3@1.63	1.63	0.0008-0.0019	0.0014-0.0025	0.2742-0.2748	0.2737-0.2742
	1.8 (1803)	8	45	45.5	37.3@1.25	1.25	0.0010-0.0024	0.0012-0.0026	0.2350-0.2356	0.2348-0.2354

93061CV8

CRANKSHAFT AND CONNECTING ROD SPECIFICATIONS

All measurements are given in inches.

Year	Engine Displacement Liters (cc)	Engine ID/VIN	Crankshaft				Connecting Rod		
			Main Brg. Journal Dia.	Main Brg. Oil Clearance	Shaft End-play	Thrust on No.	Journal Diameter	Oil Clearance	Side Clearance
1997	1.0 (993)	6	①	0.00008-0.00015	0.0044-0.0122	NA	1.6529-1.6535	0.0012-0.0019	0.0039-0.0078
	1.3 (1300)	9	①	0.00008-0.00015	0.0044-0.0122	NA	1.6529-1.6535	0.0012-0.0019	0.0039-0.0078
	1.6 (1590)	6	②	0.0006-0.0013	0.0006-0.0087	3	1.5742-1.5748	0.0008-0.0020	0.0050-0.0150
	1.8 (1803)	8	②	0.0006-0.0013	0.0006-0.0087	3	1.8893-1.8898	0.0008-0.0019	0.0050-0.0150
1998	1.0 (993)	6	①	0.00008-0.00015	0.0044-0.0122	NA	1.6529-1.6535	0.0012-0.0019	0.0039-0.0078
	1.3 (1300)	9	①	0.00008-0.00015	0.0044-0.0122	NA	1.6529-1.6535	0.0012-0.0019	0.0039-0.0078
	1.8 (1803)	8	②	0.0006-0.0013	0.0006-0.0087	3	1.8893-1.8898	0.0008-0.0019	0.0050-0.0150
1999	1.0 (993)	6	①	0.00008-0.00015	0.0044-0.0122	NA	1.6529-1.6535	0.0012-0.0019	0.0039-0.0078
	1.3 (1300)	9	①	0.00008-0.00015	0.0044-0.0122	NA	1.6529-1.6535	0.0012-0.0019	0.0039-0.0078
	1.8 (1803)	8	②	0.0006-0.0013	0.0006-0.0087	3	1.8893-1.8898	0.0008-0.0019	0.0050-0.0150
2000-01	1.0 (993)	6	①	0.00008-0.00015	0.0044-0.0122	NA	1.6529-1.6535	0.0012-0.0019	0.0039-0.0078
	1.3 (1300)	9	①	0.00008-0.00015	0.0044-0.0122	NA	1.6529-1.6535	0.0012-0.0019	0.0039-0.0078
	1.8 (1803)	8	②	0.0006-0.0013	0.0006-0.0087	3	1.8893-1.8898	0.0008-0.0019	0.0050-0.0150

NA: Not Available

① 1 Stamping: 1.7714-1.7716
2 Stamping: 1.7712-1.7714
3 Stamping: 1.7710-1.7712

② 0 Stamping: 1.8895-1.8898
1 Stamping: 1.8893-1.8895
2 Stamping: 1.8891-1.8893

93061CV9

Refer to the model specific sections for driveline service procedures

PISTON AND RING SPECIFICATIONS
All measurements are given in inches.

Year	Engine Displacement Liters (cc)	Engine ID/VIN	Piston Clearance	Ring Gap			Ring Side Clearance		
				Top Compression	Bottom Compression	Oil Control	Top Compression	Bottom Compression	Oil Control
1997	1.0 (993)	6	0.0008-0.0015	0.0079-0.0118	0.0079-0.0118	0.0079-0.0275	0.0012-0.0027	0.0008-0.0023	—
	1.3 (1300)	9	0.0008-0.0015	0.0079-0.0118	0.0079-0.0012	0.0079-0.0275	0.0014-0.0027	0.0008-0.0023	—
	1.6 (1590)	6	0.0033-0.0041	0.0098-0.0138	0.0138-0.0197	0.0039-0.0157	0.0018-0.0033	0.0012-0.0028	—
	1.8 (1803)	8	0.0033-0.0041	0.0098-0.0138	0.0138-0.0197	0.0039-0.0157	0.0018-0.0033	0.0012-0.0028	—
1998	1.0 (993)	6	0.0008-0.0015	0.0079-0.0118	0.0079-0.0118	0.0079-0.0275	0.0012-0.0027	0.0008-0.0023	—
	1.3 (1300)	9	0.0008-0.0015	0.0079-0.0118	0.0079-0.0012	0.0079-0.0275	0.0014-0.0027	0.0008-0.0023	—
	1.8 (1803)	8	0.0033-0.0041	0.0098-0.0138	0.0138-0.0197	0.0039-0.0157	0.0018-0.0033	0.0012-0.0028	—
1999	1.0 (993)	6	0.0008-0.0015	0.0079-0.0118	0.0079-0.0118	0.0079-0.0275	0.0012-0.0027	0.0008-0.0023	—
	1.3 (1300)	9	0.0008-0.0015	0.0079-0.0118	0.0079-0.0012	0.0079-0.0275	0.0014-0.0027	0.0008-0.0023	—
	1.8 (1803)	8	0.0033-0.0041	0.0098-0.0138	0.0138-0.0197	0.0039-0.0157	0.0018-0.0033	0.0012-0.0028	—
2000-01	1.0 (993)	6	0.0008-0.0015	0.0079-0.0118	0.0079-0.0118	0.0079-0.0275	0.0012-0.0027	0.0008-0.0023	—
	1.3 (1300)	9	0.0008-0.0015	0.0079-0.0118	0.0079-0.0012	0.0079-0.0275	0.0014-0.0027	0.0008-0.0023	—
	1.8 (1803)	8	0.0033-0.0041	0.0098-0.0138	0.0138-0.0197	0.0039-0.0157	0.0018-0.0033	0.0012-0.0028	—

93061CV0

TORQUE SPECIFICATIONS
All readings in ft. lbs.

Year	Engine Displacement Liters (cc)	Engine ID/VIN	Cylinder Head Bolts	Main Bearing Bolts	Rod Bearing Bolts	Crankshaft Damper Bolt	Flywheel Bolts	Manifold		Spark Plugs	Lug Nuts
								Intake	Exhaust		
1997	1.0 (993)	6	54	40	26	81 ①	45	17	17	21	44
	1.3 (1300)	9	54	40	26	79 ①	45	17	17	21	44
	1.6 (1590)	6	②	44	②	87 ①	③	14	25	21	76
	1.8 (1803)	8	②	44	18	87 ①	③	14	25	21	76
1998	1.0 (993)	6	54	40	26	81 ①	45	17	17	21	44
	1.3 (1300)	9	54	40	26	79 ①	45	17	17	21	44
	1.8 (1803)	8	②	44	18	87 ①	③	14	25	21	76
1999	1.0 (993)	6	54	40	26	81 ①	45	17	17	21	44
	1.3 (1300)	9	54	40	26	79 ①	45	17	17	21	44
	1.8 (1803)	8	②	44	18	87 ①	③	14	25	21	76
2000-01	1.0 (993)	6	54	40	26	81 ①	45	17	17	21	44
	1.3 (1300)	9	54	40	26	79 ①	45	17	17	21	44
	1.8 (1803)	8	②	44	18	87 ①	③	14	25	21	76

① Crankshaft timing belt sprocket

② Step 1: 22 ft. lbs.
   Step 2: Plus 90 degrees

③ Manual transaxle: 36 ft. lbs. Plus 90 degrees
   Automatic transaxle: 61 ft. lbs.

93061CW1

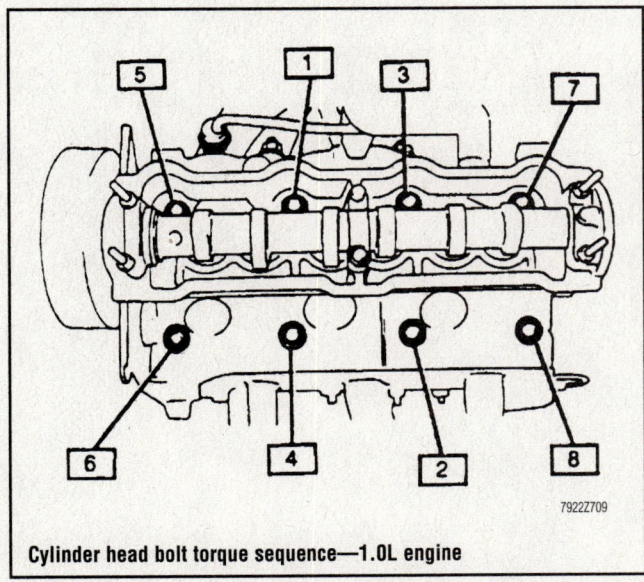

Cylinder head bolt torque sequence—1.0L engine

7922Z709

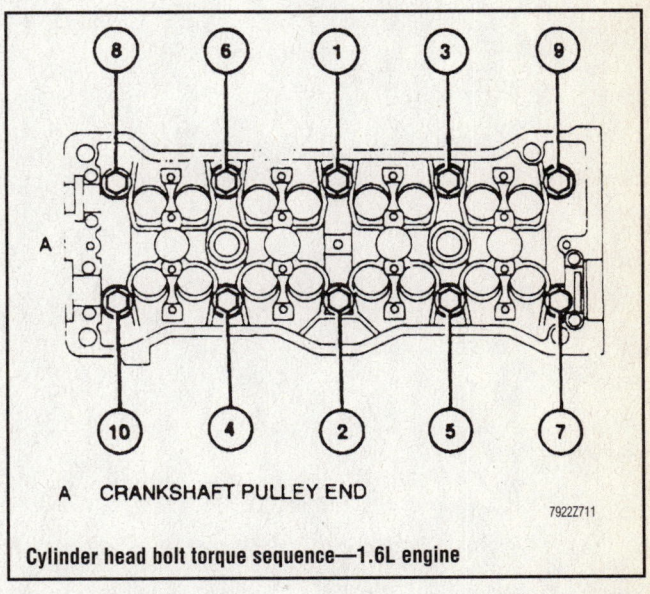

A   CRANKSHAFT PULLEY END

Cylinder head bolt torque sequence—1.6L engine

7922Z711

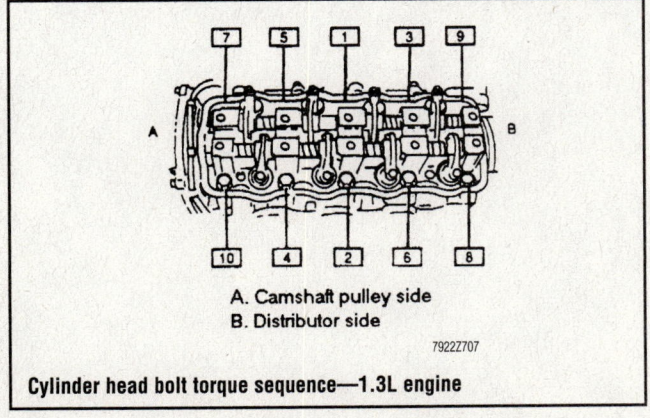

A. Camshaft pulley side
B. Distributor side

Cylinder head bolt torque sequence—1.3L engine

7922Z707

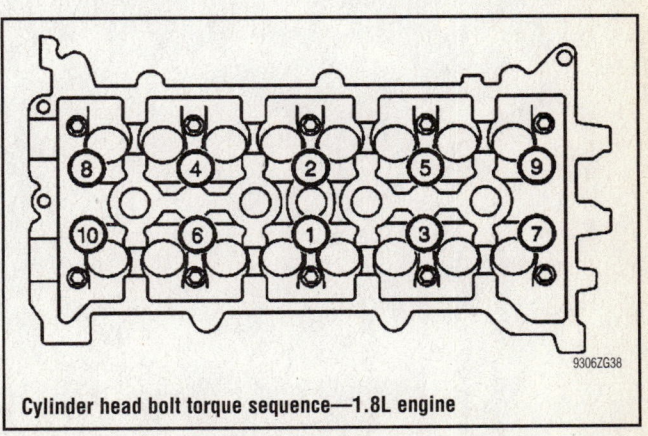

Cylinder head bolt torque sequence—1.8L engine

9306ZG38

For exhaust manifold replacement procedures, see the model specific sections of this manual

BRAKE SPECIFICATIONS
GEO/CHEVROLET
All measurements in inches unless noted

Year	Model	Brake Disc			Brake Drum Diameter			Minimum Lining Thickness ①		Brake Caliper	
		Original Thickness	Minimum Thickness	Maximum Runout	Original Inside Diameter	Max. Wear Limit	Maximum Machine Diameter	Front	Rear	Bracket Bolts (ft. lbs.)	Mounting Bolts (ft. lbs.)
1997	Metro	0.670	0.590	0.004	②	②	②	0.236	0.111	—	18
	Prizm	0.866	0.787	0.003	7.87	7.91	7.91	0.390	0.390	—	③
1998	Metro	0.670	0.590	0.004	②	②	②	0.236	0.111	—	18
	Prizm	0.866	0.787	0.003	7.87	7.91	7.91	0.390	0.390	—	③
1999	Metro	0.670	0.590	0.004	②	②	②	0.236	0.111	—	18
	Prizm	0.866	0.787	0.003	7.87	7.91	7.91	0.390	0.390	—	③
2000-01	Metro	0.670	0.590	0.004	②	②	②	0.236	0.111	—	18
	Prizm	0.866	0.787	0.003	7.87	7.91	7.91	0.390	0.390	—	③

① Minimum lining thickness includes pad/shoe backing
② 2 door: 7.09
   4 door: 7.87

③ Front: 18 ft. lbs.
   Rear: 14 ft. lbs.

93061CW2

SCHEDULED MAINTENANCE INTERVALS
(GEO METRO & PRIZM)

TO BE SERVICED	TYPE OF SERVICE	VEHICLE MILEAGE INTERVAL (x1000)												
		7.5	15	22.5	30	37.5	45	52.5	60	67.5	75	82.5	90	97.5
Engine oil & filter	R	✓	✓	✓	✓	✓	✓	✓	✓	✓	✓	✓	✓	✓
Chassis lubrication (Metro)	S/I	✓	✓	✓	✓	✓	✓	✓	✓	✓	✓	✓	✓	✓
Locking front hubs (Metro)	S/I	✓	✓	✓	✓	✓	✓	✓	✓	✓	✓	✓	✓	✓
Lubricate parking brake cable guides, underbody contact points & linkage	S/I	✓	✓	✓	✓	✓	✓	✓	✓	✓	✓	✓	✓	✓
Rotate tires	S/I	✓	✓	✓	✓	✓	✓	✓	✓	✓	✓	✓	✓	✓
Brake system	S/I	✓		✓		✓		✓		✓		✓		✓
Engine idle speed (Prizm)	S/I	✓		✓		✓		✓		✓		✓		✓
Exhaust system	S/I	✓		✓		✓		✓		✓		✓		✓
Chassis lubrication (Prizm)	S/I		✓		✓		✓		✓		✓		✓	
Fuel tank, cap & lines (Metro)	S/I		✓		✓		✓		✓		✓		✓	
Fuel tank, cap & lines (Prizm)	S/I				✓				✓					
Valve clearance (Prizm)	S/I								✓					
Air cleaner filter	R				✓				✓				✓	
Engine coolant	R				✓				✓				✓	
Fuel filter (Metro)	R				✓				✓				✓	
Fuel tank cap gasket (Prizm)	R				✓				✓				✓	
Manual transaxle oil	R				✓				✓				✓	
Spark plugs	R				✓				✓				✓	
Accessory drive belt(s) (Prizm)	S/I								✓				✓	✓
Accessory drive belt(s) (except Prizm)	S/I				✓				✓				✓	

93061CW3

Refer to the model specific sections for cooling system service procedures

SCHEDULED MAINTENANCE INTERVALS
(GEO METRO & PRIZM) (Cont.)

TO BE SERVICED	TYPE OF SERVICE	VEHICLE MILEAGE INTERVAL (x1000)												
		7.5	15	22.5	30	37.5	45	52.5	60	67.5	75	82.5	90	97.5
Cooling system (Metro)	S/I				✓				✓				✓	
Cooling system (Prizm)	S/I						✓				✓			
Automatic transaxle fluid & filter	S/I				✓				✓				✓	
EGR system	S/I				✓				✓				✓	
Engine timing (Metro)	S/I								✓					
Ignition cables	S/I								✓					
PCV system	S/I				✓				✓				✓	
Brake fluid (Metro)	R								✓					
PCV valve (Metro) ①	R													
Timing belt	R								✓					
EVAP canister (Prizm)	S/I								✓					
Throttle body unit mount bolt torque ②	S/I	✓												

R: Replace S/I: Service or Inspect

① PCV valve: replace at 50,000 miles.

② Torque to 16 ft. lbs. (22 Nm) at 6000 miles.

FREQUENT OPERATION MAINTENANCE (SEVERE SERVICE)

If a vehicle is operated under any of the following conditions it is considered severe service:

- Extremely dusty areas.

- 50% or more of the vehicle operation is in 32°C (90°F) or higher temperatures, or constant operation in temperatures below 0°C (32°F).

- Prolonged idling (vehicle operation in stop and go traffic).

- Frequent short running periods (engine does not warm to normal operating temperatures).

- Police, taxi, delivery usage or trailer towing usage.

Oil & oil filter: change every 3000 miles.

Chassis lubrication: lubricate every 6000 miles.

Throttle body mount bolt torque: torque to 16 ft. lbs. (22 Nm) at 6000 miles.

Air cleaner filter: service or inspect every 15,000 miles.

Differential fluid (Prizm): replace every 15,000 miles.

Rotate tires: rotate at 6000 miles and then every 15,000 miles thereafter.

Automatic transaxde fluid & filter (Prizm): replace every 15,000 miles.

Automatic transaxde fluid & filter (Metro): replace every 50,000 miles.

93061CW4

SCHEDULED MAINTENANCE INTERVALS
GENERAL MOTORS CORPORATION
CHEVROLET/GEO METRO, PRIZM

The following should be used as a guide when determining the amount of work required for a particular service. In estimating how long a particular Scheduled Maintenance Service should take, please observe the following:

- Labor Time is time based on field research and data supplied by the vehicle manufacturer.
- Labor time operations are given in hours and tenths of an hour.
- All labor operations are to be used as a guide.

Mechanic Skill Level Codes:
(A) PRECISION: Highly skilled with multiple certification.
(B) GENERAL: Normally skilled with certification.
(C) MAINTENANCE: Semi-skilled working on certification.

	LABOR TIME
7500 Mile Service (C)	
All Models	1.8
15000 Mile Service (C)	
All Models	.7
Rotate tires add	.5
22500 Mile Service (C)	
All Models	1.6
30000 Mile Service (B)	
All Models	2.7
Rotate tires add	.5

	LABOR TIME
37500 Mile Service (C)	
All Models	1.6
45000 Mile Service (C)	
All Models	.7
Rotate tires add	.5
60000 Mile Service (B)	
All Models	4.9
67500 Mile Service (C)	
All Models	1.6

	LABOR TIME
75000 Mile Service (C)	
All Models	.7
Rotate tires add	.5
82500 Mile Service (C)	
All Models	1.6
90000 Mile Service (B)	
All Models	2.8
97500 Mile Service (C)	
All Models	1.6

93061CW5

TIRE, WHEEL AND BALL JOINT SPECIFICATIONS
GEO

| Year | Model | OEM Tires | | Tire Pressures (psi) | | Wheel Size | Ball Joint Inspection |
		Standard	Optional	Front	Rear		
1997	Metro	P155/80R13	None	32	32	4.5-B	①
	Prizm	P175/65R14	P185/65R14	30	30	4.5-JB	①
1998	Metro	P155/80R13	None	32	32	4.5-B	①
	Prizm	P175/65R14	P185/65R14	30	30	4.5-JB	①

OEM: Original Equipment Manufacturer

PSI: Pounds Per Square Inch

STD: Standard

OPT: Optional

① Replace if any measurable movement is found.

93061CW7

SATURN
LS • LS1 • LS2 • LW1 • LW2 • SC1 • SC2 • SL • SL1 • SL2 • SW1 • SW2

ENGINE AND VEHICLE IDENTIFICATION

			Engine					Model Year	
Code ①	Liters (cc)	Cu. In.	Cyl.	Fuel Sys.	Engine Type	Eng. Mfg.		Code ②	Year
7	1.9 (1901)	116	4	MFI	DOHC	Saturn		V	1997
8	1.9 (1901)	116	4	MFI	SOHC	Saturn		W	1998
F	2.2 (2199)	134	4	SFI	DOHC	Saturn		X	1999
R	3.0 (3000)	183	6	SFI	DOHC	Saturn		Y	2000
								1	2001

MFI: Multi-point Fuel Injection
SFI: Sequential Fuel Injection
DOHC: Double Overhead Camshafts
SOHC: Single Overhead Camshaft
① 8th digit of VIN
② 10th digit of VIN

93061CX1

GENERAL ENGINE SPECIFICATIONS

Year	Model	Engine Displacement Liters (cc)	Engine ID/VIN	Fuel System Type	Net Horsepower @ rpm	Net Torque @ rpm (ft. lbs.)	Bore x Stroke (in.)	Compression Ratio	Oil Pressure @ rpm
1997	Coupe	1.9 (1901)	7	MFI	124@5600	122@4800	3.23x3.54	9.5:1	29@2000
	Coupe	1.9 (1901)	8	MFI	100@5000	114@2400	3.23x3.54	9.3:1	36@2000
	Sedan	1.9 (1901)	7	MFI	124@5600	122@4800	3.23x3.54	9.5:1	29@2000
	Sedan	1.9 (1901)	8	MFI	124@5600	114@2400	3.23x3.54	9.3:1	36@2000
	Wagon	1.9 (1901)	7	MFI	124@5600	122@4800	3.23x3.54	9.5:1	29@2000
	Wagon	1.9 (1901)	8	MFI	100@5000	114@2400	3.23x3.54	9.3:1	36@2000
1998	Coupe	1.9 (1901)	7	MFI	124@5600	122@4800	3.23x3.54	9.5:1	29@2000
	Coupe	1.9 (1901)	8	MFI	100@5000	114@2400	3.23x3.54	9.3:1	36@2000
	Sedan	1.9 (1901)	7	MFI	124@5600	122@4800	3.23x3.54	9.5:1	29@2000
	Sedan	1.9 (1901)	8	MFI	100@5000	114@2400	3.23x3.54	9.3:1	36@2000
	Wagon	1.9 (1901)	7	MFI	124@5600	122@4800	3.23x3.54	9.5:1	29@2000
	Wagon	1.9 (1901)	8	MFI	100@5000	114@2400	3.23x3.54	9.3:1	36@2000
1999	Coupe	1.9 (1901)	7	MFI	124@5600	122@4800	3.23x3.54	9.5:1	29@2000
	Coupe	1.9 (1901)	8	MFI	100@5000	114@2400	3.23x3.54	9.3:1	36@2000
	Sedan	1.9 (1901)	7	MFI	124@5600	122@4800	3.23x3.54	9.5:1	29@2000
	Sedan	1.9 (1901)	8	MFI	100@5000	114@2400	3.23x3.54	9.3:1	36@2000
	Wagon	1.9 (1901)	7	MFI	124@5600	122@4800	3.23x3.54	9.5:1	29@2000
	Wagon	1.9 (1901)	8	MFI	100@5000	114@2400	3.23x3.54	9.3:1	36@2000
2000-01	Sedan	1.9 (1901)	7	MFI	124@5600	122@4800	3.23x3.54	9.5:1	29@2000
	Sedan	1.9 (1901)	8	MFI	100@5000	114@2400	3.23x3.54	9.3:1	36@2000
	Wagon	1.9 (1901)	7	MFI	124@5600	122@4800	3.23x3.54	9.5:1	29@2000
	Wagon	1.9 (1901)	8	MFI	100@5000	114@2400	3.23x3.54	9.3:1	36@2000
	Sedan	2.2 (1901)	F	SFI	137@5800	147@4400	3.38x3.5	9.5:1	50@1000
	Wagon	2.2 (1901)	F	SFI	137@5800	147@4400	3.38x3.50	9.5:1	50@1000
	Sedan	3.0 (3000)	R	SFI	182@6000	190@3600	3.38x3.50	10.0:1	22@1000
	Wagon	3.0 (3000)	R	SFI	182@6000	190@3600	3.38x3.50	10.0:1	22@1000

MFI: Multi-port Fuel Injection
SFI: Sequential Ful Injection

93061CX2

Timing chain and gear service is covered in the model specific sections of this manual

ENGINE TUNE-UP SPECIFICATIONS

Year	Engine Displacement Liters (cc)	Engine ID/VIN	Spark Plug Gap (in.)	Ignition Timing (deg.)		Fuel Pump (psi) ①	Idle Speed (rpm)		Valve Clearance	
				MT	AT		MT ②	AT ②	In.	Ex.
1997	1.9 (1901)	7	0.040	③	③	31–36	850	750	HYD	HYD
	1.9 (1901)	8	0.040	③	③	26–31	750	650	HYD	HYD
1998	1.9 (1901)	7	0.040	③	③	31–36	850	750	HYD	HYD
	1.9 (1901)	8	0.040	③	③	31–36	750	650	HYD	HYD
1999	1.9 (1901)	7	0.040	③	③	31–36	850	750	HYD	HYD
	1.9 (1901)	8	0.040	③	③	31–36	750	650	HYD	HYD
2000-01	1.9 (1901)	7	0.040	③	③	31–36	850	750	HYD	HYD
	1.9 (1901)	8	0.040	③	③	31–36	750	650	HYD	HYD
	2.2 (2199)	F	0.043	③	③	55–65	④	④	HYD	HYD
	3.0 (3000)	R	0.043	③	③	39–49	④	④	HYD	HYD

NOTE: The Vehicle Emission Control Information label often reflects specification changes made during production. The label figures must be used if they differ from those in this chart.

HYD: Hydraulic

① Pressure measured at idle.

② Idle speed measured with manual transmission in Neutral; automatic transmission in D (drive).

③ Engines equipped with Distributorless Ignition System (DIS). Ignition timing is not adjustable.

④ Refer to the Vehicle Emission Control Information label

93061CX3

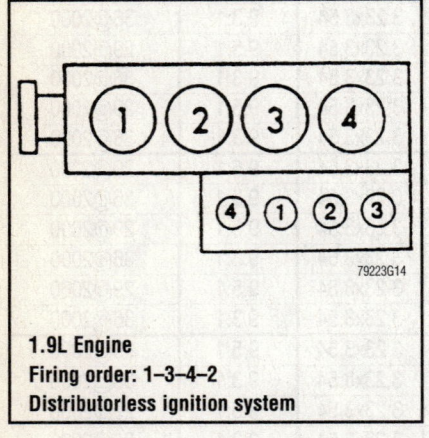

1.9L Engine
Firing order: 1–3–4–2
Distributorless ignition system

79223G14

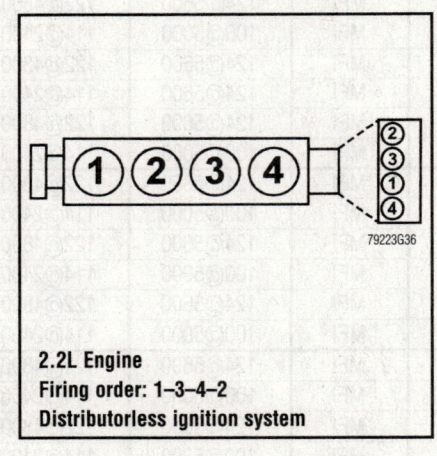

2.2L Engine
Firing order: 1–3–4–2
Distributorless ignition system

79223G36

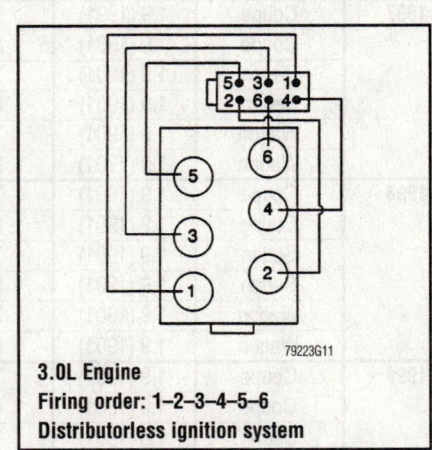

3.0L Engine
Firing order: 1–2–3–4–5–6
Distributorless ignition system

79223G11

CAPACITIES

Year	Model	Engine Displacement Liters (cc)	Engine ID/VIN	Engine Oil with Filter (qts.)	Transaxle (pts.)		Fuel Tank (gal.)	Cooling System (qts.)
					Manual	Auto. ①		
1997	Coupe	1.9 (1901)	7	4.0	5.2	7.5	12.8	7.0
	Coupe	1.9 (1901)	8	4.0	5.2	7.5	12.8	7.0
	Sedan	1.9 (1901)	8	4.0	5.2	7.5	12.8	7.0
	Sedan	1.9 (1901)	8	4.0	5.2	7.5	12.8	7.0
	Wagon	1.9 (1901)	7	4.0	5.2	7.5	12.8	7.0
	Wagon	1.9 (1901)	8	4.0	5.2	7.5	12.8	7.0
1998	Coupe	1.9 (1901)	7	4.0	5.2	7.5	12.8	7.0
	Coupe	1.9 (1901)	8	4.0	5.2	7.5	12.8	7.0
	Sedan	1.9 (1901)	7	4.0	5.2	7.5	12.8	7.0
	Sedan	1.9 (1901)	8	4.0	5.2	7.5	12.8	7.0
	Wagon	1.9 (1901)	7	4.0	5.2	7.5	12.8	7.0
	Wagon	1.9 (1901)	8	4.0	5.2	7.5	12.8	7.0
1999	Coupe	1.9 (1901)	7	4.0	5.2	7.5	12.8	7.0
	Coupe	1.9 (1901)	8	4.0	5.2	7.5	12.8	7.0
	Sedan	1.9 (1901)	7	4.0	5.2	7.5	12.8	7.0
	Sedan	1.9 (1901)	8	4.0	5.2	7.5	12.8	7.0
	Wagon	1.9 (1901)	7	4.0	5.2	7.5	12.8	7.0
	Wagon	1.9 (1901)	8	4.0	5.2	7.5	12.8	7.0
2000-01	Coupe	1.9 (1901)	7	4.0	5.2	7.5	12.1	7.0
	Coupe	1.9 (1901)	8	4.0	5.2	7.5	12.1	7.0
	Sedan	1.9 (1901)	7	4.0	5.2	7.5	12.1	7.0
	Sedan	1.9 (1901)	8	4.0	5.2	7.5	12.1	7.0
	Wagon	1.9 (1901)	7	4.0	5.2	7.5	12.1	7.0
	Wagon	1.9 (1901)	8	4.0	5.2	7.5	12.1	7.0
	Sedan	2.2 (2199)	F	5.0	8.0	9.5	13.1	7.3
	Sedan	2.2 (2199)	F	5.0	8.0	9.5	13.1	7.3
	Wagon	3.0 (3000)	R	5.0	8.0	9.5	13.1	7.4
	Wagon	3.0 (3000)	R	5.0	8.0	9.5	13.1	7.4

NOTE: All capacities are approximate. Add fluid gradually and ensure a proper fluid level is obtained.

① Specification is for overhaul. 8.4 pts. with fluid and filter change

93061CX4

Ignition system service is covered in the model specific sections of this manual

VALVE SPECIFICATIONS

Year	Engine Displacement Liters (cc)	Engine ID/VIN	Seat Angle (deg.)	Face Angle (deg.)	Spring Test Pressure (lbs. @ in.)	Spring Free-Length (in.)	Stem-to-Guide Clearance (in.)		Stem Diameter (in.)	
							Intake	Exhaust	Intake	Exhaust
1997	1.9 (1901)	7	44.5-45.4	45-45.5	163-180@ 0.984	1.6100	0.0010- 0.0025	0.0015- 0.0032	0.2736- 0.2740	0.2729- 0.2736
	1.9 (1901)	8	44.5-45.4	45-45.5	202-211@ 1.280	1.8898- 1.9134	0.0010- 0.0025	0.0015- 0.0032	0.2736- 0.2741	0.2736- 0.2740
1998	1.9 (1901)	7	44.5-45.4	45-45.5	163-180@ 0.984	1.6100	0.0010- 0.0025	0.0015- 0.0032	0.2736- 0.2740	0.2729- 0.2736
	1.9 (1901)	8	44.5-45.4	45-45.25	202-211@ 1.280	1.8898- 1.9134	0.0010- 0.0025	0.0015- 0.0032	0.2736- 0.2741	0.2736- 0.2740
1999	1.9 (1901)	7	44.5-45.4	45-45.5	163-180@ 0.984	1.6100	0.0010- 0.0025	0.0015- 0.0032	0.2736- 0.2740	0.2729- 0.2736
	1.9 (1901)	8	44.5-45.4	45-45.25	202-211@ 1.280	1.8898- 1.9134	0.0010- 0.0025	0.0015- 0.0032	0.2736- 0.2741	0.2736- 0.2740
2000-01	1.9 (1901)	7	44.5-45.4	45-45.5	163-180@ 0.984	1.6100	0.0010- 0.0025	0.0015- 0.0032	0.2736- 0.2740	0.2729- 0.2736
	1.9 (1901)	8	44.5-45.4	45-45.25	202-211@ 1.280	1.8898- 1.9134	0.0010- 0.0025	0.0015- 0.0032	0.2736- 0.2741	0.2736- 0.2740
	2.2 (2199)	F	44.5-45.4	45-45.5	① ②	1.6100	0.0012 0.0022	0.0016 0.0026	0.2344 0.2355	0.2341 0.2347
	3.0 (3000)	R	44.5-45.4	45-45.25	56.6@1.338	NA	0.0012 0.0022	0.0016 0.0026	0.2344 0.2350	0.2341 0.2346

NA: Not available

① Valve spring load @32.mm closed: 245-271 N.

② Valve spring load @32.5mm open: 525-575 N.

93061CX5

CRANKSHAFT AND CONNECTING ROD SPECIFICATIONS
All measurements are given in inches.

Year	Engine Displacement Liters (cc)	Engine ID/VIN	Crankshaft				Connecting Rod		
			Main Brg. Journal Dia.	Main Brg. Oil Clearance	Shaft End-play	Thrust on No.	Journal Diameter	Oil Clearance	Side Clearance
1997	1.9 (1901)	7	2.2438-2.2444	0.0002-0.0020	0.0020-0.0079	3	1.9761-1.9767	0.0001-0.0021	0.0065-0.0171
	1.9 (1901)	8	2.2444-2.2444	0.0002-0.0020	0.0020-0.0079	3	1.9761-1.9767	0.0001-0.0021	0.0065-0.0171
1998	1.9 (1901)	7	2.2438-2.2444	0.0002-0.0020	0.0020-0.0079	3	1.9761-1.9767	0.0001-0.0021	0.0065-0.0171
	1.9 (1901)	8	2.2438-2.2444	0.0002-0.0020	0.0020-0.0079	3	1.9761-1.9767	0.0001-0.0021	0.0065-0.0171
1999	1.9 (1901)	7	2.2438-2.2444	0.0002-0.0020	0.0020-0.0079	3	1.9761-1.9767	0.0001-0.0021	0.0065-0.0171
	1.9 (1901)	8	2.2438-2.2444	0.0002-0.0020	0.0020-0.0079	3	1.9761-1.9767	0.0001-0.0021	0.0065-0.0171
2000-01	1.9 (1901)	7	2.2438-2.2444	0.0002-0.0020	0.0020-0.0079	3	1.9761-1.9767	0.0001-0.0021	0.0065-0.0171
	1.9 (1901)	8	2.2438-2.2444	0.0002-0.0020	0.0020-0.0079	3	1.9761-1.9767	0.0001-0.0021	0.0065-0.0171
	2.2 (2199)	F	2.2045-2.2050	0.0040-0.0040	0.0012-0.0150	NA	1.9291-1.9297	0.0001-0.0021	0.0028-0.0146
	3.0 (3000)	R	2.6763-2.6766	0.0040-0.0040	0.0004-0.0300	NA	1.927-1.9280	0.0001-0.0021	0.0027-0.0110

NA: Not available

93061CX6

PISTON AND RING SPECIFICATIONS
All measurements are given in inches.

Year	Engine Displacement Liters (cc)	Engine ID/VIN	Piston Clearance	Ring Gap			Ring Side Clearance		
				Top Compression	Bottom Compression	Oil Control	Top Compression	Bottom Compression	Oil Control
1997	1.9 (1901)	7	①	0.0098-0.0157	0.0098-0.0197	0.0098-0.0429	0.0016-0.0032	0.0012-0.0031	SNUG
	1.9 (1901)	8	①	0.0098-0.0157	0.0098-0.0197	0.0098-0.0429	0.0016-0.0032	0.0012-0.0031	SNUG
1998	1.9 (1901)	7	①	0.0098-0.0157	0.0098-0.0197	0.0098-0.0429	0.0016-0.0032	0.0012-0.0031	SNUG
	1.9 (1901)	8	①	0.0098-0.0157	0.0098-0.0197	0.0098-0.0429	0.0016-0.0032	0.0012-0.0031	SNUG
1999	1.9 (1901)	7	①	0.0098-0.0157	0.0098-0.0197	0.0098-0.0429	0.0016-0.0032	0.0012-0.0031	SNUG
	1.9 (1901)	8	①	0.0098-0.0157	0.0098-0.0197	0.0098-0.0429	0.0016-0.0032	0.0012-0.0031	SNUG
2000-01	1.9 (1901)	7	①	0.0098-0.0157	0.0098-0.0197	0.0098-0.0429	0.0016-0.0032	0.0012-0.0031	SNUG
	1.9 (1901)	8	①	0.0098-0.0157	0.0098-0.0197	0.0098-0.0429	0.0016-0.0032	0.0012-0.0031	SNUG
	2.2 (2199)	F	0.0001-0.0005	0.0060-0.015	0.0012-0.0027	NA	0.0028-0.0146	0.0005-0.0024	SNUG
	3.0 (3000)	R	0.0027-0.0110	0.0008-0.0015	0.0118-0.0196	NA	0.0027-0.0110	0.0005-0.0024	SNUG

NA: Not available

① Pistion No. 1, 2 and 3: 0.0002-0.0017
  Piston No. 4: 0.0002-0.0021

93061CX7

TORQUE SPECIFICATIONS
All readings in ft. lbs.

Year	Engine Displacement Liters (cc)	Engine ID/VIN	Cylinder Head Bolts	Main Bearing Bolts	Rod Bearing Bolts	Crankshaft Damper Bolts	Flywheel Bolts	Manifold Intake	Manifold Exhaust	Spark Plugs	Lug Nuts
1997	1.9 (1901)	7	①	37	33	159	59 ②	22 ③	22 ③	20	103
	1.9 (1901)	8	④	37	33	159	59 ②	22 ③	22 ③	20	103
1998	1.9 (1901)	7	①	37	33	159	59 ②	22 ③	19 ③	20	103
	1.9 (1901)	8	④	37	33	159	59 ②	22 ③	16 ③	20	103
1999	1.9 (1901)	7	①	37	33	159	59 ②	22 ③	19 ③	20	103
	1.9 (1901)	8	④	37	33	159	59 ②	22 ③	16 ③	20	103
2000-01	1.9 (1901)	7	①	37	33	159	59 ②	22 ③	19 ③	20	103
	1.9 (1901)	8	④	37	33	159	59 ②	22 ③	16 ③	20	103
	2.2 (2199)	F	⑤	37	18	⑦	59 ②	15	13	15	138
	3.0 (3000)	R	⑥	37	26	NA	59 ②	15	18	18	139

① Step 1: 22 ft. lbs.
  Step 2: 37 ft. lbs.
  Step 3: 90 degrees

② Flexplate specification: 44 ft. lbs.

③ Studs: 106 inch lbs.

④ Step 1: 22 ft. lbs.
  Step 2: 33 ft. lbs.
  Step 3: 90 degrees

⑤ Step 1: 22 ft. lbs
  Step 2: 155 degrees

⑥ Refer to the torquence sequence chart for specifications

⑦ 74 ft. lbs. Plus 75 degrees

93061CX8

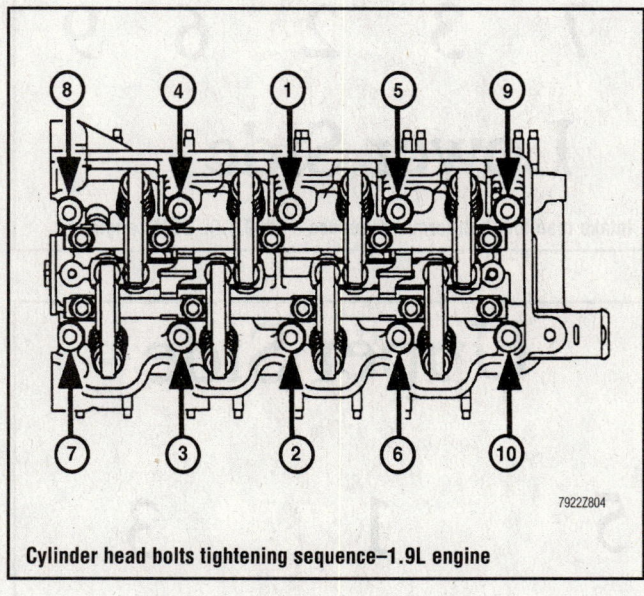

Cylinder head bolts tightening sequence–1.9L engine

7922Z804

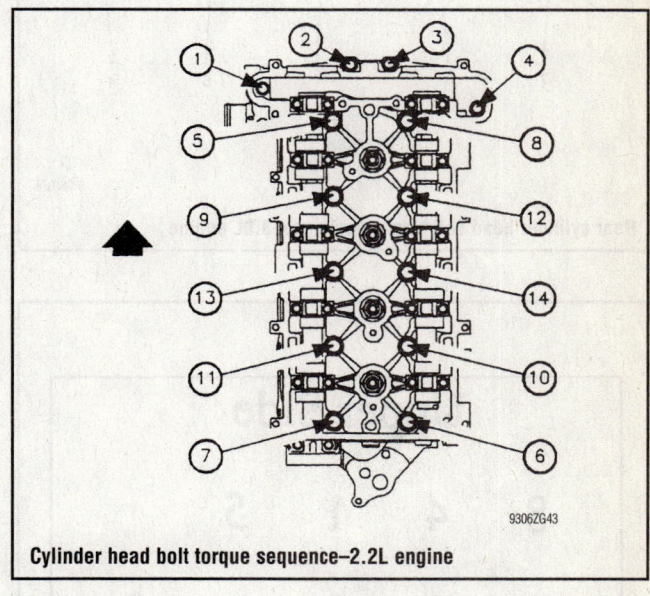

Cylinder head bolt torque sequence–2.2L engine

9306ZG43

Refer to the model specific sections for engine mechanical service procedures

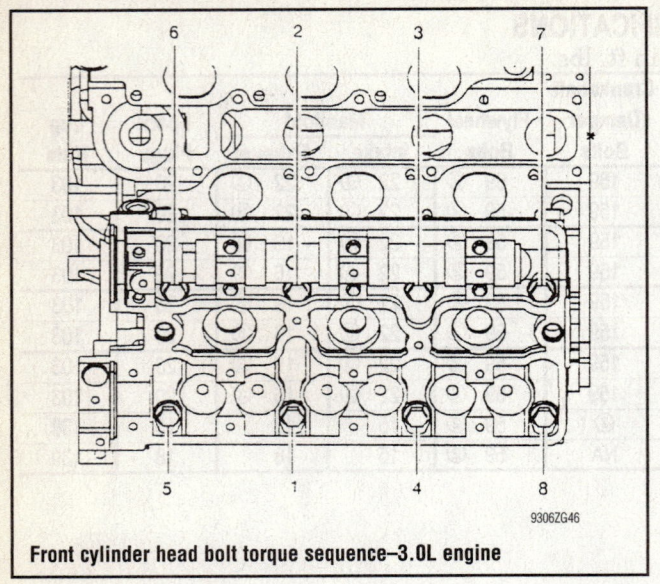

Front cylinder head bolt torque sequence–3.0L engine

9306ZG46

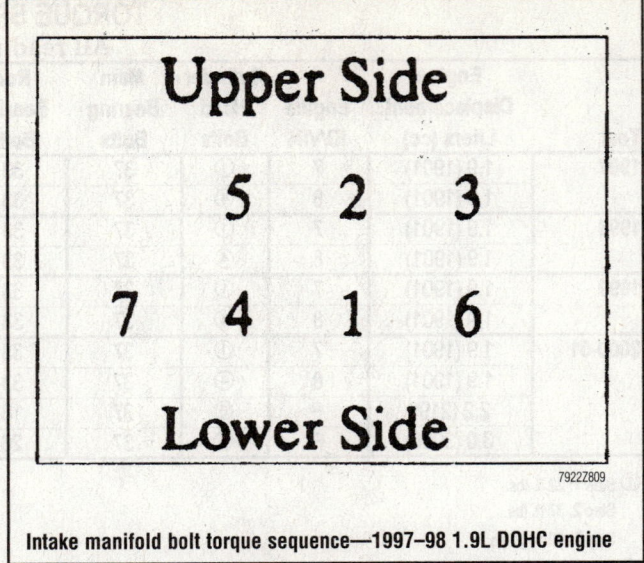

Intake manifold bolt torque sequence—1997–98 1.9L DOHC engine

7922Z809

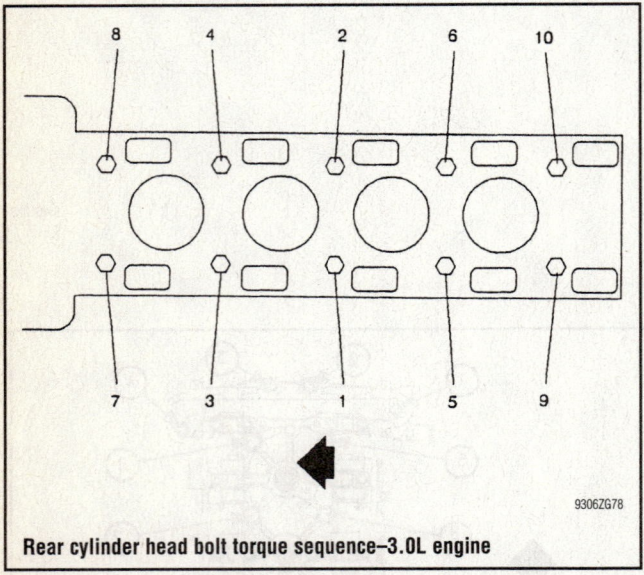

Rear cylinder head bolt torque sequence–3.0L engine

9306ZG78

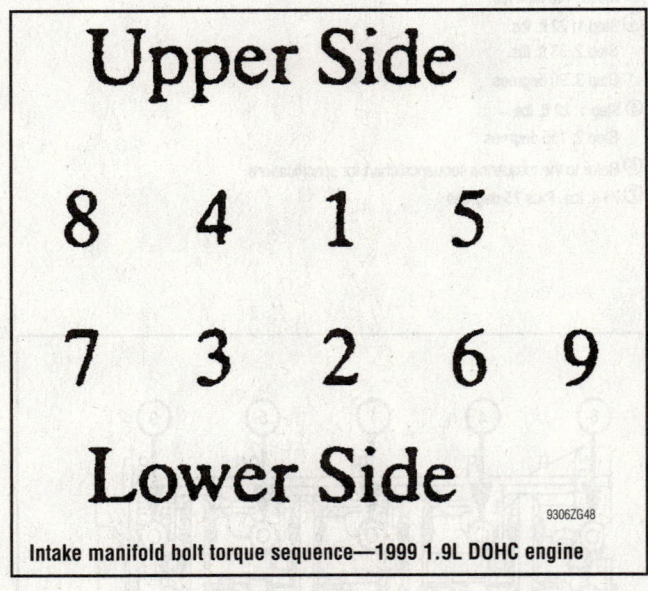

Intake manifold bolt torque sequence—1999 1.9L DOHC engine

9306ZG48

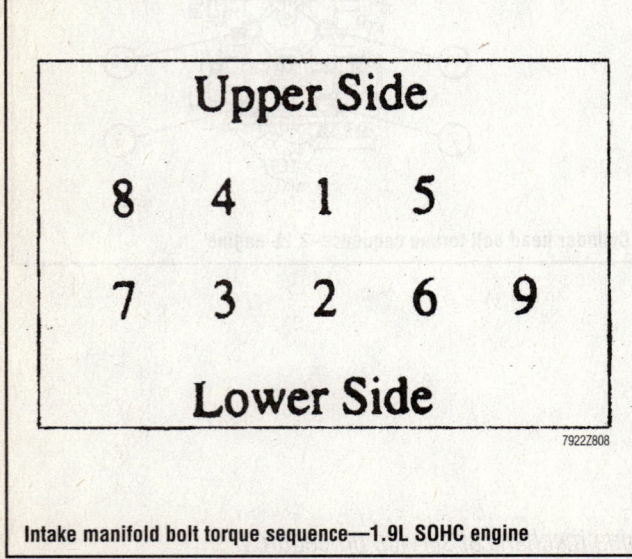

Intake manifold bolt torque sequence—1.9L SOHC engine

7922Z808

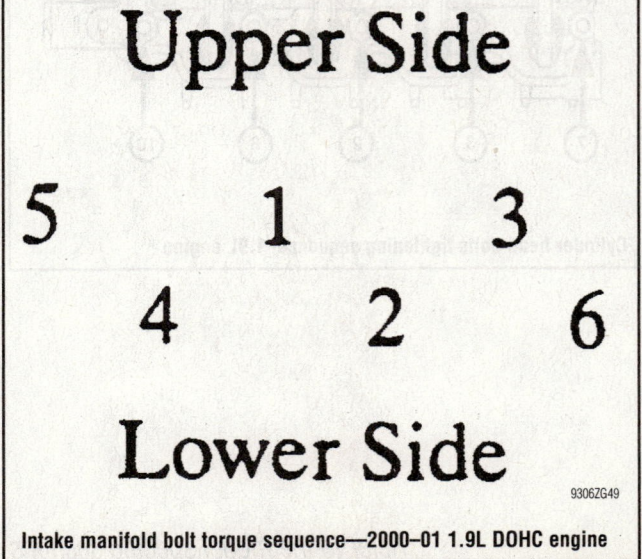

Intake manifold bolt torque sequence—2000–01 1.9L DOHC engine

9306ZG49

BRAKE SPECIFICATIONS
SATURN COUPES, SEDANS, WAGONS
All measurements in inches unless noted

Year	Model	Brake Disc			Brake Drum			Minimum Lining Thickness		Brake Caliper	
		Original Thickness	Minimum Thickness	Maximum Run-out	Original Inside Diameter	Max. Wear Limit	Maximum Machine Diameter	Pads	Shoes	Bracket Bolts (ft. lbs.)	Mounting Bolts (ft. lbs.)
1997	Coupe	①	②	0.0024	7.87	7.93	7.91	0.080	0.040	③	27
	Sedan	①	②	0.0024	7.87	7.93	7.91	0.080	0.040	③	27
	Wagon	①	②	0.0024	7.87	7.93	7.91	0.080	0.040	③	27
1998	Coupe	①	②	0.0024	7.87	7.93	7.91	0.080	0.040	③	27
	Sedan	①	②	0.0024	7.87	7.93	7.91	0.080	0.040	③	27
	Wagon	①	②	0.0024	7.87	7.93	7.91	0.080	0.040	③	27
1999	Coupe	①	②	0.0024	7.87	7.93	7.91	0.080	0.040	③	27
	Sedan	①	②	0.0024	7.87	7.93	7.91	0.080	0.040	③	27
	Wagon	①	②	0.0024	7.87	7.93	7.91	0.080	0.040	③	27
2000-01	Coupe	①	②	0.0024	7.87	7.93	7.91	0.080	0.040	③	27
	Sedan	①	②	0.0024	7.87	7.93	7.91	0.080	0.040	③	27
	Wagon	①	②	0.0024	7.87	7.93	7.91	0.080	0.040	③	27
	Coupe	③	⑤	0.006	7.87	7.93	7.91	0.080	0.040	81	27
	Sedan	④	⑥	0.005	9.05	9.09	9.08	0.090	0.035	70	22
	Wagon	④	⑥	0.005	9.05	9.09	9.08	0.090	0.035	70	22

① Front: 0.710
  Rear: 0.430

② Front: 0.633
  Rear: 0.370

③ Front: 81 ft. lbs.
  Rear: 63 ft. lbs

③ Front: 0.43
  Rear: 0.16

93061CX9

SCHEDULED MAINTENANCE INTERVALS
(SATURN LS2 & LW2)

TO BE SERVICED	TYPE OF SERVICE	VEHICLE MILEAGE INTERVAL (x1000)																			
		5	10	15	20	25	30	35	40	45	50	55	60	65	70	75	80	85	90	95	100
Engine oil & filter	R	✓	✓	✓	✓	✓	✓	✓	✓	✓	✓	✓	✓	✓	✓	✓	✓	✓	✓	✓	✓
Rotate tires	S/I	✓		✓		✓		✓		✓		✓		✓		✓		✓		✓	
Brake hoses	S/I	✓				✓		✓		✓		✓		✓		✓		✓		✓	
Passenger Compartment Air Filter (Pollen Filter)	R			✓			✓			✓			✓			✓			✓		
Air filter element	S/I			✓			✓			✓			✓			✓			✓		
	R						✓						✓						✓		
Fuel tank, cap and lines	S/I						✓						✓								
Rear axle fluid level	S/I						✓						✓								
Automatic transaxle fluid & filter ①	R										✓										✓
Accessory drive belt(s)	S/I												✓								
Spark plugs ②	R																				✓
Ignition cables	S/I																				✓
Camshaft timing belt ③	R												✓								✓
Fuel filter	R																				✓
Engine coolant ④	R																				

R: Replace   S/I: Service or Inspect

① Automatic transaxle fluid & filter: replace at 50,000 miles (83,000 km) if the vehicle has experienced severe service usage.

② Platinum tip spark plugs: replace every 100,000 miles.

③ Replace at 60,000 miles (96,000 km) if the engine was driven without an engine coolant heater being used and where temperatures fall below -20°F (-28°C).
Otherwise, replace the belt at 100,000 miles (160,000 km).

④ Engine coolant: replace every 150,000 miles. Use O.E. specified (DEX-COOL™) coolant only. If any silicate coolant is used, the service interval is every 30,000 miles.

FREQUENT OPERATION MAINTENANCE (SEVERE SERVICE)

If a vehicle is operated under any of the following conditions it is considered severe service:

- Extremely dusty areas.
- 50% or more of the vehicle operation is in 32°C (90°F) or higher temperatures, or constant operation in temperatures below 0°C (32°F).
- Prolonged idling (vehicle operation in stop and go traffic).
- Frequent short running periods (engine does not warm to normal operating temperatures).
- Police, taxi, delivery usage or trailer towing usage.

Oil & oil filter: change every 5000 miles

Rotate tires at 5000 miles, then every 10,000 miles.

Air filter element: service or inspect every 15,000 miles.

Camshaft timing belt: change every 60,000 miles for severe service.

93061CW8

SCHEDULED MAINTENANCE INTERVALS
(SATURN LS, LS1, LW1, SC, SC1, SC2, SL, SL1, SL2, SW1 & SW2)

TO BE SERVICED	TYPE OF SERVICE	VEHICLE MILEAGE INTERVAL (x1000)												
		3	6	9	12	15	18	21	24	27	30	33	36	39
Engine oil & filter	R		✓		✓		✓		✓		✓		✓	
Lubricate chassis, suspension, steering linkage, transaxle shift linkage, parking brake cable guides, underbody contact points & linkage	S/I		✓		✓		✓		✓		✓		✓	
Driveshaft boots, suspension bushings & ball joint seals	S/I		✓				✓		✓		✓		✓	
Exhaust system & throttle linkage	S/I		✓		✓		✓		✓		✓		✓	
Rotate tires	S/I		✓		✓		✓							
Brake hoses & brake lining	S/I		✓				✓				✓			
Accessory drive belt(s)	S/I						✓						✓	
Engine coolant level, hoses & clamps	S/I						✓						✓	
Air filter element	R										✓			
Engine coolant	R												✓	
Manual transaxle oil	R		✓											
Spark plugs ①	R										✓			
Automatic transaxle fluid & filter	S/I										✓			
Ignition cables & fuel systems	S/I										✓			
Vacuum line/hose	S/I										✓			
Fuel filter ②	R													

R: Replace S/I: Service or Inspect

① Platinum tip spark plugs: replace every 100,000 miles.

② Replace every 60,000 miles.

FREQUENT OPERATION MAINTENANCE (SEVERE SERVICE)

If a vehicle is operated under any of the following conditions it is considered severe service:

- Extremely dusty areas.

- 50% or more of the vehicle operation is in 32°C (90°F) or higher temperatures, or constant operation in temperatures below 0°C (32°F).

- Prolonged idling (vehicle operation in stop and go traffic).

- Frequent short running periods (engine does not warm to normal operating temperatures).

- Police, taxi, delivery usage or trailer towing usage.

Engine oil & oil filter: change every 3000 miles

93061CW9

Refer to the model specific sections for engine electrical system service procedures

SCHEDULED MAINTENANCE INTERVALS
SATURN
LS, LS1, LS2, LW1, LW2,
SC1, SC2, SL, SL1, SL2
SW1, SW2

The following should be used as a guide when determining the amount of work required for a particular service.
In estimating how long a particular Scheduled Maintenance Service should take, please observe the following:

- Labor Time is time based on field research and data supplied by the vehicle manufacturer.
- Labor time operations are given in hours and tenths of an hour.
- All labor operations are to be used as a guide.

Mechanic Skill Level Codes:
(A) PRECISION: Highly skilled with multiple certification.
(B) GENERAL: Normally skilled with certification.
(C) MAINTENANCE: Semi-skilled working on certification.

	LABOR TIME		LABOR TIME		LABOR TIME
6000 Mile Service (B)		**18000 Mile Service (C)**		**30000 Mile Service (B)**	
All Models	2.4	All Models	1.9	All Models	3.3
12000 Mile Service (C)		**24000 Mile Service (C)**		**36000 Mile Service (C)**	
All Models	.9	All Models	.9	All Models	2.3

93061CW0

TIRE, WHEEL AND BALL JOINT SPECIFICATIONS
Saturn

Year	Model	OEM Tires		Tire Pressures (psi)		Wheel Size	Ball Joint Inspection
		Standard	Optional	Front	Rear		
1997	SC1, SL, SL1, SW1	P175/70R14	None	30	28	5-JJ	NS
	SL2, SW2	P185/65R15	None	30	28	5-JJ	NS
	SC2	P195/60R15	None	30	28	5-JJ	NS
1998	SC1, SL, SL1, SW1	P175/70R14	None	30	28	5-JJ	NS
	SL2, SW2	P185/65R15	None	30	28	5-JJ	NS
	SC2	P195/60R15	None	30	28	5-JJ	NS
1999	SC1, SL, SL1, SW1	P175/70R14	None	30	28	5-JJ	NS
	SL2, SW2	P185/65R15	None	30	28	5-JJ	NS
	SC2	P195/60R15	None	30	28	5-JJ	NS
2000-01	SC1, SL, SL1, SW1	P175/70R14	None	30	28	5-JJ	NS
	SL2, SW2	P185/65R15	None	30	28	5-JJ	NS
	SC2	P195/60R15	None	30	28	5-JJ	NS
	L-Series	P195/65R15	None	30	30	6-J	NS

OEM: Original Equipment Manufacturer

PSI: Pounds Per Square Inch

STD: Standard

OPT: Optional

NS: Not specified by manufacturer

93061CY1

MAINTENANCE INDICATOR LIGHT (MIL) RESETTING

This section describes reset procedures for maintenance indicator lights. Maintenance indicator lights are used to indicate to the operator that some type of routine maintenance should be performed. Unlike a Check Engine light that will be displayed when there is a fault with the engine management system, the maintenance light will be displayed when an engine or transmission oil change is recommended according to driving conditions. Also, the light will be displayed to indicate when the emission control system is in need of maintenance service.

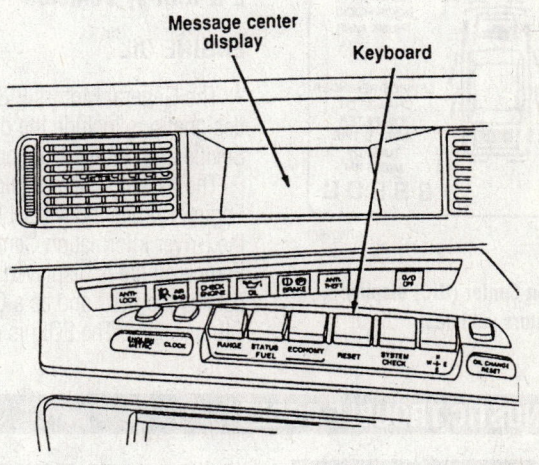

Message center display **Keyboard**

79222G02

The electronic message center control button locations—1997 Mark VIII

Ford Motor Co.

RESETTING

1997 Mark VIII

The 1997 Mark VIII continues to use the CHANGE OIL SOON or OIL CHANGE REQUIRED light. When the oil life left is between 5% and 0%, CHANGE OIL SOON will be displayed on the message center. When oil life reaches 0%, the OIL CHANGE REQUIRED message will be displayed. The message center indicator will indicate the percentage of oil life left during the System Check (during start up). This percentage is based on the driver's driving history and the amount of time since the last oil change. In order to ensure oil life left indications, the driver should only perform the OIL CHANGE RESET procedure after every oil change.

Reset the system by pressing the **OIL CHANGE RESET** switch and hold for 5 seconds. After a successful reset the message center will display oil life indicators. The CHANGE OIL SOON or OIL CHANGE REQUIRED message will disappear after the 5 second interval.

General Motors

RESETTING

C & H and G Body Vehicles

The General Motors C & H body class designations include the LeSabre, Park Ave., Eighty Eight, Ninety Eight, Bonneville, Regency and the LSS. The G body designation refers to the Riviera and Aurora.

These vehicles may be equipped with an ENGINE OIL LIFE INDEX (EOLI) in the display located on the Drivers Information Center (DIC). The Powertrain Control Module (PCM) determines approximately when the engine oil should be changed by calculating information based on vehicle speed, coolant temperature and engine RPM. Once the PCM determines it is time to change the engine oil, it will illuminate the CHANGE OIL SOON light on the DIC. This indicates that the remaining oil life is below 10%, (not to be confused with oil level). On a new vehicle, or one that has just been reset, the oil life is 100%. This percentage will slowly decrease based on inputs the PCM receives. When oil life reaches the 0% mark, the PCM

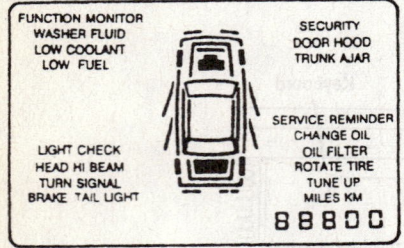

Driver Information Center (DIC) display—most General Motors vehicles

will illuminate the CHANGE OIL NOW light on the DIC. At this time both messages will be displayed accompanied by a slow 5 second audible chime. The reset button must be pressed to acknowledge each of these messages. If a steady CHANGE OIL SOON light persists, Diagnostic Trouble Code (DTC) 61 has been set, indicating a possible shorted switch. Remaining oil life percentage can be displayed by pressing the **OIL** button on the DIC and advancing through the messages until the oil life index is displayed. The oil life index will not detect abnormal conditions, such as excessively dusty conditions or engine malfunctions that could otherwise affect engine oil life.

Reset the EOLI as follows:

1. Acknowledge all diagnostic messages in the Drivers Information Center by pressing the **RESET** button.

2. Press the **SEL** button on the left to select OIL. Press the **SEL** button on the right, if necessary, to display oil life.

3. Press and hold the **RESET** button for about 5 seconds. Once the oil life index has been reset, a RESET message will be displayed, then oil life will change to 100%. Be careful not reset the oil life accidentally at any time other than when the oil has just been changed. It can not be reset accurately until the next oil change.

E & K Body Vehicles

ENGINE OIL

The General Motors E & K body class designations include the deVille, Eldorado, Seville and deVille Concours.

These vehicles are equipped with an Engine Oil Life Index (EOLI) feature as part of the Driver Information Center (DIC) display. Engine oil life is displayed through engine data as the EOLI and as a CHANGE ENGINE OIL message. The EOLI is displayed follow-

ing a number between 0 (zero) and 100. This is the percentage of oil life remaining, based on driving conditions, engine oil temperature, and mileage driven since the last time the oil life indicator was reset. When the oil life index reaches 10% or less a CHANGE OIL SOON message will appear as a reminder to schedule an oil change. When the oil life index reaches 0, the CHANGE ENGINE OIL message will appear indicating that the oil should be changed within the next 200 miles (320 km). After the oil has been changed, display the EOLI message by pressing the **INFORMATION** button several times. Press and hold the **RESET** button until the display shows 100. This will reset the oil life index. The CHANGE ENGINE OIL message will remain off until the next oil change is needed. The percentage of oil life remaining may be checked at any time by pressing the **INFORMATION** button several times until the EOLI appears.

Y Body Vehicles

The 1997–01 Corvette is equipped with an Oil Life Monitor. The Oil Life Monitor is used to inform the driver when the next service is required. A scan tool can be used to monitor and display the amount of oil life left (shown as a percentage).

➡**Repair any Throttle Position (TP) or Accelerator Pedal Position (APP) sensor diagnostic trouble codes before resetting the oil life monitor.**

1. Turn the ignition **ON** but do not start the engine.

2. Depress the accelerator pedal to the Wide Open Throttle (WOT) position and release it 3 times within 5 seconds.

3. If the Oil Life Monitor is not reset, perform this procedure again.

4. Change the oil and the filter.

OBD II DIAGNOSTIC TROUBLE CODES

Introduction

To comply with On-Board Diagnostics Second Generation (OBD II) regulations, the Powertrain Control Module (PCM) is equipped with software designed to allow it to monitor vehicle emission control systems and components. Once the ignition is turned on or the engine is started, and certain test conditions are met, the PCM runs a series of monitors to test the emission control systems and components. Test conditions include different inputs such as time since

startup, run-time, engine speed and temperature, transaxle gear position, and the engine open or closed loop status. Once the monitor is started, the control module attempts to run it to completion. If a particular monitor fails a test, a code is set and operating conditions at that time are recorded in memory. If the same component or system fails twice in succession, the Malfunction Indicator Lamp (MIL) is activated.

Monitors are divided into 2 types: Main Monitors and the Comprehensive Component Monitors.

- Catalyst monitor
- Exhaust Gas Recirculation (EGR) monitor
- Evaporative (EVAP) emissions monitor
- Fuel system monitor
- Misfire monitor
- Oxygen (O_2) sensor monitor
- O_2 sensor heater monitor

Certain monitors, in particular the fuel system and misfire monitors, have limitations that are different from any of the other monitors. The first time either of these monitors fail, the MIL is activated, and engine conditions at the time of the fault are recorded. In order for the control module to turn off an MIL related to these 2 monitors, it must determine that no faults are present with engine operating conditions similar to when it detected the fault. To qualify, the engine must be operated within a specified speed range, engine load range and temperature range.

A warm-up cycle is considered to be vehicle operation after the engine has been turned off for a period of time, with the Engine Coolant Temperature (ECT) input rising a specified amount and reaching normal operating temperature. When the MIL is turned off because a fault is no longer present, most OBD II codes will be erased after a minimum of 40 warm-up cycles. Misfire and fuel system codes require a minimum of 80 warm-up cycles before they clear.

OBD II Systems use a standardized test connector, called the Data Link Connector (DLC). It is usually located under the left side of the instrument panel. The DLC is located out of the line of sight of vehicle passengers, but is easily viewable from a kneeling position outside the vehicle. The connector is rectangular in design and contains up to 16 terminals. It has keying features to allow for easy connection. Both the DLC and Scan Tool connectors have latching features that ensure the scan tool will remain properly connected.

Some common uses of the Scan Tool are to identify and clear Diagnostic Trouble Codes (DTC's) and to read control module freeze frame.

The Malfunction Indicator Lamp (MIL)

looks similar to the "Check Engine" lamp. However, on OBD II Systems, it is controlled under a strict set of guidelines that dictate when the MIL is illuminated. If any of the control module monitors detects a fault that could impact vehicle emissions, a fault code is set. A One-Trip Monitor requires that a test fail once, a Two-Trip Monitor requires a test fail twice in succession, and a Three-Trip Monitor requires that a test fail 3 times in succession to activate the MIL.

The MIL is mounted in the instrument panel and has 2 functions: To act as a bulb check at key on and to inform the driver that an emissions fault has occurred.

Once the engine is started, if no faults are detected, the control module should extinguish the MIL after a few seconds. If the MIL remains on or flashes with the engine running a driveability symptom is present.

Federal law required all vehicle manufacturers to meet On Board Diagnostics, Second Generation or OBD II standards by 1996. In order to meet this standard, the automobile's on-board computer must monitor and perform diagnostic tests on vehicle emissions to ensure that the vehicle is operating at an acceptable (legal) emission level. The maximum allowable emission level is set by the Federal Test Procedure (FTP).

All 1997–01 vehicles are OBD II compliant. All OBD II vehicles have the same 16-pin diagnostic connector or DLC. This eliminates the need to have a manufacturer specific connector to plug a scan tool into your vehicle.

TROUBLE CODE DESCRIPTION

In the past, trouble code numbers varied between manufacturers, years, makes and models. OBD II requires that all vehicle manufacturers use a common Diagnostic Trouble Code (DTC) numbering system. Since the generic listing was not specific enough, most manufacturers came up with their own DTC listings which are called manufacturer specific codes. Both generic and manufacturer specific codes are 5 digits. The numbers can be decoded as follows:

The first digit is a letter which identifies the function of the device or circuit which has the fault. This digit can be either:

- P—Powertrain
- B—Body
- C—Chassis
- U—Network or data link code

The second digit is either a 0 or 1 and indicates whether the code is generic or manufacturer specific.

- 0—Generic
- 1—Manufacturer specific

The third digit represents the specific vehicle circuit or system that has the fault. Listed below are the number identifiers for the powertrain system.

- 1—Fuel and air metering
- 2—Fuel and air metering (injector circuit malfunctions only)
- 3—Ignition system or misfire
- 4—Auxiliary emission control
- 5—Vehicle speed control and idle control system
- 6—Computer and auxiliary outputs
- 7—Transmission
- 8—Transmission

The last 2 digits indicate the specific trouble code.

On OBD II vehicles there are 2 different types of DTC's: Stored and Pending. For a DTC to become stored, certain malfunction conditions must occur. The condition(s) required to store codes are different for every DTC and vary by vehicle manufacturer.

In order for some DTC's to become stored, a malfunction condition has to happen more than once. If the malfunction conditions are required to occur more than once, the potential malfunction is called a pending DTC. The DTC remains pending until the malfunction condition occurs the required number of times to make the code stored. If the malfunction condition does not occur again after a set time the pending DTC will be cleared.

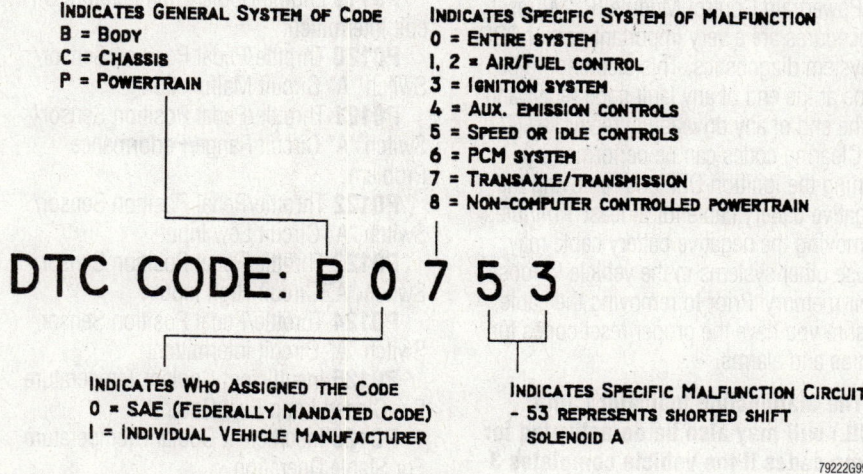

INDICATES GENERAL SYSTEM OF CODE
B = BODY
C = CHASSIS
P = POWERTRAIN

INDICATES SPECIFIC SYSTEM OF MALFUNCTION
0 = ENTIRE SYSTEM
1, 2 = AIR/FUEL CONTROL
3 = IGNITION SYSTEM
4 = AUX. EMISSION CONTROLS
5 = SPEED OR IDLE CONTROLS
6 = PCM SYSTEM
7 = TRANSAXLE/TRANSMISSION
8 = NON–COMPUTER CONTROLLED POWERTRAIN

DTC CODE: P 0 7 5 3

INDICATES WHO ASSIGNED THE CODE
0 = SAE (FEDERALLY MANDATED CODE)
1 = INDIVIDUAL VEHICLE MANUFACTURER

INDICATES SPECIFIC MALFUNCTION CIRCUIT
- 53 REPRESENTS SHORTED SHIFT SOLENOID A

79222G99

On Board Diagnostic II trouble code break-down

Chrysler Corp.

READING CODES

With Scan Tool

Reading the Powertrain Control Module (PCM) memory is one of the first steps in OBD II system diagnostics. This step should be initially performed to determine the general nature of the fault. Subsequent readings will determine if the fault has been cleared.

Reading codes can be performed by any of the methods below:

• Read the control module memory with the Generic Scan Tool (GST)

• Read the control module memory with the vehicle manufacturer's specific tester

To read the fault codes, connect the scan tool or tester according to the manufacturer's instructions. Follow the manufacturer's specified procedure for reading the codes.

Without Scan Tool

On all 1997 vehicles, as well as the 1998 Sebring coupe and Avenger models with a 2.0L engine, Diagnostic Trouble Codes (DTC's) can be accessed by observing the 2-digit number (referred to as an OBD II equivalent code) displayed by the Malfunction Indicator Lamp (MIL). The MIL is shown on the instrument panel as the check engine lamp. This method should be used as a "quick test" only; always use a scan tool to get the most detailed information.

➡ **Be advised that the MIL can only perform a limited number of functions and it is a good idea to have the system checked with a scan tool to double check the circuit function.**

Within a period of 5 seconds, cycle the ignition key **ON—OFF—ON—OFF—ON**.

1. Count the number of times the MIL (check engine lamp) on the instrument panel flashes on and off.

The number of flashes represents the trouble code. There is a short pause between the flashes representing the 1st and 2nd digits of the code. Longer pauses are used to separate individual 2-digit trouble codes.

An example of a flashed DTC is as follows:

• Lamp flashes 4 times, pauses, then

flashes 6 more times. This denotes a DTC number 46.

• Lamp flashes 5 times, pauses, then flashes 5 more times. This indicates a DTC number 55.

DTC 55 will always be the last code to be displayed.

CLEARING CODES

With Scan Tool

Powertrain Control Module (PCM) reset procedures are a very important part of OBD II system diagnostics. This step should be done at the end of any fault code repair and at the end of any driveability repair.

Clearing codes can be performed by any of the methods below:

• Clear the control module memory with the Generic Scan Tool (GST)

• Clear the control module memory with the vehicle manufacturer's specific tester

• Turn the ignition **OFF** and disconnect the negative battery cable for at least 1 minute.

Disconnecting the negative battery cable may cause other systems in the vehicle to loose their memory. Prior to removing the cable, ensure you have the proper reset codes for radios and alarms.

➡ **The Malfunction Indicator Lamp (MIL) will may also be de-activated for some codes if the vehicle completes 3 consecutive trips without a fault detected with vehicle conditions similar to those present during the fault.**

Without Scan Tool

Powertrain Control Module (PCM) reset procedures are a very important part of OBD II system diagnostics. This step should be done at the end of any fault code repair and at the end of any driveability repair.

Clearing codes can be performed by turning the ignition OFF and removing the negative battery cable for at least 1 minute. Removing the negative battery cable may cause other systems in the vehicle to loose their memory. Prior to removing the cable, ensure you have the proper reset codes for radios and alarms.

➡ **The Malfunction Indicator Lamp (MIL) will may also be de-activated for some codes if the vehicle completes 3 consecutive trips without a fault detected with vehicle conditions similar to those present during the fault.**

OBD II TROUBLE CODES

P0100 Mass or Volume Air Flow Circuit Malfunction

P0101 Mass or Volume Air Flow Circuit Range/Performance Problem

P0102 Mass or Volume Air Flow Circuit Low Input

P0103 Mass or Volume Air Flow Circuit High Input

P0104 Mass or Volume Air Flow Circuit Intermittent

P0105 Manifold Absolute Pressure/Barometric Pressure Circuit Malfunction

P0106 Manifold Absolute Pressure/Barometric Pressure Circuit Out Of Range

P0107 Manifold Absolute Pressure/Barometric Pressure Circuit Low Input

P0108 Manifold Absolute Pressure/Barometric Pressure Circuit High Input

P0109 Manifold Absolute Pressure/Barometric Pressure Circuit Intermittent

P0110 Intake Air Temperature Circuit Malfunction

P0111 Intake Air Temperature Circuit Range/Performance Problem

P0112 Intake Air Temperature Circuit Low Input

P0113 Intake Air Temperature Circuit High Input

P0114 Intake Air Temperature Circuit Intermittent

P0115 Engine Coolant Temperature Circuit Malfunction

P0116 Engine Coolant Temperature Circuit Range/Performance Problem

P0117 Engine Coolant Temperature Circuit Low Input

P0118 Engine Coolant Temperature Circuit High Input

P0119 Engine Coolant Temperature Circuit Intermittent

P0120 Throttle/Pedal Position Sensor/Switch "A" Circuit Malfunction

P0121 Throttle/Pedal Position Sensor/Switch "A" Circuit Range/Performance Problem

P0122 Throttle/Pedal Position Sensor/Switch "A" Circuit Low Input

P0123 Throttle/Pedal Position Sensor/Switch "A" Circuit High Input

P0124 Throttle/Pedal Position Sensor/Switch "A" Circuit Intermittent

P0125 Insufficient Coolant Temperature For Closed Loop Fuel Control

P0126 Insufficient Coolant Temperature For Stable Operation

P0130 O_2 Circuit Malfunction (Bank #1 Sensor #1)

P0131 O_2 Sensor Circuit Low Voltage (Bank #1 Sensor #1)

P0132 O_2 Sensor Circuit High Voltage (Bank #1 Sensor #1)

P0133 O_2 Sensor Circuit Slow Response (Bank #1 Sensor #1)

P0134 O_2 Sensor Circuit No Activity Detected (Bank #1 Sensor #1)

P0135 O_2 Sensor Heater Circuit Malfunction (Bank #1 Sensor #1)

P0136 O_2 Sensor Circuit Malfunction (Bank #1 Sensor #2)

P0137 O_2 Sensor Circuit Low Voltage (Bank #1 Sensor #2)

P0138 O_2 Sensor Circuit High Voltage (Bank #1 Sensor #2)

P0139 O_2 Sensor Circuit Slow Response (Bank #1 Sensor #2)

P0140 O_2 Sensor Circuit No Activity Detected (Bank #1 Sensor #2)

P0141 O_2 Sensor Heater Circuit Malfunction (Bank #1 Sensor #2)

P0142 O_2 Sensor Circuit Malfunction (Bank #1 Sensor #3)

P0143 O_2 Sensor Circuit Low Voltage (Bank #1 Sensor #3)

P0144 O_2 Sensor Circuit High Voltage (Bank #1 Sensor #3)

P0145 O_2 Sensor Circuit Slow Response (Bank #1 Sensor #3)

P0146 O_2 Sensor Circuit No Activity Detected (Bank #1 Sensor #3)

P0147 O_2 Sensor Heater Circuit Malfunction (Bank #1 Sensor #3)

P0150 O_2 Sensor Circuit Malfunction (Bank #2 Sensor #1)

P0151 O_2 Sensor Circuit Low Voltage (Bank #2 Sensor #1)

P0152 O_2 Sensor Circuit High Voltage (Bank #2 Sensor #1)

P0153 O_2 Sensor Circuit Slow Response (Bank #2 Sensor #1)

P0154 O_2 Sensor Circuit No Activity Detected (Bank #2 Sensor #1)

P0155 O_2 Sensor Heater Circuit Malfunction (Bank #2 Sensor #1)

P0156 O_2 Sensor Circuit Malfunction (Bank #2 Sensor #2)

P0157 O_2 Sensor Circuit Low Voltage (Bank #2 Sensor #2)

P0158 O_2 Sensor Circuit High Voltage (Bank #2 Sensor #2)

P0159 O_2 Sensor Circuit Slow Response (Bank #2 Sensor #2)

P0160 O_2 Sensor Circuit No Activity Detected (Bank #2 Sensor #2)

P0161 O_2 Sensor Heater Circuit Malfunction (Bank #2 Sensor #2)

P0162 O_2 Sensor Circuit Malfunction (Bank #2 Sensor #3)

P0163 O_2 Sensor Circuit Low Voltage (Bank #2 Sensor #3)

P0164 O_2 Sensor Circuit High Voltage (Bank #2 Sensor #3)

P0165 O_2 Sensor Circuit Slow Response (Bank #2 Sensor #3)

P0166 O_2 Sensor Circuit No Activity Detected (Bank #2 Sensor #3)

P0167 O_2 Sensor Heater Circuit Malfunction (Bank #2 Sensor #3)

P0170 Fuel Trim Malfunction (Bank #1)

P0171 System Too Lean (Bank #1)

P0172 System Too Rich (Bank #1)

P0173 Fuel Trim Malfunction (Bank #2)

P0174 System Too Lean (Bank #2)

P0175 System Too Rich (Bank #2)

P0176 Fuel Composition Sensor Circuit Malfunction

P0177 Fuel Composition Sensor Circuit Range/Performance

P0178 Fuel Composition Sensor Circuit Low Input

P0179 Fuel Composition Sensor Circuit High Input

P0180 Fuel Temperature Sensor "A" Circuit Malfunction

P0181 Fuel Temperature Sensor "A" Circuit Range/Performance

P0182 Fuel Temperature Sensor "A" Circuit Low Input

P0183 Fuel Temperature Sensor "A" Circuit High Input

P0184 Fuel Temperature Sensor "A" Circuit Intermittent

P0185 Fuel Temperature Sensor "B" Circuit Malfunction

P0186 Fuel Temperature Sensor "B" Circuit Range/Performance

P0187 Fuel Temperature Sensor "B" Circuit Low Input

P0188 Fuel Temperature Sensor "B" Circuit High Input

P0189 Fuel Temperature Sensor "B" Circuit Intermittent

P0190 Fuel Rail Pressure Sensor Circuit Malfunction

P0191 Fuel Rail Pressure Sensor Circuit Range/Performance

P0192 Fuel Rail Pressure Sensor Circuit Low Input

P0193 Fuel Rail Pressure Sensor Circuit High Input

P0194 Fuel Rail Pressure Sensor Circuit Intermittent

P0195 Engine Oil Temperature Sensor Malfunction

P0196 Engine Oil Temperature Sensor Range/Performance

P0197 Engine Oil Temperature Sensor Low

P0198 Engine Oil Temperature Sensor High

P0199 Engine Oil Temperature Sensor Intermittent

P0200 Injector Circuit Malfunction

P0201 Injector Circuit Malfunction—Cylinder #1

P0202 Injector Circuit Malfunction—Cylinder #2

P0203 Injector Circuit Malfunction—Cylinder #3

P0204 Injector Circuit Malfunction—Cylinder #4

P0205 Injector Circuit Malfunction—Cylinder #5

P0206 Injector Circuit Malfunction—Cylinder #6

P0207 Injector Circuit Malfunction—Cylinder #7

P0208 Injector Circuit Malfunction—Cylinder #8

P0209 Injector Circuit Malfunction—Cylinder #9

P0210 Injector Circuit Malfunction—Cylinder #10

P0211 Injector Circuit Malfunction—Cylinder #11

P0212 Injector Circuit Malfunction—Cylinder #12

P0213 Cold Start Injector #1 Malfunction

P0214 Cold Start Injector #2 Malfunction

P0215 Engine Shutoff Solenoid Malfunction

P0216 Injection Timing Control Circuit Malfunction

P0217 Engine Over Temperature Condition

P0218 Transmission Over Temperature Condition

P0219 Engine Over Speed Condition

P0220 Throttle/Pedal Position Sensor/Switch "B" Circuit Malfunction

P0221 Throttle/Pedal Position Sensor/Switch "B" Circuit Range/Performance Problem

P0222 Throttle/Pedal Position Sensor/Switch "B" Circuit Low Input

P0223 Throttle/Pedal Position Sensor/Switch "B" Circuit High Input

P0224 Throttle/Pedal Position Sensor/Switch "B" Circuit Intermittent

P0225 Throttle/Pedal Position Sensor/Switch "C" Circuit Malfunction

P0226 Throttle/Pedal Position Sensor/Switch "C" Circuit Range/Performance Problem

P0227 Throttle/Pedal Position Sensor/Switch "C" Circuit Low Input

P0228 Throttle/Pedal Position Sensor/Switch "C" Circuit High Input

P0229 Throttle/Pedal Position Sensor/Switch "C" Circuit Intermittent

P0230 Fuel Pump Primary Circuit Malfunction

P0231 Fuel Pump Secondary Circuit Low

P0232 Fuel Pump Secondary Circuit High

P0233 Fuel Pump Secondary Circuit Intermittent

P0234 Engine Over Boost Condition

P0261 Cylinder #1 Injector Circuit Low

P0262 Cylinder #1 Injector Circuit High

P0263 Cylinder #1 Contribution/Balance Fault

P0264 Cylinder #2 Injector Circuit Low

P0265 Cylinder #2 Injector Circuit High

P0266 Cylinder #2 Contribution/Balance Fault

P0267 Cylinder #3 Injector Circuit Low

P0268 Cylinder #3 Injector Circuit High

P0269 Cylinder #3 Contribution/Balance Fault

P0270 Cylinder #4 Injector Circuit Low

P0271 Cylinder #4 Injector Circuit High

P0272 Cylinder #4 Contribution/Balance Fault

P0273 Cylinder #5 Injector Circuit Low

P0274 Cylinder #5 Injector Circuit High

P0275 Cylinder #5 Contribution/Balance Fault

P0276 Cylinder #6 Injector Circuit Low

P0277 Cylinder #6 Injector Circuit High

P0278 Cylinder #6 Contribution/Balance Fault

P0279 Cylinder #7 Injector Circuit Low

P0280 Cylinder #7 Injector Circuit High

P0281 Cylinder #7 Contribution/Balance Fault

P0282 Cylinder #8 Injector Circuit Low

P0283 Cylinder #8 Injector Circuit High

P0284 Cylinder #8 Contribution/Balance Fault

P0285 Cylinder #9 Injector Circuit Low

P0286 Cylinder #9 Injector Circuit High

P0287 Cylinder #9 Contribution/Balance Fault

P0288 Cylinder #10 Injector Circuit Low

P0289 Cylinder #10 Injector Circuit High

P0290 Cylinder #10 Contribution/Balance Fault

P0291 Cylinder #11 Injector Circuit Low

P0292 Cylinder #11 Injector Circuit High

P0293 Cylinder #11 Contribution/Balance Fault

P0294 Cylinder #12 Injector Circuit Low

P0295 Cylinder #12 Injector Circuit High

P0296 Cylinder #12 Contribution/Balance Fault

P0300 Random/Multiple Cylinder Misfire Detected

P0301 Cylinder #1—Misfire Detected
P0302 Cylinder #2—Misfire Detected
P0303 Cylinder #3—Misfire Detected
P0304 Cylinder #4—Misfire Detected
P0305 Cylinder #5—Misfire Detected
P0306 Cylinder #6—Misfire Detected
P0307 Cylinder #7—Misfire Detected
P0308 Cylinder #8—Misfire Detected
P0309 Cylinder #9—Misfire Detected
P0310 Cylinder #10—Misfire Detected
P0311 Cylinder #11—Misfire Detected
P0312 Cylinder #12—Misfire Detected

P0320 Ignition/Distributor Engine Speed Input Circuit Malfunction

P0321 Ignition/Distributor Engine Speed Input Circuit Range/Performance

P0322 Ignition/Distributor Engine Speed Input Circuit No Signal

P0323 Ignition/Distributor Engine Speed Input Circuit Intermittent

P0325 Knock Sensor #1—Circuit Malfunction (Bank #1 or Single Sensor)

P0326 Knock Sensor #1—Circuit Range/Performance (Bank #1 or Single Sensor)

P0327 Knock Sensor #1—Circuit Low Input (Bank #1 or Single Sensor)

P0328 Knock Sensor #1—Circuit High Input (Bank #1 or Single Sensor)

P0329 Knock Sensor #1—Circuit Input Intermittent (Bank #1 or Single Sensor)

P0330 Knock Sensor #2—Circuit Malfunction (Bank #2)

P0331 Knock Sensor #2—Circuit Range/Performance (Bank #2)

P0332 Knock Sensor #2—Circuit Low Input (Bank #2)

P0333 Knock Sensor #2—Circuit High Input (Bank #2)

P0334 Knock Sensor #2—Circuit Input Intermittent (Bank #2)

P0335 Crankshaft Position Sensor "A" Circuit Malfunction

P0336 Crankshaft Position Sensor "A" Circuit Range/Performance

P0337 Crankshaft Position Sensor "A" Circuit Low Input

P0338 Crankshaft Position Sensor "A" Circuit High Input

P0339 Crankshaft Position Sensor "A" Circuit Intermittent

P0340 No Camshaft Position Sensor Signal At PCM

P0341 Camshaft Position Sensor Circuit Range/Performance

P0342 Camshaft Position Sensor Circuit Low Input

P0343 Camshaft Position Sensor Circuit High Input

P0344 Camshaft Position Sensor Circuit Intermittent

P0350 Ignition Coil Primary/Secondary Circuit Malfunction

P0351 Ignition Coil "1" Primary/Secondary Circuit Malfunction

P0352 Ignition Coil "2" Primary/Secondary Circuit Malfunction

P0353 Ignition Coil "3" Primary/Secondary Circuit Malfunction

P0354 Ignition Coil "4" Primary/Secondary Circuit Malfunction

P0355 Ignition Coil "5" Primary/Secondary Circuit Malfunction

P0356 Ignition Coil "6" Primary/Secondary Circuit Malfunction

P0357 Ignition Coil "7" Primary/Secondary Circuit Malfunction

P0358 Ignition Coil "8" Primary/Secondary Circuit Malfunction

P0359 Ignition Coil "9" Primary/Secondary Circuit Malfunction

P0360 Ignition Coil "10" Primary/Secondary Circuit Malfunction

P0361 Ignition Coil "11" Primary/Secondary Circuit Malfunction

P0362 Ignition Coil "12" Primary/Secondary Circuit Malfunction

P0370 Timing Reference High Resolution Signal "A" Malfunction

P0371 Timing Reference High Resolution Signal "A" Too Many Pulses

P0372 Timing Reference High Resolution Signal "A" Too Few Pulses

P0373 Timing Reference High Resolution Signal "A" Intermittent/Erratic Pulses

P0374 Timing Reference High Resolution Signal "A" No Pulses

P0375 Timing Reference High Resolution Signal "B" Malfunction

P0376 Timing Reference High Resolution Signal "B" Too Many Pulses

P0377 Timing Reference High Resolution Signal "B" Too Few Pulses

P0378 Timing Reference High Resolution Signal "B" Intermittent/Erratic Pulses

P0379 Timing Reference High Resolution Signal "B" No Pulses

P0380 Glow Plug/Heater Circuit "A" Malfunction

P0381 Glow Plug/Heater Indicator Circuit Malfunction

P0382 Glow Plug/Heater Circuit "B" Malfunction

P0385 Crankshaft Position Sensor "B" Circuit Malfunction

P0386 Crankshaft Position Sensor "B" Circuit Range/Performance

P0387 Crankshaft Position Sensor "B" Circuit Low Input

P0388 Crankshaft Position Sensor "B" Circuit High Input

P0389 Crankshaft Position Sensor "B" Circuit Intermittent

P0400 Exhaust Gas Recirculation Flow Malfunction

P0401 Exhaust Gas Recirculation Flow Insufficient Detected

P0402 Exhaust Gas Recirculation Flow Excessive Detected

P0403 Exhaust Gas Recirculation Circuit Malfunction

P0404 Exhaust Gas Recirculation Circuit Range/Performance

P0405 Exhaust Gas Recirculation Sensor "A" Circuit Low

P0406 Exhaust Gas Recirculation Sensor "A" Circuit High

P0407 Exhaust Gas Recirculation Sensor "B" Circuit Low

P0408 Exhaust Gas Recirculation Sensor "B" Circuit High

P0410 Secondary Air Injection System Malfunction

P0411 Secondary Air Injection System Incorrect Flow Detected

P0412 Secondary Air Injection System Switching Valve "A" Circuit Malfunction

P0413 Secondary Air Injection System Switching Valve "A" Circuit Open

P0414 Secondary Air Injection System Switching Valve "A" Circuit Shorted

P0415 Secondary Air Injection System Switching Valve "B" Circuit Malfunction

P0416 Secondary Air Injection System Switching Valve "B" Circuit Open

P0417 Secondary Air Injection System Switching Valve "B" Circuit Shorted

P0418 Secondary Air Injection System Relay "A" Circuit Malfunction

P0419 Secondary Air Injection System Relay "B" Circuit Malfunction

P0420 Catalyst System Efficiency Below Threshold (Bank #1)

P0421 Warm Up Catalyst Efficiency Below Threshold (Bank #1)

P0422 Main Catalyst Efficiency Below Threshold (Bank #1)

P0423 Heated Catalyst Efficiency Below Threshold (Bank #1)

P0424 Heated Catalyst Temperature Below Threshold (Bank #1)

P0430 Catalyst System Efficiency Below Threshold (Bank #2)

P0431 Warm Up Catalyst Efficiency Below Threshold (Bank #2)

P0432 Main Catalyst Efficiency Below Threshold (Bank #2)

P0433 Heated Catalyst Efficiency Below Threshold (Bank #2)

P0434 Heated Catalyst Temperature Below Threshold (Bank #2)

P0440 Evaporative Emission Control System Malfunction

P0441 Evaporative Emission Control System Incorrect Purge Flow

P0442 Evaporative Emission Control System Leak Detected (Small Leak)

P0443 Evaporative Emission Control System Purge Control Valve Circuit Malfunction

P0444 Evaporative Emission Control System Purge Control Valve Circuit Open

P0445 Evaporative Emission Control System Purge Control Valve Circuit Shorted

P0446 Evaporative Emission Control System Vent Control Circuit Malfunction

P0447 Evaporative Emission Control System Vent Control Circuit Open

P0448 Evaporative Emission Control System Vent Control Circuit Shorted

P0449 Evaporative Emission Control System Vent Valve/Solenoid Circuit Malfunction

P0450 Evaporative Emission Control System Pressure Sensor Malfunction

P0451 Evaporative Emission Control System Pressure Sensor Range/Performance

P0452 Evaporative Emission Control System Pressure Sensor Low Input

P0453 Evaporative Emission Control System Pressure Sensor High Input

P0454 Evaporative Emission Control System Pressure Sensor Intermittent

P0455 Evaporative Emission Control System Leak Detected (Gross Leak)

P0460 Fuel Level Sensor Circuit Malfunction

P0461 Fuel Level Sensor Circuit Range/Performance

P0462 Fuel Level Sensor Circuit Low Input

P0463 Fuel Level Sensor Circuit High Input

P0464 Fuel Level Sensor Circuit Intermittent

P0465 Purge Flow Sensor Circuit Malfunction

P0466 Purge Flow Sensor Circuit Range/Performance

P0467 Purge Flow Sensor Circuit Low Input

P0468 Purge Flow Sensor Circuit High Input

P0469 Purge Flow Sensor Circuit Intermittent

P0470 Exhaust Pressure Sensor Malfunction

P0471 Exhaust Pressure Sensor Range/Performance

P0472 Exhaust Pressure Sensor Low

P0473 Exhaust Pressure Sensor High

P0474 Exhaust Pressure Sensor Intermittent

P0475 Exhaust Pressure Control Valve Malfunction

P0476 Exhaust Pressure Control Valve Range/Performance

P0477 Exhaust Pressure Control Valve Low

P0478 Exhaust Pressure Control Valve High

P0479 Exhaust Pressure Control Valve Intermittent

P0480 Cooling Fan #1 Control Circuit Malfunction

P0481 Cooling Fan #2 Control Circuit Malfunction

P0482 Cooling Fan #3 Control Circuit Malfunction

P0483 Cooling Fan Rationality Check Malfunction

P0484 Cooling Fan Circuit Over Current

P0485 Cooling Fan Power/Ground Circuit Malfunction

P0500 Vehicle Speed Sensor Malfunction

P0501 Vehicle Speed Sensor Range/Performance

P0502 Vehicle Speed Sensor Circuit Low Input

P0503 Vehicle Speed Sensor Intermittent/Erratic/High

P0505 Idle Control System Malfunction

P0506 Idle Control System RPM Lower Than Expected

P0507 Idle Control System RPM Higher Than Expected

P0510 Closed Throttle Position Switch Malfunction

P0520 Engine Oil Pressure Sensor/Switch Circuit Malfunction

P0521 Engine Oil Pressure Sensor/Switch Range/Performance

P0522 Engine Oil Pressure Sensor/Switch Low Voltage

P0523 Engine Oil Pressure Sensor/Switch High Voltage

P0530 A/C Refrigerant Pressure Sensor Circuit Malfunction

P0531 A/C Refrigerant Pressure Sensor Circuit Range/Performance

P0532 A/C Refrigerant Pressure Sensor Circuit Low Input

P0533 A/C Refrigerant Pressure Sensor Circuit High Input

P0534 A/C Refrigerant Charge Loss

P0550 Power Steering Pressure Sensor Circuit Malfunction

P0551 Power Steering Pressure Sensor Circuit Range/Performance

P0552 Power Steering Pressure Sensor Circuit Low Input

P0553 Power Steering Pressure Sensor Circuit High Input

P0554 Power Steering Pressure Sensor Circuit Intermittent

P0560 System Voltage Malfunction

P0561 System Voltage Unstable

P0562 System Voltage Low

P0563 System Voltage High

P0565 Cruise Control On Signal Malfunction

P0566 Cruise Control Off Signal Malfunction

P0567 Cruise Control Resume Signal Malfunction

P0568 Cruise Control Set Signal Malfunction

P0569 Cruise Control Coast Signal Malfunction

P0570 Cruise Control Accel Signal Malfunction

P0571 Cruise Control/Brake Switch "A" Circuit Malfunction

P0572 Cruise Control/Brake Switch "A" Circuit Low

P0573 Cruise Control/Brake Switch "A" Circuit High

P0574 Through P0580 Reserved for Cruise Codes

P0600 Serial Communication Link Malfunction

P0601 Internal Control Module Memory Check Sum Error

P0602 Control Module Programming Error

P0603 Internal Control Module Keep Alive Memory (KAM) Error

P0604 Internal Control Module Random Access Memory (RAM) Error

P0605 Internal Control Module Read Only Memory (ROM) Error

P0606 PCM Processor Fault

P0608 Control Module VSS Output "A" Malfunction

P0609 Control Module VSS Output "B" Malfunction

P0620 Generator Control Circuit Malfunction

P0621 Generator Lamp "L" Control Circuit Malfunction

P0622 Generator Field "F" Control Circuit Malfunction

P0650 Malfunction Indicator Lamp (MIL) Control Circuit Malfunction

P0654 Engine RPM Output Circuit Malfunction

P0655 Engine Hot Lamp Output Control Circuit Malfunction

P0656 Fuel Level Output Circuit Malfunction

P0700 Transmission Control System Malfunction

P0701 Transmission Control System Range/Performance

P0702 Transmission Control System Electrical

P0703 Torque Converter/Brake Switch "B" Circuit Malfunction

P0704 Clutch Switch Input Circuit Malfunction

P0705 Transmission Range Sensor Circuit Malfunction (PRNDL Input)

P0706 Transmission Range Sensor Circuit Range/Performance

P0707 Transmission Range Sensor Circuit Low Input

P0708 Transmission Range Sensor Circuit High Input

P0709 Transmission Range Sensor Circuit Intermittent

P0710 Transmission Fluid Temperature Sensor Circuit Malfunction

P0711 Transmission Fluid Temperature Sensor Circuit Range/Performance

P0712 Transmission Fluid Temperature Sensor Circuit Low Input

P0713 Transmission Fluid Temperature Sensor Circuit High Input

P0714 Transmission Fluid Temperature Sensor Circuit Intermittent

P0715 Input/Turbine Speed Sensor Circuit Malfunction

P0716 Input/Turbine Speed Sensor Circuit Range/Performance

P0717 Input/Turbine Speed Sensor Circuit No Signal

P0718 Input/Turbine Speed Sensor Circuit Intermittent

P0719 Torque Converter/Brake Switch "B" Circuit Low

P0720 Output Speed Sensor Circuit Malfunction

P0721 Output Speed Sensor Circuit Range/Performance

P0722 Output Speed Sensor Circuit No Signal

P0723 Output Speed Sensor Circuit Intermittent

P0724 Torque Converter/Brake Switch "B" Circuit High

P0725 Engine Speed Input Circuit Malfunction

P0726 Engine Speed Input Circuit Range/Performance

P0727 Engine Speed Input Circuit No Signal

P0728 Engine Speed Input Circuit Intermittent

P0730 Incorrect Gear Ratio

P0731 Gear #1 Incorrect Ratio

P0732 Gear #2 Incorrect Ratio

P0733 Gear #3 Incorrect Ratio

P0734 Gear #4 Incorrect Ratio

P0735 Gear #5 Incorrect Ratio

P0736 Reverse Incorrect Ratio

P0740 Torque Converter Clutch Circuit Malfunction

P0741 Torque Converter Clutch Circuit Performance or Stuck Off

P0742 Torque Converter Clutch Circuit Stuck On

P0743 Torque Converter Clutch Circuit Electrical

P0744 Torque Converter Clutch Circuit Intermittent

P0745 Pressure Control Solenoid Malfunction

P0746 Pressure Control Solenoid Performance or Stuck Off

P0747 Pressure Control Solenoid Stuck On

P0748 Pressure Control Solenoid Electrical

P0749 Pressure Control Solenoid Intermittent

P0750 Shift Solenoid "A" Malfunction

P0751 Shift Solenoid "A" Performance or Stuck Off

P0752 Shift Solenoid "A" Stuck On

P0753 Shift Solenoid "A" Electrical

P0754 Shift Solenoid "A" Intermittent

P0755 Shift Solenoid "B" Malfunction

P0756 Shift Solenoid "B" Performance or Stuck Off

P0757 Shift Solenoid "B" Stuck On

P0758 Shift Solenoid "B" Electrical

P0759 Shift Solenoid "B" Intermittent

P0760 Shift Solenoid "C" Malfunction

P0761 Shift Solenoid "C" Performance Or Stuck Off

P0762 Shift Solenoid "C" Stuck On

P0763 Shift Solenoid "C" Electrical

P0764 Shift Solenoid "C" Intermittent

P0765 Shift Solenoid "D" Malfunction

P0766 Shift Solenoid "D" Performance Or Stuck Off

P0767 Shift Solenoid "D" Stuck On

P0768 Shift Solenoid "D" Electrical

P0769 Shift Solenoid "D" Intermittent

P0770 Shift Solenoid "E" Malfunction

P0771 Shift Solenoid "E" Performance Or Stuck Off

P0772 Shift Solenoid "E" Stuck On

P0773 Shift Solenoid "E" Electrical

P0774 Shift Solenoid "E" Intermittent

P0780 Shift Malfunction

P0781 1–2 Shift Malfunction

P0782 2–3 Shift Malfunction

P0783 3–4 Shift Malfunction

P0784 4–5 Shift Malfunction

P0785 Shift/Timing Solenoid Malfunction

P0786 Shift/Timing Solenoid Range/Performance

P0787 Shift/Timing Solenoid Low

P0788 Shift/Timing Solenoid High

P0789 Shift/Timing Solenoid Intermittent

P0790 Normal/Performance Switch Circuit Malfunction

P0801 Reverse Inhibit Control Circuit Malfunction

P0803 1–4 Upshift (Skip Shift) Solenoid Control Circuit Malfunction

P0804 1–4 Upshift (Skip Shift) Lamp Control Circuit Malfunction

P1195 1/1 O₂ Sensor Slow During Catalyst Monitor

P1196 2/1 O₂ Sensor Slow During Catalyst Monitor

P1197 1/2 O₂ Sensor Slow During Catalyst Monitor

P1198 Radiator Temp Sensor Voltage Too High

P1199 Radiator Temp Sensor Voltage Too Low

P1281 Engine Is Cold Too Long

P1282 Fuel Pump Relay Control Circuit

P1288 Intake Manifold Short Runner Solenoid Circuit

P1289 Manifold Tune Valve Solenoid Circuit

P1290 CNG Fuel System Pressure Too High—3.3L CNG vehicles only

P1291 No Temp Rise Seen From Intake Air Heaters

P1292 CNG Pressure Sensor Voltage Too High—3.3L CNG vehicles only

P1293 CNG Pressure Sensor Voltage Too Low—3.3L CNG vehicles only

P1294 Target Idle Not Reached

P1295 No 5-Volts To TP Sensor

P1296 No 5-Volts To MAP Sensor

P1297 No Change In MAP From Start To Run

P1298 Lean Operation At Wide Open Throttle

P1299 Vacuum Leak Found (IAC Fully Seated)

P1388 ASD Relay Control Circuit

P1389 No ASD Relay Output Voltage At PCM

P1390 Timing Belt Skipped 1 Tooth or More

P1391 Intermittent Loss Of CMP Or CKP

P1398 Misfire Adaptive Numerator At Limit (Possible Defective Crank Sensor)

P1399 Wait To Start Lamp Circuit

P1403 No 5-Volts to EGR Sensor

P1476 Too Little Secondary Air

P1477 Too Much Secondary Air

P1478 Battery Temp Sensor Volts Out of Limits

P1479 Transmission Fan Relay Circuit

P1480 PCV Solenoid Circuit

P1482 Catalyst Temp Sensor Circuit Shorted Low

P1483 Catalyst Temp Sensor Circuit Shorted High

P1484 Catalytic Converter Overheat Detected

P1485 Air Injection Solenoid Circuit

P1486 EVAP Leak Monitor Pinched Hose Or Obstruction Found

P1487 High Speed Rad Fan CTRL Circuit

P1488 Auxiliary 5-Volt Supply Output Too Low

P1489 High Speed Fan CTRL Relay Circuit

P1490 Low Speed Rad Fan CTRL Circuit

P1491 Radiator Fan Control Relay Circuit

P1492 Battery Temp Sensor Voltage Too High

P1493 Battery Temp Sensor Voltage Too Low

P1494 Leak Detection Pump Pressure Switch Or Mechanical Fault

P1495 Leak Detection Pump Solenoid Circuit

P1496 5-Volt Supply, Output Too Low

P1498 Auxiliary 5-Volt Supply Output Too Low

P1594 Charging System Voltage Too High

P1595 Speed Control Solenoid Circuits

P1596 Speed Control Switch Always High

P1597 Speed Control Switch Always Low

P1598 A/C Pressure Sensor Voltage Too High

P1599 A/C Pressure Sensor Voltage Too Low

P1680 Clutch Release Switch Circuit

P1681 No I/P Cluster CCD/J1850 Messages Received

P1682 Charging System Voltage Too Low

P1683 Speed Control Power Relay or Driver Circuit

P1684 Battery Has Been Disconnected Within the Last 50 Starts

P1685 (SKIM) Smart Key Immobilizer Module Invalid Key

P1686 No SKIM Bus Messages Received

P1697 PCM Failure SRI Mile Not Stored

P1698 PCM Failure EEPROM Write Denied

P1756 Governor Pressure Not Equal To Target @ 15–20 PSI

P1757 Governor Pressure Above 3 PSI In Gear With 0 MPH

P1762 Governor Pressure Sensor Offset Volts Too Low Or High

P1763 Governor Pressure Sensor Volts Too High

P1764 Governor Pressure Sensor Volts Too Low

P1765 Trans 12-Volt Supply Relay Control Circuit

P1899 P/N Switch Stuck In Park Or In Gear

Refer to the model specific sections for fuel system service procedures

OBD II TROUBLE CODE EQUIVALENTS

11 No crank reference signal at PCM
11 Timing belt skipped 1 tooth or more
11 Intermittent loss of CMP or CKP
11 Misfire adaptive numerator at limit
12 Battery disconnect
13 Slow change in idle MAP sensor signal (VIN N engine)
13 No change in MAP from start to run
14 MAP sensor voltage too low
14 MAP sensor voltage too high
14 No 5-volts to MAP sensor
15 5-volt supply output too low
16 No vehicle speed sensor signal
16 Knock sensor signal
17 Engine cold too long
17 Closed loop temperature not reached
21 Front O₂S shorted to voltage
21 Front O₂S stays at center
21 Rear O₂S shorted to voltage
21 Rear O₂S stays at center
21 Upstream O₂S shorted to ground
21 Upstream O₂S shorted to voltage
21 Upstream O₂S response
21 Upstream O₂S stays at center
21 Upstream O₂S heater failure
21 Downstream O₂S shorted to ground
21 Downstream O₂S shorted to voltage
21 Downstream O₂S response
21 Downstream O₂S signal inactive
21 Downstream O₂S heater failure
21 Front bank upstream O₂S shorted to ground (6-cylinder)
21 Front bank upstream O₂S shorted to voltage (6-cylinder)
21 Front bank upstream O₂S slow response 6-cylinder)
21 Front bank upstream O₂S stays at center (6-cylinder)
21 Front bank upstream O₂S heater failure (6-cylinder)
21 Front bank downstream O₂S shorted to ground (6-cylinder)
21 Front bank downstream O₂S shorted to voltage (6-cylinder)
21 Front bank downstream O₂S stays at center (6-cylinder)
21 Front bank downstream O₂S heater failure (6-cylinder)
22 ECT sensor voltage too low
22 ECT sensor voltage too high
23 Intake air temperature voltage low
23 Intake air temperature voltage high
24 TPS voltage does not agree with MAP
24 Throttle position sensor voltage low
24 Throttle position sensor voltage high

24 No 5-volts to TPS
25 Idle air control motor circuits
25 Target idle not reached
25 Vacuum leak found (IAC fully seated)
27 Injector #1 control circuit
27 Injector #2 control circuit
27 Injector #3 control circuit
27 Injector #4 control circuit
27 Injector #5 control circuit (6-cylinder)
27 Injector #6 control circuit (6-cylinder)
31 EVAP purge flow monitor failure
31 EVAP system small leak
31 EVAP solenoid circuit
31 EVAP system large leak
31 EVAP leak monitor pinched hose
31 Leak detection pump pressure switch
31 EVAP emission vent solenoid switch or mechanical failure
31 Leak detection pump solenoid circuit
31 EVAP emission vent solenoid circuit
31 High speed radiator fan ground control relay circuit
32 EGR system failure
32 EGR solenoid circuit
33 A/C pressure sensor volts too high
33 A/C pressure sensor volts too low
33 A/C clutch relay circuit
34 Speed control switch always low
34 Speed control switch always high
34 Speed control solenoid circuit
35 High speed condenser fan control relay circuit
35 High fan and high fan ground control relay circuit
35 High speed radiator fan control relay circuit
35 High speed fan control relay circuit
35 Low speed fan control relay circuit
37 Park/Neutral switch failure
41 Alternator field not switching properly
42 Auto shutdown relay circuit
42 No ASD relay output voltage at PCM
42 Fuel level sending unit volts too low
42 Fuel level sending unit volts too high
42 Fuel level unit no change over miles
42 Fuel pump relay control circuit
43 Multiple cylinder misfire
43 Cylinder #1 misfire
43 Cylinder #2 misfire
43 Cylinder #3 misfire
43 Cylinder #4 misfire
43 Cylinder #5 misfire
43 Cylinder #6 misfire
43 Ignition coil #1 primary circuit
43 Ignition coil #2 primary circuit
44 Ambient temperature sensor

44 Battery temperature sensor volts out of limit
44 Battery temperature sensor voltage too high
44 Battery temperature sensor voltage too low
45 Transaxle fault present
46 Charging system voltage too high
47 Charging system voltage too low
51 Fuel system lean (4-cylinder)
51 Rear bank fuel system lean (6-cylinder)
51 Front bank fuel system lean (6-cylinder)
52 Fuel system rich (4-cylinder)
52 Rear bank fuel system rich (6-cylinder)
52 Front bank fuel system rich (6-cylinder)
53 Internal controller failure
53 PCM failure SPI communications
53 Internal controller failure
53 PCM failure SPI communications
54 No cam signal at PCM
55 Completion or fault code display on Check Engine Lamp
62 PCM failure SRI mile not stared
63 PCM failure EEPROM write denied
64 Catalytic converter efficiency failure
64 Rear bank catalytic converter efficiency failure
65 Power steering switch failure
65 Brake switch performance circuit
66 No CCD message from body controller
66 No CCD message from TCM
71 5-volt output low speed control power circuit
72 Catalytic Converter efficiency failure
72 Front bank catalytic converter efficiency failure
77 Malfunction detected with power feed to speed control servo

Ford Motor Co.

READING CODES

Reading the Powertrain Control Module (PCM) memory is one of the first steps in OBD II system diagnostics. This step should be initially performed to determine the general nature of the fault. Subsequent readings will determine if the fault has been cleared.

Reading codes can be performed by any of the methods below:
- Read the control module memory with the Generic Scan Tool (GST)
- Read the control module memory with the vehicle manufacturer's specific tester

To read the fault codes, connect the scan

tool or tester according to the manufacturer's instructions. Follow the manufacturer's specified procedure for reading the codes.

CLEARING CODES

Powertrain Control Module (PCM) reset procedures are a very important part of OBD II system diagnostics. This step should be done at the end of any fault code repair and at the end of any driveability repair.

Clearing codes can be performed by any of the methods below:

• Clear the control module memory with the Generic Scan Tool (GST)

• Clear the control module memory with the vehicle manufacturer's specific tester

• Turn the ignition **OFF** and disconnect the negative battery cable for at least 1 minute

Disconnecting the negative battery cable may cause other systems in the vehicle to loose their memory. Prior to removing the cable, ensure you have the proper reset codes for radios and alarms.

➡ **The Malfunction Indicator Lamp (MIL) may also be de-activated for some codes if the vehicle completes 3 consecutive trips without a fault detected with vehicle conditions similar to those present during the fault.**

OBD II TROUBLE CODES

P0000 No Failures
P0100 Mass or Volume Air Flow Circuit Malfunction
P0101 Mass or Volume Air Flow Circuit Range/Performance Problem
P0102 Mass or Volume Air Flow Circuit Low Input
P0103 Mass or Volume Air Flow Circuit High Input
P0104 Mass or Volume Air Flow Circuit Intermittent
P0105 Manifold Absolute Pressure/Barometric Pressure Circuit Malfunction
P0106 Manifold Absolute Pressure/Barometric Pressure Circuit Range/Performance Problem
P0107 Manifold Absolute Pressure/Barometric Pressure Circuit Low Input
P0108 Manifold Absolute Pressure/Barometric Pressure Circuit High Input

P0109 Manifold Absolute Pressure/Barometric Pressure Circuit Intermittent
P0110 Intake Air Temperature Circuit Malfunction
P0111 Intake Air Temperature Circuit Range/Performance Problem
P0112 Intake Air Temperature Circuit Low Input
P0113 Intake Air Temperature Circuit High Input
P0114 Intake Air Temperature Circuit Intermittent
P0115 Engine Coolant Temperature Circuit Malfunction
P0116 Engine Coolant Temperature Circuit Range/Performance Problem
P0117 Engine Coolant Temperature Circuit Low Input
P0118 Engine Coolant Temperature Circuit High Input
P0119 Engine Coolant Temperature Circuit Intermittent
P0120 Throttle/Pedal Position Sensor/Switch "A" Circuit Malfunction
P0121 Throttle/Pedal Position Sensor/Switch "A" Circuit Range/Performance Problem
P0122 Throttle/Pedal Position Sensor/Switch "A" Circuit Low Input
P0123 Throttle/Pedal Position Sensor/Switch "A" Circuit High Input
P0124 Throttle/Pedal Position Sensor/Switch "A" Circuit Intermittent
P0125 Insufficient Coolant Temperature For Closed Loop Fuel Control
P0126 Insufficient Coolant Temperature For Stable Operation
P0130 O_2 Circuit Malfunction (Bank #1 Sensor #1)
P0131 O_2 Sensor Circuit Low Voltage (Bank #1 Sensor #1)
P0132 O_2 Sensor Circuit High Voltage (Bank #1 Sensor #1)
P0133 O_2 Sensor Circuit Slow Response (Bank #1 Sensor #1)
P0134 O_2 Sensor Circuit No Activity Detected (Bank #1 Sensor #1)
P0135 O_2 Sensor Heater Circuit Malfunction (Bank #1 Sensor #1)
P0136 O_2 Sensor Circuit Malfunction (Bank #1 Sensor #2)
P0137 O_2 Sensor Circuit Low Voltage (Bank #1 Sensor #2)
P0138 O_2 Sensor Circuit High Voltage (Bank #1 Sensor #2)
P0139 O_2 Sensor Circuit Slow Response (Bank #1 Sensor #2)
P0140 O_2 Sensor Circuit No Activity Detected (Bank #1 Sensor #2)

P0141 O_2 Sensor Heater Circuit Malfunction (Bank #1 Sensor #2)
P0142 O_2 Sensor Circuit Malfunction (Bank #1 Sensor #3)
P0143 O_2 Sensor Circuit Low Voltage (Bank #1 Sensor #3)
P0144 O_2 Sensor Circuit High Voltage (Bank #1 Sensor #3)
P0145 O_2 Sensor Circuit Slow Response (Bank #1 Sensor #3)
P0146 O_2 Sensor Circuit No Activity Detected (Bank #1 Sensor #3)
P0147 O_2 Sensor Heater Circuit Malfunction (Bank #1 Sensor #3)
P0150 O_2 Sensor Circuit Malfunction (Bank #2 Sensor #1)
P0151 O_2 Sensor Circuit Low Voltage (Bank #2 Sensor #1)
P0152 O_2 Sensor Circuit High Voltage (Bank #2 Sensor #1)
P0153 O_2 Sensor Circuit Slow Response (Bank #2 Sensor #1)
P0154 O_2 Sensor Circuit No Activity Detected (Bank #2 Sensor #1)
P0155 O_2 Sensor Heater Circuit Malfunction (Bank #2 Sensor #1)
P0156 O_2 Sensor Circuit Malfunction (Bank #2 Sensor #2)
P0157 O_2 Sensor Circuit Low Voltage (Bank #2 Sensor #2)
P0158 O_2 Sensor Circuit High Voltage (Bank #2 Sensor #2)
P0159 O_2 Sensor Circuit Slow Response (Bank #2 Sensor #2)
P0160 O_2 Sensor Circuit No Activity Detected (Bank #2 Sensor #2)
P0161 O_2 Sensor Heater Circuit Malfunction (Bank #2 Sensor #2)
P0162 O_2 Sensor Circuit Malfunction (Bank #2 Sensor #3)
P0163 O_2 Sensor Circuit Low Voltage (Bank #2 Sensor #3)
P0164 O_2 Sensor Circuit High Voltage (Bank #2 Sensor #3)
P0165 O_2 Sensor Circuit Slow Response (Bank #2 Sensor #3)
P0166 O_2 Sensor Circuit No Activity Detected (Bank #2 Sensor #3)
P0167 O_2 Sensor Heater Circuit Malfunction (Bank #2 Sensor #3)
P0170 Fuel Trim Malfunction (Bank #1)
P0171 System Too Lean (Bank #1)
P0172 System Too Rich (Bank #1)
P0173 Fuel Trim Malfunction (Bank #2)
P0174 System Too Lean (Bank #2)
P0175 System Too Rich (Bank #2)
P0176 Fuel Composition Sensor Circuit Malfunction

Refer to the model specific sections for engine electrical system service procedures

P0177 Fuel Composition Sensor Circuit Range/Performance

P0178 Fuel Composition Sensor Circuit Low Input

P0179 Fuel Composition Sensor Circuit High Input

P0180 Fuel Temperature Sensor "A" Circuit Malfunction

P0181 Fuel Temperature Sensor "A" Circuit Range/Performance

P0182 Fuel Temperature Sensor "A" Circuit Low Input

P0183 Fuel Temperature Sensor "A" Circuit High Input

P0184 Fuel Temperature Sensor "A" Circuit Intermittent

P0185 Fuel Temperature Sensor "B" Circuit Malfunction

P0186 Fuel Temperature Sensor "B" Circuit Range/Performance

P0187 Fuel Temperature Sensor "B" Circuit Low Input

P0188 Fuel Temperature Sensor "B" Circuit High Input

P0189 Fuel Temperature Sensor "B" Circuit Intermittent

P0190 Fuel Rail Pressure Sensor Circuit Malfunction

P0191 Fuel Rail Pressure Sensor Circuit Range/Performance

P0192 Fuel Rail Pressure Sensor Circuit Low Input

P0193 Fuel Rail Pressure Sensor Circuit High Input

P0194 Fuel Rail Pressure Sensor Circuit Intermittent

P0195 Engine Oil Temperature Sensor Malfunction

P0196 Engine Oil Temperature Sensor Range/Performance

P0197 Engine Oil Temperature Sensor Low

P0198 Engine Oil Temperature Sensor High

P0199 Engine Oil Temperature Sensor Intermittent

P0200 Injector Circuit Malfunction

P0201 Injector Circuit Malfunction—Cylinder #1

P0202 Injector Circuit Malfunction—Cylinder #2

P0203 Injector Circuit Malfunction—Cylinder #3

P0204 Injector Circuit Malfunction—Cylinder #4

P0205 Injector Circuit Malfunction—Cylinder #5

P0206 Injector Circuit Malfunction—Cylinder #6

P0207 Injector Circuit Malfunction—Cylinder #7

P0208 Injector Circuit Malfunction—Cylinder #8

P0209 Injector Circuit Malfunction—Cylinder #9

P0210 Injector Circuit Malfunction—Cylinder #10

P0213 Cold Start Injector #1 Malfunction

P0214 Cold Start Injector #2 Malfunction

P0215 Engine Shutoff Solenoid Malfunction

P0216 Injection Timing Control Circuit Malfunction

P0217 Engine Over Temperature Condition

P0218 Transmission Over Temperature Condition

P0219 Engine Over Speed Condition

P0220 Throttle/Pedal Position Sensor/Switch "B" Circuit Malfunction

P0221 Throttle/Pedal Position Sensor/Switch "B" Circuit Range/Performance Problem

P0222 Throttle/Pedal Position Sensor/Switch "B" Circuit Low Input

P0223 Throttle/Pedal Position Sensor/Switch "B" Circuit High Input

P0224 Throttle/Pedal Position Sensor/Switch "B" Circuit Intermittent

P0225 Throttle/Pedal Position Sensor/Switch "C" Circuit Malfunction

P0226 Throttle/Pedal Position Sensor/Switch "C" Circuit Range/Performance Problem

P0227 Throttle/Pedal Position Sensor/Switch "C" Circuit Low Input

P0228 Throttle/Pedal Position Sensor/Switch "C" Circuit High Input

P0229 Throttle/Pedal Position Sensor/Switch "C" Circuit Intermittent

P0230 Fuel Pump Primary Circuit Malfunction

P0231 Fuel Pump Secondary Circuit Low

P0232 Fuel Pump Secondary Circuit High

P0233 Fuel Pump Secondary Circuit Intermittent

P0234 Engine Over Boost Condition

P0261 Cylinder #1 Injector Circuit Low

P0262 Cylinder #1 Injector Circuit High

P0263 Cylinder #1 Contribution/Balance Fault

P0264 Cylinder #2 Injector Circuit Low

P0265 Cylinder #2 Injector Circuit High

P0266 Cylinder #2 Contribution/Balance Fault

P0267 Cylinder #3 Injector Circuit Low

P0268 Cylinder #3 Injector Circuit High

P0269 Cylinder #3 Contribution/Balance Fault

P0270 Cylinder #4 Injector Circuit Low

P0271 Cylinder #4 Injector Circuit High

P0272 Cylinder #4 Contribution/Balance Fault

P0273 Cylinder #5 Injector Circuit Low

P0274 Cylinder #5 Injector Circuit High

P0275 Cylinder #5 Contribution/Balance Fault

P0276 Cylinder #6 Injector Circuit Low

P0277 Cylinder #6 Injector Circuit High

P0278 Cylinder #6 Contribution/Balance Fault

P0279 Cylinder #7 Injector Circuit Low

P0280 Cylinder #7 Injector Circuit High

P0281 Cylinder #7 Contribution/Balance Fault

P0282 Cylinder #8 Injector Circuit Low

P0283 Cylinder #8 Injector Circuit High

P0284 Cylinder #8 Contribution/Balance Fault

P0285 Cylinder #9 Injector Circuit Low

P0286 Cylinder #9 Injector Circuit High

P0287 Cylinder #9 Contribution/Balance Fault

P0288 Cylinder #10 Injector Circuit Low

P0289 Cylinder #10 Injector Circuit High

P0290 Cylinder #10 Contribution/Balance Fault

P0300 Random/Multiple Cylinder Misfire Detected

P0301 Cylinder #1—Misfire Detected

P0302 Cylinder #2—Misfire Detected

P0303 Cylinder #3—Misfire Detected

P0304 Cylinder #4—Misfire Detected

P0305 Cylinder #5—Misfire Detected

P0306 Cylinder #6—Misfire Detected

P0307 Cylinder #7—Misfire Detected

P0308 Cylinder #8—Misfire Detected

P0309 Cylinder #9—Misfire Detected

P0310 Cylinder #10—Misfire Detected

P0320 Ignition/Distributor Engine Speed Input Circuit Malfunction

P0321 Ignition/Distributor Engine Speed Input Circuit Range/Performance

P0322 Ignition/Distributor Engine Speed Input Circuit No Signal

P0323 Ignition/Distributor Engine Speed Input Circuit Intermittent

P0325 Knock Sensor #1—Circuit Malfunction (Bank #1 or Single Sensor)

P0326 Knock Sensor #1—Circuit Range/Performance (Bank #1 or Single Sensor)

P0327 Knock Sensor #1—Circuit Low Input (Bank #1 or Single Sensor)

P0328 Knock Sensor #1—Circuit High Input (Bank #1 or Single Sensor)

P0329 Knock Sensor #1—Circuit Input Intermittent (Bank #1 or Single Sensor)

P0330 Knock Sensor #2—Circuit Malfunction (Bank #2)

P0331 Knock Sensor #2—Circuit Range/Performance (Bank #2)

P0332 Knock Sensor #2—Circuit Low Input (Bank #2)

P0333 Knock Sensor #2—Circuit High Input (Bank #2)

P0334 Knock Sensor #2—Circuit Input Intermittent (Bank #2)

P0335 Crankshaft Position Sensor "A" Circuit Malfunction

P0336 Crankshaft Position Sensor "A" Circuit Range/Performance

P0337 Crankshaft Position Sensor "A" Circuit Low Input

P0338 Crankshaft Position Sensor "A" Circuit High Input

P0339 Crankshaft Position Sensor "A" Circuit Intermittent

P0340 Camshaft Position Sensor Circuit Malfunction

P0341 Camshaft Position Sensor Circuit Range/Performance

P0342 Camshaft Position Sensor Circuit Low Input

P0343 Camshaft Position Sensor Circuit High Input

P0344 Camshaft Position Sensor Circuit Intermittent

P0350 Ignition Coil Primary/Secondary Circuit Malfunction

P0351 Ignition Coil "A" Primary/Secondary Circuit Malfunction

P0352 Ignition Coil "B" Primary/Secondary Circuit Malfunction

P0353 Ignition Coil "C" Primary/Secondary Circuit Malfunction

P0354 Ignition Coil "D" Primary/Secondary Circuit Malfunction

P0355 Ignition Coil "E" Primary/Secondary Circuit Malfunction

P0356 Ignition Coil "F" Primary/Secondary Circuit Malfunction

P0357 Ignition Coil "G" Primary/Secondary Circuit Malfunction

P0358 Ignition Coil "H" Primary/Secondary Circuit Malfunction

P0359 Ignition Coil "I" Primary/Secondary Circuit Malfunction

P0360 Ignition Coil "J" Primary/Secondary Circuit Malfunction

P0361 Ignition Coil "K" Primary/Secondary Circuit Malfunction

P0362 Ignition Coil "L" Primary/Secondary Circuit Malfunction

P0370 Timing Reference High Resolution Signal "A" Malfunction

P0371 Timing Reference High Resolution Signal "A" Too Many Pulses

P0372 Timing Reference High Resolution Signal "A" Too Few Pulses

P0373 Timing Reference High Resolution Signal "A" Intermittent/Erratic Pulses

P0374 Timing Reference High Resolution Signal "A" No Pulses

P0375 Timing Reference High Resolution Signal "B" Malfunction

P0376 Timing Reference High Resolution Signal "B" Too Many Pulses

P0377 Timing Reference High Resolution Signal "B" Too Few Pulses

P0378 Timing Reference High Resolution Signal "B" Intermittent/Erratic Pulses

P0379 Timing Reference High Resolution Signal "B" No Pulses

P0380 Glow Plug/Heater Circuit "A" Malfunction

P0381 Glow Plug/Heater Indicator Circuit Malfunction

P0382 Glow Plug/Heater Circuit "B" Malfunction

P0385 Crankshaft Position Sensor "B" Circuit Malfunction

P0386 Crankshaft Position Sensor "B" Circuit Range/Performance

P0387 Crankshaft Position Sensor "B" Circuit Low Input

P0388 Crankshaft Position Sensor "B" Circuit High Input

P0389 Crankshaft Position Sensor "B" Circuit Intermittent

P0400 Exhaust Gas Recirculation Flow Malfunction

P0401 Exhaust Gas Recirculation Flow Insufficient Detected

P0402 Exhaust Gas Recirculation Flow Excessive Detected

P0403 Exhaust Gas Recirculation Circuit Malfunction

P0404 Exhaust Gas Recirculation Circuit Range/Performance

P0405 Exhaust Gas Recirculation Sensor "A" Circuit Low

P0406 Exhaust Gas Recirculation Sensor "A" Circuit High

P0407 Exhaust Gas Recirculation Sensor "B" Circuit Low

P0408 Exhaust Gas Recirculation Sensor "B" Circuit High

P0410 Secondary Air Injection System Malfunction

P0411 Secondary Air Injection System Incorrect Flow Detected

P0412 Secondary Air Injection System Switching Valve "A" Circuit Malfunction

P0413 Secondary Air Injection System Switching Valve "A" Circuit Open

P0414 Secondary Air Injection System Switching Valve "A" Circuit Shorted

P0415 Secondary Air Injection System Switching Valve "B" Circuit Malfunction

P0416 Secondary Air Injection System Switching Valve "B" Circuit Open

P0417 Secondary Air Injection System Switching Valve "B" Circuit Shorted

P0418 Secondary Air Injection System Relay "A" Circuit Malfunction

P0419 Secondary Air Injection System Relay "B" Circuit Malfunction

P0420 Catalyst System Efficiency Below Threshold (Bank #1)

P0421 Warm Up Catalyst Efficiency Below Threshold (Bank #1)

P0422 Main Catalyst Efficiency Below Threshold (Bank #1)

P0423 Heated Catalyst Efficiency Below Threshold (Bank #1)

P0424 Heated Catalyst Temperature Below Threshold (Bank #1)

P0430 Catalyst System Efficiency Below Threshold (Bank #2)

P0431 Warm Up Catalyst Efficiency Below Threshold (Bank #2)

P0432 Main Catalyst Efficiency Below Threshold (Bank #2)

P0433 Heated Catalyst Efficiency Below Threshold (Bank #2)

P0434 Heated Catalyst Temperature Below Threshold (Bank #2)

P0440 Evaporative Emission Control System Malfunction

P0441 Evaporative Emission Control System Incorrect Purge Flow

P0442 Evaporative Emission Control System Leak Detected (Small Leak)

P0443 Evaporative Emission Control System Purge Control Valve Circuit Malfunction

P0444 Evaporative Emission Control System Purge Control Valve Circuit Open

P0445 Evaporative Emission Control System Purge Control Valve Circuit Shorted

P0446 Evaporative Emission Control System Vent Control Circuit Malfunction

P0447 Evaporative Emission Control System Vent Control Circuit Open

P0448 Evaporative Emission Control System Vent Control Circuit Shorted

P0449 Evaporative Emission Control System Vent Valve/Solenoid Circuit Malfunction

P0450 Evaporative Emission Control System Pressure Sensor Malfunction

P0451 Evaporative Emission Control System Pressure Sensor Range/Performance

P0452 Evaporative Emission Control System Pressure Sensor Low Input

P0453 Evaporative Emission Control System Pressure Sensor High Input

P0454 Evaporative Emission Control System Pressure Sensor Intermittent

P0455 Evaporative Emission Control System Leak Detected (Gross Leak)

P0460 Fuel Level Sensor Circuit Malfunction

P0461 Fuel Level Sensor Circuit Range/Performance

P0462 Fuel Level Sensor Circuit Low Input

P0463 Fuel Level Sensor Circuit High Input

P0464 Fuel Level Sensor Circuit Intermittent

P0465 Purge Flow Sensor Circuit Malfunction

P0466 Purge Flow Sensor Circuit Range/Performance

P0467 Purge Flow Sensor Circuit Low Input

P0468 Purge Flow Sensor Circuit High Input

P0469 Purge Flow Sensor Circuit Intermittent

P0470 Exhaust Pressure Sensor Malfunction

P0471 Exhaust Pressure Sensor Range/Performance

P0472 Exhaust Pressure Sensor Low

P0473 Exhaust Pressure Sensor High

P0474 Exhaust Pressure Sensor Intermittent

P0475 Exhaust Pressure Control Valve Malfunction

P0476 Exhaust Pressure Control Valve Range/Performance

P0477 Exhaust Pressure Control Valve Low

P0478 Exhaust Pressure Control Valve High

P0479 Exhaust Pressure Control Valve Intermittent

P0480 Cooling Fan #1 Control Circuit Malfunction

P0481 Cooling Fan #2 Control Circuit Malfunction

P0482 Cooling Fan #3 Control Circuit Malfunction

P0483 Cooling Fan Rationality Check Malfunction

P0484 Cooling Fan Circuit Over Current

P0485 Cooling Fan Power/Ground Circuit Malfunction

P0500 Vehicle Speed Sensor Malfunction

P0501 Vehicle Speed Sensor Range/Performance

P0502 Vehicle Speed Sensor Circuit Low Input

P0503 Vehicle Speed Sensor Intermittent/Erratic/High

P0505 Idle Control System Malfunction

P0506 Idle Control System RPM Lower Than Expected

P0507 Idle Control System RPM Higher Than Expected

P0510 Closed Throttle Position Switch Malfunction

P0520 Engine Oil Pressure Sensor/Switch Circuit Malfunction

P0521 Engine Oil Pressure Sensor/Switch Range/Performance

P0522 Engine Oil Pressure Sensor/Switch Low Voltage

P0523 Engine Oil Pressure Sensor/Switch High Voltage

P0530 A/C Refrigerant Pressure Sensor Circuit Malfunction

P0531 A/C Refrigerant Pressure Sensor Circuit Range/Performance

P0532 A/C Refrigerant Pressure Sensor Circuit Low Input

P0533 A/C Refrigerant Pressure Sensor Circuit High Input

P0534 A/C Refrigerant Charge Loss

P0550 Power Steering Pressure Sensor Circuit Malfunction

P0551 Power Steering Pressure Sensor Circuit Range/Performance

P0552 Power Steering Pressure Sensor Circuit Low Input

P0553 Power Steering Pressure Sensor Circuit High Input

P0554 Power Steering Pressure Sensor Circuit Intermittent

P0560 System Voltage Malfunction

P0561 System Voltage Unstable

P0562 System Voltage Low

P0563 System Voltage High

P0565 Cruise Control On Signal Malfunction

P0566 Cruise Control Off Signal Malfunction

P0567 Cruise Control Resume Signal Malfunction

P0568 Cruise Control Set Signal Malfunction

P0569 Cruise Control Coast Signal Malfunction

P0570 Cruise Control Accel Signal Malfunction

P0571 Cruise Control/Brake Switch "A" Circuit Malfunction

P0572 Cruise Control/Brake Switch "A" Circuit Low

P0573 Cruise Control/Brake Switch "A" Circuit High

P0574 Through P0580 Reserved for Cruise Codes

P0600 Serial Communication Link Malfunction

P0601 Internal Control Module Memory Check Sum Error

P0602 Control Module Programming Error

P0603 Internal Control Module Keep Alive Memory (KAM) Error

P0604 Internal Control Module Random Access Memory (RAM) Error

P0605 Internal Control Module Read Only Memory (ROM) Error

P0606 PCM Processor Fault

P0608 Control Module VSS Output "A" Malfunction

P0609 Control Module VSS Output "B" Malfunction

P0620 Generator Control Circuit Malfunction

P0621 Generator Lamp "L" Control Circuit Malfunction

P0622 Generator Field "F" Control Circuit Malfunction

P0650 Malfunction Indicator Lamp (MIL) Control Circuit Malfunction

P0654 Engine RPM Output Circuit Malfunction

P0655 Engine Hot Lamp Output Control Circuit Malfunction

P0656 Fuel Level Output Circuit Malfunction

P0700 Transmission Control System Malfunction

P0701 Transmission Control System Range/Performance

P0702 Transmission Control System Electrical

P0703 Torque Converter/Brake Switch "B" Circuit Malfunction

P0704 Clutch Switch Input Circuit Malfunction

P0705 Transmission Range Sensor Circuit Malfunction (PRNDL Input)

P0706 Transmission Range Sensor Circuit Range/Performance

P0707 Transmission Range Sensor Circuit Low Input

P0708 Transmission Range Sensor Circuit High Input

P0709 Transmission Range Sensor Circuit Intermittent

P0710 Transmission Fluid Temperature Sensor Circuit Malfunction

P0711 Transmission Fluid Temperature Sensor Circuit Range/Performance

P0712 Transmission Fluid Temperature Sensor Circuit Low Input

P0713 Transmission Fluid Temperature Sensor Circuit High Input

P0714 Transmission Fluid Temperature Sensor Circuit Intermittent

P0715 Input/Turbine Speed Sensor Circuit Malfunction

P0716 Input/Turbine Speed Sensor Circuit Range/Performance

P0717 Input/Turbine Speed Sensor Circuit No Signal

P0718 Input/Turbine Speed Sensor Circuit Intermittent

P0719 Torque Converter/Brake Switch "B" Circuit Low

P0720 Output Speed Sensor Circuit Malfunction

P0721 Output Speed Sensor Circuit Range/Performance

P0722 Output Speed Sensor Circuit No Signal

P0723 Output Speed Sensor Circuit Intermittent

P0724 Torque Converter/Brake Switch "B" Circuit High

P0725 Engine Speed Input Circuit Malfunction

P0726 Engine Speed Input Circuit Range/Performance

P0727 Engine Speed Input Circuit No Signal

P0728 Engine Speed Input Circuit Intermittent

P0730 Incorrect Gear Ratio

P0731 Gear #1 Incorrect Ratio

P0732 Gear #2 Incorrect Ratio

P0733 Gear #3 Incorrect Ratio

P0734 Gear #4 Incorrect Ratio

P0735 Gear #5 Incorrect Ratio

P0736 Reverse Incorrect Ratio

P0740 Torque Converter Clutch Circuit Malfunction

P0741 Torque Converter Clutch Circuit Performance or Stuck Off

P0742 Torque Converter Clutch Circuit Stuck On

P0743 Torque Converter Clutch Circuit Electrical

P0744 Torque Converter Clutch Circuit Intermittent

P0745 Pressure Control Solenoid Malfunction

P0746 Pressure Control Solenoid Performance or Stuck Off

P0747 Pressure Control Solenoid Stuck On

P0748 Pressure Control Solenoid Electrical

P0749 Pressure Control Solenoid Intermittent

P0750 Shift Solenoid "A" Malfunction

P0751 Shift Solenoid "A" Performance or Stuck Off

P0752 Shift Solenoid "A" Stuck On

P0753 Shift Solenoid "A" Electrical

P0754 Shift Solenoid "A" Intermittent

P0755 Shift Solenoid "B" Malfunction

P0756 Shift Solenoid "B" Performance or Stuck Off

P0757 Shift Solenoid "B" Stuck On

P0758 Shift Solenoid "B" Electrical

P0759 Shift Solenoid "B" Intermittent

P0760 Shift Solenoid "C" Malfunction

P0761 Shift Solenoid "C" Performance Or Stuck Off

P0762 Shift Solenoid "C" Stuck On

P0763 Shift Solenoid "C" Electrical

P0764 Shift Solenoid "C" Intermittent

P0765 Shift Solenoid "D" Malfunction

P0766 Shift Solenoid "D" Performance Or Stuck Off

P0767 Shift Solenoid "D" Stuck On

P0768 Shift Solenoid "D" Electrical

P0769 Shift Solenoid "D" Intermittent

P0770 Shift Solenoid "E" Malfunction

P0771 Shift Solenoid "E" Performance Or Stuck Off

P0772 Shift Solenoid "E" Stuck On

P0773 Shift Solenoid "E" Electrical

P0774 Shift Solenoid "E" Intermittent

P0780 Shift Malfunction

P0781 1–2 Shift Malfunction

P0782 2–3 Shift Malfunction

P0783 3–4 Shift Malfunction

P0784 4–5 Shift Malfunction

P0785 Shift/Timing Solenoid Malfunction

P0786 Shift/Timing Solenoid Range/Performance

P0787 Shift/Timing Solenoid Low

P0788 Shift/Timing Solenoid High

P0789 Shift/Timing Solenoid Intermittent

P0790 Normal/Performance Switch Circuit Malfunction

P0801 Reverse Inhibit Control Circuit Malfunction

P0803 1–4 Upshift (Skip Shift) Solenoid Control Circuit Malfunction

P0804 1–4 Upshift (Skip Shift) Lamp Control Circuit Malfunction

P1000 OBD II Monitor Testing Not Complete More Driving Required

P1001 Key On Engine Running (KOER) Self-Test Not Able To Complete, KOER Aborted

P1100 Mass Air Flow (MAF) Sensor Intermittent

P1101 Mass Air Flow (MAF) Sensor Out Of Self-Test Range

P1111 System Pass 49 State Except Econoline

P1112 Intake Air Temperature (IAT) Sensor Intermittent

P1116 Engine Coolant Temperature (ECT) Sensor Out Of Self-Test Range

P1117 Engine Coolant Temperature (ECT) Sensor Intermittent

P1120 Throttle Position (TP) Sensor Out Of Range (Low)

P1121 Throttle Position (TP) Sensor Inconsistent With MAF Sensor

P1124 Throttle Position (TP) Sensor Out Of Self-Test Range

P1125 Throttle Position (TP) Sensor Circuit Intermittent

P1127 Exhaust Not Warm Enough, Downstream Heated Oxygen Sensors HO2S) Not Tested

P1128 Upstream Heated Oxygen Sensors (HO2S) Swapped From Bank To Bank

P1129 Downstream Heated Oxygen Sensors (HO2S) Swapped From Bank To Bank

P1130 Lack Of Upstream Heated Oxygen Sensor (HO2S 11) Switch, Adaptive Fuel At Limit (Bank #1)

P1131 Lack Of Upstream Heated Oxygen Sensor (HO2S 11) Switch, Sensor Indicates Lean (Bank #1)

P1132 Lack Of Upstream Heated Oxygen Sensor (HO2S 11) Switch, Sensor Indicates Rich (Bank #1)

P1137 Lack Of Downstream Heated Oxygen Sensor (HO2S 12) Switch, Sensor Indicates Lean (Bank #1)

P1138 Lack Of Downstream Heated Oxygen Sensor (HO2S 12) Switch, Sensor Indicates Rich (Bank #1)

P1150 Lack Of Upstream Heated Oxygen Sensor (HO2S 21) Switch, Adaptive Fuel At Limit (Bank #2)

P1151 Lack Of Upstream Heated Oxygen Sensor (HO2S 21) Switch, Sensor Indicates Lean (Bank #2)

P1152 Lack Of Upstream Heated Oxygen Sensor (HO2S 21) Switch, Sensor Indicates Rich (Bank #2)

P1157 Lack Of Downstream Heated Oxygen Sensor (HO2S 22) Switch, Sensor Indicates Lean (Bank #2)

Ignition system service is covered in the model specific sections of this manual

P1158 Lack Of Downstream Heated Oxygen Sensor (HO2S 22) Switch, Sensor Indicates Rich (Bank #2)

P1169 (HO2S 12) Signal Remained Unchanged For More Than 20 Seconds After Closed Loop

P1170 (HO2S 11) Signal Remained Unchanged For More Than 20 Seconds After Closed Loop

P1173 Feedback A/F Mixture Control (HO2S 21) Signal Remained Unchanged For More Than 20 Seconds After Closed Loop

P1184 Engine Oil Temp Sensor Circuit Performance

P1195 Barometric (BARO) Pressure Sensor Circuit Malfunction (Signal Is From EGR Boost Sensor)

P1196 Starter Switch Circuit Malfunction

P1209 Injection Control Pressure (ICP) Peak Fault

P1210 Injection Control Pressure (ICP) Above Expected Level

P1211 Injection Control Pressure (ICP) Not Controllable—Pressure Above/Below Desired

P1212 Injection Control Pressure (ICP) Voltage Not At Expected Level

P1218 Cylinder Identification (CID) Stuck High

P1219 Cylinder Identification (CID) Stuck Low

P1220 Series Throttle Control Malfunction (Traction Control System)

P1224 Throttle Position Sensor "B" (TP-B) Out Of Self-Test Range (Traction Control System)

P1230 Fuel Pump Low Speed Malfunction

P1231 Fuel Pump Secondary Circuit Low With High Speed Pump On

P1232 Low Speed Fuel Pump Primary Circuit Malfunction

P1233 Fuel Pump Driver Module Off-line (MIL DTC)

P1234 Fuel Pump Driver Module Disabled Or Off-line (No MIL)

P1235 Fuel Pump Control Out Of Range (MIL DTC)

P1236 Fuel Pump Control Out Of Range (No MIL)

P1237 Fuel Pump Secondary Circuit Malfunction (MIL DTC)

P1238 Fuel Pump Secondary Circuit Malfunction (No DMIL)

P1250 Fuel Pressure Regulator Control (FPRC) Solenoid Malfunction

P1260 THEFT Detected—Engine Disabled

P1261 High To Low Side Short—Cylinder #1 (Indicates Low side Circuit Is Shorted To B+ Or To The High Side Between The IDM And The Injector)

P1262 High To Low Side Short—Cylinder #2 (Indicates Low side Circuit Is Shorted To B+ Or To The High Side Between The IDM And The Injector)

P1263 High To Low Side Short—Cylinder #3 (Indicates Low side Circuit Is Shorted To B+ Or To The High Side Between The IDM And The Injector)

P1264 High To Low Side Short—Cylinder #4 (Indicates Low side Circuit Is Shorted To B+ Or To The High Side Between The IDM And The Injector)

P1265 High To Low Side Short—Cylinder #5 (Indicates Low side Circuit Is Shorted To B+ Or To The High Side Between The IDM And The Injector)

P1266 High To Low Side Short—Cylinder #6 (Indicates Low side Circuit Is Shorted To B+ Or To The High Side Between The IDM And The Injector)

P1267 High To Low Side Short—Cylinder #7 (Indicates Low side Circuit Is Shorted To B+ Or To The High Side Between The IDM And The Injector)

P1268 High To Low Side Short—Cylinder #8 (Indicates Low side Circuit Is Shorted To B+ Or To The High Side Between The IDM And The Injector)

P1270 Engine RPM Or Vehicle Speed Limiter Reached

P1271 High To Low Side Open—Cylinder #1 (Indicates A High To Low Side Open Between The Injector And The IDM)

P1272 High To Low Side Open—Cylinder #2 (Indicates A High To Low Side Open Between The Injector And The IDM)

P1273 High To Low Side Open—Cylinder #3 (Indicates A High To Low Side Open Between The Injector And The IDM)

P1274 High To Low Side Open—Cylinder #4 (Indicates A High To Low Side Open Between The Injector And The IDM)

P1275 High To Low Side Open—Cylinder #5 (Indicates A High To Low Side Open Between The Injector And The IDM)

P1276 High To Low Side Open—Cylinder #6 (Indicates A High To Low Side Open Between The Injector And The IDM)

P1277 High To Low Side Open—Cylinder #7 (Indicates A High To Low Side Open Between The Injector And The IDM)

P1278 High To Low Side Open—Cylinder #8 (Indicates A High To Low Side Open Between The Injector And The IDM)

P1280 Injection Control Pressure (ICP) Circuit Out Of Range Low

P1281 Injection Control Pressure (ICP) Circuit Out Of Range High

P1282 Injection Control Pressure (ICP) Excessive

P1283 Injection Pressure Regulator (IPR) Circuit Failure

P1284 Injection Control Pressure (ICP) Failure—Aborts KOER Or CCT Test

P1285 Cylinder Head Temperature (CHT) Over Temperature Sensed

P1288 Cylinder Head Temperature (CHT) Sensor Out Of Self-Test Range

P1289 Cylinder Head Temperature (CHT) Sensor Circuit Low Input

P1290 Cylinder Head Temperature (CHT) Sensor Circuit High Input

P1291 IDM To Injector High Side Circuit #1 (Right Bank) Short To GND Or B+

P1292 IDM To Injector High Side Circuit #2 (Right Bank) Short To GND Or B+

P1293 IDM To Injector High Side Circuit Open Bank #1 (Right Bank)

P1294 IDM To Injector High Side Circuit Open Bank #2 (Left Bank)

P1295 Multiple IDM/Injector Circuit Faults On Bank #1 (Right)

P1296 Multiple IDM/Injector Circuit Faults On Bank #2 (Left)

P1297 High Sides Shorted Together

P1298 IDM Failure

P1299 Engine Over Temperature Condition

P1309 Misfire Detection Monitor Is Not Enabled

P1316 Injector Circuit/IDM Codes Detected

P1320 Distributor Signal Interrupt

P1336 Crankshaft Position Sensor (Gear)

P1345 No Camshaft Position Sensor Signal

P1351 Ignition Diagnostic Monitor (IDM) Circuit Input Malfunction

P1351 Indicates Ignition System Malfunction

P1352 Indicates Ignition System Malfunction

P1353 Indicates Ignition System Malfunction

P1354 Indicates Ignition System Malfunction

P1355 Indicates Ignition System Malfunction

P1356 PIPs Occurred While IDM Pulse width Indicates Engine Not Turning

P1357 Ignition Diagnostic Monitor (IDM) Pulse width Not Defined

P1358 Ignition Diagnostic Monitor (IDM) Signal Out Of Self-Test Range

P1359 Spark Output Circuit Malfunction

P1364 Spark Output Circuit Malfunction

P1390 Octane Adjust (OCT ADJ) Out Of Self-Test Range

P1391 Glow Plug Circuit Low Input Bank #1 (Right)

P1392 Glow Plug Circuit High Input Bank #1 (Right)

P1393 Glow Plug Circuit Low Input Bank #2 (Left)

P1394 Glow Plug Circuit High Input Bank #2 (Left)

P1395 Glow Plug Monitor Fault Bank #1

P1396 Glow Plug Monitor Fault Bank #2

P1397 System Voltage Out Of Self Test Range

P1400 Differential Pressure Feedback EGR (DPFE) Sensor Circuit Low Voltage Detected

P1401 Differential Pressure Feedback EGR (DPFE) Sensor Circuit High Voltage Detected/EGR Temperature Sensor

P1402 EGR Valve Position Sensor Open Or Short

P1403 Differential Pressure Feedback EGR (DPFE) Sensor Hoses Reversed

P1405 Differential Pressure Feedback EGR (DPFE) Sensor Upstream Hose Off Or Plugged

P1406 Differential Pressure Feedback EGR (DPFE) Sensor Downstream Hose Off Or Plugged

P1407 Exhaust Gas Recirculation (EGR) No Flow Detected (Valve Stuck Closed Or Inoperative)

P1408 Exhaust Gas Recirculation (EGR) Flow Out Of Self-Test Range

P1409 Electronic Vacuum Regulator (EVR) Control Circuit Malfunction

P1410 Check That Fuel Pressure Regulator Control Solenoid And The EGR Check Solenoid Connectors Are Not Swapped

P1411 Secondary Air Injection System Incorrect Downstream Flow Detected

P1413 Secondary Air Injection System Monitor Circuit Low Voltage

P1414 Secondary Air Injection System Monitor Circuit High Voltage

P1442 Evaporative Emission Control System Small Leak Detected

P1443 Evaporative Emission Control System—Vacuum System, Purge Control Solenoid Or Purge Control Valve Malfunction

P1444 Purge Flow Sensor (PFS) Circuit Low Input

P1445 Purge Flow Sensor (PFS) Circuit High Input

P1449 Evaporative Emission Control System Unable To Hold Vacuum

P1450 Unable To Bleed Up Fuel Tank Vacuum

P1455 Evaporative Emission Control System Control Leak Detected (Gross Leak)

P1460 Wide Open Throttle Air Conditioning Cut-Off Circuit Malfunction

P1461 Air Conditioning Pressure (ACP) Sensor Circuit Low Input

P1462 Air Conditioning Pressure (ACP) Sensor Circuit High Input

P1463 Air Conditioning Pressure (ACP) Sensor Insufficient Pressure Change

P1464 Air Conditioning (A/C) Demand Out Of Self-Test Range/A/C On During KOER Or CCT Test

P1469 Low Air Conditioning Cycling Period

P1473 Fan Secondary High, With Fan(s) Off

P1474 Low Fan Control Primary Circuit Malfunction

P1479 High Fan Control Primary Circuit Malfunction

P1480 Fan Secondary Low, With Low Fan On

P1481 Fan Secondary Low, With High Fan On

P1483 Power To Fan Circuit Over current

P1484 Open Power/Ground To Variable Load Control Module (VLCM)

P1485 EGR Control Solenoid Open Or Short

P1486 EGR Vent Solenoid Open Or Short

P1487 EGR Boost Check Solenoid Open Or Short

P1500 Vehicle Speed Sensor (VSS) Circuit Intermittent

P1501 Vehicle Speed Sensor (VSS) Out Of Self-Test Range/Vehicle Moved During Test

P1502 Invalid Self Test—Auxiliary Powertrain Control Module (APCM) Functioning

P1504 Idle Air Control (IAC) Circuit Malfunction

P1505 Idle Air Control (IAC) System At Adaptive Clip

P1506 Idle Air Control (IAC) Over-speed Error

P1507 Idle Air Control (IAC) Under-speed Error

P1512 Intake Manifold Runner Control (IMRC) Malfunction (Bank #1 Stuck Closed)

P1513 Intake Manifold Runner Control (IMRC) Malfunction (Bank #2 Stuck Closed)

P1516 Intake Manifold Runner Control (IMRC) Input Error (Bank #1)

P1517 Intake Manifold Runner Control (IMRC) Input Error (Bank #2)

P1518 Intake Manifold Runner Control (IMRC) Malfunction (Stuck Open)

P1519 Intake Manifold Runner Control (IMRC) Malfunction (Stuck Closed)

P1520 Intake Manifold Runner Control (IMRC) Circuit Malfunction

P1521 Variable Resonance Induction System (VRIS) Solenoid #1 Open Or Short

P1522 Variable Resonance Induction System (VRIS) Solenoid #2 Open Or Short

P1523 High Speed Inlet Air (HSIA) Solenoid Open Or Short

P1530 Air Condition (A/C) Clutch Circuit Malfunction

P1531 Invalid Test—Accelerator Pedal Movement

P1536 Parking Brake Applied Failure

P1537 Intake Manifold Runner Control (IMRC) Malfunction (Bank #1 Stuck Open)

P1538 Intake Manifold Runner Control (IMRC) Malfunction (Bank #2 Stuck Open)

P1539 Power To Air Condition (A/C) Clutch Circuit Over-current

P1549 Problem In Intake Manifold Tuning (IMT) Valve System

P1550 Power Steering Pressure (PSP) Sensor Out Of Self-Test Range

P1601 Serial Communication Error

P1605 Powertrain Control Module (PCM)—Keep Alive Memory (KAM) Test Error

P1608 PCM Internal Circuit Malfunction

P1609 PCM Internal Circuit Malfunction (2.5L Only)

P1625 B+ Supply To Variable Load Control Module (VLCM) Fan Circuit Malfunction

P1626 B+ Supply To Variable Load Control Module (VLCM) Air Conditioning (A/C) Circuit

P1650 Power Steering Pressure (PSP) Switch Out Of Self-Test Range

P1651 Power Steering Pressure (PSP) Switch Input Malfunction

P1660 Output Circuit Check Signal High

P1661 Output Circuit Check Signal Low

P1662 Injection Driver Module Enable (IDM EN) Circuit Failure

P1663 Fuel Delivery Command Signal (FDCS) Circuit Failure

P1667 Cylinder Identification (CID) Circuit Failure

P1668 PCM—IDM Diagnostic Communication Error

P1670 EF Feedback Signal Not Detected

P1701 Reverse Engagement Error

P1701 Fuel Trim Malfunction (Villager)

P1703 Brake On/Off (BOO) Switch Out Of Self-Test Range

P1704 Digital Transmission Range (TR) Sensor Failed To Transition State

P1705 Transmission Range (TR) Sensor Out Of Self-Test Range

P1705 TP Sensor (AT) Villager

P1705 Clutch Pedal Position (CPP) Or Park Neutral Position (PNP) Problem

P1706 High Vehicle Speed In Park

P1709 Park Or Neutral Position (PNP) Or Clutch Pedal Position (CPP) Switch Out Of Self-Test Range

P1709 Throttle Position (TP) Sensor Malfunction (Aspire 1.3L, Probe 2.5L)

P1711 Transmission Fluid Temperature (TFT) Sensor Out Of Self-Test Range

P1714 Shift Solenoid "A" Inductive Signature Malfunction

P1715 Shift Solenoid "B" Inductive Signature Malfunction

P1716 Transmission Malfunction

P1717 Transmission Malfunction

P1719 Transmission Malfunction

P1720 Vehicle Speed Sensor (VSS) Circuit Malfunction

P1727 Coast Clutch Solenoid Inductive Signature Malfunction

P1728 Transmission Slip Error—Converter Clutch Failed

P1729 4x4 Low Switch Error

P1731 Improper 1–2 Shift

P1732 Improper 2–3 Shift

P1733 Improper 3–4 Shift

P1734 Improper 4–5 Shift

P1740 Torque Converter Clutch (TCC) Inductive Signature Malfunction

P1741 Torque Converter Clutch (TCC) Control Error

P1742 Torque Converter Clutch (TCC) Solenoid Failed On (Turns On MIL)

P1743 Torque Converter Clutch (TCC) Solenoid Failed On (Turns On TCIL)

P1744 Torque Converter Clutch (TCC) System Mechanically Stuck In Off Position

P1744 Torque Converter Clutch (TCC) Solenoid Malfunction (2.5L Only)

P1746 Electronic Pressure Control (EPC) Solenoid Open Circuit (Low Input)

P1747 Electronic Pressure Control (EPC) Solenoid Short Circuit (High Input)

P1748 Electronic Pressure Control (EPC) Malfunction

P1749 Electronic Pressure Control (EPC) Solenoid Failed Low

P1751 Shift Solenoid #1 (SS1) Performance

P1754 Coast Clutch Solenoid (CCS) Circuit Malfunction

P1756 Shift Solenoid #2 (SS2) Performance

P1760 Overrun Clutch SN

P1761 Shift Solenoid #3 (SS3) Performance

P1762 Transmission Malfunction

P1765 3–2 Timing Solenoid Malfunction (2.5L Only)

P1779 TCIL Circuit Malfunction

P1780 Transmission Control Switch (TCS) Circuit Out Of Self-Test Range

P1781 4x4 Low Switch, Out Of Self-Test Range

P1783 Transmission Over Temperature Condition

P1784 Transmission Malfunction

P1785 Transmission Malfunction

P1786 Transmission Malfunction

P1787 Transmission Malfunction

P1788 3–2 Timing/Coast Clutch Solenoid (3–2/CCS) Circuit Open

P1789 3–2 Timing/Coast Clutch Solenoid (3–2/CCS) Circuit Shorted

P1792 Idle (IDL) Switch (Closed Throttle Position Switch) Malfunction

P1794 Loss Of Battery Voltage Input

P1795 EGR Boost Sensor Malfunction

P1797 Clutch Pedal Position (CPP) Switch Or Neutral Switch Circuit Malfunction

P1900 Cooling Fan

U1021 SCP Indicating The Lack Of Air Conditioning (A/C) Clutch Status Response

U1039 Vehicle Speed Signal (VSS) Missing Or Incorrect

U1051 Brake Switch Signal Missing Or Incorrect

U1073 SCP Indicating The Lack Of Engine Coolant Fan Status Response

U1131 SCP Indicating The Lack Of Fuel Pump Status Response

U1135 SCP Indicating The Ignition Switch Signal Missing Or Incorrect

U1256 SCP Indicating A Communications Error

U1451 Lack Of Response From Passive Anti-Theft System (PATS) Module—Engine Disabled

General Motors Corporation

READING CODES

Reading the Diagnostic Trouble Codes (DTC's) is one of the first steps in OBD II system diagnostics. This step should be initially performed to determine the general nature of the fault. Subsequent readings will determine if the fault has been cleared.

Reading codes can be performed by any of the methods below:

- Read the control module memory with the Generic Scan Tool (GST)
- Read the control module memory with the vehicle manufacturer's specific tester

To read the fault codes, connect the scan tool or tester according to the manufacturer's instructions. Follow the manufacturer's specified procedure for reading the codes.

CLEARING CODES

Powertrain Control Module (PCM) reset procedures are a very important part of OBD II System diagnostics. This step should be done at the end of any fault code repair and at the end of any driveability repair.

Clearing codes can be performed by any of the methods below:

- Clear the control module memory with the Generic Scan Tool (GST)
- Clear the control module memory with the vehicle manufacturer's specific tester
- Turn the ignition OFF and disconnect the negative battery cable for at least 1 minute

Disconnecting the negative battery cable may cause other systems in the vehicle to loose their memory. Prior to removing the cable, ensure you have the proper reset codes for radios and alarms.

➡**The Malfunction Indicator Lamp (MIL) will may also be de-activated for some codes if the vehicle completes 3 consecutive trips without a fault detected with vehicle conditions similar to those present during the fault.**

OBD II TROUBLE CODES

P0100 Mass or Volume Air Flow Circuit Malfunction

P0101 Mass or Volume Air Flow Circuit Range/Performance Problem

P0102 Mass or Volume Air Flow Circuit Low Input

P0103 Mass or Volume Air Flow Circuit High Input

P0104 Mass or Volume Air Flow Circuit Intermittent

P0105 Manifold Absolute Pressure/Barometric Pressure Circuit Malfunction

P0106 Manifold Absolute Pressure/Barometric Pressure Circuit Range/Performance Problem

P0107 Manifold Absolute Pressure/Barometric Pressure Circuit Low Input

P0108 Manifold Absolute Pressure/Barometric Pressure Circuit High Input

P0109 Manifold Absolute Pressure/Barometric Pressure Circuit Intermittent

P0110 Intake Air Temperature Circuit Malfunction

P0111 Intake Air Temperature Circuit Range/Performance Problem

P0112 Intake Air Temperature Circuit Low Input

P0113 Intake Air Temperature Circuit High Input

P0114 Intake Air Temperature Circuit Intermittent

P0115 Engine Coolant Temperature Circuit Malfunction

P0116 Engine Coolant Temperature Circuit Range/Performance Problem

P0117 Engine Coolant Temperature Circuit Low Input

P0118 Engine Coolant Temperature Circuit High Input

P0119 Engine Coolant Temperature Circuit Intermittent

P0120 Throttle/Pedal Position Sensor/Switch "A" Circuit Malfunction

P0121 Throttle/Pedal Position Sensor/Switch "A" Circuit Range/Performance Problem

P0122 Throttle/Pedal Position Sensor/Switch "A" Circuit Low Input

P0123 Throttle/Pedal Position Sensor/Switch "A" Circuit High Input

P0124 Throttle/Pedal Position Sensor/Switch "A" Circuit Intermittent

P0125 Insufficient Coolant Temperature For Closed Loop Fuel Control

P0126 Insufficient Coolant Temperature For Stable Operation

P0130 O_2 Circuit Malfunction (Bank #1 Sensor #1)

P0131 O_2 Sensor Circuit Low Voltage (Bank #1 Sensor #1)

P0132 O_2 Sensor Circuit High Voltage (Bank #1 Sensor #1)

P0133 O_2 Sensor Circuit Slow Response (Bank #1 Sensor #1)

P0134 O_2 Sensor Circuit No Activity Detected (Bank #1 Sensor #1)

P0135 O_2 Sensor Heater Circuit Malfunction (Bank #1 Sensor #1)

P0136 O_2 Sensor Circuit Malfunction (Bank #1 Sensor #2)

P0137 O_2 Sensor Circuit Low Voltage (Bank #1 Sensor #2)

P0138 O_2 Sensor Circuit High Voltage (Bank #1 Sensor #2)

P0139 O_2 Sensor Circuit Slow Response (Bank #1 Sensor #2)

P0140 O_2 Sensor Circuit No Activity Detected (Bank #1 Sensor #2)

P0141 O_2 Sensor Heater Circuit Malfunction (Bank #1 Sensor #2)

P0142 O_2 Sensor Circuit Malfunction (Bank #1 Sensor #3)

P0143 O_2 Sensor Circuit Low Voltage (Bank #1 Sensor #3)

P0144 O_2 Sensor Circuit High Voltage (Bank #1 Sensor #3)

P0145 O_2 Sensor Circuit Slow Response (Bank #1 Sensor #3)

P0146 O_2 Sensor Circuit No Activity Detected (Bank #1 Sensor #3)

P0147 O_2 Sensor Heater Circuit Malfunction (Bank #1 Sensor #3)

P0150 O_2 Sensor Circuit Malfunction (Bank #2 Sensor #1)

P0151 O_2 Sensor Circuit Low Voltage (Bank #2 Sensor #1)

P0152 O_2 Sensor Circuit High Voltage (Bank #2 Sensor #1)

P0153 O_2 Sensor Circuit Slow Response (Bank #2 Sensor #1)

P0154 O_2 Sensor Circuit No Activity Detected (Bank #2 Sensor #1)

P0155 O_2 Sensor Heater Circuit Malfunction (Bank #2 Sensor #1)

P0156 O_2 Sensor Circuit Malfunction (Bank #2 Sensor #2)

P0157 O_2 Sensor Circuit Low Voltage (Bank #2 Sensor #2)

P0158 O_2 Sensor Circuit High Voltage (Bank #2 Sensor #2)

P0159 O_2 Sensor Circuit Slow Response (Bank #2 Sensor #2)

P0160 O_2 Sensor Circuit No Activity Detected (Bank #2 Sensor #2)

P0161 O_2 Sensor Heater Circuit Malfunction (Bank #2 Sensor #2)

P0162 O_2 Sensor Circuit Malfunction (Bank #2 Sensor #3)

P0163 O_2 Sensor Circuit Low Voltage (Bank #2 Sensor #3)

P0164 O_2 Sensor Circuit High Voltage (Bank #2 Sensor #3)

P0165 O_2 Sensor Circuit Slow Response (Bank #2 Sensor #3)

P0166 O_2 Sensor Circuit No Activity Detected (Bank #2 Sensor #3)

P0167 O_2 Sensor Heater Circuit Malfunction (Bank #2 Sensor #3)

P0170 Fuel Trim Malfunction (Bank #1)

P0171 System Too Lean (Bank #1)

P0172 System Too Rich (Bank #1)

P0173 Fuel Trim Malfunction (Bank #2)

P0174 System Too Lean (Bank #2)

P0175 System Too Rich (Bank #2)

P0176 Fuel Composition Sensor Circuit Malfunction

P0177 Fuel Composition Sensor Circuit Range/Performance

P0178 Fuel Composition Sensor Circuit Low Input

P0179 Fuel Composition Sensor Circuit High Input

P0180 Fuel Temperature Sensor "A" Circuit Malfunction

P0181 Fuel Temperature Sensor "A" Circuit Range/Performance

P0182 Fuel Temperature Sensor "A" Circuit Low Input

P0183 Fuel Temperature Sensor "A" Circuit High Input

P0184 Fuel Temperature Sensor "A" Circuit Intermittent

P0185 Fuel Temperature Sensor "B" Circuit Malfunction

P0186 Fuel Temperature Sensor "B" Circuit Range/Performance

P0187 Fuel Temperature Sensor "B" Circuit Low Input

P0188 Fuel Temperature Sensor "B" Circuit High Input

P0189 Fuel Temperature Sensor "B" Circuit Intermittent

P0190 Fuel Rail Pressure Sensor Circuit Malfunction

P0191 Fuel Rail Pressure Sensor Circuit Range/Performance

P0192 Fuel Rail Pressure Sensor Circuit Low Input

P0193 Fuel Rail Pressure Sensor Circuit High Input

P0194 Fuel Rail Pressure Sensor Circuit Intermittent

P0195 Engine Oil Temperature Sensor Malfunction

Refer to the model specific sections for fuel system service procedures

P0196 Engine Oil Temperature Sensor Range/Performance

P0197 Engine Oil Temperature Sensor Low

P0198 Engine Oil Temperature Sensor High

P0199 Engine Oil Temperature Sensor Intermittent

P0200 Injector Circuit Malfunction

P0201 Injector Circuit Malfunction—Cylinder #1

P0202 Injector Circuit Malfunction—Cylinder #2

P0203 Injector Circuit Malfunction—Cylinder #3

P0204 Injector Circuit Malfunction—Cylinder #4

P0205 Injector Circuit Malfunction—Cylinder #5

P0206 Injector Circuit Malfunction—Cylinder #6

P0207 Injector Circuit Malfunction—Cylinder #7

P0208 Injector Circuit Malfunction—Cylinder #8

P0209 Injector Circuit Malfunction—Cylinder #9

P0210 Injector Circuit Malfunction—Cylinder #10

P0211 Injector Circuit Malfunction—Cylinder #11

P0212 Injector Circuit Malfunction—Cylinder #12

P0213 Cold Start Injector #1 Malfunction

P0214 Cold Start Injector #2 Malfunction

P0215 Engine Shutoff Solenoid Malfunction

P0216 Injection Timing Control Circuit Malfunction

P0217 Engine Over Temperature Condition

P0218 Transmission Over Temperature Condition

P0219 Engine Over Speed Condition

P0220 Throttle/Pedal Position Sensor/Switch "B" Circuit Malfunction

P0221 Throttle/Pedal Position Sensor/Switch "B" Circuit Range/Performance Problem

P0222 Throttle/Pedal Position Sensor/Switch "B" Circuit Low Input

P0223 Throttle/Pedal Position Sensor/Switch "B" Circuit High Input

P0224 Throttle/Pedal Position Sensor/Switch "B" Circuit Intermittent

P0225 Throttle/Pedal Position Sensor/Switch "C" Circuit Malfunction

P0226 Throttle/Pedal Position Sensor/Switch "C" Circuit Range/Performance Problem

P0227 Throttle/Pedal Position Sensor/Switch "C" Circuit Low Input

P0228 Throttle/Pedal Position Sensor/Switch "C" Circuit High Input

P0229 Throttle/Pedal Position Sensor/Switch "C" Circuit Intermittent

P0230 Fuel Pump Primary Circuit Malfunction

P0231 Fuel Pump Secondary Circuit Low

P0232 Fuel Pump Secondary Circuit High

P0233 Fuel Pump Secondary Circuit Intermittent

P0234 Engine Over Boost Condition

P0261 Cylinder #1 Injector Circuit Low

P0262 Cylinder #1 Injector Circuit High

P0263 Cylinder #1 Contribution/Balance Fault

P0264 Cylinder #2 Injector Circuit Low

P0265 Cylinder #2 Injector Circuit High

P0266 Cylinder #2 Contribution/Balance Fault

P0267 Cylinder #3 Injector Circuit Low

P0268 Cylinder #3 Injector Circuit High

P0269 Cylinder #3 Contribution/Balance Fault

P0270 Cylinder #4 Injector Circuit Low

P0271 Cylinder #4 Injector Circuit High

P0272 Cylinder #4 Contribution/Balance Fault

P0273 Cylinder #5 Injector Circuit Low

P0274 Cylinder #5 Injector Circuit High

P0275 Cylinder #5 Contribution/Balance Fault

P0276 Cylinder #6 Injector Circuit Low

P0277 Cylinder #6 Injector Circuit High

P0278 Cylinder #6 Contribution/Balance Fault

P0279 Cylinder #7 Injector Circuit Low

P0280 Cylinder #7 Injector Circuit High

P0281 Cylinder #7 Contribution/Balance Fault

P0282 Cylinder #8 Injector Circuit Low

P0283 Cylinder #8 Injector Circuit High

P0284 Cylinder #8 Contribution/Balance Fault

P0285 Cylinder #9 Injector Circuit Low

P0286 Cylinder #9 Injector Circuit High

P0287 Cylinder #9 Contribution/Balance Fault

P0288 Cylinder #10 Injector Circuit Low

P0289 Cylinder #10 Injector Circuit High

P0290 Cylinder #10 Contribution/Balance Fault

P0300 Random/Multiple Cylinder Misfire Detected

P0301 Cylinder #1—Misfire Detected

P0302 Cylinder #2—Misfire Detected

P0303 Cylinder #3—Misfire Detected

P0304 Cylinder #4—Misfire Detected

P0305 Cylinder #5—Misfire Detected

P0306 Cylinder #6—Misfire Detected

P0307 Cylinder #7—Misfire Detected

P0308 Cylinder #8—Misfire Detected

P0309 Cylinder #9—Misfire Detected

P0310 Cylinder #10—Misfire Detected

P0320 Ignition/Distributor Engine Speed Input Circuit Malfunction

P0321 Ignition/Distributor Engine Speed Input Circuit Range/Performance

P0322 Ignition/Distributor Engine Speed Input Circuit No Signal

P0323 Ignition/Distributor Engine Speed Input Circuit Intermittent

P0325 Knock Sensor #1—Circuit Malfunction (Bank #1 or Single Sensor)

P0326 Knock Sensor #1—Circuit Range/Performance (Bank #1 or Single Sensor)

P0327 Knock Sensor #1—Circuit Low Input (Bank #1 or Single Sensor)

P0328 Knock Sensor #1—Circuit High Input (Bank #1 or Single Sensor)

P0329 Knock Sensor #1—Circuit Input Intermittent (Bank #1 or Single Sensor)

P0330 Knock Sensor #2—Circuit Malfunction (Bank #2)

P0331 Knock Sensor #2—Circuit Range/Performance (Bank #2)

P0332 Knock Sensor #2—Circuit Low Input (Bank #2)

P0333 Knock Sensor #2—Circuit High Input (Bank #2)

P0334 Knock Sensor #2—Circuit Input Intermittent (Bank #2)

P0335 Crankshaft Position Sensor "A" Circuit Malfunction

P0336 Crankshaft Position Sensor "A" Circuit Range/Performance

P0337 Crankshaft Position Sensor "A" Circuit Low Input

P0338 Crankshaft Position Sensor "A" Circuit High Input

P0339 Crankshaft Position Sensor "A" Circuit Intermittent

P0340 Camshaft Position Sensor Circuit Malfunction

P0341 Camshaft Position Sensor Circuit Range/Performance

P0342 Camshaft Position Sensor Circuit Low Input

P0343 Camshaft Position Sensor Circuit High Input

P0344 Camshaft Position Sensor Circuit Intermittent

P0350 Ignition Coil Primary/Secondary Circuit Malfunction

P0351 Ignition Coil "A" Primary/Secondary Circuit Malfunction

P0352 Ignition Coil "B" Primary/Secondary Circuit Malfunction

P0353 Ignition Coil "C" Primary/Secondary Circuit Malfunction

P0354 Ignition Coil "D" Primary/Secondary Circuit Malfunction

P0355 Ignition Coil "E" Primary/Secondary Circuit Malfunction

P0356 Ignition Coil "F" Primary/Secondary Circuit Malfunction

P0357 Ignition Coil "G" Primary/Secondary Circuit Malfunction

P0358 Ignition Coil "H" Primary/Secondary Circuit Malfunction

P0359 Ignition Coil "I" Primary/Secondary Circuit Malfunction

P0360 Ignition Coil "J" Primary/Secondary Circuit Malfunction

P0361 Ignition Coil "K" Primary/Secondary Circuit Malfunction

P0362 Ignition Coil "L" Primary/Secondary Circuit Malfunction

P0370 Timing Reference High Resolution Signal "A" Malfunction

P0371 Timing Reference High Resolution Signal "A" Too Many Pulses

P0372 Timing Reference High Resolution Signal "A" Too Few Pulses

P0373 Timing Reference High Resolution Signal "A" Intermittent/Erratic Pulses

P0374 Timing Reference High Resolution Signal "A" No Pulses

P0375 Timing Reference High Resolution Signal "B" Malfunction

P0376 Timing Reference High Resolution Signal "B" Too Many Pulses

P0377 Timing Reference High Resolution Signal "B" Too Few Pulses

P0378 Timing Reference High Resolution Signal "B" Intermittent/Erratic Pulses

P0379 Timing Reference High Resolution Signal "B" No Pulses

P0380 Glow Plug/Heater Circuit "A" Malfunction

P0381 Glow Plug/Heater Indicator Circuit Malfunction

P0382 Glow Plug/Heater Circuit "B" Malfunction

P0385 Crankshaft Position Sensor "B" Circuit Malfunction

P0386 Crankshaft Position Sensor "B" Circuit Range/Performance

P0387 Crankshaft Position Sensor "B" Circuit Low Input

P0388 Crankshaft Position Sensor "B" Circuit High Input

P0389 Crankshaft Position Sensor "B" Circuit Intermittent

P0400 Exhaust Gas Recirculation Flow Malfunction

P0401 Exhaust Gas Recirculation Flow Insufficient Detected

P0402 Exhaust Gas Recirculation Flow Excessive Detected

P0403 Exhaust Gas Recirculation Circuit Malfunction

P0404 Exhaust Gas Recirculation Circuit Range/Performance

P0405 Exhaust Gas Recirculation Sensor "A" Circuit Low

P0406 Exhaust Gas Recirculation Sensor "A" Circuit High

P0407 Exhaust Gas Recirculation Sensor "B" Circuit Low

P0408 Exhaust Gas Recirculation Sensor "B" Circuit High

P0410 Secondary Air Injection System Malfunction

P0411 Secondary Air Injection System Incorrect Flow Detected

P0412 Secondary Air Injection System Switching Valve "A" Circuit Malfunction

P0413 Secondary Air Injection System Switching Valve "A" Circuit Open

P0414 Secondary Air Injection System Switching Valve "A" Circuit Shorted

P0415 Secondary Air Injection System Switching Valve "B" Circuit Malfunction

P0416 Secondary Air Injection System Switching Valve "B" Circuit Open

P0417 Secondary Air Injection System Switching Valve "B" Circuit Shorted

P0418 Secondary Air Injection System Relay "A" Circuit Malfunction

P0419 Secondary Air Injection System Relay "B" Circuit Malfunction

P0420 Catalyst System Efficiency Below Threshold (Bank #1)

P0421 Warm Up Catalyst Efficiency Below Threshold (Bank #1)

P0422 Main Catalyst Efficiency Below Threshold (Bank #1)

P0423 Heated Catalyst Efficiency Below Threshold (Bank #1)

P0424 Heated Catalyst Temperature Below Threshold (Bank #1)

P0430 Catalyst System Efficiency Below Threshold (Bank #2)

P0431 Warm Up Catalyst Efficiency Below Threshold (Bank #2)

P0432 Main Catalyst Efficiency Below Threshold (Bank #2)

P0433 Heated Catalyst Efficiency Below Threshold (Bank #2)

P0434 Heated Catalyst Temperature Below Threshold (Bank #2)

P0440 Evaporative Emission Control System Malfunction

P0441 Evaporative Emission Control System Incorrect Purge Flow

P0442 Evaporative Emission Control System Leak Detected (Small Leak)

P0443 Evaporative Emission Control System Purge Control Valve Circuit Malfunction

P0444 Evaporative Emission Control System Purge Control Valve Circuit Open

P0445 Evaporative Emission Control System Purge Control Valve Circuit Shorted

P0446 Evaporative Emission Control System Vent Control Circuit Malfunction

P0447 Evaporative Emission Control System Vent Control Circuit Open

P0448 Evaporative Emission Control System Vent Control Circuit Shorted

P0449 Evaporative Emission Control System Vent Valve/Solenoid Circuit Malfunction

P0450 Evaporative Emission Control System Pressure Sensor Malfunction

P0451 Evaporative Emission Control System Pressure Sensor Range/Performance

P0452 Evaporative Emission Control System Pressure Sensor Low Input

P0453 Evaporative Emission Control System Pressure Sensor High Input

P0454 Evaporative Emission Control System Pressure Sensor Intermittent

P0455 Evaporative Emission Control System Leak Detected (Gross Leak)

P0460 Fuel Level Sensor Circuit Malfunction

P0461 Fuel Level Sensor Circuit Range/Performance

P0462 Fuel Level Sensor Circuit Low Input

P0463 Fuel Level Sensor Circuit High Input

P0464 Fuel Level Sensor Circuit Intermittent

P0465 Purge Flow Sensor Circuit Malfunction

P0466 Purge Flow Sensor Circuit Range/Performance

P0467 Purge Flow Sensor Circuit Low Input

P0468 Purge Flow Sensor Circuit High Input

P0469 Purge Flow Sensor Circuit Intermittent

P0470 Exhaust Pressure Sensor Malfunction

P0471 Exhaust Pressure Sensor Range/Performance

P0472 Exhaust Pressure Sensor Low

P0473 Exhaust Pressure Sensor High

P0474 Exhaust Pressure Sensor Intermittent

P0475 Exhaust Pressure Control Valve Malfunction

P0476 Exhaust Pressure Control Valve Range/Performance

P0477 Exhaust Pressure Control Valve Low

P0478 Exhaust Pressure Control Valve High

P0479 Exhaust Pressure Control Valve Intermittent

P0480 Cooling Fan #1 Control Circuit Malfunction

P0481 Cooling Fan #2 Control Circuit Malfunction

P0482 Cooling Fan #3 Control Circuit Malfunction

P0483 Cooling Fan Rationality Check Malfunction

P0484 Cooling Fan Circuit Over Current

P0485 Cooling Fan Power/Ground Circuit Malfunction

P0500 Vehicle Speed Sensor Malfunction

P0501 Vehicle Speed Sensor Range/Performance

P0502 Vehicle Speed Sensor Circuit Low Input

P0503 Vehicle Speed Sensor Intermittent/Erratic/High

P0505 Idle Control System Malfunction

P0506 Idle Control System RPM Lower Than Expected

P0507 Idle Control System RPM Higher Than Expected

P0510 Closed Throttle Position Switch Malfunction

P0520 Engine Oil Pressure Sensor/Switch Circuit Malfunction

P0521 Engine Oil Pressure Sensor/Switch Range/Performance

P0522 Engine Oil Pressure Sensor/Switch Low Voltage

P0523 Engine Oil Pressure Sensor/Switch High Voltage

P0530 A/C Refrigerant Pressure Sensor Circuit Malfunction

P0531 A/C Refrigerant Pressure Sensor Circuit Range/Performance

P0532 A/C Refrigerant Pressure Sensor Circuit Low Input

P0533 A/C Refrigerant Pressure Sensor Circuit High Input

P0534 A/C Refrigerant Charge Loss

P0550 Power Steering Pressure Sensor Circuit Malfunction

P0551 Power Steering Pressure Sensor Circuit Range/Performance

P0552 Power Steering Pressure Sensor Circuit Low Input

P0553 Power Steering Pressure Sensor Circuit High Input

P0554 Power Steering Pressure Sensor Circuit Intermittent

P0560 System Voltage Malfunction

P0561 System Voltage Unstable

P0562 System Voltage Low

P0563 System Voltage High

P0565 Cruise Control On Signal Malfunction

P0566 Cruise Control Off Signal Malfunction

P0567 Cruise Control Resume Signal Malfunction

P0568 Cruise Control Set Signal Malfunction

P0569 Cruise Control Coast Signal Malfunction

P0570 Cruise Control Accel Signal Malfunction

P0571 Cruise Control/Brake Switch "A" Circuit Malfunction

P0572 Cruise Control/Brake Switch "A" Circuit Low

P0573 Cruise Control/Brake Switch "A" Circuit High

P0574 **Through P0580** Reserved for Cruise Codes

P0600 Serial Communication Link Malfunction

P0601 Internal Control Module Memory Check Sum Error

P0602 Control Module Programming Error

P0603 Internal Control Module Keep Alive Memory (KAM) Error

P0604 Internal Control Module Random Access Memory (RAM) Error

P0605 Internal Control Module Read Only Memory (ROM) Error

P0606 PCM Processor Fault

P0608 Control Module VSS Output "A" Malfunction

P0609 Control Module VSS Output "B" Malfunction

P0620 Generator Control Circuit Malfunction

P0621 Generator Lamp "L" Control Circuit Malfunction

P0622 Generator Field "F" Control Circuit Malfunction

P0650 Malfunction Indicator Lamp (MIL) Control Circuit Malfunction

P0654 Engine RPM Output Circuit Malfunction

P0655 Engine Hot Lamp Output Control Circuit Malfunction

P0656 Fuel Level Output Circuit Malfunction

P0700 Transmission Control System Malfunction

P0701 Transmission Control System Range/Performance

P0702 Transmission Control System Electrical

P0703 Torque Converter/Brake Switch "B" Circuit Malfunction

P0704 Clutch Switch Input Circuit Malfunction

P0705 Transmission Range Sensor Circuit Malfunction (PRNDL Input)

P0706 Transmission Range Sensor Circuit Range/Performance

P0707 Transmission Range Sensor Circuit Low Input

P0708 Transmission Range Sensor Circuit High Input

P0709 Transmission Range Sensor Circuit Intermittent

P0710 Transmission Fluid Temperature Sensor Circuit Malfunction

P0711 Transmission Fluid Temperature Sensor Circuit Range/Performance

P0712 Transmission Fluid Temperature Sensor Circuit Low Input

P0713 Transmission Fluid Temperature Sensor Circuit High Input

P0714 Transmission Fluid Temperature Sensor Circuit Intermittent

P0715 Input/Turbine Speed Sensor Circuit Malfunction

P0716 Input/Turbine Speed Sensor Circuit Range/Performance

P0717 Input/Turbine Speed Sensor Circuit No Signal

P0718 Input/Turbine Speed Sensor Circuit Intermittent

P0719 Torque Converter/Brake Switch "B" Circuit Low

P0720 Output Speed Sensor Circuit Malfunction

P0721 Output Speed Sensor Circuit Range/Performance

P0722 Output Speed Sensor Circuit No Signal

P0723 Output Speed Sensor Circuit Intermittent

P0724 Torque Converter/Brake Switch "B" Circuit High

P0725 Engine Speed Input Circuit Malfunction

P0726 Engine Speed Input Circuit Range/Performance

P0727 Engine Speed Input Circuit No Signal

P0728 Engine Speed Input Circuit Intermittent

P0730 Incorrect Gear Ratio
P0731 Gear #1 Incorrect Ratio
P0732 Gear #2 Incorrect Ratio
P0733 Gear #3 Incorrect Ratio
P0734 Gear #4 Incorrect Ratio
P0735 Gear #5 Incorrect Ratio
P0736 Reverse Incorrect Ratio
P0740 Torque Converter Clutch Circuit Malfunction

P0741 Torque Converter Clutch Circuit Performance or Stuck Off

P0742 Torque Converter Clutch Circuit Stuck On

P0743 Torque Converter Clutch Circuit Electrical

P0744 Torque Converter Clutch Circuit Intermittent

P0745 Pressure Control Solenoid Malfunction

P0746 Pressure Control Solenoid Performance or Stuck Off

P0747 Pressure Control Solenoid Stuck On

P0748 Pressure Control Solenoid Electrical

P0749 Pressure Control Solenoid Intermittent

P0750 Shift Solenoid "A" Malfunction
P0751 Shift Solenoid "A" Performance or Stuck Off

P0752 Shift Solenoid "A" Stuck On
P0753 Shift Solenoid "A" Electrical
P0754 Shift Solenoid "A" Intermittent
P0755 Shift Solenoid "B" Malfunction

P0756 Shift Solenoid "B" Performance or Stuck Off

P0757 Shift Solenoid "B" Stuck On
P0758 Shift Solenoid "B" Electrical
P0759 Shift Solenoid "B" Intermittent

P0760 Shift Solenoid "C" Malfunction

P0761 Shift Solenoid "C" Performance Or Stuck Off

P0762 Shift Solenoid "C" Stuck On
P0763 Shift Solenoid "C" Electrical
P0764 Shift Solenoid "C" Intermittent

P0765 Shift Solenoid "D" Malfunction

P0766 Shift Solenoid "D" Performance Or Stuck Off

P0767 Shift Solenoid "D" Stuck On
P0768 Shift Solenoid "D" Electrical
P0769 Shift Solenoid "D" Intermittent

P0770 Shift Solenoid "E" Malfunction

P0771 Shift Solenoid "E" Performance Or Stuck Off

P0772 Shift Solenoid "E" Stuck On
P0773 Shift Solenoid "E" Electrical
P0774 Shift Solenoid "E" Intermittent

P0780 Shift Malfunction
P0781 1–2 Shift Malfunction
P0782 2–3 Shift Malfunction
P0783 3–4 Shift Malfunction
P0784 4–5 Shift Malfunction
P0785 Shift/Timing Solenoid Malfunction

P0786 Shift/Timing Solenoid Range/Performance

P0787 Shift/Timing Solenoid Low
P0788 Shift/Timing Solenoid High
P0789 Shift/Timing Solenoid Intermittent

P0790 Normal/Performance Switch Circuit Malfunction

P0801 Reverse Inhibit Control Circuit Malfunction

P0803 1–4 Upshift (Skip Shift) Solenoid Control Circuit Malfunction

P0804 1–4 Upshift (Skip Shift) Lamp Control Circuit Malfunction

P1106 MAP Sensor Voltage Intermittently High

P1107 MAP Sensor Voltage Intermittently Low

P1111 IAT Sensor Circuit Intermittent High Voltage

P1112 IAT Sensor Circuit Intermittent Low Voltage

P1114 ECT Sensor Circuit Intermittent Low Voltage

P1115 ECT Sensor Circuit Intermittent High Voltage

P1121 TP Sensor Voltage Intermittently High

P1122 TP Sensor Voltage Intermittently Low

P1133 HO$_2$S Insufficient Switching Bank #1, Sensor #1

P1134 HO$_2$S Transition Time Ratio Bank #1, Sensor #1

P1153 HO$_2$S Insufficient Switching Sensor Bank #2, Sensor #1

P1154 HO$_2$S Transition Time Ratio Bank #2, Sensor #1

P1171 Fuel system lean during acceleration

P1200 Injector control circuit
P1222 Injector control circuit intermittent

P1345 Crankshaft/Camshaft (CKP/CMP) Correlation

P1350 Ignition Control (IC) Circuit Malfunction

P1351 Ignition Control (IC) Circuit High Voltage

P1361 Ignition Control (IC) Circuit Not Toggling

P1361 Ignition Control (IC) Circuit Low Voltage

P1374 3X Reference circuit
P1380 Electronic Brake Control Module (EBCM) DTC Detected Rough Road Data Unusable

P1381 Misfire Detected, No EBCM/PCM/VCM Serial Data

P1406 EGR Pintle Position Circuit Fault

P1415 AIR System Bank #1
P1416 AIR System Bank #2
P1441 EVAP Control System Flow During Non-Purge

P1442 EVAP Vacuum Switch Circuit
P1450 Barometric Pressure Sensor Circuit Fault

P1451 Barometric Pressure Sensor Performance

P1460 Cooling Fan Control System Fault

P1500 Starter Signal Circuit Fault
P1508 IAC System Low RPM
P1509 IAC System High RPM
P1510 Back-up Power Supply Fault
P1520 PNP Circuit
P1530 Ignition Timing Adjustment Switch Circuit

P1554 Cruise control status circuit
P1600 PCM Battery Circuit Fault

P1626 Theft Deterrent System Fuel Enable Circuit

P1629 Theft Deterrent Crank Signal Malfunction

P1635 5-Volt Reference "A" Circuit

P1639 5-Volt Reference "B" Circuit

P1641 MIL Control Circuit

P1642 FC Relay 2 and Relay 3 Control Circuit

P1643 Engine Speed Output Circuit

P1651 Fan #1 Relay Control Circuit

P1652 Fan #2 Relay Control Circuit

P1654 A/C Relay Control

P1655 EVAP Purge Solenoid Control Circuit

P1657 Skip Shift Solenoid Control Circuit

P1661 MIL Control Circuit

P1662 Cruise Control Inhibit Control Circuit

P1664 Skip Shift Lamp Control Circuit

P1667 Reverse Inhibit Solenoid Control Circuit

P1672 Low Engine Oil Level Light Control Circuit

ACCESSORY DRIVE BELTS

3

ACCESSORY DRIVE BELTS

Accessory drive belts are usually divided into two basic types: V-belts (conventional, cogged and flat multi-ribbed) and serpentine (multi-ribbed) belts. The flat multi-ribbed V-belt actually resembles a serpentine belt, however, unlike a serpentine belt, only the inner surface of the belt makes contact with the components' pulleys. (Rarely, the back of multi-ribbed V-belts may ride against an idler or tensioner pulley, however.) V-belts ride in pulleys with V-shaped groove(s) to rotate various accessories, such as the power steering pump, air conditioner compressor, alternator/generator, water pump, and air pump. Only the inside of a V-belt is used, unlike a serpentine belt which utilizes both sides. V-belts typically operate one or two accessories per belt, whereas a single serpentine belt can drive all of the accessories. V-belts and a few serpentine belts require periodic adjustment because the belts are under tension and stretch over time. Most serpentine belts utilize an automatic belt tensioner that constantly provides the proper tension to the belt.

V-Belts

INSPECTION

Although different maintenance intervals are given by each manufacturer, it is a good rule of thumb to inspect the drive belts every 15,000 miles (24,000 km) or 12 months (whichever occurs first). Determine the belt tension at a point half-way between the pulleys by pressing on the belt with moderate thumb pressure. The belt should deflect about ¼–½ in. (6–13mm) at this point. Note that "deflection" is not play, but the ability of the belt, under actual tension, to stretch slightly and give.

Inspect the belts for the following signs of damage or wear: glazing, cracking, fraying, crumbling or missing chunks. A glazed belt will be perfectly smooth from slippage, while a good belt will have a slight texture of fabric visible. Cracks will usually start at the inner edge of the belt and run outward. A belt that is fraying will have the fabric backing de-laminating itself from the belt. A belt that is crumbling or missing chunks will have voids in the cross-section of the belt, some times the section missing chunks will be in the pulley groove and not easily seen. All worn or

CONVENTIONAL "V" BELT   COGGED "V" BELT

"V" RIBBED BELT

TCCS1218

Typical accessory drive belts found on vehicles today

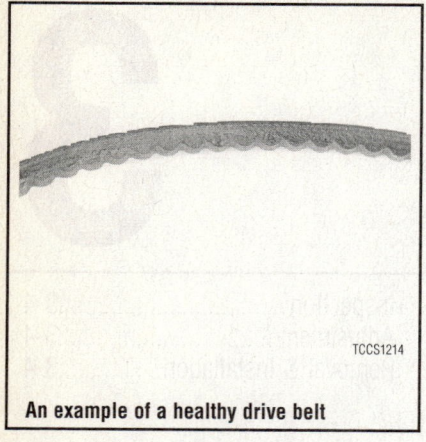

TCCS1214

An example of a healthy drive belt

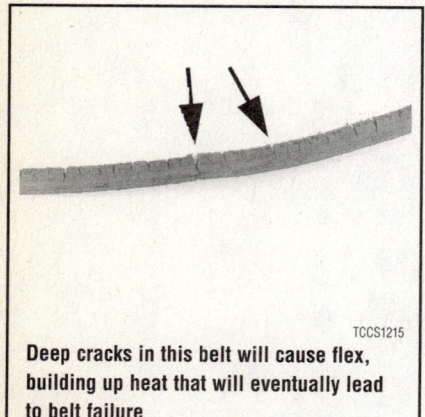

TCCS1215

Deep cracks in this belt will cause flex, building up heat that will eventually lead to belt failure

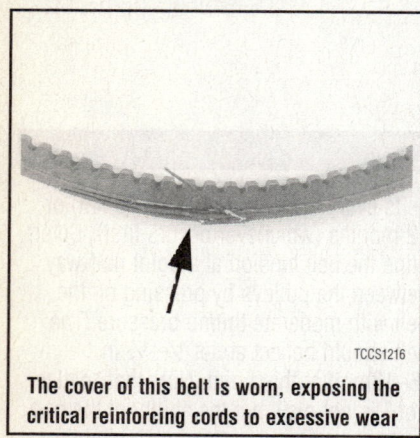

TCCS1216

The cover of this belt is worn, exposing the critical reinforcing cords to excessive wear

TCCS1217

Installing too wide a belt can result in serious belt wear and/or breakage

damaged drive belts should be replaced immediately. It is best to replace all drive belts at one time, as a preventive maintenance measure.

Although it is generally easier on the component to have the belt too loose than too tight, a very loose belt may place a high impact load on a bearing due to the whipping or snapping action of the belt. A belt that is slightly loose may slip, especially when component loads are high. This slippage may be hard to identify. For example, the generator belt may run okay during the day, then slip at night when headlights are turned on. Slipping belts wear quickly not only due to the direct effect of slippage but also because of the heat the slippage generates. Extreme slippage may even cause a belt to burn. A very smooth, glazed appearance on the belt's sides, as opposed to the obvious pattern of a fabric cover, indicates that the belt has been slipping.

ADJUSTMENT

> **☀☀ CAUTION**
>
> **On vehicles with an electric cooling fan, disable the power to the fan by disengaging the fan motor wiring connector or removing the negative battery cable before replacing or adjusting the drive belts. Otherwise, the fan may engage even though the ignition is OFF.**

Belt tension can be checked by pressing on the belt at the center point of its longest straight span. The belt should give approximately ¼ – ½ in. (6–13mm). If the belt is loose it will slip, whereas if the belt is too tight it will damage the bearings in the driven unit.

For the purposes of V-belt tensioning, there are generally three types of mounting for the various components driven by the drive belt. The first method, referred to as pivoting type without adjuster, is designed so that the component is secured by at least 2 bolts. One of the bolts is a pivoting bolt and the other is the lockbolt. When both bolts are loosened so that the component may move, the component pivots on the pivoting bolt. The lockbolt passes through the component and a slotted bracket, so that when the lockbolt's nut is tightened the component is held in that position. There are not automatic adjusting mechanisms used with this type of mounting.

The second method of component

mounting, referred to as pivoting type with adjuster, is almost identical except for the addition of an adjuster of some sort. Usually the adjuster is composed of a bracket attached to the component and a threaded adjusting bolt. After loosening the pivoting and lockbolts, the adjusting bolt can be tightened or loosened to increase or decrease the drive belt's tension. With this type of mounting, you do not have to hold the component in a tensioned position and tighten the pivoting and lockbolts; the adjusting bolt does the job for you.

Some versions of this method of mounting use an adjuster which is built into one of the components mounting braces. The brace attaches the component to the engine and incorporates a threaded adjuster in its mid-span, so that when the threaded adjuster is turned the brace shortens or lengthens. This in turn increases or decreases the amount of tension on the component.

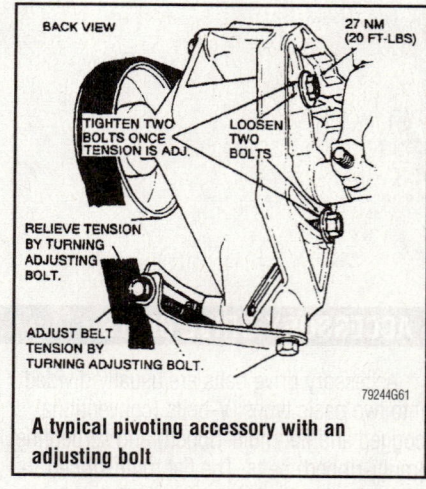

79244G61

A typical pivoting accessory with an adjusting bolt

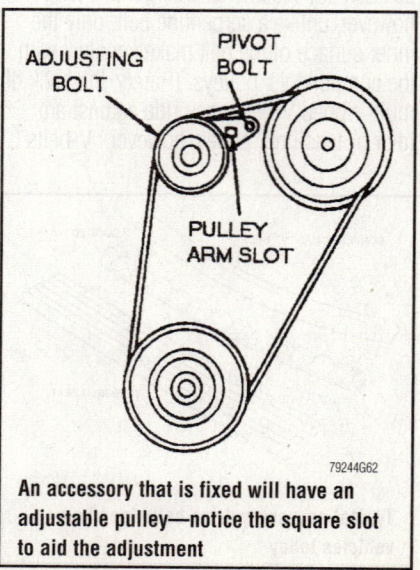

79244G62

An accessory that is fixed will have an adjustable pulley—notice the square slot to aid the adjustment

The third type of mounting, referred to as stationary type, is designed so that the component is mounted on its brackets. There are no pivoting or lockbolts, and the component is not designed to be moved. Rather, this type of mounting uses an extra tensioner idler pulley assembly. The drive belt is tensioned by adjusting the position of the idler pulley, usually accomplished by turning the adjuster bolt on the idler mechanism.

Pivoting Type

WITHOUT ADJUSTER

1. Disconnect the negative battery cable.

2. Loosen the component's lockbolt and pivoting bolt only enough for the component to move.

3. Using a strong wooden, plastic or metal prytool, move the component either closer to, or farther away from, the engine to provide the correct tension on the belt.

✳ WARNING

If using a metal prytool, always wrap the end with a rag or towel to prevent accidentally damaging the component from undue stress.

4. Once the proper amount of tension is applied to the drive belt, hold the prytool with one hand while tightening the lockbolt securely with the other hand.

5. Release the pressure from the prytool and tighten the pivoting bolt securely.

6. Double check the drive belt's tension, in case the component moved slightly while tightening the bolts.

7. Connect the negative battery cable.

WITH ADJUSTER

This type of drive belt is tensioned by a tensioner, which makes precise tension adjustment easy.

1. Disconnect the negative battery cable.

2. Loosen the component's pivot and lockbolts.

3. Inspect the tensioner assembly on the component; the tensioner adjusting bolt may use a locknut or screw to prevent it from loosening over time. On the type of adjuster with a threaded mounting brace, there may be two jam nuts used on either side of the threaded coupling. If such locking fasteners are found, loosen them.

4. Turn the tensioner adjusting bolt or threaded coupling to increase or decrease the amount of tension on the drive belt, as necessary.

5. When the belt tension is correct, tighten the lockbolt and the pivot bolt.

6. If equipped, tighten the tension adjusting bolt locknut or screw to prevent the adjuster from slowly loosening over time. If equipped, tighten the two jam nuts.

7. Connect the negative battery cable.

Stationary Type

IDLER PULLEY WITH ADJUSTING BOLT

1. Loosen the idler bracket pivot bolt and locking bolts.

2. Adjust the belt tension by inserting the proper size ratchet in the square slot of the idler bracket and rotating the bracket until tension is applied.

3. While holding the tension on the belt with the ratchet, tighten the locking bolts, then the pivot bolt.

IDLER PULLEY WITHOUT ADJUSTING BOLT

1. Loosen the mounting/pivot bolt behind the idler pulley.

2. Swivel the idler pulley with a pair of pliers or a wrench on the bearing mounting until the proper tension is achieved.

3. While holding the idler pulley, at the proper tension, tighten the mounting/pivot bolt.

REMOVAL & INSTALLATION

If a belt must be replaced, the driven unit or idler pulley must be loosened and moved to its extreme loosest position, generally by moving it toward the center of the motor. After removing the old belt, check the pulleys for dirt or built-up material which could affect belt contact. Carefully install the new belt, remembering that it is new and unused; it may appear to be just a little too small to fit over the pulley flanges. Fit the belt over the largest pulley (usually the crankshaft pulley at the bottom center of the motor) first, then work on the smaller one(s). Gentle pressure in the direction of rotation is helpful. Some belts run around a third, or idler pulley, which acts as an additional pivot in the belt's path. It may be possible to loosen the idler pulley as well as the main component, making your job much easier. Depending on which belt(s) you are changing, it may be necessary to loosen or remove other interfering belts to get at the one(s) you want.

When buying replacement belts, remember that the fit is critical according to the length of the belt ("diameter"), the width of the belt, the depth of the belt and the angle or profile of the V shape or the ribs. The belt shape should match the shape of the pulley exactly; belts that are not an exact match can cause noise, slippage and premature failure.

After the new belt is installed, draw tension on it by moving the driven unit or idler pulley away from the motor and tighten its mounting bolts. This is sometimes a three or four-handed job; you may find an assistant helpful. Be sure that all the bolts you loosened get retightened and that any other loosened belts also have the correct tension. A new belt can be expected to stretch a bit after installation so be prepared to readjust your new belt, if needed, within the first two hundred miles of use.

Pivoting Type

✳ CAUTION

On vehicles with an electric cooling fan, disable the power to the fan by disengaging the fan motor wiring connector or removing the negative battery cable before replacing or adjusting the drive belts. Otherwise, the fan may engage even though the ignition is OFF.

WITHOUT ADJUSTER

1. Disconnect the negative battery cable.

2. Loosen the accessory's slotted adjusting bracket bolt. If the hinge bolt is excessively tight, it too will have to be loosened.

3. Push the component toward the engine to provide enough slack in the belt so that it will slide over one of the accessory drive pulleys. Remove the drive belt from the accessory drive pulleys and from the vehicle.

To install:

4. Position the new drive belt over the component pulleys. Be sure that it is routed correctly.

5. Adjust the tension of the belt, as described earlier in this section.

6. Connect the negative battery cable.

WITH ADJUSTER

1. Disconnect the negative battery cable.

2. Loosen the component's pivot and lockbolts.

3. Inspect the tensioner assembly on the component; the tensioner adjusting bolt may use a locknut or screw to prevent it from loosening over time. On the type of adjuster with a threaded mounting brace, there may be two jam nuts used on either side of the threaded coupling. If such locking fasteners are found, loosen them.

4. Turn the tensioner adjusting bolt or threaded coupling to relieve all tension from the drive belt until the most possible slack is gained from the component.

5. Slip the belt off of the accessory pulley, then remove it from the other pulleys. Remove the belt from the vehicle.

To install:

6. Route the new belt on the component pulleys. Make certain that it is routed correctly; incorrect routing could cause a components to spin backward, possibly damaging it.

7. Once the belt is correctly positioned on all of the pulleys, adjust the tension as described earlier in this section.

8. Connect the negative battery cable.

Stationary Type

IDLER PULLEY WITH ADJUSTING BOLT

1. Disconnect the negative battery cable.

2. Loosen the idler bracket pivot bolt and locking bolts.

3. Move the idler pulley until the most amount of slack is gained.

4. Remove the drive belt from the accessory pulley, then from the other applicable pulleys.

To install:

5. Position the new belt over the crankshaft pulley, the idler pulley and the accessory pulley. Make certain that it is correctly routed, otherwise it could cause the accessory to be rotated backwards. This could cause damage to the accessory.

6. Adjust the belt tension, as described earlier in this section.

7. While holding the tension on the belt with the ratchet, tighten the locking bolts, then the pivot bolt.

8. Connect the negative battery cable.

IDLER PULLEY WITHOUT ADJUSTING BOLT

1. Disconnect the negative battery cable.

2. Loosen the mounting/pivot bolt behind the idler pulley.

3. Remove the drive belt from the accessory pulley, then from the other applicable pulleys.

To install:

4. Position the new belt over the crankshaft pulley, the idler pulley and the accessory pulley. Make certain that it is correctly routed, otherwise it could cause the accessory to be rotated backwards. This could cause damage to the accessory.

5. Swivel the idler pulley with a pair of pliers or a wrench on the bearing mounting until the proper tension is achieved.

6. While holding the idler pulley, at the proper tension, tighten the mounting/pivot bolt.

7. Connect the negative battery cable.

Serpentine Belts

INSPECTION

Although many manufacturers recommend that the drive belt(s) be inspected every 30,000 miles (48,000 km) or more, it is really a good idea to check them at least once a year, or at every major fluid change. Whichever interval you choose, the belts should be checked for wear or damage. Obviously, a damaged drive belt can cause problems should it give way while the vehicle is in operation. But, improper length belts (too short or long), as well as excessively worn belts, can also cause problems. Loose accessory drive belts can lead to poor engine cooling and diminished output from the alternator, air conditioning

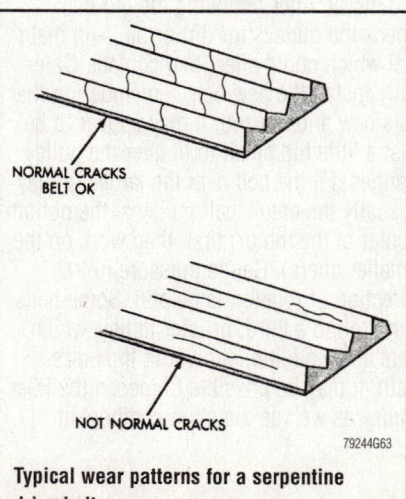

Typical wear patterns for a serpentine drive belt

compressor or power steering pump. A belt that is too tight places a severe strain on the driven unit and can wear out bearings quickly.

Serpentine drive belts should be inspected for rib chunking (pieces of the ribs breaking off), severe glazing, frayed cords or other visible damage. Any belt which is missing sections of 2 or more adjacent ribs which are ½ in. (13mm) or longer must be replaced. You might want to note that serpentine belts do tend to form small cracks across the backing. If the only wear you find is in the form of one or more cracks are across the backing and NOT parallel to the ribs, the belt is still good and does not need to be replaced.

ADJUSTMENT

Periodic drive belt tensioning is not necessary, because an automatic spring-loaded tensioner is used with these belts to maintain proper adjustment at all times. The tensioner is also useful as a wear indicator. When the belt is properly installed, the arrow on the tensioner housing must point within the acceptable range lines on the tensioner's face. If the arrow falls outside the range, either an improper belt has been installed or the belt is worn beyond its useful life span. In either case, a new belt must be installed immediately to assure proper engine operation and to prevent possible accessory damage.

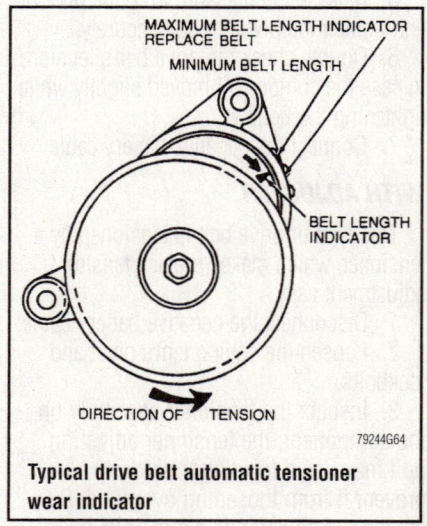

Typical drive belt automatic tensioner wear indicator

REMOVAL & INSTALLATION

Because serpentine belts use a spring loaded tensioner for adjustment, belt replacement tends to be somewhat easier than it used to be on engines where acces-

Troubleshooting the Serpentine Drive Belt

Problem	Cause	Solution
Tension sheeting fabric failure (woven fabric on outside circumference of belt has cracked or separated from body of belt)	• Grooved or backside idler pulley diameters are less than minimum recommended • Tension sheeting contacting (rubbing) stationary object • Excessive heat causing woven fabric to age • Tension sheeting splice has fractured	• Replace pulley(s) not conforming to specification • Correct rubbing condition • Replace belt • Replace belt
Noise (objectional squeal, squeak, or rumble is heard or felt while drive belt is in operation)	• Belt slippage • Bearing noise • Belt misalignment • Belt-to-pulley mismatch • Driven component inducing vibration • System resonant frequency inducing vibration	• Adjust belt • Locate and repair • Align belt/pulley(s) • Install correct belt • Locate defective driven component and repair • Vary belt tension within specifications. Replace belt.
Rib chunking (one or more ribs has separated from belt body)	• Foreign objects imbedded in pulley grooves • Installation damage • Drive loads in excess of design specifications • Insufficient internal belt adhesion	• Remove foreign objects from pulley grooves • Replace belt • Adjust belt tension • Replace belt
Rib or belt wear (belt ribs contact bottom of pulley grooves)	• Pulley(s) misaligned • Mismatch of belt and pulley groove widths • Abrasive environment • Rusted pulley(s) • Sharp or jagged pulley groove tips • Rubber deteriorated	• Align pulley(s) • Replace belt • Replace belt • Clean rust from pulley(s) • Replace pulley • Replace belt
Longitudinal belt cracking (cracks between two ribs)	• Belt has mistracked from pulley groove • Pulley groove tip has worn away rubber-to-tensile member	• Replace belt • Replace belt
Belt slips	• Belt slipping because of insufficient tension • Belt or pulley subjected to substance (belt dressing, oil, ethylene glycol) that has reduced friction • Driven component bearing failure • Belt glazed and hardened from heat and excessive slippage	• Adjust tension • Replace belt and clean pulleys • Replace faulty component bearing • Replace belt
"Groove jumping" (belt does not maintain correct position on pulley, or turns over and/or runs off pulleys)	• Insufficient belt tension • Pulley(s) not within design tolerance • Foreign object(s) in grooves	• Adjust belt tension • Replace pulley(s) • Remove foreign objects from grooves

TCCS3C09

Troubleshooting the Serpentine Drive Belt

Problem	Cause	Solution
"Groove jumping" (belt does not maintain correct position on pulley, or turns over and/or runs off pulleys)	• Excessive belt speed • Pulley misalignment • Belt-to-pulley profile mismatched • Belt cordline is distorted	• Avoid excessive engine acceleration • Align pulley(s) • Install correct belt • Replace belt
Belt broken (Note: identify and correct problem before replacement belt is installed)	• Excessive tension • Tensile members damaged during belt installation • Belt turnover • Severe pulley misalignment • Bracket, pulley, or bearing failure	• Replace belt and adjust tension to specification • Replace belt • Replace belt • Align pulley(s) • Replace defective component and belt
Cord edge failure (tensile member exposed at edges of belt or separated from belt body)	• Excessive tension • Drive pulley misalignment • Belt contacting stationary object • Pulley irregularities • Improper pulley construction • Insufficient adhesion between tensile member and rubber matrix	• Adjust belt tension • Align pulley • Correct as necessary • Replace pulley • Replace pulley • Replace belt and adjust tension to specifications
Sporadic rib cracking (multiple cracks in belt ribs at random intervals)	• Ribbed pulley(s) diameter less than minimum specification • Backside bend flat pulley(s) diameter less than minimum • Excessive heat condition causing rubber to harden • Excessive belt thickness • Belt overcured • Excessive tension	• Replace pulley(s) • Replace pulley(s) • Correct heat condition as necessary • Replace belt • Replace belt • Adjust belt tension

TCCS3C10

Ignition system service is covered in the model specific sections of this manual

sories were pivoted and bolted in place for tension adjustment. Basically, all belt replacement involves is to pivot the tensioner to loosen the belt, then slide the belt off of the pulleys. The two most important points are to pay CLOSE attention to the proper belt routing (since serpentine belts tend to be "snaked" all different ways through the pulleys) and to be sure the V-ribs are properly seated in all the pulleys.

Although belt routing diagrams have been included in this section, the first places you should check for proper belt routing are the labels in your engine compartment. These should include a belt routing diagram which may reflect changes made during a production run.

1. Disconnect the negative battery cable for safety. This will help assure that no one mistakenly cranks the engine over with your hands between the pulleys, and that the cooling fan cannot activate while servicing the belt(s).

➡**Take a good look at the installed belt and make a note of the routing. Before**

removing the belt, be sure the routing matches that of the belt routing label or one of the diagrams in this book. If for some reason a diagram does not match (you may not have the original engine or it may have been modified), carefully note the changes on a piece of paper.

2. For tensioners equipped with a ½ in. (13mm) square hole, insert the drive end of a large breaker bar into the hole. Use the breaker bar to pivot the tensioner away from the drive belt. For tensioners not equipped with this hole, use the proper-sized socket and breaker bar (or a large handled wrench) on the tensioner idler pulley center bolt to pivot the tensioner away from the belt. This will loosen the belt sufficiently so it can be pulled off of one or more of the pulleys. It is usually easiest to carefully pull the belt out from under the tensioner pulley itself.

3. Once the belt is off one of the pulleys, gently pivot the tensioner back into position. DO NOT allow the tensioner to snap back, as this could damage the tensioner's internal parts.

4. Now finish removing the belt from the other pulleys and remove it from the engine.
To install:

5. While referring to the proper routing diagram (which you identified earlier), begin to route the belt over the pulleys, leaving whichever pulley you first released it from for last.

6. Once the belt is mostly in place, carefully pivot the tensioner and position the belt over the final pulley. As you begin to allow the tensioner back into contact with the belt, run your hand around the pulleys and be sure the belt is properly seated in the ribs. If not, release the tension and seat the belt.

7. Once the belt is installed, take another look at all the pulleys to double check your installation.

8. Connect the negative battery cable, then start and run the engine to check belt operation.

9. Once the engine has reached normal operating temperature, turn the ignition **OFF** and check that the belt tensioner arrow is within the proper adjustment range.

Often the underhood label will display the serpentine drive belt routing

Relieve the belt tension by pivoting the automatic tensioner away from the belt, then remove the belt

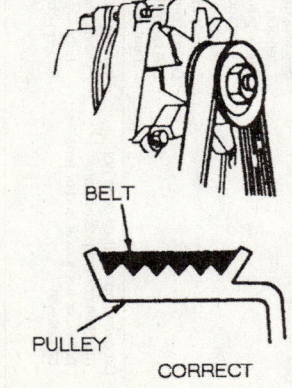

BELT

PULLEY

CORRECT

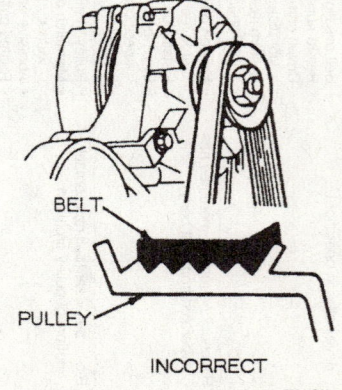

BELT

PULLEY

INCORRECT

Verifying serpentine belt alignment in the pulley

ACCESSORY DRIVE BELT ROUTING INDEX

MANUFACTURER

ENGINES	DESCRIPTION	FIGURE
Chrysler Corp.		
2.0L (VIN C, Y) Neon engine	Accessory drive belt routing	1
2.0L (VIN Y) except Neon engine	Accessory drive belt routing	2
2.0L (VIN F) turbo engine	Accessory drive belt routing	3
2.4L engine	Accessory drive belt routing	4
2.5L engine	Accessory drive belt routing	5
2.7L engine	Accessory drive belt routing	6
3.2L engine	Accessory drive belt routing	7
3.3L engine	Accessory drive belt routing	8
3.5L engine	Accessory drive belt routing	9
Ford Motor Co.		
1.3L Aspire engine	Accessory drive belt routing	10
1.8L engine	Accessory drive belt routing	11
1.9L engine	Serpentine accessory drive belt routing	12
2.0L Probe engine	Accessory drive belt routing	13
2.0L (VIN 3) engine	Accessory drive belt routing	14
2.0L (VIN P) Escort/Tracer engine with A/C	Accessory drive belt routing	15
2.0L (VIN P) Escort/Tracer engine without A/C	Accessory drive belt routing	16
2.0L (VIN 3) 1998-00 Escort/Tracer engine	Accessory drive belt routing	17
2.5L (VIN B) Probe engine without A/C	Alternator drive belt routing	18
2.5L (VIN B) Probe engine with A/C	Alternator drive belt routing	19
2.5L (VIN B) Probe engine	Power steering and water pump drive belts	20
2.5L (VIN L) engine	Water pump drive belt routing	21
2.5L (VIN L) engine with A/C	Accessory drive belt routing	22
2.5L (VIN L) engine without A/C	Accessory drive belt routing	23
3.0L (VIN U) OHV engine	Accessory drive belt routing	24
3.0L (VIN S) DOHC engine	Serpentine drive belt routing	25
3.4L SHO engine	Serpentine drive belt routing	26
3.4L SHO engine	Water pump drive belt routing	27
3.8L (VIN 4) engine	Accessory drive belt routing	28
3.8L supercharged engine	Accessory drive belt routing	29
4.6L (VIN W) engine	Serpentine drive belt routing	30
4.6L (VIN V) Continental engine	Serpentine drive belt routing	31
4.6L (VIN X) Mustang engine	Serpentine drive belt routing	32
General Motors		
2.2L engines		
1997 engines	Serpentine drive belt routing	33
1998-01 engines with A/C	Serpentine drive belt routing	34
1998-01 engines without A/C	Serpentine drive belt routing	35
2.4L engines	Serpentine drive belt routing	36
3.1L engines		
Except L/N body models	Serpentine drive belt routing	37
L/N body models	Serpentine drive belt routing	38
3.4L engines		
Except F body models	Serpentine drive belt routing	39
F body models	Serpentine drive belt routing	40

93063C01

ACCESSORY DRIVE BELT ROUTING INDEX

MANUFACTURER

ENGINES	DESCRIPTION	FIGURE
General Motors (cont.)		
3.8L engines		
C & H bodies 3.8L (VIN K) engines	Serpentine drive belt routing	41
C & H bodies 3.8L (VIN 1) engines	Serpentine drive belt routing	42
F body models	Serpentine drive belt routing	43
G body 3.8L (VIN 1) engines	Serpentine drive belt routing	44
G body 3.8L (VIN K) engines	Serpentine drive belt routing	45
W body models	Serpentine drive belt routing	46
4.0L engines	Serpentine drive belt routing	47
4.6L engines	Serpentine drive belt routing	48
5.7L engines		
5.7L (VIN G) except F body engines	Serpentine drive belt routing	49
5.7L 1997 F body engines	Serpentine drive belt routing	50
5.7L 1998-01 F body engines	Serpentine drive belt routing	51
5.7L 1998-01 F body engines	A/C drive belt routing	52
Geo/Chevrolet		
All engines	Accessory drive belt routing	53
Saturn		
All engines	Serpentine drive belt routing	54

93063C02

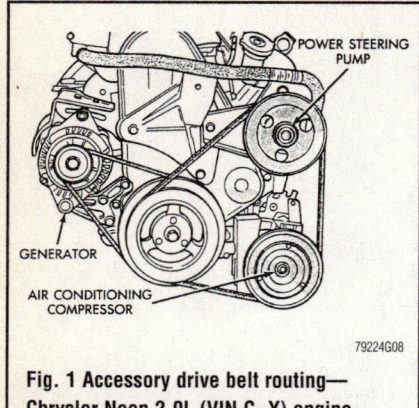

Fig. 1 Accessory drive belt routing—
Chrysler Neon 2.0L (VIN C, Y) engine

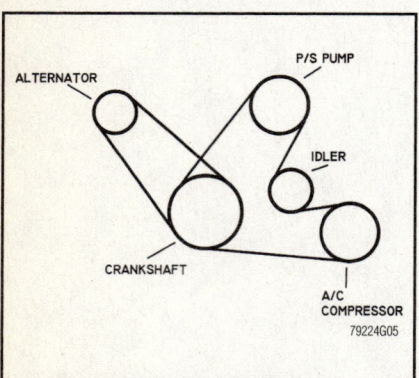

Fig. 2 Accessory drive belt routing—
Chrysler 2.0L (VIN Y) engine except Neon

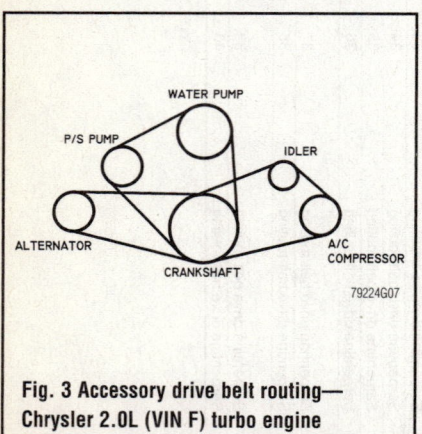

Fig. 3 Accessory drive belt routing—
Chrysler 2.0L (VIN F) turbo engine

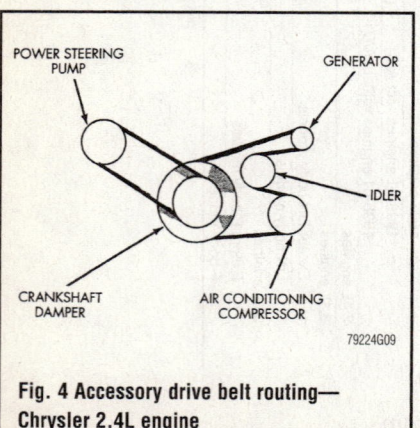

Fig. 4 Accessory drive belt routing—
Chrysler 2.4L engine

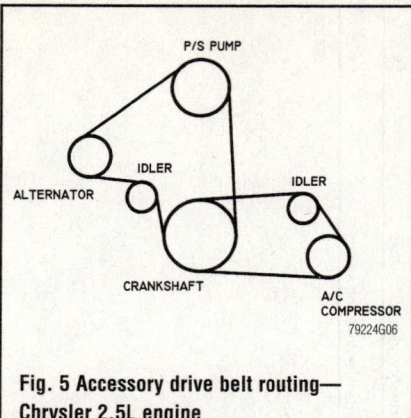

Fig. 5 Accessory drive belt routing—
Chrysler 2.5L engine

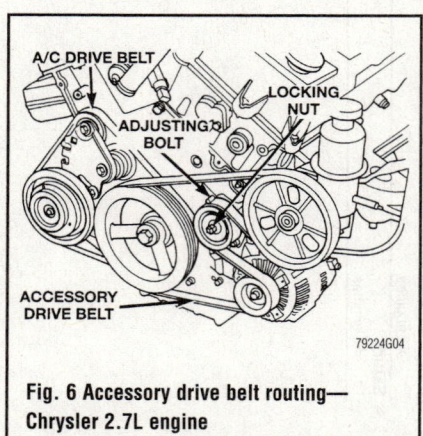

Fig. 6 Accessory drive belt routing—
Chrysler 2.7L engine

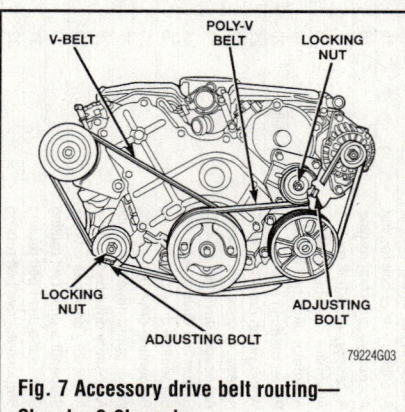

Fig. 7 Accessory drive belt routing—
Chrysler 3.2L engine

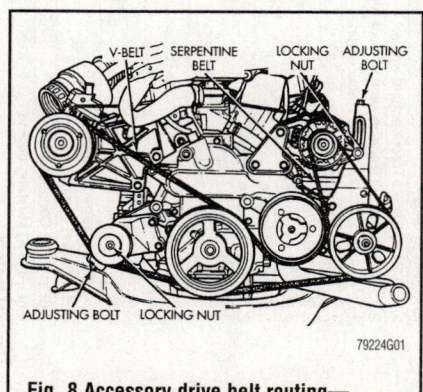
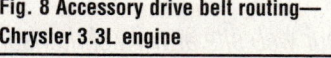

Fig. 8 Accessory drive belt routing—
Chrysler 3.3L engine

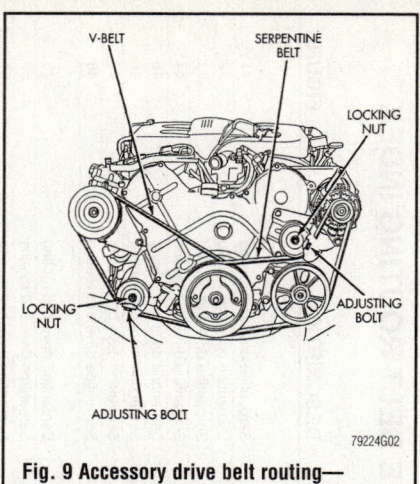

Fig. 9 Accessory drive belt routing—
Chrysler 3.5L engine

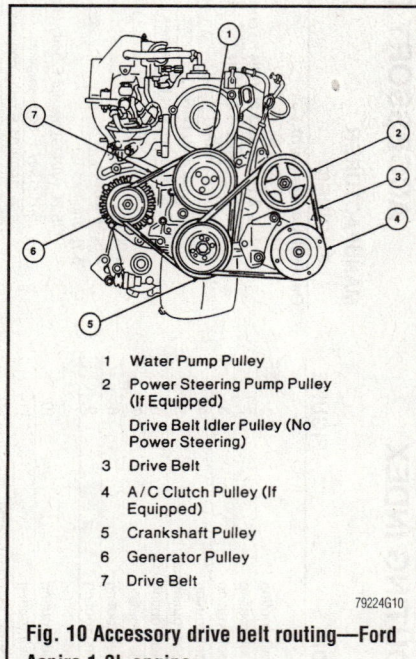

1 Water Pump Pulley
2 Power Steering Pump Pulley
   (If Equipped)
   Drive Belt Idler Pulley (No
   Power Steering)
3 Drive Belt
4 A/C Clutch Pulley (If
   Equipped)
5 Crankshaft Pulley
6 Generator Pulley
7 Drive Belt

Fig. 10 Accessory drive belt routing—Ford
Aspire 1.3L engine

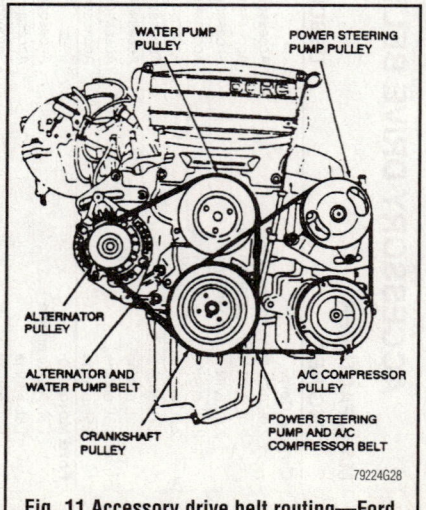

Fig. 11 Accessory drive belt routing—Ford
1.8L engine

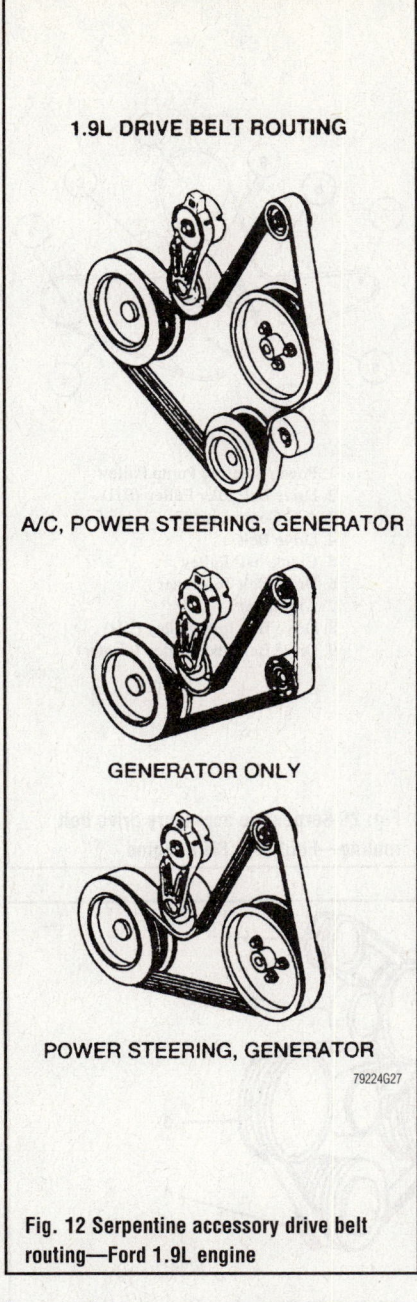

1.9L DRIVE BELT ROUTING

A/C, POWER STEERING, GENERATOR

GENERATOR ONLY

POWER STEERING, GENERATOR

79224G27

Fig. 12 Serpentine accessory drive belt routing—Ford 1.9L engine

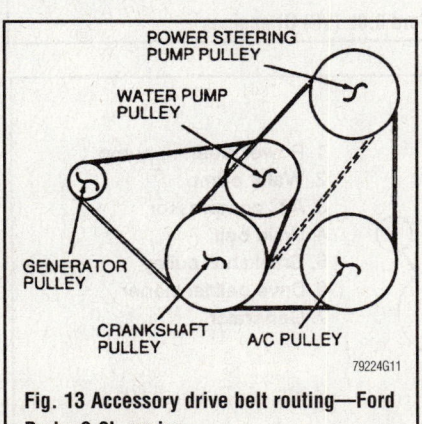

POWER STEERING PUMP PULLEY

WATER PUMP PULLEY

GENERATOR PULLEY

CRANKSHAFT PULLEY

A/C PULLEY

79224G11

Fig. 13 Accessory drive belt routing—Ford Probe 2.0L engine

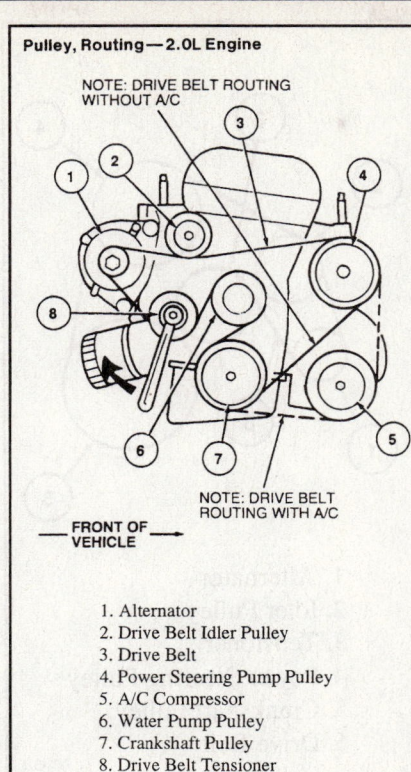

Pulley, Routing—2.0L Engine

NOTE: DRIVE BELT ROUTING WITHOUT A/C

NOTE: DRIVE BELT ROUTING WITH A/C

FRONT OF VEHICLE →

1. Alternator
2. Drive Belt Idler Pulley
3. Drive Belt
4. Power Steering Pump Pulley
5. A/C Compressor
6. Water Pump Pulley
7. Crankshaft Pulley
8. Drive Belt Tensioner

79224G18

Fig. 14 Accessory drive belt routing — Ford/Mercury 2.0L (VIN 3) engine

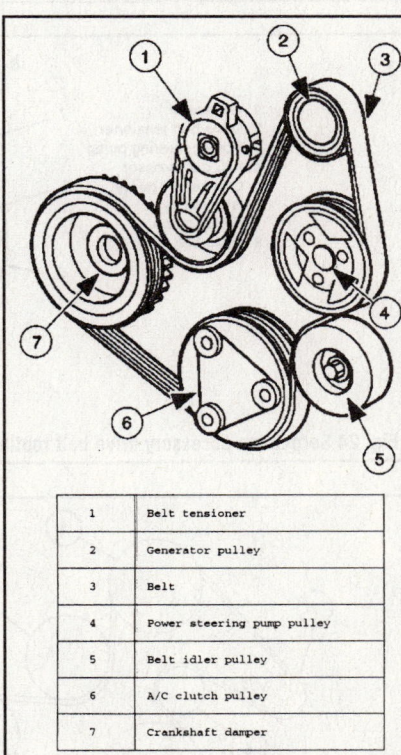

1	Belt tensioner
2	Generator pulley
3	Belt
4	Power steering pump pulley
5	Belt idler pulley
6	A/C clutch pulley
7	Crankshaft damper

93004G03

Fig. 15 Accessory drive belt routing — Ford/Mercury 2.0L (VIN P) SOHC engine with A/C—1997–01 Escort/Tracer

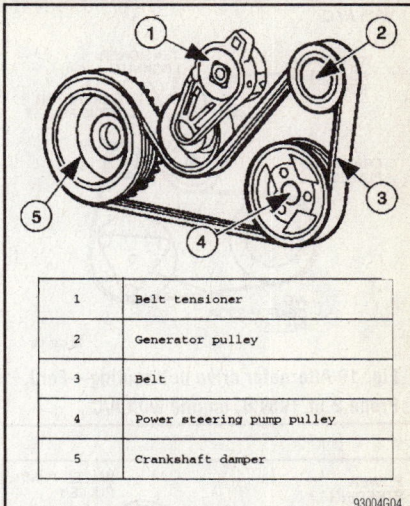

1	Belt tensioner
2	Generator pulley
3	Belt
4	Power steering pump pulley
5	Crankshaft damper

93004G04

Fig. 16 Accessory drive belt routing — Ford/Mercury 2.0L (VIN P) SOHC engine without A/C—1997–01 Escort/Tracer

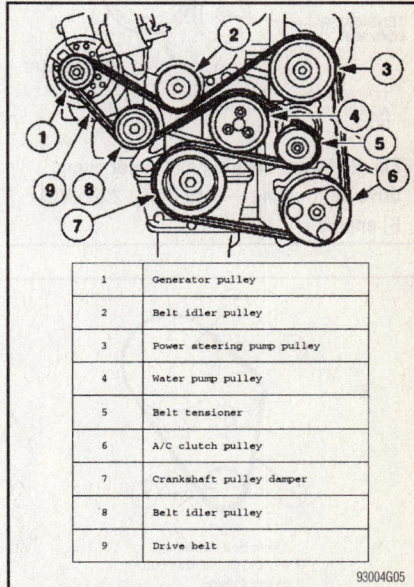

1	Generator pulley
2	Belt idler pulley
3	Power steering pump pulley
4	Water pump pulley
5	Belt tensioner
6	A/C clutch pulley
7	Crankshaft pulley damper
8	Belt idler pulley
9	Drive belt

93004G05

Fig. 17 Accessory drive belt routing — Ford/Mercury 2.0L (VIN 3) DOHC engine— 1998–01 Escort/Tracer

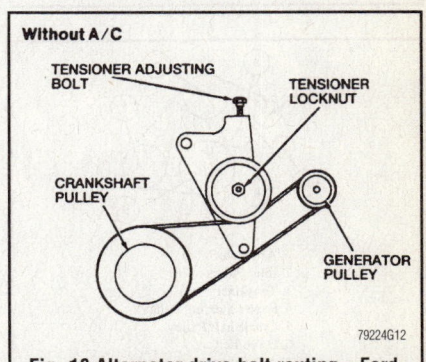

Without A/C

TENSIONER ADJUSTING BOLT

TENSIONER LOCKNUT

CRANKSHAFT PULLEY

GENERATOR PULLEY

79224G12

Fig. 18 Alternator drive belt routing—Ford Probe 2.5L (VIN B) engine without A/C

Refer to the model specific sections for engine electrical system service procedures

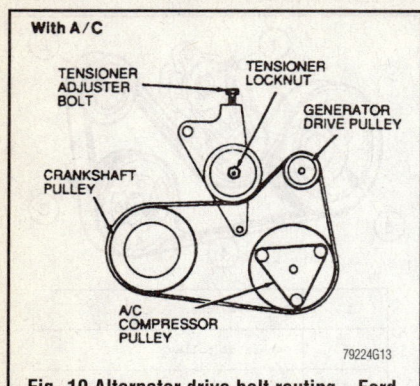

Fig. 19 Alternator drive belt routing—Ford Probe 2.5L (VIN B) engine with A/C

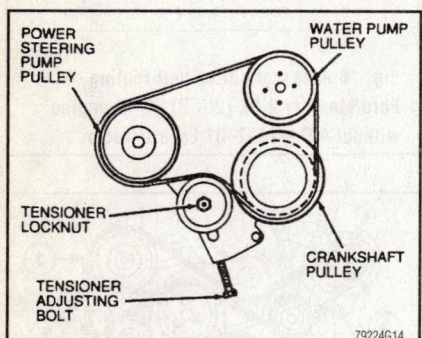

Fig. 20 Power steering and water pump drive belt routing —Ford Probe 2.5L (VIN B) engine

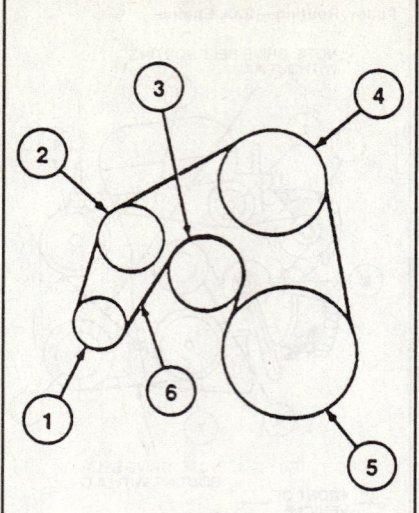

1. Alternator
2. Idler Pulley
3. Tensioner
4. Power Steering Pulley
5. Crankshaft Pulley
6. Drive Belt

Fig. 23 Accessory drive belt routing—Ford/Mercury 2.5L (VIN L) engine without A/C

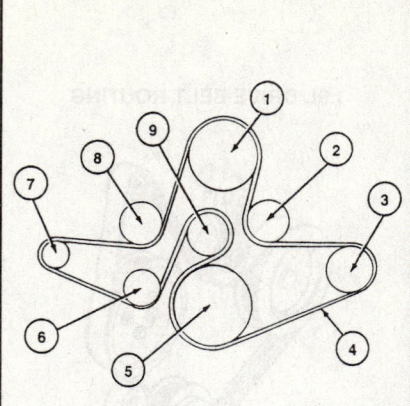

1. Power Steering Pump Pulley
2. Drive Belt Idler Pulley (RH)
3. A/C Compressor
4. Drive Belt
5. Crankshaft Pulley
6. Drive Belt Tensioner
7. Alternator
8. Drive Belt Idler Pulley (LH)
9. Drive Belt Idler Pulley (Center)

Fig. 26 Serpentine accessory drive belt routing—Ford 3.4L SHO engine

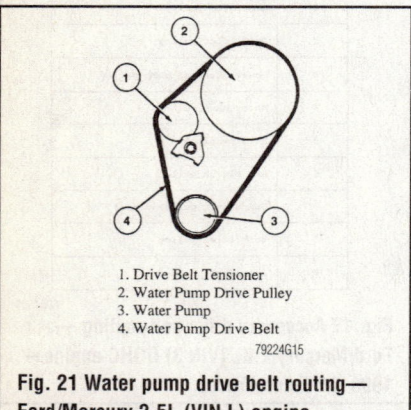

1. Drive Belt Tensioner
2. Water Pump Drive Pulley
3. Water Pump
4. Water Pump Drive Belt

Fig. 21 Water pump drive belt routing—Ford/Mercury 2.5L (VIN L) engine

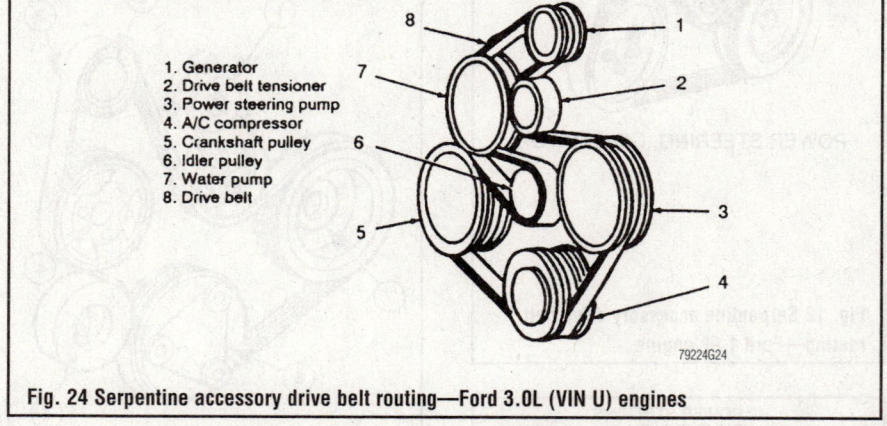

1. Generator
2. Drive belt tensioner
3. Power steering pump
4. A/C compressor
5. Crankshaft pulley
6. Idler pulley
7. Water pump
8. Drive belt

Fig. 24 Serpentine accessory drive belt routing—Ford 3.0L (VIN U) engines

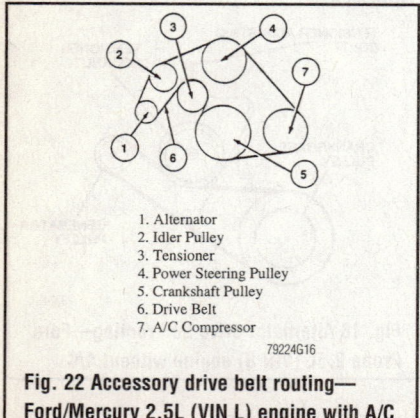

1. Alternator
2. Idler Pulley
3. Tensioner
4. Power Steering Pulley
5. Crankshaft Pulley
6. Drive Belt
7. A/C Compressor

Fig. 22 Accessory drive belt routing—Ford/Mercury 2.5L (VIN L) engine with A/C

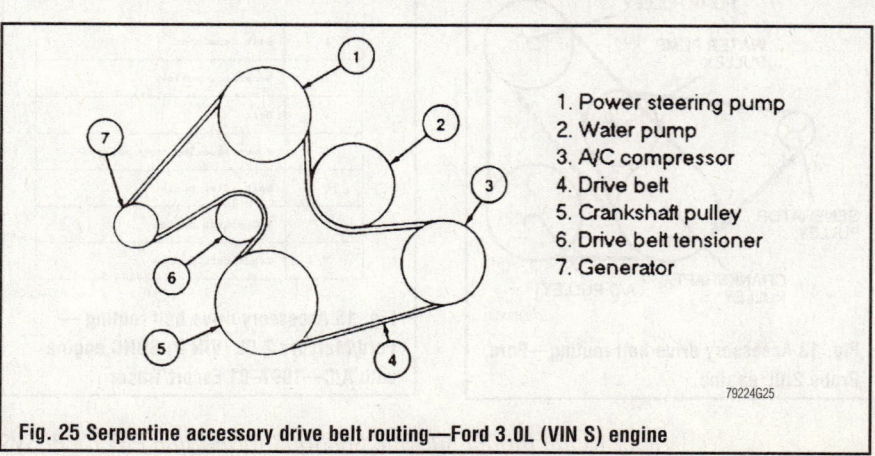

1. Power steering pump
2. Water pump
3. A/C compressor
4. Drive belt
5. Crankshaft pulley
6. Drive belt tensioner
7. Generator

Fig. 25 Serpentine accessory drive belt routing—Ford 3.0L (VIN S) engine

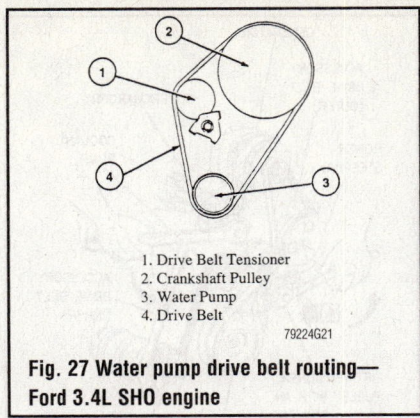

1. Drive Belt Tensioner
2. Crankshaft Pulley
3. Water Pump
4. Drive Belt

79224G21

Fig. 27 Water pump drive belt routing—Ford 3.4L SHO engine

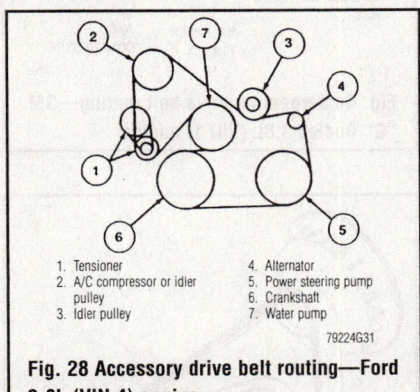

1. Tensioner
2. A/C compressor or idler pulley
3. Idler pulley
4. Alternator
5. Power steering pump
6. Crankshaft
7. Water pump

79224G31

Fig. 28 Accessory drive belt routing—Ford 3.8L (VIN 4) engine

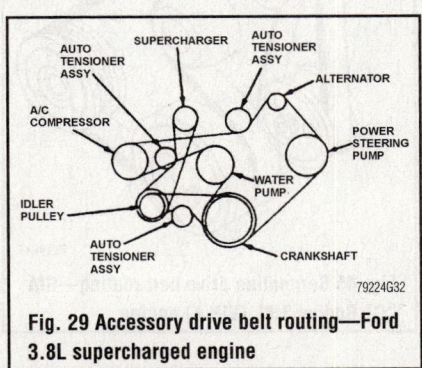

79224G32

Fig. 29 Accessory drive belt routing—Ford 3.8L supercharged engine

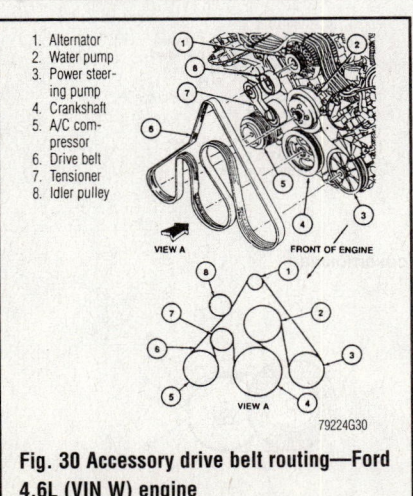

1. Alternator
2. Water pump
3. Power steering pump
4. Crankshaft
5. A/C compressor
6. Drive belt
7. Tensioner
8. Idler pulley

79224G30

Fig. 30 Accessory drive belt routing—Ford 4.6L (VIN W) engine

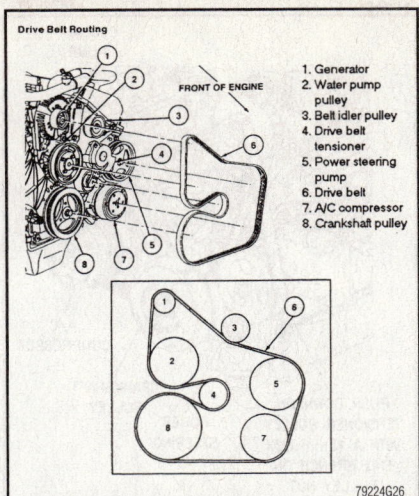

Drive Belt Routing

1. Generator
2. Water pump pulley
3. Belt idler pulley
4. Drive belt tensioner
5. Power steering pump
6. Drive belt
7. A/C compressor
8. Crankshaft pulley

79224G26

Fig. 31 Serpentine accessory drive belt routing— 4.6L (VIN V) engine—1999–01 Mustang and Lincoln Continental

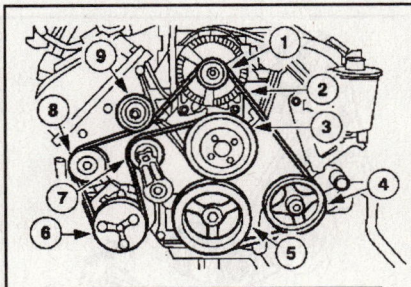

1	Generator pulley
2	Drive belt
3	Water pump pulley
4	Power steering pump pulley
5	Crankshaft vibration damper
6	A/C clutch pulley
7	Drive belt tensioner
8	Belt idler pulley
9	Belt idler pulley

93004G06

Fig. 32 Accessory drive belt routing—Ford 4.6L (VIN X) engine—1999–01 Mustang

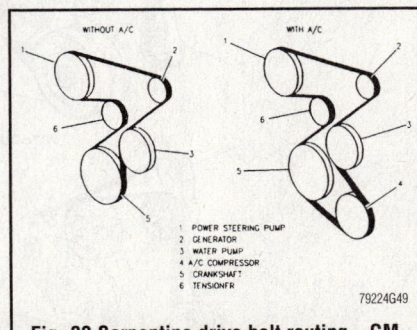

1. POWER STEERING PUMP
2. GENERATOR
3. WATER PUMP
4. A/C COMPRESSOR
5. CRANKSHAFT
6. TENSIONER

79224G49

Fig. 33 Serpentine drive belt routing—GM 1997 2.2L engine

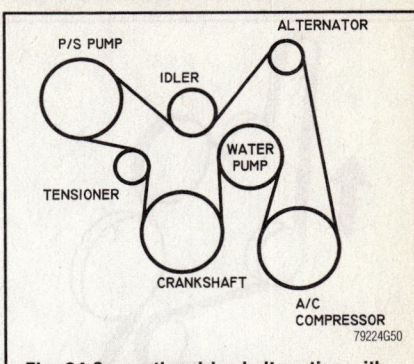

79224G50

Fig. 34 Serpentine drive belt routing with A/C—GM 1998–01 2.2L engine

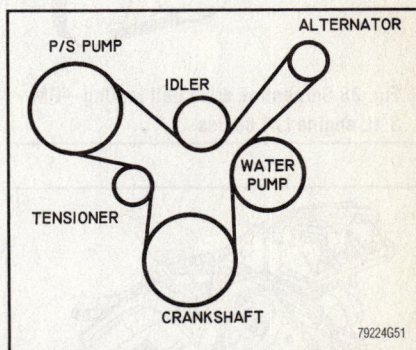

79224G51

Fig. 35 Serpentine drive belt routing without A/C—GM 1998–01 2.2L engine

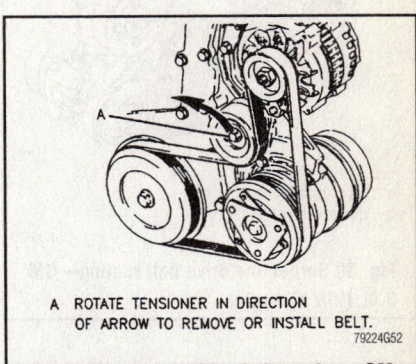

A ROTATE TENSIONER IN DIRECTION OF ARROW TO REMOVE OR INSTALL BELT.

79224G52

Fig. 36 Serpentine drive belt routing—GM 2.4L engine

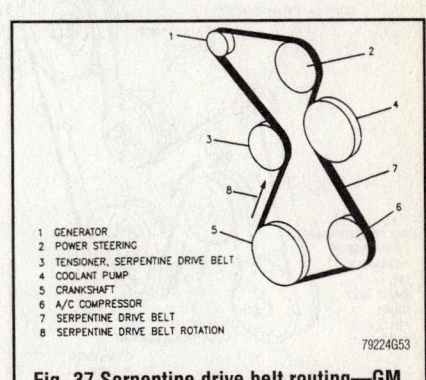

1 GENERATOR
2 POWER STEERING
3 TENSIONER, SERPENTINE DRIVE BELT
4 COOLANT PUMP
5 CRANKSHAFT
6 A/C COMPRESSOR
7 SERPENTINE DRIVE BELT
8 SERPENTINE DRIVE BELT ROTATION

79224G53

Fig. 37 Serpentine drive belt routing—GM 3.1L engine except L/N bodies

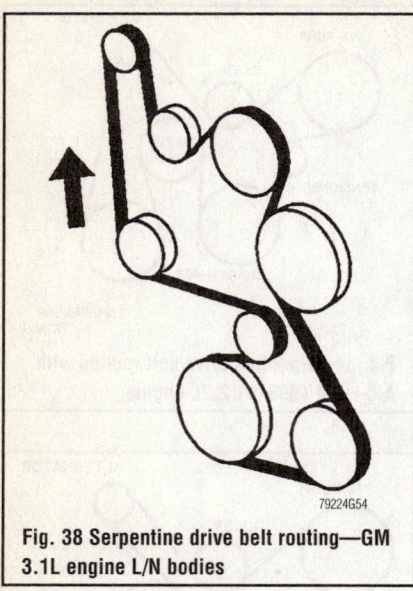

Fig. 38 Serpentine drive belt routing—GM 3.1L engine L/N bodies

79224G54

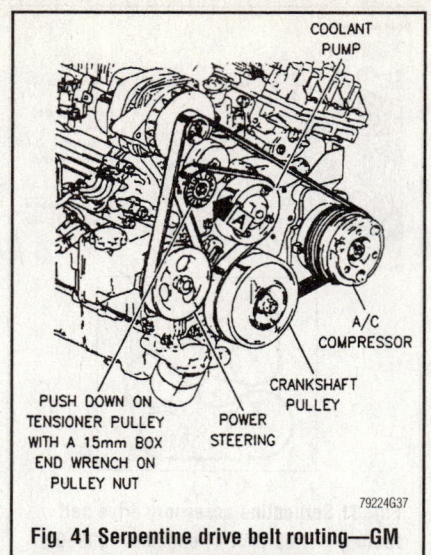

COOLANT PUMP

A/C COMPRESSOR

CRANKSHAFT PULLEY

POWER STEERING

PUSH DOWN ON TENSIONER PULLEY WITH A 15mm BOX END WRENCH ON PULLEY NUT

Fig. 41 Serpentine drive belt routing—GM "C and H" Bodies 3.8L (VIN K) engine

79224G37

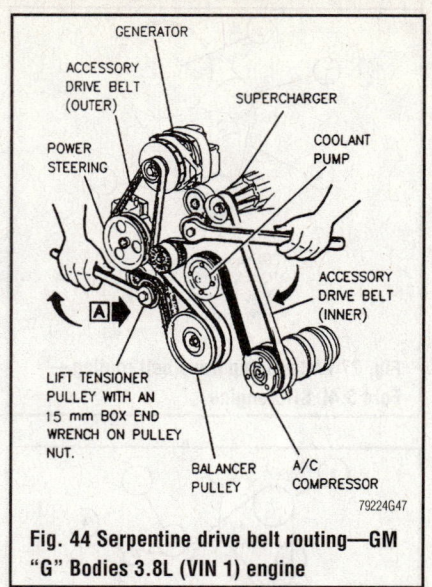

GENERATOR

ACCESSORY DRIVE BELT (OUTER)

SUPERCHARGER

POWER STEERING

COOLANT PUMP

ACCESSORY DRIVE BELT (INNER)

LIFT TENSIONER PULLEY WITH AN 15 mm BOX END WRENCH ON PULLEY NUT.

BALANCER PULLEY

A/C COMPRESSOR

Fig. 44 Serpentine drive belt routing—GM "G" Bodies 3.8L (VIN 1) engine

79224G47

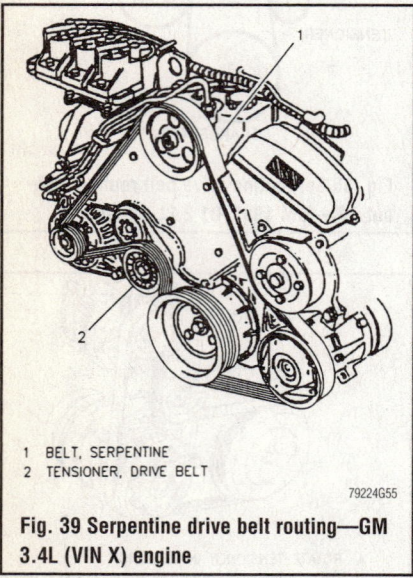

1 BELT, SERPENTINE
2 TENSIONER, DRIVE BELT

79224G55

Fig. 39 Serpentine drive belt routing—GM 3.4L (VIN X) engine

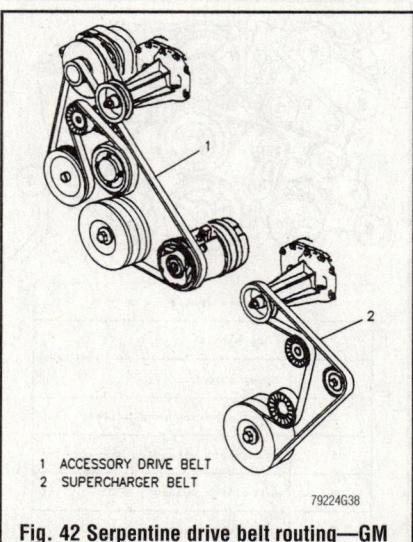

1 ACCESSORY DRIVE BELT
2 SUPERCHARGER BELT

79224G38

Fig. 42 Serpentine drive belt routing—GM "C and H" Bodies 3.8L (VIN 1) engine

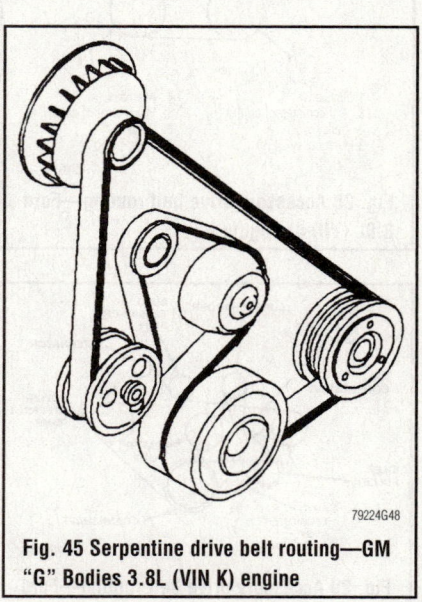

79224G48

Fig. 45 Serpentine drive belt routing—GM "G" Bodies 3.8L (VIN K) engine

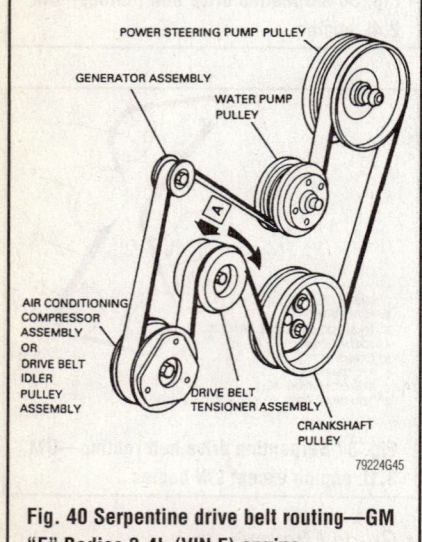

POWER STEERING PUMP PULLEY

GENERATOR ASSEMBLY

WATER PUMP PULLEY

AIR CONDITIONING COMPRESSOR ASSEMBLY OR DRIVE BELT IDLER PULLEY ASSEMBLY

DRIVE BELT TENSIONER ASSEMBLY

CRANKSHAFT PULLEY

79224G45

Fig. 40 Serpentine drive belt routing—GM "F" Bodies 3.4L (VIN E) engine

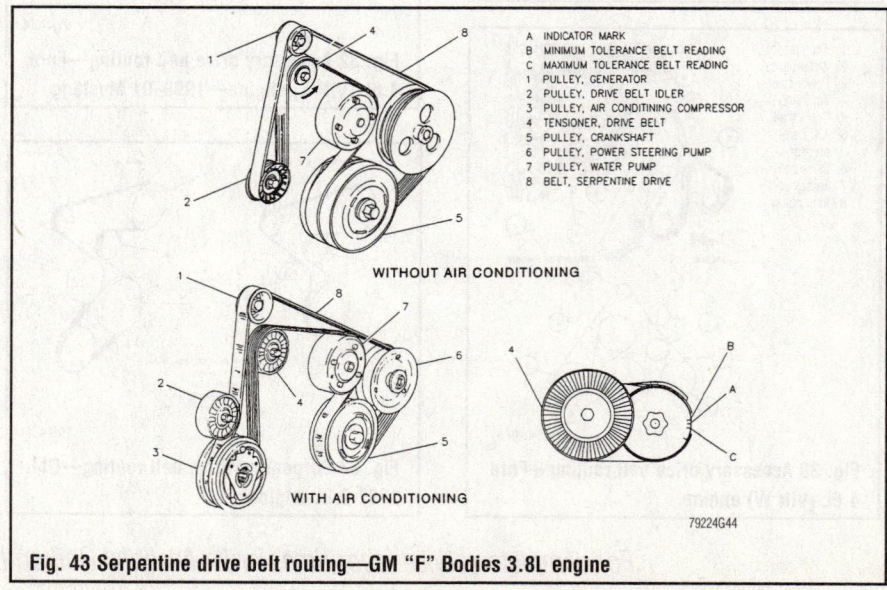

A INDICATOR MARK
B MINIMUM TOLERANCE BELT READING
C MAXIMUM TOLERANCE BELT READING
1 PULLEY, GENERATOR
2 PULLEY, DRIVE BELT IDLER
3 PULLEY, AIR CONDITINING COMPRESSOR
4 TENSIONER, DRIVE BELT
5 PULLEY, CRANKSHAFT
6 PULLEY, POWER STEERING PUMP
7 PULLEY, WATER PUMP
8 BELT, SERPENTINE DRIVE

WITHOUT AIR CONDITIONING

WITH AIR CONDITIONING

79224G44

Fig. 43 Serpentine drive belt routing—GM "F" Bodies 3.8L engine

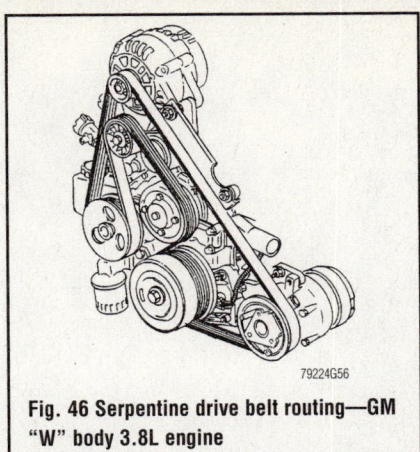

Fig. 46 Serpentine drive belt routing—GM "W" body 3.8L engine

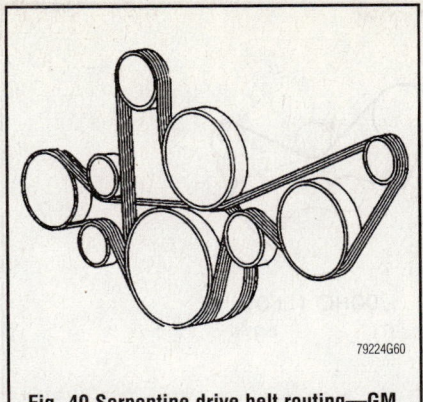

Fig. 49 Serpentine drive belt routing—GM 5.7L (VIN G) engine

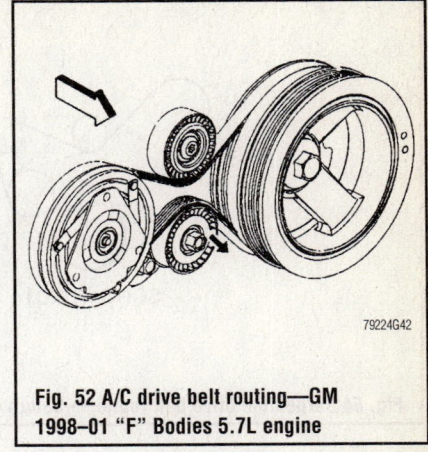

Fig. 52 A/C drive belt routing—GM 1998–01 "F" Bodies 5.7L engine

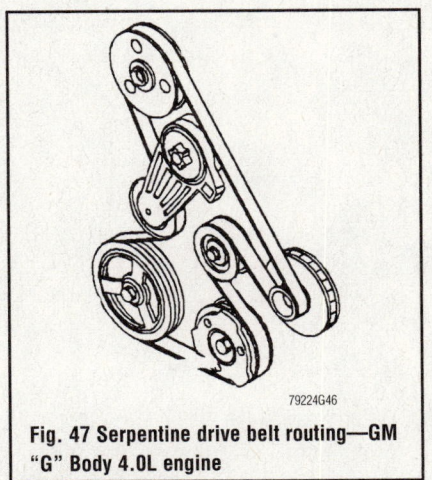

Fig. 47 Serpentine drive belt routing—GM "G" Body 4.0L engine

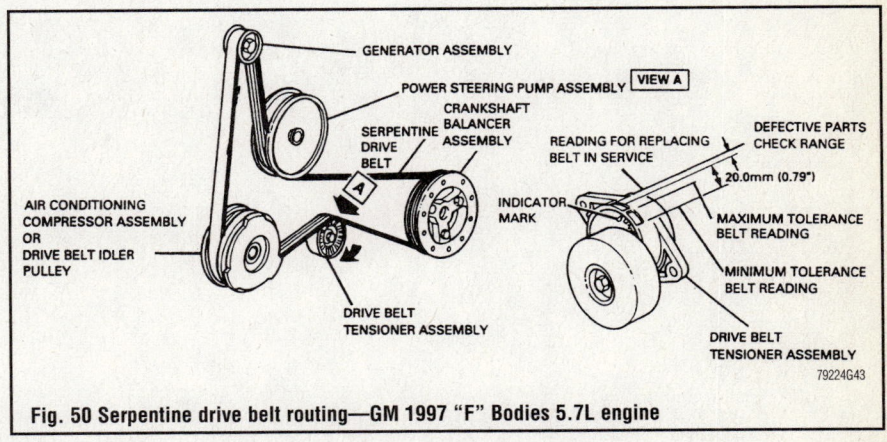

Fig. 50 Serpentine drive belt routing—GM 1997 "F" Bodies 5.7L engine

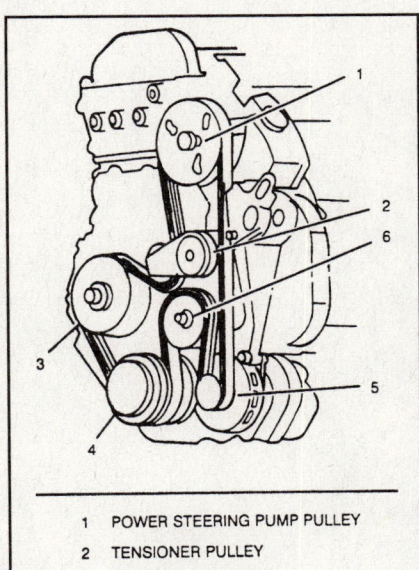

1 POWER STEERING PUMP PULLEY
2 TENSIONER PULLEY
3 CRANKSHAFT PULLEY
4 A/C COMPRESSOR PULLEY
5 GENERATOR PULLEY
6 IDLER PULLEY

Fig. 48 Serpentine drive belt routing—GM "E and K" Bodies 4.6L engine

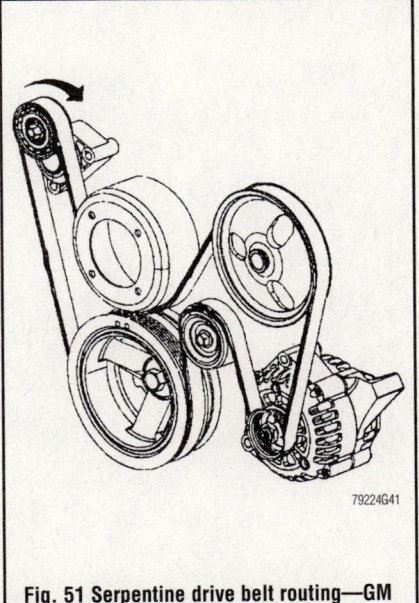

Fig. 51 Serpentine drive belt routing—GM 1998–01 "F" Bodies 5.7L engine

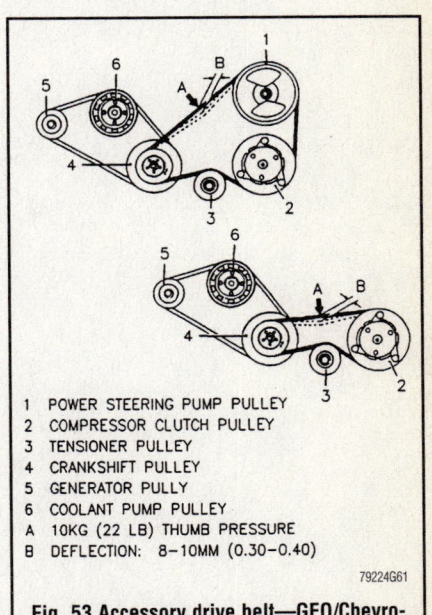

1 POWER STEERING PUMP PULLEY
2 COMPRESSOR CLUTCH PULLEY
3 TENSIONER PULLEY
4 CRANKSHIFT PULLEY
5 GENERATOR PULLY
6 COOLANT PUMP PULLEY
A 10KG (22 LB) THUMB PRESSURE
B DEFLECTION: 8–10MM (0.30–0.40)

Fig. 53 Accessory drive belt—GEO/Chevrolet engines

Ignition system service is covered in the model specific sections of this manual

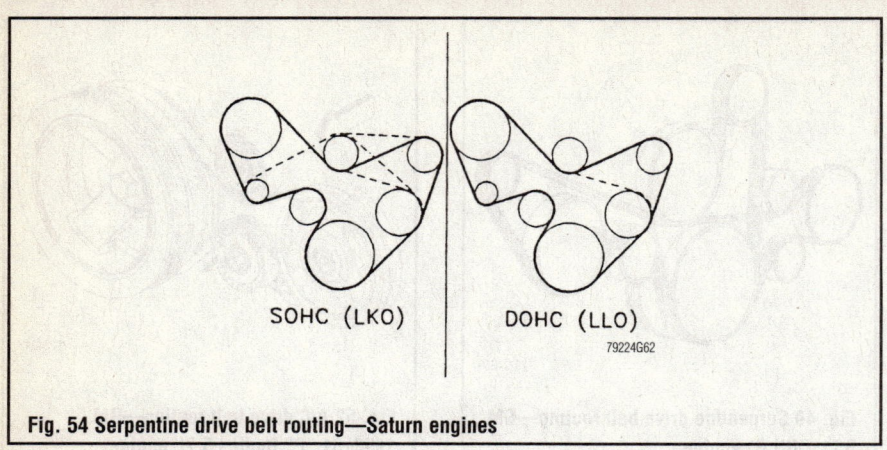

SOHC (LKO)　　DOHC (LLO)

79224G62

Fig. 54 Serpentine drive belt routing—Saturn engines

TIMING BELTS

GENERAL INFORMATION

Timing belts are typically only used on overhead camshaft engines. Timing belts are used to synchronize the crankshaft with the camshaft, similar to a timing chain on an overhead valve (pushrod) engine. Unlike a timing belt, a timing chain will normally last the life of the engine without needing service or replacement. Timing belts use raised teeth to mesh with sprockets to operate the valvetrain of an overhead camshaft engine.

Whenever a vehicle with an unknown service history comes into your repair facility or is recently purchased, here are some points that should be asked to help prevent costly engine damage:

• Does the owner know if or when the belt was replaced?

• If the vehicle purchased is used or the condition and mileage of the last timing belt replacement are unknown, it is recommended to inspect, replace or at least inform the owner that the vehicle is equipped with a timing belt.

• Note the mileage of the vehicle. The average replacement interval for a timing belt is approximately 60,000 miles (96,000 km).

Interference Engines

Engines, chain- or belt-driven, can be classified as either free-running or interference, depending on what would happen if the piston-to-valve timing is disrupted. A free-running engine is designed with enough clearance between the pistons and valves to allow the crankshaft to rotate (pistons still moving) while the camshaft stays in one position (several valves fully open). If this condition occurs normally, no internal engine damage will result. In an interference engine, there is not enough clearance between the pistons and valves to allow the crankshaft to turn without the camshaft being in time.

An interference engine can suffer extensive internal damage if a timing belt fails. The piston design does not allow clearance for the valve to be fully open and the piston to be at the top of its stroke. If the belt fails, the piston will collide with the valve and will bend or break the valve, damage the piston, and/or bend a connecting rod. When this type of failure occurs, the engine will need to be replaced or disassembled for further internal inspection; either choice costing many times that of replacing the timing belt.

TIMING BELT SERVICE

Inspection

→For manufacturer's recommended service interval, refer to the maintenance interval chart located in this manual.

The average replacement interval for a timing belt is approximately 60,000 miles (96,000km). If, however, the timing belt is inspected earlier or more frequently than suggested, and shows signs of wear or defects, the belt should be replaced at that time.

✳✳ WARNING

Never allow antifreeze, oil or solvents to come into with a timing belt. If this occurs immediately wash the solution from the timing belt. Also, never excessive bend or twist the timing belt; this can damage the belt so that its lifetime is severely shortened.

Never bend or twist a timing belt excessively, and do not allow solvents, antifreeze, gasoline, acid or oil to come into contact with the belt

Inspect both sides of the timing belt. Replace the belt with a new one if any of the following conditions exist:
- Hardening of the rubber—back side is glossy without resilience and leaves no indentation when pressed with a fingernail
- Cracks on the rubber backing
- Cracks or peeling of the canvas backing
- Cracks on rib root
- Cracks on belt sides
- Missing teeth or chunks of teeth
- Abnormal wear of belt sides—the sides are normal if they are sharp, as if cut by a knife.

If none of these conditions exist, the belt does not need replacement unless it is at the recommended interval. The belt MUST be replaced at the recommended interval.

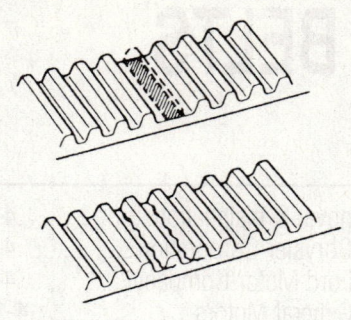

Broken tooth may be due to a damaged pulley

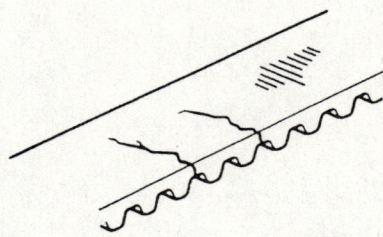

Back surface worn or cracked from a possible overheated engine or interference with the belt cover

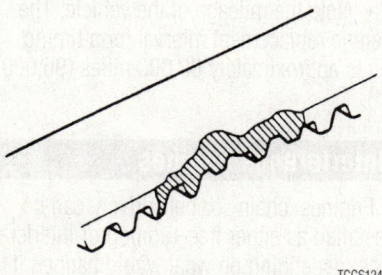

Side wear from improper installation

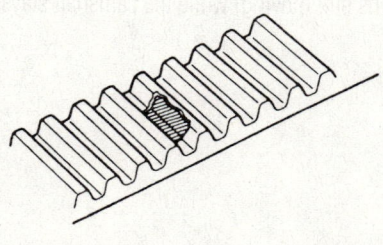

Worn teeth from excessive belt tension, camshaft or distributor not turning properly or fluid leaking on the belt

✳✳ WARNING

On interference engines, it is very important to replace the timing belt at the recommended intervals, otherwise expensive engine damage will likely result if the belt fails.

Removal & Installation

CHRYSLER CORPORATION

2.0L (VIN C) SOHC Engine

1. On Cirrus, Stratus, Breeze, and Sebring Convertible models, disconnect the negative battery cable from the left strut tower. The ground cable is equipped with a insulator grommet which should be placed on the stud to prevent the negative battery cable from accidentally grounding.
2. On Neon models, disconnect the negative battery cable.
3. Remove the drive belts and accessories.
4. Remove the right inner splashshield.
5. Remove the crankshaft damper.
6. Remove the right engine mount.
7. Place a support under the engine.
8. Remove the engine mount bracket.
9. Remove the timing belt cover.
10. Loosen the timing belt tensioner bolts.
11. Remove the timing belt and the tensioner.

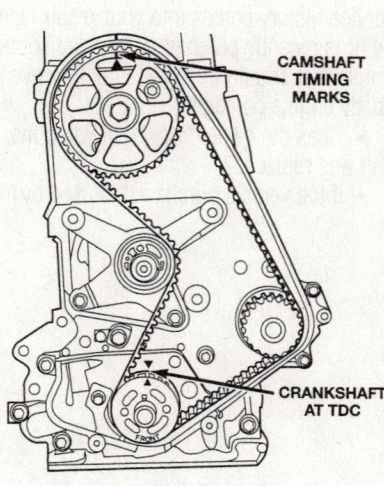

TDC alignment for timing belt installation—2.0L (VIN C) SOHC Engine

➡**When tensioner is removed from the engine it is necessary to compress the plunger into the tensioner body.**

12. Place the tensioner in a soft-jawed vise to compress the tensioner.

13. After compressing the tensioner place a pin (a ⁵⁄₆₄ in. Allen wrench will work) into the plunger side hole to retain the plunger until installation.

To install:

14. Set the crankshaft sprocket to Top Dead Center (TDC) by aligning the notch on the sprocket with the arrow on the oil pump housing, then back off the sprocket three notches before TDC.

15. Set the camshaft to align the timing marks.

16. Move the crankshaft to ½ notch before TDC.

17. Install the timing belt starting at the crankshaft, around the water pump, then around the camshaft last.

18. Move the crankshaft to TDC to take up the belt slack.

19. Reinstall the tensioner to the block but do not tighten it.

20. Using a torque wrench apply 250 inch lbs. (28 Nm) of torque to the tensioner pulley.

21. With torque being applied to the tensioner pulley, move the tensioner up against the tensioner bracket and tighten the fasteners to 275 inch lbs. (31 Nm).

22. Remove the tensioner plunger pin, the tension is correct when the plunger pin can be removed and replaced easily.

23. Rotate the crankshaft two revolutions and recheck the timing marks.

24. Reinstall the timing belt cover.

25. Reinstall the engine mount bracket.

26. Reinstall the right engine mount.

27. Remove the engine support.

28. Reinstall the crankshaft damper and tighten to 105 ft. lbs. (142 Nm).

29. Reinstall the drive belts and accessories.

30. Reinstall the right inner splashshield.

31. Perform the crankshaft and camshaft relearn alignment procedure using the DRB scan tool or equivalent.

2.0L (VIN F) Engine

1. Disconnect the negative battery cable.

2. Remove the engine undercover.

3. Remove the engine mount bracket.

4. Remove the drive belts.

5. Remove the belt tensioner pulley.

6. Remove the water pump pulleys.

7. Remove the crankshaft pulley.

8. Remove the stud bolt from the engine support bracket and remove the timing belt covers.

9. Rotate the crankshaft clockwise to align the camshaft timing marks. Always turn the crankshaft in the forward direction only.

10. Loosen the tension pulley center bolt.

➡**If the timing belt is to be reused, mark the direction of rotation on the flat side of the belt with an arrow.**

11. Move the tension pulley towards the water pump and remove the timing belt.

12. Remove the crankshaft sprocket center bolt using special tool MB990767 to hold the crankshaft sprocket while removing the center bolt. Then, use MB998778 puller to remove the sprocket.

13. Mark the direction of rotation on the timing belt "B" with an arrow.

14. Loosen the center bolt on the tensioner and remove the belt.

15. To remove the camshaft sprocket, remove the cylinder head cover. Use a wrench to hold the hexagonal part of the camshaft and remove the sprocket mounting bolt.

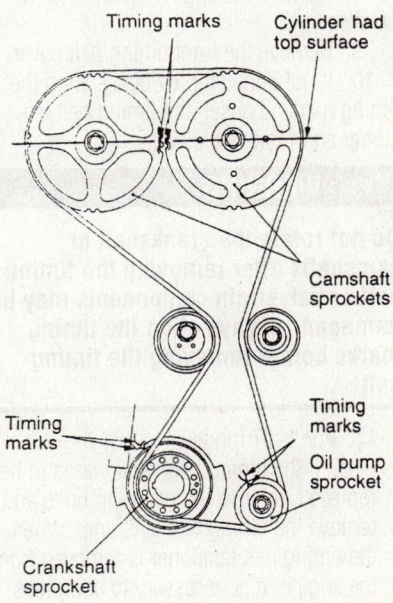

Notice the timing mark on the oil pump drive sprocket—Chrysler 2.0L (VIN F) engines

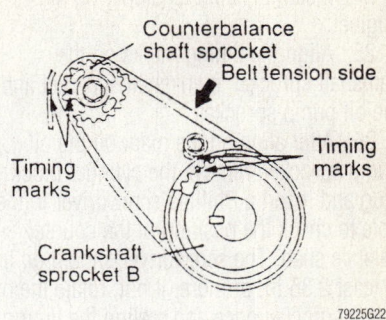

Timing belt "B" timing marks locations—Chrysler 2.0L (VIN F) engines

° **✳✳ WARNING**

Do not rotate the camshafts or the crankshaft while the timing belt is removed.

To install:

16. Use a wrench to hold the camshaft, then install the sprocket and mounting bolt. Tighten the bolt(s) to 65 ft. lbs. (88 Nm).

17. Install the cylinder head cover.

18. Place the crankshaft sprocket on the crankshaft. Use tool MB990767 to hold the crankshaft sprocket while tightening the center bolt. Tighten the center bolt to 80–94 ft. lbs. (108–127 Nm).

19. Align the timing marks on the crankshaft sprocket "B" and the balance shaft.

20. Install timing belt "B" on the sprockets. Position the center of the tensioner pulley to the left and above the center of the mounting bolt.

21. Push the pulley clockwise toward the crankshaft to apply tension to the belt and tighten the mounting bolt to 14 ft. lbs. (19 Nm). Do not let the pulley turn when tightening the bolt because it will cause excessive tension on the belt. The belt should deflect 0.20–0.28 in. (5–7mm) when finger pressure is applied between the pulleys.

22. Install the crankshaft sensing blade and the crankshaft sprocket. Apply engine oil to the mounting bolt and tighten the bolt to 80–94 ft. lbs. (108–127 Nm).

23. Use a press or vise to compress the auto tensioner pushrod. Insert a set pin when the holes are aligned.

✳✳ WARNING

Do not compress the pushrod too quickly, damage to the pushrod can occur.

24. Install the auto tensioner on the engine.

25. Align the timing marks on the camshaft sprocket, crankshaft sprocket and the oil pump sprocket.

26. After aligning the mark on the oil pump sprocket, remove the cylinder block plug and insert a Phillips screwdriver in the hole to check the position of the counter balance shaft. The screwdriver should go in at least 2.36 in. or more. If not, rotate the oil pump sprocket once and realign the timing mark so the screwdriver goes in. Do not remove the screwdriver until the timing belt is installed.

27. Install the timing belt on the intake camshaft and secure it with a clip.

28. Install the timing belt on the exhaust camshaft. Align the timing marks with the cylinder head top surface using two wrenches. Secure the belt with another clip.

29. Install the belt around the idler pulley, oil pump sprocket, crankshaft sprocket and the tensioner pulley.

30. Turn the tension pulley so the pinholes are at the bottom. Press the pulley lightly against the timing belt.

31. Screw the special tool into the left engine support bracket until it contacts the tensioner arm, then screw the tool in a little more and remove the pushrod pin from the auto tensioner. Remove the special tool and tighten the center bolt to 35 ft. lbs. (48 Nm).

32. Turn the crankshaft ¼ turn counterclockwise, then clockwise until the timing marks are aligned.

33. Loosen the center bolt. Install special tool MD998767 on the tension pulley. Turn the tension pulley counterclockwise with a torque of 2.6 ft. lbs. (3.5 Nm) and tighten the center bolt to 35 ft. lbs. (48 Nm). Do not let the tension pulley turn with the bolt.

34. Turn the crankshaft two revolutions to the right and align the timing marks. After 15 minutes, measure the protrusion of the pushrod on the auto tensioner. The standard measurement is 0.150–0.177 in. (3.8–4.5mm). If the protrusion is out of specification, loosen the tension pulley, apply the proper torque to the belt and retighten the center bolt.

35. Install the crankshaft pulley. Tighten the mounting bolts to 18 ft. lbs. (25 Nm).

36. Install the water pump. Tighten the mounting bolts to 6.5 ft. lbs. (8.8 Nm).

37. Install and adjust the drive belts.

38. Install the engine mount bracket.

39. Install the engine undercover.

40. Connect the negative battery cable.

2.0L (VIN Y) Engine

Valve timing is critical to engine operation. Use care when servicing the timing belt. There are a number of timing marks that must be properly aligned or engine damage will result. If the timing belt has not broken or jumped teeth, it is recommended that the crankshaft be turned by hand (clockwise) to Top Dead Center (TDC) No.1 cylinder compression stroke (firing position) before beginning work. This should align all the timing marks and serve as a reference for later work. Some technicians will apply a small amount of white paint to all timing marks. This helps make them more visible under the low-light conditions found underhood.

1. Disconnect the negative battery cable.

2. Remove the accessory drive belts.

3. Using C 3281 crankshaft holding tool, remove the crankshaft pulley center retaining bolt.

4. Using puller tools 1026 and 6827, remove the crankshaft pulley.

5. Remove the power steering pump from the bracket and position it aside. Do not disconnect the hoses.

6. Remove the power steering pump bracket from the engine.

7. Use a floor jack with a piece of wood on it and raise the engine to take the weight off of the engine mount.

8. Remove the engine mount and bracket.

9. Remove the front timing belt cover.

10. If not done so previously, align the timing marks. Loosen the timing belt tensioner and remove the belt.

✻✻ WARNING

Do not rotate the crankshaft or camshafts after removing the timing belt or valvetrain components may be damaged. Always align the timing marks before removing the timing belt.

11. For 1997 models:

a. If the timing belt tensioner is to be replaced, remove the retaining bolts and remove the timing belt tensioner. When the timing belt tensioner is removed from the engine, it is necessary to compress the plunger into the tensioner body.

b. Place the tensioner in a vise and slowly compress the plunger.

➡**Position the tensioner in the vise the same way it will be installed on the engine. This is to ensure proper pin**

orientation for when the tensioner is installed on the engine.

c. When the plunger is compressed into the tensioner body, install a pin through the body and plunger to hold the plunger in place until the tensioner is installed.

12. For 1998–01 models:

a. Place an 8mm Allen wrench into the belt tensioner, then using the long end of a ⅛ in. (3mm) Allen wrench, rotate the tensioner counterclockwise until it slides into the locking hole.

13. Remove the timing belt.

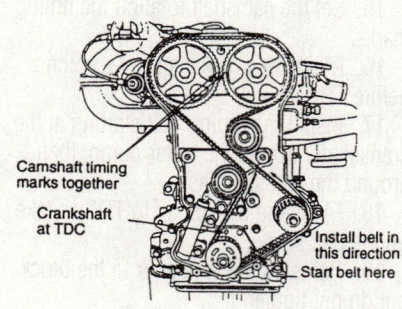

Install the timing belt by starting at the crankshaft sprocket and working around the other pulleys in a counterclockwise direction—Chrysler 2.0L (VIN Y) engine

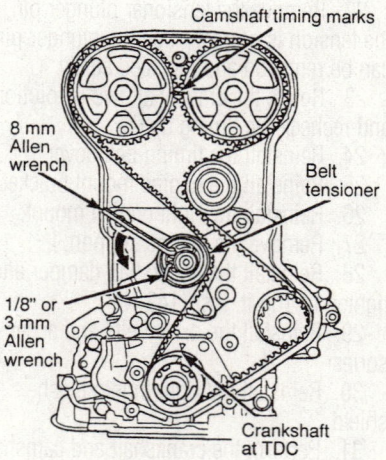

Wrench position for properly locking the tensioner on 1998–01 Chrysler 2.0L (VIN Y) engine

To install:

14. Check that all timing marks are still aligned. Bring the crankshaft sprocket to ½ a notch before TDC.

15. Install the timing belt. Starting at the crankshaft, route the belt around the water

pump sprocket, idler pulley, camshaft sprockets, then around the tensioner pulley.

16. Move the crankshaft to TDC to take up the slack in the belt. Install the tensioner to the block but do not tighten the retaining bolts.

17. For 1997 models:

a. Using a torque wrench on the tensioner pulley, apply 21 ft. lbs. (28 Nm) of torque to the pulley.

b. With the torque being applied to the tensioner pulley, move the tensioner up against the tensioner pulley bracket and tighten the retaining bolts to 23 ft. lbs. (31 Nm).

c. Remove the tensioner plunger pin. Pretension is correct when the pin can be removed and installed.

18. For 1998–01 models, remove the wrenches from the tensioner.

19. Rotate the crankshaft two revolutions and check the timing marks. If the timing marks are not properly aligned, remove the belt and reinstall it as described.

20. Install the front timing belt cover.

21. Lower the engine enough to install the engine mount bracket.

22. Install the bracket and remove the floor jack.

23. Install the power steering pump bracket and pump.

24. Install the crankshaft pulley using C-4685-C pulley installer.

25. Tighten the mounting bolt to 105 ft. lbs. (142 Nm).

26. Install the accessory drive belts.

27. Connect the negative battery cable.

28. Start the engine. Check for leaks and proper engine operation.

2.4L (VIN X) Engine

1. Disconnect the negative battery cable from the left strut tower. The ground cable is equipped with a insulator grommet which should be placed on the stud to prevent the negative battery cable from accidentally grounding.

2. Remove the right inner splash-shield.

3. Remove the accessory drive belts.

4. Remove the crankshaft damper.

5. Remove the right engine mount.

6. Place a suitable floor jack under the vehicle to support the engine.

7. Remove the engine mount bracket.

8. Remove the timing belt cover.

➡**Do not rotate the crankshaft or the camshafts after the timing belt has been removed. Damage to the valve components may occur. Before removing the timing belt, always align the timing marks.**

9. Align the timing marks of the timing belt sprockets to the timing marks on the rear timing belt cover and oil pump cover. Loosen the timing belt tensioner bolts.

10. Remove the timing belt and the tensioner.

11. Remove the camshaft timing belt sprockets.

12. Remove the crankshaft timing belt sprocket using special removal tool No. 6793.

13. Place the tensioner into a soft-jawed vise to compress the tensioner.

14. After compressing the tensioner, place a pin (a 5/64 in. Allen wrench will work) into the plunger side hole to retain the plunger until installation.

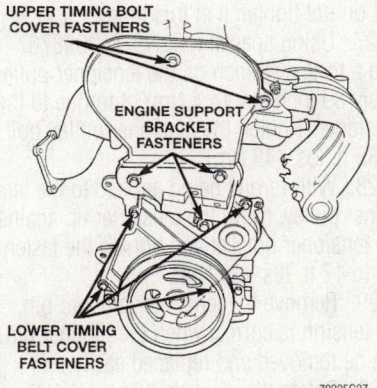

Timing belt cover bolt locations—2.4L (VIN X) Engine

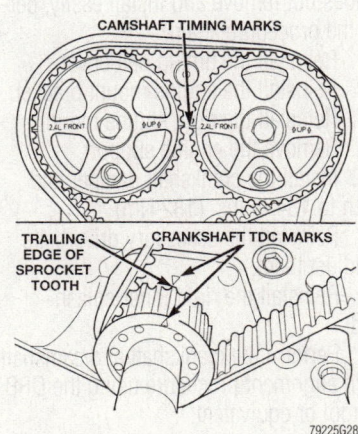

Crankshaft and camshaft alignment marks—2.4L (VIN X) Engine

To install:

15. Using special tool No. 6792, install the crankshaft timing belt sprocket onto the crankshaft.

16. Install the camshaft sprockets onto the camshafts. Install and tighten the camshaft sprocket bolts to 75 ft. lbs. (101 Nm).

17. Set the crankshaft sprocket to Top Dead Center (TDC) by aligning the notch on the sprocket with the arrow on the oil pump housing.

18. Set the camshafts to align the timing marks on the sprockets.

19. Move the crankshaft to ½ notch before TDC.

20. Install the timing belt starting at the crankshaft, then around the water pump sprocket, idler pulley, camshaft sprockets and the tensioner pulley.

21. Move the crankshaft sprocket to TDC to take up the belt slack.

22. Reinstall the tensioner to the block but do not tighten it at this time.

23. Using a torque wrench on the tensioner pulley, apply 250 inch lbs. (28 Nm) of torque to the tensioner pulley.

24. With torque being applied to the tensioner pulley, move the tensioner up against the tensioner pulley bracket and tighten the fasteners to 275 inch lbs. (31 Nm).

25. Remove the tensioner plunger pin, the tension is correct when the plunger pin can be removed and replaced easily.

26. Rotate the crankshaft two revolutions and recheck the timing marks. Wait several minutes, then recheck that the plunger pin can easily be removed and installed.

27. Reinstall the front timing belt cover.

28. Reinstall the engine mount bracket.

29. Reinstall the right engine mount.

30. Remove the floor jack from under the vehicle.

31. Install the crankshaft damper and tighten to 105 ft. lbs. (142 Nm).

32. Install and adjust the accessory drive belts.

33. Install the right inner splash-shield.

34. Reconnect the negative battery cable.

35. Perform the crankshaft and camshaft relearn alignment procedure using the DRB scan tool or equivalent.

2.5L (VIN H) Engine

1. Disconnect the negative battery cable from the left strut tower. The ground cable is equipped with a insulator grommet which should be placed on the stud to prevent the

negative battery cable from accidentally grounding.

2. Remove the right inner splash-shield.

3. Remove the accessory drive belts.

4. Remove the crankshaft damper.

5. Remove the right engine mount.

6. Place a suitable floor jack under the vehicle to support the engine.

7. Remove the right engine mount bracket.

8. Remove the timing belt upper left cover, upper right cover and lower cover.

9. Loosen the timing belt tensioner bolts.

➡**Before removing timing belt, be sure to align the sprocket timing marks to the timing marks on the rear timing belt cover.**

10. If the present timing belt is going to be reused, mark the running direction of the timing belt for installation. Remove the timing belt and the tensioner.

11. Remove the camshaft timing belt sprockets from the camshaft, if necessary.

12. Remove the crankshaft timing belt sprocket and key.

13. Place the tensioner into a soft-jawed vise to compress the tensioner.

14. After compressing the tensioner place a pin into the plunger side hole to retain the plunger until installation.

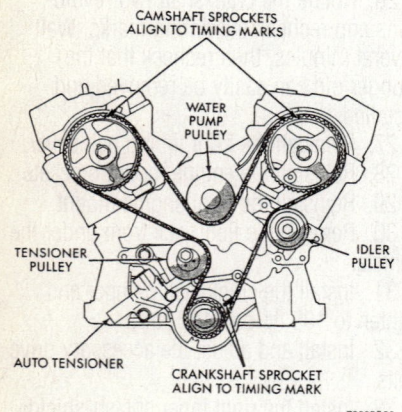

Timing belt engine sprocket timing—2.5L (VIN H) Engine

To install:

15. If removed, reinstall the camshaft sprockets onto the camshaft. Install the camshaft sprocket bolt and tighten to 65 ft. lbs. (88 Nm).

16. If removed, reinstall the crankshaft timing belt sprocket and key onto the crankshaft.

17. Set the crankshaft sprocket to Top

Dead Center (TDC) by aligning the notch on the sprocket with the arrow on the oil pump housing, then back off the sprocket three notches before TDC.

18. Set the camshafts to align the timing marks on the sprockets with the marks on the rear timing belt cover.

19. Install the belt on the rear camshaft sprocket first.

20. Install a binder clip on the belt to the sprocket so it won't slip out of position.

21. Keeping the belt taut, install it under the water pump pulley and around the front camshaft sprocket.

22. Install a binder on the front sprocket and belt.

23. Rotate the crankshaft to TDC.

24. Continue routing the belt by the idler pulley and around the crankshaft sprocket to the tensioner pulley.

25. Move the crankshaft sprocket clockwise to TDC to take up the belt slack. Check that all timing marks are in alignment.

26. Reinstall the tensioner to the block but do not tighten it at this time.

27. Using special tool No. MD998767 and a torque wrench on the tensioner pulley, apply 39 inch lbs. (4.4 Nm) of torque to tensioner. Tighten the tensioner pulley bolt to 35 ft. lbs. (48 Nm).

28. With torque being applied to the tensioner pulley, move the tensioner up against the tensioner bracket and tighten the fasteners to 17 ft. lbs. (23 Nm).

29. Remove the tensioner plunger pin, the tension is correct when the plunger pin can be removed and replaced easily.

30. Rotate the crankshaft two revolutions clockwise and recheck the timing marks. Check to be sure the tensioner plunger pin can be easily installed and removed. If the pin does not remove and install easily, perform the procedure again.

31. Reinstall the timing belt cover.

32. Reinstall the engine mount bracket.

33. Reinstall the right engine mount.

34. Remove the engine support.

35. Install the crankshaft damper and tighten to 134 ft. lbs. (182 Nm).

36. Reinstall the accessory drive belts and adjust them.

37. Reinstall the right inner splash-shield.

38. Perform the crankshaft and camshaft relearn alignment procedure using the DRB scan tool or equivalent.

2.5L (VIN N) Engine

1. Disconnect the negative battery cable.

2. Remove the accessory drive belts.

3. Using Crankshaft Holding Tools MB990767 and MB998754, remove the crankshaft bolt and remove the pulley.

4. Remove the heated oxygen sensor connection.

5. Remove the power steering pump with the hose attached and position it aside.

6. Remove the power steering pump bracket.

7. Place a floor jack under the engine oil pan, with a block of wood in between, and raise the engine so that the weight of the engine is no longer being applied to the engine support bracket.

8. Remove the upper engine mount. Spraying lubricant, slowly remove the reamer (alignment) bolt and remaining bolts and remove the engine support bracket.

➡**The reamer bolt is sometimes heat-seized on the engine support bracket.**

9. Remove the front timing belt covers.

10. If the timing belt is to be reused, draw an arrow indicating the direction of rotation on the back of the belt for reinstallation.

11. Align the timing marks by turning the crankshaft with MD998769 Crankshaft Turning tool. Loosen the center bolt on the timing belt tensioner pulley and remove the belt.

❄❄ WARNING

Do not rotate the crankshaft or camshaft after removing the timing belt or valvetrain components may be damaged. Always align the timing marks before removing the timing belt.

12. Check the belt tensioner for leaks and check the pushrod for cracks.

13. If the timing belt tensioner is to be replaced, remove the retaining bolts and remove the timing belt tensioner. When the timing belt tensioner is removed from the engine, it is necessary to compress the plunger into the tensioner body.

14. Place the tensioner in a vise and slowly compress the plunger. Take care not to damage the pushrod.

➡**Position the tensioner in the vise the same way it will be installed on the engine. This is to ensure proper pin orientation for when the tensioner is installed on the engine.**

15. When the plunger is compressed into the tensioner body, install a pin through the body and plunger to hold the plunger in place until the tensioner is installed.

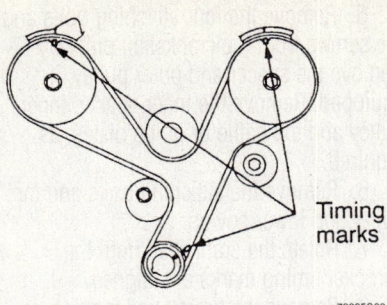

Camshaft and crankshaft alignment marks—Chrysler 2.5L (VIN N) engines

To install:

16. Install the timing belt tensioner and tighten the retaining bolts to 17 ft. lbs. (24 Nm), but do not remove the pin at this time.

17. Check that all timing marks are still aligned.

18. Use bulldog clips (large paper binder clips) or other suitable tool to secure the timing belt and to prevent it from slacking. Install the timing belt. Starting at the crankshaft, go around the idler pulley, then the front camshaft sprocket, the water pump pulley, the rear camshaft sprocket and the tensioner pulley.

19. Be sure the belt is tight between the crankshaft and front camshaft sprocket, between the camshaft sprockets and the water pump. Gently raise the tensioner pulley, so that the belt does not sag, and temporarily tighten the center bolt.

20. Move the crankshaft ¼ turn counterclockwise, then turn it clockwise to the position where the timing marks are aligned.

21. Loosen the center bolt of the tensioner pulley. Using MD998767 tensioner tool, and a torque wrench apply 3.3 ft. lbs. (4.4 Nm) tensional torque to the timing belt and tighten the center bolt to 35 ft. lbs. (48 Nm). When tightening the bolt, be sure that the tensioner pulley shaft does not rotate with the bolt.

22. Remove the tensioner plunger pin. Pretension is correct when the pin can be removed and installed easily. If the pin cannot be easily removed and installed it is still satisfactory as long as it is within its standard value.

23. Check that the tensioner pushrod is within the standard value. When the tensioner is engaged the pushrod should measure 0.149–0.177 in. (3.8–4.5mm).

24. Rotate the crankshaft two revolutions and check the timing marks. If the timing

marks are not properly aligned remove the belt and repeat Steps 17 through 23.

25. Install the timing belt covers.

26. Install the engine mounting bracket.

27. Lower the engine enough to install the engine mount onto bracket and remove the floor jack.

28. Install the power steering pump bracket and pump.

29. Install the crankshaft pulley and tighten the retaining bolt to 13 ft. lbs. (18 Nm).

30. Install the accessory drive belts.

31. Properly fill the cooling system.

32. Connect the negative battery cable.

33. Check for leaks and proper engine and cooling system operation.

3.2L (VIN J) and 3.5L (VIN F) Engines

Use care when servicing a timing belt. Valve timing is absolutely critical to engine performance. If the valve timing marks on all drive sprockets are not properly aligned, engine damage will result. If only the belt and tensioner are being serviced, do not loosen the camshaft drive sprockets unless they are to be replaced. The sprockets have oversized openings and can be rotated several degrees in each direction on their shafts. This means the sprockets must be retimed, requiring some special tools.

✳✳ CAUTION

Fuel injection systems remain under pressure, even after the engine has been turned off. The fuel system pressure must be relieved before disconnecting any fuel lines. Failure to do so may result in fire and/or personal injury.

1. Disconnect the negative battery cable.

2. Rotate the engine to Top Dead Center (TDC) on the compression stroke for cylinder No. 1.

3. Release the fuel system pressure using the recommended procedure.

4. Place a pan under the radiator and drain the coolant.

5. Remove the radiator and cooling fan assemblies.

6. Remove the accessory drive belts.

7. Remove the upper radiator hose.

8. Remove the crankshaft damper with a quality puller tool gripping the inside of the pulley.

9. Remove the stamped steel cover. Do not remove the sealer on the cover; it may be reusable.

10. Remove the left side cast cover. If necessary, remove the lower belt cover, located behind the crankshaft damper.

11. If the timing belt is to be reused, mark the timing belt with the running direction for installation.

12. Align the camshaft sprockets with the marks on the rear covers.

13. Remove the timing belt and tensioner.

14. If it is necessary to service the camshaft sprockets, use the following procedure:

   a. Hold the camshaft sprocket with a 36mm box end wrench, loosen and remove the sprocket retaining bolt and washer.

➡**To remove the camshaft sprocket retainer bolt while the engine is in the vehicle, it may be necessary to raise that side of the engine due to the length of the retainer bolt. The right bolt is 8⅜ in. (213mm) long, while the left bolt is 10 in. (254mm) long. These bolts are not interchangeable and their original location during removal should be noted.**

   b. Remove the camshaft sprocket from the camshaft. The camshaft sprockets are not interchangeable from side-to-side.

   c. Remove the crankshaft sprocket using Puller L-4407A.

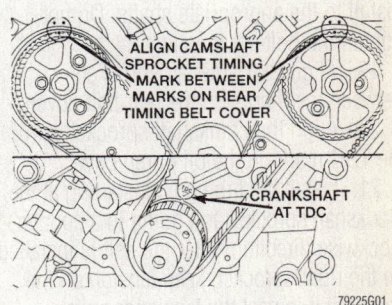

Timing belt alignment marks—Chrysler 3.2L and 3.5L engines

To install:

15. If it was necessary to remove the camshaft sprockets, use the following procedure:

➡**This procedure can only be used when the camshaft sprockets have been loosened or removed from the camshafts. Each sprocket has a D shaped hole that allows it to be rotated** several degrees in each direction on its shaft. **This design must be timed with the engine to ensure proper performance.**

a. Install the crankshaft sprocket, using tool C-4685-C1, thrust bearing, washer and 12mm bolt.

b. When the camshaft sprockets are loosened or removed, the camshafts must be timed to the engine. Install the Camshaft Alignment tools 6642-A, to the rear of the cylinder heads. These tools lock the camshafts in the proper position.

16. Preload the belt tensioner as follows:

a. Place the tensioner in a vise the same way it is mounted on the engine.

b. Slowly compress the plunger into the tensioner body.

c. When the plunger is compressed into the tensioner body, install a pin through the body and plunger to retain the plunger in place until the tensioner is installed.

17. Install both camshaft sprockets to the appropriate shafts. The left camshaft sprocket has the Distributorless Ignition System (DIS) pick-up as part of the sprocket.

➡**The right bolt is 8⅜ in. (213mm) long, while the left bolt is 10 in. (254mm) long. These bolts are not interchangeable.**

18. Apply Loctite® 271, to the threads of the camshaft sprocket retainer bolts and install to the appropriate shafts. Do not tighten the bolts at this time.

19. Align the camshaft sprockets between the marks on the rear belt covers.

20. Align the crankshaft sprocket with the TDC mark on the oil pump cover.

21. Install the timing belt, starting at the crankshaft sprocket and going in a counter-clockwise direction. After the belt is installed on the right sprocket, keep tension on the belt until it is past the tensioner pulley.

22. Holding the tensioner pulley against the belt, install the timing belt tensioner into the housing and tighten to 21 ft. lbs. (28 Nm).

23. When the tensioner is in place, pull the retainer pin out to allow tensioner to extend to the pulley bracket.

➡**Be sure that the timing marks on the cam sprockets are still between the marks on the rear cover.**

24. Remove the spark plug in the No.1 cylinder and install a dial indicator to check for TDC of the piston. Rotate the crankshaft until the piston is exactly at TDC.

25. Hold the camshaft sprocket hex with a 36mm wrench and tighten the right camshaft sprocket bolt to 75 ft. lbs. (102 Nm) plus an additional 90 degree turn. Tighten the left camshaft sprocket bolt to 85 ft. lbs. (115 Nm) plus an additional 90 degree turn.

26. Remove the dial indicator. Install the spark plug and tighten to 20 ft. lbs. (28 Nm).

27. Remove the camshaft alignment tools from the back of the cylinder heads and install the cam covers with new O-rings.

28. Tighten the fasteners to 20 ft. lbs. (27 Nm). Repeat this procedure on the other camshaft.

29. Rotate the crankshaft sprocket two revolutions and check for proper alignment of the timing marks on the camshaft and the crankshaft. If the timing marks do not align, repeat the procedure.

30. Before installing, inspect the sealer on the stamped steel cover. If some sealer is missing, use MOPAR Silicone Rubber Adhesive sealant to replace the missing sealer.

31. Install the lower belt cover behind the crankshaft damper, if necessary.

32. Install the stamped steel cover and the left side cast cover. Tighten the 6mm bolts to 105 inch lbs. (12 Nm), the 8mm bolts to 250 inch lbs. (28 Nm) and the 10mm bolts to 40 ft. lbs. (54 Nm).

33. Install the crankshaft damper using special tool L-4524, a 5.9 in. long bolt, thrust bearing and washer. Tighten the center bolt to 85 ft. lbs. (115 Nm).

34. Install the upper radiator hose.

35. Install the accessory drive belts and adjust them to the proper tension.

36. Install the radiator and cooling fan assemblies.

37. Refill and bleed the cooling system.

38. Connect the negative battery cable.

39. With the radiator cap off so coolant can be added, run the engine. Watch for leaks and listen for unusual engine noises.

FORD MOTOR COMPANY

1.3L (VIN H) Engine

1. Disconnect the negative battery cable.

2. Remove the accessory drive belts.

3. Remove the three water pump pulley attaching bolts and remove the water pump pulley.

4. Remove the right front wheel and tire assembly and the right inner fender panel.

5. Remove the four attaching bolts and the screws from the crankshaft pulley. Remove the spacer and outer pulley, if equipped. Remove the inner spacer, inner pulley and the baffle or guide plates, as required.

6. Remove the attaching bolts and the upper and lower covers.

7. Rotate the crankshaft until the sprocket timing marks are aligned.

8. Remove the timing belt tensioner spring, spring cover and timing belt tensioner bolt. Remove the timing belt.

➡**If the timing belt is to be reused, mark the direction of rotation on the belt, using a crayon, so the belt can be reinstalled in the same direction.**

9. If the camshaft sprocket requires removal, proceed as follows:

a. Hold the camshaft stationary with an open end wrench and remove the camshaft sprocket retaining bolt.

b. Pull the camshaft sprocket with the dowel pin off of the camshaft. Use care not to drop the dowel pin.

10. If the crankshaft sprocket requires removal, proceed as follows:

a. Remove the crankshaft pulley retaining bolt.

b. Pull the crankshaft pulley hub, sprocket and key from the crankshaft. Be sure not to drop the crankshaft key.

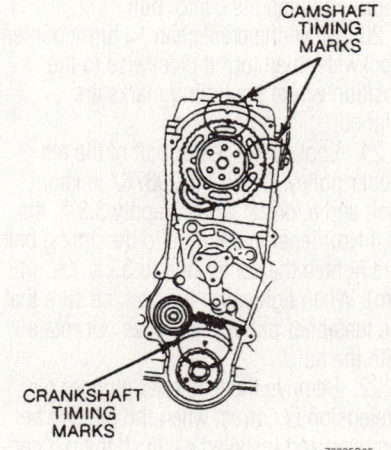

Before removing or installing the timing belt, be sure the crankshaft and both camshaft matchmarks are aligned as shown—Ford 1.3L (VIN H) engine

To install:

11. If removed, install the crankshaft sprocket as follows:

a. Install the sprocket with the key onto the crankshaft.

b. Install the crankshaft pulley hub.

c. Clean the threads of the crankshaft pulley bolt and coat with a non-hardening sealer.

d. Install the bolt and tighten to 80–85 ft. lbs. (108–118 Nm).

12. If removed, install the camshaft sprocket as follows:

a. Position the sprocket and dowel pin to the camshaft and install the retaining bolt.

b. Hold the camshaft stationary with an open end wrench and tighten the retaining bolt to 36–45 ft. lbs. (49–61 Nm).

13. Align the camshaft and crankshaft timing marks with the marks located on the cylinder head and oil pump housing.

14. If reusing the original timing belt, install the timing belt with the mark made indicating the direction of rotation.

15. Install the timing belt tensioner spring and cover on the tensioner. Position the tensioner and spring assembly on the engine and install the attaching bolt. Do not tighten the bolt at this time.

16. Rotate the crankshaft two turns in the direction of normal rotation and align the timing marks. Ensure all marks are still correctly aligned.

17. Reconnect the free end of the spring to the spring anchor. Tighten the tensioner bolt to 14–19 ft. lbs. (19–26 Nm).

18. Install the upper and lower covers. Install the attaching bolts and tighten to 71–97 inch lbs. (8–11 Nm).

19. Install the crankshaft pulley baffle with the curved lip facing outward or install the large guide plate, then the small guide plate, as required.

20. Install the inner pulley with the deep recess facing outward. Install the spacer, then the outer pulley, spacer and screws. Install the pulley bolts and tighten to 109–152 inch lbs. (12–17 Nm).

21. Install the inner fender panel.

22. Install the wheel and tire assembly. Tighten the lug bolts to 65–87 ft. lbs. (88–118 Nm).

23. Install the water pump pulley and tighten the bolts to 36–45 ft. lbs. (49–61 Nm).

24. Install the accessory drive belts.

25. Connect the negative battery cable.

26. Run the engine and check for proper operation.

1.8L (VIN 8) Engine

1. Disconnect the negative battery cable.

2. Remove the timing belt upper cover and gasket.

3. Remove the accessory drive belts.

4. Remove the water pump pulley bolts and remove the pulley.

5. Remove the right front wheel and tire assembly.

6. Remove the right upper and lower splash-shields.

7. Remove the timing belt middle and lower covers along with the gaskets.

8. Remove the crankshaft pulley hub bolt and hub.

9. Rotate the crankshaft and align the timing marks located on the camshaft sprockets and seal plate.

10. Check that the crankshaft sprocket and the oil pump are aligned.

➡️**If the timing belt is to be reused, mark an arrow on the belt to indicate it's rotational direction for installation reference.**

11. Loosen the timing belt tensioner bolt.

12. Turn the timing belt tensioner counterclockwise and hand-tighten the tensioner bolt to relieve the tension on the timing belt.

13. Remove the timing belt.

14. If the camshaft sprockets are to be removed, continue as follows:

a. Disconnect and tag the ignition wires and vacuum lines blocking the removal of the cylinder head cover.

b. Remove the cylinder head cover retaining bolts and remove the cover and gasket.

c. While holding the camshaft with a wrench, remove the camshaft sprocket retaining bolt.

d. Remove the camshaft sprocket.

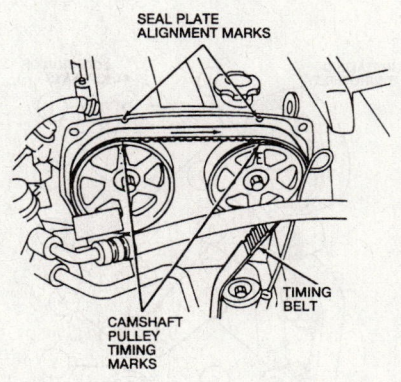

Camshaft timing alignment marks—Ford 1.8L (VIN 8) engines

79225G13

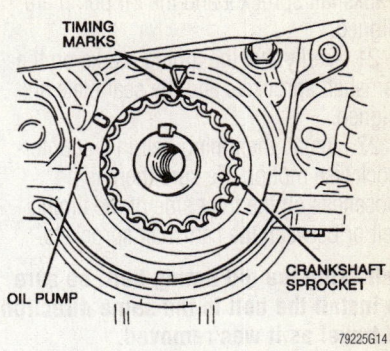

79225G14

Crankshaft timing mark position—Ford 1.8L (VIN 8) engines

e. If removing both camshaft sprockets, tag the sprockets for identification at reassembly.

15. If removing the crankshaft sprocket, remove the crankshaft pulley bolt and hub, if not already done. Slide the crankshaft sprocket off the crankshaft.

16. Inspect the timing belt tensioner and spring, replace if necessary.

To install:

17. If the crankshaft sprocket was removed, install the crankshaft key with the tapered end facing the oil pump. Install the crankshaft sprocket onto the crankshaft while making sure to match the alignment grooves.

18. If removed, install the camshaft sprockets as follows

a. Turn the camshaft until the dowel pins face straight up.

b. Install the camshaft sprocket with the **I** mark straight up for the intake camshaft or with the **E** mark straight up for the exhaust camshaft.

c. Align the camshaft sprockets with the timing marks on the seal plate.

d. While holding each camshaft with a wrench, install the camshaft sprocket retaining bolts. Tighten the bolts to 36–45 ft. lbs. (49–61 Nm).

e. Install a new cylinder head cover gasket onto the cylinder head.

f. Place the cylinder head cover into its mounting position and install the retaining bolts. Tighten the cylinder head cover bolts to 43–78 inch lbs. (4.9–8.8 Nm).

g. Install the ignition wires to the spark plugs and connect the vacuum hoses to the cylinder head cover.

19. Temporarily secure the timing belt tensioner in the far left position.

20. Verify that the timing marks on the

crankshaft sprocket and the oil pump are aligned.

21. Verify that the timing marks on the camshaft sprockets and the seal plate are aligned.

22. Install the timing belt in a counter-clockwise motion. Be sure there is no looseness on the idler side of the timing belt or between the camshaft sprockets.

➡ **If using the old timing belt, be sure to install the belt in the same direction of travel as it was removed.**

23. Loosen the timing belt tensioner bolt. Allow the tensioner spring to apply tension to the timing belt.

24. Rotate the crankshaft 1⅝ turns clockwise and align the timing belt pulley mark with the tension set mark which is located at approximately the 10 o'clock position.

25. Turn the crankshaft two turns clockwise and align the crankshaft sprocket with the tension set mark on the oil pump.

26. Verify that all timing marks are aligned. If not, remove the timing belt and repeat the installation procedures.

27. Apply tension to the timing belt tensioner and tighten the tensioner lockbolt to 27–38 ft. lbs. (37–52 Nm).

28. Rotate the crankshaft 2⅙ (780 degrees) turns clockwise and verify that the camshaft and crankshaft timing marks are aligned.

29. Measure the timing belt deflection by applying 22 lbs. (98 N) of pressure on the timing belt between the camshaft sprockets. The timing belt deflection should be 0.35–0.45 in. (9–11.5mm). If necessary to adjust the timing belt deflection, rotate the crankshaft two turns clockwise and ensure that the timing marks are still aligned. If the timing marks are not aligned, repeat the installation procedure.

30. Install the crankshaft pulley hub and tighten the retaining bolt to 80–87 ft. lbs. (108–118 Nm).

31. Install the crankshaft pulley and washer. Install the retaining bolts and tighten to 109–152 inch lbs. (12–17 Nm).

32. Install the timing belt middle and lower covers with the gaskets. Tighten the middle and lower timing belt cover retaining bolts to 65–95 inch lbs. (7.8–11 Nm).

33. Install the power steering drive belt.

34. Install the water pump pulley and retaining bolts. Tighten the bolts to 69–95 inch lbs. (7.8–11.0 Nm).

35. Install the alternator/water pump drive belt.

36. Install the splash-shields. Tighten the bolts to 69–95 inch lbs. (7.8–11.0 Nm).

37. Install the right wheel and tire assembly. Tighten the lug nuts to 65–87 ft. lbs. (88–118 Nm).

38. Install the timing belt upper cover and gasket. Tighten the bolts to 69–95 inch lbs. (7.8–11.0 Nm).

39. Connect the negative battery cable.

40. Run the engine and check for leaks.

41. Road test the vehicle and check for proper engine operation.

1.9L (VIN J) Engine

1. Disconnect the negative battery cable.

2. Remove the accessory drive belt automatic tensioner and the accessory drive belt.

3. Remove the timing belt cover.

4. Align the timing mark on the camshaft sprocket with the timing mark on the cylinder head.

5. Confirm that the timing mark on the crankshaft sprocket is aligned with the timing mark on the oil pump housing.

6. Loosen the belt tensioner attaching bolt, pry the tensioner away from the timing belt and retighten the bolt.

7. Remove the spark plugs. Remove the right engine mount.

8. Remove the right side splash-shield.

9. Remove the flywheel inspection shield.

10. Use a suitable tool to hold the flywheel in place.

11. Remove the crankshaft damper bolt and washer and remove the bolt.

12. Remove the timing belt.

➡ **With the timing belt removed and the No. 1 piston at Top Dead Center (TDC), do not rotate the camshaft. If the camshaft must be rotated, align the crankshaft damper 90 degrees BTDC.**

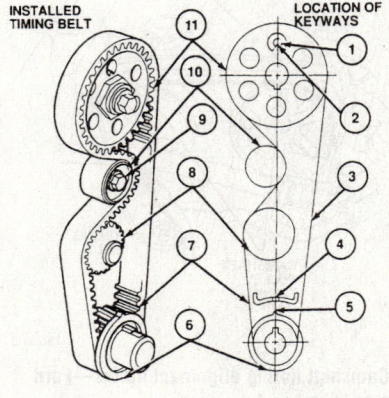

INSTALLED TIMING BELT / LOCATION OF KEYWAYS

79225G98

View of timing belt and alignment positions—Ford 1.9L (VIN J) Engine

To install:

13. Install the timing belt over the sprockets in a counterclockwise direction starting at the crankshaft. Keep the belt span from the crankshaft to the camshaft tight while installing over the remaining sprocket.

14. Loosen the belt tensioner attaching bolt, allowing the tensioner to snap against the belt.

15. Rotate the crankshaft clockwise two complete revolutions, stopping at TDC. This will allow the tensioner spring to load the timing belt.

➡ **Do not turn the engine counterclockwise to align the timing marks. Do not rotate the crankshaft with the spark plugs installed.**

16. Recheck the camshaft and crankshaft timing marks for alignment, to be sure the timing belt has not skipped a tooth during rotation. Repeat the procedure if the timing marks are not aligned.

17. Tighten the tensioner attaching bolt to 17–22 ft. lbs. (23–30 Nm).

18. Install the crankshaft dampener and the bolt and washer. Tighten the bolt to 81–96 ft. lbs. (110–130 Nm).

19. Install the flywheel inspection shield.

20. Install the splash-shield and lower the vehicle.

21. Install the right engine mount. Install the spark plugs.

22. Install the timing belt cover.

23. Install the accessory drive belt automatic tensioner and the accessory drive belt.

24. Connect the negative battery cable.

2.0L (VIN 3) Engine

When installing a timing belt, tensioner spring (6L277) and retaining bolt (W700001-S309) must be purchased and properly installed on the engine. First, check to see if these parts are already installed. The tensioner spring will adjust the timing belts tension and should not require further adjustments.

1. Disconnect the negative battery cable.

2. Remove the engine air intake resonators.

3. Label and remove the ignition wires from the spark plugs. Move the ignition wires aside.

4. Remove the spark plugs.

5. Manually rotate the crankshaft to Top Dead Center (TDC) for the No. 1 piston on its compression stroke. Be sure to align the timing marks.

6. Disconnect the retaining bracket for

the power steering pressure hose from the engine lifting eye.

7. Install the Three Bar Engine Support D88L-6000-A, onto the engine lifting eyes and slightly raise the engine.

8. Remove the upper camshaft timing belt cover retaining bolts and the cover from the engine.

➡**Mark the location of the upper front engine support bracket before removing it from the engine support bracket.**

9. Remove the upper front engine support bracket retainer nuts, the bracket and the upper front engine support insulator.

10. If equipped, remove the wiring harness connector from the low coolant level sensor at the radiator coolant recovery reservoir.

11. Remove the radiator coolant recovery reservoir retainers and move the reservoir aside.

12. Remove the upper front engine support insulator.

13. Set the coolant recovery reservoir back into position temporarily.

14. Loosen the water pump pulley retaining bolts. Do not remove the bolts completely.

15. Remove the accessory drive belt.

16. Remove the drive belt idler pulley retaining bolt and pulley from the alternator mounting bracket.

17. Finish removing the water pump retaining bolts and remove the water pump pulley.

18. Remove the center camshaft timing belt cover retaining bolts and the cover from the engine.

19. Remove the crankshaft pulley.

20. Remove the lower camshaft timing belt cover bolts and the cover from the engine.

21. Remove the valve cover as follows:

 a. Disconnect the crankcase ventilation tube from the valve cover.

 b. Remove the retaining bolt and nut for the power steering pressure hose retaining bracket and move the hose aside.

 c. Remove the valve cover retaining bolts in a standard removal sequence starting from the outside of the valve cover and working toward the inside of the valve cover.

 d. Remove the valve cover and gasket from the engine.

22. Place Camshaft Alignment Timing Tool T94P-6256-CH, into the slots of both

camshafts at the rear of the cylinder head to lock the camshafts into position.

23. Loosen the camshaft timing belt tensioner pulley retaining bolt and move the tensioner pulley to relieve the tension on the timing belt.

24. Temporarily tighten the tensioner in this position.

➡**If the timing belt is to be reused, mark the belt for the direction of rotation before removing to prevent premature wear or failure.**

25. Remove the timing belt.

26. If required, remove the sprockets as follows:

 a. Hold the camshaft with the Camshaft Sprocket Holding Tool T74P-6256-B.

 b. Loosen and remove the camshaft sprocket retaining bolt.

 c. Remove the sprocket from the camshaft.

 d. Repeat the procedure for the 2nd camshaft sprocket.

 e. Remove the crankshaft sprocket.

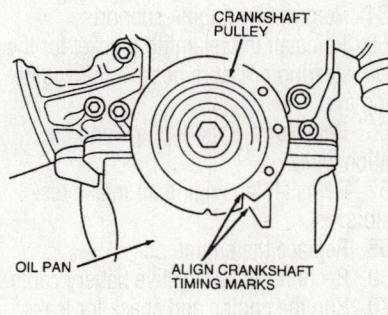

Crankshaft alignment position—Ford 2.0L (VIN 3) engines

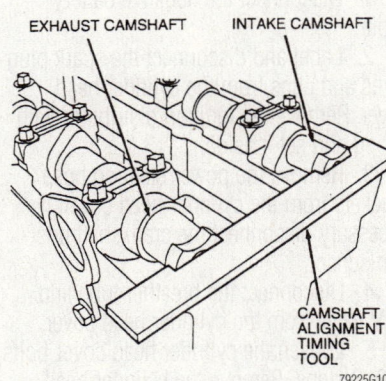

Placement of Camshaft Alignment Timing Tool T94P-6256-CH—Ford 2.0L (VIN 3) engines

To install:

27. Slide the crankshaft sprocket onto the crankshaft aligning the keyway.

28. Align the camshafts using the Camshaft Alignment Timing Tool T94P-6256-CH.

29. Reinstall the sprockets onto the camshafts and loosely install the camshaft retaining bolts.

30. Tighten the camshaft sprocket retaining bolts to 47–53 ft. lbs. (64–72 Nm).

31. Loosely install the crankshaft pulley to verify that the engine is at TDC. Realign the marks if they have moved.

32. Verify that the camshafts are aligned.

➡**It is recommended to purchase a tensioner spring and retaining bolt through the dealer parts to apply the proper tension for used or new belt installations. The spring is bolted to the tensioner assembly and becomes a part of the engine. Ignore this notice if the tensioner spring is already installed.**

33. Reinstall the retaining bolt (W700001-S309) into the hole provided in the cylinder block and place the tensioner spring (6L277) between the bolt and the camshaft timing belt tensioner pulley.

34. Tighten the retainer bolt to 71–97 inch lbs. (8–11 Nm).

35. Remove the crankshaft pulley and install the timing belt onto the crankshaft sprocket, then onto the camshaft sprockets working in a counterclockwise direction.

36. Tighten the camshaft sprocket retaining bolts to 47–53 ft. lbs. (64–72 Nm).

37. Be sure that the span of the camshaft timing belt between the crankshaft sprocket and the exhaust camshaft sprocket is not loose.

38. Be sure that the camshaft timing belt is securely aligned on all sprockets.

39. Reinstall the lower timing belt cover and tighten the retaining bolts to 53–71 inch lbs. (6–8 Nm).

40. Apply silicone sealer to the keyway of the crankshaft pulley and install. Tighten the retaining bolt to 81–89 ft. lbs. (110–120 Nm).

41. Inspect the timing mark on the crankshaft pulley to verify that the engine is still at TDC.

42. Loosen the camshaft timing belt tensioner pulley retaining bolt and allow the tensioner spring attached to the pulley to draw the tensioner pulley against the camshaft timing belt.

43. Remove the camshaft alignment tim-

ing tool from the camshafts at the rear of the engine.

44. Turn the crankshaft two revolutions in a clockwise direction.

45. Tighten the camshaft timing belt tensioner pulley retaining bolt to 26–30 ft. lbs. (35–40 Nm).

46. Recheck that the crankshaft timing mark is at TDC for the No. 1 piston, and that both camshafts are in alignment using the camshaft alignment timing tool.

➡A slight adjustment of the camshafts to allow the insertion of the camshaft alignment timing tool is permissible as long as the crankshaft stays at the TDC location.

47. Camshaft Sprocket Holding Tool T74P-6256-b can be used to move the camshaft sprocket(s) if a slight adjustment is required.

48. If a camshaft is not properly aligned, perform the following procedure:

a. Loosen the retaining bolt securing the sprocket to the camshaft while holding the camshaft sprocket from turning with the sprocket holding tool.

b. Turn the camshaft until the camshaft alignment timing tool can be installed.

c. Verify that the crankshaft timing mark is at TDC for the No. 1 cylinder.

d. While holding the camshaft sprocket with the camshaft sprocket holding tool, tighten the retaining bolt to 47–53 ft. lbs. (64–72 Nm).

e. Remove the tool and rotate the crankshaft two revolutions (clockwise).

f. Verify that the camshafts are aligned and that the crankshaft is at TDC for the No. 1 cylinder.

49. Reinstall the valve cover as follows:

a. Clean the gasket sealing surfaces.

b. Inspect the valve cover gasket and O-rings; replace as required.

c. Reinstall the valve cover retaining bolts and tighten them in a standard sequence starting from the center and working towards the outside of the valve cover to 53–71 inch lbs. (6–8 Nm).

d. Reinstall the power steering hose retaining bracket and the power steering hose.

e. Reinstall the crankcase ventilation tube to the valve cover.

50. Position the center camshaft timing belt cover.

51. Reinstall the center camshaft timing belt cover retaining bolts and tighten them to 53–71 inch lbs. (6–8 Nm).

52. Reinstall the water pump pulley and

the retaining bolts. Reinstall the bolts, finger-tight.

53. Reinstall the drive belt idler pulley.

54. Reinstall the drive belt idler pulley retaining bolt and tighten it to 35 ft. lbs. (48 Nm).

55. Reinstall the accessory drive belt.

56. Tighten the water pump pulley retaining bolts to 89–124 inch lbs. (10–14 Nm).

57. Move the radiator coolant recovery reservoir aside.

58. Reinstall the upper front engine support insulator.

59. Position the radiator coolant recovery reservoir and install the retainers.

60. If equipped, install the wiring harness to the low coolant level sensor on the coolant recovery reservoir.

61. Reinstall the upper front engine support bracket to the engine and the upper front engine support insulator using the mark made during the removal procedure for reference.

62. Install the upper camshaft timing belt cover.

63. Reinstall the upper camshaft timing belt cover retaining bolts and tighten to 27–44 inch lbs. (3–5 Nm).

64. Remove the engine support.

65. Reinstall the retaining bracket for the power steering pressure hose to the engine lifting eye.

66. Reinstall the spark plugs and the ignition wires.

67. Reinstall the engine air intake resonators.

68. Replace the engine oil.

69. Reconnect the negative battery cable.

70. Run the engine and check for leaks and proper operation.

2.0L (VIN A) Engine

1. Disconnect the negative battery cable.

2. Label and disconnect the spark plug wires and clips from the cylinder head cover. Remove the ignition distributor with wiring and set it aside.

3. Remove the power steering hose brackets from the cylinder head cover. If necessary disconnect the crankshaft position sensor.

4. Disconnect the breather tube and PCV valve from the cylinder head cover.

5. Loosen the cylinder head cover bolts in 2–3 steps. Remove the cylinder head cover.

6. Remove the power steering belt shield. Loosen the power steering adjusting bolt, lockbolt and through-bolt and remove the power steering belt.

7. Loosen the alternator adjusting bolt and upper mounting bolt. Remove the alternator belt.

8. Support the engine with Engine Support Tool 014–00750. Raise the engine slightly with a jack and remove the right side engine support insulator (mount).

9. Remove the oil level indicator bolt and four upper timing belt cover bolts and remove the upper timing belt cover.

10. Remove the splash-shields. Using Holder Tool T92C-6316-AH, hold the crankshaft pulley and remove the pulley bolt. Use a suitable puller to remove the pulley, then remove the guide plate.

11. Remove the four lower timing belt cover bolts and remove the lower timing belt cover.

12. Temporarily install the crankshaft pulley bolt.

13. Turn the crankshaft until the timing mark on the crankshaft sprocket aligns with the timing mark on the oil pump and the camshaft sprocket timing marks, **E** and **I**, align on the camshaft sprockets.

14. Insert camshaft sprocket holding tool T92C-6256-AH, between the camshaft sprockets.

15. Turn the timing belt tensioner with an Allen wrench and remove the tensioner spring from the tensioner spring pin.

16. If the timing belt is to be reused, mark the direction of rotation on the timing belt. Remove the timing belt.

17. If necessary to remove the sprockets, remove the camshaft sprocket holding tool. Hold the camshaft by placing a suitable wrench on the hexagon which is cast into the camshaft. Place another wrench onto the camshaft sprocket retaining bolt and loosen the bolt.

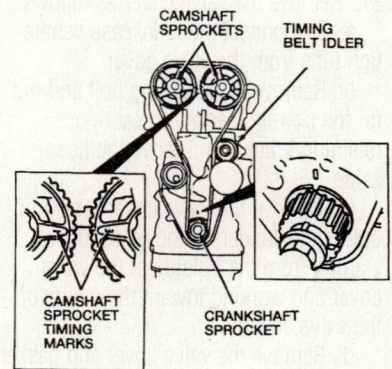

79225G06

Be sure that the intake and exhaust camshaft timing marks align so that they face each other—Ford 2.0L (VIN A) engines

➡️**Before removing the camshaft sprocket(s), be sure that the camshafts are still in alignment and tag each sprocket to the camshaft from which it was removed.**

18. Remove the camshaft sprocket bolt and the camshaft sprocket from the camshaft.

19. Repeat the camshaft sprocket removal procedure for the opposite camshaft if required.

20. Slide off the crankshaft sprocket and remove the crankshaft key.

To install:

21. Install the crankshaft key and slide the crankshaft sprocket into position.

22. Install the camshaft sprocket onto the proper camshaft, making sure to align the dowel pin.

23. Be sure that the **I** and **E** are in alignment.

24. Install the camshaft sprocket bolt. Hold the hexagon on the camshaft with a suitable wrench and tighten the sprocket bolt to 35–48 ft. lbs. (47–65 Nm). Be sure the camshaft sprockets are still properly aligned and reinstall the sprocket holding tool.

25. Be sure the timing marks on the camshaft and crankshaft sprockets are still aligned.

26. Install the timing belt. If reusing the original timing belt, be sure it is installed in the same direction of rotation.

27. Turn the tensioner clockwise with an Allen wrench and install the tensioner spring. Remove the holding tool from between the camshaft sprockets.

28. Rotate the crankshaft clockwise two turns and align the timing marks. Be sure all marks are still correctly aligned.

➡️**The timing chain tensioner automatically adjusts the tension on the timing belt.**

29. Install the timing belt lower cover and tighten the four bolts to 71–88 inch lbs. (8–10 Nm).

30. Install the guide plate, crankshaft pulley and pulley bolt. Secure the pulley with the holder tool and tighten the bolt to 116–123 ft. lbs. (157–167 Nm).

31. Install the splash-shields and lower the vehicle.

32. Raise the engine slightly with the jack and install the right side engine mount. Tighten the mount through-bolt to 63–86 ft. lbs. (86–116 Nm) and the mount attaching nuts to 54–75 ft. lbs. (74–103 Nm). Remove the engine support tool.

33. Install the upper timing belt cover and tighten the bolts to 71–88 inch lbs. (8–10 Nm).

34. Clean the cylinder head and valve cover mating surfaces thoroughly.

35. Apply silicone sealant to the cylinder head surface in the area adjacent to the front camshaft bearing caps. Apply sealant to a new gasket and install it on the cylinder head cover.

36. Install the cylinder head cover and tighten the bolts.

37. Install the power steering hose brackets and tighten the bolts to 71–88 inch lbs. (8–10 Nm). Connect the spark plug wires and wire clips. Connect the breather tube and PCV valve. If necessary, connect the crankshaft position sensor.

38. Install the alternator belt and adjust the tension. Tighten the upper mounting bolt to 14–18 ft. lbs. (19–25 Nm) and the lower through-bolt to 27–38 ft. lbs. (37–52 Nm).

39. Install the power steering belt and adjust the tension. Tighten the through-bolt to 32–45 ft. lbs. (43–61 Nm) and the lock-bolt to 23–34 ft. lbs. (31–46 Nm). Install the power steering belt shield and tighten the bolts to 61–86 inch lbs. (7–9 Nm).

40. Connect the negative battery cable.

41. Run the engine and check for leaks and proper engine operation.

2.0L (VIN P) Engine

1. Unfasten the three nuts and three bolts from the timing belt cover.

2. Remove the cover.

3. Remove the right-hand splash shield and the crankshaft pulley.

4. Align the timing marks as illustrated in the accompanying illustration.

5. Refer to the accompanying illustration and remove the timing belt as follows:

    a. Loosen the timing belt tensioner bolt (1).

    b. Use an 8mm Allen wrench, and turn the tensioner (2) counterclockwise ¼ turn.

    c. Insert a ⅛ inch drill bit in the hole (3) to lock the belt tensioner in place.

    d. Remove the timing belt (4).

    e. Inspect the belt for damage and signs of oil leakage.

To install:

➡️**Install the timing belt over the sprocket in a counterclockwise direction starting at the crankshaft. Keep the belt span between the crankshaft and camshaft tight when installing the belt over the camshaft.**

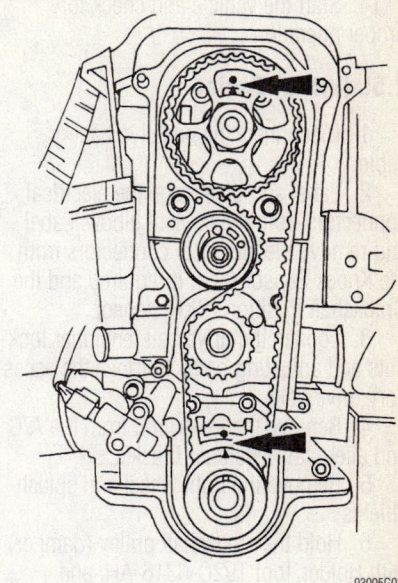

The timing marks on both the camshaft and crankshaft pulleys must be aligned like this before removing or installing the timing belt—2.0L (VIN P) SOHC engines

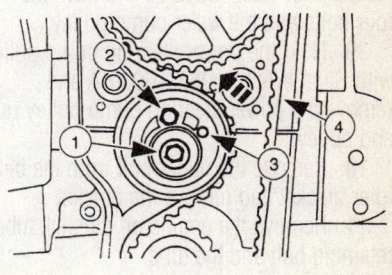

Remove the timing belt by following these 4 numbered steps (refer to the text for an explanation)—2.0L (VIN P) SOHC engine

6. Install the timing belt and remove the drill bit.

7. Tighten the tensioner bolt to 15–22 ft. lbs. (20–30 Nm).

8. Rotate the engine two complete revolutions and make sure the timing marks are aligned.

9. Install the timing belt cover and tighten the nuts and bolts to 71–97 inch lbs. (8–11 Nm).

10. Install the pulley and the bolt. Tighten the bolt to 81–98 ft. lbs. (110–120 Nm).

11. Install the splash shield(s).

12. Lower the vehicle and install the drive belt.

13. Connect the negative battery cable.

Refer to the model specific sections for cooling system service procedures

14. Start the vehicle and check for proper operation.

2.5L (VIN B) Engine

1. Disconnect the negative battery cable.

2. Label and disengage the electrical connectors from the coolant elbow. Label and remove the electrical connectors from the Knock Sensor (KS), if required and the Crankshaft Position (CKP) sensor.

3. Loosen the drive belt tensioner locknuts and adjusting bolts. Remove the accessory drive belts.

4. Remove the lower bolt from the A/C and alternator tensioner bracket.

5. Remove the right wheel and splashshields.

6. Hold the crankshaft pulley (damper) with Holder Tool T92C-6316-AH, and remove the crankshaft pulley bolt. Remove the crankshaft pulley, using a puller if needed.

7. Remove the 5 front timing belt cover bolts.

8. Hold the water pump pulley with Holder Tool T92C-6312-AH, remove the four bolts and the water pump pulley.

9. Hold the power steering pump pulley with Strap Wrench D85L-6000-A and remove the power steering pump pulley nut and pulley.

10. Remove the upper bolt from the belt idler bracket and remove the bracket.

11. Remove the engine oil dipstick tube retaining bolt and the tube.

12. Remove the 8 rear timing belt cover retaining bolts and remove the timing belt covers.

13. Temporarily reinstall the crankshaft pulley bolt.

14. Remove the three nuts and throughbolt from the right-hand engine support insulator and remove the support insulator. Remove the support insulator bracket.

15. Turn the crankshaft to Top Dead Center (TDC) No. 1 cylinder in the direction of normal rotation. Be sure that the timing mark on the crankshaft sprocket aligns with the timing mark on the oil pump.

16. Remove the two bolts from the timing belt tensioner arm, removing the lower bolt first.

17. Remove the timing belt tensioner arm.

18. If the timing belt is to be reused, mark the direction of rotation on the timing belt.

19. Loosen the Allen bolt on the timing belt tensioner.

20. Remove the timing belt.

21. If the timing belt sprockets are to be removed, proceed as follows:

   a. Remove the intake manifold.

   b. Label and disconnect the necessary hoses from the cylinder head covers.

   c. Label and disconnect the spark plug wires from the spark plugs.

   d. Remove the cylinder head cover retaining bolts and remove the cylinder head covers.

   e. Hold the camshaft using a suitable wrench on the hexagon cast into the camshaft. Remove the camshaft sprocket bolts and the camshaft sprockets.

   f. Use Crankshaft Damper Puller T74P-6316-A, to remove the crankshaft sprocket. Remove the crankshaft sprocket key.

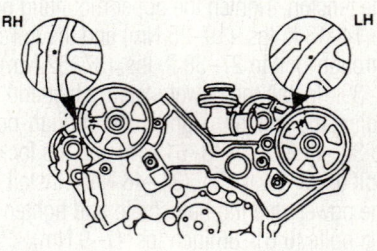

Left and right camshaft timing position—Ford 2.5L (VIN B) engines

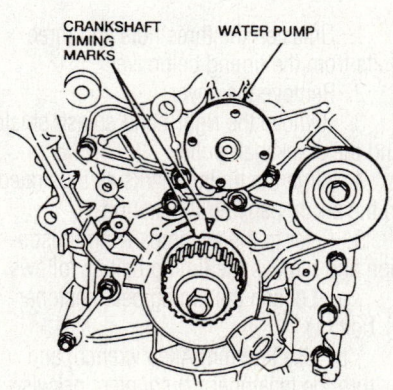

TDC alignment for the crankshaft—Ford 2.5L (VIN B) engines

To install:

22. If the timing belt sprockets were removed, proceed as follows:

   a. Install the crankshaft sprocket key and crankshaft sprocket.

   b. Install the camshaft sprockets on the camshafts with the retaining bolts.

   c. Hold the camshaft using a suitable wrench on the hexagon cast into the camshaft. Tighten the camshaft sprocket bolts to 90–103 ft. lbs. (123–140 Nm).

   d. Be sure the cylinder head cover and cylinder head contact surfaces are clean and free of dirt, oil and old sealant and gasket material.

   e. Apply silicone sealant to the cylinder heads in the area adjacent to the front and rear camshaft caps. Install new gaskets on the cylinder heads.

   f. Install the cylinder head covers and tighten the retaining bolts.

   g. Connect the spark plug wires to the spark plugs and connect the hoses to the cylinder head covers.

   h. Install the intake manifold.

23. Position the timing belt tensioner arm in a suitable press.

24. Compress the tensioner until the hole in the piston is aligned with the 2nd hole in the tensioner case. Insert a 0.060 in. (1.6mm) diameter wire or pin through the 2nd hole to keep the piston compressed.

25. Align the camshaft sprockets to TDC.

26. Turn the crankshaft counterclockwise until the crankshaft sprocket is offset from TDC by one tooth.

27. Install the timing belt.

28. If the original belt is being reused, be sure it is installed in the same direction of rotation.

29. Turn the crankshaft in the direction of normal engine rotation until the crankshaft sprocket timing mark is at TDC. This should place all of the belt slack in the timing belt tensioner portion of the timing belt.

30. Install the timing belt tensioner arm and two bolts. Tighten the bolts to 14–18 ft. lbs. (19–25 Nm).

31. Remove the wire or pin from the tensioner.

➡ **When properly timed, the crankshaft timing marks will align and the crankshaft sprocket timing mark will no longer be one tooth off.**

32. Rotate the crankshaft two complete turns in the direction of normal rotation and align the timing marks. Be sure all marks are still correctly aligned. This will also set the timing belt tension.

➡ **The timing belt tensioner will automatically adjust the timing belt tension.**

33. Tighten the timing belt tensioner Allen bolt to 28–32 ft. lbs. (35–51 Nm).

34. Install the right-hand engine support insulator. Tighten the three nuts to 54–76 ft. lbs. (74–103 Nm) and the through-bolt to 50–68 ft. lbs. (67–93 Nm).

35. Remove the crankshaft damper bolt.

36. Install the timing belt covers with the rear 8 bolts. Tighten to 71–88 inch lbs. (8–10 Nm).

37. Install the engine oil dipstick tube and retaining nut.

38. Install the belt idler bracket and the upper retaining bolt.

39. Install the power steering pump pulley and nut. Tighten the nut to 36–43 ft. lbs. (49–59 Nm) while holding the pulley with a strap wrench.

40. Install the water pump pulley and four bolts. Secure the pulley with the holder tool and tighten the bolts to 71–88 inch lbs. (8–10 Nm).

41. Install the 5 front timing belt cover bolts and tighten to 71–88 inch lbs. (8–10 Nm).

42. Install the crankshaft pulley (damper) with the bolt. Hold the crankshaft pulley with the holding tool and tighten to 116–122 ft. lbs. (157–166 Nm).

43. Install the splash-shields.

44. Install the wheel and tighten the lug nuts to 65–87 ft. lbs. (88–118 Nm).

45. Install the lower bolt into the A/C and alternator tensioner bracket.

46. Install the accessory drive belts and adjust the tension.

47. Engage the electrical connectors to the sensors at the coolant elbow and the KS and CKP sensors.

48. Connect the negative battery cable.

49. Run the engine and check for leaks and proper engine operation.

GENERAL MOTORS

1.0L (VIN 6) and 1.3 (VIN 9) Engines

➡️**Timing belts must always be completely free of dirt, grease, fluids and lubricants. This includes the sprockets and contact surfaces on which the belt rides. The belt must never be crimped, twisted or bent. Never use tools to pry or wedge the belt.**

1. Disconnect the negative battery cable.
2. Remove the clips and right side splash-shield.
3. Remove the lower alternator cover plate.
4. Remove the alternator drive belt, if equipped, the A/C drive belt.
5. Remove the water pump pulley.

➡️**It is not necessary to remove the crankshaft timing sprocket bolt (center bolt) to remove the crankshaft pulley.**

6. Remove the crankshaft pulley bolts and crankshaft pulley.
7. Remove the retaining bolts and nut from the timing belt outside cover.

8. Remove the timing belt outside cover.

9. Turn the crankshaft to align the timing marks. The mark on the crankshaft sprocket should align with the arrow mark on the oil pump housing. The mark on the camshaft sprocket should align with the **V** mark on the timing belt inner cover or cylinder head cover.

10. If the timing belt is to be reused, mark the direction of rotation on the belt.

11. Remove the timing belt tensioner, tensioner plate, tensioner spring, spring damper and timing belt.

➡️**Never turn the camshaft or crankshaft independently after the timing belt has been removed. Interference may occur between the pistons and valves, and parts may be damaged.**

12. Inspect the timing belt for wear or cracks, and replace as necessary. Check the tensioner for smooth rotation.

13. If the timing belt sprockets are to be removed, proceed as follows:

a. Using a 0.39 in. (10mm) rod inserted into the camshaft, hold the camshaft and remove the retaining bolt and camshaft sprocket.

✹✹ WARNING

Be careful not to damage the cylinder head or cylinder head cover mating surfaces. Place a clean shop cloth between the rod and cylinder head. Do not bump the rod hard against the cylinder head when loosening the bolt.

b. If equipped with a manual transaxle, lock the crankshaft in position by inserting a suitable flat-bladed tool into the hole in the bottom of the bell housing to engage the flywheel teeth.

c. If equipped with an automatic transaxle, lock the crankshaft in position by inserting a suitable flat-bladed tool between the flywheel teeth and against the engine block.

d. Remove the crankshaft sprocket bolt and crankshaft sprocket.

To install:

14. If the timing belt sprockets were removed, proceed as follows:

a. Install the crankshaft sprocket, aligning the keyway. Lock the crankshaft in place and tighten the crankshaft sprocket bolt to 81 ft. lbs. (110 Nm).

b. Install the camshaft sprocket and

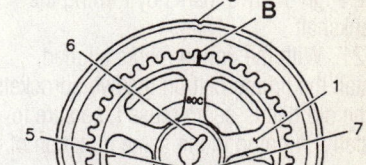

1	CAMSHAFT TIMING PULLEY	5	SLOT NO. 1
2	TIMING MARK	6	SLOT NO. 2
3	"V" MARK	7	PULLEY PIN
4	BELT INSIDE COVER		

79225G16

Upper timing pulley position—GM 1.0L (VIN 6) and 1.3L (VIN 9) engines

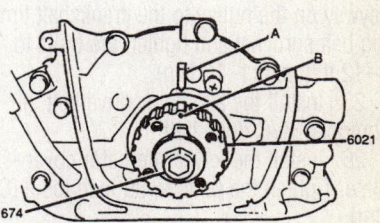

A	ARROW MARK ON OIL PUMP CASE
B	PUNCH MARK ON CRANKSHAFT TIMING GEAR
674	CRANKSHAFT PULLEY TIMING GEAR BOLT
6021	CRANKSHAFT TIMING GEAR

79225G17

Crankshaft timing mark—GM 1.0L (VIN 6) and 1.3L (VIN 9) engines

retaining bolt. Lock the camshaft in place using the rod, and tighten the bolt to 44 ft. lbs. (60 Nm). Remove the locking rod.

15. Install the tensioner plate to the tensioner.

16. Insert the lug of the tensioner plate into the hole of the tensioner.

17. Install the tensioner, tensioner plate and spring. Do not fully tighten the tensioner bolt and stud at this time.

18. Move the tensioner plate in a counterclockwise direction. This should cause the tensioner to move in the same direction. If it does not, remove the tensioner and tensioner plate, and reinsert the tensioner plate lug in the timing plate tensioner hole.

19. Check that the camshaft timing marks are aligned. If not, align the two marks by turning the camshaft.

20. Check that the punch mark on the crankshaft timing belt sprocket is aligned

with the arrow mark on the oil pump case. If not, align the two marks by turning the crankshaft.

21. With the timing marks aligned, install the timing belt on the two sprockets. If the old belt is being reused, be sure to install it running in the same direction of original rotation.

22. Install the tensioner spring and spring damper. Turn the timing belt two rotations clockwise after installing the tensioner spring and damper to remove any belt slack. Tighten the tensioner stud to 8 ft. lbs. (11 Nm), then the tensioner bolt to 20 ft. lbs. (27 Nm).

➡ **Confirm that both sets of timing marks are aligned properly.**

23. Using a new seal, install the timing belt cover and tighten the bolts and nut to 97 inch lbs. (11 Nm).

24. Install the crankshaft pulley. Fit the keyway on the pulley to the crankshaft timing belt sprocket and tighten the bolts to 8–12 ft. lbs. (11–16 Nm).

25. Install the alternator drive belt, if equipped, A/C drive belt.

26. Install the lower alternator cover plate. Tighten the bolts to 89 inch lbs. (10 Nm).

27. Install the right side splash-shield and clips.

28. Connect the negative battery cable.

29. Run the engine. Check for leaks.

1.6L (VIN 6) and 1.8L (VIN 8) Engines

1. Disconnect the negative battery cable.

2. Remove the windshield washer reservoir from the engine compartment.

3. If equipped with cruise control, proceed as follows:

   a. Remove the cruise control actuator cover.

   b. Disconnect the cruise control harnesses.

   c. Disconnect the control cable.

   d. Remove the bolts and actuator from the vehicle.

4. Remove the right front wheel.

5. Remove the bolts and plastic clips and the right front wheel housing.

6. Remove the alternator/water pump drive belt.

7. If equipped with A/C, proceed as follows:

   a. Remove the A/C compressor drive belt.

   b. Disconnect the compressor harness.

   c. Remove the bolts and compressor,

without disconnecting the refrigerant lines. Suspend the compressor aside.

   d. Remove the compressor mounting bracket.

8. Remove the power steering pump drive belt.

9. Disconnect the wiring from the alternator and oil pressure switch.

10. Remove the engine wiring harness cover.

11. Remove the wiring harness from the cylinder head cover.

12. Disconnect the ignition wires from the spark plugs, then remove the spark plugs.

13. Remove the PCV hoses from the valve cover.

14. Remove the cap nuts, the seal washers and the cylinder head cover with the gasket.

15. Turn the crankshaft to align the timing mark on the crankshaft pulley at **0**, setting the piston in the No. 1 cylinder at Top Dead Center (TDC) on the compression stroke. Check that the valve lash adjusters on the No. 1 cylinder are loose. If not, turn the crankshaft pulley one complete revolution (360 degrees).

16. Remove the engine ground wire from the right fender apron.

17. Install a suitable support under the engine and remove the engine mount.

18. Remove the water pump pulley.

19. Remove the crankshaft pulley using a suitable puller.

20. Remove the 9 retaining bolts and the timing belt covers.

21. Slide the timing belt guide from the crankshaft.

22. Be sure the timing belt sprockets are properly aligned.

✳✳ WARNING

Do not turn the crankshaft or camshaft independently after removal of the timing belt; binding or damage to engine components could result. If the timing belt is to be reused, mark the belt with an arrow showing the direction of engine revolution.

23. Remove the timing belt tensioner bolt, tensioner and tension spring.

24. Remove the timing belt from the sprockets. Inspect the timing belt for cracked or damaged teeth. Replace as necessary.

✳✳ WARNING

Do not bend, twist or turn the timing belt.

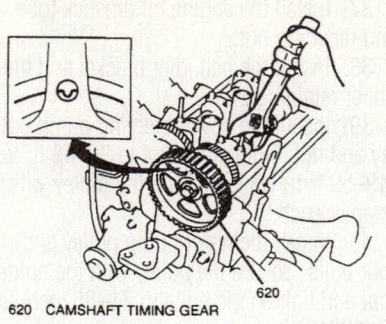

Aligning the camshaft timing marks—GM 1.6L (VIN 6) and 1.8L (VIN 8) engines

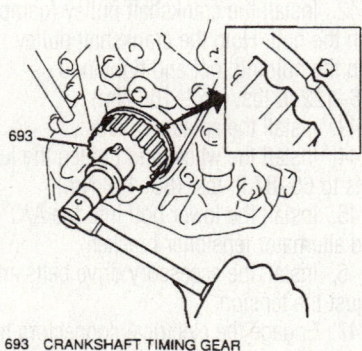

Crankshaft pulley alignment indicator— GM 1.6L (VIN 6) and 1.8L (VIN 8) engines

25. If the camshaft sprocket is to be removed, hold the camshaft stationary using a wrench positioned on the hexagon cast into the camshaft, and remove the sprocket retaining bolt and sprocket.

✳✳ WARNING

Be careful not to damage the cylinder head when holding the camshaft in place.

26. If the crankshaft sprocket is to be removed, pry it from the crankshaft using two flat-bladed prybars.

To install:

27. Align the camshaft key with the groove on the sprocket and slide the sprocket on. Hold the camshaft with the wrench at the hexagonal portion of the camshaft, and tighten the camshaft timing sprocket bolt to 43 ft. lbs. (59 Nm).

28. Be sure the sprocket is still properly aligned.

29. Install the crankshaft timing sprocket. Align the crankshaft key with the groove on the sprocket and slide it on.

30. Reinstall the timing belt tensioner and the tension spring. Pry the tensioner to the left as far as it will go and temporarily tighten the retaining bolt.

31. Install the timing belt. If installing the old belt, observe the matchmarks made during removal.

32. Loosen the retaining bolt for the timing belt tensioner and allow it to tension the belt.

33. Temporarily install the crankshaft pulley bolt and turn the crankshaft clockwise two full revolutions. Be sure each timing mark realigns exactly.

34. Tighten the timing belt tensioner bolt to 27 ft. lbs. (37 Nm).

35. Measure the timing belt deflection. Correct deflection should be 0.20–0.24 in. (5–6mm) at 4 lbs. (20 Nm) of pressure. If the deflection is not correct, adjust it with the timing belt tensioner.

36. Install the timing belt guide, with the cup side facing outward.

37. Install the timing belt covers, installing the bottom one first. Tighten the 9 cover bolts to 62 inch lbs. (7 Nm).

38. Install the crankshaft pulley after aligning the pulley key with the slot on the pulley. Hold the pulley with tool J-8614-01, and tighten the pulley bolt to 87 ft. lbs. (118 Nm).

39. Temporarily install the water pump pulley.

40. Install the engine mount.

41. Install or connect the remaining components.

42. If equipped with A/C, proceed as follows:

  a. Install the compressor mounting bracket and tighten the bolts to 35 ft. lbs. (47 Nm).

  b. Install the compressor and tighten the bolts to 18 ft. lbs. (25 Nm).

  c. Engage the compressor wiring connector.

  d. Install the compressor drive belt and adjust the tension.

43. If equipped with cruise control, proceed as follows:

  a. Install the cruise control actuator and tighten the bolts to 89 inch lbs. (10 Nm).

  b. Connect the cruise control cable.

  c. Install the cruise control actuator cover.

44. Connect the negative battery cable.

45. Start the engine and check vehicle operation.

3.0L (VIN R) Engine

➡ The steps in this procedure are critical in preventing catastrophic engine damage, adhering to this sequence is imperative. There are special tools needed to perform this procedure. It is a good idea to read this procedure several times before attempting to perform this job. This is an interference engine.

TIMING BELT INSTALLATION AND ADJUSTMENT TABLE

Step	Action	Value	Yes	No
1	Install the timing belt and align marks on the belt with the marks on the camshaft gears and the crankshaft gear. Check the timing belt deflection between the idler pulley for camshafts 3 & 4 and camshaft number 4. Is the timing belt installed, the marks aligned and the timing belt deflection adjusted?	1 cm (0.4 in) maximum	Go to Step 2	—
2	Set the initial timing belt tension at the timing belt tensioner. Is the initial timing belt tension set?	—	Go to Step 3	—
3	Rotate the engine two complete revolutions and secure the crankshaft at Top Dead Center (TDC) with the J 42069-10. Has the engine been rotated and the crankshaft secured to TDC?	—	Go to Step 4	—
4	Starting with camshafts 3 and 4, check the alignment of the marks on the camshaft gears with the marks on the J 42069-20 checking gauge. Do the marks on the camshaft gears align exactly with the marks on J 42069-20?	—	Go to Step 5	Go to Step 6
5	Check the alignment of the marks on camshafts gears 1 and 2 with the marks on the J 42069-20 checking gauge. Do the marks on the camshaft gears align exactly with the marks on J 42069-20?	—	Go to Step 14	Go to Step 10
6	Do the camshaft gear marks line up to the left (BTDC) of the marks on the J 42069-20 checking gauge?	—	Go to Step 8	Go to Step 7
7	Do the camshaft gear marks line up to the right (ATDC) of the marks on the J 42069-20 checking gauge?	—	Go to Step 9	—
8	Turn the idler pulley eccentric, for camshafts 3 and 4, counterclockwise until the marks on the camshaft gear align exactly with the marks on J 42069-20. Rotate the engine two complete revolutions, lock the crankshaft at TDC with J 42069-10 and recheck the alignment of the camshaft gear marks to the marks on J 42069-20. Do the marks on the camshaft gears align exactly with the marks on J 42069-20?	—	Go to Step 5	Go to Step 6
9	Turn the idler pulley eccentric, for camshafts 3 and 4, clockwise until the marks on the camshaft gear align exactly with the marks on J 42069-20. Rotate the engine two complete revolutions, lock the crankshaft at TDC with J 42069-10 and recheck the alignment of the camshaft gear marks to the marks on J 42069-20. Do the marks on the camshaft gears align exactly with the marks on J 42069-20?	—	Go to Step 5	Go to Step 6

79225G35

Timing belt installation and adjustment table—GM 3.0L (VIN R) engine

Step	Action	Value	Yes	No
10	Do the camshaft gear marks line up to the left (BTDC) of the marks on the J 42069-20 checking gauge?	—	Go to Step 12	Go to Step 11
11	Do the camshaft gear marks line up to the right (ATDC) of the marks on the J 42069-20 checking gauge?	—	Go to Step 13	—
12	Turn the idler pulley eccentric, for camshafts 1 and 2, counterclockwise until the marks on the camshaft gear align exactly with the marks on J 42069-20. Rotate the engine two complete revolutions, lock the crankshaft at TDC with J 42069-10 and recheck the alignment of the camshaft gear marks to the marks on J 42069-20. Do the marks on the camshaft gears align exactly with the marks on J 42069-20?	—	Go to Step 14	Go to Step 10
13	Turn the idler pulley eccentric, for camshafts 1 and 2, clockwise until the marks on the camshaft gear align exactly with the marks on J 42069-20. Rotate the engine two complete revolutions, lock the crankshaft at TDC with J 42069-10 and recheck the alignment of the camshaft gear marks to the marks on J 42069-20. Do the marks on the camshaft gears align exactly with the marks on J 42069-20?	—	Go to Step 14	Go to Step 10
14	Set the final timing belt tension at the timing belt tensioner. Is the final timing belt tension set?	—	Go to Step 15	—
15	Again, rotate the engine two complete revolutions and lock the crankshaft at TDC. Do a final inspection of the camshaft gear marks' relationship to the J 42069-20 marks. The marks must align exactly. Do the marks on the camshaft gears align exactly with the marks on the J 42069-20?	—	Go to Step 16	Go to Step 2
16	Remove all checking tools and ensure all idler pulleys and the tensioner locking nut are tightened to specifications. Continue with re-assembly of the engine.	—	—	—

79225G36

Timing belt installation and adjustment table (continued)—GM 3.0L (VIN R) engine

Always turn the crankshaft in the direction of rotation (clockwise), never against engine rotation. Never remove the timing belt without first setting the camshaft gears and crankshaft drive gear to Top Dead Center (TDC) and locking them in place with tool J42069.

The "Timing Belt Installation and Adjustment Table" provides an overview of the steps needed to properly install and adjust the timing belt. Use this table as a reference, not as a substitution, for the steps in this procedure.

1. Disconnect the negative battery cable.

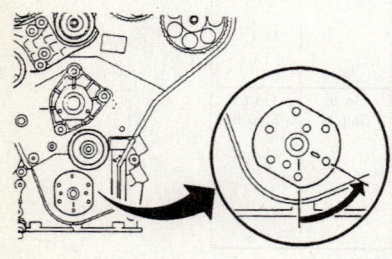

79225G30

Crankshaft alignment to 60 degrees BTDC—GM 3.0L (VIN R) engine

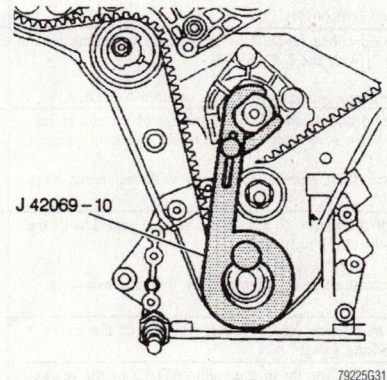

79225G31

Securing the crankshaft—GM 3.0L (VIN R) engine

J 42069-10

2. Remove the resonance chamber.

3. Remove the front timing belt cover.

4. Remove the harmonic balancer from the crankshaft.

5. Rotate the crankshaft clockwise to 60 degrees Before Top Dead Center (BTDC).

6. Install J42069-10 to the crankshaft drive gear with knurled bolt.

7. Turn the engine clockwise, with J42098, until the lever of J42069-10 firmly contacts the water pump pulley flange. Secure the lever to the water pump.

➡**Be sure the engine is not 180 degrees off. The camshaft marks must align with the rear timing cover.**

8. Lock the camshaft gears, using J42069-1 and J42069-2. It may be necessary to loosen the relevant idler pulley to lock the gears, then tighten the idler pulley bolt to 30 ft. lbs. (40 Nm).

9. Loosen the timing belt tensioner and remove the belt.

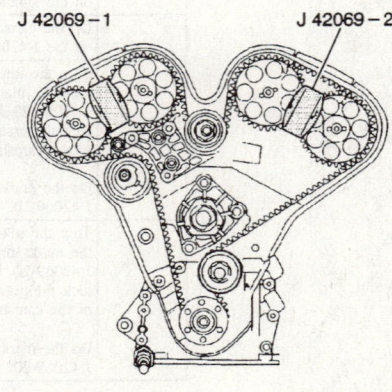

J 42069-1   J 42069-2

79225G32

Locking the camshaft—GM 3.0L (VIN R) engine

⁑ WARNING

With the belt removed, do not rotate the camshaft or crankshaft or remove the locking tools, because the pistons may contact the valves and cause internal engine damage.

To install:

10. Remove J42069-10.

11. Install the timing belt, starting at the crankshaft gear and aligning the double dash (TDC) mark on the belt with the oil pump and belt drive gear.

12. Using J42069-30, secure the belt to prevent the splines from jumping.

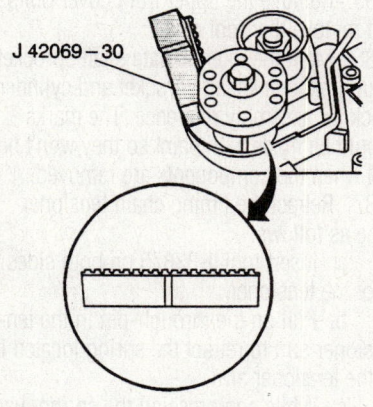

Using the tool to pin the timing belt—GM 3.0L (VIN R) engine

13. Route the belt between the idler pulley for camshafts 3 and 4, then between the gears for 3 and 4.

14. If the dash marks on the belt do not align with the camshaft and rear timing cover marks, loosen the idler pulley or move the cam gears slightly, with the camshaft gears still locked in place, until the timing belt can be properly installed. Temporally tighten the idler pulley locking bolt; the locking bolt will be tightened to specification after final adjustments are made.

➡The timing belt deflection must be no more than 0.4 in. (10mm) between camshaft gear 4 and the idler pulley. To adjust the deflection, rotate the timing belt idler pulley for camshafts 3 and 4 counterclockwise with tool J42069-40.

15. Route the belt between the idler pulley for camshafts 1 and 2, then between gears for 1 and 2.

16. If the dash marks on the belt do not align with the camshaft and rear timing cover marks, loosen the idler pulley or move the cam gears slightly, with the camshaft gears still locked in place, until the timing belt can be installed. Temporally tighten the idler pulley; the locking bolt will be tightened to specification after final adjustments are made.

17. Apply tension to the belt to keep it from slipping off the gears by turning the timing belt idler pulley for camshafts 1 and 2 counterclockwise with J42069-40. Temporally tighten the idler pulley; the locking bolt will be tightened to specification after final adjustments are made.

18. Complete the routing of the timing belt through the belt tensioner.

19. Apply initial tension by turning the timing belt tensioner counterclockwise, with a 5mm Allen wrench, until the marks are set as shown in the initial timing belt adjustment illustration.

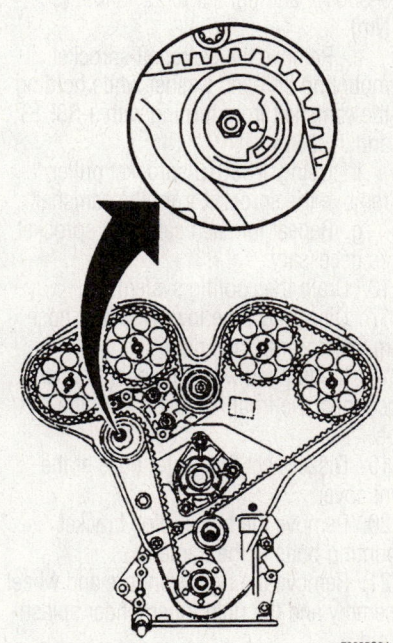

Initial timing belt tension adjustment—GM 3.0L (VIN R) engine

20. Tighten the tensioner locking nut to 15 ft. lbs. (20 Nm).

21. Ensure that the alignment marks are at their specific reference points.

22. Remove J42069-30, J42069-1 and J42069-2.

23. Rotate the engine two revolutions clockwise, stopping at 60 degrees BTDC.

24. Install J42069-10 to the crankshaft gear with the knurled bolt.

25. Turn the engine clockwise, with J42098, until the lever of J42069-10 firmly contacts the water pump pulley flange. Secure the lever to the water pump.

➡The alignment marks on the timing belt will no longer match the marks on the camshaft gears after one or more revolutions. The marks on the camshaft gears must align with the notches on the rear timing cover, and the crankshaft drive gear and the oil pump housing should match up to their mark.

26. If timing belt adjustment is necessary, first adjust camshafts 3 and 4.

27. Check the alignment of camshafts 3 and 4, 1 and 2 with gauge J42069-20.

28. If alignment is OK, then set final belt tension as follows:

   a. Loosen the timing belt tensioner locking nut.

   b. Adjust the timing belt tensioner by turning the eccentric cam, with a 5mm hex wrench, until the marks are set.

29. Tighten the tensioner locking nut to 15 ft. lbs. (20 Nm).

30. Remove J42069-10 and J42069-20.

31. Rotate the engine clockwise two revolutions, stopping at 60 degrees BTDC.

32. If further adjustment is needed, then repeat the applicable steps.

33. Tighten the idler pulley bolts for the camshafts to 30 ft. lbs. (40 Nm).

34. Be sure all tools are removed from the engine.

35. Install the harmonic balancer and tighten the bolts to 15 ft. lbs. (20 Nm).

36. Install the timing belt covers.

37. Install the resonance chamber.

38. Connect the negative battery cable, and reprogram applicable accessories.

3.4L (VIN X) Engine

The 3.4L (VIN X) engine uses a timing chain and camshaft timing belts.

1. Disconnect the negative battery cable.

2. Disconnect and remove the power steering pump from the pump mounting bracket.

3. Remove the left, right and center timing belt covers.

4. Rotate the engine clockwise to align the timing marks, TDC on the No.1 exhaust stroke, on the camshaft sprockets and intermediate shaft.

5. Loosely clamp the two camshaft

sprockets on each side of the engine together using clamping pliers or the equivalent. Secure the belt to the right side cam sprocket with a C-clamp and a wide pad on the belt.

➡ **When clamping the sprockets no deflection should be noticed. If any deflection is noticed, loosen the clamping devices. DO NOT mar the camshaft sprockets with the clamping device.**

6. Remove the tensioner side plate retaining bolts from the tensioner and remove the side plate from the actuator and base.

7. Rotate the actuator assembly around the arm pivot and out of the base. Removal of the tensioner from the base allows it to extend to its maximum travel.

8. Set the actuator aside on a table in a vertical position to allow the oil to drain into the boot end. The tensioner should be allowed to sit for 5 minutes prior to refilling with oil.

9. Reset the timing belt actuator as follows:

a. Straighten out a paper clip or a piece of stiff wire 0.032 in. (0.75mm) diameter to a minimum straight length of 1.85 in. (47mm). Form a double loop in the remaining end.

b. Remove the rubber end plug from the rear of the tensioner assembly. This will aid in allowing the oil in the tensioner to escape.

c. Hold the tensioner in your hand with the rubber boot end of the tensioner pointing down.

d. DO NOT remove the vent plug. Push the paper clip through the center hole in the vent plug and into the pilot hole.

e. Insert a small screwdriver into the screw slot inside the end of the tensioner.

f. Retract the tensioner by rotating the tensioner plunger in a clockwise direction while pushing the rod tip against a table top.

g. Align the screw slot to align with the vent hole, and push the straight section of the wire into the screw slot to retain the plunger in the retracted position.

h. If tensioner oil has been lost, fill the tensioner with SAE 5W30 Mobil 1®. Fill the tensioner to the bottom of the plug. The tensioner **MUST** be fully retracted before being filled with oil.

10. If the belt is being reused, mark the direction of rotation on the belt.

11. Remove the timing belt tensioner pulley mounting bolt and pulley.

12. Remove the timing belt after first removing the C-clamp retaining the belt to the right side camshaft sprocket.

13. Remove the Torx® head bolts securing the idler pulleys, if the idlers need to be replaced.

14. Remove the intermediate shaft sprocket using the following procedure:

a. Use a suitable tool to hold the engine from turning.

b. Remove the intermediate shaft sprocket mounting bolt and washer.

c. Using J-38616 sprocket puller, remove the sprocket from the intermediate shaft.

15. If the camshaft sprockets need to be removed, proceed as follows:

a. Remove the camshaft carrier cover(s).

b. Remove the camshaft sprocket clamping pliers.

c. Rotate the camshaft being serviced so the flats on the camshaft are face up.

d. Install a camshaft hold-down tool J-38613, and tighten to 22 ft. lbs. (30 Nm).

e. Remove the camshaft sprocket mounting bolt and washer while holding the camshaft from turning with J-38613 and J-38614.

f. Using J-38616 sprocket puller, remove the sprocket from the camshaft.

g. Repeat for each camshaft sprocket as necessary.

16. Drain the cooling system.

17. Disconnect the lower radiator hose from water pump inlet pipe.

18. If equipped with a manual transaxle, disconnect the front AIR hose from the AIR pipe.

19. Disconnect the heater hose at the front cover.

20. Remove the heater pipe bracket mounting bolts at the frame.

21. Remove the right front tire and wheel assembly and the right inner fender splashshield.

22. Remove the crankshaft pulley mounting bolts and remove the pulley from the damper.

23. Remove the crankshaft damper as follows:

a. While holding the crankshaft from turning using a suitable tool, remove the damper mounting bolt and washer.

b. Install tool J-24420-B and remove the damper from the crankshaft.

24. Place an oil catch pan under the oil filter and remove the oil filter.

25. Remove the A/C compressor mounting bracket bolts.

26. Remove the lower front cover bolts.

27. On automatic transaxle vehicles, remove the halfshaft following the recommended procedure.

28. Remove the rear alternator bracket.

29. Disconnect and remove the starter following the recommended procedure.

30. Remove the intermediate shaft drive belt sprocket retaining bolt and remove the intermediate shaft drive belt sprocket using puller J38616.

31. Remove the upper alternator mounting bolts.

32. Remove the forward light relay center screws and position the relay center aside.

33. Disconnect the oil cooler hose from the front cover.

34. Remove the water pump pulley.

35. Remove the upper front cover bolts and remove the front cover.

36. Mark the intermediate shaft sprocket, chain link, crankshaft sprocket and cylinder block for assembly reference. The marks should be made with paint so they won't be lost when the components are removed.

37. Retract the timing chain tensioner shoe as follows:

a. Insert tool J-33875 on both sides of the tensioner.

b. Pull on the through-pin in the tensioner arm to retract the spring located in the tensioner arm.

c. While compressing the spring, use a suitable tool, a cotter pin or nail, and insert the pin in the hole in the tensioner assembly to hold the tensioner compressed. The tool used must be strong enough to hold the tensioner compressed.

➡ **The timing chain, crankshaft sprocket and intermediate shaft sprocket will be removed at the same time. If, when removing the assembly, the intermediate shaft sprocket does not easily come off the intermediate shaft, rotate the crankshaft back and forth to loosen the intermediate shaft sprocket.**

38. Install a suitable puller, J-38611 and J-8433.

39. Tighten the bolt on the puller and slowly pull the crankshaft sprocket off the crankshaft. Be sure the intermediate shaft sprocket is moving along with the crankshaft sprocket.

40. Remove the timing chain and sprockets.

41. Remove the tensioner mounting bolts and remove the tensioner assembly.

To install:

42. Install the tensioner assembly and tensioner assembly mounting bolts finger-

A LOCATION OF TIMING MARKS WITH CAM HOLD
   DOWN TOOLS J 38613 INSTALLED
   (#4 TDC COMPRESSION STROKE)
B FRONT COVER TIMING MARK
C LOCATION OF TIMING MARKS WITH DRIVE
   BELT INSTALLED
D LOCATION WHERE CAM HOLD DOWN TOOLS
   ARE INSTALLED
1 RH EXHAUST CAMSHAFT SPROCKET
2 RH INTAKE CAMSHAFT SPROCKET
3 LH INTAKE CAMSHAFT SPROCKET
4 LH EXHAUST CAMSHAFT SPROCKET
5 PERMANENT MARKS PAINTED DOTS REMOVE
   PREVIOUS MARKS IF TIMING IS BEING CHANGED
   AND MARKS AGAIN IN THESE LOCATIONS
6 CRANKSHAFT BALANCER
7 INTERMEDIATE SHAFT SPROCKET

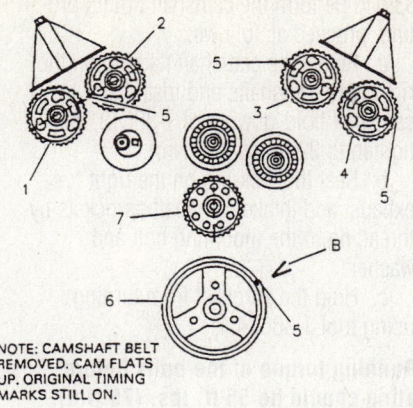

NOTE: CAMSHAFT BELT
REMOVED. CAM FLATS
UP. ORIGINAL TIMING
MARKS STILL ON.

79225G15

Timing marks with hold-down tool in place—GM 3.4L (VIN X) engines

tight first. Tighten the bolt in the slotted hole first to 18 ft. lbs. (25 Nm), then tighten the remainder of the bolts to 18 ft. lbs. (25 Nm).

43. Check to ensure that the crankshaft key is fully seated in the crankshaft cutout and the tensioner assembly is fully retracted.

44. Assemble the timing chain, intermediate shaft sprocket and crankshaft sprocket on a work bench. The timing marks made should be in alignment. The large chamfer and counterbore of the crankshaft sprocket are installed facing toward the engine and the intermediate shaft spline sockets are installed facing away from the engine.

45. Install the sprocket and chain assembly onto the engine. As the sprockets are installed, parallel alignment must be maintained.

46. The crankshaft sprocket will have to be pressed on the final 0.31 in. (8mm). This can be done using J-38612 or an equivalent puller.

47. Ensure timing was maintained.

48. Remove the retaining pin from tensioner. Clean all gasket surfaces completely.

49. Apply GM Sealer 1052080 to the lower edges of the sealing surface of the front cover. Install a new gasket on the front cover.

50. Install the front cover on the engine. Apply thread sealant to the large bolts and tighten the bolts enough to pull the front cover against the engine block.

51. Install the water pump pulley.

52. Connect the oil cooler hose to the front cover.

53. Position the forward light relay center and install the mounting screws.

54. Install the upper alternator mounting bolt and tighten it to 22 ft. lbs. (30 Nm).

55. Install the intermediate shaft drive belt sprocket. The sprocket must lock into the intermediate shaft timing chain sprocket. Install the mounting bolt and washer. While holding the engine from turning, tighten the bolt to 95 ft. lbs. (130 Nm).

56. Connect and install the starter. Tighten the starter mounting bolts to 32 ft. lbs. (43 Nm).

57. Install the halfshaft following the recommended procedure.

58. Install the rear alternator bracket. Tighten the mounting bolt to 22 ft. lbs. (30 Nm) and the mounting stud to 41 ft. lbs. (55 Nm) and the lower bolt to 61 ft. lbs. (83 Nm).

59. Install the lower front cover bolts and tighten the small bolts to 18 ft. lbs. (25 Nm).

60. Install the A/C compressor mounting bolts and tighten the mounting bolts to 37 ft. lbs. (50 Nm).

61. Install a new oil filter.

62. Install the crankshaft damper as follows:

a. Coat the seal contact area on the damper with clean engine oil.

b. Align the notch inside the damper with the crankshaft key and slide the damper on until the key is started into the notch.

c. Using J-29113 puller, press the damper into position on the crankshaft.

d. Install the crankshaft pulley and pulley mounting bolts. Tighten the pulley mounting bolts to 37 ft. lbs. (50 Nm).

e. Install the crankshaft damper mounting bolt and washer, and tighten to 78 ft. lbs. (105 Nm).

63. Install the right side inner fender splash-shield.

64. Install the tire and wheel assembly.

65. Tighten the upper front cover small bolts to 18 ft. lbs. (25 Nm) and the large bolts to 35 ft. lbs. (47 Nm).

66. Connect the heater hose to the front cover.

67. Install the heater pipe bracket mounting bolts.

68. If equipped with a manual transaxle, connect the front AIR hose to the AIR pipe.

69. Connect the lower radiator hose to the water pump.

70. Install the right side cooling fan. Install the upper radiator support.

71. Position the torque strut mounting bracket and install the mounting bolts and tighten to 52 ft. lbs. (70 Nm).

72. Install the front engine lift hook and tighten the mounting bolt to 52 ft. lbs. (70 Nm).

73. To install the camshaft sprockets, proceed as follows:

a. Wipe the camshaft noses with clean engine oil.

b. Install the camshaft sprocket onto the nose of the camshaft.

c. Install the lockring and shim ring.

d. Install, but DO NOT tighten, the camshaft sprocket mounting bolts at this time.

74. Install the intermediate shaft sprocket as follows:

a. Lubricate the seal contact area on the intermediate shaft sprocket with clean engine oil.

b. Slide the sprocket through the intermediate shaft sprocket seal and engage the locking tangs into the sockets of the chain sprocket.

c. Lightly lubricate the shaft seal and place it in position on the end of the intermediate shaft.

d. Install the intermediate shaft sprocket mounting bolt and washer. Tighten the bolt to 96 ft. lbs. (130 Nm) while holding the crankshaft from turning.

75. Install the timing belt idler pulleys and tighten the Torx® bolts to 37 ft. lbs. (50 Nm).

76. Install the actuator assembly and side plate. Tighten the actuator mounting bracket bolts to 37 ft. lbs. (50 Nm).

77. Install the belt, taking note of direction of rotation if the old belt was used.

78. Install the tensioner pulley to the mounting base. Tighten the bolt to 37 ft. lbs. (50 Nm).

79. Rotate the tensioner pulley counter-

clockwise into the belt using the cast square lug on the body and engage the ball end of the actuator into the socket on the pulley arm.

80. Remove the tensioner lockpin allowing the tensioner shaft to extend and the pulley to move into the belt.

81. Rotate the tensioner pulley counterclockwise, applying 14 ft. lbs. (18 Nm) of torque.

82. Rotate the engine clockwise three times to seat the belt. Align the crankshaft reference marks during the final rotation to TDC. Do not allow the crankshaft to spring back or reverse its direction of rotation.

➡**The timing flats on the camshafts should be 180 degrees apart from the left side to the right side. Both camshafts on the same side should be the same.**

83. To perform the camshaft timing procedure, proceed as follows:

a. Rotate the camshaft flats up on the right side camshafts and install a camshaft hold-down tool J-38613, and tighten to 22 ft. lbs. (30 Nm).

b. Seat the lockring on the right exhaust and intake camshaft sprockets by threading in the mounting bolt and washer.

c. Hold the sprocket from turning using tool J-38614.

➡**Running torque of the bolts before seating should be 55 ft. lbs. (75 Nm).**

d. If less torque is required, replace the shim ring and lockring.

e. If more torque is required, replace the shim ring and lockring and inspect the bolts for burrs.

f. Seating of the lockring is accomplished when the edge is flush with the sprocket hub.

g. With the lockring seated tighten the bolt to final torque of 81 ft. lbs. (110 Nm).

h. Remove J-38613.

i. Rotate the engine clockwise one full revolution or any number of odd revolutions. DO NOT rotate the engine backward.

j. Be sure the timing mark on the damper aligns with the mark on the front cover.

k. Repeat Substeps a through i for the left side.

84. Install the camshaft carrier covers.

85. Install timing the belt left, right and center covers and retaining bolts.

86. Connect the negative battery cable.

87. Start the engine and verify proper operation and engine performance.

BRAKES

5

CHRYSLER CORP.

Caliper

REMOVAL & INSTALLATION

**Chrysler Concorde, New Yorker, LHS
Dodge Intrepid
Eagle Vision**

FRONT

1. Remove the appropriate wheel and tire assemblies.

2. Remove the 2 caliper guide pin bolts and remove the caliper assembly. If the caliper is not being removed from the vehicle as during brake pad renewal, simply hang the caliper with a piece of wire to take the weight off the brake hose. If the caliper is being removed for rebuild or replacement, continue to Step 5.

3. Remove the bolt retaining the brake hose to the caliper. Be sure to plug the end of the brake hose or cover it with a plastic

bag to prevent contamination from entering the hydraulic system. Remove the caliper from the vehicle.

To install:

4. Reconnect the brake hose to the

caliper, if removed, using new sealing washers.

5. If new linings are being installed, the caliper pistons must be pushed back into their bore to accommodate the thickness of

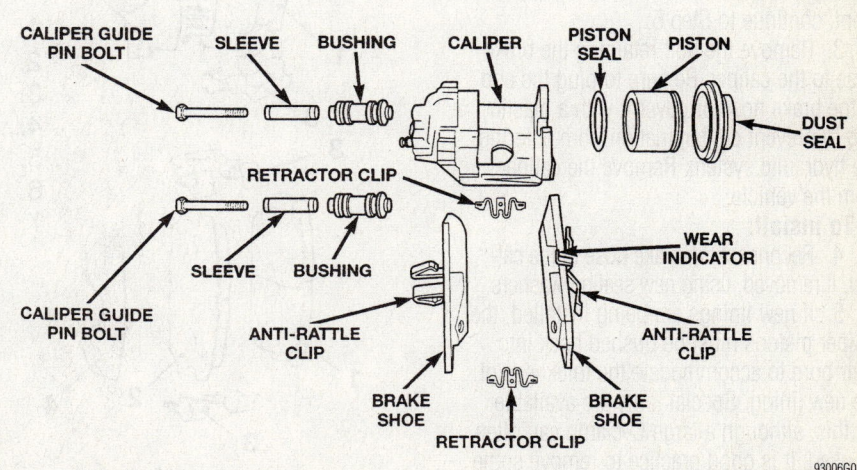

Front brake caliper and related components—Concorde, New Yorker, LHS, Intrepid, Vision

93006G01

the new lining. Special tools are available for pushing the piston back although a large C-clamp can often be used. It is good practice to remove some (⅓–½) brake fluid from the master cylinder reservoir. This prevents overflow caused by brake fluid being forced through the lines as the piston is pushed back.

6. Install the brake pads into the caliper.

7. Install the caliper to the steering knuckle in the correct position. Lightly lubricate the machined areas that support the caliper with high-temperature grease.

8. Install and torque the caliper guide pin bolts. Use care not to cross the threads of the caliper pin bolts. Torque the guide pin bolts to 15 ft. lbs. (20 Nm).

9. Torque the brake hose fittings to 35 ft. lbs. (48 Nm).

10. Be sure to bleed the brake system.

11. Install the wheels and lug nuts. Torque the wheel lug nuts in a star pattern sequence to 95–100 ft. lbs. (129–135 Nm).

12. Before attempting to move the vehicle, pump the brake pedal to seat the pads against the rotors. Make sure the vehicle has a firm brake pedal. Check the level of the brake fluid and add DOT 3 brake fluid, if necessary.

13. Road test the vehicle and make several stops to wear off any foreign material on the brakes and to seat the brake linings, if replaced.

REAR

1. Remove the appropriate wheel and tire assemblies.

2. Remove the 2 caliper guide pin bolts and remove the caliper assembly. If the caliper is not being removed from the vehicle as during brake pad renewal, simply hang the caliper with a piece of wire to take the weight off the brake hose. If the caliper is being removed for rebuild or replacement, continue to Step 5.

3. Remove the bolt retaining the brake hose to the caliper. Be sure to plug the end of the brake hose or cover it with a plastic bag to prevent contamination from entering the hydraulic system. Remove the caliper from the vehicle.

To install:

4. Reconnect the brake hose to the caliper, if removed, using new sealing washers.

5. If new linings are being installed, the caliper pistons must be pushed back into their bore to accommodate the thickness of the new lining. Special tools are available for this, although a large C-clamp can often be used. It is good practice to remove some brake fluid from the master cylinder reservoir. This prevents overflow caused by brake

fluid being forced through the lines as the piston is pushed back.

6. Install the brake pads into the caliper.

7. Install the brake caliper to the caliper adapter. Lightly lubricate machined areas that support the caliper with high-temperature grease.

8. Install and tighten the caliper guide pin bolts. Use care not to cross the threads of the caliper pin bolts. Torque the guide pin bolts to 17 ft. lbs. (22 Nm).

9. Torque the brake hose fittings to 35 ft. lbs. (48 Nm).

10. Be sure to bleed the brake system.

11. Install the wheels and lug nuts. Torque the wheel lug nuts in a star pattern sequence to 95–100 ft. lbs. (129–135 Nm).

12. Before attempting to move the vehicle, pump the brake pedal to seat the pads against the rotors. Make sure the vehicle has a firm brake pedal.

13. Check the level of the brake fluid and add DOT 3 brake fluid, if necessary.

14. Road test the vehicle and make several stops to wear off any foreign material on the brakes and to seat the brake linings, if replaced.

Chrysler Sebring
Dodge Avenger

FRONT

1. Remove about half of the brake fluid from the master cylinder.

2. Position a C-clamp, or other suitable

tool, over the caliper. Smoothly apply pressure, forcing the caliper piston into the caliper bore until it bottoms. Remove the C-clamp, if used.

3. If the caliper is to be completely removed from the vehicle, remove the brake hose attaching bolt, disconnect the brake hose from the caliper and plug the hose to prevent fluid contamination or loss.

4. Remove the caliper mounting bolts and lift the caliper off of the support bracket.

5. Remove the caliper from the vehicle. If the caliper is only removed for access to other components, support the caliper, with the brake hose attached, so that there is no strain on the brake hose.

To install:

6. Position the caliper to the steering knuckle. Lubricate and install the mounting bolts. Torque the bolts to 54 ft. lbs. (74 Nm).

7. If removed, unplug and install the brake line hose to the caliper and torque the inlet fitting bolt to 22 ft. lbs. (29 Nm).

8. Fill the master cylinder with fresh brake fluid and, if the brake hose was removed, bleed the brake system.

9. Install the wheel assembly.

10. Depress the brake pedal 3–4 times to seat the brake linings and to restore pressure in the system.

> **✳✳ CAUTION**
>
> **Do not move the vehicle until a firm pedal is obtained.**

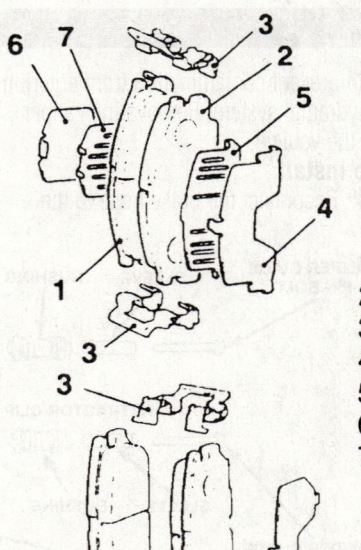

1. Pad & wear indicator assembly
2. Pad assembly
3. Clip
4. Outer shim (stainless)
5. Outer shim (coated with rubber)
6. Inner shim (stainless)
7. Inner shim (coated with rubber)

93006G02

Exploded view of the front brake pads and related components—Sebring, Avenger

REAR

Unlike many rear disc brake designs, this system does not incorporate the parking brake system, into the rear brake caliper. The rear brake system is serviced the same as the front system.

1. Remove about half of the brake fluid from the master cylinder.
2. Remove the wheel assembly.
3. Position a C-clamp, or other suitable tool, over the caliper. Smoothly apply pressure, forcing the caliper piston into the caliper bore until it bottoms. Remove the C-clamp, if used.
4. If the caliper is to be completely removed from the vehicle, remove the brake hose attaching bolt, disconnect the brake hose from the caliper and plug the hose to prevent fluid contamination or loss.
5. Remove the caliper mounting bolts and lift the caliper off of the support bracket.
6. Remove the caliper from the vehicle. If the caliper is only removed for access to other components, support the caliper, with the brake hose attached, so that there is no strain on the brake hose.

To install:
7. Position the caliper on the support bracket, lubricate and install the mounting bolts. Torque the bolts to 54 ft. lbs. (74 Nm).
8. If removed, unplug and install the brake line hose to the caliper and torque the inlet fitting bolt to 22 ft. lbs. (29 Nm).
9. Fill the master cylinder with fresh brake fluid and, if the brake hose was removed, bleed the brake system.
10. Install the wheel assembly.
11. Depress the brake pedal 3–4 times to seat the brake linings and to restore pressure in the system.

✻✻ CAUTION

Do not move the vehicle until a firm pedal is obtained.

Eagle Talon

FRONT

1. Remove the appropriate tire and wheel assembly.
2. To disconnect the front brake hose, hold the nut on the brake hose side and loosen the flared brake line nut. Remove the brake hose from the caliper.
3. Remove the caliper guide and lock pins and lift the caliper assembly from the caliper support.

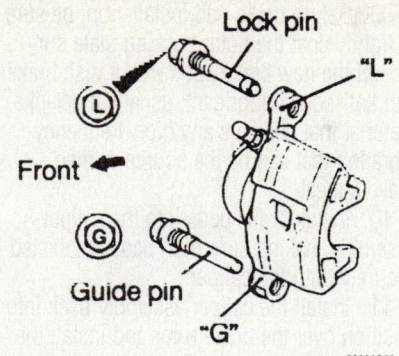

Caliper locking pin and guide pin description—Talon

To install:
4. Position caliper onto the caliper support. Install the guide pin and lock pin. Torque guide and locking pins to 54 ft. lbs. (75 Nm).
5. Reconnect the brake hose.
6. Bleed the brake system.
7. Apply brake pedal and inspect system. Ensure proper operation and no leakage.
8. Reinstall tire and wheel assembly. Torque lug nuts to 87–101 ft. lbs. (120–140 Nm).

REAR

1. Disconnect the battery negative cable.
2. Remove the appropriate tire and wheel assemblies. Loosen the parking brake cable adjustment from inside the vehicle.
3. Disconnect the parking brake cable end installed to the rear brake caliper assembly.
4. Remove the caliper lock and guide pins. Lift the caliper assembly from the caliper support.
5. Remove the rear brake hose from the caliper. Remove the caliper from the vehicle.

To install:
6. Install the rear brake hose onto the caliper with new washers in place. If equipped with brake hose retainer bolt, torque bolt to 25 ft. lbs. (35 Nm) torque. If no bolt is used, torque the brake hose fitting to 12 ft. lbs. (17 Nm).
7. Install the caliper over the brake pads. Lubricate and install the lock pin and torque to 23 ft. lbs. (32 Nm). Reinstall the guide pin and torque to 23 ft. lbs. (32 Nm).
8. Bleed the brake system.
9. Inspect the brake system for leaks and ensure proper operation.
10. Install tire and wheel assemblies. Torque wheels to 87–101 ft. lbs. (120–140 Nm).
11. Properly adjust parking brake cable.

Dodge/Plymouth Neon

1. On 1999–01 models, isolate the master cylinder as follows:
   a. Use a brake pedal holding tool and depress the brake pedal past its first one inch of travel and hold it in this position. (This will keep brake fluid from draining from the master cylinder).
2. Remove the front wheels.
3. Remove the 2 caliper guide pin bolts.
4. Disconnect the brake hose from the caliper.
5. Remove the caliper from the steering spindle.

To install:
6. Reconnect the brake hose to the caliper and torque to 35 ft. lbs. (48 Nm).
7. Reinstall the caliper to the steering spindle.
8. Reinstall the caliper guide pin bolts and torque to 16 ft. lbs. (22 Nm).
9. Properly bleed the brake system.
10. Reinstall the front wheels and lower the vehicle.
11. Pump the brake pedal to seat the front brake pads before moving the vehicle.
12. Road test the vehicle and check for proper operation.

Chrysler Cirrus, Sebring
Dodge Stratus
Plymouth Breeze

1. Remove the front wheels.
2. Remove the 2 caliper-to-steering knuckle guide pin bolts.
3. If the caliper is to be removed from the vehicle completely, for example, for overhaul perform the following procedure.
   a. Disconnect the brake hose from the caliper.
   b. Cover the opening of the brake hose so the hydraulic system does not become contaminated.
4. Remove the caliper from the steering knuckle.

To install:
5. Clean and lubricate both steering knuckle abutments with a coating of multi-purpose grease.
6. Position the caliper and brake pad assembly over the brake rotor. Be sure to properly install the caliper assembly into the abutments of the steering knuckle. Be sure the caliper guide pin bolts, rubber bushings and sleeves are clear of the steering knuckle bosses.
7. Reinstall the caliper guide pin bolts

and torque to 16 ft. lbs. (22 Nm). On Sebring and Avenger models, torque the caliper guide pin bolts to 54 ft. lbs. (74 Nm).

8. If removed, connect the brake hose to the caliper and torque to 35 ft. lbs. (48 Nm).

9. Properly bleed the brake system.

10. Reinstall the wheel and tire and torque the lug nuts in a star pattern sequence to half specification. Repeat the tightening procedure to full specified torque of 95–100 ft. lbs. (129–135 Nm).

11. Pump the brake pedal to seat the front brake pads before moving the vehicle.

12. Road test the vehicle and check for proper operation.

Disc Brake Pads

REMOVAL & INSTALLATION

Chrysler Concorde, New Yorker, LHS
Dodge Intrepid
Eagle Vision

FRONT AND REAR

1. Remove some of the fluid from the master cylinder.

2. Remove the appropriate wheels.

3. Remove the 2 caliper guide pin bolts. Remove the caliper assembly by swinging the top part of the caliper away from the brake rotor edge, then lift the caliper assembly up.

4. Prevent strain or other damage to the brake hose by supporting the caliper assembly with a strong piece of wire hanging from the strut.

5. Remove the outboard brake pad by prying the brake pad retaining clip over raised area on the caliper. Then slide the pad down and off the caliper.

6. Before removing the inboard brake pad, use a large C-clamp to press the piston back into the caliper. This will prevent possible damage to the caliper piston. It is good practice to remove some (1/3–1/2) of the brake fluid from the reservoir. This is because as the caliper piston is pushed back into the caliper, brake fluid will be pushed back through the lines, back into the master cylinder and fluid reservoir, possibly causing the reservoir to overflow.

7. Remove the inboard brake pad by pulling away from piston until the retainer clip is free from the cavity in the piston.

To install:

8. Lubricate both the caliper mating surface and the machined abutment surfaces with multi-purpose lubricant.

9. Before brake pad installation, be sure to lightly coat the outer backing plate surface of the new brake pads with a disc brake pad anti-squeal lubricant, usually a gel-like material that deadens any high-frequency vibration that can be the source of disc brake squeal.

10. Install brake pads into the caliper assembly making sure both pads are seated securely onto the caliper.

11. Install the caliper assembly back into position over the brake rotor and install the caliper guide pin bolts. Torque the front and rear caliper guide pin bolts to 17 ft. lbs. (23 Nm).

12. Install the wheels and lug nuts. Torque the lug nuts, in a star pattern sequence, to 95–100 ft. lbs. (129–135 Nm).

13. Top off the master cylinder to the appropriate level, using Dot 3 type brake fluid only.

14. Before moving the vehicle, pump the brakes until a firm pedal is obtained. Road test the vehicle to make sure the brake operation is normal.

Chrysler Sebring
Dodge Avenger

FRONT

1. Remove some of the brake fluid from the master cylinder reservoir. The reservoir should be no more than ½ full. When the pistons are depressed into the calipers, excess fluid will flow up into the reservoir.

2. Remove the appropriate tire and wheel assemblies.

3. Remove the caliper guide and lock pins and lift the caliper assembly from the caliper support. Tie the caliper out of the way using wire. Do not allow the caliper to hang by the brake line.

➡ On some models the caliper can be flipped up by leaving the upper pin in place, using it as a pivot point.

4. Remove the brake pads, spring clip and shims. Take note of positioning to aid installation.

5. Install the wheel lug nuts onto the studs and lightly tighten. This is done to hold the disc on the hub.

To install:

6. Use a large C-clamp to compress the piston(s) back into the caliper bore.

7. Lubricate the slide points and install the brake pads, shims and spring clip onto the caliper support. Install the caliper over the brake pads.

8. Lubricate and install the caliper guide and lock pins in their original positions.

tions. Torque guide and locking pins to 54 ft. lbs. (74 Nm).

9. Install the tire and wheel assemblies.

✳✳ CAUTION

Pump brake pedal several times, until firm, before attempting to move the vehicle.

10. Road test the vehicle and check brakes for proper operation.

REAR

Unlike many rear disc brake designs, this system does not incorporate the parking brake system, into the rear brake caliper, therefore, the rear brake system is serviced the same as the front system.

1. Remove some of the brake fluid from the master cylinder reservoir. The reservoir should be no more than ½ full. When the pistons are depressed into the calipers, excess fluid will flow up into the reservoir.

2. Remove the appropriate tire and wheel assemblies.

3. Remove the caliper guide and lock pins and lift the caliper assembly from the caliper support. Tie the caliper out of the way using wire. Do not allow the caliper to hang by the brake hose.

➡ On some models, the caliper can be flipped up by leaving the upper pin in place, using it as a pivot point.

4. Remove the brake pads, spring clip and shims. Take note of positioning to aid installation.

5. Install the wheel lug nuts onto the studs and lightly tighten. This is done to hold the brake disc on the hub.

To install:

6. Use a large C-clamp to compress the piston(s) back into the caliper bore.

7. Lubricate the slide points and install the brake pads, shims and spring clip onto the caliper support. Install the caliper over the brake pads.

8. Lubricate and install the caliper guide and lock pins in their original positions. Torque guide and locking pins to 54 ft. lbs. (74 Nm).

9. Install the tire and wheel assemblies.

✳✳ CAUTION

Pump brake pedal several times, until firm, before attempting to move the vehicle.

10. Road test the vehicle and check brakes for proper operation.

Eagle Talon

FRONT

1. Remove some of the brake fluid from the master cylinder reservoir. The reservoir should be no more than half full. When the pistons are pressed into the calipers, excess fluid will flow up into the reservoir.

2. Remove the appropriate tire and wheel assemblies.

3. Remove the caliper guide and lock pins and lift the caliper assembly from the caliper support. Tie the caliper out of the way using wire. Do not allow the caliper to hang by the brake line.

➡**On some vehicles, the caliper can be flipped up by leaving the upper pin in place and using it as a pivot point.**

4. Remove the brake pads, spring clip and shims. Take note of positioning to aid installation.

5. Install the wheel lug nuts onto the studs and lightly tighten. This is done to hold the disc on the hub.

To install:

6. Use a large C-clamp to compress piston(s) back into caliper bore. On 2 piston calipers both pistons will have to be retracted together.

7. Lubricate slide points and install the brake pads, shims and spring clip onto the caliper support. Install the caliper over the brake pads.

8. Lubricate and install the caliper guide and lock pins in their original positions. Torque guide and locking pins to 54 ft. lbs. (75 Nm).

9. Reinstall the tire and wheel assemblies.

➡**Pump brake pedal several times, until firm, before attempting to move vehicle.**

10. Road test the vehicle and check brakes for proper operation.

REAR

1. Remove some of the brake fluid from the master cylinder reservoir. The reservoir should be no more than half full. When the pistons are depressed into the calipers, excess fluid will flow up into the reservoir.

2. Remove the appropriate tire and wheel assemblies. Loosen the parking brake cable adjustment from inside the vehicle.

3. Disconnect the parking brake cable end installed to the rear brake caliper assembly.

4. Remove the caliper lock and guide pins and lift the caliper assembly from the caliper support. Tie the caliper out of the way using wire. Do not allow the caliper to hang by the brake line.

5. Remove the outer shim, brake pads and spring clips from the caliper support. Take note of positioning of each to aid in installation.

6. Reinstall the wheel lug nuts onto the studs and lightly tighten. This is done to hold the disc on the hub.

7. Clean the caliper piston. Using rear disc brake driver tool MB990652, thread the piston into the caliper bore. Be sure, at this point, that the stopper groove of the piston correctly fits into the projection on the replacement brake pads rear surface.

To install:

8. Lubricate all sliding and pivot points. Install the brake pads, shims and spring clip to the caliper support. Install the caliper over the brake pads.

9. Lubricate and install the caliper guide and lock pins. Torque the pins to 23 ft. lbs. (32 Nm). Attach the parking brake cable to the rear brake assembly.

10. Start the engine and forcefully depress the brake pedal 5–6 times. Apply the parking brake and make sure the adjustment is within specifications. Adjust the parking brake cable, as required.

11. Reinstall the tire and wheel assemblies.

12. Test the brakes for proper operation.

Dodge/Plymouth Neon

1. Remove the front wheels.

2. Remove the 2 caliper to steering knuckle guide pin bolts.

3. Lift the caliper away from the steering knuckle by first rotating the free end of the caliper away from the steering knuckle. Then, slide the opposite end of the caliper out from under the machined end of the steering knuckle.

4. Support the caliper from the upper control arm to prevent the weight of the caliper from being supported by the brake flex hose that will damage the hose.

5. Remove the brake pads from the caliper. Remove the outboard brake pad by prying the pad retaining clip over the raised area on the caliper. Then, slide the pad down and off the caliper. Pull the inboard brake pad away from the piston until the retaining clip is free from the cavity in the piston.

6. If required, the rotor can be removed by pulling it straight off the wheel mounting studs.

To install:

7. Clean all parts well. Inspect the caliper for piston seal leaks (brake fluid in and around the boot area and inboard lining) and for any ruptures of the piston dust boot. If the boot is damaged or fluid leak is visible, disassemble the caliper and install a new seal and boot (and piston, if scored).

8. Inspect the caliper pin bushings. Replace if damaged, dry or brittle.

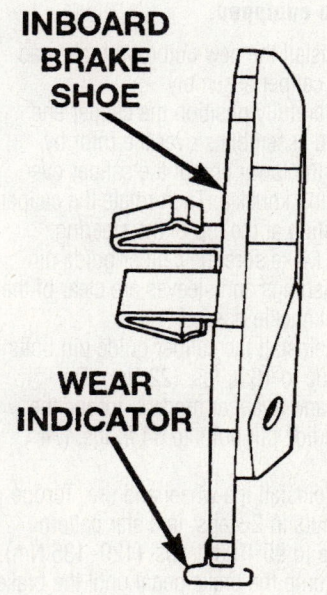

INBOARD BRAKE SHOE

WEAR INDICATOR

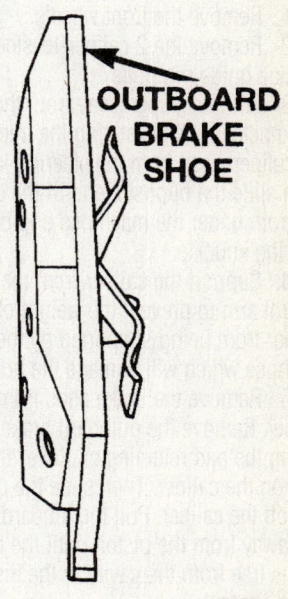

OUTBOARD BRAKE SHOE

93006G05

Disc brake pad identification—Neon

Timing chain and gear service is covered in the model specific sections of this manual

9. Completely compress the piston into the caliper using a large C-clamp or other suitable tool.

10. Lubricate the area on the steering knuckle where the caliper slides with high temperature grease.

11. Reinstall the rotor if removed.

12. Reinstall the brake pads into the caliper. Note that the inboard and outboard pads are different. Make sure the inboard brake shoe assembly is positioned squarely against the face of the caliper piston.

➡ **Be sure to remove the noise suppression gasket paper cover if the pads come so equipped.**

13. Carefully position the caliper and brake shoe assemblies over the rotor by hooking the lower end of the caliper over the steering knuckle. Then, rotate the caliper into position at the top of the steering knuckle. Make sure the caliper guide pin bolts, bushings and sleeves are clear of the steering knuckle bosses.

14. Reinstall the caliper guide pin bolts and torque to 16 ft. lbs. (22 Nm).

15. Reinstall the wheels and torque the mounting bolts to 100 ft. lbs. (135 Nm).

16. Pump the brake pedal until the brake pads are seated and a firm pedal is achieved before attempting to move the vehicle.

17. Road test the vehicle for proper operation.

**Chrysler Cirrus, Sebring
Dodge Stratus
Plymouth Breeze**

1. Remove the front wheels.

2. Remove the 2 caliper-to-steering knuckle guide pin bolts.

3. Lift the caliper away from the steering knuckle by first rotating the free end of the caliper away from the steering knuckle. Then slide the opposite end of the caliper out from under the machined end of the steering knuckle.

4. Support the caliper from the upper control arm to prevent the weight of the caliper from being supported by the brake flex hose which will damage the hose.

5. Remove the brake pads from the caliper. Remove the outboard brake pad by prying the pad retaining clip over the raised area on the caliper. Then slide the pad down and off the caliper. Pull the inboard brake pad away from the piston until the retaining clip is free from the cavity in the piston.

To install:

6. Completely depress the piston into the caliper using a large C-clamp or other suitable tool.

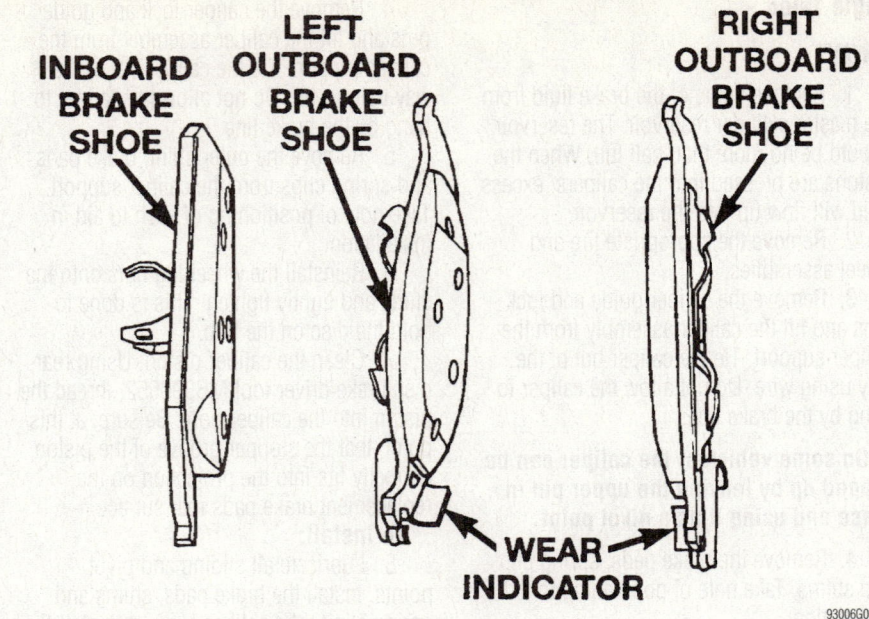

INBOARD BRAKE SHOE **LEFT OUTBOARD BRAKE SHOE** **RIGHT OUTBOARD BRAKE SHOE**

WEAR INDICATOR

93006G06

‡ **Disc brake pad identification—Cirrus, Sebring, Stratus, Breeze**

7. Lubricate the area on the steering knuckle where the caliper slides with high temperature grease.

8. Install the new inboard brake pad into the caliper piston by firmly pressing into the piston bore. Install the brake pads into the caliper. Note that the inboard and outboard pads are different. Make sure the inboard brake pad assembly is positioned squarely against the face of the caliper piston.

➡ **Be sure to remove the noise suppression gasket paper cover if the pads come so equipped.**

9. Install the new outboard brake pad onto the caliper assembly.

10. Carefully position the caliper and brake pad assemblies over the rotor by hooking the lower end of the caliper over the steering knuckle. Then rotate the caliper into position at the top of the steering knuckle. Make sure the caliper guide pin bolts, bushings and sleeves are clear of the steering knuckle bosses.

11. Reinstall the caliper guide pin bolts and torque to 16 ft. lbs. (22 Nm). On Sebring and Avenger models, torque the caliper guide pin bolts to 54 ft. lbs. (74 Nm).

12. Reinstall the wheel and tire. Torque the lug nuts in 2 steps, in a star pattern sequence to 95–100 ft. lbs. (129–135 Nm).

13. Pump the brake pedal until the brake pads are seated and a firm pedal is achieved before attempting to move the vehicle.

14. Road test the vehicle to check for proper operation.

Brake Drums

REMOVAL & INSTALLATION

**Chrysler Concorde, New Yorker, LHS
Dodge Intrepid
Eagle Vision**

1. Remove the rear wheels.

2. Remove the brake drum from the rear hub and bearing assembly. If the drum is difficult to remove, increase the clearance between the brake shoes and the drum as follows:

   a. Remove the rubber plug from the top of the brake support plate.

   b. Rotate the automatic shoe adjuster screw with an upward motion using a medium size flat tipped tool.

3. Remove the brake drum from the rear hub and bearing.

4. Inspect the brake shoe linings and drums for wear, contamination and scoring.

To install:

5. Install the rear brake drum onto the rear hub and bearing assembly.

6. Adjust the brake shoes as follows:

   a. Rotate the automatic shoe adjuster in a downward motion using a medium size flat tip tool. Turn the adjuster until there is a slight drag felt while turning the drum.

   b. Install the rubber plug back into the top part of the brake support plate.

7. Install the rear wheels and lug nuts. Torque the lug nuts in a star pattern sequence to 95–100 ft. lbs. (129–135 Nm).

Chrysler Sebring
Dodge Avenger

1. Remove the wheel assembly.

2. Remove the brake drum detent (retaining) screw and remove the drum from the axle.

3. If difficulty is encountered in removing the drum:

a. Verify the parking brake is released.

b. Loosen the parking brake cable.

c. Remove the access hole plug from the backing plate and move the parking brake lever until the lever stop rests on the brake shoe.

d. If necessary, turn the adjuster so that it draws in to allow more clearance between the shoe and drum.

To install:

4. Inspect all parts. Check the drum for cracks or excessive wear.

5. Turn the adjuster until it is drawn all the way in to the stop. Check that the adjuster turns freely. The nut must NOT lock at the end of the adjuster. Check that the parking brake lever stops are against the edge of the shoe web.

6. Install the brake drum and detent screw.

7. Install the wheel assembly.

8. Apply the foot brake at least 10 times until clicking of the adjustment actuator can no longer be heard. This procedure will automatically adjust the clearance between the shoe and drum.

Dodge/Plymouth Neon

1. Remove the rear wheels.

a. Locate and remove the rubber plug from the top of the brake support plate (backing plate).

b. Insert a small prying tool through the adjuster access hole and engage the teeth on the adjuster wheel.

c. Rotate the adjuster wheel so it is moved toward the front of the vehicle. This will back off the adjustment of the rear brake shoes.

d. Continue moving the adjuster wheel toward the front of the vehicle until it stops moving.

2. Remove the rear brake drum from the hub assembly.

To install:

3. Inspect the brake drums for cracks or signs of overheating. Measure the drum runout and diameter. If not to specification, resurface the drum. Runout should not exceed 0.006 inch (0.152mm). The diameter

variation (oval shape) of the drum braking surface must not exceed either 0.0025 inch (0.0635mm) in 30° or 0.0035 inch (0.089mm) in 360°. All brake drums are marked with the maximum allowable brake drum diameter on the face of the drum.

4. Install the rear brake drum onto the hub assembly.

5. Reinstall the wheels and properly adjust the brakes.

6. Road test vehicle to check brake operation.

Chrysler Cirrus, Sebring
Dodge Stratus
Plymouth Breeze

All vehicles except Sebring Convertible, are equipped with rear wheel, 2-shoe leading/trailing, internal expanding type of drum brakes with automatic self-adjuster mechanisms. The automatic self-adjuster mechanisms used on these vehicles are new designs and function differently than the screw type adjusters used in the past. These new self-adjusters are still actuated each time the vehicle's service brakes are applied. The new adjusters are located directly below the wheel cylinders.

The Sebring Convertible's rear wheel drum brake is a 2-shoe leading/trailing internal expanding type with an automatic self-adjuster mechanism. The automatic self-adjuster mechanism used on this vehicle is the screw type adjuster. The self-adjuster mechanism is actuated each time the vehicle service brakes are applied. Generally, drum brakes with a self-adjusting mechanism do not require manual brake shoe adjustment. Although, in the event that the brake shoes are replaced, it is advisable to make the initial adjustment manually to speed up the initial adjustment time. The initial adjustment procedure must be done prior to driving the vehicle.

1. Remove the rear wheel assembly.

2. For all vehicles, except Sebring Convertible, use the following procedure:

a. Locate and remove the rubber plug from the brake support plate (backing plate).

b. Insert a brake adjuster tool or similarly shaped prytool through the automatic adjuster access hole and engage the teeth on the adjuster wheel. Rotate the adjuster wheel so it is moved toward the front of the vehicle. Continue moving the adjuster until it stops; this will back off the adjustment of the rear brake shoes.

3. For the Sebring Convertible, use the following procedure for releasing the self-adjusting mechanism:

a. Locate and remove the rubber plug from the brake support plate (backing plate).

b. Insert a brake adjuster tool or similarly shaped prytool through the automatic adjuster access hole and carefully push the adjuster actuating lever out of engagement with the adjuster starwheel. While holding the lever away from the starwheel, insert a second prytool through the access hole and engage the teeth on the adjuster wheel. Rotate the adjuster wheel upward away from the ground; this will back off the adjustment of the rear brake shoes.

4. Remove the rear brake drum from the hub assembly.

To install:

5. Inspect the brake drums for cracks or signs of overheating. Measure the drum run-out and diameter. If not to specification, resurface the drum. Run-out should not exceed 0.006 in. (0.15mm). The diameter variation (oval shape) of the drum braking surface must not exceed either 0.0025 in. (0.064mm) in 30 degrees rotation, or 0.0035 in. (0.089mm) in 360 degrees rotation. All brake drums are marked with the maximum allowable brake drum diameter on the face of the drum.

6. Install the rear brake drum onto the hub assembly.

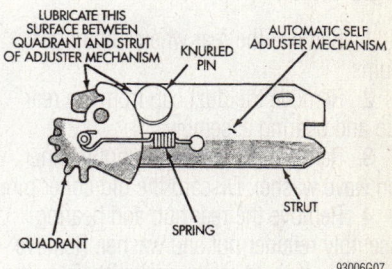

Automatic self-adjuster mechanism—Cirrus, Sebring Coupe, Stratus, Breeze

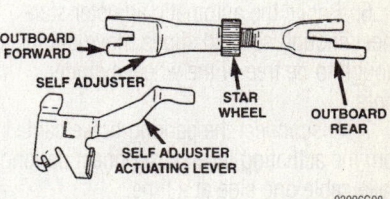

Rear brake shoe automatic self-adjuster mechanism and actuating lever—Sebring Convertible

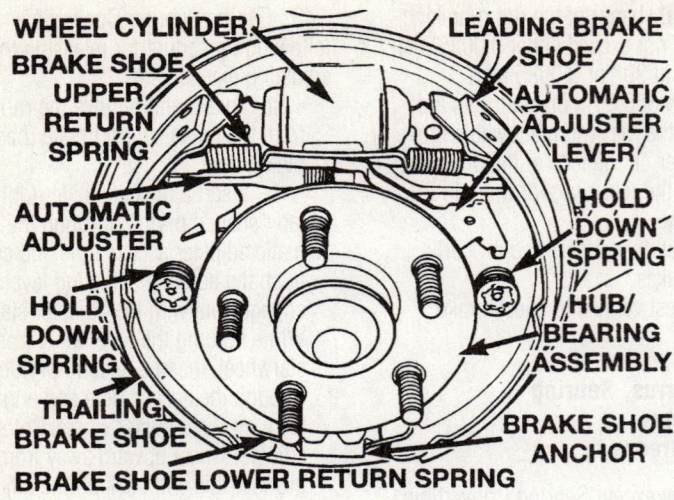

WHEEL CYLINDER
BRAKE SHOE
UPPER RETURN SPRING
AUTOMATIC ADJUSTER
HOLD DOWN SPRING
TRAILING BRAKE SHOE
BRAKE SHOE LOWER RETURN SPRING
LEADING BRAKE SHOE
AUTOMATIC ADJUSTER LEVER
HOLD DOWN SPRING
HUB/BEARING ASSEMBLY
BRAKE SHOE ANCHOR

93006G09

Kelsey Hayes rear brake assembly—Sebring Convertible

7. Reinstall the wheel and tire. Torque the lug nuts in a star pattern sequence to about 45 ft. lbs. (61 Nm); then, repeat the pattern and final torque to 95–100 ft. lbs. (129–135 Nm).

8. Properly adjust the rear brakes.

9. Road test vehicle to check for proper brake operation.

Brake Shoes

REMOVAL & INSTALLATION

Chrysler Concorde, New Yorker, LHS
Dodge Intrepid
Eagle Vision

1. Remove the rear wheels and brake drums.

2. Remove the dust cap from the rear hub and bearing assembly.

3. Remove the cotter pin, nut retainer and wave washer. Discard the old cotter pin.

4. Remove the rear hub and bearing assembly retainer nut and washer. Remove the rear hub and bearing assembly from the spindle.

5. Remove the automatic adjuster spring from the adjuster lever.

6. Rotate the automatic adjuster starwheel enough so both shoes move out far enough to be free of the wheel cylinder boots.

7. Disconnect the parking brake cable from the actuating lever. Disconnect parking brake cable one side at a time.

8. Remove the both lower brake shoe to anchor springs.

9. Remove the 2 brake shoe hold-down springs from the brake shoes.

10. Remove the brake shoes, upper shoe-to-shoe return spring, automatic adjuster and automatic adjuster lever from the backing plate as an assembly.

11. Separate the brake shoes from the automatic adjuster mechanism.

12. Remove the brake shoe automatic adjuster lever from the leading brake shoe.

To install:

13. Thoroughly clean and dry the backing plate. To prepare the backing plate, lubricate the bosses, anchor pin and parking brake actuating lever pivot surface lightly with lithium based grease.

14. Remove, clean and dry all parts still on the old shoes. Lubricate the starwheel shaft threads with anti-seize lubricant.

15. Assemble both brake shoes, the top shoe to shoe return spring, automatic adjuster and automatic adjuster lever before mounting on vehicle. Make sure the ends of the automatic adjusters are positioned above the extruded pins in the webbing of the brake shoes prior to installation.

16. Install the brake shoe assembly onto the brake support plate and install the hold-down springs.

17. Install the lower anchor springs and reconnect the parking brake cable to the park brake lever of the trailing brake shoe.

18. Rotate the serrated adjuster nut to remove the free-play from the adjuster assembly.

19. Install the automatic adjuster lever spring on the lead brake shoe assembly and the automatic adjuster lever.

20. Install the rear hub and bearing assembly. Install washer and retainer nut and torque to 124 ft. lbs. (168 Nm).

21. Install the wave washer, nut retainer and a new cotter pin onto the spindle. Install dust cap.

22. Adjust brake shoes so not to interfere with brake drum installation. Install the rear brake drum.

☛ **After installing the brake drums, pump the brake pedal several times to partially adjust the brake shoes. To verify proper operation of the self-adjusting parking brake, be sure that both rear brakes are not dragging when the parking brake pedal is released.**

23. Install the rear wheels and lug nuts. Torque the lug nuts, in a star pattern sequence, to 95 ft. lbs. (129 Nm).

24. Road test the vehicle. The automatic adjusters will continue brake adjustment during the road test of the vehicle.

Chrysler Sebring
Dodge Avenger

1. Remove the wheel assembly.

2. Remove the detent screw and brake drum. If difficulty is encountered in removing the drum:

    a. Verify the parking brake is released.

    b. Loosen the parking brake cable.

    c. Remove the access hole plug from the backing plate and move the parking brake lever until the lever stop rests on the brake shoe.

    d. If necessary, turn the adjuster so that it draws in to allow more clearance between the shoe and drum.

☛ **Note the location of all springs and clips for proper reassembly.**

3. Remove the shoe-to-lever spring and remove the adjuster lever.

4. Remove the auto adjuster assembly.

5. Remove the retainer spring.

6. Remove the hold-down springs, washers and pins.

7. Remove the shoe-to-shoe spring.

8. Remove the brake shoes from the backing plate.

9. Using a flat-tipped tool, open up the parking brake lever retaining clip. Remove the clip and washer from the pin on the shoe assembly and remove the shoe from the lever assembly.

To install:

10. Thoroughly clean and dry the backing plate. Lubricate the backing plate at the brake shoe contact points.

11. Lubricate backing plate bosses, anchor pin, and parking brake actuating mechanism with a lithium-based grease.

12. Install the parking brake lever assembly on the lever pin. Install the wave washer and a new retaining clip. Use pliers

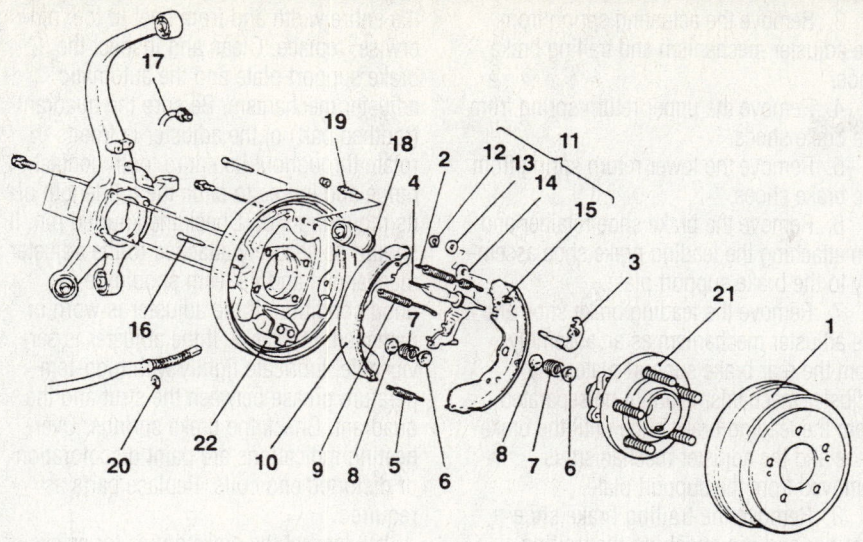

1. Brake drum
2. Shoe-to-lever spring
3. Adjuster lever
4. Auto adjuster assembly
5. Retainer spring
6. Shoe hold-down cup
7. Shoe hold-down spring
8. Shoe hold-down cup
9. Shoe-to-shoe spring
10. Shoe and lining assembly
11. Shoe and lever assembly
12. Retainer
13. Wave washer
14. Parking lever
15. Shoe and lining assembly
16. Shoe hold-down pin
17. Brake pipe connection
18. Wheel cylinder
19. Bleeder screw
20. Snap ring
21. Rear hub assembly
22. Backing plate

93006G10

Exploded view of the drum brake assembly—Sebring, Avenger

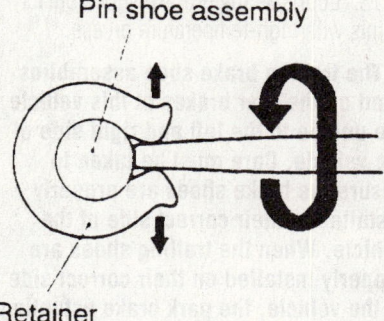

Pin shoe assembly

Retainer

93006G11

Opening the retainer clip—Sebring, Avenger

or the like to install the retainer on the pin. If removed, connect the parking brake lever to the parking brake cable and verify that the cable is properly routed.

13. Clean and lubricate the adjuster assembly. Make sure the nut-adjuster is drawn all the way to the stop, but the nut must NOT lock firmly at the end of the assembly.

14. Install the brake shoes on the backing plate with the hold-down springs, washers and pins.

15. Install the shoe-to-shoe spring.

16. Install the retainer spring.

17. Install the auto adjuster assembly and install the adjuster lever and the shoe-to-lever spring.

18. Pre-adjust the shoes so the drum slides on with a light drag and install the brake drum.

19. Adjust the rear brake shoes and install the rear wheels.

20. Adjust the parking brake cable.

21. Check for proper brake operation.

Dodge/Plymouth Neon

1. Remove the rear wheels.

2. Remove the drums.

3. Remove the automatic adjuster spring and lever.

4. Remove the hold-down clips and pins.

5. Rotate the automatic adjuster starwheel enough so both shoes move out far enough to be free of the wheel cylinder boots.

6. Disconnect the parking brake cable from the actuating lever.

7. Remove the lower shoe to shoe spring.

8. With the shoes held together by the upper shoe to shoe spring, remove them from the backing plate.

To install:

9. Thoroughly clean and dry the backing plate. To prepare the backing plate, lubricate the bosses, anchor pin and parking brake actuating lever pivot surface lightly with lithium based grease.

10. Remove, clean and dry all brake components. Lubricate the starwheel shaft threads with anti-seize lubricant and transfer all parts to their proper locations on the new shoes.

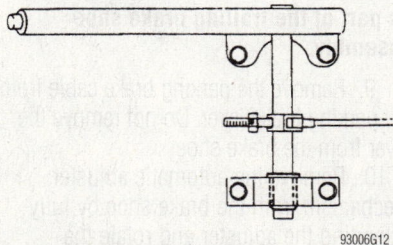

93006G12

Adjusting nut and nut holder—Sebring, Avenger

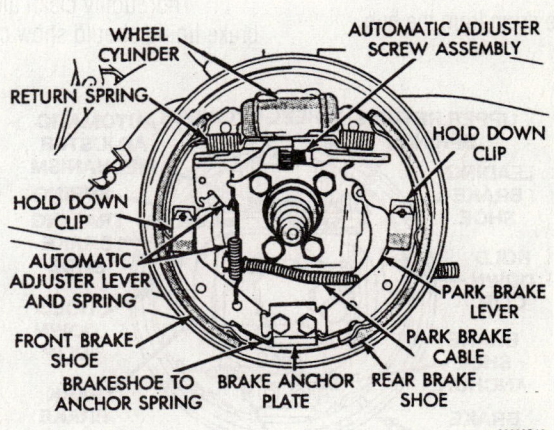

WHEEL CYLINDER
AUTOMATIC ADJUSTER SCREW ASSEMBLY
RETURN SPRING
HOLD DOWN CLIP
HOLD DOWN CLIP
AUTOMATIC ADJUSTER LEVER AND SPRING
PARK BRAKE LEVER
FRONT BRAKE SHOE
PARK BRAKE CABLE
BRAKESHOE TO ANCHOR SPRING
BRAKE ANCHOR PLATE
REAR BRAKE SHOE

93006G13

Kelsey Hayes rear brake assembly (left side shown)—Neon

Refer to the model specific sections for engine mechanical service procedures

11. Reinstall the lower spring.

12. Reconnect the parking brake cable.

13. Reinstall the automatic adjuster lever and spring.

14. Adjust the starwheel.

15. Remove any grease from the linings and install the drum.

16. Reinstall the wheels and properly adjust the brakes.

17. Check for proper brake system operation.

Chrysler Cirrus, Sebring Coupe Dodge Stratus Plymouth Breeze

All vehicles except Sebring Convertible, are equipped with rear wheel, 2 shoe leading/trailing, internal expanding type of drum brakes with automatic self-adjuster mechanisms. The automatic self-adjuster mechanisms used on these vehicles are new designs and function differently than the screw type adjusters used in the past. These new self-adjusters are still actuated each time the vehicles' service brakes are applied. The new adjusters are located directly below the wheel cylinders.

1. Remove the rear wheel assembly.

   a. Locate and remove the rubber plug from the top of the brake support plate (backing plate).

   b. Insert a brake adjuster tool or similarly shaped prytool through the automatic adjuster access hole and engage the teeth on the adjuster quadrant. Then rotate the quadrant so the teeth of the quadrant are moved toward the front of the vehicle. This will back off the adjustment of the rear brake shoes.

   c. Continue moving the quadrant toward the front of the vehicle until it stops moving.

2. Remove the drum from the hub assembly.

3. Remove the actuating spring from the adjuster mechanism and trailing brake shoe.

4. Remove the upper return spring from the brake shoes.

5. Remove the lower return spring from the brake shoes.

6. Remove the brake shoe retainer and pin attaching the leading brake shoe assembly to the brake support plate.

7. Remove the leading brake shoe and the adjuster mechanism as an assembly from the rear brake support plate. The adjuster mechanism cannot be separated from the leading brake shoe until the brake shoe and the adjuster mechanism is removed from the support plate.

8. Remove the trailing brake shoe retainer and pin attaching the trailing brake shoe assembly to the brake support plate. Remove the trailing brake shoe assembly.

➡**On this vehicle, the parking brake actuating lever is permanently attached to the trailing brake shoe assembly. Do not attempt to remove it from the original brake shoe assembly or reuse the original actuating lever on a replacement brake shoe assembly. All replacement brake shoe assemblies for this vehicle must have the actuating lever as part of the trailing brake shoe assembly.**

9. Remove the parking brake cable from the parking brake lever. Do not remove the lever from the brake shoe.

10. Remove the automatic adjuster mechanism from the brake shoe by fully extending the adjuster and rotate the adjuster out to release from the brake shoe.

To inspect:

11. Thoroughly clean all parts. The brake lining should show contact across the entire width and from heel to toe; otherwise, replace. Clean and inspect the brake support plate and the automatic adjuster mechanism. Be sure the quadrant (toothed part) of the adjuster is free to rotate throughout its entire tooth contact range and is free to slide the full length of its mounting slot. Check the knurled pin. It should be securely attached to the adjuster mechanism and its teeth should be in good condition. If the adjuster is worn or damaged, replace it. If the adjuster is serviceable, lubricate lightly with high-temperature grease between the strut and the quadrant. Check the brake springs. Overheating indications are paint discoloration or distorted end coils. Replace parts as required.

12. Inspect the brake drums for cracks or signs of overheating. Measure the drum run-out and diameter. If not to specification, reface the drum. Run-out should not exceed 0.006 in. (0.15mm). The diameter variation (oval shape) of the drum braking surface must not exceed either 0.0025 in. (0.064mm) in 30 degrees rotation, or 0.0035 in. (0.089mm) in 360 degrees rotation. All brake drums are marked with the maximum allowable brake drum diameter on the face of the drum.

To install:

13. Lubricate the 8 brake shoe contact points with high-temperature grease.

➡**The trailing brake shoe assemblies used on the rear brakes of this vehicle are unique to the left and right side of the vehicle. Care must be taken to ensure the brake shoes are properly installed in their correct side of the vehicle. When the trailing shoes are properly installed on their correct side of the vehicle, the park brake actuating lever will be positioned under the brake shoe web.**

14. Reinstall the parking brake cable onto the parking brake lever and install the trailing brake shoe and attaching pin.

15. Reinstall the automatic self-adjuster on the leading brake shoe by rotating it inward to attach. Install the leading shoe and adjuster assembly to the brake support plate.

16. Make sure the leading brake shoe is squarely seated on the brake support plate shoe contact areas, and install the brake retainer on the retainer pin.

17. Reinstall the lower return spring.

➡**The upper brake shoe return spring and adjuster mechanism actuating spring are unique to the side of the**

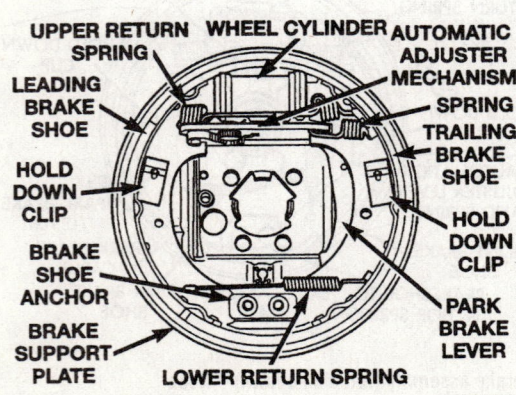

UPPER RETURN SPRING — WHEEL CYLINDER — AUTOMATIC ADJUSTER MECHANISM — LEADING BRAKE SHOE — SPRING — HOLD DOWN CLIP — TRAILING BRAKE SHOE — BRAKE SHOE ANCHOR — HOLD DOWN CLIP — BRAKE SUPPORT PLATE — LOWER RETURN SPRING — PARK BRAKE LEVER

93006G14

Varga rear wheel brake assembly (left side shown)—Cirrus, Sebring Coupe, Stratus, Breeze

vehicle they are used on. **The springs are colored for identification. The left side springs are green and the right side springs are blue.**

18. Reinstall the upper return spring (blue, right side; green, left side) on the leading brake shoe first, then on the trailing brake shoe.

19. Reinstall the self-adjuster spring on the trailing brake shoe first then attach it to the adjuster.

20. Reinstall the rear brake drums.

21. Reinstall the wheel and tire. Torque the lug nuts in a star pattern sequence to about 45 ft. lbs. (61 Nm), then repeat the pattern and final torque to 95–100 ft. lbs. (129–135 Nm).

22. Adjust the rear brakes by depressing the brake pedal. Brake shoe adjustment will occur the first time the brake pedal is depressed, pushing the rear brake shoes against the braking surface of the rear brake drums. Brake shoes should now be correctly adjusted and will not require any type of manual adjustment.

23. Road test vehicle to check for proper brake operation.

Sebring Convertible

The Sebring Convertible's rear wheel drum brake is a 2-shoe leading/trailing internal expanding type with an automatic self-adjuster mechanism. The automatic self-adjuster mechanism used on this vehicle is the screw type adjuster. The self-adjuster mechanism is actuated each time the vehicle service brakes are applied. Generally, drum brakes with a self-adjusting mechanism do not require manual brake shoe adjustment. Although, in the event that the brake shoes are replaced, it is advisable to make the initial adjustment manually to speed up the initial adjustment time. The initial adjustment procedure must be done prior to driving the vehicle.

➡**When removing the rear brake shoes, replace the brake shoes from only one side of the vehicle at a time. This is due to the automatic adjustment feature of the parking brake system. If the brake shoes are removed from both sides of the vehicle at the same time, the automatic adjuster will remove all slack from the parking brake cables, which will make brake shoe installation extremely difficult.**

1. Remove the rear wheel assembly.

   a. Locate and remove the rubber plug from the brake support plate (backing plate).

   b. Insert a brake adjuster tool or similarly shaped prytool through the automatic adjuster access hole and carefully push the adjuster actuating lever out of engagement with the adjuster starwheel. While holding the lever away from the starwheel, insert a second prytool through the access hole and engage the teeth on the adjuster wheel. Rotate the adjuster wheel upward away from the ground. This will back off the adjustment of the rear brake shoes.

2. Remove the drum from the hub assembly.

3. Remove the adjusting lever actuating spring from the leading brake shoe. Remove the automatic adjuster actuating lever from the leading brake shoe.

4. Thread the adjuster starwheel all the way into the adjuster, which will remove all tension from the adjuster.

5. Remove the upper and lower return springs from the brake shoes.

6. Remove the brake shoe hold-down spring and pin attaching the leading brake shoe assembly to the brake support plate.

7. Remove the leading brake shoe from the support plate.

8. Remove the automatic adjuster from the parking brake actuating lever and trailing brake shoe.

9. Remove the retaining clip securing the parking brake actuating lever to the trailing brake shoe.

10. Remove the trailing brake shoe hold-down spring and pin attaching the trailing brake shoe assembly to the brake support plate.

11. Remove the trailing brake shoe from the brake support plate and separate the shoe from the parking brake actuating lever.

To inspect:

12. Clean all parts well. The brake lining should show contact across the entire width and from heel to toe; otherwise, replace. Clean and inspect the brake support plate and the automatic adjuster mechanism. Be sure the adjuster is free to rotate throughout its entire range. If the adjuster is worn or damaged, replace it. If the adjuster is serviceable, lightly lubricate the threaded portion with high-temperature grease. Check the brake springs. Overheating indications are paint discoloration or

distorted end coils. Replace parts as required.

13. Inspect the brake drums for cracks or signs of overheating. Measure the drum run-out and diameter. If not to specification, reface the drum. Run-out should not exceed 0.006 in. (0.15mm). The diameter variation (oval shape) of the drum braking surface must not exceed either 0.0025 in. (0.064mm) in 30° rotation, or 0.0035 in. (0.089mm) in 360° rotation. All brake drums are marked with the maximum allowable brake drum diameter on the face of the drum.

To install:

14. Lubricate the 6 brake shoe contact points and the brake shoe anchor points with high-temperature grease.

15. Reinstall the wave washer on the pivot pin of the parking brake actuating lever.

16. Install the trailing brake shoe onto the attaching pin of the parking brake actuating lever.

17. Position the trailing brake shoe onto the brake support plate and be sure the trailing brake shoe is squarely seated on the support plate shoe contact areas and install the brake shoe hold-down spring on the hold-down pin.

18. Reinstall the parking brake actuating lever-to-trailing brake shoe retaining clip.

19. Reinstall the automatic adjuster on the trailing brake shoe and the parking brake actuating lever.

20. Place the leading brake shoe onto the brake support plate in proper position and install the attaching pin and hold-down spring.

21. Reinstall the lower and upper return springs.

22. Reinstall the automatic adjuster actuating lever and spring onto the leading brake shoe.

23. Manually adjust the brake shoes to the furthest adjusted position but not so far as to interfere with the installation of the brake drum.

24. Reinstall the rear brake drums. Check and adjust the brake shoes as necessary.

25. Reinstall the wheel and tire. Torque the lug nuts in a star pattern sequence to about 45 ft. lbs. (61 Nm), then repeat the pattern and final torque to 100 ft. lbs. (135 Nm).

26. Road test vehicle to check for proper brake operation.

FORD MOTOR COMPANY

Brake Caliper

REMOVAL & INSTALLATION

Ford Aspire

1. Remove the wheel and tire assembly.
2. Remove the brake pads.
3. Remove the banjo bolt securing the brake hose to the caliper and plug the hose end. Discard the 2 copper sealing washers.
4. Remove the 2 caliper retaining bolts.
5. Remove the caliper and the anti-squeak caps from the vehicle.

To install:

6. Install the anti-squeak caps.
7. Position the caliper on the steering knuckle and install the 2 caliper retaining bolts. Torque the caliper retaining bolts to 29–36 ft. lbs. (39–49 Nm).
8. Connect the brake hose to the caliper using the banjo bolt and 2 new copper sealing washers. Torque the banjo bolt to 16–22 ft. lbs. (22–29 Nm).
9. Install the brake pads.
10. Bleed the brake system.
11. Install the wheel and tire assembly.
12. Apply the brake pedal several times to position the brake pads, before attempting to move the vehicle.
13. Check for proper brake operation.

Ford Probe

FRONT

1. Remove the wheel.
2. Remove the banjo bolt attaching the brake hose to the caliper and discard the 2 sealing washers. Plug the hose to prevent fluid leakage.
3. Remove the caliper mounting bolt and pivot the caliper upward and off the brake pads.
4. Slide the caliper from the guide pin and remove from the vehicle.

To install:

5. Remove the guide pin bushing dust boots and push out the caliper guide pin bushing.
6. Lubricate the guide pin bushings with high temperature grease and install them in the caliper. Install the guide pin bushing dust boots.
7. Slide the caliper onto the guide pin and pivot the caliper down onto the brake pads. To provide the necessary clearance, it may be necessary to pull slightly outward on the caliper.

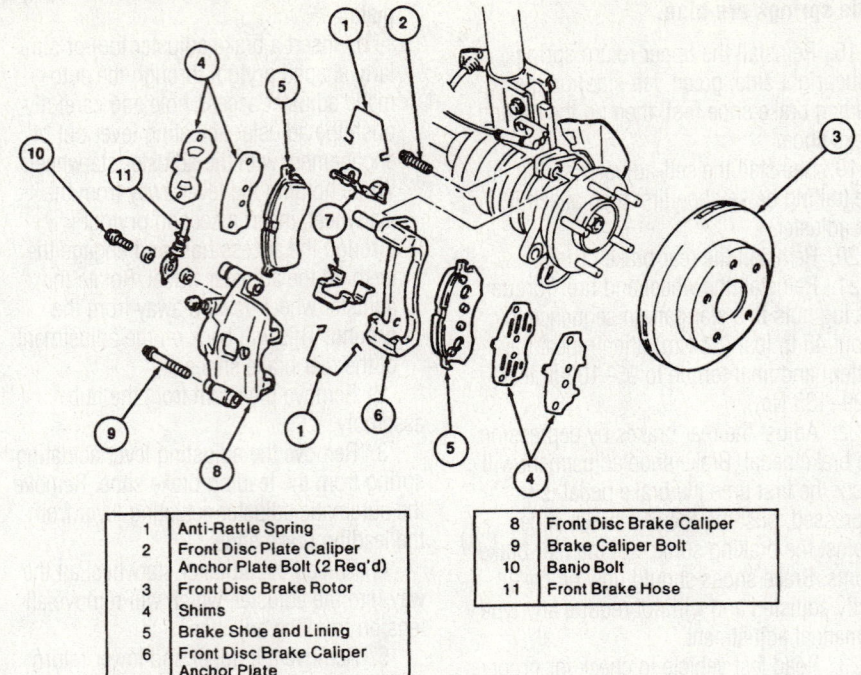

1	Anti-Rattle Spring
2	Front Disc Plate Caliper Anchor Plate Bolt (2 Req'd)
3	Front Disc Brake Rotor
4	Shims
5	Brake Shoe and Lining
6	Front Disc Brake Caliper Anchor Plate
7	Clips

8	Front Disc Brake Caliper
9	Brake Caliper Bolt
10	Banjo Bolt
11	Front Brake Hose

93006G15

Front brake caliper (exploded view)—Probe

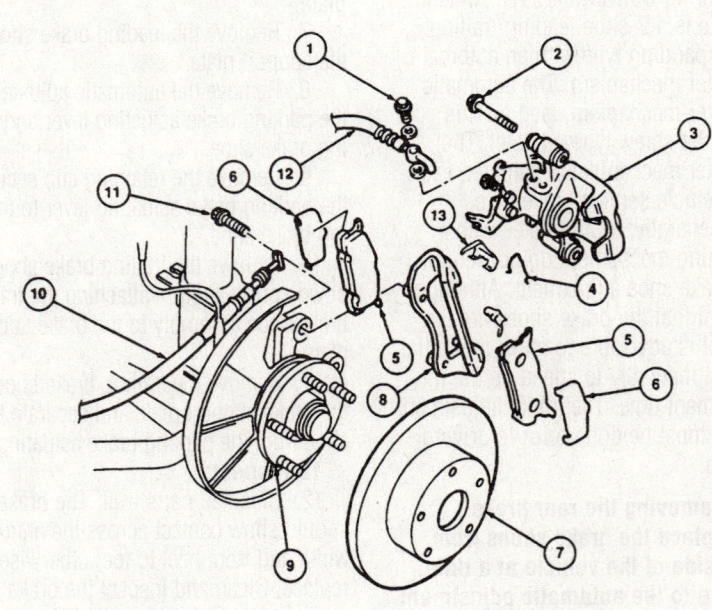

1	Banjo Bolt
2	Brake Caliper Bolt
3	Rear Disc Brake Caliper
4	Anti-Rattle Spring
5	Rear Brake Shoe and Lining
6	Shim
7	Rear Disc Brake Rotor
8	Rear Disc Brake Caliper Anchor Plate
9	Wheel Hub

10	Parking Brake Rear Cable and Conduit
11	Rear Disc Brake Caliper Anchor Plate Bolt (2 Req'd)
12	Rear Wheel Brake Hose
13	Clip

93006G16

Rear brake caliper—Probe

8. Install the caliper mounting bolt and torque to 33–36 ft. lbs. (44–49 Nm).

9. Install 2 new copper washers and the banjo bolt on the brake hose banjo fitting.

10. Position the brake hose on the caliper and install the banjo bolt. Torque the bolt to 16–22 ft. lbs. (22–29 Nm).

11. Bleed the brake system.

12. Install the wheel and torque the lug nuts to 65–87 ft. lbs. (80–118 Nm).

13. Check the brake system for proper operation.

REAR

1. Remove the wheel.

2. Remove the parking brake cable retaining clip.

3. Loosen the parking brake cable housing adjustment nut. Remove the cable housing from the bracket and the parking brake lever.

4. Remove the banjo bolt mounting the brake hose to the caliper.

5. Remove and discard the copper washers from the banjo fitting.

6. Remove the caliper mounting bolt.

7. Pivot the caliper off the brake pads and slide the caliper off the guide pin.

To install:

8. Lubricate the guide pin bushings with high temperature grease. Install the caliper onto the guide pin and pivot the caliper over the brake pads. Torque the caliper attaching bolt to 25–29 ft. lbs. (34–39 Nm).

9. Install new copper washers and the banjo bolt mounting the brake hose to the caliper. Torque the banjo bolt to 16–22 ft. lbs. (23–29 Nm).

10. Position the parking brake cable into the parking brake lever and bracket. Install the retaining clip.

11. Adjust the parking brake cable so there is no clearance between the cable end and the parking brake lever. Tighten the parking brake cable locknut.

12. Bleed the brake system.

13. Install the wheel and torque the lug nuts to 65–87 ft. lbs. (80–118 Nm).

14. Check the brake system for proper operation.

Ford Contour
Mercury Mystique

FRONT

1. Remove the wheel and tire assembly.

2. Remove the outer disc brake pad spring clip (anti-rattle clip).

3. Remove the 2 locator pin covers and remove the locator pins.

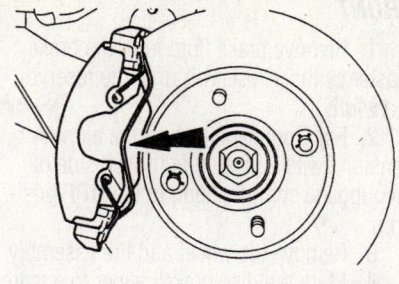

Position of disc brake pad (brake shoe and lining) spring clip—Contour, Mystique

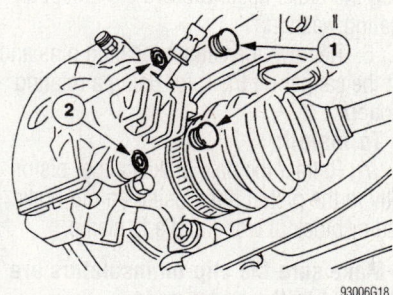

View of disc brake caliper locating pins—Contour, Mystique

4. Free the hose from its mounting on the strut.

5. Lift the caliper off of the brake rotor.

6. Remove the inboard disc brake pad from the caliper.

7. If the brake caliper is to be removed from the vehicle, place a pan under the caliper to catch the brake fluid for proper disposal. Disconnect the brake hose at the caliper and allow to drain.

8. Remove the brake caliper.

9. If the caliper is not to be serviced, tie off the caliper to prevent strain on the brake hose.

To install:

10. If removed, install the brake hose

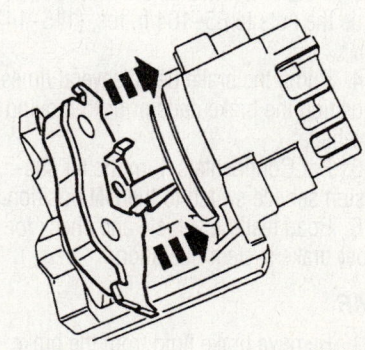

View of inboard disc brake pad (brake shoe and lining)—Contour, Mystique

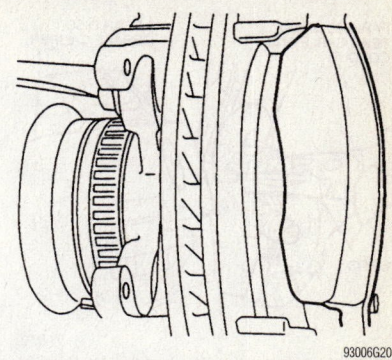

Positioning the outboard disc brake pad (brake shoe and lining)–Contour, Mystique

onto the caliper. Torque the fitting to 10 ft. lbs. (14 Nm).

11. Position the inboard disc brake pad into the caliper.

12. Make sure that the outboard disc brake pad is positioned properly.

13. Reinstall the caliper over the brake rotor and position onto the caliper anchor plate.

14. Reinstall the 2 caliper locator pins and torque to 20 ft. lbs. (28 Nm).

15. Reinstall the caliper locator pin covers.

16. Reinstall the outer disc brake pad spring clip.

17. Reconnect the brake hose to the front strut.

18. Bleed the brake system of air. Top off the master cylinder when complete.

19. If the brake pedal feels spongy, repeat the brake bleeding procedure.

20. Reinstall the wheel and tire assembly. Torque the lug nuts to 62 ft. lbs. (85 Nm).

21. Pump the brake pedal several times to position the brake pads before attempting to move the vehicle.

22. Road test the vehicle and check for proper brake system operation.

REAR

1. Remove the wheel and tire assembly.

2. Remove the parking brake rear cable and conduit from the parking brake lever at the disc brake caliper, using a pair of pliers.

3. Remove the cotter pin and guide pin.

4. Remove the caliper locating pin cover and remove the locating pin.

5. Lift the rear disc brake caliper off of the anchor plate.

6. Place a pan under the caliper to catch any lost brake fluid. Dispose of properly.

7. Crack open the rear brake hose fitting and allow the brake fluid to drain.

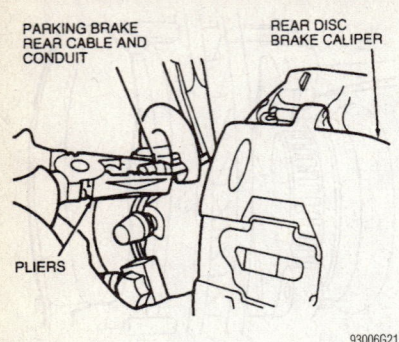

PARKING BRAKE
REAR CABLE AND
CONDUIT

REAR DISC
BRAKE CALIPER

PLIERS

93006G21

**Method of removing the parking brake
cable—Contour, Mystique**

8. Finish removing the rear brake hose and washers from the caliper. Discard the washers.

9. Remove the disc brake caliper.

To install:

10. Retract the piston fully into the caliper using service tool T87P–2588–A.

11. Reconnect the rear brake hose to the caliper using new washers.

12. Fit the rear disc brake caliper over the rotor and position onto the anchor plate.

13. Reinstall the caliper locating pin and torque to 30 ft. lbs. (41 Nm).

14. Reinstall the caliper locating pin cover.

15. Reinstall the guide pin and the cotter pin.

16. Reinstall the parking brake rear cable and conduit onto the parking brake lever.

17. Adjust the parking brake by operating the parking brake control several times.

18. Properly bleed the brake system of air. Top off the master cylinder when complete.

19. If the brake pedal feels spongy, repeat the brake bleeding procedure.

20. Reinstall the wheel and tire assembly. Torque the lug nuts to 94 ft. lbs. (128 Nm).

21. Pump the brake pedal several times to position the brake pads before attempting to move the vehicle.

22. Road test the vehicle and check for proper brake system operation.

**Ford Taurus
Lincoln Continental
Mercury Sable**

❉❉ CAUTION

On Continentals, the air suspension switch, located in the left side of the luggage compartment, must be turned OFF before raising the vehicle. Failure to do so may result in unexpected inflation or deflation of the air springs that may result in shifting of the vehicle during service.

FRONT

1. Remove brake fluid from the brake master cylinder reservoir until the reservoir is ½ full.

2. For Continentals, turn the air suspension switch, located in the left side of the luggage compartment, to the **OFF** position.

3. Remove the wheel and tire assembly.

4. Mark the disc brake caliper to ensure that it is reinstalled in the correct location.

5. Remove the hollow bolt connecting the brake hose to the disc brake caliper and plug the brake hose. Discard the 2 copper sealing washers.

6. Remove the caliper locating pins and lift the caliper off the rotor using a rotating motion.

To install:

7. Retract the disc brake caliper piston fully in the piston bore, using an old brake pad or block of wood and a C-clamp.

➡**Make sure the clip-on insulators are attached to the brake pads.**

8. Install the disc brake pads to the caliper. Make sure the brake pad insulators are correctly attached to the brake pad plate.

9. Position the disc brake caliper and pad assembly above the rotor and install it with a rotating motion. Make sure the inner and outer pads are properly positioned and the outer anti-rattle spring is properly positioned.

10. Lubricate the locating pins and the inside of the insulators with silicone grease. Torque the locating pins to 25 ft. lbs. (34 Nm).

11. Remove the plug and install the brake hose to the disc brake caliper. Use 2 new copper washers and torque the hollow bolt to 30–40 ft. lbs. (41–54 Nm).

12. Bleed the brake system, filling the master cylinder as required.

13. Install the wheel and tire assembly; torque the nuts to 85–104 ft. lbs. (115–142 Nm).

14. Pump the brake pedal several times to position the brake pads prior to moving the vehicle.

15. For Continentals, turn the air suspension service switch to the **ON** position.

16. Road test the vehicle and check for proper brake system operation.

REAR

1. Remove brake fluid from the brake master cylinder reservoir until the reservoir is ½ full.

2. For Continentals, turn the air suspension switch, located in the left side of

the luggage compartment, to the **OFF** position.

3. Remove the wheel and tire assembly.

4. Remove the retaining bolt and disconnect the brake hose from the caliper assembly. Discard the copper sealing washers.

5. Remove the retaining clip from the parking brake at the caliper. Disengage the parking brake cable end from the lever arm.

6. Lift the rear disc brake caliper away from the rear disc support bracket.

7. Remove the disc brake caliper locating pins and boots from the rear disc support bracket.

To install:

8. Using rear caliper piston adjuster tool T87P-2588-A, rotate the rear disc brake piston and adjuster clockwise until fully seated.

➡**Make sure one of the 2 slots in the rear disc brake piston and adjuster face is positioned so it will engage the nib on the disc brake pad.**

9. Apply silicone dielectric compound to the inside of the slider pin boots and the slider pins.

10. Position the slider pins and boots in the support bracket. Position the caliper assembly on the support bracket. Make sure the brake pads are installed correctly.

11. Remove the residue from the pin retainer threads and apply 1 drop of threadlock and sealer. Install the pin retainers and torque to 23–26 ft. lbs. (31–35 Nm).

12. Attach the cable end to the parking brake lever. Install the cable retaining clip on the caliper assembly.

13. Using new washers, connect the brake flex hose to the caliper. Torque the retaining bolt to 40 ft. lbs. (54 Nm).

14. Bleed the brake system, filling the master cylinder as required.

15. Install the wheel and tire assembly; torque the nuts to 85–104 ft. lbs. (115–142 Nm).

16. Pump the brake pedal several times to position the brake pads prior to moving the vehicle.

17. For Continentals, turn the air suspension service switch to the **ON** position.

18. Road test the vehicle and check for proper brake system operation.

**Ford Escort
Mercury Tracer**

FRONT

1. Remove the wheel and tire assembly.

2. Remove the disc brake pads.

3. Remove the banjo bolt securing the brake hose to the brake caliper. Discard 2 copper sealing washers.

4. Remove 2 brake caliper retaining bolts and remove the brake caliper.

To install:

5. Place the brake caliper in position and install 2 brake caliper retaining bolts. Torque the bolts to 29–36 ft. lbs. (39–49 Nm).

6. Install the brake hose to the brake caliper and install the banjo bolt with 2 new copper sealing washers. Torque the banjo bolt to 16–22 ft. lbs. (22–29 Nm).

7. Install the disc brake pads.

8. Bleed the brake system.

9. Install the wheel and tire assembly. Torque the lug nuts to 65–87 ft. lbs. (88–118 Nm).

10. Pump the brake pedal several times to position the brake pads to the brake rotor.

11. Road test the vehicle and check the brake system for proper operation.

REAR

1. Remove the wheel and tire assembly.

2. Remove the disc brake pads.

3. Remove the parking brake cable bracket bolt and position the bracket aside.

4. Remove the parking brake cable from the operating lever.

5. Remove the banjo bolt securing the brake hose to the brake caliper. Discard 2 copper sealing washers.

6. Remove the upper brake caliper retaining bolt.

7. Slide the brake caliper off the mounting bracket and remove from the vehicle.

To install:

8. Place the brake caliper on the mounting bracket and slide into position.

9. Install the upper brake caliper retaining bolt. Torque the bolt to 33–43 ft. lbs. (45–59 Nm).

10. Install the brake hose to the brake caliper and secure with the banjo bolt using 2 new copper sealing washers. Torque the banjo bolt to 16–22 ft. lbs. (22–29 Nm).

11. Connect the parking brake cable to the operating lever. Position the bracket and install the bracket bolt.

12. Install the disc brake pads.

13. Bleed the brake system.

14. Install the wheel and tire assembly. Torque the lug nuts to 65–87 ft. lbs. (88–118 Nm).

15. Pump the brake pedal several times to position the brake pads to the brake rotor.

16. Road test the vehicle and check the brake system for proper operation.

Ford Mustang

FRONT

1. Remove the wheel and tire assembly.

2. Mark the disc brake caliper to ensure that it will be installed to the same side if both calipers are being removed.

3. Remove the banjo bolt that connects the brake hose fitting to the disc brake caliper. Remove and plug the brake hose. Discard 2 copper sealing washers.

4. On single piston calipers, remove the lower brake caliper locating pin.

5. Rotate the brake caliper approximately 90° away from the anchor assembly.

6. Slide the brake caliper away from anchor assembly until the brake caliper disengages from the upper locating pin and remove from the vehicle.

7. On dual piston calipers, remove the clip and washer with the locating pin and remove the disc brake caliper.

To install:

8. If required, compress the caliper piston(s) using a C-clamp and an old disc brake pad or block of wood.

9. On single piston calipers, engage the upper disc brake caliper locating pin into the insulator.

10. Make sure the anti–rattle is properly installed on caliper.

11. Make sure the brake pads are properly installed.

12. Rotate the brake caliper assembly into place on the anchor plate.

➡ **New locating pins are recommended due to the thread locking compound on the threads.**

13. Install the lower disc brake caliper locating pin and torque to 23 ft. lbs. (31 Nm).

14. On dual piston calipers, place the disc brake caliper over the brake rotor with the brake pads installed and lower the caliper onto the brake rotor.

15. Install the disc brake caliper locating pin and clip by pressing the caliper down to compress the bias springs and the locating pin into position and secure with the washer and clip.

16. Unplug and install the brake hose to the disc brake caliper using 2 new copper sealing washers, 1 on each side of the fitting. Install the banjo bolt and torque to 30 ft. lbs. (40 Nm).

17. Bleed the brake system and check for leaks. Replace the bleeder screw rubber cap.

18. Install the wheel and tire assembly. Torque the lug nuts in a star pattern to 85–105 ft. lbs. (115–142 Nm).

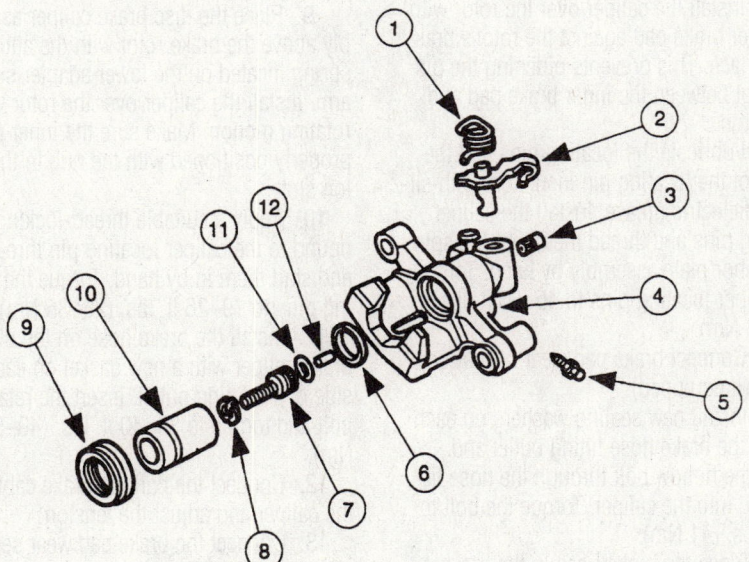

93006G22

1	Rear Wheel Brake Caliper Spring	7	Rear Disc Brake Adjuster Spindle
2	Rear Brake Operating Lever	8	Snap Ring
3	Brake Adjuster Screw	9	Dust Seal
4	Rear Disc Brake Caliper	10	Piston
5	Wheel Cylinder Bleeder Screw	11	O-Ring
6	Piston Seal	12	Brake Connecting Link

Rear disc brake assembly—Escort, Tracer

Timing chain and gear service is covered in the model specific sections of this manual

19. Pump the brake pedal several times to position the brake pads before the vehicle is moved.

20. Road test the vehicle and check for proper brake system operation.

REAR

1. Remove the wheel and tire assembly.

2. Remove the banjo bolt securing the brake hose to the disc brake caliper. Separate the brake hose from the caliper and plug the hose. Discard 2 copper sealing washers.

3. Remove the retaining clip from the parking brake rear cable at the disc brake caliper. Release the tension from the parking brake cable and disengage the cable end from the parking brake lever on the brake caliper.

4. Hold the disc brake caliper locating pin hex-heads with an open-end wrench and remove 2 brake pin retainer bolts.

5. Lift the disc brake caliper assembly away from the disc support bracket and remove the disc brake caliper from the vehicle.

6. Remove the brake caliper locating pins and boots from support bracket.

To install:

7. If required, use Caliper Piston Adjuster T87P-2588-A to rotate the caliper piston into the caliper bore. Align the tool tips with the slots in the piston and rotate the tool clockwise until the piston is seated.

8. Apply a suitable silicone dielectric compound to the inside of the locating pin boots and the caliper locating pins.

9. Install the brake caliper locating pins and boots in the disc support bracket.

10. Properly install the disc brake pads and anti-rattle clips.

11. Apply a drop of suitable thread locking compound to the threads of the brake pin retainer bolts and install the brake pin retainers. Torque the brake pin retainer bolts to 23–26 ft. lbs. (31–35 Nm) while holding the brake caliper locating pins with an open-end wrench.

12. Attach the end of the parking brake cable to the parking brake lever on the disc brake caliper.

13. Unplug and install the brake hose to the disc brake caliper using 2 new copper sealing washers on the fitting. Insert the banjo bolt through both washers and the brake line fitting and torque to 30 ft. lbs. (40 Nm).

14. Properly bleed the brake system and check for leaks.

15. Install the wheel and tire assembly. Torque the lug nuts in a star pattern to 85–105 ft. lbs. (115–142 Nm).

16. Pump the brake pedal several times to position the brake pads before moving the vehicle.

17. Road test the vehicle and check the brake system for proper operation.

Ford Thunderbird
Lincoln Mark VIII
Mercury Cougar (1997–98 Model)

FRONT

1. Remove the wheel and tire assembly.

2. Loosen the brake line fitting that connects the brake hose to the brake line at the frame bracket. Plug the brake line. Remove the retaining clip from the hose and bracket and disengage the hose from the bracket.

3. Remove the hollow bolt attaching the brake hose to the caliper and remove the brake hose. Discard the sealing washers.

4. Disconnect the brake pad wear sensor connector (if equipped).

5. Remove the caliper locating pins and remove the caliper. If removing both calipers, mark the right and left sides so they may be reinstalled correctly.

To install:

6. Fully retract piston into caliper bore.

7. Install the caliper over the rotor with the outer brake pad against the rotor's braking surface. This prevents pinching the piston boot between the inner brake pad and the piston.

8. Lubricate the locating pins and the inside of the locating pin insulators with silicone dielectric grease. Install the caliper locating pins and thread them into the spindle/anchor plate assembly by hand. Torque the caliper locating pins to 45–65 ft. lbs. (61–88 Nm).

9. Connect brake pad wear sensor connector (if equipped).

10. Install new sealing washers on each side of the brake hose fitting outlet and install the hollow bolt through the hose fitting and into the caliper. Torque the bolt to 30 ft. lbs. (41 Nm).

11. Place the brake hose in the bracket and install the retaining clip. Make sure the hose is not twisted.

12. Remove the plug from the brake line, connect the brake line to the brake hose and torque the fitting nut to 10–18 ft. lbs. (13–24 Nm).

13. Bleed the brake system using clean DOT 3 brake fluid from a closed container.

14. Install the wheel and tire assembly. Torque the lug nuts to 85–105 ft. lbs. (115–142 Nm).

15. Apply the brake pedal several times before moving the vehicle, to position the brake pads.

16. Road test the vehicle and check for proper brake system operation.

REAR

1. Remove the wheel and tire assembly.

2. Disconnect brake pad wear sensor connector (if equipped).

3. Remove the brake fitting retaining bolt from the disc brake caliper and disconnect the flexible brake hose from the caliper. Plug the hose and the caliper fitting.

4. Release the tension from the parking brake cable. Disconnect the cable from the caliper.

5. Remove the disc brake caliper locating pins. Lift the caliper off the brake rotor and anchor plate using a rotating motion.

6. Remove the disc brake pads.

To install:

7. Place the Rear Caliper Piston Adjuster T87P-2588-A in the caliper. Be sure the pins on the tool are meshed with the slots on the piston. Rotate the tool clockwise until the piston is seated in the caliper bore.

8. Install the disc pads in the support bracket. Make sure that the pads are on the correct side.

9. Place the disc brake caliper assembly above the brake rotor with the anti-rattle spring located on the lower adapter support arm. Install the caliper over the rotor with a rotating motion. Make sure the inner pad is properly positioned with the nub in the piston slot.

10. Apply a suitable thread-locking compound to the caliper locating pin threads and start them in by hand. Torque the locating pins to 19–26 ft. lbs. (26–35 Nm).

11. Install the brake hose on the disc brake caliper with a new gasket on each side of the fitting outlet. Insert the retaining bolt and torque to 30–40 ft. lbs. (40–54 Nm).

12. Connect the parking brake cable to the caliper and adjust the tension.

13. Connect the brake pad wear sensor connector (if equipped).

14. Bleed the brake system using clean DOT 3 brake fluid from a closed container.

15. Install the wheel and tire assembly. Torque the lug nuts to 85–105 ft. lbs. (115–142 Nm).

16. Apply the brake pedal several times before moving the vehicle, to position the brake pads.

17. Verify proper parking brake system operation.

18. Road test the vehicle and check for proper brake system operation.

Ford Crown Victoria
Lincoln Town Car
Mercury Grand Marquis

FRONT

➡**Before continuing with this procedure, make sure to have available, 2 new disc brake caliper guide pin bolts and 2 banjo bolt sealing washers, per caliper. Once removed, these parts loose their torque holding ability or retention capability and must not be reused.**

1. If equipped with air suspension, the air suspension switch, located on the right-hand side of the luggage compartment, must be turned to the **OFF** position before raising the vehicle.

2. Remove the front wheel and tire assembly.

3. Loosen and remove the banjo bolt securing the brake hose from the disc brake caliper. Plug the brake hose. Discard the sealing washers.

4. Remove 2 disc brake caliper guide pin bolts and discard. If removing both calipers, mark the right and left sides so they may be reinstalled correctly.

5. Lift the disc brake caliper off of the anchor plate.
   To install:

6. Retract the disc brake caliper piston fully in the piston bore, using an old brake pad or block of wood and a C-clamp.

7. Install the disc brake pads to the caliper. Make sure that the brake pad insulators are correctly attached to the brake pad plate.

8. Position the disc brake caliper onto the anchor plate. Make sure the inner and outer pads are properly positioned and the anti-rattle spring is properly positioned. The caliper bleed screw should be positioned on top of the caliper when assembled on the vehicle.

9. Install 2 new caliper guide pin bolts. Torque the bolts to 21–26 ft. lbs. (28–26 Nm).

10. Unplug and install the brake hose to the disc brake caliper using 2 new copper sealing washers on the banjo bolt. Torque the bolt to 30–40 ft. lbs. (41–54 Nm).

11. Bleed the brake system, filling the master cylinder as required. Only use clean DOT 3 brake fluid from a sealed container.

12. Install the wheel and tire assembly. Torque the lug nuts in a star pattern to 85–104 ft. lbs. (115–142 Nm).

13. If equipped with air suspension, turn the air suspension switch to the **ON** position.

14. Pump the brake pedal several times to position the brake pads prior to moving the vehicle.

15. Road test the vehicle and check for proper brake system operation.

REAR

➡**Before continuing with this procedure, make sure to have available, 2 banjo bolt sealing washers, per caliper. Once removed, these parts loose their torque holding ability or retention capability and must not be reused.**

1. If equipped with air suspension, the air suspension switch, located on the right-hand side of the luggage compartment, must be turned to the **OFF** position before raising the vehicle.

2. Remove the rear wheel and tire assembly.

3. Loosen and remove the banjo bolt securing the brake hose to the disc brake caliper. Plug the brake hose and discard both sealing washers.

4. Remove 2 disc brake caliper locating bolts. Lift the disc brake caliper off the rotor and anchor plate using a rotating motion.
   To install:

5. Retract the disc brake caliper piston fully in the piston bore, using an old brake pad or block of wood and a C-clamp.

6. Install the disc brake pads on the caliper. Make sure that the pads are on the correct side.

7. Position the disc brake caliper assembly above the rotor with the anti-rattle spring located on the lower adapter support arm. Install the caliper over the rotor with a rotating motion.

8. Clean the inner surface of the caliper bushings and locating bolts. Lubricate the caliper locating bolts with a suitable silicone dielectric compound. Install and start the locating bolts by hand only. Torque both bolts to 16–20 ft. lbs. (22–27 Nm).

9. Unplug and install the brake hose to the disc brake caliper using 2 new copper sealing washers on the banjo bolt. Torque the bolt to 30–40 ft. lbs. (41–54 Nm).

10. Bleed the brake system, filling the master cylinder as required. Only use clean DOT 3 brake fluid from a sealed container.

11. Replace the rubber rear disc brake bleeder screw cap.

12. Install the wheel and tire assembly. Torque the lug nuts in a star pattern to 85–104 ft. lbs. (115–142 Nm).

13. If equipped with air suspension, turn the air suspension switch to the **ON** position.

14. Pump the brake pedal several times to position the brake pads prior to moving the vehicle.

15. Road test the vehicle and check for proper brake system operation.

Disc Brake Pads

REMOVAL & INSTALLATION

Ford Aspire

1. Remove brake fluid from the master cylinder reservoir to lower the level by approximately⅓ preventing brake fluid overflow when the caliper piston is pressed back into its bore.

2. Remove the tire and wheel assembly.

3. Use the proper brake tool or a C-clamp to move the caliper piston into its bore approximately ⅛ in. (3mm) to allow removal of the disc brake pads.

4. Remove the brake pad anti-rattle clip. Disengage the M-shaped anti-rattle spring from the brake pads.

5. Remove the 2 disc brake caliper locating pins and the M-shaped anti-rattle spring.

6. Remove the brake pads and shims. Do not discard the shims found behind the brake pads.
   To install:

7. Use the proper brake tool or a C-clamp and one of the old brake pads to push the caliper piston back into the caliper bore. Do not push directly against the caliper piston or damage to the piston may result.

8. Apply suitable grease, normally supplied with the brake pad set, to both surfaces of the inner shim and to the back of the brake pads. Be careful not to get grease on the friction surface of the brake pads.

9. Install the brake pads, making sure the shims are installed.

10. Install the 2 disc brake caliper locating pins and the M-shaped anti-rattle spring.

11. Install the disc brake pad anti-rattle clip.

12. Install the wheel and tire assembly. Torque the lug bolts to 65–87 ft. lbs. (88–118 Nm).

13. Apply the brake pedal several times to seat the pads, before moving the vehicle. Check the brake fluid level in the master cylinder and add fluid as necessary.

14. Check for proper brake operation.

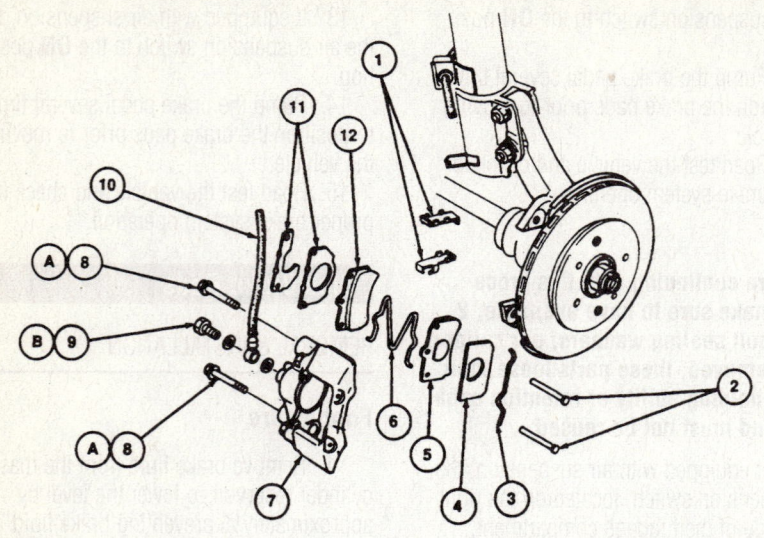

1	Anti-Squeak Caps
2	Disc Brake Caliper Locating Pins (2 Req'd)
3	Disc Brake Pad Anti-Rattle Clip
4	Brake Pad Shim
5	Brake Shoe and Lining
6	M-Shaped Anti-Rattle Spring
7	Disc Brake Caliper, Front

8	Brake Caliper Bolt (2 Req'd)
9	Banjo Bolt
10	Front Brake Hose
11	Brake Pad Shims (Part of 2001)
12	Brake Shoe and Lining

93006G23

Disc brake assembly—Aspire

Ford Probe

FRONT

1. Remove brake fluid from the master cylinder reservoir until the reservoir is approximately ½ full. Discard the removed fluid.

2. Remove the wheel.

3. If necessary, clean the brake assembly with brake cleaner and allow it to dry.

4. Using an appropriate tool, pry the caliper outboard.

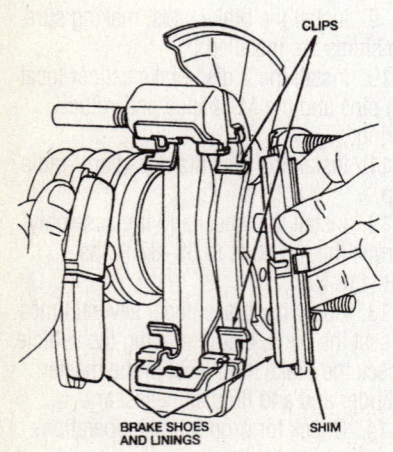

93006G24

Front disc brake pads—Probe

5. Remove the caliper mounting bolt. Pivot the caliper upward on the fixed guide pin and secure it out of the way.

6. Remove the 2 anti-rattle springs.

7. Remove the shims. Tag the shims so they can be reinstalled in their original position.

8. Remove the brake pads and retaining clips from the caliper anchor.

9. Inspect the disc brake rotor for wear and/or damage. Machine or replace, as necessary. If machining, observe the minimum thickness specification.

To install:

10. Install the retaining clips.

11. Install the brake pads into the caliper anchor. The pad with the wear indicator is the inboard pad.

12. Install the shims in their original position.

13. Compress the caliper piston into its bore using a large C-clamp and one of the old brake pads. Do not allow the clamp to push directly on the caliper piston.

14. Pivot the caliper down over the brake pads. Install the anti-rattle springs. Install the caliper mounting bolt and torque the bolt to 33–36 ft. lbs. (44–49 Nm).

15. Install the wheel. Torque the lug nuts to 65–87 ft. lbs. (80–118 Nm).

16. Pump the brake pedal several times to position the caliper piston.

17. Check the fluid level in the master cylinder reservoir and add fluid as necessary.

18. Road test the vehicle for proper brake operation.

REAR

1. Remove brake fluid from the master cylinder reservoir until the reservoir is approximately ½ full. Discard the removed fluid.

2. Remove the wheel.

3. Remove the parking brake cable retaining clip.

4. Loosen the parking brake cable housing adjusting nut. Remove the cable housing from the bracket and the parking brake lever.

5. Insert an Allen wrench into the back of the caliper and turn the manual adjustment gear counterclockwise to pull the caliper piston inward. Turn the gear until it stops.

6. Remove the caliper mounting bolt and pivot the caliper to clear the brake pads. Remove the caliper and suspend it with wire from the rear strut.

7. Remove the anti-rattle spring from the disc brake pads. Remove the disc brake pads, the shims and retaining clips. If the brake pads and shims are to be reused, tag them so they can be installed in their original positions.

8. Inspect the disc brake rotor for wear

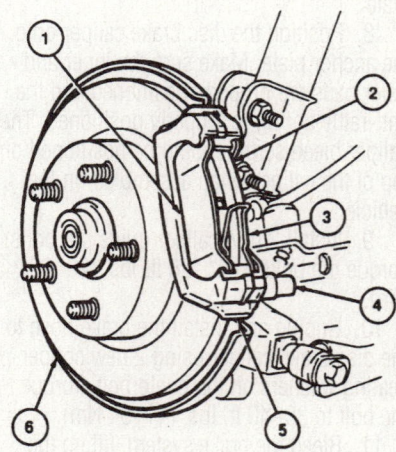

1	Shim
2	Rear Brake Shoe and Lining
3	Anti-Rattle Spring
4	Guide Pin
5	Rear Disc Brake Caliper Anchor Plate
6	Rear Disc Brake Rotor

93006G25

Rear disc brake pads—Probe

and/or damage. Machine or replace, as necessary. If machining, observe the minimum thickness specification.

To install:

9. Install the retaining clips. Position the shims on the disc brake pads and install the pads into the caliper anchor bracket.

10. Install the anti-rattle spring onto the disc brake pads.

11. Lightly lubricate the guide pin bushings with high temperature grease and install the caliper onto the guide pin. Pivot the caliper over the disc brake pads.

12. Install the caliper mounting bolt and torque to 25–29 ft. lbs. (34–39 Nm).

13. Install the parking brake cable into the parking brake lever and bracket. Install the parking brake cable retaining clip.

14. Adjust the cable so there is no clearance between the cable end and the parking brake lever. Tighten the parking brake cable locknut.

15. Turn the caliper manual adjustment gear clockwise with an Allen wrench until the brake pads just touch the rotor, then back off ⅓ turn.

16. Install the wheel and torque the lug nuts to 65–87 ft. lbs. (80–118 Nm).

17. Pump the brake pedal several times to position the caliper piston. Check the fluid level in the master cylinder reservoir and add clean brake fluid, if necessary.

18. Road test and check for proper brake operation.

Ford Contour
Mercury Mystique
Mercury Cougar (1999–01 model)

FRONT

1. Remove ½ of the brake fluid from the master cylinder reservoir.

2. Remove the wheel and tire assembly.

3. Remove the outer disc brake pad spring clip (anti-rattle clip).

4. Remove the 2 locating pin covers and remove the locating pins.

5. Free the hose from its mounting on the strut.

6. Lift the caliper off of the brake rotor and tie it off to prevent damage to the brake hose.

7. Remove the outboard disc brake pad from the anchor plate.

8. Remove the inboard disc brake pad from the brake caliper.

To install:

9. If installing new disc brake pads, use a C-clamp or similar tool to push the caliper piston into the caliper bore. This will allow room for the new pads.

10. Place the inboard disc brake pad into the caliper.

11. Place the outboard disc brake pad into position in the anchor plate.

12. Position the disc brake caliper onto the rotor.

13. Reinstall the 2 locating pins and torque to 20 ft. lbs. (28 Nm).

14. Reinstall the caliper locating pin covers.

15. Secure the brake hose to its support on the strut.

16. Reinstall the disc brake pad spring clip.

17. Reinstall the wheel and tire assembly. Torque the lug nuts to 62 ft. lbs. (85 Nm).

18. Pump the brake pedal several times to achieve a good pedal before attempting to move the vehicle.

19. Check the brake fluid level in the master cylinder fluid reservoir and add fluid as necessary.

20. Road test the vehicle and check for proper brake system operation.

REAR

1. Remove ½ of the brake fluid from the master cylinder reservoir.

2. Remove the wheels.

3. Remove the cotter pin and guide pin.

4. Remove the caliper locating pin cover and remove the locating pin.

5. Swing the rear disc brake caliper away from the brake rotor and anchor plate. There is no need to remove the parking brake cable or brake hose.

6. Remove the inner and outer disc brake pads.

To install:

7. If installing new disc brake pads, use rear caliper piston adjuster T87P-2588-A or similar tool, to rotate the rear disc brake piston clockwise, retracting the caliper piston. This will allow room for the new brake pads.

8. Install the inner and outer disc brake pads.

9. Swing the rear disc brake caliper back into position over the disc brake pads.

10. Clean the locating pin threads and apply 1 drop of a thread locking agent or similar sealer.

11. Apply a small amount of disc brake caliper slide grease to the shaft of the locating pin.

12. Reinstall the locating pin and torque to 30 ft. lbs. (41 Nm).

13. Reinstall the guide pin and the cotter pin.

14. Adjust the parking brake by operating the parking brake control several times.

15. Reinstall the wheel and tire assembly. Torque the lug nuts to 62 ft. lbs. (85 Nm).

16. Adjust the parking brake by operating the parking brake control several times.

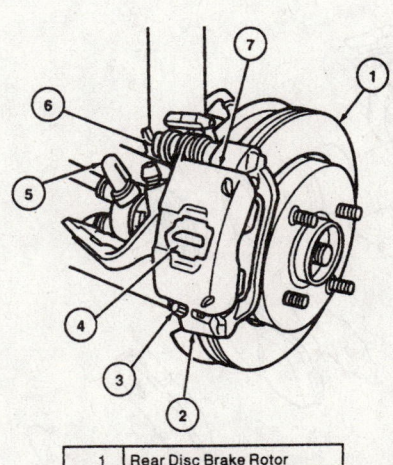

1	Rear Disc Brake Rotor
2	Rear Disc Brake Caliper Anchor Plate
3	Guide Pin
4	Anti-Rattle Clip
5	Parking Brake Lever

93006G26

Rear disc brake components—Contour, Mystique

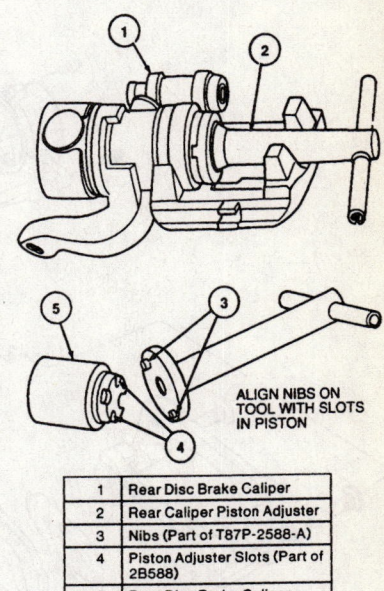

ALIGN NIBS ON TOOL WITH SLOTS IN PISTON

1	Rear Disc Brake Caliper
2	Rear Caliper Piston Adjuster
3	Nibs (Part of T87P-2588-A)
4	Piston Adjuster Slots (Part of 2B588)
5	Rear Disc Brake Caliper Piston and Adjuster

93006G27

Diagram of rear caliper piston and the adjuster tool—Contour, Mystique

Refer to the model specific sections for engine mechanical service procedures

17. Pump the brake pedal several times to achieve a good pedal before attempting to move the vehicle.

18. Check the brake fluid level in the master cylinder fluid reservoir and add fluid as necessary.

19. Road test the vehicle and check for proper brake system operation.

Ford Taurus
Lincoln Continental
Mercury Sable

✳✳ CAUTION

For Continentals, the air suspension switch, located in the left side of the luggage compartment, must be turned OFF before raising the vehicle. Failure to do so may result in unexpected inflation or deflation of the air springs that may result in shifting of the vehicle during service.

FRONT

1. Remove the master cylinder reservoir cap and check the fluid level in the reservoir. Remove brake fluid until the reservoir is ½ full. Discard the removed fluid.

2. On Continentals, turn the air suspension switch, located in the left side of the luggage compartment, to the **OFF** position.

3. Remove the wheel and tire assembly.

4. Remove the disc brake caliper locating pins. Lift the caliper assembly from the anchor plate and rotor using a rotating motion.

5. Suspend the caliper inside the fender housing with wire. Do not allow the caliper to hang from the brake hose.

6. Remove the inner and outer brake pads. Inspect the rotor braking surfaces for scoring and machine as necessary.

To install:

7. Use a C-clamp and an old brake pad or block of wood to seat the caliper piston in its bore.

8. Remove any rust buildup from the inside of the caliper in the brake pad contact area.

9. Install the inner pad in the caliper piston.

10. Install the outer pad onto the anchor plate. Make sure the clips are properly seated.

➡**Make sure the insulators are installed on the brake pads.**

11. Install the disc brake caliper onto the anchor plate.

12. Install caliper locating pins and torque to 23–28 ft. lbs. (31–38 Nm).

13. Install wheel and tire assembly and torque lugs nuts to 85–104 ft. lb. (115-142 Nm)

14. Pump the brake pedal several times prior to moving the vehicle to position the brake pads to the rotor.

15. Refill the master cylinder reservoir as necessary, using only clean DOT 3 brake fluid from a closed container.

16. On Continentals, turn the air suspension service switch to the **ON** position.

17. Road test the vehicle and check the brake system for proper operation.

REAR

1. Remove the master cylinder reservoir cap and check the fluid level in the reservoir. Remove brake fluid until the reservoir is ½ full. Discard the removed fluid.

2. On Continentals, turn the air suspension switch, located in the left side of the luggage compartment, to the **OFF** position.

3. Remove the wheel and tire assembly.

4. Remove the screw retaining the brake hose bracket to the frame side rail.

5. Remove the retaining clip from the parking brake cable at the disc brake caliper. Remove the cable end from the parking brake lever.

6. Remove the upper disc brake caliper locating pin at the support bracket. Rotate the caliper away from the rotor.

7. Remove the disc brake pads.

8. Inspect the rotor braking surfaces for scoring and machine as necessary.

To install:

9. Using Rear Caliper Piston Adjuster T87P-2588-A, rotate the piston clockwise until it is fully seated. Make sure one of the slots in the piston face is positioned so it will engage the nib on the brake pad.

10. Install the brake pads in the support bracket. Rotate the caliper assembly over the rotor into position on the support bracket. Make sure the brake pads are installed correctly.

11. Remove the residue from the rear brake pin retainer bolt threads and apply 1 drop of a suitable threadlock sealer. Install and torque the disc brake caliper locating pin to 23–26 ft. lbs. (31–35 Nm).

12. Attach the cable end to the parking brake lever. Install the cable retaining clip on the caliper assembly. Position the brake flex hose and bracket assembly to the side rail, and install the retaining screw. Torque to 11 ft. lbs. (16 Nm).

13. Install the wheel and tire assembly and torque lug nuts to 85–104 ft. lbs. (115–142 Nm).

14. Pump the brake pedal several times prior to moving the vehicle, to position the brake pads to the rotor.

15. Refill the master cylinder reservoir if necessary, using only clean DOT 3 brake fluid from a closed container.

16. On Continentals, turn the air suspension service switch to the **ON** position.

17. Road test the vehicle and check the brake system for proper operation.

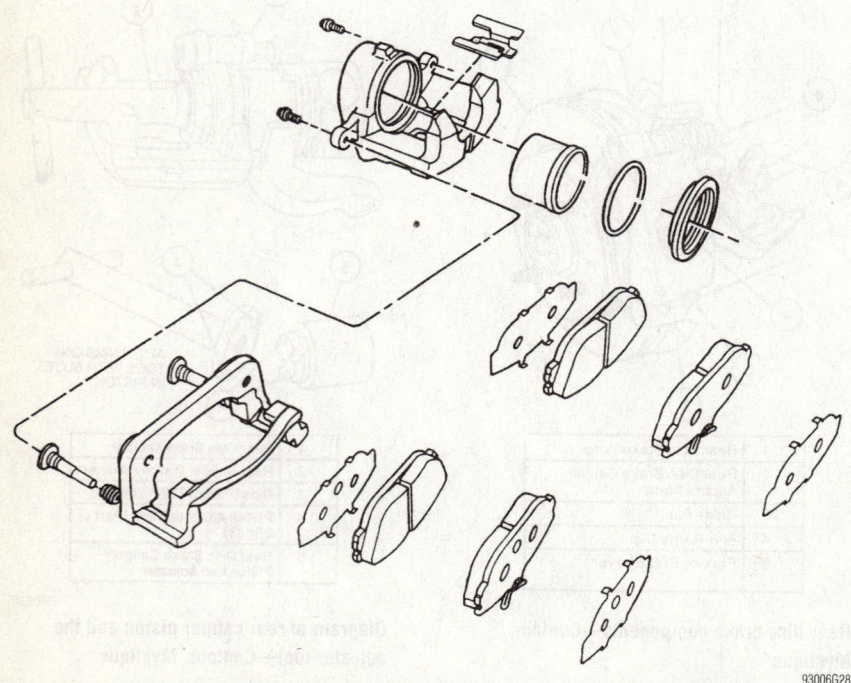

93006G28

Front disc brake caliper, pads and related components—Taurus, Continental, Sable

Ford Escort
Mercury Tracer

FRONT

1. Remove the master cylinder reservoir cap and check the fluid level in the reservoir. Remove brake fluid until the reservoir is ½ full. Discard the removed fluid.

2. Remove the wheel and tire assembly.

3. Remove the W-spring.

4. Remove 2 disc brake pad locating pins and remove the M-spring.

5. Remove the brake pads and shims from the brake caliper.

6. Inspect the brake rotor. Resurface or replace if needed.

To install:

7. Use a suitable tool to push the piston into the brake caliper bore.

8. Apply a suitable grease between the shims and the disc brake pad guide plates and position the brake pads and shims to the brake caliper.

9. Install the W-spring and 2 brake pad locating pins.

10. Install the M-spring.

11. Install the wheel and tire assembly. Torque the lug nuts to 65–87 ft. lbs. (88–118 Nm).

12. Pump the brake pedal several times prior to moving the vehicle to position the brake pads.

13. Check the fluid level in the master cylinder reservoir and fill as needed.

14. Road test the vehicle and check for proper brake system operation.

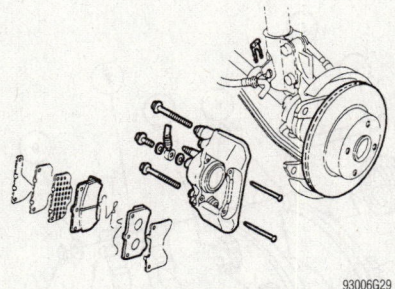

93006G29

Front disc brake pads—Escort, Tracer

REAR

1. Remove the master cylinder reservoir cap and check the fluid level in the reservoir. Remove brake fluid until the reservoir is ½ full. Discard the removed fluid.

2. Remove the wheel and tire assembly.

3. If necessary, remove the screw plug and turn the adjustment gear counterclock-

wise with an Allen® wrench to pull the piston fully inward.

4. Remove the lower brake caliper bolt.

5. Using a small prybar, pivot the caliper on its mounting bracket to access the brake pads. If the upper lock bolt requires lubrication or service, remove it and suspend the caliper with mechanics wire.

6. Remove the brake pads, shims, spring and guides.

7. Inspect the brake rotor. Resurface or replace if needed.

To install:

8. Apply an appropriate brake pad grease between the shims and the brake pads.

9. Pivot the caliper on its mounting bracket and position the brake pads, shims, spring and guides to the brake rotor.

10. Lubricate and install the lower caliper bolt. Tighten the bolt to 33–43 ft. lbs. (45–59 Nm).

11. Turn the adjustment gear clockwise with an Allen wrench until the brake pads just touch the rotor, then loosen the gear ⅓ of a turn. Install the screw plug and torque to 12 ft. lbs. (16 Nm).

12. Install the wheel and tire assembly. Torque the lug nuts to 65–87 ft. lbs. (88–118 Nm).

13. Pump the brake pedal several times prior to moving the vehicle to position the brake pads.

14. Check the brake fluid level in the master cylinder reservoir and fill if needed.

15. Road test the vehicle and check for proper brake system operation.

Mustang

FRONT WITH SINGLE PISTON CALIPER

1. Remove and discard ½ of the brake fluid from the brake master cylinder reservoir. Properly dispose of the used brake fluid.

2. Remove the wheel and tire assembly.

3. Remove 2 anchor plate mounting bolts and lift the disc brake caliper from the anchor plate and rotor using a rotating motion. Hang the disc brake caliper from the body with wire. Do not let the disc brake caliper hang by the brake hose.

4. Remove the outer and inner disc brake pads and the anti-rattle clip from the disc brake caliper.

5. Clean any residue from the caliper anchor plate and disc brake pad contact areas.

6. Inspect the disc brake rotor for scoring and wear. Replace or machine, as necessary.

7. Inspect the piston boot and the caliper pin boots for damage. Replace as necessary.

To install:

8. Use a large C-clamp and a wood block to push the caliper piston back into its bore.

9. Remove the protective paper from the insulators on the back of the disc brake pads, if equipped.

10. Install the inner and outer disc brake pads and the anti-rattle clip in the disc brake caliper.

11. Install the disc brake caliper and pads over the rotor and onto the anchor plate using a rotating motion. Hand-start 2 anchor plate mounting bolts. Torque the bolts to 95 ft. lbs. (130 Nm).

12. Install the wheel and tire assembly and torque the lug nuts in a star pattern to 85–105 ft. lbs. (115–142 Nm).

13. Repeat the procedure for the opposite disc brake caliper assembly.

14. Pump the brake pedal prior to moving the vehicle to seat the brake pads.

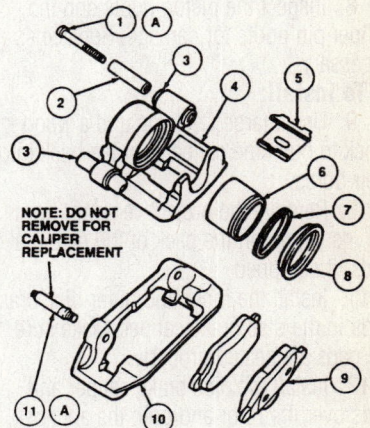

NOTE: DO NOT REMOVE FOR CALIPER REPLACEMENT

1	Upper Caliper Brake Bolt
2	Front Caliper Sleeve
3	Insulator
4	Caliper Housing (Part of 2B119)
5	Disc Brake Pad Anti-Rattle Clip
6	Caliper Piston
7	Piston Seal
8	Dust Boot
9	Brake Shoe and Lining
10	Front Disc Brake Caliper Anchor Plate
11	Disc Brake Caliper Locating Pin
A	Tighten to 88 N-m (65 Lb-Ft)

93006G30

Disc brake pads and related components—Mustang with single piston caliper

For accessory drive belt replacement procedures see the model specific sections of this manual

15. Fill the brake master cylinder reservoir with clean DOT 3 brake fluid from a closed container.

16. If the disc brake calipers were replaced or repaired, be sure to bleed the system.

17. Road test the vehicle and check the brake system for proper operation.

FRONT WITH DUAL PISTON CALIPER

1. Remove and discard ½ of the brake fluid from the brake master cylinder reservoir. Properly dispose of the used brake fluid.

2. Remove the wheel and tire assembly.

3. Remove the clip, washer and disc brake caliper locating pin.

4. Remove the disc brake caliper from the brake rotor and the caliper anchor plate. Hang the disc brake caliper from the body with wire. Do not let the disc brake caliper hang by the brake hose.

5. Remove the outer and inner disc brake pads from the disc brake caliper.

6. Clean any residue from the caliper anchor plate and disc brake pad contact areas.

7. Inspect the disc brake rotor for scoring and wear. Replace or machine, as necessary.

8. Inspect the piston boots and the caliper pin boots for damage. Replace as necessary.

To install:

9. Use a large C-clamp and a wood block to push the caliper pistons back into their bores.

10. Remove the protective paper from the insulators on the back of the disc brake pads, if equipped.

11. Install the inner and outer disc brake pads in the disc brake caliper. Make sure the pads are seated properly.

12. Install the disc brake caliper and pads over the rotor and onto the anchor plate using a rotating motion. Make sure that the guiding surfaces of the disc brake pads and the anchor bracket are seating correctly.

13. Press the disc brake caliper down by hand to compress the bias spring and slide the disc brake caliper locating pin into position.

14. Install the washer and clip.

15. Install the wheel and tire assembly. Torque the lug nuts in a star pattern to 85–105 ft. lbs. (115–142 Nm).

16. Repeat the procedure for the opposite disc brake caliper assembly.

17. Pump the brake pedal prior to moving the vehicle to position the brake pads.

18. Fill the brake master cylinder reservoir with clean DOT 3 brake fluid from a closed container.

19. If the disc brake calipers were replaced or repaired, be sure to bleed the system.

20. Road test the vehicle and check the brake system for proper operation.

REAR

1. Remove and discard ½ of the brake fluid from the brake master cylinder reservoir. Properly dispose of the used brake fluid.

2. Remove the wheel and tire assembly.

3. Remove the screw retaining the brake hose bracket to the shock absorber bracket.

4. Remove the retaining clip from the parking brake cable at the disc brake caliper.

5. Release the tension from the parking brake cable and disengage the parking brake cable end from the parking brake lever on the disc brake caliper.

6. Hold the disc brake caliper locating pin hex-head with an open-end wrench. Remove the upper brake pin retainer.

7. Rotate the disc brake caliper away from the brake rotor.

8. Remove the inner and outer disc brake pads and the anti-rattle clip from the disc support bracket.

9. Inspect the disc brake rotor for scoring and wear. Replace or machine, as necessary.

To install:

10. Using Rear Caliper Piston Adjuster T87P-2588-A, rotate the caliper piston clockwise until the piston is fully seated.

➡ **Ensure that one of the 2 slots in the rear brake piston face is positioned so it will engage the nib on the back of the inner brake pad.**

11. Install the disc brake pad anti-rattle clips and install the inner and outer disc brake pads on the rear disc support bracket.

12. Rotate the disc brake caliper over the brake rotor into position on the disc support bracket. Make sure the disc brake pads and anti-rattle clips are correctly installed.

13. Apply a suitable thread-locking compound to the threads of the upper brake pin retainer.

14. Install the brake pin retainer and tighten to 23–26 ft. lbs. (31–35 Nm) while holding the disc brake caliper locating pin with an open-end wrench.

15. Install the parking brake cable end to the parking brake lever on the disc brake caliper. Install the retaining clip to the disc brake caliper.

16. Install the wheel and tire assembly. Torque the lug nuts in a star pattern to 85–105 ft. lbs. (115–142 Nm).

17. Repeat the procedure for the opposite disc brake caliper assembly.

18. Pump the brake pedal prior to moving the vehicle to position the brake pads.

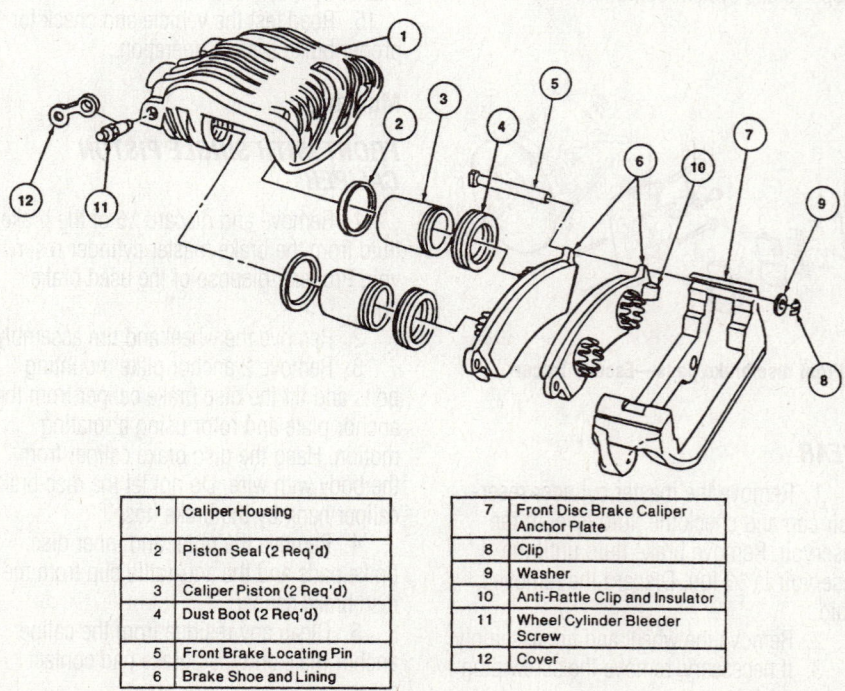

1	Caliper Housing
2	Piston Seal (2 Req'd)
3	Caliper Piston (2 Req'd)
4	Dust Boot (2 Req'd)
5	Front Brake Locating Pin
6	Brake Shoe and Lining
7	Front Disc Brake Caliper Anchor Plate
8	Clip
9	Washer
10	Anti-Rattle Clip and Insulator
11	Wheel Cylinder Bleeder Screw
12	Cover

93006G31

Disc brake pads and related components—Mustang with dual piston caliper

19. Fill the brake master cylinder reservoir with clean DOT 3 brake fluid from a closed container.

20. If the disc brake calipers were replaced or repaired, be sure to bleed the system.

21. Road test the vehicle and check the brake system for proper operation.

Ford Thunderbird
Mercury Cougar (1997–98 Model)

FRONT

1. If equipped with air suspension, the air suspension switch, located on the right-hand side of the luggage compartment, must be turned to the **OFF** position before raising the vehicle.

2. Remove and properly dispose ½ of the brake fluid from the master cylinder.

3. Remove the front wheel and tire assembly.

4. Remove 2 disc brake caliper locating pins and remove the caliper from the anchor plate and rotor. Suspend the caliper inside the fender housing with a length of wire. Do not let the caliper hang by the brake hose.

5. Remove the disc brake pads from the caliper.

6. Inspect the disc brake rotor for scoring and wear. Replace or machine as necessary. Observe the minimum thickness specification stamped on the rotor if machining is required.

To install:

7. Use a C-clamp and an old brake pad, wood block to seat the caliper piston in its bore. Do not allow metal or sharp objects to come into direct contact with the caliper piston surface or damage will result.

8. Install the correct inner disc brake pad to the caliper piston using care not to bend the anti-rattle clips.

9. Install the correct outer disc brake pad to the caliper making sure to properly install the anti-rattle clip. The outer pads are marked for left-hand or right-hand installation.

10. Install the disc brake caliper over the rotor with the outer brake pad against the rotor's braking surface. This prevents pinching the piston boot between the inner brake pad and the piston.

11. If worn, install 2 new locating pin insulators in the disc brake caliper by fabricating a tool for this purpose.

12. Lubricate the locating pins and the inside of the locating pin insulators with silicone dielectric grease. Install the caliper locating pins and thread them into the spindle/anchor plate assembly by hand.

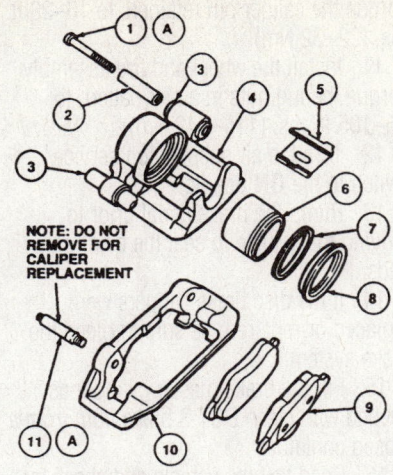

NOTE: DO NOT REMOVE FOR CALIPER REPLACEMENT

1	Brake Caliper Bolt
2	Front Caliper Sleeve
3	Insulator
4	Disc Brake Caliper
5	Disc Brake Pad Anti-Rattle Clip
6	Caliper Piston
7	Piston Seal
8	Dust Boot
9	Brake Shoe and Lining
10	Front Disc Brake Caliper Anchor Plate
11	Disc Brake Caliper Locating Pin
A	Tighten to 81 N·m (60 Lb-Ft)

93006G32

Front Disc brake pads and related components (15 inch wheel)—Thunderbird and Cougar

13. Torque the caliper locating pins to 45–65 ft. lbs. (61–88 Nm).

14. Install the wheel and tire assembly. Torque the lug nuts in a star pattern to 85–104 ft. lbs. (115–142 Nm).

15. If equipped with air suspension, turn the air suspension switch to the **ON** position.

16. Pump the brake pedal prior to moving the vehicle to seat the brake pads.

17. If the disc brake calipers were replaced or repaired be sure to bleed the hydraulic brake system.

18. Fill the master cylinder reservoir with clean DOT 3 brake fluid from a closed container.

19. Road test the vehicle and check for proper brake system operation.

REAR

1. If equipped with air suspension, the air suspension switch, located on the right-hand side of the luggage compartment, must be turned to the **OFF** position before raising the vehicle.

2. Remove and properly dispose ½ of the brake fluid from the master cylinder.

3. Remove the rear wheel and tire assembly.

4. Release the tension from the parking brake cable and disconnect the parking brake cable from the disc brake caliper.

5. Remove 2 caliper locating pins. Lift the disc brake caliper off the rotor and anchor plate using a rotating motion.

6. Remove the inner and outer disc brake pads.

7. Inspect the disc brake rotor for scoring and wear. Replace or machine, as necessary. Observe the minimum thickness specification stamped on the rotor if machining is required.

To install:

8. Use a C-clamp and an old brake pad, wood block to seat the caliper piston in its bore. Do not allow metal or sharp objects to come into direct contact with the plastic caliper piston surface or damage will result.

9. Position Caliper Piston Tool T87P-2588-A on the rear disc brake caliper. Be sure the pins on the tool are meshed with the slots on the piston. Rotate the tool clockwise until the piston is seated in the caliper.

10. Install the inner and outer disc brake pads in the support bracket. Make sure the pads are on the correct sides.

11. Position the disc brake caliper above the rotor with the anti-rattle spring located on the lower adapter support arm. Install the caliper over the rotor with a rotating motion. Make sure the inner pad is properly positioned.

12. Insert 2 disc brake caliper locating pins and thread them in by hand. Torque the pins to 19–26 ft. lbs. (26–35 Nm).

13. Install the wheel and tire assembly. Torque the lug nuts in a star pattern to 85–104 ft. lbs. (115–142 Nm).

14. If equipped with air suspension, turn the air suspension switch to the **ON** position.

15. Pump the brake pedal prior to moving the vehicle to seat the brake pads.

16. If the disc brake caliper was repaired or replaced, make sure to bleed the hydraulic brake system.

17. Fill the master cylinder reservoir with clean DOT 3 brake fluid from a closed container.

18. Road test the vehicle and check for proper brake system operation.

Lincoln Mark VIII

FRONT

1. Remove and discard ½ of the brake fluid from the brake master cylinder.

2. Turn the air suspension service switch to the **OFF** position.

3. Remove the wheel and tire assembly.

4. Remove the disc brake caliper pin retainers from the locating pins and remove the caliper from the anchor plate and disc brake rotor. Suspend the caliper inside the fender housing with a length of wire. Do not let the caliper hang by the brake hose.

5. Remove the outer, then inner disc brake pads from the caliper.

6. Inspect the disc brake rotor for scoring, runout and wear. Replace or machine as necessary. Do not exceed the minimum allowable thickness stamped on each disc brake rotor.

To install:

7. Using a C-clamp and a block of wood press the disc brake caliper piston into the caliper housing to allow for the new disc brake pads to fit the brake rotor.

8. Install the inner, then outer disc brake pads in the caliper.

9. Install the disc brake caliper over the rotor with the outer brake pad against the rotor's braking surface. This prevents pinching the piston boot between the inner brake pad and the piston.

10. Install the disc brake caliper pin retainers to the locating pins, by hand.

Torque the caliper pin retainers to 16–23 ft. lbs. (22–32 Nm).

11. Install the wheel and tire assembly. Torque the lug nuts in a star pattern to 85–105 ft. lbs. (115–142 Nm).

12. Turn the air suspension service switch to the **ON** position.

13. Pump the brake pedal prior to moving the vehicle to seat the disc brake pads.

14. If the disc brake calipers were replaced or repaired, be sure to bleed the brake system.

15. Fill the brake master cylinder as needed with clean DOT 3 brake fluid from a closed container.

16. Road test the vehicle and check for proper brake system operation.

REAR

1. Remove and discard ½ of the brake fluid from the brake master cylinder.

2. Verify that the parking brake control is released.

3. Turn the air suspension service switch to the **OFF** position.

4. Remove the wheel and tire assembly.

5. Remove the retaining clip from the parking brake cable at the disc brake caliper.

6. Release the parking brake cable tension and disengage the cable end from the caliper lever.

7. Remove the disc brake caliper pin retainers securing the caliper to the locating pins.

8. Rotate the caliper away from the disc brake rotor.

9. Remove the inner and outer disc brake pads from the disc brake support bracket.

10. Inspect the disc brake rotor for scoring, runout and wear. Replace or machine as necessary. Do not exceed the minimum allowable thickness stamped on each disc brake rotor.

To install:

11. Using Caliper Piston Adjuster T87P-2588-A, rotate the disc brake caliper piston until it is fully seated in the caliper. Be sure the pins on the tool are meshed with the slots on the piston.

12. Install the inner and outer disc brake pads in the rear disc support bracket. Check to be sure the pads are on the correct sides, and that the nib on the inner disc brake pad is correctly installed to the slot in the caliper piston.

13. Rotate the disc brake caliper over the rotor into position on the support bracket. Install the caliper pin retainers to the caliper locating pins and thread them in by hand. Torque the pin retainers to 23–26 ft. lbs. (31–35 Nm).

14. Install the wheel and tire assembly. Torque the lug nuts in a star pattern to 85–105 ft. lbs. (115–142 Nm).

15. Turn the air suspension service switch to the **ON** position.

16. Pump the brake pedal prior to moving the vehicle to seat the disc brake pads.

17. If the disc brake calipers were replaced or repaired, be sure to bleed the brake system.

18. Fill the brake master cylinder as needed with clean DOT 3 brake fluid from a closed container.

19. Road test the vehicle and check for proper brake system operation.

Ford Crown Victoria
Lincoln Town Car
Mercury Grand Marquis

➡Before continuing with this procedure, make sure to have available, 2 new disc brake caliper anchor bracket mounting bolts, per caliper. Once removed, these parts lose their torque holding ability or retention capability and must not be reused.

FRONT

1. If equipped with air suspension, the air suspension switch, located on the right-

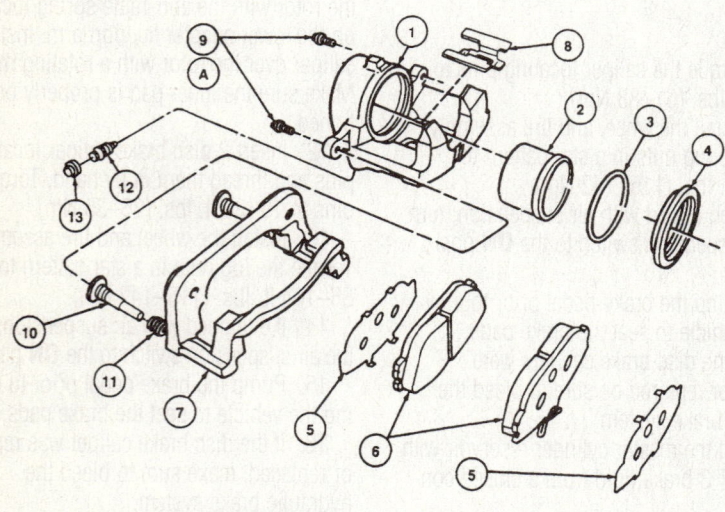

1	Disc Brake Caliper Housing
2	Caliper Piston
3	Brake Piston Seal
4	Piston Boot
5	Front Wheel Disc Brake Shoe Insulator (2 Req'd)
6	Brake Shoe and Lining
7	Front Disc Brake Caliper Anchor Plate
8	Brake Shoe Hold-Down Spring

9	Rear Brake Pin Retainer (2 Req'd)
10	Disc Brake Caliper Locating Pin
11	Caliper Guide Pin Excluder
12	Wheel Cylinder Bleeder Screw
13	Bleed Screw Cap
A	Tighten to 31-38 N·m (23-28 Lb-Ft)

93006G33

Front disc brake pads and related components—Mark VIII

hand side of the luggage compartment, must be turned to the **OFF** position before raising the vehicle.

2. Remove ½ of the brake fluid from the brake master cylinder reservoir. Properly dispose of the used brake fluid.

3. Remove the front wheel and tire assembly.

4. Remove 2 disc brake caliper anchor bracket mounting bolts and discard. Lift the caliper assembly from the disc brake rotor using a rotating motion. Suspend the caliper inside the fender housing with wire. Do not allow the caliper to hang from the brake hose.

5. Remove the inner and outer disc brake pads. Inspect the rotor braking surfaces for scoring and machine as necessary. Refer to the minimum rotor thickness specification when machining. If machining is not necessary, hand-sand the glaze from the braking surfaces with medium grit sandpaper. Make sure to wear an approved respirator.

To install:

6. Use a C-clamp and an old brake pad, wood block to seat the caliper piston in its bore. Do not allow metal or sharp

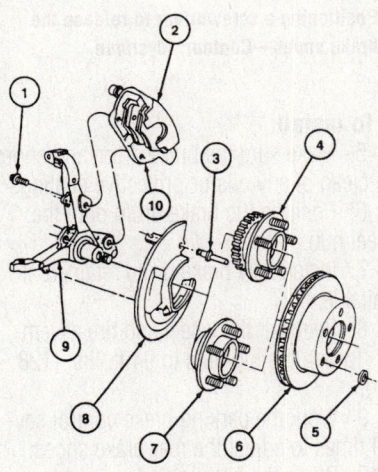

Item	Description
1	Bolt (2 Req'd)
2	Disc Brake Caliper
3	Rivet (3 Req'd)
4	Wheel Hub with ABS
5	Washer (2 Req'd)
6	Front Disc Brake Rotor
7	Wheel Hub Without ABS
8	Front Disc Brake Rotor Shield
9	Front Wheel Spindle
10	Front Disc Brake Caliper Anchor Plate Assembly

93006G83

Exploded view of the front disc assembly—Crown Victoria, Town Car, Grand Marquis

objects to come into direct contact with the plastic caliper piston surface or damage will result.

7. Remove all rust buildup from the inside of the caliper legs.

8. Make sure the anti-rattle spring is seated in the caliper lining inspection opening and that it is installed from the lining side.

9. Install the inner disc brake pad to the caliper piston. Do not bend the pad clips during installation in the piston or distortion and rattles can occur. Install the outer disc brake pad. Make sure the clips are properly seated.

10. Install the disc brake caliper over the rotor and install 2 new anchor bracket mounting bolts. Torque the bolts to 126–169 ft. lbs. (170–230 Nm).

11. Install the wheel and tire assembly. Torque the lug nuts in a star pattern to 85–104 ft. lbs. (115–142 Nm).

12. If equipped with air suspension, turn the air suspension switch to the **ON** position.

13. Pump the brake pedal prior to moving the vehicle to seat the brake pads.

14. Fill the master cylinder reservoir with clean DOT 3 brake fluid from a closed container.

15. If the disc brake calipers were replaced or repaired be sure to bleed the system.

16. Road test the vehicle and check for proper brake system operation.

REAR

1. If equipped with air suspension, the air suspension switch, located on the right-hand side of the luggage compartment, must be turned to the **OFF** position before raising the vehicle.

2. Remove ½ of the brake fluid from the brake master cylinder reservoir. Properly dispose of the used brake fluid.

3. Remove the rear wheel and tire assembly.

4. Remove 2 disc brake caliper retaining bolts.

5. Lift the disc brake caliper off the disc brake rotor and anchor plate using a rotating motion.

6. Remove the inner and outer disc brake pads.

7. Inspect the disc brake rotor for scoring and wear. Inspect the rotor braking surfaces for scoring and machine as necessary. Refer to the minimum rotor thickness specification when machining. If machining is not necessary, hand-sand the glaze from the

braking surfaces with medium grit sandpaper. Make sure to wear an approved respirator.

To install:

8. Use a C-clamp and an old brake pad, wood block to seat the caliper piston in its bore. Do not allow metal or sharp objects to come into direct contact with the plastic caliper piston surface or damage will result.

9. Remove all rust buildup from the inside of the caliper legs.

10. Install the inner disc brake pad to the caliper piston. Do not bend the pad clips during installation in the piston or distortion and rattles can occur. Install the outer disc brake pad. Make sure the clips are properly seated.

➡ **Make sure the insulators are installed on the brake pads.**

11. Install the disc brake caliper over the disc brake rotor and install 2 caliper retaining bolts. Torque to 16–20 ft. lbs. (22–27 Nm).

12. Install the wheel and tire assembly. Torque the lug nuts in a star pattern to 85–104 ft. lbs. (115–142 Nm).

13. If equipped with air suspension, turn the air suspension switch to the **ON** position.

14. Pump the brake pedal prior to moving the vehicle to seat the disc brake pads.

15. Fill the master cylinder reservoir with clean DOT 3 brake fluid from a closed container.

16. If the disc brake calipers were replaced or repaired be sure to bleed the system.

17. Road test the vehicle and check for proper brake system operation.

Brake Drums

REMOVAL & INSTALLATION

Ford Aspire

1. Remove the tire and wheel assembly.

2. Remove the hub grease cap.

3. Remove the cotter pin and wheel bearing nut cover. Discard the cotter pin.

4. Remove the wheel bearing nut.

➡ **A left-hand threaded locknut is used on the vehicle's right rear wheel spindle. Turn this locknut clockwise to loosen.**

5. Remove the brake drum, washer and bearings as an assembly. Be careful not to

let the outer wheel bearing fall out of the hub during removal.

6. If the brake drum is to be machined or replaced, remove the inner wheel bearing and grease seal.

To install:

7. If removed, install the inner wheel bearing and a new grease seal.

8. Make sure the bearings and hub contain an adequate amount of clean wheel bearing grease.

9. Adjust the distance between the brake shoes to match the inner diameter of the brake drum if the brake drum has been machined or replaced.

10. Position the brake drum on the spindle. Keep the drum centered on the spindle to prevent damage to the grease seal and spindle threads.

11. Install the outer wheel bearing, washer and wheel bearing nut.

12. Properly adjust the wheel bearing preload.

13. Install the wheel bearing nut cover and a new cotter pin.

14. Install the tire and wheel assembly. Torque the lug bolts to 65–87 ft. lbs. (88–118 Nm).

15. Check the brake system for proper operation.

Ford Probe

1. Remove the wheel.
2. Remove the hub grease cap.
3. Remove the 2 brake drum screws and remove the brake drum.
4. Inspect the brake drum for wear, scoring, cracks or other damage. Machine or replace the drum, as necessary. If machining, observe the maximum drum diameter specification.

To install:

5. If the brake drum has been machined and/or the brake shoes replaced, measure the inside diameter of the brake drum using adjustment gauge D81L-1103-A.

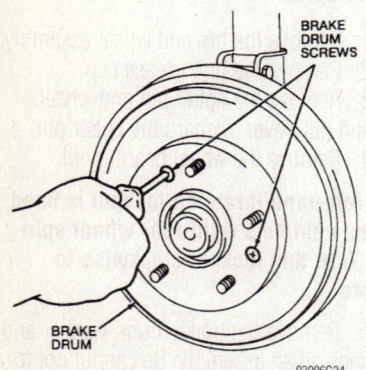

Removing the brake drum—Probe

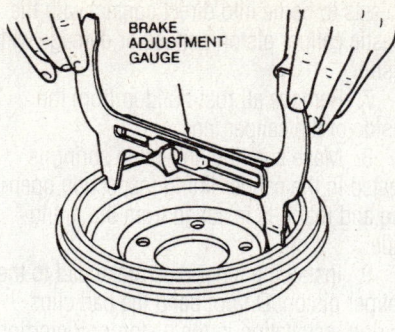

Measuring the drum with the brake adjustment gauge—Probe

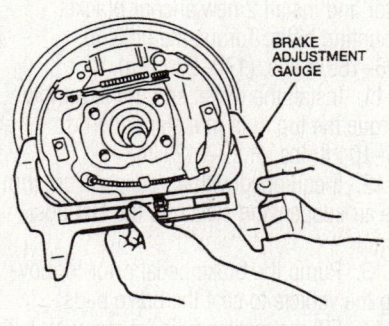

Measuring the brake shoes with the brake adjustment gauge—Probe

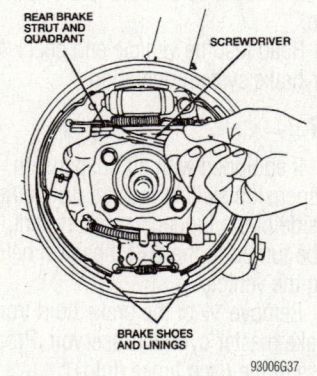

Adjusting the brake shoes—Probe

6. Insert a suitable tool into the knurled quadrant of the rear brake strut and quadrant. Adjust the shoes to the same measurement as the brake drum.

7. Install the brake drum.

8. Install the brake drum screws and torque to 89–123 inch lbs. (10–14 Nm).

9. Install the hub grease cap.

10. Install the wheel and torque the lug nuts to 65–87 ft. lbs. (88–118 Nm).

11. Complete the brake adjustment by sharply applying the brakes several times while driving the vehicle alternately forward and reverse.

Ford Contour
Mercury Mystique

1. Remove the wheel and tire assembly.
2. Remove the brake drum retainers, if installed.
3. Grasp the brake drum and remove.
4. If the drum will not slide off with light force, then the brake shoes will need to be backed off as follows:

   a. Remove the rubber plug on the backing plate and insert a screwdriver or small brake adjusting tool into the slot to contact the brake strut and quadrant.

   b. A forward motion of the tool will separate the quadrant from the knurled wheel and allow the brake shoes to retract.

   c. Remove the brake drum.

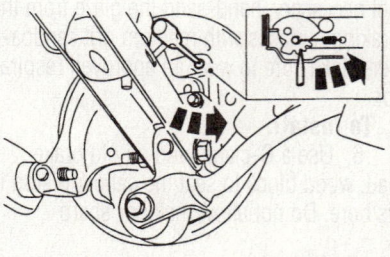

Positioning a screwdriver to release the brake shoes—Contour, Mystique

To install:

5. Make sure the brake drum and shoes are clean of any oils or protective coatings.

6. Position the brake drum onto the wheel hub.

7. Install new brake drum retainers if available.

8. Reinstall the wheel and tire assembly. Torque the lug nuts to 94 ft. lbs. (128 Nm).

9. Work the parking brake control several times to adjust the rear brake shoes.

10. Pump the brake pedal several times to assure a good pedal before attempting to move the vehicle.

11. Road test the vehicle and check for proper brake system operation.

Ford Taurus
Mercury Sable

1. Remove the wheel and tire assembly.
2. Remove the brake drum.

➡**If the brake drum cannot be removed easily, remove the brake tube-to-axle retention bracket and pry rubber plug from rear brake backing plate inspection hole. This will allow sufficient**

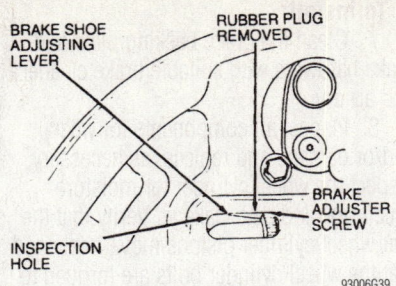

Retracting the brake shoes to allow drum removal—Taurus and Sable

room for insertion of a screwdriver and brake tools to disengage brake shoe adjusting lever and back off the brake adjuster screw.

3. Inspect the drum for scoring and/or other wear. Machine or replace, as necessary.

To install:

4. Measure the brake drum inside diameter using D81L-1103-A brake adjustment gauge.

5. Using the brake adjustment gauge, adjust the brake shoes to the same dimensions as the brake drum.

6. Position the brake drum over the brake shoes on the axle hub.

7. Install the wheel and tire assembly. Torque the lug nuts to 85–104 ft. lbs. (115–141 Nm).

8. Pump the brake pedal several times to position the brake shoes and complete the adjustment.

9. Road test the vehicle and check for proper brake system operation.

Ford Escort
Mercury Tracer

1. Remove the wheel and tire assembly.

2. Remove 2 brake drum retaining screws.

3. Pull the brake drum from the hub. Inspect the drum and refinish or replace, as necessary. If refinishing, check the maximum inside diameter specification.

To install:

4. If needed, adjust the brake shoes to fit the brake drum.

5. Place the brake drum on the hub.

6. Install 2 brake drum retaining screws. Torque to 89–123 inch lbs. (10–14 Nm).

7. Install the wheel and tire assembly. Torque the lug nuts to 73–100 ft. lbs. (100–135 Nm).

8. Check the brake system for proper operation.

Ford Mustang, Thunderbird
Mercury Cougar

1. Remove the wheel and tire assembly.

2. Remove the drum retaining nuts, if equipped, and remove the brake drum.

3. Inspect the brake drum for scoring and wear. Check the drums for conditioning and wear. Replace or machine as necessary. If machining, observe the maximum diameter specification.

To install:

4. If a new brake drum is being installed, remove the protective coating from the drum using brake cleaner.

5. Adjust the brake shoes to the brake drum using Brake Adjusting Gauge D81L-1103-A.

6. Install the brake drum.

7. Install the wheel and tire assembly.

8. Complete the brake adjustment by carefully backing the vehicle up several times while applying the brakes with a minimum force of 25 lbs. (111 N).

9. Road test the vehicle and check the brake system for proper operation.

Brake Shoes

REMOVAL & INSTALLATION

Ford Aspire

1. Remove the wheel and tire assembly.

2. Remove the brake drum.

3. Remove the brake shoe hold-down springs and pins.

4. Remove the brake shoe retracting springs and the right hand anti-rattle spring.

5. Pull the brake shoes away from the backing plate and remove.

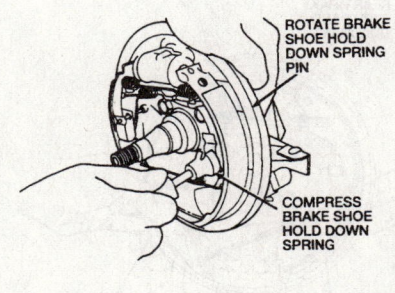

Brake shoe hold-down spring and pin removal—Ford Aspire

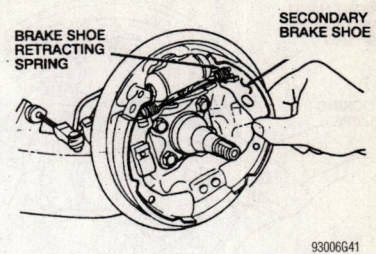

Removing the secondary brake shoe—Ford Aspire

To install:

6. Clean the brake backing plate.

7. Lubricate the backing plate shoe pads with a suitable high temperature grease.

8. Install the brake shoe upper retracting spring on the primary brake shoe. Position the primary brake shoe on the backing plate and install the hold-down pin and spring.

9. Connect the upper retracting spring to the secondary brake shoe and position the shoe against the backing plate. Install the secondary brake shoe hold-down pin and spring.

10. Install the right hand anti-rattle spring and the lower brake shoe retracting spring.

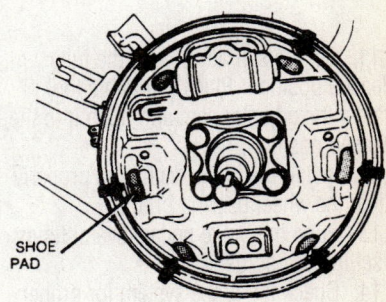

Lubricate the brake shoe pads with high temperature grease—Ford Aspire

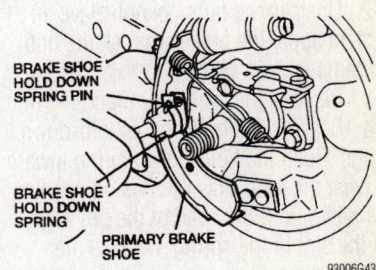

Securing the primary brake shoe with the hold-down pin and spring—Ford Aspire

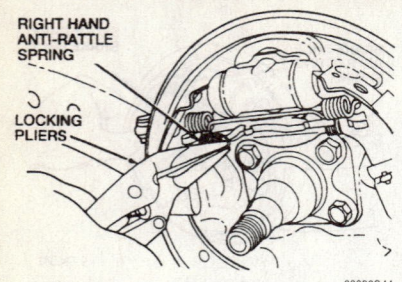

Installing the anti-rattle spring—Ford Aspire

RIGHT HAND ANTI-RATTLE SPRING

LOCKING PLIERS

93006G44

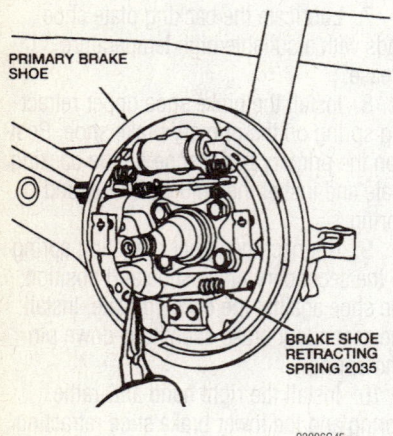

PRIMARY BRAKE SHOE

BRAKE SHOE RETRACTING SPRING 2035

93006G45

Installing the lower brake shoe return spring—Ford Aspire

11. Set the self adjuster to the fully released position. Place a suitable tool against the adjuster cam and push it to the released position.

12. Install the brake drum and properly adjust the wheel bearing preload.

13. Push the brake pedal several times to set the self adjuster.

14. Check the brake system for proper operation.

Ford Probe

1. Remove the wheel and dust cap.

2. Unstake the hub locknut. Have an assistant apply the brakes to lock the hub, then remove the locknut.

3. Remove the brake drum and the hub.

4. Remove the brake shoe hold-down springs. Push the hold-down spring inward and twist the hold-down pin using needle-nose pliers until the head of the pin aligns with the slot in the spring. Release the spring and pin.

5. Remove the parking brake cable from the parking brake anchor plate.

6. Remove the brake shoe return springs and remove the brake shoes.

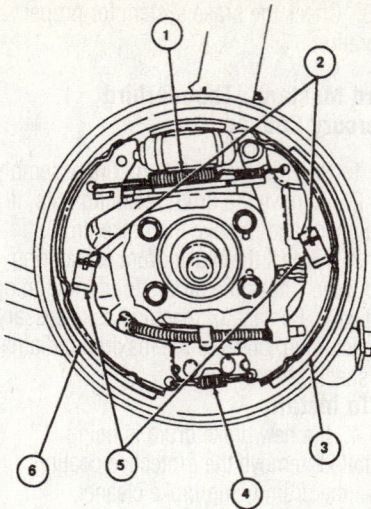

1	Brake Shoe Retracting Spring, Upper
2	Brake Shoe Hold Down Spring Pin
3	Trailing Brake Shoe and Lining
4	Brake Shoe Retracting Spring, Lower
5	Brake Shoe Hold-Down Spring
6	Leading Brake Shoe and Lining

93006G46

Brake shoes and related components—Ford Probe

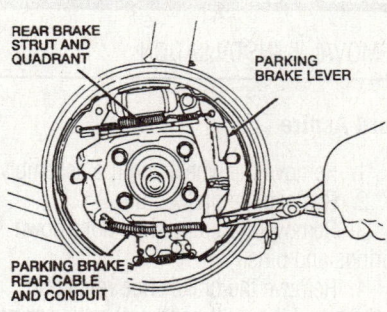

REAR BRAKE STRUT AND QUADRANT

PARKING BRAKE LEVER

PARKING BRAKE REAR CABLE AND CONDUIT

93006G47

Removing the parking brake cable from the parking brake lever—Ford Probe

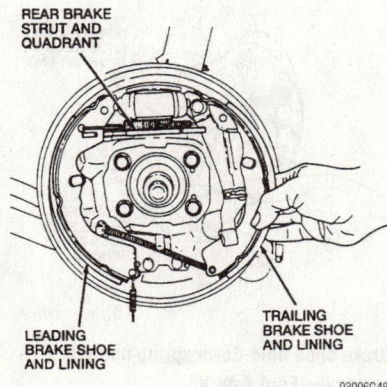

REAR BRAKE STRUT AND QUADRANT

LEADING BRAKE SHOE AND LINING

TRAILING BRAKE SHOE AND LINING

93006G48

Removing the trailing brake shoe—Ford Probe

To install:

7. Clean the brake backing plate and brake hardware with suitable brake cleaner and air dry.

8. Inspect all components for wear and/or damage and replace, as necessary. Inspect the wheel cylinder for moisture which may indicate leakage. Verify that the rear wheel cylinder pistons move freely and that the wheel cylinder bolts are torqued to 84–108 inch lbs. (10–13 Nm).

9. Inspect the brake drum for wear, scoring cracks or other damage; machine or replace as necessary. If the drum is to be machined, be sure to observe the maximum drum diameter specification.

10. Using high temperature grease, lubricate the 6 shoe contact pads on the brake backing plate.

11. Position the trailing brake shoe in the parking brake strut and install the rear hold-down pin and spring.

12. Position the leading brake shoe against the parking brake strut and backing plate and install the hold-down pin and spring.

13. Install the brake shoe return springs. Connect the parking brake cable.

14. Measure the drum inside diameter using gauge tool D81L-1103-A. Insert a small prybar or screwdriver into the knurled quadrant of the parking brake strut and adjust the brake shoes to the same measurement as the brake drum. The brake shoes should just touch the brake drum when properly adjusted.

15. Install the hub and the brake drum. Install a new locknut and torque to 130–174 ft. lbs. (177–235 Nm). Stake the locknut using a dull bladed chisel. Install the dust cap.

16. Install the wheel and torque the lug nuts to 65–87 ft. lbs. (88–118 Nm).

17. Complete the brake adjustment by sharply applying the brakes several times while driving the vehicle alternately forward and reverse.

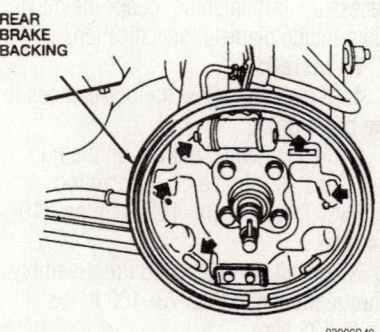

REAR BRAKE BACKING

93006G49

Apply lubricant to the brake backing plate at these locations—Ford Probe

**Ford Contour
Mercury Mystique**

1. Remove the rear wheel and tire assembly.

2. Remove the brake drum retainers, if equipped.

3. Grasp the brake drum and remove.

4. If the drum will not slide off with light force, then the brake shoes will need to be backed off:

   a. Remove the rubber plug on the backing plate and insert a screwdriver or small brake adjusting tool into the slot to contact the brake strut and quadrant.

b. A forward motion of the screwdriver will separate the quadrant from the knurled wheel and allow the brake shoes to retract.

   c. Remove the brake drum.

5. Remove the brake shoe hold down springs and the brake shoe hold down pins.

6. Remove the brake shoe retracting springs.

7. Disengage the parking brake cable and conduit from the parking brake lever.

8. Remove the brake shoes.

9. Disengage the rear brake strut and quadrant from the rear brake shoe.

10. Remove the parking brake rear cable and conduit from the parking brake cable anchor on the trailing brake shoe.

To install:

11. Lubricate the rear brake shoe contact points on the backing plate with an appropriate grease.

12. Engage the parking brake rear cable and conduit into the parking brake cable anchor on the trailing brake shoe.

13. Position the trailing brake shoe on the backing plate.

14. Engage the rear brake strut and quadrant.

15. Reinstall the parking brake rear spring.

16. Reinstall the brake shoe hold down spring pin and the hold down spring.

17. Insert the leading brake shoe into the slot on the rear brake strut and quadrant.

18. Reinstall the brake shoe hold down pin and hold down spring.

19. Reinstall the brake shoe retracting springs.

20. Adjust the brake shoes by first measuring the inside drum diameter with an appropriate brake adjustment gauge.

21. Insert a small screwdriver or similar tool into the knurled quadrant of the brake strut and quadrant to adjust the brake shoes to the same measurement of the brake drum by expanding the brake strut and quadrant.

22. Trial fit the brake drum. The shoes should just contact the drum surface when properly adjusted.

23. Make sure that the brake drum and brake shoes are clean of any oils or protective coatings.

24. Reinstall the brake drum.

25. Reinstall new drum retainers, if available.

26. Reconnect the parking brake rear cable and conduit to the parking brake lever.

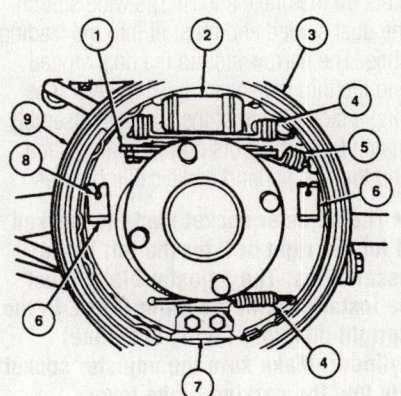

1	Rear Brake Strut and Quadrant
2	Rear Wheel Cylinder
3	Rear Brake Shoe and Lining
4	Brake Shoe Retracting Spring
5	Parking Brake Return Spring
6	Brake Shoe Hold Down Spring
7	Anchor Block
8	Brake Shoe Hold Down Spring Pin
9	Rear Brake Backing Plate

93006G50

Location of brake components—Contour/Mystique

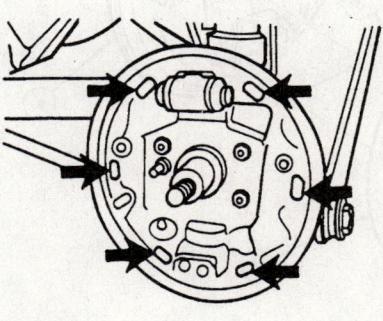

93006G52

Lubricating points on backing plate—Contour/Mystique

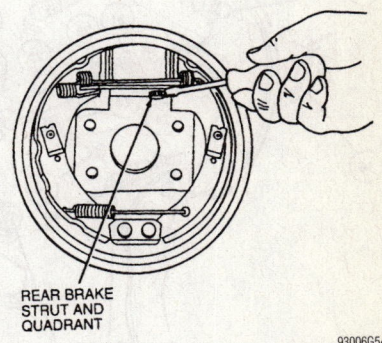

REAR BRAKE STRUT AND QUADRANT

93006G54

Adjusting the brake shoes to fit the drum—Contour/Mystique

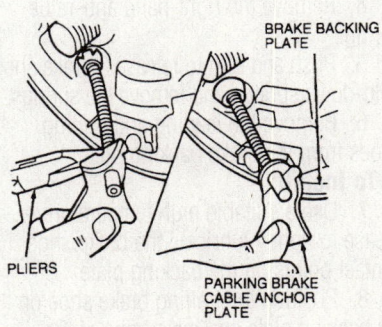

BRAKE BACKING PLATE

PLIERS

PARKING BRAKE CABLE ANCHOR PLATE

93006G51

Removal of parking brake cable—Contour/Mystique

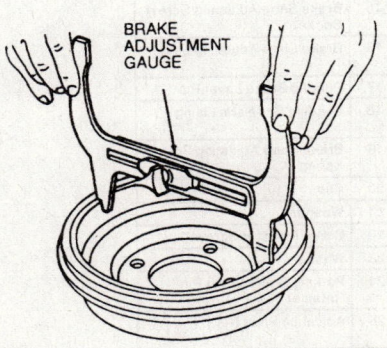

BRAKE ADJUSTMENT GAUGE

93006G53

Measuring the brake drum inner diameter—Contour/Mystique

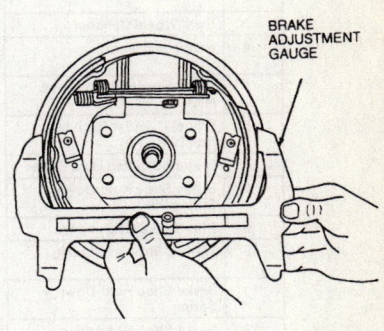

BRAKE ADJUSTMENT GAUGE

93006G55

Measuring the brake shoe adjustment—Contour/Mystique

Refer to the model specific sections for engine mechanical service procedures

It may be necessary to back off on the parking brake cable adjustment to allow for the new brake shoes.

27. Reinstall the wheel and tire assembly. Torque the lug nuts to 62 ft. lbs. (85 Nm).

28. Work the parking brake control several times to complete the brake shoe adjustment and to check the parking brake adjustment as well.

29. Pump the brake pedal several times to assure a good pedal.

30. Road test the vehicle and check for proper brake system operation.

Ford Taurus
Mercury Sable

1. Remove the wheel and tire assembly.
2. Remove the brake drum.
3. Remove the parking brake cable from the parking brake lever.

4. Remove the 2 brake shoe hold-down springs and pins.

5. Lift the brake shoes, springs and adjuster assembly off the backing plate and wheel cylinder assembly. When removing the assembly, be careful not to bend the adjusting lever.

6. Remove the retracting springs from the lower brake attachments and upper shoe-to-adjusting lever attachment points.

7. Remove the horseshoe retaining clip and spring washer and slide the lever off the parking brake lever pin on the trailing shoe. Discard the horseshoe clip.

To install:

8. Apply a light coating of disc brake caliper slide grease at the points where the brake shoes contact the backing plate.

9. Apply a thin coat of lubricant to the adjuster screw threads and socket end of the adjusting screw. Install the stainless steel

washer over the socket end of the adjusting screw and install the socket. Turn the adjusting screw into the adjusting pivot nut to the limit of the threads and then back off ½ turn.

10. Assemble the parking brake lever to the trailing shoe by installing the spring washer and a new horseshoe retaining clip. Crimp the clip until it retains the lever to the shoe securely.

11. Position the trailing shoe on the backing plate and attach the rear parking brake cable.

12. Position the leading shoe on the backing plate and attach the lower brake shoe adjusting spring to the brake shoes.

13. Install the adjuster assembly in the slots on the brake shoes. The wide slot on the dual slotted end must fit into the leading shoe. The narrow slot on the dual slotted end fits into the shoe adjusting lever. The single slotted side of the adjuster assembly must fit into the slots on the trailing shoe and the rear parking brake cable bracket.

➡ **The adjuster socket blade is marked R for the right or L for the left brake assemblies. The adjuster blade must be installed with the letter R or L in the upright position, facing the wheel cylinder. Make sure the adjuster socket fits into the parking brake lever.**

14. Complete the installation by reversing the removal procedures.

15. Pump the brake pedal several times to position the brake shoes and finish the brake shoe adjustment.

16. Road test the vehicle and check the brake system for proper operation.

Ford Escort
Mercury Tracer

1. Remove the wheel and tire assembly.
2. Remove 2 brake drum retaining screws and remove the brake drum.
3. Remove 2 brake shoe return springs.
4. Remove the right-hand anti-rattle spring.
5. Push and turn to release 2 brake shoe hold-down springs and remove the springs.
6. Remove the leading and trailing shoes from the brake backing plate.

To install:

7. Use a suitable high temperature grease to lightly lubricate the brake shoe contact points on the backing plate.

8. Position the trailing brake shoe on the backing plate and install one of the brake shoe hold-down springs.

9. Position the leading brake shoe on the backing plate and install the other brake shoe hold-down spring.

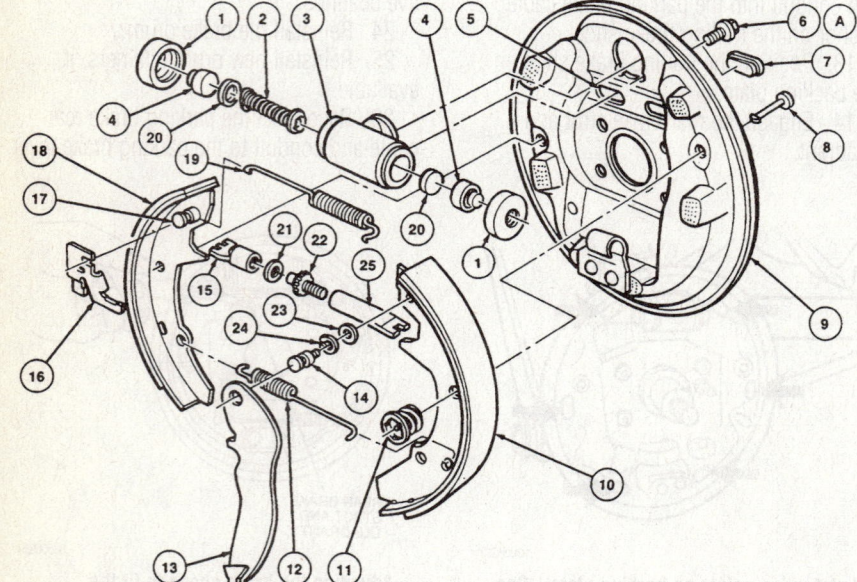

1	Boot
2	Spring Expander
3	Rear Wheel Cylinder
4	Piston and Insert
5	Shoe Adjustment Access Hole
6	Wheel Cylinder Retaining Bolt (2 Req'd)
7	Brake Adjusting Hole Cover
8	Brake Shoe Hold-Down Spring Pin
9	Rear Brake Backing Plate
10	Trailing Shoe and Lining
11	Brake Shoe Hold-Down Spring
12	Brake Shoe Retracting Spring
13	Parking Brake Lever
14	Parking Brake Lever Pin (Inner)
15	Brake Shoe Adjusting Screw Socket
16	Brake Shoe Adjusting Lever
17	Parking Brake Lever Pin
18	Leading Shoe and Lining
19	Brake Shoe Adjusting Screw Spring
20	Cup
21	Washer
22	Brake Adjuster Screw
23	Washer
24	Parking Brake Lever Pin Retainer
25	Adjusting Pivot Nut
A	Tighten to 12-18 N·m (107-159 Lb-In)

93006G56

Brake shoes and related components—Taurus and Sable

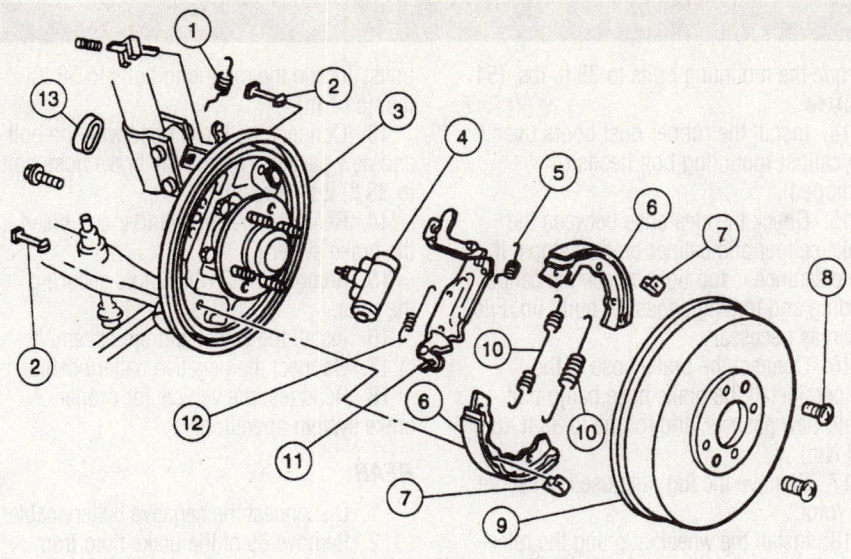

1	Parking Brake Link Spring
2	Brake Shoe Hold-Down Spring Pin
3	Rear Brake Backing Plate
4	Rear Wheel Cylinder
5	Right Hand Anti-Rattle Spring
6	Rear Brake Shoe and Lining

7	Brake Shoe Hold-Down Spring
8	Brake Drum Screw (2 Req'd)
9	Brake Drum
10	Brake Shoe Retracting Spring
11	Parking Brake Lever
12	Parking Brake Return Spring
13	Brake Adjusting Hole Cover

93006G57

Brake shoes and related components—Escort/Tracer

10. Install the right-hand anti-rattle spring.

11. Install 2 brake shoe return springs.

12. Using a brake adjusting gauge, measure the inside diameter of the brake drum.

13. Compare the brake drum measurement to the brake shoes.

14. Adjust the brake shoes by inserting a screwdriver into the knurled quadrant of the rear quad operating lever and adjust the shoes to the same measurement as the brake drum.

15. Install the brake drum.

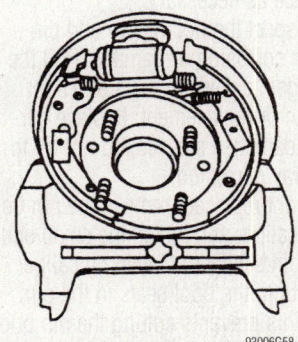

93006G58

Checking the adjustment of the brake shoes—Escort/Tracer

16. Install 2 brake drum retaining screws.

17. Install the wheel and tire assembly. Torque the lug nuts to 65–87 ft. lbs. (88–118 Nm).

18. Complete the brake shoe adjustment by sharply applying the brakes several times while driving the vehicle alternating between forward and reverse gears.

19. Check the brake system operation by making several stops while driving forward.

Ford Thunderbird
Mercury Cougar (1997–98 Model)

1. Remove the wheel and tire assembly.

2. Remove the brake drum.

3. Disconnect the parking brake rear cable from the parking brake lever.

4. Remove 2 brake shoe hold-down retainers, brake shoe hold-down springs and hold-down pins.

5. Lift the brake shoes, springs and adjuster off of the brake backing plate as an assembly using care not to bend the brake shoe adjusting lever.

6. Remove the brake shoe adjusting screw spring.

7. Separate the brake shoes by removing the brake shoe retracting springs.

8. Remove the parking brake lever pin retainer and spring washer, then remove the brake shoe adjusting lever from the adapter.

To install:

9. Apply a light coating of caliper slide grease to the brake backing plate brake shoe contact areas as well as the adjuster screw threads.

10. Assemble the adjuster screw and the brake shoe adjusting screw socket and washer. Turn the brake shoe adjusting screw socket all the way down, then back off ½ turn.

11. Install the parking brake lever to the trailing shoe with the spring washer and a new parking brake lever pin retainer. Crimp the retainer to securely retain the parking brake lever.

12. Place the trailing shoe on the brake backing plate and attach the parking brake cable.

13. Install the brake shoe hold-down pin, spring and retainers on the trailing brake shoe.

14. Place the leading shoe on the brake backing plate and attach the lower brake shoe retracting spring between both brake shoes.

15. Install the leading brake shoe hold-down pin, spring and retainers.

16. Install the brake adjuster assembly to the slots between the brake shoes. The brake shoe adjusting screw socket end must fit into the slot in the leading shoe and the adjuster nut end must fit into the slots of the trailing brake shoe and parking brake lever.

17. Install the brake shoe adjusting lever on the pin of the leading shoe and to the slot in the brake shoe adjusting screw socket.

18. Install the upper brake shoe retracting spring in the slot on the trailing shoe and the slot in the brake shoe adjusting lever. Verify that the brake shoe adjusting lever is contacting the starwheel on the adjuster assembly.

19. Adjust the brake shoes to the brake drum.

20. Install the brake drum.

21. Install the wheel and tire assembly. Using a torque wrench, torque the lug nuts in a star pattern to 85–105 ft. lbs. (115–142 Nm).

22. Apply the brakes several times while backing up the vehicle. After each stop, the vehicle must be moved forward.

23. Road test the vehicle and check for proper brake system operation by making several stops from varying forward speeds.

For accessory drive belt replacement procedures see the model specific sections of this manual

GENERAL MOTORS

Brake Caliper

REMOVAL & INSTALLATION

GM C- and H-Bodies:
Buick LeSabre, Park Avenue
Oldsmobile Eighty Eight Royale,
Ninety Eight, Regency
Pontiac Bonneville

→The Bosch 2U ABS system cannot increase brake pressure above master cylinder pressure applied by during braking. There is no need to depressurize the system prior to service.

1. Remove brake fluid from the master cylinder reservoir until the reservoir is approximately ⅓ full.
2. Remove the front wheel. Mark the position of the wheel to the wheel studs, prior to removal, for installation reference.
3. Install 2 lug nuts to retain the rotor once the caliper is removed.
4. Using a large C-clamp, bottom the piston in the caliper bore by positioning the C-clamp on the outboard pad and on the round portion of the brake caliper where the piston is housed.
5. Remove the banjo bolt that fastens the brake hose to the brake caliper. Discard the gaskets.
6. Cap the brake line to avoid excessive fluid loss or fluid contamination.
7. Remove the rubber dust boots from the caliper mounting bolt heads (if equipped).
8. Remove the caliper mounting bolts.
9. Remove the caliper from the vehicle.
10. Remove the brake pads.
   To install:
11. Install the brake pads. Lubricate the slides where the caliper mounts on the steering knuckle with silicone grease.
12. Install the caliper over the rotor.
13. Install the caliper mounting bolts.

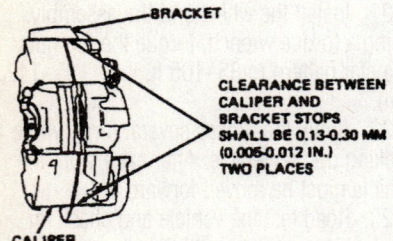

BRACKET

CLEARANCE BETWEEN CALIPER AND BRACKET STOPS SHALL BE 0.13-0.30 MM (0.005-0.012 IN.) TWO PLACES

CALIPER

93006G60

Measuring the caliper clearance—LeSabre, Park Avenue, Eighty Eight Royale, Ninety Eight, Regency, Bonneville

Torque the mounting bolts to 38 ft. lbs. (51 Nm).
14. Install the rubber dust boots over the caliper mounting bolt heads (if equipped).
15. Check the clearance between the brake caliper and caliper bracket stops. If the clearance is too tight, check the caliper leading and trailing edges for build up. File down as necessary.
16. Connect the brake hose to the caliper. Install the brake hose banjo bolt, using new gaskets, and torque to 33 ft. lbs. (45 Nm).
17. Remove the lug nuts used to secure the rotor.
18. Install the wheel, aligning the reference marks made during removal, and torque the lug nuts to 100 ft. lbs. (140 Nm).
19. Refill the master cylinder and bleed the brake system using the recommended procedure.
20. Road test the vehicle and check for proper braking performance.

GM E-, K- and V-Bodies:
Cadillac Catera, deVille, Eldorado, Seville

FRONT

1. Disconnect the negative battery cable.
2. Remove ⅔ of the brake fluid from the master cylinder.
3. Remove the front wheel. Mark the relationship between the wheel and the wheel stud for re-installation purposes.
4. Install 2 wheel nuts to keep the rotor in place.
5. Using a large C-clamp against the inboard pad, compress the caliper piston into the caliper to provide clearance during removal.
6. Place a catch pan under the caliper.
7. Disconnect the brake hose from the caliper. Cap the line to prevent excessive fluid loss or contamination.
8. Remove the caliper mounting bolts and remove the caliper from the vehicle.
9. Inspect the mounting bolts; sleeves and boots for wear and/or damage. Replace parts as necessary.
   To install:
10. Before installing the caliper, make sure the piston is fully seated in the bore and the brake pads are properly seated.
11. Lubricate the mounting bolt shafts and inner diameter of the sleeves with silicone grease.
12. Install the caliper in the caliper mounting bracket and install the mounting

bolts. Torque the mounting bolts to 38 ft. lbs. (51 Nm).
13. Connect the brake hose with the bolt and new gaskets. Torque the brake hose bolt to 33 ft. lbs. (45 Nm).
14. Refill the master cylinder and bleed the brake system.
15. Remove the 2 wheel nuts securing the rotor.
16. Install the wheel and tire assembly.
17. Connect the negative battery cable.
18. Road test the vehicle for proper brake system operation.

REAR

1. Disconnect the negative battery cable.
2. Remove ⅔ of the brake fluid from the master cylinder.
3. Remove the rear wheel.
4. Install 2 wheel nuts to keep the rotor in place.
5. Place a catch pan under the caliper.
6. Disconnect the brake hose from the caliper. Cap the line to prevent fluid loss or contamination.
7. Loosen the tension on the parking brake at the equalizer.
8. Remove the parking brake cable mounting lever, and remove the cable end by lifting up and disengaging the end.
9. Remove the caliper sleeve bolt.
10. Lift the caliper up and slide the caliper inboard off of the pin sleeve to remove the caliper from the vehicle.
11. Use a suitable tool in the caliper piston slots to turn the piston and thread it into the caliper. After bottoming the piston, lift the inner edge of the boot next to the piston and press out any trapped air the boot must lay flat.
   To install:
12. Inspect the pin boot, bolt boot and sleeve boot for cuts, tears or deterioration and replace as necessary.
13. Inspect the bolt sleeve and pin sleeve for corrosion or damage. Pull the boots to gain access to the sleeves for inspection or replacement. Replace corroded or damaged sleeves; do not try to polish away corrosion.
14. If not replaced, remove the pin boot from the caliper and install the small end over the pin sleeve (installed on caliper support) until the boot seats in the pin groove. This prevents cutting the pin boot when sliding the caliper onto the pin sleeve.
15. Hold the caliper in the position as removed and start it over the end of the pin sleeve. As the caliper approaches the pin boot, work the large end of the pin boot in

the caliper groove, then push the caliper fully onto the pin.

16. Pivot the caliper down, being careful not to damage the piston boot on the inboard disc brake pad. Compress the sleeve boot by hand as the caliper moves into position to prevent boot damage.

17. After the caliper is in position, recheck the position of the pad clips. If necessary, use a small prybar to reseat or enter the pad clips on the bracket abutments.

18. Install the sleeve bolt and torque to 20 ft. lbs. (27 Nm).

19. Install the parking brake cable bracket, with the cable attached, and torque the bolt to 32 ft. lbs. (43 Nm).

20. Install the parking brake cable onto the parking brake lever and the retaining clip onto the parking brake cable.

21. Connect the brake hose with the bolt and new gaskets and torque the bolt to 32 ft. lbs. (43 Nm).

22. Adjust the parking brake cable.

23. Refill the master cylinder and bleed the brake system.

24. Remove the wheel nuts retaining the rotor and install the wheel.

25. Connect the negative battery cable.

26. Road test the vehicle for proper brake system operation.

GM F-BODY:
Chevrolet Camaro
Pontiac Firebird

FRONT W/SINGLE PISTON

1. Remove ⅔ of the brake fluid from the master cylinder.

2. Matchmark the relationship between the wheel and hub, then remove the wheel and tire assembly.

3. Reinstall 2 of the lug nuts in order to retain the rotor.

4. Position a C-clamp over the outboard brake pad and the caliper housing, then use the C-clamp to bottom the piston into the caliper bore.

5. If completely removing the caliper from the vehicle for replacement or service, remove the brake hose bolt from the caliper housing and discard the copper washers.

6. Plug the openings in the inlet fitting and caliper housing to prevent system contamination or excessive fluid loss.

7. Remove the caliper mounting bolts.

8. Remove the caliper assembly from the rotor and bracket. If the caliper is not being completely removed, it must be suspended from the vehicle using a wire hook

in order to prevent damage to the brake lines.

To install:

9. Inspect the mounting bolts and sleeves for damage or corrosion and replace as necessary. Do not attempt to polish away corrosion. Ensure all caliper-to-bracket contact points are rust free and clean. Check the inlet fitting bolt for blockage.

10. Lubricate the sleeves, bushings and slide points with a suitable silicone grease.

11. Install the sleeves into the caliper housing, then install the caliper assembly onto the rotor and bracket assembly. Install the mounting bolts and torque to 38 ft. lbs. (51 Nm).

12. Attach brake hose to caliper using new copper washers. Torque the bolt to 32 ft. lbs. (44 Nm).

13. Replace the brake fluid in the master cylinder and, if the caliper was removed, bleed the caliper.

14. Align the marks made earlier and install the wheel and tire assembly.

15. Lower the vehicle, then with the engine running pump the brake pedal slowly and firmly 3 times to seat then brake pads.

FRONT W/DUAL PISTON

1. Remove ⅔ of the brake fluid from the master cylinder.

2. Matchmark the relationship of the wheel and hub, then remove the wheel and tire assembly.

3. If completely removing the caliper from the vehicle for replacement or service, remove the bolt, inlet fitting and 2 gaskets from the caliper housing. Plug the openings in the caliper housing and inlet fitting to prevent system contamination or excessive fluid loss.

4. Remove the circlip and retainer pin.

5. Remove the caliper housing from the rotor and mounting bracket. If the caliper is not being completely removed, it must be suspended from the vehicle using a wire hook in order to prevent damage to the brake lines.

To install:

6. Check the inlet fitting bolt for blockage, clear or replace as necessary.

7. Install the caliper housing over the rotor and onto the mounting bracket. Ensure the guiding surfaces on the inboard and outboard disc brake pads and mounting bracket are seated correctly.

8. Press the caliper housing down to compress the bias springs. Slide a new retainer pin into position and install a new circlip.

9. If removed, install the inlet fitting, bolt and 2 new gaskets. Torque the bolt to 30 ft. lbs. (40 Nm).

10. Fill the master cylinder and bleed the brake system.

11. Align the matchmarks made earlier and install the wheel and tire assembly.

12. Lower the vehicle, then with the engine running pump the brake pedal slowly and firmly 3 times to seat then brake pads.

REAR

1. Matchmark the relationship between the wheel and hub, then remove the wheel and tire assembly. Install 2 wheel nuts to retain the rotor.

2. If completely removing the caliper from the vehicle for replacement or service, remove the brake hose bolt inlet fitting and 2 gaskets from the caliper housing.

3. Plug the openings in the caliper housing and inlet fitting to prevent system contamination or excessive fluid loss.

4. Remove the 2 caliper guide pin bolts.

5. Remove the caliper housing from the rotor and mounting bracket. If the caliper is not being completely removed, it must be suspended from the vehicle using a wire hook in order to prevent damage to the brake lines.

To install:

6. Inspect the guide pins and boots and replace if corroded, worn or damaged. Check the inlet fitting bolt for blockage, clear or replace as necessary.

7. Install the caliper housing over the rotor and into the mounting bracket.

8. Install 2 caliper guide pin bolts starting with the upper pin and torque the bolts to 27 ft. lbs. (37 Nm).

9. Attach the brake hose to the caliper using 2 new copper gaskets. Torque the bolt to 22 ft. lbs. (30 Nm).

10. If the hose fitting was removed, bleed the entire brake system.

11. Lower the vehicle sufficiently and cycle the parking brake.

12. Raise and safely support the vehicle.

13. Inspect the caliper parking brake levers and ensure they are against the stops on the caliper housing. If the levers are not on their stops, check the parking brake adjustment.

14. Remove the 2 nuts securing the rotor, then align the matchmarks made earlier and install the wheel assembly.

15. Lower the vehicle, then with the engine running pump the brake pedal slowly and firmly 3 times to seat then brake pads.

16. Check the hydraulic system for leaks.

GM G-BODY:
Buick Riviera
Oldsmobile Aurora

FRONT

1. Siphon ⅔ of the brake fluid out of the master cylinder reservoir.

2. Remove the tire and wheel assembly.

3. Install 2 wheel nuts loosely to secure the rotor when the caliper is removed.

4. Remove the bolts securing the brake hose to the caliper and disconnect the brake hose from the caliper.

5. Plug the hose to prevent excessive fluid loss and possible fluid contamination.

6. Compress the piston into the caliper bore to provide clearance for removal.

7. Remove the caliper mounting bolts.

8. Remove the caliper from the anchor bracket.

9. If the caliper is being replaced remove the brake pads from the caliper or anchor bracket.

To install

10. Seat the caliper piston fully in its bore.

11. Install the brake pads in the caliper or anchor bracket.

12. Install the caliper on the anchor bracket and install the mounting bolts.

13. Torque the caliper mounting bolts to 38 ft. lbs. (51 Nm). Torque the mounting bolts to 63 ft. lbs. (85 Nm).

14. Reconnect the brake hose to the caliper using new washers. Torque the fitting bolt to 33 ft. lbs. (45 Nm).

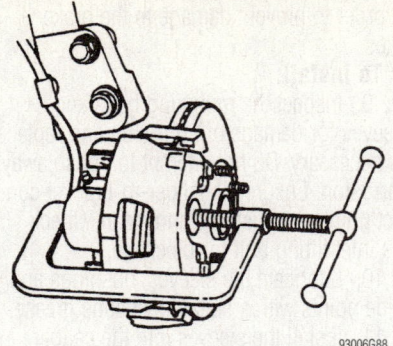

Compressing the front caliper piston—Riviera, Aurora

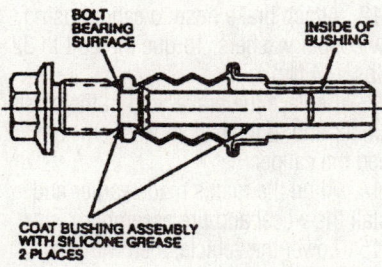

Caliper mounting bolt and sleeve lubrication points—Riviera, Aurora

15. Remove the 2 lug nuts securing the brake rotor.

16. Install the wheel and tire assembly and torque the wheel nuts to 100 ft. lbs. (140 Nm).

17. Refill the master cylinder with fluid and bleed the brake system.

18. Pump the brake pedal several times to seat the brake pads against the rotor. Verify no hydraulic leaks and a good firm brake pedal.

REAR

1. Siphon ⅔ of the brake fluid out of the master cylinder reservoir.

2. Remove the tire and wheel assembly.

3. Install 2 wheel nuts loosely to secure the rotor when the caliper is removed.

4. Remove the bolt securing the brake hose to the caliper and disconnect the brake hose from the caliper.

5. Plug the hose to prevent excessive fluid loss and possible fluid contamination.

6. The following steps are required for 1997 models:

   a. Compress the parking brake actuator lever on the caliper and disconnect the parking brake cable.

   b. Remove the bolt and washer securing the parking brake cable bracket to the caliper.

   c. Remove the lower caliper mounting bolt.

   d. Pivot the caliper upwards until it clears the brake rotor. Push the caliper inward to remove it from the upper mounting pin.

7. For 1998–01 later models, remove upper and lower caliper bolts and lift caliper from mounting bracket.

To install:

8. Seat the caliper piston fully in its bore.

9. Make sure the notches in the caliper piston are at 6 and 12 o'clock.

10. The following steps are required for 1997 models:

   a. Install the caliper onto the upper pivot pin. Turn the caliper downward until it is seated over the rotor.

   b. Reinstall the sleeve bolt and torque to 20 ft. lbs. (27 Nm).

   c. Reinstall the parking brake cable bracket and torque the mounting bolt to 32 ft. lbs. (43 Nm).

   d. Pivot the parking brake actuator lever and connect the cable end to the actuator arm.

11. On 1998–01 models, mount caliper onto anchor bracket. Install the 2 mounting bolts and torque bolts to 63 ft. lbs. (85 Nm)

12. Reconnect the brake hose to the caliper using new copper washers. Torque the mounting bolt to 33 ft. lbs. (45 Nm).

13. Remove the wheel nuts securing the rotor.

14. Reinstall the tire and wheel assembly and torque the wheel nuts to 100 ft. lbs. (140 Nm).

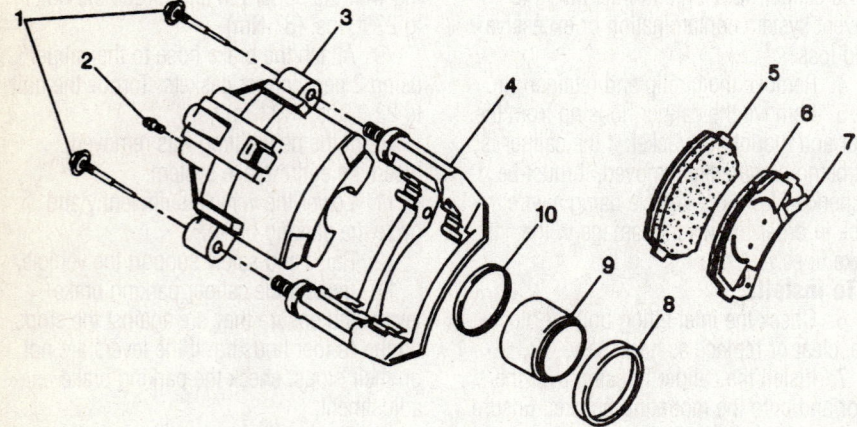

(1) Pin Bolts
(2) Outboard Pad
(3) Caliper Boot
(4) Inboard Pad
(5) Piston Seal
(6) Piston
(7) Anchor bracket
(8) Bleeder Valve
(9) Caliper Housing
(10) Caliper Anchor Bracket

Front caliper and brake pad components—Riviera, Aurora

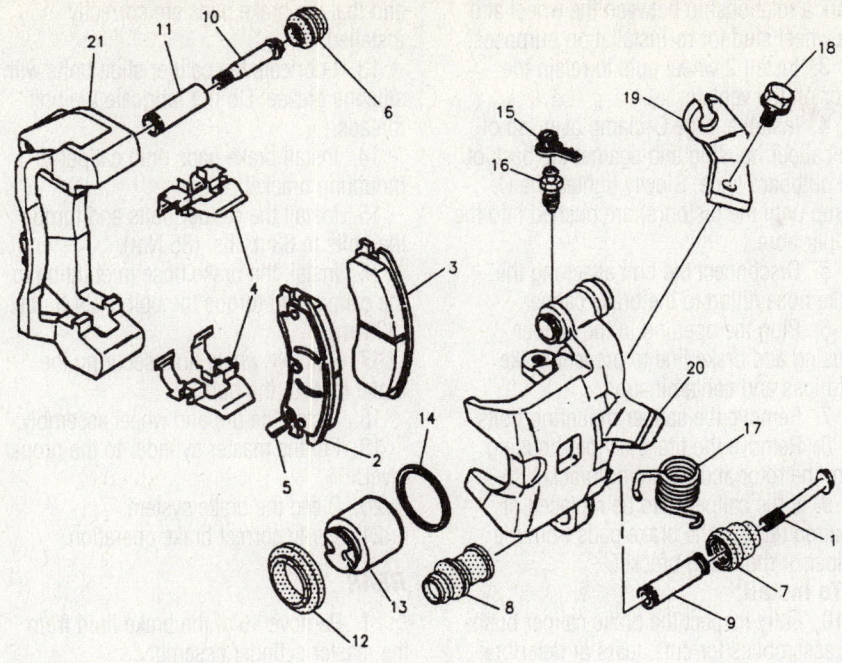

1	SLEEVE BOLT	12	PISTON BOOT
2	OUTBOARD SHOE & LINING	13	PISTON ASSEMBLY
3	INBOARD SHOE & LINING	14	PISTON SEAL
4	PAD CLIP	15	BLEEDER VALVE CAP
5	WEAR SENSOR	16	BLEEDER VALVE
6	PIN BOOT	17	LEVER RETURN SPRING
7	BOLT BOOT	18	BOLT AND WASHER
8	SLEEVE BOLT	19	CABLE SUPPORT BRACKET
9	BOLT SLEEVE	20	CALIPER BODY ASSEMBLY
10	PIN BOLT	21	CALIPER SUPPORT
11	PIN SLEEVE		

93006G90

Rear caliper and brake pad components—Riviera, Aurora

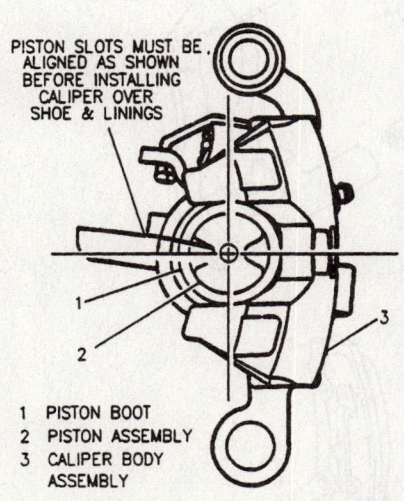

PISTON SLOTS MUST BE
ALIGNED AS SHOWN
BEFORE INSTALLING
CALIPER OVER
SHOE & LININGS

1 PISTON BOOT
2 PISTON ASSEMBLY
3 CALIPER BODY
  ASSEMBLY

93006G91

Aligning the notches in the piston—Riviera, Aurora

15. Refill the master cylinder with fluid and bleed the brake system.

16. Pump the brake pedal several times to seat the brake pads against the rotor. Verify no hydraulic leaks and a good firm brake pedal.

GM J-BODY:
Chevrolet Cavalier
Pontiac Sunfire

1. Siphon ⅔ of the brake fluid out of the master cylinder.

2. Remove the tire and wheel assembly.

3. Compress the caliper piston back into the caliper bore using a large pair of pliers, C-clamp or special piston retracting tool.

4. If the caliper is to be completely removed from the vehicle for bench service, disconnect and cap the brake line from the caliper. Discard the old washers.

5. Remove the caliper mounting bolts and sleeves.

6. Remove the caliper from the knuckle.

7. Remove the brake pads from the caliper, if caliper is being replaced.

To install:

8. Install the brake pads in the caliper.

9. Install the caliper on the steering knuckle.

10. Install the mounting bolts and sleeves and torque to 40 ft. lbs. (51 Nm).

11. If the caliper brake line was disconnected, uncap and connect the brake hose to the caliper using new copper washers. Torque the mounting bolt to 35 ft. lbs. (44 Nm).

12. Refill the master cylinder and bleed the brake system.

13. Install the tire and wheel assembly and tighten to specification.

14. Verify correct brake operation.

GM L/N and N-BODY:
Buick Skylark
Chevrolet Malibu
Oldsmobile Achieva, Cutlass
Pontiac Grand Am

1. Siphon ⅔ of the brake fluid out of the master cylinder.

2. Remove the tire and wheel assembly.

3. Compress the caliper piston back into the caliper bore using a large pair of pliers, C-clamp or special piston retracting tool.

4. Remove the brake hose from the caliper and discard the copper washers.

5. Plug the hose to prevent excessive fluid loss and possible fluid contamination.

6. Remove the caliper mounting bolts and remove the caliper from the knuckle.

7. Remove the brake pads from the caliper, if the caliper is being replaced.

To install:

8. Inspect the condition of the caliper support for rust and corrosion that will hinder the travel of the caliper.

9. Inspect the caliper mounting hardware. New bolts are usually recommended.

10. Lubricate the mounting bushings and sleeves with silicone grease as required.

11. Install the brake pads in the caliper.

12. Install the caliper on the steering knuckle.

13. Install the mounting bolts and torque to 40 ft. lbs. (51 Nm).

14. Connect the brake hose to the caliper using new copper washers and torque the mounting bolt to 35 ft. lbs. (44 Nm).

Timing chain and gear service is covered in the model specific sections of this manual

15. Refill the master cylinder and bleed the brake system.

16. Install the tire and wheel assembly.

17. Verify correct brake operation.

GM W-BODY:
Buick Century, Regal
Chevrolet Lumina, Monte Carlo
Oldsmobile Cutlass Supreme, Intrigue
Pontiac Grand Prix

FRONT

1. Remove ⅔ of the brake fluid from the master cylinder assembly.

2. Remove the tire and wheel assembly.

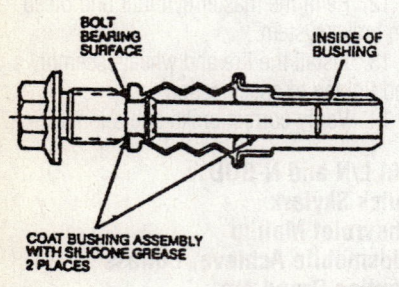

Slide bolts lubrication points—Century, Regal, Lumina, Monte Carlo, Cutlass Supreme, Intrigue, Grand Prix

Mark a relationship between the wheel and the wheel stud for re-installation purposes.

3. Install 2 wheel nuts to retain the rotor on the vehicle.

4. Install a large C-clamp over top of the caliper housing and against the back of the outboard shoe. Slowly tighten the C-clamp until the piston(s) are pushed into the caliper bore.

5. Disconnect the bolt attaching the brake hose fitting to the brake caliper.

6. Plug the opening in the caliper housing and brake line to prevent brake fluid loss and contamination.

7. Remove the caliper mounting bolts.

8. Remove the brake caliper housing from the rotor and mounting bracket.

9. If the caliper is to be replaced or repaired remove the brake pads from the caliper or mounting bracket.

To install:

10. Fully inspect the brake caliper bushing assemblies for cuts, tears or deterioration and replace parts as needed.

11. Inspect the slide bolts for corrosion. If corrosion is found, replace the slide bolts and bushings before installing the brake caliper assembly.

12. Before installing the caliper, make sure the piston(s) are seated in the bore,

and that the brake pads are correctly installed.

13. Lubricate the caliper slide bolts with silicone grease. Do not lubricate the bolt threads.

14. Install brake pads onto caliper or mounting bracket.

15. Install the caliper bolts and torque the bolts to 63 ft. lbs. (85 Nm).

16. Install the brake hose inlet fitting to the caliper and torque the bolt to 24 ft. lbs. (32 Nm).

17. Remove wheel nuts securing the brake rotor to the hub.

18. Install the tire and wheel assembly.

19. Fill the master cylinder to the proper level.

20. Bleed the brake system.

21. Verify correct brake operation.

REAR

1. Remove ⅔ of the brake fluid from the master cylinder assembly.

2. Remove the tire and wheel assembly. Mark a relationship between the wheel and the wheel stud for re-installation purposes.

3. Install 2 wheel nuts to retain the rotor.

4. Remove the brake hose from the caliper and discard the copper washers.

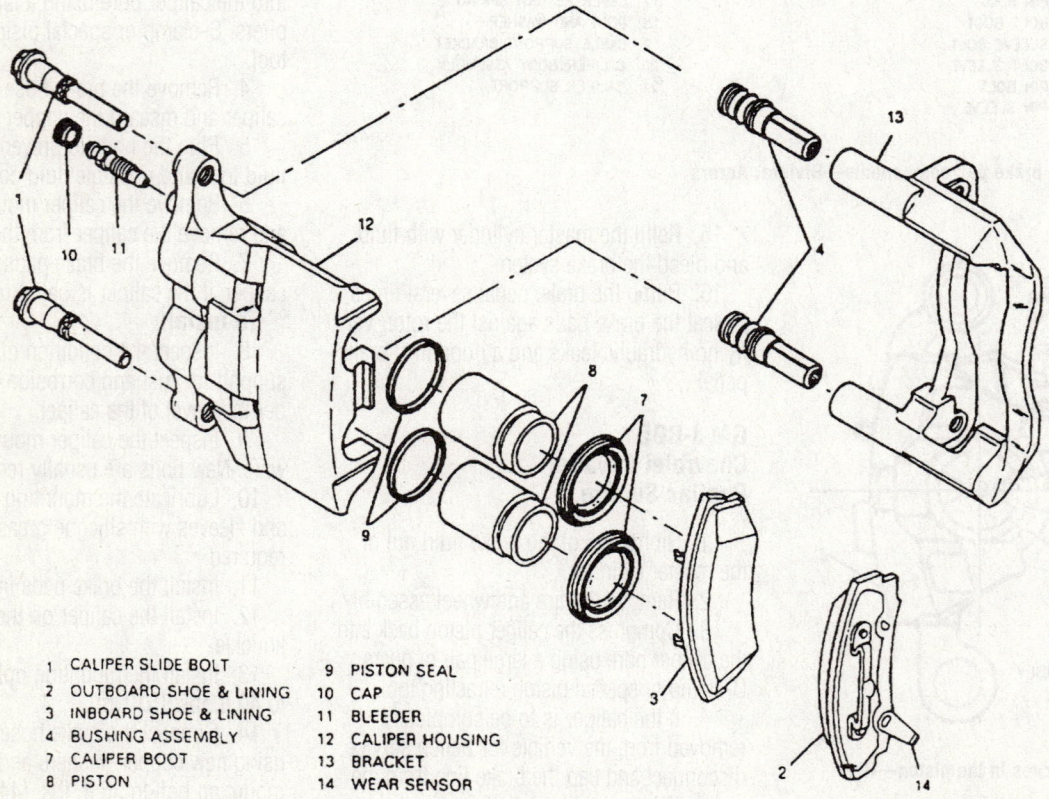

1 CALIPER SLIDE BOLT	9 PISTON SEAL
2 OUTBOARD SHOE & LINING	10 CAP
3 INBOARD SHOE & LINING	11 BLEEDER
4 BUSHING ASSEMBLY	12 CALIPER HOUSING
7 CALIPER BOOT	13 BRACKET
8 PISTON	14 WEAR SENSOR

Caliper attachments—Century, Regal, Lumina, Monte Carlo, Cutlass Supreme, Intrigue, Grand Prix

5. Plug the openings in the caliper and the brake hose to prevent brake fluid loss and contamination.

6. The following steps are for models with the park brake cable attached to the caliper:

a. Disconnect the parking brake cable from the parking brake lever on the caliper. Lift up one end of the cable spring clip free end of the cable from the lever.

b. Remove the bolt and washer attaching the cable support bracket to the caliper body assembly.

c. Remove the caliper sleeve bolts.

7. For all others, remove the two caliper mounting bolts.

8. Remove the caliper body assembly from the vehicle. Pivot the caliper assembly up to clear the rotor and then slide it inboard off the pin sleeve.

To install:

9. Inspect the caliper bolt boots, pins and sleeve bolt for cuts, tears or deterioration. Replace as necessary.

10. Lubricate the mounting surfaces and the mounting sleeves.

11. Hold the caliper body assembly in the position from which it was removed, and start it over the end of the pin sleeve.

12. As the caliper body assembly approaches the pin boot, work the large end of the pin boot in the caliper body groove. Push the caliper body fully onto the pin.

13. Pivot the caliper body assembly down, using care not to damage the piston boot on the inboard shoe. Compress the sleeve boot by hand as the caliper body moves into position to prevent boot damage.

14. After installing the caliper assembly into position, recheck the installation of the pad clips. If necessary, use a small prying tool to reset or center the pad clips.

15. Install the brake caliper sleeve bolts and torque to 20 ft. lbs. (27 Nm).

16. On models without caliper mounted park brake cable, torque caliper mounting bolts to 32 ft. lbs. (43 Nm)

17. To install the park brake cable, the following steps apply (some models).

a. Install the cable support bracket with the cable attached. Torque bolt to 32 ft. lbs. (43 Nm).

b. Lift up on the end of the cable spring clip and work the end of the parking brake cable into the notch of the parking brake lever.

18. Connect the brake hose to the brake caliper and torque the bolt to 32 ft. lbs. (44 Nm).

19. Remove the wheel nuts securing the rotor to the hub and bearing assembly.

20. Install the tire and wheel assembly.

21. Fill the master cylinder to the proper level with clean brake fluid.

22. Bleed the brake system using the recommended procedure.

23. Apply approximately 175 lbs. (79 kg) of force, 3 times, to properly seat the brake shoe and linings against the rotor.

24. Adjust the parking brake cable as necessary (some models).

GM Y-BODY:
Chevrolet Corvette

FRONT

1. Disconnect the negative battery cable and remove ⅔ of the brake fluid from the master cylinder reservoir.

2. Mark the relationship between the wheel and axle flange, then remove the tire and wheel assembly.

3. Install 2 wheel nuts to retain the brake rotor.

4. Depress the caliper pistons into the caliper bores in order to provide clearance between the pads and the rotor.

5. Disconnect the brake hose fitting at the caliper by removing the bolt. Discard the 2 copper washers.

6. Plug all openings to prevent fluid contamination or loss.

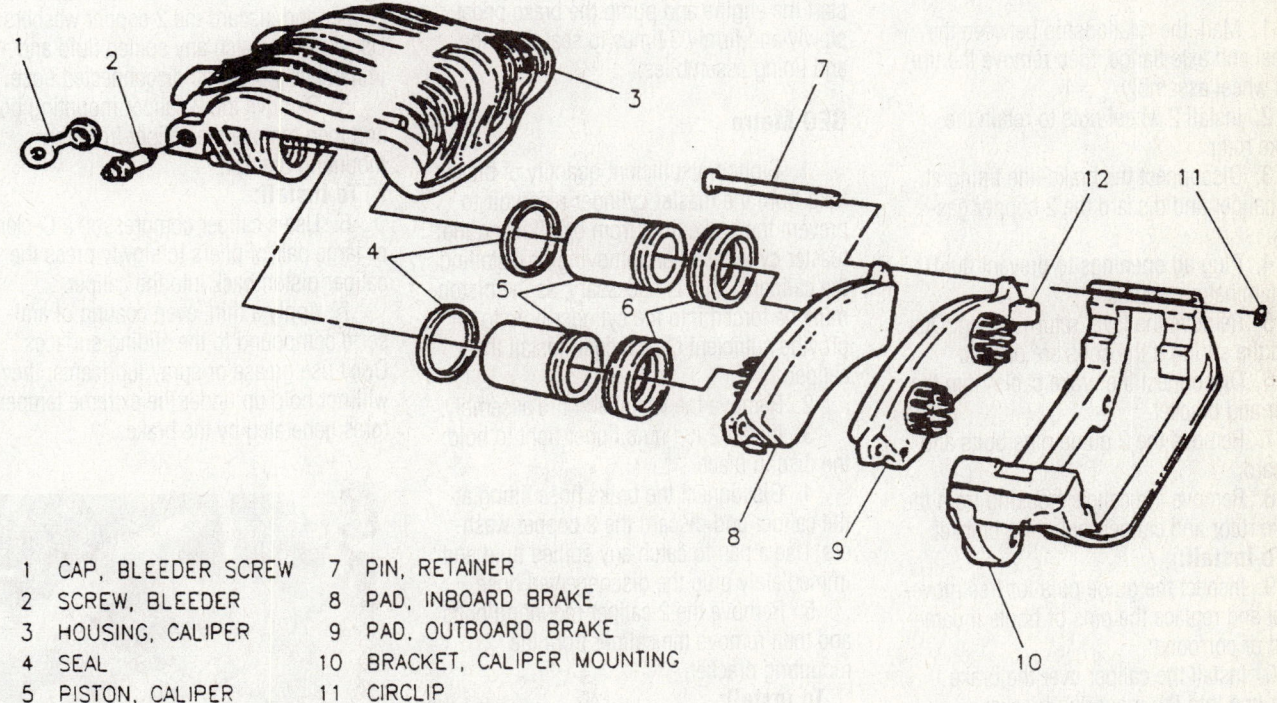

1	CAP, BLEEDER SCREW	7	PIN, RETAINER
2	SCREW, BLEEDER	8	PAD, INBOARD BRAKE
3	HOUSING, CALIPER	9	PAD, OUTBOARD BRAKE
4	SEAL	10	BRACKET, CALIPER MOUNTING
5	PISTON, CALIPER	11	CIRCLIP
6	BOOT	12	SPRING, BIAS

93006G63

Exploded view of the front caliper assembly—Corvette

➡️**Do not allow the fluid to come into contact with the front transverse spring, as damage to the spring may occur.**

7. For Corvette, remove the 2 caliper mounting bolts.

8. Remove the caliper housing from the rotor and the caliper mounting bracket.

To install:

9. Install the caliper over the brake rotor and into the caliper mounting bracket. Make sure the shoe lining guiding surfaces are correctly seated in the bracket.

10. Compress the bias springs by applying pressure to the mounting bracket, then install the new retainer pin.

11. Connect the brake hose inlet fitting using 2 new copper washers and the inlet fitting bolt. Torque the bolt to 30 ft. lbs. (40 Nm).

12. Properly bleed the entire brake system.

13. Remove the wheel nuts retaining the rotor, align the marks made earlier and install the tire and wheel assembly.

14. Check the brake fluid and add as necessary.

15. Connect the negative battery cable, start the engine and pump the brake pedal slowly and firmly 3 times to seat the shoe and lining assemblies.

REAR

1. Mark the relationship between the wheel and axle flange, then remove the tire and wheel assembly.

2. Install 2 wheel nuts to retain the brake rotor.

3. Disconnect the brake line fitting at the caliper and discard the 2 copper gaskets.

4. Plug all openings to prevent fluid contamination or loss.

5. Remove the lever return spring. Discard the spring if the coils are opened.

6. Disconnect the brake cable from the lever and bracket.

7. Remove the 2 guide pins bolts and discard.

8. Remove the caliper housing from the brake rotor and caliper mounting bracket.

To install:

9. Inspect the guide pins for free movement and replace the pins or boots if damaged or corroded.

10. Install the caliper over the brake rotor and into the mounting bracket.

11. Install the caliper mounting bolts and torque to 23 ft. lbs. (31 Nm).

12. Install the cable to the bracket and parking brake lever.

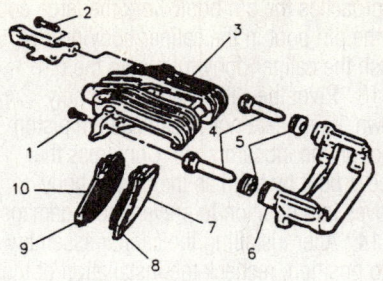

1 BOLT, UPPER GUIDE PIN
2 BOLT, LOWER GUIDE PIN
3 HOUSING, CALIPER
4 PIN, GUIDE
5 BOOT
6 BRACKET, MOUNTING
7 INSULATOR
8 PAD, OUTBOARD BRAKE
9 SENSOR, WEAR
10 PAD, INBOARD BRAKE

93006G64

Exploded view of the rear caliper assembly—Corvette

13. Connect the brake line fitting using 2 new copper washers and the inlet fitting bolt. Torque the bolt to 30 ft. lbs. (40 Nm).

14. Properly bleed the entire hydraulic brake system.

15. Remove the 2 nuts securing the rotor to the hub.

16. Align the marks made earlier and install the tire and wheel assembly.

17. Check the brake fluid level.

18. Connect the negative battery cable, start the engine and pump the brake pedal slowly and firmly 3 times to seat the shoe and lining assemblies.

GEO Metro

1. Siphon a sufficient quantity of brake fluid from the master cylinder reservoir to prevent the brake fluid from overflowing the master cylinder when removing or installing the calipers. This is necessary, as the piston must be forced into the cylinder bore to provide sufficient clearance to install the caliper.

2. Remove the wheel and tire assembly.

3. Install 2 lug nuts finger tight to hold the disc in place.

4. Disconnect the brake hose fitting at the caliper and discard the 2 copper washers. Use a pan to catch any spilled fluid and immediately plug the disconnected hose.

5. Remove the 2 caliper mounting bolts and then remove the caliper from the mounting bracket.

To install:

6. Use a caliper compressor, a C-clamp or large pair of pliers to slowly press the caliper piston back into the caliper.

7. Apply a thin, even coating of anti-

seize compound to the sliding surfaces. Don't use grease or spray lubricants; they will not hold up under the extreme temperatures generated by the brakes.

8. Install the caliper assembly to the mounting plate.

9. Install caliper mounting bolts and torque to 22 ft. lbs. (30 Nm).

10. Install the brake hose to the caliper using 2 new copper washers. Torque the bolt to 17 ft. lbs. (23 Nm).

11. Bleed the brake system.

12. Remove the 2 lugs holding the disc in place and install the wheel and tire assembly.

13. Check the level of the brake fluid in the master cylinder reservoir; it should be at least to the middle of the reservoir.

GEO Prizm

FRONT

1. Siphon a sufficient quantity of brake fluid from the master cylinder reservoir to prevent the brake fluid from overflowing the master cylinder when removing or installing the calipers. This is necessary, as the piston must be forced into the cylinder bore to provide sufficient clearance to install the caliper.

2. Remove the wheel and tire assembly.

3. Install 2 lug nuts finger tight to hold the brake rotor in place.

4. Disconnect the brake hose at the caliper and discard the 2 copper washers. Use a pan to catch any spilled fluid and immediately plug the disconnected hose.

5. Remove the 2 caliper mounting bolts and then remove the caliper from the mounting bracket.

To install:

6. Use a caliper compressor, a C-clamp or large pair of pliers to slowly press the caliper piston back into the caliper.

7. Apply a thin, even coating of anti-seize compound to the sliding surfaces. Don't use grease or spray lubricants; they will not hold up under the extreme temperatures generated by the brakes.

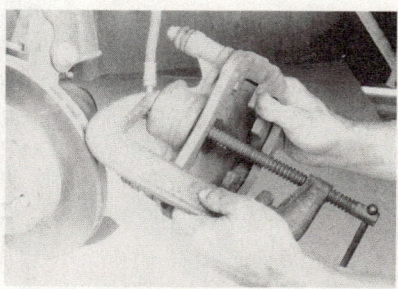

84229044

Using a large C-clamp to compress the piston back into the caliper bore

8. Install the caliper assembly to the mounting plate.

9. Install the caliper mounting bolts and torque to 25 ft. lbs. (34 Nm).

10. Install the brake hose to the caliper using 2 new copper washers. Torque the brake hose bolt to 22 ft. lbs. (30 Nm).

11. Bleed the brake system.

12. Remove the 2 lugs holding the disc in place and install the wheel.

13. Check the level of the brake fluid in the master cylinder reservoir; it should be at least to the middle of the reservoir.

Saturn

FRONT

1. Remove the front wheel and tire assembly.

2. Disconnect the brake hose from the caliper and discard the 2 copper washers.

3. Plug the openings to prevent system contamination or excessive fluid loss.

4. Remove the lock pin and guide pin from the caliper.

5. Remove the caliper from the support, being careful not to damage the pin boots.

6. Remove the pin boots from the caliper support and inspect for damage.

To install:

7. If necessary, bottom the caliper piston by hand, or by using a C-clamp.

8. If removed, install the brake pads and clips to the caliper support.

9. Lubricate the pin boots and guide pins with silicone grease.

10. Install the pin boots into the caliper support, using the pin to assure that the boot passes all the way through the support.

11. Position the caliper onto the support and over the brake pads.

12. Lubricate the non-threaded portion of the guide and lock pins with silicone grease.

13. Install the pins through the caliper and torque to 27 ft. lbs. (36 Nm).

➡**Make sure the brake line is properly routed with loop to the rear and that the hose is not twisted.**

14. Install the brake hose using 2 new copper washers. Torque the fitting bolt to 36 ft. lbs. (49 Nm).

15. Properly bleed the hydraulic brake system.

16. Install the wheel and tire assembly.

REAR

1. Remove the rear wheel and tire assembly.

2. Disconnect the brake hose from the caliper and discard the 2 copper washers.

3. Plug the openings to prevent system contamination or excessive fluid loss.

4. Slip the end of the parking cable off the parking brake lever.

5. Remove the cable outer housing from the cable bracket with SA9151BR cable release tool.

6. Remove the lock pin and guide pin.

7. Remove the caliper from the support, being careful not to damage the pin boots.

8. Remove the pin boots from the caliper support for inspection and lubrication.

To install:

9. Make sure the piston is bottomed in the bore. Do not compress the piston using a C-clamp; instead the piston must be rotated into the caliper on its threads using a piston driver tool.

10. If removed, install the brake pads and clips to the caliper support.

11. Lubricate the pin boots and guide pins with silicone grease.

12. Install the pin boots into the caliper support, using the pin to assure that the boot passes all the way through the support.

13. Position the caliper onto the caliper support.

14. Lubricate the non-threaded portion of the guide and lock pins. Install the pins and torque to 27 ft. lbs. (36 Nm).

15. Install the brake hose using new copper washers and torque the fitting bolt to 36 ft. lbs. (49 Nm).

16. Connect the parking brake cable.

17. Properly bleed the hydraulic brake system.

18. Install the wheel and tire assembly.

Disc Brake Pads

REMOVAL & INSTALLATION

GM C- and H-BODIES:
Buick LeSabre, Park Avenue
Oldsmobile Eighty Eight Royale,
Ninety Eight, Regency
Pontiac Bonneville

1. Remove brake fluid from the master cylinder reservoir until the reservoir is approximately 1/3 full. Discard the removed fluid.

2. Remove the front wheel. Mark the position of the wheel to the wheel studs, prior to removal, for installation reference.

3. Install 2 lug nuts to retain the rotor once the caliper is removed.

4. Remove the caliper mounting sleeve bolts. Support the caliper out of the way using wire. DO NOT disconnect the brake hose or allow the caliper to hang from the brake hose.

5. Remove the outboard pad by pushing it in toward the piston until the mounting tabs clear the holes in the caliper body. With the tabs clear of the holes, push the pad out the bottom of the caliper.

6. Remove the inboard pad from the piston by pulling the top of the pad out to disengage the retainer spring.

To install:

7. Before installing the pads in the caliper, the piston must be fully seated in the bore. A large C-clamp can be used to compress the piston.

8. Install the inboard pad in the caliper by inserting the top pad ears in first, then sliding the bottom of the pad into place until the spring clip snaps into place. Make sure the inboard pad seats flush against the caliper piston.

9. Install the outboard pad by lining up the tabs on the rear of the pad with the mounting holes in the caliper body. Press the pad firmly down into the caliper until the tabs snap into the mounting holes.

10. Clean and lubricate the caliper bolt and sleeve assemblies and install them into the caliper. Lubricate the caliper slides and mountings.

11. Install the caliper over the rotor and torque the mounting bolts to 38 ft. lbs. (51 Nm).

12. Remove the 2 lug nuts used to secure the rotor in place.

13. Install the wheel, aligning the marks made during removal, and torque the lug nuts to 100 ft. lbs. (140 Nm).

14. Pump the brake pedal several times to seat the pads against the rotor.

15. Refill the master cylinder using DOT 3 brake fluid only and road test to verify proper brake operation.

GM E-, K- and V-BODIES:
Cadillac Catera, deVille, Eldorado,
Seville

FRONT

1. Remove 2/3 of the brake fluid from the master cylinder reservoir.

2. Remove the front wheel.

3. Remove the caliper mounting bolts.

4. Remove the caliper from the steering knuckle without disconnecting the brake hose.

5. Suspend the caliper from the coil spring with wire. Do not let the caliper hang from the brake hose.

Refer to the model specific sections for engine mechanical service procedures

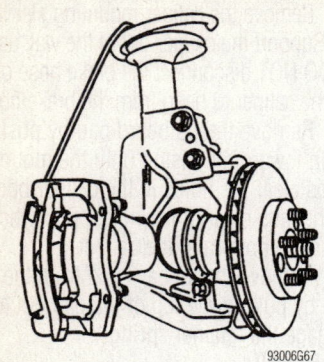

Supporting the front caliper—Catera, deVille, Eldorado, Seville

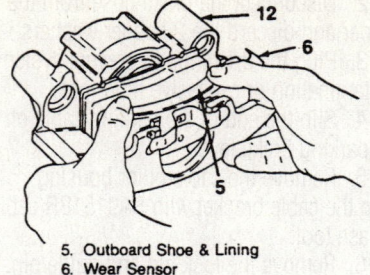

Installing the outboard disc brake pad in the front caliper—Catera, deVille, Eldorado, Seville

5. Outboard Shoe & Lining
6. Wear Sensor
12. Caliper Housing

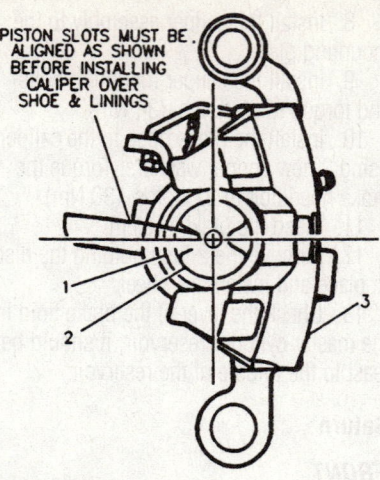

PISTON SLOTS MUST BE ALIGNED AS SHOWN BEFORE INSTALLING CALIPER OVER SHOE & LININGS

1 PISTON BOOT
2 PISTON ASSEMBLY
3 CALIPER BODY ASSEMBLY

Aligning the slots on the rear caliper—Catera, deVille, Eldorado, Seville

6. The following steps apply to 1997 models:

a. Remove the outboard pad by pushing in enough to unseat the back of the pad from the caliper housing. Once the button on the back of the pad is clear of the caliper, push the pad out the bottom of the caliper.

b. Remove the inboard pad by unsnapping the shoe spring from the piston.

7. On 1998–models, remove brake pads from anchor bracket.

To install:

8. Fully seat the caliper piston into the bore using a large C-clamp.

9. Lubricate the brake caliper mounting surfaces.

10. The following steps apply to 1997 models:

a. Install the inboard pad by snapping the pad retainer spring into the caliper piston. The pad must lie flat against the piston.

b. Install the outer pad by pushing the pad straight in from the bottom of the caliper. A click will be heard when the button on the back of the pad seats in the recess in the caliper. Take care when installing the new pad, not to distort the

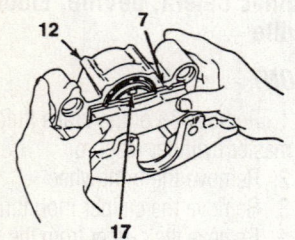

7. Inboard Shoe & Lining
12. Caliper Housing
17. Shoe Retainer Spring

Installing the inboard disc brake pad into the front caliper—Catera, deVille, Eldorado, Seville

spring clip on the outside of the pad. Make sure the wear indicator is at the trailing edge of the pad during forward wheel rotation.

c. Install the caliper on the steering knuckle and install the bolts. Torque the mounting bolts to 38 ft. lbs. (51 Nm).

11. On 1998–01 models:

a. Install the brake pads onto the anchor bracket using new shims and clips.

b. Place the caliper onto the anchor bracket and install mounting bolts.

c. Torque the mounting bolts to 63 ft. lbs. (85 Nm).

12. Install the wheel and tire assembly and torque to specification.

13. Lower the vehicle.

14. Pump the brake pedal several times to seat the brake pads.

15. Check the fluid level in the master cylinder and fill as necessary.

16. Road test the vehicle for proper brake operation.

REAR

1. Remove ⅔ of the brake fluid from the master cylinder reservoir.

2. Remove the rear wheel.

3. Remove the park brake cable from the caliper.

➡**Some models use a brake pad wear sensor. Disconnect the sensor connector from the vehicle harness.**

4. Remove the caliper mounting bolts and position and suspend the caliper from the strut with a wire. Do not let the caliper hang from the brake hose.

5. Remove the inboard and the outboard brake pads from the caliper mounting bracket.

To install:

6. Lubricate mounting surfaces and install new brake pad clips.

7. The caliper piston must be fully seated in the bore. A spanner type tool can

be used to bottom the piston into its bore by turning it in. Make sure the slots in the piston are straight across from each other so the notches on the brake pad will seat.

8. Install the inboard pad by inserting the pad into the straight tabs on the retainer, then pressing down and snapping the pad under the S-shaped tabs. The pad should lay flat against the rotor. Make sure the D-shaped notches are in line with the buttons on the back of the pad lining. If they are not in alignment, rotate the piston until the D-shaped notches face the caliper mounting bolt holes.

9. Install the outer pad into the brake pad clips. Make sure the wear indicator is at the leading edge of the pad during forward wheel rotation.

10. Install the caliper on the mounting bracket and install the bolts. Torque the mounting bolts to 63 ft. lbs. (85 Nm).

11. Install the parking brake cable onto the caliper.

12. Install the wheel and tire assembly and torque to specification.

13. Fill the master cylinder reservoir to the FULL mark and pump the brake pedal several times to seat the brake pads.

14. Check the fluid level in the master cylinder again and fill as necessary.

15. Road test the vehicle for proper brake operation.

GM F-BODY:
Chevrolet Camaro
Pontiac Firebird

FRONT

1. Remove the caliper assembly from the rotor and mounting bracket without discon-

necting the brake line, then position aside. Do not allow the caliper to hang by the brake hose, suspend it with a length of wire or a fabricated hook.

2. Remove the outer pad assembly using a small prytool, if necessary, to disengage the show buttons from the caliper assembly.

3. Remove the inner pad.

To install:

4. If not done already, bottom the piston into the caliper using a large C-clamp positioned on the housing and inside the piston well.

5. With the piston bottomed in the caliper bore, lift the inner edge of the boot next to the piston and press out any trapped air. Make sure the boot is flat.

6. Install the inner pad assembly by positioning the retainer spring into the piston. The pad must lay flat against the piston and the boot must not touch the pad. If the boot and pad are in contact, remove the pad and reposition the boot.

7. Install the outer pad assembly, making sure the back of the pad is flat against the caliper. The wear sensor should be at the trailing lower edge of the outer pad during forward wheel rotation or the outer pad has been installed on the wrong side.

8. Install the caliper assembly to the rotor and mounting bracket.

REAR

1. Remove ⅔ of the brake fluid from the master cylinder reservoir.

2. Matchmark the relationship of the wheel to the axle flange, then remove the wheel and tire assembly. Install 2 wheel nuts to retain the rotor.

3. Position a C-clamp and tighten until the piston bottoms in the base of the caliper housing. Make sure 1 end of the C-clamp rests on the inlet fitting bolt and the other against the outboard disc brake pad.

➡ **It is not necessary to remove the parking brake caliper lever return spring to replace the disc brake pads.**

4. Remove the upper caliper guide pin bolt and discard.

5. Rotate the caliper housing on the lower caliper mounting bolt. Be careful not to strain the hose or cable conduit. It may be necessary to loosen the lower caliper guide pin slightly.

6. Remove the disc brake pads and discard the shim.

To install:

7. Clean all residue from the pad guide surfaces on the mounting bracket and

caliper housing. Inspect the guide pins for free movement in the mounting bracket. Replace the guide pins or boots, if they are corroded or damaged.

8. Install a new shim, then install the disc brake pads. The outboard pad with insulator is installed toward the caliper housing. The inboard pad with the wear sensor is installed nearest the caliper piston. The wear sensor must be on the leading edge with forward wheel rotation or the pad has been installed on the wrong side.

9. Rotate the caliper housing into its operating position. The springs on the outboard brake pad must not stick through the inspection hole in the caliper housing. If the springs are sticking through the inspection hole in the caliper housing, lift the caliper housing and make the necessary corrections to the outboard brake pad positions.

10. Install a new upper caliper guide pin bolt and torque to 27 ft. lbs. (37 Nm). Ensure that the lower caliper guide bolt is torqued to 27 ft. lbs. (37 Nm).

11. With the engine running, pump the brake pedal slowly and firmly to seat the brake pads.

12. Check the caliper parking brake levers to make sure they are against the stops on the caliper housing. If the levers are not on their stops, check the parking brake adjustment.

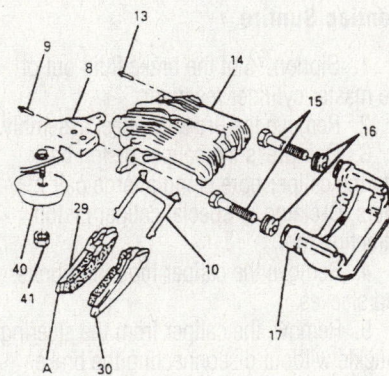

A   WEAR SENSOR
8   BRACKET, PARKING BRAKE CABLE
9   BOLT/SCREW, LOWER CALIPER GUIDE PIN
10 SHIM
13 BOLT/SCREW, UPPER CALIPER GUIDE PIN
14 HOUSING, REAR BRAKE CALIPER
15 PIN, REAR BRAKE CALIPER GUIDE
16 BOOT, REAR BRAKE CALIPER GUIDE PIN
17 BRACKET, REAR BRAKE CALIPER ANCHOR
29 PAD, REAR DISC BRAKE INNER
30 PAD, REAR DISC BRAKE OUTER
40 DAMPENER, REAR BRAKE VIBRATION
41 NUT, REAR BRAKE VIBRATION DAMPENER

93006G92

Exploded view of the rear caliper assembly—Camaro, Firebird

13. Remove the 2 wheel nuts from the rotor, then align the marks and install the wheel assembly.

14. Check the master cylinder fluid level and road test the vehicle.

GM G-BODY:
Buick Riviera
Oldsmobile Aurora

FRONT

1. Siphon ⅔ of the brake fluid from the master cylinder.

2. Remove the tire and wheel assembly.

3. Install 2 wheel nuts to secure the rotor on the hub.

4. Remove the caliper mounting bolts and sleeves.

5. Remove the caliper from the mounting bracket and support the caliper. DO NOT allow the caliper to hang unsupported from the brake hose.

6. Remove the outboard brake pad from the caliper by pushing the pad inward toward the piston to unseat the buttons on the back of pad from the holes in the caliper. Once the buttons are unseated push the pad out of the caliper.

7. Remove the inboard pad from the caliper by pulling the top of the pad away from the piston and disengaging the spring clip from the caliper.

8. Compress the piston back into the bore using a C-Clamp.

To install:

9. Install the inboard pad into the caliper so the spring clip seats in the piston. Make sure lower edge of the spring clip is engaged in the piston and the pad is even against the base of the piston. Push the pad flat against caliper piston.

10. Install the outboard pad into the caliper so the wear indicator is at the trailing edge of the pad during forward wheel rotation. Push the pad the straight down into the caliper so the spring clips rode along the outside of the caliper. The buttons

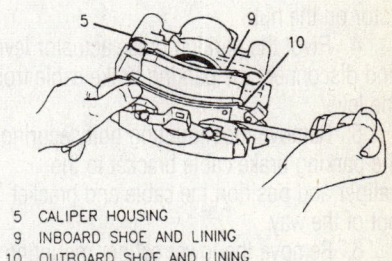

5   CALIPER HOUSING
9   INBOARD SHOE AND LINING
10 OUTBOARD SHOE AND LINING

93006G93

Removing the outboard front pad—Riviera, Aurora

For accessory drive belt replacement procedures see the model specific sections of this manual

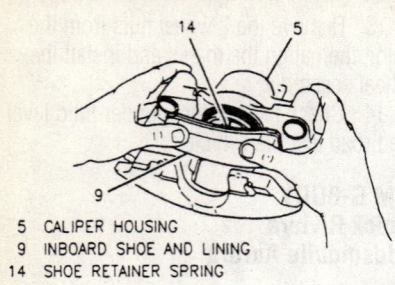

5 CALIPER HOUSING
9 INBOARD SHOE AND LINING
14 SHOE RETAINER SPRING

93006G94

Installing the inboard front pad—Riviera, Aurora

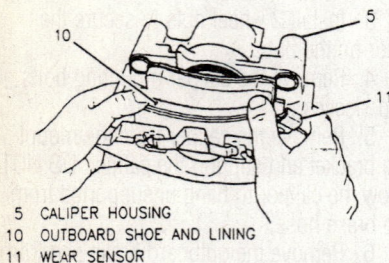

5 CALIPER HOUSING
10 OUTBOARD SHOE AND LINING
11 WEAR SENSOR

93006G95

Installing the outboard front pad—Riviera, Aurora

on the pad will snap into the mounting holes when the pad is correctly installed.

11. Reinstall the caliper onto the steering knuckle and torque the mounting bolts to 38 ft. lbs. (51 Nm).

12. Remove the 2 wheel nuts securing the rotor.

13. Reinstall the tire and wheel assembly and torque the wheel nuts to 100 ft. lbs. (140 Nm).

14. Refill the master cylinder. Pump the brake pedal several times to seat the pads against the rotor.

15. Check the master cylinder level and add fluid as necessary.

REAR

1. Siphon ⅔ of the brake fluid from the master cylinder.

2. Remove the tire and wheel assembly.

3. Install 2 wheel nuts to secure the rotor on the hub.

4. Pivot the parking brake actuator level and disconnect the parking brake cable from the lever.

5. Remove the mounting bolt securing the parking brake cable bracket to the caliper and position the cable and bracket out of the way.

6. Remove the lower caliper mounting bolt.

7. Pivot the caliper upward and secure the caliper in a position over the mounting bracket. DO NOT remove the caliper from the upper pivot pin.

8. Remove the inboard and outboard pads from the caliper bracket.

9. Remove the brake pad clips from the mounting bracket.

To install:

10. Spin the caliper piston back into the bore. Make sure the piston notches are at 6 and 12 o'clock after the piston is compressed.

11. Install new brake pad clips in the caliper mounting bracket.

12. Install the inboard and outboard pads in the mounting bracket.

13. Pivot the caliper down over the pads.

14. Reinstall the lower mounting bolt and torque to 20 ft. lbs. (27 Nm).

15. Reinstall the parking brake cable bracket on the caliper and torque the mounting bolt to 32 ft. lbs. (43 Nm).

16. Pivot the actuator lever and connect the cable end to the actuator.

17. Remove the 2 wheel nuts securing the rotor.

18. Reinstall the tire and wheel assembly and torque the wheel nuts to 100 ft. lbs. (140 Nm).

19. Refill the master cylinder. Pump the brake pedal several times to seat the pads against the rotor.

20. Check the master cylinder level and add fluid as necessary.

GM J-BODY:
Chevrolet Cavalier
Pontiac Sunfire

1. Siphon ⅔ of the brake fluid out of the master cylinder reservoir.

2. Remove the tire and wheel assembly.

3. Compress the caliper piston back into the caliper bore using a large pair of pliers, C-clamp or special caliper piston retracting tool.

4. Remove the caliper mounting bolts and sleeves.

5. Remove the caliper from the steering knuckle without disconnecting the brake hose. Do not allow the caliper to hang from the brake hose. Support the caliper with a piece of wire.

6. Remove the outboard pad by pushing in on the outside edge of the pad to release the mounting dowel from the hole in the caliper. When both dowels are unseated, push the pad out the bottom of the caliper.

7. Remove the inboard pad from the caliper by pulling it out of the caliper.

To install:

8. Inspect the caliper for any signs of leakage. If the caliper is leaking, new brake pads will be damaged. Also inspect the condition of the caliper support for rust and

corrosion which will hinder the travel on the caliper.

9. Inspect the caliper mounting hardware. New bolts are usually recommended. Clean all parts well. Lubricate the mounting bushings and sleeves with silicone grease as required.

10. Install the inboard pad in the caliper so the spring clip on the pad back engages in the caliper piston.

11. Install the outboard pad over the caliper end until the mounting dowels snap into the mounting holes in the caliper.

12. Install the caliper over the rotor onto the steering knuckle.

13. Install the mounting bolts and sleeves and torque to 40 ft. lbs. (51 Nm).

14. Install the tire and wheel assembly.

15. Pump the brake pedal several times to seat the pads against the rotor before attempting to move the vehicle.

16. Check the master cylinder level and add fluid as necessary.

GM L/N and N-BODY:
Buick Skylark
Chevrolet Malibu
Oldsmobile Achieva, Cutlass
Pontiac Grand Am

1. Siphon ⅔ of the brake fluid out of the master cylinder reservoir.

2. Remove the tire and wheel assembly.

3. Remove the caliper from the steering knuckle without disconnecting the brake hose. DO NOT allow the caliper to hang from the brake hose. Support the caliper with a piece of wire.

4. Remove the outboard pad by pushing in on the outside edge of the pad to release the mounting dowel from the hole in the caliper. When both dowels are unseated push the pad out the bottom of the caliper.

5. Remove the inboard pad from the caliper by pulling it out of the caliper.

To install:

6. Install the inboard pad in the caliper so the spring clip on the pad back engages in the caliper piston.

7. Install the outboard pad over the caliper end until the mounting dowels snap into the mounting holes in the caliper.

8. Install the caliper over the rotor onto the steering knuckle. Install the mounting bolts and sleeves and torque to 40 ft. lbs. (51 Nm).

9. Install the tire and wheel assembly.

10. Pump the brake pedal several times to seat the pads against the rotor before attempting to move the vehicle.

11. Check the master cylinder level and add fluid as necessary.

GM W-BODY:
Buick Century, Regal
Chevrolet Lumina, Monte Carlo
Oldsmobile Cutlass Supreme,
Intrigue
Pontiac Grand Prix

FRONT

1. Siphon ⅔ of the brake fluid out of the master cylinder.

2. Mark the relationship of the wheel to the wheel stud for re-installation purposes. Remove the tire and wheel assembly.

3. Install 2 lug nuts to secure the rotor in place when the caliper is removed.

4. Install a large C-clamp over the top of the caliper housing and against the back of the outboard shoe. Slowly tighten the C-clamp until the caliper pistons are pushed into the caliper bore enough to slide the caliper assembly off the rotor. Use care not to tighten the C-clamp too far or the outboard shoe retaining spring will be deformed and require replacement.

5. Remove the caliper mounting bolts and remove the brake caliper from the mounting bracket.

6. DO NOT disconnect the brake hose from the caliper or allow the brake hose to support the weight of the caliper. Support the caliper on a piece of wire out of the way.

7. Remove the outer brake pad from the caliper using a suitable prying tool to lift the outboard shoe retaining spring so that it will clear the caliper center lug and pull the brake pad out of the caliper.

8. Remove the inner brake pad by unsnapping the shoe springs from the piston.

To install:

9. Clean all parts well. If the brake pads were worn so badly that the brake rotor is damaged, it must be replaced. Light scoring of the rotor surfaces not exceeding 0.060 inch (1.5mm) in depth is not harmful to

brake operation and may result from normal use. Brake rotors may be refinished. Do not use a rotor that, after refinishing, will not meet the thickness specification cast in the rotor. Always replace with a new rotor.

10. If not done at removal, now use a C-clamp and clamp both pistons at the same time with a metal plate or wooden block across the face of both pistons. Take care not to damage the pistons or caliper boots.

➡ **After bottoming the pistons into the caliper bore, lift the inner edge of each caliper boot next to the piston and press out any trapped air. Make sure each boot convolution is tucked back into place. Boots must lay flat.**

11. Inspect the caliper bushings for wear. Replace as necessary. Carefully inspect the slide bolts for corrosion. If corrosion if found, use new parts including the bushing assemblies when installing the caliper. Do not attempt to polish away corrosion. Lubricate caliper slide bolts with silicone grease.

12. Install the new inner disc brake pad in the caliper by snapping the shoe retainer springs into the piston making sure both sets of locking tabs are seated in the caliper pistons. The pad must seat flat against the pistons.

13. Install the outer pad into the caliper by snapping the outboard shoe retaining spring over the caliper center lug and into the housing slot. The pad will slide up onto the caliper and the retaining ring will lock into place on the groove in the caliper.

14. The outer pad wear sensor should be at the trailing edge of the shoe during forward wheel rotation.

15. Install the caliper mounting bolts and torque to 80 ft. lbs. (108 Nm).

16. Remove the 2 nuts temporarily securing the rotor.

17. Install the tire and wheel assembly and tighten to specification.

18. Pump the brake pedal several times to seat the pads against the rotor.

19. Check the brake fluid level and top off as necessary.

20. Road test the vehicle to ensure the proper brake performance.

REAR

1. Siphon ⅔ of the brake fluid out of the master cylinder.

2. Remove the tire and wheel assembly.

3. Install 2 lug nuts to secure the rotor in place when the caliper is removed.

4. Remove bolt and washer attaching cable support bracket to caliper body assem-

bly. It is not necessary to disconnect the parking brake lever or disconnect the brake hose.

5. Remove the caliper retaining bolt.

6. Pivot the caliper body assembly up from the rotor and remove from the bracket. Do not completely remove the caliper assembly body.

7. Remove the outboard and inboard shoe and linings from the caliper support assembly.

8. Remove 2 brake lining clips from the caliper support.

To install:

➡ **In order for the rear pads to seat in the caliper properly, the cut outs in the caliper piston must be at the 6 and 12 o'clock positions. Failure to align the piston correctly can lead to brake drag, premature brake wear and possible brake failure.**

9. Using a suitable type spanner tool turn the piston in to bottom the piston fully into the caliper bore. Once the caliper is fully seated make sure the cutouts in the piston are at the 6 and 12 o'clock positions.

10. After bottoming the piston into the caliper bore, lift the inner edge of boot next to the piston assembly and press out any trapped air.

11. Install 2 pad clips in the caliper support.

12. Lubricate the inner pad where it contacts the piston and mounting surfaces.

13. Install outboard and inboard shoe and linings in caliper support. Position the wear sensors downward at the leading edge of the rotor during forward wheel rotation.

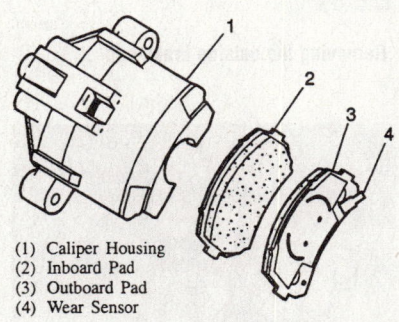

(1) Caliper Housing
(2) Inboard Pad
(3) Outboard Pad
(4) Wear Sensor

93006G71

Front brake pads and caliper—Century, Regal, Lumina, Monte Carlo, Cutlass Supreme, Intrigue, Grand Prix

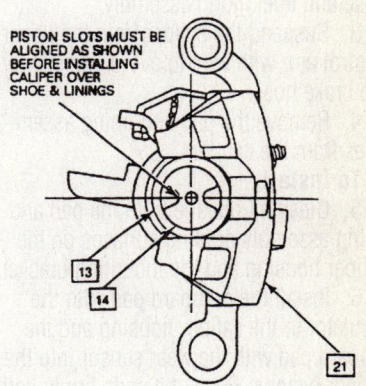

PISTON SLOTS MUST BE ALIGNED AS SHOWN BEFORE INSTALLING CALIPER OVER SHOE & LININGS

13	PISTON BOOT
14	PISTON ASSEMBLY
21	CALIPER BODY ASSEMBLY

93006G72

Positioning rear caliper piston slots—Century, Regal, Lumina, Monte Carlo, Cutlass Supreme, Intrigue, Grand Prix

14. Hold the metal shoe edge against the spring end of clips in the caliper support. Push brake pad in towards the hub, bending spring ends slightly and engage shoe notches with support abutments.

15. Pivot the caliper body assembly down over the brake pad. Compress the sleeve boot by hand as the caliper body moves into position to prevent boot damage.

➡ **After the caliper body assembly is in position, recheck installation of the brake pad clips. If necessary, use a small prying tool to reseat or center the pad clip on the support abutments.**

16. Install the sleeve bolts and torque bolt to 20 ft. lbs. (27 Nm).

17. Install the cable support bracket with the cable attached and bolt washer. Torque bolt to 32 ft. lbs. (43 Nm).

18. Remove the 2 lug nuts securing the rotor.

19. Install the tire and wheel assembly and tighten to specification.

20. Pump the brake pedal several times to seat the pads against the rotor.

21. Check the brake fluid level and top off as necessary.

22. Adjust parking brake as necessary.

23. Road test the vehicle for proper brake performance.

GM Y-BODY:
Chevrolet Corvette

FRONT

1. Disconnect the negative battery cable.

2. Remove the caliper from the mounting bracket but do not disconnect the brake hose and inlet fitting assembly.

3. Suspend the caliper from the upper control arm with wire to avoid damage to the brake hose.

4. Remove the pad and lining assemblies from the caliper.

To install:

5. Clean all residue from the pad and lining assembly guiding surfaces on the caliper housing and the mounting bracket.

6. Install the outboard pad with the insulator to the caliper housing and the inboard pad with the wear sensor into the caliper pistons. Press the pads firmly until they are they are fully seated.

7. Remove the support and install the caliper to the mounting bracket.

8. Connect the negative battery cable.

REAR

1. Disconnect the negative battery cable and remove ⅔ of the brakes fluid from the master cylinder reservoirs.

2. Mark the relationship between the wheel to the axle flange.

3. Remove the tire and wheel assembly. Install 2 wheel nuts to retain the brake rotor.

4. Use a C-clamp to depress the caliper pistons into the caliper bores to provide clearance between the pads and the rotor. Make sure 1 end of the clamp rests on the inlet fitting bolt while the other end rests on the outboard pad.

5. Remove the caliper upper guide pin bolt and discard, then rotate the caliper on the lower guide pin to access the pad linings. Be careful not to strain the cable conduit or the hoses.

6. Remove the pads from the caliper.

To install:

7. Install the outboard pad with the insulator to the caliper housing and the inboard pad with the wear sensor nearest the caliper pistons. The wear sensor must be in the trailing position during forward wheel rotation. Press the pads firmly until they are they are fully seated.

8. Rotate the caliper housing into position, then install a new upper guide pin bolt and torque 26 ft. lbs. (35 Nm).

9. Remove the wheel nuts securing the rotor to the hub and install the tire and wheel assembly.

10. Fill the master cylinder to the proper level with clean brake fluid.

11. Connect the negative battery cable, start the engine and pump the brake pedal slowly and firmly 3 times to seat the shoe and lining assemblies.

GEO Metro

1. Set the parking brake and block the rear wheels.

2. Siphon a sufficient quantity of brake

Front disc brake assembly

Removing caliper mounting bolts

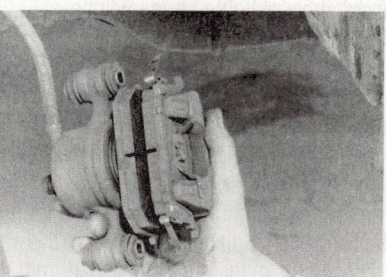

Removing the caliper from the rotor

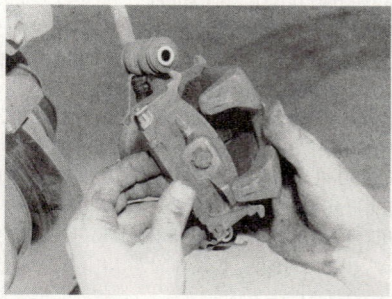

Removing the outside brake pad

Removing the inside brake pad

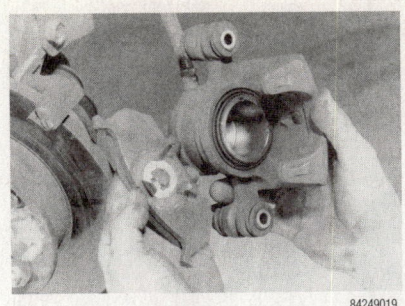

The inside brake pad is attached to the caliper piston with a spring clip

fluid from the master cylinder reservoir to prevent the brake fluid from overflowing from the master cylinder when removing or installing the brake pads. This is necessary, as the piston must be forced into the cylinder bore to provide sufficient clearance to install the pads.

3. Remove the wheel, then reinstall 2 lug nuts finger tight to hold the disc in place.

4. Remove the 2 caliper mounting bolts and then remove the caliper from the mounting bracket. Position the caliper out of the way and support it with wire so it doesn't hang by the brake line.

5. Remove the brake pads, the wear indicators, the anti-squeal shims, the support plates and the anti squeal springs (if so equipped). Disassemble slowly and take note of how the parts fit together. This will save much time during reassembly.

6. Inspect the brake disc for scoring or gouging. Measure the disc for both thickness and run-out.

7. Inspect the pads for remaining thickness and condition. Any sign of uneven wear, cracking, heat checking or spotting is cause for replacement. Compare the wear of the inner pad to the outer pad. While they will not wear at exactly the same rate, the

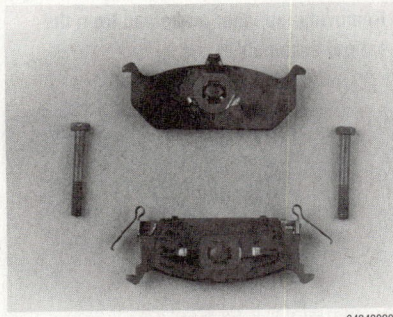

Inside pad is at top and outside pad is on bottom. Note wear indicator springs protruding from sides of outside pad

remaining thickness should be about the same on both pads. If one is heavily worn and the other is not, suspect either a binding caliper piston or dirty slides in the caliper mount.

Removing the anti-squeal springs from the caliper wear indicators

Using a C-clamp to compress the caliper piston

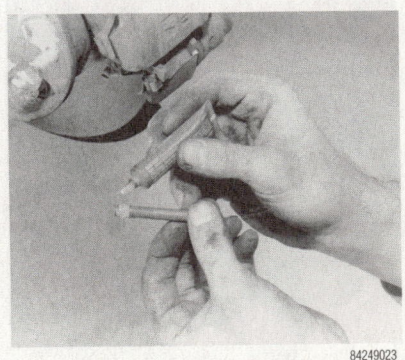

Coat the caliper mounting bolts with anti-seize during installation

8. Examine the 2 caliper retaining bolts and the slide bushings in which they run. Everything should be clean and dry. If cleaning is needed, use spray solvents and a clean cloth. Do not wire brush or sand the bolts. This will cause grooves in the metal which will trap more dirt. Check the condition of the rubber dust boots and replace them if damaged.

To install:

9. Install the pad support plates onto the mounting bracket.

10. Install new pad wear indicators onto each pad, making sure the arrow on the tab points in the direction of disc rotation.

11. Install new anti-squeal pads to the back of the pads.

12. Install the pads into the mounting bracket and install the anti-squeal springs.

13. Use a caliper compressor, or a C-clamp to slowly press the caliper piston back into the caliper. If the piston is frozen, or if the caliper is leaking hydraulic fluid, the caliper must be overhauled or replaced.

14. Install the caliper assembly to the mounting plate. Before installing the retaining bolts, apply a thin, even coating of anti-seize compound to the threads and slide surfaces. Don't use grease or spray lubricants; they will not hold up under the extreme temperatures generated by the brakes. Torque the bolts to specification.

15. Remove the 2 lugs holding the disc in place and install the wheel.

16. Check the level of the brake fluid in the master cylinder reservoir; it should be at least to the middle of the reservoir.

17. Depress the brake pedal several times and make sure that the movement feels normal. The first brake pedal application may result in a very "long" pedal due to the pistons being retracted. Always make several brake applications before starting the vehicle. Bleeding is not usually necessary after pad replacement.

18. Recheck the fluid level and add to the **MAX** line if necessary.

GEO Prizm

FRONT

1. Siphon a sufficient quantity of brake fluid from the master cylinder reservoir to prevent the brake fluid overflowing from the master cylinder when removing or installing the brake pads. This is necessary, as the piston must be forced into the cylinder bore to provide sufficient clearance to install the pads.

2. Remove the wheel and tire assembly.

Timing chain and gear service is covered in the model specific sections of this manual

3. Install 2 lug nuts finger tight to hold the disc in place.

4. Remove the 2 caliper mounting bolts and then remove the caliper from the mounting bracket. Position the caliper out of the way and support it with wire so it doesn't hang by the brake line.

5. Remove the 2 brake pads, the 2 wear indicators, the 4 anti-squeal shims, the 4 support plates (anti-rattle springs) and the 2 anti squeal springs, if so equipped. Disassemble slowly and take note of how the parts fit together. This will save much time during reassembly.

6. Inspect the brake disc for scoring or gouging. Measure the disc for both thickness and run-out. Complete inspection procedures are given later in this section.

7. Inspect the pads for remaining thickness and condition. Any sign of uneven wear, cracking, heat checking or spotting is cause for replacement. Compare the wear of the inner pad to the outer pad. While they will not wear at exactly the same rate, the remaining thickness should be about the same on both pads. If one is heavily worn and the other is not, suspect either a binding caliper piston or dirty slides in the caliper mount.

8. Examine the 2 caliper retaining bolts and the slide bushings in which they run. Everything should be clean and dry. If cleaning is needed, use spray solvents and a clean cloth. Do not wire brush or sand the bolts. This will cause grooves in the metal which will trap more dirt. Check the condition of the rubber dust boots and replace them if damaged.

To install:

9. Install the 4 pad support plates (anti-rattle springs) onto the mounting bracket.

10. Install new pad wear indicators onto each pad, making sure the arrow on the tab points in the direction of disc rotation.

11. Install new anti-squeal pads to the back of the pads.

12. Install the pads into the mounting bracket and install the anti-squeal springs, if so equipped.

13. Use a caliper compressor, a C-clamp or large pair of pliers to slowly press the caliper piston back into the caliper. If the piston is frozen, or if the caliper is leaking hydraulic fluid, the caliper must be overhauled or replaced.

14. Install the caliper assembly to the mounting plate. Before installing the retaining bolts, apply a thin, even coating of anti-seize compound to the threads and slide surfaces. Don't use grease or spray lubricants; they will not hold up under the extreme temperatures generated by the

brakes. Torque the bolts to 25 ft. lbs. (34 Nm).

15. Remove the 2 lugs holding the disc in place and install the wheel.

16. Check the level of the brake fluid in the master cylinder reservoir; it should be at least to the middle of the reservoir.

17. Depress the brake pedal several times and make sure that the movement feels normal. The first brake pedal application may result in a very "long" pedal due to the pistons being retracted. Always make several brake applications before starting the vehicle. Bleeding is not usually necessary after pad replacement.

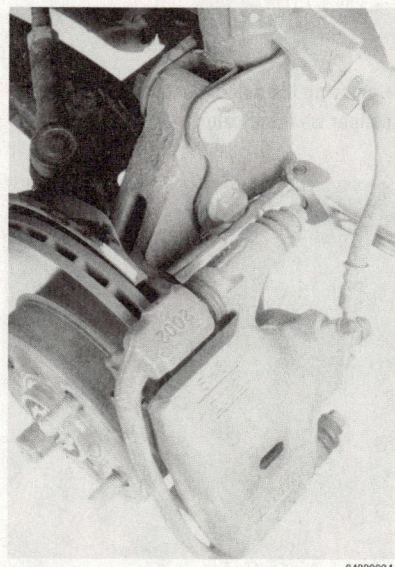
84229034

You will need a short extension to remove the front caliper mounting bracket bolts

84229035

Carefully remove the caliper assembly from the rotor

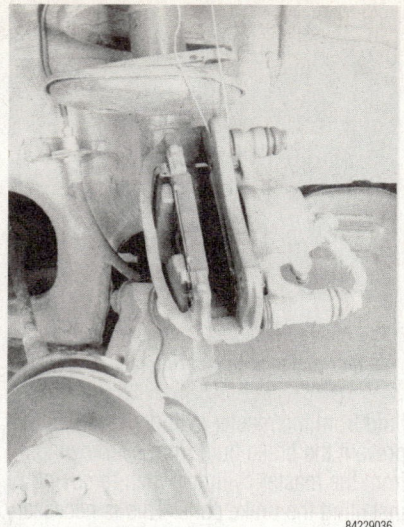
84229036

Suspend the caliper assembly out of the way to avoid hanging from the hose

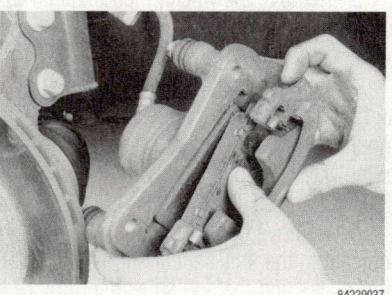
84229037

Removing the outer brake pad from the caliper assembly

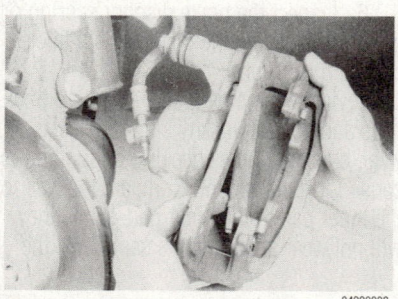
84229038

Removing the inner brake pad from the caliper assembly

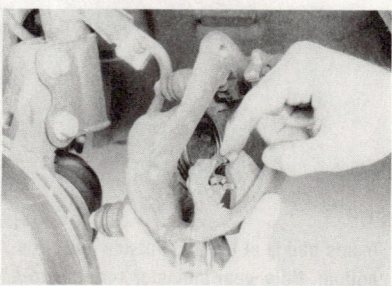
84229039

Note the correct position support plates (anti-rattle springs)

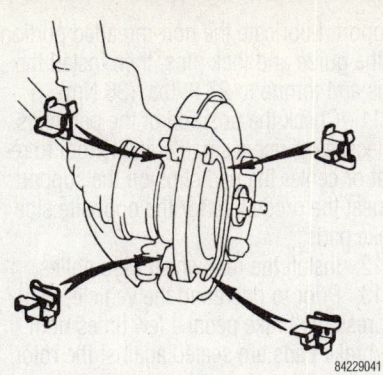

Correct placement of the support plates (anti-rattle springs)

18. Recheck the fluid level and add to the "MAX" line if necessary.

REAR

1. Raise and safely support the rear of the vehicle on jackstands. Block the front wheels.

2. Siphon a sufficient quantity of brake fluid from the master cylinder reservoir to prevent the brake fluid from overflowing the

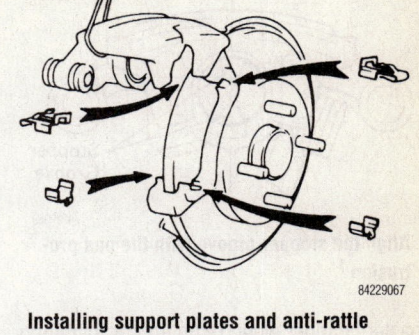

Installing support plates and anti-rattle shims

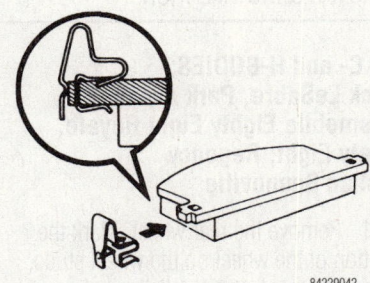

Make certain the brake wear indicators are correctly installed

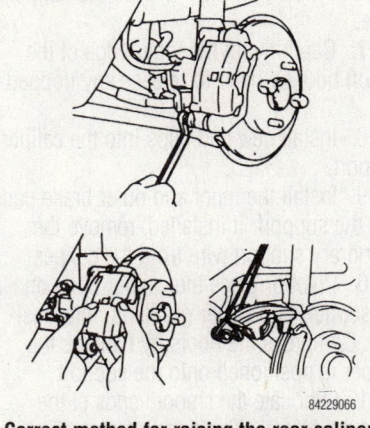

Correct method for raising the rear caliper to gain access to the pads

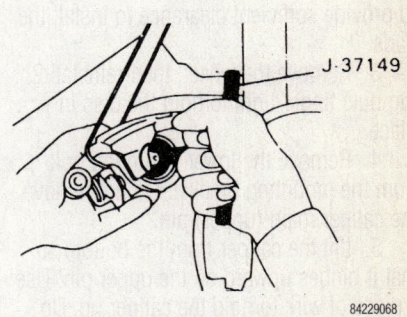

Using the GM tool to retract the rear caliper piston

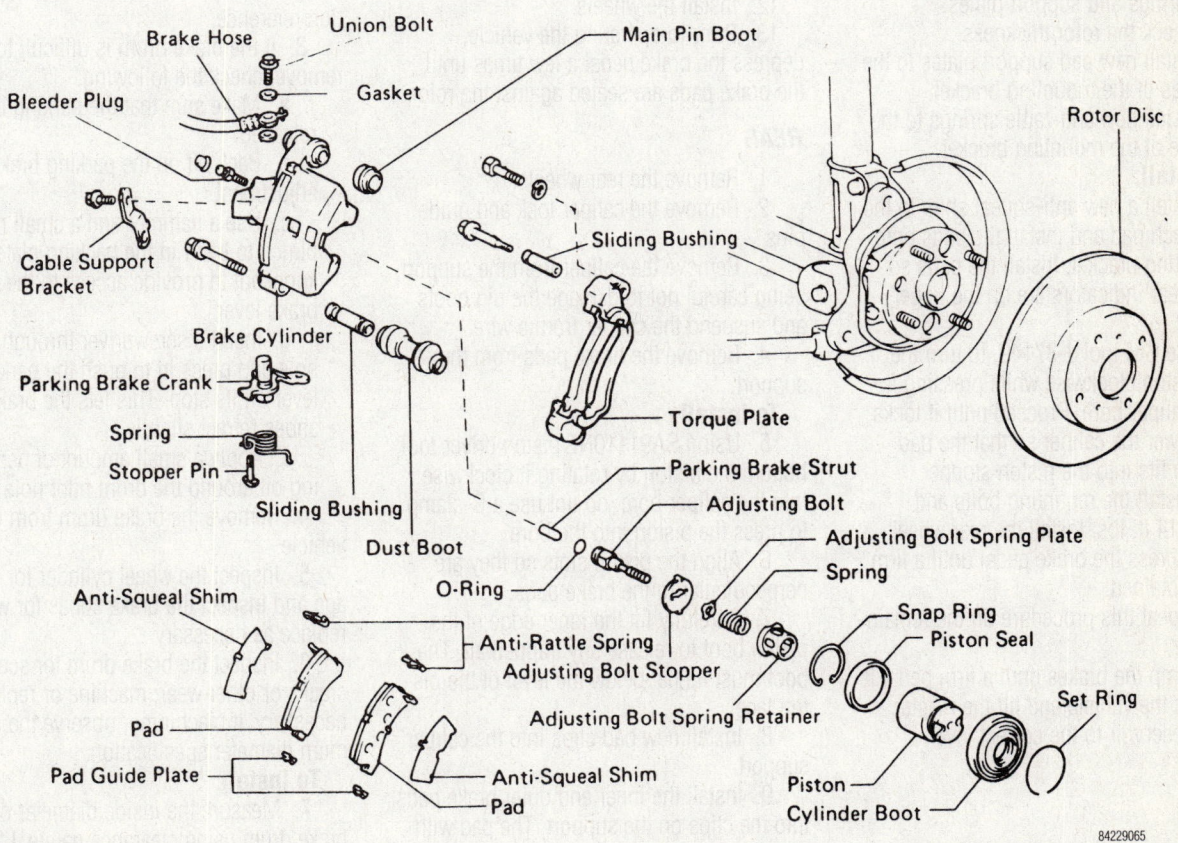

Rear disc brake components

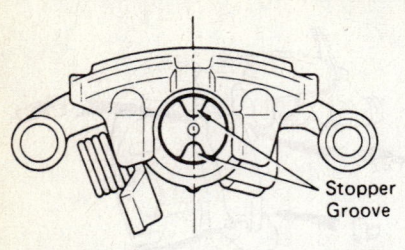

Align the stopper groove with the pad protrusion

84229069

master cylinder when removing or installing the brake pads. This is necessary, as the piston must be forced into the cylinder bore to provide sufficient clearance to install the pads.

3. Remove the wheel, then reinstall 2 lug nuts finger tight to hold the disc in place.

4. Remove the lower mounting bolt from the mounting bracket. Do not remove the caliper main (upper) pin.

5. Lift the caliper from the bottom so that it hinges upward on the upper pin. Use a piece of wire to hold the caliper up. Do not allow the brake hose to become twisted or kinked during this operation.

6. Remove the brake pads with their shims, springs and support plates.

7. Check the rotor thickness.

8. Install new pad support plates to the lower sides of the mounting bracket.

9. Install new anti-rattle springs to the upper side of the mounting bracket.

To install:

10. Install a new anti-squeal shim to the back of each pad and install the pads onto the mounting bracket. Install the pads so that the wear indicators are on the uppermost side.

11. Use GM tool J-37149, to turn the caliper piston clockwise while pressing it into the caliper bore. Proceed until it locks.

12. Lower the caliper so that the pad protrusion fits into the piston stopper groove. Install the mounting bolts and torque to 14 ft. lbs. Install the rear wheel.

13. Depress the brake pedal until a firm pedal is obtained.

14. Repeat this procedure on the remaining caliper.

15. Pump the brakes until a firm pedal is felt. Lower the vehicle and fill the master cylinder reservoir to the correct level.

Saturn

FRONT

1. Remove the front wheels.
2. Remove the caliper lower lock pins.
3. Either pivot the caliper up on the guide pin or remove the upper guide pin and support the caliper from the strut using a coat hanger or length of wire.

4. Remove the 2 brake pads and the pad clips from the caliper support. Discard the old pad clips.

5. Check the caliper pins, pin boots and the piston boot for deterioration or damage.

To install:

6. By hand or using a C-clamp, bottom the piston all the way into the caliper bore.

7. Carefully lift the inner edge of the piston boot by hand to release any trapped air.

8. Install new pad clips into the caliper support.

9. Install the inner and outer brake pads into the support. If installed, remove the temporary support wire from the caliper.

10. Pivot or place the caliper body on the support and upper guide pin into position. Compress the boots by hand as the caliper is positioned onto the support.

11. Lubricate the smooth ends of the removed pin(s) with silicone grease, then install the pin(s) and torque to 27 ft. lbs. (36 Nm). Do not get grease on the pin threads.

12. Install the wheels.

13. Prior to operating the vehicle, depress the brake pedal a few times until the brake pads are seated against the rotor.

REAR

1. Remove the rear wheels.
2. Remove the caliper lock and guide pins.
3. Remove the caliper from the support, being careful not to damage the pin boots and suspend the caliper from a wire.
4. Remove the brake pads from the support.

To install:

5. Using SA91110NE piston driver tool, bottom the piston by rotating it clockwise into the caliper bore; do not use a C-clamp to press the piston into the bore.

6. Align the piston slots so they are perpendicular to the brake pads.

7. Carefully lift the inner edge of the piston boot to release any trapped air. The boot must lie flat below the level of the piston face.

8. Install new pad clips into the caliper support.

9. Install the inner and outer brake pads into the clips on the support. The pad with the wear sensor should be located outboard. The piston indentation slots should be positioned to correctly accept the brake pads.

10. Position the caliper body onto the support. Lubricate the non-threaded portion of the guide and lock pins, then install the pins and torque to 27 ft. lbs. (36 Nm).

11. Check the position of the pad clips. If necessary, use a small suitable tool to re-seat or center the pad clips on the support. Repeat the procedure for the opposite side brake pads.

12. Install the rear wheel assemblies.

13. Prior to operating the vehicle, depress the brake pedal a few times until the brake pads are seated against the rotor.

Brake Drums

REMOVAL & INSTALLATION

GM C- and H-BODIES:
Buick LeSabre, Park Avenue
Oldsmobile Eighty Eight Royale,
Ninety Eight, Regency
Pontiac Bonneville

1. Remove the rear wheel. Mark the position of the wheel on the wheel studs, prior to removal, for installation reference.

2. Remove the brake drum from the hub. Mark the position of the drum on the wheel studs, prior to removal, for installation reference.

3. If the brake drum is difficult to remove, check the following:

   a. Make sure that the parking brake is released.

   b. Back off on the parking brake cable adjustment.

   c. Use a hammer and a small metal punch to bend in the backing plate knockout to provide access to the park brake lever.

   d. Insert a screwdriver through the hole and press in to push the park brake lever off its stop. This lets the brake shoes retract slightly.

   e. Apply a small amount of penetrating oil around the drum pilot hole.

4. Remove the brake drum from the vehicle.

5. Inspect the wheel cylinder for leakage and inspect the brake shoes for wear; replace as necessary.

6. Inspect the brake drum for scoring, cracks or other wear; machine or replace as necessary. If machining, observe the maximum diameter specification.

To install:

7. Measure the inside diameter of the brake drum using clearance gauge J 21177-A.

8. Turn the starwheel on the adjusting screw assembly until the brake shoe diame-

ter is 0.050 in. (1.27mm) less than the drum inside diameter.

9. Install the brake drum onto the wheel hub, aligning the marks made during removal.

10. Install the wheel, aligning the marks made during removal. Torque the lug nuts to 100 ft. lbs. (140 Nm).

11. Road test the vehicle and check brake operation.

GM F-BODY:
Chevrolet Camaro
Pontiac Firebird

1. Matchmark the relationship of the wheel to the axle flange, then remove the wheel and tire assembly.

2. Matchmark the relationship of the drum to the axle flange and remove the brake drum. If the brake drum is difficult to remove, try the following:

   a. Ensure the parking brake is released.

   b. Back off the parking brake cable adjustment.

   c. Remove the adjusting hole cover or knockout plate from the backing plate. Back off the adjustment screw, using suitable brake adjusting tools.

   d. Use a rubber mallet to tap gently on the outer rim of the drum and/or around the inner drum diameter by the spindle. Be careful not to deform the drum by excessive use of force.

To install:

3. Adjust the brake shoes. The outside diameter of the shoe and linings should be 0.050 inch (1.27mm) less than the inside diameter of the brake drum on each wheel.

4. Install the drum, aligning the marks on the drum and the axle flange.

5. Install the wheel and tire assembly, aligning the marks on the wheel and axle flange.

GM J-BODY:
Chevrolet Cavalier
Pontiac Sunfire

1. Remove the wheel and tire assembly.

2. Pull the brake drum off. It may be necessary to gently tap the rear edge of the drum to start it off the studs. If extreme resistance to removal is encountered, it will be necessary to retract the brake shoe self-adjuster screw, sometimes called the star-wheel. Knock out the access hole in the brake drum and turn the adjuster to retract the linings from the drum. Install a replacement hole cover before reinstalling the drum.

➡**Do not hammer on the brake drum to remove it.**

To install:

3. Inspect the inside of the brake drum. If worn, heavily grooved or if the opening is distorted, the drum should be refinished or replaced. If refinishing, observe the maximum drum diameter specification.

4. Inspect the wheel cylinder for signs of brake fluid leakage. Inspect the brake shoe springs and self-adjuster mechanism. The adjuster should usually be disassembled, cleaned and lubricated when the drum is removed for brake service.

5. Install the drum over the brake shoes.

6. Install the wheel and tire assembly.

7. Adjust the brakes.

8. Check brake operation.

GM L/N and N-BODY:
Buick Skylark
Chevrolet Malibu
Oldsmobile Achieva, Cutlass
Pontiac Grand Am

1. Remove the wheel.

2. Pull the brake drum off. It may be necessary to gently tap the rear edge of the drum to start it off the studs. If extreme resistance to removal is encountered, it will be necessary to retract the brake shoe self-adjuster screw, sometimes called the star-wheel. Knock out the access hole in the brake drum and turn the adjuster to retract the linings from the drum. Install a replacement hole cover before reinstalling the drum.

➡**DO NOT hammer on the brake drum to remove it.**

To install:

3. Inspect the inside of the brake drum. If worn, heavily grooved or if the opening is distorted, the drum should be refinished or replaced. If refinishing, observe the maximum drum diameter specification.

4. Inspect the wheel cylinder for signs of brake fluid leakage. Inspect the brake shoe

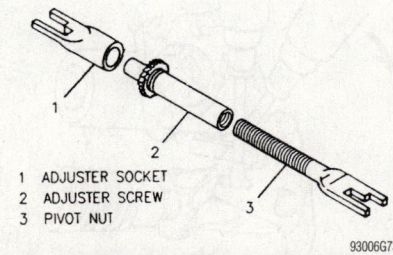

1 ADJUSTER SOCKET
2 ADJUSTER SCREW
3 PIVOT NUT

93006G73

Brake adjuster—Skylark, Malibu, Achieva, Cutlass, Grand Am

springs and self-adjuster mechanism. The adjuster should usually be disassembled, cleaned and lubricated when the drum is removed for brake service.

5. Install the drum over the brake shoes.

6. Install the wheel. Adjust the brakes.

7. Check brake operation.

GM W-BODY:
Buick Century, Regal
Chevrolet Lumina, Monte Carlo
Oldsmobile Cutlass Supreme, Intrigue
Pontiac Grand Prix

1. Mark the relationship of the wheel to the axle flange to help maintain wheel balance after assembly.

2. Remove the tire and wheel assembly.

3. Mark the relationship of the brake drum to the axle flange.

4. If difficulty is encountered in removing the brake drum, the following steps may be of assistance.

   a. Make sure the parking brake is released.

   b. Back off the parking brake cable adjustment.

   c. Remove the access hole plug from the backing plate.

   d. Using a screwdriver, back off the adjusting screw.

   e. Install the access hole plug to prevent dirt or contamination from entering the drum brake assembly.

   f. Use a small amount of penetrating oil applied around the brake drum pilot hole.

   g. Carefully remove the brake drum from the vehicle.

5. After removing the brake drum it should be checked for the following:

   a. Inspecting for cracks and deep grooves.

   b. Inspect for out of round and taper.

   c. Inspecting for hot spots (black in color).

To install:

6. Install the brake drum onto the vehicle aligning the reference marks on the axle flange.

7. Install the tire and wheel assembly, torquing it to specifications.

8. Road test for proper brake operation.

GEO Metro

1. Make sure the parking brake is fully released.

2. Remove the rear wheels.

3. Without ABS, perform the following:

Refer to the model specific sections for engine mechanical service procedures

a. Remove the dust cap. Using a hammer and punch, unstake the spindle nut.

b. Remove the spindle nut and washer. Discard the spindle nut.

4. If equipped with ABS, perform the following:

a. Remove the 2 brake drum retaining screws.

b. Install 2, 8mm screws in the 2 opposite threaded holes on the brake drum.

c. Alternately rotate each screw slowly until the 2 screws pull the drum from the hub and wheel studs.

5. Remove the drum from the vehicle. Remove the 2, 8mm screws from the drum.

6. Remove the rear brake drum assembly from the vehicle.

7. Remove the brake drum. If the drum is frozen on the hub, tap the drum with a rubber mallet or wooden hammer handle to loosen it.

8. Inspect the brake shoes for wear and/or damage; replace as necessary. Inspect the wheel cylinder for signs of brake fluid leakage; replace as necessary.

9. Inspect the drum for cracks, scoring or other wear; machine or replace as necessary. If machining, observe the maximum drum diameter specification.

To install:

10. Install the brake drum assembly onto the spindle.

11. On non-ABS equipped models;

a. Install the washer and a new spindle nut.

b. Torque the spindle nut to 74 ft. lbs. (100 Nm).

c. Stake the spindle nut.

d. Install the dust cap.

12. On ABS equipped models, install the brake drum and tighten the brake drum retaining screws.

13. Install the wheel.

14. To adjust the brakes, depress the brake pedal 3–5 times with approximately 66 lbs. (30 kg) of pressure.

15. Road test and check brake operation.

GEO Prizm

1. Make sure the parking brake is fully released.

2. Remove the rear wheel.

3. Without ABS, perform the following:

a. Remove the dust cap. Using a hammer and punch, unstake the spindle nut.

b. Remove the spindle nut and washer. Discard the spindle nut.

4. If equipped with ABS, perform the following:

a. Remove the 2 brake drum retaining screws.

b. Install 2, 8mm screws in the 2 opposite threaded holes on the brake drum.

c. Alternately rotate each screw slowly until the 2 screws pull the drum from the hub and wheel studs.

5. Remove the drum from the vehicle. Remove the 2, 8mm screws from the drum.

6. Remove the rear brake drum assembly from the vehicle.

7. Mark the position of 1 wheel lug stud in relation to a hole in the drum. This will allow the drum to be reinstalled in the original position.

8. Remove the brake drum. If the drum is frozen on the hub, tap the drum with a rubber mallet or wooden hammer handle to loosen it.

9. Inspect the brake shoes for wear and/or damage and replace as necessary. Inspect the wheel cylinder for signs of brake fluid leakage; replace as necessary.

10. Inspect the drum for cracks, scoring or other wear; machine or replace as necessary. If machining, observe the maximum drum diameter specification.

To install:

11. Install the brake drum assembly onto the spindle.

12. On non-ABS equipped models;

a. Install the washer and a new spindle nut.

b. Torque the spindle nut to 74 ft. lbs. (100 Nm).

c. Stake the spindle nut.

d. Install the dust cap.

13. On ABS equipped models, install the brake drum and tighten the brake drum retaining screws.

14. Install the drum, observing the matchmarks made earlier. Keep the drum straight while installing it, or it could damage the brake shoes.

15. Install the wheel.

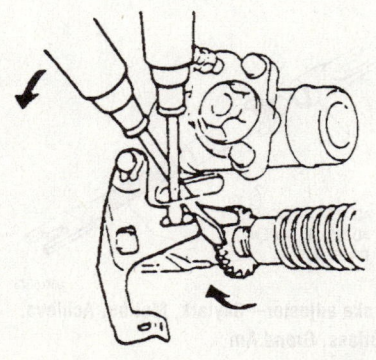

Backing off the rear brake adjuster—Prizm

16. To adjust the brakes, depress the brake pedal 3–5 times with approximately 66 lbs. (30 kg) of pressure.

17. Road test and check brake operation.

Saturn

1. Remove the rear wheel and tire assembly.

2. Remove the brake drum.

3. If necessary, turn the starwheel of the brake adjuster assembly to loosen the brake shoes and allow for drum removal.

To install:

4. Install brake drum over brake shoes and onto hub.

5. Install tire and wheel assembly. Torque to the proper specification.

6. Adjust brakes following the proper procedure.

7. Road test for braking operation.

Brake Shoes

REMOVAL & INSTALLATION

GM C- and H-BODIES:
Buick LeSabre, Park Avenue
Oldsmobile Eighty Eight Royale,
Ninety Eight, Regency
Pontiac Bonneville

1. Remove the rear wheel. Mark the position of the wheel to the wheel studs, prior to removal, for installation reference.

2. Remove the brake drum. Mark the position of the brake drum to the wheel studs, prior to removal, for installation reference.

3. Using tool J 38400 brake spanner tool and remover, remove the actuator spring from the adjuster lever. Use care not to distort the spring when removing it.

4. Lift the end of the retractor spring from the adjuster shoe assembly. Insert the hook end of the J-38400 between the retractor spring and the shoe. Pry slightly to remove the spring end from the hole in the shoe.

5. Pry the end of the retractor spring toward the axle with the flat end of the tool until the spring snaps down off the shoe web onto the backing plate.

6. Remove the one brake shoe and remove the adjuster assembly.

7. Disconnect the parking brake lever from the shoe. DO NOT remove the parking brake lever from the cable end unless it is being replaced.

8. Using J 38400, lift the end of the retractor spring from the adjuster shoe assembly. Insert the hook end of the tool

A ACCESS HOLE PLUG.

1 ADJUSTER SOCKET
2 ADJUSTER SCREW
3 PIVOT NUT

4 RETRACTOR SPRING
5 ADJUSTER SHOE AND LINING
6 WHEEL CYLINDER
7 BLEEDER VALVE
8 BOLT

9 BACKING PLATE
10 PARK BRAKE SHOE AND LINING
11 PARK BRAKE LEVER
12 ACTUATOR SPRING
13 ADJUSTER ACTUATOR

93006G77

Exploded view of the drum brake components—LeSabre, Park Avenue, Eighty Eight, Royale, Ninety Eight, Regency, Bonneville

between the retractor spring and the shoe. Pry slightly to remove the spring end from the hole in the shoe. Pry the end of the retractor spring toward the axle with the flat end of the tool, until the spring snaps down off the shoe web onto the backing plate. Leave the spring there. Do not remove it.

9. Remove the brake shoe.

To install:

10. Check the backing plate attaching bolts to make sure that they are tight. Use fine emery cloth to clean all rust and dirt from the shoe contact surfaces on the plate and lubricate with high temperature grease. Check the wheel cylinder for signs of leakage.

11. Clean all parts completely in brake solvent and air dry.

12. Clean the backing plate shoe contact points.

13. Inspect the inside of the brake drum. If worn, heavily grooved or if the opening is distorted, the drum should be machined or replaced. If machining, observe the maximum drum diameter specification.

14. Disassemble, clean and lubricate the adjuster screw.

15. Position the brake shoe that connects to the parking brake lever, on the backing plate. Using J-38400, pull the end of the retractor spring up to rest on the web of the shoe. Pull the end of the retractor spring up until it snaps into the slot in the brake shoe.

16. Connect the parking brake lever.

17. Install the remaining shoe and the adjuster screw assembly.

18. Position the brake shoe using J-38400 and pull the end of the retractor spring up to rest on the web of the shoe. Pull the end of the retractor spring up until it snaps into the slot in the brake shoe.

19. Using J-38400, spread the brake shoes and work the adjuster screw into position.

20. Install the actuator spring with the U-shaped end going through the web.

21. Measure the inside diameter of the brake drum using clearance gauge J 21177-A.

22. Turn the starwheel on the adjusting screw assembly until the brake shoe diameter is 0.050 in. (1.27mm) less than the drum inside diameter.

23. Install the brake drum onto the wheel hub, aligning the marks made during removal.

24. Install the wheel, aligning the marks made during removal. Torque the lug nuts to 100 ft. lbs. (140 Nm).

25. Repeat the procedure for the brake shoe assembly on the opposite side of the vehicle.

26. Apply and release the brake pedal 30–35 times with normal pedal force. Pause about 1 second between applications.

27. Road test the vehicle and check brake operation.

GM F-BODY:
Chevrolet Camaro
Pontiac Firebird

1. Matchmark the relationship of the wheel to the axle flange, then remove the wheel and tire assembly.

2. Matchmark the relationship of the drum to the axle flange and remove the brake drum.

3. Remove the return springs using a suitable tool.

4. Remove the hold-down springs and pins. Remove the actuator pivot.

5. Remove the actuator link while lifting up on the actuator.

6. Remove the actuator lever and lever return spring.

7. Remove the shoe guide, parking brake strut and strut spring.

8. Remove the brake shoes and disconnect the parking brake lever from the appropriate shoe.

9. Remove the adjusting screw assembly and spring.

To install:

10. Install the parking brake lever on the appropriate shoe by hooking the lever tab into the slot.

11. Install the adjusting screw and spring. Lubricate the adjusting screw with suitable brake grease.

12. Clean and lubricate the contact points of the backing plate, then install the brake shoe assemblies and the parking brake cable to the backing plate.

13. Install the parking brake strut and strut spring by spreading the shoes apart. The strut end with the spring engages the parking brake lever and shoe. The other end engages the opposite shoe.

14. Install the shoe guide, actuator lever and lever return spring.

15. Install the hold-down pins, actuator pivot and springs.

16. Install the actuator link on the anchor pin. Install the actuator link into the actuator lever while holding up on the lever.

17. Install the shoe return springs and adjust the brakes. When properly adjusted, the brake shoe linings will be approximately 0.050 inch (1.27mm) less than the inner diameter of the brake drum.

18. Align and install the brake drum, then the wheel and tire assembly.

GM J-BODY:
Chevrolet Cavalier
Pontiac Sunfire

1. Remove the tire and wheel assembly.

2. Remove the brake drum. It may be necessary to gently tap the rear edge of the drum to start it off the studs. If extreme resistance to removal is encountered, it will be necessary to retract the brake shoe self-adjuster screw, sometime called the star-

wheel. Turn the adjuster to retract the linings from the drum.

➡ **Do not hammer on the brake drum to remove it.**

3. Remove the upper return springs from the shoes using tool J-8057 brake spring tool.

4. Remove the hold-down springs using J-8049 brake spring tool.

5. Remove the shoe hold-down pins from behind the brake backing plate.

6. Lift up the actuator lever for the self-adjusting mechanism and remove the actuating link. Remove the actuator lever, pivot, and the pivot return spring.

7. Spread the shoes apart to clear the wheel cylinder pistons, then remove the parking brake strut and spring.

8. Disconnect the parking brake cable from the lever. Remove the shoes, still connected by their adjusting screw spring.

9. With the shoes removed, note the position of the adjusting spring and remove the spring and adjusting screw.

10. Remove the C-clip from the parking brake lever and remove the lever from the secondary shoe.

11. Use a damp cloth to remove all dirt and dust from the backing plate and brake parts.

To install:

12. Check the backing plate attaching bolts to make sure they are tight. Use fine emery cloth to clean all rust and dirt from the shoe contact surfaces on the plate and lubricate with brake grease. Check the wheel cylinder for signs of leakage.

13. Clean all parts completely in brake solvent and air dry.

14. Clean the backing plate shoe contact points.

15. Inspect the inside of the brake drum. If worn, heavily grooved or if the opening is distorted, the drum should be refinished or replaced.

16. Inspect the brake shoe springs and self-adjuster mechanism. Disassemble the adjuster mechanism and clean the threads and coat with grease. Make sure the

adjuster assembly turns freely before installing in the vehicle.

17. Install the parking brake lever on the secondary shoe and secure with C-clip.

18. Install the adjusting screw and spring on the shoes, connecting them together. The coils of the spring must not be over the star-wheel on the adjuster. The left and right hand springs are not interchangeable.

19. Spread the shoe assemblies apart and connect the parking brake cable. Install the shoes on the backing plate, engaging the shoes at the top temporarily with the wheel cylinder pistons. Make sure the starwheel on the adjuster is lined up with the adjusting hole in the backing plate, if equipped.

20. Spread the shoes apart slightly and install the parking brake strut and spring. Make sure the end of the strut without the spring engages the parking brake lever. The end with the spring engages the primary shoe (the one with the shorter lining).

21. Install the actuator pivot, lever and return spring. Install the actuating link in the shoe retainer. Lift up the actuator lever and hook the link into the lever.

22. Install the hold-down pins through the back of the plate using J-8057. Install the lever pivots and hold-down springs. Install the shoe return springs using J-8049. Be careful not to stretch or distort the springs.

23. Make sure the linings are in the right place, the self-adjusting mechanism is correctly installed, and the parking brake parts are hooked up.

24. Measure the distance from the edge of the primary lining to the edge secondary lining, then measure the inside width of the drum. Adjust the linings by means of the adjuster so the drum will fit onto the linings.

25. Install the hub and bearing assembly onto the axle if removed. Torque the retaining bolts to 35 ft. lbs. (55 Nm.).

26. Install the drum.

27. Install the wheel and tire assembly.

28. Adjust the brakes. Install a rubber hole cover in the adjustment knock-out hole after the adjustment is complete. Adjust the parking brake.

29. Road test the vehicle and verify proper brake operation.

GM L/N and N-BODY:
Buick Skylark
Chevrolet Malibu
Oldsmobile Achieva, Cutlass
Pontiac Grand Am

1. Remove the tire and wheel assembly. Remove the brake drum.

2. Remove the upper return springs

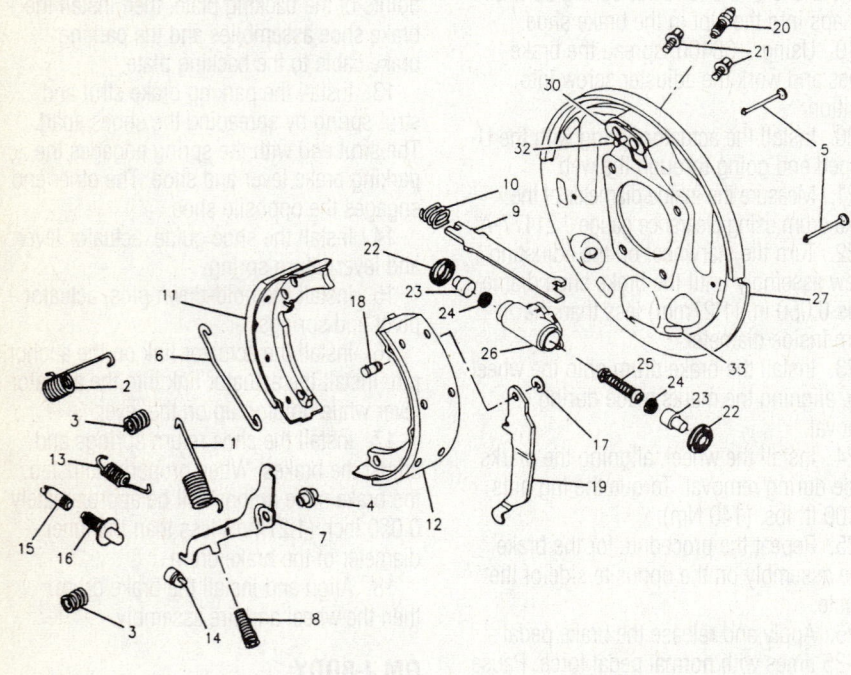

#		#		#	
1	RETURN SPRING	11	PRIMARY SHOE AND LINING	21	BOLT
2	RETURN SPRING	12	SECONDARY SHOE AND LINING	22	BOOT
3	HOLD DOWN SPRING	13	ADJUSTING SCREW SPRING	23	PISTON
4	BEARING SLEEVE	14	SOCKET	24	SEAL
5	HOLD-DOWN PIN	15	PIVOT NUT	25	SPRING ASSEMBLY
6	ACTUATOR LINK	16	ADJUSTING SCREW	26	WHEEL CYLINDER
7	ACTUATOR LEVER	17	RETAINING RING	27	BACKING PLATE
8	LEVER RETURN SPRING	18	PIN	30	SHOE RETAINER
9	PARKING BRAKE STRUT	19	PARKING BRAKE LEVER	32	ANCHOR PIN
10	STRUT SPRING	20	BLEEDER VALVE	33	SHOE PADS

Exploded view of drum brake components—Cavalier, Sunfire

93006G97

from the shoes using tool J-8057 brake spring tool.

3. Remove the hold-down springs using J-8049 brake spring tool.

4. Remove the shoe hold-down pins from behind the brake backing plate.

5. Lift up the actuator lever for the self-adjusting mechanism and remove the actuating link. Remove the actuator lever, pivot, and the pivot return spring.

6. Spread the shoes apart to clear the wheel cylinder pistons and remove the parking brake strut and spring.

7. Disconnect the parking brake cable from the lever. Remove the shoes, still connected by their adjusting screw spring.

8. With the shoes removed, note the position of the adjusting spring and remove the spring and adjusting screw.

9. Remove the C-clip from the parking brake lever and the lever from the secondary shoe.

10. Use a damp cloth to remove all dirt and dust from the backing plate and brake parts.

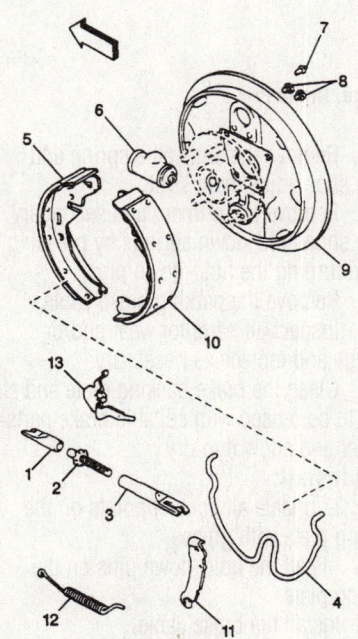

(1) Socket, Brake Adjuster
(2) Screw, Brake Adjuster
(3) Nut, Brake Pivot
(4) Spring, Retractor
(5) Brake Shoe and Lining
(6) Cylinder, Wheel Brake
(7) Valve, Bleeder
(8) Bolts, Wheel Cylinder
(9) Plate, Brake Backing
(10) Brake Shoe and Lining
(11) Lever, Park Brake
(12) Spring
(13) Adjuster Actuator

93006G78

Drum brake components, exploded view—Skylark, Malibu, Achieva, Cutlass, Grand Am

To install:

11. Check the backing plate attaching bolts to make sure they are tight. Use fine emery cloth to clean all rust and dirt from the shoe contact surfaces on the plate and lubricate with brake grease. Check the wheel cylinder for signs of leakage.

12. Clean all parts completely in brake solvent and air dry. Clean the backing plate shoe contact points.

13. Inspect the inside of the brake drum. If worn, heavily grooved or if the opening is distorted, the drum should be refinished or replaced.

14. Inspect the brake shoe springs and self-adjuster mechanism. Disassemble the adjuster mechanism and clean the threads and coat with grease. Make sure the adjuster assembly turns freely before installing in the vehicle.

15. Install the parking brake lever on the secondary shoe and secure with C-clip.

16. Install the adjusting screw and spring on the shoes, connecting them together. The coils of the spring must not be over the starwheel on the adjuster. The left and right hand springs are not interchangeable.

17. Spread the shoe assemblies and connect the parking brake cable. Install the shoes on the backing plate, engaging the shoes at the top temporarily with the wheel cylinder pistons. Make sure the starwheel on the adjuster is lined up with the adjusting hole in the backing plate, if equipped.

18. Spread the shoes slightly and install the parking brake strut and spring. Make sure the end of the strut without the spring engages the parking brake lever. The end with the spring engages the primary shoe (the one with the shorter lining).

19. Install the actuator pivot, lever and return spring. Install the actuating link in the shoe retainer. Lift up the actuator lever and hook the link into the lever.

20. Install the hold-down pins through the back of the plate using J-8057. Install the lever pivots and hold-down springs. Install the shoe return springs using J-8049. Be careful not to stretch or distort the springs.

21. Make sure the linings are in the right place, the self-adjusting mechanism is correctly installed, and the parking brake parts are hooked up.

22. Measure the distance from the edge of the primary lining to the edge secondary lining, then measure the inside width of the drum. Adjust the linings by means of the

adjuster so the drum will fit onto the linings.

23. Install the hub and bearing assembly onto the axle if removed. Torque the retaining bolts to 35 ft. lbs. (55 Nm).

24. Install the drum and the wheels.

25. Adjust the brakes. Install a rubber hole cover in the adjustment knock-out hole after the adjustment is complete. Adjust the parking brake.

26. Road test the vehicle and verify proper brake operation.

GM W-BODY:
Buick Century, Regal
Chevrolet Lumina, Monte Carlo
Oldsmobile Cutlass Supreme, Intrigue
Pontiac Grand Prix

1. Remove the tire and wheel assembly.
2. Remove the brake drum.
3. Using tool J-38400 brake spanner and remover, remove the actuator spring from the adjuster lever. Use care not to distort the spring when removing it.

✳✳ CAUTION

During the following steps when removing the retractor spring from either shoe and lining assembly, do not over stretch the spring. This will reduce its effectiveness. Keep fingers away from retractor spring to prevent fingers from being pinched between the spring and shoe web or spring and the backing plate.

4. Lift the end of the retractor spring from the adjuster shoe assembly. Insert the hook end of the J-38400, between the retractor spring and the shoe. Pry slightly to remove the spring end from the hole in the shoe.

5. Pry the end of the retractor spring toward the axle with the flat end of the tool until the spring snaps down off the shoe web onto the backing plate.

6. Remove the one brake shoe and remove the adjuster assembly.

7. Disconnect the parking brake lever from the shoe. DO NOT remove the parking brake lever from the cable end unless it is being replaced.

8. Using J-38400, lift the end of the retractor spring from the adjuster shoe assembly. Insert the hook end of the J-38400, between the retractor spring and the shoe. Pry slightly to remove the spring end from the hole in the shoe. Pry the end of the retractor spring toward the axle with the flat

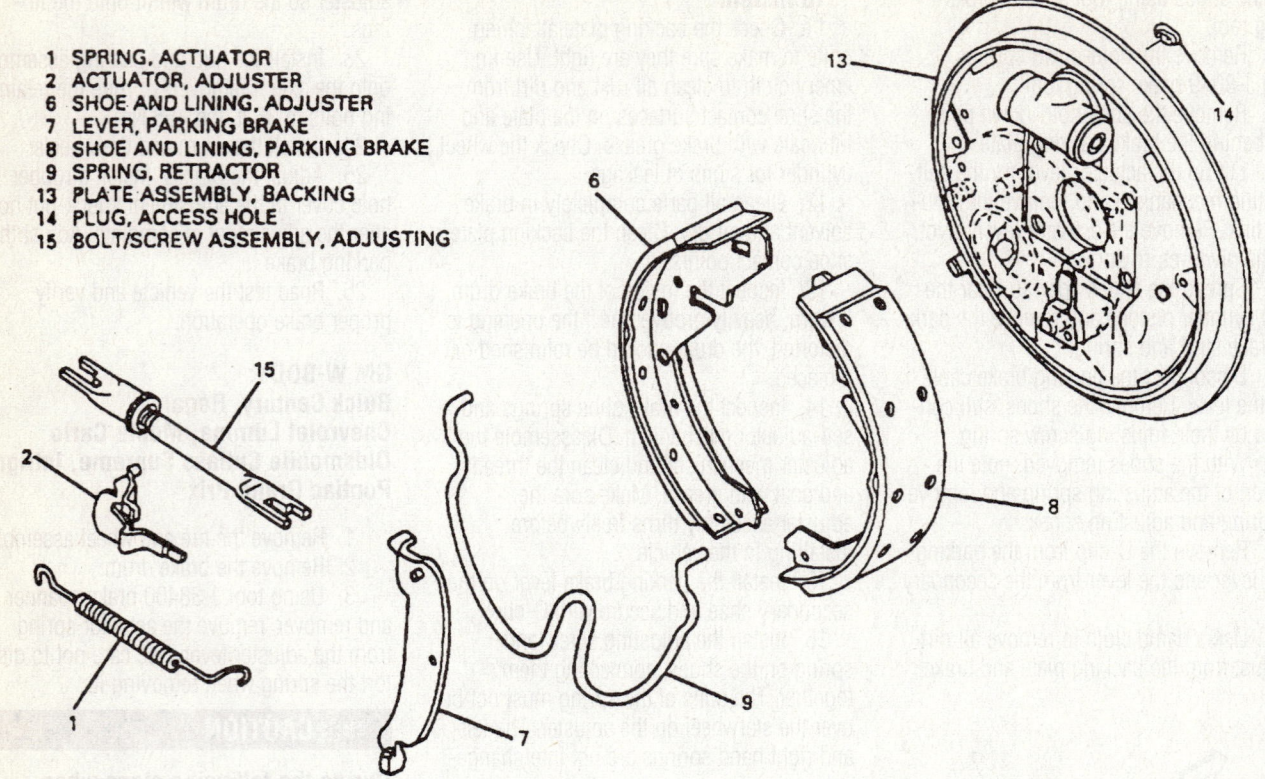

1 SPRING, ACTUATOR
2 ACTUATOR, ADJUSTER
6 SHOE AND LINING, ADJUSTER
7 LEVER, PARKING BRAKE
8 SHOE AND LINING, PARKING BRAKE
9 SPRING, RETRACTOR
13 PLATE ASSEMBLY, BACKING
14 PLUG, ACCESS HOLE
15 BOLT/SCREW ASSEMBLY, ADJUSTING

93006G79

Rear brake assembly component alignment—Century, Regal, Lumina, Monte Carlo, Cutlass Supreme, Intrigue, Grand Prix

end of the tool until the spring snaps down off the shoe web onto the backing plate.

9. Remove the brake shoe.

To install:

10. Clean all the brake spring completely with brake solvent and allow to air dry.

11. Disassemble, clean and lubricate the adjuster screw. Once lubricated, reassemble.

12. Clean the backing plate and after it is dry apply a thin coat of brake grease to the brake shoe contact points on the backing plate.

13. Position the brake shoe that connects to the parking brake lever, on the backing plate. Using J-38400, pull the end of the retractor spring up to rest on the web of the shoe. Pull the end of the retractor spring up until it snaps into the slot in the brake shoe.

14. Connect the parking brake lever.

15. Install the remaining shoe and the adjuster screw assembly.

16. Position the brake shoe, using J-38400, pull the end of the retractor spring up to rest on the web of the shoe. Pull the end of the retractor spring up until it snaps into the slot in the brake shoe.

17. Using J-38400, spread the brake shoes and work the adjuster screw into position.

18. Install the actuator spring with the U-shaped end going through the web.

19. Install the brake drum.

20. Install the tire and wheel assembly.

21. Adjust the brakes.

22. Road test for proper brake operation.

GEO Metro

1. Remove the rear wheels.

2. Remove the brake drum.

3. Remove the upper and lower return springs from the brake shoes.

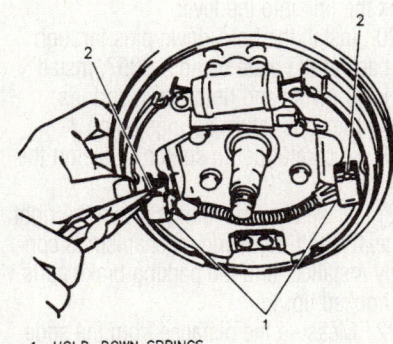

1 HOLD-DOWN SPRINGS
2 HOLD-DOWN PINS

93006G80

Removing the shoe hold-down springs—Metro

4. Remove the anti-rattle spring and brake shoe adjustment strut.

5. Remove the primary and secondary brake shoe hold-down springs by pressing in and turning the hold-down pins.

6. Remove the parking brake cable.

7. Inspect all parts for wear and/or damage and replace as necessary.

8. Clean the brake backing plate and all parts to be reused with suitable brake parts cleaner and allow it to dry.

To install:

9. Lubricate all contact points on the backing plate with grease.

10. Install the hold-down pins on the backing plate.

11. Install the brake cable.

12. Install the primary and secondary brake shoes to the vehicle and secure with the hold-down springs.

13. Install the brake adjustment strut and anti-rattle spring.

14. Install the upper and lower return springs to the primary and secondary brake shoes.

15. Install the brake drum.

16. Install the rear wheels.

17. Press the brake pedal 3–5 times with approximately 66 lbs. (30 kg) pressure to adjust the brake shoe clearance.

18. Check to ensure the brake drum is

free from dragging and proper braking is obtained.

GEO Prizm

1. Remove the rear wheels.

2. Remove the brake drum. Inspect the drum for wear and/or damage. Replace or machine the drum as necessary.

3. Remove the upper return spring.

4. Remove the front brake shoe hold-down spring, retainers and pin.

5. Remove the anchor spring from the front brake shoe and remove the front brake shoe.

6. Remove the rear brake shoe hold-down spring, retainers and pin.

7. Remove the automatic adjusting lever spring and the adjuster.

8. Remove the parking brake cable.

9. Use a suitable tool to spread the C-clips and remove the automatic adjuster lever and parking brake lever from the rear brake shoe.

10. Clean all parts and the brake backing plate with an approved brake parts cleaner.

To install:

11. Before reinstallation, apply grease to the contact points on the backing plate and pivot points on the adjuster lever.

12. Install the parking brake and automatic adjuster levers to the rear brake shoe.

13. Install new C-clips and use pliers to install them. Do not bend more than necessary to hold in place.

14. Check the clearance between the parking brake lever and the brake shoe using a feeler gauge. The clearance must be at least 0.0138 in. (0.35mm). If the clearance is not as specified, replace the shim between the lever and shoe.

15. Connect the parking brake cable.

16. Install the adjuster and the lever spring.

17. Install the rear brake shoe on the backing plate with the end of the shoe inserted in the wheel cylinder and the adjuster in place. Install the hold-down spring, retainer and pin.

18. Install the anchor spring between the front and rear shoe.

19. Install the front brake shoe with the end of the shoe inserted in the wheel cylinder and the adjuster in place.

20. Install the hold-down spring, retainers and pin.

21. Connect the return spring.

22. Adjust the brake shoes. When

adjusted properly, the outside diameter of the brake shoes will be approximately 0.024 in. (0.6mm) less than the inner diameter of the brake drum.

23. Install the brake drum and the wheel.

24. Road test and check for proper brake operation.

Saturn

1. Remove the wheels and brake drums.

2. Remove the lower return and adjuster springs using a universal brake spring remover. Do not over extend the springs or they will damaged and will need to be replaced.

3. Compress the leading brake shoe hold-down cup and spring while removing the pin from the rear of the backing plate. Release spring compression, then remove the hold-down cup and spring.

4. Pull the leading shoe towards the front of the vehicle and remove the adjuster assembly and lever. It may be necessary to turn the adjuster starwheel to shorten the adjuster's length.

5. Remove the leading shoe by twisting the shoe out of engagement with the upper return spring.

6. Remove the upper return spring from the park brake shoe, then remove the park brake shoe hold-down cup, spring and pin assembly.

7. Push the park brake shoe lever into the cable spring while disengaging the cable from the end lever and remove the parking brake shoe, lever and cable spring from the vehicle.

8. Remove the retainer and wave washer, then remove the park brake lever from the shoe.

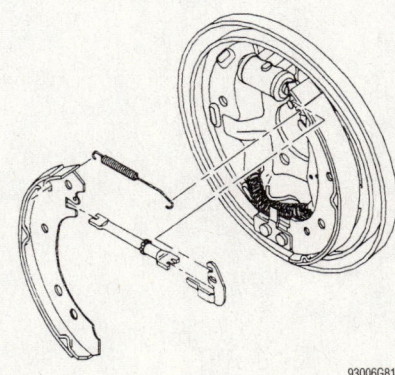

Rear brake shoe and adjuster installation—Saturn

9. Disassemble the brake adjuster socket, screw and nut, then clean the components in denatured alcohol. Inspect the assembly, making sure the screw threads smoothly into the adjusting nut over the full threaded length.

10. Inspect the wheel cylinder for signs of leakage and for cut or damaged boots. Do not attempt to repair a damaged cylinder, the assembly must be replaced.

To install:

11. Lubricate the adjuster assembly, the 6 backing plate raised shoe contact pads, the brake lever pin and surfaces which contact brake shoe webs with brake lubricant.

12. Install the park brake lever onto the pin on the brake shoe and secure with the wave washer and retainer clip. Crimp the ends of the retainer to secure the brake lever.

13. Install the cable spring into the cage on the park brake lever, then install the cable through the spring and onto the lever.

14. Install the park brake shoe using the hold-down cup assembly; use a universal spring cup remover/installer tool. Make sure the shoe is correctly engaged into the wheel cylinder (top) and the anchor (bottom).

15. Install the long straight end of the upper return spring into the back hole in the park brake shoe, position the other brake shoe and install the other end of the spring into the back of the leading shoe.

16. Pull the lead shoe toward the front of the vehicle and install the adjuster between the park and leading brake shoes. Verify that the adjuster notches properly engage the brake shoe notches and that the shoe is properly aligned in the wheel cylinder and anchor.

17. Install the adjuster lever and adjuster spring. Make sure the notch on the lever engages the pin on the park shoe and the notch on the adjusting socket. The lower leg of the lever should engage the teeth of the starwheel adjuster assembly.

18. Secure the leading brake shoe using the hold-down cup assembly.

19. Install the adjuster spring to the upper side of the brake shoes with the short end to the lead shoe and the long end to the adjuster lever. Then install the lower return spring into the lower holes of the shoes.

20. Verify the correct location of all

brake components, if necessary, use the other side brake assembly for comparison.

21. Using a suitable drum clearance gauge, measure the inner diameter of the brake drum and adjust the outside diameter of the brake shoes to 0.02 inch

(0.50mm) less than the inner diameter of the drum.

22. Repeat the procedure for the opposite brake shoes and install the brake drums.

23. If the wheel cylinders have been replaced, bleed the hydraulic brake system.

24. Install the rear wheels.

25. Apply and release the brake pedal 20 times to allow the adjuster to properly position the brake shoes.

26. Check and adjust the parking brake cable, as necessary.

WINDSHIELD WIPER SYSTEMS

6

Avenger, Breeze, Cirrus, Sebring, Stratus and Talon

GENERAL DESCRIPTION

Front Windshield Wiper and Washer

When the wiper switch is placed in the **LO** position with the ignition switch in the **ACC** or **ON** position, wipers operate continuously at low speed. Placing the wiper switch in the **HI** position causes the wipers to operate at high speed.

When the wiper switch is placed in the **OFF** position, the cam contacts of the wiper motor causing current to flow through the auto wiper stop circuit, allowing the wiper blades to cycle before they reach the stop position.

When the wiper switch is placed in the **INT** position, with the ignition switch in **ACC** or **ON** position, the intermittent wiper relay is energized, causing the intermittent wiper relay contacts to close and open repeatedly. When the contacts are closed, the wiper motor is energized. When the wiper motor is energized, the relay contacts open; however the cam contacts keep the wiper motor energized until the wiper blades return to the **PARK** position.

When the washer switch is turned **ON**, the intermittent wiper relay contacts close causing the wipers to cycle 2–3 times.

Rear Window Wiper and Washer

When the rear wiper switch is placed in the **ON** position with the ignition switch in the **ACC** or **ON** position, the wiper will operate continuously at low speed.

When the rear wiper switch is placed in the **OFF** position, the cam closes the contacts of the wiper motor causing current to flow through the auto wiper stop circuit, allowing the wiper blade to cycle before reaching the **PARK** position.

When the rear window wiper switch is placed in the **INT** position, with the ignition switch in the **ACC** or **ON** position, the rear intermittent wiper relay is energized causing the rear intermittent wiper relay contacts to close and open repeatedly. When the contacts are closed, the wiper motor is energized. When the rear wiper motor is energized, the rear intermittent wiper relay contacts open. However, the cam contacts keep the rear wiper motor energized until the wiper blades return to their **PARK** position.

TROUBLESHOOTING

Front Windshield Wiper/Washer System

1. Neither wipers nor washer operate.
   - Check fuse.
   - Check for good ground.
2. Only **LOW** or **HIGH** inoperative.
   - Check for problem in switch.
3. Wipers do not stop.
   - Check the wiper motor.
   - Check the intermittent wiper relay.
   - Check the wiper switch.
4. Intermittent wiper inoperative. The intermittent relay is built into the switch
   - Check the voltage of steering-column combination switch, terminal **7** for Talon, Stratus, Cirrus, Sebring and Avenger with the intermittent relay energized.
   - If 0 volts, check wiper relay or switch.
   - If 12 volts, steadily, check intermittent wiper relay.
   - If 0–12 volts, alternating, this is normal operation.
5. Length of intermittent pause cannot be varied.
   - Check the variable intermittent wiper control switch.
   - Check the intermittent wiper relay, built into the switch.
6. Washer is inoperative but wipers operate when washer switch is engaged.
   - Check the washer motor.
7. Washer is inoperative and wipers do not engage when washer switch is operated.
   - Check the washer switch.
8. Washer-wiper operation is inoperative.
   - Check the intermittent wiper relay, built into the switch.

Rear Window Wiper/Washer System

1. Neither wipers nor washer operate.
   - Check the fuse.
   - Check for a good ground.
2. Only **LOW** inoperative.
   - Check for a problem in rear wiper switch.
3. Wipers do not stop.
   - Check the wiper motor.
   - Check the intermittent wiper relay
   - Check the rear wiper switch. Intermittent relay is built into the switch
4. Intermittent wiper inoperative.
   - Check terminal voltage of terminal **2** or **8** (except Talon, Cirrus, Stra-

tus, Sebring and Avenger) or terminal **6** (Talon, Sebring and Avenger) of the rear intermittent wiper relay which is behind the rear trim panel, with the intermittent relay energized.
   a. If 0 volts, check rear intermittent wiper relay or rear wiper switch.
   b. If 12 volts, check intermittent wiper relay.
   c. If 0–12 volts, alternating, this is normal operation.
5. Washer is inoperative.
   - Check washer motor.
   - Check washer switch.

TESTING

Front Wiper and Washer System

FRONT WIPER MOTOR

1. Check the wiper motor after first disconnecting the wiring harness connector and with the wiper motor remaining installed to the body. Inspect the wiring connector. With the notch at the top, note that there are either 4 or 6 terminals.
2. Using jumper wires, connect battery voltage to the upper left terminal. The motor, still installed, should complete the ground circuit. The motor should run at low speed.
3. Using jumper wires, connect battery voltage to the upper right terminal on the 4 terminal version, or to the upper middle ter-

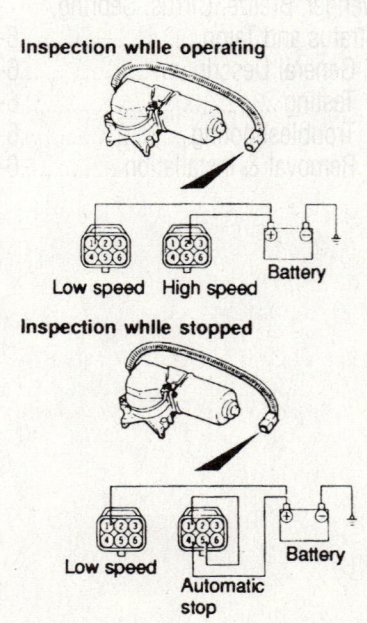

Inspection while operating

Low speed   High speed   Battery

Inspection while stopped

Low speed   Battery
Automatic stop

8838XG01

Wiper motor testing—Talon, Sebring and Avenger

minal on the 6 terminal versions. The motor, still installed, should complete the ground circuit. The motor should run at high speed.

4. Run the motor at low speed, disconnect the jumper wire from the battery and stop the motor. Using jumper wires, connect the battery to the lower left terminal and bridge the upper left to the lower right terminal (4 terminal version) or to the lower middle terminal (6 terminal versions). The motor should start turning at low speed, then stop at the automatic stop position.

5. If the motor does not pass these tests, replace it.

WIPER/WASHER SWITCH

1. Remove the lower dash panel and the steering column cover.

2. Disconnect the wiper/washer switch connector and check for continuity between the terminals.

3. If continuity checks are not as specified, replace the wiper/washer switch.

WASHER MOTOR

1. Prior to testing the washer motor, make sure it is mounted on the washer tank and that the washer tank is filled.

2. Disconnect the wiring harness connector from the washer motor.

3. Connect a jumper wire from the positive battery post to the lower of the two washer motor terminals (with the locking tab of the connector being on top), then connect a jumper wire from the negative battery post to the other washer motor terminal.

4. The washer motor should pump water out. If not, replace the washer pump.

Rear Wiper and Washer System

WIPER MOTOR

1. Check the wiper motor after first disconnecting the wiring harness connector and with the wiper motor remaining installed to the body. Inspect the wiring connector. With the notch at the top, note that there are 3 terminals.

2. Using a jumper wire, connect battery voltage to the left terminal. The motor, still installed, should complete the ground circuit. The motor should run at low speed.

3. Run the motor at low speed, then disconnect the jumper wire from the battery and stop the motor.

4. Using jumper wires, connect battery voltage to the right terminal. Connect a 2nd jumper wire to the left and center terminals. The motor, still installed, should complete

the ground circuit. The motor should start turning, then stop at the automatic **PARK** position.

5. If the motor is defective, remove and replace.

6. On Talon, fill the tank. With the notch of the connector on top, connect battery voltage to the left terminal and ground the right terminal. The washer motor should run and water should spray from the nozzle at the top of the liftgate glass.

WIPER AND WASHER SWITCH

1. Remove the wiper/washer switch.

2. Check for continuity between the terminals.

3. If continuity checks are not as specified, replace the wiper/washer switch.

INTERMITTENT WIPER RELAY

1. With the wiper relay connected to the wire harness connector, operate the intermittent wipers.

2. Using a voltmeter, check the voltage at terminal **2**.

    a. With the wiper stationary, there should be 0 volts.

    b. With the wiper operating, there should be 12 volts.

WASHER MOTOR

1. Prior to testing the washer motor, make sure it is mounted on the washer tank and that the washer tank is filled.

2. Disconnect the wiring harness connector from the washer motor.

3. Connect the positive and negative battery leads to the washer motor terminals.

4. The washer motor should pump water out. If not, replace the washer pump.

REMOVAL & INSTALLATION

Front Washer Reservoir and Pump

TALON, SEBRING AND AVENGER— NON-TURBO MODELS

1. Disconnect the negative battery cable.

2. On non-turbo models, remove the brake fluid reservoir mounting bolt to gain access to the washer tank bolts.

3. Disconnect the fluid hose and electrical connector from the washer motor.

4. Remove the washer fluid tank mounting bolts.

5. Remove the washer tank from the vehicle.

6. Remove the washer pump motor from the washer tank.

Switch position		Terminal				
		5	6	7	8	9
Wiper switch	OFF		O—O			
	1 (LO)			O————————O		
	2 (HI)				O——O	
Washer switch	ON	O				O

8838XG02

Front wiper and washer switch testing—Talon, Sebring and Avenger

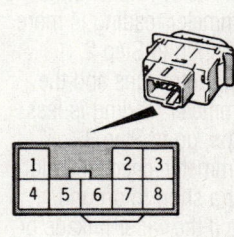

Switch position	Terminal	2	4	5	6	7	8	3	1
Wiper switch	OFF		O—O						
	ON				O—O				
	INT	O		O—O			O		
Washer switch						O—O		Illumination light	

NOTE
O—O indicates that there is continuity between the terminals.

8470V009

Rear wiper and washer switch testing—Talon, Sebring and Avenger

To install:

7. Installation is the reverse of the removal procedure.

Rear Washer Reservoir and Pump

TALON, SEBRING AND AVENGER

1. Remove the rear side trim panel.
2. Remove the washer cap.
3. Disconnect the electrical connector from the pump.
4. Disconnect the hose and drain the reservoir.
5. Remove the 3 nuts and the reservoir and pump assembly.
6. Remove the pump from the reservoir.

To install:

7. Installation is the reverse of the removal procedure.

Concorde, Intrepid, and Vision

GENERAL DESCRIPTION

The windshield wipers will only operate with the ignition switch in the **ACC** or **IGN** position. A fuse, located in the fuse block, protects the circuitry of the wiper system and the vehicle.

The wiper motor has permanent magnet fields. The speeds are determined by current flow to the appropriate set of brushes.

The intermittent wiper system, in addition to low and high speed, has a delay mode. The delay mode has a range of ½–18 seconds. The wiper delay will double to a range of 1–36 seconds when the vehicle speed is less than 10 MPH. The delay is performed by a variable resistor in the wiper switch and 2 relays. One relay operates the **ON/OFF** and the other changes the speeds.

The wiper system completes the wipe cycle when the switch is turned **OFF**. The blades park in the lowest portion of the wiping pattern.

TROUBLESHOOTING

Wiper and Washer System

WIPER MOTOR WILL NOT RUN IN ANY SWITCH POSITION

1. Check fuse **10** in the junction block and fuse **C** in the power distribution center.
- If the fuse(s) are good, go to Step 2.
- If the fuse(s) are defective, replace them and check the wiper motor operation in all switch positions.
- If the motor is still inoperative and fuses do not blow, go to Step 2.
- If the fuse blows, go to Step 11.

2. Disconnect the wiper motor connector.

3. Check the wiper motor low speed. Connect a jumper wire from the positive battery terminal to terminal **3** of the motor connector. Connect a 2nd jumper wire from terminal **2** to a suitable ground. Check the wiper motor high speed. Move the grounded jumper wire from terminal **2** to terminal **4**.
- If motor runs; go to Step 5.
- If motor does not run in high or low speed, go to Step 4.

4. Using an ohmmeter, check for a good ground at terminal **4** of the wiper motor wire harness connector.
- If OK, replace the motor.
- If not, repair the ground as necessary.

5. Using a voltmeter, check for battery voltage at terminal **D** of the intermittent wiper relay in the power distribution center.
- If no voltage is found, check fuse **C**.
- If OK, go to Step 6.

6. Using an ohmmeter, check from terminal **D** to the **HI-LO** wiper relay to terminal **2** of the wiper motor wiring harness connector for continuity. Check from terminal **E** of the **HI-LO** wiper relay to terminal **3** of the wiper motor wiring harness connector for continuity.
- If OK, go to Step 7.
- If not, repair as necessary.

7. Using an ohmmeter, check for continuity from terminal **B** of the **HI-LO** wiper relay to terminal **B** of the intermittent wiper relay.

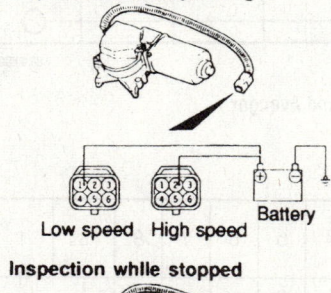
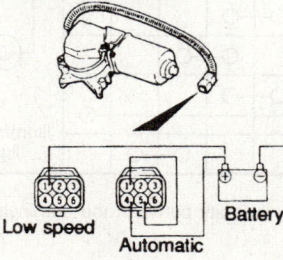

Inspection while operating

Low speed   High speed   Battery

Inspection while stopped

Low speed   Automatic stop   Battery

8838XG01

Wiper motor wire harness connector—Concorde, Intrepid, and Vision

- If OK, check for faulty relays.
- If not, repair as necessary.

8. Disconnect the connector from the body controller located on the right lower kick panel behind the trim panel.

9. Using an ohmmeter, check for continuity between terminal **1** of the body controller connector and terminal **C** of the intermittent wiper relay.
- If OK, go to Step 10.
- If not, repair as necessary.

10. Using a voltmeter, with the wiper switch connected, connect the positive lead to terminal **1** of the wiper switch. Turn the ignition switch to the **ON** position. Slowly move the wiper switch from the **OFF** position through each position to **HIGH**.
- If no voltage is present, replace the wiper switch.
- If OK, check for continuity between terminal **1** of the wiper switch and terminal **16** of the body controller connector.

11. Turn the ignition switch **OFF**. Using an ohmmeter, check for continuity between fuse **10** and terminal **1** and **18** of the body controller connector.
- If there is no continuity; check the **HI-LO** and intermittent relays.
- If OK, repair the wiring as necessary.
- If voltage increased from 0 to approximately 10 volts in the **HIGH** position, replace the body controller.

MOTOR RUNS SLOWLY AT ALL SPEEDS

1. Disconnect the wiper motor connector from the motor. Remove the wiper arms and blades. Disconnect the wiper motor drive link from the motor. Connect an ammeter from the positive battery terminal to terminal **3** of the wiper motor connector. Connect a ground wire from terminal **4** of the wiper motor connector to a suitable ground.
- If the wiper motor runs and the average ammeter reading is more than 6 amps, go to Step 2.
- If the wiper motor runs and the average ammeter reading is less than 6 amps, go to Step 3.

2. Using an ohmmeter, check the high and low circuits for a short to ground.

3. Check to see if the wiper linkage or pivots are binding or caught.

MOTOR WILL RUN AT HIGH SPEED, BUT NOT LOW; MOTOR WILL RUN AT LOW SPEED, BUT NOT HIGH

1. Disconnect the wiper motor electrical connector.

2. If the wiper motor will not run on **LOW** speed, connect a jumper wire from the positive battery terminal to terminal **3** of the motor connector. Connect a 2nd jumper wire from terminal **4** of the motor connector to a suitable ground.
- If the motor runs, go to Step 3.
- If the motor does not run, replace the motor.

3. If the motor will not run on **HIGH** speed, connect a jumper wire from the positive battery terminal to terminal **2** of the motor connector. Connect a 2nd jumper wire from terminal **4** of the motor connector to a suitable ground.
- If the motor runs, go to Step 4.
- If the motor does not run, replace the motor.

4. If the motor will not run at **LOW** speed, check for an open circuit using an ohmmeter. Check between terminal **E** of the **HI-LO** wiper relay and terminal **3** of the wiper motor wire harness for continuity.
- If OK, go to Step 5.
- If no continuity, repair wiring as necessary.

5. If the motor will not run at **LOW** speed, check for an open circuit using an ohmmeter. Check between terminal **D** of the **HI-LO** wiper relay and terminal **2** of the wiper motor wire harness for continuity.
- If OK, go to Step 6.
- If no continuity, repair wiring as necessary.

6. Check for **HI-LO** wiper relay malfunction.

WIPERS WILL OPERATE AT HIGH SPEED WITH THE SWITCH IN THE LOW POSITION; WIPERS WILL OPERATE IN INTERMITTENT MODE, BUT EACH WIPING CYCLE IS IN HIGH SPEED

1. Disconnect the wiper motor connector.
2. Connect a jumper wire from the positive battery terminal to terminal **3** of the wiper motor wire harness connector. Connect a 2nd jumper wire from the negative battery terminal to terminal **4** of the wiper motor wire harness connector.
- If wiper motor runs at **LOW** speed, go to Step 3.
- If the motor runs at **HIGH** speed, check for crossed wires in the wiper motor pigtail connector.
3. Check for a faulty **HI-LO** wiper relay.
- If faulty, replace it.
- If OK, go to Step 4.
4. Check for crossed wires in the harness from the **HI-LO** relay to the motor.

- If crossed, repair the circuit.
- If OK, go to Step 5.

5. Disconnect the connector from the body controller and remove the intermittent wiper relay and check for a short to ground.
- If short is found, repair it.
- If OK, go to Step 6.

6. If none of the above malfunctions are present, replace the body controller.

WIPERS RUN AT LOW SPEED WITH THE SWITCH IN THE HIGH SPEED POSITION

1. Check for a faulty **HI-LO** wiper relay.
- If faulty, replace the relay.
- If OK, go to Step 2.

2. Using an ohmmeter, check for an open circuit between terminal **C** of the **HI-LO** wiper relay and terminal **18** of the body controller 24–way connector.
- If OK, go to Step 3.
- If open circuit is found; repair as necessary.

3. Check the wiper switch.

MOTOR WILL KEEP RUNNING WITH THE SWITCH IN THE OFF POSITION

1. Check the wiper motor wiring harness for shorts between the low speed motor feed terminal **3** or high speed motor feed terminal **2** and the battery or ignition switch.
- If short is found, repair it.
- If OK, go to Step 2.

2. Check for a faulty **HI-LO** or intermittent relay.
- If faulty, replace the relay.
- If OK, go to Step 3.

3. Check the circuit from terminal **C** of the intermittent relay and terminal **B** of the **HI-LO** relay to the battery or ignition.
- If no voltage is found at the relay, repair the short.
- If OK, go to Step 4.

4. Disconnect the connector from the body controller. Check the circuit from terminal **1** of the connector to terminal **C** of the intermittent wiper relay for a short to ground.
- If short is found, repair the circuit.
- If OK, go to Step 5.

5. Using a voltmeter, connect the positive lead to terminal **16** of the body controller connector. Connect the negative lead to ground.
- If the voltmeter reads greater than 0 volts, check the wiper switch and wiring.
- If no voltage is found, go to Step 6.

6. Using a voltmeter, connect the positive lead to terminal **10** of the body controller connector.

- If the voltmeter reads 10–15 volts, check the circuit for a short to the battery or ignition.
- If the voltmeter reads 0 volts, replace the body controller.

WIPERS WILL RUN CONTINUOUSLY WITH THE SWITCH IN THE INTERMITTENT POSITION; WHEN THE SWITCH IS TURNED OFF, WIPERS STOP WHEREVER THEY ARE WITHOUT GOING TO THE PARK POSITION

1. Check for ground at the wiper motor wire connector terminal **4**.
2. Using an ohmmeter, with the wiper motor in the **PARK** position, check for continuity between terminal **1** and terminal **4** of the motor connector.
- If OK, go to Step 3.
- If no continuity is found; replace the wiper motor.
3. Check for continuity between terminal **1** of the wiper motor harness connector and terminal **2** of the body controller connector.
- If continuity is not found, check for a short between the battery or ignition feed in the circuit.

WIPERS DO NOT OPERATE WHEN THE WASHER MOTOR IS ENGAGED

1. Disconnect the connector from the body controller.
2. Using a voltmeter, connect the positive lead to terminal **10** of the body controller connector.
3. Engage the washer switch so the washer motor runs continuously.
- If voltage is 0, check the wiring between the washer motor and the body controller.
- If the voltage is 10–15 volts, replace the body controller.

TESTING

Intermittent Wiper Switch Test

❄❄ CAUTION

If equipped with the air bag restraint system, follow the manufacturer's instructions when removing the steering wheel or column.

Disconnect the wires from the body wiring in the steering column. Using an ohmmeter, test for continuity between the terminals of the switch. For test purposes, the 1st position is the **OFF** position, the

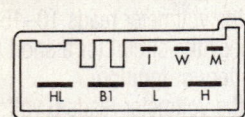

SWITCH POSITION		TERMINALS	RESISTANCE VALUE
OFF		PIN I to M	OPEN ≥ 300 K OHMS
DELAY LEVEL	1	PIN I to M	9.72 K OHMS
	2	PIN I to M	8.22 K OHMS
	3	PIN I to M	6.61 K OHMS
	4	PIN I to M	5.12 K OHMS
	5	PIN I to M	3.67 K OHMS
	6	PIN I to M	2.22 K OHMS
LOW		PIN I to M	1.02 K OHMS
HIGH		PIN I to M	0.51 K OHMS
WASH		PIN I to W	OPEN
RESISTANCE AT MAXIMUM DELAY POSITION SHOULD BE			9,720 K OHMS
RESISTANCE AT MINIMUM DELAY POSITION SHOULD BE			2,220 K OHMS

8470V015

Intermittent wiper switch testing—Concorde, Intrepid, and Vision

next 6 are for the delay wiping, 7th is the **LOW** position and 8th is the **HIGH** position. In any wiping mode, if the knob is pushed all the way in, the washer circuit will be completed.

REMOVAL & INSTALLATION

Washer Reservoir and Pump

1. Disconnect the hose from the washer pump and drain the system.
2. Disconnect the negative and positive battery cables.
3. Remove the battery heat shield, battery and tray.
4. Remove the 2 mounting nuts and the screw retaining the reservoir.
5. Disconnect the electrical connectors from the pump and float sensor.
6. Remove the reservoir.
7. Pry the pump away from the reservoir and out of the grommet.

Care must be taken not to puncture the reservoir.

To install:

8. Installation is the reverse of the removal procedure.
9. Torque the mounting nuts and the screw to 80–124 inch lbs. (9–14 Nm).

Washer Fluid Level Sensor

1. Raise and support the vehicle safely.
2. Disconnect the electrical connector from the sensor.
3. Press the sensor lock upwards and remove the sensor.

➡ **There will be no fluid loss because there is no hole in the housing.**

To install:

4. Clean the connector and seal.

5. Slide the sensor in until it locks.
6. Connect the electrical connector.

Neon

GENERAL DESCRIPTION

The windshield wipers will only operate with the ignition switch in the **ACC** or **IGN** position. A fuse, located in the fuse block and a circuit breaker located in the wiper motor, protects the circuitry of the wiper system and the vehicle.

The wiper motor has permanent magnet fields. The speeds are determined by current flow to the appropriate set of brushes.

The intermittent wiper system (if equipped), in addition to low and high speed, has a delay mode. The delay mode has a range of 1–15 seconds. Pulse wipe is accomplished by momentarily moving the stalk lever into the **WASH** position while the wiper switch is in either **OFF** or **DELAY** positions.

The intermittent wiper function is integral to the wiper switch. All electronics and relay are contained within the switch assembly. The wiper system completes the wipe cycle when the switch is turned **OFF**. The blades park in the lowest portion of the wiping pattern.

TROUBLESHOOTING

Wiper and Washer System

WIPER MOTOR WILL NOT RUN IN ANY SWITCH POSITION

1. Check fuse **15** in the fuse block.
   - If the fuse(s) are good, go to Step 2.
   - If the fuse(s) are defective, replace them and check the wiper motor operation in all switch positions.
   - If the motor is still inoperative and fuses do not blow, go to Step 2.
   - If the fuse blows, go to Step 10.

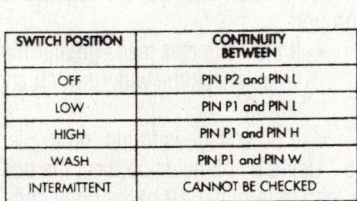

SWITCH POSITION	CONTINUITY BETWEEN
OFF	PIN P2 and PIN L
LOW	PIN P1 and PIN L
HIGH	PIN P1 and PIN H
WASH	PIN P1 and PIN W
INTERMITTENT	CANNOT BE CHECKED

8838XG05

Wiper motor wire harness connector—Neon

2. Disconnect the wiper motor connector.
3. Check the wiper motor low speed. Connect a jumper wire from the positive battery terminal to terminal **2** of the motor connector. Connect a 2nd jumper wire from ground to motor ground strap. Check the wiper motor high speed. Connect the positive wire to **1** and other to ground strap.
   - If motor runs; go to Step 5.
   - If motor does not run in high or low speed, go to Step 4.
4. Using an ohmmeter, check for a good ground at the ground strap connector.
   - If OK, replace the motor.
   - If not, repair the ground as necessary.
5. Using an ohmmeter, check at terminal **E** and ground for continuity. If OK, go to next Step. If not OK, repair ground circuit.
6. Using a voltmeter, with the switch connected, connect a negative lead to motor ground and connect positive lead to terminal **P1** of the switch connector.
   - If no voltage, repair wiring.
   - If OK, go to next step.
7. Check switch low speed by connecting voltmeter positive lead to terminal **L** of switch connector. Move stalk to **LOW**. If no voltage, replace switch.
8. Check switch high speed by connecting voltmeter positive lead to terminal **H** of switch connector. Move stalk to **HIGH**. If no voltage, replace switch.
9. Disconnect motor connector and replace fuse 15.
   - If fuse does not blow, replace motor.
   - If fuse blows, disconnect switch and replace fuse. If fuse does not blow, replace switch. If fuse blows, repair wiring.

MOTOR RUNS SLOWLY AT ALL SPEEDS

Disconnect the wiper motor connector from the motor. Remove the wiper arms and blades. Disconnect the wiper motor drive

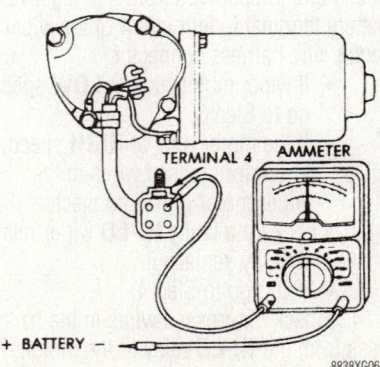

Wiper motor ammeter testing—Neon

link from the motor. Connect an ammeter from the positive battery terminal to terminal **4** of the wiper motor connector. Connect a ground wire from to ground strap.

• If the wiper motor runs and the average ammeter reading is more than 6 amps, check the high and low circuits for a short to ground.

• If the wiper motor runs and the average ammeter reading is less than 6 amps, check to see if the linkage is not binding.

MOTOR WILL RUN AT HIGH SPEED WITH SWITCH IN LOW SPEED POSITION, OR WIPERS RUN AT LOW SPEED WITH SWITCH IN HIGH SPEED POSITION

Check for crossed wires in the motor pigtail or switch connectors.

WIPERS WILL OPERATE CONTINUOUSLY WITH SWITCH IN THE INTERMITTENT POSITION; WHEN WIPER SWITCH IS TURNED OFF, WIPERS STOP WHEREVER THEY ARE, WITHOUT RETURNING TO PARK POSITION

1. Check motor ground strap connection.
2. Turn the ignition **OFF**. Using an ohmmeter, with the motor in **PARK** position, check for continuity between terminal **3** and ground strap. If continuity, replace switch. If no continuity, repair wiring.

WIPERS DO NOT OPERATE WHEN WASHER MOTOR IS ENGAGED, OR WIPERS DO NOT OPERATE IN INTERMITTENT POSITION

1. 2-speed wiper—check for ground at motor strap. If OK, replace switch.

2. Intermittent wiper—check for ground at motor strap and terminal **E** of switch. If OK, replace switch. If not, repair wiring.

TESTING

Intermittent Wiper Switch Test

❊❊ CAUTION

If equipped with the air bag restraint system, follow the manufacturer's instructions when removing the steering wheel or column.

Disconnect the wires from the body wiring in the steering column. Using an ohmmeter, test for continuity between the terminals of the switch.

REMOVAL & INSTALLATION

Washer Reservoir and Pump

1. Disconnect the hose from the washer pump and drain the system.
2. Disconnect the negative and positive battery cables.
3. Remove the mounting nuts and the screw retaining the reservoir.
4. Disconnect the electrical connectors from the pump.
   Care must be taken not to puncture the reservoir.
5. Remove the reservoir.
6. Pry the pump away from the reservoir and out of the grommet.

To install:

7. Installation is the reverse of the removal procedure.

8. Torque the mounting screws to 20–29 inch lbs. (2–3 Nm).

Wiper Switch

1. Disconnect the negative battery cable and wait 90 seconds.
2. Remove the upper half of steering column shroud.
3. Remove mounting screw and switch. Disconnect the harness.
4. Installation is the reverse of removal.

Wiper Module

1. Disconnect the negative battery cable and wait 90 seconds.
2. Remove the wiper arms and blades.
3. Remove the rear hood seal with cowl top plastic screen.
4. Disconnect the motor connector and remove the mounting screws and module.
5. Installation is the reverse of removal. Torque the screws to 60–80 inch lbs. (7–9 Nm).

Wiper Motor

1. Disconnect the negative battery cable and wait 90 seconds.
2. Remove the wiper module assembly as previously outlined.
3. Remove the linkage from motor crank. Insert suitable prybar between crank and linkage then twist and lift straight up.
4. Installation is the reverse of removal. Add Unilube®grease to the socket. Torque the motor screws to 45–55 inch lbs. (5–6 Nm) and drive link nut to 98–106 inch lbs. (11–12 Nm).

FORD MOTOR COMPANY

Wiper and Washer System

GENERAL DESCRIPTION

Continental, Crown Victoria, Grand Marquis, Mark VIII, Taurus, Town Car and Sable, Cougar, Mustang and Thunderbird

The wiper motor is located under the wiper assembly. A drive link connects the motor directly to the lever of the right hand pivot shaft.

The 2-speed, permanent magnet, 3 brush electric windshield wiper motor has

a brush rigging that permits a selection of low or high speeds. When the control lever is in the **LO** position, the common brush and blue/orange wire brushes are used. When the control lever is in the **HI** position, the common brush and white wire brushes are used. Current bypasses a portion of the armature winding, causing the motor to run faster. When the control lever is moved to the **OFF** position, the motor will continue to run at low speed until the motor switch outer contacts open, signaling the motor to park and activates the depressed park mechanism which is part of the output arm.

Escort, Tempo, Tracer and Topaz

The wiper motor is located under the wiper assembly. A drive link connects the motor directly to the lever of the right hand pivot shaft.

The 2-speed, permanent magnet, 3 brush electric windshield wiper motor has a brush rigging that permits a selection of low or high speeds. When the control lever is in the **LO** position, the common brush and the white wire brushes are used. When the control lever is in the **HI** position, the common brush and blue/orange wire brushes are used. Current bypasses a portion of the armature winding, causing the motor to run faster. When the control lever is moved to the **OFF** position, the motor will continue to run at low speed until the motor switch grounds the low speed brush, stopping the motor in the park position.

Aspire and Probe

The windshield wipers are operated by an electric motor mounted in the left rear corner of the engine compartment. The motor is attached to an access plate that is in turn attached to the dash panel. To prevent metal-to-metal contact and transmissions to the body, the motor is mounted on rubber insulators.

The rotary motion of the motor is transferred to the wiper arms through a linkage and pivot assembly. The wiper arm pivots

extend through the cowl sheet metal and are held in position with attaching nuts. The ends of the pivot shafts are serrated and cone shaped to prevent the wiper arm from slipping on the shaft.

DIAGNOSTIC TESTING

• On all vehicles, when trouble shooting the wiper system, test the motor first, then work back towards the switch to test the interval governor or module (depending on the vehicle), power circuits and the switch itself.

• In most of the tests, a volt-ohmmeter is required, although a test light can also be useful. For testing the motor, a 0–15 amp DC ammeter is required.

• When the test calls for a voltage

check, the ignition switch must be in the **ON** position.

• When testing for continuity or resistance values, turn the ignition switch to the **OFF** position and/or disconnect the negative battery cable.

• Improper or careless testing can cause permanent damage to the vehicle's electronic circuits and to test equipment. Carefully follow the test equipment manufacturer's instructions.

TESTING

Wiper Motor Operation

EXCEPT ASPIRE AND PROBE

The motors in these vehicles contain permanent magnets made of ceramic, which

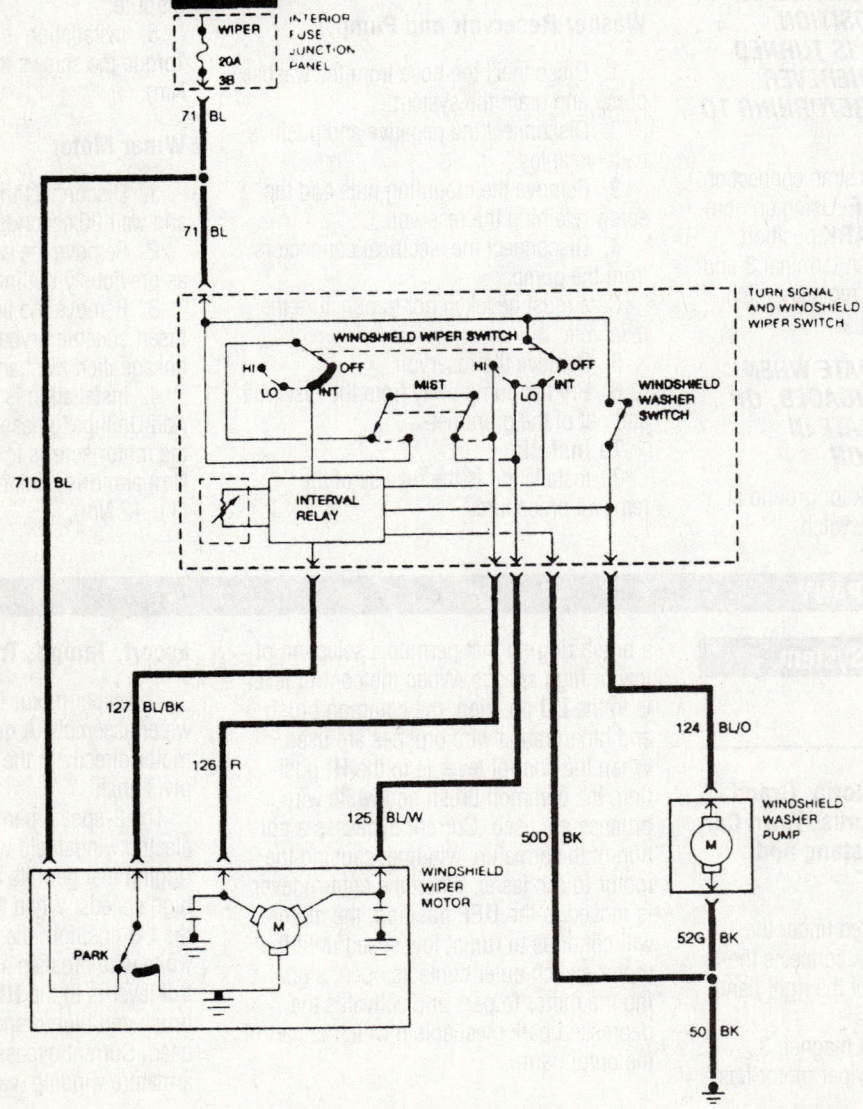

Wiper/washer schematic (interval wipers)—Probe

8838XG18

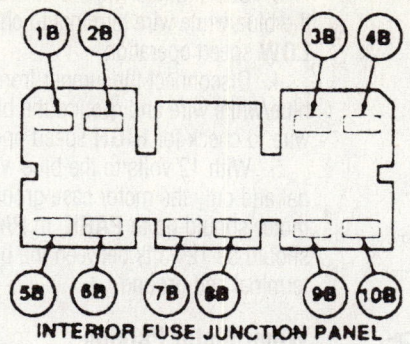

INTERIOR FUSE JUNCTION PANEL

Pin	Circuit	Circuit Function
1B	42 (BK/GN)	START/ON Power
2B	40 (BK/W)	START/ON Power
3B	71 (BL)	ON Power
4B	73 (BL/BK)	ACC/ON Power
5B	303 (BL/Y)	Ignition Key Reminder Switch Signal
6B	304 (PK)	Ignition/Door Lock Cylinder Illumination Ground
7B	80 (O)	Instrument Illumination Power
8B	117 (GN/W)	Right Front Turn Signal Lamp
9B	116 (GN/BK)	Left Front Turn Signal Lamp
10B	84G (BL/R)	Hot At All Times Power

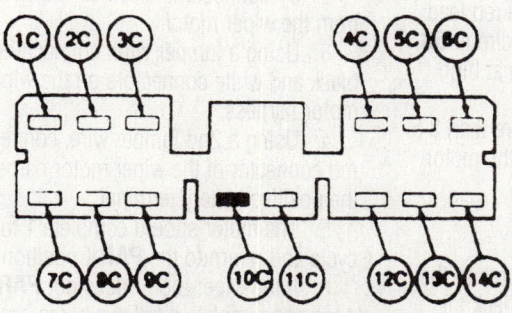

INTERIOR FUSE JUNCTION PANEL

Pin	Circuit	Circuit Function
1C	117 (GN/W)	Right Rear Turn Signal
2C	80 (O)	Instrument Illumination Power
3C	116 (GN/BK)	Left Rear Turn Signal
4C	41E (BK/Y)	START/ON Power
5C	73 (BL/BK)	ACC/ON Power
6C	307 (BR/BK)	Safety Belt Warning Indicator
7C	31 (BL/W)	ACC/ON Power
8C	85 (GN/R)	Hot At All Times Power
9C	81 (BR)	Hot At All Times Power
10C	—	NOT USED

Wiper/washer connector description—Probe

Pin	Circuit	Circuit Function
11C	84D (BL/R)	Hot At All Times Power
12C	70 (BL/GN)	ON Power
13C	300A (R/W)	Door Ajar Warning Indicator
14C	108 (R/BK)	Backup Lamps

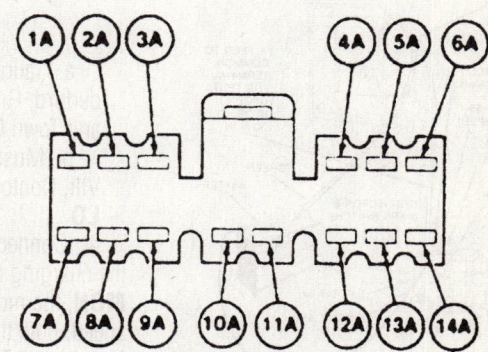

TURN SIGNAL AND WINDSHIELD WIPER SWITCH

Pin	Circuit	Circuit Function
1A	84J (BL/R)	Ignition Switch Lock Cylinder Illumination Power
2A	79 (LG)	Parking Lamp Relay Control
3A	50C (BK)	Headlamp Switch Ground
4A	127 (BL/BK)	Intermittent Mode Output
5A	124 (BL/O)	Windshield Washer Pump Output
6A	115 (GN/R)	Hazard Flasher Switch Power
7A	304 (PK)	Ignition Switch Lock Cylinder Illumination Control
8A	262 (W/R)	Headlamp Switch Power
9A	42 (BK/GN)	Turn Signal Switch Power
10A	50D (BK)	Windshield Wiper/Washer Switch Ground
11A	71 (BL)	Windshield Wiper/Washer Switch Power
12A	126 (R)	High-Speed Output
13A	125 (BL/W)	Low-Speed Output
14A	50F (BK)	Hazard Flasher Switch Ground

8838XG19

can shatter like glass if the motor is dropped or hit with a hammer. When removing the wiper motor, handle with care.

1. Remove the wiper motor linkage and electrical connectors from the windshield wiper motor.

➡ **If the electrical connector is not accessible, the motor may need to be removed.**

2. Using a suitable charging tester, connect the power lead of the tester to the positive battery terminal.

3. Connect a jumper wire from the negative battery terminal to the circuit as follows:

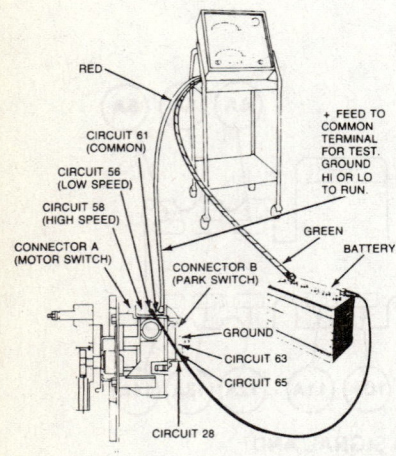

Wiper motor testing—Type C—Cougar and Thunderbird, Crown Victoria, Grand Marquis, Sable, Taurus, and Town Car

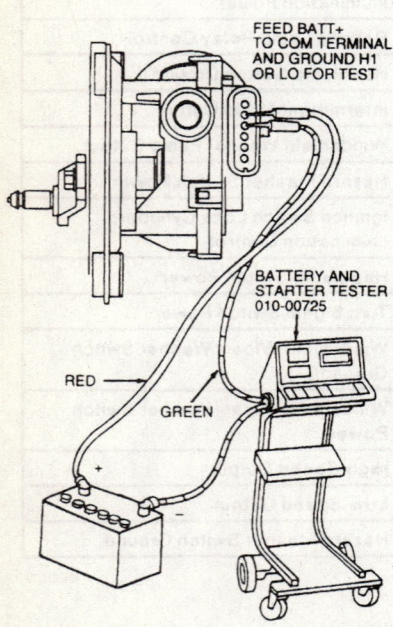

Wiper motor testing—Type E—Continental, Mark VIII and Mustang

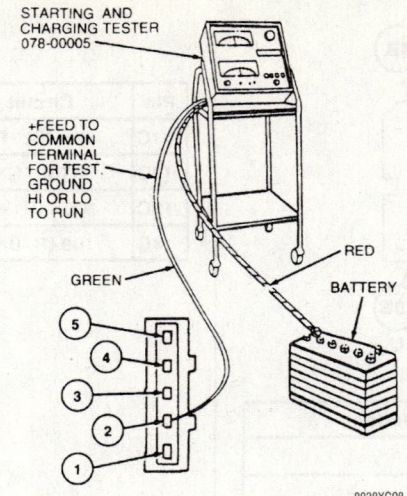

Wiper motor testing—Type F—Contour and Mystique

   a. Taurus, Sable, Cougar and Thunderbird, Grand Marquis, Crown Victoria, and Town Car—**61**

   b. Mustang and Continental, Mark VIII, Contour and Mystique—**HI or LO**

4. Connect the other power lead from the charging tester to circuit **56** or **COMMON**, the motor should operating at low speed, note the draw. Remove the red lead from circuit **56** and connect it to circuit **58**, the motor should begin operating at high speed, note the draw.

5. The draw should be no more than 3.5 amps at either speed. Repairs to the motor itself are not possible.

PROBE

Connect the 12 volt power source to the motor electrical connections to check for proper motor operation. Repairs to the motor itself are not possible.

ASPIRE

On this motor, the blue wire is a common 12 volts and is powered whenever the ignition switch is **ON**. The blue/white and blue/red wires are ground circuits for the low and high speeds. The blue/black wire connects to the motor's internal park switch and, when the wipers are in the **PARK** position, should have continuity with the blue wire terminal on the motor to feed 12 volts to the wiper switch.

1. To test the motor, turn the ignition switch **OFF** and unplug the wiper motor connector.

2. Carefully use a jumper wire to feed 12 volts to the blue wire terminal on the motor plug.

3. Use a jumper wire to carefully ground the blue/white wire terminal to check for **LOW** speed operation.

4. Disconnect the jumper from the blue/white wire and ground the blue/red wire to check for **HIGH** speed operation.

5. With 12 volts to the blue wire terminal and only the motor case grounded, the motor should go to **PARK**. In **PARK**, there should be 12 volts between the blue/black terminal and ground.

Wiper Motor Parking

EXCEPT ESCORT, MARK VIII, CONTINENTAL, MUSTANG, CONTOUR AND MYSTIQUE

1. Connect a jumper wire from the positive battery terminal to terminal 63.

2. Connect terminals **G1** and **G2** to a suitable body ground with jumper wires.

3. The wipers should complete 1 cycle and return to **PARK**.

4. If the wipers do not **PARK**, replace the motor.

ESCORT

1. Stop the wipers, when they are not in the **PARK** position, by turning the ignition switch to the **OFF** position.

2. Disconnect the electrical connector from the wiper motor.

3. Using a jumper wire, connect the black and white connectors on the wiper motor harness.

4. Using a 2nd jumper wire, connect the red connector of the wiper motor harness to the positive battery terminal.

5. The motor should complete 1 full cycle and return to the **PARK** position.

6. If the wiper motor does not **PARK** or does not complete a full cycle, replace the motor.

MARK VIII, CONTINENTAL AND MUSTANG

1. Unplug connector at motor and check ground circuit 57 (**BLK**).

2. Turn ignition switch to **RUN** and multi-function switch **OFF**. Check battery voltage between circuits 65 (**DARK GREEN**) and 57 (**BLK**) at the motor connector. Should be voltage.

3. With multi-function switch **OFF**, check for continuity between circuit 28 (**BK/PK**) and 56 (**DB/O**) and circuits 61 (**Y/R**) and 63 ® or 57 (**BK**) from the motor-to-wiper control module. If present, replace the wiper control module.

4. Check that the mounting arm and pivot shaft and linkage is not bent, cracked or misaligned.

CONTOUR AND MYSTIQUE

1. With wiper and ignition switch **OFF**, check for short to ground at motor harness circuit **32 (W/BK)** and ground. Resistance should be greater then 10K ohms.

2. Disconnect fuse junction panel connector **K**. Check for open in circuit **32** between wiper connector pin 4 and fuse panel connector pin **K4**. The resistance should be less than 3 ohms.

3. Measure circuit **14 (P)** resistance between wiper motor connector pin 5 and fuse panel connector pin **K8**. Resistance should be less than 3 ohms.

4. Remove the central timer module from fuse panel. Measure resistance from timer module pin S13 and fuse panel connector pin **K4**. Resistance should be less than 1 ohm.

5. Connect fuse panel connector **K**. Turn ignition switch to **RUN** and measure voltage at motor connector pin 5. Should be voltage.

6. With ignition in **RUN** position, measure voltage between motor connector pins **3** and **5**. Should be battery voltage.

7. The resistance through motor connector pin **3** and **5** should be 3 ohms or less.

Circuit Breaker

Some vehicles have an 8.25 amp circuit breaker located in the fuse panel. Two separate tests are necessary to check for correct circuit breaker operation.

1. Remove the circuit breaker from the fuse panel.

2. Using a suitable volt-amp tester, touch the test leads together and adjust the current draw until it equals the circuit breaker rating.

3. Connect the test leads to the circuit breaker, hold the current reading on the ammeter at the rated current and leave it connected for 10 minutes.

4. If the circuit breaker opens during the 10 minutes, replace the circuit breaker.

5. Touch the testers leads together and adjust the current draw until it is twice the rated current.

6. Connect the circuit breaker to the tester and hold the current rating on twice the rated current.

7. The current reading on the ammeter should drop to 0 within 30 seconds.

8. If it takes longer than 30 seconds for the ammeter to drop to 0 (circuit breaker to open), replace the circuit breaker.

Washer Pump Draw

1. Connect a suitable volt-amp tester to the washer pump.

2. Run the washer pump using the column switch.

3. The current draw should not exceed 4 amps nor indicate below 2 amps while in use.

Wiper Switch

On all vehicles, the switch can be tested independently using a powered test light to

TO TEST	Connect Self-Powered Test Lamp or Ohmmeter to Terminals	Move Switch to These Positions	A Good Switch Will Indicate
Wiper Speed "LO"	C225 (Pin J) and C225 (Pin N)	Off Lo Hi	Open Circuit Open Circuit Closed Circuit
Wiper Speed "HI"	C225 (Pin J) and C225 (Pin L)	Off Lo Hi	Open Circuit Closed Circuit Open Circuit
Park Switch Circuit	C225 (Pin N) and C225 (Pin K)	Off Lo Hi	Closed Circuit Open Circuit Open Circuit

```
 O  M  K      ▯     E  C  A
 ⊠  ⊠  ⊠   ▯  ▯  ▯  ⊠  ⊠  ⊠
 P  N  L      J  H     F  D  B
 ⊠  ⊠  ⊠   ▯  ⊠  ⊠  ⊠  ⊠  ⊠
```

Wiper switch test—Probe

TO TEST	Connect Self-Powered Test Lamp or Ohmmeter to Terminals	Move Switch to These Positions	A Good Switch Will Indicate
Wiper Speed "LO"	C225 (Pin J) and C225 (Pin N)	Off Int Lo Hi	Open Circuit Open Circuit Closed Circuit Open Circuit
Wiper Speed "HI"	C225 (Pin J) and C225 (Pin L)	Off Int Lo Hi	Open Circuit Open Circuit Open Circuit Closed Circuit
Park Switch Circuit	C225 (Pin N) and C225 (Pin K)	Off Int Lo Hi	Closed Circuit Closed Circuit Open Circuit Open Circuit
"MIST" Circuit	C225 (Pin J) and C225 (Pin L)	Mist Switch On Mist Switch Off	Closed Circuit Open Circuit

8470V026

TO TEST	Connect Self-Powered Test Light or Ohmmeter to Terminals	Move Switch to These Positions	A Good Switch Will Indicate
Washer Switch Circuit	590, 590 (DB/W) and 993, 993 (BR/W)	With Wiper Switch OFF: Push washer switch in Release washer switch	Closed Circuit 103.3K ohm
Wiper Switch Circuit	589, 589 (O) and 993, 993 (BR/W)	OFF INT LO HI	47.6K ohm 11.33K ohm 4.08K ohm Closed Circuit
Interval Time Adjust	590, 590 (DB/W) and 993, 993 (BR/W)	INT and OFF	Rotate Control toward OFF; Ohmmeter will show smoothly increasing resistance from 3.3K ohm min. to 103.3K ohm max.
		LO and HI	3.3K ohm

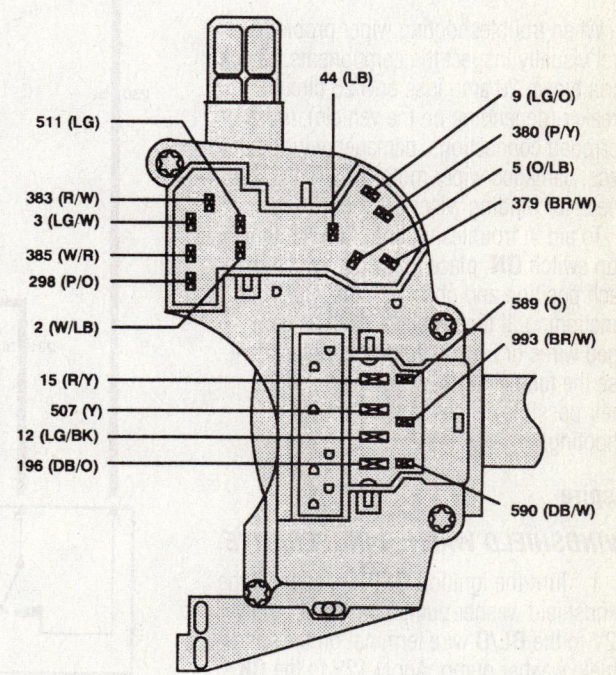

Wiper switch test—Continental, Crown Victoria, Grand Marquis, Mark VIII, Sable, Taurus, Mustang and Town Car

8470V020

Please visit our web site at www.chiltononline.com

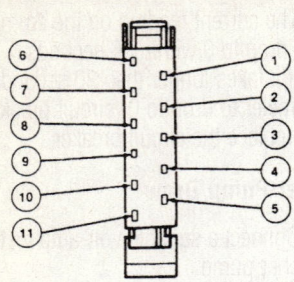

WINDSHIELD WIPER SWITCH CONNECTOR

Pin Number	Circuit	Circuit Function
1	32 (W/GN)	Wiper Motor Low Speed Output
2	32 (W/BK)	Wiper Motor High Speed Output
3	—	Not Used
4	32 (W/BK)	Wiper Motor Intermittent Timer Input
5	8 (W/BK)	Wiper Motor Intermittent Timer Reference Signal
6	8 (W)	Wiper Motor Intermittent Timer Signal
7	—	Not Used
8	14 (P/O)	Switch Supply
9	33 (Y/BK)	Washer Timer Input
10	31 (BK)	Ground
11	14 (P·W)	Washer Motor Output

8838XG09

Wiper switch test—Contour and Mystique

check for continuity. Interval systems must be tested with an ohmmeter. Locate the correct schematic and follow the switch testing procedure indicated. A defective switch or interval governor cannot be repaired and must be replaced.

MALFUNCTION CHART

When troubleshooting wiper problems, first visually inspect the components. Check for a blown 20 amp fuse or 8.25 circuit breaker (depending on the vehicle), loose or corroded connections, damaged wiring harness, damaged wiper motor or switch. Also check for binding wiper arms or linkage.

To aid in troubleshooting, turn the ignition switch **ON**, place the wiper switch in each position and observe if the wiper is functioning. If the problem, such as damaged wires or broken linkage is not evident, use the following list of conditions with their possible causes to start troubleshooting.

Aspire

WINDSHIELD WASHER INOPERATIVE

1. Turn the ignition **OFF**. Disconnect the windshield washer pump connector. Apply 12V to the **BL/O** wire terminal on the windshield washer pump. Apply 12V to the **BK** wire terminal on the windshield washer pump.

   a. If the windshield washer pump operates, go to Step 2.

   b. If the windshield washer pump does not operate, replace the windshield washer pump.

2. Turn the ignition **OFF**. Disconnect the windshield washer pump connector. Measure resistance of **BK** wire between the windshield washer pump connector and ground.

   a. If the resistance is less than 5 ohms, go to Step 3.

   b. If the resistance is greater than 5 ohms, service the **BK** wire.

3. Turn the ignition **OFF**. Disconnect the turn signal/windshield wiper switch connector.

   a. Measure resistance of the following wire terminals of the turn signal/windshield wiper switch under the following conditions:

- With the switch in the **OFF** position, the resistance of terminals 1-to-5 should be less than 5 ohms.
- With the switch in the **INT** position, the resistance of terminals 1-to-5 should be less than 5 ohms.
- With the switch in the **LO** position, the resistance of terminals 15-to-5 should be less than 5 ohms.
- With the switch in the **HIGH** position, the resistance of terminals 15-to-4 should be less than 5 ohms.
- With the switch in the **MIST** position, the resistance of terminals 15-to-4 should be less than 5 ohms.
- With the switch in the **WASH** position, the resistance of terminals 15-to-3 should be less than 5 ohms.

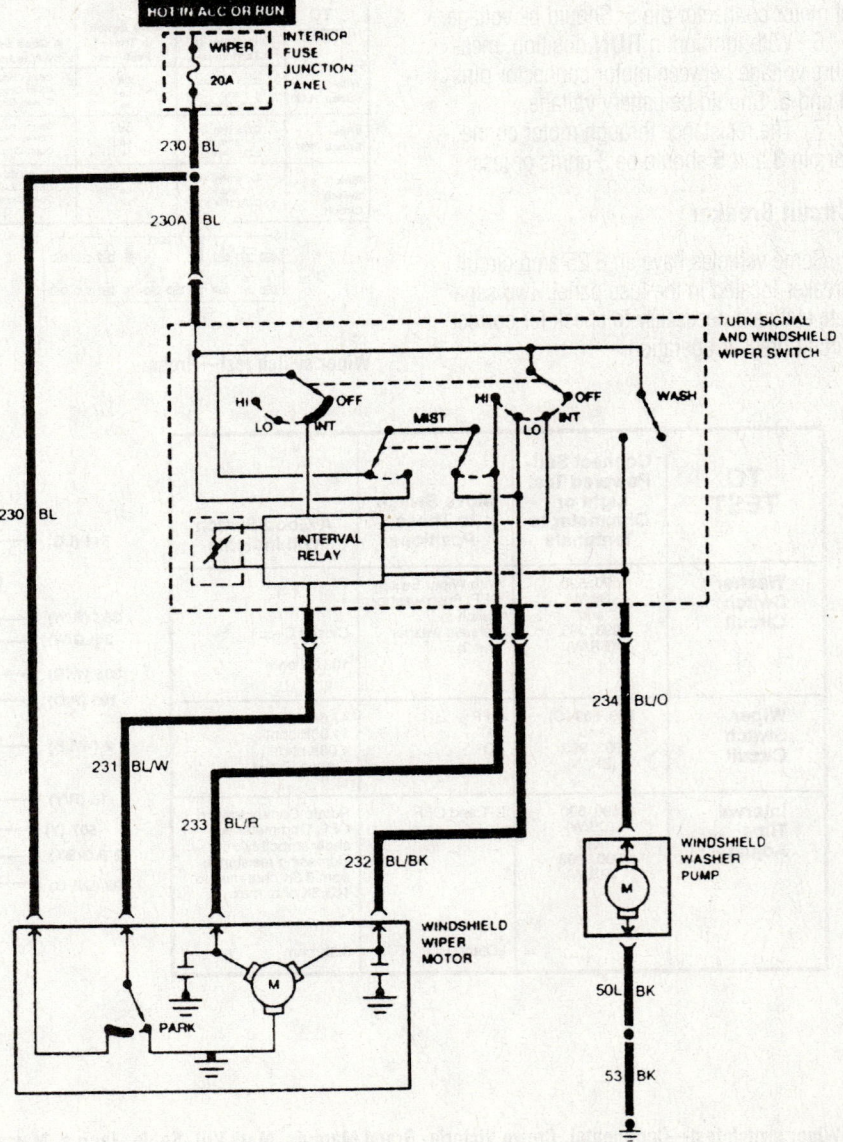

Electrical schematic—Front wiper/washer system (with interval function)—Aspire

8838XG10

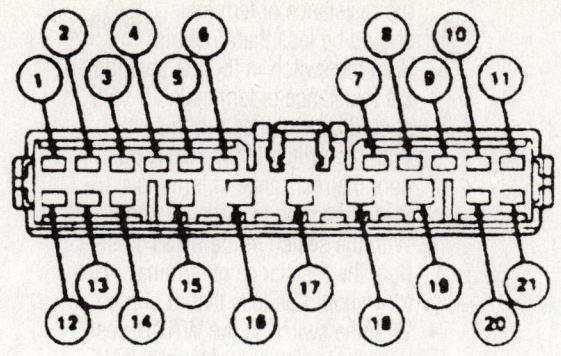

**TURN SIGNAL AND WINDSHIELD
WIPER SWITCH**

Pin	Circuit	Circuit Function
1	231 (BL - W)	Windshield Wiper Motor Park Input
2	500 (BK)	Ground
3	234 (BL - O)	Windshield Washer Motor Output
4	233 (BL / R)	High Speed Wiper Output
5	232 (BL / BK)	Low Speed Wiper Output
6	50K (BK)	Ground
7	367 (GN)	Left Turn Signal Output
8	368 (Y)	Right Turn Signal Output
9	160H (BK / Y)	Power Supply
10	13 (R - W)	Parking Lamp Relay Control

Pin	Circuit	Circuit Function
11	388 (O)	Hazard Flasher Switch Output
12	227 (BL / Y)	Rear Window Washer Motor Control
13	50E (BK)	Ground
14	226 (BK / BL)	Rear Window Wiper Motor Control
15	230A (BL)	ACC / ON Power
16	12 (R / GN)	Headlamp Relay Input
17	7 (R)	Hot At All Times Power
18	281 (R / W)	High Beam Output
19	282 (R / BL)	Low Beam Output
20	11 (R / BL)	Headlamp Relay Control
21	50V (BK)	Ground

8838XG11

Wiper switch connector description—Aspire

- The resistance of all other terminals not listed under the conditions should be greater than 10,000 ohms.
b. If the switch's resistance requirements are:
- Okay, service the **BL/O** wire.
- Not okay, replace the turn signal/windshield wiper switch.

REAR WINDOW WASHER INOPERATIVE

1. Turn the ignition **OFF**. Disconnect the rear window washer pump connector. Apply 12V to the **BL/GN** wire terminal on the rear window washer pump. Apply ground to the **BL/Y** wire terminal on the rear window washer pump.
a. If the windshield washer pump operates, go to Step 2.
b. If the windshield washer pump does not operate, replace the rear window washer pump.
2. Turn the ignition **OFF**. Disconnect the rear window washer pump connector. Turn

the ignition **ON**. Measure the voltage on the **BL/GN** wire at the rear window washer pump connector. Apply ground to the **BL/Y** wire terminal on the rear window washer pump.
a. If the voltage is greater than 10 volts, go to Step 3.
b. If the voltage is less than 10 volts, service the **BL/GN** wire.
3. Turn the ignition **OFF**. Disconnect the turn signal/windshield wiper switch connector.
a. Measure the resistance between the **BL/Y** and **BK** wire terminals on the turn signal/windshield wiper switch connector under the following conditions:
- With the switch in the **ON** position, the resistance should be less than 5 ohms.
- With the switch in the **OFF** position, the resistance should be greater than 10,000 ohms.
b. Measure the resistance between the **BL/Y** and **BK** wire terminals on the turn signal/windshield wiper switch connector under the following conditions:

- If the resistances meet specifications, go to Step 4.
- If the resistances do not meet specifications, replace the turn signal/windshield wiper switch.
4. Turn the ignition **OFF**. Disconnect the turn signal/windshield wiper switch connector. Measure the resistance between the **BK** wire terminal between the turn signal/windshield wiper switch connector and ground:
a. If the resistance is less than 5 ohms, service the **BL/Y** wire terminal between the rear window washer pump and the turn signal/windshield wiper switch.
b. If the resistance is greater than 5 ohms, service the **BK** wire.

WINDSHIELD WIPERS INOPERATIVE IN ALL SWITCH POSITIONS

1. Turn the ignition **OFF**. In the interior fuse panel, check the **20A WIPER** fuse.
a. If the fuse is okay, go to Step 4.
b. If the fuse is not okay, go to Step 2.

For brake related suspension and axle service, refer to the model specific sections of this manual

2. Turn the ignition **OFF**. In the interior fuse panel, install the **20A WIPER** fuse. Turn the ignition **ON**.

   a. If the fuse is okay, go to Step 4.

   b. If the fuse is not okay, go to Step 3.

3. Turn the ignition **OFF**. Remove the **20A WIPER** fuse. Disconnect the windshield wiper motor connector and the turn signal/windshield wiper switch connector. Measure the resistance of the **BL** wire between the bottom terminal of the **20A WIPER** fuse holder and ground:

   a. If the resistance is less than 5 ohms, service the **BL** wire.

   b. If the resistance is greater than 5 ohms, replace the **20A WIPER** fuse and go the Step 4.

4. Turn the ignition **OFF**. Disconnect the windshield wiper motor connector and the turn signal/windshield wiper switch connector. Turn the ignition **ON**. Measure the voltage of the **BL** wire at the windshield wiper motor connector and the turn signal/windshield wiper switch connector:

   a. If the voltage is less than 10 volts, service the **BL** wire.

   b. If the voltage is greater than 10 volts, go the Step 5.

5. Turn the ignition **OFF**. Disconnect the windshield wiper motor connector. Apply 12 volts to terminal **2** of the windshield wiper motor; the wiper should operate at low speed.

6. Apply 12 volts to terminal **1** of the windshield wiper motor; the wiper should operate at high speed.

   a. To check the interval park switch, measure the resistance between the wire terminals **3** and **4** of the windshield wiper motor, under the following conditions:

- With the wipers in the park position, the resistance should be less than 5 ohms.
- With the wipers not in the park position, the resistance should be greater than 10,000 ohms.

   b. If the windshield wiper motor test are:

- Okay, go to Step 7.
- Not okay, replace the windshield wiper motor.

7. Turn the ignition **OFF**. Disconnect the turn signal/windshield wiper switch connector.

   a. Measure resistance of the following wire terminals of the turn signal/windshield wiper switch under the following conditions:

- With the switch in the **OFF** position, the resistance of terminals 1-to-5 should be less than 5 ohms.
- With the switch in the **INT** position,

the resistance of terminals 1-to-5 should be less than 5 ohms.
- With the switch in the **LO** position, the resistance of terminals 15-to-5 should be less than 5 ohms.
- With the switch in the **HIGH** position, the resistance of terminals 15-to-4 should be less than 5 ohms.
- With the switch in the **MIST** position, the resistance of terminals 15-to-4 should be less than 5 ohms.
- With the switch in the **WASH** position, the resistance of terminals 15-to-3 should be less than 5 ohms.
- The resistance of all other terminals not listed under the conditions should be greater than 10,000 ohms.

   b. If the switch's resistance requirements are:

- Okay, service the **BL/W**, **BL/R** and/or **BL/BK** wires between the turn signal/windshield wiper switch and the windshield wiper motor.
- Not okay, replace the turn signal/windshield wiper switch.

WINDSHIELD WIPERS INOPERATIVE AT HIGH SPEED

1. Turn the ignition **OFF**. Disconnect the windshield wiper motor connector. Apply 12 volts to terminal **2** of the windshield wiper motor; the wiper should operate at low speed. Apply 12 volts to terminal **1** of the windshield wiper motor; the wiper should operate at high speed.

   a. To check the interval park switch, measure the resistance between the wire terminals **3** and **4** of the windshield wiper motor, under the following conditions:

- With the wipers in the park position, the resistance should be less than 5 ohms.
- With the wipers not in the park position, the resistance should be greater than 10,000 ohms.

   b. If the windshield wiper motor test are:

- Okay, go to Step 2.
- Not okay, replace the windshield wiper motor.

2. Turn the ignition **OFF**. Disconnect the turn signal/windshield wiper switch connector.

   a. Measure resistance of the following wire terminals of the turn signal/windshield wiper switch under the following conditions:

- With the switch in the **OFF** position, the resistance of terminals 1-to-5 should be less than 5 ohms.
- With the switch in the **INT** position,

the resistance of terminals 1-to-5 should be less than 5 ohms.
- With the switch in the **LO** position, the resistance of terminals 15-to-5 should be less than 5 ohms.
- With the switch in the **HIGH** position, the resistance of terminals 15-to-4 should be less than 5 ohms.
- With the switch in the **MIST** position, the resistance of terminals 15-to-4 should be less than 5 ohms.
- With the switch in the **WASH** position, the resistance of terminals 15-to-3 should be less than 5 ohms.
- The resistance of all other terminals not listed under the conditions should be greater than 10,000 ohms.

   b. If the switch's resistance requirements are:

- Okay, service the **BL/R** wire between the turn signal/windshield wiper switch and the windshield wiper motor.
- Not okay, replace the turn signal/windshield wiper switch.

WINDSHIELD WIPERS INOPERATIVE AT LOW SPEED

1. Turn the ignition **OFF**. Disconnect the windshield wiper motor connector. Apply 12 volts to terminal **2** of the windshield wiper motor; the wiper should operate at low speed. Apply 12 volts to terminal **1** of the windshield wiper motor; the wiper should operate at high speed.

   a. To check the interval park switch, measure the resistance between the wire terminals **3** and **4** of the windshield wiper motor, under the following conditions:

- With the wipers in the park position, the resistance should be less than 5 ohms.
- With the wipers not in the park position, the resistance should be greater than 10,000 ohms.

   b. If the windshield wiper motor test are:

- Okay, go to Step 2.
- Not okay, replace the windshield wiper motor.

2. Turn the ignition **OFF**. Disconnect the turn signal/windshield wiper switch connector.

   a. Measure resistance of the following wire terminals of the turn signal/windshield wiper switch under the following conditions;

- With the switch in the **OFF** position, the resistance of terminals 1-to-5 should be less than 5 ohms.
- With the switch in the **INT** position,

the resistance of terminals 1-to-5 should be less than 5 ohms.

- With the switch in the **LO** position, the resistance of terminals 15-to-5 should be less than 5 ohms.
- With the switch in the **HIGH** position, the resistance of terminals 15-to-4 should be less than 5 ohms.
- With the switch in the **MIST** position, the resistance of terminals 15-to-4 should be less than 5 ohms.
- With the switch in the **WASH** position, the resistance of terminals 15-to-3 should be less than 5 ohms.
- The resistance of all other terminals not listed under the conditions should be greater than 10,000 ohms.

b. If the switch's resistance requirements are:

- Okay, service the **BL/BK** wire between the turn signal/windshield wiper switch and the windshield wiper motor.
- Not okay, replace the turn signal/windshield wiper switch.

WINDSHIELD WIPERS WILL NOT PARK BELOW WINDSHIELD

1. Turn the ignition **OFF**. Disconnect the windshield wiper motor connector. Apply 12 volts to terminal **2** of the windshield wiper motor; the wiper should operate at low speed. Apply 12 volts to terminal **1** of the windshield wiper motor; the wiper should operate at high speed.

a. To check the interval park switch, measure the resistance between the wire terminals **3** and **4** of the windshield wiper motor, under the following conditions:

- With the wipers in the park position, the resistance should be less than 5 ohms.
- With the wipers not in the park position, the resistance should be greater than 10,000 ohms.

b. If the windshield wiper motor test are:

- Okay, go to Step 2.
- Not okay, replace the windshield wiper motor.

2. Turn the ignition **OFF**. Disconnect the turn signal/windshield wiper switch connector. Disconnect the windshield wiper motor connector. Measure resistance of the **BL/W** wire between the turn signal/windshield wiper switch connector and the windshield wiper motor connector.

a. If the resistance is less than 5 ohms, replace the turn signal/windshield wiper switch.

b. If the resistance is greater than 5 ohms, service the **BL/W** wire.

WINDSHIELD WIPERS WILL NOT TURN OFF

1. Turn the ignition **OFF**. Disconnect the turn signal/windshield wiper switch connector.

2. Measure resistance of the following wire terminals of the turn signal/windshield wiper switch under the following conditions:

- With the switch in the **OFF** position, the resistance of terminals 1-to-5 should be less than 5 ohms.
- With the switch in the **INT** position, the resistance of terminals 1-to-5 should be less than 5 ohms.
- With the switch in the **LO** position, the resistance of terminals 15-to-5 should be less than 5 ohms.
- With the switch in the **HIGH** position, the resistance of terminals 15-to-4 should be less than 5 ohms.
- With the switch in the **MIST** position, the resistance of terminals 15-to-4 should be less than 5 ohms.
- With the switch in the **WASH** position, the resistance of terminals 15-to-3 should be less than 5 ohms.
- The resistance of all other terminals not listed under the conditions should be greater than 10,000 ohms.

3. If the switch's resistance requirements are:

- Okay, replace the windshield wiper motor.
- Not okay, replace the turn signal/windshield wiper switch.

REAR WINDOW WIPER INOPERATIVE

1. Turn the ignition **OFF**. In the interior fuse panel, check the **15A R.WIPER** fuse.
    a. If the fuse is okay, go to Step 4.
    b. If the fuse is not okay, go to Step 2.

2. Turn the ignition **OFF**. In the interior fuse panel, install the **15A R.WIPER** fuse. Turn the ignition **ON**.
    a. If the fuse is okay, go to Step 4.
    b. If the fuse is not okay, go to Step 3.

3. Turn the ignition **OFF**. Remove the **15A WIPER** fuse. Disconnect the rear window wiper motor connector and the rear window washer motor connector. Measure the resistance of the **BL/GN** wire between the bottom terminal of the **15A R.WIPER** fuse holder and ground:
    a. If the resistance is less than 5 ohms, service the **BL/GN** wire.
    b. If the resistance is greater than 5

ohms, replace the **15A R.WIPER** fuse and go the Step 4.

4. Turn the ignition **OFF**. Disconnect the rear window wiper motor connector. Turn the ignition **ON**.

5. Measure the voltage of the **BL/GN** wire at the rear window wiper motor connector:
    a. If the voltage is less than 10 volts, service the **BL/GN** wire.
    b. If the voltage is greater than 10 volts, go the Step 5.

6. Turn the ignition **OFF**. Disconnect the rear window wiper motor connector. Apply 12 volts to the **BL/GN** terminal of the rear window wiper motor. Apply ground to the **BK/BL** wire terminal of the rear window wiper motor.
    a. If the rear window wiper motor operates, go to Step 6.
    b. If the rear window wiper motor does not operate, replace the rear window wiper motor.

7. Turn the ignition **OFF**. Disconnect the turn signal/windshield wiper switch connector.

a. Measure resistance between the **BK/BL** and **BK** wire terminals of the turn signal/windshield wiper switch under the following conditions:

- With the rear wiper switch in the **ON** position, the resistance should be less than 5 ohms.
- With the rear wiper switch in the **OFF** position, the resistance should be greater than 10,000 ohms.

b. If the switch's resistance requirements are:

- Okay, go to Step 7.
- Not okay, replace the turn signal/windshield wiper switch.

8. Turn the ignition **OFF**. Disconnect the turn signal/windshield wiper switch connector. Measure the resistance of the **BK** wire between pin **13** of the turn signal/windshield wiper switch connector and ground:
    a. If the resistance is less than 5 ohms, service the **BK/BL** wire between the turn signal/windshield wiper switch and the rear window wiper motor.
    b. If the resistance is greater than 5 ohms, service the **BK** wire.

REAR WINDOW WIPER WILL NOT TURN OFF

1. Turn the ignition **OFF**. Disconnect the turn signal/windshield wiper switch connector.

2. Measure resistance between the

BK/BL and **BK** wire terminals of the turn signal/windshield wiper switch under the following conditions:

- With the rear wiper switch in the **ON** position, the resistance should be less than 5 ohms.
- With the rear wiper switch in the **OFF** position, the resistance should be greater than 10,000 ohms.

3. If the switch's resistance requirements are:

- Okay, service the **BK/BL** wire between the turn signal/windshield wiper switch and the rear window wiper motor.
- Not okay, replace the turn signal/windshield wiper switch.

Escort and Tracer

WINDSHIELD WASHER INOPERATIVE

1. Turn the key to the **OFF** position. Disconnect the turn signal/windshield wiper switch connector.

a. Measure the resistance between the turn signal/windshield wiper switch terminals under the following conditions:

- With the switch in the **HI** position, terminals **BL**-to-**R** should be less than 5 ohms.
- With the switch in the **LO** position, terminals **BL**-to-**BL/W** should be less than 5 ohms.
- With the switch in the **MIST (OFF and pushed)** position, terminals **BL**-to-**R** should be less than 5 ohms.
- With the switch in the **WASH (pulled)** position, terminals **BL**-to-**BL/O** should be less than 5 ohms.
- With the switch in the **OFF** position, terminals **BL/Y**-to-**BL/W** should be less than 5 ohms.

b. Perform the following procedures:

- If the resistances are okay, go to Step 2.
- If the resistances are not okay, replace the turn signal/windshield wiper switch.

2. Check power to windshield washer pump. Turn the key to the **OFF** position. Disconnect the windshield washer pump connector. Turn the key to the **ON** position. Turn the washer **ON**. Measure the voltage on the **BL/O** wire at the windshield wiper/washer pump connector:

a. If the voltage is greater than 10 volts, go to Step 3.

b. If the voltage is less than 10 volts, service the **BL/O** wire.

3. Check the windshield washer pump ground. Turn the key to the **OFF** position. Disconnect the windshield washer pump connector. Measure the resistance on the **BK** wire between the windshield washer pump connector and ground:

a. If the resistance is less than 5 ohms, replace the windshield washer pump.

b. If the resistance is greater than 5 ohms, service the **BK** wire.

REAR WINDOW WASHER INOPERATIVE

1. Turn the key to the **OFF** position. Disconnect the rear window wiper/washer switch connector.

a. Measure the resistance of the rear window wiper/washer switch terminals, under the following conditions:

- With the switch in the **REST** position, check terminals **BK**-to-**BL/BK**; the resistance should be greater than 10,000 ohms.
- With the switch in the **REST** position, check terminals **BK**-to-**O**; the resistance should be greater than 10,000 ohms.
- With the switch in the **WIPER ON** position, check terminals **BK**-to-**BL/BK**; the resistance should be less than 5 ohms.
- With the switch in the **WIPER ON** position, check terminals **BK**-to-**O**; the resistance should be greater than 10,000 ohms.
- With the switch in the **WASHER ON** position, check terminals **BK**-to-**BL/BK**; the resistance should be less than 5 ohms.
- With the switch in the **WASHER ON** position, check terminals **BK**-to-**O**; the resistance should be less than 5 ohms.

b. Perform the following procedures:
- If the resistances are okay, go to Step 2.
- If the resistances are not okay, replace the rear window wiper/washer switch.

2. Check rear window washer pump. Turn the key to the **OFF** position. Disconnect the rear window washer pump connector. Apply 12 volts to the **BL/GN** wire at the rear window washer pump. Ground the **O** wire terminal at the rear window washer pump; the pump should operate:

a. If the tests are okay, go to Step 3.

b. If the tests are not okay, replace the rear window washer pump.

3. Check power to rear window washer pump. Turn the key to the **OFF** position.

Disconnect the rear window washer pump connector. Turn the key to the **ON** position. Measure the voltage on the **BL/GN** wire at the rear window washer pump connector:

a. If the voltage is greater than 10 volts, go to Step 4.

b. If the voltage is less than 10 volts, service the **BL/GN** wire.

4. Check rear window wiper/washer switch ground. Turn the key to the **OFF** position. Disconnect the rear window wiper/washer pump connector. Measure the resistance on the **BK** wire between the rear window wiper/washer pump connector and ground:

a. If the resistance is less than 5 ohms, service the **O** wire between the rear window wiper/washer pump and rear window wiper/washer pump connector.

b. If the resistance is greater than 5 ohms, service the **BK** wire.

WINDSHIELD WIPERS INOPERATIVE IN ALL SWITCH POSITIONS

1. Turn the key to the **OFF** position. Check **20A WIPER** fuse.

a. If fuse is okay, go to Step 4.

b. If fuse is bad, go to Step 2.

2. Turn the key to the **OFF** position. Install and confirm fuse is good. Turn ignition switch **ON** and check that **20A WIPER** fuse does not blow.

a. If fuse is okay, go to Step 4.

b. If fuse is bad, go to Step 3.

3. Check for short to ground. Turn ignition switch **OFF**. Disconnect the interior fuse junction panel, the wiper motor switch and the wiper motor connectors. Measure the resistance of the **BL** wire between the interior fuse junction panel connector and ground.

a. If resistance is greater then 5 ohms, install the interior fuse junction panel connector and go to Step 4.

b. If resistance is less than 5 ohms, service the **BL** wire.

4. Check washer switch. Turn the key to the **OFF** position. Disconnect the turn signal/windshield wiper switch connector.

a. Measure the resistance between the turn signal/windshield wiper switch terminals under the following conditions:

- With the switch in the **HI** position, terminals **BL**-to-**R** should be less than 5 ohms.
- With the switch in the **LO** position, terminals **BL**-to-**BL/W** should be less than 5 ohms.
- With the switch in the **MIST (OFF and pushed)** position, terminals **BL**-to-**R** should be less than 5 ohms.

- With the switch in the **WASH (pulled)** position, terminals **BL**-to-**BL/O** should be less than 5 ohms.
- With the switch in the **OFF** position, terminals **BL/Y**-to-**BL/W** should be less than 5 ohms.

5. Perform the following procedures:
- If the resistances are okay, go to Step 5.
- If the resistances are not okay, replace the turn signal/windshield wiper switch.

6. Check windshield wiper motor. Turn the key to the **OFF** position. Disconnect the windshield wiper motor connectors.

a. To check for **LO** wiper operation, perform the following procedures:
- Apply 12 volts to terminal **BL** of one connector and **BL/W** of the other connector.
- Apply ground to terminal **BK** of one connector and **BK** of the other connector.
- The wiper should operate in **LO** speed.

b. To check for **HI** wiper operation, perform the following procedures:
- Apply 12 volts to terminal **BL** of one connector and **R** of the other connector.
- Apply ground to terminal **BK** of one connector and **BK** of the other connector.
- The wiper should operate in **HI** speed.

c. Perform the following procedure:
- If the motor tests okay, go to Step 6.
- If the motor does not test okay, replace the windshield wiper motor.

7. Check power to turn signal/windshield wiper switch. Turn the key to the **OFF** position. Disconnect the turn signal/windshield wiper switch connector. Turn the key to the **ON** position. Measure the voltage on the **BL** wire at the turn signal/windshield wiper switch connector:

a. If the voltage is greater than 10 volts, go to Step 7.

b. If the voltage is less than 10 volts, service the **BL** wire.

8. Check turn signal/windshield wiper switch ground. Turn the key to the **OFF** position. Disconnect the turn signal/windshield wiper switch connector. Measure the resistance on the **BK** wire between the turn signal/windshield wiper switch connector and ground:

a. If the resistance is less than 5 ohms, go to Step 8.

b. If the resistance is greater than 5 ohms, service the **BK** wire.

9. Check windshield wiper motor power feed. Turn the key to the **OFF** position. Disconnect the windshield wiper motor connectors. Turn the key to the **ON** position. Measure the voltage on the **BL** wire at the windshield wiper motor connector:

a. If the voltage is greater than 10 volts, service the **BK** wire(s) between the windshield wiper motor and ground.

b. If the voltage is less than 10 volts, service the **BL** wire.

WINDSHIELD WIPERS INOPERATIVE AT HIGH SPEED

1. Turn the key to the **OFF** position. Disconnect the turn signal/windshield wiper switch connector.

a. Measure the resistance between the turn signal/windshield wiper switch terminals under the following conditions:
- With the switch in the **HI** position, terminals **BL**-to-**R** should be less than 5 ohms.
- With the switch in the **LO** position, terminals **BL**-to-**BL/W** should be less than 5 ohms.
- With the switch in the **MIST (OFF and pushed)** position, terminals **BL**-to-**R** should be less than 5 ohms.
- With the switch in the **WASH (pulled)** position, terminals **BL**-to-**BL/O** should be less than 5 ohms.
- With the switch in the **OFF** position, terminals **BL/Y**-to-**BL/W** should be less than 5 ohms.

b. Perform the following procedures:
- If the resistances are okay, go to Step 2.
- If the resistances are not okay, replace the turn signal/windshield wiper switch.

2. Check the windshield wiper motor high speed input, Turn the key to the **OFF** position. Disconnect the windshield wiper motor connector. Turn the key to the **ON** position and place the wipers on **HI**. Measure the voltage on the **R** wire at the windshield wiper motor connector:

a. If the voltage is greater than 10 volts, replace windshield wiper motor.

b. If the voltage is less than 10 volts, service the **R** wire.

WINDSHIELD WIPERS INOPERATIVE AT LOW SPEED

1. Turn the key to the **OFF** position. Disconnect the turn signal/windshield wiper switch connector.

a. Measure the resistance between the turn signal/windshield wiper switch terminals under the following conditions:
- With the switch in the **HI** position, terminals **BL**-to-**R** should be less than 5 ohms.
- With the switch in the **LO** position, terminals **BL**-to-**BL/W** should be less than 5 ohms.
- With the switch in the **MIST (OFF and pushed)** position, terminals **BL**-to-**R** should be less than 5 ohms.
- With the switch in the **WASH (pulled)** position, terminals **BL**-to-**BL/O** should be less than 5 ohms.
- With the switch in the **OFF** position, terminals **BL/Y**-to-**BL/W** should be less than 5 ohms.

b. Perform the following procedures:
- If the resistances are okay, go to Step 2.
- If the resistances are not okay, replace the turn signal/windshield wiper switch.

2. Check the windshield wiper motor low speed input. Turn the key to the **OFF** position. Disconnect the windshield wiper motor connector. Turn the key to the **ON** position and place the wipers on **LO**. Measure the voltage on the **BL/W** wire at the windshield wiper motor connector:

a. If the voltage is greater than 10 volts, replace windshield wiper motor.

b. If the voltage is less than 10 volts, service the **BL/W** wire.

WINDSHIELD WIPERS INOPERATIVE AT INTERVAL SETTING

1. Turn the key to the **OFF** position. Disconnect the turn signal/windshield wiper switch connector.

2. Measure the resistance between the turn signal/windshield wiper switch terminals under the following conditions:
- With the switch in the **HI** position, terminals **BL**-to-**R** should be less than 5 ohms.
- With the switch in the **LO** position, terminals **BL**-to-**BL/W** should be less than 5 ohms.
- With the switch in the **MIST (OFF and pushed)** position, terminals **BL**-to-**R** should be less than 5 ohms.
- With the switch in the **WASH (pulled)** position, terminals **BL**-to-**BL/O** should be less than 5 ohms.

- With the switch in the **OFF** position, terminals **BL/Y**-to-**BL/W** should be less than 5 ohms.
3. Perform the following procedures:
  - If the resistances are okay, service the **BL/Y** wire.
  - If the resistances are not okay, replace the turn signal/windshield wiper switch.

WINDSHIELD WIPERS WILL NOT TURN OFF

1. Turn the key to the **OFF** position. Disconnect the turn signal/windshield wiper switch connector.
2. Measure the resistance between the turn signal/windshield wiper switch terminals under the following conditions:
  - With the switch in the **HI** position, terminals **BL**-to-**R** should be less than 5 ohms.
  - With the switch in the **LO** position, terminals **BL**-to-**BL/W** should be less than 5 ohms.
  - With the switch in the **MIST (OFF and pushed)** position, terminals **BL**-to-**R** should be less than 5 ohms.
  - With the switch in the **WASH (pulled)** position, terminals **BL**-to-**BL/O** should be less than 5 ohms.
  - With the switch in the **OFF** position, terminals **BL/Y**-to-**BL/W** should be less than 5 ohms.
3. Perform the following procedures:
  - If the resistances are okay, replace the windshield wiper motor.
  - If the resistances are not okay, replace the turn signal/windshield wiper switch.

REAR WINDOW WIPER INOPERATIVE

1. Turn the key to the **OFF** position. Check **10A REAR WIPER** fuse.
  a. If fuse is okay, go to Step 4.
  b. If fuse is bad, go to Step 2.
2. Check the system. Turn the key to the **OFF** position. Install and confirm fuse is good. Turn ignition switch **ON** and check that **10A REAR WIPER** fuse does not blow.
  a. If fuse is okay, go to Step 4.
  b. If fuse is bad, go to Step 3.
3. Check for short to ground. Turn ignition switch **OFF**. Disconnect the interior fuse junction panel, the rear window washer pump and the rear window wiper motor connectors. Measure the resistance of the **BL/GN** wire between the interior fuse junction panel connector and ground.
  a. If resistance is greater then 10,000

ohms, install the interior fuse junction panel connector and go to Step 4.
  b. If resistance is less than 10,000 ohms, service the **BL/GN** wire.
4. Check the rear window wiper switch. Turn the key to the **OFF** position. Disconnect the rear window wiper/washer switch connector.
  a. Measure the resistance of the rear window wiper/washer switch terminals, under the following conditions:
    - With the switch in the **REST** position, check terminals **BK**-to-**BL/BK**; the resistance should be greater than 10,000 ohms.
    - With the switch in the **REST** position, check terminals **BK**-to-**O**; the resistance should be greater than 10,000 ohms.
    - With the switch in the **WIPER ON** position, check terminals **BK**-to-**BL/BK**; the resistance should be less than 5 ohms.
    - With the switch in the **WIPER ON** position, check terminals **BK**-to-**O**; the resistance should be greater than 10,000 ohms.
    - With the switch in the **WASHER ON** position, check terminals **BK**-to-**BL/BK**; the resistance should be less than 5 ohms.
    - With the switch in the **WASHER ON** position, check terminals **BK**-to-**O**; the resistance should be less than 5 ohms.
  b. Perform the following procedures:
    - If the resistances are okay, go to Step 5.
    - If the resistances are not okay, replace the rear window wiper/washer switch.
5. Check the rear window wiper motor. Turn the key to the **OFF** position. Disconnect the rear window wiper motor connector. Apply 12 volts to terminal **BL/GN** wire terminal at the rear window wiper motor. Ground the **BL/BK** terminal of at the rear window wiper motor. Perform the following procedure:
  a. If the motor tests okay, go to Step 6.
  b. If the motor does not test okay, replace the rear window wiper motor.
6. Check the rear window wiper motor power supply. Turn the key to the **OFF** position. Disconnect the rear window wiper motor connector. Turn the key to the **ON** position. Measure the voltage on the **BL/GN** wire at the rear window wiper motor connector:
  a. If the voltage is greater than 10 volts, go to Step 7.

  b. If the voltage is less than 10 volts, service the **BL/GN** wire.
7. Check the rear window wiper switch ground. Turn the key to the **OFF** position. Disconnect the rear window wiper/washer switch. Measure the resistance on the **BK** wire between the rear window wiper/washer switch connector and ground:
  a. If the resistance is less than 5 ohms, service the **BL/BK** wire between the rear window wiper motor and rear window wiper/washer switch.
  b. If the resistance is greater than 5 ohms, service the **BK** wire.

REAR WINDOW WIPER WILL NOT SHUT OFF

1. Turn the key to the **OFF** position. Disconnect the rear window wiper/washer switch connector.
2. Measure the resistance of the rear window wiper/washer switch terminals, under the following conditions:
  - With the switch in the **REST** position, check terminals **BK**-to-**BL/BK**; the resistance should be greater than 10,000 ohms.
  - With the switch in the **REST** position, check terminals **BK**-to-**O**; the resistance should be greater than 10,000 ohms.
  - With the switch in the **WIPER ON** position, check terminals **BK**-to-**BL/BK**; the resistance should be less than 5 ohms.
  - With the switch in the **WIPER ON** position, check terminals **BK**-to-**O**; the resistance should be greater than 10,000 ohms.
  - With the switch in the **WASHER ON** position, check terminals **BK**-to-**BL/BK**; the resistance should be less than 5 ohms.
  - With the switch in the **WASHER ON** position, check terminals **BK**-to-**O**; the resistance should be less than 5 ohms.
3. Perform the following procedures:
  - If the resistances are okay, service the **BL/BK** wire between the rear window wiper motor and the rear window wiper/washer switch.
  - If the resistances are not okay, replace the rear window wiper/washer switch.

Probe

WINDSHIELD WASHER INOPERATIVE

1. Check the front wiper fuse. Turn the ignition switch **OFF**.
2. Check the **20A WIPER** fuse.

a. If the fuse is okay, go the Step 4

b. If the fuse is not okay, go the Step 2

3. Check system. Turn the ignition switch **OFF**. Install the **20A WIPER** fuse.

a. If the fuse is okay, go the Step 4

b. If the fuse is not okay, go the Step 3

4. Check the short to ground check. Turn the ignition switch **OFF**. Disconnect the turn signal/windshield wiper switch, the windshield wiper motor and the interior fuse junction panel connectors. Measure the resistance of the **BL** wire between the fuse junction panel and ground:

a. If the resistance is less than 5 ohms, service the **BL** wire.

b. If the resistance is greater than 5 ohms, replace the **20A WIPER** fuse and go the Step 4.

5. Check the windshield washer switch power supply. Turn the ignition switch **OFF**. Reconnect the windshield wiper motor and the interior fuse junction panel connectors. Disconnect the turn signal/windshield wiper switch (harness side). Turn the ignition switch **ON**. Measure the voltage of the **BL** wire at the turn signal/windshield wiper switch connector:

a. If the voltage is less than 10 volts, service the **BL** wire.

b. If the voltage is greater than 10 volts, go the Step 5.

6. Check the windshield wiper/washer switch. Turn the ignition switch **OFF**. Reconnect the turn signal/windshield wiper switch connector. Turn the ignition switch **ON**. Depress the windshield washer switch. Measure the voltage of the **BL/O** wire at the turn signal/windshield wiper switch connector. Release the windshield washer switch. Measure the voltage of the **BL/O** wire at the turn signal/windshield wiper switch connector:

a. If the voltage is less than 10 volts with the switch depressed and/or greater than 1 volt with the switch released, replace the turn signal/windshield wiper switch.

b. If the voltage is greater than 10 volts with the switch depressed and less than 1 volt with the switch released, go the Step 6.

7. Check the windshield wiper/washer switch and windshield washer pump wire. Turn the ignition switch **OFF**. Disconnect the turn signal/windshield wiper switch and the windshield washer pump connector. Measure the resistance of the **BL/O** wire

between the turn signal/windshield wiper switch connector and the windshield washer pump connector. Measure the resistance of the **BL/O** wire between the turn signal/windshield wiper switch connector and ground:

a. If the resistance is less than 5 ohms between the turn signal/windshield wiper switch connector and the windshield washer pump connector and greater than 10,000 ohms between the turn signal/windshield wiper switch connector and ground, go the Step 7.

b. If the resistance is greater than 5 ohms between the turn signal/windshield wiper switch connector and the windshield washer pump connector and less than 10,000 ohms between the turn signal/windshield wiper switch connector and ground, service the **BL/O** wire.

8. Check the windshield washer pump ground. Turn the ignition switch **OFF**. Disconnect the windshield washer pump connector. Measure the resistance of the **BK** wire between the windshield washer pump connector and ground:

a. If the resistance is less than 5 ohms, replace the windshield washer pump.

b. If the resistance is greater than 5 ohms, service the **BK** wire.

REAR WINDOW WASHER INOPERATIVE

1. Check the rear wiper fuse. Turn the ignition switch **OFF**. Check the **15A REAR WIPER** fuse.

a. If the fuse is okay, go the Step 4.

b. If the fuse is not okay, go the Step 2.

2. Check the system. Turn the ignition switch **OFF**. Install the **15A REAR WIPER** fuse. Turn the ignition switch **ON**.

a. If the fuse is okay, go the Step 3.

b. If the fuse is not okay, go the Step 4.

3. Check the short to ground. Turn the ignition switch **OFF**. Disconnect the rear window washer switch, the rear window wiper motor and the interior fuse junction panel connectors. Measure the resistance of the **BL/GN** wire between the fuse junction panel and ground:

a. If the resistance is less than 5 ohms, service the **BL/GN** wire.

b. If the resistance is greater than 5 ohms, replace the **15A REAR WIPER** fuse and go the Step 4.

4. Check the rear window washer pump power supply. Turn the ignition switch **OFF**. Reconnect the rear window wiper motor and

the interior fuse junction panel connectors. Disconnect the rear window washer pump connector. Turn the ignition switch **ON**. Measure the voltage of the **BL/GN** wire at the rear window washer pump connector:

a. If the voltage is less than 10 volts, service the **BL/GN** wire.

b. If the voltage is greater than 10 volts, go the Step 5.

5. Check the rear window washer pump ground. Turn the ignition switch **OFF**. Disconnect the rear window washer pump connector. Depress the rear window washer switch. Measure the resistance of the **BL/Y** wire between the rear window washer pump connector and ground. Release the rear window washer switch. Measure the resistance of the **BL/Y** wire between the rear window washer pump connector and ground:

a. If the resistance is less than 5 ohms with the rear window washer switch depressed and greater than 10,000 ohms with the rear window washer switch released, replace the rear window washer switch.

b. If the resistance is greater than 5 ohms with the rear window washer switch depressed and less than 1 ohm with the rear window washer switch released, go the Step 6.

6. Check the rear window washer switch and pump wire. Turn the ignition switch **OFF**. Disconnect the rear window washer pump and the rear window washer switch connectors. Measure the resistance of the **BL/Y** wire between the rear window washer pump connector and the rear window washer switch connectors. Measure the resistance of the **BL/Y** wire between the rear window washer pump connector and ground:

a. If the resistance is less than 5 ohms between the rear window washer pump and the rear window washer switch and greater than 10,000 ohms between the rear window washer pump and ground, go the Step 7.

b. If the resistance is greater than 5 ohms between the rear window washer pump and the rear window washer switch and less than 10,000 ohms between the rear window washer pump and ground, service the **BL/O** wire.

7. Check the rear window washer switch. Turn the ignition switch **OFF**. Disconnect the rear window washer switch connector. Depress the rear window washer switch. Measure the resistance between the **BL/Y** wire terminal and the **BK** wire terminal on the rear window washer switch. Release the

rear window washer switch. Measure the resistance between the **BL/Y** wire terminal and the **BK** wire terminal on the rear window washer switch:

    a. If the resistance is less than 5 ohms with the rear window washer switch depressed and greater than 10,000 ohms with rear window washer switch released, service the **BK** wire.

    b. If the resistance is greater than 5 ohms with the rear window washer switch depressed and/or less than 10,000 ohms with rear window washer switch released, replace the rear window washer switch.

WINDSHIELD WIPERS INOPERATIVE IN ALL SWITCH POSITIONS

1. Check the fuse. Turn the ignition switch **OFF**. Check the **20A WIPER** fuse.

    a. If the fuse is okay, go the Step 4.

    b. If the fuse is not okay, go the Step 2.

2. Check the system. Turn the ignition switch **OFF**. Install the **20A WIPER** fuse. Turn the ignition switch **ON**.

    a. If the fuse is okay, go the Step 4.

    b. If the fuse is not okay, go the Step 3.

3. Check for the short to ground. Turn the ignition switch **OFF**. Disconnect the turn signal/windshield wiper switch, the windshield wiper motor and the interior fuse junction panel connectors. Measure the resistance of the **BL** wire between the fuse junction panel and ground:

    a. If the resistance is less than 5 ohms, service the **BL** wire.

    b. If the resistance is greater than 5 ohms, replace the **20A WIPER** fuse and go the Step 4.

4. Check the windshield wiper motor and turn signal/windshield wiper switch power supply. Turn the ignition switch **OFF**. Reconnect the interior fuse junction panel connectors. Disconnect the turn signal/windshield wiper switch and the windshield wiper motor connectors. Turn the ignition switch **ON**. Measure the voltage of the **BL** wire at the turn signal/windshield wiper switch connector and the voltage of the **BL** wire at the windshield wiper motor connector:

    a. If the voltages are less than 10 volts, service the **BL** wire.

    b. If the voltages are greater than 10 volts, go the Step 5.

5. Check the windshield wiper/washer switch. Turn the ignition switch **OFF**. Disconnect the turn signal/windshield wiper switch connector.

6. Measure the resistance of the wire terminals at the switch side of the turn signal/windshield wiper switch connector:

- With the switch in the **OFF** position, the resistance between terminals **BL/BK**-to-**BL/W** should be 5 ohms.
- With the switch in the **INT** position, the resistance between terminals **BL/BK**-to-**BL/W** should be 5 ohms.
- With the switch in the **LO** position, the resistance between terminals **BL**-to-**BL/W** should be 5 ohms.
- With the switch in the **HI** position, the resistance between terminals **BL**-to-**R** should be 5 ohms.
- With the switch in the **MIST** position, the resistance between terminals **BL**-to-**R** should be 5 ohms.
- With the switch in the **WASH** position, the resistance between terminals **BL**-to-**BL/O** should be 5 ohms.

7. Perform the following procedures:

- If the resistances meet the specifications, go the Step 6.
- If the resistances do not meet the specifications, replace the turn signal/windshield wiper switch.

8. Check the windshield wiper/washer switch and windshield washer motor wire. Turn the ignition switch **OFF**. Disconnect the turn signal/windshield wiper switch and the windshield washer motor connector. Measure the resistances between the turn signal/windshield wiper switch connector and the windshield washer motor connector wires: **BL/BK**, **R** and **BL/W**. Measure the resistances between the turn signal/windshield wiper switch connector and ground wires: **BL/BK**, **R** and **BL/W**. Perform the following procedures:

    a. If the resistance is less than 5 ohms between the turn signal/windshield wiper switch connector and the windshield washer motor connector and greater than 10,000 ohms between the turn signal/windshield wiper switch connector and ground, check the **BK** wire between the windshield wiper motor case and ground. If okay, replace the windshield wiper motor.

    b. If the resistance is greater than 5 ohms between the turn signal/windshield wiper switch connector and the windshield washer motor connector and/or less than 10,000 ohms between the turn signal/windshield wiper switch connector and ground, service the wires in question.

WINDSHIELD WIPERS INOPERATIVE AT HIGH SPEED

1. Turn the ignition switch **OFF**. Disconnect the turn signal/windshield wiper switch connector.

    a. Measure the resistance of the wire terminals at the switch side of the turn signal/windshield wiper switch connector:

- With the switch in the **OFF** position, the resistance between terminals **BL/BK**-to-**BL/W** should be 5 ohms.
- With the switch in the **INT** position, the resistance between terminals **BL/BK**-to-**BL/W** should be 5 ohms.
- With the switch in the **LO** position, the resistance between terminals **BL**-to-**BL/W** should be 5 ohms.
- With the switch in the **HI** position, the resistance between terminals **BL**-to-**R** should be 5 ohms.
- With the switch in the **MIST** position, the resistance between terminals **BL**-to-**R** should be 5 ohms.
- With the switch in the **WASH** position, the resistance between terminals **BL**-to-**BL/O** should be 5 ohms.

    b. Perform the following procedures:

- If the resistances meet the specifications, go the Step 2.
- If the resistances do not meet the specifications, replace the turn signal/windshield wiper switch.

2. Check the circuit. Turn the ignition switch **OFF**. Disconnect the windshield wiper motor connector. Turn the windshield wiper switch to **HIGH**. Measure the voltage of the **R** wire at the windshield wiper motor connector:

- If the voltage is less than 10 volts, service the **R** wire.
- If the voltage is greater than 10 volts, service the windshield motor.

WINDSHIELD WIPERS INOPERATIVE AT LOW SPEED

1. Turn the ignition switch **OFF**. Disconnect the turn signal/windshield wiper switch connector.

    a. Measure the resistance of the wire terminals at the switch side of the turn signal/windshield wiper switch connector:

- With the switch in the **OFF** position, the resistance between terminals **BL/BK**-to-**BL/W** should be 5 ohms.
- With the switch in the **INT** position, the resistance between terminals **BL/BK**-to-**BL/W** should be 5 ohms.
- With the switch in the **LO** position, the resistance between terminals **BL**-to-**BL/W** should be 5 ohms.

- With the switch in the **HI** position, the resistance between terminals **BL**-to-**R** should be 5 ohms.
- With the switch in the **MIST** position, the resistance between terminals **BL**-to-**R** should be 5 ohms.
- With the switch in the **WASH** position, the resistance between terminals **BL**-to-**BL/O** should be 5 ohms.
b. Perform the following procedures:
- If the resistances meet the specifications, go the Step 2.
- If the resistances do not meet the specifications, replace the turn signal/windshield wiper switch.

2. Check the circuit. Turn the ignition switch **OFF**. Disconnect the windshield wiper motor connector. Turn the ignition switch to **ON**. Turn the windshield wiper switch to **LOW**. Measure the voltage of the **BL/W** wire at the windshield wiper motor connector:

a. If the voltage is less than 10 volts, service the **BL/W** wire.

b. If the voltage is greater than 10 volts, service the windshield motor.

WINDSHIELD WIPERS INOPERATIVE AT INTERVAL SETTINGS

1. Turn the ignition switch **OFF**. Disconnect the windshield wiper motor connector. Measure the resistance between the windshield wiper motor case and ground to ensure the resistance is less than 5 ohms. Apply 12 volts to terminal **BL/W** of the windshield wiper motor; **LO** speed wiper operation should result. Apply 12 volts to terminal **R** of the windshield wiper motor; **HI** speed wiper operation should result. Perform the following procedures:

2. If the testing specifications are met, replace the turn signal/windshield wiper switch.

3. If the testing specifications are not met, replace the windshield wiper motor.

WINDSHIELD WIPERS WILL NOT PARK BELOW THE GLASS

1. Turn the ignition switch **OFF**. Disconnect the windshield wiper motor connector. Turn the ignition switch to **ON**. Measure the voltage of the **BL** wire at the windshield wiper motor connector:

a. If the voltage is less than 10 volts, service the **BL** wire.

b. If the voltage is greater than 10 volts, go to Step 2.

2. Check the windshield wiper motor. Turn the ignition switch **OFF**. Disconnect

the windshield wiper motor connector. Measure the resistance between the windshield wiper motor case and ground to ensure the resistance is less than 5 ohms. Apply 12 volts to terminal **BL/W** of the windshield wiper motor; **LO** speed wiper operation should result. Apply 12 volts to terminal **R** of the windshield wiper motor; **HI** speed wiper operation should result. Perform the following procedures:

a. If the testing specifications are met, go to Step 3.

b. If the testing specifications are not met, replace the windshield wiper motor.

3. Check the windshield wiper/washer switch and windshield washer motor wire. Turn the ignition switch **OFF**. Disconnect the turn signal/windshield wiper switch and the windshield washer motor connector. Measure the resistance of the **BL/BK** wire between the turn signal/windshield wiper switch connector and the windshield washer motor connector wires. Measure the resistance of the **BL/BK** wire between the turn signal/windshield wiper switch connector and ground wires. Perform the following procedures:

a. If the resistance is less than 5 ohms between the turn signal/windshield wiper switch connector and the windshield washer motor connector and greater than 10,000 ohms between the turn signal/windshield wiper switch connector and ground, replace the turn signal/windshield wiper switch.

b. If the resistance is greater than 5 ohms between the turn signal/windshield wiper switch connector and the windshield washer motor connector and/or less than 10,000 ohms between the turn signal/windshield wiper switch connector and ground, service the **BL/BK** wire.

WINDSHIELD WIPERS WILL NOT TURN OFF

1. Turn the ignition switch **OFF**. Disconnect the turn signal/windshield wiper switch connector.

2. Measure the resistance of the wire terminals at the switch side of the turn signal/windshield wiper switch connector:

- With the switch in the **OFF** position, the resistance between terminals **BL/BK**-to-**BL/W** should be 5 ohms.
- With the switch in the **INT** position, the resistance between terminals **BL/BK**-to-**BL/W** should be 5 ohms.
- With the switch in the **LO** position,

the resistance between terminals **BL**-to-**BL/W** should be 5 ohms.
- With the switch in the **HI** position, the resistance between terminals **BL**-to-**R** should be 5 ohms.
- With the switch in the **MIST** position, the resistance between terminals **BL**-to-**R** should be 5 ohms.
- With the switch in the **WASH** position, the resistance between terminals **BL**-to-**BL/O** should be 5 ohms.

3. Perform the following procedures:
- If the resistances meet the specifications, service the **R** or **BL/W** wire between the turn signal/windshield wiper switch and windshield motor for short.
- If the resistances do not meet the specifications, replace the turn signal/windshield wiper switch.

REAR WINDOW WIPER INOPERATIVE

1. Turn the ignition switch **OFF**. Check the **15A REAR WIPER** fuse.

a. If the fuse is okay, go the Step 4.

b. If the fuse is not okay, go the Step 2.

2. Check the system. Turn the ignition switch **OFF**. Install the **15A REAR WIPER** fuse. Turn the ignition switch **ON**.

a. If the fuse is okay, go the Step 4.

b. If the fuse is not okay, go the Step 3.

3. Check the short to ground. Turn the ignition switch **OFF**. Disconnect the rear window wiper pump, the rear window wiper motor and the interior fuse junction panel connectors. Measure the resistance of the **BL/GN** wire between the fuse junction panel and ground:

a. If the resistance is less than 5 ohms, service the **BL/GN** wire.

b. If the resistance is greater than 5 ohms, replace the **15A REAR WIPER** fuse and go the Step 4.

4. Check the rear window wiper motor power supply. Turn the ignition switch **OFF**. Disconnect the fuse junction panel connector. Disconnect the rear window wiper motor connector. Turn the ignition switch to **ON**. Measure the voltage of the **BL/GN** wire at the rear window wiper motor connector:

a. If the voltage is less than 10 volts, service the **BL/GN** wire.

b. If the voltage is greater than 10 volts, go to Step 5.

5. Check the rear window wiper motor ground. Turn the ignition switch **OFF**. Disconnect the rear window wiper motor

switch. Depress the rear window wiper motor connector. Measure the resistance of the **BK/BL** wire between the rear window wiper motor connector and ground. Perform the following procedures:

a. If the resistance is less than 5 ohms with the rear window wiper motor switch depressed and greater than 10,000 ohms with the rear window wiper motor switch released, replace the rear window wiper motor.

b. If the resistance is greater than 5 ohms with the rear window wiper motor switch depressed and/or less than 10,000 ohms with the rear window wiper motor switch released, go to Step 6.

6. Check the rear window wiper motor-to-rear window switch wire. Turn the ignition switch **OFF**. Disconnect the rear window wiper motor switch connector and the rear window wiper motor connector. Measure the resistance of the **BK/BL** wire between the rear window wiper motor connector and the rear window wiper motor switch connector. Measure the resistance of the **BK/BL** wire between the rear window wiper motor connector and ground. Perform the following procedures:

a. If the resistance is less than 5 ohms between the rear window wiper motor and the rear window wiper motor switch and greater than 10,000 ohms between the rear window wiper motor and ground, go to Step 7.

b. If the resistance is greater than 5 ohms between the rear window wiper motor and the rear window wiper motor switch and/or less than 10,000 ohms between the rear window wiper motor and ground, service the **BK/BL** wire.

7. Check the rear window wiper switch. Turn the ignition switch **OFF**. Disconnect the rear window wiper switch connector.

8. Depress the rear window wiper switch. Measure the resistance of the **BK/BL** wire terminal and the **BK** wire terminal on the rear window wiper switch. Release the rear window wiper switch. Measure the resistance of the **BK/BL** wire terminal and the **BK** wire terminal on the rear window wiper switch. Perform the following procedures:

a. If the resistance is less than 5 ohms with the rear window wiper switch depressed and greater than 10,000 ohms with the rear window wiper switch released, service the **BK** wire between the rear window wiper switch connector and ground.

b. If the resistance is greater than 5 ohms with the rear window wiper switch depressed and/or less than 10,000 ohms

with the rear window wiper switch released, replace the rear window wiper switch.

REAR WINDOW WIPER WILL NOT PARK

1. Turn the ignition switch **ON**. Turn the rear window wiper **ON**. Turn the ignition switch **OFF** when the rear window wiper is not in the park position. Disconnect the rear window wiper switch connector. Measure the resistance between the **BK/BL** wire terminal at the rear window wiper motor connector and the rear window wiper motor ground terminal. Perform the following procedures:

a. If the resistance is less than 5 ohms with the rear window wiper out of the park position, go to Step 2.

b. If the resistance is greater than 5 ohms with the rear window wiper out of the park position, replace the rear window wiper motor.

2. Check the rear window wiper park position. Turn the ignition switch **OFF**. Reconnect the rear window wiper motor connector. Turn the ignition switch **ON**. Turn the ignition switch **OFF** when the rear window wiper reaches the park position. Disconnect the rear window wiper motor connector. Measure the resistance between the **BK/BL** wire terminal at the rear window wiper motor connector and the rear window wiper motor ground terminal. Perform the following procedures:

a. If the resistance is less than 10,000 ohms with the rear window wiper in the park position, replace the rear window wiper motor.

b. If the resistance is greater than 10,000 ohms with the rear window wiper in the park position, service the rear window wiper motor ground wire and/or the rear window wiper motor ground wire terminal.

REAR WINDOW WIPER WILL NOT TURN OFF

1. Turn the ignition switch **OFF**. Disconnect the rear window wiper switch connector. Depress the rear window wiper switch. Measure the resistance of the **BK/BL** wire terminal and the **BK** wire terminal on the rear window wiper switch. Release the rear window wiper switch. Measure the resistance of the **BK/BL** wire terminal and the **BK** wire terminal on the rear window wiper switch. Perform the following procedures:

a. If the resistance is less than 5 ohms with the rear window wiper switch depressed and greater than 10,000 ohms with the rear window wiper switch released, go to Step 2.

b. If the resistance is greater than 5 ohms with the rear window wiper switch depressed and/or less than 10,000 ohms with the rear window wiper switch released, replace the rear window wiper switch.

2. Check the circuit. Turn the ignition switch **OFF**. Disconnect the rear window wiper motor connector. Measure the resistance the **BK/BL** wire between the rear window wiper motor connector and ground. Perform the following procedures:

a. If the resistance is less than 10,000 ohms, service the **BK/BL** wire.

b. If the resistance is greater than 10,000 ohms, replace the rear window wiper motor.

Cougar and Thunderbird

WINDSHIELD WASHERS DO NOT OPERATE

1. Check the fluid level of the windshield washer reservoir.

a. If empty, fill the reservoir.

b. If OK, go to Step 2.

2. Activate the turn signal/windshield wiper switch and check the washer pump operation.

a. If the windshield washer pump will squirt fluid, go to Step 11.

b. If the windshield washer pump will not squirt fluid, go to Step 3.

3. Activate the turn signal/windshield wiper switch and check the washer operation.

a. If the windshield washer runs and will squirt fluid, go to Step 4.

b. If the windshield washer runs but will not squirt fluid, go to Step 9.

4. Check windshield washer hoses and nozzles for kinks or blockage.

a. If the hoses and nozzles are kinked or blocked, clean, repair or replace as necessary.

b. If the hoses and nozzles are OK, go to Step 5.

5. Check the washer hose at the windshield washer pump outlet for blockage.

a. If the washer pump is blocked, remove the washer pump from reservoir and clean or replace it.

b. If the washer pump is not blocked, replace the windshield washer pump.

6. Using an voltmeter or test lamp, check for voltage at the windshield washer pump by operating the turn signal/windshield washer switch.

a. If voltage is found, go to Step 7.

b. If no voltage is found, go to Step 8.

7. Using an ohmmeter, check the ground at the windshield washer pump.

a. If ground is found, replace the pump.

b. If no ground is found, repair the wiring.

8. Check the power at the switch by operating the turn signal/windshield wiper switch.

a. If wipers operate, go to Step 9.

b. If wipers do not operate, go to Step 10.

9. Using an voltmeter or test lamp, activate the turn signal/windshield washer switch and check for voltage at terminal **BK/W** (circuit **941**) of the wiper switch.

a. If voltage is found, go to Step 11.

b. If voltage is not found, go to Step 12.

10. Activate the heater blower.

a. If the heater blower motor runs, go to Step 11.

b. If the heater blower motor will not run, service the open circuit in the power feed wiring.

11. Check the windshield wiper/washer fuse.

a. If the circuit breaker is operational, go to Step 12.

b. If the circuit breaker is not operational, replace the fuse.

12. Check the turn signal/windshield wiper switch.

a. If the turn signal/windshield wiper switch circuits are functional, go to Step 13.

b. If the turn signal/windshield wiper switch circuits are not functional, replace the turn signal/windshield wiper switch.

13. Using an ohmmeter, perform the following tests on the windshield wiper switch:

- With the wash switch turned **OFF**, the resistance of pin **4**-to-**2** should be 3.3 kilo-ohms.
- With the wash switch turned **ON**, the resistance is closed to pin **4**-to-**2**.
- With the wiper switch turned **OFF** and the wash switch turned **OFF**, the resistance of pin **4**-to-**2** should be 103.3 kilo-ohms and the resistance of pin **4**-to-**6** should be 47.6 kilo-ohms.
- With the wiper interval switch at **MAX** delay (closest position to OFF) to **MIN** delay (closest position to **LO**), the resistance is of pin **4**-to-**2** should be 11.33 kilo-ohms and linearly decreasing from 103.3 kilo-ohms to 3.3 kilo-ohms.
- With the wiper switch turned **LO** and the wash switch turned **OFF**,

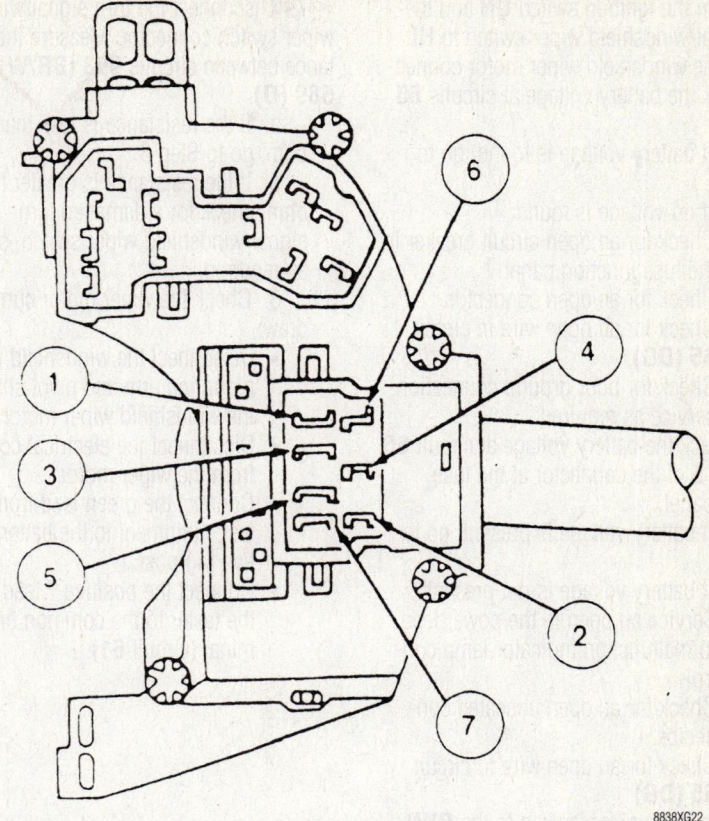

Windshield wiper test—terminal identification—Cougar and Thunderbird

8838XG22

the resistance of pin **4**-to-**2** should be 3.3 kilo-ohms and the resistance of pin **4**-to-**6** should be 4.08 kilo-ohms.

- With the wiper switch turned **HI** and the wash switch turned **OFF**, the resistance of pin **4**-to-**2** should be 3.3 kilo-ohms and closed to pin **4**-to-**6**.

a. If the switch test are OK, service the wiper/washer wiring and connectors.

b. If the switch test are not OK, service the switch.

WIPERS DO NOT WORK IN ANY SWITCH POSITION

1. Unplug the wiper motor connector, set the turn signal/windshield wiper switch on **HIGH**, and check for battery voltage at circuits **65 (DG)** and **56 (DB/O)**.

a. If voltage is found, go to Step 2.

b. If no voltage is found:

- Check for a malfunctioning turn signal/windshield wiper switch.
- Check for an open connector.
- Check for an open wire in circuit **56 (DB/O)** or **65 (DG)**.

2. Check the wiper motor current draw:

- Disconnect the windshield wiper

mounting arm and pivot shaft from the windshield wiper motor.

- Disconnect the electrical connector from the wiper motor.
- Connect the green lead from the test equipment to the battery positive **(+)** post.
- Connect the positive ® lead from the tester to the common brush terminal (circuit **61**).
- Attach a ground first to the low speed connection (circuit **56**) and then to the high speed connection (circuit **58**) at the connector plug.
- In either case, the current draw should not exceed 3.5 amps.

a. If the tests are performed OK, check the linkage for binding and service as necessary.

b. If the tests are not performed OK, repair motor as necessary.

WIPERS DO NOT WORK IN HIGH SPEED SWITCH POSITION

1. Turn the turn signal/windshield wiper switch to **LOW**.

a. If the low speed works, go to Step 4.

b. If the low speed does not work, go to Step 2.

2. Turn the ignition switch **ON** and the turn signal/windshield wiper switch to **HI**. Unplug the windshield wiper motor connector. Check the battery voltage at circuits **65 (DG)**.

   a. If battery voltage is found, go to Step 3.

   b. If no voltage is found:

- Check for an open circuit breaker in the fuse junction panel.
- Check for an open connector.
- Check for an open wire in circuit **65 (DG)**.
- Check for poor ground connection, service as required.

3. Check the battery voltage at circuit **65 (DG)** pin 5 of the connector at the fuse junction panel.

   a. If battery voltage is present, go to Step 4.

   b. If battery voltage is not present:

- Service an open in the power feed to malfunction indicator lamp control.
- Check for an open unseated connector.
- Check for an open wire in circuit **65 (DG)**.

4. Turn the ignition switch to the **RUN** position. Turn the turn signal/windshield wiper switch to **HI**. Disconnect windshield wiper motor connector. Check the battery voltage at circuit **61 (Y/R)** and **58 (W)**.

   a. If battery voltage is present, go to Step 7.

   b. If battery voltage is not present, go to Step 5.

5. Check for battery voltage between the malfunction indicator lamp control and pin **2** of the fuse junction panel.

   a. If battery voltage is present, check for an open wire, an open connector and/or an unseated connector, service as necessary.

   b. If battery voltage is not present, go to Step 6.

6. Disconnect the malfunction indicator lamp control connector. Measure the resistance between circuits **993 (BR/W)** and **589 (O)**.

   a. If the resistance is less than 1.0 ohm, replace the malfunction indicator lamp control.

   b. If the resistance is greater than 1.0 ohm:

- Check for an open wire between the turn signal/windshield wiper switch and the malfunction indicator lamp control.
- Check for a damaged turn signal/windshield wiper switch, service as required.

7. Disconnect the turn signal/windshield wiper switch connector. Measure the resistance between circuits **993 (BR/W)** and **589 (O)**.

   a. If the resistance is less than 1.0 ohm, go to Step 8.

   b. If the resistance is greater than 1.0 ohm, check for a damaged turn signal/windshield wiper switch, service as required.

8. Check the wiper motor current draw:

- Disconnect the windshield wiper mounting arm and pivot shaft from the windshield wiper motor.
- Disconnect the electrical connector from the wiper motor.
- Connect the green lead from the test equipment to the battery positive **(+)** post.
- Connect the positive ® lead from the tester to the common brush terminal (circuit **61**).
- Attach a ground first to the low speed connection (circuit **56**) and then to the high speed connection (circuit **58**) at the connector plug.
- In either case, the current draw should not exceed 3.5 amps.

   a. If the tests are performed OK, check the linkage for binding and service as necessary.

   b. If the tests are not performed OK, repair motor as necessary.

WIPERS DO NOT WORK IN LOW SPEED SWITCH POSITION

1. Turn the turn signal/windshield wiper switch to **HIGH**.

   a. If the low speed works, go to Step 4.

   b. If the low speed does not work, go to Step 2.

2. Turn the ignition switch to the **RUN** position and the turn signal/windshield wiper switch to **HI**. Unplug the windshield

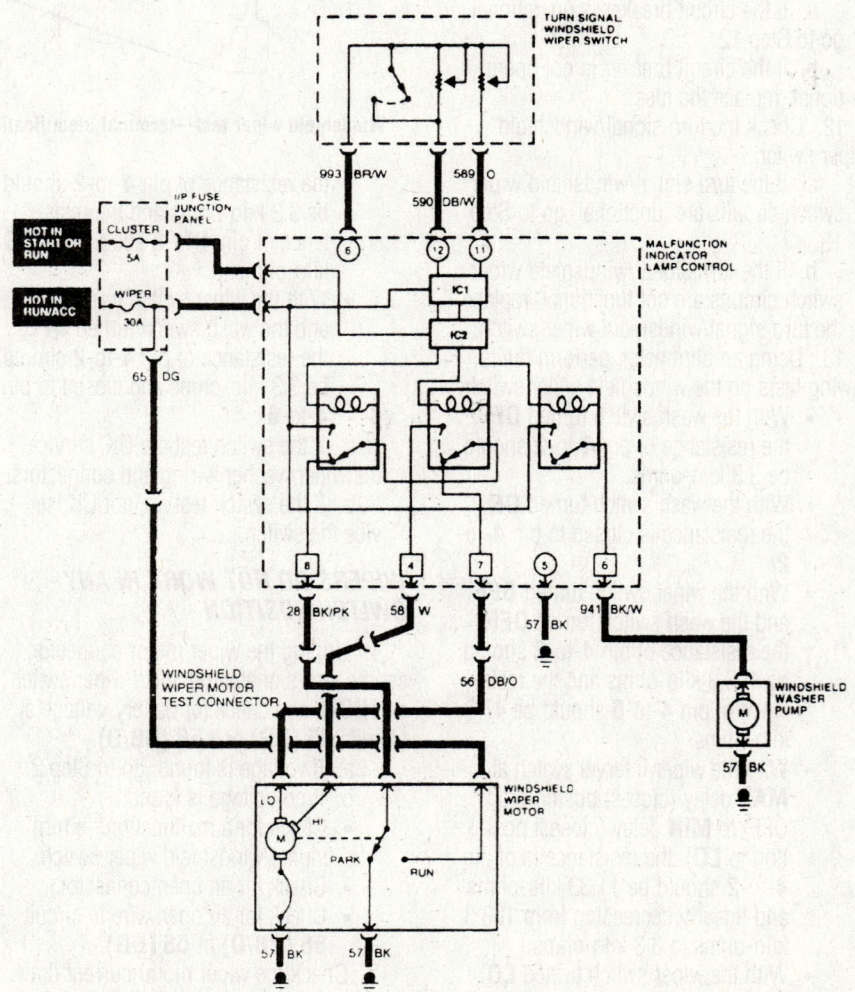

Windshield wiper/washer system—Cougar and Thunderbird

wiper motor connector. Check the battery voltage at circuits **65 (DG)**.

   a. If battery voltage is found, go to Step 3.

   b. If no voltage is found:

- Check for an open circuit breaker in the fuse junction panel.
- Check for an open connector.
- Check for an open wire in circuit **65 (DG)**.
- Check for poor ground connection, service as required.

3. Check the battery voltage at circuit **65**

(DG) pin 5 of the connector at the fuse junction panel.

   a. If battery voltage is present, go to Step 4.

   b. If battery voltage is not present:

- Service an open in the power feed to malfunction indicator lamp control.
- Check for an open unseated connector.
- Check for an open wire in circuit **65 (DG)**.

4. Turn the ignition switch to the **RUN**

position. Turn the turn signal/windshield wiper switch to **LO**. Disconnect windshield wiper motor connector. Check the battery voltage at circuit **56 (DB/O)** and **58 (W)**.

   a. If battery voltage is present, go to Step 7.

   b. If battery voltage is not present, go to Step 5.

5. Check for battery voltage between circuit **56 (DB/O)** and **58 (W)** of the malfunction indicator lamp control connector.

   a. If battery voltage is present, check for an open wire in circuit **56 (DB/O)** or

Connector End Views

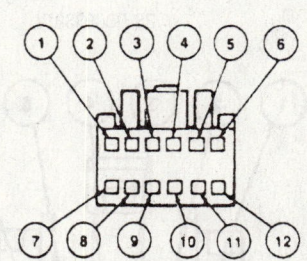

MALFUNCTION INDICATOR LAMP
CONTROL 12-PIN LC-12 CONNECTOR

Pin Number	Circuit	Circuit Function
1	993 (BR/W)	Wiper Switch Return
2	57 (BK)	Ground
3	—	Not Used
4	159 (R/PK)	Driver's Door Switch
5	85 (BR/LB)	Seat Belt Switch
6	450 (DG/LG)	Seat Belt Warning Lamp
7	590 (DB/W)	Wiper Switch—Delay
8	589 (O)	Wiper Switch—Mode
9	462 (P)	MIL Warning
10	465 (W/LB)	Door Handle Switch
11	257 (W/R)	Headlamp Switch
12	158 (BK/PK)	Key In Switch

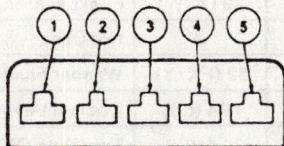

MALFUNCTION INDICATOR LAMP CONTROL
5-PIN J/B CONNECTOR

Pin Number	Circuit	Circuit Function
1	296 (W/P)	ACC-RUN
2	54 (LG/Y)	+Battery
3	53 (BK/LB)	Courtesy Lamps
4	640 (R/Y)	RUN-START
5	65 (DG)	ACC-RUN

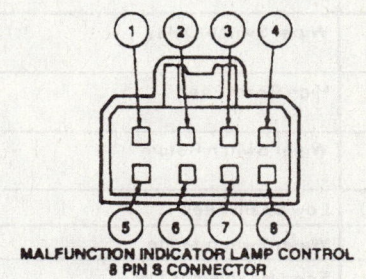

MALFUNCTION INDICATOR LAMP CONTROL
8 PIN S CONNECTOR

Pin Number	Circuit	Circuit Function
1	58 (W)	Wiper Motor—HI
2	705 (LG/O)	Engine Compartment Lamp
3	705 (LG/O)	+Battery
4	705 (LG/O)	Glove Compartment Lamp
5	28 (BK/PK)	Wiper PARK—RUN Switch
6	941 (BK/WH)	Washer Motor
7	56 (DB/O)	Wiper Motor—LO
8	—	Not Used

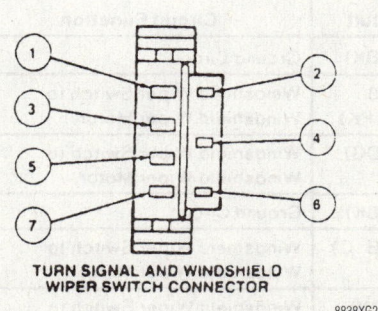

TURN SIGNAL AND WINDSHIELD
WIPER SWITCH CONNECTOR

8838XG24

Description and identification of the electrical connectors—Cougar and Thunderbird

For brake related suspension and axle service, refer to the model specific sections of this manual

58 (W), an open connector and/or an unseated connector, service as necessary.

b. If battery voltage is not present, go to Step 6.

6. Disconnect the malfunction indicator lamp control connector. Measure the resistance between circuits **993 (BR/W)** and **589 (O)**.

a. If the resistance is between 3.5–4.5 ohms, replace the malfunction indicator lamp control.

b. If the resistance is not between 3.5–4.5 ohms:

- Check for an open wire between the turn signal/windshield wiper switch and the malfunction indicator lamp control.

- Check for a damaged turn signal/windshield wiper switch, service as required.

7. Disconnect the turn signal/windshield wiper switch connector. Measure the resistance between circuits **993 (BR/W)** and **589 (O)**.

a. If the resistance is between 3.5–4.5 ohms, go to Step 8.

b. If the resistance is not between 3.5–4.5 ohms, check for a damaged turn signal/windshield wiper switch, service as required.

8. Check the wiper motor current draw:

- Disconnect the windshield wiper mounting arm and pivot shaft from the windshield wiper motor.

- Disconnect the electrical connector from the wiper motor.

- Connect the green lead from the test equipment to the battery positive (+) post.

- Connect the positive ® lead from the tester to the common brush terminal (circuit **61**).

- Attach a ground first to the low speed connection (circuit **56**) and then to the high speed connection (circuit **58**) at the connector plug.

- In either case, the current draw should not exceed 3.5 amps.

a. If the tests are performed OK, check the linkage for binding and service as necessary.

Pin Number	Circuit	Circuit Function
1	196 (DB O)	Supply-Hot At All Times
2	590 (DB W)	Wiper Switch-Delay
3	12 (LG BK)	High Beam Feed
4	993 (BR W)	Wiper Switch Return
5	13 (R BK)	Low Beam Feed
6	589 (O)	Wiper Switch-Mode
7	15 (R Y)	Feed-Headlamps ON

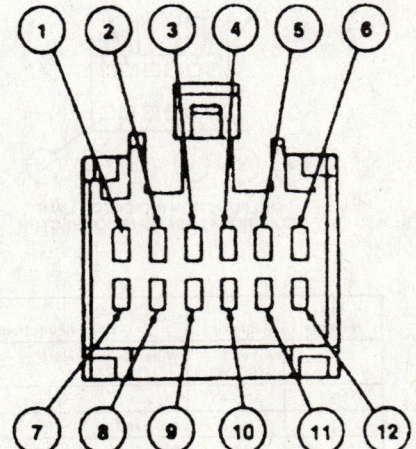

VEHICLE MAINTENANCE MONITOR CONNECTOR

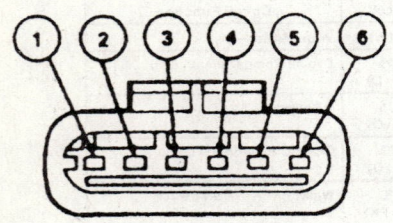

WINDSHIELD WIPER MOTOR

Pin Number	Circuit	Circuit Function
1	57 (BK)	Ground Circuit
2	28 (BK PK)	Windshield Wiper Switch to Windshield Wiper Motor
3	65 (DG)	Windshield Wiper Switch to Windshield Wiper Motor
4	57 (BK)	Ground Circuit
5	56 (DB O)	Windshield Wiper Switch to Windshield Wiper Motor
6	58 (W)	Windshield Wiper Switch to Windshield Wiper Motor

Pin Number	Circuit	Circuit Function
1	57 (BK)	Ground
2	—	Not Used
3	—	Not Used
4	29 (Y W)	Fuel Level
5	—	Not Used
6	82 (PK Y)	Washer Fluid Level
7	794 (LB)	Coolant Level Sensor
8	419 (DG LG)	Firm Ride ON Input
9	627 (BK O)	Door Ajar Input
10	960 (BK LB)	Traction ON Indicator Input
11	298 (P O)	Ignition Power
12	959 (G Y)	Traction Assist Switch Output

Description and identification of the electrical connectors—Cougar and Thunderbird, Cont.

8838XG25

b. If the tests are not performed OK, repair motor as necessary.

WIPERS DO NOT WORK AT INTERVAL SETTING POSITIONS

1. Set the wiper switch to interval.

a. If the slow(s) speed work(s), go to Step 2.

b. If the slow(s) speed do not work(s), go to Wipers do not Work in Low Speed Position procedure.

2. Disconnect the connector from the malfunction indicator lamp control. Measure the resistance between terminals for circuits **993 (BR/W)** and **589 (O)**.

a. If the resistance is between 10.5 kilo-ohms and 12.0 kilo-ohms, go to Step 4.

b. If the resistance is not between 10.5 kilo-ohms and 12.0 kilo-ohms, go to Step 3.

3. Disconnect the connector from the turn signal/windshield wiper switch. Measure the resistance between circuits **993 (BR/W)** and **589 (O)**.

a. If the resistance is between 10.5 kilo-ohms and 12.0 kilo-ohms, check for an open wire between the turn signal/windshield wiper switch and the windshield wiper governor, service as required.

b. If the resistance is not between 10.5 kilo-ohms and 12.0 kilo-ohms, check for a damaged turn signal/windshield wiper switch, service as required.

4. Rotate the interval control on the turn signal/windshield wiper switch from **S** to **F**. Measure the resistance between circuits **993 (BR/W)** and **590 (DB/W)**.

a. If the resistance is between 3.3–103.3 kilo-ohms, replace the windshield wiper governor.

b. If the resistance is not between 3.3–103.3 kilo-ohms, go to Step 5.

5. Disconnect the harness from the turn signal/windshield wiper switch. Rotate the interval control on the turn signal/windshield wiper switch from **S** to **F**. Measure the resistance between terminals of circuits **993 (BR/W)** and **590 (DB/W)**.

a. If the resistance is between 3.3–103.3 kilo-ohms, check for open wires between turn signal/windshield wiper switch and windshield wiper governor, serviced as required.

b. If the resistance is not between 3.3–103.3 kilo-ohms, check for a damaged turn signal/windshield wiper switch, serviced as required.

WIPERS WILL NOT PARK AT PROPER POSITION

1. Turn the ignition switch to the **OFF** position and the turn signal/windshield wiper switch to **OFF**. Unplug the windshield wiper motor connector. Check for continuity between circuits **28 (BK/PK)** and **56 (DB/O)**.

a. If continuity is found, go to Step 4.

b. If continuity is not found, go to Step 2.

2. Locate the malfunction indicator lamp control at the fuse junction panel and disconnect its electrical connector. Check for continuity between pins **7** and **8**.

a. If continuity is found, check for an unseated connector or an open circuit between the malfunction indicator lamp control and the windshield wiper motor, service as required.

b. If continuity is not found, go to Step 3.

3. Measure the resistance between circuits **993 (BR/W)** and **589 (O)**.

a. If the resistance is between 45 kilo-ohms and 50 kilo-ohms, replace the malfunction indicator lamp control.

b. If the resistance is not between 45 kilo-ohms and 50 kilo-ohms:

• Check for a damaged turn signal/windshield wiper switch, service as required.

• Check for an open unseated turn signal/windshield wiper switch connector.

• Check for an open wire in circuit **993 (BR/W)** and **589 (O)**.

4. Turn the ignition switch to the **RUN** position. Disconnect the windshield wiper motor connector. Using a voltmeter, connect 1 lead to a good ground and the other lead to circuit **65 (DG)**; then, read the voltage.

a. If battery voltage is present, go to Step 5.

b. If battery voltage is not present, service circuit **65 (DG)**, restore vehicle and retest system.

5. Using a voltmeter at the windshield wiper motor connector, connect 1 lead to circuit **65 (DG)** and the other lead to circuit **57 (BK)**; then, read the voltage.

a. If battery voltage is present, go to Step 6.

b. If battery voltage is not present, service circuit **57 (BK)**, restore vehicle and retest system.

6. Connect its electrical connector to the windshield wiper motor. Using an ohmmeter at the windshield wiper motor connector,

connect 1 lead to circuit **28 (BK/PK)** and the other lead to the ground terminal; then, read the ohmmeter.

a. If continuity is found, go to Step 7.

b. If continuity is not found, replace the windshield wiper motor, restore vehicle and retest system.

7. Inspect the windshield wiper mounting arm and pivot shaft.

a. If the windshield wiper mounting arm is bent or cracked, service as required, restore vehicle and retest system.

b. If the windshield wiper mounting arm is not bent or cracked, go to Step 8.

8. Using an ohmmeter, perform the following tests on the windshield wiper switch:

• With the wash switch turned **OFF**, the resistance of pin **4**-to-**2** should be 3.3 kilo-ohms.

• With the wash switch turned **ON**, the resistance is closed to pin **4**-to-**2**.

• With the wiper switch turned **OFF** and the wash switch turned **OFF**, the resistance of pin **4**-to-**2** should be 103.3 kilo-ohms and the resistance of pin **4**-to-**6** should be 47.6 kilo-ohms.

• With the wiper interval switch at **MAX** delay (closest position to **OFF**) to **MIN** delay (closest position to **LO**), the resistance is of pin **4**-to-**2** should be 11.33 kilo-ohms and linearly decreasing from 103.3 kilo-ohms to 3.3 kilo-ohms.

• With the wiper switch turned **LO** and the wash switch turned **OFF**, the resistance of pin **4**-to-**2** should be 3.3 kilo-ohms and the resistance of pin **4**-to-**6** should be 4.08 kilo-ohms.

• With the wiper switch turned **HI** and the wash switch turned **OFF**, the resistance of pin **4**-to-**2** should be 3.3 kilo-ohms and closed to pin **4**-to-**6**.

a. If the switch test are OK, replace the malfunction indicator lamp control, restore the vehicle and retest the system.

b. If the switch test are not OK, replace the turn signal/windshield wiper switch, restore the vehicle and retest the system.

WIPERS RUN WHEN SWITCH IS TURNED OFF

1. Disconnect the electrical connector from the windshield wiper motor and the wires at the malfunction indicator lamp control. Check for continuity of circuit **28 (BK/PK)**.

a. If continuity is found, go to Step 2.

b. If continuity is not found, check for an unseated component or a damaged windshield wiper motor, service as required.

2. Measure the continuity of circuits **28 (BK/PK)** and **56 (DB/O)** at the malfunction indicator lamp control.

a. If continuity is found, check for an open circuit between the malfunction indicator lamp control and windshield wiper motor, service as required.

b. If continuity is not found, go to Step 3.

3. Measure the resistance between circuits **589 (O)** and **993 (BR/W)** at the wiper switch.

a. If resistance is between 45 kilo-ohms and 50 kilo-ohms, replace the malfunction indicator lamp control.

b. If resistance is not between 45 kilo-ohms and 50 kilo-ohms, check for and open circuit at **589 (O)** or **993 (BR/W)** between the turn signal/windshield wiper switch and malfunction indicator lamp control or a damaged turn signal/windshield wiper switch. Service as required.

Crown Victoria, Grand Marquis and Town Car

WINDSHIELD WIPERS INOPERATIVE

1. Check the fluid level in the reservoir.

a. If the fluid level is OK, go to Step 2.

b. If the fluid level is low, fill the reservoir.

2. Activate the turn signal/windshield wiper switch and check the washer pump operation.

a. If the washer pump squirts fluid, go to Step 11.

b. If the washer pump does not squirt fluid, go to Step 3.

3. Activate the turn signal/windshield wiper switch and check the washer pump operation.

a. If the washer pump runs but not squirt fluid, go to Step 9.

b. If the washer pump and squirts fluid, go to Step 4.

4. Turn the ignition switch **ON**, depress the turn signal/windshield wiper switch and check for battery voltage at circuit **941 (BK/W)** at the windshield wiper motor.

a. If the battery voltage is present, go to Step 8.

b. If the battery voltage is not present, go to Step 5.

5. Check for battery voltage at circuit **65 (DG)** at the windshield wiper governor pin **J1-2**.

a. If battery voltage is present, go to Step 6.

b. If battery voltage is not present, check for an open circuit breaker, an open connector and/or an open wire circuit **65 (DG)**, service as required.

6. Disconnect the windshield wiper governor connector, depress the turn signal/windshield wiper switch and measure the resistance between circuits **993 (BR/W)** and **590 (DB/W)**.

a. If there is continuity, go to Step 7.

b. If there is no continuity:
- Check for an open wire between the turn signal/windshield wiper switch and the windshield wiper governor.
- Check for a damaged turn signal/windshield wiper switch, service or replace as required.

7. Connect the windshield wiper governor connector, turn the ignition switch to **RUN**, depress the turn signal/windshield wiper switch and measure the voltage at circuit **58 (W)** at the windshield wiper governor connector.

a. If battery voltage is present, check for an open circuit **58 (W)** between the windshield wiper governor and windshield wiper motor.

b. If battery voltage is not present, replace the damaged windshield wiper governor.

8. Using an ohmmeter, check the ground at the windshield washer pump.

a. If the ground is functional, replace the windshield washer pump.

b. If the ground is functional, service the ground.

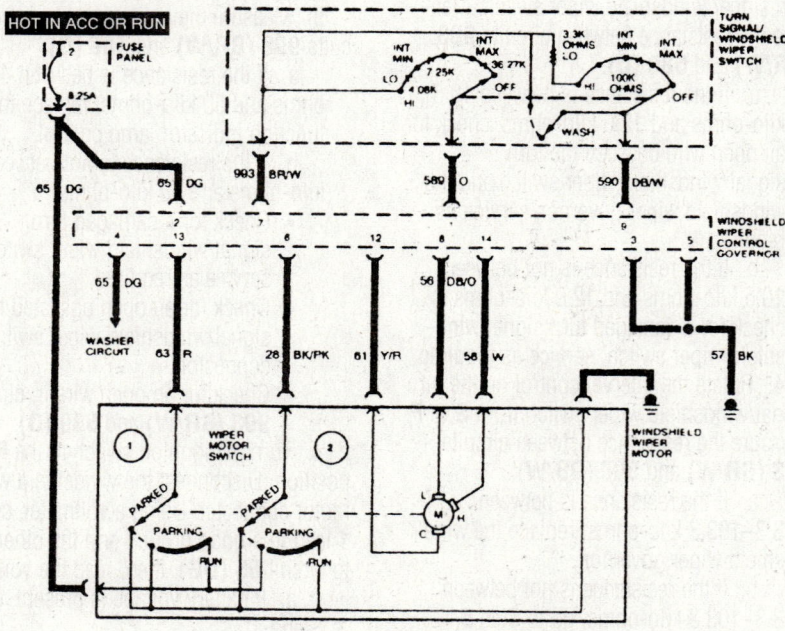

Wiper Circuit

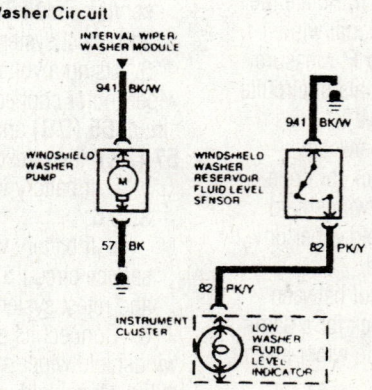

Washer Circuit

Windshield wiper/washer electrical schematic—Continental, Crown Victoria, Grand Marquis and Town Car—Continental, Mark VIII, Sable and Taurus are similar

8838XG26

9. Inspect window washer hose and windshield washer nozzle jet and bracket for blockage or window washer hose kinks.

a. If the window washer hose is bent or kinked, clean, repair or replace as necessary.

b. If the window washer hose is not bent or kinked, go to Step 10.

10. Disconnect window washer hose at windshield washer reservoir and check for blockage at the windshield washer pump outlet.

a. If the window washer hose is blocked at the washer pump outlet, remove the windshield washer pump from the windshield washer reservoir and clean.

b. If the window washer hose is not blocked, replace the windshield washer pump.

11. Disconnect windshield wiper motor connector, turn the ignition switch to **RUN**, depress and release the turn signal/windshield wiper switch; then, check for battery voltage between circuits **58 (W)** and **61 (Y/R)**.

a. If battery voltage is present, perform the windshield wiper motor current draw test, service as required.

b. If battery voltage is not present, go to Stop 12.

12. Turn the ignition switch to **RUN**, depress and release the turn signal/windshield wiper switch; then, check for battery voltage between circuits **58 (W)** and **61**

(Y/R) at the windshield wiper governor connector.

a. If battery voltage is present, check for an unseated connector. Check for an open circuit **58 (W)** between the windshield wiper governor and the windshield wipe motor.

b. If battery voltage is not present, replace the windshield wiper governor.

WINDSHIELD WIPERS INOPERATIVE IN ALL SWITCH POSITIONS

1. Turn the ignition switch to **RUN** and the turn signal/windshield wiper switch to **HI**. Unplug the windshield wiper motor and check for battery voltage at circuit **65 (DG)**.

a. If battery voltage is present, go to Step 2.

b. If battery voltage is not present;
- Check for an open circuit breaker in the fuse junction panel.
- Check for an open connector.
- Check for an open wire circuit **65 (DG)**.
- Check for poor ground connection, service as required.

2. Check for battery voltage at circuit **65 (DG)** pin **2** of the connector.

a. If battery voltage is present, go to Step 3.

b. If battery voltage is not present, service the open in the power feed to windshield wiper governor;
- Check for an open unseated connector.

- Check for an open wire circuit **65 (DG)**.

3. Turn the ignition switch to **RUN** and the turn signal/windshield wiper switch to **HI**. Disconnect the connector from the windshield washer pump. Check for battery voltage between circuits **61 (Y/R)** and **58 (W)**.

a. If battery voltage is present, go to Step 6.

b. If battery voltage is not present, go to Step 4.

4. Check for battery voltage between pin **12**, circuit **61 (Y/R)** and pin **14,** circuit **58 (W)** of the windshield wiper governor connector.

a. If battery voltage is not present, go to Step 5.

b. If battery voltage is present;
- Check for an unseated connector.
- Check for an open connector.
- Check for an open wire circuits **58 (W)** or **61 (Y/R)**.

5. Disconnect the connector from the windshield wiper governor. Measure the resistance between circuits **993 (BR/W)** and circuit **589 (O)**.

a. If resistance is present, replace the windshield wiper governor.

b. If resistance is not present;
- Check for damaged turn signal/windshield wiper switch, service as required.
- Check for an open wire between the turn signal/windshield wiper switch and windshield wiper governor.

6. Disconnect the connector from the turn signal/windshield wiper switch. Check the resistance between terminals for circuits **993 (BR/W)** and circuit **589 (O)**.

a. If resistance is less than 1.0 ohm, check for an open wire between the turn signal/windshield wiper switch and the windshield wiper windshield wiper governor, then, go to Step 7.

b. If resistance is greater than 1.0 ohm, check for a damaged turn signal/windshield wiper switch, service as required.

7. Check the wiper motor current draw:
- Disconnect the windshield wiper mounting arm and pivot shaft from the windshield wiper motor.
- Disconnect the electrical connector from the wiper motor.
- Connect the green lead from the test equipment to the battery positive **(+)** post.
- Connect the positive ® lead from the tester to the common brush terminal (circuit **61**).

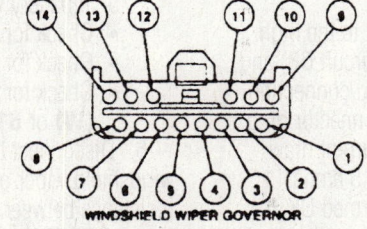

Wire Harness Connector End View

WINDSHIELD WIPER GOVERNOR

Pin Number	Circuit	Circuit Function
1	589 (O)	Turn Signal and Windshield Wiper Switch
2	65 (DG)	Hot in ACC or RUN
3	57 (BK)	Ground
4	941 (BK·W)	Windshield Washer Pump
5	57 (BK)	Ground
6	28 (BK·PK)	Windshield Wiper Motor
7	993 (BR·W)	Windshield Wiper Governor to Turn Signal and Windshield Wiper Switch

Pin Number	Circuit	Circuit Function
8	56 (DB/O)	Windshield Wiper Motor-Lo
9	500 (DB/W)	Interval Switch
10	—	Not Used
11	—	Not Used
12	61 (Y/R)	Windshield Wiper Motor Switch-Parked Position
13	83 (R)	Turn Signal and Windshield Wiper Switch
14	58 (W)	Windshield Wiper Motor-Hi

8838XG27

Windshield wiper governor electrical terminal description—Continental, Crown Victoria, Mark VIII, Grand Marquis and Town Car

- Attach a ground first to the high speed connection (circuit **58**) and then to the low speed connection (circuit **56**) at the connector plug.
- In either case, the current draw should not exceed 3.5 amps.

a. If the tests are performed OK, check the linkage for binding and service as necessary.

b. If the tests are not performed OK, repair motor as necessary.

WINDSHIELD WIPERS INOPERATIVE AT HIGH SPEED

1. Check the windshield wiper operation.

a. If the low speed works, go to Step 4.

b. If the low speed does not work, go to Step 2.

2. Turn the ignition switch **ON** and the turn signal/windshield wiper switch to **HI**. Unplug the windshield wiper motor and check for battery voltage at circuit **65 (DG)**.

a. If battery voltage is present, go to Step 3.

b. If battery voltage is not present;
- Check for an open circuit breaker in the fuse junction panel.
- Check for an open connector.
- Check for an open wire circuit **65 (DG)**.
- Check for poor ground connection, service as required.

3. Check for battery voltage at circuit **65 (DG)** pin **2** of the connector.

a. If battery voltage is present, go to Step 4.

b. If battery voltage is not present, service the open in the power feed to windshield wiper governor;
- Check for an open unseated connector.
- Check for an open wire circuit **65 (DG)**.

4. Turn the ignition switch to **RUN** and the turn signal/windshield wiper switch to **HI**. Disconnect the connector from the windshield wiper motor. Check for battery voltage between circuits **61 (Y/R)** and **56 (DB/O)**.

a. If battery voltage is present, go to Step 7.

b. If battery voltage is not present, go to Step 5.

5. Check for battery voltage between pin **12**, circuit **61 (Y/R)** and pin **14**, circuit **56 (DB/O)** of the windshield wiper governor connector.

a. If battery voltage is not present, go to Step 6.

b. If battery voltage is present;
- Check for an unseated connector.
- Check for an open connector.
- Check for an open wire circuits **56 (DB/O)** or **61 (Y/R)**.

6. Disconnect the connector from the windshield wiper governor. Measure the continuity between circuits **993 (BR/W)** and circuit **589 (O)**.

a. If continuity is present, replace the windshield wiper governor.

b. If continuity is not present;
- Check for damaged turn signal/windshield wiper switch, service as required.
- Check for an open wire between the turn signal/windshield wiper switch and windshield wiper governor.

7. Disconnect the connector from the turn signal/windshield wiper switch. Check the continuity between terminals for circuits **993 (BR/W)** and circuit **589 (O)**.

a. If continuity is present, go to Step 8.

b. If continuity is not present, check for a damaged turn signal/windshield wiper switch, service as required.

8. Check the wiper motor current draw:
- Disconnect the windshield wiper mounting arm and pivot shaft from the windshield wiper motor.
- Disconnect the electrical connector from the wiper motor.
- Connect the green lead from the test equipment to the battery positive **(+)** post.
- Connect the positive ® lead from the tester to the common brush terminal (circuit **61**).
- Attach a ground first to the high speed connection (circuit **58**) and then to the low speed connection (circuit **56**) at the connector plug.
- In either case, the current draw should not exceed 3.5 amps.

a. If the tests are performed OK, check the linkage for binding and service as necessary.

b. If the tests are not performed OK, service the windshield wiper motor as necessary.

WINDSHIELD WIPERS INOPERATIVE AT LOW SPEED

1. Check the windshield wiper operation.

a. If the high speed works, go to Step 4.

b. If the high speed does not work, go to Step 2.

2. Turn the ignition switch **ON** and the turn signal/windshield wiper switch to **HI**.

Unplug the windshield wiper motor and check for battery voltage at circuit **65 (DG)**.

a. If battery voltage is present, go to Step 3.

b. If battery voltage is not present;
- Check for an open circuit breaker in the fuse junction panel.
- Check for an open connector.
- Check for an open wire circuit **65 (DG)**.
- Check for poor ground connection, service as required.

3. Check for battery voltage at circuit **65 (DG)** pin **2** of the connector.

a. If battery voltage is present, go to Step 4.

b. If battery voltage is not present, service the open in the power feed to windshield wiper governor;
- Check for an open unseated connector.
- Check for an open wire circuit **65 (DG)**.

4. Turn the ignition switch to **RUN** and the turn signal/windshield wiper switch to **LO**. Disconnect the connector from the windshield wiper motor. Check for battery voltage between circuits **61 (Y/R)** and **58 (W)**.

a. If battery voltage is present, go to Step 7.

b. If battery voltage is not present, go to Step 5.

5. Check for battery voltage between pin **12**, circuit **61 (Y/R)** and pin **8**, circuit **58 (W)** of the windshield wiper governor connector.

a. If battery voltage is not present, go to Step 6.

b. If battery voltage is present;
- Check for an unseated connector.
- Check for an open connector.
- Check for an open wire circuits **58 (W)** or **61 (Y/R)**.

6. Disconnect the connector from the windshield wiper governor. Measure the resistance between circuit **993 (BR/W)** and circuit **589 (O)**.

a. If resistance is 4.08 kilo-ohms, replace the windshield wiper governor.

b. If resistance is not 4.08 kilo-ohms;
- Check for damaged turn signal/windshield wiper switch, service as required.
- Check for an open wire between the turn signal/windshield wiper switch and windshield wiper governor.

7. Disconnect the connector from the turn signal/windshield wiper switch. Measure the resistance between circuit **993 (BR/W)** and circuit **589 (O)**.

a. If resistance is 4.08 kilo-ohms, go to Step 8.

b. If resistance is not 4.08 kilo-ohms, service the damaged turn signal/windshield wiper switch.

8. Check the wiper motor current draw:
   - Disconnect the windshield wiper mounting arm and pivot shaft from the windshield wiper motor.
   - Disconnect the electrical connector from the wiper motor.
   - Connect the green lead from the test equipment to the battery positive (+) post.
   - Connect the positive ® lead from the tester to the common brush terminal (circuit 61).
   - Attach a ground first to the high speed connection (circuit 58) and then to the low speed connection (circuit 56) at the connector plug.
   - In either case, the current draw should not exceed 3.5 amps.

   a. If the tests are performed OK, check the linkage for binding and service as necessary.

   b. If the tests are not performed OK, service the windshield wiper motor as necessary.

WINDSHIELD WIPERS INOPERATIVE AT INTERVAL SETTING

1. Check the windshield wiper operation.

   a. If the low speed works, go to Step 2.

   b. If the low speed does not work, go to Windshield Wipers Inoperative at Low Speed.

2. Disconnect the connector from the windshield wiper governor. Measure the resistance between circuit 993 (BR/W) and circuit 589 (O).

   a. If resistance is 11.3 kilo-ohms, go to Step 4.

   b. If resistance is not 11.3 kilo-ohms, go to Step 3.

3. Disconnect the connector from the turn signal/windshield wiper switch. Measure the resistance between circuit 993 (BR/W) and circuit 589 (O).

   a. If resistance is 11.3 kilo-ohms, check for an open wire between the turn signal/windshield wiper switch and the windshield wiper governor.

   b. If resistance is not 11.3 kilo-ohms, check for a damaged turn signal/windshield wiper switch, service as required.

4. Rotate the interval control on the turn signal/windshield wiper switch. Measure the resistance between circuit 993 (BR/W) and circuit 590 (DB/W).

   a. If resistance is 3.3 kilo-ohms to 11.3 kilo-ohms, replace the windshield wiper governor.

   b. If resistance is not 3.3 kilo-ohms to 11.3 kilo-ohms, go to Step 5.

5. Disconnect the connector from the turn signal/windshield wiper switch. Rotate the interval control on the turn signal/windshield wiper switch from MIN to MAX. Measure the resistance between terminals of the turn signal/windshield wiper switch for circuit 993 (BR/W) and circuit 590 (DB/W).

   a. If resistance is 3.3 kilo-ohms to 11.3 kilo-ohms, check for an open wire(s) between the turn signal/windshield wiper switch and the windshield wiper governor.

   b. If resistance is not 3.3 kilo-ohms to 11.3 kilo-ohms, check for a damaged turn signal/windshield wiper switch, service as required.

WINDSHIELD WIPERS WILL NOT PARK

1. Turn the turn signal/windshield wiper switch to OFF position. Unplug the windshield wiper motor and check for continuity between circuit 28 (BK/PK) and circuit 58 (W).

   a. If continuity is present, perform the windshield wiper motor parking test.

   b. If continuity is not present, go to Step 2.

2. Turn the ignition switch to OFF position. Unplug the windshield wiper governor and check for continuity between pin J1-6 and J1-8 of the windshield wiper governor.

   a. If continuity is present:
   - Check for unseated connectors.
   - Check for an open circuit between the windshield wiper governor and windshield wiper motor, service as required.

   b. If continuity is not present, go to Step 3.

3. Turn the turn signal/windshield wiper switch to OFF position. Measure the resistance between circuit 589 (O) and circuit 993 (BR/W).

   a. If resistance is not approximately 47.6 kilo-ohms:
   - Check for open circuit 589 (O) or 993 (BR/W).
   - Check for a damaged turn signal/windshield wiper switch, service as required.
   - Check for an unseated turn signal/windshield wiper switch connector.

   b. If resistance is approximately 47.6 kilo-ohms, replace the windshield wiper governor.

WINDSHIELD WIPERS WILL NOT TURN OFF

1. Disconnect the connector from the windshield wiper motor. Turn the ignition switch to RUN position and the turn signal/windshield wiper switch to OFF position. Measure the continuity between circuits 28 (BK/PK) and between circuits 61 (Y/R) and 63 ®.

   a. If continuity is present:
   - Check for unseated connectors.
   - Check for a damaged windshield wiper motor, service as required.

   b. If continuity is not present, go to Step 2.

2. Measure the continuity between circuits 28 (BK/PK) and 58 (W) and between circuits 61 (Y/R) and 63 ® at the windshield wiper governor.

   a. If continuity is present, service the open circuit between the windshield wiper governor and windshield wiper motor.

   b. If continuity is not present, go to Step 3.

3. Measure the resistance between circuit 589 (O) and circuit 993 (BR/W).

   a. If resistance is not approximately 47.6 kilo-ohms:
   - Check for open circuit 589 (O) or 993 (BR/W) between turn signal/windshield wiper switch and the windshield wiper governor.
   - Check for a damaged turn signal/windshield wiper switch, service as required.

   b. If resistance is approximately 47.6 kilo-ohms, replace the windshield wiper governor.

Mustang

WINDSHIELD WASHER INOPERATIVE

1. Check the fluid level in the reservoir.
   a. If the level is OK, go to Step 2.
   b. If the level is not OK, fill the reservoir.

2. Turn the windshield washer switch ON. Check the fluid level in the reservoir.
   a. If the windshield washer pump runs, go to Step 3.
   b. If the windshield washer pump does not run, go to Step 6.

3. Inspect the windshield washer nozzle jet and bracket for blockage.
   a. If the windshield washer nozzle jet

and bracket are blocked, clean and replace the windshield washer nozzle jet and bracket.

b. If the windshield washer nozzle jet and bracket are not blocked, go to Step 4.

4. Inspect the windshield washer hose, filter and/or check valve for blockage or kinks.

a. If blockage or kinks are present, clean, service or replace as necessary.

b. If blockage or kinks are not present, go to Step 5.

5. Inspect the windshield washer pump outlet for blockage.

a. If the windshield washer pump outlet is blockage or obstructed, remove and clean the washer pump.

b. If windshield washer pump outlet is not blockage or obstructed, Replace the washer pump and retest the system.

6. Using a voltmeter, actuate the turn signal/windshield wiper switch and check for voltage at the windshield washer pump.

a. If battery voltage is present, go to Step 7.

b. If battery voltage is not present, go to Step 8.

7. Using an ohmmeter, check for ground at the pump connector.

a. If the connector is properly grounded, replace the windshield washer pump.

b. If the connector is not properly grounded, service the ground.

8. Turn the windshield wiper **ON** and check the operation.

a. If wipers operate, go to Step 9.

b. If wipers do not operate, go to Windshield Wipers Inoperative in All Switch Positions.

9. Disconnect the connector from the

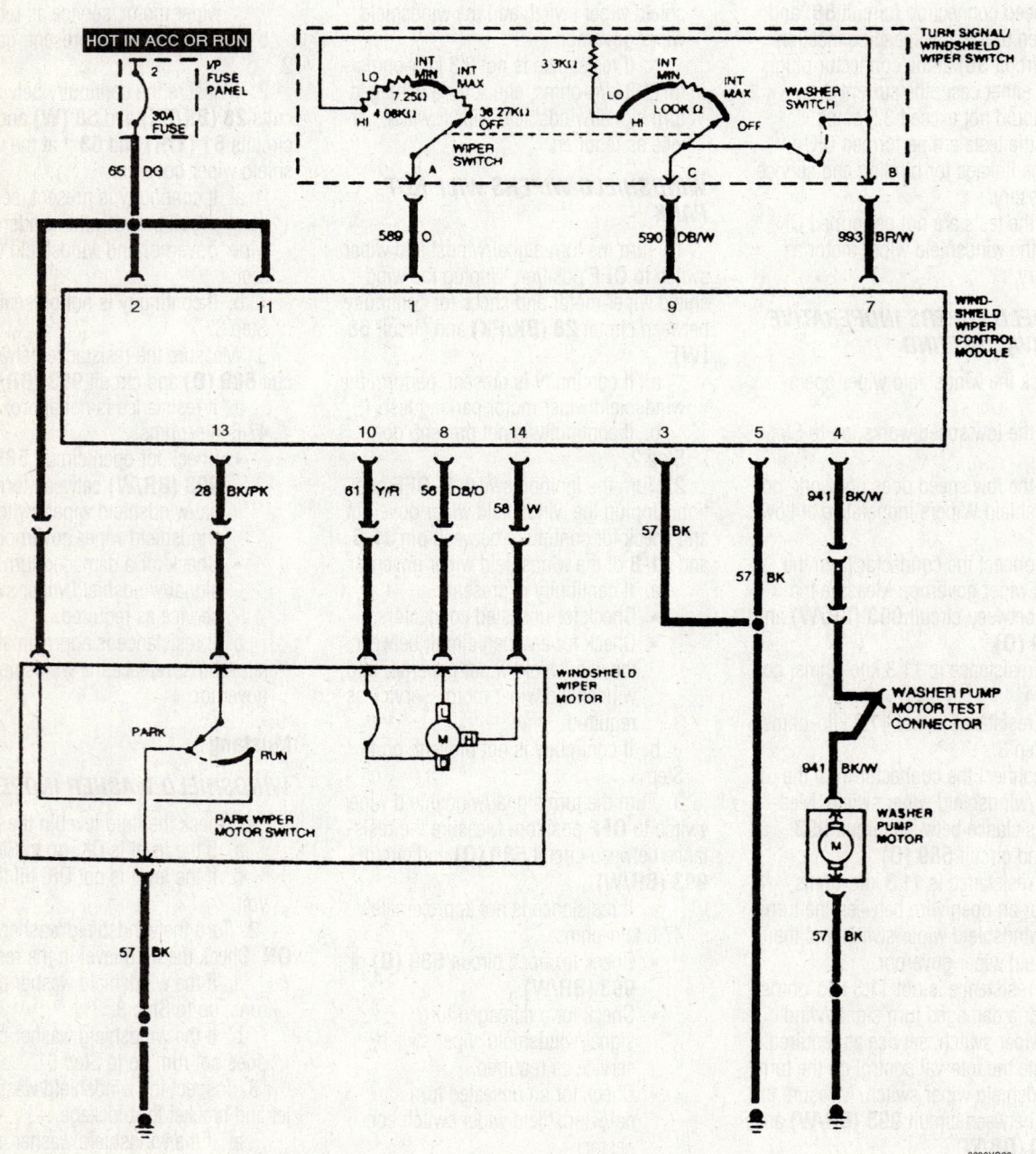

Windshield wiper electrical schematic—Mustang

8838XG28

Connector End Views

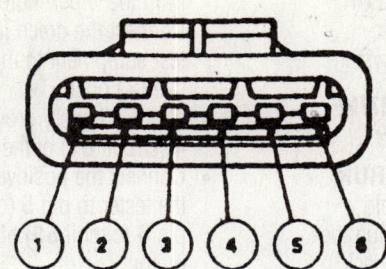

WINDSHIELD WIPER MOTOR

Pin Number	Circuit	Circuit Function
1	57 (BK)	Wiper Motor Ground (Park)
2	28 (BK/PK)	Wiper Module to Wiper Motor (Park Switch)
3	65 (DG)	Wiper Motor Power (Park Feed)
4	61 (Y/R)	Wiper Motor Common (RUN)
5	56 (DB/O)	Wiper Motor LO
6	58 (W)	Wiper Motor HI

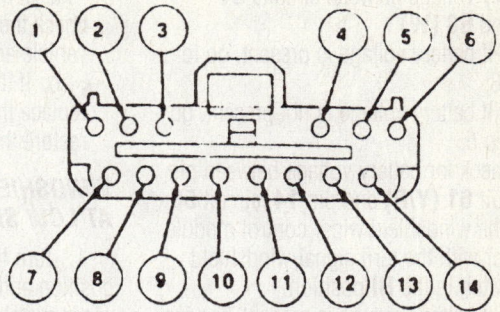

WINDSHIELD WIPER CONTROL MODULE

Pin Number	Circuit	Circuit Function
1	58 (W)	Windshield Wiper Motor HI
2	28 (BK/PK)	Windshield Wiper Motor Park Switch
3	—	Not Used
4	65 (DG)	Power (Hot In ACC or RUN)
5	61 (Y/R)	Windshield Wiper Motor Connector
6	590 (DB/W)	Interval Wiper/Washer Reference Voltage
7	56 (DB/O)	Windshield Wiper Motor LO
8	993 (BR/W)	Interval Wiper/Washer Reference Voltage
9	—	Not Used
10	57 (BK)	Ground
11	941 (BK/W)	Windshield Washer Pump Motor
12	57 (BK)	Ground
13	65 (DG)	Power (Hot In ACC or RUN)
14	589 (O)	Windshield Wiper Switch

8838XG29

Windshield wiper motor terminal identification—Mustang

windshield wiper control module. Depress the washer switch on the end of the turn signal/windshield wiper switch. Check the continuity between circuits **993 (BR/W)** and **590 (DB/W)**.

  a. If continuity is present, go to Step 11.

  b. If continuity is not present, go to Step 10.

10. Disconnect the connector from the windshield wiper switch. Depress the turn signal/windshield wiper switch. Check continuity between terminated **B** and **W**.

  a. If continuity is present, service for an open circuit between the turn signal/windshield wiper switch and the wiper control module.

  b. If continuity is not present, service the turn signal/windshield wiper switch.

11. Check the continuity of circuit **941 (BK/W)** from the wiper control module to the windshield washer pump.

  a. If continuity is present, replace the wiper control module.

  b. If continuity is not present, service for an open circuit.

WINDSHIELD WIPERS INOPERATIVE IN ALL SWITCH POSITIONS

1. Turn the ignition switch **RUN** and the turn signal/windshield wiper switch to **HI**. Unplug the windshield wiper motor. Check for battery voltage at circuit **65 (DG)**.

  a. If battery voltage is present, go to Step 2.

  b. If battery voltage is not present, go to Step 3.

2. Check for battery voltage at circuit **65 (DG)** pin **2** of the connector.

  a. If battery voltage is present, go to Step 4.

  b. If battery voltage is not present, service circuit **65 (DG)** for an open circuit, restore vehicle and retest the system.

3. Using a test lamp, check for battery voltage at fuse **2** (30 amp).

  a. If voltage is present on both sides of the circuit breaker, service the circuit **65 (DG)** for an open circuit, restore vehicle and retest the system.

  b. If voltage is not present, replace the fuse.

4. Turn the ignition switch **RUN** and the turn signal/windshield wiper switch to **HI**. Unplug the windshield wiper motor. Check

for battery voltage between circuits **61 (Y/R)** and **58 (W)**.

a. If battery voltage is present, go to Step 8.

b. If battery voltage is not present, go to Step 5.

5. Check for battery voltage between pin **10**, circuit **61 (Y/R)** and pin **14**, circuit **58 (W)** of the windshield wiper control module connector with the turn signal/windshield wiper switch in the **HI** position.

a. If battery voltage is present, service circuit **61 (Y/R)** or circuit **58 (W)** for an open circuit, restore the vehicle and retest the system.

b. If battery voltage is not present, go to Step 6.

6. Disconnect the connector from the windshield wiper control module. Measure the resistance between circuits **993 (BR/W)** and **589 (O)** with the turn signal/windshield wiper switch in the **HI** position.

a. If resistance is less than 1.0 ohm, replace the windshield wiper control module, restore the vehicle and retest the system.

b. If resistance is greater than 1.0 ohm, go to Step 7.

7. Disconnect the connector from the turn signal/windshield wiper switch. Check the continuity between terminals for circuits **993 (BR/W)** and **589 (O)** with the turn signal/windshield wiper switch in the **HI** position.

a. If resistance is less than 1.0 ohm, service circuits **993 (BR/W)** or **589 (O)** for an open circuit, restore the vehicle and retest the system.

b. If resistance is greater than 1.0 ohm, replace the turn signal/windshield wiper switch, restore the vehicle and retest the system.

8. Check the wiper motor current draw:
- Disconnect the starter relay cable from the battery.
- Disconnect the windshield wiper mounting arm and pivot shaft from the windshield wiper motor.
- Disconnect the electrical connector from the wiper motor.
- Connect the green lead from the test equipment to the battery positive **(+)** post.
- Attach a battery ground wire to pin **4** (circuit **61**) of the wiper motor.
- Connect the positive ® lead from the tester to pin **5** (circuit **56**) or pin **6** (circuit **58**) of the wiper motor.
- In either case, the current draw should not exceed 3.0 amps.

a. If the tests are performed OK, check the linkage for binding, restore the vehicle and retest the system.

b. If the tests are not performed OK, replace the windshield wiper motor, restore the vehicle and retest the system.

WINDSHIELD WIPERS INOPERATIVE AT LOW SPEED

1. Turn the ignition switch to the **RUN** position and the turn signal/windshield wiper switch to the **LO** position. Unplug the windshield wiper motor connector. Check for battery voltage between circuits **61 (Y/R)** and **56 (DB/O)**.

a. If battery voltage is present, go to Step 5.

b. If battery voltage is not present, go to Step 2.

2. Check for battery voltage between pin **10**, circuit **61 (Y/R)** and pin **8**, circuit **56 (DB/O)** of the windshield wiper control module connector.

a. If battery voltage is present, service circuit **61 (Y/R)** or circuit **56 (DB/O)** for an open circuit, restore the vehicle and retest the system.

b. If battery voltage is not present, go to Step 3.

3. Disconnect the connector from the windshield wiper control module. Measure the resistance between circuits **993 (BR/W)** and **589 (O)** with the turn signal/windshield wiper switch in the **LO** position.

a. If the resistance is between 3.5 kilo-ohms and 4.5 kilo-ohms, replace the windshield wiper control module, restore the vehicle and retest the system.

b. If the resistance is not between 3.5 kilo-ohms and 4.5 kilo-ohms, go to Step 4.

4. Disconnect the connector from the turn signal/windshield wiper switch. Measure the continuity between terminals for circuits **993 (BR/W)** and **589 (O)** with the turn signal/windshield wiper switch in the **LO** position.

a. If the resistance is between 3.5 kilo-ohms and 4.5 kilo-ohms, service circuits **993 (BR/W)** or **589 (O)** for an open circuit, restore the vehicle and retest the system.

b. If the resistance is not between 3.5 kilo-ohms and 4.5 kilo-ohms, replace the damaged turn signal/windshield wiper switch, restore the vehicle and retest the system.

5. Check the wiper motor current draw:
- Disconnect the starter relay cable from the battery.
- Disconnect the windshield wiper

mounting arm and pivot shaft from the windshield wiper motor.
- Disconnect the electrical connector from the wiper motor.
- Connect the green lead from the test equipment to the battery positive **(+)** post.
- Attach a battery ground wire to pin **4** (circuit **61**) of the wiper motor.
- Connect the positive **(R)** lead from the tester to pin **5** (circuit **56**) or pin **6** (circuit **58**) of the wiper motor.
- In either case, the current draw should not exceed 3.0 amps.

a. If the tests are performed OK, check the linkage for binding, restore the vehicle and retest the system.

b. If the tests are not performed OK, replace the windshield wiper motor, restore the vehicle and retest the system.

WINDSHIELD WIPERS INOPERATIVE AT INTERVAL SETTING

1. Disconnect the connector from the wiper control module. Measure the resistance between circuit **993 (BR/W)** and circuit **589 (O)** with the turn signal/windshield wiper switch at the interval setting.

a. If the resistance is between 10.5 kilo-ohms and 12.0 kilo-ohms, go to Step 3.

b. If the resistance is not between 10.5 kilo-ohms and 12.0 kilo-ohms, go to Step 2

2. Disconnect the connector from the turn signal/windshield wiper switch. Measure the resistance between terminals for circuits **993 (BR/W)** and **589 (O)** with the turn signal/windshield wiper switch at the interval setting.

a. If the resistance is between 10.5 kilo-ohms and 12.0 kilo-ohms, service circuit **993 (BR/W)** or circuit **589 (O)** for an open circuit, restore the vehicle and retest the system.

b. If the resistance is not between 10.5 kilo-ohms and 12.0 kilo-ohms, replace the damaged wiper/washer switch, restore the vehicle and retest the system.

3. Rotate the interval control on the turn signal/windshield wiper switch from **MIN** to **MAX**. Measure the resistance between circuits **993 (BR/W)** and circuit **590 (DB/W)**.

a. If the resistance is less than 104 kilo-ohms, replace the wiper control module, restore the vehicle and retest the system.

b. If the resistance is greater than 104 kilo-ohms, go to Step 4.

4. Disconnect the connector from the turn signal/windshield wiper switch. Rotate the interval control on the turn signal/windshield wiper switch from **MIN** to **MAX**. Measure the resistance between terminals of the wiper switch for circuits **993 (BR/W)** and circuit **590 (DB/W)**.

a. If the resistance is less than 104 kilo-ohms, service circuit **993 (BR/W)** or circuit **589 (O)** for an open circuit, restore the vehicle and retest the system.

b. If the resistance is greater than 104 kilo-ohms, replace the damaged wiper/washer switch, restore the vehicle and retest the system.

WINDSHIELD WIPERS WILL NOT PARK AT PROPER POSITION

1. Unplug the wiper motor connector. Check for ground at circuit **57 (BK)**.

a. If ground is okay, go to Step 2.

b. If ground is not okay, service the open circuit.

2. Turn the ignition switch to the **RUN** position and the wiper switch to the **OFF** position. Check for battery voltage between circuit **65 (DG)** and **57 (BK)**.

a. If battery voltage is present, go to Step 3.

b. If battery voltage is not present, service the open circuits.

3. Turn the wiper switch to the **OFF** position. Check for continuity of circuit **28 (BK/PK)** to **56 (DB/O)** and circuit **61 (Y/R)** to **57 (BK)**.

a. If continuity is okay, go to Step 5.

b. If continuity is not okay, go to Step 4.

4. Check continuity of circuits **28 (BK/PK)**, **56 (DB/O)**, **61 (Y/R)** and **57 (BK)** from the wiper motor to the wiper control module.

a. If continuity is okay, replace the wiper control module.

b. If continuity is not okay, service the open circuits.

5. Check that the wiper linkage is not bent, cracked or out of position from the motor shaft.

a. If the linkage is okay, replace the wiper motor.

b. If the linkage is not okay, service linkage.

WIPERS WILL NOT STOP IN INTERVAL OR STOP MODE

1. Check that the wiper motor and the wiper control module connectors are fully seated.

a. If connections are is okay, go to Step 2.

b. If connections are not okay, service as required and recheck the system.

2. Disconnect the connector from the wiper motor. Turn the wiper switch to the **OFF** position. Check the continuity of circuits **28 (BK/PK)** to **56 (DB/O)** and between circuits **61 (Y/R)** and **57 (BK)** at the motor connector.

a. If the continuity exists, replace the damaged wiper motor.

b. If the continuity does not exist, go to Step 3.

3. Check the continuity of circuits **28 (BK/PK)**, **56 (DB/O)**, **61 (Y/R)** and **57 (BK)** from the wiper motor to wiper control module.

a. If the continuity is okay, go to Step 4.

b. If the continuity is not okay, service circuit as required.

4. Turn the wiper switch to the **OFF** position. Measure the resistance between circuits **589 (O)** and **933 (BR/W)** at the wiper control module.

a. If resistance is between 45 kilo-ohms and 50 kilo-ohms, replace the wiper control module.

b. If resistance is not between 45 kilo-ohms and 50 kilo-ohms:, go to Step 5

5. Check the continuity of circuits **589 (O)** and **993 (BR/W)** between the wiper switch and wiper control module.

a. If the continuity is okay, replace the wiper switch.

b. If the continuity is not okay, service open circuit(s).

Mark VIII, Sable and Taurus

WINDSHIELD WASHERS INOPERATIVE IN ALL SWITCH POSITIONS

1. Check the fluid level in the reservoir.

a. If the level is OK, go to Step 2.

b. If the level is not OK, fill the reservoir.

2. Activate the washer switch. Check the fluid level in the reservoir.

a. If the motor is inoperative, go to Step 3.

b. If the motor operates but fluid will not squirt, go to Step 8.

c. If fluid squirts but the wipers do not operate, go to Step 10.

3. Turn the ignition switch **ON**. Depress the washer switch. Check for battery voltage at circuit **941 (BK/W)** at the washer pump.

a. If battery voltage is present, go to Step 7.

b. If battery voltage is not present, go to Step 4.

4. Check for battery voltage at circuits **65 (DG)** of the wiper control module.

a. If battery voltage is present, go to Step 5.

b. If battery voltage is not present:
- Check for circuit breakers.
- Check for an open connector.
- Check for an open wire circuit **65 (DG)**, service as required.

5. Disconnect the connector from the windshield control module. Depress the washer switch. Measure the resistance between circuit **993 (BR/W)** and between circuit **590 (DB/W)**.

a. If continuity is present, go to Step 6.

b. If continuity is not present:
- Check for an open wire between the wiper switch and the wiper control module.
- Check for a damaged windshield wiper/washer switch, service as required.

6. Connect the connector to the wiper control module. Turn the ignition switch to the **RUN** position. Depress the washer switch. Measure the voltage at circuit **56 (DB/O)** at the wiper control module connector.

a. If battery voltage is present, check for an open circuit **56 (DB/O)** between the wiper control module and wiper motor.

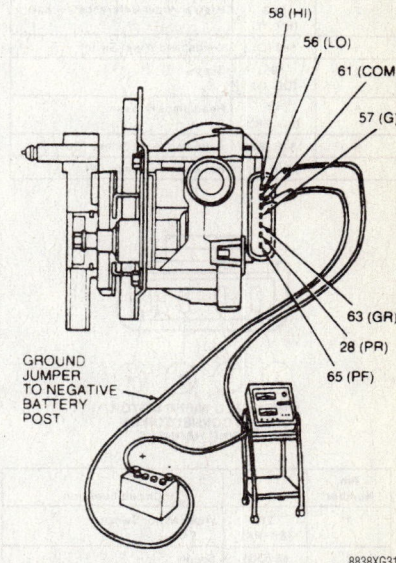

Windshield wiper motor terminal identification and motor testing—Mark VIII, Sable and Taurus

58 (HI)
56 (LO)
61 (COM)
57 (G)
63 (GR)
28 (PR)
65 (PF)

GROUND JUMPER TO NEGATIVE BATTERY POST

8838XG31

b. If continuity is not present, replace the damaged wiper control module.

7. Using an ohmmeter, check the ground at the pump.

a. If the ground is functional, replace the washer pump.

b. If the ground is not functional, service the ground.

8. Inspect the washer hose and nozzle for blockage or hose kinks.

a. If the hose is blocked or kinked, clean, replace or service the nozzle of hoses.

b. If the hose is not blocked or kinked, go to Step 9.

9. Disconnect the hose at the reservoir and check for blockage at the washer pump outlet.

a. If the hose is blocked at the washer outlet, remove and clean the nozzle water pump.

b. If the hose is not blocked at the washer outlet, replace the washer pump.

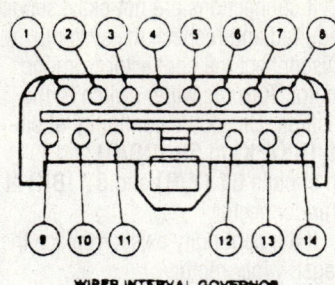

WIPER INTERVAL GOVERNOR

Pin Number	Circuit	Circuit Function
1	589 (O)	Turn Signal and Windshield Wiper Switch
2	65 (DG)	Power (Hot in ACC or RUN)
3	26 (W/P)	Ground
4	941 (BK·W)	Windshield Washer Pump
5	57 (BK)	Ground
6	28 (BK·PK)	Turn Signal and Windshield Wiper Switch
7	993 (BR/W)	Windshield Wiper Governor to Turn Signal and Windshield Wiper Switch
8	56 (DB·O)	Windshield Wiper Motor—LO
9	590 (DB/W)	Windshield Wiper Governor to Turn Signal and Windshield Wiper Switch
10	—	Not Used
11	—	Not Used
12	61 (Y/R)	Windshield Wiper Motor Common
13	63 (R)	Turn Signal and Windshield Wiper Switch
14	58 (W)	Windshield Wiper Motor—Hi

8838XG33

Windshield wiper interval governor connector terminal identification—Sable and Taurus

10. Disconnect the connector from the wiper motor. Turn the ignition switch to the

RUN position. Depress and release the washer switch. Check for battery voltage between circuit **56 (DB/O)** and **61 (Y/R)**.

a. If battery voltage is present, perform the wiper motor current draw test, service as required.

b. If battery voltage is not present, go to Step 11.

11. Turn the ignition switch to the **RUN** position. Depress and release the washer switch. Check for battery voltage between circuit **56 (DB/O)** and **61 (Y/R)** at the wiper control module connector.

a. If battery voltage is present:
- Check for an unseated connector.
- Check for an open circuit **56 (DB/O)** between the wiper control module and wiper motor.

b. If battery voltage is not present, replace the wiper control module.

WINDSHIELD WIPERS INOPERATIVE AT HIGH SPEED

1. Check the low speed operation.
a. If the low speed works, go to Step 4.
b. If the low speed does not work, go to Step 2.

2. Turn the ignition switch to the **ON** position and the wiper switch to the **HI** position. Unplug the wiper motor connector. Check for battery voltage at circuit **65 (DG)**.

a. If battery voltage is present, go to Step 3.

b. If battery voltage is not present:
- Check for an open circuit breaker in the fuse panel.
- Check for an open wire circuit **65 (DG)**.
- Check for an open wire connector.

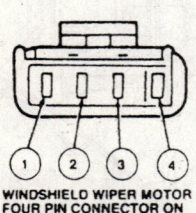

WINDSHIELD WIPER SWITCH CONNECTOR ON 14401 WIRING ASSY

Pin Number	Circuit	Circuit Function
1	590 (DB·W)	Interval Switch
2	993 (BR·W)	Interval Wiper Reference Voltage
3	589 (O)	Windshield Wiper Switch
4	196 (DB·O)	Supply
5	12 (LG·BK)	Headlamps Hi Beam
6	13 (R·BK)	Autolamp Auto Dimmer Control
7	15 (R·Y)	Hot with Headlamps ON

WINDSHIELD WIPER MOTOR FOUR PIN CONNECTOR ON 14401 WIRING HARNESS

Pin Number	Circuit	Circuit Function
1	28 (BK·PK)	Wiper Motor Switch
2	65 (DG)	Supply
3	63 (R)	Wiper Motor Switch
4	57 (BK)	Ground

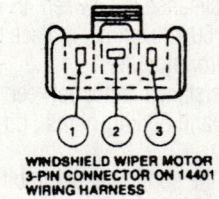

WINDSHIELD WIPER MOTOR 3-PIN CONNECTOR ON 14401 WIRING HARNESS

Pin Number	Circuit	Circuit Function
1	61 (Y·R)	Motor Common
2	56 (DB·O)	Motor Low Speed Supply
3	58 (W)	Motor High Speed Supply

Washer

8838XG32

Windshield wiper motor and switch connectors terminal identification and washer electrical schematic—Continental

- Check for a poor ground connection, service as required.

3. Check for battery voltage at circuit 65 (DG) pin 2 of the connector.

a. If battery voltage is present, go to Step 4.

b. If battery voltage is not present, service the open in the power feed to module:

- Check for an open in circuit 65 (DG).
- Check for an open unseated connector.

4. Turn the ignition switch to the RUN position and the wiper switch to the HI position. Disconnect the connector from the wiper motor. Check for battery voltage between circuit 58 (W) and 61 (Y/R).

a. If battery voltage is present, go to Step 7.

b. If battery voltage is not present, go to Step 5.

5. Check for battery voltage between pin 12 circuit 61 (Y/R) and pin 14 circuit 58 (W) of the wiper control module connector.

a. If battery voltage is present:

- Check for open wire circuits 58 (W) or 61 (Y/R).
- Check for an unseated connector.
- Check for an open unseated connector.

b. If battery voltage is not present, go to Step 6.

6. Disconnect the connector from the wiper control module. Measure the resistance between circuit 993 (BR/W) and circuit 589 (O).

a. If the resistance is less than 1.0 ohm, replace the wiper control module.

b. If the resistance is greater than 1.0 ohm:

- Check for an open wire between the wiper switch and the wiper control module.
- Check for a damaged wiper/washer switch, service as required.

7. Disconnect the connector from the wiper switch. Measure the resistance between terminals for circuit 993 (BR/W) and circuit 589 (O).

a. If the resistance is less than 1.0 ohm, check for an open wire between the switch and the wiper control module.

b. If the resistance is greater than 1.0 ohm, check for a damaged wiper/washer switch, service as required.

8. Check the wiper motor current draw:

- Disconnect the windshield wiper mounting arm and pivot shaft from the windshield wiper motor.

- Disconnect the electrical connector from the wiper motor.
- Connect the green lead from the test equipment to the battery positive (+) post.
- Connect the positive ® lead from the tester to the common brush terminal (circuit 61).
- Attach a ground first to the low speed connection (circuit 56) and then to the high speed connection (circuit 58) at the connector plug.
- In either case, the current draw should not exceed 3.5 amps.

a. If the tests are performed OK, check the linkage for binding and service as necessary.

b. If the tests are not performed OK, service the wiper motor as necessary.

WINDSHIELD WIPERS INOPERATIVE AT LOW SPEED

1. Check the high speed operation.

a. If the high speed works, go to Step 4.

b. If the high speed does not work, go to Step 2.

2. Turn the ignition switch to the ON position and the wiper switch to the HI position. Unplug the wiper motor connector. Check for battery voltage at circuit 65 (DG).

a. If battery voltage is present, go to Step 3.

b. If battery voltage is not present:

- Check for an open circuit breaker in the fuse panel.
- Check for an open wire circuit 65 (DG).
- Check for an open connector.
- Check for a poor ground connection, service as required.

3. Check for battery voltage at circuit 65 (DG) pin 2 of the connector.

a. If battery voltage is present, go to Step 4.

b. If battery voltage is not present, service the open in the power feed to module:

- Check for an open wire in circuit 65 (DG).
- Check for an open unseated connector.

4. Turn the ignition switch to the RUN position and the wiper switch to the LO position. Disconnect the connector from the wiper motor. Check for battery voltage between circuit 56 (DB/O) and 61 (Y/R).

a. If battery voltage is present, go to Step 7.

b. If battery voltage is not present, go to Step 5.

5. Check for battery voltage between pin 12 circuit 61 (Y/R) and pin 8 circuit 56 (DB/O) of the wiper control module connector.

a. If battery voltage is present:

- Check for open wire circuits 56 (DB/O) or 61 (Y/R).
- Check for an unseated connector.
- Check for an open connector.

b. If battery voltage is not present, go to Step 6.

6. Disconnect the connector from the wiper control module. Measure the resistance between circuit 993 (BR/W) and circuit 589 (O).

a. If the resistance is between 3.5–4.5 kilo-ohms, replace the wiper control module.

b. If the resistance is not between 3.5–4.5 kilo-ohms:

- Check for an open wire between the wiper switch and the wiper control module.
- Check for a damaged wiper/washer switch, service as required.

7. Disconnect the connector from the wiper switch. Measure the resistance between terminals for circuit 993 (BR/W) and circuit 589 (O).

a. If the resistance is between 3.5–4.5 kilo-ohms, check for an open wire between the switch and the wiper control module.

b. If the resistance is not between 3.5–4.5 kilo-ohms, check for a damaged wiper/washer switch, service as required.

8. Check the wiper motor current draw:

- Disconnect the windshield wiper mounting arm and pivot shaft from the windshield wiper motor.
- Disconnect the electrical connector from the wiper motor.
- Connect the green lead from the test equipment to the battery positive (+) post.
- Connect the positive ® lead from the tester to the common brush terminal (circuit 61).
- Attach a ground first to the low speed connection (circuit 56) and then to the high speed connection (circuit 58) at the connector plug.
- In either case, the current draw should not exceed 3.5 amps.

a. If the tests are performed OK, check the linkage for binding and service as necessary.

b. If the tests are not performed OK, service the wiper motor as necessary.

For brake related suspension and axle service, refer to the model specific sections of this manual

WINDSHIELD WIPERS INOPERATIVE AT SLOW SPEED INTERVAL

1. Check the slow speed operation.
   a. If the slow(s) speed works, go to Step 2.
   b. If the slow(s) speed does not work, go to Windshield Wipers Inoperative at High Speed.
2. Disconnect the connector from the wiper control module. Measure the resistance between circuit **993 (BR/W)** and circuit **589 (O)**.
   a. If the resistance is between 10.5 kilo-ohms and 12.0 kilo-ohms, go to Step 4.
   b. If the resistance is not between 10.5 kilo-ohms and 12.0 kilo-ohms, go to Step 3
3. Disconnect the connector from the wiper switch. Measure the resistance between terminals for circuit **993 (BR/W)** and circuit **589 (O)**.
   a. If the resistance is between 10.5 kilo-ohms and 12.0 kilo-ohms, check for an open wire between the switch and the wiper control module.
   b. If the resistance is not between 10.5 kilo-ohms and 12.0 kilo-ohms, check for a damaged wiper/washer switch, service as required.
4. Rotate the interval control on the wiper switch from **S** to **F**. Measure the resistance between circuit **993 (BR/W)** and circuit **590 (DB/W)**.
   a. If the resistance is between 3.3 kilo-ohms and 104 kilo-ohms, replace the wiper control module.
   b. If the resistance is not between 3.3 kilo-ohms and 104 kilo-ohms, go to Step 5
5. Disconnect the connector from the wiper switch. Rotate the interval control on the wiper switch from **S** to **F**. Measure the resistance between terminals of the wiper switch for circuit **993 (BR/W)** and circuit **590 (DB/W)**.
   a. If the resistance is between 3.3 kilo-ohms and 104 kilo-ohms, check for open wires between the wiper switch and the wiper control module.
   b. If the resistance is not between 3.3 kilo-ohms and 104 kilo-ohms, Check for a damaged wiper switch, service as required.

WINDSHIELD WIPERS WILL NOT PARK

1. Turn the wiper switch to the **OFF** position. Unplug the wiper motor connector. Check for continuity between circuit **28 (BK/PK)** and **56 (DB/O)**.

a. If continuity is present, perform the motor parking test.
   b. If continuity is not present, go to Step 2.
2. Turn the ignition switch to the **OFF** position. Unplug the wiper control module. Check for continuity between pin **6** and pin **8** of the wiper control module.
   a. If continuity is present:
   • Check for an open circuit breaker between the wiper control module and the wiper motor.
   • Check for an open unseated connector.
   b. If continuity is not present, go to Step 3.
3. Turn the wiper switch to the **OFF** position. Measure the resistance between circuit **589 (O)** and **993 (BR/W)**.
   a. If resistance is between 45 kilo-ohms to 50 kilo-ohms, replace the wiper control module.
   b. If resistance is not between 45 kilo-ohms to 50 kilo-ohms:
   • Check for an unseated wiper switch connector.
   • Check for an open circuit **589 (O)** and **993 (BR/W)**.
   • Check for a damaged wiper switch, service as required.

WIPERS WILL NOT STOP IN INTERVAL OR STOP MODE

1. Disconnect the connector from the wiper motor. Turn the ignition switch to the **RUN** position and the wiper switch to the **OFF** position. Measure the continuity between circuits **28 (BK/PK)** and between circuits **61 (Y/R)** and **63** ®.
   a. If the continuity exists, check for an unseated component and/or a damaged wiper motor, service as required.
   b. If the continuity does not exist, go to Step 2.
2. Measure the continuity between circuits **28 (BK/PK)** and **56 (DB/O)** and between circuits **61 (Y/R)** and **63** ® at the wiper control module connector.
   a. If the continuity exists, check open circuit between the wiper control module and the wiper motor.
   b. If the continuity does not exist, go to Step 3.
3. Measure the resistance between circuit **589 (O)** and **993 (BR/W)**.
   a. If resistance is between 45 kilo-ohms and 50 kilo-ohms, replace the wiper control module.
   b. If resistance is not between 45 kilo-ohms to 50 kilo-ohms:
   • Check for an open circuit **589 (O)** and **993 (BR/W)** between the

wiper switch and the wiper control module.
   • Check for a damaged wiper switch, service as required.

REAR WINDSHIELD WIPER DIAGNOSIS

1. Locate the interior fuse junction panel. Check the 10 amp window wiper motor fuse.
   a. If the fuse is OK, go to Step 4.
   b. If the fuse is not OK, go to Step 2.
2. Replace the fuse. Turn the ignition switch to the **RUN** position. Check the 10 amp window wiper motor fuse.
   a. If the fuse is OK, go to Step 3.
   b. If the fuse is not OK, service the **DB/DG** wire for a short to ground.
3. Turn the ignition switch to the **RUN** position and the window wiper motor to the **ON** position. Check the 10 amp window wiper motor fuse.
   a. If the fuse is OK, the system is OK.
   b. If the fuse is not OK, replace the window wiper motor.
4. Disconnect the connector from the wiper motor. Turn the ignition switch to the **ON** position. Measure the voltage on the **DB/DG** wire.
   a. If the voltage is greater than 10 volts, go to Step 5.
   b. If the voltage is less than 10 volts, service the **DB/DG** wire.
5. Connect the connector to the wiper motor. Disconnect the connector from the wiper switch. Turn the ignition switch to the **ON** position. Measure the voltage on the **DB/BK** wire at the rear window wiper/washer switch connector.
   a. If the voltage is greater than 10 volts, go to Step 6.
   b. If the voltage is less than 10 volts, service the **DB/BK** wire.
6. Turn the ignition switch to the **OFF** position. Measure the resistance between the **BK** wire at the rear window wiper/washer switch connector and ground.
   a. If the resistance is greater than 5 ohms, service the **BK** wire.
   b. If the resistance is less than 5 ohms, go to Step 7.
7. Disconnect the connector from the rear window wiper switch. Jumper the **DB/BK** wire at the rear window wiper switch connector to ground. Turn the ignition switch to the **ON** position.
   a. If the rear window wiper switch operates, replace the rear wiper switch.
   b. If the rear window wiper switch operates, replace the rear window wiper motor.

Continental

WINDSHIELD WASHER INOPERATIVE

1. Make sure fluid level is full. If pump runs but no spray, check for clogged hoses or nozzles.

2. Check for voltage and ground at washer pump when activating switch.

3. Check for voltage at switch by operating the wiper motor.

4. Unplug connector from wiper control module, depress washer switch and check continuity between circuits **993 (BR/W and 590 (DB/W)**.

5. Unplug switch connector and depress switch. Check continuity between terminals **C2-4** and **C2-6**. If not continuity, replace switch. If continuity, repair open in circuit.

6. Check continuity of circuit **941 (BK/W)** from control module to washer pump. If continuity, replace control module. If not, repair open circuit.

WINDSHIELD WIPERS INOPERATIVE AT ALL SWITCH POSITIONS

1. Turn ignition switch to **RUN** and wiper switch to **HI**. Unplug wiper motor and check for voltage at circuit **65 (DG)**. If not, check circuit breaker, open connector, open **65 (DG)** or **297 (BK/LG)** circuits.

2. Unplug control module connector and check for voltage at circuit **65 (DG)** pin **13**. If not, repair open circuit.

3. Turn ignition switch to **RUN** and wiper switch to **HI**. Check for voltage between circuits **61 (Y/R)** and **58 (W)**. If voltage, check for motor current draw or go to next step.

4. Check for voltage between **pins 3** and **1** of control module connector with switch in **HI** position. If voltage, check for opens in circuits **58 (W)** and **61 (Y/R)**. If not, go to next step.

5. Disconnect connector from control module. Measure resistance between circuits **993 (BR/W)** and **589 (O)** with switch on **HI**. If resistance is less than 5 ohms, replace control module. If greater, go to next step.

6. Disconnect harness from switch and check continuity between terminals **C2-4** and **C2-1** with switch on **HI**. If less than 1 ohm, check for open wire. If greater, replace switch.

WINDSHIELD WIPERS INOPERATIVE AT LOW SPEED

1. Check for voltage at motor connector circuits **61 (Y/R)** and **56 (DB/O)**. If present, check motor current draw. If not, go to next step.

2. Check for voltage at wiper control module. Place switch on **LOW** and check circuits **61 (Y/R)** and **56 (DB/O)** of module connector for battery voltage. If voltage, check for opens. If not, go to next step.

3. Disconnect control module and measure resistance between circuits **993 (BR/W)** and **589 (O)** with switch on **LOW**. If resistance is 3.5–4.5 ohms, replace control module. If not, go to next step.

4. Disconnect switch and check continuity between switch terminals **993 (BR/W)** and **589 (O)** with switch on **LOW**. If resistance is 3.5–4.5 ohms, service open between switch and control module. If not, replace switch.

WINDSHIELD WIPERS INOPERATIVE AT INTERVAL SETTINGS

1. Disconnect control module connector and measure resistance between circuits **993 (BR/W)** and **589 (O)** with switch at **INTERVAL**. If resistance is 10.5–12.0 kilo-ohms, check interval select input signal at switch (step 3). If not, go to next step.

2. Disconnect wiper switch and measure resistance between circuits **993 (BR/W)** and **589 (O)**. If resistance is 10.5–12.0 kilo-ohms, check for open circuit. If not, check for defective switch.

3. Disconnect wiper switch and rotate interval control counterclockwise. Measure resistance between switch terminal circuits **590 (DB/W)** and **993 (BR/W)**. If resistance is 3.3–103.3 kilo-ohms, check for opens. If not, check for defective switch.

4. Check continuity of circuits **590 (DB/W)** and **993 (BR/W)**. If continuity, replace control module. If not, repair opens.

Contour and Mystique

WINDSHIELD WASHER INOPERATIVE

1. Make sure fluid level is full. If pump runs but no spray, check for clogged hoses or nozzles.

2. Check for voltage and ground at washer pump when activating switch.

3. Check for voltage at switch by operating the wiper motor.

4. Unplug connector from wiper switch and measure resistance of circuits **32 (W/R)** to washer pump connector **W/BK**. If circuit **32** resistance is less than 5 ohms, go to next step. If not, repair circuit **32**.

5. Remove circuit breaker in **F20** position of fuse block and check continuity. If not, replace circuit breaker.

6. Disconnect connector **N** from fuse panel and measure resistance of circuits **14 (P/O) pin 1** and **pin 8** (wiper switch). Resistance should be less than 3 ohms. If not, repair circuit **14**.

7. Check for voltage at connector **N, pin N1** with ignition on **RUN**. If voltage, install new switch. If not, install new fuse and retest.

8. Press washer switch, disconnect switch connector and measure resistance of circuit **31 (BK)** between **pin 10** of switch connector and ground. Resistance should be 5 ohms or less. If so, go to next step. If not, repair circuit **31**.

9. Disconnect fuse panel connector **N**, measure resistance between circuit **33 (Y/BK)** from **pin 9** of switch to **pin N10**. Go to next step if resistance is less than 3 ohms. If not, repair circuit **33**.

10. Disconnect central timer module from fuse panel and measure resistance between **pin N10** and **pin 3** of timer module. If resistance is less than 3 ohms, replace timer module. If not, install new fuse.

WINDSHIELD WIPERS INOPERATIVE AT ALL SWITCH POSITIONS

1. Turn ignition switch to **RUN** and wiper switch to **HI**. Unplug wiper motor and check for voltage at circuit **32 (W/BK)**. If not, go to step 3. If voltage, check wiper motor current draw.

2. Disconnect wiper switch connector and measure resistance of circuit **32 (W/BK)** from switch connector **pin 2** to motor connector **pin 1**. If resistance is less than 3 ohms, go to next step. If not, service circuit **32**.

3. Disconnect switch and place ignition switch to **RUN**. Check for voltage of **pin 8** of switch connector. If present, install new switch. If not, go to next step.

4. Remove circuit breaker **F20** from fuse panel and check continuity. If OK, reinstall and go to next step. If not, replace circuit breaker.

5. Disconnect connector **N** from fuse panel and measure resistance of circuits **14 (P/O)** from **pin 1** of connector **N** to **pin 8** of wiper switch connector. If less than 3 ohms, go to next step. If not, repair circuit **14**.

6. At connector **N** and ignition in **RUN** position, measure voltage from pin **N1** to ground. If voltage, install new switch. If not, install new fuse.

WINDSHIELD WIPERS INOPERATIVE AT HIGH SPEED

1. Turn ignition switch **ON**, wiper switch to **HIGH** and disconnect wiper motor. Check for voltage at circuit **32 (W/BK)**. If

voltage, check motor draw. If not, go to next step.

2. Disconnect switch connector and measure resistance of circuit **32 (W/BK)** from switch connector **pin 2** to motor connector **pin 1**. If circuit resistance is less than 3 ohms, go to next step. If not, repair circuit **32**.

3. Disconnect wiper switch and turn ignition to **RUN**. Check voltage on **pin 8** of switch connector. If voltage, install new switch. If not, go to next step.

4. Check **F20** circuit breaker in the fuse block for continuity. If not, replace circuit breaker. If continuity, install and go to next step.

5. Disconnect connector **N** from fuse panel and measure resistance between circuit **14 (P/O)** from **pin 1** of connector **N** to **pin 8** of switch connector. If resistance is less than 3 ohms, go to next step. If not, repair circuit **14**.

6. Disconnect connector **N** from fuse panel and place ignition switch to **RUN**. Measure voltage from **pin N1** to ground. If voltage at pin **N1**, install new switch. If not, install new fuse.

WINDSHIELD WIPERS INOPERATIVE AT LOW SPEED

1. Check for voltage at motor connector circuits **32 (W/GN)**. If present, check motor current draw. If not, go to next step.

2. Disconnect switch connector and measure resistance of circuit **32 (W/BK)** from switch connector **pin 1** to motor connector **pin 2**. If circuit resistance is less than 3 ohms, go to next step. If not, repair circuit **32**.

3. Disconnect wiper switch and turn ignition to **RUN**. Check voltage on **pin 8** of switch connector. If voltage, install new switch. If not, go to next step.

4. Check **F20** circuit breaker in the fuse block for continuity. If not, replace circuit breaker. If continuity, install and go to next step.

5. Disconnect connector **N** from fuse panel and measure resistance between circuit **14 (P/O)** from **pin 1** of connector **N** to **pin 8** of switch connector. If resistance is less than 3 ohms, go to next step. If not, repair circuit **14**.

6. Disconnect connector **N** from fuse panel and place ignition switch to **RUN**. Measure voltage from **pin N1** to ground. If voltage at pin **N1**, install new switch. If not, install new fuse.

WINDSHIELD WIPERS INOPERATIVE AT INTERVAL SETTINGS

1. With ignition switch **OFF**, disconnect timer module at fuse panel. Connect ohm-

meter to timer module **pin S14** and **S17**. Set ohmmeter to 20K range and go from **SLOW** to **FAST** while observing meter. Resistance should be 10–12 kilo-ohms. If within range, check wiper relay output. If not, go to next step.

2. Does ohmmeter read an open in the previous step? If yes, go to next step. If no, check for short circuit between connector **N** terminals **N3** and **N4**.

3. Disconnect wiper switch and measure resistance from **pin S17** to **pin 6**. If less than 3 ohms, go to step after next. If not, go to next step.

4. Check fuse pins **S17** and **N3** for continuity. If less than 1 ohm, service open circuit **8 (W)**. If not, install new fuse.

5. Measure resistance between **pin S14** and **pin 5** of switch connector. If less than 3 ohms, go to step after next. If not, go to next step.

6. Check fuse pins **S14** and **N4** for continuity. If less than 1 ohm, service open circuit **8 (W/BK)**. If not, install new fuse.

7. Measure resistance between fuse panel **pin N4** and **pin 4** of switch connector. If less than 3 ohms, go to next step. If not, repair open circuit **32 (W/GN)**.

8. Remove wiper relay from fuse panel and connect ohmmeter between terminals as shown in illustration. Replace relay if necessary.

9. Disconnect fuse panel connector **N** and check for a short circuit between **N3** and **N4**. If yes, repair short circuit. If no, install new wiper switch.

REMOVAL & INSTALLATION

Front Washer Reservoir and Pump

COUGAR AND THUNDERBIRD

1. Drain the reservoir.
2. Remove the bolts and the reservoir.
3. Disconnect the washer hose and the electrical connector.
4. Remove the pump from the reservoir.
To install:
5. Install the pump into the reservoir.
6. Connect the hose and electrical connector to the pump.
7. Position the reservoir and torque the bolts to 48–60 inch lbs. (5.4–6.8 Nm).
8. Fill the reservoir and check for proper operation.

CROWN VICTORIA, GRAND MARQUIS AND TOWN CAR

1. Remove the left front wheel well apron shield.
2. Remove the air cleaner.
3. Remove the retaining screws from the reservoir and disconnect the reservoir from the apron.
4. Disconnect the washer hose from the pump and drain the system.
5. Disconnect the electrical connector from the pump.
6. Carefully pry the pump from the reservoir.
7. Remove the seal/filter and inspect for damage.
To install:
8. Insert the seal into the reservoir.

Relay Terminal	Relay Energized	Relay Not Energized
3 and 5	Closed	Open
3 and 6	Open	Closed

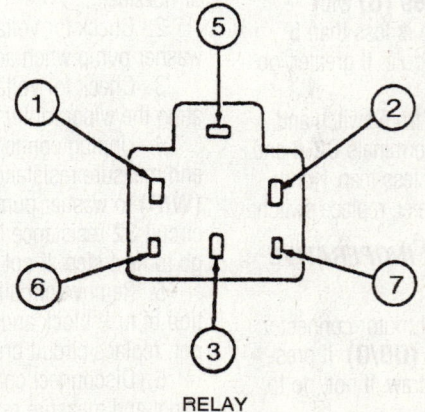

8838XG36

Wiper relay terminal schematic—Contour and Mystique

9. Lubricate the inside diameter of the seal with soapy water and insert the pump until it is firmly seated.

10. Installation of the reservoir is the reverse of the removal procedure.

11. Fill the washer system slowly to avoid an air lock.

12. Check for system leaks.

CONTOUR, MYSTIQUE, CONTINENTAL, TAURUS AND SABLE

1. On SHO, Contour and Mystique vehicles, remove the 2 reservoir retaining screws and the right front inner splash shield.

2. All others, remove the reservoir retaining screw.

3. Remove the left or right front wheel well apron shield.

4. Disconnect the hose from the washer pump and drain the reservoir.

5. Disconnect the electrical connector.

6. Carefully pry the pump from the reservoir.

7. Remove the seal/filter and inspect for damage.

To install:

8. Insert the seal into the reservoir.

9. Lubricate the inside diameter of the seal with soapy water and insert the pump until it is firmly seated.

10. Installation of the reservoir is the reverse of the removal procedure.

11. Fill the washer system slowly to avoid air lock.

12. Check for system leaks.

ESCORT AND TRACER—1.8L ENGINE

1. Disconnect the negative battery cable.

2. Remove the 2 power steering fluid reservoir bolts and position the reservoir to the side.

3. Loosen the 2 cruise control bracket mounting bolts and position the bracket to the side.

4. Remove the 2 washer reservoir mounting bolts.

5. Disconnect the electrical connector from the washer pump.

6. Disconnect the hose from the washer pump and drain the system.

7. Carefully pry the washer reservoir with the motor attached.

To install:

8. Installation is the reverse of removal procedure.

9. Torque the washer reservoir mounting bolts to 61–87 inch lbs. (7–9 Nm).

ESCORT AND TRACER—1.9L ENGINE

1. Disconnect the negative battery cable.

2. Remove the 2 bolts and nut and the washer reservoir.

3. Disconnect the electrical connector from the washer pump.

4. Disconnect the hose from the washer pump and drain the system.

5. Carefully pry the washer reservoir with the motor attached.

To install:

6. Installation is the reverse of the removal procedure.

7. Torque the washer reservoir mounting bolts to 61–87 inch lbs. (7–9 Nm).

ASPIRE

1. Disconnect the negative battery cable.

2. Remove the filler neck-to-vehicle attaching bolt and the filler neck from the reservoir.

3. Raise and support the vehicle safely.

4. Remove the left front wheel and tire assembly.

5. Remove the left front fender splash shield and the front splash shield.

6. Remove the 2 washer reservoir bolts.

7. Disconnect the filler tube from the reservoir and remove the reservoir.

8. Disconnect the windshield washer electrical connector and hose.

9. Remove the washer pump.

To install:

10. Install the pump onto the reservoir. Connect the hose and electrical connector to the washer.

11. Install the reservoir and connect the filler neck to it,

12. Position the reservoir and tighten the 2 reservoir-to-vehicle bolts.

13. Install the left front splash shield and the front fender splash shield.

14. Install the tire and wheel assembly and torque the lug bolts to 65–87 ft. lbs. (88–118 Nm).

15. Lower the vehicle.

16. Install the filler neck to the reservoir and filler neck-to-vehicle attaching bolt.

17. Connect the negative battery cable.

18. Fill the system and check for leaks.

MUSTANG

1. Disconnect the negative battery cable.

2. Remove the left front inner fender splash shield.

3. Disconnect the lock-tab wire connector and hose.

4. Remove the screw and disconnect the reservoir and pump assembly from the fender apron.

5. Disconnect the washer hose from the pump and drain the reservoir.

6. Remove the reservoir and pump assembly.

7. Pry the washer pump retaining ring from the reservoir.

8. Remove the pump by carefully pulling it from the reservoir with pliers around 1 side of the electrical terminal wall.

➡**If the impeller and seal come off during removal, reassemble them onto the pump.**

To install:

9. Clean the reservoir pump chamber thoroughly before installation.

10. Lubricate the outer diameter of the pump seal with a dry lubricant.

11. Align the projection of the motor end cap with the slot in the reservoir, and insert the pump so the seal seats against the bottom of the motor cavity.

12. Using a 1 inch 12 point socket or equivalent, press the pump retaining ring securely against the motor endplate.

13. Connect the hose and electrical connector to the pump.

14. Install the reservoir and tighten the mounting screw.

15. Install the splash shield.

16. Fill the reservoir and check for leaks.

MARK VIII

1. Disconnect the negative battery cable.

2. Remove the radiator sight shield.

3. Remove the reservoir filler tube support bracket bolt.

4. Raise and support the vehicle safely.

5. Open the access panel above the headlamp.

6. Remove the nuts attaching the cornering lamps to the grill.

7. Remove the screws attaching the lamps to the fender.

8. Disconnect the lamps from the body and bulbs from the lamps.

9. Remove the lamps.

10. Remove the 8 bolts and the upper radiator grill molding.

11. Remove the 6 screws (3 on each side) attaching the bumper cover to the fender splash shields at the front fender wheel opening.

12. Remove the 4 screws (2 on each side) attaching the bottom of the cover to the front fender splash shield.

13. Remove the 4 nuts (2 on each side) through the front cornering lamp opening attaching the front cover to the fenders.

14. Remove the 2 bolts attaching the grill support rods to the grill opening reinforcement.

15. Remove the screw attaching the cover to the "Z" brace.

16. Remove the 4 push pins attaching the bottom of the cover to the radiator support.

17. Carefully remove the cover and grille assembly.

18. Remove the power steering cooler and position it aside.

19. Remove the daytime running lamp and position it aside.

20. Disconnect the electrical connectors.

21. Remove the reservoir retaining screws.

22. Disconnect the pump supply hose and drain the system.

23. Remove the reservoir from the vehicle.

24. Carefully pry the pump from the reservoir.

25. Remove the seal/filter from the reservoir and inspect for damage.

To install:

26. Insert the seal into the reservoir.

27. Lubricate the inside diameter of the seal with soapy water and insert the pump until it is firmly seated.

28. Connect the hose and electrical connector to the assembly.

29. Install the reservoir and torque the screws to 41–55 inch lbs. (4.6–6.2 Nm).

30. Install the bumper cover onto the body.

31. Install the 4 push pins into the radiator support.

32. Connect the "Z" brace to the cover and torque the bolt to 12–15 inch lbs. (1.3–1.7 Nm).

33. Connect the grill support rods to the grill opening reinforcement and torque the bolts to 49–66 inch lbs. (5.5–7.4 Nm).

34. Install the 4 nuts connecting the cover to the fender and torque them to 5.8–8.2 inch lbs. (57–72 Nm).

35. Install the 4 screws connecting the cover to the splash shields and torque them to 12–15 inch lbs. (1.3–1.7 Nm).

36. Install the 6 screws connecting the cover to the splash shields and torque them to 12–15 inch lbs. (1.3–1.7 Nm).

37. Install the headlamp and grill mounting.

38. Install the radiator sight shield panel.

39. Install the bulbs into the cornering lamp sockets.

40. Install the lamps and torque the screws to 15–20 inch lbs. (1.6–2.2 Nm).

41. Install the lamp mounting nuts and torque them to 46–64 inch lbs. (5.2–7.2 Nm).

42. Lower the vehicle.

43. Install the filler neck support bracket bolt.

44. Fill the system and check for leaks.

PROBE

1. Disconnect the negative battery cable.

2. Remove the reservoir filler tube retaining bolt and tube.

3. Raise and support the vehicle safely.

4. Remove the screws and the right front inner fender splash shield.

5. Remove the 2 reservoir mounting bolts.

6. Disconnect the hose from the pump and drain the system.

7. Disconnect the pump and washer fluid lever sensor connectors.

8. Remove the reservoir and pump assembly.

9. Pry the pump away from the reservoir.

To install:

10. Installation is the reverse of the removal procedure.

Rear Washer Reservoir and Pump

ESCORT AND TRACER

1. Disconnect the negative battery cable.

2. Remove the right rear lower quarter trim panel.

3. Remove the 3 reservoir mounting bolts.

4. Disconnect the washer pump electrical connector.

5. Disconnect the hose from the pump and drain the reservoir.

6. Remove the reservoir.

7. Pry the pump from the reservoir.

To install:

8. Installation is the reverse of the removal procedure.

ASPIRE

1. Disconnect the negative battery cable.

2. Remove the right luggage compartment side cover.

3. Remove the right rear quarter trim panel.

4. Remove the 2 reservoir mounting bolts.

5. Remove the hose from the wire duct. Pull the reservoir away from the quarter panel.

6. Disconnect the washer pump electrical connector.

7. Disconnect the hose from the pump and drain the reservoir.

8. Remove the reservoir.

9. Remove the 2 washer pump-to-reservoir screws and the pump.

To install:

10. Installation is the reverse of the removal procedure.

➡ **When installing the filler neck, ensure that it is properly seated in the body grommet.**

11. Check for system leaks.

PROBE

1. Remove the left rear lower side trim panel.

2. Remove the filler cap.

3. Loosen the reservoir filler tube attaching clamp and remove the tube.

4. Lift the reservoir from the mounting bracket.

5. Disconnect the hose from the washer pump and drain the system.

6. Disconnect the electrical connector from the washer pump.

7. Remove the reservoir and pump assembly.

8. Pry the washer pump from the reservoir.

To install:

9. Installation is the reverse of the removal procedure.

TAURUS AND SABLE

1. Remove the right rear quarter panel trim.

2. Disconnect the electrical connector from the washer reservoir.

3. Disconnect the hose from the washer reservoir pump and the washer nozzle jet and the bracket; drain the system.

4. Remove the reservoir-to-vehicle screws and the reservoir/pump assembly.

5. Using a prybar, pry the washer pump from the reservoir; be careful not to damage the plastic housing.

To install:

6. Installation is the reverse of the removal procedure.

7. Inspect the seal/filter for damage.

8. Lubricate the inside seal with soapy water and insert the pump into the reservoir until firmly seated.

9. Connect the electrical connector and the hoses.

10. Install the reservoir and the screws.

11. Refill the reservoir and install the quarter trim panel.

Wiper Control Module (WCM)

CROWN VICTORIA, GRAND MARQUIS AND TOWN CAR

1. Disconnect the negative battery cable.

2. Remove the split steering column cover retaining screws and separate the 2 halves.

3. Disconnect the multiple connector at the rear of the wiper switch.

4. Disconnect the multiple connector at the main wiring loom.

5. Remove the **WCM** from the bracket.

To install:

6. Installation is the reverse of the removal procedure.

MARK VIII

➡The wiper control module is located on the far left side of the instrument panel and is attached to the lower panel flange.

1. Disconnect the negative battery cable.

2. Remove the left lower hush panel.

3. Remove the bolt and the **WCM** assembly.

4. Disconnect the electrical connector.

To install:

5. Installation is the reverse of the removal procedure.

6. Torque the bolt to 2.3–3.2 ft. lbs. (3.1–4.3 Nm).

MUSTANG

➡The wiper control module is located at the instrument panel fuse panel.

1. Disconnect the negative battery cable.

2. Disconnect the electrical harness connector.

3. Remove the **WCM** assembly from the bracket.

To install:

4. Installation is the reverse of the removal procedure.

TAURUS AND SABLE

➡On Taurus and Sable, the wiper control module is located on the right side of the steering column support bracket and is attached to a bracket.

1. Disconnect the negative battery cable.

2. Disconnect the harness connector.

3. Remove the both retaining screws and the **WCM** assembly.

To install:

4. Installation is the reverse of the removal procedure.

5. Torque the bolt to 2.3–3.2 ft. lbs. (3.1–4.3 Nm).

CONTINENTAL

➡The wiper control module is located on the left side of steering column support bracket.

1. Disconnect the negative battery cable.

2. Disconnect the harness connector.

3. Remove the both retaining screws and the **WCM** assembly.

To install:

4. Installation is the reverse of the removal procedure.

5. Torque the bolt to 2.3–3.2 ft. lbs. (3.1–4.3 Nm).

Central Timer Module

CONTOUR AND MYSTIQUE

The timer module is located in the fuse panel. It is removed by pulling straight out of the fuse panel.

GENERAL MOTORS CORPORATION MODELS WITH A 4-TERMINAL WIPER MOTOR

All Equipped Models

GENERAL INFORMATION

Models equipped with this type of wiper motor have 4 terminals and a roughly square-type cover, along with a separate, remote washer motor.

Based on the type of control switch used and whether an optional electronic printed circuit board is attached to the wiper cover, the system can serve as either a pulse-type wiper-washer system or a standard 2-speed type windshield wiper. Pulse timing and demand wash functions are controlled electronically on pulse windshield wipers.

Wiper System

This wiper motor is a 2-speed motor designed for a non-depressed wiper park system. It uses a permanent magnet positive park wiper motor with a dynamic brake and separate washer pump assembly.

When equipped for delay or pulse type operation, the pulse windshield wiper and washer system uses a turn signal type wiper/washer switch. The pulse and demand wash functions are controlled by a plug-in printed circuit board enclosed in the wiper's die-cast aluminum housing cover.

Internal parts such as field magnet, armature, drive gear, park switch actuator and brush holder assembly are enclosed in the aluminum housing. The cover is attached with rivets. A radio interference suppressor is located in the terminal connector on the wiper motor. A strap attached to one of the motor bolt hole grommets provides a ground for the suppressor. An automatic reset-type circuit breaker located on the motor brush holder assembly protects the motor while a fuse in the fuse block protects the vehicle wiring.

Power and control are through a 4-terminal connector. Use care when disconnecting the lock-type connectors that attach the vehicle wiring to the wiper.

The wiper motor has 3 brushes: common, low speed and high speed. When the ignition switch is **ON**, a 12V **(+)** circuit is applied to both the low and high speed fixed contacts in the multi-function lever. The low and high speed brushes are connected to the multi-function lever through terminals **C** and **D**. The armature is grounded through the common brush via the ground strap.

Washer System

The washer system consists of a solvent container, pump, washer hose and nozzle.

The fluid washer system is controlled by a small plastic element designed into the washer nozzle. As water is forced through this insert, the design of the mechanism creates an oscillating power stream, designed to more widely disperse the washer fluid for better cleaning. A correctly operating wiper-washer system has a spray pattern that cleans 75 percent of the wipe pattern within 10 wiper cycles.

If the nozzle becomes plugged, apply air pressure. If nozzle remains plugged, the nozzle must be replaced. If the spray pattern is too low or too high on the windshield, wedge-type adjustment shims can be used. Placement of a shim under the nozzle mounting bracket will raise the pattern about 3 degrees. Reverse installation of the same shim will lower the pattern 3 degrees.

WIPER AND WASHER OPERATION

The electronic printed circuit board controls all the timing and washer commands. When the wash button is pushed for more than 0.3 second, a demand wash is performed in 1½ second intervals for as long as the button is held, followed by approximately 6 seconds of dry wipes and a shut **OFF**.

Rotating the switch to either the **LOW** or

HIGH speed position completes the respective brush circuit to 12V DC **(+)** at the multi-function lever and the wiper motor runs at that speed.

An instantaneous wipe can be obtained by rotating the switch to the mist position and a continuous wipe will be performed if the switch is held.

To have the blades stop in their normal **PARK** position and to have the wiper motor shut off properly when the wiper is turned **OFF** at the multi-function lever, the motor operates at low speed at the shut-down cycle. This is accomplished as follows: the low speed brush circuit is completed to 12V DC **(+)** at the multi-function lever through a park switch located on the brush assembly (terminals **A** and **B**). The park switch contacts are normally closed and this permits the wiper to continue running. When the blades reach the park position, a cam on the large gear moves the park switch actuator that opens the normally closed positive park switch and grounds the wiper motor. This accomplishes a reversal of the motor flux path which causes a no-coast positive park, shutting off the wiper.

The wiper motor can be operated only when the ignition switch is in the **RUN** or **ACCESSORY** position.

CIRCUIT OPERATION

In addition to the features of a conventional (non-pulse) wiper system, (2-speed, **LOW** and **HIGH**), the pulse-type wiper/washer system includes an operating mode in which the wipers make a single stroke with an adjustable time interval between stokes. The time interval is controlled by a solid state Pulse/Speed/Wash Control in the wiper motor assembly. The duration of the delay interval is determined by the delay rheostat in the wiper switch.

The wiper motor has a built-in self-resetting circuit breaker which opens to protect the motor when the wipers are blocked, as from ice on the windshield, for example. The circuit breaker will reset upon cooling.

Low Speed

In the **LOW** position, the wiper switch supplies voltage to the gray wire and the Pulse/Speed/Wash Control grounds the Park/Run relay which closes its contacts, supplying voltage to the low speed brush of the wiper motor. The wipers run at low speed.

High Speed

With the wiper switch in the **HIGH** position, battery voltage is supplied from the purple wire directly to a 2nd armature terminal of the wiper motor. The wipers run at high speed. When the wiper switch is turned to **OFF**, the wipers complete the last sweep at low speed and return to the **PARK** position.

Park

When the wiper switch is 1st turned to **OFF**, voltage is still applied to the wiper motor through contacts in the Park/Run relay. The wiper motor runs at low speed. When the wipers reach the park position, the Park/Run relay opens and shunts the wiper motor to stop it quickly. The wiper blades remain in the **PARK** position.

Mist

When the wiper switch is moved to **MIST** and released, the wipers make 1 sweep at low speed and return to **PARK**. The circuit operation is the same as **LOW** speed.

Pulse

With the wiper switch in **PULSE**, voltage is applied to the gray wire and the solid state Pulse/Speed/Wash control. The Pulse/Speed/Wash control momentarily supplies ground to the Park/Run relay which closes its contacts, applying voltage to the wiper motor. When the wipers return to park, the Park/Run switch opens and ground is removed from the Park/Run relay. The wipers remain in park until the Pulse/Speed/Wash control again supplies ground to the Park/Run relay to start another sweep. The delay time between sweeps is controlled by the variable resistor and can be adjusted from 0–20 seconds.

Washer

When the washer switch is depressed, voltage is applied to the Pulse/Speed/Wash control. The Pulse/Speed/Wash control supplies battery voltage to the washer pump through the orange and pink wires. It also starts the wiper cycle through the low speed brush of the wiper motor. The washer pump continues to run as long as the switch is held down. The Pulse/Speed/Wash control keeps the wipers on for approximately 6 seconds after the washer pump goes **OFF**. If the washer pump is switched **ON** during the pulse operation, the wipers run in low speed for 6 seconds. The wash cycle is completed before the wipers return to the pulse operation.

CHEVROLET Cavalier; PONTIAC Sunfire

TROUBLESHOOTING

Symptom Tests

The following procedures assume that the technician has checked the following:

1. Check fuse **14**. If open, check for short to ground through circuit **143** and replace fuse.
2. Continuity of all harness wires.
3. Wiper motor and wiper/washer switch connectors are mated correctly.
4. If the wiper motor operates but the wipers do not; check the wiper linkage and wiper motor crank arm.
5. Wiper motor-to-dash mounting screws tight for good ground.
6. Washer hoses clear, fluid in tank.

➡ **Prior to starting the diagnosis procedure, it is very important to confirm the reported condition with a complete operational check including the washer system.**

WIPERS DO NOT OPERATE IN ANY MODE

1. With ignition to **RUN**, backprobe with test light to switch connector **C215** terminal **D** to ground. If light, go to next step. If not, repair open in circuit **243**. If fuse **A25** is blown, check for short in related circuits.
2. Wiper switch to **HI** and connect test light from connector **C215** terminal **G**. If light, go to next step. If not, check for poor connections at **C215** or open in pigtail **143**. If OK, replace wiper switch.
3. Disconnect wiper motor connector and test light connector terminal **C** to ground. If light, go to next step. If not, repair open in circuit **92** between connector **C215** and motor.
4. Connect test light from motor connector terminal **C** to ground. If light, go to next step. If not, repair open or poor connection in ground circuit **150**.

WIPERS RUN WHEN SWITCH IS IN "OFF" POSITION

1. Ignition switch to **RUN**, wiper switch **OFF** and disconnect wiper switch connector **C215**
2. If motor keeps running, use a voltmeter to measure voltage from connector **C215** terminal **E** to ground. If more than 1 volt, reconnect **C215**, disconnect motor connector and measure voltage from motor connector terminal **D** to ground. If more

than 1 volt, repair battery connection to circuit **113**. If less than 1 volt, replace wiper motor cover assembly.

3. If motor parks, check for shorted wires in pigtail to wiper switch assembly. If OK, replace switch.

NO HIGH SPEED MODE

1. Ignition switch to **RUN**, wiper switch **HI**.

2. Do wipers operate at all with switch on **HI**. If not, replace switch.

3. If yes, test light between switch connector **C215** terminal **G** and ground. If light, go to next step. If not, repair open or poor connection in connector **215** or switch pigtail. If OK, replace switch.

4. Disconnect motor connector and test light between motor connector terminal **C** and ground. If light, check for poor connection to motor. If OK, replace motor. If no light, repair open in circuit **92**

LOW SPEED, PULSE DELAY AND MIST MODES INOPERATIVE (HIGH SPEED MODE OK)

1. Ignition switch to **RUN**, wiper switch **LO**. Measure voltage from wiper switch connector **C215** to ground. If more than 1 volt, go to next step. If not, check for poor connection at connector **C215** or open pigtail to switch. If OK, replace switch.

2. Disconnect motor connector and measure voltage from terminal **D** to ground. If more than 1 volt, replace motor cover. If less than 1 volt, repair open in circuit **113**.

PULSE DELAY OPERATES INCORRECTLY OR NOT AT ALL

1. Ignition switch **OFF**, disconnect wiper switch connector **C215**, wiper switch to **DELAY**. Measure resistance of switch connector **C215** terminal **D** to **F**. Move the delay button through the delay range, one notch at a time. The resistance should vary 39–680 kilo-ohms. If not, replace switch. If OK, go to next step.

2. Reconnect switch connector and disconnect motor connector. With ignition in **RUN**, measure voltage from motor connector terminal **E** to ground. If voltage, replace motor cover assembly. If not, check circuit **112**. If OK, replace motor cover.

WIPERS STOP RANDOMLY AND DO NOT PARK WHEN SWITCH IS MOVED TO "OFF"

1. Ignition switch **RUN**, disconnect wiper switch connector **C215**, wiper switch to **OFF**. Do wipers park?

2. If not, measure voltage from **C215** terminal **E** to ground. If more than 1 volt, go to next step. If less, replace motor cover assembly.

3. Reconnect switch and disconnect motor connector. Measure voltage from motor connector terminal **D** to ground. If more than 1 volt, repair short to battery in circuit **113**. If less, replace motor cover assembly.

WIPERS DO NOT OPERATE WHEN WASHER SWITCH IS ACTIVATED

Ignition switch **RUN**, connect test light between switch connector **C215** terminal **E** and ground. Activate washer switch. If light, check for open in circuit **113** or poor connection. If OK, replace motor cover assembly. If no light, check for open in switch. If OK, replace switch.

WASHER DOES NOT OPERATE

1. Disconnect pump connector and connect test light between terminals **A** and **B**. If no light, go to next step. If yes, check for poor connection to washer pump. If OK, replace pump.

2. Connect test light between pump connector terminal **A** and ground. If no light, go to next step. If light, repair open in circuit **150**.

3. Connect test light between switch connector terminal **H** and ground. If no light, check for poor connection at connector **C215** terminal **H**. If OK, replace switch. If light, check for open in circuit **228**.

REMOVAL & INSTALLATION

Repairs can be made to the wiper motor cover and pulse board only.

Wiper Motor Cover

1. Remove wiper motor from vehicle.
2. Remove the bolt or rivets.
3. Remove cover.
To assemble:
4. Install the cover and torque the bolt to 26 inch lbs. (3 Nm).
5. Install the wiper motor.

Pulse Circuit Board Replacement

1. Disconnect the negative battery cable and wait 90 seconds.
2. Remove wiper arms, 4 screws, 5 retainers and screen assembly.
3. Disconnect motor connector and remove wiper drive system.
4. Remove 3 screws and pulse circuit board and cover assembly.

5. Installation is the reverse of removal. Torque the cover screws to 18 inch lbs. (2 Nm).

> **BUICK LeSabre, Park Avenue, Regal, CADILLAC deVille, Eldorado, Seville; CHEVROLET Lumina, Monte Carlo; OLDSMOBILE Cutlass Supreme; PONTIAC Bonneville, Grand Prix**

TROUBLESHOOTING

Diagnostic Tests

WIPERS DO NOT OPERATE IN ANY MODE

1. Disconnect the wiper/washer switch connector. Turn the ignition switch to the **RUN** position. Connect a test light between the connector's, white wire terminal and ground.
   a. If the test light is **ON,** go to Step 2.
   b. If the test light is **OFF,** check for an open in the wiper fuse or in circuit **93 (WHITE)**. If okay, check for an open in the power feed circuit **4**.

2. Disconnect the wiper motor connector **C2**. Connect a test light between the connector, terminal **C (BLACK)** to the battery's positive **(+)** terminal.
   a. If the test light is **ON,** go to Step 3.
   b. If the test light is **OFF,** repair the open in the ground circuit **150**, **151** or **152**.

3. Connect the wiper/washer switch connector. Disconnect the wiper motor connector **C1**. Connect a test light between the connector terminal **C (DARK GREEN)** and ground.
   a. If the test light is **ON,** go to Step 4.
   b. If the test light is **OFF,** check for a poor connection at the wiper/washer switch connector or for an open in circuit **95 (DARK GREEN)**. If okay, replace the wiper/washer switch.

4. Turn the wiper switch to the **LO** position. Connect a test light between the connector **C1**, terminal **B (GREY)** and ground.
   a. If the test light is **ON,** go to Step 5.
   b. If the test light is **OFF,** check for a poor connection at the wiper/washer switch connector or for an open in circuit **91 (GREY)**. If okay, replace the wiper/washer switch.

5. Check for continuity between the wiper motor connector **C1**, terminal **A**

(YELLOW) and connector **C2**, terminal **B** (YELLOW).

    a. If there is continuity, go to Step 6.

    b. If there is no continuity, repair the open in circuit **196 (YELLOW)**.

    6. Check for a poor connection at the wiper motor connectors.

    a. If okay, replace the wiper motor cover assembly.

    b. If trouble is not corrected, replace the wiper motor.

WIPERS RUN AT HIGH SPEED ONLY—LOW SPEED INOPERATIVE

    1. Disconnect the wiper motor connector **C1**. Turn the ignition switch to the **RUN** position and the wiper switch to the **LO** position. Connect a test light between the connector **C1**, terminal **B (GREY)** and ground.

    a. If the test light is **ON**, go to Step 2.

    b. If the test light is **OFF**, check for an open in circuit **91 (GREY)** or a poor connection at the wiper/washer switch connector. If okay, replace the wiper/washer switch.

    2. Connect a test light between the connector **C1**, terminal **C (DARK GREEN)** and ground.

    a. If the test light is **ON**, go to Step 3.

    b. If the test light is **OFF**, check circuit **95 (DARK GREEN)** for poor connections or open. If okay, replace the wiper/washer switch.

    3. Check for continuity through circuit **196 (YELLOW)**.

    a. If there is continuity, go to Step 4.

    b. If there is no continuity, repair the open in circuit **196 (YELLOW)**.

    4. Check for a poor connection at connector **C1**.

    a. If okay, replace the wiper motor cover assembly.

    b. If trouble is not corrected, replace the wiper motor.

WIPERS RUN AT LOW SPEED ONLY—HIGH SPEED INOPERATIVE

    1. Disconnect the wiper motor connector **C2**. Turn the ignition switch to the **RUN** position and the wiper switch to the **HI** position. Connect a test light between the connector **C2**, terminal **A (PURPLE)** and ground.

    a. If the test light is **ON**, go to Step 2.

    b. If the test light is **OFF**, check for an open in circuit **92 (PURPLE)** or a poor connection at the wiper/washer switch connector. If okay, replace the wiper/washer switch.

    2. Check for a poor connection at connector **C2**, terminal **A (PURPLE)**.

    a. If okay, replace the wiper motor cover assembly.

    b. If trouble is not corrected, replace the wiper motor.

WIPERS RUN INTERMITTENTLY IN LOW OR HIGH SPEED SETTINGS

    1. Remove the wiper fuse and connect an ammeter (0–30 amp) across the fuse block terminals. Turn the ignition switch to the **RUN** position and the wiper switch to the **LO** position. Observe the lowest current draw while the wipers are running on dry glass (current draw will fluctuate).

    a. If the lowest current draw is less than 3.5 amps, replace the wiper motor.

    b. If the current draw is 3.5–6.5 amps, end test.

    c. If the lowest current draw is more than 6.5 amps, go to Step 2.

    2. Replace the wiper blade elements and repeat the test.

    a. If the lowest current draw is still more than 6.5 amps, go to Step 3.

    b. If the lowest current draw is less than 6.5 amps, end test.

    3. Disconnect the wiper transmission drive link from the wiper motor crank arm and repeat test.

    a. If the lowest current draw is still more than 6.5 amps, replace the wiper motor.

    b. If the lowest current draw is less than 6.5 amps, the wiper transmission

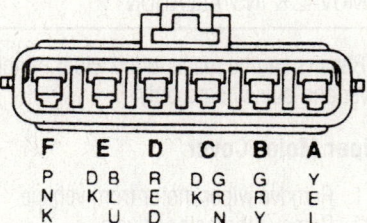

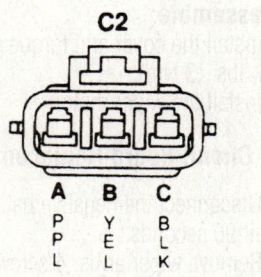

Windshield wiper motor wiring harness electrical connectors—BUICK LeSabre, Park Avenue, Regal; CADILLAC deVille, Eldorado, Seville; CHEVROLET Lumina, Monte Carlo; OLDSMOBILE Cutlass Supreme; PONTIAC Bonneville, Grand Prix

8838XG41

assembly is binding, repair or replace as required.

WIPERS WILL NOT TURN OFF

    1. Disconnect the wiper motor connector **C1**. Turn the ignition switch to the **RUN** position and the wiper switch to the **OFF** position. Using a digital multimeter, measure the voltage from connector **C1**, terminal **B (GREY)** to ground.

    a. If the voltage is 0 volts, go to Step 2.

    b. If battery voltage is present, check for a short to **B+** in circuit **91 (GREY)**. If okay, replace the wiper/washer switch.

    2. Disconnect the wiper motor connector **C2**. Using a digital multimeter, measure the voltage from connector **C2**, terminal **A (PURPLE)** to ground.

    a. If the voltage is 0 volts, repair the short to **B+** in circuit **196 (YELLOW)**.

    b. If battery voltage is present, check for a short to **B+** in circuit **92 (PURPLE)**. If okay, replace the wiper/washer switch.

WIPERS CYCLE IN AND OUT OF PARK AFTER WIPERS ARE SHUT OFF

    1. Turn the ignition switch to the **RUN** position. Operate the wiper switch and return it to the **OFF** position.

    a. If the wiper motor continues to operate in low speed, go to Step 2.

    b. If the wiper motor continues to operate in high speed, go to Wipers Run At High Speed Only chart.

    2. Replace the park switch assembly.

    a. If the trouble is corrected, end test.

    b. If the trouble is not corrected, replace the wiper motor assembly.

PULSE DELAY OPERATES INCORRECTLY OR NOT AT ALL

    1. Disconnect the wiper/washer switch connector. Turn the ignition switch to the **OFF** position and the wiper switch to the **DELAY** position. Using a digital multimeter, measure the resistance through the wiper/washer switch at connector, from white wire terminal to pink wire terminal; then, move the wiper switch through the entire **DELAY** range.

    a. If the resistance varies from 1.244 Mega-ohms to 0.024 Mega-ohms, go to Step 2.

    b. If the resistance does not vary from 1.244 Mega-ohms to 0.024 Mega-ohms, replace the wiper/washer switch assembly.

    2. Measure the resistance through the wiper/washer switch at connector, from gray wire terminal to white wire terminal.

a. If the resistance is less than 3 ohms, go to Step 3.

b. If the resistance is greater than 3 ohm, replace the wiper/washer switch assembly.

3. Check circuits **91 (GREY)** and **94 (PINK)** for an open or poor connection. If okay, remove the wiper motor cover assembly.

a. If the park switch pulse contacts are touching the pads on the circuit board, replace the wiper motor cover assembly.

b. If the park switch pulse contacts are not touching the pads on the circuit board, replace the park switch spring contacts.

WASHER WILL NOT OPERATE

1. Disconnect the washer pump connector. Turn the ignition switch to the **RUN** position. Connect a test light between terminals **A (RED)** and **B (DARK BLUE)** of the washer pump connector; then, activate the washer switch while observing the test light.

a. If the test light is **OFF,** go to Step 2.

b. If the test light is **ON,** check for a poor connection at the washer pump connector. If okay, replace the washer pump.

2. Connect a test light between connector, terminal **A (RED)** and ground; then, activate the washer switch while observing the test light.

a. If the test light is **OFF,** go to Step 3.

b. If the test light is **ON,** check for a poor connection or open in circuit **227 (DARK BLUE)**. If okay, replace the wiper motor assembly (internal ground circuit open).

3. Connect a test light between wiper motor connector **C1**, terminal **D (RED)** and ground.

a. If the test light is **OFF,** go to Step 4.

b. If the test light is **ON,** check for a poor connection or open in circuit **228 (RED)**.

4. Turn the ignition switch to the **RUN** position. Using a digital multimeter, backprobe the wiper/washer switch connector, from pink wire terminal to ground; then, activate the washer switch while observing the digital multimeter.

a. If 0 voltage is present, replace the wiper/washer switch assembly.

b. If battery voltage is present, check for a poor connection at the wiper/washer

switch connector(s) and wiper motor assembly; or open in circuit **94 (PINK)**. If okay, replace the wiper motor assembly.

WASHER WILL NOT SHUT OFF

1. Turn the ignition switch to the **RUN** position and the wiper switch to the **LO** position. Disconnect the wiper motor connector **C1**. Connect a test light between connector **C1**, terminal **F (PINK)** and ground at the wiper motor case. Momentarily, activate the washer switch while observing the test light.

2. If the test light is **OFF** when the washer switch is released, replace the wiper motor cover assembly.

3. If the test light is **ON** when the washer switch is released, replace the wiper/washer switch assembly.

REMOVAL & INSTALLATION

Wiper Motor Cover

1. Remove the wiper arm assemblies from the vehicle. Disconnect the negative battery cable from the battery. At the center or the cowl, remove the washer hose from the nipple.

➡**The air inlet shroud is 2 pieces; be careful not to break it.**

2. Remove the screws and the air inlet shroud.

3. At the wiper motor cover's electrical connector, pull the retainer from the connector; then, disconnect the electrical connector from the wiper motor cover assembly.

4. Remove the wiper motor cover-to-wiper motor screws and the cover.

To install:

5. With the wiper motor in the park position, align the wiper motor cover's cam slot with the drive pin. Install the cover and torque the screws to 18 inch lbs. (2 Nm).

6. Install the electrical connector and secure with the retainer. Install the air inlet shroud.

7. Lubricate the washer hose and install onto the nipple. Connect the negative battery cable. Install the wiper arm assemblies.

Park Switch Assembly

1. Remove the wiper motor cover assembly.

➡**If the wiper motor is in the park position, operate the motor (as required) to remove the pawl from the relay slot.**

2. Remove the screw and the park switch from the wiper motor assembly.

To install:

3. Install the park switch and screw onto the wiper motor assembly.

4. When the pawl is in the relay slot, operate the wiper motor back into the park position.

5. Install the wiper motor cover assembly.

Wiper Drive System Module

1. Remove the wiper arm assemblies from the vehicle. Disconnect the negative battery cable from the battery. At the center or the cowl, remove the washer hose from the nipple.

➡**The air inlet shroud is 2 pieces; be careful not to break it.**

2. Remove the screws and the air inlet shroud.

3. At the wiper motor electrical connectors, pull the retainers from the connectors; then, disconnect the electrical connectors from the wiper motor assembly.

4. Remove the wiper drive system module-to-cowl screws and the module from the vehicle.

To install:

5. Install the wiper drive system module and torque the module-to-cowl screws to 106 inch lbs. (12 Nm).

6. Connect the electrical connectors to the wiper motor and secure with the retainers.

7. Install the air inlet shroud.

8. Lubricate the washer hose and install onto the nipple. Connect the negative battery cable. Install the wiper arm assemblies.

CHEVROLET Corvette

TROUBLESHOOTING

Diagnostic Tests

WIPERS DO NOT OPERATE IN ANY MODE

1. Disconnect the wiper/washer switch connector **C236**. Turn the ignition switch to the **ACCY** or **RUN** position. Connect a test light between the connector **C236**, terminal **B (YELLOW)** and ground.

a. If the test light is **ON,** go to Step 2.

b. If the test light is **OFF,** check for an open in the wiper fuse or in circuit **143 (YELLOW)**. If okay, check for an open in the power feed circuit **4**.

2. Connect the wiper/washer switch connector **C1**. Disconnect all 3 wiper motor connectors. Connect a test light between the connector **C2**, terminal **C (GREY)** and ground.

    a. If the test light is **ON,** go to Step 3.

    b. If the test light is **OFF,** check for an open in circuit **91 (GREY)**. If okay, replace the wiper/washer switch.

3. Turn the wiper switch to the **LO** position. Connect a test light between the connector **C2**, terminal **B (LIGHT BLUE)** and ground.

    a. If the test light is **ON,** go to Step 4.

    b. If the test light is **OFF,** check for an open in circuit **97 (LIGHT BLUE)**. If okay, replace the wiper/washer switch.

4. Reconnect the wiper motor connectors **C1** and **C2**. With the wiper switch still in the **LO** position, connect a test light between connector **C3**, terminal **B (YELLOW)** and ground.

    a. If the test light is **ON,** go to Step 5.

    b. If the test light is **OFF,** check for an open in circuit **196 (GREY)**. If okay, replace the wiper motor assembly.

5. Connect a test light between connector **C3**, terminal **A (PURPLE)** and ground. Turn the wiper switch to the **HI** position.

    a. If there is continuity, check for an open or short to battery voltage in ground circuit **150**. If okay, replace the wiper motor assembly.

    b. If there is no continuity, check the open in circuit **92 (YELLOW)**. If okay, replace the wiper/washer switch.

WIPERS RUN AT HIGH SPEED ONLY—LOW SPEED INOPERATIVE

1. Disconnect the wiper motor connectors **C2** and **C3**. Turn the ignition switch to the **ACCY** or **RUN** position and the wiper switch to the **LO** position. Connect a test light between the connector **C2**, terminal **C (GREY)** and ground.

    a. If the test light is **ON,** go to Step 2.

    b. If the test light is **OFF,** check for an open in circuit **91 (GREY)**. If okay, replace the wiper/washer switch.

2. Connect a test light between the connector **C2**, terminal **B (LIGHT BLUE)** and ground.

    a. If the test light is **ON,** go to Step 3.

    b. If the test light is **OFF,** check for an open in circuit **97 (LIGHT BLUE)**. If okay, replace the wiper/washer switch.

3. Reconnect connector **C2**. Connect a test light between the connector **C2**, terminal **B (LIGHT BLUE)** and ground.

    a. If the test light is **ON,** replace the wiper motor.

    b. If the test light is **OFF,** check for

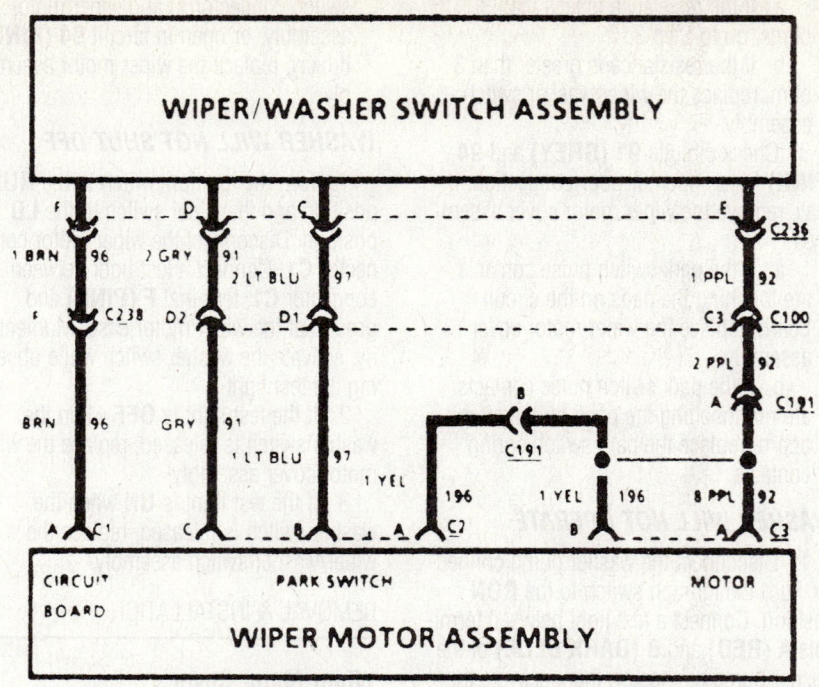

Windshield wiper/washer system electrical schematic—Corvette

an open in circuit **196 (YELLOW)**. If okay, replace the wiper motor.

WIPERS WILL NOT TURN OFF

1. Disconnect the 3 wiper motor connectors. Turn the ignition switch to the **ACCY** or **RUN** position and the wiper switch to the **OFF** position. Connect a test light between connector **C1**, terminal **A (BROWN)** to ground.

    a. If the test light is **OFF,** go to Step 2.

    b. If the test light is **ON,** check for an short to B+ in circuit **96 (BROWN)**. If okay, replace the wiper/washer switch.

2. Connect a test light between connector **C2**, terminal **B (LIGHT BLUE)** and ground.

    a. If the test light is **OFF,** go to Step 3.

    b. If the test light is **ON,** check for an short to B+ in circuit **97 (LIGHT BLUE)**. If okay, replace the wiper/washer switch.

3. Reconnect connectors **C1** and **C2**. Connect a test light between connector **C3**, terminal **B (YELLOW)** and ground.

    a. If the test light is **OFF,** go to Step 4.

    b. If the test light is **ON,** check for an short to B+ in circuit **196 (YELLOW)**. If okay, replace the wiper motor.

4. Connect a test light between connector **C3**, terminal **A (BROWN)** and ground.

    a. If the test light is **OFF,** replace the wiper motor.

    b. If the test light is **ON,** check for an short to B+ in circuit **92 (PURPLE)**. If okay, replace the wiper/washer switch.

WIPERS RUN AT LOW SPEED ONLY— HIGH SPEED INOPERATIVE

1. Disconnect the wiper motor connector **C3**. Turn the ignition switch to the **ACCY** or **RUN** position and the wiper switch to the **HI** position. Connect a test light between the connector **C3**, terminal **A (PURPLE)** and ground.

2. If the test light is **ON,** replace the wiper motor.

3. If the test light is **OFF,** check for an open in circuit **92 (PURPLE)**. If okay, replace the wiper/washer switch.

PULSE DELAY OPERATES INCORRECTLY OR NOT AT ALL

1. Disconnect the wiper motor connectors **C1** and **C2**. Turn the ignition switch to the **OFF** position and the wiper switch to the **LO** position. Using a digital multimeter, measure the resistance across connector **C1**, from terminal **A (BROWN)** and connector **C2**, terminal **B (LIGHT BLUE)**.

    a. If the resistance is more than 24 kilo-ohms, go to Step 2.

    b. If the resistance is less than 24 kilo-ohms, check for an open in circuit **96 (BROWN)** or **97 (LIGHT BLUE)**. If okay, replace the wiper/washer switch assembly.

2. Move the wiper switch through the

entire pulse **DELAY** range and measure the resistance.

a. If the resistance increases to approximately 1.2 Mega-ohms, replace the wiper motor assembly.

b. If the resistance does not increase to approximately 1.2 Mega-ohms, replace the wiper/washer switch assembly.

WASHER WILL NOT OPERATE

1. Disconnect the washer pump connector. Turn the ignition switch to the **ACCY** or **RUN** position. Connect a test light between terminals **A (PINK)** and **B (BLACK)** of the washer pump connector; then, activate the washer switch while observing the test light.

a. If the test light is **OFF,** go to Step 2.

b. If the test light is **ON,** replace the washer pump.

2. Connect a test light between connector, terminal **A (PINK)** and ground; then, activate the washer switch while observing the test light.

a. If the test light is **OFF,** go to Step 3.

b. If the test light is **ON,** repair the open in circuit **150 (BLACK);** terminal of the pump connector.

3. Disconnect the wiper motor connectors **C1** and **C2.** Connect a test light between wiper motor connector **C1,** terminal **C (PINK)** and ground; then, activate the washer switch while observing the test light.

a. If the test light is **OFF,** go to Step 4.

b. If the test light is **ON,** repair the open in circuit **94 (PINK).**

4. Connect a test light between wiper motor connector **C1,** terminal **A (PINK)** and ground; then, activate the washer switch while observing the test light.

a. If the test light is **OFF,** check for an open in circuit **96 (BROWN).**

b. If the test light is **ON,** go to Step 5.

5. Connect a test light between wiper motor connector **C2,** terminal **B (LIGHT BLUE)** and ground; then, activate the washer switch while observing the test light.

a. If the test light is **OFF,** check for an open in circuit **97 (LIGHT BLUE).** If okay, replace the wiper/washer switch assembly.

b. If the test light is **ON,** replace the wiper motor.

REMOVAL & INSTALLATION

Wiper Motor Cover

1. Disconnect the negative battery cable from the battery.

2. Disconnect the electrical connector from the wiper motor cover and the wiper motor.

3. Remove the wiper motor cover-to-wiper motor screws and the cover.

To install:

4. With the wiper motor in the park position, align the wiper motor cover's cam slot with the drive pin. Install the cover and torque the screws to 18 inch lbs. (2 Nm).

5. Install the electrical connectors.

6. Connect the negative battery cable.

Park Switch Assembly

1. Remove the wiper motor assembly.

2. Remove the wiper motor cover assembly.

➡**If the wiper motor is in the park position, operate the motor (as required) to remove the pawl from the relay slot.**

3. Remove the screw and the park switch from the wiper motor assembly.

To install:

4. Install the park switch and screw onto the wiper motor assembly.

5. When the pawl is in the relay slot, operate the wiper motor back into the park position.

6. Install the wiper motor cover assembly.

7. Install the wiper motor assembly.

CHEVROLET Camaro; PONTIAC Firebird

TROUBLESHOOTING

Diagnostic Tests

WIPERS DO NOT OPERATE IN ANY MODE

1. Turn the ignition switch to the **RUN** position. Backprobe with a test light from the wiper/washer switch connector **C215,** terminal **D (YELLOW)** and ground.

a. If the test light is **ON,** go to Step 2.

b. If the test light is **OFF,** check for an open in circuit **143 (YELLOW).** If fuse **14** is open, check for a short to ground in the related circuits.

2. Turn the wiper switch to the **HI** posi-

tion. Connect a test light between the connector **C215,** terminal **G (PURPLE)** to ground.

a. If the test light is **ON,** go to Step 3.

b. If the test light is **OFF,** check for a poor connection at connector **C215,** terminal **D (YELLOW)** or an open in circuit **143 (YELLOW)** to the wiper/washer switch.

3. Disconnect the wiper motor connector. Connect a test light between the connector, terminal **C (PURPLE)** and ground.

a. If the test light is **ON,** go to Step 4.

b. If the test light is **OFF,** check for an open or a poor connection in circuit **92 (PURPLE)** between connector **C215** and the wiper motor.

4. Connect a test light between the wiper motor connector, terminal **C (PURPLE)** and terminal **A (BLACK).**

a. If the test light is **ON,** check for a poor connection to the wiper motor assembly. If okay, replace the wiper motor assembly.

b. If the test light is **OFF,** repair the open or poor connection in the ground circuit **150 (BLACK).**

WIPERS RUN WHEN SWITCH IS OFF

1. Turn the ignition switch to the **RUN** position and the wiper switch to the **OFF** position. Disconnect the wiper/washer switch connector **C215.**

a. If the wiper motor keeps running, go to Step 2.

b. If the wiper motor parks, check for shorted wires in the pigtail to the wiper/washer switch assembly. If okay, replace the wiper/washer switch assembly.

2. Using a digital multimeter, measure the voltage from connector **C215** (vehicle side), terminal **E (DARK GREEN)** to ground.

a. If more than 1.0 volt is present, go to Step 3.

b. If less than 1.0 volt is present (approx. 0 volts), go to Step 4.

3. Reconnect the wiper/washer switch connector **C215.** Disconnect the wiper motor connector. Using a digital multimeter, measure the voltage from the wiper motor connector, terminal **D (DARK GREEN)** to ground.

a. If more than 1.0 volt is present, repair **B+** connection to circuit **113 (DARK GREEN).**

b. If less than 1.0 volt is present, replace the wiper motor cover assembly.

4. Reconnect the wiper/washer switch connector **C215**. Disconnect the wiper motor connector. Using a digital multimeter, measure the voltage from the wiper motor connector, terminal **C (PURPLE)** to ground.

    a. If 0 volts is present, replace the wiper motor cover assembly.

    b. If **B+** voltage is present, repair the short to the **B+** in circuit **92 (PURPLE)**.

NO HIGH SPEED MODE

1. Turn the ignition switch to the **RUN** position and the wiper/washer switch to the **HI** position.

    a. If the wipers work some, go to Step 2.

    b. If the do not work at all, replace the wiper/washer switch.

2. With the ignition switch in the **RUN** position and the wiper switch in the **HI** position. Connect a test light between the wiper/washer switch connector **C215**, terminal **G (PURPLE)** and ground.

    a. If the test light is **ON,** go to Step 3.

    b. If the test light is **OFF,** check for a poor connection at the wiper/washer switch connector **C215** or for an open in the pigtail to the wiper/washer switch assemble. If okay, replace the wiper/washer switch.

3. Disconnect the wiper motor connector. Connect a test light between the harness terminal **C (PURPLE)** and ground.

    a. If the test light is **ON,** check for a poor connection at the wiper motor assembly. If okay, replace the wiper motor cover assembly.

    b. If the test light is **OFF,** repair the open in circuit **92 (PURPLE)**.

LOW SPEED, PULSE DELAY AND MIST MODES INOPERATIVE—HIGH SPEED MODE OK

1. Turn the ignition switch to the **RUN** position and the wiper switch to the **LO** position. Using a digital multimeter, measure the voltage from the wiper/washer switch connector **C215**, terminal **E (DARK GREEN)** to ground.

    a. If more than 1.0 volt is present, go to Step 2.

    b. If less than 1.0 volt is present (approx. 0 volt), check for a poor connection at the wiper/washer switch connector **C215** or for an open pigtail to the wiper/washer switch assembly. If okay, replace the wiper/washer switch.

2. Disconnect the wiper motor connector. Using a digital multimeter, measure the voltage from the wiper motor connec-

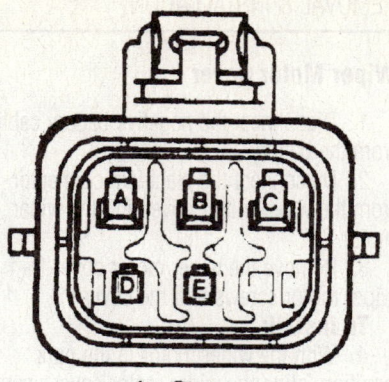

A	BLK
B	YEL
C	PPL
D	DK GRN
E	GRY

8838XG47

Windshield wiper motor wiring harness electrical connector—Camaro and Firebird

tor, terminal **D (DARK GREEN)** to ground.

    a. If more than 1.0 volt is present, replace the wiper motor cover assembly.

    b. If less than 1.0 volt is present (approx. 0 volt), repair the open in circuit **113 (DARK GREEN)**.

PULSE DELAY OPERATES INCORRECTLY OR NOT AT ALL

1. Disconnect the wiper/washer switch connector **C215**. Turn the ignition switch to the **OFF** position and the wiper switch to the **DELAY** position. Using a digital multimeter, measure the resistance through the wiper/washer switch assembly from connector **C215**, terminal **D (YELLOW)** to terminal **F (GREY)**. Move the wiper switch through the entire **DELAY** range, one notch at a time.

    a. If the resistance varies from 39 kilo-ohms to 680 kilo-ohms, go to Step 2.

    b. If the resistance does not vary from 39 kilo-ohms to 680 kilo-ohms, replace the wiper/washer switch assembly.

2. Reconnect the wiper/washer switch connector **C215**. Disconnect the wiper motor connector. Turn the ignition switch to the **RUN** position. Using a digital multimeter, measure the voltage from the wiper motor connector, terminal **E (GREY)** to ground.

    a. If **B+** is present, replace the wiper motor cover assembly.

    b. If approx. 0 volts is present, check circuit **112 (GREY)** for an open or poor connection. If okay, replace the wiper motor cover assembly.

WIPERS STOP RANDOMLY AND DO NOT PARK WHEN SWITCH IS MOVED TO OFF

1. Turn the ignition switch to the **RUN** position and the wiper switch to the **OFF** position. Disconnect the wiper/washer switch connector **C215**.

    a. If the wipers do not park, go to Step 2.

    b. If the wipers park, replace the wiper/washer switch assembly.

2. Using a digital multimeter, measure the voltage from connector **C215** (vehicle side), terminal **E (GREY)** to ground.

    a. If more than 1.0 volt is present, go to Step 3.

    b. If less than 1.0 volt is present (approx. 0 volt), replace the wiper motor cover assembly.

3. Reconnect the wiper/washer switch connector **C215**. Disconnect the wiper motor connector. Using a digital multimeter, measure the voltage from connector, terminal **D (DARK GREEN)** to ground.

    a. If more than 1.0 volt is present, repair the short to **B+** in circuit **113 (DARK GREEN)**.

    b. If less than 1.0 volt is present (approx. 0 volt), replace the wiper motor cover assembly.

WIPERS DO NOT OPERATE WHEN WASHER SWITCH IS ACTIVATED

1. Turn the ignition switch to the **RUN** position. Connect a test light between the wiper/washer switch connector **C215**, terminal **E (DARK GREEN)** and ground; then activate the washer switch and observe the test light.

    a. If the light turns **ON,** check for an open in circuit **113 (DARK GREEN)** or for a poor connection at connector **C215** or at the wiper motor assembly.

    b. If the light does not turn **ON,** check for an open in the wiper/washer switch assembly pigtail and connection. If okay, replace the wiper/washer switch assembly.

2. Reconnect the wiper/washer switch connector **C215**. Disconnect the wiper motor connector. Turn the ignition switch to the **RUN** position. Using a digital multimeter, measure the voltage from the wiper motor connector, terminal **E (GREY)** to ground.

    a. If **B+** is present, replace the wiper motor cover assembly.

    b. If approx. 0 volts is present, check circuit **112 (GREY)** for an open or poor connection. If okay, replace the wiper motor cover assembly.

WASHER DOES NOT OPERATE

1. Disconnect the washer pump connector. Connect a test light between terminals **A (RED)** and **B (BLACK)** of the washer pump connector; then, activate the washer switch while observing the test light.

   a. If the test light is **OFF,** go to Step 2.

   b. If the test light is **ON,** check for a poor connection to the washer pump. If okay, replace the washer pump.

2. Connect a test light between the washer pump connector, terminal **A (RED)** and ground.

   a. If the test light is **OFF,** go to Step 3.

   b. If the test light is **ON,** repair the open in circuit **150 (BLACK)**; terminal of the pump connector.

3. Connect a test light between wiper/washer switch connector **C215**, terminal **H (PINK)** and ground.

   a. If the test light is **OFF,** check for a poor connection at connector **C215**, terminal **H (PINK)**. If okay, replace the wiper/washer switch assembly.

   b. If the test light is **ON,** check for an open in circuit **94 (PINK)**, circuit **228 (RED)** or isolation diode.

REMOVAL & INSTALLATION

Wiper Motor Cover

1. Disconnect the negative battery cable from the battery.

2. Disconnect the electrical connector from the wiper motor cover and the wiper motor.

3. Remove the wiper motor cover-to-wiper motor screws and the cover.

To install:

4. With the wiper motor in the park position, align the wiper motor cover's cam slot with the drive pin. Install the cover and torque the screws to 18 inch lbs. (2 Nm).

5. Install the electrical connectors.

6. Connect the negative battery cable.

PONTIAC Grand Am

TROUBLESHOOTING

Diagnostic Tests

WIPERS DO NOT OPERATE IN ANY MODE

1. Disconnect the wiper/washer switch connector. Turn the ignition switch to the **RUN** position. Connect a test light between the connector, terminal **B. (WHITE)** and ground.

   a. If the test light is **ON,** go to Step 2.

   b. If the test light is **OFF,** check for an open in the wiper fuse or in circuit **93 (WHITE)**. If okay, check for an open in the power feed circuit **4**.

2. Disconnect the wiper motor connector **C2**. Connect a test light between the connector, terminal **C (BLACK)** to the battery's positive **(+)** terminal.

   a. If the test light is **ON,** go to Step 3.

   b. If the test light is **OFF,** repair the open in the ground circuit **150**.

3. Connect the wiper/washer switch connector. Disconnect the wiper motor connector **C1**. Connect a test light between the connector, terminal **C (GREY)** and ground.

   a. If the test light is **ON,** go to Step 4.

   b. If the test light is **OFF,** check for an open in circuit **91 (GREY)**. If okay, replace the wiper/washer switch.

4. Turn the wiper switch to the **LOW** position. Connect a test light between the connector **C1**, terminal **B (BROWN)** and ground.

   a. If the test light is **ON,** go to Step 5.

   b. If the test light is **OFF,** check for an open in circuit **96 (BROWN)**. If okay, replace the wiper/washer switch.

5. Check for continuity between the

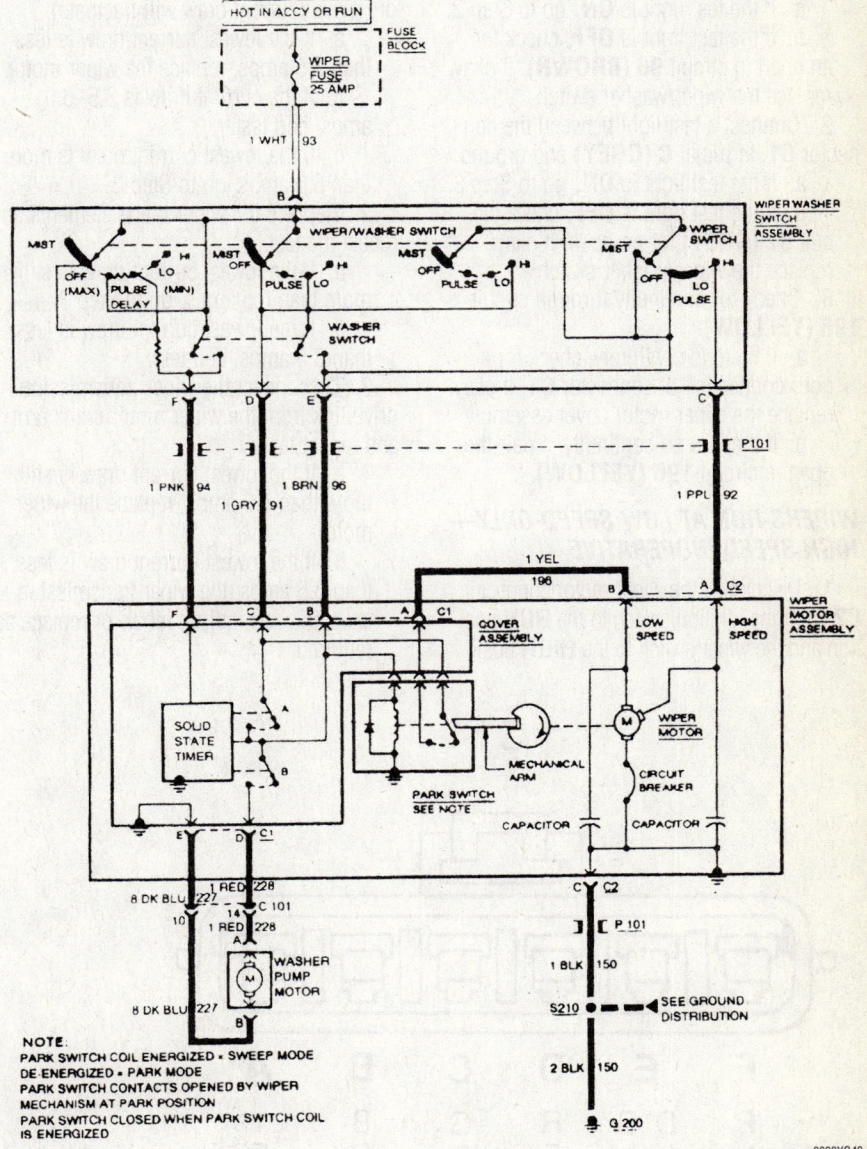

NOTE:
PARK SWITCH COIL ENERGIZED = SWEEP MODE
DE-ENERGIZED = PARK MODE
PARK SWITCH CONTACTS OPENED BY WIPER
MECHANISM AT PARK POSITION
PARK SWITCH CLOSED WHEN PARK SWITCH COIL
IS ENERGIZED

Windshield wiper/washer electrical schematic—Grand Am

wiper motor connector **C1**, terminal **A (YELLOW)** and connector **C2**, terminal **B (YELLOW)**.

a. If there is continuity, check for a poor connection at the wiper motor connectors. If okay, replace the wiper motor assembly.

b. If there is no continuity, repair the open in circuit **196 (YELLOW)**.

WIPERS RUN AT HIGH SPEED ONLY—LOW SPEED INOPERATIVE

1. Disconnect the wiper motor connector **C1**. Turn the ignition switch to the **RUN** position and the wiper switch to the **LOW** position. Connect a test light between the connector **C1**, terminal **B (BROWN)** and ground.

a. If the test light is **ON,** go to Step 2.

b. If the test light is **OFF,** check for an open in circuit **96 (BROWN)**. If okay, replace the wiper/washer switch.

2. Connect a test light between the connector **C1**, terminal **C (GREY)** and ground.

a. If the test light is **ON,** go to Step 3.

b. If the test light is **OFF,** check circuit **91 (GREY)** for an open. If okay, replace the wiper/washer switch.

3. Check for continuity through circuit **196 (YELLOW)**.

a. If there is continuity, check for a poor connection at connector **C1**. If okay, replace the wiper motor cover assembly.

b. If there is no continuity, repair the open in circuit **196 (YELLOW)**.

WIPERS RUN AT LOW SPEED ONLY—HIGH SPEED INOPERATIVE

1. Disconnect the wiper motor connector **C2**. Turn the ignition switch to the **RUN** position and the wiper switch to the **HIGH** posi-

tion. Connect a test light between the connector **C2**, terminal **A (PURPLE)** and ground.

2. If the test light is **ON,** check for a poor connection at connector **C2**, terminal **A (PURPLE)**. If okay, replace the wiper motor assembly.

3. If the test light is **OFF,** check for an open in circuit **92 (PURPLE)**. If okay, replace the wiper/washer switch.

WIPERS RUN INTERMITTENTLY IN LOW OR HIGH SPEED SETTINGS

1. Remove the wiper fuse and connect an ammeter (0–30 amp) across the fuse block terminals. Turn the ignition switch to the **RUN** position and the wiper switch to the **LOW** position. Observe the lowest current draw while the wipers are running on dry glass (current draw will fluctuate).

a. If the lowest current draw is less than 3.5 amps, replace the wiper motor.

b. If the current draw is 3.5–6.5 amps, end test.

c. If the lowest current draw is more than 6.5 amps, go to Step 2.

2. Replace the wiper blade elements and repeat the test.

a. If the lowest current draw is still more than 6.5 amps, go to Step 3.

b. If the lowest current draw is less than 6.5 amps, end test.

3. Disconnect the wiper transmission drive link from the wiper motor crank arm and repeat test.

a. If the lowest current draw is still more than 6.5 amps, replace the wiper motor.

b. If the lowest current draw is less than 6.5 amps, the wiper transmission assembly is binding, repair or replace as required.

WIPERS WILL NOT TURN OFF

1. Disconnect the wiper motor connector **C1**. Turn the ignition switch to the **RUN** position and the wiper switch to the **OFF** position. Using a digital multimeter, measure the voltage from connector **C1**, terminal **B (GREY)** to ground.

a. If the voltage is 0 volts, go to Step 2.

b. If battery voltage is present, check for a short to **B+** in circuit **96 (BROWN)**. If okay, replace the wiper/washer switch.

2. Disconnect the wiper motor connector **C2**. Using a digital multimeter, measure the voltage from connector **C2**, terminal **A (PURPLE)** to ground.

a. If the voltage is 0 volts, repair the short to **B+** in circuit **196 (YELLOW)**.

b. If battery voltage is present, check for a short to **B+** in circuit **92 (PURPLE)**. If okay, replace the wiper/washer switch.

WIPERS CYCLE IN AND OUT OF PARK AFTER WIPERS ARE SHUT OFF

1. Turn the ignition switch to the **RUN** position. Operate the wiper switch and return it to the **OFF** position.

a. If the wiper motor continues to operate in low speed, go to Step 2.

b. If the wiper motor continues to operate in high speed, go to Wipers Run At High Speed Only chart.

2. Replace the park switch assembly.

a. If the trouble is corrected, end test.

b. If the trouble is not corrected, replace the wiper motor assembly.

PULSE DELAY OPERATES INCORRECTLY OR NOT AT ALL

1. Disconnect the wiper/washer switch connector. Turn the ignition switch to the

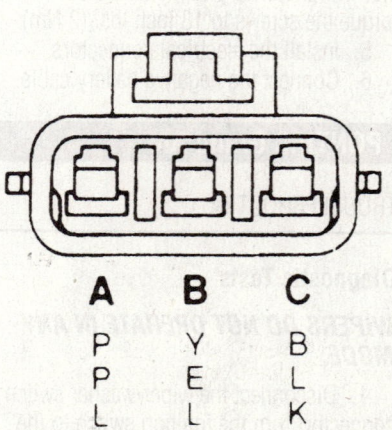

C1

F	E	D	C	B		A
P	D	B	R	G	B	Y
N	K	L	E	R	R	E
K	U	U	D	Y	N	L

C2

A	B	C
P	Y	B
P	E	L
L	L	K

Windshield wiper motor wiring harness electrical connectors—Grand Am

8838XG49

OFF position and the wiper switch to the **DELAY** position. Using a digital multimeter, measure the resistance through the wiper/washer switch at connector, from terminal **B (WHITE)** to terminal **F (PINK)**; then, move the wiper switch through the entire **DELAY** range.

a. If the resistance varies from 1.244 Mega-ohms to 0.024 Mega-ohms, go to Step 2.

b. If the resistance does not vary from 1.244 Mega-ohms to 0.024 Mega-ohms, replace the wiper/washer switch assembly.

2. Measure the resistance through the wiper/washer switch at connector, from terminal **B (WHITE)** to terminal **E (BROWN)**.

a. If the resistance is less than 3 ohms, go to Step 3.

b. If the resistance is greater than 3 ohm, replace the wiper/washer switch assembly.

3. Check circuits **96 (BROWN)** and **94 (PINK)** for an open or poor connection. If okay, remove the wiper motor cover assembly.

a. If the park switch pulse contacts are touching the pads on the circuit board, replace the wiper motor cover assembly.

b. If the park switch pulse contacts are not touching the pads on the circuit board, replace the park switch spring contacts.

WASHER WILL NOT OPERATE

1. Disconnect the washer pump connector. Turn the ignition switch to the **RUN** position. Connect a test light between terminals **A (RED)** and **B (DARK BLUE)** of the washer pump connector; then, activate the washer switch while observing the test light.

a. If the test light is **OFF,** go to Step 2.

b. If the test light is **ON,** check for a poor connection at the washer pump connector. If okay, replace the washer pump.

2. Connect a test light between connector, terminal **A (RED)** and ground; then, activate the washer switch while observing the test light.

a. If the test light is **OFF,** go to Step 3.

b. If the test light is **ON,** check for a poor connection or open in circuit **227 (DARK BLUE)**. If okay, replace the wiper motor assembly (internal ground circuit open).

3. Connect a test light between wiper motor connector **C1**, terminal **D (RED)** and ground.

a. If the test light is **OFF,** go to Step 4.

b. If the test light is **ON,** check for a poor connection or open in circuit **228 (RED)**.

4. Turn the ignition switch to the **RUN** position. Using a digital multimeter, back-probe the wiper/washer switch connector, from terminal **B (WHITE)** to ground; then, activate the washer switch while observing the digital multimeter.

a. If 0 voltage is present, replace the wiper/washer switch assembly.

b. If battery voltage is present, check for a poor connection at the wiper/washer switch and wiper motor assembly connectors; or open in circuit **94 (PINK)**. If okay, replace the wiper motor assembly.

WASHER WILL NOT SHUT OFF

1. Turn the ignition switch to the **RUN** position and the wiper switch to the **LOW** position. Disconnect the wiper motor connector **C1**. Connect a test light between connector **C1**, terminal **F (PINK)** and ground, at the wiper motor case. Momentarily, activate the washer switch while observing the test light.

2. If the test light is **OFF** when the washer switch is released, replace the wiper motor cover assembly.

3. If the test light is **ON** when the washer switch is released, replace the wiper/washer switch assembly.

REMOVAL & INSTALLATION

Wiper Motor Cover

1. Disconnect the negative battery cable from the battery. At the center or the cowl, remove the washer hose from the nipple.

2. At the wiper motor cover's electrical connector, pull the retainer from the connector; then, disconnect the electrical connector from the wiper motor cover assembly.

3. Remove the wiper motor cover-to-wiper motor screws and the cover.

To install:

4. With the wiper motor in the park position, align the wiper motor cover's cam slot with the drive pin. Install the cover and torque the screws to 18 inch lbs. (2 Nm).

5. Install the electrical connector and secure with the retainer.

6. Connect the negative battery cable.

Park Switch Assembly

1. Remove the wiper motor cover assembly.

➡ **If the wiper motor is in the park position, operate the motor (as required) to remove the pawl from the relay slot.**

2. Remove the screw and the park switch from the wiper motor assembly.

To install:

3. Install the park switch and screw onto the wiper motor assembly.

4. When the pawl is in the relay slot, operate the wiper motor back into the park position.

5. Install the wiper motor cover assembly.

BUICK Riviera; OLDSMOBILE Aurora

TROUBLESHOOTING

Troubleshooting Hints

WIPERS DO NOT OPERATE IN ANY MODE

1. Disconnect the wiper switch connector **C202**, ignition switch to **RUN** and connect test light from connector terminal **E5** to ground. If light, go to next step. If no light, check for open in fuse, circuit **93** or power circuit **4**.

2. Disconnect motor connector **C2** and connect test light from terminal **C** to battery positive. If light go to next step. If no light, repair open in ground circuit **151**.

3. Reconnect switch connector and disconnect motor connector **C1**. Connect test light from **C1** terminal **C** and ground. If light, go to next step. If no light, check for open in circuit **95**. If OK, replace wiper switch.

4. Wiper switch to **LO** and connect test light from connector **C1** terminal **B** to ground. If light, go to next step. If no light, check for open in circuit **91**. If OK, replace wiper switch.

5. Check for continuity between motor connector **C1** terminal **A** and connector **C2** terminal **B**. If continuity, check for poor connections. If OK, replace wiper motor cover assembly. If still not corrected, replace motor assembly. If no continuity, repair open in circuit **196**.

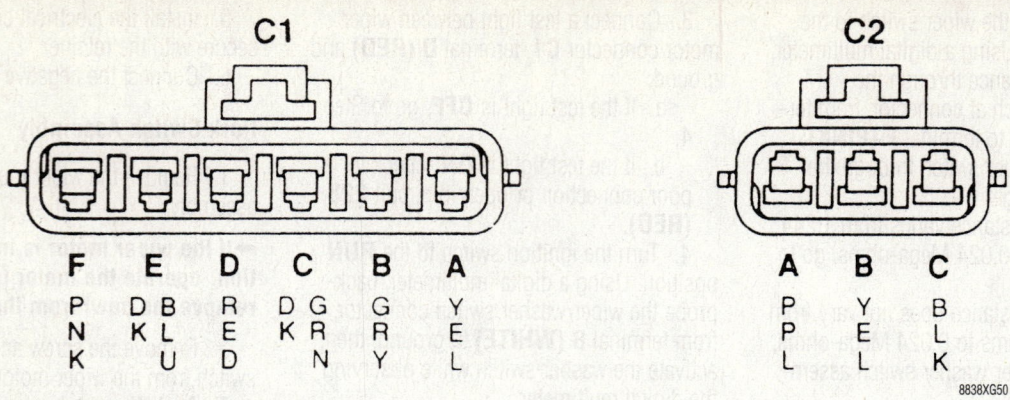

C1

F	E	D	C	B	A
P	D	B	R	D	G	G	Y
N	K	L	E	K	R	R	E
K	U	D		N	Y	L

C2

A	B	C
P	Y	B
P	E	L
L	L	K

8838XG50

Windshield wiper motor harness connector—Aurora/Riviera

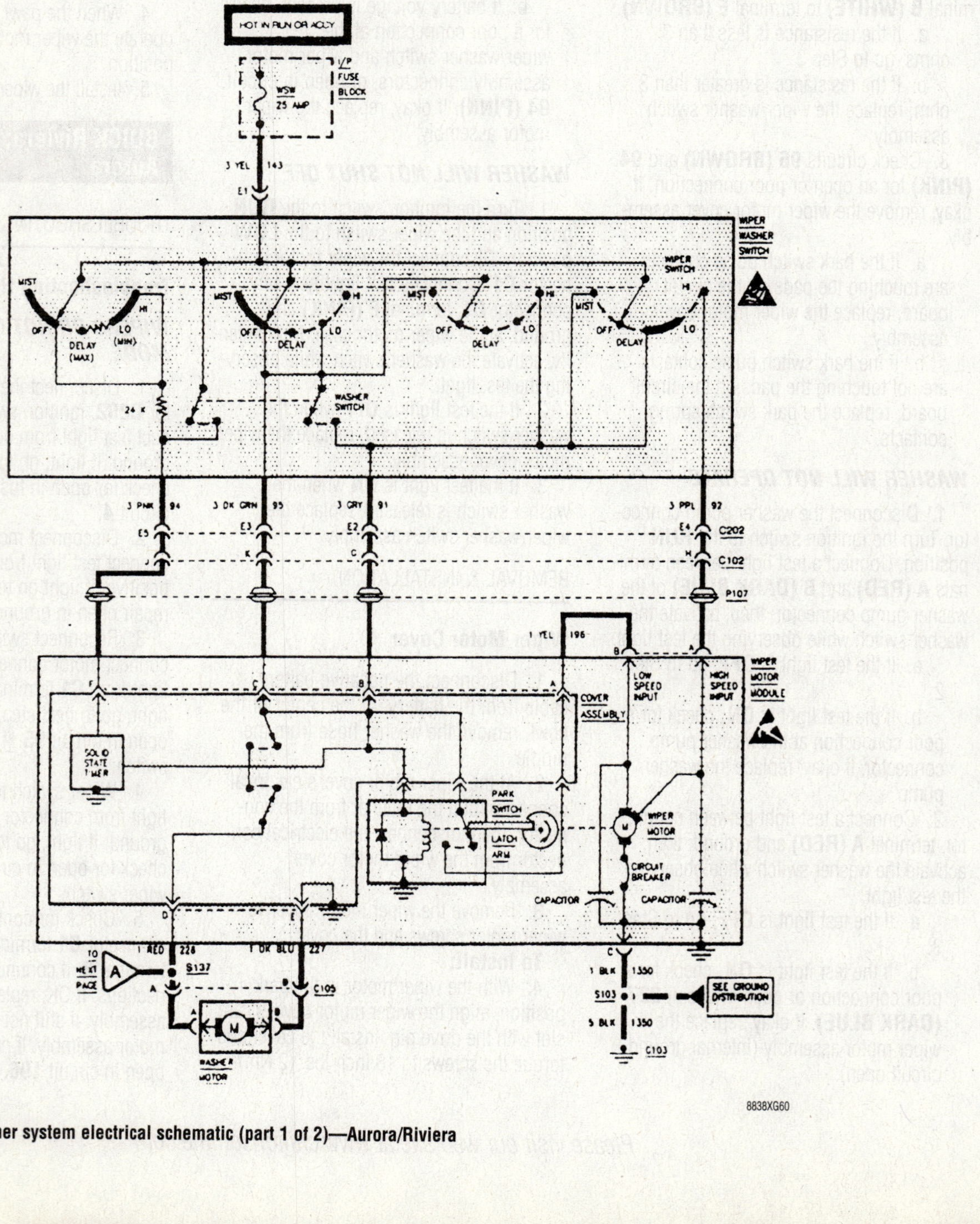

Windshield wiper/washer system electrical schematic (part 1 of 2)—Aurora/Riviera

8838XG60

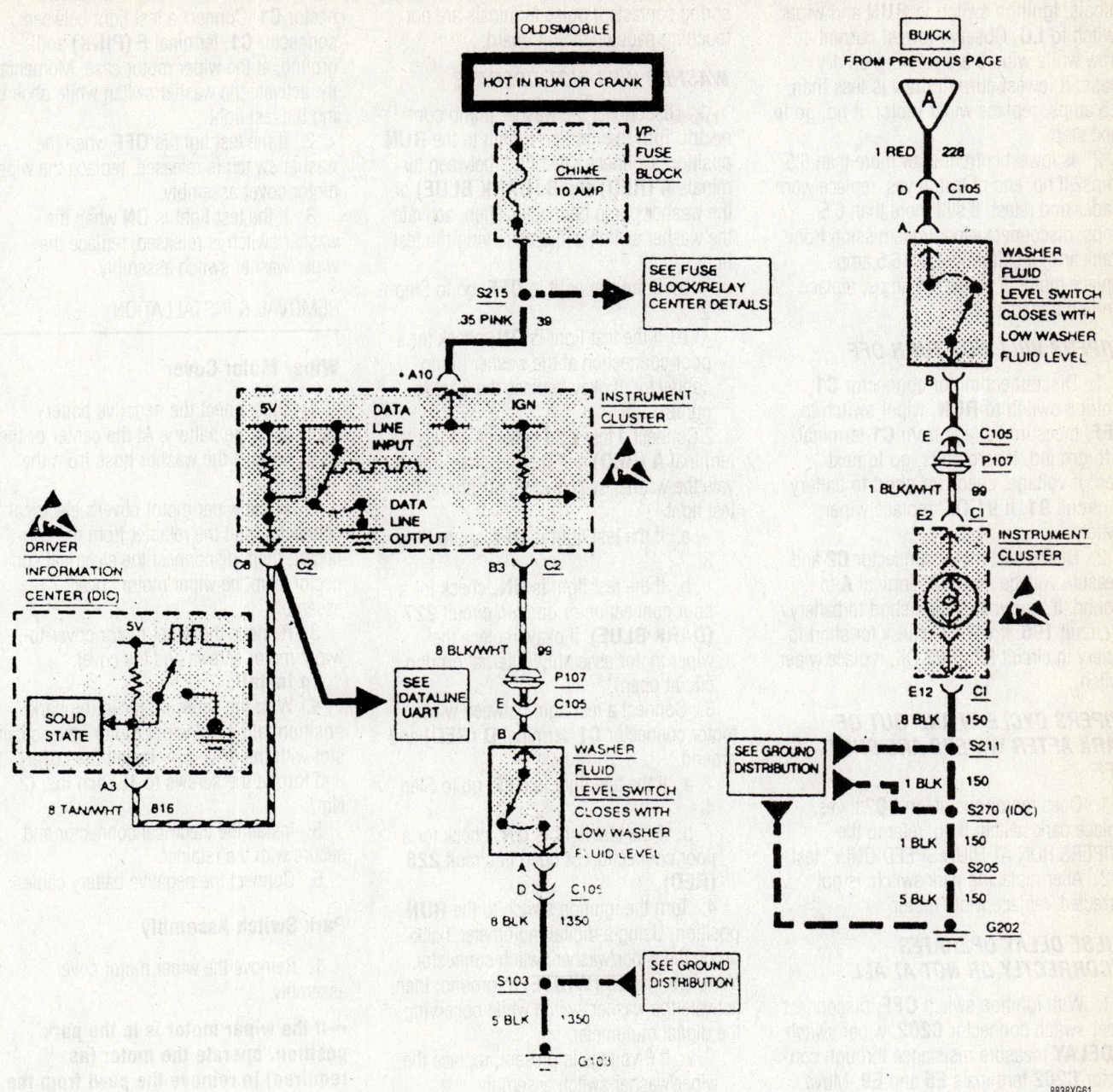

Windshield wiper/washer system electrical schematic (part 2 of 2)—Aurora/Riviera

WIPERS RUN AT HIGH SPEED ONLY (LOW SPEED INOPERATIVE)

1. Disconnect motor connector **C1**, ignition to **RUN**, wiper switch to **LO** and connect test light from **C1** terminal **B** to ground. If light, go to next step. If no light, check for open in circuit **91** or poor connection.

2. Connect test light from **C1** terminal **C** to ground. If light, check for continuity through circuit **196**. If no light, check for open in circuit **95**. If **95** OK, replace wiper switch.

3. If circuit **196** has continuity, check for poor connection at motor connector **C1**. If **(C1)** OK, replace wiper motor cover. If still not corrected, replace wiper motor. If circuit **95** is not OK, repair as needed.

WIPERS RUN AT LOW SPEED ONLY (HIGH SPEED INOPERATIVE)

1. Disconnect motor connector **C2**, ignition to **RUN**, wiper switch to **HI** and connect

test light from **C2** terminal **A** to ground. If light, go to next step. If no light, check for open in circuit **92** or poor connection. If circuit **92** OK, replace wiper switch.

2. Check for poor connection at motor connector **C2** terminal **A**. If OK, replace wiper motor.

WIPERS RUN INTERMITTENTLY IN LOW OR HIGH SPEED

1. Remove wiper fuse and connect ammeter with 0–30 amps across fuse ter-

---

For brake related suspension and axle service, refer to the model specific sections of this manual

minals. Ignition switch to **RUN** and wiper switch to **LO**. Observe lowest current draw while wipers are running on dry glass. If lowest current draw is less than 3.5 amps, replace wiper motor. If no, go to next step.

2. Is lowest current draw more than 6.5 amps? If no, end of test. If yes, replace worn blades and retest. If still more than 6.5 amps, disconnect wiper transmission from crank arm. If still more than 6.5 amps, replace motor. If below 6.5 amps, replace binding transmission.

WIPERS WILL NOT TURN OFF

1. Disconnect motor connector **C1**, ignition switch to **RUN**, wiper switch to **OFF**, measure voltage from **C1** terminal **B** to ground. If zero volts, go to next step. If voltage, check for short to battery in circuit **91**. If **91** OK, replace wiper switch.

2. Disconnect motor connector **C2** and measure voltage from **C2** terminal **A** to ground. If zero volts, repair short to battery in circuit **196**. If voltage, check for short to battery in circuit **92**. If **92** OK, replace wiper switch.

WIPERS CYCLE IN AND OUT OF PARK AFTER WIPERS ARE SHUT OFF

1. Does motor operate in **LO**? If yes, replace park switch. If no, refer to the "WIPERS RUN AT HIGH SPEED ONLY" test.

2. After replacing park switch, is not corrected, replace wiper motor.

PULSE DELAY OPERATES INCORRECTLY OR NOT AT ALL

1. With ignition switch **OFF**, disconnect wiper switch connector **C202**, wiper switch to **DELAY** measure resistance through connector **C202** terminals **E5** and **E9**. Move the switch through the delay range. If the resistance varies from 1.224–0.024 M ohms, go to next step. If not, replace switch.

2. Measure resistance through connector **C202** terminals **E5** and **E6**. If less than 3 ohms, go to next step. If not, replace wiper switch.

3. Check circuits **91** and **94** for opens or poor connections. If circuits OK, replace wiper motor cover. Replace park switch

spring contacts if pulse terminals are not touching pads on circuit board.

WASHER WILL NOT OPERATE

1. Disconnect the washer pump connector. Turn the ignition switch to the **RUN** position. Connect a test light between terminals **A (RED)** and **B (DARK BLUE)** of the washer pump connector; then, activate the washer switch while observing the test light.

   a. If the test light is **OFF**, go to Step 2.

   b. If the test light is **ON**, check for a poor connection at the washer pump connector. If okay, replace the washer pump.

2. Connect a test light between connector, terminal **A (RED)** and ground; then, activate the washer switch while observing the test light.

   a. If the test light is **OFF**, go to Step 3.

   b. If the test light is **ON**, check for a poor connection or open in circuit **227 (DARK BLUE)**. If okay, replace the wiper motor assembly (internal ground circuit open).

3. Connect a test light between wiper motor connector **C1**, terminal **D (RED)** and ground.

   a. If the test light is **OFF**, go to Step 4.

   b. If the test light is **ON**, check for a poor connection or open in circuit **228 (RED)**.

4. Turn the ignition switch to the **RUN** position. Using a digital multimeter, back-probe the wiper/washer switch connector, from terminal **E9 (WHITE)** to ground; then, activate the washer switch while observing the digital multimeter.

   a. If 0 voltage is present, replace the wiper/washer switch assembly.

   b. If battery voltage is present, check for a poor connection at the wiper/washer switch and wiper motor assembly connectors; or open in circuit **94 (PINK)**. If okay, replace the wiper motor assembly.

WASHER WILL NOT SHUT OFF

1. Turn the ignition switch to the **RUN** position and the wiper switch to the **LOW** position. Disconnect the wiper motor con-

nector **C1**. Connect a test light between connector **C1**, terminal **F (PINK)** and ground, at the wiper motor case. Momentarily, activate the washer switch while observing the test light.

2. If the test light is **OFF** when the washer switch is released, replace the wiper motor cover assembly.

3. If the test light is **ON** when the washer switch is released, replace the wiper/washer switch assembly.

REMOVAL & INSTALLATION

Wiper Motor Cover

1. Disconnect the negative battery cable from the battery. At the center or the cowl, remove the washer hose from the nipple.

2. At the wiper motor cover's electrical connector, pull the retainer from the connector; then, disconnect the electrical connector from the wiper motor cover assembly.

3. Remove the wiper motor cover-to-wiper motor screws and the cover.

To install:

4. With the wiper motor in the park position, align the wiper motor cover's cam slot with the drive pin. Install the cover and torque the screws to 18 inch lbs. (2 Nm).

5. Install the electrical connector and secure with the retainer.

6. Connect the negative battery cable.

Park Switch Assembly

1. Remove the wiper motor cover assembly.

➡**If the wiper motor is in the park position, operate the motor (as required) to remove the pawl from the relay slot.**

2. Remove the screw and the park switch from the wiper motor assembly.

To install:

3. Install the park switch and screw onto the wiper motor assembly.

4. When the pawl is in the relay slot, operate the wiper motor back into the park position.

5. Install the wiper motor cover assembly.

GENERAL MOTORS CORPORATION MODELS WITH A 9-TERMINAL WIPER MOTOR

All Equipped Models

GENERAL INFORMATION

The basic 9-terminal windshield wiper/washer system is available with the washer pump mounted remotely on the solvent container.

Depending on the type of control switch used and whether an optional electronic printed circuit board is attached to the wiper cover, the system can serve as either a pulse-type wiper/washer system or a standard type 2-speed windshield wiper. Pulse timing and demand wash functions are controlled electronically on pulse windshield wipers.

Standard wound field (non-pulse) motors are about 4½ in. (114mm) in length. The wiper motor and gearbox assembly electrical leads (black and black with a pink stripe) are routed internally through a cavity in the gearbox casting. These leads, formerly exposed on a past model design, are routed through a grommet in the motor casting.

Both standard system and multiplex pulse system styles use similar motors. Multiplex pulse wipers use a green pulse relay case. Multiplex pulse wipers can also be identified by a single electrical lead **(BLACK/PINK)** leading to the timing circuit.

The multiplex pulse wiper system provides a controlled wiping action. It uses a wound field motor and wiper blades that park below the hood line. The wiper switch in the **DELAY** mode can be turned from a **MIN** (minimum) to a **MAX** (maximum) position. Turning the control knob from the **MIN** to **MAX** position varies the amount of time the wiper will delay between each wipe. The delay ranges between 0–12 seconds depending on the position of the knob. Minimum delay or 0 seconds between wipes provides the equivalent of low speed continuous operation.

WIPER AND WASHER OPERATION

Standard Wiper/Washer System

The standard system is controlled by the multi-function lever switch and the wipers can be driven at 2 speeds, either **HIGH** or **LOW**. When pushed, the **WASH** switch on the lever energizes the washer motor to drive the pump and deliver washer fluid to the windshield as long as the switch is pressed.

Multiplex Pulse Wiper/Washer System

The dash switch is a combination of switches and a variable resistor controlled by a single knob and a wash button switch. Two relays control motor operation:

1. Parking relay (gearbox relay) located in the gearbox.
2. Pulse relay (part of the timing circuit) located on the washer pump frame.

Both relays must be energized to complete 12V DC circuit to the wiper motor windings.

> **BUICK, LeSabre, Park Avenue, Regal, Riviera, Skylark; CADILLAC deVille, Eldorado, Seville; CHEVROLET Camaro, Corvette, Lumina, Monte Carlo; OLDSMOBILE Achieva, Aurora, Cutlass Supreme; PONTIAC Bonneville, Firebird, Grand Am, Grand Prix**

TROUBLESHOOTING

Wiper Motor System Operation

To help find problems, it's important to understand normal operation. The following should be used as a guide:
1. With the ignition switch in **ACCY** or **RUN**, press the washer switch to **ON** for less than 1 second. Look for:
   a. Normal operation is for the washer to spray the windshield for approximately 2½ seconds.
   b. The wiper should run at low speed and continue to run at low speed until the washer button is released.
   c. After the button is released, wipers run for approximately 6 seconds and then return to park.
2. With the wiper switch turned to **PULSE** or **DELAY** Mode, look for:
   a. Wipers should make 1 complete stroke, then pause for 0–25 seconds before making the next stroke.
   b. The wait time should be adjustable by turning the wiper switch through the delay range.
3. With the wiper switch in **PULSE**, hold the washer switch **ON** for 1–2 seconds. Look for:
   a. Washer should spray windshield as long as washer button is held **ON**.
   b. Pulse function is overridden and the wipers run at low speed during the spray period.
   c. After the washer stops, the wipers continue to run for 6 seconds.
   d. Wipers return to Pulse operation.
4. With the wiper switch in **HIGH**, hold the washer switch for 1–2 seconds. Look for: Same operation at low speed wash except that wipers run at high speed.
5. Turn wiper switch to **LOW**. Look for: Wipers should run continuously at low speed.
6. Turn wiper switch to **HIGH**. Look for: Wipers should run continuously at high speed.
7. Turn wiper switch **OFF**. Look for: Wipers should return to the park position at **LOW** speed, then shut **OFF**.
8. Turn the wiper switch to **MIST**. Look for: Wipers should make 1 complete stroke and then park.

In addition, check the following:
9. Check the wiper fuse.
10. Check that the wiper/washer switch connector and wiper/washer motor connectors are mated correctly.
11. If the washer does not operate check that:
   a. The washer reservoir is filled.
   b. The hoses are not pinched or kinked.
   c. The hoses are correctly attached.
   d. The nozzles are not clogged.
12. If the wipers cycle in and out of park position in **HIGH** but do not operate in **LOW, MIST** or **PULSE**, check the yellow wire of an open.
13. If the wiper motor runs but the wiper blades do not, check the wiper linkage at the wiper crank arm.

CIRCUIT OPERATION

In addition to the features of a conventional non-pulse wiper system (2-speed, low and high) the pulse-type windshield wiper/washer system includes an operating mode in which the wipers make a single stroke with an adjustable time interval between strokes. The time interval is controlled by a solid state timer in the wiper motor assembly. The duration of the delay interval is determined by the delay rheostat in the wiper switch assembly.

The wiper motor is protected by a circuit breaker. If the wipers are blocked (by snow or ice, for example) the circuit breaker will open the circuit. The circuit breaker resets automatically when it cools.

TESTING

Symptom Test—Wiper Motor: Pulse

1. Wipers do not operate in any mode.
   a. Perform Test A: Wiper/Washer Switch Voltage.
   b. Perform Test B: Wiper Motor Module Input Voltage.
   c. Perform Test E: Wiper Motor Module Current Draw.
2. Wipers run at **LOW** speed only (no **HIGH** speed). Perform Test B: Wiper Motor Module Input Voltage.
3. Wipers cycle in and out of park when in **HIGH**.
   a. Perform Test B: Wiper Motor Module Input Voltage.

b. Perform Test C: Wiper Motor Module Resistance.
4. Wipers cycle in and out of park when in **OFF** and operate in **LOW**. Replace the Park Switch.
5. Wipers will not shut off. Perform Test B: Wiper Motor Module Input Voltage.
6. No delay in **PULSE** mode or **PULSE** mode does not operate correctly.
   a. Perform Test B: Wiper Motor Module Input Voltage.
   b. Perform Test D: Wiper/Washer Pulse Control Resistance.
7. Wipers operate very slowly or intermittently. Perform Test E: Wiper Motor Module Current Draw.
8. Wipers do not park. Perform Test F: Complete Mechanical Inspection.
9. Washer will not operate or runs continuously.
   a. Perform Test B: Wiper Motor Module Input Voltage.
   b. Perform Test G: Washer Motor Voltage.
10. Wipers stay in delay during wash cycle. Replace cover assembly.

TROUBLESHOOTING TESTS

Test A: Wiper/Washer Switch Voltage

1. Measure the voltage at the wiper/washer switch connector (disconnected).
2. Turn the ignition switch to **RUN**.
3. Measure the voltage between terminal **D (WHITE)** and ground. It should read battery voltage.
   a. If voltage is correct, recheck symptoms.
   b. If no voltage is present, check the white wire and the wiper fuse for an open.

Test B: Wiper Motor Module Input Voltage

1. Measure the voltage at the wiper motor module connectors C1 (DARK BLUE) and C2 (BLACK) disconnected.
2. Turn the ignition switch to **RUN**.
3. With the wiper switch in position **OFF**, connect between connector **C2**

	SWITCH MODE / TERMINAL #	MIST	OFF	PULSE	LO	HI	WASH
PULSE	1	C TO 8	C TO 8	C TO 8	C TO 8	C TO 8	C TO 8
	2	B(+)	—	B(+)	B(+)	C TO 3	C TO 3
	3	B(+)	B(+)	—	B(+)	C TO 2	C TO 2
	4	—	—	—	—	—	—
	5	—	—	—	—	—	B(+)
	6	10-12V	10-12V	10-12V	10-12V	10-12V	B(+)
	7	GROUND	GROUND	GROUND	GROUND	GROUND	GROUND
	8	C TO 1	C TO 1	C TO 1	C TO 1	C TO 1	C TO 1
	9	—	—	—	—	B(+)	—
STANDARD	1	C TO 8	C TO 8	//////	C TO 8	C TO 8	C TO 8
	2	B(+)	—	//////	B(+)	C TO 3	C TO 3
	3	B(+)	B(+)	//////	B(+)	C TO 2	C TO 2
	4	—	—	//////	—	—	—
	5	—	—	//////	—	—	B(+)
	6	—	—	//////	—	—	—
	7	GROUND	GROUND	//////	GROUND	GROUND	GROUND
	8	C TO 1	C TO 1	//////	C TO 1	C TO 1	C TO 1
	9	—	—	//////	—	B(+)	—

C = CONTINUITY

9-Terminal wiper motor wiper/washer switch check chart—General Motors except Chevrolet Cavalier, Pontiac Sunbird and Sunfire

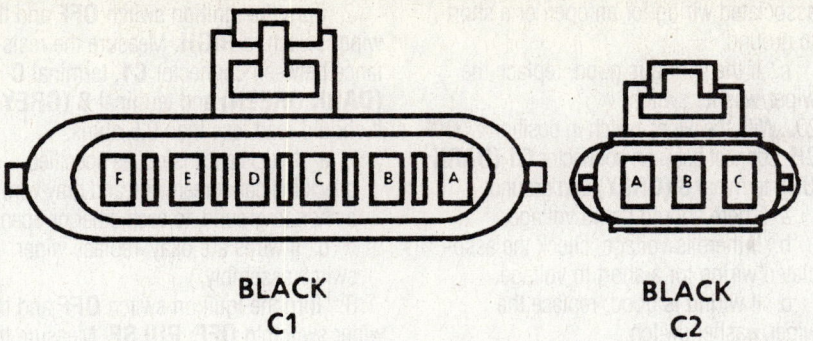

BLACK C1 **BLACK C2**

8470V038

9-Terminal wiper motor assembly electrical connectors—General Motors except Chevrolet Cavalier, Pontiac Sunbird and Sunfire

(BLACK), terminal **A (PURPLE)** and ground.

   a. There should be no voltage.

   b. If there is voltage, check the associated wiring for a short to voltage.

   c. If wiring is good, replace the wiper/washer switch.

   4. With the wiper switch in position **OFF**, connect between connector **C1 (DARK BLUE)**, terminal **B (GREY)** and ground.

   a. There should be no voltage.

   b. If there is voltage, check the associated wiring for a short to voltage.

   c. If wiring is good, replace the wiper/washer switch.

   5. With the wiper switch in position **OFF**, connect between connector **C1**

(DARK BLUE), terminal **C (DARK GREEN)** and ground.

   a. There should be battery voltage.

   b. If there is no voltage, check the associated wiring to the wiper/washer switch for an open or short to ground.

   c. If the wiring is good, replace the wiper/washer switch.

   6. With the wiper switch in position **OFF**, connect between connector **C1 (DARK BLUE)**, terminal **F (PINK)** and ground.

   a. There should be battery voltage.

   b. If there is no voltage, check the associated wiring to the wiper/washer switch for an open or short to ground.

   c. If the wiring is good, replace the wiper/washer switch.

TERMINAL #1
TERMINAL #2
TERMINAL #3
TERMINAL #4
TERMINAL #5
TERMINAL #6
TERMINAL #7
TERMINAL #8
TERMINAL #9

8470V040

9-Terminal wiper motor wiper terminal identification—General Motors except Chevrolet Cavalier, Pontiac Sunbird and Sunfire

   7. With the wiper switch in position **MIST**, connect between connector **C2 (BLACK)**, terminal **A (PURPLE)** and ground.

   a. There should be no voltage.

   b. If there is voltage, check the associated wiring for a short to voltage.

   c. If the wiring is good, replace the wiper/washer switch.

   8. With the wiper switch in position **MIST**, connect between connector **C1 (DARK BLUE)**, terminal **B (GREY)** and ground.

   a. There should be battery voltage.

   b. If there is no voltage, check the associated wiring for an open or a short to ground.

   c. If the wiring is good, replace the wiper/washer switch.

   9. With the wiper switch in position **MIST**, connect between connector **C1 (DARK BLUE)**, terminal **C (DARK GREEN)** and ground.

   a. There should be battery voltage.

   b. If there is no voltage, check the associated wiring for an open or a short to ground.

   c. If the wiring is good, replace the wiper/washer switch.

   10. With the wiper switch in position **MIST**, connect between connector **C1 (DARK BLUE)**, terminal **F (PINK)** and ground.

   a. There should be battery voltage.

   b. If there is no voltage, check the associated wiring for an open or a short to ground.

   c. If the wiring is good, replace the wiper/washer switch.

   11. With the wiper switch in position **PULSE**, connect between connector **C2 (BLACK)**, terminal **A (PURPLE)** and ground.

   a. There should be no voltage.

   b. If there is voltage, check the associated wiring for a short to voltage.

   c. If the wiring is good, replace the wiper/washer switch.

   12. With the wiper switch in position **PULSE**, connect between connector **C1 (DARK BLUE)**, terminal **B (GREY)** and ground.

   a. There should be battery voltage.

   b. If there is no voltage, check the associated wiring for an open or a short to ground.

   c. If the wiring is good, replace the wiper/washer switch.

   13. With the wiper switch in position **PULSE**, connect between connector **C1**

(DARK BLUE), terminal C (DARK GREEN) and ground.

   a. There should be no voltage.

   b. If there is voltage, check the associated wiring for a short to voltage.

   c. If wiring is good, replace the wiper/washer switch.

14. With the wiper switch in position PULSE, connect between connector C1 (DARK BLUE), terminal F (PINK) and ground.

   a. There should be battery voltage.

   b. If there is no voltage, check the associated wiring for an open or a short to ground.

   c. If the wiring is good, replace the wiper/washer switch.

15. With the wiper switch in position LOW, connect between connector C2 (BLACK), terminal A (PURPLE) and ground.

   a. There should be no voltage.

   b. If there is voltage, check the associated wiring for a short to voltage.

   c. If wiring is good, replace the wiper/washer switch.

16. With the wiper switch in position LOW, connect between connector C1 (DARK BLUE), terminal B (GREY) and ground.

   a. There should be battery voltage.

   b. If there is no voltage, check the associated wiring for an open or a short to ground.

   c. If the wiring is good, replace the wiper/washer switch.

17. With the wiper switch in position LOW, connect between connector C1 (DARK BLUE), terminal C (DARK GREEN) and ground.

   a. There should be battery voltage.

   b. If there is no voltage, check the associated wiring for an open or a short to ground.

   c. If the wiring is good, replace the wiper/washer switch.

18. With the wiper switch in position LOW, connect between connector C1 (DARK BLUE), terminal F (PINK) and ground.

   a. There should be battery voltage.

   b. If there is no voltage, check the associated wiring for an open or a short to ground.

   c. If the wiring is good, replace the wiper/washer switch.

19. With the wiper switch in position HIGH, connect between connector C2 (BLACK), terminal A (PURPLE) and ground.

   a. There should be battery voltage.

   b. If there is no voltage, check the

associated wiring for an open or a short to ground.

   c. If the wiring is good, replace the wiper/washer switch.

20. With the wiper switch in position HIGH, connect between connector C1 (DARK BLUE), terminal B (GREY) and ground.

   a. There should be no voltage.

   b. If there is voltage, check the associated wiring for a short to voltage.

   c. If wiring is good, replace the wiper/washer switch.

21. With the wiper switch in position OFF and washer switch ON, connect between connector C2 (BLACK), terminal A (PURPLE) and ground.

   a. There should be no voltage.

   b. If there is voltage, check the associated wiring for a short to voltage.

   c. If wiring is good, replace the wiper/washer switch.

22. With the wiper switch in position OFF and washer switch ON, connect between connector C1 (DARK BLUE), terminal B (GREY) and ground.

   a. There should be battery voltage.

   b. If there is no voltage, check the associated wiring for an open or a short to ground.

   c. If the wiring is good, replace the wiper/washer switch.

23. With the wiper switch in position OFF and washer switch ON, connect between connector C1 (DARK BLUE), terminal C (DARK GREEN) and ground.

   a. There should be battery voltage.

   b. If there is no voltage, check the associated wiring for an open or a short to ground.

   c. If the wiring is good, replace the wiper/washer switch.

24. With the wiper switch in position OFF and washer switch ON, connect between connector C1 (DARK BLUE), terminal F (PINK) and ground.

   a. There should be battery voltage.

   b. If there is no voltage, check the associated wiring for an open or a short to ground.

   c. If the wiring is good, replace the wiper/washer switch.

   d. If all measurements are correct and the wiper motor is ON all the time, replace the cover assembly. Otherwise, review symptoms.

Test C: Wiper Motor Module Resistance

1. Measure the resistance at the wiper motor assembly connectors C1 and C2 (disconnected).

2. Turn the ignition switch OFF and the wiper switch to HIGH. Measure the resistance between connector C1, terminal C (DARK GREEN) and terminal B (GREY). It should read less than 0.5 ohms.

   a. If resistance is not as specified, check the dark green wire and gray wire for a short to ground, to each other or opens.

   b. If wires are okay, replace wiper switch assembly.

3. Turn the ignition switch OFF and the wiper switch to OFF, PULSE. Measure the resistance between connector C1, terminal C (DARK GREEN) and terminal B (GREY). It should read infinite resistance.

   a. If resistance is not as specified, check the dark green wire and gray wire for a short to ground, to each other or opens.

   b. If wires are okay, replace wiper switch assembly.

4. Turn the ignition switch OFF and the wiper switch to OFF, PULSE. Measure the resistance between connector C1, terminal A (YELLOW) which is a jumper between the connectors and connector C2, terminal B of the other end of the yellow wire. It should read less than 0.5 ohms. If resistance is not as specified, check the yellow wire an open.

5. Turn the ignition switch OFF and the wiper switch to OFF, PULSE. Measure the resistance between connector C1, terminal A (YELLOW) and ground. It should read infinite resistance. If resistance is not as specified, check the yellow wire for a short to ground.

Test D: Wiper/Washer Pulse Control Resistance

1. Measure the resistance at the wiper motor assembly connector C1 (disconnected).

2. Turn the ignition switch OFF, disconnect the negative battery cable and turn the wiper switch to LOW. Measure the resistance between terminal B (GREY) and terminal F (PINK). It should read approximately 24 kilo-ohms.

   a. If resistance is not as specified, check the pink wire and gray wire for an open.

   b. If the wires are okay, replace wiper switch assembly.

3. Turn the ignition switch OFF, disconnect the negative battery cable and turn the wiper switch through the delay range to the maximum delay position. Measure the resistance between terminal B (GREY) and terminal F (PINK). It should read approximately 1.2 mega-ohms.

   a. If resistance is not as specified,

check the pink wire and gray wire for an open.

   b. If the wires are okay, replace wiper switch assembly.

   c. If both resistances are correct, but the pulse mode does not operate, replace the cover assembly.

Test E: Wiper Motor Module Current Draw

1. Remove the wiper fuse.
2. Connect an ammeter (30 amp range or higher) across fuse terminals.
3. Turn the ignition switch to **RUN**, wet the windshield and turn the wiper switch to **HIGH**.
4. Read the ammeter. Current will vary. Look for the lowest reading. If the lowest reading is less than 3.5 amps or if the reading cycles between any value and 0, check:

   a. Motor grounds.

   b. Brush/commutator condition.

   c. Circuit breaker, which should be closed.

   d. Armature.

5. If the ammeter reading is greater than 6.5 amps:

   a. Replace the wiper blades.

   b. Retest.

6. After replacing the wiper blades and retesting, if the reading is less then 6.5 amps system is okay. The wiper blades were causing the problem.

7. After replacing the wiper blades and retesting, if the reading is greater then 6.5 amps:

   a. Disconnect the linkage from the motor crank.

   b. Retest.

   c. If current draw is still greater than 6.5 amps, remove the wiper motor assembly for repair.

   d. If the current draw is now less than 6.5 amps, the linkage is binding. Remove and repair as required.

Test F: Mechanical Inspection

1. Remove the wiper motor cover.
2. Reconnect the motor without the cover.
3. Turn the wiper switch to **LOW**.
4. Observe the spring loaded latch arm and drive pawl which rotates with the big gear.
5. Turn the wiper switch **OFF**.
6. Does the latch arm spring out and catch drive pawl to shift to park?

   a. If latch arm doesn't spring out, replace the park switch.

   b. If latch arm does spring out, check for bent pawl or shaft end.

Test G: Washer Motor Voltage

1. Measure the voltage at the washer motor connector (disconnected).
2. Turn the ignition switch to **ACCY** and the washer switch to **ON** and hold.
3. Measure the voltage between terminal **A (RED)** and terminal **B (DARK BLUE)**. It should read battery voltage.

   a. If measurement does not read battery voltage, check the red wire and dark blue wire for an open.

   b. If the wires are okay, check the terminal control between the park switch and cover assembly.

   c. If the contact is good, replace the cover assembly.

4. Turn the ignition switch to **ACCY** and turn the washer switch to **OFF**.
5. Measure the voltage between terminal **A (RED)** and terminal **B (DARK BLUE)**. It should read 0 voltage.

   a. If voltage is present, check the red wire for a short to voltage.

   b. If the wire is okay, replace the cover assembly.

   c. If all voltage checks are okay and washer does not work, replace washer motor.

REMOVAL & INSTALLATION

Washer Pump (Standard Wiper Motor)

1. Remove the washer hoses from the pump.
2. Disconnect the wires from the pump relay.
3. Remove the plastic pump cover.
4. Remove the attaching screws securing the pump frame to the motor gearbox and remove the pump and frame.

  To install:

5. Installation is the reverse of the removal procedure.
6. The wiper motor gear must be in park position to assemble the pump to the wiper motor.
7. Rotate the 4-lobe cam until the index hole in the cam is aligned with the hole in the pump mounting plate. Insert a pin through both holes to maintain cam in position.
8. Position the pump on the wiper so the slot in the 4-lobe cam fits over the gear drive pin which is part of the lock pawl. Secure the pump to gear housing and remove the locator pin. Temporarily connect the wiring connector.

9. Turn the wiper motor **ON** and use the washer pump to check pump operation. A loud knocking noise would indicate that the pump cam has not engaged the drive pin properly.
10. Install pump cover.

Multiplex Pulse Wiper Motor

1. Remove the complete wiper/washer assembly from the vehicle.
2. Pull the plastic cover off the mounting post.
3. Disconnect the green lead from terminal **1A**, the yellow and red leads from the pulse relay terminals and unsolder the black with pink stripe wire from the remaining relay terminal.
4. If just the pump assembly is being removed from the motor and gearbox (wiper motor still on vehicle), cut the black with pink stripe lead 4 in. from the motor grommet.

➡**Depending on the type of repair required, it will be necessary to splice this lead to the replacement relay lead or to the original relay lead after the pump is reinstalled.**

5. Remove the 3 screws that attach the pump to the gearbox.

  To install:

6. Installation is the reverse of the removal procedure. Make sure the wiper gearbox is in the park position.
7. Install a locator pin in the pump mechanism through the hole in the 4-lobe cam.

➡**If it is necessary to rotate the cam to install the locator pin, be sure to turn the cam counterclockwise.**

8. Position the pump assembly on the gearbox and install the 3 attaching screws. Remove the locator pin.
9. Route and attach the leads. Solder the black and pink stripe wire back into place.
10. Position the cover on the washer pump and mechanism and snap it over the mounting pin.
11. Reinstall wiper in vehicle, attach wiring and hoses. Test system.

Relay Switch and Terminal Board Assembly (Multiplex Pulse Wiper Motor)

1. Remove the washer pump.
2. The wiper gear mechanism must be out of the park position to remove the relay

---

For brake related suspension and axle service, refer to the model specific sections of this manual

switch and terminal board assembly. If the wiper gear mechanism is not in the park position, drive pawl away from the latch arm, use the following procedure:

a. To move the wiper gear drive pawl out of the park position, manually trip the latch arm toward the coil and apply feed current to the center terminal of the relay switch and terminal board and ground the motor case. The wiper motor should turn the gear, moving the drive pawl out of the park position in the relay switch slot.

b. If applying feed current to the center terminal does not energize the motor, it is possible to remove some of the insulation from the black with pink stripe wire between the motor and the relay switch and apply feed current at this point. Be sure to cover the exposed wire with tape after the repair is complete.

3. Remove the relay switch and terminal board attaching screw and carefully lift the assembly out of the gearbox. Unsolder leads as required.

To install:

4. Installation is the reverse of the removal procedure.

5. Resolder leads to relay switch and terminal board assembly as required.

a. Solder the black wire to terminal 3 and the black with pink stripe wire to the fixed contact post.

Use care to route the wires in such a manner as to avoid having them pinched between the relay switch and wiper housing.

6. Position the relay switch and terminal board assembly in the housing and attach with screw.

7. Install the washer pump to the wiper motor.

8. Install assembly into vehicle and test system.

Park Switch Replacement

1. Remove the wiper motor cover.

2. If the motor is in the park position, operate the motor as required to remove the pawl from the relay slot.

3. Remove the park switch assembly.

To install:

4. Installation is the reverse of the removal procedure.

5. Install the new park switch assembly.

➡️ **When installing the new wiper cover, always install the cover assembly with the wiper in the park position and the**

drive pin in the large angled open area of the cam. Do not try to put the drive pin in the slot of the cam. Place it in the open area only.

6. Torque the cover screws to 18 inch lbs. (2 Nm).

Wiper Motor Replacement

1. Raise the hood and remove the cowl screen.

2. Loosen the transmission drive link-to-motor crank arm attaching nuts.

3. Remove the transmission drive link from the motor crank arm.

4. Disconnect the wiring and washer hoses.

5. Remove the 3 motor attaching screws.

6. Remove the motor while guiding crank arm through hole.

To install:

7. Installation is the reverse of the removal procedure.

➡️ **The motor must be in the park position before assembling the crank arm to the transmission.**

8. Connect wiring and hoses.

SATURN

General Information

Saturn uses single wiper motor which is located in the cowl (on the driver's side) attached to the wiper transmission. The wiper control module is attached to the wiper motor assembly. An underhood junction block is located in the engine compartment on the left wheel housing; it houses a 30 amp fuse that supplies power to the ignition switch. Power is directed from the ignition switch to an instrument panel junction block (located under the driver's side of the instrument panel); it houses a 25 amp fuse that directs power to the wiper control module and windshield wiper switch.

SYSTEM PERFORMANCE TEST

1. Turn the ignition switch to the **ACC** position the wiper switch to the **INTERMITTENT 1** position; the wipers should activate. On the **INTERMITTENT 1** position, the time interval between cycles (1 cycle being 1 back/forth motion of the blades) should be 2 seconds.

- On the **INTERMITTENT 1** position, the time intverval between cycles (1 cycle being 1 back/forth

motion of the blades) should be 2 seconds.

- On the **INTERMITTENT 2** position, the time interval between cycles should be 7 seconds.
- On the **INTERMITTENT 3** position, the time interval between cycles should be 12 seconds.

2. Start the engine.

3. Place the wiper switch in the **LOW** speed position; the wipers should activate and the speed should be 42–52 cycles/min.

4. Place the wiper switch in the **HIGH** speed position; the wipers should activate (within 1 second) and the speed should be 61–73 cycles/min. on a wet windshield.

5. Push the wiper switch down to the **MIST** position; the wipers should cycle once as long as the switch is being held in that position.

6. Pull the wiper switch to the **WASH** position; the washer pump and wipers should both activate within 1 second. The wipers should cycle twice and the washer pump should remain **ON** as long as the switch lever is pulled into the position. The wipers will complete 2 cycles before parking after wash; do not operate the washer pump without fluid in the washer reservoir.

7. With the wipers on the **LOW** speed, crank the engine. The wipers should shop moving and start again once the ignition is back in the run position.

FRONT WIPER TROUBLESHOOTING

Wiper Switch

1. Disconnect the electrical connector from the wiper switch. Using an ohmmeter, measure the resistance of the switch between pins **C** and **A**.

a. With column switch in the **OFF** position, the resistance should be open.

b. With column switch in the **LOW** position, the resistance should be 300 ohms.

c. With column switch in the **HIGH** position, the resistance should be 300 ohms.

d. With column switch in the **MIST** position, the resistance should be 300 ohms.

e. With column switch in the **INTERMITTENT 1** position, the resistance should be 2.09 kilo-ohms.

f. With column switch in the **INTERMITTENT 2** position, the resistance should be 990 ohms.

g. With column switch in the **INTER-MITTENT 3** position, the resistance should be 560 ohms.

h. With column switch in the **WASH** position, the resistance should be 130 ohms.

2. Using an ohmmeter, measure the continuity of the switch between pins **B** and **A**; there should be less than 1.0 ohms when the switch is in the **HIGH** position, and **OPEN** when the switch is in any other position.

Fuse Tests

• **IGN4 Fuse**: A 30 amp fuse located in the underhood junction block and feeds circuit **202**.

• **Wiper Fuse**: A 25 amp fuse located in the instrument panel junction block and feeds circuit **143**.

Ground Circuit Tests

Before checking the ground circuit from the faulty component all the way to the ground stud, check the circuit from the splice pack to ground by testing some of the other subsystems grounded by the same splice pack. If the other subsystems function properly, it is most likely that the path from the splice pack to ground is good.

INSTRUMENT PANEL SPLICE PACK #1

It is taped to the harness behind the instrument cluster. If subsystems Perf/Norm switch, instrument panel dimmer, cruise module, headlight switch or cigar lighter work properly, ground circuit is most likely OK.

RIGHT SIDE FORWARD LAMP SPLICE PACK

Located behind front right headlight. If subsystems coolant level switch, washer pump or right forward lights work properly, ground circuit is most likely OK.

INSTRUMENT PANEL SPLICE PACK #2

It is taped to the harness behind the instrument cluster. If subsystems fuel sensor, park brake switch, wiper motor or radio work properly, ground circuit is most likely OK.

CIRCUIT 350R

Connects the wiper module connector cavity **B** to instrument panel ground splice pack #2 cavity **G** (black 16 gauge wire). It provides ground for the wiper motor and control module.

CIRCUIT 350F

Connects the column switch connector cavity **A** to instrument panel ground splice pack #1 cavity **G** (black 22 gauge wire). It provides ground for the column switch.

CIRCUIT 150J

Connects the washer pump connector cavity **2** to forward light splice pack cavity **D** (black 20 gauge wire). It provides ground for the washer pump.

CIRCUIT 150Y

Connects the forward light ground splice pack cavity **K** to right forward light ground ring terminal (black **14** gauge wire). It provides ground for the fog light switch.

CIRCUIT 350Y

Connects the instrument panel ground splice pack #1 cavity **A** to chassis ground ring (black 18 gauge wire). It provides ground for the instrument panel ground splice pack #1.

CIRCUIT 350Z

Connects the instrument panel ground splice pack #2 cavity **A** to chassis ground ring (black 18 gauge wire). It provides ground for the instrument panel ground splice pack #2.

CIRCUIT 350AA

Connects the instrument panel ground splice pack #2 cavity **A** to ground splice pack #1 cavity **A** (black 18 gauge wire). It provides ground for the instrument panel ground splice pack #1 and 2.

Power Circuit Tests

CIRCUIT 202/4/143

The circuit provides power to the windshield wiper motor/control module through the ignition switch.

CIRCUIT 202

Connects the underhood junction block connector cavity **A** to ignition switch connector cavity **H** (red 12 gauge wire). Should have voltage at all times.

CIRCUIT 4

Connects the ignition switch cavity **G** to instrument panel junction connector cavity

F12 (brown 14 gauge wire). Should have voltage at ignition **ACC** or **RUN** positions.

CIRCUIT 143

Connects the instrument panel junction block connector cavity **E12** to wiper module cavity **E** (yellow 16 gauge wire). Should have voltage at ignition **ACC** or **RUN** positions.

CIRCUIT 92

Connects the wiper module connector cavity **C** to column switch cavity **F** (purple 22 gauge wire). Should have voltage at ignition **ACC** or **RUN** positions.

CIRCUIT 96

Connects the wiper module connector cavity **D** to column switch cavity **E** (brown 22 gauge wire). Should have voltage at ignition **ACC** or **RUN** positions.

CIRCUIT 94A/94

Power for washer pump. Connects the wiper module connector cavity **A** to underhood junction block connector cavity **C3** (pink 16 gauge wire). Should have voltage at ignition **ACC** or **RUN** positions with the column switch on **WASH**.

REAR WIPER TROUBLESHOOTING

Fuse Tests

• **SUN Fuse**: A 15 amp fuse located in the instrument panel junction block and feeds circuit **580**. This fuse powers the sunroof and rear wiper.

• **Power Convenience Fuse**: A 30 amp fuse located in the underhood junction block and feeds circuit **302**. This fuse powers the power windows, sunroof and rear wiper.

Ground Circuit Tests

Before checking the ground circuit from the faulty component all the way to the ground stud, check the circuit from the splice pack to ground by testing some of the other subsystems grounded by the same splice pack. If the other subsystems function properly, it is most likely that the path from the splice pack to ground is good.

REAR BODY SPLICE PACK

Located above left rear shock tower. It provides ground for the rear body, deck lid and hatch. If subsystems license, cargo lights, fuel pump, or washer pump work properly, ground circuit is most likely OK.

CIRCUIT 550EB

Connects rear wiper motor connector cavity **C** to inline connector cavity **E** (black 20 gauge wire). It provides ground for the rear wiper motor.

CIRCUIT 550AG

Connects inline connector cavity **E** to rear body ground (black 20 gauge wire). It provides ground for the rear wiper motor.

CIRCUIT 550AH

Connects rear washer pump connector cavity **2** to rear body ground splice pack cavity **E** (black 20 gauge wire). It provides ground for the rear washer pump.

CIRCUIT 550AS

Connects left rear body splice pack cavity **J** to left rear body ground ring terminal (black 14 gauge wire). It provides ground for the left rear body splice pack.

Power Circuit Tests

CIRCUIT 302

Connects underhood junction block connector cavity **A** to instrument panel junction block connector cavity **A10** (red **14** gauge wire). It provides power to the instrument panel junction block.

CIRCUIT 580A

Connects underhood junction block connector cavity **A2** to inline connector cavity **B** (orange/black 20 gauge wire). It provides power to the rear wiper motor.

CIRCUIT 580F

Connects inline connector cavity **B** to rear wiper motor connector cavity **A** (orange 20 gauge wire). It provides power to the rear wiper motor.

CIRCUIT 580D

Connects instrument panel junction block connector cavity **B** to rear wiper switch connector cavity **D** (orange 20 gauge wire). It provides power to the rear wiper switch.

CIRCUIT 393C

Connects inline connector cavity **C** to rear wiper motor connector cavity **B** (white 20 gauge wire). It provides power to the rear wiper motor.

CIRCUIT 393A

Connects rear wiper switch connector cavity **C** to instrument panel inline connector cavity **B** (white 20 gauge wire). It provides power to the rear wiper motor.

CIRCUIT 392A

Connects rear wiper switch connector cavity **B** to instrument panel body inline connector cavity **A** (dark green 20 gauge wire). It provides power to the rear washer pump.

CIRCUIT 392B

Connects instrument panel body inline connector cavity **A** to rear washer pump connector cavity **1** (dark green 20 gauge wire). It provides power to the rear washer pump.

CIRCUIT 393B

Connects instrument panel body inline connector cavity **B** to inline connector cavity **C** (white 20 gauge wire). It provides power to the rear wiper motor.

OXYGEN (O₂S) SENSORS

7

OXYGEN (O₂S) SENSORS

General Information

An Oxygen (O₂S) sensor is an input device used by the engine control computer to monitor the amount of oxygen in the exhaust gas stream. This information is used by the computer, along with other inputs, to fine-tune the air/fuel mixture so that the engine can run with the greatest efficiency in all conditions. The O₂S sensor sends this information to the computer in the form of a 100–900 millivolt (mV) reference signal, which is actually created by the O₂S sensor itself through chemical interactions between the sensor tip material (zirconium dioxide in almost all cases) and the oxygen levels in the exhaust gas stream and ambient atmosphere gas. At operating tem-

peratures, approximately 1100°F (600°C), the element becomes a semiconductor. Essentially, through the differing levels of oxygen in the exhaust gas stream and in the surrounding atmosphere, the sensor creates a voltage signal that is directly and consistently related to the concentration of oxygen in the exhaust stream. Typically, a higher than normal amount of oxygen in the exhaust stream indicates that not all of the available oxygen was used in the combustion process, because there was not enough fuel (lean condition) present. Inversely, a lower than normal concentration of oxygen in the exhaust stream indicates that a large amount was used in the combustion process, because a larger than necessary amount of fuel was present (rich condition). Thus, the engine control computer can correct the amount of fuel introduced into the combustion chambers.

Since the control computer uses the O₂S sensor output voltage as an indication of

the oxygen concentration, and the oxygen concentration directly affects O₂S sensor output, the signal voltage from the sensor to the computer fluctuates constantly. This fluctuation is caused by the nature of the interaction between the computer and the O₂S sensor, which follows a general pattern: detect, compare, compensate, detect, compare, compensate, etc. This means that when the computer detects a lean signal from the O₂S sensor, it compares the reading with known parameters stored within its memory. It calculates that there is too much oxygen present in the exhaust gases, so it compensates by adding more fuel to the air/fuel mixture. This, in turn, causes the O₂S sensor to send a rich signal to the computer, which then compares this new signal, and adjusts the air/fuel mixture again. This pattern constantly repeats itself: detect rich, compare, compensate lean, detect lean, compare, compensate rich, etc. Since the O₂S sensor fluctuates between

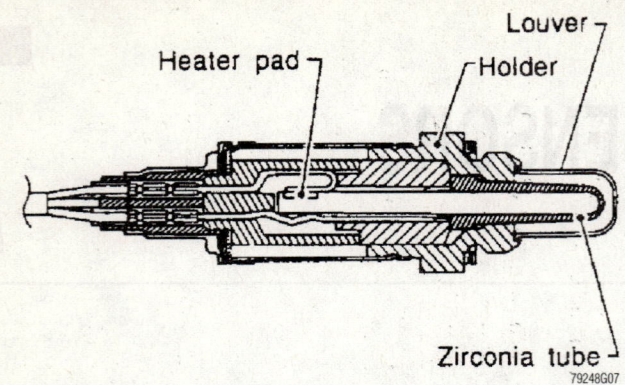

A cut away view of a heated oxygen sensor

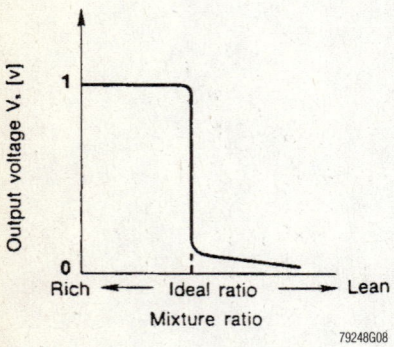

O2S sensor output voltage vs. mixture ratio

rich and lean, and because the lean limit for sensor output is 100 mV and the rich limit is 900 mV, the proper voltage signal from a normally functioning O2S sensor consistently fluctuates between 100–300 and 700–900 mV.

➡ **The sensor voltage may never quite reach 100 or 900 mV, but it should fluctuate from at least below 300 mV to above 700 mV, and the mid-point of the fluctuations should be centered around 500 mV.**

To improve O2S sensor efficiency, newer O2S sensors were designed with a built-in heating element, and were called Heated O2S (HO2) sensors. This heating element was incorporated into the sensor so that the sensor would reach optimal operating temperature quicker, meaning that the O2S sensor output signal could be used by the engine control computer sooner. Because the sensor reaches optimal temperature quicker, modern vehicles enjoy improved driveability and fuel economy even before the engine reaches normal operating temperature.

On-Board Diagnostics second generation (OBD-II), an updated system based on the former OBD-I, calls for additional O2S sensors to be used after the catalytic converter, so that catalytic converter efficiency can be measured by the vehicle's engine control computer. The O2S sensors mounted in the exhaust system after the catalytic converters are not used to affect air/fuel mixture; they are used solely to monitor catalytic converter efficiency.

O2 (Oxygen Sensors) Service

PRECAUTIONS

When testing or servicing an O2S sensor you will need to start and warm the engine to operating temperature in order to either perform the necessary testing procedures or to easily remove the sensor from its fitting. This will create a situation in which you will be working around a **HOT** exhaust system. The following is a list of precautions to consider during this service:

• Do not pierce any wires when testing an O2S sensor, as this can lead to wiring harness damage. Backprobe the connector, when necessary.

• While testing the sensor, be sure to keep out of the way of moving engine components, such as the cooling fan. Refrain from wearing loose clothing which may become tangled in moving engine components.

• Safety glasses must be worn at all times when working on or near the exhaust system. Older exhaust systems may be covered with loose rust particles which can shower you when disturbed. These particles are more than a nuisance and can injure your eye.

• Be cautious when working on and around the hot exhaust system. Painful burns will result if skin is exposed to the exhaust system pipes or manifolds.

• The O2S sensor may be difficult to remove when the engine temperature is below 120°F (48°C). Excessive force may damage the threads in the exhaust manifold or pipe, therefore always start the engine and allow it to reach normal operating temperature prior to removal.

• Since O2S sensors are usually designed with a permanently-attached wiring pigtail (this allows the wiring harness and sensor connectors to be positioned away from the hot exhaust system), it may be necessary to use a socket or wrench that is designed specifically for this purpose. Before purchasing such a socket, be sure that you can't save some money by using a box end wrench for sensor removal.

TESTING

The best, and most accurate method to test the operation of an O2S sensor is with the use of either an oscilloscope or a Diagnostic Scan Tool (DST), following their specific instructions for testing. It is possible, however, to test whether the O2S sensor is functioning properly within general parameters using a Digital Volt-Ohmmeter (DVOM), also referred to as a Digital Multi-Meter (DMM). Newer DMM's are often designed to perform many advanced diagnostic functions, and some are even constructed to be used as an oscilloscope. Two in-vehicle testing procedures, and one bench test procedure, will be provided for the common zirconium dioxide oxygen sensor. The first in-vehicle test makes use of a standard DVOM with a 10 megohm impedance, whereas the second in-vehicle test presented necessitates the usage of an advanced DMM with MIN/MAX/Average functions. Both of these in-vehicle test procedures are likely to set Diagnostic Trouble Codes (DTC's) in the engine control computer. Therefore, after testing, be sure to clear all DTC's before retesting the sensor, if necessary.

These are some of the common DTC's which may be set during testing:

• Open in the O2S sensor circuit
• Constant low voltage in the O2S sensor circuit
• Constant high voltage in the O2S sensor circuit
• Other fuel system problems could set a O2S sensor code

➡ **Because an improperly functioning fuel delivery and/or control system can adversely affect the O2S sensor voltage output signal, testing only the O2S sensor is an inaccurate method for diagnosing an engine driveability problem.**

If after testing the sensor, the sensor is thought to be defective because of high or low readings, be sure to check that the fuel delivery and engine management system is working properly before condemning the O₂S sensor. Otherwise, the new O₂S sensor may continue to register the same high or low readings.

Often, by testing the O₂S sensor, another problem in the engine control management system can be diagnosed. If the sensor appears to be defective while installed in the vehicle, perform the bench test. If the sensor functions properly during the bench test, chances are that there may be a larger problem in the vehicle's fuel delivery and/or control system.

Many things can cause an O₂S sensor to fail, including old age, antifreeze contamination, physical damage, prolonged exposure to overly-rich exhaust gases, and exposure to silicone sealant fumes. Be sure to remedy any such condition prior to installing a new sensor, otherwise the new sensor may be damaged as well.

➡**Perform a visual inspection of the sensor. Black sooty deposits may indicate a rich air/fuel mixture, brown deposits may indicate an oil consumption problem, and white gritty deposits may indicate an internal coolant leak. All of these conditions can destroy a new sensor if not corrected before installation.**

O₂S sensor Terminal Identification

The easiest method for determining sensor terminal identification is to use a wiring diagram for the vehicle and engine in question. However, if a wiring diagram is not available there is a method for determining terminal identification. Throughout the testing procedures, the following terms will be used for clarity:

• Vehicle harness connector—this refers to the connector on the wires which are attached to the vehicle; NOT the connector at the end of the sensor pigtail.

• Sensor pigtail connector—this refers to the connector attached to the sensor itself.

• O₂S circuit—this refers to the circuit in a Heated O₂S (HO₂) sensor which corresponds to the oxygen-sensing function of the sensor; NOT the heating element circuit.

• Heating circuit—this refers to the circuit in a HO₂S sensor which is designed to warm the HO₂S sensor quickly to improve driveability.

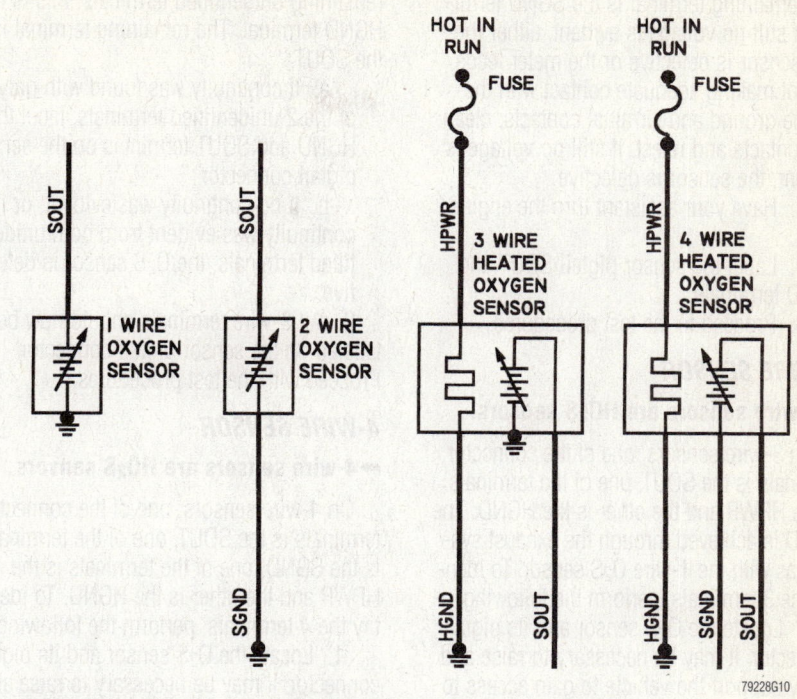

Wiring schematic of typical 1-, 2-, 3- and 4-wire oxygen sensor circuits

• Sensor Output (SOUT) terminal—this is the terminal which corresponds to the O₂S circuit output. This is the terminal which will register the millivolt signals created by the sensor based upon the amount of oxygen in the exhaust gas stream.

• Sensor Ground (SGND) terminal—when a sensor is so equipped, this refers to the O₂S circuit ground terminal. Many O₂S sensors are not equipped with a ground wire, rather they utilize the exhaust system for the ground circuit.

• Heating Power (HPWR) terminal—this terminal corresponds to the circuit which provides the O₂S sensor heating circuit with power when the ignition key is turned to the **ON** or **RUN** positions.

• Heating Ground (HGND) terminal—this is the terminal connected to the heating circuit ground wire.

1-WIRE SENSOR

1-wire sensors are by far the easiest to determine sensor terminal identification, but this is self-evident. On 1-wire O₂S sensors, the single wire terminal is the SOUT and the exhaust system is used to provide the sensor ground pathway. Proceed to the test procedures.

2-WIRE SENSOR

On 2-wire sensors, one of the connector terminals is the SOUT and the other is the

SGND. To determine which one is which, perform the following:

1. Locate the O₂S sensor and its pigtail connector. It may be necessary to raise and safely support the vehicle to gain access to the connector.

2. Start the engine and allow it to warm up to normal operating temperature, then turn the engine **OFF**.

3. Using a DVOM set to read 100–900 mV (millivolts) DC, backprobe the positive DVOM lead to one of the unidentified terminals and attach the negative lead to a good engine ground.

✳✳ CAUTION

While the engine is running, keep clear of all moving and hot components. Do not wear loose clothing. Otherwise severe personal injury or death may occur.

4. Have an assistant restart the engine and allow it to idle.

5. Check the DVOM for voltage.

6. If no voltage is evident, check your DVOM leads to ensure that they are properly connected to the terminal and engine ground. If still no voltage is evident at the first terminal, move the positive meter lead to backprobe the second terminal.

7. If voltage is now present, the positive meter lead is attached to the SOUT terminal.

The remaining terminal is the SGND terminal. If still no voltage is evident, either the O_2S sensor is defective or the meter leads are not making adequate contact with the engine ground and terminal contacts; clean the contacts and retest. If still no voltage is evident, the sensor is defective.

8. Have your assistant turn the engine **OFF**.
9. Label the sensor pigtail SOUT and SGND terminals.
10. Proceed to the test procedures.

3-WIRE SENSOR

➡3-wire sensors are HO_2S sensors.

On 3-wire sensors, one of the connector terminals is the SOUT, one of the terminals is the HPWR and the other is the HGND. The SGND is achieved through the exhaust system, as with the 1-wire O_2S sensor. To identify the 3 terminals, perform the following:

1. Locate the O_2S sensor and its pigtail connector. It may be necessary to raise and safely support the vehicle to gain access to the connector.
2. Disengage the sensor pigtail connector from the vehicle harness connector.
3. Using a DVOM set to read 12 volts, attach the DVOM ground lead to a good engine ground.
4. Have an assistant turn the ignition switch **ON** without actually starting the engine.
5. Probe all 3 terminals in the vehicle harness connector. One of the terminals should exhibit 12 volts of power with the ignition key **ON**; this is the HPWR terminal.
   a. If the HPWR terminal was identified, note which of the sensor harness connector terminals is the HPWR, then match the vehicle harness connector to the sensor pigtail connector. Label the corresponding sensor pigtail connector terminal with HPWR.
   b. If none of the terminals showed 12 volts of power, locate and test the heater relay or fuse. Then, perform Steps 3–6 again.
6. Start the engine and allow it to warm up to normal operating temperature, then turn the engine **OFF**.
7. Have your assistant turn the ignition **OFF**.
8. Using the DVOM set to measure resistance (ohms), attach one of the leads to the HPWR terminal of the sensor pigtail connector. Use the other lead to probe the 2 remaining terminals of the sensor pigtail connector, one at a time. The DVOM should show continuity with only one of the remaining unidentified terminals; this is the HGND terminal. The remaining terminal is the SOUT.
   a. If continuity was found with only 1 of the 2 unidentified terminals, label the HGND and SOUT terminals on the sensor pigtail connector.
   b. If no continuity was evident, or if continuity was evident from both unidentified terminals, the O_2S sensor is defective.
9. All 3-wire terminals should now be labeled on the sensor pigtail connector. Proceed with the test procedures.

4-WIRE SENSOR

➡4-wire sensors are HO_2S sensors.

On 4-wire sensors, one of the connector terminals is the SOUT, one of the terminals is the SGND, one of the terminals is the HPWR and the other is the HGND. To identify the 4 terminals, perform the following:

1. Locate the O_2S sensor and its pigtail connector. It may be necessary to raise and safely support the vehicle to gain access to the connector.
2. Disengage the sensor pigtail connector from the vehicle harness connector.
3. Using a DVOM set to read 12 volts, attach the DVOM ground lead to a good engine ground.
4. Have an assistant turn the ignition switch **ON** without actually starting the engine.
5. Probe all 4 terminals in the vehicle harness connector. One of the terminals should exhibit 12 volts of power with the ignition key **ON**; this is the HPWR terminal.
   a. If the HPWR terminal was identified, note which of the sensor harness connector terminals is the HPWR, then match the vehicle harness connector to the sensor pigtail connector. Label the corresponding sensor pigtail connector terminal with HPWR.
   b. If none of the terminals showed 12 volts of power, locate and test the heater relay or fuse. Then, perform Steps 2–6 again.
6. Have your assistant turn the ignition **OFF**.
7. Using the DVOM set to measure resistance (ohms), attach one of the leads to the HPWR terminal of the sensor pigtail connector. Use the other lead to probe the 3 remaining terminals of the sensor pigtail connector, one at a time. The DVOM should show continuity with only one of the remaining unidentified terminals; this is the HGND terminal.
   a. If continuity was found with only one of the 2 unidentified terminals, label the HGND terminal on the sensor pigtail connector.
   b. If no continuity was evident, or if continuity was evident from all unidentified terminals, the O_2S sensor is defective.
   c. If continuity was found at 2 of the other terminals, the sensor is probably defective. However, the sensor may not necessarily be defective, because it may have been designed with the 2 ground wires joined inside the sensor in case one of the ground wires is damaged; the other circuit could still function properly. Though, this is highly unlikely. A wiring diagram is necessary in this particular case to know whether the sensor was so designed.
8. Reattach the sensor pigtail connector to the vehicle harness connector.
9. Start the engine and allow it to warm up to normal operating temperature, then turn the engine **OFF**.
10. Using a DVOM set to read 100–900 mV (millivolts) DC, backprobe the negative DVOM lead to one of the unidentified terminals and the positive lead to the other unidentified terminal.

⁂ CAUTION

While the engine is running, keep clear of all moving and hot components. Do not wear loose clothing. Otherwise severe personal injury or death may occur.

11. Have an assistant restart the engine and allow it to idle.
12. Check the DVOM for voltage.
   a. If no voltage is evident, check your DVOM leads to ensure that they are properly connected to the terminals. If still no voltage is evident at either of the terminals, either the terminals were accidentally marked incorrectly or the sensor is defective.
   b. If voltage is present, but the polarity is reversed (the DVOM will show a negative voltage amount), turn the engine **OFF** and swap the 2 DVOM leads on the terminals. Start the engine and ensure that the voltage now shows the proper polarity.
   c. If voltage is evident and is the proper polarity, the positive DVOM lead is attached to the SOUT and the negative lead to the SGND terminals.
13. Have your assistant turn the engine **OFF**.

14. Label the sensor pigtail SOUT and SGND terminals.

In-Vehicle Tests

✳✳ WARNING

Never apply voltage to the O₂S circuit of the sensor, otherwise it may be damaged. Also, never connect an ohmmeter (or a DVOM set on the ohm function) to both of the O₂S circuit terminals (SOUT and SGND) of the sensor pigtail connector; it may damage the sensor.

Test 1 makes use of a standard DVOM with a 10 megohm impedance, whereas Test 2 necessitates the usage of an advanced Digital Multi-Meter (DMM) with MIN/MAX/Average functions or a sliding bar graph function. Both of these in-vehicle test procedures are likely to set Diagnostic Trouble Codes (DTC's) in the engine control computer. Therefore, after testing, be sure to clear all DTC's before retesting the sensor, if necessary. The third in-vehicle test is designed for the use of a scan tool or oscilloscope. The 4th test (Heating Circuit Test) is designed to check the function of the heating circuit in a HO₂S sensor.

➡**If the O₂S sensor being tested is designed to use the exhaust system for the SGND, excessive corrosion between the exhaust and the O₂S sensor may affect sensor functioning.**

The in-vehicle tests may be performed for O₂S sensors located in the exhaust system after the catalytic converter. However, the O₂S sensors located behind the catalytic converter will not fluctuate like the sensors mounted before the converter, because the

To test the O₂S sensor, locate it and its connector (inset), which should be positioned away from the exhaust system to prevent heat damage.

converter, when functioning properly, emits a steady amount of oxygen. If the O₂S sensor mounted after the catalytic converter exhibits a fluctuating signal (like other O₂S sensors), the catalytic converter is most likely defective.

TEST 1—DIGITAL VOLT-OHMMETER

This test will not only verify proper sensor functioning, but is also designed to ensure the engine control computer and associated wiring is functioning properly as well.

1. Start the engine and allow it to warm up to normal operating temperature.

➡**If you are using the opening of the thermostat to gauge normal operating temperature, be forewarned: a defective thermostat can open too early and prevent the engine from reaching normal operating temperature. This can cause a slightly rich condition in the exhaust, which can throw the O₂S sensor readings off slightly.**

2. Turn the ignition switch **OFF**, then locate the O₂S sensor pigtail connector.
3. Perform a visual inspection of the connector to ensure it is properly engaged and all terminals are straight, tight and free from corrosion or damage.
4. Disengage the sensor pigtail connector from the vehicle harness connector.
5. On sensors equipped with a SGND terminal (sensors which do not use the exhaust system for the sensor ground pathway), connect a jumper wire to the SGND terminal and to a good, clean engine ground (preferably the negative terminal of the battery).
6. Using a DVOM set to read DC voltage, attach the positive lead to the SOUT terminal of the sensor pigtail connector, and the DVOM negative lead to a good engine ground.

✳✳ CAUTION

While the engine is running, keep clear of all moving and hot components. Do not wear loose clothing. Otherwise severe personal injury or death may occur.

7. Have an assistant start the engine and hold it at approximately 2000 rpm. Wait at least 1 minute before commencing with the test to allow the O₂S sensor to sufficiently warm up.
8. Using a jumper wire, connect the SOUT terminal of the **vehicle harness**

connector to a good engine ground. This will fool the engine control computer into thinking it is receiving a lean signal from the O₂S sensor, and, therefore, the computer will enrichen the air/fuel ratio. With the SOUT terminal so grounded, the DVOM should register at least 800 mV, as the control computer adds additional fuel to the air/fuel ratio.

9. While observing the DVOM, disconnect the vehicle harness connector SOUT jumper wire from the engine ground. Use the jumper wire to apply slightly less than 1 volt to the SOUT terminal of the vehicle harness connector. One method to do this is by grasping and squeezing the end of the jumper between your forefinger and thumb of one hand while touching the positive terminal of the battery post with your other hand. This allows your body to act as a resistor for the battery positive voltage, and fools the engine control computer into thinking it is receiving a rich signal. Or, use a mostly-drained AA battery by connecting the positive terminal of the AA battery to the jumper wire and the negative terminal of the battery to a good engine ground. (Another jumper wire may be necessary to do this.) The computer should lean the air/fuel mixture out. This lean mixture should register as 150 mV or less on the DVOM.

10. If the DVOM did not register millivoltages as indicated, the problem may be either the sensor, the engine control computer or the associated wiring. Perform the following to determine which is the defective component:

   a. Remove the vehicle harness connector SOUT jumper wire.
   b. While observing the DVOM, artificially enrich the air/fuel charge using propane. The DVOM reading should register higher than normal millivoltages. (Normal voltage for an ideal air/fuel mixture is approximately 450–550 mV DC). Then, lean the air/fuel intake charger by either disconnecting one of the fuel injector wiring harness connectors (to prevent the injector from delivering fuel) or by detaching 1 or 2 vacuum lines (to add additional non-metered air into the engine). The DVOM should now register lower than normal millivoltages. If the DVOM functioned as indicated, the problem lies elsewhere in the fuel delivery and control system. If the DVOM readings were still unresponsive, the O₂S sensor is defective; replace the sensor and retest.

➥Poor wire connections and/or ground circuits may shift a normal O₂S sensor's millivoltage readings up into the rich range or down into the lean range. It is a good idea to check the wire condition and continuity before replacing a component which will not fix the problem. A voltage drop test between the sensor case and ground which reveals 14–16 mV or more, indicates a probable bad ground.

11. Turn the engine **OFF**, remove the DVOM and all associated jumper wires. Reattach the vehicle harness connector to the sensor pigtail connector. If applicable, reattach the fuel injector wiring connector and/or the vacuum line(s).

12. Clear any DTC's present in the engine control computer memory, as necessary.

TEST 2—DIGITAL MULTI-METER

This test method is a more straight-forward O₂S sensor test, and does not test the engine control computer's response to the O₂S sensor signal. The use of a DMM with the MIN/MAX/Average function or sliding bar graph/wave function is necessary for this test. Don't forget that the O₂S sensor mounted after the catalytic converter (if equipped) will not fluctuate like the other O₂S sensor(s) will.

1. Start the engine and allow it to warm up to normal operating temperature.

➥If you are using the opening of the thermostat to gauge normal operating temperature, be forewarned: a defective thermostat can open too early and prevent the engine from reaching normal operating temperature. This can cause a slightly rich condition in the exhaust, which can throw the O₂S sensor readings off slightly.

2. Turn the ignition switch **OFF**, then locate the O₂S sensor pigtail connector.

3. Perform a visual inspection of the connector to ensure it is properly engaged and all terminals are straight, tight and free from corrosion or damage.

4. Backprobe the O₂S sensor connector terminals. Attach the DMM positive test lead to the SOUT terminal of the sensor pigtail connector and the negative lead to either the SGND terminal of the sensor pigtail connector (if equipped—refer to the terminal identification procedures earlier in this section for clarification) or to a good, clean engine ground.

5. Activate the MIN/MAX/Average or sliding bar graph/wave function on the DMM.

✳✳ CAUTION

While the engine is running, keep clear of all moving and hot components. Do not wear loose clothing. Otherwise severe personal injury or death may occur.

6. Have an assistant start the engine and wait a few minutes before commencing with the test to allow the O₂S sensor to sufficiently warm up.

7. Read the minimum, maximum and average readings exhibited by the O₂S sensor or observe the bar graph/wave form. The average reading for a properly functioning O₂S sensor is be approximately 450–550 mV DC. The minimum and maximum readings should vary more than 300–600 mV. A typical O₂S sensor can fluctuate from as low as 100 mV to as high as 900 mV; if the sensor range of fluctuation is not large enough, the sensor is defective. Also, if the fluctuation range is biased up or down in the scale. For example, if the fluctuation range is 400 mV to 900 mV the sensor is defective, because the readings are pushed up into the rich range (as long as the fuel delivery system is functioning properly). The same goes for a fluctuation range pushed down into the lean range. The midpoint of the fluctuation range should be around 400–500 mV. Finally, if the O₂S sensor voltage fluctuates too slowly (usually the voltage wave should oscillate past the mid-way point of 500 mV several times per second) the sensor is defective. (Technician's refer to this state as "lazy.")

➥Poor wire connections and/or ground circuits may shift a normal O₂S sensor's millivoltage readings up into the rich range or down into the lean range. It is a good idea to check the wire condition and continuity before replacing a component which will not fix the problem. A voltage drop test between the sensor case and ground which reveals 14–16 mV or more, indicates a probable bad ground.

8. Using the propane method, enrichen the air/fuel mixture and observe the DMM readings. The average O₂S sensor output signal voltage should rise into the rich range.

9. Lean the air/fuel mixture by either disconnecting a fuel injector wiring harness connector or by disconnecting a vacuum line. The O₂S sensor average output signal voltage should drop into the lean range.

10. If the O₂S sensor did not react as

---

indicated, the sensor is defective and should be replaced.

11. Turn the engine **OFF**, remove the DMM and all associated jumper wires. Reattach the vehicle harness connector to the sensor pigtail connector. If applicable, reattach the fuel injector wiring connector and/or the vacuum line(s).

12. Clear any DTC's present in the engine control computer memory, as necessary.

TEST 3—OSCILLOSCOPE

This test is designed for the use of an oscilloscope to test the functioning of an O₂S sensor.

➥This test is only applicable for O₂S sensors mounted in the exhaust system before the catalytic converter.

1. Start the engine and allow it to reach normal operating temperature.

2. Turn the engine **OFF**, and locate the O₂S sensor connector. Backprobe the scope lead to the O₂S sensor connector SOUT terminal. Refer to the manufacturer's instructions for more information on attaching the scope to the vehicle.

3. Turn the scope ON.

4. Set the oscilloscope amplitude to 200 mV per division, and the time to 1 second per division. Use the 1:1 setting of the probe, and be sure to connect the scope's ground lead to a good, clean engine ground. Set the signal function to automatic or internal triggering.

5. Start the engine and run it at 2000 rpm.

6. The oscilloscope should display a wave form, representative of the O₂S sensor switching between lean (100–300 mV) and rich (700–900 mV). The sensor should switch between rich and lean, or lean and rich (crossing the mid-point of 500 mV) several times per second. Also, the range of each wave should reach at least above 700 mV and below 300 mV. However, an occasional low peak is acceptable.

7. Force the air/fuel mixture rich by introducing propane into the engine, then observe the oscilloscope readings. The fluctuating range of the O₂S sensor should climb into the rich range.

8. Lean the air/fuel mixture out by either detaching a vacuum line or by disengaging one of the fuel injector's wiring connectors. Watch the scope readings; the O₂S sensor wave form should drop toward the lean range.

9. If the O₂S sensor's wave form does not fluctuate adequately, is not centered around 500 mV during normal engine oper-

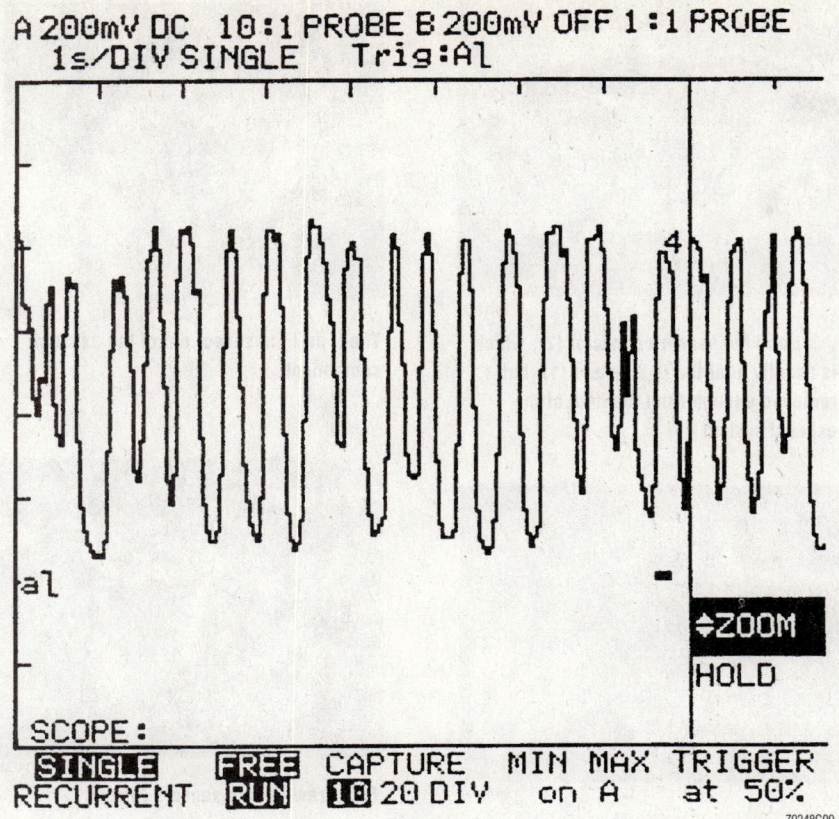

A 200mV DC 10:1 PROBE B 200mV OFF 1:1 PROBE
1s/DIV SINGLE   Trig:A1

ZOOM
HOLD

SCOPE:
SINGLE   FREE   CAPTURE   MIN MAX TRIGGER
RECURRENT RUN 10 20 DIV   on A   at 50%

79248G09

An oscilloscope wave form of a typical good O₂S sensor as it fluctuates from rich to lean

ation, does not climb toward the rich range when propane is added to the engine, or does not drop toward the lean range when a vacuum hose or fuel injector connector is detached, the sensor is defective.

10. Reattach the fuel injector connector or vacuum hose.

11. Disconnect the oscilloscope from the vehicle.

HEATING CIRCUIT TEST

The heating circuit in an O₂S sensor is designed only to heat the sensor quicker than a non-heated sensor. This provides an advantage of increased engine driveability and fuel economy while the engine temperature is still below normal operating temperature, because the fuel management system can enter closed loop operation (more efficient than open loop operation) sooner.

Therefore, if the heating element goes bad, the O₂S sensor may still function properly once the sensor warms up to its normal temperature. This will take longer than normal and may cause mild driveability-related problems while the engine has not reached normal operating temperature.

If the heating element is found to be defective, replace the O₂S sensor without wasting your time testing the O₂S circuit; if necessary, you can perform the O₂S circuit test with the new O₂S sensor and save yourself some time.

1. Locate the O₂S sensor pigtail connector.

2. Perform a visual inspection of the connector to ensure it is properly engaged and all terminals are straight, tight and free from corrosion or damage.

3. Disengage the sensor pigtail connector from the vehicle harness connector.

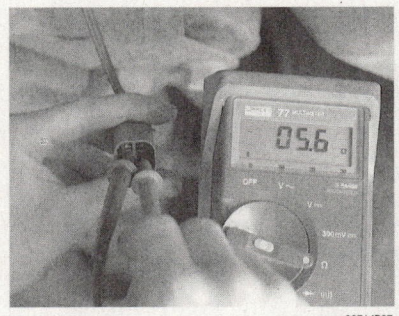

89714P27

The heating circuit of the O₂S sensor can be tested with a DMM set to measure resistance

4. Using a DVOM set to read resistance (ohms), attach 1 DVOM test lead to the HPWR terminal, and the other lead to the HGND terminal, of the sensor pigtail connector, then observe the resistance readings.

a. If there is no continuity between the HPWR and HGND terminals, the sensor is defective. Replace it with a new one and retest.

b. If there is continuity between the 2 terminals, but the resistance is greater than approximately 20 ohms, the sensor is defective. Replace it with a new one and retest.

➡For the following step, the HO₂S sensor should be approximately 75°F (23°C) for the proper resistance values.

c. If there is continuity between the 2 terminals and it is less than 20 ohms, the sensor is probably not defective. Because of the large diversity of engine control systems used in vehicles today, O₂S sensor heating circuit resistance specifications change often. Generally, the amount of resistance an O₂S sensor heating circuit should exhibit is between 2–9 ohms. However, some manufacturer's O₂S sensors may show resistance as high as 15–20 ohms. As a rule of thumb, 20 ohms of resistance is the upper limit allowable.

5. Turn the engine **OFF**, remove the DVOM and all associated jumper wires. Reattach the vehicle harness connector to the sensor pigtail connector.

6. Clear any DTC's present in the engine control computer memory, as necessary.

Bench Test

➡**Utilize one of the in-vehicle tests before performing this test.**

This test is designed to test an O₂S sensor which does not seem to fluctuate fully beyond 400–700 mV. The sensor is to be secured in a table-mounted vise.

✳✳ CAUTION

This test can be very dangerous. Take the necessary precautions when working with a propane torch. Ensure that all combustible substances are removed from the work area and have a fire extinguisher ready at all times. Be sure to wear the appropriate protective clothing as well.

1. Remove the O₂S sensor.

➡ **Perform a visual inspection of the sensor. Black sooty deposits may indicate a rich air/fuel mixture, brown deposits may indicate an oil consumption problem, and white gritty deposits may indicate an internal coolant leak. All of these conditions can destroy a new sensor if not corrected before installation.**

2. Position the sensor in a vise so that the vise holds the sensor by the hex portion of its case.

3. Attach 1 lead of a DVOM set to read DC millivoltages to the sensor case and the other lead to the SOUT terminal of the sensor pigtail connector.

4. Carefully use a propane torch to heat the tip (and ONLY the tip) of the sensor. Once the sensor reaches close to normal operating temperature range, alternately heat the sensor up and allow it to cool down; the sensor output voltage signal should change with the temperature change.

➡ **This may also clean a sensor covered with a heavy coat of carbon.**

5. If the sensor voltage does not change with the fluctuation in temperature, replace the sensor with a new one. Install the new sensor and perform one of the in-vehicle tests to rule out additional fuel management system faults.

REMOVAL & INSTALLATION

1. Start the engine and allow it to reach normal operating temperature, then turn the ignition switch **OFF**.

2. Disconnect the negative battery cable.

3. Open the hood and locate the O₂S sensor connector. It may be necessary to raise and safely support the vehicle for access to the sensor and its connector.

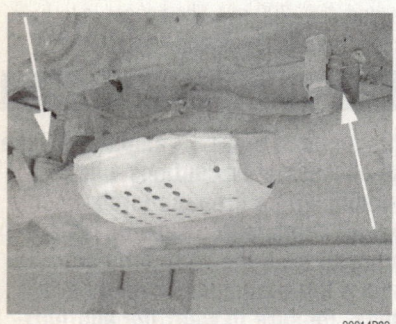

Since sensor locations vary between vehicles, the first step in removal is to locate the O₂S sensors (arrows) . . .

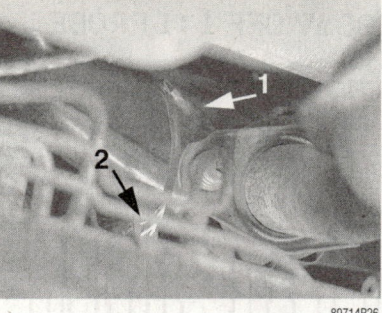

. . . and the sensor connector (2), which is usually near the O₂S sensor (1), but removed enough from the heat of the exhaust system

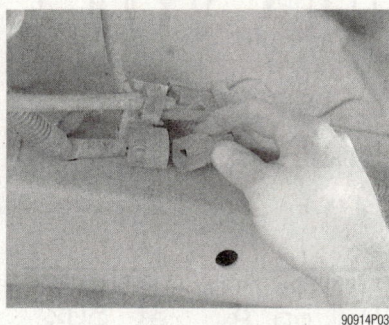

Disengage the sensor pigtail connector half from the vehicle harness connector half

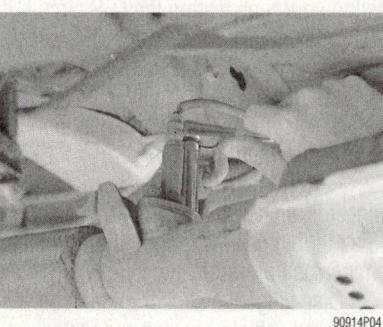

For flange type sensors, loosen the hold-down fasteners . . .

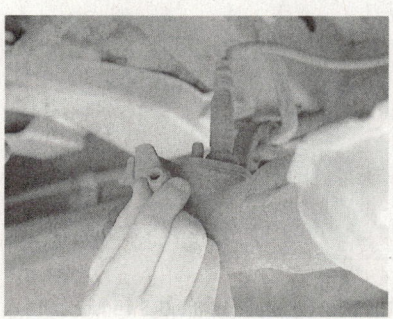

. . . which happen to be nuts in this particular case—some models may use bolts rather than nuts

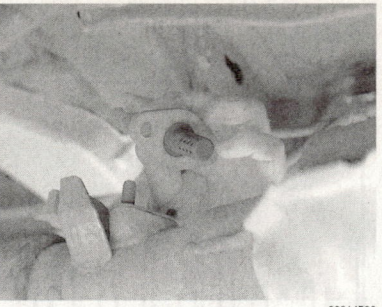

Then, pull the sensor out of the exhaust component

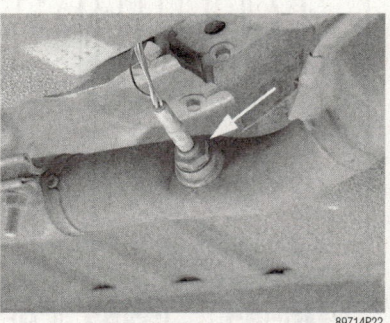

For screw-in type sensors (arrow) . . .

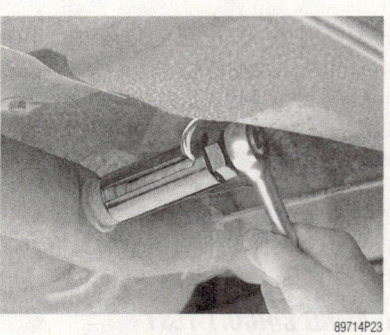

. . . either use a box end wrench to loosen the sensor or a socket designed expressly for this purpose . . .

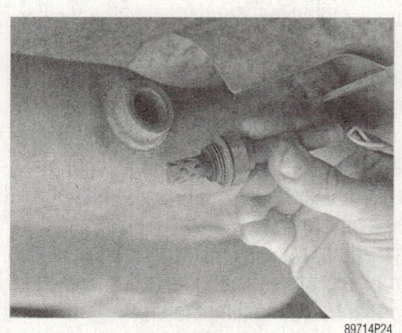

. . . then remove the sensor from the exhaust component

➡ **On a few models, it may be necessary to remove the passenger seat and lift the carpeting in order to access the connector for a downstream O₂S sensor.**

4. Disengage the O₂S sensor pigtail connector from the vehicle harness connector.

➡ **There are generally 2 methods used to mount an O₂S sensor in the exhaust system: either the O₂S sensor is threaded directly into the exhaust component (screw-in type) or the O₂S sensor is retained by a flange and 2 nuts or bolts (flange type).**

✳✳ WARNING

To prevent damaging a screw-in type O₂S sensor, if excessive force is needed to remove the sensor lubricate it with penetrating oil prior to removal. Also, be sure to protect the tip of the sensor; O₂S sensor tips are very sensitive and may be easily damaged if allowed to strike or come in contact with other objects.

5. Remove the sensor, as follows:
- Screw-in type sensors—Since O₂S sensors are usually designed with a permanently-attached wiring pigtail (this allows the wiring harness and sensor connectors to be positioned away from the hot exhaust system), it may be necessary to use a socket or wrench that is designed specifically for this purpose. Before purchasing such a socket, be sure that you can't save some money by using a box end wrench for sensor removal.
- Flange type sensors—Loosen the hold-down nuts or bolts and pull the sensor out of the exhaust component. Be sure to remove and discard the old sensor gasket, if equipped. You will need a new gasket for installation.

6. Perform a visual inspection of the sensor. Black sooty deposits may indicate a rich air/fuel mixture, brown deposits may indicate an oil consumption problem, and white gritty deposits may indicate an internal coolant leak. All of these conditions can destroy a new sensor if not corrected before installation.

To install:

7. Install the sensor, as follows:

➡ **A special anti-seize compound is used on most screw-in type O₂S sensor threads, and is designed to ease O₂S sensor removal. New sensors usually have the compound already applied to the threads. However, if installing the old O₂S sensor or the new sensor did not come with compound, apply a thin coating of electrically-conductive anti-seize compound to the sensor threads.**

✳✳ WARNING

Be sure to prevent any of the anti-seize compound from coming in contact with the O₂S sensor tip. Also, take precautions to protect the sensor tip from physical damage during installation.

- Screw-in type sensors—Install the sensor in the mounting boss, then tighten it securely.
- Flange type sensors—Position a new sensor gasket on the exhaust component and insert the sensor. Tighten the hold-down fasteners securely and evenly.

8. Reattach the sensor pigtail connector to the vehicle harness connector.

9. Lower the vehicle.

10. Connect the negative battery cable.

11. Start the engine and ensure no Diagnostic Trouble Codes (DTC's) are set.

LOCATIONS

There are different locations in the exhaust system where O₂S sensors are positioned. The locations have been given numbers and will be used in the accompanying charts to identify the positions of O₂S sensors in most vehicles.

Due to mid-year production changes or factory inconsistencies, all models may not be covered. If a vehicle being serviced is not covered in the charts, inspect the exhaust system (while cold!) in the general locations to find the applicable O₂S sensors.

➡ **If equipped with dual exhaust systems, there may be up to 4 or 5 O₂S sensors in the exhaust system. Be sure to locate all of them before commencing with any testing or service.**

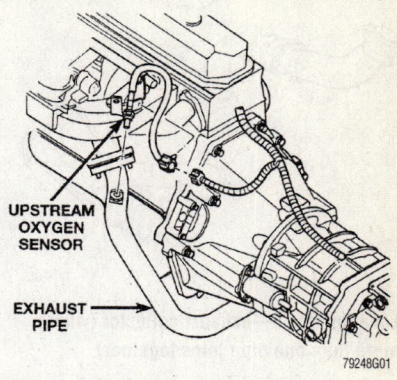

Location No. 1—down pipe or exhaust manifold

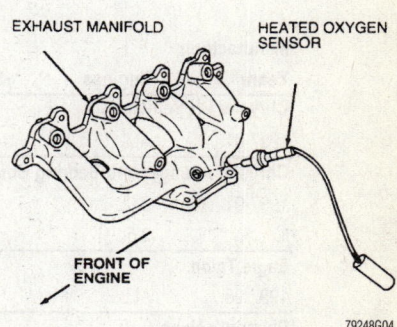

Location No. 1—typical O₂S sensor located in the exhaust manifold

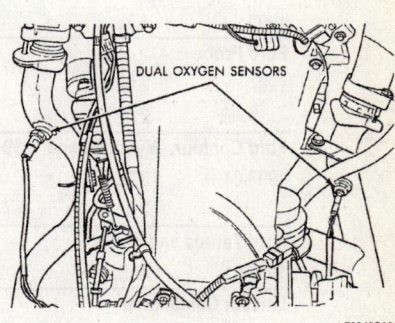

Location No. 2—left and right banks of a V-type engine

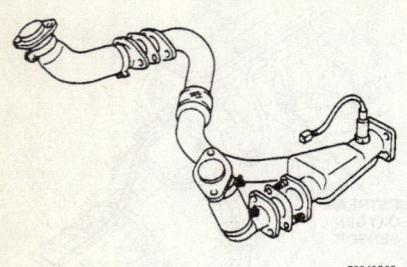

Location No. 3—exhaust collector (where more than one pipe joins together)

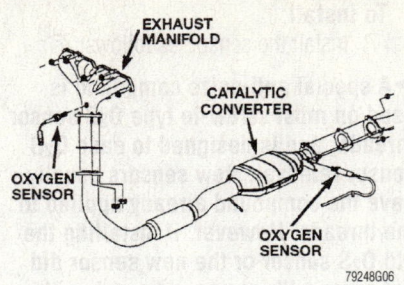

Location No. 4—outlet of the catalytic converter

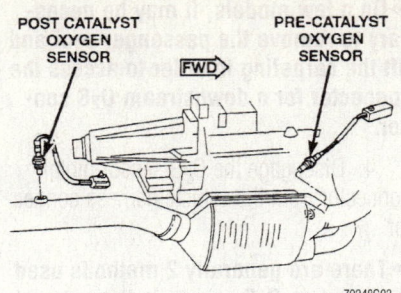

Location No. 5—inlet and outlet of the catalytic converter

OXYGEN SENSOR LOCATIONS

Manufacturer Years	Engines	No. of Sensors	Location	Manufacturer Years	Engines	No. of Sensors	Location
Chrysler LH Vehicles ①				**Ford Full-size**			
1997-01	ALL	4	2, 4	1997-01	4.6L	4	5
Chrysler Avenger and Sebring Coupe				**General Motors C & H Body**			
1997-01	2.0L	2	1, 4	1997-01	3.8L	2	1, 4
	2.5L	3	2, 4	**General Motors E & K Bodies**			
Eagle Talon				1997-01	4.6L	4	1, 5
1997-98	ALL	2	1, 4	**General Motors F Body**			
Plymouth Neon				1997-01	3.8L	3	5
1997-01	ALL	2	1, 4		5.7L	4	5
Chrysler JA/JX Vehicles ②				**General Motors G Body**			
1997-01	ALL	2	1, 4	1997-01	3.8L	2	1, 4
Ford Aspire					4.0L	2	1, 4
1997	1.3L	2	1, 4	**General Motors J Body**			
Ford Probe				1997-01	2.2L	2	5
1997	2.0L	2	1, 4		2.4L	2	5
	2.5L	4	2, 4	**General Motors L/N Body**			
Ford Contour, Mystique and 1999-00 Cougar				1997-01	2.4L	2	1, 4
1997-01	2.0L	2	1, 4		3.1L	2	1, 4
	2.5L	3	1, 4	**General Motors N Body**			
Ford Taurus and Sable				1997-01	2.4L	2	1, 4
1997-01	ALL	4	2, 4		3.1L	2	1, 4
Lincoln Continental				**General Motors V Body**			
1997-01	4.6L	4	5	1997-01	3.0L	4	5
Ford Escort, Tracer and ZX2				**General Motors W Body**			
1997	1.8L	2	1, 4	1997-01	3.1L	2	5
	1.9L	2	1, 4		3.4L	2	5
1998-01	2.0L	2	1, 4		3.8L	2	5
Ford Mustang				**General Motors Y Body**			
1997-01	ALL	4	2, 4	1997-01	5.7L	4	5
Lincoln Mark VIII				**GEO/Chevrolet**			
1997-01	4.6L	4	5	1997-01	ALL	2	1, 4
Ford Cougar (1997)				**Saturn**			
1997	3.8L	2	1, 4	1997-01	1.9L	2	1, 4
	4.6L	4	5				

① Chrysler LH class designation refers to the Chrysler 300M, Concorde, LHS, New Yorker, Dodge Intrepid and Eagle Vision.

② Chrysler JA class designation refers to the Chrysler Cirrus, Plymouth Breeze and Dodge Stratus.

    Chrysler JX class designation refers to the Chrysler Sebring Convertible.

93068C01

ELECTRIC COOLING FANS

8

ELECTRIC COOLING FANS

General Information

A basic vehicle cooling system consists of a radiator, water pump, thermostat, electric or engine-driven cooling fan, and hoses. Electric cooling fans are common on today's vehicles due to engine compartment space limitations or engine layout. Electric cooling fans operate in either a pusher or a puller capacity. A pusher type fan is typically mounted on the front of the radiator assembly and forces air through the radiator, whereas a puller type fan is mounted on the engine side of the radiator and draws air through the grill and radiator assembly. Vehicles that utilize a transversely-mounted engine will always be equipped with at least one electric cooling fan (most having two), because none of the engine pulleys are inline with the radiator air-flow.

There are generally two types of electric cooling fans: primary cooling fans and secondary cooling fans. Primary cooling fans are typically of the puller style. Vehicles that do not incorporate an engine-driven mechanical cooling fan will utilize a primary cooling fan. The secondary cooling fan, also known as a A/C condenser fan or auxiliary cooling fan by certain manufacturers, could be of either a pusher or a puller style. Vehicles equipped with A/C will either utilize the radiator cooling fan or a separate fan as the A/C condenser cooling fan (which performs the same function as an auxiliary cooling fan on vehicles with a primary mechanical fan). The engine control computer that receives inputs from various sensors in the engine compartment commonly controls electric cooling fans. The engine control computer receives inputs from the engine coolant temperature sensors and A/C system pressure switches, then actuates the necessary cooling fan relays to engage the applicable cooling fan for the condition. On models equipped with only one electric primary cooling fan, the fan can operate at two speeds: low speed and high speed. The low speed condition is enabled when the engine begins to heat up or when the A/C is engaged. As the engine demands more cooling, the cooling fan will be stepped-up to high speed.

Electric Cooling Fan Service

Due to the wide variety of vehicle manufacturers and suppliers of electric cooling fans it is almost impossible to cover every specific combination of cooling fan and model. The following procedures will cover the most common types of mountings and troubleshooting techniques.

REMOVAL & INSTALLATION

Puller Type

➡It may be simpler to remove the cooling fan(s) with the radiator as an assembly.

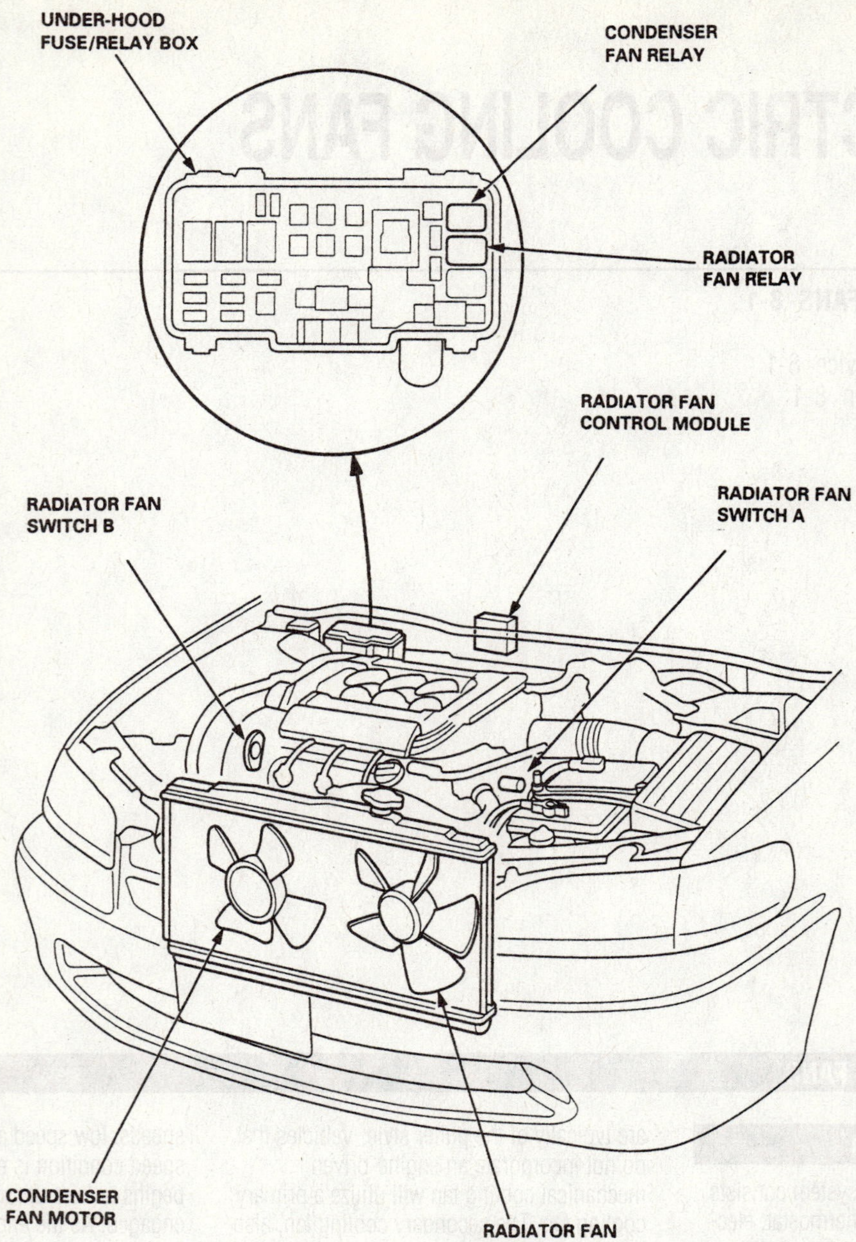

UNDER-HOOD
FUSE/RELAY BOX

CONDENSER
FAN RELAY

RADIATOR
FAN RELAY

RADIATOR FAN
CONTROL MODULE

RADIATOR FAN
SWITCH B

RADIATOR FAN
SWITCH A

CONDENSER
FAN MOTOR

RADIATOR FAN
MOTOR

79229G01

Typical dual fan set-up, showing common cooling fan system control components used on many vehicles with A/C

1. Disconnect the negative battery cable.

2. Inspect the cooling fan and take note of any wires, hoses or A/C lines which may hamper fan removal. Also at this time, decide whether it is necessary to remove the fan along with the radiator or not.

3. Position aside all wires, hoses and A/C lines for fan removal. It may not always be possible to create enough clearance for fan removal by simply moving these obstructions aside; often they must be disconnected. If any cooling system lines must be disconnected, drain and recycle the engine coolant. If any of the A/C lines must be disconnected, the A/C system will need to be discharged and evacuated by a MVAC-trained technician using an approved recovery machine.

4. Disengage the cooling fan wiring harness connector.

5. If the fan can be removed without the radiator, perform the following:

a. Loosen the mounting fasteners. Usually there are two nuts or bolts along the top edge of the cooling fan shroud and either two retaining clips or bolts along the bottom edge.

b. Carefully lift the fan up and out of the engine compartment, making sure that no wires or hoses get hung up on it.

6. If it is necessary to remove the radiator for fan removal, perform the following:

a. Disconnect all cooling system hoses from it after draining the cooling system.

b. Locate all of the radiator mounting fasteners (usually two or more nuts or bolts along the top, possibly two along the bottom).

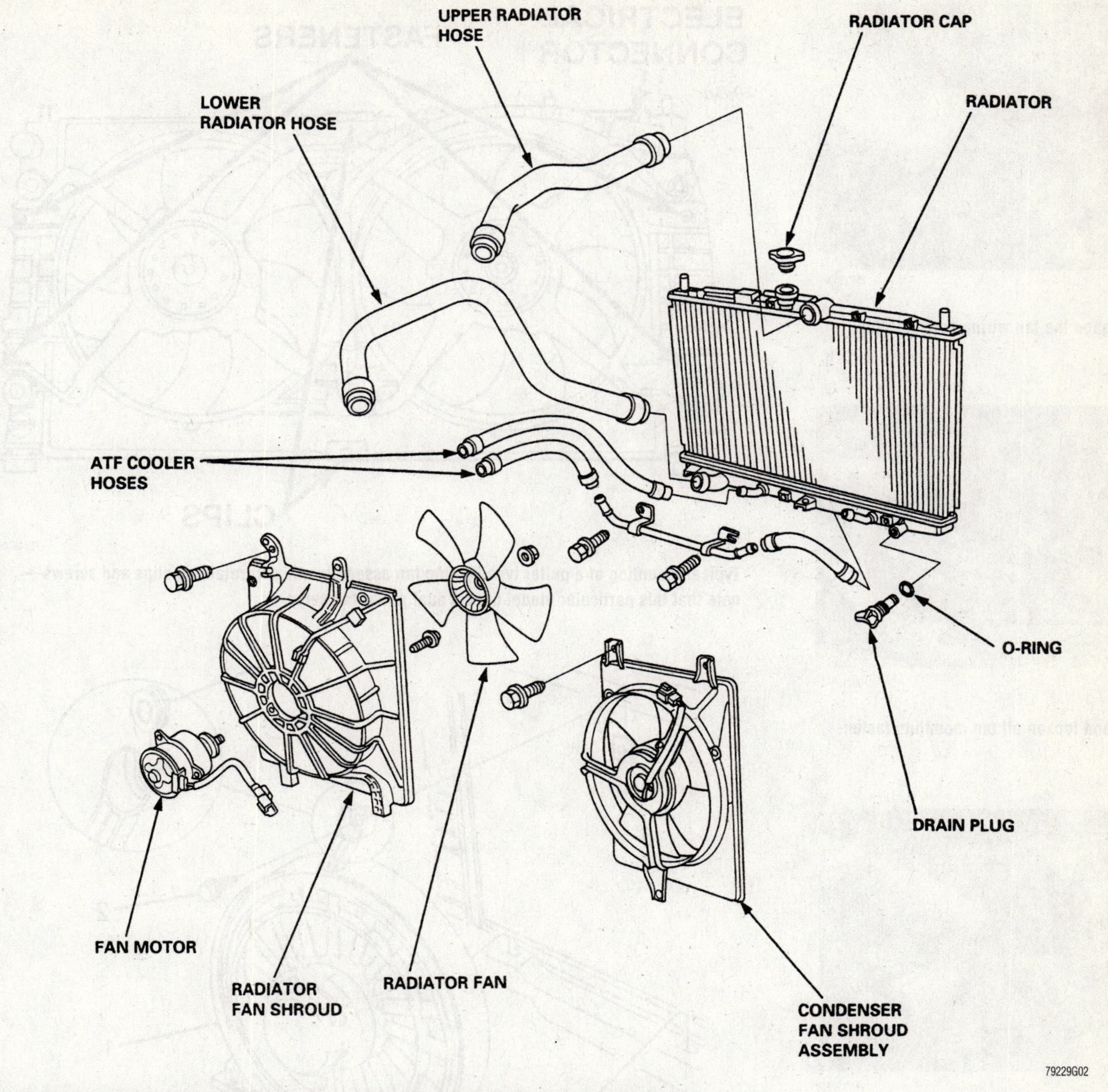

UPPER RADIATOR HOSE

RADIATOR CAP

RADIATOR

LOWER RADIATOR HOSE

ATF COOLER HOSES

O-RING

DRAIN PLUG

FAN MOTOR

RADIATOR FAN SHROUD

RADIATOR FAN

CONDENSER FAN SHROUD ASSEMBLY

79229G02

Exploded view of a typical dual cooling fan set-up and related cooling system components

➠Quite a few radiators are secured along the bottom by two posts which fit into rubber grommets. The rubber grommets help isolate the radiator from harsh vibrations in the frame. If no nuts or bolts can be located along the bottom of the radiator, chances are that the radiator is secured with the posts and grommets.

c. Lift the radiator and cooling fan up and out of the engine compartment together.

d. Separate the cooling fan from the radiator by removing the attaching fasteners.

89713P96

To remove a puller type cooling fan, first detach any braces (1), wires (2) or other obstructions . . .

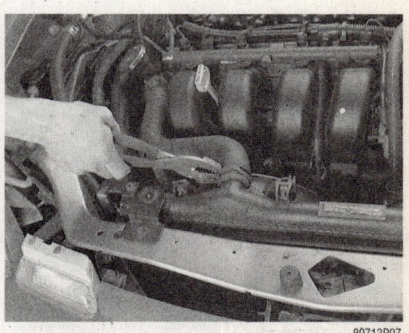

89713P97

. . . including cooling system hoses, to allow fan removal

For complete service labor times order Nichols' Chilton Labor Guide Manual

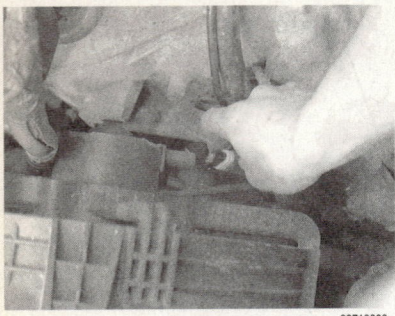

Disengage the fan wiring connector(s) . . .

. . . and loosen all fan mounting fasteners

Separate the fan from the radiator . . .

. . ., then lift the fan up and out of the engine compartment

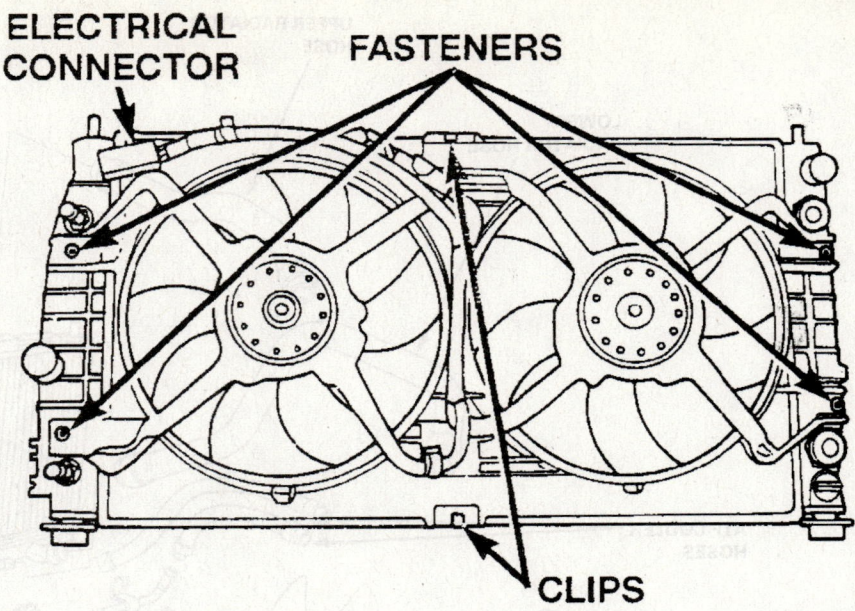

Typical mounting of a puller type cooling fan assembly utilizing retaining clips and screws— note that this particular model uses a dual puller fan setup

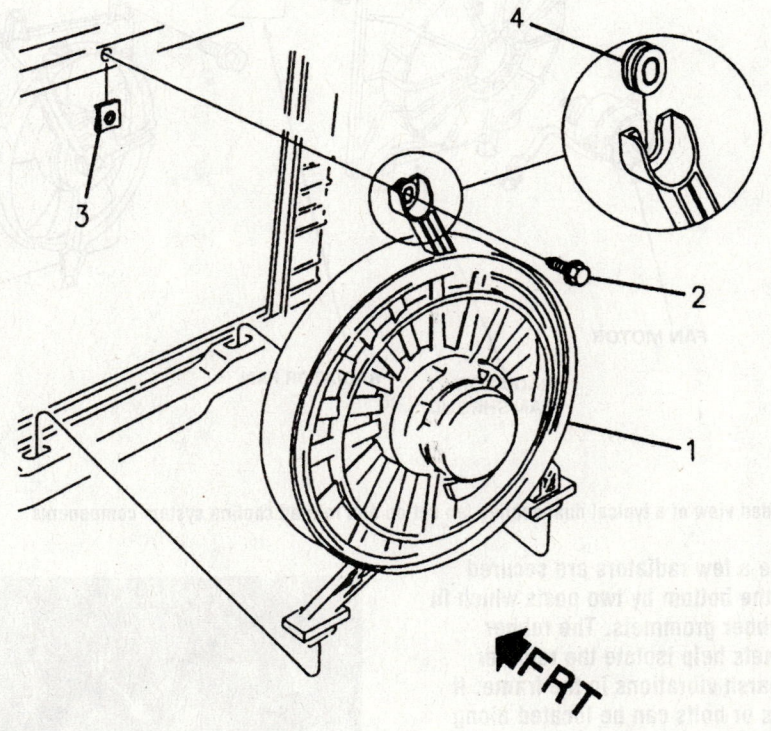

1   FAN ASSEMBLY
2   BOLT
3   CLIP
4   INSULATOR, ENGINE COOLING FAN

Notice the slots in the bottom of the radiator, in which the fan housing posts rest—common mounting of a puller type cooling fan

To install:

7. If applicable, install the cooling fan on the radiator.

8. Install the cooling fan and shroud assembly (also the radiator if necessary). Tighten the fan shroud mounting bolts.

9. Reattach all wires, hoses and A/C lines as applicable. If the A/C lines were detached, the system must be evacuated and recharged by a MVAC-trained technician.

10. If drained, refill and bleed the cooling system.

11. Reattach the cooling fan electrical harness connector.

12. Connect the negative battery cable.

13. Start the engine and check for leaks.

14. Verify the operation of the cooling fan(s).

Pusher Type

Vehicles that utilize the pusher type of electric cooling fan, may require the removal of the grilles and/or upper radiator shroud in order to gain access the fasteners that mount the fan assembly in the vehicle.

1. Disconnect the negative battery cable.

2. Access the cooling fan.

3. Label and disconnect the cooling fan electrical harness.

➡ **It may be necessary to loosen the mounting bolts for the A/C condenser to the body**

4. Remove the fasteners that mount the cooling fan to the A/C condenser or radiator.

5. Lift the cooling fan out of the vehicle.

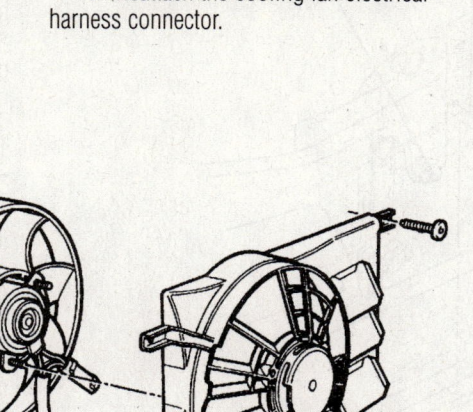

This fan mounts to the fan shroud, then the shroud mounts to the radiator—molded clips in the radiator hold the bottom in place and screws at the top

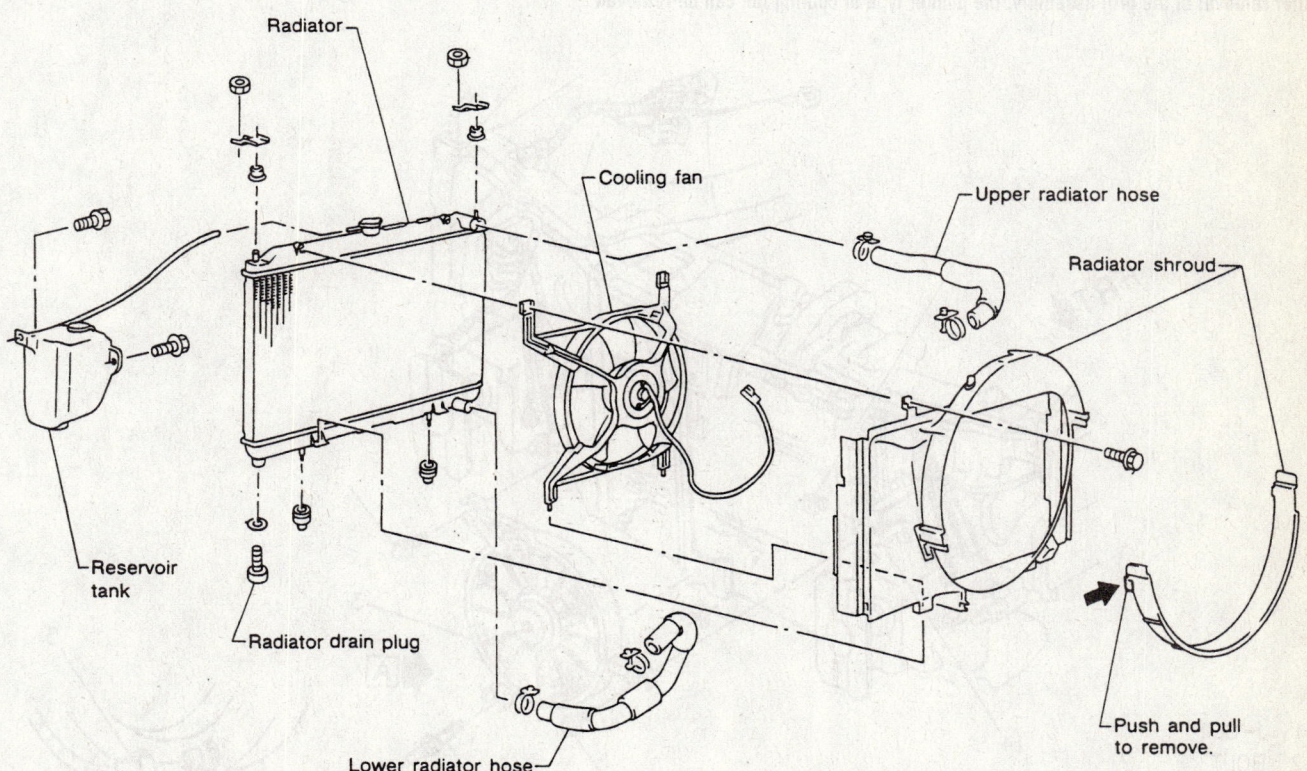

Typically the cooling fan is rubber mounted to isolate vibration and noise—usually the rubber grommets are located at the mount, verify their position before installation

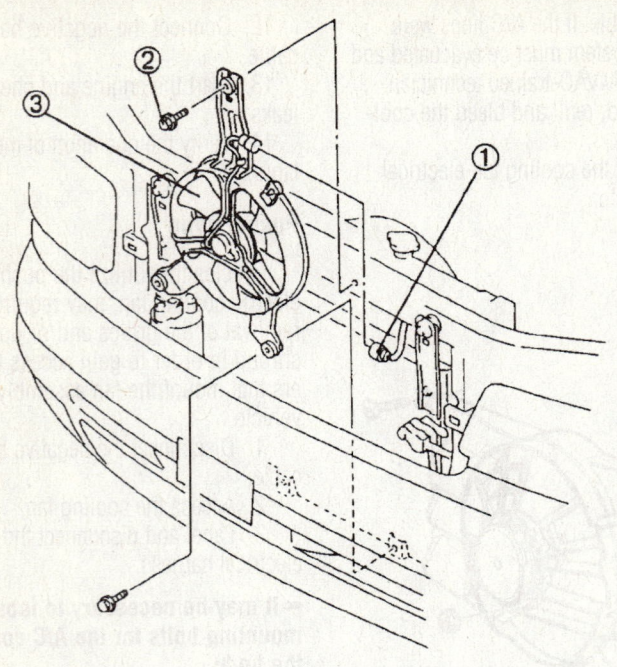

1	Connector
2	Bolt
3	Condenser fan

79249G13

After removal of the grill assembly, the pusher type of cooling fan can be removed

To install:

6. Insert the cooling fan into the vehicle.

7. Mount the cooling fan to the A/C condenser or radiator

8. Connect the cooling fan electrical harness.

9. If removed, install any shrouding or grills.

10. Connect the negative battery cable.

TROUBLESHOOTING

When diagnosing an inoperative cooling fan it may be necessary to use a diagnostic scan tool to monitor engine coolant temperature and the engine control computer.

1. Perform a visual inspection of the cooling fan. If the fan does not turn with ease, the fan motor is seized and needs to be replaced.

2. Check all the fuses and fusible links related to the cooling fan circuit.

3. Check the integrity of the electrical connections related to the cooling fan circuit.

4. Check the cooling fan motor.

5. Check the relays associated with the cooling fan circuit.

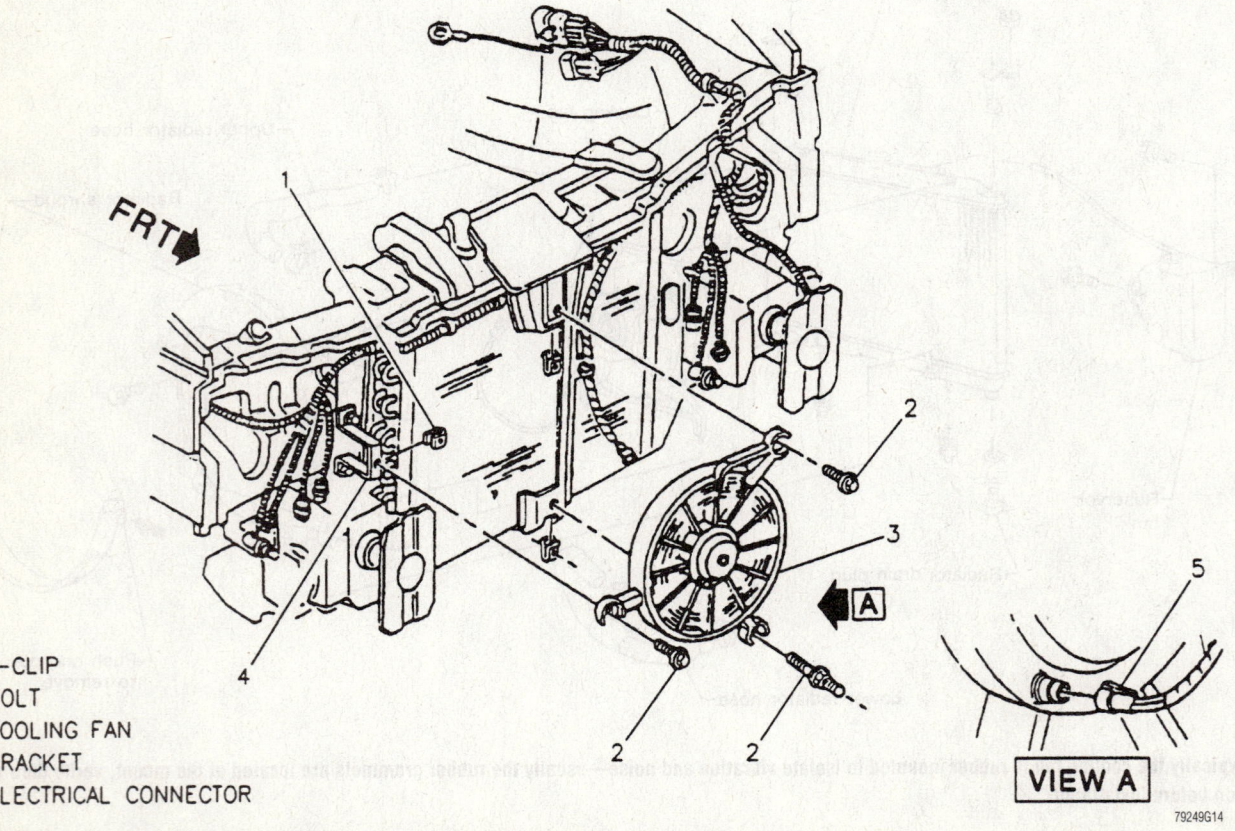

FRT

1 J—CLIP
2 BOLT
3 COOLING FAN
4 BRACKET
5 ELECTRICAL CONNECTOR

VIEW A

79249G14

It may be necessary to remove the grill assembly to access the A/C condenser cooling fan—pusher type

6. Using a scan tool, determine if the engine control computer is calling for the fan to activate.

Cooling Fan Motor

1. Disconnect the negative battery cable.
2. Disengage the cooling fan motor connector.
3. Identify and label the ground and the power terminals of the cooling fan connector using the wiring diagrams provided.
4. Using jumper leads with a fuse in series, apply battery voltage to the appropriate terminals of the cooling fan.
5. The cooling fan should operate. If not, replace the cooling fan.

If the cooling fan functions properly during this test, proceed to the cooling fan relay test.

Cooling Fan Relay

1. Turn the ignition **OFF**.
2. Remove the relay.

3. Locate the two terminals on the relay, which are connected to the coil windings. Check the relay coil for continuity. Connect the common meter lead to terminal 85 and positive meter lead to terminal 86. There should be continuity. If not, replace the relay.

4. Check the operation of the internal relay contacts.

   a. Connect the meter leads to terminals 30 and 87. Meter polarity does not matter for this step.

   b. Apply positive battery voltage to terminal 86 and ground to terminal 85. The relay should click as the contacts are drawn toward the coil and the meter should indicate continuity. Replace the relay if your results are different.

If the relay functions properly during this test, inspect the coolant temperature sensor and the cooling fan system wiring for defects.

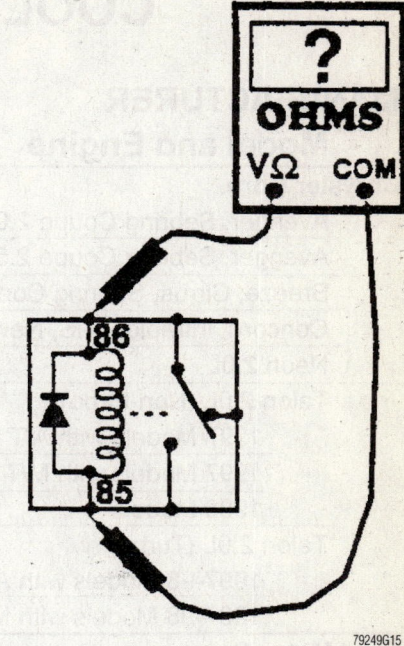

Use an ohmmeter to check for circuit continuity of the coil in the relay

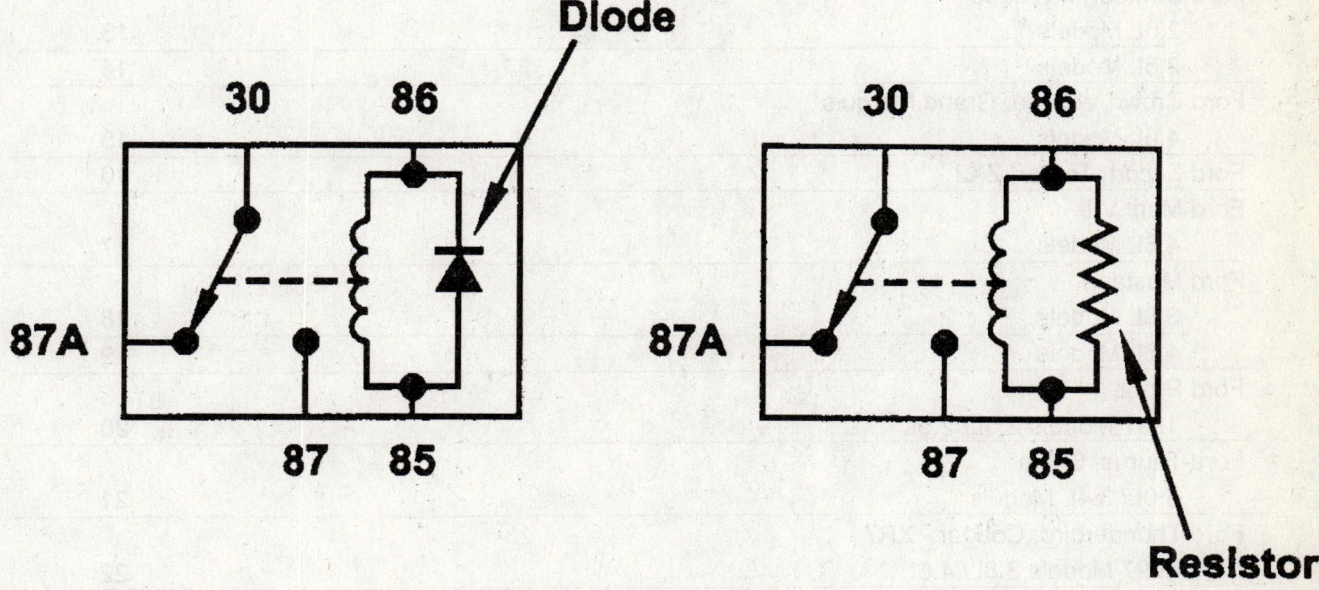

Terminal identification of the most common types of relays. Diodes and resistors in the relay prevent voltage spikes induced when the current is removed from the coil from damaging electronic components

Refer to the model specific sections for engine mechanical service procedures

COOLING FAN DIAGRAM INDEX

COOLING FAN DIAGRAM INDEX

MANUFACTURER
Model and Engine

	Diagram
General Motors (cont.)	
C & H Bodies (Bonneville, Eighty-Eight, Ninety-Eight, Park Ave., Le Sabre, LSS) 3.8L	24
E & K Bodies (DeVille, Eldorado, Seville) 4.6L	
1997 Models	25
1998-01 Models	26
F Body (Camaro, Firebird) 3.8L	27
F Body (Camaro, Firebird) 5.7L	
1997 Models	27
1998-01 Models	28
G Body (Aurora, Riviera)	
3.8L Models	29
4.0L Models	30
J Body (Cavalier, Sunfire) 2.2L/ 2.3L/ 2.4L	31
L/N Bodies (Cutlass, Malibu) 2.4L/ 3.1L	32
N Body (Acheiva, Grand Am, Skylark) 2.3L/ 2.4L/ 3.1L	33
V Body (Catera) 3.0L	34
W Body (Lumina, Monte Carlo, Grand Prix, Cutlass Supreme, Regal, Intrigue) 3.1L/ 3.4L/ 3.8L	
1997 Cutlass Supreme	35
1997-01 Models (except Cutlass Supreme and Intrigue)	36
1998-01 Models (Intrigue)	36
Y Body (Corvette) 5.7L	37
Geo/Chevrolet	
Metro 1.0L/ 1.3L (w/o A/C)	38
Metro 1.0L/ 1.3L (w/ A/C)	39
Prism 1.6L/ 1.8L (w/ A/C)	40
Prism 1.6L/ 1.8L (w/o A/C)	41
Saturn	
1.9L	42

93068C02

Refer to the model specific sections for cooling system service procedures

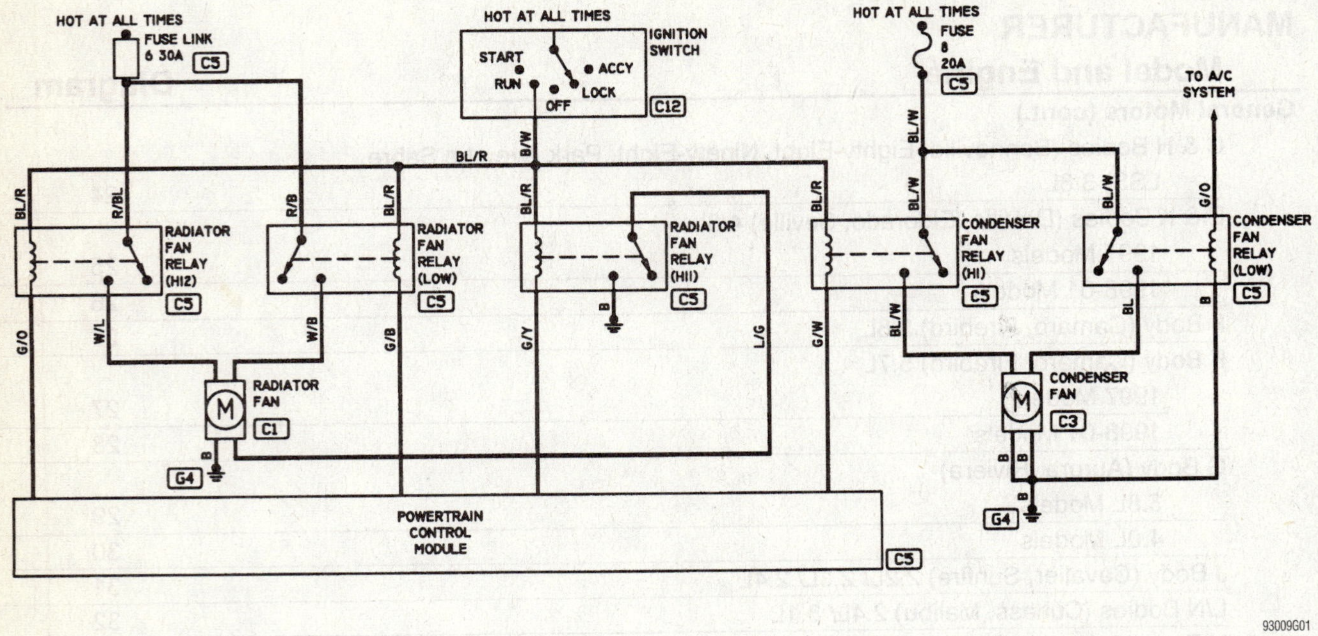

DIA. 1—Chrysler Avenger/Sebring Coupe 2.0L

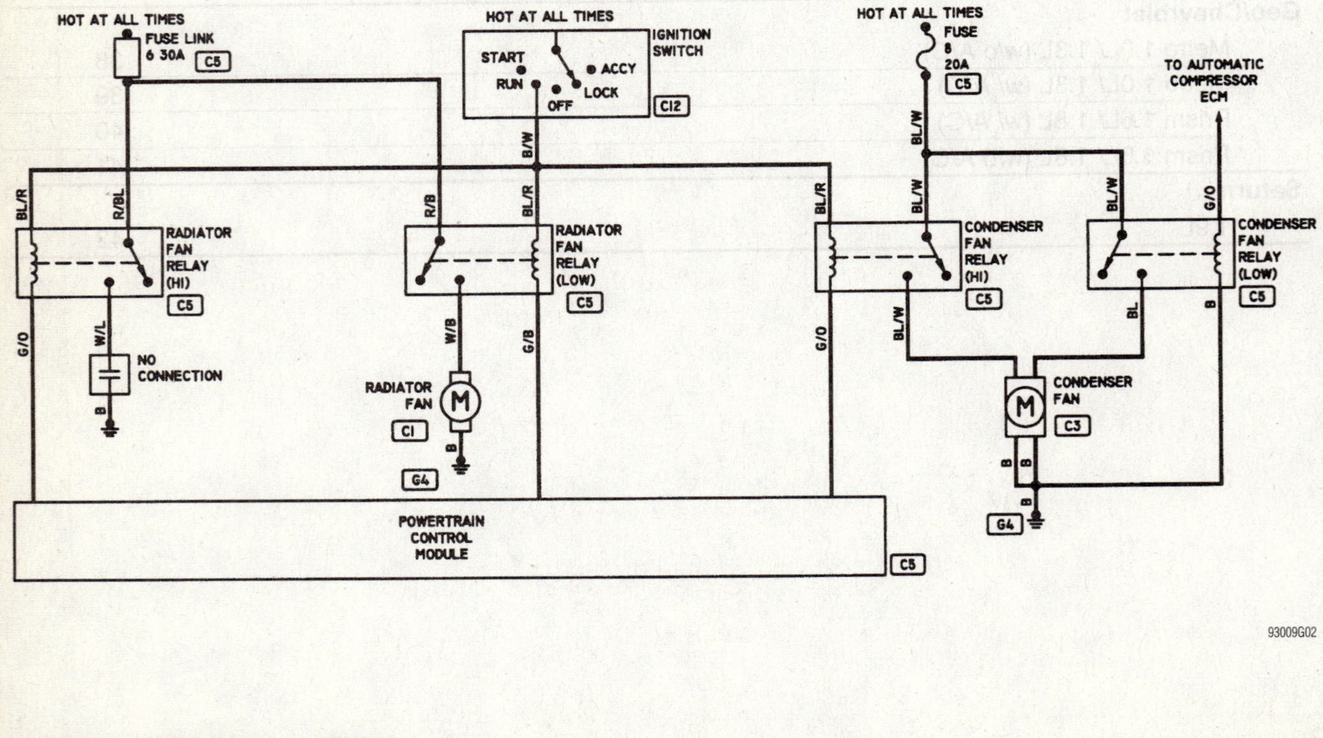

DIA. 2—Chrysler Avenger/Sebring Coupe 2.5L

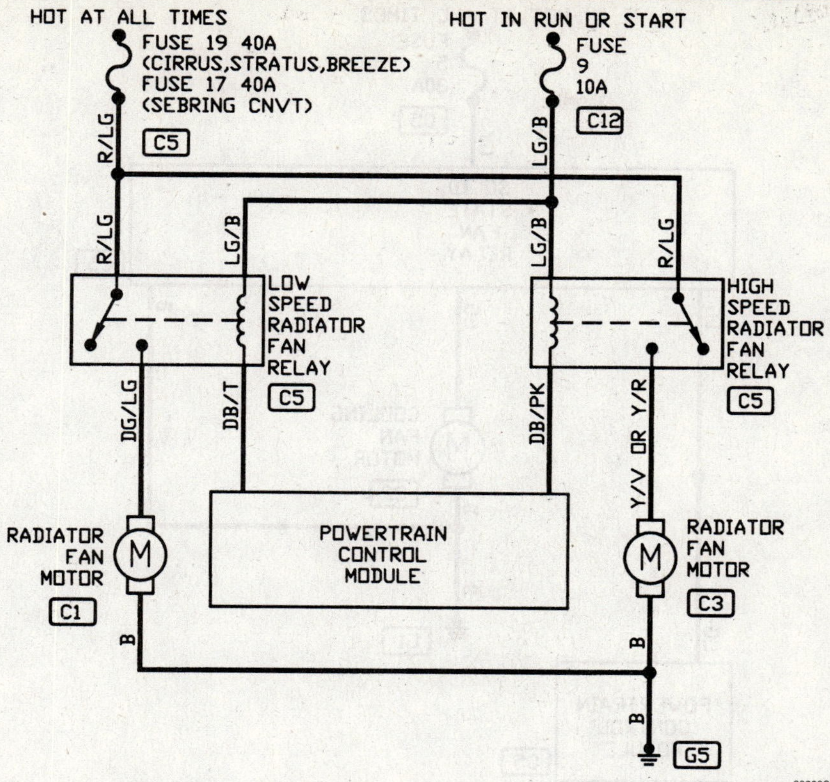

DIA. 3—Chrysler Breeze/Cirrus/Sebring Convertible/Stratus 2.0L/2.4L/2.5L

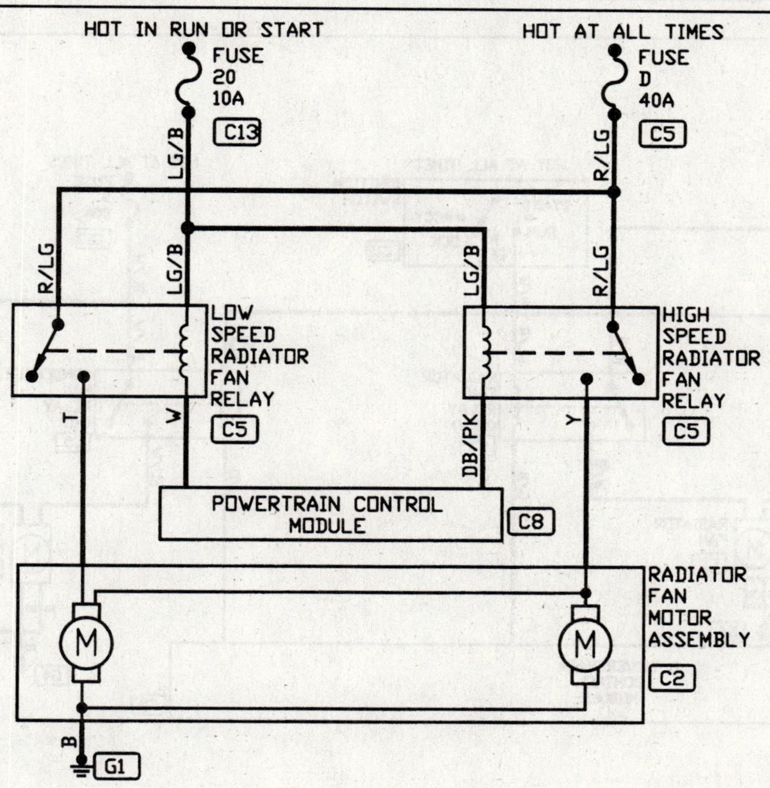

DIA. 4—Chrysler Concorde/Intrepid/LHS/New Yorker/Vision 2.7L/3.2L/3.3L/3.5L

For complete service labor times order Nichols' Chilton Labor Guide Manual

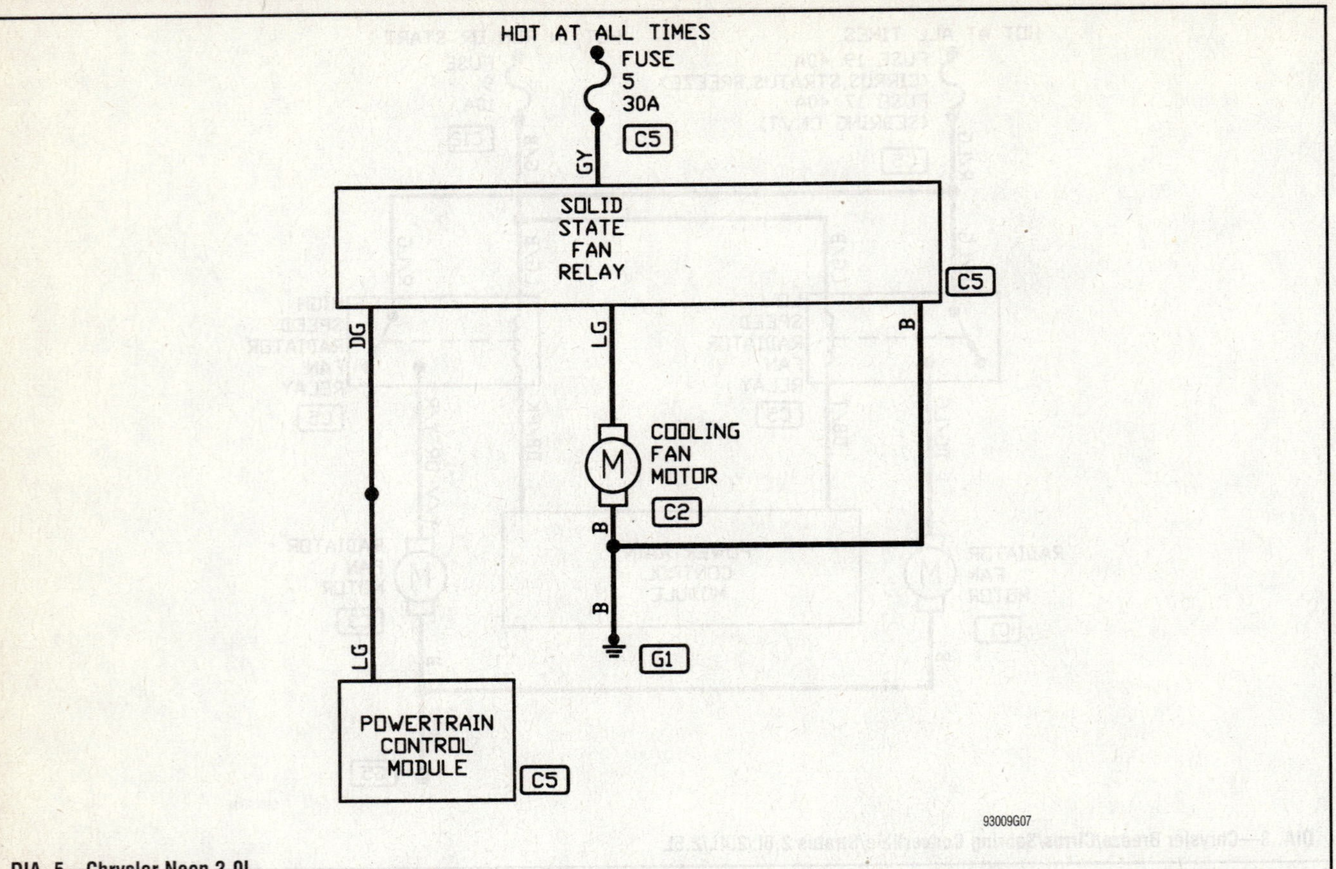

HOT AT ALL TIMES

FUSE
5
30A

C5

GY

SOLID
STATE
FAN
RELAY

C5

DG

LG

B

COOLING
FAN
MOTOR

M

C2

B

B

G1

LG

POWERTRAIN
CONTROL
MODULE

C5

93009G07

DIA. 5—Chrysler Neon 2.0L

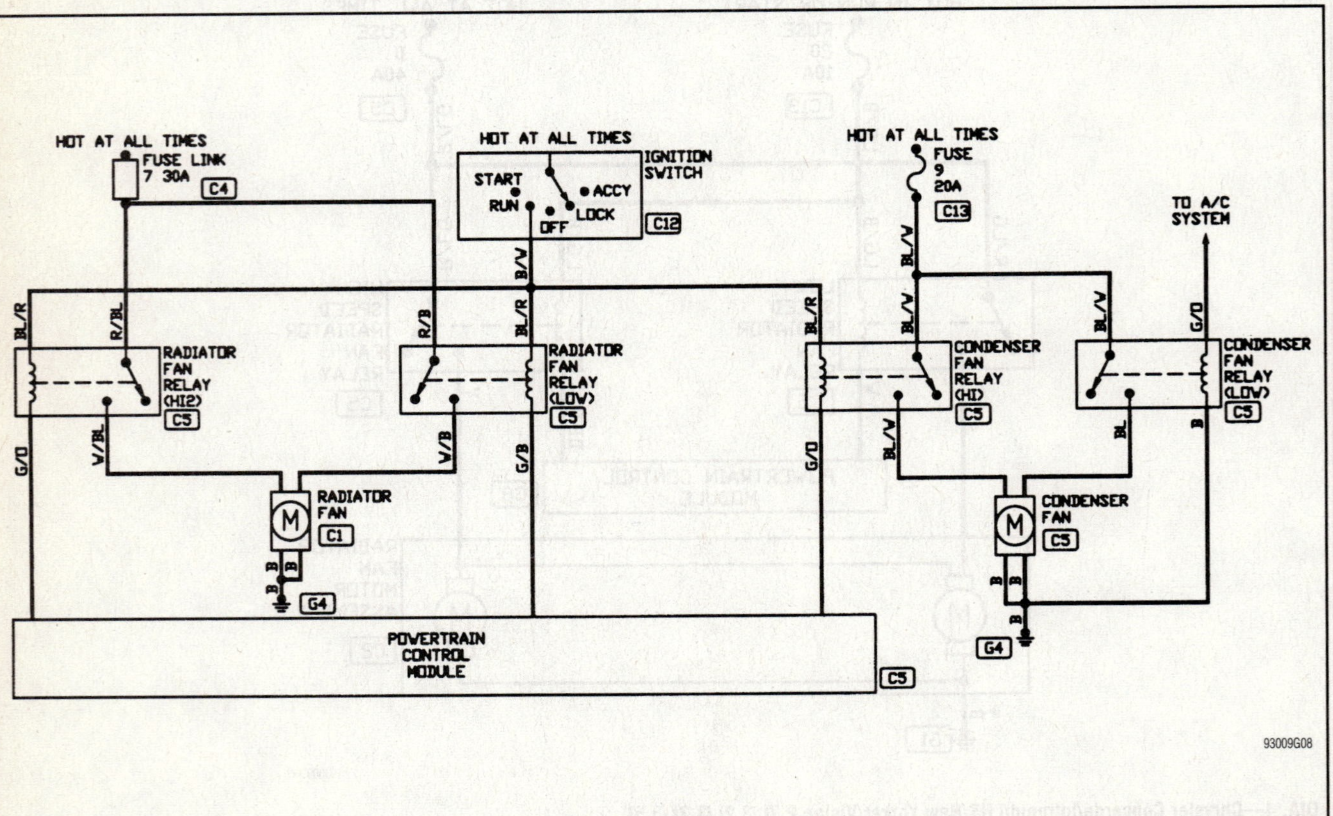

HOT AT ALL TIMES

FUSE LINK
7 30A   C4

HOT AT ALL TIMES

IGNITION
SWITCH

START   ACCY
RUN   LOCK
OFF   C12

HOT AT ALL TIMES

FUSE
9
20A

C13

TO A/C
SYSTEM

BL/R

R/BL

RADIATOR
FAN
RELAY
(HI)   C5

B/V

R/B

B/R

RADIATOR
FAN
RELAY
(LOW)   C5

B/R

BL/V

BL/V

CONDENSER
FAN
RELAY
(HI)   C5

BL/V

G/O

CONDENSER
FAN
RELAY
(LOW)   C5

G/O

V/BL

V/B

G/B

G/O

BL/V

BL

B

RADIATOR
FAN
C1

M

B   B

G4

CONDENSER
FAN
C5

M

B   B

G4

POWERTRAIN
CONTROL
MODULE

C5

93009G08

DIA. 6—1997 Chrysler Neon 2.0L (Non-Turbo—A/T)

PRECAUTIONS

Test Equipment

Never use jumper wires made from a thinner gauge wire than the circuit being tested. If the jumper wire is of too small a gauge, it may overheat and possibly melt. Never use jumpers to bypass high resistance loads in a circuit. Bypassing resistances, in effect, creates a short circuit. This may, in turn, cause damage and fire. Jumper wires should only be used to bypass lengths of wire or to simulate switches.

Do not use a test light to probe electronic ignition, spark plug or coil wires. Never use a pick-type test light to probe wiring on computer controlled systems unless specifically instructed to do so. Any wire insulation that is pierced by the test light probe should be taped and sealed with silicone after testing.

Never use an ohmmeter to check the resistance of a component or wire while there is voltage applied to the circuit.

A self-powered test light should not be used on any computer controlled system or component. The small amount of electricity transmitted by the test light is enough to damage many electronic automotive components.

Never disengage any sensor while the ignition is ON.

Always replace fuses, circuit breakers and fusible links with identically rated components. Under no circumstances should a component of higher or lower amperage rating be substituted.

Electronic Control Systems

Electronic control systems are very delicate and complicated. To save yourself aggravation, money and time, be sure to adhere to the following points when working on a vehicle's control system:

• Unless otherwise instructed, always disconnect the battery cables when servicing the electronic system.

• When disconnecting the battery, always be sure to detach the negative battery cable FIRST, then the positive cable. This simple practice will almost completely prevent the chance of arcing or shorting the system.

• Never pierce, or cut the insulation off of, a wire for testing purposes. Many of the control system's wires are designed to handle a precise amount of electrical resistance, and the computer expects to see a certain predetermined amount of resistance. If you pierce, or cut the insulation off of a wire, corrosion can build up in the wiring, leading to decreased control system efficiency, DTC storing or possibly even component damage.

• Never subject any control computer to excessive jolts (such as dropping).

• If welding on the vehicle, always disconnect the computer from the vehicle's wiring harness.

• Never detach a wiring harness connector when the ignition switch is turned ON.

Handling Electrostatic Discharge (ESD) Sensitive Parts

Electronic modules are very sensitive to Electrostatic Static Discharge (ESD). If the modules are exposed to these charges, they may be damaged. While most vehicles display a label informing you that their electronic components may be damaged by ESD, some do not have labels, but they may be damaged also. To avoid possible damage to any of these components, follow the steps outlined below.

1. Body movement produces an electrostatic charge. To discharge personal static electricity, touch a ground point (metal) on the vehicle. This should be performed any time you:

• Slide across the vehicle seat
• Sit down or get up
• Do any walking
• Touch an ESD sensitive part

2. Do not touch any exposed terminals on components or connectors with your fingers or any tools.

3. Never use jumper wires, ground a terminal on a component, use test equipment on any component or terminal unless instructed to in a diagnostic or testing procedure. When using test equipment, always connect the ground lead first.

4. Do not remove the part from its protective packing until it's time to install it.

5. Before removing the part from its protective packing, ground the packing to a known good ground on the vehicle.

Air Bags

When working on the air bag system or any components which require the removal of the air bag, adhere to all of the following precautions to minimize the risks of personal injury or component damage:

1. Before attempting to diagnose, remove or install air bag system components, you must first disconnect and isolate the negative (-) battery cable. Failure to do so could result in accidental deployment and possible personal injury.

2. When an undeployed air bag assembly is to be removed from the steering wheel, after disconnecting the negative battery cable, allow the system capacitor to discharge for two minutes before commencing with the air bag system component removal.

3. Replace the air bag system components only with specified replacement parts, or equivalent. Substitute parts may visually appear interchangeable, but internal differences may result in inferior occupant protection.

4. The fasteners, screws, and bolts originally used for the air bag system have special coatings and are specifically designed for the system. They must never be replaced with any substitutes. Anytime a new fastener is needed, replace with the correct fasteners provided in the service package or fasteners listed in the parts books.

BLACK	B	PINK	PK
BROWN	BR	PURPLE	P
RED	R	GREEN	G
ORANGE	O	WHITE	W
YELLOW	Y	LIGHT BLUE	LBL
GRAY	GY	LIGHT GREEN	LG
BLUE	BL	DARK GREEN	DG
VIOLET	V	DARK BLUE	DBL
NO COLOR AVAILABLE			NCA

WIRE COLOR ABREVIATIONS

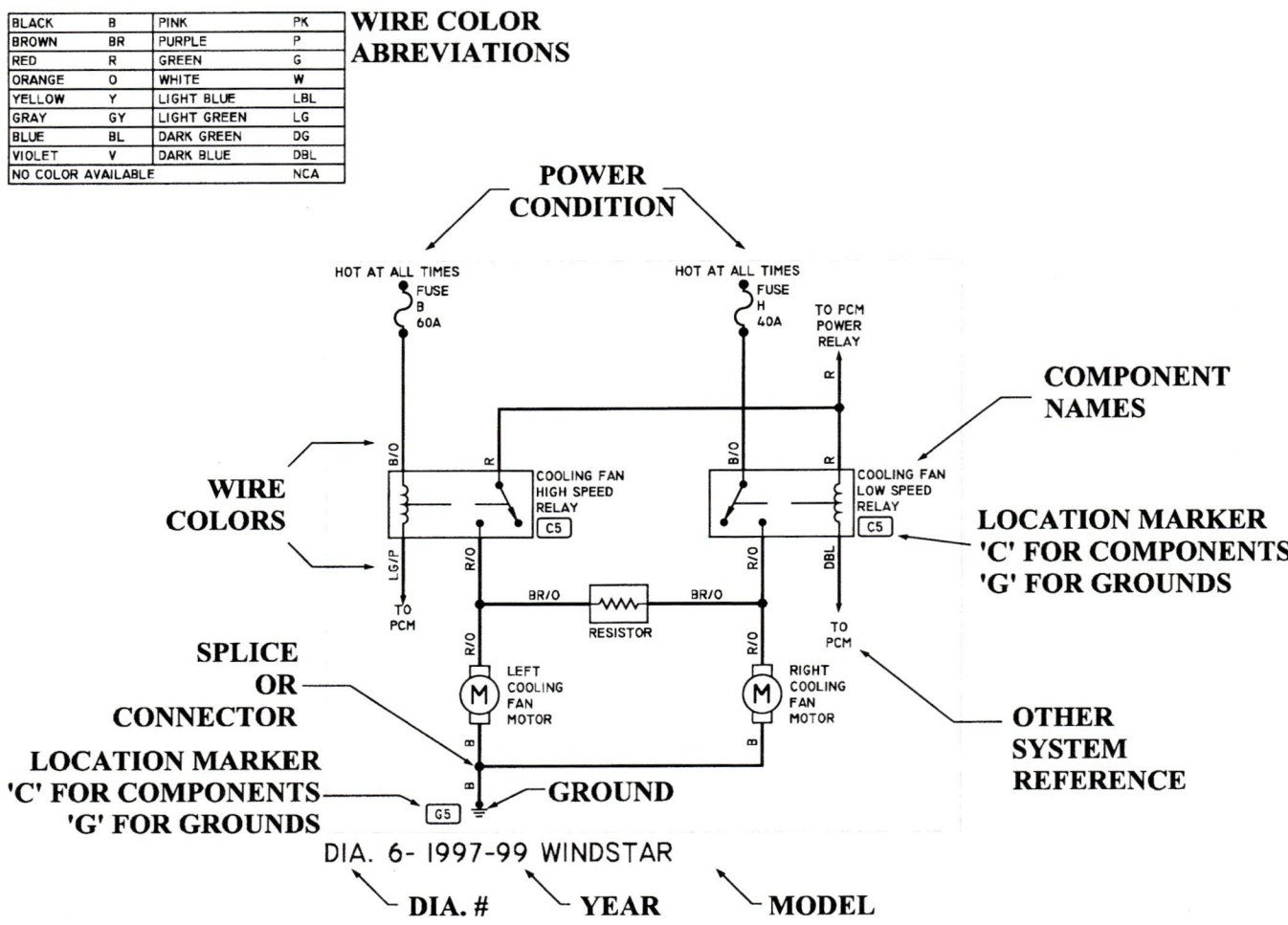

POWER CONDITION

COMPONENT NAMES

WIRE COLORS

LOCATION MARKER 'C' FOR COMPONENTS 'G' FOR GROUNDS

SPLICE OR CONNECTOR

LOCATION MARKER 'C' FOR COMPONENTS 'G' FOR GROUNDS

GROUND

OTHER SYSTEM REFERENCE

DIA. 6- 1997-99 WINDSTAR

DIA. #   **YEAR**   **MODEL**

LOCATION SCHEMATIC

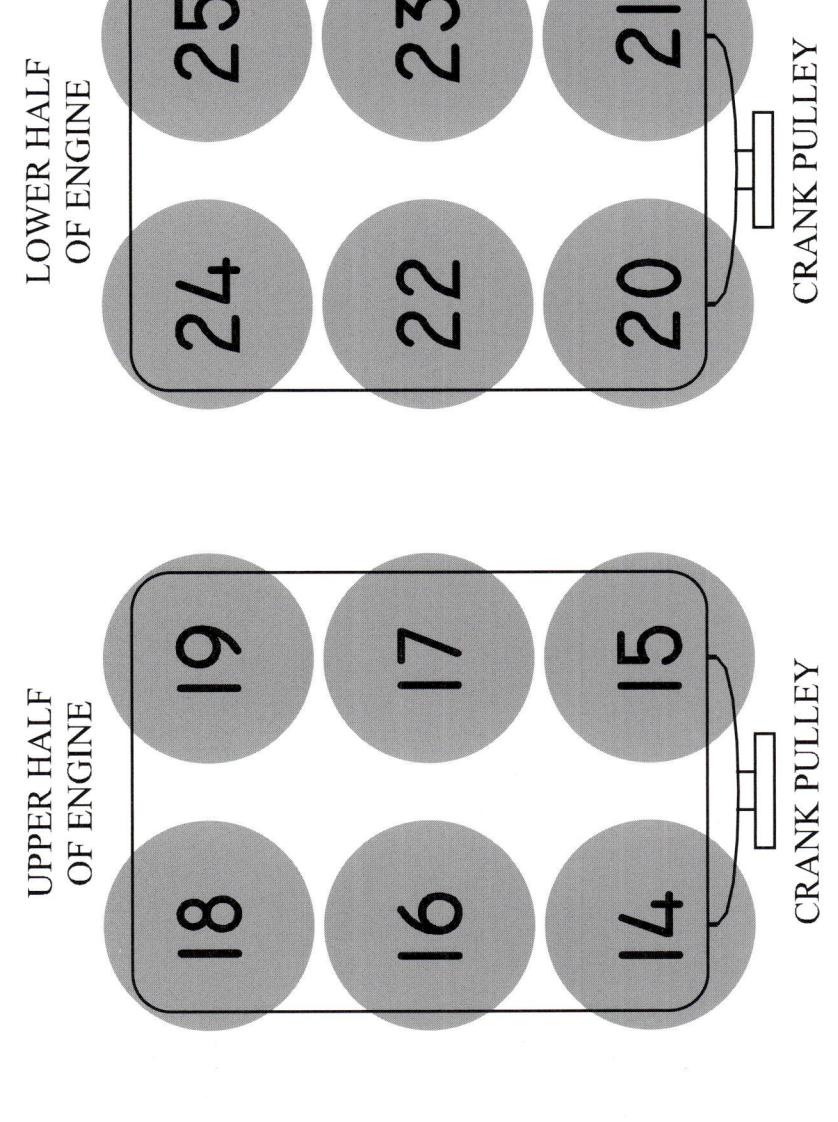

UPPER HALF OF ENGINE

18	19
16	17
14	15

CRANK PULLEY

LOWER HALF OF ENGINE

24	25
22	23
20	21

CRANK PULLEY

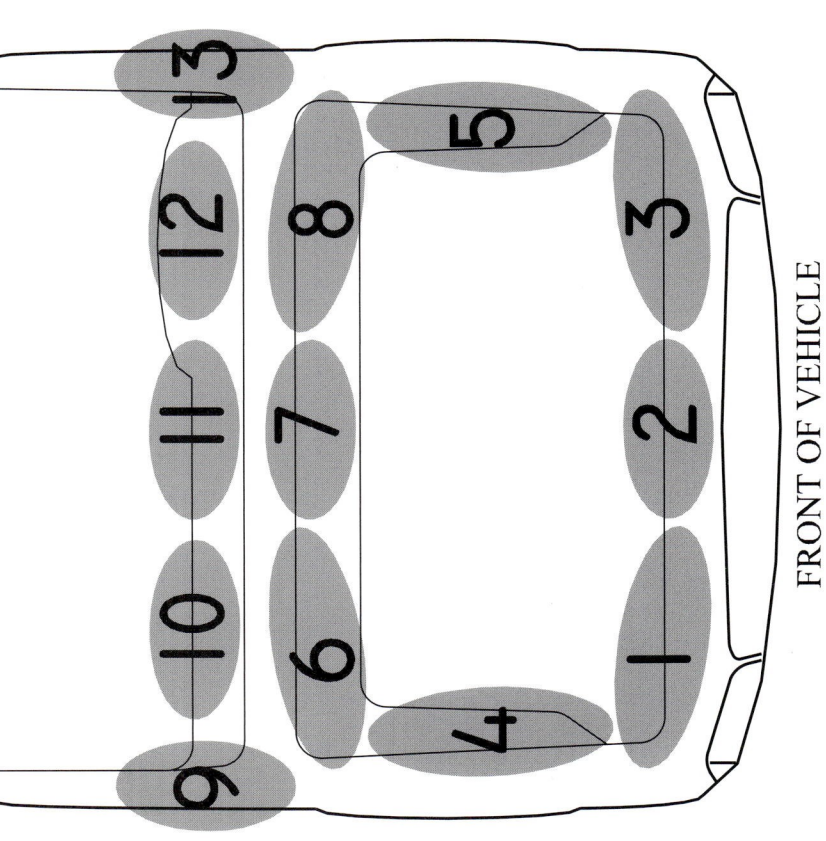

FRONT OF VEHICLE

DIAGRAM X

Location Number	Location Description
1	Engine compartment – Front right
2	Engine compartment – Front middle
3	Engine compartment – Front left
4	Engine compartment – Right inner fender
5	Engine compartment – Left inner fender
6	Engine compartment – Firewall right
7	Engine compartment – Firewall middle
8	Engine compartment – Firewall left
9	Passenger compartment – Right kick panel
10	Passenger compartment – Underdash right
11	Passenger compartment – Underdash middle
12	Passenger compartment – Underdash left
13	Passenger compartment – Left kick panel
14	Facing Crank Pulley – Upper Engine – Front left
15	Facing Crank Pulley – Upper Engine – Front right
16	Facing Crank Pulley – Upper Engine – Middle left
17	Facing Crank Pulley – Upper Engine – Middle right
18	Facing Crank Pulley – Upper Engine – Rear left
19	Facing Crank Pulley – Upper Engine – Rear right
20	Facing Crank Pulley – Lower Engine – Front left
21	Facing Crank Pulley – Lower Engine – Front right
22	Facing Crank Pulley – Lower Engine – Middle left
23	Facing Crank Pulley – Lower Engine – Middle right
24	Facing Crank Pulley – Lower Engine – Rear left
25	Facing Crank Pulley – Lower Engine – Rear right

WIRING DIAGRAM SYMBOLS

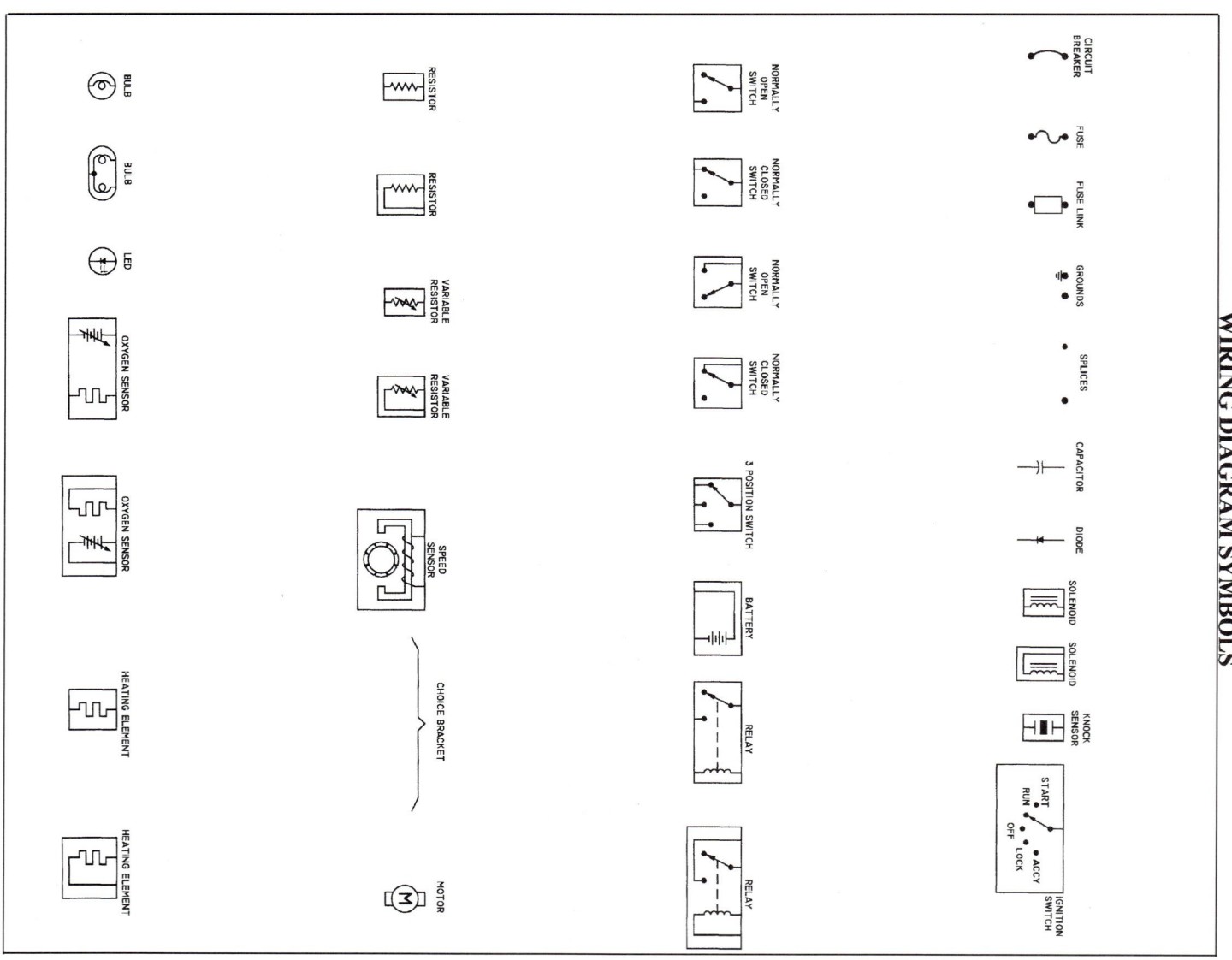

NOTES

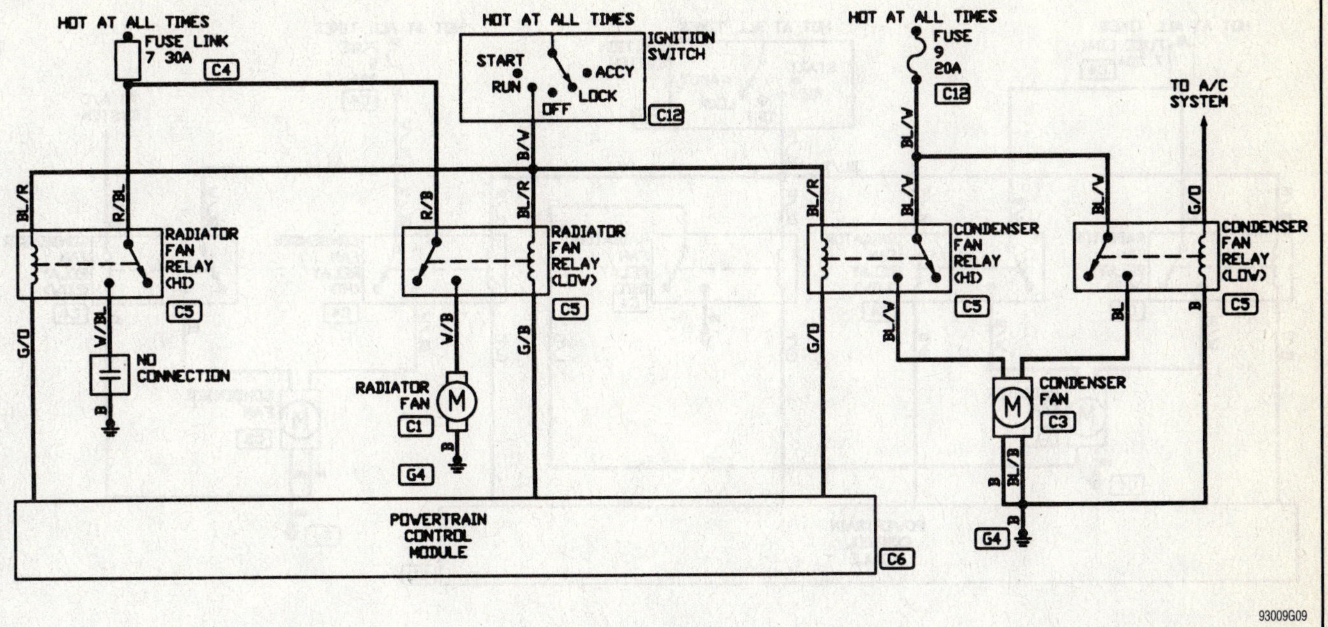

DIA. 7—1997-98 Chrysler Neon 2.0L (Non-Turbo—M/T)

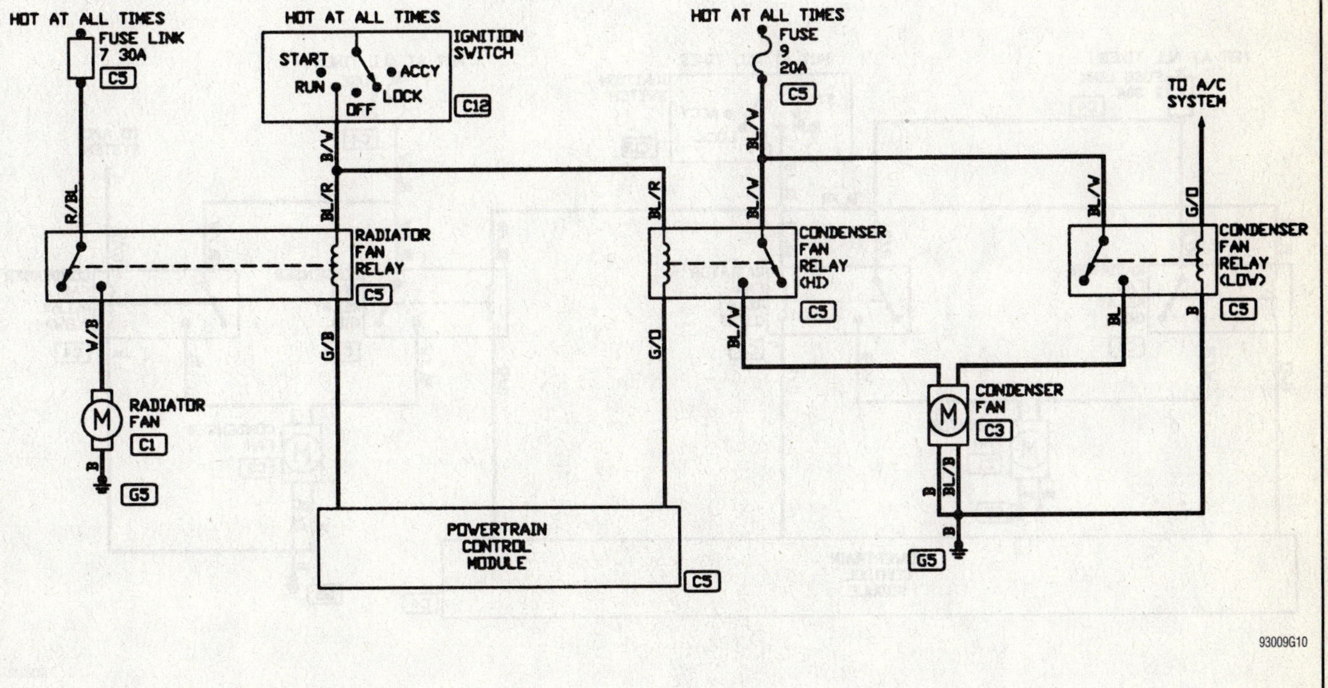

93009G09

DIA. 8—1998 Chrysler Neon 2.0L (Non-Turbo)

93009G10

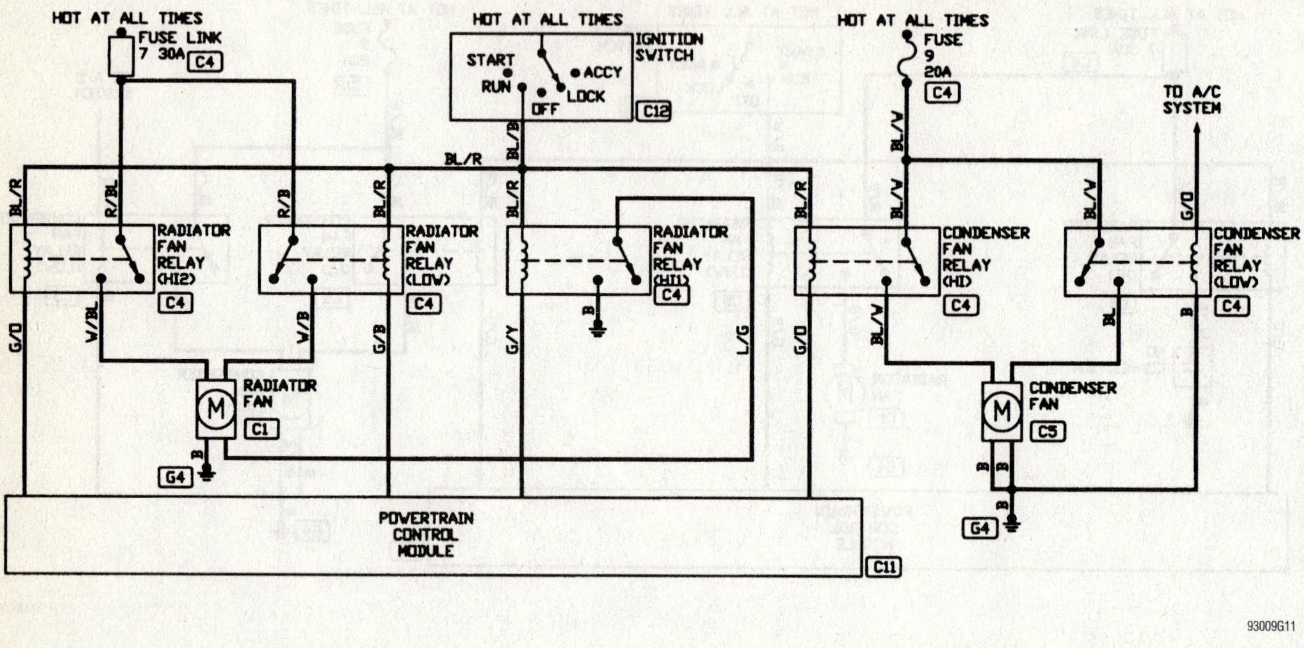

DIA. 9—1997–98 Chrysler Neon 2.0L (Turbo—A/T)

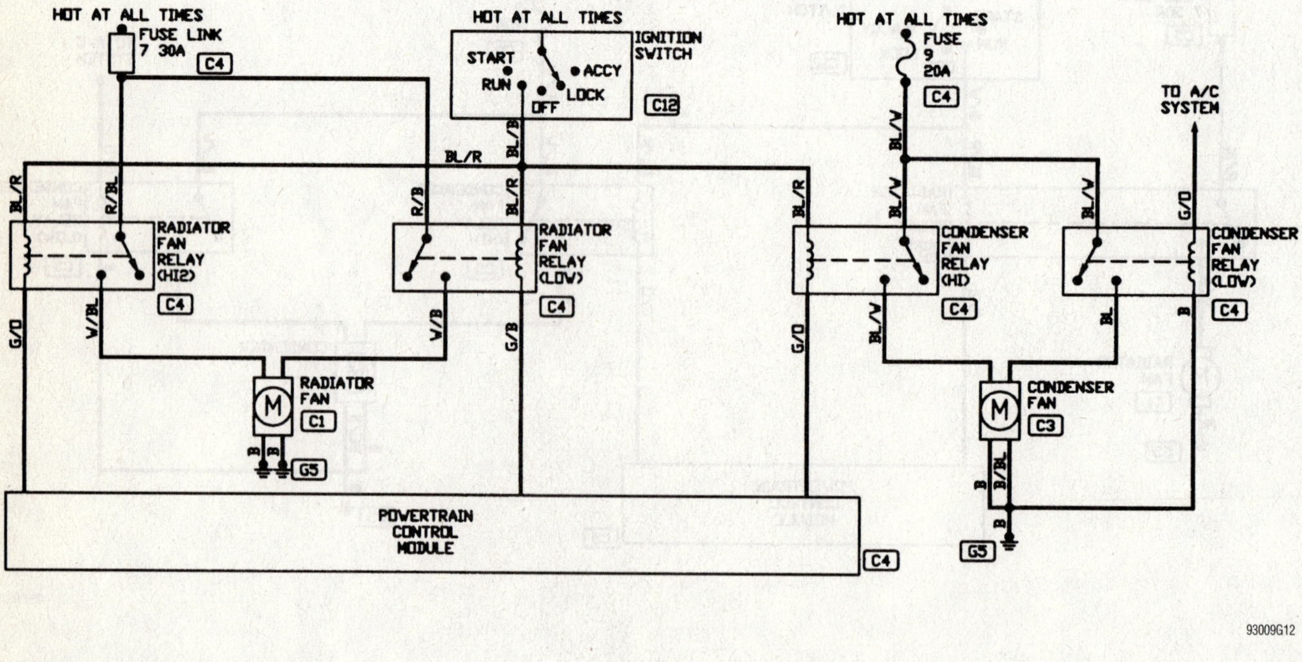

93009G11

DIA. 10—1997–98 Chrysler Neon 2.0L (Turbo—M/T)

93009G12

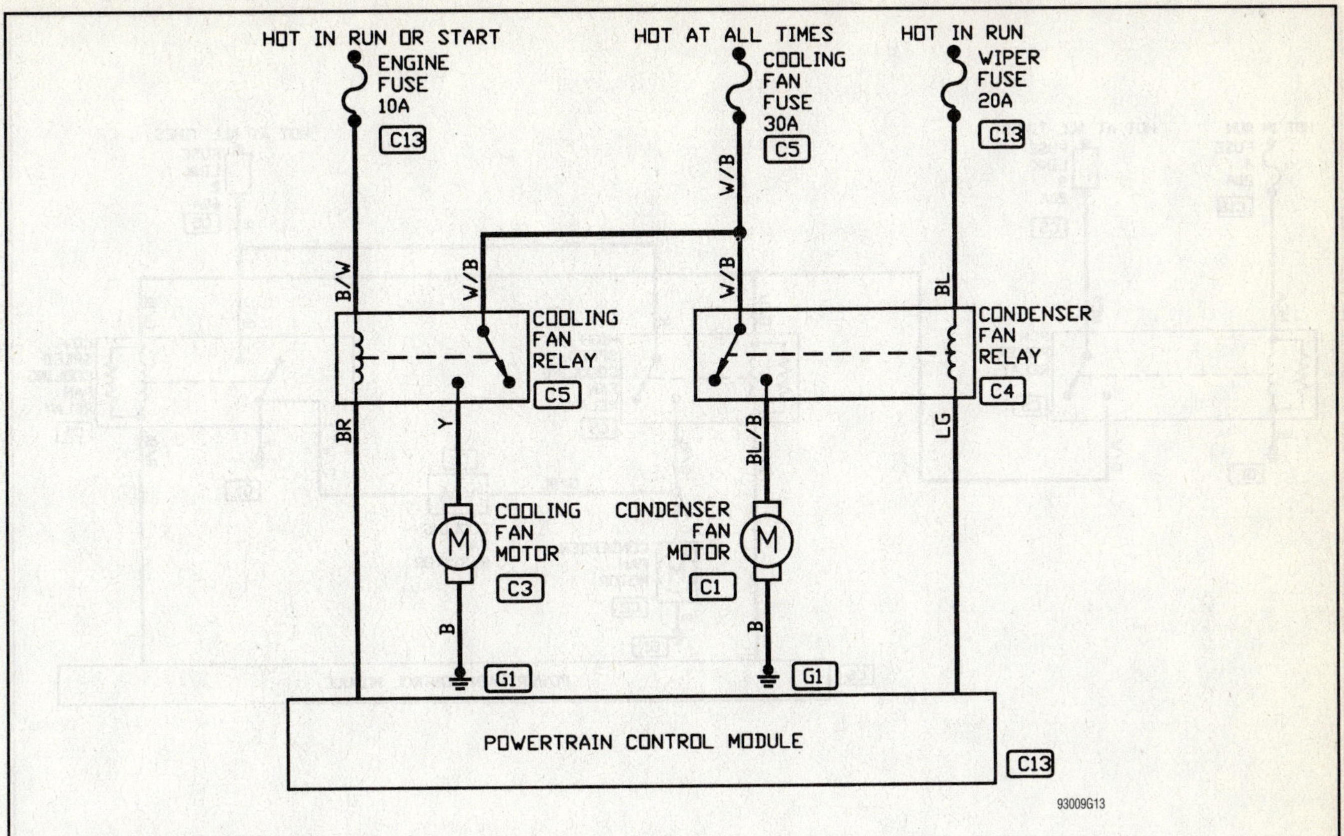

HOT IN RUN OR START
ENGINE
FUSE
10A
C13

HOT AT ALL TIMES
COOLING
FAN
FUSE
30A
C5

HOT IN RUN
WIPER
FUSE
20A
C13

B/W

W/B

W/B

BL

COOLING
FAN
RELAY
C5

CONDENSER
FAN
RELAY
C4

BR

Y

BL/B

LG

COOLING
FAN
MOTOR
C3

CONDENSER
FAN
MOTOR
C1

B

B

G1

G1

POWERTRAIN CONTROL MODULE

C13

93009G13

DIA. 11—1997 Ford Aspire 1.3L

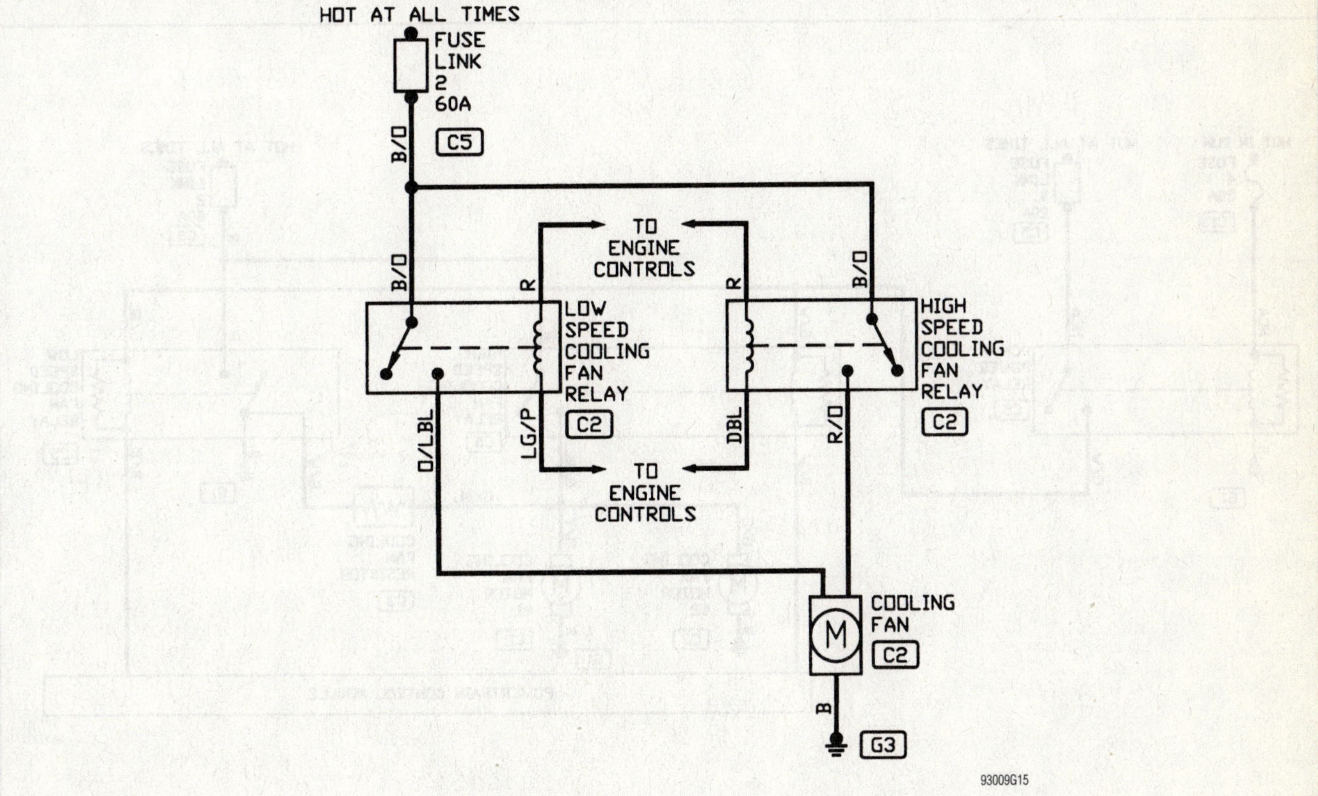

HOT AT ALL TIMES
FUSE
LINK
2
60A

B/O
C5

B/O

R

R

B/O

TO
ENGINE
CONTROLS

LOW
SPEED
COOLING
FAN
RELAY
C2

HIGH
SPEED
COOLING
FAN
RELAY
C2

O/LBL

LG/P

DBL

R/O

TO
ENGINE
CONTROLS

COOLING
FAN
C2

B

G3

93009G15

DIA. 12—Ford Continental 4.6L

Refer to the model specific sections for engine mechanical service procedures

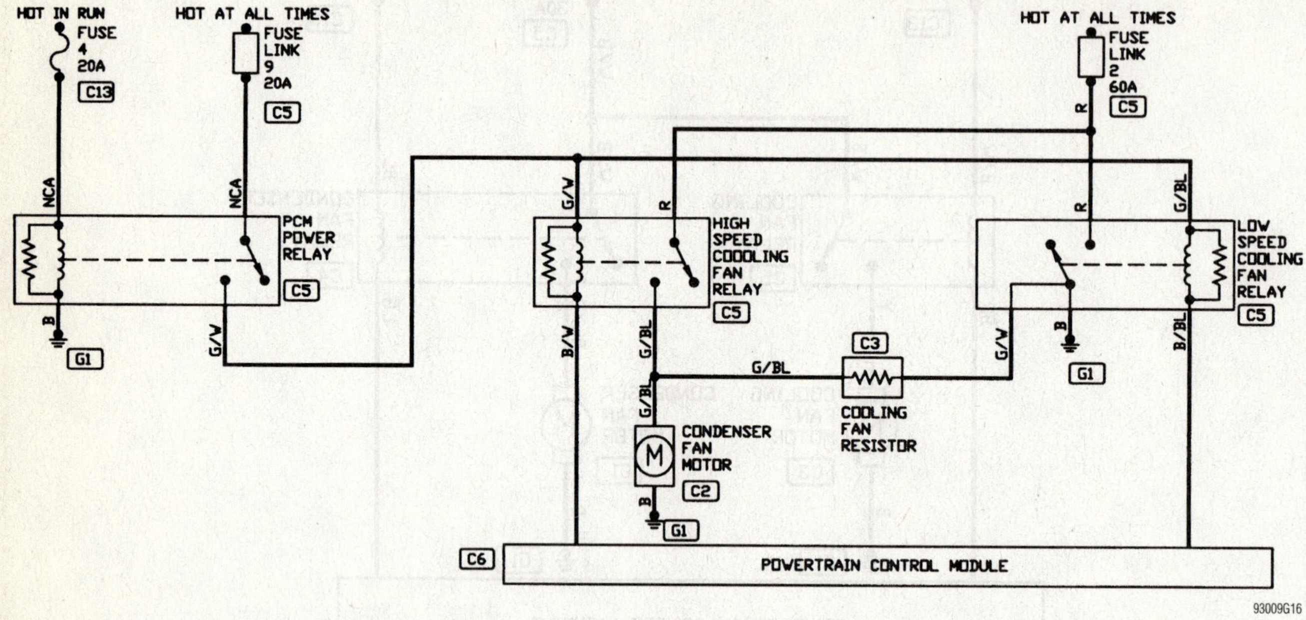

DIA. 13—Ford Contour/Mystique 2.0L

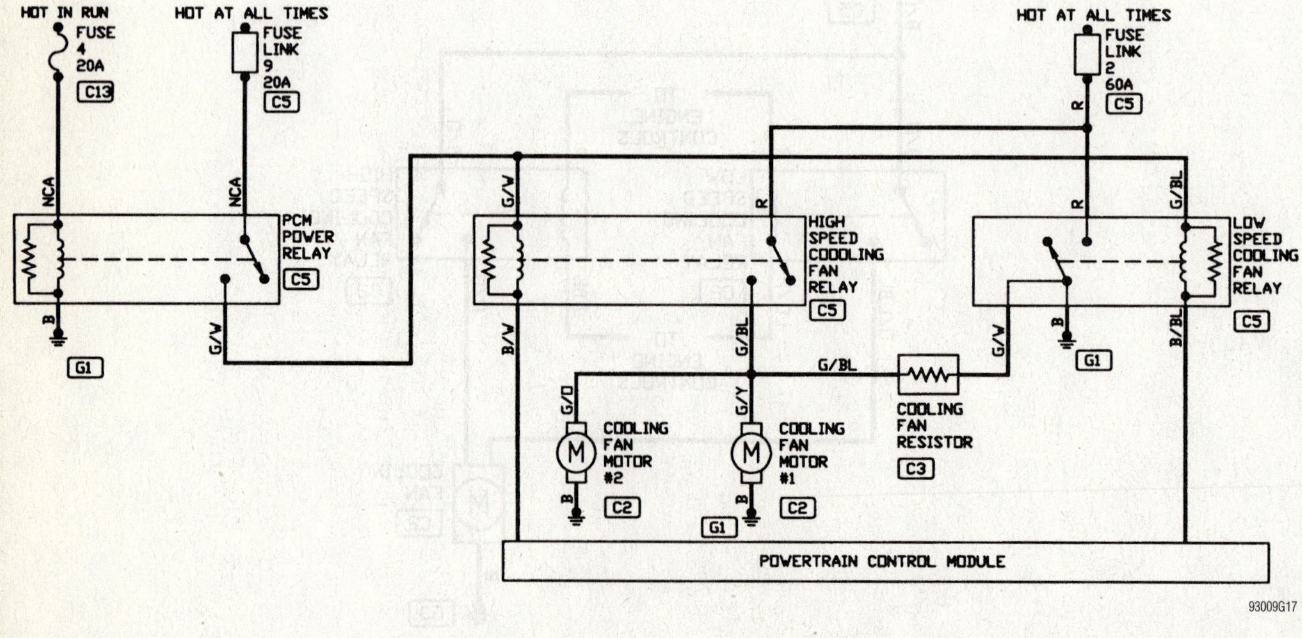

DIA. 14—Ford Contour/Mystique 2.5L

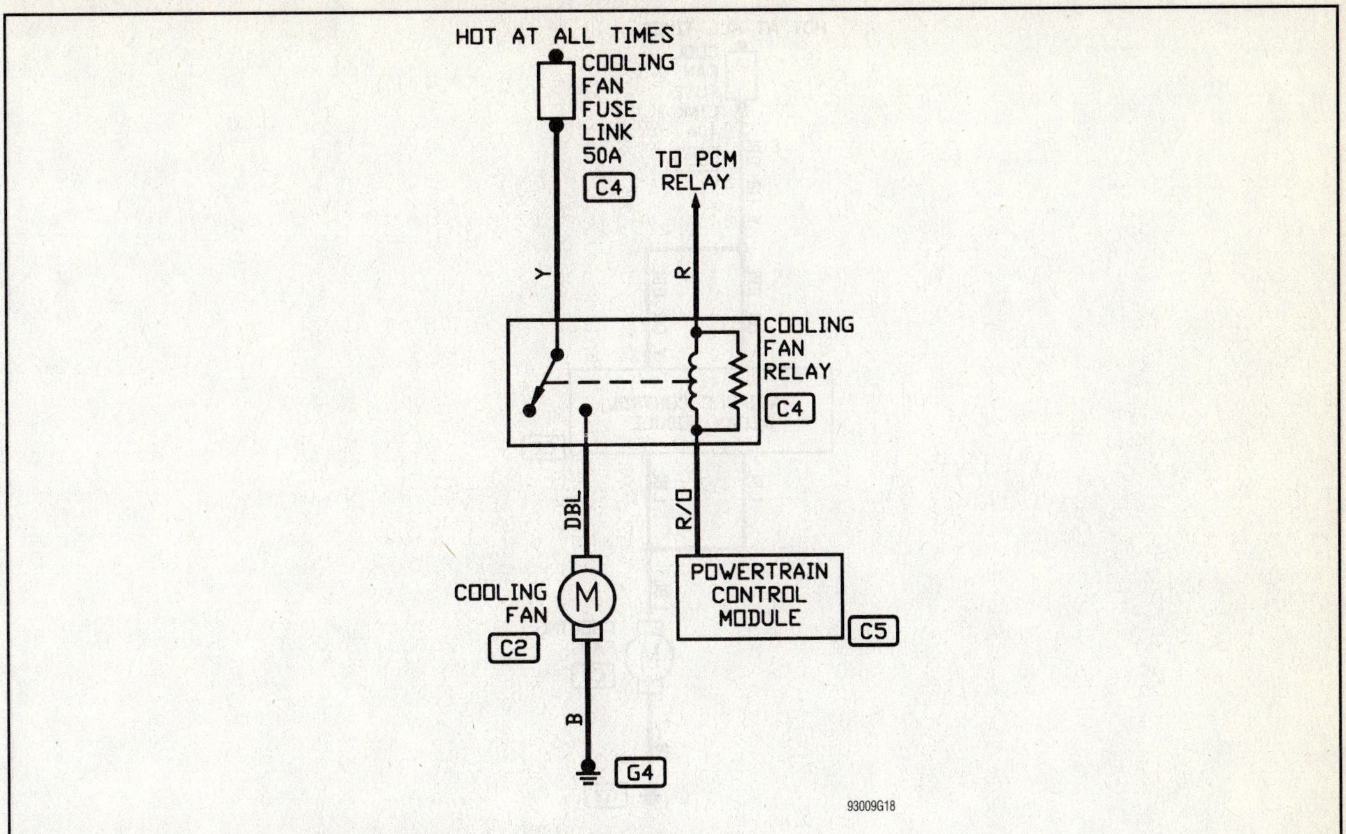

HOT AT ALL TIMES

COOLING
FAN
FUSE
LINK
50A
C4

TO PCM
RELAY

Y

R

COOLING
FAN
RELAY
C4

DBL

R/O

COOLING
FAN
C2

M

POWERTRAIN
CONTROL
MODULE
C5

B

G4

93009G18

DIA. 15—Ford Crown Victoria/Grand Marquis 4.6L

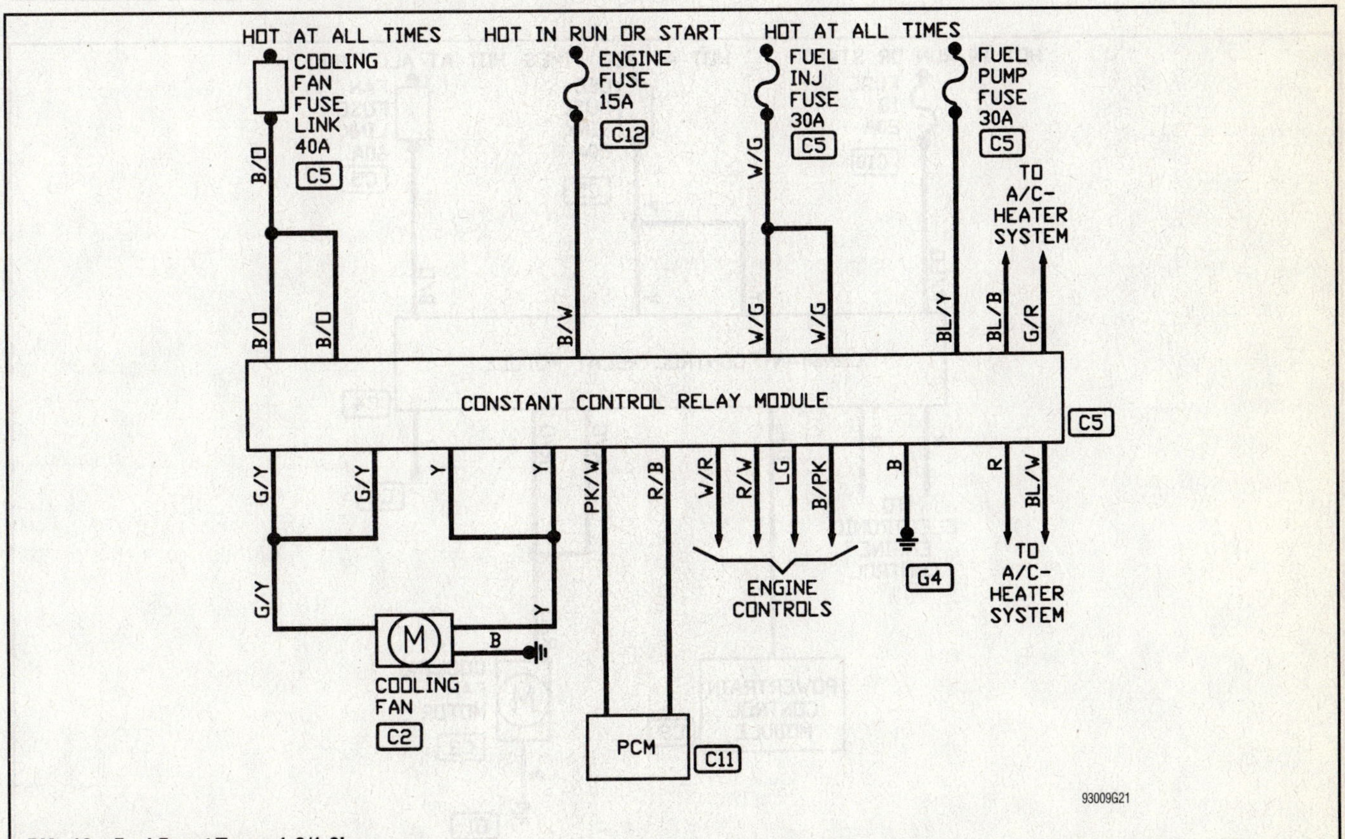

HOT AT ALL TIMES

COOLING
FAN
FUSE
LINK
40A
C5

B/O

HOT IN RUN OR START

ENGINE
FUSE
15A
C12

HOT AT ALL TIMES

FUEL
INJ
FUSE
30A
C5

HOT AT ALL TIMES

FUEL
PUMP
FUSE
30A
C5

TO
A/C-
HEATER
SYSTEM

B/O   B/O   B/W   W/G   W/G   BL/Y   BL/B   G/R

CONSTANT CONTROL RELAY MODULE   C5

G/Y   G/Y   Y   Y   PK/W   R/B   W/R   R/W   LG   B/PK   B   R   BL/W

G/Y   Y

M   B

COOLING
FAN
C2

PCM   C11

ENGINE
CONTROLS

G4

TO
A/C-
HEATER
SYSTEM

93009G21

DIA. 16—Ford Escort/Tracer 1.8/1.9L

Refer to the model specific sections for cooling system service procedures

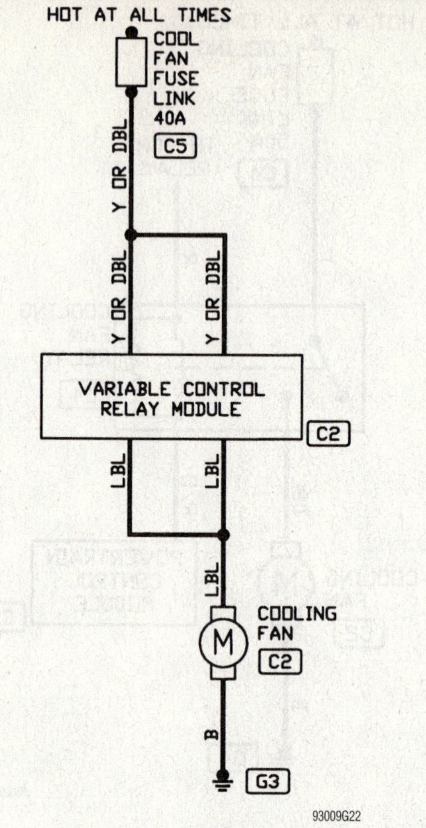

HOT AT ALL TIMES

COOL
FAN
FUSE
LINK
40A

C5

Y OR DBL

Y OR DBL

Y OR DBL

VARIABLE CONTROL
RELAY MODULE

C2

LBL

LBL

LBL

COOLING
FAN

M

C2

B

G3

93009G22

DIA. 17—1997–98 Ford Mark VIII 4.6L

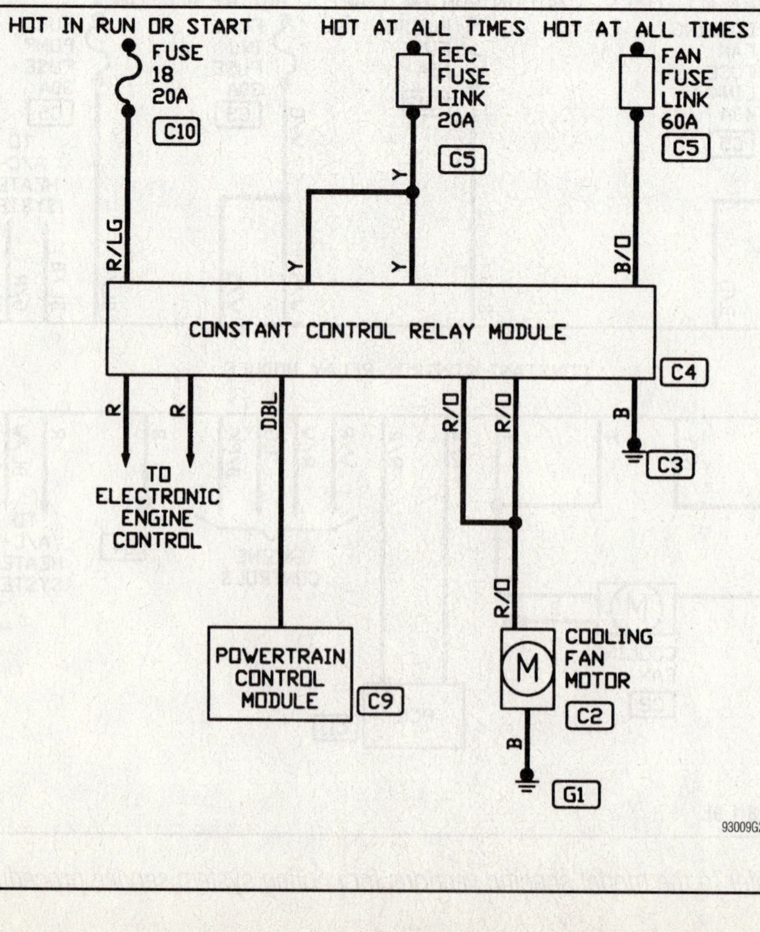

HOT IN RUN OR START

FUSE
18
20A

C10

HOT AT ALL TIMES

EEC
FUSE
LINK
20A

C5

HOT AT ALL TIMES

FAN
FUSE
LINK
60A

C5

R/LG

Y

Y

Y

B/O

CONSTANT CONTROL RELAY MODULE

C4

R

R

DBL

R/O

R/O

B

C3

TO
ELECTRONIC
ENGINE
CONTROL

POWERTRAIN
CONTROL
MODULE

C9

R/O

COOLING
FAN
MOTOR

M

C2

B

G1

93009G23

DIA. 18—Ford Mustang 3.8L

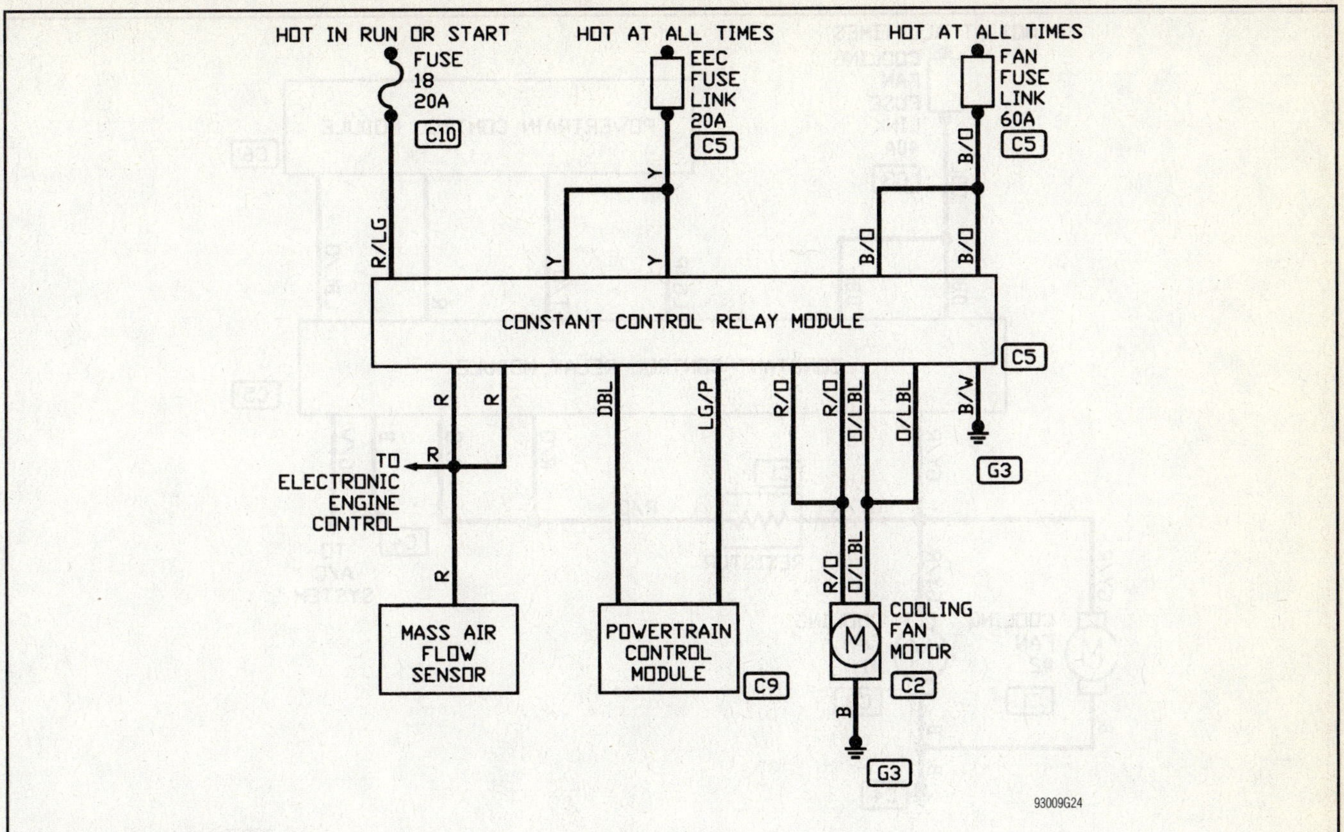

HOT IN RUN OR START
FUSE
18
20A
C10

HOT AT ALL TIMES
EEC
FUSE
LINK
20A
C5

HOT AT ALL TIMES
FAN
FUSE
LINK
60A
C5

R/LG

Y

Y   Y

B/O

B/O   B/O

CONSTANT CONTROL RELAY MODULE
C5

R   R

DBL   LG/P   R/O   R/O   O/LBL   O/LBL   B/W

G3

TO
ELECTRONIC
ENGINE
CONTROL   R

R/O
O/LBL

R

MASS AIR
FLOW
SENSOR

POWERTRAIN
CONTROL
MODULE
C9

M   COOLING
FAN
MOTOR
C2

B

G3

93009G24

DIA. 19—Ford Mustang 4.6L

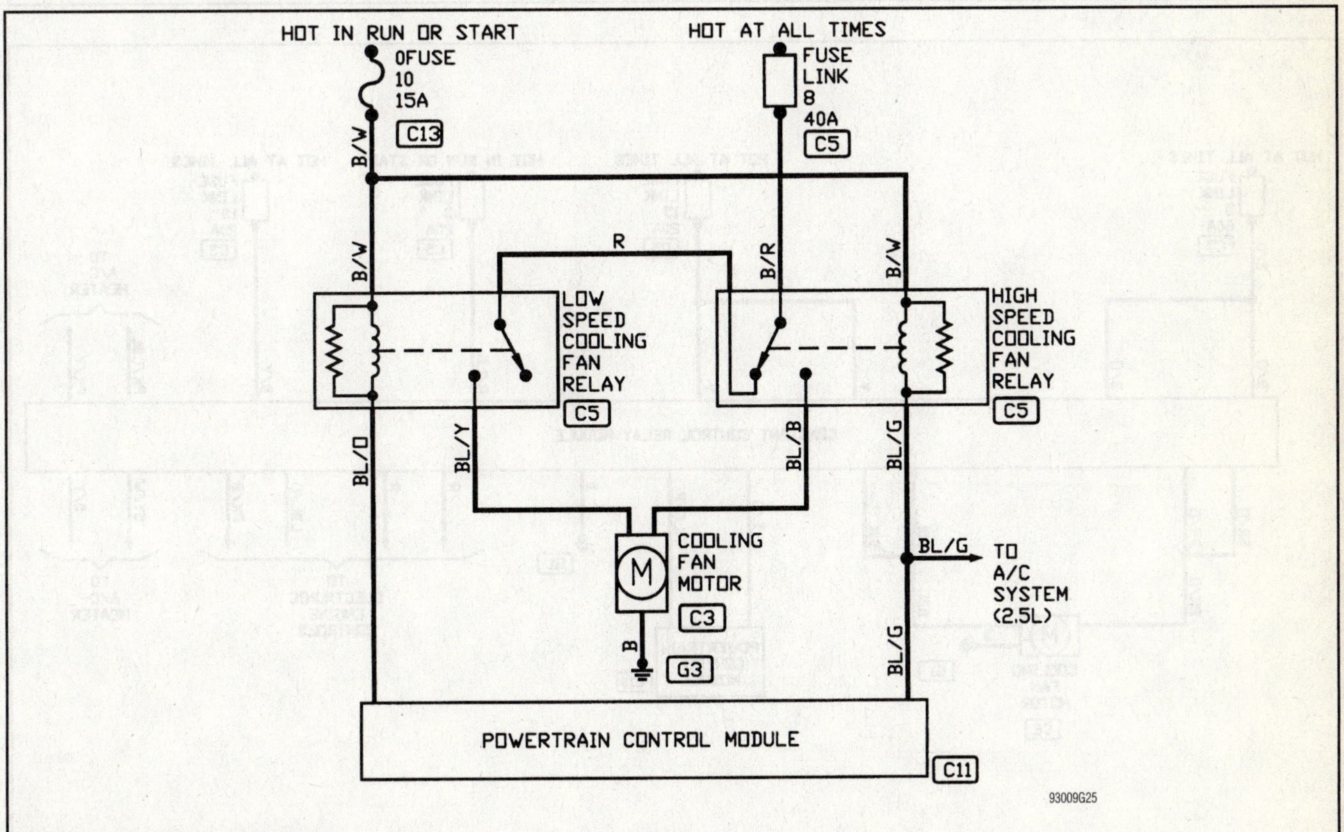

HOT IN RUN OR START
0FUSE
10
15A
C13

HOT AT ALL TIMES
FUSE
LINK
8
40A
C5

B/W

B/W   R   B/R   B/W

LOW
SPEED
COOLING
FAN
RELAY
C5

HIGH
SPEED
COOLING
FAN
RELAY
C5

BL/O   BL/Y   BL/B   BL/G

M   COOLING
FAN
MOTOR
C3

BL/G   TO
A/C
SYSTEM
(2.5L)

B

G3

BL/G

POWERTRAIN CONTROL MODULE
C11

93009G25

DIA. 20—1997 Ford Probe 2.0L/2.5L

For complete service labor times order Nichols' Chilton Labor Guide Manual

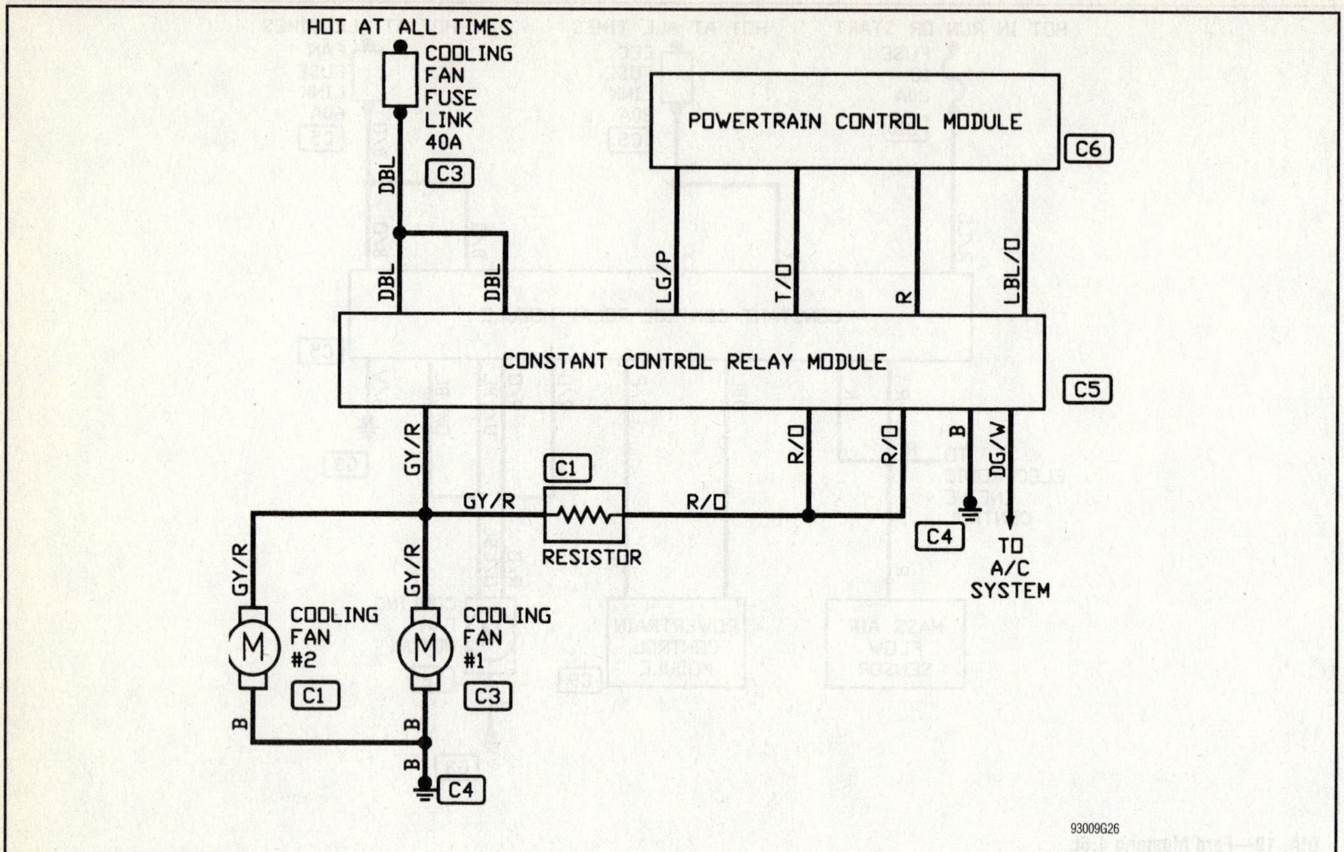

HOT AT ALL TIMES

COOLING
FAN
FUSE
LINK
40A
C3

DBL

POWERTRAIN CONTROL MODULE
C6

DBL DBL

LG/P T/O R LBL/O

CONSTANT CONTROL RELAY MODULE
C5

GY/R

GY/R

R/O R/O B DG/W

C1

GY/R RESISTOR R/O

C4

TO
A/C
SYSTEM

GY/R GY/R

M COOLING
FAN
#2
C1

M COOLING
FAN
#1
C3

B B

B

C4

93009G26

DIA. 21—Ford Taurus/Sable 3.0L/3.4L

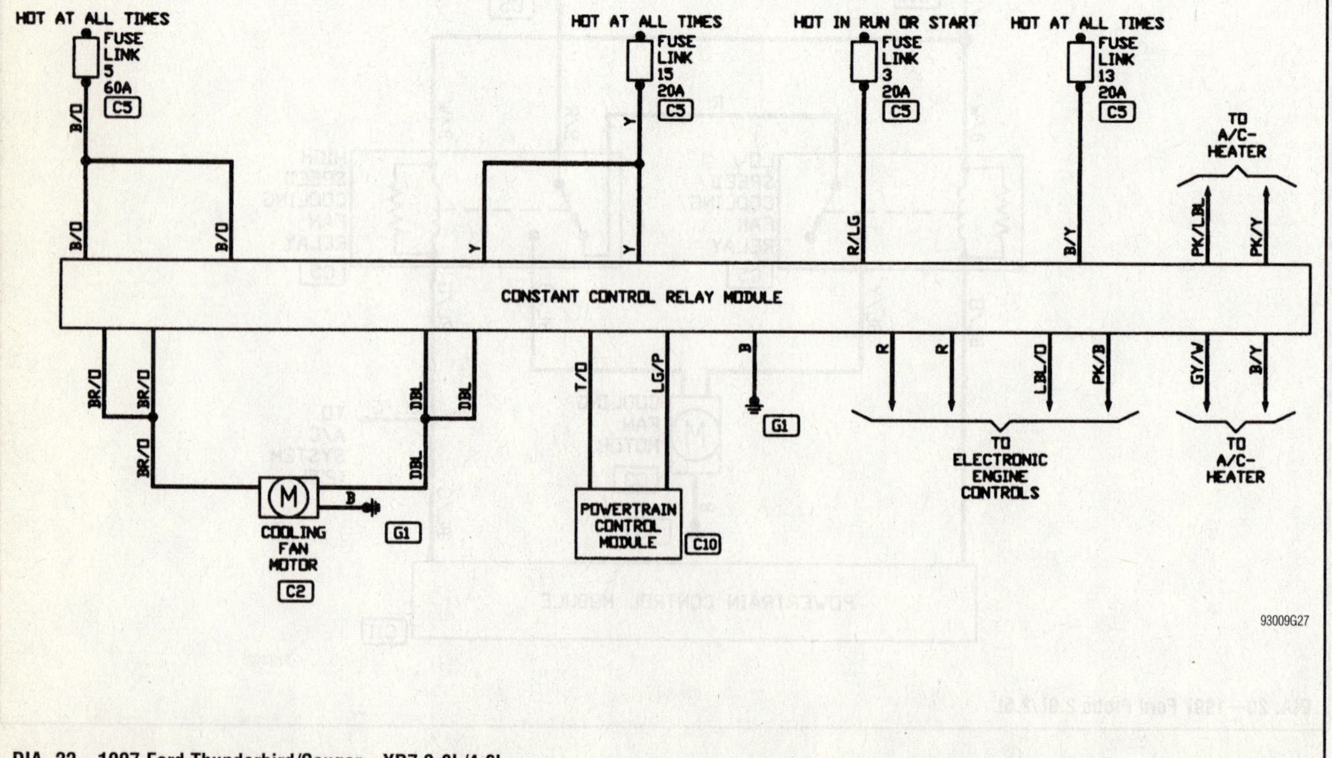

HOT AT ALL TIMES

FUSE
LINK
5
60A
C5

B/O

HOT AT ALL TIMES

FUSE
LINK
15
20A
C5

Y

HOT IN RUN OR START

FUSE
LINK
3
20A
C5

R/LG

HOT AT ALL TIMES

FUSE
LINK
13
20A
C5

B/Y

TO
A/C-
HEATER

B/O B/O

Y Y

PK/LBL PK/Y

CONSTANT CONTROL RELAY MODULE

BR/O BR/O

DBL DBL

T/O LG/P

B

G1

R R LBL/O PK/B GY/W B/Y

BR/O DBL

M COOLING
FAN
MOTOR
C2

B

G1

POWERTRAIN
CONTROL
MODULE
C10

TO
ELECTRONIC
ENGINE
CONTROLS

TO
A/C-
HEATER

93009G27

DIA. 22—1997 Ford Thunderbird/Cougar—XR7 3.8L/4.6L

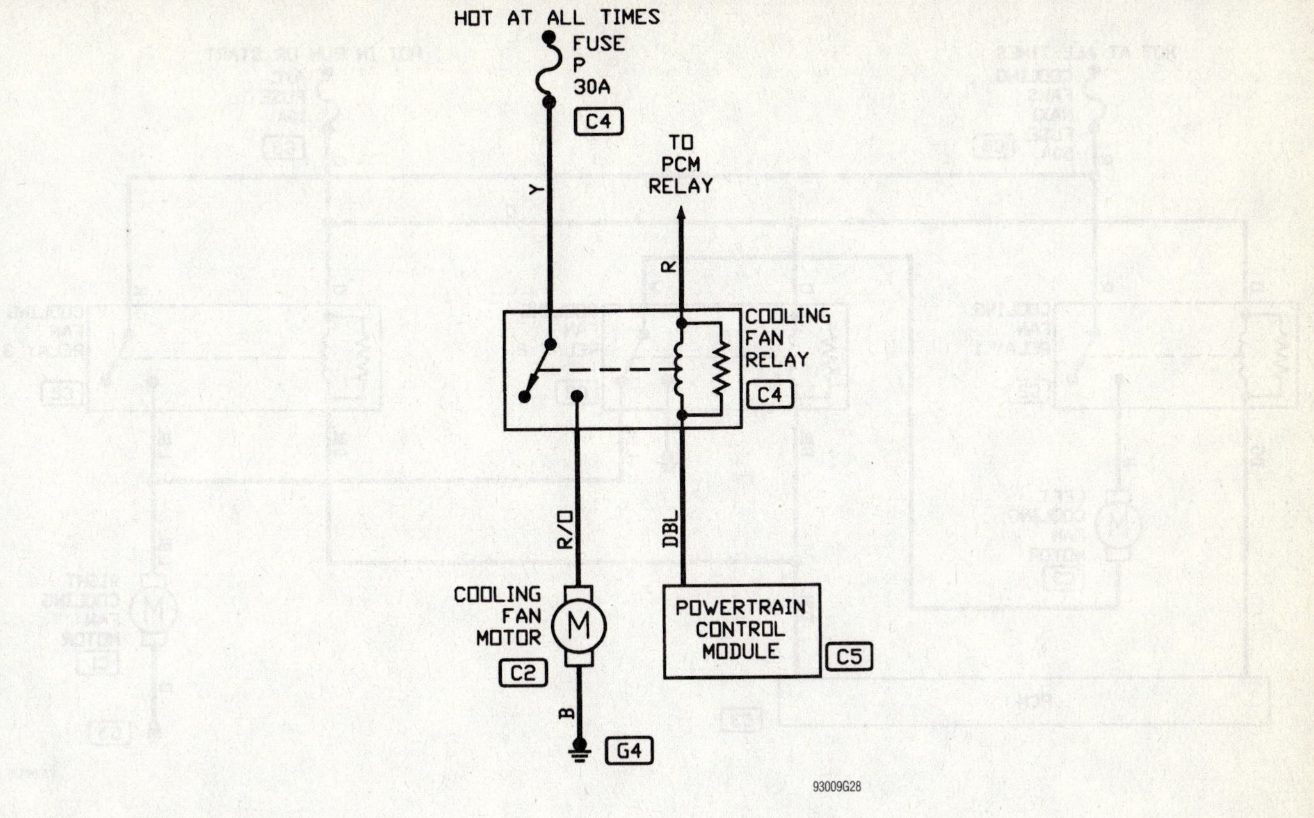

HOT AT ALL TIMES

FUSE
P
30A

C4

TO
PCM
RELAY

R

Y

COOLING
FAN
RELAY

C4

R/O

DBL

COOLING
FAN
MOTOR

M

C2

POWERTRAIN
CONTROL
MODULE

C5

B

G4

93009G28

DIA. 23—Lincoln Town Car 4.6L

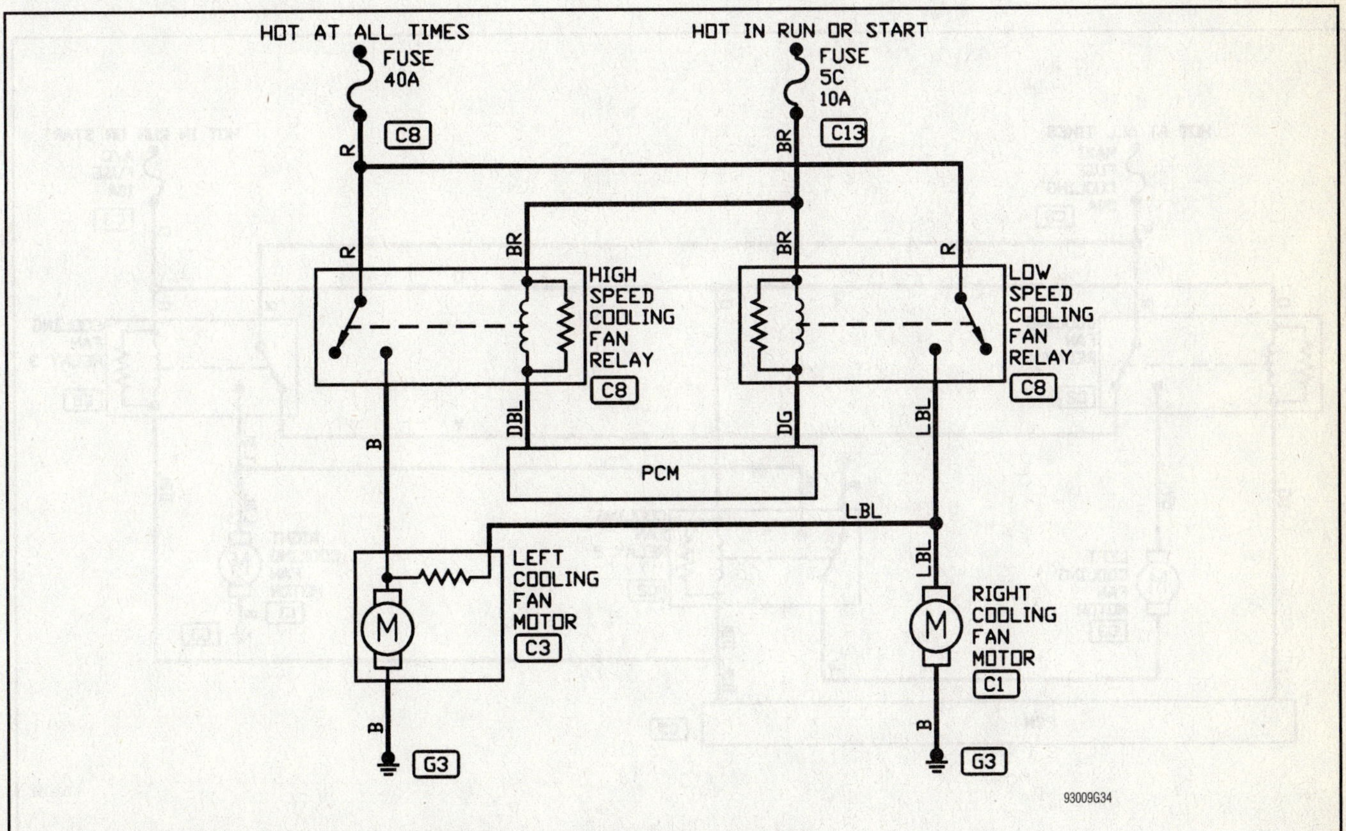

HOT AT ALL TIMES

FUSE
40A

C8

R

HOT IN RUN OR START

FUSE
5C
10A

C13

BR

R

BR

BR

BR

R

HIGH
SPEED
COOLING
FAN
RELAY

C8

LOW
SPEED
COOLING
FAN
RELAY

C8

B

DBL

DG

LBL

PCM

LBL

LBL

LBL

LEFT
COOLING
FAN
MOTOR

M

C3

RIGHT
COOLING
FAN
MOTOR

M

C1

B

G3

B

G3

93009G34

DIA. 24—1997–99 Bonneville/88/98/Le Sabre/LSS/Regency and 1997–01 Park Avenue 3.8L

Please visit our web site at www.chiltonsonline.com

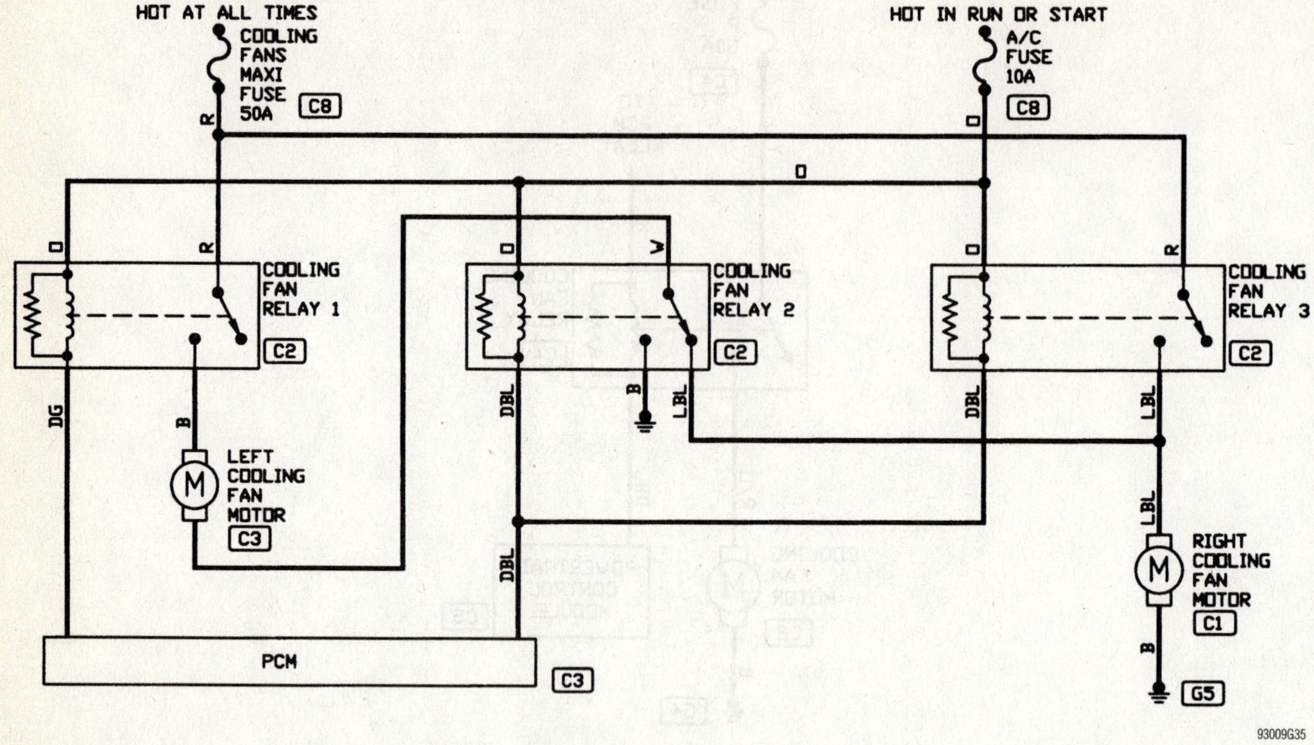

DIA. 25—1997 DeVille/Eldorado/Seville 4.6L

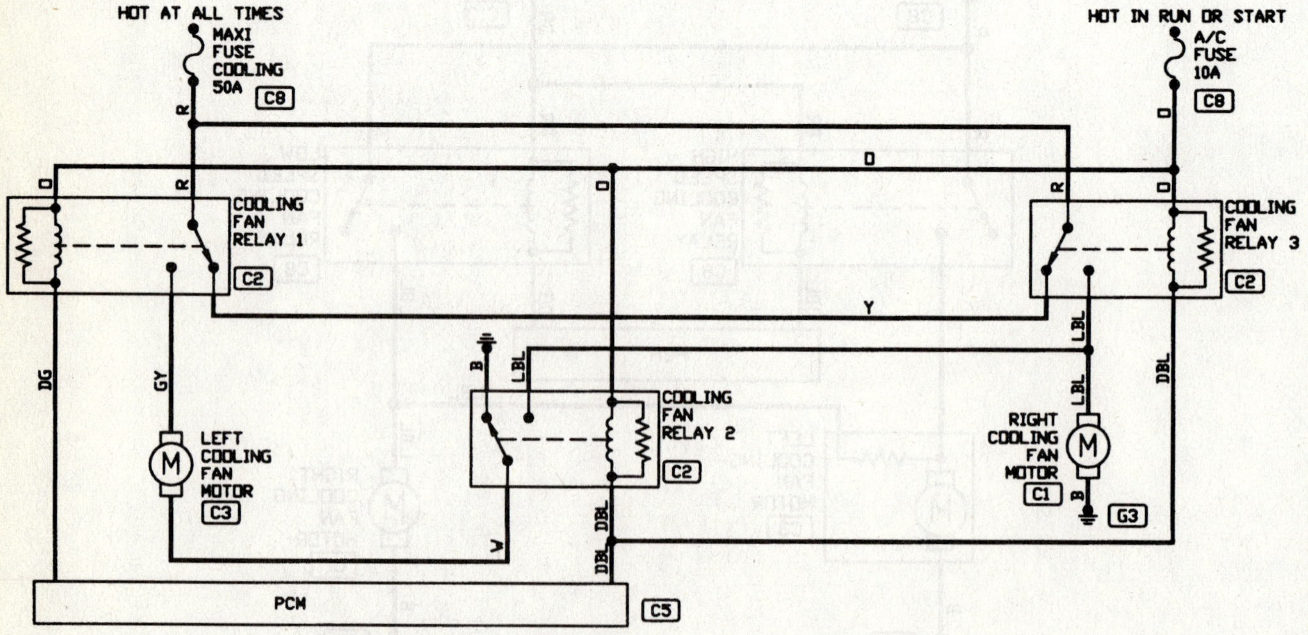

DIA. 26—1998–01 DeVille/Eldorado/Seville 4.6L

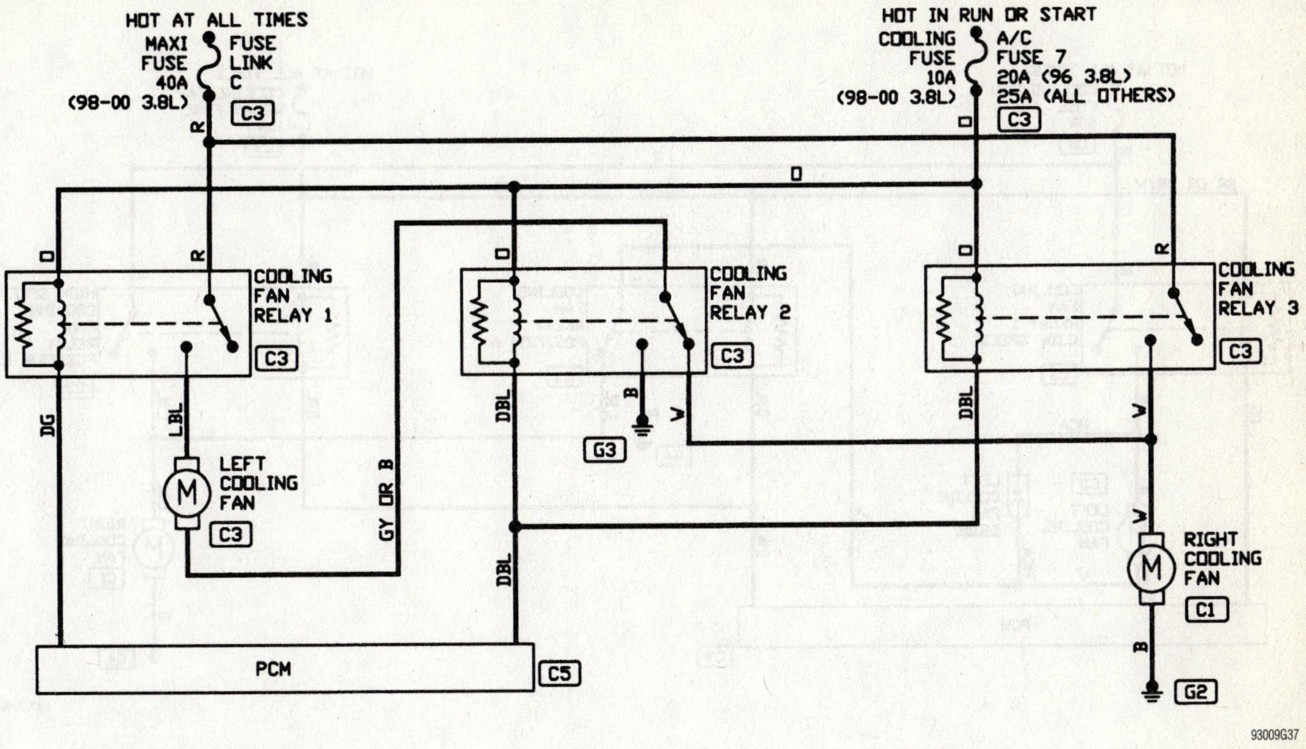

DIA. 27—Camaro/Firebird 3.8L/5.7L

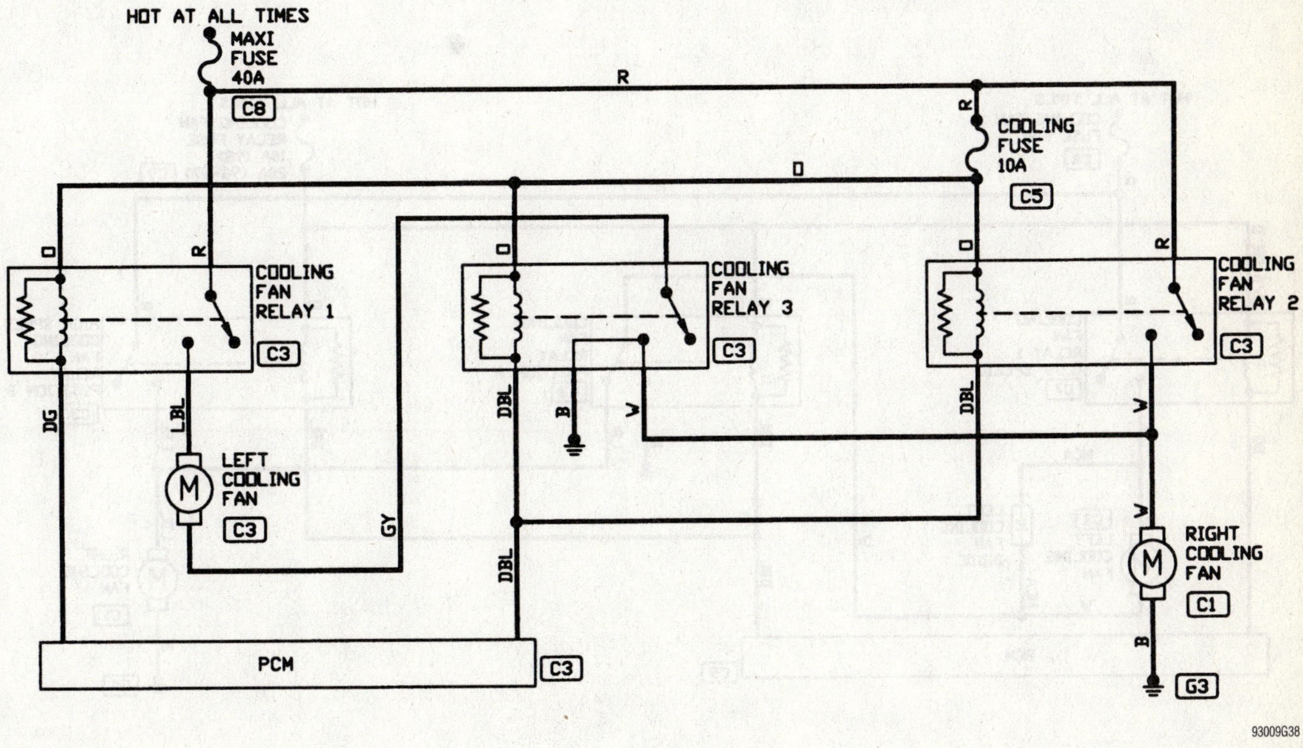

DIA. 28—1998–01 Camaro/Firebird 5.7L

Refer to the model specific sections for engine mechanical service procedures

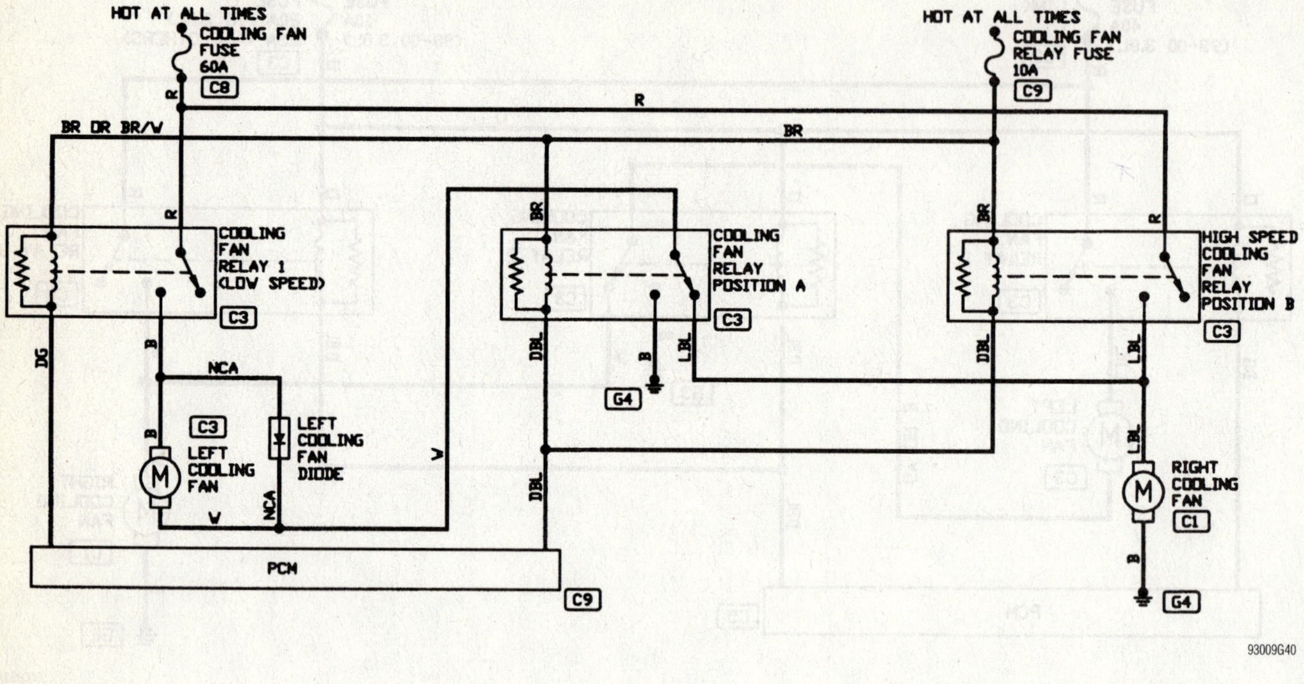

DIA. 29—Aurora/Riviera 3.8L

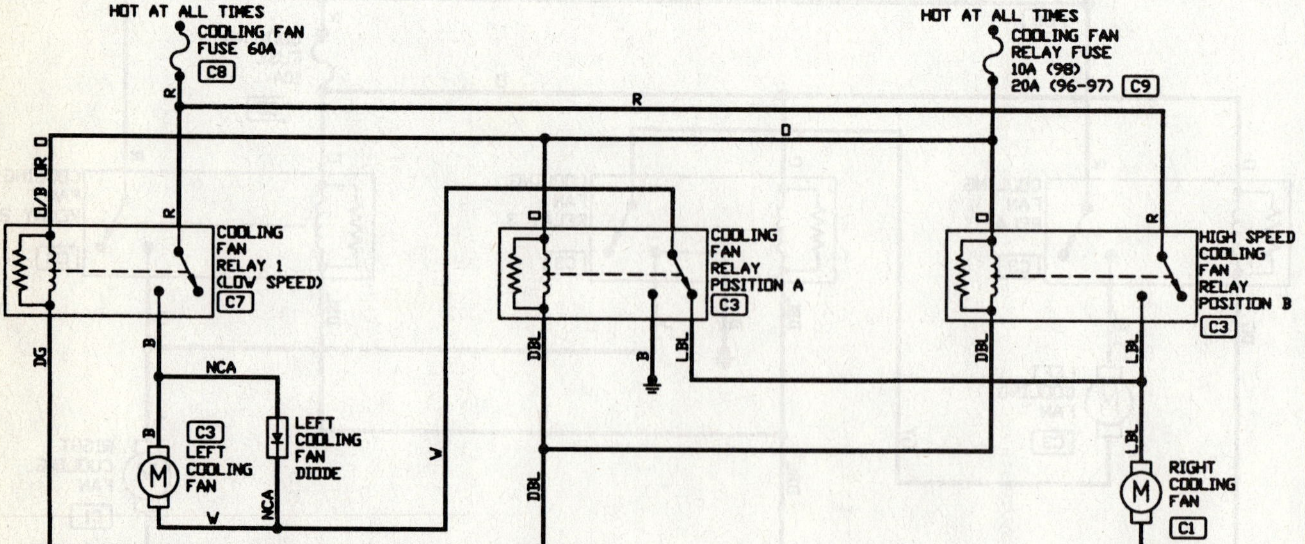

DIA. 30—Aurora/Riviera 4.0L

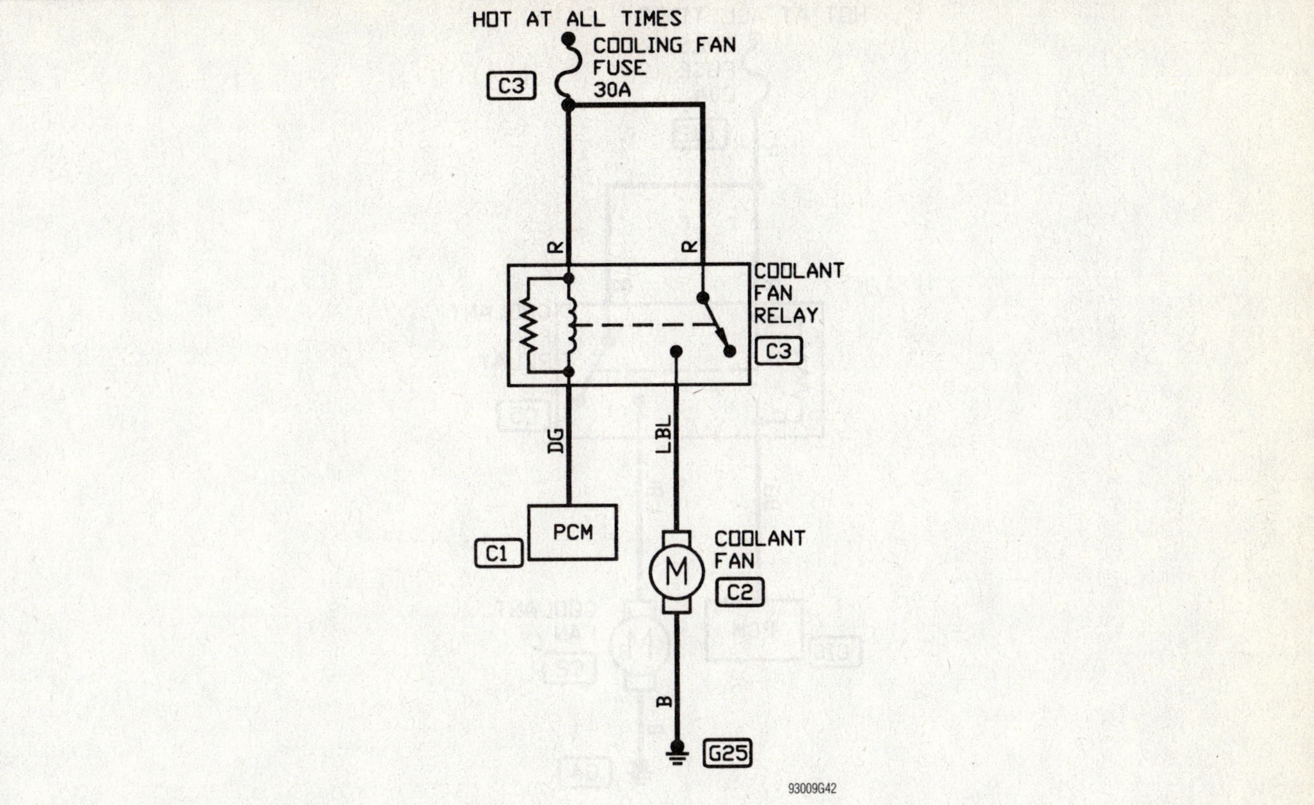

HOT AT ALL TIMES

COOLING FAN
FUSE
30A

C3

R   R   COOLANT
              FAN
              RELAY

              C3

DG   LBL

C1 PCM   COOLANT
             FAN
         M   C2

             B

             G25

93009G42

DIA. 31—Cavalier/Sunfire 2.2L/2.3L/2.4L

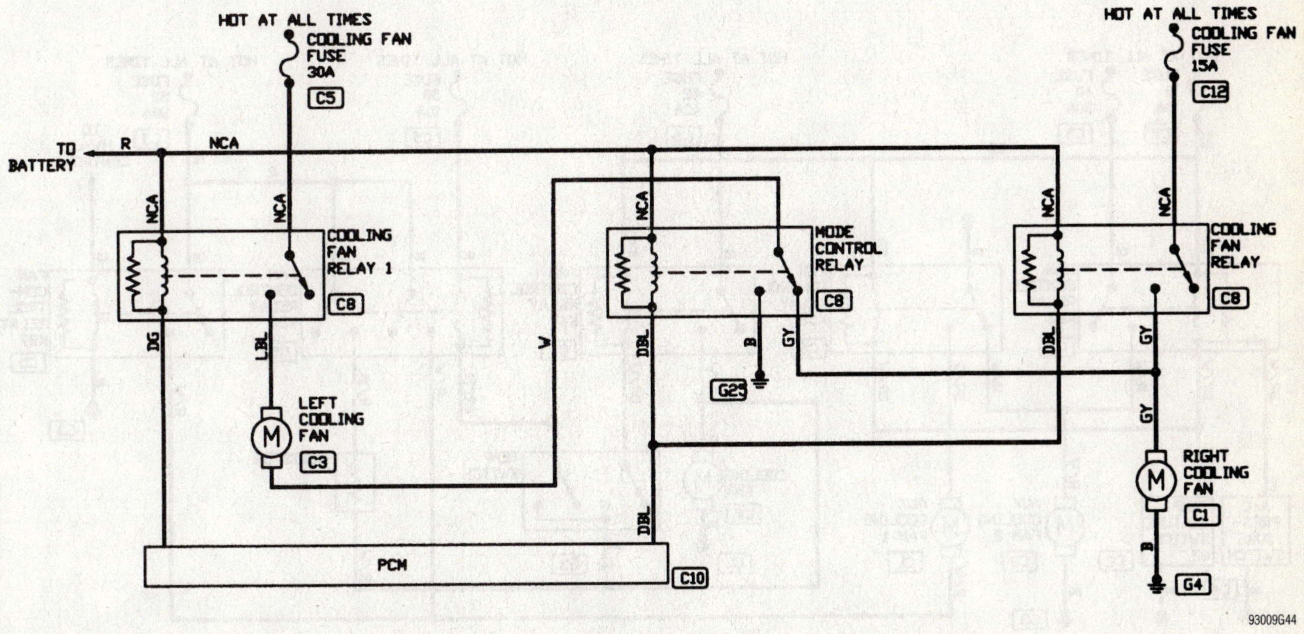

HOT AT ALL TIMES   HOT AT ALL TIMES

COOLING FAN   COOLING FAN
FUSE   FUSE
30A   15A

C5   C12

TO   R   NCA   NCA
BATTERY

NCA   NCA   NCA   NCA   NCA

              COOLING   MODE   COOLING
              FAN   CONTROL   FAN
              RELAY 1   RELAY   RELAY

              C8   C8   C8

DG   LBL   V   DBL   B   GY   DBL   GY

      LEFT   GY
      COOLING
  M   FAN   G25   RIGHT
      C3   M   COOLING
                                                          FAN
                                                          C1

                                                          B
              DBL
PCM   C10   G4

                                                   93009G44

DIA. 32—Cutlass/Malibu 2.4L/3.1L

Refer to the model specific sections for cooling system service procedures

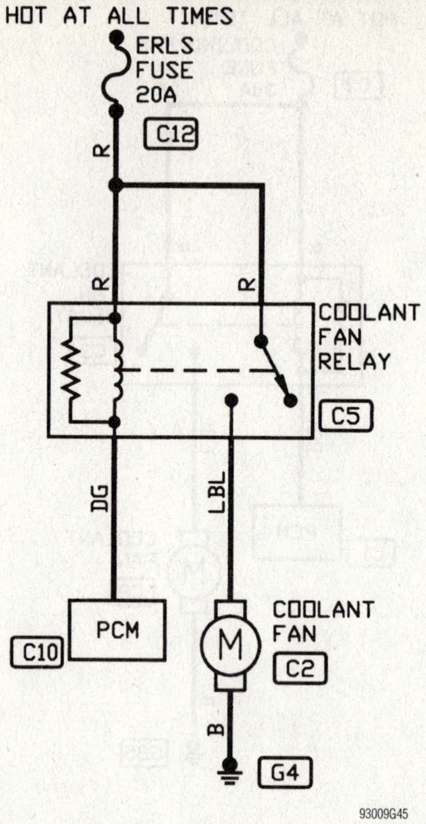

HOT AT ALL TIMES

ERLS
FUSE
20A

C12

R

R   R

COOLANT
FAN
RELAY

C5

DG   LBL

C10 PCM

COOLANT
FAN

C2

M

B

G4

93009G45

DIA. 33—Achieva/Grand Am/Skylark 2.3L/2.4L/3.1L

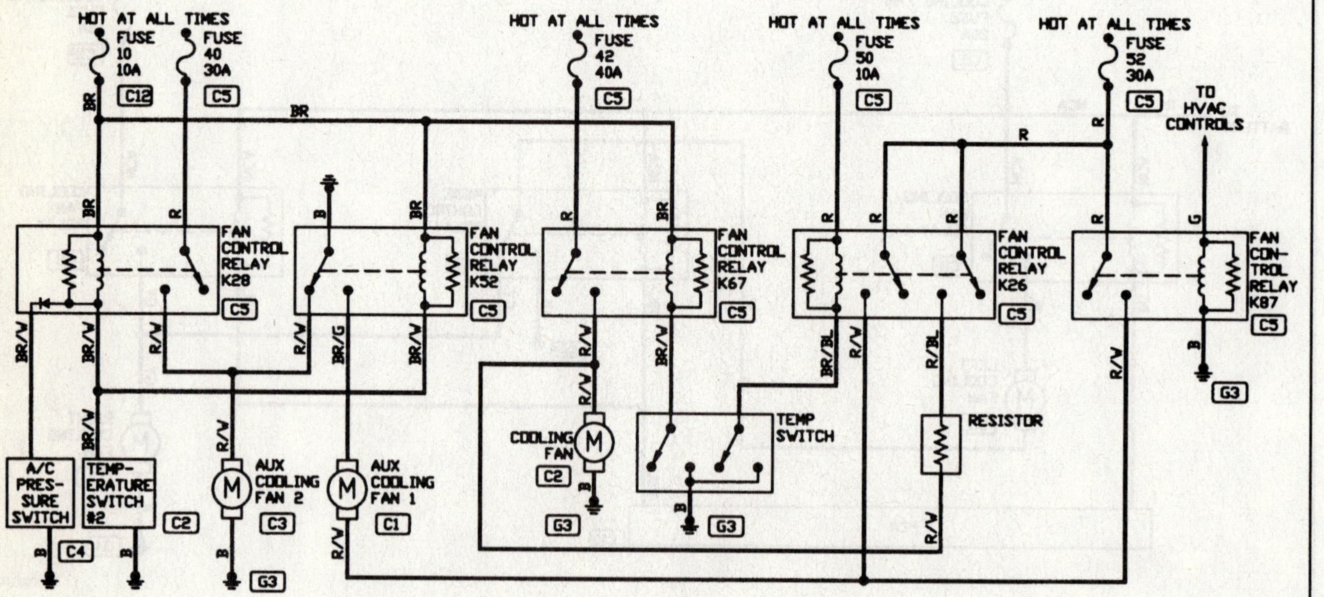

HOT AT ALL TIMES   HOT AT ALL TIMES   HOT AT ALL TIMES   HOT AT ALL TIMES

FUSE   FUSE   FUSE   FUSE   FUSE
10   40   42   50   52
10A   30A   40A   10A   30A

C12   C5   BR   C5   C5   R   C5
                                                                                     TO
BR   R   R   HVAC
                                                                                     CONTROLS

BR   R   B   BR   BR   R   R   R   G

FAN   FAN   FAN   FAN   FAN
CONTROL   CONTROL   CONTROL   CONTROL   CON-
RELAY   RELAY   RELAY   RELAY   TROL
K28   K52   K67   K26   RELAY
                                                                                                 K87
C5   C5   C5   C5   C5

BR/V   BR/V R/V   R/V   BR/G BR/V   R/V R/V BR/V   BR/BL R/V R/BL   R/V   B

                                                                                                 G3

A/C   TEMP-   AUX   AUX   COOLING   TEMP   RESISTOR
PRES- ERATURE   COOLING   COOLING   FAN   SWITCH
SURE   SWITCH   FAN 2   FAN 1   R/V
SWITCH #2   C2
       C2   M   C3   M   C1   R/V
C4   G3   G3
                    B   B   B
B   G3   R/V
                                                                              R/V
                                                  R/V

93009G46

DIA. 34—Catera 3.0L

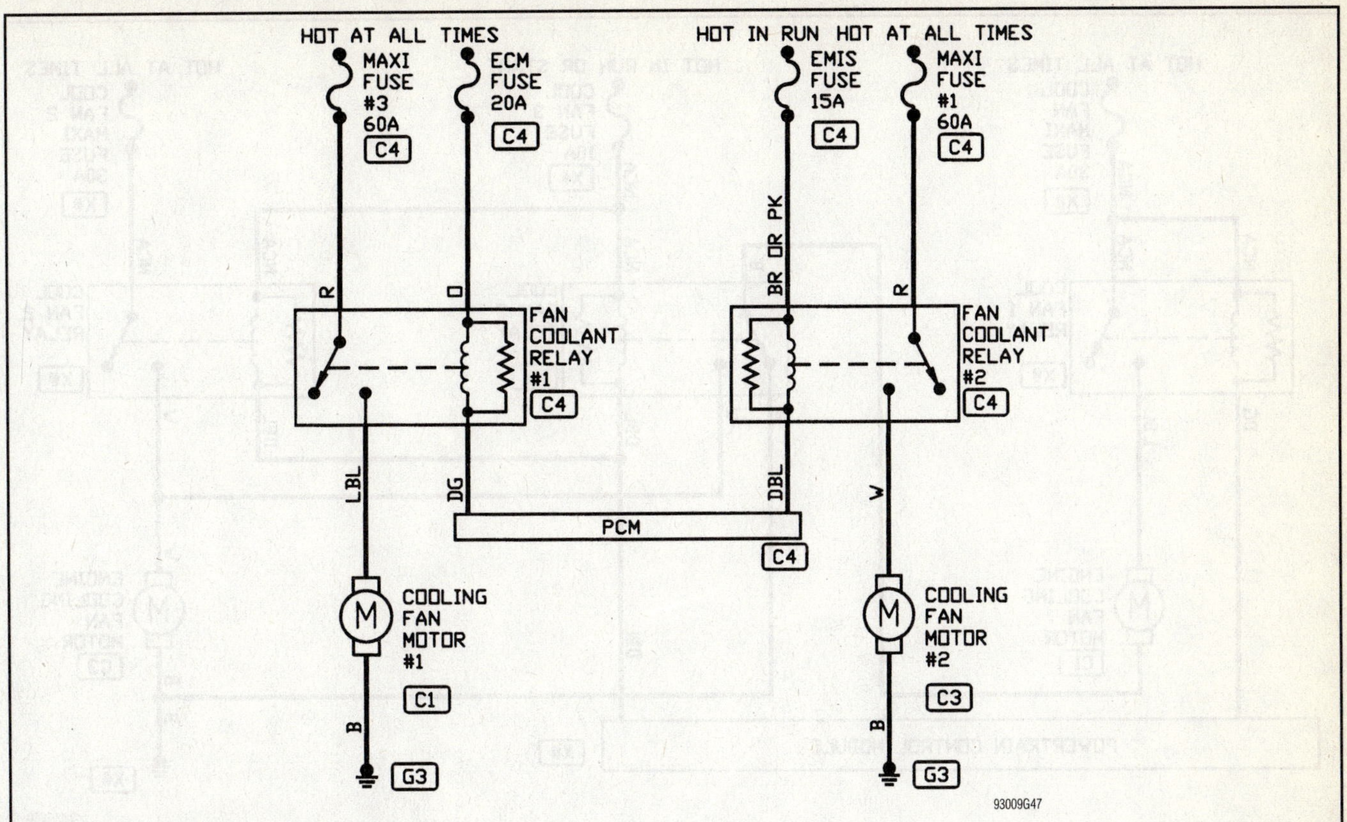

HOT AT ALL TIMES

HOT IN RUN   HOT AT ALL TIMES

MAXI FUSE #3 60A
C4

ECM FUSE 20A
C4

EMIS FUSE 15A
C4

MAXI FUSE #1 60A
C4

R

O

BR OR PK

R

FAN COOLANT RELAY #1
C4

FAN COOLANT RELAY #2
C4

LBL

DG

DBL

W

PCM
C4

M COOLING FAN MOTOR #1
C1

M COOLING FAN MOTOR #2
C3

B
G3

B
G3

93009G47

DIA. 35—1997 Cutlass Supreme 3.1L/3.4L

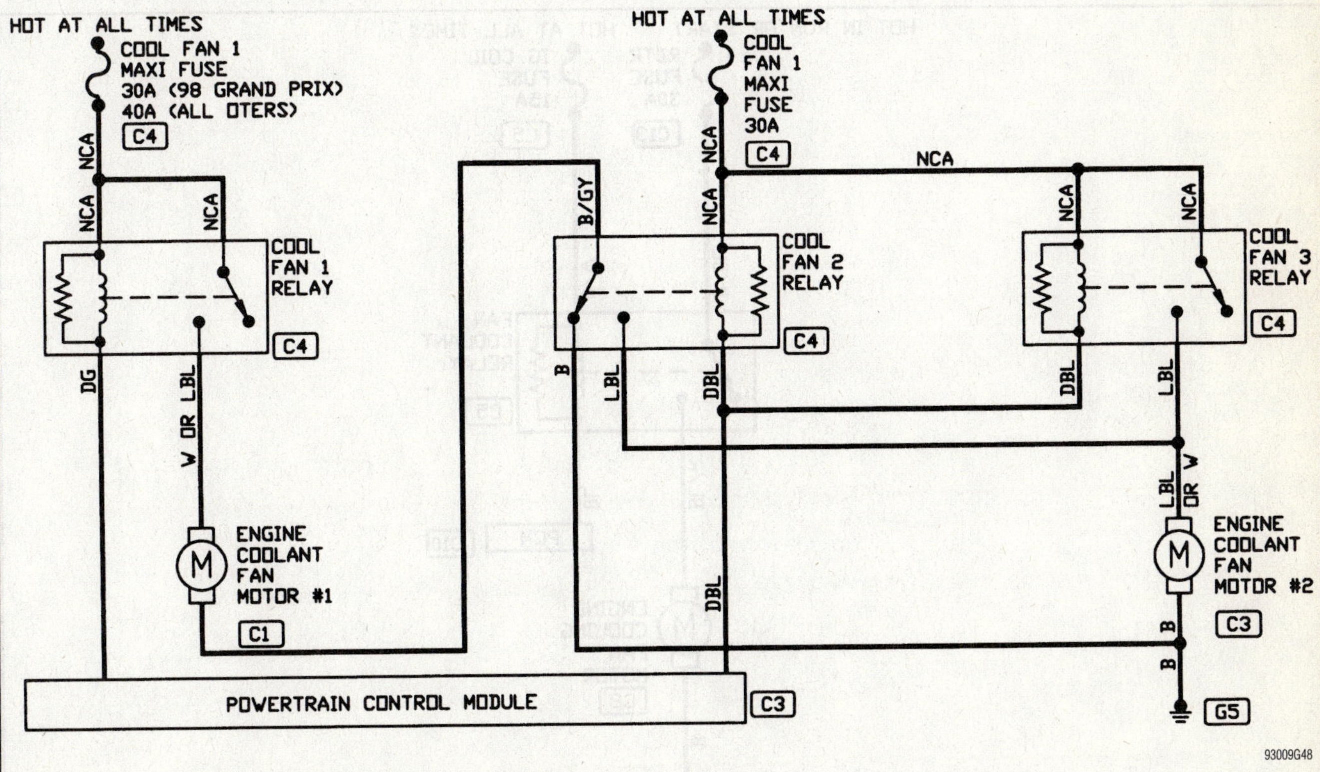

HOT AT ALL TIMES

HOT AT ALL TIMES

COOL FAN 1 MAXI FUSE 30A (98 GRAND PRIX) 40A (ALL OTERS)
C4

COOL FAN 1 MAXI FUSE 30A
C4

NCA   NCA

NCA

NCA

NCA

NCA

NCA

NCA   NCA

B/GY

COOL FAN 1 RELAY
C4

COOL FAN 2 RELAY
C4

COOL FAN 3 RELAY
C4

DG

W OR LBL

B

LBL

DBL

DBL

LBL

LBL OR V

M ENGINE COOLANT FAN MOTOR #1
C1

M ENGINE COOLANT FAN MOTOR #2
C3

DBL

B

B
G5

POWERTRAIN CONTROL MODULE
C3

93009G48

DIA. 36—Century/Grand Prix/Regal and 1998–01 Intrigue 3.1L/3.8L

For complete service labor times order Nichols' Chilton Labor Guide Manual

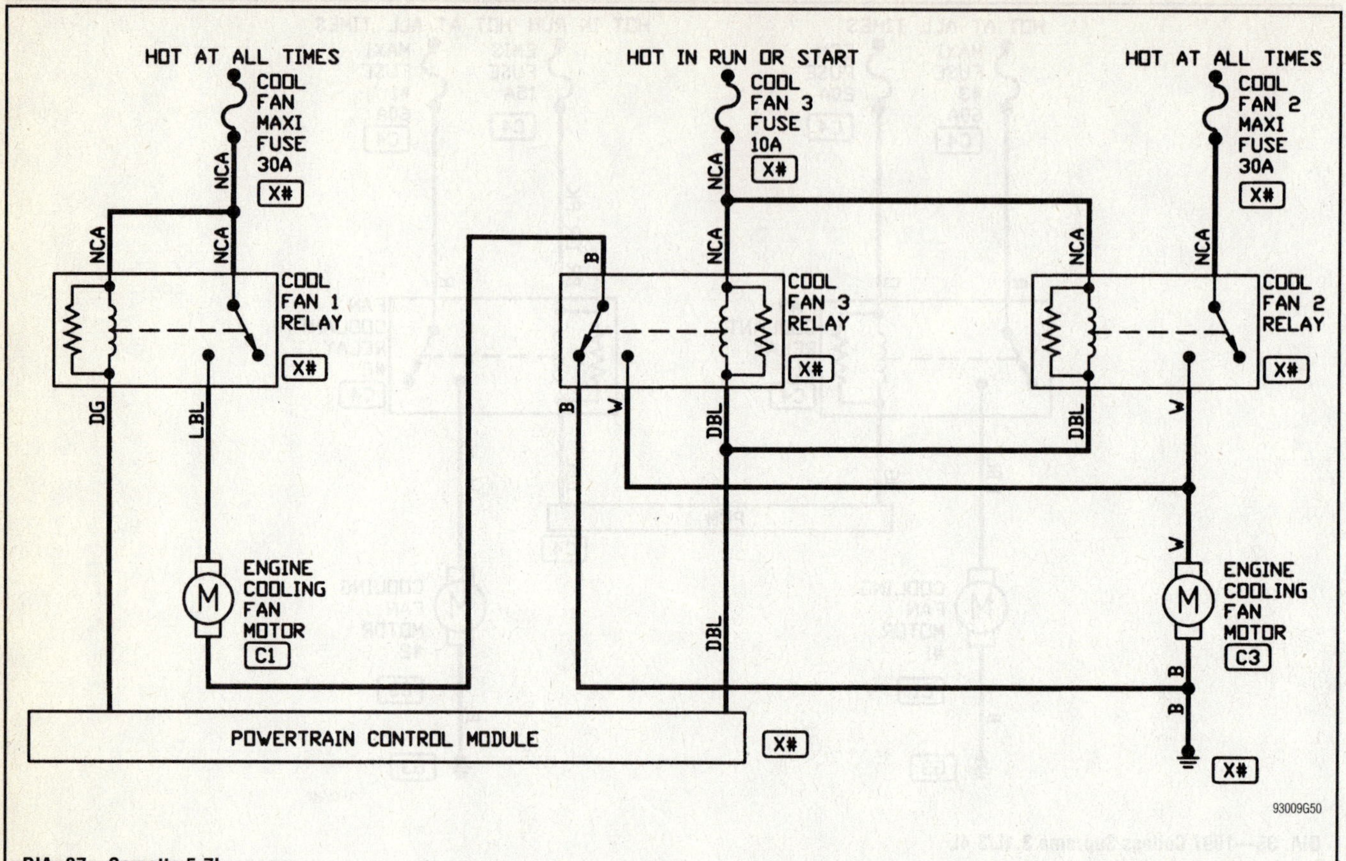

DIA. 37—Corvette 5.7L

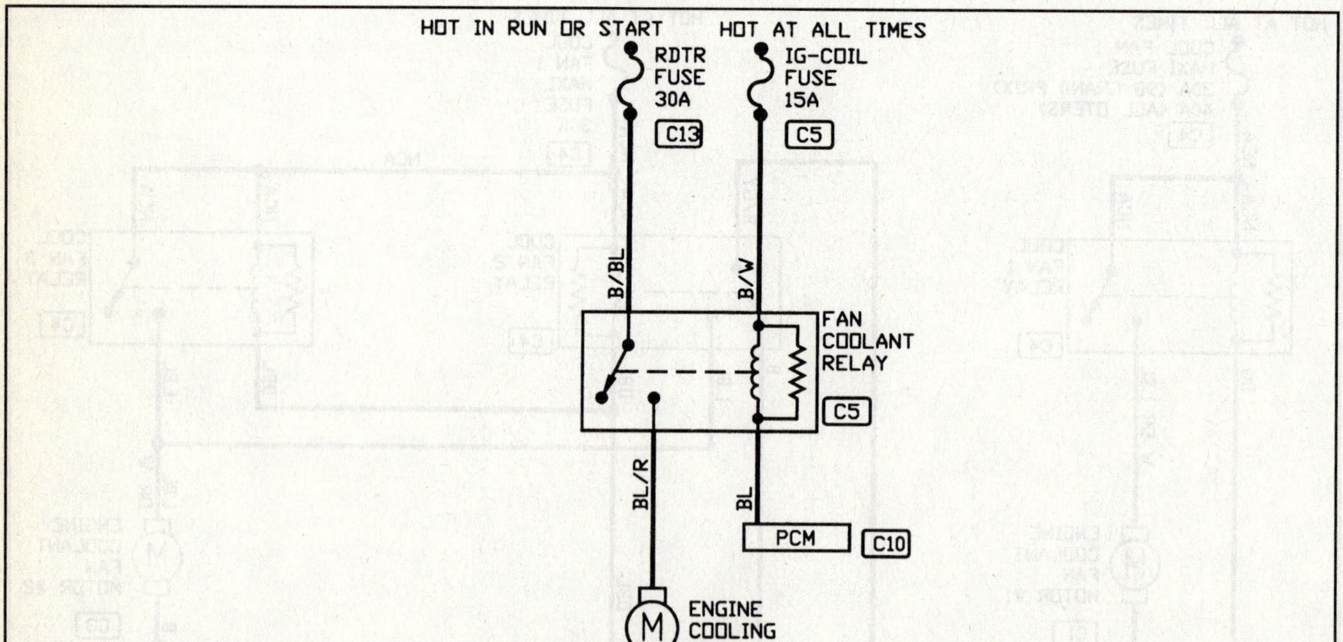

DIA. 38—Metro 1.0L/1.3L (w/o A/C)

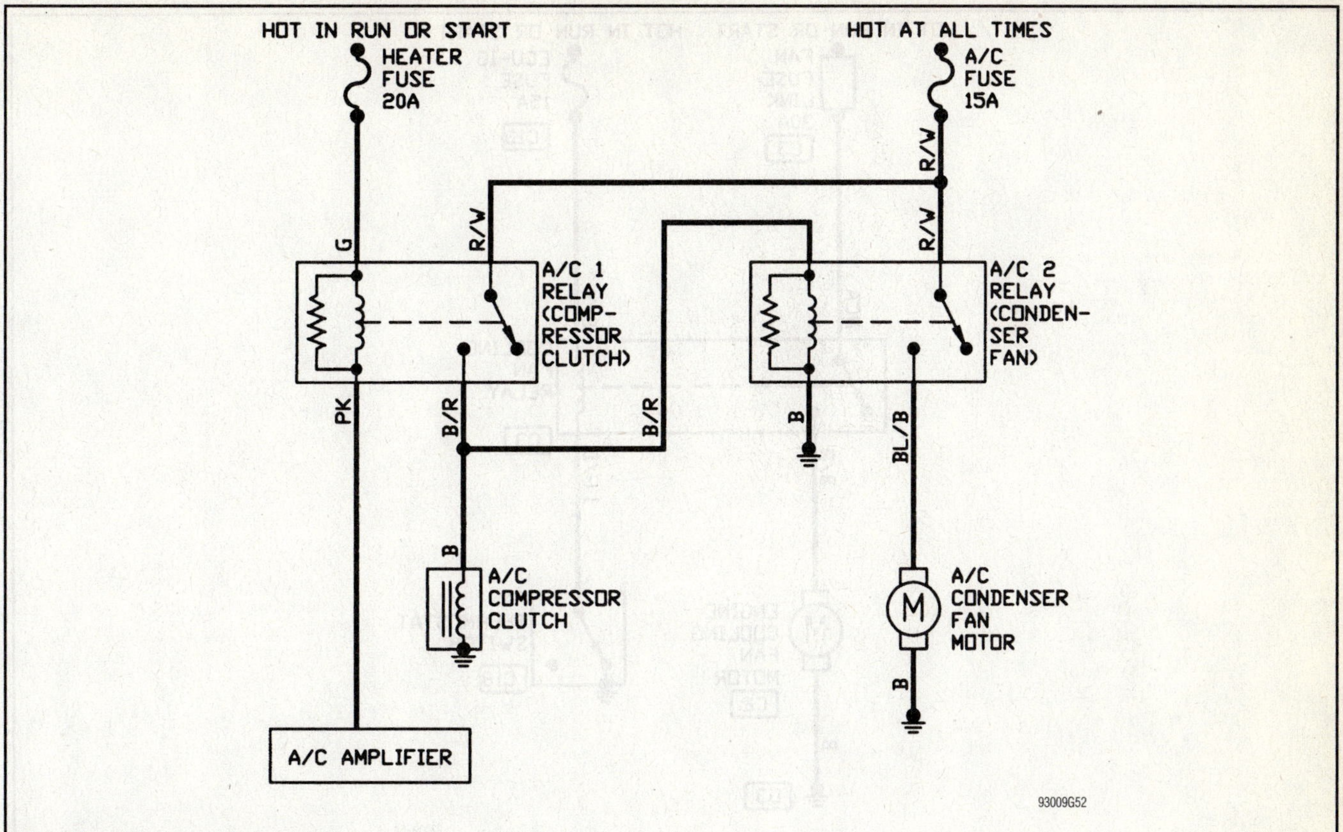

HOT IN RUN OR START

HEATER
FUSE
20A

HOT AT ALL TIMES

A/C
FUSE
15A

G

R/W

R/W

R/W

A/C 1
RELAY
(COMP-
RESSOR
CLUTCH)

A/C 2
RELAY
(CONDEN-
SER
FAN)

PK

B/R

B/R

B

BL/B

B

A/C
COMPRESSOR
CLUTCH

M

A/C
CONDEN-
SER
FAN
MOTOR

B

A/C AMPLIFIER

93009G52

DIA. 39—Metro 1.0L/1.3L (w/ A/C)

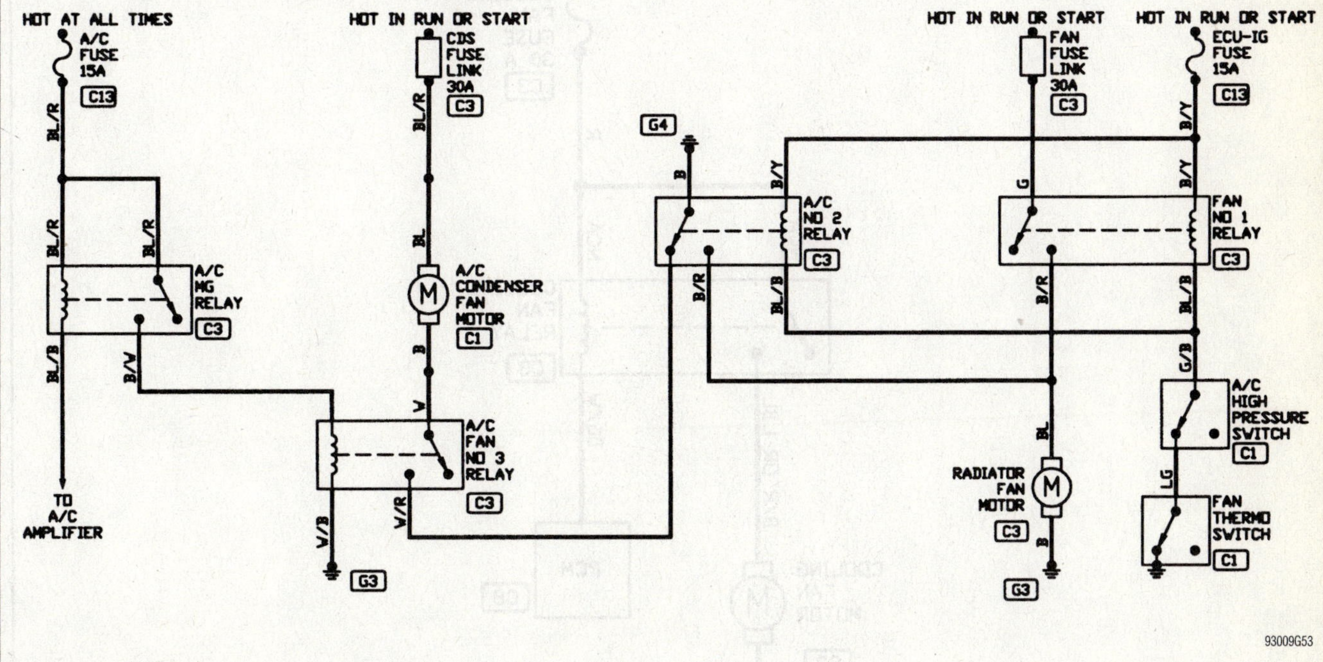

HOT AT ALL TIMES

A/C
FUSE
15A
C13

BL/R

BL/R

BL/R

A/C
MG
RELAY
C3

BL/B

B/V

TO
A/C
AMPLIFIER

HOT IN RUN OR START

CDS
FUSE
LINK
30A
C3

BL/R

BL

M

A/C
CONDENSER
FAN
MOTOR
C1

B

V

A/C
FAN
NO 3
RELAY
C3

V/B

V/R

V/B

V/R

G3

G4

B

B/Y

A/C
NO 2
RELAY
C3

B/R

BL/B

HOT IN RUN OR START

FAN
FUSE
LINK
30A
C3

B/Y

G

B/R

FAN
NO 1
RELAY
C3

BL/B

HOT IN RUN OR START

ECU-IG
FUSE
15A
C13

B/Y

B/Y

G/3

BL/B

A/C
HIGH
PRESSURE
SWITCH
C1

LG

FAN
THERMO
SWITCH
C1

BL

RADIATOR
FAN
MOTOR
C3

M

B

G3

93009G53

DIA. 40—Prism 1.6L/1.8L (w/ A/C)

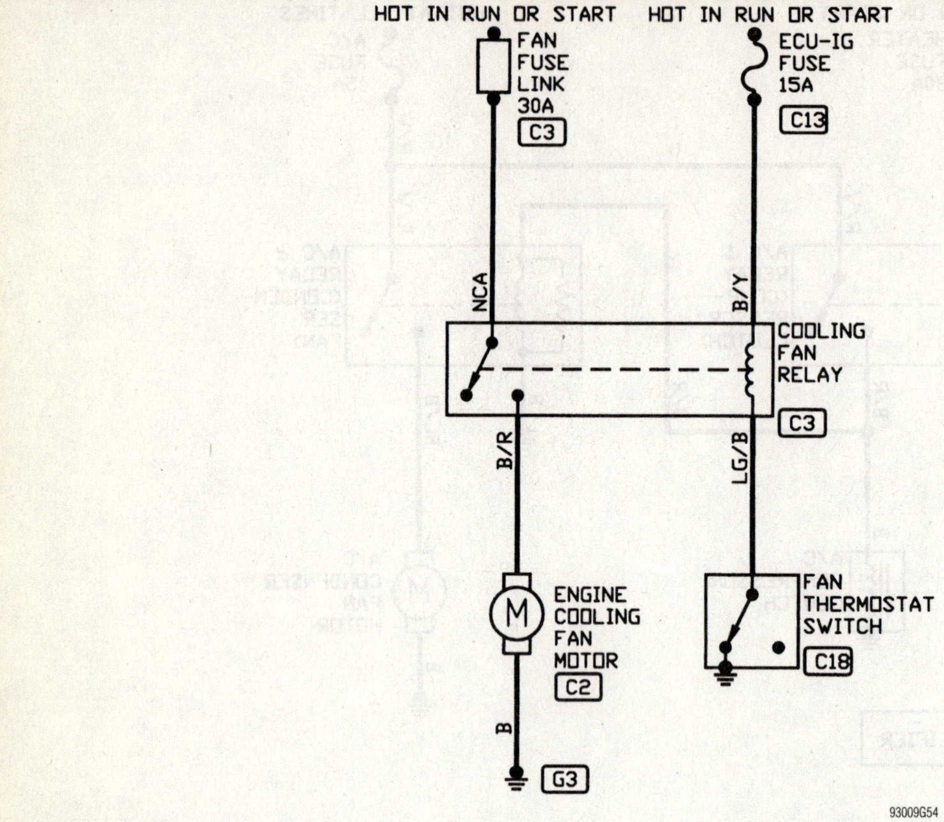

HOT IN RUN OR START   HOT IN RUN OR START

FAN
FUSE
LINK
30A
C3

ECU-IG
FUSE
15A
C13

NCA

B/Y

COOLING
FAN
RELAY
C3

B/R

LG/B

ENGINE
COOLING
FAN
MOTOR
C2

M

FAN
THERMOSTAT
SWITCH
C18

B

G3

93009G54

DIA. 41—Prism 1.6L/1.8L (w/o A/C)

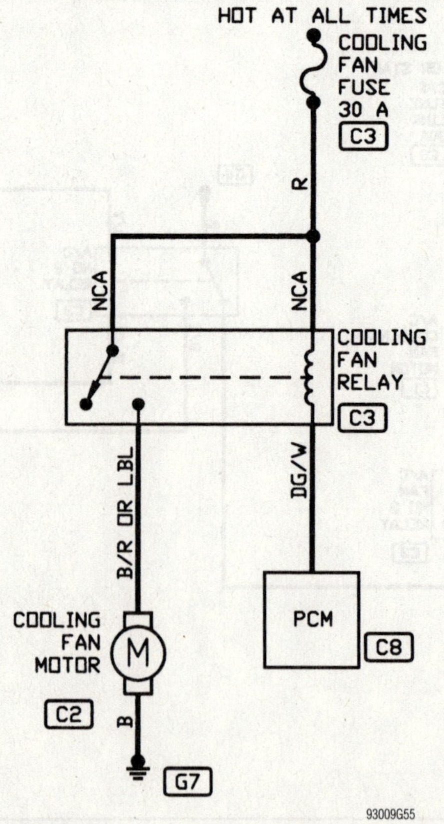

HOT AT ALL TIMES

COOLING
FAN
FUSE
30 A
C3

R

NCA   NCA

COOLING
FAN
RELAY
C3

B/R OR LBL

DG/W

COOLING
FAN
MOTOR
C2

M

PCM
C8

B

G7

93009G55

DIA. 42—Saturn 1.9L (w/o A/C)

HEATER CORES

9

CHRYSLER CORPORATION

Concorde, Intrepid, LHS and Vision

REMOVAL & INSTALLATION

1997 Models

➡ **The heater/air conditioning assembly must be removed in order to remove the heater core or the evaporator core.**

1. Disconnect the negative battery cable. Properly discharge the air conditioning system into an approved R-134a recovery machine.

➡ **If any refrigerant lines are opened, they must be capped immediately to avoid system contamination**

2. Remove the air cleaner hose and air duct from the engine. Properly drain the cooling system. Detach and plug the heater hoses from the firewall.

3. Remove or disconnect the following:
   - Quick-fit connectors for the refrigerant lines at the expansion valve
   - 3 nuts from the studs in the engine compartment

4. Carefully pry off the right and left end caps from the instrument panel.

5. Remove or disconnect the following:
   - Right and left interior door post kick panel
   - Right side bezel from the instrument panel
   - Radio center bezel (6 clips)
   - Radio assembly and the climate control panel (protect from scratching the face plates)
   - Center horizontal panel bezel (4 clips)
   - Center floor console, if equipped

6. If equipped with a passenger's air bag, press in on the sides of the glove box and lower it down. Remove the 4 air bag mounting screws, then close the glove box.

7. Remove or disconnect the following:
   - Lower bolster screws and lower the bolster
   - Trunk release, glove box light wiring. Remove bolster
   - Right and left A-pillar trim covers
   - 5 bolts holding the instrument panel in place (bolts are at the base of the windshield)
   - DRB II scan tool connector from the brace. Instrument panel ground strap at the lower left of the center console
   - Left knee panel support bracket, under column duct and left floor duct
   - 60-way wiring connector and all related connectors
   - Fuse panel connectors and the brake light switch
   - Steering column covers, the column bolts and lower the column to the floor
   - Steering column wiring
   - Air bag connectors
   - Right floor air duct
   - 10-way connector, blower module connector and blower motor connector
   - Body control module. Right wiring harness connector and the antenna connector
   - Right and left upper instrument panel screws in the door jam
   - Upper instrument panel with all harnesses and gauges attached (requires and assistant for removal)
   - Rear heater air duct
   - Air bag module

   - 3 bolts holding the heater housing in place. Carefully roll the heater housing out of the vehicle
   - Drain tube
   - Recirc door actuator, door and housing
   - Upper heater-evaporator housing screws and the upper half of the housing
   - Heater core out of the housing

To install:

8. Install or connect the following:
   - Heater core into the heater-evaporator housing and reassemble the housing
   - Drain tube. Carefully roll the heater housing into the vehicle
   - 3 bolts holding the heater housing in place
   - Air bag module (handle carefully)
   - Rear heater air duct
   - Upper instrument panel with all harnesses and gauges attached (requires and assistant)
   - Right and left upper instrument panel screws in the door jam
   - Right wiring harness connector and the antenna connector
   - Body control module
   - 10-way connector, blower module connector and blower motor connector
   - Right floor air duct
   - Air bag connectors
   - Steering column wiring
   - Steering column, steering column bolts and covers
   - Fuse panel connectors and the brake light switch
   - All related connectors
   - 60-way wiring connector
   - Under column duct and left floor duct, then the left knee panel support bracket
   - Instrument panel ground strap at the lower left of the center console
   - DRB II scan tool connector to the brace
   - 5 bolts holding the instrument panel in place (bolts are at the base of the windshield)
   - Right and left A-pillar trim covers
   - Bolster
   - Trunk release and glove box light wiring
   - Lower bolster and screws
   - Passengers air bag (if equipped), the 4 air bag mounting screws, then close the glove box

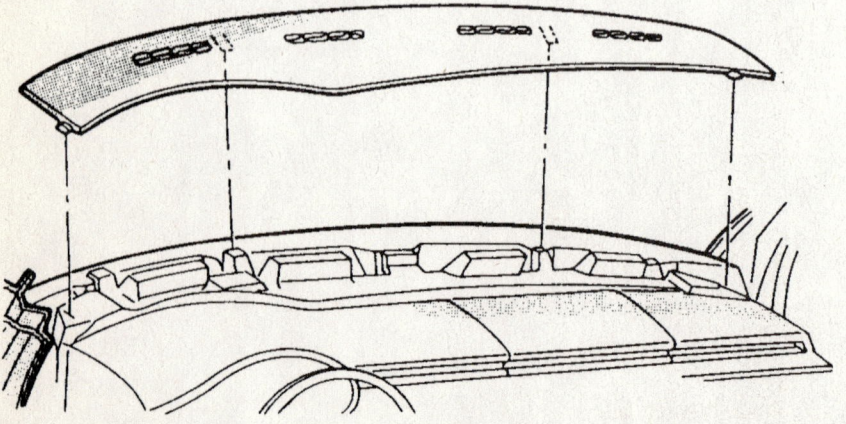

Top cover installation—1997 Concorde, Intrepid, LHS and Vision

88170G15

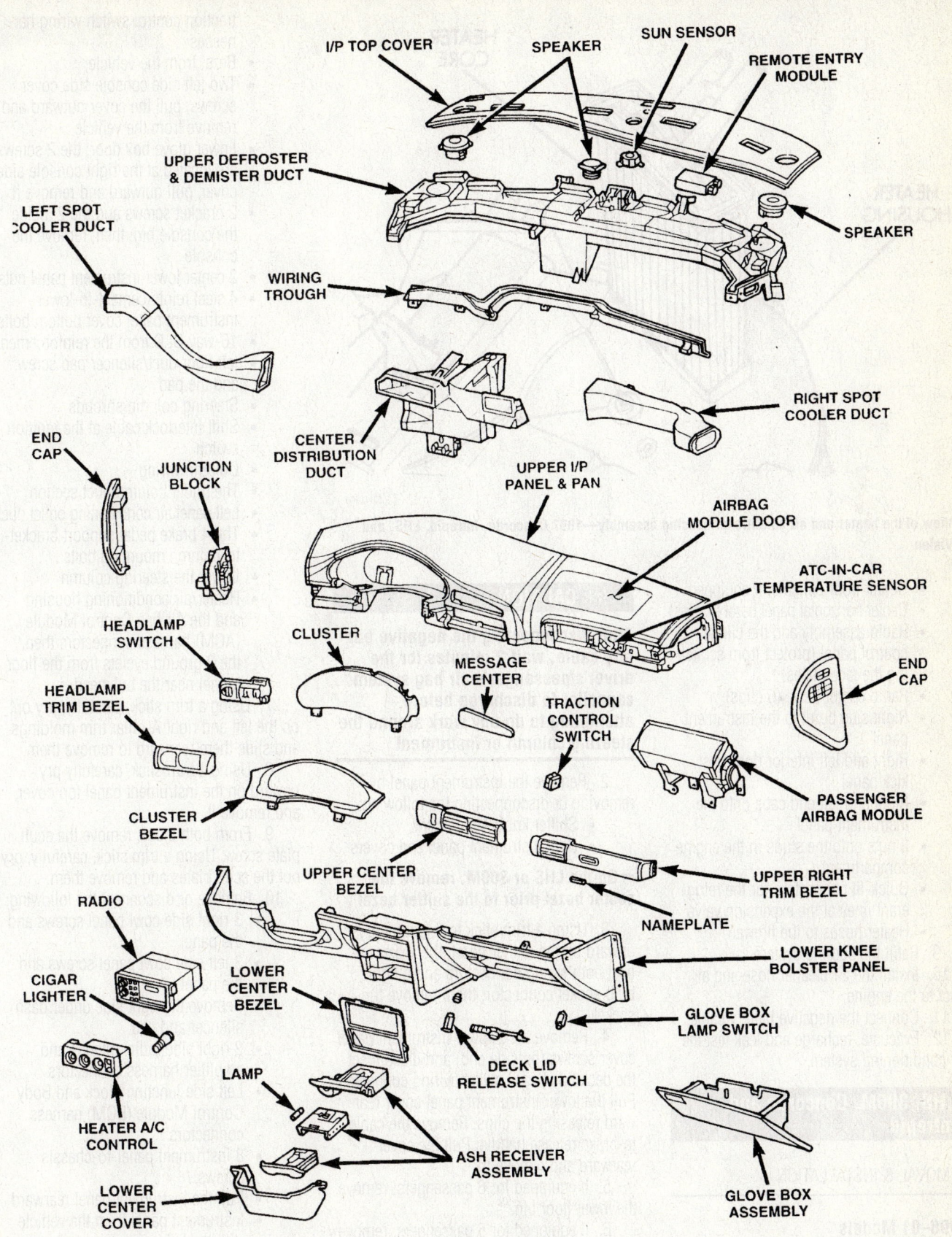

I/P TOP COVER
SPEAKER
SUN SENSOR
REMOTE ENTRY MODULE
UPPER DEFROSTER & DEMISTER DUCT
LEFT SPOT COOLER DUCT
SPEAKER
WIRING TROUGH
RIGHT SPOT COOLER DUCT
END CAP
JUNCTION BLOCK
CENTER DISTRIBUTION DUCT
UPPER I/P PANEL & PAN
AIRBAG MODULE DOOR
ATC-IN-CAR TEMPERATURE SENSOR
HEADLAMP SWITCH
CLUSTER
MESSAGE CENTER
END CAP
HEADLAMP TRIM BEZEL
TRACTION CONTROL SWITCH
PASSENGER AIRBAG MODULE
CLUSTER BEZEL
UPPER CENTER BEZEL
UPPER RIGHT TRIM BEZEL
NAMEPLATE
RADIO
LOWER KNEE BOLSTER PANEL
CIGAR LIGHTER
LOWER CENTER BEZEL
GLOVE BOX LAMP SWITCH
DECK LID RELEASE SWITCH
LAMP
HEATER A/C CONTROL
ASH RECEIVER ASSEMBLY
LOWER CENTER COVER
GLOVE BOX ASSEMBLY

88170G16

Exploded view of the instrument panel—1997 Concorde, Intrepid, LHS and Vision

For complete service labor times order Nichols' Chilton Labor Guide Manual

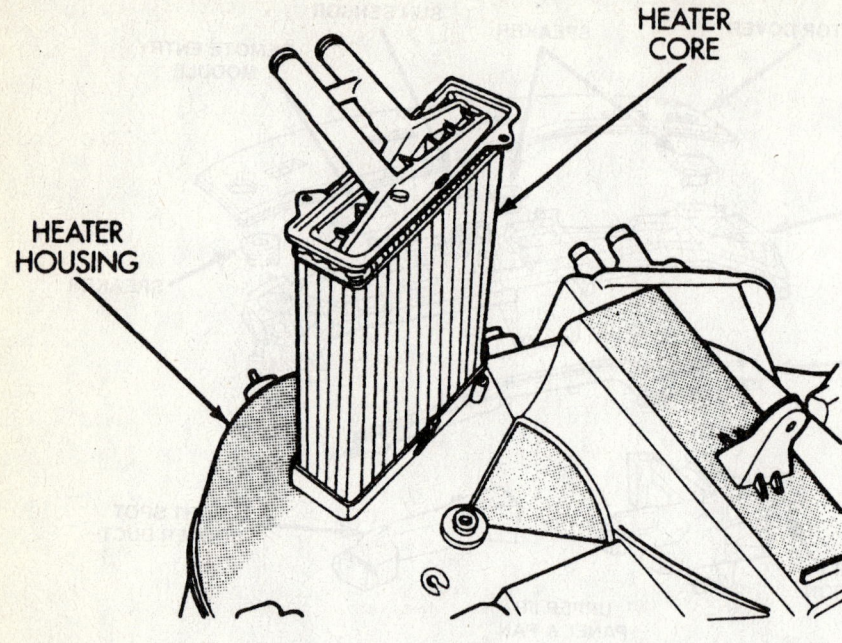

HEATER CORE

HEATER HOUSING

93111GC6

View of the heater and air conditioner housing assembly—1997 Concorde, Intrepid, LHS, and Vision

- Center floor console, if equipped
- Center horizontal panel bezel (4 clips)
- Radio assembly and the climate control panel (protect from scratching the face plates)
- Radio center bezel (6 clips)
- Right side bezel to the instrument panel
- Right and left interior door post kick panel
- Right and left end caps onto the instrument panel
- 3 nuts onto the studs in the engine compartment
- Quick-fit connectors for the refrigerant lines at the expansion valve
- Heater hoses to the firewall

9. Refill the cooling system.

10. Install the air cleaner hose and air duct to the engine.

11. Connect the negative battery cable.

12. Evacuate, recharge and leak test the air conditioning system.

LHS, 300M, Concorde and Intrepid

REMOVAL & INSTALLATION

1998–01 Models

1. Disconnect the negative battery cable from the remote battery post located near the right strut tower.

❋❋ CAUTION

After disconnecting the negative battery cable, wait 2 minutes for the driver's/passenger's air bag system capacitor to discharge before attempting to do any work around the steering column or instrument

2. Remove the instrument panel by removing or disconnecting the following:
- Shifter knob Allen screw
- Both instrument panel end covers

➡ **On the LHS or 300M, remove the center bezel prior to the shifter bezel**

3. Using a trim stick tool, gently pry upward on the shifter bezel; then, disconnect both wiring connectors and a light bulb socket connector; then, remove the socket.

4. Remove the 2 lower instrument panel cover screws (outside end) and disconnect the deck lid release switch wiring connector. Pull the lower instrument panel cover rearward releasing the clips. Remove the cable-to-brake release handle. Pull the cover rearward and remove it.

5. If equipped for 6 passengers, remove the lower floor bin.

6. If equipped for 5 passengers, remove or disconnect the following items:
- Center bezel using the trim stick
- Heater/air conditioning housing assembly control switch and the

traction control switch wiring harnesses
- Bezel from the vehicle
- Two left side console side cover screws, pull the cover outward and remove from the vehicle
- Lower glove box door; the 2 screws are located at the right console side cover, pull outward and remove it
- 2 bracket screws and the 2 inside the console bin; then, remove the console
- 2 center lower instrument panel nuts
- 4 steel reinforcement-to-lower instrument panel cover bottom bolts
- 16-way DLC from the reinforcement
- left floor duct/silencer pad screw and the pad
- Steering column shrouds
- Shift interlock cable at the ignition switch
- Column wiring
- The under column duct section
- Left panel air conditioning outlet duct
- The 4 brake pedal support bracket-to-column mounting bolts
- Lower the steering column
- Heater/air conditioning housing and the Air bag Control Module (ACM) harness connectors then, the 2 ground eyelets from the floor tunnel near the bulkhead

7. Using a trim stick, carefully, pry out on the left and right A-pillar trim moldings and slide them rearward to remove them.

8. Using a trim stick, carefully pry upward on the instrument panel top cover, and remove it.

9. From both sides, remove the scuff plate screw. Using a trim stick, carefully, pry out the scuff plates and remove them.

10. Remove or disconnect the following:
- 3 right side cowl panel screws and the panel
- 3 left side cowl panel screws and the panel
- Remove the right side under dash silencer and pad
- 2 right side radio antenna and amplifier harness connectors
- Left side junction block and Body Control Module (BCM) harness connectors
- 8 instrument panel-to-chassis screws
- Pull the instrument panel rearward
- Instrument panel from the vehicle with the help of an assistant

11. Discharge and recover the air conditioning system refrigerant.

12. Drain the cooling system into a clean container for reuse.

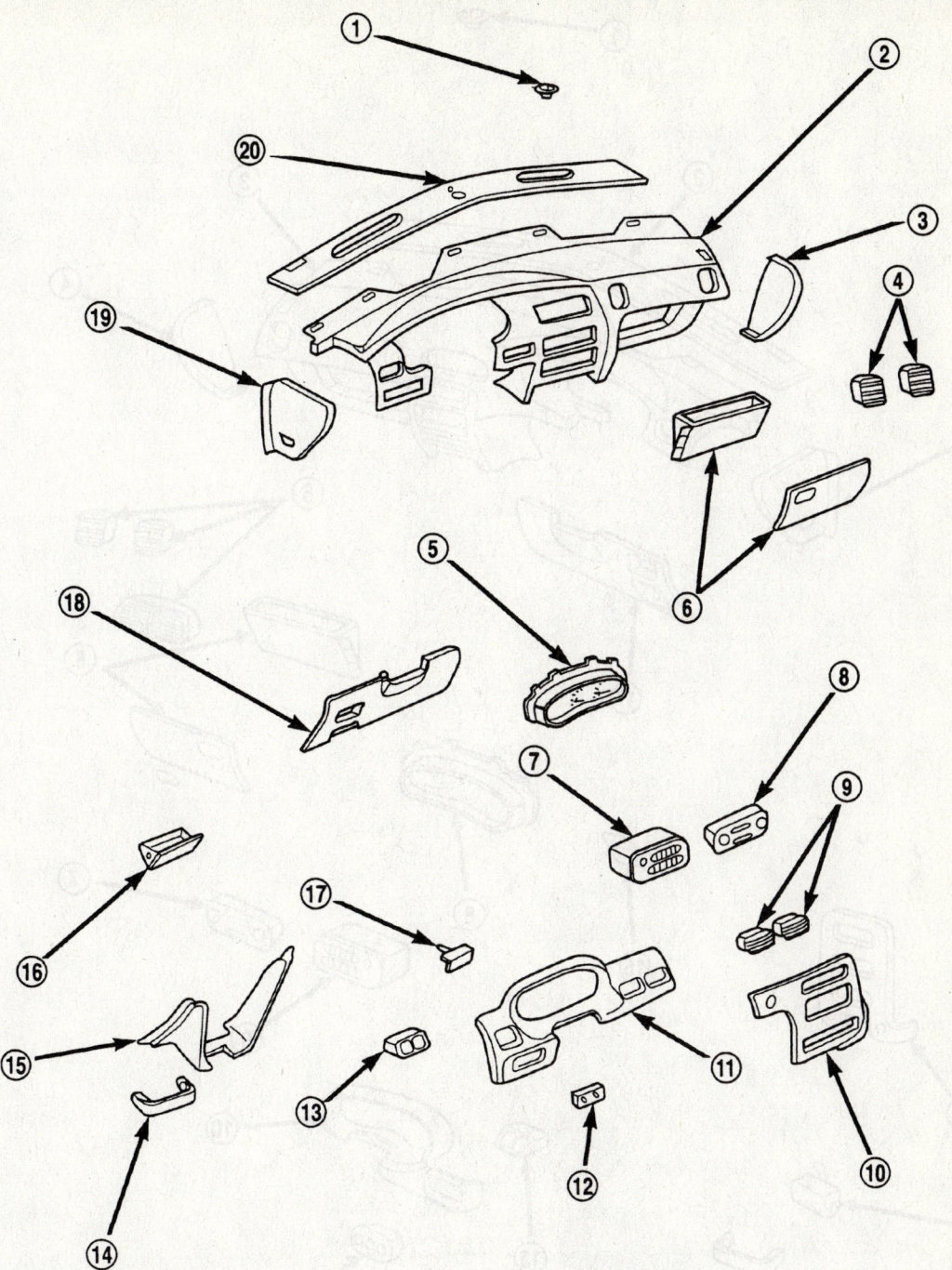

1 – SPEAKER, INSTRUMENT PANEL CENTER
2 – INSTRUMENT PANEL ASSEMBLY
3 – BEZEL, INSTRUMENT PANEL END CAP
4 – LOUVER, AIR OUTLET
5 – HOUSING INSTRUMENT CLUSTER
6 – GLOVE BOX ASSEMBLY
7 – RADIO
8 – CONTROL ASSEMBLY, INSTRUMENT PANEL
9 – LOUVER, AIR OUTLET
10 – BEZEL, INSTRUMENT PANEL TRIM-CENTER
11 – BEZEL INSTRUMENT CLUSTER

12 – SWITCH HEADLAMP
13 – LOUVER, AIR OUTLET
14 – COVER, INSTRUMENT PANEL CENTER SUPPORT/BIN (6 PASS. ONLY)
15 – 6 PASS. ONLY
16 – ASH RECEIVER
17 – LEVER, PARKING BRAKE
18 – COVER, LOWER INSTRUMENT PANEL
19 – BEZEL, INSTRUMENT PANEL END CAP
20 – COVER, UPPER INSTRUMENT PANEL

93111G81

Exploded view of the instrument panel—1998–01 Intrepid

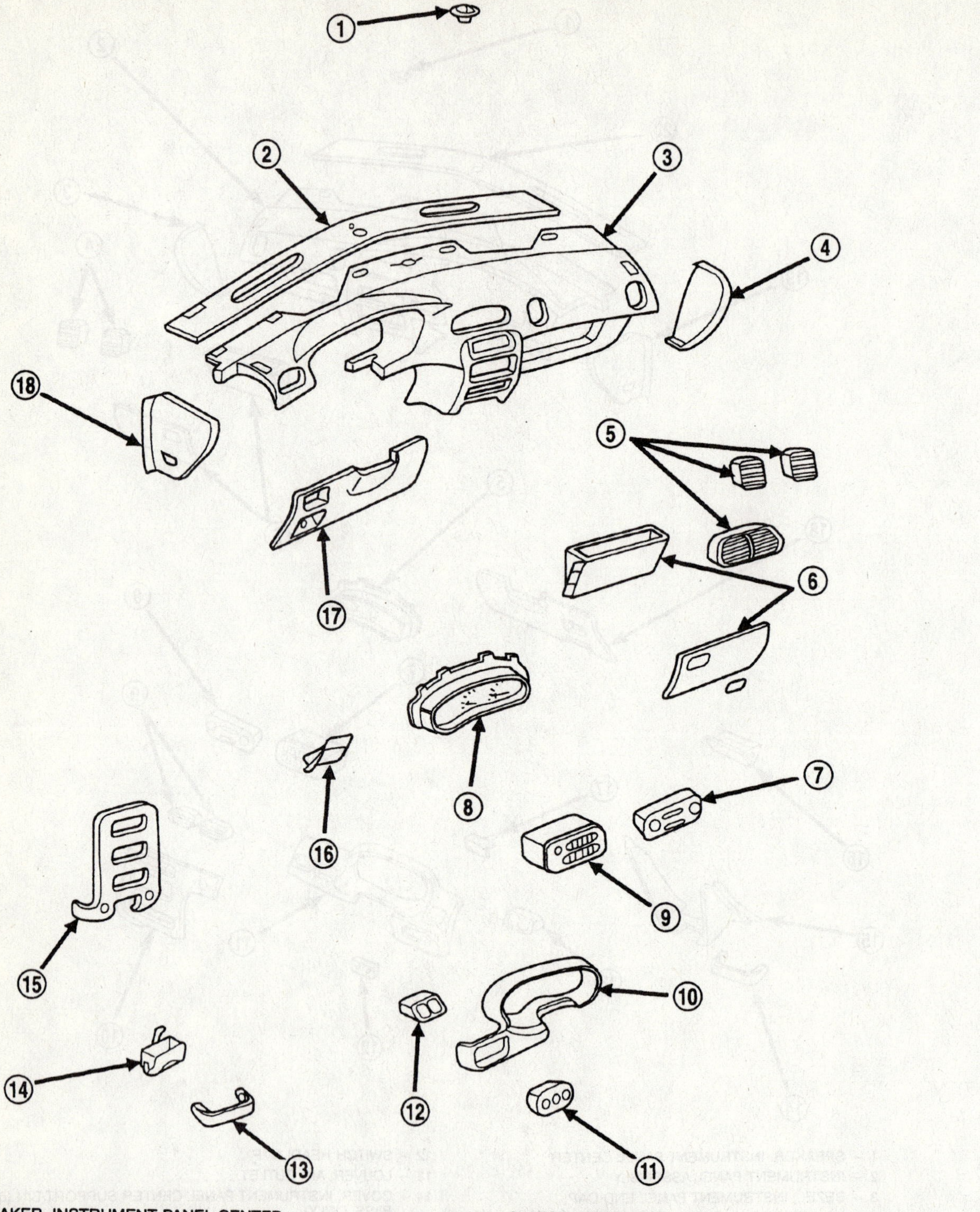

1 – SPEAKER, INSTRUMENT PANEL CENTER
2 – COVER, UPPER INSTRUMENT PANEL
3 – INSTRUMENT PANEL ASSEMBLY
4 – BEZEL, INSTRUMENT PANEL END CAP
5 – LOUVER, AIR OUTLET
6 – GLOVE BOX ASSEMBLY
7 – CONTROL ASSEMBLY, INSTRUMENT PANEL
8 – HOUSING, INSTRUMENT CLUSTER
9 – RADIO
10 – BEZEL, INSTRUMENT CLUSTER

11 – SWITCH, HEADLAMP
12 – LOUVER, AIR OUTLET
13 – COVER, INSTRUMENT PANEL CENTER SUPPORT/BIN (6 PASS. ONLY)
14 – ASH RECEIVER
15 – BEZEL, INSTRUMENT PANEL TRIM-CENTER
16 – LEVER, PARKING BRAKE
17 – COVER, LOWER INSTRUMENT PANEL
18 – BEZEL, INSTRUMENT PANEL END CAP

Exploded view of the instrument panel—1998–01 Concorde

93111G82

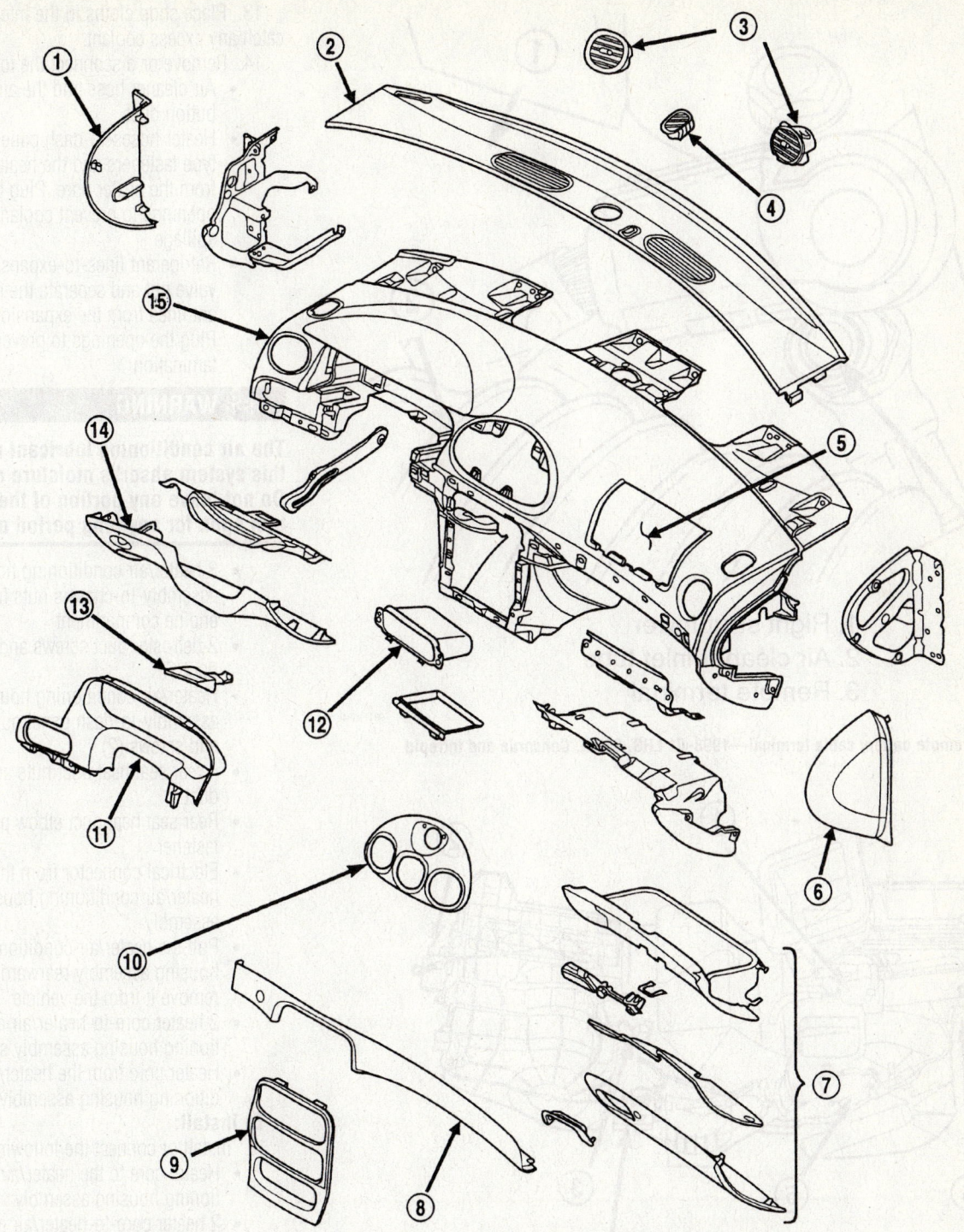

1 – BEZEL, INSTRUMENT PANEL END CAP
2 – COVER, UPPER INSTRUMENT PANEL
3 – LOUVER, AIR OUTLET
4 – LOUVER/DEMISTER SIDE WINDOW
5 – MODULE, PASSENGER SIDE AIRBAG
6 – BEZEL, INSTRUMENT PANEL END CAP
7 – GLOVE BOX ASSEMBLY, INSTRUMENT PANEL
8 – BEZEL, INSTRUMENT PANEL UPPER RIGHT TRIM

9 – BEZEL, INSTRUMENT PANEL TRIM-CENTER
10 – BEZEL, INSTRUMENT PANEL AIR DISTRIBUTION OUTLET
11 – BEZEL, INSTRUMENT CLUSTER
12 – STORAGE COMPARTMENT CUBBY BOX
13 – LEVER, PARKING BRAKE
14 – COVER, LOWER INSTRUMENT PANEL-LEFT SIDE
15 – INSTRUMENT PANEL ASSEMBLY

93111G83

Exploded view of the instrument panel—1998–01 LHS and 300M

Refer to the model specific sections for engine mechanical service procedures

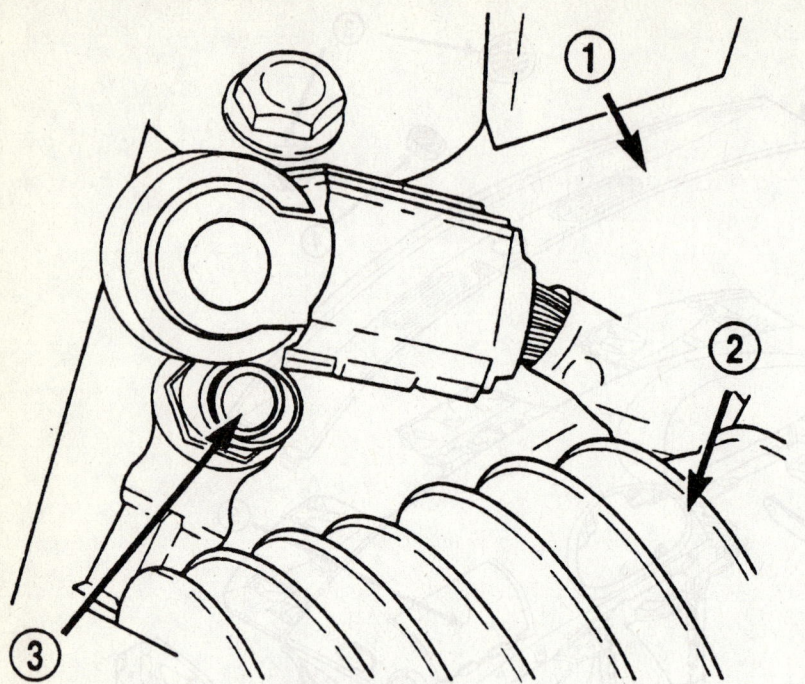

1. Right strut tower
2. Air cleaner inlet tube
3. Remote terminal

93111G84

View of the remote battery cable terminal—1998–01 LHS, 300M, Concorde and Intrepid

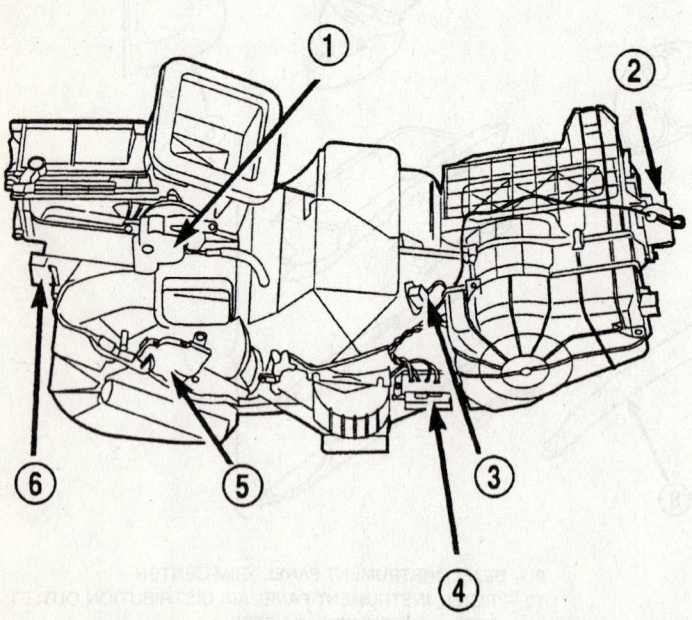

1 – MODE DOOR ACTUATOR
2 – RECIRCULATION DOOR ACTUATOR
3 – EVAPORATOR TEMPERATURE SENSOR
4 – POWER MODULE OR BLOWER RESISTOR
5 – BLEND DOOR ACTUATOR

93111G85

View of the heater/air conditioning housing assembly—1998–01 LHS, 300M, Concorde and Intrepid

13. Place shop cloths in the interior to catch any excess coolant.
14. Remove or disconnect the following:
   - Air cleaner hose and the air distribution duct
   - Heater hoses-to-dash panel spring type fasteners and the heater hoses from the heater core. Plug the openings to prevent coolant spillage
   - Refrigerant lines-to-expansion valve nut and separate the refrigerant lines from the expansion valve. Plug the openings to prevent contamination

✳✳ WARNING

The air conditioning lubricant used in this system absorbs moisture readily. Do not leave any portion of the system open for any long period of time.

   - 3 heater/air conditioning housing assembly-to-chassis nuts from the engine compartment
   - 2 defroster duct screws and the duct
   - Heater/air conditioning housing assembly-to-dash panel nuts (2) and screws (2)
   - 4 rear seat heat duct nuts and the duct
   - Rear seat heat duct elbow push-pin fastener
   - Electrical connector from the heater/air conditioning housing assembly
   - Pull the heater/air conditioning housing assembly rearward and remove it from the vehicle
   - 2 heater core-to-heater/air conditioning housing assembly screws
   - Heater core from the heater/air conditioning housing assembly

To install:
15. Install or connect the following:
   - Heater core to the heater/air conditioning housing assembly
   - 2 heater core-to-heater/air conditioning housing assembly screws
   - Push the heater/air conditioning housing assembly forward (carefully) and install it to the vehicle
   - Electrical connector to the heater/air conditioning housing assembly
   - Rear seat heat duct elbow push pin fastener
   - Duct and the 4 rear seat heat duct nuts
   - Heater/air conditioning housing

assembly-to-dash panel nuts (2) and screws (2)
- 2 defroster duct and the duct screws
- In the engine compartment, the 3 heater/air conditioning housing assembly-to-chassis nuts
- Refrigerant lines to the expansion valve
- Refrigerant lines-to-expansion valve nut
- Heater hoses to the heater core and the heater hoses-to-dash panel spring type fasteners
- Air cleaner hose and the air distribution duct

16. Refill the cooling system.

17. Evacuate, charge and leak-test the air conditioning system refrigerant.

18. Install the instrument panel by installing or connecting the following:
- Instrument panel to the vehicle
- Push the instrument panel forward
- 8 instrument panel-to-chassis screws
- Left side junction block and Body Control Module (BCM) harness connectors
- 2 right side radio antenna and amplifier harness connectors
- Right side under dash silencer and pad
- Left side cowl panel and the 3 panel screws
- Right side cowl panel and the 3 panel screws
- Install the scuff plate and the screw (both sides)
- Instrument panel top cover
- Left and right A-pillar trim moldings
- Heater/air conditioning housing and the Air bag Control Module (ACM) harness connectors then, the 2 ground eyelets to the floor tunnel near the bulkhead
- Raise the steering column
- The 4 brake pedal support bracket-to-column mounting bolts
- Left panel air conditioning outlet duct
- The under column duct section
- Column wiring
- Shift interlock cable at the ignition switch
- Steering column shrouds
- Left floor duct/silencer pad and the pad screw
- 4 steel reinforcement-to-lower instrument panel cover bottom bolts
- 6-way Diagnostic Link Connector (DLC) to the reinforcement
- 2 center lower instrument panel nuts

- The 2 bracket screws and the 2 inside the console bin; then, the console (5 passenger models only)
- 2 screws are located at the right console side cover (5 passenger models only)
- Two left side console side cover screws (5 passenger models only)
- Bezel to the vehicle (5 passenger models only).
- Heater/air conditioning housing assembly control switch and the traction control switch wiring harnesses.
- Center bezel using the trim stick.
- Lower floor bin (6 passenger models only).
- 2 lower instrument panel cover screws (outside end) and connect the deck lid release switch wiring connector. Install the cable-to-brake release handle
- Light bulb socket. Both wiring connectors and a light bulb socket connector
- Shifter bezel
- Center bezel prior to the shifter bezel (LHS or 300M models)

- Both instrument panel end covers
- Shifter knob Allen screw

19. Connect the negative battery cable to the remote battery post located near the right strut tower.

20. Operate the engine to normal operating temperatures; then, check the climate control operation and check for leaks.

Avenger and Sebring Coupe°

REMOVAL & INSTALLATION

1997–01 Models

1. Disconnect the negative battery cable. Properly drain the cooling system.

2. Disconnect the heater hoses from the heater core.

3. Remove the floor console by removing or disconnecting the following:
- Center console panel
- Shift knob
- Accessory box or ashtray
- Floor console panel assembly
- Shift lever cover assembly
- Floor console assembly

4. From under the steering wheel,

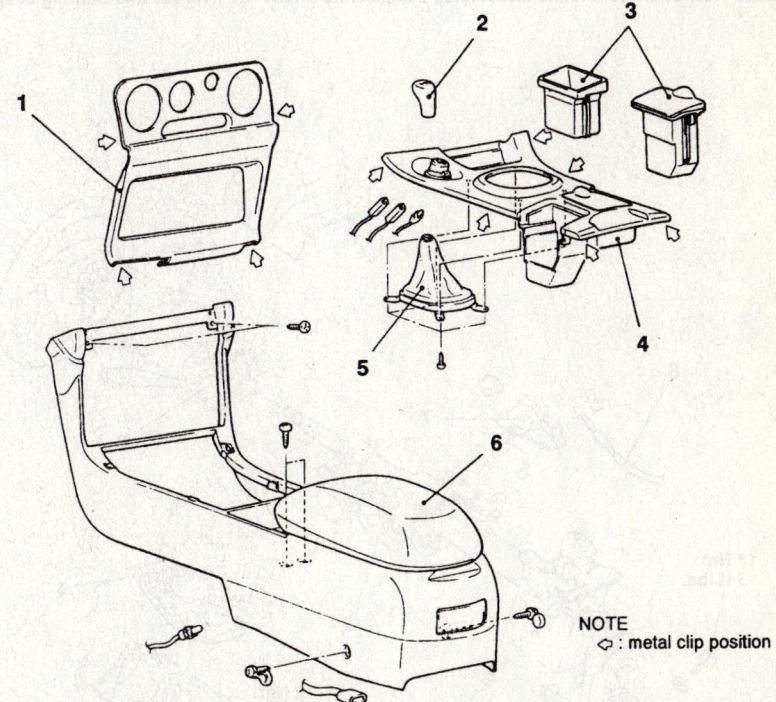

NOTE
◇ : metal clip position

1. Center console panel
2. Shift knob
3. Accessory box or ashtray
4. Floor console panel assembly
5. Shift lever cover assembly
6. Floor console assembly

93111G52

Exploded view of the center console—1997–01 Avenger and Sebring coupe

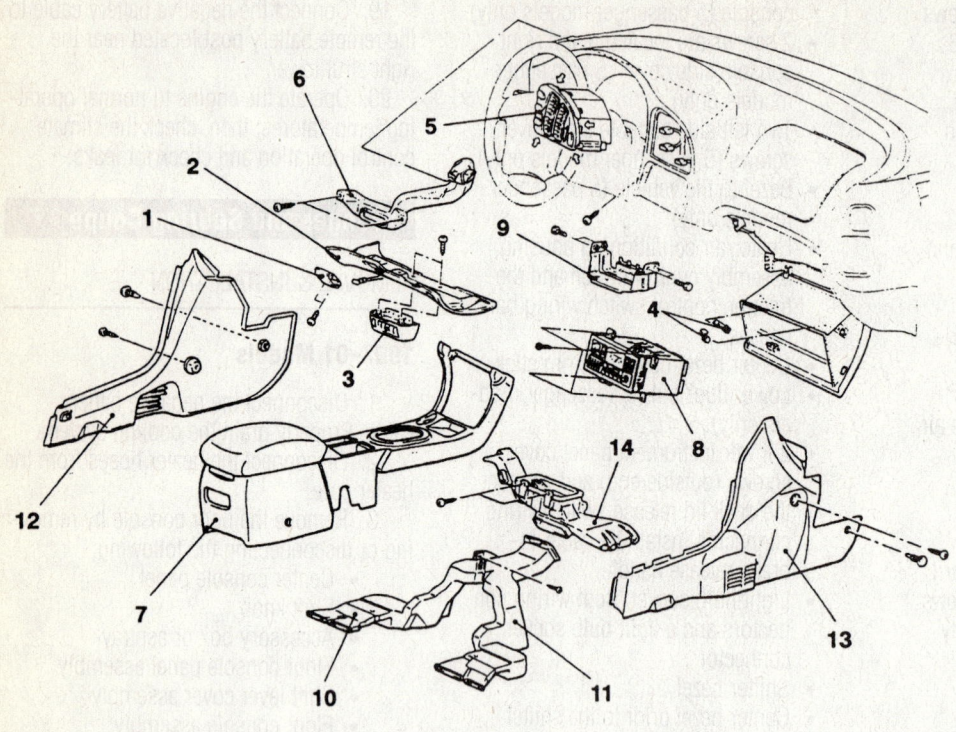

1. Hood lock release handle
2. Driver's side under cover
3. Lap cooler grille
4. Stopper
5. Center air outlet
6. Lap cooler duct
7. Floor console
8. Radio and tape player
9. Relay bracket
10. Rear heater duct (L.H.)
11. Rear heater duct (R.H.)
12. Console side cover (L.H.)
13. Console side cover (R.H.)
14. Foot distribution duct

93111G53

Exploded view of the ventilators and related components—1997–01 Avenger and Sebring coupe

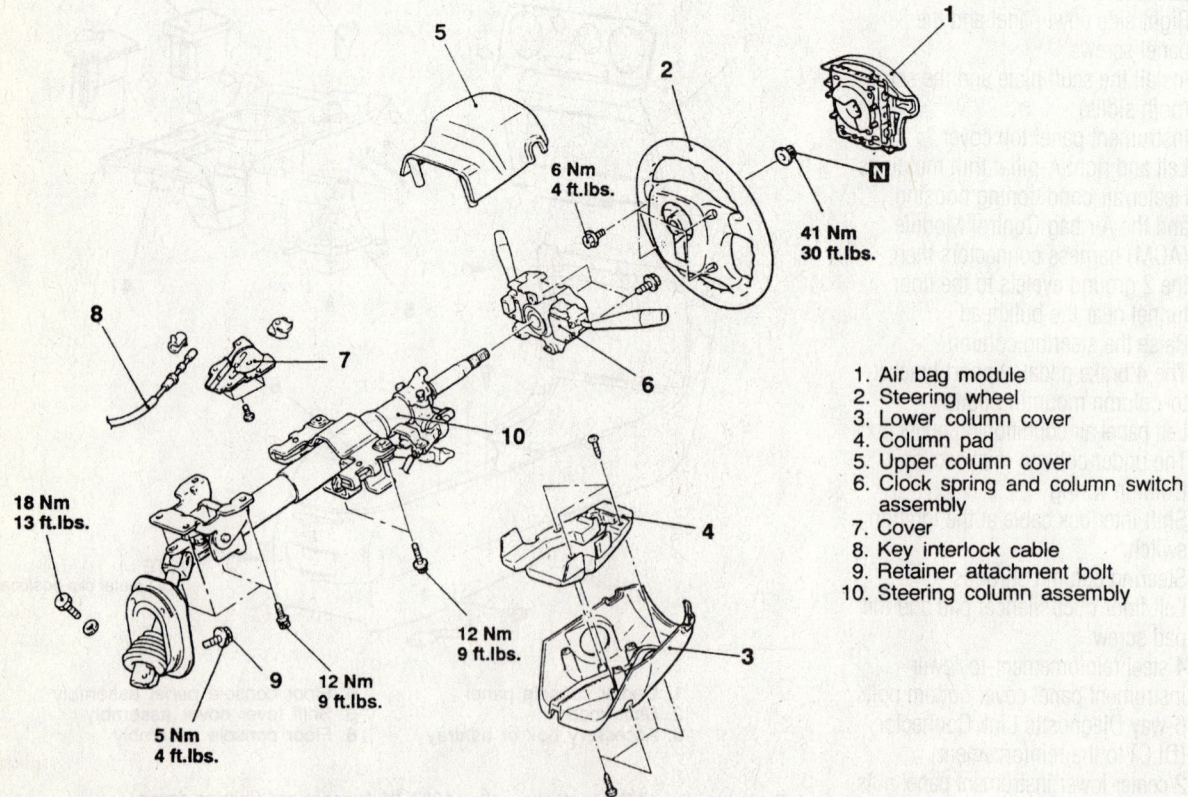

6 Nm
4 ft.lbs.

41 Nm
30 ft.lbs.

18 Nm
13 ft.lbs.

12 Nm
9 ft.lbs.

5 Nm
4 ft.lbs.

12 Nm
9 ft.lbs.

1. Air bag module
2. Steering wheel
3. Lower column cover
4. Column pad
5. Upper column cover
6. Clock spring and column switch assembly
7. Cover
8. Key interlock cable
9. Retainer attachment bolt
10. Steering column assembly

93111G54

Exploded view of the steering column and related components—1997–01 Avenger and Sebring coupe

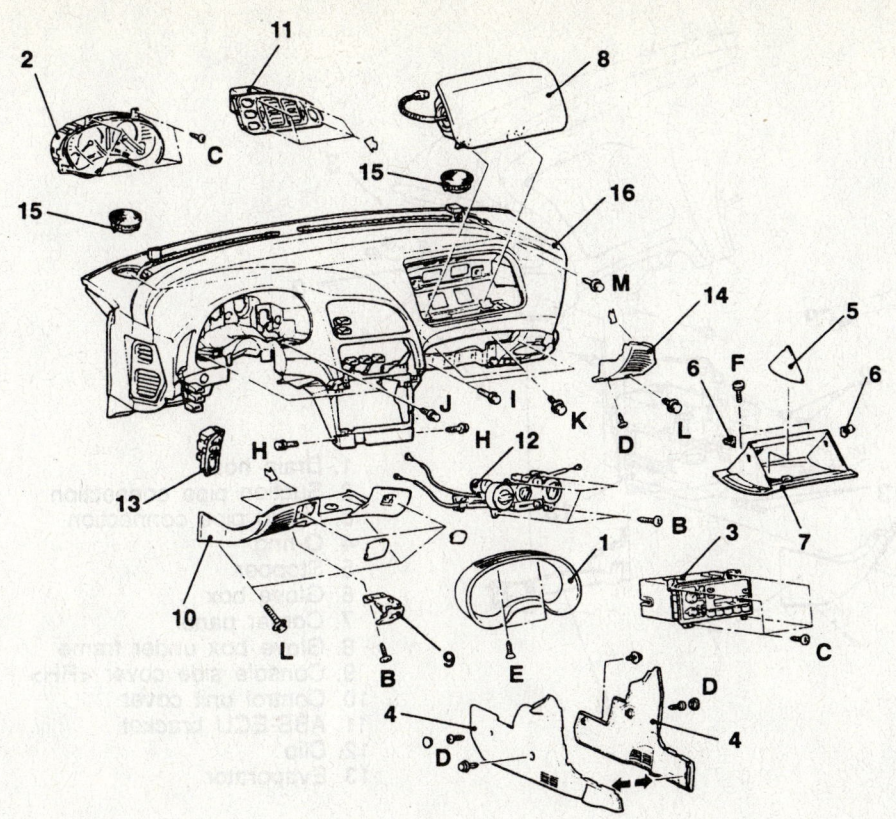

1. Meter bezel
2. Combination meter
3. Radio and tape player
4. Console side cover
5. Sunglasses holder
6. Stopper
7. Glove box
8. Passenger's side air bag module assembly
9. Hood lock release handle
10. Instrument under cover L.H.
11. Center air outlet assembly
12. Heater control assembly
13. Instrument panel switch
14. Instrument under cover R.H.
15. Front speaker
16. Instrument panel assembly

93111G55

Exploded view of the instrument panel and related components—1997–01 Avenger and Sebring coupe

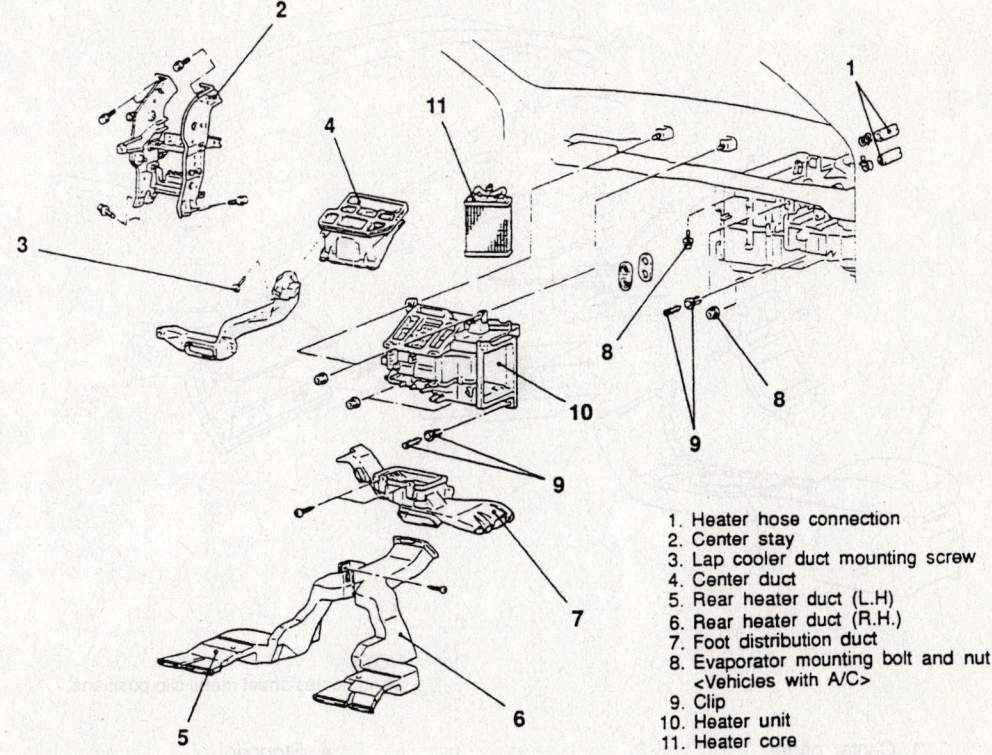

1. Heater hose connection
2. Center stay
3. Lap cooler duct mounting screw
4. Center duct
5. Rear heater duct (L.H)
6. Rear heater duct (R.H.)
7. Foot distribution duct
8. Evaporator mounting bolt and nut <Vehicles with A/C>
9. Clip
10. Heater unit
11. Heater core

93111G31

Exploded view of the heater core housing and related components—1997–01 Avenger and Sebring coupe

For complete service labor times order Nichols' Chilton Labor Guide Manual

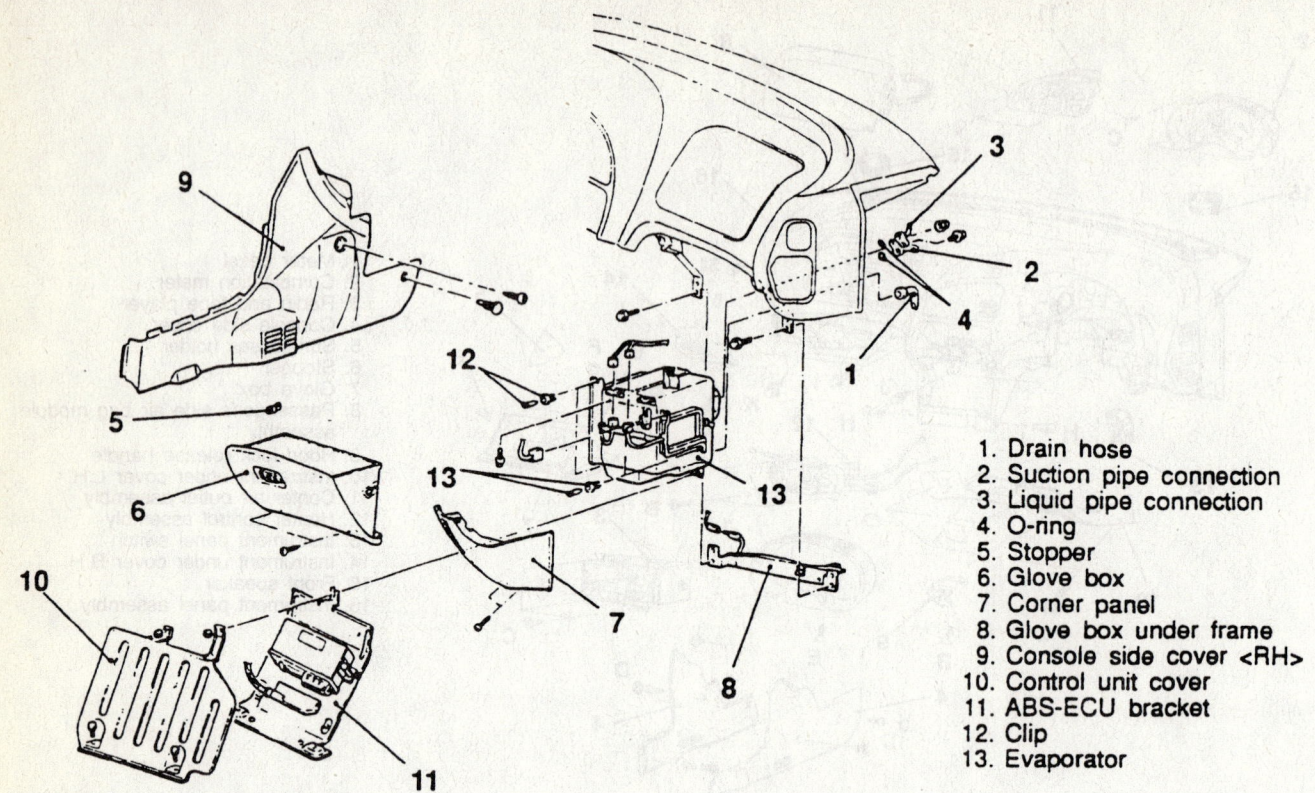

1. Drain hose
2. Suction pipe connection
3. Liquid pipe connection
4. O-ring
5. Stopper
6. Glove box
7. Corner panel
8. Glove box under frame
9. Console side cover <RH>
10. Control unit cover
11. ABS-ECU bracket
12. Clip
13. Evaporator

93111G32

Exploded view of the evaporator core housing and related components—1997–01 Avenger and Sebring coupe

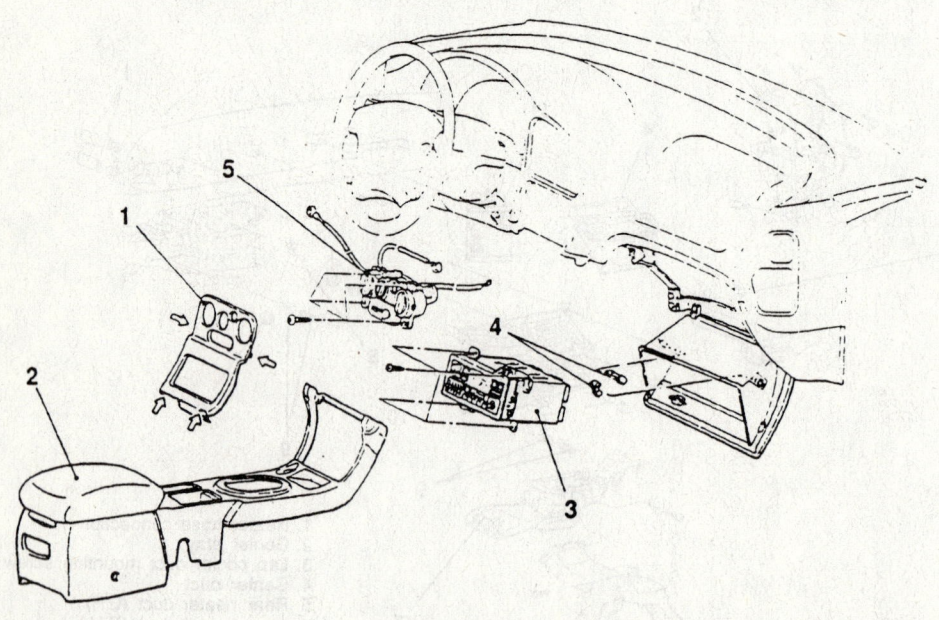

NOTE
⟸ indicates sheet metal clip positions.

1. Center panel
2. Floor console
3. Radio and tape player

4. Stopper
5. Heater control assembly

93111G33

Exploded view of the manual control head and related components—1997–01 Avenger and Sebring coupe remove the hood lock release handle, the driver's side under cover and the lap cooler grille.

5. Remove the steering wheel by removing or disconnecting the following:
- Air bag module-to-steering wheel screws (rear of the steering wheel) and the air bag module
- Steering wheel-to-column nut and press the steering wheel from the column
- Lower steering column cover screws, the lower cover, the upper cover and the column pad

6. Remove the instrument panel by removing or disconnecting the following:
- Meter bezel and the combination meter
- Radio and tape player
- Console side cover
- Sunglass holder
- Glove box stopper and the glove box
- Passenger's side air bag module
- Passenger's side air bag module electrical connector
- Center air outlet assembly
- Instrument panel switch
- Instrument panel switch electrical connectors
- Right side instrument panel under cover
- Front speaker
- Instrument panel

7. Remove the attaching clip and nuts and remove the heater unit.

8. Remove the heater core from the heater unit.

To install:

9. Install or connect the following components:
- Heater core into the heater unit
- Heater unit and attach the nuts and clip
- Instrument panel by reversing the removal procedures
- Steering column pad, the upper cover, the lower cover and the lower steering column cover screws
- Steering wheel by reversing the removal procedure
- Lap cooler grille, the driver's side under cover and the hood lock release handle
- Floor console by reversing the removal procedure
- Heater hoses to the heater core

10. Refill the cooling system.

11. Connect the negative battery cable. Check for leaks.

Talon

REMOVAL & INSTALLATION

1997–98 Models

➡ **The evaporator housing can be removed by it self, without removing** the console, instrument panel or heater core. **The heater core, though, cannot be removed without removing the evaporator.**

1. Disconnect the negative battery cable.
2. Drain the cooling system and properly discharge the air conditioning system and disconnect the refrigerant lines from the

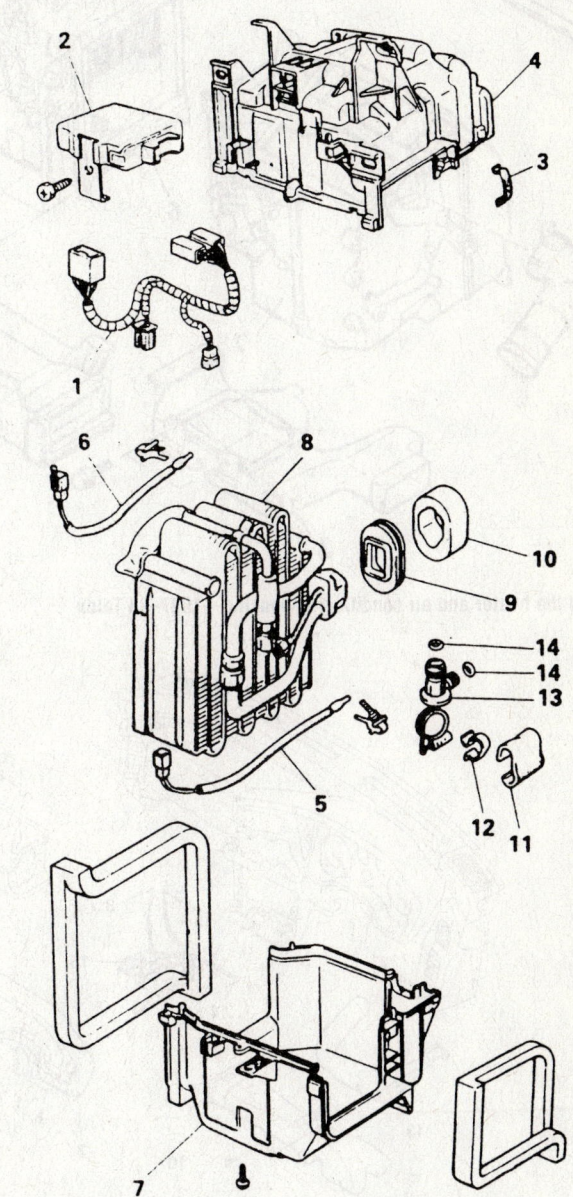

1. Wiring harness
2. Air conditioning control unit
3. Clips
4. Upper evaporator case
5. Air inlet sensor
6. Air thermo sensor
7. Lower evaporator case
8. Evaporator assembly
9. Grommet
10. Insulator
11. Rubber insulator
12. Clip
13. Expansion valve
14. O-ring

93111G26

Exploded view of the evaporator and related components—1997–98 Talon

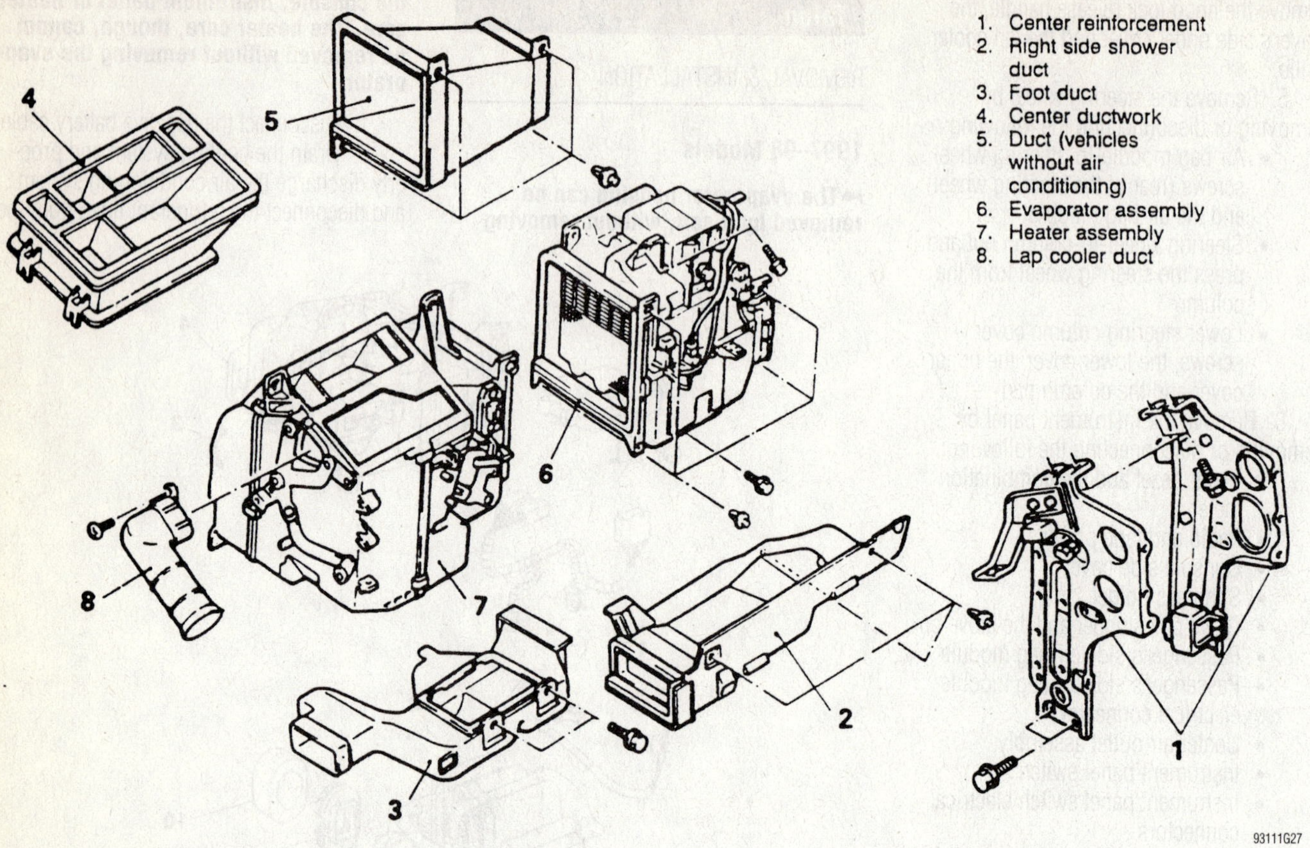

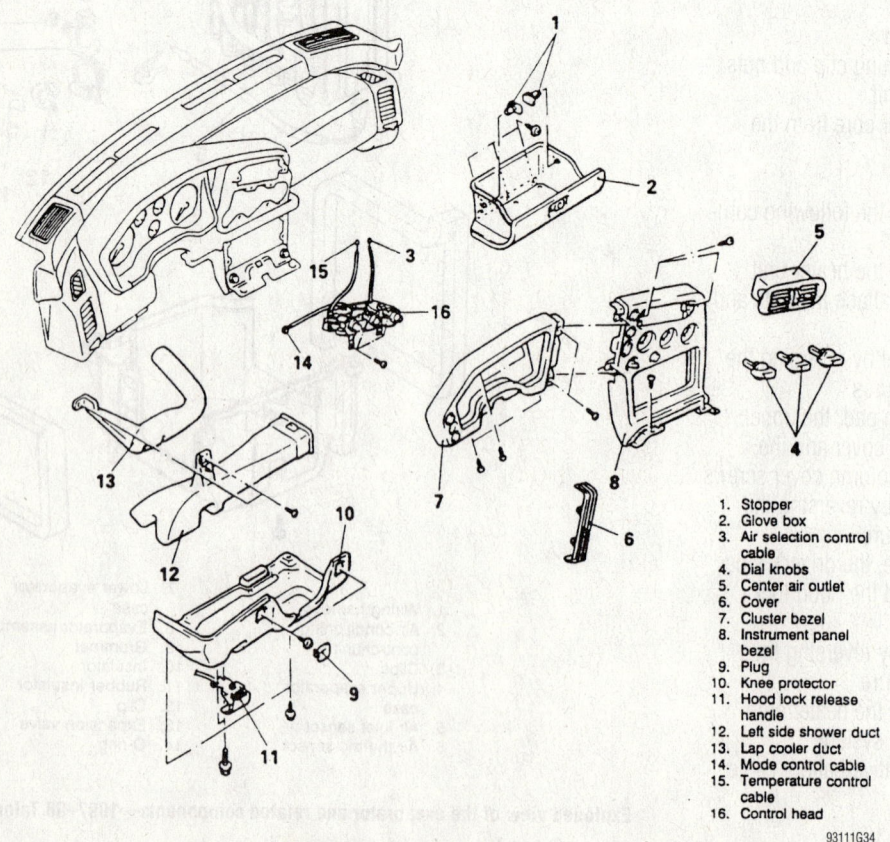

1. Center reinforcement
2. Right side shower duct
3. Foot duct
4. Center ductwork
5. Duct (vehicles without air conditioning)
6. Evaporator assembly
7. Heater assembly
8. Lap cooler duct
1
2
3
4
5
6
7
8
93111G27

Exploded view of the heater and air conditioning housing—1997–98 Talon

1. Stopper
2. Glove box
3. Air selection control cable
4. Dial knobs
5. Center air outlet
6. Cover
7. Cluster bezel
8. Instrument panel bezel
9. Plug
10. Knee protector
11. Hood lock release handle
12. Left side shower duct
13. Lap cooler duct
14. Mode control cable
15. Temperature control cable
16. Control head
1
2
3
4
5
6
7
8
9
10
11
12
13
14
15
16
93111G34

Exploded view of the manual control head and related components—1997–98 Talon

evaporator, if equipped. Cover the exposed ends of the lines to minimize contamination.

3. Remove the floor console by first removing the plugs, then the screws retaining the side covers and the small cover piece in front of the shifter. Remove the shifter knob, for manual transmission, and the cup holder. Remove both small pieces of upholstery to gain access to the retainer screws. Disconnect both electrical connectors at the front of the console. Remove the shoulder harness guide plates and the console assembly.

4. Remove the instrument panel assembly by performing the following procedure:

 a. Locate the rectangular plugs in the knee protector on either side of the steering column.

 b. Pry these plugs out and remove the screws.

 c. Remove the screws from the hood lock release lever and the knee protector.

5. Remove or disconnect the following:
- Upper and lower column covers
- Narrow panel covering the instrument cluster cover screws and the cover
- Radio panel and the radio
- Center air outlet assembly by reaching through the grille and pushing the side clips out with a small flat-tipped tool while carefully prying the outlet free
- Heater control knobs (pull off) and the heater control panel assembly
- Open the glove box, remove the plugs from the sides and the glove box assembly
- Instrument gauge cluster and the speedometer adapter by disconnecting the speedometer cable from the transaxle, pulling the cable slightly towards the vehicle interior, then giving a slight twist on the adapter to release it
- Left and right speaker covers from the top of the instrument panel
- Center plate below the heater controls
- Lower air ducts
- Steering column bolts and lower the column
- Instrument panel mounting screws, bolts and the instrument panel assembly
- Both stamped steel reinforcement pieces
- Lower duct work from the heater box
- Upper center duct

6. Vehicles without air conditioning will have a square duct in place of the evapora-

tor. Remove this duct if present. If equipped with air conditioning, remove the evaporator assembly by removing or disconnecting the following:
- Wiring harness connectors and the electronic control unit
- Drain hose and lift out the evaporator unit

7. If servicing the assembly, disassemble the housing and remove the expansion valve and evaporator.

8. With the evaporator removed, remove the heater unit. To prevent bolts from falling inside the blower assembly, set the inside/outside air-selection damper to the position that permits outside air introduction.

9. Remove the cover plate around the heater tubes and remove the core fastener clips. Pull the heater core from the heater box, being careful not to damage the fins or tank ends.

To install:

10. Install the heater core to the heater box. Install the clips and cover.

11. Install the heater box and connect the duct work.

12. Assemble the housing, evaporator and expansion valve, making sure the gaskets are in good condition. Install the evaporator housing.

13. Using new lubricated O-rings, connect the refrigerant lines to the evaporator.

14. Install or connect the following:
- Electronic transmission ELC box
- All wire and control cables

- Instrument panel assembly and the console by reversing their removal procedures

15. Evacuate, charge and leak-test the air conditioning system. If the evaporator was replaced, add 2 oz. of refrigerant oil during the recharge.

16. Refill the cooling system.

17. Connect the negative battery cable and check the entire climate control system for proper operation. Check the system for leaks.

Neon

REMOVAL & INSTALLATION

1997–01 Models

1. Disconnect the negative battery cable.
2. Discharge and recover the air conditioning system refrigerant.
3. Remove the instrument panel from the vehicle by removing or disconnecting the following:
- Push the seats back all the way
- Pry out the left and right A-pillar trim moldings and remove (using a trim stick tool)
- Upper instrument panel cover
- Pull up on the cluster bezel (carefully), and remove it from the vehicle
- Pull the instrument panel cover rearward (carefully), and remove it from the vehicle

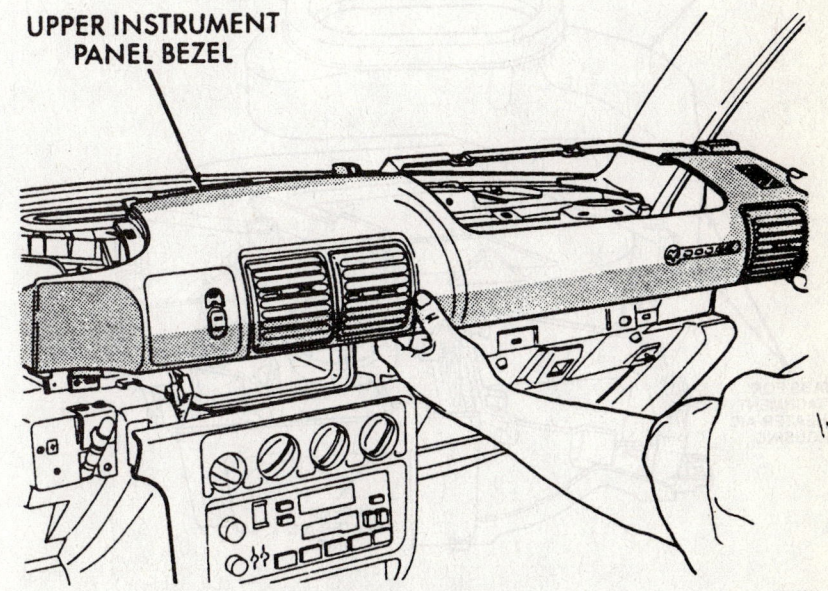

UPPER INSTRUMENT PANEL BEZEL

Remove the right side upper instrument panel bezel—Neon

89716G11

Refer to the model specific sections for engine mechanical service procedures

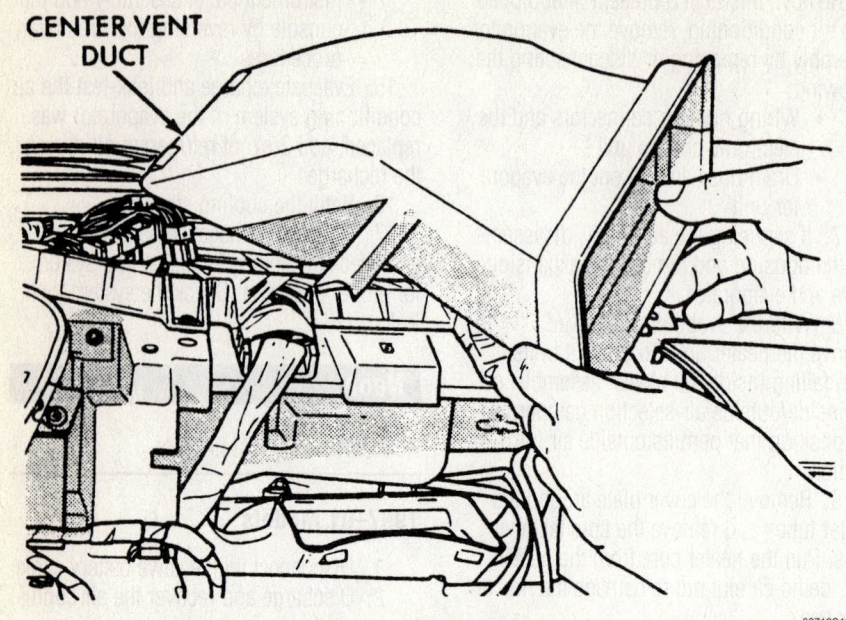

CENTER VENT DUCT

You must remove the instrument panel center vent duct—Neon

89716G12

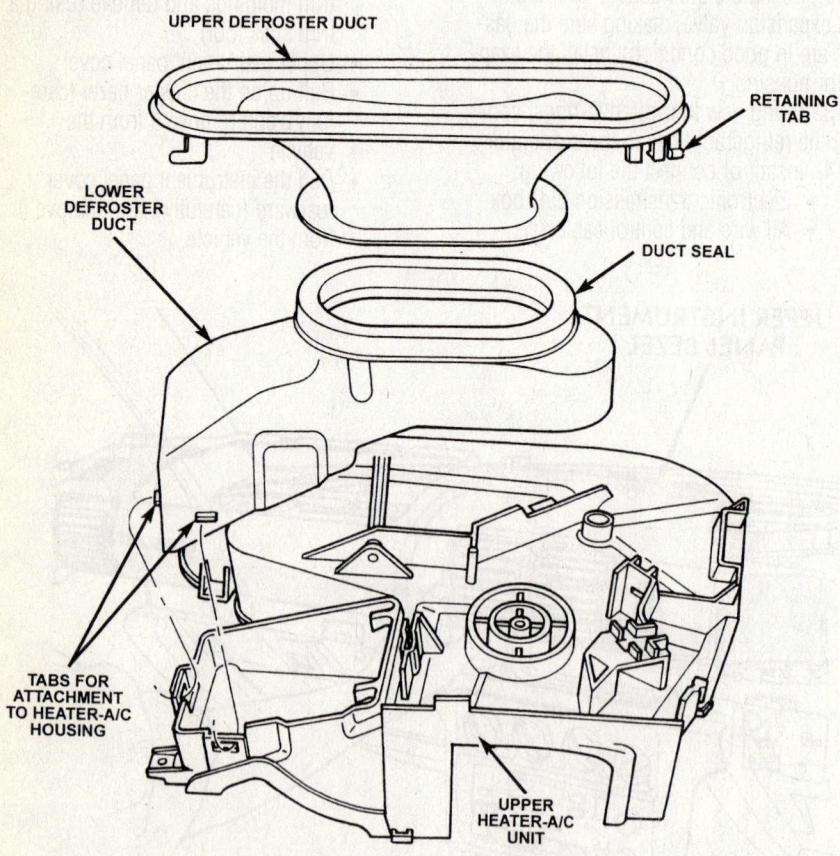

UPPER DEFROSTER DUCT

RETAINING TAB

LOWER DEFROSTER DUCT

DUCT SEAL

TABS FOR ATTACHMENT TO HEATER-A/C HOUSING

UPPER HEATER-A/C UNIT

89716G13

The upper defrost duct is secured with retaining tabs—Neon

✳✳ WARNING

Lock the steering wheel in the straight-ahead position; this will prevent damage to the clockspring

- Steering column as an assembly
- Left and right instrument panel end caps
- Center console
- Depress the Data Link Connector (DLC) sides and remove the DLC from the instrument panel reinforcement
- 4 bulkhead instrument panel screws
- 2 brake pedal support bracket bolts
- 2 center support mounting bolts
- Left and right A-pillar bolts; there are 2 on each side
- Antenna connector from the right side
- Left and right A-pillar door harness connectors
- 2 HVAC wiring harness connectors from the top right of the instrument panel
- Left side wiring harness connector from the top left of the instrument panel for the vanity and rear view mirrors
- Pull off the HVAC control head knobs
- 2 top front center bezel screws
- Using a trim stick, carefully pry out the instrument panel center bezel and remove it
- 2 HVAC control head screws
- Instrument panel wiring harness connector
- Vacuum harness connector

4. Pull the HVAC control head out of the instrument panel, twist it 90 degrees and push it back through the opening; do not disconnect the control cables.

5. Remove or disconnect the following:
- Air bag Control Module (ACM) from the center console
- Parking Brake Warning Lamp Switch from the center console
- Transmission Range Indicator Lamp from the center console

6. Using an assistant, pull the instrument panel rearward and remove it from the vehicle.

7. Drain the cooling system and remove the heater hoses at the dash panel. Place plugs in the heater core outlets to prevent coolant spillage during the unit housing removal.

8. Remove the suction line at the expansion valve. Place a piece of tape over the open refrigerant line to prevent moisture and/or dirt from entering the line.

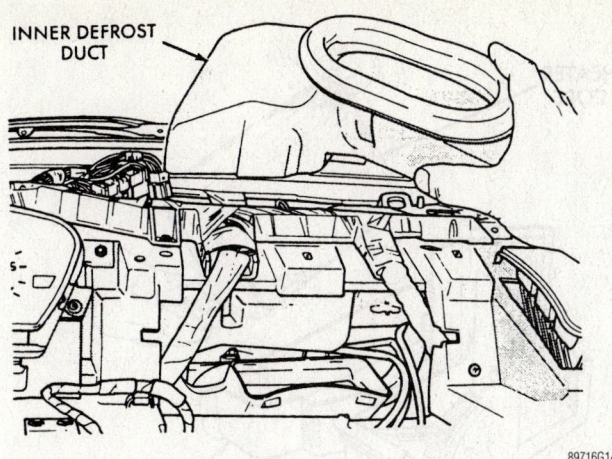

Remove the inner defrost duct—Neon

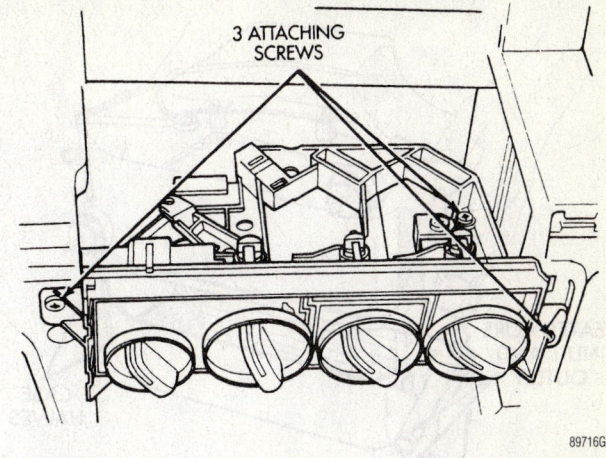

Exploded view of the control panel retainer locations—Neon

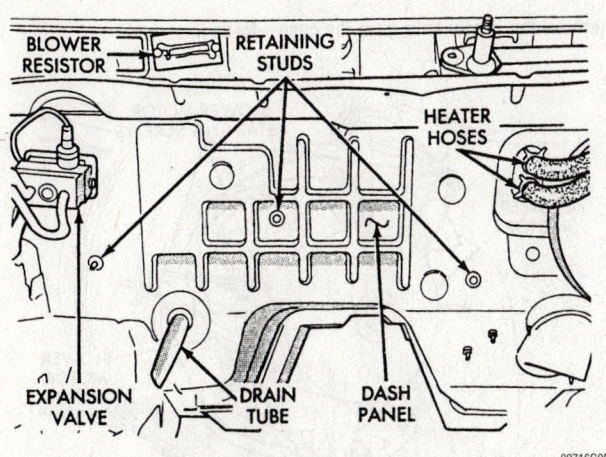

Location of the 3 dash panel retaining studs—Neon

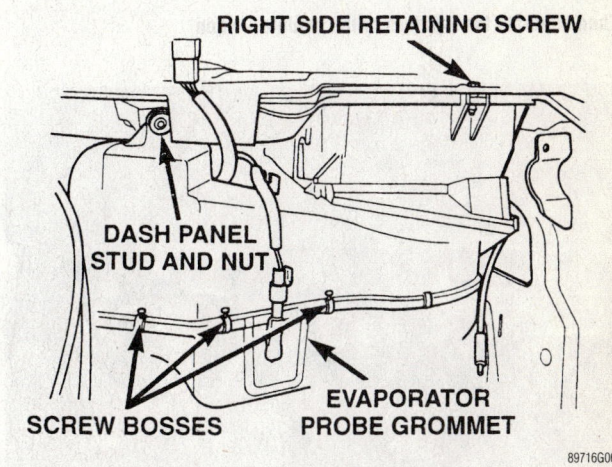

Unit housing retaining screw location—Neon

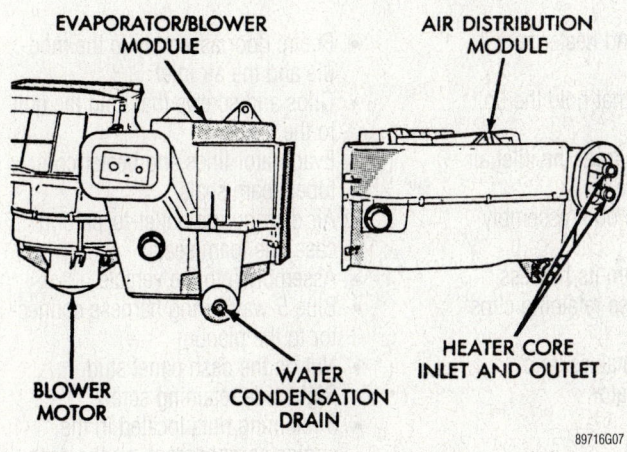

You must remove the retainers, then separate the air distribution module from the evaporator/blower module—Neon

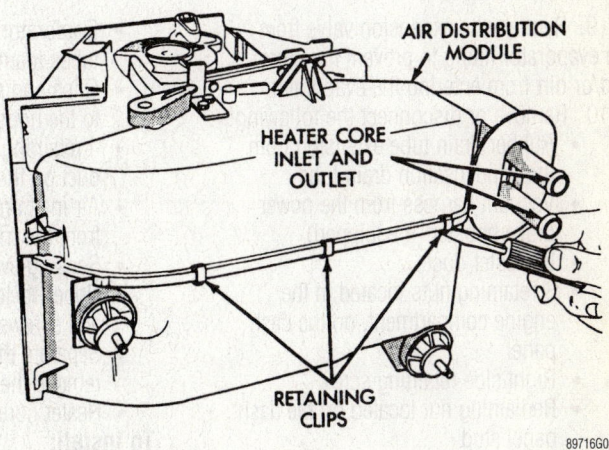

Remove the upper-to-lower housing retaining clips and screws—Neon

Refer to the model specific sections for cooling system service precautions

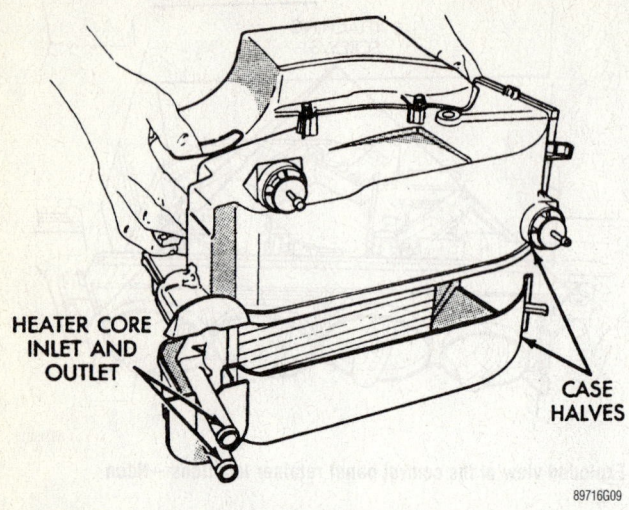

89716G09

Then separate the 2 halves of the module—Neon

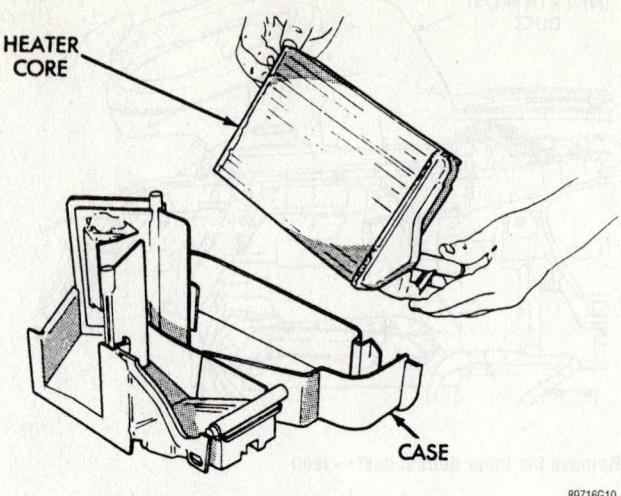

89716G10

Remove the heater core from the case—Neon

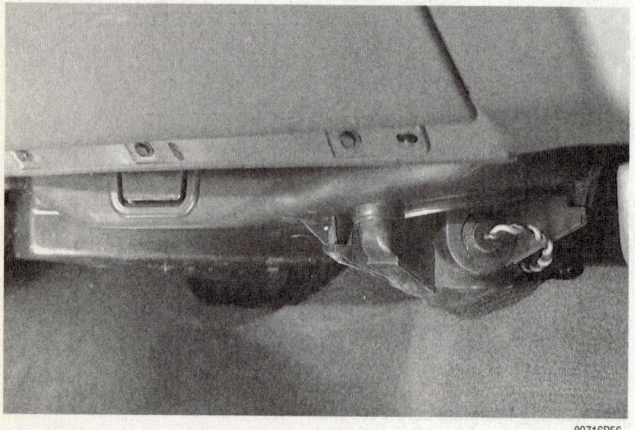

89716P56

The blower motor assembly is located under the passenger's side dash panel—1997–01 Neon

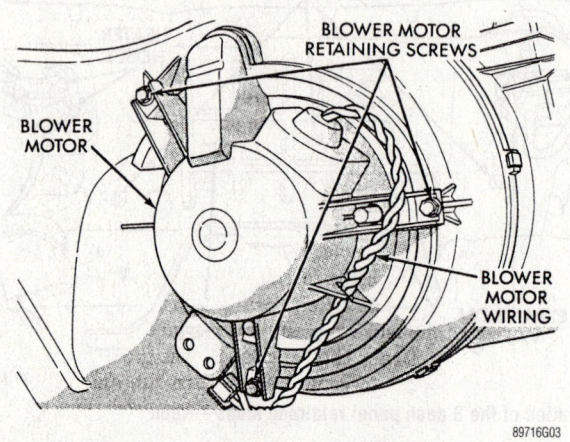

89716G03

Blower motor mounting and location of the retaining screws and wiring—1997–01 Neon vehicles with air conditioning

9. Remove the expansion valve from the evaporator fitting to prevent moisture and/or dirt from entering the evaporator.

10. Remove or disconnect the following:
- Rubber drain tube extension from the condensation drain tube
- Vacuum harness from the power brake booster (if equipped)
- Defroster duct
- 3 retaining nuts located in the engine compartment, on the dash panel
- Right side retaining screw
- Remaining nut located on the dash panel stud
- Blue 5-way wiring harness connector from the plenum
- Heater/air conditioning assembly from the vehicle
- Separate the air distribution outlet-to-parting case line foam seals

- Evaporator lines and heater core tubes foam seals
- Clips and screws that hold the unit to the housing
- 4 retaining screws from the inlet air duct on the module
- Air inlet and recirc door assembly from the module
- Sensing switch from its harness
- Upper-to-lower case retaining clips and screws
- Separate the case halves, and remove the evaporator
- Heater core

To install:

11. Install or connect the following:
- Heater core into the heater/air conditioning unit.
- Evaporator and the upper-to-lower case retaining clips and screws
- Sensing switch to its harness

- Recirc door assembly to the module and the air inlet
- Clips and screws that hold the unit to the housing
- Evaporator lines and heater core tubes foam seals.
- Air distribution outlet-to-parting case line foam seals
- Assembly into the vehicle
- Blue 5-way wiring harness connector to the plenum
- Nut on the dash panel stud
- Right side retaining screw
- 3 retaining nuts located in the engine compartment, on the dash panel
- Defroster duct
- If equipped, the vacuum harness to the power brake booster
- Rubber drain tube extension to the condensation drain tube

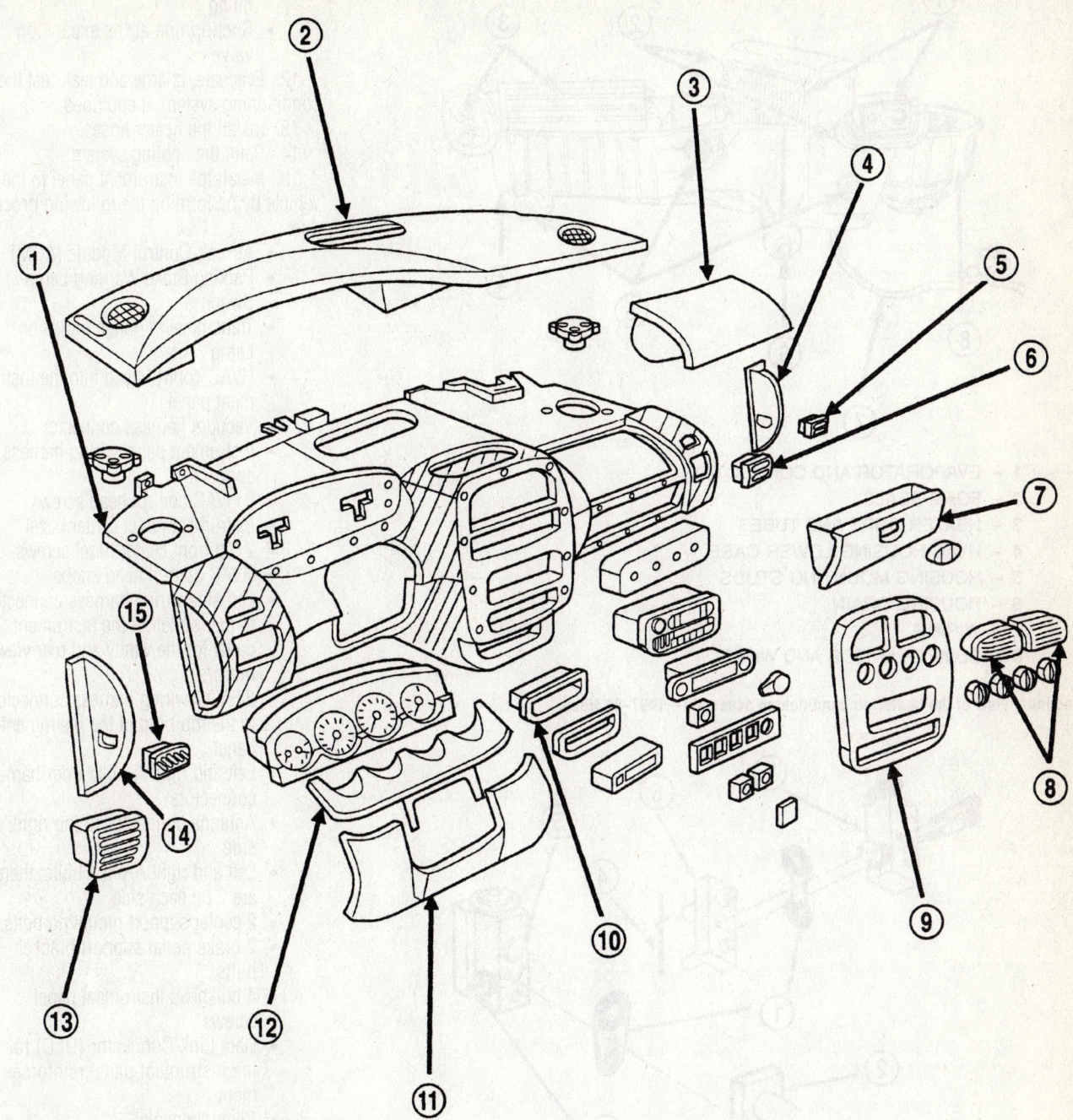

1 – INSTRUMENT PANEL ASSEMBLY
2 – UPPER COVER INSTRUMENT PANEL
3 – MODULE, PASSENGER SIDE AIRBAG
4 – END CAP, RIGHT
5 – DEMISTER GRILLE, RIGHT
6 – LOUVER, AIR OUTLET, RIGHT
7 – DOOR, GLOVE BOX
8 – LOUVER, AIR OUTLET, CENTER

9 – BEZEL INSTRUMENT PANEL, CENTER
10 – BIN, LOWER STORAGE
11 – COVER, LOWER INSTRUMENT PANEL
12 – CLUSTER BEZEL
13 – LOUVER, AIR OUTLET, LEFT
14 – END CAP, LEFT
15 – DEMISTER GRILLE, LEFT

93111G86

Exploded view of the instrument panel—1997–01 Neon

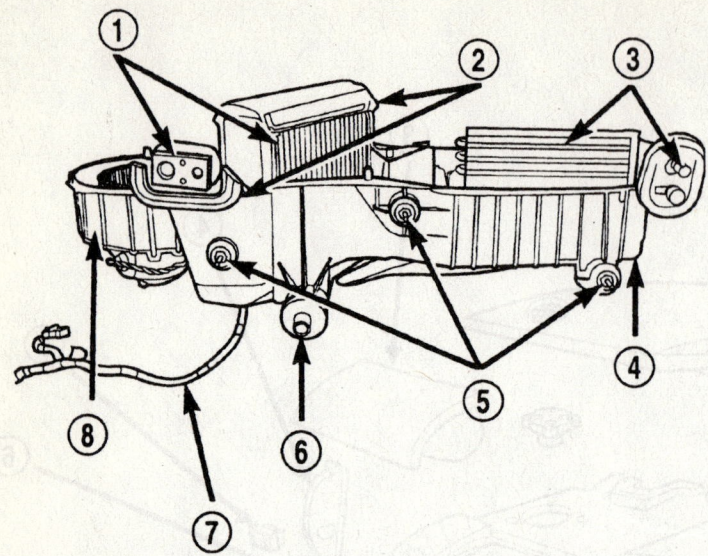

1 – EVAPORATOR AND CONNECTION
2 – FOAM SEALS
3 – HEATER CORE AND TUBES
4 – HVAC HOUSING LOWER CASE
5 – HOUSING MOUNTING STUDS
6 – HOUSING DRAIN
7 – WIRING
8 – BLOWER MOTOR AND WHEEL

93111G87

Sectional view of the heater/air conditioning assembly—1997–01 Neon

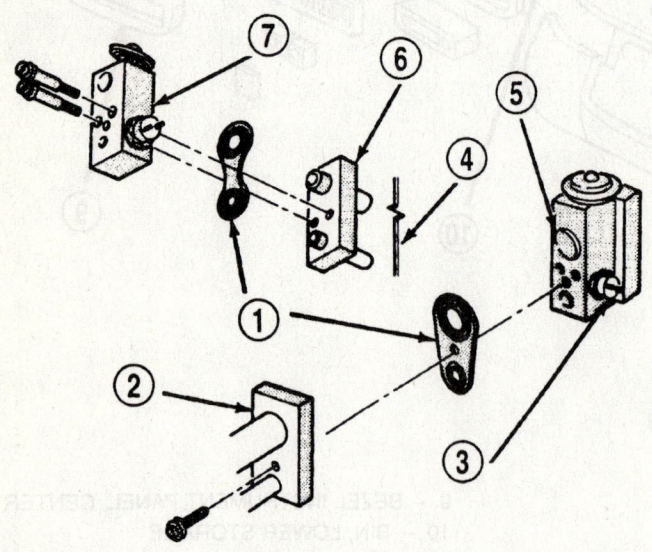

1 – ALUMINUM N-GASKET
2 – PLUMBING SEALING PLATE
3 – LOW/DIFFERENTIAL PRESSURE CUT-OFF SWITCH
4 – DASH PANEL
5 – H-VALVE
6 – EVAPORATOR SEALING PLATE
7 – H-VALVE

93111G88

Exploded view of the expansion valve—1997–01 Neon

- Expansion valve to the evaporator fitting
- Suction line at the expansion valve

12. Evacuate, charge and leak-test the air conditioning system, if equipped.

13. Install the heater hoses.

14. Refill the cooling system.

15. Install the instrument panel to the vehicle by performing the following procedure:

- Air bag Control Module (ACM)
- Parking Brake Warning Lamp Switch
- Transmission Range Indicator Lamp
- HVAC control head into the instrument panel
- Vacuum harness connector
- Instrument panel wiring harness connector
- 2 HVAC control head screws
- Instrument panel center bezel
- 2 top front center bezel screws
- HVAC control head knobs
- Left side wiring harness connector to the top left of the instrument panel for the vanity and rear view mirrors
- 2 HVAC wiring harness connectors to the top right of the instrument panel
- Left and right A-pillar door harness connectors
- Antenna connector to the right side
- Left and right A-pillar bolts; there are 2 on each side
- 2 center support mounting bolts
- 2 brake pedal support bracket bolts
- 4 bulkhead instrument panel screws
- Data Link Connector (DLC) to the instrument panel reinforcement
- Center console
- Left and right instrument panel end caps
- Steering column as an assembly
- Instrument panel cover
- Cluster bezel
- Upper instrument panel cover
- Left and right A-pillar trim moldings
- Move seats forward
- Negative battery cable

16. Operate the engine to normal operating temperatures; then, check the climate control operation and check for leaks.

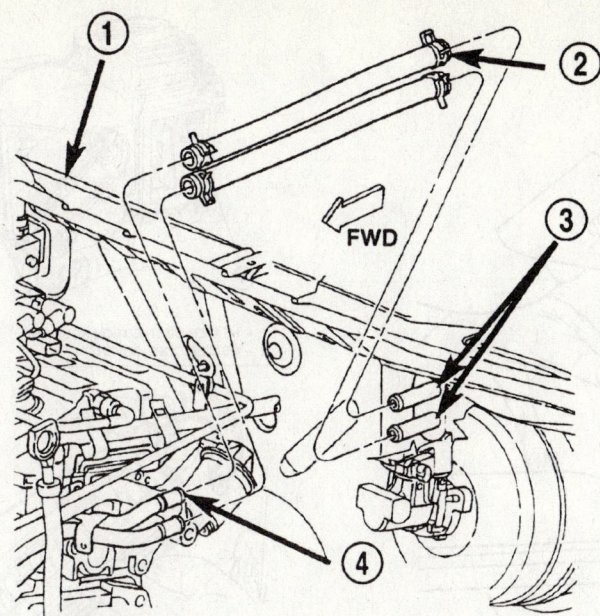

1 – COWL PANEL
2 – HEATER HOSE AND CLAMPS
3 – HEATER CORE TUBES
4 – HEATER HOSE SUPPLY AND RETURN TUBES

93111G89

View of the heater hoses and clamps—1997–01 Neon

Cirrus, Sebring Convertible, Breeze, Stratus

REMOVAL & INSTALLATION

1997–01 Models

1. Disconnect the negative battery cable.
2. Drain the cooling system into a clean container for reuse.
3. From the center of the instrument panel, grasp and pull to remove the radio/control module bezel.
4. At the right side of the instrument panel, remove the side trim.
5. Remove or disconnect the following:

- 2 lower right side support beam screws
- Instrument panel support-to-A-pillar bolt
- On left side of the instrument panel, remove the side trim
- Upper instrument panel bezel
- Lower knee bolster
- Console-to-instrument panel screws
- Gearshift knob and the shifter bezel

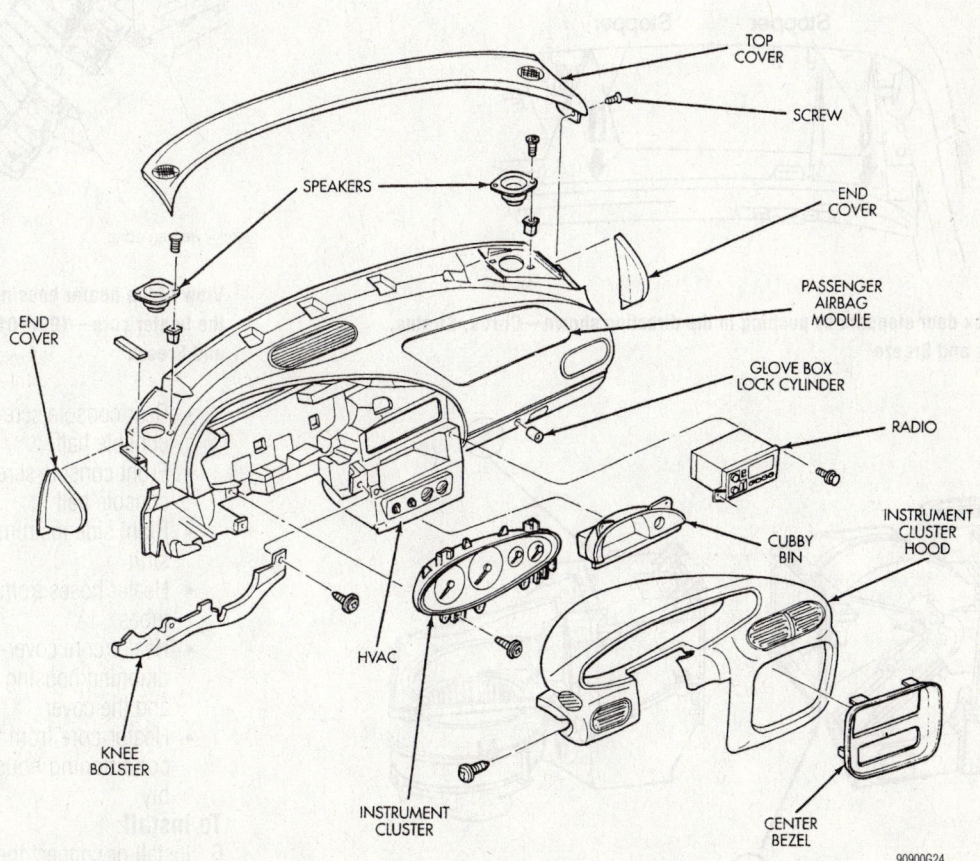

90900G24

Exploded view of the instrument panel assembly—Cirrus, Stratus, Sebring convertible and Breeze

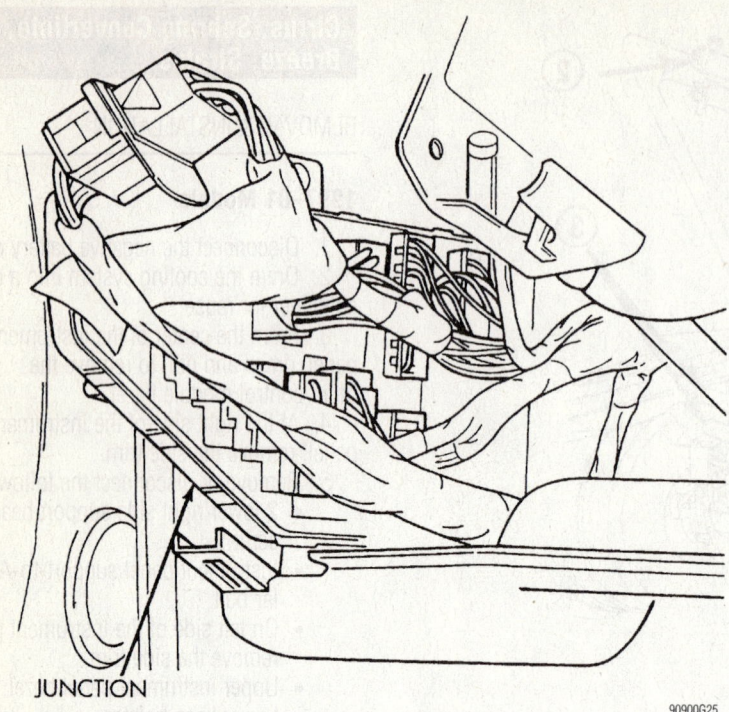

JUNCTION

Junction block location—Cirrus, Stratus, Sebring convertible and Breeze

90900G25

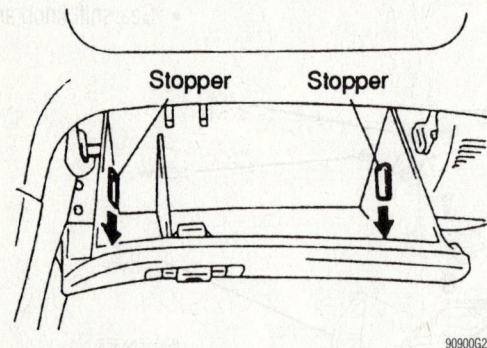

Stopper   Stopper

Unlock the glove box door stoppers by pushing in the direction shown—Cirrus, Stratus, Sebring convertible and Breeze

90900G27

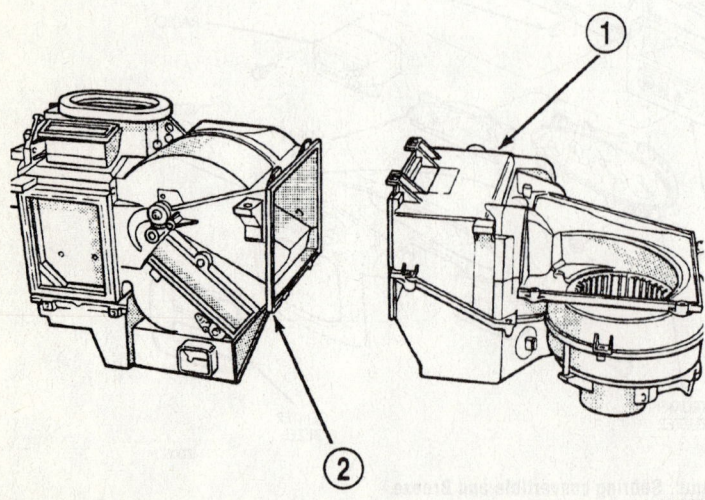

View of the heater/air conditioning housing assembly—1997-01 Cirrus, Stratus and Breeze

93111G79

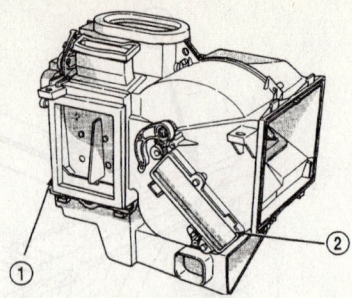

1 – HEATER DISTRIBUTION HOUSING
2 – HEATER CORE COVER

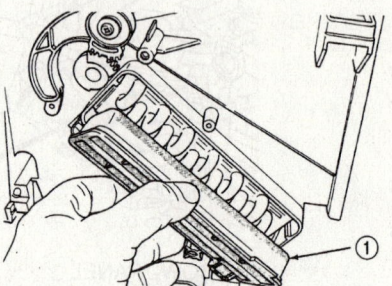

1 – HEATER CORE COVER

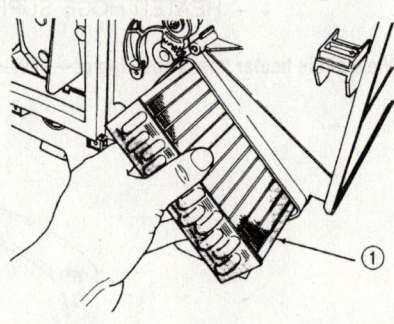

1 – HEATER CORE

93111G80

View of the heater housing assembly and the heater core—1997-01 Cirrus, Stratus and Breeze

- Rear console screws and the rear console half
- Front console screws and the front console half
- Right side instrument panel support strut
- Heater hoses from the heater core tubes
- Heater core cover-to-heater/air conditioning housing assembly screws and the cover
- Heater core from the heater/air conditioning housing assembly

To install:

6. Install or connect the following:
- Heater core to the heater/air conditioning housing assembly
- Heater core cover and the cover-to-

heater/air conditioning housing assembly screws
- Heater hoses to the heater core tubes
- Right side instrument panel support strut
- Front console half and the front console screws
- Rear console half and the rear console screws

- Shifter bezel and the gearshift knob
- Console-to-instrument panel screws
- Lower knee bolster
- Upper instrument panel bezel
- On left side of the instrument panel, install the side trim
- Instrument panel support-to-A-pillar bolt
- 2 lower right side support beam screws

- Right side of the instrument panel, install the side trim
- On center of the instrument panel, install the radio/control module bezel
7. Refill the cooling system.
8. Connect the negative battery cable.
9. Operate the engine to normal operating temperatures; then, check the climate control operation and check for leaks.

FORD MOTOR COMPANY

Aspire

REMOVAL & INSTALLATION

1. Disconnect the negative battery cable.

⁂ **CAUTION**

Never open, service or drain the radiator or cooling system when hot; serious burns can occur from the steam and hot coolant. Also, when draining engine coolant, keep in mind that cats and dogs are attracted to ethylene glycol antifreeze and

could drink any that is left in an uncovered container or in puddles on the ground. This will prove fatal in sufficient quantities. Always drain coolant into a sealable container. Coolant should be reused unless it is contaminated or is several years old.

2. Drain and recycle the engine coolant.
3. Disable the air bag system.
4. Remove the instrument panel by removing or disconnecting the following:
   - Driver's side air bag module retainers from the back side of the steering wheel

- Air bag/horn electrical connection and the air bag from the steering wheel
- Steering wheel
- Multi-function switch and the ignition switch
- Lower steering column shaft lower bolt
- Lower steering column bracket nuts
- 2 upper steering column bracket bolts
- Matchmark the juncture of the column intermediate shaft coupling and the lower column shaft
- Steering column
- Instrument cluster
- Fuse panel cover, loosen the fuse panel screws and push the panel forward, but do not remove it
- Parking brake console and the shift console
- If not already done, the shift console panel
- 2 air bag diagnostic monitor electrical connections
- Monitor retaining nuts and slide the monitor from its mounting bracket
- Climate control panel assembly
- Open the glove compartment door, loosen the compartment retaining screws and remove the glove compartment
- Passenger side air bag module bolts

➡ **Do not pull the wiring when handling the module.**

⁂ **CAUTION**

Always carry the module with the deployment doors facing away from the body.

- Passenger side air bag module by pushing on the module from inside the instrument panel

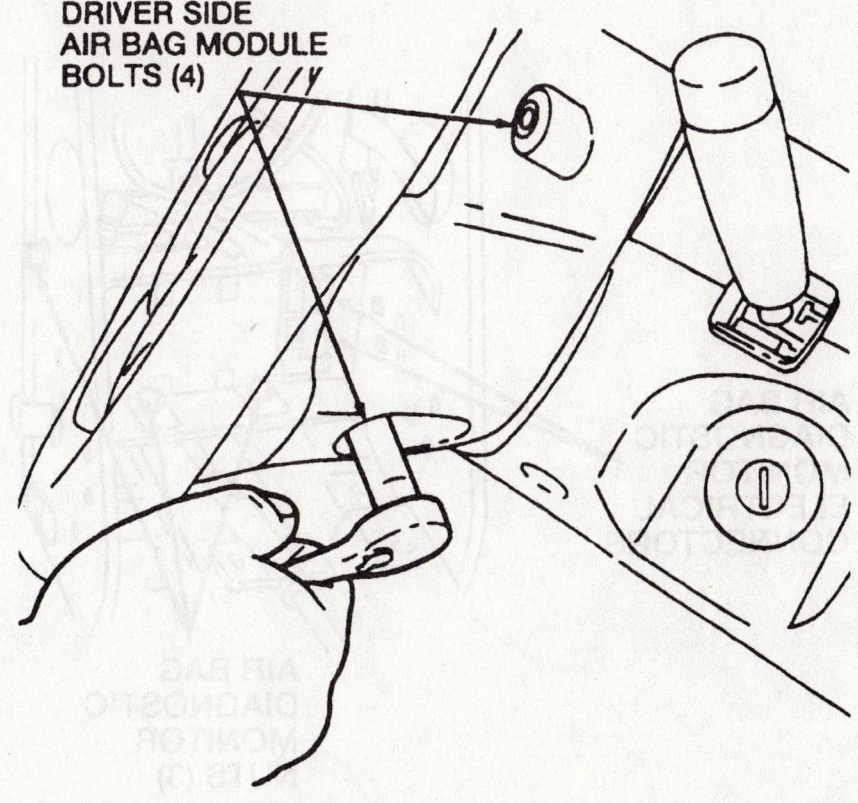

DRIVER SIDE AIR BAG MODULE BOLTS (4)

89720G02

Loosen the driver's side air bag module retaining bolts—Aspire

Refer to the model specific sections for engine mechanical service procedures

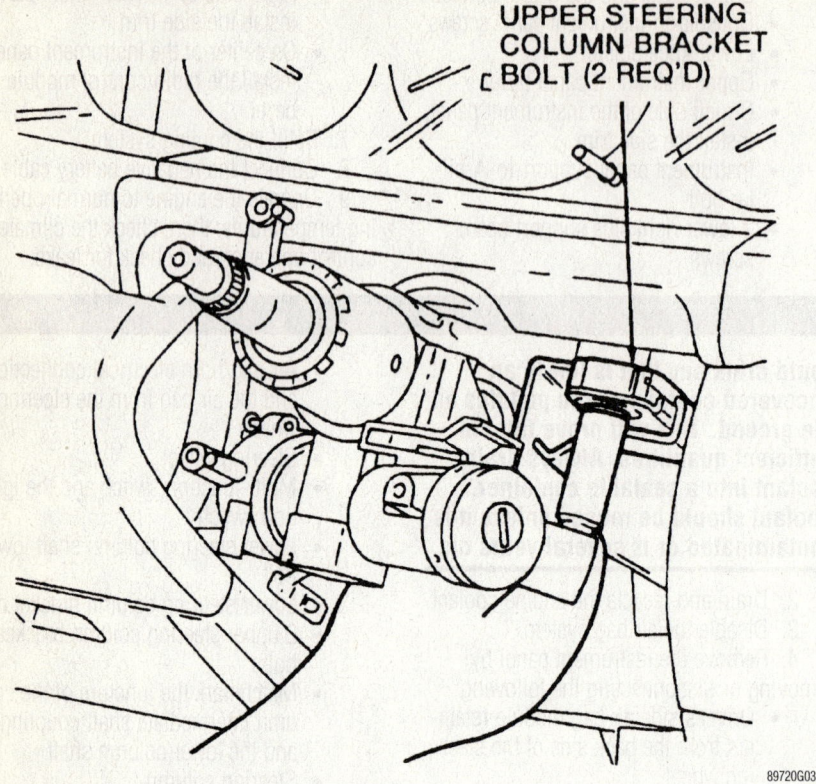

UPPER STEERING
COLUMN BRACKET
BOLT (2 REQ'D)

89720G03

Loosen the upper column bracket bolts—Aspire

- Press the orange tab and unplug the orange connector
- Press the blue tab and unplug the blue connector
- White ground electrical connection and the module
- Instrument panel control opening cover and loosen the tapping screw, which is located in the center of the panel
- Panel lower mounting bolts
- Panel side covers and loosen the side bolts
- Hood release handle locknut and lower the handle until it is out of the way
- Electrical connections from the rear of the instrument panel and remove the instrument panel

5. Remove or disconnect the following:

- Inlet and outlet heater water hoses in the engine compartment.
- Wiring harness and antenna lead from the bracket on the front of the heater core case
- Air conditioning evaporator register duct-to-heater core case retaining screw

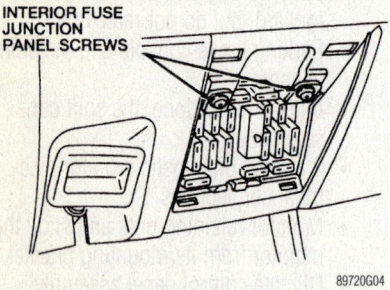

INTERIOR FUSE
JUNCTION
PANEL SCREWS

89720G04

Loosen the fuse panel screws and push the panel forward, but do not remove it— Aspire

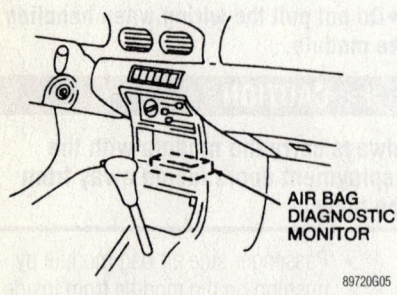

AIR BAG
DIAGNOSTIC
MONITOR

89720G05

The air bag diagnostic monitor is located behind the shift console—Aspire

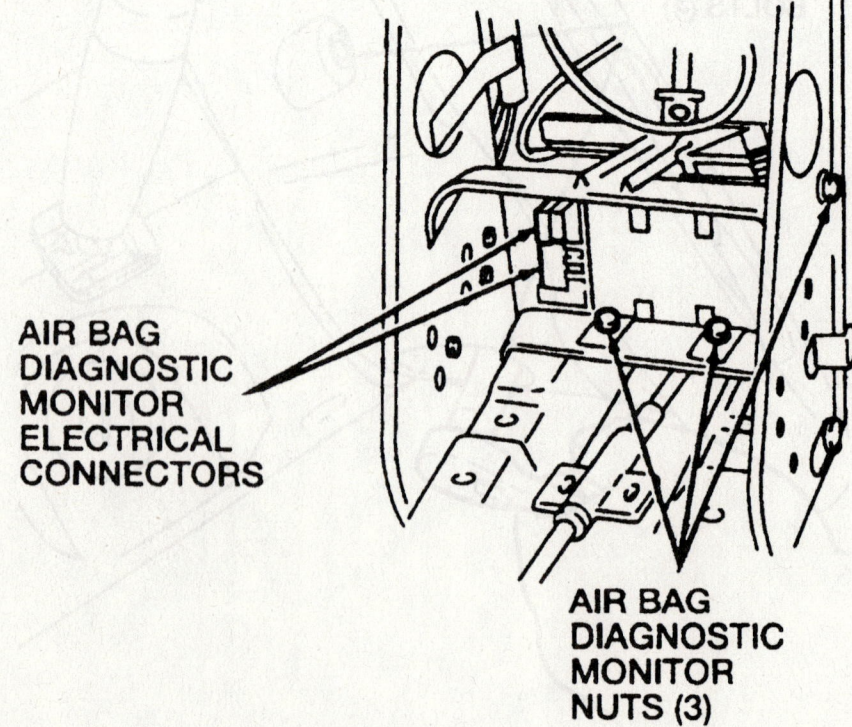

AIR BAG
DIAGNOSTIC
MONITOR
ELECTRICAL
CONNECTORS

AIR BAG
DIAGNOSTIC
MONITOR
NUTS (3)

89720G06

Disengage the diagnostic monitor, loosen the nuts and remove the monitor—Aspire

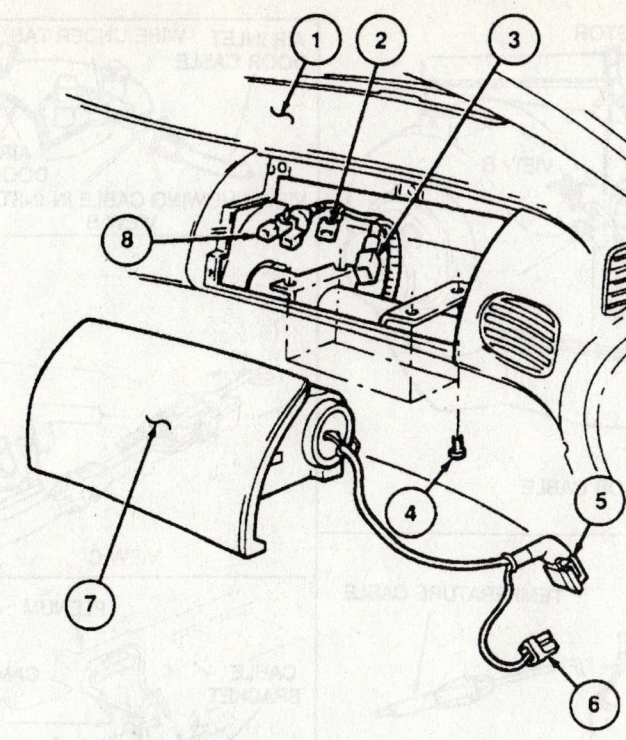

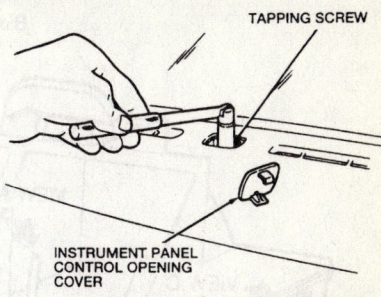

89720G11

Fig. 24 Remove the cover and loosen the tapping screw which is located in the center of the panel—Aspire

- 2 nuts from the upper and lower right side of the case
- Nut on the lower left side, and disengage the case from the windshield defroster nozzle connectors
- Heater core cover seal retaining screws, then remove the seal
- Heater core from the case

To install:

6. Install or connect the following:
   - Heater core into its case
   - Seal and the case retaining screws

➡ **Make sure the windshield defroster nozzle connectors and the air conditioning evaporator register duct are properly seated on the heater core case before installing the case.**

- Heater core case and tighten the retaining nuts
- Air conditioning evaporator register duct-to-heater core case retaining screw
- Antenna and wiring harness to the bracket on the front of the case

7. Install the instrument panel by installing or connecting the following:
   - Electrical connections to the rear of the instrument panel
   - Place the panel in position, connect the hood release handle and tighten its locknut
   - Loosely tighten the tapping screw which is located in the center of the panel
   - Tighten the panel side bolts to 14–18 ft. lbs. (19–25 Nm)
   - Tapping screw located in the center of the panel to 71–97 inch lbs. (8–11 Nm)
   - Panel side covers

Item	Description
1	Instrument Panel
2	Ground Electrical Connector (WHITE)
3	Electrical Connector (ORANGE)
4	Passenger Side Air Bag Module Bolts (4 Req'd)
5	Electrical Connector (BLUE)
6	Ground Electrical Connector (WHITE)
7	Passenger Side Air Bag Module
8	Electrical Connector (BLUE)

89720G07

Exploded view of the passenger side air bag assembly—Aspire

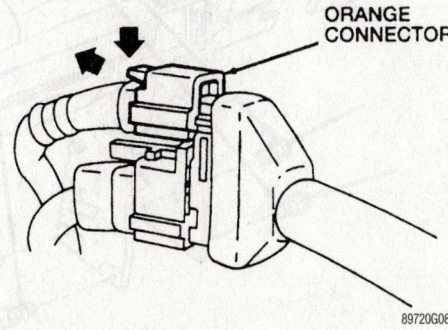

89720G08

Press on the tab and disengage the orange connector—Aspire

Refer to the model specific sections for cooling system service precautions

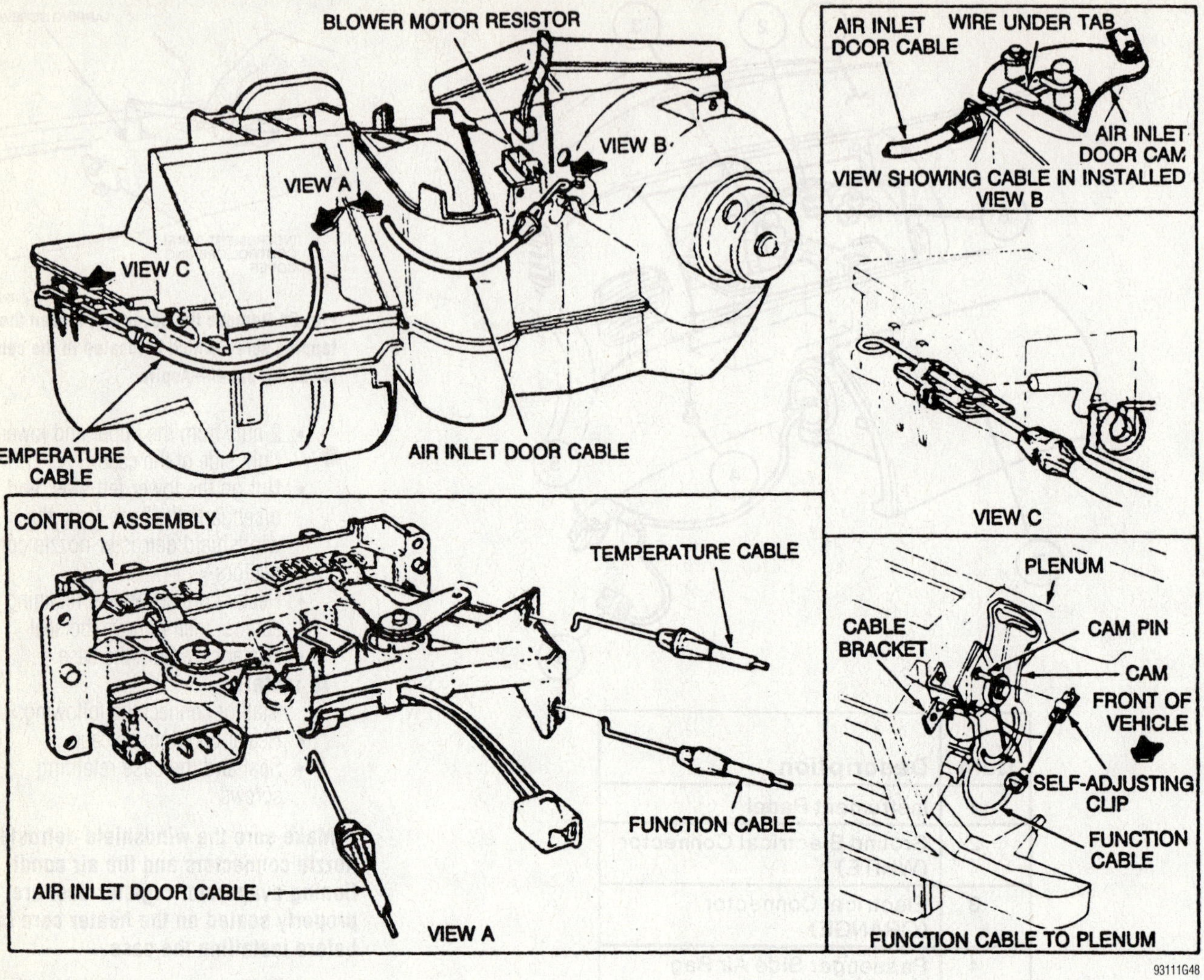

BLOWER MOTOR RESISTOR

VIEW B

VIEW A

VIEW C

AIR INLET DOOR CABLE — WIRE UNDER TAB

AIR INLET DOOR CAM

VIEW SHOWING CABLE IN INSTALLED
VIEW B

TEMPERATURE CABLE

AIR INLET DOOR CABLE

VIEW C

CONTROL ASSEMBLY

TEMPERATURE CABLE

FUNCTION CABLE

AIR INLET DOOR CABLE

VIEW A

PLENUM

CABLE BRACKET

CAM PIN

CAM

FRONT OF VEHICLE

SELF-ADJUSTING CLIP

FUNCTION CABLE

FUNCTION CABLE TO PLENUM

93111G48

View of the heater/air conditioning housing and control cables—Aspire

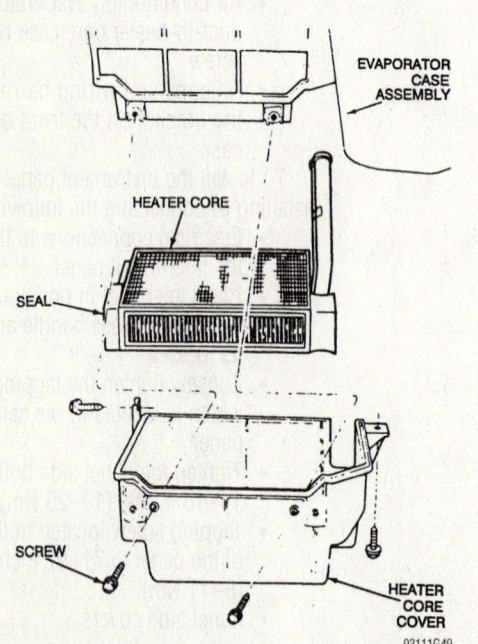

EVAPORATOR CASE ASSEMBLY

HEATER CORE

SEAL

SCREW

HEATER CORE COVER

93111G49

Exploded view of the heater core and housing components—Aspire

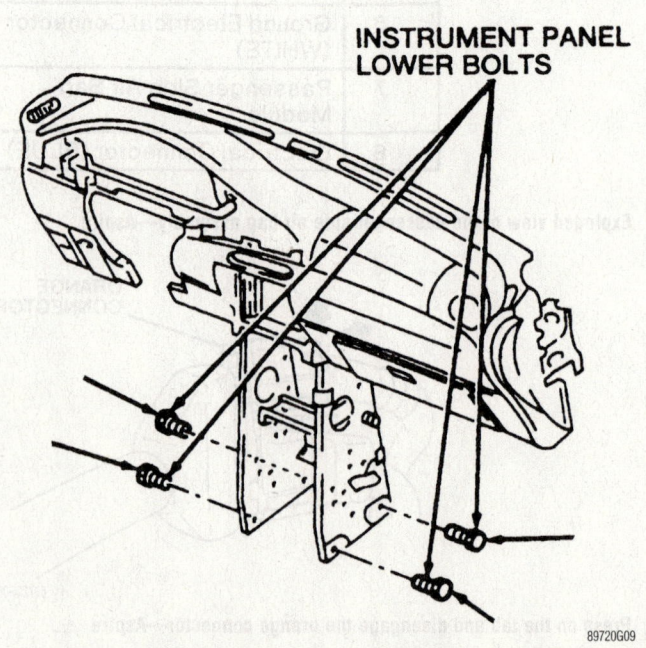

INSTRUMENT PANEL LOWER BOLTS

89720G09

Loosen the instrument panel's lower mounting bolts—Aspire

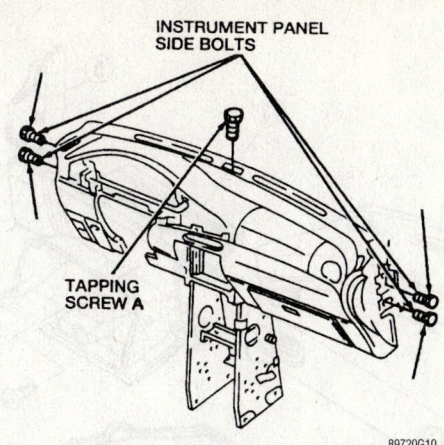

After the instrument panel side covers have been removed, loosen the side bolts—Aspire

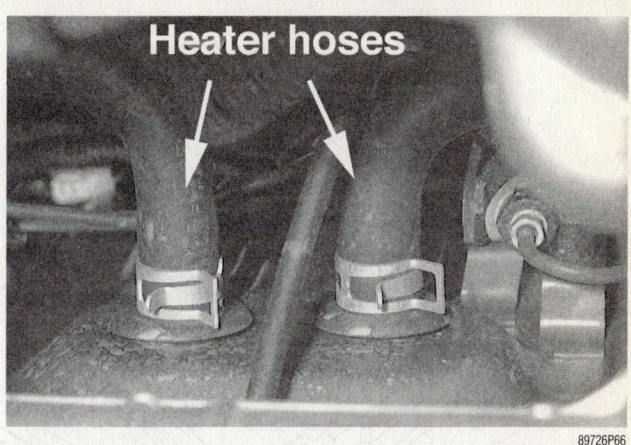

Tag and disconnect the inlet and outlet heater hoses in the engine compartment—Aspire

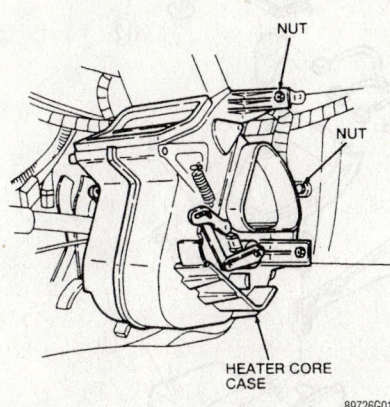

Remove the nuts from the upper and lower right side of the heater core case—Aspire

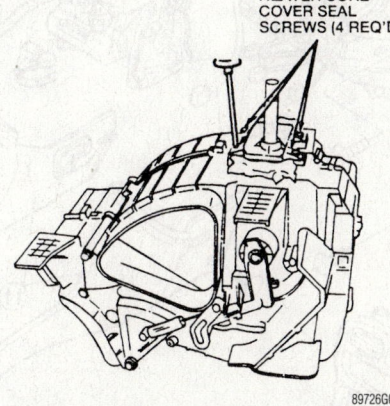

Remove the heater core cover seal screws and seal—Aspire

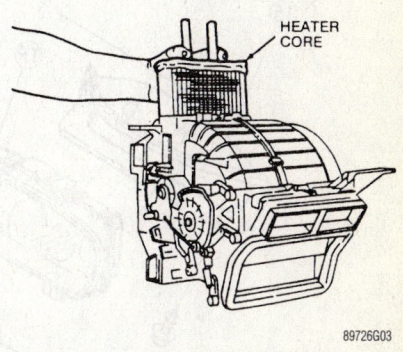

Withdraw the heater core from the case assembly—Aspire

- Tighten the panel lower bolts to 14–18 ft. lbs. (19–25 Nm)
- Passenger side air bag module's electrical connections
- Module in the panel, then tighten the module retaining bolts to 80–91 inch lbs. (9–12 Nm)
- Glove compartment and tighten its retaining screws
- Climate control panel assembly
- Slide the air bag diagnostic monitor onto its bracket and tighten the retaining nuts
- Electrical connections and install the shift console panel
- Shift console, parking brake console and instrument cluster
- Steering column and align the marks made on the juncture of the column intermediate shaft coupling and the lower column shaft
- Upper column bracket bolts to 13–20 ft. lbs. (18–26 Nm)

- Lower column bracket nuts to 13–20 ft. lbs. (18–26 Nm)
- Lower column shaft lower bolt to 12–17 ft. lbs. (16–23 Nm)
- Ignition switch and multi-function switch
- Steering wheel
- Driver's side air bag module its electrical connections
- Module retaining bolts at the back of the steering wheel and tighten them to 80–115 inch lbs. (9–13 Nm)
- Inlet and outlet heater hoses

8. Fill the cooling system to its proper level with the proper mixture of coolant.

9. Connect the negative battery cable.

10. Start the engine, let it idle until it reaches normal operating temperature, and check for cooling system leaks.

Probe

REMOVAL & INSTALLATION

1997 Models

1. Disconnect the negative battery cable.

2. Remove the instrument panel by removing or disconnecting the following:

- Upper and lower steering column covers. Detach the steering column and lower it to the seat
- Instrument cluster
- Floor console
- Glove compartment
- Hush panel, console kick panels and side kick panels
- Climate control assembly
- Radio assembly and trip computer, if equipped

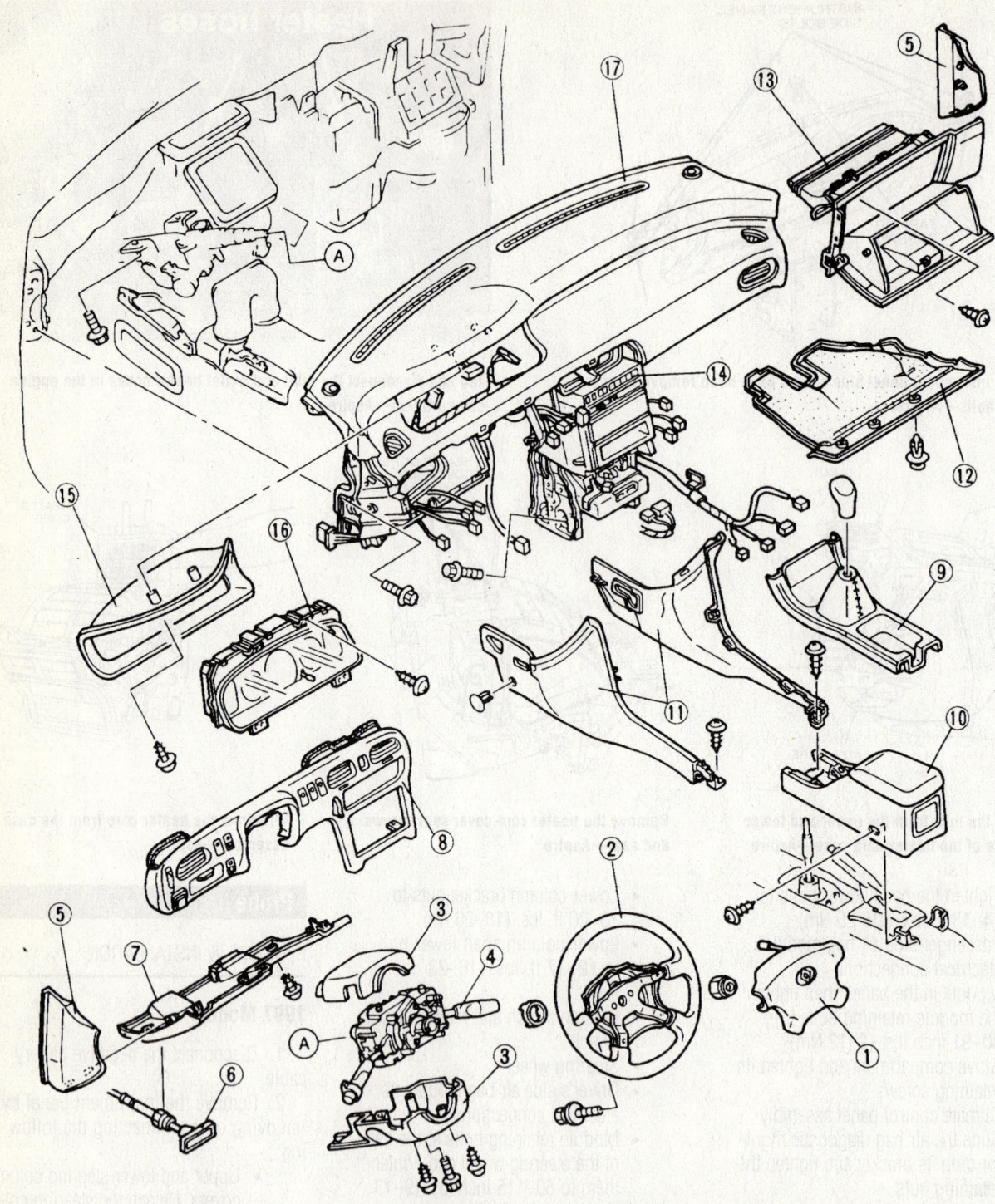

1. Steering wheel cover
2. Steering wheel
3. Column cover
4. Combination switch
5. Side panel
6. Hood release knob
7. Lower panel
8. Switch panel
9. Front console
10. Rear console
11. Side wall
12. Undercover
13. Glove compartment
14. Heater control unit assembly
15. Meter/gauge hood
16. Instrument cluster
17. Dashboard

89540G32

Instrument panel mounting—1997 Probe

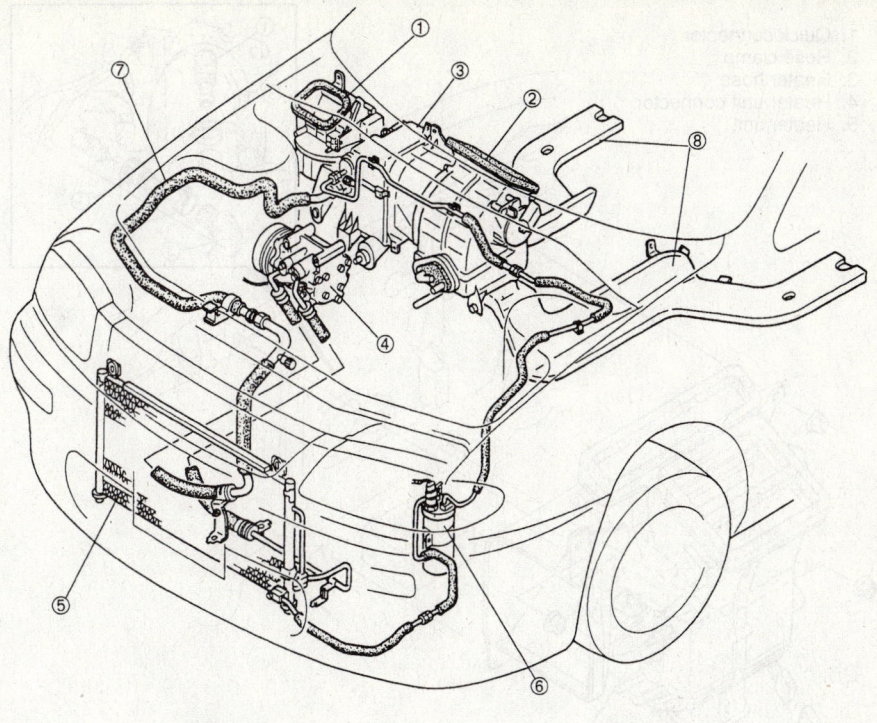

1. Blower unit
2. Heater unit
3. Cooling unit
4. A/C compressor
5. Condenser
6. Receiver/drier
7. Refrigerant lines
8. Rear heat duct

89546GA1

View of the heating and air conditioning system components and relative locations—1997 Probe

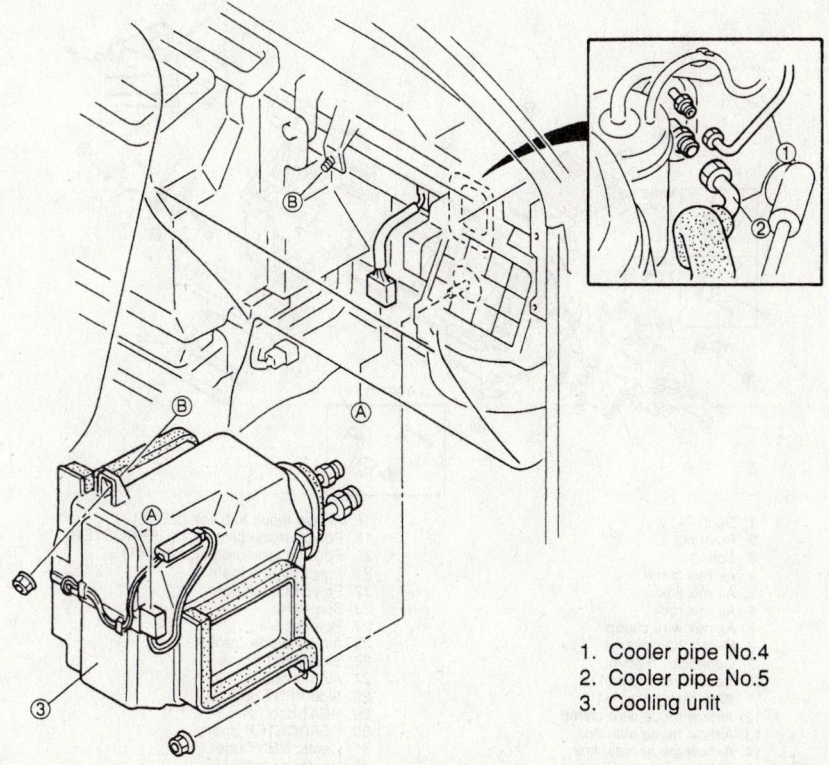

1. Cooler pipe No.4
2. Cooler pipe No.5
3. Cooling unit

89546GA2

Before the heater core can be removed, you must first remove the air conditioning unit from the firewall—1997 Probe

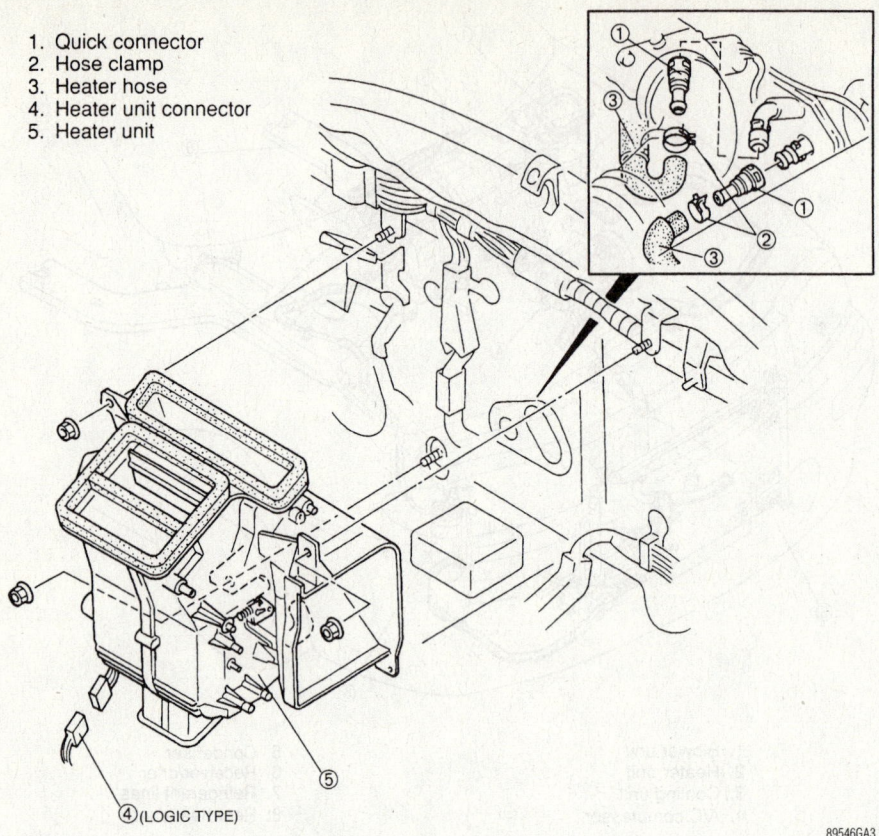

1. Quick connector
2. Hose clamp
3. Heater hose
4. Heater unit connector
5. Heater unit

(LOGIC TYPE)

89546GA3

View of the heater unit mounting and hose/electrical connections—1997 Probe

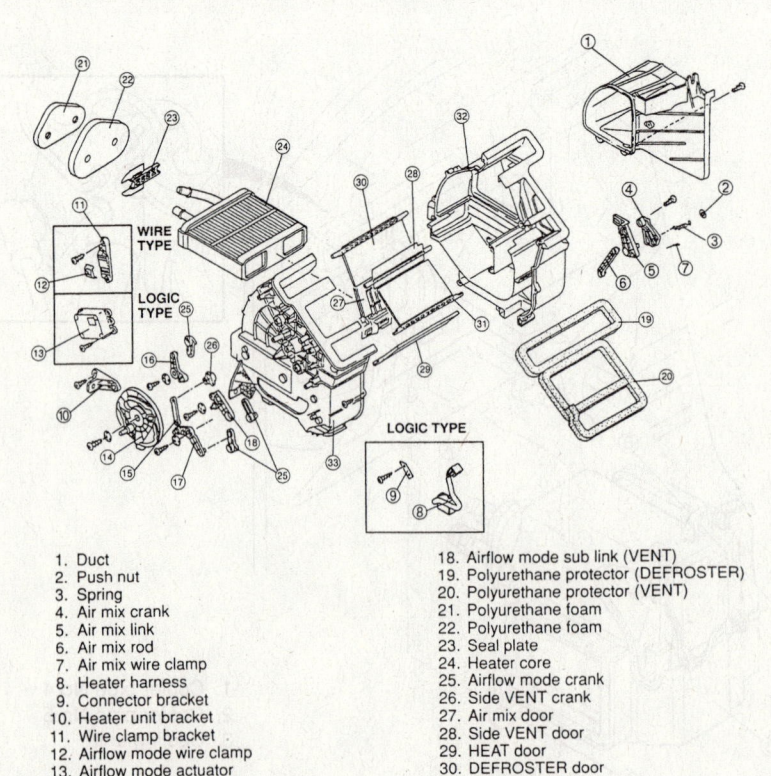

1. Duct
2. Push nut
3. Spring
4. Air mix crank
5. Air mix link
6. Air mix rod
7. Air mix wire clamp
8. Heater harness
9. Connector bracket
10. Heater unit bracket
11. Wire clamp bracket
12. Airflow mode wire clamp
13. Airflow mode actuator
14. Airflow mode main link
15. Airflow mode rod
16. Airflow mode sub link (DEFROSTER)
17. Airflow mode sub link (HEAT)
18. Airflow mode sub link (VENT)
19. Polyurethane protector (DEFROSTER)
20. Polyurethane protector (VENT)
21. Polyurethane foam
22. Polyurethane foam
23. Seal plate
24. Heater core
25. Airflow mode crank
26. Side VENT crank
27. Air mix door
28. Side VENT door
29. HEAT door
30. DEFROSTER door
31. Center VENT door
32. Heater case (1)
33. Heater case (2)

89546GA4

Exploded view of the typical heater unit and core assembly. When disassembling, only remove the case half fasteners—1997 Probe

- 2 instrument panel side covers
- Instrument panel mounting bolts
- Door pillar trim
- Lift the panel up and to the rear, disconnect all remaining electrical harness and remove the panel from the vehicle

3. Drain the cooling system to a level below the heater core.

4. Remove or disconnect the following:

- Hoses from the heater core. Plug the hoses to avoid system contamination
- Loosen the upper left evaporator/blower unit nut to allow for removal of the heater case. Remove the heater wire harness screw
- Heater case attaching screws and pull the heater case straight out; be careful not to damage the heater core extension tubes
- Heater core tube braces-to-heater case screws and the tube braces. Lift the heater core straight up and from the heater case

To install:

5. Install or connect the following:

- Heater core to the heater case
- Tube braces and the heater core tube braces-to-heater case screws
- Heater case attaching screws
- Heater wire harness screw
- Hoses to the heater core

6. Install the instrument panel by installing or connecting the following:

- All electrical harness to the rear of the instrument panel and install the panel to the vehicle
- Door pillar trim

- Instrument panel mounting bolts
- Install the 2 instrument panel side covers
- Radio assembly and trip computer, if equipped
- Climate control assembly
- Hush panel, console kick panels and side kick panels
- Glove compartment
- Floor console
- Instrument cluster
- Steering column and the upper and lower steering column covers

7. Connect the negative battery cable.

8. Refill the cooling system and check for leaks.

1997–01 Contour, Mystique and 1999–01 Cougar

REMOVAL & INSTALLATION

1. Disconnect the negative battery cable.

2. Remove the center console.

3. Disarm the air bag system and remove the air bag diagnostic monitor and bracket.

4. Remove or disconnect the following:

- Screw retaining the air transfer duct to the heater outlet floor duct. Push the transfer duct inside of the heater outlet floor duct
- 3 screws retaining the heater outlet floor duct to the heater core cover and release the retaining tabs on each side of the duct and remove the duct

---

- Heater hoses from the heater core, and plug the heater core tubes and the hoses to prevent coolant loss.
- Vacuum supply hose (the black hose) from the vacuum source in the engine compartment
- Vacuum supply hose (the black hose) from the air conditioning vacuum reservoir tank
- Release the 4 retaining tabs and remove the 2 clips and the heater core cover containing the heater core
- Heater dash panel seal and the vacuum hose from the heater core cover
- Retaining screw and the heater core bracket from the cover
- Heater core from the cover
- Heater core case seal from the heater core

To install:

5. Install or connect the following:

- Heater core case seal on the heater core
- Heater core into the cover
- Retaining screw and the heater core bracket onto the cover
- Heater dash panel seal and the vacuum hose onto the heater core cover
- 4 retaining tabs, 2 clips and the heater core cover containing the heater core
- Vacuum supply hose (the black hose) to the air conditioning vacuum reservoir tank
- Vacuum supply hose (the black hose) to the vacuum source in the engine compartment

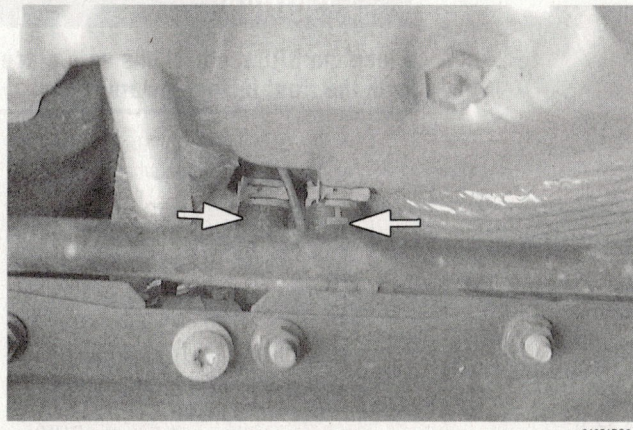

The heater hoses are best accessed from underneath the vehicle—1997–01 Contour and Mystique

91051PC8

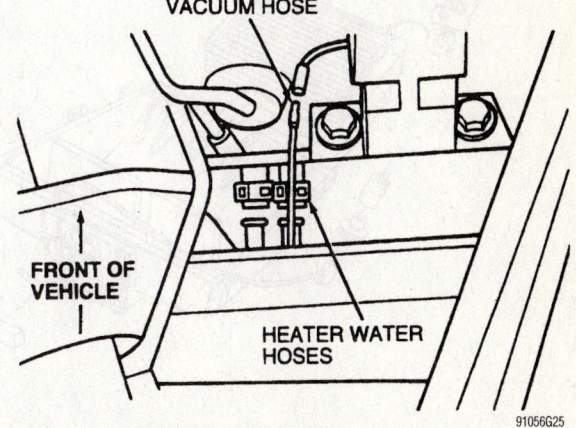

VACUUM HOSE

FRONT OF VEHICLE

HEATER WATER HOSES

Disconnect the heater hose and vacuum line from underneath the vehicle—1997–01 Contour and Mystique

91056G25

Refer to the model specific sections for engine mechanical service procedures

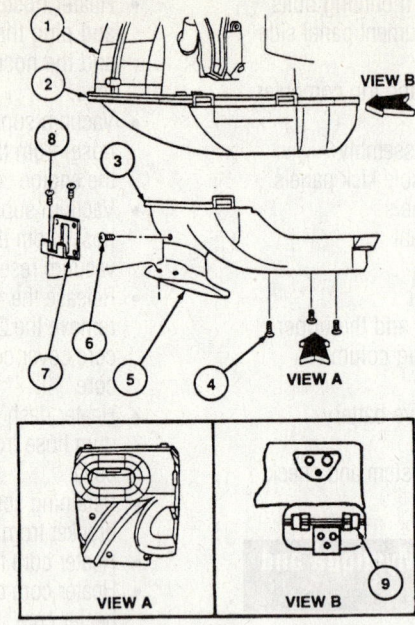

Item	Description
1	A/C Evaporator Housing
2	Heater Core Cover (Part of 19850)
3	Heater Outlet Floor Duct
4	Screw (3 Req'd)
5	Air Transfer Duct (Part of 18C433)
6	Screw (1 Req'd)
7	Air Bag Diagnostic Monitor Bracket
8	Screw (2 Req'd)
9	Clip (2 Req'd)

91056G26

Exploded view of the heater outlet floor duct and related components—1997–01 Contour and Mystique

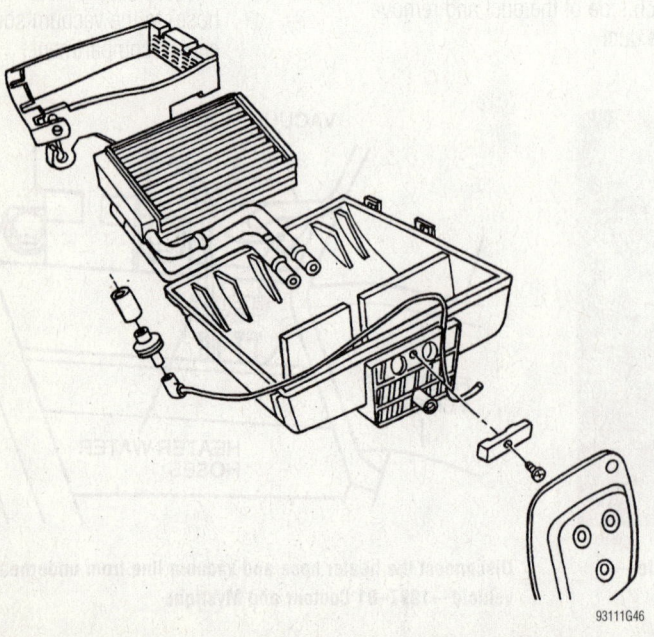

93111G46

Exploded view of the heater core and related components—1997–01 Contour and Mystique

- Unplug the hoses and the core tubes (if installing old core)
- Heater hoses onto the heater core
- Heater outlet floor duct, engage the retaining tabs and tighten the 3 screws retaining the heater outlet floor duct to the heater core cover
- Push the transfer duct out of the heater outlet floor duct
- Tighten the screw retaining the air transfer duct to the heater outlet floor duct
- Air bag diagnostic monitor and bracket
- Center console

6. Connect the negative battery cable.

Taurus and Sable

REMOVAL & INSTALLATION

1. Disconnect the negative battery cable.

✳✳ CAUTION

After disconnecting the negative battery cable, wait for at least 1 minute for the SRS or air bag module to deplete its energy.

2. Place the front wheels in the straight-ahead position.
3. Lock the steering column.
4. Remove the steering wheel by removing or disconnecting the following:

- SRS bolt covers from both sides of the steering wheel
- SRS module-to-steering wheel bolts
- SRS module and disconnect the electrical connector

✳✳ CAUTION

Place the SRS module in a safe place with the front facing upward.

- Steering wheel bolt and discard it
- Press the steering wheel from the steering column

5. Remove the steering column by removing or disconnecting the following:

- Lower steering column shaft bolt
- 2 lower instrument panel cover-to-instrument panel screws and unsnap the lower cover from the instrument panel
- Turn ignition switch to the RUN position

➡Insert a ⅛ in. (3mm) wire or pin punch in the lower steering column

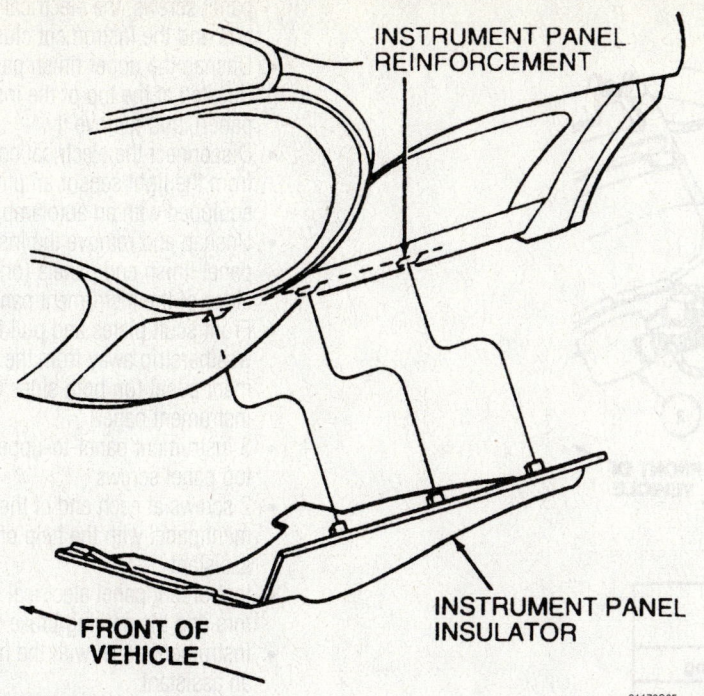

Remove the instrument panel insulator from the instrument panel reinforcement—1997–01 Taurus and Sable

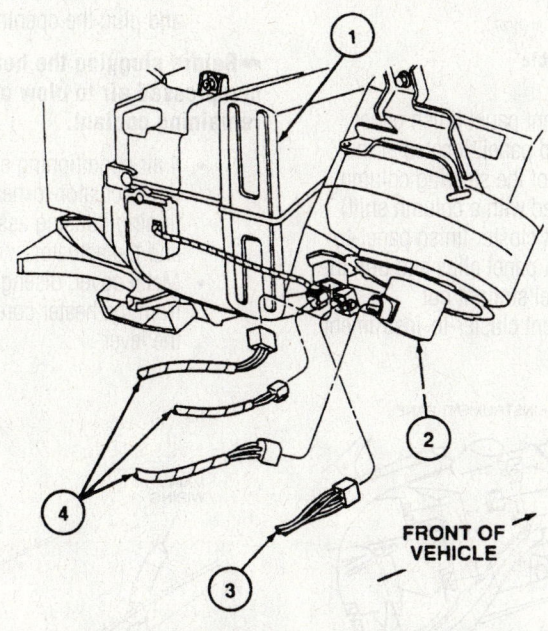

Item	Description
1	A/C Evaporator Housing
2	Blower Motor
3	Vacuum Hose Harness
4	Main Wiring

Manual air conditioning/heater equipped vehicles disconnection points—1997–01 Taurus and Sable

shroud hole, under the ignition switch; then, press on the pin while pulling out on the ignition switch lock cylinder and remove it from the steering column lock cylinder housing.

- 3 steering column shroud screws and the shrouds
- Unsnap and slide the shift control selector lever boot upward, (if equipped with a column shift)
- Gearshift lever pin from the manual control lever and remove the lever
- Wiring connector at the bottom of the steering column and remove the wiring from the column, (if equipped with an overdrive lockout switch on the manual control lever)
- Electrical connectors
- Multi-function switch screws and move it aside
- Shift indicator cable from the shifter tube
- Shifter indicator-to-column adjustment cable screw
- Interlock cable and actuator (if equipped with a column shift)
- 4 steering column-to-instrument panel bracket nuts and steering column

6. Remove the instrument panel by removing or disconnecting the following:
- Push pins and the lower instrument cover from the instrument panel reinforcement (at the passenger's side)
- Console finish panel

7. Under the steering column, 2 instrument panel brace screws, the courtesy lamp socket, the 2 Diagnostic Link Connector (DCL) screws and the instrument panel brace.

8. If not equipped with an Electronic Automatic Temperature Control (EATC), disconnect the electrical connectors and the vacuum harness from the evaporator housing and the blower motor.

9. If equipped with an Electronic Automatic Temperature Control (EATC), remove the sensor hose/elbow and disconnect the electrical harness connectors and the vacuum hose harness from the evaporator housing.

10. Insert the Radio Removing tools 415-001 into the integrated control panel faceplate; then, push the tools in approximately 1½ in. (38mm) to release the retaining clips. Spread the tools slightly and pull the integrated control panel from the instrument panel.

Refer to the model specific sections for cooling system service precautions

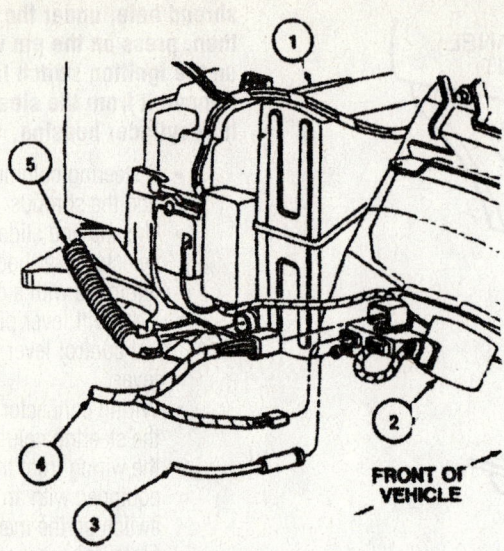

Item	Description
1	A/C Evaporator Housing
2	Blower Motor
3 & 4	Main Wiring
5	Automatic Temperature Control Sensor Hose and Elbow

91170G07

EATC equipped vehicles disconnection points—1997-01 Taurus and Sable

11. Remove or disconnect the following:

- Electrical connectors and the automatic temperature control sensor hose and elbow, if equipped
- 6 console center finish panel screws and the panel, (if equipped with a floor shift)

- 4 instrument panel finish panel screws and panel, located at the right side of the steering column, (if equipped with a column shift)
- Instrument cluster finish panel-to-instrument panel clips and pull the finish panel straight out
- 4 instrument cluster-to-instrument

panel screws, the electrical connectors and the instrument cluster

- Unsnap the upper finish panel (located at the top of the instrument panel), and remove it
- Disconnect the electrical connector from the light sensor amplifier (if equipped with an autolamp)
- Unsnap and remove the instrument panel finish end panels (on both sides of the instrument panel)
- Front scuff plates and pull the door weatherstrip away from the instrument panel (on both sides of the instrument panel)
- 3 instrument panel-to-upper cowl top panel screws
- 2 screws at each end of the instrument panel with the help of an assistant
- Instrument panel electrical connectors and the parking brake switch
- Instrument panel with the help of an assistant

12. Drain the cooling system into a clean container for reuse

13. Remove or disconnect the following:

- Heater hoses from the heater core and plug the openings

➡ **Before plugging the heater core, use compressed air to blow out any remaining coolant.**

- 4 air conditioning electronic blend door actuator-to-heater/air conditioning housing assembly screws and the actuator
- Metal cover, disengage the spring from the heater core cover and from the lever

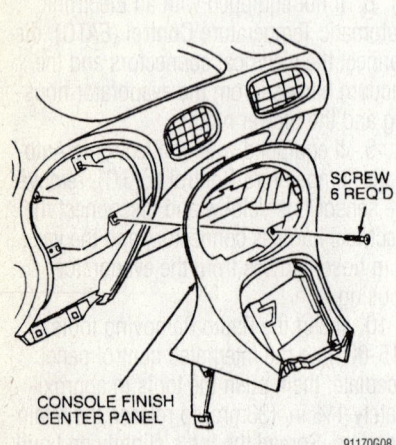

SCREW 6 REQ'D

CONSOLE FINISH CENTER PANEL

91170G08

On floor shift vehicles, remove the console center finish panel—1997-01 Taurus and Sable

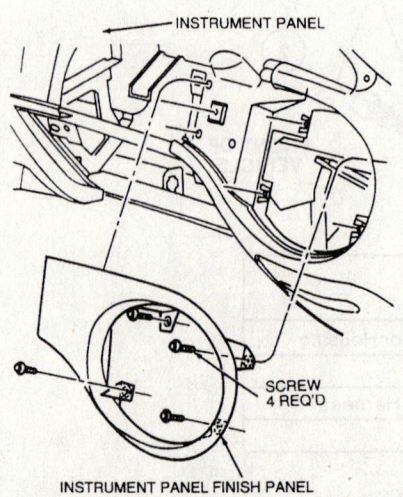

INSTRUMENT PANEL

SCREW 4 REQ'D

INSTRUMENT PANEL FINISH PANEL

91170G09

On floor shift vehicles, remove the finish panel from around the integrated control panel—1997-01 Taurus and Sable

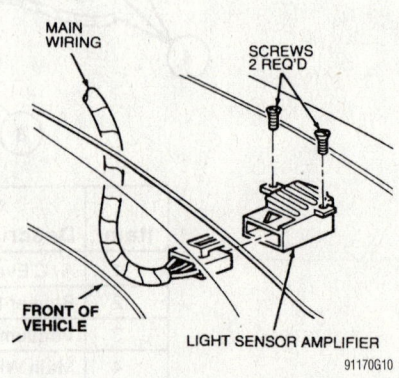

MAIN WIRING

SCREWS 2 REQ'D

FRONT OF VEHICLE

LIGHT SENSOR AMPLIFIER

91170G10

If equipped with autolamps, detach the light sensor amplifier—1997-01 Taurus and Sable

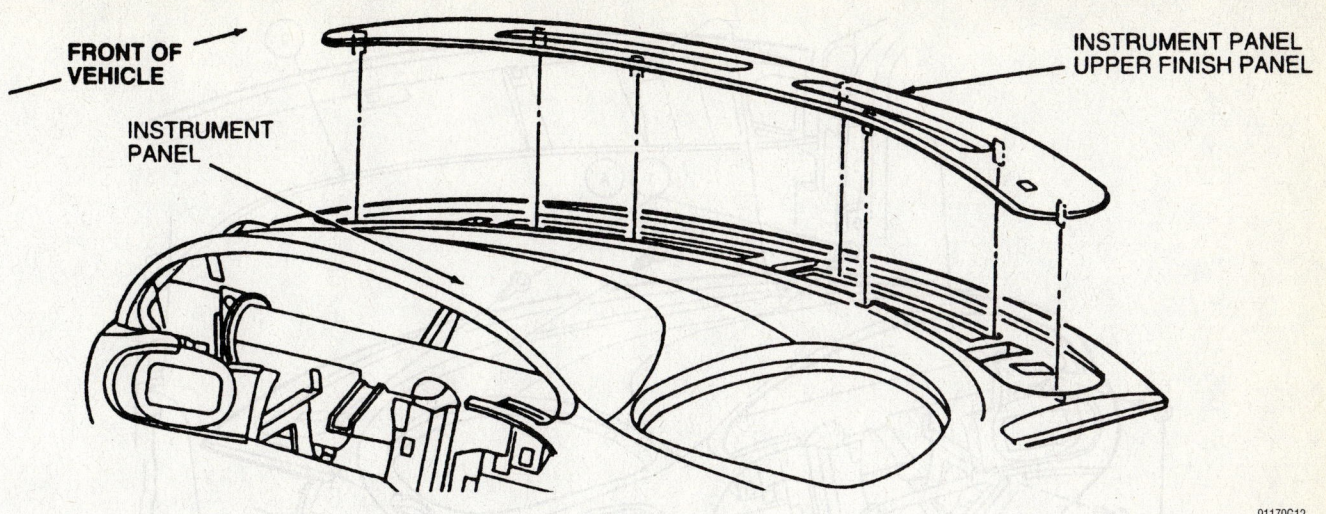

Unsnap the upper finish panel from the instrument panel—1997–01 Taurus and Sable

91170G12

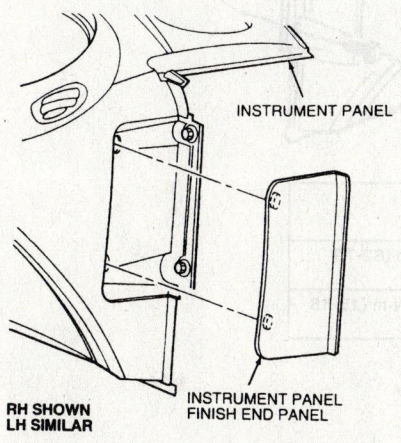

RH SHOWN
LH SIMILAR

91170G11

Remove the instrument panel finish end panel—1997–01 Taurus and Sable

- Gently, depress the locking ramp and remove the lever from the secondary air temperature control door end

✳✳ WARNING

Do not attempt to bend any part of the lever, for it is brittle and will break.

14. Rotate the primary air conditioning air temperature control door shaft downward, swing the metal link counterclockwise and remove it from the pin.

15. Remove the 3 heater core cover-to-heater/air conditioning housing assembly screws, the cover and the seal.

16. Press on the heater core tubes and remove the heater core from the heater/air conditioning housing assembly.

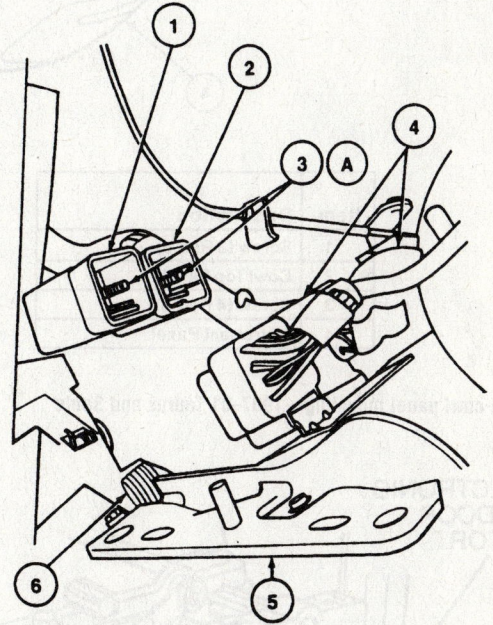

Item	Description
1	Wiring Assy Electrical Connector
2	Wiring Assy Electrical Connector
3	Bolt (Part of 14290 and 14A005)
4	Wiring Assy Electrical Connector
5	Instrument Panel
6	Parking Brake Control
A	Tighten to 4-6 N·m (36-53 Lb-In)

91170G13

Detach the electrical connectors—1997–01 Taurus and Sable

For complete service labor times order Nichols' Chilton Labor Guide Manual

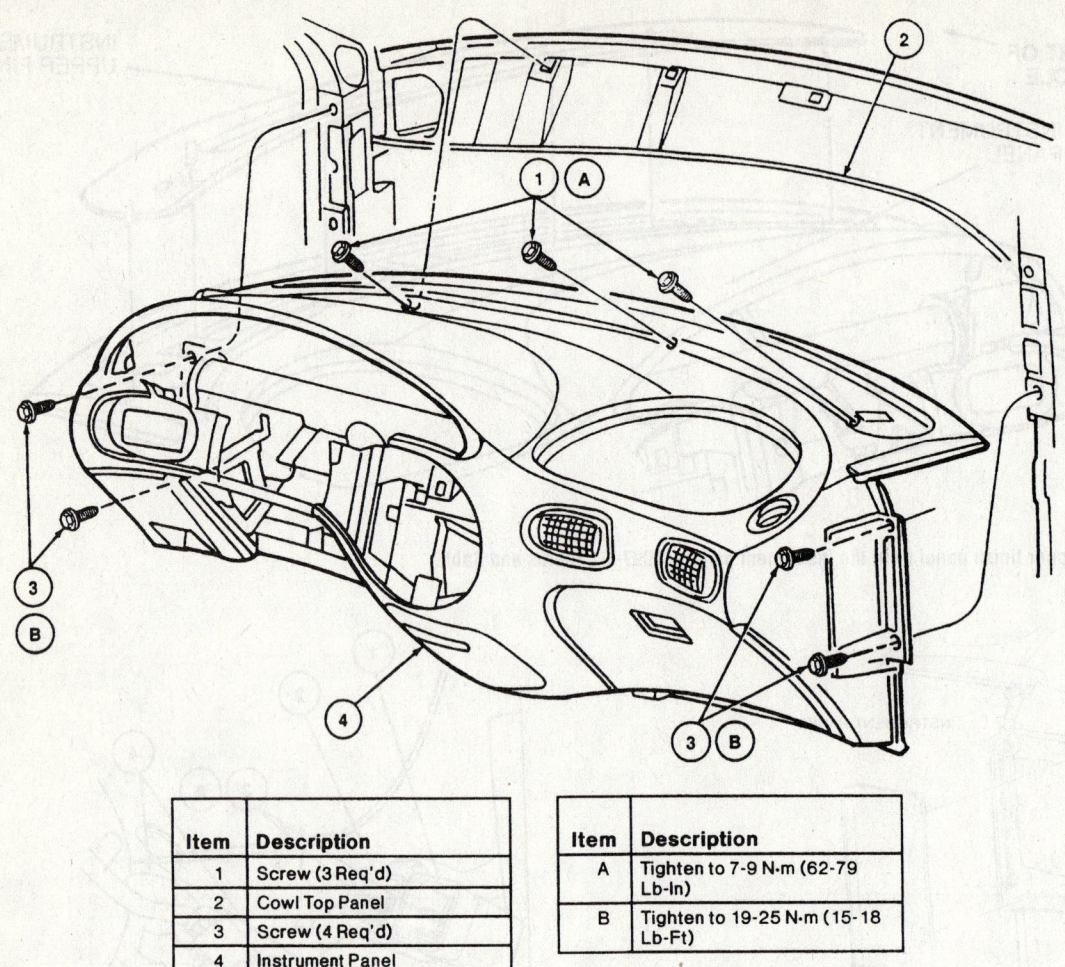

Item	Description
1	Screw (3 Req'd)
2	Cowl Top Panel
3	Screw (4 Req'd)
4	Instrument Panel

Item	Description
A	Tighten to 7-9 N·m (62-79 Lb-In)
B	Tighten to 19-25 N·m (15-18 Lb-Ft)

91170G14

Instrument panel-to-cowl panel mounting—1997–01 Taurus and Sable

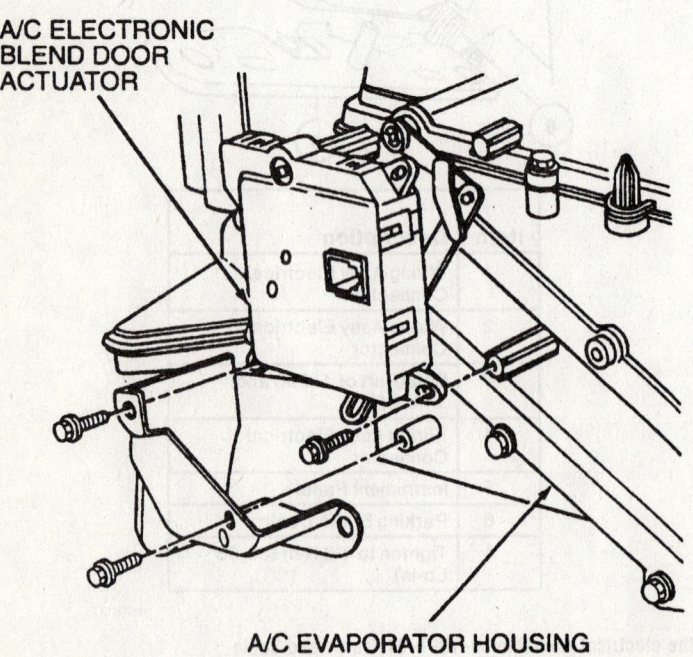

A/C ELECTRONIC BLEND DOOR ACTUATOR

A/C EVAPORATOR HOUSING

91176G05

Remove the 4 blend door actuator retaining screws—1997–01 Taurus and Sable

To install:

17. Install or connect the following:
- Heater core to the heater/air conditioning housing assembly
- Heater core cover, the seal and the 3 heater core cover-to-heater/air conditioning housing assembly screws
- Lever to the secondary air conditioning air temperature control door end

※ WARNING

Do not attempt to bend any part of the lever, for it is brittle and will break.

- Spring to the lever, engage the spring to the heater core cover and install the metal cover
- Air conditioning electronic blend door actuator and the 4 actuator-to-heater/air conditioning housing assembly screws
- Heater hoses to the heater core

18. Refill the cooling system.

19. Install the instrument panel by installing or connecting the following:

• Instrument panel with the help of an assistant

• Instrument panel electrical connectors and the parking brake switch

• 2 screws at each end of the instrument panel with the help of an assistant

• 3 instrument panel-to-upper cowl top panel screws

• Front scuff plates and the door weatherstrip (on both sides of the instrument panel)

• Instrument panel finish end panels (on both sides of the instrument panel)

• Electrical connector to the light sensor amplifier (if equipped with an autolamp)

• Upper finish panel (at the top of the instrument panel)

• Instrument cluster, electrical connectors and the 4 instrument cluster-to-instrument panel screws

• Instrument cluster finish panel and engage the finish panel-to-instrument panel clips

• Instrument panel finish panel and 4 panel screws, located at the right side of the steering column (if equipped with a column shift)

• Console center finish panel and the 6 panel screws (if equipped with a floor shift)

• Electrical connectors and the automatic temperature control sensor hose and elbow, if equipped

• Integrated control panel faceplate

⁎⁎ WARNING

Do not use excessive force when installing the radio, the retaining clips can become damaged.

• Sensor hose/elbow, the electrical harness connectors and the vacuum hose harness to the evaporator housing (if equipped with an Electronic Automatic Temperature Control (EATC)

• Connect the electrical connectors and the vacuum harness to the evaporator housing and the blower motor (if not equipped with an EATC)

• Instrument panel brace and the 2 Diagnostic Link Connector (DCL) screws; then, the courtesy lamp socket and install the 2 instrument panel brace screws

• Console finish panel (if equipped with a floor shift)

• Lower instrument cover to the instrument panel reinforcement (located on the passenger's side)

To install:

20. Install the steering column by installing or connecting the following:

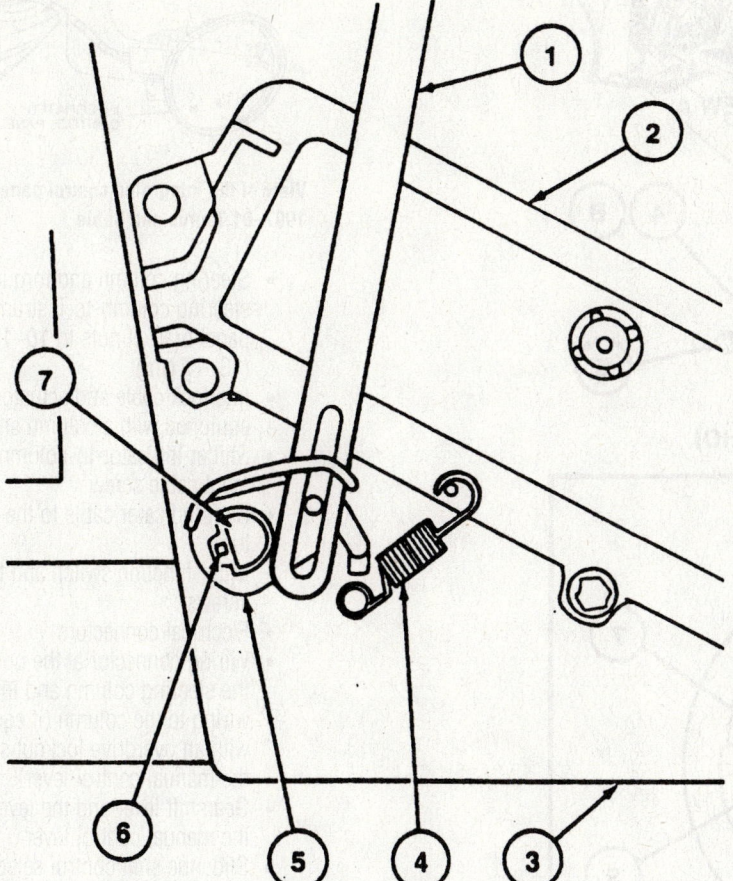

Item	Description
1	Metal Link (Part of 19B555)
2	Heater Core Cover
3	A/C Evaporator Housing
4	Spring (Part of 19B555)
5	Lever (Part of 19B555)
6	Locking Ramp (Part of Secondary A/C Air Temperature Control Door Shaft)
7	Secondary A/C Air Temperature Control Door Shaft (Part of 19B555)

91176G06

Secondary air temperature door connections—1997–01 Taurus and Sable

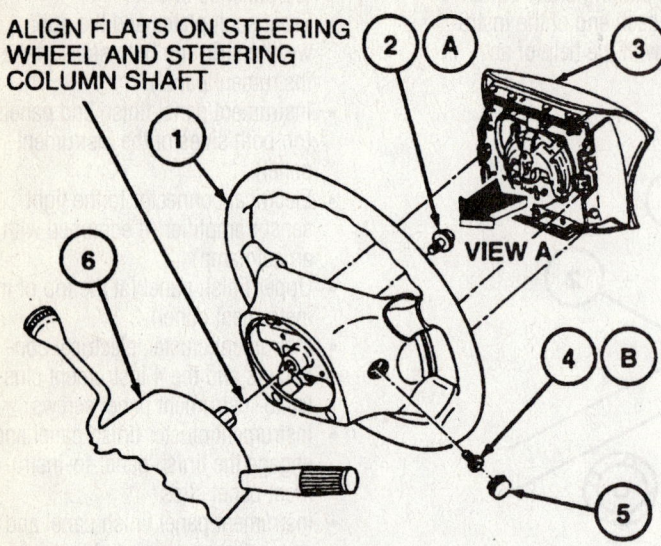

ALIGN FLATS ON STEERING
WHEEL AND STEERING
COLUMN SHAFT

VIEW A

TAURUS, SABLE (EXCEPT SHO)

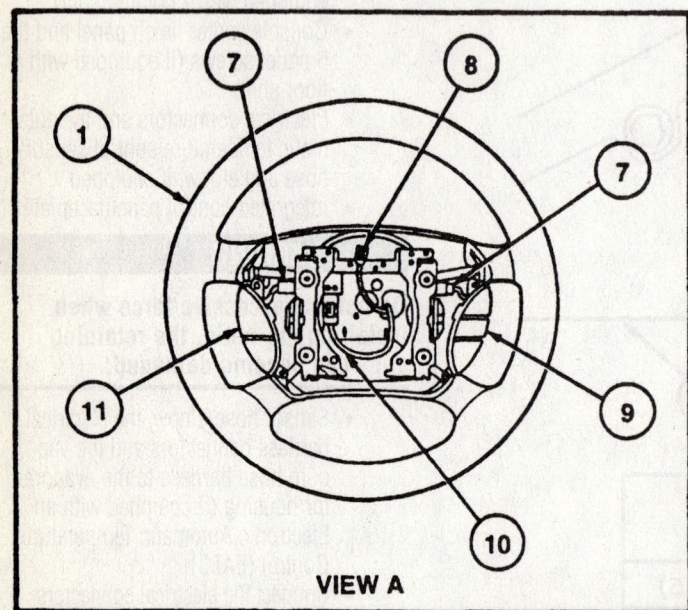

VIEW A

1 Steering Wheel
2 Bolt
3 Driver Side Air Bag Module
4 Screw (2 Req'd)
5 Steering Wheel Spoke Cover
6 Steering Column Tube
7 Electrical Connector
8 Air Bag Electrical Connector
9 Speed Control Actuator Switch (Right Hand)

10 Speed Control / Horn Wire Connector
11 Speed Control Actuator Switch (Left Hand)
A Tighten to 34-46 N·m (26-33 Lb-Ft)
B Tighten to 10-14 N·m (89-123 Lb-In)

Exploded view of the SRS module and the steering wheel assembly—1997–01 Taurus and Sable

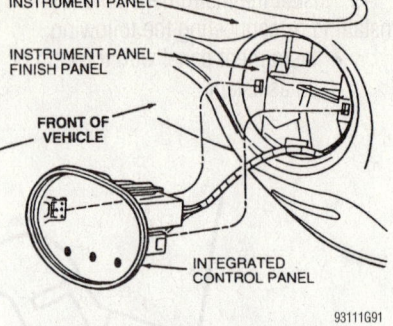

INSTRUMENT PANEL
INSTRUMENT PANEL FINISH PANEL
FRONT OF VEHICLE
INTEGRATED CONTROL PANEL

93111G91

**View of the integrated control panel—
1997–01 Taurus and Sable**

- Steering column and torque the 4 steering column-to-instrument panel bracket nuts to 10–13 ft. lbs. (13–17 Nm)
- Interlock cable and actuator (if equipped with a column shift)
- Shifter indicator-to-column adjustment cable screw
- Shift indicator cable to the shifter tube
- Multi-function switch and the screws
- Electrical connectors
- Wiring connector at the bottom of the steering column and install the wiring to the column (if equipped with an overdrive lockout switch on the manual control lever)
- Gearshift lever and the lever pin to the manual control lever
- Slide the shift control selector lever boot downward (if equipped with a column shift)
- 3 steering column shroud screws and the shrouds
- Ignition switch to the steering column lock cylinder housing
- Lower instrument panel cover and the 2 lower cover-to-instrument panel screws
- Lower steering column shaft bolt and torque it to 17–20 ft. lbs. (22–26 Nm)

21. Install the steering wheel by installing or connecting the following:

- Steering wheel to the steering column
- New steering wheel bolt and torque it to 26–33 ft. lbs. (34–46 Nm)
- SRS module and connect the electrical connector
- SRS module-to-steering wheel bolts and torque the bolts to 89–123 inch lbs. (10–14 Nm)
- SRS bolt covers

22. Connect the negative battery cable

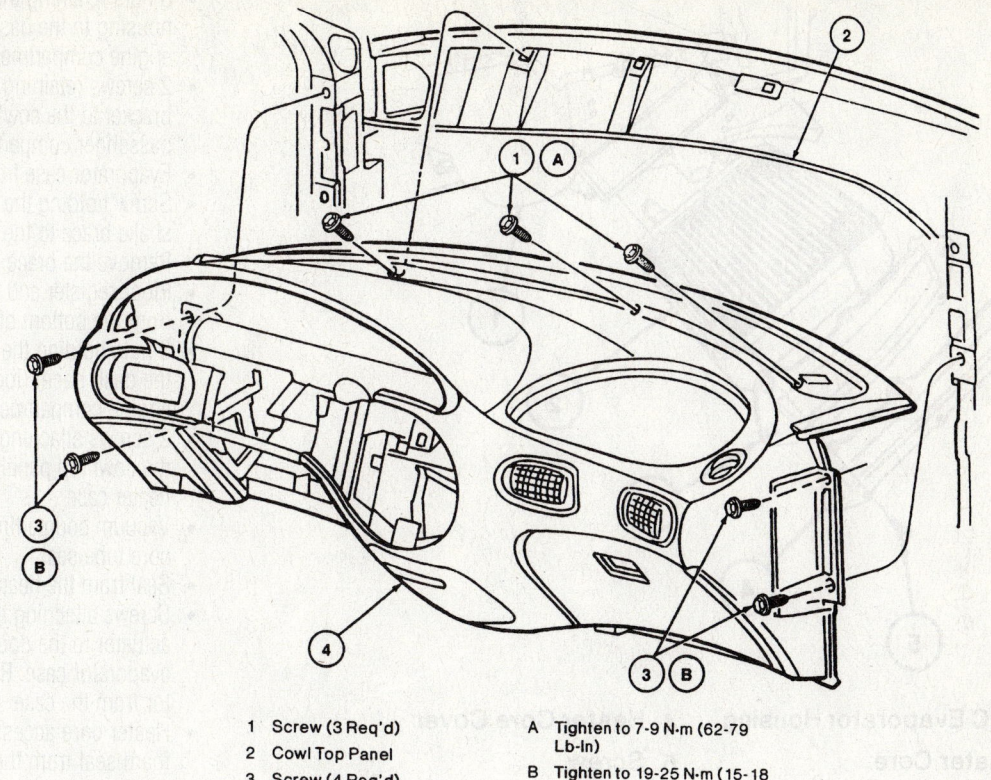

1 Screw (3 Req'd)
2 Cowl Top Panel
3 Screw (4 Req'd)
4 Instrument Panel

A Tighten to 7-9 N·m (62-79 Lb-In)
B Tighten to 19-25 N·m (15-18 Lb-Ft)

93111G92

Exploded view of the instrument panel—1997-01 Taurus and Sable

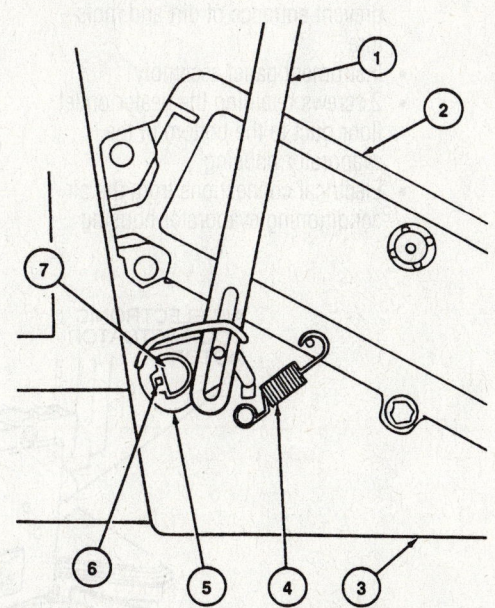

1 Metal Link
2 Heater Core Cover
3 A/C Evaporator Housing
4 Spring
5 Lever

6 Locking Ramp (Part of Secondary A/C Air Temperature Control Door Shaft)
7 Secondary A/C Air Temperature Control Door Shaft

93111G93

View of the temperature control mechanism—1998-01 Taurus and Sable

Refer to the model specific sections for engine mechanical service procedures

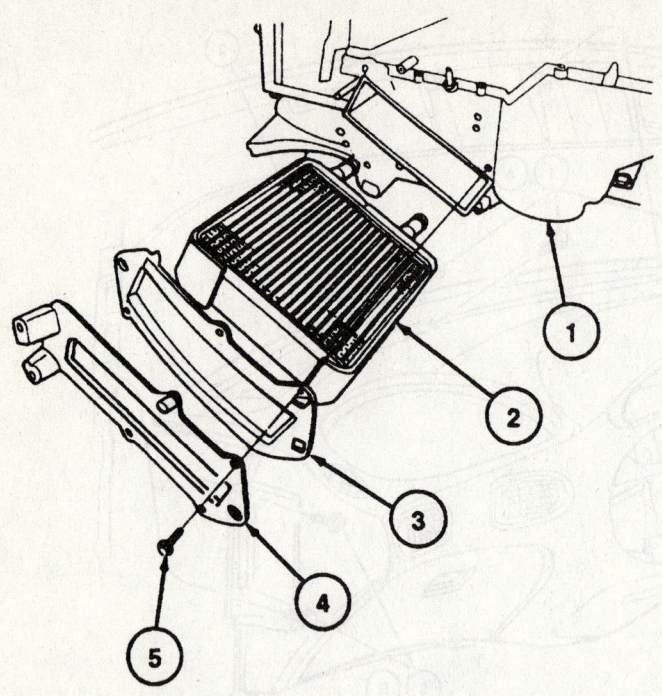

1 A/C Evaporator Housing   4 Heater Core Cover

2 Heater Core   5 Screw

3 Heater Core Cover Seal

93111G94

Exploded view of the heater core—1997–01 Taurus and Sable

23. Operate the engine to normal operating temperatures; then, check the climate control operation and check for leaks.

Continental

REMOVAL & INSTALLATION

1997 Models

➡ **Record the User 1 and User 2 preset radio frequencies for reprogramming following the installation.**

1. Disconnect the negative battery cable.
2. Properly drain the cooling system.
3. Properly discharge the air conditioning system.
4. Remove or disconnect the following:
   - Heater hoses from the heater core. Plug the heater core tubes
   - Vacuum supply hose (black) from the in-line air conditioning vacuum check valve in the engine compartment
   - Condenser-to-evaporator tube and evaporator-to-accumulator tube from the evaporator core at the dash panel. Cap the refrigerant lines and the evaporator core to prevent entrance of dirt and moisture
   - Instrument panel assembly
   - 2 screws retaining the heater outlet floor duct to the bottom of the evaporator housing
   - Electrical connections from the air conditioning evaporator housing

   - 3 nuts retaining the evaporator housing to the dash panel in the engine compartment
   - 2 screws retaining the support bracket to the cowl top panel in the passenger compartment
   - Evaporator case from the vehicle
   - Screw holding the instrument panel shake brace to the heater case. Remove the brace
   - Floor register and rear floor ducts from the bottom of the heater case
   - 3 nuts holding the heater case to the dash panel (located in the engine compartment)
   - 2 screws attaching the bracket to the cowl top panel. Remove the heater case
   - Vacuum source line from the heater core tube seal
   - Seal from the heater core tubes
   - Screws attaching the blend door actuator to the door shaft on the evaporator case. Remove the actuator from the case
   - Heater core access cover and the foam seal from the evaporator case

5. Lift the heater core with the 3 foam seals from the evaporator case. Transfer the foam seals to the new heater core.

To install:

6. Install or connect the following:
   - Heater core with the 3 foam seals into the evaporator case
   - Actuator to the case
   - Screws attaching the blend door actuator to the door shaft on the evaporator case
   - Foam seal and the heater core

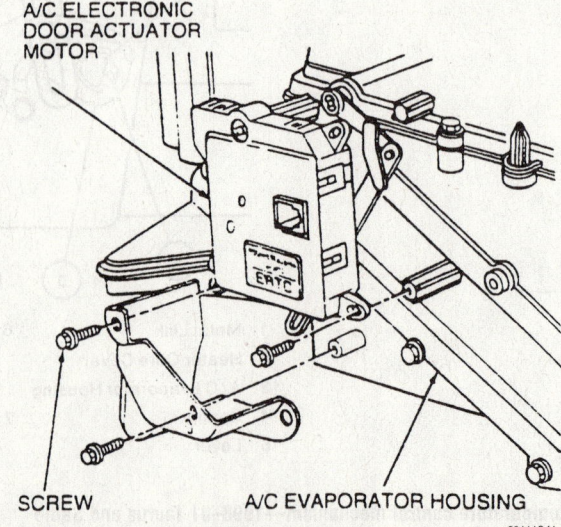

SCREW   A/C EVAPORATOR HOUSING

93111G41

View of the electronic door actuator motor—1997 Continental

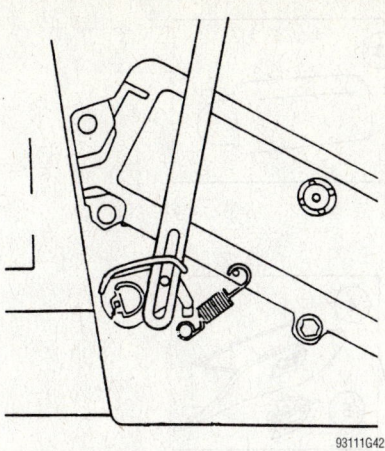

View of the heater core lever—1997 Continental

access cover onto the evaporator case
- Seal onto the heater core tubes
- Vacuum source line onto the heater core tube seal
- Air conditioning evaporator housing assembly

7. Position the evaporator housing assembly against the dash panel and cowl top panel at the air inlet opening.

8. Install or connect the following:
- 2 screws retaining the support brackets to the cowl top panel
- 3 nuts in the engine compartment retaining the evaporator housing to the dash panel
- Heater outlet floor duct to the evaporator housing and tighten the screws
- Instrument panel shake brace and screw it to the evaporator case
- Air conditioning refrigerant lines to the evaporator
- Instrument panel assembly
- Heater hoses to the heater core

9. Evacuate, charge and leak test the air conditioning system.

10. Refill the cooling system.

11. Connect the negative battery cable.

12. Reprogram the radio frequencies and the set the clock.

1998–01 Models

1. Disconnect the negative battery cable.

> **✳✳ CAUTION**
>
> **After disconnecting the negative battery cable, wait for at least 1 minute for the SRS or air bag module to deplete its energy.**

2. Drain the cooling system into a clean container for reuse.

3. Remove the driver's side air bag module by removing or disconnecting the following:
- SRS module-to-steering wheel bolts, (located at both sides of the steering wheel)
- SRS module (carefully) and disconnect the electrical connector
- Horn switch electrical connector

> **✳✳ CAUTION**
>
> **Place the SRS module in a safe place with the front facing upward.**

4. Remove the passenger's side SRS module by removing or disconnecting the following:
- Push inward on the 2 glove box door tabs and lower it
- SRS module's electrical connector
- SRS module-to-instrument panel bolts and the module

> **✳✳ CAUTION**
>
> **Place the SRS module in a safe place with the front facing upward**

5. Remove the instrument panel by removing or disconnecting the following:
- Floor or mini console (if equipped)
- Rear seat climate control air duct sleeve (if equipped)
- Left side instrument panel insulator pushpins and the insulator; then, disconnect the courtesy lamp
- Instrument panel steering column cover screws and the cover
- Pull the hood release handle, remove the screws and move it aside
- Pull the parking brake handle, remove the bolts, the parking brake release handle and the cable
- Steering column opening cover reinforcement-to-instrument panel bolts and the cover reinforcement
- Release the cable and the conduit from the parking brake actuator
- Steering column
- Loosen the bolt and disconnect the left side outboard bulkhead electrical connector
- Loosen the bolt and disconnect the left side inboard bulkhead electrical connector
- Heated seat switch electrical connectors (if equipped)

- 2 steering column mounting support-to-instrument cowl brace bolts
- Instrument panel dash brace-to-instrument panel bolt
- Instrument panel dash brace nut and move the brace aside
- Right side instrument panel insulator pushpins and the insulator; then, disconnect the courtesy lamp
- Vacuum harness connector
- In-line electrical harness connector
- Scuff plate and the cowl trim panel (located on the right side)
- Antenna connector
- Brake shift interlock actuator cable
- Pry out the instrument panel defroster opening grille assembly, disconnect the 2 electrical connectors and remove the assembly
- Upper instrument panel-to-cowl screws
- Instrument panel support-to-cowl side nut (located on the right side)
- Instrument panel support-to-cowl side bolts (located on the left side); then, loosen the instrument panel support-to-cowl side captive bolt
- Pull the instrument panel rearward; then, disconnect the Electronic Air Temperature Control (EATC) hose from the heater plenum and make sure all electrical connectors are disconnected
- Instrument panel with the help of an assistant

➡ **Check the upper cowl clips for damage; if necessary, replace them.**

6. Loosen the screw and disconnect the PCM electrical connector.

7. Disconnect the heater hoses from the heater core.

8. Remove or disconnect the following:
- 2 metal cover-to-heater/air conditioning housing screws and the metal cover (located below the heater core cover)
- Electrical harness connector (at the heater core cover); then, remove the air conditioning electronic blend door actuator-to-heater/air conditioning housing screws and the actuator
- Air conditioning air intake flue damper assist spring

> **✳✳ WARNING**
>
> **Do not bend any part of the air conditioning damper door shaft for it is brittle and will break.**

Refer to the model specific sections for cooling system service precautions

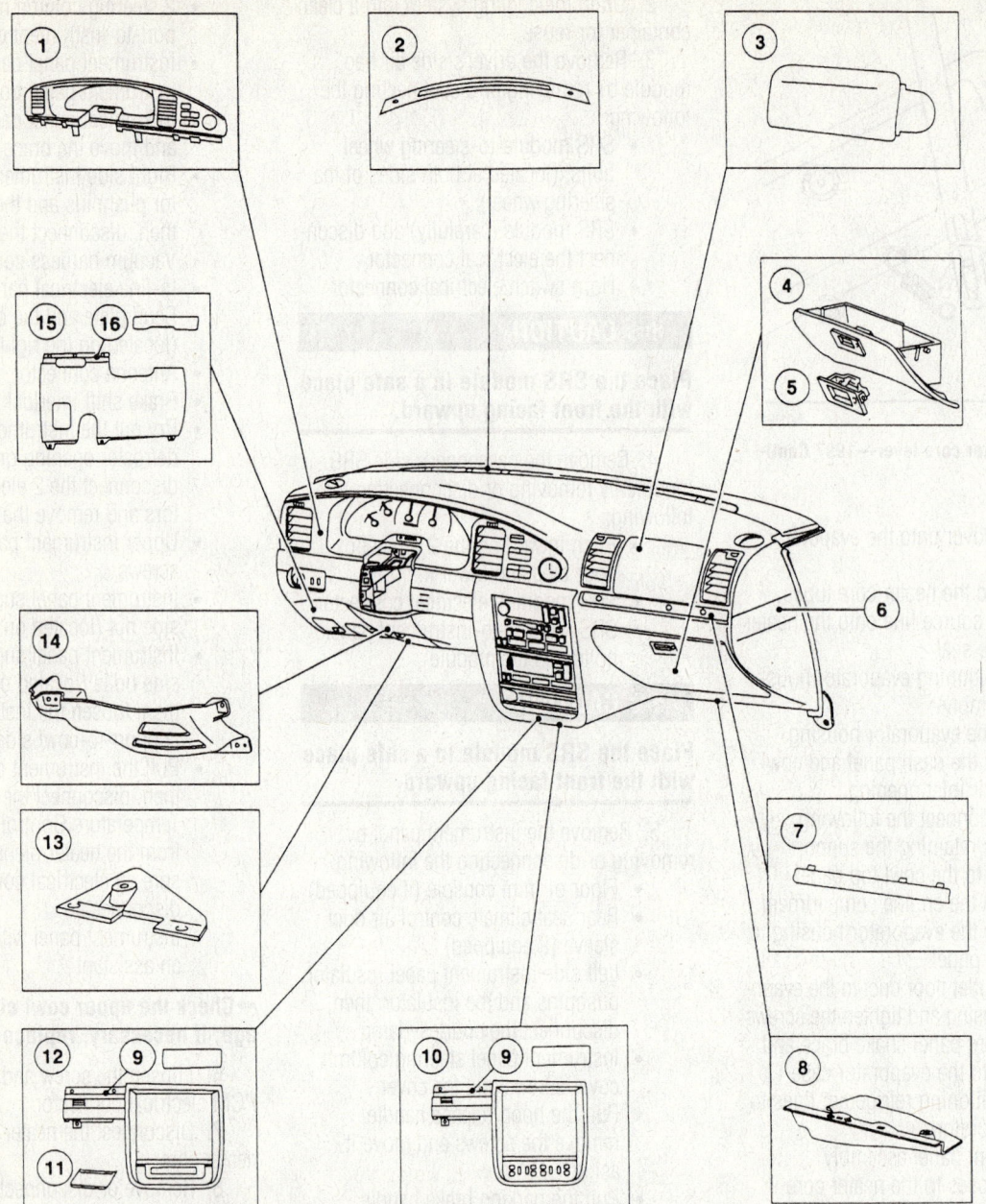

1 Instrument Panel Cluster
   Finish Panel

2 Instrument Panel Defroster
   Opening Grille

3 Passenger Side Air Bag
   Module

4 Glove Compartment

5 Glove Compartment Door
   Latch

6 Instrument Panel

7 Instrument Panel Finish Panel
   (RH) (Wood)

8 Instrument Panel Insulator
   (RH)

9 Instrument Panel Finish Panel
   (Wood)

10 Instrument Panel Center Finish
   Panel (Service, Heated Seat)

11 Utility Compartment Lower
   Mat

12 Instrument Panel Center Finish
   Panel (Base)

13 Instrument Panel Insulator
   (LH)

14 Instrument Panel Steering
   Column Opening Cover
   Reinforcement

15 Instrument Panel Steering
   Column Cover

16 Instrument Panel Finish Panel
   (LH) (Wood)

93111G99

Exploded view of the instrument panel and related components—1998–01 Continental

9. Depress the air conditioning damper door shaft locking ramp, disconnect it from the air temperature control door shaft, swing the locking ramp counterclockwise and remove it from the air conditioning damper door shaft.

10. Move the air conditioning damper door shaft counterclockwise and remove it.

11. Remove or disconnect the following:
- Heater core cover-to-heater/air conditioning housing screws and the cover
- Heater core cover seal
- Heater core from the heater/air conditioning housing

To install:

12. Install or connect the following:
- Heater core to the heater/air conditioning housing
- Heater core cover seal
- Heater core cover and the cover-to-heater/air conditioning housing screws
- Air conditioning damper door shaft and move it clockwise and install it
- Air conditioning damper door shaft locking ramp, swing the locking ramp clockwise and connect it to the air temperature control door shaft
- Air conditioning air intake flue damper assist spring

✻✻ WARNING

Do not bend any part of the air conditioning damper door shaft for it is brittle and will break.

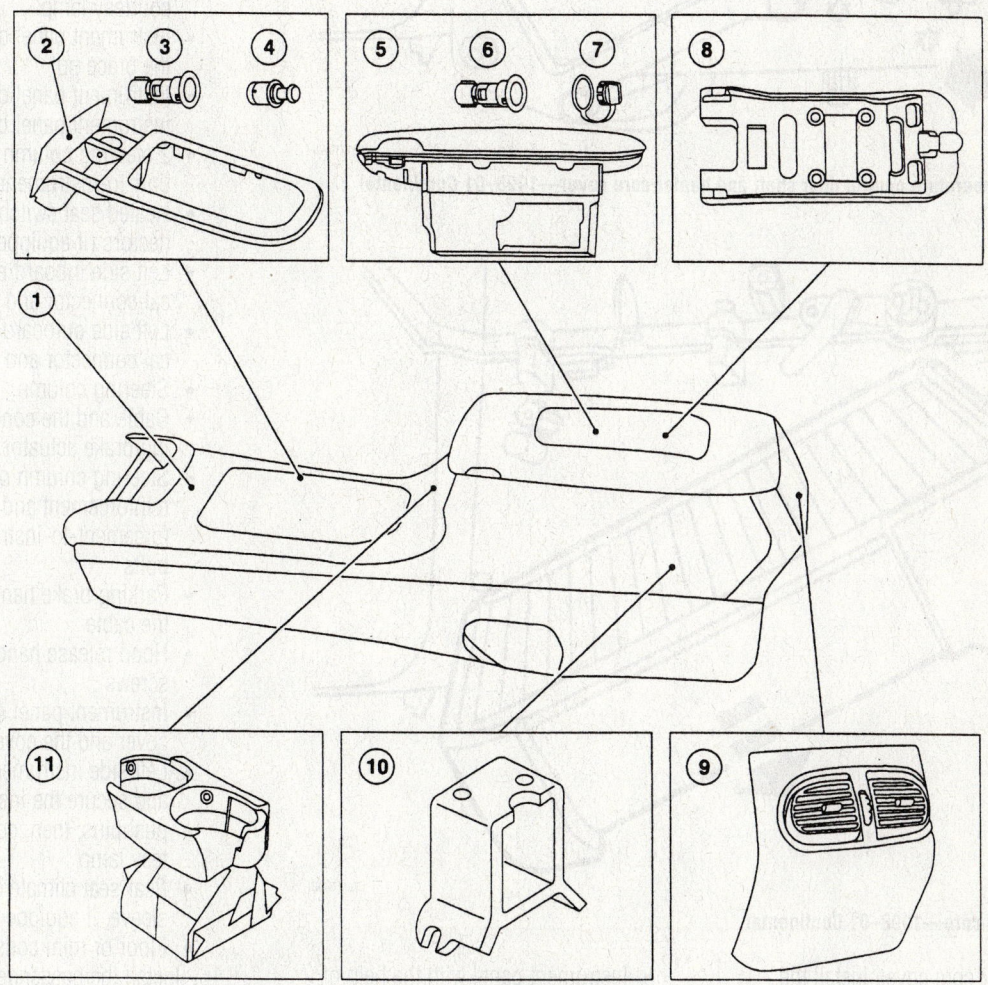

1. Console Panel
2. Console Top Panel
3. Cigar Lighter Socket and Retainer
4. Cigar Lighter Knob and Element
5. Glove Compartment
6. Auxiliary Electric Power Socket
7. Auxiliary Electrical Power Socket Cap
8. Handset Cradle
9. A/C Register
10. Instrument Panel Console Bracket
11. Utility Tray Beverage Holder

93111G00

Exploded view of the floor console and related components—1998–01 Continental

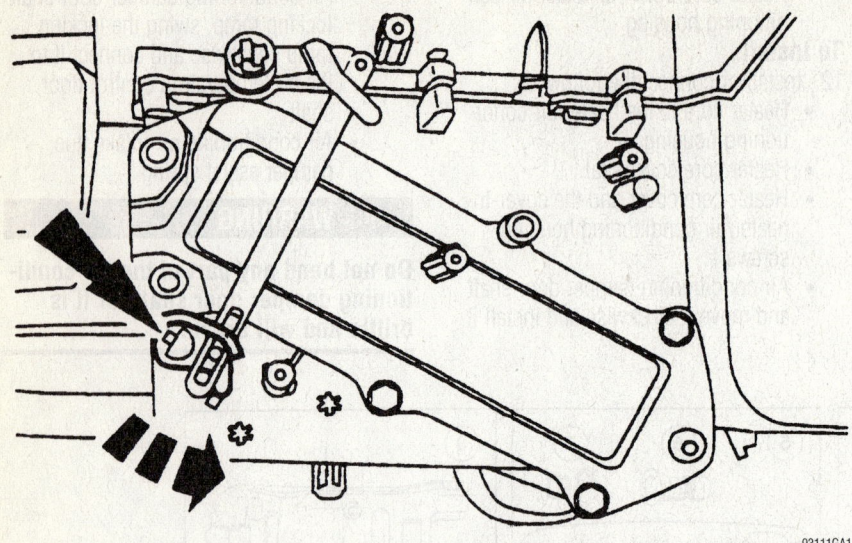

View of the air temperature control door shaft and heater core cover—1998–01 Continental

93111GA1

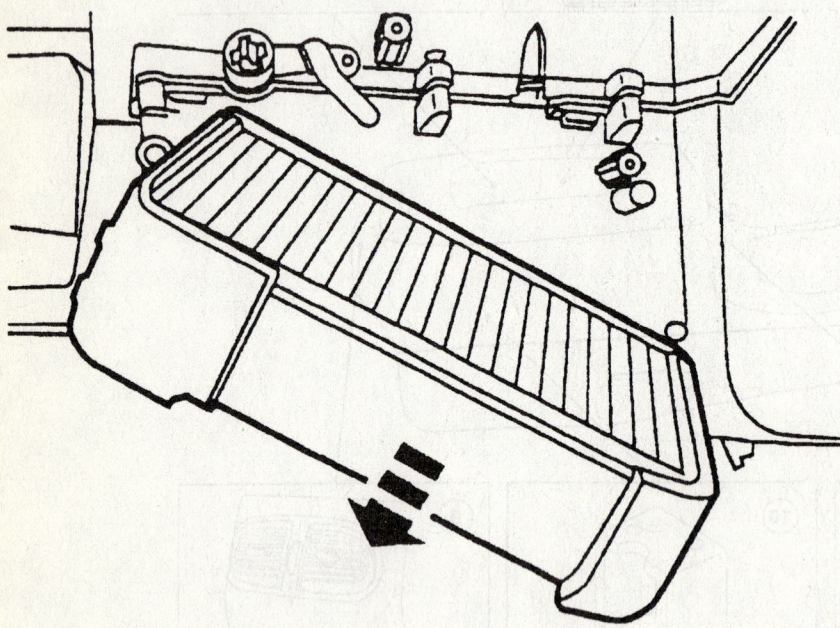

View of the heater core—1998–01 Continental

93111GA2

13. At the heater core cover, install the air conditioning electronic blend door actuator and the actuator-to-heater/air conditioning housing screws; then, connect the electrical harness connector.

14. Install or connect the following:
- Metal cover and the 2 metal cover-to-heater/air conditioning housing screws (located below the heater core cover)
- Heater hoses to the heater core
- PCM electrical connector and tighten the screw

15. Install the instrument panel by installing or connecting the following:

- Instrument panel with the help of an assistant
- Pull the instrument panel rearward; then, connect the Electronic Air Temperature Control (EATC) hose to the heater plenum and make sure all electrical connectors are connected
- Instrument panel support-to-cowl side bolts and the instrument panel support-to-cowl side captive bolt (located on the left side)
- Instrument panel support-to-cowl side nut (located on the right side)
- Upper instrument panel-to-cowl screws
- 2 electrical connectors and the instrument panel defroster opening grille assembly
- Brake shift interlock actuator cable
- Antenna connector
- Scuff plate and the cowl trim panel (located on the right side)
- In-line electrical harness connector
- Vacuum harness connector
- Right side instrument panel insulator and secure the insulator with the pushpins; then, connect the courtesy lamp
- Instrument panel dash brace and the brace nut
- Instrument panel dash brace-to-instrument panel bolt
- 2 steering column mounting support-to-instrument cowl brace bolts
- Heated seat switch electrical connectors (if equipped)
- Left side inboard bulkhead electrical connector and tighten the bolt
- Left side outboard bulkhead electrical connector and tighten the bolt
- Steering column
- Cable and the conduit to the parking brake actuator
- Steering column opening cover reinforcement and the cover reinforcement-to-instrument panel bolts
- Parking brake handle, the bolts and the cable
- Hood release handle and the screws
- Instrument panel steering column cover and the cover screws
- Left side instrument panel insulator and secure the insulator with the pushpins; then, connect the courtesy lamp
- Rear seat climate control air duct sleeve, if equipped
- Floor or mini console, if equipped

16. Install the passenger's side SRS module by installing or connecting the following:

- SRS module and torque the module-to-instrument panel bolts to 62–97 inch lbs. (7–11 Nm)
- SRS module's electrical connector
- Glove box door

17. Install the driver's side air bag module by installing or connecting the following:

- Horn switch electrical connector
- Electrical connector and install the SRS module
- SRS module-to-steering wheel bolts

(located at both sides of the steering wheel), and torque the bolts to 90–122 inch lbs. (10–14 Nm)

18. Refill the cooling system.

19. Connect the negative battery cable.

20. Operate the engine to normal operating temperatures; then, check the climate control operation and check for leaks.

Escort, ZX2 and Tracer

REMOVAL & INSTALLATION

1997 Models

1. Disconnect the negative battery cable and drain the cooling system.

2. Disconnect the heater hoses at the bulkhead.

3. Remove the instrument panel by removing or disconnecting the following:

- 4 bolts securing the steering column to the instrument panel frame. Lower the steering column
- Cap screws securing the instrument cluster bezel to the instrument panel and remove the instrument cluster bezel
- Speedometer cable at the transaxle by pulling the cable out of the vehicle speed sensor
- Screws and bolts securing the instrument cluster to the instrument panel. Pull the instrument cluster out slightly and disconnect the electrical connectors from the rear of the instrument cluster
- Speedometer cable from the instrument cluster
- Instrument cluster from the instrument panel
- Hood release cable from the left lower dash trim panel. Carefully, pry out both dash side panels
- 4 retaining screws and the left lower dash trim panel. Disconnect all necessary electrical connectors
- 2 hinge-to-instrument panel retaining screws and remove the glove compartment
- Climate control assembly and the ashtray
- 7 accessory console retaining screws. Disconnect the radio antenna, radio wire connectors and cigarette lighter connector
- Retaining screws and the right lower dash trim panel. Disconnect the 3 amplifier wire connectors
- 4 bolts attaching the instrument panel frame to the floor pan. Remove the bolt from both of the lower instrument panel mounts
- 2 bolts from both of the upper instrument panel mounts. Remove the retaining screw and the defroster duct bezel
- 3 mounting bolts that attach the upper instrument panel to the cowl and remove the instrument panel from the vehicle

➡**Use care to prevent any damage to the instrument panel or the surrounding interior trim.**

- Mode selector and temperature control cables from the cams and retaining clips
- Necessary defroster duct screws and loosen the capscrew that secures the heater-to-blower clamp
- 3 heater unit mounting nuts, and disconnect the antenna lead from

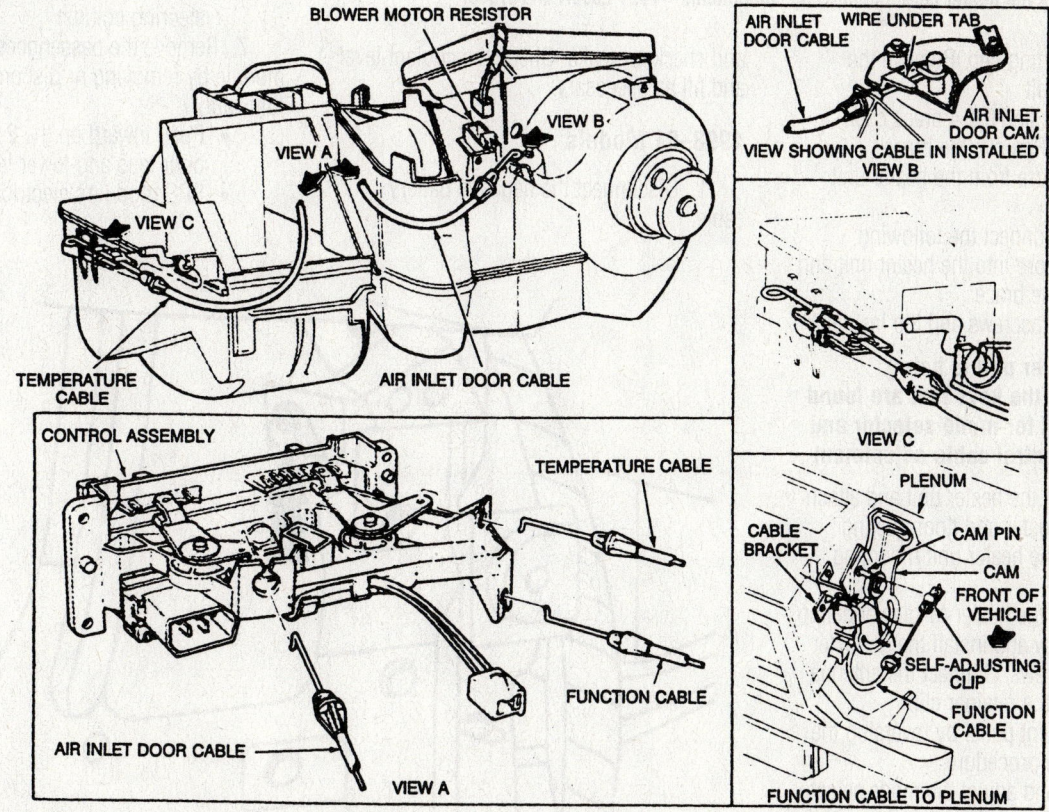

View of the heater/air conditioning housing and control cables—1997 Escort, Tracer

93111G48

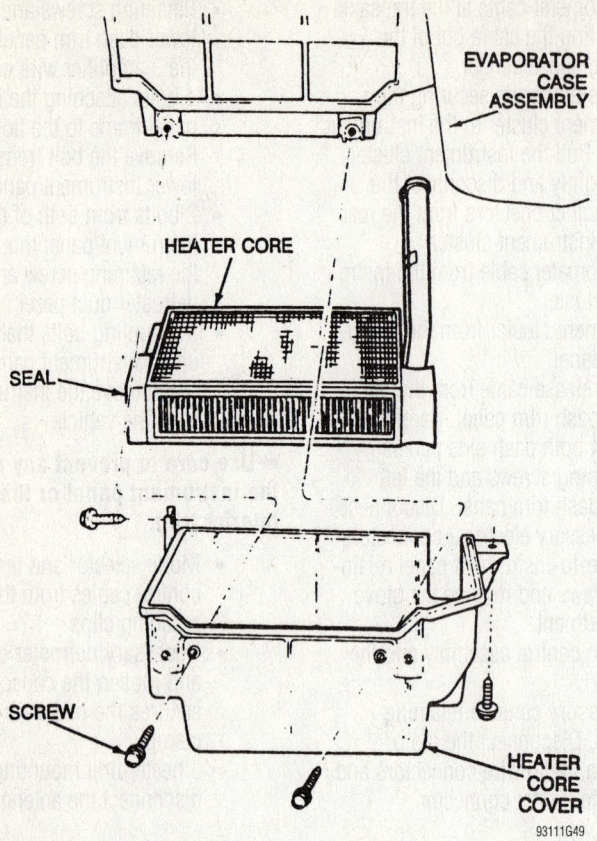

Exploded view of the heater core and housing components—1997 Escort and Tracer

the retaining clip. Remove the heater unit
- Insulator and the 4 brace cap-screws. Remove the brace
- Heater core from the heater unit

To install:

4. Install or connect the following:
- Heater core into the heater unit and install the brace
- Brace capscrews and the insulator

➡ **If a new heater unit is being installed, save the keys that are found on the new unit for mode selector and temperature control cable adjustment**

- Position the heater unit and attach the defroster and floor ducting. Install the heater unit mounting nuts
- Tighten the heater-to-blower clamp capscrew and install the defroster duct screws. Connect the antenna lead to the retainer clip
- Instrument panel by reversing the removal procedure

5. Connect and adjust the mode selector and temperature control cables. Connect the heater hoses at the bulkhead.

6. Refill the cooling system and connect the negative battery cable. Start the engine

and check for leaks. Check the coolant level and fill as necessary.

1998–01 Models

1. Disconnect the negative battery cable.

After disconnecting the negative battery cable, wait for at least 1 minute for the SRS or air bag module to deplete its energy.

2. Drain the cooling system into a clean container for reuse.

3. On the Coupe, remove the air cleaner outlet tube.

4. Disconnect the heater hoses from the heater core.

5. Place the front wheels in the straight-ahead position. Lock the steering column.

6. Remove the steering wheel by removing or disconnecting the following:
- SRS module-to-steering wheel bolts
- SRS module (carefully), and disconnect the horn switch and the SRS electrical connectors

Place the SRS module in a safe place with the front facing upward

- Steering wheel bolt and discard it
- Press the steering wheel from the steering column

7. Remove the passenger's side SRS module by removing or disconnecting the following:
- Push inward on the 2 glove box door tabs and lower it
- SRS module's electrical connector

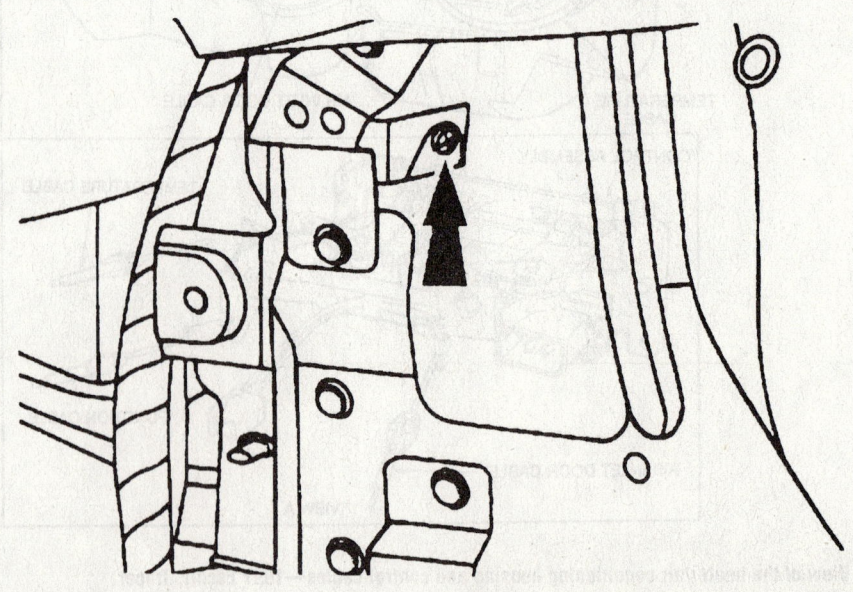

Remove the screw from the center instrument panel finish panel—1998–01 Escort and Tracer

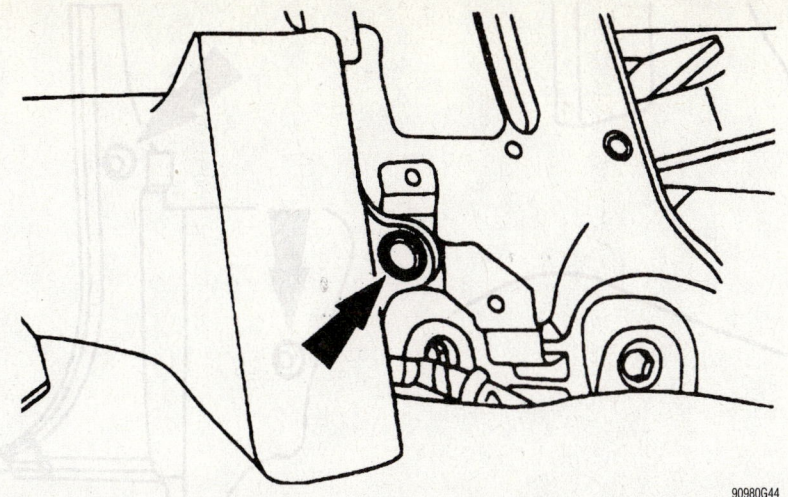

Unfasten the pushpins, then remove the left-hand and right-hand control box covers—1998–01 Escort and Tracer

90980G44

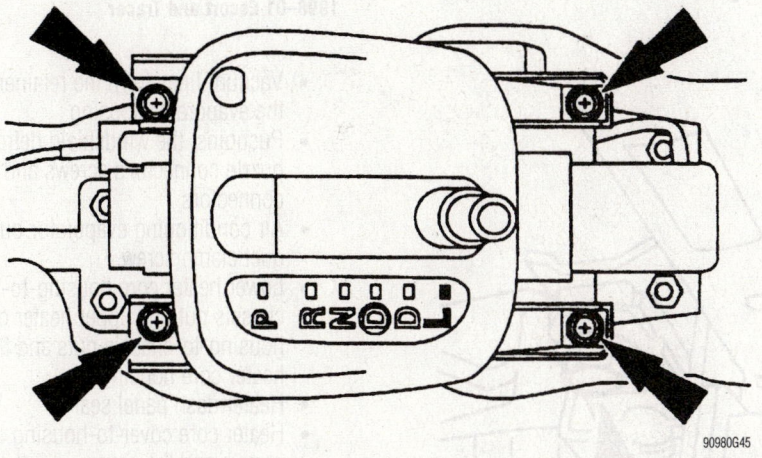

Unfasten the retaining screws and position the transaxle control selector dial bezel sideways—1998–01 Escort and Tracer

90980G45

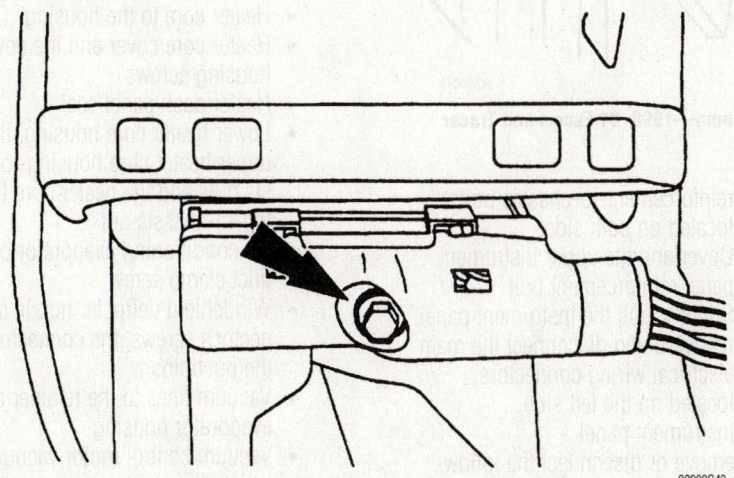

Unfasten the PCM electrical connector bolt, unplug the connector and move it aside—1998–01 Escort and Tracer

90980G43

- SRS module-to-instrument panel bolts and the module

⁜⁜ CAUTION

Place the SRS module in a safe place with the front facing upward.

8. Remove the instrument panel by removing or disconnecting the following:
- Floor console
- Screw located at the center instrument panel finish panel
- Pull the center instrument panel finish panel straight out from the instrument panel reinforcement (Coupe models only)
- Power point socket electrical connectors and remove the center instrument panel finish panel, if equipped
- Control box side cover pushpins and the covers located on both sides
- Radio antenna lead-in cable, located at the instrument panel reinforcement
- Radio antenna lead-in cable
- Transmission control selector dial bezel screws; then, place the transmission control selector dial bezel sideways
- PCM electrical connector bolt and move the PCM aside
- 2 rear side PCM bracket nuts, the 2 bolts; then, the PCM and bracket as an assembly
- Rotate the temperature control switch to the COOL position and disconnect the heater control cable
- Hood latch control handle nut; then, position the hood latch control handle and cable aside
- Instrument panel steering column cover screw and release the cover
- Light switch rheostat resistor electrical connector and remove the instrument panel steering column cover (Coupe models only)
- Steering column shroud screws and remove the shrouds
- Steering column bracket bolts and lower the steering column
- Pull upward on the front door scuff plates
- Cowl side trim panel pushpins and the panels, located on both sides
- Interior fuse junction panel electrical connector

Refer to the model specific sections for engine mechanical service procedures

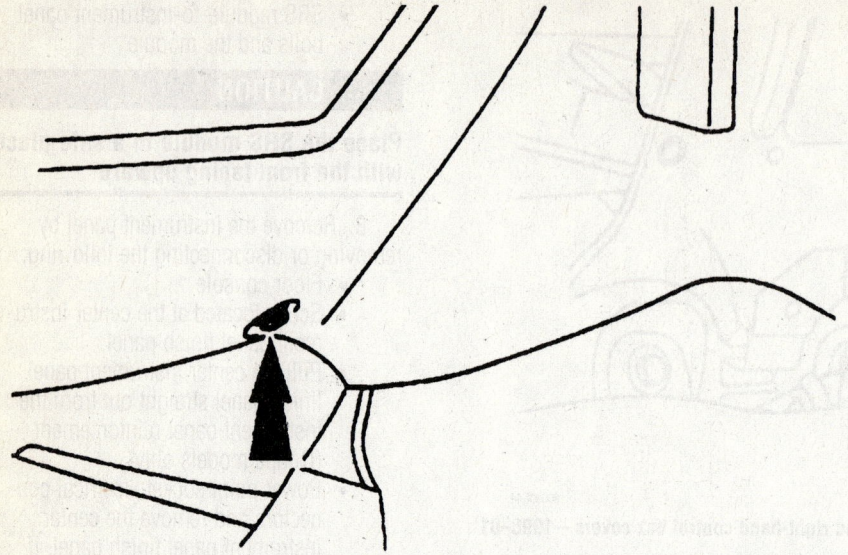

90980G46

Unfasten the screw and remove the instrument panel steering column cover—1998–01 Escort and Tracer

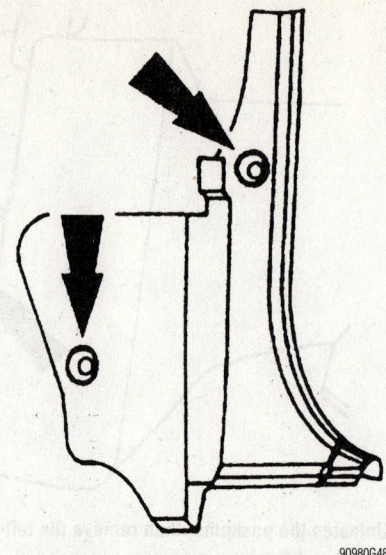

90980G48

Remove the pushpins from each cowl side trim panel, and remove the panels—1998–01 Escort and Tracer

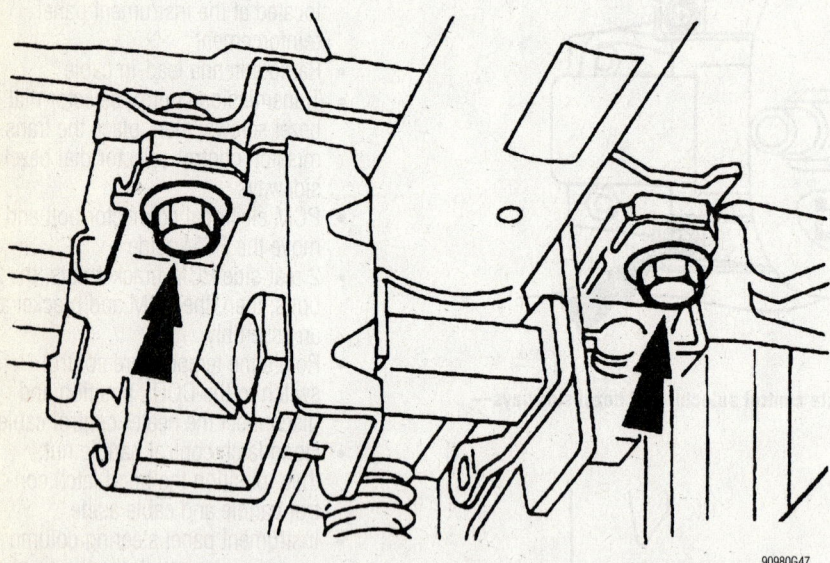

90980G47

Remove the steering column bracket bolts and lower the column—1998–01 Escort and Tracer

- Lower instrument panel reinforcement in-line electrical connector, located on the left side
- Vacuum line harness connector
- Lower instrument panel reinforcement in-line electrical connector, located on the right side
- Blower motor resistor electrical connector
- Instrument panels end panels, located on both sides
- Upper and lower instrument panel-to-chassis bolts, located on both sides
- Upper and lower instrument panel

reinforcement-to-chassis bolts, located on both sides
- Cover and the upper instrument panel reinforcement bolt
- Slightly, pull the instrument panel rearward and disconnect the main electrical wiring connectors, located on the left side
- Instrument panel

9. Remove or disconnect the following:

- Antenna lead from the heater core housing
- Vacuum control motor vacuum connector

- Vacuum lines from the retainer at the evaporator housing
- Pushpins, the windshield defroster nozzle connector's screws and the connectors
- Air conditioning evaporator outlet duct clamp screw
- Lower heater core housing-to-chassis nut, the upper heater core housing-to-chassis nuts and the heater core housing
- Heater dash panel seal
- Heater core cover-to-housing screws and the cover
- Heater core from the housing

To install:

10. Install or connect the following:

- Heater core to the housing
- Heater core cover and the cover-to-housing screws
- Heater dash panel seal
- Lower heater core housing, the upper heater core housing-to-chassis nuts and the heater core housing-to-chassis nut
- Air conditioning evaporator outlet duct clamp screw
- Windshield defroster nozzle connector's screws, the connectors and the pushpins
- Vacuum lines to the retainer at the evaporator housing
- Vacuum control motor vacuum connector
- Antenna lead to the heater core housing

11. Install the instrument panel by installing or connecting the following:

- Instrument panel
- Main electrical wiring connectors (located on the left side), and install the instrument panel
- Upper instrument panel reinforcement bolt and the cover
- Upper and lower instrument panel reinforcement-to-chassis bolts (both sides)
- Upper and lower instrument panel-to-chassis bolts (both sides)
- Instrument panels end panels (both sides)
- Blower motor resistor electrical connector
- Lower instrument panel reinforcement in-line electrical connector, located on the right side
- Vacuum line harness connector.
- Lower instrument panel reinforcement in-line electrical connector, located on the left side
- Interior fuse junction panel electrical connector
- Cowl side trim panels and secure the panels with the pushpins, located on both sides
- Front door scuff plates, located on both sides
- Steering column and the steering column bracket bolts
- Steering column shrouds and the shroud screws
- Light switch rheostat resistor electrical connector and install the instrument panel steering column cover (coupe models only)
- Instrument panel steering column cover and the cover screw
- Hood latch control handle and cable and tighten the hood latch control handle nut

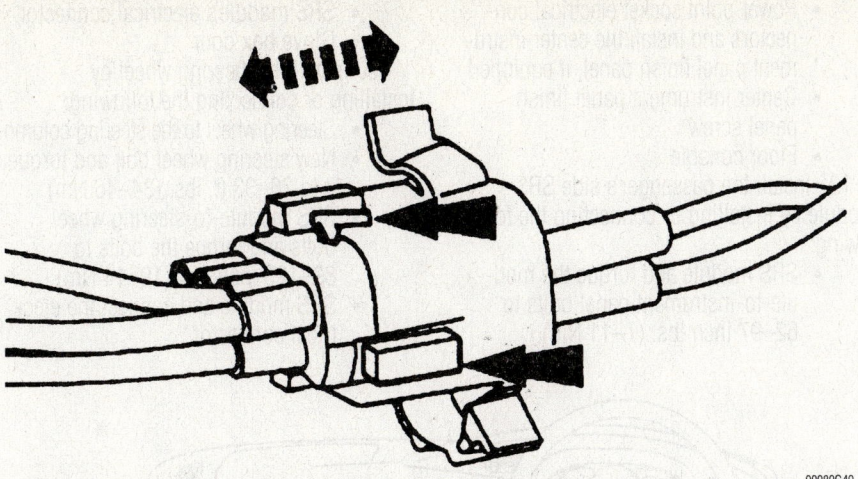

Unplug the vacuum line harness connector—1998–01 Escort and Tracer

90980G49

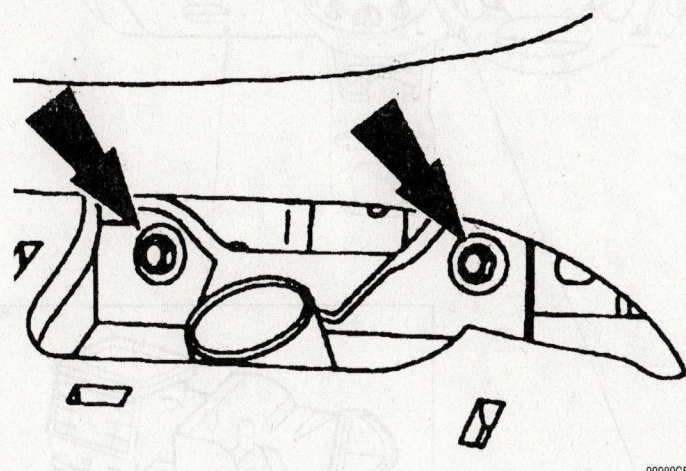

Unfasten both the left-hand and right-hand center instrument panel reinforcement bolts— 1998–01 Escort and Tracer

90980G50

Unfasten both the left-hand and right-hand lower instrument panel reinforcement bolts— 1998–01 Escort and Tracer

90980G51

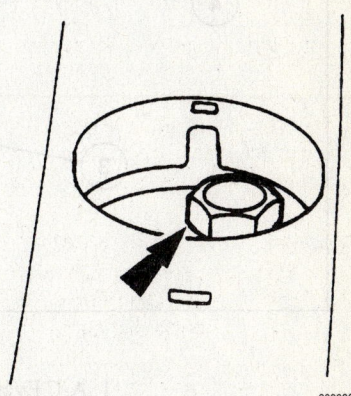

Remove the cover and unfasten the upper instrument panel reinforcement bolt— 1998–01 Escort and Tracer

90980G52

Refer to the model specific sections for cooling system service precautions

- Heater control cable
- PCM/bracket, the 2 PCM/bracket nuts and the 2 bolts
- PCM electrical connector and the bolt
- Transmission control selector dial bezel screws
- Radio antenna lead-in cable
- Radio antenna lead-in cable
- Control box side covers and secure with the pushpins, located at both sides

- Power point socket electrical connectors and install the center instrument panel finish panel, if equipped
- Center instrument panel finish panel screw
- Floor console

12. Install the passenger's side SRS module by installing or connecting the following:

- SRS module and torque the module-to-instrument panel bolts to 62–97 inch lbs. (7–11 Nm)

- SRS module's electrical connector
- Glove box door

13. Install the steering wheel by installing or connecting the following:

- Steering wheel to the steering column
- New steering wheel bolt and torque it to 26–33 ft. lbs. (34–46 Nm)
- SRS module-to-steering wheel bolts and torque the bolts to 89–123 inch lbs. (10–14 Nm)
- SRS module and connect the electrical connector

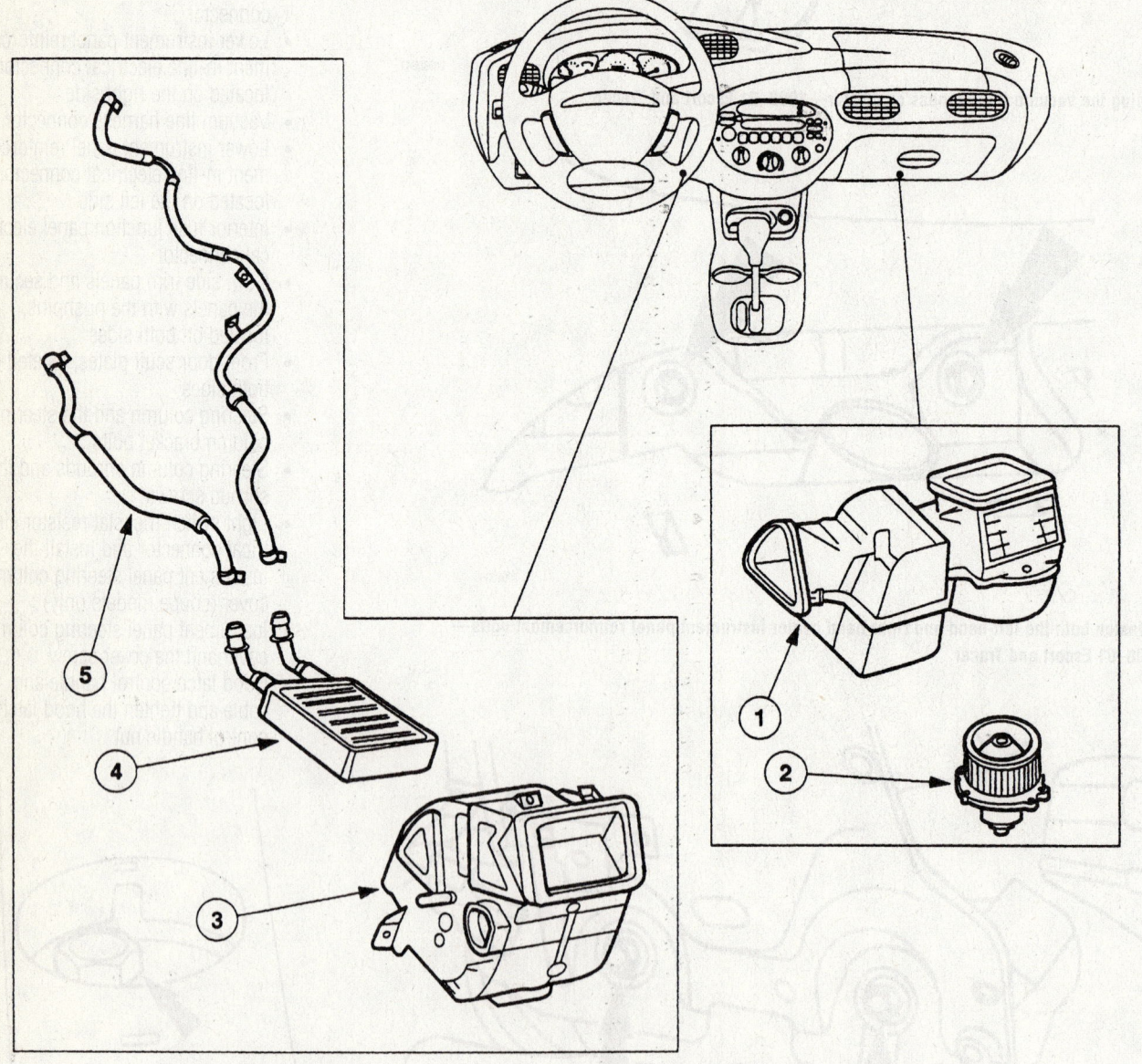

1 A/C Evaporator Housing
2 Blower Motor
3 Heater Core Housing
4 Heater Core
5 Heater Water Hoses

Exploded view of the heater core, heater housing and related components—1998–01 Escort and Tracer

93111GB3

14. Connect the heater hoses to the heater core.

15. On the Coupe, install the air cleaner outlet tube.

16. Refill the cooling system.

17. Connect the negative battery cable.

18. Operate the engine to normal operating temperatures; then, check the climate control operation and check for leaks.

Mustang

REMOVAL & INSTALLATION

1997 Models

WITHOUT AIR CONDITIONING

1. Disconnect the negative battery cable.

2. Remove the floor console and instrument panel by removing or disconnecting the following:

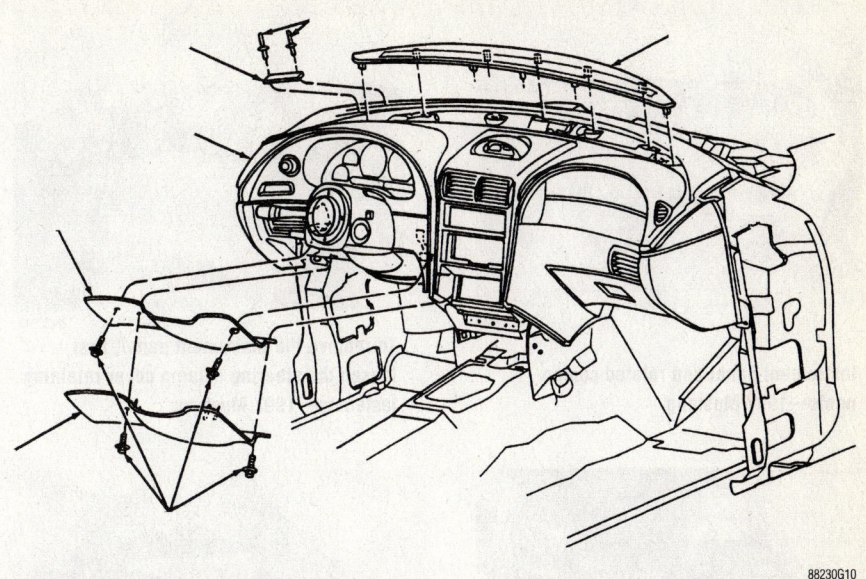

88230G10

Exploded view of the steering column cover and reinforcement mounting—1997 Mustang

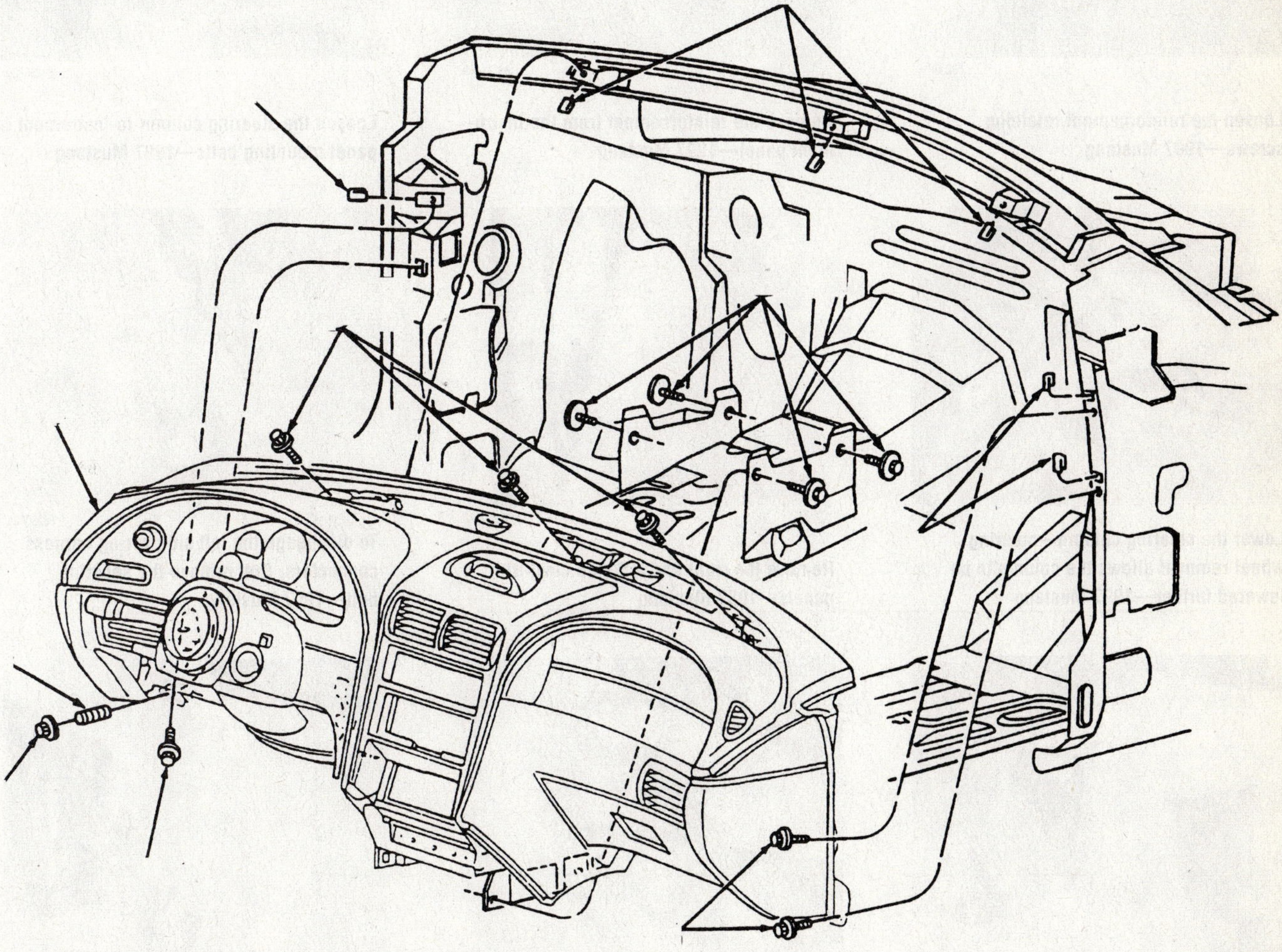

Exploded view of the instrument panel mounting—1997 Mustang

88230G09

For complete service labor times order Nichols' Chilton Labor Guide Manual

Instrument panel and related components—1997 Mustang

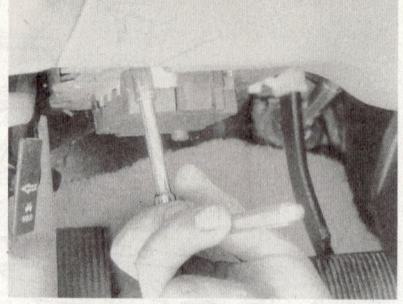

To remove the instrument panel, first loosen the steering column cover retaining fasteners—1997 Mustang

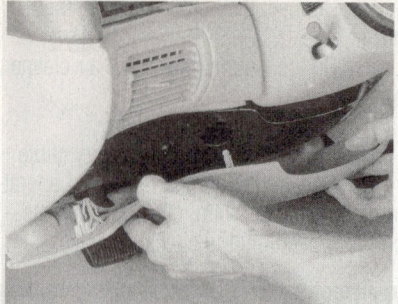

Lower the steering column cover—1997 Mustang

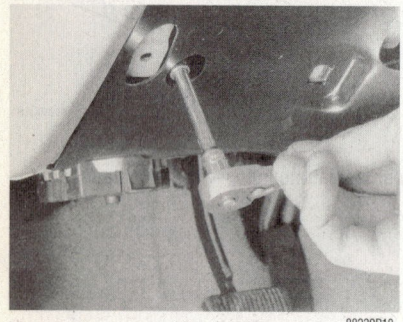

Loosen the reinforcement retaining screws—1997 Mustang

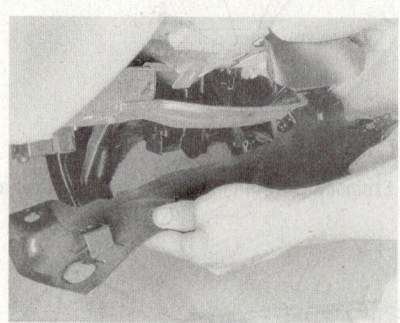

Remove the reinforcement from the instrument panel—1997 Mustang

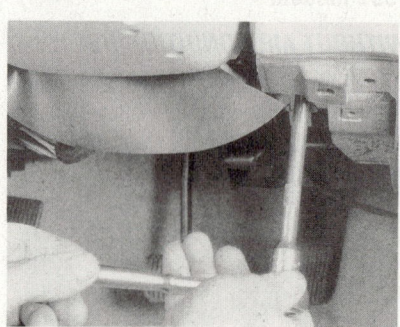

Loosen the steering column-to-instrument panel mounting bolts—1997 Mustang

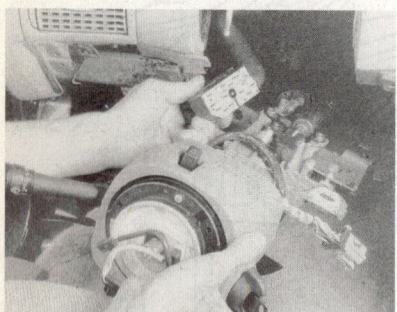

Lower the steering column—steering wheel removal allows the column to be lowered further—1997 Mustang

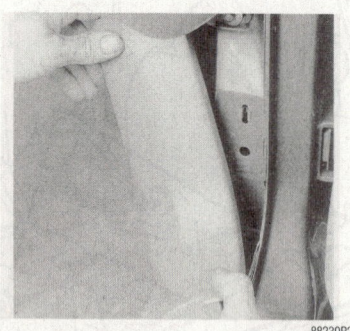

Remove the right and left side cowl trim panels—1997 Mustang

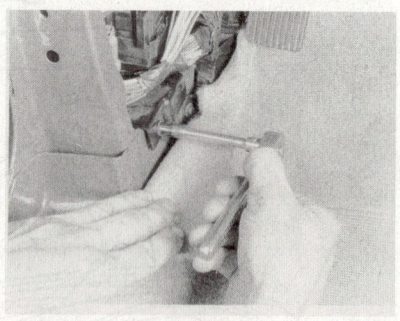

To disengage the left side wiring harness connectors, first remove the securing bolt—1997 Mustang

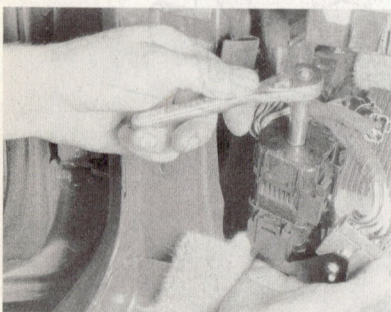

Pull the connectors out from the panel recess and loosen the connector retaining bolt—1997 Mustang

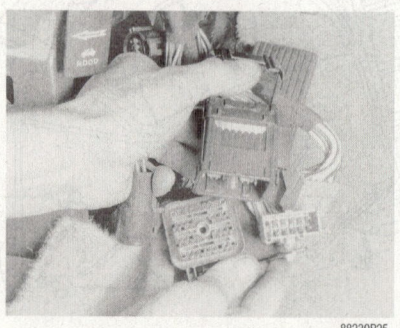

Separate the connector halves—1997 Mustang

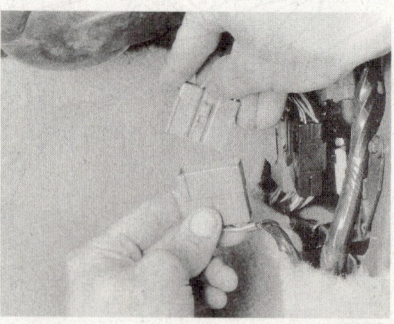

Disengage the wiring connectors from the right-hand side as well—1997 Mustang

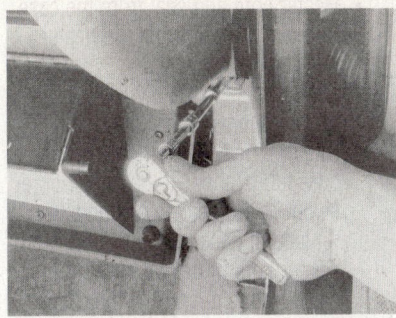

Remove the instrument panel's side mounting fasteners—1997 Mustang

Be sure not to miss the fastener located in the glove box opening—1997 Mustang

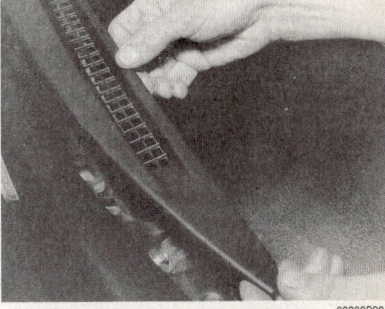

Remove the defroster grille from the top of the instrument panel—1997 Mustang

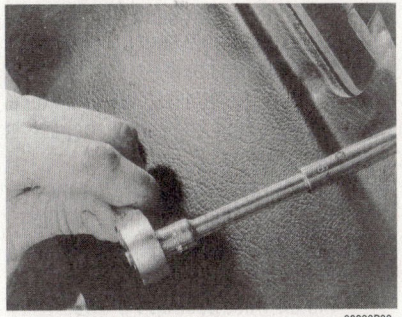

Loosen the upper instrument panel mounting screws—1997 Mustang

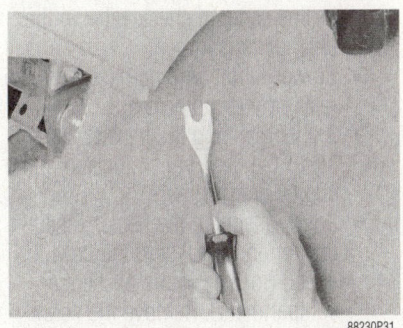

Carefully pry out the retainers, then pull back the carpet to expose the diagnostic monitor—1997 Mustang

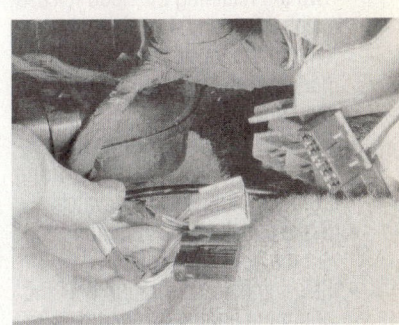

Disengage the diagnostic monitor's electrical connectors—1997 Mustang

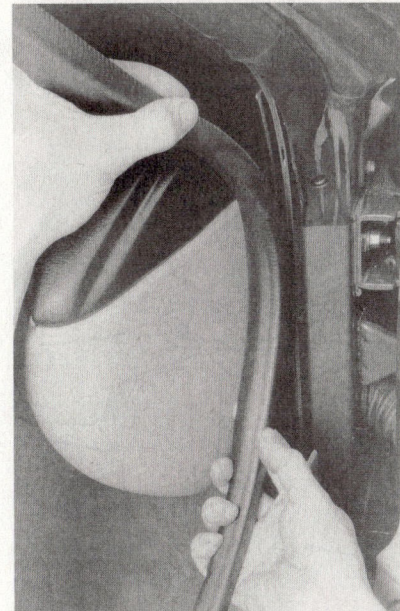

Remove the door opening weatherstripping—1997 Mustang

- 2 covers at the rear of the console, the armrest retaining bolts and the armrest
- Gearshift opening trim panel (snap-

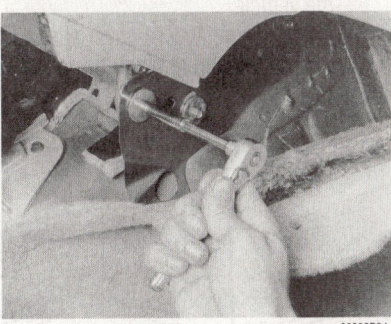

Remove the 4 instrument panel lower mounting screws—1997 Mustang

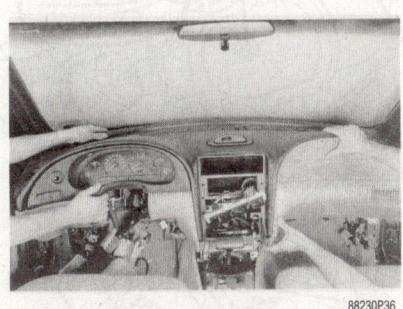

With the help of an assistant, remove the instrument panel from the vehicle—1997 Mustang

Detach the vacuum hose connector from the air conditioning housing hoses—1997 Mustang

fit). On manual transmission models, the shift boot is attached to the bottom of the finish panel; remove the shift knob and slide the boot and finish panel up and off the lever
- Pull the emergency brake handle up, remove the 4 screws and lift up the top finish panel. Detach the wiring
- Radio chassis (if installed) or pry the radio cover finish panel out of the console
- Flex the glove box bin tabs inward, lower the glove box assembly and

remove the 2 console-to-instrument panel screws
- 4 console bracket retaining screws and the console panel
- 3 bolts attaching the steering column opening cover and reinforcement panel. Remove the cover
- Steering column opening reinforcement by removing the 2 bolts. Remove the 2 bolts retaining the lower steering column opening reinforcement and remove the reinforcement
- 6 steering column retaining nuts. Two are retaining the hood release mechanism and 4 retain the column to the lower brake pedal support. Lower the steering column to the floor
- Steering column upper and lower shrouds and disconnect the wiring from the multi-function switch.
- Brake pedal support nut and snap out the defroster grille
- Steering column through bolt and nut in the engine compartment. Remove the steering column from the vehicle
- Screws from the speaker covers. Snap out the speaker covers. Remove the front screws retaining the right and left scuff plates at the cowl trim panel. Remove the right and left side cowl trim panels

- Wiring at the right and left cowl sides. Remove the cowl side retaining bolts, 1 on each side
- 5 cowl top screw attachments. Gently pull the instrument panel away from the cowl. Disconnect the speedometer cable and wire connectors

3. Drain the coolant from the cooling system and remove the hoses from the heater core. Plug the hoses and the core.

4. Remove or disconnect the following:
- Screw attaching the air inlet duct and blower housing assembly support bracket to the cowl top panel
- Black vacuum supply hose from the in-line vacuum check valve in the engine compartment
- Blower motor wire harness from the resistor and motor head
- 2 nuts retaining the heater assembly to the dash panel, located in the engine compartment
- Screw attaching the heater assembly support bracket to the cowl top panel, (located in the passenger compartment). Remove the screw retaining the bracket below the heater assembly to the dash panel
- Pull the heater assembly away from the dash panel and remove from the vehicle
- 4 heater core access cover attaching screws and remove the access cover from the case

- Heater core and seal from the case. Remove the seal from the heater core tubes

To install:

5. Install or connect the following:
- Heater core tube seal on the heater core tubes. Inspect the heater core sealer in the heater case and replace, if necessary
- Heater core in the case with the seals on the outside of the case. Position the heater core access cover on the case and install the 4 attaching screws
- Heater assembly in the vehicle. Install the screw attaching the heater assembly support bracket to the cowl top panel

6. Check the heater assembly drain tube to ensure it is through the dash panel and is not pinched or kinked.

7. Install or connect the following:
- 2 nuts retaining the heater assembly to the dash panel (located in the engine compartment). Install the air inlet duct and blower housing support bracket attaching screw. Install 1 screw to the retainer bracket below the heater assembly to the dash pane
- Blower motor ground wire to ground and the harness to the resistor and blower motor lead
- Black vacuum supply hose to the

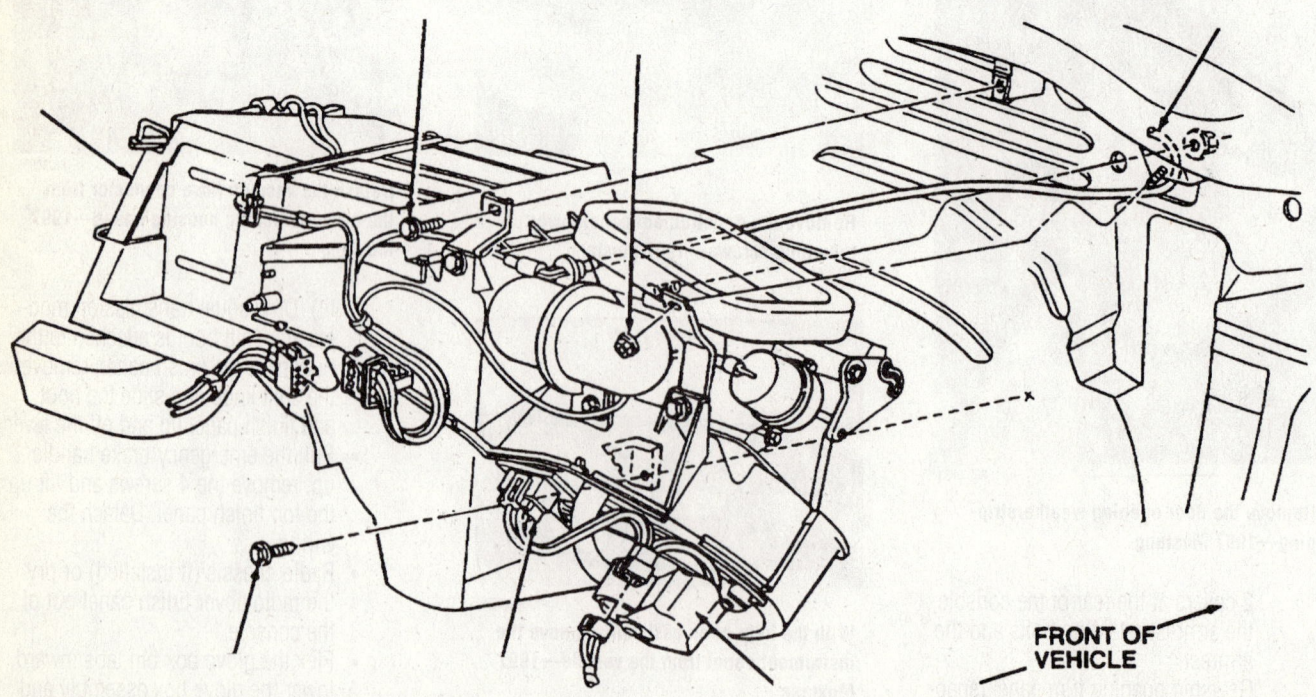

FRONT OF VEHICLE

Exploded view of the heater case assembly mounting—1997 Mustang

88236G06

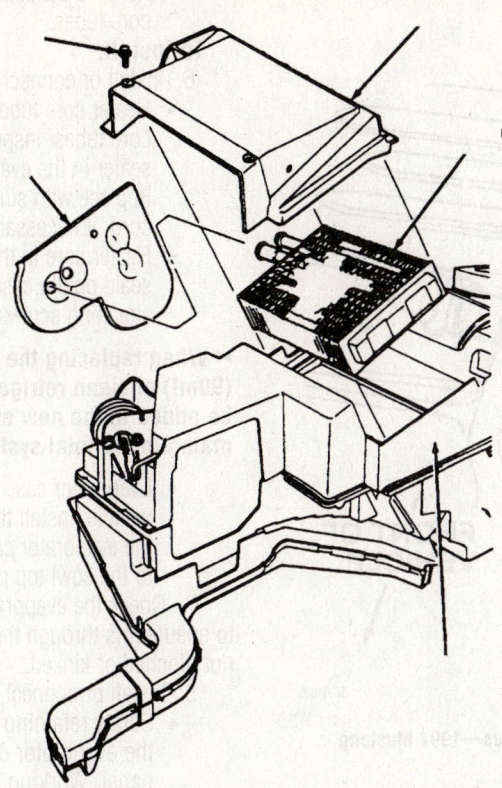

Exploded view of the heater core mounting in the heater case assembly—1997 Mustang

88236G05

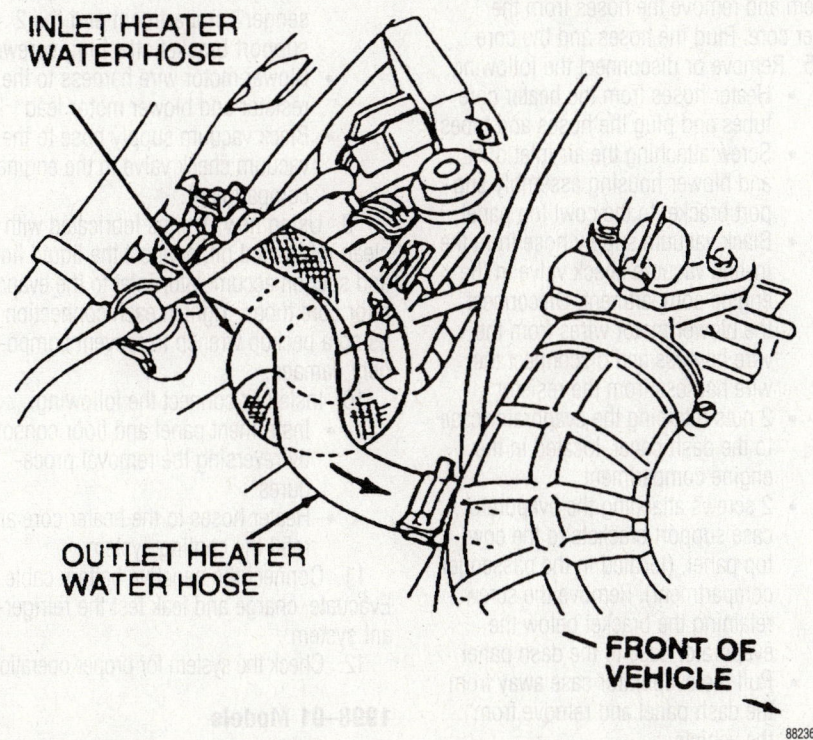

INLET HEATER
WATER HOSE

OUTLET HEATER
WATER HOSE

FRONT OF
VEHICLE

88236G08

To remove the heater core, first disconnect the water hoses from the heater core tubes—3.8L engine hose routing shown—1997 Mustang

vacuum check valve in the engine compartment
- Instrument panel and floor console by reversing the removal procedures
- Heater hoses to the heater core and refill the cooling system. Check the system for proper operation

WITH AIR CONDITIONING

1. Disconnect the negative battery cable.
2. Discharge and recover the air conditioning system refrigerant.
3. Remove the floor console and instrument panel by removing or disconnecting the following:

- 2 covers at the rear of the console and remove the armrest retaining bolts and remove the armrest
- Gearshift opening trim panel (snap-fit). On manual transmission models, the shift boot is attached to the bottom of the finish panel; remove the shift knob and slide the boot and finish panel up and off the lever
- Pull the emergency brake handle up, remove the 4 screws and lift up the top finish panel. Detach the wiring
- Radio chassis (if installed) or pry the radio cover finish panel out of the console
- Flex the glove box bin tabs inward, lower the glove box assembly and remove the 2 console-to-instrument panel screws
- 4 console bracket retaining screws and remove the console panel
- 3 bolts attaching the steering column opening cover and reinforcement panel. Remove the cover
- Steering column opening reinforcement by removing the 2 bolts. Remove the 2 bolts retaining the lower steering column opening reinforcement and remove the reinforcement
- 6 steering column retaining nuts. Two are retaining the hood release mechanism and 4 retain the column to the lower brake pedal support. Lower the steering column to the floor
- Steering column upper and lower shrouds and disconnect the wiring from the multi-function switch
- Brake pedal support nut and snap out the defroster grille

Refer to the model specific sections for engine mechanical service procedures

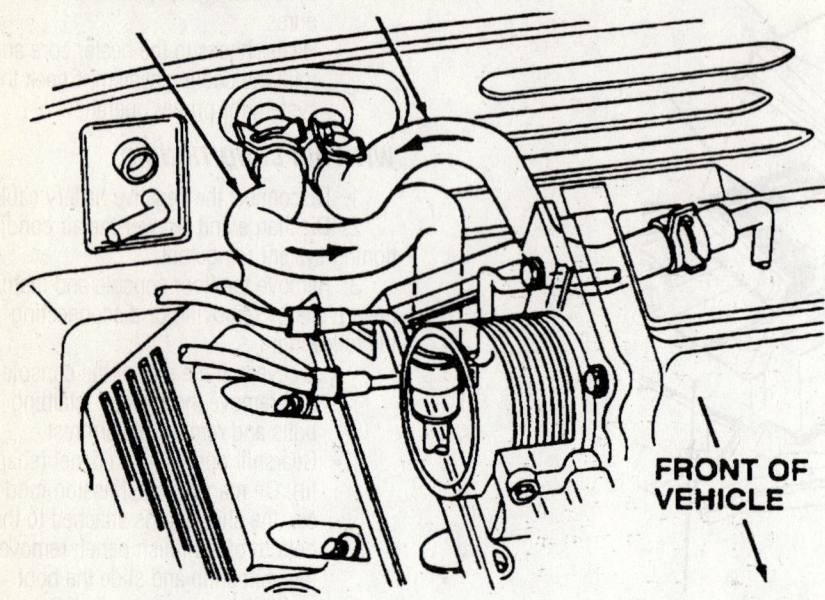

OUTLET HEATER WATER HOSE

INLET HEATER WATER HOSE

FRONT OF VEHICLE

88236G09

Heater core water hose routing on vehicles equipped with the 4.6L engines—1997 Mustang

- Steering column through bolt and nut in the engine compartment. Remove the steering column from the vehicle
- Screws from the speaker covers. Snap out the speaker covers. Remove the front screws retaining the right and left scuff plates at the cowl trim panel. Remove the right and left side cowl trim panels
- Wiring at the right and left cowl sides. Remove the cowl side retaining bolts, 1 on each side
- Open the glove compartment door and flex the glove compartment bin tabs inward. Lower the glove compartment door assembly
- 5 cowl top screw attachments. Gently pull the instrument panel away from the cowl. Disconnect the speedometer cable and wire connectors

➡ **Whenever an evaporator case is replace, it will be necessary to replace the suction accumulator/drier.**

- Liquid line and the accumulator/drier inlet tube for the evaporator core at the dash panel. Cap the refrigerant lines and evaporator core tube to prevent the entrance of dirt and excessive

moisture. Remove the high and low pressure hoses. Cap the openings
4. Drain the coolant from the cooling system and remove the hoses from the heater core. Plug the hoses and the core.
5. Remove or disconnect the following:
- Heater hoses from the heater core tubes and plug the hoses and tubes
- Screw attaching the air inlet duct and blower housing assembly support bracket to the cowl top panel
- Black vacuum supply hose from the in-line vacuum check valve in the engine compartment. Disconnect the blower motor wires from the wire harness and disconnect the wire harness from the resistor
- 2 nuts retaining the evaporator case to the dash panel, located in the engine compartment
- 2 screws attaching the evaporator case support brackets to the cowl top panel, (located in the passenger compartment). Remove the screw retaining the bracket below the evaporator case to the dash panel
- Pull the evaporator case away from the dash panel and remove from the vehicle
- 4 heater core access cover attaching screws and remove the access cover from the case

- Heater core and seal from the case. Remove the seal from the heater core tubes
To install:
6. Install or connect the following:
- Heater core tube seal on the heater core tubes. Inspect the heater core sealer in the evaporator case. Replace with suitable caulking cord, if necessary
- Heater core in the case with the seals on the case and install the 4 attaching screws

➡ **When replacing the evaporator, 3 oz. (90ml) of clean refrigerant oil should be added to the new evaporator to maintain the total system oil charge**

- Evaporator case assembly in the vehicle. Install the screw attaching the evaporator case support bracket to the cowl top panel
7. Check the evaporator case drain tube to ensure it is through the dash panel and is not pinched or kinked.
8. Install or connect the following:
- Screw retaining the bracket below the evaporator case to the dash panel. Working under the hood, install the 2 nuts retaining the evaporator case to the dash panel. Tighten the 2 screws in the passenger compartment and the 2 support bracket attaching screws
- Blower motor wire harness to the resistor and blower motor lead
- Black vacuum supply hose to the vacuum check valve in the engine compartment
9. Using new O-rings lubricated with clean refrigerant oil, connect the liquid line and suction accumulator inlet to the evaporator core tubes. Tighten each connection using a backup wrench to prevent component damage.
10. Install or connect the following:
- Instrument panel and floor console by reversing the removal procedures
- Heater hoses to the heater core and refill the cooling system
11. Connect the negative battery cable. Evacuate, charge and leak test the refrigerant system.
12. Check the system for proper operation.

1998–01 Models

➡ **Record the USER 1 and USER 2 preset radio frequencies for reprogramming purposes.**

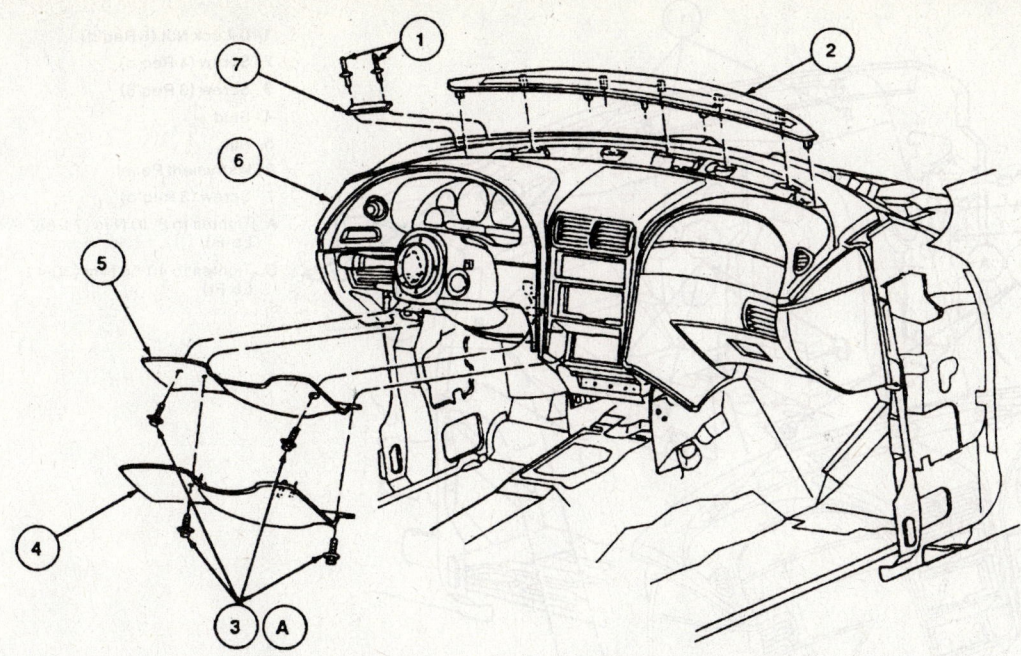

1 Rivet (2 Req'd)
2 Instrument Panel Upper Finish Panel
3 Screw (4 Req'd)
4 Instrument Panel Steering Column Cover
5 Instrument Panel Reinforcement
6 Instrument Panel
7 Vehicle Identification Plate
A Tighten to 8-10 N·m (71-88 Lb-In)

93111GA3

Exploded view of the instrument panel, cover and reinforcement—1998–01 Mustang

1. Disconnect the negative battery cable.

✳✳ CAUTION

After disconnecting the negative battery cable, wait for at least 1 minute for the SRS or air bag module to deplete its energy.

2. Drain the cooling system into a clean container for reuse.
3. Disconnect the heater hoses from the heater core.
4. Place the front wheels in the straight-ahead position.
5. Lock the steering column.
6. Remove the steering wheel by removing or disconnecting the following:
   - SRS bolt covers, located on both sides of the steering wheel
   - SRS module-to-steering wheel bolts
   - SRS module and disconnect the electrical connector

✳✳ CAUTION

Place the SRS module in a safe place with the front facing upward.

- Steering wheel bolt and discard it
- Press the steering wheel from the steering column

7. Remove the instrument panel by removing or disconnecting the following:

- 2 instrument panel steering column cover screws and the cover
- 2 instrument panel reinforcement screws and the reinforcement
- 2 lower instrument panel reinforcement screws and the reinforcement
- Console panel
- Instrument cluster finish panel
- Ignition switch lock cylinder and the tilt column lever
- 4 steering column shroud screws and the shrouds
- Electrical connectors from the ignition switch and the shift lock actuator
- 2 multi-function switch screws and the switch
- Cowl side trim panels (on both sides), and disconnect the electrical connectors
- 4 steering column-to-instrument panel reinforcement nuts
- Electrical connectors and lower the steering column to the floor
- 2 ignition/shifter interlock cable screws, (models with a automatic transmission only)
- Lower steering column pinch bolt and the steering column
- Electrical connectors from the air bag diagnostic monitor
- Open the glove box; then, disconnect the antenna lead cable, the

heater/air conditioning housing electrical connectors and vacuum harness
- Pull back the weatherstrips at both front doors
- 4 instrument panel-to-floor bracket screws
- Instrument panel-to-cowl fasteners (2 screws on the right side; 1 screw and 1 nut of the left side), located on both sides
- Finish panel at the top of the instrument panel using a suitable prytool
- 3 instrument panel-to-upper cowl panel screws
- Pull instrument panel rearward and disconnect the control cable from the heater/air conditioning housing
- Instrument panel

8. If equipped with air conditioning, perform the following procedure:
   a. Discharge and recover the air conditioning system refrigerant.
   b. Disconnect the refrigerant lines from the evaporator core. Discard the O-rings and plug the openings to prevent contamination.
   c. Remove the suction accumulator/drier.
   d. Remove the 2 accumulator bracket-to-cowl nuts and the bracket.

9. Remove or disconnect the following:

Refer to the model specific sections for cooling system service precautions

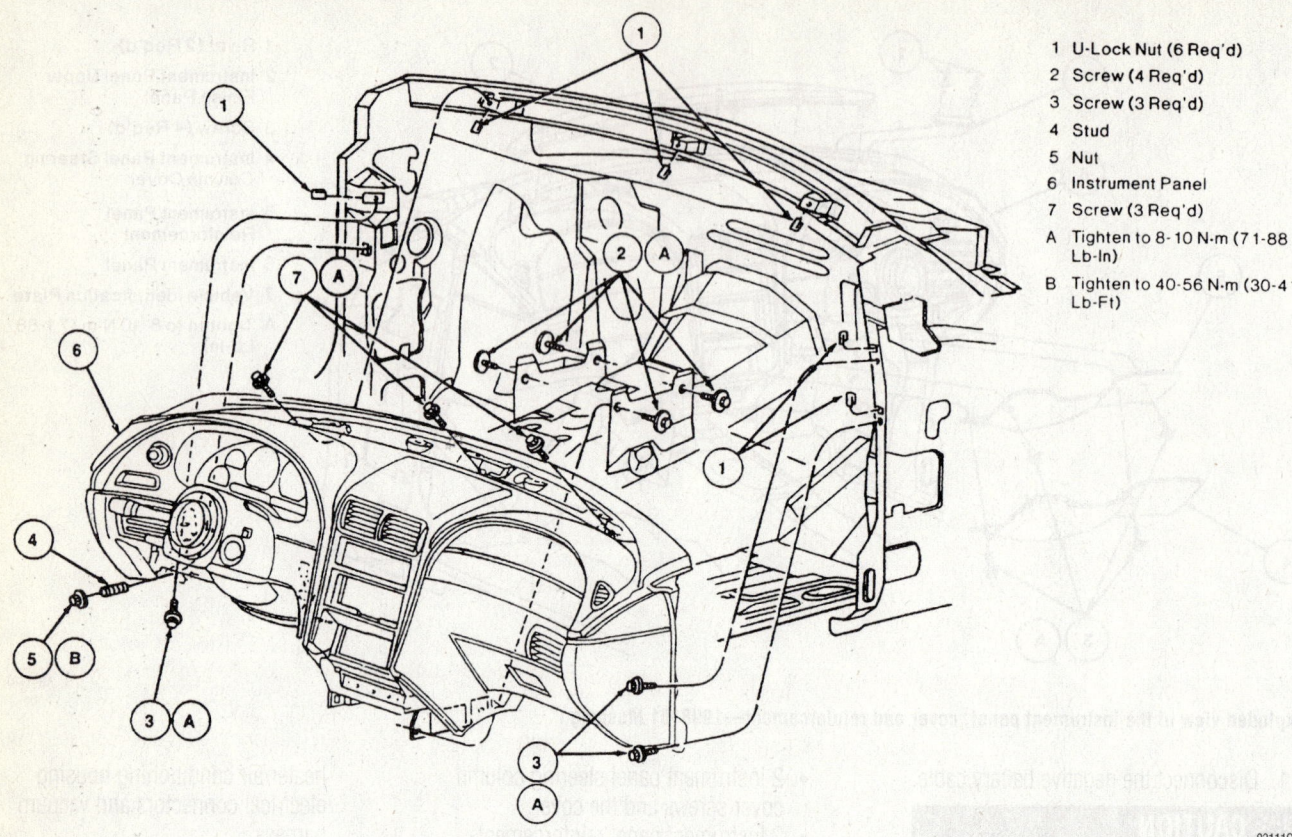

1 U-Lock Nut (6 Req'd)
2 Screw (4 Req'd)
3 Screw (3 Req'd)
4 Stud
5 Nut
6 Instrument Panel
7 Screw (3 Req'd)
A Tighten to 8-10 N·m (71-88 Lb-In)
B Tighten to 40-56 N·m (30-41 Lb-Ft)

93111GA5

Exploded view of the instrument panel and related components—1998–01 Mustang

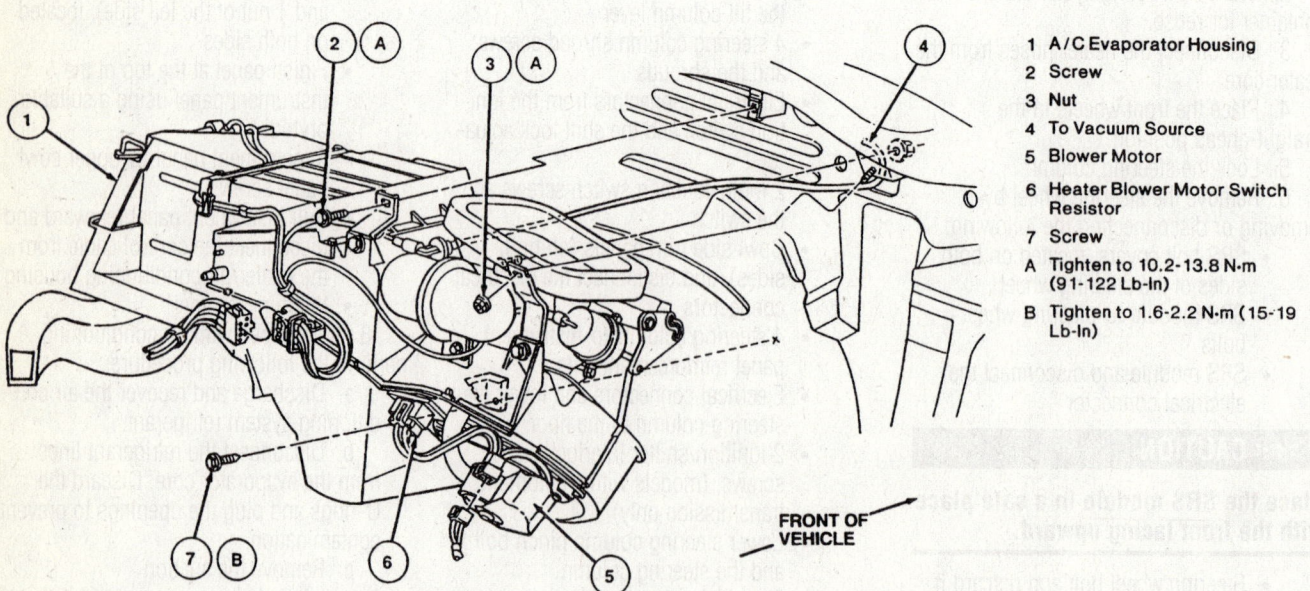

1 A/C Evaporator Housing
2 Screw
3 Nut
4 To Vacuum Source
5 Blower Motor
6 Heater Blower Motor Switch Resistor
7 Screw
A Tighten to 10.2-13.8 N·m (91-122 Lb-In)
B Tighten to 1.6-2.2 N·m (15-19 Lb-In)

FRONT OF VEHICLE

93111GA4

Exploded view of the heater/air conditioning housing assembly—1998–01 Mustang

- Disconnect the vacuum supply hose from the vacuum source, located in the engine compartment
- Heater/air conditioning evaporator housing-to-cowl nut
- Bottom heater/air conditioning evaporator housing-to-cowl screw, located in the passenger compartment
- Upper heater/air conditioning evaporator housing support bracket-to-cowl nut and screw
- Wiring harness from the blower motor
- Heater/air conditioning housing assembly from the vehicle
- Vacuum harness from the heater/air conditioning housing and move it aside
- 4 heater core cover-to-heater/air conditioning housing screws and the cover
- Seal from the heater core tubes
- Heater core from the heater/air conditioning housing

To install:

10. Install or connect the following:
- Heater core to the heater/air conditioning housing
- Seal to the heater core tubes
- Heater core cover-to-heater/air conditioning housing and the 4 cover screws
- Vacuum harness to the heater/air conditioning housing
- Heater/air conditioning housing assembly to the vehicle
- Wiring harness to the blower motor
- Upper heater/air conditioning evaporator housing support bracket-to-cowl nut and screw
- Bottom heater/air conditioning evaporator housing-to-cowl screw, located in the passenger compartment
- Heater/air conditioning evaporator housing-to-cowl nut
- vacuum supply hose to the vacuum source, located in the engine compartment

11. If equipped with air conditioning, perform the following procedure:
a. Install the accumulator bracket and 2 bracket-to-cowl nuts.
b. Install the suction accumulator/drier.
c. Using new O-rings, connect the refrigerant lines to the evaporator core.

12. Install the instrument panel by installing or connecting the following:

- Instrument panel
- Control cable to the heater/air conditioning housing and push the instrument panel forward
- 3 instrument panel-to-upper cowl panel screws
- Finish panel to on the instrument panel
- Instrument panel-to-cowl fasteners (2 screws on the right side, 1 screw and 1 nut of the left side), on both sides
- 4 instrument panel-to-floor bracket screws
- Weatherstrips on both front doors
- Antenna lead cable, the heater/air conditioning housing electrical connectors and vacuum harness
- Electrical connectors to the air bag diagnostic monitor
- Lower steering column and the steering column pinch bolt
- 2 ignition/shifter interlock cable screws, if equipped with an automatic transmission
- Steering column and connect the electrical connectors
- 4 steering column-to-instrument panel reinforcement nuts and tighten to 10–12 ft. lbs. (13–17 Nm)
- Electrical connectors and install the cowl side trim panels, on both sides
- Multi-function switch and the 2 switch screws
- Electrical connectors to the ignition switch and the shift lock actuator
- Steering column shrouds and the 4 shroud screws
- Ignition switch lock cylinder and the tilt column lever
- Instrument cluster finish panel
- Console panel
- Lower instrument panel reinforcement and the 2 reinforcement screws
- Instrument panel reinforcement and the 2 reinforcement screws
- Instrument panel steering column cover and the 2 cover screws

13. Install the steering wheel by installing or connecting the following:
- Steering wheel to the steering column
- Use a new steering wheel bolt and torque it to 26–33 ft. lbs. (34–46 Nm)
- SRS module and connect the electrical connector

- SRS module-to-steering wheel bolts and torque the bolts to 89–123 inch lbs. (10–14 Nm)
- SRS bolt covers

14. Connect the heater hoses to the heater core.

15. Refill the cooling system.

16. Connect the negative battery cable.

17. Evacuate, charge and leak test the air conditioning system.

18. Operate the engine to normal operating temperatures. Check the climate control operation and check for leaks.

Mark VIII

REMOVAL & INSTALLATION

1997–01 Models

1. Disconnect the negative battery cable.

✳✳ CAUTION

After disconnecting the negative battery cable, wait for at least 1 minute for the air bag module to deplete its energy.

2. Drain the cooling system into a clean container for reuse.

3. Disconnect the heater hoses from the heater core.

4. Discharge and recover the air conditioning system refrigerant.

5. Disconnect the refrigerant lines from the evaporator core; then, plug the lines to prevent contamination.

6. Place the front wheels in the straight-ahead position.

7. Lock the steering column.

8. Remove the SRS module and the steering wheel by removing or disconnecting the following:
- SRS bolt covers, both sides of the steering wheel
- 2 SRS module-to-steering wheel screws and washers
- SRS module and disconnect the electrical connector

✳✳ CAUTION

Place the SRS module in a safe place with the front facing upward.

- Steering wheel bolt and discard it.

9. Press the steering wheel from the steering column.

10. Remove the passenger's side SRS module by removing or disconnecting the following:
- Instrument cluster finish panel
- Instrument panel finish panel, located on the right side

11. Lower the glove compartment.

12. Remove or disconnect the following:
- Evaporator register duct screws and the duct
- SRS module's electrical connector
- SRS module-to-instrument panel bolts and the module

✳✳ CAUTION

Place the SRS module in a safe place with the front facing upward.

- Instrument panel by performing the following procedure:
- Transmission electrical connectors, located at the transmission cross-member.
- Bulkhead electrical connector bolt and disconnect the electrical connector
- Bulkhead electrical connector from the dash, located on the left side
- Steering column
- Floor console
- Radio chassis
- Electronic Automatic Temperature Control (EATC) module screws and move the module aside
- Electrical connectors and the vacuum harness connector (located at the rear of the EATC module); then, remove the EATC module nuts and the module
- Heater outlet duct
- Front door weatherstrips, the cowl side trim panels and the roof side, inner, front moldings from both sides
- Mobile phone speaker electrical connector, located on the left side inner front molding, (if equipped)

13. Lift the rear edge of the instrument panel defroster opening grille, disconnect the air conditioning sunload sensor electrical connector and remove the instrument panel defroster opening grille.

14. Remove or disconnect the following:
- Electrical connector; then, remove the windshield wiper control module/bracket screw, the module and bracket
- Bulkhead electrical connector bolt and disconnect the electrical connectors, located on the left side
- Ignition/shifter interlock cable from

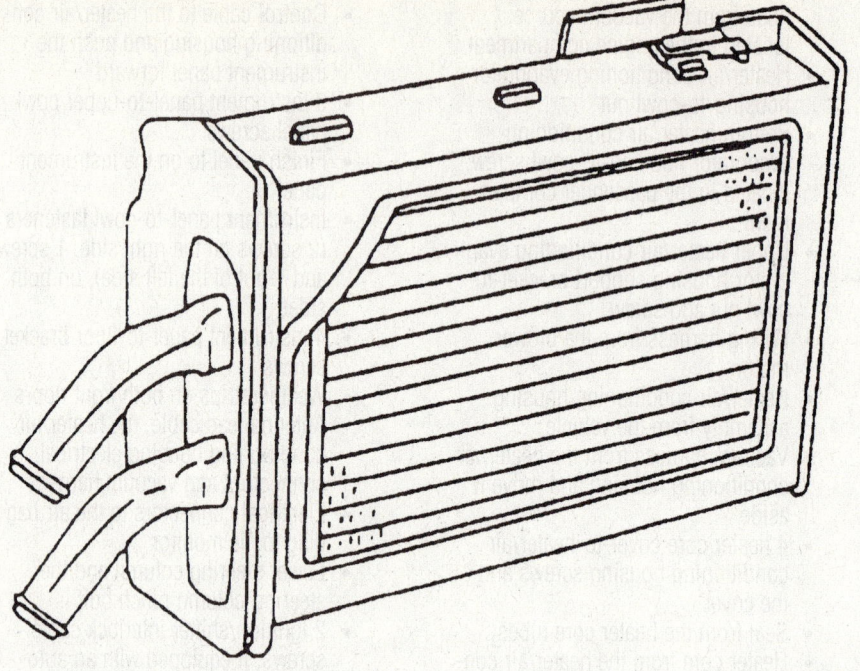

View of the heater core—1997–01 Mark VIII

the pawl by depressing the locking tab
- Instrument panel insulator push-pins, the courtesy lamp/socket and the insulator, located on the right side
- Glove compartment
- EATC sensor hose and elbow
- Climate control vacuum harness connector
- In-line electrical connector accessed through the glove box opening
- Insulator pad pushpin and the pad, located on the right side
- Electrical harness connectors, located on the right side
- Antenna connector
- Unseat the transmission electrical harness grommet from the floorpan
- Instrument panel cowl side nuts, located on the left side
- Instrument panel center support nuts
- Instrument panel-to-floor bracket bolts and the bracket
- Instrument panel cowl side nut, located on the right side
- 6 upper instrument panel cowl bolts
- Instrument panel with the help of an assistant

15. Remove the evaporator housing by performing the following procedure:

a. Loosen the accumulator bracket clamp screw.

b. Remove the nuts and rotate the accumulator bracket away from the cowl.

16. Remove or disconnect the following:
- Vacuum supply hose
- Floor outlet ventilation duct extension screw and the duct extension
- Floor outlet ventilation duct screws and the duct
- 3 evaporator housing-to-cowl nuts
- Evaporator housing-to-chassis screw and the evaporator housing

17. Remove the heater core from the evaporator housing by removing or disconnecting the following:
- Electrical connector from the air conditioning electric blend door actuator
- Air conditioning electric blend door actuator-to-evaporator housing screws and the actuator
- 13 evaporator case screws
- 4 heater core cover-to-evaporator housing screws

✳✳ WARNING

Do not bend any part of the levers for they are brittle and will break.

- Upper evaporator case from the lower half
- Depress the air conditioning air

temperature control door lever locking ramp and disengage the lever
- Levers from the control door ends
- Heater core

To install:

18. Install the heater core to the evaporator housing by installing or connecting the following:
- Heater core
- Levers to the control door ends
- Air conditioning air temperature control doors lever and the locking ramp
- Upper evaporator case to the lower half
- 4 heater core cover-to-evaporator housing screws

❊❊ WARNING

Do not bend any part of the levers for they are brittle and will break.

- 13 evaporator case screws
- Air conditioning electric blend door actuator and the actuator-to-evaporator housing screws
- Electrical connector to the air conditioning electric blend door actuator

19. Install the evaporator housing by installing or connecting the following:
- Evaporator housing-to-chassis and the evaporator housing screw
- 3 evaporator housing-to-cowl nuts
- Floor outlet ventilation duct and the duct screws
- Floor outlet ventilation duct extension and the duct extension screw
- Vacuum supply hose
- Accumulator bracket; then, tighten the accumulator bracket clamp screw and the nuts

20. Install the instrument panel by installing or connecting the following:
- Instrument panel with the help of an assistant
- 6 upper instrument panel cowl bolts
- Instrument panel cowl side nut, located on the right side
- Instrument panel-to-floor bracket and the bracket bolts
- Instrument panel center support nuts
- Instrument panel cowl side nuts, located on the left side
- Transmission electrical harness grommet to the floorpan
- Antenna connector

- Electrical harness connectors, located on the right side
- Insulator pad and the pad pushpin, located on the right side
- In-line electrical connector, accessed through the glove box opening
- Climate control vacuum harness connector
- EATC sensor hose and elbow
- Glove compartment
- Instrument panel insulator pushpins, the courtesy lamp/socket and the insulator, located on the right side
- Ignition/shifter interlock cable to the pawl
- Electrical connectors and tighten the bulkhead electrical connector bolt, located on the left side
- Electrical connector; then, install the windshield wiper control module/bracket and the module/bracket screw
- Air conditioning sunload sensor electrical connector and install the instrument panel defroster opening grille
- Mobile phone speaker electrical connector, located on the left side inner front molding, if equipped
- Front door weatherstrips, the cowl side trim panels and the roof side inner front moldings
- Heater outlet duct
- Electrical connectors and the vacuum harness connector to the rear of the Electronic Automatic Temperature Control (EATC) module; then, install the EATC module and the module nuts
- EATC module and the module screws
- Radio chassis
- Floor console
- Steering column
- Bulkhead electrical connector to the dash, located on the left side
- Bulkhead electrical connector and tighten the bolt, located on the left side
- Electrical connector and tighten the bulkhead electrical connector bolt
- Transmission electrical connectors, located at the transmission crossmember

21. Install the passenger's side SRS module by installing or connecting the following:

- SRS module and torque the module-to-instrument panel screws to 9–17 inch lbs. (1–2 Nm)
- SRS module's electrical connector
- Evaporator register duct and the duct screws
- Glove compartment
- Instrument panel finish panel, located on the right side
- Instrument cluster finish panel

22. Install the SRS module and the steering wheel by installing or connecting the following:
- Steering wheel to the steering column
- New steering wheel bolt and torque it to 26–33 ft. lbs. (34–46 Nm)
- SRS module and connect the electrical connector
- 2 SRS module-to-steering wheel screws and washers; then, and torque the screws to 89–123 inch lbs. (10–13 Nm)
- SRS bolt covers, located on both sides of the steering wheel
- Refrigerant lines to the evaporator core
- Heater hoses to the heater core

23. Refill the cooling system.
24. Connect the negative battery cable.
25. Evacuate, charge and leak test the air conditioning system.
26. Operate the engine to normal operating temperatures; then, check the climate control operation and check for leaks.

1997–98 Thunderbird and 1997 Cougar

REMOVAL & INSTALLATION

❊❊ CAUTION

To avoid accidental air bag deployment and possible personal injury, disconnect both battery cables and wait 1 minute for the air bag diagnostic monitor to deplete the air bag back-up power supply.

1. Disconnect the negative battery cable.
2. Disconnect the positive battery cable and wait 1 minute for the back-up power supply to be de-energized.
3. Partially drain the cooling system.
4. Discharge and recover the air conditioning system.
5. Remove the instrument panel by removing or disconnecting the following:

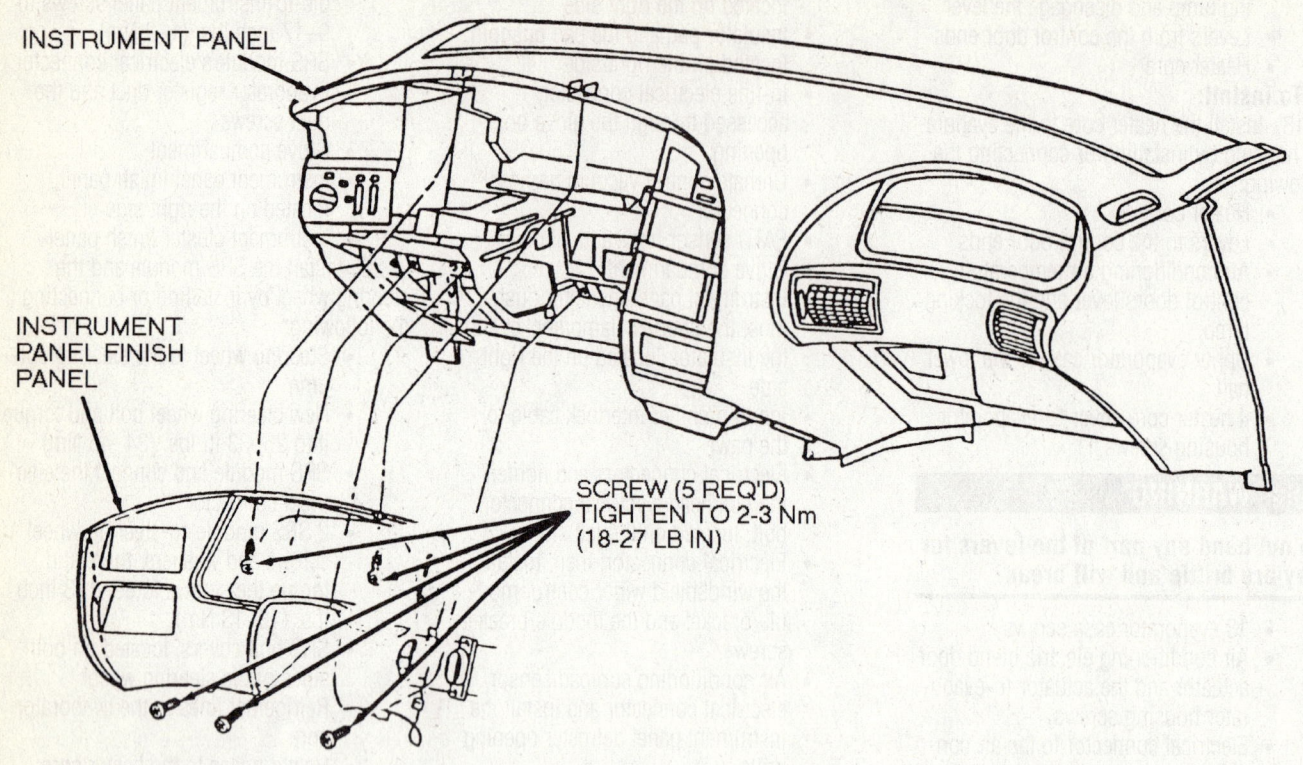

INSTRUMENT PANEL

INSTRUMENT PANEL FINISH PANEL

SCREW (5 REQ'D) TIGHTEN TO 2-3 Nm (18-27 LB IN)

88180GA3

Exploded view of the instrument panel finish panel mounting screws for the cluster—1997–98 Thunderbird and 1997 Cougar shown

- Main wiring connector bolt in the engine compartment at the left side of the dash panel and separate the connectors
- Radio antenna stanchion and the radio antenna lead-in cable from the base of the stanchion
- Both windshield side garnish moldings
- Both door scuff plates and weatherstrip
- Both kick panels
- 3 steering column cover retaining screws and pull on the steering column cover to unsnap the 3 clips across the top of the cover
- Instrument panel steering column cover
- Ignition switch lock cylinder
- 4 steering column shroud retaining screws and the shrouds
- Ignition switch lock cylinder to prevent the steering wheel from turning
- Wiring connectors at the multifunction switch
- Screw and the evaporator register duct from under the steering column tube
- Wiring connectors at the bottom of the steering column tube

- Steering column lower yoke pinch bolt. Using a suitable prytool, spread the yoke slightly
- 4 steering column tube retaining nuts (while supporting the steering column tube)
- Interlock cable retaining screws and the shift actuator cable fitting
- Steering column tube
- Main wiring connector bolt at the left side of the steering column opening and separate the connectors
- Stoplight switch wiring connector and the clutch pedal switch wiring connector (manual transmission only)
- Pull back the floor carpet on both sides
- Window regulator safety relay switch wiring and the Powertrain Control Module (PCM)
- Unsnap the glove compartment door check, remove the 3 door hinge retaining screws and the glove compartment from the instrument panel
- Wiring and vacuum connectors from the evaporator housing (accessed through the glove com-

partment opening)
- Main wiring from the speed control amplifier
- Amplifier and bracket assembly

6. Open the console glove compartment door.

7. Remove the 2 screws from the console finish panel and lift the rear of the console finish panel to unsnap the retainers.

8. Reach under the console finish panel and disconnect the wires to the fog lamp switch, the air suspension drive switch (if equipped) and the cigar lighter.

9. Lift the rear of the console finish panel, slide the panel rearward to release and lift off.

10. Remove or disconnect the following:

- Mat and the center screw from the console glove compartment. Lift the glove compartment from the console panel
- Luggage compartment and fuel filler door switches (if equipped)
- 2 screws from the bottom of the console glove compartment and the cap and screw from each side
- Front sides of the floor console
- 2 screws retaining the front of the console to the instrument panel

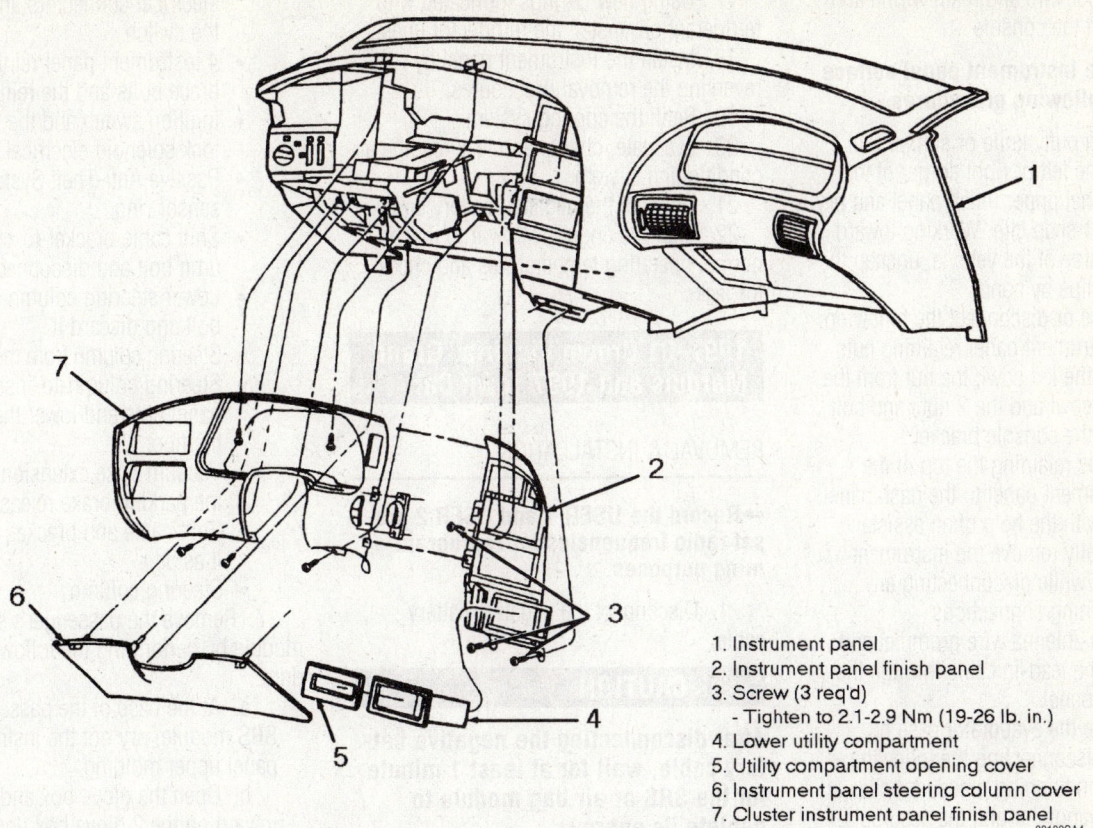

1. Instrument panel
2. Instrument panel finish panel
3. Screw (3 req'd)
   - Tighten to 2.1-2.9 Nm (19-26 lb. in.)
4. Lower utility compartment
5. Utility compartment opening cover
6. Instrument panel steering column cover
7. Cluster instrument panel finish panel

88180GA4

Exploded view of the instrument panel finish panel center—1997–98 Thunderbird and 1997 Cougar shown

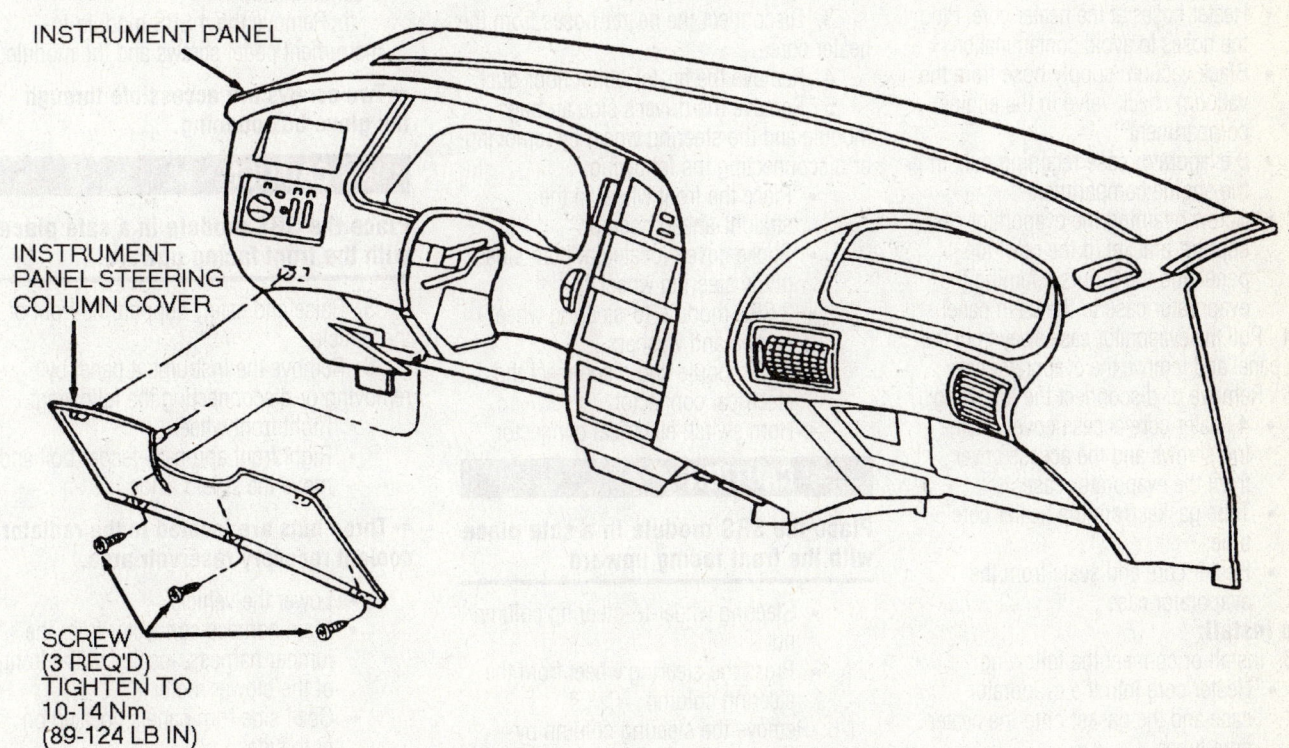

INSTRUMENT PANEL

INSTRUMENT
PANEL STEERING
COLUMN COVER

SCREW
(3 REQ'D)
TIGHTEN TO
10-14 Nm
(89-124 LB IN)

88180GA5

Instrument panel steering column cover mounting—1997–98 Thunderbird and 1997 Cougar shown

Refer to the model specific sections for engine mechanical service procedures

- Jumper wire and main wiring and lift off the console

➡ **Protect the instrument panel surface during the following procedures.**

11. Insert a putty knife or similar tool under either the left or right corner of the instrument panel upper finish panel and pry up to release 1 snap clip. Working toward the opposite side of the vehicle, unsnap the remaining 4 clips by hand.

12. Remove or disconnect the following:

- 2 instrument panel retaining nuts from the left cowl, the nut from the right cowl and the 2 nuts and bolt from the console bracket
- 6 bolts retaining the top of the instrument panel to the dash panel and with the help of an assistant carefully remove the instrument panel while disconnecting any remaining connections
- Radio antenna wire grommet and pull the lead-in cable through the dash panel

13. Remove the evaporator case by removing or disconnecting the following:

- Air conditioning pressure hoses at the evaporator and the accumulator/drier inlet tube. Cap the hoses to avoid contamination
- Accumulator/drier and the bracket
- Heater hoses at the heater core. Plug the hoses to avoid contamination
- Black vacuum supply hose from the vacuum check valve in the engine compartment
- 3 evaporator case retaining nuts in the engine compartment
- Screw retaining the evaporator case support bracket to the cowl top panel and the 2 nuts retaining the evaporator case to the dash panel

14. Pull the evaporator case away from the dash panel and remove the evaporator case.

15. Remove or disconnect the following:

- 4 heater core access cover retaining screws and the access cover from the evaporator case
- Tube gasket from the heater core tubes
- Heater core and seals from the evaporator case

To install:

16. Install or connect the following:

- Heater core into the evaporator case and the gasket onto the heater core tubes
- Access cover onto the evaporator case and secure with the screws
- Evaporator case by reversing the removal procedures

17. Using new O-rings lubricated with refrigerant oil, install the refrigerant lines.

18. Install the instrument panel by reversing the removal procedures.

19. Refill the cooling system.

20. Evacuate, charge and leak test the air conditioning system.

21. Connect the negative battery cable.

22. Start the engine, allow it to reach normal operating temperatures and check for leaks.

1997–01 Crown Victoria, Grand Marquis and 1997 Town Car

REMOVAL & INSTALLATION

➡ **Record the USER 1 and USER 2 preset radio frequencies for reprogramming purposes.**

1. Disconnect the negative battery cable.

✳✳ CAUTION

After disconnecting the negative battery cable, wait for at least 1 minute for the SRS or air bag module to deplete its energy.

2. Drain the cooling system into a clean container for reuse.

3. Disconnect the heater hoses from the heater core.

4. Remove the heater outlet floor duct.

5. Remove the driver's side air bag module and the steering wheel by removing or disconnecting the following:

- Place the front wheel in the straight-ahead position
- Spoke cover, located at both sides of the steering wheel
- 2 SRS module-to-steering wheel screws and washers
- SRS module and disconnect the electrical connector
- Horn switch electrical connector

✳✳ CAUTION

Place the SRS module in a safe place with the front facing upward.

- Steering wheel-to-steering column nut
- Press the steering wheel from the steering column

6. Remove the steering column by removing or disconnecting the following:

- Air bag sliding contact
- 2 multi-function switch-to-steering column bolts, disconnect the 2

electrical connectors and remove the switch

- 4 instrument panel reinforcement brace bolts and the reinforcement
- Ignition switch and the brake interlock solenoid electrical connectors
- Passive Anti-Theft System (PATS) sensor ring
- Shift cable bracket-to-steering column bolt and disconnect the cable
- Lower steering column shaft pinch bolt and discard it
- Steering column from the lower yoke
- Steering column-to-instrument panel nuts and lower the column to the floor
- Vacuum hose extension, located at the parking brake release switch
- Shift cable and bracket; then, move it aside
- Steering column

7. Remove the passenger's side SRS module by performing the following procedure:

a. At the base of the passenger's side SRS module, pry out the instrument panel upper molding.

b. Open the glove box and push inward on the 2 glove box door tabs and lower it.

c. Disconnect the SRS module's electrical connector.

d. Remove the 4 SRS module-to-instrument panel screws and the module.

➡ **Two screws are accessible through the glove box opening.**

✳✳ CAUTION

Place the SRS module in a safe place with the front facing upward.

8. Raise and safely support the front of the vehicle.

9. Remove the instrument panel by removing or disconnecting the following:

- Right front wheel
- Right front apron-to-fender bolt and move the shield aside

➡ **Three nuts are located in the radiator coolant recovery reservoir area.**

- Lower the vehicle
- Main harness connector from the jumper harness, located at the front of the blower motor
- Cowl side trim panels, located on both sides
- Electrical wiring connectors, located on both sides
- Ground wire, located at the left cowl side

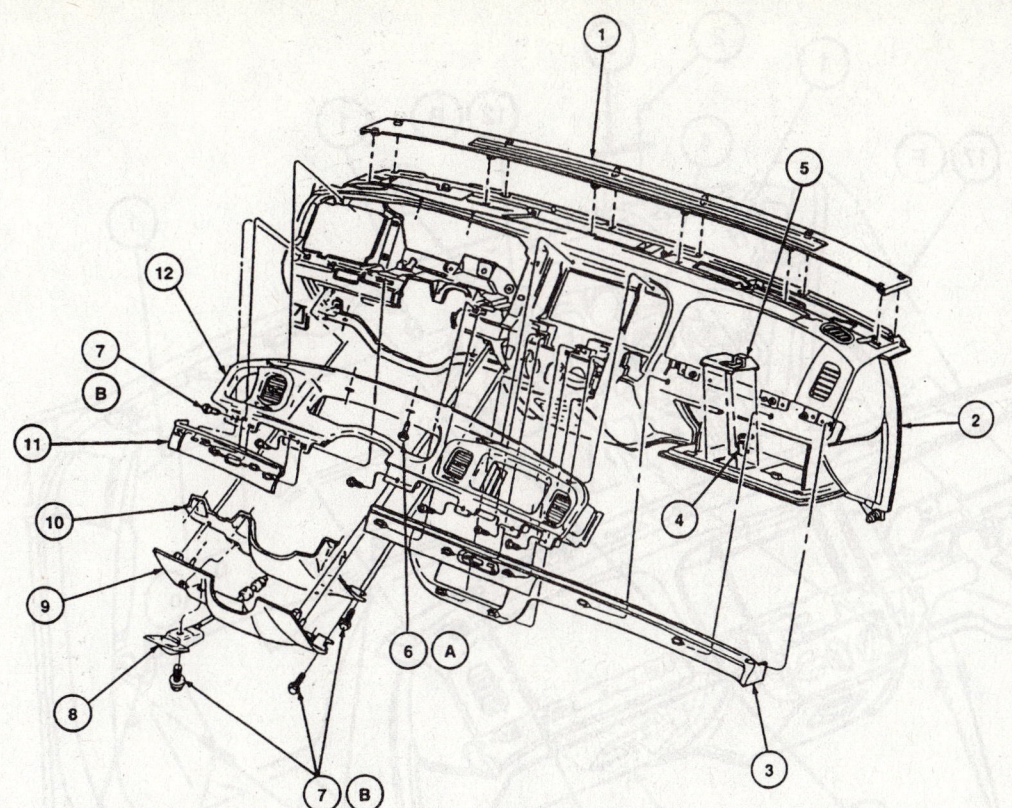

1 Instrument Panel Upper Finish Panel
2 Instrument Panel
3 Instrument Panel Upper Moulding , RH
4 Glove Compartment Lock Set
5 Glove Compartment Door Cover
6 Screw (2 Req'd)
7 Screw (10 Req'd)
8 Parking Brake Release Handle (Part of 2780)
9 Instrument Panel Steering Column Cover
10 Instrument Panel Steering Column Opening Cover Reinforcement
11 Instrument Panel Moulding , LH
12 Instrument Panel Cluster Finish Panel
A Tighten to 2.1-2.9 N·m (19-25 Lb-In)
B Tighten to 4-6 N·m (36-53 Lb-In)

93111GA9

View of the instrument panel finish panels—1997–01 Crown Victoria, Grand Marquis and 1997 Town Car

- Snap out the instrument panel mouldings (on both sides); then, disconnect any necessary electrical connectors
- Glove compartment
- Instrument panel upper finish panel using a suitable prytool
- Air conditioning sunload sensor and the anti-theft indicator, if equipped
- 5 upper instrument panel-to-cowl screws
- Automatic temperature control sensor hose and elbow, located at the evaporator housing
- Vacuum hose harness assembly
- Electrical connectors (located at the left side of the engine compartment), and push the harness through the bulkhead
- Instrument panel-to-cowl nut and bolt, located at the left side
- Instrument panel-to-cowl panel, located at the right side
- Instrument panel with the help of an assistant

10. Remove the heater air plenum chamber by removing or disconnecting the following:

- Upper left side corner of the evaporator housing-to-dash panel nut
- 2 vacuum supply hoses at the vacuum source; then, push the grommet and hoses into the passenger's compartment
- Electrical connectors from the air conditioning electronic blend door actuator
- White vacuum hose from the heater and air conditioning air inlet duct door vacuum control motor
- Nuts from the studs, located along the lower heater air plenum chamber flange
- Air conditioning electronic blend door actuator and the electronic module electrical connectors, located at the side of the heater air plenum chamber
- Pull the heater air plenum chamber rearward and remove it
- 4 heater core cover-to-heater plenum chamber screws and the cover seal and the heater core

To install:

11. Install or connect the following:
- Seal and the heater core

- 4 heater core cover-to-heater plenum chamber and the cover screws

12. Install the heater air plenum chamber by removing or disconnecting the following:

- Move the heater air plenum chamber forward and install it
- Air conditioning electronic blend door actuator and the electronic module electrical connectors, located at the side of the heater air plenum chamber
- Nuts to the studs, located along the lower heater air plenum chamber flange
- White vacuum hose to the heater and air conditioning air inlet duct door vacuum control motor
- Electrical connectors to the air conditioning electronic blend door actuator

13. Push the grommet and hoses into the passenger's compartment and connect the 2 vacuum supply hoses at the vacuum source.

14. Install the upper left side corner of the evaporator housing-to-dash panel nut.

Refer to the model specific sections for cooling system service precautions

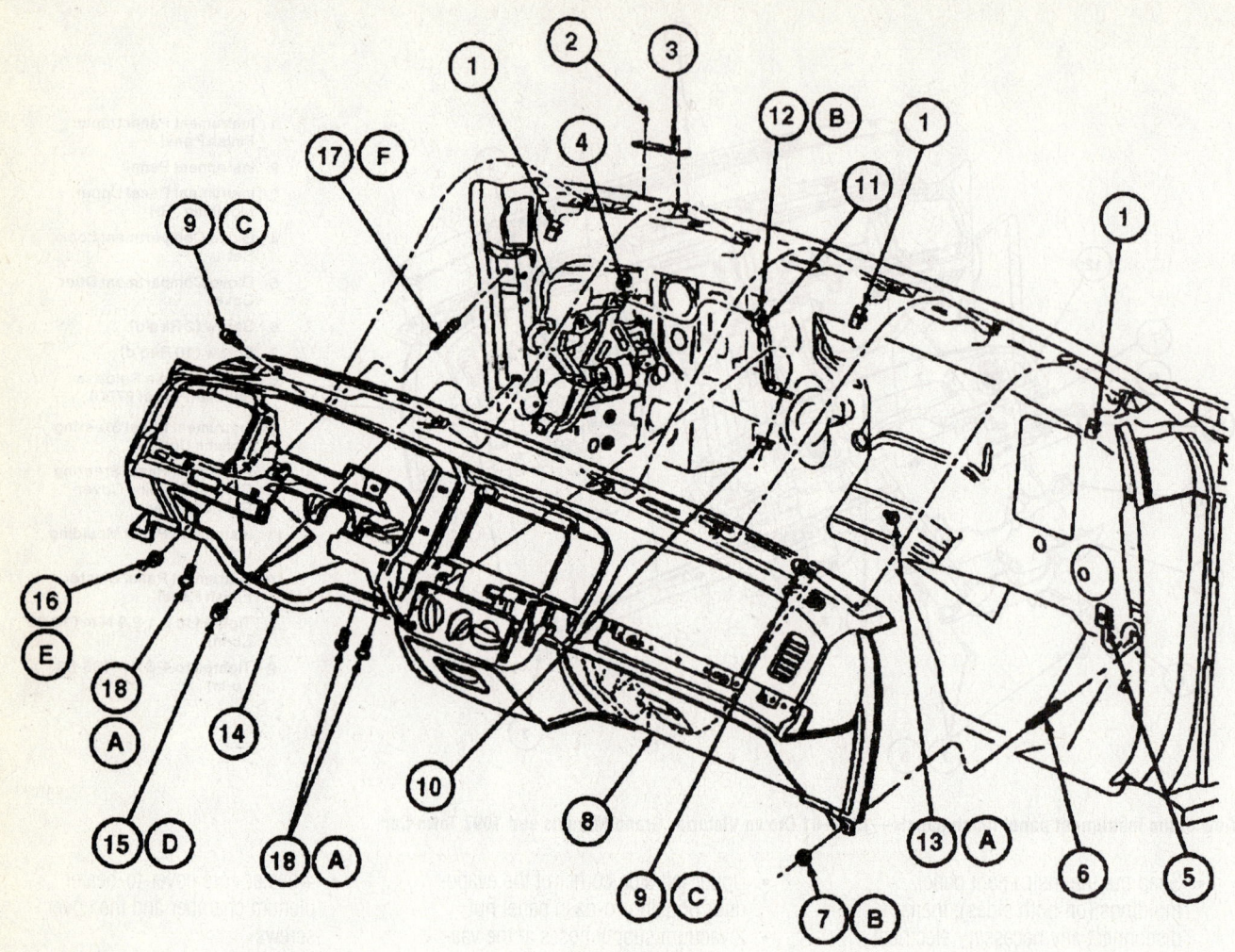

1 Nut (3 Req'd)
2 Rivet (2 Req'd)
3 Vehicle Identification Plate
4 Brake Pedal Support
5 J Nut
6 Stud
7 Nut
8 Instrument Panel
9 Screw (3 Req'd)
10 Steering Column Retaining Nut
11 Bolt (Part of 3F659)
12 Brake Pedal Support Steering Column Brace
13 Bolt (2 Req'd)
14 Instrument Panel Steering Column Opening Cover Reinforcement
15 Bolt (2 Req'd)
16 Nut
17 Stud
18 Bolt (3 Req'd)
A Tighten to 9-14 N·m (80-123 Lb-In)
B Tighten to 10-14 N·m (89-123 Lb-In)
C Tighten to 2-3 N·m (18-26 Lb-In)
D Tighten to 47-63 N·m (35-46 Lb-Ft)
E Tighten to 45-70 N·m (34-51 Lb-Ft)
F Tighten to 22-34 N·m (17-25 Lb-Ft)

93111GA0

Exploded view of the instrument panel—1997-01 Crown Victoria, Grand Marquis and 1997 Town Car

15. Install the instrument panel by installing or connecting the following:
- Instrument panel
- Instrument panel-to-cowl panel, located on the right side
- Instrument panel-to-cowl nut and bolt, located on the left side
- Push the harness through the bulkhead on the left side of the engine compartment and connect the electrical connectors
- Vacuum hose harness assembly

- Automatic temperature control sensor hose and elbow, located at the evaporator housing
- 5 upper instrument panel-to-cowl screws
- Air conditioning sunload sensor and the anti-theft indicator, if equipped
- Instrument panel upper finish panel
- Glove compartment
- All necessary electrical connectors

and install the instrument panel moldings on both sides
- Ground wire on the left cowl side
- Electrical wiring connectors on both sides
- Cowl side trim panels on both sides
- Main harness connector to the jumper harness at the front of the blower motor

16. Install or connect the following:

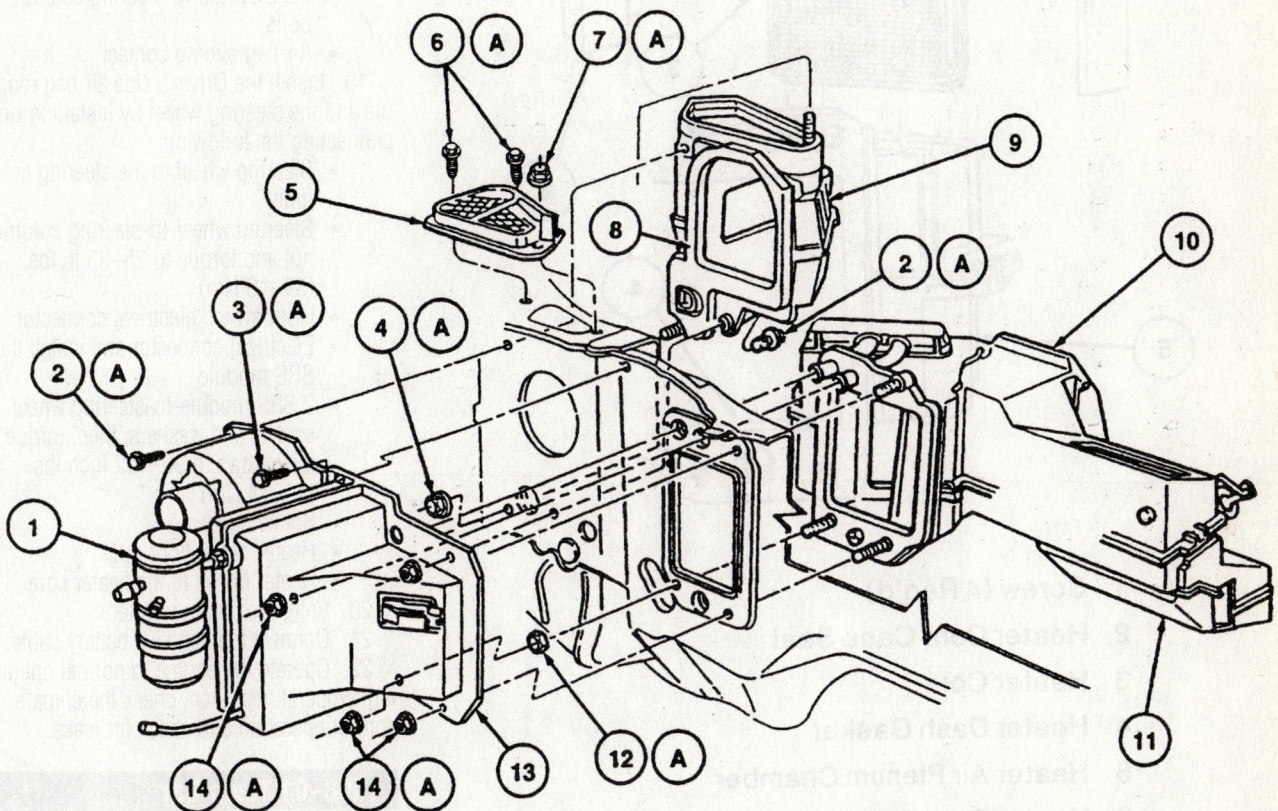

1	Suction Accumulator / Drier
2	Screw (2 Req'd)
3	Screw
4	Nut and Washer Assy
5	A / C Recirculating Air Duct Screen
6	Screw (2 Req'd)
7	Nut and Washer
8	A / C Air Inlet Door Inner Seal
9	A / C Recirculating Air Duct
10	Heater Air Plenum Chamber
11	Heater Outlet Floor Duct
12	Nut
13	A / C Evaporator Core Housing
14	Nut and Washer
A	Tighten to 2.5-3.2 N·m (23-28 Lb-In)

93111GB1

Exploded view of the heater air plenum chamber, the evaporator housing and the air inlet duct—1997–01 Crown Victoria, Grand Marquis and 1997 Town Car

For complete service labor times order Nichols' Chilton Labor Guide Manual

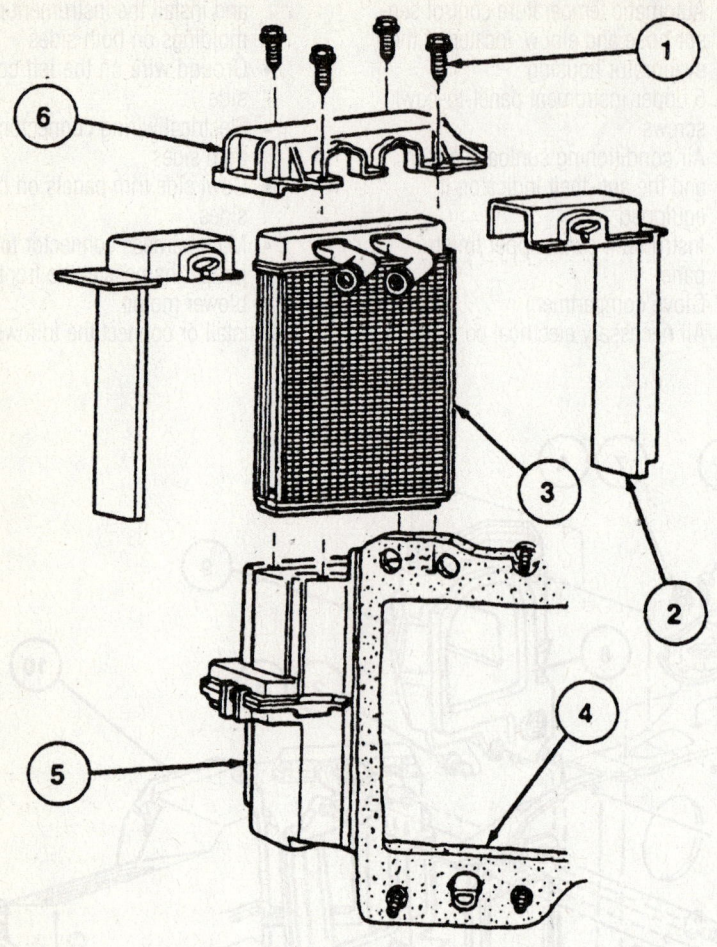

1 Screw (4 Req'd)
2 Heater Core Case Seal
3 Heater Core
4 Heater Dash Gasket
5 Heater Air Plenum Chamber
6 Heater Core Cover

93111GB2

View of the heater core—1997–01 Crown Victoria, Grand Marquis and 1997 Town Car

- Install the right front apron and the shield-to-fender bolt.

➡**Three nuts are located in the radiator coolant recovery reservoir area.**

- Install the right front wheel.
- Lower the vehicle.

17. Install the passenger's side SRS module by installing or connecting the following:

- SRS module and the 4 module-to-instrument panel screws; torque the 2 in the glove box to 68 inch lbs. (7.6–10.4 Nm) and the 2 at the retainer to 19–25 inch lbs. (2.1–2.9 Nm).

➡**Two screws are accessible through the glove box opening.**

- SRS module's electrical connector
- Glove box
- Instrument panel upper molding

18. Install the steering column by installing or connecting the following:

- Steering column
- Shift cable and bracket
- Vacuum hose extension at the parking brake release switch.
- Steering column and torque the column-to-instrument panel nuts to 10–13 ft. lbs. (13–17 Nm)

- Steering column to the lower yoke
- New lower steering column shaft pinch bolt and torque it to 19–25 ft. lbs. (26–34 Nm)
- Cable and install the shift cable bracket-to-steering column bolt
- Passive Anti-Theft System (PATS) sensor ring
- Ignition switch and the brake interlock solenoid electrical connectors
- Instrument panel reinforcement brace and the 4 reinforcement bolts
- Multi-function switch, connect the 2 electrical connectors and install the 2 switch-to-steering column bolts
- Air bag sliding contact

19. Install the Driver's side air bag module and the steering wheel by installing or connecting the following:

- Steering wheel to the steering column
- Steering wheel-to-steering column nut and torque to 25–33 ft. lbs. (34–46 Nm)
- Horn switch electrical connector
- Electrical connector and install the SRS module
- 2 SRS module-to-steering wheel screws and washers; then, torque the screws to 90–122 inch lbs. (10–14 Nm)
- Spoke cover
- Heater outlet floor duct
- Heater hoses to the heater core

20. Refill the cooling system.
21. Connect the negative battery cable.
22. Operate the engine to normal operating temperatures; then, check the climate control operation and check for leaks.

1998–01 Town Car

REMOVAL & INSTALLATION

1. Disconnect the negative battery cable.

✹✹ CAUTION

After disconnecting the negative battery cable, wait for at least 1 minute for the SRS or air bag module to deplete its energy.

2. Drain the cooling system into a clean container for reuse.
3. Disconnect the heater hoses from the heater core.
4. Remove the rear seat airflow duct.
5. Remove the driver's side air bag module by removing or disconnect the following:

- SRS module-to-steering wheel bolts, from both sides of the steering wheel.
- SRS module and disconnect the electrical connector
- Horn switch electrical connector

✻✻ CAUTION

Place the SRS module in a safe place with the front facing upward.

6. Remove the passenger's side SRS module by removing or disconnecting the following:

- Open the glove box and disconnect the glove compartment isolator
- Push inward on the 2 glove box door tabs and lower it
- SRS module's electrical connector
- SRS module-to-instrument panel bolts and the module

✻✻ CAUTION

Place the SRS module in a safe place with the front facing upward.

7. Remove the instrument panel by removing or disconnecting the following:

- Speed control servo nuts and move the servo aside
- Bolt and disconnect the left side bulkhead connector
- Left side bulkhead connector from the dash panel
- Windshield washer fluid reservoir screw, and position the reservoir aside
- Blower motor electrical connector
- Air conditioning pressure cut-off switch electrical connector
- In-line electrical harness connector
- Electronic Automatic Temperature

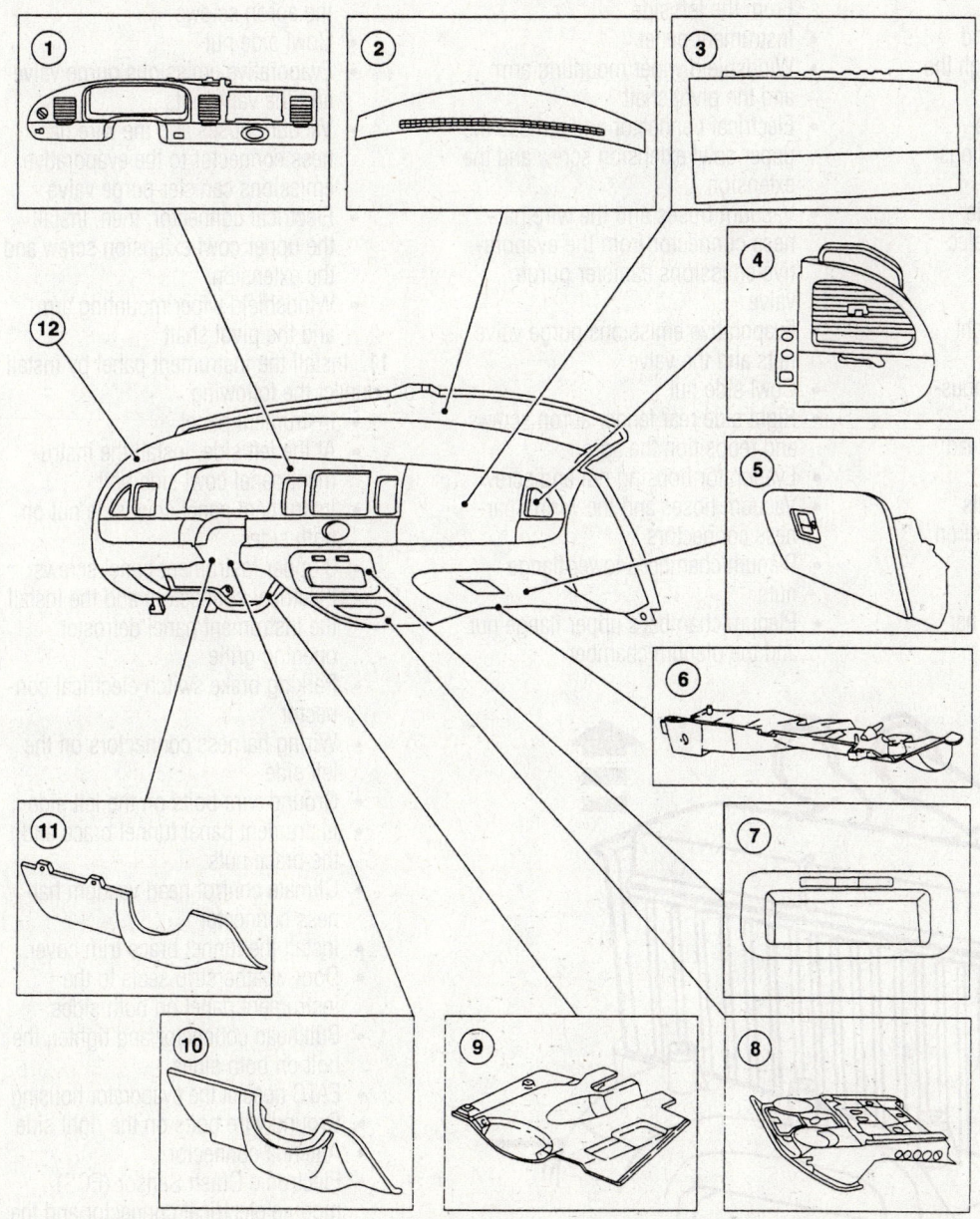

1 Instrument Panel Finish Panel
2 Instrument Panel Defroster Opening Grille
3 Passenger Side Air Bag Module
4 Instrument Panel Finish Panel
5 Glove Compartment
6 Instrument Panel Lower Insulator (RH)
7 Instrument Panel Finish Panel
8 Instrument Panel Ash Receptacle
9 Instrument Panel Lower Insulator (LH)
10 Instrument Panel Steering Column Cover
11 Instrument Panel Steering Column Opening Cover Reinforcement
12 Instrument Panel

93111GA7

Exploded view of the instrument panel and related components—1998–01 Town Car

Control (EATC) variable blower motor controller electrical connector

8. Remove or disconnect the following:
- Right front wheel
- Right front fender splash shield bolts and move the shield away from the cowl
- Wiring harness from the evaporator case
- Wiring harness from the cowl
- Right side instrument panel lower insulator pushpins, disconnect the power point electrical connector, remove the courtesy lamp from the socket and remove the insulator
- Unseat the wiring grommet and feed the wiring harness through the cowl
- Cowl side trim panels and the windshield side garnish moldings from both sides
- Locking clip and the Electronic Crash Sensor (ECS) module electrical connector
- Antenna connector
- Ground wire bolts from the right side
- EATC hose at the evaporator housing
- Bolt and disconnect the bulkhead connector from the right side
- Pull the door weatherstrip seals away from the instrument panel on both sides
- Tunnel brace trim cover
- Climate control head vacuum harness connector

- Instrument panel tunnel brace nuts and the brace
- Ground wire bolts from the left side
- Wiring harness connectors from the left side
- Parking brake switch electrical connector

c. Pry out the instrument panel defroster opening grille, disconnect the electrical connectors and the remove the grille.

9. Remove or disconnect the following:
- 3 upper instrument panel screws
- Instrument panel cowl side nut from both sides
- Instrument panel cowl side bolt. From the left side
- Instrument panel
- Windshield wiper mounting arm and the pivot shaft
- Electrical connector and remove the upper cowl extension screw and the extension
- Vacuum hoses and the wire harness connector from the evaporative emissions canister purge valve
- Evaporative emissions purge valve nuts and the valve
- Cowl side nut
- Right side rear fender apron screws and reposition the apron
- Evaporator housing nut and screw
- Vacuum hoses and the wiring harness connectors
- Plenum chamber's lower flange nuts
- Plenum chamber's upper flange nut and the plenum chamber

- Heater core cover-to-heater plenum chamber screws and the cover
- Seal and the heater core

To install:
10. Install or connect the following:
- Seal and the heater core
- Heater core cover and the cover-to-heater plenum chamber screws
- Plenum chamber and the plenum chamber's upper flange nut
- Plenum chamber's lower flange nuts
- Vacuum hoses and the wiring harness connectors
- Evaporator housing nut and screw
- Right side rear fender apron and the apron screws
- Cowl side nut
- Evaporative emissions purge valve and the valve nuts
- Vacuum hoses and the wire harness connector to the evaporative emissions canister purge valve
- Electrical connector; then, install the upper cowl extension screw and the extension
- Windshield wiper mounting arm and the pivot shaft

11. Install the instrument panel by install or connect the following:
- Instrument panel
- At the left side, install the instrument panel cowl side bolt
- Instrument panel cowl side nut on both sides
- 3 upper instrument panel screws
- Electrical connectors and the install the instrument panel defroster opening grille
- Parking brake switch electrical connector
- Wiring harness connectors on the left side
- Ground wire bolts on the left side
- Instrument panel tunnel brace and the brace nuts
- Climate control head vacuum harness connector
- Install the tunnel brace trim cover.
- Door weatherstrip seals to the instrument panel on both sides
- Bulkhead connector and tighten the bolt on both sides
- EATC hose at the evaporator housing
- Ground wire bolts on the right side
- Antenna connector
- Electronic Crash Sensor (ECS) module electrical connector and the locking clip
- Cowl side trim panels and the windshield side garnish moldings on both sides

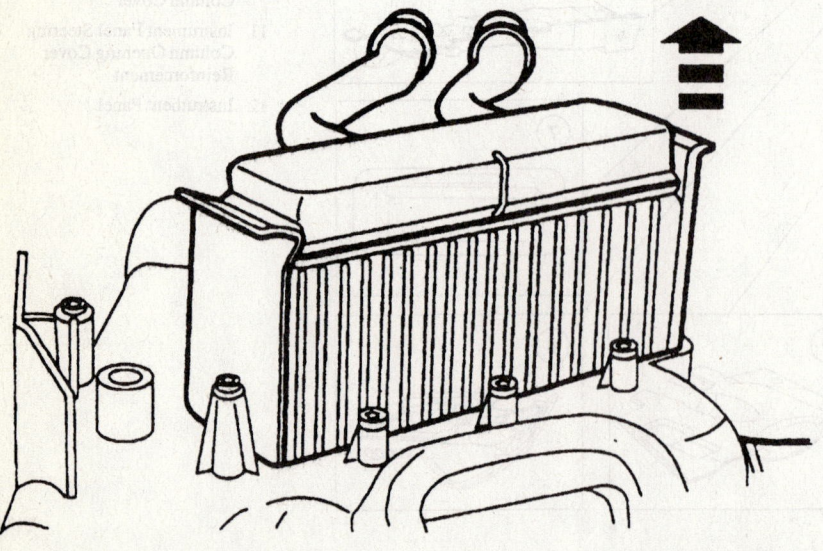

93111GA8

View of the heater core—1998–01 Town Car

- Feed the wiring harness through the cowl and seat the wiring grommet
- Right side instrument panel lower insulator, connect the power point electrical connector, install the courtesy lamp to the socket and secure the insulator with push-pins
- Wiring harness from the cowl
- Wiring harness to the evaporator case
- Right front fender splash shield and the shield bolts
- Right front wheel
- Electronic Automatic Temperature Control (EATC) variable blower motor controller electrical connector
- In-line electrical harness connector

- Air conditioning pressure cut-off switch electrical connector
- Blower motor electrical connector
- Windshield washer fluid reservoir and the reservoir screw
- Left side bulkhead connector to the dash panel
- Left side bulkhead connector and tighten the bolt
- Speed control servo and the servo nuts

12. Install the passenger's side SRS module by installing or connecting the following:

- SRS module and torque the module-to-instrument panel bolts to 62–97 inch lbs. (7–11 Nm)
- SRS module's electrical connector

- Glove compartment isolator
- Glove box door

13. Install the driver's side air bag module by installing or connecting the following:

- Horn switch electrical connector
- Electrical connector and install the SRS module
- SRS module-to-steering wheel bolts on both sides of the wheel, and torque the bolts to 90–122 inch lbs. (10–14 Nm)

14. Install the rear seat airflow duct.
15. Connect the heater hoses to the heater core.
16. Refill the cooling system.
17. Connect the negative battery cable.
18. Operate the engine to normal operating temperatures; then, check the climate control operation and check for leaks.

GENERAL MOTORS

Bonneville, Eighty-Eight, LeSabre and Park Avenue

REMOVAL & INSTALLATION

1997–01 Models

BONNEVILLE AND LESABRE

1. Disconnect the negative battery cable.
2. Drain the cooling system into a clean container for reuse.
3. Remove or disconnect the following:

- Heater hoses from the heater core
- Right sound insulator
- All necessary electrical connectors and remove the instrument panel compartment
- Temperature valve actuator
- Electrical connector and remove the HVAC programmer
- Heater core cover-to-heater assembly screws and the cover
- Heater core-to-heater assembly screws and the heater core

To install:

4. Install or connect the following:

- Heater core and the heater core-to-heater assembly screws, then, tighten the screws to 12 inch lbs. (1.4 Nm)
- Heater core cover and the cover-to-heater assembly screws, then,

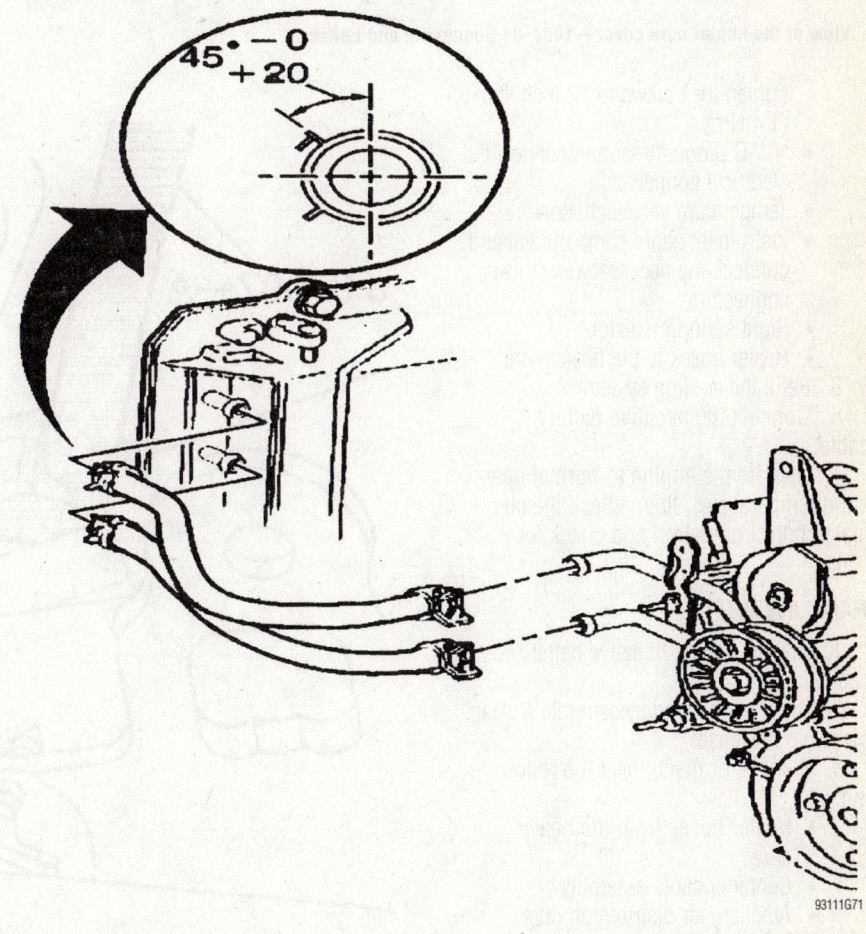

View of the heater hoses and clamp positions—1997-01 Bonneville and LeSabre

93111G71

Refer to the model specific sections for engine mechanical service procedures

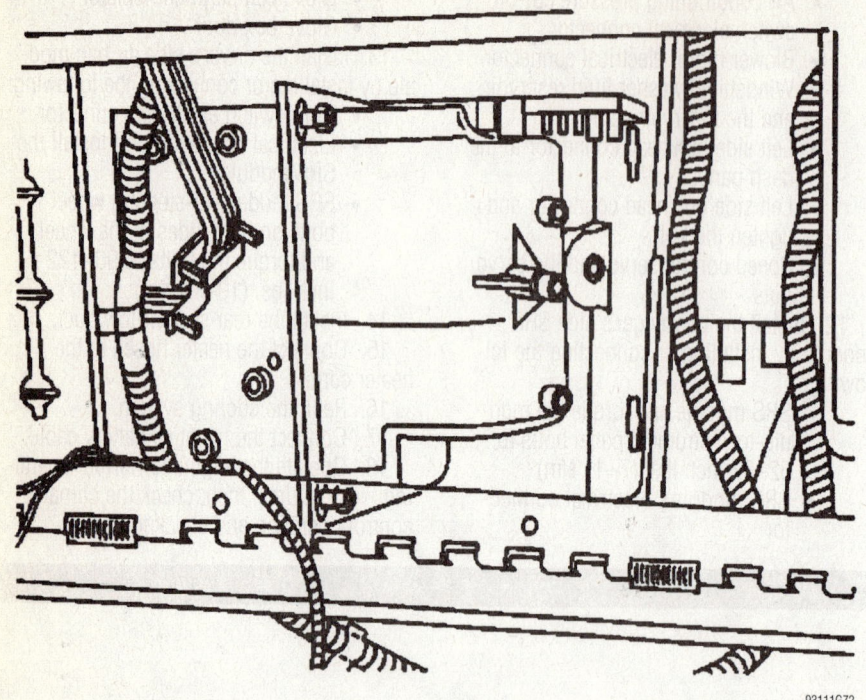

View of the heater core cover—1997–01 Bonneville and LeSabre

93111G72

tighten the screws to 12 inch lbs. (1.4 Nm)

- HVAC programmer and connect the electrical connector
- Temperature valve actuator
- Instrument panel compartment and connect any necessary electrical connectors
- Right sound insulator
- Heater hoses to the heater core

5. Refill the cooling system.
6. Connect the negative battery cable.
7. Operate the engine to normal operating temperatures; then, check the climate control operation and check for leaks.

PARK AVENUE

1. Disconnect the negative battery cable.
2. Drain the cooling system into a clean container for reuse.
3. Remove or disconnect the following:

- Heater hoses from the heater core
- Center console assembly
- Auxiliary air distribution duct
- Heater core heat shield cover from the HVAC module
- Air filter access cover and the heater core cover screws
- Heater core cover to obtain access

to remove the heater core
- Heater core retaining bolts and straps
- Heater core

To install:

4. Install or connect the following:

- Heater core
- Heater core straps and retaining bolts, then, tighten to 18 inch lbs. (1.5 Nm)
- Heater core cover
- Air filter access cover and the heater core cover screws, then tighten to 12 inch lbs. (1.4 Nm)
- Heater core heat shield cover to the HVAC module
- Auxiliary air distribution duct
- Center console assembly
- Heater hoses to the heater core

5. Refill the cooling system.
6. Connect the negative battery cable.
7. Operate the engine to normal operating temperatures; then, check the climate control operation and check for leaks.

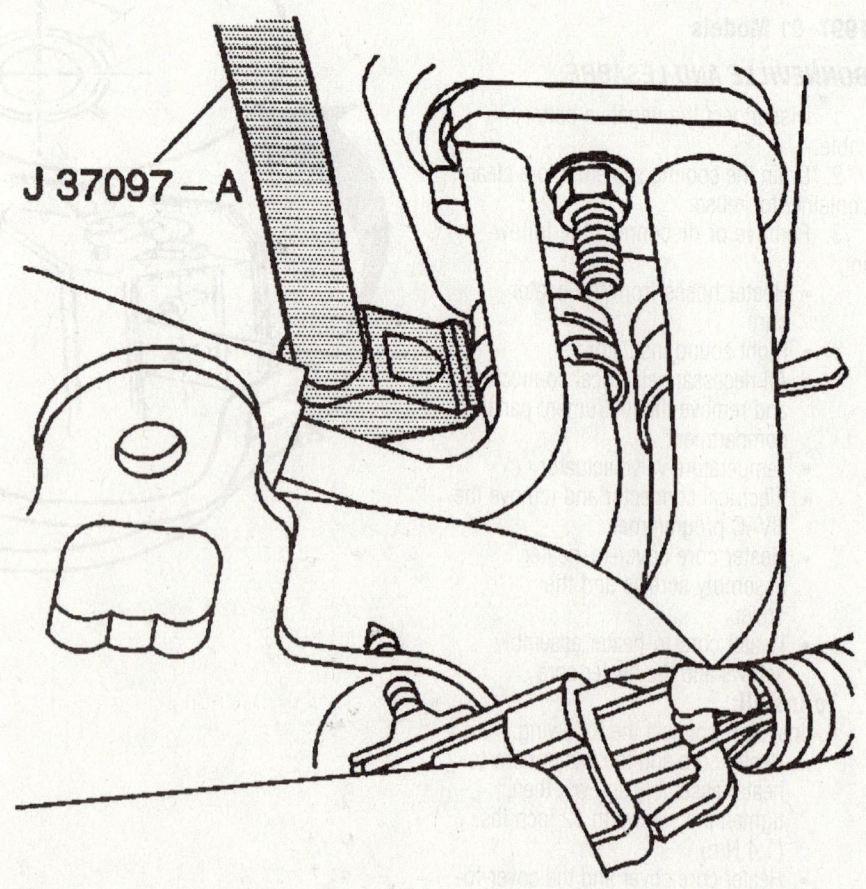

Using Hose Clamp Pliers tool J-37097-A remove the heater hoses clamp—1997–01 Park Avenue

93111G73

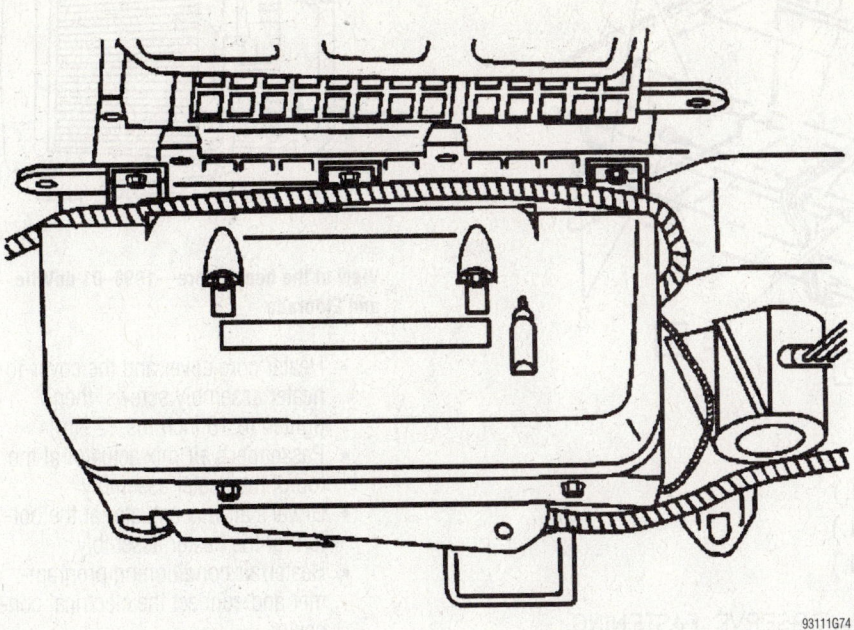

View of the heater core cover—1997–01 Park Avenue

View of the heater core—1997–01 Park Avenue

Concours, deVille, Eldorado and Seville

REMOVAL & INSTALLATION

1997 Models

1. Disconnect the negative battery cable.
2. Drain the cooling system into a clean container for reuse.
3. Remove the glove box compartment by removing or disconnecting the following:

- Open the trap door in the rear of the glove compartment and remove the passenger's side SIR wiring connector from the retaining clip on the rear of the glove compartment assembly.
- Glove compartment switches
- 6 glove compartment-to-instrument panel screws
- Glove compartment assembly
- Right sound insulator
- Heater/air conditioning programmer
- Heater hoses from the heater core
- Heater core-to-heater case screws
- Heater core

To install:

4. Install or connect the following:

- Heater core
- Heater core-to-heater case screws
- Heater hoses to the heater core
- Heater/air conditioning programmer
- Right sound insulator

5. Install the glove box compartment by installing or connecting the following:

- Glove compartment assembly
- 6 glove compartment-to-instrument panel screws
- Glove compartment switches
- Passenger's side SIR wiring connector to the retaining clip on the rear of the glove compartment assembly

6. Refill the cooling system.
7. Connect the negative battery cable.
8. Operate the engine to normal operating temperatures; then, check the climate control operation and check for leaks.

Refer to the model specific sections for cooling system service precautions

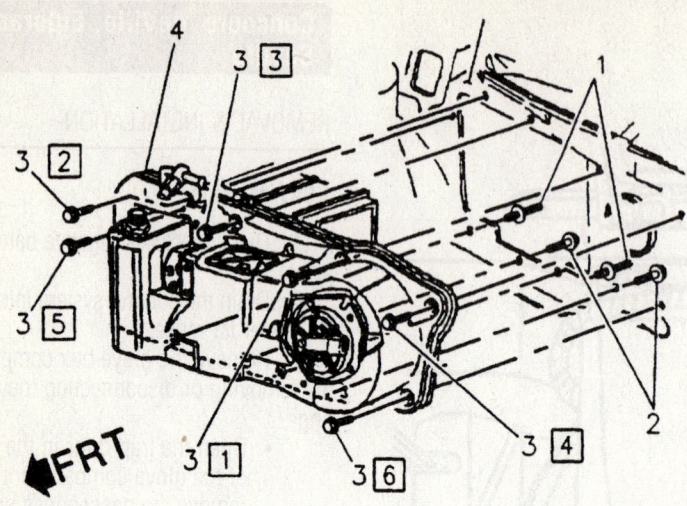

1 STUDS, 5 N•m (44 LB. IN.)
2 BOLTS, 5 N•m (44 LB. IN.)
3 BOLTS, 8 N•m (71 LB. IN.)
4 HVAC MODULE

☐ OBSERVE FASTENING SEQUENCE

93111GB5

View of the heater/air conditioning housing assembly—1997 deVille, Concours, Eldorado and Seville

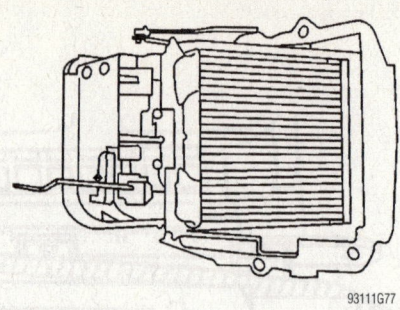

93111G77

View of the heater core—1998–01 deVille and Eldorado

- Heater core cover and the cover-to-heater assembly screws, then, tighten to 18 inch lbs. (2 Nm)
- Passenger's air mix actuator at the top of the heater assembly
- Driver's air mix actuator at the bottom of the heater assembly
- Heater/air conditioning programmer and connect the electrical connector
- Sound insulator on the right side
- Instrument panel compartment
5. Refill the cooling system.
6. Connect the negative battery cable.

1998–01 Models

1. Disconnect the negative battery cable.
2. Drain the cooling system into a clean container for reuse.
3. Remove or disconnect the following:
- Instrument panel compartment
- Sound insulator from the right side
- Electrical connector and remove the heater/air conditioning programmer
- Driver's air mix actuator from the bottom of the heater assembly
- Passenger's air mix actuator from the bottom of the heater assembly
- Heater core cover-to-heater assembly screws and the cover
- Heater hoses from the heater core, located in the engine compartment
- Heater core-to-heater assembly screws
- Heater core

To install:
4. Install or connect the following:
- Heater core
- Heater core-to-heater assembly screws, then, tighten to 18 inch lbs. (2 Nm)
- Heater hoses to the heater core

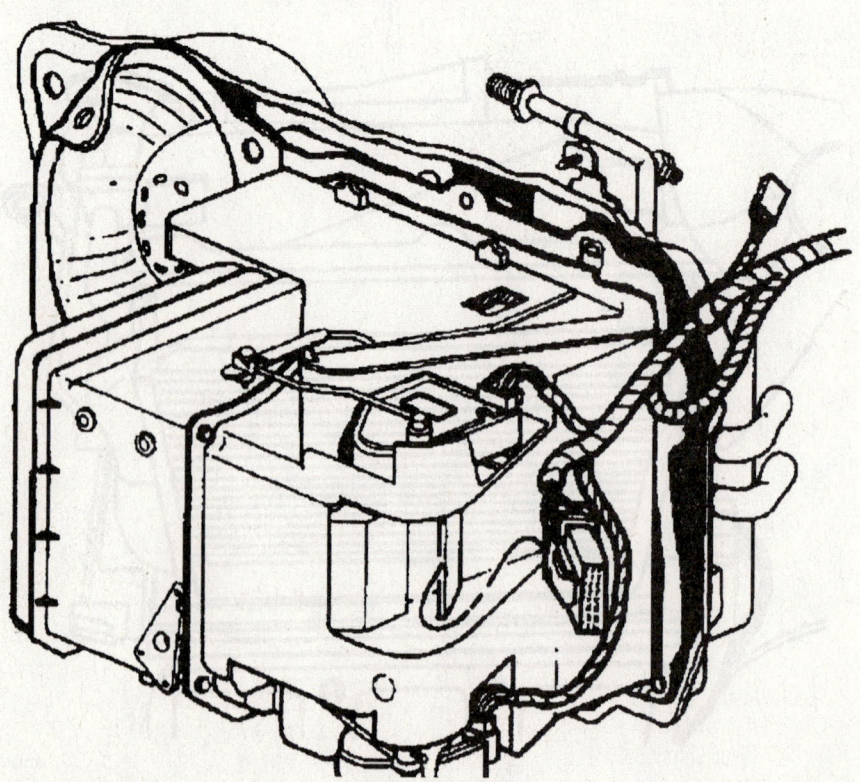

93111G76

View of the heater assembly with the driver's and passenger's air mix actuators—1998–01 deVille and Eldorado

Seville

REMOVAL & INSTALLATION

1998–01 Models

1. Disconnect the negative battery cable.
2. Drain the cooling system into a clean container for reuse.
3. Disconnect the heater hoses from the heater core.
4. Disable the SIR system.
5. Remove the instrument panel by removing or disconnecting the following:
   - Console
   - Right insulator panel
   - Instrument panel end caps from both sides
   - Side windows air outlets
   - Upper instrument panel trim pad
   - Passenger's side SIR module
   - Instrument panel trim plate from the right side
   - Instrument panel cluster
   - Center instrument panel trim plate
   - Radio
   - Lap cooler duct
   - Knee bolster.
   - Steering column
   - Headlight switch.
   - Fuel door/rear compartment release switch.
   - Instrument panel storage compartment
   - 10 instrument panel retainer-to-instrument panel carrier fasteners

➡**One fastener is located in the fuel/rear compartment release switch opening.**

   - Instrument panel retainer from the carrier and feed the wiring through the openings, as necessary
   - Inside air temperature sensor electrical connector
   - Instrument panel
   - Heater core-to-heater housing cover screws
   - Heater core-to-heater housing screws
   - Heater core retaining straps
   - Heater core
   - Heater core seals

To install:

6. Install or connect the following:
   - Heater core seals
   - Heater core
   - Heater core retaining straps

   - Heater core-to-heater housing screws
   - Heater core-to-heater housing cover screws
7. Install the instrument panel by installing or connecting the following:
   - Instrument panel
   - Inside air temperature sensor electrical connector
   - Instrument panel retainer to the carrier and feed the wiring through the openings, as necessary
   - 10 instrument panel retainer-to-instrument panel carrier fasteners

➡**One fastener is located in the fuel/rear compartment release switch opening.**

   - Instrument panel storage compartment
   - Fuel door/rear compartment release switch
   - Headlight switch
8. Install or connect the following:
   - Steering column
   - Knee bolster
   - Lap cooler duct
   - Radio
   - Center instrument panel trim plate
   - Instrument panel cluster
   - Install the instrument panel trim plate on the right side
   - Passenger's side SIR module
   - Upper instrument panel trim pad
   - Side windows air outlets
   - Instrument panel end caps on both sides
   - Right insulator panel
   - Console
9. Enable the SIR system.
10. Connect the heater hoses to the heater core.
11. Refill the cooling system.
12. Connect the negative battery cable.
13. Operate the engine to normal operating temperatures; then, check the climate control operation and check for leaks.

Camaro, Z28, Firebird and Trans AM

✳✳ CAUTION

Some vehicles are equipped an SIR or air bag system. The air bag system must be disabled before performing service on or around the air bag, instrument panel components, wiring and sensors. Failure to follow safety and disabling procedures could result in accidental air bag deployment, possible personal injury and unnecessary air bag system repairs.

REMOVAL & INSTALLATION

1997–01 Models

1. With the ignition key removed, disconnect the negative battery cable.
2. Disable the SIR system by removing or disconnecting the following:
   - SIR fuse from the fuse panel
   - Left side sound insulator
   - Connector Positive Assurance (CPA) from the yellow 2-way SIR harness connector at the base of the steering column and separate the connector
   - Squeeze the sides of the glove box and release it to access the heater core assembly
3. Drain the cooling system.
4. Remove or disconnect the following:
   - 2 heater module cover retaining screws and remove the cover
   - Clamp at the left side of the heater core

➡**Do not apply excessive pressure on the tubes or the heater core will be damaged.**

   - Clamp from the heater core tubes on the engine compartment side. Carefully, remove the heater hoses from the core tubes. Plug the hoses to prevent leakage
   - Pull heater core toward the rear of the vehicle to remove it

To install:

5. Install or connect the following:
   - Position the heater core into place and then attach the heater hoses to the heater core tubes. Install the hose clamp

➡**Lubricate the heater tubes with petroleum jelly for best sealing. Be sure the seals around the heater pipes remain in place.**

   - Heater core clamp, then install the heater core module cover
6. Properly, refill the cooling system, then operate the system and check for leaks.
7. If equipped, enable the SIR system by installing connecting the following:
   - Yellow 2-way SIR connector and insert the Connector Positive

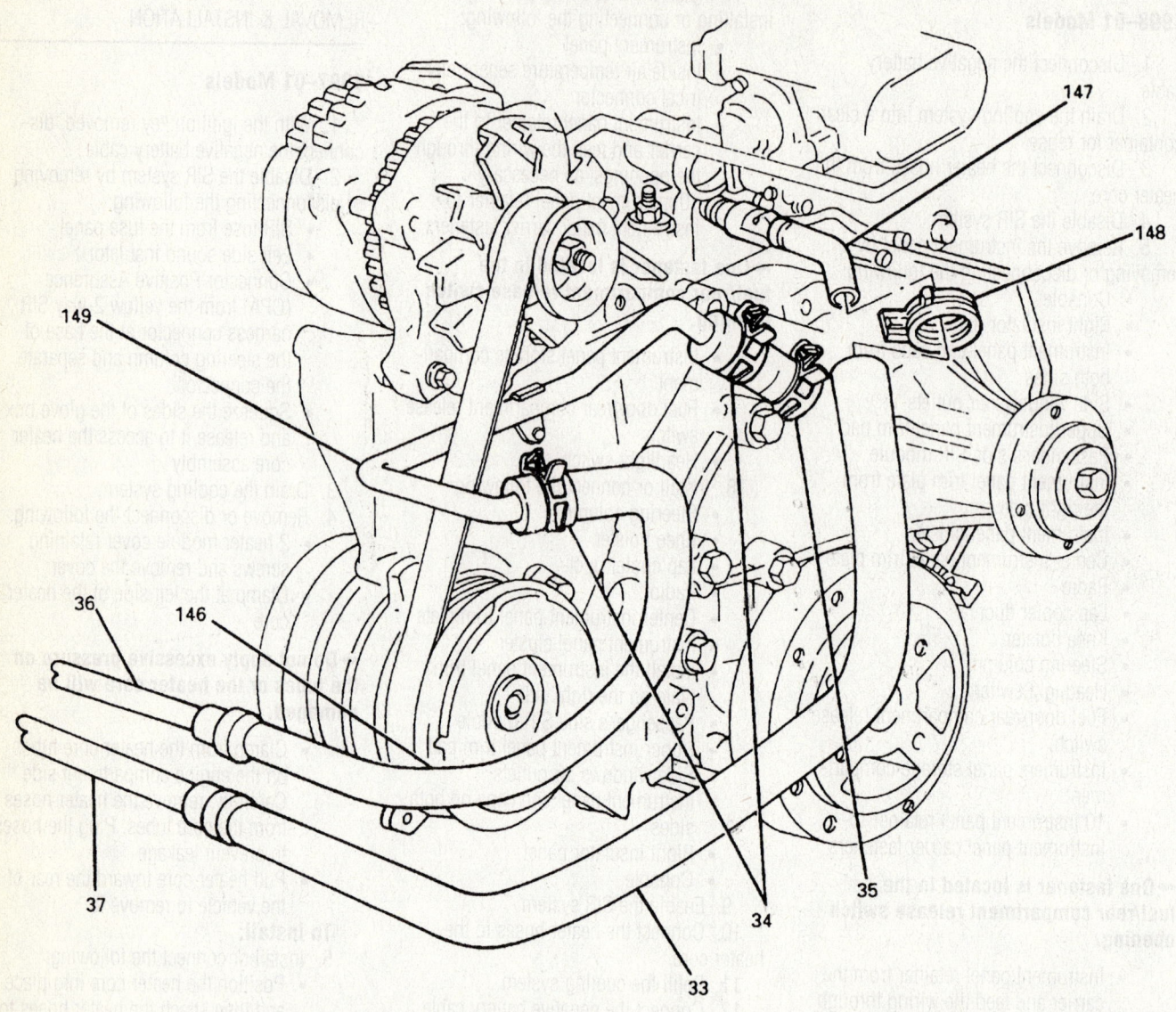

33 HOSE ASSEMBLY, HEATER INLET
34 CLAMP, HEATER OUTLET FRONT HOSE
35 CLAMP, HEATER INLET FRONT HOSE
36 PIPE, HEATER HOSE OUTLET
37 PIPE, HEATER HOSE INLET
146 HOSE ASSEMBLY, HEATER OUTLET
147 HOSE, THROTTLE BODY HEATER RETURN
148 CLAMP, THROTTLE BODY HEATER RETURN HOSE
149 PIPE, HEATER OUTLET

88146G08

Heater hose and pipe routing—1997–01 Camaro/Firebird with the 3.4L engine

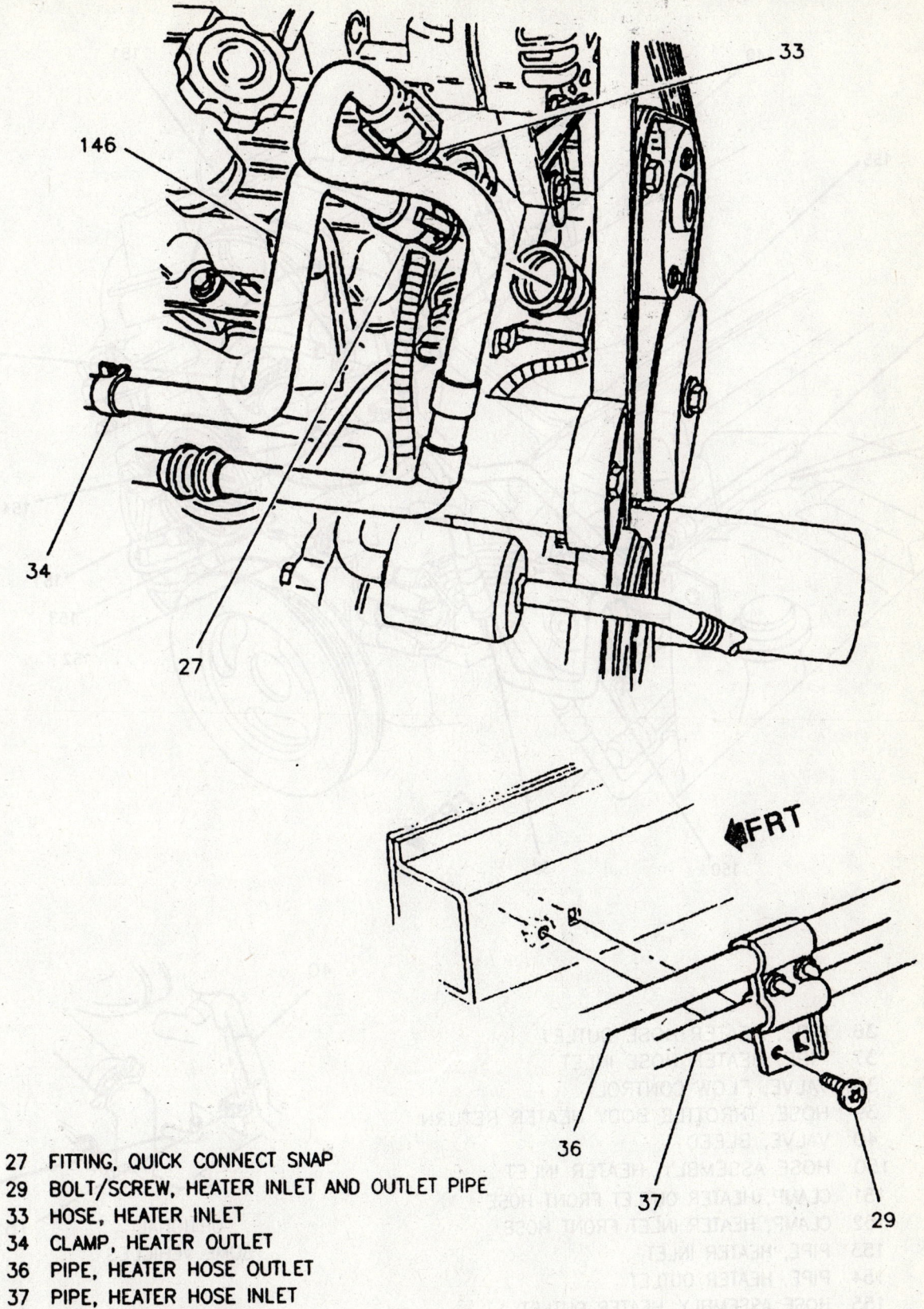

27 FITTING, QUICK CONNECT SNAP
29 BOLT/SCREW, HEATER INLET AND OUTLET PIPE
33 HOSE, HEATER INLET
34 CLAMP, HEATER OUTLET
36 PIPE, HEATER HOSE OUTLET
37 PIPE, HEATER HOSE INLET
146 HOSE, HEATER OUTLET

88146G09

Heater hose and pipe routing—1997–01 Camaro/Firebird with the 3.8L engine

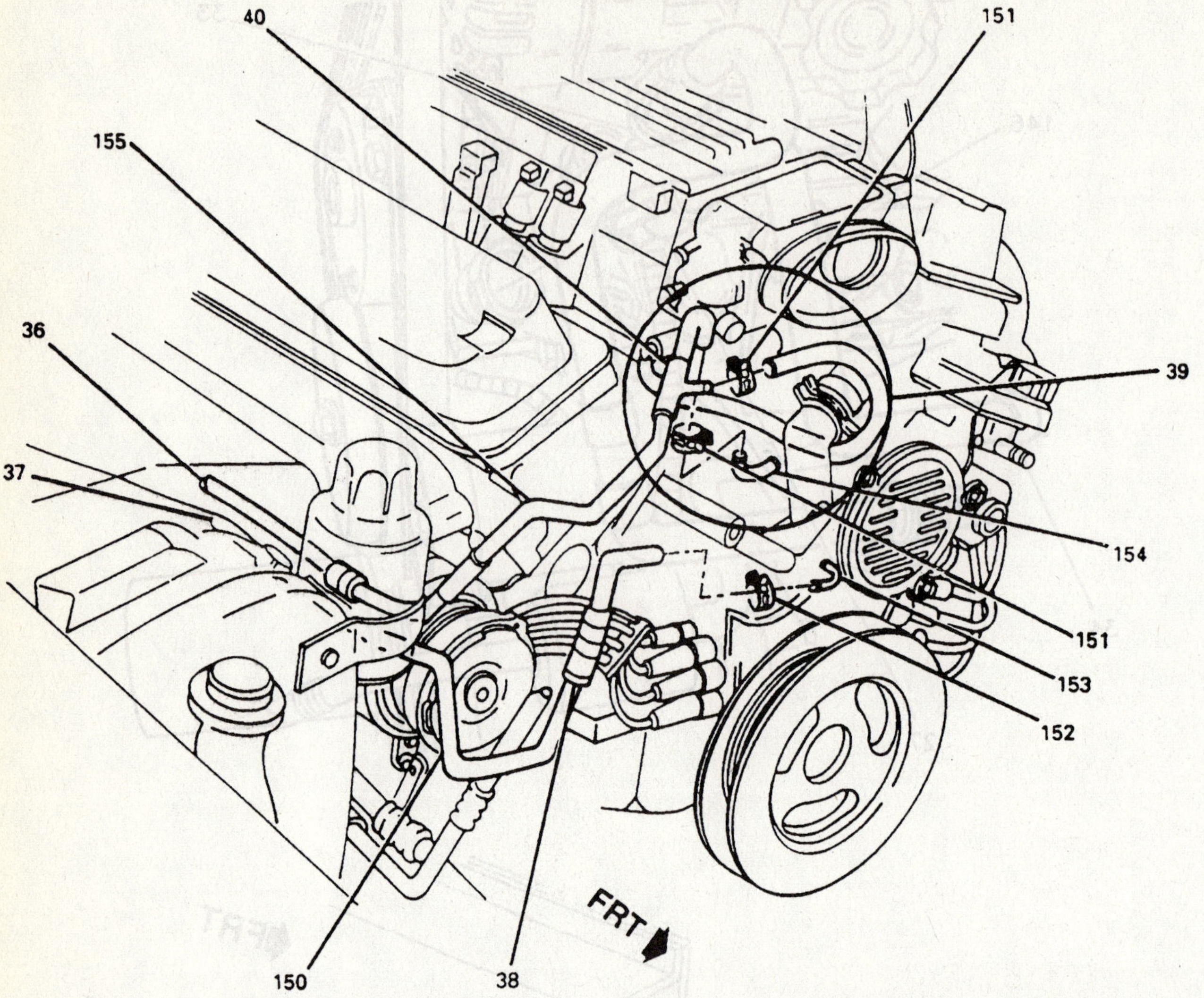

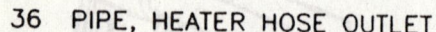

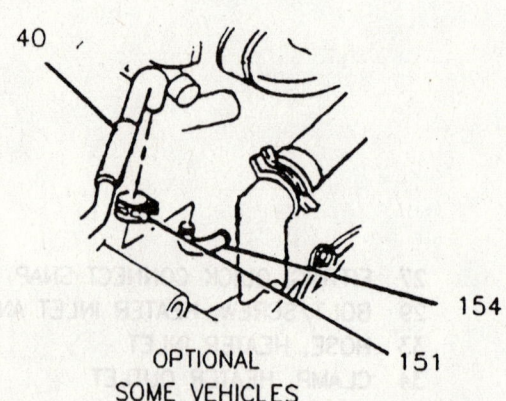

FRT

36 PIPE, HEATER HOSE OUTLET
37 PIPE, HEATER HOSE INLET
38 VALVE, FLOW CONTROL
39 HOSE, THROTTLE BODY HEATER RETURN
40 VALVE, BLEED
150 HOSE ASSEMBLY, HEATER INLET
151 CLAMP, HEATER OUTLET FRONT HOSE
152 CLAMP, HEATER INLET FRONT HOSE
153 PIPE, HEATER INLET
154 PIPE, HEATER OUTLET
155 HOSE ASSEMBLY, HEATER OUTLET

OPTIONAL
SOME VEHICLES

Heater hose and pipe routing—1997–01 Camaro/Firebird with the 5.7L engine

88146G10

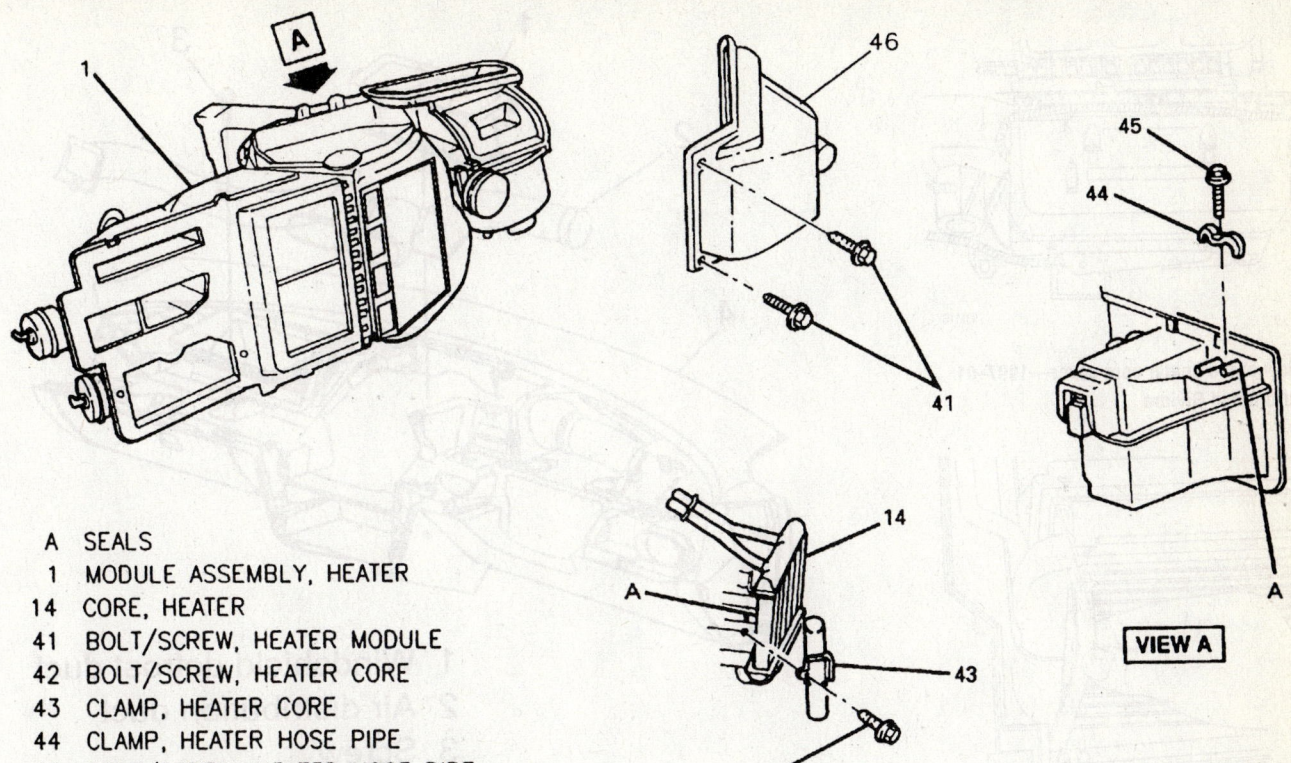

A   SEALS
1   MODULE ASSEMBLY, HEATER
14 CORE, HEATER
41 BOLT/SCREW, HEATER MODULE
42 BOLT/SCREW, HEATER CORE
43 CLAMP, HEATER CORE
44 CLAMP, HEATER HOSE PIPE
45 BOLT/SCREW, HEATER HOSE PIPE
46 COVER, HEATER MODULE ASSEMBLY

88146G07

Exploded view of the heater core removed from the heater module assembly—1997–01 Camaro/Firebird

Assurance (CPA) at the base of the steering column
- Left side sound insulator
- SIR fuse in the fuse panel
- Negative battery cable

Aurora and Riviera

REMOVAL & INSTALLATION

1997–01 Models

1. Disconnect the negative battery cable.
2. Drain the cooling system into a clean container for reuse.
3. Remove or disconnect the following:
   - Heater hoses from the heater core
   - Center console assembly
   - Auxiliary air duct connector
   - Right sound insulator
   - Heater core heat shield-to-heating, HVAC module screws and the shield
   - Heater core cover-to-HVAC module screws and the cover
   - Heater core-to-HVAC module screws and straps
   - Heater core

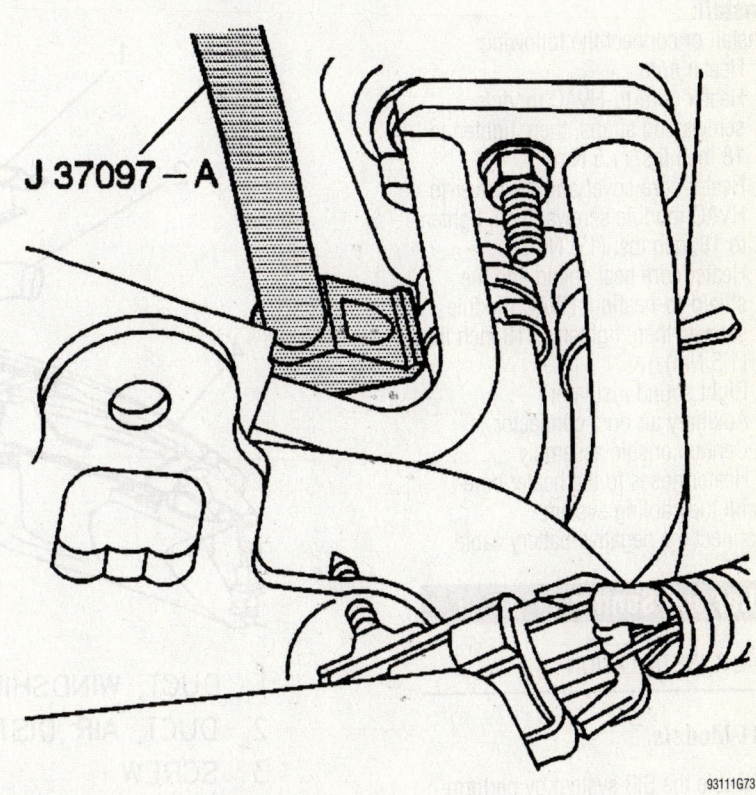

J 37097 – A

93111G73

Remove the heater hoses clamp—1997–01 Aurora and Riviera

Refer to the model specific sections for engine mechanical service procedures

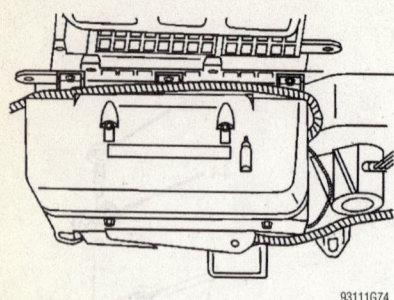

View of the heater core cover—1997–01 Aurora and Riviera

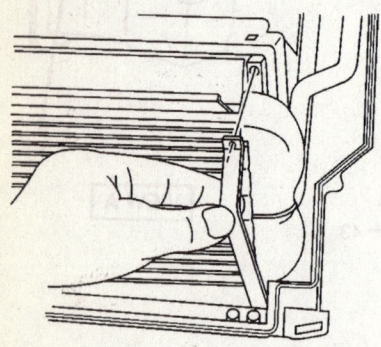

View of the heater core retaining straps—1997–01 Aurora and Riviera

To install:

4. Install or connect the following:
   - Heater core
   - Heater core-to-HVAC module screws and straps, then, tighten to 18 inch lbs. (1.5 Nm)
   - Heater core cover and the cover-to-HVAC module screws, then, tighten to 18 inch lbs. (1.5 Nm)
   - Heater core heat shield and the shield-to-heating, HVAC module screws, then, tighten to 18 inch lbs. (1.5 Nm)
   - Right sound insulator
   - Auxiliary air duct connector
   - Center console assembly
   - Heater hoses to the heater core
5. Refill the cooling system.
6. Connect the negative battery cable.

Cavalier and Sunfire

REMOVAL & INSTALLATION

1997–01 Models

1. Disable the SIR system by performing the following procedure:
   a. Point the wheel in the straight-ahead position.

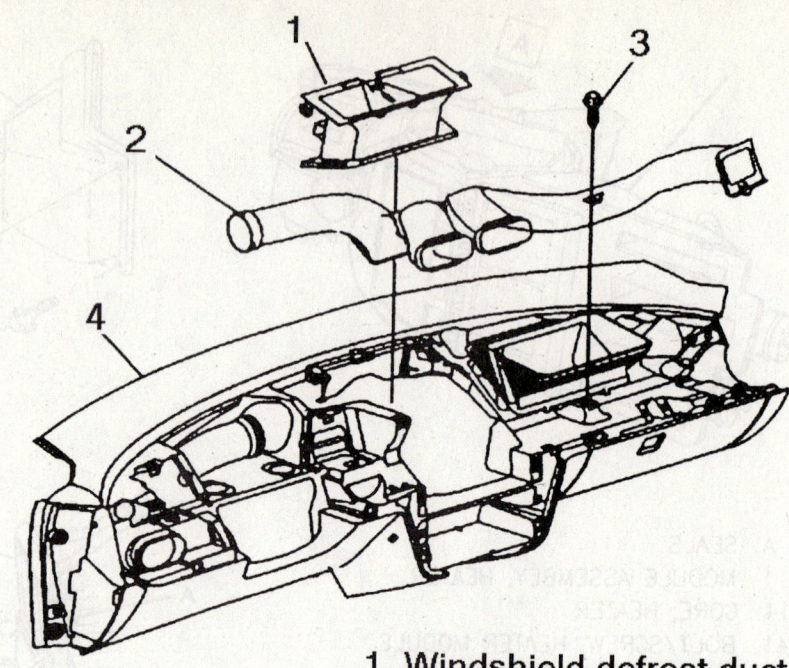

1 Windshield defrost duct
2 Air distribution duct
3 Screw
4 Lower I/P

Air distribution duct mounting—1997–01 Cavalier shown

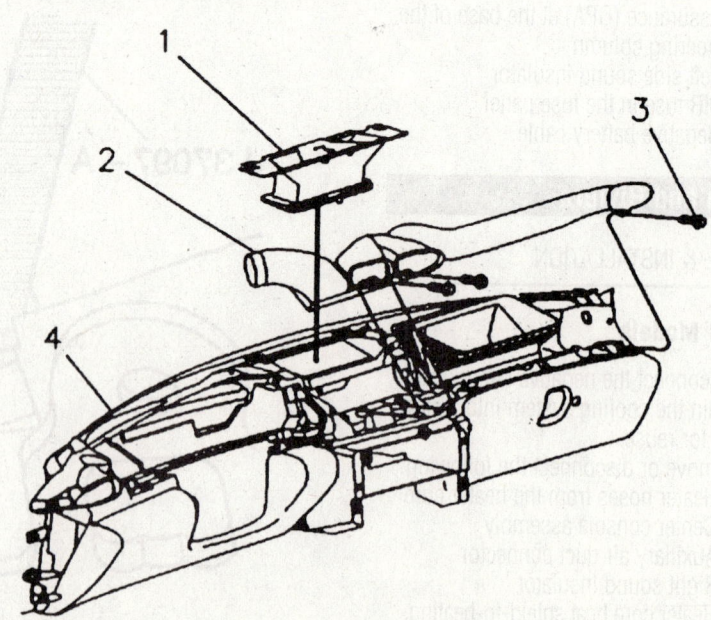

1 DUCT, WINDSHIELD DEFROST
2 DUCT, AIR DISTRIBUTION
3 SCREW
4 LOWER I/P

Location of the air distribution duct mounting—1997–01 Sunfire shown

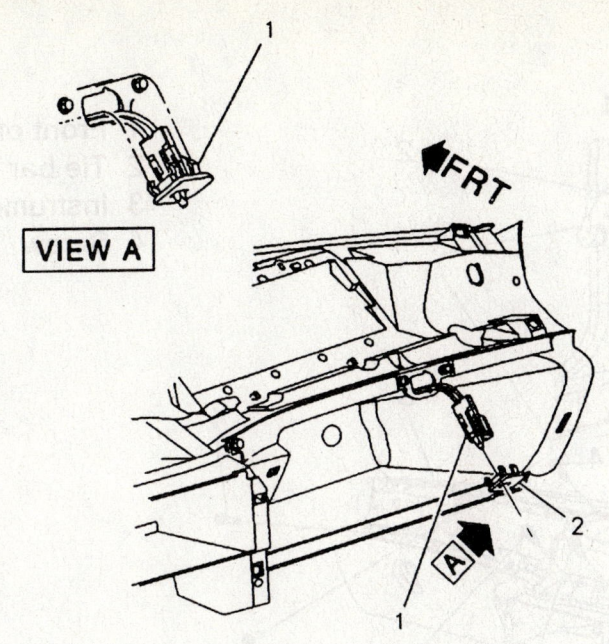

1 LAMP, I/P COMPARTMENT
2 RETAINER

87950085

Detach the instrument panel lamp connector—1997–01 Cavalier and Sunfire

b. Turn the ignition switch to the LOCK position.

c. Remove the AIR BAG fuse from the fuse block.

d. At the base of the steering column, remove the left sound insulator.

e. At the base of the steering column, disconnect the Connector Position Assurance (CPA), the yellow 2-way electrical connectors and the passenger's side module electrical connector.

2. Disconnect the negative battery cable.

3. Drain the cooling system into a clean container for reuse.

4. Disconnect the heater hoses from the heater core.

5. If equipped, remove the Diagnostic Energy Reserve Module (DERM) with attaching brackets.

6. Remove the steering wheel by removing or disconnecting the following:

- SIR module-to-steering wheel screws
- SIR module and disconnect the electrical connector

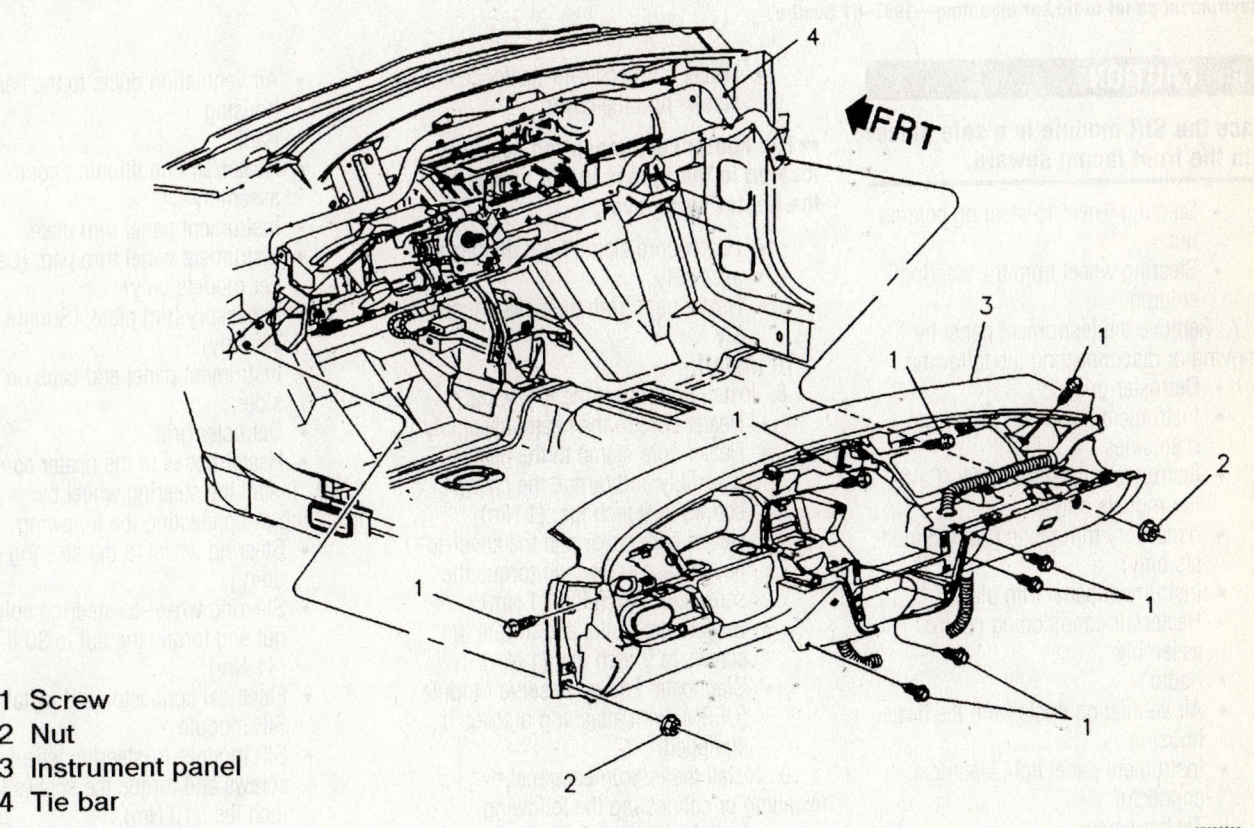

1 Screw
2 Nut
3 Instrument panel
4 Tie bar

87950086

Instrument panel-to-tie bar attachments—1997–01 Cavalier

Refer to the model specific sections for cooling system service precautions

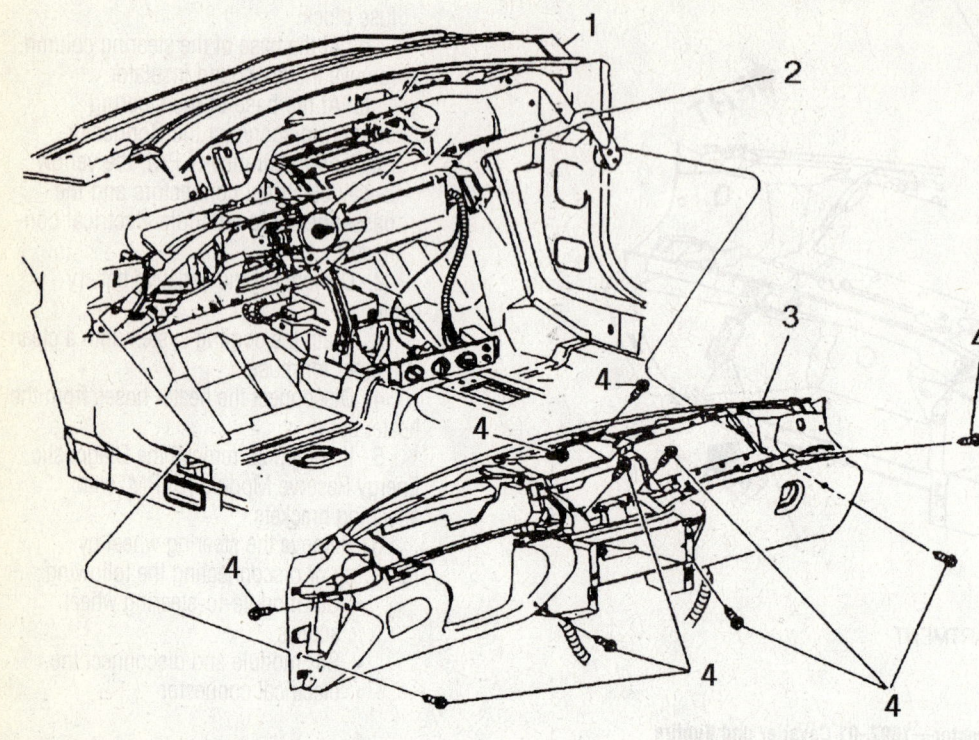

1 Front of dash
2 Tie bar
3 Instrument panel
4 Screw

Instrument panel-to-tie bar mounting—1997–01 Sunfire

87950087

※※ CAUTION

Place the SIR module in a safe place with the front facing upward.

- Steering wheel-to-steering column nut
- Steering wheel from the steering column

7. Remove the instrument panel by removing or disconnecting the following:
- Defroster grille
- Instrument panel end caps from both sides
- Instrument panel trim pad, (Cavalier models only)
- Accessory trim plate, (Sunfire models only)
- Instrument panel trim plate
- Heater/air conditioning control assembly
- Radio
- Air ventilation ducts from the heater housing
- Instrument panel light electrical connector
- Tie bar screws
- Instrument panel from the tie bar
- Heater core outlet screws and the outlet

- Heater core cover-to-heater case screws and the cover.

➡The heater core mounting screw is located in the recess in the center of the heater core cover.

- Heater core clamp from the heater assembly
- Heater core from the heater assembly

To install:

8. Install or connect the following:
- Heater core to the heater assembly
- Heater core clamp to the heater assembly and torque the clamp screws to 9 inch lbs. (1 Nm)
- Heater core cover and the cover-to-heater case screw and torque the screws to 9 inch lbs. (1 Nm)
- Heater core outlet and torque the screws to 9 inch lbs. (1 Nm)
- Diagnostic Energy Reserve Module (DERM) with attaching bracket, if equipped

9. Install the instrument panel by installing or connecting the following:
- Instrument panel to the tie bar
- Tie bar screws
- Instrument panel light electrical connector

- Air ventilation ducts to the heater housing
- Radio
- Heater/air conditioning control assembly
- Instrument panel trim plate
- Instrument panel trim pad, (Cavalier models only)
- Accessory trim plate, (Sunfire models only)
- Instrument panel end caps on both sides
- Defroster grill
- Heater hoses to the heater core

10. Install the steering wheel by installing or connecting the following:
- Steering wheel to the steering column
- Steering wheel-to-steering column nut and torque the nut to 30 ft. lbs. (41 Nm)
- Electrical connector and install the SIR module
- SIR module-to-steering wheel screws and torque the screws to 89 inch lbs. (10 Nm)

11. Refill the cooling system.
12. Connect the negative battery cable.
13. Enable the SIR system by performing the following procedure:

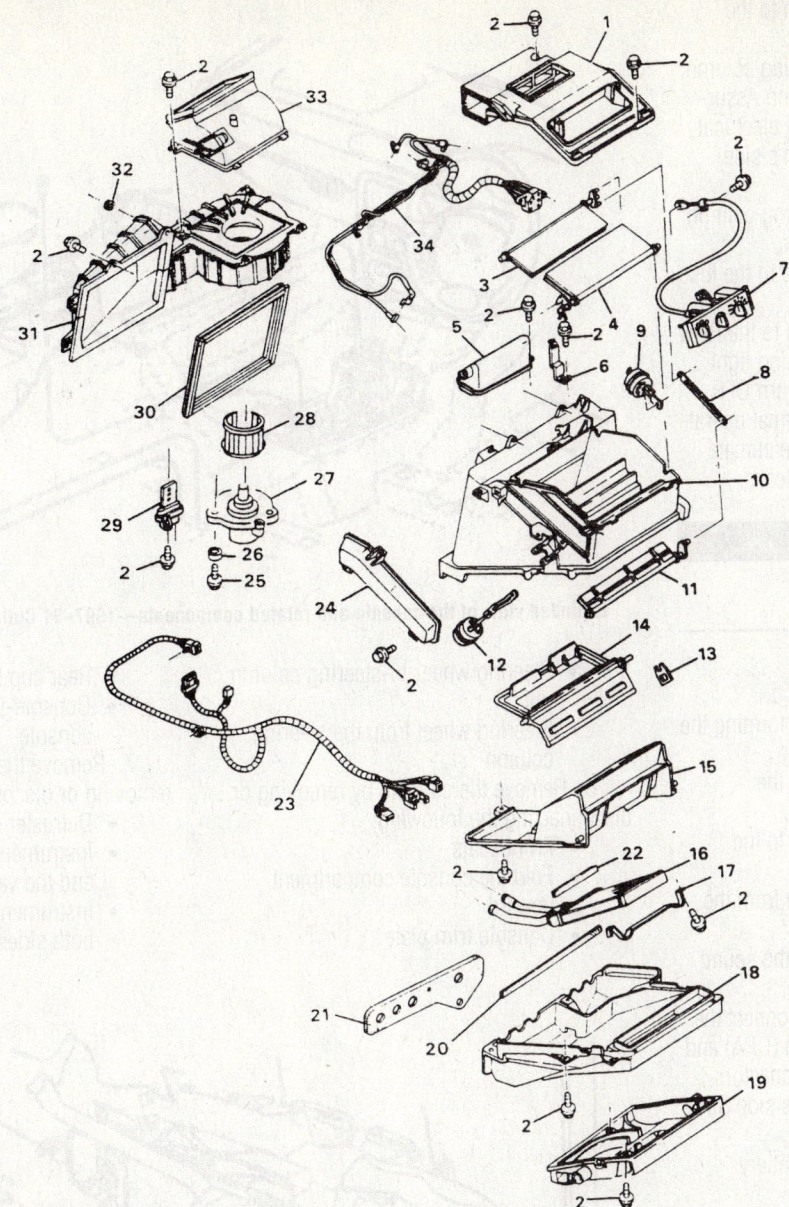

1 VALVE HOUSING COVER
2 HEATER/BLOWER MODULE BOLT
3 DEFROSTER VALVE
4 MODE VALVE
5 HEATER–VACUUM TANK
6 HEATER MODULE MOUNTING BRACKET
7 HEATER–CONTROL
8 HEATER VALVE LEVER LINK
9 DEFROSTER VALVE ACTUATOR
10 HEATER CASE
11 HEATER VALVE
12 MODE VALVE ACTUATOR
13 TEMPERATURE VALVE CLIP
14 TEMPERATURE VALVE
15 HEATER CORE SHROUD
16 HEATER CORE
17 HEATER CORE STRAP
18 HEATER COVER
19 HEATER OUTLET
20 HEATER CORE SHROUD SEAL
21 HEATER CORE TUBE AND MOUNT SEAL
22 HEATER CORE SEAL
23 HEATER AND A/C CONTROL SWITCH HARNESS
24 DEFROSTER DUCT
25 BLOWER MOTOR BOLTS
26 BLOWER MOTOR ISOLATOR
27 BLOWER MOTOR
28 BLOWER FAN
29 BLOWER RESISTOR
30 HEATER CASE SEAL
31 BLOWER AND AIR INLET CASE
32 MOUNTING SEAL
33 AIR INLET HOUSING
34 VACUUM HARNESS

93111GB4

Exploded view of the heater/evaporator housing assembly—1997–01 Cavalier and Sunfire

a. Turn the ignition switch to the LOCK position.

b. At the base of the steering column, connect the Connector Position Assurance (CPA), the yellow 2-way electrical connectors and the passenger's side module electrical connector.

c. At the base of the steering column, install the left sound insulator.

d. Install the AIR BAG fuse to the fuse block.

e. Turn the ignition switch to the RUN position; the INFL REST warning light should flash 7–9 times then turn OFF.

14. Operate the engine to normal operating temperatures; then, check the climate control operation and check for leaks.

Cutlass and Malibu

REMOVAL & INSTALLATION

1997–01 Models

1. Disable the air bag by performing the following procedure:

a. Place the front wheel in the straight-ahead position.

b. Turn the ignition switch to the LOCK position.

c. Remove the air bag fuse from the fuse block.

d. At the left side, remove the sound insulator.

e. At the driver's side, disconnect the Connector Position Assurance (CPA) and the yellow 2-way electrical connectors and the lead to the passenger's side SIR module.

2. Disconnect the negative battery cable.

3. Drain the cooling system into a clean container for reuse.

4. Disconnect the heater hoses from the heater core and remove the drain tube from the heater/air conditioning housing.

5. Remove the steering wheel by removing or disconnecting the following:

- 2 SIR module-to-steering wheel screws (located at the rear of the steering wheel), and the module
- SIR module and disconnect the electrical connector and remove the SIR module

❊❊ CAUTION

Place the SIR module in a safe place with the front facing upward.

- Horn and cruise control electrical connectors

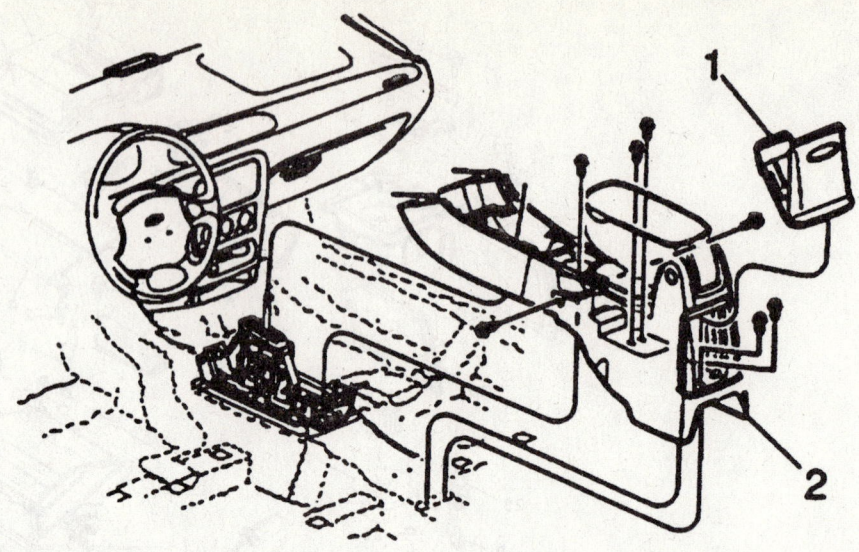

93111GB9

Exploded view of the console and related components—1997–01 Cutlass and Malibu

- Steering wheel-to-steering column nut
- Steering wheel from the steering column

6. Remove the console by removing or disconnecting the following:
- Front seats
- Fold the console compartment upward
- Console trim plate
- Rear cup holder
- Console-to-chassis screws and the console

7. Remove the instrument panel by removing or disconnecting the following:
- Defroster grille
- Instrument panel valance screws and the valance
- Instrument panel end caps from both sides

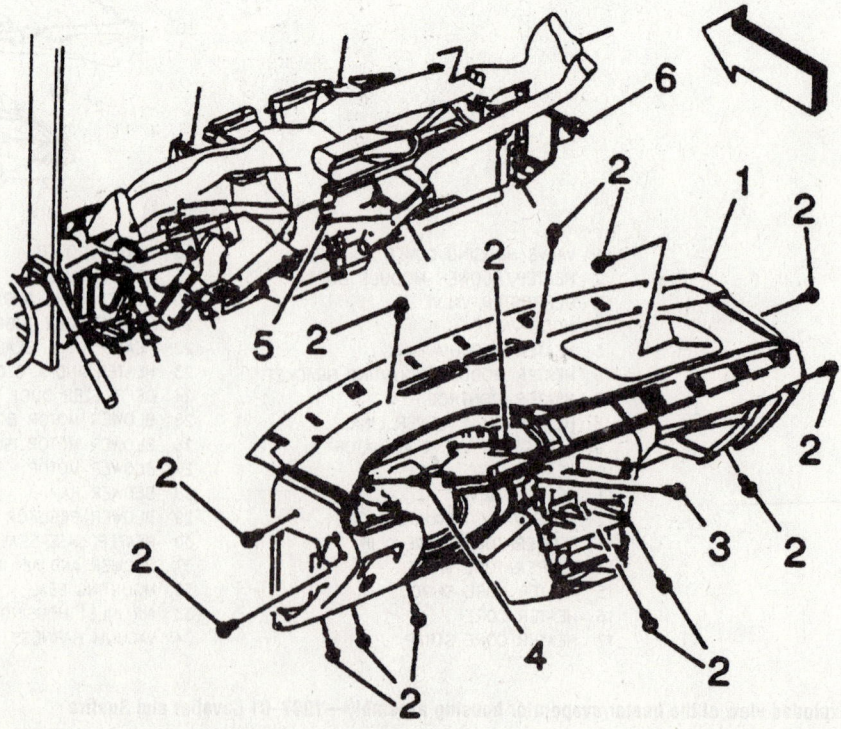

93111GB0

View of instrument panel—1997–01 Cutlass and Malibu

- Screws located under the instrument panel end caps
- Instrument panel compartment
- Steering column covers
- Steering column stalks
- Instrument cluster and accessory trim plates
- Instrument cluster fasteners, disconnect the electrical connectors and remove the cluster
- Heater/air conditioning control assembly

- Stereo/tape deck assembly
- Ignition switch
- Upper windshield side garnish molding
- Loosen the center console, pull it rearward to disengage it from the instrument panel
- Instrument panel-to-tie bar screws
- Instrument panel
- Outlet from the heater/air conditioning housing

- Heater core cover-to-heater/air conditioning housing

➡ **There is a screw located in the recess in the center of the cover.**

- Heater core-to-heater/air conditioning housing clamps
- Heater core

To install:

8. Install or connect the following:
- Heater core
- Heater core-to-heater/air conditioning housing clamps

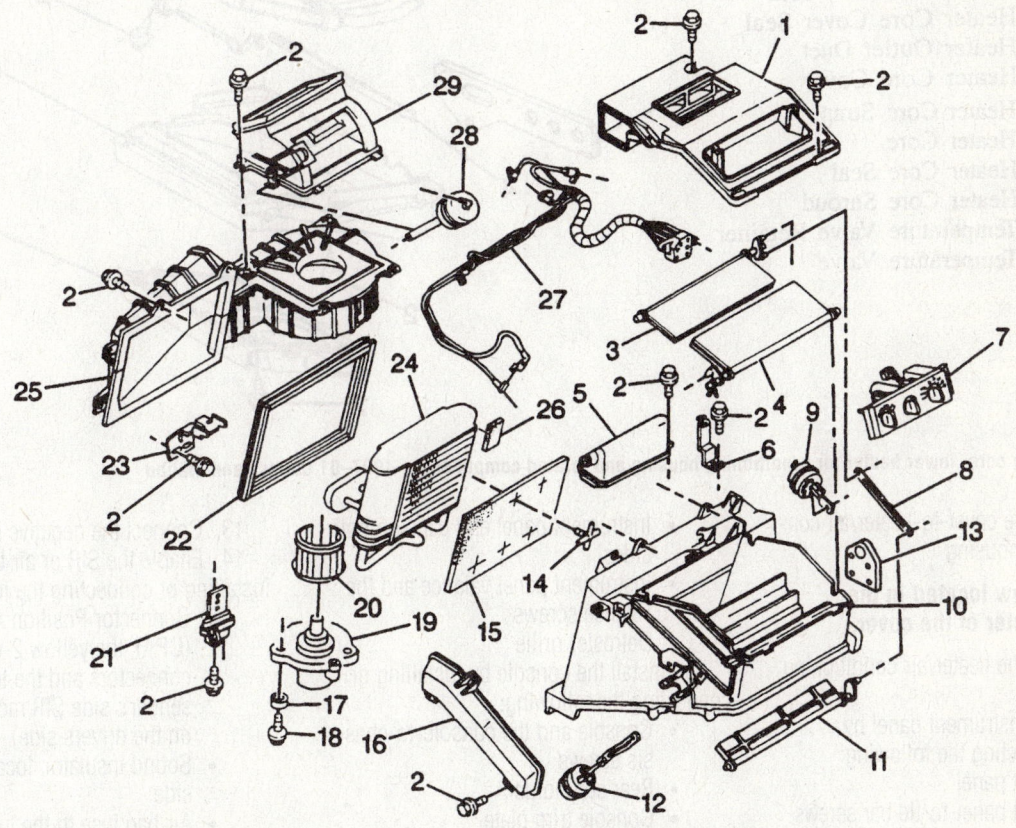

1 Valve Housing Cover	16 Defroster Case
2 Bolt	17 Blower Motor Bolt Insulator
3 Defroster Valve	18 Blower Motor Bolt
4 Mode Valve	19 Blower Motor
5 Vacuum Tank	20 Blower Motor Fan
6 HVAC Module Bracket	21 Blower Motor Resistor
7 HVAC Control Assembly	22 Evaporator Core Seal
8 Heater Valve Link	23 Evaporator Core Bracket
9 Defroster Valve Actuator	24 Evaporator Core
10 Evaporator Case	25 Blower and Air Inlet Case
11 Heater Valve	26 Evaporator Core Spacer
12 Mode Valve Actuator	27 HVAC Vacuum Harness
13 Temperature Control Motor	28 Air Inlet Valve Actuator
14 Water Filter Retainer	29 Air Inlet Case
15 Water Filter	

93111GC1

View of the evaporator core, upper heater/air conditioning housing and related components—1997–01 Cutlass and Malibu

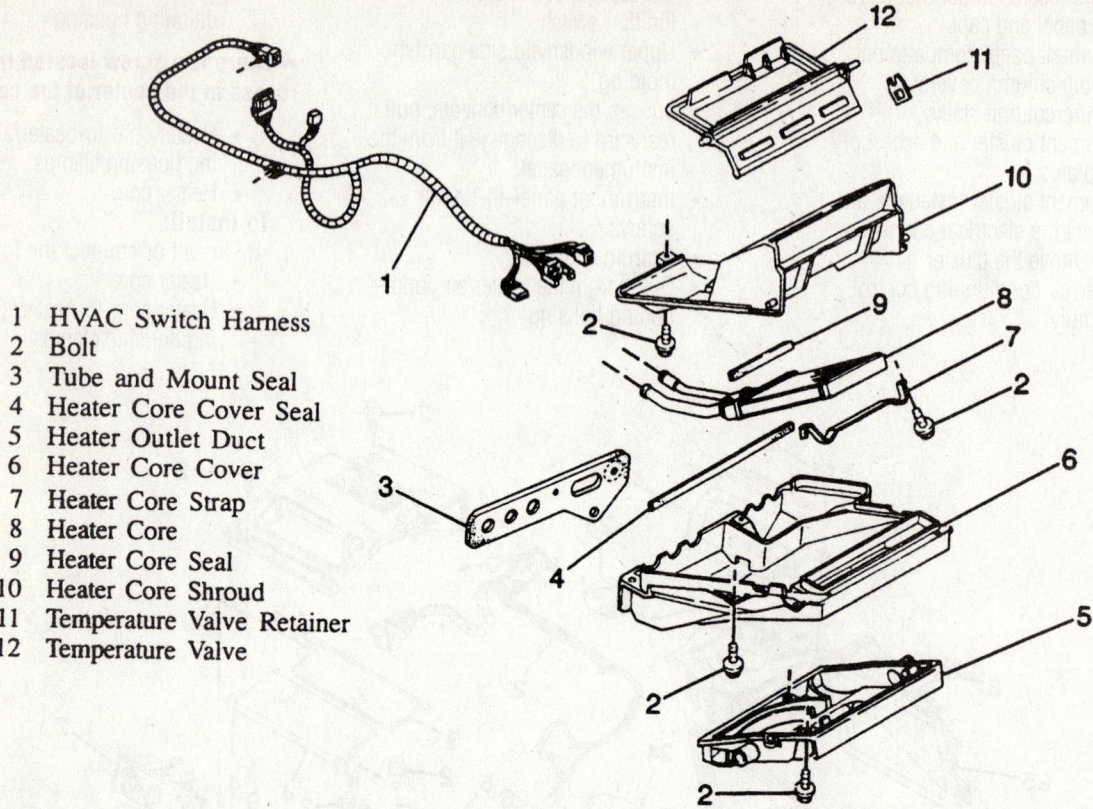

1 HVAC Switch Harness
2 Bolt
3 Tube and Mount Seal
4 Heater Core Cover Seal
5 Heater Outlet Duct
6 Heater Core Cover
7 Heater Core Strap
8 Heater Core
9 Heater Core Seal
10 Heater Core Shroud
11 Temperature Valve Retainer
12 Temperature Valve

93111GC2

View of the heater core, lower heater/air conditioning housing and related components—1997–01 Cutlass and Malibu

- Heater core cover-to-heater/air conditioning housing

➡**There is a screw located in the recess in the center of the cover.**

- Outlet to the heater/air conditioning housing

9. Install the instrument panel by installing or connecting the following:
- Instrument panel
- Instrument panel-to-tie bar screws
- Move the center console forward and engage it to the instrument panel
- Upper windshield side garnish molding
- Ignition switch
- Stereo/tape deck assembly
- Heater/air conditioning control assembly
- Instrument cluster, connect the electrical connectors and install the cluster fasteners
- Instrument cluster accessory trim plates
- Steering column stalks
- Steering column covers
- Instrument panel compartment
- Instrument panel end caps, install the screws

- Instrument panel end caps on both sides
- Instrument panel valance and the valance screws
- Defroster grille

10. Install the console by installing or connecting the following:
- Console and the console-to-chassis screws
- Rear cup holder
- Console trim plate
- Front seats

11. Install the steering wheel by installing or connecting the following:
- Steering wheel to the steering column
- Steering wheel-to-steering column nut and torque to 30 ft. lbs. (41 Nm)
- Horn and cruise control electrical connectors
- SIR module and connect the electrical connector
- SIR module and torque the 2 module-to-steering wheel screws to 89 inch lbs. (10 Nm)
- Heater hoses to the heater core and install the drain tube to the heater/air conditioning housing

12. Refill the cooling system.

13. Connect the negative battery cable.

14. Enable the SIR or air bag by installing or connecting the following:
- Connector Position Assurance (CPA), the yellow 2-way electrical connectors and the lead to the passenger's side SIR module (located on the drivers side)
- Sound insulator, located on the left side
- Air bag fuse to the fuse block

a. Turn the ignition switch to RUN and verify that the Air Bag Warning light flashes 7–9 times and turns OFF.

➡**If the SIR system does not operate as described, perform the SIR diagnostic system check.**

15. Operate the engine to normal operating temperatures; then, check the climate control operation and check for leaks.

Achieva, Grand Am and Skylark

REMOVAL & INSTALLATION

1997–01 Models

1. Disconnect the negative battery cable.

2. Drain the cooling system into a clean container for reuse.

3. Raise and safely support the vehicle.

4. Remove the drain tube from the heater housing.

5. Disconnect the heater hoses from the heater core.

6. Lower the vehicle.

7. Remove or disconnect the following:

- Console, if equipped
- Sound insulators from both sides

- Steering column opening filler
- Air outlet duct
- Rear floor air outlet screws and the outlet
- Heater core cover
- Heater core-to-housing mounting clamps and the heater core

To install:

8. Install or connect the following:

- Heater core and the heater core-to-housing mounting clamps
- Heater core cover

- Rear floor air outlet and the outlet screws
- Air outlet duct
- Steering column opening filler
- Sound insulators, if equipped
- Console, if equipped
- Heater hoses to the heater core.
- Drain tube to the heater housing.

9. Refill the cooling system.

10. Connect the negative battery cable.

11. Operate the engine to normal operat-

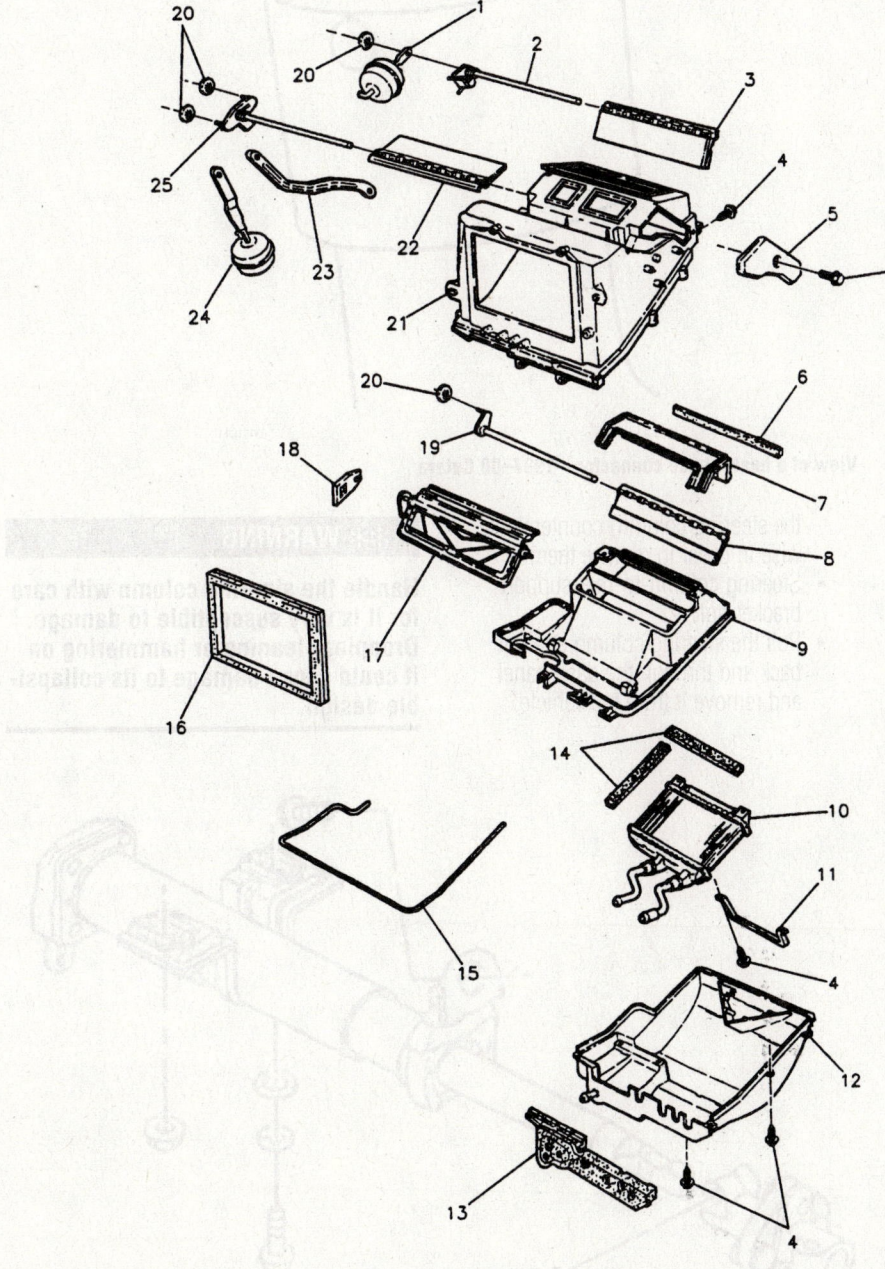

1	ACTUATOR, MODE VALVE
2	SHAFT, MODE VALUE
3	VALVE, MODE
4	BOLT
5	DUCT, DEFROSTER
6	SEAL, DEFROSTER VALVE
7	SEAT, DEFROSTER VALVE
8	VALVE, HEATER
9	SHROUD, HEATER CORE
10	CORE, HEATER
11	STRAP, HEATER CORE
12	COVER, HEATER CORE
13	SEAL, TUBE MOUNTING
14	SEAL, HEATER CORE
15	GASKET, EVAPORATOR CASE
16	SEAL, EVAPORATOR TO CASE
17	VALVE, TEMPERATURE
18	CLIP, TEMPERATURE VALVE
19	SHAFT, HEATER VALVE
20	CLIP, PUSH ON
21	CASE, A/C EVAPORATOR
22	VALVE, DEFROSTER
23	LINK, DEFROSTER VALVE
24	ACTUATOR, DEFROSTER VALVE
25	SHAFT, DEFROSTER VALVE

93111GB8

Exploded view of the heater core, heater housing and related components—1997–01 Grand Am, Achieva and Skylark

Refer to the model specific sections for engine mechanical service procedures

ing temperatures. Check the climate control operation and check for leaks.

Catera

REMOVAL & INSTALLATION

1997–00 Models

1. Disable the SIR system.
2. Disconnect the negative battery cable.
3. Drain the cooling system by performing the following procedures:

   a. Position the vehicle on a level surface.

   b. With the engine cool, remove the radiator cap.

   c. Install a piece of ⅜ in. hose to the radiator drain cock outlet and place the other end in a clean container.

   d. Open the radiator drain cock and drain the cooling system.

   e. Close the drain cock and remove the drain hose.

4. Remove the heater hose quick connects from the heater core pipes by performing the following procedure:

   a. At the passenger side, raise the air inlet screen and open the access door near the pollen filter.

   b. Unlock the quick connect collars by squeezing the tabs and carefully pulling back on the tabs to disconnect the sleeve.

   c. If green assembly marks are attached, discard them.

✳✳ WARNING

The front wheels must be maintained in the straight-ahead position and the steering column must be in the LOCK position. Failure to do so will cause improper alignment of some components during installation and may result to damage to the SIR coil assembly.

5. Remove the steering column by removing or disconnecting the following:

- Instrument panel driver knee bolster energy absorber and sound insulator
- Steering column electrical connector(s)
- Coupler bolt from the lower steering column connection and slightly separate the coupler to aid in the shaft removal
- Using a chisel and a hammer, rotate the forward support strap shear nut and bolt (located under

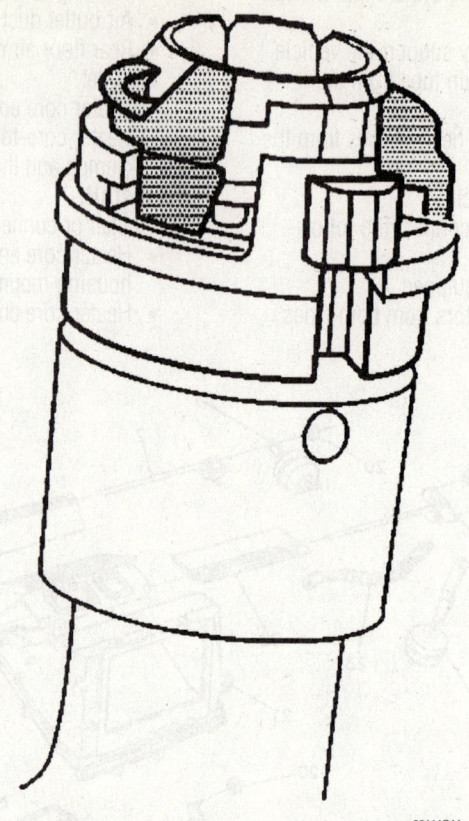

View of a heater hose connector—1997–00 Catera

the steering column) counterclockwise in order to remove them
- Steering column-to-rear support bracket bolt
- Pull the steering column straight back and through the dash panel and remove it from the vehicle.

✳✳ WARNING

Handle the steering column with care for it is very susceptible to damage. Dropping, leaning or hammering on it could cause damage to its collapsible design.

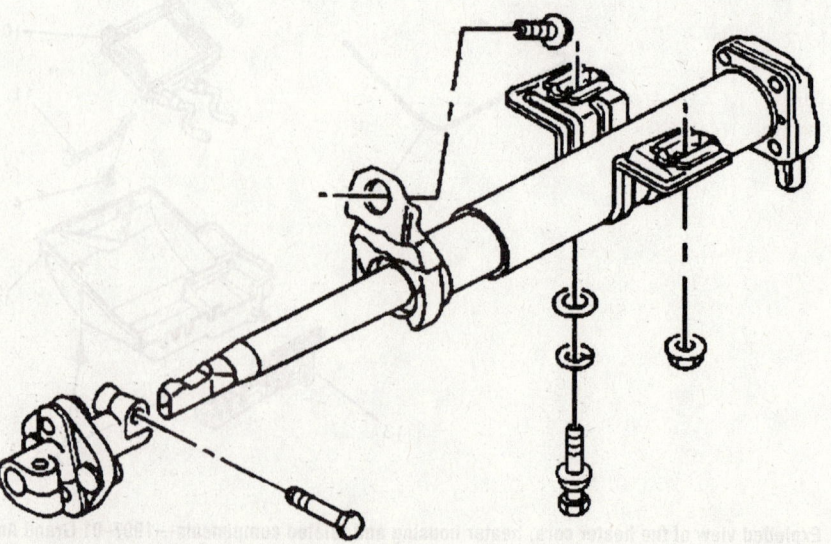

View of the steering column assembly—1997–01 Catera

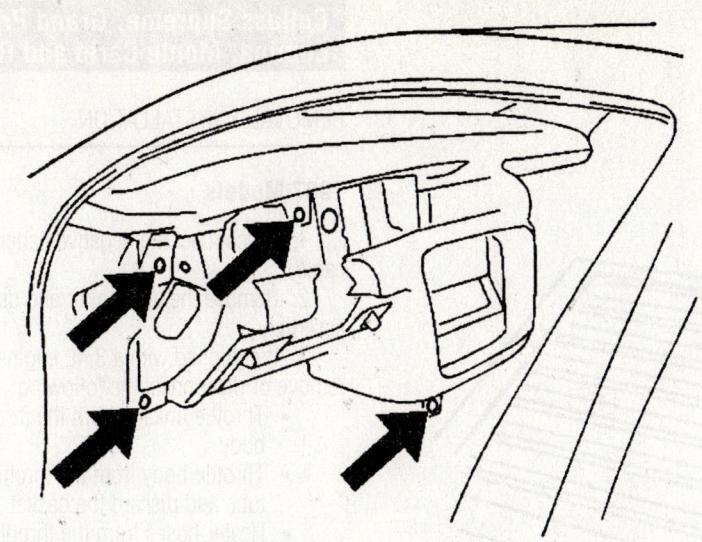

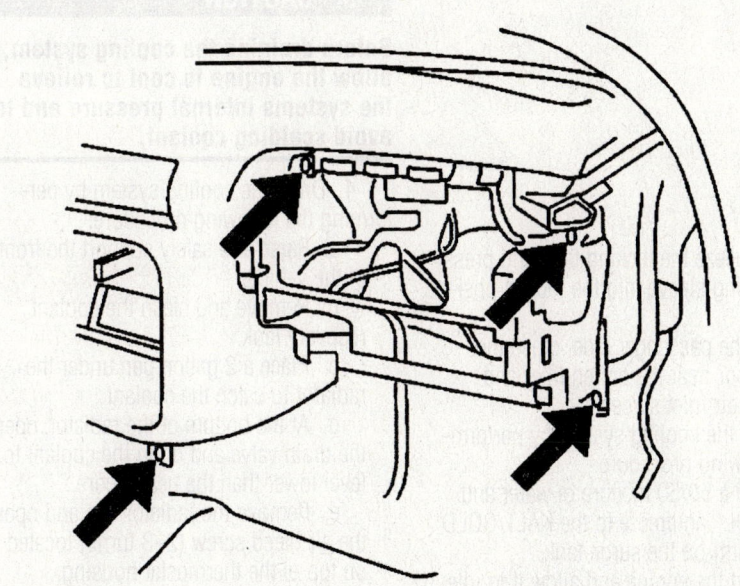

93111G09

View of the instrument panel carrier bolt locations—1997–01 Catera

- Instrument cluster
- Fuse and relay panel screws and the panels
- Instrument panel carrier bolts
- Electrical connectors from the instrument panel and/or the wiring harness clips from the instrument panel carrier, if necessary
- Instrument panel carrier

➡**It is not necessary to physically remove the instrument panel but it is necessary to pull the carrier rearward to enable the heater core to be removed from its housing.**

- Blower motor housing screws and the housing with the motor
- Heater core pipe bracket-to-chassis screw and the bracket
- Heater core inlet/outlet pipe bracket-to-heater core screw and the inlet/outlet pipe bracket
- Instrument panel support brace bolts from the instrument panel and the transmission well, then remove the brace
- Heater core-to-housing retaining screw. Plug the heater core pipes and protect the interior from coolant spills
- Heater core and the rubber seal from the heater housing

To install:

7. Install or connect the following:
- Rubber seal and heater core into the heater housing; be careful not to damage the fins
- Heater core-to-housing retainer screw
- Instrument panel support brace to the transmission well and instrument panel, then torque the bolts to 16 ft. lbs. (22 Nm)
- Heater core inlet/outlet pipe bracket to the heater core (using a new O-ring lightly coated with coolant), and torque the screw to 44 inch lbs. (5 Nm)
- Heater core pipe bracket with the screw to the chassis, be careful not to strip the screw
- Blower motor/housing assembly and torque the screws to 35 inch lbs. (4 Nm)
- Instrument panel carrier
- Instrument panel carrier by reversing the removal procedures and torque the instrument panel carrier bolts to 16 ft. lbs. (22 Nm)

6. Remove the instrument panel carrier by removing or disconnecting the following:
- Windshield pillar moldings
- Access panel, the air deflector outlet screw, the air deflector outlet and the air outlet duct, located at the right-side of the instrument panel
- Instrument panel SIR (air bag) module cover, the instrument panel compartment and the SIR module
- Upper center console and the lower center console
- Center console air duct screw and the center console air duct
- Radio tape player bezel and the radio
- Climate control head
- Center air outlet deflector, the outlet screws and the outlet housing
- Driver's side access panel
- Driver's side air outlet deflector, the outlet screw and the outlet housing
- Driver's side lower outlet duct

Refer to the model specific sections for cooling system service precautions

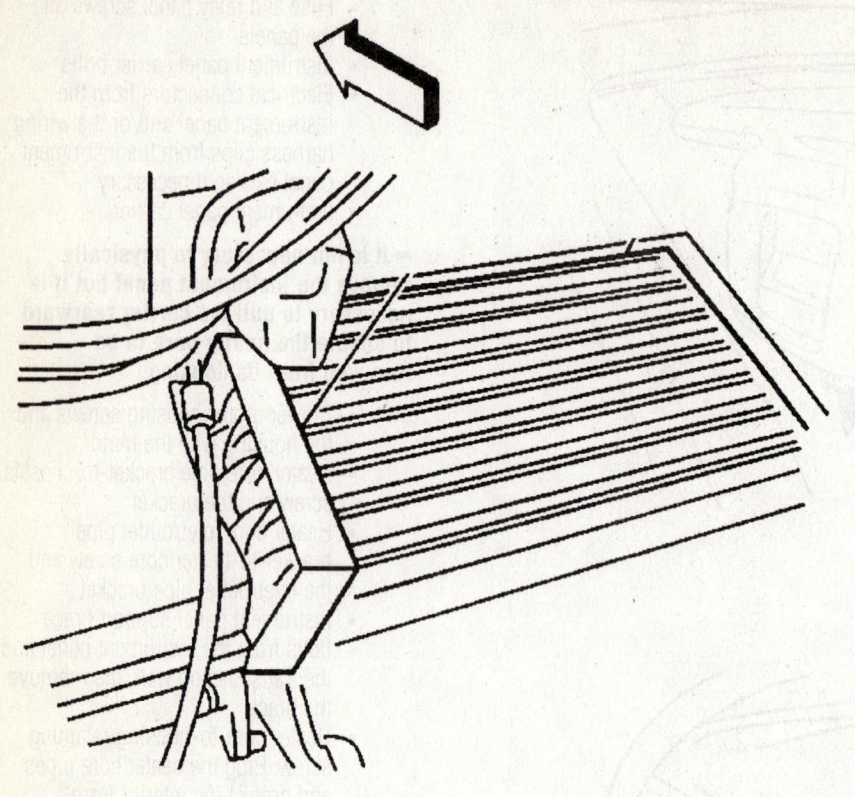

View of a heater core and seal—1997–01 Catera

93111G12

8. Remove the steering column by installing or connecting the following:
- Steering column into the vehicle, through the dash panel and into the lower steering coupling
- Hand start the rear support bracket bolt, the forward support strap nut and shear bolt
- Rear support bracket bolt. Torque to 16 ft. lbs. (22 Nm)
- Forward support strap nut. Torque to 16 ft. lbs. (22 Nm)
- New forward support shear bolt. Torque to 15 ft. lbs. (21 Nm)
- Lower steering column shaft bolt and torque to 16 ft. lbs. (22 Nm)
- Steering column electrical connector(s)
- Sound insulator and the instrument panel driver knee bolster energy absorber

9. Connect the heater hoses to the heater core pipes by performing the following procedure:
  a. If not attached to the quick connect, discard the green assembly marker(s).
  b. Push the quick connects into the pipes until they are fully seated.

  c. Squeeze the locking tabs and press the retaining sleeve into the locked position.
  d. At the passenger side, close the access door near the pollen filter and lower the air inlet screen.
10. Refill the cooling system by performing the following procedure:
  a. Add a 50/50 mixture of water and DEX-COOL® antifreeze to the KALT/COLD mark (seam) on the surge tank.
  b. Start the engine and allow it to idle for 1 min.
  c. Add more coolant to the surge tank as necessary.
  d. Install the radiator sure tank cap.
  e. Cycle the engine, from idle to 3000 rpm, in 30 second intervals, until the engine reaches normal operating temperatures.

➡**The cooling system will bleed itself automatically during warm-up.**

  f. Turn the engine OFF and recheck the coolant level when the engine is cool
11. Connect the negative battery cable.
12. Enable the SIR system.
13. Reprogram the necessary accessories.

Cutlass Supreme, Grand Prix, Lumina, Monte Carlo and Regal

REMOVAL & INSTALLATION

1997 Models

1. Disconnect the negative battery cable.
2. Remove the air cleaner and duct assembly.
3. If equipped with a 3.4L engine, remove or disconnect the following:
- Throttle linkage from the throttle body
- Throttle body from the throttle body tube and discard the gasket
- Heater hoses from the throttle body tube connectors
- Throttle body tube from the intake manifold and discard the gasket

✳✳ CAUTION

Before draining the cooling system, allow the engine to cool to relieve the systems internal pressure and to avoid scalding coolant.

4. Drain the cooling system by performing the following procedure:
  a. Raise and safely support the front of the vehicle.
  b. Remove and clean the coolant recovery tank.
  c. Place a 2 gallon pan under the radiator to catch the coolant.
  d. At the bottom of the radiator, open the drain valve and drain the coolant to a level lower than the heater core.
  e. Remove the radiator cap and open the air bleed screw (2–3 turns) located on top of the thermostat housing.
  f. After sufficient coolant has been drained from the system, close the drain valve.

✳✳ CAUTION

Engine coolant is a hazardous waste; it should be stored for reuse or submitted for recycling. NEVER dispose of it by dumping it into the environment.

5. Disconnect and plug the heater hoses at the heater core.
6. If equipped, remove the lower center console by removing or disconnect the following:
- Cigarette lighter
- Automatic transaxle shift handle

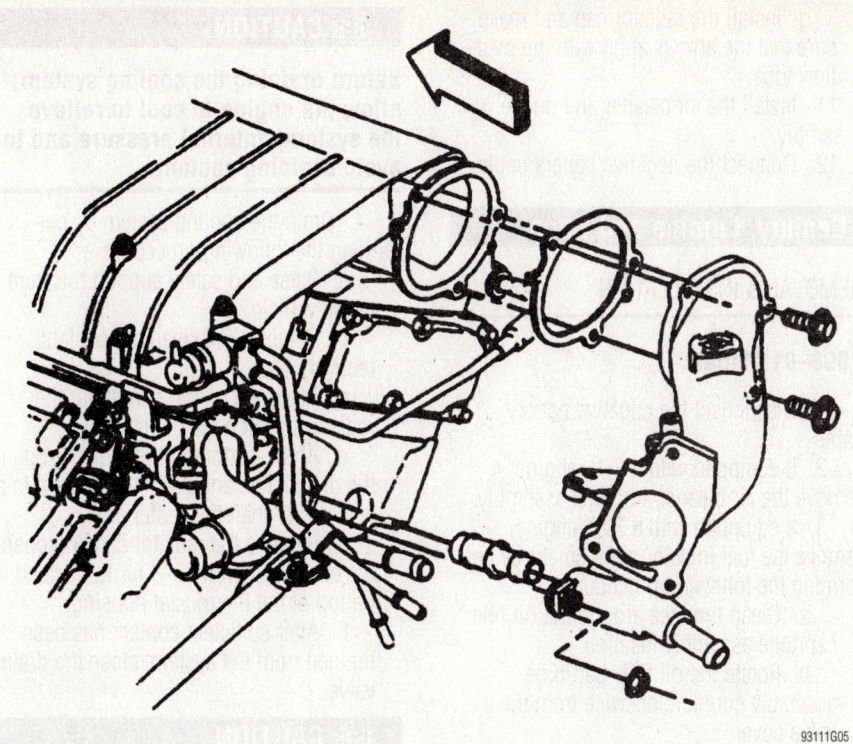

Exploded view of the throttle body tube with coolant passages—1997 3.4L engine Lumina and Monte Carlo

- Upper console trim plate from the front floor console by unsnapping it
- Electrical connectors from the upper console trim plate and remove the trim plate
- C/D storage compartment from the front floor console
- Raise the front floor console armrest and remove the compartment mat
- Console-to-chassis bolts and screws
- Electrical connectors from the console and remove the console from the vehicle
- Sound insulators from under both sides of the instrument panel
- Ashtray and bracket, if necessary
- Lower heater duct
- Heater core cover
- Heater core mounting clip and bracket
- Heater core

To install:
7. Install or connect the following:
- Heater core in the vehicle
- Heater core mounting clip and bracket

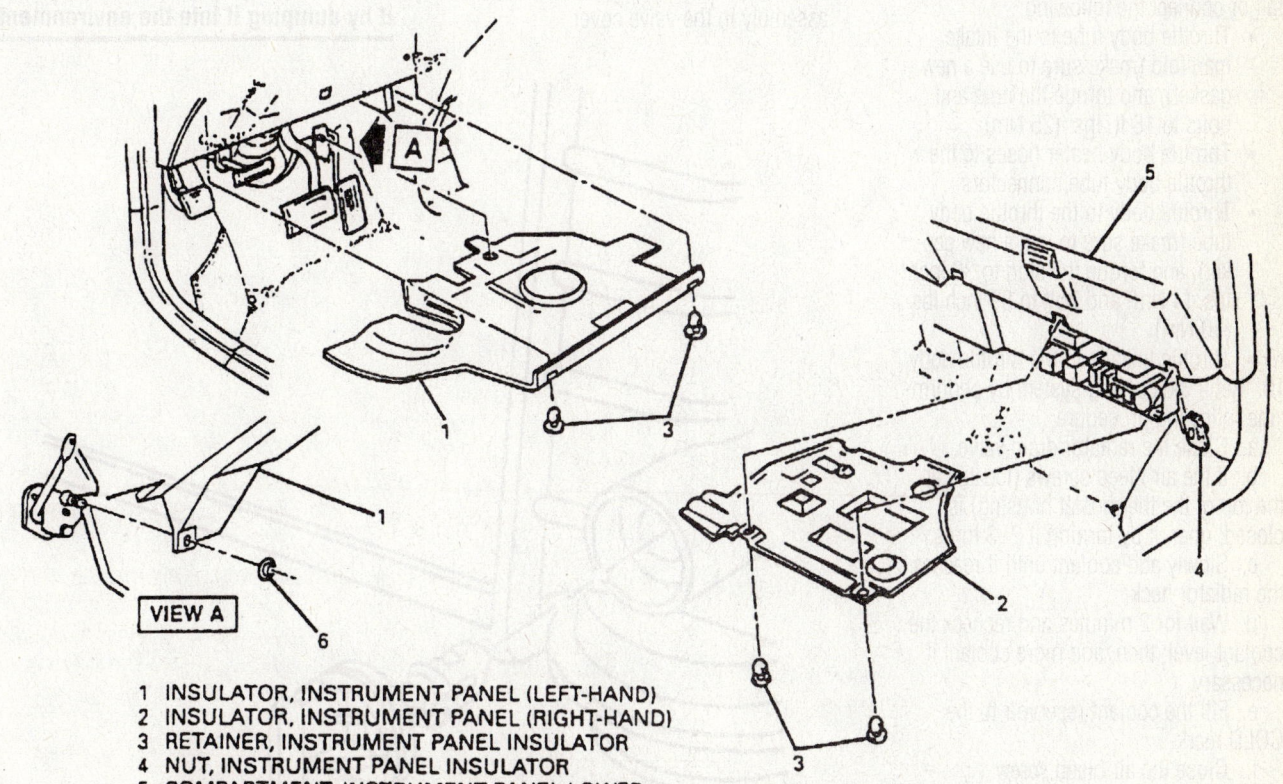

1 INSULATOR, INSTRUMENT PANEL (LEFT-HAND)
2 INSULATOR, INSTRUMENT PANEL (RIGHT-HAND)
3 RETAINER, INSTRUMENT PANEL INSULATOR
4 NUT, INSTRUMENT PANEL INSULATOR
5 COMPARTMENT, INSTRUMENT PANEL LOWER
6 NUT, INSTRUMENT PANEL INSULATOR

View of the sound insulator panels—1995–97 Cutlass Supreme, Grand Prix, Lumina, Monte Carlo and Regal

- Heater core cover and torque the bolts to 27 inch lbs. (3 Nm)
- Lower heater duct
- Ashtray and bracket, if removed
- Sound insulators, located under both sides of the instrument panel

8. If equipped, install the lower center console by installing or connecting the following:

- Console in the vehicle and connect the electrical connectors
- Console-to-chassis bolts and screws. Tighten in sequence beginning at the front right and continue in a clockwise order to 106 inch lbs. (12 Nm)
- Armrest compartment mat and lower the front floor console armrest
- Snap C/D storage compartment into the front floor console
- Electrical connectors to the upper console trim plate and snap the trim plate onto the console
- Automatic transaxle shift handle and the cigarette lighter
- Heater hoses to the heater core and secure with the clamps

9. If equipped with a 3.4L engine, install or connect the following:

- Throttle body tube to the intake manifold (make sure to use a new gasket), and torque the nuts and bolts to 18 ft. lbs. (25 Nm)
- Throttle body heater hoses to the throttle body tube connectors
- Throttle body to the throttle body tube (make sure to use a new gasket), and torque the stud to 36 inch lbs. (4 Nm) and bolt to 89 inch lbs. (10 Nm)
- Throttle linkage to the throttle body

10. Refill the cooling system by performing the following procedure:

a. Close the radiator drain valve.

b. If the air bleed screws (located at the top of the thermostat housing) is closed, open it by turning it 2–3 turns.

c. Slowly add coolant until it reaches the radiator neck.

d. Wait for 2 minutes and recheck the coolant level; then, add more coolant if necessary.

e. Fill the coolant reservoir to the COLD mark.

f. Close the air bleed screw.

❊❊ WARNING

Do not over-tighten the air bleed screw for it is made of brass.

g. Install the radiator cap and make sure that the arrows align with the overflow tube.

11. Install the air cleaner and duct assembly.

12. Connect the negative battery cable.

Century, Lumina and Regal

REMOVAL & INSTALLATION

1998–01 Models

1. Disconnect the negative battery cable.

2. If equipped with a 3.1L engine, remove the air cleaner and duct assembly.

3. If equipped with a 3.8L engine, remove the fuel injector sight shield by performing the following procedures:

a. Clean the area around the oil filler cap/tube assembly location.

b. Rotate the oil filler cap/tube assembly counterclockwise from the valve cover.

c. Lift the fuel injector sight shield up at the front and slide it from the rear engine bracket.

d. Reinstall the oil filler cap/tube assembly in the valve cover.

❊❊ CAUTION

Before draining the cooling system, allow the engine to cool to relieve the systems internal pressure and to avoid scalding coolant.

4. Drain the cooling system by performing the following procedure:

a. Raise and safely support the front of the vehicle.

b. Remove and clean the coolant recovery tank.

c. Place a 2 gallon pan under the radiator to catch the coolant.

d. At the bottom of the radiator, open the drain valve and drain the coolant to a level lower than the heater core.

e. Remove the radiator cap and open the air bleed screw (2–3 turns) located on top of the thermostat housing.

f. After sufficient coolant has been drained from the system, close the drain valve.

❊❊ CAUTION

Engine coolant is a hazardous waste; it should be stored for reuse or submitted for recycling. NEVER dispose of it by dumping it into the environment.

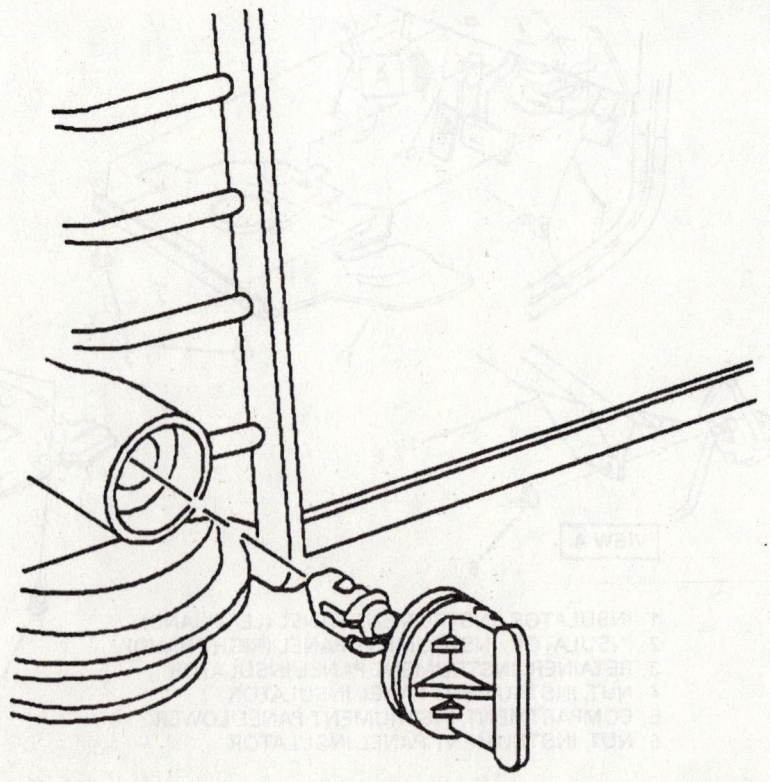

View of the radiator drain valve—1998–01 Century, Grand Prix, Intrigue, Lumina, Monte Carlo and Regal

93111G01

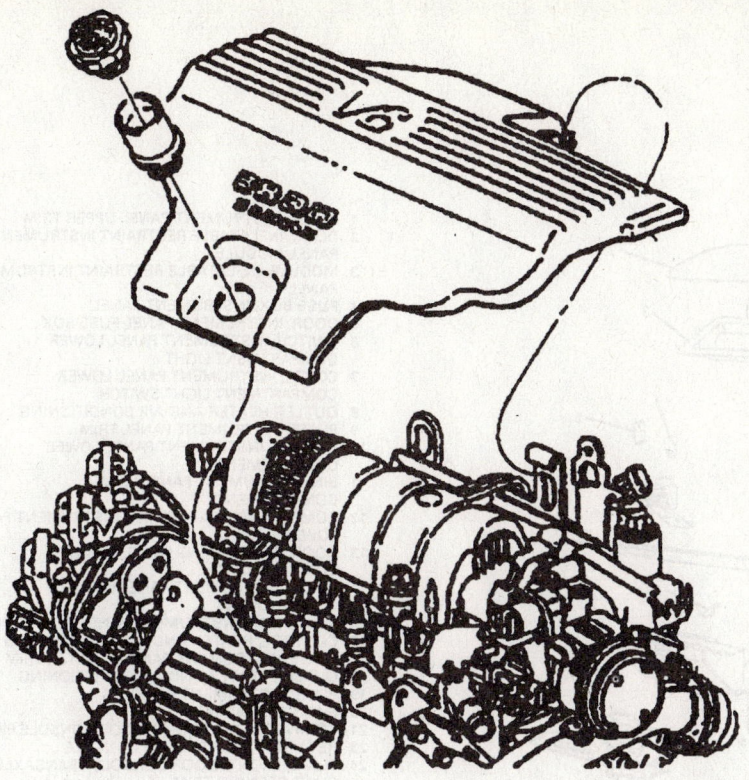

View of the fuel injector sight shield—1998–01 Century, Grand Prix, Intrigue, Lumina, Monte Carlo and Regal

5. Disconnect and plug the heater hoses at the heater core.

6. If equipped, remove the lower center console by removing or disconnecting the following:
- Cigarette lighter
- Automatic transaxle shift handle
- Upper console trim plate from the front floor console by unsnapping it
- Electrical connectors from the upper console trim plate and remove the trim plate
- CD storage compartment from the front floor console by unsnapping it
- Raise the front floor console armrest and remove the compartment mat
- Console-to-chassis bolts and screws
- Electrical connectors from the console and remove the console from the vehicle

7. Remove the lower instrument panel lower compartment by removing or disconnecting the following:
- Lower right instrument panel insulator

- Compartment-to-panel bolts and screws, from under the instrument panel compartment
- Instrument panel compartment door screws and the door
- Instrument panel compartment screws and plastic clips; then slide the compartment from the instrument panel
- Electrical connector from the compartment
- Ashtray and bracket, if necessary
- Lower heater duct
- Heater core cover and discard the cover seals
- Heater core mounting clip and bracket
- Heater core

To install:

8. Install and connect the following:
- Heater core in the vehicle
- Heater core mounting clip and bracket
- New seals on the heater core cover
- Heater core cover and torque the bolts to 13 inch lbs. (1.5 Nm)
- Lower heater duct, if removed
- Ashtray and bracket, if removed

9. Install the lower instrument panel lower by installing or connecting the following:
- Electrical connector to the compartment
- Slide the compartment into the instrument panel; then, secure it with screws and plastic clips
- Instrument panel compartment door and screws
- Compartment-to-panel bolts and screws, located under the instrument panel compartment
- Lower right instrument panel insulator

10. If equipped, install the lower center console install or connect the following:
- Console in the vehicle and connect the electrical connectors
- Console-to-chassis bolts and screws, tighten in sequence beginning at the front right and continue in a clockwise order to 106 inch lbs. (12 Nm)
- Armrest compartment mat and lower the front floor console armrest
- C/D storage compartment into the front floor console
- Electrical connectors to the upper console trim plate and snap the trim plate onto the console
- Automatic transaxle shift handle and the cigarette lighter
- Heater hoses to the heater core and secure with the clamps

11. Refill the cooling system by performing the following procedure:
  a. Close the radiator drain valve.
  b. If the air bleed screws (located at the top of the thermostat housing) is closed, open it by turning it 2–3 turns.
  c. Slowly add coolant until it reaches the radiator neck.
  d. Wait for 2 minutes and recheck the coolant level; then, add more coolant if necessary.
  e. Fill the coolant reservoir to the COLD mark.
  f. Close the air bleed screw.

✴✴ WARNING

Do not over-tighten the air bleed screw for it is made of brass.

  g. Install the radiator cap and make sure that the arrows align with the overflow tube.

12. If equipped with a 3.8L engine,

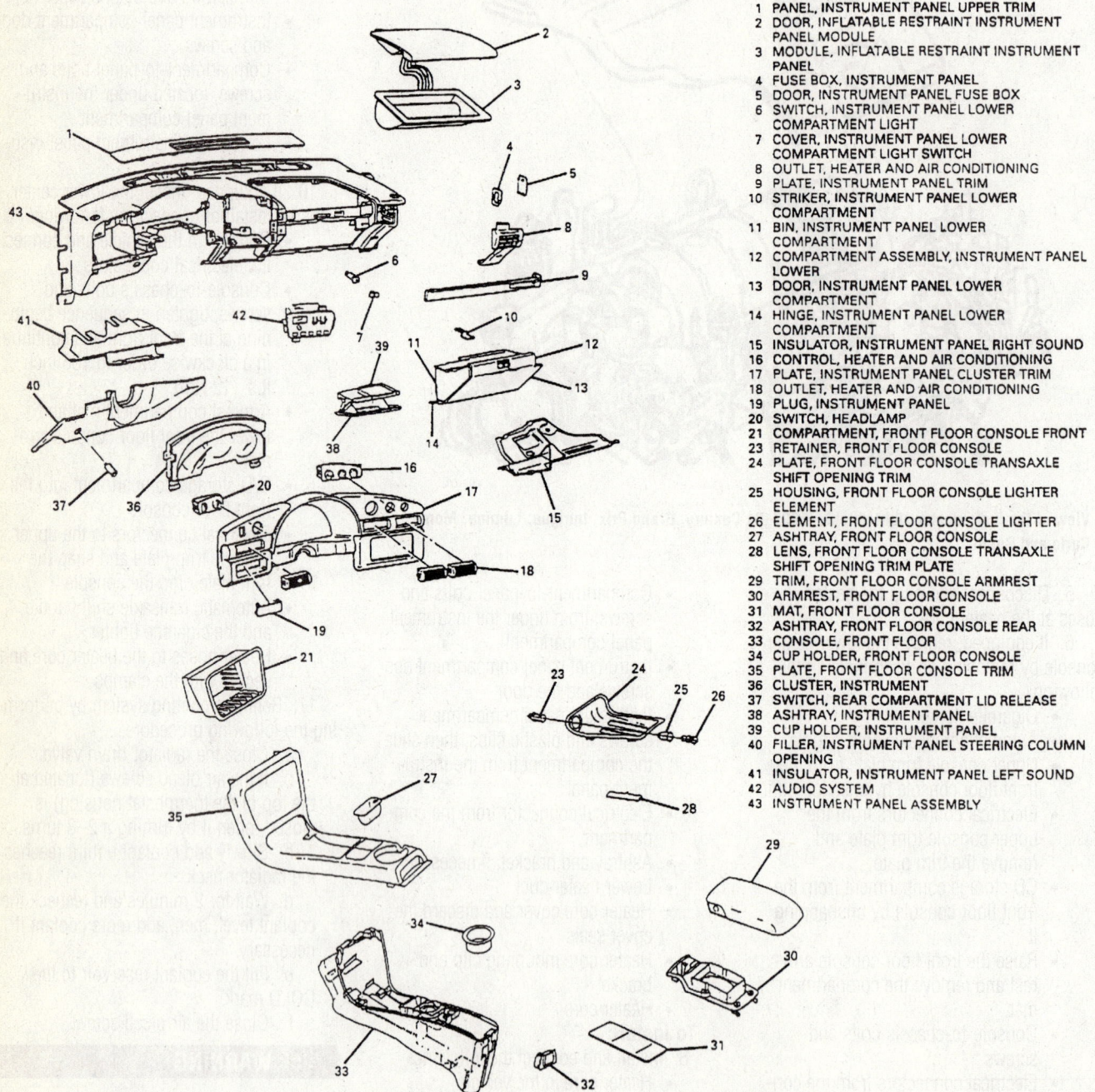

1 PANEL, INSTRUMENT PANEL UPPER TRIM
2 DOOR, INFLATABLE RESTRAINT INSTRUMENT
   PANEL MODULE
3 MODULE, INFLATABLE RESTRAINT INSTRUMENT
   PANEL
4 FUSE BOX, INSTRUMENT PANEL
5 DOOR, INSTRUMENT PANEL FUSE BOX
6 SWITCH, INSTRUMENT PANEL LOWER
   COMPARTMENT LIGHT
7 COVER, INSTRUMENT PANEL LOWER
   COMPARTMENT LIGHT SWITCH
8 OUTLET, HEATER AND AIR CONDITIONING
9 PLATE, INSTRUMENT PANEL TRIM
10 STRIKER, INSTRUMENT PANEL LOWER
   COMPARTMENT
11 BIN, INSTRUMENT PANEL LOWER
   COMPARTMENT
12 COMPARTMENT ASSEMBLY, INSTRUMENT PANEL
   LOWER
13 DOOR, INSTRUMENT PANEL LOWER
   COMPARTMENT
14 HINGE, INSTRUMENT PANEL LOWER
   COMPARTMENT
15 INSULATOR, INSTRUMENT PANEL RIGHT SOUND
16 CONTROL, HEATER AND AIR CONDITIONING
17 PLATE, INSTRUMENT PANEL CLUSTER TRIM
18 OUTLET, HEATER AND AIR CONDITIONING
19 PLUG, INSTRUMENT PANEL
20 SWITCH, HEADLAMP
21 COMPARTMENT, FRONT FLOOR CONSOLE FRONT
23 RETAINER, FRONT FLOOR CONSOLE
24 PLATE, FRONT FLOOR CONSOLE TRANSAXLE
   SHIFT OPENING TRIM
25 HOUSING, FRONT FLOOR CONSOLE LIGHTER
   ELEMENT
26 ELEMENT, FRONT FLOOR CONSOLE LIGHTER
27 ASHTRAY, FRONT FLOOR CONSOLE
28 LENS, FRONT FLOOR CONSOLE TRANSAXLE
   SHIFT OPENING TRIM PLATE
29 TRIM, FRONT FLOOR CONSOLE ARMREST
30 ARMREST, FRONT FLOOR CONSOLE
31 MAT, FRONT FLOOR CONSOLE
32 ASHTRAY, FRONT FLOOR CONSOLE REAR
33 CONSOLE, FRONT FLOOR
34 CUP HOLDER, FRONT FLOOR CONSOLE
35 PLATE, FRONT FLOOR CONSOLE TRIM
36 CLUSTER, INSTRUMENT
37 SWITCH, REAR COMPARTMENT LID RELEASE
38 ASHTRAY, INSTRUMENT PANEL
39 CUP HOLDER, INSTRUMENT PANEL
40 FILLER, INSTRUMENT PANEL STEERING COLUMN
   OPENING
41 INSULATOR, INSTRUMENT PANEL LEFT SOUND
42 AUDIO SYSTEM
43 INSTRUMENT PANEL ASSEMBLY

93111G03

Exploded view of the instrument panel—1998–01 Century, Grand Prix, Intrigue, Lumina, Monte Carlo and Regal

install the fuel injector sight shield by performing the following procedures:

   a. Remove the oil filler cap/tube assembly from the valve cover.

   b. Slide the fuel injector sight shield into the rear engine bracket and lower it into place.

   c. Reinstall the oil filler cap/tube assembly in the valve cover. Twist it clockwise to lock the detent on the tube into the notch in the valve cover.

13. If equipped with a 3.1L engine, install the air cleaner and duct assembly.

14. Connect the negative battery cable.

Grand Prix, Intrigue and Regal

REMOVAL & INSTALLATION

1998–01 Models

   1. Disconnect the negative battery cable.

   2. Drain the engine coolant into a clean container for reuse.

   3. On Grand Prix or Regal equipped with a 3.1L engine, remove the air cleaner and duct assembly.

   4. On Grand Prix or Regal equipped

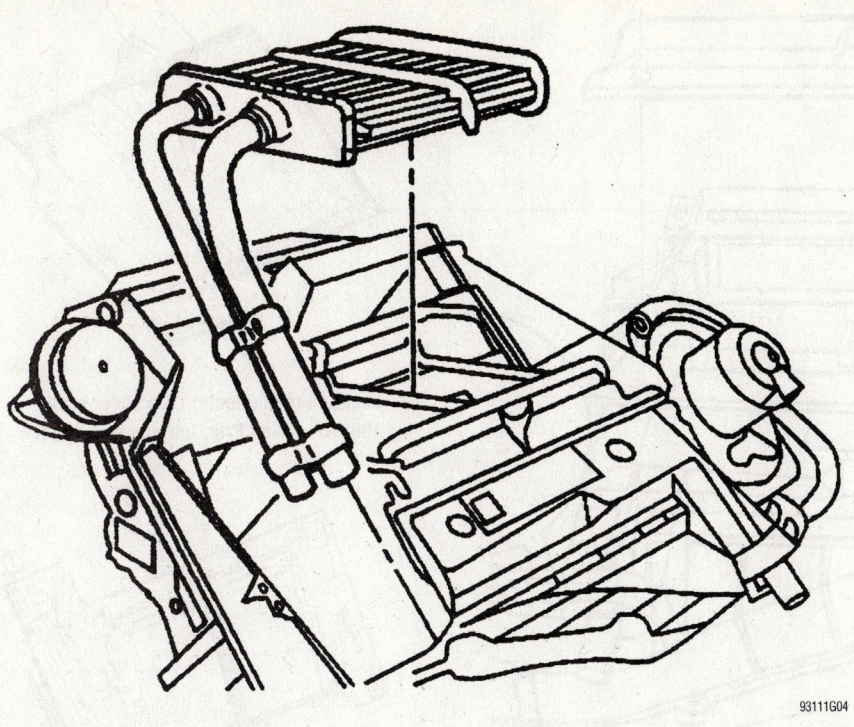

View of the heater core—1998–01 Century, Grand Prix, Intrigue, Lumina, Monte Carlo and Regal

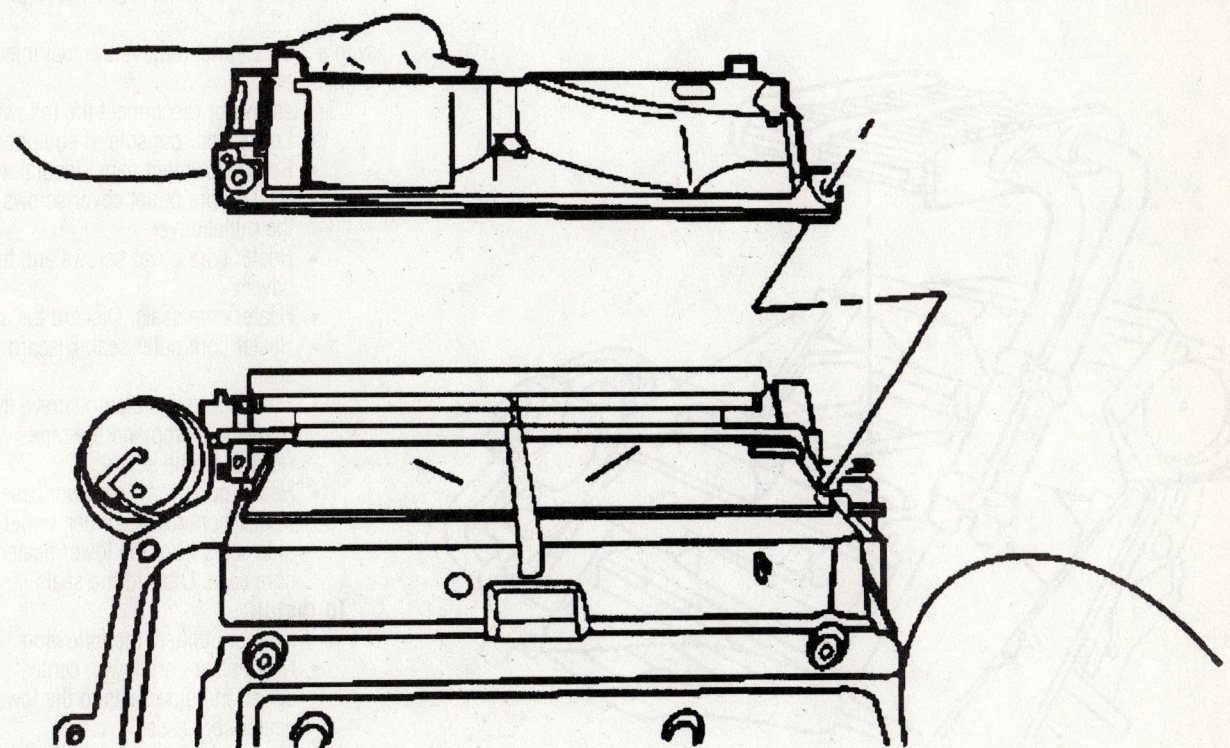

View of the heater core outlet cover—1998–01 Grand Prix, Intrigue and Regal

Refer to the model specific sections for engine mechanical service procedures

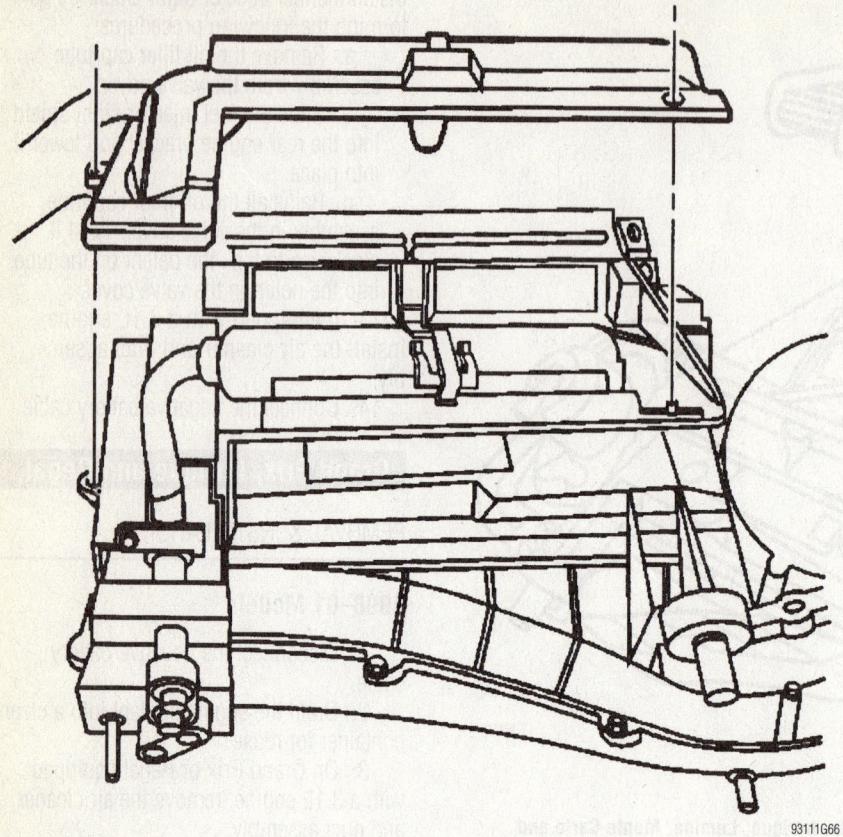

View of the heater core cover—1998–01 Grand Prix, Intrigue and Regal

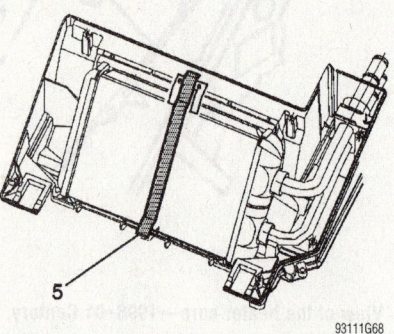

Location of the heater core cover seals—
1998–01 Grand Prix, Intrigue and Regal

View of the heater core outer seal—
1998–01 Grand Prix, Intrigue and Regal

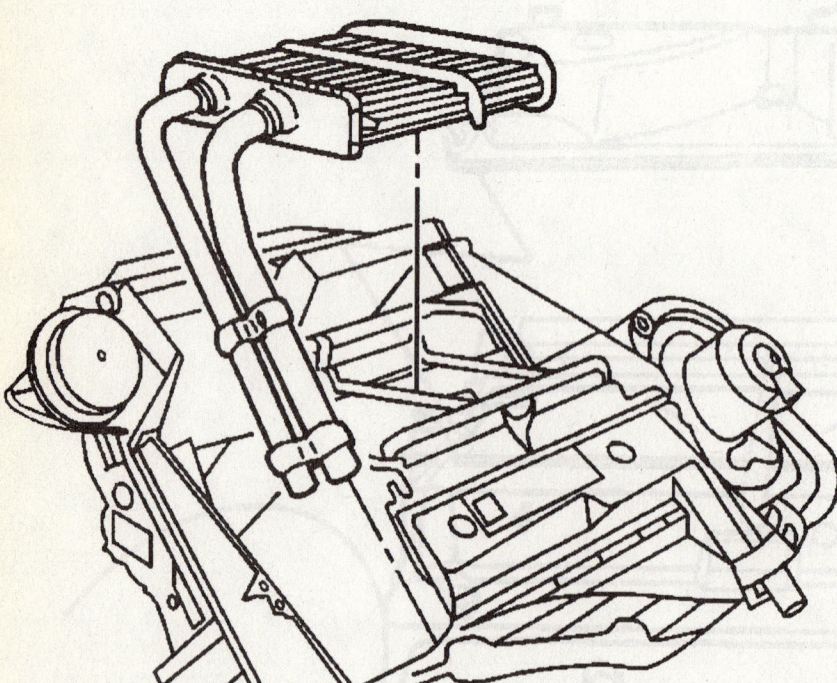

View of the heater core—1998–01 Grand Prix, Intrigue and Regal

with a 3.8L engine, remove the fuel injector sight shield.

5. Remove or disconnect the following:
- Lower floor console, if equipped
- Both instrument panel insulators
- Heater core outlet cover screws and the outlet cover
- Heater core cover screws and the cover
- Heater core seals. Discard the seals
- Heater core outer seal. Discard the seal
- Heater core line clamp screw, the retaining clamp and the pipe retainer clamp screw
- Heater core from the lower case
- Heater core lower, center, upper and side seals from the lower heater core case. Discard the seals

To install:
6. Install or connect the following:
- New heater core lower, center, upper and side seals to the lower heater core case
- Heater core to the lower case
- Pipe retainer clamp screw, the retaining clamp and the heater core line clamp screw
- Heater core outer seal

- Heater core seals
- Heater core cover and the outlet cover screws, then, tighten the screws to 13 inch lbs. (1.5 Nm)
- Heater core outlet cover and the outlet cover screws, then, tighten the screws to 13 inch lbs. (1.5 Nm)
- Both instrument panel insulators
- Lower floor console, if equipped

7. On Grand Prix or Regal equipped with a 3.8L engine, install the fuel injector sight shield.

8. On Grand Prix or Regal equipped with a 3.1L engine, install the air cleaner and duct assembly.

9. Refill the engine cooling system.

10. Connect the negative battery cable.

11. Operate the engine to normal operating temperatures; then, check the climate control operation and check for leaks.

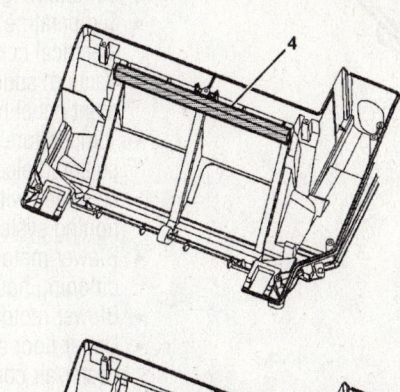

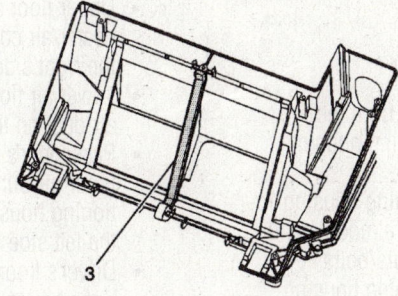

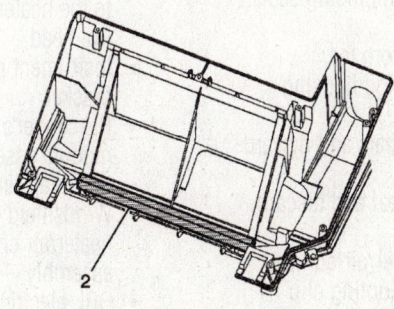

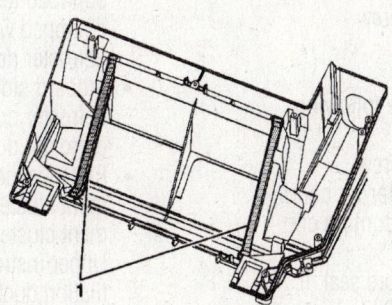

93111G70

View of the heater core lower, center, upper and side seals of the lower heater core case— 1998–01 Grand Prix, Intrigue and Regal

Corvette

✵✵ CAUTION

Some vehicles are equipped an SIR or air bag system. The air bag system must be disabled before performing service on or around the air bag, instrument panel components, wiring and sensors. Failure to follow safety and disabling procedures could result in accidental air bag deployment, possible personal injury and unnecessary air bag system repairs.

REMOVAL & INSTALLATION

1997–01 Models

1. If equipped, disable the SIR system by using the following procedure:

a. Remove the SIR fuse from the fuse panel.

b. Remove the left side sound insulator.

c. Disconnect the Connector Positive Assurance (CPA) from the yellow 2-way SIR harness connector at the base of the steering column and separate the connector.

d. Disconnect the negative battery cable.

2. Discharge and recover the air conditioning system refrigerant.

3. Drain the cooling system into a clean container for reuse.

4. Remove the heater/air conditioning housing assembly by removing or disconnecting the following:

- Intake manifold
- Heater hoses from the heater core
- Refrigerant lines from the evaporator core
- Drain tube from the heater/air conditioning housing assembly
- Upper instrument pad and the ventilation duct assembly
- Electrical connector from the instrument cluster and remove the instrument cluster
- Inboard side window glass defroster duct from the windshield defroster duct on both sides
- DRL electrical connector and the sun load temperature sensor from the windshield defroster duct, if equipped
- Windshield defroster duct from the

Refer to the model specific sections for cooling system service precautions

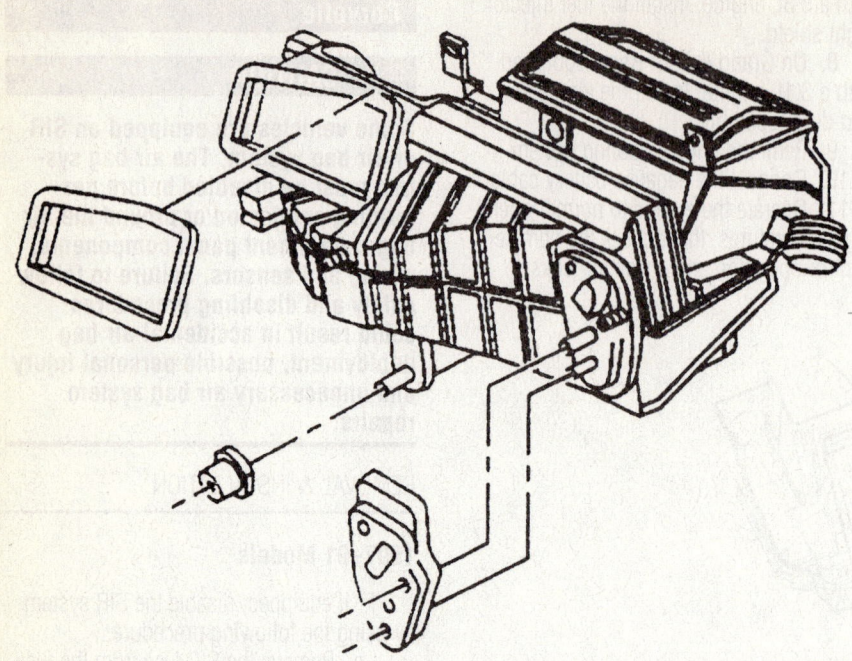

View of the heater/air conditioning housing assembly—1997–01 Corvette

heater/air conditioning housing assembly
- Inside air temperature sensor duct from the heater/air conditioning housing assembly
- Passenger's side SIR module electrical connector
- Passenger's side SIR bracket and module assembly
- Instrument panel center support bracket.
- Electrical and vacuum connectors from the heater/air conditioning control head
- Knee bolster
- Driver's floor hush panel
- Floor air outlet-to-heater/air conditioning housing assembly duct from the left side
- Passenger's side floor hush panel
- Lower air floor air duct from the upper air duct from the right side
- Upper floor air duct from the heater/air conditioning housing from the right side
- Blower motor electrical connector
- Blower motor from the heater/air conditioning housing
- Temperature door and the vacuum solenoid electrical connectors, if equipped with the CJ2 air conditioning system
- Vacuum source line from the instrument panel harness connection
- Temperature door control motor electrical connector

- Rear floor air ducts from the heater/air conditioning housing from both side
- Heater/air conditioning housing-to-bulkhead/heater core module and instrument panel nuts/bolts
- Heater/air conditioning housing assembly
- Air inlet, drain and plumbing seals. Discard the seals
- Heater core cover from the heater/air conditioning housing assembly
- Heater core cover seals and discard the seals
- Outer heater core seal and discard the seal
- Heater core-to-heater/air conditioning housing mounting clip screws
- Heater core pipe screw
- Heater core

To install:
5. Install or connect the following:
- Heater core
- Heater core pipe screw
- Heater core-to-heater/air conditioning housing mounting clip screws
- New outer heater core seal, if equipped with the CJ2 air conditioning system
- New heater core cover seals
- Heater core cover to the heater/air conditioning housing assembly
6. Install the heater/air conditioning

housing assembly by installing or connecting the following:
- New air inlet, drain and plumbing seals
- Heater/air conditioning housing assembly
- Heater/air conditioning housing-to-bulkhead/heater core module and instrument panel nuts/bolts
- Rear floor air ducts to the heater/air conditioning housing on both sides
- Temperature door control motor electrical connector
- Vacuum source line to the instrument panel harness connection
- Temperature door and the vacuum solenoid electrical connectors, if equipped with the CJ2 air conditioning system
- Blower motor to the heater/air conditioning housing
- Blower motor electrical connector
- Upper floor air duct to the heater/air conditioning housing on the right side
- Lower air floor air duct to the upper air duct on the right side
- Passenger's side floor hush panel
- Floor air outlet-to-heater/air conditioning housing assembly duct on the left side
- Driver's floor hush panel
- Knee bolster
- Electrical and vacuum connectors to the heater/air conditioning control head
- Instrument panel center support bracket
- Passenger's side SIR bracket and module assembly
- Inside air temperature sensor duct
- Windshield defroster duct to the heater/air conditioning housing assembly
- DRL electrical connector and the sun load temperature sensor, if equipped with a windshield defroster duct
- Inboard side window glass defroster duct to the windshield defroster duct on both sides
- Electrical connector to the instrument cluster and install the instrument cluster
- Upper instrument pad and the ventilation duct assembly
- Drain tube to the heater/air conditioning housing assembly
- Refrigerant lines to the evaporator core
- Heater hoses to the heater core
- Intake manifold

7. Refill the cooling system.

8. Evacuate, charge and leak test the air conditioning system refrigerant.

9. Connect the negative battery cable.

10. If equipped, enable the SIR system by performing the following procedure:

a. Connect the Connector Positive Assurance (CPA) to the yellow 2-way SIR harness connector at the base of the steering column.

b. Install the left side sound insulator.

c. Install the SIR fuse to the fuse panel.

11. Operate the engine to normal operating temperatures; then, check the climate control operation and check for leaks.

GEO

Metro

REMOVAL & INSTALLATION

1997 Models

1. Disconnect the negative battery cable.

2. Properly drain the cooling system into a clean container for reuse.

3. Remove the instrument panel by removing or disconnect the following:

※ CAUTION

The Supplemental Inflatable Restraint (SIR) system must be disabled prior to performing this service.

- Inflator module from the steering wheel, convertible models only
- Lower steering column trim panel
- Steering wheel, convertible models only
- SIR coil/combination switch assembly, convertible models only
- Combination switch from the steering wheel, hardtop models only

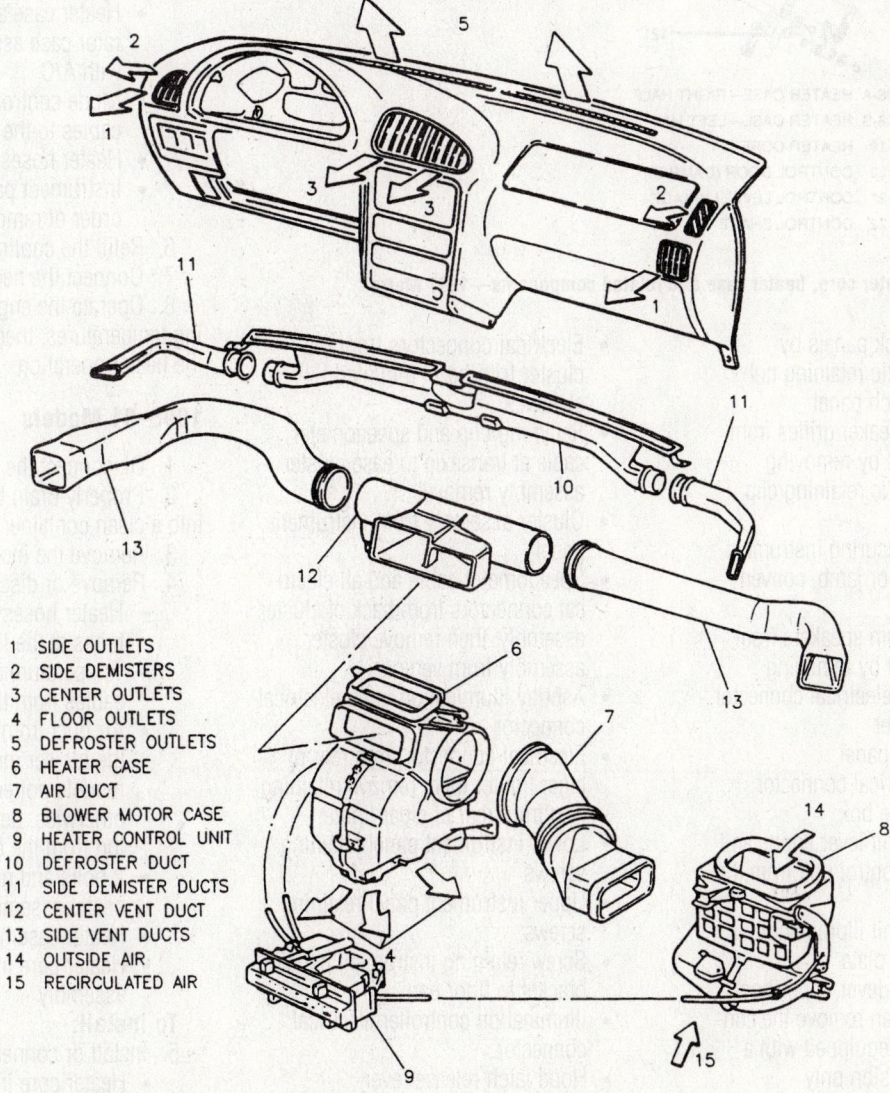

1 SIDE OUTLETS
2 SIDE DEMISTERS
3 CENTER OUTLETS
4 FLOOR OUTLETS
5 DEFROSTER OUTLETS
6 HEATER CASE
7 AIR DUCT
8 BLOWER MOTOR CASE
9 HEATER CONTROL UNIT
10 DEFROSTER DUCT
11 SIDE DEMISTER DUCTS
12 CENTER VENT DUCT
13 SIDE VENT DUCTS
14 OUTSIDE AIR
15 RECIRCULATED AIR

93111GC3

Exploded view of the instrument panel, heater housing, ventilation ducts and related components

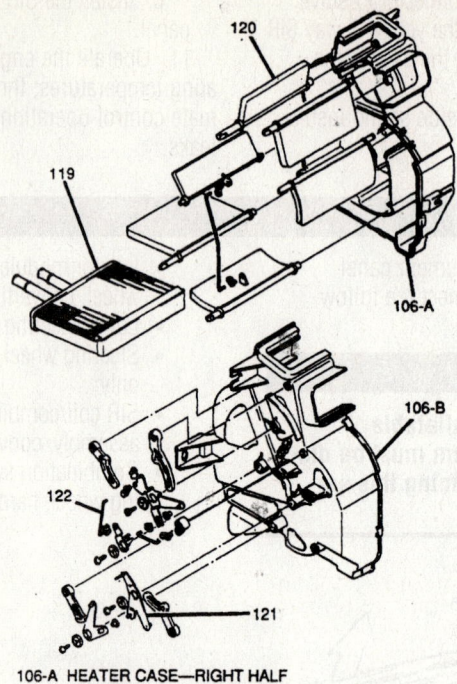

106-A HEATER CASE—RIGHT HALF
106-B HEATER CASE—LEFT HALF
119 HEATER CORE
120 CONTROL DOOR (DAMPER)
121 CONTROL LEVEL LINKAGE
122 CONTROL SHAFT

93111GC4

Exploded view of the heater core, heater case and related components—1997 Metro

- Right and left kick panels by removing a plastic retaining nut and clip from each panel
- Right and left speaker grilles from instrument panel by removing screws and plastic retaining clip from each grille
- Retaining clip securing instrument panel to each door jamb, convertible models only
- Right and left from speakers from instrument panel by removing screws and one electrical connector from each speaker
- Glove box inner panel
- A/C switch electrical connector through the glove box
- Heater control unit lever knobs and pull the heater control unit from the instrument panel
- Heater control unit illumination lamp from cover plate
- Gearshift control lever upper boot from console, then remove the console, on models equipped with a manual transmission only
- Ashtray
- Center console trim bezel and instrument panel center trim bezel. Remove the radio

- Electrical connectors from the cluster trim bezel mounted switches
- Retaining clip and speedometer cable at transaxle to ease cluster assembly removal
- Cluster assembly from instrument panel
- Speedometer cable and all electrical connectors from back of cluster assembly, then remove cluster assembly from vehicle
- Ashtray illumination lamp electrical connector
- Electrical connector from rear of cigar lighter then, remove retaining ring from rear of cigar lighter
- Lower instrument panel retaining screws
- Upper instrument panel retaining screws
- Screw retaining instrument panel bracket to floor pan
- Illumination controller electrical connector
- Hood latch release lever
- Instrument panel from vehicle
4. Remove or disconnect the following:
   - Heater hoses from the heater core tubes at the firewall

- Temperature and mode control cables from the heater housing
- Air duct from the heater housing to the blower motor assembly (on models not equipped with air conditioning); otherwise, detach the heater housing from the evaporator assembly
- 2 bolts and nuts and remove the heater assembly
- Heater case halves
- Heater core from the heater case assembly

To install:
5. Install or connect the following:
   - Heater core into the heater case assembly
   - Assemble heater case assembly
   - Heater assembly and install the 2 bolts and nuts
   - Heater case assembly to the evaporator case assembly, if equipped with A/C
   - Mode control and the temperature cables to the heater housing
   - Heater hoses to the heater core
   - Instrument panel in the reverse order of removal
6. Refill the cooling system.
7. Connect the negative battery cable.
8. Operate the engine to normal operating temperatures; then, check for leaks and the heater operation.

1998–01 Models

1. Disconnect the negative battery cable.
2. Properly drain the cooling system into a clean container for reuse.
3. Remove the instrument panel.
4. Remove or disconnect the following:
   - Heater hoses from the heater core tubes at the firewall
   - Temperature and mode control cables from the heater housing
   - Air duct from the heater housing to the blower motor assembly (on models not equipped with A/C); otherwise, detach the heater housing from the evaporator assembly
   - 2 bolts and nuts and remove the heater assembly
   - Heater case halves
   - Heater core from the heater case assembly

To install:
5. Install or connect the following:
   - Heater core into the heater case assembly
   - Assemble the heater case assembly
   - Heater assembly and install the 2 bolts and nuts

- Heater case assembly to the evaporator case assembly, if equipped with A/C
- Mode control and the temperature cables to the heater housing
- Heater hoses to the heater core

6. Install the instrument panel.
7. Refill the cooling system.
8. Connect the negative battery cable.
9. Operate the engine to normal operating temperatures; then, check for leaks and the heater operation.

Prizm

REMOVAL & INSTALLATION

1997 Models

1. Disconnect the negative battery cable.
2. Drain the cooling system into a clean container for reuse.
3. Remove or disconnect the following:
   - Steering wheel
   - Trim bezel from the instrument panel
   - Cup holder from the console
   - Radio
4. Remove the instrument cluster, instrument panel, console and all console trim by removing or disconnecting the following:
   - Disable the SRS system
   - A-pillar lower trim panel from both sides
   - 1 nut from each kick panel and panels from the vehicle

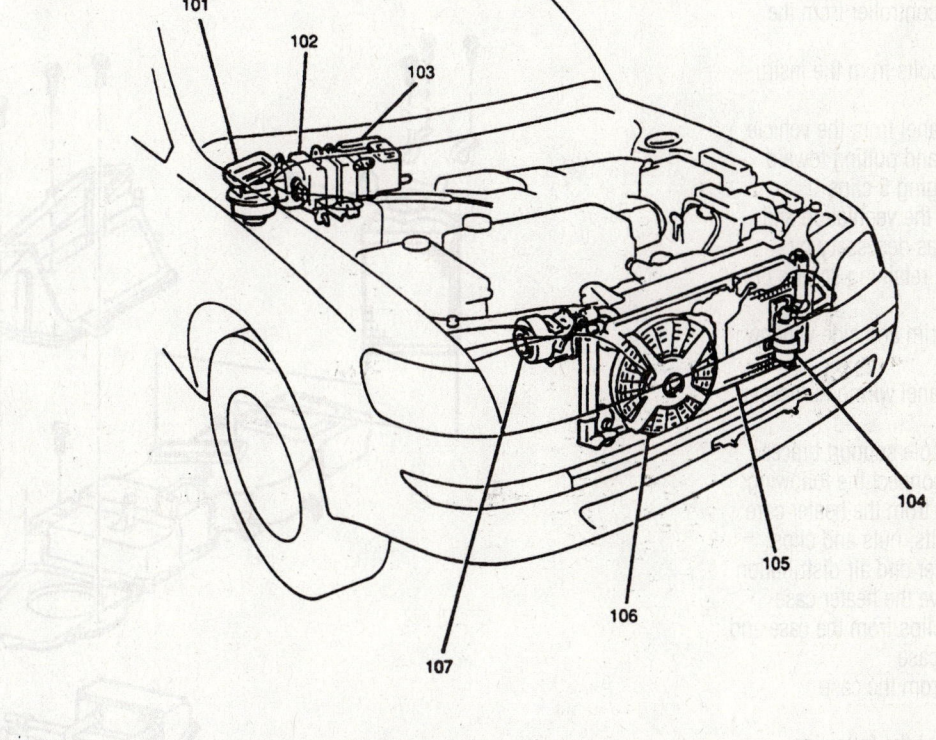

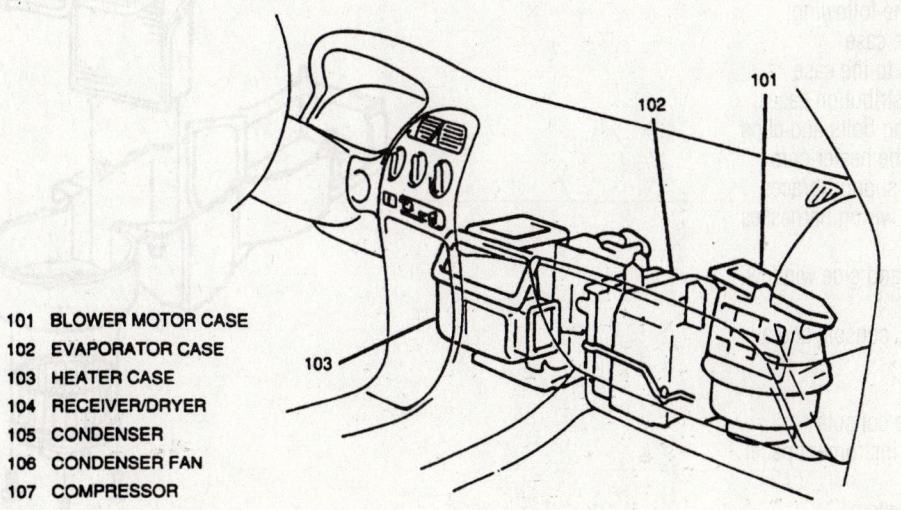

101	BLOWER MOTOR CASE
102	EVAPORATOR CASE
103	HEATER CASE
104	RECEIVER/DRYER
105	CONDENSER
106	CONDENSER FAN
107	COMPRESSOR

93111G64

View of the climate control system—1997 Prizm

- Steering wheel
- 5 screws and steering column upper and lower trim panels
- Center console
- 2 screws and the instrument cluster trim panel, disengaging 2 lower clips
- 4 screws and the instrument cluster assembly, disconnecting 3 electrical connectors
- Illumination control knob
- 1 nut from illumination controller
- 4 clips and the instrument panel left side outlet trim bezel
- Illumination controller electrical connector
- Illumination controller from the vehicle
- 4 mounting bolts from the instrument panel
- Instrument panel from the vehicle by lifting up and pulling toward rear, disengaging 5 clips
- Disassemble the ventilation and heater ducts as necessary by removing the retaining screws or clips
- Lower dash trim and side window air deflectors
- Instrument panel wiring harnesses and cables
- 2 center console support braces

5. Remove or disconnect the following:
- Heater hoses from the heater core
- Mounting bolts, nuts and clips from the heater and air distribution cases. Remove the heater case
- Screws and clips from the case and separate the case
- Heater core from the case

To install:

6. Install or connect the following:
- Heater core to the case
- Screws and clips to the case
- Heater and air distribution cases; then, the mounting bolts and clips
- Heater hoses to the heater core
- 2 center console support braces
- Instrument panel wiring harnesses and cables
- Lower dash trim and side window air deflectors
- Instrument panel, console and all console trim
- Radio
- Cup holder to the console
- Trim bezel to the instrument panel
- Steering wheel

7. Refill the cooling system.
8. Connect the negative battery cable.
9. Operate the engine to normal operating temperatures; then, check the heating system operation and check for leaks.

1998–01 Models

1. Disconnect the negative battery cable.
2. Drain the cooling system into a clean container for reuse.
3. Discharge and recover the air conditioning system refrigerant.
4. Remove the heater hoses from the heater core.
5. Remove the instrument panel by removing or disconnecting the following:
- Steering wheel-disarm air bag system if so equipped
- Right and left front pillar garnish trim
- Floor console bin

- Engine hood release lever
- Lower finish No. 1 trim panel
- Steering column cover
- Center cluster finish panel
- Cluster finish panel
- Radio
- Stereo opening cover or center differential control switch if so equipped
- Combination meter assembly
- Lower finish No. 2 panel with glove compartment door
- Heater control assembly
- Lower center finish panel

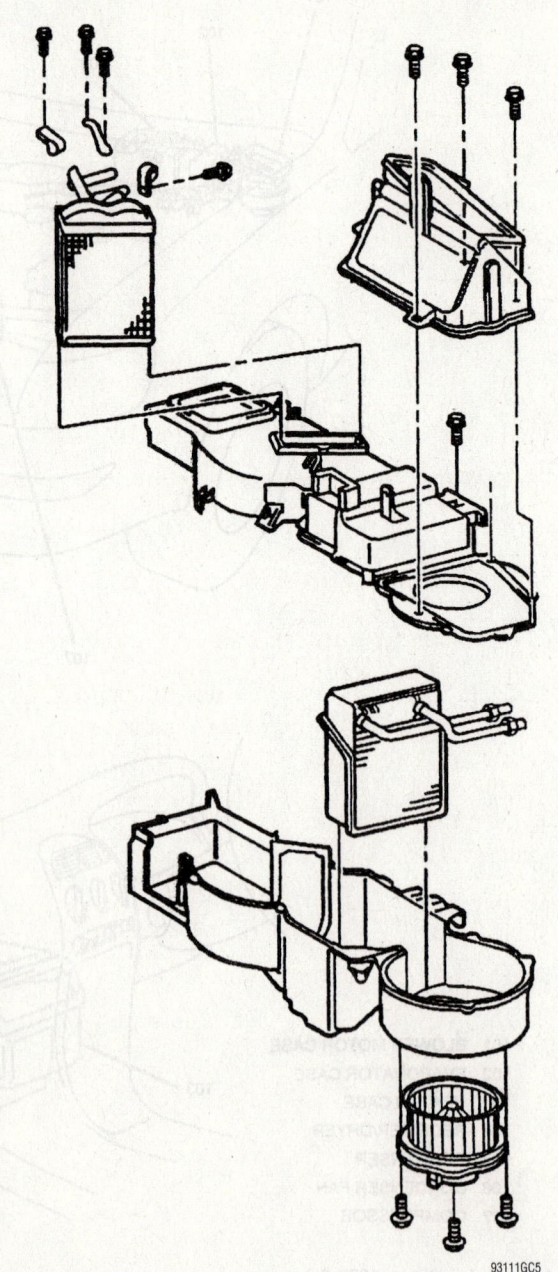

Exploded view of the heater core, the evaporator core, the heater/air conditioning housing and related components—1998–01 Prizm

93111GC5

➡**The defroster nozzle has a boss on the reverse side for clamping onto the clip on the body side. When removing, pull upward at an angle.**

- No. 1 and No. 2 side defroster nozzles
- Safety pad assembly from the vehicle

6. Remove or disconnect the following:
- Instrument panel reinforcement
- Blower motor electrical connector and resistor electrical connector
- Air conditioning compressor control module electrical connector, if equipped
- Cruise control servo
- Refrigerant lines from the evaporator core; then, plug the openings to prevent contamination
- Ventilation ducts from the heater/air conditioning housing
- 6 heater/air conditioning housing assembly-to-chassis nuts and the assembly
- Heater core-to-heater/air conditioning housing clamp screws and the clamps
- Heater core

To install:

7. Install or connect the following:
- Heater core
- Heater core-to-heater/air conditioning housing clamps and the clamp screws

8. Install the heater/air conditioning housing assembly by installing or connecting the following:
- Heater/air conditioning housing assembly and the 6 assembly-to-chassis nuts
- Ventilation ducts to the heater/air conditioning housing
- Refrigerant lines to the evaporator core
- Cruise control servo, if equipped
- Air conditioning compressor control module electrical connector
- Blower motor electrical connector and resistor electrical connector
- Instrument panel reinforcement

9. Install the instrument panel by installing or connecting the following:
- Safety pad assembly in the vehicle
- No. 1 and No. 2 side defroster nozzles
- Lower center finish panel
- Heater control assembly
- Lower finish No. 2 panel with glove compartment door
- Combination meter assembly

- Stereo opening cover or center differential control switch if so equipped
- Radio
- Cluster finish panel
- Center cluster finish panel
- Steering column covers
- No. 1 lower finish panel
- Engine hood release lever
- Floor console box
- Right and left front pillar garnish trim
- Steering wheel

10. Install the heater hoses to the heater core.

11. Evacuate, charge and leak test the air conditioning system refrigerant.

12. Refill the cooling system.

13. Connect the negative battery cable.

Saturn

REMOVAL & INSTALLATION

1997–01 Models

1. Disconnect the negative battery cable.
2. Drain the cooling system into a clean container for reuse.
3. Raise and safely support the vehicle.
4. Move the heater hose-to-heater core clamps up the heater hoses.

➡**Carefully, use compressed air to blow the remainder of the coolant from the heater core to prevent spillage of coolant in the interior when removing the heater core.**

5. Remove or disconnect the following
- Lower trim panel extensions (located at both sides of the console-to-center instrument panel), by pulling outward at the dual lock locations; then, rotate the panels outward to disengage the hinges at the console
- Lower instrument panel closeout panel (located on the right side of the heater/air conditioning housing), by pulling it out at the top edge and rotating the top downward
- Lower heater duct-to-heater/air conditioning housing 2 screws and 2 clips (located at the bottom of the heater/air conditioning housing); then, drop the duct down and carefully, slide it out sideways

✳✳ WARNING

Be careful not to damage the heater duct-to-rear floor heater duct seal.

- Release the retaining clip and disconnect the temperature control cable from the heater door hook

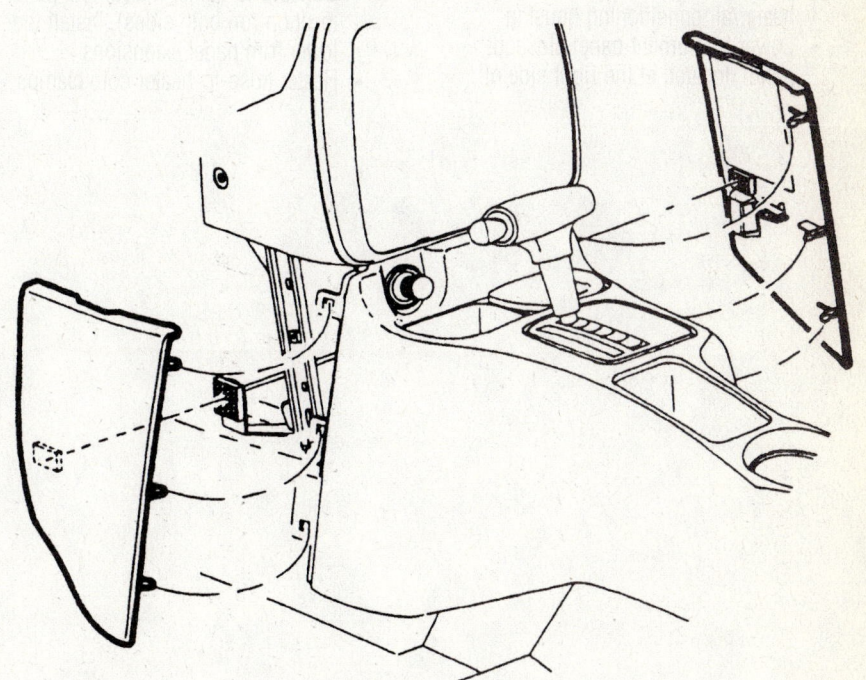

View of the lower trim panel extensions—1997–01 Saturn

93111G97

Refer to the model specific sections for engine mechanical service procedures

- Heater core side cover screw and the cover, located at the left side of the heater/air conditioning housing assembly
- 4 lower heater core cover-to-heater/air conditioning housing assembly screws and the cover
- Heater core-to-heater/air conditioning housing assembly screw, the clamp and the heater core

To install:

6. Install or connect the following:
   - Heater core, the clamp and the heater core-to-heater/air conditioning housing assembly screw
   - Lower heater core cover and the 4 cover-to-heater/air conditioning housing assembly screws
   - Heater core side cover and the cover screw, located at the left side of the heater/air conditioning housing assembly
   - Temperature control cable to the heater door hook and secure with the retaining clip

❄❄ WARNING

Be careful not to damage the heater duct-to-rear floor heater duct seal

- Lower heater duct; then, the lower heater duct-to-heater/air conditioning housing 2 screws and 2 clips, located at the bottom of the heater/air conditioning housing
- Lower instrument panel closeout panel, located at the right side of

the heater/air conditioning housing
- Console-to-center instrument panel location (on both sides), install the lower trim panel extensions
- Heater hose-to-heater core clamps

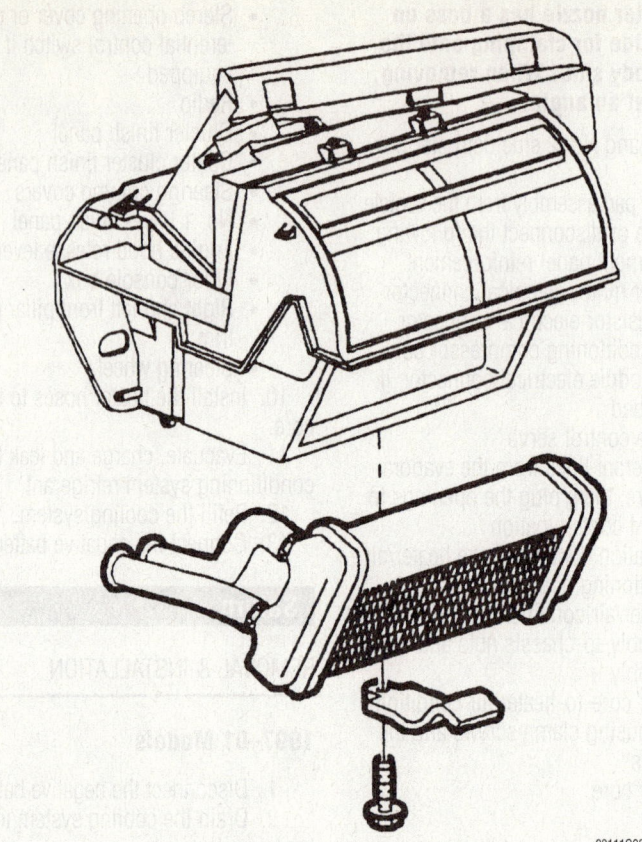

Exploded view of the heater core and heater case—1997–01 Saturn

93111G98

7. Lower the vehicle.
8. Refill the cooling system.
9. Connect the negative battery cable.
10. Operate the engine to normal operating temperatures; then, check the climate control operation and check for leaks.

CHRYSLER CORPORATION

Chrysler-Concorde • LHS • 300M • **Dodge**-Intrepid • **Eagle**-Vision

PRECAUTIONS

Before servicing any vehicle, please be sure to read all of the following precautions, which deal with personal safety, prevention of component damage, and important points to take into consideration when servicing a motor vehicle:

• Never open, service or drain the radiator or cooling system when the engine is hot; serious burns can occur from the steam and hot coolant.

• Observe all applicable safety precautions when working around fuel. Whenever servicing the fuel system, always work in a well-ventilated area. Do not allow fuel spray or vapors to come in contact with a spark, open flame or excessive heat (a hot drop light, for example). Keep a dry chemical fire extinguisher near the work area. Always keep fuel in a container specifically designed for fuel storage; also, always properly seal fuel containers to avoid the possibility of fire or explosion. Refer to the additional fuel system precautions later in this section.

• Fuel injection systems often remain pressurized, even after the engine has been turned **OFF**. The fuel system pressure must be relieved before disconnecting any fuel lines. Failure to do so may result in fire and/or personal injury.

• Brake fluid often contains polyglycol ethers and polyglycols. Avoid contact with the eyes and wash your hands thoroughly after handling brake fluid. If you do get brake fluid in your eyes, flush your eyes with clean, running water for 15 minutes. If eye irritation persists, or if you have taken brake fluid internally, IMMEDIATELY seek medical assistance.

• The EPA warns that prolonged contact with used engine oil may cause a number of skin disorders, including cancer! You should make every effort to minimize your exposure to used engine oil. Protective gloves should be worn when changing oil. Wash your hands and any other exposed skin areas as soon as possible after exposure to used engine oil. Soap and water, or waterless hand cleaner should be used.

• All new vehicles are now equipped with an air bag system. The system must be disabled before performing service on or around system components, steering column, instrument panel components, wiring

and sensors. Failure to follow safety and disabling procedures could result in accidental air bag deployment, possible personal injury and unnecessary system repairs.

• Always wear safety goggles when working with, or around, the air bag system. When carrying a non-deployed air bag, be sure the bag and trim cover are pointed away from your body. When placing a non-deployed air bag on a work surface, always face the bag and trim cover upward, away from the surface. This will reduce the motion of the module if it is accidentally deployed. Refer to the additional air bag system precautions later in this section.

• Clean, high quality brake fluid from a sealed container is essential to the safe and proper operation of the brake system. You should always buy the correct type of brake fluid for your vehicle. If the brake fluid becomes contaminated, completely flush the system with new fluid. Never reuse any brake fluid. Any brake fluid that is removed from the system should be discarded. Also, do not allow any brake fluid to come in contact with a painted surface; it will damage the paint.

• Never operate the engine without the proper amount and type of engine oil; doing so WILL result in severe engine damage.

• Timing belt maintenance is extremely important! Many models utilize an interference-type, non-freewheeling engine. If the timing belt breaks, the valves in the cylinder head may strike the pistons, causing potentially serious (also time-consuming and expensive) engine damage. Refer to the maintenance interval charts in the front of this manual for the recommended replacement interval for the timing belt, and to the timing belt section for belt replacement and inspection.

• Disconnecting the negative battery cable on some vehicles may interfere with the functions of the on-board computer system(s) and may require the computer to undergo a relearning process once the negative battery cable is reconnected.

• When servicing drum brakes, only disassemble and assemble one side at a time, leaving the remaining side intact for reference.

• Only an MVAC-trained, EPA-certified automotive technician should service the air conditioning system or its components.

ENGINE REPAIR

Alternator

REMOVAL

2.7L Engine

1. Remove or disconnect the following:
   • Negative battery cable
   • Lower plastic splash shield
   • Transmission cooler and position it aside
   • Lower radiator crossmember support
2. Loosen:
   • Adjusting "T" bolt and the pivot bolt
   • Drive belt adjusting bolt
3. Remove or disconnect the following:
   • Drive belt
   • Alternator field circuit plug
   • Alternator B+ terminal nut and wire
   • Pivot bolt; be careful not to lose the spacer
   • Alternator

3.3L Engine

1. Remove or disconnect the following:
   • Negative battery cable
   • Alternator field circuit plug
   • Alternator B+ terminal nut and wire
2. Loosen:
   • Adjusting "T" bolt and the pivot bolt
   • Drive belt tension bolt
3. Remove or disconnect the following:
   • Drive belt
   • Adjusting "T" bolt and the pivot bolt; be careful not to lose the spacer
   • Alternator

3.2L and 3.5L Engines

1. Disconnect the negative battery cable.
2. Loosen:
   • Lower mounting bolt and pivot bolt
   • Drive belt tension bolt
3. Remove or disconnect the following:
   • Drive belt
   • Bracket, lower mounting bolt and pivot bolt
   • Alternator
   • Alternator field circuit plug
   • Alternator B+ terminal nut and wire

INSTALLATION

2.7L Engine

1. Install or connect the following:
   - Alternator
   - Pivot bolt with the spacer and leave loose
   - Alternator field circuit plug
   - Alternator B+ wire and terminal nut; then, torque the nut to 90 inch lbs. (10 Nm)
   - Drive belt.
2. Using a belt tension gauge, tighten the adjusting "T" bolt until the tension gauge reads 120 lbs. (534 N) for a used belt or 180–200 lbs. (792–880 N) for new belt.
3. Install:
   - Lower radiator crossmember support
   - Transmission cooler
   - Lower plastic splash shield
   - Negative battery cable
4. Torque:
   - Pivot bolt to 40 ft. lbs. (54 Nm)
   - 8mm mounting bolt to 30 ft. lbs. (41 Nm)
   - 10mm mounting bolt to 40 ft. lbs. (54 Nm)

3.3L Engine

1. Install or connect the following:
   - Alternator
   - Pivot bolt (with spacer) and adjusting "T" bolt
   - Drive belt
2. Using a belt tension gauge, tighten the adjusting "T" bolt until the tension gauge reads 120 lbs. (534 N) for a used belt or 140–160 lbs. (623–711 N) for new belt.
3. Torque the pivot and adjusting bolts to 40 ft. lbs. (54 Nm).
4. Install or connect the following:
   - Alternator B+ wire and terminal nut; then, torque the nut to 90 inch lbs. (10 Nm)
   - Alternator field circuit plug
   - Negative battery cable

3.5L (VIN F) Engine

1. Install or connect the following:
   - Alternator B+ wire and terminal nut; then, torque the nut to 90 inch lbs. (10 Nm)
   - Alternator field circuit plug
   - Alternator
   - Drive belt
   - Pivot bolt and lower mounting bolt

2. Using a belt tension gauge, tighten the drive belt until the tension gauge reads 120 lbs. (534 N) for a used belt or 140–160 lbs. (623–711 N) for new belt.
3. Torque the pivot and lower mounting bolts to 40 ft. lbs. (54 Nm).
4. Connect or install:
   - Bracket
   - Negative battery cable

3.2L and 3.5L (VIN G) Engines

1. Install or connect the following:
   - Alternator B+ wire and terminal nut; then, torque the nut to 90 inch lbs. (10 Nm)
   - Alternator field circuit plug
   - Alternator
   - Drive belt
   - Pivot bolt and lower mounting bolt
2. Using a belt tension gauge, tighten the "V" drive belt until the tension gauge reads 120 lbs. (534 N) for a used belt or 140–160 lbs. (623–711 N) for new belt.
3. Using a belt tension gauge, tighten the Poly "V" belt until the tension gauge reads 120 lbs. (534 N) for a used belt or 180–200 lbs. (792–880 N) for new belt.
4. Install the bracket.

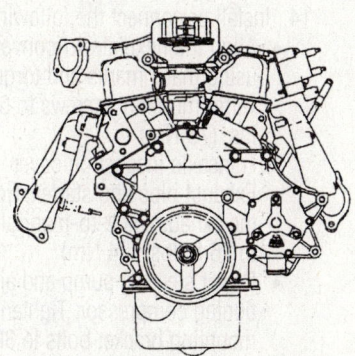
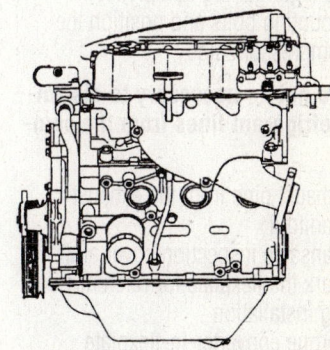

Engine front and side views—3.3L engines

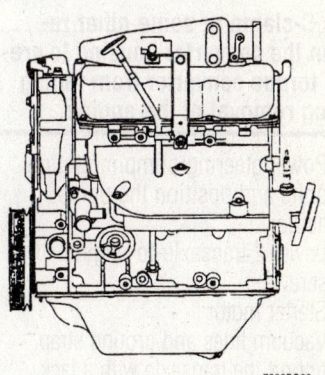

Engine front and side views—1997 3.5L engines

5. Torque:
   - Pivot bolt to 40 ft. lbs. (54 Nm)
   - 8mm mounting bolt to 30 ft. lbs. (41 Nm)
   - 10mm mounting bolt to 40 ft. lbs. (54 Nm)
6. Connect the negative battery cable.

Ignition Timing

ADJUSTMENT

All models utilize a Distributorless Ignition System (DIS). It is a fixed ignition timing system, which means that basic ignition timing cannot be adjusted. All spark advance is permanently set by the Powertrain Control Module (PCM).

Engine Assembly

REMOVAL & INSTALLATION

1997 Models

1. Before servicing the vehicle, refer to the precautions in the beginning of this section.

2. Properly relieve the fuel system pressure.

3. Drain the cooling system.

4. Drain the engine oil.

5. Remove or disconnect the following:
- Hood
- Negative battery cable
- Radiator and cooling fan assemblies
- All electrical connections
- Coolant hoses from the engine

6. Disconnect the fuel lines using the following procedure:

a. At the fuel rail, push the quick-connect fitting toward the fuel tube while depressing the built-in disconnect tool with Quick-Connect Fitting tool 6751 or equivalent.

b. Slightly, twist the fitting while maintaining downward pressure on tool 6751.

c. Wrap shop towels around the fuel hoses to absorb any fuel spillage and be sure to cover the openings to prevent system contamination.

7. Remove or disconnect the following:

- Accelerator and cruise control cables from the throttle body
- Air cleaner assembly
- Air conditioning compressor mounting bolts and position the compressor aside

➡ It should not be necessary to disconnect the refrigerant lines from the compressor.

- Exhaust pipe from the exhaust manifold
- Transaxle inspection cover and mark the flexplate for reference during installation
- Torque converter-to-flexplate screws

❋❋ WARNING

Attach a C-clamp or some other restraint on the converter housing to prevent the torque converter from falling out during removal of the engine.

- Power steering pump mounting bolts and position the pump aside
- Lower 2 transaxle-to-engine screws
- Starter motor
- Vacuum lines and ground strap.

8. Support the transaxle with a jack.

9. Attach an engine lifting hoist to the engine and support it.

10. Remove or disconnect the following:
- Upper transaxle mounting bolts

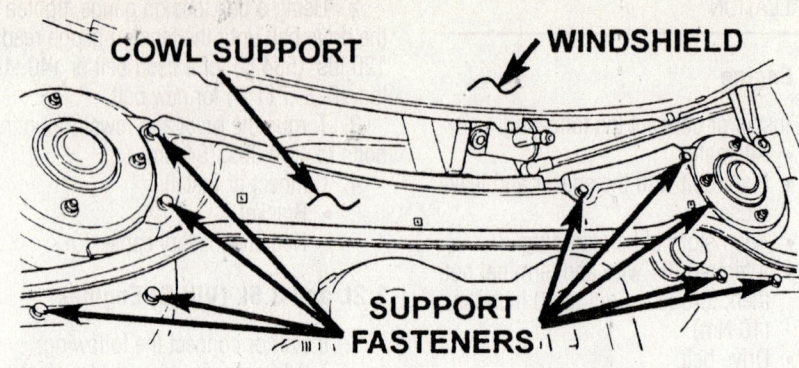

Remove the cowl support for clearance to remove the engine—2.7L engine

- Insulator mounting nuts from the engine mounts
- Engine

To install:

11. Install or connect the following:
- Engine. Align the engine mounts and tighten the mount fasteners to 45 ft. lbs. (61 Nm)
- Transaxle and tighten transaxle-to-engine bolts to 75 ft. lbs. (102 Nm)

12. Remove the engine hoist and the transaxle holding fixture.

13. Remove the C-clamp from the converter housing, if installed.

14. Install or connect the following:
- Align the flexplate-to-converter using matchmarks and torque converter mounting screws to 55 ft. lbs. (75 Nm)
- Transaxle inspection cover
- Exhaust pipe and starter. Tighten the exhaust pipe-to-manifold bolts to 25 ft. lbs. (34 Nm)
- Power steering pump and air conditioning compressor. Tighten the mounting bracket bolts to 30 ft. lbs. (41 Nm)
- All vacuum lines
- All electrical connectors and ground strap

15. Connect the fuel lines to the fuel rail as follows:

a. Be sure that the black plastic release ring in the quick-connect fitting is in the OUT position. Place Special tool 6751 under the largest diameter of the quick-connect fitting.

b. Pull tool 6751 toward the fuel rail until the quick-connect fitting clicks into place.

c. Place the special tool between the shoulder of the built-in disconnect tool and the top of the quick-connect fitting, then inspect the security of the fitting by applying a slight downward force against the fitting. It should be locked in place.

16. Install or connect the following:
- Accelerator and cruise control cables to the throttle lever
- Radiator and cooling fan assemblies
- Negative battery cable
- Hood

17. Refill crankcase and replace the oil filter, if necessary.

18. Refill and bleed the cooling system.

19. Check to be sure that all hoses, wiring connectors, cables, vacuum and fluid lines are reconnected.

20. Check all fluid levels.

21. Start the engine and allow it to reach normal operating temperatures. Inspect all fluid systems for leaks and correct level.

22. Road test the vehicle. Adjust the transaxle linkage, as necessary.

1998–01 Models

2.7L ENGINE

1. Before servicing the vehicle, refer to the precautions in the beginning of this section.

2. Relieve the fuel system pressure.

3. Drain the cooling system.

4. Drain the crankcase.

5. Remove or disconnect the following:
- Hood
- Negative battery cable at the remote terminal near the right strut tower.
- Wiper arms, cowl covers and cowl support
- Air intake duct and air cleaner assembly
- Upper radiator crossmember
- Hood release cable from the latch
- Cooling fan assembly
- Upper and lower radiator hoses
- Air conditioning condenser-to-radiator fasteners
- Radiator
- Accessory drive belts

- Power steering pump and position it aside without disconnecting the lines

➡ **Remove the alternator with the engine.**

- Air conditioning compressor and position it aside without disconnecting the lines
- V-band clamps at the exhaust manifolds
- Speed control and throttle cables from the throttle body
- Heater hoses and the coolant hoses at the recovery tank
- All vacuum lines, electrical connectors and ground straps from the engine
- Catalytic converter down pipes-to-rear mount fasteners
- Structural collar mounting bolts and collar

6. Matchmark the flexplate-to-torque converter and remove the torque converter bolts.

7. Remove or dicsonnect the following:
- Both transaxle cooler line-to-engine brackets
- Starter and Crankshaft Position (CKP) sensor
- 2 lower transaxle-to-engine bolts
- Exhaust Gas Recirculation (EGR) valve assembly
- Fuel line and engine harness from the throttle body bracket

8. Remove the following brackets from the double-ended transaxle-to-engine bolts:
- Wiring harness bracket
- Transaxle shift cable bracket
- Throttle body support bracket
- Upper transaxle-to-engine bolts
- Both (right and left) engine mount isolators-to-engine mount bracket fasteners

---

⁕⁕ **WARNING**

Be careful not to damage the intake manifold or cylinder head covers when lifting the engine.

9. Attach an engine lifting fixture to the engine.

10. Support the transaxle with a jack and remove the engine.

To install:

11. Install the engine.

12. Align the engine mounts and install the fasteners, but do not tighten them at this time.

⁕⁕ **WARNING**

Do not tighten the transaxle-to-engine bolts until all of the bolts have been hand-started and the engine is flush against the transaxle.

13. Install the transaxle-to-engine bolts. Tighten the bolts to 75 ft. lbs. (102 Nm).

14. Remove the engine support fixture.

15. Tighten the engine mount isolator-to-bracket fasteners to 45 ft. lbs. (61 Nm).

16. Align the matchmarks and install the flexplate-to-torque converter bolts. Tighten the bolts to 55 ft. lbs. (75 Nm).

17. Install the starter and the CKP sensor.

18. Install the structural collar using the following sub-steps:

   a. Torque the vertical collar-to-oil pan bolts to 10 inch lbs. (1.1 Nm).

   b. Torque the collar-to-transaxle bolts to 40 ft. lbs. (55 Nm).

   c. Torque the center vertical bolt to 40 ft. lbs. (55 Nm); then, the remaining vertical bolts to the same torque.

19. Complete the installation by reversing the removal procedure. Keep the following in mind:
- Use new V-band clamps and tighten them to 100 inch lbs. (11 Nm)
- Tighten the air conditioning compressor and power steering pump fasteners to 21 ft. lbs. (28 Nm)
- Negative battery cable

20. Refill the cooling system and the engine oil to the correct levels.

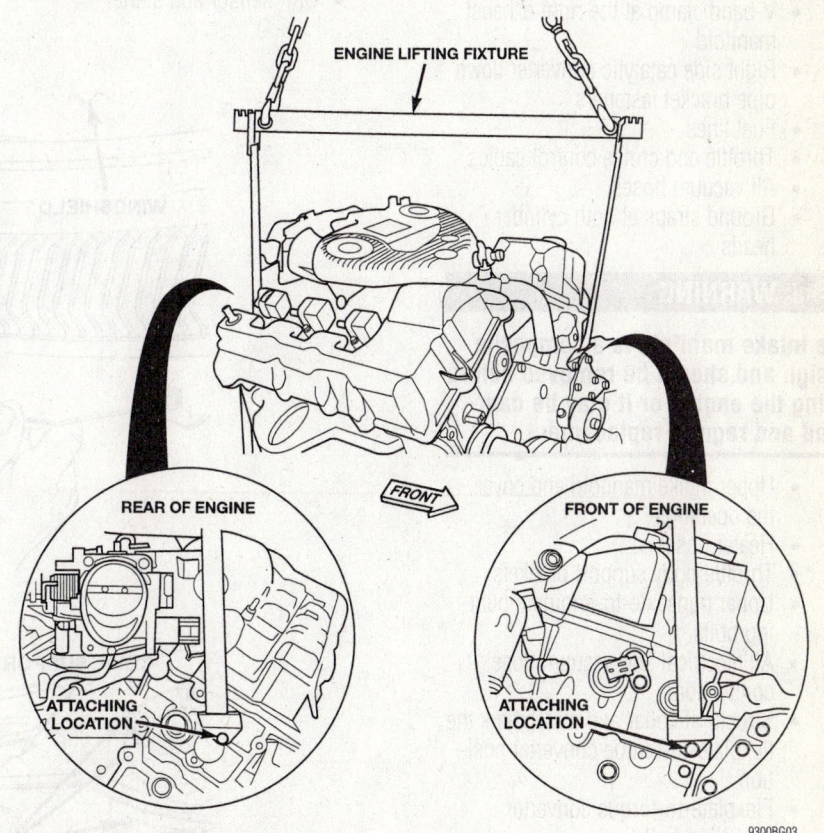

Engine support fixture attaching points—2.7L engine

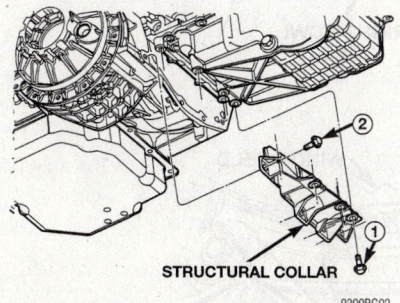

Removing the structural collar—2.7L engine

Timing belt service is covered in Section 4 of this manual

3.2L AND 3.5L ENGINES

1. Before servicing the vehicle, refer to the precautions in the beginning of this section.

2. Drain the engine oil.

3. Drain the engine coolant.

4. Properly relieve the fuel system pressure.

5. Remove or disconnect the following:

- Hood
- Negative battery cable
- Wiper arms
- Cowl covers and supports
- Air cleaner and air inlet duct
- Upper radiator support and hood release cable
- Fan module
- Accessory drive belts
- Upper and lower radiator hoses
- Engine oil and transmission cooler lines at the radiator
- Alternator, if necessary
- Air conditioning compressor mounting bolts and position it aside with the lines connected
- Power steering pump mounting bolts and position the pump aside
- V-band clamp at the right exhaust manifold
- Right side catalytic converter down pipe bracket fasteners
- Fuel lines
- Throttle and cruise control cables
- All vacuum hoses
- Ground straps at both cylinder heads

※※ WARNING

The intake manifold is a composite design and should be removed before lifting the engine or it may be damaged and require replacement.

- Upper intake manifold and cover the openings
- Heater hoses
- Throttle body support brackets
- Upper transaxle-to-engine mounting bolts
- All electrical and vacuum hose connections
- Structural collar and matchmark the flexplate-to-torque converter position
- Flexplate-to-torque converter mounting bolts
- Left exhaust manifold V-band clamp and left catalytic converter support brackets

- Starter
- Left and right engine mounting bolts
- Crankshaft Position (CKP) sensor
- Lower engine-to-transaxle mounting bolts

6. Attach a suitable lifting device to the engine.

7. Support the transaxle using a floor jack with a small block of wood in between.

8. Slowly lift the engine from the vehicle.

To install:

9. Install the engine.

10. Align the engine mounts and install the fasteners, but do not tighten them until all of the mounting bolts have been installed.

11. Install the engine-to-transaxle mounting bolts and tighten to 75 ft. lbs. (102 Nm).

12. Remove the engine lifting device.

13. Tighten the engine mount nuts/bolts 45 ft. lbs. (61 Nm).

14. Align the flexplate-to-torque converter matchmarks and install the mounting bolts, then tighten to 55 ft. lbs. (75 Nm).

15. Install or connect the following:

- CKP sensor and starter

- Left-side exhaust manifold V-band clamp and tighten to 100 inch lbs. (11 Nm).
- Left-side catalytic converter mounting bracket fasteners

16. Install the structural collar using the following procedure:

a. Install the vertical collar-to-oil pan bolts and tighten, temporarily to 10 inch lbs. (1.1 Nm).

b. Install the collar-to-transaxle bolts and tighten to 40 ft. lbs. (55 Nm).

c. Starting with the center vertical bolt and working outward, tighten the bolts to 40 ft. lbs. (55 Nm).

17. Install or connect the following:

- Throttle body support bracket
- Heater hoses, all ground straps and vacuum hoses
- Upper intake manifold
- All engine wiring harnesses
- Adjust the throttle and cruise control cables
- Fuel lines
- V-band clamp on the right exhaust manifold and tighten to 100 inch lbs. (11 Nm)
- Right-side catalytic converter mounting bracket fasteners
- Air conditioning compressor and

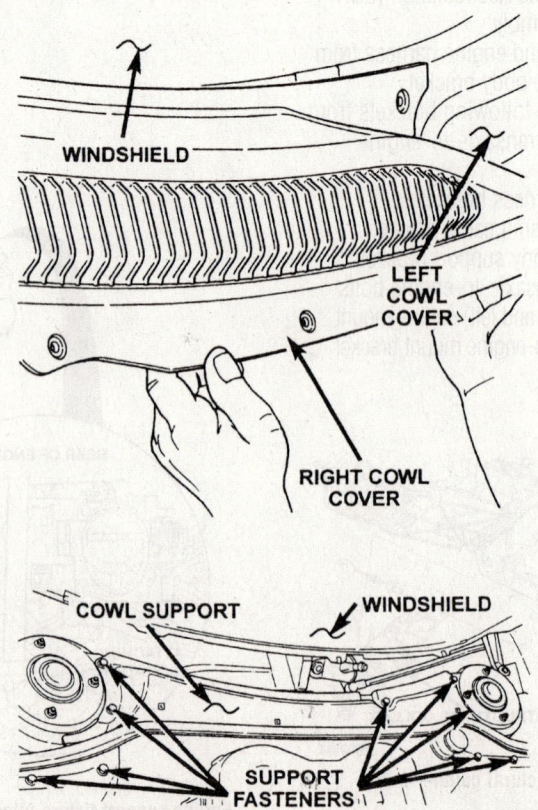

Be careful not to damage the windshield when removing the cowl covers and supports— 1998–01 3.2L and 3.5L models

7922BG03

tighten the mounting bolts to 21 ft. lbs. (28 Nm)

- Alternator and its wiring harness
- Radiator
- Power steering pump
- Engine oil and transaxle cooler lines
- Radiator hoses and accessory drive belt
- Hood release cable and upper radiator support
- Air cleaner and inlet hose
- Cowl covers, supports and wiper arms
- Hood
- Negative battery cable

18. Refill the cooling system and the crankcase to the proper level.

Water Pump

REMOVAL & INSTALLATION

The water pump has a die cast aluminum body and a stamped steel impeller. It bolts directly to the chain case cover using an O-ring for sealing. It is driven by the back side of the serpentine belt.

It is normal for a small amount of coolant to drip from the weep hole located on the water pump body (small black spot). If this condition exists, DO NOT replace the water pump. Only replace the water pump if a heavy deposit or steady flow of brown/green coolant is visible on the water pump body from the weep hole, which would indicate shaft seal failure. Before replacing the water pump, be sure to perform a thorough inspection. A defective pump will not be able to circulate heated coolant through the long heater hose.

2.7L Engine

1. Before servicing the vehicle, refer to the precautions in the beginning of this section.
2. Disconnect the negative battery cable.
3. Drain the coolant from the engine.
4. Remove or disconnect the following:
   - Upper radiator crossmember
   - Fan module
   - Accessory drive belts

➡**The water pump is driven by the primary timing chain.**

- Crankshaft damper, timing chain cover, timing chain and all guides
- Water pump mounting bolts
- Water pump, then clean the mounting surface

To install:
5. Install or connect the following:
   - Water pump and gasket, then tighten the bolts to 105 inch lbs. (12 Nm)
   - Guides, timing chain and timing chain cover
   - Crankshaft damper and tighten the center bolt to 125 ft. lbs. (170 Nm)
   - Accessory drive belts
   - Fan module and upper radiator crossmember
   - Negative battery cable
6. Refill the cooling system.

3.2L and 3.5L Engines

1. Before servicing the vehicle, refer to the precautions in the beginning of this section.
2. Drain the coolant from the engine.

✸✸ WARNING

Do not use pliers to open the plastic drain.

3. Remove or disconnect the following:
   - Negative battery cable
   - Coolant recovery cap and open the thermostat bleed valve
   - Timing belt

➡**It is good practice to turn the crankshaft until the No. 1 cylinder is at TDC of its compression stroke (firing position).**

- Water pump mounting bolts and pump. Discard the O-ring seal.
4. Clean the gasket sealing surfaces. Do not scratch the aluminum surfaces.

To install:
5. Install or connect the following:
   - New O-ring and wet with clean coolant. Be sure to keep the new O-ring free of any oil or grease.
   - Water pump, O-ring and torque water pump-to-engine bolts to 105 inch lbs. (12 Nm)

✸✸ WARNING

Rotate the pump and check for freedom of movement.

- Timing belt
6. Refill the cooling system by performing the following procedure:
   a. Close the radiator drain.
   b. Open the thermostat bleed valve. Install a ¼ in. (6mm) clear hose about 48 in. (1.2m) long to the end of the bleed valve and the other end into a clean con-

tainer. The intent is to keep coolant off of the drive belt(s).
   c. Slowly, refill the coolant recovery bottle until a steady stream of coolant flows out of the thermostat bleed valve. Gently squeeze the upper radiator hose until all of the air is removed from the system.
   d. Close the bleed valve and continue to fill the coolant recovery bottle to the proper level. Install the cap on the bottle and remove the hose from the bleed valve.
7. Reconnect the negative battery cable. Start the engine and allow it to reach normal operating temperatures.
8. Check the cooling system for leaks and correct coolant level. Be sure that the thermostat bleed valve is closed once the cooling system has been bled of any trapped air.

3.3L Engines

1. Before servicing the vehicle, refer to the precautions in the beginning of this section.
2. Drain the coolant from the engine.

✸✸ WARNING

Do not use pliers to open the plastic drain.

3. Remove or disconnect the following:
   - Negative battery cable
   - Coolant recovery bottle cap and open the thermostat bleed valve
   - Serpentine belt. If necessary, remove the right front lower fender shield
   - Water pump pulley bolts and pulley
   - Water pump-to-engine bolts and pump. Discard the O-ring seal.
4. Clean the gasket sealing surfaces. Do not scratch the aluminum surfaces.

To install:
5. Install or connect the following:
   - New O-ring into the O-ring groove and the water pump to the timing chain case. Be sure to keep the O-ring free of any oil or grease.
   - Water pump-to-engine bolts to 105 inch lbs. (12 Nm)
6. Rotate the pump and check for freedom of movement.
7. Install or connect the following:
   - Water pump pulley and tighten to 21 ft. lbs. (30 Nm)
   - Serpentine belt and right lower fender shield
8. Refill the cooling system by performing the following procedure:

a. Close the radiator drain.

b. Open the thermostat bleed valve. Install a ¼ in. (6mm) diameter clear hose about 48 in. (1.2m) long to the end of the bleed valve and the other end into a clean container. The intent is to keep coolant off the drive belt(s).

c. Slowly refill the coolant recovery bottle until a steady stream of coolant flows out of the thermostat bleed valve. Gently squeeze the upper radiator hose until all of the air is removed from the system.

d. Close the bleed valve and continue to fill the coolant recovery bottle to the proper level. Install the cap on the bottle and remove the hose from the bleed valve.

9. Reconnect the negative battery cable. Start the engine and allow it to reach normal operating temperatures.

10. Check the cooling system for leaks and correct coolant level. Be sure that the thermostat bleed valve is closed once the cooling system has been bled of any trapped air.

Cylinder Head

REMOVAL & INSTALLATION

2.7L Engine

1. Before servicing the vehicle, refer to the precautions in the beginning of this section.

2. Properly relieve the fuel system pressure.

3. Drain and recycle the engine coolant.

4. Remove or disconnect the following:
- Negative battery cable
- Accessory drive belts
- Crankshaft damper
- Intake plenum, lower intake manifold and exhaust manifold

➡Place shop rags in the openings to prevent debris from entering the engine.

- Valve and timing chain covers
- Coolant connections for the cylinder heads

5. Rotate the crankshaft until the crankshaft timing mark aligns with the timing mark on the oil pump.

6. Remove or disconnect the following:

- Primary timing chain.
- Camshaft bearing caps, gradually, in the reverse order of the tightening sequence
- Camshafts

✳✳ WARNING

Be sure the head bolts 9–11 are removed before attempting to remove the cylinder head, the head and/or block may be damaged.

- Cylinder head bolts in reverse order of installation starting with bolts 11–9, then 8–1
- Cylinder head(s)

To install:

7. Thoroughly clean and dry the mating surfaces of the head and block. Check the cylinder head for cracks, damage or engine coolant leakage. Remove scale, sealing compound and carbon. Clean the oil passages thoroughly.

8. Place a new head gasket on the cylinder block over the locating dowels.

9. Inspect the cylinder head bolts for necking (stretching) by holding a straightedge against the threads of each bolt. If all of the threads are not contacting the straightedge, the bolt should be replaced. New head bolts are recommended.

✳✳ WARNING

Due to the cylinder head bolt torque method used, it is imperative that the bolt threads be inspected for necking (stretching) prior to installation. If the threads are necked down, the bolt

should be replaced. Failure to do so may result in parts failure or damage.

10. Lubricate the bolt threads with clean engine oil, then install them.

➡**Refer to Section one of this manual for the cylinder head torque sequence illustration. The illustration is located after the Torque Specification Chart.**

11. Tighten the head bolts in the sequence as shown in the illustration, utilizing the following steps and tightening values:

a. Step 1: bolts 1 thru 8: 35 ft. lbs. (48 Nm).

b. Step 2: bolts 1 thru 8: 55 ft. lbs. (75 Nm).

c. Step 3: bolts 1 thru 8: 55 ft. lbs. (75 Nm).

d. Step 4: bolts 1 thru 8: plus 90 degree turn. Do not use a torque wrench for this step.

e. Step 5: bolts 9 thru 11: 21 ft. lbs. (28 Nm).

12. Install or connect the following:

- Camshafts, timing chain and sprockets
- Water connections to the cylinder head
- Valve and timing chain covers
- Crankshaft damper and tighten the center bolt to 125 ft. lbs. (170 Nm)
- Lower intake manifold and intake plenum
- Exhaust manifolds
- Accessory drive belts
- Negative battery cable

13. Refill the cooling system.

3.2L and 3.5L Engines

1. Before servicing the vehicle, refer to the precautions in the beginning of this section.

This engine uses aluminum alloy cylinder heads. Use care when working with light alloy components. The heads are common to either cylinder bank, but in practice a cylinder head should be returned to the side of the engine from which it was removed. Removal of a cylinder head involves removal of the timing belt. Great care is required to install the belt, paying attention to all valve timing marks. Please note that camshaft removal on this engine does require the removal of the cylinder head.

2. Release the fuel system pressure.

3. Drain the cooling system.

4. Remove or disconnect the following:

- Negative battery cable
- Radiator and cooling fan assemblies
- Air cleaner assembly and intake manifold plenum

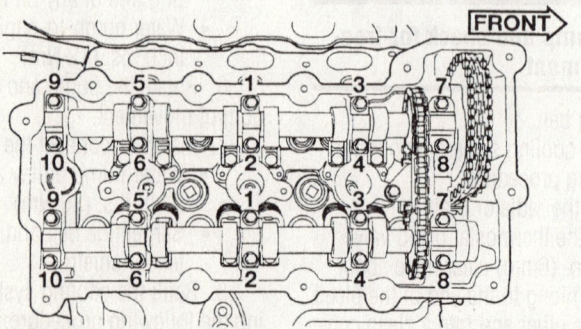

FRONT ▷

7922BG05

Camshaft bolt tightening sequence—2.7L engine

➡Cover the lower intake manifold during service.

- Accessory drive belts
- Crankshaft damper using the proper puller
- Engine valve covers
- Timing belt covers

➡**Mark the timing belt running direction for installation. Align the camshaft sprockets with the marks on the rear covers.**

- Timing belt and tensioner

5. Pre-load the timing belt tensioner as follows:

   a. Place tensioner in a vise the same way it is mounted on the engine.

   b. Slowly compress the plunger into the tensioner body.

   c. Once the plunger is compressed, install a pin through the body and plunger to retain it in place until the tensioner is installed.

6. Hold the camshaft sprocket with a 36mm box wrench, loosen and remove the sprocket retaining bolt and washer.

➡**To remove the camshaft sprocket retainer bolt while the engine is in the vehicle, it may be necessary to raise that side of the engine due to the length of the retainer bolt. The right bolt is 8.370 in. (212.6mm) long, while the left bolt is 10.0 in. (253mm) long. These bolts are not interchangeable and their original location during removal should be noted.**

7. Remove or disconnect the following:

- Camshaft sprocket from the camshaft

➡**The camshaft sprockets are not interchangeable.**

- Intake manifold assembly using the recommended procedure
- Rear timing belt cover-to-cylinder head fasteners

➡**If the right timing belt cover is to be removed, there are O-rings located behind it for the water pump passages.**

- Cylinder head mounting bolts in the reverse order of the tightening sequence
- Cylinder head

To install:

8. Thoroughly clean and dry the mating surfaces of the head and block.

⁂ **WARNING**

When cleaning the cylinder head and block mating surfaces, do not use a metal scraper because the soft aluminum surfaces could be cut or damaged. Instead, use a scraper made of wood or plastic.

9. Check the cylinder head for cracks, damage or engine coolant leakage. Check the head for flatness. End-to-end, the head should be within 0.002 in. (0.051mm) normally with 0.008 in. (0.203mm) the maximum allowed out of true. The resurface limit is 0.008 in. (0.203mm) maximum, the combined total dimension of stock removal from the cylinder head, if any, and block top surface.

10. Place a new head gasket on the cylinder block locating dowels, being sure the gasket is on the correct side.

11. Inspect the cylinder head bolts for necking (stretching) by holding a straight-edge against the threads of each bolt. If all of the threads are not contacting the scale, the bolt should be replaced.

⁂ **WARNING**

Due to the cylinder head bolt torque method used, it is imperative that the threads of the bolts be inspected for necking prior to installation. If the threads are necked down, the bolt should be replaced. Failure to do so may result in parts failure or damage. New bolts are always recommended.

➡**Refer to Section one of this manual for the cylinder head torque sequence illustration. The illustration is located after the Torque Specification Chart.**

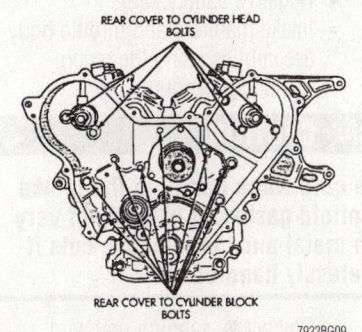

Remove the rear timing belt cover-to-cylinder head bolts, noting the bolt locations—3.2L and 3.5L engines

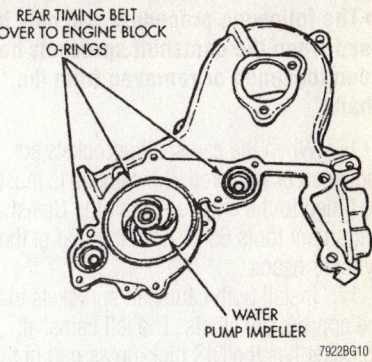

Right side belt cover, water pump and O-rings—3.2L and 3.5L engines

12. Install the cylinder head into position on the engine block and over the dowels. Install the cylinder head bolts, lubricating the threads with clean engine oil prior to installation.

13. Tighten the cylinder head bolts using the proper sequence as follows:

   a. Step 1: tighten in sequence to 45 ft. lbs. (61 Nm).

   b. Step 2: tighten in sequence to 65 ft. lbs. (88 Nm).

   c. Step 3: tighten in sequence to 65 ft. lbs. (88 Nm).

   d. Step 4: tighten in sequence an additional ¼ turn.

➡**Do not use a torque wrench for Step 4. Inspect the bolt torque after tightening. The torque should be over 90 ft. lbs. (122 Nm). If not, replace the cylinder head bolt.**

14. Install the rear timing belt cover bolts and tighten as follows:

- M6 bolts: 105 inch lbs. (12 Nm)
- M8 bolts: 21 ft. lbs. (28 Nm)
- M10 bolts: 40 ft. lbs. (54 Nm)

15. Install the intake manifold assembly and tighten the bolts following the proper sequence to 21 ft. lbs. (28 Nm).

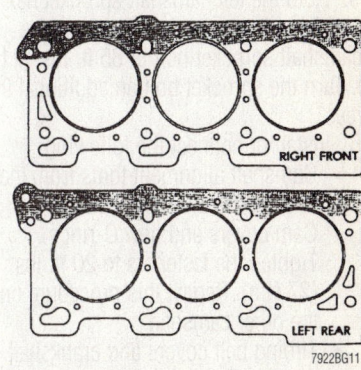

Correct positioning for the head gaskets—3.2L and 3.5L engines

Refer to Section 1 for engine rebuilding specifications

➡️**The following procedure can only be used when the camshaft sprockets have been loosened or removed from the shafts.**

16. When the camshaft sprockets are loosened or removed, the camshafts must be timed to the engine. Install the Camshaft Alignment tools 6642-A, to the rear of the cylinder heads.

17. Install both camshaft sprockets to the appropriate shafts. The left camshaft sprocket has the DIS pick-up as part of the sprocket.

18. Apply thread locking compound to the threads of the camshaft sprocket retainer bolts and install to the appropriate shafts. The right bolt is 8.380 in. (21.3cm) long, while the left bolt is 10.0 in. (25.4cm) long. These bolts are not interchangeable. Do not tighten the bolts at this time. The camshaft marks should be positioned between the marks on the cover.

19. Place the crankshaft sprocket to the TDC mark on the oil pump housing. Install the timing belt starting at the crankshaft sprocket and working in a counterclockwise direction.

20. After the belt is installed around the last sprocket keep tension on the belt until it is past the tensioner pulley.

21. Holding the tensioner pulley against the belt, install the tensioner housing and tighten to 21 ft. lbs. (28 Nm).

22. When the tensioner is in place pull the retainer pin to allow the tensioner to extend to the pulley bracket.

23. Install a dial indicator in the spark plug hole of the No. 1 cylinder to check TDC of the piston. Rotate the crankshaft until the piston is exactly at TDC.

24. Hold the right camshaft sprocket hex with a 36mm box wrench and tighten the right camshaft sprocket bolt to 75 ft. lbs. (102 Nm). Turn the sprocket bolt an additional 90 degrees.

25. Hold the left camshaft sprocket hex with a 36mm box wrench and tighten the left camshaft sprocket bolt to 85 ft. lbs. (115 Nm). Turn the sprocket bolt an additional 90 degrees.

26. Install or connect the following:
- Camshaft alignment tools from the back of the cylinder heads
- Cam covers and new O-rings. Tighten the fasteners to 20 ft. lbs. (27 Nm). Repeat this procedure on the other camshaft.
- Timing belt covers and crankshaft damper. Tighten the crankshaft damper bolt to 85 ft. lbs. (115 Nm).
- Valve covers and tighten bolts to 105 inch lbs. (12 Nm)

- Spark plug tube nut and O-ring. Tighten the nut to 60 inch lbs. (7 Nm).
- Spark plug and tighten to 20 ft. lbs. (28 Nm)
- Air conditioning compressor and tighten the mounting bracket bolts to 30 ft. lbs. (41 Nm)
- Spark plug wires
- Accessory drive belts and adjust to the proper tension
- Intake manifold plenum using the recommended procedure
- Air cleaner assembly
- Radiator and cooling fan assemblies
- Negative battery cable

27. Check to be sure that all hoses, wiring connectors, cables, fluid and vacuum lines are reconnected.

28. Change the engine oil and oil filter.

29. Refill and bleed the cooling system.

30. Run the vehicle with the radiator cap off so coolant can be added as required until the thermostat opens. Watch for leaks and for unusual engine noises. Refill the radiator completely as required.

31. Once the vehicle has cooled, recheck the coolant and oil level.

3.3L Engines

1. Before servicing the vehicle, refer to the precautions in the beginning of this section.

The cylinder heads on this engine are aluminum alloy, retained by 9 bolts. Valve seats and guides are inserts. Use care when handling alloy parts. In addition, the cylinder head bolts are torque-to-yield type which stretch during the torque process. Head bolts must be checked carefully before reuse. New head bolts are recommended.

2. Release the fuel system pressure.

3. Drain the cooling system.

4. Remove or disconnect the following:
- Negative battery cable
- Intake manifold and throttle body assemblies using the recommended procedure

✳✳ CAUTION

Use care when handling the intake manifold gasket. It is made of very thin metal and could cause cuts if carelessly handled.

- Coil wires, sending unit wire, heater hoses and bypass hose
- Evaporation control system, closed ventilation system and cylinder head covers
- Exhaust manifold(s)

- Rocker arm and shaft assemblies. Remove the pushrods and identify to assure installation in their original locations
- 9 head bolts in the reverse order of the tightening sequence from the cylinder head
- Cylinder head

To install:

5. Thoroughly clean and dry the mating surfaces of the head and block. Check the cylinder head for cracks, damage or engine coolant leakage. Remove scale, sealing compound and carbon. Clean the oil passages thoroughly. Check the head for flatness. End-to-end, the head should be within 0.002 in. (0.051mm) normally with 0.008 in. (0.203mm) the maximum allowed out of true. The total thickness allowed to be removed from the head and block is 0.008 in. (0.203mm) maximum.

6. Place a new head gasket on the cylinder block with the identification marks facing upward. Do not use sealer on factory type gaskets.

7. Inspect the cylinder head bolts for necking (stretching) by holding a straightedge against the threads of each bolt. If all of the threads are not contacting the straightedge, the bolt should be replaced. New head bolts are recommended.

✳✳ WARNING

Due to the cylinder head bolt torque method used, it is imperative that the bolt threads be inspected for necking (stretching) prior to installation. If the threads are necked down, the bolt should be replaced. Failure to do so may result in parts failure or damage.

➡️**Refer to Section one of this manual for the cylinder head torque sequence illustration. The illustration is located after the Torque Specification Chart.**

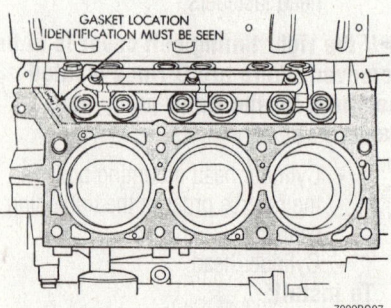

When installing the end gasket, the markings on the gasket must be seen—3.3L engine

7922BG07

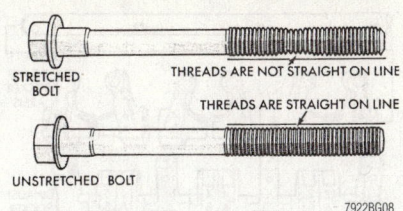

STRETCHED BOLT — THREADS ARE NOT STRAIGHT ON LINE

THREADS ARE STRAIGHT ON LINE

UNSTRETCHED BOLT

7922BG08

Inspect the cylinder head bolts for stretching—all engines

8. Install the cylinder head bolts. Tighten bolts Nos. 1 through 8 using the proper sequence as follows:

    a. Step 1: tighten in sequence to 45 ft. lbs. (61 Nm).

    b. Step 2: tighten in sequence to 65 ft. lbs. (88 Nm).

    c. Step 3: tighten in sequence to 65 ft. lbs. (88 Nm).

    d. Step 4: tighten in sequence an additional ¼ turn.

9. Tighten bolts No. 9 to 25 ft. lbs. (33 Nm) only after bolts 1–8 have been tightened to specification.

➡**Do not use a torque wrench for Step 4. Inspect the bolt torque after tightening. The torque should be over 90 ft. lbs. (122 Nm). If not, replace the cylinder head bolt.**

10. Inspect the pushrods and replace worn or bent rods. Install the pushrods, rocker arm and shaft assemblies with the stamped steel retainers in the forward positions. Tighten the rocker shaft retainers to 21 ft. lbs. (28 Nm).

✳✳ WARNING

The rocker arm shaft should be tightened down slowly, starting with the centermost bolts. Allow 20 minutes tappet bleed down time after installation of the rocker shafts before engine operation.

11. Install the cylinder head covers with new gaskets in place. Tighten the retainers to 105 inch lbs. (12 Nm).

✳✳ CAUTION

The factory-type intake manifold gasket is made of very thin metal and is very sharp. Handle with care or personal injury may occur.

12. Using all new gaskets, install the intake manifold, throttle body, air intake plenum and exhaust manifold, using the recommended procedure and following the proper torque sequences.

13. Install or connect the following:
- Exhaust and fuel connections
- Coil wires, sending unit wire, heater hoses and bypass hose
- Air intake hose
- Negative battery cable

14. Change the engine oil and oil filter.

15. Refill and bleed the cooling system.

16. Run the vehicle with the radiator cap off so coolant can be added as required until the thermostat opens. Watch for leaks and unusual engine noises that might indicate a problem. Fill the radiator completely.

17. Once the vehicle has cooled, recheck the coolant and oil level.

Rocker Arm/Shafts

REMOVAL & INSTALLATION

2.7L Engine

1. Before servicing the vehicle, refer to the precautions in the beginning of this section.

2. Remove or disconnect the following:
- Negative battery cable
- Valve covers

3. Position the camshaft so that the base circle (heel) is facing the rocker arm being serviced.

✳✳ WARNING

Depress the valve spring only enough to remove the rocker arm or damage to the spring may result.

4. Using Valve Spring tool 8215 and Adapter 8216, depress the valve spring enough to release the tension on the rocker arm.

➡**If the rocker arms are to be reused, identify their positions for reassembly in their original positions.**

5. Repeat this procedure for each rocker arm being removed.

To install:

6. Lubricate the rocker arms with clean engine oil, prior to installation.

7. Position the camshaft so that the base circle (heel) is facing the rocker arm being installed.

✳✳ WARNING

Depress the valve spring only enough to install the rocker arm or damage to the spring may result.

8. Using Valve Spring tool 8215 and Adapter 8216, depress the valve spring enough to install the rocker arm.

9. Install the rocker arm in the original position (if reused) over the valve and lash adjuster

➡**Inspect the rocker arm for proper engagement into the lash adjuster and valve tip.**

10. Release the tension on the valve spring and remove the tools.

11. Install the valve covers and connect the negative battery cable.

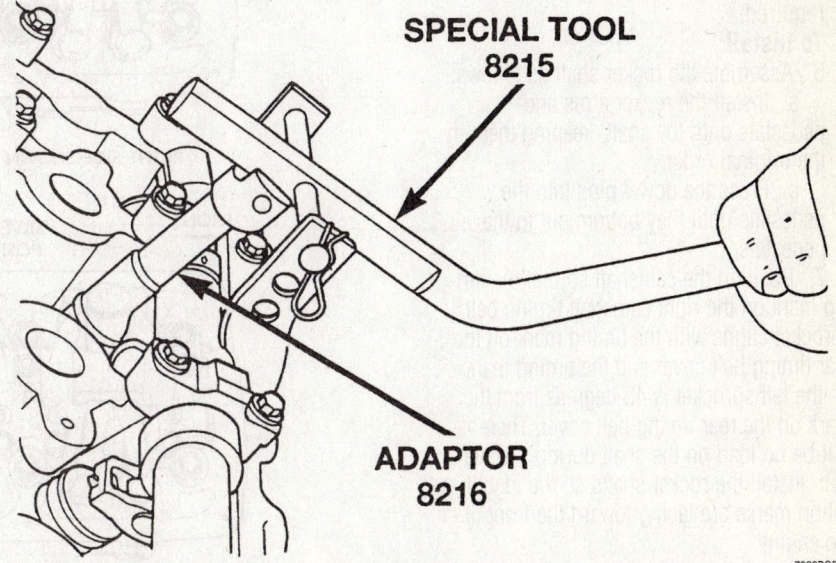

SPECIAL TOOL 8215

ADAPTOR 8216

7922BG59

Only depress the valve spring enough to remove the rocker arm—2.7L engine

For engine torque specifications, refer to Section 1 of this manual

3.2L and 3.5L Engines

1. Before servicing the vehicle, refer to the precautions in the beginning of this section.

2. Relieve the fuel system pressure.

3. Remove or disconnect the following:
- Negative battery cable
- Air cleaner assembly and the intake manifold plenum

➡ **Cover the lower intake manifold during service.**

- Cylinder head covers
- Rocker arm assembly

4. Inspect the rocker arms for wear or damage. Inspect the roller for scuffing or wear. Replace assembly as necessary.

✳✳ WARNING

Do not remove the lash adjusters from the rocker arm assembly. The rocker arm and the adjuster are serviced as an assembly.

5. Identify the rocker arm assemblies and rocker arms and disassemble the shaft as follows:

a. Thread a nut, washer and spacer onto a 4mm screw.

b. Insert and tighten the 4mm screw into the dowel pin on the shaft.

c. Loosen the nut on the screw. This will pull the dowel pin from the shaft support.

d. Remove the rocker arms and pedestals, keeping them in order.

e. Check the oil holes for restrictions with a small wire and clean as required.

To install:

6. Assemble the rocker shaft as follows:

a. Install the rocker arms and pedestals onto the shaft, keeping them in the original order.

b. Press the dowel pins into the pedestals until they bottom out in the pedestals.

7. Position the camshaft so that the timing mark on the right camshaft timing belt sprocket aligns with the timing mark on the rear timing belt cover and the timing mark on the left sprocket is 45 degrees from the mark on the rear timing belt cover. There will be no load on the shaft during installation. Install the rocker shafts so the identification marks are facing toward the front of the engine.

8. Install the oil feed bolt in the correct location on the rocker shaft retainer. Tighten the bolts in proper sequence to 23 ft. lbs. (31 Nm).

9. Install or connect the following:
- Valve covers and tighten bolts to 105 inch lbs. (12 Nm)
- Intake manifold plenum
- Air cleaner assembly
- Negative battery cable

3.3L Engines

1. Before servicing the vehicle, refer to the precautions in the beginning of this section.

2. Relieve the fuel system pressure.

3. Remove or disconnect the following:
- Negative battery cable
- Upper intake manifold assembly
- Spark plug wires from the plugs

➡ **Remove by first twisting, then pulling on the boot, in line with the spark plug.**

- Closed crankcase ventilation system and the evaporative control system from the cylinder head cover
- Cylinder head cover and gasket
- 4 rocker shaft bolts and retainers
- Rocker arms and shafts

4. Inspect the rocker arm and compo-

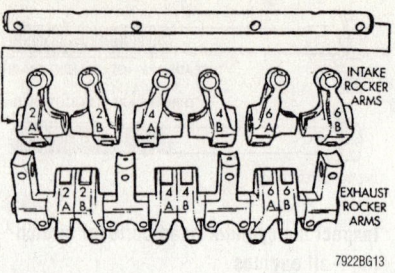

Left bank rocker arm and shaft identification—3.2L and 3.5L engines

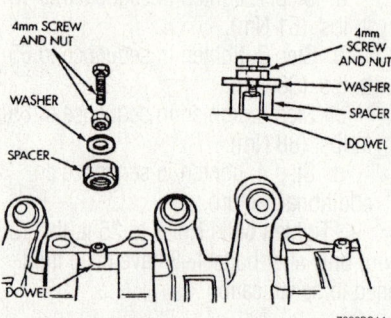

Remove the dowel pin using a 4mm screw, nut, spacer and washer installed into the pin—3.2L and 3.5L engines

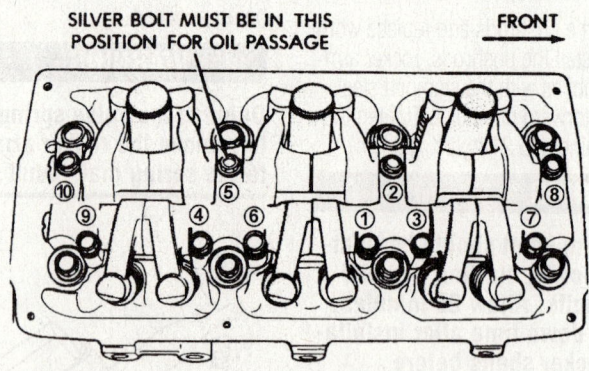

SILVER BOLT MUST BE IN THIS POSITION FOR OIL PASSAGE

FRONT →

RIGHT SIDE SHOWN

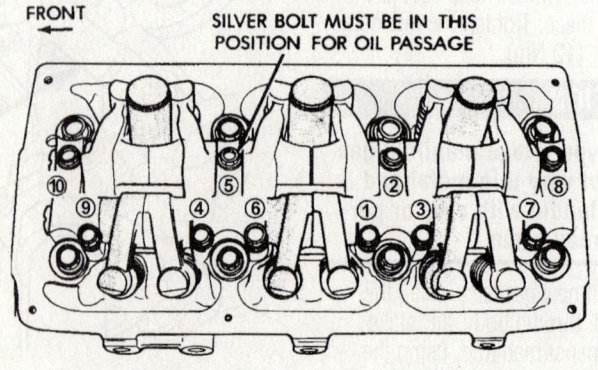

FRONT ←

SILVER BOLT MUST BE IN THIS POSITION FOR OIL PASSAGE

LEFT SIDE SHOWN

Proper torque sequence for the rocker arm and shaft assemblies—3.2L and 3.5L engines

nents for wear or damage and replace as required. If the rocker shaft is disassembled for cleaning or replacement, be sure to install the components in their original locations.

To install:

5. Install the rocker arms and shaft assemblies with the stamped steel retainers in the 4 positions. Tighten the retainer bolts slowly to 21 ft. lbs. (28 Nm), in 3 even steps starting at the centermost bolts and working outward.

✳✳ WARNING

After installation, allow the tappets to bleed down for 20 minutes before operating the engine or damage to the valves may occur.

6. Clean the mating surfaces of the cylinder head cover gasket. Inspect the cylinder head cover and straighten out if distorted.

7. Install or connect the following:
  - Cylinder head cover with new gasket and tighten the fasteners to 105 inch lbs. (12 Nm)
  - Closed crankcase ventilation system
  - Evaporative control system
  - Spark plug wires

➡ **Make sure that each wire is connected to the correct spark plug.**

  - Upper intake manifold assembly
  - Negative battery cable

Intake Manifold

REMOVAL & INSTALLATION

2.7L and 3.3L Engines

1. Before servicing the vehicle, refer to the precautions in the beginning of this section.

2. Disconnect the negative battery cable.

3. Remove the fuel filler cap. Release the fuel system pressure.

4. Drain the cooling system.

5. Disconnect the air tube from the air cleaner and the throttle body.

6. Hold the throttle lever in the wide-open position and remove the throttle cable and the speed control cable from the lever. Compress the locking tabs on the cables and remove them from the mounting brackets.

7. Unplug the electrical connections from the following:
  - Solenoid on the Exhaust Gas Recirculation (EGR) valve transducer
  - Manifold Absolute Pressure (MAP) sensor
  - Throttle Position (TP) sensor
  - Iadle Air Control (IAC) motor

8. Remove or disconnect the following:
  - Vacuum hose from the PCV valve as well as the power brake booster at the intake manifold nipple
  - Vacuum line at the fuel pressure regulator
  - Purge hose from the throttle body
  - Electrical connector from the TP sensor and the idle air control motor
  - EGR tube-to-intake manifold plenum screws
  - Intake manifold plenum (upper part of the manifold)

➡ **Cover the lower part of the intake manifold to prevent foreign material from entering the engine.**

  - Fuel supply and return tubes from the fuel rail at the rear of the intake manifold

9. Disconnect the fuel/return tubes by pushing the quick-connect fitting toward the fuel tube while depressing the built-in disconnect tool with Quick-Connect Fitting tool 6751. To disconnect the fitting from the fuel rail, slightly twist the fitting while maintaining downward pressure on tool 6751. Wrap shop towels around the fuel hoses to absorb any fuel spillage.

10. Plug the fuel line openings to prevent system contamination.

11. Remove or disconnect the following:
  - Fuel clamp screw and tubes from the bracket
  - Electrical harness from the injectors and turn toward the center of the engine
  - Fuel rail mounting bolts and lift the fuel rail with the injectors attached straight up and off the engine

12. Cover the injector openings.

13. On the 3.3L engine, remove the upper radiator hose, heater hose and the rear intake manifold hose.

14. Remove or disconnect the following:
  - Intake manifold bolts and the manifold
  - Intake manifold seal retainer screws and intake manifold gasket

15. Clean all mating surfaces.

16. Inspect the manifold for damage,

cracks or clogged passages. Repair, clean or replace the manifold as required.

To install:

17. Verify that all intake manifold and cylinder head sealing surfaces are clean. Place a drop of sealant onto each of the 4 corners of the intake manifold gasket, where the cylinder head meets the engine block.

18. On the 3.3L engine, carefully install the intake manifold gasket and tighten the end seal retainers to 105 inch lbs. (12 Nm).

✳✳ CAUTION

The intake manifold gasket is made of very thin metal and can cause cuts if handled carelessly.

➡ **Refer to Section one of this manual for the intake manifold torque sequence illustration. The illustration is located after the torque specification chart.**

19. Install the intake manifold and 8 mounting bolts. Snug down evenly to just 10 inch lbs. (1.1 Nm).

20. On the 3.3L engine, tighten the lower intake manifold bolts in the proper sequence to 16 ft. lbs. (22 Nm). Once all bolts are tightened, repeat the sequence again tightening the bolts to 16 ft. lbs. (22 Nm). Inspect to be sure all seals are still in place.

21. On the 2.7L engine, tighten the lower intake manifold bolts in the proper sequence to 105 inch lbs. (12 Nm).

22. Install the fuel injectors by performing the following procedure:
  a. Apply a light coat of clean engine oil to the O-ring on the nozzle end of each injector.
  b. Insert the fuel injector nozzles into the openings in the intake manifold. Seat the injectors in place and install the fuel rail mounting bolts, tightening to 16 ft. lbs. (22 Nm).

23. Install or connect the following:
  - Electrical connectors to each fuel injector. Rotate the injectors toward the cylinder head covers.
  - Fuel supply and return tubes to the fuel rail. Be sure that the black plastic release ring to the quick-connect fitting is in the OUT position. Place special tool 6751 under the largest diameter of the quick-connect fitting.

24. Pull tool 6751 toward the fuel rail until the quick-connect fitting clicks into place. Place the special tool between the shoulder of the built-in disconnect tool and top of the quick-connect fitting, then inspect

the security of the fitting by applying a slight downward force against the fitting. It should be locked in place.

25. Install or connect the following:
- Intake plenum with new gasket onto the intake manifold. Loosely install the mounting bolts.
- EGR tube to the manifold with a new gasket in place. Loosely install the mounting screws.

➡ **Refer to Section one of this manual for the intake plenum torque sequence illustration. The illustration is located after the torque specification chart.**

26. On the 3.3L engine, tighten the intake manifold plenum mounting bolts to 21 ft. lbs. (28 Nm) following the outlined sequence.

27. On the 2.7L engine, install or connect the following:
- Tighten the intake manifold plenum mounting bolts to 105 inch lbs. (12 Nm) following the outlined sequence
- Left and right support brackets to the manifold. Tighten the lower fasteners to 50 inch lbs. (6 Nm) and the upper fasteners to 105 inch lbs. (12 Nm).

28. Install or connect the following:
- EGR tube mounting bolts
- PCV valve hose and power brake booster hose
- Electrical connectors to the EGR transducer solenoid, idle air control motor, MAP and TP sensors
- Throttle cable and speed control cable to the mounting bracket and connect to the throttle body lever while holding lever in the wide-open position
- Purge hose to the throttle body
- Reconnect the air tube to the air cleaner and the throttle body
- Negative battery cable

29. Drain the engine oil and replace the oil and filter.

30. Refill the crankcase and cooling system. Run the vehicle with the radiator cap removed until the thermostat opens, adding coolant as required. Watch for fuel and coolant leaks and for correct engine operation.

31. Once the vehicle has cooled, recheck the coolant level and add, if necessary.

3.2L and 3.5L Engines

1. Before servicing the vehicle, refer to the precautions in the beginning of this section.

2. Drain the cooling system.
3. Remove or disconnect the following:
- Negative battery cable
- Fuel filler cap. Release the fuel system pressure using the recommended procedure.
- Engine cover from the top of the intake manifold
- Accelerator and the speed control cable from the throttle lever
- Idle Air Control (IAC) motor
- Intake Air Temperature (IAT) sensor
- Manifold Absolute Pressure (MAP) sensor
- Ground screw from the intake manifold
- Electrical connector from the Throttle Position (TP) sensor
- Vacuum hoses from the manifold tuning valve, PCV make-up air hose, IAC motor supply hose and the purge hose from the throttle bodies
- Brake booster hose, PCV hose and the remaining vacuum hoses from the intake manifold
- Exhaust Gas Recirculation (EGR) tube-to-intake manifold plenum bolts
- Plenum support bracket mounting bolts on each side of the plenum
- Intake plenum mounting bolts

➡ **The intake manifold plenum (upper half of the intake manifold assembly) uses 2 different length bolts. Take note of their position and be sure they are installed in the same location during installation.**

- Intake manifold plenum from the intake manifold

➡ **Discard the old gasket. Cover the intake manifold openings with tape to keep debris from entering the engine.**

- Upper radiator hose from the thermostat housing
- Heater hose from the rear of the intake manifold
- Lower intake manifold bolts and manifold

➡ **Clean all gasket mating surfaces and inspect for distortion with a good straightedge.**

To install:

➡ **Verify that all intake manifold and cylinder head sealing surfaces are clean.**

➡ **Refer to Section one of this manual for the intake manifold torque sequence illustration. The illustration**

is located after the torque specification chart.

4. Install or connect the following:
- Intake manifold gasket, then the lower manifold. Tighten the bolts in the proper sequence to 21 ft. lbs. (28 Nm).
- Upper radiator hose to the thermostat housing
- Heater hose to the rear of the intake manifold

➡ **Ensure the ignition cables are routed out of the way of the intake plenum.**

➡ **Refer to Section one of this manual for the intake manifold plenum torque sequence illustration. The illustration is located after the torque specification chart.**

- Intake manifold plenum with a new gasket in place. Tighten the mounting bolts, working from the center outward, to 21 ft. lbs. (28 Nm).

➡ **Do not overtighten bolts when working with light alloys.**

- Support bracket bolts
- Electrical connectors to the MAP sensor, TP sensor, IAC motor and IAT sensor
- Vacuum hose to the manifold tuning valve
- EGR tube. Tighten the EGR tube-to-intake manifold plenum screws to 17 ft. lbs. (22 Nm).

➡ **Be sure that the insulation on the EGR tube aligns with and contacts the insulation on the vacuum harness at the rear of the engine. Rotate the throttle lever to the wide-open position and reconnect the speed control and throttle cables.**

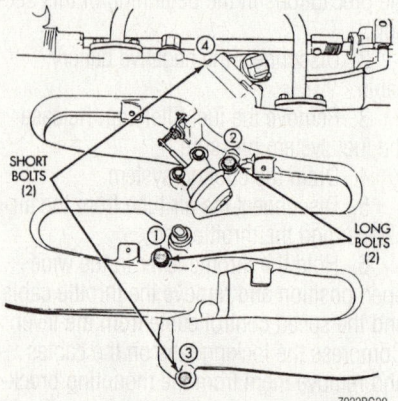

Note the positions of the 4 plenum bolts (they are 2 different sizes)—1997 3.5L engines

- PCV valve hose
- Air cleaner plenum and plenum hose
- Ground wire to the intake manifold plenum
- Brake booster hose to intake manifold plenum fitting
- Throttle body purge tubes
- Intake manifold plenum cover
- Negative battery cable

5. Refill and bleed the cooling system.
6. Change the engine oil and filter.
7. Test run the engine, check for fuel and coolant leaks and verify correct engine operation.

Exhaust Manifold

REMOVAL & INSTALLATION

2.7L Engine

RIGHT MANIFOLD

1. Before servicing the vehicle, refer to the precautions in the beginning of this section.
2. Remove or disconnect the following:

- Negative battery cable
- Air intake plenum and the air filter housing
- Battery cable housing tube-to-transaxle bolt
- Ehaust Gas Recirculation (EGR) valve and tube
- Oxygen (O_2S) sensor
- V-band clamp from the manifold

➡**Do not reuse the V-band clamps.**

- Heat shield
- Exhaust manifold

3. Remove all traces of the old manifold gasket and clean both gasket mating surfaces.

To install:

4. Install or connect the following:

- Exhaust manifold and new gasket. Tighten the bolts to 17 ft. lbs. (23 Nm) working from the center outward.
- Heat shields and tighten the mounting bolts to 105 inch lbs. (12 Nm)
- New V-band clamp and tighten to 100 inch lbs. (11.3 Nm)
- O_2S sensor
- EGR valve and tube using new gaskets, then tighten to 95 inch lbs. (11 Nm)

- Battery cable tube-to-transaxle bolt and tighten bolt to 75 ft. lbs. (101 Nm).
- Air inlet plenum and air filter housing
- Negative battery cable

LEFT MANIFOLD

1. Before servicing the vehicle, refer to the precautions in the beginning of this section.
2. Disconnect the negative battery cable.
3. Remove or disconnect the following:

- Exhaust system
- V-band clamps and left catalytic converter

➡**Do not reuse the V-band clamps.**

4. Loosen and rotate the transaxle dipstick tube out of the way.
5. Remove or disconnect the following:

- Engine wiring harness support bracket from the cylinder head
- Oxygen (O_2S) sensor
- Engine oil dipstick tube and manifold heat shield
- Exhaust manifold bolts and manifold

To install:

6. Remove all traces of the old manifold gasket and clean both gasket mating surfaces.
7. Install or connect the following:

- Exhaust manifold and new gasket. Tighten the bolts to 17 ft. lbs. (23 Nm) working from the center outward.
- Heat shields and tighten the mounting bolts to 105 inch lbs. (12 Nm)
- O_2S sensor
- Transaxle dipstick tube
- O-ring for the engine oil dipstick tube and tube
- Catalytic converter, new V-band clamp and tighten to 100 inch lbs. (10 Nm)
- Engine wiring harness support bracket to the cylinder head
- Exhaust system
- Negative battery cable

3.2L and 3.5L Engines

1. Before servicing the vehicle, refer to the precautions in the beginning of this section.

2. Remove or disconnect the following:
- Negative battery cable
- Exhaust pipes from the exhaust manifold
- Heated Oxygen (HO_2S) sensor electrical wiring
- Heat shield-to-exhaust manifold screws
- Exhaust manifold bolts and manifold

3. Inspect the manifold for damage or cracks. Check for distortion against a straight-edge or thickness gauge. Replace manifold if required.
4. Remove all traces of the old manifold gasket and clean both gasket mating surfaces.

To install:

5. Install or connect the following:
- New manifold gasket and exhaust manifold to the cylinder head. Install the retainer bolts and tighten to 15 ft. lbs. (20 Nm).
- Exhaust pipe to the exhaust manifold and tighten the nuts to 21 ft. lbs. (28 Nm)
- Install the heat shield and tighten the manifold retaining screws to 11 ft. lbs. (15 Nm)
- HO_2S sensor electrical connector
- Negative battery cable

6. Operate the vehicle and inspect for exhaust leaks.

3.3L Engines

1. Before servicing the vehicle, refer to the precautions in the beginning of this section.

2. Remove or disconnect the following:

- Negative battery cable
- Exhaust pipe from the exhaust manifold
- Heated Oxygen (HO_2S) sensor lead wire
- Exhaust Gas Recirculation (EGR) tube from the exhaust manifold
- Heat shield to the exhaust manifold screws
- Manifold from the cylinder head

3. These manifolds are thin-wall designs to save weight. Inspect the manifold carefully for cracks or other damage. Check for distortion against a straightedge or thickness gauge. Replace the manifold if required.
4. Remove all traces of the old manifold gasket and clean both gasket mating surfaces.

Please refer to Section 8 for electric cooling fan wiring schematics

To install:

5. Install or connect the following:
- Exhaust manifold and a new manifold gasket and tighten the bolts to 17 ft. lbs. (23 Nm)
- Exhaust pipe to the exhaust manifold and tighten the nuts to 21 ft. lbs. (28 Nm)
- EGR tube
- Heat shield to the manifold
- HO_2S sensor electrical connector
- Negative battery cable

6. Operate the vehicle and inspect for exhaust leaks.

Front Crankshaft Seal

➡ The front crankshaft seal procedures are for timing belt equipped engines only. For engines that utilize timing chains, please refer to the applicable procedure later in this section.

REMOVAL & INSTALLATION

3.2L and 3.5L Engines

Note that the timing belt must be removed from the vehicle to perform this service. Use care to be sure all valve timing marks are carefully aligned both before removing the belt and after belt installation and all service has been completed. It may be good practice to set the engine to TDC No. 1 cylinder compression stroke (firing position) and aligning all timing marks before removing the timing belt. This serves as a reference for all work that follows.

1. Before servicing the vehicle, refer to the precautions at the beginning of this section.
2. Release the fuel system pressure.
3. Remove or disconnect the following:
- Negative battery cable

- Radiator and cooling fan module assembly
- Accessory drive belts
- Crankshaft damper bolt
- Timing belt front cover

➡ The sealer on the timing belt front cover may be reusable and should not be removed. Use silicone rubber adhesive sealant to replace any missing sealer.

- Timing belt and tensioner using the recommended procedure
- Crankshaft timing belt sprocket

4. Locate the small dowel pin in the crankshaft. With a small punch, carefully tap out the dowel from the end of the crankshaft.

5. Remove the crankshaft seal using tool 6341A, taking care not to nick the shaft seal surface or seal bore during removal.

To install:

6. Inspect the crankshaft seal lip surface for varnish and dirt. Polish the area using 400 grit sandpaper to remove varnish as necessary.

7. Install or connect the following:
- Crankshaft seal using seal installer tool 6342
- Rear lower timing belt cover
- Dowel into the crankshaft so that it protrudes 0.047 in. (1.2mm)
- Timing belt sprocket at the crankshaft using tool C-4685C1, thrust bearing, washer and 12mm bolt or an equivalent setup to pull the sprocket onto crankshaft. Do not hammer on the sprocket.

8. Verify that all valve timing marks are aligned.

- Timing belt and tensioner using the recommended procedure

9. Rotate the crankshaft 2 complete turns and recheck the timing marks on the

camshafts and crankshaft. The marks must align with their respective locations. If the marks do not align, repeat the timing belt installation procedure. When correct valve timing has been verified, install the timing belt covers.

10. Install or connect the following:
- Crankshaft damper. Hold the crankshaft damper, using tool L-3281, and tighten the crankshaft bolt to 85 ft. lbs. (115 Nm).
- Accessory drive belts and adjust to the proper tension
- Radiator and cooling fan assemblies
- Negative battery cable

11. Refill and bleed the cooling system.

Camshaft and Valve Lifters

REMOVAL & INSTALLATION

2.7L Engine

1. Before servicing the vehicle, refer to the precautions in the beginning of this section.

✲✲ WARNING

When the timing chain is removed and the cylinder heads are installed, DO NOT turn the crankshaft or camshaft without first locating the proper crankshaft position. Failure to do so will result in piston-to-valve contact.

2. Remove or disconnect the following:
- Primary timing chain
- Second chain tensioner mounting bolts

3. Slowly loosen the camshaft bearing cap retaining bolts in the reverse order of the tightening sequence.

4. Remove or disconnect the following:
- Bearing caps

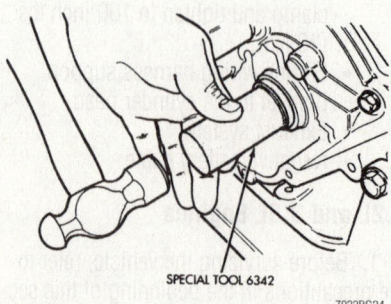

Removing the timing belt sprocket dowel pin from the crankshaft—3.2L and 3.5L engines

Installing the crankshaft oil seal—3.2L and 3.5L engines

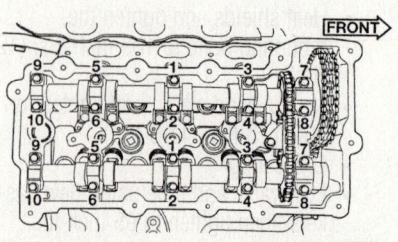

Camshaft bearing cap tightening sequence—2.7L engine

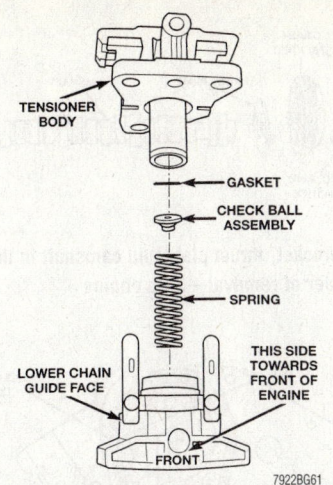

Exploded view of the camshaft (secondary) chain tensioner, early build—2.7L engine

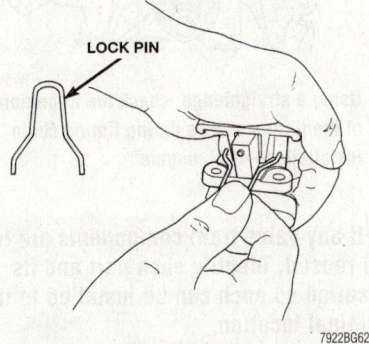

Fabricate a lockpin, as shown, to keep the tensioner compressed—2.7L engine

- Camshafts, secondary chain and tensioner as an assembly
- Tensioner and chain from the crankshaft

To install:

5. Assemble the chain on the camshafts. Ensure the plated links are facing toward the front. Align the plated links to the dots on the camshaft sprockets.

➡There are 2 different styles of camshaft (secondary) chain tensioners. The Early Build tensioners will separate into sub-components, the Later Build tensioners will not. Compress the camshaft (secondary) chain as follows:

6. For early build vehicles:
a. Separate the tensioner cylinder from the tensioner housing.
b. Carefully drain the oil from the housing using care not to remove the internal tensioner components.
c. Assemble the tensioner housing as shown.

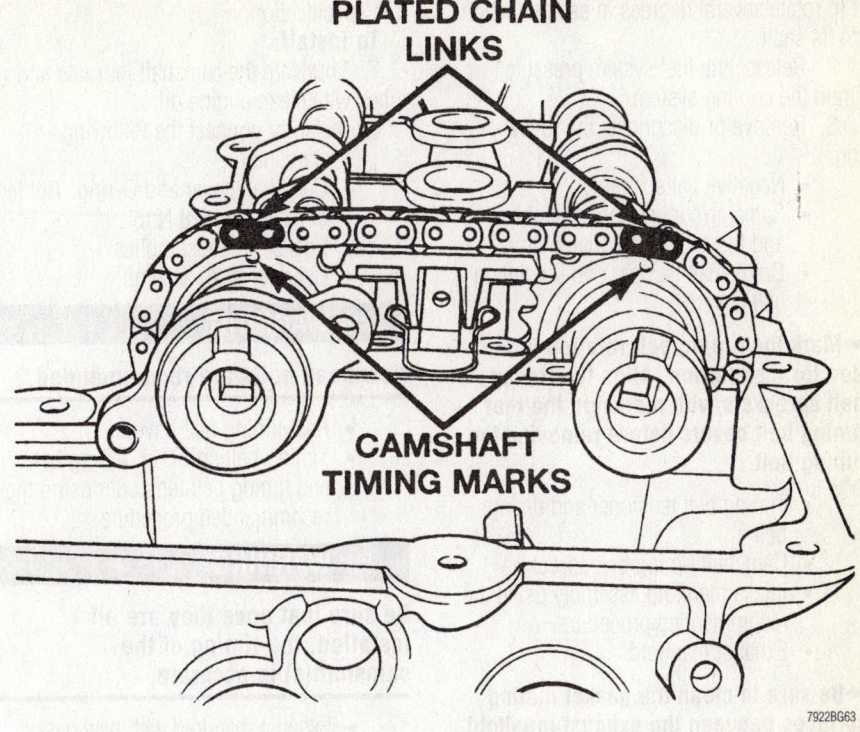

Proper camshaft (secondary) chain alignment—2.7L engine

d. Using hand pressure, compress and lock the tensioner using a fabricated lockpin.

7. For late build vehicles:
a. Place the tensioner in a soft-jawed vise.
b. Slowly compress the tensioner until the fabricated lockpin can be installed.
c. Remove the compressed and locked tensioner from the vise.

8. Insert the compressed and locked camshaft chain tensioner in between the camshafts and chain.

9. Position the camshafts so that the plated links and dots are facing 12:00 o'clock.

10. Install or connect the following:
- Camshafts

✳✳ WARNING

Ensure that the rocker arms are correctly seated and in proper positions.

- Camshaft bearing caps. Tighten the camshaft bearing cap bolts gradually, in sequence, to 105 inch lbs. (12 Nm).
- Secondary chain tensioner bolts and tighten to 105 inch lbs. (12 Nm)

- Primary timing chain
- Negative battery cable

11. Remove the lockpin from the secondary chain tensioner.

3.2L and 3.5L Engines

1. Before servicing the vehicle, refer to the precautions in the beginning of this section.

Camshafts are serviced from the rear of the cylinder head. Although the engine does not need to be removed for camshaft service, the cylinder head must be removed from the vehicle. Note too, that the camshaft

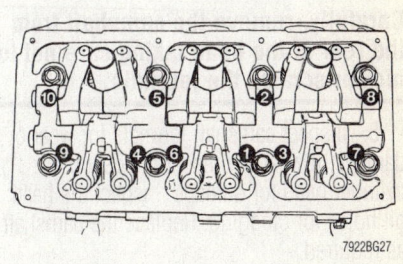

Rocker arm/shaft tightening sequence—3.2L and 3.5L engines

sprockets have a D-shaped hole that allows it to rotate several degrees in each direction on its shaft.

2. Release the fuel system pressure. Drain the cooling system.

3. Remove or disconnect the following:

- Negative battery cable
- Radiator/cooling fan assemblies and the accessory drive belts
- Crankshaft damper and the timing belt covers

➡ Mark the timing belt rotation direction for installation. Align the timing belt sprockets with marks on the rear timing belt covers before removing the timing belt.

- Timing belt tensioner and timing belt
- Camshaft timing belt sprockets
- Intake manifold assembly using the recommended procedure
- Exhaust manifold

➡ Be sure to clean the gasket mating surfaces between the exhaust manifold and the cylinder head.

4. The rear timing belt cover must be removed to remove the cylinder heads. Remove the rear timing belt cover-to-cylinder head bolts. Remove the rear timing belt covers.

➡ The right-hand side timing belt cover has O-rings located behind it for the water pump passages.

- Cylinder head bolts and cylinder head

➡ Mark the rocker arm assembly to note component locations before disassembly.

- Rocker arm and shaft assemblies
- Rear camshaft cover and O-ring

✹✹ WARNING

Carefully, remove the camshaft from the rear of the head taking care not to nick or scratch the journals.

5. Inspect camshaft journals for wear or damage. If wear is present, inspect the cylinder head for damage. Inspect the head oil holes for clogging. Replace the camshaft as required.

6. Measure the height of the cam using a micrometer. Measure in 2 places: the unworn area and in the wear zone. Subtract the figures to get cam wear. The standard specification is 0.001 in. (0.0254mm) with the wear limit being 0.010 in. (0.254mm).

Replace the camshaft if it is worn beyond this specification.

To install:

7. Lubricate the camshaft journals and lobes with clean engine oil.

8. Install or connect the following:

- Camshaft
- Camshaft cover and O-ring. Tighten to 21 ft. lbs. (28 Nm).
- Rocker arm assemblies
- Cylinder head assembly

✹✹ WARNING

New head bolts are recommended.

- Rear timing belt covers
- Timing belt sprocket, timing belt and timing belt tensioner using the recommended procedure.

✹✹ WARNING

Be sure that once they are all installed, the timing of the camshaft(s) is accurate.

- Exhaust manifold with new gasket
- Intake manifold assembly
- Timing belt covers and crankshaft damper
- Accessory drive belts and set them to the proper tension
- Radiator and cooling fan assembly
- Negative battery cable

9. Refill and bleed the cooling system. An oil and filter change is recommended.

3.3L Engines

1. Before servicing the vehicle, refer to the precautions in the beginning of this section.

➡ To remove and replace the camshaft on this engine, the engine assembly must be removed from the vehicle.

2. Drain the engine oil and remove the oil filter.

3. Relieve the fuel system pressure.

4. Remove or disconnect the following:

- Negative battery cable
- Radiator and cooling fan assemblies
- Engine
- Cylinder head covers, rocker arm and rocker arm shaft assemblies
- Intake manifold assembly and cylinder heads
- Harmonic balancer
- Timing chain case cover and timing chain
- Pushrods and tappets

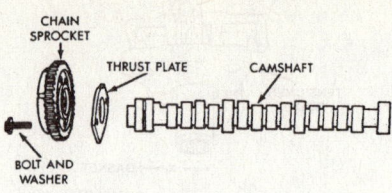

Sprocket, thrust plate and camshaft in the order of removal—3.3L engine

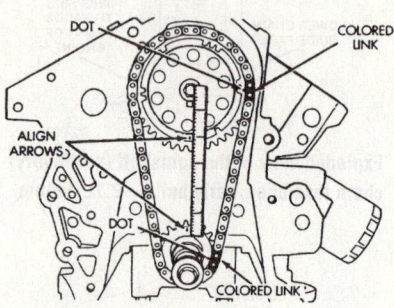

Using a straightedge, check the alignment of the timing arrows during timing chain installation—3.3L engine

➡ If any valve train components are to be reused, identify each part and its location so each can be installed in its original location.

➡ If the camshaft is being removed to replace it with a new one, new valve lifters MUST be installed.

- Camshaft thrust plate

➡ Install a long bolt into the front of the camshaft to act as a handle and aid in removal.

- Camshaft

✹✹ WARNING

Be careful not to damage the cam bearings with the cam lobes.

5. Inspect the bearing journals and the lobes on the shaft for wear, replace the camshaft if required. Remember, new lifters must be installed with a new camshaft.

To install:

6. Lubricate the camshaft lobes and the camshaft bearing journals. Inspect the bearing journals on the camshaft and install the shaft within 2 in. (5cm) of its final position in the cylinder block.

➡ Chrysler recommends 1 pint (0.473L) of Chrysler Crankcase Conditioner, be added to the crankcase when the camshaft has been replaced. This will

aid during break-in. Leave the oil mixture in the engine for a minimum of 500 miles (804 km) and drain at the next normal oil change.

7. Install the camshaft thrust plate with the 2 screws and tighten to 105 inch lbs. (12 Nm).

8. Rotate the crankshaft so the timing arrow is in the 12 o'clock position.

9. Position the camshaft sprocket so the timing arrow is at the 6 o'clock position. Place the timing chain around the camshaft sprocket aligning the dark colored link of the chain with the dot on the camshaft sprocket.

10. Place the timing chain around the crankshaft sprocket aligning the dot on the crankshaft sprocket with the dark colored link on the chain. Install the camshaft sprocket in position on the shaft.

11. Using a straight-edge, check the alignment of the timing arrows. Install the camshaft bolt and washer and tighten to 40 ft. lbs. (54 Nm).

12. Rotate the crankshaft 2 revolutions in the direction of engine rotation. Check the alignment of the timing arrows, which should align with each other.

   a. If they do not align, remove the camshaft sprocket and re-time the engine.

   b. Again, rotate the crankshaft 2 revolutions in the direction of rotation, and confirm alignment of the timing marks.

13. Check the camshaft end-play. With a new thrust plate the specification is 0.005–0.012 in. (0.0127–0.3040mm) or 0.012 in. (0.3040mm) for an old thrust plate. If not within specifications, replace the thrust plate.

14. Lubricate and install the valve lifters (tappets) in their original positions. If the camshaft was replaced, all lifters must be replaced with new parts.

15. Install or connect the following:
   • Timing chain front cover using new seals and O-rings
   • Cylinder heads and intake manifold assemblies onto the engine using the recommended procedures
   • Pushrods in their original positions
   • Rocker arm and rocker arm shaft assemblies
   • Cylinder head covers

16. Tighten the oil pan drain plug and install a new oil filter.

17. Install or connect the following:
   • Engine

   • Radiator and cooling fan assemblies
   • All fluid lines, cables, hoses and electrical connectors
   • Negative battery cable

18. Refill the engine with the correct amount of clean SAE 5W-30 or SAE 10W-30 engine oil only. Do not mix the two grades of oil.

19. Refill and bleed the cooling system.

20. Start the engine and inspect for leaks. Test drive the vehicle.

21. Check engine fluid levels and top off, if necessary.

Valve Lash

ADJUSTMENT

These engines use hydraulic roller lifters to take up the free-play in the valve train system, therefore no lash adjustments are necessary.

Starter Motor

REMOVAL & INSTALLATION

2.7L Engine

1. On 1998, at the catalyst support bracket, remove the bracket nut and the 2 bracket mounting nuts.

2. Remove or disconnect the following:
   • Negative battery cable from the remote ground post
   • Battery feed and posi-lock connectors
   • Starter heat shield nut and 2 bolts
   • 3 starter-to-engine/transaxle bolts
   • Starter by rotating it toward the engine and sliding it rearward between the catalyst and the engine mount

To install:

3. Install or connect the following:
   • Starter by sliding it forward between the catalyst and the engine mount and rotating it away from the engine
   • Starter and torque the 3 starter-to-engine/transaxle bolts 40 ft. lbs. (54 Nm)
   • Starter heat shield nut and 2 bolts
   • Positive battery cable and torque the nut to 90 inch lbs. (10 Nm)

   • Posi-lock connectors
   • Negative battery cable to the remote ground post

4. On 1998, at the catalyst support bracket, install the bracket nut and the 2 bracket mounting nuts.

3.2L and 3.5L (VIN G) Engines

1. On 1998, at the catalyst support bracket, remove the bracket nut and the 2 bracket mounting nuts.

2. Remove or disconnect the following:
   • Negative battery cable from the remote ground post
   • Starter-to-engine/transaxle nut and bolts
   • Positive battery feed wire from the starter
   • Starter and position it to gain access to the posi-lock connector

3. Place a support under the engine and slightly relieve the pressure from the left engine mount.

4. Remove the 3 left engine mount-to-engine bolts.

5. Slightly, raise the engine to provide more room.

6. Remove the starter by sliding it rearward between the catalyst and the engine mount.

7. Remove or disconnect the following:
   • Posi-lock connector
   • Starter

To install:

8. Install or connect the following:
   • Starter
   • Posi-lock connector
   • Starter by sliding it forward between the catalyst and the engine mount

9. Slightly, lower the engine.
   • 3 left engine mount-to-engine bolts
   • Positive battery feed wire to the starter and torque the nut to 90 inch lbs. (10 Nm)
   • Starter and torque the starter-to-engine/transaxle bolts 40 ft. lbs. (54 Nm)
   • Negative battery cable to the remote ground post

10. On 1998, at the catalyst support bracket, install the bracket nut and the 2 bracket mounting nuts.

3.3L and 3.5L (VIN F) Engines

1. Disconnect the negative battery cable.

2. Remove the starter-to-engine/transaxle bolts.

3. Position the starter to gain access to the wiring connectors.

4. Remove or disconnect the following:
- Positive battery cable-to-starter nut and cable
- Solenoid wire connector
- Starter

To install:

5. Install or connect the following:
- Starter

6. Position the starter to gain access to the wiring connectors.
- Solenoid wire connector
- Positive battery cable and torque the nut to 90 inch lbs. (10 Nm)
- Starter and torque the starter-to-engine/transaxle bolts 40 ft. lbs. (54 Nm)
- Negative battery cable

Oil Pan

REMOVAL & INSTALLATION

2.7L, 3.2L, and 1998–01 3.5L (VIN G) Engines

1. Before servicing the vehicle, refer to the precautions in the beginning of this section.

2. Drain the engine oil and remove the oil filter.

3. Remove or disconnect the following:
- Negative battery cable
- Dipstick and housing
- Structural collar from the rear of the oil pan and transmission housing
- Engine oil cooler lines from the oil pan, if equipped
- Transmission oil cooler line clips, if necessary
- Oil pan mounting bolts, oil pan and gasket

4. Clean the oil pan and all gasket surfaces.

To install:

5. Apply a ⅛ in. (3mm) bead of sealer at the parting line of the oil pump body and the rear seal retainer.

6. Install or connect the following:
- Oil pan to the engine block and tighten the M8 nuts/bolts to 21 ft. lbs. (28 Nm) and the M6 nuts/bolts to 105 inch lbs. (12 Nm)

7. Install the structural collar using the following procedure:
   a. Install the vertical collar to the oil

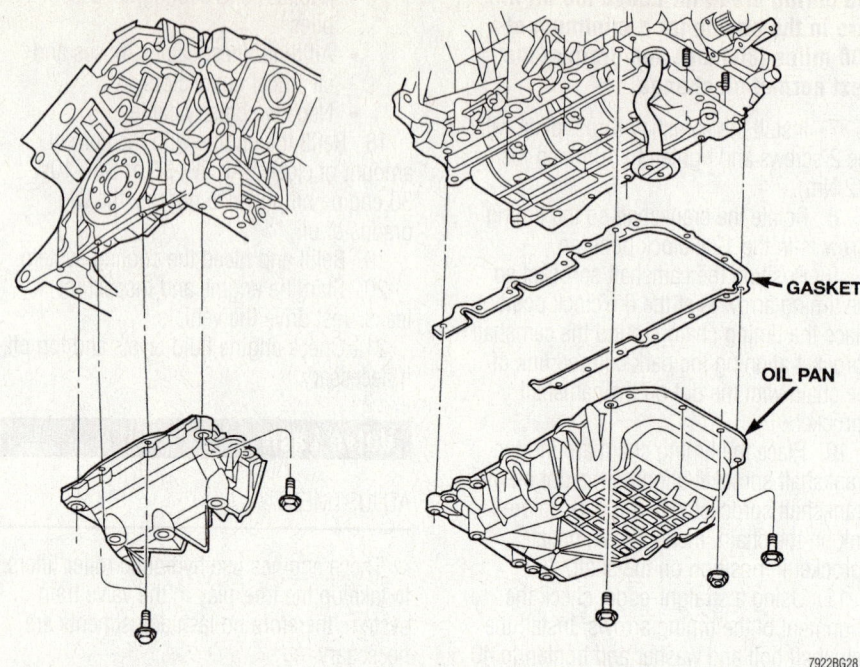

Exploded view of the oil pan removal and installation—2.7L and 1998–01 3.5L (VIN G) engines

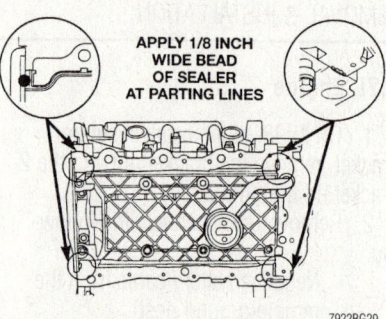

APPLY 1/8 INCH WIDE BEAD OF SEALER AT PARTING LINES

To ensure a proper seal, apply sealer as shown—2.7L and 1998–01 3.5L engines

pan mounting bolts and tighten, temporarily to 10 inch lbs. (1.1 Nm).

   b. Install the collar-to-transaxle bolts and tighten to 40 ft. lbs. (55 Nm).

   c. Starting with the center vertical bolt and working outward, tighten the bolts to 40 ft. lbs. (55 Nm).

8. Install or connect the following:
- Negative battery cable
- Dipstick and housing

9. Refill the engine with the proper amount of clean SAE 5W-30 or SAE 10W-30 engine oil only. Do not mix the two grades of oil.

10. Start the engine and check for leaks.

3.3L Engines

1. Before servicing the vehicle, refer to the precautions in the beginning of this section.

2. Drain the engine oil.

3. Remove or disconnect the following:
- Negative battery cable
- Engine oil dipstick
- Oil filter
- Sway bar and move to the rear of the vehicle, if necessary
- Transaxle support bracket and inspection cover
- Oil pan bolts and oil pan
- Oil pickup tube, if necessary. Discard the old oil pickup tube O-ring.

To install:

4. Thoroughly clean and dry the oil pan, cylinder block bolts and bolt holes. Inspect the oil pan flange for bends or distortion. Straighten the flange if necessary. Clean the oil screen and pipe in clean solvent. Inspect the condition of the screen and replace if necessary.

5. Apply a ⅛ in. (3mm) bead of sealer at the parting line of the chain case cover and the rear seal retainer.

6. Install or connect the following:
- New O-ring on the oil pickup tube and install it into the pump body. Tighten the screws to 20 ft. lbs. (28 Nm), if removed.
- New oil pan gasket
- Oil pan and tighten bolts to 108 inch lbs. (12 Nm)
- Transaxle support bracket and inspection cover
- Sway bar

- Oil pan drain plug and new oil filter
- Oil dipstick.
- Negative battery cable

7. Refill the engine with the proper amount of clean SAE 5W-30 or SAE 10W-30 engine oil only. Do not mix the two grades of oil.

8. Start the engine and check for leaks.

1997 3.5L (VIN F) Engine

1. Before servicing the vehicle, refer to the precautions in the beginning of this section.

2. Drain the engine oil.

3. Remove or disconnect the following:
- Negative battery cable
- Engine oil dipstick
- Oil filter
- Sway bar and move to the rear of the vehicle, if necessary
- Transaxle support bracket and inspection cover
- Oil pan screws and oil pan
- Oil pick-up tube, if necessary and the windage tray/oil pan gaskets

➡The windage tray and oil pan gasket are integral. The silicone rubber gaskets are bonded directly to both sides of the windage tray. This assembly is reusable if it is not damaged upon removal. Discard the old oil pickup tube O-ring.

➡Any old sealant must be carefully removed if the gasket is going to be used again.

To install:

4. Thoroughly clean and dry the oil pan, cylinder block bolts and bolt holes. Inspect the oil pan flange for bends or distortion. Straighten the flange if necessary. Clean the oil screen and pipe in clean solvent. Inspect the condition of the screen and replace if necessary.

5. Apply a ⅛ in. (3mm) bead of sealer at the parting line of the oil pump body and the rear seal retainer.

6. Install or connect the following:
- New O-ring on the oil pickup tube and tube into the pump body. Tighten the screws to 20 ft. lbs. (28 Nm), if removed.
- Windage tray/oil pan gasket
- Oil pan and retaining bolts. Tighten the screws to 108 inch lbs. (12 Nm).

- Transaxle support bracket and inspection cover
- Sway bar
- Oil pan drain plug and new oil filter
- Oil dipstick.
- Negative battery cable

7. Refill the engine with the proper amount of clean SAE 5W-30 or SAE 10W-30 engine oil only. Do not mix the two grades of oil.

8. Start the engine and check for leaks.

Oil Pump

REMOVAL & INSTALLATION

2.7L Engine

1. Before servicing the vehicle, refer to the precautions in the beginning of this section.

2. Remove or disconnect the following:

- Crankshaft damper
- Timing chain cover
- Timing chain
- Crankshaft sprocket
- Oil pan
- Oil pick-up tube and O-ring
- Oil pump

To install:

3. Fill the oil pump rotor cavity with clean engine oil.

4. Carefully, install the oil pump over the crankshaft and into position.

5. Install the oil pump mounting bolts and tighten to 21 ft. lbs. (28 Nm).

6. Lubricate the new pickup tube O-ring with clean engine oil and tighten the pickup tube mounting bolts to 21 ft. lbs. (28 Nm).

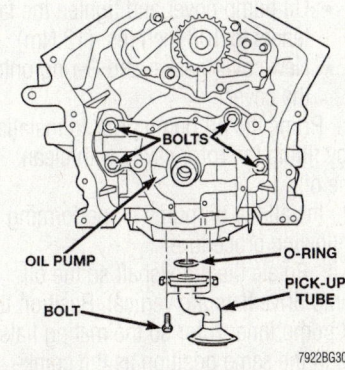

Oil pump mounting bolt locations—2.7L engine

7. Install or connect the following:
- Oil pan
- Crankshaft sprocket
- Timing chain
- Timing chain cover
- Crankshaft damper

8. Refill the crankcase with clean engine oil.

3.2L and 3.5L Engines

The timing belt must be removed to access the oil pump located behind the crankshaft drive sprocket. It is good practice to turn the crankshaft to TDC No. 1 cylinder compression stroke (firing position) before starting disassembly. This should align all timing marks and be a good point of reference for all work to follow.

1. Before servicing the vehicle, refer to the precautions in the beginning of this section.

2. Drain the cooling system and the radiator.

3. Drain the engine oil.

4. Remove or disconnect the following:

- Negative battery cable
- Accessory drive belts
- Oil filter
- Oil pan
- Oil pump pick-up tube
- Windage tray/oil pan gasket
- Crankshaft damper using a suitable puller tool
- Timing belt covers

5. Place matchmarks on the timing belt to aid installation. Align the matchmarks on the camshaft sprockets to marks on the rear timing belt covers before removing the timing belt.

6. Timing belt and inspect the belt for cracks or excessive wear; then, replace, if necessary.

7. Remove or disconnect the following:

- Crankshaft sprocket using a suitable puller tool
- Oil pump-to-engine screws and pump
- Oil pump cover screws and cover
- Oil pump rotors

8. Wash all parts in solvent and inspect carefully for damage or wear.

To install:

9. Clean all parts well. There should be no traces of old gasket/sealer on any components.

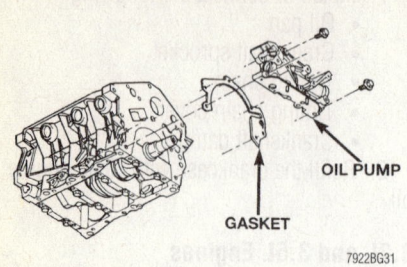

OIL PUMP

GASKET

7922BG31

Prime the oil pump before installation, because a dry pump will wear prematurely and cause low oil pressure—3.2L and 3.5L engines

10. Assemble the oil pump with new parts as required.

11. Install the pump cover and tighten the fasteners to 108 inch lbs. (12 Nm).

12. Prime the oil pump prior to installation by filling the rotor cavity with clean engine oil.

13. Install the oil pump and tighten the oil pump-to-engine screws as follows:
- M8 screws: 21 ft. lbs. (28 Nm)
- M10 screws: 40 ft. lbs. (55 Nm)

14. Tighten the oil pan drain plug and install a new oil filter.

15. Install or connect the following:
- Oil pump pick-up tube
- Windage tray/oil pan gasket
- Oil pan. Tighten the oil pan fasteners to 108 inch lbs. (12 Nm). Pay attention to sealing the oil pan gasket and its integral windage tray.
- Crankshaft sprocket using tool C-4685C1, thrust bearing, washer and 12mm bolt to draw the sprocket onto the crankshaft
- Timing belt
- Timing belt covers, thrust bearing, washer plate and vibration damper using tool L-4524
- Accessory drive belts
- Radiator and radiator hoses
- Negative battery cable

16. Refill and bleed the cooling system.

17. Refill the engine with the correct amount of clean SAE 5W-30 or SAE 10W-30 engine oil only. Do not mix the two grades of oil.

18. Run the engine. Check for leaks and proper oil pressure.

3.3L Engines

1. Before servicing the vehicle, refer to the precautions in the beginning of this section.

2. Drain the cooling system.

3. Raise and safely support the vehicle.

4. Drain the engine oil.

5. Remove or disconnect the following:
- Negative battery cable
- Radiator
- Oil filter
- Sway bar and place it to the rear of the vehicle to gain access to the oil pan
- Transmission support brackets and inspection cover
- Oil pan and pickup tube
- Accessory drive belts and tensioner pulley bracket
- Power steering pump and set aside
- Air compressor and set it aside
- Air compressor bracket

➡ **It is not necessary to disconnect the refrigerant lines or evacuate the refrigerant system.**

- Crankshaft pulley using a puller
- Tensioner pulley bracket
- Camshaft sensor from the chain case cover
- Timing chain case cover bolts and cover

6. Clean the gasket material from the mating surfaces of the cover and the block.

7. Remove or disconnect the following:
- Oil pump cover screws and cover
- Oil pump rotors
- Crankshaft oil seal from the front cover

8. Wash all parts in solvent and inspect carefully for damage or wear.

To install:

9. Clean all parts well. Assemble the oil pump with new parts as required.

10. Install or connect the following:
- Inner rotor with the chamfer facing the oil pump cover
- Oil pump cover and tighten the fasteners to 108 inch lbs. (12 Nm)
- New cover gasket and O-ring onto the cover

11. Prime the oil pump prior to installation by filling the rotor cavity with clean engine oil.

12. Install the oil pump by performing the following procedure:

a. Rotate the crankshaft so the oil pump drive flats are vertical. Position the oil pump inner rotor so the mating flats are in the same position as the crankshaft drive flats.

b. Install the front cover making sure the pump is correctly engaged on the crankshaft or severe damage may result.

13. Install the timing chain case cover screws and snug the 2 bottom screws and the top center screw. Ensure the cover is seated to the block, then tighten all screws to 20 ft. lbs. (27 Nm).

14. Install or connect the following:
- Crankshaft damper
- Tensioner pulley bracket
- Cam sensor
- Air conditioning compressor
- Accessory drive belt

15. Tighten the oil pan drain plug and install a new oil filter.

16. Install or connect the following:
- Oil pump pickup tube
- Oil pan
- Transaxle inspection cover, if removed
- Negative battery cable

17. Refill the crankcase with clean engine oil to the proper level. Install a new oil filter.

18. Install the radiator assembly. Check the condition of the radiator hoses. Refill and bleed the cooling system.

19. Run the engine and check for leaks. Verify correct oil pressure with a gauge.

Rear Main Seal

REMOVAL & INSTALLATION

1. Before servicing the vehicle, refer to the precautions in the beginning of this section.

2. Remove or disconnect the following:
- Negative battery cable
- Transaxle, inspection cover and flywheel/flexplate

3. Using a small prytool, carefully pry out the rear oil seal. Be careful not to nick or damage the crankshaft flange seal surface or the retainer bore.

To install:

4. Place the Seal Pilot tool C-4681 or equivalent, onto the crankshaft.

5. Lightly coat the oil seal outside diameter with Loctite® Stud N' Bearing Mount® or the equivalent.

6. Apply a light coating of engine oil to the entire circumference of the oil seal lip.

7. Place the seal over the special tool and tap the seal in place with a plastic mallet.

8. Install or connect the following:
- Flexplate/flywheel
- Transaxle
- Negative battery cable

Timing Chain, Sprockets, Front Cover and Seal

REMOVAL & INSTALLATION

2.7L Engine

❋❋ WARNING

When aligning the timing marks, rotate the crankshaft, not the camshafts. DO NOT rotate the camshafts or crankshaft with the timing chain removed without locating the crankshaft position, piston and/or valve damage may occur.

1. Before servicing the vehicle, refer to the precautions in the beginning of this section.

2. Remove or disconnect the following:

- Upper intake manifold and valve covers
- Upper radiator crossmember
- Fan module
- Accessory drive belts

3. Using Crankshaft Damper Holder

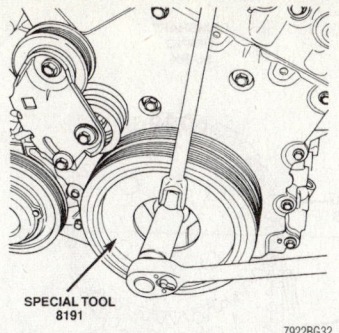

SPECIAL TOOL 8191

Removing the crankshaft center bolt using the Crankshaft Damper Holder tool—2.7L engine

tool 8191 or equivalent, hold the crankshaft and remove the center bolt.

4. Remove or disconnect the following:

- Damper using a 3-jaw puller
- Power steering pump and position it aside without disconnecting the hydraulic lines
- Accessory drive belt tensioner pulley
- Timing chain cover bolts

5. Clean and inspect the sealing surfaces.

6. Align the crankshaft sprocket timing mark with the oil pump housing mark.

➡ **The mark on the oil pump housing is 60 degrees ATDC.**

7. Remove or disconnect the following:

- Primary timing chain tensioner from the right cylinder head
- Camshaft Position (CKP) sensor and timing chain access plug from the left cylinder head

➡ **The camshafts will rotate clockwise, when the camshaft sprocket bolts are removed.**

- Right camshaft sprocket mounting bolts, camshaft damper and sprocket
- Left camshaft sprocket bolts and sprocket
- Lower timing chain guide, tensioner arm and primary timing chain

To install:

➡ **Lubricate the timing chain and guides with clean engine oil before installation.**

8. Install the timing chain by performing the following procedure:

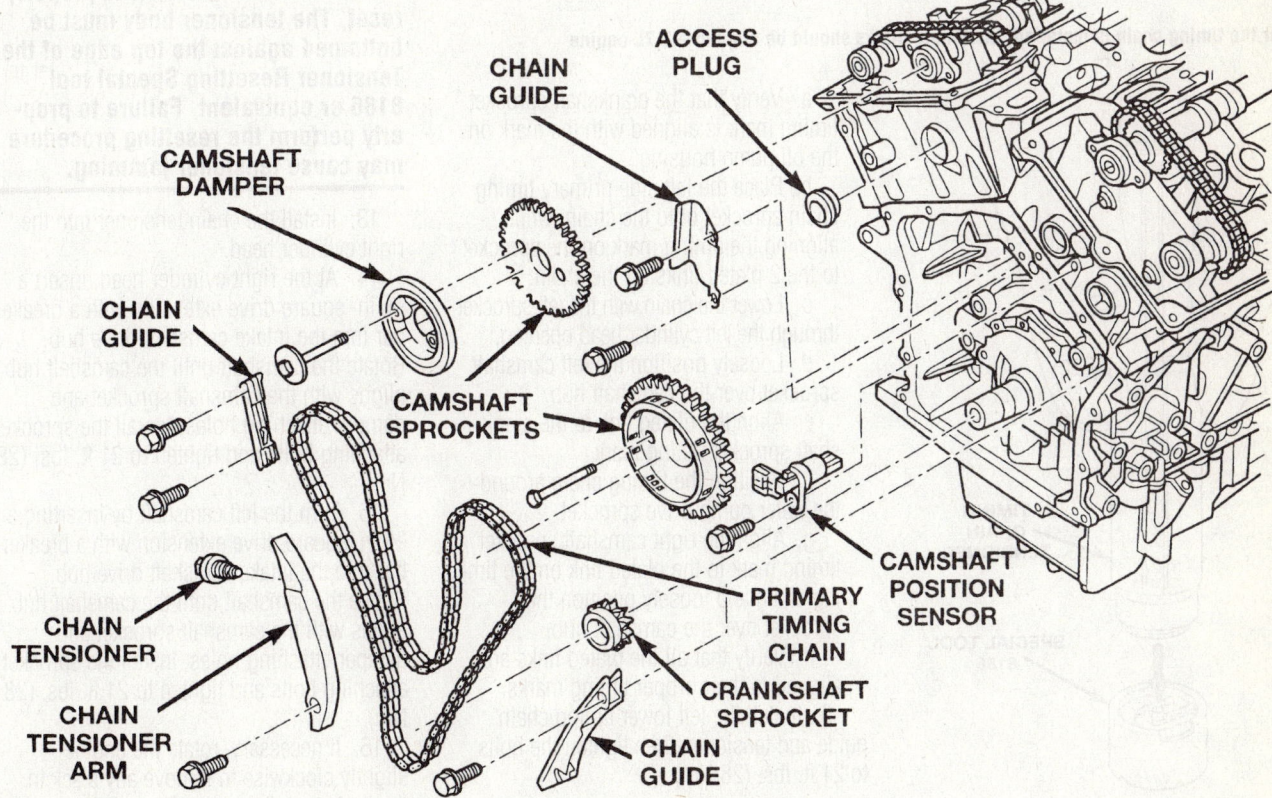

CHAIN GUIDE

ACCESS PLUG

CAMSHAFT DAMPER

CHAIN GUIDE

CAMSHAFT SPROCKETS

CHAIN TENSIONER

CHAIN TENSIONER ARM

PRIMARY TIMING CHAIN

CRANKSHAFT SPROCKET

CHAIN GUIDE

CAMSHAFT POSITION SENSOR

Exploded view of the timing chain drive assembly—2.7L engine

Refer to Section 1 for engine rebuilding specifications

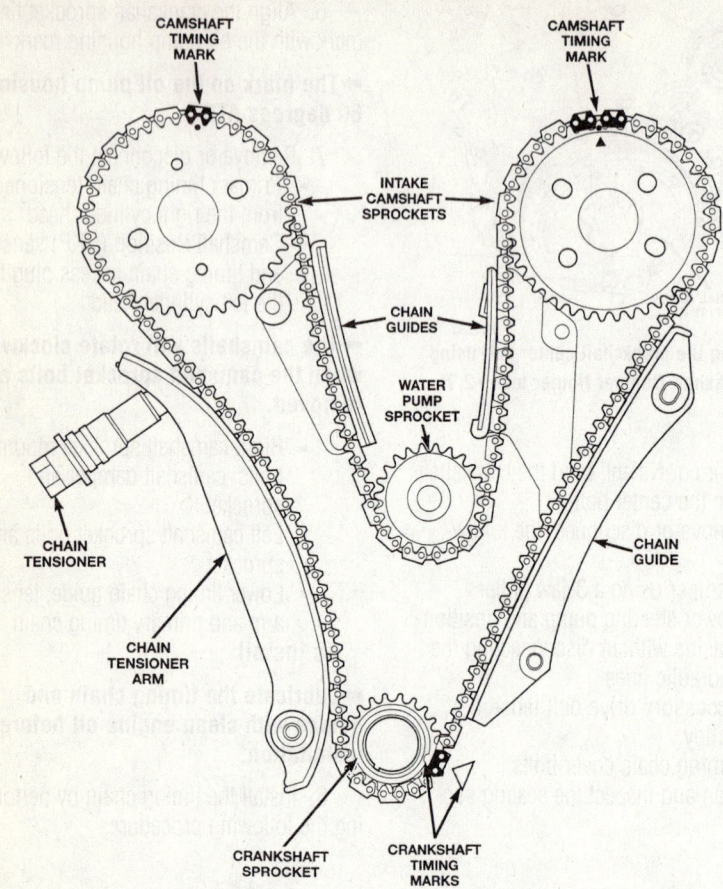

After the timing chain is installed, the timing marks should be aligned—2.7L engine

7922BG34

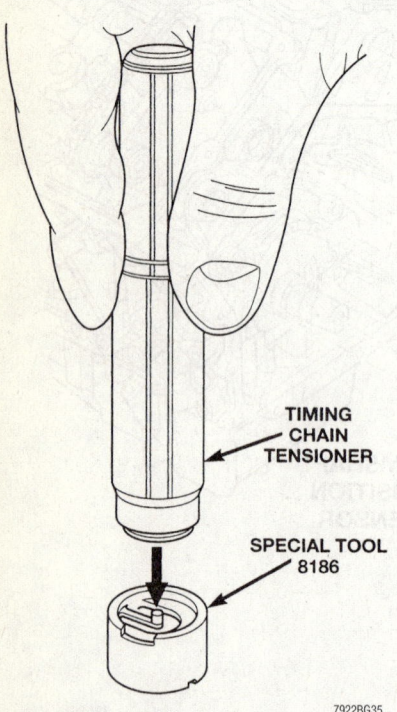

TIMING CHAIN TENSIONER

SPECIAL TOOL 8186

7922BG35

Using the Tensioner Resetting Special tool or equivalent, to purge the oil from the tensioner—2.7L engine

a. Verify that the crankshaft sprocket timing mark is aligned with the mark on the oil pump housing.

b. Place the left side primary timing chain sprocket onto the chain, while aligning the timing mark on the sprocket to the 2 plated links on the chain.

c. Lower the chain with the left sprocket through the left cylinder head opening.

d. Loosely position the left camshaft sprocket over the camshaft hub.

e. Align the plated link to the crankshaft sprocket timing mark.

f. Position the timing chain around the water pump drive sprocket.

g. Align the right camshaft sprocket timing mark to the plated link on the timing chain and loosely position the sprocket over the camshaft hub.

h. Verify that all the plated links are aligned to their proper timing marks.

9. Install the left lower timing chain guide and tensioner, then tighten the bolts to 21 ft. lbs. (28 Nm).

➡**Inspect the timing chain guide access plug O-rings before installing. Replace damaged O-rings as necessary.**

10. Install the timing chain guide access plug to the left cylinder head and tighten to 15 ft. lbs. (20 Nm).

➡**To reset the timing chain tensioner, oil will first need to be purged from the tensioner.**

11. Purge oil from the timing chain tensioner using the following procedure:

a. Remove the tensioner from the tensioner housing.

b. Place the check ball end of the tensioner into the shallow end of the Tensioner Resetting Special tool 8186 or equivalent.

c. Using hand pressure, slowly depress the tensioner until oil is purged from the cylinder.

d. Reinstall the tensioner into the tensioner housing.

12. Reset the timing chain tensioner using the following procedure:

a. Position the cylinder plunger into the deeper side of the Tensioner Resetting special tool 8186 or equivalent.

b. Apply a downward force until the tensioner is reset.

❋❋ WARNING

Ensure that the tensioner is properly reset. The tensioner body must be bottomed against the top edge of the Tensioner Resetting Special tool 8186 or equivalent. Failure to properly perform the resetting procedure may cause tensioner jamming.

13. Install the chain tensioner into the right cylinder head.

14. At the right cylinder head, insert a ⅜ in. square drive extension with a breaker bar into the intake camshaft drive hub. Rotate the camshaft until the camshaft hub aligns with the camshaft sprocket and damper attaching holes. Install the sprocket attaching bolts and tighten to 21 ft. lbs. (28 Nm).

15. Turn the left camshaft by inserting a ⅜ in. square drive extension with a breaker bar into the intake camshaft drive hub. Rotate the camshaft until the camshaft hub aligns with the camshaft sprocket and damper attaching holes. Install the sprocket attaching bolts and tighten to 21 ft. lbs. (28 Nm).

16. If necessary, rotate the engine slightly clockwise to remove any slack in the timing chain.

17. To arm the timing chain tensioner: Use a flat-bladed prytool to gently pry the tensioner arm towards the tensioner slightly.

Then, release the tensioner arm. Verify the tensioner extends.

18. Inspect and replace the timing chain cover gasket and oil seal.

19. Apply a ⅛ in. (3mm) bead of sealer at the parting line of the oil pan and engine block.

➡**When installing the timing cover, guide the seal over the crankshaft to prevent damage to the seal's lip.**

20. Install or connect the following:
- Timing cover and gasket. Tighten the M10 bolts to 40 ft. lbs. (54 Nm) and the M6 bolts to 105 inch lbs. (12 Nm)
- Crankshaft damper
- Accessory drive belt tensioner pulley
- Power steering pump
- Crankshaft damper
- Crankshaft center bolt to 125 ft. lbs. (170 Nm) using tool 8191
- Accessory drive belts
- Fan module and electrical wiring harness
- Upper radiator crossmember
- Negative battery cable

3.3L Engines

1. Before servicing the vehicle, refer to the precautions in the beginning of this section.

2. Drain the cooling system.

3. Drain the engine oil.

4. Relieve the fuel system pressure.

5. Rotate the engine to Top Dead Center (TDC) on No. 1 cylinder. This provides a reference point.

6. Remove or disconnect the following:
- Negative battery cable
- Remove the radiator and cooling fan assemblies

- Sway bar to gain access to the oil pan
Negative battery cable
- Transaxle support brackets and inspection cover
- Engine oil pan and oil pump pick-up
- Accessory drive belt(s)
- Power steering pump and set aside
- Air conditioning compressor and set aside, if necessary
- Crankshaft damper using a puller
- Tensioner pulley bracket
- Camshaft Position (CMP) sensor from the chain case cover
- Timing chain cover and oil seal

7. If the chain is out of specification, remove the camshaft sprocket bolt and the timing chain with the sprocket.

8. Remove the crankshaft sprocket using a puller. Be careful not to damage the crankshaft surface.

To install:

9. Install the timing chain by performing the following procedure:

a. Position a new crankshaft sprocket onto the shaft, then install the sprocket with a suitably-sized socket and a rubber or plastic mallet. Be sure that the sprocket is seated in position.

b. Rotate the crankshaft, if needed, until the timing mark is in the 12 o'clock position.

c. Situate the timing chain on the camshaft sprocket and hold the camshaft sprocket so that the timing mark is in the 6 o'clock position.

d. Align the dark links with the camshaft sprocket dot, place the timing chain around the crankshaft sprocket with the dark link aligned with the sprocket dot and install the camshaft sprocket onto the camshaft.

e. Using a straightedge, check the alignment of the crankshaft and camshaft timing marks.

f. Install the camshaft bolt and washer. Tighten the bolt to 40 ft. lbs. (54 Nm).

g. Rotate the crankshaft 2 full revolutions. The timing marks should align. If the timing marks do not align, remove the camshaft sprocket and realign it.

10. Check the camshaft end-play. With a new thrust plate, the specification is 0.005–0.012 in. (0.0127–0.304mm). The old thrust plate specification is 0.012 in. (0.31mm) maximum. If not within these limits install a new thrust plate.

11. Install the timing chain snubbers. Tighten the retaining screws to 108 inch lbs. (12 Nm).

✳✳ WARNING

Each model year engine may use different length bolts, therefore do not use bolts from any other model year engine.

12. Clean all parts well. Use care to remove all old sealer and gasket material from the timing chain cover.

➡**The crankshaft oil seal must be removed to insure correct oil pump engagement.**

13. Remove the old oil seal from the timing case cover. Be sure that the mating surfaces for the timing chain cover gasket are clean and free of any burrs. Rotate the crankshaft so that the oil pump drive flats are vertical. Position the oil pump inner rotor so the mating flats are in the same position as the crankshaft drive flats. Install the timing chain front cover using new gasket and O-rings.

✳✳ WARNING

Be sure the oil pump is engaged on the crankshaft correctly or severe damage may result.

14. Install the chain case cover screws. Snug the 2 bottom screws and the top center screw. Be sure the cover is seated on the block, then tighten all the other screws to 20 ft. lbs. (27 Nm).

15. Install or connect the following:
- New front cover oil seal
- Crankshaft damper and tighten the center bolt to 40 ft. lbs. (54 Nm)
- Tensioner pulley bracket

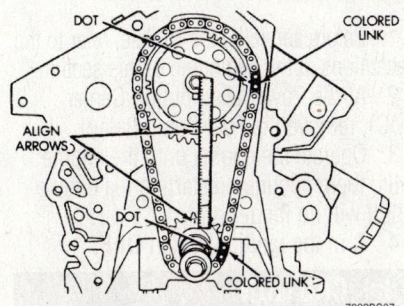

Using a straightedge to align the timing marks during installation—3.3L engine

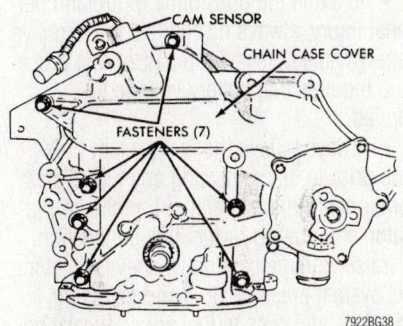

Timing cover mounting bolt locations— 3.3L engine

For engine torque specifications, refer to Section 1 of this manual

- CMP sensor
- Accessory drive belt(s)
- Oil pump pick-up tube and oil pan
- Transaxle support brackets and inspection cover
- Power steering pump and air conditioning compressor, if removed
- Sway bar
- Radiator and cooling fan assemblies
- Negative battery cable

16. Refill the engine with the correct amount of clean SAE 5W-30 or SAE 10W-30 engine oil only. Do not mix the two grades of oil. A filter change is recommended.

17. Refill and bleed the cooling system.

18. Test run the engine and check for leaks.

Piston and Rings

POSITIONING

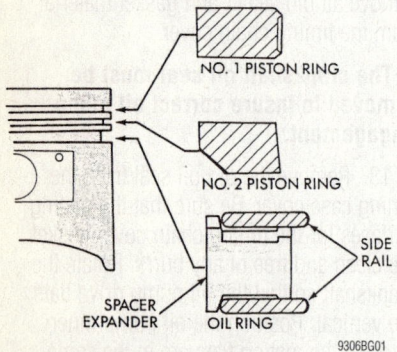

Cross-sectional view of the piston rings—2.7L, 3.3L, 3.5L (VIN F) Engines

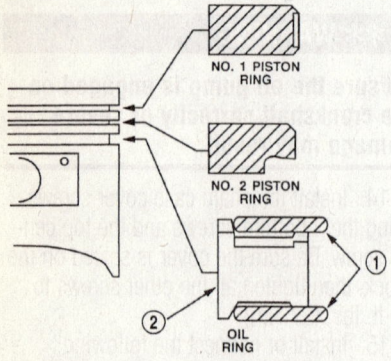

1 – SIDE RAIL
2 – SPACER EXPANDER

Cross-sectional view of the piston rings—3.5L (VIN G) Engine

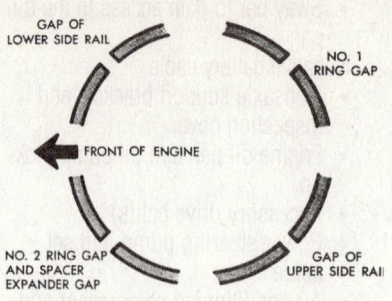

Piston ring gap positions—3.3L Engine

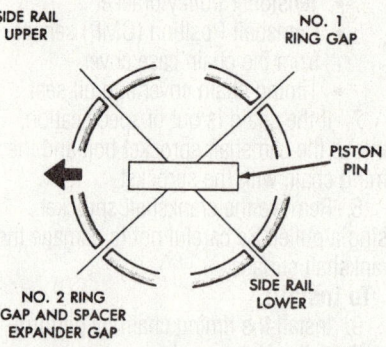

Piston ring gap positions—2.7L, 3.2L, 3.5L Engines

FUEL SYSTEM

Fuel System Service Precautions

Safety is the most important factor when performing not only fuel system maintenance but any type of maintenance. Failure to conduct maintenance and repairs in a safe manner may result in serious personal injury or death. Maintenance and testing of the vehicle's fuel system components can be accomplished safely and effectively by adhering to the following rules and guidelines:

- To avoid the possibility of fire and personal injury, always disconnect the negative battery cable unless the repair or test procedure requires that battery voltage be applied.

- Always relieve the fuel system pressure prior to disconnecting any fuel system component (injector, fuel rail, pressure regulator, etc.), fitting or fuel line connection. Exercise extreme caution whenever relieving fuel system pressure, to avoid exposing skin, face and eyes to fuel spray. Please be advised that fuel under pressure may penetrate the skin or any part of the body that it contacts.

- Always place a shop towel or cloth

around the fitting or connection prior to loosening to absorb any excess fuel due to spillage. Ensure that all fuel spillage (should it occur) is quickly removed from engine surfaces. Ensure that all fuel soaked cloths or towels are deposited into a suitable waste container.

- Always keep a dry chemical (Class B) fire extinguisher near the work area.

- Do not allow fuel spray or fuel vapors to come into contact with a spark or open flame.

- Always use a back-up wrench when loosening and tightening fuel line connection fittings. This will prevent unnecessary stress and torsion to fuel line piping.

- Always replace worn fuel fitting O-rings with new. Do not substitute fuel hose or equivalent, where fuel pipe is installed.

Before servicing the vehicle, also make sure to refer to the precautions in the beginning of this section as well.

Fuel System Pressure

RELIEVING

1997 Models

1. Before servicing the vehicle, refer to the precautions in the beginning of this section.

2. Remove or disconnect the following:
- Negative battery cable
- Fuel filler cap
- Fuel pressure test port safety cap located on the fuel rail

3. Place the open end of the fuel pressure release hose tool C-4799–1 or equivalent, into a proper gasoline container.

4. Connect the other end of the hose to the fuel pressure test port.

5. Open fuel pressure test port and bleed off fuel.

1998–01 Models

1. Before servicing the vehicle, refer to the precautions in the beginning of this section.

2. At the Power Distribution Center (PDC), remove the Fuel Pump Relay.

3. Operate the engine until the engine stalls; then, continue restarting the engine until it will no longer run.

4. Turn the ignition switch **OFF**.

✷✷ CAUTION

The previous steps must be performed to relieve the high pressure fuel from the fuel rail. The following steps must be performed to remove

excess fuel from the fuel rail. Do not use the following steps to relieve high pressure for excessive fuel will be forced into a cylinder chamber.

5. Disconnect the electrical connector from any injector.

6. Connect 1 end of a jumper wire (with an alligator clips) to either injector terminal and the other end to the positive side of the battery.

7. Connect 1 end of a second jumper wire to the other injector terminal.

✳✳ WARNING

Applying power to an injector for more than a few seconds will damage the injector.

8. Momentarily, touch the other end of the jumper wire to a ground for no more than a few seconds.

9. At the Power Distribution Center (PDC), install the fuel pump relay.

➡**When the fuel pump relay is removed, 1 or more Diagnostic Trouble Codes (DTC's) may be stored in the PCM memory. A DRB scan tool must by used to clear the DTC's.**

Fuel Filter

The fuel filter mounts to the frame rail in front of the fuel tank. The inlet and outlet ends of the filter are marked for installation purposes.

REMOVAL & INSTALLATION

1997 Models

1. Before servicing the vehicle, refer to the precautions in the beginning of this section.

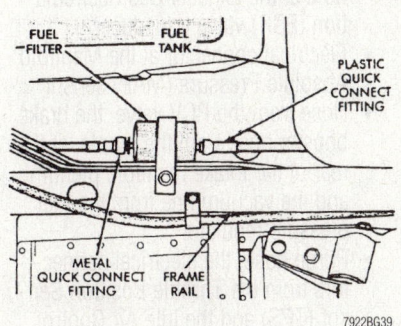

The fuel filter mounts to the frame rail in front of the fuel tank—1997 models

2. Relieve the fuel system pressure.

3. Disengage the quick-connect fittings from the filter.

4. Remove the filter mounting bracket, then the filter.

To install:

➡**The inlet and outlet sides of the filter are marked, install the filter with the inlet side to the fuel tank.**

5. Place the filter into the bracket. Place the bracket against the frame rail, tighten the mounting screw to 110 inch lbs. (12 Nm).

6. Apply a light coat of clean 30 weight engine oil to the fuel filter nipples. Install the fuel lines.

7. Start the engine and check for leaks.

1998–01 Models

➡**The fuel filter is part of the fuel pressure regulator mounted on the fuel pump module.**

1. Before servicing the vehicle, refer to the precautions in the beginning of this section.

2. Properly relieve the fuel system pressure.

3. Lower the fuel tank.

4. Remove or disconnect the following:
- Negative battery cable
- Purge and vent lines
- Fuel line from the pressure regulator
- Filter/regulator by pushing in the locking tab, turning the regulator to unlock it and pulling the it straight up

To install:

5. Push the fuel filter/regulator into the fuel pump module and turn to lock it into position.

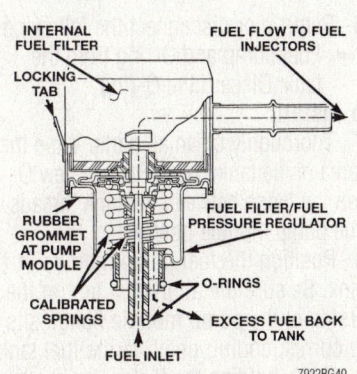

Cut away view of the fuel filter/pressure regulator—1998–01 models

6. Connect the fuel lines and install the tank.

7. Start the engine and check for leaks.

Fuel Pump

REMOVAL & INSTALLATION

1997 Models

An electric fuel pump is used with fuel injection systems and is located in the fuel tank. To perform the testing or servicing, use a DRB III or equivalent, scan tool.

1. Before servicing the vehicle, refer to the precautions in the beginning of this section.

2. Release the fuel system pressure.

3. Remove or disconnect the following:
- Negative battery cable
- Trunk liner
- Access panel fasteners
- Access panel and gasket. Inspect the gasket for damage. If necessary, replace the gasket.
- Electrical wiring from the top of fuel pump module

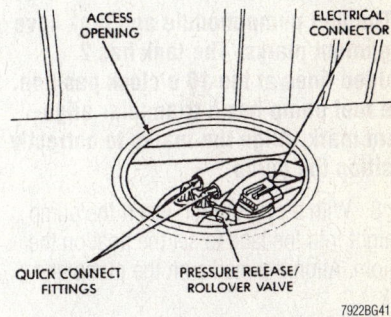

Once the cover is removed, access to the pump is obtained—1997 models

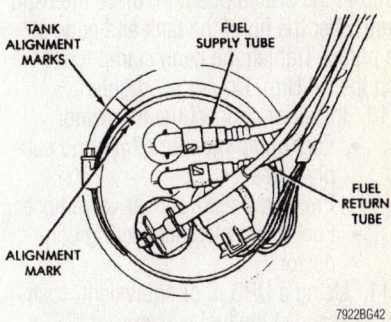

Note that the alignment marks must be aligned to install the pump correctly—1997 models

For complete service labor times order Nichols' Chilton Labor Guide Manual

- Fuel supply and return tubes from fuel pump module
- Pressure relief/rollover valve hose

➡ **A band clamp fastens the pump module to the tank. The module rises up from the tank after loosening the clamp.**

4. Loosen the band clamp until the pump module rises up from the tank.

❋❋ CAUTION

The pump reservoir may contain fuel. Do not spill fuel while removing the module.

5. To absorb any possible spillage, place a shop towel around the access opening. Without removing the module, tip it backwards to allow fuel in the reservoir to run down the side and back into the tank.

6. Remove the pump module and gasket from the tank.

➡ **The float arm of the sensor catches on the inside of the tank while removing the module. Tilt the module to the one side when removing it from the tank.**

7. Drain the remainder of fuel from the reservoir before servicing the pump module.

To install:

➡ **The fuel pump module and tank have alignment marks. The tank has 2 molded lines at the 10 o'clock position. The fuel pump has a triangular alignment mark. Align the marks to correctly position the pump.**

8. With a new gasket, insert the pump straight into the tank to set the float on the bottom. Align the marks on the pump and tank.

9. Seat the pump to the tank by pushing the top downward. Be sure the gasket does not slip over the outside or inside edge of the tank lip. While holding the pump in the seated position, place the band clamp over the lip of the tank and edge of the pump. Tighten the band clamp to 31 inch lbs. (4 Nm). Do not overtighten.

10. Install or connect the following:
- Fuel pump module return and supply tubes
- Pressure relief/rollover valve hose
- Fuel pump electrical wiring connector

11. Using a DRB III or equivalent, scan tool, pressurize the fuel system.

12. Check for leaks.

13. Install or connect the following:
- Access cover and gasket
- Trunk liner
- Negative battery cable

1998–01 Models

The in-tank fuel pump module contains the fuel pump and pressure regulator which adjusts fuel system pressure. Fuel pump voltage is supplied through the fuel pump relay.

The fuel pump is serviced as part of the fuel pump module. The fuel pump module is installed in the top of the fuel tank and contains the electric fuel pump, fuel pump reservoir, inlet strainer fuel gauge sending unit, fuel supply and return line connections and the pressure regulator. The inlet strainer, fuel pressure regulator and level sensor are the only serviceable items. If the fuel pump requires service, replace the fuel pump module.

1. Before servicing the vehicle, refer to the precautions in the beginning of this section.

2. Remove or disconnect the following:
- Fuel filler cap and properly relieve the fuel system pressure
- Negative battery cable
- Fuel tank

3. Clean the top of the tank to remove any loose dirt.

4. Remove or disconnect the following:
- Fuel lines from the fuel pump module by squeezing the quick-connect fitting with thumb and forefinger
- Fuel pump module electrical connector from the top of the fuel pump module

5. Using special tool 6856 or equivalent, remove the fuel pump locknut by turning it counterclockwise.

❋❋ CAUTION

The fuel reservoir of the fuel pump module does not empty out when the tank is drained. The fuel in the reservoir may spill out when the module is removed.

6. Remove or disconnect the following:
- Fuel pump and O-ring from the tank. Discard the O-ring.

To install:

7. Thoroughly clean all parts. Wipe the seal area of the tank clean. Place a new O-ring on the ledge between the tank threads and the pump module opening.

8. Position the fuel pump module in the tank. Be sure the alignment tab on the underside of the pump module flange sits in the corresponding notch in the fuel tank.

9. While holding the fuel pump module in place install the locking ring and tighten to 40 inch lbs. (5 Nm) using special tool 6856 or equivalent, spanner-type tool.

10. Install or connect the following:

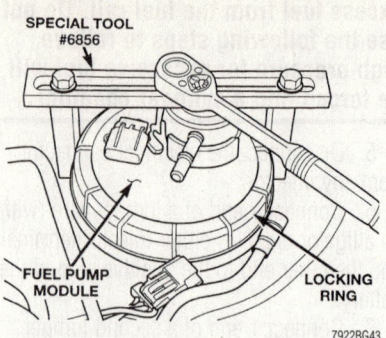

Using special tool 6856 or equivalent, remove the fuel pump module locknut—1998–01 models

- Fuel tank
- Fuel pump module electrical connector
- Negative battery cable

11. Fill the fuel tank with fuel. Install the fuel filler cap. Turn the ignition switch to the **ON** position to pressurize the system. Check the fuel system for leaks.

Fuel Injector

REMOVAL & INSTALLATION

3.3L Engine

1. Relieve the fuel system pressure.
2. Remove or disconnect the following:
- Negative battery cable
- Air plenum from the air cleaner and the throttle body

3. Move the throttle lever to the wide-open position; then, disconnect the throttle cable and the speed control cable from the lever.

4. At the cable bracket, compress the throttle cable and speed control cable locking tabs and remove them from the bracket.

5. Remove or disconnect the following:
- Electrical connector from the solenoid at the Exhaust Gas Recirculation (EGR) valve transducer
- Electrical connector at the Manifold Absolute Pressure (MAP) sensor
- Hose from the PCV valve, the brake booster hose from the nipple, at the rear of the intake manifold plenum and the vacuum line from the fuel pressure regulator
- Purge hose, the electrical connectors from the Throttle Position Sensor (TPS) and the Idle Air Control (IAC) motor at the throttle body
- EGR tube mounting screws at the intake manifold plenum
- Intake manifold plenum mounting bolts; then, lift the plenum off the

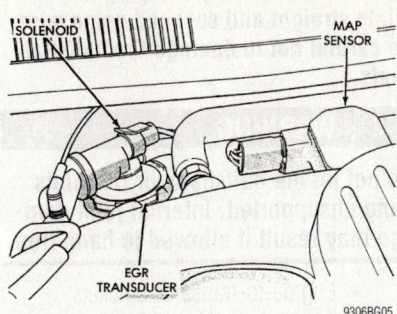

View of the EGR transducer and MAP sensor–3.3L engine

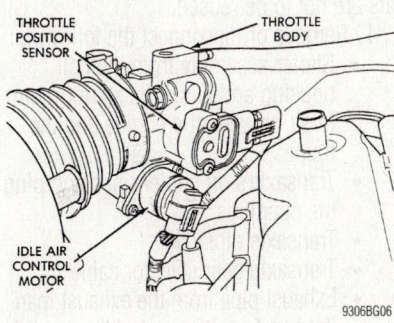

View of the throttle position sensor and idle air control motor–3.3L engine

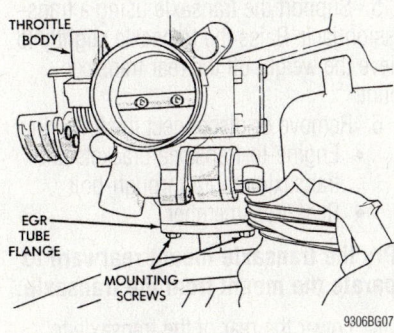

View of the EGR tube–3.3L engine

engine and cover the opening with a clean rag

6. Place a shop rag under the fuel rail's quick-connect fittings; then, squeeze the quick-connect fittings retainer tabs together and pull the fitting assemblies off of the fuel tube nipples.

7. Remove or disconnect the following:
- Fuel tube clamp screw and fuel tubes from the bracket
- Rotate the fuel injectors toward the center of the engine
- Fuel injector electrical connectors

- Fuel rail and cover the injector openings with a clean cloth

To install:

8. Lubricate the injector O-rings with clean engine oil.

9. Install or connect the following:
- Fuel injectors
- Fuel rail. Seat the injectors into the fuel rail; then, install the fuel rail bolts and torque to 200 inch lbs. (22 Nm).
- Fuel injector electrical connectors and rotate them toward the cylinder head covers

10. Lubricate the quick-connect fittings O-rings with clean engine oil; then, push the connectors together until the retainer seats and a click is heard.

11. Place the clamp over the fuel tubes and secure with the bolt.

12. Using a new gasket, position the intake manifold plenum on the intake manifold and loosely install the bolts.

13. Using a new gasket, install the EGR tube and loosely install the bolts.

14. Tighten the intake manifold plenum bolts in sequence; then, tighten the EGR tube mounting bolts.

15. Install or connect the following:
- PCV valve and brake booster hoses
- MAP sensor and EGR transducer solenoid electrical connectors
- TPS and IAC motor electrical connectors
- Throttle and speed control cables to throttle body bracket
- Throttle cable and speed control cable to the throttle lever when at wide-open position
- Air cleaner-to-throttle body air plenum
- Negative battery cable

3.5L (VIN F) Engine

1. Relieve the fuel system pressure.
2. Remove or disconnect the following:
- Negative battery cable
- Intake manifold plenum and cover the opening with a clean cloth
- Fuel supply and return tubes from fuel rail using tool 6751

3. Connect a Fuel Gauge Adapter tool 6631 to the fuel supply tube end of the fuel rail. Connect a fuel hose to the fuel return side of the fuel rail and place the other end into an approved gasoline container.

4. Using 55 psi (379 kPa) of compressed air at the adapter tool 6631, purge the excess fuel from the fuel rail.

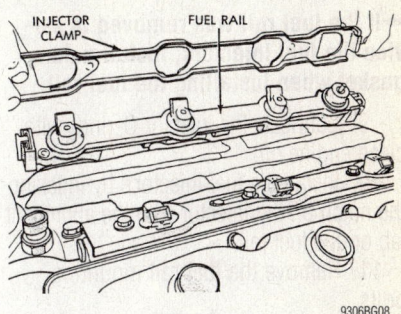

View of the injector clamp–3.5L (VIN F) engine

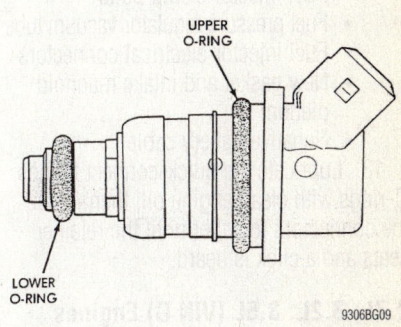

View of the fuel injector–3.5L (VIN F) engine

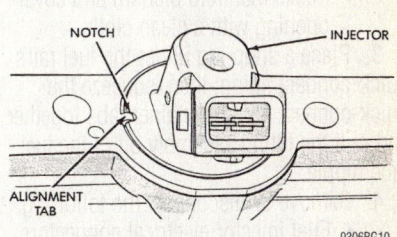

View of the fuel injector alignment tab–3.5L (VIN F) engine

5. Remove or disconnect the following:
- Fuel injector electrical connectors
- Fuel pressure regulator's vacuum tube
- Fuel rail-to-engine bolts and fuel injector clamp bolts
- Fuel injector clamps from the fuel rail by moving them rearward

6. Install the fuel rail mounting bolts finger-tight.

7. Using a small prybar, pry the fuel injector's out of the fuel rail.

8. Make sure the upper and lower O-rings were removed with the injectors; if not, remove them from the fuel rail.

To install:

➡️ **If the fuel rail was removed to service the fuel injectors, install a new gasket when installing the fuel rail.**

9. Lubricate the injector O-rings with clean engine oil.

10. Install the fuel injector's by indexing the notch on the injector with the alignment tab on the fuel rail.

11. Remove the fuel rail mounting bolts

12. Install or connect the following:
- Fuel injector clamps
- Fuel rail bolts and torque to 100 inch lbs. (11 Nm)
- Fuel injector clamp bolts
- Fuel pressure regulator vacuum tube
- Fuel injector electrical connectors
- New gasket and intake manifold plenum
- Negative battery cable

13. Lubricate the quick-connect fittings O-rings with clean engine oil; then, push the connectors together until the retainer seats and a click is heard.

2.7L, 3.2L, 3.5L (VIN G) Engines

1. Relieve the fuel system pressure.
2. Remove or disconnect the following:
- Negative battery cable
- Intake manifold plenum and cover opening with a clean cloth

3. Place a shop rag under the fuel rail's quick-connect fitting; then, squeeze the quick-connect fitting's retainer tabs together and pull the fitting assembly off of the fuel tube nipple.

4. Remove or disconnect the following:
- Fuel injector electrical connectors
- Fuel rail-to-engine bolts and fuel rail
- Fuel injector-to-fuel rail retainer clip's
- Fuel injector's

To install:

5. Lubricate the injector O-rings with clean engine oil.

6. Install or connect the following:
- Fuel injector's and secure with retaining clips
- Fuel rail onto cylinder head and press rail into place
- Fuel rail-to-cylinder head bolts and torque bolts to 100 inch lbs. (11 Nm)
- Intake plenum
- Negative battery cable

7. Lubricate the quick-connect fitting's O-rings with clean engine oil; then, push the connector together until the retainer seats and a click is heard.

DRIVE TRAIN

Transaxle Assembly

REMOVAL & INSTALLATION

The 42LE four speed transaxle uses fully-adaptive controls. Adaptive controls are those which perform their functions based on real-time feedback sensor information. The transaxle is conventional in the use of hydraulically applied clutches to shift a planetary gear train. However, it uses electronics to control virtually all other functions. The following components are serviceable in the vehicle: valve body assembly, solenoid pack, manual valve lever position sensor, input and output speed sensors, transfer chain and sprockets, short (right side) stub shaft seal and the long (left side) stub shaft and ball bearing. Note that the factory recommends that before attempting any repair on the 42LE four-speed automatic transaxle, always check for proper shift linkage adjustment. Also, check for diagnostic trouble codes with the Chrysler DRB scan tool or equivalent.

Use MOPAR Type 7176 Automatic Transmission Fluid only. Do not substitute transaxle fluid. If the differential sump requires fluid, use 80W-90 petroleum based Hypoid gear lubricant.

1. Before servicing the vehicle, refer to the precautions in the beginning of this section.

2. Remove or disconnect the following:
- Negative battery cable
- Engine air inlet tube
- Crankshaft Position (CKP) sensor connector and remove the sensor from the located on the upper right side of the transaxle bell housing
- Transaxle wiring connector block located on the right shock tower. To free the connector from the harness, remove the wire ties.
- Front wheels
- Strut-to-steering knuckle bolts on both sides of the vehicle and/or tie rod ends, if required
- ABS wheel speed sensor, if equipped
- Halfshafts

➡️ **Remove the halfshafts by inserting a prybar between the halfshaft and the transaxle case and prying the shafts from the transaxle housing. Swing the**

shafts out of the way, keeping the joints straight and suspend using wire. Be careful not to damage the halfshaft seals.

✳✳ WARNING

Do not let the halfshafts or CV-joints hang unsupported. Internal joint damage may result if allowed to hang free.

- Engine-to-transaxle brackets
- Transaxle bell housing cover

3. Mark the driveplate to the torque converter and remove the torque converter bolts. The driveplate-to-torque converter bolts are not to be reused.

4. Remove or disconnect the following:
- Starter assembly from the bell housing and allow the starter motor to sit between the engine and the frame
- Transaxle's oil cooler lines and plug the openings
- Transaxle dipstick
- Transaxle gear selector cable
- Exhaust pipe from the exhaust manifold and position out of the way

➡️ **If the clearance will not allow for transaxle removal, remove the exhaust system from the vehicle.**

5. Support the transaxle using a transmission jack. Raise the transaxle slightly to relieve the weight off the rear transaxle mount.

6. Remove or disconnect the following:
- Engine-to-transaxle brackets and transaxle mount through-bolt
- Rear crossmember

➡️ **Pry the transaxle mount rearward to separate the mount from the transaxle.**

7. Lower the rear of the transaxle to gain access to the bell housing bolts. Remove the bell housing bolts.

8. Place a drain pan under the dipstick in the transaxle to catch transaxle fluid that will drain out of the case.

9. Remove or disconnect the following:
- Transaxle dipstick tube and plug hole
- Engine-to-transaxle bolts and transaxle

➡️ **The driveplate-to-torque converter bolts and the driveplate-to-crankshaft bolts must not be reused. Install new bolts whenever these bolts are removed.**

10. Inspect the driveplate for cracks. If cracks are present, replace the driveplate.

To install:

➡ **Apply a light coating of grease to the pilot hole of the crankshaft if the torque converter is being replaced.**

✳✳ WARNING

When installing the transaxle, be careful that the fuel tubes at the rear of the engine do not contact the following:

11. Install or connect the following:
   - Tie rod attachment plate at the power steering rack
   - EGR tube
   - Transaxle wiring harness
   - Driveplate and tighten the fastener to 75 ft. lbs. (101 Nm)
   - Transaxle and tighten engine-to-transaxle case bolts to 75 ft. lbs. (101 Nm)
   - Rear transaxle case mount and rear crossmember in position and secure all fasteners
   - Transaxle dipstick tube
   - Exhaust pipe to engine exhaust manifold
   - Transaxle gear selector cable and oil cooler lines
   - Starter and tighten bolts to 40 ft. lbs. (54 Nm). Be sure that the starter ground strap is installed correctly
   - Align torque converter matchmarks and torque new torque converter-to-driveplate bolts to 60 ft. lbs. (81 Nm)
   - Bell housing cover and engine-to-transaxle brackets

12. While pulling the top of the steering knuckle outward, install the inner CV-joint, with new retainer clip in place, into the transaxle.

13. Install or connect the following:
   - ABS wheel sensor (if removed) and strut-to-steering knuckle bolts
   - Front wheels and tighten the lug nuts, in a star pattern sequence, to 95–100 ft. lbs. (129–135 Nm)
   - Transaxle's dipstick
   - Transaxle's wiring harness connector on the right shock tower
   - CKP sensor
   - Air inlet tube and negative battery cable

14. Start the engine and allow it to idle for 2 minutes. Apply the parking brake and move the selector through each gear posi-

tion, ending in **N**. Recheck the fluid level and add if necessary. Be sure the vehicle is level when refilling the transaxle. Use Mopar Type 7176 Automatic Transmission Fluid (ATF) only. Do not substitute transaxle fluid. If the differential sump requires fluid, use 80W-90 petroleum based Hypoid gear lubricant.

15. Check the transaxle or proper operation. Adjust the shift linkage, if necessary. Be sure the reverse lamps come on when in reverse.

Halfshaft

REMOVAL & INSTALLATION

✳✳ WARNING

Allowing the CV-joint assemblies to dangle unsupported, or pulling or pushing the ends, can damage boots or CV-joints. Always support both ends of the halfshaft to prevent damage or disengagement of the Tri-pot joint.

1. Before servicing the vehicle, refer to the precautions in the beginning of this section.

2. Remove or disconnect the following:
   - Negative battery cable
   - Front wheels
   - Front caliper assembly from steering knuckle
   - Front brake rotor from the hub
   - Speed sensor cable routing bracket from strut assembly
   - Hub and bearing-to-stub axle retainer nut

3. Install a puller tool onto the hub and bearing assembly and secure it into place using the wheel lug nuts.

4. Protect wheel stud threads by installing a wheel lug nut onto a wheel stud. Use a flat-bladed prying tool to prevent the hub from turning. Using the puller tool, force the halfshaft outer stub axle from the hub and bearing assembly.

5. Dislodge the inner Tri-pot joint from the stub shaft retaining snapring on the transaxle. To do this, insert a pry-bar between the transaxle case and the inner Tri-pot joint and pry on Tri-pot joint.

➡ **Do not try to remove the inner Tri-pot joint from the transaxle stub shaft at**

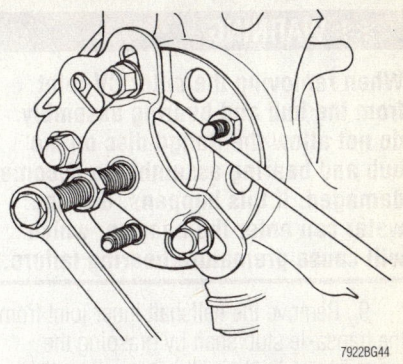

Removing the stub axle from the front hub/bearing assembly—halfshaft service

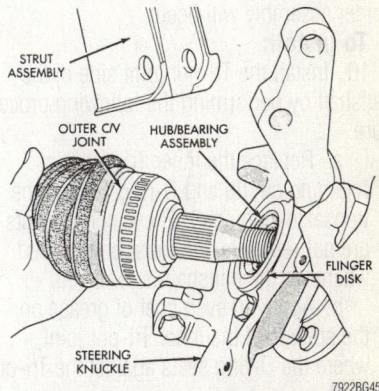

STRUT ASSEMBLY
OUTER CV JOINT
HUB/BEARING ASSEMBLY
FLINGER DISK
STEERING KNUCKLE
7922BG45

Be careful not to damage the threads for the axle nut when removing the outer CV-joint from the steering knuckle—halfshaft service

this time. Only disengage the inner Tri-pot joint from the retainer snapring.

6. Remove the strut assembly-to-steering knuckle attaching bolts from the strut assembly.

✳✳ WARNING

The strut assembly-to-steering knuckle bolts are serrated (toothed) where they go through the strut assembly and steering knuckle. When removing the bolts, turn the nuts off the bolt; do not turn the bolts in the steering knuckle or damage to the steering knuckle will result.

7. Separate the top of the steering knuckle from the lower end of the strut.

8. Hold the outer joint assembly with one hand. Grasp the steering knuckle with the other hand and rotate it out and to the rear of the vehicle, until the outer CV-joint clears the hub and bearing assembly.

❊❊ WARNING

When removing the outer CV-joint from the hub and bearing assembly, do not allow the flange disc on the hub and bearing assembly to become damaged. If this happens, dirt and water can enter the bearing, which will cause premature bearing failure.

9. Remove the halfshaft inner joint from the transaxle stub shaft by grasping the inner Tri-pot joint and the interconnecting shaft and pulling both pieces at the same time. Take care not to pull on the interconnecting shaft to remove or separation of the spider assembly will occur.

To install:

10. Install the Tri-pot joint side of the halfshaft by performing the following procedure:

　a. Replace the inner Tri-pot joint retaining circlip and O-ring seal on the transaxle stub shaft. These components are not reusable and must be replaced whenever the halfshaft is removed.

　b. Apply an even coat of grease on the splines of the inner Tri-pot joint, where the O-ring seats against the Tri-pot joint.

　c. Install the halfshaft through the hole in the splash shield. Grasp the inner joint in 1 hand and interconnecting shaft in the other. Align the inner Tri-pot joint spline with the stub shaft spline on the transaxle. Use a rocking motion with the inner Tri-pot joint to get it past the circlip on the transaxle stub shaft.

　d. Continue pushing the Tri-pot joint onto transaxle stub shaft until it stops moving. The O-ring on the stub shaft should not be visible when the inner Tri-pot joint is fully installed. Check that the inner Tri-pot joint is locked in position by grasping the inner joint and pulling. If locked in position, the joint will not move on the stub shaft.

11. Hold the outer CV-joint assembly with one hand. Grasp the steering knuckle with the other and rotate it out and to the rear of the vehicle. Install the outer CV-joint into the hub and bearing assembly.

12. Install or connect the following:

• Top of the steering knuckle into the strut assembly. Align the steering knuckle-to-strut assembly mounting holes.

• Strut assembly-to-steering knuckle attaching bolts. Install the nuts to the attaching bolts and while holding the bolt heads, tighten the nuts

to 125 ft. lbs. (170 Nm). Turn the nuts on the bolts. DO NOT turn the bolts.

• New hub and bearing assembly-to-stub shaft retainer nut. Tighten but do not torque the nut at this time.

• Speed sensor cable routing bracket and screw

• Brake rotor and caliper assembly; then, tighten the caliper guide pin bolts to 30 ft. lbs. (41 Nm).

• Front wheels and lug nuts

• Negative battery cable

13. Pump the brakes until a firm pedal is obtained.

14. Apply the brakes and tighten the new stub shaft-to-hub and bearing assembly retainer nut to 120 ft. lbs. (163 Nm).

❊❊ WARNING

When tightening the stub shaft retaining nut, be careful not to exceed the maximum torque specification of 120 ft. lbs. (163 Nm). If this specification is exceeded, failure of the halfshaft could result.

15. Road test the vehicle to check for noise or vibration.

CV-Joints

OVERHAUL

Inner (Tri-pot) Joint

1. Remove or disconnect the following:

• Negative battery cable
• Halfshaft
• Large and small boot retaining clamps

2. Slide the boot down the shaft away from the tri-pot housing.

➡**When separating the spider joint from the tri-pot joint housing, hold the rollers in place on the trunions to prevent the rollers and needle bearings from falling away.**

3. Carefully, slide the shaft/spider assembly from the tri-pot housing.

4. Remove the spider assembly-to-shaft snapring; then, slide the spider assembly off the shaft.

❊❊ WARNING

If necessary, tap the spider assembly off the shaft using a brass drift; be careful not to hit the outer bearings.

5. Slide the boot off the shaft.

6. Throughly, inspect all parts for signs of excessive wear; if necessary, replace the halfshaft.

➡**Component parts are not serviceable and must be replaced as an assembly.**

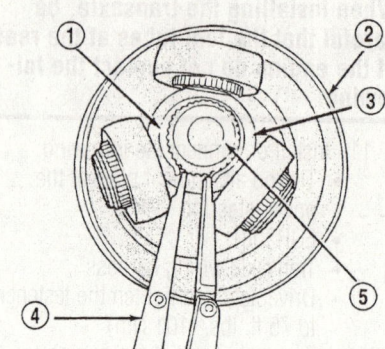

1 – SNAP RING
2 – SEALING BOOT
3 – SPIDER ASSEMBLY
4 – SNAP RING PLIERS
5 – INTERCONNECTING SHAFT

9306BG11

View of the halfshaft inner tri-pot joint and snapring

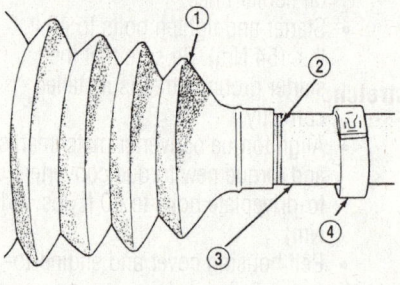

1 – SEALING BOOT
2 – INTERCONNECTING SHAFT THINNEST GROOVE
3 – INTERCONNECTING SHAFT
4 – BOOT CLAMP

9306BG12

View of the halfshaft boot, shaft and boot clamp

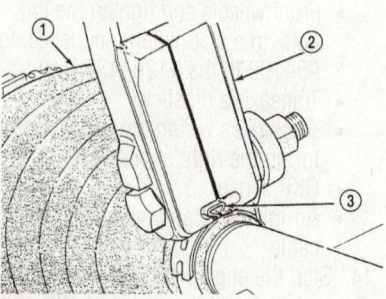

1 – SEALING BOOT
2 – SPECIAL TOOL C-4975
3 – CLAMP BRIDGE

9306BG13

Securing the halfshaft boot clamp

To install:

7. Slide the inner tri-pot boot clamp and boot onto the shaft; then, position the boot so that only the thinnest (sight) groove is visible on the shaft.

8. Install the spider assembly onto the shaft just far enough so that the snapring can be installed.

✳✳ WARNING

If necessary, tap the spider assembly onto the shaft using a brass drift; be careful not to hit the outer bearings.

9. Install the snapring onto the shaft; make sure that the snapring is fully seated in the groove.

10. If installing a new boot, distribute ½ of the grease in the service package inside the tri-pot housing and the other ½ inside the boot.

11. Carefully, slide the spider assembly and shaft into the tri-pot housing.

12. Position the inner boot clamp evenly on the sealing boot.

13. Using the Crimper tool C-4975, place the tool over the clamp bridge, tighten the tool nut until the jaws are completely closed (face-to-face).

✳✳ WARNING

The seal must not be dimpled, stretched or out of shape. If necessary, equalize the seal pressure and shape it by hand.

14. Position the boot onto the tri-pot housing retaining groove and install the retaining clamp evenly on the boot.

15. Using the Crimper tool C-4975, place the tool over the clamp bridge, tighten the tool nut until the jaws are completely closed (face-to-face).

16. Install the halfshaft into the vehicle.

Outer CV-Joint

1. Remove or disconnect the following:

- Negative battery cable
- Halfshaft
- Large and small boot retaining clamps

2. Slide the boot down the shaft away from the CV-joint housing.

3. Remove the grease to expose the CV-joint-to-shaft retaining ring.

4. Spread the snapring ears apart and slide the CV-joint assembly off of the shaft.

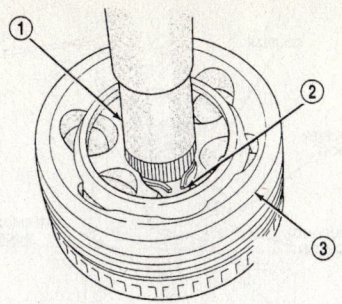

1 – INTERCONNECTING SHAFT
2 – RETAINING SNAP RING
3 – OUTER C/V JOINT ASSEMBLY

9306BG14

View of the halfshaft outer CV-joint and snapring

5. Slide the boot off the shaft.

6. Throughly, clean and inspect all parts for signs of excessive wear; if necessary, replace the halfshaft.

➡ **Component parts are not serviceable and must be replaced as an assembly.**

To install:

7. Slide the outer CV-joint boot clamp and boot onto the shaft; then, position the boot so that only the thinnest (sight) groove is visible on the shaft.

8. Slide the outer CV-joint assembly on the shaft, spread the snapring ears, position the CV-joint and verify that the snapring is fully seated in the shaft groove.

9. If installing a new boot, distribute ½ of the grease in the service package into the CV-joint housing and the other ½ inside the boot.

10. Position the outer boot clamp evenly on the sealing boot.

11. Using the Crimper tool C-4975, place the tool over the clamp bridge, tighten the tool nut until the jaws are completely closed (face-to-face).

✳✳ WARNING

The seal must not be dimpled, stretched or out of shape. If necessary, equalize the seal pressure and shape it by hand.

12. Position the boot onto the CV-joint housing retaining groove and install the retaining clamp evenly on the boot.

13. Using the Crimper tool C-4975, place the tool over the clamp bridge, tighten the tool nut until the jaws are completely closed (face-to-face).

14. Install the halfshaft into the vehicle.

STEERING AND SUSPENSION

Air Bag

✳✳ CAUTION

Some vehicles are equipped with an air bag system. The system must be disabled before performing service on or around system components, steering column, instrument panel components, wiring and sensors. Failure to follow safety and disabling procedures could result in accidental air bag deployment, possible personal injury and unnecessary system repairs.

PRECAUTIONS

Several precautions must be observed when handling the inflator module to avoid accidental deployment and possible personal injury.

- Never carry the inflator module by the wires or connector on the underside of the module.
- When carrying a live inflator module, hold securely with both hands, and ensure that the bag and trim cover are pointed away.
- Place the inflator module on a bench or other surface with the bag and trim cover facing up.
- With the inflator module on the bench, never place anything on or close to the module which may be thrown in the event of an accidental deployment.

Before servicing the vehicle, also make sure to refer to the precautions in the beginning of this section as well.

DISARMING

✳✳ CAUTION

The Air Bag system must be disarmed before repair and/or removal of any component in its immediate area including the air bag itself. Failure to do so may cause accidental deployment of the air bag, resulting in unnecessary system repairs and/or personal injury.

1. Disconnect the negative battery cable and isolate the cable using an appropriate insulator (wrap with quality electrical tape).

2. Allow the system capacitor to discharge for 2 minutes before starting any repair on any air bag system or related components. This will disable the air bag system.

❊❊ CAUTION

Always wear safety goggles when working with or around the air bag system. When carrying a live air bag, be sure the bag and trim cover are pointed away from the body. In the unlikely event of an accidental deployment, the bag will, then deploy with minimal chance of injury. When placing a live air bag on a bench or other surface, always face the bag and trim cover up, away from the surface. This will reduce the motion of the module if it is accidentally deployed.

Power Rack and Pinion Steering Gear

REMOVAL & INSTALLATION

1997 Models

1. Before servicing the vehicle, refer to the precautions in the beginning of this section.

2. Disconnect the negative battery cable. Disarm the air bag system.

3. Remove or disconnect the following:
- Transaxle gearshift cable from the shifter lever
- Loosen the gearshift cable-to-transaxle mount bolt
- Gearshift cable from the transaxle
- Throttle cable from the throttle body, if necessary

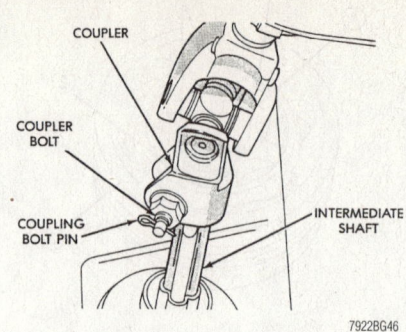

Matchmark the steering coupler to the intermediate shaft for proper alignment

- Throttle cable bracket
- Both wiper arm assemblies from the wiper arm pivots
- Cowl closure panel and weather-stripping as an assembly from the cowl
- Wiper module wiring harness from the vehicle wiring harness
- Wiper module assembly from the cowl panel
- Air plenum from the throttle body, PCV make up air tube and the idle air control motor. Remove the plenum from the right side of the vehicle through the wiper module area.
- Power brake booster vacuum connector at the intake manifold

4. Turn the front wheels to the full left position. Then, turn the wheels back in the other direction until the roll pin in the lower steering coupler is accessible. Turn the ignition key switch to the **LOCK** position to keep the steering column from rotating after the coupler is removed from the steering gear. If the steering column shaft rotates beyond the normal number of turns in either direction, the air bag clock spring will be damaged.

5. Using paint, mark the steering cou-

pling and steering gear shaft for orientation. Using the correct size punch, remove the roll pin from the steering coupling.

6. If equipped, remove the pedal travel sensor from the brake booster as follows:

a. Pump the brake pedal approximately 20 times. This will bleed the vacuum stored in the booster.

b. Remove the wiring harness connector from the sensor.

c. Using a small flat-tipped tool, lift the retainer ring from the notch. Then, remove the retaining ring from the grommet.

d. Remove the pedal travel sensor from the brake booster by carefully pulling it straight out of its mounting grommet. Do not twist the sensor.

7. Remove or disconnect the following:
- Master cylinder from brake booster with the brake lines connected and position aside
- Power steering pressure hose and return hose from the power steering gear
- Bend back the tie rods-to-steering gear bolt retaining tabs and remove the bolts

8. Lay the tie rods, bolts and plate as an assembly on the bell housing of the transaxle.

9. If the rack and pinion steering gear unit being removed is a speed proportional steering gear, disconnect the vehicle wiring harness from the solenoid control module.

10. Remove or disconnect the following:
- 4 bolts attaching the steering gear assembly to the crossmember. Slide the steering gear forward in the vehicle to disengage the steering coupler from the steering gear shaft. After the gear is disengaged, do not rotate the steering gear shaft
- Steering gear assembly from the vehicle through the area in the cowl from which the windshield wiper module was previously removed

To install:

11. If a replacement rack is being installed, grasp the shaft of the steering gear and rotate it until the steering gear center take off is in a full left turn position. Install the steering gear into the vehicle through the wiper module opening in the cowl.

12. If the original gear is being installed, align the paint mark on the steering coupler with the mark on the steering gear shaft and install the steering gear shaft into the steering gear coupler.

13. If a replacement rack is being installed, the steering gear shaft and steering coupler must be aligned. Rotate the steering gear shaft back from the full left turn position until the master spline on the steering

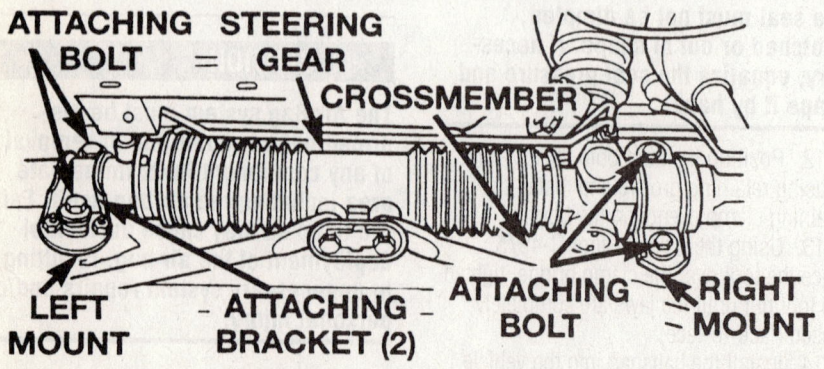

Steering rack-to-subframe attaching bolt locations—replace mounts if worn

gear shaft is aligned with the master spline on the steering coupler. At this point, install the steering gear into the coupler.

14. Align the steering gear with the mounting holes in the crossmember and install the bolts. Be sure the brake line routing clip is installed under the left steering gear mounting bracket. Tighten the mounting bolts to 50 ft. lbs. (68 Nm).

15. Install the steering coupler-to-steering gear shaft retaining roll pin until it is flush with the top edge of the steering coupler.

16. If equipped with the 3.5L engine, correct orientation of the power steering pressure hose at the power steering pump must be maintained. Be sure the power steering hose is installed in the orientation clip at the power steering pump prior to tightening the tube fitting. Attach the power steering pressure and return lines onto the proper ports of the power steering gear. Tighten both fittings to 23 ft. lbs. (31 Nm).

17. Align the center take off on the steering gear with the tie rod assemblies. Install the tie rod attaching bolts and washers into the steering gear assembly. Be sure the washers are installed between the tie rods and the steering gear. Tighten the tie rod-to-steering gear attaching bolts to 55 ft. lbs. (75 Nm). Bend the retaining tabs against the heads of the bolts.

18. Install the pedal travel sensor retainer ring on the travel sensor grommet in the vacuum booster. The tab on the retaining ring should be located in the top notch of the mounting grommet.

19. Sparingly lubricate the pedal travel sensor O-ring with fresh brake fluid. Install the pedal travel O-ring into the pedal travel sensor mounting grommet. Coat the end of the sensor with fresh brake fluid and install it by pushing straight into the mounting grommet on the brake booster until the tab on the sensor is past the retaining ring on grommet.

20. Install or connect the following:
- Pedal travel sensor wiring harness connector
- Master cylinder and tighten nuts to 21 ft. lbs. (28 Nm)
- Power booster vacuum hose to the intake manifold
- Windshield wiper module to the cowl panel
- Module's electrical harness
- Air intake plenum (if removed) to idle air control motor, PCV air tube and throttle body
- Windshield wiper module assembly into the vehicle cowl area

- Wiring harness from the wiper module to the vehicle wiring harness
- Cowl closure panel and tighten the 6 mounting screws
- Weather strip on the shock towers
- Windshield washer hoses on the wiper arms
- Windshield wiper arms on the pivots
- Throttle cable to the bracket, if removed
- Bracket to the throttle body
- Solenoid control valve wiring harness onto the solenoid control module

➡ **Be sure that the harness connector seal is in good condition before installation.**

- Gearshift cable onto the transaxle's shift lever
- Gearshift cable on the transaxle's cable mounting bracket and tighten the bolt
- Negative battery cable

21. Refill the pump reservoir to the correct lever with Mopar Power Steering Fluid, or equivalent. Do not use any type of automatic transmission fluid. Start the engine and turn the steering wheel several times from stop-to-stop to bleed air from the fluid in the system. Check and add fluid as required.

22. Adjust the front suspension toe setting.

1998–01 Models

1. Before servicing the vehicle, refer to the precautions in the beginning of this section.

2. Turn the front wheels to the straight-ahead position.

3. Remove or disconnect the following:
- Negative battery cable.
- Wiper arms
- Wiper module cover and cowl cover
- Reinforcement from the strut towers and wiper module
- Throttle body's intake air duct and resonator

4. Clamp the steering wheel in the center position with some type of holding device.

5. Remove or disconnect the following:

- Intermediate shaft from the steering column coupler

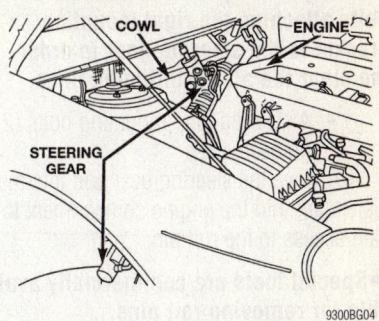

The steering gear is removed or installed through the right side of the vehicle

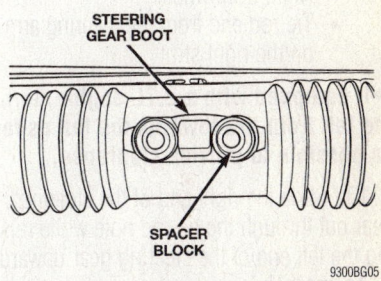

Center the spacer block in the steering gear before installing the tie rods

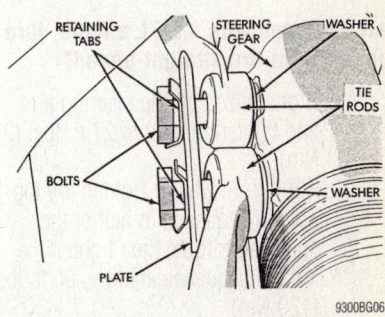

Be sure to position the washers between the tie rods and the steering gear as shown

- Both tie rods from the steering gear and place them on the transaxle bell housing
- Siphon the power steering fluid from the reservoir
- Power steering gear fluid lines

6. If equipped with speed proportional steering, disconnect the wiring from the solenoid control valve on the end of the steering gear under the master cylinder.

7. Remove or disconnect the following:
- Master cylinder from the booster and position it to the side without disconnecting the fluid lines
- Booster vacuum line

➡It may be helpful to loosen the 2 bolts attaching the right mounting bracket to the steering gear in order the clear the air conditioning lines.

- 4 steering gear mounting bolts (2 on each side)

8. Move the steering gear and intermediate shaft into the engine compartment to gain access to the roll pin.

➡Special tools are commercially available for removing roll pins.

9. Remove or disconnect the following:
- Roll pin and separate the intermediate shaft from the steering gear
- Right front wheel
- Tie rod end from the steering arm on the right strut

➡If equipped with a 2.7L engine, turn the left front tire towards the left as far as possible to provide clearance.

10. Slide the right end of the steering gear out through the tie rod hole while raising the left end of the steering gear upward.

To install:

11. Position the tie rod attaching points at the center of the steering gear travel.

12. Install or connect the following:
- Steering gear

➡If equipped with a 2.7L engine, turn the left front tire straight-ahead.

- Right tie rod on the steering arm and tighten the nut to 27 ft. lbs. (37 Nm)
- Right front wheel. Tighten the lug nuts in sequence to half of the specified torque, then tighten the nuts in sequence again to 95 ft. lbs. (129 Nm).
- Intermediate shaft to the steering gear using the roll pin. Be sure the pin is centered in the joint.
- 4 steering gear mounting bolts and tighten the bolts to 43 ft. lbs. (58 Nm)
- Bracket bolts; tighten them (if loosened) to 27 ft. lbs. (37 Nm)
- Steering gear fluid lines; tighten the nuts to 35 ft. lbs. (47 Nm)
- Solenoid valve, if equipped with speed proportional steering

✳✳ WARNING

Be sure the spacer block in the rack is centered before connecting the tie rods to the steering gear.

- Tie rods to the steering gear with the washers between the rods and

the steering gear. Tighten the bolts to 60 ft. lbs. (82 Nm).
- Remaining components in the reverse order of the removal steps
- Negative battery cable

13. Add Mopar® power steering fluid to the reservoir and let it settle for at least 2 minutes. Start the engine for a few seconds and turn it **OFF**. Add fluid as necessary. Repeat this procedure until the fluid level remains constant.

14. Raise the front wheels off the floor and start the engine. Turn the steering from lock-to-lock several times. Do not hold the wheel in the locked position for more than 2 seconds at a time. Refill the reservoir as needed.

15. Lower the vehicle and repeat the procedure. If the fluid is extremely foamy, allow the vehicle to stand with the engine **OFF** for a few minutes, then repeat the procedure.

Strut

REMOVAL & INSTALLATION

Front

1. Before servicing the vehicle, refer to the precautions in the beginning of this section.

➡Service of the coil spring requires the use of a coil spring compressor tool. It is required that 5 coils be captured within the jaws of the compressor tool.

➡Do not support the vehicle by placing supports under the suspension arms. The suspension arms must hang freely.

2. Remove or disconnect the following:
- Negative battery cable.
- Front wheel(s)
- Stabilizer bar attaching link at the strut assembly

3. Loosen, but do not remove the outer tie rod end-to-strut assembly steering arm attaching nut. Then, remove the outer tie rod end from the steering arm using puller MB-990635 or equivalent.

4. Remove or disconnect the following:
- Speed sensor wiring harness mounting bracket from the strut, if equipped with ABS
- Brake caliper assembly. Support the caliper assembly from the vehicle frame with a strong piece of wire. Do not allow the assembly to hang by the brake hose. Remove the front brake rotor disc.

✳✳ WARNING

The strut assembly-to-steering knuckle bolts are serrated where they go through the strut and steering knuckle. Do not turn the bolts during removal. If the bolts are turned, damage to the steering knuckle will result.

5. The strut assembly-to-steering knuckle bolts must not be turned during strut removal. Hold the bolt head with a wrench and turn the nuts off the bolts.

6. Remove the 3 strut assembly upper mount-to-shock tower mounting nuts and washers. Remove the strut from the vehicle.

7. Disassemble the strut by performing the following procedure:

a. Securely mount the strut assembly into a vise. Using paint, mark the strut unit, lower spring isolator, spring and upper strut mount for indexing of the parts at assembly.

b. Position the spring compressor tool onto the strut. Compress the coil spring until all load is off the upper strut mount assembly.

c. Install Strut Rod Socket tool L-4558A on the strut shaft nut and a 10mm socket on the end of the strut shaft to prevent it from turning. Remove the strut shaft nut.

d. Remove the upper mount assembly, jounce bumper and seat bearing and dust shield as an assembly.

e. Remove the coil spring and compressor as an assembly from the strut. Remove the lower spring isolator from the strut assembly lower spring seat.

f. Inspect all components for abnormal wear, oil leakage or failure. Replace parts as required.

To install:

8. Assemble the strut by performing the following procedure:

a. Inspect the strut assembly for signs of leakage. Actual leakage will be a stream of fluid running down the side and dripping off the lower end of the strut. A slight amount of seepage between the strut rod and strut shaft seal is not unusual and does not affect performance of the strut assembly.

b. Install the lower spring isolator on the strut unit. Install the compressed coil spring onto the strut assembly aligning the paint marks made during removal.

c. Install the strut bearing into the bearing seat. The bearing must be installed into the seat with the notches on the bearings facing down.

d. Lower the seat bearing and dust shield onto the strut and spring assembly. Align the paint marks made during removal.

e. Install the jounce bumper and upper mount on the strut shaft, aligning the paint marks.

f. Install the strut mount-to-shaft retainer nut. Inspect all alignment marks made during removal and align as required. While holding the strut shaft from turning with a 10mm socket, tighten the strut shaft nut to 70 ft. lbs. (94 Nm).

g. Equally loosen the spring compressor tool until all tension is released. Remove the spring compressor tool.

9. Install the front strut into the strut tower and install the 3 upper mount nuts and washers. Tighten the mounting nuts to 25 ft. lbs. (33 Nm).

10. Position the steering knuckle neck into the strut assembly. Install the strut assembly-to-steering knuckle bolts. Install the nuts onto the attaching bolts and tighten to 125 ft. lbs. (169 Nm). Do not turn the serrated bolt heads during installation. Turn only the nuts.

❋❋ WARNING

The strut assembly-to-steering knuckle bolts are serrated (toothed) where they go through the strut and steering knuckle. Do not turn the bolts during removal. If bolts are turned, damage to the steering knuckle will result

11. Install or connect the following:
- Brake rotor and caliper assembly to adapter; then, tighten the caliper mounting bolts to 14 ft. lbs. (19 Nm)
- Front speed sensor cable routing bracket onto the front strut, if equipped
- Outer tie rod on the steering arm and tighten the attaching nut to 27 ft. lbs. (37 Nm)
- Stabilizer link assembly onto the strut assembly and tighten the attaching nut to 70 ft. lbs. (95 Nm)
- Front wheel and lug nuts. Tighten the lug nuts, in sequence, to 95–100 ft. lbs. (129–135 Nm)
- Negative battery cable

Rear

1. Before servicing the vehicle, refer to the precautions in the beginning of this section.

The rear strut assemblies support the weight of the vehicle using coil springs positioned around the struts. The coil springs are contained between the upper mount of the strut assembly and a lower spring seat on the body of the strut assembly. The strut is attached to the spindle by a split collar on the rear spindle with a pinch bolt to hold the spindle to the strut.

2. Remove or disconnect the following:
- Rear wheel
- Caliper assembly and rotor from the hub, if equipped with rear disc brakes
- Brake flex hose from the support bracket and wheel cylinder, if equipped with rear drum brakes. Plug the brake flex hose to prevent system contamination. Do not allow the rear caliper to hang by the brake hose. Support the caliper off of the frame with a strong piece of wire.
- Speed sensor cable routing bracket and tube, if equipped with ABS
- Lateral links to the rear spindle assembly bolts
- Rear strut assembly-to-stabilizer bar attaching link at the stabilizer bar

➥Hold the hex on the attaching link stud while breaking the nut loose. The attaching link does not have to be removed from the strut.

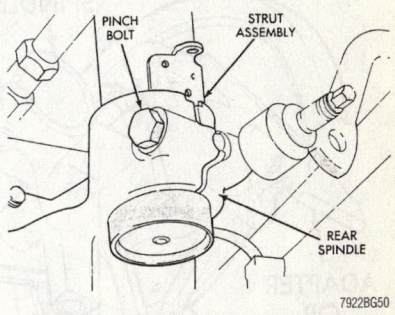

Loosen, then remove the rear spindle-to-strut pinch bolt—rear strut service

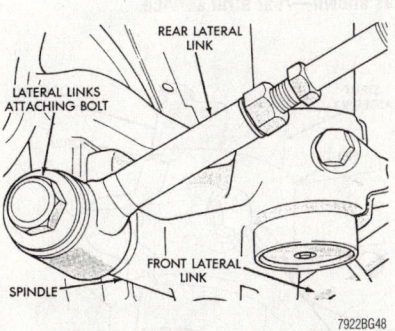

Separate the lateral links from the spindle—rear strut service

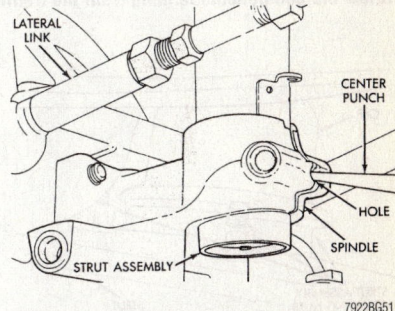

Insert a center punch into the hole on the spindle and tap until the casting is spread—rear strut service

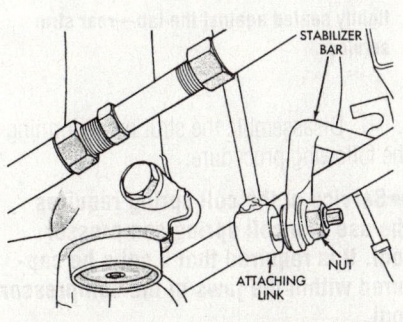

Remove the nut from the stabilizer-to-strut attaching link stud at the bar—rear strut service

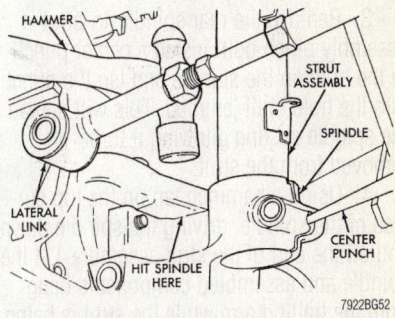

Tap with a hammer on the surface of the spindle driving it down and off the end of the strut—rear strut service

Turn to Section 5 for brake system applications

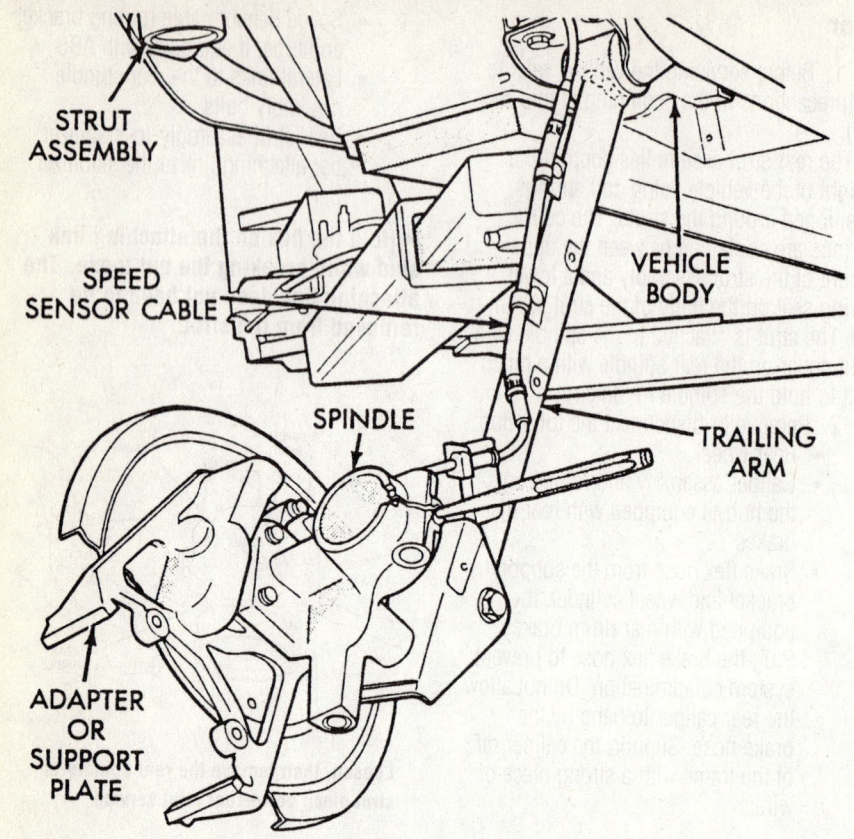

Allow the components to hang from the trailing arm as shown—rear strut service

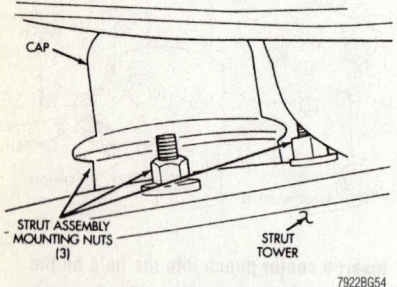

Access the 3 upper strut mounting nuts through the trunk—rear strut service

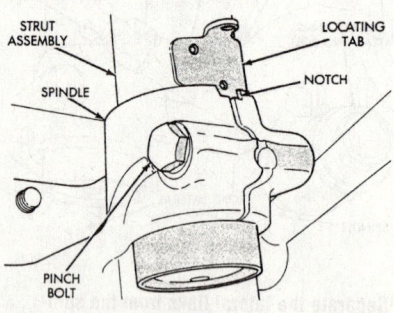

During reassembly, tap the spindle onto the strut until the notch in the spindle is tightly seated against the tab—rear strut service

3. Remove the rear spindle-to-strut assembly pinch bolt. Install a center punch in the hole on the spindle and tap the punch into the hole until jammed. This will spread the spindle casting allowing it to be removed from the strut.

4. Using a hammer, tap on the top surface of the spindle, driving the spindle down and off the end of the strut assembly. Let the spindle and assembled components hang from the trailing arm while the strut is being serviced.

5. From inside the trunk of the vehicle, remove the 3 upper strut mounting bolts and remove the strut from the vehicle.

6. Disassemble the strut by performing the following procedure:

➡ **Service of the coil spring requires the use of a coil spring compressor tool. It is required that 5 coils be captured within the jaws of the compressor tool.**

a. Securely mount the strut assembly into a vise. Using paint, mark the strut assembly, lower spring isolator, spring and upper strut mount for indexing of the parts at reassembly.

b. Position a spring compressor tool onto the coil spring. Compress the coil spring until all load is off of the upper strut mount assembly.

c. Install the strut rod socket tool L-4558 on the strut shaft nut and an 8mm Allen wrench on the end of the strut shaft to prevent it from turning. Remove the strut shaft nut.

d. Remove the upper strut mount assembly off of the strut shaft. Remove the coil spring and compressor tool as an assembly from the strut.

e. Remove the plate, dust shield and jounce bumper off of the strut unit.

f. Inspect all components for abnormal wear, oil leakage or failure. Replace parts as required.

To install:

7. Assemble the strut by performing the following procedure:

a. Install the lower spring isolator on the strut unit. If it is the original isolator, align the paint marks.

b. Install the jounce bumper into the dust shield. Install the plate on top of the dust shield and into the jounce bumper.

c. Install the dust shield, jounce bumper and the top plate onto the strut unit as an assembly.

d. Install the coil spring and compressor tool onto the strut unit and align the paint marks on the spring to that of the strut unit.

e. Install the upper strut mount assembly onto the strut shaft. Align the paint marks and install the strut shaft retaining nut.

f. Using the strut rod socket tool L-4558 and the 8mm Allen wrench to prevent the strut shaft from turning, tighten the strut shaft nut to 70 ft. lbs. (95 Nm).

g. Equally loosen the spring compressor tool until all tension is released. Remove the spring compressor tool.

8. Position the strut in the vehicle and install the 3 upper mounting nuts to 20 ft. lbs. (28 Nm).

9. Install the spindle assembly onto the bottom of the strut. Push or tap the spindle assembly onto the strut, until the notch in the spindle is tightly seated against the locating tap on the strut assembly. Remove the center punch from the hole in the spindle.

10. Install or connect the following:
- Strut-to-spindle pinch bolt and tighten to 40 ft. lbs. (55 Nm)
- Lateral link-to-spindle attaching bolt and tighten to 105 ft. lbs. (140 Nm)

- Stabilizer bar attaching link and torque the stabilizer link-to-stabilizer bar attaching nut to 70 ft. lbs. (95 Nm), while holding the stabilizer link stud at the hex with a wrench
- Rear speed sensor cable routing tube and bracket, if equipped with ABS.
- Rotor and caliper assembly (if equipped with rear disc brakes) and tighten the caliper mounting bolts to 16 ft. lbs. (22 Nm)
- Install the rear brake flex hose to the wheel cylinder and support plate, if equipped with rear drum brakes
- Rear wheel(s) and tighten the lug nuts, in sequence, to 95 ft. lbs. (129 Nm).

11. Bleed the brake system, if equipped with rear drum brakes.

12. Have the rear wheel toe set to specifications.

Coil Springs

REMOVAL & INSTALLATION

Front

Refer to the front strut removal and installation procedure for coil spring service information.

Rear

Refer to the rear strut removal and installation procedure for coil spring service information.

Lower Ball Joint

➡**The lower ball joints on this vehicle are not serviced separately. The lower ball joints operate with no free-play. If defective, the entire lower control arm must be replaced.**

Lower Control Arm

REMOVAL & INSTALLATION

The front lower control arm is a steel forging with 2 rubber bushings isolating the lower control arm from the front cradle assembly. The isolator bushings consist of a metal encased pivot bushing and a solid rubber tension strut bushing. The lower control arm is bolted to the cradle assembly

using a pivot bolt through the center of the rubber pivot bushing at the tension strut isolator bushing. The ball joint is built into the lower control arm and is non-serviceable. If the ball joint becomes worn, the entire lower control arm must be replaced. The ball joint seal, however, is replaceable as well as the lower control arm inner bushing. If the lower control arm is damaged, do not attempt to repair or straighten a broken or bent lower control arm.

1. Before servicing the vehicle, refer to the precautions in the beginning of this section.

2. Remove or disconnect the following:

- Front wheel(s)
- Ball joint stud-to-steering knuckle clamp nut and bolt

3. Carefully insert a prybar between the lower control arm and the steering knuckle and separate ball joint from knuckle. Be sure the ball joint seal does not get damaged during separation.

✳✳ WARNING

Pulling the steering knuckle out from the vehicle after releasing from the ball joint can separate the inner CV-joint. Do not separate the inner CV-joint or it can be damaged.

4. Remove the tension strut-to-cradle attaching nut and washer from the end of the tension strut. When removing the nut, keep the strut from turning by holding the tension strut at the flats using an open end

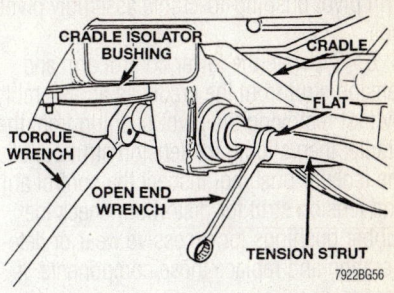

Remove the tension strut-to-cradle nut and washer—lower control arm service

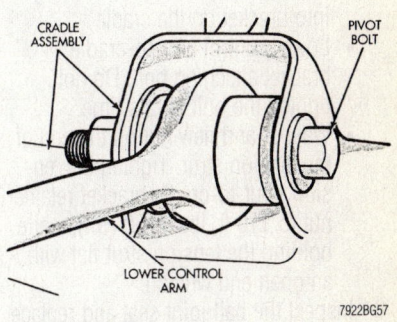

Loosen the pivot bolt and remove it— lower control arm service

wrench. Discard the tension strut-to-cradle retainer nut. A new nut must be used during installation.

➡**A new tension strut-to-cradle attaching nut must be used when installing the tension strut.**

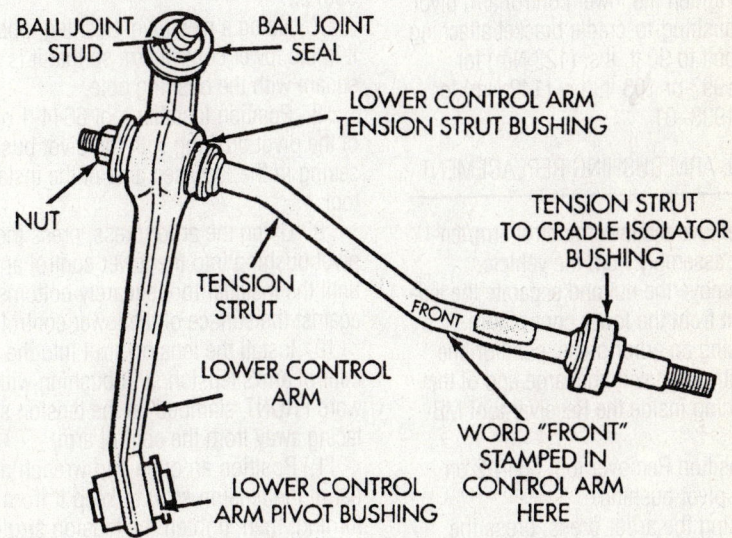

Inspect the control arm and tension strut for distortion—lower control arm service

5. Loosen and remove the lower control arm pivot bushing-to-cradle assembly pivot bolt.

6. Separate the lower control arm and tension strut from the cradle as an assembly by first removing the pivot bushing from the cradle, then sliding the tension strut out of the isolator bushing. Inspect the control arm and tension strut for distortion, check the rubber bushings for excessive wear or deterioration and replace these components, if necessary.

To install:

7. Install or connect the following:
- Tension strut and isolator bushing into the cradle first, then install lower control arm pivot bushing into bracket on the cradle
- Lower control arm-to-cradle bracket attaching bolt. Do not tighten the bolt at this time.
- Washer and new nut on the end of the tension strut. Tighten the tension strut-to-cradle bracket retainer nut to 110 ft. lbs. (150 Nm), while holding the tension strut flat with an open end wrench.

8. Inspect the ball joint seal and replace it if damaged. Install the lower ball joint stud into the steering knuckle and install the clamp bolt and nut. Tighten the bolt to 40 ft. lbs. (55 Nm).

9. Install or connect the following:
- Front wheel and lug nuts. Tighten the lug nuts, in a star pattern, to 95–100 ft. lbs. (129–135 Nm). Lower the vehicle so the suspension is supporting the weight of the vehicle
- Tighten the lower control arm pivot bushing-to-cradle bracket attaching bolt to 90 ft. lbs. (123 Nm) for 1997 or 105 ft. lbs. (142 Nm) for 1998–01

CONTROL ARM BUSHING REPLACEMENT

1. Remove the lower control arm/tension strut assembly from the vehicle.
2. Remove the nut and separate the tensions strut from the lower control arm.
3. Using an arbor press, position the lower control arm with the large end of the pivot bushing inside the Receiver tool MB-990799.
4. Position Remover tool 6644-2 on top of the pivot bushing.
5. Using the arbor press, press pivot bushing out of the lower control arm.

To install:

6. Turn the lower control arm over and

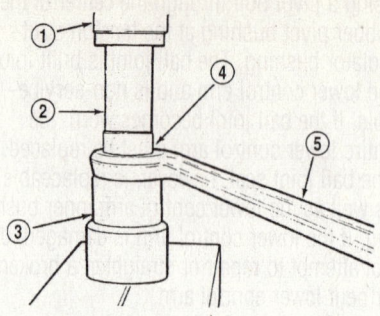

1 – ARBOR PRESS RAM
2 – SPECIAL TOOL 6644-2
3 – SPECIAL TOOL MB990799
4 – PIVOT BUSHING
5 – LOWER CONTROL ARM

9306BG25

Removing the lower control arm pivot bushing

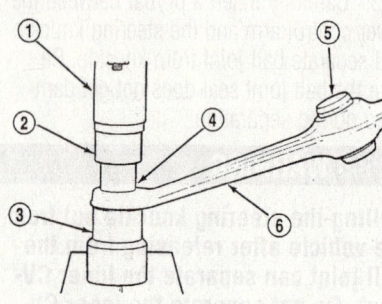

1 – ARBOR PRESS RAM
2 – SPECIAL TOOL 6644-1
3 – SPECIAL TOOL MB990799
4 – PIVOT BUSHING
5 – TENSION STRUT BUSHING
6 – LOWER CONTROL ARM

9306BG22

Installing the lower control arm pivot bushing

reposition it on the Receiver tool MB-990799.

7. Using a new pivot bushing, position it in the lower control arm so that it is square with the bushing hole.

8. Position Installer tool 6644-1 on top of the pivot bushing with the pivot bushing setting in the recessed area of the installer tool.

9. Using the arbor press, press the pivot bushing into the lower control arm until the installer tool squarely bottoms against the surface of the lower control arm.

10. Install the tension strut into the lower control arm's tension strut bushing with the word FRONT, stamped on the tension strut, facing away from the control arm.

11. Position an open end wrench on the flat of the tension strut to keep it from turning; then, tighten the tension strut-to-lower control arm nut to 110 ft. lbs. (150 Nm) for 1997 or 95 ft. lbs. (130 Nm) for 1998–01.

TENSION STRUT BUSHING REPLACEMENT

1. Remove the lower control arm/tension strut assembly from the vehicle.
2. Remove the nut and separate the tensions strut from the lower control arm.
3. Using an arbor press, position the lower control arm with the tension strut bushing inside the Receiver tool MB-990799.
4. Position Remover tool 6644-4 on top of the tension strut bushing.
5. Using the arbor press, press the tension strut bushing out of the lower control arm.

➡ **As the Remover tool is press through the tension strut bushing, it will cut the bushing into 2 pieces.**

6. Remove the lower control arm, both bushing pieces and the Remover tool.

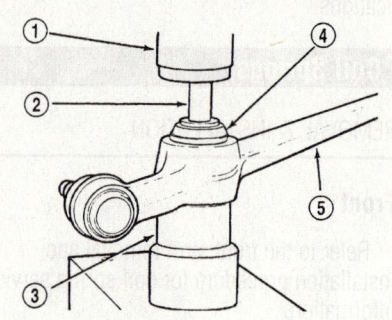

1 – ARBOR PRESS RAM
2 – SPECIAL TOOL 6644-4
3 – SPECIAL TOOL MB990799
4 – TENSION STRUT BUSHING
5 – LOWER CONTROL ARM

9306BG23

Removing the lower control arm's tension strut bushing

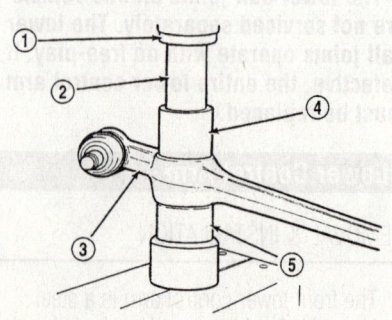

1 – ARBOR PRESS
2 – SPECIAL TOOL 6644-2
3 – LOWER CONTROL ARM
4 – SPECIAL TOOL 6644-3
5 – SPECIAL TOOL MB990799

9306BG24

Installing the lower control arm's tension strut bushing

To install:

7. Thoroughly, lubricate the new tension strut bushing, the lower control arm and the Installer tool 6644-3 with Rubber Bushing Installation Lube.

8. Press the new tension strut bushing by hand, into the large end of the Installer tool 6644-3 as far as it will go.

9. Position the lower control arm onto on the arbor press so that the tension strut hole is centered on the Receiver tool MB-990799.

10. Position Installer tool 6644-3, with the bushing installed, inside the tension strut bushing hole in the lower control arm.

11. Position Installer tool 6644-2 on top of the tension strut bushing.

12. Using the arbor press, press the tension strut bushing into the lower control arm.

➡**As the bushing is being installed, a pop will be heard and Installer tool 6644-3 will move slightly up off the control arm.**

13. Remove the control arm assembly from the arbor press and remove Installer tool 6644-3 from the tension strut bushing; the tension strut bushing is now installed.

14. Install the tension strut into the lower control arm's tension strut bushing with the word FRONT, stamped on the tension strut, facing away from the control arm.

15. Position an open end wrench on the flat of the tension strut to keep it from turning; then, tighten the tension strut-to-lower control arm nut to 110 ft. lbs. (150 Nm) for 1997 or 95 ft. lbs. (130 Nm) for 1998–01.

Wheel Bearings

ADJUSTMENT

These front wheel drive vehicles are equipped with permanently sealed front and rear wheel bearings. There is no periodic lubrication or maintenance recommended for these units.

REMOVAL & INSTALLATION

Front

1. Before servicing the vehicle, refer to the precautions in the beginning of this section.

2. Remove or disconnect the following:
   • Front wheel

• Front caliper assembly from the steering knuckle by removing the 2 guide pin bolts, then rotating the top of the caliper away from the knuckle and lifting the caliper off the machined abutment on the steering knuckle

3. Suspend the caliper out of the way with a piece of wire.

4. Remove or disconnect the following:
   • Front brake rotor from the hub by pulling it straight off of the wheel mounting stud

5. Remove the hub and bearing-to-stub axle retainer nut.

➡**This hub nut is a torque prevailing retaining nut and can not be reused. A NEW retaining nut MUST be used when assembling the hub.**

6. Remove or disconnect the following:
   • Attaching bolts that mount the hub and bearing assembly to the steering knuckle assembly

➡**If the metal seal on the hub and bearing assembly is seized to the steering knuckle and becomes dislodged on the hub and bearing during removal, the hub and bearing must be replaced. If the flinger disc becomes damaged during the removal procedure, the hub and bearing assembly must be replaced.**

• Hub and bearing assembly from the steering knuckle by sliding it straight out of the knuckle and off the ends of the stub shaft

7. Gently pry the assembly out with a prybar or tap it out with a soft-faced hammer, if necessary. Be very careful not to damage the hub and bearing assembly.

To install:

8. Clean the hub and bearing mounting surfaces of dirt and be sure there are no nicks present.

9. Install or connect the following:
   • Hub and bearing squarely onto the stub shaft and the steering knuckle
   • Bearing assembly mounting bolts and tighten equally until the bearing assembly is seated squarely against the front of the steering knuckle. Tighten the mounting bolts to 80 ft. lbs. (110 Nm).
   • New hub and bearing assembly-to-stub shaft retainer nut. A NEW retaining nut MUST be used when assembling the hub. Tighten but do not torque the nut at this time.
   • Brake rotor and the caliper assembly. Tighten the brake caliper guide bolts to 16 ft. lbs. (22 Nm).
   • Wheel and lug nuts. Tighten the lug nuts in a star pattern to 95–100 ft. lbs. (129–135 Nm).

10. Pump the brakes until a firm pedal is obtained.

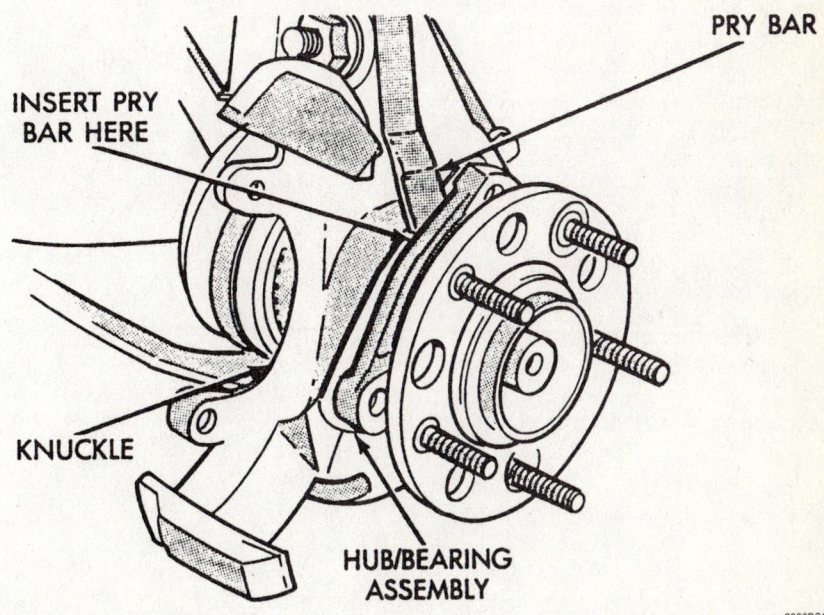

Carefully pry the front bearing/hub assembly away from the steering knuckle

9300BG07

11. With the weight on the vehicle on its wheels, apply the brakes to keep the vehicle from moving. Tighten the hub and bearing assembly-to-stub shaft retaining nut to 120 ft. lbs. (163 Nm).

✳✳ WARNING

When tightening the hub and bearing assembly to stub shaft retaining nut, do not exceed the maximum torque of 120 ft. lbs. (163 Nm). If the maximum torque is exceeded this may result in a failure of the halfshaft.

12. Inspect the toe setting on the vehicle and adjust, if necessary.

Rear

1. Before servicing the vehicle, refer to the precautions in the beginning of this section.

2. Remove or disconnect the following:

- Rear wheel
- Brake caliper and rotor, if equipped with rear disc brakes
- Brake drum, if equipped with drum brakes
- Bearing dust cap
- Cotter pin, nut retainer, nut, washer and bearing/hub assembly from the spindle

To install:

3. Install or connect the following:

- Bearing/hub assembly, the bearing/hub assembly washer and tighten the nut to 124 ft. lbs. (168 Nm).
- Nut retainer and a new cotter pin
- Dust cap
- Brake drum or rotor and caliper assembly
- Rear wheel and tighten the lug nuts, in a star pattern, to 95–100 ft. lbs. (129–135 Nm)

4. Road test the vehicle to verify no excessive noise from the rear wheel bearing area.

CHRYSLER CORPORATION

Chrysler-Sebring Coupe • **Dodge**-Avenger

PRECAUTIONS

Before servicing any vehicle, please be sure to read all of the following precautions, which deal with personal safety, prevention of component damage, and important points to take into consideration when servicing a motor vehicle:

• Never open, service or drain the radiator or cooling system when the engine is hot; serious burns can occur from the steam and hot coolant.

• Observe all applicable safety precautions when working around fuel. Whenever servicing the fuel system, always work in a well-ventilated area. Do not allow fuel spray or vapors to come in contact with a spark, open flame or excessive heat (a hot drop light, for example). Keep a dry chemical fire extinguisher near the work area. Always keep fuel in a container specifically designed for fuel storage; also, always properly seal fuel containers to avoid the possibility of fire or explosion. Refer to the additional fuel system precautions later in this section.

• Fuel injection systems often remain pressurized, even after the engine has been turned **OFF**. The fuel system pressure must be relieved before disconnecting any fuel lines. Failure to do so may result in fire and/or personal injury.

• Brake fluid often contains polyglycol ethers and polyglycols. Avoid contact with the eyes and wash your hands thoroughly after handling brake fluid. If you do get brake fluid in your eyes, flush your eyes with clean, running water for 15 minutes. If eye irritation persists, or if you have taken brake fluid internally, IMMEDIATELY seek medical assistance.

• The EPA warns that prolonged contact with used engine oil may cause a number of skin disorders, including cancer! You should make every effort to minimize your exposure to used engine oil. Protective gloves should be worn when changing oil. Wash your hands and any other exposed skin areas as soon as possible after exposure to used engine oil. Soap and water, or waterless hand cleaner should be used.

• All new vehicles are now equipped with an air bag system, often referred to as a Supplemental Restraint System (SRS) or Supplemental Inflatable Restraint (SIR) system. The system must be dis-abled before performing service on or around system components, steering column, instrument panel components, wiring and sensors. Failure to follow safety and disabling procedures could result in accidental air bag deployment, possible personal injury and unnecessary system repairs.

• Always wear safety goggles when working with, or around, the air bag system. When carrying a non-deployed air bag, be sure the bag and trim cover are pointed away from your body. When placing a non-deployed air bag on a work surface, always face the bag and trim cover upward, away from the surface. This will reduce the motion of the module if it is accidentally deployed. Refer to the additional air bag system precautions later in this section.

• Clean, high quality brake fluid from a sealed container is essential to the safe and proper operation of the brake system. You should always buy the correct type of brake fluid for your vehicle. If the brake fluid becomes contaminated, completely flush the system with new fluid. Never reuse any brake fluid. Any brake fluid that is removed from the system should be discarded. Also, do not allow any brake fluid to come in contact with a painted surface; it will damage the paint.

• Never operate the engine without the proper amount and type of engine oil; doing so WILL result in severe engine damage.

• Timing belt maintenance is extremely important! Many models utilize an interference-type, non-freewheeling engine. If the timing belt breaks, the valves in the cylinder head may strike the pistons, causing potentially serious (also time-consuming and expensive) engine damage. Refer to the maintenance interval charts in the front of this manual for the recommended replacement interval for the timing belt, and to the timing belt section for belt replacement and inspection.

• Disconnecting the negative battery cable on some vehicles may interfere with the functions of the on-board computer system(s) and may require the computer to undergo a relearning process once the negative battery cable is reconnected.

• When servicing drum brakes, only disassemble and assemble one side at a time, leaving the remaining side intact for reference.

• Only an MVAC-trained, EPA-certified automotive technician should service the air conditioning system or its components.

ENGINE REPAIR

Distributor

REMOVAL

2.5L Engine

The 2.5L engine is equipped with a camshaft driven mechanical distributor. This engine uses a fixed ignition timing system, in which the basic ignition timing is not adjustable. The Powertrain Control Module (PCM) determines spark advance. The Crankshaft Position (CKP) sensor and Camshaft Position (CMP) sensor are Hall effect devices. The CKP sensor is mounted remotely from the distributor, while the CMP sensor is mounted inside the distributor housing. Both sensors generate pulses that serve as inputs to the PCM; the PCM determines crankshaft position from these sensors, then calculates injector sequence and ignition timing, based on the data.

1. Before servicing the vehicle, refer to the precautions in the beginning of this section.

2. Disconnect the negative battery cable.

3. Remove or disconnect, if necessary for access:
   • Air inlet resonator to the intake manifold bolt
   • Air cleaner cover to air cleaner housing cover clamps
   • PCV make-up air hose from the air inlet tube
   • Throttle body hose clamp
   • Air cleaner cover, resonator and inlet tube
   • Exhaust Gas Recirculation (EGR) tube

4. Remove or disconnect the following:
   • Spark plug wires from the distributor cap
   • Distributor cap

5. Matchmark the rotor-to-distributor and the distributor-to-engine positioning to help with installation.

6. Remove or disconnect the following:
   • Rotor

- Distributor's 2 electrical harness connectors
- Distributor hold-down nuts and washers
- Spark plug cable mounting bracket (if necessary)
- Transaxle dipstick tube
- Distributor

INSTALLATION

2.5L Engine

TIMING NOT DISTURBED

➡**Before servicing the vehicle, refer to the precautions in the beginning of this section.**

1. Inspect the rotor for cracks or burned electrodes, and replace if defective. Install the rotor onto the distributor.

2. Inspect the O-ring seal. If nicked or cracked, replace with a new one. Be sure the O-ring is properly seated on the distributor.

3. Install or connect the following:
- Distributor drive with the slotted end of the camshaft

➡**When the distributor is installed properly, the rotor will be aligned with the previously made mark.**

- Distributor hold-down nuts/washers and tighten to 108 inch lbs. (13 Nm)
- Spark plug cable bracket
- Both distributor wiring connectors
- Distributor cap
- Spark plug cables
- Transaxle dipstick tube

4. Install or connect the following, if removed:
- EGR tube and tighten the bolts to 95 inch lbs. (11 Nm)

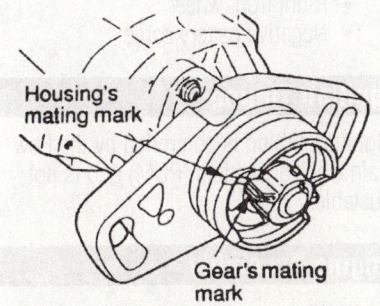

Prior to installation, align the distributor shaft with the distributor housing—2.5L engine

Housing's mating mark

Gear's mating mark

7922CG01

- Air cleaner cover, resonator and inlet tube
- Throttle body hose clamp
- PCV hose
- Air cleaner housing cover clamps
- Air inlet resonator to intake manifold bolt
- Negative battery cable

TIMING DISTURBED

1. Rotate the crankshaft until the No. 1 piston is at Top Dead Center (TDC) of the compression stroke.

2. Align the rotor with the distributor housing matchmark.

3. Install or connect the following:
- Distributor

➡**With the distributor fully seated, the rotor should align the No. 1 terminal of the distributor cap.**

- Distributor hold-down nuts/washers and tighten the nuts to 108 inch lbs. (13 Nm)
- Spark plug cable bracket
- Both distributor wiring connectors
- Distributor cap
- Spark plug cables
- Transaxle dipstick tube

4. Install or connect the following, if removed:
- EGR tube and tighten the bolts to 95 inch lbs. (11 Nm)
- Air cleaner cover, resonator and inlet tube
- Throttle body hose clamp

- PCV hose
- Air cleaner housing cover clamps
- Air inlet resonator to intake manifold bolt
- Negative battery cable

REMOVAL

2.0L Engine

1. Remove or disconnect the following:

- Negative battery cable
- Right front wheel
- Wheel well side cover
- Auto-cruise speed control assembly
- Alternator drive belt
- Alternator electrical connectors
- Alternator bracket
- Alternator

2.5L Engine

1. Remove or disconnect the following:

- Negative battery cable
- Right front wheel
- Wheel well side cover
- Auto-cruise control reservoir assembly
- Power steering pump drive belt cover
- A/C compressor drive belt
- Power steering pump/alternator drive belt

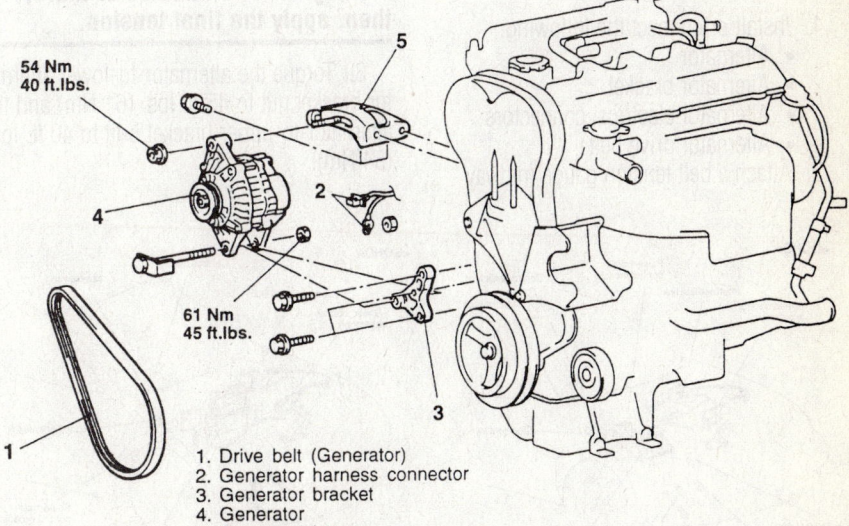

54 Nm
40 ft.lbs.

61 Nm
45 ft.lbs.

1. Drive belt (Generator)
2. Generator harness connector
3. Generator bracket
4. Generator
5. Generator brace

9306CG02

Exploded view of the alternator and related components—2.0L engine

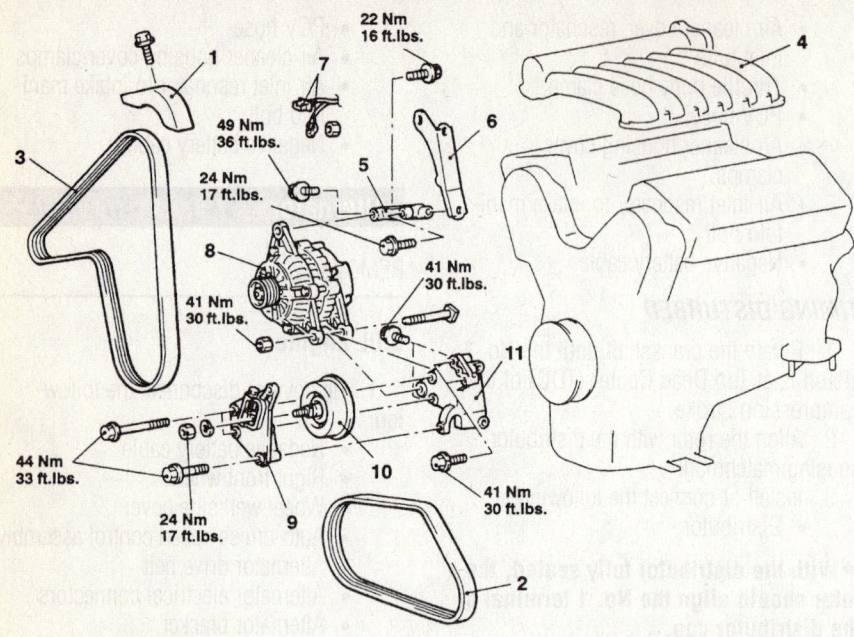

22 Nm
16 ft. lbs.

49 Nm
36 ft. lbs.

24 Nm
17 ft. lbs.

41 Nm
30 ft. lbs.

44 Nm
33 ft. lbs.

24 Nm
17 ft. lbs.

41 Nm
30 ft. lbs.

41 Nm
30 ft. lbs.

9306CG01

1. Pump cover
2. Drive belt (A/C compressor)
3. Drive belt (Power steering oil pump and generator)
4. Intake manifold plenum (Refer to GROUP 11 – Intake Manifold.)
5. Generator bracket
6. Intake manifold plenum stay
7. Generator harness connector
8. Generator
9. Tensioner pulley bracket
10. Tensioner pulley
11. Generator bracket

Exploded view of the alternator and related components—2.5L engine

- Intake manifold plenum
- Alternator bracket
- Intake manifold plenum stay
- Alternator electrical connectors
- Alternator

INSTALLATION

2.0L Engine

1. Install or connect the following:
   - Alternator
   - Alternator bracket
   - Alternator electrical connectors
   - Alternator drive belt
2. Attach a belt tension gauge midway on the drive belt; then, adjust the drive belt tension to 90–110 lbs. (400–490 N) for a used belt or 110–160 lbs. (490–712 N) for a new belt.

✳✳ WARNING

If installing a new belt, tension the belt to 70 lbs. (310 N) and operate the engine for 5 minutes or more; then, apply the final tension.

3. Torque the alternator-to-lower alternator bracket nut to 45 ft. lbs. (61 Nm) and the alternator-to-upper bracket bolt to 40 ft. lbs. (54 Nm).

4. Install or connect the following:
   - Auto-cruise speed control assembly
   - Wheel well side cover
   - Right front wheel
   - Negative battery cable

2.5L Engine

1. Install or connect the following:
   - Alternator
   - Alternator electrical connectors
   - Intake manifold plenum stay
   - Alternator bracket
2. Torque the alternator-to-lower alternator bracket nut to 30 ft. lbs. (41 Nm) and the alternator-to-upper bracket bolt to 16 ft. lbs. (22 Nm).
3. Install or connect the following:
   - Intake manifold plenum
   - Power steering pump/alternator drive belt
4. Attach a belt tension gauge midway on the drive belt, between the alternator and power steering pump pulleys; then, adjust the drive belt tension to 99–121 lbs. (440–540 N) for a used belt or 143–187 lbs. (642–838 N) for a new belt.
5. Torque the tension pulley bracket nut to 17 ft. lbs. (24 Nm).
6. Install the A/C compressor's drive belt.
7. Attach a belt tension gauge midway on the drive belt, between the crankshaft and tension pulleys; then, adjust the drive belt tension to 66–86 lbs. (295–385 N) for a used belt or 110–132 lbs. (490–590 N) for a new belt.
8. Torque the tension pulley bracket nut to 17 ft. lbs. (24 Nm).
9. Install or connect the following:
   - Power steering pump drive belt cover
   - Auto-cruise control reservoir assembly
   - Wheel well side cover
   - Right front wheel
   - Negative battery cable

Ignition Timing

Ignition timing is controlled by the Powertrain Control Module (PCM) and is not adjustable.

Engine Assembly

REMOVAL & INSTALLATION

1. Before servicing the vehicle, refer to the precautions in the beginning of this section.

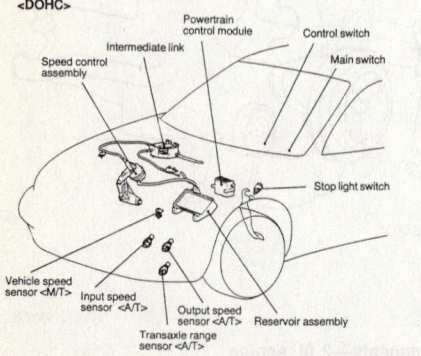

<DOHC>

Speed control assembly
Intermediate link
Powertrain control module
Control switch
Main switch
Stop light switch
Vehicle speed sensor <M/T>
Input speed sensor <A/T>
Output speed sensor <A/T>
Reservoir assembly
Transaxle range sensor <A/T>

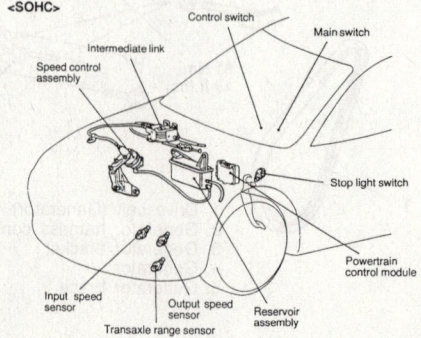

<SOHC>

Speed control assembly
Intermediate link
Control switch
Main switch
Stop light switch
Input speed sensor
Output speed sensor
Reservoir assembly
Transaxle range sensor
Powertrain control module

9306CG03

View of the auto-cruise speed control and related components—2.0L and 2.5L engines

➡**The transaxle must be removed before removing the engine. They will not come out as a unit.**

2. Drain the engine coolant.

3. Drain the engine oil and the transmission oil.

4. Safely relieve the pressure within the fuel injection system.

5. Remove or disconnect the following:

- Hood
- Negative battery cable

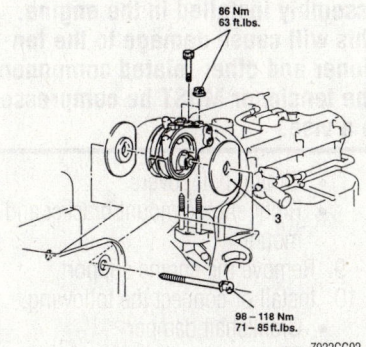

Exploded view of the right-side engine mount—2.0L engine

- Engine under cover
- Transaxle assembly
- Radiator by disconnecting the hoses at the engine
- Accelerator cable and bracket
- Heater hoses
- Brake booster vacuum hose at the engine
- Vacuum hoses running to the bulkhead
- High pressure fuel line and discard the O-ring
- Fuel return hose from the fuel supply rail
- Electrical connectors from the engine components

➡**All wires and connectors should be labeled at the time of engine removal. This will save time during assembly.**

- Accessory drive belts
- Power steering pump move aside

✳✳ WARNING

Do not disconnect the hoses or allow the pump to hang by the hoses.

- Power steering pump bracket
- A/C compressor and move aside

✳✳ CAUTION

Do not loosen or remove the A/C hoses or discharge the system.

- Exhaust system joint bolts just below the manifold and discard the gasket and nuts

6. Install the engine hoist equipment and make certain the attaching points on the engine are secure. Draw tension on the hoist just enough to support the engine's weight but no more. Do not disturb the placement of the vehicle on the stands.

7. Remove or disconnect the following:

- Rear (bulkhead side) roll stopper through-bolt
- Front engine roll stopper through-bolt
- Upper (right-side) engine mount-to-engine nuts/bolts, through-bolt and mount assembly
- Support bracket below the mount
- Engine

✳✳ WARNING

Immediately place it on an engine stand or support it with wooden blocks. Do not allow it to rest on the oil pan or lie on its side. Do not leave the engine hanging from the hoist.

To install:

8. Installation is the reverse of the removal procedure. Please note the following important steps:

a. Connect the exhaust system to the manifold, using a new gasket. Tighten the bolts to 33 ft. lbs. (44 Nm).

b. Tighten the engine mount nuts and bolts as follows:

- Right-side mount-to-engine nut and bolt: 63 ft. lbs. (86 Nm)
- Right-side mount through-bolt: 71–85 ft. lbs. (98–118 Nm)
- Rear roll stopper through-bolt: 32 ft. lbs. (44 Nm)
- Front roll stopper through-bolt: 41 ft. lbs. (56 Nm)

➡**Allow the mounts to support the engine weight before final tightening of the front roll stopper through-bolt.**

c. Tighten the power steering pump bracket bolts to 16 ft. lbs. (22 Nm) for 2.0L engine or to 29 ft. lbs. (39 Nm) for 2.5L engine.

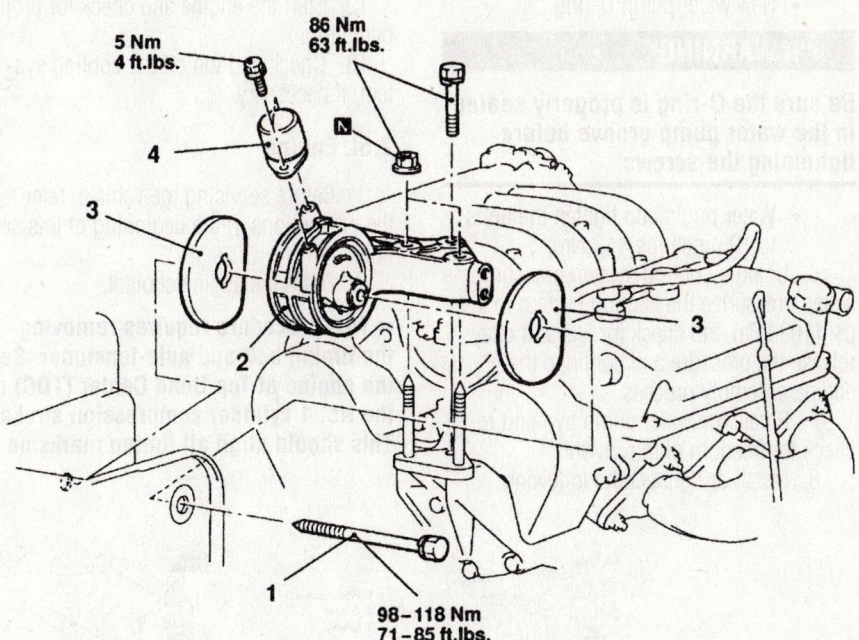

1. Engine mount insulator mounting bolt
2. Engine mount bracket
3. Engine mount stopper
4. Dynamic damper

Exploded view of the right-side engine mount—2.5L engine

Timing belt service is covered in Section 4 of this manual

d. Connect the wiring harness connectors to the engine.

✳✴ WARNING

Make certain each terminal is clean and the connector is firmly seated. Do not route wires near hot surfaces or moving parts.

e. Using a new O-ring lightly lubricated with clean engine oil, connect the high pressure fuel line and tighten the bolts to 22 inch lbs. (2.5 Nm).

f. Check the engine oil drain plug and secure it if necessary, and refill the crankcase.

g. Check the transaxle drain plug, tightening it if needed, and refill the transaxle.

h. Check the radiator and engine drain cocks, closing them if necessary, and refill the cooling system.

i. Double check all installation items, paying particular attention to loose hoses or hanging wires, loosened nuts, poor routing of hoses and wires.

9. Connect the negative battery cable. Start the engine and check for leaks.

10. Attend to all leaks immediately. Adjust the drive belts to the correct tension. Adjust all cables (transaxle, throttle, shift selector) and check the fluid levels. Check the operation of all gauges and dashboard lights.

11. Road test the vehicle.

Water Pump

REMOVAL & INSTALLATION

2.0L Engine

1. Before servicing the vehicle, refer to the precautions in the beginning of this section.

✳✴ WARNING

This procedure requires removing the timing belt and auto-tensioner. The factory specifies that the timing marks should always be aligned before removing the timing belt. Set the engine at Top Dead Center (TDC) on the No. 1 cylinder compression stroke. This should align all timing marks on the crankshaft sprocket and both camshaft sprockets.

2. Drain the engine coolant.
3. Remove or disconnect the following:

- Negative battery cable
- Right inner splash shield
- Accessory drive belts
- Properly support the engine and remove the right motor mount
- Timing belt, tensioner and camshaft sprockets

✳✴ WARNING

With the timing belt removed, DO NOT rotate the camshaft or crankshaft or damage to the engine may occur.

- Rear timing belt cover
- Water pump

To install:

4. Thoroughly clean all sealing surfaces.

✳✴ WARNING

Replace the water pump if there are any cracks, signs of coolant leakage from the shaft seal, loose or rough turning bearings, damaged impeller or sprocket or loose or damaged sprocket flange.

5. Install or connect the following:
- New water pump O-ring

✳✴ WARNING

Be sure the O-ring is properly seated in the water pump groove before tightening the screws.

- Water pump and tighten the bolts to 105 inch lbs. (12 Nm)

6. Using a cooling system pressure tester, pressurize the cooling system to 15 psi (103 kPa) and check for leaks. If okay, release the pressure and continue the engine assembly process.

7. Rotate the water pump by hand to check for freedom of movement.

8. Install or connect the following:

- Rear timing belt cover
- Camshaft sprocket(s), timing belt and tensioner

✳✴ WARNING

DO NOT allow the camshafts to turn while the sprocket bolts are being tightened.

✳✴ WARNING

Do not attempt to compress the tensioner plunger with the tensioner assembly installed in the engine. This will cause damage to the tensioner and other related components. The tensioner MUST be compressed in a vise.

- Timing belt covers
- Right engine mount bracket and mount

9. Remove the engine support.

10. Install or connect the following:
- Crankshaft damper
- Right inner splash shield
- Accessory drive belts

11. Refill and bleed the cooling system.

12. Start the engine and check for proper operation.

13. Check and top off the cooling system, if necessary.

2.5L Engine

1. Before servicing the vehicle, refer to the precautions in the beginning of this section.

2. Drain the engine coolant.

➡ **This procedure requires removing the timing belt and auto-tensioner. Set the engine at Top Dead Center (TDC) on the No. 1 cylinder compression stroke. This should align all timing marks on**

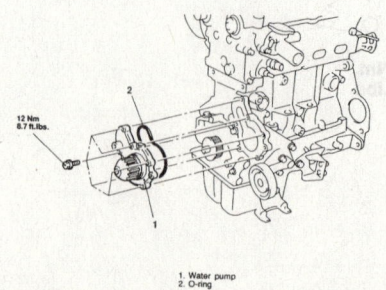

1. Water pump
2. O-ring

7922CG04

Exploded view of the water pump mounting—2.0L engine

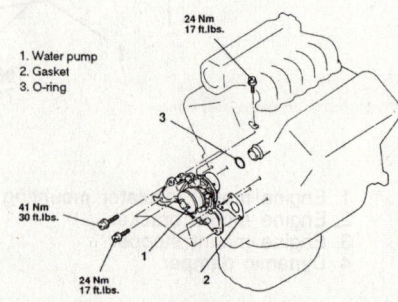

1. Water pump
2. Gasket
3. O-ring

24 Nm
17 ft.lbs.

41 Nm
30 ft.lbs.

24 Nm
17 ft.lbs.

7922CG05

Exploded view of the water pump mounting—2.5L engine

the crankshaft sprocket and both camshaft sprockets.

3. Remove or disconnect the following:
- Negative battery cable
- Accessory drive belts and crank-shaft damper
- Support the engine and remove the right engine mount
- Timing belt covers
- Timing belt and tensioner
- Water pump mounting bolts
- Water pump

To install:

4. Thoroughly clean all sealing surfaces. Inspect the pump for damage or cracks, signs of coolant leakage at the vent and excessive looseness or rough turning bearing. Any problems require a new pump.

5. Install or connect the following:
- New water inlet pipe O-ring.

❊❊ WARNING

Wet the O-ring with water to make installation easier; DO NOT use oil or grease.

- New water pump gasket

➡**Fit the pump inlet opening over the water pipe and press the assembly together to force the pipe into the water pump.**

- Water pump and tighten the pump-to-engine bolts to 20 ft. lbs. (27 Nm)
- Timing belt and timing belt tensioner. Set the timing belt tension.
- Timing belt covers
- Right engine mount. Remove the floor jack and engine block from underneath the engine.
- Crankshaft damper
- Accessory drive belts and adjust tension
- Negative battery cable

6. Refill and bleed the engine cooling system.

7. Start the engine and verify proper operation.

Cylinder Head

REMOVAL & INSTALLATION

2.0L Engine

1. Before servicing the vehicle, refer to the precautions in the beginning of this section.

2. Properly relieve the fuel system pressure.

3. Drain the engine coolant.

4. Remove or disconnect the following:
- Negative battery cable
- Air cleaner assembly
- All vacuum hoses, lines and wiring harness connections required for cylinder head removal
- Fuel line
- Throttle linkage
- Accessory drive belt(s)
- Power steering pump and move aside
- Coil pack wiring connector
- Spark plug wires from the spark plugs
- Ignition coil pack unit
- Cylinder head cover
- Intake and exhaust manifolds, if necessary
- Timing belt cover, timing belt, camshaft sprocket and rear timing belt cover
- Rocker arm/rocker arm shaft assemblies
- Cylinder head bolts and cylinder head

To install:

❊❊ WARNING

Stretch-type bolts are used. New head bolts are recommended.

5. Thoroughly clean all parts. Clean all sealing surfaces. Use care not to scratch the aluminum cylinder head sealing surface. Check the cylinder head for flatness using a feeler gauge and a straight-edge. The cylinder head must be flat within 0.004 in. (0.1mm).

6. Check the cylinder head for cracks or other damage.

7. Install or connect the following:
- New gasket and the cylinder head

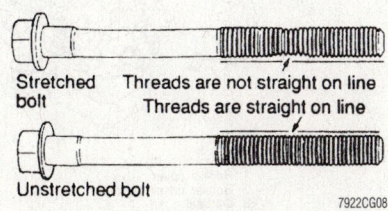

Stretched bolt — Threads are not straight on line
Threads are straight on line
Unstretched bolt
7922CG08

Checking the cylinder head bolts for necking (stretching)—2.0L engine

- Lubricate the cylinder head bolt threads with clean engine oil

➡**Refer to Section one of this manual for the cylinder head torque sequence illustration. The illustration is located after the Torque Specification Chart.**

- Cylinder head bolts, the short bolts (110mm) are to be installed in positions 7, 8, 9 and 10.

8. Tighten the cylinder head bolts in 4 steps as follows:
- a. Step 1: 25 ft. lbs. (34 Nm).
- b. Step 2: 50 ft. lbs. (68 Nm).
- c. Step 3: Again to 50 ft. lbs. (68 Nm).
- d. Step 4: Plus ¼ (90 degree) turn.

➡**Do not use a torque wrench for the 4th step.**

9. Install or connect the following:
- Rocker arm/rocker arm shaft assemblies
- Cylinder head cover
- Timing belt rear cover, camshaft sprocket and timing belt
- Timing belt cover
- Intake and exhaust manifolds, if removed
- Ignition coil pack
- Coil pack wiring connector and spark plug wires
- Power steering pump
- Accessory drive belts
- Throttle linkage
- All ducts, hoses, fuel lines and wiring harness connectors
- Air cleaner assembly
- Negative battery cable

10. Refill the cooling system.

➡**A complete oil and filter change is recommended.**

11. Start the engine and check for leaks. Run the engine with the radiator cap off so as the engine warms and the thermostat opens, coolant can be added to the radiator. When the cooling system is full, shut the engine **OFF**, install the radiator cap and allow the engine to cool.

12. With the engine cool, check all fluid levels. Add coolant and oil as required. Restart the engine and test drive vehicle to check for proper operation.

2.5L Engine

1. Before servicing the vehicle, refer to the precautions in the beginning of this section.

2. Release the fuel system pressure.

3. Drain the engine cooling system.

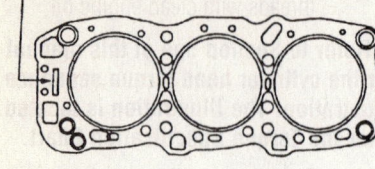

Identification mark

7922CG07

Install the head gasket with the identification mark at the front facing upward—2.5L engine

4. Remove or disconnect the following:
- Negative battery cable
- Timing belt and camshaft sprockets
- Wiring harnesses, vacuum hoses and lines that may inhibit cylinder head removal
- Intake manifold assembly
- Water pump inlet pipe retaining bolt from the inner rear of the front cylinder head
- Valve covers and rocker arm assemblies
- Distributor assembly
- Ground strap from the left end of the front cylinder head
- Exhaust manifolds and crossover pipe
- Cylinder head bolts; keep them in numbered order
- Cylinder head

To install:

5. Thoroughly clean and dry the mating surfaces of the head and block. Check the cylinder head for cracks, damage or engine coolant leakage. Remove scale, sealing compound and carbon. Clean the oil passages thoroughly. Check the head for flatness. End-to-end, the head should be no more than 0.008 in. (0.2mm) out-of-true. If the service limit is exceeded, correct to meet specifications. Note that the maximum amount from stock allowed to be removed from the cylinder head and mating cylinder block is 0.0079 in. (0.2mm). If the cylinder head cannot be made serviceable by removing this amount, replace it.

6. Check that the head gaskets have the proper identification marks for the engine. Lay the head gasket with the identification mark at the front top.

➡**Do not apply sealant to the head gasket or mating surfaces. Stretch-type cylinder head bolts are used. All new head bolts are recommended.**

7. Install or connect the following:
- Cylinder head straight down onto the block
- Lubricate the bolts with clean engine oil

- Bolts and the special washers by hand and just start each bolt one or 2 turns on the threads

➡**The washers must be installed correctly. The rounded shoulder of the washer denotes the face in contact with the bolt. The flat side of the washer contacts the head.**

➡**Refer to Section one of this manual for the cylinder head torque sequence illustration. The illustration is located after the Torque Specification Chart.**

8. Tighten the head bolts in the proper sequence as follows:
- a. Step 1: 62 ft. lbs. (84 Nm).
- b. Step 2: 70 ft. lbs. (95 Nm).
- c. Step 3: 80 ft. lbs. (108 Nm).
9. Install or connect the following:
- Valve cover and gasket
- Exhaust manifolds and crossover pipe
- Distributor
- Intake manifold
- All wiring harnesses, vacuum hoses and lines
- Negative battery cable
10. Refill the cooling system. Changing the oil and filter is recommended to eliminate pollutants such as coolant in the oil.

11. With the radiator cap off, start the engine and check for leaks of fuel, vacuum, oil or coolant. Check the operation of all engine electrical systems as well as dashboard gauges and lights. Add coolant as the engine warms.

12. Perform necessary adjustments to the accelerator cable and drive belts. Allow the engine to cool and once again check and adjust the coolant level.

Rocker Arm/Shafts

REMOVAL & INSTALLATION

2.5L Engine

1. Before servicing the vehicle, refer to the precautions in the beginning of this section.
2. Disconnect the negative battery cable.
3. Properly relieve the fuel system pressure.
4. If removing the right (firewall) side rocker arm/shaft assembly, remove the upper intake manifold (air intake plenum), which is a 2-piece unit of aluminum alloy.
5. Remove the valve cover(s).

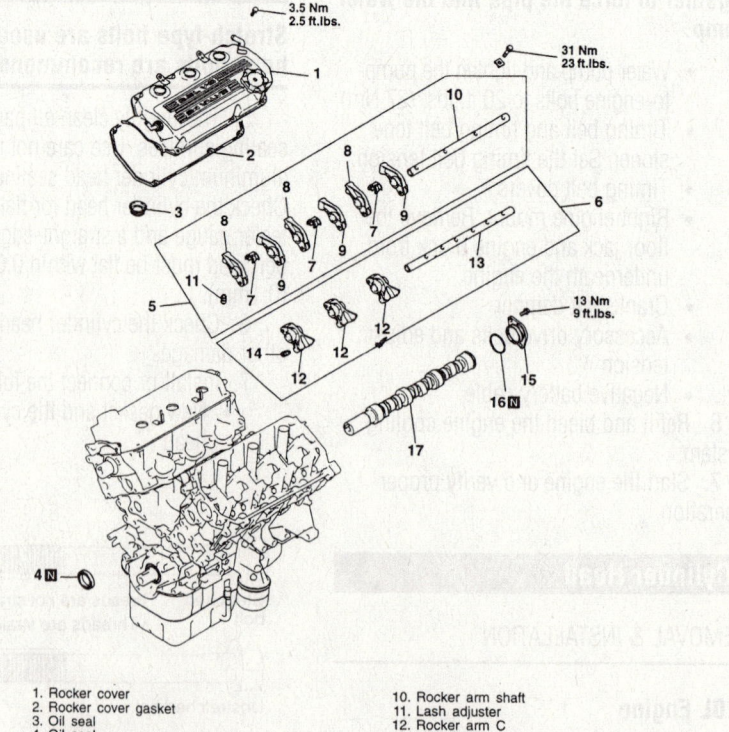

3.5 Nm 2.5 ft.lbs.
31 Nm 23 ft.lbs.
13 Nm 9 ft.lbs.

1. Rocker cover
2. Rocker cover gasket
3. Oil seal
4. Oil seal
5. Rocker arm and rocker arm shaft
6. Rocker arm and rocker arm shaft
7. Rocker shaft spring
8. Rocker arm A
9. Rocker arm B
10. Rocker arm shaft
11. Lash adjuster
12. Rocker arm C
13. Rocker arm shaft
14. Lash adjuster
15. Thrust case
16. O-ring
17. Camshaft

Exploded view of the cylinder head valve train assembly—2.5L engine

7922CG10

6. Identify the rocker arm shaft assemblies before removal.

7. Install the auto lash adjuster retainers Special Tool MD 998443 or equivalent to keep the auto lash adjusters from falling out of the rocker arms when the rocker arm assembly is removed.

8. Remove the rocker arm shaft assemblies.

➡The hydraulic automatic lash adjusters are precision units installed in the machined openings in the rocker arm units. Do not disassemble the auto lash adjusters.

To install:

9. The rocker arm shafts are hollow and used as a lubrication oil duct. Ensure all valve train parts are clean. Check the rocker arm mounting portion of the shafts for wear or damage. Replace if necessary. Check all oil holes for clogging with a small wire and clean as required. If any rockers were removed, lubricate and install them on the shafts in their original positions.

10. For the right cylinder head, install the rocker arm and shaft assemblies with the FLAT in the rocker arm shafts facing toward the timing belt side of the engine.

11. For the left cylinder head, install the rocker arm and shaft assembly with the FLAT in the rocker arm shaft facing toward the transaxle side of the engine.

12. Install the retainers and spring clips in their original positions on the exhaust and intake shafts. Tighten the retainer bolts to 23 ft. lbs. (31 Nm) working from the center, outward. Remove the valve lash retainer tools that may have been installed at disassembly.

13. Inspect the spark plug tube seals located on the ends of each tube. These seals slide onto each tube to seal the cylinder head cover to the spark plug tube. If these seals show signs of hardness and/or cracks, they should be replaced.

14. Install or connect the following:
- Valve cover(s)
- Upper intake manifold (plenum), if necessary
- All remaining electrical connectors and tighten the air tube connections
- Negative battery cable

15. An oil and filter change is recommended.

16. Start the engine and check for leaks, abnormal noises and vibrations.

Intake Manifold

REMOVAL & INSTALLATION

2.0L Engine

This engine uses a 2-piece aluminum intake manifold. A non-reusable gasket joins the 2 halves.

➡Be sure to observe all cautions and warnings in the beginning of the section that may be related to this procedure.

1. Relieve the fuel system pressure.
2. Drain the cooling system.
3. Remove or disconnect the following:
- Negative battery cable
- Accelerator cable, breather hose and air intake hose
- Vacuum connection at the power brake booster and the PCV valve
- All remaining vacuum hoses and pipes, as necessary. Tag for identification, if necessary, to save time at assembly.
- Fuel line(s), the throttle control cable and brackets

✳✳ CAUTION

Do not use conventional fuel filters, hoses or clamps when servicing fuel injection systems. They are not compatible with the injection system and could fail, causing personal injury or damage to the vehicle. Use only hoses and clamps specifically designed for fuel injection.

- Alternator wiring harness
- Manifold Absolute Pressure (MAP) sensor and Intake Air Temperature (IAT) sensor connectors
- Throttle Position (TP) sensor connector and position the engine wiring harness aside
- Exhaust Gas Recirculation (EGR) pipe connection
- Intake manifold stay and engine hanger
- Fuel injector connectors
- Throttle body assembly
- Intake manifold plenum and gasket
- Fuel rail assembly

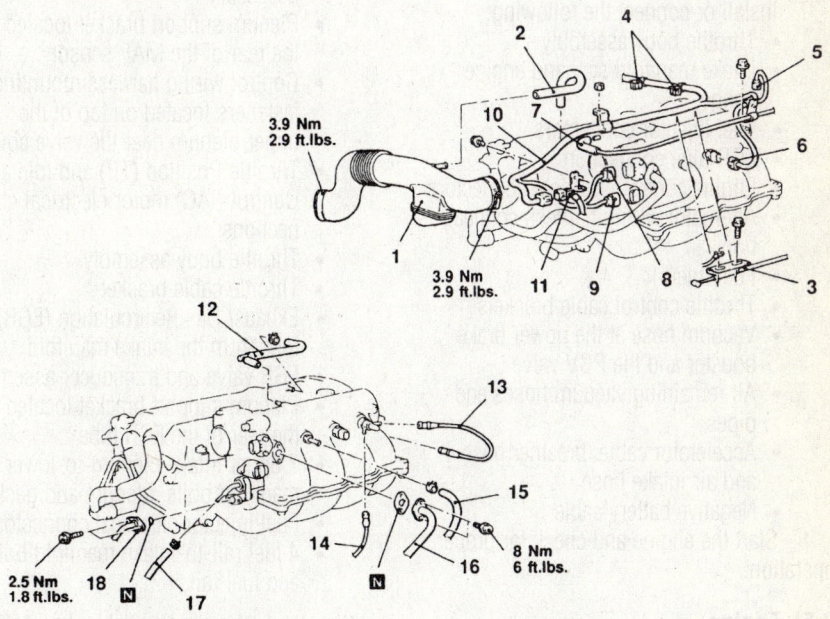

1. Air intake hose
2. Breather hose
3. Accelerator cable connection
4. Clip
5. MAP sensor connector
6. Intake air temperature sensor connector
7. Vacuum hose connection
8. TPS connector
9. Idle air control motor connector
10. Control wiring harness
11. Generator wiring harness connection
12. PCV hose assembly
13. Vacuum hose
14. Vacuum hose connection
15. Brake booster vacuum hose connection
16. EGR pipe connection
17. Fuel return hose connection
18. High-pressure fuel hose connection
Ⓝ. use new components

3.9 Nm
2.9 ft.lbs.

3.9 Nm
2.9 ft.lbs.

8 Nm
6 ft.lbs.

2.5 Nm
1.8 ft.lbs.

7922CG11

Intake manifold hose, cable and wire attachment identification—2.0L engine

Refer to Section 1 for engine rebuilding specifications

➡**Use care since the fuel injectors can drop out of the fuel rail as it is being removed.**

- Intake manifold and gasket

To install:

4. Clean all gasket material from the cylinder head and intake manifold assembly. Check both surfaces for cracks or other damage. Check the intake manifold water passages and air passages for clogging. Clean if necessary. Check the gasket surface of the intake manifold for flatness using a straight-edge and feeler gauge. It should be 0.006 in. (0.15mm) or less. The limit is 0.008 in. (0.20mm).

5. Install or connect the following:

- New gasket and the manifold. Tighten the manifold in a crisscross pattern, starting from the inside and working outwards to 17 ft. lbs. (23 Nm).
- Lubricate fuel injector O-rings with clean engine oil
- Fuel rail, injector and pressure regulator assembly

6. Thoroughly clean the mating surfaces and install the intake manifold plenum with a new gasket.

7. Install or connect the following:

- Throttle body assembly
- Intake manifold stay and engine hanger
- Fuel injector connectors
- EGR pipe connection
- Engine control electrical connectors
- Alternator wiring harness connection
- Fuel line(s)
- Throttle control cable brackets
- Vacuum hose at the power brake booster and the PCV valve
- All remaining vacuum hoses and pipes
- Accelerator cable, breather hose and air intake hose
- Negative battery cable

8. Start the engine and check for proper operation.

2.5L Engine

1. Before servicing the vehicle, refer to the precautions in the beginning of this section.

2. Disconnect the negative battery cable.

3. Properly relieve the fuel system pressure.

4. Disconnect the fuel line(s) from the fuel rail assembly. For quick-connect fittings, squeeze the fitting retainer tabs together and separate the connection.

✳✳ CAUTION

To prevent fuel from getting in your eyes, wrap shop towels around the connection to catch any gasoline spillage.

5. Remove or disconnect the following:

- Throttle body air inlet hose clamp
- Air cleaner cover and inlet hose
- Vacuum connection from the power brake booster and the PCV valve
- All remaining vacuum hoses and pipes, as necessary. Tag for identification, if necessary, to save time at assembly.

➡**It may be helpful to identify and tag each sensor connector and vacuum connection as it is being removed or disengaged. This may save time at assembly.**

- Manifold Absolute Pressure (MAP) sensor and Intake Air Temperature (IAT) sensor connectors
- Power steering pressure switch and Oxygen (O₂S) sensor connectors, if necessary.
- Plenum support bracket located to the rear of the MAP sensor
- Control wiring harness mounting fasteners located on top of the upper plenum near the valve cover
- Throttle Position (TP) and Idle air Control (IAC) motor electrical connections
- Throttle body assembly
- Throttle cable bracket
- Exhaust Gas Recirculation (EGR) tube from the intake manifold
- EGR valve and transducer assembly
- Plenum support bracket located to the rear of the EGR tube
- 7 upper intake plenum-to-lower manifold bolts, plenum and gasket
- Fuel injector electrical connectors
- 4 fuel rail-to-intake manifold bolts and fuel rail

➡**Use care, there are spacers under each fuel rail bolt.**

➡**It may be necessary to remove the power steering fluid reservoir and mounting bracket to access all of the lower intake manifold fasteners.**

- Lower intake manifold bolts, intake manifold and discard the gaskets

To install:

6. Clean all gasket sealing surfaces. Check both surfaces for cracks or other

---

damage. Check the intake manifold air passages for clogging. Clean if necessary.

7. Check upper and lower manifold gasket surfaces for flatness using a straight-edge and feeler gauge.

8. The surfaces must be flat within 0.006 in. (0.15mm) per 12 in. (30.5cm) of manifold length. The limit is 0.008 in. (0.20mm).

9. Properly position the new gaskets on the heads and install the lower intake manifold. Tighten the nuts as follows:

   a. Front bank: 60 inch lbs. (7 Nm).
   b. Rear bank: 14–17 ft. lbs. (20–23 Nm).
   c. Front bank: 14–17 ft. lbs. (20–23 Nm).
   d. Repeat once more.

10. Lubricate the fuel injector O-rings with clean engine oil.

11. Install or connect the following:

- Fuel injectors
- Seat the injectors and tighten the fuel rail bolts to 96 inch lbs. (12 Nm)
- Fuel injector electrical connectors
- Fuel line(s) to the fuel rail assembly

➡**Exert a slight tug on the fuel line away from the fuel rail to verify positive engagement.**

- Upper intake plenum with new gaskets and tighten the bolts to 13 ft. lbs. (18 Nm)
- Plenum support brackets and tighten to 13 ft. lbs. (18 Nm)
- EGR valve and transducer assembly
- EGR tube and tighten the screws to 95 inch lbs. (11 Nm)
- Throttle cable bracket
- Throttle body assembly
- TPS and IAC electrical connections
- Control wiring harness and tighten the mounting fasteners
- Power steering pressure switch and oxygen sensor connectors, if disconnected.
- MAP sensor and IAT sensor connectors
- Vacuum hose at the power brake booster and the PCV valve
- All remaining vacuum hoses and pipes
- Remaining engine control system electrical connectors
- Air cleaner cover and air inlet hose. Tighten the intake hose-to-throttle body hose clamp.
- Negative battery cable

12. Start the engine and check for leaks.

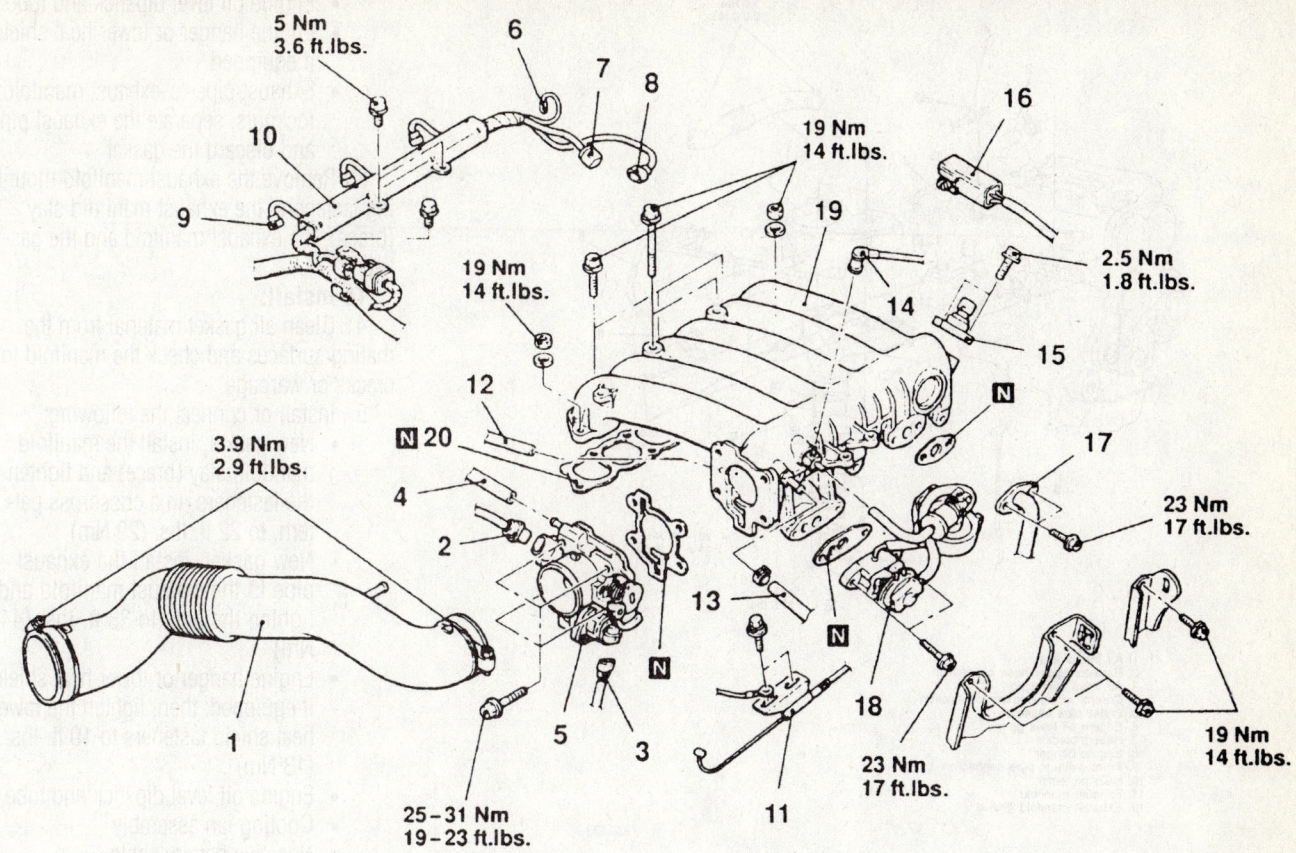

1. Air intake hose
2. TPS connector
3. Idle air control motor connector
4. Vacuum hose connection
5. Throttle body assembly
6. Power steering oil pressure switch connector
7. Heated oxygen sensor connector
8. Intake air temperature sensor connector
9. Injector connector
10. Control wiring harness
11. Accelerator cable connection
12. Vacuum hose connection
13. Brake booster vacuum hose connection
14. Vacuum hose connection
15. MAP sensor
16. Heated oxygen sensor harness
17. EGR pipe connection
18. EGR valve and EGR transducer assembly
19. Intake manifold plenum
20. Intake manifold plenum gasket

7922CG12

Exploded view of the plenum and intake manifold—2.5L engine

Exhaust Manifold

REMOVAL & INSTALLATION

2.0L Engine

1. Before servicing the vehicle, refer to the precautions in the beginning of this section.

2. Properly drain the engine coolant.

3. Remove or disconnect the following:

- Negative battery cable
- Air intake hose and small air hose connection
- Upper radiator hose from the thermostat housing
- Control wiring harness connection
- Water pipe assembly and engine oil level dipstick
- Heat shield and engine hanger
- Pulsed secondary air injection valve, if equipped
- Exhaust pipe-to-exhaust manifold locknuts, separate the exhaust pipe and discard the gasket

4. Loosen the mounting fasteners and remove the exhaust manifold.

To install:

5. Clean all gasket material from the mating surfaces and check the manifold for cracks or warpage.

6. Install or connect the following:

- New gasket, the manifold and tighten the fasteners, in a criss-

For engine torque specifications, refer to Section 1 of this manual

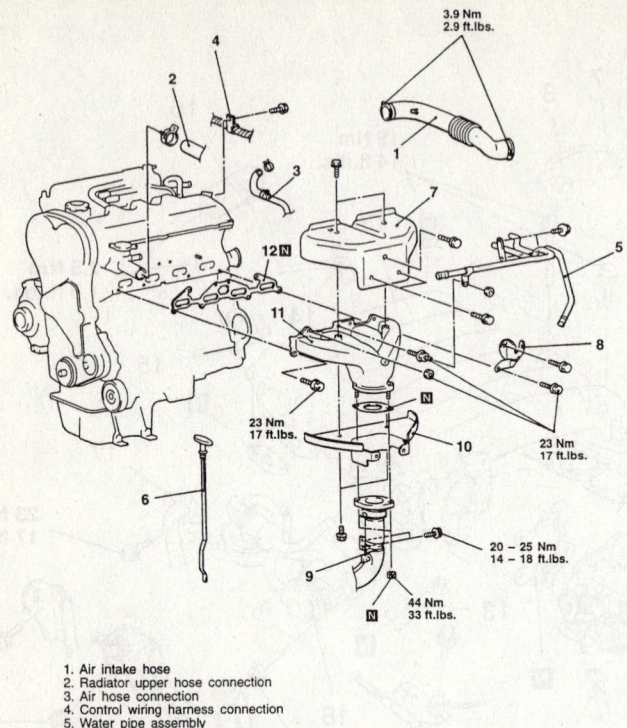

1. Air intake hose
2. Radiator upper hose connection
3. Air hose connection
4. Control wiring harness connection
5. Water pipe assembly
6. Engine oil level gauge
7. Heat protector
8. Engine hanger
9. Front exhaust pipe connection
10. Heat protector
11. Exhaust manifold
12. Exhaust manifold gasket

7922CG13

Exploded view of the exhaust manifold and related components—2.0L engine

- Engine oil level dipstick and tube
- Engine hanger or lower heat shield, if equipped
- Exhaust pipe-to-exhaust manifold locknuts, separate the exhaust pipe and discard the gasket

3. Remove the exhaust manifold mounting fasteners, the exhaust manifold stay (brace), the exhaust manifold and the gasket.

To install:

4. Clean all gasket material from the mating surfaces and check the manifold for cracks or warpage.

5. Install or connect the following:

- New gasket, install the manifold, manifold stay (brace) and tighten the fasteners, in a crisscross pattern, to 22 ft. lbs. (29 Nm)
- New gasket, install the exhaust pipe to the exhaust manifold and tighten the nuts to 33 ft. lbs. (44 Nm)
- Engine hanger or lower heat shield, if equipped; then, tighten the lower heat shield fasteners to 10 ft. lbs. (13 Nm)
- Engine oil level dipstick and tube
- Cooling fan assembly
- Negative battery cable

cross pattern, to 17 ft. lbs. (23 Nm)

- Exhaust pipe to the exhaust manifold with a new gasket and new locknuts. Tighten the nuts to 33 ft. lbs. (44 Nm).
- Pulsed secondary air injection valve, if equipped
- Heat shield and the engine hanger
- Control wiring harness connection
- Upper radiator hose to the thermostat housing
- Air intake hose and small air hose
- Negative battery cable.

7. Refill the cooling system.

8. Start the engine and check for exhaust leaks.

2.5L Engine

FRONT BANK

1. Before servicing the vehicle, refer to the precautions in the beginning of this section.

2. Remove or disconnect the following:

- Negative battery cable
- Cooling fan assembly

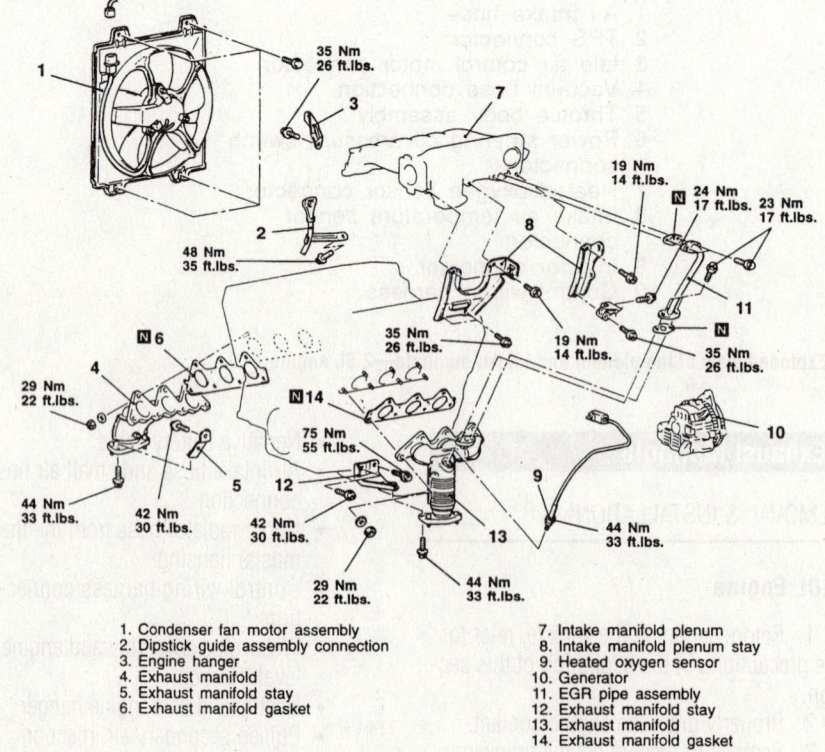

1. Condenser fan motor assembly
2. Dipstick guide assembly connection
3. Engine hanger
4. Exhaust manifold
5. Exhaust manifold stay
6. Exhaust manifold gasket
7. Intake manifold plenum
8. Intake manifold plenum stay
9. Heated oxygen sensor
10. Generator
11. EGR pipe assembly
12. Exhaust manifold stay
13. Exhaust manifold
14. Exhaust manifold gasket

7922CG14

Exploded view of the exhaust manifold assembly and related components—2.5L engine

6. Operate the engine and check for exhaust leaks.

REAR BANK

1. Before servicing the vehicle, refer to the precautions in the beginning of this section.

2. Remove or disconnect the following:

- Negative battery cable
- Intake manifold plenum and plenum stay
- Heated Oxygen (HO2S) sensor
- Alternator
- Exhaust Gas Recirculation (EGR) pipe assembly
- Exhaust pipe-to-exhaust manifold locknuts, separate the exhaust pipe and discard the gasket
- Manifold heat shield, if equipped
- Exhaust manifold bolts, the exhaust manifold brace, the exhaust manifold and the gasket

To install:

3. Clean all gasket material from the mating surfaces and check the manifold for cracks or warpage.

4. Install or connect the following:

- New gasket, the manifold and manifold brace; then, tighten the nuts, in a crisscross pattern, to 22 ft. lbs. (30 Nm)
- Manifold heat shield, if equipped
- Exhaust pipe-to-exhaust manifold using a new gasket, and tighten the nuts to 33 ft. lbs. (44 Nm)
- EGR pipe assembly
- Alternator and HO2S sensor
- Intake manifold plenum and plenum stay (brace)
- Negative battery cable

5. Start the engine and check for exhaust leaks.

Front Crankshaft Seal

REMOVAL & INSTALLATION

2.0L Engine

1. Before servicing the vehicle, refer to the precautions in the beginning of this section.

2. Drain the engine oil.

3. Remove or disconnect the following:

- Negative battery cable

- Accessory drive belts
- Crankshaft damper/pulley
- Timing belt cover
- Timing belt
- Crankshaft sprocket

✳✳ WARNING

Be careful not to nick the seal surface of the crankshaft or the seal bore.

- Front crankshaft seal using a seal puller tool

✳✳ WARNING

Be careful not to damage the seal contact area of the crankshaft.

To install:

4. Lubricate the new seal with clean engine oil. Install the new front crankshaft oil seal by using Oil Seal Installer tool No. 6780-1 or equivalent seal tool.

5. Place a new oil seal into the opening with the seal spring facing the inside of the engine. Be sure the oil seal is installed flush with the front cover.

6. Install or connect the following:

- Crankshaft timing belt sprocket
- Timing belt
- Timing belt cover
- Crankshaft damper/pulley
- Accessory drive belts
- Negative battery cable

7. Change the oil filter and refill the crankcase.

8. Start the engine and check for leaks.

2.5L Engine

1. Before servicing the vehicle, refer to the precautions in the beginning of this section.

2. Drain the engine oil.

3. Remove or disconnect the following:

- Negative battery cable
- Accessory drive belts
- Crankshaft damper/pulley
- Front timing belt covers
- Timing belt
- Crankshaft sprocket and key
- Front crankshaft seal by prying it out with a flat tipped prytool; be sure to cover the end of the prytool tip with a shop towel

✳✳ WARNING

Be careful not to nick the seal surface of the crankshaft or the seal bore.

To install:

4. Apply a light coating of clean engine oil to the lip of the new oil seal. Install the new front crankshaft oil seal into the oil pump housing by using oil seal installer tool No. MD998717 or equivalent. Be sure the oil seal is installed flush with the oil pump cover.

5. Install or connect the following:

- Crankshaft timing belt sprocket and key
- Timing belt
- Timing belt covers
- Crankshaft damper/pulley
- Accessory drive belts
- Negative battery cable

6. Change the oil filter and refill the crankcase.

7. Start the engine and check for leaks.

Camshaft and Valve Lifters

REMOVAL & INSTALLATION

2.0L Engine

1. Before servicing the vehicle, refer to the precautions in the beginning of this section.

2. Properly relieve the fuel system pressure.

3. Remove or disconnect the following:

- Negative battery cable
- Spark plug wires
- Ignition coil pack with spark plug wires
- Cylinder head cover and discard the gasket
- Ground strap
- Timing belt covers, timing belt and camshaft sprockets

➡ **The camshaft bearing caps are numbered for correct location during installation.**

- Outer camshaft bearing caps, first

4. Loosen, but do not remove, the camshaft bearing cap retaining fasteners in the correct sequence, inside working outward. Perform this step on one camshaft at a time.

5. Identify the camshafts, if they are to be reused, for later installation. The camshafts are not interchangeable.

6. Remove or disconnect the following:

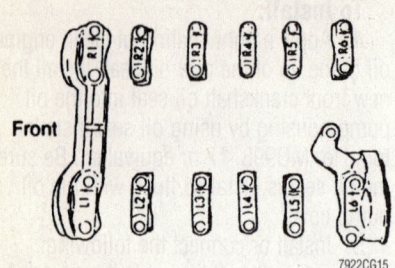

Camshaft bearing cap identification—2.0L engine

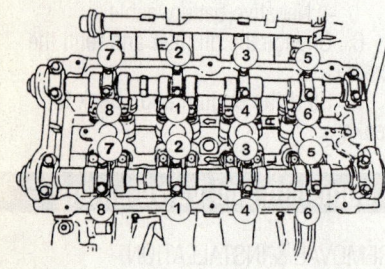

Camshaft bearing cap retaining bolt removal sequence—2.0L engine

- Camshaft bearing caps
- Camshafts
- Camshaft followers

❊❊ WARNING

Any components that are to be reused must be installed in their original locations. Use care to identify and mark the positions of any removed valve train components so they may be reinstalled correctly.

7. Inspect the camshaft bearing oil feed holes in the cylinder head for clogging. Inspect the camshaft bearing journals for wear or scoring. Check the cam surface for abnormal wear and damage. A visible worn groove in the roller path or on the cam lobes is cause for replacement.

To install:

8. Thoroughly clean all camshaft and related parts.

9. If the fit and condition of the camshafts are acceptable, remove the camshafts for installation of the cam followers.

10. The hydraulic valve lash adjusters are inside the roller cam followers. Be sure they are clean, well lubricated with clean engine oil and properly positioned. Install the cam followers in their original positions on the hydraulic adjuster and valve stem.

❊❊ WARNING

To avoid valve to piston contact, be sure NONE of the pistons are at Top Dead Center when installing the camshafts.

11. Lubricate the camshaft bearing journals and cam followers with clean engine oil.

12. Install or connect the following:
- Camshafts
- Right and left camshaft bearing caps No. 2 through No. 5 and right side No. 6
- Tighten the M6 fasteners to 105 inch lbs. (12 Nm) in correct sequence

13. Apply Mopar® Gasket Maker or equivalent, sealer to the No. 1 and left-side No. 6 bearing caps.

14. Install or connect the following:
- Bearing caps
- Tighten the M8 fasteners to 21 ft. lbs. (28 Nm)

➡ The end caps must be installed before the seals may be installed.

- Camshaft end seals
- Camshaft sprockets, if removed
- Timing belt

➡ Make sure all timing marks are properly aligned, using the recommended procedure.

- Timing belt covers

❊❊ WARNING

Verify that all timing marks are correct. If the timing belt or sprockets are incorrectly installed, engine damage will occur.

15. Clean all sealing surfaces. Make certain the rails are flat.

16. Install or connect the following:
- New cylinder head cover gaskets

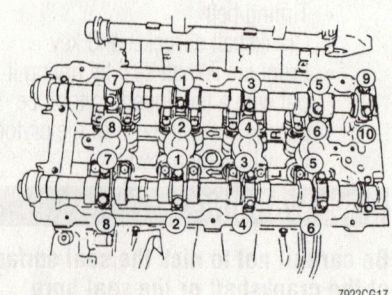

Camshaft bearing cap retaining bolt tightening sequence—2.0L engine

❊❊ WARNING

DO NOT allow oil or solvents to contact the timing belt as they can deteriorate the rubber and cause tooth skipping. Apply Mopar Silicone Rubber Adhesive Sealant or equivalent, at the camshaft cap corners and at the top edge of the ½ round seal.

➡ Inspect the spark plug well seals for cracking and/or swelling and replace, if necessary.

- Cylinder head cover assembly

17. Tighten the cylinder head cover fasteners, in sequence, using the following 3 steps:
- a. Step 1: 40 inch lbs. (4.5 Nm).
- b. Step 2: 80 inch lbs. (9 Nm).
- c. Step 3: 105 inch lbs. (12 Nm).

18. Install or connect the following:
- Ignition coil pack and tighten the fasteners to 105 inch lbs. (12 Nm)
- Spark plug wires
- Ground strap
- All vacuum lines and remaining wiring

➡ An oil and filter change is recommended to wash out any sealant or gasket material that may have fallen into the engine.

- Negative battery cable

19. Test run the vehicle. Check for leaks and for proper operation.

2.5L Engine

➡ For camshaft service, the cylinder head must be removed.

1. Relieve the fuel system pressure.
2. Drain the cooling system.
3. Drain the oil.
4. Remove or disconnect the following:

- Negative battery cable
- Timing belt covers, timing belt and camshaft sprockets
- Upper intake manifold plenum
- Lower intake manifold
- Cylinder head bolts and cylinder head
- Thrust case from the left head assembly
- Left camshaft from the rear of the head
- Distributor from the right cylinder head
- Right camshaft from the rear of the head

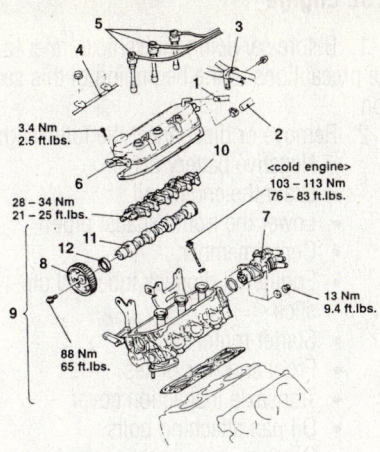

3.4 Nm
2.5 ft.lbs.

<cold engine>
103 – 113 Nm
76 – 83 ft.lbs.

28 – 34 Nm
21 – 25 ft.lbs.

13 Nm
9.4 ft.lbs.

88 Nm
65 ft.lbs.

1. Breather hose connection
2. Blow-by hose
3. Fuel hose assembly connection
4. Vacuum pipe connection
5. Spark plug cable
6. Rocker cover
7. Distributor
8. Camshaft sprocket
9. Cylinder head assembly
10. Rocker arm and rocker shaft assembly
11. Camshaft
12. Camshaft oil seal

7922CG18

Exploded view of the rear cylinder head and camshaft mounting—2.5L engine

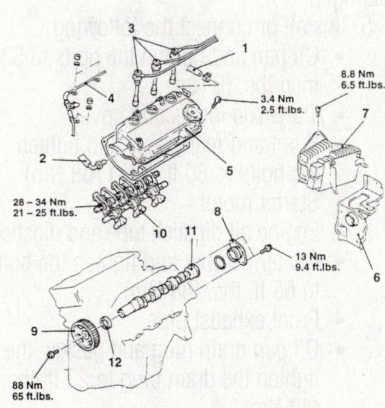

8.8 Nm
6.5 ft.lbs.

3.4 Nm
2.5 ft.lbs.

28 – 34 Nm
21 – 25 ft.lbs.

13 Nm
9.4 ft.lbs.

88 Nm
65 ft.lbs.

1. Blow-by hose
2. PCV valve and hose assembly connection
3. Spark plug cable
4. Vacuum pipe and hose asembly
5. Rocker cover
6. Relay box bracket assembly
7. Control module and bracket assembly
8. Thrust case
9. Camshaft sprocket
10. Rocker arm and rocker shaft assembly
11. Camshaft
12. Camshaft oil seal

7922CG19

Exploded view of the front cylinder head and camshaft mounting—2.5L engine

To install:

5. Lubricate the camshaft journals
6. Install or connect the following:
   • Camshaft into the cylinder head
   • Thrust case and tighten the fasteners to 108 inch lbs. (13 Nm)

➡Lubricate the camshaft oil seal lip with clean engine oil.

   • Camshaft seal

➡The camshaft must be installed before installing the seal. Be sure the seal is installed flush with the cylinder head surface.

   • Camshaft sprocket and tighten to 65 ft. lbs. (88 Nm)
   • Cylinder head
   • Lower intake manifold using new gaskets
   • Rocker arm and shaft assemblies
   • Timing belt

7. Inspect the spark plug tube seals located on the ends of each tube. These seals slide onto each tube to seal the cylinder head cover to the spark plug tube. If these seals show signs of hardness and/or cracks, they should be replaced.

8. Install or connect the following:
   • Cylinder head cover
   • Spark plug wires
   • Intake manifold plenum
   • Throttle and speed control cables
   • Air inlet resonator, air inlet hose and air cleaner housing cover
   • All remaining electrical connectors
   • Tighten the air tube connections
   • Negative battery cable

9. Refill the cooling system.
10. Change the oil filter and refill the crankcase.
11. Start the engine and check for leaks, abnormal noises and vibrations.
12. Bleed the cooling system.

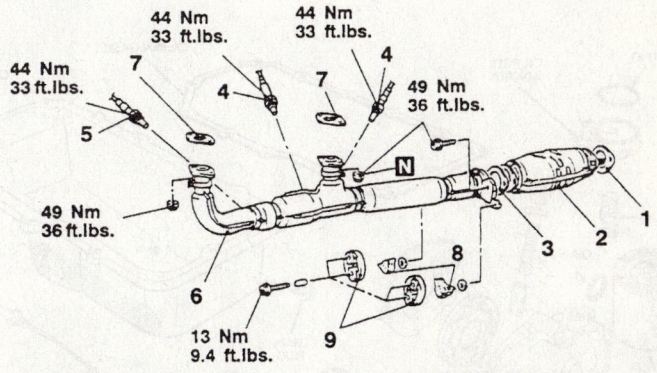

44 Nm
33 ft.lbs.

44 Nm
33 ft.lbs.

44 Nm
33 ft.lbs.

49 Nm
36 ft.lbs.

49 Nm
36 ft.lbs.

13 Nm
9.4 ft.lbs.

N

1. Gasket
2. Catalytic converter
3. Gasket
4. Heated oxygen sensor <Except vehicles for California>
5. Heated oxygen sensor
6. Front exhaust pipe
7. Gasket
8. Protector
9. Hanger

9306CG04

Exploded view of the front exhaust pipe and related components—2.5L engine

Valve Lash

ADJUSTMENT

The engines in these vehicles do not require periodic valve lash adjustment.

Starter Motor

REMOVAL & INSTALLATION

1. Remove or disconnect the following:
   • Negative battery cable
   • Engine under cover
   • Heated Oxygen (H2OS) sensor electrical connector
   • Front exhaust pipe
   • Starter motor electrical connectors
   • Starter motor

To install:

2. Install or connect the following:
   • Starter motor. Torque starter-to-transaxle bolts to 40 ft. lbs. (54 Nm) for 2.0L engine or 20–25 ft. lbs. (26–33 Nm) for 2.5L engine.
   • Starter motor electrical connectors

➡Use new gaskets when installing the front exhaust pipe.

   • Front exhaust pipe. Torque the front exhaust pipe-to-exhaust manifold nuts to 36 ft. lbs. (49 Nm) and the front exhaust pipe-to-catalytic converter bolts to 36 ft. lbs. (49 Nm).
   • HO_2 sensor electrical connector
   • Engine under cover
   • Negative battery cable

Please refer to Section 8 for electric cooling fan wiring schematics

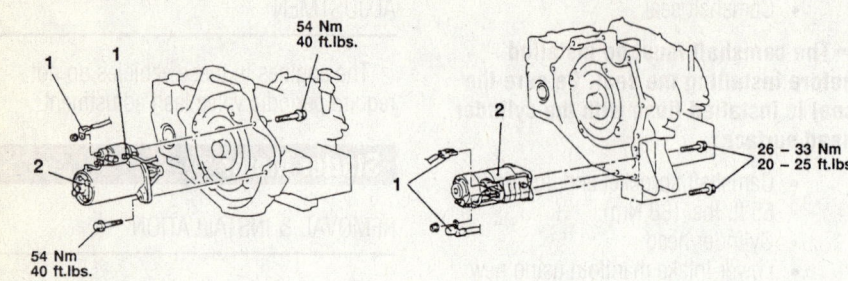

<DOHC>

<SOHC>

Removal steps
1. Starter terminal and connector
2. Starter motor

9306CG05

View of the starter motor—2.0L (DOHC) engine and 2.5L (SOHC) engine

Oil Pan

REMOVAL & INSTALLATION

2.0L Engine

1. Before servicing the vehicle, refer to the precautions in the beginning of this section.
2. Drain the engine oil.
3. Remove or disconnect the following:

- Negative battery cable
- Oil dipstick and tube
- Front plate
- Front exhaust pipe
- Oil pan bolts
- Oil pan

To install:

4. Inspect the oil pan for damage and cracks; replace, if necessary. While the pan is removed, inspect the oil screen for clogging, damage and cracks. Clean and/or replace, if necessary.

5. Thoroughly, clean the mating surfaces of the cylinder block and the oil pan.

6. Apply sealant to the seams between the oil pump and the engine block.

7. Install or connect the following:

- Oil pan and tighten bolts to 108 inch lbs. (12 Nm)
- Front exhaust pipe
- Oil dipstick and tube
- Oil drain plug and tighten to 25 ft. lbs. (34 Nm)
- Negative battery cable

8. Refill the crankcase.

9. Start the engine and check for leaks.

2.5L Engine

1. Before servicing the vehicle, refer to the precautions in the beginning of this section.

2. Remove or disconnect the following:

- Negative battery cable
- Drain the engine oil
- Lower the front exhaust pipe
- Centermember
- Engine oil dipstick tube and dipstick
- Starter motor
- Front and rear plates
- Transaxle inspection cover
- Oil pan attaching bolts
- Oil pan

To install:

3. Thoroughly clean and dry the oil pan, cylinder block and cylinder block bolts and bolt holes.

4. Apply a continuous 3/16 inch (4mm) bead of silicone adhesive sealant to the oil pan gasket surface. Be sure to circle all mounting bolt holes as well. Install the oil pan within a 10–15 minute period of applying the gasket material to ensure proper sealing.

5. Install or connect the following:

- Oil pan and tighten the bolts to 53 inch lbs. (6 Nm)
- Transaxle inspection cover
- Front and rear plates and tighten the bolts to 80 ft. lbs. (108 Nm)
- Starter motor
- Engine oil dipstick tube and dipstick
- Centermember and tighten the bolts to 65 ft. lbs. (88 Nm)
- Front exhaust pipe
- Oil pan drain plug and gasket; then, tighten the drain plug to 29 ft. lbs. (40 Nm)
- Negative battery cable

6. Refill the crankcase and install a new oil filter.

7. Start the engine and check for leaks.

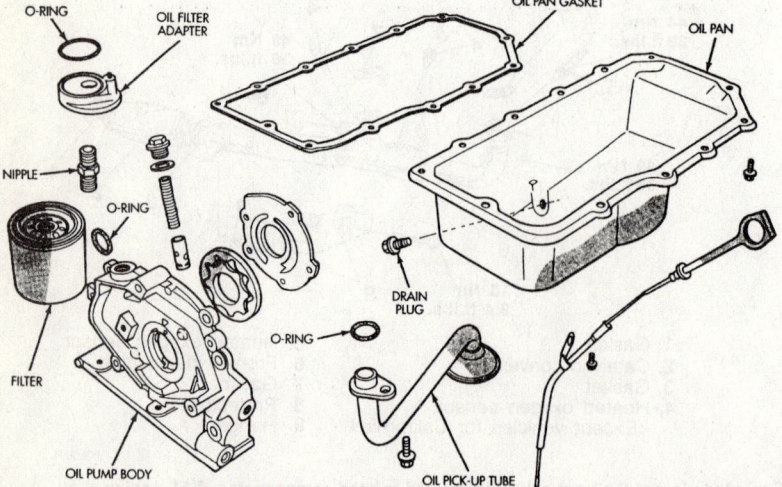

Exploded view of the engine lubricating components—2.0L engine

7922CG21

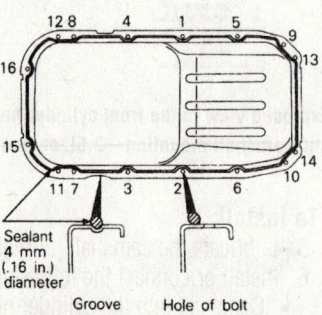

7922CG22

To ensure a leak-free seal, apply sealer as shown and tighten the bolts following the specified sequence—2.5L engine

Oil Pump

REMOVAL & INSTALLATION

2.0L Engine

1. Before servicing the vehicle, refer to the precautions in the beginning of this section.

2. Remove or disconnect the following:
- Negative battery cable
- Timing belt
- Oil pan
- Crankshaft sprocket
- Oil pump pick-up tube and O-ring
- Oil pump and front crankshaft seal

✳✳ WARNING

The front cover/oil pump mounting bolts may be different sizes and must be reinstalled in their original locations. Remove and tag the front cover mounting bolts.

3. Inspect the oil pump case for damage and remove the rear cover.

4. Remove the pump rotors and inspect the inside of the case for excessive wear.

5. Check that the oil relief plunger slides smoothly and check for a broken spring.

To install:

6. Clean all parts well. Be sure the block and pump surfaces are clean and free of old sealer.

7. Assemble the pump using new parts as required with clean oil. Align the marks on the inner and outer rotors when assembling.

8. Install the pump back cover and tighten the screws to 88 inch lbs. (10 Nm).

9. Reinstall the pump relief valve, spring, gasket and valve cap. Tighten the valve cap to 30–33 ft. lbs. (41–44 Nm).

10. Apply gasket maker to the engine block mounting surface of the oil pump body.

11. Install the oil ring into the discharge passage of the pump body.

12. Prime the oil pump before installation by filling the rotor cavity with clean engine oil.

13. Align the flats of the oil pump rotor with the flats on the crankshaft as you install the pump to the engine block.

14. Install or connect the following:
- Oil pump-to-engine block bolts to 17–21 ft. lbs. (23–28 Nm)

- New front oil seal
- Crankshaft sprocket
- Oil pump pickup tube and O-ring; then, tighten the oil pump pickup tube screw to 21 ft. lbs. (28 Nm)
- Oil pan
- Timing belt and covers
- Cankshaft damper
- New oil filter

15. Refill the engine with new, clean engine oil and coolant.

16. Test run the vehicle to check for leaks. An oil pressure gauge should be installed to verify proper engine oil pressure.

2.5L Engine

1. Before servicing the vehicle, refer to the precautions in the beginning of this section.

2. Drain the engine coolant.
3. Drain the engine oil.
4. Remove or disconnect the following:
- Negative battery cable
- Drive belts and accessories
- Crankshaft damper
- Timing belt upper and lower covers
- Crankshaft sprocket
- Oil pump

5. Inspect the oil pump case for damage and remove the rear cover.

6. Remove the pump rotors and inspect the inside of the case for excessive wear.

7. Check that the oil relief plunger slides smoothly and check for a broken spring.

To install:

8. Clean all parts well. Be sure the block and pump surfaces are clean and free of old sealer.

9. Assemble the pump using new parts as required with clean oil. Align the marks on the inner and outer rotors when assembling.

10. Install the pump back cover and tighten the screws to 88 inch lbs. (10 Nm).

11. Reinstall the pump relief valve, spring, gasket and valve cap. Tighten the valve cap to 30–33 ft. lbs. (41–44 Nm).

12. Prime the pump before installation by filling the rotor cavity with clean engine oil.

13. Apply gasket maker or equivalent sealer on the pump. Install the O-ring into the counterbore on the pump body discharge passage. Position the pump onto the crankshaft until seated on the block. Tighten

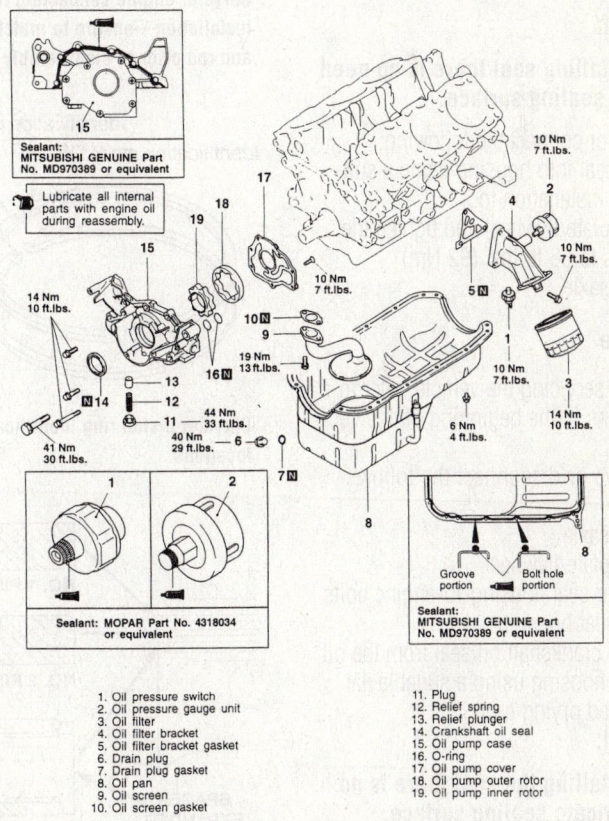

1. Oil pressure switch
2. Oil pressure gauge unit
3. Oil filter
4. Oil filter bracket
5. Oil filter bracket gasket
6. Drain plug
7. Drain plug gasket
8. Oil pan
9. Oil screen
10. Oil screen gasket
11. Plug
12. Relief spring
13. Relief plunger
14. Crankshaft oil seal
15. Oil pump case
16. O-ring
17. Oil pump cover
18. Oil pump outer rotor
19. Oil pump inner rotor

7922CG20

Exploded view of the oil pan and pump assembly—2.5L engine

the size M8 fasteners to 10 ft. lbs. (14 Nm) and size M10 fasteners to 30 ft. lbs. (41 Nm).

14. Install or connect the following:
- Timing belt and crankshaft sprocket
- Timing belt cover
- Crankshaft damper
- Drive belts and accessories

15. Refill the cooling system. Install a new oil filter and refill the engine with oil.

16. Road test the vehicle. Check for proper operation as well as leaks.

Rear Main Seal

REMOVAL & INSTALLATION

2.0L Engine

➡ Be sure to observe all cautions and warnings in the beginning of the section that may be related to this procedure.

1. Remove or disconnect the following:
- Transaxle
- Flexplate/flywheel
- Rear crankshaft oil seal

➡ Pry the oil seal from the housing using a suitable flat bladed prying tool.

To install:

➡ When installing seal there is no need to lubricate sealing surface.

2. Install or connect the following:
- Oil seal into housing using a suitable installation tool
- Flexplate/flywheel and tighten the bolts to 68 ft. lbs. (92 Nm)
- Transaxle

2.5L Engine

1. Before servicing the vehicle, refer to the precautions in the beginning of this section.

2. Remove or disconnect the following:
- Transaxle
- Flexplate/flywheel
- 5 rear seal housing-to-engine bolts
- Oil seal housing
- Rear crankshaft oil seal from the oil seal housing using a suitable flat bladed prying tool

To install:

➡ When installing the seal there is no need to lubricate sealing surface.

3. Install the seal into the housing using a suitable seal and bearing driver.

4. Apply silicone rubber adhesive

sealant to the mating surface of the seal housing.

5. Apply a light coating of engine oil to the entire oil seal lip circumference.

6. Install or connect the following:
- Oil seal and housing; then, tighten the mounting bolts to 96 inch lbs. (11 Nm)
- Flexplate/flywheel and tighten the bolts to 68 ft. lbs. (92 Nm)
- Transaxle

Piston and Ring

POSITIONING

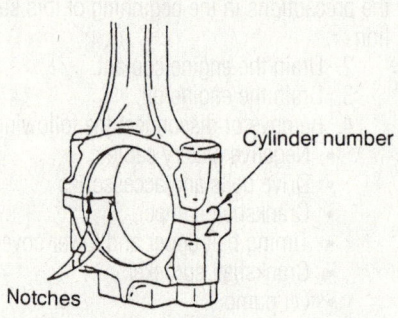

Chrysler engine connecting rod and cap installation—ensure to matchmark the cap and rod prior to disassembly

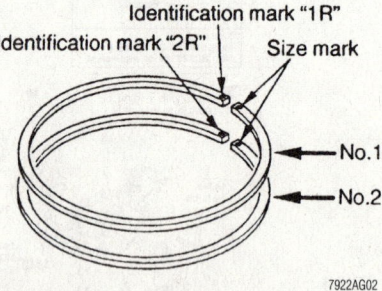

Chrysler piston ring identification mark locations

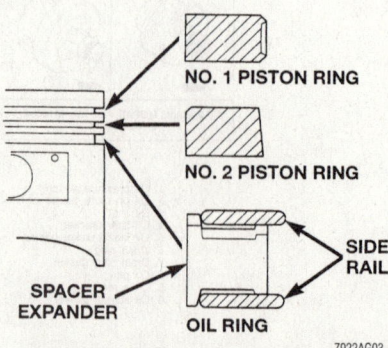

Piston ring orientation—2.0L (VIN Y) and 2.5L (VIN N) engines

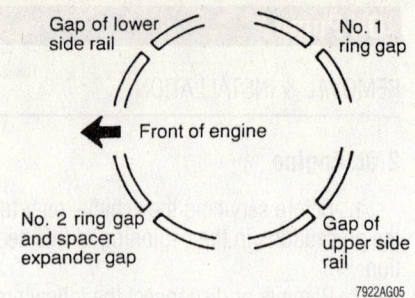

Piston ring end-gap spacing—2.0L (VIN Y) engine

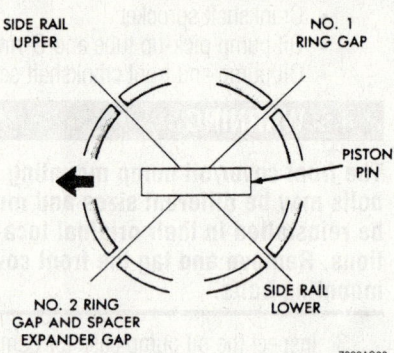

Piston ring end-gap spacing—2.5L (VIN N) engine

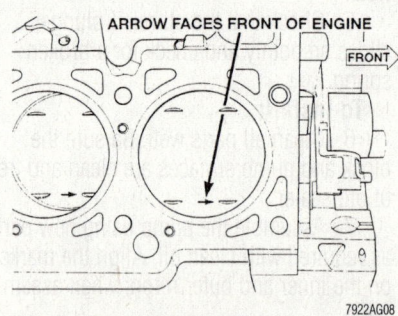

Piston positioning. The small arrows on the crown of the pistons must point toward the front of the engine—2.0L (VIN Y) and 2.5L (VIN N) engines

FUEL SYSTEM

Fuel System Service Precautions

Safety is the most important factor when performing not only fuel system maintenance but any type of maintenance. Failure to conduct maintenance and repairs in a safe manner may result in serious personal injury or death. Maintenance and testing of the vehicle's fuel system components can be accomplished safely and effectively by adhering to the following rules and guidelines.

• To avoid the possibility of fire and personal injury, always disconnect the negative battery cable unless the repair or test procedure requires that battery voltage be applied.

• Always relieve the fuel system pressure before disconnecting any fuel system component (injector, fuel rail, pressure regulator, etc.), fitting or fuel line connection. Exercise extreme caution whenever relieving fuel system pressure, to avoid exposing skin, face and eyes to fuel spray. Please be advised that fuel under pressure may penetrate the skin or any part of the body that it contacts.

• Always place a shop towel or cloth around the fitting or connection prior to loosening to absorb any excess fuel due to spillage. Ensure that all fuel spillage (should it occur) is quickly removed from engine surfaces. Ensure that all fuel soaked cloths or towels are deposited into a suitable waste container.

• Always keep a dry chemical (Class B) fire extinguisher near the work area.

• Do not allow fuel spray or fuel vapors to come into contact with a spark or open flame.

• Always use a back-up wrench when loosening and tightening fuel line connection fittings. This will prevent unnecessary stress and torsion to fuel line piping.

• Always replace worn fuel fitting O-rings with new. Do not substitute fuel hose or equivalent, where fuel pipe is installed.

Fuel System Pressure

RELIEVING

1. Before servicing the vehicle, refer to the precautions in the beginning of this section.

2. Remove the fuel filler cap to release fuel tank pressure.

3. Remove the rear seat cushion.

4. At the fuel tank, disconnect the fuel pump harness connector.

5. Start the vehicle and allow it to run until it stalls from lack of fuel. Turn the key to the **OFF** position.

6. Disconnect the negative battery cable, then reconnect the fuel pump connector.

7. Install the rear seat cushion and the fuel filler cap.

❋❋ CAUTION

Always wrap shop towels around a fitting that is being disconnected to absorb residual fuel in the lines.

Fuel Filter

REMOVAL & INSTALLATION

A replaceable fuel filter is located in the engine compartment, on the bulkhead, next to the brake booster.

1. Before servicing the vehicle, refer to the precautions in the beginning of this section.

2. Following proper procedures, relieve the fuel system residual pressure.

3. Remove or disconnect the following:

• Negative battery cable
• Air intake hose for access

4. Hold the fuel filter housing securely with a wrench. Cover the hoses with shop towels and remove the eyebolt. Discard the gaskets.

5. Separate the flare nut connection at the bottom of the filter.

6. Remove the mounting bolts and the fuel filter from the vehicle.

❋❋ CAUTION

Do not use conventional fuel filters, hoses or clamps when servicing fuel injection systems. They are not compatible with the injection system and the high pressures in fuel injection systems, and could cause substandard parts to fail, causing personal injury or damage to the vehicle. Use only hoses and clamps specifically designed for fuel injection.

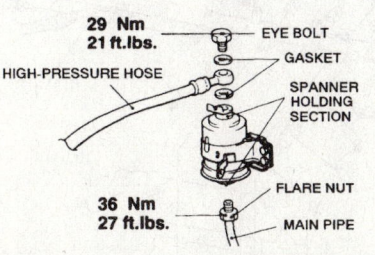

29 Nm
21 ft.lbs.   EYE BOLT
              GASKET
HIGH-PRESSURE HOSE
              SPANNER
              HOLDING
              SECTION

              FLARE NUT
36 Nm
27 ft.lbs.   MAIN PIPE

7922CG23

Exploded view of the fuel line-to-filter connection

To install:

7. Tighten the flare nut fitting by hand before mounting the filter on the bracket.

8. Install the filter on its bracket only finger-tight. Movement of the filter will ease attachment of the fuel lines.

9. Using new gaskets, connect the high pressure hose and eye bolt. While holding the fuel filter housing, tighten the eye bolt to 21 ft. lbs. (29 Nm). Tighten the flare nut to 27 ft. lbs. (36 Nm).

10. Tighten the filter mounting bolts fully.

11. Install the intake air hose.

12. Connect the negative battery cable, turn the key to the **ON** position to pressurize the fuel system and check for leaks.

13. If necessary, release the fuel pressure and repair leaks.

Fuel Pump

REMOVAL & INSTALLATION

1. Before servicing the vehicle, refer to the precautions in the beginning of this section.

Do not use conventional fuel filters, hoses or clamps when servicing fuel injection systems. They are not compatible with the injection system and could fail, causing personal injury or damage to the vehicle. Use only hoses and clamps specifically designed for fuel injection.

2. Relieve the fuel system pressure.

➡**The rear seat cushion must be removed in order to gain access to the fuel pump.**

3. Remove or disconnect the following:
• Negative battery cable
• Rear seat cushion

➡**Remove the seat cushion by pulling the stopper outward and lifting the lower cushion upward. There are 2 access covers underneath the seat. The panel on the far right side is for the fuel pump.**

• Access cover
• Fuel pump wiring
• Return hose and high pressure fuel hose
• Fuel pump nuts and pump

To install:

➡**Align the seal position projections with the holes in the fuel pump assembly**

4. Install or connect the following:
• Fuel pump assembly and tighten the nuts to 22 inch lbs. (2.5 Nm)

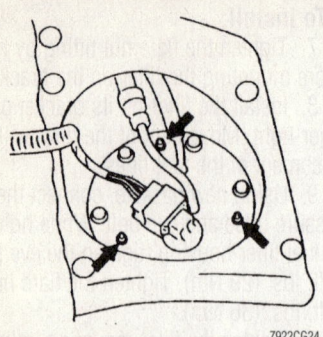

Position the fuel pump for installation by aligning the seal projections (arrows) with the fuel pump holes

- High pressure hose, return hose and fuel pump wiring
- Negative battery cable

5. Check the fuel pump for proper pressure and inspect the entire system for leaks.

6. Apply sealant to the access cover and install the cover.

7. Install the rear seat cushion.

8. Pressurize the fuel system by turning the ignition key to the **ON** position. Check for leaks. Start the engine to verify proper fuel pump performance.

Fuel Injector

REMOVAL & INSTALLATION

2.0L Engine

1. Before servicing the vehicle, refer to the precautions in the beginning of this section.

2. Relieve the fuel system pressure.

3. Remove or disconnect the following:

1. High-pressure fuel hose connection
2. O-ring
3. Injector harness connector
4. Fuel rail
5. Injector connectors
6. Retainers
7. Injectors
8. O-rings
9. O-rings

- Battery
- Air intake hose
- High pressure fuel hose connection and discard O-ring
- Fuel injector harness connector
- Fuel rail
- Fuel injector electrical connectors
- Fuel injector-to-fuel rail retainer(s)
- Fuel injectors and discard the O-rings

To install:

4. Install or connect the following:
- New fuel injector O-rings
- Fuel injectors

5. Lubricate the O-rings with clean engine oil; then, install the injectors into the fuel rail by twisting them (left and right) to make sure that they turn smoothly in the seat.

✳✳ WARNING

Do not allow engine oil to get into the fuel rail.

- Fuel injector-to-fuel rail retainer(s)
- Fuel injector electrical connectors
- Fuel rail
- Fuel injector harness connector
- New high-pressure fuel hose O-ring

6. Lubricate the O-ring with clean engine oil.

✳✳ WARNING

Do not allow engine oil to get into the fuel rail.

- High pressure fuel hose connection and torque the fuel hose-to-fuel rail bolts to 1.8 ft. lbs. (2.5 Nm)
- Air intake hose
- Battery

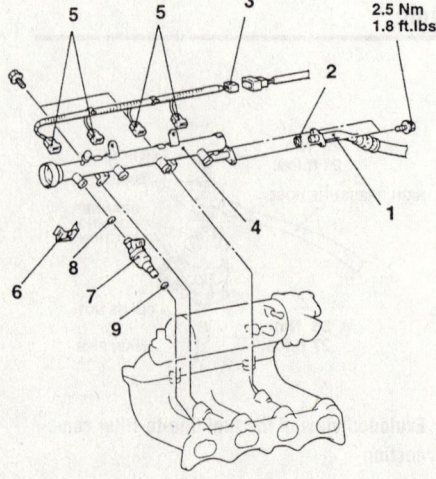

2.5 Nm
1.8 ft.lbs.

Exploded view of the fuel injector, fuel rail and related components—2.0L engine

2.5L Engine

1. Before servicing the vehicle, refer to the precautions in the beginning of this section.

2. Relieve the fuel system pressure.

3. Remove or disconnect the following:
- Power steering oil pressure switch connector
- Heated Oxygen (HO$_2$) sensor connector
- Intake Air Temperature (IAT) sensor connector
- Injector connectors
- Control wiring harness
- Intake manifold plenum
- Fuel injector electrical connectors
- High pressure fuel hose connection
- O-ring from the high pressure fuel hose connection
- Fuel rail
- Fuel injector retainer(s)
- Fuel injector(s) and discard the O-rings and grommet

To install:

4. Install or connect the following:
- New fuel injector O-rings and grommet(s)
- Fuel injectors

5. Lubricate the O-rings and grommet(s) with clean engine oil; then, install the injectors into the fuel rail by twisting them (left and right) to make sure that they turn smoothly in the seat.

✳✳ WARNING

Do not allow engine oil to get into the fuel rail.

6. Install or connect the following:
- Fuel injector-to-fuel rail retainer(s)
- Fuel injector electrical connectors
- Fuel rail and torque the fuel rail-to-intake manifold bolts to 7.2–9.4 ft. lbs. (10–13 Nm)
- New high-pressure fuel hose O-ring

7. Lubricate the O-ring with clean engine oil.

✳✳ WARNING

Do not allow engine oil to get into the fuel rail.

8. Install or connect the following:
- High pressure fuel hose connection and torque the fuel hose-to-fuel rail bolts to 1.8 ft. lbs. (2.5 Nm)
- Intake manifold plenum
- Control wiring harness
- Injector connectors
- IAT sensor connector
- HO$_2$ sensor connector

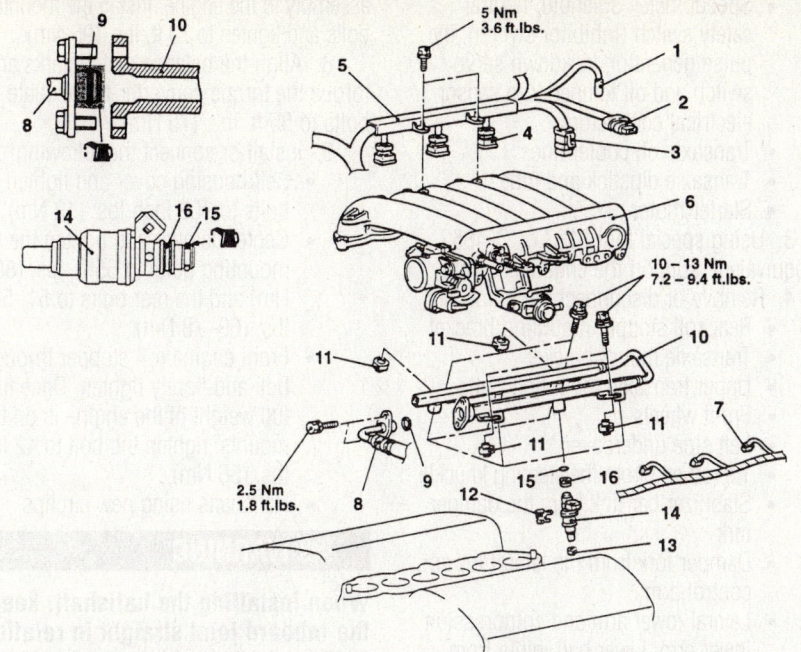

1. Power steering oil pressure switch connector
2. Heated oxygen sensor connector
3. Intake air temperature sensor connector
4. Injector connectors
5. Control wiring harness
6. Intake manifold plenum
7. Injector connectors
8. High-pressure fuel hose connection
9. O-ring
10. Fuel rail
11. Insulators
12. Injector supports
13. Insulators
14. Injectors
15. O-rings
16. Grommets

9306CG07

Exploded view of the fuel injector, fuel rail and related components—2.5L engine

- Power steering oil pressure switch connector

DRIVE TRAIN

Transaxle Assembly

REMOVAL & INSTALLATION

Manual

1. Before servicing the vehicle, refer to the precautions in the beginning of this section.
2. Remove or disconnect the following:
- Battery and battery tray
- Battery brace
- Air cleaner and intake hoses
- Drain the transaxle fluid
- Select and shift cable cotter pins and the cable ends from the transaxle
- Back-up light switch harness and position it aside.

- Speedometer electrical connector, from the transaxle assembly
- Starter motor

3. Using special tool 7137 or C-4852 or equivalent, support the engine assembly.
4. Remove or disconnect the following:
- Rear roll stopper mounting bracket
- Transaxle mount bracket
- Upper transaxle mounting bolts
- Front wheels
- Under cover
- Cotter pin and tie rod end from the steering knuckle
- Stabilizer bar link from the damper fork
- Damper fork from the lateral lower control arm
- Lateral lower arm, compression lower arm and lower ball joints from the steering knuckle
- Halfshafts from the transaxle and secure aside
- Clutch release cylinder connection and move aside without disconnecting the hydraulic line
- Bell housing cover

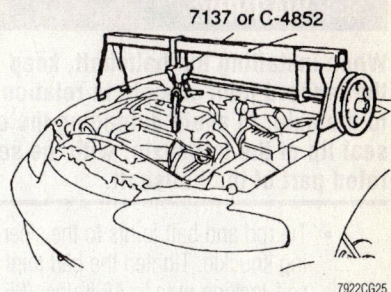

For transaxle removal, properly support the engine assembly as shown

7922CG25

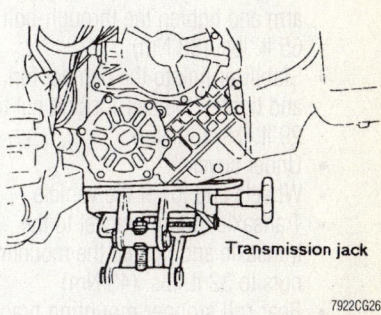

Transmission jack

7922CG26

Also, use a transmission jack to support the transaxle assembly

- Engine front roll stopper through-bolt
- Centermember

5. Support the transaxle, using a transmission jack, and remove the transaxle lower coupling bolt.

➡The coupling bolt threads from the engine side, into the transaxle, and is located just above the halfshaft opening.

6. Slide the transaxle rearward and carefully lower it from the vehicle.

To install:

7. Install or connect the following:
- Transaxle and tighten transaxle-to-engine bolts to 70 ft. lbs. (95 Nm)
- Bell housing cover and tighten the bolts to 84 inch lbs. (9 Nm)
- Centermember and tighten the front mounting bolts to 65 ft. lbs. (88 Nm) and the rear bolt to 54 ft. lbs. (73 Nm)
- Front engine roll stopper through-bolt and lightly tighten. Once the full weight of the engine is on the mounts, tighten the bolt to 42 ft. lbs. (57 Nm).
- Clutch release cylinder
- Halfshafts using new circlips

✳✳ WARNING

When installing the halfshaft, keep the inboard joint straight in relation to the axle, to avoid damaging the oil seal lip of the transaxle, with the serrated part of the halfshaft.

- Tie rod and ball joints to the steering knuckle. Tighten the ball joint self-locking nuts to 48 ft. lbs. (65 Nm). Tighten the tie rod end nut to 21 ft. lbs. (28 Nm) and secure with a new cotter pin.
- Damper fork to the lower control arm and tighten the through-bolt to 65 ft. lbs. (88 Nm)
- Stabilizer link to the damper fork and tighten the self-locking nut to 29 ft. lbs. (39 Nm)
- Under cover
- Wheels and lower the vehicle
- Transaxle mount bracket to the transaxle and tighten the mounting nuts to 32 ft. lbs. (43 Nm)
- Rear roll stopper mounting bracket

8. Remove the engine support. Tighten the transaxle mount through-bolt to 51 ft. lbs. (69 Nm) and tighten the front engine roll stopper through-bolt.

9. Install or connect the following:
- Upper transaxle mounting bolts and tighten to 35 ft. lbs. (48 Nm)
- Starter motor
- Back-up light switch and speedometer connector
- Select and shift cables and new cotter pins
- Air cleaner and air intake hose
- Battery tray and battery
- Battery stay

10. Be sure the vehicle is level, and refill the transaxle with Mopar® MS9417 MTX fluid, part number 4773167.

11. Check the transaxle for proper operation. Be sure the reverse lights come ON when in reverse.

Automatic

1. Before servicing the vehicle, refer to the precautions in the beginning of this section.

2. Remove or disconnect the following:
- Battery and battery tray
- Battery brace
- Air cleaner and intake hoses
- Drain the transaxle fluid
- Shifter lever-to-transaxle nut, cable retaining clip and cable from the transaxle
- Shifter cable mounting bracket

- Speedometer, solenoid, neutral safety switch (inhibitor switch), the pulse generator, kickdown servo switch and oil temperature sensor electrical connectors
- Transaxle oil cooler lines
- Transaxle dipstick and tube
- Starter motor

3. Using special tool 7137 or C-4852 or equivalent, support the engine assembly.

4. Remove or disconnect the following:
- Rear roll stopper mounting bracket
- Transaxle mount bracket
- Upper transaxle mounting bolts
- Front wheels
- Left side undercover
- Tie rod end from the steering knuckle
- Stabilizer bar link from the damper fork
- Damper fork from the lateral lower control arm
- Lateral lower arm and compression lower arm, lower ball joints from the steering knuckle
- Halfshafts from the transaxle and secure aside
- Bell housing cover
- Engine front roll stopper through-bolt
- Centermember
- Flexplate-to-torque converter bolts. Rotate the crankshaft to bring the bolts into a position for removal, one at a time.

➡ **To make installation easier, use chalk or paint to make matchmarks on the torque converter and flexplate. These marks will be used at assembly to realign the assembly, keeping these parts in balance.**

✳✳ WARNING

After removing the bolts, push the torque converter toward the transaxle. This will prevent the converter from remaining in contact with the engine, possibly damaging the converter.

5. Support the transaxle using a transmission jack (at the side of the case, NOT at the pan), and remove the transaxle lower coupling bolt.

➡ **The coupling bolt is inserted from the engine side into the transaxle and is located just above the halfshaft opening.**

6. Slide the transaxle rearward and carefully lower it from the vehicle.

To install:

7. After the torque converter has been mounted on the transaxle, install the transaxle

assembly to the engine. Install the mounting bolts and tighten to 70 ft. lbs. (95 Nm).

8. Align the balance matchmarks and torque the torque converter-to-flexplate bolts to 55 ft. lbs. (75 Nm).

9. Install or connect the following:
- Bell housing cover and tighten the bolts to 108 inch lbs. (12 Nm)
- Centermember and tighten the front mounting bolts to 65 ft. lbs. (88 Nm) and the rear bolts to 51–58 ft. lbs. (69–78 Nm)
- Front engine roll stopper through-bolt and lightly tighten. Once the full weight of the engine is on the mounts, tighten the bolt to 42 ft. lbs. (56 Nm).
- Halfshafts using new circlips

✳✳ WARNING

When installing the halfshaft, keep the inboard joint straight in relation to the axle to avoid damaging the oil seal lip of the transaxle with the splined part of the halfshaft.

- Tie rod and ball joints to the steering knuckle. Tighten the ball joint self-locking nuts to 48 ft. lbs. (65 Nm), the tie rod end nut to 21 ft. lbs. (28 Nm) and secure with a new cotter pin.
- Damper fork to the lower control arm and tighten the through-bolt to 65 ft. lbs. (88 Nm)
- Stabilizer link to the damper fork and tighten the self-locking nut to 29 ft. lbs. (39 Nm)
- Left side undercover
- Wheels and lower the vehicle
- Transaxle mount bracket and tighten the mounting nuts to 32 ft. lbs. (43 Nm)
- Rear roll stopper mounting bracket

10. Remove the engine support.

11. Install or connect the following:
- Transaxle mount through-bolt to 51 ft. lbs. (69 Nm) and tighten the front engine roll stopper through-bolt.
- Upper transaxle mounting bolts and tighten to 35 ft. lbs. (48 Nm)
- Starter motor
- Dipstick tube and dipstick
- Shifter cable mounting bracket
- Shifter lever and tighten the nut to 14 ft. lbs. (19 Nm)
- Oil cooler lines and secure with clamps
- Speedometer, solenoid, neutral safety switch (inhibitor switch), the pulse generator, kickdown servo

switch and oil temperature sensor electrical connectors
- Air cleaner and air intake hose
- Battery tray and battery

12. Refill the transaxle with MOPAR® ATF PLUS or equivalent, transmission fluid. Start the engine and allow it to idle for 2 minutes. Apply the parking brake and move the selector through each gear position, ending in **N**. Recheck fluid level and add if necessary. Fluid level should be between the marks in the **HOT** range on the dipstick.

13. Check the transaxle for proper operation.

Clutch

ADJUSTMENT

Pedal Height and Free-Play

1. Measure the clutch pedal height from the face of the pedal pad to the bulkhead. Compare the measured value with the desired distance of 7.0–7.09 in. (175–180mm).

2. Measure the clutch pedal clevis pin play at the face of the pedal pad. Press the pedal lightly until resistance is met, and measure this distance. The clutch pedal clevis pin play should be within 0.040–0.120 in. (1–3mm).

3. If the clutch pedal height or clevis pin play, is not within the standard values, adjust as follows:

   a. If not equipped with cruise control, turn and adjust the stop bolt so the pedal height is the standard value, then tighten the locknut.

   b. If equipped with cruise control system, disconnect the clutch switch connector and turn the switch to obtain the standard clutch pedal height. Then, lock by tightening the locknut.

   c. Turn the pushrod to adjust the clutch pedal clevis pin play to agree with the standard value and secure the pushrod with the locknut.

➡ **When adjusting the clutch pedal height or the clutch pedal clevis pin play, be careful not to push the pushrod toward the master cylinder.**

   d. Check that when the clutch pedal is depressed all the way, the interlock switch switches over from ON to OFF.

4. Move the clutch pedal until the resistance begins to increase; measure between this point and the pedal resting point to determine the clutch pedal free-play. The clutch pedal free-play measurement should be between 0.240–0.510 in. (6–13mm). With the pedal fully disengaged, check the distance between the bulkhead and the top of the pedal pad. The measurement should be 2.760 in. (70mm) or more.

5. If the measurements are not within specification, bleed the clutch hydraulic system. If after bleeding the measurements are still not within specified range, there is a faulty component in the system, which must be replaced.

REMOVAL & INSTALLATION

1. Before servicing the vehicle, refer to the precautions in the beginning of this section.

2. Remove or disconnect the following:
- Negative battery cable
- Transaxle
- Pressure plate-to-flywheel bolts, pressure plate and clutch disc

➡ **If the pressure plate is to be reused, loosen the bolts in a diagonal pattern, one or 2 turns at a time. This will prevent warping the clutch cover assembly.**

- Return clip and the pressure plate release bearing. Do not use solvent to clean the bearing.

3. Inspect the clutch release fork and fulcrum for damage or wear. If necessary, remove the release fork and the fulcrum from the transaxle.

4. Carefully inspect the condition of the clutch components and replace any worn or damaged parts.

To install:

5. Inspect the flywheel for heat damage or cracks. Resurface or replace the flywheel as required.

6. Install or connect the following:
- Flywheel using new bolts
- Fulcrum, if removed, and tighten
- Release fork

➡ **Apply a coating of multi-purpose grease to the point of contact with the fulcrum and the point of contact with the release bearing. Apply a coating of multi-purpose grease to the end of the release cylinder's pushrod and the pushrod hole in the release fork.**

✳✳ WARNING

When installing the clutch, apply grease to each part, but be careful not to apply excessive grease. Exces-

1. Oil tube
2. Clutch release cylinder
3. Clutch & flywheel assembly
4. Clutch release bearing
5. Clutch release lever
6. Clutch control equip stud
7. Boot

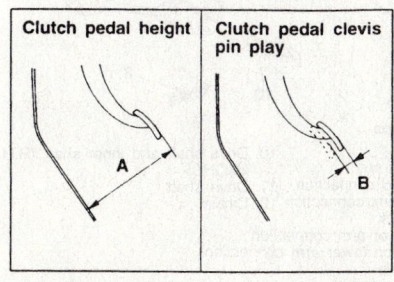

Clutch pedal height and free-play adjustment measurements

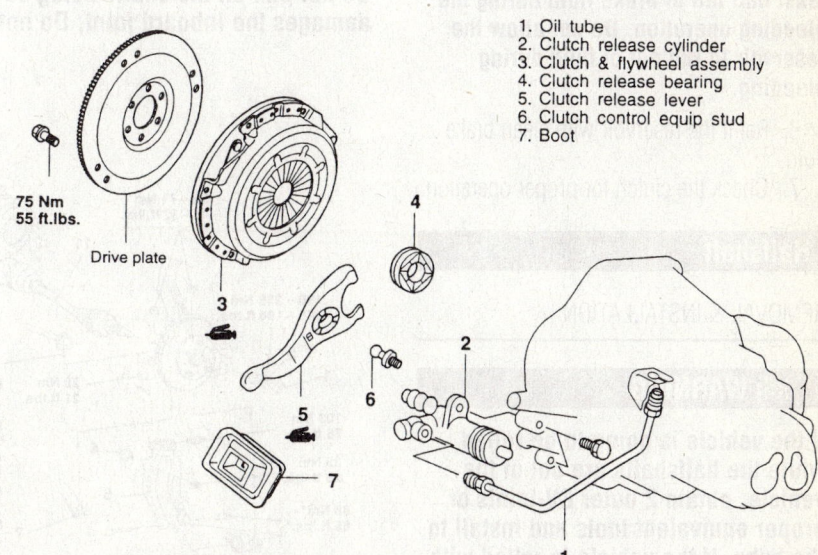

Exploded view of the clutch assembly

75 Nm
55 ft.lbs.

Drive plate

Clutch pedal height | Clutch pedal clevis pin play

A

B

9300CG01

7922CG28

sive grease will cause clutch slippage and shudder.

7. Apply multi-purpose grease to the clutch release bearing. Pack the bearing inner surface and the groove with grease. Do not apply grease to the resin portion of the bearing. Place the bearing in position and install the return clip.

8. Apply a coating of grease to the clutch disc splines, then use a brush to rub it in the grooves. Using a clutch disc alignment tool, position the clutch disc on the flywheel. Install the retainer bolts and tighten a little at a time, in a diagonal sequence.

9. Install the transaxle assembly and check the fluid level.

10. Verify proper clutch operation.

Hydraulic Clutch System

BLEEDING

1. Before servicing the vehicle, refer to the precautions in the beginning of this section.

2. Fill the reservoir with clean DOT 3 or DOT 4 brake fluid.

3. Loosen the bleed screw, then have the clutch pedal pressed to the floor.

4. Tighten the bleed screw, then release the clutch pedal.

5. Repeat the procedure until the fluid is free of air bubbles.

➡**It is suggested that a hose be attached to the bleed screw with the other end immersed in a container at least half full of brake fluid during the bleeding operation. Do not allow the reservoir to run out of fluid during bleeding.**

6. Refill the reservoir with clean brake fluid.

7. Check the clutch for proper operation.

Halfshaft

REMOVAL & INSTALLATION

✳✳ WARNING

If the vehicle is going to be rolled while the halfshafts are out of the vehicle, obtain 2 outer CV-joints or proper equivalent tools and install to the hubs. If the vehicle is rolled without the proper torque applied to the front wheel bearings, the bearings will no longer be usable.

1. Before servicing the vehicle, refer to the precautions in the beginning of this section.

2. Remove or disconnect the following:
- Negative battery cable
- Cotter pin, halfshaft nut and washer
- Front wheel
- Tie rod end from the steering knuckle using Joint Separation tool MB991113 or equivalent

✳✳ WARNING

Use of improper methods of joint separation can result in damage to the joint, leading to possible fail-ure.

- Sway bar link from the damper fork
- Damper fork lower through-bolts, upper pinch bolt and damper fork assembly
- Lateral arm and the compression arm from the steering knuckle using a joint separation tool
- Halfshaft from the hub/knuckle by setting up a puller on the outside wheel hub and pushing the halfshaft from the front hub
- Halfshaft from the transaxle by inserting a prybar between the transaxle case and the halfshaft

3. If equipped with a center bearing on the right halfshaft, remove the center bearing bracket-to-chassis bolts; then, tap lightly on the center bearing bracket to separate the inner shaft from the transaxle.

✳✳ WARNING

Do not pull on the shaft. Doing so damages the inboard joint. Do not

insert the prybar too far or the oil seal in the case may be damaged.

To install:

4. Inspect the halfshaft boot for damage or deterioration. Check the ball joints and splines for wear.

5. Replace the circlips on the ends of the halfshaft(s).

6. Insert the halfshaft into the transaxle. Be sure it is fully seated.

7. If equipped with a center bearing on the right halfshaft, install the center bearing bracket-to-chassis bolts and torque to 30 ft. lbs. (40 Nm).

8. Pull the knuckle assembly outward and install the other end of the halfshaft into the hub.

9. Install or connect the following:
- Washer so the chamfered edge faces outward.
- Halfshaft nut and tighten temporarily.
- Lateral arm and the compression arm to the steering knuckle. Tighten the self-locking nuts to 43–52 ft. lbs. (59–71 Nm).
- Damper fork; then, tighten the lower through-bolt/nut to 65 ft. lbs. (88 Nm) and the upper pinch bolt to 76 ft. lbs. (103 Nm)
- Tie rod end to the steering knuckle and tighten the nut to 17–25 ft. lbs. (24–33 Nm) and install a new cotter pin
- Sway bar link to the damper fork and tighten the link nut to 29 ft. lbs. (39 Nm)
- Lockwasher and axle nut; then, tighten the axle nut with the spe-

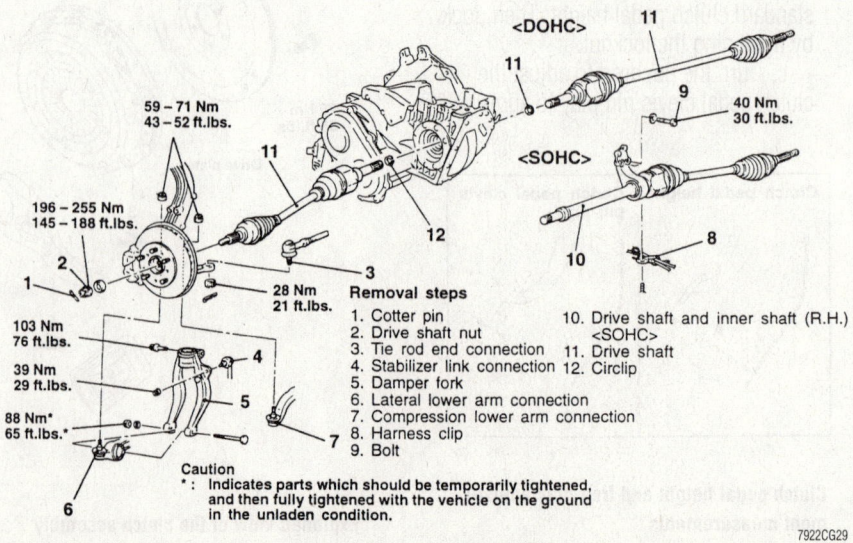

Removal steps
1. Cotter pin
2. Drive shaft nut
3. Tie rod end connection
4. Stabilizer link connection
5. Damper fork
6. Lateral lower arm connection
7. Compression lower arm connection
8. Harness clip
9. Bolt
10. Drive shaft and inner shaft (R.H.) <SOHC>
11. Drive shaft
12. Circlip

Caution
*: Indicates parts which should be temporarily tightened, and then fully tightened with the vehicle on the ground in the unladen condition.

7922CG29

Exploded view of the left and right halfshaft assemblies' mounting

cial tool MB990767 to hold the hub from turning to 145–188 ft. lbs. (200–260 Nm)

➡ **Before securely tightening the axle nut, make sure there is no load on the wheel bearings.**

- New cotter pin
- Front wheel
- Negative battery cable

10. Refill the transaxle.

11. Test drive the vehicle and check for proper operation.

CV-Joints

OVERHAUL

❄ WARNING

The Birfield joint assembly, located on the wheel side of the halfshaft, is not to be disassembled; repair of this joint is only by replacement of the halfshaft.

Tri-Pot Joint

2.0L (DOHC) ENGINE

1. Remove halfshaft and place it in a soft jawed vise.

2. Disassemble or remove:

- Tri-pot boot bands
- Tri-pot case

➡ **Wipe the grease from the tri-pot case.**

- Halfshaft snapring
- Tri-pot spider assembly

❄ WARNING

Do not disassemble the spider assembly.

- Tri-pot boot

❄ WARNING

If the boot is to be reused, wrap plastic tape around the shaft splines to protect the boot from damage.

3. If necessary, remove the dynamic damper bands and slide the damper from the halfshaft.

To install:

4. If removed, install the dynamic damper by performing the following procedure:

a. Slide the damper onto the halfshaft with new bands.

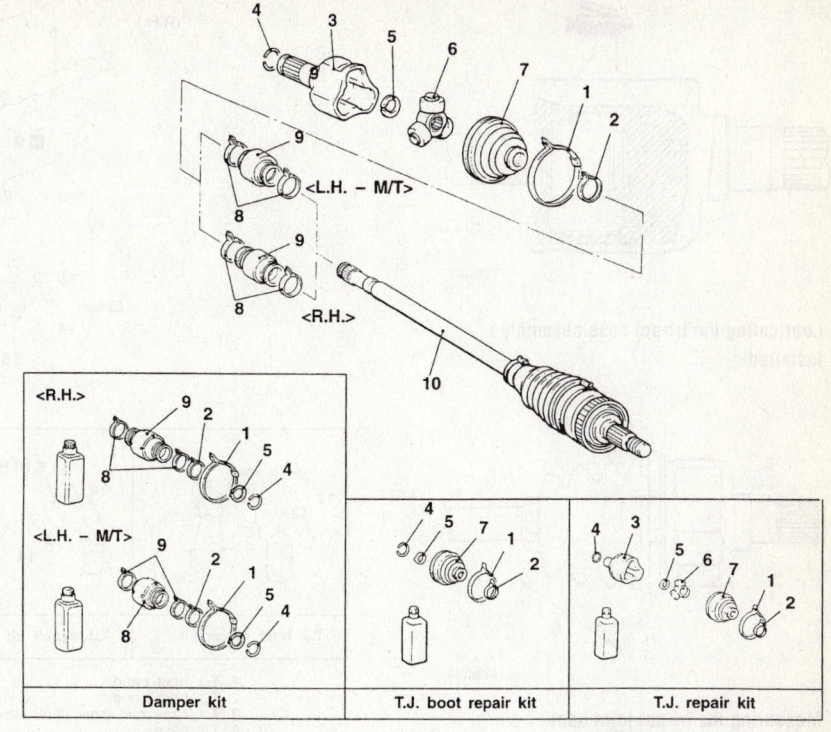

Exploded view of the halfshaft assemblies—2.0L (DOHC) Engine

1. T.J. boot band
2. T.J. boot band
3. T.J. case
4. Circlip
5. Snap ring
6. Spider assembly
7. T.J. boot
8. Damper band
9. Dynamic damper
10. B.J. assembly

b. Position the damper so the distance from the front of the birfield joint to the front edge of the damper assembly is 14.60–14.84 in. (371–377mm) for the right halfshaft or 7.52–7.76 in. (191–197mm) for the left halfshaft.

c. Tighten and secure the damper bands.

❄ WARNING

Wrap plastic tape around the shaft splines to protect the boot from damage.

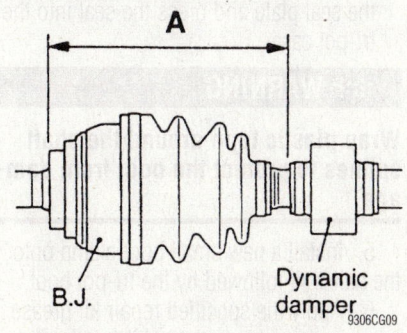

Positioning the dynamic damper on the halfshaft assemblies—2.0L (DOHC) Engine

5. Install a new small boot clamp onto the halfshaft followed by the tri-pot boot.

6. Apply the specified repair kit grease between the spider axle and the roller.

7. Install the tri-pot spider assembly onto the shaft from the spline beveled section direction and secure with the snapring.

8. Distribute a portion of the 3.7 oz. (105 g) specified repair kit grease into the tri-pot case, insert the spider assembly and add the remaining grease.

9. Install the tri-pot boot by performing the following procedure:

a. Position the boots large end on the tri-pot case.

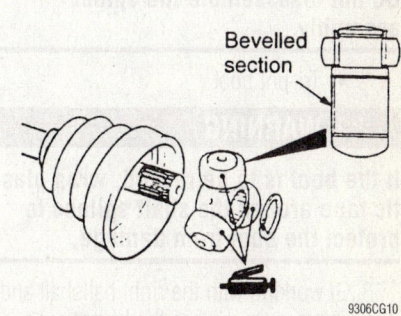

Lubricating the tri-pot spider assembly

Turn to Section 5 for brake system applications

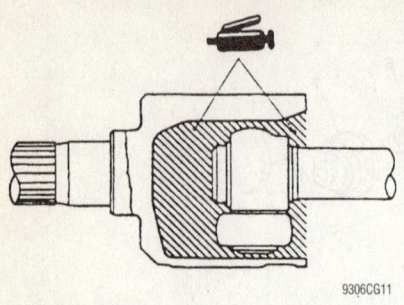

Lubricating the tri-pot case assembly installed

9306CG11

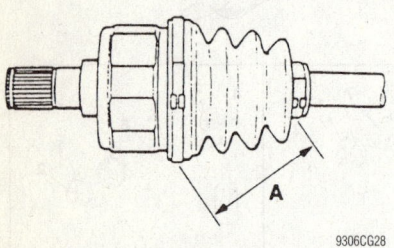

9306CG28

Measuring the tri-pot joint boot

b. Position the large and small boot clamps onto the boot.

c. Adjust the boot so that the bands are spaced at 3.03–3.27 in. (77–83mm).

d. Tighten the band securely.

2.5L (SOHC) ENGINE

1. Remove halfshaft and place it in a soft jawed vise.

2. Disassemble or remove:
- Tri-pot boot bands
- Tri-pot case for left halfshaft or tri-pot case/inner shaft assembly for right halfshaft.

➡ **Wipe the grease from the tri-pot case.**
- Halfshaft snapring
- Tri-pot spider assembly

✳✳ WARNING

Do not disassemble the spider assembly.

- Tri-pot boot

✳✳ WARNING

If the boot is to be reused, wrap plastic tape around the shaft splines to protect the boot from damage.

3. If working with the right halfshaft and it is necessary to replace the tri-pot case, press the case from the inner shaft assembly.

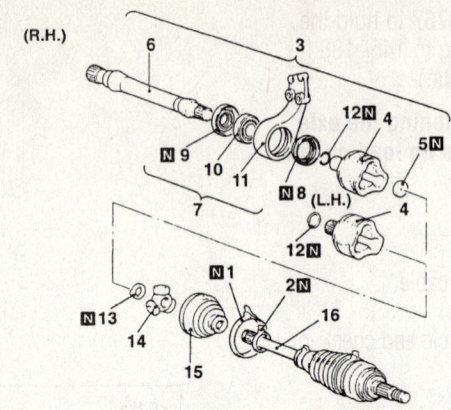

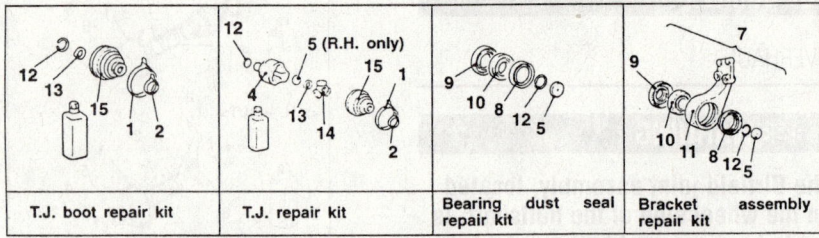

| T.J. boot repair kit | T.J. repair kit | Bearing dust seal repair kit | Bracket assembly repair kit |

1. T.J. boot band
2. T.J. boot band
3. T.J. case and inner shaft assembly
4. T.J. case
5. Seal plate
6. Inner shaft
7. Bracket assembly
8. Dust seal outer
9. Dust seal inner
10. Center bearing
11. Center bearing bracket
12. Circlip
13. Snap ring
14. Spider assembly
15. T.J. boot
16. B.J. assembly

9306CG12

Exploded view of the halfshaft assemblies—2.5L (SOHC) Engine

To install:

4. If installing a new tri-pot case onto the right halfshaft, perform the following procedure:

a. Lubricate the inner shaft splines with Multi-Mileage Grease No. 2525035 or equivalent.

b. Press the inner shaft assembly into tri-pot case.

c. Secure the tri-pot case with special tool MB991248 on a hydraulic press with the case facing upward.

d. Position a new seal plate in the center of the tri-pot case.

e. Place a 1.18 in. (30mm) pipe on the seal plate and press the seal into the tri-pot case.

✳✳ WARNING

Wrap plastic tape around the shaft splines to protect the boot from damage.

5. Install a new small boot clamp onto the halfshaft followed by the tri-pot boot.

6. Apply the specified repair kit grease between the spider axle and the roller.

7. Install the tri-pot spider assembly onto the shaft from the spline beveled section direction and secure with the snapring.

8. Distribute a portion of the 4.23 oz. (120 g) specified repair kit grease into the tri-pot case, insert the spider assembly and add the remaining grease.

9. Install the tri-pot boot by performing the following procedure:

a. Position the boots large end on the tri-pot case.

b. Position the large and small boot clamps onto the boot.

c. Adjust the boot so that the bands are spaced at 3.03–3.27 in. (77–83mm).

d. Tighten the band securely.

Center Bearing

2.5L (SOHC) ENGINE

1. Remove the right halfshaft and place it in a soft-jawed vise.

2. Remove the tri-pot spider assembly from the tri-pot case.

3. Remove the tri-pot case by performing the following procedure:

a. Position the inner shaft/tri-pot case assembly on a hydraulic press supported by tool MB991248 with the tri-pot case facing upward.

b. Position a bar inside the tri-pot case, on the end of the inner shaft and press the case from the inner shaft assembly.

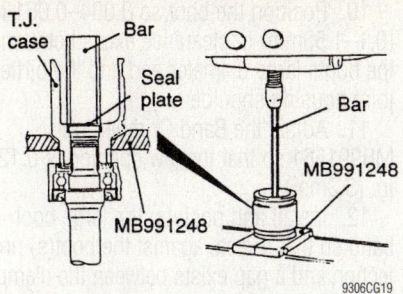

Removing the tri-pot case from the inner shaft assembly—Right halfshaft with 2.5L (SOHC) Engine

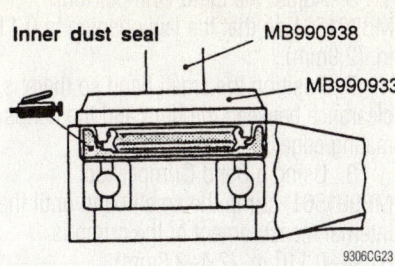

Installing the inner dust seal to the center bearing bracket—Right halfshaft with 2.5L (SOHC) Engine

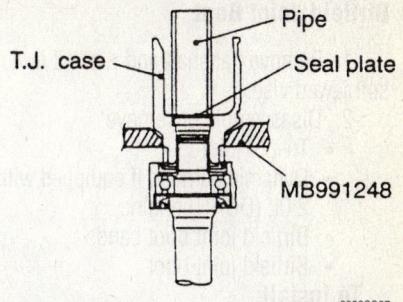

Installing the seal plate into the tri-pot case—Right halfshaft with 2.5L (SOHC) Engine

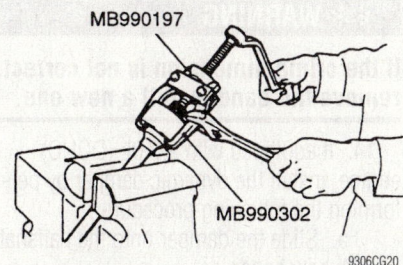

Removing the center bearing bracket from the inner shaft assembly—Right halfshaft with 2.5L (SOHC) Engine

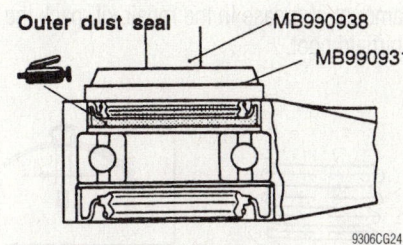

Installing the outer dust seal to the center bearing bracket—Right halfshaft with 2.5L (SOHC) Engine

4. Place the inner shaft assembly in a soft-jawed vise.

5. Using a wheel puller, press the center bearing bracket from the inner shaft.

6. Using a hydraulic press, Installer Adapter tool MB990932 and Snap-in Bar tool MB990938, press the center bearing and inner dust seal from the center bearing bracket.

To install:

7. Using a hydraulic press, Installer Adapter tool MB990932 and Snap-in Bar tool MB990938, press the center bearing into the center bearing bracket.

8. Using a hydraulic press, Installer Adapter tool MB990933 and Snap-in Bar tool MB990938, press the inner duct seal into the center bearing bracket.

9. Using a hydraulic press, Installer Adapter tool MB990931 and Snap-in Bar tool MB990938, press the outer duct seal into the center bearing bracket.

10. Using a hydraulic press and Adapter tool MB991172, press the inner shaft into the center bearing bracket.

11. Install the tri-pot case onto the right halfshaft by performing the following procedure:

a. Lubricate the inner shaft splines with Multi-Mileage Grease No. 2525035 or equivalent.

b. Press the inner shaft assembly into tri-pot case.

c. Secure the tri-pot case with special tool MB991248 on a hydraulic press with the case facing upward.

d. Position a new seal plate in the center of the tri-pot case.

e. Place a 1.18 in. (30mm) pipe on the seal plate and press the seal into the tri-pot case.

12. Assemble the tri-pot joint assembly.

13. Install the right halfshaft.

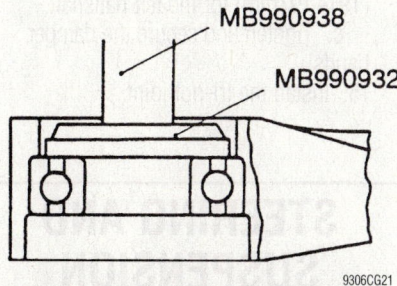

Removing the center bearing from the center bearing bracket—Right halfshaft with 2.5L (SOHC) Engine

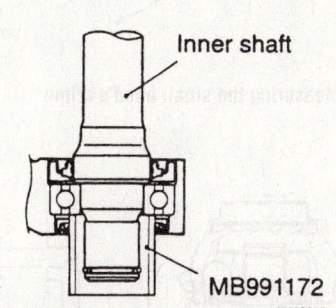

Installing the inner shaft into the center bearing bracket—Right halfshaft with 2.5L (SOHC) Engine

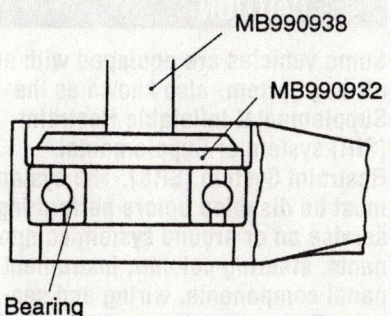

Installing the center bearing to the center bearing bracket—Right halfshaft with 2.5L (SOHC) Engine

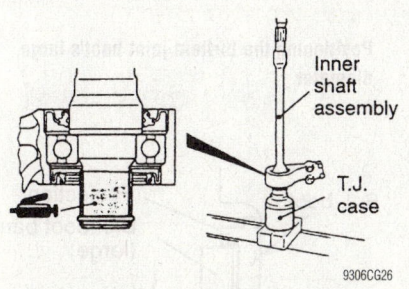

Installing the inner shaft assembly into the tri-pot case—Right halfshaft with 2.5L (SOHC) Engine

Birfield Joint Boot

1. Remove halfshaft and place it in a soft jawed vise.
2. Disassemble or remove:
   - Tri-pot joint
   - Dynamic damper, if equipped with a 2.0L (DOHC) engine
   - Birfield joint boot bands
   - Birfield joint boot

To install:

3. Assemble or install:
   - Birfield joint boot
   - Birfield joint boot small band
4. Place the halfshaft in a soft jawed vise so that the birfield joint is standing vertically.
5. Position the boots small diameter so that only 1 groove is exposed on the shaft.

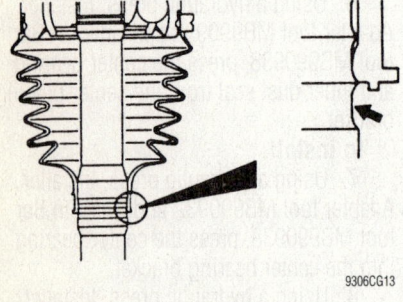

Positioning the birfield joint boot's small diameter

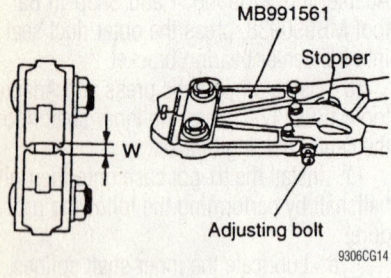

View of the band crimper tool

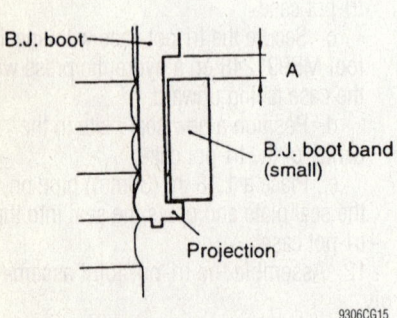

Positioning the birfield joint boot's small band

6. Adjust the Band Crimper tool MB991561 so that the jaw opening is 0.114 in. (2.9mm).
7. Position the small band so there is clearance between the boot and the bands mating edge.
8. Using a Band Crimper tool MB991561, crimp the small band until the internal measurement of the crimp is 0.094–0.110 in. (2.4–2.8mm).

9. Using 5.47 oz. (155g) specified amount of grease in the repair kit, pack the birfield boot.

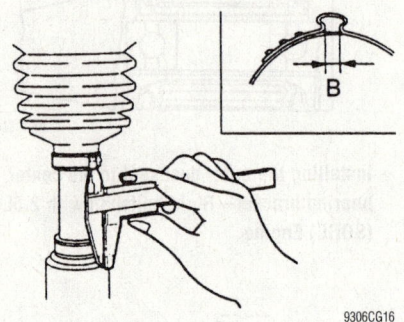

Measuring the small band's crimp

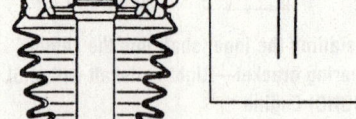

Positioning the birfield joint boot's large diameter

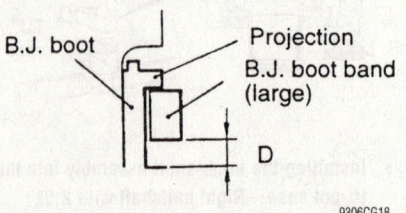

Positioning the birfield joint boot's large band

10. Position the boot so 0.004–0.061 in. (0.1–1.55mm) of clearance exists between the boots large diameter end and the birfield joint housing shoulder.
11. Adjust the Band Crimper tool MB991561 so that the jaw opening is 0.126 in. (3.2mm).
12. Install and position the large boot band so that it rests against the boot(s) projection and a gap exists between the clamp and the boot.
13. Using a Band Crimper tool MB991561, crimp the small band until the internal measurement of the crimp is 0.094–0.110 in. (2.4–2.8mm).

14. If equipped with a 2.0L (DOHC) engine, install the dynamic damper by performing the following procedure:
   a. Slide the damper onto the halfshaft with new bands.
   b. Position the damper so the distance from the front of the birfield joint to the front edge of the damper assembly is 14.60–14.84 in. (371–377mm) for the right halfshaft or 7.52–7.76 in. (191–197mm) for the left halfshaft.
   c. Tighten and secure the damper bands.
15. Install the tri-pot joint.

STEERING AND SUSPENSION

Air Bag

PRECAUTIONS

Several precautions must be observed when handling the inflator module to avoid accidental deployment and possible personal injury. Along with the precautions in the beginning of this section, observe the following:

• Never carry the inflator module by the wires or connector on the underside of the module.

• When carrying a live inflator module, hold securely with both hands, and ensure that the bag and trim cover are pointed away.

• Place the inflator module on a bench or other surface with the bag and trim cover facing up.

• With the inflator module on the bench, never place anything on or close to the module which may be thrown in the event of an accidental deployment.

1. Do not attempt to repair any of the air bag system wiring harness connectors. If any of the connectors or wires are faulty, replace that harness.

• Air bag components should not be subjected to heat over 200°F (93°C). Remove the SRS-ECU, the air bag modules themselves and the clock spring before drying or baking the vehicle after painting.

• After air bag system service, check the SRS warning light operation to be sure that the system functions properly.

• Make certain that the ignition switch is in the **OFF** position when a scan tool is connected or disconnected.

DO NOT use any electrical test equipment on or near any SRS components except those specified by Chrysler corporation:

• Use a digital multi-meter for which the maximum test current is 2mA or less at the minimum range of resistance measurement for use with the Chrysler SRS Check Harness when checking the SRS electrical circuitry.

• Chrysler special tool MB991613 SRS Check Harness acts like a "break-out box" for checking SRS wiring. There are other factory special tool wiring adapters that are available and may be used.

• DRB III or equivalent scan tool for reading and erasing air bag diagnostic codes.

NEVER ATTEMPT TO REPAIR THE FOLLOWING COMPONENTS:

• Air Bag Control Unit (SRS-ECU)
• Air Bag Modules
• If any of these components are diagnosed as faulty, they should only be replaced.

DISARMING

The system consists of 2 air bag modules, one located in the center of the steering wheel and another located above the glove box, which contains the folded air bag and an inflator unit. The air bag Electronic Control Unit (SRS-ECU) located under the floor console assembly monitors the system and which contains a safing G sensor and analog G sensor. An SRS warning light is located on the instrument panel which indicates the status of the air bag system. A clock spring interconnection is located within the steering column.

To deploy the air bags, the SRS-ECU must respond to the output signal from the analog G sensor and the safing G sensor must be ON. The SRS-ECU, then causes the air bag modules to ignite and deploy.

Service technicians should use care when working around any vehicle equipped with an air bag system, to avoid injury to the technician by inadvertent deployment of the air bag or to the driver by rendering the air bag system inoperative.

The SRS-ECU not only controls the air bag system, it can provide diagnostic information. The SRS-ECU monitors the air bag system and stores data concerning any detected faults in the system. When the ignition key is turned to the **ON** or **START** position, the SRS warning light should illuminate for about 7 seconds, then turn off. That indicates that the SRS system is in operating condition. If the SRS warning light does not illuminate as described or stays on for more than 7 seconds or if the SRS light illuminates while driving, immediate inspection is required. If the vehicle's SRS warning light is in any of these 3 conditions, the SRS system must be inspected, diagnosed and serviced.

To avoid injury from accidental deployment of the air bag during vehicle servicing, refer to all service precautions.

✳✳ CAUTION

The Air Bag system must be disarmed before removing many components. Failure to do so may cause

accidental deployment of the air bag, resulting in unnecessary system repairs and/or personal injury.

1. Disarm the air bag system using the following procedure:

a. Position the front wheels in the straight-ahead position and place the key in the **LOCK** position. Remove the key from the ignition lock cylinder.

b. Disconnect the negative battery cable and insulate the cable end with high-quality electrical tape or similar non-conductive wrapping.

c. Wait at least one minute before working on the vehicle. The air bag system is designed to retain enough voltage to deploy the air bag for a short period of time even after the battery has been disconnected.

Power Rack and Pinion Steering Gear

REMOVAL & INSTALLATION

✳✳ CAUTION

Prior to removal of the steering rack and pinion unit, center the front wheels and remove the ignition key. Failure to do so may damage the SRS (air bag system) clock spring under the steering wheel and render SRS system inoperative, risking serious driver injury.

1. Before servicing the vehicle, refer to the precautions in the beginning of this section.

2. Drain the power steering fluid using the following procedure:

a. Disconnect the power steering return (low side) hose.

b. Connect a suitable container to the hose.

c. Properly disable the ignition system by removing the connector from the ignition coil.

d. While cranking the engine, turn the wheels, several times, from side-to-side, until the fluid is removed.

3. Disarm the SRS system.

4. Remove or disconnect the following:

• Both front wheels
• Lower steering column joint-to-rack and pinion input shaft bolt
• Stabilizer bar and washer tank

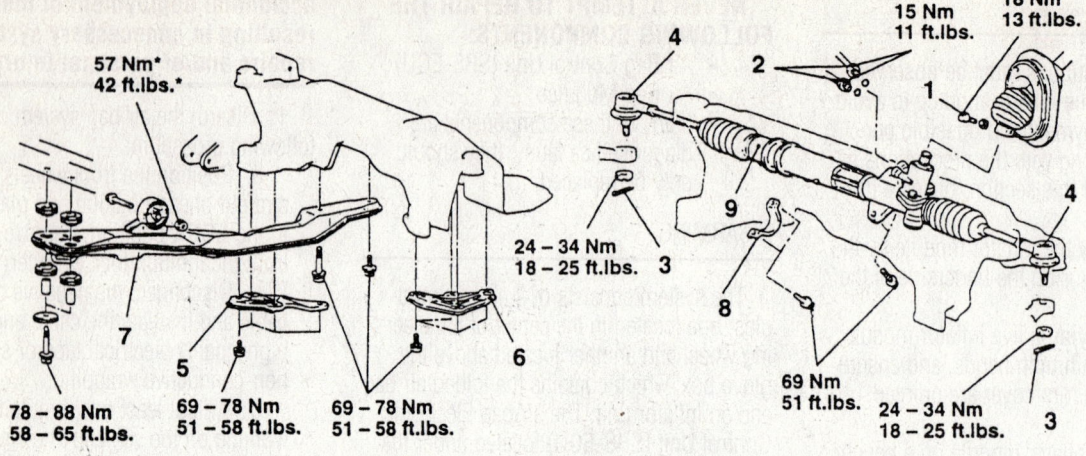

1. Joint assembly and gear box connecting bolt
2. Power steering pipe connection
3. Cotter pin
4. Tie rod end and knuckle connection
5. Stay (L.H.)
6. Stay (R.H.)
7. Center member assembly
8. Clamp
9. Gear box assembly

Caution
The fasteners marked * should be temporarily tightened before they are finally tightened once the total weight of the engine has been placed on the vehicle body.

7922CG30

Exploded view of the power rack and pinion steering gear mounting

- Cotter pins and tie rod ends from the steering knuckles
- Solenoid's wiring harness connector, if equipped with Electronic Control Power Steering (EPS)
- Both triangular braces near the crossmember

5. Support the center crossmember. Remove the through-bolt from the front round roll stopper and remove the 3 bolts securing the center crossmember.
6. Remove or disconnect the following:
   - Center crossmember
7. Properly support the engine and remove the rear roll stopper through-bolt. Lower the engine slightly.

❉❉ WARNING

In order to prevent damage to the engine, when supporting and jacking the engine, place a block of wood between the jack and the oil pan.

8. Remove or disconnect the following:
   - Power steering fluid pressure pipe and return hose from the rack fittings; then, plug the fittings to prevent excessive fluid leakage
   - Rack assembly clamp bolts and the 2 rack assembly-to-chassis bolts

- Rack and pinion steering assembly and its rubber mounts

➡**When removing the rack and pinion assembly, tilt the assembly to the inner side of the compression lower arm, and remove from the left side of the vehicle. Use caution to avoid damaging the boots.**

To install:

9. Align the rack assembly so the splines are inserted into the steering column shaft.
10. Install or connect the following:
    - Rack and tighten the mounting bolts to 51 ft. lbs. (69 Nm)
    - Pinch bolt and tighten the bolt to 13 ft. lbs. (18 Nm)
    - Power steering fluid lines; tighten the high side fitting to 11 ft. lbs. (15 Nm) and secure the low side hose with the clamp
11. Raise the engine into position.
12. Install or connect the following:
    - Rear roll stopper through-bolt and tighten to 32 ft. lbs. (43 Nm)
    - Crossmember; then, tighten the front bolts to 58–65 ft. lbs. (78–88 Nm) and the rear bolt to 51–58 ft. lbs. (69–78 Nm)
    - Front roll stopper bolt and tighten the nut to 32 ft. lbs. (43 Nm)

- Both triangular braces and tighten the bolts to 50–56 ft. lbs. (69–78 Nm)
- Stabilizer bar
- Tie rod ends and tighten the nuts to 20 ft. lbs. (27 Nm)
- Solenoid's wiring harness connector, if equipped with EPS
- Front wheels and lower the vehicle

13. Refill the reservoir with power steering fluid and properly bleed the power steering system.
14. Perform a front end alignment.

Shock Absorber

REMOVAL & INSTALLATION

Front

1. Before servicing the vehicle, refer to the precautions in the beginning of this section.
2. Remove or disconnect the following:
   - Negative battery cable.
   - Wheel
   - Sway bar link from the damper fork
   - Damper fork lower through-bolt, upper pinch bolt and damper fork assembly
   - Shock absorber

✳✳ CAUTION

DO NOT remove the large center nut.

To install:

3. Install or connect the following:
- Shock absorber and tighten the upper mounting nuts to 32 ft. lbs. (44 Nm)

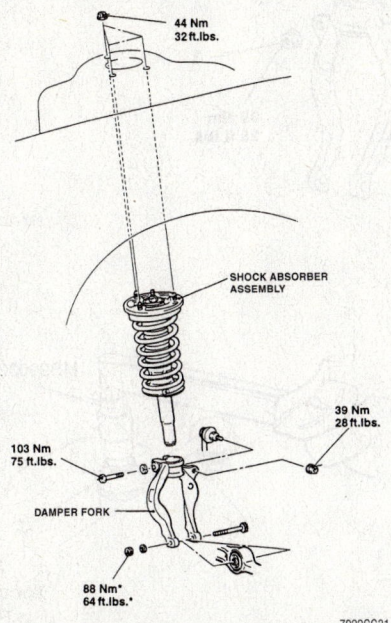

Exploded view of the front shock absorber assembly mounting

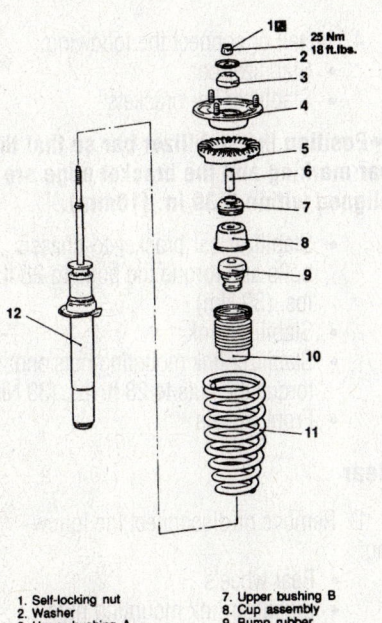

Exploded view of the front shock absorber

1. Self-locking nut
2. Washer
3. Upper bushing A
4. Upper bracket assembly
5. Upper spring pad
6. Collar
7. Upper bushing B
8. Cup assembly
9. Bump rubber
10. Dust cover
11. Coil spring
12. Shock absorber assembly

7922CG32

- Damper fork; then, tighten the lower through-bolt/nut to 65 ft. lbs. (88 Nm) and the upper pinch bolt to 76 ft. lbs. (103 Nm)
- Sway bar link and tighten the link-to-damper fork nut to 29 ft. lbs. (39 Nm)
- Wheel

4. Perform a front end alignment.

Rear

➡ **The shock absorber assembly is a load bearing component; therefore, the vehicle chassis and axle weight must be supported separately, requiring the use of 2 separate lifting devices.**

The rear package shelf front cover(s) must be removed to access the top mounting nuts. Most connections are plastic clips. Use care when removing these components to avoid unnecessary damage.

1. Remove or disconnect the following:
- Rear shelf speaker covers
- Rear shelf top assembly
- Front cover(s) to access the shock absorber top mounting nuts

2. Raise and support lower control arm assembly slightly.

3. Remove or disconnect the following:
- Shock absorber upper mounting nuts
- Shock absorber lower mounting bolt
- Shock absorber

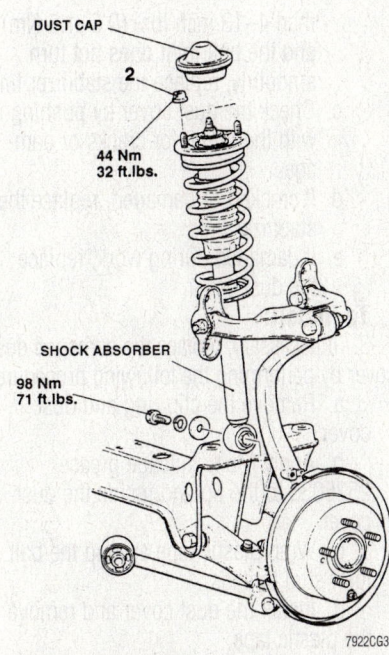

Exploded view of the rear shock absorber assembly mounting

7922CG33

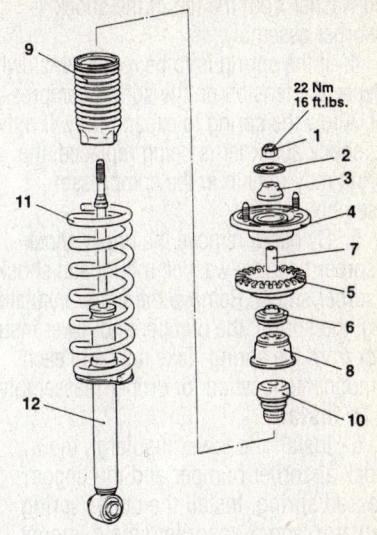

1. Self-locking nut
2. Washer
3. Upper bushing A
4. Bracket
5. Spring pad
6. Upper bushing B
7. Collar
8. Cup
9. Dust cover
10. Bump rubber
11. Coil spring
12. Shock absorber assembly

7922CG34

Exploded view of the rear shock absorber

To install:

4. Position the shock absorber assembly so that the lower mounting bolt can be installed and lightly tightened.

5. Use a jack to raise or lower the lower control arm, so that the top shock absorber plate studs align through the body. Raise the jack to hold the shock absorber assembly in position.

6. Install or connect the following:
- Top plate nuts and tighten the mounting nuts to 32 ft. lbs. (44 Nm)
- Lower mounting bolt to 71 ft. lbs. (98 Nm)
- Interior trim pieces

Coil Spring

REMOVAL & INSTALLATION

1. Before servicing the vehicle, refer to the precautions in the beginning of this section.

2. Place the shock absorber assembly in a MB991237 and MB991238 spring compressor assembly or equivalent. Tighten the compressor and compress the spring slowly. Make certain the compressor is properly engaged before tightening.

3. After tension has been removed from the shock absorber assembly and shock absorber plate, remove the piston rod nut

and washer from the top of the shock absorber assembly.

4. If the spring is to be replaced, slowly release the tension on the spring compressor. Allow the spring to expand fully. If only the shock absorber is being replaced, the spring may remain in the compressor assembly.

5. By hand, remove the upper shock absorber bearing, washer, mount and shock absorber shield. Remove the upper insulator ring, the spring, the bumper and lower insulator from the spring. Take notice to each components location for proper reassembly.

To install:

6. Install the lower insulator, the shock absorber bumper and the uncompressed spring. Install the upper spring insulator, shock absorber shield, mount and washer.

7. Install or align the spring compressor. Make certain the spring is correctly positioned relative to the upper and lower insulator rings. Smoothly compress the spring.

8. Install the washer and piston rod nut. Tighten the nut on the front strut to 18 ft. lbs. (25 Nm) or 16 ft. lbs. (22 Nm) on the rear strut. Install the dust cap.

9. Carefully release the spring compressor, watching the spring position as it seats. When the spring is properly seated, release/remove the compressor tools.

10. Reinstall the shock absorber assembly.

Stabilizer Bars

REMOVAL & INSTALLATION

Front

1. Remove or disconnect the following:
   - Front wheels
   - Stabilizer link mounting nuts
   - Stabilizer link
   - Stabilizer bar bracket-to-chassis bolts
   - Stabilizer bar brackets
   - Stabilizer bar

2. Inspect the stabilizer link ball joint by performing the following procedure:
   a. Shake the ball joint stud several times; then, install the stud nut and Preload Wrench tool MB990326.
   b. Using a torque wrench, measure the ball joints breakaway torque.
   - If the breakaway torque is higher than 4–13 inch lbs. (0.5–1.5 Nm), replace the stabilizer link
   - If the breakaway torque is lower

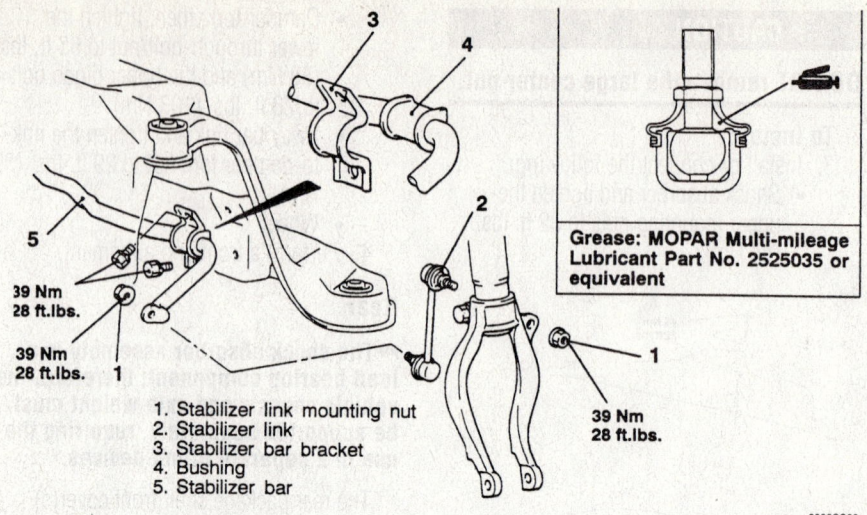

1. Stabilizer link mounting nut
2. Stabilizer link
3. Stabilizer bar bracket
4. Bushing
5. Stabilizer bar

39 Nm
28 ft.lbs.

39 Nm
28 ft.lbs.

39 Nm
28 ft.lbs.

Grease: MOPAR Multi-mileage Lubricant Part No. 2525035 or equivalent

9306CG29

Exploded view of the front stabilizer bar assembly

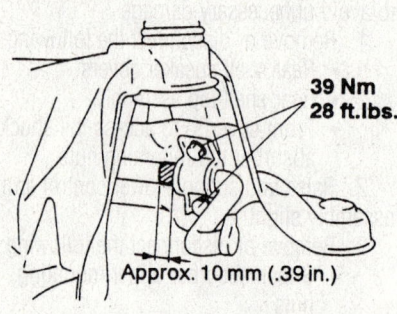

39 Nm
28 ft.lbs.

Approx. 10 mm (.39 in.)

9306CG30

Aligning the front stabilizer bar with the bracket

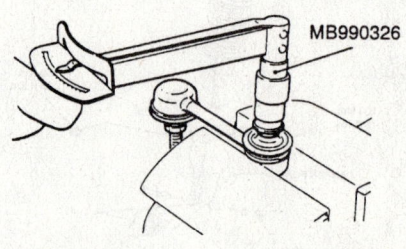

MB990326

9306CG31

Inspecting the front stabilizer link ball joint turning torque—Rear stabilizer link ball joint is similar

than 4–13 inch lbs. (0.5–1.5 Nm) and the ball joint does not turn smoothly, replace the stabilizer link
   c. Check the dust cover by pushing in with the finger for cracks or damage.
   d. If cracked or damaged, replace the stabilizer link.
   e. If damaged during work, replace the dust cover.

To install:

3. If necessary, replace the damaged dust cover by performing the following procedure:
   a. Remove the clip ring and dust cover.
   b. Apply Multi-mileage grease 2525035 to the lip and inside the dust cover.
   c. Wrap plastic tape around the ball joint stud threads.
   d. Install the dust cover and remove the plastic tape.
   e. Install the clip ring and secure the dust cover by aligning the clip ring ends at 90 degrees from the stabilizer link axis.

4. Install or connect the following:
   - Stabilizer bar
   - Stabilizer bar brackets

➡️**Position the stabilizer bar so that the bar marking and the bracket edge are aligned within 0.39 in. (10mm).**

   - Stabilizer bar bracket-to-chassis bolts and torque the bolts to 28 ft. lbs. (39 Nm)
   - Stabilizer link
   - Stabilizer link mounting nuts and torque the nuts to 28 ft. lbs. (39 Nm)
   - Front wheels

Rear

1. Remove or disconnect the following:
   - Rear wheels
   - Stabilizer link mounting nuts
   - Stabilizer link
   - Stabilizer bar bracket-to-chassis bolts
   - Stabilizer bar brackets
   - Stabilizer bar

2. Inspect the stabilizer link ball joint by performing the following procedure:

a. Shake the ball joint stud several times; then, install the stud nut and Pre-load Wrench tool MB990326.

b. Using a torque wrench, measure the ball joints breakaway torque.

- If the breakaway torque is higher than 4–13 inch lbs. (0.5–1.5 Nm), replace the stabilizer link
- If the breakaway torque is lower than 4–13 inch lbs. (0.5–1.5 Nm) and the ball joint does not turn smoothly, replace the stabilizer link

c. Check the dust cover by pushing in with the finger for cracks or damage.

d. If cracked or damaged, replace the stabilizer link.

e. If damaged during work, replace the dust cover.

To install:

3. If necessary, replace the damaged dust cover by performing the following procedure:

a. Remove the clip ring and dust cover.

b. Apply Multi-Mileage grease 2525035 to the lip and inside the dust cover.

c. Wrap plastic tape around the ball joint stud threads.

d. Install the dust cover and remove the plastic tape.

e. Install the clip ring and secure the dust cover by aligning the clip ring ends at 90 degrees from the stabilizer link axis.

4. Install or connect the following:
- Stabilizer bar
- Stabilizer bar brackets

➡**Position the stabilizer bar so that the bar marking and the bracket edge are aligned within 0.39 in. (10mm).**

- Stabilizer bar bracket-to-chassis bolts and torque the bolts to 7–10 ft. lbs. (9–14 Nm)
- Stabilizer link

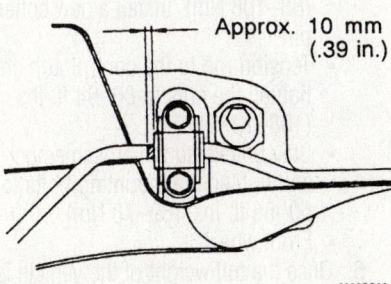

Approx. 10 mm (.39 in.)

9306CG33

Aligning the rear stabilizer bar with the bracket

- Stabilizer link mounting nuts and torque the nuts to 28 ft. lbs. (39 Nm)
- Rear wheels

Upper Ball Joint

REMOVAL & INSTALLATION

The upper ball joint is an integrated part of the upper control arm assembly, and cannot be serviced separately. A worn or damaged ball joint requires replacement of the upper control arm assembly.

Lower Ball Joint

REMOVAL & INSTALLATION

The front suspension is called a Multi-Link Suspension. There are 2 lower arms used in this front suspension; a curved arm called the Compression Lower Arm and also a straight arm called the Lateral Lower Arm. Both arms contain lower ball joints since there are 2 sockets in the steering knuckle. Ball joints and lower arms are removed and replaced as an assembly. A front end alignment is required after these procedures.

Upper Control Arm

REMOVAL & INSTALLATION

1. Before servicing the vehicle, refer to the precautions in the beginning of this section.

2. Remove or disconnect the following:
- Front wheel
- Ball joint stud from the steering knuckle, using the Joint Separation tool MB991113 or equivalent

3. The ball joint can be checked using the following procedure:

a. An adapter (MB 990326) is available that fits onto the ball joint stud and adapts to an inch-pound torque wrench. If this tool is not available, a shop-made substitute can be fabricated.

b. Turn the ball joint stud with the torque wrench. The factory standard for breakaway torque is 3–13 inch lbs. (0.34–1.45 Nm).

c. If the ball joint stud is out of specification (turns too easily or is too stiff), continue with the ball joint/control arm assembly replacement.

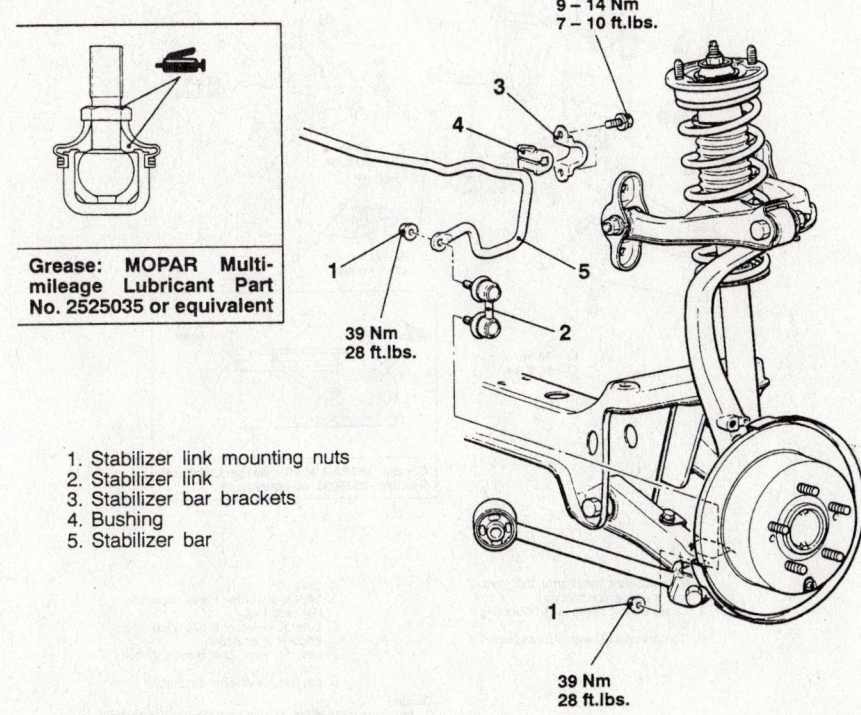

Grease: MOPAR Multi-mileage Lubricant Part No. 2525035 or equivalent

9 – 14 Nm
7 – 10 ft.lbs.

39 Nm
28 ft.lbs.

39 Nm
28 ft.lbs.

1. Stabilizer link mounting nuts
2. Stabilizer link
3. Stabilizer bar brackets
4. Bushing
5. Stabilizer bar

9306CG32

Exploded view of the rear stabilizer bar assembly

Turn to Section 5 for brake system applications

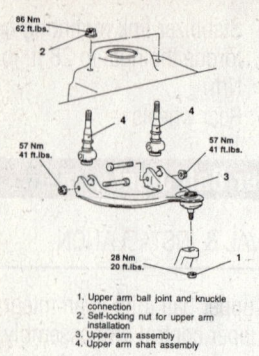

1. Upper arm ball joint and knuckle connection
2. Self-locking nut for upper arm installation
3. Upper arm assembly
4. Upper arm shaft assembly

7922CG35

Exploded view of the upper control arm mounting

➡ **The upper ball joint boot can be removed and the joint greased. A new replacement ball joint boot is recommended.**

4. Inside the engine compartment, at the shock absorber tower, locate the upper control arm mounting nuts. Remove the nuts and using the joint separation tool, separate the upper arm shafts from the shock absorber tower.

5. Remove or disconnect the following:

- Upper control arm assembly
- Upper arm shaft assembly-to-upper control arm nuts/bolts and the shaft(s)

To install:

6. Install the upper arm shaft assemblies to the upper control arm and torque the nuts and bolts to 41 ft. lbs. (57 Nm).

7. Align the upper control arm shafts to the shock absorber tower and secure it with the mounting nuts. Tighten the mounting nuts to 62 ft. lbs. (86 Nm).

8. Install or connect the following:

- Ball joint to the knuckle and tighten the locking nut to 20 ft. lbs. (28 Nm)
- Front wheel

9. Check the wheel alignment and adjust, if necessary.

Lower Control Arm

REMOVAL & INSTALLATION

Lateral Lower Arm

1. Before servicing the vehicle, refer to the precautions in the beginning of this section.

2. Remove or disconnect the following:

- Front wheel
- Stay bracket from the crossmember
- Ball joint stud from the steering

knuckle, using joint separator MB991113

- Damper fork-to-lower control arm through-bolt
- Lower control arm-to-crossmember bolt
- Lower control arm

To install:

3. When installing the control arm, temporarily tighten the nuts and/or bolts securing the control arm to the suspension crossmember. Tighten them fully only after the vehicle is sitting on its wheels.

4. Install or connect the following:

- Damper fork and tighten the fork-to-lower control arm through-bolt to 64 ft. lbs. (88 Nm)
- Ball joint stud to the knuckle and tighten the nut to 65–80 ft. lbs. (88–108 Nm). Install a new cotter pin.
- Tension rod to the control arm and tighten the nuts to 80–94 ft. lbs. (108–127 Nm)
- Stay bracket to the crossmember and tighten the mounting bolts to 50–56 ft. lbs. (69–78 Nm).
- Front wheel

5. Once the full weight of the vehicle is on the suspension, tighten the inner lower arm mounting bolt nut to 71–85 ft. lbs. (98–118 Nm).

6. Check the front end alignment and adjust as required.

Compression Lower Arm

1. Before servicing the vehicle, refer to the precautions in the beginning of this section.

2. Remove or disconnect the following:

- Front wheel
- Ball joint stud from the steering knuckle, using joint separator MB991113
- Lower control arm-to-crossmember bolt
- Lower control arm

To install:

3. Install or connect the following:

- Control arm to the crossmember and tighten the bolts to 60 ft. lbs. (83 Nm)
- Ball joint stud to the knuckle and tighten the nut to 43–51 ft. lbs. (59–71 Nm)
- Front wheel

4. Check the front end alignment and adjust as required.

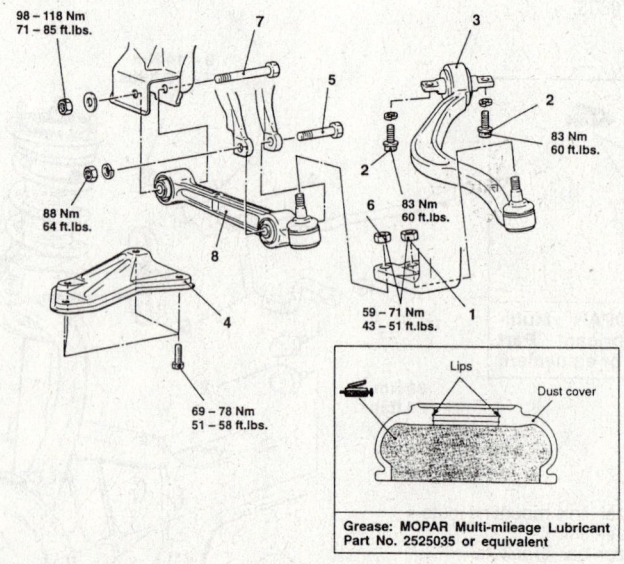

Grease: MOPAR Multi-mileage Lubricant Part No. 2525035 or equivalent

1. Compression lower arm ball joint and knuckle connection
2. Compression lower arm mounting bolt
3. Compression lower arm assembly
4. Stay
5. Shock absorber lower mounting bolt and nut
6. Lateral lower arm ball joint and knuckle connection
7. Lateral lower arm mounting bolt and nut
8. Lateral lower arm assembly

Caution
*: Indicates parts which should be temporarily tightened, and then fully tightened with the vehicle on the ground in the unladen condition.

7922CG36

Exploded view of the lateral lower arm and the compression lower arm mounting

Wheel Bearings

ADJUSTMENT

Front

To check hub and bearing assembly end-play, remove the caliper and rotor. Position a dial indicator to bear against the hub flange near the center ridge. Wiggle the hub back and forth. If end-play exceeds 0.002 in. (0.05mm), replace the front hub and bearing assembly.

Rear

The rear hub and wheel bearing assembly is designed for the life of the vehicle and requires no type of adjustment or periodic maintenance. The bearing is a sealed unit with the wheel hub and can only be removed and/or replaced as one unit.

REMOVAL & INSTALLATION

Front

1. Before servicing the vehicle, refer to the precautions in the beginning of this section.
2. Remove the cotter pin, halfshaft nut and washer.
3. Remove or disconnect the following:
   - Front wheel
   - Vehicle Speed Sensor (VSS), if equipped with ABS
   - Caliper and brake pads; then, sup-

port the caliper out of the way using wire
   - Brake rotor from the hub assembly
   - Upper ball joint from the steering knuckle using a press type tool and pull the knuckle outward

✳✳ WARNING

Use of improper methods of joint separation can result in damage to joint, leading to possible failure. Never use wedge-type tools or the ball joint can be damaged.

   - 4 hub-to-steering knuckle bolts
   - Hub and bearing assembly from the knuckle

➡**The hub and wheel bearing assembly is not serviceable and should not be disassembled.**

To install:
4. Install or connect the following:
   - Hub to the steering knuckle and tighten the bolts to 65 ft. lbs. (88 Nm)
   - Upper ball joint to the steering knuckle and tighten the self-locking nut to 21 ft. lbs. (28 Nm)
5. Position the rotor on the hub. Install a couple of lug nuts and lightly tighten to hold the rotor on the hub.
6. Install the caliper holder and place the brake pads in the holder. Slide the caliper over the brake pads and install the

guide pins. Once the caliper is secured, the lug nuts can be removed.
7. Install or connect the following:
   - VSS, if equipped with ABS
   - Front wheel
   - New cotter pin and bend to secure
8. Examine the driveshaft (halfshaft) hub washer. Locate the chamfered side. This side is installed outward, away from the hub. Install the washer and hub nut. Tighten the axle nut with the brakes applied. Tighten the nut to 145–188 ft. lbs. (200–260 Nm).

✳✳ WARNING

Pump the brake pedal until hard, before attempting to move the vehicle.

Rear

WITH DRUM BRAKES

1. Before servicing the vehicle, refer to the precautions in the beginning of this section.
2. Remove or disconnect the following:
   - Rear wheel
   - Vehicle Speed Sensor (VSS), if equipped with Anti-Lock Brake System (ABS)
   - Brake drum
   - 4 hub to the knuckle bolts
   - Hub and bearing assembly from the knuckle

➡**The hub assembly is not serviceable and should not be disassembled.**

3. If replacing the hub, use special socket MB991248 and a press, to remove the wheel sensor rotor from the hub.
To install:
4. Press the wheel sensor rotor onto the hub.
5. Install or connect the following:
   - Hub to the knuckle and tighten the bolts to 54–65 ft. lbs. (74–88 Nm)
   - Brake drum
   - VSS, if equipped with ABS
   - Rear wheel and lower the vehicle

WITH DISC BRAKES

1. Before servicing the vehicle, refer to the precautions in the beginning of this section.
2. Remove or disconnect the following:
   - Rear wheel
   - Vehicle Speed Sensor (VSS), if equipped with Anti-Lock Brake System (ABS)

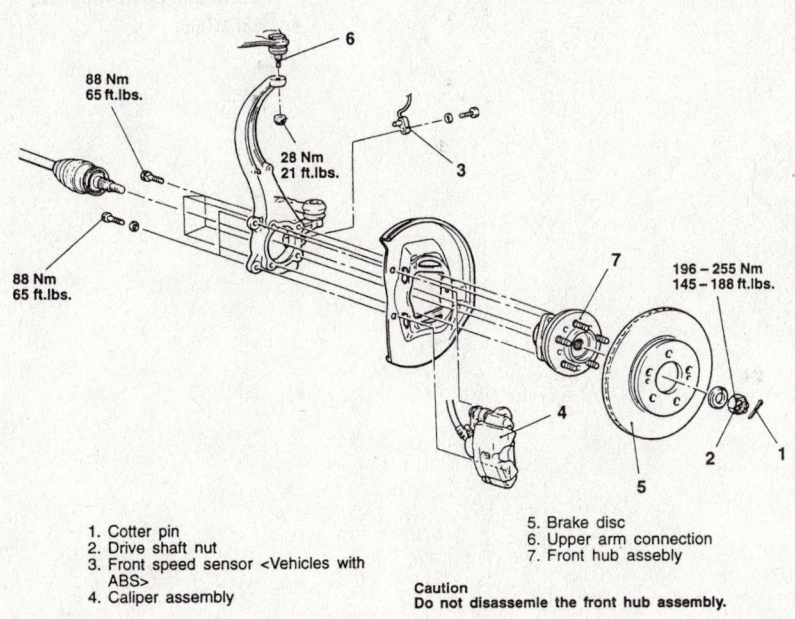

88 Nm
65 ft.lbs.

28 Nm
21 ft.lbs.

88 Nm
65 ft.lbs.

196 – 255 Nm
145 – 188 ft.lbs.

1. Cotter pin
2. Drive shaft nut
3. Front speed sensor <Vehicles with ABS>
4. Caliper assembly

5. Brake disc
6. Upper arm connection
7. Front hub assebly

Caution
Do not disassemie the front hub assembly.

7922CG37

Exploded view of the front hub assembly mounting and related components

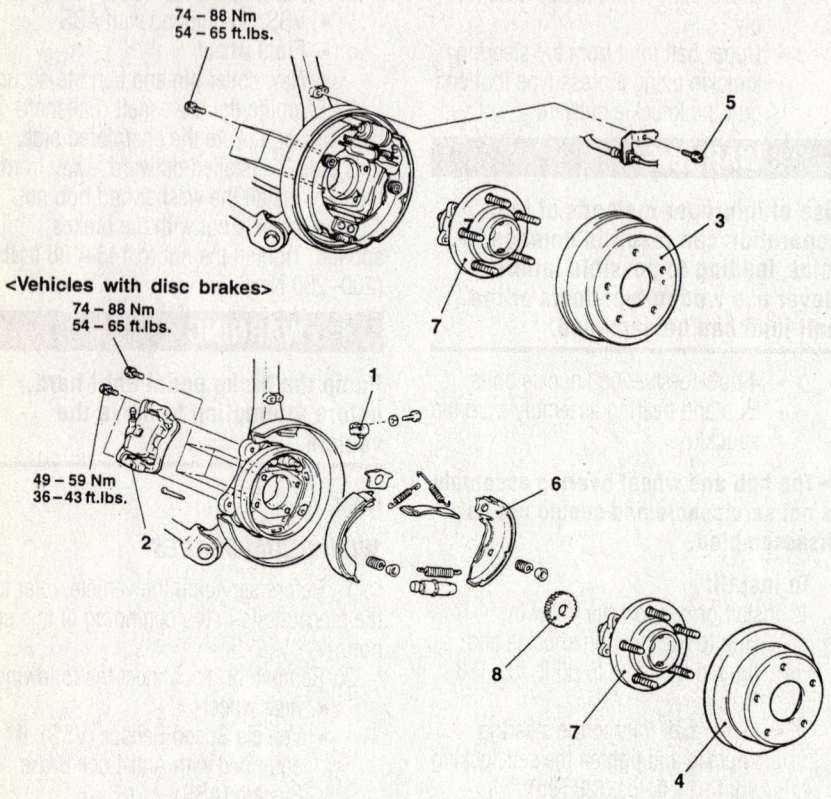

<Vehicles with drum brakes>

74 – 88 Nm
54 – 65 ft.lbs.

5

<Vehicles with disc brakes>

74 – 88 Nm
54 – 65 ft.lbs.

1

49 – 59 Nm
36 – 43 ft.lbs.

2

6

8

7

4

1. Rear speed sensor <Vehicles with ABS>
2. Caliper assembly
3. Brake drum
4. Brake disc
5. Clip mounting bolt

6. Shoe and lining assembly <Drum in disc brake>
7. Rear hub assembly
8. ABS-rotor <Vehicles with ABS>

Caution
Do not disassemble the rear hub assembly.

7922CG38

Exploded view of the rear hub assembly mounting

- Caliper and brake pads; then, support the caliper out of the way using wire
- Brake rotor
3. Remove the parking brake shoes as follows:
  - Upper shoe-to-anchor springs
  - Lower shoe-to-shoe spring
  - Brake shoe hold-down springs
  - Parking brake cable from the actuating lever
4. Remove or disconnect the following:
  - 4 hub-to-knuckle bolts
  - Hub and bearing assembly from the knuckle

➡**The hub assembly is not serviceable and should not be disassembled.**

5. If replacing the hub, use special socket MB991248 and a press, to remove the wheel sensor rotor from the hub.

To install:
6. Press the wheel sensor rotor onto the hub.
7. Install or connect the following:
  - Hub to the knuckle and tighten the bolts to 54–65 ft. lbs. (74–88 Nm)
  - Parking brake shoes
8. Position the rotor on the hub. Install a couple of lug nuts and lightly tighten to hold rotor on hub.
9. Install the caliper holder and place brake pads in holder. Slide the caliper over brake pads and install guide pins. Once caliper is secured, lug nuts can be removed.
  - VSS, if equipped with ABS
  - Rear wheel

CHRYSLER CORPORATION

Eagle-Talon

12

PRECAUTIONS

Before servicing any vehicle, please be sure to read all of the following precautions, which deal with personal safety, prevention of component damage, and important points to take into consideration when servicing a motor vehicle:

• Never open, service or drain the radiator or cooling system when the engine is hot; serious burns can occur from the steam and hot coolant.

• Observe all applicable safety precautions when working around fuel. Whenever servicing the fuel system, always work in a well-ventilated area. Do not allow fuel spray or vapors to come in contact with a spark, open flame or excessive heat (a hot drop light, for example). Keep a dry chemical fire extinguisher near the work area. Always keep fuel in a container specifically designed for fuel storage; also, always properly seal fuel containers to avoid the possibility of fire or explosion. Refer to the additional fuel system precautions later in this section.

• Fuel injection systems often remain pressurized, even after the engine has been turned **OFF**. The fuel system pressure must be relieved before disconnecting any fuel lines. Failure to do so may result in fire and/or personal injury.

• Brake fluid often contains polyglycol ethers and polyglycols. Avoid contact with the eyes and wash your hands thoroughly after handling brake fluid. If you do get brake fluid in your eyes, flush your eyes with clean, running water for 15 minutes. If eye irritation persists, or if you have taken brake fluid internally, IMMEDIATELY seek medical assistance.

• The EPA warns that prolonged contact with used engine oil may cause a number of skin disorders, including cancer! You should make every effort to minimize your exposure to used engine oil. Protective gloves should be worn when changing oil. Wash your hands and any other exposed skin areas as soon as possible after exposure to used engine oil. Soap and water, or waterless hand cleaner should be used.

• All new vehicles are now equipped with an air bag system. The system must be disabled before performing service on or around system components, steering column, instrument panel components, wiring and sensors. Failure to follow safety and disabling procedures could result in accidental air bag deployment, possible personal injury and unnecessary system repairs.

• Always wear safety goggles when working with, or around, the air bag system. When carrying a non-deployed air bag, be sure the bag and trim cover are pointed away from your body. When placing a non-deployed air bag on a work surface, always face the bag and trim cover upward, away from the surface. This will reduce the motion of the module if it is accidentally deployed. Refer to the additional air bag system precautions later in this section.

• Clean, high quality brake fluid from a sealed container is essential to the safe and proper operation of the brake system. You should always buy the correct type of brake fluid for your vehicle. If the brake fluid becomes contaminated, completely flush the system with new fluid. Never reuse any brake fluid. Any brake fluid that is removed from the system should be discarded. Also, do not allow any brake fluid to come in contact with a painted surface; it will damage the paint.

• Never operate the engine without the proper amount and type of engine oil; doing so WILL result in severe engine damage.

• Timing belt maintenance is extremely important! Many models utilize an interference-type, non-freewheeling engine. If the timing belt breaks, the valves in the cylinder head may strike the pistons, causing potentially serious (also time-consuming and expensive) engine damage. Refer to the maintenance interval charts in the front of this manual for the recommended replacement interval for the timing belt, and to the timing belt section for belt replacement and inspection.

• Disconnecting the negative battery cable on some vehicles may interfere with the functions of the on-board computer system(s) and may require the computer to undergo a relearning process once the negative battery cable is reconnected.

• When servicing drum brakes, only disassemble and assemble one side at a time, leaving the remaining side intact for reference.

• Only an MVAC-trained, EPA-certified automotive technician should service the air conditioning system or its components.

ENGINE REPAIR

Alternator

REMOVAL

Non-Turbo

1. Disconnect the negative battery cable.
2. Remove or disconnect the following:
   • Right wheel
   • Under cover side panel
   • Speed control assembly
   • Alternator drive belt
   • Alternator electrical connector
   • Alternator bracket
   • Alternator

Turbo

1. Disconnect the negative battery cable.
2. Remove or disconnect the following:
   • Right wheel
   • Under cover side panel
   • Alternator drive belt
   • Power steering pump drive belt
   • Power steering pump

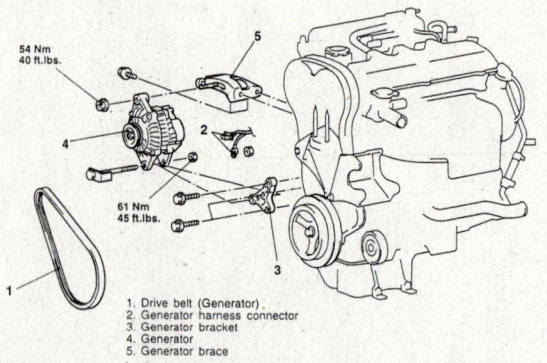

54 Nm
40 ft.lbs.

61 Nm
45 ft.lbs.

1. Drive belt (Generator)
2. Generator harness connector
3. Generator bracket
4. Generator
5. Generator brace

9306DG01

Exploded view of the alternator and related components—Non-turbo

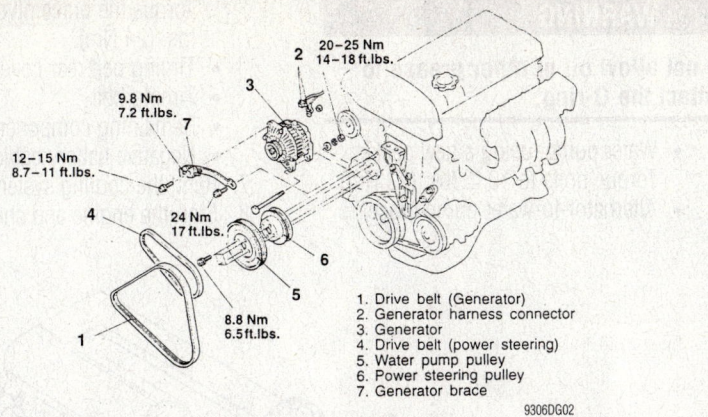

9306DG02

Exploded view of the alternator and related components—Turbo

20–25 Nm
14–18 ft.lbs.

9.8 Nm
7.2 ft.lbs.

12–15 Nm
8.7–11 ft.lbs.

24 Nm
17 ft.lbs.

8.8 Nm
6.5 ft.lbs.

1. Drive belt (Generator)
2. Generator harness connector
3. Generator
4. Drive belt (power steering)
5. Water pump pulley
6. Power steering pulley
7. Generator brace

➡**Support the power steering pump above the engine without disconnecting the hoses.**

- Alternator electrical connector
- Alternator

INSTALLATION

Non-Turbo

1. Install or connect the following:
   - Alternator
   - Alternator bracket
   - Alternator electrical connector
   - Alternator drive belt
2. Adjust the alternator drive belt:
   - Used belt deflection: 0.35–0.47 in. (9.0–12.0mm)
   - New belt deflection: 0.30–0.41 in. (7.5–10.5mm)
   - Used belt tension: 90–110 lbs. (400–490 N)
   - New belt tension: 110–160 lbs. (490–712 N)
3. Torque the alternator-to-upper bracket nut to 40 ft. lbs. (54 Nm) and the alternator-to-lower bracket nut to 45 ft. lbs. (61 Nm).
4. Install or connect the following:
   - Speed control assembly
   - Under cover side panel
   - Right wheel
   - Negative battery cable

Turbo

1. Install or connect the following:
   - Alternator
   - Alternator electrical connector
   - Alternator drive belt
2. Adjust the alternator drive belt:
   - Used belt deflection: 0.35–0.45 in. (9.0–11.5mm)

- New belt deflection: 0.30–0.35 in. (7.5–9.0mm)
- Used belt tension: 55.1–110.2 lbs. (245–490 N)
- New belt tension: 110.2–154.3 lbs. (490–686 N)

3. Torque the alternator-to-upper bracket bot to 8.7–11 ft. lbs. (12–15 Nm) and the alternator-to-lower bracket nut/bolt to 14–18 ft. lbs. (20–25 Nm).
4. Adjust the power steering drive belt:
   - Used belt deflection: 0.22–0.32 in. (5.5–8.0mm)
   - New belt deflection: 0.18–0.22 in. (4.5–5.5mm)
   - Used belt tension: 55.1–110.2 lbs. (245–490 N)
   - New belt tension: 110.2–154.3 lbs. (490–686 N)
5. Install or connect the following:
   - Under cover side panel
   - Right wheel
   - Negative battery cable

Ignition Timing

It is not necessary to check the ignition timing, because the crankshaft position is detected directly and the ignition timing is controlled electronically.

Engine Assembly

REMOVAL & INSTALLATION

The following procedure can be used on all vehicles. Slight variations may occur due to extra connections, etc., but the basic procedure should cover all models.

1. Before servicing the vehicle, refer to the precautions in the beginning of this section.

2. Drain the cooling system and the crankcase.
3. Relieve the fuel system pressure.
4. Remove or disconnect the following:
   - Negative battery cable
   - Engine undercover, if equipped
   - Hood assembly, matchmark it
   - Air cleaner assembly and air intake ducts
   - Radiator, coolant reservoir and intercooler
   - Transaxle and transfer case, if equipped with All Wheel Drive (AWD)
   - Accelerator cable
   - Heater hoses
   - Brake vacuum hose
   - Connection for vacuum hoses
   - High pressure fuel line
   - Fuel return line
   - Oxygen (O2S) sensor connection
   - Coolant temperature gauge connection
   - Coolant Temperature Sensor (CTS) connector
   - Connection for thermo switch sensor
   - Automatic transaxle, if equipped
   - Idle speed control connection
   - Motor Position (MP) sensor connector
   - Throttle Position (TP) sensor connector
   - Exhaust Gas Recirculation (EGR) temperature sensor connection (California vehicles)
   - Fuel injector connectors
   - Power transistor connector
   - Ignition coil connector
   - Condenser and noise filter connector
   - Distributor and control harness
   - Alternator and oil pressure switch connectors.
   - Drive belt and compressor, if equipped with A/C. DO NOT discharge the system or disconnect the refrigerant lines. Wire the compressor aside.
   - Power steering pump and wire aside
   - Exhaust manifold-to-pipe nuts and discard the gasket

5. Attach a hoist to the engine and support the engine weight.
6. Remove or disconnect the following:

   - Engine mount bracket
   - Torque control brackets (roll stoppers)

➡**Some engine mount pieces have arrows on them for proper assembly.**

- Engine

To install:

7. Install or connect the following:
- Engine. Torque the engine mount bolts to 50 ft. lbs. (69 Nm).

➡**The front lower mount through-bolt nut should not be tightened until the full weight of the engine is on the mount.**

- Exhaust pipe
- Power steering pump
- Air conditioning compressor
- All electrical and vacuum connections
- Transaxle. Torque the upper mounting bolts to 65 ft. lbs. (90 Nm).
- Starter. Torque the bolts to 54–65 ft. lbs. (75–90 Nm).
- Radiator and intercooler
- Air cleaner assembly
- Control brackets
- Hood
- Negative battery cable

8. Refill the crankcase and cooling system

9. Start the engine, allow it to reach normal operating temperature and check for leaks.

10. Check the ignition timing and adjust, if necessary.

11. Road test the vehicle and check all functions for proper operation.

Water Pump

REMOVAL & INSTALLATION

1. Be sure to observe all cautions and warnings in the beginning of the section that may be related to this procedure.
2. Drain the cooling system.
3. Remove or disconnect the following:
- Timing belt
- Alternator-to-water pump brace
4. Unfasten the retainers, then remove any brackets for access to the rear cover.
5. Remove or disconnect the following:
- Timing belt rear cover, if necessary
- Water pump bolts
- Water pump, gasket and O-ring. Discard the gasket and O-ring.

To install:

6. Install or connect the following:
- New water inlet pipe O-ring

➡**Coat the O-ring with water or coolant.**

✳✳ WARNING

Do not allow oil or other grease to contact the O-ring.

- Water pump, using a new gasket. Torque bolts to 10 ft. lbs. (13 Nm).
- Alternator-to-water pump brace.

Torque the brace pivot bolt to 17 ft. lbs. (24 Nm).
- Timing belt rear cover, if removed
- Timing belt
- Remaining components
- Negative battery cable

7. Refill the cooling system
8. Start the engine and check for leaks.

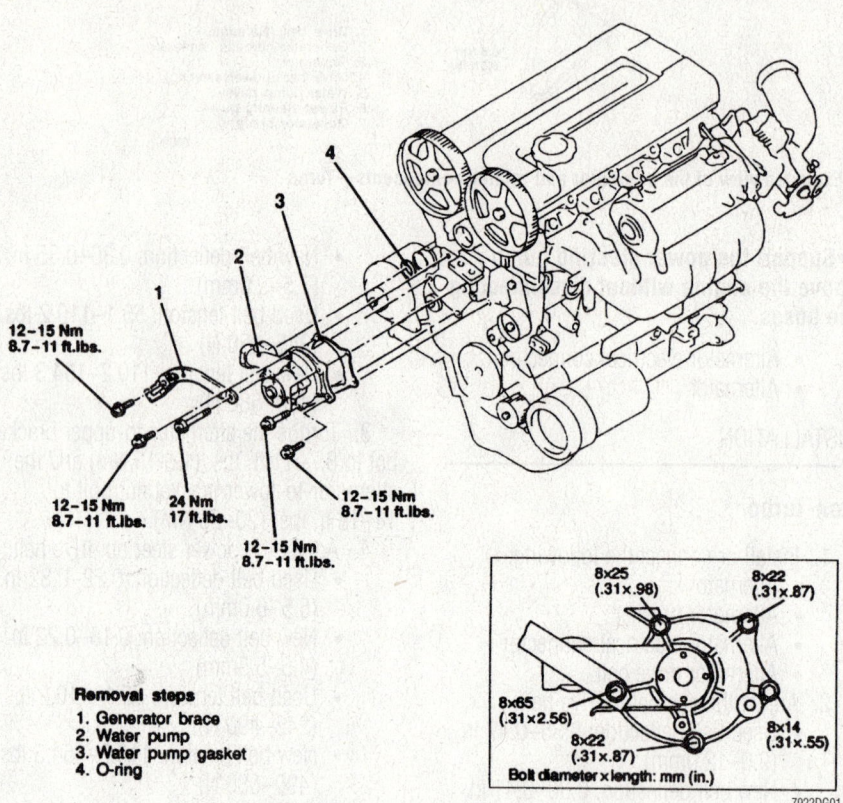

Removal steps
1. Generator brace
2. Water pump
3. Water pump gasket
4. O-ring

Bolt diameter × length: mm (in.)

Water pump mounting and bolt locations—2.0L (VIN F) engine

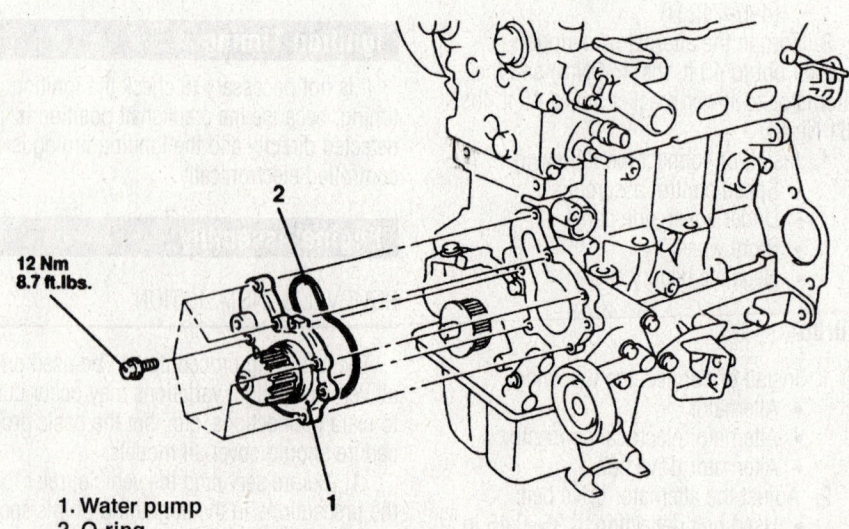

1. Water pump
2. O-ring

Exploded view of the water pump and O-ring mounting—2.0L (VIN Y) engine

Cylinder Head

REMOVAL & INSTALLATION

2.0L (VIN F) Engine

1. Be sure to observe all cautions and warnings in the beginning of the section that may be related to this procedure.
2. Drain the cooling system and crankcase
3. Remove or disconnect the following:
   - Negative battery cable
   - Accelerator cable and mounting bracket
   - Intake air duct (hose) from the throttle body
4. Label and disconnect the following:
   - Idle Air Control (IAC) motor
   - Knock Sensor (KS)
   - Heated Oxygen Sensor (HO$_2$S)
   - Engine coolant temperature gauge sender
   - Engine Coolant Temperature (ECT) sensor
   - Ignition module (power transistor)
   - Throttle Position (TP) sensor
   - Condenser
   - Manifold differential pressure sensor
   - Fuel injectors
   - Ignition coil
   - Camshaft Position (CMP) sensor
   - Crankshaft Position (CKP) sensor
   - Air conditioning compressor
   - Engine control wiring harness
5. Remove or disconnect the following:
   - Engine center cover
   - Spark plug wires
   - Brake booster vacuum hose
   - Fuel lines from the fuel supply rail
   - Bypass hose and water hose connections
   - Vacuum hoses, breather hose and PCV hose
   - Timing belt
   - Power steering pump
   - Cylinder head cover and semi-circular packing
   - Heat protector
   - Water and radiator hoses
   - Thermostat housing and O-ring
   - Intake manifold stay
   - Turbocharger assembly from exhaust manifold
6. Gradually, loosen and remove the cylinder head bolts, in 2–3 steps, using the specified sequence.
   - Cylinder head and discard the gasket

To install:

7. Thoroughly, clean the deck surface of the engine block and the sealing surface of the cylinder head. Check the cylinder head for warpage.
8. Measure the length of the cylinder head bolts from below the head to the end; if the bolt measures more than 3.913 in. (9.94cm), replace the bolt.
9. Install or connect the following:
   - New cylinder head gasket, with identification mark facing upwards
   - Cylinder head. Apply clean engine oil to the bolts and install them finger-tight.

➡ **Refer to Section one of this manual for the cylinder head torque sequence illustration. The illustration is located after the Torque Specification Chart.**

10. Tighten the bolts in sequence, using the following procedure:
    a. Tighten the bolts in sequence to 58 ft. lbs. (78 Nm).
    b. Loosen the bolts completely in the reverse order.
    c. Tighten the bolts in sequence to 15 ft. lbs. (20 Nm).
    d. Tighten the bolt ¼ turn (90 degrees) from the mark.
    e. Tighten the bolt an additional 90 degree or (¼) turn.
11. Install or connect the following:
    - Turbocharger, using a new gasket
    - Intake manifold stay
    - Thermostat housing
    - Radiator and water hoses
    - Heat protector
    - Cylinder head, by applying sealant to the semi-circular packing
12. Apply sealant at the front of the cylinder head where the camshaft oil seal retainer and the cylinder head come together
13. Install or connect the following:
    - Cylinder head cover, using a new gasket
    - Power steering pump
    - Timing belt
    - Pollution Control Valve (PCV), breather and vacuum hoses
    - Water hose and bypass hose
    - Fuel lines to fuel supply rail, using a new O-ring. Apply a small amount of engine oil to the new O-ring.
    - Brake booster vacuum hose
    - Spark plug wires and center cover
    - All removed connectors
    - Intake air hose, at the throttle body

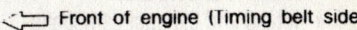
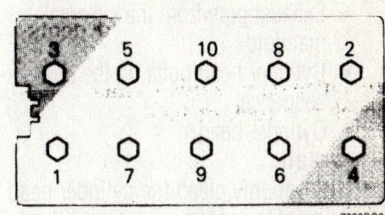

⬅ Front of engine (Timing belt side)

7922DG04

Cylinder head bolt removal sequence— 2.0L (VIN F and Y) engines

    - Accelerator cable, connect and adjust
    - Negative battery cable.
14. Refill the cooling system
15. Replace the oil filter and refill the crankcase.
16. Start the engine and check for fuel, coolant and oil leaks.

2.0L (VIN Y) Engine

1. Be sure to observe all cautions and warnings in the beginning of the section that may be related to this procedure.
2. Drain the cooling system and crankcase.
3. Remove or disconnect the following:
   - Negative battery cable
   - Air cleaner and air intake duct
   - Air conditioning compressor
   - Power Steering Pump (PSP) switch
   - Heated Oxygen Sensor (HO$_2$S)
   - Engine coolant temperature gauge sender
   - Engine Coolant Temperature (ECT) sensor
   - Manifold Absolute Pressure (MAP) sensor
   - Intake Air Temperature (IAT) sensor
   - Throttle Position (TP) sensor
   - Idle Air Control (IAC) motor
   - Injector harness
   - Ignition coil
   - Camshaft Position (CMP) sensor
   - Exhaust Gas Recirculation (EGR) solenoid valve
   - Accelerator cable from the throttle body
   - Heater hoses from the rear of the engine
   - Fuel lines from the fuel supply rail
   - Purge air hose and brake booster vacuum hose connections
   - Overflow tube connection
   - Upper radiator hose and water hose connections
   - Timing belt

Timing belt service is covered in Section 4 of this manual

- Intake manifold stay
- Intake and exhaust camshafts
- Exhaust pipe from the exhaust manifold
- Cylinder head bolts, in the proper sequence
- Cylinder head

To install:

4. Thoroughly clean the cylinder head and engine block sealing surfaces. Check the deck and the cylinder head for warpage.

5. Clean the cylinder head bolts and inspect them for stretching. If a bolt appears to be stretched, replace it.

6. Install or connect the following:
- New head gasket
- Cylinder head

7. Coat the threads of the bolts with clean engine oil and install the bolts finger-tight in the engine block. The short bolts go in the corners.

➡️**Refer to Section one of this manual for the cylinder head torque sequence illustration. The illustration is located after the Torque Specification Chart.**

8. Tighten the cylinder head bolts in the proper sequence, in the following steps:
a. Center bolts 1 through 6: 25 ft. lbs. (33 Nm).
b. Outer bolts 7 through 10: 20 ft. lbs. (27 Nm).
c. Center bolts 1 through 6: 50 ft. lbs. (67 Nm).
d. Outer bolts 7 through 10: 20 ft. lbs. (27 Nm).
e. Center bolts 1 through 6: 50 ft. lbs. (67 Nm).
f. Outer bolts 7 through 10: 20 ft. lbs. (27 Nm).
g. Turn all fasteners 1 through 10: 1/4 turn (90 degrees) more in sequence. Do not use a torque wrench for this step.

9. Install or connect the following:
- Front exhaust pipe-to-exhaust manifold using a new gasket
- Camshafts
- Timing belts
- Intake manifold stay
- Upper radiator hose
- Water hose at the water pipe
- Overflow tube
- Brake booster vacuum hose and purge air hose
- Fuel lines-to-fuel supply rail using a new gasket
- Heater hose
- All electrical connectors
- Accelerator cable and adjust as necessary

- Air intake duct and air cleaner assembly
- Oil filter

10. Refill the crankcase and cooling system

11. Turn the ignition to the **ON** position and check for fuel leaks. Then, start the engine and check for coolant leaks and proper operation.

Rocker Arm/Shafts

REMOVAL & INSTALLATION

The DOHC engines do not use rocker arm shafts; the valves are directly actuated by rocker arms. To remove the arms, the camshaft must first be removed. It is recommended that all rocker arms and lash adjusters be replaced together. Refer the camshaft procedure for details.

Turbocharger

REMOVAL & INSTALLATION

1. Be sure to observe all cautions and warnings in the beginning of the section that may be related to this procedure.

2. Drain the crankcase and cooling system.

3. Remove or disconnect the following:
- Negative battery cable.
- Radiator
- Condenser fan/radiator assembly, if equipped with A/C
- Oxygen (O2S) sensor
- Oil dipstick and tube
- Air intake bellows hose
- Wastegate vacuum hose
- Air outlet hose connections
- Upper and lower heat shield
- Power steering pump and bracket assembly

➡️**Leave the hoses connected, wire the pump aside.**

- Exhaust manifold self-locking nuts
- Triangular engine hanger bracket
- Oil feed line-to-turbo eyebolt and gaskets
- Water cooling lines

➡️**The water line under the turbo has a threaded connection.**

- Exhaust pipe nuts and discard the gasket
- Exhaust manifold
- Exhaust manifold-to-turbocharger through-bolts/nuts
- Oil return line capscrews and gasket from under the turbo
- Turbocharger

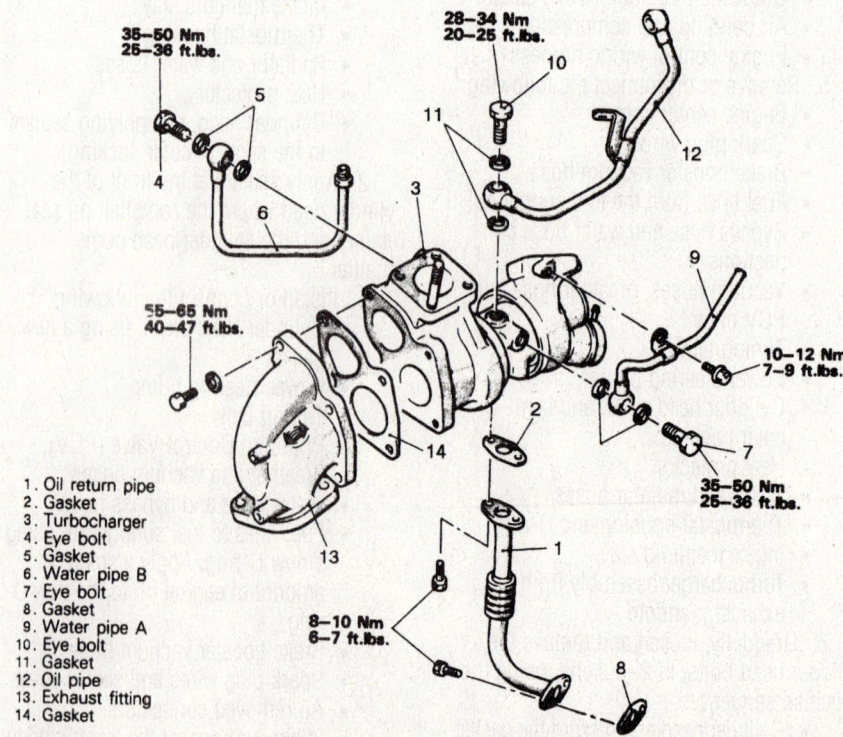

1. Oil return pipe
2. Gasket
3. Turbocharger
4. Eye bolt
5. Gasket
6. Water pipe B
7. Eye bolt
8. Gasket
9. Water pipe A
10. Eye bolt
11. Gasket
12. Oil pipe
13. Exhaust fitting
14. Gasket

35–50 Nm
25–36 ft.lbs.

28–34 Nm
20–25 ft.lbs.

55–65 Nm
40–47 ft.lbs.

10–12 Nm
7–9 ft.lbs.

35–50 Nm
25–36 ft.lbs.

8–10 Nm
6–7 ft.lbs.

Exploded view of the turbocharger assembly—2.0L (VIN F) engine

7922DG06

➤**Both water pipes and oil feed line can remain attached.**

4. Inspect the following items:
   - Turbine (hot side) and compressor (cold side) wheels for cracking or other damage
   - Turbine and compressor wheels for ease of movement
   - Oil leakage
   - Wastegate valve operation. If any problem is found, replace the part
   - Oil passages for restriction or deposits, clean as required

5. Pressure test the wastegate valve by applying approximately 9 psi (62 kPa) to the actuator to make sure the rod moves.

✴✴ WARNING

Do not apply more than 10 psi (71 kPa) for the wastegate diaphragm may be damaged.

➤**The wastegate actuator should maintain vacuum; if not, replace it.**

✴✴ WARNING

Do not attempt to adjust the wastegate valve.

To install:

6. Prime the oil return line with clean engine oil. Replace all locking nuts. Before installing the threaded connection for the water inlet pipe, apply light oil to the inner pipe flange surface.

7. Install or connect the following:
   - Turbocharger
   - Exhaust manifold using a new gasket
   - Water cooling lines
   - Oil feed line
   - Engine hanger
   - Power steering pump and bracket, if removed
   - Heat shields
   - Air outlet hose
   - Wastegate hose
   - Air intake bellows
   - Oil dipstick tube and dipstick
   - O_2S sensor
   - Radiator assembly
   - Negative battery cable

8. Refill the crankcase and cooling system

Intake Manifold

REMOVAL & INSTALLATION

2.0L (VIN F) Engine

1. Be sure to observe all cautions and warnings in the beginning of the section that may be related to this procedure.
2. Relieve the fuel system pressure.
3. Drain the cooling system.
4. Remove or disconnect the following:
   - Negative battery cable
   - Accelerator cable, breather hose and air intake hose
   - Upper radiator hose, heater hose and water bypass hose
   - All necessary vacuum hoses and pipes
   - Brake booster vacuum line
   - High pressure fuel line and fuel return hose
5. Label and disconnect the following the electrical connectors:
   - Oxygen (O_2S) sensor
   - Engine Coolant Temperature (ECT) sensor
   - Thermo switch
   - Idle speed control
   - Exhaust Gas Recirculation (EGR) temperature sensor
   - Spark plug wires
6. Remove or disconnect the following:
   - Fuel rail, with injectors and pressure regulator attached
   - Intake manifold bracket
   - Throttle body water hose
   - Water inlet and heater connections
   - Thermostat housing, if necessary
   - Power brake booster and PCV valve vacuum lines, if connected
   - Intake manifold

To install:

7. Inspect the intake manifold's:
   - Mounting surfaces for cleanliness, cracks or other damage
   - Water passages and air passages, for clogging
8. Install or connect the following:
   - Intake manifold, using a new gasket. Torque the manifold-to-cylinder head bolts in a crisscross pattern, starting from the inside and working outwards, to 11–14 ft. lbs. (15–19 Nm).
   - Fuel rail, with injectors and pressure regulator, lubricate all seals lightly with oil. Torque the retaining

bolts to 84–108 inch lbs. (10–13 Nm).
   - Thermostat housing, if removed
   - Intake manifold brace bracket
   - Throttle body bracket
   - All hoses, cables and electrical connectors
   - Negative battery cable
9. Refill the cooling system
10. Run the engine until the thermostat opens, refill the radiator completely and check for leaks.
11. Adjust the accelerator cable. Check and adjust the ignition timing. Once the vehicle has cooled, recheck the coolant level.

2.0L (VIN Y) Engine

1. Be sure to observe all cautions and warnings in the beginning of the section that may be related to this procedure.
2. Properly relieve the fuel system pressure.
3. Drain the cooling system.
4. Remove or disconnect the following:
   - Negative battery cable
   - Vacuum reservoir, if equipped with cruise control
   - Air intake and breather hoses
   - Accelerator cable from the bracket
   - Engine harness retaining clips
   - Manifold Absolute Pressure (MAP) sensor
   - Coolant Temperature (CT) sensor connector
   - Throttle Position (TP) sensor connector
   - Air Injector Service (AIS) motor connector
   - Engine control wiring harness and move it aside
   - Alternator wiring harness
   - Pollution Control Valve (PCV) hose assembly
   - Vacuum hoses
   - Exhaust Gas Recirculation (EGR) pipe
   - Fuel lines from the fuel rail
   - Intake manifold stay and engine hanger
   - Throttle body
   - Intake manifold plenum and gasket
   - Injector connectors
   - Fuel rail with injectors
   - Intake manifold

To install:

5. Install or connect the following:
   - Intake manifold using a new gasket. Tighten the retainers in a crisscross pattern to 17 ft. lbs. (23 Nm).

- Fuel rail assembly
- Injector connectors
- Intake plenum using a new gasket
- Throttle body using a new gasket
- Intake manifold stay and engine hanger
- Fuel rail fuel lines using new O-rings
- EGR pipe
- Vacuum hoses and PCV hose assembly
- Alternator wiring harness
- Engine control wiring harness and reposition and secure with brackets/clips
- AIS motor and TP sensor
- Vacuum hose at throttle body
- MAP and CT sensors
- Accelerator cable at the bracket and throttle body
- Breather and air intake hoses
- Vacuum reservoir, if equipped
- Negative battery cable
6. Refill the cooling system.
7. Adjust the accelerator cable.

Exhaust Manifold

REMOVAL & INSTALLATION

2.0L (VIN F) Engine

1. Be sure to observe all cautions and warnings in the beginning of the section that may be related to this procedure.
2. Drain the cooling system.
3. Drain the crankcase.
4. Remove or disconnect the following:

- Negative battery cable
- Condenser cooling fan, if equipped with A/C
- Power steering pump and move it aside
- Oxygen (O₂S) sensor harness
- Dipstick tube
- Exhaust pipe-to-turbocharger nuts, separate the exhaust pipe and discard the gasket
- Air intake and vacuum hose connections
- Heat shields at exhaust manifold and turbocharger
- Exhaust manifold-to-turbocharger bolts and nut
- Engine hanger, water and oil lines from the turbocharger, if necessary
- Exhaust manifold and discard gasket

To install:
5. Clean all gasket material from the

mating surfaces and check the manifold for damage.
6. Install or connect the following:

- Exhaust manifold, using a new gasket. Torque the manifold-to-head nuts in a crisscross pattern to 18–22 ft. lbs. (25–30 Nm) and the manifold-to-turbocharger nut/bolts to 40–47 ft. lbs. (55–65 Nm).
- Engine hanger, water and oil lines at the turbocharger
- Heat shields
- Exhaust pipe using a new gasket
- Condenser cooling fan
- Power steering pump
- O₂S sensor harness
- Oil level indicator and tube using a new O-ring
- Negative battery cable

7. Refill the crankcase and cooling system
8. Operate the engine until the thermostat opens.
9. Check for fluid and exhaust leaks. Top off the engine coolant.

2.0L (VIN Y) Engine

1. Be sure to observe all cautions and warnings in the beginning of the section that may be related to this procedure.
2. Drain the cooling system.
3. Remove or disconnect the following:

- Negative battery cable
- Air intake hose
- Upper radiator hose from water outlet
- Air hose connection
- Engine control wiring harness from the rear of the engine
- Water pipe assembly
- Oil dipstick
- Upper heat shield
- Engine hanger
- Pulsed Secondary Air Injection (PAIR) valve from exhaust pipe (manual transaxle)
- Front exhaust pipe from the manifold
- Lower heat shield
- Exhaust manifold and discard gasket

To install:
4. Install or connect the following:

- Exhaust manifold using a new gasket. Torque the nuts and bolts to 17 ft. lbs. (23 Nm).
- Lower heat shield
- Front exhaust pipe using a new gasket
- PAIR valve, if equipped with a manual transaxle
- Engine hanger

- Upper heat shield
- Oil dipstick and water pipe
- Engine wiring harness to the rear of the engine
- Air hose and upper radiator hose
- Air intake hose
- Negative battery cable

5. Refill the cooling system, start the engine and check for leaks.

Front Crankshaft Seal

REMOVAL & INSTALLATION

2.0L (VIN F) Engine

1. Be sure to observe all cautions and warnings in the beginning of the section that may be related to this procedure.
2. Remove or disconnect the following:

- Negative battery cable
- Engine undercover
- Timing belts

➡If reusing the timing belt, be sure to mark the direction of rotation on the belt. This will ensure the same direction of rotation, thereby extending belt life.

- Crankshaft pulley
- Timing belt crankshaft sprocket

➡If the sprocket is difficult to remove, an appropriate puller may be used.

- Crankshaft seal by prying it out

To install:
3. Install or connect the following:

- New crankshaft seal using a driver tool
- Crankshaft sprocket
- Timing belt and remaining components
- Engine undercover
- Negative battery cable

4. Start the engine and check for leaks.

2.0L (VIN Y) Engine

1. Be sure to observe all cautions and warnings in the beginning of the section that may be related to this procedure.
2. Remove or disconnect the following:

- Timing belt
- Crankshaft sprocket using Crankshaft Sprocket Removal tool MB995027
- Crankshaft oil seal using Crankshaft Oil Seal Removal tool MB995020

➡Be careful not the scratch the oil seal bore or the crankshaft sealing surface.

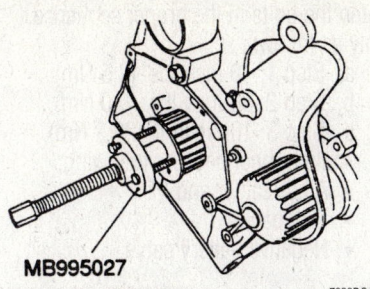

MB995027

To prevent damaging the end of the crankshaft, use the proper sprocket removal tool—2.0L (VIN Y) engine

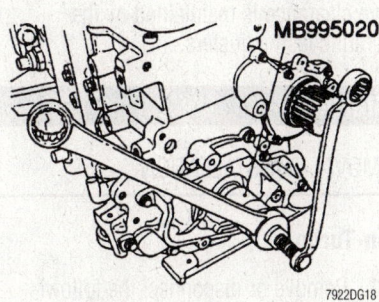

MB995020

Using the special tool to remove the front crankshaft seal—2.0L (VIN Y) engine

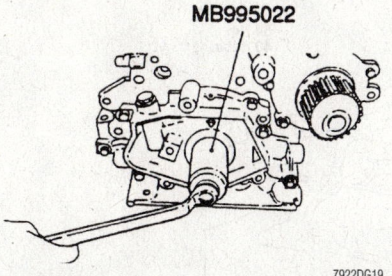

MB995022

To avoid damaging the front seal, use the Front Oil Seal Installer tool MB995022—2.0L (VIN Y) engine

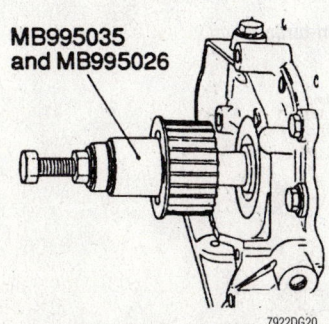

MB995035 and MB995026

Installing the front crankshaft sprocket using the Crankshaft Sprocket Installer tools MB995035 and MB995026—2.0L (VIN Y) engine

To install:

3. Apply clean engine oil to the oil seal.
4. Install or connect the following:
   - Oil seal using a seal driver
   - Crankshaft sprocket using Crankshaft Sprocket Installer tools MB995035 and MB995026
   - Timing belt

Camshaft and Valve Lifters

REMOVAL & INSTALLATION

2.0L (VIN F) Engine

1. Be sure to observe all cautions and warnings in the beginning of the section that may be related to this procedure.
2. Remove or disconnect the following:
   - Negative battery cable
   - Accelerator cable from the throttle body
   - Cable bracket from intake plenum
   - Engine center cover
   - Spark plug cables
   - Breather hose and Pollution Control Valve (PCV) hose from the rocker cover
   - Rocker cover
3. Position the No. 1 piston at Top Dead Center (TDC) on the compression stroke.
4. Remove or disconnect the following:
   - Timing belt
   - Camshaft sprockets

➡ **Use a wrench on the hex shaped part of the camshaft to hold the cam when removing the sprockets.**

   - Bearing caps. Loosen the bearing cap bolts in 2–3 steps.

➡ **If the bearing caps are hard to remove, tap the rear of the camshaft with a plastic hammer.**

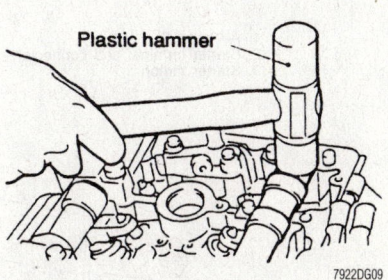

Plastic hammer

Tap the camshaft with a plastic hammer to loosen the bearing caps—2.0L (VIN F) engine

Intake side   Exhaust side

Slits

Identifying the rocker arm shafts—notice the slits in the intake side

✳✳ WARNING

Bearing caps and rocker arms must be installed in the same location from which they were removed.

   - Camshaft(s) and seals

To install:

5. Install or connect the following:
   - Camshafts, lubricate with engine oil and position with the dowels facing up

✳✳ WARNING

If new camshaft(s) are being installed, remove the rocker arms and install the camshaft(s) and bearing caps. Be sure the camshaft(s) can be turned by hand. After checking, remove the camshafts and install the rocker arms.

   - Bearing caps. Torque the bolts evenly, in 2–3 steps to 14 ft. lbs. (20 Nm).
6. Lubricate the seal lip with engine oil.
7. Install or connect the following:
   - Front oil seal using Seal Installer MB998713
   - Camshaft sprockets
   - Timing belt
   - Cylinder head by applying sealant to the semi-circular packing

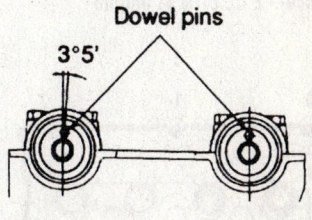

Dowel pins

3°5'

Exhaust side   Intake side

For installation, position the camshafts with the dowels facing up, as shown—2.0L (VIN F) engine

Refer to Section 1 for engine rebuilding specifications

8. Apply sealant to the lower part of the front and rear bearing caps where they meet the cylinder head.

9. Install or connect the following:
- Rocker cover using a new gasket
- Pollution Control Valve (PCV) hose and breather hose
- Spark plug wires
- Center cover
- Accelerator cable and adjust it
- Negative battery cable

2.0L (VIN Y) Engine

1. Be sure to observe all cautions and warnings in the beginning of the section that may be related to this procedure.

2. Remove or disconnect the following:
- Negative battery cable
- Ignition coil pack
- Pollution Control Valve (PCV) hose and breather hose from cylinder head cover
- Semi-circular packing from the rear of the head
- Camshaft Position (CMP) sensor
- Timing belt
- Camshaft sprockets

➡ **Use tool MB990767 and MB998719 to secure the camshaft sprockets when removing the sprocket mounting bolt.**

- Rear timing belt cover and bracket
- Outside camshaft bearing cap

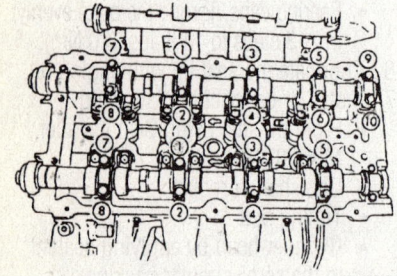

Camshaft bearing cap bolt tightening sequence—2.0L (VIN Y) engine

7922DG03

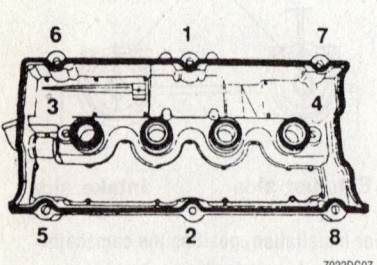

Cylinder head cover bolt tightening sequence—2.0L (VIN Y) engine

7922DG07

- Bearing caps. Gradually, loosen the camshaft bearing caps in the reverse of the tightening sequence, one camshaft at a time.

➡ **Keep the bearing caps in order. They must be installed in the location from which they were removed.**

- Camshafts

➡ **The camshafts are not interchangeable. Mark the camshafts for later identification.**

To install:

3. Install or connect the following:
- Camshafts, lubricate with engine oil
- Bearing caps. Tighten the bolts evenly and in sequence.
- Outside camshaft bearing caps, lubricate them with Loctite 518®
- Camshaft oil seal
- Rear timing belt cover and bracket
- Camshaft sprockets using special tools
- Timing belt
- Semi-circular packing, lubricate with Loctite 5699® at rear of cylinder head
- CMP sensor

4. Install the cylinder head cover.

Tighten the bolts in the proper sequence, evenly as follows:
  a. Step 1: 40 inch lbs. (4.5 Nm).
  b. Step 2: 80 inch lbs. (9.0 Nm).
  c. Step 3: 106 inch lbs. (12 Nm).

5. Install or connect the following:
- Air, breather and PCV
- Coil pack
- Negative battery cable

Valve Lash

ADJUSTMENT

Valve clearance is not adjustable. Proper valve clearance is maintained by the hydraulic lash adjusters.

Starter

REMOVAL & INSTALLATION

Non-Turbo

1. Remove or disconnect the following:
- Negative battery cable
- Starter electrical connectors
- Starter

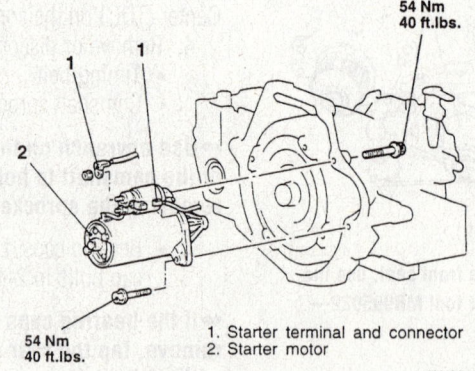

1. Starter terminal and connector
2. Starter motor

9306DG03

Exploded view of the starter and related components—Non-turbo

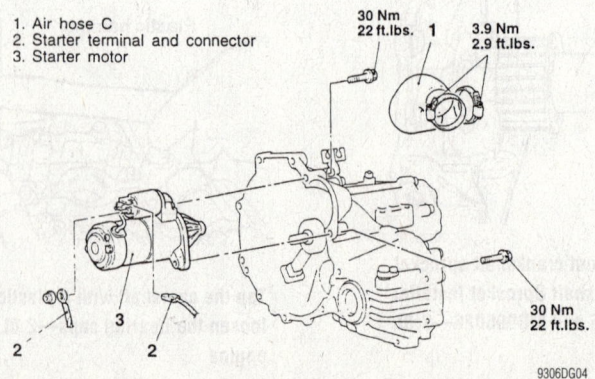

1. Air hose C
2. Starter terminal and connector
3. Starter motor

9306DG04

Exploded view of the starter and related components—Turbo

To install:

2. Install or connect the following:
- Starter. Torque the starter-to-transaxle bolts to 40 ft. lbs. (54 Nm).
- Starter electrical connectors
- Negative battery cable

Turbo

1. Remove or disconnect the following:
- Battery
- Air hose "C"
- Starter electrical connectors
- Starter

To install:

2. Install or connect the following:
- Starter. Torque the starter-to-transaxle bolts to 22 ft. lbs. (30 Nm).
- Starter electrical connectors
- Air hose "C"
- Battery

Oil Pan

REMOVAL & INSTALLATION

2.0L (VIN F) Engine

1. Be sure to observe all cautions and warnings in the beginning of the section that may be related to this procedure.
2. Drain the crankcase.
3. Remove or disconnect the following:
- Negative battery cable
- Exhaust pipe, lower it from the engine manifold
- Transfer assembly and right driveshaft, on All Wheel Drive (AWD) models.
4. Using the appropriate equipment, support the weight of the engine.
5. Remove or disconnect the following:
- Crossmember
- Turbocharger return pipe from the side of the oil pan
- Oil pan bolts. Tap a thin prytool between the engine block and oil pan to break the seal.
6. Inspect the oil pan for damage and cracks. Replace if faulty. While the pan is removed, inspect the oil screen for clogging, damage and cracks. Replace if faulty.

To install:

7. Using a wire brush or other tool, clean all gasket surfaces of the cylinder block and the oil pan so that all loose mate-

rial is removed. Clean sealing surfaces of all dirt and oil.

8. Apply sealant around the gasket surfaces of the oil pan in such a manner that all bolt holes are circled and there is a continuous bead of sealer around the entire perimeter of the oil pan.

➡ **The continuous bead of sealer should be applied in a bead approximately 0.16 in. (4mm) in diameter.**

9. Install or connect the following:
- Oil pan. Install within 15 minutes after applying sealant. Torque bolts to 48–72 inch lbs. (6–8 Nm).
- Oil return pipe using a new gasket. Torque the retainers to 62–88 inch lbs. (7–10 Nm).
- Crossmember. Torque the bolts to 72 ft. lbs. (100 Nm).
- Left member. Torque the forward retainer bolts to 72 ft. lbs. (100 Nm) and the rearward left member bolts to 58 ft. lbs. (80 Nm).
- Transfer assembly and right driveshaft
- Exhaust pipe using a new gasket. Torque the exhaust pipe-to-manifold flange nuts to 43 ft. lbs. (60 Nm).
- Oil drain plug. Torque to 33 ft. lbs. (42 Nm).
- Negative battery cable
10. Refill the crankcase.
11. Start the engine and check for leaks.

2.0L (VIN Y) Engine

1. Be sure to observe all cautions and warnings in the beginning of the section that may be related to this procedure.
2. Drain the engine oil.
3. Remove or disconnect the following:
- Negative battery cable
- Front exhaust pipe
- Dipstick and tube assembly
- Front plate
- Oil pan bolts
- Oil pan and discard the gasket

To install:

4. Clean all traces of old gasket or sealer material from the oil pan and engine block mating surfaces.
5. Apply sealant at the point where the engine block meets the oil pump.
6. Install or connect the following:
- Oil pan using a new gasket. Tighten the bolts to 107 inch lbs. (12 Nm).

- Front plate
- Front exhaust pipe
- Dipstick and tube assembly
- Negative battery cable
7. Refill the crankcase.
8. Start the engine and check for leaks.

Oil Pump

REMOVAL & INSTALLATION

2.0L (VIN F) Engine

✳✳ WARNING

Whenever the oil pump is disassembled or the cover is removed, the gear cavity must be filled with petroleum jelly. This seals the pump and acts like a primer so the oil pump draws oil as soon as the engine turns. Do not use grease.

1. Be sure to observe all cautions and warnings in the beginning of the section that may be related to this procedure.
2. Disconnect the negative battery cable. Rotate the engine so that the No. 1 cylinder is at Top Dead Center (TDC) of its compression stroke. The timing marks should be aligned at this point.
3. Drain the engine oil.
4. Using the proper equipment, support the weight of the engine.
5. Remove or disconnect the following:
- Front engine mount bracket and accessory drive belts
- Timing belt upper and lower covers
- Timing belt and crankshaft sprocket
- Oil pressure sending unit electrical connector
- Oil pressure sensor
- Oil filter and bracket
- Oil pan, oil screen and discard gasket
- Plug cap in the engine front cover, using Special Plug Removal tool MD998162
- Plug on the side of the engine block. Insert a suitable tool with a shaft diameter of 0.32 in. (8mm) into the plug hole. This will hold the silent shaft in position.
- Oil pump driven gear-to-silent shaft bolt
- Front cover mounting bolts

For engine torque specifications, refer to Section 1 of this manual

➡**Note the lengths of the mounting bolts as they are removed for proper installation.**

- Front case cover and oil pump assembly

➡**If necessary, the silent shaft can come out with the cover assembly.**

- Oil pump cover at the rear of the engine front cover
- Oil pump drive and driven gears

6. After disassembling the oil pump, clean all components and remove all residual gasket material from the mating surfaces.

7. Assemble the oil pump gears into the front case and rotate it to ensure smooth movement and no looseness. Be sure there is no ridge wear on the contact surface between the front case and the gear surface of the oil pump front cover.

To install:

8. Install or connect the following:
- Oil pump, by aligning the oil pump drive gear with the driven gear timing marks. Lubricate the gears with engine oil.
- Oil pump cover. Torque the bolts to 13 ft. lbs. (18 Nm).
- New crankshaft seal using an appropriate driver
- New front case gasket. Position Seal Guide tool MD998285 on the front end of the crankshaft to protect the seal from damage. Apply a thin coat of oil to the outer circumference of the seal pilot tool.
- Front case assembly, through a new front case gasket and temporarily tighten the flange bolts
- Oil filter on the bracket using a new oil filter bracket gasket. Torque the bolts to 25 ft. lbs. (34 Nm).

9. Insert a suitable tool into the hole in the left side of the engine block to lock the silent shaft in place.

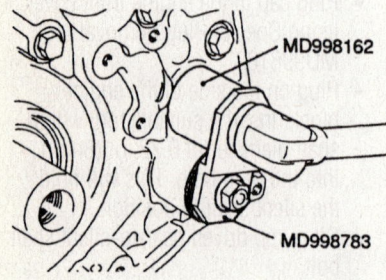

Using the special tool to tighten the plug cap—2.0L (VIN F) engine

10. Secure the oil pump drive gear onto the left silent shaft by installing and tightening the driven gear bolt to 29 ft. lbs. (40 Nm).

11. Install or connect the following:
- Plug cap using a new O-ring in the front case groove. Using the special tool MD998162, tighten the cap to 20 ft. lbs. (27 Nm).
- Oil screen using a new gasket

12. Clean the oil pan and cylinder block mating surfaces. Apply sealant in the oil pan flange groove, keeping towards the inside of the bolt holes. The width of the sealant bead applied is to be about 0.16 in. (4mm) wide.

➡**Install the oil pan within 15 minutes of sealant application.**

13. Install or connect the following:
- Oil pan. Secure with the retainers and torque the bolts to 108 inch lbs. (12 Nm).
- Oil pressure gauge unit and oil pressure switch
- Oil pressure gauge unit and oil pressure switch
- Electrical harness
- Oil cooler. Torque the bolt to 33 ft. lbs. (45 Nm).
- Oil filter and refill the crankcase
- Negative battery cable

14. Start the engine. Verify oil pressure and inspect for leaks.

2.0L (VIN Y) Engine

1. Be sure to observe all cautions and warnings in the beginning of the section that may be related to this procedure.

2. Drain the engine oil.

3. Remove or disconnect the following:
- Negative battery cable
- Rear plate
- Oil filter and adapter
- Oil pan
- Oil pick-up tube
- Timing belt
- Crankshaft sprocket using the Crankshaft Sprocket Removal tool MB995027

✳✳ WARNING

Do not nick the crankshaft sealing surface or the seal bore.

- Crankshaft oil seal using Crankshaft Oil Seal tool MB995020
- Oil pump mounting bolts
- Oil pump

To install:

4. Apply a bead of sealant to the sealing surface of the oil pump and install a new O-ring into the counterbore on the oil pump discharge passage.

5. Install or connect the following:
- Oil pump. Torque the bolts to 17 ft. lbs. (23 Nm).
- New crankshaft oil seal in the oil pump
- Crankshaft sprocket using the proper installation tools
- Timing belt and related components
- Oil pickup tube

6. Apply Loctite® 18718 at the point where the oil pump meets the engine block.

7. Install or connect the following:
- Oil pan using a new gasket. Torque the bolts to 108 inch lbs. (12 Nm).
- Oil filter adapter using a new O-ring. Align the roll pin with the hole and torque the assembly to 40 ft. lbs. (55 Nm).
- New oil filter
- Rear plate
- Negative battery cable

8. Refill the crankcase.

9. Start the engine and check for leaks.

Rear Main Seal

REMOVAL & INSTALLATION

1. Be sure to observe all cautions and warnings in the beginning of the section that may be related to this procedure.

2. Remove or disconnect the following:
- Negative battery cable
- Transaxle
- Transfer case, if equipped
- Drive plate, if equipped with an automatic transaxle
- Bell housing cover and flywheel, if equipped with a manual transaxle
- Crankshaft rear oil seal case, if leaking; otherwise, the oil seal

➡**Some engines have a separator that should also be removed.**

To install:

3. Lubricate the inner diameter of the new seal with clean engine oil.

4. Install or connect the following:
- Oil seal in the crankshaft rear oil seal case using Seal Installer tool MD998376.

➡**Press the seal all the way in without tilting it.**

5. If removed, drive the oil separator into the oil seal case so the its oil hole is facing downward.

6. Install or connect the following:
- Seal case using a new gasket, if removed
- Flywheel or drive plate
- Transfer case, if equipped
- Transaxle
- Negative battery cable

7. Refill the crankcase. Start the engine and check for leaks.

Piston and Ring

POSITIONING

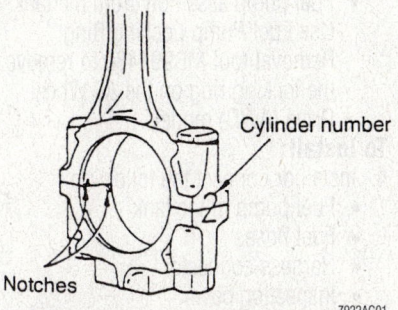

Chrysler engine connecting rod and cap installation—ensure to matchmark the cap and rod prior to disassembly

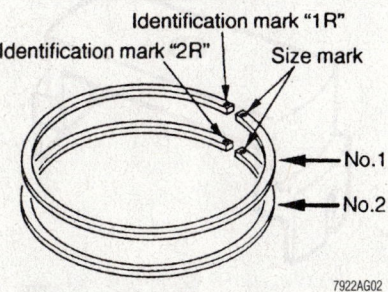

Chrysler piston ring identification mark locations

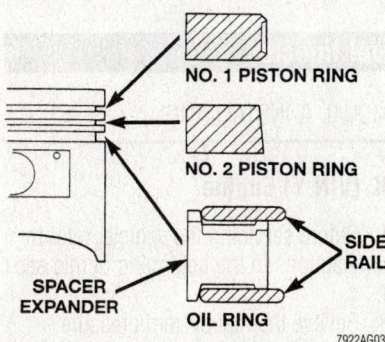

Piston ring orientation—2.0L Engine

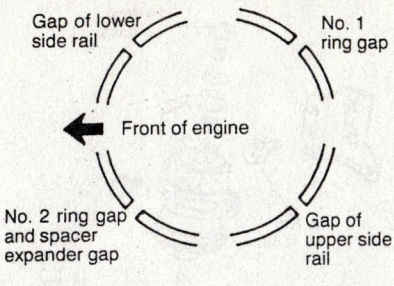

Piston ring end-gap spacing—2.0L (VIN Y) engine

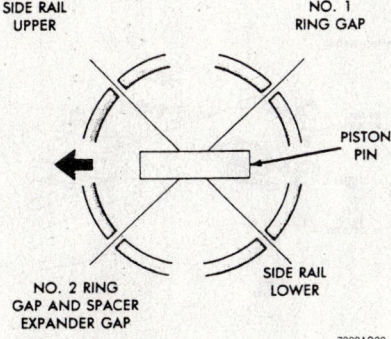

Piston ring end-gap spacing—2.0L (VIN F) engine

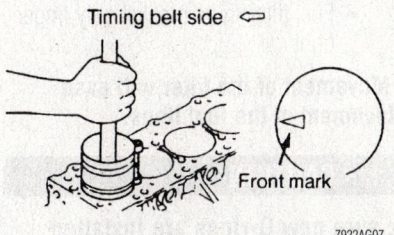

Piston positioning—2.0L (VIN F) engine

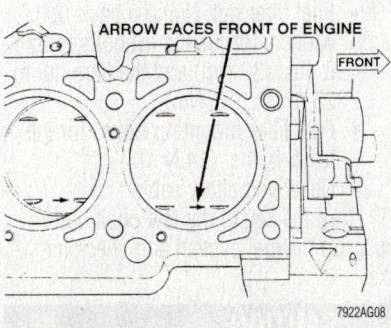

Piston positioning—2.0L (VIN Y) engine. The small arrows on the crown of the pistons must point toward the front of the engine

FUEL SYSTEM

Fuel System Service Precautions

Safety is an important factor when servicing the fuel system. Failure to conduct maintenance and repairs in a safe manner may result in serious personal injury. Maintenance and testing of the vehicle's fuel system components can be accomplished safely and effectively by adhering to the following rules and guidelines.

- To avoid the possibility of fire and personal injury, always disconnect the negative battery cable unless the repair or test procedure requires that battery voltage be applied.
- Always relieve the fuel system pressure prior to disconnecting any fuel system component (injector, fuel rail, pressure regulator, etc.), fitting or fuel line connection. Exercise extreme caution whenever relieving fuel system pressure, to avoid exposing skin, face and eyes to fuel spray. Please be advised that fuel under pressure may penetrate the skin or any part of the body that it contacts.
- Always place a shop towel or cloth around the fitting or connection prior to loosening to absorb any excess fuel due to spillage. Ensure that all fuel spillage is quickly removed from engine surfaces. Ensure that all fuel soaked cloths or towels are deposited into a suitable waste container.
- Always keep a dry chemical (Class B) fire extinguisher near the work area.
- Do not allow fuel spray or fuel vapors to come into contact with a spark or open flame.
- Always use a back-up wrench when loosening and tightening fuel line connection fittings. This will prevent unnecessary stress and torsion to fuel line piping.
- Always replace worn fuel fitting O-rings. Do not substitute fuel hose where fuel pipe is installed.

Fuel System Pressure

RELIEVING

1. Be sure to observe all cautions and warnings in the beginning of the section that may be related to this procedure.

2. Remove or disconnect the following:
- Rear seat cushion
- Protector
- Fuel pump connector

3. Start the engine and allow it to run until it stops, due to lack of fuel. Turn the ignition switch to the **OFF** position.
- Disconnect the negative battery cable.

After relieving fuel pressure:

4. Install or connect the following:
- Fuel pump connector
- Protector
- Rear seat cushion

Fuel Filter

REMOVAL & INSTALLATION

On most vehicles, the fuel filter is located in the engine compartment, mounted on the firewall. On some non-turbo engines, the fuel filter is mounted under the vehicle near the fuel tank.

✳✳ CAUTION

Do not use conventional fuel filters, hoses or clamps when servicing fuel injection systems. They are not compatible with the injection system and could fail, causing personal injury or damage to the vehicle. Use only hoses and clamps specifically designed for fuel injection systems.

1. Properly relieve the fuel system pressure.
2. On non-turbo engines, raise and safely support the vehicle to gain access to the filter.

➡**Wrap shop towels around the fitting that is being disconnected to absorb residual fuel in the lines.**

3. Cover the hose connection with shop towels to prevent any splash of fuel that could be caused by residual pressure in the fuel pipe line.
4. Remove or disconnect the following:
- Negative battery cable
- Eye bolt, by holding the fuel filter nut securely with a back-up wrench
- High-pressure fuel line from the filter and discard gaskets
- Main pipe flare nut, loosen it while holding the fuel filter nut securely with a back-up wrench
- Flare nut connection from the filter and discard gaskets

5. If equipped with a fuel tank mounted filter, remove or disconnect the following:
- Eyebolt, gasket and connector
- Pressure regulator
- Fuel filter bolts and filter
- Fuel filter bracket, if necessary

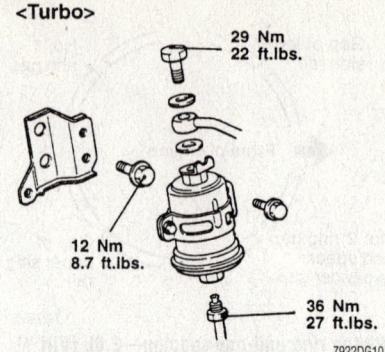

<Turbo>

29 Nm
22 ft.lbs.

12 Nm
8.7 ft.lbs.

36 Nm
27 ft.lbs.

7922DG10

Exploded view of the fuel filter mounting—2.0L (VIN F) engine

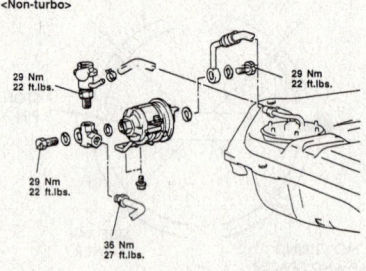

<Non-turbo>

29 Nm
22 ft.lbs.

29 Nm
22 ft.lbs.

29 Nm
22 ft.lbs.

36 Nm
27 ft.lbs.

7922DG11

Exploded view of the fuel filter mounting—2.0L (VIN Y) engine

To install:

6. Install or connect the following:
- Fuel filter in its bracket only finger-tight

➡**Movement of the filter will ease attachment of the fuel lines.**

✳✳ CAUTION

Be sure new O-rings are installed prior to assembly.

- Main pipe at the filter. Manually, screw in the main pipe's flare nut.
- Fuel filter nut. Using a back-up wrench, torque the eyebolts to 22 ft. lbs. (30 Nm) and the flare nut to 25 ft. lbs. (35 Nm).
- Fuel filter mounting bolts. Torque to 10 ft. lbs. (14 Nm).
- Negative battery cable

7. Turn the key to the **ON** position to pressurize the fuel system and check for leaks.

✳✳ CAUTION

If repairs of a leak are required, remember to release the fuel pressure before opening the fuel system.

Fuel Pump

REMOVAL & INSTALLATION

1. Be sure to observe all cautions and warnings in the beginning of the section that may be related to this procedure.
2. Relieve the fuel system pressure.
3. Remove or disconnect the following:
- Negative battery cable
- Rear seat cushion, by pulling the seat stopper near the floor and lifting the cushion up
- Inspection cover on the right side of the vehicle
- Harness connector
- Fuel lines
- Fuel pump assembly from the tank. Use Fuel Pump Locking Ring Removal tool MB991480 to remove the locking ring on the All Wheel Drive (AWD) model.

To install:

4. Install or connect the following:
- Fuel pump in the tank
- Fuel hoses
- Harness connector
- Inspection cover
- Rear seat
- Negative battery cable

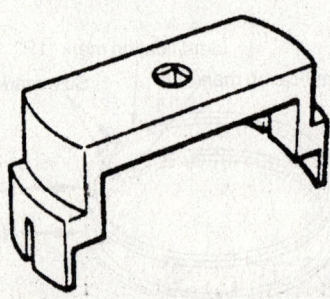

7922DG22

To service the fuel pump on AWD vehicles, a Fuel Pump Locking Ring Removal tool MB991480 is needed

Fuel Injector

REMOVAL & INSTALLATION

2.0L (VIN Y) Engine

1. Before servicing the vehicle, refer to the precautions in the beginning of this section.
2. Relieve the fuel system pressure.
3. Remove or disconnect the following:
- Battery
- Air intake hose

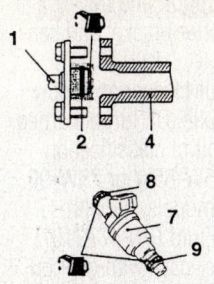

1. High-pressure fuel hose connection
2. O-ring
3. Injector harness connector
4. Fuel rail
5. Injector connectors
6. Retainers
7. Injectors
8. O-rings
9. O-rings

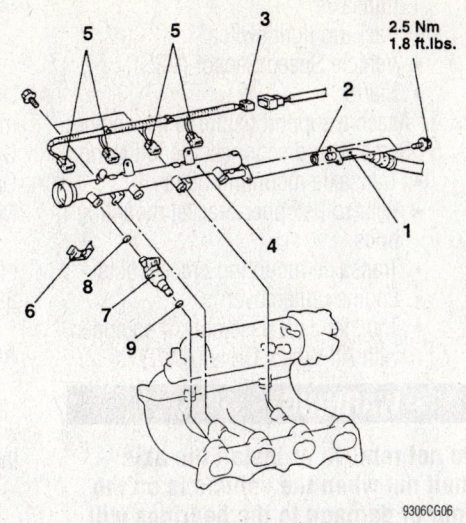

2.5 Nm
1.8 ft.lbs.

9306CG06

Exploded view of the fuel injector, fuel rail and related components—2.0L (VIN Y) engine

- High pressure fuel hose connection
- Discard O-ring
- Fuel injector harness connector
- Fuel rail
- Fuel injector electrical connectors
- Fuel injector-to-fuel rail retainer(s)
- Fuel injectors and discard the O-rings

To install:
4. Install or connect the following:
- New fuel injector O-rings
- Fuel injectors

➡**Lubricate the O-rings with clean engine oil; then, install the injectors into the fuel rail by twisting them (left and right) to make sure that they turn smoothly in the seat.**

❋❋ WARNING

Do not allow engine oil to get into the fuel rail.

- Fuel injector-to-fuel rail retainer(s)
- Fuel injector electrical connectors
- Fuel rail
- Fuel injector harness connector
- New high-pressure fuel hose O-ring

➡**Lubricate the O-ring with clean engine oil.**

❋❋ WARNING

Do not allow engine oil to get into the fuel rail.

- High pressure fuel hose connection. Torque the fuel hose-to-fuel rail bolts to 1.8 ft. lbs. (2.5 Nm).
- Air intake hose
- Battery

2.0L (VIN F) Engine

1. Before servicing the vehicle, refer to the precautions in the beginning of this section.
2. Relieve the fuel system pressure.
3. Remove or disconnect the following:
- Negative battery cable
- Spark plug cables
- High pressure fuel line connection
- O-ring and discard it
- Fuel return line connection
- Vacuum hose connection
- Fuel pressure regulator
- O-ring and discard it
- PCV hose
- Fuel injector connectors
- Fuel rail
- Insulators
- Fuel injector(s)
- O-rings and discard them
- Grommets and discard them

To install:
4. Install or connect the following:
- New grommets
- New O-rings

➡**Lubricate the O-rings with clean engine oil.**

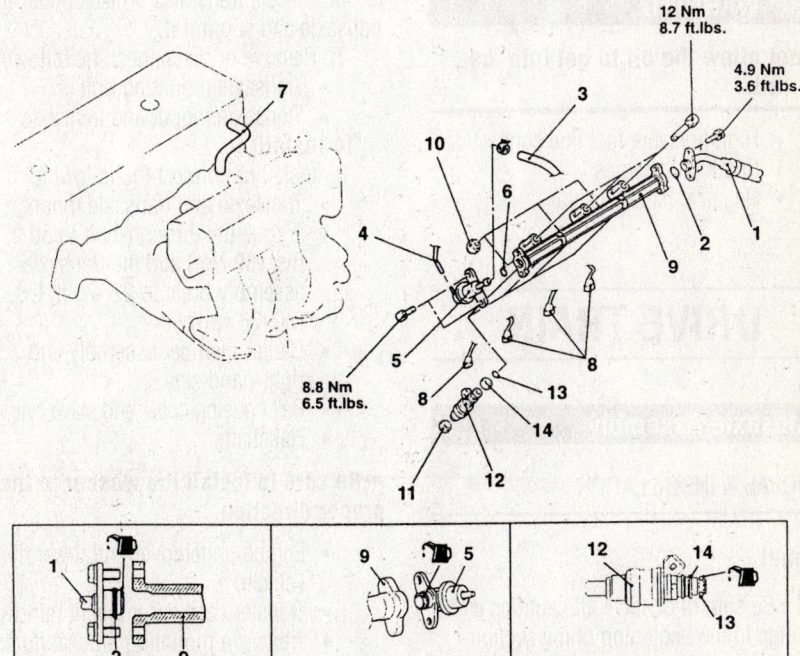

12 Nm
8.7 ft.lbs.

4.9 Nm
3.6 ft.lbs.

8.8 Nm
6.5 ft.lbs.

1. High-pressure fuel hose connection
2. O-ring
3. Fuel return hose connection
4. Vacuum hose connection
5. Fuel pressure regulator
6. O-ring
7. PCV hose

8. Injector connectors
9. Fuel rail
10. Insulators
11. Insulators
12. Injectors
13. O-rings
14. Grommets

9306DG05

Exploded view of the fuel injector, fuel rail and related components—2.0L (VIN F) engine

❉❉ WARNING

Do not allow the oil to get into the fuel rail. Make sure the fuel injector turns smoothly.

- Fuel injector(s)
- New insulators
- Fuel rail
- Fuel injector connectors
- PCV hose
- New O-ring

➡️**Lubricate the O-ring with clean engine oil.**

❉❉ WARNING

Do not allow the oil to get into the fuel rail. Make sure the fuel pressure regulator turns smoothly.

- Fuel pressure regulator. Torque to 6.5 ft. lbs. (8.8 Nm).
- Vacuum hose connection
- Fuel return line connection
- New O-ring

➡️**Lubricate the O-ring with clean engine oil.**

❉❉ WARNING

Do not allow the oil to get into the fuel rail.

- High pressure fuel line connection
- Spark plug cables
- Negative battery cable

DRIVE TRAIN

Transaxle Assembly

REMOVAL & INSTALLATION

Manual

1. Be sure to observe all cautions and warnings in the beginning of the section that may be related to this procedure.
2. Drain the transaxle and transfer case fluid, if equipped.
3. Remove or disconnect the following:
   - Battery
   - Air intake hoses
   - Battery tray and support
   - Auto-cruise actuator and bracket, if equipped with cruise control
   - Charcoal canister and bracket

- Shift and select cables from the transaxle
- Back-up light switch
- Vehicle Speed Sensor (VSS)
- Starter

4. Attach a support fixture to the engine.
5. Remove or disconnect the following:
   - Transaxle mounting bolts
   - Rear roll stopper bracket mounting bolts
   - Transaxle mounting bracket nuts
   - Engine undercover
   - Transfer case assembly, if equipped with All Wheel Drive (AWD)

❉❉ WARNING

Do not remove or install the axle shaft nut when the vehicle is on the floor or damage to the bearings will occur.

- Halfshafts
- Slave cylinder from the bell housing. Do not disconnect the fluid line and position it aside.
- Bell housing cover
- Right-hand center member stay (support)
- Center member

6. Place a transmission jack under the transaxle and support it.
7. Remove or disconnect the following:
   - Transaxle mounting bolt
   - Transaxle mount and transaxle

To install:

8. Install or connect the following:
   - Transaxle and transaxle mount. Torque the through-bolt to 50 ft. lbs. (69 Nm) and the transaxle assembly bolts to 22–25 ft. lbs. (30–34 Nm).
   - Center member assembly and right-hand stay
   - Bell housing cover and slave cylinder
   - Halfshafts

➡️**Be sure to install the washer in the proper direction.**

- Engine undercover and lower the vehicle.
- Transfer case assembly, if removed
- Transaxle mounting bracket nuts
- Rear roll stopper bracket mounting bolts
- Transaxle assembly mounting bolts. Torque the mounting bolts to 35 ft. lbs. (48 Nm).

9. Remove the engine support fixture.
10. Install or connect the following:
    - Starter
    - VSS and back-up light connectors
    - Cruise control actuator, if removed

- Battery tray support and tray
- Charcoal canister bracket and canister
- Air duct and air cleaner assembly

11. Refill the transaxle. On turbocharged models, fill with gear oil of classification GL-4 or higher, SAE 75W-85W or 75W-90. On non-turbocharged models, fill with Mopar MS9417 MTX Fluid P/N 4773167.
12. Refill the transfer case with gear oil of classification GL-4 or higher, SAE 75W-85W or 75W-90.

Automatic

1. Be sure to observe all cautions and warnings in the beginning of the section that may be related to this procedure.
2. Drain the transaxle fluid.
3. Remove or disconnect the following:
   - Negative battery cable
   - Battery and battery tray
   - Control actuator and bracket, if equipped with auto-cruise
   - Air cleaner assembly, intercooler and air hose, as required
4. Mark the shift cable's location.
5. Remove or disconnect the following:
   - Adjusting nut and shift cable
   - Dipstick and tube assembly
   - Solenoid connector
   - Neutral safety switch (inhibitor switch) connector
   - Pulse generator kickdown servo switch connector
   - Oil temperature sensor connector
   - Speedometer cable and oil cooler lines
   - Starter
   - Upper transaxle-to-engine bolts
   - Transaxle mounting bracket supporting the transaxle
   - Sheet metal undercover
   - Tie rod ends and ball joints from steering knuckle
   - Halfshafts
   - Exhaust pipe and transfer case, on All Wheel Drive (AWD) vehicles
   - Lower bell housing cover
   - Flexplate-to-torque converter special bolts

➡️**To remove the bolts, turn the engine crankshaft with a box wrench and bring the bolts into a position appropriate for removal, one at a time.**

❉❉ WARNING

After removing the bolts, push the torque converter toward the transaxle so it doesn't stay on the engine, allowing oil to pour out of the con-

verter hub or cause damage to the converter.

- Lower transaxle-to-engine bolts and transaxle

To install:

6. Install or connect the following:
- Transaxle. Torque the transaxle-to-engine bolts to 35 ft. lbs. (48 Nm) and the torque converter-to-drive-plate bolts to 34–38 ft. lbs. (46–53 Nm).
- Bell housing cover
- Transfer case and exhaust pipe, using a new gasket, for AWD models
- Circlips and halfshafts
- Tie rods and ball joint
- Transaxle mounting bracket
- Under-guard
- Starter
- Speedometer cable and oil cooler lines
- Solenoid connector
- Neutral safety switch (inhibitor switch) connector
- Pulse generator kickdown servo switch connector
- Oil temperature sensor connector
- All remaining components

7. Refill with Dexron®II, Mopar ATF Plus type 7176, Mitsubishi Plus ATF automatic transaxle fluid. If equipped with AWD, check and fill the transfer case.

8. Start the engine and allow it to idle for 2 minutes. Apply the parking brake and move the selector through each gear position, ending in **N** (neutral). Recheck the fluid level and add, if necessary.

➡ **If the vehicle has run for less than 15 minutes but more than one minute, the fluid is considered warm and should be above the ADD mark on the dipstick. Do not add fluid unless the level is at or below the ADD mark.**

Clutch

ADJUSTMENTS

Clutch Pedal Free-Play

1. Measure the clutch pedal height from the face of the pedal pad to the firewall.

2. Compare the measured value with the proper distance of 6.93–7.17 in. (176–182mm).

3. Measure the clutch pedal clevis pin play at the face of the pedal pad. Press the pedal lightly until resistance is met, and measure this distance. The clutch pedal clevis pin play should be within 0.04–0.12 in. (1–3mm).

4. If the clutch pedal height or clevis pin play are not within the standard values, adjust as follows:

a. If not equipped with cruise control, turn and adjust the stop bolt so the pedal height is the standard value, then tighten the locknut.

b. If equipped with cruise control, detach the clutch switch connector and turn the switch to obtain the standard clutch pedal height. Then, lock by tightening the locknut.

c. Turn the pushrod to adjust the clutch pedal clevis pin play to agree with the standard value and secure the pushrod with the locknut.

➡ **When adjusting the clutch pedal height or the clutch pedal clevis pin play, be careful not to push the pushrod toward the master cylinder.**

d. Check that when the clutch pedal is depressed all the way, the interlock switch changes from ON to OFF.

REMOVAL & INSTALLATION

2.0L (VIN F) Engine

1. Be sure to observe all cautions and warnings in the beginning of the section that may be related to this procedure.

2. Remove or disconnect the following:
- Transaxle
- Clutch oil tubes by unscrewing the fittings
- Clutch oil fluid chamber
- Clutch release (slave) cylinder union bolt, gaskets and union
- Valve plate and valve plate spring
- Clutch release (slave) cylinder, without disconnecting the fluid line
- Pressure plate
- Clutch disc
- Clutch release bearing by unfastening the return clip
- Release fork by sliding it away from the fulcrum

❄ WARNING

Be careful not to cause damage to the clip by pushing the fork in any other direction or removing it with force.

- Release fork boot and fulcrum

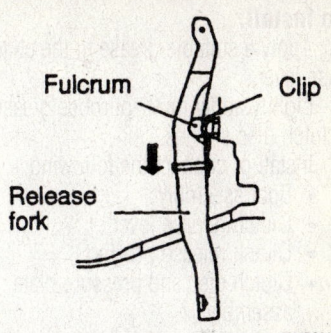

Fulcrum   Clip

Release fork

9300DG04

Slide the release fork in the direction of the arrow to disengage it from the pivot ball

To install:

3. Install or connect the following:
- Fulcrum and release fork boot
- Clutch release fork
- Return clip

4. Apply grease to the clutch release fork contact areas.

5. Lubricate the clutch release bearing.

6. Lightly apply multi-purpose grease to the clutch disc splines.

7. Install or connect the following:
- Clutch disc using a suitable guide to position the disc on the flywheel
- Pressure plate
- Clutch release (slave) cylinder. Tighten the bolts to 13 ft. lbs. (18 Nm).
- Valve plate spring and valve plate
- Gasket, union, gasket and union bolt, on the release cylinder
- Clutch oil fluid chamber. Uncap or unplug the clutch oil tubes, then attach them and tighten the fittings to 11 ft. lbs. (15 Nm).
- Transaxle

2.0L (VIN Y) Engine

1. Be sure to observe all cautions and warnings in the beginning of the section that may be related to this procedure.

2. Remove or disconnect the following:
- Transaxle
- Clutch oil tube by unscrewing the fitting

➡ **Plug or cap the ends to prevent contamination from entering the line.**

- Release (slave) cylinder
- Pressure plate and clutch disc
- Clutch release bearing
- Clutch release lever
- Boot

To install:

3. Apply a suitable grease to the clutch release lever.

4. Lightly apply multi-purpose grease to the clutch disc splines.

5. Install or connect the following:
- Boot assembly
- Clutch release lever
- Clutch release bearing
- Clutch disc and pressure plate assembly
- Clutch release (slave) cylinder

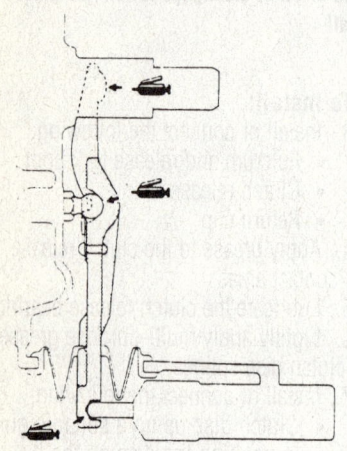

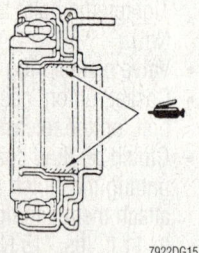

Lubrication points for the clutch release lever and bearing

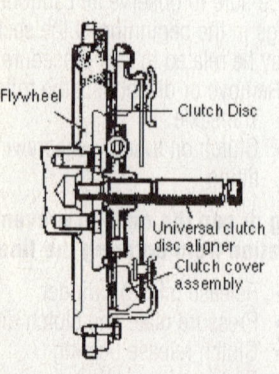

Cross-sectional view of proper clutch disc and pressure plate alignment, showing the alignment tool

- Clutch oil tube
- Transaxle

Hydraulic Clutch System

BLEEDING

➡**Do not allow the reservoir to run out of fluid during bleeding, otherwise the entire procedure must be repeated.**

1. Fill the reservoir with clean brake fluid meeting DOT 3 specifications.

2. Attach a hose to the bleeder valve on the slave cylinder with the other end of the hose submerged in a container at least half full of fresh DOT 3 brake fluid from a sealed container.

3. Have an assistant press the clutch pedal to the floor, then loosen the bleed screw on the slave cylinder.

4. Tighten the bleed screw and have your helper release the clutch pedal.

5. Repeat the procedure until the fluid is free of air bubbles.

Transfer Case Assembly

REMOVAL & INSTALLATION

1. Be sure to observe all cautions and warnings in the beginning of the section that may be related to this procedure.

2. Drain the transfer oil.

3. Remove or disconnect the following:
- Negative battery cable
- Front exhaust pipe
- Transfer case assembly

➡**Be careful not to damage the transfer case's output housing oil seal. Do not let the rear driveshaft hang; suspend it from the body with a piece of wire. Cover the opening in the transaxle and transfer case to keep oil from dripping and to keep dirt out.**

To install:

4. Lubricate the driveshaft sleeve yoke and oil seal lip on the transfer extension housing with clean engine oil.

5. Install or connect the following:
- Transfer case assembly. Torque the transfer case-to-transaxle bolts to 40–43 ft. lbs. (55–60 Nm) on manual transaxle or 43–58 ft. lbs. (60–80 Nm) on automatic transaxle.

➡**Use care when installing the rear driveshaft to the transfer case output shaft.**

- Front exhaust pipe using a new gasket

6. Refill the transfer case with gear oil of classification GL-4 or higher, SAE 75W-85W or 75W-90. Check the fluid level in the transaxle and add, as required.

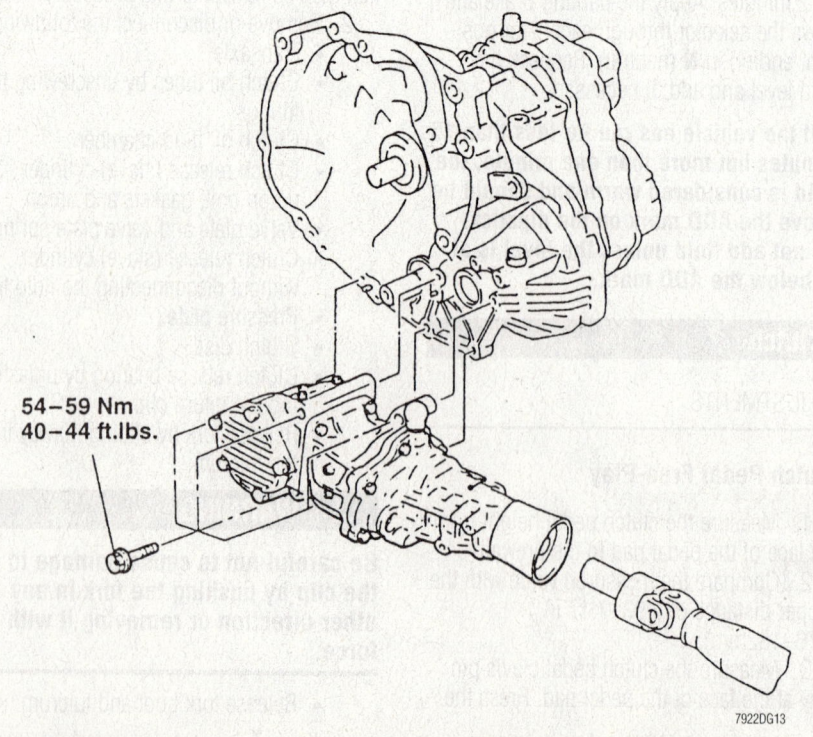

54–59 Nm
40–44 ft.lbs.

Exploded view of the transfer case assembly mounting—Vehicles with manual transaxle

Halfshaft

REMOVAL & INSTALLATION

Front

1. Be sure to observe all cautions and warnings in the beginning of the section that may be related to this procedure.

❊❊ WARNING

If the vehicle is going to be rolled with the halfshafts removed, install 2 outer CV-joints or equivalent tools in the hubs. Also, if proper torque is not applied to the front wheel bearings, the bearings will no longer be usable.

2. Remove or disconnect the following:
   - Negative battery cable.
   - Cotter pin, halfshaft nut and washer
   - Speedometer drive from the right extension housing if removing the right halfshaft
   - Tie rod from the steering knuckle
   - Stabilizer link from the damper fork
   - Damper fork from the lateral lower arm
   - Lateral lower arm from the steering knuckle

❊❊ WARNING

Use of improper methods of joint separation can result in damage to the joint, leading to possible failure.

   - Center support bearing bracket bolts, if equipped with an inner shaft on All Wheel Drive (AWD) vehicles
   - Halfshaft by pressing it from the hub
   - Halfshaft/inner shaft assembly by tapping it from the transaxle with a plastic hammer on AWD vehicles
   - Halfshafts by prying it from the transaxle on FWD vehicles

❊❊ WARNING

Do not pull on the shaft to dislodge it from the transaxle; doing so damages the inboard joint. Do not insert the prybar too far or the oil seal in the case may be damaged.

To install:

3. Inspect the halfshaft boot for damage or deterioration. Check the ball joints and splines for wear.

4. Install or connect the following:
   - Circlips on the halfshaft ends
   - Halfshaft into the transaxle

➡ Be sure it is fully seated.

   - Halfshaft into the hub
   - Center bearing bracket, if equipped. Torque the bolts to 33 ft. lbs. (45 Nm).
   - Washer, face the chamfered edge outward
   - Halfshaft nut, temporarily tighten
   - Tie rod end and ball joint, to the steering knuckle. Torque the ball joint nut to 21 ft. lbs. (28 Nm) and the tie rod nut to 17–25 ft. lbs. (24–33 Nm).
   - Wheel. Torque the axle nut to 145–188 ft. lbs. (200–260 Nm) with the brakes applied.
   - New cotter pin

Rear

1. Be sure to observe all cautions and warnings in the beginning of the section that may be related to this procedure.

2. Install or connect the following:
   - Rear wheel(s)
   - Wheel speed sensor, if equipped with Anti-Lock Brake System (ABS)
   - Brake caliper and rotor or brake drum
   - Parking brake shoes (disc brakes) or shoe/lever assembly (drum brakes)
   - Parking brake cable from the backing plate
   - Wheel cylinder brake line, if equipped with drum brakes
   - Shock absorber from the steering knuckle
   - Trailing arm and lower arm from the steering knuckle
   - Toe control arm from the steering knuckle
   - Cotter pin, nut and washer from the halfshaft
   - Differential mount support.
   - Halfshaft by prying it from the differential housing
   - Halfshaft from the hub assembly

To install:

3. Install or connect the following:
   - Halfshaft in the hub assembly

   - New circlip on the inner shaft
   - Halfshaft into the differential
   - Differential mount support
   - Washer on the halfshaft in the correct direction
   - Halfshaft nut. Torque it to 145–188 ft. lbs. (196–255 Nm).

➡ If the cotter pin hole does not align, tighten the nut to 188 ft. lbs. (255 Nm) and install the cotter pin in the first hole that aligns.

   - Toe control arm, trailing arm and lower arm. Torque the toe control arm nut to 20 ft. lbs. (28 Nm), trailing arm nut to 85–99 ft. lbs. (118–137 Nm) and lower arm nut to 71 ft. lbs. (98 Nm).
   - Lower shock mount to the steering knuckle
   - Wheel cylinder brake line, if removed
   - Parking brake cable
   - Remaining brake components
   - ABS wheel speed sensor, if removed
   - Rear wheel
   - Brake drums, if equipped
4. Bleed the brake system.

CV-Joints

OVERHAUL

❊❊ WARNING

The Birfield joint assembly, located on the wheel side of the halfshaft, is not to be disassembled; repair of this joint is only by replacement of the halfshaft.

Tri-Pot Joint

FRONT WHEEL DRIVE (FWD)

1. Remove halfshaft and place it in a soft jawed vise.
2. Disassemble or remove the following:
   - Tri-pot boot bands
   - Tri-pot case

➡ Wipe the grease from the tri-pot case.

   - Halfshaft snapring
   - Tri-pot spider assembly

❊❊ WARNING

Do not disassemble the spider assembly.

   - Tri-pot boot

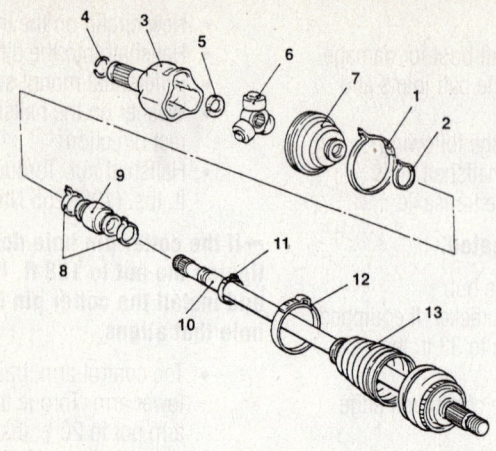

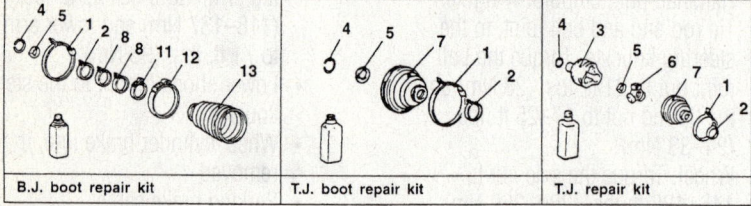

1. T.J. boot band (large)
2. T.J. boot band (small)
3. T.J. case
4. Circlip
5. Snap ring
6. Spider assembly
7. T.J. boot
8. Damper band
9. Dynamic damper

10. B.J. assembly
11. B.J.boot band (small)
12. B.J.boot band (large)
13. B.J. boot

Caution
Do not disassemble the B.J. assembly except replacement of the B.J. boot.

9306DG06

Exploded view of the front halfshaft assemblies—Front wheel drive

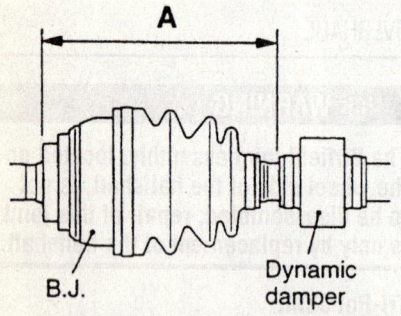

9306CG09

Positioning the dynamic damper on the front halfshaft assemblies—Front wheel drive

✳✳ WARNING

If the boot is to be reused, wrap plastic tape around the shaft splines to protect the boot from damage.

- Dynamic damper bands from the halfshaft, if necessary

To install:

3. If removed, install the dynamic damper by performing the following procedure:

   a. Slide the damper onto the halfshaft with new bands.

b. Position the damper so the distance from the front of the Birfield joint to the front edge of the damper assembly is 14.60–14.84 in. (371–377mm) for the right halfshaft (non-turbo)/left halfshaft (turbo) or 7.52–7.76 in. (191–197mm) for the left halfshaft (non-turbo, M/T).

   c. Tighten and secure the damper bands.

✳✳ WARNING

Wrap plastic tape around the shaft splines to protect the boot from damage.

4. Install a new small boot clamp onto the halfshaft followed by the tri-pot boot.

5. Apply the specified repair kit grease between the spider axle and the roller.

6. Install the tri-pot spider assembly onto the shaft from the spline beveled section direction and secure with the snapring.

7. Distribute a portion of the 3.7 oz. (105 g) for non-turbo or 4.23 oz. (120 g) for turbo specified repair kit grease into the tri-pot case, insert the spider assembly and add the remaining grease.

8. Install the tri-pot boot by performing the following procedure:

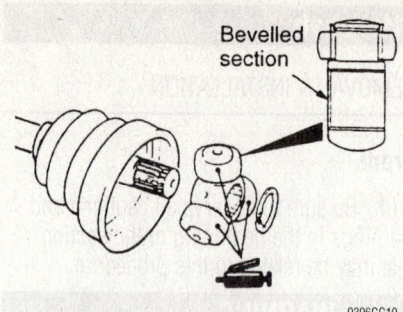

9306CG10

Lubricating the tri-pot spider assembly

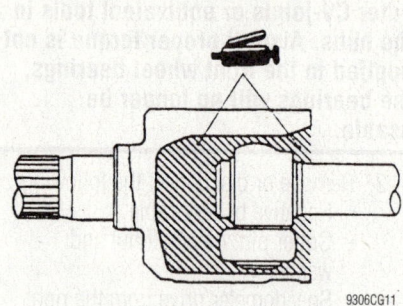

9306CG11

Lubricating the tri-pot case assembly installed

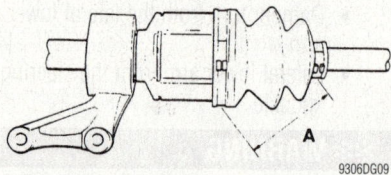

9306DG09

Measuring the tri-pot joint boot

   a. Position the boots large end on the tri-pot case.

   b. Position the large and small boot clamps onto the boot.

   c. Adjust the boot so that the bands are spaced at 3.03–3.27 in. (77–83mm).

   d. Tighten the band securely.

ALL WHEEL DRIVE (AWD): FRONT

1. Remove halfshaft and place it in a soft jawed vise.

2. Disassemble or remove the following:
   - Tri-pot boot bands
   - Tri-pot case (right halfshaft) or tri-pot case/inner shaft assembly (left halfshaft)

➡ Wipe the grease from the tri-pot case.

   - Halfshaft snapring
   - Tri-pot spider assembly

❈❈ WARNING

Do not disassemble the spider assembly.

- Tri-pot boot

❈❈ WARNING

If the boot is to be reused, wrap plastic tape around the shaft splines to protect the boot from damage.

3. If working with the left halfshaft and it is necessary to replace the tri-pot case, press the case from the inner shaft assembly.

To install:

4. If installing a new tri-pot case onto the left halfshaft, perform the following procedure:

a. Lubricate the inner shaft splines with Multi-Mileage Grease No. 2525035.

b. Press the inner shaft assembly into tri-pot case.

c. Secure the tri-pot case with special tool MB991248 on a hydraulic press with the case facing upward.

d. Position a new seal plate in the center of the tri-pot case.

e. Place a 1.18 in. (30mm) pipe on the seal plate and press the seal into the tri-pot case.

❈❈ WARNING

Wrap plastic tape around the shaft splines to protect the boot from damage.

5. Install a new small boot clamp onto the halfshaft followed by the tri-pot boot.

6. Apply the specified repair kit grease between the spider axle and the roller.

7. Install the tri-pot spider assembly onto the shaft from the spline beveled section direction and secure with the snapring.

8. Distribute a portion of the 3.70 oz. (105 g) specified repair kit grease into the tri-pot case, insert the spider assembly and add the remaining grease.

9. Install the tri-pot boot by performing the following procedure:

a. Position the boots large end on the tri-pot case.

b. Position the large and small boot clamps onto the boot.

c. Adjust the boot so that the bands are spaced at 3.03–3.27 in. (77–83mm).

d. Tighten the band securely.

ALL WHEEL DRIVE (AWD): REAR

1. Remove halfshaft and place it in a soft jawed vise.

2. Disassemble or remove the following:
- Tri-pot boot bands
- Tri-pot case

➡ **Wipe the grease from the tri-pot case.**

- Halfshaft snapring
- Tri-pot spider assembly

❈❈ WARNING

Do not disassemble the spider assembly.

- Tri-pot boot

❈❈ WARNING

If the boot is to be reused, wrap plastic tape around the shaft splines to protect the boot from damage.

To install:

❈❈ WARNING

Wrap plastic tape around the shaft splines to protect the boot from damage.

3. Install a new small boot clamp onto the halfshaft followed by the tri-pot boot.

4. Apply the specified repair kit grease between the spider axle and the roller.

5. Install the tri-pot spider assembly onto the shaft from the spline beveled section direction and secure with the snapring.

6. Distribute a portion of the specified repair kit grease into the tri-pot case, insert the spider assembly and add the remaining grease.

- Conventional: 3.35 oz. (95 g)
- Limited slip: 3.70 oz. (105 g)

7. Install the tri-pot boot by performing the following procedure:

a. Position the boots large end on the tri-pot case.

b. Position the large and small boot clamps onto the boot. Be sure to check the boot band identification numbers:

- Large band: 20-98 No. BJ 82

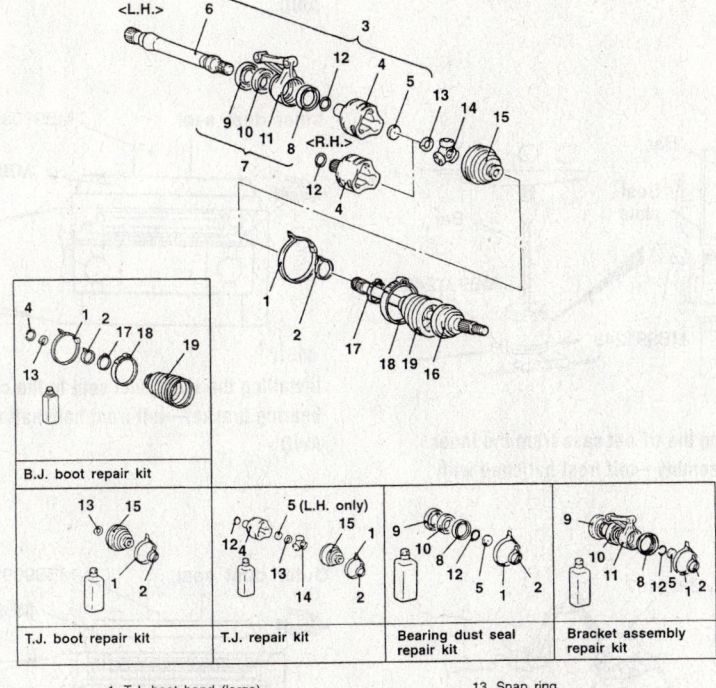

B.J. boot repair kit

T.J. boot repair kit

T.J. repair kit

Bearing dust seal repair kit

Bracket assembly repair kit

1. T.J. boot band (large)
2. T.J. boot band (small)
3. T.J. case and inner shaft assembly
4. T.J. case
5. Seal plate
6. Inner shaft
7. Bracket assembly
8. Dust seal (outer)
9. Dust seal (inner)
10. Center bearing
11. Center bearing bracket
12. Circlip
13. Snap ring
14. Spider assembly
15. T.J. boot
16. B.J. assembly
17. B.J. boot band (small)
18. B.J. boot band (large)
19. B.J. boot

Caution
Do not disassemble the B.J. assembly except replacement of the B.J. boot.

9306DG07

Exploded view of the front halfshaft assemblies—AWD

Turn to Section 5 for brake system applications

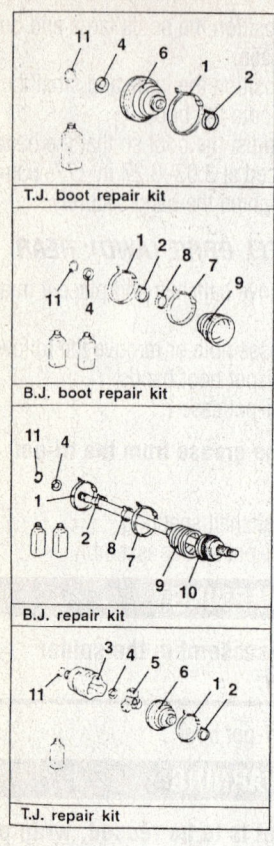

T.J. boot repair kit

B.J. boot repair kit

B.J. repair kit

T.J. repair kit

Exploded view of the rear halfshaft assemblies—AWD

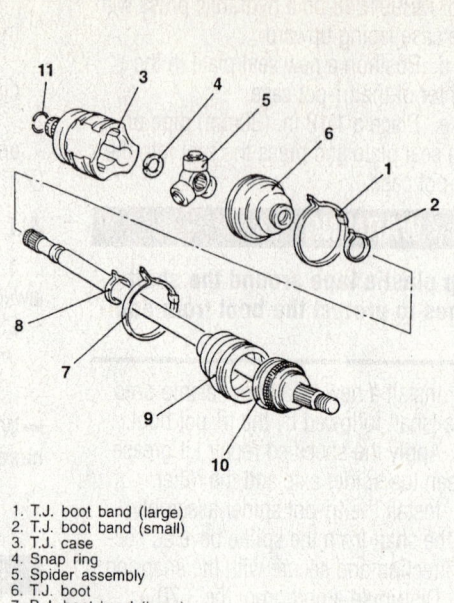

1. T.J. boot band (large)
2. T.J. boot band (small)
3. T.J. case
4. Snap ring
5. Spider assembly
6. T.J. boot
7. B.J. boot band (large)
8. B.J. boot band (small)
9. B.J. boot
10. B.J. assembly
11. Circlip

Caution
Do not disassemble the B.J. assembly.

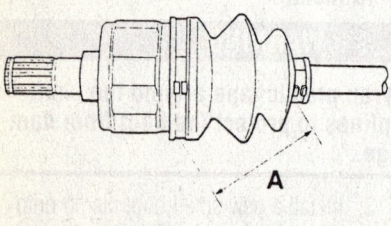

Positioning the tri-pot boot bands—Rear halfshaft assemblies with AWD

- Small band: 20-83 No. BJ 82
c. Adjust the boot so that the bands are spaced at:
- Conventional: 2.99–3.23 in. (76–82mm)
- Limited slip: 3.19–3.43 in. (81–87mm)
d. Tighten the band securely.

Center Bearing

ALL WHEEL DRIVE (AWD)

1. Remove and disconnect the following:
- Left halfshaft, place it in a soft-jawed vise
- Tri-pot spider assembly from the tri-pot case

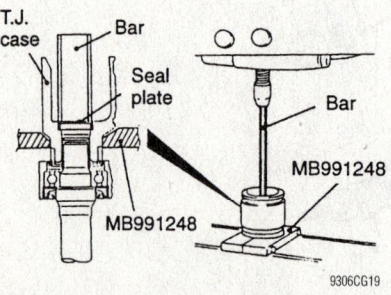

Removing the tri-pot case from the inner shaft assembly—left front halfshaft with AWD

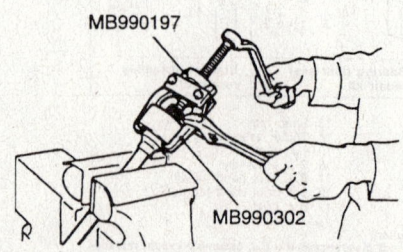

Removing the center bearing bracket from the inner shaft assembly—left front halfshaft with AWD

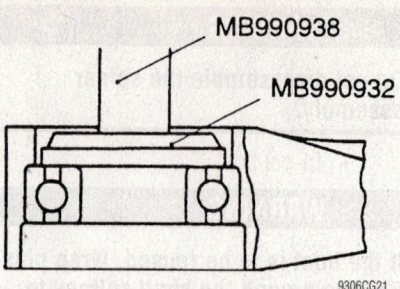

Removing the center bearing from the center bearing bracket—left front halfshaft with AWD

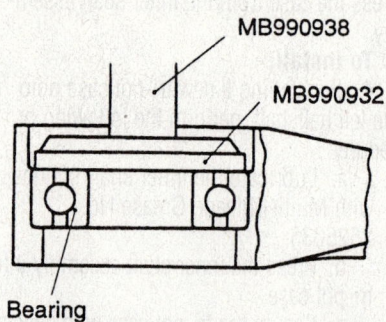

Bearing

Installing the center bearing to the center bearing bracket—left front halfshaft with AWD

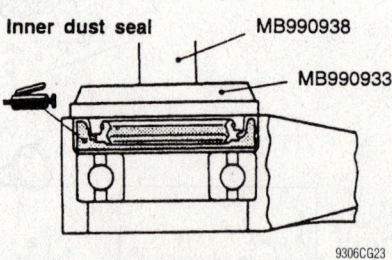

Inner dust seal

Installing the inner dust seal to the center bearing bracket—left front halfshaft with AWD

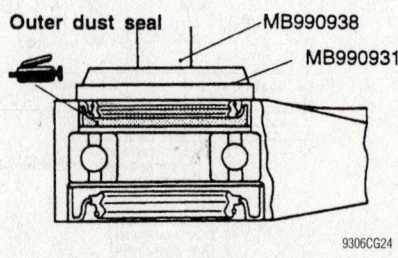

Outer dust seal

Installing the outer dust seal to the center bearing bracket—left front halfshaft with AWD

2. Remove the tri-pot case by performing the following procedure:

a. Position the inner shaft/tri-pot case assembly on a hydraulic press supported by tool MB991248 with the tri-pot case facing upward.

b. Position a bar inside the tri-pot case, on the end of the inner shaft and press the case from the inner shaft assembly.

3. Remove and disconnect the following:
- Inner shaft assembly, place it in a soft-jawed vise

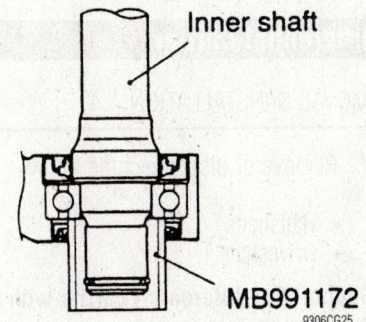

Installing the inner shaft into the center bearing bracket—left front halfshaft with AWD

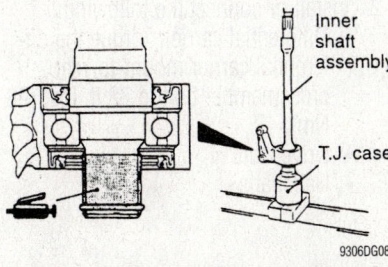

Installing the inner shaft assembly into the tri-pot case—left front halfshaft with AWD

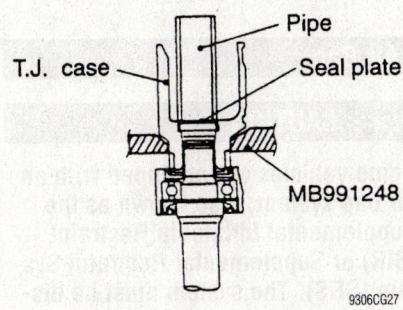

Installing the seal plate into the tri-pot case—left front halfshaft with AWD

- Center bearing bracket, press it from the inner shaft with a wheel puller
- Center bearing and inner dust seal from the center bearing bracket using a hydraulic press, Installer Adapter tool MB990932 and Snap-in Bar tool MB990938

To install:

4. Install or connect the following:
- Center bearing into the center bearing bracket using a hydraulic press, Installer Adapter tool MB990932 and Snap-in Bar tool MB990938
- Inner duct seal into the center bearing bracket using a hydraulic press, Installer Adapter tool MB990933 and Snap-in Bar tool MB990938
- Outer duct seal into the center bearing bracket using a hydraulic press, Installer Adapter tool MB990931 and Snap-in Bar tool MB990938
- Inner shaft into the center bearing bracket using a hydraulic press and Adapter tool MB991172

5. Install the tri-pot case onto the left halfshaft by performing the following procedure:

a. Lubricate the inner shaft splines with Multi-Mileage Grease No. 2525035.

b. Press the inner shaft assembly into tri-pot case.

c. Secure the tri-pot case with special tool MB991248 on a hydraulic press with the case facing upward.

d. Position a new seal plate in the center of the tri-pot case.

e. Place a 1.18 in. (30mm) pipe on the seal plate and press the seal into the tri-pot case.

6. Install or connect the following:
- Tri-pot joint assembly
- Left halfshaft

Birfield Joint Boot

FRONT

1. Remove the halfshaft and place it in a soft jawed vise.

2. Disassemble or remove the following:

- Tri-pot joint
- Dynamic damper, for Front Wheel Drive (FWD) models
- Birfield joint boot bands
- Birfield joint boot

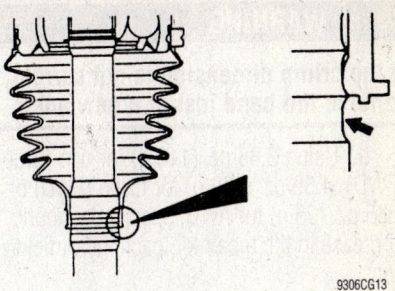

Positioning the Birfield joint boot's small diameter

To install:

3. Assemble or install the following:
- Birfield joint boot
- Birfield joint boot small band

4. Place the halfshaft in a soft jawed vise so that the Birfield joint is standing vertically.

5. Position the boots small diameter so that only 1 groove is exposed on the shaft.

6. Adjust the Band Crimper tool MB991561 so that the jaw opening is 0.114 in. (2.9mm).

7. Position the small band so there is clearance between the boot and the bands mating edge.

8. Using a Band Crimper tool MB991561, crimp the small band until the internal measurement of the crimp is 0.094–0.110 in. (2.4–2.8mm).

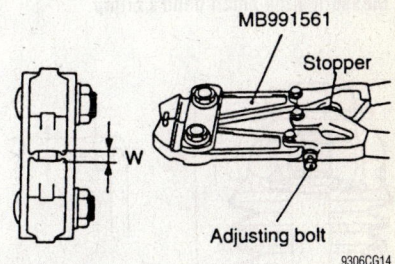

View of the band crimper tool

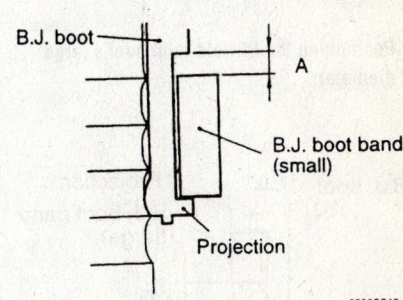

Positioning the Birfield joint boot's small band

✲✲ WARNING

If the crimp dimension is not correct, remove the band install a new one.

9. Using 3.88 oz. (110 g) for non-turbo (FWD), 4.59 oz. (130 g) for turbo (FWD) or 3.35 oz. (95 g) for AWD, specified amount of grease in the repair kit, pack the Birfield boot.

10. Position the boot so 0.004–0.061 in. (0.1–1.55mm) of clearance exists between the boots large diameter end and the Birfield joint housing shoulder.

11. Adjust the Band Crimper tool MB991561 so that the jaw opening is 0.126 in. (3.2mm).

12. Install and position the large boot band so that it rests against the boot(s) projection and a gap exists between the clamp and the boot.

13. Using a Band Crimper tool

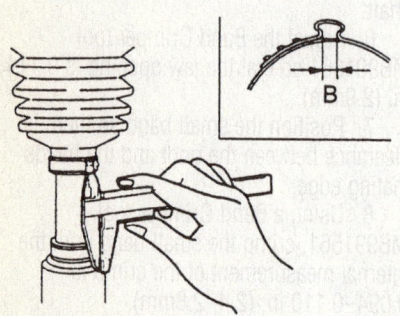

Measuring the small band's crimp

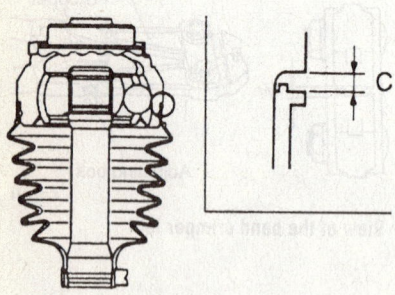

Positioning the Birfield joint boot's large diameter

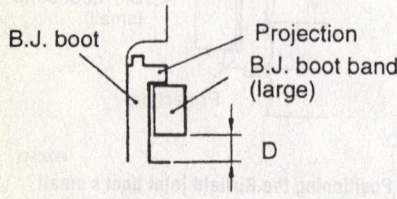

Positioning the Birfield joint boot's large band

MB991561, crimp the small band until the internal measurement of the crimp is 0.094–0.110 in. (2.4–2.8mm).

✲✲ WARNING

If the crimp dimension is not correct, remove the band install a new one.

14. If equipped with FWD, install the dynamic damper by performing the following procedure:

a. Slide the damper onto the halfshaft with new bands.

b. Position the damper so the distance from the front of the Birfield joint to the front edge of the damper assembly is 14.60–14.84 in. (371–377mm) for the right halfshaft (non-turbo)/left halfshaft (turbo) or 7.52–7.76 in. (191–197mm) for the left halfshaft (non-turbo, M/T).

c. Tighten and secure the damper bands.

15. Install the tri-pot joint.

REAR

1. Remove the halfshaft and place it in a soft jawed vise.

2. Disassemble or remove the following:
- Tri-pot joint
- Birfield joint boot bands
- Birfield joint boot

To install:

3. Assemble or install the following:
- Birfield joint boot
- Birfield joint boot small band

4. Position the large and small boot clamps onto the boot. Be sure to check the boot band identification numbers:
- Large band: 20-110 No. BJ 87
- Small band: 20-83 No. BJ 82

5. Install the tri-pot joint.

Pinion Seal

REMOVAL & INSTALLATION

1. Remove or disconnect the following:
- Driveshaft
- Companion flange nut. Use End Yoke Holder tool MB990850 to secure the companion flange.

➡**Matchmark the companion flange to the drive pinion.**

- Companion flange. Use a bearing puller to pull the companion flange from the drive pinion.
- Pinion oil seal

To install:

2. Install or connect the following:

- New pinion oil seal. Use an Oil Seal Installer tool to drive the new seal into the axle housing.
- Grease oil seal lip and companion flange. Lubricate with Multi-Mileage grease No. 2525035.
- Align the companion flange-to-drive pinion matchmarks
- New companion flange-to-drive pinion nut. Use an End Yoke Holder tool MB990850 to secure the flange and torque the nut to 137 ft. lbs. (186 Nm).
- Driveshaft. Torque the driveshaft-to-companion flange nuts/bolts to 22–25 ft. lbs. (29–34 Nm).

Differential Carrier

REMOVAL & INSTALLATION

1. Remove or disconnect the following:
- Halfshafts
- Driveshaft

➡**Support the differential carrier with a jack.**

- Differential carrier mount-to-rear crossmember bolt
- Differential carrier

To install:

2. Install or connect the following:
- Differential carrier. Torque the differential carrier mount-to-rear crossmember bolt to 72 ft. lbs. (98 Nm).
- Driveshaft
- Halfshafts

STEERING AND SUSPENSION

Air Bag

✲✲ CAUTION

Some vehicles are equipped with an air bag system, also known as the Supplemental Inflatable Restraint (SIR) or Supplemental Restraint System (SRS). The system must be disabled before performing service on or around system components, steering column, instrument panel components, wiring and sensors. Failure to follow safety and disabling proce-

dures could result in accidental air bag deployment, possible personal injury and unnecessary system repairs.

PRECAUTIONS

Several precautions must be observed when handling the inflator module to avoid accidental deployment and possible personal injury.

• Never carry the inflator module by the wires or connector on the underside of the module.

• When carrying a live inflator module, hold securely with both hands, and ensure that the bag and trim cover are pointed away from you.

• Place the inflator module on a bench or other surface with the bag and trim cover facing up.

• With the inflator module on the bench, never place anything on or close to the module that may be thrown in the event of an accidental deployment.

DISARMING

1. Position the front wheels in the straight-ahead position and place the ignition key in the **LOCK** position. Remove the key from the ignition lock cylinder.

2. Disconnect the negative battery cable and insulate the cable end with high-quality electrical tape or similar non-conductive wrapping.

3. Wait at least one minute before working on the vehicle. The air bag system is designed to retain enough voltage to deploy the air bag for a short period of time after the battery has been disconnected.

To arm:

4. Reconnect the negative battery cable, turn the ignition switch to the **ON** position and check the air bag warning light for proper operation.

Power Rack and Pinion Steering Gear

REMOVAL & INSTALLATION

1. Be sure to observe all cautions and warnings in the beginning of the section that may be related to this procedure.

2. Drain the power steering fluid into a suitable container.

3. For 2.0L turbocharged engines, remove or disconnect the following:

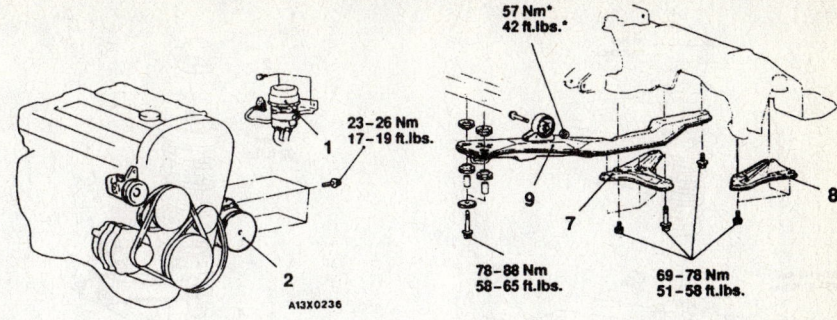

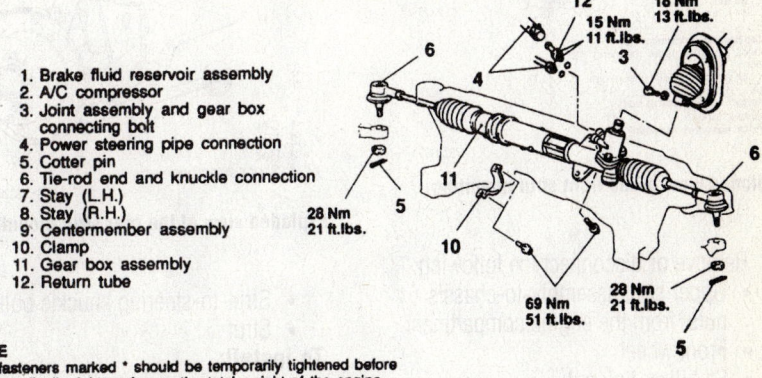

1. Brake fluid reservoir assembly
2. A/C compressor
3. Joint assembly and gear box connecting bolt
4. Power steering pipe connection
5. Cotter pin
6. Tie-rod end and knuckle connection
7. Stay (L.H.)
8. Stay (R.H.)
9. Centermember assembly
10. Clamp
11. Gear box assembly
12. Return tube

NOTE
The fasteners marked * should be temporarily tightened before they are finally tightened once the total weight of the engine has been placed on the vehicle body.

Exploded view of the power steering gear assembly and related components

• Negative battery cable
• Windshield washer fluid reservoir
• Brake fluid reservoir
• Air conditioning compressor. Position it aside; DO NOT disconnect the refrigerant lines.

4. Remove or disconnect the following:

• Stabilizer bar
• Joint assembly and gear body connecting bolt
• Power steering pipe connection
• Tie rod end from the steering knuckle
• Left and right side stays
• Center member assembly retainers
• Center member
• Power steering gear retaining clamp
• Power steering gear assembly

To install:

5. Install or connect the following:
• Power steering gear assembly
• Power steering gear retaining clamp. Torque the bolts to 51 ft. lbs. (69 Nm).
• Center member
• Center member assembly retainers.

Torque the bolts to 58–65 ft. lbs. (78–88 Nm).

• Left and right side stays. Torque the bolts to 51–58 ft. lbs. (69–78 Nm).

• Tie rod end to the steering knuckle. Torque the nut to 21 ft. lbs. (28 Nm).

• Power steering pipe connection. Torque the nuts to 13 ft. lbs. (18 Nm).

• Joint assembly and gear body connecting bolt. Torque the bolt to 11 ft. lbs. (15 Nm).

• Stabilizer bar

6. Refill the reservoir with power steering fluid and bleed the system.

7. Check the front end alignment and adjust, if necessary.

Strut

REMOVAL & INSTALLATION

Front

1. Be sure to observe all cautions and warnings in the beginning of the section that may be related to this procedure.

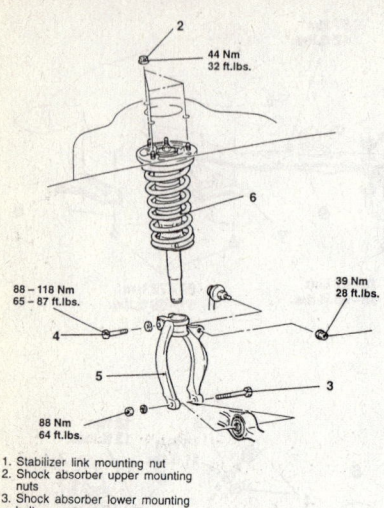

1. Stabilizer link mounting nut
2. Shock absorber upper mounting nuts
3. Shock absorber lower mounting bolt
4. Damper fork mounting bolt
5. Damper fork
6. Shock absorber assembly

7922DG23

Exploded view of the front strut mounting

2. Remove or disconnect the following:
- Upper strut assembly-to-chassis nuts, from the engine compartment
- Front wheel
- Stabilizer link nut
- Strut assembly lower mounting bolts
- Damper fork
- Strut

To install:

3. Install or connect the following:
- Strut
- Damper fork. Torque the damper fork-to-lower arm nut/bolt to 64 ft. lbs. (88 Nm).
- Strut assembly lower mounting bolts. Torque the strut-to-damper fork bolt to 65–87 ft. lbs. (88–118 Nm).
- Stabilizer link nut. Torque the nut to 28 ft. lbs. (39 Nm).
- Front wheel
- Upper strut assembly-to-chassis nuts, in the engine compartment. Torque the nuts to 32 ft. lbs. (44 Nm).

Rear

1. Be sure to observe all cautions and warnings in the beginning of the section that may be related to this procedure.
2. Remove or disconnect the following:
- Service lid, in the luggage compartment
- Upper mounting bracket-to-body cap and flange nuts

➡**Do not remove the large nut in the center of the strut assembly.**

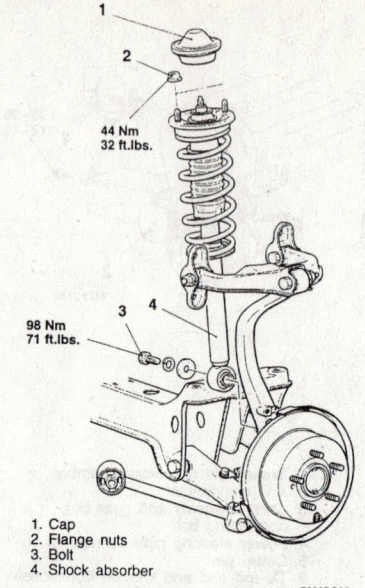

1. Cap
2. Flange nuts
3. Bolt
4. Shock absorber

7922DG26

Exploded view of the rear strut mounting

- Strut-to-steering knuckle bolt
- Strut

To install:

3. Install or connect the following:
- Strut. Tighten the upper strut-to-chassis nuts to 32 ft. lbs. (44 Nm).
4. Raise the suspension up with a jack or adjustable stand to align the strut lower mounting holes.
5. Install or connect the following:

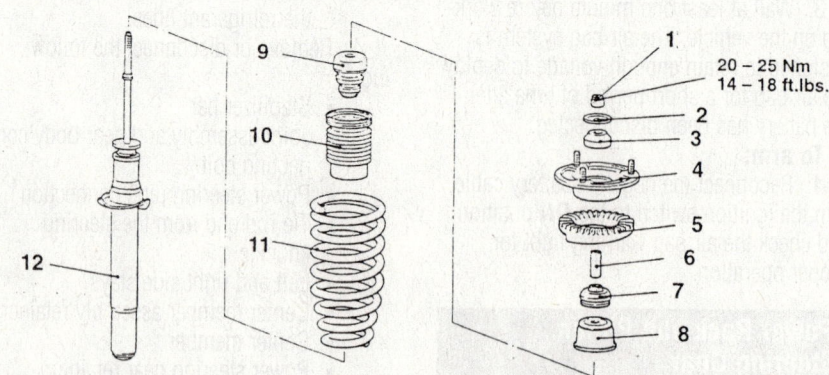

Disassembly steps
1. Self-locking nut
2. Washer
3. Upper bushing A
4. Upper bracket assembly
5. Upper spring pad
6. Collar

7. Upper bushing B
8. Cup assembly
9. Bump rubber
10. Dust cover
11. Coil spring
12. Shock absorber assembly

7922DG28

Exploded view of the front strut assembly

- Lower strut mounting bolt. Tighten the bolt to 71 ft. lbs. (97 Nm).
- Cap and service lid

OVERHAUL

Front

1. Be sure to observe all cautions and warnings in the beginning of the section that may be related to this procedure.
2. Remove or disassemble the following:
- Strut

✳✳ CAUTION

Do not use air tools to tighten the compressor tool bolt.

- Compress the coil spring, using Spring Compressing tools MB991237 and MB991239.

✳✳ WARNING

Be sure to install the tools evenly so the maximum length will be attained within the installation range.

- Self-locking nut, by holding the piston rod
- Washer
- Upper bushing **A**
- Upper bracket assembly
- Upper spring pad
- Collar

- Upper bushing **B**
- Cup assembly
- Rubber bumper
- Dust cover
- Coil spring

To assemble:

3. Use the compressor tools to compress the coil spring, then install it to the strut. Align the edge of the coil spring to the stepped portion of the strut spring seat.

4. Install or assemble the following:
- Dust cover
- Rubber bumper
- Cup
- Upper bushing **B**
- Collar
- Upper spring pad
- Upper bracket assembly

➡**Install the assembly so the position of the 3 bolts are in the proper orientation with the damper fork.**

- Upper bushing **A**
- Washer and self-locking nut. Temporarily, tighten the self-locking nut, then remove the spring compressor tools and tighten the nut to 14–18 ft. lbs. (20–25 Nm) using a torque wrench.

❋❋ WARNING

Do not use air tools to tighten the self-locking nut!

- Strut

Rear

1. Be sure to observe all cautions and warnings in the beginning of the section that may be related to this procedure.

2. Remove or disassemble the following:
- Strut
- Compress the spring using a coil spring compressor
- Self-locking nut by holding the piston rod
- Upper bracket assembly and spring pad
- Collar
- Upper bushing
- Cup assembly
- Bump rubber
- Dust cover
- Coil spring

To assemble:

3. Align the end of the coil spring with the stepped part of the spring seat and install the compressed coil spring on the strut.

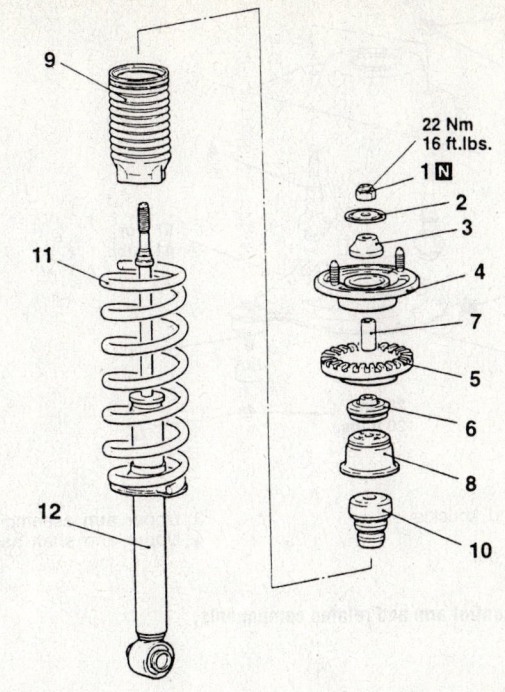

Disassembly steps
1. Self-locking nut
2. Washer
3. Upper bushing A
4. Upper bracket assembly
5. Upper spring pad
6. Upper bushing B

7. Collar
8. Cup assembly
9. Dust cover
10. Bump rubber
11. Coil spring
12. Shock absorber assembly

7922DG27

Exploded view of the rear strut assembly

4. Install or assemble the following:
- Dust cover
- Bump rubber
- Cup assembly
- Upper bushing
- Collar
- Upper spring pad
- Bracket assembly
- Upper bushing and washer
- New self-locking nut on the piston rod. Temporarily, tighten the nut.
5. Carefully, remove the spring compressor from the spring. Tighten the self-locking nut to 16 ft. lbs. (25 Nm).
6. Install the strut.

Upper Ball Joint

REMOVAL & INSTALLATION

The upper ball joint is an integral part of the upper control arm. If the upper ball joint is to be serviced, the upper control arm will have to be replaced.

Lower Ball Joint

REMOVAL & INSTALLATION

The lower ball joint is an integral part of the lower control arm assembly; and cannot be serviced separately. A worn or damaged ball joint, requires replacement of the lower control arm assembly.

Upper Control Arm

REMOVAL & INSTALLATION

1. Be sure to observe all cautions and warnings in the beginning of the section that may be related to this procedure.
2. Remove or disconnect the following:
- Front wheel(s)
- Upper ball joint from the steering knuckle
- Upper shaft mounting nuts from the body

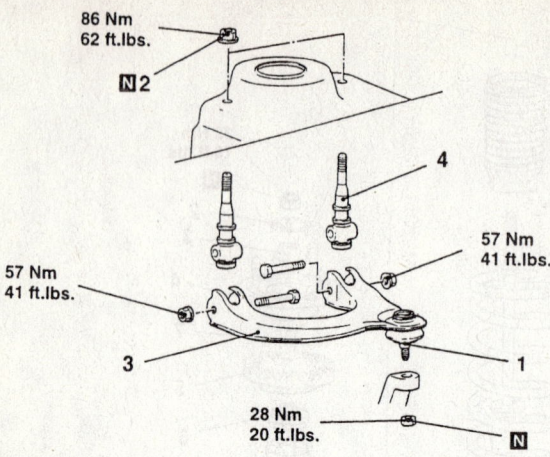

Removal steps

1. Upper arm ball joint and knuckle connection
2. Upper arm self-locking nut
3. Upper arm assembly
4. Upper arm shaft assembly

9300DG01

Exploded view of the upper control arm and related components

A : 299.9 mm (11.8 in.)
B : 234.0 mm (9.2 in.)

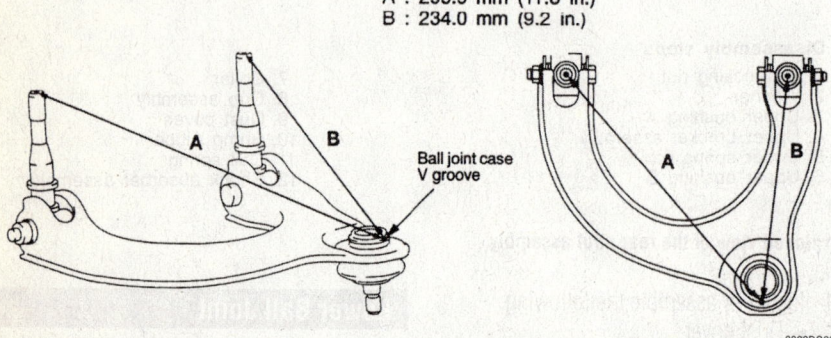

9300DG02

Be sure to install the shafts on the control arm at the correct angle

- Upper arm
- Upper arm-to-shafts through-bolts

To install:

3. Assemble the upper arm to the shafts at the proper angle. Tighten the through-bolts and nuts to 41 ft. lbs. (57 Nm). The proper angle is 84–86 degrees. After the arm and the shafts are connected at the correct angle, measure dimensions A and B to insure correct assembly.
- A—11.8 in. (299.9mm)
- B—9.2 in. (234.0mm)
4. Install or connect the following:
- Control arm assembly. Torque the self-locking nuts to 62 ft. lbs. (86 Nm).
- Upper ball joint-to-steering knuckle. Torque the new locking nut to 20 ft. lbs. (28 Nm).
- Front wheel(s)
5. Perform front wheel alignment and adjust, if necessary.

Lower Control Arm

REMOVAL & INSTALLATION

Compression Lower Arm

1. Be sure to observe all cautions and warnings in the beginning of the section that may be related to this procedure.
2. Remove or disconnect the following:
- Wheel
- Compression lower arm ball joint at the steering knuckle
- Both compression lower arm bolts
- Compression lower arm

To install:

3. Install or connect the following:
- Compression lower arm. Tighten the 2 mounting bolts to 60 ft. lbs. (81 Nm).

- Ball joint to the knuckle assembly. Tighten the new self-locking nut to 43–51 ft. lbs. (59–71 Nm).
- Wheel
4. Check and adjust the front wheel alignment, if necessary.

Lateral Lower Arm

1. Be sure to observe all cautions and warnings in the beginning of the section that may be related to this procedure.
2. Remove or disconnect the following:
- Wheel
- Stay (bracket)
- Strut lower mounting bolts
- Lateral lower arm at the knuckle assembly
- Lateral lower arm mounting bolts
- Lateral arm

To install:

3. Install or connect the following:
- Lateral lower arm. Temporarily, install the mounting bolts; do not tighten the bolt until the vehicle is on the floor at normal riding height.
- Ball joint to the knuckle assembly. Tighten the new self-locking nut to 43–51 ft. lbs. (59–71 Nm).
- Strut lower mounting bolts. Torque the nut to 64 ft. lbs. (88 Nm).
- Stay. Torque the bolts to 51–58 ft. lbs. (69–78 Nm).
- Wheel
4. Torque the lateral lower arm through-bolt and nut to 71–85 ft. lbs. (97–118 Nm).
5. Check and adjust the front wheel alignment, if necessary.

Wheel Bearings

ADJUSTMENT

Front

The front wheel bearing is a sealed and not adjustable. If the wheel bearing shows signs of play, the hub assembly must be replaced.

Rear

The wheel bearing play is not adjustable. If the wheel bearing play is not within specifications, the hub assembly must be replaced.

FRONT WHEEL DRIVE (FWD)

1. Release the parking brake and if equipped, remove the brake drum.
2. If equipped with rear disc brakes,

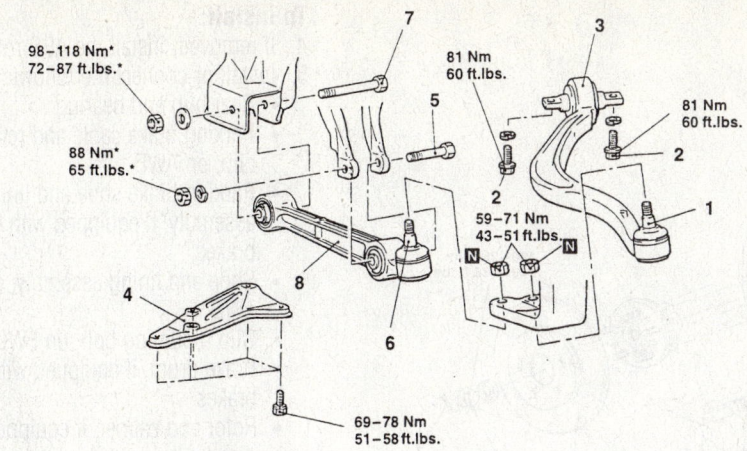

98–118 Nm*
72–87 ft.lbs.*

88 Nm*
65 ft.lbs.*

81 Nm
60 ft.lbs.

81 Nm
60 ft.lbs.

59–71 Nm
43–51 ft.lbs.

69–78 Nm
51–58 ft.lbs.

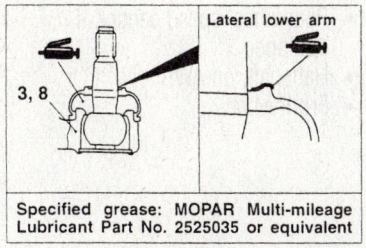

Lateral lower arm

3, 8

Specified grease: MOPAR Multi-mileage
Lubricant Part No. 2525035 or equivalent

**Compression lower arm assembly
removal steps**

1. Compression lower arm ball joint
   and knuckle connection
2. Compression lower arm mounting
   bolts
3. Compression lower arm assembly

**Lateral lower arm assembly
removal steps**

4. Stay
5. Shock absorber lower mounting
   bolt
6. Lateral lower arm ball joint and
   knuckle connection
7. Lateral lower arm mounting bolt
8. Lateral lower arm assembly

Caution
*: Indicates parts which should be temporarily tightened,
    and then fully tightened with the vehicle on the ground
    in the unladen condition.

9300DG03

Exploded view of the lower arms and related components

remove the caliper assembly and the brake
disc (rotor).

3. Place a dial gauge against the hub surface, then move the hub in the axial direction
and check whether or not there is end-play.
Specification is 0.002 in (0.05mm).

4. To check for rotary sliding resistance,
turn the hub a few times to seat the bearing.
Wind a rope around the hub bolts and turn
the hub by pulling at a 90° angle with a
spring scale. Measure to determine whether
or not the rotary sliding resistance of the
rear hub is at the limit value. Specification
is 3.9 lbs. (1.8 kg) or less.

ALL WHEEL DRIVE (AWD)

1. Remove the caliper assembly and the
brake disc (rotor).

2. Place a dial gauge against the hub
surface, then move the hub in the axial
direction and check whether or not there is
end-play. Specification is 0.002 in.
(0.05mm).

REMOVAL & INSTALLATION

Front

➡**The front hub assembly is a sealed
unit and should not be disassembled.**

1. Before servicing the vehicle, refer to
the precautions in the beginning of this section.

2. Remove or disconnect the following:

- Wheel
- Halfshaft nut cotter pin and discard
  it
- Halfshaft nut by holding the rotor in
  place with a suitable tool
- Front wheel speed sensor, if
  equipped with Anti-lock Brake System (ABS).
- Caliper and suspend it out of the
  way with a piece of wire

➡**Do not disconnect the fluid line.**

- Upper control arm ball joint from
  the steering knuckle
- Front hub assembly

➡**Shift the knuckle to the outside in
order to keep the clearance between
the front hub mounting bolts and halfshaft.**

✳✳ WARNING

**Be careful not to damage the ball
joint boot. If equipped with ABS, be
careful not to damage the rotor.**

3. If necessary to remove the steering
knuckle, remove or disconnect the following:

- Dust shield
- Tie rod end from the steering
  knuckle and discard the cotter
  pin
- Compression and lateral lower control arm ball joints from the steering knuckle
- Damper fork and lateral lower
  control arm from the steering
  knuckle
- Steering knuckle

To install:

4. If the steering knuckle was removed,
install or connect the following:

- Steering knuckle. Hand-tighten the
  bolt and nut.
- Lateral and compression lower
  control arm ball joints into the
  steering knuckle
- Tie rod end ball joint to the steering
  knuckle. Torque the retaining nut
  and tighten to 17–25 ft. lbs.
  (24–33 Nm).
- New cotter pin
- Dust shield. Torque the bolt to 78
  inch lbs. (8.5 Nm).

5. Install or connect the following:

- Front hub assembly. Torque the
  bolts to 65 ft. lbs. (88 Nm).
- Upper control arm ball joint to the
  steering knuckle
- Brake disc (rotor) and caliper
- Front wheel speed sensor, if
  equipped
- Halfshaft nut. Hold the rotor in
  position while torquing the nut to
  145–188 ft. lbs. (196–255 Nm).

➡**If the cotter pin holes do not align,
tighten the nut to 188 ft. lbs. (225 Nm)
maximum. Install a new cotter pin in
the first matching holes.**

- Wheel

Turn to Section 5 for brake system applications

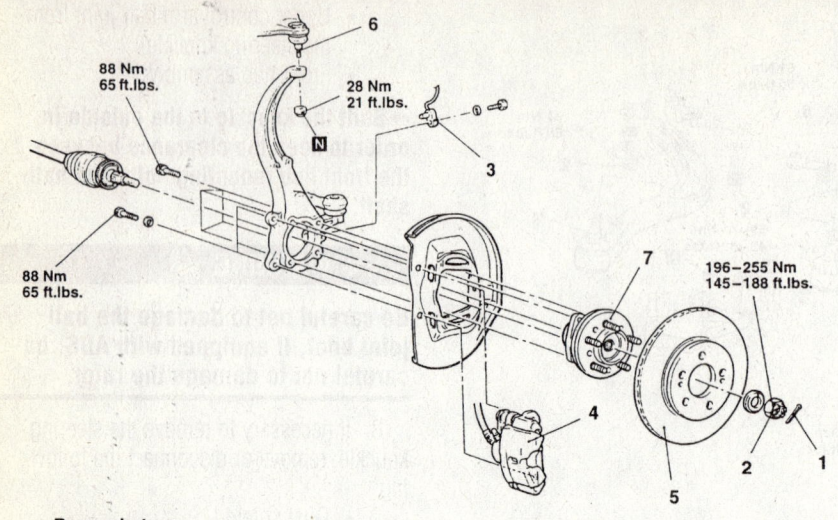

Removal steps
1. Cotter pin
2. Drive shaft nut
3. Front wheel speed sensor <Vehicles with ABS>
4. Caliper assembly
5. Brake disc
6. Upper arm ball joint and knuckle connection
7. Front hub assembly

7922DG25

Exploded view of the front hub assembly

Rear

1. Be sure to observe all cautions and warnings in the beginning of the section that may be related to this procedure.

2. Remove or disconnect the following:

- Wheel
- Halfshaft, on All Wheel Drive (AWD) vehicles
- Rear wheel speed sensor, if equipped with Anti-lock Brake System (ABS)
- Caliper, if equipped with rear disc brakes and suspend the caliper on a suitable piece of wire.

➡**Do not disconnect the fluid line.**

- Brake drum, if equipped with drum brakes
- Clip mounting bolt, on Front Wheel Drive (FWD)
- Brake shoe and lining assembly, on AWD
- Parking brake shoe and lining assembly, if equipped with disc brakes
- Parking brake cable clip and cable, on AWD
- Rear hub and bearing assembly

3. On FWD vehicles equipped with ABS, use a suitable inner shaft remover to press off the ABS rotor.

To install:

4. If removed, install the ABS rotor.
5. Install or connect the following:

- Rear hub and bearing
- Parking brake cable and retaining clip, on AWD
- Parking brake shoe and lining assembly, if equipped with disc brakes
- Shoe and lining assembly, on AWD
- Clip mounting bolt, on FWD
- Brake drum, if equipped with drum brakes
- Rotor and caliper, if equipped with disc brakes
- Rear wheel speed sensor, if equipped
- Halfshaft, on AWD
- Front wheel

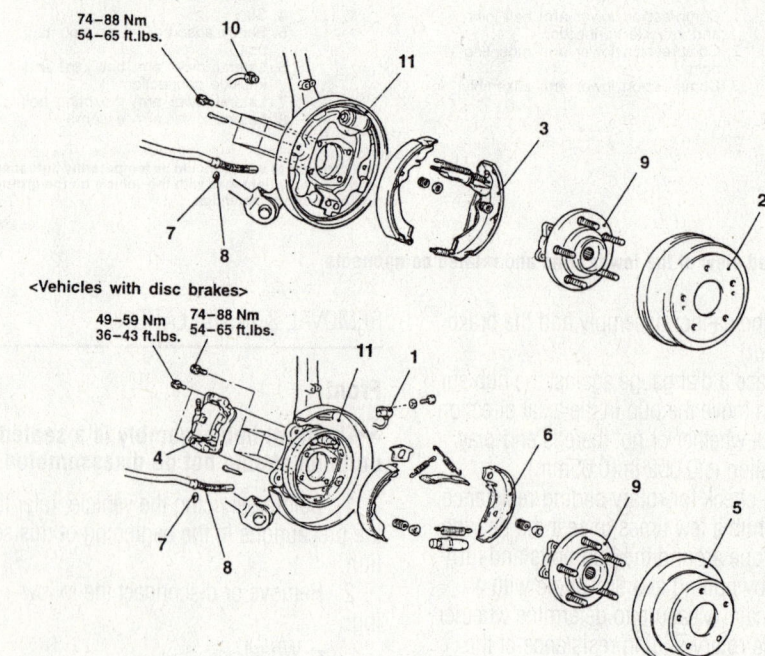

<Vehicles with drum brakes>

<Vehicles with disc brakes>

1. Rear wheel speed sensor <Vehicles with ABS>
2. Brake drum
3. Shoe and lever assembly
4. Caliper assembly
5. Brake disc
6. Shoe and lining assembly
7. Clip
8. Parking brake cable
9. Rear hub assembly
10. Brake pipe connection
11. Dust seal

7922DG24

Exploded view of the rear hub assembly

CHRYSLER CORP.

Dodge/Plymouth-Neon

PRECAUTIONS

Before servicing any vehicle, please be sure to read all of the following precautions, which deal with personal safety, prevention of component damage, and important points to take into consideration when servicing a motor vehicle:

• Never open, service or drain the radiator or cooling system when the engine is hot; serious burns can occur from the steam and hot coolant.

• Observe all applicable safety precautions when working around fuel. Whenever servicing the fuel system, always work in a well-ventilated area. Do not allow fuel spray or vapors to come in contact with a spark, open flame, or excessive heat (a hot drop light, for example). Keep a dry chemical fire extinguisher near the work area. Always keep fuel in a container specifically designed for fuel storage; also, always properly seal fuel containers to avoid the possibility of fire or explosion. Refer to the additional fuel system precautions later in this section.

• Fuel injection systems often remain pressurized, even after the engine has been turned **OFF**. The fuel system pressure must be relieved before disconnecting any fuel lines. Failure to do so may result in fire and/or personal injury.

• Brake fluid often contains polyglycol ethers and polyglycols. Avoid contact with the eyes and wash your hands thoroughly after handling brake fluid. If you do get brake fluid in your eyes, flush your eyes with clean, running water for 15 minutes. If eye irritation persists, or if you have taken brake fluid internally, IMMEDIATELY seek medical assistance.

• The EPA warns that prolonged contact with used engine oil may cause a number of skin disorders, including cancer! You should make every effort to minimize your exposure to used engine oil. Protective gloves should be worn when changing oil. Wash your hands and any other exposed skin areas as soon as possible after exposure to used engine oil. Soap and water, or waterless hand cleaner should be used.

• All new vehicles are now equipped with an air bag system, often referred to as a Supplemental Restraint System (SRS) or Supplemental Inflatable Restraint (SIR) system. The system must be disabled before performing service on or around system components, steering column, instrument panel components, wiring and sensors. Failure to follow safety and disabling procedures could result in accidental air bag deployment, possible personal injury and unnecessary system repairs.

• Always wear safety goggles when working with, or around, the air bag system. When carrying a non-deployed air bag, be sure the bag and trim cover are pointed away from your body. When placing a non-deployed air bag on a work surface, always face the bag and trim cover upward, away from the surface. This will reduce the motion of the module if it is accidentally deployed. Refer to the additional air bag system precautions later in this section.

• Clean, high quality brake fluid from a sealed container is essential to the safe and proper operation of the brake system. You should always buy the correct type of brake fluid for your vehicle. If the brake fluid becomes contaminated, completely flush the system with new fluid. Never reuse any brake fluid. Any brake fluid that is removed from the system should be discarded. Also, do not allow any brake fluid to come in contact with a painted surface; it will damage the paint.

• Never operate the engine without the proper amount and type of engine oil; doing so WILL result in severe engine damage.

• Timing belt maintenance is extremely important! Many models utilize an interference-type, non-freewheeling engine. If the timing belt breaks, the valves in the cylinder head may strike the pistons, causing potentially serious (also time-consuming and expensive) engine damage. Refer to the maintenance interval charts in the front of this manual for the recommended replacement interval for the timing belt, and to the timing belt section for belt replacement and inspection.

• Disconnecting the negative battery cable on some vehicles may interfere with the functions of the on-board computer system(s) and may require the computer to undergo a relearning process once the negative battery cable is reconnected.

• When servicing drum brakes, only disassemble and assemble one side at a time, leaving the remaining side intact for reference.

• Only an MVAC-trained, EPA-certified automotive technician should service the air conditioning system or its components.

ENGINE REPAIR

Alternator

REMOVAL

1997–99 Models

1. Remove or disconnect the following:
   • Negative battery cable
   • Alternator's adjustment nut, loosen only
   • Plastic lower splash shield
   • Alternator field circuit wiring connector, push **RED** locking tab to release
   • Alternator pivot bolt, loosen only
   • Alternator drive belt

➡ **The alternator spill shield does not need to be removed.**

   • 3 pivot bracket-to-engine bolts
   • Pivot bracket
   • Alternator, by sliding it off the "T" bolt and out through the wheel well

➡ **It is not necessary to remove the "T" bolt.**

2000–01 Models

1. Remove or disconnect the following:
   • Negative battery cable
   • Alternator jam nut, loosen only
   • Alternator adjustment nut, loosen only
   • Accessory drive splash shield
   • Alternator lower bolt, loosen only
   • Alternator drive belt
   • Alternator field circuit wiring connector, push **RED** locking tab to release
   • Battery positive terminal
   • Upper and lower bolts, move alternator off pivot bracket
   • Pivot bracket
   • Alternator

INSTALLATION

1997–99 Models

1. Install or connect the following:
   • Alternator, by moving it through the wheel well and sliding it onto the "T" bolt
   • Pivot bracket

- 3 pivot bracket-to-engine bolts. Torque the bolts to 40 ft. lbs. (54 Nm).
- Alternator drive belt
- Alternator pivot bolt
- Alternator field circuit wiring connector, push **RED** locking tab in until it snaps in place
- Plastic lower splash shield
- Tension the drive belt to 100 lbs. (used) or 135 lbs. (new)
- Alternator adjustment nut. Torque all nuts/bolts to 40 ft. lbs. (54 Nm).
- Negative battery cable

2000–01 Models

1. Install or connect the following:
- Alternator
- Pivot bracket. Torque the bolts to 40 ft. lbs. (54 Nm).
- Alternator, move it onto pivot bracket
- Alternator field circuit wiring connector, push **RED** locking tab in until it snaps in place
- Battery positive terminal
- Alternator drive belt
- Tension the drive belt to 100 lbs. (used) or 135 lbs. (new)
- Alternator adjustment bolt.
- Alternator jam nut. Torque nut to 40 ft. lbs. (54 Nm).
- Alternator mount bolts. Torque bolts to 40 ft. lbs. (54 Nm).
- Accessory drive splash shield
- Negative battery cable

Ignition Timing

ADJUSTMENT

Ignition timing is controlled by the Powertrain Control Module (PCM). No adjustment is necessary or possible.

Engine Assembly

REMOVAL & INSTALLATION

1997–99 Models

➡**After all components are installed on the engine, a DRB or equivalent, scan tool is necessary to perform the camshaft and crankshaft timing relearn procedure.**

1. Before servicing the vehicle, refer to the precautions in the beginning of this section.

2. Properly recover the air conditioning system refrigerant.
3. Drain the engine oil.
4. Drain the cooling system.
5. Properly relieve the fuel system pressure.
6. Remove or disconnect the following:
- Battery and battery tray
- Powertrain Control Module (PCM) and move it aside
- Upper radiator hose
- Radiator
- Fan module assembly
- Lower radiator hose
- Automatic transaxle cooler lines and plug them, if equipped
- Clutch cable, for manual transaxle
- Transaxle shift linkage
- Throttle body linkage
- Engine wiring harness
- Heater hoses
- Right inner splash shield
- Accessory drive belts
- Halfshafts
- Exhaust pipe from the manifold
7. Support the engine and transaxle assembly with a jack.
8. Remove or disconnect the following:
- Front engine mount
- Power hop damper, if equipped with manual transaxle
- Air cleaner assembly
- Power steering pump/reservoir assembly and move them aside
- Air conditioning compressor, if equipped
- Chassis ground straps
9. Raise the vehicle enough to allow a suitable engine dolly and cradle to be placed under the engine.
10. Loosen the engine support posts in order to allow movement for positioning onto the engine locating holes and flange on the engine bedplate. Lower the vehicle and position the cradle until the engine is resting on the support posts. Tighten the mounts to the cradle frame. This will keep the support posts from moving when removing or installing the engine and transaxle.
11. Install safety straps around the engine to the cradle; tighten the straps and lock them into position.
12. Raise the vehicle enough to see if the straps are tight enough to hold the cradle assembly to the engine.
13. Lower the vehicle so the weight of the engine and transaxle ONLY is on the cradle.
14. Remove the engine and transaxle mount through-bolts.

15. Raise the vehicle slowly, it might be necessary to move the engine/transaxle assembly with the cradle to allow removal around the body flanges.

To install:
16. Install or connect the following:
- Engine/transaxle assembly, lower the vehicle over the assembly
- Engine and transaxle mounts
17. Tighten the front engine mount bracket retainers as follows:
   a. Bolt 1: 20 inch lbs. (3 Nm).
   b. Bolts 2, 3 and 4: 80 ft. lbs. (108 Nm).
   c. Bolts 5 and 1: 40 ft. lbs. (54 Nm).
18. Install or connect the following:
- Engine mount bracket-to-insulator through-bolt: 40 ft. lbs. (54 Nm)
- Insulator assembly-to-lower radiator crossmember nuts: 40 ft. lbs. (54 Nm)
- Mass damper bolt: 40 ft. lbs. (54 Nm)
19. Tighten the left engine mount as follows:
   a. **A** fasteners: 40 ft. lbs. (54 Nm).
   b. **B** fasteners: 80 ft. lbs. (108 Nm).
20. Tighten the right engine mount as follows:
   a. Engine mount-to-rail fasteners: 40 ft. lbs. (54 Nm).
   b. Engine mount-to-engine bracket: 80 ft. lbs. (108 Nm).
21. Remove the engine/transaxle assembly safely straps; then, raise the vehicle to remove the dolly and cradle.
22. Install or connect the following:
- Power hop damper, if equipped. Torque retainers to 40 ft. lbs. (54 Nm).
- Exhaust pipe to the manifold
- Halfshafts
- Accessory drive belts
- Right inner splash shield
- Heater hoses
- Engine wiring harness
- Throttle body linkage
- Transaxle shift linkage
- Clutch cable, for manual transaxle
- Automatic transaxle cooler lines, if equipped
- Lower radiator hose
- Fan module assembly
- Radiator
- Upper radiator hose
- PCM
- Battery and battery tray
23. Refill the crankcase.
24. Refill the cooling system.

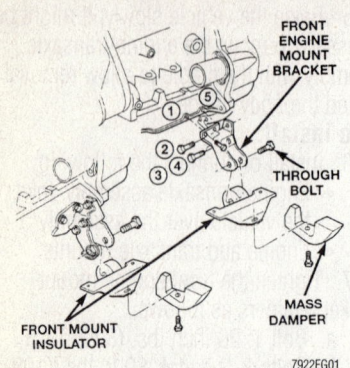

Front engine mount location and bolt identification—1997–99 models

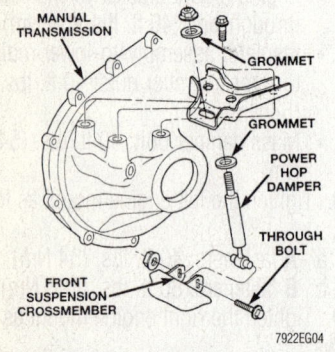

View of the power hop damper—1997–99 models—manual transaxle

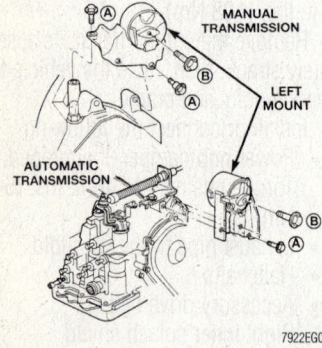

Exploded view of the left engine mount—1997–99 models

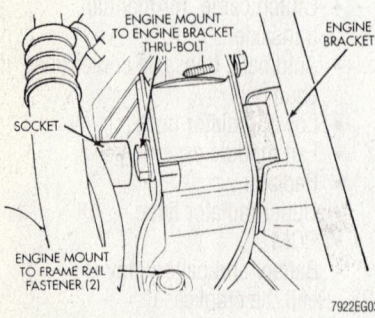

Location of the right engine mount—1997–99 models

25. Perform the camshaft and crankshaft timing relearn procedure as follows:

   a. Connect a DRB or equivalent, scan tool to the DLC (located under the instrument panel, near the steering column).

   b. Turn the ignition switch **ON** and access the "miscellaneous" screen.

   c. Select "re-learn cam/crank" option and follow the directions on the scan tool screen.

26. If equipped with air conditioning, recharge the system.

2000–01 Models

➡**After all components are installed on the engine, a DRB or equivalent, scan tool is necessary to perform the camshaft and crankshaft timing relearn procedure.**

1. Before servicing the vehicle, refer to the precautions in the beginning of this section.

2. Properly recover the air conditioning system refrigerant.

3. Properly relieve the fuel system pressure.

4. Drain the cooling system.

5. Drain the crankcase.

6. Remove or disconnect the following:
  • Battery and battery tray
  • Air intake duct from the intake manifold
  • Throttle cables
  • Electrical connectors
  • Air cleaner assembly
  • Upper radiator hose
  • Fan module assembly
  • Lower radiator hose
  • Automatic transaxle cooler lines (if equipped), plug the lines
  • Clutch cable (manual transaxle)
  • Shift linkage from the transaxle
  • Engine wiring harness
  • Power Distribution Center (PDC)
  • Ground wires
  • Heater hoses
  • Brake booster vacuum hose
  • Coolant recovery hose
  • Accessory drive belts
  • Power steering pump and reservoir, move them aside
  • Right inner splash shield
  • Front wheels
  • Halfshafts
  • Exhaust pipe from the manifold
  • Downstream Oxygen Sensor (O_2S) connector
  • Lower engine torque strut
  • Structural collar
  • Air conditioning compressor, if equipped

7. Raise the vehicle enough to allow an Engine Dolly tool 6135 and Cradle tool 6710 to be placed under the engine.

8. Loosen the engine support posts in order to allow movement for positioning onto the engine locating holes and flange on the engine bedplate. Lower the vehicle and position the cradle until the engine is resting on the support posts. Tighten the mounts to the cradle frame. This will keep the support posts

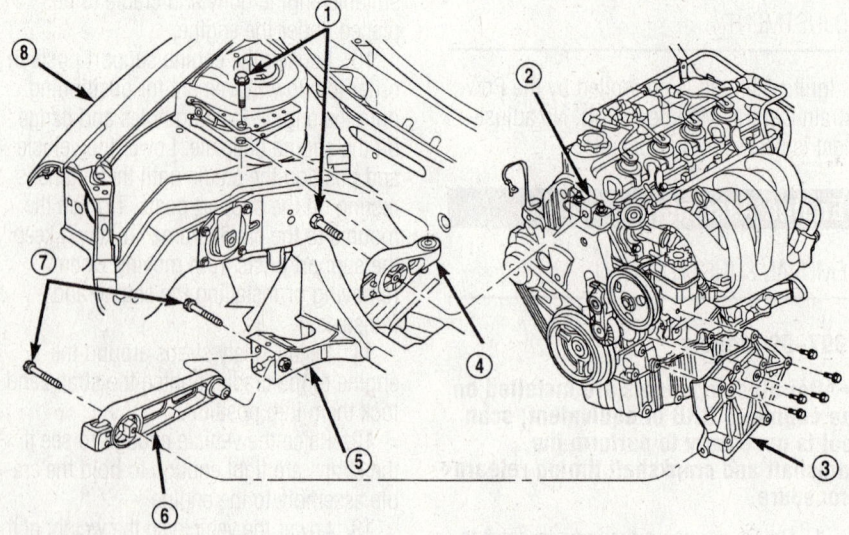

1 – BOLTS
2 – ENGINE MOUNT BRACKET
3 – TORQUE STRUT BRACKET
4 – UPPER TORQUE STRUT
5 – CROSSMEMBER
6 – LOWER TORQUE STRUT
7 – BOLTS
8 – RIGHT FENDER

Exploded view of the torque struts and bracket—2000–01 models

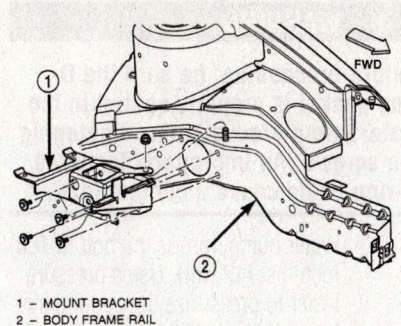

1 – MOUNT BRACKET
2 – BODY FRAME RAIL

9306EG14

Exploded view of the left mount bracket—2000–01 models

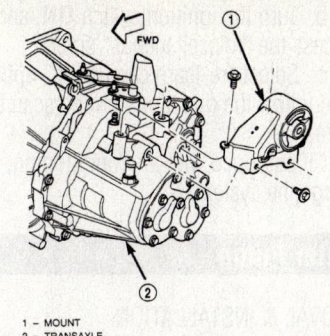

1 – MOUNT
2 – TRANSAXLE

9306EG16

Exploded view of the left mount—Manual transaxle 2000–01 models

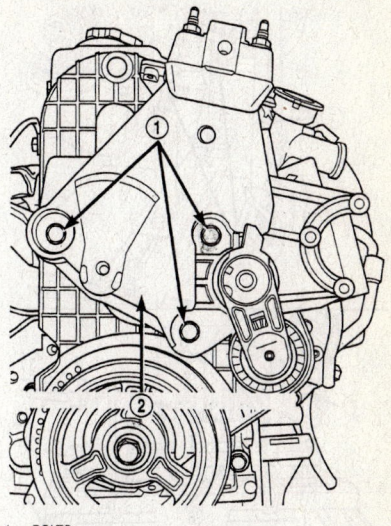

1 – BOLTS
2 – ENGINE MOUNT BRACKET ASSEMBLY

9306EG19

Exploded view of the right mount bracket—2000–01 models

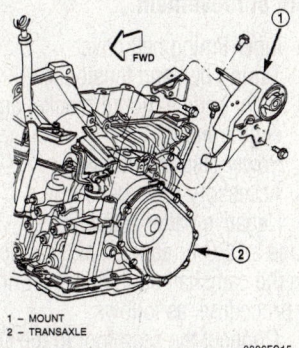

1 – MOUNT
2 – TRANSAXLE

9306EG15

Exploded view of the left mount—Automatic transaxle 2000–01 models

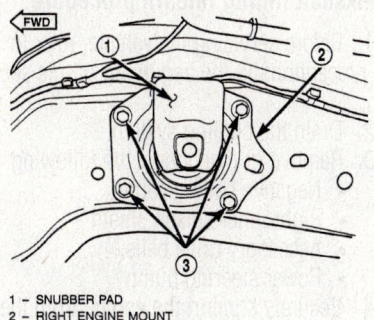

1 – SNUBBER PAD
2 – RIGHT ENGINE MOUNT
3 – BOLTS

9306EG17

Exploded view of the right mount—2000–01 models

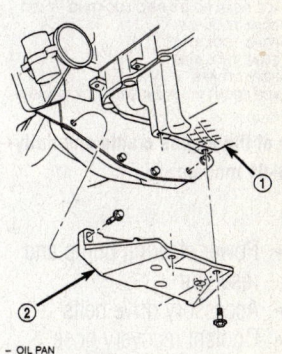

1 – OIL PAN
2 – STRUCTURAL COLLAR

9306EG18

Exploded view of the structural collar—2000–01 models

from moving when removing or installing the engine and transaxle.

9. Install safety straps around the engine to the cradle; tighten the straps and lock them into position.

10. Raise the vehicle enough to see if the straps are tight enough to hold the cradle assembly to the engine.

11. Lower the vehicle so the weight of the engine and transaxle ONLY is on the cradle.

12. Remove or disconnect the following:
- Upper engine torque strut
- Right and left engine/transaxle mount through-bolts

13. Raise the vehicle slowly, until it is about 6 in. (15cm) above normal engine mount locations.

14. Remove or disconnect the following:
- Alternator
- Lower bracket and upper mounting bolt

15. Continue raising the vehicle until the engine/transaxle assembly clears the compartment.

➡**If may be necessary to joggle the engine/transaxle assembly with the cradle to clear the body flanges.**

To install:

16. If removed, torque the left engine mount as follows:
   a. Engine mount-to-rail fasteners: 21 ft. lbs. (28 Nm).
   b. Engine mount bracket-to-engine bolts: 50 ft. lbs. (68 Nm).

17. If removed, torque the right engine mount as follows:
   a. Engine mount-to-rail fasteners: 21 ft. lbs. (28 Nm).
   b. Engine mount bracket-to-engine bolts: 45 ft. lbs. (61 Nm).

18. Position the engine/transaxle assembly and lower the vehicle slowly, until the vehicle is within 6 in. (15cm) of the engine mount locations.

19. Install or connect the following:
- Lower bracket and upper mounting bolt
- Alternator

20. Continue lowering the vehicle until the right and left engine/transaxle mount holes align; then, install and torque the through-bolts to 87 ft. lbs. (118 Nm).

21. Install the upper engine torque strut. Torque the through-bolt to 87 ft. lbs. (118 Nm).

22. Remove the engine/transaxle safety straps and the dolly and cradle.

23. Install the structural collar and torque the bolts, in 3 steps, using the following procedure:
   a. Step 1: Collar-to-oil pan bolts to 30 inch lbs. (3 Nm).
   b. Step 2: Collar-to-transaxle bolts to 80 ft. lbs. (108 Nm).
   c. Step 3: Collar-to-oil pan bolts to 40 ft. lbs. (54 Nm).

24. Install or connect the following:
- Lower engine torque strut. Torque the through-bolts to 87 ft. lbs. (118 Nm).
- Downstream O2S connector
- Exhaust pipe, to the manifold
- Halfshafts
- Right inner splash shield
- Front wheels

Timing belt service is covered in Section 4 of this manual

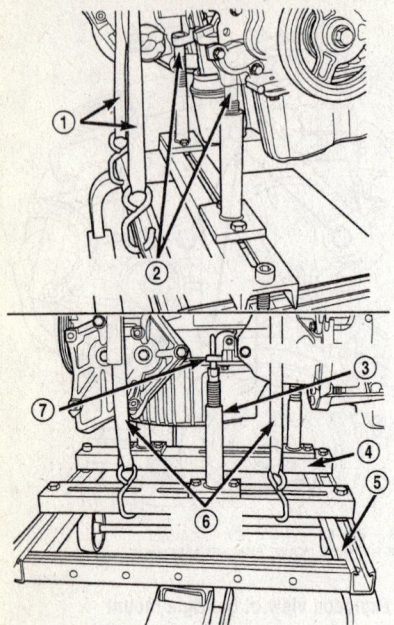

1 – SAFETY STRAPS
2 – PLACE REAR POSTS INTO LOCATING HOLES
3 – SPECIAL TOOL 6848
4 – SPECIAL TOOL 6710
5 – SPECIAL TOOL 6135
6 – SAFETY STRAPS
7 – PLACE FRONT POST UNDER BLOCK FLANGE

9306EG20

View of the engine cradle and dolly—2000–01 models

- Power steering pump and reservoir
- Accessory drive belts
- Coolant recovery hose
- Brake booster vacuum hose
- Heater hoses
- Ground wires
- PDC
- Engine wiring harness
- Shift linkage to the transaxle
- Clutch cable (manual transaxle)
- Automatic transaxle cooler lines, if equipped
- Lower radiator hose
- Fan module assembly
- Upper radiator hose
- Air cleaner assembly
- Electrical connectors
- Throttle cables
- Air intake duct to the intake manifold
- Battery and battery tray

25. Refill the crankcase.
26. Refill the cooling system.
27. After all components are installed, perform the camshaft and crankshaft timing relearn procedure as follows:

    a. Connect a DRB or equivalent, scan tool to the DLC (located under the instrument panel, near the steering column).

    b. Turn the ignition switch **ON**, and access the "miscellaneous" screen.

    c. Select "re-learn cam/crank" option and follow the directions on the scan tool screen.

28. If equipped with air conditioning, recharge the system.

Water Pump

REMOVAL & INSTALLATION

➡**After all components are installed on the engine, a DRB scan tool is necessary to perform the camshaft and crankshaft timing relearn procedure.**

1. Before servicing the vehicle, refer to the precautions in the beginning of this section.
2. Drain the cooling system.
3. Remove or disconnect the following:
   - Negative battery cable
   - Right inner splash shield
   - Accessory drive belts
   - Power steering pump
4. Securely support the engine from the bottom with a jack.
5. Remove or disconnect the following:
   - Right engine mount
   - Power steering pump bracket bolts, move the pump/bracket assembly aside

➡**It is not necessary to disconnect the power steering lines.**

   - Right engine mount bracket
   - Timing belt tensioner and timing belt
   - Camshaft sprocket(s)
   - Inner timing belt cover
   - Water pump and discard the O-ring

To install:
6. Install or connect the following:
   - New O-ring, in the water pump groove

➡**Hold the O-ring in place with a few small dabs of suitable silicone sealant.**

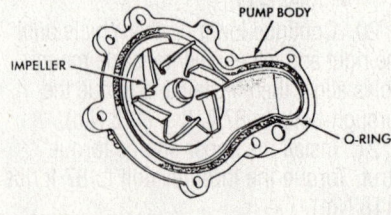

7922EG05

Be sure the O-ring is seated in the groove before installing the new pump

Before proceeding, be sure the O-ring gasket is properly seated in the water pump groove before tightening the screws. An improperly installed O-ring could cause a coolant leak.

- Water pump, torque the bolt to 108 inch lbs. (12 Nm). Use a pressure tester to pressurize the cooling system to 15 psi (103 kPa) and check the water pump shaft seal and O-ring for leaks.

➡**Rotate the pump by hand to check for freedom of movement.**

- Inner timing belt cover
- Timing belt and tensioner
- Right engine mount bracket and engine mount
- Power steering pump
- Accessory drive belts
- Negative battery cable

7. Use a DRB or equivalent, scan tool to perform the camshaft and crankshaft timing relearn procedure, as follows:

    a. Connect the scan tool to the DLC, located under the instrument panel near the steering column.

    b. Turn the ignition switch **ON**, and access the "miscellaneous" screen.

    c. Select the "re-learn cam/crank" option, then follow the instructions on the scan tool screen.

Cylinder Head

REMOVAL & INSTALLATION

1997–99 Models

➡**After all components are installed on the engine, a DRB scan tool is necessary to perform the camshaft and crankshaft timing relearn procedure.**

1. Before servicing the vehicle, refer to the precautions in the beginning of this section.
2. Properly relieve the fuel system pressure.
3. Drain the cooling system.
4. Remove or disconnect the following:

- Negative battery cable
- Air cleaner inlet duct and air cleaner
- Vacuum lines and electrical wiring
- Fuel lines from the throttle body
- Throttle linkage

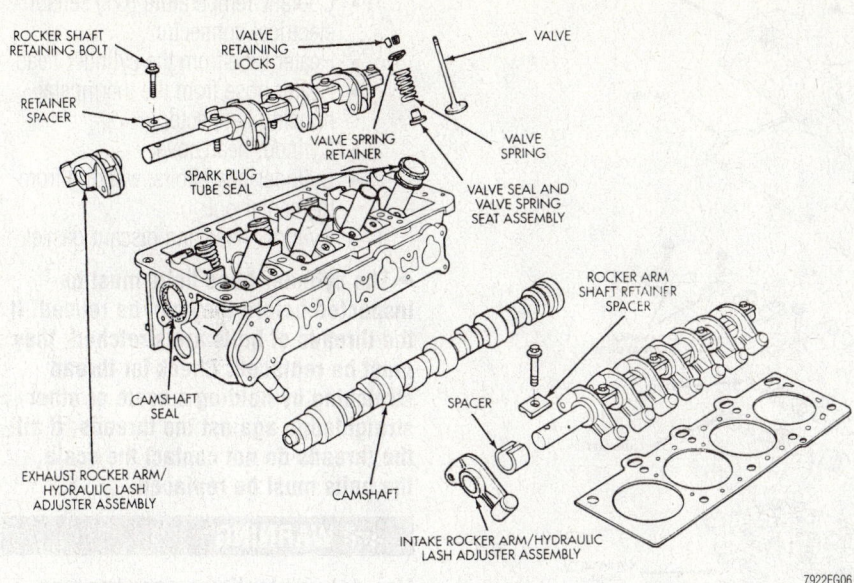

Exploded view of the cylinder head and valvetrain components—SOHC engine

7922EG06

- Accessory drive belts
- Power brake vacuum hose from the intake manifold
- Exhaust pipe from the manifold
- Power steering pump, move it aside. DO NOT disconnect the fluid lines.
- Ignition coil pack wiring connector
- Ignition coil pack and bracket
- Cam sensor electrical connector
- Fuel injector electrical connector
- Intake manifold
- Timing belt
- Timing belt tensioner, for DOHC engine
- Camshaft sprocket
- Inner timing belt cover
- Rocker arm (valve) cover
- Camshaft and cam follower assemblies, for DOHC engine

5. For SOHC engine, remove or disconnect the following:
- Rocker arm shaft assemblies
- Oil separator, if necessary
- Heater hoses
- Any remaining hoses or lines

6. Remove or disconnect the following:
- Cylinder head bolts, working from the center outward
- Cylinder head

➡The cylinder head bolts must be inspected before they can be reused. If the threads of bolts are stretched, they must be replaced. Check for thread stretching by holding a scale or other straightedge against the threads. If all the threads do not contact the scale, the bolts must be replaced.

✳✳ WARNING

Use only a plastic scraper to clean the mating surfaces. NEVER use metal, as this may gouge the surfaces and cause leaks!

7. Cover the combustion chambers, then use a plastic scraper to thoroughly and carefully clean the engine block and cylinder head mating surfaces.

To install:

8. Install or connect the following:
- New head gasket
- Cylinder head

➡Refer to Section 1 of this manual for the cylinder head torque sequence illustration. The illustration is located after the Torque Specification Chart.

9. Lubricate the cylinder head bolt threads. The 4 short bolts (110mm for 1997–98 or 164mm for 1999) are installed in positions 7, 8, 9 and 10.

10. For SOHC engines, torque the cylinder head bolts, in the sequence, to:
   a. Step 1: 25 ft. lbs. (34 Nm).
   b. Step 2: 50 ft. lbs. (68 Nm).
   c. Step 3: 50 ft. lbs. (68 Nm).
   d. Step 4: An additional ¼ turn. DO NOT use a torque wrench for this step.

11. For DOHC engines, torque the cylinder head bolts, in the sequence, in the following order:
   a. Bolts 1–6: 25 ft. lbs. (34 Nm) and bolts 7–10: 20 ft. lbs. (28 Nm).
   b. Bolts 1–6: 50 ft. lbs. (68 Nm) and bolts 7–10: 20 ft. lbs. (28 Nm).
   c. Bolts 1–6: 50 ft. lbs. (68 Nm) and bolts 7–10: 20 ft. lbs. (28 Nm).
   d. Tighten all bolts an additional ¼ turn. DO NOT use a torque wrench for this step.

12. For SOHC engine, install or connect the following:
- Heater hoses
- Any removed hoses or lines
- Oil separator, if necessary
- Rocker arm shaft assemblies

13. Install or connect the following:
- Camshaft and cam follower assemblies, for DOHC engine
- Rocker arm (valve) cover
- Inner timing belt cover
- Camshaft sprocket
- Timing belt tensioner, for DOHC engine
- Timing belt
- Intake manifold
- Fuel injector electrical connector
- Cam sensor electrical connector
- Ignition coil pack and bracket
- Ignition coil pack wiring connector
- Power steering pump
- Exhaust pipe to the manifold
- Power brake vacuum hose to the intake manifold
- Accessory drive belts
- Throttle linkage
- Fuel lines to the throttle body
- Vacuum lines and electrical wiring
- Air cleaner inlet duct and air cleaner
- Negative battery cable

14. Refill the cooling system.

15. Use a DRB or equivalent, scan tool to perform the camshaft and crankshaft timing relearn procedure, as follows:
   a. Connect the scan tool to the DLC, located under the instrument panel near the steering column.
   b. Turn the ignition switch **ON**, and access the "miscellaneous" screen.
   c. Select the "re-learn cam/crank" option, then follow the instructions on the scan tool screen.

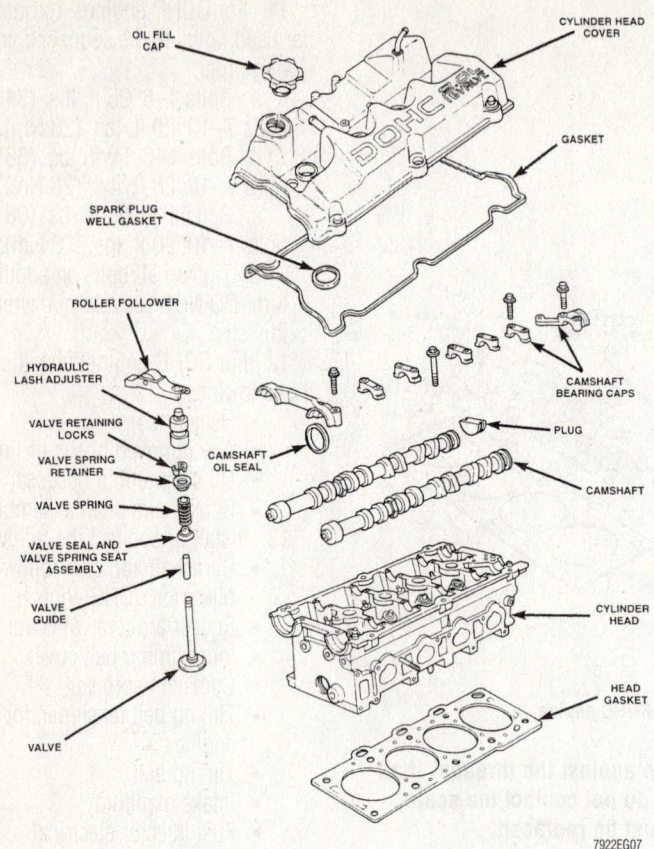

Exploded view of the cylinder head and valvetrain components—DOHC engine

2000–01 Models

➡After all components are installed on the engine, a DRB scan tool is necessary to perform the camshaft and crankshaft timing relearn procedure.

1. Before servicing the vehicle, refer to the precautions in the beginning of this section.

2. Properly relieve the fuel system pressure.

3. Drain the cooling system.

4. Remove or disconnect the following:
- Negative battery cable
- Power steering/air conditioning drive belt
- Exhaust pipe from the manifold
- Right front wheel
- Right side splash shield
- Alternator drive belt
- Crankshaft damper
- Lower torque strut
- Upper torque strut
- Ground strap from the engine mount bracket
- Power steering hose support clip from the engine mount bracket
- Power steering pump, move it aside

5. Place a jack under the engine and support it.

6. Remove or disconnect the following:
- Right side engine mount-to-bracket through-bolt
- Lower engine mount bracket bolt

7. Slightly, raise the engine.

8. Remove or disconnect the following:
- Upper engine mount bracket bolts
- Engine mount bracket

➡It may be necessary to raise and lower the engine until the bracket clears the engine components.

- Front timing belt cover

9. Rotate the crankshaft and align the timing marks.

10. Remove or disconnect the following:
- Timing belt and tensioner
- Camshaft sprocket
- Rear timing belt cover
- Fuel line from the fuel rail
- Coolant recovery container
- Ground wire from the cylinder head
- Upper radiator hose
- Intake manifold
- Ignition coil electrical connector
- Coil pack
- Spark plug wires
- Crankcase Closed Ventilation (CCV) hose from the valve cover
- Cam sensor electrical connector
- Coolant Temperature (CT) sensor electrical connector
- Heater tube from the cylinder head
- Heater hose from the thermostat housing connector
- Cylinder head cover
- Cylinder head bolts, working from the center out
- Cylinder head and discard gasket

➡The cylinder head bolts must be inspected before they can be reused. If the threads of bolts are stretched, they must be replaced. Check for thread stretching by holding a scale or other straightedge against the threads. If all the threads do not contact the scale, the bolts must be replaced.

✳✳ WARNING

Use only a plastic scraper to clean the mating surfaces. NEVER use metal, as this may gouge the surfaces and cause leaks!

11. Cover the combustion chambers, then use a plastic scraper to thoroughly and carefully clean the engine block and cylinder head mating surfaces.

To install:

12. Install or connect the following:
- New head gasket, apply Mopar Gasket Sealant to both sides of the gasket
- Cylinder head

➡Refer to Section 1 of this manual for the cylinder head torque sequence illustration. The illustration is located after the Torque Specification Chart.

13. Lubricate the cylinder head bolt threads. The 4 short bolts (164mm) are installed in positions 7, 8, 9 and 10.

14. For SOHC engines, torque the cylinder head bolts, in the sequence, to:
   a. Step 1: 25 ft. lbs. (34 Nm).
   b. Step 2: 50 ft. lbs. (68 Nm).
   c. Step 3: 50 ft. lbs. (68 Nm).
   d. Step 4: An additional ¼ turn. DO NOT use a torque wrench for this step.

15. Install or connect the following:
- Cylinder head cover
- Heater hose to the thermostat housing connector
- Heater tube to the cylinder head
- CT sensor electrical connector
- Cam sensor electrical connector
- CCV hose to the valve cover
- Coil pack
- Spark plug wires
- Ignition coil electrical connector
- Intake manifold

- Upper radiator hose
- Ground wire to the cylinder head
- Coolant recovery container
- Fuel line to the fuel rail
- Rear timing belt cover
- Camshaft sprocket
- Timing belt and tensioner
- Front timing belt cover
- Engine mount bracket
- Upper engine mount bracket bolts
- Lower engine mount bracket bolt
- Right side engine mount-to-bracket through-bolt. Torque it to 87 ft. lbs. (118 Nm)

16. Remove the jack from under the engine.

17. Install or connect the following:
- Power steering pump
- Power steering hose support clip to the engine mount bracket
- Ground strap, to the engine mount bracket
- Upper torque strut
- Lower torque strut
- Crankshaft damper. Torque bolt to 100 ft. lbs. (136 Nm).
- Alternator drive belt
- Right side splash shield
- Right front wheel
- Exhaust pipe to the manifold
- Power steering/air conditioning drive belt
- Negative battery cable

18. Refill the cooling system.

19. Use a DRB or equivalent, scan tool to perform the camshaft and crankshaft timing relearn procedure, as follows:

a. Connect the scan tool to the DLC, located under the instrument panel near the steering column.

b. Turn the ignition switch **ON**, and access the "miscellaneous" screen.

c. Select the "re-learn cam/crank" option, then follow the instructions on the scan tool screen.

Rocker Arms/Shafts

REMOVAL & INSTALLATION

This procedure applies to Single Overhead Camshaft (SOHC) engines only. On Dual Overhead Camshaft (DOHC) engines, the valves are actuated directly by the camshafts and no rocker arms are used.

1. Before servicing the vehicle, refer to the precautions in the beginning of this section.

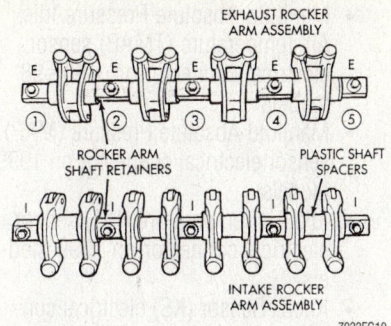

Be sure to note the rocker arm shaft component positions before disassembling the rocker arm shafts

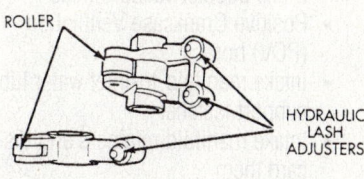

Disassembled view of an intake and exhaust rocker arm

2. Remove or disconnect the following:
- Negative battery cable
- Cylinder head cover

➡Be sure to note the installed positions of the rocker arm shaft assemblies before removal.

- Rocker arm shaft attaching fasteners, loosen them
- Rocker arm shaft assembly from the cylinder head
- Rocker arm assemblies, slide the rocker arms and spacers off the shaft

➡Be sure to keep the spacers and rocker arms in their original locations for installation.

3. Inspect the rocker arm for scoring, wear on the roller or damage to the rocker arm; replace any components showing damage. Check the location where the rocker arms mount to the shafts for wear or damage. Replace if damaged or worn. The rocker arm shaft is hollow and is used as a lubrication oil duct. Check the oil holes for clogs with a small piece of wire, and clean as required. Lubricate the rocker arms and spacers. Be sure to install in their original locations.

To install:

✳✳ WARNING

Set the crankshaft to 3 notches before Top Dead Center (TDC) before installing the rocker arm shafts, otherwise valvetrain damage may occur when the mounting bolts are tightened.

4. Set the crankshaft sprocket to TDC by aligning the mark on the sprocket with the arrow on the oil pump housing, then back off to 3 notches before TDC.

5. Install the rocker arm/hydraulic lash adjuster assembly making sure that the adjusters are at least partially full of oil. This is indicated by little or no plunger travel when the lash adjuster is depressed. If there is excessive plunger travel, submerge the rocker arm assembly into clean engine oil and pump the plunger until the lash adjuster travel is taken up. If travel is not reduced, replace the assembly. The hydraulic lash adjuster and rocker arm are serviced as an assembly.

6. Install or connect the following:
- Rocker arm and shaft assemblies. Position the rocker arm shafts with the **NOTCH FACING UP** and toward the timing belt side of the engine.

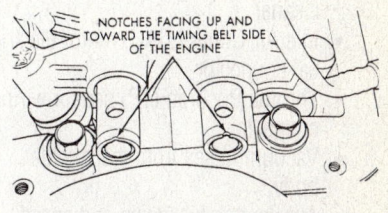

Be sure the notches in the rocker arm shafts point up and toward the timing belt side of the engine

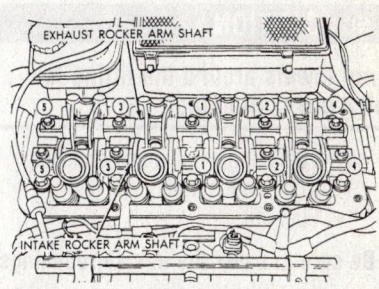

Rocker arm shaft assembly bolt tightening sequence

Refer to Section 1 for engine rebuilding specifications

- Retainers in their original positions on the exhaust and intake shafts. Tighten the bolts, in the sequence, to 21 ft. lbs. (28 Nm).
- Rocker arm (valve) cover
- Negative battery cable

✳✳ WARNING

When installing the intake rocker arm shaft assembly, be sure the plastic spacers do not interfere with the spark plug tubes. If the spacers do interfere, rotate them until they are at the proper angle. To avoid damaging the spark plug tubes, do not try to rotate the spacers by forcing the shaft down.

Intake Manifold

REMOVAL & INSTALLATION

SOHC Engine

1997–99 MODELS

1. Before servicing the vehicle, refer to the precautions in the beginning of this section.
2. Properly relieve the fuel system pressure.
3. Remove or disconnect the following:
   - Negative battery cable
   - Fresh air inlet duct from the air cleaner
   - Idle Air Control (IAC) motor electrical connector
   - Throttle Position (TP) sensor wiring connector
   - Vacuum hoses from the throttle body
   - Accelerator, kickdown and speed control cables from the brackets and throttle lever
   - Throttle body
   - Air duct and upper air filter housing

✳✳ CAUTION

Wrap towels around the fitting to catch any spilled fuel.

- Fuel supply line quick-connect, from the fuel rail
- Fuel rail

➡ **Be sure to cover the injector openings.**

✳✳ WARNING

DO NOT set the fuel injectors on their tips, as this may damage them.

- Manifold Absolute Pressure/Idle Air Temperature (TMAP) sensor electrical connector on 1997–98 models
- Manifold Absolute Pressure (MAP) sensor electrical connector on 1999 models
- Idle Air Temperature (IAT) sensor electrical connector on 1999 models
- Knock Sensor (KS) electrical connector
- Starter electrical connectors and move aside
- Exhaust Gas Recirculation (EGR) tube from the intake manifold and discard the gasket
- Brake booster vacuum hose
- Positive Crankcase Ventilation (PCV) hose
- Intake manifold-to-inlet water tube support fastener
- Intake manifold retainers and discard them
- Intake manifold and discard the gaskets and seals

4. Thoroughly, clean the gasket mating surfaces.

To install:

➡ **Refer to Section 1 of this manual for the intake manifold torque sequence illustration. The illustration is located after the Torque Specification Chart.**

5. Install or connect the following:
   - New gaskets and seals
   - Intake manifold. Torque the new retainers, in sequence, to 108 inch lbs. (12 Nm).
   - Intake manifold-to-water inlet support fastener. Torque to 108 inch lbs. (12 Nm).
   - Fuel rail. Torque the screws to 17 ft. lbs. (23 Nm)
   - PCV hose
   - Brake booster hose

6. Inspect the fuel line quick-connect fittings for damage and replace if necessary. Apply a small amount of clean engine oil to the fuel inlet tube.

7. Install or connect the following:
   - Fuel supply hose to the fuel rail assembly. Ensure the connection is fastened securely by pulling on the connector.
   - Throttle body. Torque the fasteners to 16 ft. lbs. (22 Nm).
   - Transaxle-to-throttle body support bracket. Torque to 108 inch lbs. (12 Nm) at the throttle body first; then, the bracket at the transaxle.

- TMAP sensor electrical connector on 1997–98 models
- MAP sensor electrical connector on 1999 models
- IAT sensor electrical connector on 1999 models
- KS and starter electrical connectors
- IAC motor and TP sensor connectors
- Throttle body vacuum hoses
- Accelerator, kickdown and speed control cables to their bracket and throttle lever
- EGR tube to the intake manifold. Torque the retainers to 95 inch lbs. (11 Nm).
- Air duct to the air filter housing. Torque the clamp to 30 inch lbs. (3 Nm).
- Negative battery cable

2000–01 MODELS

1. Before servicing the vehicle, refer to the precautions in the beginning of this section.
2. Properly relieve the fuel system pressure.
3. Remove or disconnect the following:
   - Negative battery cable
   - Throttle body-to-intake manifold air duct
   - Fuel supply line quick-connect from the fuel tube assembly

✳✳ CAUTION

Wrap towels around the fitting to catch any spilled fuel.

- Fuel rail from the engine

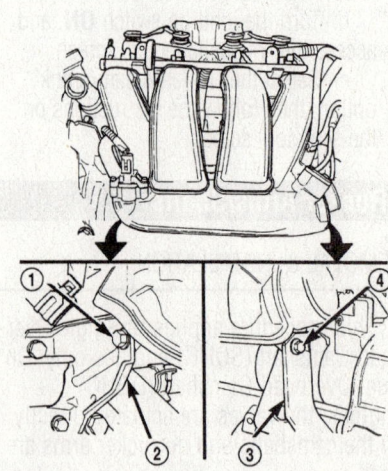

1 – BOLT
2 – BRACKET
3 – BRACKET
4 – BOLT

9306EG21

View of the intake manifold lower supports—2000–01 SOHC engines

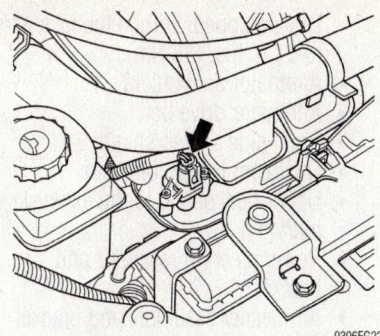

View of the Manifold Absolute Pressure (MAP) sensor—2000–01 SOHC engines

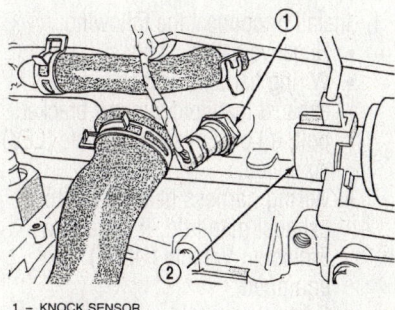

1 – KNOCK SENSOR
2 – STARTER MOTOR

View of the Knock Sensor (KS)—2000–01 SOHC engines

✲✲ WARNING

Cover the fuel injector openings. DO NOT set the fuel injectors on their tips, as this may damage them.

- Manifold Absolute Pressure (MAP) sensor electrical connector
- Knock Sensor (KS) electrical connector
- Starter electrical connectors, move it aside
- Brake booster vacuum hose
- Positive Crankcase Ventilation (PCV) hose
- Intake manifold-to-lower support bracket bolts
- Intake manifold fasteners and discard them
- Intake manifold and discard the gaskets and seals

4. Thoroughly clean the gasket mating surfaces.

To install:

➡Refer to Section 1 of this manual for the intake manifold torque sequence illustration. The illustration is located after the Torque Specification Chart.

5. Install or connect the following:
- New gaskets and seals
- Intake manifold. Torque the new retainers in sequence to 105 inch lbs. (12 Nm).
- Intake manifold-to-lower support bracket bolts. Torque the bolts to 95 inch lbs. (11 Nm).
- PCV hose
- Brake booster vacuum hose
- Starter electrical connectors
- Knock Sensor (KS) electrical connector
- Manifold Absolute Pressure (MAP) sensor electrical connector
- Fuel rail. Torque the bolts to 16 ft. lbs. (23 Nm).
- Fuel supply line quick-connect to the fuel tube assembly
- Throttle body-to-intake manifold air duct
- Negative battery cable

DOHC Engine

1. Before servicing the vehicle, refer to the precautions in the beginning of this section.
2. Relieve the fuel system pressure.
3. Remove or disconnect the following:
- Negative battery cable
- Air inlet duct from the intake manifold

✲✲ CAUTION

Wrap towels around the fitting to catch any spilled fuel.

- Fuel supply line quick-connect from the fuel rail
- Air inlet duct
- Engine Coolant Temperature (ECT) sensor connector
- Heater hose from the intake manifold
- Heater tube from the bottom of the intake manifold
- Upper radiator and coolant recovery hoses

✲✲ WARNING

Do not allow the injectors to rest on their tips as this may damage them.

- Fuel rail

➡**Cover the injector openings to prevent debris from entering the ports.**

- Accelerator, kickdown and speed control (if equipped) cables from the throttle lever and bracket
- Idle Air Control (IAC) motor electrical connector
- Throttle Position (TP) sensor electrical connector
- Throttle body vacuum hoses
- Throttle body
- Manifold Absolute Pressure/Idle Air Temperature (TMAP) sensor electrical connector on 1997–98 models
- Manifold Absolute Pressure (MAP) sensor electrical connector on 1999 models
- Idle Air Temperature (IAT) sensor electrical connector on 1999 models
- Positive Crankcase Ventilation (PCV) hose
- Brake booster hose
- Knock Sensor (KS) electrical connector. Detach the wiring harness from the tab located on the heater tube.
- Starter electrical connectors
- Exhaust Gas Recirculation (EGR) tube
- Upper and lower intake manifold assemblies and discard the gaskets

➡**If necessary, separate the upper and lower manifolds.**

4. Thoroughly clean all of the gasket mating surfaces.

To install:

➡**Refer to Section 1 of this manual for the intake manifold torque sequence illustration. The illustration is located after the Torque Specification Chart.**

5. Install or connect the following:
- Upper and lower manifold, using a new gasket. Torque the bolts to 21 ft. lbs. (28 Nm) in the sequence.
- Intake manifold using a new gasket. Torque the fasteners to 21 ft. lbs. (28 Nm).
- Fuel rail onto the intake manifold. Torque the screws to 17 ft. lbs. (23 Nm).
- PCV hose
- Brake booster vacuum hose

6. Inspect the fuel line quick-connect fittings for damage and replace, if necessary. Apply a small amount of clean engine oil to the fuel inlet tube.

7. Install or connect the following:
- Fuel supply hose to the fuel rail assembly

➡**Ensure the connection is fastened securely by pulling on the connector.**

- Heater tube and hose to the intake manifold
- Upper radiator and coolant recovery reservoir hoses
- ECT sensor electrical connector
- Throttle body. Torque the fastener to 16 ft. lbs. (22 Nm).
- TMAP sensor electrical connector on 1997–98 models
- MAP sensor electrical connector on 1999 models
- IAT sensor electrical connector on 1999 models
- KS and starter electrical connectors
- Wiring harness to the heater tube tab
- IAC motor and TP sensor electrical connectors
- Throttle body vacuum hoses
- Accelerator, kickdown and speed control cables to their bracket and throttle lever
- EGR tube. Torque to 95 inch lbs. (11 Nm).
- Intake manifold side retainers. Torque to 95 inch lbs. (11 Nm).
- Air duct to the air filter housing. Torque the clamp to 25 inch lbs. (3 Nm).
- Negative battery cable

Exhaust Manifold

REMOVAL & INSTALLATION

1997–98 Models

1. Before servicing the vehicle, refer to the precautions in the beginning of this section.
2. Remove or disconnect the following:
   - Negative battery cable
   - Air cleaner assembly and bracket
   - Power steering pump reservoir, move it aside. DO NOT disconnect the fluid lines.
   - Exhaust manifold heat shield
   - Upstream Heated Oxygen Sensor (HO2S) connector

➡️ **It may be necessary to loosen the alternator bracket bolt to remove the outer exhaust manifold bolt.**

   - Exhaust manifold and discard the gasket
3. Thoroughly clean the mating surfaces.
To install:
4. Install or connect the following:
   - New gasket
   - Exhaust manifold. Apply Mopar Stud and Bearing Mount or equiva-

lent, to the fasteners. Torque to 17 ft. lbs. (23 Nm), starting at the center and working outward in both directions.

➡️ **Repeat this procedure until all fasteners are tightened to specifications.**

- Alternator bracket bolt, if loosened
- Exhaust manifold heat shield
- Power steering pump reservoir
- Upstream HO2S
- Air cleaner bracket and assembly
- Exhaust pipe to the manifold. Torque the fasteners to 21 ft. lbs. (28 Nm).
- Negative battery cable

1999 Models

1. Before servicing the vehicle, refer to the precautions in the beginning of this section.
2. Release the fuel pressure.
3. Remove or disconnect the following:
   - Negative battery cable
   - Fuel supply line from the fuel rail
   - Air cleaner assembly and bracket
   - Power steering reservoir bracket and move the reservoir aside
   - Upper heat shield from the exhaust manifold
   - Upstream Heated Oxygen Sensor (HO2S) connector
   - Right side splash shield
   - Alternator drive belt
   - Alternator spill shield
   - Exhaust pipe from the manifold. If Low Emission Vehicle (LEV) equipped, discard the manifold-to-flex joint gasket.
   - Lower heat shield from the exhaust manifold
   - Lower exhaust manifold fasteners
   - Upper exhaust manifold fasteners
   - Exhaust manifold and discard the gasket
4. Thoroughly clean the mating surfaces.
To install:
5. Install or connect the following:
   - New gasket
   - Exhaust manifold. Apply Mopar Stud and Bearing Mount or equivalent, to the fasteners. Install the fasteners and tighten to 17 ft. lbs. (23 Nm), starting at the center and working outward in both directions. Repeat this procedure until all fasteners are tightened to specifications.
   - Lower heat shield to the exhaust manifold
   - Exhaust pipe to the manifold. Use a new manifold-to-flex joint gasket, if

LEV equipped. Torque the fasteners to 21 ft. lbs. (28 Nm).
- Alternator spill shield
- Alternator drive belt
- Right side splash shield
- Upstream HO2S connector
- Upper heat shield to the exhaust manifold
- Power steering reservoir and bracket
- Air cleaner assembly and bracket
- Fuel supply line to the fuel rail
- Negative battery cable

2000–01 Models

1. Install or connect the following:
   - Negative battery cable
   - Wiring harness heat shield-to-exhaust manifold support bracket bolt, if Low Emission Vehicle (LEV) equipped
   - Wiring harness heat shield-to-exhaust manifold, if Ultra Low Emission Vehicle (ULEV) equipped
   - Exhaust manifold support bracket bolt, if LEV equipped
   - Flex joint-to-exhaust manifold flange fasteners and move the exhaust system rearward
   - Cylinder head-to-exhaust manifold support bracket bolt, if ULEV equipped
   - CCV hose from the rear of the cylinder head cover
   - Oxygen Sensor (O2S) connector and harness clip
   - Upper heat shield
   - Exhaust manifold bolts
   - Cylinder head cover, if ULEV equipped

➡️ **Cover the cylinder head opening.**

   - Exhaust manifold and discard gasket.

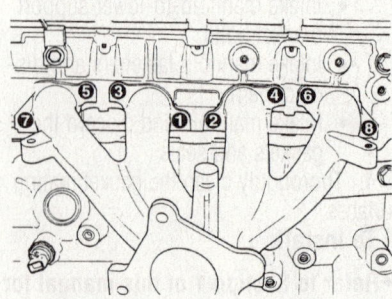

(14) Lower vehicle.
(15) Connect negative cable to battery.

9306EG25

Exhaust manifold tightening sequence–2000–01 models

- Manifold from the top of the vehicle

To install:

2. Install or connect the following:
- New gasket
- Exhaust manifold. Torque the bolts, in sequence, to 16 ft. lbs. (23 Nm).
- Upper heat shield, if ULEV equipped. Torque bolts to 16 ft. lbs. (23 Nm).
- Upper and lower heat shields. Torque bolts to 95 inch lbs. (11 Nm).
- O₂S connector and harness clip
- Cylinder head cover, if ULEV equipped
- CCV hose to the rear of the cylinder head cover
- Flex joint-to-exhaust manifold flange using a new gasket. Torque the fasteners to 21 ft. lbs. (28 Nm).
- Exhaust manifold support bracket bolt, if LEV equipped. Torque the M10 bolt to 40 ft. lbs. (54 Nm), M12 bolt to 70 ft. lbs. (95 Nm) and the nut to 21 ft. lbs. (28 Nm).
- Cylinder head-to-exhaust manifold support bracket bolt, if ULEV equipped. Torque the bolts to 40 ft. lbs. (54 Nm).
- Wiring harness heat shield-to-exhaust manifold, if ULEV equipped
- Wiring harness heat shield-to-exhaust manifold support bracket bolt, if LEV equipped
- Negative battery cable

Front Crankshaft Seal

REMOVAL & INSTALLATION

1. Before servicing the vehicle, refer to the precautions in the beginning of this section.

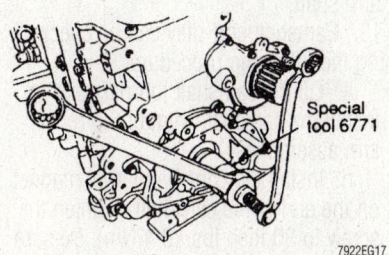

Removing the front crankshaft oil seal

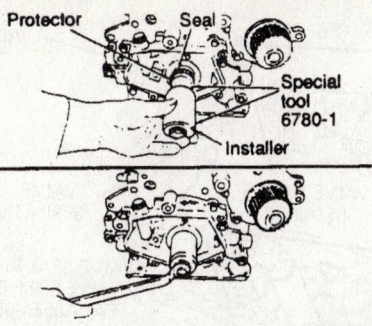

Installing a new seal using Seal Installer 6780-1—proceed with caution if using substitute tools

2. Remove or disconnect the following:
- Negative battery cable
- Accessory drive belts
- Crankshaft damper bolt
- Crankshaft damper, using Puller tool 1026 and Insert tool 6827-A
- Outer timing belt cover

3. Turn the crankshaft clockwise until the engine is at Top Dead Center (TDC) No. 1 cylinder compression stroke (firing position).

4. Remove or disconnect the following:
- Timing belt
- Crankshaft sprocket, using Crankshaft Sprocket Remover tool 6793 and Insert tool C-4685-C2
- Crankshaft key
- Crankshaft oil seal, using a Seal Puller tool 6771

➡Be careful not to damage the seal surface of the cover.

To install:

5. Install or connect the following:
- New front crankshaft oil seal, using Crankshaft Installer tool 6780–1 or equivalent
- Crankshaft key
- Crankshaft timing belt sprocket, using Installer tool 6792

➡Make sure the word FRONT on the crankshaft sprocket is facing outward.

- Timing belt

※※ WARNING

Make sure that all timing marks are properly aligned or engine damage will result.

- Timing belt covers
- Crankshaft damper using thrust bearing washer and bolt from Installer tool 6792. Torque the

damper bolt to 105 ft. lbs. (142 Nm) for 1997–99 models or 100 ft. lbs. (136 Nm) for 2000–01 models.
- Accessory drive belts
- Negative battery cable

Camshaft and Lifters

REMOVAL & INSTALLATION

SOHC Engine

This engine uses a camshaft running in an aluminum cylinder head. Rocker arm shafts mount directly to the cylinder head. Care must be taken to ensure all valve timing marks align after cylinder head and valvetrain service. Please note that the cylinder head must be removed from the vehicle to service the camshaft.

➡After all components are installed on the engine, a DRB scan tool is necessary to perform the camshaft and crankshaft timing relearn procedure.

1. Before servicing the vehicle, refer to the precautions in the beginning of this section.
2. Relieve the fuel system pressure.
3. Remove or disconnect the following:
- Negative battery cable
- Cylinder head cover

➡Mark the rocker arm shaft assemblies to identify them for later installation.

- Rocker arm shaft bolts
- Rocker arm assemblies
- Timing belt and tensioner
- Camshaft sprocket
- Rear timing belt cover
- Cylinder head
- Camshaft Position (CMP) sensor
- Camshaft from the rear of the cylinder head

To install:

➡The cylinder head bolts should be checked for stretching before reuse. If the thread area of the bolt is necked down the bolts must be replaced with new. New head bolts are recommended.

4. Clean all parts well. Inspect the camshaft journals for scoring. Check the oil feed holes in the head for blockage. Check the camshaft bearing journals for scoring. If light scratches are present, they may be removed with 400 grit abrasive paper. If deep

For complete mechanical specifications, refer to Section 1 of this manual

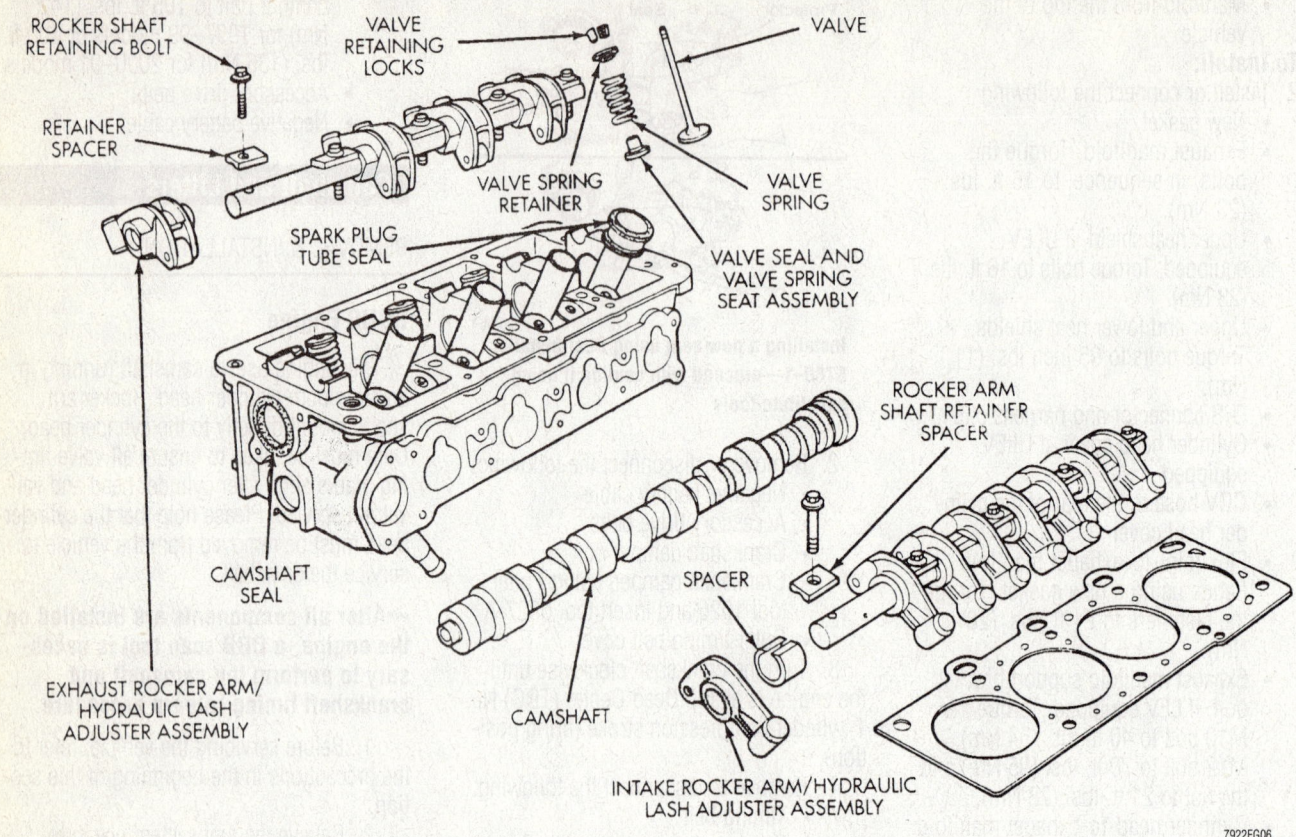

Exploded view of the cylinder head and valvetrain assembly—SOHC engine

scratches are present, replace the camshaft and check the cylinder head for damage. Replace the cylinder head if worn or damaged.

5. If the camshaft lobes show signs of wear, check the corresponding rocker arm roller for wear or damage. Replace rocker arms/hydraulic lash adjuster if worn or damaged. If the camshaft lobes show signs of pitting on the nose, flank or base circle, replace the camshaft.

6. If the rocker arms and shaft are to be serviced, mark the rocker arms so any that are to be returned to service will be installed in their original locations. Slide the rocker arms off the shaft. Keep the spacers and rocker arms in the same location for reassembly.

7. Inspect the rocker arms for scoring, wear on the roller or damage to the shaft. Replace parts as necessary.

8. The rocker arm shaft is hollow and used as a lubrication oil duct. Check that the shaft is clean inside and out.

9. Check all oil holes for clogging with a small wire and clean as required.

10. To assemble, thoroughly lubricate all rocker arm components and spacers, then install them on the rocker arm shaft in their original locations.

11. If the vehicle exhibited a tappet-like

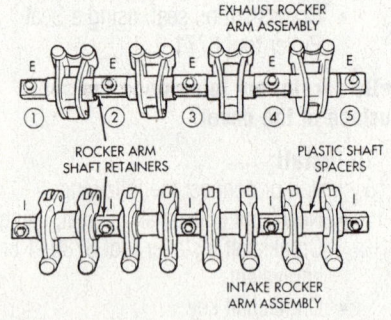

Rocker arm shaft identification—SOHC engine

noise, the valve lash adjusters built into the rocker arms should be cleaned and checked. Lash adjusters removed from a rocker arm should be returned to their original locations. Replace worn or defective lash adjusters.

12. To install a lash adjuster, use the following procedure:

a. Lubricate the lash adjuster thoroughly with clean engine oil.

b. Install the adjuster into the rocker arm making sure the adjuster is at least partially filled with oil.

c. Submerge the rocker arm in clean

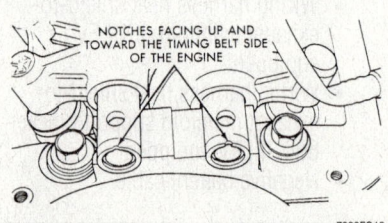

Rocker arm shaft notch location—SOHC engine

engine oil and pump the plunger until the lash adjuster travel is taken up. If travel is not reduced, replace the adjuster.

d. Install the rocker arm on the rocker arm shaft.

13. Camshaft end-play can be checked, using the following procedure:

a. Oil the camshaft journals and install the camshaft without the rocker arm assemblies.

b. Install the camshaft target magnet on the end of the camshaft. Tighten the screw to 30 inch lbs. (3.4 Nm). Be sure to fit the dowels on the magnet in the holes on the camshaft.

c. Install the CMP sensor and tighten the screws to 80 inch lbs. (9 Nm).

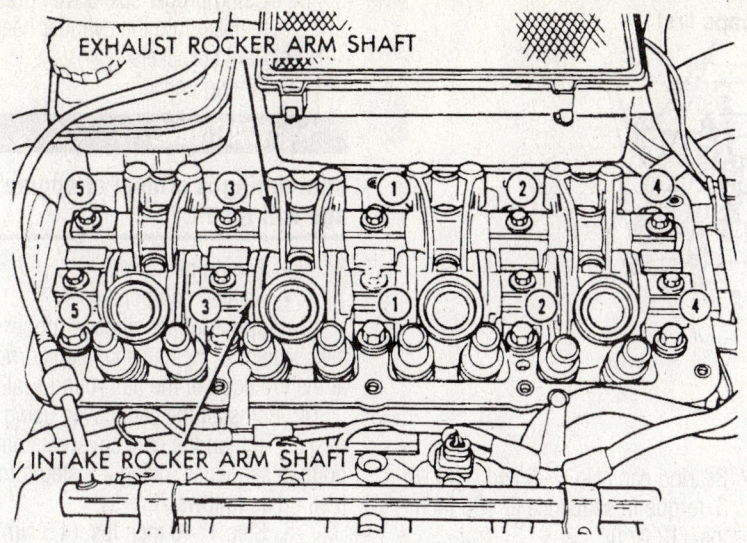

EXHAUST ROCKER ARM SHAFT

INTAKE ROCKER ARM SHAFT

7922EG13

Rocker arm shaft tightening sequence—SOHC engine

d. Setup a dial indicator to touch on the nose of the camshaft.

e. Using a suitable tool, move the camshaft as far rearward as it will go. Be sure the dial indicator probe is in contact with the camshaft.

f. Zero the dial indicator.

g. Move the camshaft as far forward as it will go.

h. Read the end-play on the dial indicator. Specification is 0.005–0.013 inch (0.13–0.33mm).

14. Install or connect the following:
• Camshaft, lubricate the bearing journals thoroughly

➡**Be sure it turns freely.**

• CMP sensor and torque the screws to 85 inch lbs. (9.6 Nm)
• Camshaft seal flush with the cylinder head
• Camshaft sprocket and torque the bolt to 85 ft. lbs. (115 Nm)
• Cylinder head

15. Before installing the rocker arm and shaft assemblies, set the crankshaft to 3 notches before TDC on the crankshaft sprocket.

16. Install or connect the following:
• Rocker arm and shaft assemblies. Position the rocker shafts pointing up and toward the timing belt side of the engine.
• Rocker arm shaft retainers in their original positions. Torque the bolts to 17 ft. lbs. (23 Nm).
• Timing belt

• All electrical, vacuum and fluid connections
• Negative battery cable

17. Refill the cooling system.

➡**An oil and filter change are recommended.**

18. Use a DRB or equivalent, scan tool to perform the camshaft and crankshaft timing relearn procedure, as follows:

a. Connect the scan tool to the DLC (located under the instrument panel, near the steering column).

b. Turn the ignition switch **ON**, and access the "miscellaneous" screen.

c. Select the "re-learn cam/crank" option, then follow the instructions on the scan tool screen.

19. Start the engine and check for leaks. Run the engine with the radiator cap off so as the engine warms and the thermostat opens, coolant can be added to the radiator. Test drive vehicle to check for proper operation.

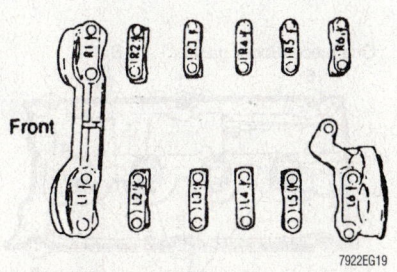

Front

7922EG19

Identifying the camshaft bearing caps—DOHC engine

DOHC Engine

➡**After all components are installed on the engine, a DRB scan tool is necessary to perform the camshaft and crankshaft timing relearn procedure.**

1. Be sure to observe all precautions in the beginning of this section.

2. Remove or disconnect the following:
• Negative battery cable
• Cam cover

➡**Always rotate the crankshaft in a clockwise direction. Make a mark on the back of the timing belt indicating the direction of rotation so it may be reassembled in the same direction if it is to be reused.**

3. Rotate the crankshaft clockwise and align the timing marks so the No. 1 piston will be at Top Dead Center (TDC) of the compression stroke.

4. Remove or disconnect the following:
• Timing belt cover
• Timing belt
• Both camshaft sprockets
• Camshaft bearing caps, loosen the bearing caps in sequence, one camshaft at a time.

➡**The bearing caps are identified for location. Remove the outside bearing caps first. If the bearing caps are difficult to remove, use a plastic hammer to gently tap the rear part of the camshaft.**

• Intake and exhaust camshafts
• Cam follower assemblies from the cylinder head

➡**Keep the cam followers in the order they have been removed from the head for reassembly.**

• Lash adjusters, mark them for reassembly in their original positions

5. Check the camshaft end-play, by performing the following procedure:

a. Oil the camshaft journals and install the camshaft **WITHOUT** cam follower assemblies.

b. Install the rear cam caps.

c. Using a suitable tool, move the camshaft as far rearward as it will go.

d. Attach a dial indicator and zero it.

e. Move the camshaft as far forward as it will go.

f. Measure and record the end-play. End-play specs are: 0.002–0.06 inches (0.05–0.15mm).

Please refer to Section 8 for electric cooling fan wiring schematics

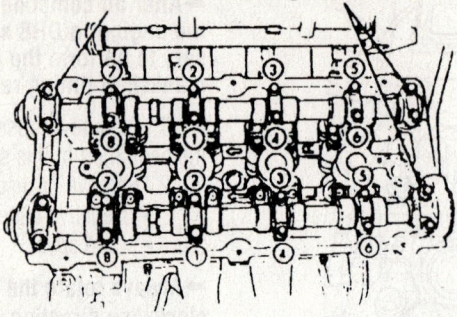

Remove outside bearing caps first

Bearing cap removal sequence—DOHC engine

7922EG20

✳✳ WARNING

The camshafts and their components are NOT interchangeable. Place an identifying mark on each component. Be sure to keep all parts organized for proper reassembly in their original positions.

To install:

6. Before installation, clean the cylinder head and cover mating surfaces. Make certain that the rails are flat.

7. Install or connect the following:
- Lash adjuster assembly, make sure the adjusters are at least partially full of oil.

➡ Lash adjuster oil level is indicated by little or no plunger travel when the adjuster is depressed.

- Cam followers, lubricate them with clean engine oil

8. Check the camshaft journals on the cylinder head and the cam bearings for wear or damage. Check the cam lobes and rocker rollers for damage. Also, check the cylinder head oil holes for clogging.

9. Inspect the cam followers for wear or damage. Replace as necessary.

10. Install or connect the following:
- Camshafts, lubricate with heavy engine oil and position them on the cylinder head

✳✳ WARNING

The pistons should not be at top dead center when installing the camshafts since some valves will be open depending on camshaft position.

➡ Be sure the dowel pin on each camshaft sprocket end is located on the top.

- Bearing caps No. 2–5 and right No. 6, torque in sequence to 108 inch lbs. (12 Nm).

➡ Check the markings on the caps to identify the cap number and intake/exhaust symbol. Be sure the rocker arm is correctly mounted on the lash adjuster and the valve stem end.

11. Apply Mopar Gasket Maker® to the No. 1 and No. 6 bearing caps.

12. Install or connect the following:
- Bearing caps. Torque the bolts, using the same sequence as when removed, to 18 ft. lbs. (24 Nm).
- Oil seal, lubricate with engine oil.

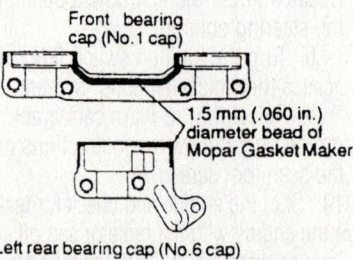

Front bearing cap (No.1 cap)

1.5 mm (.060 in.) diameter bead of Mopar Gasket Maker:

Left rear bearing cap (No.6 cap)

7922EG21

To prevent leaking from the bearing cap ends, apply sealant as shown—DOHC engine

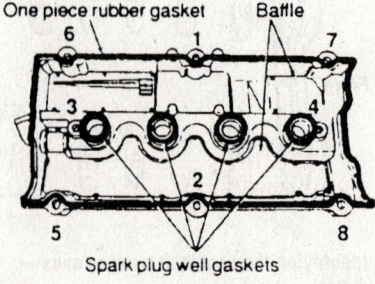

One piece rubber gasket   Baffle

Spark plug well gaskets

7922EG22

Cam cover tightening sequence—DOHC engine

Using proper size driver, press-fit the seal into the cylinder head.
- Cam sprockets
- Timing belt

✳✳ WARNING

Cam timing is critical or engine damage will result.

- Timing belt cover
- Related components

13. Apply Mopar® silicone rubber adhesive sealant at the camshaft cap corners and at the top edge of the half round seal.

14. Reinstall the cam cover, using a new gasket. Tighten the cam cover retaining bolts in sequence, using a 3 step torque method as follows:
a. Step 1: 40 inch lbs. (4.5 Nm).
b. Step 2: 78 inch lbs. (9 Nm).
c. Step 3: 108 inch lbs. (12 Nm).

15. Replace the oil and filter.

➡ If a camshaft had failed, metal particles may be spread throughout the engine, so an oil and filter change should be mandatory.

16. Connect the negative battery cable.

17. Use a DRB or equivalent, scan tool to perform the camshaft and crankshaft timing relearn procedure, as follows:
a. Connect the scan tool to the DLC (located under the instrument panel, near the steering column).
b. Turn the ignition switch **ON**, and access the "miscellaneous" screen.
c. Select the "re-learn cam/crank" option, then follow the instructions on the scan tool screen.

18. Start the engine and check for proper operation and leaks.

Valve Lash

ADJUSTMENT

The engines in these vehicles do not require periodic valve lash adjustment.

➡ Refer to the rocker arm removal and installation procedure for additional information.

Starter Motor

REMOVAL & INSTALLATION

1997–99 Models

1. Remove the negative battery cable.
2. If equipped with Air Conditioning (A/C), perform the following procedure:

a. Support the engine/transaxle assembly with a jack.

b. Remove the front engine mount bolt from the mount/crossmember bracket.

c. Lower and rotate the engine/transaxle assembly forward to provide starter clearance.

➡ **Do not remove the wiring at this time.**

3. Remove or disconnect the following:
- Both starter-to-transaxle bolts
- Starter electrical connectors
- Starter by positioning it vertically and lowering it

➡ **If equipped, move the A/C lines aside.**

To install:

4. Install or connect the following:
- Starter
- Starter electrical connectors
- Starter-to-transaxle bolts. Torque the bolts to 40 ft. lbs. (54 Nm).
- Negative battery cable

5. If equipped with A/C, perform the following steps:

a. Raise and support the engine/transaxle assembly.

b. Install the front engine mount-to-mount/crossmember bracket bolt. Torque the bolt to 40 ft. lbs. (54 Nm).

2000–01 Models

1. Remove or disconnect the following:
- Negative battery cable
- Starter electrical connectors
- Starter-to-engine bolts
- Starter

To install:

2. Install or connect the following:
- Starter. Torque bolts to 40 ft. lbs. (54 Nm).
- Starter electrical connectors
- Negative battery cable

Oil Pan

REMOVAL & INSTALLATION

1997 Models

1. Before servicing the vehicle, refer to the precautions in the beginning of this section.

2. Drain the crankcase.

3. Support the engine and transaxle assembly.

4. Remove or disconnect the following:
- Transaxle bending bracket
- Front engine mount and bracket

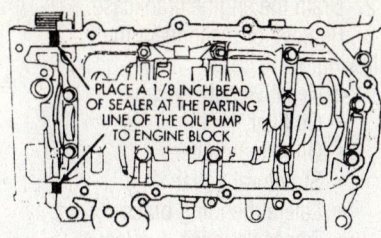

Silicone sealer application locations—oil pan service

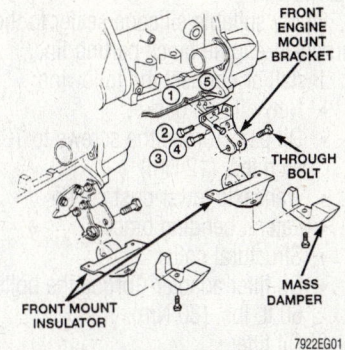

Front engine mount location and bolt identification

- Transaxle inspection cover
- Oil filter and adapter, if equipped with air conditioning
- Oil pan

5. Thoroughly, clean the gasket mating surfaces.

To install:

6. Apply silicone sealer to the oil pump-to-engine block parting line.

7. Install or connect the following:
- New gasket on the oil pan
- Oil pan. Torque the retainers to 105 inch lbs. (12 Nm)
- Oil filter and adapter, if removed
- Transaxle inspection cover
- Front engine mount and bracket

8. Torque the front engine mount retainers, as follows:

a. Engine mount bracket bolt 1: 20 inch lbs. (3 Nm).

b. Engine mount bracket bolts 2, 3 and 4: 80 ft. lbs. (108 Nm).

c. Engine mount bracket bolts 5 and 1: 40 ft. lbs. (54 Nm).

d. Engine mount bracket-to-insulator assembly through-bolt: 40 ft. lbs. (54 Nm).

e. Insulator assembly-to-lower radiator crossmember nuts: 40 ft. lbs. (54 Nm).

f. Mass damper bolt: 40 ft. lbs. (54 Nm).

9. Install the transaxle bending bracket.

10. Refill the crankcase.

11. Start the engine and check for leaks; then, recheck the fluid level and add as necessary.

1998–99 Models

1. Before servicing the vehicle, refer to the precautions in the beginning of this section.

2. Drain the crankcase.

3. Properly support the engine and transaxle assembly.

4. Remove or disconnect the following:
- Front engine mount bracket
- Powertrain bending strut
- Oil pan-to-transaxle structural collar
- Transaxle lower dust cover
- Oil filter and adapter, if equipped with air conditioning
- Oil pan

5. Thoroughly, clean the gasket mating surfaces.

To install:

6. Apply suitable silicone sealer to the oil pump-to-engine block parting line.

7. Install or connect the following:
- New oil pan gasket
- Oil pan. Torque the retainers to 105 inch lbs. (12 Nm).
- Oil filter and adapter, if removed
- Transaxle lower dust cover
- Power train bending strut
- Front engine mount and bracket

8. Torque the front engine mount retainers as follows:

a. Engine mount bracket bolt 1: 20 inch lbs. (3 Nm).

b. Engine mount bracket bolts 2, 3 and 4: 80 ft. lbs. (108 Nm).

c. Engine mount bracket bolts 5 and 1: 40 ft. lbs. (54 Nm).

d. Engine mount bracket-to-insulator

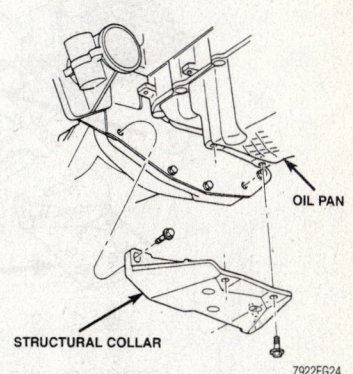

Exploded view of the structural collar mounting—1998–99 models

assembly through-bolt: 40 ft. lbs. (54 Nm).

e. Insulator-to-lower radiator cross-member nuts: 40 ft. lbs. (54 Nm).

f. Mass damper bolt: 40 ft. lbs. (54 Nm).

☀☀ WARNING

Follow the proper tightening sequence for the structural collar or damage to the collar or oil pan may occur!

9. Install the structural collar and torque the retainers as follows:

a. Collar-to-oil pan bolts: 30 inch lbs. (3 Nm).

b. Collar-to-transaxle bolts: 80 ft. lbs. (108 Nm).

c. Collar-to-oil pan bolts: 40 ft. lbs. (54 Nm), final torque.

10. Refill the crankcase.

11. Start the engine and check for leaks; then, recheck the fluid level and add as necessary.

2000–01 Models

1. Before servicing the vehicle, refer to the precautions in the beginning of this section.

2. Drain the engine crankcase.

3. Remove or disconnect the following:

- Negative battery cable
- Oil filter
- Oil filter adapter
- Structural collar
- Lateral bending brace
- Transaxle lower dust cover
- Oil pan

4. Thoroughly, clean the gasket mating surfaces.

To install:

5. Apply suitable silicone sealer to the oil pump-to-engine block parting line.

6. Install or connect the following:

- New oil pan gasket
- Oil pan. Torque the screws to 105 inch lbs. (12 Nm).
- Transaxle lower dust cover
- Lateral bending brace
- Structural collar
- Oil filter adapter. Torque the bolts to 60 ft. lbs. (80 Nm).
- Oil filter

7. Refill the crankcase.

8. Start the engine and check for leaks; then, recheck the fluid level and add as necessary.

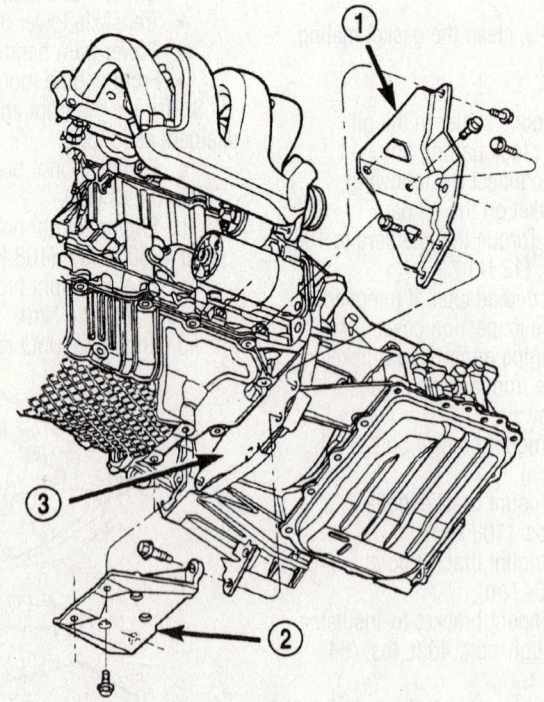

1 – LATERAL BENDING BRACE
2 – STRUCTURAL COLLAR
3 – DUST COVER

9306EG26

Exploded view of the bending brace, structural collar and dust cover—2000–01 models

Oil Pump

REMOVAL & INSTALLATION

1. Before servicing the vehicle, refer to the precautions in the beginning of this section.

2. Drain the crankcase.

3. Remove or disconnect the following:

- Negative battery cable
- Crankshaft damper
- Timing belt
- Timing belt tensioner, on 2000–01 models
- Oil pan
- Crankshaft sprocket, using tool 6795 and Insert tool C-4685-C2
- Oil pickup tube
- Oil pump
- Front crankshaft seal
- Oil pump cover screws and lift the cover off
- Oil pump rotors

4. Wash all parts in a suitable solvent; then, inspect carefully for damage or wear, as follows:

a. Inspect the mating surface of the oil pump should be smooth. Replace the pump cover, if scratched or grooved.

b. Lay a straightedge across the pump cover surface. If a 0.003 in. (0.076mm) feeler gauge can be inserted between the cover and the straightedge, the cover should be replaced.

c. Measure the thickness and diameter of the outer rotor. If the outer rotor thickness measures 0.301 in. (7.64mm) or less, or if the diameter is 3.148 in. (79.95mm) or less, replace the outer rotor.

d. If the inner rotor measures 0.301 in. (7.64mm) or less, replace the inner rotor.

e. Slide the outer rotor into the pump housing, press to one side with your fingers and measure the clearance between the rotor and the housing. If the measurement is 0.015 in. (0.39mm) or more, replace the housing only if the outer rotor is within specification.

f. Install the inner rotor into the pump housing, If the clearance between the inner and outer rotors is 0.008 in. (0.203mm) or more, replace both rotors.

g. Place a straightedge across the face of the pump housing, between the bolt holes. If a feeler gauge of 0.004 in. (0.102mm) or more can be inserted between the rotors and the straightedge, replace the pump assembly.

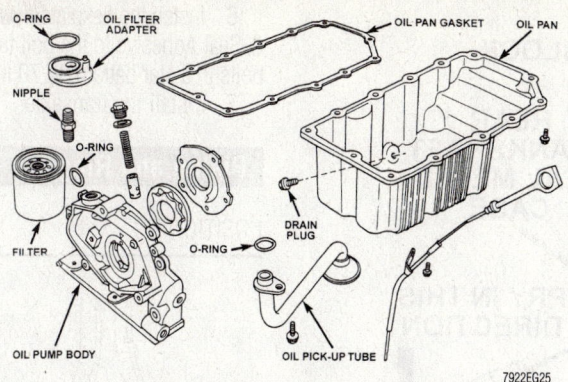

Exploded view of the oil pump and related component mounting

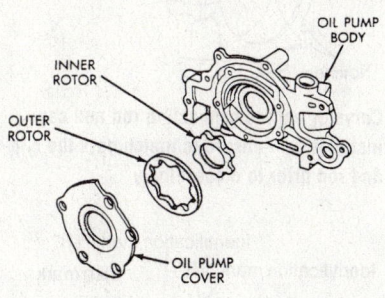

Exploded view of the oil pump assembly

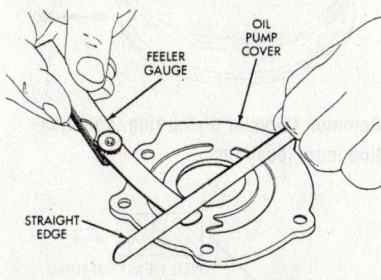

Use a feeler gauge and straightedge to check the oil pump cover for warpage

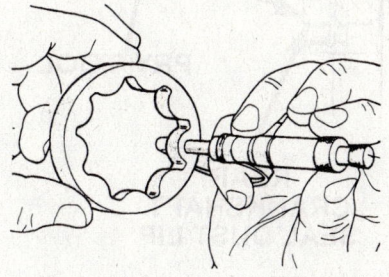

Use calipers to measure the outer rotor thickness . . .

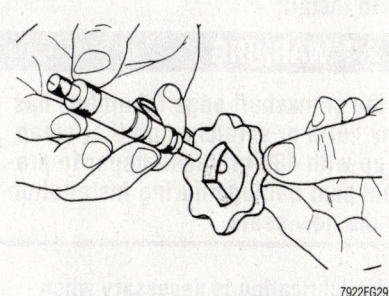

. . . and the inner rotor thickness

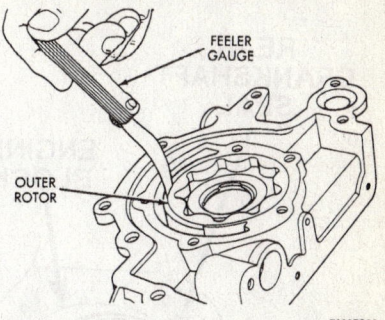

Measure the outer rotor clearance in the housing

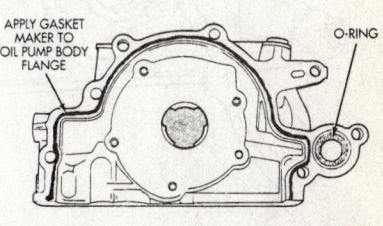

Apply a small amount of gasket maker to the pump body cover mounting surface

---

h. Inspect the oil pressure relief valve plunger for scoring and free operation in its bore. Small marks may be removed with 400 grit wet or dry sandpaper.

i. The relief valve spring has a free length of about 2.39 in. (60.7mm) and should test between 18–19 lbs. (8.1–8.6 kg) when compressed to 1.60 in. (40.6mm). Replace the spring if, it falls outside of specifications.

j. If the oil pressure is low and the pump is within specifications, inspect for worn engine bearings or for other reasons for oil pressure loss.

To install:

5. Assemble the pump, using new parts as required, as follows:

a. Install the inner rotor with the chamfer facing the cast iron oil pump cover.

b. Apply Mopar or equivalent, gasket maker to the oil pump.

c. Install the oil ring into the oil pump body discharge passage.

6. Prime the oil pump before installation by filling the rotor cavity with engine oil.

7. Install or connect the following:

- Oil pump, align the rotor flats with the crankshaft flats. Torque the pump bolts to 21 ft. lbs. (28 Nm).

※※ WARNING

The front crankshaft seal MUST be out of the pump to align or damage may result.

- New front crankshaft seal, using Seal Driver tool 6780
- Crankshaft sprocket, using a Crankshaft Sprocket Installer tool 6792
- Oil pump pickup tube
- Oil pan
- Timing belt tensioner, on 2000–01 models
- Timing belt
- Front timing belt cover
- Crankshaft damper
- Accessory drive belts
- Negative battery cable

8. Refill the crankcase.

9. Start the engine and check for leaks; then, recheck the fluid level and add as necessary.

Rear Main Seal

REMOVAL & INSTALLATION

1. Before servicing the vehicle, refer to the precautions in the beginning of this section.

2. Remove or disconnect the following:

Timing belt service is covered in Section 4 of this manual

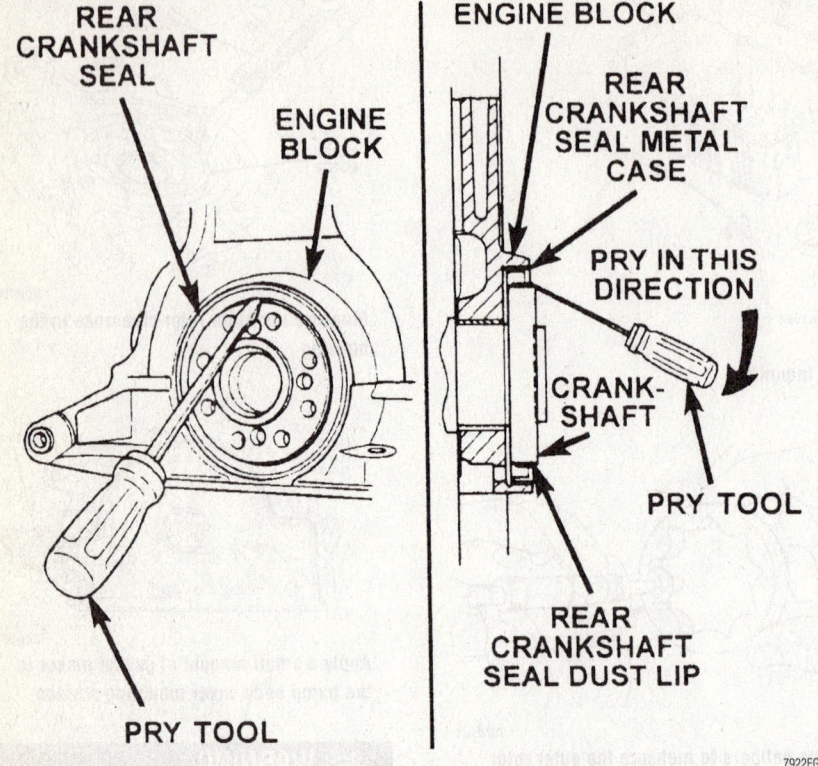

When prying the seal out, be sure to use the prytool at the proper angle

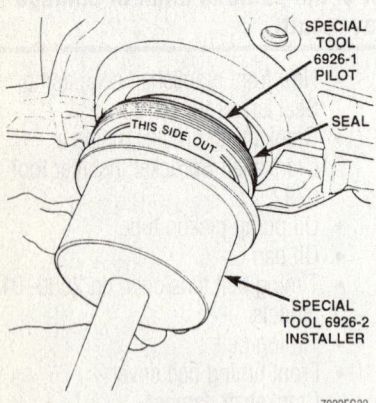

Place a proper size pilot tool with a magnetic base on the crankshaft

- Transaxle
- Flexplate/flywheel
- Rear main seal. Insert a seal remover between the dust lip and the metal case of the crankshaft seal. Angle the tool through the dust lip against the metal case of the seal. Pry out the seal.

✳✳ WARNING

DO NOT let the prytool contact the crankshaft seal surface. Contact of the tool blade against the crankshaft edge (chamfer) is permitted.

To install:

✳✳ WARNING

If the crankshaft edge (chamfer) has any burrs or scratches on the, clean it up with 400 grit sand paper to prevent seal damage during installation of the new seal.

➡ No lubrication is necessary when installing the seal.

3. Place Crankcase Seal Pilot tool 6926–1 or equivalent, on the crankshaft; this is a pilot tool with a magnetic base.

4. Position the seal over the pilot tool; be sure the words THIS SIDE OUT on the seal can be read.

➡ The pilot tool should stay on the crankshaft during installation of the seal. Be sure the seal lip faces the crankcase during installation.

✳✳ WARNING

If the seal is driven in the block past flush, this may cause an oil leak.

5. Drive the seal into the block, using Crankshaft Seal tool 6926-2 and handle C-4171, until the tool bottoms out against the block.

6. Install the flexplate/flywheel. Apply Lock & Seal Adhesive to the bolt treads. Torque the bolts in a star pattern, to 70 ft. lbs. (95 Nm).

7. Install the transaxle.

Piston and Ring

POSITIONING

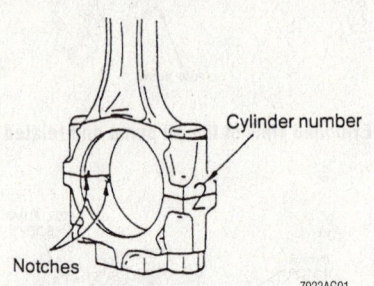

Chrysler engine connecting rod and cap installation—ensure to matchmark the cap and rod prior to disassembly

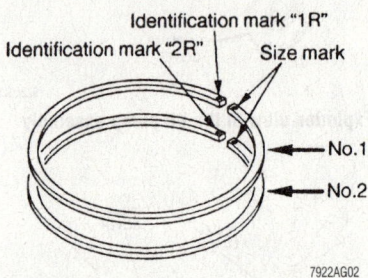

Common Chrysler piston ring identification mark locations

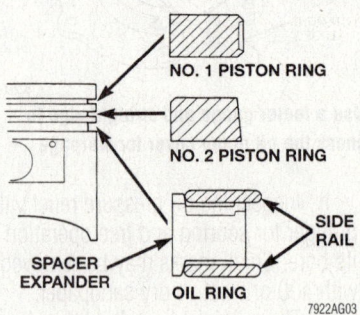

2.0L Engine—piston ring orientation

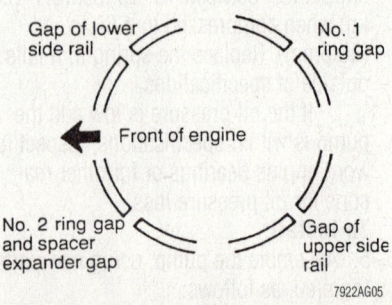

2.0L (VIN C and Y) engines—piston ring end-gap spacing

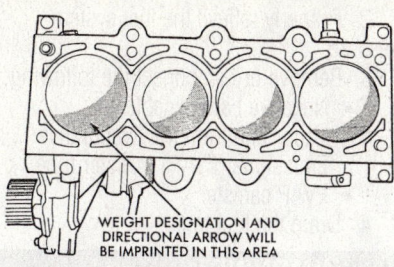

2.0L (VIN C) Engine—piston positioning. The arrow or weight marking (L or H) must face the timing belt side of the engine

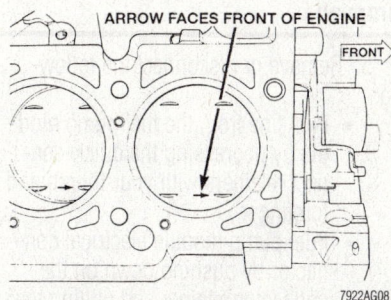

2.0L (VIN Y) Engine—piston positioning. The small arrows on the crown of the pistons must point toward the front of the engine

FUEL SYSTEM

Fuel System Service Precautions

Safety is an important factor when servicing the fuel system. Failure to conduct maintenance and repairs in a safe manner may result in serious personal injury. Maintenance and testing of the vehicle's fuel system components can be accomplished safely and effectively by adhering to the following rules and guidelines:

• To avoid the possibility of fire and personal injury, always disconnect the negative battery cable unless the repair or test procedure requires that battery voltage be applied.

• Always relieve the fuel system pressure prior to disconnecting any fuel system component (injector, fuel rail, pressure regulator, etc.), fitting or fuel line connection. Exercise extreme caution whenever relieving fuel system pressure, to avoid exposing skin, face and eyes to fuel spray. Please be advised that fuel under pressure may penetrate the skin or any part of the body that it contacts.

• Always place a shop towel or cloth around the fitting or connection prior to loosening to absorb any excess fuel due to spillage. Ensure that all fuel spillage is quickly removed from engine surfaces. Ensure that all fuel soaked cloths or towels are deposited into a suitable waste container.

• Always keep a dry chemical (Class B) fire extinguisher near the work area.

• Do not allow fuel spray or fuel vapors to come into contact with a spark or open flame.

• Always use a back-up wrench when loosening and tightening fuel line connection fittings. This will prevent unnecessary stress and torsion to fuel line piping.

• Always replace worn fuel fitting O-rings. Do not substitute fuel hose where fuel pipe is installed.

Fuel System Pressure

RELIEVING

✳✳ CAUTION

Relieve the fuel system pressure before servicing any components of the fuel system. Service vehicles in well ventilated areas and avoid ignition sources. NEVER smoke while servicing the vehicle!

1. Before servicing the vehicle, refer to the precautions in the beginning of this section.

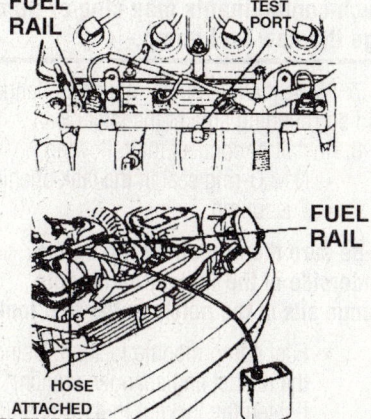

Relieve the fuel system, allowing the pressure to bleed off through the hose into the container

2. Remove or disconnect the following:
   • Negative battery cable
   • Fuel filler cap
   • Protective cap from the fuel rail's pressure port

3. Place the open end of a suitable fuel pressure release hose (tool C-4799–1 or equivalent) into an approved gasoline container. Connect the other end of the hose to the fuel pressure test port. The fuel pressure will bleed off through the hose into the gasoline container.

➡**Fuel pressure gauge kit C-4799-B contains hose C-4799–1.**

4. The vehicle is now safe for servicing.
5. When finished working on the fuel system, install the fuel filler cap.

Fuel Filter

A combination fuel filter/pressure regulator assembly is used, which is located on the top of the fuel pump module.

REMOVAL & INSTALLATION

✳✳ CAUTION

Do not allow fuel spray or fuel vapors to come in contact with a spark or open flame. Keep a dry chemical fire extinguisher nearby. Never store fuel in an open container due to risk of fire or explosion.

1. Before servicing the vehicle, refer to the precautions in the beginning of this section.

2. Properly relieve the fuel system pressure.

3. Remove or disconnect the following:
   • Negative battery cable
   • Quick-connect fuel supply line from the filter/regulator nipple

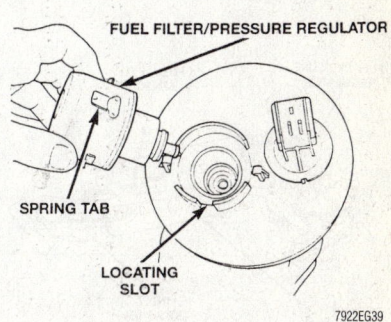

Depress the spring tab, then rotate and pull the fuel filter assembly out

4. Depress the locking spring tab, located on the side of the fuel filter/regulator, then rotate 90 degrees and pull out. Be sure the upper and lower O-rings are still on the filter assembly.

To install:

5. Lightly coat the filter O-rings with clean engine oil. Insert the filter into the opening in the fuel pump module, then align the 2 hold-down tabs with the flange.

6. While applying downward pressure, rotate the filter clockwise until the spring tab catches in the locating slot.

7. Attach the fuel line to the filter/regulator assembly.

8. Connect the negative battery cable.

Fuel Pump

The fuel pump is integral with the pump module, which also contains the fuel reservoir, level sensor, inlet strainer and fuel pressure regulator. The inlet strainer, fuel pressure regulator and level sensor are the only serviceable items. If the fuel pump requires service, replace the entire fuel pump module.

REMOVAL & INSTALLATION

1997–99 Models

1. Before servicing the vehicle, refer to the precautions in the beginning of this section.

2. Properly relieve the fuel system pressure.

3. Drain the fuel tank.

✴✴ WARNING

The fuel reservoir of the fuel pump module does not empty out when the tank is drained. The fuel in the reservoir will spill out when the module is removed.

4. Remove or disconnect the following:

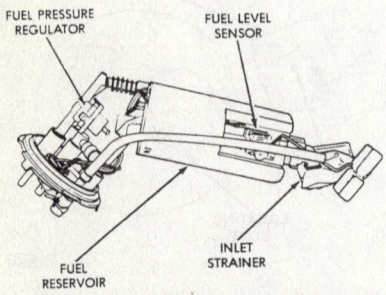

FUEL PRESSURE REGULATOR — FUEL LEVEL SENSOR — FUEL RESERVOIR — INLET STRAINER

7922EG36

The fuel module assembly contains the pump, pressure regulator, reservoir, inlet strainer and level sensor

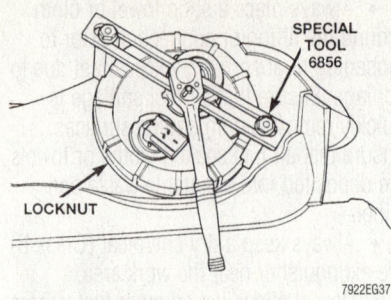

SPECIAL TOOL 6856 — LOCKNUT

7922EG37

To loosen the fuel pump module locknut, use a ratchet and spanner wrench

- Negative battery cable
- Fuel lines from the fuel pump module by depressing the quick-connect retainers with your thumb and forefinger.
- Fuel pump module electrical lock by sliding it to unlock it
- Fuel pump module electrical connector by pushing down on the connector retainer and pulling the connector off of the module

5. Support the fuel tank with a transmission jack.

6. Remove or disconnect the following:
- Fuel tank strap bolts; then, lower the tank slightly for access to the module
- Fuel pump module locknut using a ratchet and spanner wrench
- Fuel pump and discard the O-ring seal

To install:

✴✴ WARNING

Take care to avoid wiping dirt or debris into the fuel tank opening. Such contaminants may clog or damage the new fuel pump.

7. Wipe the fuel pump mounting flange and surrounding area of the tank clean.

8. Install or connect the following:
- New O-ring seal in the tank opening
- Fuel pump

➡**Be sure the alignment tab on the underside of the fuel pump module flange sits in the notch on the fuel tank.**

- Fuel pump module locknut. Using the ratchet and spanner wrench, tighten the locknut to 41 ft. lbs. (55 Nm).
- Negative battery cable

2000–01 Models

1. Before servicing the vehicle, refer to the precautions in the beginning of this section.

2. Properly relieve the fuel system pressure.

3. Remove or disconnect the following:
- Negative battery cable
- Vapor line from the Evaporative Emissions (EVAP) canister tube
- EVAP canister

4. Drain the fuel tank.

✴✴ WARNING

The fuel reservoir of the fuel pump module does not empty out when the tank is drained. The fuel in the reservoir will spill out when the module is removed.

5. Remove or disconnect the following:
- Fuel line from the fuel pump module by depressing the quick-connect retainers with your thumb and forefinger
- Fuel pump module electrical connector by pushing down on the connector retainer and pulling the connector off of the module
- Fuel filler tube and filler vent tube from the fuel tank's filler hose

6. Support the fuel tank with a transmission jack.

7. Remove or disconnect the following:
- Fuel tank strap bolts; then, lower the tank slightly for access to the module
- Fuel pump module locknut using a ratchet and spanner wrench
- Fuel pump and discard the O-ring seal

To install:

✴✴ WARNING

Take care to avoid wiping dirt or debris into the fuel tank opening. Such contaminants may clog or damage the new fuel pump.

8. Wipe the fuel pump mounting flange and surrounding area of the tank clean.

9. Install or connect the following:
- New O-ring seal in the tank opening
- Fuel pump

➡**Be sure the alignment tab on the underside of the fuel pump module flange sits in the notch on the fuel tank.**

- Fuel pump module locknut. Using the ratchet and spanner wrench, tighten the locknut to 41 ft. lbs. (55 Nm).

- Fuel tank
- Fuel filler tube and filler vent tube to the fuel tank's filler hose
- Fuel pump module electrical connector
- Fuel line, to the fuel pump module
- EVAP canister
- Vapor line to the EVAP canister tube
- Negative battery cable

10. Check for leaks.

Fuel Injector

REMOVAL & INSTALLATION

1. Before servicing the vehicle, refer to the precautions in the beginning of this section.

2. Release the fuel system pressure.

3. Remove or disconnect the following:
- Negative battery cable
- Fuel line(s) from fuel rail
- Fuel injector electrical connectors
- Fuel rail with the fuel injectors
- Fuel injector retainers
- Fuel injector(s) and discard the O-rings

To install:

4. Install or connect the following:
- Fuel injector(s) using new O-rings

➡**Lubricate the O-rings with clean engine oil.**

- Fuel injector retainers
- Fuel rail with fuel injectors. Torque the fuel rail bolts to 170–230 inch lbs. (20–25 Nm).
- Fuel injector electrical connectors
- Fuel line(s) to fuel rail
- Negative battery cable

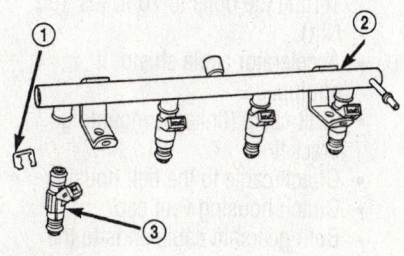

1 – RETAINER
2 – FUEL RAIL
3 – FUEL INJECTOR

9306EG01

Exploded view of the fuel rail assembly

DRIVE TRAIN

Transaxle Assembly

REMOVAL & INSTALLATION

1997–99 Models

MANUAL TRANSAXLE

1. Before servicing the vehicle, refer to the precautions in the beginning of this section.

2. Drain the transaxle fluid.

3. Remove or disconnect the following:
- Battery cables
- Power Distribution Center (PDC), pull it up and out of its bracket and move it aside
- Battery heat shield
- Battery
- Battery tray
- Cruise control, if equipped
- Vehicle Speed Sensor (VSS) wire
- Back-up lamp switch wiring from the transaxle

✻✻ WARNING

Pry with equal amounts of force on both sides of the shifter cable isolator bushing to avoid damaging the cable isolator bushing.

- Both gearshift cable ends from the transaxle shift levers, using 2 pry tools
- Clutch housing vent cap, exposing the clutch cable end and clutch release lever
- Clutch cable from the bell housing
- Shift cable (linkage) mounting bracket
- Accelerator cable shield, if equipped

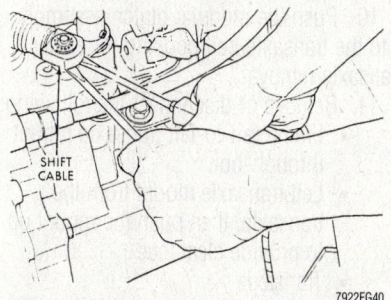

7922EG40

Use 2 prytools to disconnect the gearshift cable ends from the shift levers—1997–99 manual transaxle

- Intake manifold support bracket
- Upper starter bolt
- Upper bell housing bolt

4. Install a suitable engine bridge fixture and support the engine securely.

5. Remove or disconnect the following:
- Front wheels
- Halfshafts

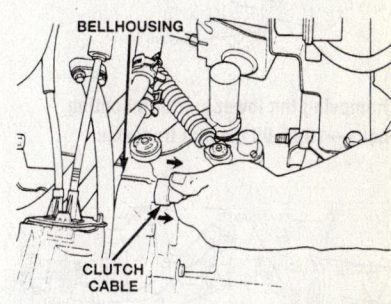

7922EG41

Pull the clutch cable backward, to disconnect the clutch cable from the bell housing—1997–99 manual transaxle

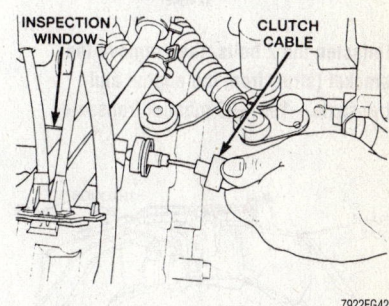

7922EG42

Remove the clutch cable from the lever—1997–99 manual transaxle

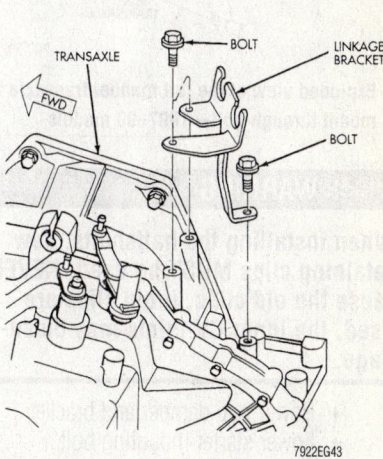

7922EG43

Exploded view of the linkage mounting bracket—1997–99 manual transaxle

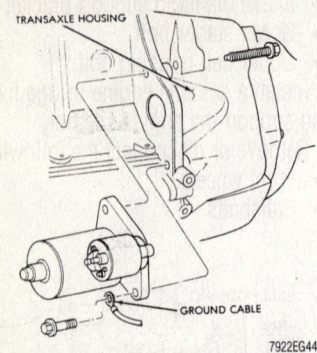

Removing the lower starter mounting bolts—1997–99 manual transaxle

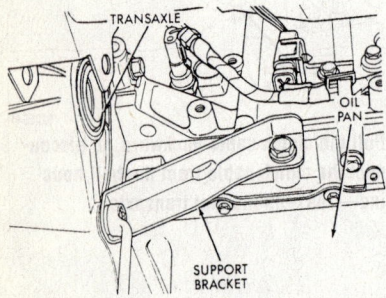

Unfasten the 2 bolts, then remove the bracket (strut) from the engine and transaxle—1997–99 manual transaxle

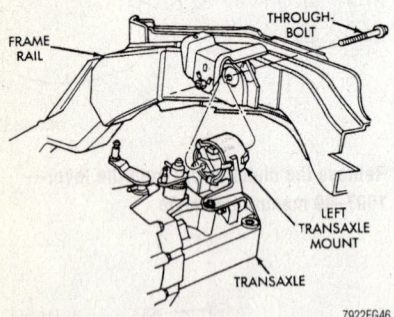

Exploded view of the left manual transaxle mount through-bolt—1997–99 models

✳✳ WARNING

When installing the halfshafts, new retaining clips MUST be used. NEVER reuse the old clips. If old clips are used, the inner CV-joints may disengage.

- Power hop damper and bracket
- Lower starter mounting bolt
- Transaxle-to-rear lateral bending strut from the engine and transaxle

6. Support the transaxle with a suitable jack.

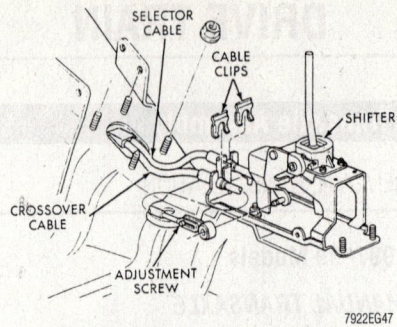

Loosen the adjustment screw on the crossover cable at the shifter—manual transaxle

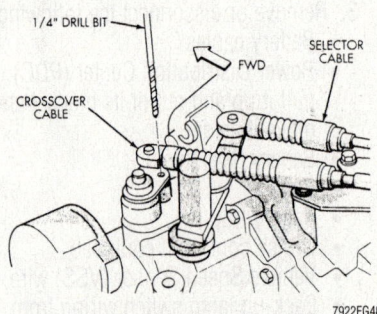

Insert a ¼ in. Diameter drill bit to pin the crossover lever in the 3–4 neutral position—1997–99 manual transaxle

7. Remove or disconnect the following:
- Front motor mount through-bolt
- Front motor mount bolts from the engine and transaxle
- Lower dust shield

8. Rotate the crankshaft clockwise in order to access the driveplate-to-modular clutch bolts.

➡ **For installation purposes, matchmark the driveplate and pressure plate before removing any bolts.**

9. Remove the driveplate-to-modular clutch bolts, to separate the driveplate from the clutch

10. Push the modular clutch assembly into the transaxle bell housing for easier transaxle removal.

11. Remove or disconnect the following:
- Frame rail-to-left transaxle mount through-bolt
- Left transaxle mount from the transaxle, then push the mount up to provide clearance
- Transaxle
- Modular clutch assembly from the transaxle input shaft

To install:

12. Install or connect the following:
- Modular clutch assembly to the transaxle input shaft

- Transaxle. Torque the transaxle-to-engine bolts to 70 ft. lbs. (95 Nm) and the lateral bending strut bolts to 40 ft. lbs. (54 Nm).

13. Support the transaxle with a jack.

14. Install or connect the following:
- Left transaxle mount to the transaxle. Torque the bolt to 40 ft. lbs. (54 Nm).
- Frame rail-to-left transaxle mount through-bolt. Torque the through-bolt to 80 ft. lbs. (108 Nm).
- 4 driveplate-to-modular clutch bolts
- Lower dust shield. Torque the bolts to 108 inch lbs. (12 Nm).
- Front engine mount bolts to the engine and transaxle. Torque the front engine mount-to-transaxle bolt to 80 ft. lbs. (108 Nm) and the front mount-to-engine bolt to 40 ft. lbs. (54 Nm).
- Front motor mount through-bolt. Torque the through-bolt to 45 ft. lbs. (61 Nm).
- Lower starter mounting bolt
- Power hop damper and bracket. Torque the damper bolts to 40 ft. lbs. (54 Nm).

✳✳ WARNING

When installing the halfshafts, new retaining clips MUST be used. NEVER reuse the old clips. If old clips are used, the inner cv-joints may disengage.

- Halfshafts
- Front wheels

15. Refill the transaxle to the bottom of the fill plug hole.

16. Remove the engine bridge fixture and support.

17. Install or connect the following:
- Upper bell housing bolt
- Upper starter bolt
- Intake manifold support bracket. Torque the bolts to 70 ft. lbs. (95 Nm).
- Accelerator cable shield, if equipped
- Shift cable (linkage) mounting bracket
- Clutch cable to the bell housing
- Clutch housing vent cap
- Both gearshift cable ends to the transaxle shift levers
- Back-up lamp switch wiring to the transaxle
- VSS wire
- Cruise control, if equipped
- Battery tray
- Battery

- Battery heat shield
- PDC
- Battery cables

18. Be sure the vehicle's back-up lights and speedometer are functioning properly.

19. Adjust the crossover cable in order to ensure proper shifter adjustment. Adjust as follows:

    a. Remove the floor shift console.

    b. Loosen the adjusting screw on the crossover cable at the shifter.

    c. Pin the transaxle crossover cable in the 3–4 neutral position using a ¼ in. drill bit. Align the hole in the crossover lever with the hole in the boss on the transaxle case. Be sure the drill bit goes into the transaxle case at least ½ in. (12mm).

    d. The shifter is spring loaded and self-centering. Allow the shifter to rest in its neutral position. Torque the adjustment screw to 70 inch lbs. (8 Nm). Be careful to avoid moving the shift mechanism off-center during screw tightening.

    e. Remove the drill bit from the transaxle case and perform a functional check by shifting the transaxle into all gears.

    f. Reinstall the center shift console. Blouse the boot out around the console. Seat the boot lip on the top of the console.

20. Road test the vehicle to be sure the transaxle is operating properly.

AUTOMATIC TRANSAXLE

The transaxle and torque converter must be removed as an assembly; otherwise the torque converter driveplate, pump bushing or oil seal may be damaged. The driveplate will not support a load; therefore, none of the weight of the transaxle should be allowed to rest on the plate during removal.

1. Before servicing the vehicle, refer to the precautions in the beginning of this section.

2. Remove or disconnect the following:
- Battery cables
- Power Distribution Center (PDC), pull it up and out of its bracket and move it aside
- Battery heat shield
- Battery
- Battery tray
- Cruise control, if equipped
- Vehicle Speed Sensor (VSS) wiring
- Neutral safety switch and torque converter control wiring, from the transaxle

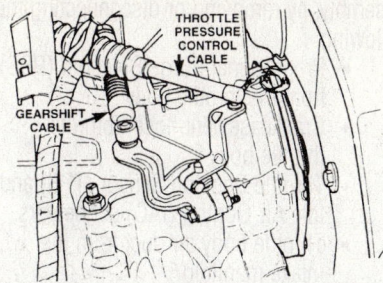

Disconnect the gearshift cable end from the transaxle shift lever—1997–99 automatic transaxle

7922EG49

> ⁕⁕ **WARNING**
>
> **Pry up on both sides of the shift cable isolator bushing, evenly, to avoid damaging the cable isolator bushing.**

- Gearshift cable end from the transaxle shift lever
- Gearshift cable bracket bolt from the transaxle
- Throttle pressure control cable from the lever
- Throttle pressure control cable bracket bolts from the transaxle
- Transaxle's dipstick tube
- Transaxle's oil cooler lines plug them to prevent contamination
- Throttle pressure control cable support bracket bolts
- Upper bell housing bolts
- Upper starter bolt

3. Install a suitable engine bridge fixture and support the engine.

4. Remove or disconnect the following:
- Front wheels
- Halfshafts

> ⁕⁕ **WARNING**
>
> **When installing the halfshafts, new retaining clips must be used. DO NOT reuse the old clips. Failure to use new clips could cause the inner CV-joints to disengage.**

> ⁕⁕ **WARNING**
>
> **On 1998–99 vehicles, the exhaust flex joint must be disconnected from the exhaust manifold anytime the engine is lowered. If the engine is lowered with the flex pipe attached, damage will occur.**

- Exhaust flex joint-to-exhaust manifold bolts, on 1998–99 vehicles
- Exhaust pipe, from the manifold, on 1998–99 vehicles
- Transaxle-to-rear lateral bending strut, from the engine and transaxle
- Front engine bracket through-bolt
- Front engine bracket bolts
- Lower starter bolt
- Lower dust shield screws

5. Rotate the engine clockwise and remove the converter bolts.

➡ **Matchmark the converter to the flexplate for alignment during installation.**

6. Support the transaxle with a transaxle jack.

7. Remove or disconnect the following:
- Left mount through-bolt
- Left mount-to-transaxle bolts
- Left mount
- Rear engine bolt from the transaxle
- Transaxle

8. Carefully work the transaxle and torque converter assembly rearward off the engine block dowels. Disengage the converter hub from the end of the crankshaft. Attach a small C-clamp to the edge of the bell housing. This will hold the torque converter in place during transaxle removal.

To install:

9. Install the transaxle. Torque the transaxle-to-cylinder block bolt: 70 ft. lbs. (95 Nm).

10. Support the transaxle with a transaxle jack.

11. Install or connect the following:
- Rear engine bolt to the transaxle
- Left mount
- Left mount-to-transaxle bolts. Torque the left motor mount bolts: 40 ft. lbs. (54 Nm).
- Left mount through-bolt

12. If the torque converter was removed from the transaxle, be sure to align the pump inner gear pilot flats with the torque converter impeller hub flats. Torque the flexplate-to-crankshaft bolts to 70 ft. lbs. (95 Nm) and the flexplate-to-torque converter bolts: 50 ft. lbs. (68 Nm).

13. Rotate the engine clockwise to get access to the converter bolts.

14. Install or connect the following:
- Lower dust shield screws. Torque the bell housing cover bolts to 108 inch lbs. (12 Nm).
- Lower starter bolt
- Front engine bracket bolts
- Front engine bracket through-bolt

- Transaxle-to-rear lateral bending strut to the engine and transaxle
- Exhaust pipe to the manifold, on 1998–99 vehicles
- Exhaust flex joint-to-exhaust manifold bolts, on 1998–99 vehicles
- Halfshafts

✳✳ WARNING

When installing the halfshafts, new retaining clips must be used. DO NOT reuse the old clips. Failure to use new clips could cause the inner CV-joints to disengage.

- Front wheels

15. Remove the engine bridge fixture and support.
16. Install or connect the following:
- Upper starter bolt
- Upper bell housing bolts
- Throttle pressure control cable support bracket bolts
- Transaxle's oil cooler lines. Torque the oil cooler line-to-radiator fitting to 108 inch lbs. (12 Nm) and transaxle oil cooler line fitting to 21 ft. lbs. (28 Nm).
- Transaxle's dipstick tube
- Throttle pressure control cable bracket bolts to the transaxle
- Throttle pressure control cable to the lever
- Gearshift cable bracket bolt to the transaxle
- Gearshift cable end to the transaxle shift lever
17. Adjust the gearshift and throttle cables.
18. Install or connect the following:
- Neutral safety switch and torque converter control wiring to the transaxle
- VSS wiring
- Cruise control, if equipped
- Battery tray
- Battery
- Battery heat shield
- PDC
- Battery cables
19. Refill the transaxle.
20. Be sure the vehicle's back-up lights and speedometer are working properly.

2000–01 Models

MANUAL TRANSAXLE

1. Before servicing the vehicle, refer to the precautions in the beginning of this section.
2. Drain the transaxle fluid.
3. Remove the battery.
4. Remove the air cleaner/throttle body assembly, by removing or disconnecting the following:
- Proportional Purge Solenoid (PSS) from the throttle body
- Crankcase vent hose from the throttle body
- Throttle Position Sensor (TPS) and Idle Air Control (IAC) connectors
- Throttle body air duct from the intake manifold
- Air cleaner assembly nuts and bolts
- Accelerator cable
- Speed control cable, if equipped
- Air cleaner assembly
5. Remove or disconnect the following:
- Battery tray from the bracket
- Ground cable from the battery tray bracket
- Back-up light switch connector
- Bell housing cap
- Clutch cable from the fork and transaxle
- Shift cable-to-bracket clips
- Shift selector and crossover cables from the levers and move aside
- Halfshafts
- Structural collar
- Left engine-to-transaxle lateral bending brace
- Bell housing dust cover
- Right engine-to-transaxle lateral bending brace
- Starter
- Driveplate-to-clutch module bolts
6. Place a jack and block of wood under the engine's oil pan and support the engine. Remove the transaxle's upper mount through-bolt
7. Lower the engine/transaxle assembly to provide clearance.
8. Remove or disconnect the following:
- Transaxle-to-engine bolts, using an assistant to support the transaxle
- Transaxle

To install:

9. If installing a new or replacement transaxle, transfer the upper mount to the new transaxle; then, torque the upper mount-to-transaxle bolts to 50 ft. lbs. (68 Nm).
10. Install or connect the following:
- Transaxle
- Transaxle-to-engine bolts, using an assistant to support the transaxle. Torque the transaxle-to-engine bolts to 70 ft. lbs. (95 Nm).
11. Raise the engine/transaxle assembly until the upper mount aligns with the mount bracket hole. Torque the upper mount-to-mount bracket through-bolt to 80 ft. lbs. (108 Nm).
12. Remove the jack and wooden block.

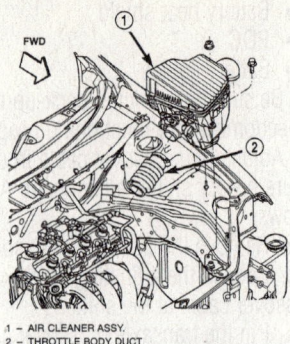

FWD

1 – AIR CLEANER ASSY.
2 – THROTTLE BODY DUCT

9306EG27

View of the air cleaner assembly and throttle body duct—2000–01 models

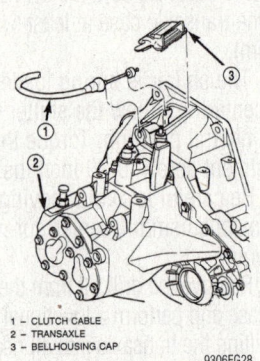

1 – CLUTCH CABLE
2 – TRANSAXLE
3 – BELLHOUSING CAP

9306EG28

View of the clutch cable and bell housing cap—2000–01 manual transaxle

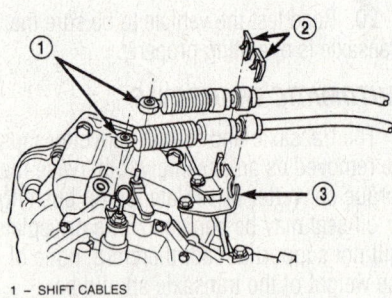

1 – SHIFT CABLES
2 – CLIPS
3 – BRACKET

9306EG29

View of the shift cables—2000–01 manual transaxle

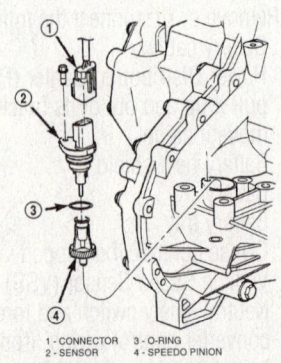

1 – CONNECTOR   3 – O-RING
2 – SENSOR   4 – SPEEDO PINION

9306EG30

View of the Vehicle Speed Sensor (VSS)—2000–01 manual transaxle

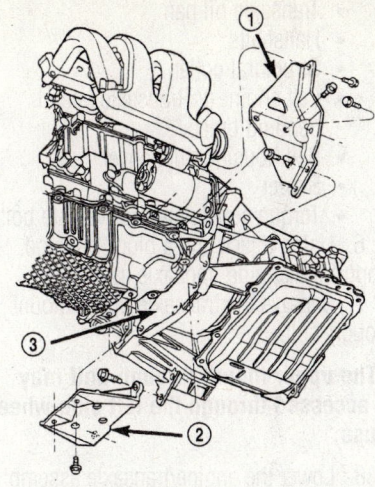

1 – LATERAL BENDING BRACE
2 – STRUCTURAL COLLAR
3 – DUST COVER

9306EG31

View of the left lateral bending brace and structural collar—2000–01 models

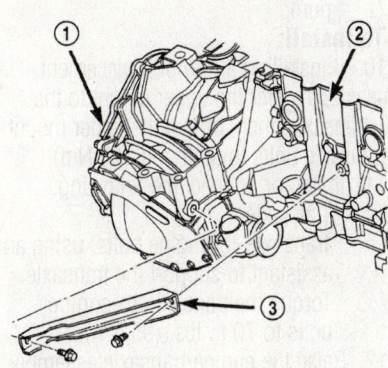

1 – TRANSAXLE
2 – ENGINE
3 – LATERAL BENDING BRACE

9306EG32

View of the right lateral bending brace—2000–01 models

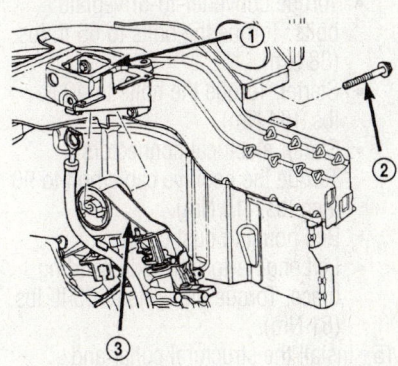

1 – MOUNT BRACKET
2 – BOLT
3 – MOUNT

9306EG33

View of the upper mount through-bolt—2000–01 models

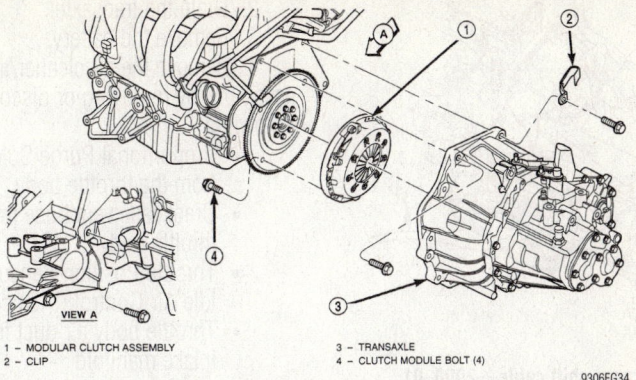

1 – MODULAR CLUTCH ASSEMBLY
2 – CLIP
3 – TRANSAXLE
4 – CLUTCH MODULE BOLT (4)

9306EG34

Exploded view of the transaxle and related components—2000–01 manual transaxle

13. Install or connect the following:
  • Driveplate-to-clutch module bolts. Torque the bolts to 65 ft. lbs. (88 Nm).
  • Starter. Torque the bolts to 40 ft. lbs. (54 Nm).
  • Starter electrical connectors. Torque the positive cable bolt to 90 inch lbs. (10 Nm).
  • Left engine-to-transaxle lateral bending brace. Torque the bolts to 60 ft. lbs. (81 Nm).
14. Install the structural collar and torque the bolts as follows:
  a. Step 1—Structural collar-to-oil pan bolts: 30 inch lbs. (3 Nm).
  b. Step 2—Structural collar-to-transaxle bolts: 80 ft. lbs. (108 Nm).
  c. Step 3—Structural collar-to-oil pan bolts: 40 ft. lbs. (54 Nm).
15. Install or connect the following:
  • Right engine-to-transaxle lateral bending brace. Torque the bolts to 60 ft. lbs. (81 Nm).
  • Halfshafts

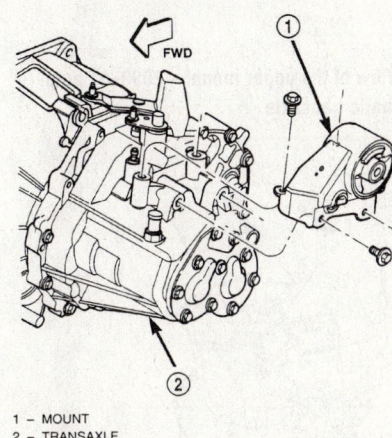

1 – MOUNT
2 – TRANSAXLE

9306EG35

View of the upper mount—2000–01 manual transaxle

  • Bell housing dust cover
  • VSS electrical connector
  • Shift selector and crossover cables to the levers
  • Shift cable-to-bracket clips
  • Clutch cable to the fork and transaxle
  • Bell housing cap
  • Back-up light switch connector
  • Ground cable to the battery tray bracket
  • Battery tray to the bracket
16. Install the air cleaner/throttle body assembly, by installing or connecting the following:
  • Air cleaner assembly
  • Accelerator cable
  • Speed control cable, if equipped
  • Air cleaner assembly. Torque the nuts and bolts to 10 ft. lbs. (14 Nm).
  • Throttle body air duct to the intake manifold
  • TPS and IAC connectors
  • Crankcase vent hose to the throttle body
  • PSS to the throttle body
  • Battery
17. Refill the transaxle.
18. Road test the vehicle and inspect for leaks.

AUTOMATIC TRANSAXLE

The transaxle and torque converter must be removed as an assembly; otherwise the torque converter driveplate, pump bushing or oil seal may be damaged. The driveplate will not support a load; therefore, none of the weight of the transaxle should be allowed to rest on the plate during removal.

1. Before servicing the vehicle, refer to the precautions in the beginning of this section.

Turn to Section 5 for brake system applications

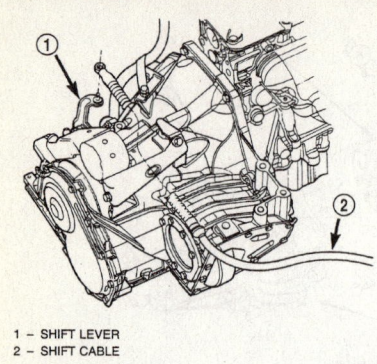

1 – SHIFT LEVER
2 – SHIFT CABLE

9306EG36

View of the gear shift cable—2000–01 automatic transaxle

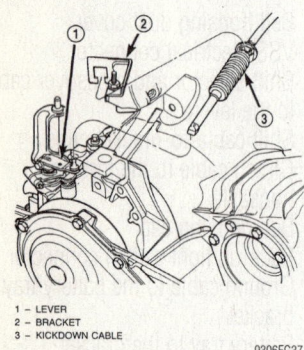

1 – LEVER
2 – BRACKET
3 – KICKDOWN CABLE

9306EG37

View of the kickdown cable—2000–01 automatic transaxle

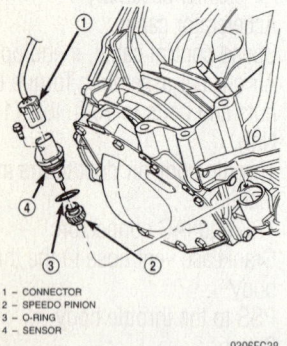

1 – CONNECTOR
2 – SPEEDO PINION
3 – O-RING
4 – SENSOR

9306EG38

View of the Vehicle Speed Sensor (VSS)— 2000–01 automatic transaxle

2. Drain the transaxle.

3. Remove the battery.

4. Remove the air cleaner/throttle body assembly, by removing or disconnecting the following:
  - Proportional Purge Solenoid (PSS) from the throttle body
  - Crankcase vent hose from the throttle body
  - Throttle Position Sensor (TPS) and Idle Air Control (IAC) connectors
  - Throttle body air duct from the intake manifold
  - Air cleaner assembly nuts and bolts
  - Accelerator cable
  - Transaxle kickdown cable
  - Speed control cable, if equipped
  - Air cleaner assembly

5. Remove or disconnect the following:
  - Battery tray from the bracket
  - Torque converter clutch solenoid connector
  - Neutral safely/back-up light switch connector
  - Transaxle oil cooler lines. Plug the lines to prevent contamination
  - Shift cable and bracket from the transaxle
  - Kickdown cable and bracket from the transaxle

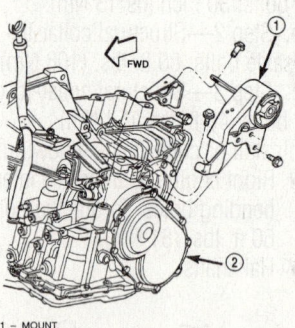

1 – MOUNT
2 – TRANSAXLE

9306EG40

View of the upper mount—2000–01 automatic transaxle

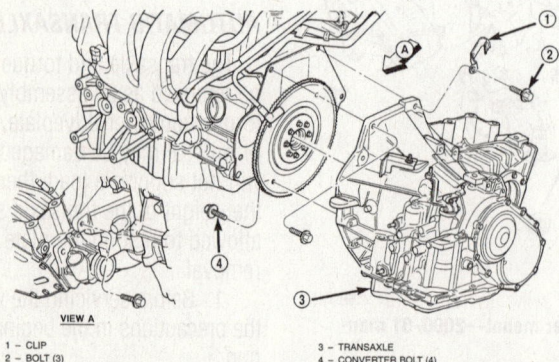

VIEW A

1 – CLIP
2 – BOLT (3)
3 – TRANSAXLE
4 – CONVERTER BOLT (4)

9306EG39

Exploded view of the transaxle and related components—2000–01 automatic transaxle

  - Transaxle oil pan
  - Halfshafts
  - Structural collar
  - Left engine-to-transaxle lateral bending brace
  - Bell housing duct cover
  - Starter
  - Torque converter-to-driveplate bolts

6. Using a jack and a block of wood, support the engine/transaxle assembly.

7. Remove the transaxle upper mount through-bolt.

➡**The upper mount through-bolt may be accessed through the left side wheel house.**

8. Lower the engine/transaxle assembly for clearance.

9. Remove or disconnect the following:
  - Transaxle-to-engine bolts, using an assistant to support the transaxle
  - Transaxle
  - Torque converter from the front pump

To install:

10. If installing a new or replacement transaxle, transfer the upper mount to the new transaxle; then, torque the upper mount-to-transaxle bolts to 50 ft. lbs. (68 Nm).

11. Install or connect the following:
  - Transaxle
  - Transaxle-to-engine bolts, using an assistant to support the transaxle. Torque the transaxle-to-engine bolts to 70 ft. lbs. (95 Nm).

12. Raise the engine/transaxle assembly until the upper mount aligns with the mount bracket hole. Torque the upper mount-to-mount bracket through-bolt to 80 ft. lbs. (108 Nm).

13. Remove the jack and wooden block.

14. Install or connect the following:
  - Torque converter-to-driveplate bolts. Torque the bolts to 65 ft. lbs. (88 Nm).
  - Starter. Torque the bolts to 40 ft. lbs. (54 Nm).
  - Starter electrical connectors. Torque the positive cable bolt to 90 inch lbs. (10 Nm).
  - Bell housing dust cover
  - Left engine-to-transaxle bending brace. Torque the bolts to 60 ft. lbs. (81 Nm).

15. Install the structural collar and torque the bolts as follows:
  a. Step 1—Structural collar-to-oil pan bolts: 30 inch lbs. (3 Nm).
  b. Step 2—Structural collar-to-transaxle bolts: 80 ft. lbs. (108 Nm).
  c. Step 3—Structural collar-to-oil pan bolts: 40 ft. lbs. (54 Nm).

16. Install or connect the following:
- Halfshafts
- Speed control cable, if equipped
- Right engine-to-transaxle lateral bending brace. Torque the bolts to 60 ft. lbs. (81 Nm).
- Transaxle oil cooler lines. Torque the oil cooler line-to-radiator fitting to 108 inch lbs. (12 Nm) and transaxle oil cooler line fitting to 21 ft. lbs. (28 Nm).
- Torque converter clutch solenoid and neutral safely/back-up light switch connectors
- Transaxle dipstick tube
- Gearshift cable bracket bolt to the transaxle
- Gearshift cable end to the transaxle shift lever
- Transaxle kickdown cable to the lever and bracket
- Battery tray
- Battery

17. Install the air cleaner/throttle body assembly, by installing or connecting the following:
- Air cleaner assembly
- Accelerator cable
- Transaxle kickdown cable
- Speed control cable, if equipped
- Air cleaner assembly. Torque the nuts and bolts to 10 ft. lbs. (14 Nm).
- TPS and IAC connectors
- Crankcase vent hose to the throttle body
- PSS to the throttle body

18. Refill the transaxle and check for leaks.
19. Be sure the vehicle's back-up lights and speedometer are working properly.

Clutch

ADJUSTMENT

1997–99 Models

The manual transaxle clutch release system has a unique self-adjusting mechanism to compensate for clutch disc wear. This adjuster mechanism is located with the clutch cable assembly. The preload spring maintains tension on the cable. This tension keeps the clutch release bearing continuously loaded against the fingers of the clutch cover assembly. No manual adjustment is obtainable.

When servicing this vehicle or if removing and installing the clutch cable, do not pull on the clutch cable housing to remove

it from the dash panel. Damage to the cable self-adjuster may occur.

To check the function of the adjuster mechanism, use the following procedure:

1. With slight pressure, pull the clutch release lever end of the cable to draw the cable taut.

2. Push the clutch cable housing toward the dash panel. With less than 25 lbs. (11kg) of effort the cable housing should move 1.2–2.0 in. (30–50mm). This indicates proper adjuster mechanism function.

3. If the cable does not adjust, determine if the mechanism is properly seated on the bracket.

REMOVAL & INSTALLATION

➡**Vehicles made at the Toluca, Mexico assembly plant have conventional clutch and flywheel assembles. Vehicles made at the Belvidere assembly plant have modular clutch assemblies. If the 11th digit of the VIN code is "D", the vehicle was produced at the Belvidere assembly plant; if the VIN code is "T", the vehicle was produced at the Toluca assembly plant.**

1997–99 Models

TOLUCA BUILT VEHICLES

1. Before servicing the vehicle, refer to the precautions in the beginning of this section.

2. Remove the transaxle assembly.

3. Matchmark the position of the clutch cover and flywheel for proper alignment during installation.

4. Install a suitable clutch alignment tool through the clutch disc hub to prevent the clutch disc from falling and damaging the facings.

5. Loosen the clutch cover attaching bolts, 1–2 turns at a time, in a crisscross

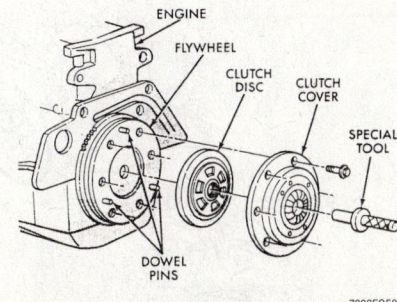

Exploded view of the conventional clutch components—1997–99 vehicles built in Toluca

7922EG50

pattern. This releases the spring pressure gradually, avoiding cover damage.

➡**DO NOT touch the clutch disc facing with oily or dirty hands. Oil or dirt transferred from your hands onto the clutch disc may cause clutch chatter.**

6. Remove or disconnect the following:
- Clutch pressure plate
- Clutch cover assembly and disc from the flywheel
- Flywheel, if necessary

To inspect:

➡**Handle the components carefully to avoid contaminating the friction surfaces.**

7. Inspect for oil leakage through the engine rear main bearing oil seal and transaxle input shaft seal. If there is leakage, it should be fixed at this time.

8. The friction faces of the flywheel and pressure plate should not have excessive discoloration, burned areas, cracks, deep grooves or ridges. Replace parts as required.

9. Clean the flywheel face with medium sandpaper, then wipe the surface with mineral spirits. If the surface is severely scored, heat checked, cracked or warped, replace the flywheel.

10. The clutch disc should be handled without touching the facings. Replace the disc if the facings show grease or oil soakage, or wear to within less than 0.008 in. (0.20mm) of the rivet heads. The splines on the disc hub and transaxle input shaft should be a snug fit without signs of excessive wear. Metallic portions of the disc assembly should be dry, clean and not discolored from excessive heat. Each of the arched springs between the facings should be tight.

11. Wipe the friction surface of the pressure plate with mineral spirits.

12. Using a straightedge, check the pressure plate for flatness. The pressure plate friction area should be flat-to-slightly concave, with the inner diameter 0.000–0.0039 in. (0.0–0.1mm) below the outer diameter. It should also be free from discoloration, burned areas, cracks, grooves or ridges.

13. Using a surface plate, test the cover for flatness. All sections around the attaching bolt holes should be in contact with the surface plate within 0.015 in. (0.381mm).

14. The cover should be a snug fit on the flywheel dowels. If the clutch assembly does not meet these requirements, it should be replaced.

To install:

➡**The heavy side of the flywheel is indicated by a white paint mark, near the outside diameter.**

15. To minimize the effects of flywheel unbalance, perform the following installation procedure:

    a. Loosely assembly the flywheel to the crankshaft. If available, use new flywheel attaching bolts which have sealant on the threads. If new bolts are not available, apply Loctite® sealant to the threads of the original bolts. This sealant is required to prevent engine oil leakage.

    b. Rotate the flywheel and crankshaft until the white paint (heavy side) is at the 12 o'clock position.

    c. Tighten the flywheel attaching bolts, in a crisscross pattern, to 70 ft. lbs. (95 Nm).

16. Mount the clutch assembly on the flywheel with the disc centered on the alignment tool, being careful to properly align the dowels and the alignment marks made before removal. The flywheel side of the clutch disc is marked for proper installation. If the new clutch or flywheel is installed, align the orange cover balance spot as close as possible to the orange flywheel balance spot. Apply pressure to the alignment tool. Center the tip of the tool into the crankshaft and the sliding cone into the clutch fingers. Tighten the clutch attaching bolts sufficiently to hold the disc in position.

17. To avoid distorting the clutch cover, tighten the bolts gradually, a few turns at a time. Use a crisscross pattern until all bolts are seated. Tighten the bolts to a final torque of 21 ft. lbs. (28 Nm).

18. Remove the clutch alignment tool.

19. Install the transaxle.

BELVIDERE BUILT VEHICLES

1. Before servicing the vehicle, refer to the precautions in the beginning of this section.

2. Remove or disconnect the following:
- Negative battery cable
- Starter motor assembly
- Rear and front transaxle brackets
- Modular clutch-driveplate bolts. Discard the bolts
- Transaxle

➡**The transaxle and modular clutch come out as an assembly.**

- Modular clutch assembly from the transaxle input shaft

➡**Handle the components carefully to avoid contaminating the friction surface.**

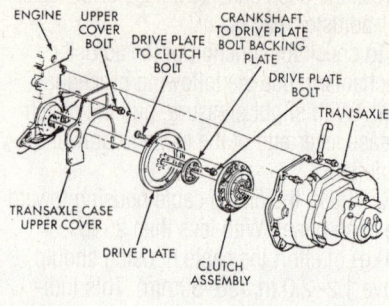

ENGINE   UPPER COVER BOLT   DRIVE PLATE TO CLUTCH BOLT   CRANKSHAFT TO DRIVE PLATE BOLT BACKING PLATE   DRIVE PLATE BOLT   TRANSAXLE

TRANSAXLE CASE UPPER COVER   DRIVE PLATE   CLUTCH ASSEMBLY

7922EG51

The transaxle and modular clutch are removed as an assembly—1997–99 vehicles

3. Inspect for oil leakage through the engine rear main bearing oil seal and transaxle input shaft seal. If any leakage is noted, it should be fixed at this time.

To install:

➡**Always use new bolts when mounting the modular clutch assembly to the driveplate.**

4. Install or connect the following:
- Modular clutch assembly onto the input shaft
- Transaxle

5. To avoid distorting the driveplate, tighten the bolts gradually a few turns at a time. Use a crisscross pattern, until all bolts are seated. Tighten the bolts to a final torque of 55 ft. lbs. (75 Nm).

6. Install or connect the following:
- Clutch inspection cover
- Transaxle lower support brackets
- Starter assembly
- Negative battery cable

2000–01 Models

1. Before servicing the vehicle, refer to the precautions in the beginning of this section.

2. Remove or disconnect the following:
- Negative battery cable

- Modular clutch-to-driveplate bolts. Discard the bolts
- Transaxle assembly
- Modular clutch assembly from the transaxle input shaft

To install:

3. Install or connect the following:
- Modular clutch assembly onto the transaxle input shaft
- Transaxle assembly. Torque the transaxle-to-engine bolts to 70 ft. lbs. (95 Nm).
- New modular clutch-to-driveplate bolts. Torque the clutch module-to-driveplate bolts to 65 ft. lbs. (88 Nm).
- Negative battery cable

Halfshafts

REMOVAL & INSTALLATION

1. Before servicing the vehicle, refer to the precautions in the beginning of this section.

2. On 1997–99 vehicles, remove the cotter pin (discard it), locknut and spring washer, from the end of the outer CV-joint stub axle.

3. With the vehicle on the ground and brakes applied, loosen, but do not remove the stub axle-to-hub and bearing retaining nut.

➡**The front hub and driveshaft are splined together and retained by the hub nut.**

4. On 2000–01 vehicles equipped with Anti-lock Brake System (ABS), disconnect the front wheel speed sensor.

5. Remove or disconnect the following:
- Front wheel
- Front caliper-to-steering knuckle bolts
- Caliper from the steering knuckle

6. Support the caliper out of the way by

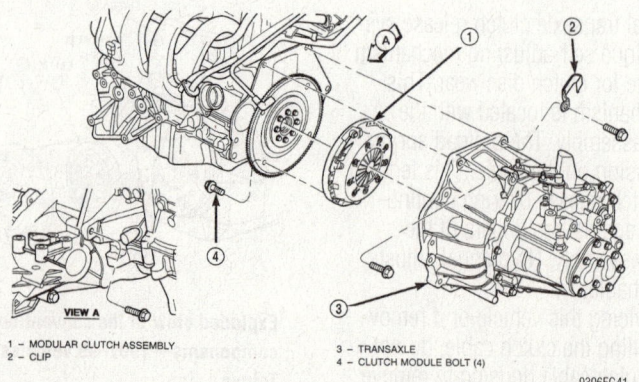

VIEW A

1 – MODULAR CLUTCH ASSEMBLY
2 – CLIP
3 – TRANSAXLE
4 – CLUTCH MODULE BOLT (4)

9306EG41

Exploded view of the manual transaxle, clutch module and related components—2000–01 vehicles

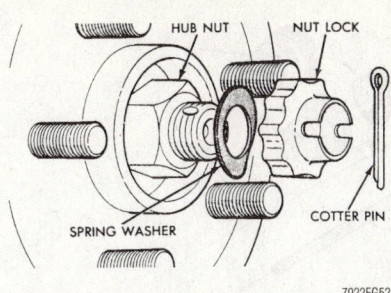

Exploded view of the cotter pin, locknut and washer—halfshaft service

suspending it with a piece of wire from the strut. DO NOT allow the caliper to hang by the brake hose.

7. Remove or disconnect the following:
- Rotor from the hub
- Outer tie rod end-to-steering knuckle nut by holding the tie rod end stud with a $1\frac{1}{32}$ in. socket while loosening the nut
- Tie rod end stud from the steering knuckle
- Ball joint stud-to-steering knuckle nut and bolt

✳✳ WARNING

Be careful when separating the ball joint stud from the steering knuckle, so the ball joint seal does not get damaged.

- Ball joint stud from the steering knuckle by prying down on the lower control arm

8. For 1998–00 vehicles, perform the following steps:
   a. Remove the hub and bearing-to-stub axle retaining nut.
   b. Install a suitable puller on the hub and bearing assembly, using the lug nuts to hold it in place.
   c. Install a wheel lug nut on wheel stud to protect the threads on the stud. Install a flat-bladed prytool to keep the hub from turning. Using the puller, force the outer stub axle from the hub and bearing.

✳✳ WARNING

Be careful when separating the inner CV-joint during this operation. Do not let the driveshaft hang by the inner CV-joint, the driveshaft must be supported.

9. Pull the steering knuckle assembly out and away from the outer CV-joint of the driveshaft assembly. Support the outer end of the driveshaft assembly.

10. Insert a prybar between the inner tripod joint and the transaxle case. Pry against the inner tripod joint until the joint retaining snapring is disengaged from the transaxle side gear.

➡ **Inner tripod joint removal is easier by applying outward pressure on the joint while hitting the punch with a hammer.**

11. Remove the inner tripod joints from the transaxle side gears using a punch to dislodge the inner tripod joint retaining ring from the transaxle side gear. If removing the

right side inner tripod joint, position the punch against the inner tripod joint. Hit the punch sharply with a hammer to dislodge the right inner joint from the side gear. If removing the left side inner tripod joint, position the punch in the groove of the inner tripod joint. Hit the punch sharply with a hammer to dislodge the left inner tripod joint from the side gear.

12. Hold the inner tripod joint and interconnecting shaft of the driveshaft assembly. Remove the inner tripod joint from the transaxle by pulling it straight out of the transaxle side gear and transaxle oil seal. When removing the tripod joint, do not let the spline or snapring drag across the sealing lip of the transaxle-to-tripod joint oil seal.

✳✳ WARNING

The driveshaft, when installed, acts as a bolt which secures the front hub and bearing assembly. If the vehicle is to be supported or moved on its wheels with a driveshaft removed, install a proper-sized bolt and nut through the front hub. Tighten the bolt and nut to 135 ft. lbs. (183 Nm). This will ensure that the hub bearing cannot loosen.

To install:

13. Thoroughly clean the spline and oil seal sealing surface on the tripod joint. Lightly lubricate the oil seal sealing surface on the tripod joint with fresh, clean transmission fluid.

14. Holding the driveshaft assembly by the tripod joint and interconnecting shaft, install the tripod joint into the transaxle side gear as far as possible by hand.

15. Carefully align the tripod joint with the transaxle side gears. Then, grasp the driveshaft interconnecting shaft and push the tripod joint into the transaxle side gear until fully seated. Be sure the snapring is fully engaged with the side gear by trying to remove the tripod joint from the transaxle by hand. If the snapring is fully seated with the side gear, the tripod joint will not be removable by hand.

16. Clean all debris and moisture out of the steering knuckle.

17. Be sure that the outer CV-joint, which fits into the steering knuckle, has no debris or moisture on it before installing into the steering knuckle.

18. Slide the driveshaft back into the front hub. Install the steering knuckle into the ball joint stud.

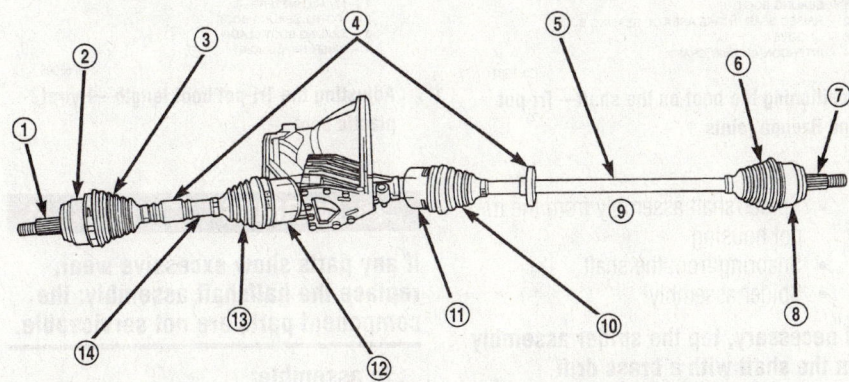

1 – STUB AXLE
2 – OUTER C/V JOINT
3 – OUTER C/V JOINT BOOT
4 – TUNED RUBBER DAMPER WEIGHT
5 – INTERCONNECTING SHAFT
6 – OUTER C/V JOINT BOOT
7 – STUB AXLE
8 – OUTER C/V JOINT
9 – RIGHT DRIVESHAFT
10 – INNER TRIPOD JOINT BOOT
11 – INNER TRIPOD JOINT
12 – INNER TRIPOD JOINT
13 – INNER TRIPOD JOINT BOOT
14 – INTERCONNECTING SHAFT LEFT DRIVESHAFT

View of the halfshaft assemblies—Typical

19. Install a NEW steering knuckle-to-ball joint stud bolt and nut. Tighten the nut and bolt to 70 ft. lbs. (95 Nm).

20. Insert the tie rod end into the steering knuckle. Start the tie rod end-to-steering knuckle nut onto the stud of the tie rod end. While holding the stud of the tie rod end stationary, tighten the nut. Then, using a crow's foot and 11⁄32 in socket, tighten the tie rod end nut to 45 ft. lbs. (61 Nm).

21. Install the rotor back onto the hub and bearing assembly.

22. Position the caliper on the steering knuckle. Slide the top of the caliper under the top abutment on the steering knuckle, then install the bottom of the caliper against the bottom abutment of the steering knuckle.

23. Install the caliper-to-knuckle bolts and tighten to 23 ft. lbs. (31 Nm).

24. On 2000–01 vehicles equipped with ABS, connect the front wheel speed sensor.

25. Clean all foreign matter from the threads of the outer CV-joint stub axle. Install hub nut and washer onto the threads of the stub axle and tighten the nut.

26. With the vehicle's brakes applied to prevent the axle shaft from turning, tighten the hub nut to 135 ft. lbs. (183 Nm) for 1997 models, 150 ft. lbs. (203 Nm) for 1998–99 models or 180 ft. lbs. (244 Nm) for 2000–01 models.

27. On 1997–99 vehicles, install the spring washer, locknut and new cotter pin into the outer CV-joint stub axle.

28. Install the front wheel and tire assembly. Install the lug nuts and tighten to 100 ft. lbs. (135 Nm) for 1997–99 models or 95 ft. lbs. (128 Nm) for 2000–01 models.

29. Check the transaxle fluid level, lowering the vehicle as necessary.

CV-Joints

OVERHAUL

Tri-Pot (Inner) Joint

1. Remove or disassemble the following:
   - Halfshaft and place it in a soft-jawed vise
   - Tri-pot joint boot clamps and slide the boot down the shaft

✳✳ WARNING

When removing the spider joint, hold the rollers in place on the trunions to keep the rollers and needle bearings in place.

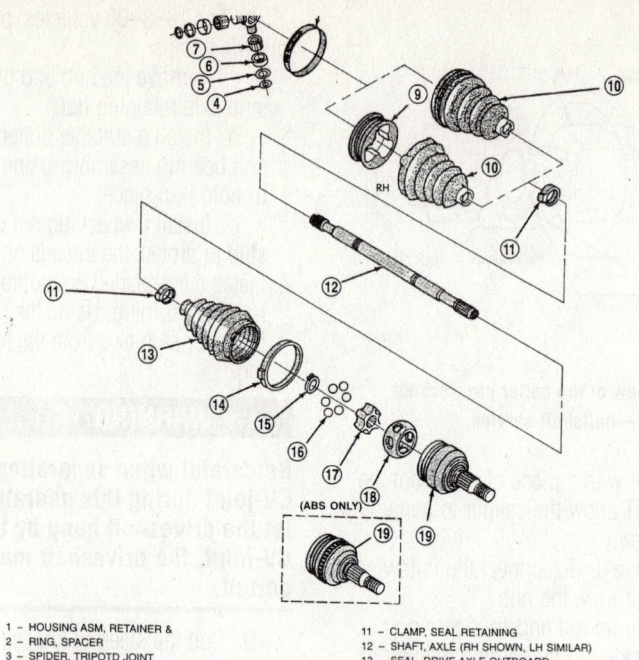

1 – HOUSING ASM, RETAINER &
2 – RING, SPACER
3 – SPIDER, TRIPOTD JOINT
4 – RING, RETAINING
5 – RETAINER, BALL & ROLLER
6 – BALL, TRIPOD JOINT
7 – ROLLER, NEEDLE
8 – CLAMP, SEAL RETAINING
9 – BUSHING, TRILOBAL TRIPOD
10 – SEAL, DRIVE AXLE INBOARD
11 – CLAMP, SEAL RETAINING
12 – SHAFT, AXLE (RH SHOWN, LH SIMILAR)
13 – SEAL, DRIVE AXLE OUTBOARD
14 – CLAMP, SEAL RETAINING
15 – RING, RACE RETAINING
16 – BALL, CHROME ALLOY
17 – RACE, C/V JOINT INNER
18 – CAGE, C/V JOINT
19 – RACE, C/V JOINT OUTER

9306EG03

Exploded view of the halfshaft assembly—Typical

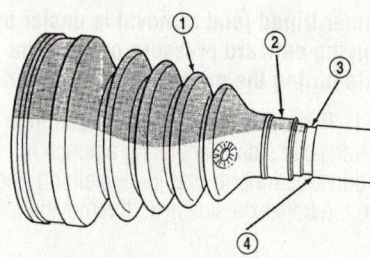

1 – SEALING BOOT
2 – RAISED BEAD IN THIS AREA OF SEALING BOOT
3 – GROOVE
4 – INTERCONNECTING SHAFT

9306EG04

Positioning the boot on the shaft—Tri-pot and Rzeppa joints

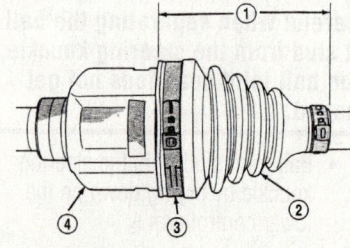

1 – 107 MILLIMETERS
2 – HYTREL SEALING BOOT
3 – SEALING BOOT CLAMP
4 – INNER TRIPOD JOINT

9306EG05

Adjusting the Tri-pot boot length—Hytrel plastic boot

- Spider/shaft assembly from the tri-pot housing
- Snapring from the shaft
- Spider assembly

➡ If necessary, tap the spider assembly from the shaft with a brass drift.

✳✳ WARNING

When removing the spider assembly, do not hit the outer bearings.

- Boot by sliding it off the shaft

✳✳ WARNING

If any parts show excessive wear, replace the halfshaft assembly; the component parts are not serviceable.

To assemble:

✳✳ WARNING

The Tri-pot sealing boots are made of 2 different types of material; silicon rubber (high temperature) which is soft and pliable or hytrel plastic

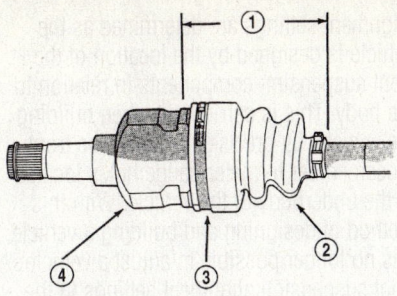

1 – 115 MILLIMETERS
2 – SILICONE SEALING BOOT
3 – CLAMP
4 – INNER TRIPOD JOINT

9306EG06

Adjusting the Tri-pot boot length—Silicone rubber boot

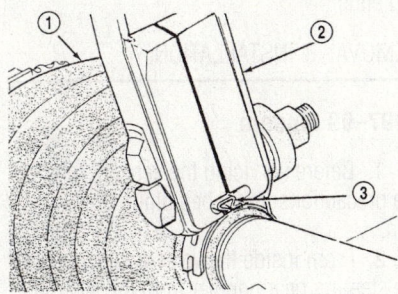

1 – SEALING BOOT
2 – SPECIAL TOOL C-4975
3 – CLAMP BRIDGE

9306BG13

Tightening the high profile boot clamp—Tri-pot joint (Hytrel plastic) boot and Rzeppa joint boots

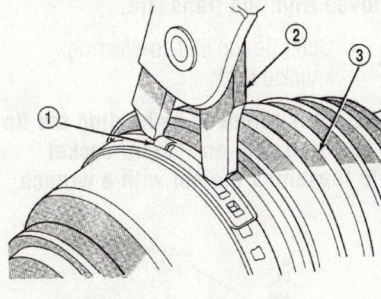

1 – CLAMP
2 – SPECIAL TOOL YA3050
3 – SEALING BOOT

9306EG07

Tightening the low profile boot clamp—Silicone rubber Tri-pot boot

(standard temperature) which is stiff and rigid. Be sure to replace the boot made of the correct material.

2. Install or assemble the following:
  • New small boot clamp and slide it on the shaft
  • Boot and slide it on the shaft
3. Position the boot so that the raised

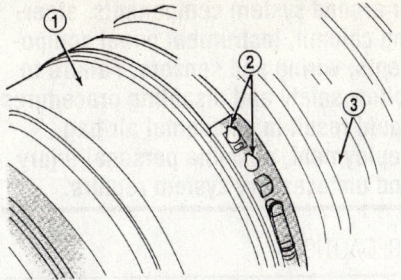

1 – INNER TRIPOD JOINT HOUSING
2 – TOP BANK OF CLAMP MUST BE RETAINED BY TABS AS SHOWN HERE TO CORRECTLY LATCH BOOT CLAMP
3 – SEALING BOOT

9306EG08

Secured the low profile boot clamp—Silicone rubber Tri-pot boot

bead on the inside the boot seal is in the shaft groove.

4. If installing a new boot, distribute ½ of the grease in the service package inside the tri-pot housing and the other ½ inside the boot.

5. Install or assemble the following
  • Spider assembly, face the chamfered side toward the shaft

✳✳ WARNING

If necessary, tap the spider assembly onto the shaft using a brass drift; be careful not to hit the outer bearings.

  • Snapring making sure it is fully seated in the groove
  • Spider/shaft assembly into the tripot housing
  • New inner boot clamp and position it evenly on the sealing boot

6. Using a trim stick, adjust the boot length to 107mm (hytrel plastic) or 115mm (silicone rubber).

7. If installing a high profile boot clamp, perform the following procedure:

  a. Using the Crimper tool C-4975-A, place the tool over the clamp bridge, tighten the tool nut until the jaws are completely closed (face-to-face).

✳✳ WARNING

The seal must not be dimpled, stretched or out of shape. If necessary, equalize the seal pressure and shape it by hand.

  b. Position the boot onto the tri-pot housing retaining groove and install the retaining clamp evenly on the boot.

  c. Using the Crimper tool C-4975-A, place the tool over the clamp bridge,

tighten the tool nut until the jaws are completely closed (face-to-face).

8. If installing a low profile latching type boot clamp, position Snap-On® Clamp Locing tool YA3050 prongs in the clamp holes and squeeze the tool until the upper clamp band is latched behind the 2 tabs on the lower clamp band.

9. Install the halfshaft.

Rzeppa (Outer) Joint

1. Remove or disassemble the following:
  • Halfshaft and place it in a soft-jawed vise
  • Rzeppa joint boot clamps and slide the boot down the shaft
  • Rzeppa joint housing by sharply hitting it with a soft-faced hammer to drive it off the shaft
  • Circlip from the shaft
  • Boot by sliding it off the shaft

✳✳ WARNING

If any parts show excessive wear, replace the halfshaft assembly; the component parts are not serviceable.

To assemble:
2. Install or assemble the following:

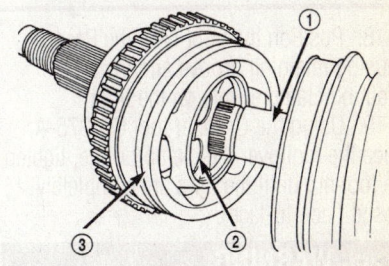

1 – INTERCONNECTING SHAFT
2 – CROSS
3 – OUTER C/V JOINT ASSEMBLY

9306EG09

Aligning the cross splines with the shaft splines—Rzeppa joint

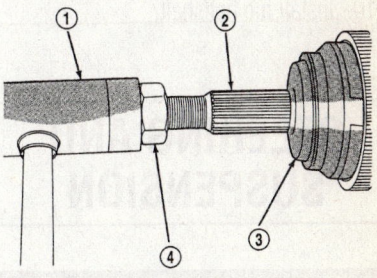

1 – SOFT FACED HAMMER
2 – STUB AXLE
3 – OUTER C/V JOINT
4 – NUT

9306EG10

Driving the Rzeppa joint onto the shaft

Turn to Section 5 for brake system applications

- New small boot and clamp and slide it onto the shaft
- Boot and slide it onto the shaft
- Circlip, if removed

3. Position the boot so that the raised bead on the inside the boot seal is in the shaft groove.

4. Install or connect the following:
- Halfshaft hub nut onto the Rzeppa joint threaded shaft so it is flush with the end
- Rzeppa joint, align the shaft splines and tap it onto the shaft with a soft-faced hammer so it locks on the circlip

5. Distribute ½ of the grease in the service package inside the Rzeppa joint housing and the other ½ inside the boot.

6. Install the new small boot clamp and position it evenly on the sealing boot

7. Using the Crimper tool C-4975-A, place the tool over the clamp bridge, tighten the tool nut until the jaws are completely closed (face-to-face).

✳✳ WARNING

The seal must not be dimpled, stretched or out of shape. If necessary, equalize the seal pressure and shape it by hand.

8. Position the boot onto the Rzeppa housing retaining groove and install the retaining clamp evenly on the boot.

9. Using the Crimper tool C-4975-A, place the tool over the clamp bridge, tighten the tool nut until the jaws are completely closed (face-to-face).

✳✳ WARNING

The seal must not be dimpled, stretched or out of shape. If necessary, equalize the seal pressure and shape it by hand.

10. Install the halfshaft.

STEERING AND SUSPENSION

Air Bag

✳✳ CAUTION

Some vehicles are equipped with an air bag system. The system MUST BE disabled before performing service on or around system components, steering column, instrument panel components, wiring and sensors. Failure to follow safety and disabling procedures could result in accidental air bag deployment, possible personal injury and unnecessary system repairs.

PRECAUTIONS

Several precautions must be observed when handling the inflator module to avoid accidental deployment and possible personal injury:

- Never carry the inflator module by the wires or connector on the underside of the module.
- When carrying a live inflator module, hold securely with both hands, and ensure that the bag and trim cover are pointed away.
- Place the inflator module on a bench or other surface with the bag and trim cover facing up.
- With the inflator module on the bench, never place anything on or close to the module which may be thrown in the event of an accidental deployment.

DISARMING

Proper SRS disarming can be obtained by disconnecting and isolating the negative battery cable. Allow the air bag system capacitor at least 2 minutes to discharge before removing any air bag system components.

Rack and Pinion Steering Gear

These vehicles are designed and assembled using NET BUILD front suspension alignment settings. This means that the alignment settings are determined as the vehicle is designed by the location of the front suspension components in relation to the body. This is carried out when building the vehicle, by precisely locating the front crossmember to meter gauge holes located in the underbody of the vehicle. With this method of designing and building a vehicle, it is no longer possible to adjust a vehicle's front suspension alignment settings to the required specifications. As a result, whenever the crossmember is removed from a vehicle, it MUST be replaced in the same location on the body of the vehicle it was removed from. The front suspension toe settings can still be adjusted by the outer tie rod ends.

REMOVAL & INSTALLATION

1997–99 Models

1. Before servicing the vehicle, refer to the precautions in the beginning of this section.

2. From inside the vehicle, disconnect the steering gear coupler from the steering column shaft coupler.

3. Remove or disconnect the following:
- Both front wheels
- Engine/transaxle bobble damper from the front suspension crossmember, if equipped

➡**The bobble strut does not have to be removed from the transaxle.**

- Outer tie rod end-to-steering knuckle nut

➡**The nut is removed by holding the tie rod end stud with an $^{11}/_{32}$ in. socket while loosening the nut with a wrench.**

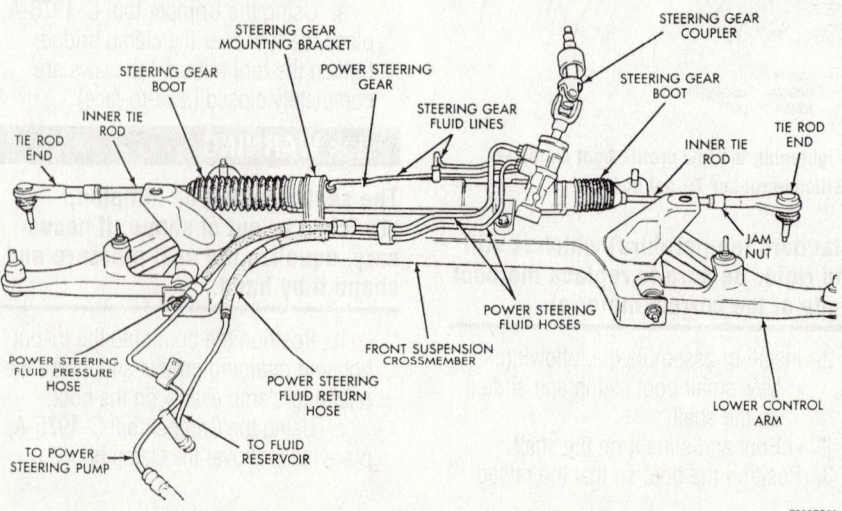

Identification of the rack and pinion steering gear components—1997–99 vehicles

7922EG53

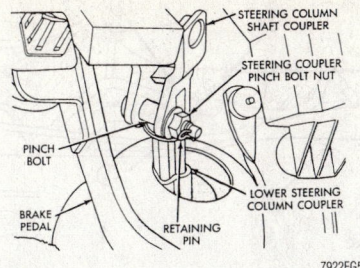

Disconnect the steering gear coupler from inside the vehicle—1997–99 vehicles

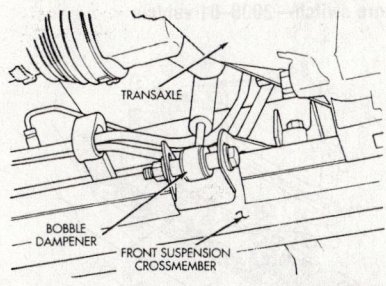

Some vehicles are equipped with a bobble damper that must be removed from the crossmember during steering gear service—1997–99 vehicles

- Tie rod ends from the steering knuckles, using a side puller, tool MB-991113.
- Power steering fluid pressure switch connector
- Power steering pressure/return hose routing bracket from the front crossmember

➡The bracket does not have to be removed from the power steering pressure and return hoses.

- Power steering fluid pressure and return hoses from the power steering gear

✳✳ WARNING

Before removing the crossmember from the vehicle, the location of the crossmember MUST be scribed or marked on the vehicle. This must be done so the crossmember can be reinstalled in its exact location. If this is not done, the proper NET BUILD alignment specifications will not be obtained and may lead to handling and/or tire wear problems.

4. Matchmark the crossmember to the chassis.

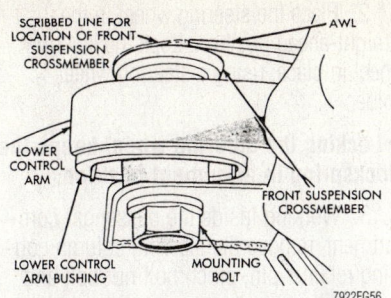

Because of the method used for aligning the vehicle, matchmark the crossmember installed position prior to steering gear removal—1997–99 vehicles

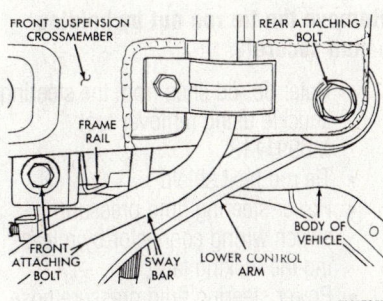

Location of the front crossmember mounting bolts—1997–99 vehicles

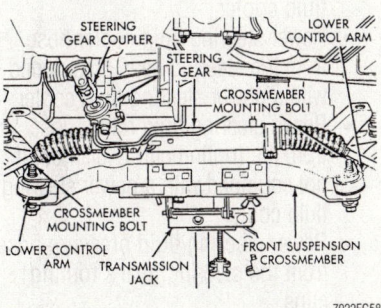

Lower the crossmember for access to the steering gear—1997–99 vehicles

5. Place a transmission jack under the center of the crossmember. The jack will be used to lower, support and raise the crossmember when removing the steering gear.

6. Remove both front crossmember-to-frame rails bolts. Then, loosen both rear crossmember/lower control arm to the body bolts. Lower the crossmember while loosening the rear bolts.

7. Using the transmission jack, lower the crossmember enough to allow the steering gear to be removed from the crossmember. When lowering the crossmember, do not let the crossmember hang from the

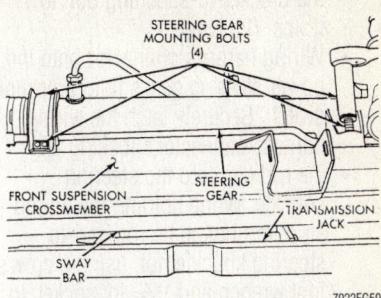

View of the steering gear mounting bolts—1997–99 vehicles

lower control arms. The weight should be supported by the jack.

8. Remove or disconnect the following:
- 4 steering gear-to-crossmember bolts
- Steering gear

➡If a new steering gear is being installed, transfer any necessary parts from the old steering gear to the new steering gear.

To install:

9. Install the steering gear on the crossmember and torque the bolts to 50 ft. lbs. (68 Nm).

10. Using the transmission jack, raise the crossmember/steering gear assembly against the chassis frame rails. Start the 2 rear crossmember-to-chassis bolts; then, the 2 front crossmember-to-frame rail volts. Tighten the 4 bolts until the crossmember is aligned with the mounting points. Torque the bolts to 20 inch lbs. (2 Nm).

➡When the crossmember is installed, it MUST align with the removal matchmarks; the purpose is maintain NET BUILD front suspension alignment settings.

11. Tap the crossmember into position, with a rubber mallet, until it is aligned with the matchmarks. Once positioned, torque both rear crossmember/lower control arm bolts to 120 ft. lbs. (163 Nm); then, both front bolts to 120 ft. lbs. (163 Nm).

12. Install or connect the following:
- Power steering fluid pressure/return hoses into the steering gear ports. Torque the line-to-steering gear tube nuts to 23 ft. lbs. (31 Nm).
- Power steering fluid pressure/return hose routing bracket and screw on the crossmember. Torque

the bracket-to-attaching bolt to 17 ft. lbs. (23 Nm).

- Wiring harness connector onto the power steering gear's fluid pressure switch. Securely latch the wiring harness connector's locking tab.
- Tie rod end into the steering knuckle. While holding the tie rod stud, torque the tie rod end-to-steering knuckle nut, using a crow's foot wrench and $^{11}/_{32}$ in. socket, to 40 ft. lbs. (55 Nm).
- Engine/transaxle bobble strut, if equipped, onto the crossmember bracket.
- Both front wheels. Torque the lug nuts, in a crisscross pattern, to 100 ft. lbs. (135 Nm).
- Steering gear coupler to the steering column shaft coupler, under the dash. Torque the bolt to 21 ft. lbs. (28 Nm).
- Upper-to-lower steering coupler retaining bolt retention pin

✵✵ WARNING

When refilling and bleeding the power steering system, always use the proper type of fluid. NEVER substitute automatic transmission fluid for the specified fluid.

13. Refill the power steering pump fluid reservoir to the FULL-COLD level with the proper type and amount of fluid. Bleed the system.

2000–01 Models

1. Before servicing the vehicle, refer to the precautions in the beginning of this section.

2. Place the steering wheel in the straight-ahead position. Lock the steering wheel in place, using a steering wheel holder.

➡ **Locking the steering wheel keeps the clockspring in alignment position.**

3. Working inside the passenger compartment, remove the steering column coupling retainer pin, pinch bolt nut/bolt and separate the couplings.

4. Remove or disconnect the following:

- Both front wheels
- Outer tie rods-to-steering knuckle nuts

➡ **Remove the tie rod nut by holding the stud securely.**

- Outer tie rod ends from the steering knuckle using remover tool MB991113
- Tie rod heat shield
- Power steering fluid pressure switch wiring connector by releasing the locking tab
- Power steering fluid pressure hose from the steering gear
- Power steering fluid return hose from the steering gear, if not equipped with a power steering fluid cooler
- Power steering fluid cooler hose from the steering gear, if equipped with a power steering fluid cooler
- Power steering fluid return hose from the routing clip C-clamps, if not equipped with a power steering fluid cooler
- Power steering fluid pressure hose from the steering gear's routing clips

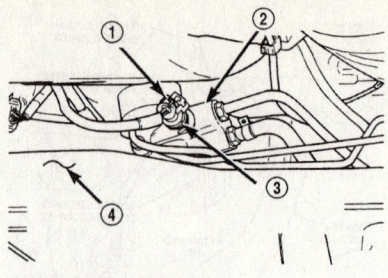

1 – WIRING HARNESS CONNECTOR
2 – POWER STEERING GEAR
3 – POWER STEERING FLUID PRESSURE SWITCH
4 – REAR OF FRONT SUSPENSION CROSSMEMBER

9306EG43

View of the power steering gear fluid pressure switch—2000–01 vehicle

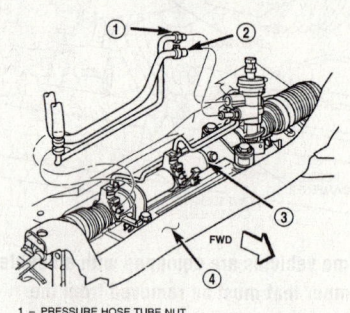

1 – PRESSURE HOSE TUBE NUT
2 – RETURN HOSE
3 – POWER STEERING GEAR
4 – FRONT SUSPENSION CROSSMEMBER

9306EG44

View of the power steering gear hoses and routing clips—2000–01 vehicle

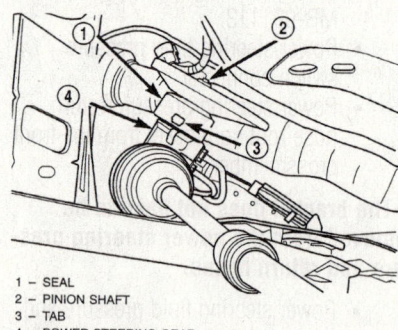

1 – SEAL
2 – PINION SHAFT
3 – TAB
4 – POWER STEERING GEAR

9306EG45

View of the pinion shaft dash cover seal—2000–01 vehicle

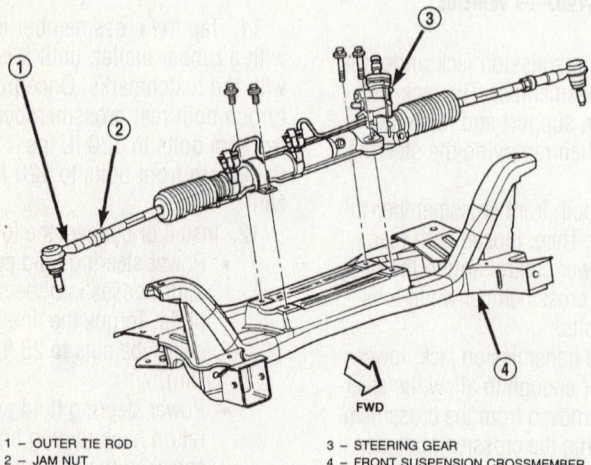

1 – OUTER TIE ROD
2 – JAM NUT
3 – STEERING GEAR
4 – FRONT SUSPENSION CROSSMEMBER

9306EG42

View of the power steering gear and crossmember—2000–01 vehicle

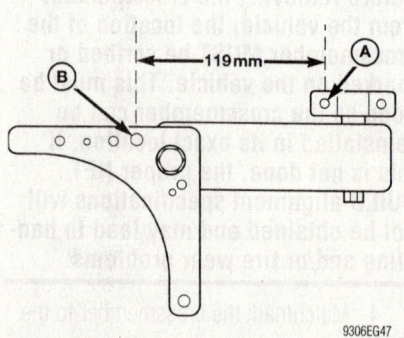

119mm

9306EG47

Measuring the engine torque bracket—2000–01 vehicle

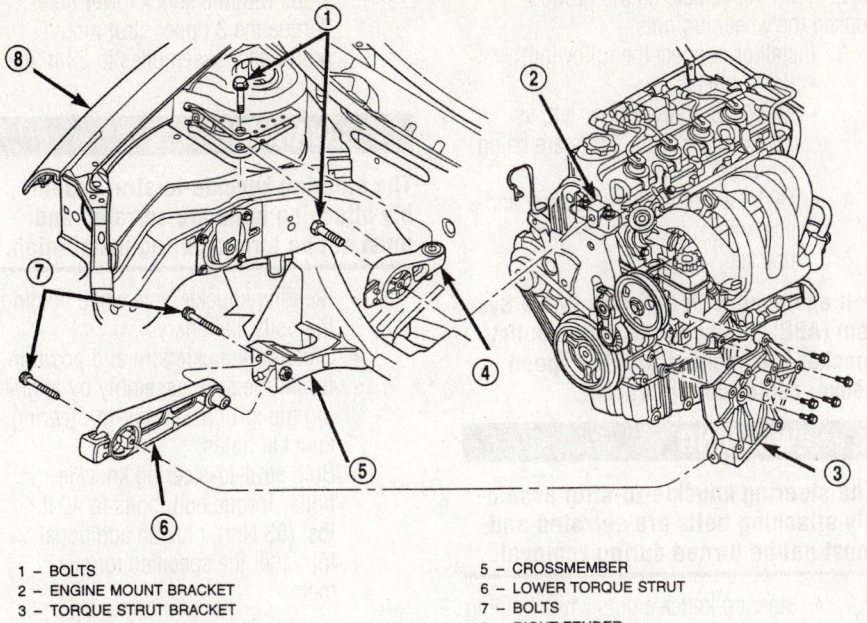

1 – BOLTS
2 – ENGINE MOUNT BRACKET
3 – TORQUE STRUT BRACKET
4 – UPPER TORQUE STRUT
5 – CROSSMEMBER
6 – LOWER TORQUE STRUT
7 – BOLTS
8 – RIGHT FENDER

9306EG46

View of the engine torque struts and related components—2000–01 vehicle

- Power steering cooler hose from the steering gear's right routing clip, if equipped
- Both power steering cooler screws from the front suspension crossmember, if equipped, and move the cooler aside

➡ **The screws are located behind the cooler and can be accessed from above.**

- Power steering cooler, if equipped, and move it aside
- Engine torque strut-to-front suspension crossmember bolt from the right forward corner of the crossmember

5. Matchmark the front suspension crossmember-to-chassis location.

✳✳ **WARNING**

If the front suspension crossmember-to-chassis location is not matchmarked, the front wheel alignment setting will be lost.

6. Place a transmission jack under the front crossmember and support it.

7. Remove both front suspension crossmember-to-frame rail bolts, one located at each side.

8. Loosen both rear suspension crossmember-to-frame rail bolts, one located at each side, until they release from the threaded tapping plates in the bolt.

✳✳ **WARNING**

Do not completely remove the rear bolts for they are designed to disengage from the body threads and will stay within the lower control arm rear isolator bushing.

➡ **The threaded tapping plates allow the lower control arm to stay in place on the crossmember.**

9. Using the transmission jack, lower the front suspension crossmember enough to allow the power steering gear to be removed form the rear of the crossmember. Use the jack to support the crossmember's weight.

10. Remove or disconnect the following:
- Lower steering column coupling-to-power steering gear pinion shaft's roll pin, using a roll pin punch
- Lower steering column coupling from the power steering column pinion shaft
- Pinion shaft dash cover seal from the tabs cast into the power steering gear housing
- Power steering gear from the front suspension crossmember.

To install:

11. Install or connect the following:
- Power steering gear onto the front suspension crossmember. Torque the bolts to 45 ft. lbs. (61 Nm).

- Pinion shaft dash cover seal over the shaft and onto the power steering gear housing

➡ **Align the seal holes with the tabs cast into the power steering gear housing.**

- Lower steering column coupling by aligning the coupling and steering gear pinion shaft flats
- Lower steering column coupling-to-pinion shaft's roll pin until it is centered

12. Center the power steering gear rack's travel.

13. Install or connect the following:
- Front suspension crossmember/ power steering gear assembly by raising it with the jack until is aligns with it's matchmarks.
- Lower steering column coupling, guide it through the dash panel hole as it is raised
- Both rear crossmember-to-tapping plate bolts
- Both front crossmember-to-frame rail bolts. Torque the 4 bolts to 20 inch lbs. (2 Nm).

✳✳ **WARNING**

Be sure to align the front suspension crossmember-to-chassis matchmarks; otherwise, the front wheel alignment setting will be lost.

- Once aligned, torque both rear crossmember-to-rear lower control arm bolts to 150 ft. lbs. (203 Nm) and both front crossmember bolts to 105 ft. lbs. (142 Nm).
- Engine torque strut to the right forward corner of the front suspension crossmember

14. Adjust the engine torque strut by performing the following procedure:

a. Loosen the upper torque strut at the shock tower bracket.

b. Position a floor jack on the forward edge of the bell housing to prevent the least amount of upward lifting of the engine.

c. Slowly, lift the assembly, allowing the engine to rotate rearward so the distance between center of the engine mount bracket's rearmost attaching stud (point A) and the center of the shock tower bracket's washer hose clip hole (point B) is 4.70 in. (119mm).

d. Torque the upper and lower torque strut bolts to 87 ft. lbs. (118 Nm).

e. Remove the floor jack.

15. Install or connect the following:

- Power steering hose-to-power steering gear using a new O-ring lubricated with power steering oil, if not equipped with a power steering cooler
- Power steering fluid cooler line-to-power steering gear, if equipped with a power steering cooler
- Power steering fluid return hose to the routing clip C-clamps, if not equipped with a power steering fluid cooler
- Power steering fluid pressure hose to the steering gear's routing clips
- Power steering cooler hose to the steering gear's right routing clip, if equipped
- Torque the power steering pressure hose-to-power steering gear nut to 25 ft. lbs. (34 Nm).
- Both power steering cooler screws to the front suspension crossmember, if equipped
- Power steering fluid pressure switch wiring connector be sure the locking tab is secure latched
- Tie rod heat shield, facing outboard
- Outer tie rod ends to the steering knuckle. Torque the nut, using a crowsfoot wrench, to 40 ft. lbs. (55 Nm), while holding the tie rod stationary
- Both front wheels. Torque the lug nuts, in a crisscross pattern, to 95 ft. lbs. (128 Nm).
- Dash-to-lower coupling seal over the lower coupling's plastic collar

➡ **Verify that the seal's lip shows grease at the coupling's plastic collar contact.**

- Steering column lower coupling-to-steering column upper coupling pinch bolt. Torque the nut to 21 ft. lbs. (28 Nm).
- Pinch bolt retainer pin

16. Remove the steering wheel holder.
17. Refill and bleed the power steering system.
18. Check for leaks.
19. Check and/or adjust the front toe setting.

Strut

REMOVAL & INSTALLATION

Front

1. Before servicing the vehicle, refer to the precautions in the beginning of this section.

2. With the vehicle on the ground, loosen the wheel lug nuts.
3. Install or connect the following:
- Front wheels
- Mark each one right or left, as applicable, if both struts are being removed.
- Hydraulic brake hose bracket and screw from the strut damper bracket.

➡ **If equipped with Anti-lock Brake System (ABS), the hydraulic hose routing bracket is combined with the speed sensor cable routing bracket.**

❋❋ WARNING

The steering knuckle-to-strut assembly attaching bolts are serrated and must not be turned during removal.

- Steering knuckle nuts while holding the bolts stationary
- Steering knuckle nuts by holding the bolts in place
- 3 upper strut mount-to-strut tower nuts

➡ **If necessary, partially lower the vehicle for access to the upper mounting nuts.**

- Strut assembly

To install:
4. Install or connect the following:
- Strut assembly into the strut tower by aligning the 3 upper strut mount

studs with the shock tower holes. Torque the 3 upper strut mount nut/washer assemblies to 23 ft. lbs. (31 Nm).

❋❋ WARNING

The steering knuckle-to-strut assembly attaching bolts are serrated and must not be turned during installation.

- Steering knuckle nuts while holding the bolts stationary
- Steering knuckle arm and position it into the strut assembly by aligning the strut assembly-to-steering knuckle holes
- Both strut-to-steering knuckle bolts. Torque both bolts to 40 ft. lbs. (53 Nm), plus an additional ¼ turn after the specified torque is met.

➡ **The bolts should be installed with the nuts facing the front of the vehicle.**

- Hydraulic brake hose routing bracket and screw onto the strut damper bracket. Torque the bracket bolts to 10 ft. lbs. (13 Nm).

➡ **If equipped with ABS, the hydraulic hose routing bracket is combined with the speed sensor cable routing bracket.**

- Front wheel

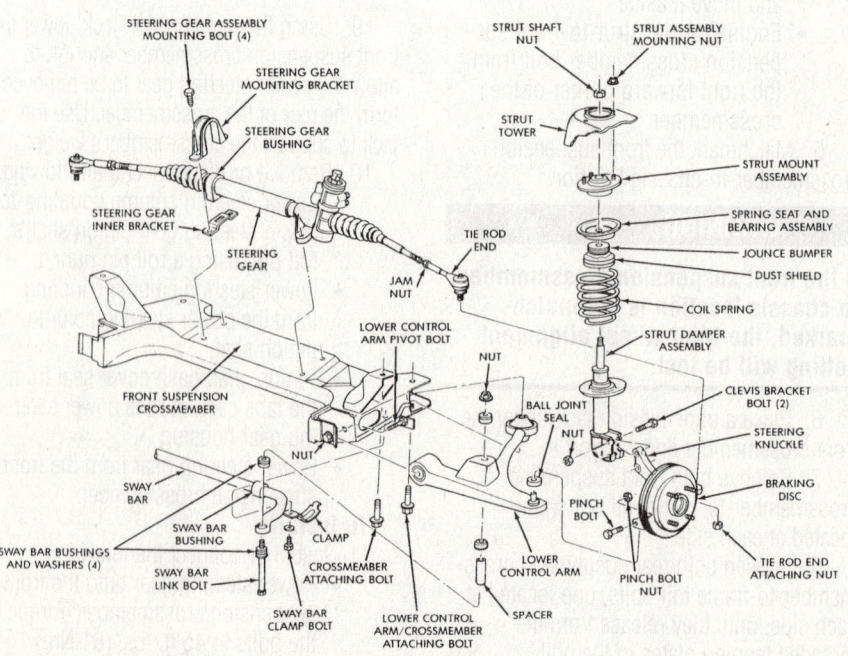

Exploded view of the front suspension—1997–99 models

7922EG60

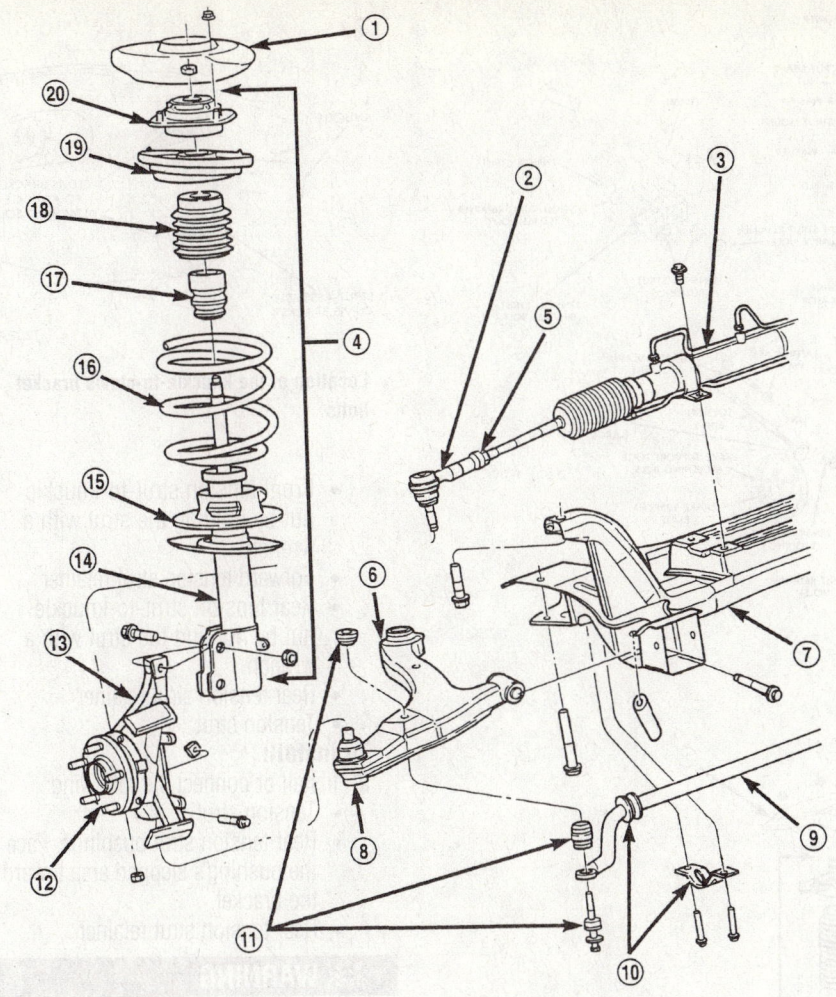

1 – VEHICLE STRUT TOWER
2 – OUTER TIE ROD
3 – STEERING GEAR
4 – STRUT ASSEMBLY
5 – JAM NUT
6 – LOWER CONTROL ARM
7 – CROSSMEMBER
8 – BALL JOINT
9 – STABILIZER BAR
10 – STABILIZER BAR CUSHION AND RETAINER
11 – STABILIZER BAR LINK
12 – HUB
13 – KNUCKLE
14 – STRUT
15 – LOWER SPRING ISOLATOR
16 – COIL SPRING
17 – JOUNCE BUMPER
18 – DUST SHIELD
19 – SPRING SEAT AND BEARING
20 – UPPER MOUNT

9306EG11

Exploded view of the front suspension—2000–01 models

5. Torque the lug nuts, in a criss-cross pattern, to 100 ft. lbs. (135 Nm) for 1997–99 or 95 ft. lbs. (128 Nm) for 2000–01.

Rear

1. Before servicing the vehicle, refer to the precautions in the beginning of this section.
2. Remove or disconnect the following:
   - Rear wheel
   - Hydraulic flex hose bracket from the strut bracket

➡If equipped with Anti-lock Brake System (ABS), the wheel speed sensor cable routing clip is also attached to the strut assembly bracket.

   - Clevis bracket-to-knuckle bolts by supporting the rear knuckle, suspension and brake components

➡DO NOT allow the weight of the knuckle and related components to hang without support when the strut is removed.

The knuckle-to-strut attaching bolts are serrated and must not be turned during removal. Remove the nuts while holding the bolts stationary in the knuckle.

   - Both strut-to-knuckle clevis bracket nuts

➡**Access to the rear upper strut mount-to-strut tower attaching bolts is through the trunk of the vehicle.**

   - Carpet from the top of the strut tower, if necessary
   - Rubber dust shield from the top of the strut tower

3. Loosen, but do not remove the 4 upper strut mounting nuts.
4. Remove or disconnect the following:
   - 4 strut-to-chassis mount nuts, by supporting it
   - Strut from the knuckle by sliding the knuckle out of the clevis bracket

To install:

5. Install or connect the following:
   - Strut. Torque the 4 strut mount-to-body nuts to 25 ft. lbs. (34 Nm).
   - Dust shield onto the top of the strut tower opening
   - Carpeting on top of the strut tower
   - Knuckle into the strut assemblies clevis bracket. Torque both clevis bracket-to-knuckle to 70 ft. lbs. (95 Nm).
   - Brake hose bracket onto to the strut bracket

➡**If equipped with ABS, attach the wheel speed sensor cable routing clip to the strut bracket.**

   - Rear wheel. Torque the lug nuts evenly, in sequence, to 100 ft. lbs. (135 Nm) for 1997–99 or 95 ft. lbs. (128 Nm) for 2000–01.
6. Check the alignment and adjust, if necessary.

Tension Strut

REMOVAL & INSTALLATION

1997–99 Models

1. Remove or disconnect the following:
   - Rear wheels

Turn to Section 5 for brake system applications

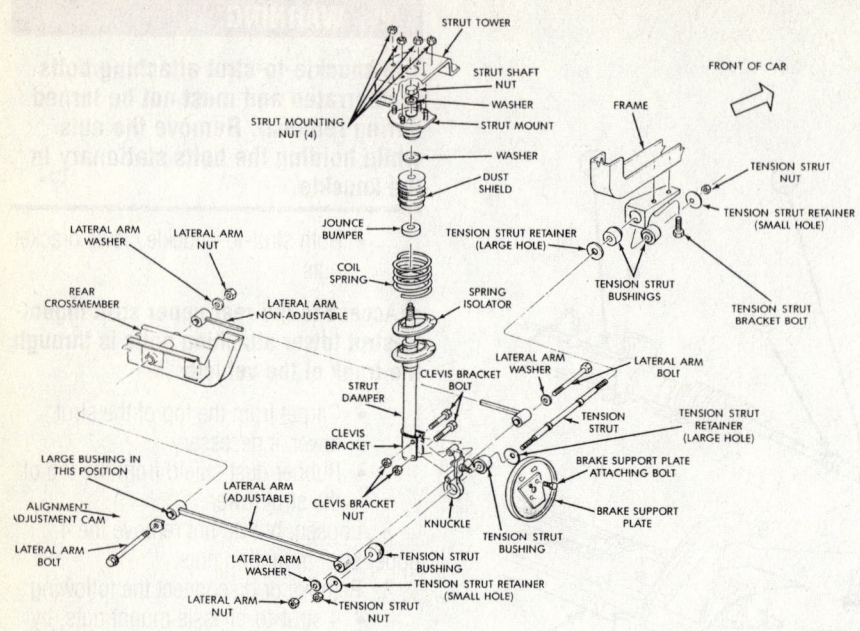

Exploded view of the rear suspension—1997–99

7922EG61

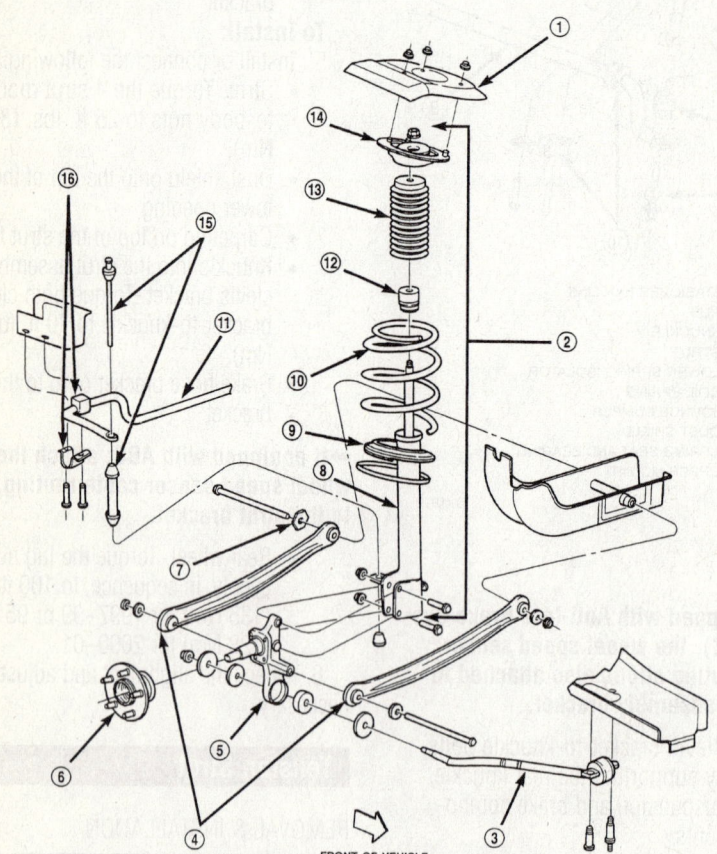

1 – VEHICLE STRUT TOWER
2 – STRUT ASSEMBLY
3 – TENSION STRUT
4 – LATERAL ARMS
5 – KNUCKLE
6 – HUB AND BEARING
7 – WHEEL ALIGNMENT ADJUSTMENT CAM
8 – STRUT

9 – LOWER SPRING ISOLATOR
10 – COIL SPRING
11 – STABILIZER BAR
12 – JOUNCE BUMPER
13 – DUST SHIELD
14 – UPPER MOUNT
15 – STABILIZER BAR LINK
16 – STABILIZER BAR CUSHION AND RETAINER

9306EG12

Exploded view of the rear suspension—2000–01

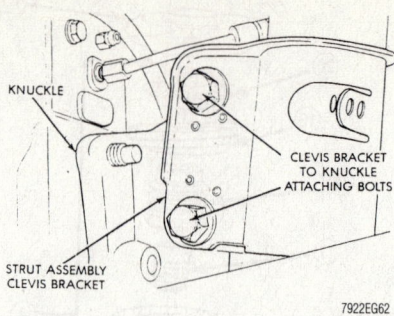

7922EG62

Location of the knuckle-to-clevis bracket bolts

- Front tension strut-to-knuckle nut by holding the strut with a wrench
- Forward tension strut retainer
- Rear tension strut-to-knuckle nut by holding the strut with a wrench
- Rear tension strut retainer
- Tension strut

To install:
2. Install or connect the following:
- Tension strut
- Rear tension strut bushings. Face the bushing's stepped area toward the bracket.
- Rear tension strut retainer

✳✳ WARNING

When installing the tension strut retainers, be sure to face the cupped surfaces away from the bracket.

- Rear tension strut-to-knuckle nut by holding the strut with a wrench. Torque the nut to 70 ft. lbs. (95 Nm).
- Forward tension strut bushings. Face the bushing's stepped area toward the knuckle.
- Forward tension strut retainer

✳✳ WARNING

When installing the tension strut retainers, be sure to face the cupped surfaces away from the knuckle.

- Forward tension strut-to-knuckle nut by holding the strut with a wrench. Torque the nut to 70 ft. lbs. (95 Nm).
- Rear wheels. Torque the lug nuts to 100 ft. lbs. (135 Nm).
3. Check and/or align the rear wheels.

2000–01 Models

1. Remove or disconnect the following:

- Rear wheels
- Tension strut-to-knuckle nut by holding the strut with a wrench
- Forward tension strut retainer
- Rear tension strut bayonet bushing
- Parking brake cable from tension strut bolt
- Tension strut from the chassis

To install:

2. Install or connect the following:

- Tension strut to the chassis. Torque the bolts to 70 ft. lbs. (95 Nm).
- Parking brake cable to tension strut nut. Torque the bolts to 21 ft. lbs. (28 Nm).

➡ **The mounting bolt with the stud on the head is installed on the inboard side.**

- Rear tension strut bayonet bushing. Face the bushing's stepped area toward the knuckle.
- Tension strut retainer
- Tension strut-to-knuckle nut by holding the strut with a wrench. Torque the nut to 70 ft. lbs. (95 Nm).
- Rear wheels. Torque the lug nuts to 100 ft. lbs. (135 Nm).

3. Check and/or align the rear wheels.

Stabilizer Bars

REMOVAL & INSTALLATION

Front

1. Remove or disconnect the following:

- Both stabilizer bar links by holding the upper nut with a wrench and turning the link bolt
- Both stabilizer bar retainer brackets
- Stabilizer bar
- Stabilizer bar retainer cushions, if necessary

To install:

2. Install or connect the following:

- Stabilizer bar retainer cushions at the end of each bar just before the curve with the slits facing forward
- Stabilizer bar

➡ **Make sure the stabilizer is not install upside down; the curve on the outboard ends must face downward to clear the control arms.**

- Both stabilizer bar retainer brackets. Torque the bolts to 21 ft. lbs. (28 Nm).
- Both stabilizer bar links

3. Torque the stabilizer bar link nuts to:
- 1997–99 models: 21 ft. lbs. (28 Nm)
- 2000–01 models: 17 ft. lbs. (23 Nm)

Rear

1. Remove or disconnect the following:
- Both rear wheels
- Both stabilizer bar link bolts and pull the bolts out through the top
- Stabilizer bar links
- Stabilizer bar retainers
- Stabilizer bar
- Stabilizer bar retainer cushions, if necessary

To install:

2. Install or connect the following:
- Stabilizer bar retainer cushions, with the slits facing forward and the flat side facing upward
- Stabilizer bar, the center dipped area must face downward
- Both stabilizer bar retainers and hand-tighten the bolts
- Both stabilizer bar links and hand-tighten the nuts
- Both rear wheels

3. Torque the wheel lug nuts to:
- 1997–99 models: 100 ft. lbs. (135 Nm)
- 2000–01 models: 95 ft. lbs. (128 Nm)

4. Torque the following items:
- Stabilizer bar retainers bolts: 25 ft. lbs. (34 Nm)
- Stabilizer bar link nuts to 25 ft. lbs. on 1997–99 models or 17 ft. lbs. (23 Nm) on 2000–01 models

5. Check and/or adjust the rear toe.

Lower Ball Joint

REMOVAL & INSTALLATION

The front suspension ball joints operate with no free-play. The ball joints are replaceable ONLY as an assembly. Do not attempt any type of repair on the ball joint assembly. The ball joint is a press fit into the lower control arm with the joint stud retained in the steering knuckle by the clamp bolt. To

check the ball joint, with the weight of the vehicle resting on the road wheels, grasp the grease fitting and without using any tools, attempt to move the grease fitting. If the ball joint is worn the grease fitting will move easily. If movement is noted, replacement of the ball joint is recommended.

1. Before servicing the vehicle, refer to the precautions in the beginning of this section.

2. Remove or disconnect the following:
- Wheel

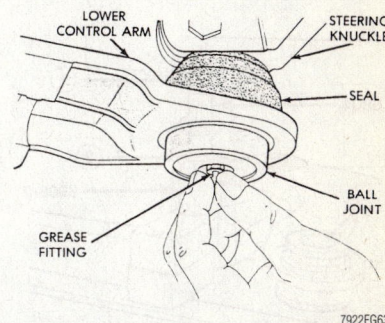

Wiggle the grease fitting with your fingers—if it moves, the ball joint should be replaced

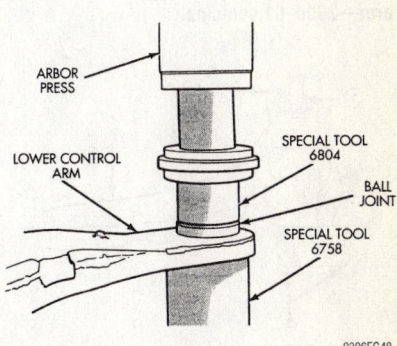

Removing the ball joint from the control arm—1997–99 vehicles

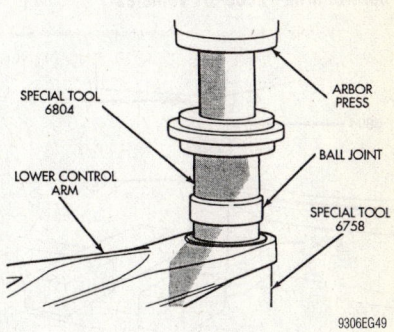

Installing the ball joint to the control arm—1997–99 vehicles

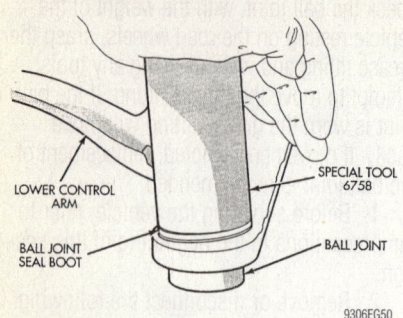

Installing the ball joint boot seal—1997–99 vehicles

9306EG50

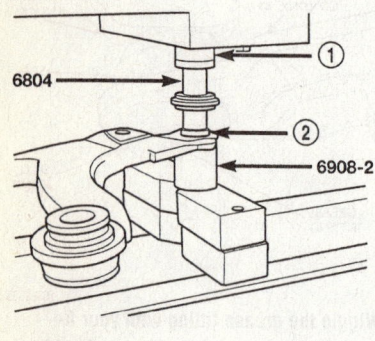

1 – PRESS
2 – BALL JOINT

9306EG51

Removing the ball joint from the control arm—2000–01 vehicles

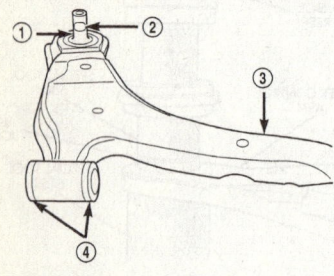

1 – BALL JOINT STUD
2 – NOTCH
3 – LOWER CONTROL ARM
4 – FRONT ISOLATOR BUSHING

9306EG52

Aligning the ball joint stud notch to the control arm—2000–01 vehicles

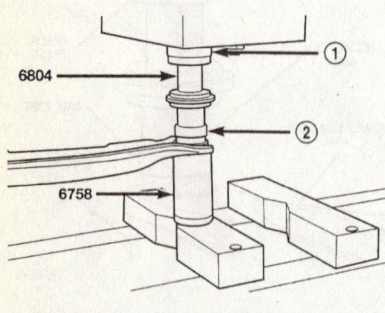

1 – PRESS
2 – BALL JOINT

9306EG53

Installing the ball joint to the control arm—2000–01 vehicles

- Steering knuckle-to-ball joint stud's pinch bolt and nut
- Stabilizer bar-to-lower control arm links

3. Loosen, but do not remove the bolts holding the stabilizer bar retainers to the crossmember. Then, rotate the stabilizer bar and attaching links away from the lower control arms.

❋❋ WARNING

Pulling the steering knuckle outward after releasing the ball joint can separate the inner CV-joint.

4. Remove or disconnect the following:
- Ball joint from the steering knuckle using a prybar

❋❋ WARNING

Be careful when separating the ball joint stud from the knuckle, so the seal does not become damaged.

- Front lower control arm bushing-to-crossmember nut and bolt
- Rear lower control arm-to-crossmember bolt
- Lower control arm
- Ball joint using a suitable prytool

5. Using a hydraulic press, press the ball joint from the lower control arm using tools:
- Receiver tool 6758: 1997–99 vehicles
- Adapter tool 6804: 1997–99 vehicles
- Receiver tool 6908-2: 2000–01 vehicles
- Adapter tool 6804: 2000–01 vehicles

To install:
6. Reinstall the ball joint into the lower control arm with the notch in the ball joint stud facing the front lower control arm bushing.

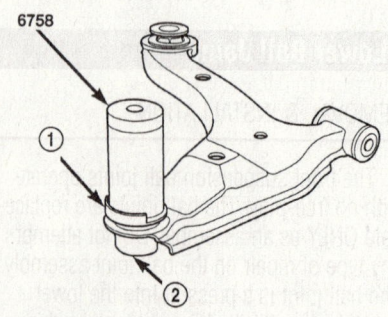

1 – SEAL BOOT UPWARD LIP
2 – BALL JOINT

9306EG54

Installing the ball joint boot seal—2000–01 vehicles

7. Using a hydraulic press, press the ball joint into the lower control arm using tools:
- Receiver tool 6758
- Adapter tool 6804

8. Install or connect the following:
- Ball joint boot seal using a driver tool such as a large socket or suitable sized piece of pipe

❋❋ WARNING

Do not use a shop press that was used to install the ball joint, for the press exerts too much force.

- Lower control arm into the front crossmember
- Rear lower control arm-to-crossmember and frame rail bolt

➡ **DO NOT tighten the rear bolt at this time.**

- Front lower control arm-to-crossmember nut and bolt

9. Torque the lower control arm fasteners to:
- Front control arm nut/bolt: 120 ft. lbs. (163 Nm) for 1997–99 models
- Rear control arm nut/bolt: 120 ft. lbs. (163 Nm) for 1997–99 models
- Rear pivot bolt: 150 ft. lbs. (203 Nm) for 2000–01 models
- Front pivot bolt: 120 ft. lbs. (163 Nm) for 2000–01 models

10. Install the ball joint stud into the steering knuckle. Torque the steering knuckle-to-ball joint stud pinch bolt and nut to 70 ft. lbs. (95 Nm).

11. Assemble the stabilizer bar-to-lower control arm link assemblies and bushings.

12. Rotate the stabilizer bar into position, installing the stabilizer bar links into the lower control arms. Install the top stabilizer bar link bushings and nuts. DO NOT tighten the link yet.

13. Install the wheel.

14. Lower the vehicle so the suspension is supporting the total weight of the vehicle.

15. Torque the stabilizer bar-to-lower control arm links to:
- 21 ft. lbs. (28 Nm) for 1997–98 models
- 17 ft. lbs. (23 Nm) for 1999–01 models

16. Torque the stabilizer bar bushing retainer-to-crossmember bolts to 21 ft. lbs. (28 Nm).

17. Check and/or adjust the toe, as necessary.

Wheel Bearings

ADJUSTMENT

Neons are equipped with sealed hub and bearing assemblies. The hub and bearing assembly is non-serviceable. If the assembly is damaged, the complete unit must be replaced.

REMOVAL & INSTALLATION

Front

1. Before servicing the vehicle, refer to the precautions in the beginning of this section.
2. Remove the steering knuckle and hub and bearing assembly.
3. Remove a wheel lug stud from the hub flange using a C-clamp and Adapter tool 4150A.
4. Rotate the hub to align the removed lug stud with the notch in the bearing retainer plate.
5. Rotate the hub so the stud hole is facing away from the brake caliper's lower rail on the steering knuckle.
6. Install ½ of a Bearing Splitter tool 1130, between the hub and the bearing retainer plate. The threaded hole in this ½ is to be aligned with the caliper rail on the steering knuckle.
7. Install the remaining pieces of the bearing splitter on the steering knuckle. Hand-tighten the nuts to hold the splitter in place on the knuckle.
8. When the bearing splitter is installed, be sure the 3 bolts attaching the bearing retainer plate to the knuckle are contacting the bearing splitter. The bearing retainer plate should not support the knuckle or contact the splitter.

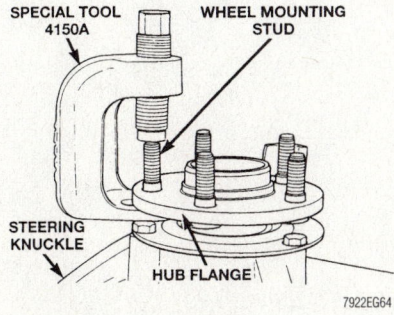

Use a proper C-clamp and adapter tool to press out one of the lug studs

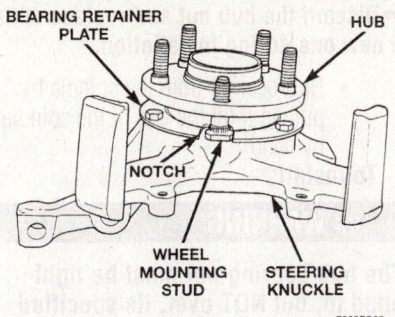

Rotate the hub in order to remove the lug stud

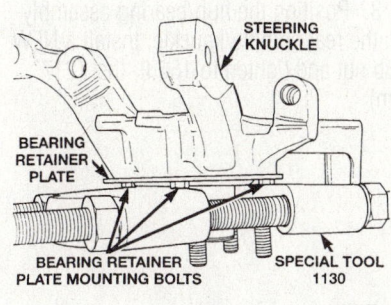

Proper installation of the bearing splitter

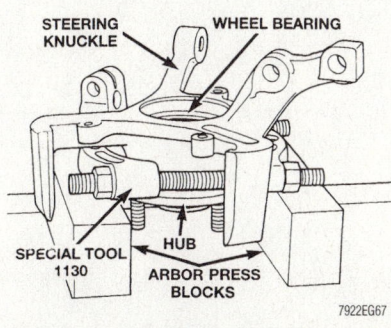

Properly support the steering knuckle for hub and bearing removal

9. Place the steering knuckle in a hydraulic press, supported by the bearing splitter.
10. Position a suitable sized driver on the small end of the hub. Using the press, remove the hub from the wheel bearing. The outer bearing race will come out of the wheel bearing when the hub is pressed out of the bearing.
11. Remove the bearing splitter tool from the knuckle.
12. Place the knuckle in a press supported by the press block. The blocks must not obstruct the bore in the steering knuckle so the wheel bearing can be pressed out of the knuckle. Place a suitable driver on the outer race of the wheel bearing, then press the bearing out of the knuckle.
13. Install the bearing splitter on the hub. The splitter is to be installed on the hub so it is between the flange of the hub and the bearing race on the hub. Place the hub, bearing race and splitter in a press. Use a driver to press the hub out of the bearing race.

To install:

14. Use clean, dry cloth to wipe and grease or dirt from the bore of the steering knuckle.
15. Clean the rust preventative from the replacement wheel bearing using a clean, dry towel.
16. Place the new wheel bearing into the bore of the steering knuckle. Be sure the bearing is placed squarely into the bore. Place the knuckle in a press with a receiver tool, C-4698–2 supporting the steering knuckle. Place a suitable driver tool on the outer race of the wheel bearing. Press the wheel bearing into the steering knuckle until it is fully bottomed in the bore of the steering knuckle.

➡️Only the original or original equipment replacement bolts should be used to mounting the bearing retainer to the knuckle. If a bolt requires replacement when installing the bearing retainer plate, be sure to get the proper type of replacement.

17. Install the bearing retainer plate on the steering knuckle. Install the 3 bearing retainer mounting bolts. Tighten the bolts to 21 ft. lbs. (28 Nm).
18. Install the removed wheel lug stud into the hub flange.
19. Place the hub with the lug stud installed, in a suitable press supported by adapter tool C-4698–1 or equivalent. Press the wheel lug stud into the hub flange until it is fully seated against the back side on the hub flange.
20. Place the steering knuckle with the wheel bearing installed, in a press with special receiver tool MB-990799 supporting the inner race of the wheel bearing. Place the hub in the wheel bearing, making sure it is square with the bearing. Press the hub into the wheel bearing until it is fully bottomed in the wheel bearing.
21. Install the steering knuckle and the wheel.
22. Check and/or adjust the front alignment.

Rear

1. Before servicing the vehicle, refer to the precautions in the beginning of this section.
2. Remove or disconnect the following:
   - Wheel
   - Rear brake drum, if equipped
   - Caliper (suspend on a wire) and the rotor, if equipped with rear disc brakes

⁂ WARNING

DO NOT allow the caliper to hang by the brake hose.

   - Dust cap from the rear hub/bearing
   - Hub/bearing assembly-to-knuckle/spindle nut

➡ **Discard the hub nut and replace with a new one during installation.**

   - Hub/bearing from the spindle by pulling it off the end of the spindle by hand

To install:

⁂ WARNING

The hub/bearing nut must be tightened to, but NOT over, its specified torque value. The proper specification is crucial to the life of the hub bearing.

3. Position the hub/bearing assembly on the rear spindle/knuckle. Install a NEW hub nut and tighten to 160 ft. lbs. (217 Nm).

4. Install or connect the following:
   - Dust cap and seat it using a soft face hammer to carefully tap it into place
   - Brake drum, if equipped with drum brakes
   - Rotor, if equipped with disc brakes
   - Caliper and 2 guide pin bolts, if equipped with disc brakes. Tighten the bolts to 16 ft. lbs. (22 Nm).

5. Install the wheel and tire assembly. Tighten the lug nuts in a crisscross pattern, to 100 ft. lbs. (135 Nm) for 1997–99 or 95 ft. lbs. (128 Nm) for 2000–01.

CHRYSLER CORP.

14

Chrysler-Cirrus • Sebring Convertible • **Dodge**-Stratus • **Plymouth**-Breeze

PRECAUTIONS

Before servicing any vehicle, please be sure to read all of the following precautions. The following precautions deal with personal safety, preventing of component damage, and important points to take into consideration when servicing a motor vehicle:

• Never open, service or drain the radiator or cooling system when the engine is hot; serious burns can occur from the steam and hot coolant.

• Observe all applicable safety precautions when working around fuel. Whenever servicing the fuel system, always work in a well-ventilated area. Do not allow fuel spray or vapors to come in contact with a spark, open flame or excessive heat (a hot drop light, for example). Keep a dry chemical fire extinguisher near the work area. Always keep fuel in a container specifically designed for fuel storage; also, always properly seal fuel containers to avoid the possibility of fire or explosion. Refer to the additional fuel system precautions later in this section.

• Fuel injection systems often remain pressurized, even after the engine has been turned **OFF**. The fuel system pressure must be relieved before disconnecting any fuel lines. Failure to do so may result in fire and/or personal injury.

• Brake fluid often contains polyglycol ethers and polyglycols. Avoid contact with the eyes and wash your hands thoroughly after handling brake fluid. If you do get brake fluid in your eyes, flush your eyes with clean, running water for 15 minutes. If eye irritation persists, or if you have taken brake fluid internally, IMMEDIATELY seek medical assistance.

• The EPA warns that prolonged contact with used engine oil may cause a number of skin disorders, including cancer! You should make every effort to minimize your exposure to used engine oil. Protective gloves should be worn when changing the oil. Wash your hands and any other exposed skin areas as soon as possible after exposure to used engine oil. Soap and water, or waterless hand cleaner should be used.

• All vehicles are equipped with an air bag system, often referred to as a Supplemental Restraint System (SRS) or as a Supplemental Inflatable Restraint (SIR) system. The system must be disabled before performing service on or around system components, steering column, instrument panel components, wiring and sensors. Failure to follow safety and disabling procedures could result in accidental air bag deployment, possible personal injury and unnecessary system repairs.

• Always wear safety goggles when working with, or around, the air bag system. When carrying a non-deployed air bag, be sure the bag and trim cover are pointed away from your body. When placing a non-deployed air bag on a work surface, always face the bag and trim cover upward, away from the surface. This will reduce the motion of the module if it is accidentally deployed.

• Clean, high quality brake fluid from a sealed container is essential for the safe and proper operation of the brake system. You should always buy the grade of fluid recommended for your vehicle. If the brake fluid becomes contaminated, drain and flush the system, then refill the master cylinder with new fluid. Never reuse any brake fluid. Any brake fluid that is removed from the system should be discarded. Also, do not allow any brake fluid to come in contact with a painted surface; it will damage the paint.

• Never operate the engine without the proper amount and type of engine oil; doing so WILL result in severe engine damage.

• Timing belt maintenance is extremely important! Many models may utilize an interference-type, non-free-wheeling engine. If the timing belt breaks, the valves in the cylinder head may strike the pistons, causing potentially serious (also time-consuming and expensive) engine damage. Refer to the maintenance interval charts in the front of this manual for the recommended replacement interval for the timing belt, and to the timing belt section for belt replacement and inspection.

• Disconnecting the negative battery cable on some vehicles may interfere with the functions of the on board computer system(s) and may require the computer to undergo a relearning process once the negative battery cable is reconnected.

• When servicing drum brakes, only disassemble and assemble one side at a time, leaving the remaining side intact for reference.

• Only an MVAC-trained, EPA-certified, automotive technician should service the air conditioning system or its components.

ENGINE REPAIR

Distributor

REMOVAL

2.5L Engine

The 2.5L engine is equipped with a camshaft driven mechanical distributor. This engine uses a fixed ignition timing system. The basic ignition timing is not adjustable. The Powertrain Control Module (PCM) determines spark advance. The Crankshaft Position (CKP) sensor and Camshaft Position (CMP) sensor are Hall Effect devices. The CKP sensor is mounted remotely from the distributor while the CMP sensor is mounted inside the distributor housing. Both sensors generate pulses that are inputs to the PCM. The PCM determines crankshaft position from these sensors. The PCM calculates injector sequence and ignition timing. There is a resistor built into the distributor cap. An ohmmeter connected between the center button and ignition coil terminal should read 5000 ohms.

1. Before servicing the vehicle, refer to the precautions in the beginning of this section.

2. Remove or disconnect the following:
   • Negative battery cable from the left shock tower

➡ **The ground cable is equipped with an insulator grommet which should be placed on the stud to prevent the negative battery cable from accidentally grounding.**

   • Air inlet resonator-to-intake manifold bolt
   • Air cleaner cover-to-air cleaner housing clamp
   • Positive Crankcase Ventilation (PCV) air hose from the air inlet tube
   • Exhaust Gas Recirculation (EGR) tube
   • Spark plug wires from the distributor cap
   • Distributor cap

➡ **Mark the rotor position. A scribe mark indicates where to position the rotor when reinstalling the distributor.**

- Rotor
- Both electrical connectors from the distributor
- Distributor hold-down nuts and washers
- Spark plug cable mounting bracket
- Transaxle dipstick tube
- Distributor

INSTALLATION

2.5L Engine

TIMING NOT DISTURBED

1. Inspect the rotor for cracks or a burned electrode. Replace if defective.
2. Install or connect the following:
   - Rotor onto the distributor
   - New O-ring on the distributor
3. Carefully, engage the distributor drive with the slotted end of the camshaft. When the distributor is installed properly, the rotor will be aligned with the previously made mark.
4. Verify proper rotor alignment with mark made at disassembly.
5. Install or connect the following:
   - Distributor hold-down nuts and washers. Torque the nuts to 108 inch lbs. (13 Nm).
   - Spark plug cable bracket
   - Both distributor wiring connectors
   - Distributor cap
   - Spark plug cables
   - Transaxle dipstick tube
   - EGR tube. Torque the bolts to 95 inch lbs. (11 Nm).
   - PCV hose
   - Air cleaner
   - Air inlet resonator
   - Negative battery cable

TIMING DISTURBED

1. Rotate the crankshaft until No. 1 piston is at Top Dead Center (TDC) of its compression stroke.
2. Rotate the rotor to the No. 1 terminal position on the distributor cap.
3. Lower the distributor into place, engaging the distributor drive with the drive on the camshaft. With the distributor fully seated on the engine, the rotor should be under the No. 1 terminal.
4. Install or connect the following:
   - Distributor hold-down nuts and washers. Torque the nuts to 108 inch lbs. (13 Nm).
   - Spark plug cable bracket
   - Both distributor wiring connectors
   - Distributor cap
   - Spark plug cables

- Transaxle dipstick tube
- EGR tube. Torque the bolts to 95 inch lbs. (11 Nm).
- PCV hose
- Air cleaner
- Air inlet resonator
- Negative battery cable

Alternator

REMOVAL

2.0L Engine

1. Before servicing the vehicle, refer to the precautions in the beginning of this section.
2. Remove or disconnect the following:
   - Negative battery cable from the shock tower
   - Belt cover
   - Alternator electrical connectors
   - Alternator adjusting and pivot bolts, loosen them
   - Alternator drive belt
   - Alternator adjusting and pivot bolts, do not drop the pivot bolt's spacer
   - Alternator, by moving it toward the head light bucket area

2.4L Engine

1. Before servicing the vehicle, refer to the precautions in the beginning of this section.
2. Remove or disconnect the following:
   - Negative battery cable from the shock tower
   - Alternator electrical connectors
   - Alternator adjusting and pivot bolts, loosen them
   - Alternator drive belt
   - Alternator adjusting and pivot bolts
   - Anti-lock Brake System (ABS) braking unit, by removing the 2 lower plate mounting bolts
   - Coolant overflow bottle
   - Alternator, by moving it under the refrigerant lines toward the passenger's side

2.5L Engine

1. Before servicing the vehicle, refer to the precautions in the beginning of this section.
2. Remove or disconnect the following:
   - Negative battery cable from the shock tower
   - Alternator electrical connectors
   - Upper mounting ear, pivot and idler adjusting bolts, loosen them
   - Alternator drive belt

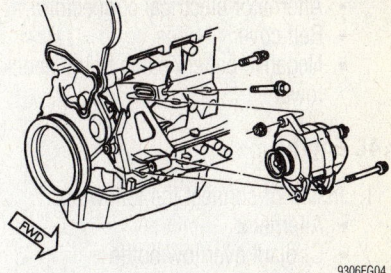

Exploded view of the alternator and related components—2.0L engine

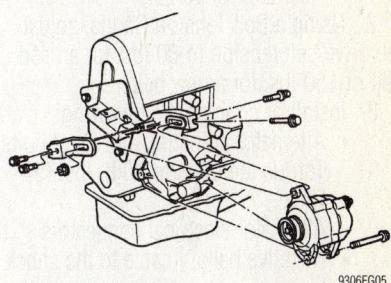

Exploded view of the alternator and related components—2.4L engine

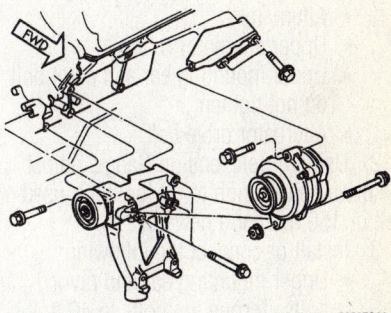

Exploded view of the alternator and related components—2.5L engine

- Alternator pivot bolt, do not drop the spacer
- Upper mounting ear bolt
- Upper alternator bracket
- Alternator

INSTALLATION

2.0L Engine

1. Install or connect the following:
   - Alternator
   - Alternator drive belt
2. Using a Belt Tension Gauge, adjust the drive belt tension to 80 lbs. for a used belt or 150 lbs. for a new belt.
3. Install or connect the following:
   - Alternator adjusting and pivot bolts. Torque the bolts to 40 ft. lbs. (54 Nm).

- Alternator electrical connectors
- Belt cover
- Negative battery cable to the shock tower

2.4L Engine

1. Install or connect the following:
   - Alternator
   - Coolant overflow bottle
   - Anti-lock Brake System (ABS) braking unit. Torque the 2 lower plate mounting bolts to 21 ft. lbs. (28 Nm).
   - Alternator drive belt
2. Using a Belt Tension Gauge, adjust the drive belt tension to 80 lbs. for a used belt or 150 lbs. for a new belt.
3. Install or connect the following:
   - Alternator adjusting and pivot bolts. Torque the bolts to 40 ft. lbs. (54 Nm).
   - Alternator electrical connectors
   - Negative battery cable to the shock tower

2.5L Engine

1. Install or connect the following:
   - Alternator
   - Upper alternator bracket
   - Upper mounting ear and pivot bolt, do not tighten
   - Alternator drive belt
2. Using a Belt Tension Gauge, adjust the drive belt tension to 80 lbs. for a used belt or 150 lbs. for a new belt.
3. Install or connect the following:
   - Upper mounting ear and pivot bolts. Torque the bolts to 40 ft. lbs. (54 Nm).
   - Alternator electrical connectors
   - Negative battery cable to the shock tower

Ignition Timing

ADJUSTMENT

These engines use a fixed ignition system. The Powertrain Control Module (PCM) regulates the ignition timing. Basic ignition timing is not adjustable.

Engine Assembly

REMOVAL & INSTALLATION

1. Before servicing the vehicle, refer to the precautions in the beginning of this section.
2. Relieve the fuel system pressure using the recommended procedure. Discon-

nect the fuel line quick-connect fitting from the fuel rail by squeezing the retainer tabs together and pulling the fuel tube/quick-connect fitting assembly off the fuel tube nipple.

3. Place the ignition switch in the **OFF** unlocked position and turn **OFF** all accessories.

4. Turn the steering wheel to the extreme left position.

5. Remove or disconnect the battery and battery tray as follows:
   - Negative battery cable from the left shock tower

➡ **The ground cable is equipped with an insulator grommet which should be placed on the stud to prevent the negative battery cable from accidentally grounding.**

   - Shield, by twisting the 4 plastic screws ¼ turn

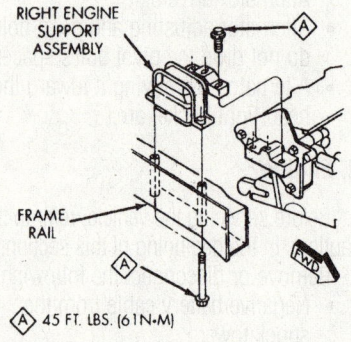

Exploded view of the right side engine mount—all engines

- Battery blanket heater, if equipped
- Battery cables
- Battery strap-to-battery hold-down bracket and hold-down bracket bolts
- Battery
- Battery tray and battery strap
6. Remove or disconnect the following:
   - Air cleaner and inlet duct assembly
   - Powertrain Control Module (PCM), move it aside
7. Drain the cooling system.
   - Upper/lower radiator hose, radiator and cooling fan
   - Automatic transaxle cooler lines, if equipped, plug the lines
   - Clutch cable and transaxle shift linkage, if equipped
   - Throttle body linkage and the engine wiring harness
   - Heater hoses
8. Discharge and recover the air conditioning refrigerant.
   - Front wheels
9. Drain the engine oil, if necessary.
10. Remove or disconnect the following:
    - Right side inner splash shield
    - Accessory drive belts
    - Both halfshafts
    - Exhaust pipe from the exhaust manifold
    - Front/rear engine mount brackets, from the body
    - Power steering pump and reservoir; move them aside
11. Remove or disconnect the air conditioning compressor as follows:
    - Compressor clutch wire lead

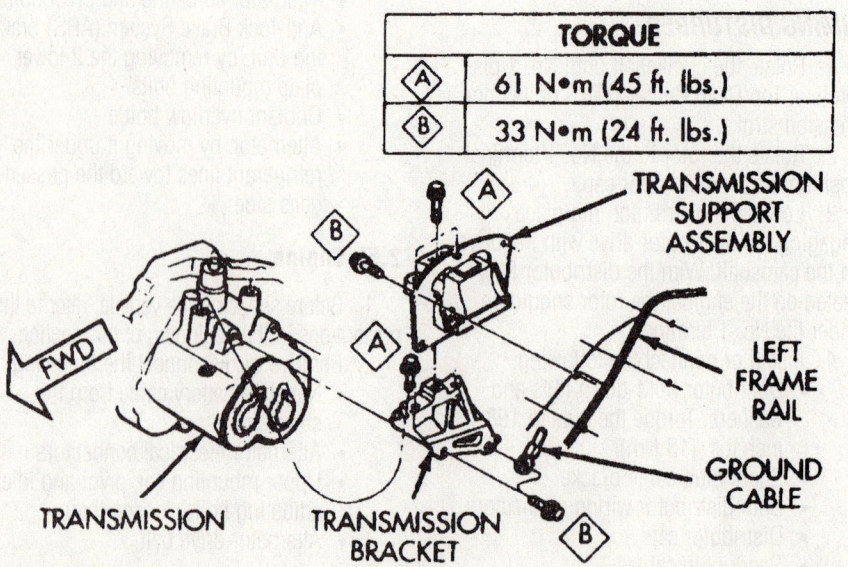

TORQUE	
Ⓐ	61 N•m (45 ft. lbs.)
Ⓑ	33 N•m (24 ft. lbs.)

Exploded view of the left side engine mount—Type 1

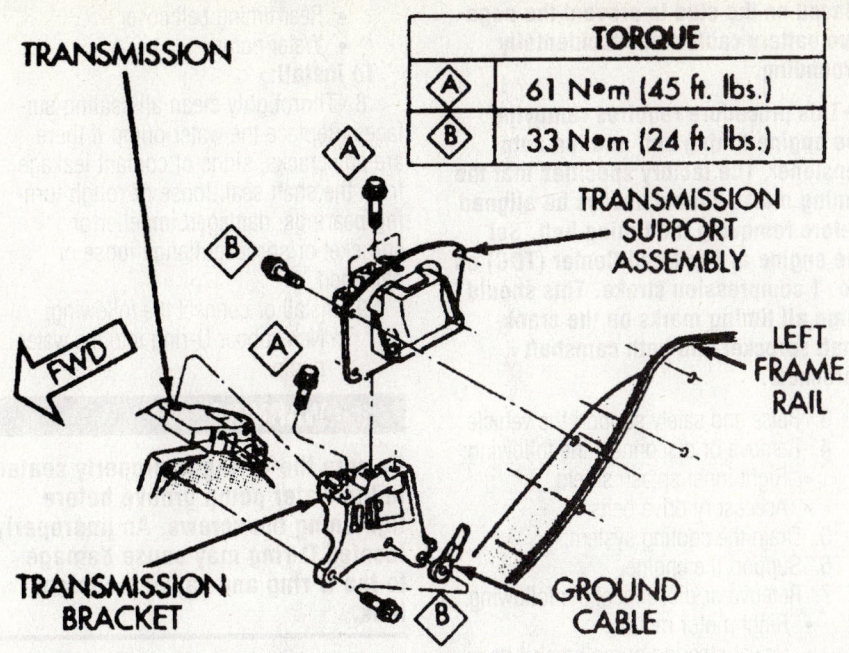

TORQUE	
Ⓐ	61 N•m (45 ft. lbs.)
Ⓑ	33 N•m (24 ft. lbs.)

Exploded view of the left side engine mount—Type 2

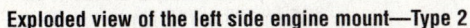

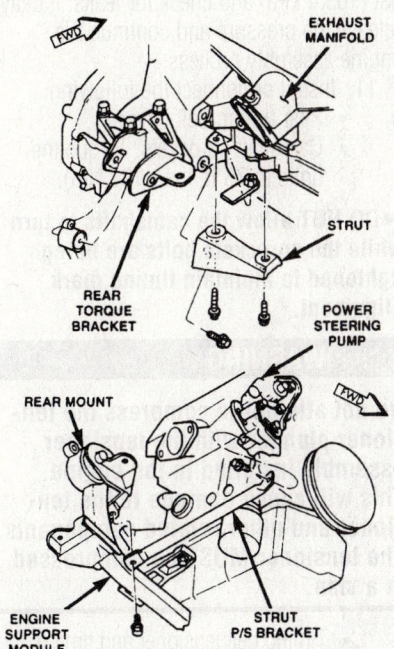

Exploded view of the rear engine mounting torque bracket—2.0L engine

- Refrigerant lines from the compressor
- Compressor mounting bolts
- Compressor, plug all openings to prevent moisture contamination
12. Remove or disconnect the following:
- Engine ground straps
13. Raise the vehicle and install an

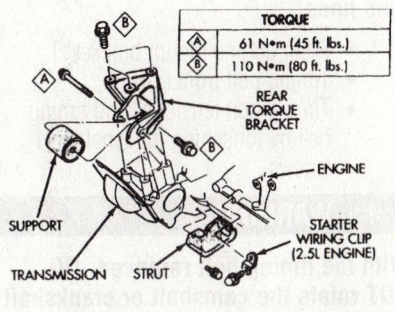

TORQUE	
Ⓐ	61 N•m (45 ft. lbs.)
Ⓑ	110 N•m (80 ft. lbs.)

Exploded view of the rear engine mounting torque bracket—2.4L and 2.5L engines

engine dolly under the vehicle and support engine.
14. Remove or disconnect the following:
- Transaxle and engine mount through-bolts
- Transaxle/engine assembly
15. Raise the vehicle slowly allowing the engine/transaxle assembly to remain on the dolly.

To install:
16. Position the engine/transaxle assembly under the vehicle and lower the vehicle onto the engine assembly.
17. Install or connect the following:
- Right and left mount bolts
- Transaxle mount
- Both halfshafts
- Transaxle and engine braces
- Splash shields

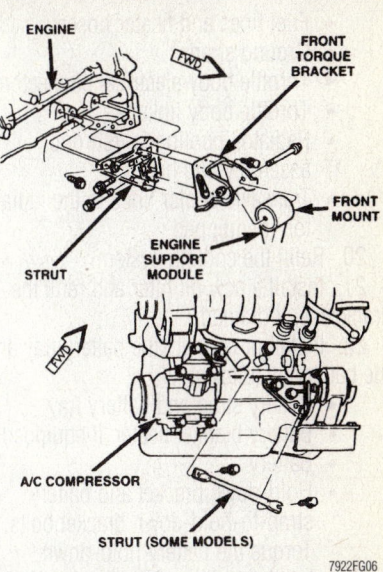

Exploded view of the front engine mounting torque bracket—2.0L and 2.4L engines

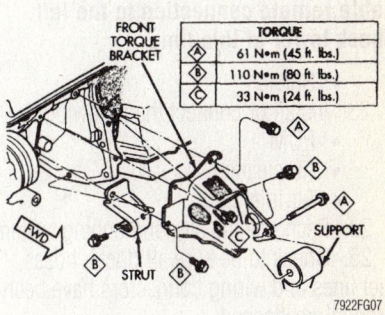

TORQUE	
Ⓐ	61 N•m (45 ft. lbs.)
Ⓑ	110 N•m (80 ft. lbs.)
Ⓒ	33 N•m (24 ft. lbs.)

Exploded view of the front engine mounting torque bracket—2.5L engine

- Exhaust pipe to the exhaust manifold
- Power steering pump and reservoir
18. Install or connect the air conditioning compressor as follows:
- Compressor. Torque the mounting bolts to 30 ft. lbs. (41 Nm).
- Refrigerant hoses using new seals
- Compressor clutch wire
19. Install or connect the following:
- Accessory drive belts and adjust them
- Front engine mount
- Inner splash shield
- Front wheels. Torque the lug nuts to 95–100 ft. lbs. (129–135 Nm).
- Clutch cable and linkages, if equipped with a manual transaxle
- Shifter and kickdown linkages, if equipped with an automatic transaxle

Timing belt service is covered in Section 4 of this manual

- Fuel lines and heater hoses
- Ground straps
- Throttle body electrical connectors
- Throttle body linkage
- Radiator, cooling fan/shroud assembly and hoses
- Transaxle cooler lines to the radiator, if equipped

20. Refill the cooling system.

21. Install a new oil filter and refill the crankcase, if drained.

22. Install or connect the battery tray and the battery as follows:

- Battery strap and battery tray
- Battery blanket heater, if equipped
- Battery
- Hold-down bracket and battery strap-to-hold-down bracket bolts. Torque the battery hold-down bracket bolt to 10 ft. lbs. (14 Nm).
- Battery cables. Torque the cables to 13 ft. lbs. (17 Nm).

➡**DO NOT reattach the negative battery cable remote connection to the left shock tower at this time.**

- Shield

23. Install or connect the following:

- PCM
- Air cleaner
- Air inlet duct

24. Recharge the air conditioning system.

25. Check to be sure all ducts, hoses, fuel lines and wiring connectors have been properly reattached.

26. Start the engine, check for oil pressure, and run until operating temperature is reached.

27. Check for leaks and proper operation.

Water Pump

REMOVAL & INSTALLATION

2.0L and 2.4L Engines

This engine uses a die-cast aluminum body water pump with a stamped steel impeller. The water pump bolts directly to the block. Cylinder block-to-water pump sealing is provided by a large rubber O-ring. The water pump is driven by the timing belt, that must be removed to service the water pump.

1. Before servicing the vehicle, refer to the precautions in the beginning of this section.

2. Disconnect the negative battery cable from the left shock tower.

➡**The ground cable is equipped with an insulator grommet which should be placed on the stud to prevent the negative battery cable from accidentally grounding.**

➡**This procedure requires removing the engine timing belt and the auto-tensioner. The factory specifies that the timing marks should always be aligned before removing the timing belt. Set the engine at Top Dead Center (TDC) on No. 1 compression stroke. This should align all timing marks on the crankshaft sprocket and both camshaft sprockets.**

3. Raise and safely support the vehicle.

4. Remove or disconnect the following:

- Right inner splash shield
- Accessory drive belts

5. Drain the cooling system.

6. Support the engine.

7. Remove or disconnect the following:

- Right motor mount
- Power steering pump bracket bolts, move the pump/bracket assembly aside

➡**Do not disconnect the power steering fluid lines.**

- Right engine mount bracket
- Timing belt front covers
- Timing belt tensioner and timing belt by loosening the tensioner screws

✳✳ WARNING

With the timing belt removed, DO NOT rotate the camshaft or crankshaft or damage to the engine could occur.

- Camshaft sprockets

➡**Do not allow the camshafts to turn when the camshaft sprockets are being removed.**

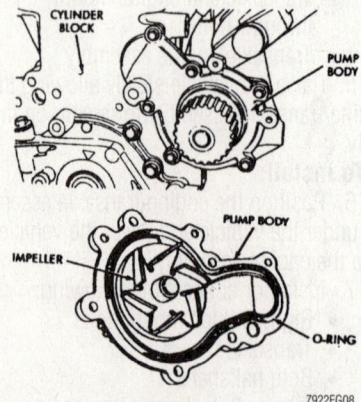

When installing the water pump, properly install the O-ring to ensure a tight seal—2.0L and 2.4L engines

- Rear timing belt cover
- Water pump

To install:

8. Thoroughly clean all sealing surfaces. Replace the water pump if there are any cracks, signs of coolant leakage from the shaft seal, loose or rough turning bearings, damaged impeller or sprocket or sprocket flange loose or damaged.

9. Install or connect the following:

- New rubber O-ring into the water pump

✳✳ WARNING

Be sure the O-ring is properly seated in the water pump groove before tightening the screws. An improperly located O-ring may cause damage to the O-ring and cause a coolant leak.

- Water pump. Torque the bolts to 105 inch lbs. (12 Nm).

10. Pressurize the cooling system to 15 psi (103.4 kPa) and check for leaks. If okay, release the pressure and continue the engine assembly process.

11. Install or connect the following:

- Rear timing belt cover
- Camshaft sprockets. Torque the bolts to 75 ft. lbs. (101 Nm).

➡**DO NOT allow the camshafts to turn while the sprockets bolts are being tightened to maintain timing mark alignment.**

✳✳ WARNING

Do not attempt to compress the tensioner plunger with the tensioner assembly installed in the engine. This will cause damage to the tensioner and other related components. The tensioner MUST be compressed in a vise.

- Timing belt tensioner and timing belt. Properly tension the timing belt.
- Front upper and lower timing belt covers
- Right engine mount bracket and engine mount
- Crankshaft damper. Torque the center bolt to 105 ft. lbs. (142 Nm).
- Right inner splash shield
- Power steering pump bracket and power steering pump. Torque the bracket mounting bolts to 40 ft. lbs. (54 Nm).
- Accessory drive belts. Properly tension the drive belts.

12. Refill and bleed the cooling system.

13. Start the engine and check for proper operation.

14. Check and top off cooling system, if necessary.

2.5L Engine

The water pump bolts directly to the engine block using a gasket for pump-to-block sealing. The pump is serviced as a unit. The 2.5L engine uses metal piping beyond the lower radiator hose to route coolant to the suction side of the water pump, located in the "V" of the cylinder banks. These pipes also have connections for thermostat bypass and heater return coolant hoses. The pipes use O-rings for sealing.

The water pump is driven by the timing belt which must be removed to service the water pump. Timing belt covers must be removed to access the timing belt.

1. Before servicing the vehicle, refer to the precautions in the beginning of this section.

2. Disconnect the negative battery cable from the left shock tower.

➡**The ground cable is equipped with an insulator grommet which should be placed on the stud to prevent the negative battery cable from accidentally grounding.**

3. Drain the cooling system.

➡**This procedure requires removing the engine timing belt and the auto-tensioner. To help assure proper alignment at assembly, it may be helpful to set the engine at Top Dead Center (TDC) on No. 1 compression stroke. This should align all timing marks on the crankshaft sprocket and both camshaft sprockets.**

4. Remove or disconnect the following:

- Accessory drive belts
- Crankshaft damper
- Right engine mount by safely supporting the engine
- Timing belt covers, in this order: upper left, upper right and lower covers
- Timing belt and tensioner
- Water pump by separating it from the water inlet pipe

To install:

5. Thoroughly clean all sealing surfaces. Inspect the pump for damage or

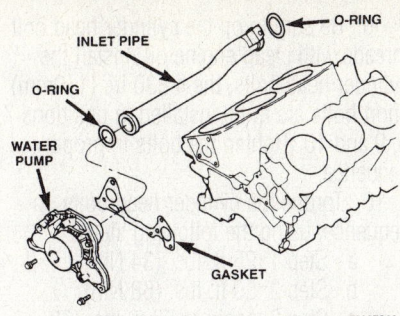

Exploded view of the water pump mounting—2.5L engine

cracks, signs of coolant leakage at the vent and excessive looseness or rough turning bearing. Any problems require a new pump.

6. Install or connect the following:

- New O-ring on the water inlet pipe by wetting it with water
- New gasket on the water pump
- Water pump. Torque the bolts to 20 ft. lbs. (27 Nm).
- Timing belt and timing belt tensioner by adjusting tension
- Timing belt covers
- Right engine mount
- Crankshaft damper
- Accessory drive belts by adjusting tension
- Negative battery cable

7. Refill and bleed the cooling system.

8. Start the engine and verify proper operation.

Cylinder Head

REMOVAL & INSTALLATION

2.0L Engine

This engine uses a Single Over Head Camshaft (SOHC) 4-valves per cylinder cross flow aluminum cylinder head. Care must be taken to be sure all valve timing marks align after cylinder head service.

1. Before servicing the vehicle, refer to the precautions in the beginning of this section.

2. Relieve the fuel system pressure using the recommended procedure.

3. Disconnect the negative battery cable from the left shock tower.

➡**The ground cable is equipped with an insulator grommet which should be placed on the stud to prevent the negative battery cable from accidentally grounding.**

4. Drain the cooling system.

5. Remove or disconnect the following:

- Air cleaner assembly
- All vacuum hoses and electrical connectors from the throttle body
- Fuel line quick-connect fitting from the fuel rail, by squeezing the retainer tabs together and pulling the fuel tube/quick-connect fitting assembly off the fuel tube nipple
- Throttle linkage
- Accessory drive belt(s)

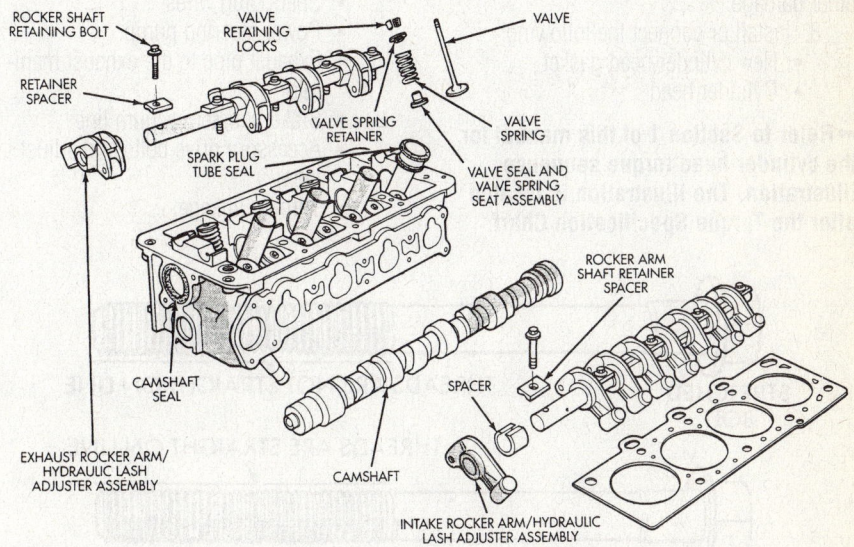

Exploded view of the cylinder head and valvetrain components—2.0L engine

- Power brake booster vacuum hose from the intake manifold
- Exhaust pipe from the exhaust manifold
- Power steering pump and move it aside
- Coil pack wiring connector
- Spark plug wires from the spark plugs
- Ignition coil pack
- Cylinder head cover
- Cam sensor and fuel injector wiring
- Intake and exhaust manifolds, if necessary
- Timing belt cover
- Timing belt
- Camshaft sprocket
- Rear timing belt cover
- Rocker arm/rocker arm shaft assemblies
- Cylinder head bolts
- Cylinder head

To install:

➡**The cylinder head bolts should be checked for stretching before reuse. If the thread area of the bolt is necked-down the bolts must be replaced with new. New head bolts are recommended.**

6. Thoroughly clean all parts. Clean all sealing surfaces. Use care not to scratch the aluminum cylinder head sealing surface. Check the cylinder head for flatness using a feeler gauge and a straightedge. The cylinder head must be flat within 0.004 in. (0.1mm).

7. Check the cylinder head for cracks or other damage.

8. Install or connect the following:
- New cylinder head gasket
- Cylinder head

➡**Refer to Section 1 of this manual for the cylinder head torque sequence illustration. The illustration is located after the Torque Specification Chart.**

9. Be sure to oil the cylinder head bolt threads with clean engine oil. Install the cylinder head bolts, the 4.330 in. (110mm) short bolts are to be installed in positions 7, 8, 9 and 10. Tighten the bolts in proper sequence.

10. Torque the cylinder head bolts, in sequence, using the following steps:
   a. Step 1: 25 ft. lbs. (34 Nm).
   b. Step 2: 50 ft. lbs. (68 Nm).
   c. Step 3: again to 50 ft. lbs. (68 Nm).
   d. Step 4: an additional ¼ turn.

➡**Do not use a torque wrench for the 4th step.**

11. Set the crankshaft to 3 notches Before Top Dead Center (BTDC) before installing the rocker arm shafts.

12. Install or connect the following:
- Rocker arm/rocker arm shaft assemblies
- Cylinder head cover using a new gasket. Torque the bolts to 105 inch lbs. (12 Nm).

➡**Be sure the cover gasket mating surfaces are clean of any dirt, oil or old gasket material.**

- Timing belt rear cover
- Camshaft sprocket
- Timing belt
- Timing belt cover
- Intake and exhaust manifolds, if removed
- Cam sensor and fuel injector electrical connectors
- Ignition coil pack
- Spark plug wires
- Power steering pump
- Exhaust pipe to the exhaust manifold
- Brake booster vacuum line
- Accessory drive belts and adjust them
- Throttle linkage

- All vacuum hoses and electrical connectors to the throttle body
- Fuel line to the fuel rail
- Air cleaner assembly
- Negative battery cable

13. Refill the cooling system and install a new oil filter.

14. Check to be sure all ducts, hoses, fuel lines and wiring connectors have been properly reattached.

15. Start the engine and check for leaks. Run the engine with the radiator cap off so as the engine warms and the thermostat opens, coolant can be added to the radiator. When satisfied that the cooling system is full, shut the engine **OFF**, install the radiator cap and allow the engine to cool.

16. With the engine cool, check all fluid levels. Add coolant and oil as required. Restart the engine and test drive the vehicle to check for proper operation.

2.4L Engine

This engine uses a Dual Over Head Camshaft (DOHC) 4-valves per cylinder cross flow aluminum cylinder head. The valves are actuated by roller cam followers which pivot on stationary hydraulic valve adjusters. Care must be taken to be sure all valve timing marks align after cylinder head and valvetrain service.

1. Before servicing the vehicle, refer to the precautions in the beginning of this section.

2. Relieve the fuel system pressure.

3. Drain the cooling system.

4. Disconnect the negative battery cable from the left shock tower.

➡**The ground cable is equipped with an insulator grommet which should be placed on the stud to prevent the negative battery cable from accidentally grounding.**

5. Remove or disconnect the following:
- Air cleaner assembly
- All vacuum lines, electrical connectors and fuel lines from the throttle body
- Throttle linkage
- Accessory drive belts
- Power brake vacuum hose from the intake manifold
- Exhaust pipe from the exhaust manifold
- Power steering pump and move it aside. Do not disconnect the fluid lines.
- Spark plug wires
- Coil pack electrical connector
- Coil pack with the spark plug wires

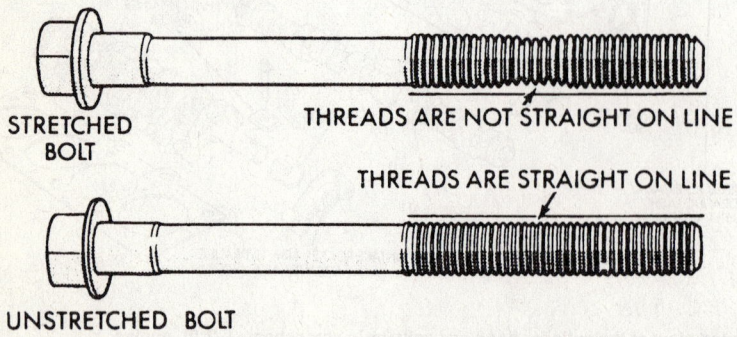

STRETCHED BOLT

THREADS ARE NOT STRAIGHT ON LINE

THREADS ARE STRAIGHT ON LINE

UNSTRETCHED BOLT

7922FG11

Before reusing old cylinder head bolts, check them for necking (stretching)—2.0L and 2.4L engines

- Cam sensor and fuel injector electrical connectors
- Timing belt covers
- Timing belt
- Camshaft sprockets
- Timing belt idler pulley
- Rear timing belt cover
- Cylinder head cover
- Ground strap

6. Identify the camshafts if they are to be reused for later installation. The camshafts are not interchangeable.

7. Remove or disconnect the following:
- Camshaft bearing cap bolts in sequence
- Camshafts

➡**Refer to the camshaft removal and installation procedure for correct bolt removal/installation sequence.**

- Camshaft followers

➡**Any components that are to be reused must be installed in their original locations. Use care to identify and mark the positions of any removed valvetrain components so they may be reinstalled correctly.**

8. Remove or disconnect the following:
- Intake and exhaust manifolds
- Cylinder head bolts
- Cylinder head

➡**Be careful not to damage the aluminum gasket surfaces.**

9. Remove all gasket material from the cylinder head and engine block. Be careful not to gouge or scratch the sealing surface of the aluminum head. The cylinder head should be checked for flatness using a good straightedge and feeler gauges. The cylinder head must be flat within 0.004 in. (0.1mm).

10. Inspect the camshaft bearing oil feed holes in the cylinder head for clogging. Inspect the camshaft bearing journals for wear or scoring. Check the cam surface for abnormal wear and damage. A visible worn groove in the roller path or on the cam lobes is cause for replacement. Valve service may be performed at this time.

To install:

11. Thoroughly clean all parts.

➡**The cylinder head bolts are stretch-type. New cylinder head bolts are recommended.**

12. Thoroughly clean all sealing surfaces.
13. Install or connect the following:
- New cylinder head gasket
- Cylinder head

➡**Refer to Section 1 of this manual for the cylinder head torque sequence illustration. The illustration is located after the Torque Specification Chart.**

14. Before installing the bolts, the threads should be oiled with clean engine oil.

15. Torque the cylinder head bolts in sequence, using the following 4 Steps:
a. Tighten all bolts to 25 ft. lbs. (34 Nm).
b. Tighten all bolts to 50 ft. lbs. (68 Nm).
c. Tighten all bolts again to 50 ft. lbs. (68 Nm).
d. Tighten all bolts and additional ¼ turn.

➡**Do not use a torque wrench for the 4th step.**

16. Check the camshaft end-play using the recommended procedure, then install the camshaft.

17. Apply Mopar Gasket Maker or equivalent sealer to the No. 1 and No. 6 bearing caps. Install the bearing caps and tighten the M8 fasteners to 21 ft. lbs. (28 Nm). The end caps must be installed before the seals may be installed.

18. Apply a light coating of clean engine oil to the lip of the new camshaft seal. Install the camshaft seal until it fits flush with the cylinder head.

19. Install or connect the following:
- Camshaft sprockets, if removed
- Rear timing belt cover
- Timing belt and properly align the timing marks
- Timing belt cover

✳✳ WARNING

Verify that all timing marks are correct. If the timing belt or sprockets are incorrectly installed, engine damage will occur. Take time to be sure all timing marks are correctly aligned.

- Intake and exhaust manifolds
- New cylinder head cover gasket
- Cylinder head cover

✳✳ WARNING

DO NOT allow oil or solvents to contact the timing belt as they can deteriorate the rubber and cause tooth skipping.

➡**Apply Mopar Silicone Rubber Adhesive Sealant or equivalent, at the**

camshaft cap corners and at the top edge of the ½ round seal.

20. Torque the cylinder head cover fasteners, in sequence, using the following Steps:
a. Step 1: 40 inch lbs. (4.5 Nm).
b. Step 2: 80 inch lbs. (9 Nm).
c. Step 3: 105 inch lbs. (12 Nm).

21. Install or connect the following:
- Ground strap
- Coil pack and spark plug wiring
- Cam sensor and fuel injector wiring
- Power steering pump assembly
- Exhaust pipe to the exhaust manifold
- All vacuum lines and electrical connectors
- Throttle linkage and fuel lines
- Accessory drive belts and adjust them
- Negative battery cable

22. Refill the cooling system.

➡**An oil and filter change is recommended since coolant can enter the oil system when a head is removed.**

23. Connect the remaining air ducting. Test run vehicle. Check for leaks and for proper operation.

2.5L Engine

This engine uses aluminum alloy cylinder heads with 4-valves per cylinder and pressed-in cast iron valve guides. The cylinders are common to either cylinder bank. Two overhead camshafts are supported by 4 bearing journals which are part of the head with the distributor driven off the right (firewall side) cylinder head. Right and left camshaft drive sprockets are interchangeable. The sprockets and engine water pump are driven by the timing belt. Care must be taken to be sure all valve timing marks align after cylinder head and valvetrain service.

➡**Please note that for camshaft service, the cylinder head must be removed.**

1. Before servicing the vehicle, refer to the precautions in the beginning of this section.

2. Disconnect the negative battery cable from the left shock tower.

➡**The ground cable is equipped with an insulator grommet which should be placed on the stud to prevent the nega-**

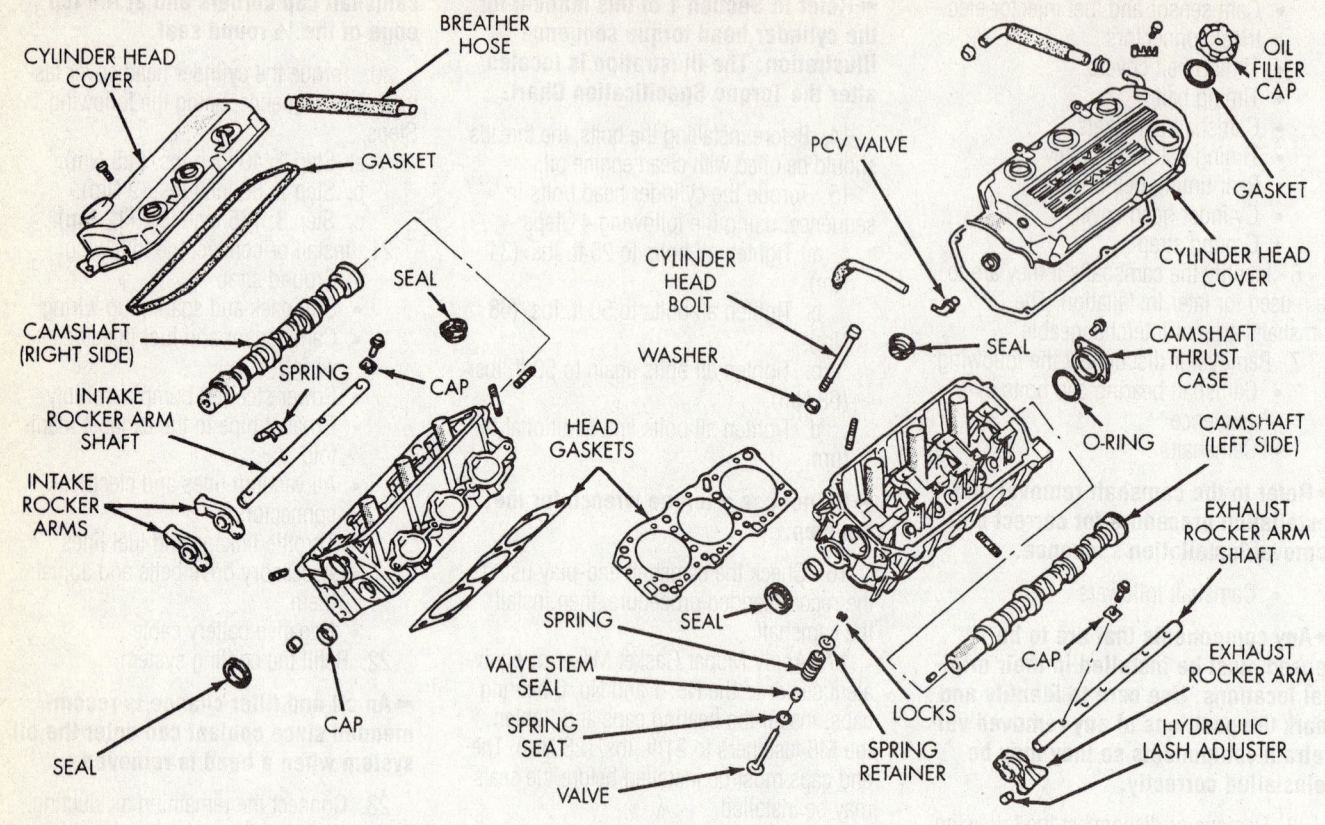

Exploded view of the cylinder head, camshafts and rocker assemblies—2.5L engine

7922FG14

tive battery cable from accidentally grounding.

3. Relieve the fuel system pressure using the recommended procedure.

4. Drain the cooling system.

5. Remove or disconnect the following:
- Accessory drive belts
- Front timing belt covers
- Timing belt
- Camshaft sprockets

➡The intake manifold is a 2-piece unit. The upper part is a large air intake plenum of aluminum alloy. Use care working with light alloy parts.

- Air intake plenum
- Lower intake manifold
- Spark plug wires and move them aside
- Cylinder head cover

6. Identify the rocker arm shaft assemblies before removal.

7. Install the Auto Lash Adjuster Retainers MD 998443 to keep the auto lash adjusters from falling out of the rocker arms when the rocker arm assembly is removed.

8. Remove or disconnect the following:
- Rocker arm shaft assemblies
- Distributor assembly

- Exhaust manifold and crossover
- Cylinder head bolts
- Cylinder head

9. If the camshaft(s) are to be serviced, remove the thrust case from the left head assembly and remove the camshaft from the rear of the head. If not already done, remove the distributor from the right cylinder head and remove the camshaft from the rear of the head.

10. Valve service may be performed at this time, if required.

To install:

11. Thoroughly clean all parts well. All sealing surfaces on the engine block, cylinder head(s) and both the upper and lower sections of the intake manifold must be clean. Check for cracks, signs of wear in the camshaft bores or other damage. With a straightedge and feeler gauge, check the head for flatness. It should be within 0.0012 in. (0.03mm) along its length. The service limit is 0.008 in. (0.2mm). If the head must be resurfaced, the grinding limit is 0.008 in. (0.2mm). Note that this dimension is a combined total dimension of stock material removal from the cylinder head, if any, and the block top surface is 0.0079 in. (0.2mm).

12. Camshaft end-play can be checked as follows:

a. Oil the camshaft journals with clean engine oil and install (if removed) the camshaft without the rocker arm assemblies.

b. Move the camshaft as far rearward as it will go.

c. Mount a dial indicator to bear on the front of the camshaft.

d. Zero the indicator.

e. Move the camshaft as far forward as it will go. End-play should be 0.004–0.008 in. (0.1–0.2mm). Maximum allowed end-play is 0.016 in. (0.4mm).

13. If the camshafts were removed, lubricate the camshaft journals and carefully reinstall the camshaft into the cylinder head. Install the thrust case and torque the thrust case mounting bolts to 108 inch lbs. (13 Nm).

14. Apply a light coating of engine oil to the lip of the camshaft seal(s).

➡Refer to Section 1 of this manual for the cylinder head torque sequence illustration. The illustration is located after the Torque Specification Chart.

15. Install or connect the following:
- Camshaft seal(s)
- Camshaft sprocket(s). Torque the bolts to 65 ft. lbs. (88 Nm).

- New cylinder head gasket
- Cylinder head
- New 10mm Allen hex cylinder head bolts, with washers. Torque the cylinder head bolts, in proper sequence, in 2–3 steps, to 80 ft. lbs. (108 Nm).
- Lower intake manifold using new gaskets
- Rocker arm assemblies
- Exhaust manifold and crossover exhaust pipe
- Timing belt, properly align the timing marks
- Timing belt covers

16. Inspect the spark plug tube seals located on the ends of each tube. These seals slide onto each tube to seal the cylinder head cover to the spark plug tube. If these seals show signs of hardness and/or cracks, they should be replaced.

17. Thoroughly clean all sealing surfaces.

18. Install or connect the following:
- Cover using a new gasket. Torque bolts to 88 inch lbs. (10 Nm).
- Distributor assembly
- Spark plug wires
- Upper intake manifold (plenum) using a new gasket. Torque the bolts to 13 ft. lbs. (18 Nm).
- Plenum support bracket bolts
- Exhaust Gas Recirculation (EGR) tube
- Speed control cable, if equipped
- Throttle cable
- Throttle Position Sensor (TPS) and Idle Air Control (IAC) motor electrical connectors
- Air cleaner cover, inlet hoses and air inlet resonator
- Manifold Absolute Pressure (MAP) and Intake Air Temperature (IAT) sensor wiring connectors
- Accessory drive belts and adjust them
- Negative battery cable

19. Refill the cooling system.

➡**An oil and filter change is recommended whenever a cylinder head has been removed since coolant can get into the oil system.**

20. Check to be sure all ducts, hoses, fuel lines and wiring connections have all been properly reattached.

21. Start the engine and check for leaks, abnormal noises and vibrations. Bleed the cooling system.

Rocker Arm/Shaft

REMOVAL & INSTALLATION

The 2.0L and 2.5L engines are equipped with rocker arms/shafts. On the 2.4L engine the camshaft acts directly on the valve, therefore, no rocker arms/shafts are used.

2.0L Engine

This engine uses an Single Over Head Camshaft (SOHC) running in an aluminum cylinder head. Rocker arm shafts mount directly to the cylinder head. Care must be taken to be sure all valve timing marks align after cylinder head and valvetrain service. The Hydraulic Lash Adjusters (HLAs) are located in the valve actuating end of the rocker arm and are serviced as an assembly.

1. Before servicing the vehicle, refer to the precautions in the beginning of this section.

2. Disconnect the negative battery cable from the left shock tower.

➡**The ground cable is equipped with an insulator grommet which should be placed on the stud to prevent the negative battery cable from accidentally grounding.**

3. Relieve the fuel system pressure using the recommended procedure.

4. Remove or disconnect the following:
- Spark plug wires
- Air inlet duct
- Ignition coil pack
- Cylinder head cover

5. Thoroughly clean the cylinder head cover and gasket mating surfaces. Be sure the gasket mating surfaces are flat.

6. Mark the rocker arm shaft assemblies to identify them for later installation.

7. Remove or disconnect the following:
- Rocker arm shaft bolts
- Rocker arm assemblies

8. Mark the rocker arm spacers and retainers to identify them for correct installation.

9. Disassemble the rocker arm/shaft assemblies as follows:
- Bolts from the rocker arm shaft assemblies
- Rocker arm/HLA assembly and rocker arm spacers, sliding them off the rocker arm shaft

✲✲ WARNING

Be sure the rocker arms and spacers are reassembled in the same positions they are removed.

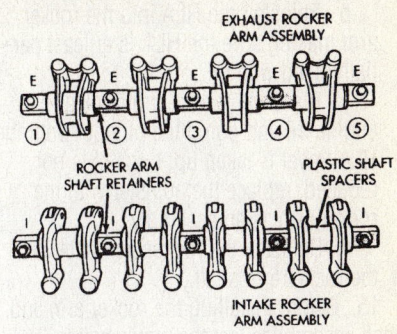

Rocker arm shaft identification—2.0L engine

To install:

➡**Inspect the rocker arms and shaft for scoring and/or wear on the rollers or damage to the rocker arm. If scoring, wear or damage is present, replace the rocker arm assemblies. The rocker arm shaft is hollow and, therefore, used as an oil lubrication duct. Inspect the oil holes for clogging, using a small wire and clean, if necessary. Inspect the location where the rocker arms mount to the shaft and replace if damaged or worn.**

10.. If the camshaft lobes show signs of wear, check the corresponding rocker arm roller for wear or damage. Replace rocker arms/HLAs if worn or damaged. If the camshaft lobes show signs of pitting on the nose, flank or base circle replace the camshaft.

11. Inspect the rocker arms for scoring, wear on the roller or damage to the shaft. Replace parts as necessary. Check that the rocker arm shaft is clean inside and out. Check all oil holes for clogging with a small wire and clean and required.

12. Thoroughly lubricate all rocker arm components and spacers and reinstall on the rocker arm shaft in the original locations.

13. If the vehicle exhibited a tappet-like noise, the valve lash adjusters built into the rocker arms should be cleaned and checked. Lash adjusters removed from a rocker arm should be returned to their original locations. Replacement of worn or defective lash adjusters would require the replacement of the rocker arm/HLAs as an assembly.

14. Install a HLA, by using the following procedure:
a. Lubricate the HLA thoroughly with clean engine oil.

b. Reinstall the HLA into the rocker arm making sure the HLA is at least partially filled with oil.

c. Place the rocker arm in clean engine oil and pump the plunger until the HLA travel is taken up. If travel is not reduced, replace the adjuster with the rocker arm as an assembly.

d. Reinstall the rocker arm back on the rocker arm shaft.

15. Before installing the rocker arm and shaft assemblies, set the crankshaft to 3 notches Before Top Dead Center (BTDC) on the crankshaft sprocket.

➡**When installing the intake rocker arm/shaft assembly, be sure the plastic rocker arm spacers do not interfere with the spark plug tubes. If there is interference, rotate the plastic spacers until they are at the proper angle. Do not rotate the spacers by forcing down on the shaft assembly or damage to the spark plug tubes will occur.**

16. Reinstall the rocker arm and shaft assemblies with the small notches in the rocker shafts pointing up and toward the timing belt side of the engine. Install the retainers in their original positions on the exhaust and intake shafts. Tighten the bolts in proper sequence to 17 ft. lbs. (23 Nm).

17. Install or connect the following:
- Cylinder head cover using a new gasket. Torque the bolts to 105 inch lbs. (12 Nm).
- Ignition coil pack. Torque the fasteners to 17 ft. lbs. (23 Nm).
- Spark plug wires
- Air cleaner inlet duct
- Negative battery cable

18. Check to be sure all electrical, vacuum and fluid connections are reattached as required.

19. An oil and filter change are recommended.

20. Start the engine and check for leaks. Test drive the vehicle to check for proper operation.

2.5L Engine

1. Before servicing the vehicle, refer to the precautions in the beginning of this section.

2. Disconnect the negative battery cable from the left shock tower.

➡**The ground cable is equipped with an insulator grommet which should be placed on the stud to prevent the negative battery cable from accidentally grounding.**

3. Relieve the fuel system pressure using the recommended procedure.

4. If removing the right (firewall) side rocker arm/shaft assembly, remove the upper intake manifold (air intake plenum), which is a 2-piece unit of aluminum alloy. Use care working with light alloy parts.

5. Remove or disconnect the air intake plenum using the following procedure:
- Fuel supply tube from the fuel rail. Squeeze the tabs together and pull the fuel tube/quick-connect fitting assembly off the fuel tube nipple.
- Manifold Absolute Pressure (MAP) sensor and Intake Air Temperature (IAT) sensor electrical connections
- Plenum support bracket bolt located rearward of the MAP sensor
- Air inlet resonator-to-intake manifold bolt
- Throttle body air inlet hose clamp
- Air cleaner housing cover and inlet hoses
- Throttle Position (TP) sensor electrical connector and Idle Air Control (IAC) motor electrical connections
- Throttle cable by sliding it out of the bracket
- Speed control cable by sliding it out of its bracket, if equipped
- Exhaust Gas Recirculation (EGR) tube from the intake manifold
- Plenum support bracket bolt from the rear of the EGR tube
- Upper intake plenum

6. Remove or disconnect the following:
- Spark plug wires
- Cylinder head cover

7. Identify the rocker arm shaft assemblies before removal.

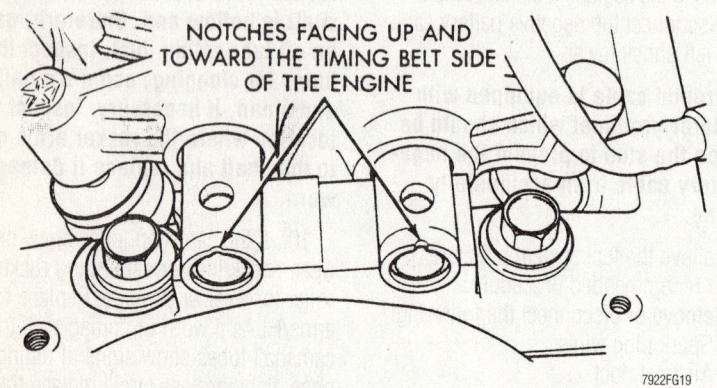

NOTCHES FACING UP AND TOWARD THE TIMING BELT SIDE OF THE ENGINE

7922FG19

Rocker arm shaft notch locations—2.0L engine

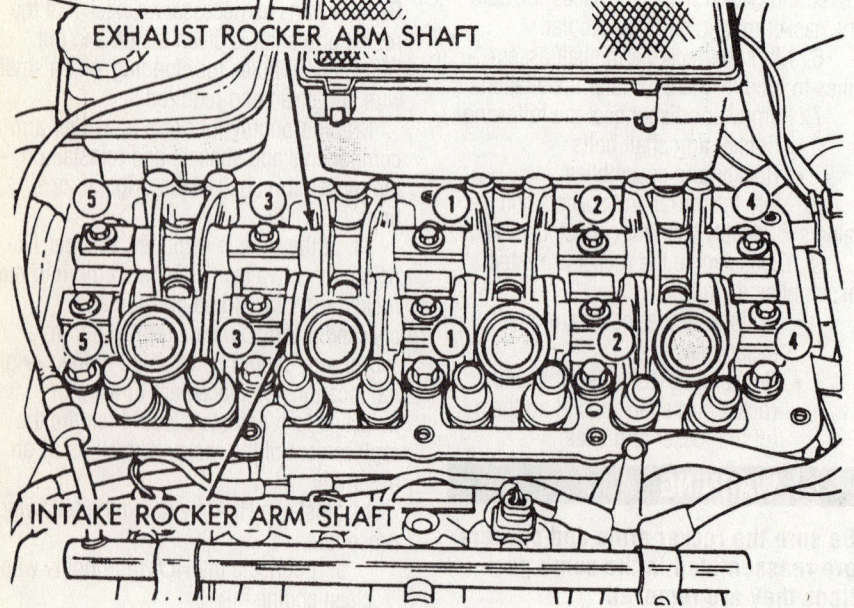

EXHAUST ROCKER ARM SHAFT

INTAKE ROCKER ARM SHAFT

7922FG20

Rocker arm shaft tightening sequence—2.0L engine

8. Install the auto lash adjuster retainers Special Tool MD 998443 to keep the auto lash adjusters from falling out of the rocker arms when the rocker arm assembly is removed.

9. Loosen the fasteners and remove the rocker arm shaft assemblies.

➡**The hydraulic automatic lash adjusters are precision units installed in the machined openings in the rocker arm units. Do not disassemble the auto lash adjusters from the rocker arms.**

To install:

10. The rocker arm shafts are hollow and used as a lubrication oil duct. Be sure all valvetrain parts are clean. Check the rocker arm mounting portion of the shafts for wear or damage. Replace if necessary. Check all oil holes for clogging with a small wire and clean as required. If any rockers were removed, lubricate and install on the shafts in their original positions.

11. For the right cylinder head, install the rocker arm and shaft assemblies with the FLAT in the rocker arm shafts facing the timing belt side of the engine. For the left cylinder head, install the rocker arm and shaft

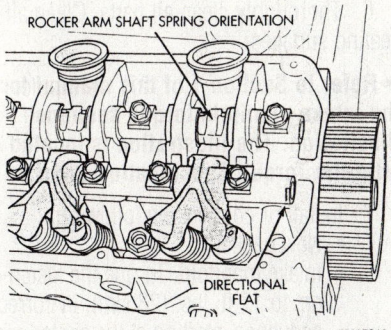

The flats on the rocker arm shaft aids proper orientation—2.5L engine

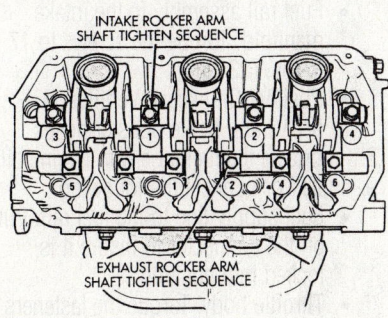

Rocker arm shaft tightening sequence— 2.5L engine

assembly with the FLAT in the rocker arm shaft facing the transaxle side of the engine. Install the retainers and spring clips in their original positions on the exhaust and intake shafts. Tighten the retainer bolts to 23 ft. lbs. (31 Nm) working from the center, outward. Remove the valve lash retainer tools that should have been installed at disassembly.

12. Inspect the spark plug tube seals located on the ends of each tube. These seals slide onto each tube to seal the cylinder head cover to the spark plug tube. If these seals show signs of hardness and/or cracking, they should be replaced.

13. Clean the cylinder head and cover mating surfaces.

14. Install or connect the following:
- Cylinder head cover using a new gasket. Torque bolts to 88 inch lbs. (10 Nm).
- Spark plug wires
- Upper intake manifold (plenum) using a new gasket. Tighten the bolts to 13 ft. lbs. (18 Nm).
- Plenum support bracket bolts
- EGR tube
- Throttle and speed control cables
- TP sensor, MAP sensor, IAT sensor and IAC motor electrical connectors
- Air inlet resonator, air inlet hose and air cleaner housing cover
- All remaining electrical connectors
- Air tube connections
- Negative battery cable

15. An oil and filter change is recommended.

✳✳ WARNING

Operating the engine without the proper amount and type of engine oil will result in severe engine damage.

16. Start the engine and check for leaks, abnormal noises and vibrations.

Intake Manifold

REMOVAL & INSTALLATION

2.0L Engine

The intake manifold is a long branch design made of a molded plastic composition. It is attached to the cylinder head with 10 fasteners. Please note that all seals are to be replaced with new seals and all fasteners are to be replaced with new fasteners.

1. Before servicing the vehicle, refer to

the precautions in the beginning of this section.

2. Disconnect the negative battery cable from the left shock tower.

➡**The ground cable is equipped with an insulator grommet which should be placed on the stud to prevent the negative battery cable from accidentally grounding.**

3. Relieve the fuel system pressure using the recommended procedure.

4. Remove the air inlet resonator as follows:
- Air inlet resonator-to-throttle body screw
- Air inlet resonator-to-air inlet tube clamp, loosen it
- Resonator

5. Remove or disconnect the following:
- Fuel supply line quick-disconnect fitting from the fuel rail. Squeeze the retainer tabs together and pull the fuel tube fitting from the fuel tube nipple. The retainer will remain on the fuel tube.

➡**Wrap shop towels around the fuel line openings to catch any spilling fuel.**

- Fuel rail

✳✳ WARNING

Use care when handling the fuel injectors. Do not set them on their tips. Cover the fuel injector openings after fuel rail removal.

- Accelerator, kickdown and speed control cables from the throttle lever and bracket
- Throttle Position (TP) sensor and Idle Air Control (IAC) motor electrical connections
- Vacuum hoses from the throttle body
- Manifold Absolute Pressure (MAP) sensor, Idle Air Control (IAC) motor and Intake Air Temperature (IAT) sensor
- Vapor and brake booster hoses
- Knock sensor electrical connector
- Starter relay electrical connector
- Wiring harness from the intake manifold tab
- Transaxle-to-throttle body support bracket fasteners at the throttle body and loosen the fastener at the transaxle end
- Throttle body assembly
- Exhaust Gas Recirculation (EGR) tube

- Intake manifold-to-inlet water tube support fastener
- Intake manifold fasteners and discard them
- Intake manifold

To install:

6. Clean all sealing surfaces. Check upper and lower manifold gasket surfaces for flatness with a straightedge. Surface must be flat within 0.006 in. (0.15mm) per foot (30cm).

➡️**Refer to Section 1 of this manual for the intake manifold torque sequence illustration. The illustration is located after the Torque Specification Chart.**

➡️**Replace all seals and fasteners with new ones.**

7. Install or connect the following:
- Intake manifold with new O-ring seals. Torque the fasteners, in proper sequence, to 105 inch lbs. (12 Nm).

8. Lubricate the fuel injector O-rings with engine oil.

9. Install or connect the following:
- Fuel injector/fuel rail assembly. Torque the fuel rail bolts to 17 ft. lbs. (23 Nm).
- Fuel injector electrical connectors

10. Lubricate the quick-connect fittings with engine oil.

11. Install or connect the following:
- Fuel supply line to the fuel rail. Pull on the connector to insure it is locked into position.
- Positive Crankcase Ventilation (PCV) and brake booster hoses
- Throttle body. Torque the fasteners to 17 ft. lbs. (23 Nm).
- Transaxle-to-throttle body support bracket. Torque the fasteners to 105 inch lbs. (12 Nm).

➡️**Tighten the support bracket at the throttle body first; then, at the transaxle.**

- MAP and IAT sensor electrical connectors
- Knock sensor electrical and starter relay connectors
- Wiring harness to the intake manifold tab
- IAC and TP sensor electrical connectors
- Throttle body vacuum hoses
- Accelerator, kickdown and speed control cables, to their bracket(s) and throttle lever
- EGR tube. Torque the fasteners to 95 inch lbs. (11 Nm).

➡️**Tighten the EGR tube-to-valve fasteners first; then, at the intake manifold.**

- Fresh air duct to the air filter housing
- Air inlet resonator to the throttle body
- Air inlet tube to the resonator. Torque the clamps to 20–30 inch lbs. (2–3 Nm).
- Negative battery cable

2.4L Engine

The intake manifold is a long branch design made of cast aluminum. It is attached to the cylinder head with 8 fasteners.

1. Before servicing the vehicle, refer to the precautions in the beginning of this section.

2. Disconnect the negative battery cable from the left shock tower.

➡️**The ground cable is equipped with an insulator grommet which should be placed on the stud to prevent the negative battery cable from accidentally grounding.**

3. Relieve the fuel system pressure using the recommended procedure.

4. Remove the air inlet resonator as follows:
- Both air inlet resonator-to-intake manifold bolts
- Resonator-to-throttle body screw, loosen it
- Air inlet resonator-to-air inlet tube clamp, loosen it
- Resonator

5. Remove or disconnect the following:
- Fuel supply line quick-disconnect at the fuel tube assembly

➡️**Squeeze the retainer tabs together and pull the fuel tube/quick-disconnect fitting assembly from the fuel tube nipple. The retainer will remain on the fuel tube. Use shop towels to catch any dripping fuel.**

- Fuel rail

✳✳ WARNING

Use care when handling the fuel injectors. Do not set them on their tips. Cover the fuel injector openings after fuel rail removal.

- Accelerator, kickdown and speed control cables, from the throttle lever and bracket
- Idle Air Control (IAC) motor and Throttle Position (TP) sensor electrical connections
- Throttle body vacuum hoses
- Manifold Absolute Pressure (MAP) sensor and Intake Air Tem-

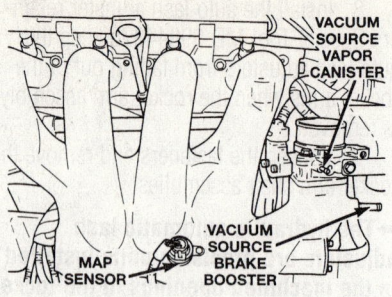

MAP sensor location—2.4L engine

perature (IAT) sensor electrical connections
- Vapor and brake booster hoses
- Knock sensor electrical connector
- Wiring harness from the intake manifold tab
- Transaxle-to-throttle body support bracket fasteners at the throttle body and loosen the fastener at the transaxle end
- Throttle body
- Exhaust Gas Recirculation (EGR) tube
- Intake manifold support bracket
- Intake manifold

To install:

6. Thoroughly clean all parts. Clean all sealing surfaces

➡️**Refer to Section 1 of this manual for the intake manifold torque sequence illustration. The illustration is located after the Torque Specification Chart.**

7. Install or connect the following:
- New gasket
- Intake manifold. Torque the fasteners to 17 ft. lbs. (23 Nm), in correct sequence, starting at the center and working outward.

➡️**Make sure the fuel injector openings clean.**

- Fuel rail assembly to the intake manifold. Torque the screws to 17 ft. lbs. (23 Nm).
- Positive Crankcase Ventilation (PCV) and brake booster hoses

8. Lubricate the fuel tube with engine oil.

9. Install or connect the following:
- Fuel supply line to the fuel rail. Pull on the connector to insure it is locked into position.
- Throttle body. Torque the fasteners to 17 ft. lbs. (23 Nm).
- Transaxle-to-throttle body support bracket. Torque the fasteners to 105 inch lbs. (12 Nm) at the throttle body first; then, at the transaxle.

- MAP and IAT electrical connectors
- Knock sensor electrical connector
- Wiring harness to the intake manifold tab
- IAC motor and TP sensor electrical connectors
- Throttle body vacuum hoses
- Accelerator, kickdown and speed control cables to the throttle lever and bracket
- EGR tube. Torque the fasteners to 95 inch lbs. (11 Nm), at the EGR valve first; then, the intake manifold.
- Air inlet resonator to the throttle body
- Air inlet tube to the resonator. Torque the clamps to 20–30 inch lbs. (2.5–3.5 Nm).
- Both air inlet resonator-to-intake manifold bolts
- Negative battery cable

2.5L Engine

The intake manifold assembly is composed of an upper plenum and lower manifold. This aluminum alloy manifold has long runners to improve airflow inertia. The plenum chamber absorbs air pulsations cre- ated during the suction phase of each cylinder. The lower intake manifold is machined for 6 injectors and the fuel rail mounts.

1. Before servicing the vehicle, refer to the precautions in the beginning of this section.

2. Disconnect the negative battery cable from the left shock tower.

➡The ground cable is equipped with an insulator grommet which should be placed on the stud to prevent the negative battery cable from accidentally grounding.

3. Relieve the fuel system pressure using the recommended procedure.

4. Disconnect the fuel supply line quick-disconnect fitting from the fuel rail. Squeeze the fitting retainer tabs together and separate the connection.

✳✳ CAUTION

Wrap shop towels around the connection to catch any gasoline spillage.

➡It may be helpful to identify and tag each sensor connector as it is being removed. This may save time at assembly.

5. Remove or disconnect the following:

- Manifold Absolute Pressure (MAP) sensor and Intake Air Temperature (IAT) sensor electrical connections
- Plenum support bracket at the rear of the MAP sensor
- Air inlet resonator bolt
- Throttle body air inlet hose clamp, loosen it
- Air cleaner cover and inlet hoses
- Throttle Position Sensor (TPS) and Idle Air Control (IAC) motor electrical connections
- Throttle cable from the bracket
- Speed control cable out of the bracket, if equipped
- Exhaust Gas Recirculation (EGR) tube from the intake manifold
- Plenum support bracket at the rear of the EGR tube
- Upper intake plenum from the intake manifold
- Fuel injector electrical connectors
- Fuel rail

➡There are spacers under each fuel rail bolt.

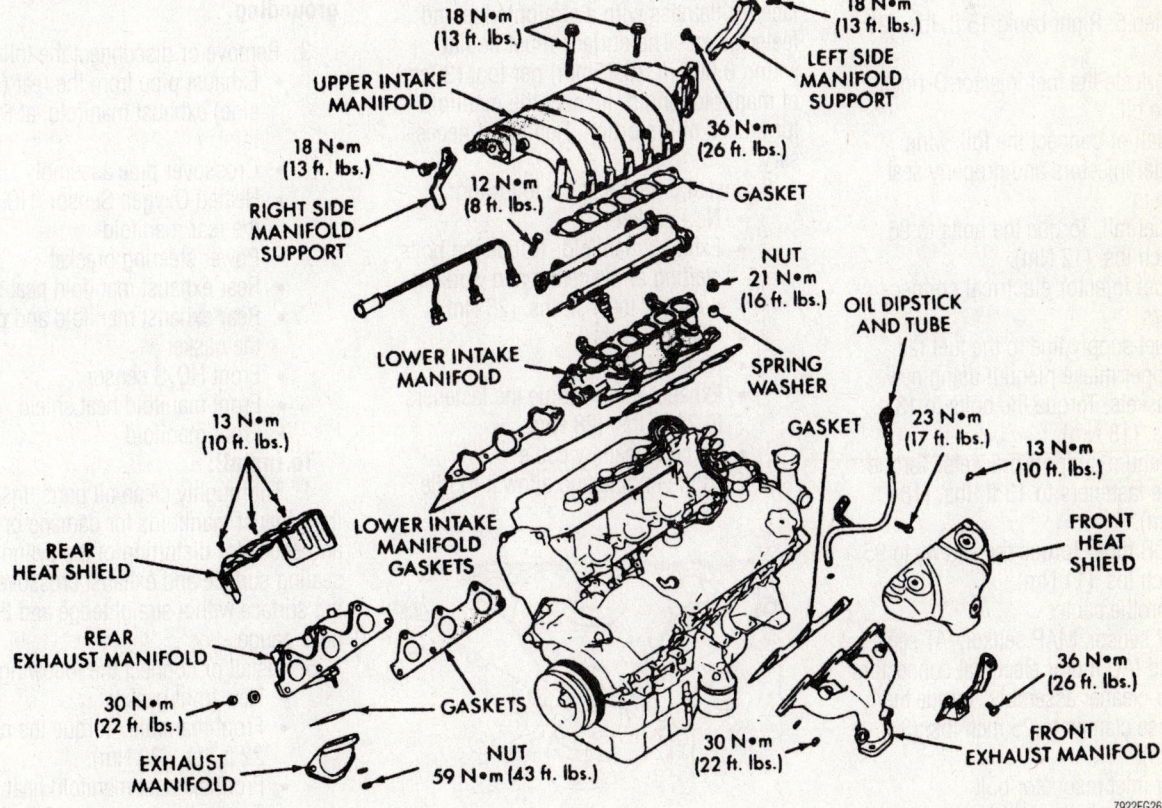

Exploded view of the intake/exhaust manifolds and related components—2.5L engine

7922FG26

Please refer to Section 8 for electric cooling fan wiring schematics

- Lower intake manifold and discard the gaskets

To install:

6. Clean all sealing surfaces.

7. Check upper and lower manifold gasket surfaces for flatness with a straightedge. Surface must be flat within 0.006 in. (0.15mm) per 12 in. (30cm) of manifold length.

➡️**Refer to Section 1 of this manual for the intake manifold torque sequence illustration. The illustration is located after the Torque Specification Chart.**

8. Install or connect the following:
- New gaskets
- Lower intake manifold

9. For 1997–99 engines, torque the nuts, in the correct sequence, to 15 ft. lbs. (21 Nm).

10. For 2000–01 engines, torque each bank nuts in the following order:
   a. Step 1: Right bank to 56 inch lbs. (6.4 Nm).
   b. Step 2: Left bank: 15 ft. lbs. (21 Nm).
   c. Step 3: Right bank: 15 ft. lbs. (21 Nm).
   d. Step 4: Left bank: 15 ft. lbs. (21 Nm).
   e. Step 5: Right bank: 15 ft. lbs. (21 Nm).

11. Lubricate the fuel injector O-rings with engine oil.

12. Install or connect the following:
- Fuel injectors and properly seat them
- Fuel rail. Torque the bolts to 96 inch lbs. (12 Nm).
- Fuel injector electrical connectors
- Fuel supply line to the fuel rail
- Upper intake plenum using new gaskets. Torque the bolts to 13 ft. lbs. (18 Nm).
- Plenum support brackets. Torque the fasteners to 13 ft. lbs. (18 Nm).
- EGR tube. Torque the screws to 95 inch lbs. (11 Nm).
- Throttle cables
- TP sensor, MAP sensor, IAT sensor and IAC motor electrical connectors
- Air cleaner assembly. Torque the hose clamps to 25 inch lbs. (3 Nm).
- Air inlet resonator bolt
- Negative battery cable

13. Start the engine and check for leaks.

Exhaust Manifold

REMOVAL & INSTALLATION

2.0L and 2.4L Engines

1. Before servicing the vehicle, refer to the precautions in the beginning of this section.

2. Disconnect the negative battery cable from the left shock tower.

➡️**The ground cable is equipped with an insulator grommet which should be placed on the stud to prevent the negative battery cable from accidentally grounding.**

3. Remove or disconnect the following:
- Exhaust pipe from the exhaust manifold
- Exhaust manifold heat shield
- Heated Oxygen Sensor (HO_2S), if necessary
- Exhaust manifold and discard the gasket

To install:

4. Thoroughly clean all parts. Clean all sealing surfaces of the manifold and cylinder head. Check the manifold gasket surface for flatness with a straightedge and feeler gauge. The surface must be flat within 0.006 in. (0.15mm) per foot (30cm) of manifold length. Inspect the manifold for cracks or distortion. Replace if necessary.

5. Install or connect the following:
- New gasket
- Exhaust manifold. Torque the bolts, starting at the center and working outward, to 17 ft. lbs. (23 Nm).
- HO_2S sensor
- Heat shield
- Exhaust pipe. Torque the fasteners to 21 ft. lbs. (28 Nm).
- Negative battery cable

6. Start the engine and allow it to idle

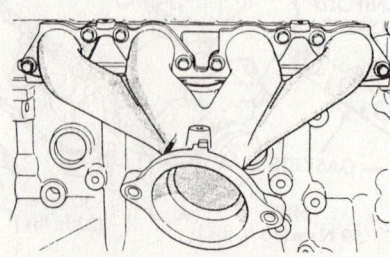

Be sure the gasket mating surfaces are clean and flat before installing the exhaust manifold—2.0L engine

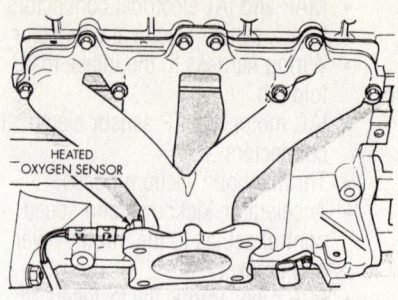

HEATED OXYGEN SENSOR

7922FG29

Be careful not to damage the oxygen sensor when servicing the manifold—2.4L engine

while inspecting the manifold for exhaust leaks.

2.5L Engine

1. Before servicing the vehicle, refer to the precautions in the beginning of this section.

2. Disconnect the negative battery cable from the left shock tower.

➡️**The ground cable is equipped with an insulator grommet which should be placed on the stud to prevent the negative battery cable from accidentally grounding.**

3. Remove or disconnect the following:
- Exhaust pipe from the rear (cowl side) exhaust manifold, at the flex joint
- Crossover pipe assembly
- Heated Oxygen Sensor (HO_2S) from the rear manifold
- Power steering bracket
- Rear exhaust manifold heat shield
- Rear exhaust manifold and discard the gasket
- Front HO_2S sensor
- Front manifold heat shield
- Front manifold

To install:

4. Thoroughly clean all parts. Inspect the exhaust manifolds for damage or cracks and check for distortion of the cylinder head sealing surface and exhaust crossover sealing surface with a straightedge and thickness gauge.

5. Install or connect the following:
- New front gasket
- Front manifold. Torque the nuts to 22 ft. lbs. (30 Nm).
- Front exhaust manifold heat shield. Torque the screws to 10 ft. lbs. (13 Nm).
- Front HO_2S sensor
- New rear gasket

- Rear exhaust manifold. Torque the nuts to 22 ft. lbs. (30 Nm).
- Power steering bracket
- Crossover pipe. Torque the nuts to 22 ft. lbs. (30 Nm).
- Rear HO2S sensor
- Exhaust pipe to the rear manifold. Torque the bolts to 21 ft. lbs. (28 Nm).
- Negative battery cable

6. Lower the vehicle.
7. Start the engine and allow the engine to idle while inspecting the vehicle for exhaust leaks at the manifold.

Front Crankshaft Seal

REMOVAL & INSTALLATION

2.0L and 2.4L Engines

The timing belt must be removed for this procedure. Use care that all timing marks are aligned after installation or the engine will be damaged.

1. Before servicing the vehicle, refer to the precautions in the beginning of this section.
2. Disconnect the negative battery cable from the left shock tower.

➡ **The ground cable is equipped with an insulator grommet which should be placed on the stud to prevent the negative battery cable from accidentally grounding.**

3. Remove the accessory drive belts.
4. Raise and safely support the vehicle. Drain the engine oil.
5. Remove or disconnect the following:
   - Crankshaft damper/pulley using a jaw puller tool
   - Timing belt
   - Crankshaft timing belt sprocket using a gear/sprocket puller

➡ **Be careful not to nick the seal surface of the crankshaft or the seal bore.**

   - Front crankshaft seal using Seal Removal tool No. 6771

➡ **Be careful not to damage the seal contact area of the crankshaft.**

To install:
6. Lubricate the new oil seal lip with engine oil.
7. Install or connect the following:
   - New crankshaft oil seal with the

spring facing inward using Oil Seal Installer tool 6780–1 until it is flush with the front cover
   - Crankshaft timing belt sprocket using tool No. 6792

➡ **Be sure the word "FRONT" on the timing belt sprocket is facing outward.**

   - Timing belt and timing belt cover
   - Crankshaft damper/pulley using the thrust bearing/washer and 12M-1.75 x 150mm bolt from special tool No. 6792. Torque the bolt to 105 ft. lbs. (142 Nm).
   - Accessory drive belts and adjust the tension
   - Negative battery cable

✳✳ WARNING

Operating the engine without the proper amount and type of engine oil will result in severe engine damage.

8. Refill the crankcase.
9. Start the engine and check for leaks.

2.5L Engine

The timing belt must be removed for this procedure. Use care to be sure all timing marks are aligned after this service or the engine will be damaged.

1. Before servicing the vehicle, refer to the precautions in the beginning of this section.
2. Disconnect the negative battery cable from the left shock tower.

➡ **The ground cable is equipped with an insulator grommet which should be placed on the stud to prevent the negative battery cable from accidentally grounding.**

3. Remove the accessory drive belts.
4. Raise and safely support the vehicle. Drain the engine oil.
5. Remove or disconnect the following:
   - Right inner splash shield
   - Crankshaft damper/pulley
   - Timing belt covers and timing belt
   - Crankshaft timing belt sprocket and key
   - Crankshaft seal by prying it out with a flat-tipped prytool

✳✳ WARNING

Be sure to cover the end of the prytool tip with a shop towel. Be careful not to nick the seal surface of the crankshaft or the seal bore.

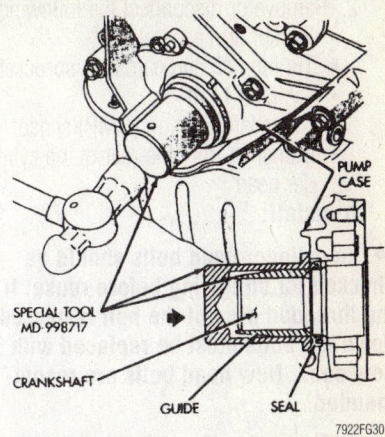

SPECIAL TOOL MD-998717
CRANKSHAFT
GUIDE   SEAL
PUMP CASE
7922FG30

To prevent damage to the end of the crankshaft, use Oil Seal Installer MD998717 or equivalent, as shown—2.5L engine

To install:
6. Lubricate the new oil seal lip with engine oil.
7. Install or connect the following:
   - New crankshaft oil seal until it is flush with the oil pump cover, using Oil Seal Installer MD998717
   - Crankshaft timing belt sprocket and key
   - Timing belt and timing belt covers

✳✳ WARNING

Verify that all timing marks are correctly aligned or the engine will be damaged.

   - Crankshaft damper/pulley. Torque the bolt to 134 ft. lbs. (182 Nm).
   - Right inner splash shield
   - Accessory drive belts and adjust the tension
   - Negative battery cable

✳✳ WARNING

Operating the engine without the proper amount and type of engine oil will result in severe engine damage.

8. Refill the crankcase.
9. Start the engine and check for leaks.

Camshaft

REMOVAL & INSTALLATION

2.0L Engine

1. Before servicing the vehicle, refer to the precautions in the beginning of this section.

2. Remove or disconnect the following:
- Rocker arm assemblies
- Timing belt and camshaft sprocket
- Cylinder head
- Camshaft Position (CMP) sensor
- Camshaft from the rear of the cylinder head

To install:

➡ **The cylinder head bolts should be checked for stretching before reuse. If the threaded area of the bolt is necked-down the bolts must be replaced with new ones. New head bolts are recommended.**

3. Thoroughly clean all parts. Inspect the camshaft journals for scoring. Check the oil feed holes in the head for blockage. Check the camshaft bearing journals for scoring. If light scratches are present, they may be removed with 400 grit abrasive paper. If deep scratches are present, replace the camshaft and check the cylinder head for damage. Replace the cylinder head if worn or damaged.

4. If the camshaft lobes show signs of wear, check the corresponding rocker arm roller for wear or damage. Replace rocker arms/Hydraulic Lash Adjuster (HLAs) if worn or damaged. If the camshaft lobes show signs of pitting on the nose, flank or base circle, replace the camshaft.

5. If the rocker arms and shaft are to be serviced, mark the rocker arms so any that are to be returned to service will be installed in their original locations.

6. Install or connect the following:
- Rocker arm on the rocker arm shaft
- Camshaft, be sure it turns freely
- Cam sensor. Torque the screws to 85 inch lbs. (10 Nm).

7. Camshaft end-play can be checked by using the following procedure:

a. Lubricate the camshaft journals and install the camshaft without the rocker arm assemblies.

b. Install the cam sensor and torque the screws to 85 inch lbs. (10 Nm).

c. Adjust a dial indicator to touch the camshaft nose.

d. Pry the camshaft rearward as far as it will go. Be sure the dial indicator probe is in contact with the camshaft.

e. Zero the dial indicator.

f. Move the camshaft forward as far as it will go.

g. Read the end-play on the dial indicator. Specification is 0.005–0.013 in. (0.13–0.33mm).

8. Install or connect the following:
- Camshaft seal until it is flush with the cylinder head

- Camshaft sprocket. Torque the bolt to 85 ft. lbs. (115 Nm).
- Cylinder head using new bolts

9. Before installing the rocker arm and shaft assemblies, position the crankshaft to 3 notches Before Top Dead Center (BTDC) on the crankshaft sprocket.

10. Install or connect the following:
- Rocker arm and shaft assemblies
- Camshaft sprocket
- Timing belt, by aligning all valve timing marks

2.4L Engine

This engine uses a DOHC, 4-valves per cylinder, cross-flow aluminum cylinder head. The valves are actuated by roller cam followers which pivot on stationary hydraulic valve adjusters. Care must be taken to ensure all valve timing marks align after cylinder head and valvetrain service.

1. Before servicing the vehicle, refer to the precautions in the beginning of this section.

2. Disconnect the negative battery cable from the left shock tower.

➡ **The ground cable is equipped with an insulator grommet which should be placed on the stud to prevent the negative battery cable from accidentally grounding.**

3. Relieve the fuel system pressure using the recommended procedure.

4. Remove or disconnect the following:

- Spark plugs cables
- Ignition coil pack with the spark plug cables
- Cylinder head cover and discard the gasket
- Ground strap

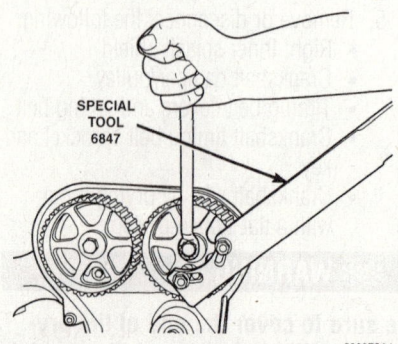

Use special tool 6847 or equivalent to hold the camshaft sprocket while removing or installing the center bolt—2.4L engine

- Timing belt covers and timing belt
- Camshaft sprockets by holding them with tool 6847, while removing the bolt

5. Take note that the camshaft bearing caps are numbered for correct location during installation. Remove the outer bearing caps first.

6. Loosen, but do not remove, the camshaft bearing cap retaining fasteners in the correct sequence, inside working outward. Perform this step on one camshaft at a time.

7. Identify the camshafts, if they are to be reused for later installation. The camshafts are not interchangeable.

8. Remove or disconnect the following:

- Camshaft bearing caps
- Camshafts
- Camshaft followers

9. Any components that are to be reused must be installed in their original locations. Use care to identify and mark the positions of any removed valvetrain components so they may be reinstalled correctly.

10. Inspect the camshaft bearing oil feed holes in the cylinder head for clogging. Inspect the camshaft bearing journals for wear or scoring. Check the cam surface for abnormal wear and damage. A visible worn groove in the roller path or on the cam lobes is cause for replacement.

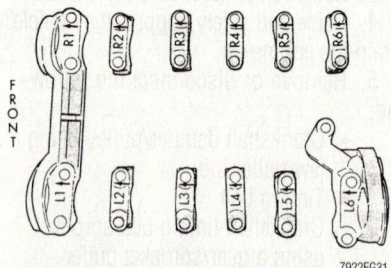

Camshaft bearing cap identification—2.4L engine

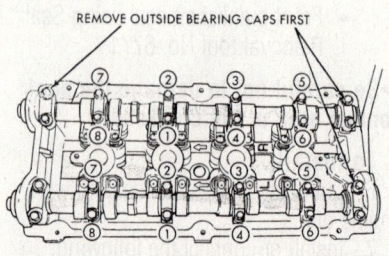

Camshaft bearing cap bolt removal sequence—2.4L engine

To install:

11. Thoroughly clean all camshaft and related parts.

12. Inspect the camshaft end-play using the following procedure:

   a. Lubricate the camshaft journals and install the camshaft **WITHOUT** the cam follower assemblies. Install the rear cam caps and tighten to 21 ft. lbs. (28 Nm).

   b. Push the camshaft rearward as far as it will go.

   c. Adjust a dial indicator to rest against the front of the camshaft (the sprocket end). Zero the indicator.

   d. Move the camshaft forward as far as it will go. Read the dial indicator. End-play specification is 0.002–0.010 in. (0.05–0.15mm).

   e. If excessive end-play is present, inspect the cylinder head and camshaft for wear; replace if necessary.

13. If the fit and condition of the camshafts are acceptable, remove the camshafts for installation of the cam followers.

14. The hydraulic valve lash adjusters are inside the roller cam followers. Be sure they are clean, well lubricated with engine oil and properly positioned. Install the cam followers in their original positions on the hydraulic adjuster and valve stem.

☀ WARNING

Be sure NONE of the pistons are at Top Dead Center (TDC) when installing the camshafts.

15. Lubricate the camshaft bearing journals and cam followers with clean engine oil

16. Install or connect the following:
   - Camshafts
   - Right/left-side camshaft bearing caps Nos. 2 through 5 and right-side No. 6. Torque the M6 fasteners

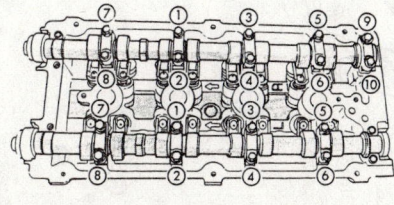

Camshaft bearing cap tightening sequence—2.4L engine

7922FG33

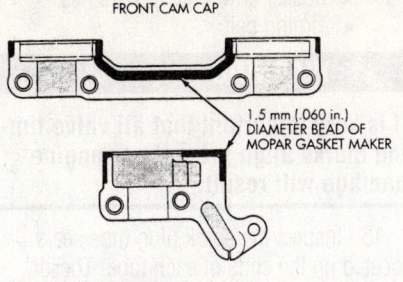

FRONT CAM CAP

1.5 mm (.060 in.) DIAMETER BEAD OF MOPAR GASKET MAKER

LEFT REAR CAM CAP

7922FG34

Apply sealer as shown to prevent oil leakage from the camshaft bearing end caps—2.4L engine

to 105 inch lbs. (12 Nm) in the correct sequence.

17. Apply Mopar® Gasket Maker or equivalent sealer to the No. 1 and left-side No. 6 bearing caps.

18. Install or connect the following:
   - Bearing caps. Torque the M8 fasteners to 21 ft. lbs. (28 Nm).
   - Camshaft end seals
   - Camshaft sprockets, if removed. Torque the bolts to 75 ft. lbs. (101 Nm).
   - Timing belt, making sure all timing marks are aligned
   - Timing belt covers

☀ WARNING

If the timing belt or sprockets are incorrectly installed, engine damage will occur. Take time to be sure all timing marks are correctly aligned.

19. Clean all sealing surfaces. Make certain the rails are flat.

20. Install new cylinder head cover gaskets. Apply Mopar® Silicone Rubber Adhesive Sealant at the camshaft cap corners and at the top edge of the ½ round seal.

➡ **Inspect the spark plug well seals for cracking and/or swelling and replace if necessary.**

21. Install the cylinder head cover and torque the fasteners, in sequence, using the following:

   a. Step 1: 40 inch lbs. (4.5 Nm).
   b. Step 2: 80 inch lbs. (9 Nm).
   c. Step 3: 105 inch lbs. (12 Nm).

22. Install or connect the following:
   - Ignition coil pack. Torque the fasteners to 105 inch lbs. (12 Nm).
   - Spark plug cables

   - Ground strap
   - All vacuum lines and wiring
   - Negative battery cable

➡ **An oil and filter change is recommended.**

23. Test run vehicle. Check for leaks and for proper operation.

2.5L Engine

This engine uses aluminum alloy cylinder heads with 4-valves per cylinder and pressed-in cast iron valve guides. The cylinders are common to either cylinder bank. Two overhead camshafts are supported by 4 bearing journals which are part of the head with the distributor driven off the right (firewall side) cylinder head. Right and left camshaft drive sprockets are interchangeable. The sprockets and engine water pump are driven by the timing belt. Care must be taken to be sure all valve timing marks align after cylinder head and valve train service. Please note that for camshaft service, the cylinder head must be removed.

1. Before servicing the vehicle, refer to the precautions in the beginning of this section.

2. Disconnect the negative battery cable from the left shock tower.

➡ **The ground cable is equipped with an insulator grommet which should be placed on the stud to prevent the negative battery cable from accidentally grounding.**

3. Relieve the fuel system pressure using the recommended procedure.

4. Drain the cooling system.

5. Remove or disconnect the following:
   - Timing belt covers and timing belt
   - Camshaft sprockets by holding them with tool 6847 while removing the bolt
   - Upper intake plenum
   - Lower intake manifold and discard the gasket
   - Spark plug cables
   - Cylinder head cover

6. Identify the rocker arm shaft assemblies.

7. Install the Auto Lash Adjuster Retainers MD 998443 to keep the auto lash adjusters from falling out of the rocker arms when the rocker arm assembly is removed.

Timing belt service is covered in Section 4 of this manual

8. Remove or disconnect the following:
- Rocker arm shaft assemblies from the cylinder head
- Distributor assembly
- Exhaust manifold and crossover pipe
- Cylinder head
- Thrust case from the left cylinder head
- Camshafts from the rear of the cylinder heads
- Camshaft oil seals and discard them

9. Inspect the camshafts for scratches or worn areas. For light scratches, remove them with 400 grit sandpaper. For deep scratches, replace the camshaft and check the cylinder head for damage. Check the oil holes to be sure they are open and free of debris. If the camshaft lobes show signs of wear, check the corresponding rocker arm roller for wear or damage. Replace the rocker arm if worn or damaged. If the camshaft shows signs of wear on the lobes, replace it.

To install:

10. Check camshaft end-play, as follows:
   a. Lubricate the camshaft journals with engine oil and install the camshaft **WITHOUT** the rocker arm assemblies.
   b. Move the camshaft rearward as far as it will go.
   c. Mount a dial indicator to rest on the front of the camshaft.
   d. Zero the indicator.
   e. Move the camshaft forward as far as it will go. End-play should be 0.004–0.008 in. (0.1–0.2mm). Maximum allowed end-play is 0.016 in. (0.4mm).

11. Lubricate the camshaft journals

12. Install or connect the following:
- Camshafts
- Thrust case to the left cylinder head. Torque the fasteners to 108 inch lbs. (13 Nm).
- New camshaft seal (lubricate the seal lip), until it is flush with the cylinder head surface
- Camshaft sprocket. Torque the bolt to 75 ft. lbs. (101 Nm).
- Cylinder head(s)
- Lower intake manifold using new gaskets

13. The rocker arm shafts are hollow and used as a lubrication oil duct. Be sure all valvetrain parts are clean. Check the rocker arm mounting portion of the shafts for wear or damage, replace if necessary. Check all oil holes for clogging with a small wire and clean as required. If any rockers were removed, lubricate and install on the shafts in their original positions.

14. Install or connect the following:

- Rocker arm/shaft assemblies
- Timing belt

✳✳ WARNING

It is very important that all valve timing marks align properly or engine damage will result.

15. Inspect the spark plug tube seals located on the ends of each tube. These seals slide onto each tube to seal the cylinder head cover to the spark plug tube. If these seals show signs of hardness and/or cracking, replace them.

16. Clean all sealing surfaces.

17. Install or connect the following:
- Cylinder head covers using new gaskets. Torque the bolts to 88 inch lbs. (10 Nm).
- Spark plug cables
- Upper intake manifold (plenum) using a new gasket. Torque the bolts to 13 ft. lbs. (18 Nm).
- Plenum support brackets
- EGR tube
- Throttle and speed control cables
- TP sensor and IAC motor electrical connectors
- MAP and IAT sensor electrical connectors
- Air inlet resonator, air inlet hose and air cleaner housing cover
- All remaining electrical connectors
- Air tube connections and tighten them
- Negative battery cable

18. Refill the cooling system.

➡An oil and filter change is recommended whenever a cylinder head has been removed since coolant can get into the oil system.

✳✳ WARNING

Operating the engine without the proper amount and type of engine oil will result in severe engine damage.

19. Start the engine and check for leaks, abnormal noises and vibrations. Bleed the cooling system.

Valve Lash

ADJUSTMENT

2.0L and 2.5L Engines

The engines are equipped with Hydraulic Lash Adjusters (HLAs) which are precision units installed in machined openings in the valve actuating ends of the rocker arms. Valve clearance adjustments are not performed.

2.4L Engine

The valves are actuated by roller cam followers which pivot on stationary Hydraulic Lash Adjusters (HLAs). The HLAs are precision units installed in machined openings of the cam follower. Valve clearance adjustments are not performed.

Starter Motor

REMOVAL & INSTALLATION

2.0L Engine

MANUAL TRANSAXLE

1. Before servicing the vehicle, refer to the precautions in the beginning of this section.

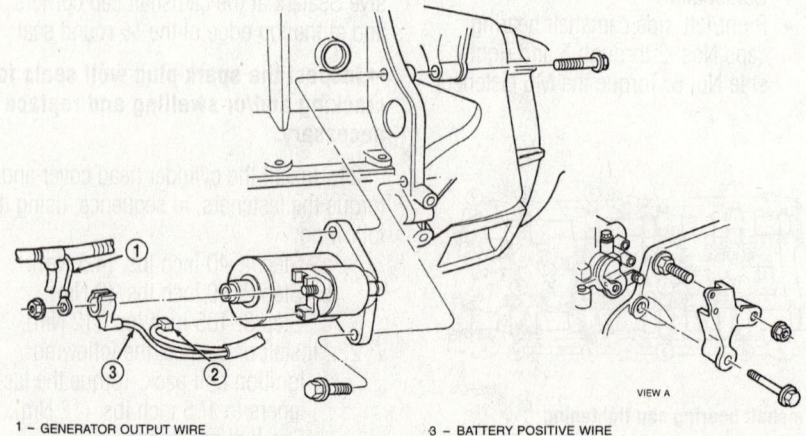

1 – GENERATOR OUTPUT WIRE
2 – PUSH ON SOLENOID CONNNECTOR
3 – BATTERY POSITIVE WIRE

VIEW A

9306FG01

Exploded view of the starter and related components—2.0L engine with a manual transaxle

2. Remove or disconnect the following:
- Negative battery cable from the shock tower
- Air cleaner resonator
- Electrical connectors from the starter
- Starter-to-transaxle bolts
- Starter

To install:
3. Install or connect the following:
- Starter. Torque the bolts to 40 ft. lbs. (54 Nm).
- Electrical connectors to the starter
- Air cleaner resonator
- Negative battery cable to the shock tower

AUTOMATIC TRANSAXLE

1. Before servicing the vehicle, refer to the precautions in the beginning of this section.
2. Remove or disconnect the following:
- Negative battery cable from the shock tower
- Air cleaner resonator

➡**Do not disconnect the TCM electrical connector(s).**

- Transmission Control Module (TCM) and move it aside
- Upper starter-to-transaxle bolt
- Battery cable from the starter
- Solenoid connector by unlocking the red tab and compressing it
- Lower starter-to-transaxle bolt
- Starter

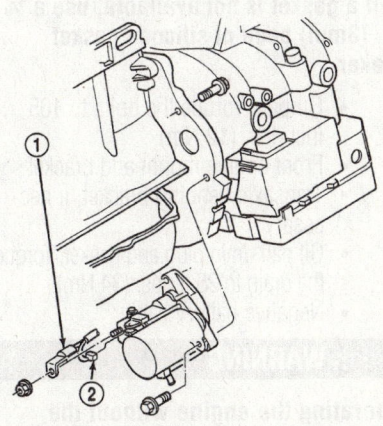

1 – BATTERY POSITIVE WIRE
2 – PUSH ON SOLENOID CONNECTOR

9306FG02

Exploded view of the starter and related components—2.0L engine with an automatic transaxle and 2.4L engine

To install:
3. Install or connect the following:
- Starter
- Lower starter-to-transaxle bolt. Torque the bolt to 40 ft. lbs. (54 Nm).
- Electrical connectors to the starter
- Upper starter-to-transaxle bolt. Torque the bolt to 40 ft. lbs. (54 Nm).
- TCM
- Air cleaner resonator
- Negative battery cable to the shock tower

2.4L Engine

1. Before servicing the vehicle, refer to the precautions in the beginning of this section.
2. Remove or disconnect the following:
- Negative battery cable from the shock tower
- Air cleaner resonator

➡**Do not disconnect the TCM electrical connector(s).**

- Transmission Control Module (TCM) and move it aside
- Upper starter-to-transaxle bolt
- Electrical connectors from the starter
- Lower starter-to-transaxle bolt
- Starter

To install:
3. Install or connect the following:
- Starter
- Lower starter-to-transaxle bolt. Torque the bolt to 40 ft. lbs. (54 Nm).
- Electrical connectors to the starter
- Upper starter-to-transaxle bolt. Torque the bolt to 40 ft. lbs. (54 Nm).
- TCM
- Air cleaner resonator
- Negative battery cable to the shock tower

2.5L Engine

1. Before servicing the vehicle, refer to the precautions in the beginning of this section.
2. Remove or disconnect the following:
- Negative battery cable from the shock tower
- Oil filter
- Electrical connectors from the starter

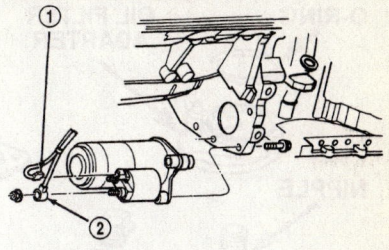

1 – PUSH ON SOLENOID CONNECTOR
2 – BATTERY POSITIVE WIRE

9306FG03

Exploded view of the starter and related components—2.5L engine

- Starter-to-transaxle bolts
- Starter

To install:
3. Install or connect the following:
- Starter. Torque the bolt to 40 ft. lbs. (54 Nm).
- Electrical connectors to the starter
- Oil filter
- Negative battery cable

Oil Pan

REMOVAL & INSTALLATION

2.0L Engine

1. Before servicing the vehicle, refer to the precautions in the beginning of this section.
2. Disconnect the negative battery cable from the left shock tower.

➡**The ground cable is equipped with an insulator grommet which should be placed on the stud to prevent the negative battery cable from accidentally grounding.**

3. Drain the crankcase.
4. Remove or disconnect the following:
- Transaxle bending bracket
- Front engine mount and bracket
- Transaxle inspection cover
- Oil filter and oil filter adapter
- Oil pan and discard the gasket
5. Clean the oil pan and gasket sealing surfaces.
To install:
6. Using a suitable rubber adhesive gasket sealant, apply a 1/8 in. (3mm) bead at the oil pump-to-engine block parting line.
7. Install or connect the following:
- New oil pan gasket

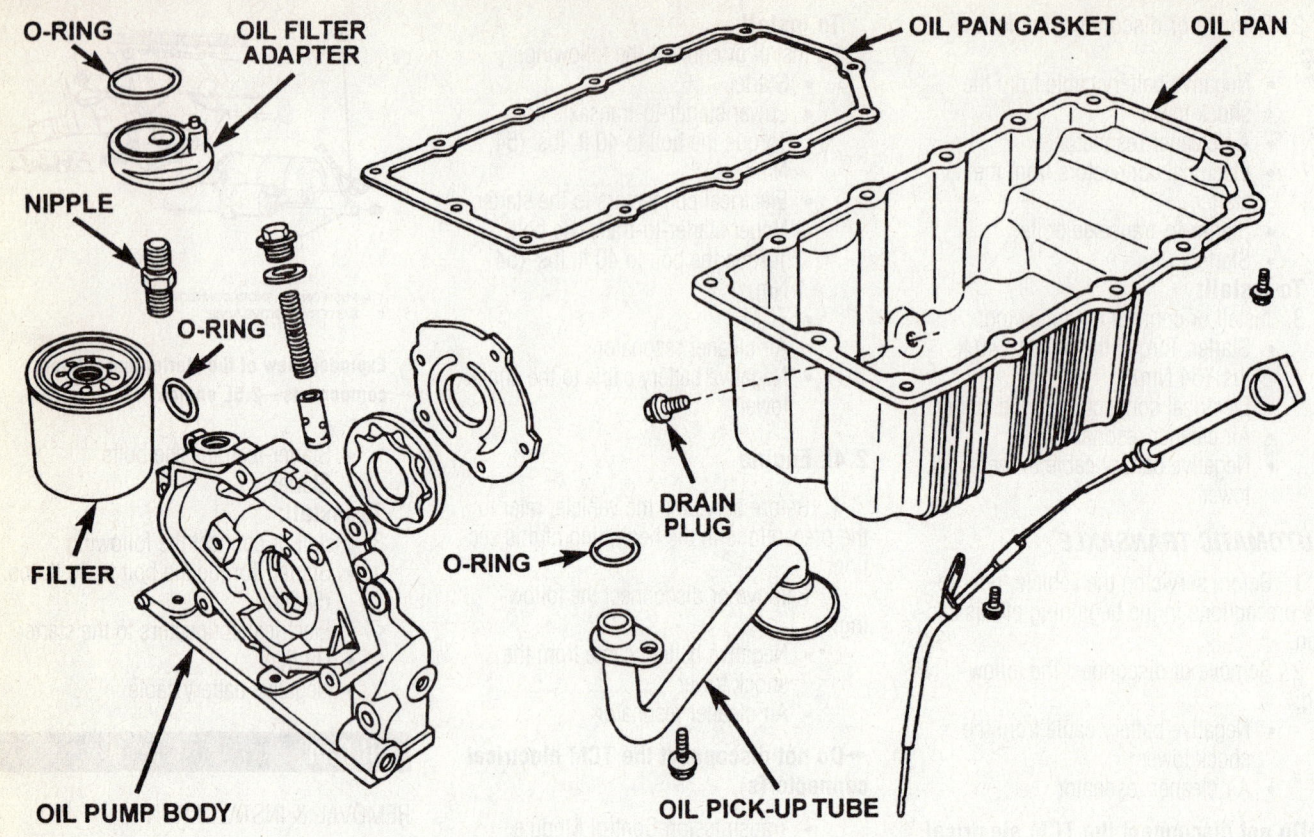

Exploded view of the oil pan and pump assembly—2.0L engine

7922FG35

➡️If a gasket is not available, use a ⅛ in. (3mm) bead of silicone gasket maker.

• Oil pan. Torque the bolts to 105 inch lbs. (12 Nm).

8. Install the oil filter adapter as follows:

a. Seat the O-ring in the adapter groove.

b. Align the locating roll pin into the engine block.

c. Torque the fastener to 60 ft. lbs. (80 Nm).

9. Reinstall a new oil filter as follows:

a. Lubricate the oil filter gasket with engine oil.

b. Be sure the gasket contact surface on the oil filter adapter is smooth, flat and clean of any debris or old pieces of rubber.

c. Install the oil filter and torque it to 15 ft. lbs. (21 Nm).

10. Install or connect the following:

• Transaxle inspection cover
• Front engine mount and bracket
• Transaxle bending bracket
• Oil pan drain plug and gasket. Torque the plug to 25 ft. lbs. (34 Nm).
• Negative battery cable

⁂ WARNING

Operating the engine without the proper amount and type of engine oil will result in severe engine damage.

11. Refill the crankcase.
12. Start the engine and check for leaks.

2.4L Engine

1. Before servicing the vehicle, refer to the precautions in the beginning of this section.

2. Disconnect the negative battery cable from the left shock tower.

➡️The ground cable is equipped with an insulator grommet which should be placed on the stud to prevent the negative battery cable from accidentally grounding.

3. Raise and safely support the vehicle.

4. Drain the crankcase.

5. Remove or disconnect the following:

• Transaxle bending bracket, if necessary
• Front engine mount and bracket

• Oil pan and discard the gasket

To install:

6. Using a suitable gasket sealant apply a ⅛ in. (3mm) bead at the oil pump-to-engine block parting line.

7. Install or connect the following:

• New gasket.

➡️If a gasket is not available, use a ⅛ in. (3mm) bead of silicone gasket maker.

• Oil pan. Torque the bolts to 105 inch lbs. (12 Nm).
• Front engine mount and bracket
• Transaxle bending bracket, if necessary
• Oil pan drain plug and gasket. Torque the drain to 25 ft. lbs. (34 Nm).
• Negative battery cable

⁂ WARNING

Operating the engine without the proper amount and type of engine oil will result in severe engine damage.

8. Refill the crankcase. A filter change is recommended.

9. Start the engine and check for leaks.

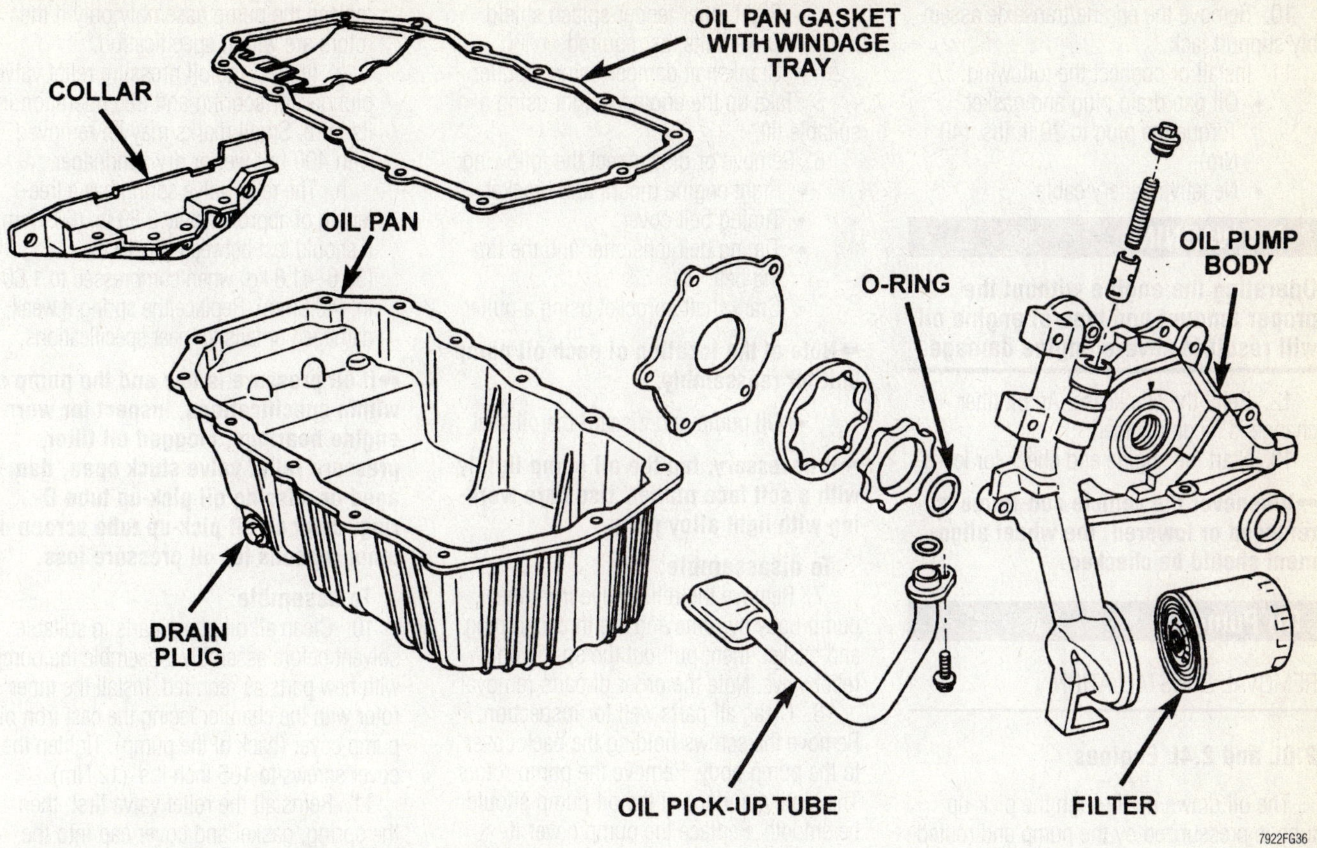

COLLAR

OIL PAN GASKET WITH WINDAGE TRAY

OIL PAN

O-RING

OIL PUMP BODY

DRAIN PLUG

OIL PICK-UP TUBE

FILTER

7922FG36

Exploded view of the oil pan and pump assembly—2.4L engine

2.5L Engine

1. Before servicing the vehicle, refer to the precautions in the beginning of this section.

2. Disconnect the negative battery cable from the left shock tower.

➡**The ground cable is equipped with an insulator grommet which should be placed on the stud to prevent the negative battery cable from accidentally grounding.**

3. Drain the crankcase.

4. Place a suitable support jack under the engine/transaxle assembly at the transaxle to prevent it from rotating.

5. Remove the engine support module as follows:

- Rear mount through-bolt
- Support module-to-crossmember bolts
- Upper mounting bolt from the rear support strut bracket
- Front support module-to-lower radiator support member bolts
- Radiator/cooling fan assembly and support it
- Lower radiator support member

- Front engine mount through-bolt
- Engine support module

6. Remove or disconnect the following:

- Engine oil dipstick tube and dipstick
- Starter motor
- Engine-to-transaxle struts
- Transaxle inspection cover
- Oil pan and discard the gasket

To install:

➡**Oil pan-to-engine block sealing is provided by using silicone adhesive sealant.**

7. Apply a continuous ⁵⁄₃₂ in. (4mm) bead of silicone adhesive sealant to the oil pan gasket surface. Be sure to circle all mounting bolt holes as well. Install the oil pan within a 10 minute period of applying the gasket material to ensure proper sealing.

8. Install or connect the following:

- Oil pan using a new gasket. Torque the bolts to 53 inch lbs. (6 Nm).
- Transaxle inspection cover
- Engine-to-transaxle struts
- Starter motor
- Engine oil dipstick tube and dipstick

9. Install the engine support module as follows:

- Engine support module
- Front mount through-bolt, do not tighten
- Lower radiator support
- Engine support module-to-lower radiator support bolts
- Upper rear support strut bracket bolt
- Rear mount through-bolt. Torque the bolt to 45 ft. lbs. (61 Nm).
- Front mount through-bolt. Torque the bolt to 45 ft. lbs. (61 Nm).

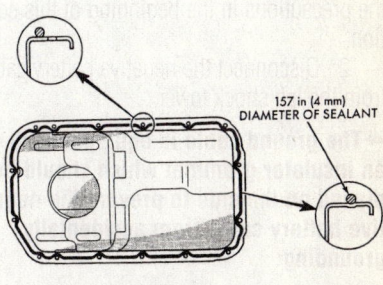

157 in (4 mm) DIAMETER OF SEALANT

7922FG37

To ensure an adequate seal, apply sealer as shown—2.5L engine

Refer to Section 1 for engine rebuilding specifications

10. Remove the engine/transaxle assembly support jack.

11. Install or connect the following:
- Oil pan drain plug and gasket. Torque the plug to 29 ft. lbs. (40 Nm).
- Negative battery cable

❄❄ WARNING

Operating the engine without the proper amount and type of engine oil will result in severe engine damage.

12. Refill the crankcase. An oil filter change is recommended.

13. Start the engine and check for leaks.

➥Whenever the vehicle sub-frame is removed or lowered, the wheel alignment should be checked.

Oil Pump

REMOVAL & INSTALLATION

2.0L and 2.4L Engines

The oil drawn up through the pick-up tube is pressurized by the pump and routed through the full flow filter to the main oil galley running the length of the cylinder block. The oil pick-up, pump and check valve provide oil flow to the main oil gallery. A vertical hole at the No. 5 bulkhead routes pressurized oil through a restrictor up past a cylinder head bolt to an oil galley running the length of the cylinder head. The camshaft journals are slotted to allow pressurized oil to pass into the bearing cap cavities. Small holes in the bearing caps direct oil to the camshaft lobes.

It is necessary to remove the oil pan, oil pick-up and oil pump housing to service the oil pump rotors. The oil pump pressure relief valve can be serviced without removing the oil pan and oil pick-up tube.

1. Before servicing the vehicle, refer to the precautions in the beginning of this section.

2. Disconnect the negative battery cable from the left shock tower.

➥The ground cable is equipped with an insulator grommet which should be placed on the stud to prevent the negative battery cable from accidentally grounding.

3. Drain the crankcase.

4. Remove or disconnect the following:
- Oil pan and discard the gasket
- Oil pump pick-up tube and O-ring

- Right inner fender splash shield
- Drive belts, as required
- Crankshaft damper using a puller

5. Take up the engine weight using a suitable lift.

6. Remove or disconnect the following:
- Right engine mount and bracket
- Timing belt cover
- Timing belt tensioner and the timing belt
- Crankshaft sprocket using a puller

➥Note of the location of each oil pump bolt for reassembly.

- Oil pump and discard the oil seal

➥If necessary, tap the oil pump lightly with a soft face mallet. Use care working with light alloy parts.

To disassemble:

7. Remove the relief valve from the pump body by removing the threaded plug and gasket; then, pull out the spring and relief valve. Note the order of parts removal.

8. Clean all parts well for inspection. Remove the screws holding the back cover to the pump body. Remove the pump rotors. The mating surface of the oil pump should be smooth. Replace the pump cover if scratched or grooved.

9. Inspect the pump using the following procedure:

a. Lay a straightedge across the pump cover surface. If a 0.003 in. (0.076mm) feeler gauge can be inserted between the cover and straightedge, the cover should be replaced.

b. Measure the thickness and diameter of the outer rotor. If the outer rotor thickness measures 0.301 in. (7.6mm) or less, or if the diameter is 3.148 in. (80mm) or less, replace the outer rotor.

c. If the inner rotor measures 0.301 in. (7.6mm) or less, replace the inner rotor.

d. Slide the outer rotor into the pump housing, press to one side with your fingers and measure the clearance between the rotor and housing. If the measurement is 0.015 in. (0.38mm) or more, replace the oil pump housing only if the outer rotor is in specification.

e. Install the inner rotor into the pump housing. If the clearance between the inner and outer rotors is 0.008 in. (0.20mm) or more, replace both rotors.

f. Place a straightedge across the face of the pump housing between the bolt holes. If a feeler gauge of 0.004 in. (0.10mm) or more can be inserted between the rotors and straightedge,

replace the pump assembly only if the rotors are within specification.

g. Inspect the oil pressure relief valve plunger for scoring and free operation in its bore. Small marks may be removed with 400 grit wet or dry sandpaper.

h. The relief valve spring has a free-length of approximately 2.39 in. (60.7mm). It should test between 18–19 lbs. (39.6–41.8 kg) when compressed to 1.60 in. (40.6mm). Replace the spring if weak, damaged or fails to meet specifications.

➥If oil pressure is low and the pump is within specifications, inspect for worn engine bearings, clogged oil filter, pressure relief valve stuck open, damaged or missing oil pick-up tube O-ring, clogged oil pick-up tube screen or other reasons for oil pressure loss.

To assemble:

10. Clean all oil pump parts in suitable solvent before assembly. Assemble the pump with new parts as required. Install the inner rotor with the chamfer facing the cast iron oil pump cover (back of the pump). Tighten the cover screws to 105 inch lbs. (12 Nm).

11. Reinstall the relief valve first, then the spring, gasket and cover cap into the pump body. Note that installing the spring first will seriously damage the engine. The relief valve goes in first. Tighten the cover cap to 30 ft. lbs. (41 Nm) for 2.0L engine or 40 ft. lbs. (55 Nm) for 2.4L engine.

12. Prime the oil pump before installation by filling the rotor cavity with clean engine oil.

13. Insert a new oil ring seal to the oil pump counterbore on the pump body discharge passage. Apply silicone gasket material to the oil pump body flange. This material cures in the absence of air when squeezed between 2 flat machined metal surfaces. For this reason, the mating surfaces of both the pump body and the engine block must be spotlessly clean so all air will be expelled when the parts are bolted together and tightened. Install the pump slowly onto the crankshaft aligning the oil pump rotor flats with the flats on the crankshaft until seated to the engine block. Tighten the fasteners to 21 ft. lbs. (28 Nm).

To install:

14. Install or connect the following:
- New front oil pump seal, spring side facing the engine, until it is flush with the cover
- Crankshaft sprocket, using a special tool to draw it onto the crankshaft
- Timing belt, by aligning the timing marks

※※ WARNING

Failure to properly align the timing marks will result in severe engine damage.

- Timing covers
- Crankshaft damper using an installer tool
- Oil pump pick-up tube and O-ring. Torque the screw to 21 ft. lbs. (28 Nm).

15. Clean the oil pan well and be sure the gasket rails are in good condition. Use Mopar® Silicone Rubber Adhesive Sealant or equivalent sealer at the oil pump-to-engine block parting line.

16. Install or connect the following:

- Oil pan using a new gasket. Torque the bolts to 105 inch lbs. (12 Nm).
- New oil filter
- Right inner fender splash shield
- Drive belts and adjust them
- Engine mount and bracket, as required
- Negative battery cable

17. Refill the crankcase and cooling system.

18. Test run the vehicle to check for leaks. An oil pressure gauge should be installed to verify proper engine oil pressure.

2.5L Engine

The oil pump assembly is mounted on the timing belt end of the cylinder block with the inner pump rotor indexed and installed on the crankshaft nose. The oil pump case also retains the crankshaft front oil seal and provides oil pan front end closure.

Oil pressure can be checked with a mechanical oil pressure gauge installed at the oil switch location. Oil pressure should be 6 psi (41.4 kPa) at idle and 35–75 psi (241.3–517.1 kPa) at 3000 rpm with the engine at operating temperature.

※※ WARNING

If an oil pressure problem is suspected or if oil pressure is zero at idle, do not run the engine up to 3000 rpm in an attempt to raise oil pressure or the engine will be severely damaged.

Because the oil pump is driven off the crankshaft, the timing belt must be removed to access the pump. Use care to properly align all valve timing marks.

1. Before servicing the vehicle, refer to the precautions in the beginning of this section.

2. Disconnect the negative battery cable from the left shock tower.

➡ **The ground cable is equipped with an insulator grommet which should be placed on the stud to prevent the negative battery cable from accidentally grounding.**

3. Remove or disconnect the following:
- Drive belts
- Accessories
4. Drain the cooling system.
- Radiator and cooling fan
5. Raise and safely support the vehicle. Drain the crankcase.
- Right inner splash shield
- Crankshaft damper
6. Support the engine.
7. Remove or disconnect the following:
- Right engine mount and bracket
- Timing belt upper and lower covers

- Timing belt and tensioner
- Crankshaft sprocket using a puller
- Oil pump
8. Inspect the oil pump case for damage and remove the rear cover.

9. Remove the pump rotors and inspect the inside of the case for excessive wear.

10. Check that the oil relief plunger slides smoothly and check for a broken spring.

To install:

11. Clean all parts well. Be sure the block and pump surfaces are clean and free of old sealer.

12. Assemble the pump using new parts as required with clean oil. Align the marks on the inner and outer rotors when assembling.

13. Reinstall the pump back cover and tighten the screws to 88 inch lbs. (10 Nm).

14. Reinstall the pump relief valve, spring, gasket and valve cap. Tighten the valve cap to 30–33 ft. lbs. (41–44 Nm).

15. Prime the pump before installation by filling the rotor cavity with clean engine oil.

16. Apply Mopar® Gasket Maker or equivalent sealer to the pump.

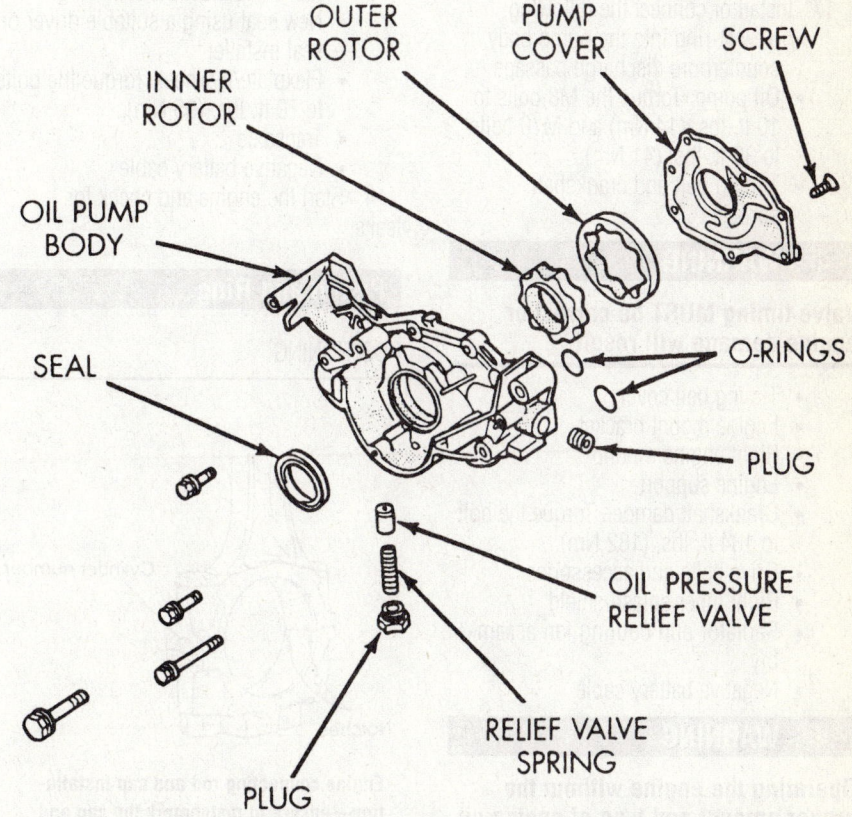

Exploded view of the oil pump assembly. Note the different bolt lengths—2.5L engine

7922FG38

For engine torque specifications, refer to Section 1 of this manual

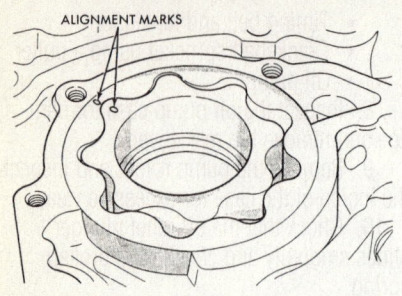

Aligning the matchmarks for the inner and outer rotor of the oil pump—2.5L engine

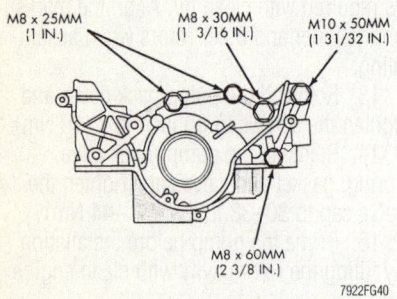

Oil pump mounting bolt locations and dimensions—2.5L engine

17. Install or connect the following:
- New O-ring into the pump body counterbore discharge passage
- Oil pump. Torque the M8 bolts to 10 ft. lbs. (14 Nm) and M10 bolts to 30 ft. lbs. (41 Nm).
- Timing belt and crankshaft sprocket

❄❄ WARNING

Valve timing MUST be correct or engine damage will result.

- Timing belt cover
- Engine mount bracket
- Right engine mount
- Engine support
- Crankshaft damper. Torque the bolt to 134 ft. lbs. (182 Nm).
- Drive belts and accessories
- Right inner splash shield
- Radiator and cooling fan assembly
- Negative battery cable

❄❄ WARNING

Operating the engine without the proper amount and type of engine oil will result in severe engine damage.

18. Refill the cooling system. Install a new oil filter and refill the crankcase.
19. Road test the vehicle. Check for proper operation as well as leaks.

Rear Main Seal

REMOVAL & INSTALLATION

1. Before servicing the vehicle, refer to the precautions in the beginning of this section.
2. Remove or disconnect the following:
- Negative battery cable from the left shock tower

➡**The ground cable is equipped with an insulator grommet which should be placed on the stud to prevent the negative battery cable from accidentally grounding.**

- Transaxle
- Flexplate/flywheel
- Rear crankshaft oil seal using a flat-bladed prying tool

To install:

➡**When installing the seal there is no need to lubricate the sealing surface.**

3. Install or connect the following:
- New seal using a suitable driver or seal installer
- Flexplate/flywheel. Torque the bolts to 70 ft. lbs. (95 Nm).
- Transaxle
- Negative battery cable
4. Start the engine and check for leaks.

Piston and Ring

POSITIONING

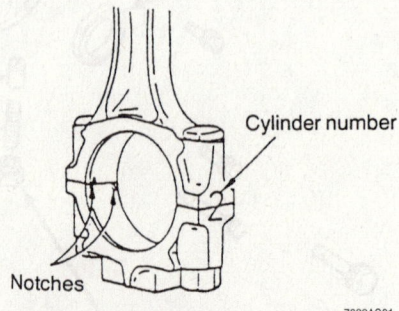

Engine connecting rod and cap installation—ensure to matchmark the cap and rod prior to disassembly

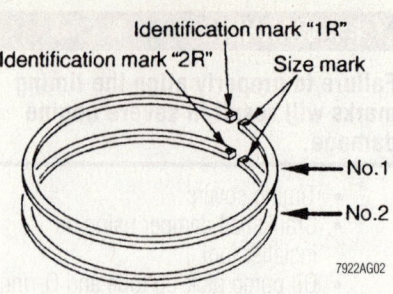

Piston ring identification mark locations

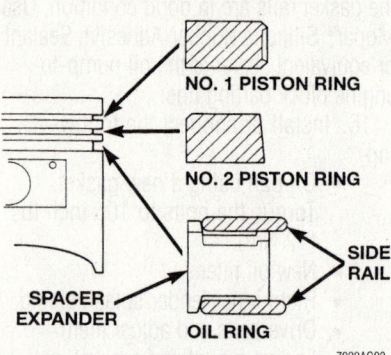

Piston ring orientation—2.0L, 2.4L and 2.5L engines

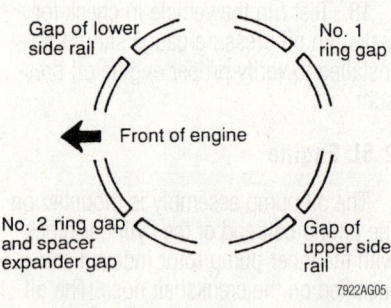

Piston ring end-gap spacing—2.0L and 2.4L engines

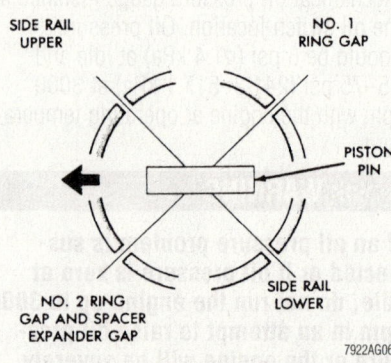

Piston ring end-gap spacing—2.5L engine

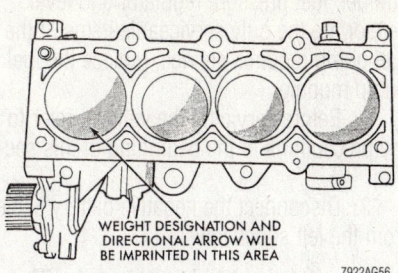

Piston positioning. The arrow or weight marking (L or H) must face toward the timing belt side of the engine—2.0L and 2.4L engines

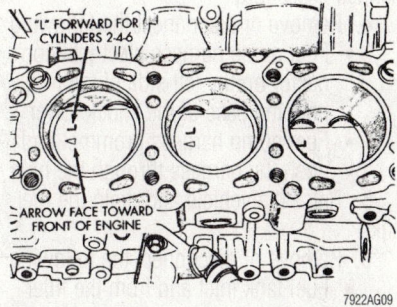

Piston positioning mark locations—2.5L engine

FUEL SYSTEM

Fuel System Service Precautions

Safety is the most important factor when performing not only fuel system maintenance but any type of maintenance. Failure to conduct maintenance and repairs in a safe manner may result in serious personal injury or death. Maintenance and testing of the vehicle's fuel system components can be accomplished safely and effectively by adhering to the following rules and guidelines.

• To avoid the possibility of fire and personal injury, always disconnect the negative battery cable unless the repair or test procedure requires that battery voltage be applied.

• Always relieve the fuel system pressure prior to disconnecting any fuel system component (injector, fuel rail, pressure regulator, etc.), fitting or fuel line connection. Exercise extreme caution whenever relieving fuel system pressure to avoid exposing skin, face and eyes to fuel spray. Please be advised

that fuel under pressure may penetrate the skin or any part of the body that it contacts.

• Always place a shop towel or cloth around the fitting or connection prior to loosening to absorb any excess fuel due to spillage. Ensure that all fuel spillage (should it occur) is quickly removed from engine surfaces. Ensure that all fuel soaked cloths or towels are deposited into a suitable waste container.

• Always keep a dry chemical (Class B) fire extinguisher near the work area.

• Do not allow fuel spray or fuel vapors to come into contact with a spark or open flame.

• Always use a back-up wrench when loosening and tightening fuel line connection fittings. This will prevent unnecessary stress and torsion to fuel line piping.

• Always replace worn fuel fitting O-rings with new. Do not substitute fuel hose or equivalent, where fuel pipe is installed.

Fuel System Pressure

RELIEVING

2.0L and 2.4L Engines

1. Before servicing the vehicle, refer to the fuel system precautions and to the precautions in the beginning of this section.
2. Remove or disconnect the following:
   • Negative battery cable from the left shock tower

➡**The ground cable is equipped with an insulator grommet which should be placed on the stud to prevent the negative battery cable from accidentally grounding.**

   • Fuel filler cap
   • Fuel pressure test port cap, from the fuel rail

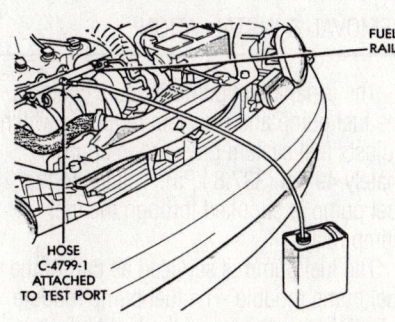

Fuel pressure test port location—2.0L and 2.4L engines

3. Place the open end of Fuel Pressure Release Hose special tool number C-4799–1 into an approved gasoline container. Connect the other end of hose C-4799–1 to the fuel pressure test port. Fuel pressure will bleed off through the hose into the gasoline container.

2.5L Engine

1. Before servicing the vehicle, refer to the fuel system precautions and to the precautions in the beginning of this section.
2. Disconnect the fuel rail electrical harness from the engine harness. This is connector C165, a black plastic connector located at the right rear of the intake manifold.
3. Circuit A142 supplies voltage for the fuel injectors while the Powertrain Control Module (PCM) controls the ground for each injector. Connect a jumper wire to the terminal for Circuit A142 (18 Ga. wire, Dark Green with Orange tracer, from ASD relay).
4. Connect the other end of the jumper wire to a 12 volt power source.
5. Connect one end of a second jumper wire to a ground source.
6. Momentarily ground each of the injectors by connecting the other end of the jumper wire to the injector terminal in the harness connector. Repeat this procedure for 2 or 3 injectors.

✳✳ WARNING

Do not attempt to start the engine for several minutes to avoid hydrostatic lock.

Fuel Filter

REMOVAL & INSTALLATION

The fuel delivery system contains a replaceable inline filter. The fuel filter mounts to the frame above the rear of the fuel tank. The fuel tank assembly must be loosened and lowered slightly to access the filter. The inlet and outlet tubes are permanently attached to the filter. Please note that the fuel system pressure must be relieved before servicing fuel system components. In addition, quick-disconnect fittings are used on fuel line connections. When the tubes are fully connected, the locking ears and the fuel tube shoulder are visible in the windows of the connector.

1. Before servicing the vehicle, refer to

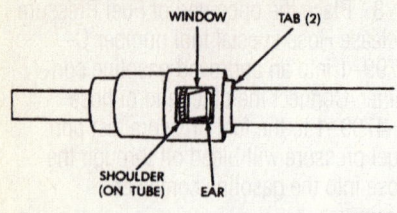

Be sure the shoulder and locking tabs are visible through the window of the connector when attached

the precautions in the beginning of this section.

2. Disconnect the negative battery cable from the left shock tower.

➡ **The ground cable is equipped with an insulator grommet which should be placed on the stud to prevent the negative battery cable from accidentally grounding.**

3. Relieve the fuel system pressure using the recommended procedure.

4. From inside the trunk, disconnect the fuel pump module wiring jumper from the main body harness. The 4-pin connector is located under the trunk mat on the left side of the trunk near the base of the shock tower. Locate the body grommet for the jumper near the base of the rear seat. Push the grommet out and feed the jumper completely through the hole in the body.

5. Remove the fuel cap slowly to release tank pressure.

6. Raise and safely support the vehicle.

7. Locate the drain plug on the bottom left of the fuel tank. Place an approved fuel container with a capacity of at least 16 gallons, under the drain plug. Remove the plug and drain the fuel tank. When finished draining, install the plug since there will be 1–2 gallons of fuel remaining. Tighten the drain plug to 32 inch lbs. (3.6 Nm).

8. Remove or disconnect the following:
- Driver's side fuel tank strap
- Passenger's side fuel tank strap loosen it

➡ **Allow the tank to lower until the fuel tank neck touches the rear suspension crossmember.**

✳✳ CAUTION

Wrap shop towels around the fuel hoses to catch any gasoline spillage.

- Fuel line quick-disconnect fittings from the fuel pump module. Squeeze fuel filter hose connector

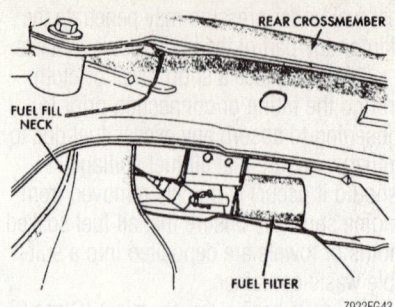

Fuel filter mounting location

releasing tabs and detach the fuel lines.
- Fuel filter

To install:

➡ **The fuel supply (to filter) tube and the return tube (to fuel pump module) are permanently attached to the fuel filter. The ends of the fuel supply and return tubes have different size quick-disconnect fittings. The large quick-disconnect fitting attaches to the large nipple (supply side) on the fuel pump module. The smaller quick-disconnect fitting attaches the small nipple (return side) on the fuel pump module.**

9. Lubricate the fuel filter nipples with engine oil.

10. Install or connect the following:
- Fuel tubes
- Fuel tank raise it into position
- Fuel tank straps. Torque the bolts to 17 ft. lbs. (23 Nm).

➡ **Be sure the fuel pump module electrical harness grommet is installed in the body as the tank is raised into position.**

- Fuel pump module connector
- Negative battery cable

11. Refill the fuel tank.

Fuel Pump

REMOVAL & INSTALLATION

The in-tank fuel pump module contains the fuel pump and pressure regulator which adjusts fuel system pressure to approximately 49 psi (337.8 kPa). Voltage to the fuel pump is supplied through the fuel pump relay.

The fuel pump is serviced as part of the fuel pump module. The fuel pump module is installed in the top of the fuel tank and contains the electric fuel pump, fuel pump reservoir, inlet strainer fuel gauge sending unit, fuel supply and return line connections and the pressure regulator. The inlet

strainer, fuel pressure regulator and level sensor are the only serviceable items. If the fuel pump requires service, replace the fuel pump module.

1. Before servicing the vehicle, refer to the precautions in the beginning of this section.

2. Disconnect the negative battery cable from the left shock tower.

➡ **The ground cable is equipped with an insulator grommet which should be placed on the stud to prevent the negative battery cable from accidentally grounding.**

3. Remove the fuel filler cap and relieve the fuel system pressure using the recommended procedure.

4. Remove or disconnect the following:
- Fuel pump harness electrical connector on the left side of the trunk near the base of the shock tower
- Fuel pump harness grommet and push the harness through the hole

5. Raise the vehicle and drain the fuel tank.

6. Remove or disconnect the following:
- Fuel tank inlet and from the filler hose
- Fuel tank straps. Support with a jack prior to loosening the straps.

7. Carefully lower the tank.

8. Clean the top of the tank to remove any loose dirt.

9. Remove or disconnect the following:
- Fuel lines from the fuel pump module
- Fuel pump locknut using Spanner wrench tool 6856

✳✳ CAUTION

The fuel reservoir of the fuel pump module does not empty out when the tank is drained. The fuel in the reservoir may spill out when the module is removed.

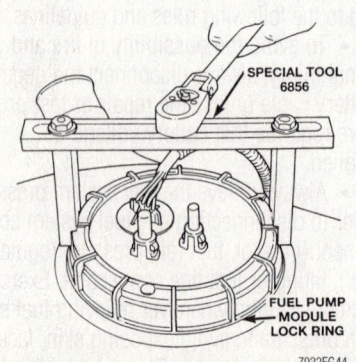

Removing the fuel pump module lock ring using special tool 6856

- Fuel pump
- Fuel tank O-ring and discard it

To install:

10. Thoroughly clean all parts. Wipe the seal area of the tank clean.

11. Install or connect the following:
   - New O-ring onto the fuel tank
   - Fuel pump module in the tank

➡**Be sure the alignment tab on the underside of the pump module flange sits in the corresponding notch in the fuel tank.**

- Locking ring. Torque it to 40–45 ft. lbs. (54–61 Nm), using Spanner Wrench tool 6856.
- Fuel tank assembly
- Negative battery cable

12. Refill the fuel tank.

13. Turn the ignition switch **ON** to pressurize the system. Check the fuel system for leaks.

Fuel Injector

REMOVAL & INSTALLATION

2.0L and 2.4L Engines

1. Before servicing the vehicle, refer to the precautions in the beginning of this section.

2. Disconnect the negative battery cable from the left shock tower.

➡**The ground cable is equipped with an insulator grommet which should be placed on the stud to prevent the negative battery cable from accidentally grounding.**

3. Relieve the fuel system pressure using the recommended procedure.

4. Remove or disconnect the following:
   - Fuel supply line quick quick-connect fitting from the fuel rail
   - Fuel injector electrical connectors
   - Fuel rail from the intake manifold

➡**Cover the fuel injector holes in the intake manifold.**

- Fuel injector clip
- Fuel injector(s) from the fuel rail and discard the O-rings

To install:

5. Install or connect the following:
   - Fuel injector to the fuel rail using new O-rings lubricated with engine oil
   - Fuel injector clip

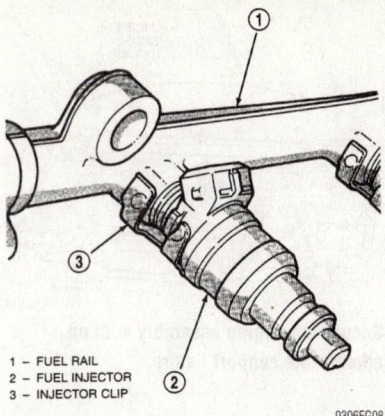

1 – FUEL RAIL
2 – FUEL INJECTOR
3 – INJECTOR CLIP

9306FG08

View of the fuel injector—2.0L, 2.4L and 2.5L engines

- Fuel rail. Torque the screws to 14–19 ft. lbs. (19.5–25.5 Nm).
- Fuel injector electrical connectors
- Fuel supply line quick quick-connect fitting to the fuel rail
- Negative battery cable

6. Use a Diagnostic Readout Box (DRB) scan tool Automatic Shutdown (ASD) fuel system test to pressurize the fuel system. Check for leaks.

2.5L Engine

1. Before servicing the vehicle, refer to the precautions in the beginning of this section.

2. Disconnect the negative battery cable from the left shock tower.

➡**The ground cable is equipped with an insulator grommet which should be placed on the stud to prevent the negative battery cable from accidentally grounding.**

3. Relieve the fuel system pressure using the recommended procedure.

4. Remove or disconnect the following:
   - Fuel supply line quick quick-connect fitting from the fuel rail

1 – FUEL RAIL BOLTS

9306FG07

View of the fuel rail assembly—2.5L engine

- Upper intake manifold plenum and discard the gasket
- Fuel injector electrical connectors
- Fuel rail from the intake manifold

➡**Cover the intake manifold openings to keep dirt from entering the system.**

- Fuel injector clip
- Fuel injector(s) from the fuel rail and discard the O-rings

To install:

5. Install or connect the following:
   - Fuel injector to the fuel rail using new O-rings lubricated with engine oil
   - Fuel injector clip
   - Fuel rail. Torque the bolts to 8 ft. lbs. (12 Nm).

➡**Be sure the spacers are located under the fuel rail.**

- Fuel injector electrical connectors
- Fuel supply line quick quick-connect fitting to the fuel rail
- Upper intake manifold plenum using a new gasket. Torque the bolts to 13 ft. lbs. (18 Nm).
- Throttle cables
- Sensor electrical connectors
- Negative battery cable

6. Use a Diagnostic Readout Box (DRB) scan tool Automatic Shutdown (ASD) fuel system test to pressurize the fuel system. Check for leaks.

DRIVE TRAIN

Transaxle Assembly

REMOVAL & INSTALLATION

Manual

✳✳ WARNING

If the vehicle is going to be rolled on its wheels while the transaxle is out of the vehicle, obtain 2 outer CV-joints to install in the hubs. If the vehicle is rolled without the proper torque applied to the front wheel bearings, the bearings will no longer be usable.

1. Before servicing the vehicle, refer to the precautions in the beginning of this section.

2. Remove or disconnect the following:
- Negative battery cable from the left shock tower.

➡ **The ground cable is equipped with an insulator grommet which should be placed on the stud to prevent the negative battery cable from accidentally grounding.**

- Air cleaner and intake hoses
- Clutch housing vent cap
- Clutch cable from the bell housing

✶✶ WARNING

Using equal force, pry up on both sides of the shifter cable isolator bushings to avoid damaging the cable isolator bushing.

- Selector lever and crossover cables from the transaxle
- Shift cable mounting bracket from the transaxle
- Accelerator cables from the throttle body
- Accelerator cable bracket from the throttle body
- Upper starter-to-throttle body support bracket bolt
- Upper bell housing-to-throttle body support bracket stud nut
- Throttle body support bracket
- Left transaxle mount upper bolts
- Upper bell housing bolts
- Vehicle Speed Sensor (VSS)
- Back-up light electrical connector from the transaxle

3. Install an engine support fixture tool and support the engine.

4. Remove or disconnect the following:
- Front wheels
- Halfshafts
- Lower splash shield/battery cover from the left side
- Lower bracket bolts, from the left transaxle mount
- Engine-to-lower crossbar bolts
- Front steel engine mount bracket
- 3 front aluminum engine mount bracket bolts
- Starter
- Rear transaxle mount bracket
- Transaxle-to-rear lateral bending strut from engine/transaxle assembly
- Transaxle bell housing cover

5. Using a transaxle jack, support the transaxle.

6. Rotate the engine clockwise to gain access to the driveplate clutch bolts.

7. Remove or disconnect the following:
- Driveplate clutch bolts

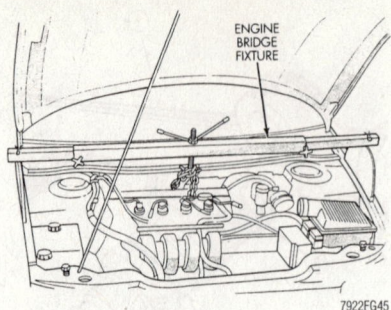

Secure the engine assembly with an appropriate support fixture

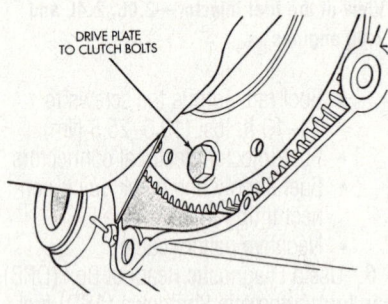

Remove the driveplate clutch bolts—rotate the engine clockwise to advance to the next bolt

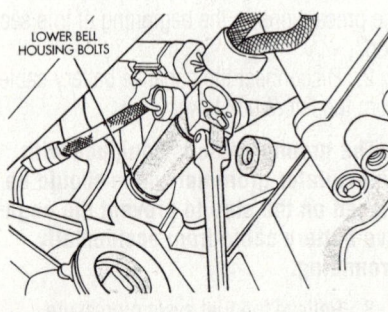

Removing the lower engine-to-transaxle mounting bolts

- Lower engine-to-transaxle bolts
- Transaxle

8. To prepare the vehicle for rolling, support the engine with a suitable support or reinstall the front motor mount to the engine. Then, reinstall the ball joints to the steering knuckle and install the retaining bolt. Install the obtained outer CV-joints to the hubs, install the washers and tighten the axle nuts to 180 ft. lbs. (244 Nm). The vehicle may now be safely rolled.

To install:

9. Install or connect the following:
- Transaxle. Torque the transaxle-to-engine bolts to 70 ft. lbs. (95 Nm).

- Driveplate clutch bolts
- Lower engine-to-transaxle bolts. Torque the bolts to 70 ft. lbs. (95 Nm).
- Transaxle bell housing cover. Torque bolts to 9 ft. lbs. (12 Nm).
- Transaxle-to-rear lateral bending strut to the engine/transaxle assembly. Torque the bolt to 40 ft. lbs. (54 Nm).
- Rear transaxle mount bracket. Torque the bolts to 40 ft. lbs. (54 Nm).
- Starter
- 3 front aluminum engine mount bracket bolts. Torque the bolts to 40 ft. lbs. (54 Nm).
- Front steel engine mount bracket. Torque the bolt to 45 ft. lbs. (61 Nm).
- Engine-to-lower crossbar bolts
- Lower bracket bolts to the left transaxle mount. Torque the bolts to 40 ft. lbs. (54 Nm).
- Lower splash shield/battery cover to the left side
- Halfshafts
- Front wheels

10. Remove engine support fixture tool.

11. Install or connect the following:
- Back-up light electrical connector, to the transaxle
- VSS sensor
- Upper bell housing bolts. Torque the bolts to 70 ft. lbs. (95 Nm).
- Left transaxle mount upper bolts. Torque the bolts to 40 ft. lbs. (54 Nm).
- Throttle body support bracket
- Upper bell housing-to-throttle body support bracket stud nut. Torque the nut to 32 ft. lbs. (43 Nm).

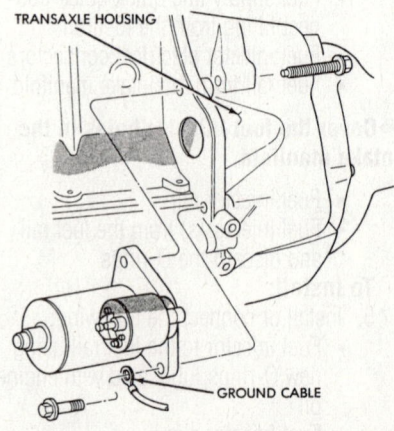

Be sure to connect the ground cable at the starter

- Upper starter-to-throttle body support bracket bolt
- Accelerator cable bracket to the throttle body
- Accelerator cables to the throttle body
- Shift cable mounting bracket to the transaxle
- Selector lever and crossover cables to the transaxle
- Clutch cable to the bell housing
- Clutch housing vent cap
- Air cleaner and intake hoses
- Negative battery cable

12. Check to be sure that all fasteners are tightened and connections made.

13. Refill the transaxle.

14. Check the transaxle for proper operation. Be sure the reverse lights turn **ON** when in reverse.

Automatic

※※ **WARNING**

If the vehicle is going to be rolled on its wheels while the transaxle is out of the vehicle, obtain 2 outer CV-joints to install to the hubs. If the vehicle is rolled without the proper torque applied to the front wheel bearings, the bearings will no longer be usable.

1. Before servicing the vehicle, refer to the precautions in the beginning of this section.

2. Drain the transaxle.

3. Remove or disconnect the following:

- Negative battery cable from the left shock tower.

➡**The ground cable is equipped with an insulator grommet which should be placed on the stud to prevent the nega-**

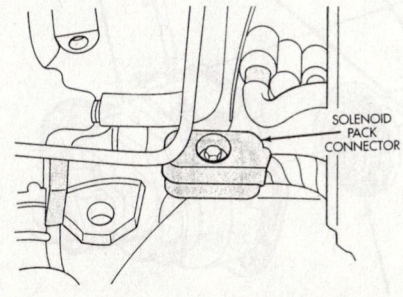

Location of the transaxle solenoid assembly 8-way connector and retaining bolt

7922FG49

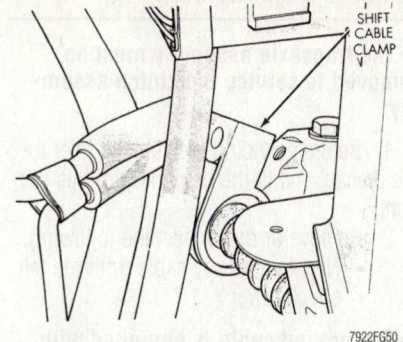

Removing the shift cable and clamp

7922FG50

tive battery cable from accidentally grounding.

- Air cleaner duct
- Transmission Control Module (TCM)
- Solenoid pack electrical connec-tor
- Dipstick tube from the transaxle
- Transaxle cooler lines
- Shift lever cable from the transaxle lever

4. Using an engine support fixture tool, support the engine assembly.

5. Remove or disconnect the following:

- Upper transaxle mount top bolts from the left side
- Front wheels
- Lower splash shields from both sides
- Exhaust pipe from the exhaust manifold
- Upper transaxle mount remaining bolts from the left side
- Engine oil filter
- Starter
- Front engine mount bracket
- Rear mount bracket through-bolt
- Centermember bolts
- Rear mount bracket
- Radiator lower crossmember
- Both lateral bending strut brackets
- Flexplate cover

6. Matchmark the converter-to-flexplate location. Rotate the crankshaft clockwise to align the converter bolts.

7. Remove or disconnect the following:

- Converter-to-flexplate bolts
- Crankshaft Position (CKP) sensor, if equipped
- Transaxle electrical connectors
- Right side steering gear and K-frame bolts
- Sway bar mounts

8. Using a transmission jack and a safety chain, secure the transaxle and support it.

9. Remove or disconnect the following:

- Bell housing-to-engine bolts
- Transaxle, by moving the K-frame rearward

10. To prepare the vehicle for rolling, support the engine with a suitable support or reinstall the front motor mount to the engine. Then, reinstall the ball joints to the steering knuckle and install the retaining bolt. Install the obtained outer CV-joints to the hubs, install the washers and tighten the axle nuts to 180 ft. lbs. (244 Nm). The vehicle may now be safely rolled.

To install:

11. Install or connect the following:

- Transaxle, by moving the K-frame rearward
- Bell housing-to-engine bolts. Torque the bolts to 70 ft. lbs. (95 Nm).
- Sway bar mounts
- Right side steering gear and K-frame bolts
- Transaxle electrical connectors
- Crankshaft Position (CKP) sensor, if equipped

12. Align the converter-to-flexplate matchmark. Rotate the crankshaft clockwise to align the converter bolts.

13. Install or connect the following:

- Torque converter. Torque the converter-to-flexplate bolts to 55 ft. lbs. (74 Nm).
- Flexplate cover. Torque the bolts to 108 inch lbs. (12 Nm).
- Both lateral bending strut brackets. Torque the bolts to 45 ft. lbs. (61 Nm).
- Radiator's lower crossmember. Torque the bolts to 45 ft. lbs. (61 Nm).
- Rear mount bracket
- Centermember bolts. Torque the bolts to 45 ft. lbs. (61 Nm).
- Rear mount bracket through-bolt. Torque the through-bolt to 45 ft. lbs. (61 Nm).
- Front engine mount bracket. Torque the bolts to 24 ft. lbs. (33 Nm).
- Starter
- New engine oil filter
- Upper transaxle mount remaining bolts, to the left side
- Exhaust pipe to the exhaust manifold
- Lower splash shields to both sides
- Front wheels
- Upper transaxle mount top bolts to the left side
- Shift lever cable to the transaxle lever. Torque the nut to 14 ft. lbs. (19 Nm).

- Transaxle cooler lines
- Dipstick tube to the transaxle
- Solenoid pack electrical connector
- TCM
- Air cleaner duct
- Negative battery cable

14. Adjust the gearshift and throttle cables.

15. Refill the transaxle.

16. Check the transaxle for proper operation. Be sure the back-up lights and speedometer are working properly.

Clutch

ADJUSTMENT

Free-Play

The manual transaxle clutch release system has a unique self-adjusting mechanism to compensate for clutch disc wear. This adjuster mechanism is located with the clutch cable assembly. The preload spring maintains tension on the cable. This tension keeps the clutch release bearing continuously loaded against the fingers of the clutch cover assembly. No manual adjustment is necessary.

When servicing this vehicle or if removing and installing the clutch cable, do not pull on the clutch cable housing to remove it from the dash panel. Damage to the cable self-adjuster may occur.

To check the function of the adjuster mechanism, use the following procedure:

1. With slight pressure, pull the clutch release lever end of the cable to draw the cable taut.

2. Push the clutch cable housing toward the dash panel. With less than 25 lbs. (11 kg) of effort, the cable housing should move 1.2–2.0 in. (30–50mm). This indicates proper adjuster mechanism function.

3. If the cable does not adjust, determine if the mechanism is properly seated on the bracket.

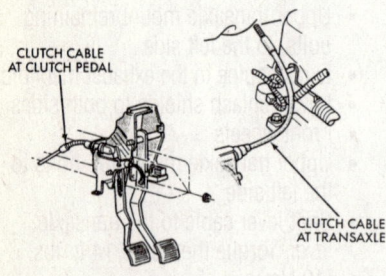

CLUTCH CABLE AT CLUTCH PEDAL

CLUTCH CABLE AT TRANSAXLE

7922FG51

Clutch cable routing

REMOVAL & INSTALLATION

➡**The transaxle assembly must be removed to service the clutch assembly.**

1. Before servicing the vehicle, refer to the precautions in the beginning of this section.

2. Remove or disconnect the following:
- Negative battery cable from the left shock tower.

➡**The ground cable is equipped with an insulator grommet which should be placed on the stud to prevent the negative battery cable from accidentally grounding.**

- Starter
- Rear and front transaxle support brackets
- Clutch inspection cover
- Modular clutch-to-flywheel bolts
- Transaxle assembly with the clutch as an assembly
- Clutch assembly from the transaxle input shaft

To install:

3. Clean all parts well. Inspect for oil leakage through the engine rear crankshaft oil seal and transaxle input shaft seal. If leakage is noted, it should be corrected at this time.

4. Examine the throwout or clutch release bearing. It is pre-lubricated and sealed and should not be washed in solvent. The bearing should turn smoothly when held in the hand with a light thrust load. A light drag caused by the lubricant fill is normal. If the bearing is noisy, rough or dry, replace the complete bearing assembly. In most cases where a clutch is being serviced, the complete clutch assembly and release bearing are usually replaced together.

5. Check the condition of the stud pivot spring clips on the back side of the clutch fork. If the clips are broken or distorted, replace the clutch fork. The pivot ball pocket in the fork is Teflon® coated and should be installed **WITHOUT** any lubricant such as grease which will break down the Teflon® coating. Be sure the ball stud and fork pocket are clean of contamination and dirt. When assembling the fork to the bearing, the small pegs on the bearing must go over the fork arms.

6. Check the flywheel for cracks, glazing or grooves. If any of these conditions exist, machine (reface) or replace the flywheel to prevent clutch chatter and premature clutch wear.

➡**The manual transaxle is equipped with a reverse brake. It functions as a synchronizer, but only if the vehicle is not moving. When the clutch pedal is depressed to the floor and held for 3 seconds, and the transaxle shifts to reverse, no gear clash should be present. If there is, the input shaft should be checked. When the transaxle is removed for clutch service, check the input clutch shaft, clutch disc splines**

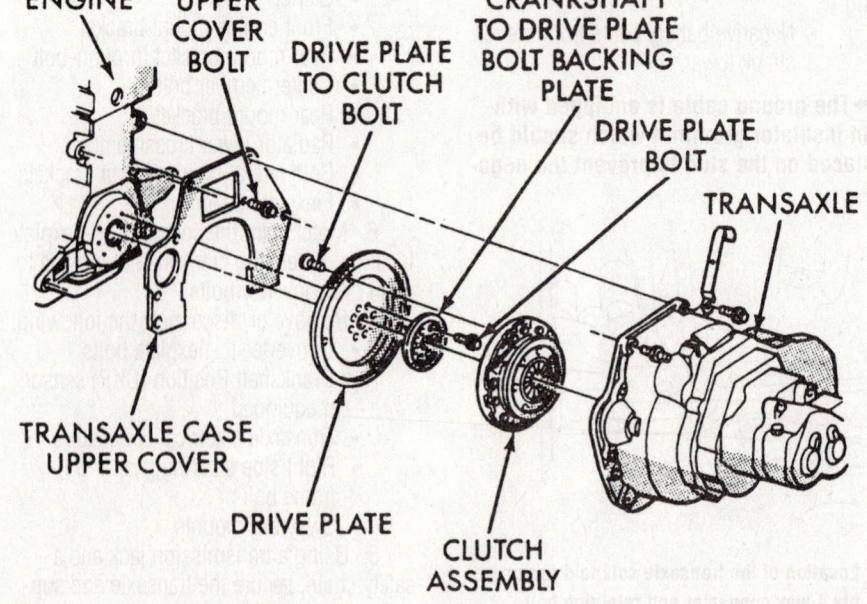

ENGINE UPPER COVER BOLT DRIVE PLATE TO CLUTCH BOLT CRANKSHAFT TO DRIVE PLATE BOLT BACKING PLATE DRIVE PLATE BOLT TRANSAXLE

TRANSAXLE CASE UPPER COVER DRIVE PLATE CLUTCH ASSEMBLY

7922FG52

Exploded view of the clutch assembly

and release bearing for dry rust. If present, clean rust off and apply a light coat of high temperature bearing grease to the input shaft splines. Apply grease on the input shaft splines only where the clutch disc slides. Verify that the clutch disc slides freely along the input shaft splines.

7. Install or connect the following:
- Modular clutch assembly onto the transaxle input shaft
- Transaxle assembly
- New clutch-to-driveplate (fly-wheel) bolts. Tighten the bolts, in a crisscross pattern, a few turns at a time to 55 ft. lbs. (75 Nm).
- Clutch inspection cover
- Transaxle lower support brackets
- Starter
- Negative battery cable

8. Road test the vehicle to check for proper clutch operation.

Halfshafts

REMOVAL & INSTALLATION

→If the vehicle is going to be rolled while the halfshafts are out of the vehicle, obtain 2 outer CV-joints or proper equivalent tools and install to the hubs.

✴✴ WARNING

If the vehicle is rolled without the proper torque applied to the front wheel bearings, the bearings will no longer be usable.

1. Before servicing the vehicle, refer to the precautions in the beginning of this section.
2. Remove or disconnect the following:
- Negative battery cable
- Cotter pin, nut lock and spring washer
- Halfshaft nut, loosen it while the vehicle is on the floor with the brakes applied
- Wheel
- Brake caliper assembly and support it on a wire
- Brake rotor
- Halfshaft nut and washer
- Tie rod end from the steering knuckle, using Joint Separation tool MB991113

✴✴ WARNING

Use of improper methods of joint separation can result in damage to the joint, leading to possible failure.

- Speed sensor cable routing bracket, if equipped with an Anti-lock Brake System (ABS)
- Sway bar link from the damper fork, if necessary
- Damper fork assembly
- Steering knuckle from the lower control arm
- Halfshaft by pressing it from the hub

→After pressing the outer shaft, insert a prybar between the transaxle case and the halfshaft and pry the shaft from the transaxle.

✴✴ WARNING

Do not pull on the shaft. Doing so damages the inboard joint. Do not insert the prybar too far or the oil seal in the case may be damaged.

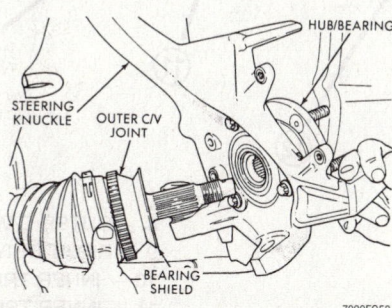

Carefully remove the outer CV-joint from the steering knuckle—be careful NOT to damage the threads or splines on the joint

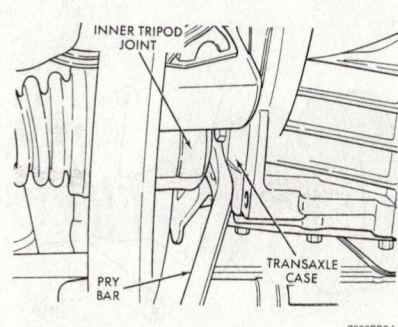

Inserting the prybar too far may damage the transaxle seal

To install:

3. Inspect the halfshaft boot for damage or deterioration. Check the ball joints and splines for wear.
4. Replace the circlips on the ends of the halfshaft(s).
5. Install or connect the following:
- Halfshaft into the transaxle until it is fully seated
- Halfshaft into the hub by pulling the knuckle assembly outward
- Washer. Make sure the chamfered edge faces outward.
- Halfshaft nut and tighten temporarily
- Control arm to the steering knuckle. Torque the nuts to 43–52 ft. lbs. (59–71 Nm).
- Damper fork. Torque the lower through-bolt/nut to 65 ft. lbs. (88 Nm) and the upper pinch bolt to 76 ft. lbs. (103 Nm).
- Tie rod end, to the steering knuckle. Torque the nut to 17–25 ft. lbs. (24–33 Nm) and install a new cotter pin.
- Sway bar link to the damper fork. Torque the link nut to 29 ft. lbs. (39 Nm).
- Lockwasher and axle nut. Torque the nut to 145–188 ft. lbs. (200–260 Nm).

→Before securely tightening the axle nut, be sure there is no load on the wheel bearings.

- Brake rotor and caliper assembly
- New cotter pin
- Wheel
- Negative battery cable

6. Refill the transaxle.
7. Test drive the vehicle and check for proper operation.

CV-Joints

OVERHAUL

Inner Tri-pot Joint

1. Remove or disassemble the following:
- Negative battery cable
- Halfshaft
- Large and small boot retaining clamps

2. Slide the boot down the shaft away from the tri-pot housing.

→When separating the spider joint from the tri-pot joint housing, hold the rollers in place on the trunions to pre-

Turn to Section 5 for brake system applications

vent the rollers and needle bearings from falling away.

3. Carefully slide the shaft/spider assembly from the tri-pot housing.

4. Remove the spider assembly-to-shaft snapring; then, slide the spider assembly off the shaft.

❋❋ WARNING

If necessary, tap the spider assembly off the shaft using a brass drift; be careful not to hit the outer bearings.

5. Slide the boot off the shaft.

6. Throughly inspect all parts for signs of excessive wear. If necessary, replace the halfshaft.

➡ **Component parts are not service-able and must be replaced as an assembly.**

To assemble:

❋❋ WARNING

The Tri-pot sealing boots are made of 2 different types of material; silicon rubber (high temperature)

which is soft and pliable or Hytrel plastic (standard temperature) which is stiff and rigid. Be sure to replace the boot made of the correct material.

7. Slide the inner tri-pot boot clamp and boot onto the shaft; then, position the boot so that only the thinnest (sight) groove is visible on the shaft.

8. Install the spider assembly onto the shaft just far enough so that the snapring can be installed.

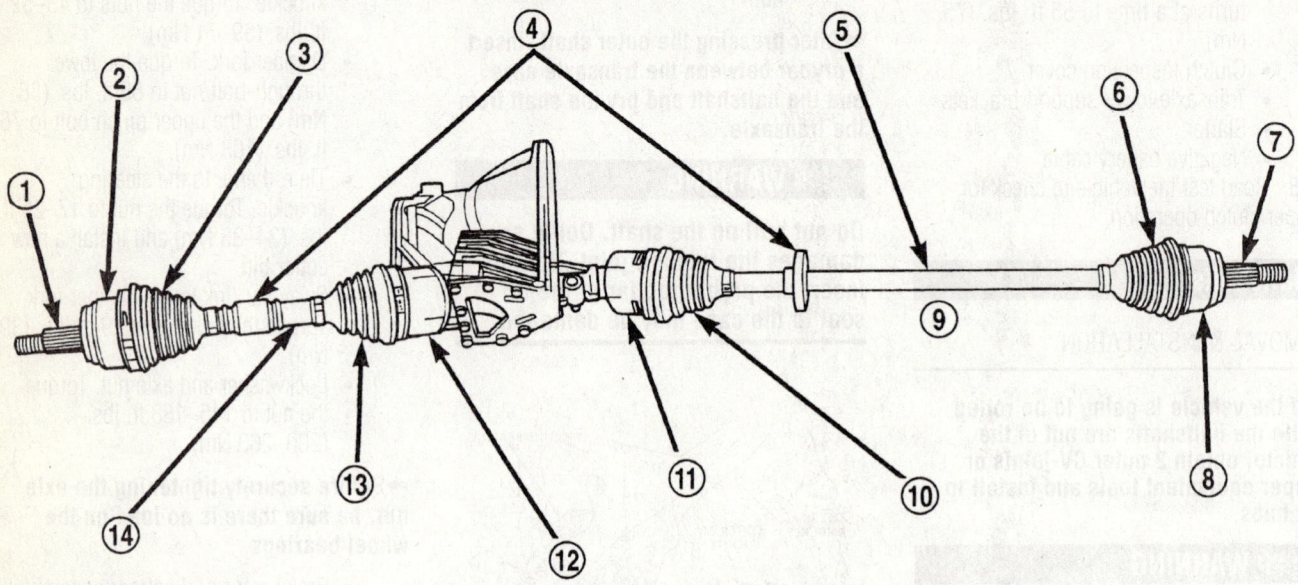

1 – STUB AXLE
2 – OUTER C/V JOINT
3 – OUTER C/V JOINT BOOT
4 – TUNED RUBBER DAMPER WEIGHT
5 – INTERCONNECTING SHAFT
6 – OUTER C/V JOINT BOOT
7 – STUB AXLE

8 – OUTER C/V JOINT
9 – RIGHT DRIVESHAFT
10 – INNER TRIPOD JOINT BOOT
11 – INNER TRIPOD JOINT
12 – INNER TRIPOD JOINT
13 – INNER TRIPOD JOINT BOOT
14 – INTERCONNECTING SHAFT LEFT DRIVESHAFT

9306EG02

View of the halfshaft assemblies—Typical

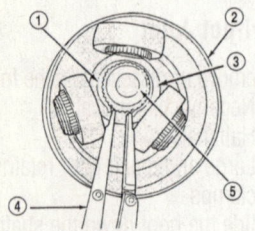

1 – SNAP RING
2 – SEALING BOOT
3 – SPIDER ASSEMBLY
4 – SNAP RING PLIERS
5 – INTERCONNECTING SHAFT

9306BG11

View of the halfshaft inner tri-pot joint and snapring

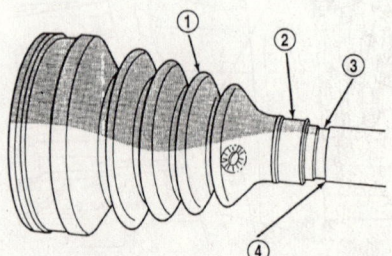

1 – SEALING BOOT
2 – RAISED BEAD IN THIS AREA OF SEALING BOOT
3 – GROOVE
4 – INTERCONNECTING SHAFT

9306EG04

View of the halfshaft boot and shaft

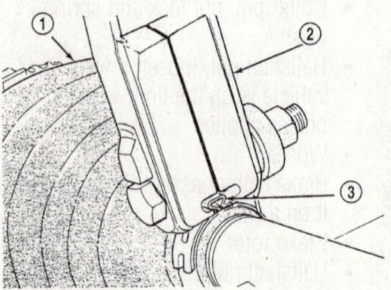

1 – SEALING BOOT
2 – SPECIAL TOOL C-4975
3 – CLAMP BRIDGE

9306BG13

Securing the halfshaft boot clamp

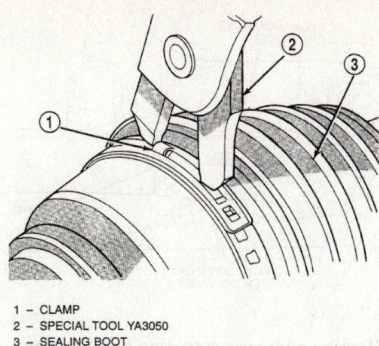

1 – CLAMP
2 – SPECIAL TOOL YA3050
3 – SEALING BOOT

9306EG07

Tightening the low profile boot clamp—Silicone rubber Tri-pot boot

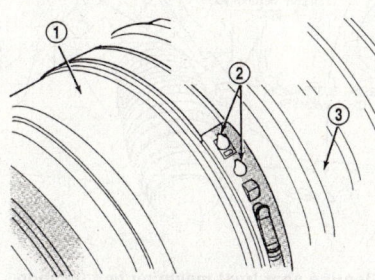

1 – INNER TRIPOD JOINT HOUSING
2 – TOP BANK OF CLAMP MUST BE RETAINED BY TABS AS SHOWN HERE TO CORRECTLY LATCH BOOT CLAMP
3 – SEALING BOOT

9306EG08

Secured the low profile boot clamp—Silicone rubber Tri-pot boot

※※ **WARNING**

If necessary, tap the spider assembly onto the shaft using a brass drift; be careful not to hit the outer bearings.

9. Install the snapring onto the shaft; make sure that the snapring is fully seated in the groove.

10. If installing a new boot, distribute ½ of the grease in the service package inside the tri-pot housing and the other ½ inside the boot.

11. Carefully, slide the spider assembly and shaft into the tri-pot housing.

12. Position the inner boot clamp evenly on the sealing boot.

※※ **WARNING**

The seal must not be dimpled, stretched or out of shape. If necessary, use a trim stick to seat and equalize the seal pressure and shape it by hand.

➡ **If using a Hytrel (hard plastic) boot, be sure the stick is inserted between the soft rubber insert and the tri-pot**

housing, not between the hard plastic sealing boot and the soft rubber insert.

13. Position the boot onto the tri-pot housing retaining groove and install the retaining clamp evenly on the boot.

14. If using a crimp type boot clamp, perform the following procedure:

a. Using the Crimper tool C-4975-A, place the tool over the clamp bridge, tighten the tool nut until the jaws are completely closed (face-to-face).

b. Using the Crimper tool C-4975-A, place the tool over the clamp bridge, tighten the tool nut until the jaws are completely closed (face-to-face).

15. If using a latching type boot clamp, perform the following procedure:

a. Position Snap-On® Clamp Locking tool YA3050 prongs in the clamp holes.

b. Squeeze the tool until the upper clamp band is latched behind the 2 tabs on the lower clamp band.

16. Install the halfshaft into the vehicle.

Rzeppa (Outer) Joint

1. Remove or disassemble the following:

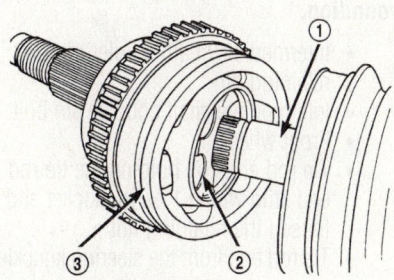

1 – INTERCONNECTING SHAFT
2 – CROSS
3 – OUTER C/V JOINT ASSEMBLY

9306EG09

Aligning the cross splines with the shaft splines—Rzeppa joint

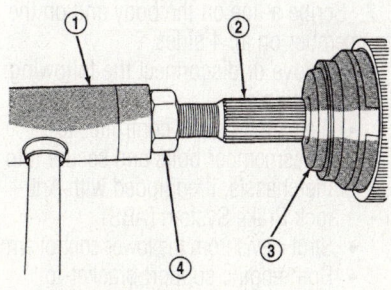

1 – SOFT FACED HAMMER
2 – STUB AXLE
3 – OUTER C/V JOINT
4 – NUT

9306EG10

Driving the Rzeppa joint onto the shaft

- Halfshaft and place it in a soft-jawed vise
- Rzeppa joint boot clamps and slide the boot down the shaft
- Rzeppa joint housing by sharply hitting it with a soft-faced hammer to drive it off the shaft
- Circlip from the shaft
- Boot by sliding it off the shaft

※※ **WARNING**

If any parts show excessive wear, replace the halfshaft assembly; the component parts are not serviceable.

To assemble:

2. Install or assemble the following:
- New small boot clamp and slide it onto the shaft
- Boot and slide it onto the shaft
- Circlip, if removed

3. Position the boot so that the raised bead on the inside the boot seal is in the shaft groove.

4. Install or assemble the following:
- Halfshaft hub nut onto the Rzeppa joint threaded shaft so it is flush with the end
- Rzeppa joint and align the shaft splines and tap it onto the shaft with a soft-faced hammer so it locks on the circlip

5. Distribute ½ of the grease in the service package inside the Rzeppa joint housing and the other ½ inside the boot.

6. Install or connect the following:
- New small boot clamp and position it evenly on the sealing boot

7. Using the Crimper tool C-4975-A, place the tool over the clamp bridge, tighten the tool nut until the jaws are completely closed (face-to-face).

※※ **WARNING**

The seal must not be dimpled, stretched or out of shape. If necessary, equalize the seal pressure and shape it by hand.

8. Position the boot onto the Rzeppa housing retaining groove and install the retaining clamp evenly on the boot.

9. Using the Crimper tool C-4975-A, place the tool over the clamp bridge, tighten the tool nut until the jaws are completely closed (face-to-face).

✳✳ WARNING

The seal must not be dimpled, stretched or out of shape. If necessary, equalize the seal pressure and shape it by hand.

9. Install the halfshaft into the vehicle.

STEERING AND SUSPENSION

Air Bag

✳✳ CAUTION

Some vehicles are equipped with an air bag system, also known as the Supplemental Inflatable Restraint (SIR) or Supplemental Restraint System (SRS). The system must be disabled before performing service on or around system components, steering column, instrument panel components, wiring and sensors. Failure to follow safety and disabling procedures could result in accidental air bag deployment, possible personal injury and unnecessary system repairs.

PRECAUTIONS

Several precautions must be observed when handling the inflator module to avoid accidental deployment and possible personal injury.

➡**Before servicing the vehicle, also refer to the precautions in the beginning of this section.**

- Never carry the inflator module by the wires or connector on the underside of the module.
- When carrying a live inflator module, hold securely with both hands, and ensure that the bag and trim cover are pointed away.
- Place the inflator module on a bench or other surface with the bag and trim cover facing up.
- With the inflator module on the bench, never place anything on or close to the module which may be thrown in the event of accidental deployment.

DISARMING

This air bag system is a sensitive, complex, electromechanical unit. Proper SRS (also called Supplemental Inflatable Restraint, or SIR, or air bag system) disarming can be obtained by disconnecting and isolating the negative battery cable (wrapping the battery cable end with electrical tape is a good method for isolating it). Failure to disconnect the battery could result in accidental air bag deployment and possible personal injury. Before beginning service work, allow the system capacitor 2 minutes to discharge after disconnecting and isolating the negative battery cable.

Power Rack and Pinion Steering Gear

REMOVAL & INSTALLATION

1. Before servicing the vehicle, refer to the precautions in the beginning of this section.
2. Remove or disconnect the following:
   - Negative battery cable from the left shock tower.

➡**The ground cable is equipped with an insulator grommet which should be placed on the stud to prevent the negative battery cable from accidentally grounding.**

- Intermediate shaft coupler pin bolt retaining pin
- Intermediate shaft coupler pin bolt
- Front wheels
- Tie rod ends by holding the tie rod end stud with a $1\frac{1}{32}$ in. socket and loosen the retaining nut
- Tie rod end from the steering knuckle

➡**Before removing the front suspension crossmember from the vehicle scribe the front suspension crossmember and the vehicle body. This must be done to retain the proper alignment. The caster and camber are not adjustable.**

3. Scribe a line on the body and on the crossmember on all 4 sides.
4. Remove or disconnect the following:
   - Stabilizer
   - 3 anti-lock brake controller-to-crossmember bolts and secure it to the chassis, if equipped with Anti-lock Brake System (ABS)
   - Strut clevis from the lower control arm
   - Both engine support bracket-to-crossmember bolts
   - Engine support bracket-to-transaxle mounting bracket bolt
5. Place a lifting device under the front suspension crossmember.
6. Remove or disconnect the following:

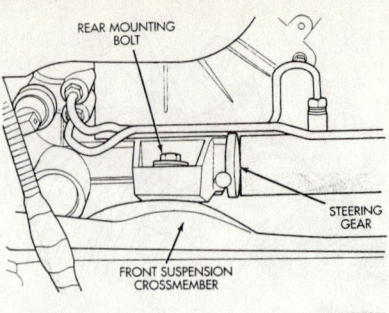

Steering gear rear mounting bolt location

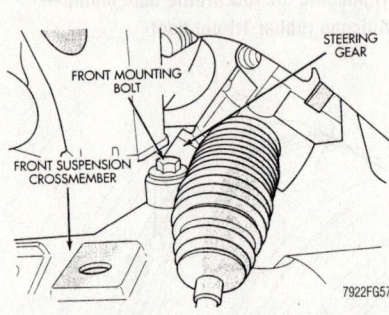

Steering gear front mounting bolt location

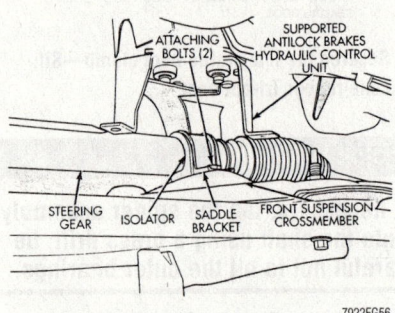

Check the condition of the isolator—if worn or oil soaked, replace

- 8 crossmember-to-chassis bolts
7. Lower the lifting device enough to gain access to the steering rack.
8. Remove or disconnect the following:
   - Power steering lines and drain the fluid
   - Power steering pressure switch electrical connector
   - Solenoid control module electrical connector, if equipped with speed proportional steering
   - Both steering rack isolator bolts
   - Both steering rack saddle bracket bolts
   - Steering rack

To install:
9. Install or connect the following:
   - Steering rack
   - Isolator and saddle bracket. Torque the bolts to 50 ft. lbs. (68 Nm).

- Power steering pressure and return lines. Torque the lines to 23 ft. lbs. (31 Nm).
- Crossmember, install the rear bolts first. Torque the bolts to 20 inch lbs. (2 Nm).

10. Using a soft faced hammer tap the crossmember into position.

➡**Be sure to align the scribed marks on the crossmember.**

11. Install or connect the following:
- Crossmember, starting with the rear bolts. Torque the bolts to 120 ft. lbs. (163 Nm).
- Both engine support bracket-to-crossmember bolts
- Engine support bracket-to-transaxle bracket bolt. Torque the 3 bolts to 55 ft. lbs. (75 Nm).
- Power steering pressure switch
- Anti-lock brake control unit. Torque the bolts to 21 ft. lbs. (28 Nm).
- Heat shield on the tie rod ends
- Shock clevis to the lower control arm
- Tie rod ends. Torque the nuts to 45 ft. lbs. (61 Nm).
- Both stabilizer clamps
- Strut clevis bolt. Torque the bolt to 68 ft. lbs. (92 Nm).
- Wheels. Torque the lug nuts to 95 ft. lbs. (129 Nm).
- Intermediate shaft pin bolt and retaining pin. Torque the pin bolt to 20 ft. lbs. (27 Nm).
- Negative battery cable

12. Refill the power steering system.
13. Start the engine and allow it to run for a few minutes.
14. Shut **OFF** the engine and check the power steering fluid.
15. Add power steering fluid if necessary.
16. Raise the front wheels off the ground.
17. Start the engine and turn the wheel from stop-to-stop to bleed any air from the system.
18. Check the fluid level and add, if necessary.
19. Check and adjust the alignment.

Strut

REMOVAL & INSTALLATION

Front

1. Before servicing the vehicle, refer to the precautions in the beginning of this section.
2. Remove or disconnect the following:

- Front wheel
- Steering knuckle
- Strut-to-shock clevis pin bolt
- Clevis-to-lower control arm through-bolt
- Clevis from the strut by tapping it with a brass drift
- 4 strut-to-shock tower bolts
- Strut/upper control arm mounting bracket as an assembly

To install:

3. Install or connect the following:
- Strut into the shock tower
- 4 upper strut mounting bolts. Torque the bolts to 23 ft. lbs. (31 Nm).
- Clevis onto the strut, using a brass drift until the clevis is fully seated against the locating tab
- Clevis pin bolt
- Clevis onto the lower control arm
- Clevis through-bolt
- Steering knuckle. Torque the clevis-to-strut pin bolt to 65 ft. lbs. (88 Nm).

4. Lower the vehicle to support the lower control arm.
5. Install or connect the following:
- Torque the clevis-to-lower control arm mounting bolt 40 ft. lbs. (54 Nm).
- Front wheel

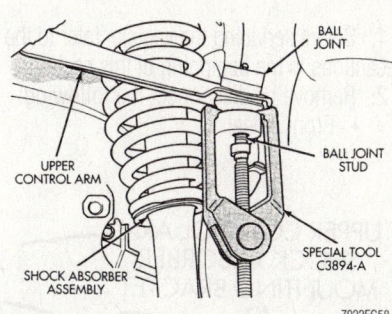

Separating the upper ball joint from the steering knuckle

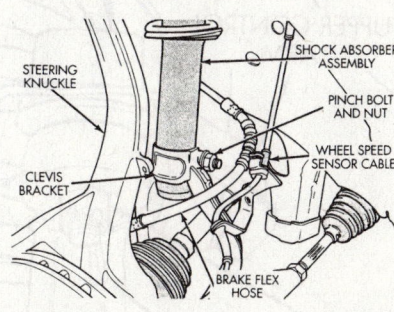

View of the front strut mount and related components

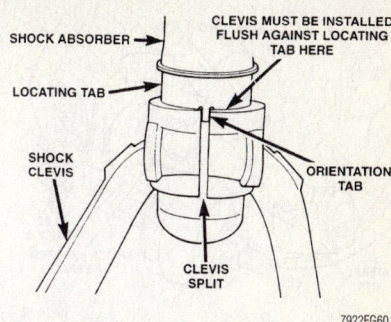

Be sure the orientation tab is situated into the clevis split

Rear

1. Before servicing the vehicle, refer to the precautions in the beginning of this section.
2. Remove or disconnect the following:
- Carpet, pull it back from the rear strut tower
- Plastic cover from the top of the strut tower
- Both strut assembly-to-chassis nuts
- Rear wheel
- Strut-to-rear knuckle bolt
- Strut by pushing the rear suspension downward and tilting the top of the strut outward

To install:

3. Install or connect the following:
- Strut by pushing the rear suspension downward and inserting the top of the strut into the vehicle
- Strut-to-rear knuckle bolt. Torque the bolt to 70 ft. lbs. (95 Nm).
- Strut upper mounting nuts. Torque the nuts to 25 ft. lbs. (34 Nm).
- Strut top cover
- Rear wheel. Torque the nuts to 95 ft. lbs. (125 Nm).

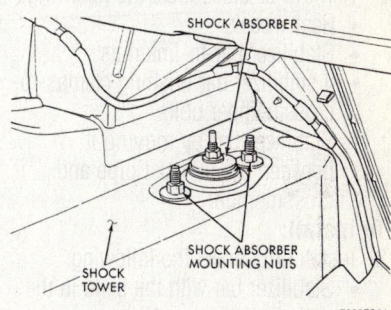

Access the rear strut upper mounting from inside the trunk

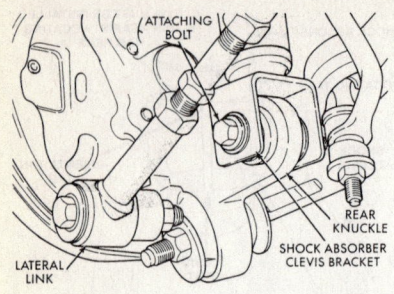

ATTACHING BOLT

REAR KNUCKLE

SHOCK ABSORBER CLEVIS BRACKET

LATERAL LINK

7922FG62

View of the rear strut lower mounting

Stabilizer Bars

REMOVAL & INSTALLATION

Front

1. Before servicing the vehicle, refer to the precautions in the beginning of this section.
2. Remove or disconnect the following:
   - Stabilizer bar link assemblies from the lower control arms
   - 4 stabilizer bushing retainer-to-crossmember/chassis bolts
   - Stabilizer bushing retainers
   - Stabilizer bar

To install:
3. Install or connect the following:
   - Stabilizer bar
   - Stabilizer bushing retainers. Torque the retainer-to-crossmember bolts to 120 ft. lbs. (163 Nm) and the retainer-to-chassis bolts to 45 ft. lbs. (61 Nm).
   - Stabilizer bar link assemblies. Torque the stabilizer bar-to-link nuts to 78 ft. lbs. (105 Nm).

Rear

1. Before servicing the vehicle, refer to the precautions in the beginning of this section.
2. Remove or disconnect the following:
   - Rear wheels
   - Stabilizer bar-to-link nuts
   - 4 stabilizer bar bushing clamps-to-crossmember bolts
   - Stabilizer bar by moving it between the exhaust pipe and crossmember

To install:
3. Install or connect the following:
   - Stabilizer bar with the bend in the ends facing upward
   - Stabilizer bar onto the links. Torque the nuts to 24 ft. lbs. (32 Nm).

➡**Position the bushings with the slits facing the front of the vehicle.**

- Stabilizer bar bushing clamps. Torque the clamp-to-crossmember bolts to 21 ft. lbs. (28 Nm).
- Rear wheels. Torque the nuts to 95 ft. lbs. (129 Nm).

Upper Ball Joint

REMOVAL & INSTALLATION

The upper ball joint is an integrated part of the upper control arm assembly, and cannot be serviced separately. A worn or damaged ball joint requires replacement of upper control arm assembly.

Lower Ball Joint

REMOVAL & INSTALLATION

On all vehicles, the ball joint cannot be serviced separately. If the ball joint is defective it will require replacement of the lower control arm.

Upper Control Arm

REMOVAL & INSTALLATION

Front

1. Before servicing the vehicle, refer to the precautions in the beginning of this section.
2. Remove or disconnect the following:
   - Front wheel

- Ball joint from the steering knuckle using the Joint Separation tool MB991113
- Strut assembly
- Upper control arm mounting bracket from the strut assembly
- Upper control arm shaft-to-bracket nuts
- Upper control arm, from the bracket using the joint separation tool
- Upper control arm assembly

To install:
3. Install or connect the following:
   - Upper control arm assembly
   - Upper control arm to the bracket. Torque the nuts to 62 ft. lbs. (86 Nm).
   - Upper control arm mounting bracket to the strut assembly
   - Strut assembly
   - Ball joint to the steering knuckle. Torque the locking nut to 20 ft. lbs. (28 Nm).
   - Front wheel
4. Check and/or adjust the wheel alignment, if necessary.

Rear

1. Before servicing the vehicle, refer to the precautions in the beginning of this section.
2. Remove or disconnect the following:
   - Both rear wheels
   - Both struts from the knuckles
   - Muffler hanger from the frame rail
   - Rear exhaust pipe hanger from the

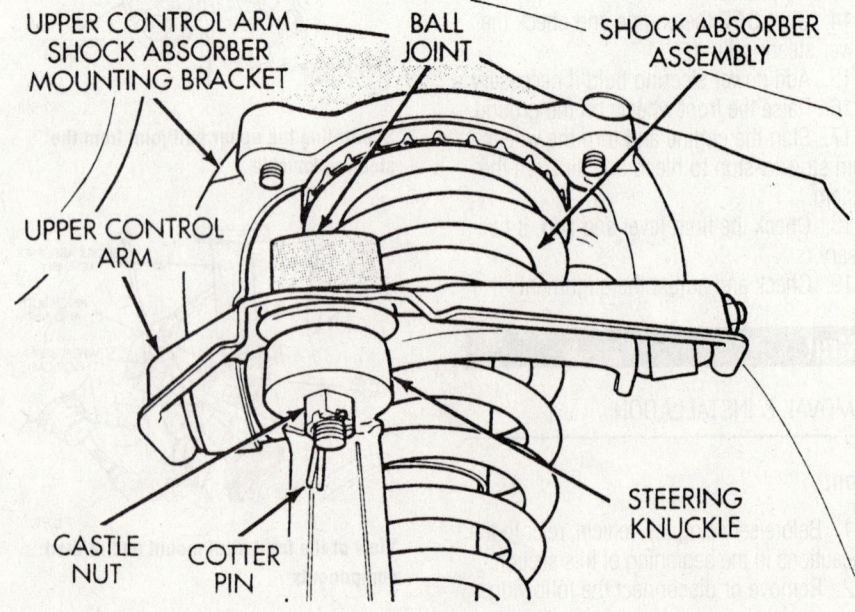

UPPER CONTROL ARM SHOCK ABSORBER MOUNTING BRACKET

BALL JOINT

SHOCK ABSORBER ASSEMBLY

UPPER CONTROL ARM

STEERING KNUCKLE

CASTLE NUT

COTTER PIN

7922FG63

Front upper control arm component identification

rear crossmember and allow it to hang

- Upper control arm ball joint stud from the knuckle

3. Support the center of the rear crossmember with a jack and a block of wood.

4. Remove or disconnect the following:
- Speed sensor wiring from the upper control arms, if equipped with an Anti-lock Brake System (ABS)
- 4 crossmember-to-frame bolts

✳✳ WARNING

Do not damage the rear brake hoses while lowering the crossmember.

5. Lower the crossmember to access the 2 upper control arm pivot bar mounting bolts.

6. Remove or disconnect the following:
- Both upper control arm-to-crossmember bolts
- Upper control arm

To install:

7. Install or connect the following:
- Upper control arm to the crossmember. Torque the bolts to 80 ft. lbs. (108 Nm).

➡Be sure to place the flat washers between the crossmember and the pivot bar.

- Crossmember using a drift to align the holes. Tighten the bolts to 80 ft. lbs. (108 Nm).

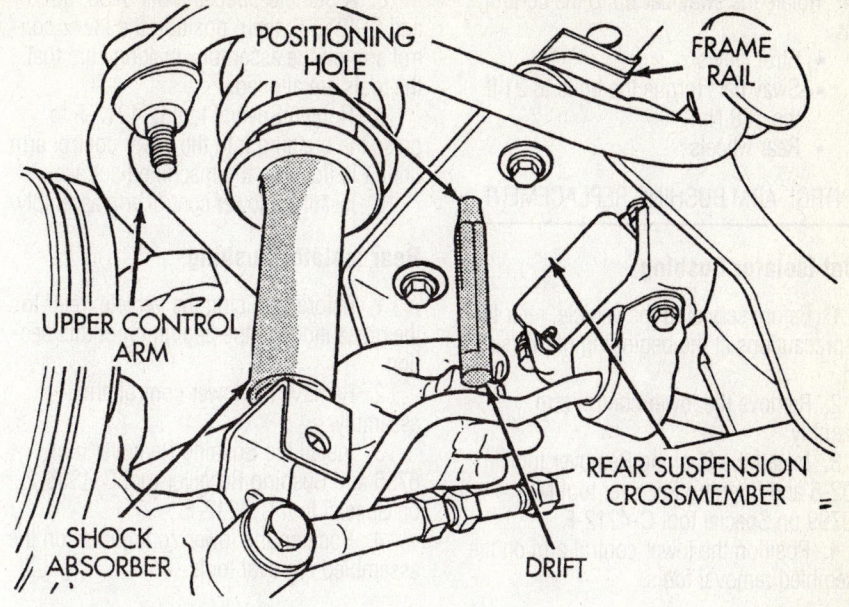

Use a drift to align the rear crossmember to the frame

8. Remove the jack
9. Install or connect the following:
- Speed sensor wiring to the upper control arms, if equipped with an Anti-lock Brake System (ABS)
- Upper control arm ball joint stud to the knuckle. Torque the ball joint stud nut to 63 ft. lbs. (85 Nm).
- Rear exhaust pipe hanger to the rear crossmember

- Muffler hanger to the frame rail
- Both struts to the knuckles. Torque the lower strut bolt to 70 ft. lbs. (95 Nm).
- Both rear wheels

Lower Control Arm

REMOVAL & INSTALLATION

Front

1. Before servicing the vehicle, refer to the precautions at the beginning of this section.

2. Remove or disconnect the following:
- Front wheels
- Heat shield, if equipped with 15 inch wheels
- Ball joint clamp nut
- Sway bar-to-control arm bolts
- Strut clevis from the lower control arm
- Sway bar-to-crossmember bolts, loosen them and rotate the sway bar away from the control arm
- Lower control arm from the steering knuckle using a prybar
- Both lower control arm bolts
- Control arm

To install:

3. Install or connect the following:
- Lower control arm. Torque the bolts to 120 ft. lbs. (163 Nm).
- Control arm to the steering knuckle. Torque the nut to 70 ft. lbs. (95 Nm).

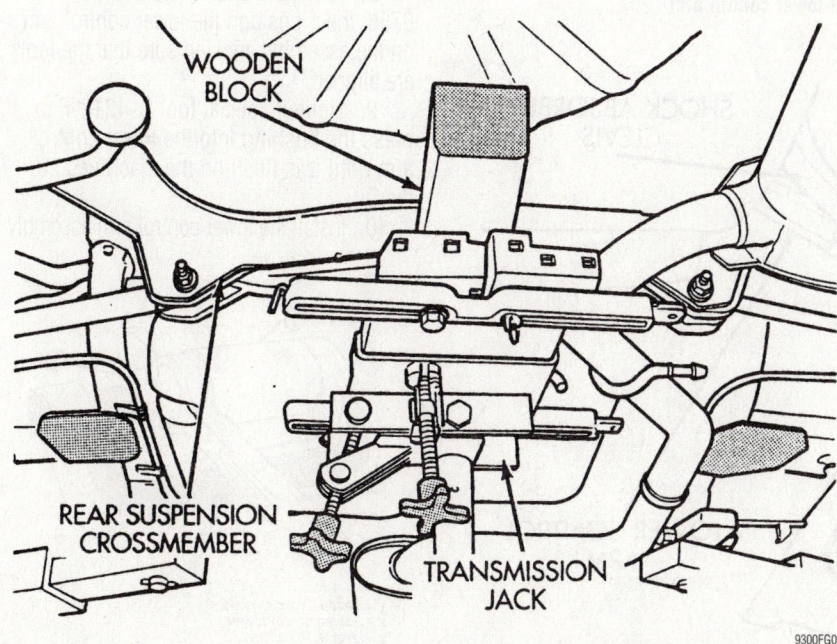

A jack with a block of wood should be used to support the rear crossmember

4. Rotate the sway bar up to the control arms.

- Strut clevis
- Sway bar. Torque the bolts to 21 ft. lbs. (28 Nm).
- Rear wheels

CONTROL ARM BUSHING REPLACEMENT

Front Isolator Bushing

1. Before servicing the vehicle, refer to the precautions at the beginning of this section.

2. Remove the lower control arm assembly

3. Install the Bushing Remover tool 6602-5 and Bushing Receiver tool MB-990799 on Special tool C-4212-F.

4. Position the lower control arm on the assembled removal tools.

➡ **Be sure the Bushing Receiver tool MB-990799 is square on the lower control arm and Bushing Remover tool 6602-5 is positioned correctly on the isolator bushing.**

5. Tighten Special tool C-4212-F to press the bushing from the lower control arm.

To assemble:

6. Position the Bushing Installer tool 6876 onto the screw portion of Special tool C-4212-F.

7. Start the new bushing into the lower control arm hole machined surface side by hand, making sure it is square with its mounting hole.

8. Assemble Special tools 6758, 6876 and C-4212-F; then, position the lower control arm on the assembly, making sure that the tools are aligned.

9. Tighten Special tool C-4212-F to press the bushing into the lower control arm until it is flush on the machined surface.

10. Install the lower control arm assembly.

Rear Isolator Bushing

1. Before servicing the vehicle, refer to the precautions at the beginning of this section.

2. Remove the lower control arm assembly

3. Install the Bushing Remover tool 6756 and Bushing Receiver tool C-4366-2 on Special tool C-4212-F.

4. Position the lower control arm on the assembled removal tools.

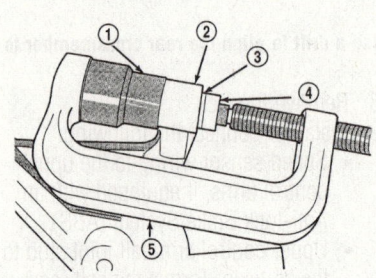

1 – SPECIAL TOOL MB-990799
2 – LOWER CONTROL ARM
3 – FRONT ISOLATOR BUSHING
4 – SPECIAL TOOL 6602-5
5 – SPECIAL TOOL C-4212-F

9306FG09

Removing the front isolator bushing from the lower control arm

1 – SPECIAL TOOL 6876
2 – ISOLATOR BUSHING
3 – MACHINED SURFACE SIDE OF LOWER CONTROL ARM
4 – SPECIAL TOOL 6758
5 – SPECIAL TOOL C-4212-F

9306FG10

Installing the front isolator bushing to the lower control arm

➡ **Be sure the bushing receiver tool C-4366-2 is square on the lower control arm and bushing remover tool 6756 is positioned correctly on the isolator bushing.**

5. Tighten Special tool C-4212-F to press the bushing from the lower control arm.

To assemble:

6. Position the bushing installer tool 6760 onto the screw portion of special tool C-4212-F.

7. Start the new bushing into the lower control arm hole's machined surface side by hand, making sure it is square with its mounting hole with the void in the rubber portion facing away from the ball joint.

8. Assemble special tools 6760 and 6756; then, position the lower control arm on the assembly, making sure that the tools are aligned.

9. Tighten special tool C-4212-F to press the bushing into the lower control arm until it is flush on the machined surface.

10. Install the lower control arm assembly.

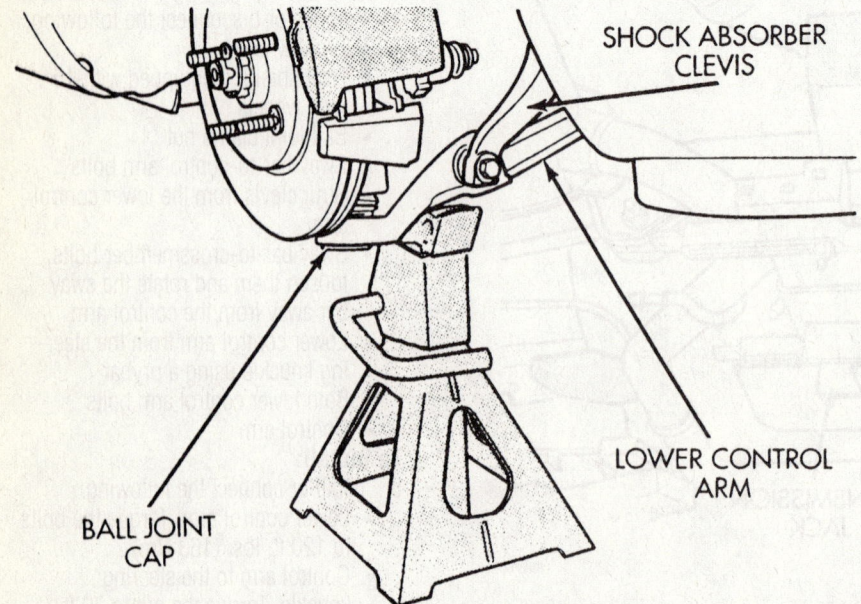

SHOCK ABSORBER CLEVIS

LOWER CONTROL ARM

BALL JOINT CAP

7922FG64

Pre-load the suspension before final tightening the control arm to the steering knuckle

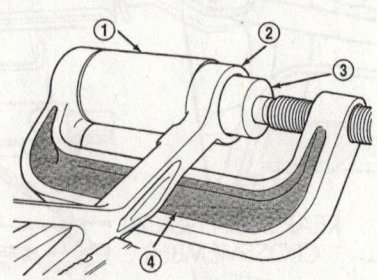

1 – SPECIAL TOOL C-4366-2
2 – LOWER CONTROL ARM
3 – SPECIAL TOOL 6756
4 – SPECIAL TOOL C-4212-F

9306FG11

Removing the rear isolator bushing from the lower control arm

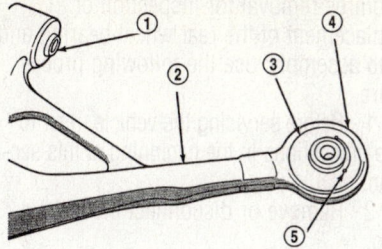

1 – FRONT ISOLATOR BUSHING
2 – LOWER CONTROL ARM
3 – REAR ISOLATOR BUSHING
4 – MACHINED SURFACE
5 – VOID IN BUSHING IN THIS DIRECTION

9306FG12

Positioning the rear isolator bushing to the lower control arm

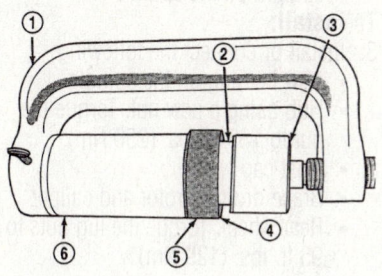

1 – SPECIAL TOOL C-4212-F
2 – REAR BUSHING
3 – SPECIAL TOOL 6760
4 – MACHINED SURFACE ON LOWER CONTROL ARM
5 – LOWER CONTROL ARM
6 – SPECIAL TOOL 6756

9306FG13

Installing the rear isolator bushing to the lower control arm

Clevis Bushing

1. Before servicing the vehicle, refer to the precautions at the beginning of this section.

2. Remove the lower control arm assembly

3. Install the bushing remover tool 6877 and bushing receiver tool 6876 on special tool C-4212-F.

4. Position the lower control arm on the assembled removal tools.

➡ **Be sure the bushing receiver tool 6876 is square on the lower control arm and bushing remover tool 6877 is positioned correctly on the clevis bushing.**

5. Tighten special tool C-4212-F to press the bushing from the lower control arm.

To assemble:

6. Position the bushing installer tool 6877 onto the screw portion of special tool C-4212-F.

7. Start the new bushing into the lower control arm hole's machined surface side by

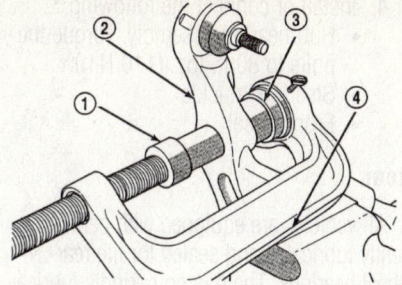

1 – SPECIAL TOOL 6877
2 – LOWER CONTROL ARM
3 – SPECIAL TOOL 6876
4 – SPECIAL TOOL C-4212-F

9306FG14

Removing the clevis bushing from the lower control arm

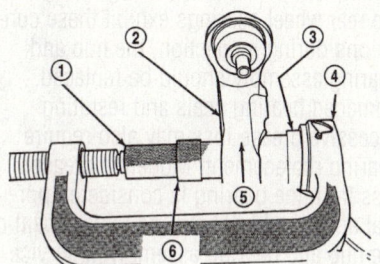

1 – SPECIAL TOOL 6877
2 – MACHINED SURFACE SIDE OF LOWER CONTROL ARM
3 – SPECIAL TOOL 6876
4 – SPECIAL TOOL C-4212-F
5 – LOWER CONTROL ARM
6 – CLEVIS BUSHING

9306FG15

Installing the clevis bushing to the lower control arm

hand, making sure it is square with its mounting hole with the void in the rubber portion facing away from the ball joint.

8. Assemble special tools 6876 and 6877; then, position the lower control arm on the assembly, making sure that the tools are aligned.

9. Tighten special tool C-4212-F to press the bushing into the lower control arm until it is flush on the machined surface.

10. Install the lower control arm assembly.

Wheel Bearings

ADJUSTMENT

Front

The front hub wheel bearing is designed for the life of the vehicle and requires no type of adjustment or periodic maintenance. The bearing is a sealed unit with the wheel hub and can only be removed and/or replaced as one unit.

Rear

The rear hub and wheel bearing assembly is designed for the life of the vehicle and requires no type of adjustment or periodic maintenance. The bearing is a sealed unit with the wheel hub and can only be removed and/or replaced as one unit.

The following procedure may be used for evaluation of bearing condition:

1. Raise and safely support the vehicle.

2. Remove the rear wheels and brake drums.

3. Turn the hub flange carefully. Excessive roughness, lateral play or resistance to rotation may indicate dirt intrusion or bearing failure.

4. If the rear wheel bearings exhibit the conditions during inspection, the hub and bearing assembly should be replaced.

5. Damaged bearing seals and resulting excessive grease loss may also require bearing replacement. Moderate grease loss from the bearing is considered normal and should not require replacement of the hub and bearing assembly.

REMOVAL & INSTALLATION

Front

The front wheel bearing used on this vehicle is a bolt-in type wheel bearing.

The wheel bearing is serviced separately from the front steering knuckle and front hub assembly. Retention of the front wheel bearing into the steering knuckle is by means of 3 bolts installed from the rear of the steering knuckle. The 3 bolts attach the hub/bearing to the front surface of the steering knuckle. Removal and installation of the hub/bearing assembly from the steering knuckle must be done with the steering knuckle removed from the vehicle.

The face of the outer CV-joint has a metal bearing shield pressed on it. This design deters direct water splash on the bearing seal while allowing any water that gets in to run out the bottom of the steering knuckle. It is important to thoroughly clean the outer CV-joint and the wheel bearing area in the steering knuckle before it is assembled after servicing the front wheel bearing or driveshaft.

At no time when servicing this vehicle, can a sheet metal screw, bolt or other metal fastener be installed in the shock tower to take the place of an original plastic clip. Also, NO holes can be drilled into the front shock tower for the installation of any metal fasteners into the shock tower. Because of

Turn to Section 5 for brake system applications

the minimum clearance in this area installation of metal fasteners could damage the coil spring's protective coating and lead to corrosion failure of the spring. If a plastic clip is missing, lost or broken during servicing a vehicle, replace only with the equivalent part listed in the Mopar parts catalog.

1. Before servicing the vehicle, refer to the precautions in the beginning of this section.

2. Remove or disconnect the following:
- Front wheel
- Steering knuckle assembly
- 3 hub/bearing assembly-to-steering knuckle bolts
- Hub/bearing assembly from the steering knuckle. If necessary, tap the bearing out, using a soft-faced hammer.

➡ **The wheel bearing is transferable to a replacement steering knuckle if the bearing is found in serviceable condition.**

To install:

3. Clean all parts well. Thoroughly, clean all the hub/bearing assembly mounting surfaces on the steering knuckle.

4. Install or connect the following:
- Hub/bearing assembly. Torque the bolts to 80 ft. lbs. (110 Nm).
- Steering knuckle
- Front wheel

Rear

All vehicles are equipped with permanently lubricated and sealed for life rear wheel bearings. There is no periodic lubrication or maintenance recommended for these units.

To evaluate the condition of the rear wheel bearings, remove the wheel and brake drum or rotor and rotate the flanged outer ring of the hub. Excessive roughness or resistance to rotation may indicate dirt intrusion or wheel bearing failure. If the rear wheel bearings exhibit these conditions during inspection, the hub and bearing assembly should be replaced. Damaged bearing seals and resulting excessive grease loss may also require bearing replacement. Moderate grease loss from the bearing is considered normal and should not require replacement of the hub and bearing assembly. If service

requires removal for inspection or replacement of the rear wheel bearing and hub assembly, use the following procedure.

1. Before servicing the vehicle, refer to the precautions in the beginning of this section.

2. Remove or disconnect the following:

- Rear wheel
- Brake drum, if equipped with drum brakes
- Brake caliper and rotor, if equipped with disc brakes
- Hub dust cap
- Hub nut and discard it
- Hub/bearing assembly by pulling straight off the spindle

To install:

3. Install or connect the following:
- New bearing on the spindle
- Hub using a new nut. Torque the nut to 185 ft. lbs. (250 Nm).
- Dust cap
- Brake drum or rotor and caliper
- Rear wheel. Torque the lug nuts to 95 ft. lbs. (129 Nm).

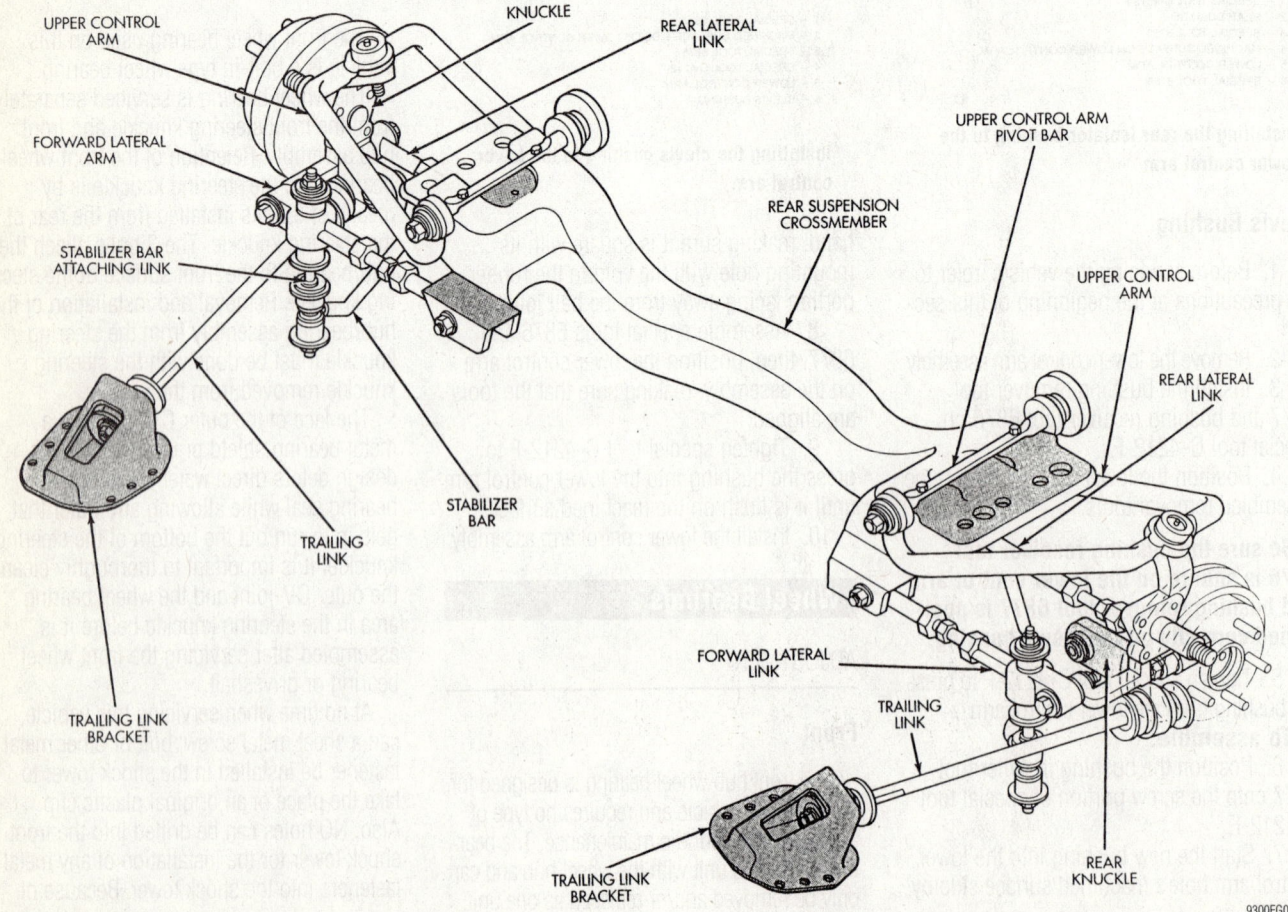

UPPER CONTROL ARM

KNUCKLE

REAR LATERAL LINK

FORWARD LATERAL ARM

STABILIZER BAR ATTACHING LINK

TRAILING LINK

STABILIZER BAR

TRAILING LINK BRACKET

UPPER CONTROL ARM PIVOT BAR

REAR SUSPENSION CROSSMEMBER

UPPER CONTROL ARM

REAR LATERAL LINK

FORWARD LATERAL LINK

TRAILING LINK

REAR KNUCKLE

TRAILING LINK BRACKET

9300FG03

Independent rear suspension component identification

CHRYSLER CORP.

PT Cruiser

PRECAUTIONS

Before servicing any vehicle, please be sure to read all of the following precautions, which deal with personal safety, prevention of component damage, and important points to take into consideration when servicing a motor vehicle:

• Never open, service or drain the radiator or cooling system when the engine is hot; serious burns can occur from the steam and hot coolant.

• Observe all applicable safety precautions when working around fuel. Whenever servicing the fuel system, always work in a well-ventilated area. Do not allow fuel spray or vapors to come in contact with a spark, open flame, or excessive heat (a hot drop light, for example). Keep a dry chemical fire extinguisher near the work area. Always keep fuel in a container specifically designed for fuel storage; also, always properly seal fuel containers to avoid the possibility of fire or explosion. Refer to the additional fuel system precautions later in this section.

• Fuel injection systems often remain pressurized, even after the engine has been turned **OFF**. The fuel system pressure must be relieved before disconnecting any fuel lines. Failure to do so may result in fire and/or personal injury.

• Brake fluid often contains polyglycol ethers and polyglycols. Avoid contact with the eyes and wash your hands thoroughly after handling brake fluid. If you do get brake fluid in your eyes, flush your eyes with clean, running water for 15 minutes. If eye irritation persists, or if you have taken brake fluid internally, IMMEDIATELY seek medical assistance.

• The EPA warns that prolonged contact with used engine oil may cause a number of skin disorders, including cancer! You should make every effort to minimize your exposure to used engine oil. Protective gloves should be worn when changing oil. Wash your hands and any other exposed skin areas as soon as possible after exposure to used engine oil. Soap and water, or waterless hand cleaner should be used.

• All new vehicles are now equipped with an air bag system, often referred to as a Supplemental Restraint System (SRS) or Supplemental Inflatable Restraint (SIR) system. The system must be disabled before performing service on or around system components, steering column, instrument panel components, wiring and sensors. Failure to follow safety and disabling procedures could result in accidental air bag deployment, possible personal injury and unnecessary system repairs.

• Always wear safety goggles when working with, or around, the air bag system. When carrying a non-deployed air bag, be sure the bag and trim cover are pointed away from your body. When placing a non-deployed air bag on a work surface, always face the bag and trim cover upward, away from the surface. This will reduce the motion of the module if it is accidentally deployed. Refer to the additional air bag system precautions later in this section.

• Clean, high quality brake fluid from a sealed container is essential to the safe and proper operation of the brake system. You should always buy the correct type of brake fluid for your vehicle. If the brake fluid becomes contaminated, completely flush the system with new fluid. Never reuse any brake fluid. Any brake fluid that is removed from the system should be discarded. Also, do not allow any brake fluid to come in contact with a painted surface; it will damage the paint.

• Never operate the engine without the proper amount and type of engine oil; doing so WILL result in severe engine damage.

• Timing belt maintenance is extremely important! Many models utilize an interference-type, non-freewheeling engine. If the timing belt breaks, the valves in the cylinder head may strike the pistons, causing potentially serious (also time-consuming and expensive) engine damage. Refer to the maintenance interval charts in the front of this manual for the recommended replacement interval for the timing belt, and to the timing belt section for belt replacement and inspection.

• Disconnecting the negative battery cable on some vehicles may interfere with the functions of the on-board computer system(s) and may require the computer to undergo a relearning process once the negative battery cable is reconnected.

• When servicing drum brakes, only disassemble and assemble one side at a time, leaving the remaining side intact for reference.

• Only an MVAC-trained, EPA-certified automotive technician should service the air conditioning system or its components.

ENGINE REPAIR

Distributor

The PT Cruiser uses a Direct Ignition System (DIS) and basic ignition timing is not adjustable.

Alternator

REMOVAL

Remove or disconnect the following:

• Negative battery cable
• Air cleaner lid
• Inlet Air Temperature (IAT) sensor and make-up hose
• Right front wheel
• Splash shield
• Lower pivot bolt, loosen only
• Drive belt T-bolt, loosen only
• Alternator field circuit wiring connector
• Battery positive terminal
• Alternator belt
• Axle retaining nut
• Lower control arm from the steering knuckle
• Axle shaft
• Lower mounting bolt from the upper adjustment bracket
• Alternator

INSTALLATION

Install or connect the following:

• Alternator
• Alternator drive belt
• Axle shaft
• Lower control arm
• Lower ball joint nut. Torque the nut to 70 ft. lbs. (95 Nm).
• Axle retaining nut. Torque the nut to 120 ft. lbs. (163 Nm).
• Support bracket
• B terminal. Torque the fastener to 100 inch lbs. (11 Nm).
• Field circuit to the alternator
• Splash shield and right front wheel
• Upper pivot nut. Torque the nut to 40 ft. lbs. (54 Nm).
• Negative battery cable

Ignition Timing

ADJUSTMENT

Ignition timing is controlled by the Powertrain Control Module (PCM). No adjustment is necessary or possible.

Engine Assembly

REMOVAL & INSTALLATION

➡️**After all components are installed on the engine, a DRB or equivalent, scan tool is necessary to perform the camshaft and crankshaft timing relearn procedure.**

1. Before servicing the vehicle, refer to the precautions in the beginning of this section.
2. Properly recover the air conditioning system refrigerant.
3. Properly relieve the fuel system pressure.
4. Drain the cooling system.
5. Drain the engine oil.
6. Remove or disconnect the following:
   - Battery and battery tray
   - Throttle and speed control cables
   - Powertrain Control Module (PCM) wiring harness
   - Positive cable from the Power Distribution Center (PDC) and ground wire
   - Ground wire from the body to engine
   - Brake booster vacuum hose
   - Proportional purge hoses from the intake manifold
   - Coolant recovery hose
   - Heater hoses
   - Upper radiator support crossmember
   - Upper and lower radiator hoses
   - A/C line from the condenser
   - Cooler lines, if equipped
   - Fan module assembly
   - Transmission shift linkage and electrical connectors
   - Clutch hydraulic lines, if equipped
   - Halfshafts
   - Heater hoses
   - Accessory drive belts
   - Alternator
   - Downstream Oxygen (O2S) sensor
   - Exhaust system from the manifold
   - Power steering pressure hose
   - Lower engine torque strut
   - Structural collar
   - Torque converter bolts

- A/C compressor
- Power steering return line
- Power steering pump

7. Raise the vehicle enough to allow an engine dolly and cradle to be placed under the engine.
8. Loosen the engine support posts in order to allow movement for positioning onto the engine locating holes and flange on the engine bedplate. Lower the vehicle and position the cradle until the engine is resting on the support posts. Tighten the mounts to the cradle frame. This will keep the support posts from moving when removing or installing the engine and transaxle.
9. Install safety straps around the engine to the cradle; tighten the straps and lock them into position.
10. Raise the vehicle enough to see if the straps are tight enough to hold the cradle assembly to the engine.
11. Lower the vehicle so the weight of the engine and transaxle ONLY is on the cradle.

12. Remove the engine and transaxle mount through-bolts.
13. Raise the vehicle slowly, it might be necessary to move the engine/transaxle assembly with the cradle to allow removal around the body flanges.

To install:
14. Install or connect the following:
   - Engine/transaxle assembly, lower the vehicle over the assembly
   - Engine and transaxle mounts. Torque the bolts to 87 ft. lbs. (118 Nm).
   - Upper torque strut and remove the support fixtures
   - Alternator
   - Halfshafts

15. Install the structural collar and torque the bolts, in 3 steps, using the following procedure:
   a. Step 1: Collar-to-oil pan bolts to 30 inch lbs. (3 Nm).

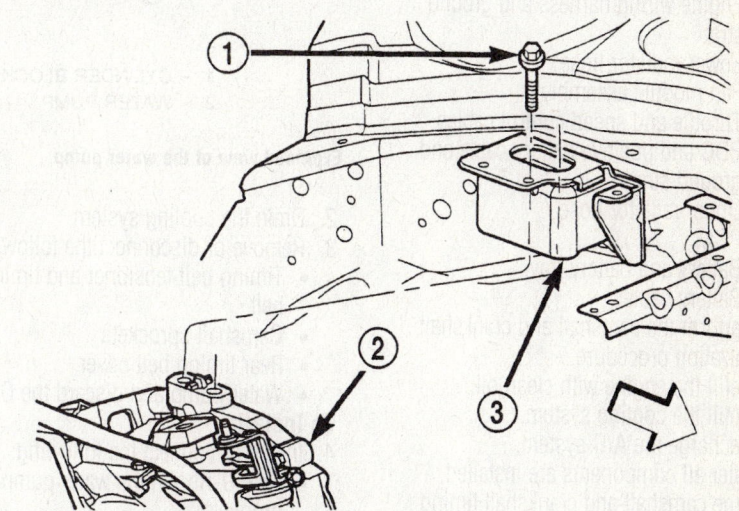

Front engine mount location and bolt identification

9306ZG83

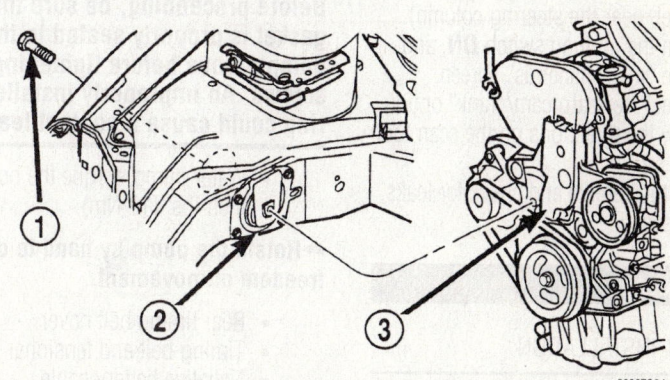

Exploded view of the left mount through bolt

9306ZG84

b. Step 2: Collar-to-transmission bolts to 80 ft. lbs. (108 Nm).

c. Step 3: Collar-to-oil pan bolts to 40 ft. lbs. (54 Nm).

16. Install or connect the following:
- Lower engine torque strut. Torque the through bolts to 87 ft. lbs. (118 Nm).
- Downstream O$_2$S sensor connector
- Exhaust pipe to the manifold
- Power steering pressure hose to the steering gear
- A/C compressor
- Power steering pump
- Drive belts
- Right inner splash shield and wheel
- Power steering return hose
- Clutch hydraulic line, electrical connectors and shift linkage, if equipped
- Shift linkage and cooler lines, if equipped
- Fuel lines
- Heater hoses
- Engine wiring harness and ground strap
- Lower radiator hose
- Fan module assembly
- Throttle and speed control cables
- PDC and positive battery cable and ground strap
- Upper radiator hose
- PCM
- Battery and battery tray
- Battery cables

17. Perform the camshaft and crankshaft synchronization procedure.

18. Refill the engine with clean oil.

19. Refill the cooling system.

20. Recharge the A/C system.

21. After all components are installed, perform the camshaft and crankshaft timing relearn procedure as follows:

a. Connect a DRB or equivalent, scan tool to the DLC (located under the instrument panel, near the steering column).

b. Turn the ignition switch **ON**, and access the "miscellaneous" screen.

c. Select "re-learn cam/crank" option and follow the directions on the scan tool screen.

22. Start the vehicle and check for leaks, repair if necessary.

Water Pump

REMOVAL & INSTALLATION

1. Before servicing the vehicle, refer to the precautions in the beginning of this section.

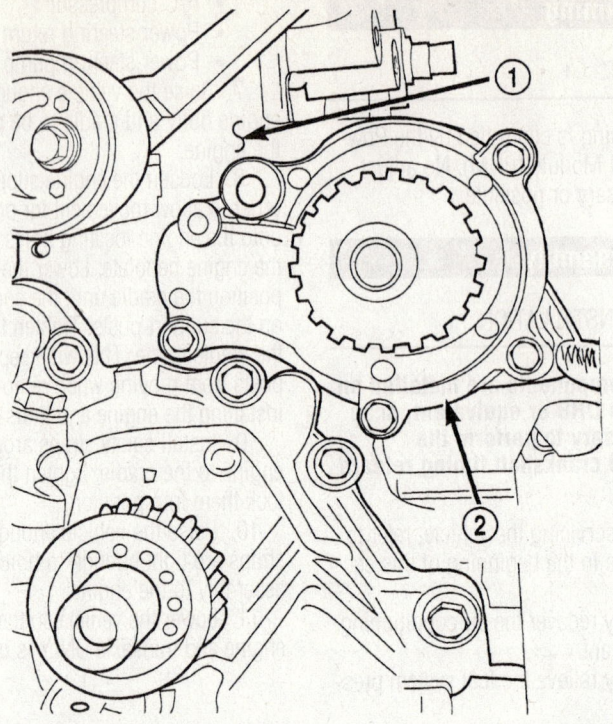

1 – CYLINDER BLOCK
2 – WATER PUMP

9306ZG85

Exploded view of the water pump

2. Drain the cooling system.
3. Remove or disconnect the following:
- Timing belt tensioner and timing belt
- Camshaft sprockets
- Rear timing belt cover
- Water pump and discard the O-ring

To install:

4. Install or connect the following:
- New O-ring in the water pump groove

✳✳ WARNING

Before proceeding, be sure the O-ring gasket is properly seated in the water pump groove before tightening the screws. An improperly installed O-ring could cause a coolant leak.

- Water pump, torque the bolt to 105 inch lbs. (12 Nm).

➡ **Rotate the pump by hand to check for freedom of movement.**

- Rear timing belt cover
- Timing belt and tensioner
- Negative battery cable

5. Refill the cooling system.
6. Start the vehicle and check for leaks, repair if necessary.

Cylinder Head

REMOVAL & INSTALLATION

➡ **After all components are installed on the engine, a DRB scan tool is necessary to perform the camshaft and crankshaft timing relearn procedure.**

1. Before servicing the vehicle, refer to the precautions in the beginning of this section.

2. Properly relieve the fuel system pressure.

3. Drain the cooling system.

4. Remove or disconnect the following:
- Negative battery cable
- Air cleaner inlet duct and air cleaner
- Inlet Air Temperature (IAT) sensor and make-up air hose
- Upper intake manifold
- Fuel lines from the throttle body
- Heater tube support bracket
- Upper radiator hose
- Accessory drive belt
- Exhaust pipe from the manifold
- Power steering pump, move it aside. DO NOT disconnect the fluid lines.

- Ignition coil pack wiring connector
- Ignition coil pack and bracket
- Cam sensor electrical connector
- Timing belt
- Timing belt idler pulley
- Camshaft sprocket
- Power steering pump reservoir and bracket
- Cylinder head cover
- Camshaft and cam followers
- Cylinder head bolts, working from the center outward
- Cylinder head

➡ **The cylinder head bolts must be inspected before they can be reused. If the threads of bolts are stretched, they must be replaced. Check for thread stretching by holding a scale or other straightedge against the threads. If all the threads do not contact the scale, the bolts must be replaced.**

❋❋ WARNING

Use only a plastic scraper to clean the mating surfaces. NEVER use metal, as this may gouge the surfaces and cause leaks!

5. Cover the combustion chambers, then use a plastic scraper to thoroughly and carefully clean the engine block and cylinder head mating surfaces.

To install:

6. Install or connect the following:
   - New head gasket with the part number facing up
   - Cylinder head

➡ **Refer to Section 1 of this manual for the cylinder head torque sequence illustration. The illustration is located after the Torque Specification Chart.**

7. Lubricate the cylinder head bolt threads
8. Torque the cylinder head bolts, in the sequence, to:
   a. Step 1: 25 ft. lbs. (34 Nm).
   b. Step 2: 50 ft. lbs. (68 Nm).
   c. Step 3: 50 ft. lbs. (68 Nm).
   d. Step 4: An additional ¼ turn.
9. Install or connect the following:
   - Camshaft and cam follower assemblies
   - Cylinder head cover
   - Rear timing belt cover and pulley
   - Cam sensor wiring connector
   - Ignition coil and spark plug wires
   - Power steering pump reservoir and bracket

- Exhaust pipe to the manifold
- Accessory drive belts
- Lower intake manifold
- Upper radiator and heater supply hose
- Heater support bracket
- Dipstick tube fastener to the intake manifold
- Power brake vacuum hose to the intake manifold
- Fuel lines to the throttle body
- Vacuum lines and electrical wiring
- Upper intake manifold
- Air cleaner inlet duct and air cleaner
- Negative battery cable

10. Refill the cooling system.
11. Turn the ignition switch **ON**, and access the "miscellaneous" screen.
12. Select the "re-learn cam/crank" option, then follow the instructions on the scan tool screen.

Intake Manifold

REMOVAL & INSTALLATION

Upper

1. Before servicing the vehicle, refer to the precautions in the beginning of this section.
2. Properly relieve the fuel system pressure.
3. Remove or disconnect the following:
   - Negative battery cable
   - Fresh air inlet duct and air cleaner
   - Engine cover
   - Throttle and speed cables from the throttle lever bracket
   - Manifold Absolute Pressure (MAP) sensor
   - Idle Air Control (IAC) motor electrical connector
   - Throttle Position (TP) sensor wiring connector
   - Proportional purge hoses
   - Brake booster vacuum hose
   - Positive Crankcase Ventilation (PCV) hose from the intake manifold
   - Throttle body support bracket bolt
   - Exhaust Gas Recirculation (EGR) tube bolts
   - Upper intake manifold
4. Clean the mating surfaces.

To install:

➡ **Refer to Section 1 of this manual for the intake manifold torque sequence**

illustration. The illustration is located after the Torque Specification Chart.

5. Install or connect the following:
   - New gaskets and seals
   - Intake manifold on the EGR tube. Torque the new retainers, in sequence, to 105 inch lbs. (12 Nm).
   - Throttle body support bracket. Torque the bolt to 28 ft. lbs. (20 Nm).
   - EGR retainer plate. Torque the smaller bolt to 95 inch lbs. (11 Nm) and the large bolt to 28 ft. lbs. (20 Nm).
   - PCV hose to the intake manifold
   - MAP sensor electrical connector
   - Proportional purge hoses
   - Brake booster hose
   - IAC motor and TP sensor connectors
   - Throttle and speed control cables
   - Air cleaner assembly
   - Engine cover
   - Inlet air temperature sensor
   - Negative battery cable

Lower

1. Before servicing the vehicle, refer to the precautions in the beginning of this section.
2. Properly relieve the fuel system pressure.
3. Drain the coolant system.
4. Remove or disconnect the following:
   - Negative battery cable
   - Inlet Air Temperature (IAT) sensor and make-up hose
   - Air cleaner
   - Upper intake manifold
   - Upper radiator hose and coolant outlet connector
   - Fuel supply line quick-connect from the fuel rail
   - Fuel injector wiring harness
   - Oil dipstick tube from the lower intake manifold
   - Intake manifold fasteners and discard them
   - Intake manifold and discard the gaskets and seals
5. Thoroughly clean the gasket mating surfaces.

To install:

➡ **Refer to Section 1 of this manual for the intake manifold torque sequence illustration. The illustration is located after the Torque Specification Chart.**

Timing belt service is covered in Section 4 of this manual

6. Install or connect the following:
- New gaskets and seals
- Intake manifold. Torque the new retainers in sequence to 105 inch lbs. (12 Nm).
- Intake manifold-to-lower support bracket bolts. Torque the bolts to 17 ft. lbs. (23 Nm).
- Fuel injector wiring harness
- Fuel supply line quick-connect to the fuel tube assembly
- Oil dipstick tube to the lower intake manifold
- Upper radiator hose
- Air cleaner assembly
- IAT sensor
- Negative battery cable

7. Fill the coolant system.
8. Pressurize the fuel system.
9. Start the vehicle and check for leaks, repair if necessary.

Exhaust Manifold

REMOVAL & INSTALLATION

1. Before servicing the vehicle, refer to the precautions in the beginning of this section.
2. Remove or disconnect the following:
- Negative battery cable
- Air cleaner assembly and bracket
- Throttle and speed control cables
- Power steering pump reservoir, move it aside. DO NOT disconnect the fluid lines.
- Exhaust manifold heat shield
- Exhaust pipe from the manifold
- Engine wiring heat shield
- Manifold support bracket
- Upstream Heated Oxygen Sensor (HO2S) connector

➡It may be necessary to loosen the alternator bracket bolt to remove the outer exhaust manifold bolt.

- Exhaust manifold and discard the gasket

3. Thoroughly clean the mating surfaces.
To install:
4. Install or connect the following:
- New gasket
- Exhaust manifold. Torque the bolts, starting at the center and working outward in both directions to 17 ft. lbs. (23 Nm).

➡Repeat this procedure until all fasteners are tightened to specifications.

- Alternator bracket bolt, if loosened
- Exhaust manifold heat shield. Torque the bolts to 105 inch lbs. (12 Nm).

- Exhaust manifold support bracket
- Engine wiring heat shield
- Upstream HO2S wiring connector
- Exhaust pipe to the manifold. Torque the fasteners to 21 ft. lbs. (28 Nm).
- Power steering pump reservoir
- Throttle and speed control cables
- Air cleaner bracket and assembly
- Negative battery cable

5. Start the vehicle and check for leaks, repair if necessary.

Front Crankshaft Seal

REMOVAL & INSTALLATION

1. Before servicing the vehicle, refer to the precautions in the beginning of this section.
2. Remove or disconnect the following:
- Negative battery cable
- Crankshaft damper bolt
- Crankshaft damper, using Puller tool 1026 and Insert tool 6827-A

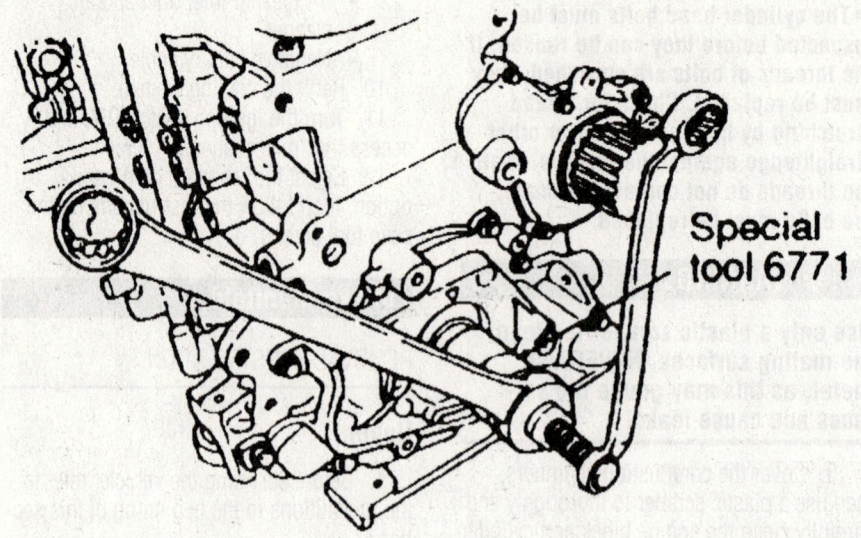

Removing the front crankshaft oil seal

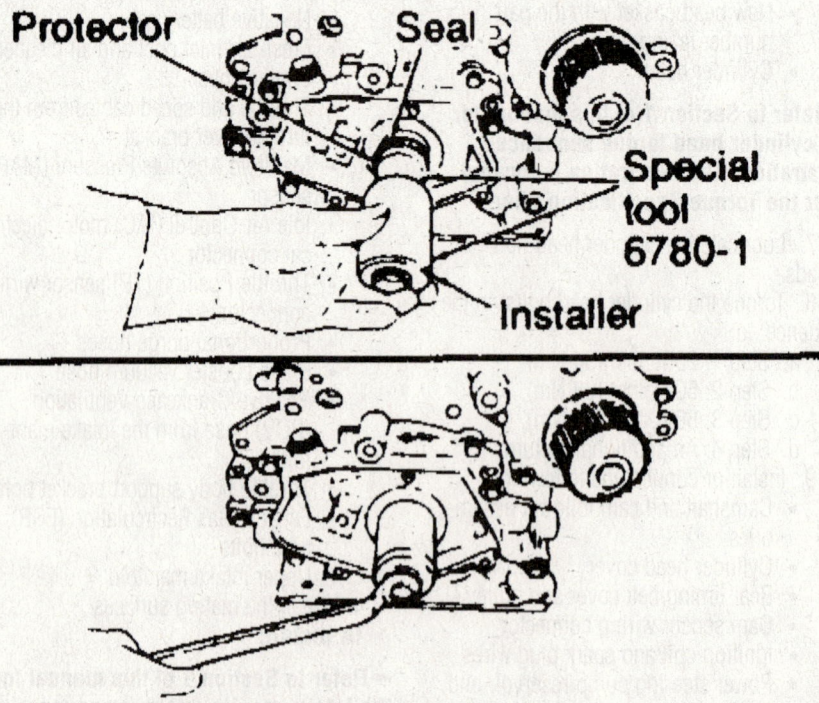

Installing a new seal using seal installer 6780-1; proceed with caution if using substitute tools

- Timing belt
- Crankshaft sprocket, using Crankshaft Sprocket Remover tool 6793 and Insert tool C-4685-C2
- Crankshaft oil seal, using a seal puller tool 6771

➡️**Be careful not to damage the seal surface of the cover.**

To install:

3. Install or connect the following:
- New front crankshaft oil seal with the seal spring facing the engine, using Crankshaft Installer tool 6780.
- Crankshaft timing belt sprocket, using Installer tool 6792

➡️**Make sure the word FRONT on the crankshaft sprocket is facing outward.**

- Timing belt
- Timing belt covers
- Crankshaft damper using thrust bearing washer and bolt from Installer tool 6792. Torque the damper bolt to 105 ft. lbs. (142 Nm).
- Negative battery cable
4. Start the vehicle and check for leaks, repair if necessary.

Camshaft and Lifters

REMOVAL & INSTALLATION

➡️**After all components are installed on the engine, a DRB scan tool is necessary to perform the camshaft and crankshaft timing relearn procedure.**

1. Before servicing the vehicle, refer to the precautions in the beginning of this section.
2. Relieve the fuel system pressure.
3. Remove or disconnect the following:
- Negative battery cable
- Cylinder head cover
- Camshaft Position (CMP) sensor and target magnet
- Timing belt and tensioner
- Camshaft sprocket
- Rear timing belt cover
- Loosen the camshaft bearing caps in sequence from the rear of the cylinder head
- Remove the camshafts

To install:

Make certain that the pistons are NOT at Top Dead Center (TDC) before installing the camshafts.

4. Install or connect the following:
- Camshaft cam followers, lubricate the bearing journals thoroughly

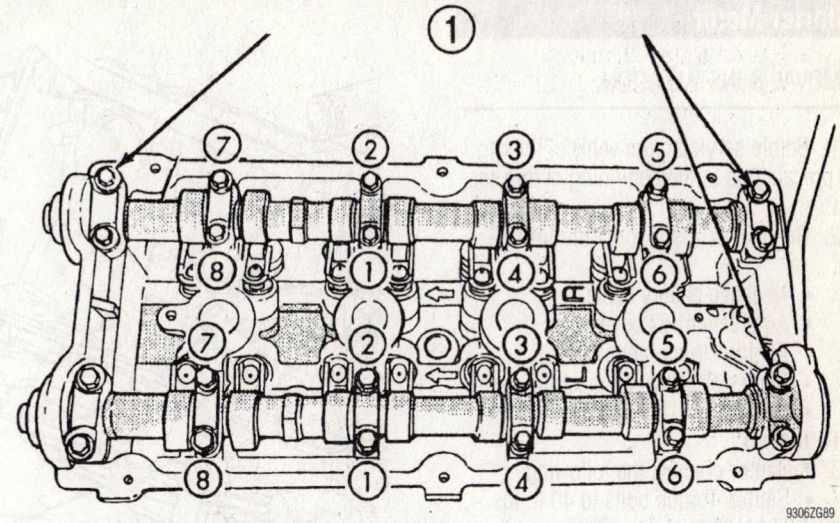

Remove the camshaft bearing caps in sequence

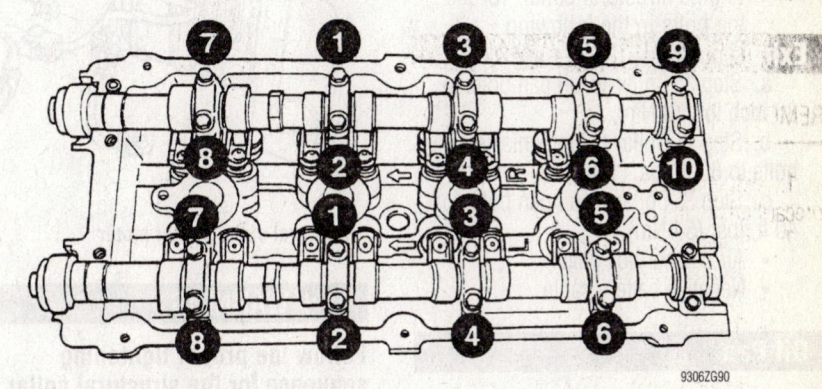

Camshaft bearing cap tightening sequence

➡️**Be sure it turns freely.**

- Left and right camshaft bearing caps, No's 2–5 and right side No. 6. Torque these fasteners to 105 inch lbs. (12 Nm). Apply Mopar® gasket maker to No.1 and left side No. 6. Torque these fasteners to 18 ft. lbs. (24 Nm).
- Camshaft seals
- Rear timing belt cover
- Camshaft sprockets. Torque the bolt to 85 ft. lbs. (115 Nm).
- Timing belt
- Target magnet
- CMP sensor. Torque the screws to 85 inch lbs. (9.6 Nm)
- Cylinder head cover
- Negative battery cable.

➡️**An oil and filter change are recommended.**

5. Use a DRB or equivalent, scan tool to perform the camshaft and crankshaft timing relearn procedure, as follows:

a. Connect the scan tool to the DLC (located under the instrument panel, near the steering column).

b. Turn the ignition switch **ON** and access the "miscellaneous" screen.

c. Select the "re-learn cam/crank" option, then follow the instructions on the scan tool screen.

6. Start the engine and check for leaks. Run the engine with the radiator cap off so as the engine warms and the thermostat opens, coolant can be added to the radiator. Test drive vehicle to check for proper operation.

Valve Lash

ADJUSTMENT

The engines in these vehicles do not require periodic valve lash adjustment.

➡️**Refer to the rocker arm removal and installation procedure for additional information.**

Starter Motor

REMOVAL & INSTALLATION

1. Before servicing the vehicle, refer to the precautions in the beginning of this section.
2. Remove or disconnect the following:
   - Negative battery cable
   - Air cleaner box cover
   - Engine structural collar
   - Starter electrical connectors
   - Starter

To install:

3. Install or connect the following:
   - Starter. Torque bolts to 40 ft. lbs. (54 Nm).
   - Starter electrical connectors
   - Engine structural collar. Torque the bolts in the following sequence:
   a. Step 1: Collar-to-oil pan bolts to 30 inch lbs. (3 Nm).
   b. Step 2: Collar-to-transmission bolts to 80 ft. lbs. (108 Nm).
   c. Step 3: Collar-to-oil pan bolts to 40 ft. lbs. (54 Nm).
   - Air cleaner box cover
   - Negative battery cable

Oil Pan

REMOVAL & INSTALLATION

1. Before servicing the vehicle, refer to the precautions in the beginning of this section.
2. Drain the engine oil.
3. Support the powertrain assembly.
4. Remove or disconnect the following:
   - Negative battery cable
   - Right inner splash shield
   - Engine structural collar
   - Lower torque strut
   - Oil filter adapter
   - Oil pan and gasket
5. Thoroughly clean the gasket mating surfaces.

To install:

6. Apply silicone sealer to the oil pump-to-engine block parting line.
7. Install or connect the following:
   - New gasket on the oil pan
   - Oil pan. Torque the retainers to 105 inch lbs. (12 Nm).
   - Oil filter and adapter. Torque the screws to 105 inch lbs. (12 Nm).
   - Structural collar

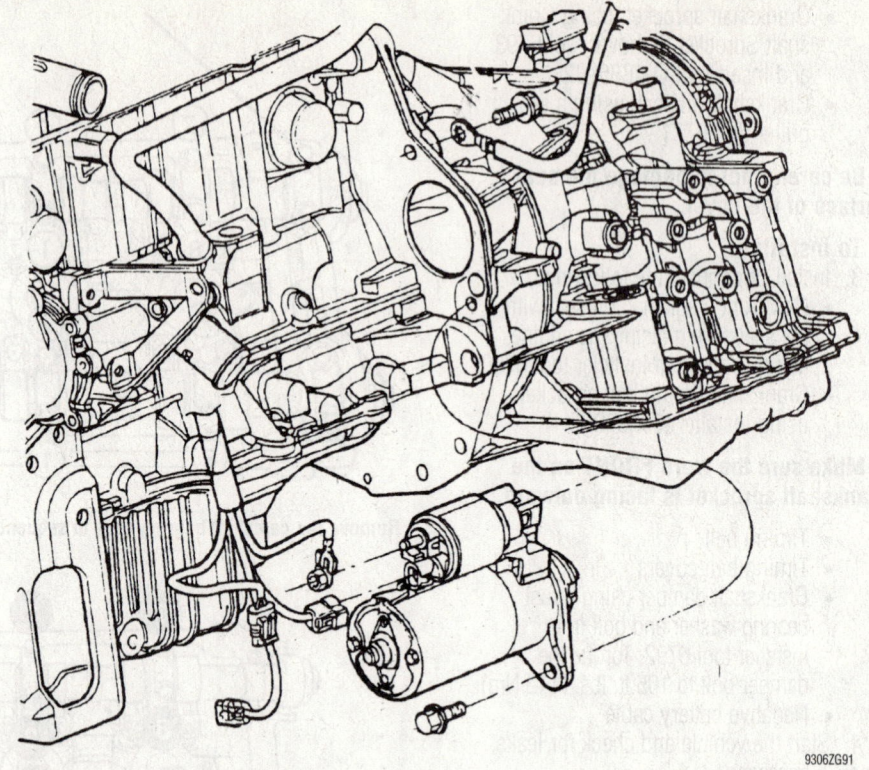

Removal of the starter motor

9306ZG91

❄ WARNING

Follow the proper tightening sequence for the structural collar or damage to the collar or oil pan may occur!

8. Install the structural collar and torque the retainers as follows:
   a. Collar-to-oil pan bolts: 30 inch lbs. (3 Nm).
   b. Collar-to-transaxle bolts: 80 ft. lbs. (108 Nm).

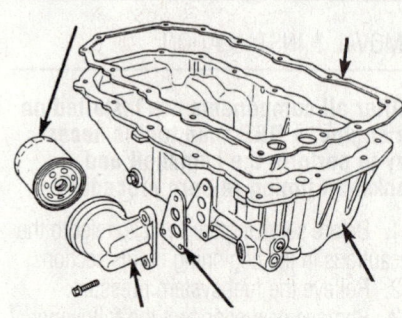

9306ZG92

Remove the oil filter adapter

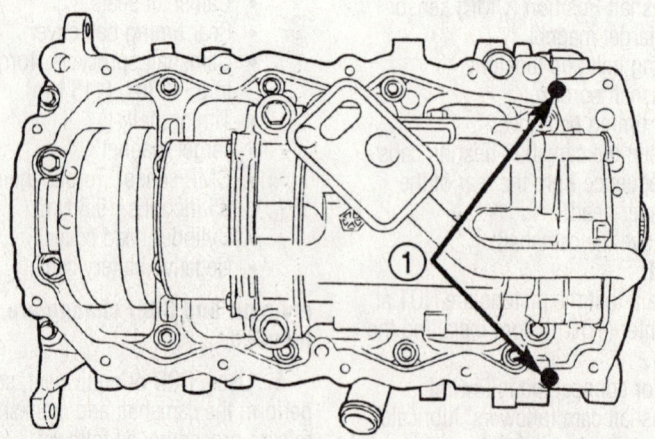

9306ZG93

Silicone sealer application locations

c. Collar-to-oil pan bolts: 40 ft. lbs. (54 Nm), final torque.

9. Install or connect the following:
- Lower torque strut
- Right inner splash shield
- Negative battery cable

10. Fill the engine with clean oil.

11. Start the vehicle and check for leaks, repair if necessary.

Oil Pump

REMOVAL & INSTALLATION

1. Before servicing the vehicle, refer to the precautions in the beginning of this section.

2. Drain the engine oil.

3. Remove or disconnect the following:
- Negative battery cable
- Timing belt
- Oil pan
- Crankshaft sprocket, using tool 6795 and Insert tool C-4685-C2
- Crankshaft key
- Oil pickup tube
- Oil pump

To install:

4. Wash all parts in a solvent; then, inspect carefully for damage or wear, as follows:

  a. Inspect the mating surface of the oil pump should be smooth. Replace the pump cover, if scratched or grooved.

  b. Apply Mopar® gasket maker to the oil pump.

  c. Install the O-ring into the oil pump body discharge passage.

5. Prime the oil pump before installation by filling the rotor cavity with engine oil.

6. Install or connect the following:
- Oil pump, align the rotor flats with the crankshaft flats. Torque the pump bolts to 21 ft. lbs. (28 Nm).

✳✳ WARNING

The front crankshaft seal MUST be out of the pump to align or damage may result.

- New front crankshaft seal, using Seal Driver tool 6780
- Crankshaft key
- Crankshaft sprocket, using a Crankshaft Sprocket Installer tool 6792

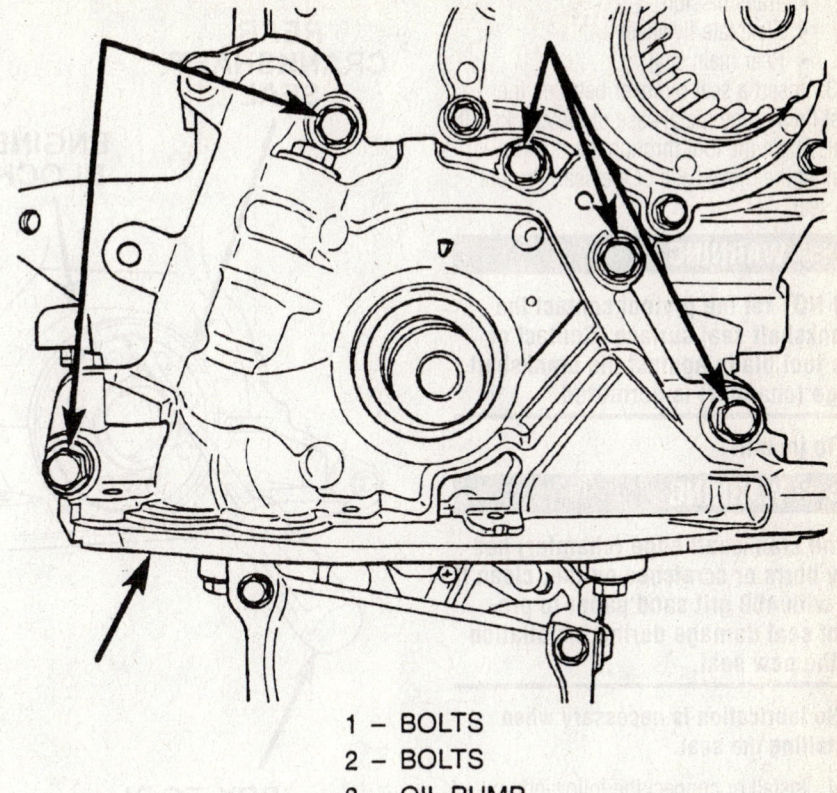

1 – BOLTS
2 – BOLTS
3 – OIL PUMP

9306ZG94

Exploded view of the oil pump mounting bolts

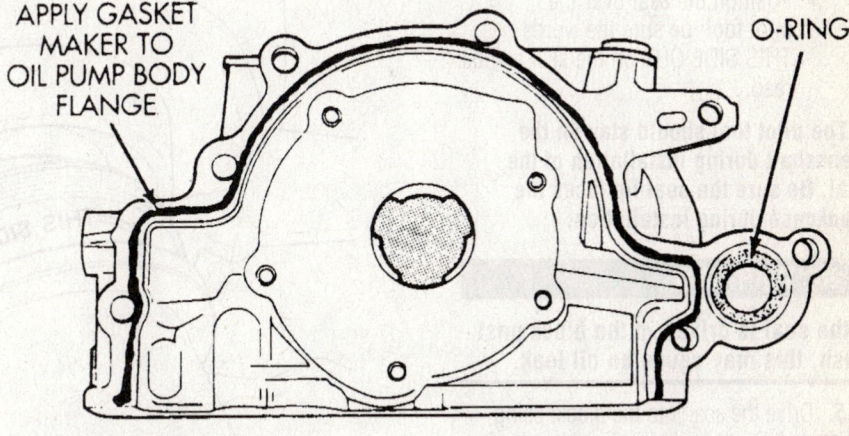

APPLY GASKET MAKER TO OIL PUMP BODY FLANGE

O-RING

7922EG31

Apply a small amount of gasket maker to the pump body cover mounting surface

- Oil pump pickup tube
- Oil pan
- Timing belt
- Rear timing belt cover
- Negative battery cable

7. Refill the engine with clean oil.

8. Start the engine and check for leaks; repair if necessary.

Rear Main Seal

REMOVAL & INSTALLATION

1. Before servicing the vehicle, refer to the precautions in the beginning of this section.

2. Remove or disconnect the following:

Refer to Section 1 for engine rebuilding specifications

- Transmission
- Flexplate/flywheel
- Rear main seal

3. Insert a seal remover between the dust lip and the metal case of the crankshaft seal. Angle the tool through the dust lip against the metal case of the seal. Pry out the seal.

✱✱ WARNING

DO NOT let the prytool contact the crankshaft seal surface. Contact of the tool blade against the crankshaft edge (chamfer) is permitted.

To install:

✱✱ WARNING

If the crankshaft edge (chamfer) has any burrs or scratches on the, clean it up with 400 grit sand paper to prevent seal damage during installation of the new seal.

➡No lubrication is necessary when installing the seal.

4. Install or connect the following:
- Place Crankcase Seal Pilot tool 6926-1 on the crankshaft; this is a pilot tool with a magnetic base
- Position the seal over the pilot tool; be sure the words THIS SIDE OUT on the seal can be read.

➡The pilot tool should stay on the crankshaft during installation of the seal. Be sure the seal lip faces the crankcase during installation.

✱✱ WARNING

If the seal is driven in the block past flush, this may cause an oil leak.

5. Drive the seal into the block, using Crankshaft Seal tool 6926-2 and handle C-4171, until the tool bottoms out against the block.
6. Install or connect the following:
- Flexplate/flywheel. Apply Lock & Seal Adhesive to the bolt treads. Torque the bolts in a star pattern, to 70 ft. lbs. (95 Nm).
- Transmission
- Negative battery cable

7. Start the vehicle and check for leaks, repair if necessary.

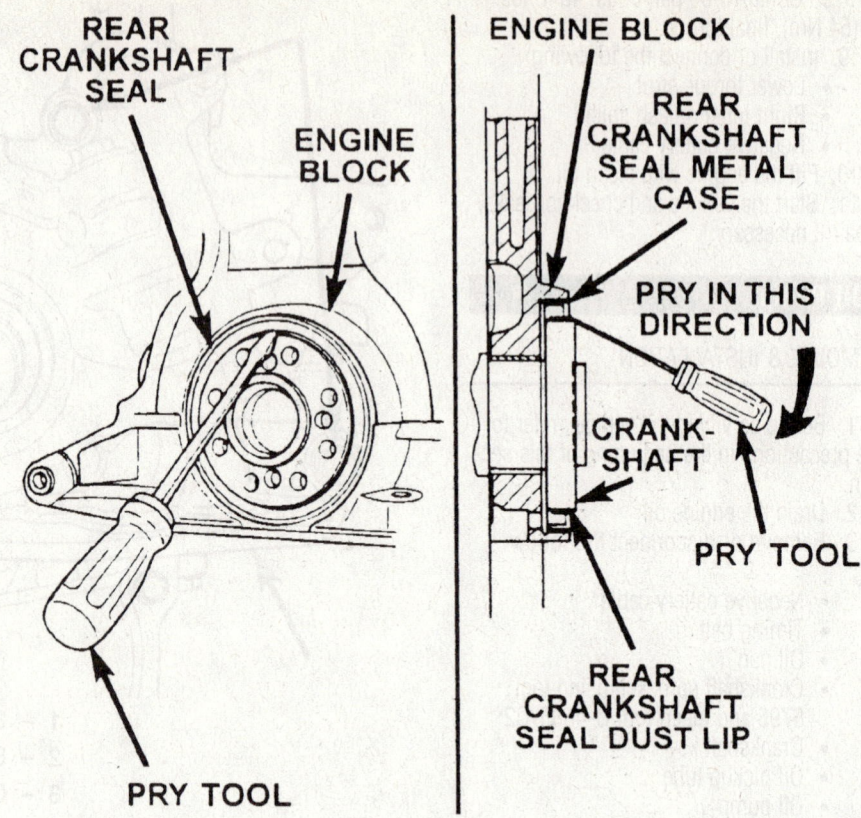

When prying the seal out, be sure to use the prytool at the proper angle

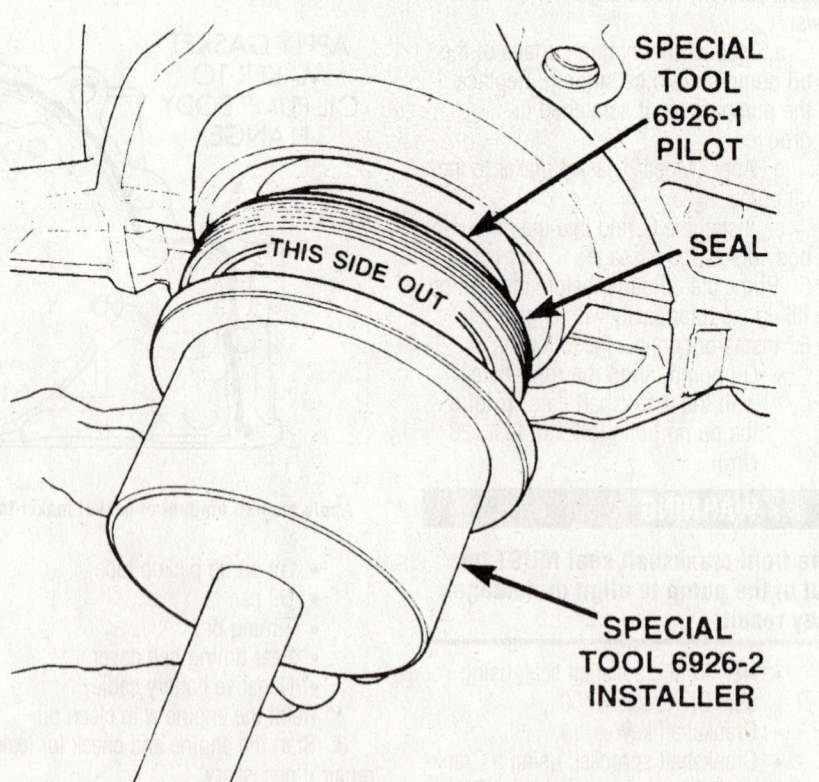

Place a proper size pilot tool with a magnetic base on the crankshaft

Piston and Ring

POSITIONING

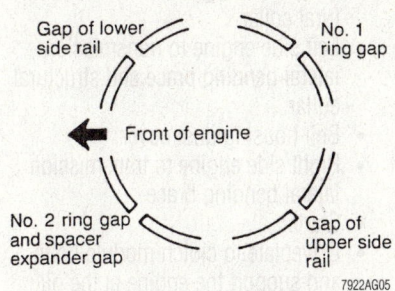

Piston ring end-gap spacing—2.4L engine

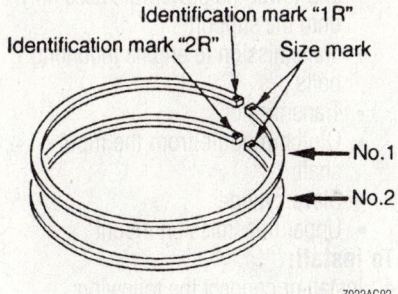

Common Chrysler piston ring identification mark locations

FUEL SYSTEM

Fuel System Service Precautions

Safety is an important factor when servicing the fuel system. Failure to conduct maintenance and repairs in a safe manner may result in serious personal injury. Maintenance and testing of the vehicle's fuel system components can be accomplished safely and effectively by adhering to the following rules and guidelines:

• To avoid the possibility of fire and personal injury, always disconnect the negative battery cable unless the repair or test procedure requires that battery voltage be applied.

• Always relieve the fuel system pressure prior to disconnecting any fuel system component (injector, fuel rail, pressure regulator, etc.), fitting or fuel line connection. Exercise extreme caution whenever relieving fuel system pressure, to avoid exposing skin, face and eyes to fuel spray. Please be advised that fuel under pressure may penetrate the skin or any part of the body that it contacts.

• Always place a shop towel or cloth around the fitting or connection prior to loosening to absorb any excess fuel due to spillage. Ensure that all fuel spillage is quickly removed from engine surfaces. Ensure that all fuel soaked cloths or towels are deposited into a suitable waste container.

• Always keep a dry chemical (Class B) fire extinguisher near the work area.

• Do not allow fuel spray or fuel vapors to come into contact with a spark or open flame.

• Always use a back-up wrench when loosening and tightening fuel line connection fittings. This will prevent unnecessary stress and torsion to fuel line piping.

• Always replace worn fuel fitting O-rings. Do not substitute fuel hose where fuel pipe is installed.

Fuel System Pressure

RELIEVING

✳✳ CAUTION

Relieve the fuel system pressure before servicing any components of the fuel system. Service vehicles in well ventilated areas and avoid ignition sources. NEVER smoke while servicing the vehicle!

1. Before servicing the vehicle, refer to the precautions in the beginning of this section.

2. Remove or disconnect the following:
• Negative battery cable
• Fuel pump relay from the Power Distribution Center (PDC)
• Start and run the engine until it stalls
• Turn the ignition key to the OFF position

Fuel Filter

The fuel filter is part of the fuel pump module located in the fuel tank.

REMOVAL & INSTALLATION

1. Before servicing the vehicle, refer to the precautions in the beginning of this section.

2. Properly relieve the fuel system pressure.

3. Remove or disconnect the following:
• Negative battery cable
• Remove the air cleaner lid
• Inlet Air Temperature (IAT) sensor and the make-up hose
• Fuel tank
• Fuel pump module and seal from the tank
• Fuel filter from the fuel pump module
• Quick-connect fuel supply line from the filter/regulator nipple

4. Depress the locking spring tab, located on the side of the fuel filter/regulator, then rotate 90 degrees and pull out. Be sure the upper and lower O-rings are still on the filter assembly.

To install:

5. Lightly coat the filter O-rings with clean engine oil. Insert the filter into the opening in the fuel pump module, then align the 2 hold-down tabs with the flange.

6. While applying downward pressure, rotate the filter clockwise until the spring tab catches in the locating slot.

7. Install or connect the following:
• Fuel line to the filter/regulator assembly
• Fuel pump module to the fuel tank
• IAT sensor and make-up hose
• Air cleaner lid
• Negative battery cable

8. Start the vehicle and check for leaks, repair if necessary.

Fuel Pump

The fuel pump is integral with the pump module, which also contains the fuel reservoir, level sensor, inlet strainer and fuel pressure regulator. The inlet strainer, fuel pressure regulator and level sensor are the only serviceable items. If the fuel pump requires service, replace the entire fuel pump module.

REMOVAL & INSTALLATION

1. Before servicing the vehicle, refer to the precautions in the beginning of this section.

2. Properly relieve the fuel system pressure.

3. Remove or disconnect the following:
• Negative battery cable
• Air cleaner lid
• Inlet Air Temperature (IAT) sensor and make up air hose

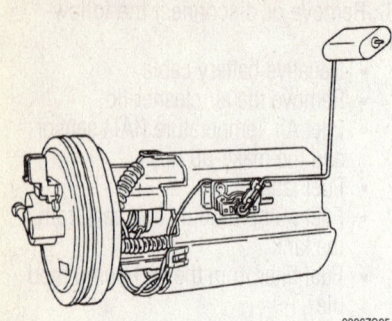

Exploded view of the fuel pump module

- Fuel tank
- Fuel pump module and seal from the tank
- Fuel filter lines from the fuel pump module
- Locknut to release the fuel pump module, using a Ring Spanner tool No. 6856
- Fuel pump and seal from the fuel tank

To install:

4. Install or connect the following:
- Fuel pump module in the tank
- Locknut while holding the fuel pump in position. Using tool 6856, torque the locknut to 56 ft. lbs. (75 Nm).
- Fuel tank
- IAT sensor and make-up hose
- Air cleaner lid
- Negative battery cable
5. Fill the fuel tank
6. Start the vehicle and check for leaks, repair if necessary.

Fuel Injector

REMOVAL & INSTALLATION

1. Before servicing the vehicle, refer to the precautions in the beginning of this section.

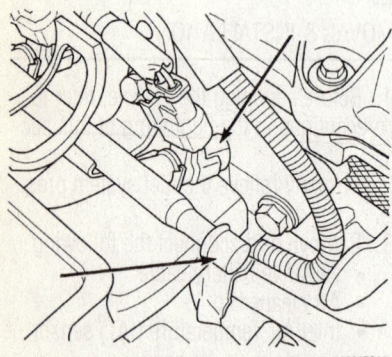

Remove the fuel rail and injectors as an assembly

2. Release the fuel system pressure.
3. Remove or disconnect the following:
- Negative battery cable
- Remove the air cleaner lid
- Inlet Air Temperature (IAT) sensor and the make-up hose
- Engine cover or throttle control shield, if equipped
- Fuel line(s) from fuel rail
- Intake manifold
- Fuel injector electrical connectors
- Fuel rail with the fuel injectors
- Fuel injector(s) and discard the O-rings

To install:

4. Install or connect the following:
- Fuel injector(s) using new O-rings

➡**Lubricate the O-rings with clean engine oil.**

- Fuel injector nozzles into the intake manifold. When seated properly, torque the fuel rail bolts to 8 ft. lbs. (12 Nm).
- Fuel injector electrical connectors
- Fuel line(s) to fuel rail
- Intake manifold
- Engine cover or throttle control shield, if equipped
- IAT sensor and make-up hose
- Air cleaner lid
- Negative battery cable

5. Start the vehicle and check for leaks, repair if necessary.

DRIVE TRAIN

Transaxle Assembly

REMOVAL & INSTALLATION

Manual Transmission

1. Before servicing the vehicle, refer to the precautions in the beginning of this section.
2. Drain the transmission fluid.
3. Remove or disconnect the following:
- Battery cables
- Battery and tray
- Air cleaner
- Back-up lamp switch wiring from the transmission
- Shift selector and crossover cable and move them out of the way
- Vehicle Speed Sensor (VSS) wire
- Clutch master cylinder hydraulic tube from the slave cylinder
- Both halfshafts
- Power steering hose from the structural collar
- Left side engine to transmission lateral bending brace and structural collar
- Bell housing dust cover
- Right side engine to transmission lateral bending brace
- Starter
- Driveplate to clutch module bolts and support the engine at the oil pan
- Transmission upper mount bolts and lower the powertrain assembly onto the support
- Transmission to engine mounting bolts
- Transmission
- Clutch module from the input shaft
- Slave cylinder
- Upper transmission mount

To install:

4. Install or connect the following:
- Clutch module to the transmission input shaft
- Upper transmission mount. Torque the bolts to 45 ft. lbs. (62 Nm).
- Transmission. Torque the transmission-to-engine bolts to 80 ft. lbs. (108 Nm).
- Driveplate to clutch module bolts. Torque the bolts to 65 ft. lbs. (88 Nm).
- Starter. Torque the bolts to 40 ft. lbs. (54 Nm).
- Ground cable to the starter
- Starter electrical connectors. Torque the nut to 89 inch lbs. (10 Nm).
- Bell housing dust cover
- Left side engine to transmission bending brace and structural brace. Torque the bolts to 60 ft. lbs. (81 Nm).
- Power steering hose to the structural collar
- Right lateral bending brace. Torque the bolts to 60 ft. lbs. (81 Nm).
- Both halfshafts
- Clutch master cylinder tube to the slave cylinder
- VSS electrical connector
- Shift crossover and selector cables to the shift lever
- Cables to the bracket and install a new retainer clip

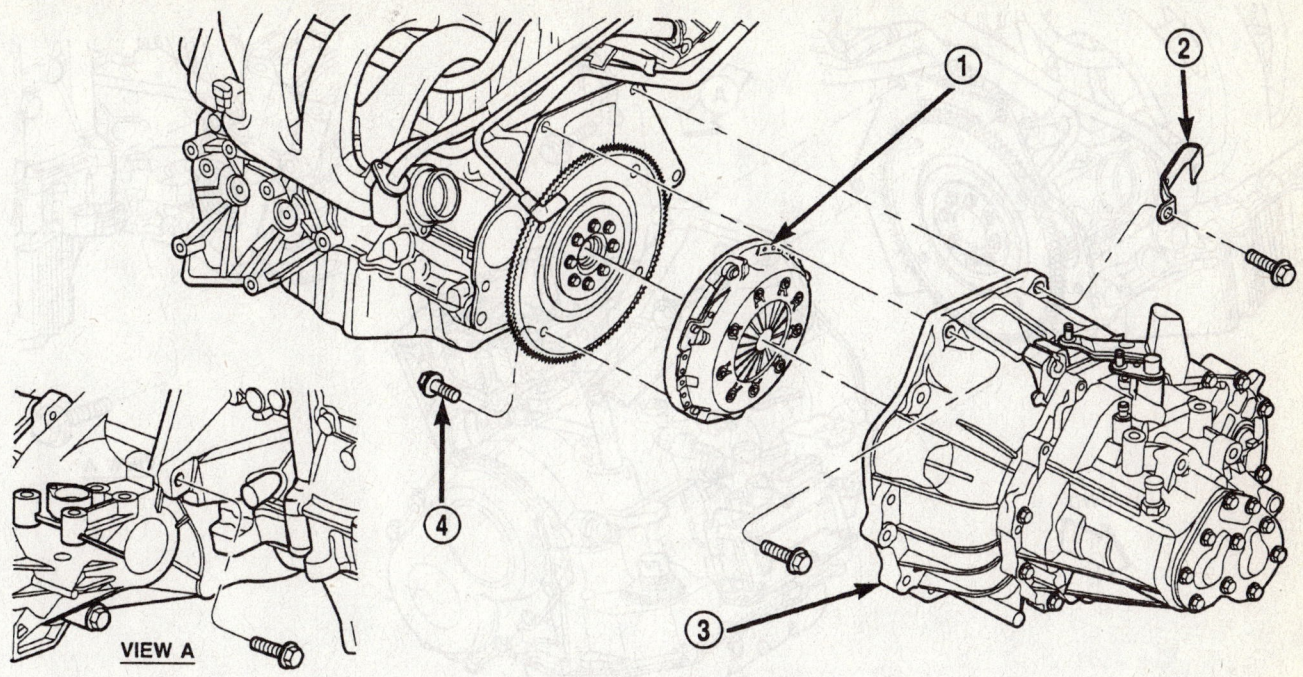

1 – MODULAR CLUTCH ASSEMBLY   3 – TRANSAXLE
2 – CLIP   4 – CLUTCH MODULE BOLT (4)

9306ZG0E

Remove the clutch module from the transmission assembly

- Back-up lamp switch connector
- Battery tray
- Battery
- Battery cables
- Air cleaner assembly

5. Fill the transmission fluid to the proper level.

6. Be sure the vehicle's back-up lights and speedometer are functioning properly.

7. Start the vehicle and check for leaks, repair if necessary.

Automatic Transmission

1. Before servicing the vehicle, refer to the precautions in the beginning of this section.

2. Remove or disconnect the following:
- Battery cables
- Air cleaner assembly
- Battery and tray
- Upper starter to transmission bell housing bolt
- Transmission dipstick and tube
- Gearshift cable end from the transmission shift lever
- Gearshift cable bracket bolt from the transmission

- Transmission oil cooler and lines. Plug the lines to prevent contamination
- Input and output speed sensor electrical connectors
- Transmission range sensor connector
- Solenoid/pressure switch assembly connector
- Both front wheels
- Left front splash shield
- Both halfshafts
- Power steering hose from the structural collar
- Left and right side engine to transmission lateral brace and structural collar
- Starter motor electrical connectors
- Starter
- Gearshift cable bracket
- Driveplate to torque converter bolts and support the powertrain assembly
- Transmission upper mount to bracket bolts and lower the powertrain assembly
- Transmission

To install:

3. Install or connect the following:

- Transmission. Torque the transmission-to-engine bolts to 80 ft. lbs. (105 Nm) and support the transmission with a jack
- Mount to transmission bracket bolts. Torque the bolts to 50 ft. lbs. (68 Nm) and remove the jack
- Driveplate to torque converter bolts. Torque the bolts to 65 ft. lbs. (88 Nm).
- Starter and hand tighten the bolts
- Dipstick tube and secure the bracket to the transmission. Torque the upper starter bolt to 40 ft. lbs. (54 Nm).
- Cable bracket to the bell housing. Torque the bolt to 45 ft. lbs. (61 Nm).
- Starter lower bolt. Torque the bolt to 40 ft. lbs. (54 Nm).
- Starter electrical connections
- Bell housing dust cover
- Lower dust shield screws. Torque the bell housing cover bolts to 108 inch lbs. (12 Nm).
- Right side lateral bending brace. Torque the bolts to 60 ft. lbs. (81 Nm).

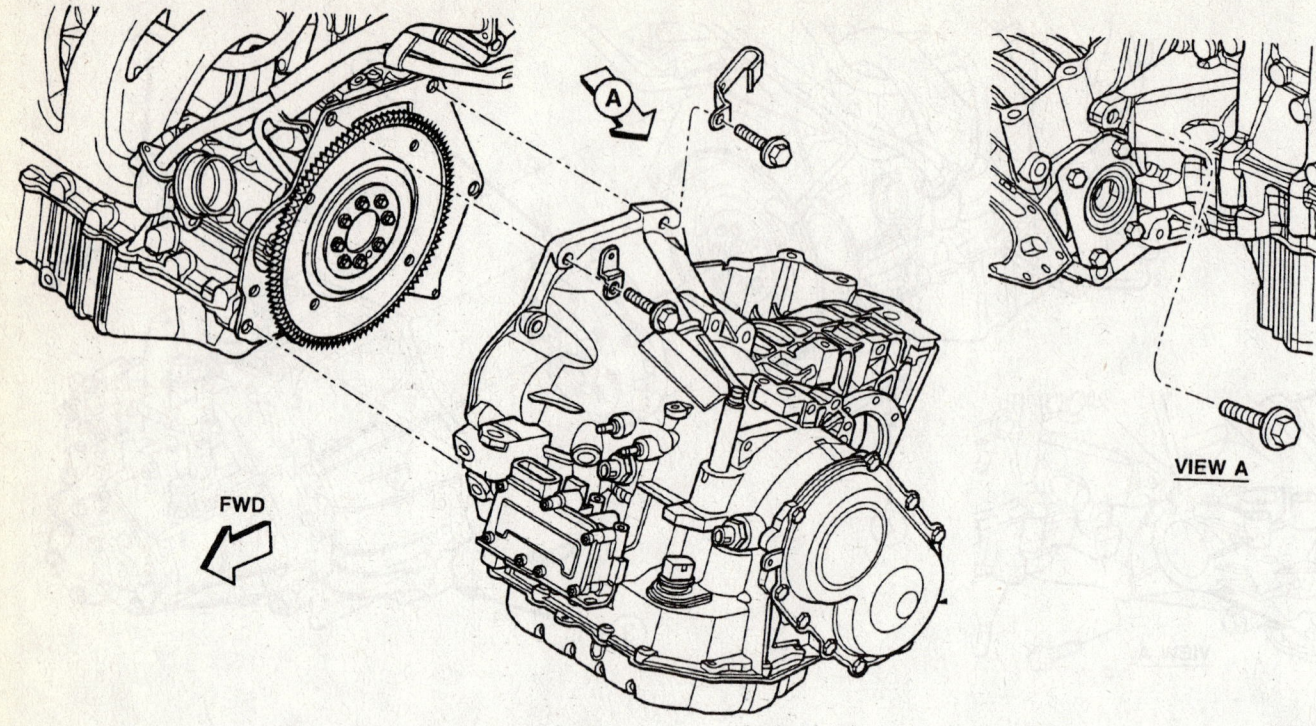

FWD

VIEW A

9306ZG97

Exploded view of automatic transmission removal

- Both halfshafts
- Left side splash shield and wheel
- Cooler lines to the transmission and secure with constant tension clamps
- Solenoid/pressure switch assembly
- Transmission range sensor connector
- Input/output sensor connectors
- Gearshift cable to the bracket and connect it to the manual valve lever
- Battery tray and battery
- Air cleaner assembly
- VSS wiring
- Battery cables

4. Refill the transmission.
5. Be sure the vehicle's back-up lights and speedometer are working properly.

Clutch

ADJUSTMENT

This vehicle utilizes a modular clutch assembly located between the engine and the transmission. The modular clutch is serviced as an assembly and is self-adjusting. The self-adjusting feature of the clutch relies on a sensor ring and adjuster ring.

REMOVAL & INSTALLATION

1. Before servicing the vehicle, refer to the precautions in the beginning of this section.
2. Remove or disconnect the following:
   - Negative battery cable
   - Air cleaner assembly
   - Battery and tray
   - Back-up lamp electrical connector
   - Shift cable to bracket clips
   - Shift lever and crossover cable from the levers. Move the cables out of the way
   - Vehicle Speed Sensor (VSS) electrical connector
   - Clutch master cylinder tube from the slave cylinder using tool 6638A
   - Both halfshafts
   - Power steering hose from the structural collar
   - Left side lateral bending brace and structural collar
   - Bell housing dust cover
   - Right side lateral bending brace
   - Starter
   - Driveplate to clutch module bolts and support the engine at the oil pan
   - Transmission upper mount bolts and lower the engine/transmission assembly
   - Modular clutch from the input shaft

To install:

3. Install or connect the following:
   - Clutch module to the input shaft
   - Transmission to engine mount bolts. Torque the bolts to 80 ft. lbs. (108 Nm).
   - Upper mount bolts. Torque the bolts to 65 ft. lbs. (88 Nm).

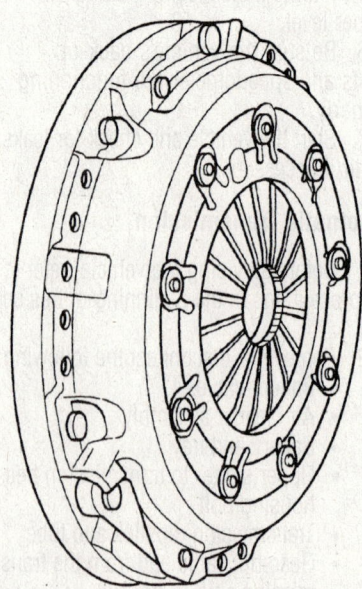

9306ZG98

Exploded view of the modular clutch assembly

- Driveplate to clutch module bolts. Torque the bolts to 65 ft. lbs. (88 Nm).
- Starter. Torque the bolts to 40 ft. lbs. (54 Nm). Make certain that the ground cable is fastened to the upper bolt
- Starter electrical connectors. Torque the positive cable nut to 89 inch lbs. (10 Nm).
- Bell housing dust cover
- Left side lateral bending brace and structural collar.
- Power steering hose to the structural collar
- Right side lateral bending brace. Torque the bolts to 60 ft. lbs. (81 Nm).
- Both halfshafts
- Clutch master cylinder tube to the slave cylinder
- VSS electrical connector
- Back-up lamp switch electrical connector
- Air cleaner assembly
- Battery and tray
- Battery cables

4. Fill the transmission to the proper level.

5. Road test the vehicle and check for proper clutch operation.

6. Check the fluid level and adjust if needed.

Halfshafts

REMOVAL & INSTALLATION

1. Before servicing the vehicle, refer to the precautions in the beginning of this section.

2. Place the transmission in the **P** position, for automatic transmission or neutral for manual transmissions.

3. Remove or disconnect the following:
- Negative battery cable
- Front wheel
- Cotter pin, locknut and spring washer from the end of the outer Constant Velocity (CV) joint stub axle
- Driveshaft to hub and bearing nut
- Front wheel speed sensor, if equipped
- Steering knuckle from the ball joint
- Driveshaft from the steering knuckle and support the outer end of the driveshaft

---

✳✳ WARNING

Be careful when separating the ball joint stud from the steering knuckle, so the ball joint seal does not get damaged.

✳✳ WARNING

Be careful when separating the inner CV-joint during this operation. Do not let the driveshaft hang by the inner CV-joint, the driveshaft must be supported.

➡**Inner Tri-Pot joint removal is easier by applying outward pressure on the joint while hitting the punch with a hammer.**

4. Inner Tri-Pot joints from the transmission side gears using a punch to dislodge the inner Tri-Pot joint retaining ring from the transmission side gear. If removing the right side inner Tri-Pot joint, position the punch against the inner Tri-Pot joint. Hit the punch sharply with a hammer to dislodge the right inner joint from the side gear. If removing the left side inner Tri-Pot joint, position the punch in the groove of the inner Tri-Pot joint. Hit the punch sharply with a hammer to dislodge the left inner Tri-Pot joint from the side gear.

5. Hold the inner Tri-Pot joint and interconnecting shaft of the driveshaft assembly. Remove the inner Tri-Pot joint from the transaxle by pulling it straight out of the transaxle side gear and transmission oil seal. When removing the Tri-Pot joint, do not let the spline or snapring drag across the sealing lip of the transmission-to-Tri-Pot joint oil seal.

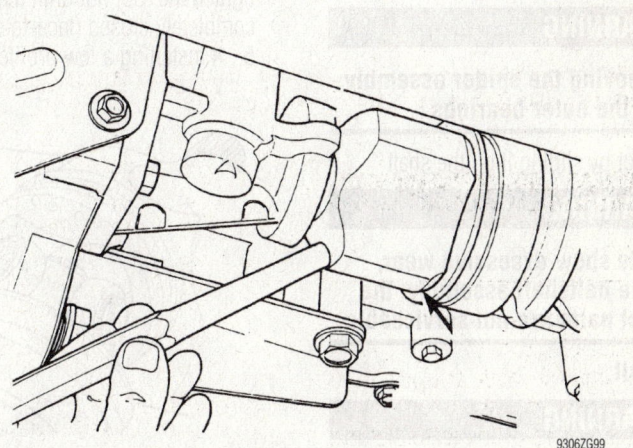

Remove the Tri-Pot joint from the transmission

✳✳ WARNING

The driveshaft, when installed, acts as a bolt which secures the front hub and bearing assembly. If the vehicle is to be supported or moved on its wheels with a driveshaft removed, install a proper-sized bolt and nut through the front hub. Tighten the bolt and nut to 135 ft. lbs. (183 Nm). This will ensure that the hub bearing cannot loosen.

To install:

6. Thoroughly clean the spline and oil seal sealing surface on the Tri-Pot joint. Lightly lubricate the oil seal sealing surface on the Tri-Pot joint with fresh, clean transmission fluid.

7. Install or connect the following:
- Holding the driveshaft assembly by the Tri-Pot joint and interconnecting shaft, install the Tri-Pot joint into the transmission side gear as far as possible by hand.
- Align the Tri-Pot joint with the transmission side gears, grasp the driveshaft interconnecting shaft and push the Tri-Pot joint into the transmission side gear until fully seated. Be sure the snapring is fully engaged with the side gear by trying to remove the Tri-Pot joint from the transaxle by hand. If the snapring is fully seated with the side gear, the Tri-Pot joint will not be removable by hand.
- Driveshaft back into the front hub. Install the steering knuckle into the ball joint stud.
- New steering knuckle-to-ball joint

stud bolt and nut. Torque the nut and bolt to 70 ft. lbs. (95 Nm).
- Washer and hub nut to the stub axle. Torque the nut to 180 ft. lbs. (244 Nm).
- Spring washer, locknut and cotter pin
- VSS, if equipped
- Front wheel
- Negative battery cable

8. Check the transmission fluid and adjust if needed.

CV-Joints

OVERHAUL

Tri-Pot (Inner) Joint

1. Before servicing the vehicle, refer to the precautions in the beginning of this section.
2. Remove or disassemble the following:
   - Negative battery cable
   - Halfshaft
   - Tri-pot joint boot clamps and slide the boot down the shaft

❋❋ WARNING

When removing the spider joint, hold the rollers in place on the trunions to keep the rollers and needle bearings in place.

- Slide the interconnecting shaft and spider assembly from the tri-pot housing
- Snapring from the shaft
- Spider assembly

➡ **If necessary, tap the spider assembly from the shaft with a brass drift.**

❋❋ WARNING

When removing the spider assembly, do not hit the outer bearings.

- Boot by sliding it off the shaft

❋❋ WARNING

If any parts show excessive wear, replace the halfshaft assembly; the component parts are not serviceable.

To install:

❋❋ WARNING

The Tri-pot sealing boots are made of 2 different types of material; silicon

rubber (high temperature) which is soft and pliable or hytrel plastic (standard temperature) which is stiff and rigid. Be sure to replace the boot made of the correct material.

3. Install or connect the following:
   - New small boot clamp and slide it on the shaft
   - Boot and slide it on the shaft
   - Position the boot so that the raised bead on the inside the boot seal is in the shaft groove.
   - Spider assembly, face the chamfered side toward the shaft
   - Snapring making sure it is fully seated in the groove
   - Spider/shaft assembly into the tri-pot housing
   - New inner boot clamp and position it evenly on the sealing boot
   - Using a trim stick, adjust the boot length to 115mm (hytrel plastic) or 115mm (silicone rubber).

4. If installing a high profile boot clamp, perform the following procedure:

   a. Using the Crimper tool C-4975-A, place the tool over the clamp bridge, tighten the tool nut until the jaws are completely closed (face-to-face).

❋❋ WARNING

The seal must not be dimpled, stretched or out of shape. If necessary, equalize the seal pressure and shape it by hand.

   b. Position the boot onto the tri-pot housing retaining groove and install the retaining clamp evenly on the boot

   c. Using the Crimper tool C-4975-A, place the tool over the clamp bridge, tighten the tool nut until the jaws are completely closed (face-to-face).

5. If installing a low profile latching type

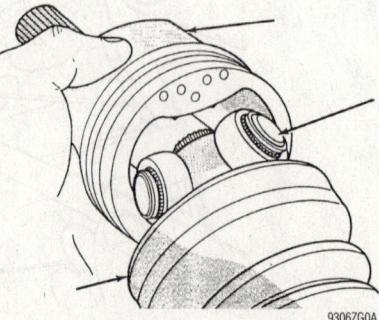

Install the Tri-Pot housing on to the spider assembly

9306ZG0A

boot clamp, position Snap-On® Clamp Locking tool YA3050 prongs in the clamp holes and squeeze the tool until the upper clamp band is latched behind the 2 tabs on the lower clamp band.

6. Install or connect the following:
   - Halfshaft
   - Negative battery cable

Outer Joint

1. Before servicing the vehicle, refer to the precautions in the beginning of this section.
2. Remove or disassemble the following:
   - Halfshaft
   - Clamps from the CV-joint boot and discard
   - Boot from the CV-joint housing and slide it down the interconnecting shaft
   - Outer CV-joint from the interconnecting shaft by sharply hitting it with a soft-faced hammer to drive it off the shaft
   - Circlip from the shaft
   - CV-joint by sliding it off the shaft

❋❋ WARNING

If any parts show excessive wear, replace the halfshaft assembly; the component parts are not serviceable.

To install:

3. Install or assemble the following:
   - New small boot clamp and slide it onto the shaft
   - Boot and slide it onto the shaft
   - Circlip
   - Position the boot so that the raised bead on the inside the boot seal is in the shaft groove
   - Halfshaft hub nut onto the joint threaded shaft so it is flush with the end
   - Align the shaft splines and tap it onto the shaft with a soft-faced hammer so it locks on the circlip

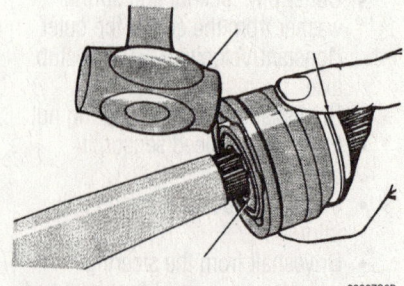

Remove the outer C/V joint from the interconnecting shaft

9306ZG0B

- Distribute ½ of the grease in the service package inside the joint housing and the other ½ inside the boot.
- New small boot clamp and position it evenly on the sealing boot

✳✳ CAUTION

Clamp the boot to the shaft using the Crimper tool C-4975-A, place the tool over the clamp bridge, tighten the tool nut until the jaws are completely closed (face-to-face).

✳✳ WARNING

The seal must not be dimpled, stretched or out of shape. If necessary, equalize the seal pressure and shape it by hand.

- Position the boot onto the retaining groove and install the retaining clamp evenly on the boot.
- Clamp the boot to the outer CV-joint housing using the Crimper tool C-4975-A, place the tool over the clamp bridge, tighten the tool nut until the jaws are completely closed (face-to-face).
- Halfshaft
- Negative battery cable

STEERING AND SUSPENSION

Air Bag

✳✳ CAUTION

Some vehicles are equipped with an air bag system. The system MUST BE disabled before performing service on or around system components, steering column, instrument panel components, wiring and sensors. Failure to follow safety and disabling procedures could result in accidental air bag deployment, possible personal injury and unnecessary system repairs.

PRECAUTIONS

Several precautions must be observed when handling the inflator module to avoid accidental deployment and possible personal injury:

- Never carry the inflator module by the wires or connector on the underside of the module.
- When carrying a live inflator module, hold securely with both hands, and ensure that the bag and trim cover are pointed away.
- Place the inflator module on a bench or other surface with the bag and trim cover facing up.
- With the inflator module on the bench, never place anything on or close to the module which may be thrown in the event of an accidental deployment.

DISARMING

Proper SRS disarming can be obtained by disconnecting and isolating the negative battery cable. Allow the air bag system capacitor at least 2 minutes to discharge before removing any air bag system components.

Rack and Pinion Steering Gear

REMOVAL & INSTALLATION

1. Before servicing the vehicle, refer to the precautions in the beginning of this section.
2. Place the steering wheel in the straight-ahead position. Lock the steering wheel in place, using a steering wheel holder.

➡**Locking the steering wheel keeps the clockspring in alignment position.**

3. Remove or disconnect the following:
- Silencer pad from below the knee blocker panel
- Knee blocker
- Steering column coupling retainer pin, pinch bolt nut/bolt and separate the couplings
- Both front wheels
- Outer tie rods-to-steering knuckle nuts
- Outer tie rod ends from the steering knuckle using remover tool MB991113
- Tie rod heat shield
- Power steering fluid pressure switch wiring connector by releasing the locking tab
- Power steering fluid pressure hose from the steering gear
- Power steering fluid return hose

from the steering gear, if not equipped with a power steering fluid cooler
- Power steering fluid cooler hose from the steering gear, if equipped with a power steering fluid cooler
- Power steering fluid return hose from the routing clip C-clamps, if not equipped with a power steering fluid cooler
- Power steering fluid pressure hose from the steering gear's routing clips
- Power steering cooler hose from the steering gear's right routing clip, if equipped
- Both power steering cooler screws from the front suspension crossmember, if equipped, and move the cooler aside
- Drive belt splash shield
- Engine torque strut-to-front suspension crossmember bolt from the right forward corner of the crossmember

4. Matchmark the front suspension crossmember-to-chassis location.

✳✳ WARNING

If the front suspension crossmember-to-chassis location is not matchmarked, the front wheel alignment setting will be lost.

5. Place a transmission jack under the front crossmember and support it.
6. Remove or disconnect the following:
- Both front suspension crossmember-to-frame rail bolts, one located at each side
- Loosen both rear suspension crossmember-to-frame rail bolts, one located at each side, until they release from the threaded tapping plates in the bolt

✳✳ WARNING

Do not completely remove the rear bolts for they are designed to disengage from the body threads and will stay within the lower control arm rear isolator bushing.

➡**The threaded tapping plates allow the lower control arm to stay in place on the crossmember.**

7. Using the transmission jack, lower the front suspension crossmember enough

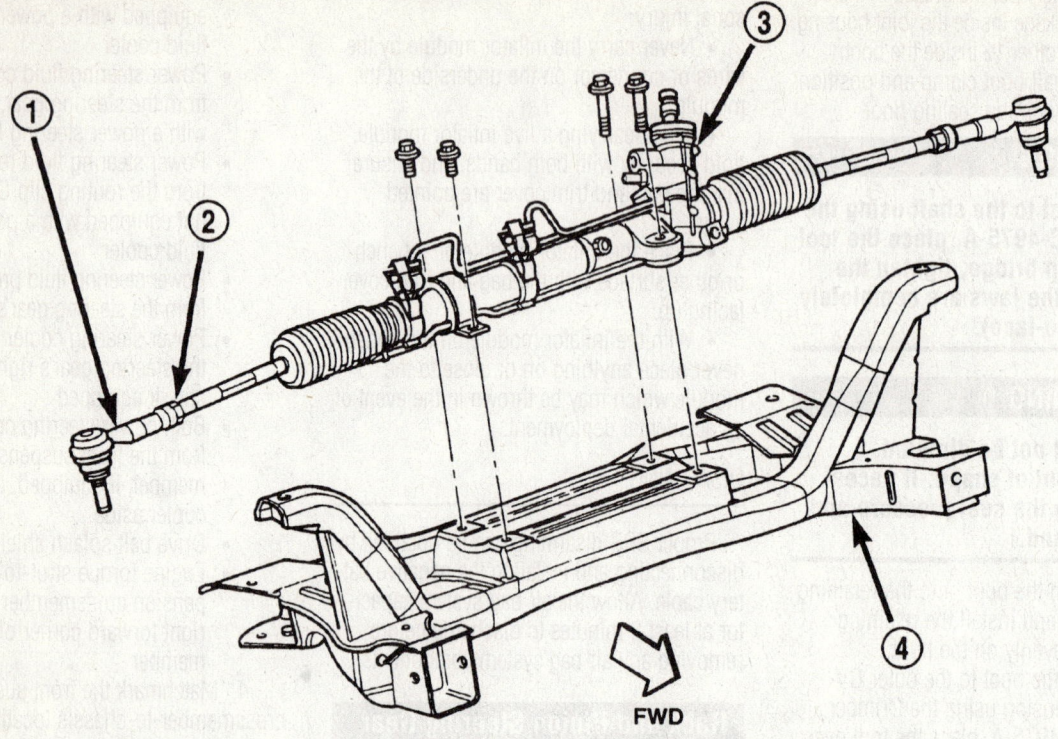

1 – OUTER TIE ROD
2 – JAM NUT

3 – STEERING GEAR
4 – FRONT SUSPENSION CROSSMEMBER

9306EG42

View of the power steering gear and crossmember—2000–01 vehicle

to allow the power steering gear to be removed form the rear of the crossmember. Use the jack to support the crossmember's weight.

8. Remove or disconnect the following:
   - Lower steering column coupling-to-power steering gear pinion shaft's roll pin, using a roll pin punch
   - Lower steering column coupling from the power steering column pinion shaft
   - Pinion shaft dash cover seal from the tabs cast into the power steering gear housing
   - Power steering gear from the front suspension crossmember

To install:

9. Install or connect the following:
   - Power steering gear onto the front suspension crossmember. Torque the bolts to 45 ft. lbs. (61 Nm).
   - Pinion shaft dash cover seal over the shaft and onto the power steering gear housing. Align the seal holes with the tabs cast into the power steering gear housing
   - Lower steering column coupling by

aligning the coupling and steering gear pinion shaft flats
   - Lower steering column coupling-to-pinion shaft's roll pin until it is centered. Center the power steering gear rack's travel
   - Front suspension crossmember/power steering gear assembly by raising it with the jack until is aligns with its matchmarks
   - Lower steering column coupling, guide it through the dash panel hole as it is raised
   - Both rear crossmember-to-tapping plate bolts
   - Both front crossmember-to-frame rail bolts. Torque the 4 bolts to 20 inch lbs. (2 Nm).

✲✲ WARNING

Be sure to align the front suspension crossmember-to-chassis matchmarks; otherwise, the front wheel alignment setting will be lost.

   - Once aligned, torque both rear crossmember-to-rear lower control arm bolts to 185 ft. lbs. (250 Nm)

and both front crossmember bolts to 113 ft. lbs. (153 Nm).
   - Engine torque strut to the right forward corner of the front suspension crossmember

10. Adjust the engine torque strut by performing the following procedure:
    a. Loosen the upper torque strut at the shock tower bracket.
    b. Position a floor jack on the forward edge of the bell housing to prevent the least amount of upward lifting of the engine.
    c. Slowly, lift the assembly, allowing the engine to rotate rearward so the distance between center of the engine mount bracket's rearmost attaching stud (point A) and the center of the shock tower bracket's washer hose clip hole (point B) is 4.70 in. (119mm).
    d. Torque the upper and lower torque strut bolts to 87 ft. lbs. (118 Nm).
    e. Remove the floor jack.

11. Install or connect the following:
    - Drive belt splash shield
    - Power steering hose-to-power steering gear using a new O-ring lubricated with power steering oil, if

not equipped with a power steering cooler
- Power steering fluid cooler line-to-power steering gear, if equipped with a power steering cooler
- Power steering fluid return hose to the routing clip C-clamps
- Tie rod ends to the steering knuckle. Torque the nut, using a crowsfoot wrench, to 40 ft. lbs. (55 Nm), while holding the tie rod stationary
- Both front wheels
- Dash-to-lower coupling seal over the lower coupling's plastic collar

➡**Verify that the seal's lip shows grease at the coupling's plastic collar contact.**

- Steering column lower coupling-to-steering column upper coupling pinch bolt. Torque the nut to 21 ft. lbs. (28 Nm).
- Pinch bolt retainer pin
- Knee blocker and silencer pad

12. Remove the steering wheel holder.
13. Refill and bleed the power steering system.
14. Start the vehicle and check for leaks, repair if necessary.
15. Check and/or adjust the front toe setting.

Strut

REMOVAL & INSTALLATION

Front

1. Before servicing the vehicle, refer to the precautions in the beginning of this section.
2. Install or connect the following:
- Negative battery cable
- Front wheels
- Mark each one right or left, as applicable, if both struts are being removed
- Ground strap from the rear of the strut
- Anti-lock Brake System (ABS) wheel speed sensor from the strut, if equipped

✳✳ WARNING

The steering knuckle-to-strut assembly attaching bolts are serrated and must not be turned during removal.

- Steering knuckle nuts while holding the bolts stationary
- Steering knuckle nuts by holding the bolts in place
- 3 upper strut mount-to-strut tower nuts
- Strut assembly

To install:
3. Install or connect the following:
- Strut assembly into the strut tower by aligning the 3 upper strut mount studs with the shock tower holes. Torque the 3 upper strut mount nut/washer assemblies to 25 ft. lbs. (34 Nm).

✳✳ WARNING

The steering knuckle-to-strut assembly attaching bolts are serrated and must not be turned during installation.

- Steering knuckle nuts while holding the bolts stationary
- Steering knuckle arm and position it into the strut assembly by aligning the strut assembly-to-steering knuckle holes
- Both strut-to-steering knuckle bolts. Torque both bolts to 40 ft.

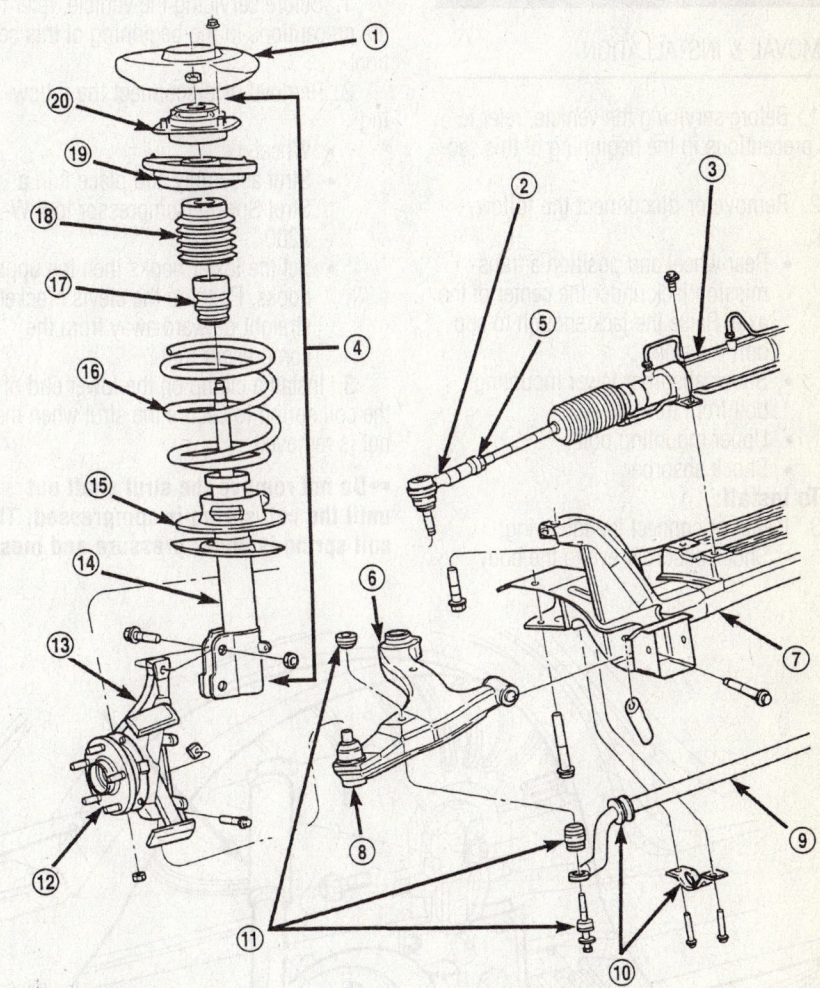

1 – VEHICLE STRUT TOWER
2 – OUTER TIE ROD
3 – STEERING GEAR
4 – STRUT ASSEMBLY
5 – JAM NUT
6 – LOWER CONTROL ARM
7 – CROSSMEMBER
8 – BALL JOINT
9 – STABILIZER BAR
10 – STABILIZER BAR CUSHION AND RETAINER
11 – STABILIZER BAR LINK
12 – HUB
13 – KNUCKLE
14 – STRUT
15 – LOWER SPRING ISOLATOR
16 – COIL SPRING
17 – JOUNCE BUMPER
18 – DUST SHIELD
19 – SPRING SEAT AND BEARING
20 – UPPER MOUNT

9306EG11

Exploded view of the front suspension

lbs. (53 Nm), plus an additional 90 degrees after the specified torque is met

➡**The bolts should be installed with the nuts facing the front of the vehicle.**

- ABS wheel sensor to the rear of the strut. Torque the screw to 120 inch lbs. (13 Nm).
- Ground strap to the rear of the strut. Torque the screw to 120 inch lbs. (13 Nm).
- Front wheel
- Negative battery cable

Shock Absorber

REMOVAL & INSTALLATION

1. Before servicing the vehicle, refer to the precautions in the beginning of this section.
2. Remove or disconnect the following:

- Rear wheel and position a transmission jack under the center of the axle. Raise the jack enough to support the axle
- Shock absorber lower mounting bolt from the axle
- Upper mounting bolt
- Shock absorber

To install:

3. Install or connect the following:
- Shock absorber eye to the body

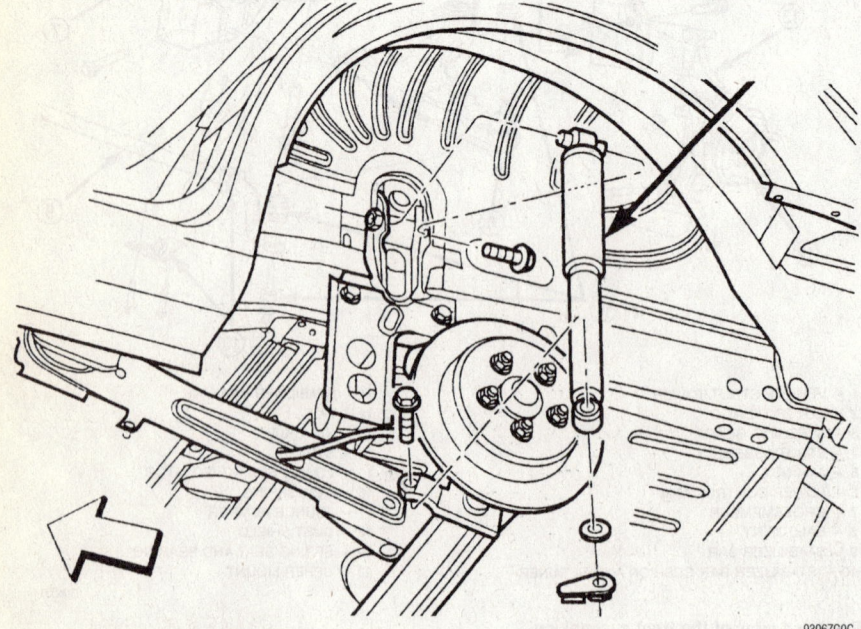

Shock absorber mounting bolts

9306ZG0C

bracket. Hand tighten the upper mounting bolt
- Lower the jack and install the lower mounting bolt through the axle flange and shock absorber. Torque the bolt to 50 ft. lbs. (68 Nm). Torque the upper mounting bolt to 73 ft. lbs. (99 Nm).
- Rear wheel and remove the jack
- Negative battery cable

Coil Spring

REMOVAL & INSTALLATION

1. Before servicing the vehicle, refer to the precautions in the beginning of this section.
2. Remove or disconnect the following:

- Wheel
- Strut assembly and place it in a Strut Spring Compressor tool W-7200
- Set the lower hooks then the upper hooks. Position the clevis bracket straight outward away from the compressor tool

3. Install a clamp on the lower end of the coil spring to secure the strut when the nut is removed.

➡**Do not remove the strut shaft nut until the coil spring is compressed. The coil spring is under pressure and must**

be compressed before the shaft nut is removed.

4. Compress the coil spring until all tension is removed from the upper mount.
5. Install a Strut Nut Socket tool 6864 once the spring is compressed.
6. Install a socket on the hex end of the strut shaft and remove the nut.
7. Remove or disconnect the following:

- Upper mount from the strut shaft
- Upper spring seat, bearing and upper isolator as an assembly
- Dust shield and jounce bumper
- Clamp from the bottom of the coil spring
- Strut through the bottom of the coil
- Release the tension from the coil spring by backing off the compressor drive completely
- Coil spring

8. Inspect the coil spring for any signs of damage

To install:

9. Install or connect the following:
- Coil spring in the compressor. Rotate the spring so that the end of the top coil is directly in the front
- Slowly compress the coil until enough room is available to install the strut
- Lower spring isolator on the lower spring seat
- Strut through the bottom of the of the coil spring until the lower spring seat contacts the lower end of the coil spring. Rotate the strut until the clevis bracket is positioned straight outward away from the compressor
- Clamp on the lower end of the coil spring and strut
- Jounce bumper on the strut shaft with the smaller end pointing downward
- Dust shield until the bottom of the shield snaps on to the retainer
- Upper spring isolator
- Upper spring seat and bearing on top of the coil spring. Position the notch formed into the edge of the upper seat straight out away from the compressor
- Strut upper mount over the strut shaft and onto the top of the upper spring seat and bearing. Position the mount so that the third mounting stud is inward toward the compressor
- Loosely install the retaining nut on the strut shaft
- Strut nut socket on the strut shaft

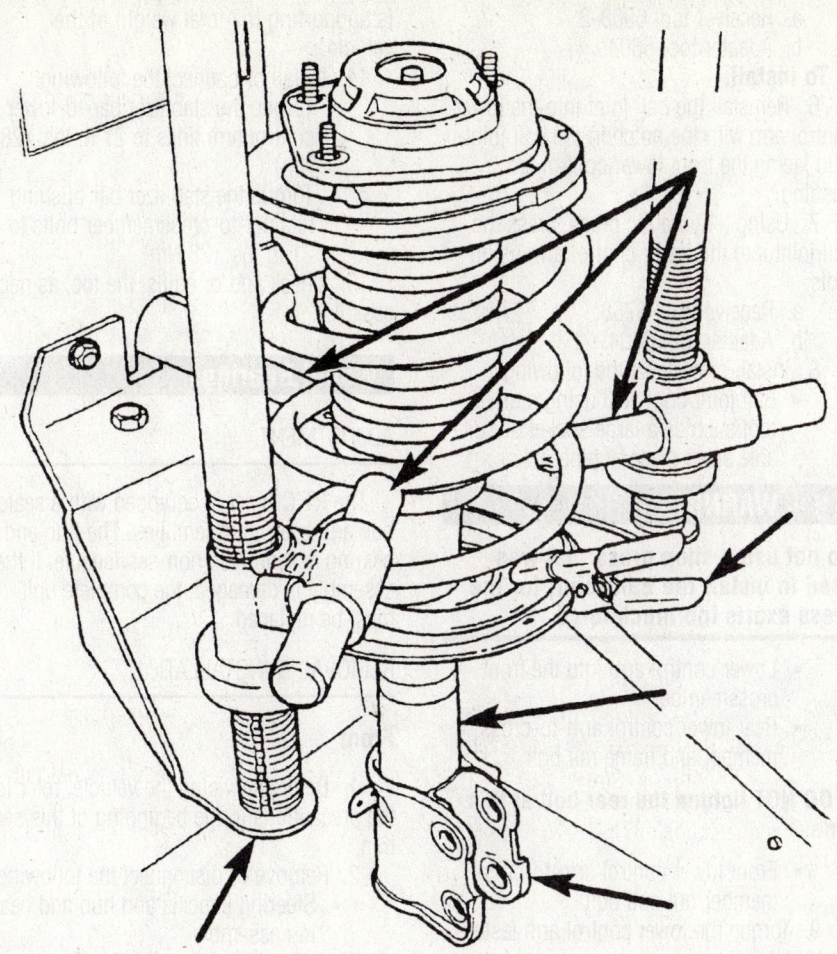

1 – LOWER HOOKS
2 – CLAMP
3 – STRUT ASSEMBLY
4 – CLEVIS BRACKET
5 – SPRING COMPRESSOR

9306ZG0D

Coil spring mounted in the coil spring compressor tool

retaining nut. Install a socket on the hex end of the shaft. Secure the strut shaft and torque the nut to 55 ft. lbs. (75 Nm).
- Slowly release the tension from the coil spring by backing off the compressor completely

10. Remove the clamp from the bottom of the coil spring and strut. Push back the spring compressor upper and lower hooks and remove the strut from the compressor

11. Install the strut assembly to the vehicle.

Lower Ball Joint

REMOVAL & INSTALLATION

The front suspension ball joints operate with no free-play. The ball joints are replaceable ONLY as an assembly. Do not attempt any type of repair on the ball joint assembly. The ball joint is a press fit into the lower control arm with the joint stud retained in the steering knuckle by the clamp bolt. To check the ball joint, with the weight of the vehicle resting on the road wheels, grasp the grease

fitting and without using any tools, attempt to move the grease fitting. If the ball joint is worn the grease fitting will move easily. If movement is noted, replacement of the ball joint is recommended.

1. Before servicing the vehicle, refer to the precautions in the beginning of this section.

2. Remove or disconnect the following:
- Wheel
- Stabilizer bar-to-lower control arm links
- Loosen, but do not remove the bolts holding the stabilizer bar retainers to the crossmember. Then, rotate the stabilizer bar and attaching links away from the lower control arms

✲✲ WARNING

Pulling the steering knuckle outward after releasing the ball joint can separate the inner CV-joint.

- Steering knuckle-to-ball joint stud's pinch bolt and nut
- Ball joint from the steering knuckle using a prybar

✲✲ WARNING

Be careful when separating the ball joint stud from the knuckle, so the seal does not become damaged.

3. If removing the right lower control arm, perform the following steps:
   a. Remove the drive belt splash shield.
   b. Remove the pencil strut from the right front corner of the crossmember
   c. Remove the engine torque strut.

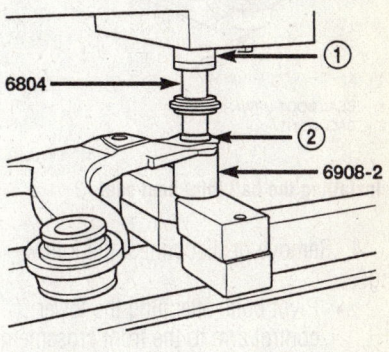

1 – PRESS
2 – BALL JOINT

9306EG51

Removing the ball joint from the control arm

Turn to Section 5 for brake system applications

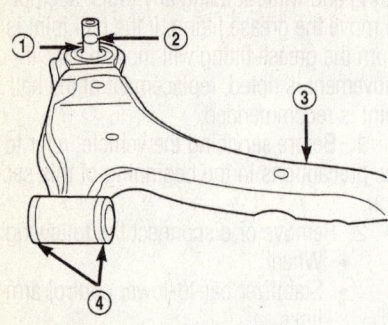

1 – BALL JOINT STUD
2 – NOTCH
3 – LOWER CONTROL ARM
4 – FRONT ISOLATOR BUSHING

9306EG52

Aligning the ball joint stud notch to the control arm

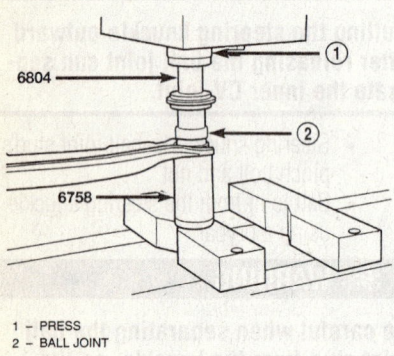

1 – PRESS
2 – BALL JOINT

9306EG53

Installing the ball joint to the control arm

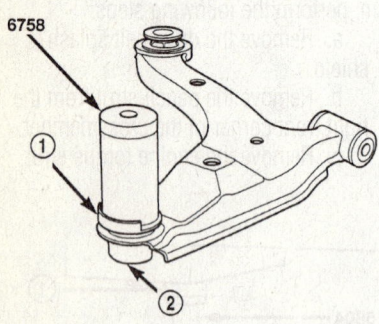

1 – SEAL BOOT UPWARD LIP
2 – BALL JOINT

9306EG54

Installing the ball joint boot seal

4. Remove or disconnect the following:
- Pivot bolts attaching the lower control arm to the front crossmember
- Lower control arm
- Ball joint using a pry tool

5. Using a hydraulic press, press the ball joint from the lower control arm using tools:

a. Receiver tool 6908-2
b. Adapter tool 6804

To install:

6. Reinstall the ball joint into the lower control arm with the notch in the ball joint stud facing the front lower control arm bushing.

7. Using a hydraulic press, press the ball joint into the lower control arm using tools:

a. Receiver tool 6758.
b. Adapter tool 6804.

8. Install or connect the following:
- Ball joint boot seal using a driver tool such as a large socket or suitable sized piece of pipe

✲✲ WARNING

Do not use a shop press that was used to install the ball joint, for the press exerts too much force.

- Lower control arm into the front crossmember
- Rear lower control arm-to-crossmember and frame rail bolt

➡**DO NOT tighten the rear bolt at this time.**

- Front lower control arm-to-crossmember nut and bolt

9. Torque the lower control arm fasteners to:

a. Rear pivot bolt: 185 ft. lbs. (250 Nm).
b. Front pivot bolt: 120 ft. lbs. (163 Nm).

10. Install the ball joint stud into the steering knuckle. Torque the steering knuckle-to-ball joint stud pinch bolt/nut to 70 ft. lbs. (95 Nm).

11. If the right side lower control arm has been service, install the following:
- Engine torque strut
- Pencil strut to the right front corner of the crossmember. Torque the nuts to 43 ft. lbs. (58 Nm).
- Drive belt splash shield
- Front fascia-to-reinforcement screws

12. Install or connect the following:
- Stabilizer bar-to-lower control arm link assemblies and bushings
- Rotate the stabilizer bar into position, installing the stabilizer bar links into the lower control arms
- Top stabilizer bar link bushings and nuts. DO NOT tighten the link yet
- Wheel

13. Lower the vehicle so the suspension is supporting the total weight of the vehicle.

14. Install or connect the following:
- Torque the stabilizer bar-to-lower control arm links to 21 ft. lbs. (28 Nm).
- Torque the stabilizer bar bushing retainer-to-crossmember bolts to 21 ft. lbs. (28 Nm).

15. Check and/or adjust the toe, as necessary.

Wheel Bearings

ADJUSTMENT

The PT Cruiser is equipped with a sealed hub and bearing assemblies. The hub and bearing assembly is non-serviceable. If the assembly is damaged, the complete unit must be replaced.

REMOVAL & INSTALLATION

Front

1. Before servicing the vehicle, refer to the precautions in the beginning of this section.

2. Remove or disconnect the following:
- Steering knuckle and hub and bearing assembly
- Wheel lug stud from the hub flange, using a C-clamp and Adapter tool 4150A

3. Rotate the hub to align the removed lug stud with the notch in the bearing retainer plate.

4. Rotate the hub so the stud hole is facing away from the brake caliper's lower rail on the steering knuckle.

5. Install ½ of a Bearing Splitter tool 1130, between the hub and the bearing retainer plate. The threaded hole in this ½ is to be aligned with the caliper rail on the steering knuckle.

6. Install the remaining pieces of the bearing splitter on the steering knuckle. Hand-tighten the nuts to hold the splitter in place on the knuckle.

7. When the bearing splitter is installed, be sure the 3 bolts attaching the bearing retainer plate to the knuckle are contacting the bearing splitter. The bearing retainer plate should not support the knuckle or contact the splitter.

8. Place the steering knuckle in a hydraulic press, supported by the bearing splitter.

9. Position a driver on the small end

of the hub. Using the press, remove the hub from the wheel bearing. The outer bearing race will come out of the wheel bearing when the hub is pressed out of the bearing.

10. Remove or disconnect the following:

- Bearing splitter tool from the knuckle
- 3 bolts mounting the bearing retainer plate to the steering knuckle

11. Place the knuckle in a press supported by the press block. The blocks must not obstruct the bore in the steering knuckle so the wheel bearing can be pressed out of the knuckle. Place a driver on the outer race of the wheel bearing, then press the bearing out of the knuckle.

12. Install the bearing splitter on the hub. The splitter is to be installed on the hub so it is between the flange of the hub and the bearing race on the hub. Place the hub, bearing race and splitter in a press. Use a driver to press the hub out of the bearing race.

To install:

13. Use clean, dry cloth to wipe and grease or dirt from the bore of the steering knuckle.

14. Install or connect the following:

- New wheel bearing into the bore of the steering knuckle. Be sure the bearing is placed squarely into the bore. Place the knuckle in a press with a receiver tool, C-4698-2 supporting the steering knuckle. Place a driver tool on the outer race of the wheel bearing. Press the wheel bearing into the steering knuckle until it is fully bottomed in the bore of the steering knuckle

➡**Only the original or original equipment replacement bolts should be used to mounting the bearing retainer to the knuckle. If a bolt requires replacement when installing the bearing retainer plate, be sure to get the proper type of replacement.**

- Bearing retainer plate on the steering knuckle. Install the 3 bearing retainer mounting bolts. Tighten the bolts to 21 ft. lbs. (28 Nm).
- Wheel lug stud into the hub flange

15. Place the hub with the lug stud installed, in a press supported by adapter

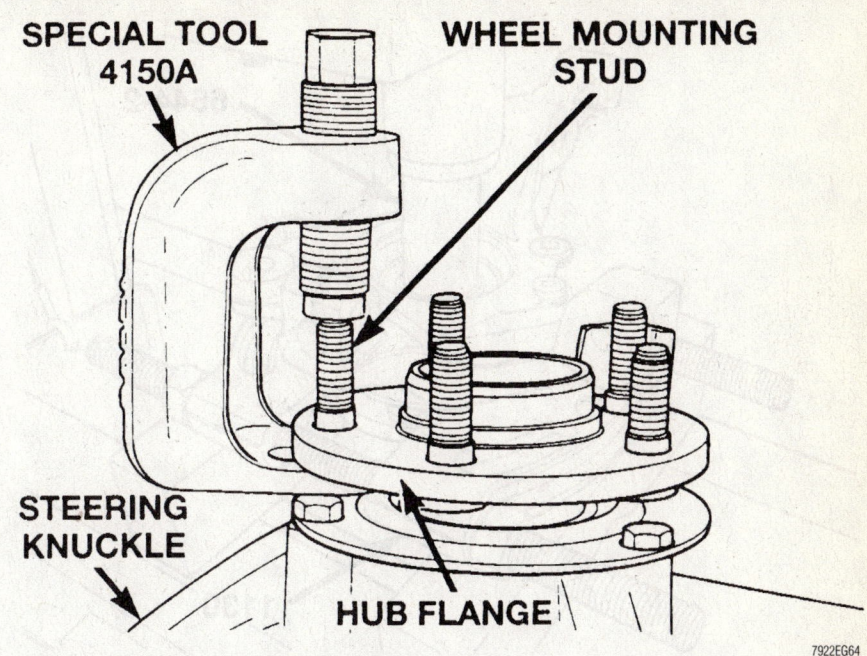

Use a proper C-clamp and adapter tool to press out one of the lug studs

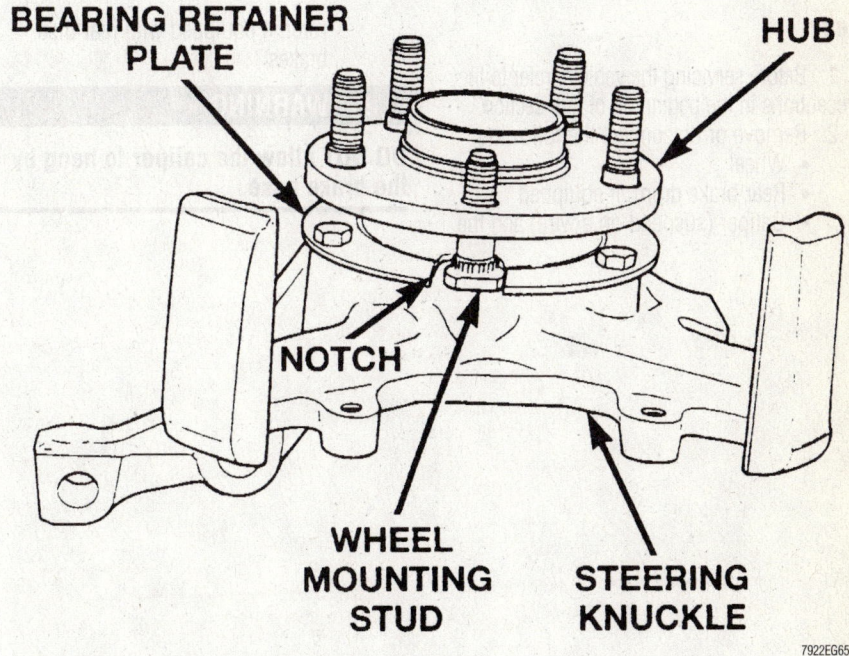

Rotate the hub in order to remove the lug stud

tool C-4698-1 and press the wheel lug stud into the hub flange until it is fully seated against the back side on the hub flange.

16. Place the steering knuckle with the wheel bearing installed, in a press with special receiver tool MB-990799 supporting the inner race of the wheel bearing. Place the

hub in the wheel bearing, making sure it is square with the bearing. Press the hub into the wheel bearing until it is fully bottomed in the wheel bearing.

17. Install the steering knuckle and the wheel.

18. Check and/or adjust the front alignment.

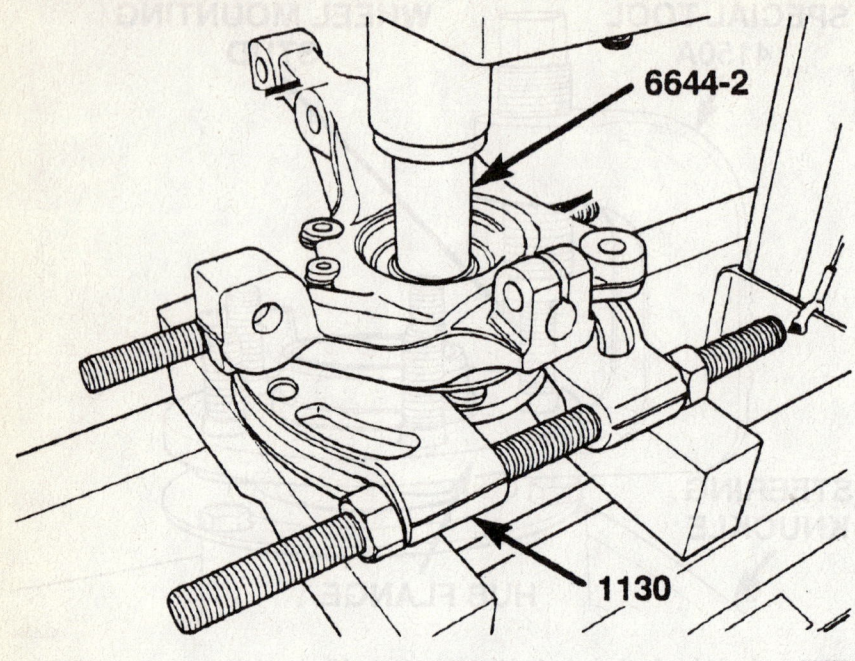

6644-2

1130

9306ZG82

Properly support the steering knuckle for hub and bearing removal

Rear

1. Before servicing the vehicle, refer to the precautions in the beginning of this section.
2. Remove or disconnect the following:
   • Wheel
   • Rear brake drum, if equipped
   • Caliper (suspend on a wire) and the rotor, if equipped with rear disc brakes

※※ WARNING

DO NOT allow the caliper to hang by the brake hose.

• Dust cap from the rear hub/bearing
• Hub/bearing assembly-to-knuckle/spindle nut

➡ **Discard the hub nut and replace with a new one during installation.**

• Hub/bearing from the spindle by pulling it off the end of the spindle by hand

To install:

※※ WARNING

The hub/bearing nut must be tightened to, but NOT over, its specified torque value. The proper specification is crucial to the life of the hub bearing.

3. Position the hub/bearing assembly on the rear spindle/knuckle. Install a NEW hub nut and tighten to 160 ft. lbs. (217 Nm).
4. Install or connect the following:
   • Dust cap and seat it using a soft face hammer to carefully tap it into place
   • Brake drum, if equipped
   • Rotor, if equipped
   • Caliper and 2 guide pin bolts, if equipped with disc brakes. Torque the bolts to 16 ft. lbs. (22 Nm).

FORD MOTOR CO.

Aspire

PRECAUTIONS

Before servicing any vehicle, please be sure to read all of the following precautions, which deal with personal safety, prevention of component damage, and important points to take into consideration when servicing a motor vehicle:

• Never open, service or drain the radiator or cooling system when the engine is hot; serious burns can occur from the steam and hot coolant.

• Observe all applicable safety precautions when working around fuel. Whenever servicing the fuel system, always work in a well-ventilated area. Do not allow fuel spray or vapors to come in contact with a spark, open flame, or excessive heat (a hot drop light, for example). Keep a dry chemical fire extinguisher near the work area. Always keep fuel in a container specifically designed for fuel storage; also, always properly seal fuel containers to avoid the possibility of fire or explosion. Refer to the additional fuel system precautions later in this section.

• Fuel injection systems often remain pressurized, even after the engine has been turned **OFF**. The fuel system pressure must be relieved before disconnecting any fuel lines. Failure to do so may result in fire and/or personal injury.

• Brake fluid often contains polyglycol ethers and polyglycols. Avoid contact with the eyes and wash your hands thoroughly after handling brake fluid. If you do get brake fluid in your eyes, flush your eyes with clean, running water for 15 minutes. If eye irritation persists, or if you have taken brake fluid internally, IMMEDIATELY seek medical assistance.

• The EPA warns that prolonged contact with used engine oil may cause a number of skin disorders, including cancer! You should make every effort to minimize your exposure to used engine oil. Protective gloves should be worn when changing oil. Wash your hands and any other exposed skin areas as soon as possible after exposure to used engine oil. Soap and water, or waterless hand cleaner should be used.

• All new vehicles are now equipped with an air bag system, often referred to as a Supplemental Restraint System (SRS) or Supplemental Inflatable Restraint (SIR) system. The system must be disabled before performing service on or around system components, steering column, instrument panel components, wiring and sensors. Failure to follow safety and disabling procedures could result in accidental air bag deployment, possible personal injury and unnecessary system repairs.

• Always wear safety goggles when working with, or around, the air bag system. When carrying a non-deployed air bag, be sure the bag and trim cover are pointed away from your body. When placing a non-deployed air bag on a work surface, always face the bag and trim cover upward, away from the surface. This will reduce the motion of the module if it is accidentally deployed. Refer to the additional air bag system precautions later in this section.

• Clean, high quality brake fluid from a sealed container is essential to the safe and proper operation of the brake system. You should always buy the correct type of brake fluid for your vehicle. If the brake fluid becomes contaminated, completely flush the system with new fluid. Never reuse any brake fluid. Any brake fluid that is removed from the system should be discarded. Also, do not allow any brake fluid to come in contact with a painted surface; it will damage the paint.

• Never operate the engine without the proper amount and type of engine oil; doing so WILL result in severe engine damage.

• Timing belt maintenance is extremely important! Many models utilize an interference-type, non-freewheeling engine. If the timing belt breaks, the valves in the cylinder head may strike the pistons, causing potentially serious (also time-consuming and expensive) engine damage. Refer to the maintenance interval charts in the front of this manual for the recommended replacement interval for the timing belt, and to the timing belt section for belt replacement and inspection.

• Disconnecting the negative battery cable on some vehicles may interfere with the functions of the on-board computer system(s) and may require the computer to undergo a relearning process once the negative battery cable is reconnected.

• When servicing drum brakes, only disassemble and assemble one side at a time, leaving the remaining side intact for reference.

• Only an MVAC-trained, EPA-certified automotive technician should service the air conditioning system or its components.

ENGINE REPAIR

Distributor

REMOVAL

1. Before servicing the vehicle, refer to the precautions in the beginning of this section.
2. Position the No. 1 piston at Top Dead Center (TDC) of the compression stroke.
3. Matchmark the distributor base flange and the cylinder head.
4. Remove or disconnect the following:
   • Negative battery cable
   • Distributor cap
5. Matchmark the rotor and distributor housing.
   • Distributor electrical connections
   • Distributor
   • O-ring, if damaged or worn

INSTALLATION

Timing Not Disturbed

➡ **When installing the distributor, be sure the offset drive tangs engage the camshaft slots.**

1. Ensure the No. 1 piston is still at Top Dead Center (TDC).
2. Install or connect the following:
   • Distributor, aligning the matchmarks
   • Hold-down bolts and tighten them to 14–19 ft. lbs. (19–25 Nm)
   • Cap
   • Electrical connections
   • Battery cable
3. Recheck the initial timing, and adjust if necessary.

Timing Disturbed

➡ **When installing the distributor, be sure the offset drive tangs engage the camshaft slots.**

1. Rotate the engine clockwise until the No. 1 piston is on the compression stroke. Align the timing marks.
2. Install or connect the following:
   • Distributor, aligning the matchmarks. If installing a new distributor, mark the location of the No. 1 tower on the distributor housing. Install the distributor and align the No.1 tower mark.

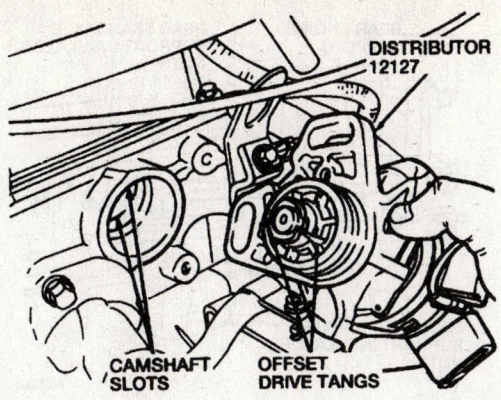

Distributor

7922GG01

View of the cylinder head and the drive side of the distributor showing the offset drive tangs and the camshaft slots

- Distributor hold-down bolts and tighten them to 14–19 ft. lbs. (19–25 Nm)
- Cap
- Electrical connections
- Negative battery cable
- Recheck the initial timing, and adjust if necessary.

Ignition Timing

ADJUSTMENT

1. Before servicing the vehicle, refer to the precautions in the beginning of this section.
2. Perform the following:
   - Start the vehicle and let it reach operating temperature.
   - Turn all accessories **OFF**.
   - Check the timing. Timing should read 10° BTDC. Set the timing as needed.

- Tighten the distributor hold-down bolts to 14–19 ft. lbs. (19–25 Nm).
- Recheck the timing.

Alternator

REMOVAL & INSTALLATION

1. Remove or disconnect the following:
   - Negative battery cable
   - Any wires, hoses or component(s) that will interfere with alternator removal
   - Alternator adjustment bolt
   - Alternator/water pump drive belt from the alternator pulley
   - **B** terminal nut and disengage the electrical connection
   - Alternator electrical connection
   - Alternator lower bolt
   - Alternator

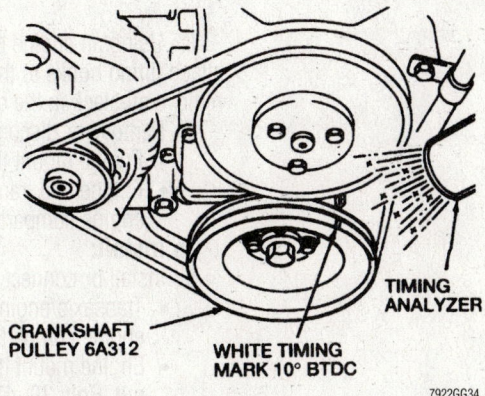

CRANKSHAFT PULLEY 6A312   **WHITE TIMING MARK 10° BTDC**   **TIMING ANALYZER**

7922GG34

Clean the timing marks with a shop rag to help view them with the timing light

To install:

2. Install or connect the following:
   - Alternator and finger-tighten the adjustment bolt
   - Alternator lower bolt and tighten until snug
   - Drive belt and adjust the belt to the proper tension
   - Alternator electrical connections and tighten the **B** terminal nut
   - Alternator lower bolt to 27–38 ft. lbs. (37–52 Nm). Lower the car
   - Alternator adjustment bolt to 14–19 ft. lbs. (19–25 Nm)
   - Negative battery cable

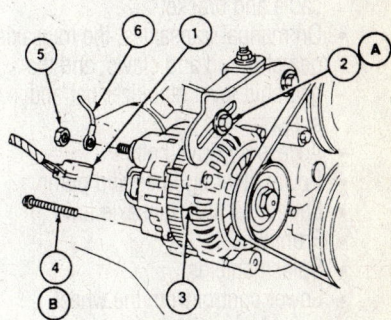

Item	Description
1	Alternator Electrical Connector
2	Alternator Adjustment Bolt
3	Alternator
4	Alternator Lower Bolt
5	B-Terminal Nut
6	B-Terminal Lead
A	Tighten to 19-25 N·m (14-19 Lb-Ft)
B	Tighten to 37-53 N·m (27-38 Lb-Ft)

89722G06

Exploded view of the alternator mounting and electrical components

Engine Assembly

REMOVAL & INSTALLATION

1. Before servicing the vehicle, refer to the precautions in the beginning of this section.
2. Remove or disconnect the following:
   - Negative battery cable
   - Fuel system pressure
   - Battery and tray
   - Hood
   - Air cleaner assembly and hoses
   - Cooling fan and the radiator
   - Accelerator cable

- Accelerator shaft bracket
- Speedometer cable from the transaxle
- Fuel tube hose and tube from the injection supply manifold
- Hoses from the heater core
- All necessary vacuum hoses
- All necessary electrical connections and grounds
- Park/Neutral safety switch connection, the kickdown solenoid electrical connection (automatic transaxle) and the transaxle ground
- Clutch cable
- On automatic transaxles, the shift-to-manual shaft boot, and the shift cable and bracket
- On manual transaxles, the transaxle gearshift rod and clevis, and the gearshift lever stabilizer bar and support
- Accessory drive belts
- Power steering lines and pump
- Engine oil and transaxle fluid
- Front wheels
- Splash shields
- Lower control from the wheel knuckles
- Halfshafts

➠Install plugs in the transaxle to avoid leakage or contamination

- Air conditioning compressor
- Exhaust inlet pipe
- Front and rear transaxle support insulator nuts
- Muffler pipe bracket
- Transaxle case-to-block front and rear brackets
- Engine rear plate
- With automatic transaxle, loosen the flywheel-to-torque converter nuts
- All necessary vacuum lines

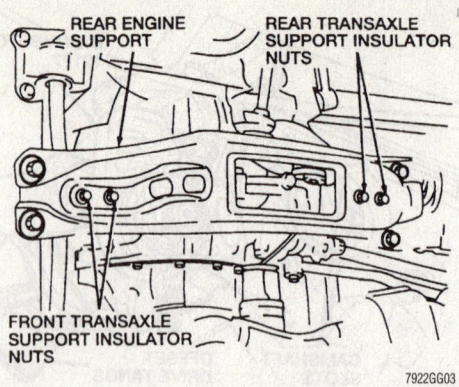

Location of the front and rear transaxle support insulator nuts

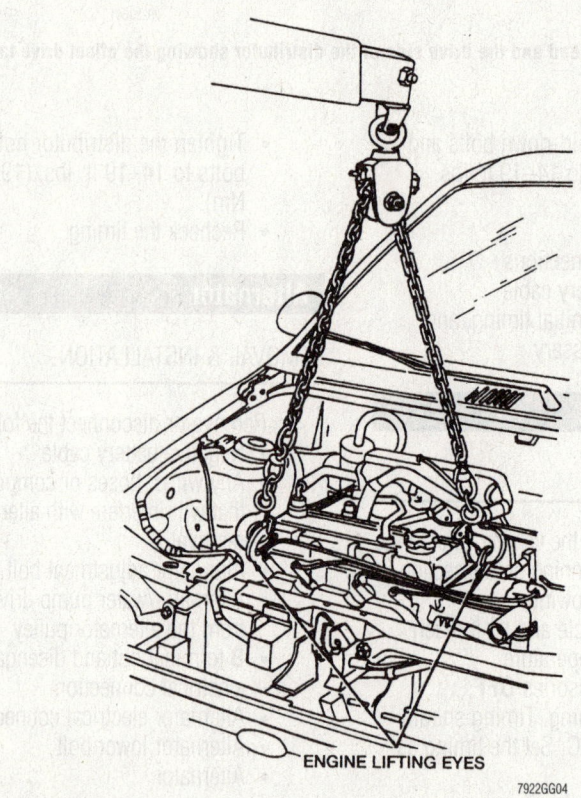

To avoid damaging the engine, attach the hoist chain to the lifting eyes as shown

3. Using an engine hoist and chain, attach lifting hooks to the lifting eyes and remove all slack in the chain.

4. Remove or disconnect the following:
- Engine mount through-bolt and nut
- Engine and transaxle from the engine compartment

To install:

5. Install or connect the following:
- Transaxle/engine assembly into the engine compartment
- Engine mount through-bolt and nut. Bolt: 39–47 ft. lbs. (53–64 Nm)
- All vacuum lines
- On automatic transaxle, the fly-

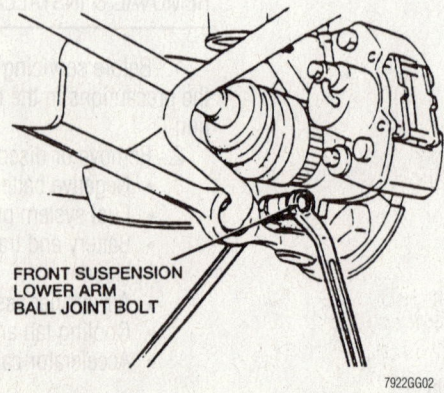

Use 2 wrenches (one as a back-up) to loosen the front suspension lower arm clamp bolts and nuts

wheel-to-torque converter nuts. Nuts: 25–36 ft. lbs. (34–49 Nm)
- Engine rear plate. Bolt to 61–87 inch lbs. (7–10 Nm)
- Transaxle case-to-engine block front brackets. Bolts: 27–38 ft. lbs. (37–52 Nm)
- Muffler pipe brackets. Bolts: 28–41 ft. lbs. (38–56 Nm)
- Front and rear transaxle support insulator nuts. Rear nuts: 21–34 ft. lbs. (28–46 Nm); front nuts: 27–38 ft. lbs. (37–52 Nm)
- Starter and exhaust inlet pipe
- Air conditioning compressor
- Power steering pump. Bolts: 27–40 ft. lbs. (36–54 Nm)
- Halfshafts
- Lower arms. Bolts and nuts: 32–40 ft. lbs. (43–54 Nm)
- Splash shields and tires. Hub nut: 65–87 ft. lbs. (88–118 Nm)
- With manual transaxle: transaxle gearshift rod and clevis, gearshift lever stabilizer bar and support, clutch cable, and starter motor electrical connections
- Park/Neutral safety switch, back-up lamp switch and the transaxle ground
- Power steering lines and drive belts
- With automatic transaxle: connect the shift cable and bracket, Park/Neutral safety switch and the kickdown solenoid electrical connections and the transaxle ground
- All wiring
- All vacuum hoses
- Heater hoses
- Fuel tube and hose
- Speedometer cable
- Accelerator shaft bracket
- Accelerator cable
- Radiator and cooling fan
- Air cleaner and hoses
- Hood
- Battery and tray
- Coolant, transmission fluid and engine oil

Water Pump

REMOVAL & INSTALLATION

1. Before servicing the vehicle, refer to the precautions in the beginning of this section.
2. Remove or disconnect the following:
   - Negative battery cable
   - Timing belt

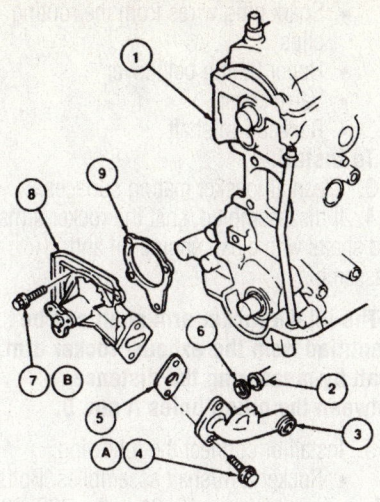

1. Cylinder Block
2. Heater Water Hose
3. Water Inlet Connection
4. Hot Water Heater Elbow Connector Bolt (2 Req'd)
5. Water Pump Inlet Gasket
6. O-Ring
7. Water Pump Bolt (4 Req'd)
8. Water Pump
9. Water Pump Housing Gasket
A. Tighten to 19-30 N·m (14-22 Lb-Ft)
B. Tighten to 19-26 N·m (14-19 Lb-Ft)

7922GG05

Exploded view of the water pump and its related components

- Coolant
- Inlet tube from the water pump housing
- Water pump
- All existing gasket material

To install:
3. Install or connect the following:
   - New water pump and inlet tube gaskets coated, both sides, with water resistant sealer
   - Water pump. Bolts: 14–19 ft. lbs. (19–26 Nm)
   - Inlet tube. Bolts to 14–22 ft. lbs. (19–30 Nm)
   - Timing belt
   - Coolant
   - Negative battery cable

Cylinder Head

REMOVAL & INSTALLATION

➡️**Refer to Section 1 of this manual for the cylinder head torque sequence illustration. The illustration is located after the Torque Specification Chart.**

1. Before servicing the vehicle, refer to the precautions in the beginning of this section.
2. Remove or disconnect the following:
   - Negative battery cable
   - Coolant
   - Spark plug wires
   - Distributor
   - Timing belt
   - Valve cover
   - Exhaust and intake manifolds
   - Front and rear engine lift hangers
   - Engine block ground wire
   - All wiring harness connectors
   - Upper radiator hose
   - Water bypass tube (or hose) and bracket
   - Cylinder head and gasket

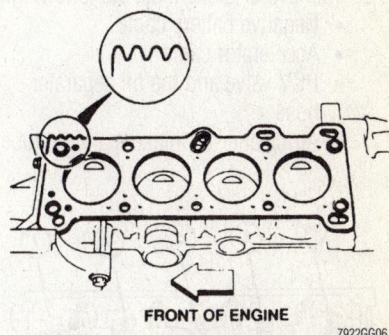

FRONT OF ENGINE

7922GG06

Be sure to position the gasket properly on the engine block before installing the cylinder head to ensure proper sealing

To install:
3. Clean any old gasket material residue from the cylinder head gasket mating surfaces.

➡️**The cylinder head gasket has marks on one of its edges that match the shape of the cylinder head, when the gasket is installed these marks must align properly before cylinder head installation.**

4. Install new gasket and cylinder head in position.
5. Install new cylinder head bolts as follows:
   a. First pass: 35–40 ft. lbs. (50–60 Nm)
   b. Second pass: 56–60 ft. lbs. (75–81 Nm)
6. Install or connect the following:
   - Water bypass tube (or hose) and bracket
   - Upper radiator hose

Timing belt service is covered in Section 4 of this manual

- All wiring harness connectors
- Engine ground wire
- Front and rear engine lift hangers
- Distributor
- Intake and exhaust manifolds
- Valve cover
- Timing belt
- Spark plug wires
- Coolant
- Negative battery cable

Rocker Arms/Shafts

REMOVAL & INSTALLATION

1. Before servicing the vehicle, refer to the precautions in the beginning of this section.
2. Remove or disconnect the following:
- Negative battery cable
- Accelerator cable
- PCV valve and the oil separator hose
- Air cleaner-to-intake manifold tube

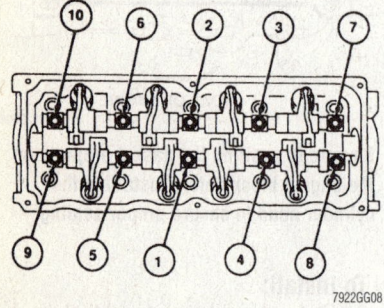

Rocker arm and shaft retaining bolt loosening and tightening sequence

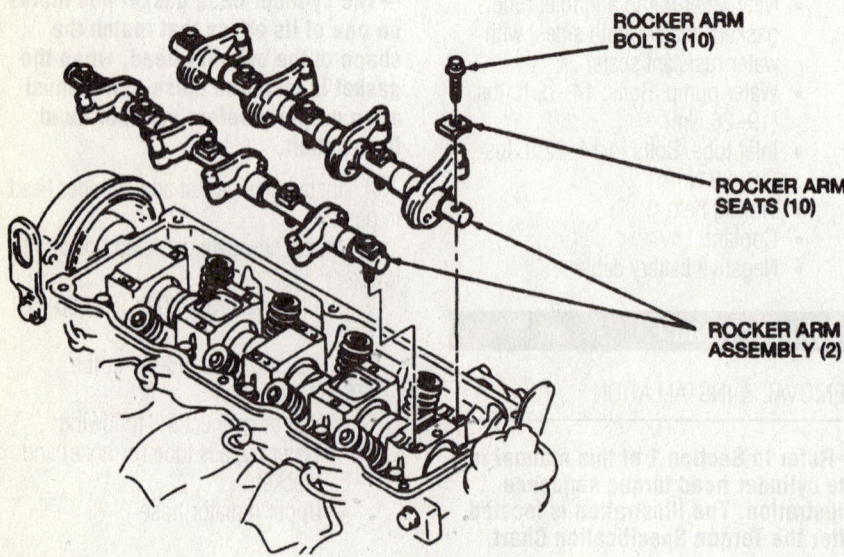

Exploded view of the rocker arm/shaft assemblies' mounting

- Spark plug wires from the routing clips
- Upper timing belt cover
- Valve cover
- Rocker arm shaft

To install:

3. Clean all gasket mating surfaces.
4. If disassembled, coat the rocker arms and shafts with clean engine oil and reassemble.

➡ **The intake rocker arm shaft can be identified from the exhaust rocker arm shaft by measuring the distance between the oiling holes A and B.**

5. Install or connect the following:
- Rocker arm/shaft assemblies. Bolts, in sequence: 16–21 ft. lbs. (22–28 Nm)
- Valve cover and new gasket. Bolts: 44–79 inch lbs. (5–9 Nm)
- Upper timing belt cover

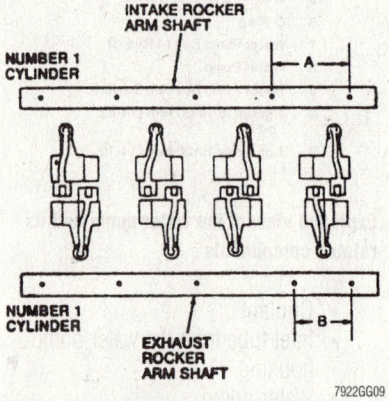

Method of identifying the intake and exhaust rocker arm shafts

- Spark plug wires
- PCV valve and oil separator hose
- Accelerator cable
- Air cleaner-to-intake manifold tube
- Negative battery cable

Intake Manifold

REMOVAL & INSTALLATION

➡ **Refer to Section 1 of this manual for the intake manifold torque sequence illustration. The illustration is located after the Torque Specification Chart.**

Upper Manifold

1. Before servicing the vehicle, refer to the precautions in the beginning of this section.
2. Remove or disconnect the following:
- Negative battery cable
- Fuel system pressure
- Coolant
- Upper intake manifold support
- Accelerator cable
- Air cleaner-to-intake manifold tube
- Coolant hoses from the upper manifold
- All necessary wiring and hoses
- Upper intake manifold and gasket

To install:

3. Use a scraper to clean any old gasket material residue from the upper and lower manifold mating surfaces.
4. Install or connect the following:
- New gasket and upper intake manifold. Bolts: 14–20 ft. lbs. (19–26 Nm)
- Coolant hoses to the upper manifold
- All wiring and hoses
- Air cleaner-to-intake manifold tube
- Accelerator cable to the throttle lever
- Upper intake manifold support. Bolts: 22–34 ft. lbs. (31–46 Nm)
- Coolant
- Negative battery cable

Lower Manifold

1. Remove or disconnect the following:
- Upper intake manifold
- All necessary wiring and hoses

➡ **You may have to raise the vehicle to unfasten the lower nut on the passenger's side of the manifold.**

- Intake manifold and gasket

To install:

2. Clean any old gasket material residue from the cylinder head and intake manifold mating surfaces.

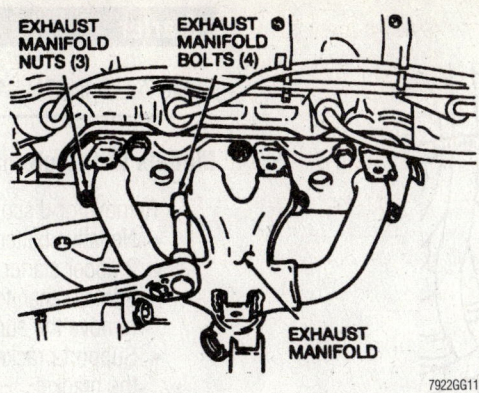

During installation, be sure the ignition wires are not pinched between the manifold and cylinder head

3. Install or connect the following:
   - New gasket and place the intake manifold. Bolts: 14–20 ft. lbs. (19–26 Nm)
   - Intake manifold support. Bolts: 22–34 ft. lbs. (31–46 Nm)
   - Upper intake manifold.

Exhaust Manifold

REMOVAL & INSTALLATION

1. Before servicing the vehicle, refer to the precautions in the beginning of this section.
2. Remove or disconnect the following:
   - Negative battery cable
   - Exhaust inlet pipe-to-exhaust manifold nuts and washers
   - Muffler pipe bracket bolts
   - Air cleaner-to-intake manifold tube
   - Exhaust manifold heat shield
   - Oxygen (O_2S) sensor wiring connector
   - O_2S sensor
   - Exhaust manifold
   - Inlet pipe and exhaust manifold gaskets

To install:

3. Remove all existing gasket material from the exhaust manifold and cylinder head inlet pipe. Clean all threaded surfaces.
4. Install or connect the following:
   - New gasket and exhaust manifold. Nuts and bolts: 12–17 ft. lbs. (16–23 Nm)
   - O_2S sensor
   - Heat shield. Bolts: to 12–17 ft. lbs. (16–23 Nm)
   - O_2S sensor electrical connector
   - Air cleaner-to-intake manifold tube
   - Muffler inlet pipe gasket and inlet

pipe. Nuts and washers: 23–34 ft. lbs. (31–46 Nm)
   - Muffler pipe bracket. Bolts: 28–47 ft. lbs. (38–56 Nm)
   - Negative battery cable

Front Crankshaft Seal

REMOVAL & INSTALLATION

The timing belt must be removed for this procedure. The crankshaft seal is located behind the crankshaft sprocket in the oil pump front housing.

1. Before servicing the vehicle, refer to the precautions in the beginning of this section.
2. Remove or disconnect the following:
   - Negative battery cable
   - Accessory drive belts
   - Timing belt cover and timing belt
   - Crankshaft sprocket and key
   - Crankshaft front seal from the oil pump housing

To install:

3. Lubricate the lip of the new seal and the crankshaft seal surface with clean engine oil
4. Install or connect the following:
   - Front crankshaft seal into the oil pump housing, using an installer
   - Crankshaft key and sprocket
   - Timing belt and cover
   - Accessory drive belts
   - Negative battery cable

Camshaft and Valve Lifters

REMOVAL & INSTALLATION

1. Before servicing the vehicle, refer to the precautions in the beginning of this section.
2. Remove or disconnect the following:
   - Battery
   - Timing belt
   - Valve cover
   - Camshaft sprocket
   - Distributor
   - Rocker arm/shaft assemblies
   - Lash adjusters
   - Camshaft thrust plate
   - Camshaft

To install:

3. Clean the camshaft and cylinder head surface. Inspect the camshaft oil seal and replace it if necessary. Coat the surfaces of the camshaft with clean engine oil.
4. Install or connect the following:
   - Camshaft
   - Camshaft thrust plate. Bolt: 71–88 inch lbs. (8–10 Nm)
5. Pour clean engine oil into the oil reservoir in the rocker arm and apply engine oil to the lash adjuster.

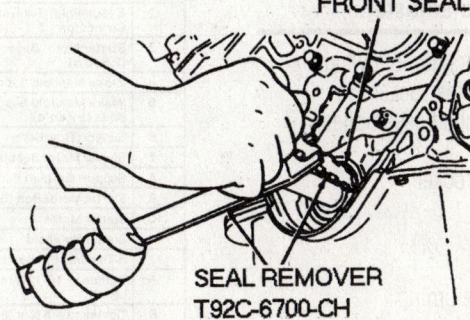

When removing the front crankshaft seal, be careful not to damage the crankshaft threads or the seal bore

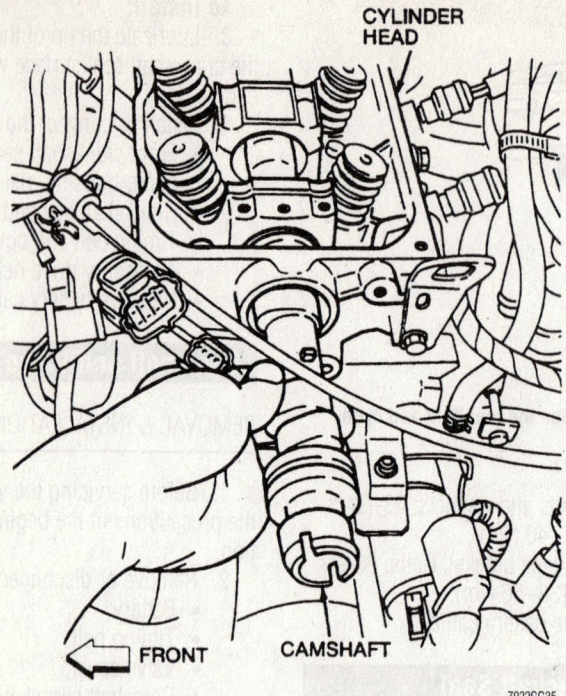

CYLINDER HEAD

FRONT

CAMSHAFT

7922GG35

Lubricate the machined surfaces of the camshaft during installation to prevent premature wear

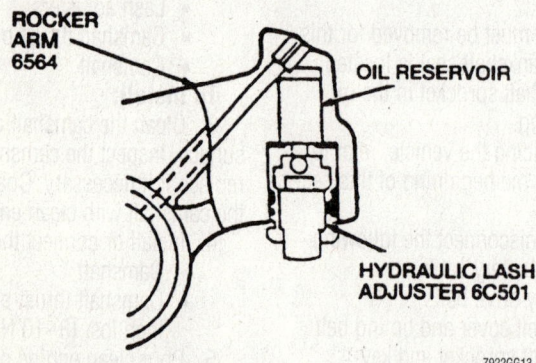

ROCKER ARM 6564

OIL RESERVOIR

HYDRAULIC LASH ADJUSTER 6C501

7922GG13

The lash adjuster is located in a bore in the underside of the rocker arm

※※ WARNING

Be careful not to damage the O-ring when installing the adjuster.

6. Install or connect the following:
   • Adjuster into the rocker arm
   • Rocker arm/shaft assemblies
   • Distributor
   • Camshaft sprocket
   • Valve cover
   • Timing belt
   • Battery
7. Adjust the valve timing

Valve Lash

ADJUSTMENT

No valve lash adjustment is necessary.

REMOVAL & INSTALLATION

Models With Automatic Transaxle

1. Remove or disconnect the following:
   • Negative battery cable
   • 2 upper starter motor retaining bolts
   • 2 intake manifold support bolts and remove the support
   • Support bracket bolts and remove the bracket
   • Starter motor support
   • **S** terminal connection from the solenoid
   • **B** terminal washer and nut, then disengage the electrical connection from the solenoid
   • Starter

To install:

2. Install or connect the following:
   • Starter.
   • Lower starter motor bolt and tighten to 23–34 ft. lbs. (31–46 Nm)
   • **S** and **B** terminal electrical connections
   • Starter motor support and tighten the retainers to 35–44 inch lbs. (4–5 Nm)
   • Support bracket and tighten the retaining bolts
   • Intake manifold support bracket and tighten the retainers to 12–14 ft. lbs. (16–22 Nm)
   • Starter motor upper retaining bolts and tighten them to 23–34 ft. lbs. (31–46 Nm)
   • Negative battery cable

Item	Description
1	B-Terminal Nut
2	S (Solenoid)-Terminal Connector
3	Starter Motor Support Nuts (2 Req'd)
4	Intake Manifold Support
5	Intake Manifold Support Bolts (2 Req'd)
6	Support Bracket
7	Starter Motor Support
8	Support Bracket Bolt
9	Starter Motor Bolt (3 Req'd)
10	Starter Motor
11	Starter Solenoid
12	B-Terminal Connector
A	Tighten to 10-12 N·m (89-106 Lb-In)
B	Tighten to 4-5 N·m (35-44 Lb-In)
C	Tighten to 16-22 N·m (12-14 Lb-Ft)
D	Tighten to 31-46 N·m (23-34 Lb-Ft)

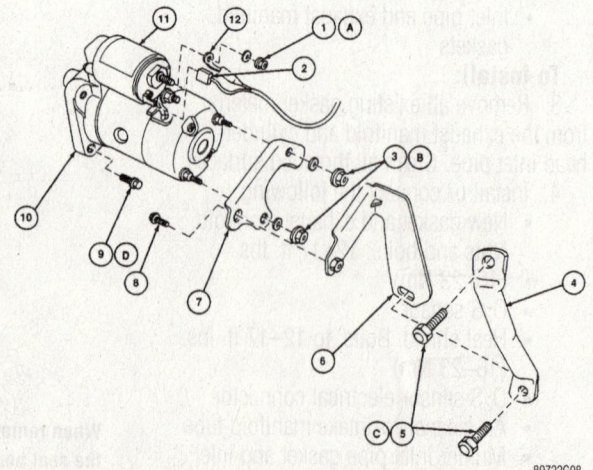

89722G08

Starter motor mounting and electrical connections—models with automatic transaxles

Models With Manual Transaxle

1. Remove or disconnect the following:

- Negative battery cable
- **B** terminal washer and nut, then disengage the electrical connection from the solenoid
- **S** terminal connection from the solenoid
- 2 starter support bolts
- Starter motor support
- Starter

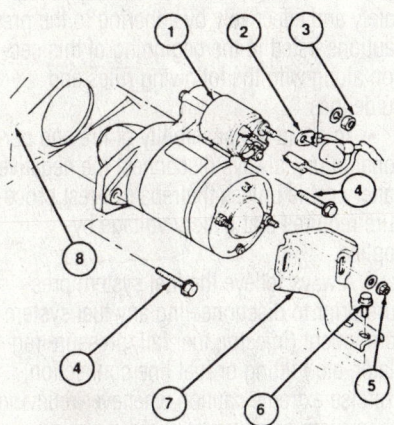

Item	Description
1	Starter Motor
2	B-Terminal
3	B-Terminal Nut
4	Starter Motor Bolts (2 Req'd)
5	Starter Motor Support Nuts
6	Starter Motor Support Bolts (2 Req'd)
7	Starter Motor Support
8	Flywheel Housing

89722G09

Starter motor mounting and electrical connections—models with manual transaxles

To install:

2. Install or connect the following:

- Starter in the vehicle. Install the starter motor bolts and tighten to 23–34 ft. lbs. (31–46 Nm).
- **S** and **B** terminal electrical connections
- Starter motor support and tighten the nuts to 35–44 inch lbs. (4–5 Nm)
- Starter motor support bolts and tighten them to 14–18 ft. lbs. (19–25 Nm)
- Negative battery cable

Oil Pan

REMOVAL & INSTALLATION

1. Before servicing the vehicle, refer to the precautions in the beginning of this section.
2. Remove or disconnect the following:

- Engine oil
- Exhaust header pipe
- Oil pan and discard the old gasket

To install:

3. Clean the oil pan and cylinder block sealing surfaces to remove all traces of gasket material. Thoroughly clean the oil pan. Apply a suitable oil resistant sealant to the joint lines formed at the cylinder block and front and rear engine covers.

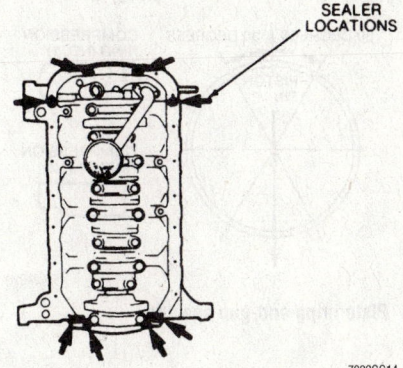

7922GG14

Apply sealer at these locations to ensure a good seal

4. Install or connect the following:

- New gasket onto the oil pan
- Oil pan and gasket. Nuts and bolts, in an alternating pattern: 69–78 inch lbs. (8–9 Nm)
- Oil pan drain plug and tighten to 22–30 ft. lbs. (29–41 Nm)
- Exhaust header pipe
- Engine oil

Oil Pump

REMOVAL & INSTALLATION

1. Before servicing the vehicle, refer to the precautions in the beginning of this section.
2. Remove or disconnect the following:

- Timing belt covers and timing belt
- Crankshaft sprocket
- Engine oil
- Oil pan
- Crankshaft Position (CKP) sensor and bracket

- Oil pump assembly and gasket
- Oil pump pick-up tube and screen

3. Disassemble the oil pump and inspect all components as necessary. Replace the oil pump if needed.

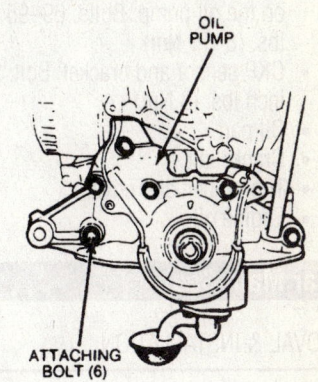

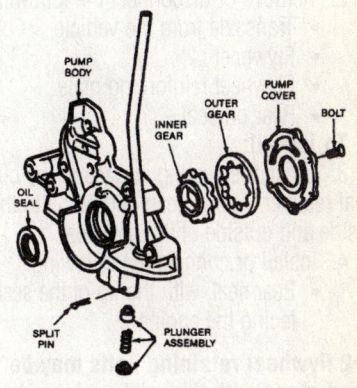

7922GG15

Exploded view of the oil pump assembly and mounting bolt locations

To install:

4. Clean all gasket mating surfaces. If disassembled, clean the oil pump housing and components with a suitable solvent and allow them to dry. Reassemble the oil pump, lubricating all components with clean engine oil.

5. Install or connect the following:

- New front crankshaft seal
- New gasket, coated with sealant, on the oil pump

➡**Do not allow the sealant compound to enter the oil pump discharge opening once the gasket is in place. This opening must be free and clear before the oil pump is installed onto the cylinder block.**

Refer to Section 1 for engine rebuilding specifications

- Oil pump on the cylinder block. Bolts: 14–19 ft. lbs. (19–25 Nm).
- New gasket on the oil pump pick-up tube
- Oil pump pick-up tube and screen on the oil pump. Bolts: 69–95 inch lbs. (8–11 Nm)
- CKP sensor and bracket. Bolt: 25 inch lbs. (3 Nm)
- Oil pan
- Crankshaft
- Timing belt and covers
- Engine oil

Rear Main Seal

REMOVAL & INSTALLATION

1. Before servicing the vehicle, refer to the precautions in the beginning of this section.
2. Remove or disconnect the following:
- Transaxle from the vehicle
- Flywheel
- Flywheel reinforcing plate
- Rear oil seal

To install:

3. Clean the sealing surface of the oil seal retainer. Apply clean engine oil to the inside and outside of the new seal.
4. Install or connect the following:
- Rear seal, with the lip of the seal facing the engine

➡ **2 flywheel retaining bolts may be used along with the seal replacer tool to install the rear crankshaft seal.**

- Flywheel reinforcing plate. Bolt: 71–97 inch lbs. (8–11 Nm)
- Flywheel. Bolts: 71–76 ft. lbs. (96–103 Nm)
- Transaxle

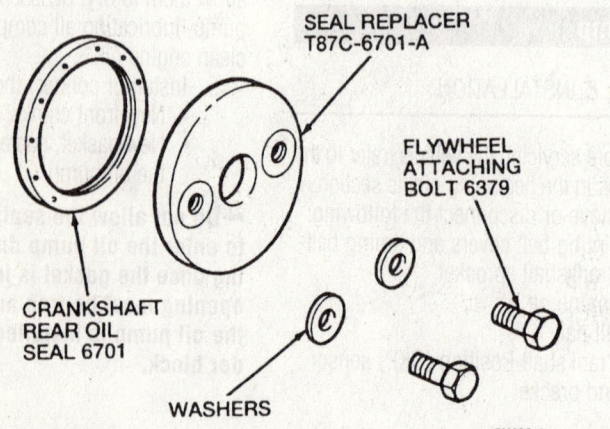

Installing a new rear main seal

Piston and Ring

POSITIONING

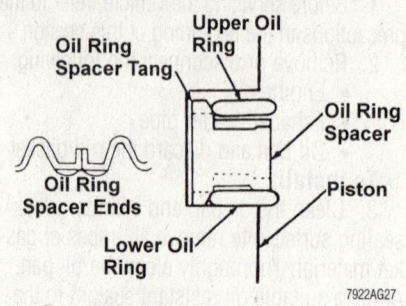

Piston ring positioning

7922AG27

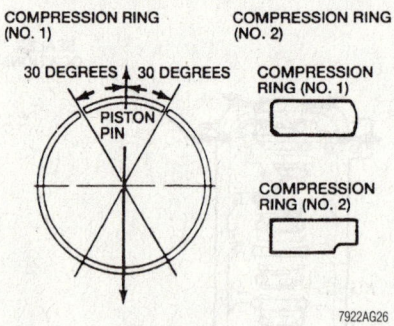

Piston ring end-gap spacing

7922AG26

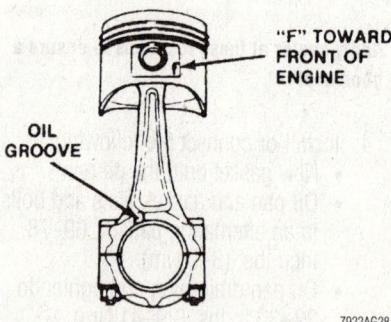

Piston and connecting rod assembly

7922AG28

7922GG16

FUEL SYSTEM

Fuel System Service Precautions

Safety is the most important factor when performing not only fuel system maintenance, but any type of maintenance. Failure to conduct maintenance and repairs in a safe manner may result in serious personal injury or death. Work on a vehicle's fuel system components can be accomplished safely and effectively by adhering to the precautions listed in the beginning of this section along with the following rules and guidelines:

- To avoid the possibility of fire and personal injury, always disconnect the negative battery cable unless the repair or test procedure requires that battery voltage by applied.
- Always relieve the fuel system pressure prior to disconnecting any fuel system component (injector, fuel rail, pressure regulator, etc.) fitting or fuel line connection. Exercise extreme caution whenever relieving fuel system pressure, to avoid exposing skin, face and eyes to fuel spray. Please be advised that fuel under pressure may penetrate the skin or any part of the body that it contacts.
- Always place a shop towel or cloth around the fitting or connection prior to loosening to absorb any excess fuel due to spillage. Ensure that all fuel spillage is quickly remove from engine surfaces. Ensure that all fuel-soaked cloths or towels are deposited into a flame-proof waste container with a lid.
- Always keep a dry chemical (Class B) fire extinguisher near the work area.
- Do not allow fuel spray or fuel vapors to come into contact with a spark or open flame.
- Always use a second wrench when loosening or tightening fuel line connections fittings. This will prevent unnecessary stress and torsion to fuel piping.
- Always replace worn fuel fitting O-rings with new ones. Do not substitute fuel hose where rigid pipe is installed.

Fuel System Pressure

RELIEVING

1. Before servicing the vehicle, refer to the precautions in the beginning of this section.

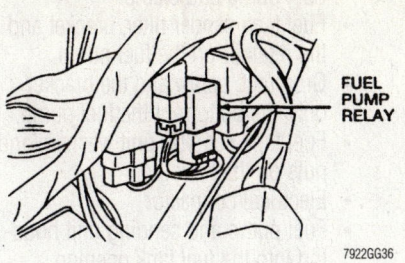

Fuel pump relay location

7922GG36

2. Perform the following:
- Remove the fuel tank filler cap.
- Unplug the fuel pump relay electrical connection, which is located behind the left-hand side of the instrument panel.
- Turn the engine **ON** and let it idle normally.
- The engine will stall, when it does, turn the ignition key **OFF** and engage the fuel pump relay electrical connection.

➡The fuel system pressure has now been relieved and will remain so until the engine is turned ON.

Fuel Filter

REMOVAL & INSTALLATION

1. Before servicing the vehicle, refer to the precautions in the beginning of this section.

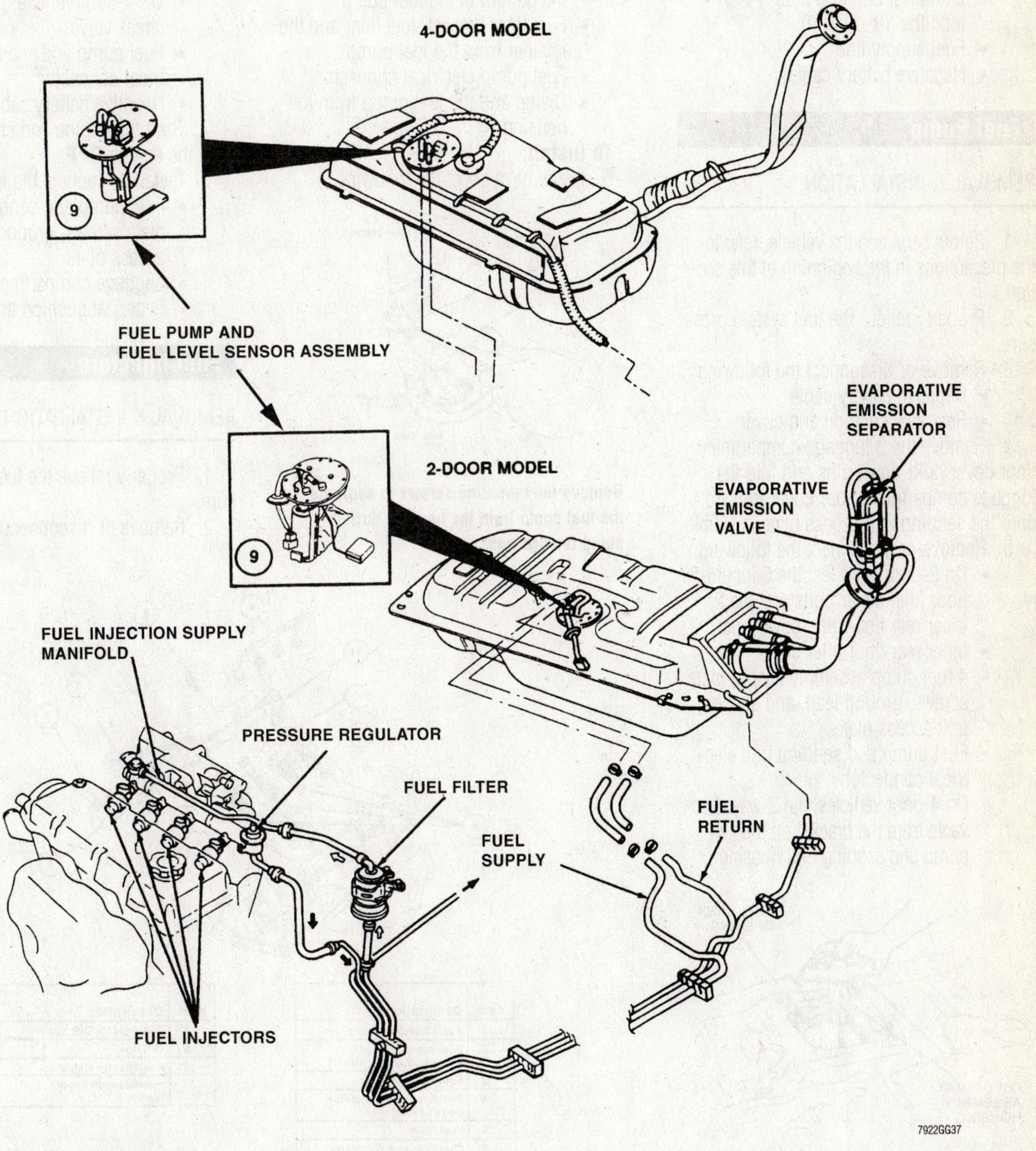

4-DOOR MODEL

9

**FUEL PUMP AND
FUEL LEVEL SENSOR ASSEMBLY**

2-DOOR MODEL

9

**EVAPORATIVE
EMISSION
SEPARATOR**

**EVAPORATIVE
EMISSION
VALVE**

**FUEL INJECTION SUPPLY
MANIFOLD**

PRESSURE REGULATOR

FUEL FILTER

FUEL SUPPLY

FUEL RETURN

FUEL INJECTORS

7922GG37

Fuel system component identification

2. Properly relieve the fuel system pressure.

3. Remove or disconnect the following:
- Negative battery cable
- Fuel supply line at the inlet of the fuel filter
- Fuel return line at the fuel filter outlet fitting
- Fuel filter and bracket

To install:

4. Install or connect the following:
- Fuel filter into the bracket
- Fuel return line to the fuel filter outlet fitting. Bolt and nuts: 71–97 inch lbs. (8–11 Nm)
- Fuel supply line
- Negative battery cable

Fuel Pump

REMOVAL & INSTALLATION

1. Before servicing the vehicle, refer to the precautions in the beginning of this section.

2. Properly relieve the fuel system pressure.

3. Remove or disconnect the following:
- Negative battery cable
- Rear seat cushion and cover

4. Remove the 3 luggage compartment floor cover hold-down pins and fold the luggage compartment floor cover forward until the sending unit access plate is visible.

5. Remove or disconnect the following:
- On 2-door vehicles, the 6 inner rear floor filler cover bolts and the 2 inner rear floor filler cover nuts
- Inner rear floor filler cover
- 4 fuel pump assembly access plate screws, ground lead, and sending unit access plate
- Fuel pump and sending unit electrical connector
- On 4-door vehicles, the 2-way check valve from the bracket on the fuel pump and sending unit housing

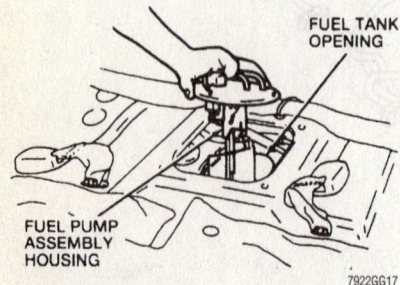

When removing the fuel pump housing from the fuel tank, slowly pull it out to prevent fuel from splashing

- 2 hoses from the fittings on the fuel pump and sending unit housing
- Matchmark the fuel pump assembly to the fuel tank.
- 4 screws (2-door) or 8 screws (4-door) and the fuel pump and sending unit housing from the fuel tank
- Fuel tank sending unit electrical connector
- 2 fuel tank sending unit washers and nuts and the fuel tank sending unit
- Fuel pump screw, fuel pump grommet and the fuel pump bracket from the bottom of the fuel pump
- Fuel filter bracket, fuel filter and the retainer from the fuel pump
- Fuel pump electrical connector
- Clamp and the fuel pump from the housing

To install:

6. Install or connect the following:

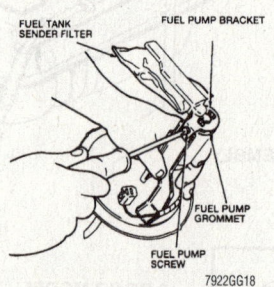

Remove the mounting screws to separate the fuel pump from the housing during pump replacement

- Fuel pump and clamp
- Fuel tank sender filter, bracket and the retainer on the fuel pump
- Grommet, screw and the bracket onto the bottom of the fuel pump
- Fuel tank sending unit washers and nuts on the housing
- Electrical connector
- Fuel pump and sending unit housing into the fuel tank opening, aligning the matchmarks
- Fuel hoses on sending unit hose fittings
- On 4-door vehicles, the 2-way check valve
- Fuel pump and sending unit electrical connector
- Negative battery cable

7. Start the engine and check for leaks. Turn the engine **OFF**.

8. Install or connect the following:
- Fuel pump and sending unit access plate screws, ground lead and access plate
- Luggage compartment floor cover
- Rear seat cushion and cover

Fuel Injectors

REMOVAL & INSTALLATION

1. Properly relieve the fuel system pressure.

2. Remove or disconnect the following:

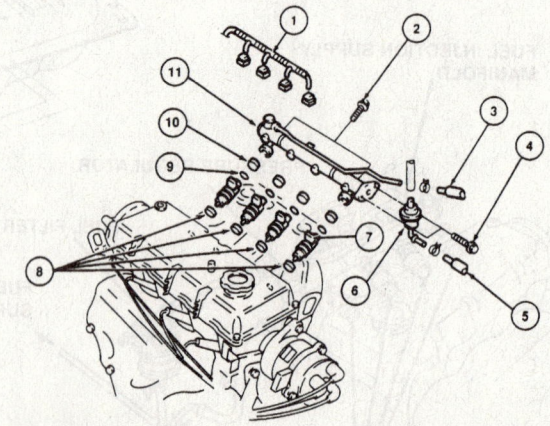

Item	Description
1	Fuel Charging Wiring
2	Fuel Injection Supply Manifold Bolts (2 Req'd)
3	Fuel Tube Hose
4	Fuel Pressure Regulator Bolts (2 Req'd)
5	Fuel Hose
6	Fuel Pressure Regulator
7	Fuel Injector

Item	Description
8	Fuel Injector O-Rings
9	O-Rings
10	Fuel Injector Insulators
11	Fuel Injection Supply Manifold

Exploded view of the fuel injectors and supply manifold assembly

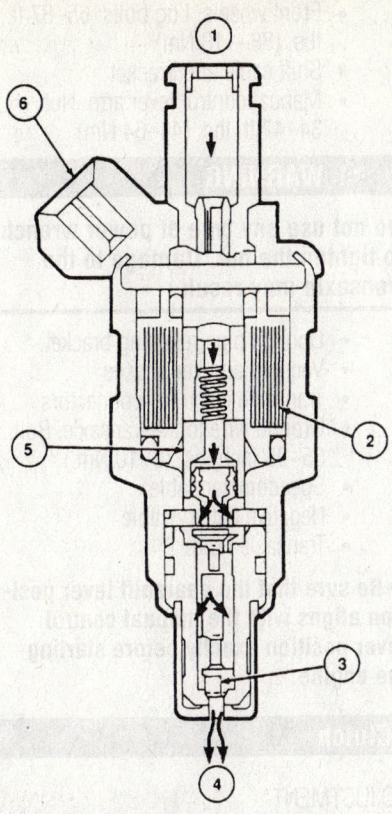

Item	Description
1	Fuel Injection Supply Manifold
2	Coil
3	Needle Valve
4	Injection
5	Armature
6	Electrical Connector

89725G06

Cross-sectional view of a typical fuel injector used in the SFI system

- Negative battery cable
- Upper intake manifold
- Fuel lines
- Fuel injector electrical connections
- Fuel supply manifold (fuel rail) retaining bolts
- Fuel injection supply manifold and the insulators
- Injectors from the fuel rail.
- Fuel injector O-rings and the insulators

To install:

3. Install or connect the following:
- New O-rings and insulators on the fuel injectors
- Injectors to the fuel supply rail
- Fuel supply manifold (rail) assembly
- Supply manifold retaining bolts and

tighten them to 14–17 ft. lbs. (19–23 Nm)
- Injector electrical connections
- Fuel lines
- Upper intake manifold
- Negative battery cable

DRIVE TRAIN

Transaxle Assembly

REMOVAL & INSTALLATION

Manual

1. Before servicing the vehicle, refer to the precautions in the beginning of this section.
2. Remove or disconnect the following:
- Negative battery cable
- Back-up light switch wiring connectors
- Clutch cable from the release lever. Pull the cable through the clutch cable bracket.
- Engine compartment wiring harness ground strap from the transaxle
- Starter
- Speedometer cable
- 2 bolts from the top of the clutch housing
3. Install an engine support tool.
4. Remove or disconnect the following:
- Halfshafts

➡**Install differential side gear plugs to prevent the side gears from moving.**

- Nut and bolt attaching the shift rod to the input shift rail
- Gearshift stabilizer bar from the control rod-to-support bar stud

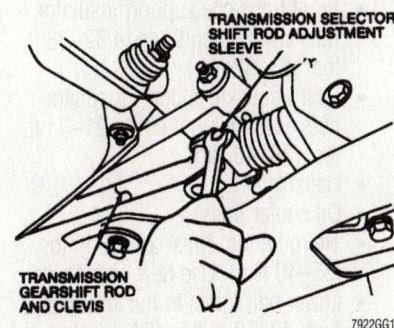

7922GG19

When removing the gearshift rod and clevis, note the position of the washers

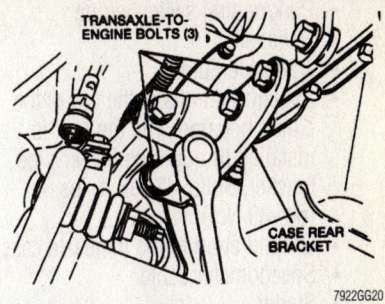

7922GG20

Support the transaxle before removing the transaxle case rear bracket

- Transaxle case rear bracket
- Transaxle case front bracket
- 2 rear and 2 front transaxle support insulator nuts from the rear engine support
- 4 rear engine support rebound insulator bolts and the rear engine support
5. Position a suitable transmission jack under the transaxle and secure it with a safety chain or strap.
6. Remove or disconnect the following:
- 4 flywheel reinforcing plate bolts
- 2 remaining transaxle-to-engine block retaining bolts
- Transaxle from the vehicle

To install:

7. Install or connect the following:
- Transaxle into position against the rear of the engine
- Flywheel reinforcing plate bolts and tighten to 62–86 inch lbs. (7–10 Nm)
- 2 lower transaxle retaining bolts and tighten to 47–66 ft. lbs. (64–89 Nm)
- Rear engine support. Support rear insulator nuts: 21–34 ft. lbs. (28–46 Nm.); front transaxle support insulator nuts: 32–38 ft. lbs. (43–52 Nm.); rear engine support rebound insulator bolts: 47–66 ft. lbs. (64–89 Nm.)
- Transaxle case-to-cylinder block front and rear brackets. Bolts: 27–38 ft. lbs. (37–52 Nm.).
- Washer and the gearshift stabilizer bar on the control rod-to-support bar stud. Nut: 28–38 ft. lbs. (38–52 Nm.).
- Gearshift rod and clevis on the main shift control shaft, and the selector shift rod adjustment sleeve. Nut: 12–17 ft. lbs. (16–23 Nm.)

- Park/neutral switch wiring
- Halfshafts
- Transaxle fluid
- 2 retaining bolts at the top of the clutch housing. The top bolt is installed through the heater pipe bracket. Bolts: 47–66 ft. lbs. (64–89 Nm)
- Ground strap to the transaxle case
- Speedometer cable
- Starter
- park/neutral and back-up light switch wiring connectors
- Clutch cable
- Negative battery cable

Automatic

1. Before servicing the vehicle, refer to the precautions in the beginning of this section.
2. Remove or disconnect the following:
   - Negative battery cable
   - Manual control lever nut and arm
   - Shift cable and bracket from the transaxle
   - Speedometer cable from the transaxle
   - Electrical connectors
   - Transaxle ground wire
   - Vacuum hose and vent hose located below the distributor cap
   - Starter
   - Coolant pipe retaining bracket, located below the distributor cap
   - 2 upper bell housing bolts
   - Support the engine
   - Front wheels
   - Transaxle fluid
   - Splash shield
   - Stabilizer bar
   - Lower control arms from the knuckles

➡ **Use care not to damage the ball joint dust boots.**

- Tie rod end from the knuckle
- Halfshafts

➡ **Install the differential plugs between the differential side gears to prevent side gear movement.**

- Front and rear transaxle support insulator nuts
- 4 rear engine support rebound insulator bolts
- Transmission support crossmember
- Front transaxle support insulator
- Front transaxle support bracket
- Rear transaxle support bracket and insulator
- Intake manifold support

- Transaxle case rear bracket
- Transaxle case-to-cylinder block front bracket
- Flywheel cover
- Torque converter-to-flywheel nuts
- Oil cooler lines

3. Position a transmission jack under the transaxle and secure it with a chain or strap.
4. Remove or disconnect the following:
   - Remaining engine-to-transaxle retaining bolts
   - Transaxle from the vehicle

To install:

5. Install or connect the following:
   - Transaxle into position
   - 2 engine-to-transaxle bolts. Be sure that the torque converter is in alignment with the flexplate. Bolts: 47–66 ft. lbs. (64–89 Nm).
   - Starter
   - Torque converter bolts and tighten to 26–36 ft. lbs. (34–49 Nm)
   - Flywheel cover. Bolts: 71–97 inch lbs. (8–11 Nm)
   - Front transaxle-to-engine support. Bolts to 27–38 ft. lbs. (37–52 Nm)
   - Intake manifold support. Bolts: 27–38 ft. lbs. (37–52 Nm)
   - Transaxle case rear bracket. Bolts: 27–38 ft. lbs. (37–52 Nm)
   - Front transaxle support insulator bracket. Bolts: 28–37 ft. lbs. (38–51 Nm)
   - Front transaxle support bracket.

➡ **Do not tighten the through-bolt and nut until the rear engine support is installed.**

- Crossmember
- Rear engine support rebound insulator bolts. Bolts: 47–66 ft. lbs. (64–89 Nm)
- Front transaxle support bracket through-bolt and nut to 69–83 ft. lbs. (93–113 Nm)
- Front transaxle support insulator nuts and tighten them to 32–38 ft. lbs. (43–52 Nm)
- Rear transaxle support insulator nuts and tighten them to 21–34 ft. lbs. (28–46 Nm)
- Halfshafts
- Oil cooler lines
- Tie rod ends. Nuts: 26–30 ft. lbs. (35–40 Nm). Use new cotter pins.
- Lower ball joints to the knuckles. Bolt: 40–50 ft. lbs. (54–68 Nm)
- Front stabilizer bar. Nuts: 43–52 ft. lbs. (58–71 Nm)
- Splash shield. Bolts: 65–95 inch lbs. (8–10 Nm.)

- Front wheels. Lug bolts: 65–87 ft. lbs. (88–118 Nm)
- Shift cable and bracket
- Manual control lever arm. Nut: 34–47 ft. lbs. (44–64 Nm)

✳✳ WARNING

Do not use any type of power wrench to tighten the nut. Damage to the transaxle may result.

- Coolant pipe retaining bracket
- Vacuum and vent hoses
- Transaxle electrical connectors
- Ground wire to the transaxle. Bolt: 65–95 inch lbs. (8–10 Nm.)
- Speedometer cable
- Negative battery cable
- Transaxle fluid

➡ **Be sure that the gearshift lever position aligns with the manual control lever position exactly before starting the engine.**

Clutch

ADJUSTMENT

Clutch Cable Free-Play

1. Before servicing the vehicle, refer to the precautions in the beginning of this section.
2. Perform the following:
   a. Carefully move the clutch pedal back and forth and measure the amount of travel before the pedal activates the clutch. If the clutch pedal free-play is 0.35–0.59 in. (9–15mm), no adjustment is necessary. If the free-play is not within specification, proceed.
   b. Pull back the transaxle release lever and measure the clearance between the lever and the cable connecting link, as shown in the accompanying graphic.

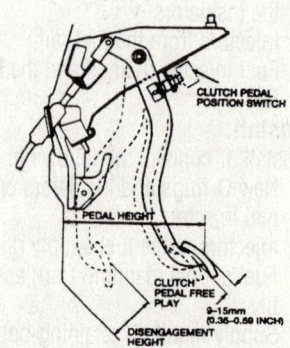

7922GG23

Clutch pedal free-play specifications

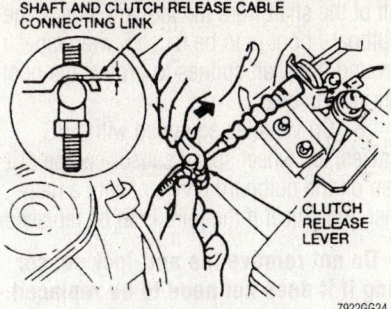

CLEARANCE BETWEEN CLUTCH RELEASE
SHAFT AND CLUTCH RELEASE CABLE
CONNECTING LINK

CLUTCH
RELEASE
LEVER

7922GG24

**Check the clearance between the release
lever and connecting link**

Thread the adjuster in or out until the
clearance between the connecting link
and the release lever is 0.06–0.10 in.
(1.5–2.5mm).

c. Check the free-play at the clutch
pedal. If it is not within specification,
inspect the clutch release components
for a problem.

d. After adjusting the clutch, be sure
the clutch disengagement height is 2.92
inches (74mm) minimum.

REMOVAL & INSTALLATION

1. Before servicing the vehicle, refer to
the precautions in the beginning of this section.

2. Remove or disconnect the follow-
ing:
  • Negative battery cable
  • Transaxle

➡ **If the pressure plate is to be reused,
paint or scribe alignment marks on the
pressure plate and flywheel for assembly reference.**

3. Install a clutch aligning tool.

4. Remove or disconnect the follow-
ing:
  • Pressure plate retaining bolts in a
    crisscross pattern, 1 turn at a time
  • Pressure plate and clutch disc

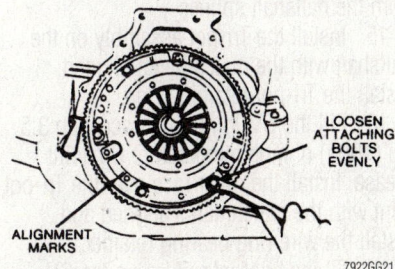

LOOSEN
ATTACHING
BOLTS
EVENLY

ALIGNMENT
MARKS

7922GG21

**Be sure to line up the matchmarks, if re-
using the pressure plate**

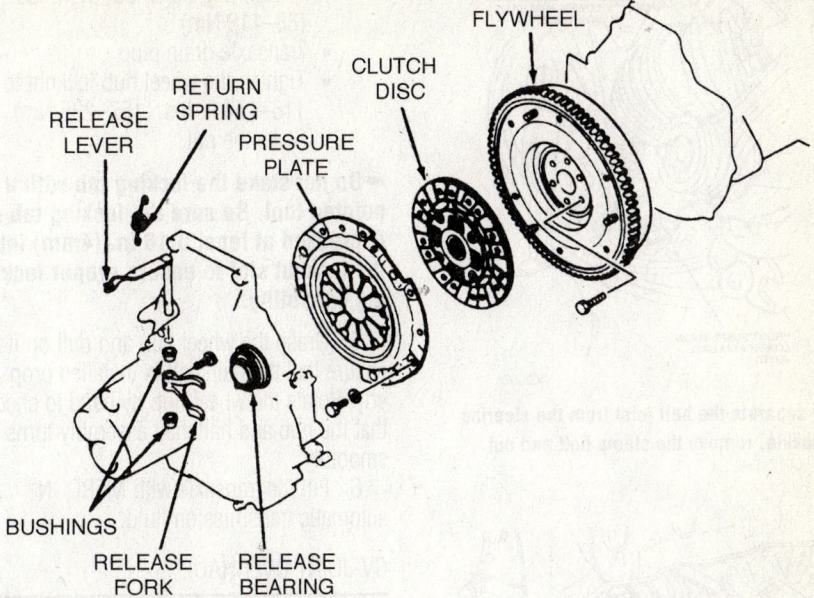

RELEASE
LEVER

RETURN
SPRING

PRESSURE
PLATE

CLUTCH
DISC

FLYWHEEL

BUSHINGS

RELEASE
FORK

RELEASE
BEARING

7922GG22

Exploded view of the clutch assembly

5. Inspect all clutch components
including the clutch release fork and release
bearing, and replace as required.

6. Inspect the flywheel for scoring,
cracks and heat checks. Resurface or
replace the flywheel, as necessary.

7. Inspect the pilot bearing for damage.
Be sure the bearing turns easily. If replacement is necessary, remove the flywheel and
remove the pilot bearing.

To install:

8. Install or connect the following:
  • New pilot bearing

➡ **Use only a driver tool that contacts
the bearing outer race. A driver tool
that contacts the inner race or the bearing area will damage the bearing.**

  • Flywheel. Coat the bolt threads with
    sealer. Bolts: 71–76 ft. lbs.
    (96–103 Nm)
  • Clutch disc and alignment tool

➡ **When installing the clutch disc, be
sure the disc dampener springs are
facing away from the flywheel. A new
disc will be stamped FLYWHEEL to
indicate the correct installation position.**

  • Pressure plate. Bolts evenly, in a
    crisscross pattern and in several
    steps: 13–20 ft. lbs. (18–26 Nm).

9. Clean the clutch disc splines on the
input shaft with a dry rag and coat the
spline surfaces with a light film of clutch
grease.

10. Install or connect the following:
  • Transaxle
  • Negative battery cable

11. Adjust the clutch pedal free-play.

Halfshaft

REMOVAL & INSTALLATION

1. Before servicing the vehicle, refer to
the precautions in the beginning of this section.

2. Remove or disconnect the following:
  • Negative battery cable
  • Loosen, but do not remove, the
    locknut
  • Transaxle fluid

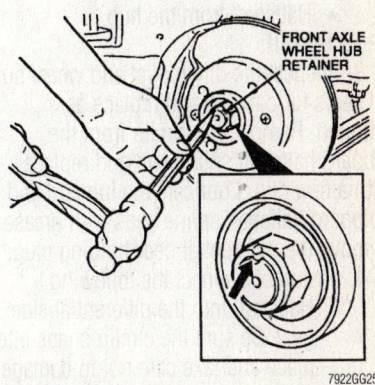

FRONT AXLE
WHEEL HUB
RETAINER

7922GG25

**Use a chisel to raise the staked edge of the
wheel hub retaining nut, then loosen the
nut**

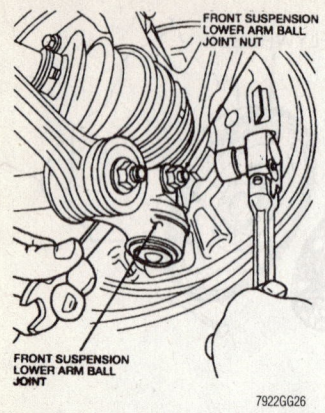

To separate the ball joint from the steering knuckle, remove the clamp bolt and nut

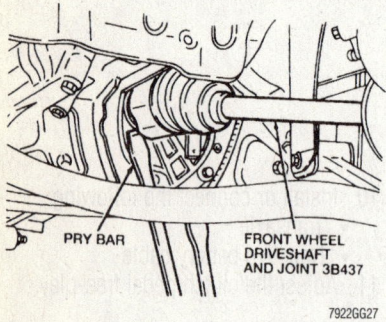

Use a small prybar to disengage the inner CV-joint from the transaxle, as shown

- Wheels
- Ball joint from the steering knuckle
- Halfshaft from the transaxle

➡**The halfshaft must be separated from the transaxle gradually. If the halfshaft is yanked out suddenly, the oil seal may be damaged. Install differential plugs to prevent the differential side gear from moving.**

- Hub nut
- Halfshaft from the hub

To install:

3. Inspect the differential and wheel hub oil seals for damage and replace as required. Remove the circlip from the inboard halfshaft spline end and replace with a new clip. Lubricate the inboard and outboard halfshaft spline ends with grease. Remove the differential gear holding plug.

4. Install or connect the following:

- Halfshaft into the differential side gear. Be sure the circlip snaps into place and take care not to damage the differential oil seal.
- Halfshaft into the wheel hub
- Hub nut, hand tight
- Ball joint. Nut: 32–40 ft. lbs. (43–54 Nm)

- Wheel. Lug bolts: 65–87 ft. lbs. (88–118 Nm)
- Transaxle drain plug
- Tighten the wheel hub locknut to 116–174 ft. lbs. (157–235 Nm). Stake the nut.

➡**Do not stake the locking tab with a pointed tool. Be sure the locking tab is depressed at least 0.16 in. (4mm) into the locknut slot to ensure proper locking capability.**

5. Grasp the wheel hub and pull on it to ensure that the halfshaft is installed properly. Rotate the wheel hub by hand to check that the hub and halfshaft assembly turns smoothly.

6. Fill the transaxle with MERCON® automatic transmission fluid.

CV-JOINT OVERHAUL

➡**On all halfshafts, the outboard CV-joint (Birfield-type) is permanently fitted onto the halfshaft and cannot be removed. To replace the outboard CV-joint boot, the inner CV-joint (Tri-pot-type) must first be removed. If a boot has failed due to age or wear, all boots should be replaced at the same time.**

1. Remove the halfshaft from the vehicle and support the assembly in a vise with protective or soft jaws.

2. Remove the large boot clamp from the inboard CV-joint and roll the boot back over the shaft.

3. Matchmark the outer race, halfshaft and Tri-pot bearing for reassembly using paint or marker. Do not use a punch or chisel.

4. Remove the wire ring bearing retainer from inside the outer race/housing and remove the outer race.

5. Matchmark the Tri-pot bearing and halfshaft. Remove the bearing snapring, then remove the bearing from the halfshaft. It may be necessary to drive the bearing off the shaft with a brass drift.

6. Remove the small clamp and the inboard CV-joint boot from the halfshaft.

➡**Test the CV-joint grease for contamination by rubbing a small amount between 2 fingers. If a gritty feeling is present, the grease is contaminated and the CV-joint must be disassembled and thoroughly cleaned and inspected before adding new grease.**

7. To remove the outboard CV-joint boot, remove the dynamic damper if applicable (right-hand halfshaft only), then

remove the boot clamps and slide the boot off of the shaft from the inboard side. If the outboard boot is to be reused, wrap tape around the shaft splines to protect the boot during removal.

8. On vehicles equipped with ABS brakes, the wheel speed sensor can be driven off the outboard CV-joint with a hammer and chisel if the joint is to be replaced.

➡**Do not remove the anti-lock sensor ring if it does not need to be replaced. If the sensor ring must be removed, replace with a new sensor ring.**

To install:

9. If not already installed, wrap smooth electrical tape around the halfshaft spline to protect and ease the installation of the CV-joint boot(s). Slide the clamps and the outboard boot onto the shaft.

10. Before positioning the boot over the CV-joint, pack the CV-joint and boot with grease. Be sure to use all of the grease in the pouch supplied with the boot kit.

11. Fit the boot into place on the CV-joint, making sure it is fully seated in the grooves in the shaft and outer race. Insert a suitable tool between the boot and the outer bearing race to allow trapped air to escape from the boot.

12. Install the boot clamps, wrapping them around the boots in the opposite direction of normal (forward) halfshaft rotation. Pull the clamps tight with a suitable tool and bend the locking tabs to secure in position.

13. After installing the outboard CV-joint boot, if applicable, install the dynamic damper onto the halfshaft at a distance of 18.99–19.27 in. (482.5–489.5mm) from the outboard end of the halfshaft. Measure this distance with the outboard CV-joint fully pushed onto the halfshaft.

➡**The dynamic damper is only used on the right-hand halfshaft assembly.**

14. Fit the inboard CV-joint boot and clamps onto the halfshaft. Remove the tape from the halfshaft splines.

15. Install the Tri-pot assembly on the halfshaft with the matchmarks aligned. Install the Tri-pot retaining ring.

16. Fill the CV-joint outer race with 3.5 oz. (100g) of high temperature CV-joint grease. Install the outer race over the Tri-pot joint with the matchmarks aligned and install the wire ring bearing retainer.

17. Fit the boot into place on the CV-joint, making sure it is fully seated in the grooves in the shaft and outer race. The distance between the CV-joint boot clamp grooves will measure about 3.5 in. (90mm).

18. Insert a suitable tool between the boot and the outer bearing race to allow trapped air to escape from the boot.

19. Install the boot clamps, wrapping them around the boots in the opposite direction of normal (forward) halfshaft rotation. Pull the clamps tight with a suitable tool and bend the locking tabs to secure in position.

20. Work the CV-joint through its full range of travel at various angles. The joint should flex, extend and compress smoothly. Wipe away any excess grease.

21. If necessary, carefully drive or press the wheel speed sensor onto the CV-joint.

STEERING AND SUSPENSION

Air Bag

✳✳ CAUTION

Some vehicles are equipped with the Supplemental Inflatable Restraint (SIR) or air bag system. The SIR system must be disabled before performing service on or around SIR system components, steering column, instrument panel components, wiring and sensors. Failure to follow safety and disabling procedures could result in accidental air bag deployment, possible personal injury and unnecessary SIR system repairs.

PRECAUTIONS

Several precautions must be observed when handling the inflator module to avoid accidental deployment and possible personal injury.

• Never carry the inflator module by the wires or connector on the underside of the module.

• When carrying a live inflator module, hold securely with both hands, and ensure that the bag and trim cover are pointed away.

• Place the inflator module on a bench or other surface with the bag and trim cover facing up.

• With the inflator module on the bench, never place anything on or close to the module which may be thrown in the event of an accidental deployment.

DISARMING

➡**Be sure to observe all air bag precautions before commencing with this procedure.**

1. Perform the following:
   a. Disconnect the negative battery cable.
   b. Wait 1 minute before proceeding with the service procedure. This is the time required for the back-up power supply in the air bag diagnostic monitor to deplete its stored energy.
   c. After service is completed, reconnect the negative battery cable.
   d. Turn the ignition switch to the **RUN** position. The air bag indicator should light continuously for approximately 6 seconds, then turn OFF. If the indicator flashes, fails to light or remains lit continuously, there is a fault in the air bag system.

Rack and Pinion Steering Gear

REMOVAL & INSTALLATION

Manual

1. Before servicing the vehicle, refer to the precautions in the beginning of this section.

2. Remove or disconnect the following:
   • Negative battery cable

➡**Matchmark the steering column lower universal joint and steering rack pinion for assembly reference.**

   • Steering column and intermediate shaft
   • Floor set plate Cut the plastic tie

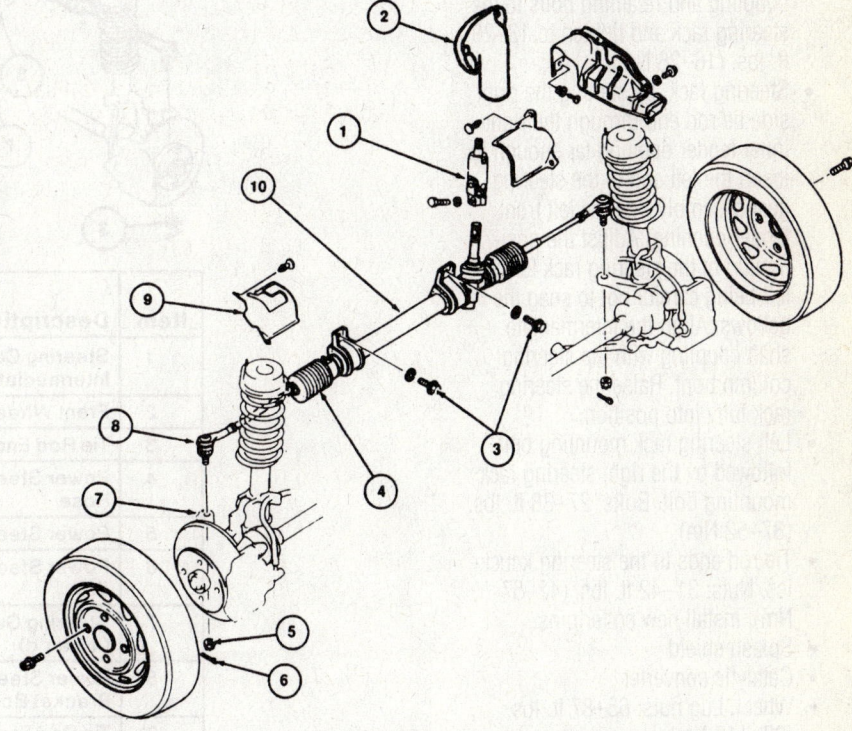

1 Steering Column Gear Input Shaft Coupling
2 Steering Column Tube Boot
3 Steering Gear Bolts
4 Front Wheel Spindle Connecting Rod Bellow
5 Front Wheel Spindle Connecting Rod End Nut
6 Front Wheel Spindle Connecting Rod End Cotter Pin
7 Front Wheel Knuckle
8 Front Wheel Spindle Connecting Rod Or End
9 Front Splash Shield
10 Steering Gear and Linkage

7922GG28

Exploded view of the manual steering gear mounting, showing related components

wrap securing the steering column boot to the steering rack.
- Front wheels
- Tie rod ends from the steering knuckles
- Catalytic converter
- Splash shield from the right inner fender
- 2 steering rack mounting bolts and lower the steering rack until it is free of the steering column boot. Slide the rack to the right, through the inner fender opening until the left tie rod is clear of the left inner fender, then lower the left end until the steering rack assembly can be withdrawn from the left side of the vehicle.
- Steering column intermediate shaft coupling bolt and the coupling from the steering rack

To install:

3. Install or connect the following:
- Steering column intermediate shaft coupling and retaining bolts to the steering rack and tighten to 13–20 ft. lbs. (18–26 Nm).
- Steering rack, by starting the right side tie rod end through the right inner fender opening far enough to insert the left end of the steering gear assembly into the left front fender opening. Adjust the positioning of the steering rack to the left being careful not to snag the bellows. Align the intermediate shaft coupling with the steering column boot. Raise the steering rack fully into position.
- Left steering rack mounting bolt followed by the right steering rack mounting bolt. Bolts: 27–38 ft. lbs. (37–52 Nm).
- Tie rod ends to the steering knuckles. Nuts: 31–42 ft. lbs. (42–57 Nm). Install new cotter pins.
- Splash shield
- Catalytic converter
- Wheel. Lug nuts: 65–87 ft. lbs. (88–118 Nm)
- New tie wrap
- Floor set plate
- Steering column
- Negative battery cable

Power

1. Before servicing the vehicle, refer to the precautions in the beginning of this section.

2. Remove or disconnect the following:
- Negative battery cable

- Steering column tube boot
- Intermediate shaft coupling bolt
- Wheels
- Power steering hose bracket
- Power steering lines
- Tie rod ends from the steering knuckles. Discard the cotter pins.
- Splash shield

➡**Lowering the exhaust system will ease access to the steering gear.**

- 3 exhaust inlet pipe nuts and 2 bracket bolts

- Muffler inlet pipe hanger posts from the exhaust hanger insulators

➡**Place alignment marks on the right tie rod end to ease installation.**

- Right tie rod end
- Steering rack mounting bolts. Lower the steering rack until it is free of the steering column boot. Slide the rack to the left and pull the right tie rod through the fender opening. Remove the steering gear by sliding it to the right.

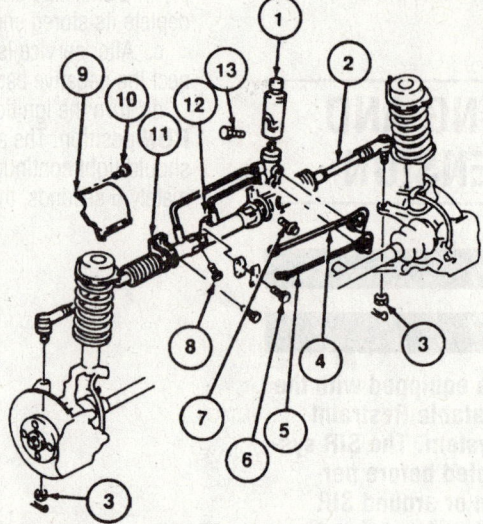

Item	Description
1	Steering Column Intermediate Shaft Coupling
2	Front Wheel Spindle Tie Rod
3	Tie Rod End Nut (2 Req'd)
4	Power Steering Pressure Hose
5	Power Steering Return Hose
6	Power Steering Hose Clamp Bolt
7	Steering Gear Bracket Bolts (4 Req'd)
8	Power Steering Hose Bracket Bolt
9	Tie Rod End Splash Shield
10	Tie Rod End Splash Shield Bolt (3 Req'd)
11	Steering Gear Mounting Bracket
12	Power Steering Hose Bracket
13	Steering Column Gear Input Shaft Coupling Bolt
A	Tighten to 42-57 N·m (31-42 Lb-Ft)

7922GG38

Exploded view of the power steering gear mounting, showing related components

To install:

3. Install the steering rack in its mounting location

4. Align the intermediate shaft with the universal joint and install the coupling bolt, but do not tighten it at this time.

5. Install or connect the following:

- Steering rack bracket bolts and tighten to 27–38 ft. lbs. (37–52 Nm)
- Intermediate shaft coupling bolt to 13–20 ft. lbs. (18–26 Nm)
- Power steering lines bracket
- Muffler inlet pipe hanger posts onto the exhaust hanger insulators
- Exhaust system. Nuts: 28–38 ft. lbs. (38–53 Nm.)
- 2 exhaust inlet pipe bracket bolts
- Right tie rod end
- Tie rod ends to the steering knuckles. Nuts: 31–42 ft. lbs. (42–57 Nm). Install new cotter pins.

- Splash shield
- Wheels. Lug bolts to 65–87 ft. lbs. (88–118 Nm)
- Negative battery cable
- Power steering fluid

Strut and Spring

REMOVAL & INSTALLATION

Front

1. Before servicing the vehicle, refer to the precautions in the beginning of this section.

2. Remove or disconnect the following:

- Wheel
- Brake line clip from the strut lower mounting bracket, and disengage the brake line
- 2 nuts and bolts securing the strut lower bracket to the steering knuckle
- 2 nuts securing the strut mounting block in the strut tower

- Strut lower bracket from the steering knuckle and lower the strut clear of the wheel well
- Coil spring using a spring compressor
- Mounting block cap, strut upper nut and lockwasher
- Strut mounting block and spacer plate
- Washer, bearing seal and bearing from the strut rod
- Upper spring seat, seat insulator and spring
- Jounce bumper/shield off the strut

➡ **If replacing the spring, release the spring compressor progressively to prevent spring arching. Open the compressor jaws wide enough to grip the new spring in the same position and tighten the compressor screws progressively, compressing the spring until the strut can be assembled without interference.**

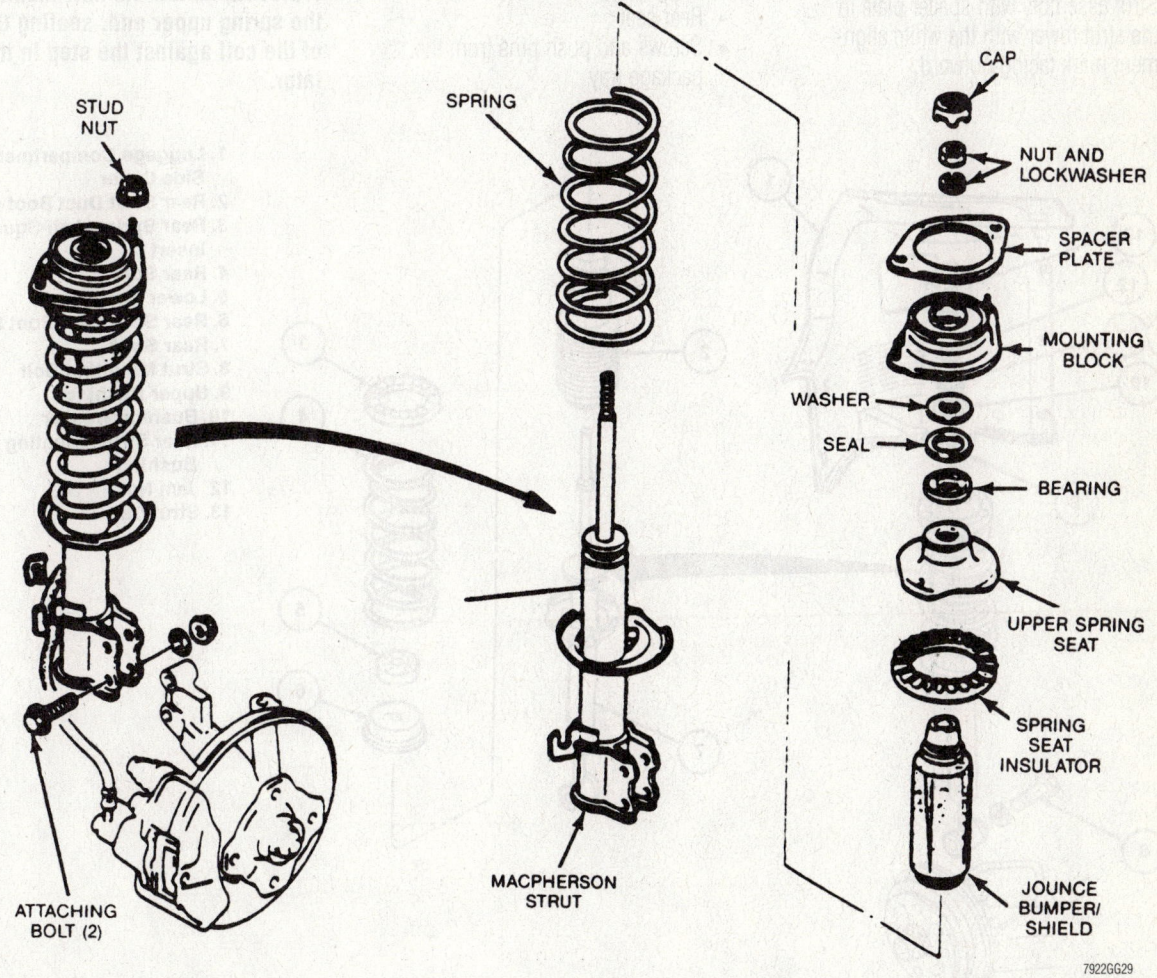

STUD NUT

SPRING

ATTACHING BOLT (2)

MACPHERSON STRUT

CAP

NUT AND LOCKWASHER

SPACER PLATE

MOUNTING BLOCK

WASHER

SEAL

BEARING

UPPER SPRING SEAT

SPRING SEAT INSULATOR

JOUNCE BUMPER/ SHIELD

7922GG29

Exploded view of the front strut assembly

To install:

3. Check the condition of the jounce bumper and spring seat insulator and replace, as necessary. Be sure the bearing operates smoothly. Check the spring for uniform coil spacing, for nicks or burrs and compare the spring length with a new spring to check for excessive spring set; replace as necessary.

4. Install or connect the following:
- Jounce bumper/shield onto the strut rod and over the body
- Compressed spring, upper spring seat insulator and upper seat, positioning the spring ends against the steps in the seats
- Bearing, seal and plain washer on the strut rod
- Strut mounting block with the white alignment spot on the same side of the strut as the steering knuckle mounting bracket
- Spacer plate and lockwasher. Nut: 40–50 ft. lbs. (54–67 Nm). Release and remove the spring compressor.
- Strut assembly with spacer plate in the strut tower with the white alignment mark facing outward.

- 2 upper mounting block stud nuts and tighten to 34–46 ft. lbs. (46–63 Nm).
- Steering knuckle in the strut tower lower bracket. Bolts: 69–86 ft. lbs. (93–117 Nm).
- Brake line and retaining clip
- Wheels lug bolts to 65–87 ft. lbs. (88–118 Nm)

Rear

✳✳ WARNING

Do not attempt to remove both left and right spring and strut assemblies at the same time. Do one side at a time to prevent damage to the rear suspension.

1. Before servicing the vehicle, refer to the precautions in the beginning of this section.

2. Remove or disconnect the following:
- Cargo compartment side cover
- Luggage compartment cover
- Rear seat
- Screws and push pins from the package tray

- Radio speaker electrical connectors
- Rear safety belt anchor bolt
- Push pins and the luggage compartment side cover
- Rear door scuff plate
- Quarter trim panel
- Strut cap, jam nut and flanged nut from the strut rod
- Bushing washer and upper bushing

➡ **Raising the vehicle will release any tension left on the coil spring.**

- Rear wheels
- Lower strut mounting bolt from the torsion beam
- Strut assembly from the vehicle and separate it from the spring and seat insulator

3. Inspect the condition of the spring, spring seat insulator and strut. Replace any damaged or deteriorated components, as required.

To install:

➡ **If the upper spring seat insulator is replaced, install the new insulator on the spring upper end, seating the end of the coil against the step in the insulator.**

1. Luggage Compartment Side Cover
2. Rear Strut Dust Boot Cover
3. Rear Spring Anti-Squeak Insert
4. Rear Spring
5. Lower Bushing
6. Rear Strut Dust Boot Seat
7. Rear Strut
8. Strut Mounting Bolt
9. Upper Bushing
10. Bushing Washer
11. Rear Strut Mounting Bushing
12. Jam Nut
13. Strut Cap

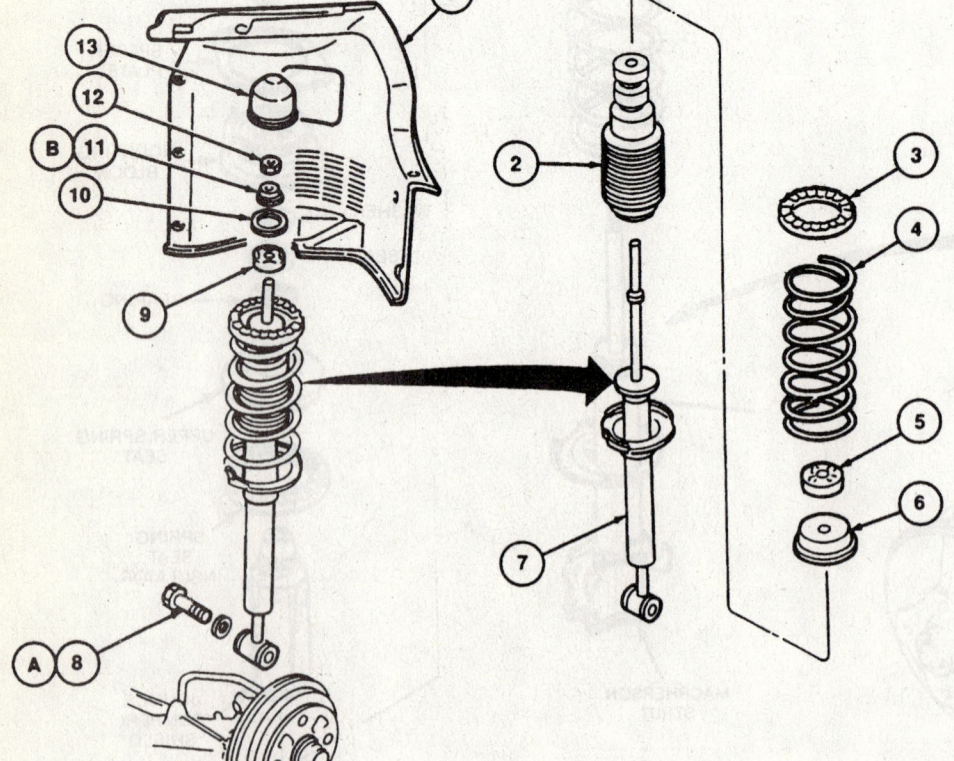

Exploded view of the rear strut assembly

7922GG39

4. Install or connect the following:
- Spring on the strut, making sure the end of the coil seats against the step in the strut spring seat.
- Strut into the upper strut mounting hole
- Strut lower end to the mounting hole in the torsion beam. Start the mounting bolt in by hand to hold the strut in position.
- Wheel. Lug nuts: 65–87 ft. lbs. (88–118 Nm)

5. Lower the vehicle. Be sure that the coil spring is positioned properly on the spring seat insulator.

6. Install or connect the following:
- Rod upper end bushing, bushing washer and flanged nut. Flanged nut: 12–18 ft. lbs. (16–24 Nm). Hold the flanged nut stationary and tighten the locknut.
- Jam nut and the strut cap
- Side cover in the cargo compartment
- Lower strut mounting bolt to 50–60 ft. lbs. (68–81 Nm)

Lower Ball Joints

REMOVAL & INSTALLATION

The lower ball joint is an integral component of the lower control arm. If the lower ball joint is defective, the entire lower control arm must be replaced.

Sway Bar

REMOVAL & INSTALLATION

1. Remove or disconnect the following:
- Stabilizer bar brackets
- Split bushings from the stabilizer bar. Replace deteriorated or worn bushings as required.
- Cotter pins and front stabilizer bar retaining nuts at the lower control arms and remove the rear washers and bushings.
- Stabilizer bar
- Front bushings and washers. Replace deteriorated or worn bushings as required.

To install:
2. Install or connect the following:
- Control arm bushing washers on the ends of the stabilizer bar and install the control arm front bushings
- Stabilizer bar and insert the ends of the bar into the lower control arms

- Rear control arm bushings and washers with the retaining nuts. Make the retaining nuts finger-tight.
- 2 split bushings on the stabilizer bar with the split side forward and position them next to the white alignment marks on the bar.
- 2 stabilizer bar brackets. Tighten the 4 bracket retaining nuts to 40–50 ft. lbs. (54–68 Nm).
- Front stabilizer bar retaining nuts to 47–57 ft. lbs. (64–77 Nm) and install new cotter pins.

Lower Control Arm

REMOVAL & INSTALLATION

The ball joint is an integral component of the lower control arm and cannot be serviced separately.

1. Before servicing the vehicle, refer to the precautions in the beginning of this section.

2. Remove or disconnect the following:
- Front wheels
- Ball joint clamp bolt and nut from the steering knuckle assembly
- Cotter pin and stabilizer bar bushing nut from the rear of the control arm
- Rear bushing washer and bushing. Discard the cotter pin.
- Ball joint stud out of the steering knuckle
- Control arm from the stabilizer bar end

3. If the lower control arm is to be reused, inspect the control arm bushings for damage or excessive wear. Verify that the ball joint swivels freely, but is not loose. Replace the lower control arm as required.

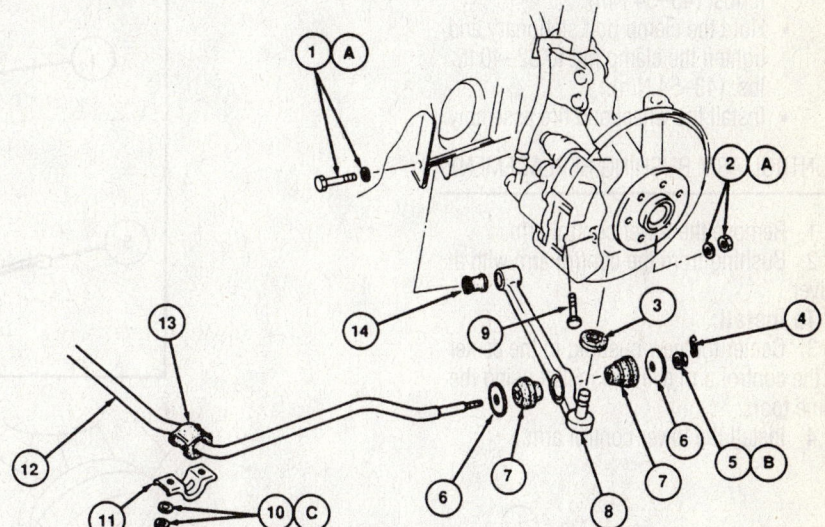

Item	Description
1	Front Suspension Lower Arm-to-Chassis Bolt and Washer
2	Front Suspension Lower Arm Ball Joint Washer and Nut
3	Front Suspension Lower Arm Ball Joint Dust Boot (Part of 3078)
4	Cotter Pin (Part of 5A486)
5	Front Stabilizer Bar Nut (Part of 5A486)
6	Front Stabilizer Bar Washers (2 Req'd) (Part of 5A486)
7	Front Stabilizer Bar Bushings (2 Req'd) (Part of 5A486)
8	Front Suspension Lower Arm

Item	Description
9	Front Suspension Lower Arm Ball Joint Bolt
10	Stabilizer Bar Bracket Washers and Nuts (2 Req'd)
11	Stabilizer Bar Bracket
12	Front Stabilizer Bar
13	Lower Suspension Arm Stabilizer Bar Insulator
14	Front Suspension Lower Arm Mounting Bolt Bushing
A	Tighten to 43-54 N·m (32-40 Lb-Ft)
B	Tighten to 64-77 N·m (47-57 Lb-Ft)
C	Tighten to 54-68 N·m (40-50 Lb-Ft)

Exploded view of the lower control arm assembly

7922GG33

Turn to Section 5 for brake system applications

To install:

4. Install or connect the following:
- Front bushing washer and bushing onto the stabilizer bar end. Engage the lower control arm with the stabilizer bar.
- Control arm inner end into the pivot bracket on the frame and start the pivot bolt to hold the control arm in place. Do not completely tighten the bolt at this time.
- Control arm ball joint stud with the clamp bore in the steering knuckle, and install the clamp bolt and nut. Do not tighten it yet.
- Stabilizer bar rear bushing and washer onto the stabilizer bar end. Nut: 47–57 ft. lbs. (64–77 Nm). Install a new cotter pin.
- Tighten the lower arm-to-chassis bolt at the frame bracket to 32–40 ft. lbs. (43–54 Nm).
- Hold the clamp bolt stationary and tighten the clamp nut to 32–40 ft. lbs. (43–54 Nm).
- Install the wheel and tire assembly.

CONTROL ARM BUSHING REPLACEMENT

1. Remove the lower control arm.
2. Bushing from the control arm with a driver

To install:

3. Center the new bushing in the center of the control arm eye and install using the same tools.
4. Install the lower control arm.

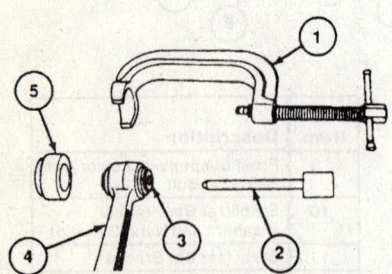

Item	Description
1	C-Frame and Clamp Assembly
2	Lower Control Arm Bushing Tool
3	Front Suspension Lower Arm Mounting Bolt Bushing
4	Front Suspension Lower Arm
5	Receiver Adapter

89728G03

Use the appropriate tools to remove or install the control arm bushing

Wheel Hub and Knuckle

REMOVAL & INSTALLATION

1. Remove or disconnect the following:
- Wheel hub retaining nut
- Wheel
- Retaining clip securing the brake hose to the strut
- Anti-lock sensor
- Tie rod end attaching nut
- Tie rod end from the steering knuckle arm
- Caliper
- Rotor
- Clamp bolt and nut at the point where the lower control arm ball joint connects to the steering knuckle
- Lower ball joint from the steering knuckle by prying downward on the lower control arm
- 2 bolts that position the steering knuckle between the strut bracket flanges
- Knuckle/hub assembly from the end of the halfshaft
- Disc brake rotor shield from the knuckle/hub assembly

To install:

2. Install a new brake rotor shield.
3. Clean the halfshaft spline end and lubricate with a coating of wheel bearing grease. Apply a thin film of clean SAE 30 weight oil to the steering knuckle/hub assembly up to the point where the uppermost arm of the steering knuckle seats into the strut bracket. Guide the steering knuckle/hub assembly onto the halfshaft and the strut.

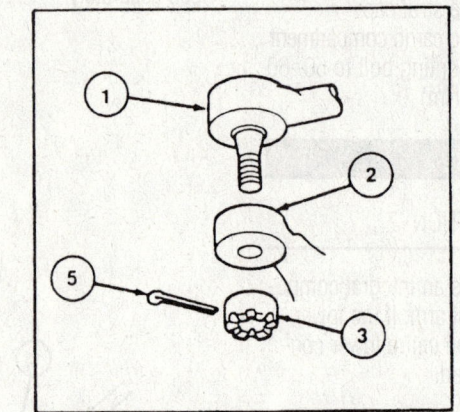

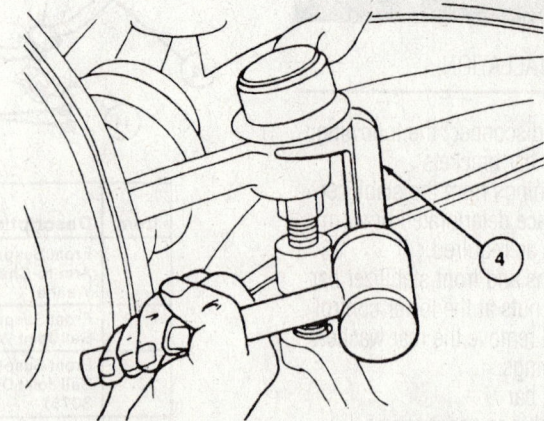

Item	Description
1	Tie Rod End
2	Front Wheel Knuckle
3	Tie Rod End Nut
4	Tie Rod End Separator
5	Cotter Pin

89728G05

Separating the tie rod end from the steering knuckle arm

4. Install or connect the following:
- Strut-to-steering knuckle bolts and attaching nuts. Tighten the nuts to 69–86 ft. lbs. (93–117 Nm).
- Lower control arm ball joint in the steering knuckle
- Lower control arm pinch bolt and attaching nut. Tighten the nut to 32–40 ft. lbs. (43–54 Nm).

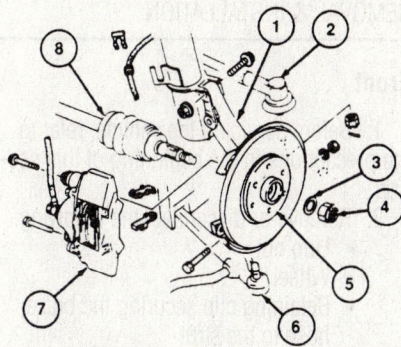

Item	Description
1	Front Wheel Knuckle
2	Tie Rod End
3	Front Axle Wheel Hub Retainer Washer
4	Front Axle Wheel Hub Retainer
5	Front Disc Brake Rotor
6	Front Suspension Lower Arm Ball Joint
7	Disc Brake Caliper
8	Front Wheel Driveshaft and Joint

89728G04

Exploded view of the wheel hub and knuckle assembly

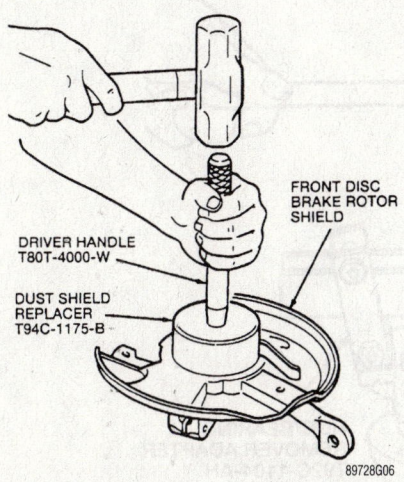

DRIVER HANDLE
T80T-4000-W

FRONT DISC
BRAKE ROTOR
SHIELD

DUST SHIELD
REPLACER
T94C-1175-B

89728G06

If the brake rotor shield was removed, install a new one using a dust shield replacer and driver

- Brake rotor
- Caliper on the steering knuckle and install the attaching bolts. Tighten the bolts to 29–36 ft. lbs. (39–49 Nm).
- Caliper hose in the strut routing bracket and install the retaining clip
- Anti-lock sensor
- New wheel hub retaining nut and tighten by hand
- Tie rod end to the steering knuckle and install the attaching nut. Tighten the attaching nut to 22–33 ft. lbs. (29–44 Nm).
- New cotter pin through the nut and ball stud
- Wheel

5. Tighten the wheel hub retaining nut to 116–174 ft. lbs. (157–235 Nm). After installation, the wheel hub assembly must rotate freely by hand. Stake the halfshaft attaching nut into the shaft groove.

➡ **Do not use a pointed tool to stake the nut. If the nut cracks even slightly during staking, replace it with another new one.**

6. Check the front wheel alignment.

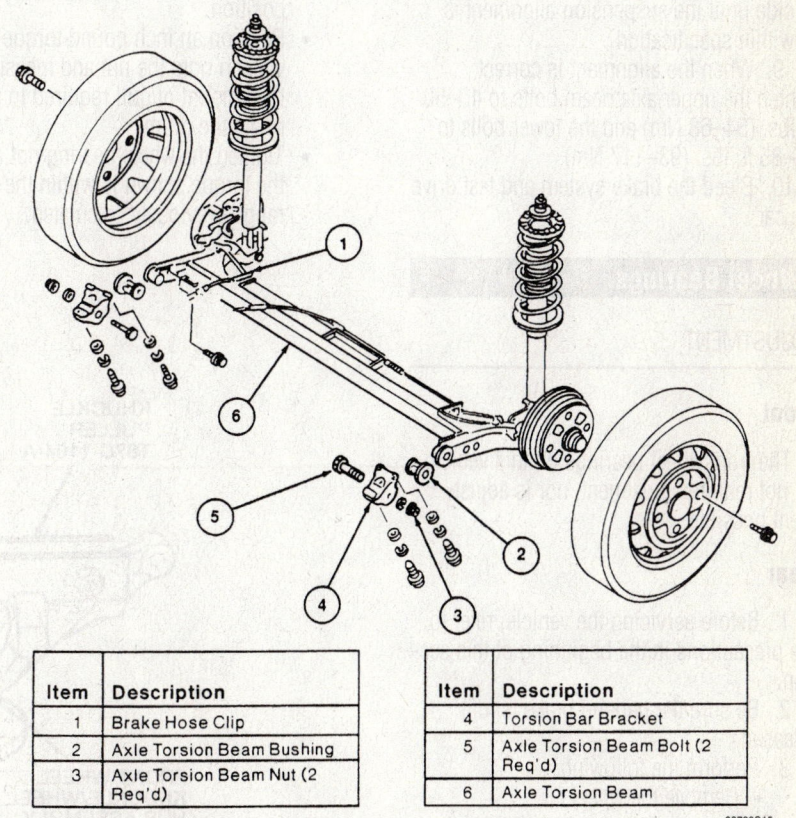

Item	Description
1	Brake Hose Clip
2	Axle Torsion Beam Bushing
3	Axle Torsion Beam Nut (2 Req'd)

Item	Description
4	Torsion Bar Bracket
5	Axle Torsion Beam Bolt (2 Req'd)
6	Axle Torsion Beam

89728G15

Exploded view of the axle torsion beam assembly

Rear Axle Torsion Beam

REMOVAL & INSTALLATION

1. Remove or disconnect the following:
- Wheel and tire assemblies
- Rear wheel spindles
- Rear brake hoses
- Front parking brake cable and conduit clevises at the brake backing plates
- Front parking brake cable and conduit from the axle torsion beam
- Rear brakes
- Backing plate and assemblies

2. Loosen the axle torsion beam retaining nuts.

3. Loosen the torsion bar retaining nuts from the brackets

4. Remove or disconnect the following:
- Torsion beam

➡ **If the torsion beam brackets are not to be replaced, leave them on the car. The brackets' mounting holes are slotted and, if removed, require alignment when the torsion beam is installed.**

To install:

5. If installing a new torsion beam, install the beam bushings.

6. Install or connect the following:
- Bushing flange washers and place the beam into position on the brackets
- Finger-tighten the retaining nuts and bolts
- Brake backing plates
- Wheel speed sensor
- Wheel spindles
- Parking brake cables and conduit
- Brake hoses
- Wheels

7. Tighten the torsion beam nuts to 69–86 ft. lbs. (93–117 Nm), with the car on the ground.

8. Check the rear suspension alignment as follows:

a. Locate and mark the center of the underbody at a point of equal distance from the inner and upper right and left axle torsion beam bolts.

b. From this point, measure the distance to the centers of both the right and left shock absorber bolts.

c. If these measurements are not within 0.2 inches (5mm) of each other, shift the torsion beam brackets side-to-side until the suspension alignment is within specification.

9. When the alignment is correct, tighten the upper axle beam bolts to 40–50 ft. lbs. (54–68 Nm) and the lower bolts to 69–86 ft. lbs. (93–117 Nm).

10. Bleed the brake system and test drive the car.

Wheel Bearings

ADJUSTMENT

Front

The front wheel bearings on this vehicle do not require adjustment, nor is adjustment possible.

Rear

1. Before servicing the vehicle, refer to the precautions in the beginning of this section.

2. Be sure the parking brake is fully released.

3. Perform the following:
- Remove the wheel.
- Remove the grease cap.
- Rotate the brake drum to be sure there is no brake drag.
- Remove the cotter pin, wheel bear-

ing nut cover. Discard the cotter pin.
- To seat the bearings, tighten the wheel bearing nut to 18–22 ft. lbs. (25–29 Nm). Rotate the brake drum by hand while tightening the nut.
- Loosen the wheel bearing nut until it can be turned by hand.
- Before the bearing preload can be set, the amount of seal drag must be measured and added to the required preload.
- To measure the seal drag, install a lug bolt and rotate the brake drum until the stud is in the 12 o'clock position. Place an inch pound torque wrench onto the bolt to measure the amount of force required to rotate the brake drum. Pull the torque wrench and record the torque reading when rotation begins.
- Add the oil seal drag value obtained to the specified value of 0.6–1.9 inch lbs. (2.6–8.5 Nm). This is the standard bearing preload.
- Loosely tighten the bearing nut and rotate the brake drum until the nut and wheel are at the 12 o'clock position.
- Position an inch pound torque wrench onto the nut and measure the amount of pull required to rotate the drum.
- Tighten the wheel bearing nut until the torque shown is within the range previously calculated.

- turn the wheel bearing nut slowly to adjust it to the standard bearing preload.
- Install the nut retaining cap and a new cotter pin.
- Install the grease cap and the wheel and tire assembly.
- Lower the vehicle.
- road test the vehicle and check for proper operation.

REMOVAL & INSTALLATION

Front

1. Before servicing the vehicle, refer to the precautions in the beginning of this section.

2. Remove or disconnect the following:
- Hub nut
- Wheel
- Retaining clip securing the brake hose to the strut
- Front brake anti-lock sensor
- Tie rod end from the steering knuckle arm
- Caliper attaching bolts and lift the caliper assembly from the steering knuckle.
- Brake rotor
- Ball joint from the steering knuckle
- 2 bolts that position the steering knuckle between the strut bracket flanges
- Knuckle/hub assembly from the end of the halfshaft
- Halfshaft
- Disc brake rotor shield from the

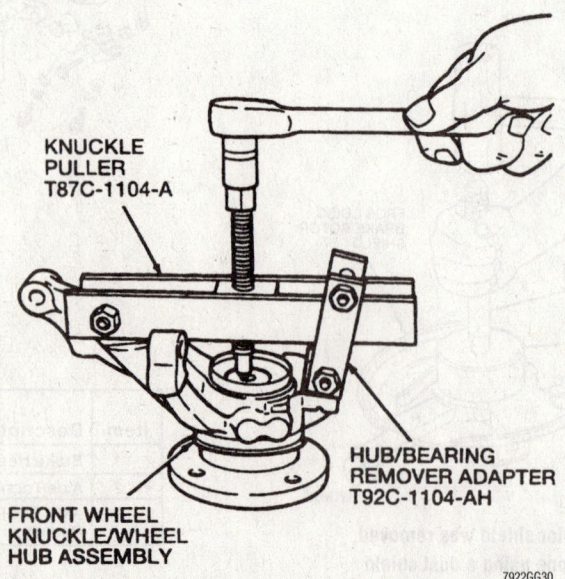

KNUCKLE PULLER T87C-1104-A

HUB/BEARING REMOVER ADAPTER T92C-1104-AH

FRONT WHEEL KNUCKLE/WHEEL HUB ASSEMBLY

7922GG30

Use a puller to separate the front wheel bearing hub from the steering knuckle

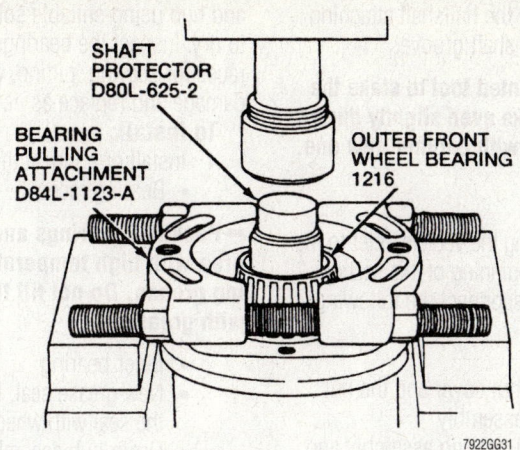

SHAFT
PROTECTOR
D80L-625-2

BEARING
PULLING
ATTACHMENT
D84L-1123-A

OUTER FRONT
WHEEL BEARING
1216

7922GG31

Use a bearing pulling attachment, driver and a press to remove the front outer wheel bearing, as shown

knuckle/hub assembly. Discard the shield.

➡**Shield replacement is not a requirement for normal bearing service.**

- Hub from the knuckle
- Outer bearing retainer washer

➡**The outer bearing retainer washer is pre-selected to yield the correct bearing preload. Save the washer for use during assembly.**

- Outer bearing from the wheel hub with a press
- Grease seals from the hub and steering knuckle bore and discard
- Inner wheel bearing
- Bearing races from the steering knuckle using a puller and slide hammer

3. Thoroughly clean the hub and knuckle. Inspect the hub and knuckle for wear and/or damage. Replace as necessary.

To install:

4. Install or connect the following:
- Brake rotor shield
- Outer bearing races in the steering knuckle
- Bearing races and bearing, coated with a thin film of clean grease, in the steering knuckle
- spacer selection tool T87C-1104-B, or equivalent, and clamp the bolt head in a vise.

5. Perform the following:
- Tighten the center bolt in increments, to 36, 72, 108 and 145 ft. lbs. (49, 98, 147 and 196 Nm). After tightening the center bolt to each specified increment, seat the

bearings by rotating the steering knuckle.
- Remove the tool/steering knuckle from the vise. Remount the assembly in the vise, clamping it where the strut mounts.
- Measure the amount of torque required to rotate the spacer selector tool, using an inch pound torque wrench. The torque wrench reading must be taken just as the tool starts to rotate.
- If the torque wrench indicates 2.2–10.4 inch lbs. (0.25–1.80 Nm), the outer bearing retainer washer is the correct thickness. If the torque wrench indicates less than 2.2 inch

Front outer wheel bearing retainer washer thickness chart

Stamped mark	Thickness
1	6.285 mm (0.2474 in)
2	6.325 mm (0.2490 in)
3	6.365 mm (0.2506 in)
4	6.405 mm (0.2522 in)
5	6.445 mm (0.2538 in)
6	6.485 mm (0.2554 in)
7	6.525 mm (0.2570 in)
8	6.565 mm (0.2586 in)
9	6.605 mm (0.2602 in)
10	6.645 mm (0.2618 in)
11	6.685 mm (0.2634 in)
12	6.725 mm (0.2650 in)
13	6.765 mm (0.2666 in)
14	6.805 mm (0.2682 in)
15	6.845 mm (0.2698 in)
16	6.885 mm (0.2714 in)
17	6.925 mm (0.2730 in)
18	6.965 mm (0.2746 in)
19	7.005 mm (0.2762 in)
20	7.045 mm (0.2778 in)
21	7.085 mm (0.2794 in)

7922GG32

lbs. (0.25 Nm), a thinner outer bearing retainer washer must be installed. If the torque wrench indicates more than 10.4 inch lbs. (1.8 Nm), a thicker outer bearing retainer washer must be installed.

- Each outer bearing retainer washer has a numerical code that identifies its thickness, which is stamped onto the outer diameter of the washer. The numbers range from 1 to 21, with 1 being the thinnest washer. If the number stamped on the washer is not legible, measure the washer with a micrometer and compare it to the thickness chart to determine the number.

➡**Changing the outer bearing retainer washer thickness by 1 number, either higher or lower, will change the bearing preload by 1.7–3.5 inch lbs. (0.2–0.4 Nm).**

- Pack the bearings and the hub area with a suitable high temperature wheel bearing grease. Place the inner wheel bearing into the steering knuckle bore.
- Lubricate the lip of the new inner grease seal with the bearing grease. Form the lubricant into a strip, concentrated along the edges of the seal lip. Install the bearing into the bore, using a suitable installation tool.
- Place the original outer bearing retainer washer, or the outer bearing retainer washer selected from the front wheel bearing adjustment procedure, in the steering knuckle bore. Position the outer wheel bearing in the steering knuckle bore.
- Lubricate the lip of the new outer grease seal with the bearing grease. Form the lubricant into a strip, concentrated along the edges of the seal lip. Install the outer seal into the bore, using a suitable installation tool.

6. Install or connect the following:
- Hub in the steering knuckle bore with a press
- Clean the halfshaft spline end and lubricate with a coating of wheel bearing grease. Apply a thin film of clean SAE 30 weight oil to the steering knuckle/hub assembly up to the point where the uppermost

arm of the steering knuckle seats into the strut bracket. Guide the steering knuckle/hub assembly onto the halfshaft and the strut.

- Strut-to-steering knuckle bolts and attaching nuts. Tighten the nuts to 69–86 ft. lbs. (93–117 Nm).
- Lower control arm ball joint in the steering knuckle. Nut: 32–40 ft. lbs. (43–54 Nm).
- Brake rotor
- Caliper. Bolts: 29–36 ft. lbs. (39–49 Nm)
- Brake hose
- ABS sensor
- Hub nut, hand tight
- Tie rod end to the steering knuckle. Nut: 22–33 ft. lbs. (29–44 Nm). Use a new cotter pin.
- Wheel
- Tighten the wheel hub retaining nut to 116–174 ft. lbs. (157–235 Nm). After installation, the wheel hub assembly must rotate freely by

hand. Stake the halfshaft attaching nut into the shaft groove.

➡**Do not use a pointed tool to stake the nut. If the nut cracks even slightly during staking, replace it with another new one.**

Rear

1. Before servicing the vehicle, refer to the precautions in the beginning of this section.
2. Remove or disconnect the following:
   - Wheel
   - Grease cap
   - Cotter pin, nut cover and the nut
   - Drum/hub assembly
   - Outer wheel bearing assembly and washer
   - Grease seal
   - Inner wheel bearing assembly

➡**If replacing the bearings, the bearing races must also be replaced.**

   - Bearing races from the hub
3. Thoroughly clean the wheel bearings

and hub using suitable solvent and allow it to dry. Inspect the bearings and bearing races for scoring, pitting, wear or other damage and replace as necessary.

To install:

4. Install or connect the following:
   - Bearing races

➡**Pack the bearings and the drum hub area with high temperature wheel bearing grease. Do not fill the entire hub with grease.**

   - Inner bearing
   - New grease seal. Lubricate the lip of the seal with wheel bearing grease.
   - Drum/hub assembly on the spindle
   - Outer wheel bearing, washer and nut. Adjust the bearing preload.
   - Bearing nut cover and a new cotter pin
   - Grease cap
   - Wheel
5. Check and adjust the brakes as required.

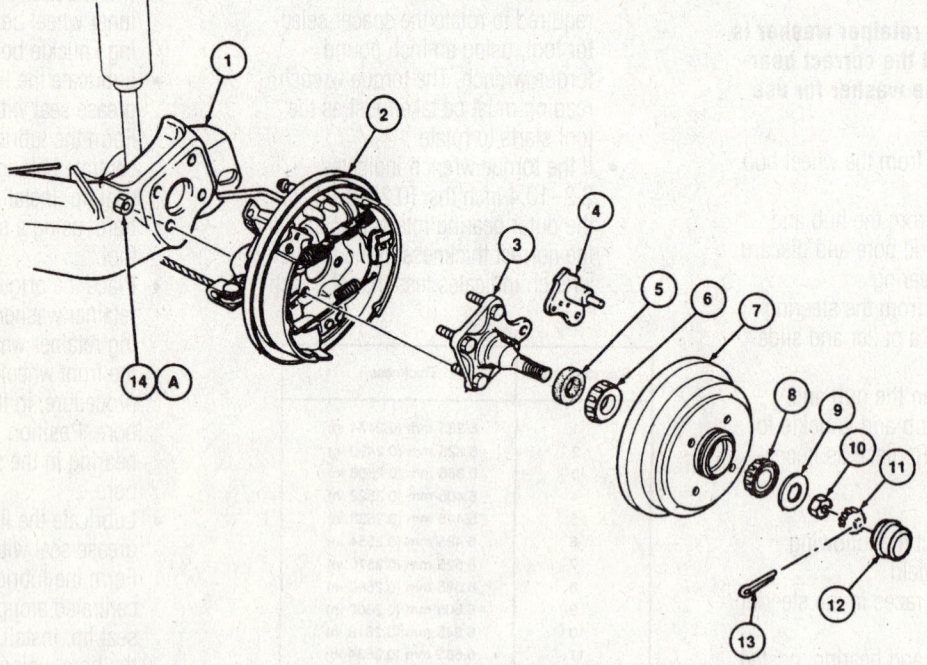

Item	Description
1	Axle Torsion Beam
2	Brake Assembly
3	Rear Wheel Spindle
4	Rear Brake Anti-Lock Sensor (If Equipped)
5	Inner Wheel Bearing Oil Seal
6	Inner Rear Wheel Bearing
7	Brake Drum
8	Outer Rear Wheel Bearing

Item	Description
9	Washer
10	Wheel Bearing Nut
11	Wheel Bearing Nut Cover
12	Hub Grease Cap
13	Cotter Pin
14	Rear Wheel Spindle Nut (4 Req'd)
A	Tighten to 43-61 N·m (31-45 Lb-Ft)

7922GG40

Exploded view of the rear wheel bearing and related components

FORD MOTOR CO.

Probe

PRECAUTIONS

Before servicing any vehicle, please be sure to read all of the following precautions, which deal with personal safety, prevention of component damage, and important points to take into consideration when servicing a motor vehicle:

• Never open, service or drain the radiator or cooling system when the engine is hot; serious burns can occur from the steam and hot coolant.

• Observe all applicable safety precautions when working around fuel. Whenever servicing the fuel system, always work in a well-ventilated area. Do not allow fuel spray or vapors to come in contact with a spark, open flame, or excessive heat (a hot drop light, for example). Keep a dry chemical fire extinguisher near the work area. Always keep fuel in a container specifically designed for fuel storage; also, always properly seal fuel containers to avoid the possibility of fire or explosion. Refer to the additional fuel system precautions later in this section.

• Fuel injection systems often remain pressurized, even after the engine has been turned **OFF**. The fuel system pressure must be relieved before disconnecting any fuel lines. Failure to do so may result in fire and/or personal injury.

• Brake fluid often contains polyglycol ethers and polyglycols. Avoid contact with the eyes and wash your hands thoroughly after handling brake fluid. If you do get brake fluid in your eyes, flush your eyes with clean, running water for 15 minutes. If eye irritation persists, or if you have taken brake fluid internally, IMMEDIATELY seek medical assistance.

• The EPA warns that prolonged contact with used engine oil may cause a number of skin disorders, including cancer! You should make every effort to minimize your exposure to used engine oil. Protective gloves should be worn when changing oil. Wash your hands and any other exposed skin areas as soon as possible after exposure to used engine oil. Soap and water, or waterless hand cleaner should be used.

• All new vehicles are now equipped with an air bag system, often referred to as a Supplemental Restraint System (SRS) or Supplemental Inflatable Restraint (SIR) system. The system must be disabled before performing service on or around system components, steering column, instrument panel components, wiring and sensors. Failure to follow safety and disabling procedures could result in accidental air bag deployment, possible personal injury and unnecessary system repairs.

• Always wear safety goggles when working with, or around, the air bag system. When carrying a non-deployed air bag, be sure the bag and trim cover are pointed away from your body. When placing a non-deployed air bag on a work surface, always face the bag and trim cover upward, away from the surface. This will reduce the motion of the module if it is accidentally deployed. Refer to the additional air bag system precautions later in this section.

• Clean, high quality brake fluid from a sealed container is essential to the safe and proper operation of the brake system. You should always buy the correct type of brake fluid for your vehicle. If the brake fluid becomes contaminated, completely flush the system with new fluid. Never reuse any brake fluid. Any brake fluid that is removed from the system should be discarded. Also, do not allow any brake fluid to come in contact with a painted surface; it will damage the paint.

• Never operate the engine without the proper amount and type of engine oil; doing so WILL result in severe engine damage.

• Timing belt maintenance is extremely important! Many models utilize an interference-type, non-freewheeling engine. If the timing belt breaks, the valves in the cylinder head may strike the pistons, causing potentially serious (also time-consuming and expensive) engine damage. Refer to the maintenance interval charts in the front of this manual for the recommended replacement interval for the timing belt, and to the timing belt section for belt replacement and inspection.

• Disconnecting the negative battery cable on some vehicles may interfere with the functions of the on-board computer system(s) and may require the computer to undergo a relearning process once the negative battery cable is reconnected.

• When servicing drum brakes, only disassemble and assemble one side at a time, leaving the remaining side intact for reference.

• Only an MVAC-trained, EPA-certified automotive technician should service the air conditioning system or its components.

ENGINE REPAIR

Distributor

REMOVAL

2.0L Engine

1. Before servicing the vehicle, refer to the precautions in the beginning of this section.
2. Remove or disconnect the following:
   • Negative battery cable.
   • Distributor cap. Before removing the distributor, mark the position of the distributor cap No. 1 spark plug wire tower on the distributor.
   • Distributor electrical harness
3. Rotate the crankshaft to No. 1 piston Top Dead Center (TDC) compression stroke.
4. Matchmark the distributor housing and cylinder head.
5. Remove or disconnect the following:
   • Distributor
   • O-ring

2.5L Engine

1. Before servicing the vehicle, refer to the precautions in the beginning of this section.
2. Remove or disconnect the following:
   • Negative battery cable.
   • Air cleaner intake tube nuts.
   • Air cleaner intake tube.
   • Air duct.
   • Vane Air Flow (VAF) meter electrical connector.
   • Evaporative emission canister vacuum hose.
   • Fuel pressure regulator control solenoid.
   • Air cleaner assembly.
   • Spark plug wires from the distributor cap.
   • 2 electrical connectors from the top of the distributor
   • Matchmark the distributor and the head. Remove the distributor.

INSTALLATION

2.0L Engine

TIMING NOT DISTURBED

1. Lubricate the distributor O-ring.
2. Align the marks.
3. Install or connect the following:
   • Distributor

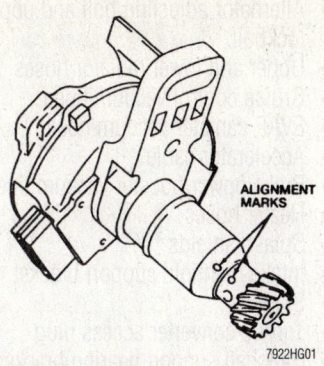

Distributor assembly alignment mark locations—2.0L engine

- Hold-down bolt
- Wiring
- Cap
- Negative battery cable

TIMING DISTURBED

Perform the following:
- Lubricate the distributor O-ring.
- Rotate the crankshaft to Top Dead Center (TDC) on the compression stroke.
- Position the rotor to align with No. 1 plug wire tower.
- Install the distributor. Align the marks.
- Tighten the hold-down bolts.
- Connect the wiring.
- Install the cap.
- Connect the negative battery cable.

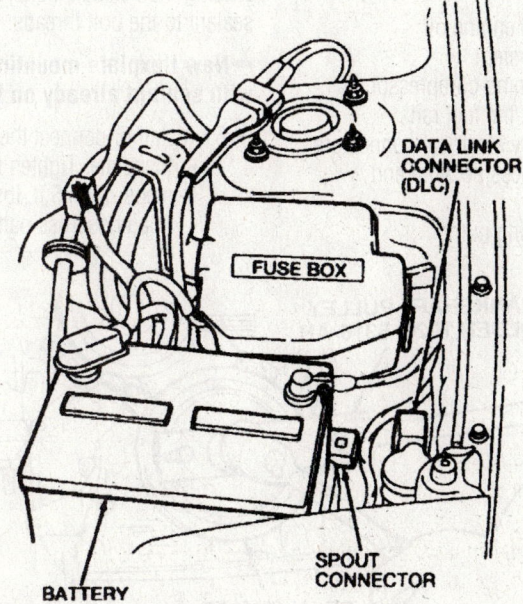

Location of the SPOUT connector—2.0L engine

2.5L Engine

➥The tangs on the distributor shaft are different sizes, allowing the distributor to be installed in only one position.

Install or connect the following:
- Distributor
- Hold-down bolts
- Wiring
- Cap
- Air cleaner assembly
- Fuel pressure regulator solenoid
- Evaporative canister vacuum hose
- Vane Air Flow (VAF) meter electrical connector
- Air duct
- Air cleaner intake tube
- Negative battery cable

Ignition Timing

ADJUSTMENT

2.0L Engine

1. Before servicing the vehicle, refer to the precautions in the beginning of this section.
2. Perform the following:
   - Apply the parking brake.
   - Be sure all accessories are OFF.
   - Remove the shorting bar from the SPOUT connector.
   - Set idle at 650–750 rpm.

- Timing should be 10 degrees Before Top Dead Center (BTDC).
- Adjust if necessary. Hold-down bolt: 14–19 ft. lbs. (19–25 Nm). Recheck the timing after the bolt has been tightened.
- Install the shorting bar.

2.5L Engine

1. Before servicing the vehicle, refer to the precautions in the beginning of this section.
2. Perform the following:
   - Locate the timing marks on the crankshaft pulley and timing belt cover.
   - Start the engine and allow it to come to normal operating temperature.
   - Be sure all accessories are **OFF**.
   - Connect a tachometer and timing light.
   - Connect terminals **STI (TEN)** and **GND** on the Data Link Connector (DLC) with a jumper wire.

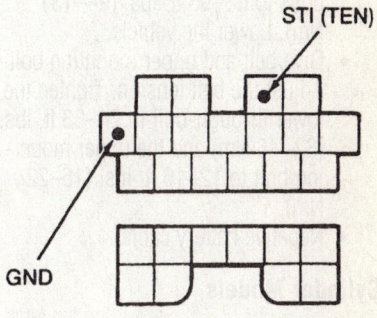

Data Link Connector terminal locations—2.5L engine

- Set the idle speed to 600–700 rpm.
- Timing should be 10 degrees Before Top Dead Center (BTDC).

➥Do not pinch the ignition coil-to-distributor high tension wiring when turning the distributor.

- Adjust, if necessary. Hold-down bolts: 14–19 ft. lbs. (19–25 Nm) and recheck the timing.

Alternator

REMOVAL & INSTALLATION

4-Cylinder Models

1. Remove or disconnect the following:
   - Negative battery cable

- Alternator upper mounting bolt
- Drive belt from the alternator pulley
- The 6 bolts and remove the transverse member
- Electrical connectors from the alternator
- Front exhaust pipe
- Alternator lower through-bolt
- Alternator

To install:

2. Install or connect the following:
- Alternator with the through-bolt
- Exhaust pipe, using new gaskets. Tighten the pipe-to-converter nuts to 28–38 ft. lbs. (38–51 Nm) and the exhaust manifold flange nuts to 28–38 ft. lbs. (38–51 Nm). Tighten the exhaust clamp nuts to 14–18 ft. lbs. (19–25 Nm).
- Oxygen sensor, and tighten to 36 ft. lbs. (49 Nm). Connect the oxygen sensor electrical connector.
- Alternator electrical connectors
- Transverse member and tighten the bolts to 68–96 ft. lbs. (94–131 Nm). Lower the vehicle.
- Dive belt and upper mounting bolt. Adjust the belt tension. Tighten the lower through-bolt to 24–33 ft. lbs. (32–46 Nm) and the upper mounting bolt to 12–16 ft. lbs. (16–22 Nm).
- Negative battery cable

6-Cylinder Models

1. Remove or disconnect the following:
- Negative battery cable
- Fresh air duct and radiator upper bracket
- Condenser fan
- Electrical connectors from the alternator

2. Loosen the belt tensioner locknut and tension adjusting bolt. Remove the alternator upper mounting bolt.
- Right splash shield
- Drive belt from the alternator pulley
- Air conditioning compressor mounting bolts and support the compressor aside, leaving the refrigerant lines connected
- Alternator through-bolt
- Alternator

To install:

3. Install or connect the following:
- Alternator and install the through-bolt. Tighten the alternator through-bolt to 24–33 ft. lbs. (32–46 Nm) on the 1.8L, and to 38

ft. lbs. (51 Nm) on the 2.5L engine.
- Air conditioning compressor mounting bolts to 26 ft. lbs. (35 Nm).
- Right splash shield, and lower the vehicle.
- Drive belt and adjust the tension
- Alternator upper mounting bolt and tighten to 18 ft. lbs. (25 Nm)

4. Tighten the belt tensioner locknut and tension adjusting bolt.
- Electrical connectors at the alternator
- Condenser fan
- Radiator upper bracket and fresh air duct
- Negative battery cable

Engine Assembly

REMOVAL & INSTALLATION

2.0L Engine

WITH AUTOMATIC TRANSAXLE

➡**The engine is lifted from the engine compartment, leaving the transaxle in the vehicle.**

1. Before servicing the vehicle, refer to the precautions in the beginning of this section.
2. Relieve the fuel system pressure using the recommended procedure.
3. Remove or disconnect the following:
- Battery and battery tray
- Hood
- Coolant and engine oil
- Air intake system
- Air conditioning compressor
- Fuel lines at the fuel rail
- All necessary electrical connectors
- Sensor harness tie wrap and retainer clip
- Power steering pump

- Alternator adjusting bolt and upper lockbolt
- Upper and lower radiator hoses
- Cruise control vacuum hose
- EVAP canister vacuum hose
- Accelerator cable
- Brake power booster vacuum line
- Heater hoses
- Splash shields
- Intake manifold support bracket.
- Starter
- Torque converter access plug
- Halfshaft support bearing bracket bolts.
- 4 torque converter-to-flexplate nuts
- 3 engine-to-transaxle bolts
- 2 transaxle-to-engine mounting bolts
- Exhaust inlet pipe-to-catalytic converter nuts.
- Exhaust pipe bracket bolts
- Exhaust pipe
- Crankshaft pulley

4. Attach a shop crane. Raise the engine slightly.
- Right-hand engine support insulator
- Remaining transaxle-to-engine mounting bolts
- Engine from the vehicle
- Flexplate from the crankshaft

To install:

5. Remove the engine from the workstand. Remove the old sealant from the flexplate mounting bolts and bolt holes. If reusing the flexplate bolts, apply silicone sealant to the bolt threads.

➡**New flexplate mounting bolts come with sealant already on them.**

6. Install or connect the following:
- Flexplate. Tighten the bolts in 2–3 steps: 70–75 ft. lbs. (96–103 Nm) in a crisscross pattern.

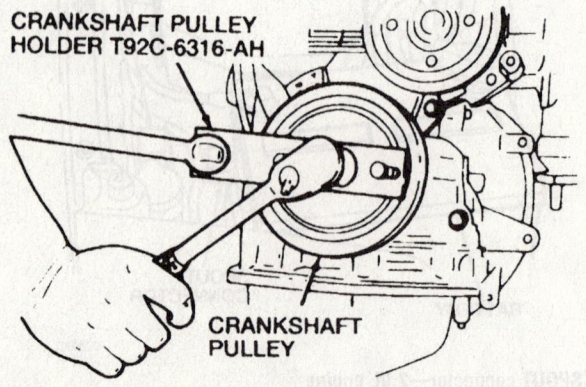

CRANKSHAFT PULLEY HOLDER T92C-6316-AH

CRANKSHAFT PULLEY

7922HG03

Hold the crankshaft while removing the pulley bolt—2.0L engine

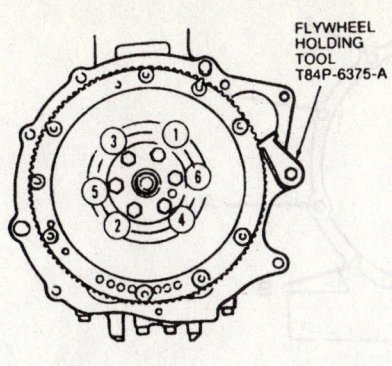

Flexplate bolt torque sequence—2.0L engine

- Engine into the vehicle and align it to the transaxle. Be sure that the torque converter studs are aligned with the holes in the flexplate.
- 4 transaxle-to-engine bolts and tighten mounting bolts marked **A** to 50–73 ft. lbs. (68–99 Nm) for vehicles equipped with the 4EAT transaxle, and 66–86 ft. lbs. (90–116 Nm) for vehicles equipped with the CD4E transaxle.

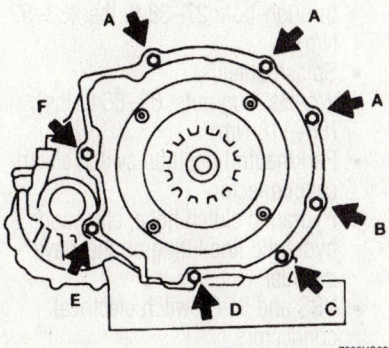

Transaxle and engine mounting bolt identification, 4EAT transaxle—2.0L engine

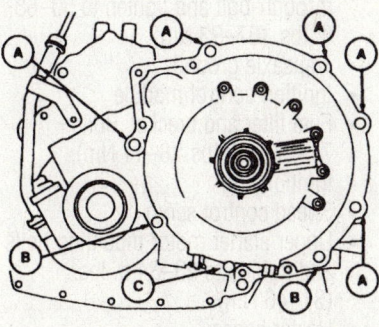

Transaxle and engine mounting bolt identification, CD4E transaxle—2.0L engine

- Right-hand engine support insulator. Through-bolt: 63–86 ft. lbs. (86–116 Nm); Nuts: 54–75 ft. lbs. (74–103 Nm).
- Torque converter-to-flexplate nuts, and tighten to 32–45 ft. lbs. (44–60 Nm).
- Remaining transaxle-to-engine mounting bolts. Bolts marked **B**: 50–73 ft. lbs. (68–99 Nm) for vehicles equipped with the 4EAT transaxle and 28–38 ft. lbs. (38–51 Nm) for vehicles equipped with the CD4E transaxle. Mounting bolt **C**: 28–38 ft. lbs. (38–51 Nm) for vehicles equipped with the 4EAT transaxle and 14–18 ft. lbs. (19–25 Nm) for vehicles equipped with the CD4E transaxle. With the 4EAT transaxle, mounting bolt **D**: 14–18 ft. lbs. (19–25 Nm), **E**: 28–38 ft. lbs. (38–51 Nm) and **F**: 50–73 ft. lbs. (68–99 Nm).
- Alternator
- Through-bolt
- Alternator wiring
- Harness bracket to the back of the alternator
- Starter. Bolts: 23–34 ft. lbs. (31–46 Nm)
- Intake manifold support bracket. Bolts: 27–38 ft. lbs. (37–52 Nm).

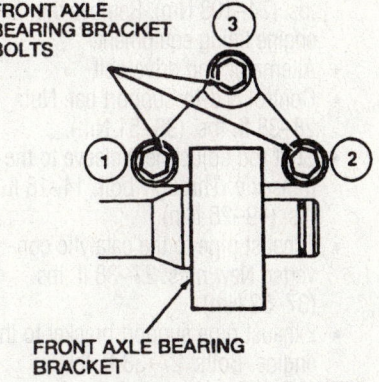

Halfshaft bearing bracket bolt torque sequence—2.0L engine with an automatic transaxle

- Halfshaft bearing bracket bolts and tighten, in sequence, to 32–45 ft. lbs. (43–61 Nm).
- All remaining wiring
- Air conditioning compressor. Bolts to 26 ft. lbs. (35 Nm).
- Crankshaft pulley. Bolt: 116–123 ft. lbs. (157–167 Nm).

- Exhaust pipe. New nuts: 27–38 ft. lbs. (37–52 Nm).
- Exhaust inlet pipe-to-exhaust manifold nuts and tighten to 27–38 ft. lbs. (37–52 Nm). @RL-BS0:•
- Alternator belt. Upper mounting bolt: 14–18 ft. lbs. (19–25 Nm); through-bolt: 27–38 ft. lbs. (37–52 Nm).
- Splash shields.
- Power steering pump support and through-bolt and lockbolt
- Power steering pump drive belt. Through-bolt: 27–38 ft. lbs. (37–52 Nm); Lockbolt: 14–18 ft. lbs. (19–25 Nm).
- Power steering pump belt shield. Bolts: 71–88 inch lbs. (8–10 Nm).
- Power steering hose brackets. Bolts: 71–88 inch lbs. (8–10 Nm).
- Heater hoses
- Cruise control vacuum line
- EVAP canister vacuum hose
- Power brake booster vacuum line to the back left-hand side of the intake manifold.
- Fuel lines to the fuel rail
- Sensor harness retainer clip
- Tie wrap to the water bypass hose.
- Accelerator cable
- Upper and lower radiator hoses
- Air intake system.
- Hood.
- Battery tray and battery
- Engine oil and coolant

WITH MANUAL TRANSAXLE

➡ **The engine and transaxle are lifted from the engine compartment as an assembly.**

1. Before servicing the vehicle, refer to the precautions in the beginning of this section.
2. Relieve the fuel system pressure.
3. Remove or disconnect the following:
   - Battery and battery tray
   - Hood
   - Coolant and engine oil
   - Air intake system
   - Upper and lower radiator hoses
   - Radiator
   - Air conditioning compressor
   - Fuel lines
   - All electrical connectors from the engine
   - Power steering pump
   - Alternator upper lockbolt
   - Cruise control vacuum hose
   - EVAP canister vacuum hose

Timing belt service is covered in Section 4 of this manual

- Accelerator cable
- Power booster vacuum hose
- Heater hoses
- Upper starter motor mounting bolts
- Speed control electrical connector
- Speed control servo aside
- Ignition coil
- Fuel filter bracket
- Ignition control module
- Ground wire bracket from the transaxle and rear transaxle support insulator
- Rear transaxle support insulator through-bolt
- Transaxle ground
- All electrical connectors from the transaxle
- Lower clutch slave cylinder tube fitting and spring clips
- Hydraulic clutch hose from the slave cylinder tube
- Park/neutral position switch
- Splash shields
- Front wheels
- Crossmember
- Lower transaxle support insulator
- Rear engine support
- Halfshafts

➡**Install transaxle plug tools into the differential side gears. If the plugs are not installed, the differential side gears may become misaligned. If the gears are misaligned, the differential may have to be removed to reposition them.**

- Intake manifold support
- Rear transaxle support bracket
- Starter
- Exhaust pipe
- Control rod-to-support bar
- Transaxle linkage
- Alternator
- Crankshaft pulley

4. Attach an engine sling to the engine lifting eyes and a suitable hoist to the sling. Raise the engine slightly.

5. Remove or disconnect the following:
- Right-hand engine support insulator
- Left-hand engine support insulator
- Engine/transaxle assembly from the vehicle
- Transaxle-to-engine bolts and the engine-to-transaxle bolts
- Transaxle from the engine
- Clutch assembly, flywheel and crankshaft rear cover plate

To install:

6. Install or connect the following:
- Crankshaft rear cover plate and tighten the bolt to 71–88 inch lbs. (8–10 Nm)
- Flywheel and clutch assembly

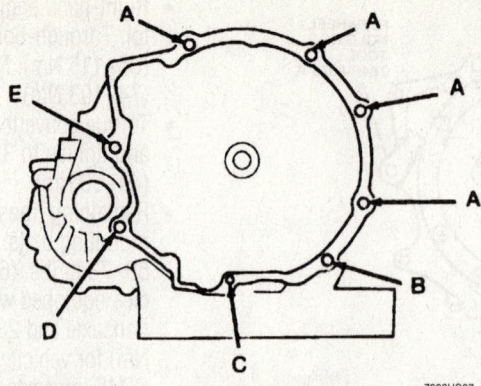

Transaxle and engine mounting bolt identification, MTX transaxle—2.0L engine

7. Tighten the bolts as follows:
   a. Bolts **A**: 66–86 ft. lbs. (90–116 Nm).
   b. Bolts **B**: 28–38 ft. lbs. (38–51 Nm).
   c. Bolts **C**: 14–18 ft. lbs. (19–25 Nm).
   d. Bolts **D**: 28–38 ft. lbs. (38–51 Nm).
   e. Bolts **E** to 66–86 ft. lbs. (90–116 Nm).

8. Install or connect the following:
- Engine/transaxle assembly into the engine compartment
- Left-hand transaxle support insulator. Nuts and bolt: 50–68 ft. lbs. (67–93 Nm). Through-bolt: 63–86 ft. lbs. (86–116 Nm).
- Right-hand engine support insulator. Through-bolt: 63–86 ft. lbs. (86–116 Nm); insulator nuts: 54–75 ft. lbs. (74–103 Nm). Remove the engine lifting equipment.
- Alternator and drive belt
- Control rod-to-support bar. Nut: 28–38 ft. lbs. (38–51 Nm).
- Shift rod adjustment sleeve to the transaxle. Through-bolt: 14–18 ft. lbs. (19–25 Nm).
- Exhaust pipe to the catalytic converter. New nuts: 27–38 ft. lbs. (37–52 Nm).
- Exhaust pipe support bracket to the engine. Bolts: 27–38 ft. lbs. (37–52 Nm).
- Exhaust pipe-to-exhaust manifold nuts and tighten to 27–38 ft. lbs. (37–52 Nm).
- HO2S and oil pressure sensor electrical connectors.
- Starter. Bolts: 23–34 ft. lbs. (31–46 Nm).
- Rear transaxle support insulator. Bolts: 50–68 ft. lbs. (67–93 Nm).
- Intake manifold support bracket. Bolts to 27–38 ft. lbs. (38–52 Nm).
- Halfshafts
- Lower transaxle support insulator. Bolts: 41–59 ft. lbs. (55–80 Nm).

- Rear engine support. Bolts and nuts **B**: 50–68 ft. lbs. (67–93 Nm); nuts **A**: 55–77 ft. lbs. (75–104 Nm); nuts **C**: 32–44 ft. lbs. (44–60 Nm).
- Crossmember. Bolts: 68–96 ft. lbs. (94–131 Nm).
- Crankshaft pulley. Bolt: 116–123 ft. lbs. (157–167 Nm).
- Air conditioning compressor. Bolts: 18–26 ft. lbs. (24–35 Nm).
- Alternator. Upper mounting bolt: 14–18 ft. lbs. (19–25 Nm); through-bolt: 27–38 ft. lbs. (38–52 Nm).
- Splash shields
- Wheels. Lug nuts: 65–86 ft. lbs. (88–118 Nm)
- Park/neutral position switch electrical connector
- Hydraulic clutch hose, clips and hydraulic line fitting on the slave cylinder
- VSS and BOO switch electrical connectors
- Ground wire bracket between the transaxle and the rear transaxle support insulator
- Rear transaxle support insulator through-bolt and tighten to 50–68 ft. lbs. (67–93 Nm)
- Transaxle ground
- Ignition control module
- Fuel filter and bracket. Bolts: 71–97 inch lbs. (8–11 Nm).
- Ignition coil
- Speed control servo
- Upper starter motor mounting bolts and tighten to 23–34 ft. lbs. (31–46 Nm)
- Heater hoses
- Power brake booster vacuum line
- Accelerator cable
- All remaining electrical connectors and hoses

- Power steering pump. Through-bolt: 32–45 ft. lbs. (43–61 Nm); lockbolt to 23–34 ft. lbs. (31–46 Nm).
- Power steering pump drive belt pulley shield. Bolts: 61–86 inch lbs. (7–9 Nm)
- Power steering hose brackets to the cylinder head cover. Bolts: 71–88 inch lbs. (8–10 Nm).
- Fuel lines.
- Radiator
- Upper and lower radiator hoses
- Air intake system
- Battery tray and battery
- Hood
- Coolant and engine oil
- Bleed the clutch hydraulic system.

2.5L Engine

WITH AUTOMATIC TRANSAXLE

➡ **The engine and transaxle are lifted from the engine compartment as an assembly.**

1. Before servicing the vehicle, refer to the precautions in the beginning of this section.
2. Relieve the fuel system pressure using the recommended procedure.
3. Remove or disconnect the following:
   - Battery and battery tray
   - Hood
   - Coolant and engine oil
   - Air intake system
   - Accessory drive belts
   - Front wheels
   - Splash shields
   - Crossmember
   - All necessary electrical connectors
   - Exhaust inlet pipe-to-exhaust manifold nuts
   - Halfshafts
   - Power steering pump
   - Air conditioning compressor
   - Upper and lower radiator hoses and overflow hose
   - Transaxle cooler lines
   - Radiator and cooling fan assembly
   - All remaining vacuum hoses
   - Heater hoses from the thermostat housing
   - Wiring harness grounds
   - Speed control servo
   - Fuel supply and return lines and discard the copper crush washer
   - Fuel line retaining bolts from the fuel line bracket
   - Accelerator cable from the throttle body

- Fuel filter bracket and position the filter aside
- Spring clip from the shift cable bracket and pull the cable from the switch
- Cooling fan relay bracket
- Front and rear transaxle support insulator through-bolts

4. Attach suitable lifting equipment to the engine lifting eyes and remove any slack using an engine hoist attached to the lifting cables.
5. Remove or disconnect the following:
   - Left-hand transaxle support insulator through-bolt
   - Right-hand transaxle support insulator through-bolt and 2 nuts
   - Right-hand engine support insulator
   - Engine/transaxle assembly from the vehicle
   - Transaxle from the engine
   - Flexplate

To install:

6. Install or connect the following:
   - Flexplate. Bolts, in 2–3 steps, in sequence: 45–49 ft. lbs. (61–67 Nm)

- Engine to the transaxle. Bolts: 50–73 ft. lbs. (68–99 Nm)
- Engine/transaxle assembly into the engine compartment
- Right-hand engine support insulator. Through-bolt to 50–68 ft. lbs. (67–93 Nm); nuts: 54–76 ft. lbs. (74–103 Nm)
- Left-hand transaxle support insulator through-bolt and tighten to 63–86 ft. lbs. (86–116 Nm)
- Front and rear transaxle support insulator through-bolts and tighten to 63–86 ft. lbs. (86–116 Nm)
- Cooling fan relay bracket. Bolts: 88 inch lbs. (10 Nm)
- Shift cable and spring clip
- Fuel filter. Nuts: 71–88 inch lbs. (8–10 Nm)
- All vacuum lines
- Accelerator cable
- Fuel line bracket. Bolts: 71–88 inch lbs. (8–10 Nm)
- Fuel supply and return lines, using new copper crush washers. Bolt to 18–25 ft. lbs. (25–34 Nm)
- Speed control servo
- Wiring harness grounds

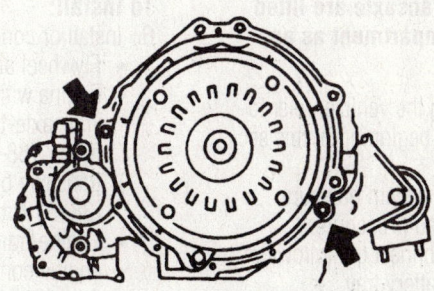

Engine-To-Transaxle Bolts

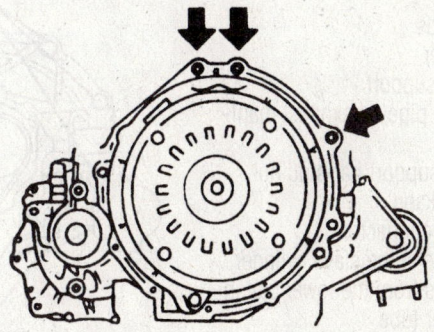

Transaxle-To-Engine Bolts

7922HG08

Engine and automatic transaxle retaining bolt locations—2.5L engine

- Heater hoses
- All electrical connectors
- Radiator and cooling fan assembly. Nuts: 71–88 inch lbs. (8–10 Nm)
- Oil cooler lines
- Upper and lower radiator hoses
- Air conditioning compressor. Bolts: 28–38 ft. lbs. (38–51 Nm)
- Power steering pump. Rear bracket bolt: to 24–34 ft. lbs. (32–46 Nm)
- Power steering hose bracket bolt and tighten to 24–34 ft. lbs. (31–46 Nm)
- 3 power steering pump bolts through the pulley and tighten to 23–34 ft. lbs. (31–46 Nm)
- Power steering pump drive belt
- Halfshafts
- Exhaust inlet pipe. Nuts: 30–41 ft. lbs. (40–55 Nm)
- Crossmember. Bolts: 69–93 ft. lbs. (94–126 Nm)
- Splash shields
- Wheels. Lug nuts: 65–87 ft. lbs. (88–118 Nm)
- Alternator drive belt
- Air intake system
- Hood
- Battery tray and battery
- Oil and coolant

WITH MANUAL TRANSAXLE

➡ The engine and transaxle are lifted from the engine compartment as an assembly.

1. Before servicing the vehicle, refer to the precautions in the beginning of this section.

2. Relieve the fuel system pressure using the recommended procedure.

3. Remove or disconnect the following:
- Battery and battery tray
- Hood
- Coolant and engine oil
- Air intake system
- Front wheels
- Splash shields
- Crossmember
- Rear engine support
- Exhaust inlet pipe-to-exhaust manifold nuts
- Control rod support bar stud nut
- Transaxle linkage
- All electrical connectors
- Hydraulic line at the slave cylinder
- 2 spring clips from the lower clutch slave cylinder tube
- Halfshafts
- Rear transaxle support bracket
- Power steering pump
- Air conditioning compressor

- Power steering hose bracket
- Alternator drive belt
- Upper and lower radiator hoses and overflow hose
- Radiator and the cooling fan as an assembly
- All vacuum hoses
- Ground-to-engine bracket bolt
- Speed control servo
- Transaxle ground and back-up lamp switch electrical connector
- Starter-to-chassis ground
- Heater hoses
- Fuel supply and return lines
- Fuel filter

4. Attach suitable engine lifting equipment to the engine lifting eyes and take up any slack.

5. Remove or disconnect the following:
- 2 left-hand transaxle support insulator nuts and through-bolt
- 3 right-hand engine support insulator nuts and the through-bolt
- Right-hand engine support insulator
- Engine/transaxle assembly from the vehicle
- Transaxle-to-engine bolts and the engine-to-transaxle bolts. Separate the transaxle from the engine
- Clutch assembly, flywheel and crankshaft rear cover plate

To install:

6. Install or connect the following:
- Flywheel and clutch assembly
- Engine with the transaxle. Transaxle-to-engine bolts: 50–73 ft. lbs. (68–99 Nm); engine-to-transaxle bolts: 28–38 ft. lbs. (38–51 Nm).
- Engine/transaxle assembly into the engine compartment
- Rear transaxle support insulator.

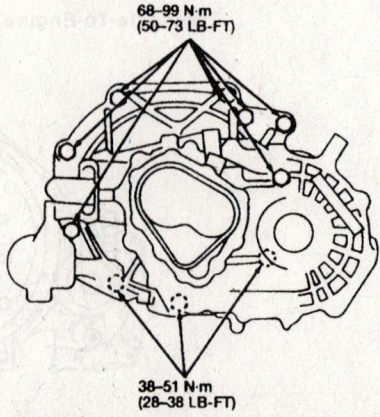

68–99 N·m (50–73 LB-FT)

38–51 N·m (28–38 LB-FT)

7922HG09

Engine and manual transaxle mounting bolt locations—2.5L engine

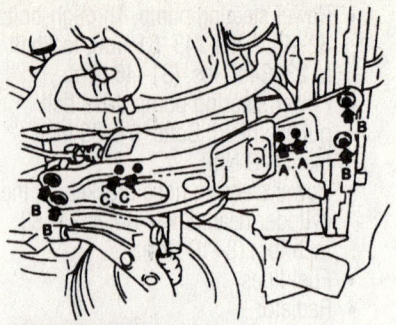

TIGHTENING TORQUE
A: 75 – 104 N·m (55 – 77 LB-FT)
B: 67 – 93 N·m (50 – 68 LB-FT)
C: 44 – 60 N·m (32 – 44 LB-FT)

7922HG10

Rear engine support mounting nut and bolt locations—2.5L engine

Nuts: 50–68 ft. lbs. (67–93 Nm); through-bolt: 63–86 ft. lbs. (86–116 Nm)
- Left-hand transaxle support insulator. Nuts: 55–77 ft. lbs. (75–104 Nm); through-bolt: 63–86 ft. lbs. (86–116 Nm)
- Right-hand transaxle support insulator. Nuts: 54–77 ft. lbs. (74–104 Nm); through-bolt: 50–68 ft. lbs. (67–93 Nm)
- Power steering pump. Bolts: 23–34 ft. lbs. (31–46 Nm)
- Tighten the power steering pump rear bracket bolt to 24–34 ft. lbs. (32–46 Nm)
- Power steering pump drive belt and adjust the tension
- Air conditioning compressor. Bolts: 28–38 ft. lbs. (38–51 Nm). Install the alternator and air conditioning drive belt
- Control rod-to-support bar. Nut: 23–33 ft. lbs. (32–46 Nm)
- Shift rod adjustment sleeve to the transaxle. Through-bolt: 12–16 ft. lbs. (16–22 Nm)
- Halfshafts
- Rear engine support. Bolts and nuts B: 50–68 ft. lbs. (67–93 Nm); nuts A: 55–77 ft. lbs. (75–104 Nm); nuts C: to 32–44 ft. lbs. (44–60 Nm)
- Exhaust inlet pipe to the exhaust manifolds. Nuts: 30–41 ft. lbs. (40–55 Nm).
- Crossmember and tighten the 6 bolts to 69–93 ft. lbs. (94–126 Nm)
- Splash shields
- Wheels. Lug nuts: 65–86 ft. lbs. (88–118 Nm)
- Power steering hose bracket bolt to the pump

- All electrical connectors
- All vacuum hoses
- Harness grounds
- Heater hoses
- Fuel supply and return lines. Fuel line bracket bolts: 71–88 inch lbs. (8–10 Nm); fuel supply line bolt: 18–25 ft. lbs. (25–34 Nm). Be sure to use new copper crush washers
- Fuel filter
- Speed control servo
- Hydraulic line to the slave cylinder and install the line bracket spring clips
- Radiator and cooling fan assembly. Bolts: 71–88 inch lbs. (8–10 Nm).
- Upper and lower radiator hoses
- Air intake system
- Hood
- Battery tray and the battery
- Coolant and engine oil
- Fill the transaxle with the proper type and quantity of oil, if needed.

Water Pump

REMOVAL & INSTALLATION

2.0L Engine

1. Before servicing the vehicle, refer to the precautions in the beginning of this section.
2. Remove or disconnect the following:
   - Battery cables
   - Coolant
   - Accessory drive belts
   - PSP switch electrical connector
   - Power steering pump drive belt idler pulley shield
   - Power steering pump through-bolt and lockbolt

- Cylinder head cover
- Water pump pulley
- Splash shields
- Timing belt
- Power steering pump lower bracket from the water pump
- 5 water pump mounting bolts and water pump

To install:

3. Clean all gasket mating surfaces.
4. Install or connect the following:
   - New gasket and the water pump. Bolts: 14–19 ft. lbs. (19–25 Nm).
   - Power steering pump lower bracket
   - Water pump pulley. Bolts: 71–88 inch lbs. (8–10 Nm)
   - Timing belt
   - Splash shields. Bolts: 71–88 inch lbs. (8–10 Nm)
   - Cylinder head cover. Bolts in 2–3 steps: 52–69 inch lbs. (6–7 Nm) in the proper sequence
   - Power steering pump. Through-bolt: 32–45 ft. lbs. (43–61 Nm); lockbolt: 23–34 ft. lbs. (31–46 Nm)
   - PSP switch electrical connector
   - Accessory drive belts and adjust the tension
   - Idler pulley shield. Bolts: 61–86 inch lbs. (7–9 Nm)
   - Battery cables
   - Fill and bleed the cooling system.

2.5L Engine

1. Before servicing the vehicle, refer to the precautions in the beginning of this section.
2. Remove or disconnect the following:
   - Negative battery cable
   - Coolant
   - Timing belt covers and the timing belt

- Water pump pulley
- Front engine support insulator mounting bracket bolts
- Water pump (5 bolts)

To install:

3. Clean the mating surfaces of the water pump and the engine block.
4. Install or connect the following:
   - New O-ring onto the water pump
   - Water pump. Bolts: 14–18 ft. lbs. (19–25 Nm)
   - Engine support mounting bracket bolts
   - Water pump pulley. Bolts: 71–88 inch lbs. (8–10 Nm)
   - Timing belt and timing belt covers
   - Negative battery cable
   - Coolant

Cylinder Head

REMOVAL & INSTALLATION

➡ **Refer to Section 1 of this manual for the cylinder head torque sequence illustration. The illustration is located after the Torque Specification Chart.**

2.0L Engine

1. Before servicing the vehicle, refer to the precautions in the beginning of this section.
2. Relieve the fuel system pressure using the recommended procedure.
3. Remove or disconnect the following:
   - Negative battery cable
   - Coolant
   - Air intake system
   - Power steering hose bracket bolts
   - PSP switch
   - Power steering pump idler pulley shield
   - Accessory drive belts
   - Power steering pump
   - Exhaust manifold
   - Spark plug wires
   - Hoses from the cylinder head cover
   - Cylinder head cover
   - Timing belt covers and timing belt
   - Intake manifold support
   - All necessary wiring
   - Coolant temperature sensor housing
   - Fuel supply and return lines
   - All vacuum hoses
   - Accelerator cable
   - Distributor
   - Camshafts
   - Cylinder head bolts in 3 steps in the proper sequence

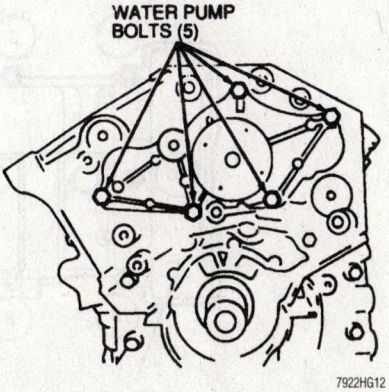

Water pump mounting bolt locations—2.0L engine

Water pump mounting bolt locations—2.5L engine

Refer to Section 1 for engine rebuilding specifications

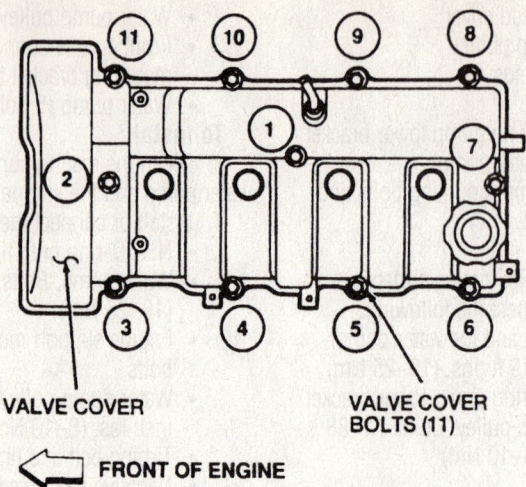

Cylinder head cover mounting bolt loosening sequence—2.0L engine

- Cylinder head and gasket

4. Clean all gasket mating surfaces. Inspect the cylinder head for damage, cracks, and fluid leakage. Check the head gasket surface for distortion (warpage) using a straight-edge and feeler gauge. Maximum allowable distortion is 0.004 in. (0.10mm).

To install:

5. Install the new gasket and the cylinder head.

➡**Measure the cylinder head bolts to determine if they are reusable or if they are stretched beyond use. If the cylinder head bolt is longer than 4 inches (105.5mm), it is stretched and must be replaced. Measurements are taken from under the shoulder to the end of the threads.**

6. Tighten the cylinder head bolts in the proper sequence as follows:

   a. Tighten each bolt to 10 ft. lbs. (13 Nm).

   b. Tighten each bolt again to 16 ft. lbs. (22 Nm).

   c. Paint a mark on the edge of each cylinder head bolt to use as a reference.

   d. Using the same torque sequence, tighten each bolt 85–95 degrees.

   e. Use the same sequence and tighten each bolt an additional 85–95 degrees.

7. Install or connect the following:

   - Camshafts

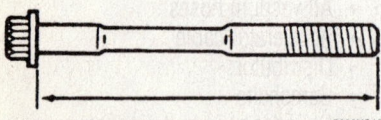

Measuring the cylinder head bolt length to check for excessive stretching—2.0L engine

➡**Be sure that none of the camshaft lobes are located directly on the hydraulic valve lifters when tightening the camshaft cap bolts.**

- Distributor
- All vacuum hoses
- Accelerator cable
- All wiring connectors
- Fuel supply and return lines
- Timing belt and covers
- Intake manifold support. Bolts: 28–38 ft. lbs. (38–51 Nm).
- Apply sealant to the cylinder head surface in the area adjacent to the front camshaft caps, then install the cover and new gasket. Bolts in 2 steps, in sequence: 52–69 inch lbs. (6–7 Nm)
- Hoses on the cylinder head cover
- Spark plug wires
- Exhaust manifold

- Alternator belt
- Power steering pump drive belt. Through-bolt: 32–45 ft. lbs. (43–61 Nm); lockbolt: 23–34 ft. lbs. (31–46 Nm).
- Power steering pump idler pulley and retaining bolts. Bolts: 61–86 inch lbs. (7–9 Nm).
- Power steering hose brackets to the cylinder head cover. Bolts: 71–88 inch lbs. (8–10 Nm).
- Coolant temperature sensor housing with a new gasket. Bolts: 14–18 ft. lbs. (19–25 Nm).
- Air intake system
- Negative battery cable
- Coolant

2.5L Engine

➡**New cylinder head bolts must be used.**

1. Before servicing the vehicle, refer to the precautions in the beginning of this section.

2. Relieve the fuel system pressure using the recommended procedure.

3. Remove or disconnect the following:

- Negative battery cable
- Coolant
- Timing belt covers belt
- Intake manifold
- Ventilation pipe
- Cylinder head covers
- Camshafts
- Timing belt tensioner and the lower idler
- Alternator-to-alternator adjusting arm bolts
- Seal plate from the front of the engine
- Coolant elbow
- Heated Oxygen (HO2S) sensor electrical connectors

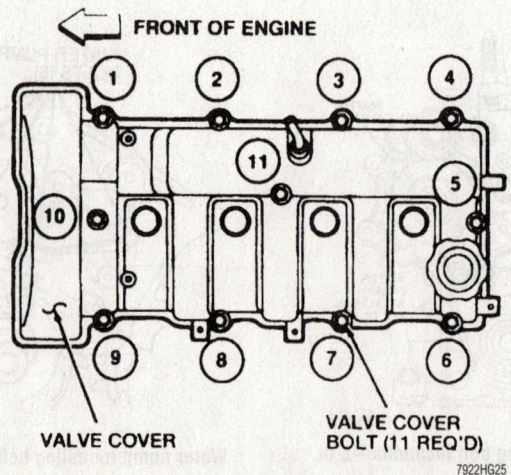

Cylinder head cover mounting bolt tightening sequence—2.0L engine

- Exhaust pipe-to-exhaust manifold nuts and lower the exhaust pipes
- If removing the rear cylinder head, the Exhaust Gas Recirculation (EGR) tube and bracket
- Lifters

➡ **If the lifters are to be reused, store them upside down in an oil filled container**

- Cylinder head bolts, in 2–3 steps in the reverse order of the tightening sequence
- Cylinder heads

4. Clean all gasket mating surfaces. Inspect the cylinder head(s) for damage, cracks, and water and oil leakage.

5. Check the cylinder head gasket surface for distortion using a straight-edge and feeler gauge. Maximum allowable distortion is 0.004 in. (0.10mm).

To install:

➡ **Refer to Section 1 of this manual for the cylinder head torque sequence illustration. The illustration is located after the Torque Specification Chart.**

6. Install or connect the following:
- New head gaskets on the cylinder block

➡ **The gaskets cannot be interchanged and are marked R and L for the right and left banks**

- Cylinder heads

➡ **Measure the cylinder head bolts from the shoulder to the end of the threads. If the length of the bolt measures more than 5.217 in. (132.5mm), it has stretched beyond its service limit and must be replaced.**

- Cylinder head bolts (oiled) and washers

7. Tighten the cylinder head bolts using the following procedure:

a. Tighten the cylinder head bolts in sequence to 10 ft. lbs. (13 Nm).

b. Tighten the bolts again in sequence to 19 ft. lbs. (26 Nm).

c. Paint a mark on the edge of the socket or each cylinder head bolt to use as a reference.

d. Turn each bolt, in sequence, 85–95 degrees.

e. Turn each bolt, in sequence, an additional 85–95 degrees.

8. Install or connect the following:
- Lifters

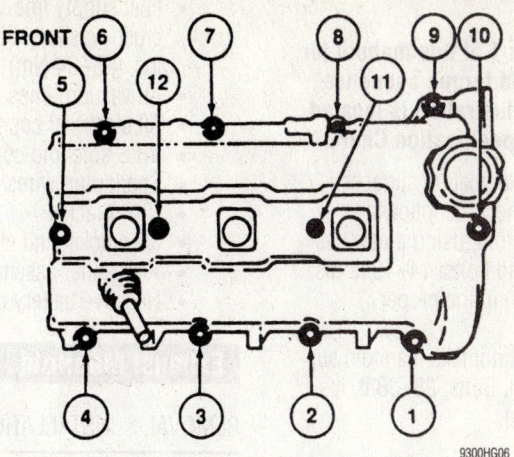

Front cylinder head cover torque sequence—2.5L engine

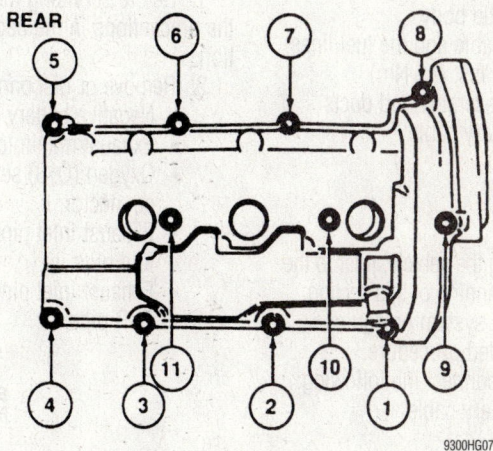

Rear cylinder head cover torque sequence—2.5L engine

- Seal plate. Bolts: 71–88 inch lbs. (8–10 Nm)
- Coolant elbow. Bolts: 14–18 ft. lbs. (19–25 Nm)
- Alternator-to-adjusting arm bolts. Bolts: 14–18 ft. lbs. (19–25 Nm)
- Lower timing belt idler. Bolt: 28–38 ft. lbs. (38–51 Nm)
- Timing belt tensioner. Bolt: 27–33 ft. lbs. (37–44 Nm)
- Camshafts
- EGR tube and bracket
- Exhaust inlet pipes. Nuts: 41 ft. lbs. (55 Nm)
- Heated oxygen sensor electrical connectors
- Cylinder head covers. Bolts in 2 steps, in sequence: 43–78 inch lbs. (5–8 Nm)
- Intake manifold
- Timing belt and covers
- Negative battery cable
- Coolant

Intake Manifold

REMOVAL & INSTALLATION

2.0L Engine

1. Before servicing the vehicle, refer to the precautions in the beginning of this section.

2. Relieve the fuel system pressure using the recommended procedure.

3. Remove or disconnect the following:
- Negative battery cable
- Air ducts and air cleaner assembly
- Fuel supply and return lines
- Accelerator cable
- Coolant lines at the IAC BPA valve and the throttle body
- All necessary vacuum lines
- All necessary electrical connectors
- PCV valve
- Intake manifold support bracket
- EGR pipe
- Intake manifold and gasket

To install:

➡ **Refer to Section 1 of this manual for the intake manifold torque sequence illustration. The illustration is located after the Torque Specification Chart.**

4. Clean all gasket mating surfaces.
5. Install or connect the following:
- Intake manifold, using a new gasket. Nuts and bolts: 14–19 ft. lbs. (19–25 Nm) in the proper sequence.
- EGR pipe and intake manifold support bracket. Bolts: 28–38 ft. lbs. (38–51 Nm).
- PCV valve
- All electrical connectors
- All vacuum lines
- Coolant lines to the IAC BPA valve and the throttle body
- Accelerator cable and the fuel lines. Bolt: 97 inch lbs. (11 Nm)
- Air cleaner assembly and ducts
- Negative battery cable
- Coolant

2.5L Engine

1. Before servicing the vehicle, refer to the precautions in the beginning of this section.
2. Relieve the fuel system pressure using the recommended procedure.
3. Remove or disconnect the following:
- Negative battery cable
- Coolant
- Air cleaner assembly
- KS bracket and CKP sensor bracket
- Right bank spark plug wires
- Variable Resonance Induction System (VRIS) solenoid connector bracket
- All necessary vacuum hoses
- TPS and fuel rail electrical connectors
- Accelerator cable
- Fuel supply line at the fuel rails and discard the copper crush washers
- Fuel and vacuum lines from the fuel pressure regulator
- EGR breather tube
- Intake manifold mounting nuts and bolts in 2–3 steps, then the intake manifold

To install:

4. Clean all gasket mating surfaces.
5. Install or connect the following:
- New gaskets and the intake manifold. Nuts and bolts in 2–3 steps: 14–18 ft. lbs. (19–25 Nm).
- EGR breather tube
- Fuel and vacuum lines to the fuel pressure regulator

- Fuel supply line, using new copper crush washers. Fittings: 18–25 ft. lbs. (25–34 Nm)
- All vacuum lines
- All electrical connectors
- VRIS solenoid connector bracket
- Spark plug wires
- CKP bracket
- KS bracket and electrical connector
- Air cleaner assembly
- Negative battery cable

Exhaust Manifold

REMOVAL & INSTALLATION

2.0L Engine

1. Before servicing the vehicle, refer to the precautions in the beginning of this section.
2. Remove or disconnect the following:
- Negative battery cable
- Exhaust manifold heat shield
- Oxygen (O$_2$S) sensor electrical connector
- Exhaust inlet pipe-to-exhaust manifold nuts
- Exhaust inlet pipe bracket bolts
- EGR pipe

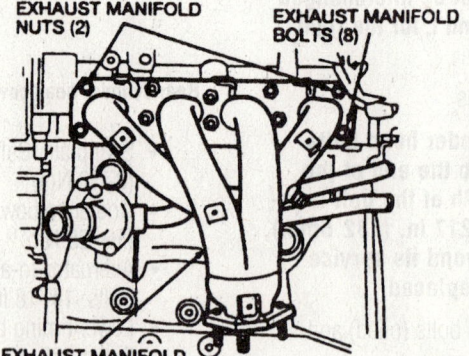

Exhaust manifold-to-cylinder head mounting bolt and nut locations—2.0L engine

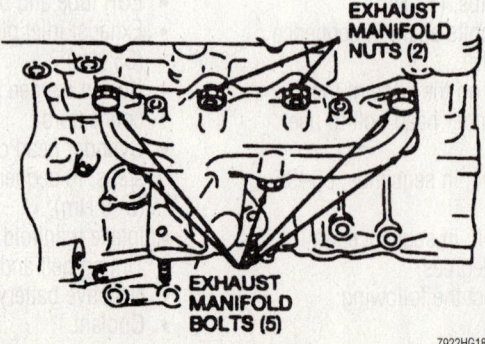

Right side exhaust manifold-to-cylinder head mounting bolt locations—2.5L engine

- Exhaust manifold

To install:

3. Clean all gasket mating surfaces.
4. Install or connect the following:
- New gasket and exhaust manifold. Bolts: 12–17 ft. lbs. (16–23 Nm).
- Exhaust pipe to the manifold. Nuts: 27–38 ft. lbs. (37–52 Nm)
- Oxygen sensor connector
- Exhaust inlet pipe bracket bolts
- EGR pipe. Nuts: 24–34 ft. lbs. (32–47 Nm)
- Exhaust manifold heat shield. Bolts: 71–88 inch lbs. (8–10 Nm)
- Negative battery cable

2.5L Engine

1. Before servicing the vehicle, refer to the precautions in the beginning of this section.
2. Remove or disconnect the following:
- Negative battery cable
- Oxygen (O$_2$S) sensor connectors
- Nuts from the front and rear exhaust pipes and lower the exhaust system.

➡ **Both pipes must be disconnected, even if only one manifold is to be removed.**

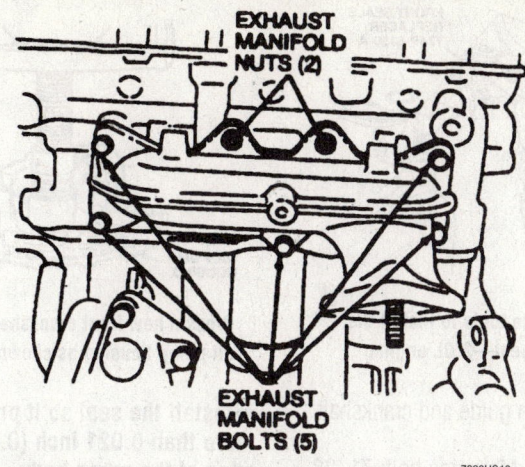

Left side exhaust manifold-to-cylinder head mounting bolt locations—2.5L engine

- EGR pipe (right side)
- Exhaust manifold shield
- Exhaust manifold(s)

To install:

3. Clean all gasket mating surfaces.
4. Install or connect the following:
   - Exhaust manifold, using a new gasket. Nuts and bolts: 14–18 ft. lbs. (19–25 Nm)
   - Exhaust manifold shield. Bolts: 71–88 inch lbs. (8–10 Nm)
   - EGR pipe
   - Exhaust pipes to the manifolds, using new gaskets. New nuts: 30–41 ft. lbs. (40–55 Nm)
   - O_2S sensor connectors
   - Negative battery cable

Starter

REMOVAL & INSTALLATION

2.0L ENGINE

1. Remove or disconnect the following:
   - Negative battery cable
   - Fresh air duct and resonance chamber
   - Electrical connectors and remove the air cleaner assembly
   - Intake manifold bracket
   - Wiring at the starter
   - Starter mounting bolts and remove the starter
2. Installation is the reverse of the removal procedure. Tighten the starter mounting bolts to 33 ft. lbs. (46 Nm) and the intake manifold bracket bolts to 38 ft. lbs. (51 Nm).

2.5L ENGINE

1. Remove or disconnect the following:
   - Negative battery cable
   - Fresh air duct
   - Electrical connector and remove the air cleaner assembly
2. If equipped with automatic transaxle, proceed as follows:
   a. Relieve the fuel system pressure. Drain the cooling system.
   b. Disconnect the accelerator cable from the throttle body. Label and disconnect the electrical connectors, vacuum hoses and coolant hoses from the throttle body.
   c. Remove the throttle body.
   d. Disconnect and plug the fuel supply and return lines.

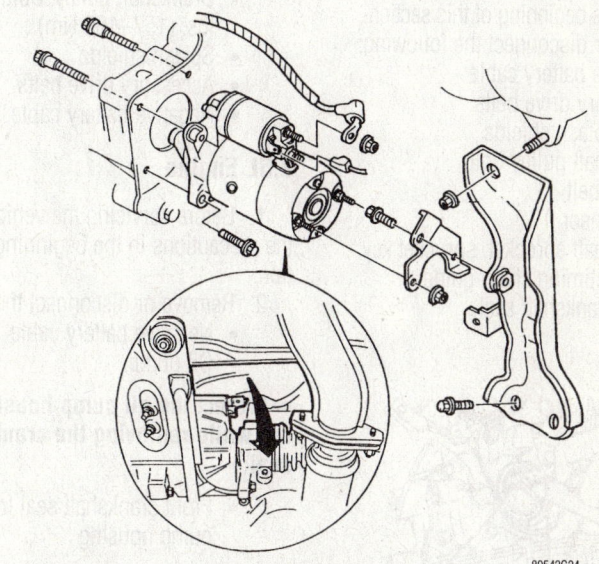

Exploded view of a typical side mounted starter assembly

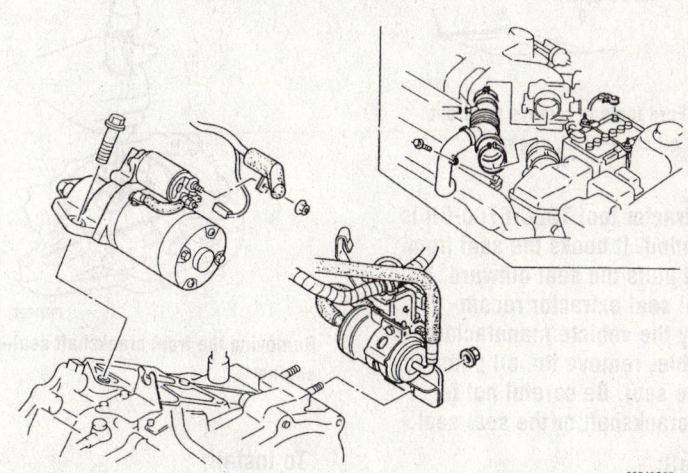

Exploded view of a typical top mounted (mostly V6 engines with automatic transmissions) starter assembly

For complete mechanical specifications, refer to Section 1 of this manual

e. Disconnect the transaxle selector cable from the transaxle and remove the cable bracket.

f. Remove the starter bracket.

3. Label and disconnect the wiring at the starter.

4. Remove the starter mounting bolts and remove the starter.

5. Installation is the reverse of the removal procedure. Tighten the starter mounting bolts to 38 ft. lbs. (51 Nm).

Front Crankshaft Seal

REMOVAL & INSTALLATION

2.0L Engine

1. Before servicing the vehicle, refer to the precautions in the beginning of this section.

2. Remove or disconnect the following:
- Negative battery cable
- Accessory drive belts
- Front splash shields
- Crankshaft pulley bolt
- Timing belt
- CKP sensor
- Crankshaft sprocket, sprocket key and the timing chain guide
- Front crankshaft seal

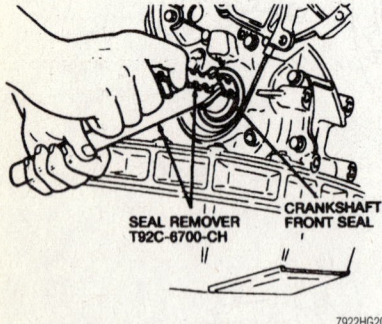

Using the Ford tools to remove the front crankshaft oil seal—2.0L engine

➡ **Seal extractor tool T92C-6700-CH is recommended. It hooks the seal from inside and pulls the seal outward. If the special seal extractor recommended by the vehicle manufacturer is not available, remove the oil pump to remove the seal. Be careful not to score the crankshaft or the seal seat.**

To install:

3. Install or connect the following:
- New seal into the oil pump cavity. Lubricate the seal lip with clean engine oil.

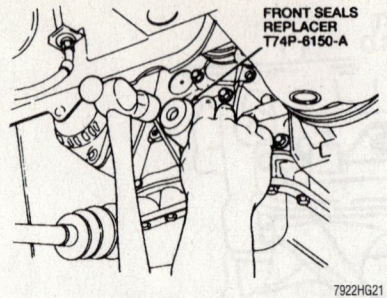

Using the appropriate tools to install the front crankshaft oil seal—2.0L engine

- Timing chain guide and crankshaft sprocket
- CKP sensor. Mounting bolt: 71–88 inch lbs. (8–10 Nm)
- Timing belt
- Crankshaft pulley. Bolt: 116–123 ft. lbs. (157–166 Nm)
- Splash shields
- Accessory drive belts
- Negative battery cable

2.5L Engine

1. Before servicing the vehicle, refer to the precautions in the beginning of this section.

2. Remove or disconnect the following:
- Negative battery cable
- Oil pump

➡ **Protect the oil pump housing with a rag while removing the crankshaft front seal.**

- Front crankshaft seal from the oil pump housing

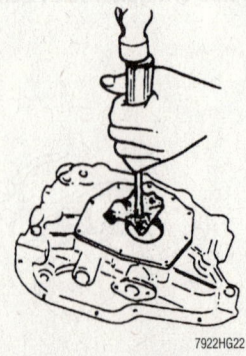

Removing the front crankshaft seal—2.5L engine

To install:

3. Install or connect the following:
- New seal into the oil pump housing. Lubricate the seal lip with clean engine oil

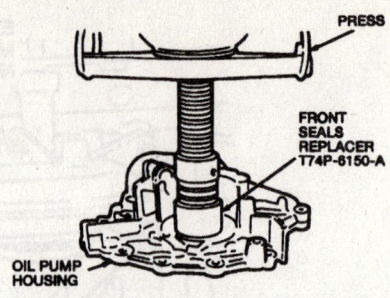

Press a new front crankshaft seal into the oil pump housing as shown—2.5L engine

➡ **Install the seal so it protrudes no more than 0.021 inch (0.7mm) from the edge of the pump body.**

- Oil pump
- Negative battery cable

Camshaft and Valve Lifters

REMOVAL & INSTALLATION

2.0L Engine

1. Before servicing the vehicle, refer to the precautions in the beginning of this section.

2. Remove or disconnect the following:
- Negative battery cable
- Spark plug wires and clips
- Distributor
- Power steering hose brackets
- Breather tube and PCV valve
- Cylinder head cover
- Accessory drive belts, timing belt covers and timing belt
- Camshaft sprockets

➡ **Loosen the camshaft cap bolts in 2 steps, in the reverse order of the tightening sequence.**

- Camshaft caps and the oil seals
- Camshafts

➡ **If they are to be removed, number each lifter with a paint marker or equivalent during removal.**

3. Inspect the camshafts and lifters for wear and/or damage and replace, as necessary.

To install:

4. Install or connect the following:
- Lifters
- Camshafts. Be sure none of the lobes are depressing any of the hydraulic lifters
- Apply silicone sealant to the cylinder head on the front camshaft cap mating surface
- Camshaft bearing caps.

TIGHTENING SEQUENCE

CAMSHAFTS

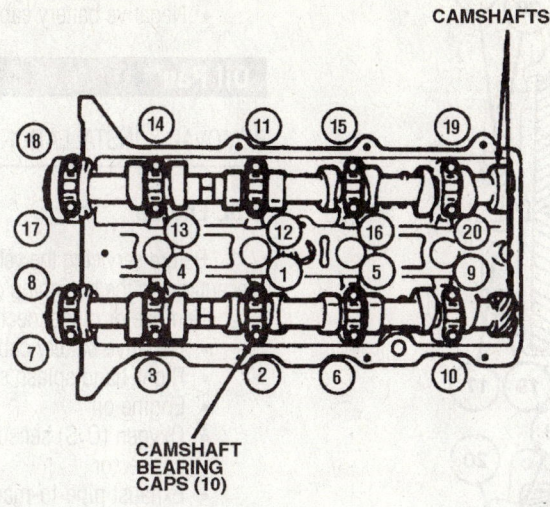

CAMSHAFT
BEARING
CAPS (10)

7922HG24

Camshaft bearing cap bolt torque sequence—2.0L engine

5. Install the bolts and tighten, in sequence, in 3 steps:
  a. Step 1: 35 inch lbs. (4 Nm)
  b. Step 2: 71 inch lbs. (8 Nm)
  c. Step 3: 100–126 inch lbs. (12–14 Nm)
6. Install or connect the following:
  • Camshaft front seals
  • Camshaft sprockets, timing belt and timing belt covers
  • Accessory drive belts

➡Apply silicone sealant to a new cylinder head cover gasket and to the cylinder head in the area adjacent to the front camshaft caps.

  • Cylinder head cover. Bolts in 2 steps: 52–69 inch lbs. (6–7 Nm).
  • Power steering hose brackets. Bolts: 71–88 inch lbs. (8–10 Nm)
  • Breather hose and PCV valve

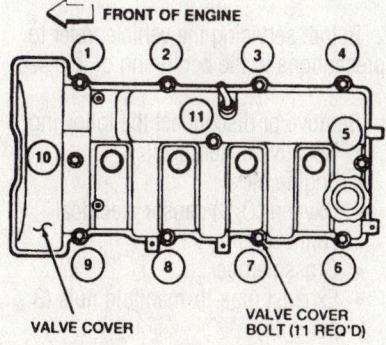

FRONT OF ENGINE

VALVE COVER

VALVE COVER
BOLT (11 REQ'D)

7922HG25

Cylinder head cover bolt torque sequence—2.0L engine

  • Distributor and spark plug wires
  • Negative battery cable

2.5L Engine

1. Before servicing the vehicle, refer to the precautions in the beginning of this section.
2. Remove or disconnect the following:

  • Negative battery cable
  • Intake manifold
  • Spark plug wires
  • Upper timing belt cover bolts
  • Ventilation pipe
  • Cylinder head covers
  • Timing belt
  • Camshaft sprockets

✳✳ WARNING

Do not remove any of the camshaft bearing caps when the camshaft lobes are depressing the valve lifters or damage to the thrust journal support or camshaft may result.

➡Turn the camshafts so the knock pins are aligned with the marks on the camshaft bearing end-caps. This will reduce the pressure on the hydraulic lifters. Note the markings on the camshaft bearing caps prior to removal, so they can be reinstalled in the same positions. The right bank (rear) caps are marked with numbers and the left bank (front) caps are marked with letters.

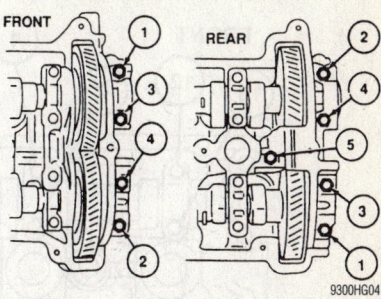

9300HG04

Camshaft bearing end-cap mounting bolt loosening sequence—2.5L engine

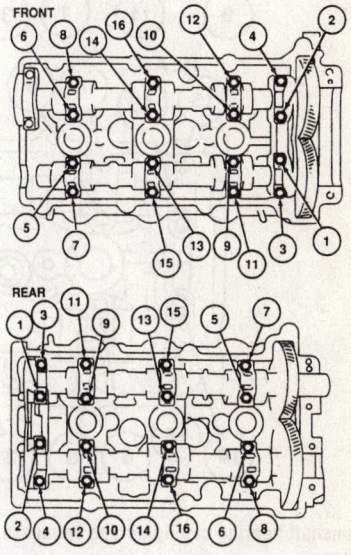

9300HG05

Camshaft bearing cap loosening sequence for the front and rear cylinder heads—2.5L engine

  • Camshaft bearing end-caps (Loosen the camshaft bearing end-cap bolts in sequence, in 5–6 steps)
  • Blind caps
  • Remove the remaining camshaft bearing cap bolts, in 5–6 steps, in the proper sequence.
  • Bearing caps (being sure to remove the thrust caps last)
  • Camshafts and oil seals
  • Lifters

3. Inspect the camshafts and lifters for wear and/or damage; replace as necessary.
To install:
4. Install or connect the following:
  • Lifters
  • Camshafts

5. Apply silicone sealant to the cylinder head surface in the area forward of the camshaft gear cavity on both cylinder heads and to the left (front) cylinder head on the

Please refer to Section 8 for electric cooling fan wiring schematics

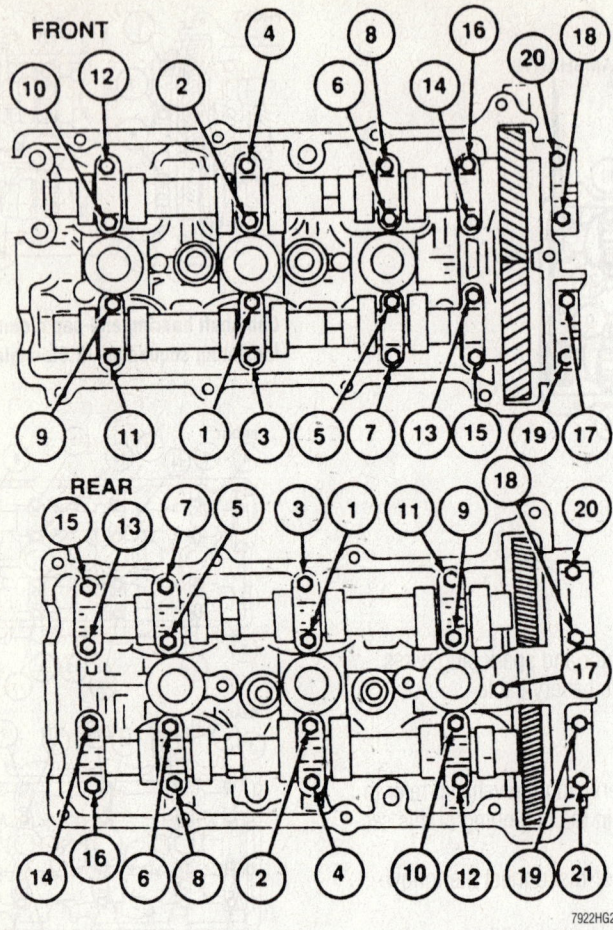

Camshaft bearing cap tightening sequence for the front and rear cylinder heads—2.5L engine

rear exhaust camshaft end-cap mating surface.

6. Install or connect the following:
- Thrust caps. Tighten the thrust cap bolts until the caps are fully seated on the cylinder head

✻✻ WARNING

Do not install any of the camshaft bearing caps when the camshaft lobes are depressing the valve lifters or damage to the thrust journal support or camshaft may result.

- Remaining camshaft bearing caps and camshaft bearing end-caps in their original positions. Tighten the caps, in sequence, in 5 equal steps, with the final step being 98–123 inch lbs. (11–14 Nm).

➡**The right bank (rear) camshaft bearing caps are marked with numbers and the left bank (front) camshaft bearing caps are marked with letters.**

7. Apply a light coat of clean engine

oil to 4 new camshaft oil seals and install the seals using a suitable socket and hammer. The camshaft oil seals should be flush with the front of the cylinder head with a maximum protrusion of 0.020 inch (0.5mm).

8. Apply sealant to 4 new blind caps.
9. Install or connect the following:
- Blind caps, using a plastic hammer
- Camshaft sprockets and retaining bolts. Tighten the retaining bolts to 90–103 ft. lbs. (123–140 Nm).
- Timing belt

10. Remove any sealant and gasket material from the cylinder head cover contact surfaces. Apply silicone sealant to the cylinder head in the area adjacent to the front and rear camshaft caps.

11. Install or connect the following:
- New gasket on the cylinder head
- Cylinder head cover following the proper torque sequence, as shown earlier in this section, to 43–78 inch lbs. (5–8 Nm).
- Upper timing cover bolts to 71–88 inch lbs. (8–10 Nm)
- Ventilation pipe

- Intake manifold
- Spark plug wires
- Negative battery cable

Oil Pan

REMOVAL & INSTALLATION

2.0L Engine

1. Before servicing the vehicle, refer to the precautions in the beginning of this section.
2. Remove or disconnect the following:
- Negative battery cable
- Right-hand splash shield
- Engine oil
- Oxygen (O_2S) sensor electrical connector
- Exhaust pipe-to-manifold nuts. Move the exhaust pipe aside
- Exhaust clamp
- Oil pan bolts
- Oil pan

To install:

3. Clean all dirt, oil and old sealant from the oil pan, cylinder block and stiffener contact surfaces.
4. Apply a continuous bead of silicone sealant around the oil pan, going on the inside of the bolt holes.
5. Install or connect the following:
- Oil pan. Bolts: 14–19 ft. lbs. (19–25 Nm)
- New exhaust clamp. Nuts: 26–34 ft. lbs. (34–47 Nm)
- Exhaust pipe with new nuts. Nuts: 27–38 ft. lbs. (37–52 Nm)
- O_2S sensor electrical connector
- Right-hand splash shield
- Oil pan drain plug to 22–30 ft. lbs. (30–41 Nm)
- Engine oil
- Negative battery cable

2.5L Engine

1. Before servicing the vehicle, refer to the precautions in the beginning of this section.
2. Remove or disconnect the following:
- Negative battery cable
- Engine oil
- Oxygen (O_2S) sensor electrical connectors
- Crossmember
- Exhaust pipe-to-manifold nuts (3 per side)
- Lower the exhaust system to gain access to the oil pan bolts

➡**The oil pan bolts are different lengths. Identify them as they are**

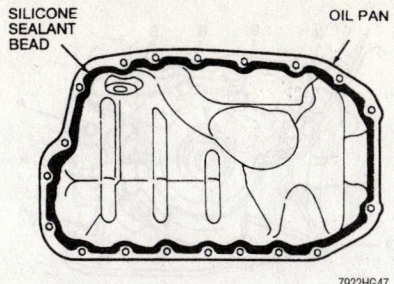

Be sure to apply the bead of sealant on the inside of the bolt holes, as shown—2.5L engine

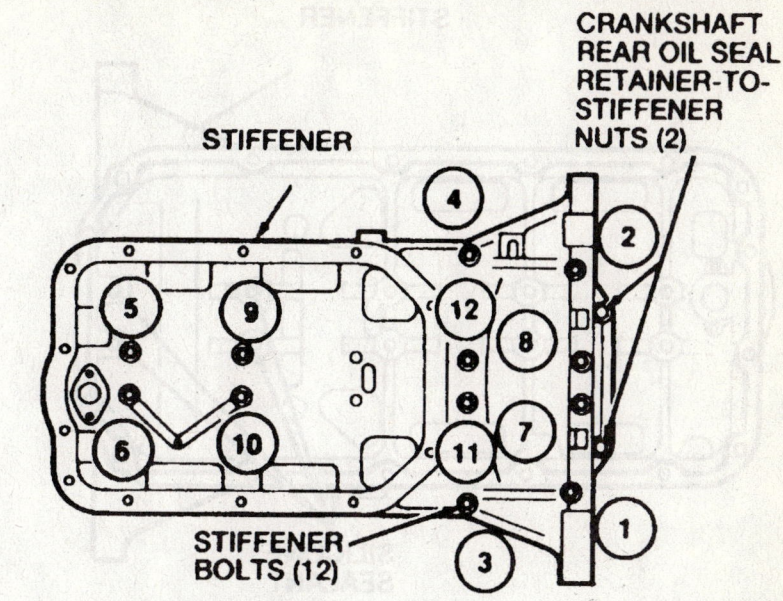

Stiffener bolt and nut loosening sequence—2.0L engine

removed so they can be reinstalled in their proper locations.

- Oil pan

To install:

3. Clean all dirt, oil and old sealant from the oil pan and cylinder block contact surfaces. Remove the old sealant from the threads of the oil pan bolts and the bolt holes in the block.

✳✳ WARNING

Failure to remove the old sealant from the bolts and bolt holes may cause the block to crack.

4. Apply a continuous bead of silicone sealant along the inside of the bolt holes, overlapping the ends. Once the new silicone sealant is applied, the oil pan must be installed within 5 minutes.

5. Install or connect the following:
- Oil pan. Long bolts: 14–18 ft. lbs. (19–25 Nm); short bolts: 71–88 inch lbs. (8–10 Nm).
- Exhaust pipes to the manifolds with new gaskets. Nuts: 30–41 ft. lbs. (40–55 Nm).
- O_2S sensor electrical connectors
- Crossmember. Bolts: 69–93 ft. lbs. (94–126 Nm)
- Oil pan drain plug to 22–30 ft. lbs. (30–41 Nm)
- Engine oil

Oil Pump

REMOVAL & INSTALLATION

2.0L Engine

1. Before servicing the vehicle, refer to the precautions in the beginning of this section.

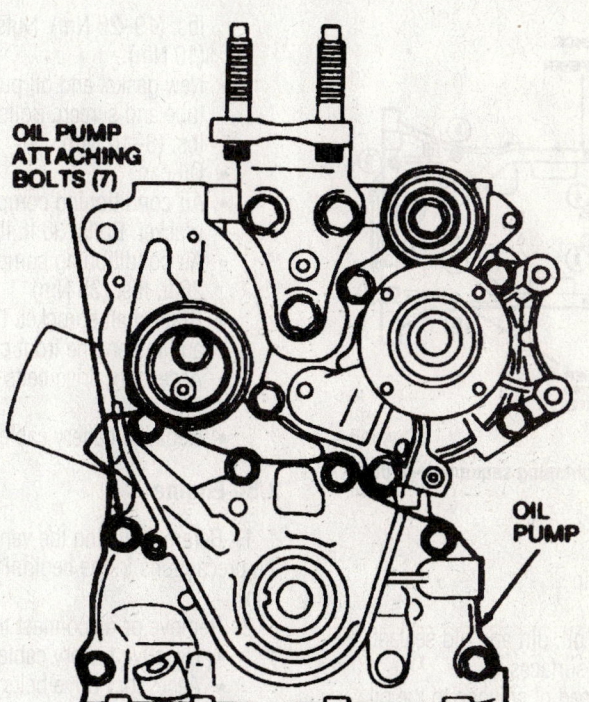

Oil pump mounting bolt locations—2.0L engine

2. Remove or disconnect the following:
- Negative battery cable
- Accessory drive belts
- Oil pan, oil pump pick-up tube and screen
- 2 rear main seal housing-to-stiff-

ener nuts and the 12 stiffener bolts in 2 steps, in the proper sequence
- Stiffener.
- Front covers, timing belt and crankshaft sprocket
- Air conditioning compressor and mounting bracket

STIFFENER

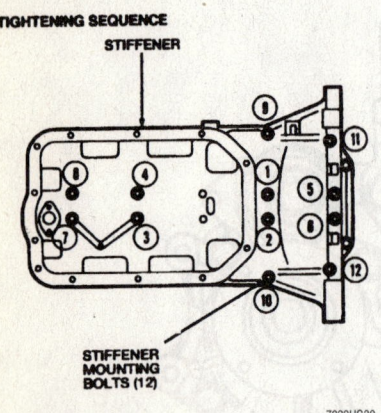

SILICONE
SEALANT

7922HG29

Apply sealant to the stiffener in the places indicated—2.0L engine

TIGHTENING SEQUENCE
STIFFENER

STIFFENER
MOUNTING
BOLTS (12)

7922HG30

Stiffener bolt tightening sequence—2.0L engine

- Oil pump

To install:

3. Clean the oil, dirt and old sealant from all contact surfaces.

4. Apply a bead of silicone to the oil pump-to-cylinder block contact surface, along the inside of the bolt holes.

5. Install or connect the following:
- Oil pump. Bolts: 14–19 ft. lbs. (19–25 Nm)

6. Clean the engine block contact area and stiffener. Apply a bead of silicone sealant to the perimeter of the stiffener, going on the inside of the bolt holes. Apply sealant to the 4 rear bolt holes.
- Stiffener and mounting bolts. Bolts in 2 steps, in sequence: 14–19 ft.

lbs. (19–25 Nm). Nuts: 88 inch lbs. (10 Nm).
- New gasket and oil pump pick-up tube and screen. Bolts: 71–88 inch lbs. (8–10 Nm)
- Oil pan
- Air conditioning compressor bracket. Bolts: 38 ft. lbs. (52 Nm)
- Air conditioning compressor. Bolts: 26 ft. lbs. (35 Nm)
- Crankshaft sprocket, timing belt and the engine front covers
- Accessory drive belts
- Engine oil
- Negative battery cable

2.5L Engine

1. Before servicing the vehicle, refer to the precautions in the beginning of this section.

2. Remove or disconnect the following:
- Negative battery cable
- Accessory drive belts
- Engine front covers and the timing belt
- Oil pan
- Air conditioning compressor and bracket
- Power steering pump and tensioner
- Crankshaft sprocket and key
- Oil pump

➡**The oil pump mounting bolts are different lengths. Identify them as they are removed so they can be reinstalled in their proper locations.**

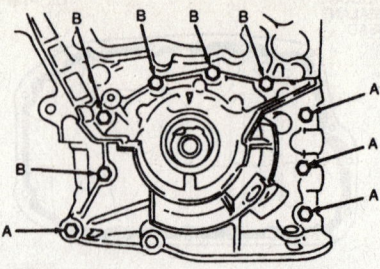

BOLT A: 40mm (1.57 IN.)
BOLT B: 25mm (0.98 IN.)

7922HG31

Notice the positions of the different length oil pump mounting bolts—2.5L engine

- Oil pump O-ring

➡**Protect the oil pump housing with a rag while removing the crankshaft front seal.**

To install:

3. Clean the oil, dirt and old sealant from all contact surfaces.

4. Install or connect the following:
- New front crankshaft seal lubricated with clean engine oil.

➡**Install the seal so it is flush with the edge of the oil pump housing or protrudes no more than 0.021 in. (0.7mm) from the edge of the pump body.**

- New O-ring onto the oil pump. Apply a continuous bead of silicone sealant to the oil pump mating surface
- Oil pump and mounting bolts. Bolts: 14–18 ft. lbs. (19–25 Nm).

➡**Be sure that the proper length bolts are placed into the correct positions.**

- Crankshaft sprocket and key
- Power steering pump and tensioner. Tensioner upper bolts and rear bracket bolt: 24–33 ft. lbs. (32–46 Nm). Tensioner lower bolt: 14–18 ft. lbs. (19–25 Nm).
- Air conditioning compressor bracket. Bolts: 28–38 ft. lbs. (38–51 Nm).
- Air conditioning compressor. Bolts: 28–38 ft. lbs. (38–51 Nm).
- Oil strainer-to-oil pump bolts and tighten to 71–88 inch lbs. (8–10 Nm).
- Oil pan, timing belt and the front engine covers
- Accessory drive belts
- Engine oil
- Negative battery cable

Piston and Ring

POSITIONING

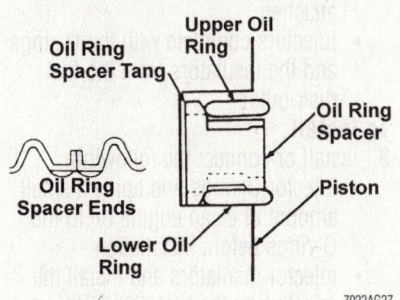

2.0L (VIN A) engines—piston ring positioning

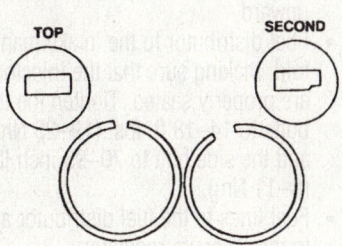

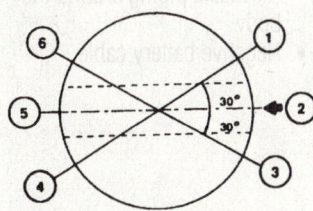

1. Top ring end gap
2. Piston pin end gap
3. Second ring end gap
4. Oil ring lower rail end gap
5. Oil ring spacer end gap
6. Oil ring upper rail end gap

2.5L (VIN B) engine—piston ring end-gap spacing

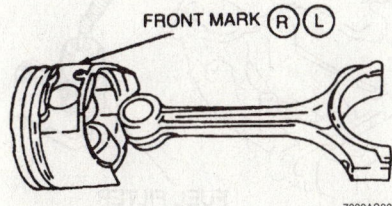

2.5L (VIN B) engine—piston and connecting rod assembly

FUEL SYSTEM

Fuel System Service Precautions

Safety is the most important factor when performing not only fuel system maintenance but any type of maintenance. Failure to conduct maintenance and repairs in a safe manner may result in serious personal injury or death. Maintenance and testing of the vehicle's fuel system components can be accomplished safely and effectively by adhering to the following rules and guidelines.

• To avoid the possibility of fire and personal injury, always disconnect the negative battery cable unless the repair or test procedure requires that battery voltage be applied.

• Always relieve the fuel system pressure prior to disconnecting any fuel system component (injector, fuel rail, pressure regulator, etc.), fitting or fuel line connection. Exercise extreme caution whenever relieving fuel system pressure to avoid exposing skin, face and eyes to fuel spray. Please be advised that fuel under pressure may penetrate the skin or any part of the body that it contacts.

• Always place a shop towel or cloth around the fitting or connection prior to loosening to absorb any excess fuel due to spillage. Ensure that all fuel spillage (should it occur) is quickly removed from engine surfaces. Ensure that all fuel soaked cloths or towels are deposited into a suitable waste container.

• Always keep a dry chemical (Class B) fire extinguisher near the work area.

• Do not allow fuel spray or fuel vapors to come into contact with a spark or open flame.

• Always use a back-up wrench when loosening and tightening fuel line connection fittings. This will prevent unnecessary stress and torsion to fuel line piping.

• Always replace worn fuel fitting O-rings with new. Do not substitute fuel hose or equivalent, where fuel pipe is installed.

Fuel System Pressure

RELIEVING

1. Before servicing the vehicle, refer to the precautions in the beginning of this section.

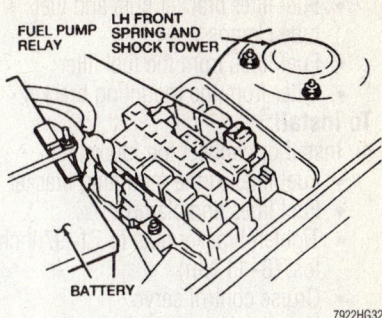

Fuel pump relay location in the fuse box

2. Perform the following:
   a. Start the engine and let it idle.
   b. Remove the fuel pump relay from the main fuse junction panel
   c. After the engine stalls, turn **OFF** the ignition switch.
   d. Disconnect the negative battery cable.
   e. Install the fuel pump relay.

Fuel Filter

REMOVAL & INSTALLATION

1. Before servicing the vehicle, refer to the precautions in the beginning of this section.
2. Properly relieve the fuel system pressure.
3. Remove or disconnect the following:
   • Negative battery cable
   • Cruise control servo

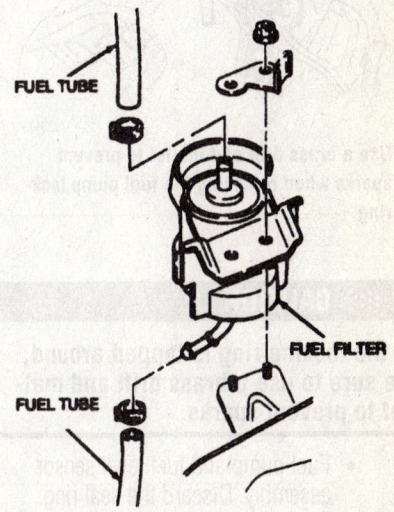

Exploded view of the fuel filter assembly mounting

- Fuel filter bracket nuts and fuel tube clamps
- Fuel lines from the fuel filter
- Filter from the mounting bracket

To install:

4. Install or connect the following:
- Fuel filter in the mounting bracket
- Fuel lines and clamps
- Tighten bracket nuts to 71–97 inch lbs. (8–11 Nm)
- Cruise control servo
- Negative battery cable

Fuel Pump

REMOVAL & INSTALLATION

1. Before servicing the vehicle, refer to the precautions in the beginning of this section.

2. Relieve the fuel system pressure using the recommended procedure.

3. Remove or disconnect the following:
- Negative battery cable
- Fuel from the tank
- Hoses attached to the fuel tank
- Fuel pump electrical connector
- Fuel tank heat shield
- Fuel tank support brackets
- Fuel tank
- Fuel pump locking ring

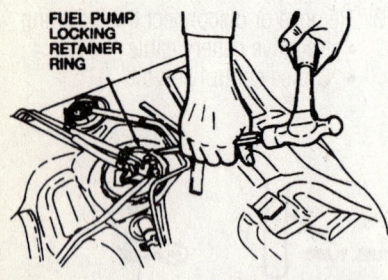

7922HG34

Use a brass drift and mallet to prevent sparks when removing the fuel pump lock-ring

❈❈ CAUTION

If the locking ring is tapped around, be sure to use a brass drift and mallet to prevent sparks.

- Fuel pump and fuel level sensor assembly. Discard the seal ring.

To install:

4. Clean the fuel pump mounting flange, fuel tank mounting surface and seal ring groove.

➡ **Apply a light coating of grease on a new seal ring.**

5. Install or connect the following:
- Seal ring
- Fuel pump and fuel level sensor assembly

➡ **Be sure the locating keys are in the keyways and the seal ring remains in the groove.**

- Locking ring
- Fuel tank. Add a minimum of 10 gallons of fuel to the tank and check for leaks.
- Negative battery cable

Fuel Injectors

REMOVAL & INSTALLATION

2.0L Engine

1. Properly relieve the fuel system pressure.

2. Remove or disconnect the following:
- Electrical connectors from the injectors and remove the wiring harness
- Vacuum hose from the pressure regulator
- Fuel lines from the fuel distributor

and remove the fuel line attaching bolt on the side of the intake manifold

- Bolts from the fuel distributor and remove the it with injectors attached
- Injectors complete with the O-rings and the insulators from the fuel distributor.

To install:

3. Install or connect the following:
- Injector O-rings and apply a small amount of clean engine oil to the O-rings before installation.
- Injector insulators and install the injectors to the fuel distributor. Make sure that the injectors are properly seated and that the electrical connector points are facing upward.
- Fuel distributor to the intake manifold, making sure that the injectors are properly seated. Tighten the top bolts to 14–18 ft. lbs. (19–25 Nm) and the side bolt to 70–95 inch lbs. (8–11 Nm).
- Fuel lines to the fuel distributor and to the pressure regulator
- Electrical harness to the injectors
- Air intake piping around the throttle body
- Negative battery cable

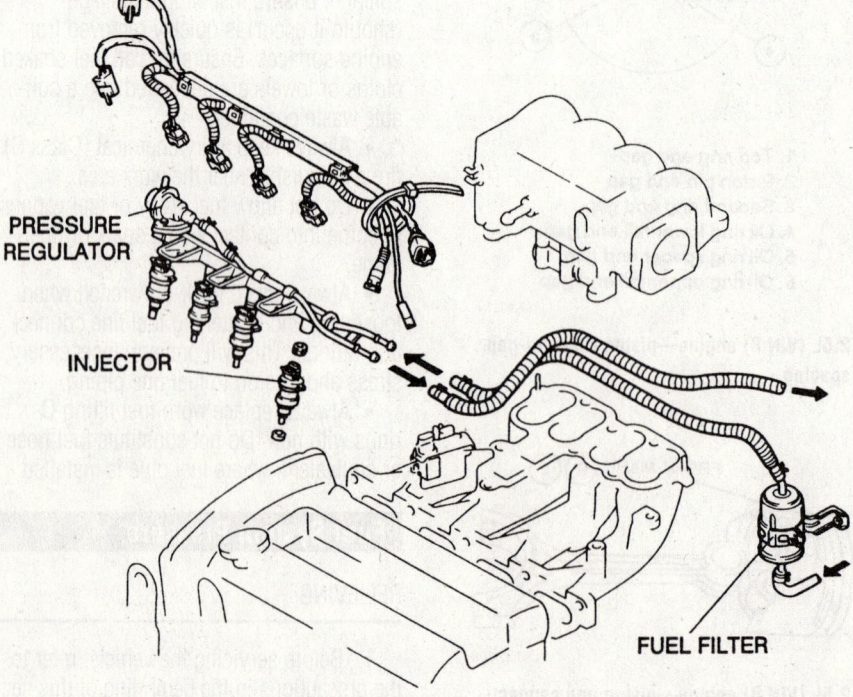

Exploded view of the typical 4-cylinder engine fuel injector and distributor assembly

89545G13

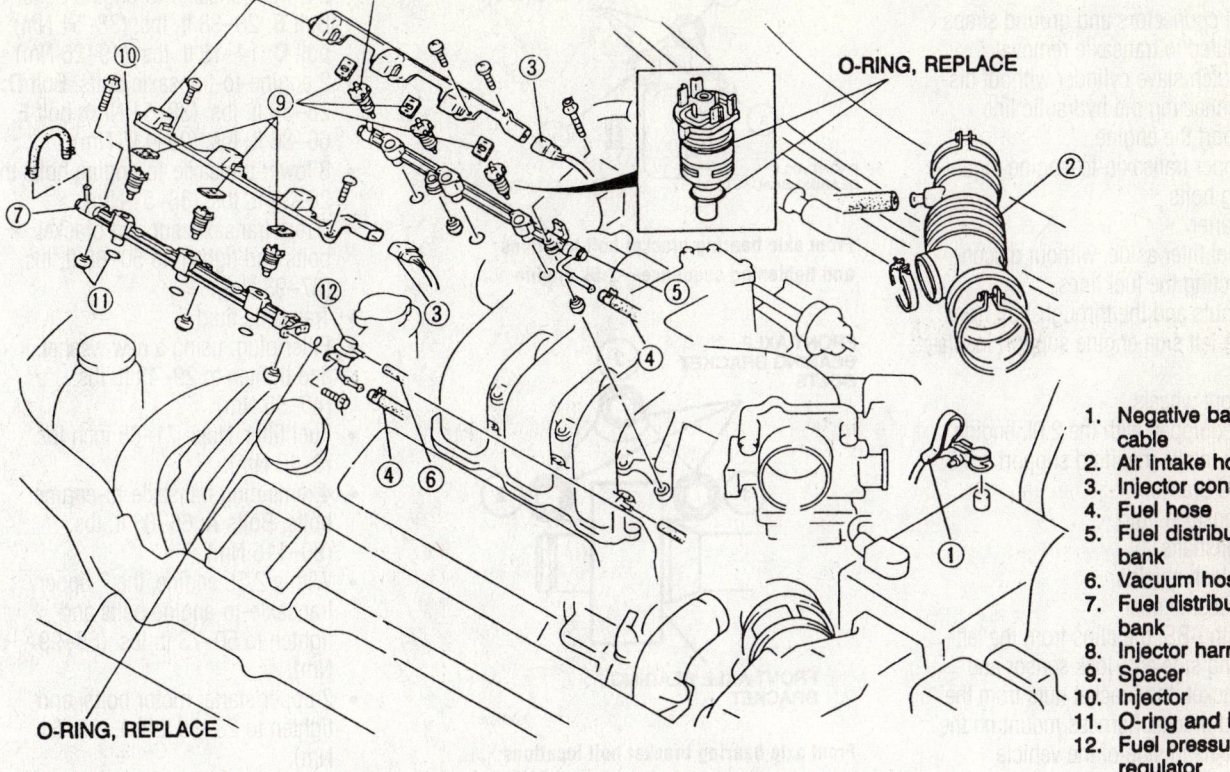

O-RING, REPLACE

O-RING, REPLACE

1. Negative battery cable
2. Air intake hose
3. Injector connector
4. Fuel hose
5. Fuel distributor/Right bank
6. Vacuum hose
7. Fuel distributor/Left bank
8. Injector harness
9. Spacer
10. Injector
11. O-ring and insulator
12. Fuel pressure regulator

89545G14

Exploded view of the typical 6-cylinder engine fuel injector and distributor assemblies

2.5L Engines

1. Relieve the fuel system pressure.
2. Remove or disconnect the following:
   - Negative battery cable
   - Air intake hose assembly
   - Injector electrical connectors from the injector harness
   - Fuel hoses from the end of the fuel distributor
   - Fuel distributor attaching screws and remove the fuel distributor

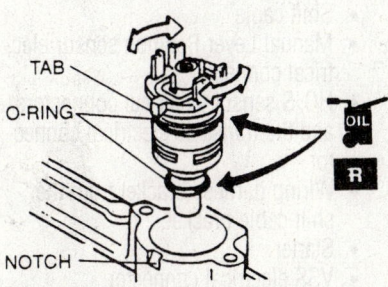

When installing the injector on V6 engines, replace the O-rings and lightly oil them with engine oil

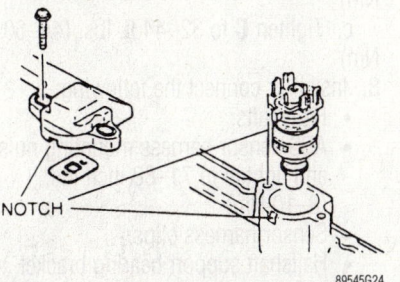

89545G24

Align the tab on the injector with the notches on the fuel distributor and wire harness connector

   - Fuel injector harnesses from the fuel distributor
   - Injectors from the distributor and remove the O-ring and spacer.

To install:
3. Install or connect the following:
   - Injector O-rings and apply a small amount of clean engine oil to the O-rings before installation.
   - Injectors to the fuel distributor. Turn until the injector is fully seated, aligning the tab on the injector with the notch in the fuel distributor.

   - Injector harness on the fuel distributor and install the assembly to the engine.
   - Fuel distributor screws to 22–31 inch lbs. (2.5–3.5 Nm).
   - Fuel hoses to the fuel distributor and attach the electrical connectors to the injector harness.
   - Intake hose
   - Negative battery cable

DRIVE TRAIN

Transaxle Assembly

REMOVAL & INSTALLATION

Manual

1. Before servicing the vehicle, refer to the precautions in the beginning of this section.
2. Remove or disconnect the following:
   - Battery and battery tray

- Air cleaner intake tube and air cleaner
- All connectors and ground straps related to transaxle removal
- Clutch slave cylinder without disconnecting the hydraulic line
3. Support the engine.
- Upper transaxle-to-engine mounting bolts
- Starter
- Fuel filter aside, without disconnecting the fuel lines
- 2 nuts and the through-bolt from the left side engine support insulator
- Front wheels
- If equipped with the 2.0L engine, the intake manifold support bolts and bracket
- Transaxle fluid
- Halfshafts
- Splash shields
- Crossmember
- With ABS, the clips from the left-hand side anti-lock sensor and bracket, the bracket nuts from the and bracket harness mount on the left-hand side of the vehicle
- Rear engine support
- Shift rod and control rod from the transaxle
- Rear transaxle support bracket bolts
4. Support the transaxle with a suitable jack.
- Rear transaxle support insulator
- Lower transaxle-to-engine mounting bolts
- Transaxle from the vehicle

To install:
5. Place the transaxle on a suitable jack. Apply a thin coating of molybdenum grease to the input shaft splines. Raise the transaxle into position and align it with the engine.
6. Install or connect the following:
- Lower transaxle-to-engine bolts
- Nuts and bolts to the engine support insulator. Nuts: 32–44 ft. lbs. (44–60 Nm); bolts: 63–86 ft. lbs. (86–116 Nm).
- Rear transaxle support insulator with the 3 bolts. Bolts: 50–68 ft. lbs. (67–93 Nm).
- Control rod and shift rod to the transaxle. Control rod nut: 28–38 ft. lbs. (38–51 Nm); shift rod bolt and nut: 14–18 ft. lbs. (19–25 Nm).
7. Install the rear engine support, and tighten the bolts and nuts as follows:
    a. Tighten **A** to 55–77 ft. lbs. (75–104 Nm)

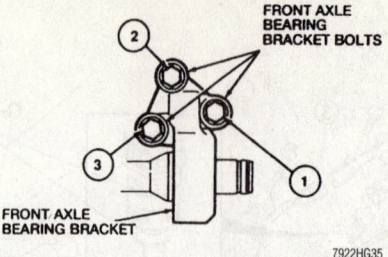

Front axle bearing bracket bolt locations and tightening sequence—2.5L engine

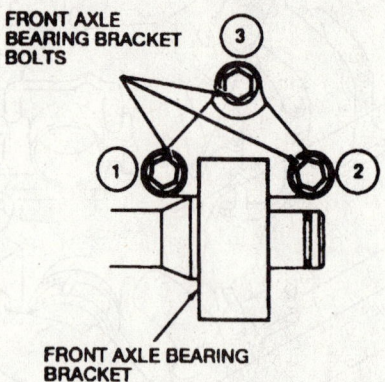

Front axle bearing bracket bolt locations and tightening sequence—2.0L engine

    b. Tighten **B** to 50–68 ft. lbs. (67–93 Nm)
    c. Tighten **C** to 32–44 ft. lbs. (44–60 Nm)
8. Install or connect the following:
- Halfshafts.
- ABS sensor harness mounting nuts and tighten to 71–88 inch lbs. (8–10 Nm)
- Sensor harness clips
- Halfshaft support bearing bracket bolts. Bolts, in sequence: 32–45 ft. lbs. (43–61 Nm).
- Exhaust pipes to the manifolds and tighten the new nuts to 30–41 ft. lbs. (40–55 Nm).
- Oxygen sensor connectors
- Crossmember. Bolts: 69–96 ft. lbs. (94–131 Nm).
- New halfshaft retaining nuts. Tighten the nuts to 174–235 ft. lbs. (235–319 Nm). Stake the nuts.
- Wheels. Lug nuts: 65–87 ft. lbs. (88–118 Nm).
- Transaxle drain plug. Tighten to 29–43 ft. lbs. (40–58 Nm).
- Starter motor and wiring. Lower retaining bolt: 28–38 ft. lbs. (35–52 Nm).
- Intake manifold support bracket. Bolts: 27–38 ft. lbs. (37–52 Nm).

- Splash shields.
- 2 lower transaxle-to-engine bolts. Bolt **B**: 28–38 ft. lbs. (38–51 Nm); bolt **C**: 14–18 ft. lbs. (19–25 Nm)
- 2 engine-to-transaxle bolts. Bolt **D**: 28–38 ft. lbs. (38–51 Nm); bolt **E**: 66–86 ft. lbs. (90–116 Nm).
- 3 lower transaxle-to-engine bolts to 28–38 ft. lbs. (38–51 Nm).
- 3 rear transaxle support bracket bolts and tighten to 50–68 ft. lbs. (67–93 Nm).
- Transaxle fluid
- Filler plug, using a new washer, and tighten to 29–43 ft. lbs. (40–58 Nm)
- Fuel filter. Nuts: 71–88 inch lbs. (8–10 Nm).
- 4 remaining transaxle-to-engine bolts. Bolts **A**: 66–86 ft. lbs. (90–116 Nm).
- With a 2.5L engine, the 7 upper transaxle-to-engine bolts and tighten to 50–73 ft. lbs. (68–99 Nm).
- 2 upper starter motor bolts, and tighten to 28–38 ft. lbs. (35–51 Nm).
- Clutch slave cylinder. Bolts: 12–16 ft. lbs. (16–22 Nm).
- Back-up lamp switch and VSS electrical connectors and the transaxle ground straps
- Battery and battery tray
- Air cleaner and the air cleaner intake tube

Automatic

4EAT TRANSAXLE

1. Before servicing the vehicle, refer to the precautions in the beginning of this section.
2. Remove or disconnect the following:
- Battery and battery tray
- Air cleaner assembly
- Shift cable
- Manual Lever Position sensor electrical connector
- HO2S sensor electrical connectors and the transaxle electrical connector
- Wiring harness bracket from the shift cable bracket.
- Starter
- VSS electrical connector
- Ground wire bracket and the ground wire
- Harness support bracket at the rear engine support insulator bracket
- Oil cooler tubes
- 3 transaxle-to-engine mounting bolts

Engine-To-Transaxle Bolts

Transaxle-To-Engine Bolts

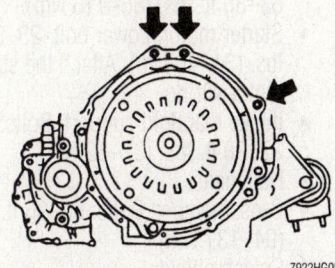

7922HG08

Engine and transaxle retaining bolt locations—2.5L engine

3. Support the engine from above.
   - 2 left-hand engine support insulator nuts and bolt and the mount through-bolt
   - Fuel filter and bracket
   - Left-hand engine support insulator bracket
   - Pulse Signal Generator electrical connector
   - Front wheels
   - Splash shields
   - Crossmember
   - Rear engine support
   - Lower transaxle support insulator
   - Halfshafts
   - Transaxle vent hose and the dipstick tube
   - Inspection cover
   - 4 torque converter nuts
4. Support the transaxle with a suitable transmission jack.
   - 2 engine-to-transaxle bolts
   - 3 rear transaxle support bracket bolts
   - Transaxle from the engine. Slightly tilt the transaxle and engine to ease removal.
   - Transaxle from the engine

To install:
5. Position the transaxle onto a suitable transmission jack and secure the transaxle to the jack.
6. Raise the transaxle into position. Align the torque converter studs with the flexplate.

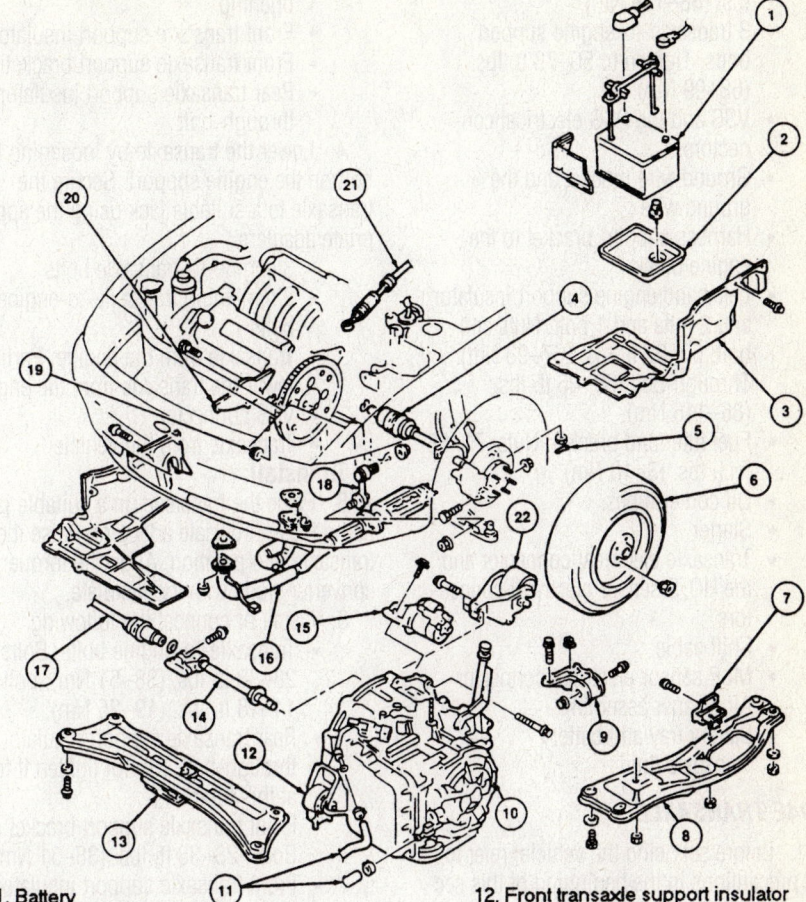

1. Battery
2. Battery tray
3. Front fender splash shield
4. LH front wheel driveshaft & joint
5. Cotter pin
6. Wheel & tire
7. Lower transaxle support insulator
8. Rear engine support
9. LH transaxle support insulator
10. Transaxle
11. Oil cooler tubes
12. Front transaxle support insulator
13. Crossmember
14. Halfshaft
15. Starter motor
16. Exhaust inlet pipe
17. RH front wheel driveshaft & joint
18. Stabilizer bar link
19. Flywheel to converter retaining nut
20. Cover plate
21. Transmission shift cable & bracket
22. Rear transaxle support insulator

7922HG49

Exploded view of all transaxle removal/installation related components—4EAT transaxle

7. Install or connect the following:
   - 2 engine-to-transaxle bolts and tighten to 50–73 ft. lbs. (68–99 Nm).
   - 3 rear transaxle support bracket bolts and tighten to 50–68 ft. lbs. (67–93 Nm).
   - Tour torque converter-to-flexplate nuts, tighten to 32–45 ft. lbs. (44–60 Nm).
   - Inspection cover
   - Vent hose and dipstick tube. Dipstick tube mounting bolts: 71–88 inch lbs. (8–10 Nm).
   - Halfshafts
   - Lower transaxle support insulator. Bolts: 41–59 ft. lbs. (55–80 Nm).
   - Rear engine support. Engine support-to-body bolts and nuts: 50–68 ft. lbs. (67–93 Nm). Rear engine support-to-front mount nuts: 55–77 ft. lbs. (75–104 Nm). Rear engine support-to-rear mount nuts: 32–44 ft. lbs. (44–60 Nm).
   - Crossmember. Bolts: 68–96 ft. lbs. (94–131 Nm).
   - Splash shields

- Front wheels. Lug nuts: 66–86 ft. lbs. (88–118 Nm).
- 3 transaxle-to-engine support bolts. Tighten to 50–73 ft. lbs. (68–99 Nm).
- VSS and the PSG electrical connectors
- Ground wire bracket and the ground wire
- Harness support bracket to the engine block
- Left-hand engine support insulator and 2 nuts and 1 bolt. Nuts and bolt: 50–68 ft. lbs. (67–93 Nm). Through-bolt: 63–86 ft. lbs. (86–116 Nm).
- Fuel filter and bracket. Nuts: 71–88 inch lbs. (8–10 Nm).
- Oil cooler tubes.
- Starter
- Transaxle electrical connector and the HO2S sensor electrical connectors
- Shift cable
- MLP sensor electrical connector
- Air cleaner assembly
- Battery tray and battery
- Transaxle fluid

CD4E TRANSAXLE

1. Before servicing the vehicle, refer to the precautions in the beginning of this section.
2. Remove or disconnect the following:
- Battery and battery tray
- Air cleaner assembly
- Manual Lever Position sensor
- Ground wire bracket and the ground wire
- Shift cable and bracket
- Transaxle electrical connector
- Oil cooler inlet and outlet hoses
- 2 upper starter bolts
3. Support the engine from above.
- Top 3 transaxle-to-engine mounting bolts
- Fuel filter and bracket
- Ignition coil and mounting straps
- Speed control servo
- Left-hand support insulator
- Front wheels
- Splash shields
- Crossmember
- Rear engine support
- Halfshafts

➡ Install transaxle plugs into the differential side gears

- Intake manifold support
- Starter
- TSS connector
- 4 torque converter-to-flywheel

retaining nuts through the starter opening
- Front transaxle support insulator
- Front transaxle support bracket
- Rear transaxle support insulator through-bolt
4. Lower the transaxle by loosening the bolt on the engine support. Secure the transaxle to a suitable jack using the appropriate adapters.
- 3 engine-to-transaxle bolts
- 2 remaining transaxle-to-engine bolts
- Transaxle from the engine. Partially lower the transaxle from the engine
- VSS connector
- Transaxle from the vehicle

To install:

5. Place the transaxle on a suitable jack using the appropriate adapters. Raise the transaxle into position. Align the torque converter studs with the flexplate.
6. Install or connect the following:
- Transaxle-to-engine bolts. Bolts **B**: 28–38 ft. lbs. (38–51 Nm); bolts **C**: 14–18 ft. lbs. (19–25 Nm).
- Rear transaxle support insulator through-bolt. Do not tighten it fully at this time.
- Front transaxle support bracket. Bolts: 28–38 ft. lbs. (38–51 Nm).
- Front transaxle support insulator and through-bolt. Do not tighten the through-bolt fully at this time.
- TSS and VSS connectors.
- 4 torque converter-to-flexplate nuts and tighten to 24–30 ft. lbs. (33–40 Nm).
- Torque converter access plug
- Left-hand engine support insulator. Through-bolt: 63–86 ft. lbs. (86–116 Nm)
- 2 left-hand engine support insulator nuts and 2 bolts. Do not tighten them fully at this time.

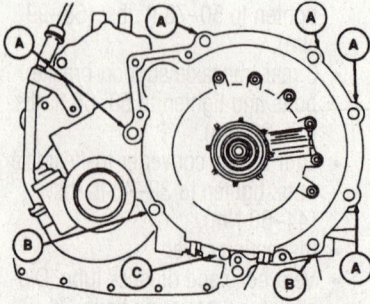

7922HG42

Transaxle-to-engine mounting bolts— CD4E transaxle

7. Install the rear engine support. Tighten the rear engine support bolts and nuts as follows:
   a. Tighten **A** to 55–77 ft. lbs. (75–104 Nm)
   b. Tighten **B** to 50–68 ft. lbs. (67–93 Nm)
   c. Tighten **C** to 32–44 ft. lbs. (44–60 Nm)
8. Install or connect the following:
- Tighten the front and rear transaxle support insulator through-bolts to 63–86 ft. lbs. (86–116 Nm).
- Starter motor. Lower bolt: 23–34 ft. lbs. (31–46 Nm). Attach the starter motor wiring.
- Intake manifold support. Bolts: 27–38 ft. lbs. (37–52 Nm).
- Halfshafts.
- Crossmember. Bolts: 68–96 ft. lbs. (94–131 Nm).
- Splash shields
- Wheels. Lug nuts: 67–86 ft. lbs. (88–118 Nm).
- Tighten the 2 left-hand support insulator nuts to 12–17 ft. lbs. (16–23 Nm). Tighten the 2 left-hand engine support insulator bolts to 28–38 ft. lbs. (38–51 Nm).
- Ignition coil
- Speed control servo
- Fuel filter bracket nuts and tighten to 71–97 inch lbs. (8–11 Nm).
- 2 upper starter motor bolts and tighten to 23–34 ft. lbs. (31–46 Nm).
- 3 remaining transaxle-to-engine bolts. Bolts: 66–86 ft. lbs. (89–117 Nm).
- Shift cable bracket and 2 bolts.
- Transaxle electrical connector.
- MLP sensor. Adjust the MLP sensor. Bolts: 96–117 inch lbs. (11–13 Nm).
- Oil cooler inlet and outlet hoses.
- Air cleaner assembly.
- Battery tray and battery.
- Ground wire bracket and the ground wire.
- Transaxle fluid

Clutch

ADJUSTMENTS

Pedal Height

1. Before servicing the vehicle, refer to the precautions in the beginning of this section.

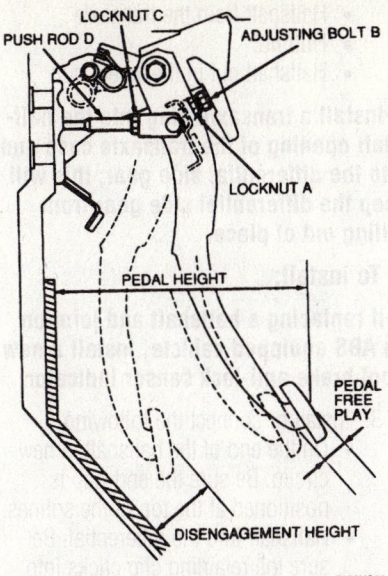

Clutch pedal adjustments and related components

2. Perform the following:

a. To determine if the clutch pedal height requires an adjustment, measure the distance from the bulkhead to the upper center of the pedal pad. The distance should be 7.32–8.31 in. (186–211mm).

b. If adjustment is required, loosen locknut **A** and turn the adjusting bolt **B** until the desired pedal height is reached.

c. Tighten the locknut to 122–156 inch lbs. (14–17 Nm).

Pedal Free-Play

1. Before servicing the vehicle, refer to the precautions in the beginning of this section.

2. Perform the following:

a. Measure the clutch pedal height at rest.

b. Depress the clutch pedal by hand and measure the height of the pedal when resistance is felt.

c. The difference should be 0.04–0.12 inch (1–3mm).

3. If adjustment is necessary, proceed as follows:

a. Loosen locknut **C** and turn clutch master cylinder pushrod **D** until the pedal play is within specifications.

b. Measure the distance from the floor to the center of the pedal pad when the pedal is fully depressed. The distance should be 2.64 inches (67mm).

c. Tighten the locknut to 105–147 inch lbs. (12–16 Nm).

REMOVAL & INSTALLATION

1. Before servicing the vehicle, refer to the precautions in the beginning of this section.

2. Remove or disconnect the following:
- Negative battery cable
- Transaxle assembly

3. Install a suitable clutch alignment tool and flywheel holding tool.

4. Remove or disconnect the following:
- Pressure plate-to-flywheel bolts evenly
- Pressure plate, clutch disc and alignment tool

5. Inspect the pressure plate and clutch disc for wear and/or damage and replace, as necessary.

6. Inspect the pilot bearing for excessive wear or scoring. Remove it using a suitable puller, only if replacement is necessary.

7. Inspect the flywheel for scoring, cracks, worn or broken teeth, or other damage. Remove the flywheel if machining or replacement is necessary. Use care when removing the last bolt to prevent dropping the flywheel.

8. Remove the release bearing and fork. Inspect them for wear or damage and replace as necessary.

To install:

9. Apply molybdenum grease to the release bearing and release fork.

10. Install or connect the following:
- Release fork and bearing
- Flywheel. Bolts, in sequence: 71–75 ft. lbs. (97–102 Nm) on the 2.0L engine or 45–49 ft. lbs. (61–67 Nm) on the 2.5L engine.
- Pilot bearing

➡**When installed, the pilot bearing should be 0–0.016 in. (0–0.4mm) below the surface of the crankshaft flange.**

11. Apply a small amount of molybdenum grease to the clutch disc and input shaft splines.

12. Install or connect the following:
- Clutch disc with the spring side of the disc toward the transaxle. Install the alignment tool to hold the disc in place.
- Pressure plate. Bolts: 13–18 ft. lbs.

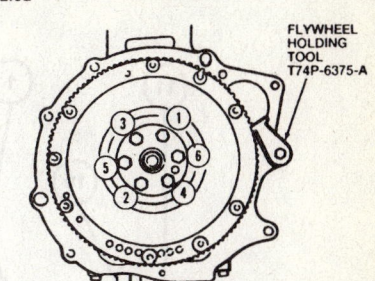

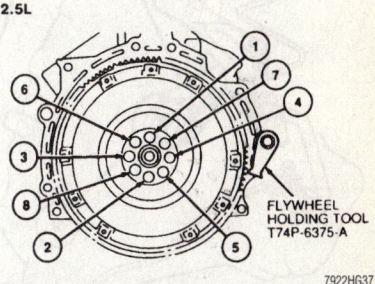

Flywheel bolt tightening sequences

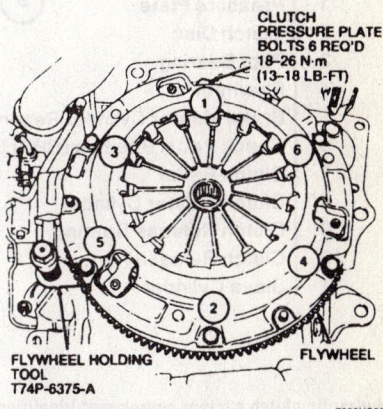

Clutch pressure plate bolt tightening sequence

(18–26 Nm) in the proper sequence.
- Transaxle assembly
- Negative battery cable

Hydraulic Clutch System

BLEEDING

➡**The fluid reservoir must be maintained at the ¾ level or higher during air bleeding.**

1. Before servicing the vehicle, refer to the precautions in the beginning of this section.

Turn to Section 5 for brake system applications

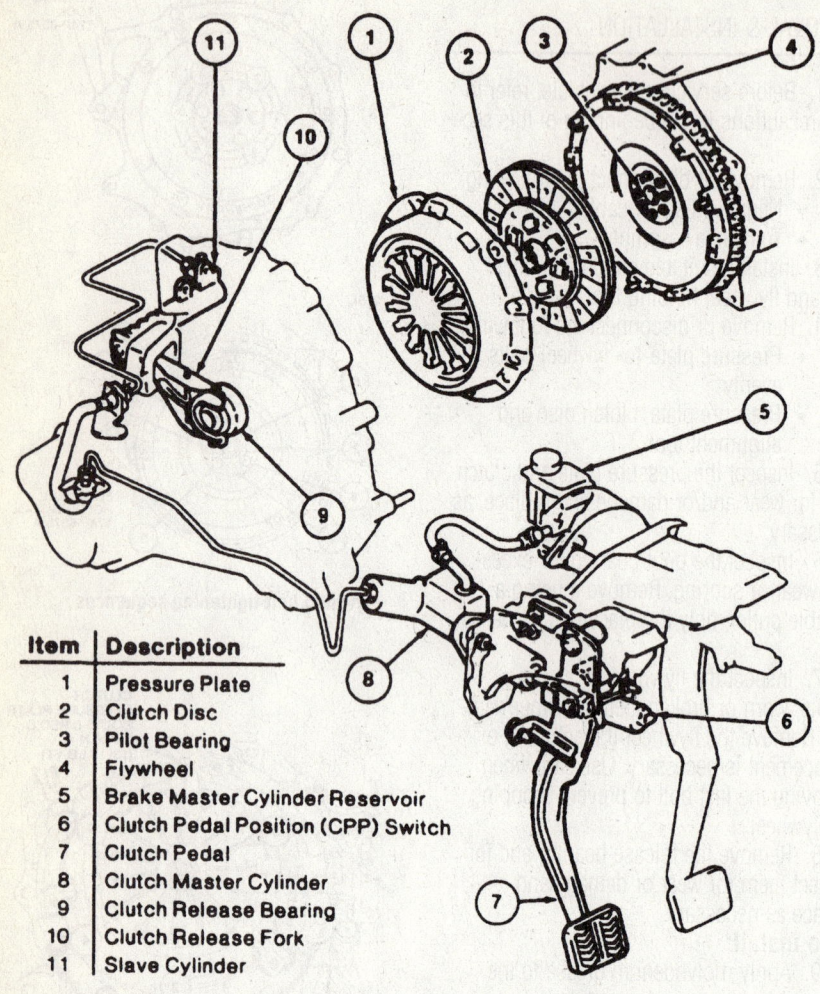

Item	Description
1	Pressure Plate
2	Clutch Disc
3	Pilot Bearing
4	Flywheel
5	Brake Master Cylinder Reservoir
6	Clutch Pedal Position (CPP) Switch
7	Clutch Pedal
8	Clutch Master Cylinder
9	Clutch Release Bearing
10	Clutch Release Fork
11	Slave Cylinder

7922HG48

Hydraulic clutch system component identification

2. Remove the bleeder cap from the slave cylinder and attach a vinyl hose to the bleeder screw.

3. Place the other end of the hose in a clear container partially filled with brake fluid.

4. Have an assistant slowly pump the clutch pedal several times.

5. With the clutch pedal depressed, loosen the bleeder screw to release the fluid and air.

6. Tighten the bleeder screw. Repeat this procedure until there are no air bubbles in the fluid in the container.

7. When complete, tighten the bleeder screw to 53–78 inch lbs. (6–8 Nm).

8. Check the fluid level and fill as required.

9. Check for leaks and proper clutch operation.

Halfshaft

REMOVAL & INSTALLATION

1. Before servicing the vehicle, refer to the precautions in the beginning of this section.

2. Remove or disconnect the following:
- Negative battery cable
- Loosen but do not remove the hub nut
- Wheel and inner fender splash guards
- Stabilizer link assembly from the lower control arm
- Ball joint from the lower control arm

➡ **If removing the right halfshaft, remove the support bearing bracket from the cylinder block.**

- Halfshaft from the transaxle
- Hub nut
- Halfshaft out of the wheel hub

➡ **Install a transaxle plug into the halfshaft opening of the transaxle case and into the differential side gear; this will keep the differential side gear from falling out of place.**

To install:

➡ **If replacing a halfshaft and joint on an ABS equipped vehicle, install a new front brake anti-lock sensor indicator.**

3. Install or connect the following:
- On the end of the halfshaft, a new circlip. Be sure the end-gap is positioned at the top of the splines.
- Halfshaft into the differential. Be sure the retaining clip clicks into the differential side gear groove.
- Halfshaft through the wheel hub and install a new attaching nut. Do not tighten the nut at this time.
- On the right halfshaft, the halfshaft support bearing. Bolts: 31–46 ft. lbs. (42–62 Nm).

➡ **The support bearing bolts must be tightened in the proper sequence, as shown earlier in this section.**

- Ball joint in the steering knuckle and install the clamp bolt/nut. Nut: 25–42 ft. lbs. (34–57 Nm).
- Stabilizer link assembly. Nuts: 27–40 ft. lbs. (36–54 Nm).
- Splash shields and wheel. Halfshaft nut: 174–235 ft. lbs. (235–319 Nm).

➡ **Stake the nut. If the nut splits or cracks after staking, it must be replaced with a new nut.**

- Negative battery cable

CV-JOINT OVERHAUL

Disassemble the driveshaft as shown in the exploded view. The clip (3) should be removed with a prytool, while the snapring (5) should be removed with snapring pliers or a similar tool.

Pull the ball bearings, inner ring and cage out of the shaft while still assembled. Then insert a prytool between the inner ring and cage to gently pry each ball out. Finally, matchmark the cage and inner ring and then turn the cage 30 degrees and pull it off the inner ring.

Assemble in reverse order, being careful to repack bearings in the grease supplied with the kit in a thorough manner.

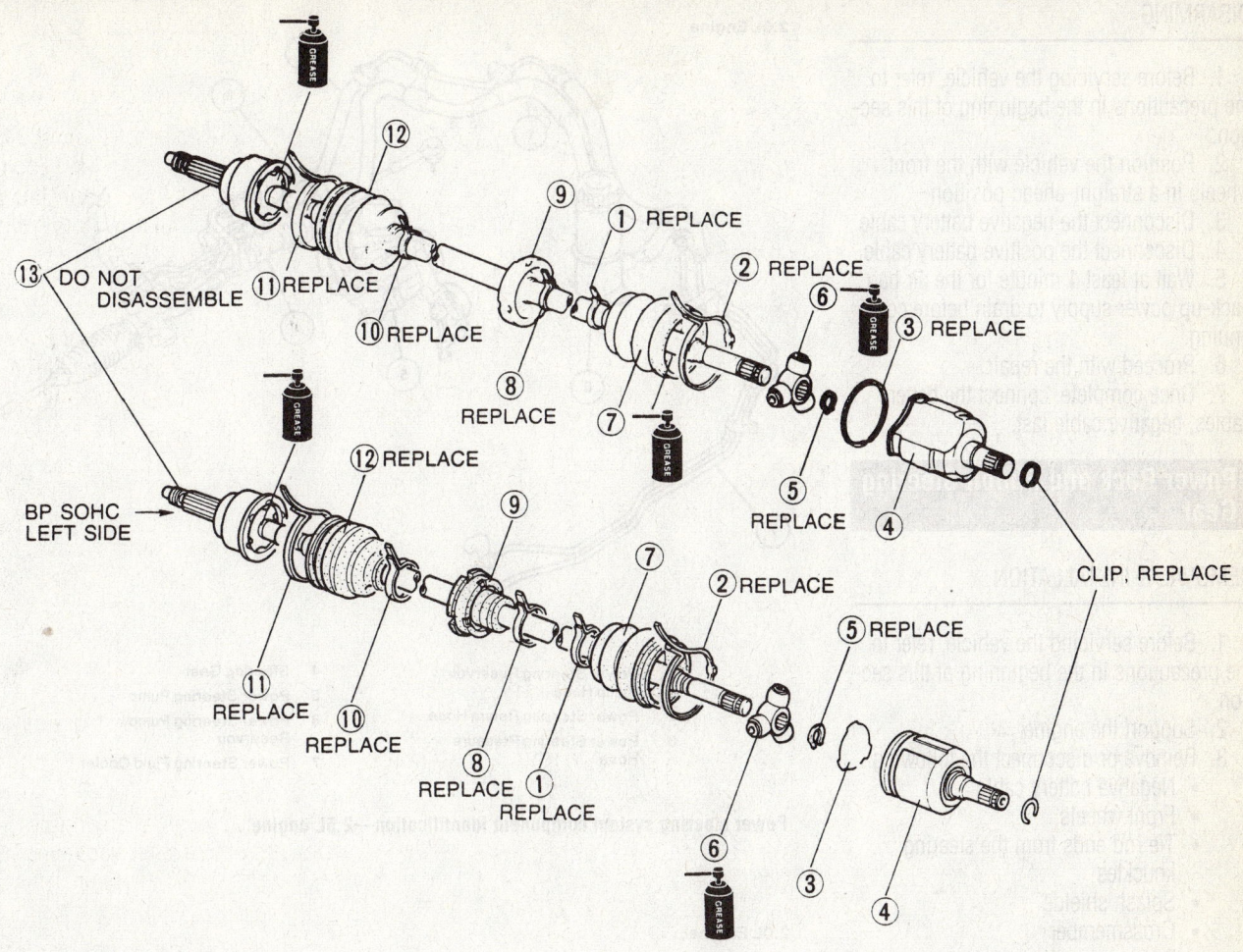

1. Boot band
2. Boot band
3. Clip
4. Outer ring
   Inspect inside bore for wear, corrosion, and scoring
5. Snap ring
6. Tripod joint
7. Boot

8. Band
9. Dynamic damper
10. Boot band
11. Boot band
12. Boot
13. Shaft and ball joint assembly
    Inspect splines for damage and wear
    Inspect wheel-side joint for excessive play and rough rotation

89547G04

Exploded view of the halfshaft assemblies

STEERING AND SUSPENSION

Air Bag

✳✳ CAUTION

The Supplemental Restraint System (SRS) must be disarmed before removing the air bag module. Failure to do so may cause accidental deployment of the air bag, resulting in unnecessary SRS repairs and/or personal injury.

PRECAUTIONS

Several precautions must be observed when handling the inflator module to avoid accidental deployment and possible personal injury.
• Never carry the inflator module by the wires or connector on the underside of the module.
• When carrying a live inflator module, hold securely with both hands, and ensure that the bag and trim cover are pointed away.
• Place the inflator module on a bench or other surface with the bag and trim cover facing up.
• With the inflator module on the bench, never place anything on or close to the module that may be thrown in the event of an accidental deployment.

DISARMING

1. Before servicing the vehicle, refer to the precautions in the beginning of this section.
2. Position the vehicle with the front wheels in a straight-ahead position.
3. Disconnect the negative battery cable.
4. Disconnect the positive battery cable.
5. Wait at least 1 minute for the air bag back-up power supply to drain before continuing.
6. Proceed with the repair.
7. Once complete, connect the battery cables, negative cable last.

Power Rack and Pinion Steering Gear

REMOVAL & INSTALLATION

1. Before servicing the vehicle, refer to the precautions in the beginning of this section.
2. Support the engine.
3. Remove or disconnect the following:
   - Negative battery cable
   - Front wheels.
   - Tie rod ends from the steering knuckles
   - Splash shields
   - Crossmember
   - Rear engine support
   - 2.5L engine, the Oxygen (O_2S) sensor connectors
   - Exhaust pipes from the manifolds
   - Power steering hoses
   - Steering shaft U-joint shield
   - Ground wire bracket from the rear transaxle support bracket
   - Transaxle support bracket (4EAT and MTX transaxles only)
   - Rack and pinion assembly mounting brackets
   - Steering column lower yoke-to-power steering gear input shaft and bolt
   - Manual transaxle control rod aside
4. Position a jack under the front subframe.
   - 6 sub-frame bolts and 2 nuts
   - Vent tube
   - Upper stabilizer bar link nuts
5. Lower the sub-frame to allow removal of the rack and pinion assembly. Remove the rack and pinion assembly from the driver's side of the vehicle.
   To install:

➡**If a new rack and pinion assembly is being installed or if the old assembly**

2.5L Engine

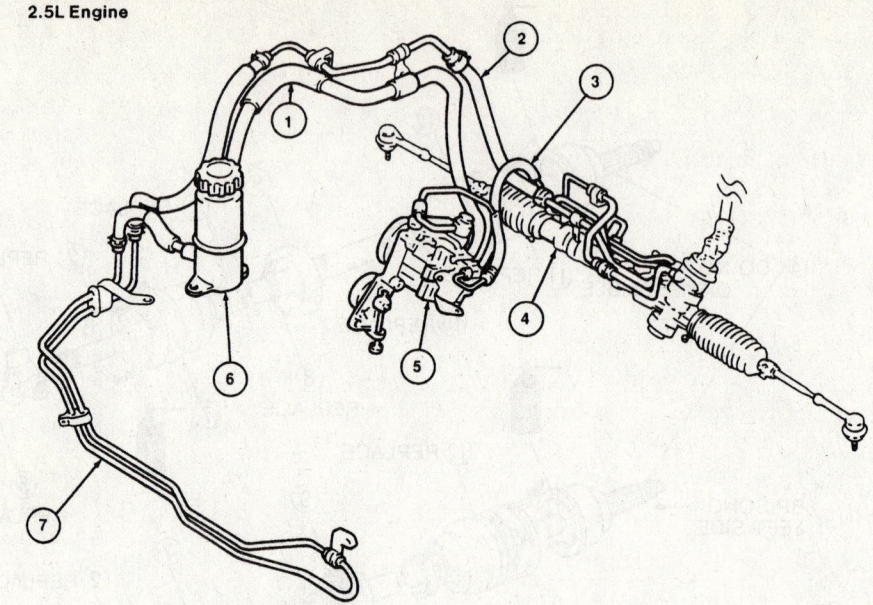

1	Power Steering Reservoir Pump Hose		4	Steering Gear
2	Power Steering Return Hose		5	Power Steering Pump
3	Power Steering Pressure Hose		6	Power Steering Pump Reservoir
			7	Power Steering Fluid Cooler

7922HG50

Power steering system component identification—2.5L engine

2.0L Engine

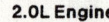
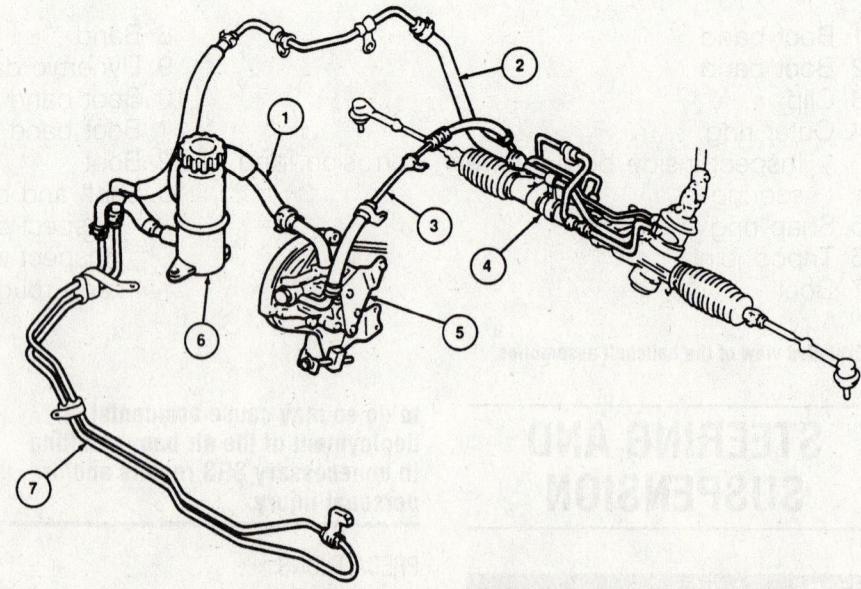

1	Power Steering Reservoir Pump Hose		4	Steering Gear
2	Power Steering Return Hose		5	Power Steering Pump
3	Power Steering Pressure Hose		6	Power Steering Pump Reservoir
			7	Power Steering Fluid Cooler

7922HG51

Power steering system component identification—2.0L engine

was turned, place the assembly into a soft-jawed vise and rotate the steering gear input shaft, counting the number of turns lock-to-lock. Back the steering gear input shaft up one-half of the number of the turns counted to center the rack and pinion. Do not damage the input shaft splines.

6. Position the rack and pinion assembly in the vehicle.

7. Install or connect the following:
- Steering column lower yoke-to-power steering gear input shaft and bolt. Bolt: 13–20 ft. lbs. (18–26 Nm)
- Sub-frame. Bolts: 69–97 ft. lbs. (93–131 Nm)
- Upper stabilizer bar link. Nuts: 27–40 ft. lbs. (36–54 Nm)
- Vent tube
- Rack and pinion assembly mounting brackets. Bolts: 28–38 ft. lbs. (38–51 Nm)
- Rear transaxle support insulator. Through-bolt: 63–86 ft. lbs. (85–117 Nm).
- Rear transaxle support bracket bolts. Tighten to 50–68 ft. lbs. (67–93 Nm)
- Ground wire bracket to the rear engine mount
- Steering shaft U-joint shield and bolt and tighten securely
- Power steering lines
- Manual transaxle: the control rod. Nut: 28–38 ft. lbs. (38–51 Nm).
- 2.5L engine: Exhaust pipes. Nuts: 38 ft. lbs. (51 Nm)
- O₂S sensor connectors

8. Install the rear engine support. Tighten the rear engine support nuts and bolts as follows:

   a. Tighten **A** to 55–77 ft. lbs. (75–104 Nm)

   b. Tighten **B** to 50–68 ft. lbs. (67–93 Nm)

   c. Tighten **C** to 32–44 ft. lbs. (44–60 Nm)

9. Install or connect the following:
- Crossmember. Bolts: 69–97 ft. lbs. (93–131 Nm)
- Tie rod ends to the steering knuckles. Nuts: 23–33 ft. lbs. (31–44 Nm).
- Splash shields
- Wheels. Lug nuts: 65–87 ft. lbs. (88–118 Nm).
- Power steering system fluid
- Negative battery cable

9. Check the front wheel alignment.

Strut and Spring

REMOVAL & INSTALLATION

Front

1. Before servicing the vehicle, refer to the precautions in the beginning of this section.

2. Remove or disconnect the following:
- Negative battery cable
- Wheel
- With ABS, the electrical harness and bracket
- U-clip from the brake line hose and slide it out of the strut bracket
- Strut-to-steering knuckle bolts and nuts
- 4 upper strut mounting bolts
- Strut from the vehicle

3. Place the strut assembly in a suitable holding fixture. Loosen, but do not remove the shock mounting nut. Compress the spring with a suitable compressor tool, then remove the shock mounting nut. Gradually release the spring compressor to relieve the spring tension.

4. Remove the strut mounting bracket, thrust bearing, upper spring seat with insulator, dust tube and bumper.

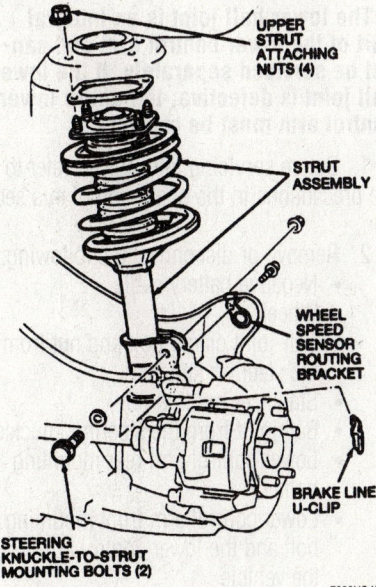

Front strut attaching nut and bolt locations

5. Remove the coil spring and the lower spring insulator. Replace components as required.

To install:

➡ Face the direction indicator on the strut mounting bracket towards the rear outboard position during reassembly. Be sure that the notch on the upper spring seat faces towards the outboard position during reassembly.

6. Perform the following:
- Compress the coil spring with the compressor and install the spring and the lower insulator onto the strut.
- Install the bumper, dust tube, upper spring seat with insulator, thrust bearing and the strut mounting bracket.
- Install the strut mounting nut and tighten to 66–86 ft. lbs. (89–117 Nm).
- Gradually release the compressor tool and remove it from the strut assembly.

7. Install or connect the following:
- Strut in the shock tower with the direction indicator facing the rear outboard position. Nuts: 34–46 ft. lbs. (46–63 Nm).
- Strut on the steering knuckle. Nuts and bolts: 68–86 ft. lbs. (93–117 Nm).
- Caliper and the brake hose in its bracket.
- With ABS: the bracket and harness. Bracket: 13–19 ft. lbs. (18–25 Nm).
- Wheel. Lug nuts to 65–87 ft. lbs. (88–118 Nm).
- Negative battery cable.

8. Check the wheel alignment.

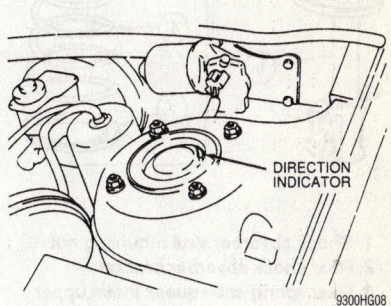

Be sure the direction indicator is positioned as shown

Rear

1. Before servicing the vehicle, refer to the precautions in the beginning of this section.
2. Remove or disconnect the following:
   - Rear wheel
   - With ABS, the speed sensor routing bracket
   - Brake line U-clip from the strut housing
   - Spindle-to-strut mounting nuts and bolts
   - Trunk side panel
   - Upper strut attaching nuts and strut

✷✷ CAUTION

Do not attempt to remove the coil spring from the strut assembly without compressing the coil spring first.

3. Use a spring compressor tool to compress the coil spring.
4. Remove the mounting nut from the strut and disassemble the strut components.

To install:

5. Assemble the strut, the compressed coil spring and related components.

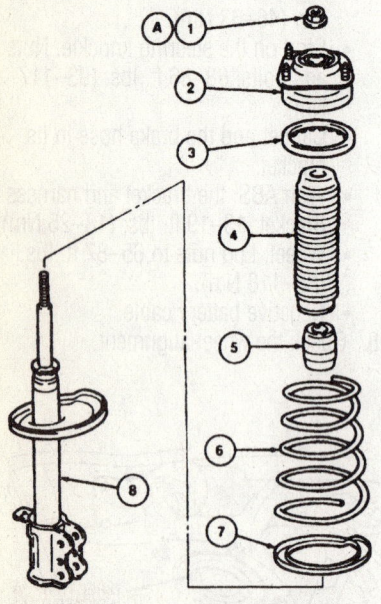

1. Shock absorber strut mounting nut
2. Rear shock absorber bracket
3. Rear spring anti-squeak insert, upper
4. Shock absorber dust tube
5. Rear shock absorber dust boot
6. Rear spring
7. Rear spring anti-squeak insert, lower
8. Rear shock absorber
A. 66–87 ft. lb. (89–117 Nm)

7922HG45

Exploded view of the rear strut assembly

6. Install the mounting nut and tighten to 66–87 ft. lbs. (89–117 Nm). Release the compressor and remove the strut.

➡**Be sure that the lower coil spring is seated properly.**

7. Install or connect the following:
   - Strut in the vehicle. Upper nuts: 34–46 ft. lbs. (46–63 Nm)
   - Trunk side panel
   - Spindle-to-strut bolts, and nuts and tighten to 69–87 ft. lbs. (93–117 Nm)
   - Brake line U-clip
   - Wheel speed sensor bracket
   - Wheel. Lug nuts: 65–87 ft. lbs. (88–118 Nm)
   - Check the wheel alignment.

Lower Ball Joint

REMOVAL & INSTALLATION

The lower ball joint is an integral part of the lower control arm and cannot be serviced separately. If the lower ball joint is defective, the entire lower control arm must be replaced.

Lower Control Arm

REMOVAL & INSTALLATION

➡**The lower ball joint is an integral part of the lower control arm and cannot be serviced separately. If the lower ball joint is defective, the entire lower control arm must be replaced.**

1. Before servicing the vehicle, refer to the precautions in the beginning of this section.
2. Remove or disconnect the following:
   - Negative battery cable
   - Wheel
   - Ball-joint clamp bolt and nut from the steering knuckle
   - Stabilizer bar link nut
   - Ball joint from the steering knuckle
   - Lower control arm rear mounting bolts
   - Lower control arm front mounting bolt and the lower control arm from the vehicle

To install:

3. Install or connect the following:
   - Lower control arm. Rear mounting bolts: 69–96 ft. lbs. (93–131 Nm).
   - Lower control arm front mounting bolt, and tighten to 58–78 ft. lbs. (78–106 Nm).
   - Ball joint stud into the steering

knuckle. Clamp bolt to 32–40 ft. lbs. (43–54 Nm).
   - Stabilizer bar link nut and tighten to 27–40 ft. lbs. (36–54 Nm).
   - Wheel. Lug nuts: 65–87 ft. lbs. (88–118 Nm).

CONTROL ARM BUSHING REPLACEMENT

1. For the front bushing, cut away the projecting rubber portion of the bushing with a knife.
2. Press out the old bushing.
3. To install a new bushing, apply soapy water to the new bushing and pull it into place.
4. For the rear bushing, remove the retaining nut on the control arm and slide the bushing, complete with bracket, from the control arm.
5. Installation is the reverse of the removal procedure.

Stabilizer Bar

REMOVAL & INSTALLATION

Front

1. Remove or disconnect the following:
   - Front wheels
   - Engine undercover
2. Install an engine support device.
3. Remove or disconnect the following:
   - Tie rod end/steering knuckle assembly
   - Transverse member from under the engine
   - Engine mount member
   - Front exhaust pipe from the manifold
   - Stabilizer nuts and insulator pad
   - Steering lines
   - Steering gear and linkage assembly
   - Lower arm and front crossmember assembly bolts and remove the assembly from the vehicle.
   - Remaining stabilizer bar bolts and remove the stabilizer bar

To install:

4. Install or connect the following:
   - Stabilizer bar and install the mounting bolts. If the mounting bushings were removed, make sure that they are replaced to the original positions and that the bushings are aligned with the marks on the bar. Tighten the stabilizer bar bolts to 32–43 ft. lbs. (43–59 Nm).
   - Lower arm and front crossmember assembly to the vehicle. Tighten the

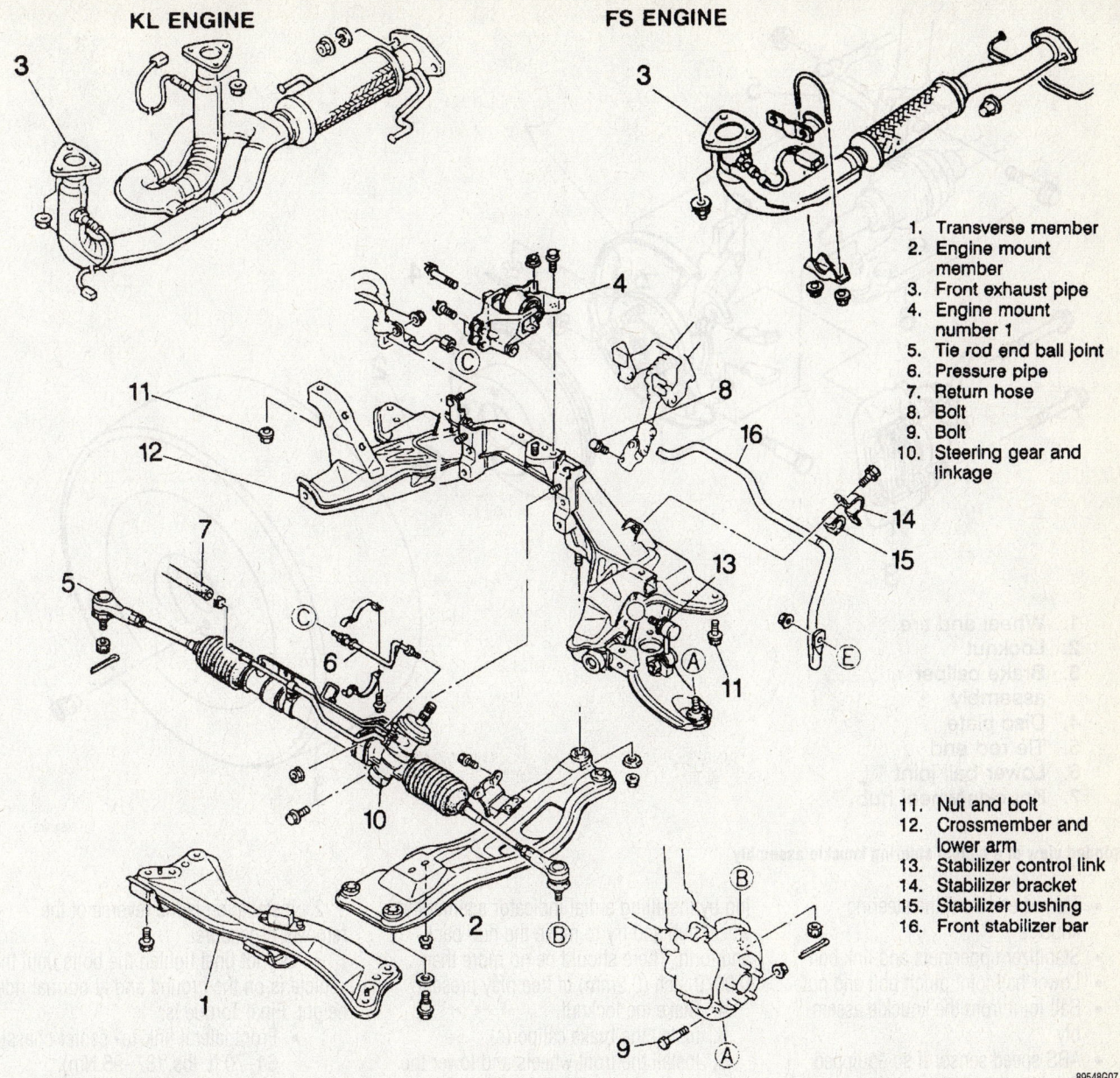

KL ENGINE

FS ENGINE

1. Transverse member
2. Engine mount member
3. Front exhaust pipe
4. Engine mount number 1
5. Tie rod end ball joint
6. Pressure pipe
7. Return hose
8. Bolt
9. Bolt
10. Steering gear and linkage

11. Nut and bolt
12. Crossmember and lower arm
13. Stabilizer control link
14. Stabilizer bracket
15. Stabilizer bushing
16. Front stabilizer bar

89548G07

Exploded view of the stabilizer bar assembly and related components

mounting bolts to 69–93 ft. lbs. (93–127 Nm).
- Steering gear and linkage. Tighten the mounting nuts to 27–38 ft. lbs. (37–52 Nm) and connect the lines to the steering gear and linkage.
- Insulator plate and install the stabilizer nuts. Tighten the stabilizer nuts to 32–45 ft. lbs. (43–61 Nm).
- Exhaust pipe gaskets and tighten the nuts to 27–38 ft. lbs. (37–52 Nm).
- Engine mount member
- Transverse member

- Tie rod end to the steering knuckle. Replace the cotter pin.
- Engine support device and install the under engine cover.
- Wheels

Rear

1. Remove or disconnect the following:
- Rear wheels
- Stabilizer bar-to-link mounting nut and protectors
- Stabilizer bracket and remove the stabilizer bar
- Stabilizer bushings and inspect the

bushing for deterioration or wear. Replace if necessary.
2. Installation is the reverse of the removal procedure.

Steering Knuckle

REMOVAL & INSTALLATION

1. Remove or disconnect the following:
- Wheels
- Center locknut and discard
- Caliper assembly
- Rotor

Turn to Section 5 for brake system applications

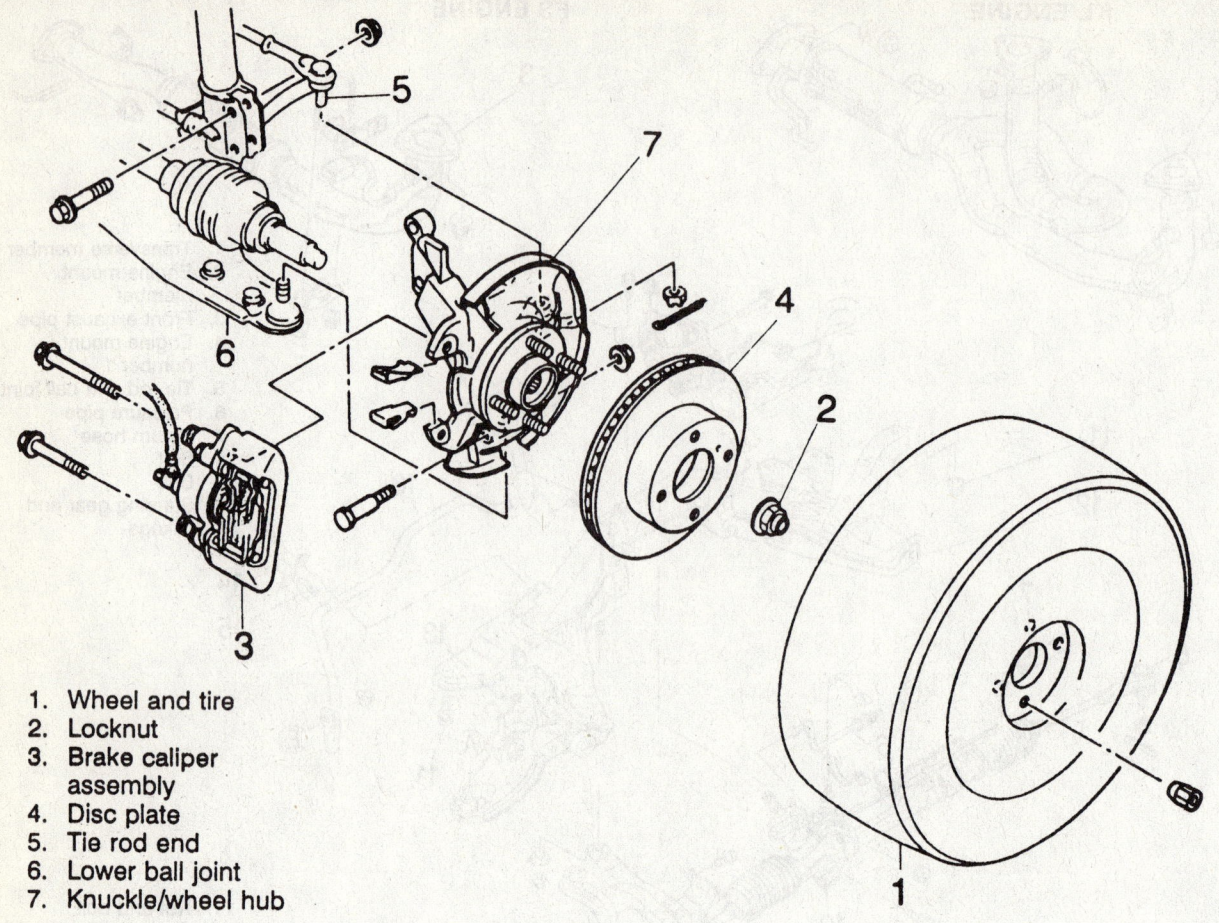

1. Wheel and tire
2. Locknut
3. Brake caliper
   assembly
4. Disc plate
5. Tie rod end
6. Lower ball joint
7. Knuckle/wheel hub

89548G08

Exploded view of a typical steering knuckle assembly

- Tie rod end from the steering knuckle
- Stabilizer upper nuts and link bolt
- Lower ball joint pinch bolt and nut
- Ball joint from the knuckle assembly
- ABS speed sensor if so equipped
- Driveshaft from the knuckle assembly
- Knuckle assembly

To install:

2. Install or connect the following:
- Knuckle assembly in place. Loosely tighten the knuckle to shock absorber bolt.
- Lower arm ball joint to the knuckle and tighten the pinch bolt
- Driveshaft
- Stabilizer control link
- ABS speed sensor and tighten the bolts to 12–17 ft. lbs. (16–23Nm).
- Tie rod ends to the knuckle. Replace the cotter pins.
- New wheel hub lock nut and tighten the locknut to 174–235 ft. lbs. (235–319 Nm).
3. Check the end play of the wheel bearing by installing a dial indicator against the wheel hub and try to move the hub back and forth. There should be no more than 0.0079 inch (0.2mm) of free play present.
4. Stake the locknut.
5. Install the brake caliper(s).
6. Install the front wheels and lower the vehicle.
7. With the vehicle lowered check all of the bolts and retorque as necessary.
8. Inspect the front end alignment and adjust as necessary.

Rear Control Arms and Links

REMOVAL & INSTALLATION

1. Remove or disconnect the following:
- Wheels
- Access cap from the underside of the rear crossmember
- Lateral links and trailing link. If removing the rear lateral link, paint an alignment mark on the cam plate and crossmember for assembly reference.

2. Installation is the reverse of the removal procedure.
3. Do not final tighten the bolts until the vehicle is on the ground and at normal ride height. Final Torque is:
- Front lateral link-to- center chassis: 64–70 ft. lbs. (87–95 Nm).
- Lateral link-to-axle through bolt: 64–86 ft. lbs. (87–116 Nm).
- Trailing arm-to-axle bolt: 69–93 ft. lbs. (94–126 Nm).
- Trailing arm-to-body bolt: 55–69 ft. lbs. (75–93 Nm).

Wheel Bearings

ADJUSTMENT

➡️**Wheel bearings are sealed units.**

1. Before servicing the vehicle, refer to the precautions in the beginning of this section.
2. Remove or disconnect the following:
- Wheel
- If equipped, the disc brake caliper

3. Rotate the drum or rotor to be sure there is no brake drag.

4. Position a suitable dial indicator.

5. Check the wheel bearing end-play. End-play should not exceed 0.002 in. (0.05mm). If the end-play exceeds specification, replace the wheel bearing or hub/bearing assembly, as required.

REMOVAL & INSTALLATION

Front

1. Before servicing the vehicle, refer to the precautions in the beginning of this section.

2. Remove or disconnect the following:
- Negative battery cable
- Wheel
- Wheel hub retaining nut. Discard the nut after removal; it must not be reused.
- With ABS, the 2 anti-lock sensor and bracket
- Tie rod end from the steering knuckle
- Lower control arm ball joint clamp nut/bolt. Using a prybar, pry the

lower control arm downward and separate the ball joint from the steering knuckle.
- Steering knuckle-to-strut attaching bolts
- Caliper and rotor
- Steering knuckle/hub assembly off of the halfshaft. Do not let the halfshaft hang on the inner CV-joint or the joint could be pulled apart.
- Steering knuckle, hub and wheel bearing assembly from the vehicle
- Grease seal from the knuckle

3. Press the hub from the knuckle. If the inner race remains on the hub, grind a section of the inner race to approximately 0.020 in. (0.5mm) and use a chisel to remove it. Wear appropriate eye protection.

4. Remove the snapring from the steering knuckle.

➡**Wheel bearings are contained within a sealed unit and are not serviceable.**

5. Press the wheel bearing from the knuckle.

➡**Unless the disc brake rotor dust shield is damaged, it should be left on the steering knuckle; it is pressed on**

and must be replaced if removed or damaged.

To install:

6. Inspect the steering knuckle and hub for cracks, wear and scoring. Replace parts as necessary.

7. Press in the wheel bearing. Be sure the press tool contacts only the outer bearing race or the bearing will be damaged. Install the snapring.

8. Press the hub into the steering knuckle. Be sure the inner bearing race is supported or the bearing will be damaged.

9. Press the seal into the knuckle.

10. Grease the halfshaft splines. Slide the hub/steering knuckle onto the halfshaft and position it into the strut bracket.

11. Install or connect the following:
- Strut-to-steering knuckle bolts and nuts and tighten to 68–86 ft. lbs. (93–117 Nm).
- Lower control arm ball joint into the steering knuckle. Clamp bolt and nut: 25–42 ft. lbs. (34–57 Nm).
- Disc brake rotor
- Caliper anchor bracket. Bolts: 58–72 ft. lbs. (78–98 Nm).

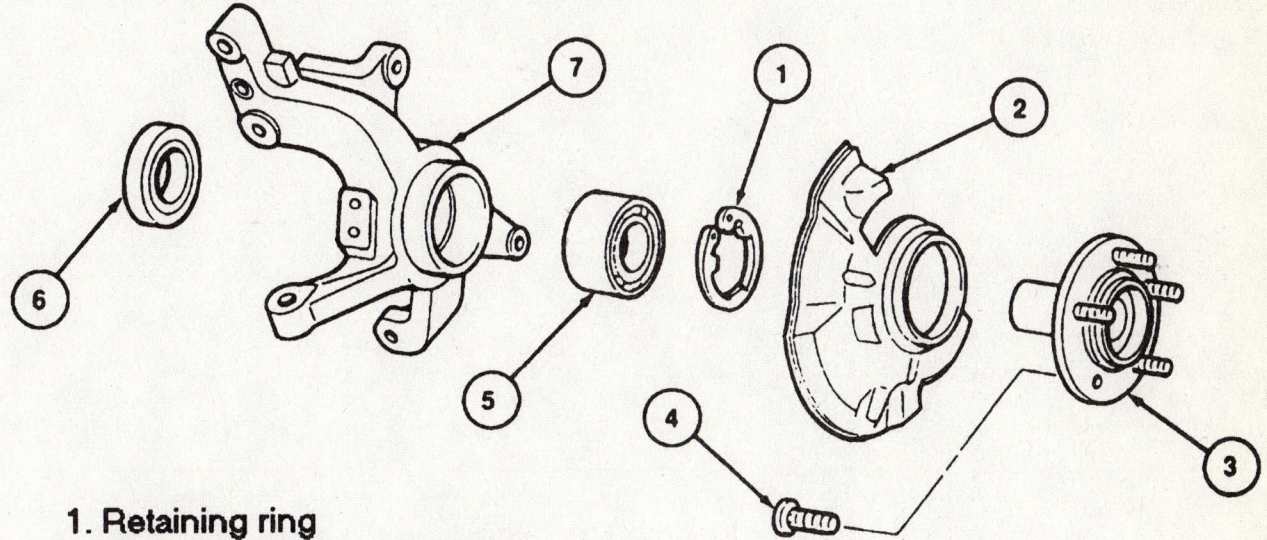

1. Retaining ring
2. Front disc brake rotor shield
3. Wheel hub
4. Wheel hub bolt
5. Front wheel bearing
6. Inner wheel bearing oil seal
7. Front wheel knuckle

7922HG44

Exploded view of the front hub and knuckle assembly, showing the wheel bearings

- Tie rod end to the steering knuckle. Nut: 22–33 ft. lbs. (29–44 Nm). Install a new cotter pin.
- With ABS, the anti-lock brake sensor and bracket. Bolts: 12–17 ft. lbs. (16–23 Nm).
- New hub nut and tighten the nut to 174–235 ft. lbs. (235–319 Nm). Stake the hub nut, using a chisel with a rounded cutting edge or similar tool.
- Wheel. Lug nuts: 65–87 ft. lbs. (88–118 Nm).
- Negative battery cable

Rear

➡ **The wheel bearing cannot be disassembled from the hub; it must be replaced as an assembly.**

1. Before servicing the vehicle, refer to the precautions in the beginning of this section.
2. Remove or disconnect the following:
   - Negative battery cable
   - Rear wheel
   - Wheel hub retainer. Discard the nut.
   - With rear disc brakes, the caliper and rotor
   - With rear drum brakes, remove the brake drum

- Wheel bearing and hub assembly from the wheel spindle

To install:

3. Install or connect the following:
   - Wheel bearing and hub assembly
   - With rear disc brakes, the rotor caliper
   - With rear drum brakes, the brake drum
   - New wheel hub retainer. Hub retainer: 130–174 ft. lbs. (177–235 Nm). Stake the nut.
   - Wheel. Lug nuts: 65–87 ft. lbs. (88–118 Nm).
   - Negative battery cable

FORD MOTOR CO.

Ford-Contour • Mercury-Mystique • 1999-01 Cougar

18

PRECAUTIONS

Before servicing any vehicle, please be sure to read all of the following precautions, which deal with personal safety, prevention of component damage, and important points to take into consideration when servicing a motor vehicle:

• Never open, service or drain the radiator or cooling system when the engine is hot; serious burns can occur from the steam and hot coolant.

• Observe all applicable safety precautions when working around fuel. Whenever servicing the fuel system, always work in a well-ventilated area. Do not allow fuel spray or vapors to come in contact with a spark, open flame, or excessive heat (a hot drop light, for example). Keep a dry chemical fire extinguisher near the work area. Always keep fuel in a container specifically designed for fuel storage; also, always properly seal fuel containers to avoid the possibility of fire or explosion. Refer to the additional fuel system precautions later in this section.

• Fuel injection systems often remain pressurized, even after the engine has been turned **OFF**. The fuel system pressure must be relieved before disconnecting any fuel lines. Failure to do so may result in fire and/or personal injury.

• Brake fluid often contains polyglycol ethers and polyglycols. Avoid contact with the eyes and wash your hands thoroughly after handling brake fluid. If you do get brake fluid in your eyes, flush your eyes with clean, running water for 15 minutes. If eye irritation persists, or if you have taken brake fluid internally, IMMEDIATELY seek medical assistance.

• The EPA warns that prolonged contact with used engine oil may cause a number of skin disorders, including cancer. You should make every effort to minimize your exposure to used engine oil. Protective gloves should be worn when changing oil. Wash your hands and any other exposed skin areas as soon as possible after exposure to used engine oil. Soap and water, or waterless hand cleaner should be used.

• All new vehicles are now equipped with an air bag system, often referred to as a Supplemental Restraint System (SRS) or Supplemental Inflatable Restraint (SIR) system. The system must be disabled before performing service on or around system components, steering column, instrument panel components, wiring and sensors. Failure to follow safety and disabling procedures could result in accidental air bag deployment, possible personal injury and unnecessary system repairs.

• Always wear safety goggles when working with, or around, the air bag system. When carrying a non-deployed air bag, be sure the bag and trim cover are pointed away from your body. When placing a non-deployed air bag on a work surface, always face the bag and trim cover upward, away from the surface. This will reduce the motion of the module if it is accidentally deployed. Refer to the additional air bag system precautions later in this section.

• Clean, high quality brake fluid from a sealed container is essential to the safe and proper operation of the brake system. You should always buy the correct type of brake fluid for your vehicle. If the brake fluid becomes contaminated, completely flush the system with new fluid. Never reuse any brake fluid. Any brake fluid that is removed from the system should be discarded. Also, do not allow any brake fluid to come in contact with a painted surface; it will damage the paint.

• Never operate the engine without the proper amount and type of engine oil; doing so WILL result in severe engine damage.

• Timing belt maintenance is extremely important. Many models utilize an interference-type, non-freewheeling engine. If the timing belt breaks, the valves in the cylinder head may strike the pistons, causing potentially serious (also time-consuming and expensive) engine damage. Refer to the maintenance interval charts in the front of this manual for the recommended replacement interval for the timing belt, and to the timing belt section for belt replacement and inspection.

• Disconnecting the negative battery cable on some vehicles may interfere with the functions of the on-board computer system(s) and may require the computer to undergo a relearning process once the negative battery cable is reconnected.

• When servicing drum brakes, only disassemble and assemble one side at a time, leaving the remaining side intact for reference.

• Only an MVAC-trained, EPA-certified automotive technician should service the air conditioning system or its components.

ENGINE REPAIR

➡ **Disconnecting the negative battery cable on some vehicles may interfere with the operation of the on-board computer system. The computer may undergo a relearning process once the negative battery cable is reconnected.**

Alternator

REMOVAL

2.0L Engine

1. Before servicing the vehicle, refer to the precautions in the beginning of this section.
2. Remove or disconnect the following:
   • Negative battery cable
   • Air intake resonator
   • Alternator electrical connections
   • Ground cable
   • Right front wheel
   • Right splash shield
   • Radiator splash shield
   • Accessory drive belt
   • Alternator. Remove the upper mounting bolt last.

➡ **There is a limited amount of space in which to remove the alternator. Do not damage any hoses or cables.**

2.5L Engine

1997–98 MODELS

1. Before servicing the vehicle, refer to the precautions in the beginning of this section.
2. Remove or disconnect the following:
   • Negative battery cable
   • Accessory drive belt
   • Right halfshaft
   • Exhaust system Y pipe
   • Right splash shield
   • Alternator wiring connectors
   • Alternator rear support bracket
   • Alternator

1999–01 MODELS

1. Before servicing the vehicle, refer to the precautions in the beginning of this section.
2. Remove or disconnect the following:
   • Negative battery cable
   • Right front wheel
   • Right splash shield
   • Accessory drive belt
   • Right outer tie rod end

- Alternator wiring connectors
- Alternator rear support bracket
- Alternator

INSTALLATION

2.0L Engine

1. Install or connect the following:
   - Alternator. Tighten the mounting bolts to 33 ft. lbs. (45 Nm).
   - Accessory drive belt
   - Radiator splash shield
   - Right splash shield
   - Right front wheel. Tighten the lug nuts to 63 ft. lbs. (86 Nm).
   - Ground cable
   - Alternator electrical connections
   - Air intake resonator
   - Negative battery cable

2.5L Engine

1997–98 MODELS

1. Install or connect the following:
   - Alternator. Tighten the mounting bolts to 33 ft. lbs. (45 Nm).
   - Alternator rear support bracket. Tighten the bracket bolts to 18 ft. lbs. (25 Nm).
   - Alternator wiring connectors
   - Right splash shield
   - Exhaust system Y pipe
   - Right halfshaft
   - Accessory drive belt
   - Negative battery cable

1999–01 MODELS

1. Install or connect the following:
   - Alternator. Tighten the mounting bolts to 33 ft. lbs. (45 Nm).
   - Alternator rear support bracket. Tighten the bracket bolts to 18 ft. lbs. (25 Nm).
   - Alternator wiring connectors
   - Right outer tie rod end. Tighten the nut to 21 ft. lbs. (28 Nm).
   - Accessory drive belt
   - Right splash shield
   - Right front wheel. Tighten the lug nuts to 63 ft. lbs. (86 Nm).
   - Negative battery cable

Ignition Timing

ADJUSTMENT

The ignition timing is set at 10 degrees Before Top Dead Center (BTDC) and is not adjustable.

Engine Assembly

REMOVAL & INSTALLATION

2.0L Engine

➡ **The engine and transaxle are removed as an assembly.**

1. Before servicing the vehicle, refer to the precautions in the beginning of this section.
2. Drain the engine oil and coolant.
3. Drain the transaxle fluid.
4. Attach an engine support fixture to the engine lifting eyes.
5. Secure the A/C condenser to the radiator support with safety wire.
6. Loosen the suspension strut lock nuts five turns.
7. Remove or disconnect the following:
   - Battery
   - Mass Air Flow (MAF) sensor connector
   - Intake Air Temperature (IAT) sensor connector
   - Air cleaner outlet tube
   - Air cleaner
   - Exhaust Gas Recirculation (EGR) vacuum supply hose, if equipped
   - EGR pressure sensor wiring, if equipped
   - EGR exhaust tube, if equipped
   - Engine wiring harness connector
   - Accelerator cable
   - Upper drive belt cover
   - Front wheels
   - Left, right and center splash shields
   - Accessory drive belt
   - Stabilizer bar links
   - Outer tie rod ends
   - Lower ball joints
   - Lower radiator retainers
   - Both Heated Oxygen (HO$_2$S) sensor connectors
   - Power steering hoses
   - Brake booster vacuum line at intake manifold
   - Steering gear and heat shield
   - Right support insulator and bracket
   - Front exhaust pipe
   - Left support insulator
   - A/C accumulator attachment bolts
   - 4 subframe bolts and the subframe
8. If equipped with a manual transaxle, place the shift lever in neutral. Lock in place with special tool Gear Lever Aligner T97P-7025-A.
9. Remove or disconnect the following:

- Clutch hydraulic line
- Shift cables
- Reverse lamp switch connector
- Vehicle Speed (VSS) sensor connector

10. If equipped with an automatic transaxle, remove or disconnect the following:
    - Torque converter
    - Transaxle control wiring connector
    - Range switch connector
    - Ground strap
    - Shift cable
    - VSS and bracket
    - Transaxle cooler lines and fluid tube
    - Turbine Shaft Speed (TSS) sensor connector

11. For all vehicles, remove or disconnect the following:
    - Halfshafts
    - Upper and lower radiator hoses
    - 2 ground cables from radiator support
    - Coolant hose bracket and power steering hose
    - Coolant hoses at the recovery tank
    - Radiator and cooling fan
    - A/C compressor
    - Power steering pump
    - Heater hoses and bracket
    - Powertrain Control Module (PCM) connector
    - Vacuum hoses at intake manifold
    - Battery cables at battery tray
    - Fuel supply and return lines

12. Support the engine and transaxle assembly from below.
13. Remove or disconnect the following:
    - Top support fixture
    - Coolant recovery tank.
    - Front and rear engine mount brackets

14. Raise the vehicle away from the engine and transaxle assembly
15. To separate the engine and transaxle, support the engine with a shop hoist, support the transaxle with a transmission jack.
16. Remove or disconnect the following:
    - Starter
    - Ground cable
    - Transaxle flange bolts
    - Engine from the transaxle.

To install:

➡ **Replace all snaprings, split pins, and self-locking nuts.**

17. Install or connect the following:
    - Transaxle flange bolts. Tighten the bolts to 35 ft. lbs. (48 Nm).
    - Ground cable
    - Starter motor. Tighten the bolts to 35 ft. lbs. (48 Nm).

18. Lower the vehicle onto the engine and transaxle assembly.

19. Install or connect the following:
- Front and rear engine mount brackets. Tighten the nuts and bolts finger-tight.
- Top support fixture
- Fuel supply and return lines
- Battery cables to battery tray. Secure with cable ties.
- Vacuum hoses to intake manifold
- PCM connector
- Heater hoses and bracket
- Power steering pump. Tighten the bolts to 35 ft. lbs. (47 Nm).
- A/C compressor. Tighten the bolts to 18 ft. lbs. (25 Nm).
- Radiator and cooling fan
- Power steering hose and coolant hose bracket
- 2 ground cables to the radiator support
- Upper and lower radiator hoses
- Halfshafts

20. If equipped with a manual transaxle, install or connect the following:
- Clutch hydraulic line
- Shift cables
- VSS connector
- Reverse lamp switch connector

21. Remove the Gear Lever Aligner.

22. If equipped with an automatic transaxle, install or connect the following:
- TSS connector
- Torque converter. Tighten the nuts to 27 ft. lbs. (36 Nm).
- Transaxle cooler lines and fluid tube
- VSS and bracket
- Shift cable
- Ground strap
- Range switch connector
- Transaxle control wiring connector
- Powertrain Alignment Gauge T94P-6000-AH to the subframe.
- Lower radiator retainers to the subframe.
- Subframe and attach the front bolts. Do not tighten the bolts at this time.
- Steering gear to the subframe. Tighten the bolts to 96 ft. lbs. (130 Nm).
- Steering gear heat shield.
- Power steering line and coolant line brackets.
- Subframe Alignment Pin Set T94P-2100-AH.
- Subframe bolts. Tighten the bolts in a diagonal pattern to 96 ft. lbs. (130 Nm).
- Center bolt to the Powertrain Alignment Tool. Tighten it to 22 ft. lbs. (30 Nm).

- Right engine support insulator. Tighten the center bolt to 88 ft. lbs. (120 Nm), and the restrictor mounting bolts to 35 ft. lbs. (48 Nm).
- Rear engine mounting bracket nuts to 61 ft. lbs. (83 Nm).

☀☀ CAUTION

Do not twist or strain the front engine mounting bracket.

- Front engine mounting bracket. Torque to 61 ft. lbs. (83 Nm).

23. Remove the Powertrain Alignment Tool.

24. Install or connect the following:
- Left engine support insulator. Tighten the center bolt to 88 ft. lbs. (120 Nm), and the restrictor mounting bolts to 35 ft. lbs. (48 Nm).
- Brake booster vacuum hose
- A/C accumulator attachment bolts
- Front exhaust pipe. Use a new gasket and tighten the fasteners to 33 ft. lbs. (45 Nm).
- Attach the power steering lines to the subframe
- HO$_2$S connectors. Secure the wiring harness with cable ties.
- Lower ball joints. Tighten to 61 ft. lbs. (83 Nm)
- Outer tie rod ends. Tighten the nuts to 19 ft. lbs. (26 Nm)
- Stabilizer bar links. Tighten to 35 ft. lbs. (47 Nm)
- Left, right and center splash shields
- Front wheels. Tighten the lug nuts to 63 ft. lbs. (86 Nm).

25. Remove the top engine support.

26. Install or connect the following:
- Coolant recovery tank and hoses
- Ground cables at the radiator support
- Accelerator cable
- Accessory drive belt
- Upper drive belt cover. Tighten the bolts to 18 ft. lbs. (24 Nm).
- EGR exhaust tube, if equipped
- EGR pressure sensor connector, if equipped
- EGR vacuum supply, if equipped
- CKP sensor connector
- ECT sensor connector
- Main wiring harness connector
- Air cleaner and air outlet tube
- IAT sensor connector
- MAF sensor connector
- Battery

27. Tighten the suspension strut locknuts to 34 ft. lbs. (46 Nm).

28. Fill the engine crankcase and cooling system.

29. Fill the transaxle.

30. Start the engine and check for leaks and proper operation.

➡Whenever the vehicle subframe is removed or lowered, the wheel alignment should be checked.

2.5L Engine

➡The engine and transaxle are removed as an assembly.

1. Before servicing the vehicle, refer to the precautions in the beginning of this section.

2. Drain the engine cooling system and engine oil.

3. Recover the A/C refrigerant.

4. Secure the radiator and fan shroud assembly to the radiator support, using safety wire.

5. Remove or disconnect the following:
- Battery cables
- Water pump pulley shield
- Steering shaft joint at cowl inside the vehicle
- Air cleaner
- Catalytic converter
- Exhaust crossover pipe
- Front wheels
- Stabilizer bar links
- Outer tie rod ends
- Lower ball joints
- Separate the halfshafts from the hubs
- A/C accumulator mounting screws
- Speedomoter cable
- Vehicle Speed (VSS) sensor connector
- Torque converter nuts (automatic)
- Accelerator cable and bracket
- Cruise control cable, if equipped
- Engine control wiring harness connectors
- Power steering pump reservoir
- Power steering return hose
- Power steering pressure hose
- Powertrain Control Module (PCM) connector and ground strap
- Coolant recovery tank
- Shift cable and bracket (automatic)
- Shift rod and stabilizer bar (manual)
- Clutch slave cylinder fluid pipe (manual)
- Transaxle range switch connector (automatic)
- Power brake booster vacuum pipe
- Radiator hoses
- Heater hoses
- Block heater wiring, if equipped

- A/C suction and discharge hoses
- Transaxle oil cooler lines (automatic)
- Lower radiator supports
- A/C compressor harness connector
- Bumper cover braces
- Front engine support insulator and bracket
- Transaxle support insulator
6. Support the powertrain from below
7. Remove or disconnect the following:
   - Subframe bolts.
   - Powertrain from the vehicle.
8. Attach an engine hoist to the engine lifting eyes.
9. Remove the left and right engine support insulators and lift the powertrain away from the subframe.
10. Support the transaxle from below.
11. Remove or disconnect the following:
   - Halfshafts.
   - Starter, wiring harness and ground cable.
   - Engine from the transaxle.

To install:

→**Replace all snaprings, split pins, and self-locking nuts.**

12. Install or connect the following:
   - Engine to the transaxle. Tighten the transaxle flange bolts to 25–34 ft. lbs. (34–46 Nm).
   - Halfshafts to the transaxle.
   - Starter, wiring harness connectors.
   - Ground cable.
   - Powertrain Alignment Gauge T94P-6000-AH to the subframe and position the powertrain. Tighten the center bolt to 20 ft. lbs. (27 Nm).
   - Right engine support insulator. Leave the bolts finger-tight.
   - Subframe Alignment Pin Set 94P-2100-AH and raise the subframe to the vehicle. Tighten the subframe bolts to 92–100 ft. lbs. (125–135 Nm).
13. Remove the alignment pins.
14. Install or connect the following:
   - Front engine support insulator and bracket. Tighten the nuts to 84 inch lbs. (10 Nm).

→**The left and right support insulators must be aligned in the middle of the support insulator brackets.**

   - Right engine support insulator-to-subframe bolts to 30–41 ft. lbs. (41–55 Nm).
   - Front engine support bracket nuts to 52–70 ft. lbs. (70–95 Nm).

- Engine and transmission support insulator. Torque nuts to 30–41 ft. lbs. (41–55 Nm) for automatic transaxles or 52–70 ft. lbs. (70–95 Nm) for manual transaxles.
- Right front engine support insulator. Torque through-bolt to 75–102 ft. lbs. (103–137 Nm).
15. Remove the powertrain alignment gauge.
16. Install or connect the following:
   - Left front engine support insulator to the subframe. Tighten the retaining bolts to 30–41 ft. lbs. (41–55 Nm). Tighten the through-bolt to 75–102 ft. lbs. (103–137 Nm).
   - A/C compressor wiring harness
   - Lower radiator supports. Tighten the retaining bolts to 71–97 inch lbs. (8–11 Nm).
   - Transaxle oil cooler lines (automatic)
   - A/C suction and discharge hoses
   - Block heater wiring, if equipped
   - Radiator hoses
   - Heater hoses
   - Power brake booster vacuum pipe
   - Transaxle range switch connector (automatic)
   - Clutch slave cylinder fluid pipe (manual)
   - Shift cable and bracket (automatic). Tighten the retaining bolts to 15–19 ft. lbs. (20–25 Nm).
   - Shift rod and stabilizer bar (manual). Tighten the shift rod bolt to 17 ft. lbs. (23 Nm) and the stabilizer nut to 41 ft. lbs. (55 Nm).
   - Coolant recovery tank
   - PCM connector and ground strap
   - Power steering pressure hose
   - Power steering return hose
   - Power steering pump reservoir
   - Engine control wiring harness connectors
   - Cruise control cable, if equipped
   - Accelerator cable and bracket. Tighten the bolts to 71–106 inch lbs. (8–12 Nm).
   - Torque converter nuts (automatic). Tighten the retaining nuts in an alternating sequence to 54–64 ft. lbs. (73–87 Nm).
   - VSS sensor connector
   - Speedometer cable
   - A/C accumulator mounting screws
   - Halfshafts to front hubs. Use new nuts and tighten to 246 ft. lbs. (340 Nm).
   - Outer tie rod ends. Tighten the nuts to 21 ft. lbs. (28 Nm).

- Lower ball joints. Tighten the bolts to 37–43 ft. lbs. (50–58 Nm).
- Stabilizer bar links. Tighten the nuts to 35 ft. lbs. (48 Nm).
- Front wheels. Tighten the lug nuts to 63 ft. lbs. (86 Nm).
- Exhaust crossover pipe
- Catalytic converter
- Air cleaner
- Steering shaft joint. Tighten the bolt to 18 ft. lbs. (24 Nm).
- Water pump pulley shield
- Battery cables
17. Fill the crankcase and cooling system.
18. Check all fluid levels.
19. Evacuate and recharge the air conditioning system.
20. Start the engine and check for leaks and proper operation.

→**Whenever the vehicle subframe is removed or lowered, the wheel alignment should be checked.**

Water Pump

REMOVAL & INSTALLATION

2.0L Engine

1. Before servicing the vehicle, refer to the precautions in the beginning of this section.
2. Drain the cooling system.
3. Remove or disconnect the following:
   - Negative battery cable
   - Lower radiator hose

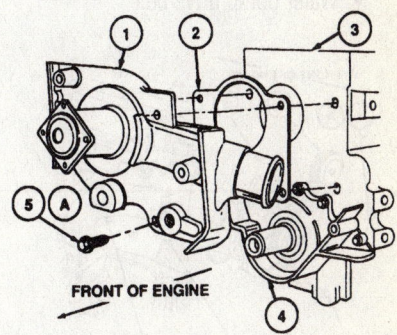

FRONT OF ENGINE

1. Water pump
2. Water pump housing gaskets
3. Cylinder block
4. Oil pump
5. Bolt(4)
A. 12-15 ft. lb.(16-20 Nm)

7922JG01

Exploded view of the water pump mounting—2.0L engine

- Accessory drive belt
- Timing belt
- Water pump

To install:

4. Install or connect the following:
- Water pump. Tighten the bolts to 12–15 ft. lbs. (16–20 Nm).
- Timing belt
- Accessory drive belt
- Lower radiator hose
- Negative battery cable

5. Fill the cooling system and inspect for leaks

2.5L Engine

➡ **The 3 water pump bolts are torque-to-yield and must be replaced.**

1. Before servicing the vehicle, refer to the precautions in the beginning of this section.
2. Drain the engine cooling system.
3. Remove or disconnect the following:
- Negative battery cable
- Water pump pulley shield
- Water pump drive belt
- Coolant hoses
- Water pump and pump housing

4. Separate the water pump from the pump housing.

To install:

5. Install the water pump to the pump housing. Tighten the fasteners to 16–18 ft. lbs. (22–25 Nm).

6. Install or connect the following:
- Water pump and pump housing. Use new bolts and tighten them to 11–13 ft. lbs. (15–18 Nm), plus 85–95 degrees.
- Coolant hoses
- Water pump drive belt

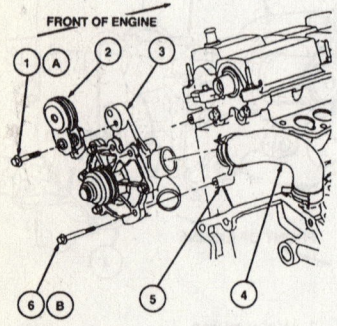

FRONT OF ENGINE

1. Bolt
2. Water pump drive belt tensioner
3. Water pump
4. Water pump outlet hose
5. LH cylinder head
6. Bolt(3)
A. 71-106 in. lb.(8-12 Nm)
B. 11-13 ft. lb.(15-18 Nm) then rotate 85-95°

7922JG02

Exploded view of the water pump mounting—2.5L engine

- Water pump pulley shield
- Negative battery cable

7. Fill the cooling system and check for leaks.

Cylinder Head

REMOVAL & INSTALLATION

2.0L Engine

➡ **The cylinder head bolts are a torque-to-yield design and must be replaced.**

1. Before servicing the vehicle, refer to the precautions in the beginning of this section.
2. Drain the cooling system.
3. Remove or disconnect the following:
- Negative battery cable
- Accessory drive belt
- Power steering pump pulley cover
- Power steering pump
- Power steering pump support bracket
- Alternator bracket
- Valve cover
- Intake manifold
- Exhaust manifold
- Timing cover and timing belt
- Camshafts and valve tappets
- Right lifting eye
- Timing belt tensioner pulley
- Thermostat housing
- Ignition coil and bracket
- Spark plugs

4. Remove the cylinder head bolts in the reverse of the installation order, and remove the cylinder head.

To install:

5. Use a new gasket and install the cylinder head.

6. Use new cylinder head bolts and oil the threads.

➡ **Refer to Section one of this manual for the cylinder head torque sequence illustration. The illustration is located after the Torque Specification Chart.**

7. Tighten the cylinder head bolts in sequence and in the following steps:
   a. Step 1: Tighten all bolts to 15–22 ft. lbs. (20–30 Nm).
   b. Step 2: Tighten all bolts to 30–37 ft. lbs. (40–50 Nm).
   c. Step 3: Rotate all bolts 90–120 degrees.

8. Install or connect the following:
- Ignition coil and bracket
- Thermostat housing
- Timing belt tensioner pulley
- Right lifting eye

- Camshafts and valve tappets
- Timing cover and timing belt
- Exhaust manifold
- Intake manifold
- Valve cover
- Alternator bracket
- Power steering pump support bracket
- Power steering pump
- Accessory drive belt
- Power steering pump pulley cover
- Spark plugs
- Negative battery cable

9. Fill the cooling system and check for leaks.

10. Start the engine and check for proper operation.

2.5L Engine

➡ **The cylinder head bolts are a torque-to-yield design and must be replaced.**

1. Before servicing the vehicle, refer to the precautions in the beginning of this section.
2. Drain the crankcase and cooling system.
3. Remove or disconnect the following:
- Negative battery cable
- Air cleaner housing
- Accessory drive belts
- Upper and lower intake manifolds
- Valve covers
- Oil pan
- Alternator and bracket
- Left and right Heated Oxygen (HO$_2$S) sensors
- Catalytic converter and exhaust crossover tube
- Water pump
- Engine front cover and timing chains
- Camshafts and valve tappets
- Exhaust Gas Recirculation (EGR) pressure sensor
- EGR transducer
- EGR tube
- Coolant bypass
- Oil dipstick tube

4. Remove the cylinder head bolts in reverse of the tightening order and remove the cylinder heads.

To install:

5. Use new gaskets and install the cylinder heads.

6. Use new cylinder head bolts and oil the threads.

➡ **Refer to Section one of this manual for the cylinder head torque sequence illustration. The illustration is located after the Torque Specification Chart.**

7. Tighten the cylinder head bolts in sequence and in the following steps:

   a. Step 1: Tighten the bolts, in sequence, to 27–32 ft. lbs. (37–43 Nm).

   b. Step 2: Rotate the bolts, in sequence, 85–95 degrees.

   c. Step 3: Loosen the bolts, in sequence, a minimum of 1 full turn.

   d. Step 4: Tighten the bolts, in sequence, to 27–32 ft. lbs. (37–43 Nm).

   e. Step 5: Rotate the bolts, in sequence, 85–95 degrees.

   f. Step 6: Rotate the bolts, in sequence, an additional 85–95 degrees.

8. Install or connect the following:

- Oil dipstick tube
- Coolant bypass
- EGR tube
- EGR transducer
- EGR pressure sensor
- Camshafts and valve tappets
- Engine front cover and timing chains
- Water pump
- Catalytic converter and exhaust crossover tube
- Left and right HO$_2$S sensors
- Alternator and bracket
- Oil pan
- Valve covers
- Upper and lower intake manifolds
- Accessory drive belts
- Air cleaner housing
- Negative battery cable

9. Fill the cooling system and the engine crankcase.

10. Start the engine and check for leaks and proper operation.

Rocker Arms

REMOVAL & INSTALLATION

The 2.0L engine is not equipped with rocker arms, the camshaft directly actuates the valves through a hydraulic lifter.

2.5L Engine

1. Before servicing the vehicle, refer to the precautions in the beginning of this section.

2. Remove or disconnect the following:

- Battery
- Upper manifold
- Intake Manifold Runner Control (IMRC) actuator
- Spark plug wires and bracket
- Coolant reservoir breather hose bracket and wiring
- Fuel injector wiring harness

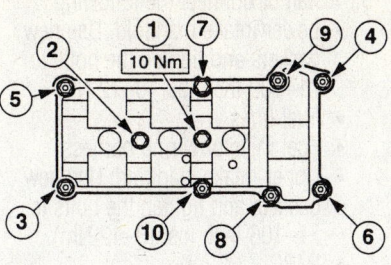

Valve cover bolt tightening sequence— 2.5L engine

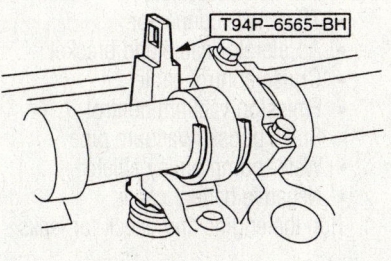

Valve spring compressor—2.5L engine

- Ignition coil
- Wiring harness brackets
- Valve covers. Remove the bolts in reverse sequence.
- Spark plugs.

3. Rotate the crankshaft so that the piston on the cylinder to be serviced is at bottom dead center with the valves closed.

4. Install an adapter in the spark plug hole and connect a compressed air supply at 102–144 psi.

5. Install special tool Valve Spring Compressor T94P-6565-BH.

6. Compress the valve spring and remove the roller finger follower. Repeat for each follower to be removed.

➡️**If the followers are to be reused, ensure that they are installed in the same position that they were removed from.**

To install:

7. Compress the valve spring and install the roller finger follower. Repeat for each follower to be installed.

8. Install or connect the following:

- Spark plugs
- Valve covers. Tighten the bolts in sequence to 88 inch lbs. (10 Nm).
- Wiring harness brackets
- Ignition coil
- Fuel injector wiring harness
- Coolant reservoir breather hose bracket and wiring

- Spark plug wires and bracket
- IMRC actuator
- Upper manifold
- Battery

9. Run the engine and check for leaks and proper operation.

Intake Manifold

REMOVAL & INSTALLATION

2.0L Engine

1. Before servicing the vehicle, refer to the precautions in the beginning of this section.

2. Remove or disconnect the following:

- Negative battery cable
- Air cleaner outlet pipe
- Cruise control cable
- Accelerator cable and bracket
- Throttle Position (TP) sensor connector
- Idle Air Control (IAC) connector
- Engine Coolant Temperature (ECT) sensor connector
- Fuel lines
- Injector wiring harness
- Fuel supply manifold with injectors attached
- Engine wiring harness
- Vacuum hoses
- Brake booster vacuum pipe
- Accessory drive belt

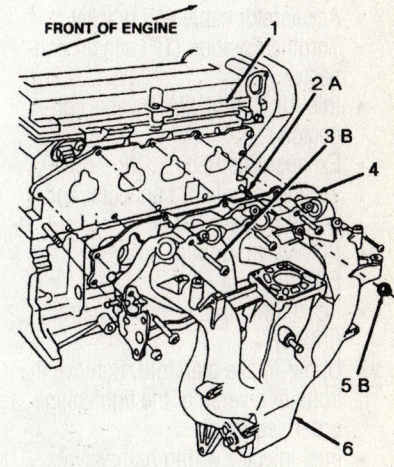

1. Cylinder head
2. Stud (2 req'd)
3. Bolt (8 req'd)
4. Intake manifold gasket
5. Nut (2 req'd)
6. Intake manifold
A. Tighten to 0-10 Nm (0-89 lb. in.)
B. Tighten to 16-20 Nm (12-15 lb. ft.)

Exploded view of the intake manifold mounting—2.0L engine

- Alternator
- Intake manifold.

To install:

3. Install or connect the following:
   - New gasket
   - Intake manifold. Tighten the fasteners to 13 ft. lbs. (18 Nm).

4. Install or connect the following:
   - Alternator
   - Accessory drive belt
   - Brake booster vacuum pipe
   - Vacuum hoses
   - Engine wiring harness
   - Fuel supply manifold with injectors attached
   - Injector wiring harness
   - Fuel lines
   - Accelerator cable and bracket
   - Cruise control cable
   - ECT sensor connector
   - IAC connector
   - TP sensor connector
   - Air cleaner outlet pipe
   - Negative battery cable

2.5L Engine

1. Before servicing the vehicle, refer to the precautions in the beginning of this section.

2. Remove or disconnect the following:
   - Negative battery cable
   - Water pump pulley shield
   - Brake booster vacuum pipe
   - Emission vacuum control
   - Cruise control cable
   - Accelerator cable and bracket
   - Throttle Position (TP) sensor connector
   - Idle Air Control (IAC) valve connector
   - Exhaust Gas Recirculation (EGR) vacuum regulator connector and vacuum hoses
   - PCV valve vacuum hose
   - EGR tube
   - Intake Manifold Runner Control (IMRC)
   - Upper intake manifold. Remove the bolts in reverse of the tightening order sequence
   - Fuel injector wiring harness
   - Fuel lines
   - Lower intake manifold. Remove the bolts in reverse of the tightening order sequence

To install:

➡Refer to Section one of this manual for the lower intake manifold torque sequence illustration. The illustration is located after the Torque Specification Chart.

3. Install or connect the following:
   - Lower intake manifold. Use new gaskets and tighten the bolts to 71–106 inch lbs. (8–12 Nm).
   - Fuel lines
   - Fuel injector wiring harness
   - Upper intake manifold. Use new gaskets and tighten the bolts to 71–106 inch lbs. (8–12 Nm).
   - IMRC
   - EGR tube
   - PCV valve vacuum hose
   - EGR vacuum regulator connector and vacuum hoses
   - IAC valve connector
   - TP sensor connector
   - Accelerator cable and bracket
   - Cruise control cable
   - Emission vacuum control
   - Brake booster vacuum pipe
   - Water pump pulley shield
   - Negative battery cable

4. Run the engine and check for leaks

Exhaust Manifold

REMOVAL & INSTALLATION

2.0L Engine

1. Before servicing the vehicle, refer to the precautions in the beginning of this section.

2. Remove or disconnect the following:

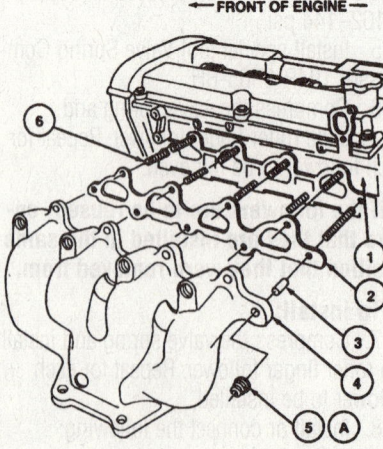

← FRONT OF ENGINE →

1 Cylinder Head
2 Exhaust Manifold Gasket
3 Spacer
4 Exhaust Manifold
5 Nut (9 Req'd)
6 Stud (9 Req'd)
A Tighten to 14-17 N·m (13-16 Lb-Ft)

7922JG09

Exhaust manifold and related components—2.0L engine

- Negative battery cable
- Air intake resonators
- Oil dipstick tube
- Exhaust manifold heat shield
- Heated Oxygen (HO2S) sensor
- Exhaust Gas Recirculation (EGR) tube and bracket, if equipped
- Catalytic converter
- 9 manifold retaining nuts and the exhaust manifold

To install:

3. Install or connect the following:
   - New gasket
   - Exhaust manifold. Tighten the nuts to 12 ft. lbs. (16 Nm).
   - Catalytic converter
   - EGR tube and bracket, if equipped
   - HO2S sensor
   - Exhaust manifold heat shield
   - Oil dipstick tube
   - Air intake resonators
   - Negative battery cable

4. Run the engine and check for leaks and proper operation

2.5L Engine

RIGHT SIDE

1. Before servicing the vehicle, refer to the precautions in the beginning of this section.

2. Remove or disconnect the following:

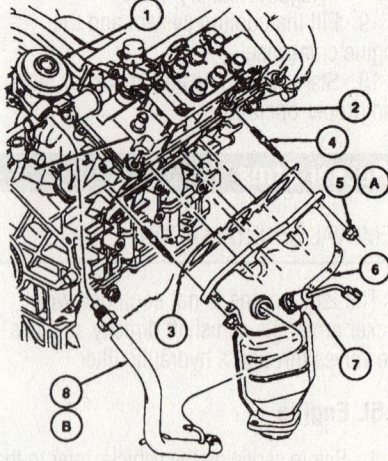

1 EGR Valve
2 RH Cylinder Head
3 Exhaust Manifold Gasket
4 Stud Bolt (6 Req'd)
5 Nut (6 Req'd)
6 RH Exhaust Manifold
7 Heated Oxygen Sensor
8 EGR Valve to Exhaust Manifold Tube
A Tighten to 18-22 N·m (13-16 Lb-Ft)
B Tighten to 35-45 N·m (26-33 Lb-Ft)

7922JG10

Exploded view of the right-side exhaust manifold mounting—2.5L engine

- Negative battery cable
- Alternator and bracket
- Heated Oxygen (HO2S) sensor
- Catalytic converter
- Halfshaft bearing support bracket
- Exhaust Gas Recirculation (EGR) tube
- Exhaust manifold

To install:

3. Install or connect the following:
- New gasket
- Exhaust manifold. Tighten the fasteners to 15 ft. lbs. (20 Nm).
- EGR tube
- Halfshaft bearing support bracket
- Catalytic converter
- HO2S sensor
- Alternator and bracket
- Negative battery cable

4. Run the engine and check for exhaust leaks and proper operation.

LEFT SIDE

1. Before servicing the vehicle, refer to the precautions in the beginning of this section.

2. Disconnect or remove:
- Negative battery cable
- Heated Oxygen (HO2S) sensor
- Exhaust crossover tube
- Radiator hose bracket
- 6 manifold retaining nuts and the exhaust manifold

To install:

3. Install or connect the following:
- New gasket
- Exhaust manifold. Tighten the nuts to 15 ft. lbs. (20 Nm).
- Radiator hose bracket
- Exhaust crossover tube
- HO2S sensor
- Negative battery cable

4. Run the engine and check for exhaust leaks and proper operation.

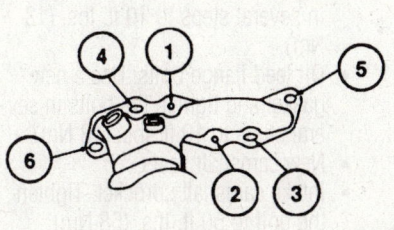

Exhaust manifold mounting bolt tightening sequence—2.5L engine

7922JG11

Front Crankshaft Seal

➡ The front crankshaft seal procedures apply only to engines equipped with timing belts. For the front seals on engines equipped with timing chains or gears, refer to the applicable procedure later in this section.

REMOVAL & INSTALLATION

2.0L Engine

1. Before servicing the vehicle, refer to the precautions in the beginning of this section.

2. Remove or disconnect the following:
- Negative battery cable
- Right splash shield
- Accessory drive belt
- Timing cover and timing belt. Refer to the timing belt unit repair section.
- Crankshaft sprocket
- Crankshaft front seal. Use a seal puller to protect the crankshaft surface from damage.

To install:

3. Lubricate and install the front crankshaft seal. Use special tool Seal Replacer T81P-6700-A and the crankshaft pulley bolt to press the seal into the oil pump housing.

4. Install or connect the following:
- Crankshaft sprocket
- Timing belt and timing cover
- Accessory drive belt
- Right splash shield
- Negative battery cable

5. Run the engine and check for leaks and proper operation.

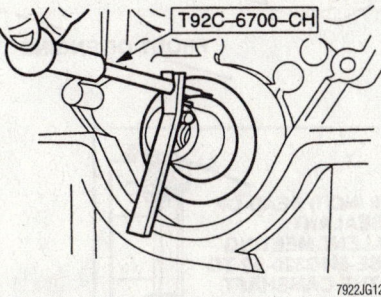

T92C-6700-CH

Removing the crankshaft front seal with Ford seal remover T92C-6700-CH—2.0L engine

7922JG12

Camshaft and Valve Lifters

REMOVAL & INSTALLATION

2.0L Engine

1997 MODELS

1. Before servicing the vehicle, refer to the precautions in the beginning of this section.

2. Remove or disconnect the following:
- Negative battery cable
- Air intake resonators
- Valve cover
- Timing cover
- Timing belt and camshaft sprockets.

➡ Mark the camshaft journal caps to the cylinder head for installation in the same position.

3. Loosen all of the camshaft journal cap bolts in pairs and in sequence 1 turn at a time.

➡ Remove the camshaft journal thrust caps last.

4. Remove or disconnect the following:
- All of the camshaft journal caps

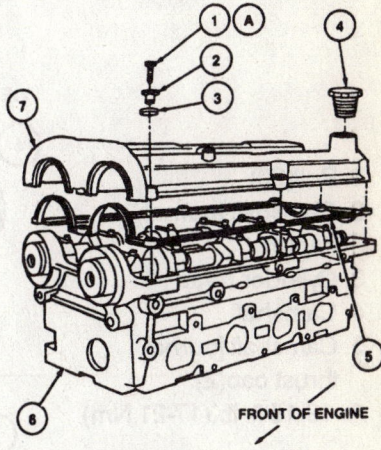

1. Bolt (10)
2. Spacer (10)
3. O-ring (10)
4. Oil filler cap
5. Valve cover gasket
6. Cylinder head
7. Valve cover
A. 53-71 in. lb. (6-8 Nm)

7922JG13

Valve cover and related components— 2.0L engine

Refer to Section 1 for engine rebuilding specifications

- Intake and exhaust camshafts and the camshaft front seals from the cylinder head

➡ If the valve lifters are to be reused, mark their locations to ensure that they will be installed into their correct positions.

- Valve lifters from the cylinder head

To install:

➡ Before installing the camshafts, the crankshaft must be positioned so that No. 1 cylinder is at TDC on its compression stroke.

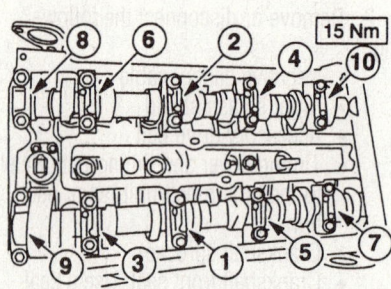

Remove the bearing cap bolts in pairs using the sequence shown—2.0L engine

1. Bolt(20)
2. Camshaft journal cap(8)
3. Cylinder head
4. Camshaft
5. Camshaft journal thrust cap(2)
A. 13-15 ft. lb.(17-21 Nm)

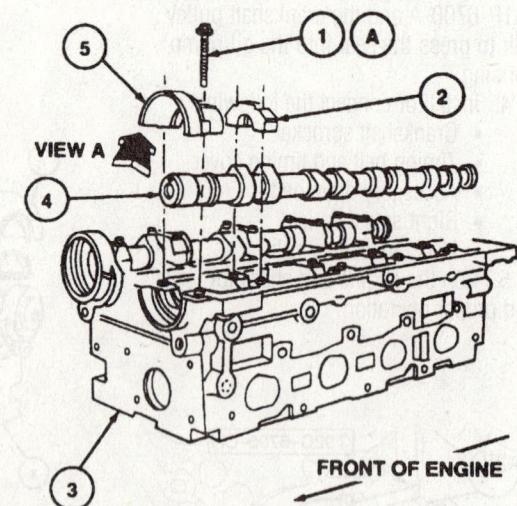

VIEW A

FRONT OF ENGINE

NOTE: APPLY A 3 mm (1/8 INCH) BEAD OF SILICONE GASKET AND SEALANT F1AZ-19562-A OR EQUIVALENT MEETING FORD SPECIFICATION WSE-M4G320-A2 TO SEALING SURFACES OF THE CAMSHAFT JOURNAL THRUST CAPS AS SHOWN.

VIEW A

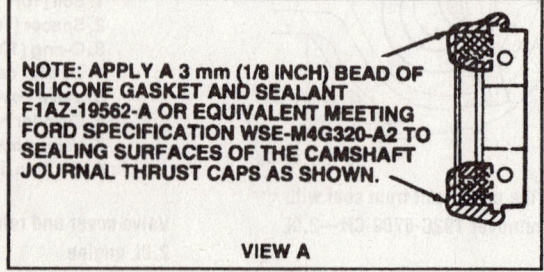

During assembly, apply sealant to the camshaft journal thrust cap as shown—2.0L engine

5. Install or connect the following:
- Valve lifters, Lubricate them
- Camshafts and journal caps. Tighten the bolts in sequence and in several steps to 11 ft. lbs. (15 Nm).
- New camshaft seals
- Camshaft sprockets. Tighten the bolts to 50 ft. lbs. (68 Nm).
- Timing belt and timing cover
- Valve cover
- Air intake resonators
- Negative battery cable

6. Run the engine and check for leaks and proper operation.

15 Nm

Camshaft journal cap retaining bolt tightening sequence—2.0L engine

1998–01 MODELS

1. Before servicing the vehicle, refer to the precautions in the beginning of this section.

2. Remove or disconnect the following:
- Negative battery cable
- Air intake resonators
- Valve cover
- Timing cover
- Timing belt
- Intake camshaft sprocket
- Exhaust gear oil plug
- Exhaust camshaft sprocket and Variable Camshaft Timing (VCT) hydraulic cylinder
- Oil feed flange bolts

➡ Mark the camshaft journal caps to the cylinder head for installation in the same position.

3. Loosen all of the camshaft journal cap bolts in pairs and in sequence 1 turn at a time.

➡ Remove the camshaft journal thrust caps last.

4. Remove or disconnect the following:
- All of the camshaft journal caps
- Intake and exhaust camshafts and the camshaft front seals from the cylinder head

➡ If the valve lifters are to be reused, mark their locations to ensure that they will be installed into their correct positions.

- Valve lifters from the cylinder head

To install:

➡ Before installing the camshafts, the crankshaft must be positioned so that No. 1 cylinder is at TDC on its compression stroke.

5. Install or connect the following:
- Valve lifters, Lubricate them
- Camshafts and journal caps. Tighten the bolts in sequence and in several steps to 10 ft. lbs. (13 Nm).
- Oil feed flange bolts. Use a new gasket and tighten the bolts in several steps to 10 ft. lbs. (13 Nm).
- New camshaft seals
- Intake camshaft sprocket. Tighten the bolt to 50 ft. lbs. (68 Nm).
- Exhaust camshaft sprocket and VCT hydraulic cylinder. Align the locating tab and bore as shown in the illustration and tighten the bolt to 88 ft. lbs. (120 Nm).
- Exhaust gear oil plug. Tighten to 27 ft. lbs. (37 Nm).

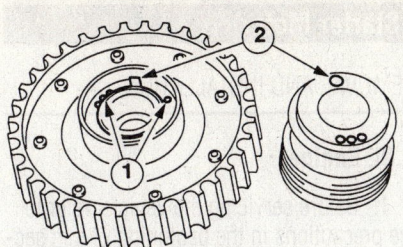

1. Oil passages and match mark
2. Locating tab and bore

9306HG03

Alignment of the exhaust camshaft sprocket and the VCT hydraulic cylinder— 1998–01 2.0L engines

- Timing belt and timing cover
- Valve cover
- Air intake resonators
- Negative battery cable

6. Run the engine and check for leaks and proper operation.

2.5L Engine

1. Before servicing the vehicle, refer to the precautions in the beginning of this section.

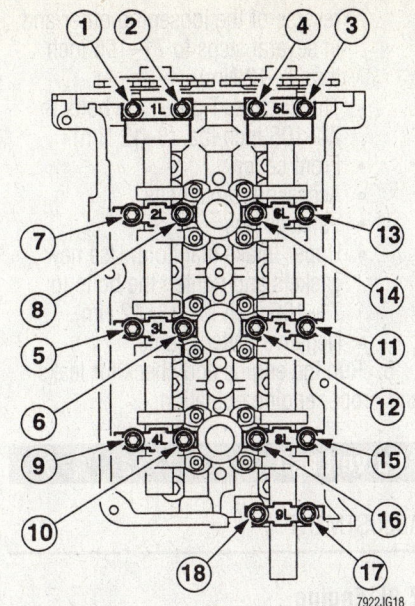

Left (front) cylinder head camshaft journal cap retaining bolt loosening sequence— 2.5L engine

7922JG18

2. Remove or disconnect the following:

- Negative battery cable

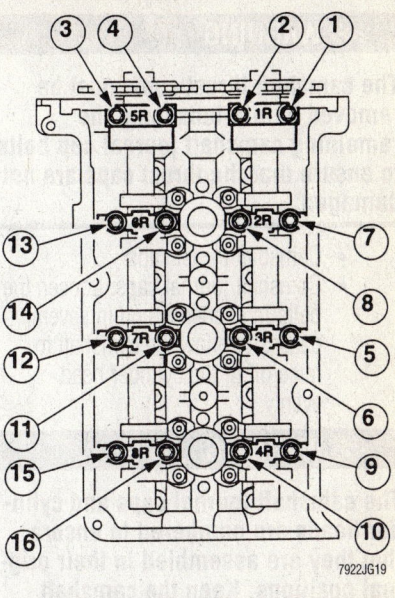

Right (rear) cylinder head camshaft journal cap retaining bolt loosening sequence—2.5L engine

7922JG19

- Upper intake manifold
- Valve covers
- Accessory drive belts
- Front cover and timing chains.

Camshafts Shown Removed From Cylinder Heads For Clarity

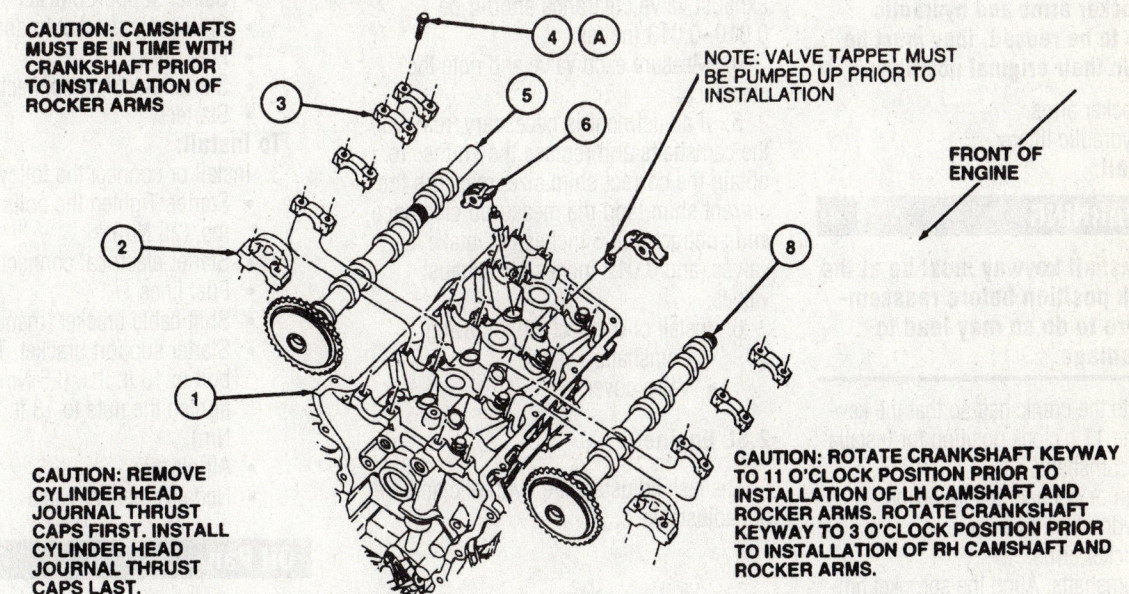

CAUTION: CAMSHAFTS MUST BE IN TIME WITH CRANKSHAFT PRIOR TO INSTALLATION OF ROCKER ARMS

NOTE: VALVE TAPPET MUST BE PUMPED UP PRIOR TO INSTALLATION

FRONT OF ENGINE

CAUTION: REMOVE CYLINDER HEAD JOURNAL THRUST CAPS FIRST. INSTALL CYLINDER HEAD JOURNAL THRUST CAPS LAST.

CAUTION: ROTATE CRANKSHAFT KEYWAY TO 11 O'CLOCK POSITION PRIOR TO INSTALLATION OF LH CAMSHAFT AND ROCKER ARMS. ROTATE CRANKSHAFT KEYWAY TO 3 O'CLOCK POSITION PRIOR TO INSTALLATION OF RH CAMSHAFT AND ROCKER ARMS.

1. Cylinder head
2. Camshaft journal thrust cap(2)
3. Camshaft journal cap(7)
4. Bolt(18)
5. LH intake camshaft
6. Rocker arm(12)
7. Valve tappet(12)
8. LH exhaust camshaft
A. 71-106 in. lb.(8-12 Nm)

7922JG17

Exploded view of camshaft mounting—2.5L engine

For engine torque specifications, refer to Section 1 of this manual

⁂ **WARNING**

The camshaft thrust caps must be removed before loosening the remaining camshaft journal cap bolts to ensure that the thrust caps are not damaged.

- Camshaft thrust caps
- Camshaft journal caps. Loosen the bolts in sequence and in several passes to allow the camshaft to raise off of the cylinder head evenly.

⁂ **WARNING**

The camshaft journal caps and cylinder heads are numbered to ensure that they are assembled in their original positions. Keep the camshaft journal caps from each cylinder head together; do not mix them with caps from another cylinder head. Failure to do so may result in engine damage.

- Camshaft journal caps with the retaining bolts installed
- Camshafts from the cylinder head.

➡ **If the rocker arms and hydraulic lifters are to be reused, they must be installed in their original positions.**

- Rocker arms.
- Hydraulic lifters

To install:

⁂ **WARNING**

The crankshaft keyway must be at the 11 o'clock position before reassembly. Failure to do so may lead to engine damage.

3. Rotate the crankshaft so that the keyway is at the 11 o'clock position for installation of the camshafts.
4. Install or connect the following:
- Hydraulic lifters
- Rocker arms.
- Camshafts. Align the sprocket timing marks.

➡ **Do not install the camshaft journal thrust caps until the rocker arms and timing chains have been installed and the camshaft journal caps are secured into position.**

- All camshaft journal caps except the thrust caps.
- Timing chains. Tighten the camshaft journal cap bolts in

reverse of the loosening order and in several steps to 71–106 inch lbs. (8–12 Nm).
- Thrust caps. Tighten the bolts to 71–106 inch lbs. (8–12 Nm).
- Front cover
- Accessory drive belts
- Valve covers
- Upper intake manifold. Use new gaskets and tighten the bolts to 71–106 inch lbs. (8–12 Nm).
- Negative battery cable

5. Run the engine and check for leaks and proper engine operation.

Valve Lash

ADJUSTMENT

2.0L Engine

1. Before servicing the vehicle, refer to the precautions in the beginning of this section.
2. Remove the valve cover.
3. Rotate the crankshaft so that the valve is closed and measure the clearance between the lifter shim and the camshaft base circle. Intake valve clearance should be 0.004–0.007 inches. Exhaust valve clearance should be 0.010–0.013 inches.
4. Measure each valve and note the clearance.
5. If adjustment is necessary, remove the camshafts and replace the shims. To obtain the correct shim size, measure the current shim, add the measured clearance, and subtract 0.006 inches for intake valves, and 0.012 inches for exhaust valves.
6. Install or connect the following:
- Camshafts
- Valve cover

2.5L Engine

The lash adjusters are hydraulic and are not adjustable.

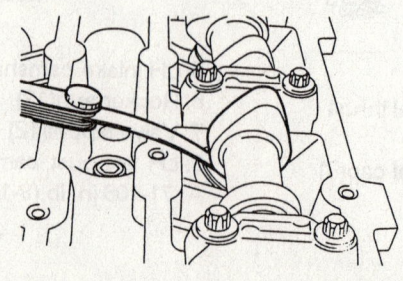

9306HG04
Checking valve clearance—2.0L engine

Starter Motor

REMOVAL AND INSTALLATION

2.0L Engine

1. Before servicing the vehicle, refer to the precautions in the beginning of this section.
2. Remove or disconnect the following:
- Negative battery cable
- Air cleaner
- Starter electrical connectors
- Starter

To install:
3. Install or connect the following:
- Starter. Tighten the bolts to 18 ft. lbs. (25 Nm).
- Starter electrical connectors
- Air cleaner
- Negative battery cable

2.5L Engine

1. Before servicing the vehicle, refer to the precautions in the beginning of this section.
2. Remove or disconnect the following:
- Negative battery cable
- Air cleaner
- Starter support bracket
- Shift cable bracket (manual)
- Fuel lines
- Starter electrical connectors
- Starter

To install:
3. Install or connect the following:
- Starter. Tighten the bolts to 18 ft. lbs. (25 Nm).
- Starter electrical connectors
- Fuel lines
- Shift cable bracket (manual)
- Starter support bracket. Tighten the bolt to 18 ft. lbs. (25 Nm), and tighten the nuts to 13 ft. lbs. (17 Nm).
- Air cleaner
- Negative battery cable

Oil Pan

REMOVAL & INSTALLATION

2.0L Engine

1. Before servicing the vehicle, refer to the precautions in the beginning of this section.
2. Drain the engine oil.
3. Attach an engine support fixture to the engine lifting eyes.

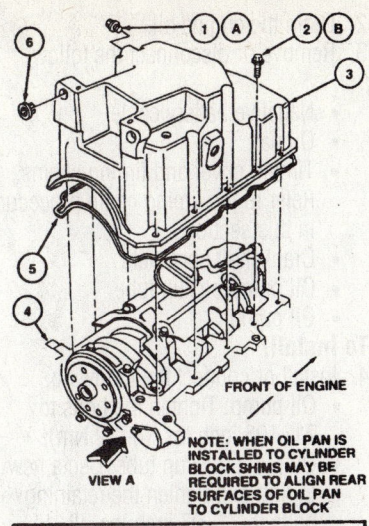

VIEW A

NOTE: WHEN OIL PAN IS INSTALLED TO CYLINDER BLOCK SHIMS MAY BE REQUIRED TO ALIGN REAR SURFACES OF OIL PAN TO CYLINDER BLOCK

FRONT OF ENGINE

3 mm (0.25 INCH)

SEALER

NOTE: APPLY A 3 mm (0.25 INCH) BEAD OF SILICONE GASKET AND SEALANT F1AZ-19562-A OR EQUIVALENT MEETING FORD SPECIFICATION WSE-M4G320-A2

VIEW A TYPICAL FOUR PLACES

1 Oil pan drain plug
2 Bolt (10 req'd)
3 Oil pan
4 Cylinder block
5 Oil pan gasket
6 Oil pan spacer (as req'd)
A Tighten to 21-28 Nm (15-21 lb-ft)
B Tighten to 20-24 Nm (15-18 lb-ft)

7922JG20

Exploded view of the oil pan mounting—2.0L engine

4. Remove or disconnect the following:
- Negative battery cable
- Catalytic converter
- Oil lever sensor connector
- Heater coolant pipe
- Lower engine rear plate
- Left and right engine support insulator center bolts

➡**Mark the location of the upper front engine support before removing it from the front engine support bracket.**

- Front engine support bracket.
5. Raise the engine to allow room for removal of the engine oil pan.
6. Remove the oil pan.

To install:

➡**Apply a bead of silicone gasket sealer to the oil pump parting lines and at the crankshaft rear main seal retainer on the cylinder block.**

7. Install or connect the following:
- Oil pan. Use a new gasket and tighten the bolts in several passes to 15–18 ft. lbs. (20–24 Nm), working from the center of the

block towards the ends. Tighten the transaxle case bolts to 25–34 ft. lbs. (34–46 Nm).
- Lower engine rear plate
8. Lower the engine and install or connect:
- Front engine support insulator
- Left and right engine support insulator center bolts
- Heater coolant pipe
- Oil lever sensor connector
- Catalytic converter
- Negative battery cable
9. Fill the crankcase with the proper amount of engine oil.
10. Run the engine and check for leaks and proper operation.

2.5L Engine

1. Before servicing the vehicle, refer to the precautions in the beginning of this section.
2. Drain the engine oil.
3. Attach an engine support fixture to the engine lifting eyes.
4. Remove or disconnect the following:
- Negative battery cable

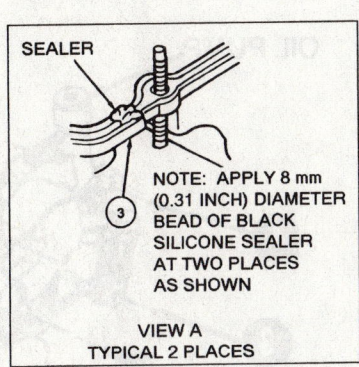

SEALER

NOTE: APPLY 8 mm (0.31 INCH) DIAMETER BEAD OF BLACK SILICONE SEALER AT TWO PLACES AS SHOWN

VIEW A TYPICAL 2 PLACES

1 Upper cylinder block
2 Lower cylinder block
3 Oil pan
4 Stud bolt (5 req'd)
5 Bolt (10 req'd)
6 Oil pan gasket
7 Engine front cover
A Tighten to 20-30 Nm (15-22 lb-ft)

- Water pump pulley shield
- Exhaust crossover pipe and bracket
- Exhaust heat shields
- Lower engine rear plate
- Left and right engine support insulator center bolts

➡**Mark the location of the upper front engine support before removing it from the front engine support bracket.**

- Front engine support bracket.
5. Raise the engine to allow room for removal of the engine oil pan.
6. Remove the oil pan.

To install:

7. Apply a bead of silicone sealer to the gasket area where the pan meets the parting lines of the lower cylinder block and the front engine cover.
8. Install or connect the following:
- Oil pan. Use a new gasket, tighten the pan bolts in several passes to 15–22 ft. lbs. (20–30 Nm) and the transaxle case bolts to 25–34 ft. lbs. (34–46 Nm).
- Lower engine rear plate
9. Lower the engine and install or connect:

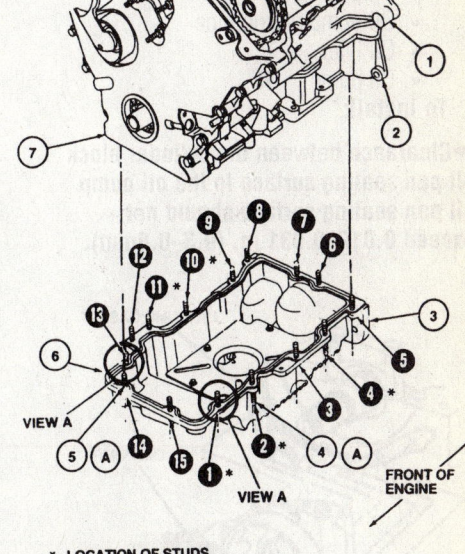

VIEW A

VIEW A

FRONT OF ENGINE

* LOCATION OF STUDS
● TIGHTEN BOLTS/STUDS IN SEQUENCE SHOWN

7922JG21

Exploded view of the oil pan mounting, showing the mounting bolt and stud tightening sequence—2.5L engine

For complete mechanical specifications, refer to Section 1 of this manual

- Front engine support insulator
- Left and right engine support insulator center bolts
- Exhaust heat shields
- Exhaust crossover pipe and bracket
- Water pump pulley shield
- Negative battery cable

10. Fill the crankcase with the proper amount of engine oil.

11. Run the engine and check for leaks and proper operation.

Oil Pump

REMOVAL & INSTALLATION

2.0L Engine

1. Before servicing the vehicle, refer to the precautions in the beginning of this section.

2. Drain the engine oil.

3. Remove or disconnect the following:
- Negative battery cable
- Accessory drive belt
- Timing belt cover and timing belt. Refer to the timing belt unit repair section.
- Crankshaft sprocket
- Catalytic converter
- Oil pan
- Oil pump pickup tube
- Oil filter
- Oil pump

To install:

➡Clearance between the cylinder block oil pan sealing surface to the oil pump oil pan sealing surface should not exceed 0.012–0.031 in. (0.3–0.8mm).

4. Install or connect the following:
- Oil pump. Use a straight-edge to align the oil pump oil pan sealing surface with the cylinder block oil pan sealing surface. Tighten the oil pump retaining bolts to 71–102 inch lbs. (8–11.5 Nm).
- Oil filter
- Oil pump pickup tube. Use a new gasket and tighten the retaining bolts to 71–97 inch lbs. (8–11 Nm). Use a new self-locking nut and tighten it to 13–15 ft. lbs. (17–21 Nm).
- Oil pan
- Catalytic converter
- Crankshaft sprocket
- Timing belt cover and timing belt
- Accessory drive belt
- Negative battery cable

5. Fill the crankcase with the proper amount of engine oil.

6. Run the engine and check for leaks and proper operation.

2.5L Engine

1. Before servicing the vehicle, refer to the precautions in the beginning of this section.

2. Drain the engine oil.

3. Remove or disconnect the following:
- Negative battery cable
- Oil pan
- Timing cover and timing chains. Refer to the timing chain procedure in this section.
- Crankshaft sprockets
- Oil pump pickup tube
- Oil pump

To install:

4. Install or connect the following:
- Oil pump. Tighten the bolts to 71–106 inch lbs. (8–12 Nm).
- Oil pump pickup tube. Use a new O-ring and tighten the retaining bolts to 71–97 inch lbs. (8–11 Nm). Use a new self-locking nut and tighten it to 15–22 ft. lbs. (20–30 Nm).
- Crankshaft sprockets
- Timing cover and timing chains
- Oil pan
- Negative battery cable

5. Fill the crankcase with the proper amount of engine oil.

6. Run the engine and check for leaks and proper operation.

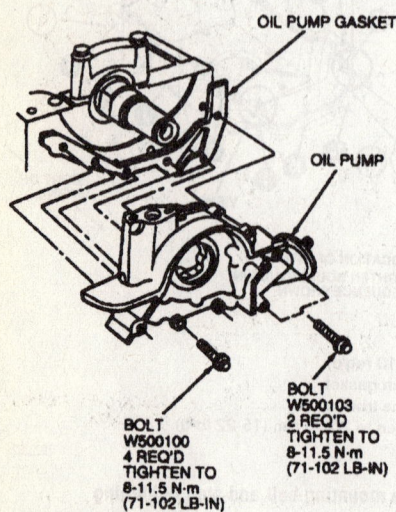

Exploded view of the oil pump mounting—2.0L engine

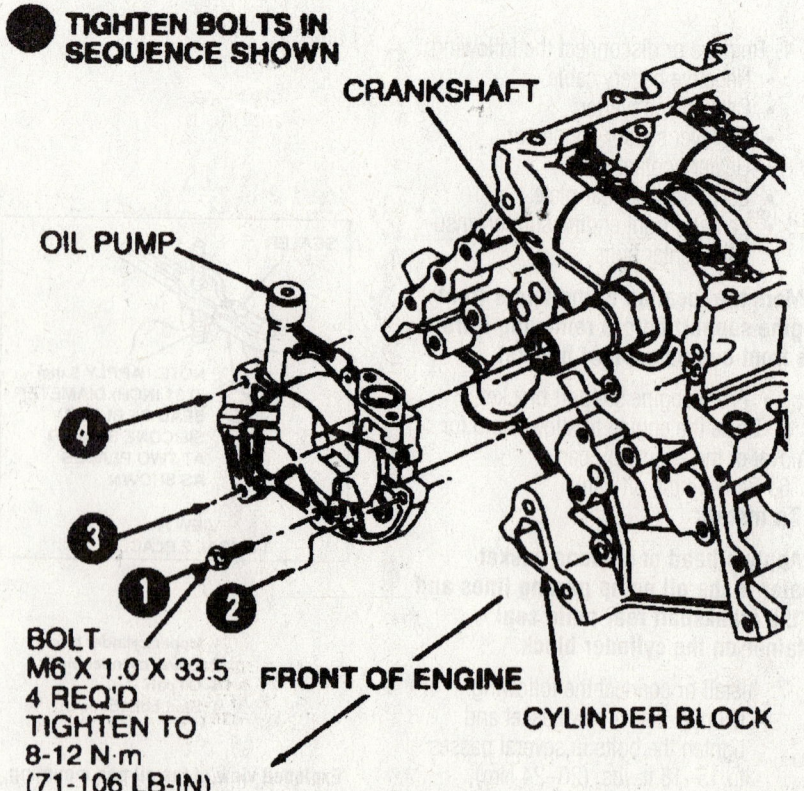

Exploded view of the oil pump mounting, showing the retaining bolt tightening sequence—2.5L engine

Rear Main Seal

REMOVAL & INSTALLATION

2.0L Engine

1. Before servicing the vehicle, refer to the precautions in the beginning of this section.
2. Remove or disconnect the following:
   - Negative battery cable
   - Transaxle and flexplate/flywheel
   - Oil seal

To install:

3. Install or connect the following:
   - Oil seal. Seat the seal flush with the rear of the crankshaft oil seal retainer.
   - Flexplate/flywheel. Tighten the bolts to 82 ft. lbs. (112 Nm).
   - Transaxle
   - Negative battery cable
4. Start the engine and check for leaks.

2.5L Engine

➡The following procedure requires a specific Ford design seal remover, or equivalent aftermarket version.

1. Before servicing the vehicle, refer to the precautions in the beginning of this section.
2. Remove or disconnect the following:
   - Negative battery cable
   - Transaxle and flexplate/flywheel
   - Oil seal. Use special tool Seal Remover T95P-6701-EH and a slide hammer to remove the seal.

To install:

3. Install or connect the following:
   - Oil seal. Press the seal in evenly until it is flush with the cylinder block.
   - Flexplate/flywheel. Tighten the bolts to 59 ft. lbs. (80 Nm).

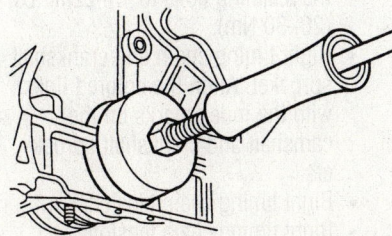

Thread the oil seal remover into the seal, then withdraw the seal using a slide hammer—2.5L engine

   - Transaxle
   - Negative battery cable
4. Start the engine and check for leaks.

Timing Chain, Sprockets, Front Cover and Seal

REMOVAL & INSTALLATION

2.5L Engine

1. Before servicing the vehicle, refer to the precautions in the beginning of this section.
2. Attach an engine support fixture to the engine lifting eyes.
3. Drain the engine oil.
4. Remove or disconnect the following:
   - Negative battery cable
   - Upper intake manifold
   - Valve covers
   - Low coolant level sensor connector
   - Coolant recovery reservoir

➡Mark the position of the upper front engine support bracket before removing.

   - Front engine support insulator and bracket
   - Engine wiring harness connectors
   - Accessory drive belt
   - Power steering pump and bracket
   - Right splash shield
   - Alternator
   - Crankshaft pulley

   - Crankshaft Position (CKP) sensor connector
   - Oil pan
   - A/C compressor
   - A/C hose bracket
   - Front cover. Remove the bolts in reverse of the installation sequence.
   - CKP sensor pulse ring
5. Rotate the crankshaft so that the keyway is at the 11 o'clock position to locate the crankshaft at Top Dead Center (TDC) for No. 1 cylinder.
6. Verify that the alignment arrows on the camshafts are aligned. If not, rotate the crankshaft 1 complete revolution and recheck.
7. Rotate the crankshaft so that the keyway is at the 3 o'clock position. This positions the right cylinder head camshafts to the neutral position.
8. Remove or disconnect the following:
   - Right timing chain tensioner

✷✷ WARNING

The camshaft thrust caps must be removed before loosening the remaining camshaft journal cap bolts to ensure that the thrust caps are not damaged.

➡The camshaft journal caps and cylinder heads are numbered to ensure that they are assembled in their original positions.

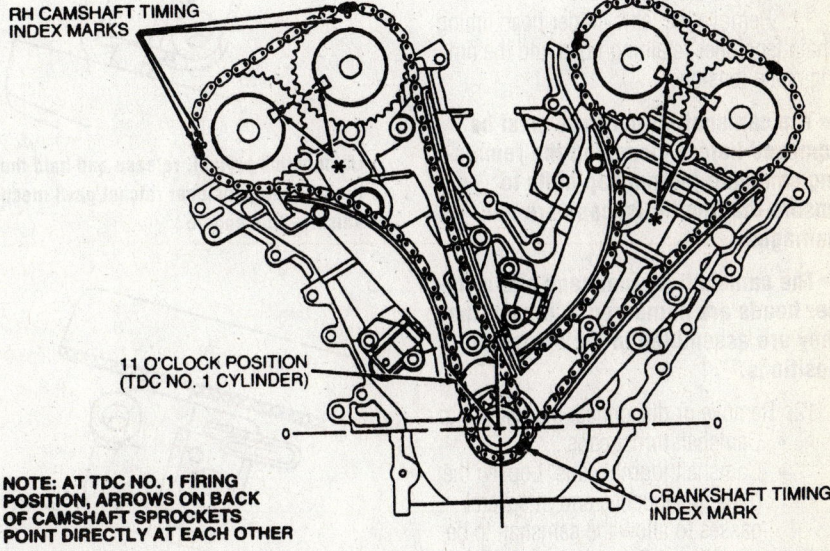

RH CAMSHAFT TIMING INDEX MARKS

11 O'CLOCK POSITION (TDC NO. 1 CYLINDER)

CRANKSHAFT TIMING INDEX MARK

*NOTE: AT TDC NO. 1 FIRING POSITION, ARROWS ON BACK OF CAMSHAFT SPROCKETS POINT DIRECTLY AT EACH OTHER

View of the timing chains and gears, showing the right timing chain alignment marks properly positioned—2.5L engine

Please refer to Section 8 for electric cooling fan wiring schematics

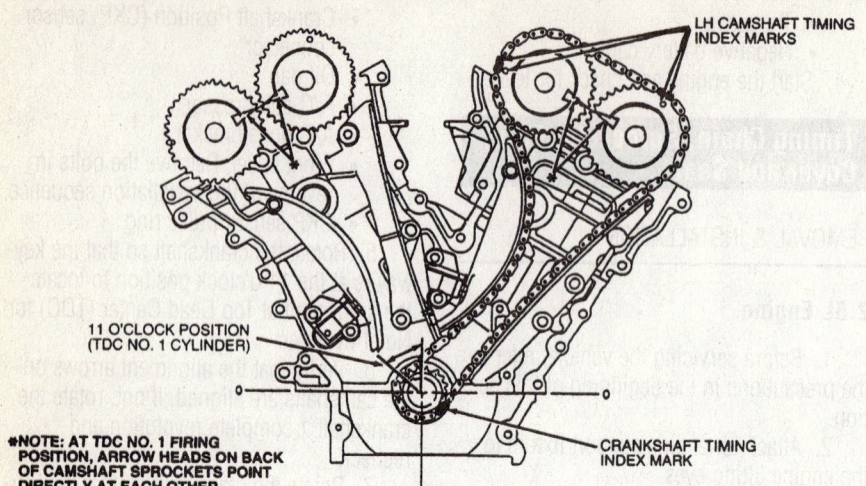

LH CAMSHAFT TIMING INDEX MARKS

11 O'CLOCK POSITION (TDC NO. 1 CYLINDER)

CRANKSHAFT TIMING INDEX MARK

#NOTE: AT TDC NO. 1 FIRING POSITION, ARROW HEADS ON BACK OF CAMSHAFT SPROCKETS POINT DIRECTLY AT EACH OTHER

7922JG26

Left timing chain alignment mark positioning for servicing the chain—2.5L engine

- Camshaft thrust caps
- Camshaft journal caps. Loosen the bolts in sequence and in several passes to allow the camshaft to be raised from the cylinder head evenly.
- Rocker arms. Keep the rocker arms in order for installation.
- Right timing chain tensioner arm
- Right timing chain and crankshaft sprocket

9. Rotate the crankshaft 2 revolutions and locate the crankshaft keyway at the 11 o'clock position. This will position the left cylinder head camshafts to their neutral position.

10. Verify that the alignment arrows on the camshafts are aligned.

11. Remove the left cylinder head timing chain tensioner retaining bolts and the timing chain tensioner.

➡The camshaft thrust caps must be removed before loosening the remaining camshaft journal cap bolts to ensure that the thrust caps are not damaged.

➡The camshaft journal caps and cylinder heads are numbered to ensure that they are assembled in their original positions.

12. Remove or disconnect the following:
- Camshaft thrust caps
- Camshaft journal caps. Loosen the bolts in sequence and in several passes to allow the camshaft to be raised from the cylinder head evenly.
- Rocker arms. Keep the rocker arms in order for installation.
- Left timing chain tensioner arm

- Left timing chain and crankshaft sprocket

To install:

13. Prepare the timing chain tensioners for installation as follows:
   a. Place the left chain tensioner in a vise.
   b. Using a small prytool, release and hold the timing chain tensioner ratchet/pawl mechanism through the

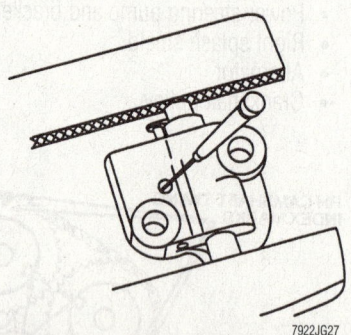

7922JG27

Using a thin prytool, release and hold the timing chain tensioner ratchet/pawl mechanism—2.5L engine

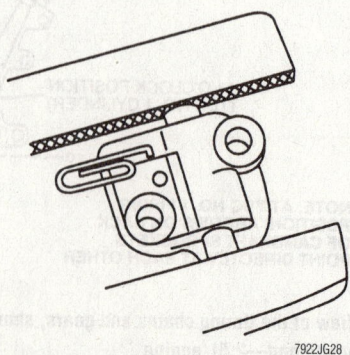

7922JG28

Retain the piston with a 1.5 mm wire or paperclip—2.5L engine

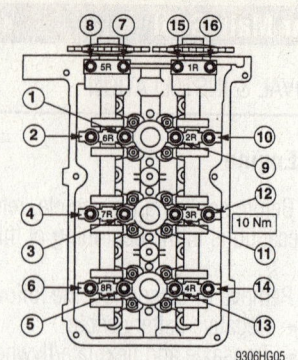

9306HG05

Camshaft journal cap tightening sequence—2.5L engine

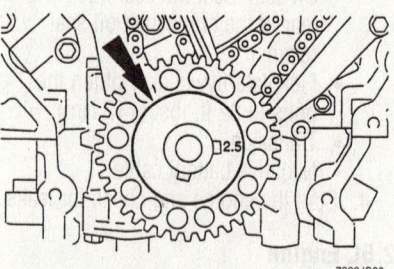

7922JG30

When installing the CKP sensor pulse ring, be sure to use the correct keyway—2.5L engine

access hole in the timing chain tensioner.
   c. Slowly compress the tensioner.
   d. Lock the piston with a 1.5 mm wire or paperclip.
   e. Repeat for the right chain tensioner.

➡Be sure that the crankshaft keyway is still at the 11 o'clock position.

14. Install or connect the following:
- Left timing chain and crankshaft sprocket. Align the colored links with the index marks on the camshaft and crankshaft sprockets.
- Left timing chain tensioner arm
- Left timing chain tensioner. Tighten the retaining bolts to 15–22 ft. lbs. (20–30 Nm).
- Right timing chain and crankshaft sprocket. Align the colored links with the index marks on the camshaft and crankshaft sprockets.
- Right timing chain tensioner arm
- Right timing chain tensioner. Tighten the retaining bolts to 15–22 ft. lbs. (20–30 Nm).

➡The crankshaft keyway must be in the 11 o'clock position to install the left cylinder head rocker arms.

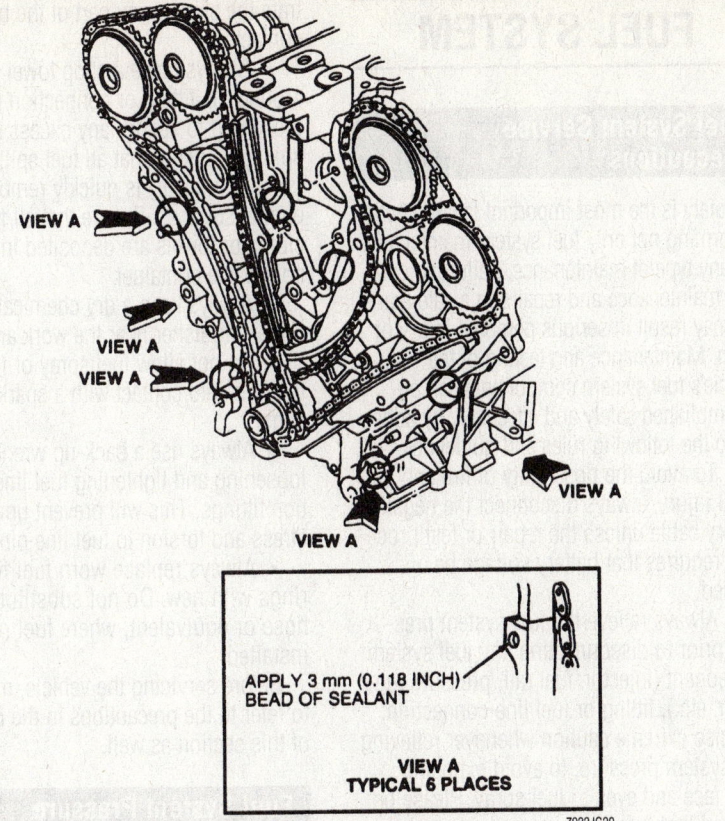

APPLY 3 mm (0.118 INCH)
BEAD OF SEALANT

**VIEW A
TYPICAL 6 PLACES**

7922JG29

To prevent oil leakage, apply sealant to the places indicated—2.5L engine

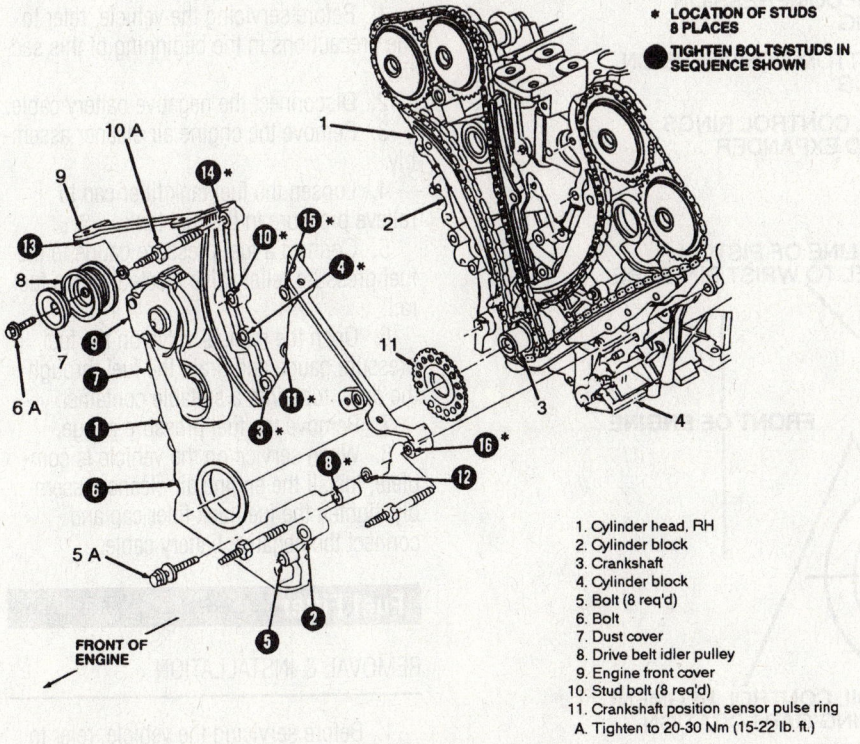

★ LOCATION OF STUDS
8 PLACES

● TIGHTEN BOLTS/STUDS IN SEQUENCE SHOWN

1. Cylinder head, RH
2. Cylinder block
3. Crankshaft
4. Cylinder block
5. Bolt (8 req'd)
6. Bolt
7. Dust cover
8. Drive belt idler pulley
9. Engine front cover
10. Stud bolt (8 req'd)
11. Crankshaft position sensor pulse ring
A. Tighten to 20-30 Nm (15-22 lb. ft.)

7922JG31

FRONT OF ENGINE

Exploded view of the front cover mounting, showing the retaining bolt and nut tightening sequence—2.5L engine

15. Install the left cylinder head rocker arms in their original positions

➡ **Do not install the camshaft journal thrust caps until the other journal caps have been installed and tightened.**

16. Tighten the left camshaft journal caps in the order shown and in several passes to 88 inch lbs. (10 Nm).

17. Install the left camshaft journal thrust caps and tighten the bolts to 88 inch lbs. (10 Nm).

18. Remove the retaining wire from the left timing chain tensioner.

➡ **The crankshaft keyway must be in the 3 o'clock position to install the right cylinder head rocker arms.**

19. Rotate the crankshaft so that the key-way is in the 3 o'clock position.

20. Install the right cylinder head rocker arms in their original positions.

➡ **Do not install the camshaft journal thrust caps until the other journal caps have been installed and tightened.**

21. Tighten the right camshaft journal caps in the order shown and in several passes to 88 inch lbs. (10 Nm).

22. Install the right camshaft journal thrust caps and tighten the bolts to 88 inch lbs. (10 Nm).

23. Remove the retaining wire from the right timing chain tensioner.

24. Install the CKP sensor pulse ring. Use the keyway for the 2.5L engine as shown.

25. Replace the crankshaft seal in the front cover with a new one. Apply clean engine oil to the seal lip.

26. Apply silicone sealer to the 6 critical areas shown in View **A**, to the cylinder block to prevent oil seepage.

27. Place new front cover gaskets onto the dowel pins on the cylinder block and heads.

28. Place the front cover into position.

29. Install the 6 front cover retaining bolts and stud bolts where the silicone sealer was applied.

30. Tighten the bolts and stud bolts until the front cover contacts the cylinder block and heads an, then turn the bolts and stud bolts an additional ¼ turn.

31. Install the remaining front cover retaining bolts and stud bolts.

32. Tighten all of the front cover retaining bolts and stud bolts in proper sequence to 15–22 ft. lbs. (20–30 Nm).

For complete service labor times order Nichols' Chilton Labor Guide Manual

33. Install or connect the following:
- A/C hose bracket
- A/C compressor
- Oil pan
- CKP sensor connector
- Crankshaft pulley
- Alternator
- Right splash shield
- Power steering pump and bracket
- Accessory drive belt
- Engine wiring harness connectors
- Front engine support insulator and bracket
- Coolant recovery reservoir
- Low coolant level sensor connector
- Valve covers
- Upper intake manifold. Use new gaskets and tighten the bolts to 71–106 inch lbs. (8–12 Nm).
- Negative battery cable

34. Fill the engine with the proper amount and grade of oil.

35. Run the engine and check for leaks and proper operation.

Piston and Ring

POSITIONING

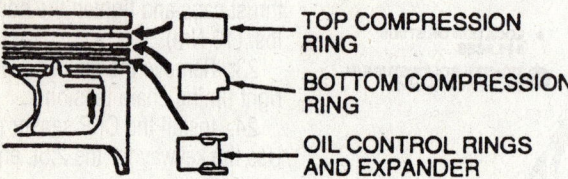

CENTER LINE OF PISTON PARALLEL TO WRIST PIN BORE

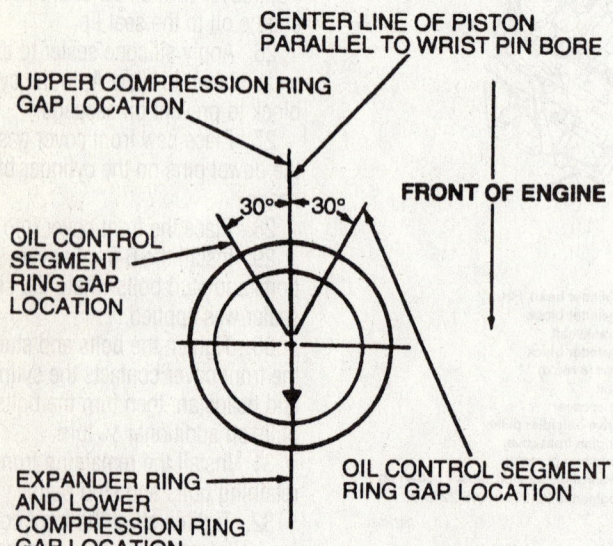

2.0L and 2.5L engines—piston ring positioning, end gap spacing, and piston positioning. The small directional arrow must face the front of the engine.

7922AG29

FUEL SYSTEM

Fuel System Service Precautions

Safety is the most important factor when performing not only fuel system maintenance but any type of maintenance. Failure to conduct maintenance and repairs in a safe manner may result in serious personal injury or death. Maintenance and testing of the vehicle's fuel system components can be accomplished safely and effectively by adhering to the following rules and guidelines.

- To avoid the possibility of fire and personal injury, always disconnect the negative battery cable unless the repair or test procedure requires that battery voltage be applied.
- Always relieve the fuel system pressure prior to disconnecting any fuel system component (injector, fuel rail, pressure regulator, etc.), fitting or fuel line connection. Exercise extreme caution whenever relieving fuel system pressure, to avoid exposing skin, face and eyes to fuel spray. Please be advised that fuel under pressure may penetrate the skin or any part of the body that it contacts.
- Always place a shop towel or cloth around the fitting or connection prior to loosening to absorb any excess fuel due to spillage. Ensure that all fuel spillage (should it occur) is quickly removed from engine surfaces. Ensure that all fuel soaked cloths or towels are deposited into a suitable waste container.
- Always keep a dry chemical (Class B) fire extinguisher near the work area.
- Do not allow fuel spray or fuel vapors to come into contact with a spark or open flame.
- Always use a back-up wrench when loosening and tightening fuel line connection fittings. This will prevent unnecessary stress and torsion to fuel line piping.
- Always replace worn fuel fitting O-rings with new. Do not substitute fuel hose or equivalent, where fuel pipe is installed.

Before servicing the vehicle, make sure to refer to the precautions in the beginning of this section as well.

Fuel System Pressure

RELIEVING

1. Before servicing the vehicle, refer to the precautions in the beginning of this section.
2. Disconnect the negative battery cable.
3. Remove the engine air cleaner assembly.
4. Loosen the fuel tank filler cap to relieve pressure in the fuel tank.
5. Connect a fuel pressure gauge to the fuel pressure relief valve located on the fuel rail.
6. Open the manual valve on the fuel pressure gauge and drain the fuel through the drain tube into a suitable container.
7. Remove the fuel pressure gauge.
8. When service on the vehicle is complete, install the engine air cleaner assembly, tighten the fuel tank filler cap and connect the negative battery cable.

Fuel Filter

REMOVAL & INSTALLATION

1. Before servicing the vehicle, refer to the precautions in the beginning of this section.
2. Relieve the fuel system pressure.
3. Remove or disconnect the following:
- Negative battery cable

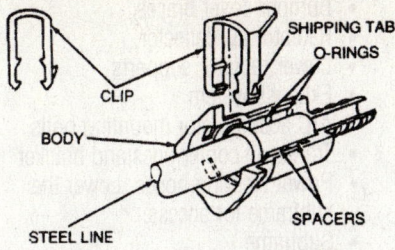

Once the retainer clip has been removed from the connector, the fuel line can be removed from the filter

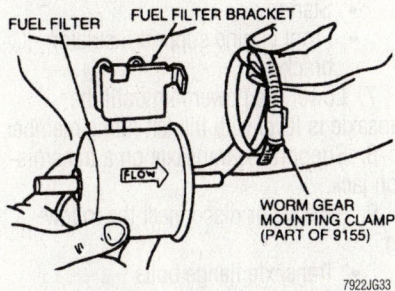

Be sure to install the fuel filter with the arrow pointing in the direction of the fuel flow

➡ The fuel filter is located underneath the vehicle, near the fuel tank.

- Retainer clips at both ends of the fuel filter.
- Fuel lines from the fuel filter
- Fuel filter

To install:

4. Install or connect the following:
- New fuel filter with the arrow pointed in the direction of flow
- New retainer clips onto the fuel line fittings before placing the lines onto the fuel filter ends.
- Fuel lines onto the fuel filter until an audible click is heard. Pull on the fitting to verify a good connection.

5. Start the engine and check for fuel leaks and proper operation.

Fuel Pump

REMOVAL & INSTALLATION

1. Before servicing the vehicle, refer to the precautions in the beginning of this section.
2. Relieve the fuel pressure.

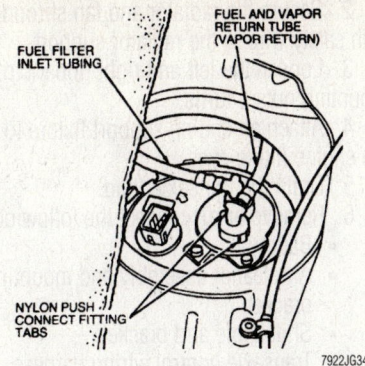

View of fuel pump fittings through the floor pan

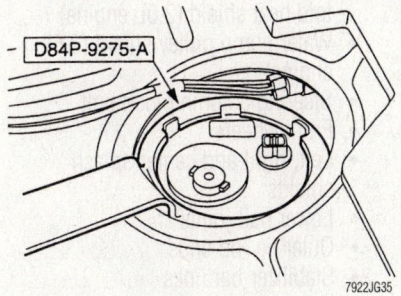

Remove the locking ring from the fuel pump sender with special tool Fuel Tank Sender Wrench D84P-9275-A

3. Remove or disconnect the following:
- Negative battery cable
- Rear seat cushion
- Plastic access panel
- Fuel pump wiring harness connector
- Fuel lines
- Fuel pump lock ring. Use special tool Fuel Tank Sender Wrench D84P-9275-A.
- Fuel pump

To install:

4. Install or connect the following:
- Fuel pump using a new O-ring seal
- Fuel pump lock ring using special tool Fuel Tank Sender Wrench D84P-9275-A
- Fuel lines
- Fuel pump wiring harness connector
- Plastic access panel
- Rear seat cushion
- Negative battery cable

5. Start the engine and check for leaks and proper operation.

Fuel Injector

REMOVAL AND INSTALLATION

2.0L Engine

1. Before servicing the vehicle, refer to the precautions in the beginning of this section.
2. Relieve fuel system pressure.
3. Remove or disconnect the following:
- Negative battery cable
- Fuel lines and retaining clip
- Pressure regulator vacuum hose
- Accelerator cable
- Fuel injector electrical connectors
- Fuel supply manifold with the injectors attached
- Injectors from the supply manifold

To install:

4. Install or connect the following:
- Fuel injectors using new O-ring seals
- Fuel supply manifold with the injectors attached. Tighten the bolts to 88 inch lbs. (10 Nm).
- Fuel injector electrical connectors
- Accelerator cable
- Pressure regulator vacuum hose
- Fuel lines and retaining clip
- Negative battery cable

2.5L Engine

WITHOUT RETURNLESS FUEL DELIVERY SYSTEM

1. Before servicing the vehicle, refer to the precautions in the beginning of this section.
2. Relieve fuel system pressure.
3. Remove or disconnect the following:
- Negative battery cable
- Air cleaner outlet tube
- Fuel lines
- Upper intake manifold
- Fuel injector electrical connectors
- Fuel pressure regulator vacuum line
- Intake Manifold Runner Control (IMRC) rod
- Fuel supply manifold with the injectors attached
- Injectors from the supply manifold

To install:

4. Install or connect the following:
- Fuel injectors using new O-ring seals
- Fuel supply manifold with the injectors attached. Tighten the bolts to 88 inch lbs. (10 Nm).
- IMRC rod

- Fuel pressure regulator vacuum line
- Fuel injector electrical connectors
- Upper intake manifold. Use new gaskets and tighten the bolts to 71–106 inch lbs. (8–12 Nm).
- Fuel lines
- Air cleaner outlet tube
- Negative battery cable

WITH RETURNLESS FUEL DELIVERY SYSTEM

1. Before servicing the vehicle, refer to the precautions in the beginning of this section.
2. Relieve fuel system pressure.
3. Remove or disconnect the following:
   - Negative battery cable
   - Air cleaner outlet tube
   - Fuel line
   - Upper intake manifold
   - Fuel injector electrical connectors
   - Fuel pressure sensor electrical connector and vacuum line
   - Intake Manifold Runner Control (IMRC) rod
   - Fuel supply manifold with the injectors attached
   - Injectors from the supply manifold

To install:

4. Install or connect the following:
   - Fuel injectors using new O-ring seals
   - Fuel supply manifold with the injectors attached. Tighten the bolts to 88 inch lbs. (10 Nm).
   - IMRC rod
   - Fuel pressure sensor electrical connector and vacuum line
   - Fuel injector electrical connectors
   - Upper intake manifold. Use new gaskets and tighten the bolts to 71–106 inch lbs. (8–12 Nm).
   - Fuel line
   - Air cleaner outlet tube
   - Negative battery cable

DRIVE TRAIN

Transaxle Assembly

REMOVAL & INSTALLATION

Automatic

1. Before servicing the vehicle, refer to the precautions in the beginning of this section.

2. Secure the radiator and fan shroud with safety wire to the radiator support.
3. Loosen the left and right upper strut mounting nuts 5 turns.
4. Attach an engine support fixture to the engine lifting eyes.
5. Drain the transaxle fluid.
6. Remove or disconnect the following:
   - Battery
   - Air cleaner assembly and mounting bracket
   - Shift cable and bracket
   - Transaxle control wiring harness connector
   - Transaxle range sensor
   - Rear transaxle support insulator
   - Oil dipstick tube and exhaust manifold heat shield (2.0L engine)
   - Water pump pulley shield (2.5L engine)
   - Steering column pinch bolt
   - Front wheels
   - Left, right and center splash shields
   - Lower ball joints
   - Outer tie rod ends
   - Stabilizer bar links
   - Left and right engine support insulators
   - Power steering oil cooler hoses

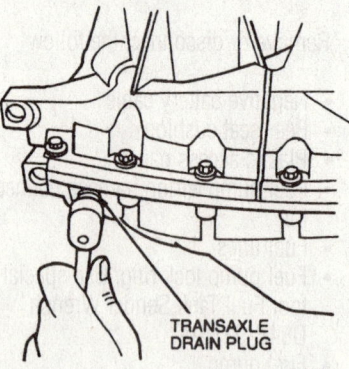

Transaxle drain plug location

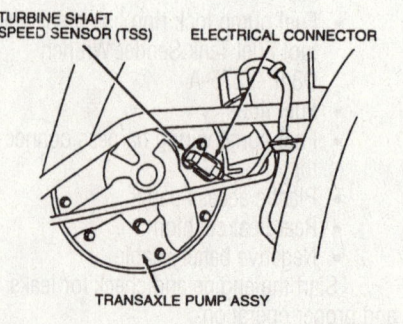

TSS sensor location

- Bumper cover braces
- Radiator air deflector
- Lower radiator supports
- Exhaust system
- A/C accumulator mounting bolts
- Transaxle cooler lines and bracket
- Power steering hoses. Lower the subframe for access.
- Subframe
- Turbine Speed (TSS) sensor connector
- Halfshafts and intermediate shaft
- Vehicle Speed (VSS) sensor connector
- Torque converter nuts (4)
- Starter
- Front engine support insulator bracket

7. Lower the powertrain until the transaxle is level with the left frame member.
8. Support the transaxle on a transmission jack.
9. Remove or disconnect the following:
   - Transaxle flange bolts
   - Transaxle engine

➡ **Use care when removing the transaxle to prevent the torque converter from falling out.**

   - Transaxle

To install:

➡ **Replace all snaprings, split pins, and self-locking nuts.**

10. Install or connect the following:
    - Transaxle Tighten the flange bolts to 41–50 ft. lbs. (55–68 Nm).
    - Torque converter. Tighten the nuts to 23–39 ft. lbs. (31–53 Nm).
    - TSS connector
    - Subframe. Attach the power steering hoses before installing the subframe bolts.
    - Special tool Subframe Alignment Pin Set T95P-2100-AH and the

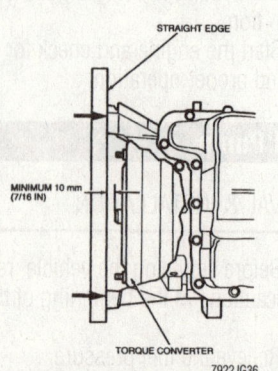

Be sure that the torque converter is properly seated in the transaxle

subframe bolts. Tighten the subframe bolts to 81–110 ft. lbs. (110–150 Nm). Remove the alignment pins.

- A/C accumulator bolts
- Power steering oil cooler lines
- Special tool Powertrain Alignment Gauge T94P-6000-AH in place of the left engine support insulator. Tighten the 2 retaining bolts to 20 ft. lbs. (27 Nm) and snug the through-bolt.

➡ **The left and right support insulators must be aligned in the middle of the support insulator brackets.**

- Right engine support insulator. Tighten the 2 subframe retaining bolts to 30–41 ft. lbs. (41–55 Nm) and the through-bolt to 75–102 ft. lbs. (103–137 Nm).
- Rear engine support insulator. Tighten the nuts to 61 ft. lbs. (83 Nm).
- Front engine support insulator. Tighten the nuts to 61 ft. lbs. (83 Nm).

11. Remove the Powertrain Alignment Tool and install the left engine support insulator. Tighten the center bolt to 88 ft. lbs. (120 Nm), and the mounting bolts to 35 ft. lbs. (48 Nm).

12. Install or connect the following:
- Transaxle oil cooler lines
- Starter. Tighten the bolts to 43–58

ft. lbs. (59–79 Nm) for the 2.5L engine or 15–20 ft. lbs. (20–27 Nm) for the 2.0L engine.
- VSS sensor connector
- Halfshafts and intermediate shaft
- Exhaust system
- Lower radiator supports
- Radiator air deflector
- Bumper cover braces
- Power steering oil cooler hoses
- Left and right engine support insulators
- Stabilizer bar links. Tighten the nuts to 35–48 ft. lbs. (47–65 Nm).
- Outer tie rod ends. Tighten the nuts to 23–35 ft. lbs. (31–47 Nm).
- Lower ball joints. Tighten the pinch bolt to 37–43 ft. lbs. (50–58 Nm) for 1997 vehicles or to 61 ft. lbs. (83 Nm) for 1998–01 vehicles.
- Left, right and center splash shields
- Front wheels. Tighten the lug nuts to 63 ft. lbs. (86 Nm).
- Steering column pinch bolt. Tighten the bolt to 15–20 ft. lbs. (20–27 Nm).
- Water pump pulley shield (2.5L engine)
- Oil dipstick tube and exhaust manifold heat shield (2.0L engine)
- Transaxle range sensor
- Transaxle control wiring harness connector
- Shift cable and bracket

- Air cleaner assembly and mounting bracket
- Battery

13. Tighten the upper strut mount nuts to 34 ft. lbs. (46 Nm).

14. Fill the transaxle.

15. Check for leaks and proper operation.

➡ **Whenever the vehicle subframe is removed or lowered, the wheel alignment should be checked.**

Manual

1. Before servicing the vehicle, refer to the precautions in the beginning of this section.

2. Attach an engine support fixture to the engine lifting eyes.

3. Secure the radiator and fan shroud to the radiator support using safety wire.

4. Loosen the front strut upper mount nuts 5 turns.

5. Remove or disconnect the following:
- Battery
- Steering column pinch bolt
- Air cleaner assembly and bracket
- Front and rear engine support insulators
- Reverse lamp switch connector
- Ground strap
- Left, right and center splash shields
- Clutch slave cylinder hydraulic line
- Accessory drive belt cover
- Power steering pulley shield (2.5L engine)
- Exhaust crossover pipe (2.5L engine)
- Catalytic converter
- Front wheels
- Vehicle Speed Sensor (VSS)
- Radiator air deflector
- Shift rod and stabilizer bar
- A/C accumulator mounting bolts.
- Halfshafts and intermediate shaft
- Left and right engine support insulators
- Lower ball joints
- Outer tie rod ends
- Stabilizer bar links
- Power steering oil cooler lines
- Lower radiator supports
- Bumper cover braces
- Power steering hoses. Lower the subframe for access.
- Subframe
- Starter

6. Lower the powertrain until the transaxle is level with the left frame member.

7. Support the transaxle on a transmission jack.

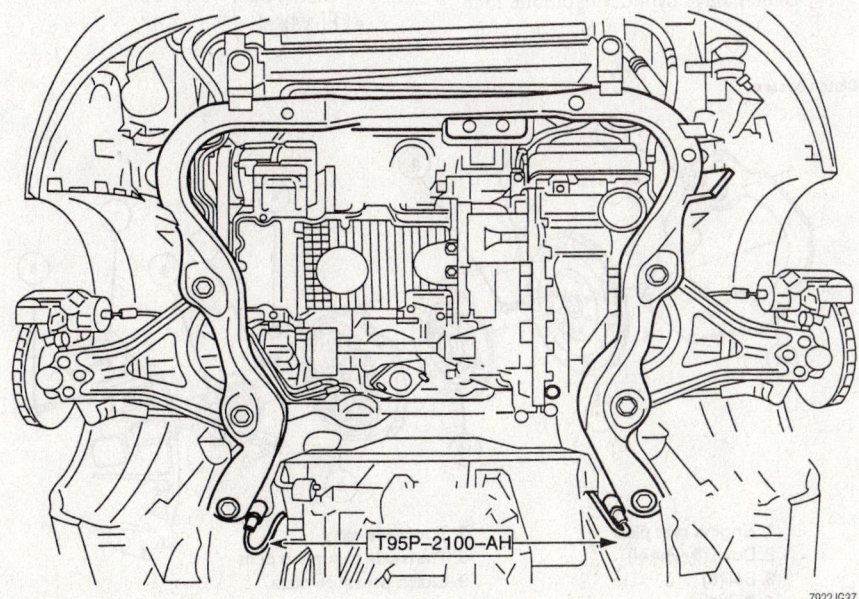

To properly align the subframe, install Subframe Alignment Pin Set T95P-2100-AH—manual and automatic transaxles

T95P-2100-AH

7922JG37

For complete service labor times order Nichols' Chilton Labor Guide Manual

8. Remove or disconnect the following:
- Transaxle flange bolts
- Transaxle from the engine

To install:

➡️**Replace all snaprings, split pins and self-locking nuts.**

9. Install the transaxle to the engine. Tighten the flange bolts to 28–38 ft. lbs. (38–51 Nm).

10. Raise the powertrain

11. Install or connect the following:
- Starter. Tighten the bolts to 35 ft. lbs. (48 Nm).
- Subframe. Attach the power steering hoses before installing the subframe bolts.
- Special tool Subframe Alignment Pin Set T95P-2100-AH and the subframe bolts. Tighten the subframe bolts to 81–110 ft. lbs. (110–150 Nm). Remove the alignment pins.
- A/C accumulator bolts
- Power steering oil cooler lines
- Special tool Powertrain Alignment Gauge T94P-6000-AH in place of the left engine support insulator. Tighten the 2 retaining bolts to 20 ft. lbs. (27 Nm) and snug the through-bolt.

➡️**The left and right support insulators must be aligned in the middle of the support insulator brackets.**

- Right engine support insulator. Tighten the 2 subframe retaining bolts to 30–41 ft. lbs. (41–55 Nm) and the through-bolt to 75–102 ft. lbs. (103–137 Nm).
- Rear engine support insulator. Tighten the nuts to 61 ft. lbs. (83 Nm).
- Front engine support insulator. Tighten the nuts to 61 ft. lbs. (83 Nm).

12. Remove the Powertrain Alignment

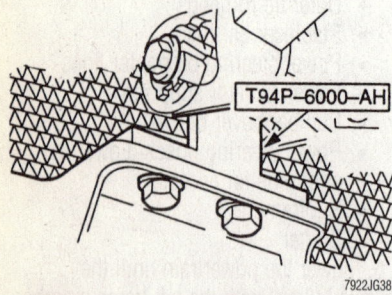

The Powertrain Alignment Gauge (T94P-6000-AH) tool must be installed in the correct position to ensure proper engine/transaxle orientation

Tool and install the left engine support insulator. Tighten the center bolt to 88 ft. lbs. (120 Nm), and the mounting bolts to 35 ft. lbs. (48 Nm).

13. Install or connect the following:
- Bumper cover braces
- Lower radiator supports. Tighten the bolts to 71–97 inch lbs. (8–11 Nm).
- Power steering oil cooler lines
- Stabilizer bar links. Tighten the fasteners to 35–48 ft. lbs. (47–65 Nm).
- Outer tie rod ends. Tighten the nuts to 23–35 ft. lbs. (31–47 Nm).
- Lower ball joints. Tighten the pinch bolt to 37–43 ft. lbs. (50–58 Nm) for 1997 vehicles or to 61 ft. lbs. (83 Nm) for 1998–01 vehicles.
- Axle halfshafts and intermediate shaft
- A/C accumulator mounting bolts
- Shift rod and stabilizer bar. Tighten the shift rod bolt to 14–18 ft. lbs. (19–25 Nm), and tighten the stabilizer bar nut to 28–38 ft. lbs. (38–51 Nm).
- Radiator air deflector
- VSS sensor
- Front wheels. Tighten the lug nuts to 63 ft. lbs. (86 Nm).
- Catalytic converter
- Exhaust crossover pipe (2.5L engine)
- Power steering pulley shield (2.5L engine
- Accessory drive belt cover
- Clutch slave cylinder hydraulic line

- Left, right and center splash shields
- Ground strap
- Reverse lamp switch connector
- Air cleaner assembly and bracket
- Steering column pinch bolt. Tighten the bolt to 15–20 ft. lbs. (20–27 Nm).
- Battery

14. Tighten the strut mounting nuts to 34 ft. lbs. (46 Nm).

15. Adjust the shift linkage and bleed the hydraulic clutch system as required.

16. Road test the vehicle and check for proper operation.

➡️**Whenever the vehicle subframe is removed or lowered, the wheel alignment should be checked.**

Clutch

ADJUSTMENTS

Because the clutch system is hydraulic, the clutch pedal free-play is self-adjusting and requires no additional maintenance.

REMOVAL & INSTALLATION

1. Before servicing the vehicle, refer to the precautions in the beginning of this section.

2. Remove or disconnect the following:
- Transaxle
- Clutch pressure plate
- Clutch disk
- Flywheel

Clutch System

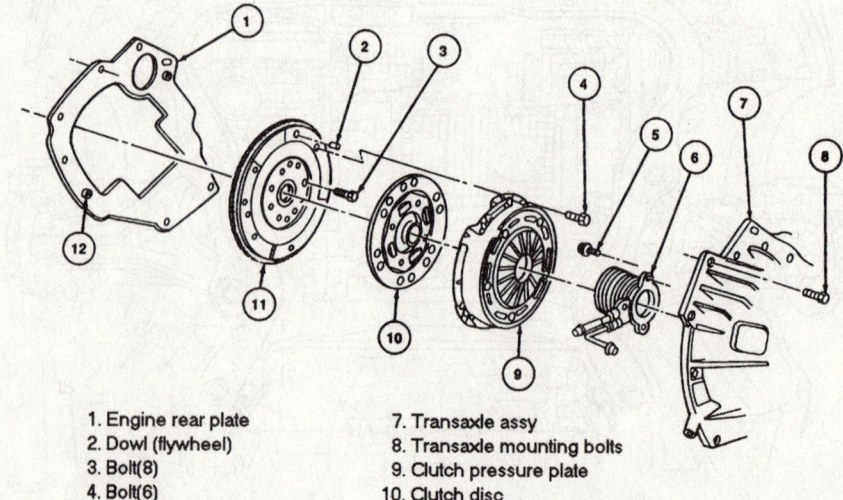

1. Engine rear plate
2. Dowl (flywheel)
3. Bolt(8)
4. Bolt(6)
5. Bolt(3)
6. Clutch slave cylinder
7. Transaxle assy
8. Transaxle mounting bolts
9. Clutch pressure plate
10. Clutch disc
11. Flywheel
12. Dowl bushing (engine plate)

Exploded view of the clutch disc, pressure plate and related component mounting

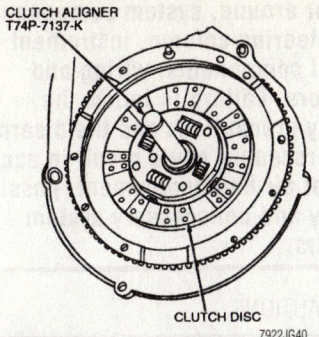

Insert an alignment tool through the clutch disc to ensure that it is centered after the pressure plate is installed

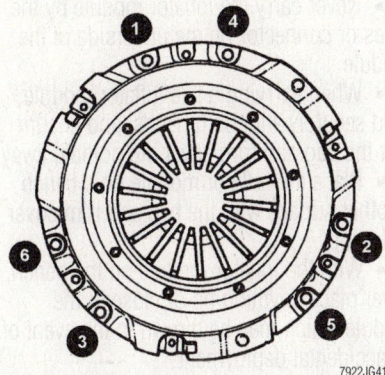

Pressure plate tightening sequence

To install:

3. Install or connect the following:
   - Flywheel. Tighten the bolts to 82 ft. lbs. (112 Nm) for 2.0L engines or to 59 ft. lbs. (80 Nm) for 2.5L engines.
   - Clutch disk and pressure plate. Tighten the pressure plate bolts evenly in several passes to 21 ft. lbs. (29 Nm).
   - Transaxle

4. Bleed the hydraulic clutch system, if required.

5. Check the clutch system for proper operation.

Hydraulic Clutch System

BLEEDING

1. Before servicing the vehicle, refer to the precautions in the beginning of this section.

2. Remove or disconnect the following:
   - Negative battery cable
   - Air cleaner outlet tube and the Mass Airflow (MAF) sensor

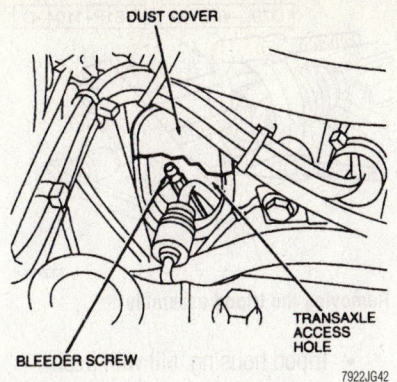

Clutch slave cylinder bleeder valve

➡**The brake master cylinder fluid reservoir is also the reservoir for the hydraulic clutch master cylinder.**

   - Rubber inspection cover from the bell housing

3. Connect a hose to the bleeder valve fitting on the clutch slave cylinder. Submerge the other end of the hose into a container of clean brake fluid.

4. Open the bleeder valve and have an assistant depress the clutch pedal.

5. Close the bleeder before releasing the clutch pedal.

6. Repeat the procedure until no more air bubbles are seen.

7. Install the rubber inspection cover to the bell housing.

8. Top off the brake master cylinder fluid reservoir and install the diaphragm and cap securely.

9. Install or connect the following:
   - MAF sensor and air cleaner outlet tube.
   - Negative battery cable.

10. Check the clutch for proper operation.

Halfshaft

REMOVAL & INSTALLATION

➡**Replace all snaprings, split pins and self-locking nuts.**

1. Before servicing the vehicle, refer to the precautions in the beginning of this section.

2. Loosen the strut upper mount nut 5 turns on the side to be serviced.

3. Remove or disconnect the following:
   - Wheel
   - Splash shield
   - Lower ball joint
   - Outer tie rod end
   - Stabilizer bar link

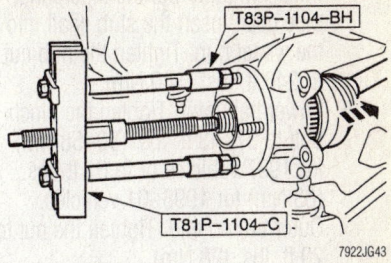

Front Hub Remover/Replacer T81P-1104-C

4. Separate the outer CV-joint and half-shaft from the wheel hub using Front Hub Remover/Replacer T81P-1104-C and its associated components, or equivalent.

5. Install CV-joint puller T86P-3514-A1 between the inner CV-joint and the transaxle case.

➡**If the intermediate shaft has already been removed, install Differential Rotator T81P-4026-A into the right side of the differential before removing the left shaft to maintain alignment within the differential.**

6. Remove the halfshaft.

To install:

7. Install or connect the following:
   - Halfshaft. A non-metallic mallet may be used to aid in seating the

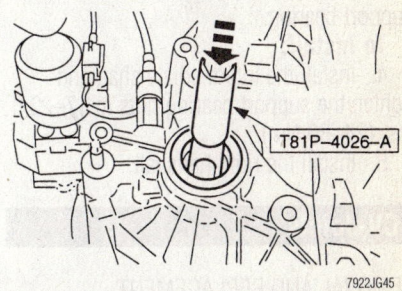

If the intermediate shaft has been removed, install Differential Rotator T81P-4026-A before removing the left halfshaft

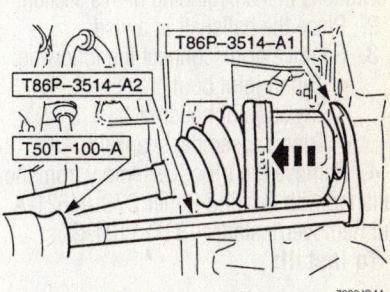

Use a slide hammer to pull the inner CV-joint from the transaxle

inner CV-joint into the differential side gear. Insert the stub shaft into the wheel hub. Tighten the hub nut to 246 ft. lbs. (340 Nm).

- Lower ball joint. Tighten the pinch bolt to 37–43 ft. lbs. (50–58 Nm) for 1997 vehicles or to 61 ft. lbs. (83 Nm) for 1998–01 vehicles.
- Outer tie rod end. Tighten the nut to 20 ft. lbs. (28 Nm).
- Stabilizer bar link. Tighten the nut to 14–23 ft. lbs. (20–32 Nm).
- Splash shield
- Wheel. Tighten the lug nuts to 63 ft. lbs. (86 Nm).

8. Tighten the strut upper mount nut to 34 ft. lbs. (46 Nm).

9. Road test the vehicle and check for proper operation.

Intermediate shaft

1. Before servicing the vehicle, refer to the precautions in the beginning of this section.

2. Remove the right halfshaft.

➡ **If the left halfshaft has already been removed, install Differential Rotator T81P-4026-A into the left side of the differential before removing the intermediate shaft to maintain alignment within the differential.**

3. Remove the intermediate shaft and support bearing.

To install:

4. Install the intermediate shaft and tighten the support bearing nuts to 17–22 ft. lbs. (24–30 Nm).

5. Install the right halfshaft.

CV-Joints

REMOVAL AND REPLACEMENT

Inner Tripod Joint

1. Before servicing the vehicle, refer to the precautions in the beginning of this section.

2. Place the halfshaft in a vise.

3. Remove or disconnect the following:
- Tripod joint boot
- Tripod joint housing
- Tripod assembly snapring

4. Remove the tripod assembly from the halfshaft with Bearing Puller D79L-4621-A and Remover/Installer T81P-1104-C

To install:

➡ **Use new snaprings and boot clamps.**

5. Install or connect the following:
- Tripod assembly and snapring

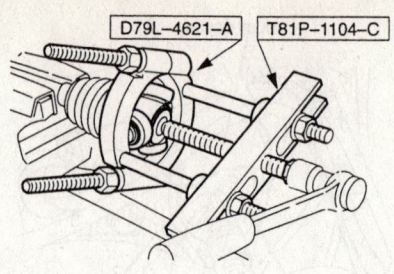

D79L–4621–A | T81P–1104–C

Removing the tripod assembly

- Tripod housing. Fill with fresh grease.
- Tripod boot and clamps

Outer CV-Joint

1. Before servicing the vehicle, refer to the precautions in the beginning of this section.

2. Place the halfshaft in a vise.

3. Remove the CV-joint boot clamps and slide the boot away from the joint.

4. Drive the CV-joint off the halfshaft with a brass drift and a hammer.

To install:

5. Replace the snapring.

6. Fill the CV-joint with fresh grease and slide the joint on to the halfshaft.

7. Use new clamps and install the CV-joint boot.

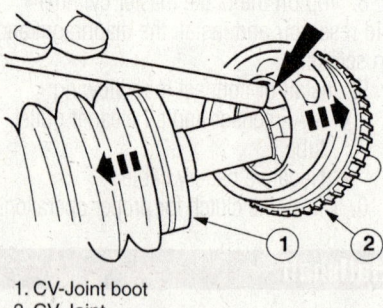

1. CV-Joint boot
2. CV-Joint

Removing the outer CV-joint

STEERING AND SUSPENSION

Air Bag

☀☀ CAUTION

Some vehicles are equipped with an air bag system. The system must be disarmed before performing service

on, or around, system components, the steering column, instrument panel components, wiring and sensors. Failure to follow the safety precautions and the disarming procedure could result in accidental air bag deployment, possible injury and unnecessary system repairs.

PRECAUTIONS

Several precautions must be observed when handling the inflator module to avoid accidental deployment and possible personal injury.

- Never carry the inflator module by the wires or connector on the underside of the module
- When carrying a live inflator module, hold securely with both hands, and ensure that the bag and trim cover are pointed away
- Place the inflator module on a bench or other surface with the bag and trim cover facing up
- With the inflator module on the bench, never place anything on or close to the module which may be thrown in the event of an accidental deployment

Before servicing the vehicle, also be sure to refer to the precautions in the beginning of this section as well

DISARMING

1. Before servicing the vehicle, refer to the precautions in the beginning of this section.

2. Position the vehicle with the front wheels in a straight-ahead position.

3. Disconnect the negative battery cable.

4. Disconnect the positive battery cable.

5. Wait at least 1 minute for the air bag back-up power supply to drain before continuing.

6. Proceed with the repair.

ARMING

1. Once complete, connect the battery cables, negative cable last.

2. Check the functioning of the air bag system by turning the ignition key to the **RUN** position and visually monitoring the air bag indicator lamp in the instrument cluster. The indicator lamp should illuminate for approximately 6 seconds, then turn **OFF**. If the indicator lamp does not illuminate, stays on, or flashes at any time, a fault has been detected by the air bag diagnostic monitor.

Power Rack and Pinion Steering Gear

REMOVAL & INSTALLATION

1. Before servicing the vehicle, refer to the precautions in the beginning of this section.

2. Attach an engine support fixture to the engine lifting eyes.

3. Secure the radiator and fan shroud to the radiator support using safety wire.

4. Remove or disconnect the following:
- Negative battery cable
- Steering gear flexible coupling
- Left, right and center splash shields
- Catalytic converter
- Front wheels
- Lower ball joints
- Outer tie rod ends
- Stabilizer bar links
- Left and right engine support insulators
- Power steering oil cooler lines
- A/C accumulator bolts
- Lower radiator supports
- Bumper cover braces
- Power steering hoses. Lower the subframe for access.

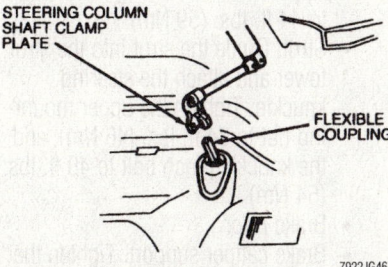

Disconnect the steering column shaft from the flexible coupling

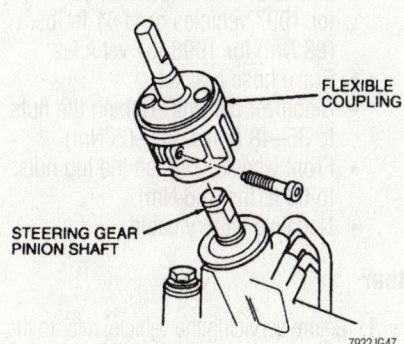

Disengage the flexible coupling from the steering gear pinion shaft

- Subframe with steering gear attached
- Steering gear cover plate
- Steering gear

To install:

5. Install or connect the following:
- Steering gear. Tighten the bolts to 101 ft. lbs. (137 Nm).
- Steering gear cover plate. Tighten the bolts to 37 ft. lbs. (50 Nm).
- Subframe. Use new seals and attach the power steering hoses before bolting the subframe in place.
- Special tool Subframe Alignment Pin Set T95P-2100-AH and the subframe bolts. Tighten the subframe bolts to 81–110 ft. lbs. (110–150 Nm). Remove the alignment pins.
- Special tool Powertrain Alignment Gauge T94P-6000-AH in place of the left engine support insulator. Tighten the 2 retaining bolts to 20 ft. lbs. (27 Nm) and snug the through-bolt.

➡ **The left and right support insulators must be aligned in the middle of the support insulator brackets.**

- Right engine support insulator. Tighten the 2 subframe retaining bolts to 30–41 ft. lbs. (41–55 Nm) and the

through-bolt to 75–102 ft. lbs. (103–137 Nm).

6. Remove the Powertrain Alignment Tool and install the left engine support insulator. Tighten the center bolt to 88 ft. lbs. (120 Nm), and the mounting bolts to 35 ft. lbs. (48 Nm).

7. Install or connect the following:
- Bumper cover braces
- Lower radiator supports
- A/C accumulator bolts
- Power steering oil cooler lines
- Stabilizer bar links
- Outer tie rod ends. Tighten the nuts to 23–35 ft. lbs. (31–47 Nm).
- Lower ball joints. Tighten the pinch bolt to 37–43 ft. lbs. (50–58 Nm) for 1997 vehicles or to 61 ft. lbs. (83 Nm) for 1998–01 vehicles.
- Front wheels. Tighten the lug nuts to 63 ft. lbs. (86 Nm).
- Catalytic converter
- Left, right and center splash shields
- Steering gear flexible coupling. Tighten the upper bolt to 21 ft. lbs. (28 Nm), and the lower bolt to 18 ft. lbs. (24 Nm).
- Negative battery cable

8. Fill the power steering system.

9. Run the engine and check for leaks and proper operation.

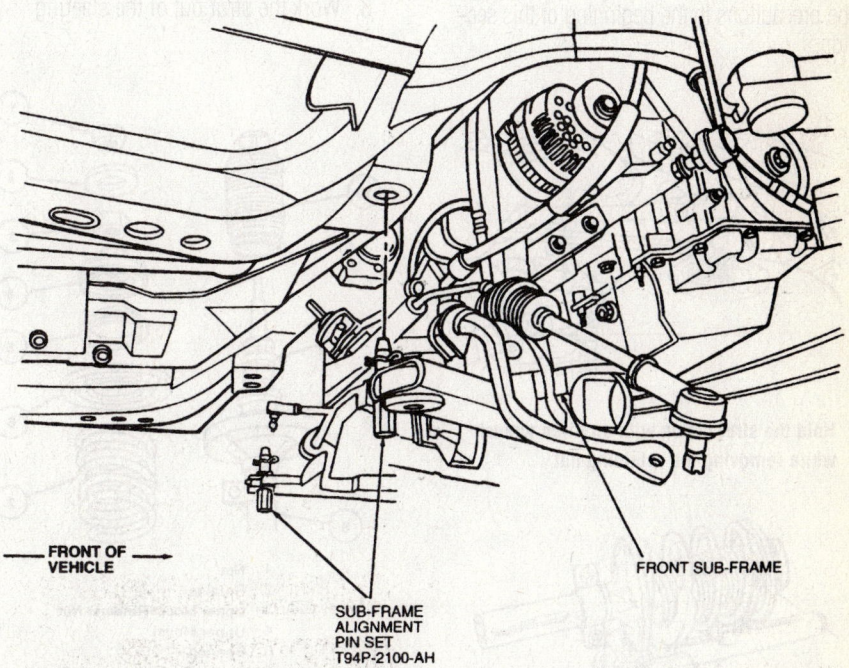

← **FRONT OF VEHICLE**

SUB-FRAME ALIGNMENT PIN SET T94P-2100-AH

FRONT SUB-FRAME

Install Subframe Alignment Pin Set T94P-2100-AH into the subframe to ensure correct positioning

Turn to Section 5 for brake system applications

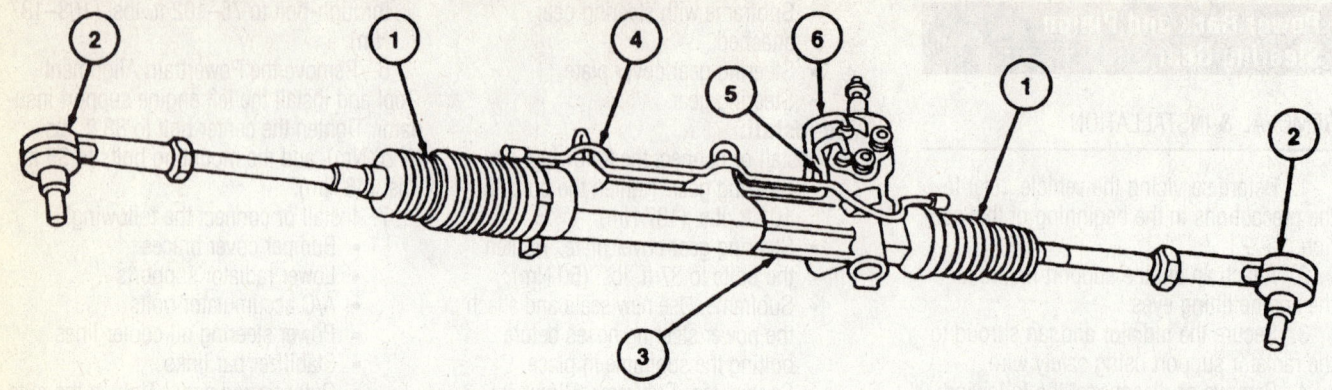

1. Front Suspension Steering Ball Dust Seal
2. Front Wheel Spindle Connecting End
3. Steering Gear
4. Power Steering Gear Rack Balance Tube
5. Power Steering Left Turn Pressure Tube
6. Power Steering Right Turn Pressure Tube

7922JG49

Power rack and pinion steering gear assembly component identification

➡ **Whenever the vehicle subframe is removed or lowered, the wheel alignment should be checked.**

Strut and Spring

REMOVAL & INSTALLATION

Front

1. Before servicing the vehicle, refer to the precautions in the beginning of this section.

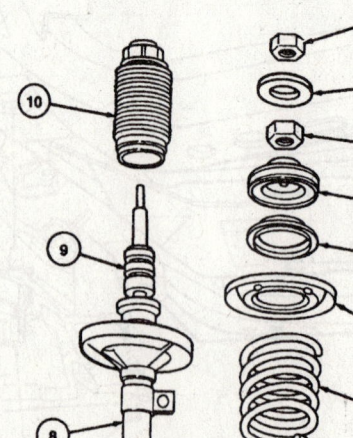

7922JG50

Hold the strut piston with an Allen wrench while removing the retaining nut

ROTUNDA SPRING COMPRESSOR

7922JG51

Compress the coil spring assembly before removing the retaining nut

2. Remove or disconnect the following:
   • Negative battery cable
   • Front wheels
   • Upper strut mount nut
   • Stabilizer bar link
   • Brake hose bracket
   • Lower ball joint
   • Wheel speed sensor
   • Brake caliper and caliper support
   • Brake rotor
   • Steering knuckle pinch bolt
3. Work the strut out of the steering

1 Nut
2 Retainer
3 Upper Mount Retainer Nut
4 Upper Mount
5 Bearing
6 Spring Seat
7 Front Coil Spring
8 Front Shock Absorber
9 Jounce Bumper
10 Dust Shield

7922JG52

Exploded view of the strut assembly

knuckle and lower the strut out of the strut tower.

4. Comrpess the spring and remove the upper strut mount.

5. Remove the spring from the strut.

To install:

6. Transfer parts as necessary, and install the spring onto the strut.

7. Install or connect the following:
   • Upper strut mount. Tighten the nut to 44 ft. lbs. (59 Nm).
   • Strut. Guide the strut into the strut tower and attach the steering knuckle. Tighten the upper mounting nut to 34 ft. lbs. (46 Nm), and the knuckle pinch bolt to 40 ft. lbs. (54 Nm).
   • Brake rotor
   • Brake caliper support. Tighten the bolts to 88 ft. lbs. (120 Nm).
   • Wheel speed sensor
   • Lower ball joint. Tighten the pinch bolt to 37–43 ft. lbs. (50–58 Nm) for 1997 vehicles or to 61 ft. lbs. (83 Nm) for 1998–01 vehicles.
   • Brake hose bracket
   • Stabilizer bar link. Tighten the nuts to 35–48 ft. lbs. (47–65 Nm).
   • Front wheels. Tighten the lug nuts to 63 ft. lbs. (86 Nm).
   • Negative battery cable

Rear

1. Before servicing the vehicle, refer to the precautions in the beginning of this section.

2. Remove or disconnect the following:
   • Negative battery cable
   • Rear wheels
   • Wheel speed sensor

- Rear brake hose
- Stabilizer bar link
- Tie rod

➡ **The front and rear control arms must be supported before the removal of the strut attachments.**

- Spindle pinch bolt

3. Separate the spindle from the strut by tapping down on the wheel spindle.

4. Compress the coil spring.

5. Remove the 2 top retaining bolts and remove the strut assembly.

6. Compress the coil spring enough to relieve the tension on the spring seat.

7. Remove the top mount nut, rear strut bracket, bushing and spring seat.

8. Remove the coil spring from the strut.

To install:

9. Transfer parts as necessary and install the spring to the strut.

10. Install the spring seat, bushing, rear strut bracket and the top mount nut. Tighten the top mount nut to 30–43 ft. lbs. (41–58 Nm).

11. With the coil spring compressed, install the strut assembly into position.

12. Install or connect the following:

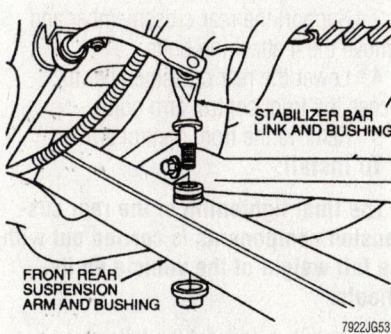

For rear strut removal, disconnect the sway bar link from the control arm

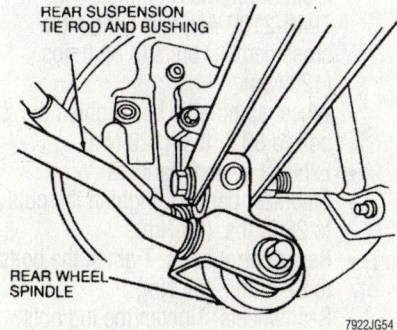

. . . and separate the tie rod from the rear wheel spindle

- Strut bracket mounting bolts. Tighten the bolts to 17–22 ft. lbs. (23–30 Nm).

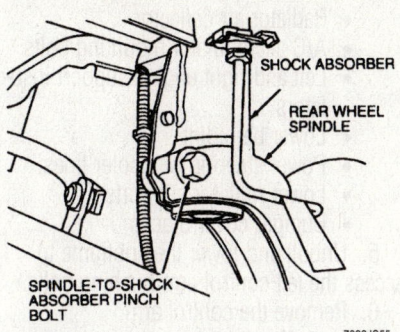

Remove the rear strut pinch bolt to release the strut assembly from the spindle

- Spindle pinch bolt. Tighten the bolt to 52–72 ft. lbs. (70–98 Nm). Remove the spring compressor.

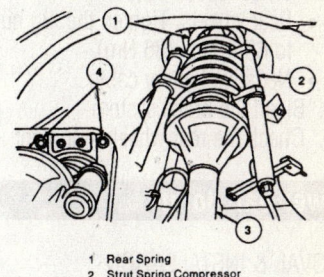

1 Rear Spring
2 Strut Spring Compressor
3 Shock Absorber
4 Mounting Nuts

Compress the coil spring, then unthread the 2 top retaining bolts and remove the strut from the vehicle

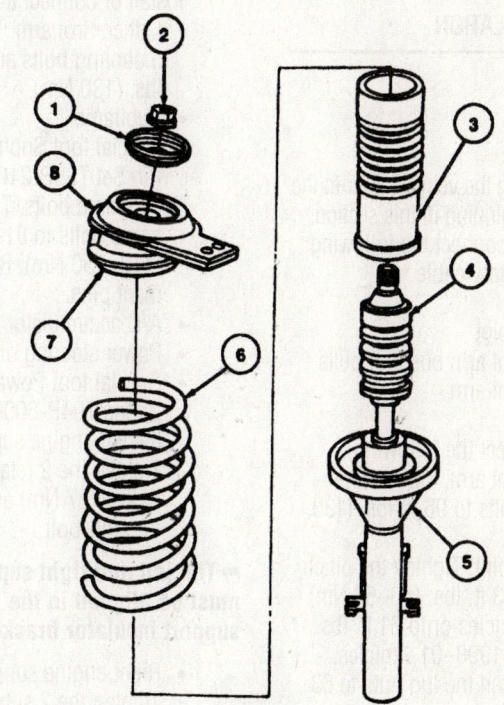

1 Rear Shock Absorber Bracket
2 Shock Absorber Mounting Nut
3 Rear Shock Absorber Dust Boot
4 Rear Suspension Jounce Bumper
5 Shock Absorber
6 Rear Spring
7 Spring Seat
8 Shock Absorber Bushing

Exploded view of the rear strut assembly

- Tie rod. Tighten the bolt to 75–102 ft. lbs. (102–138 Nm).
- Stabilizer bar link
- Rear brake hose
- Wheel speed sensor
- Rear wheels. Tighten the lug nuts to 63 ft. lbs. (86 Nm).
- Negative battery cable
13. Bleed the brake system.
14. Check the rear wheel alignment.

Lower Ball Joint

REMOVAL & INSTALLATION

The lower ball joint is serviced with the lower control arm as an assembly.

Lower Control Arm

REMOVAL & INSTALLATION

Front

RIGHT SIDE

1. Before servicing the vehicle, refer to the precautions in the beginning of this section.
2. Remove or disconnect the following:
   - Negative battery cable
   - Wheel
   - Lower ball joint
   - Lower control arm bushing bolts
   - Lower control arm
   To install:
3. Install or connect the following:
   - Lower control arm. Tighten the mounting bolts to 96 ft. lbs. (130 Nm).
   - Lower ball joint. Tighten the pinch bolt to 37–43 ft. lbs. (50–58 Nm) for 1997 vehicles or to 61 ft. lbs. (83 Nm) for 1998–01 vehicles.
   - Wheel. Tighten the lug nuts to 63 ft. lbs. (86 Nm).
   - Negative battery cable
4. Check the wheel alignment.

LEFT SIDE

1. Before servicing the vehicle, refer to the precautions in the beginning of this section.
2. Secure the radiator and fan shroud with safety wire to the radiator support.
3. Attach an engine support fixture to the engine lifting eyes.
4. Remove or disconnect the following:
   - Negative battery cable
   - Steering column pinch bolt
   - Left, right and center splash shields

- Exhaust crossover pipe (2.5L engine)
- Catalytic converter
- Front wheel
- Vehicle Speed Sensor (VSS)
- Radiator air deflector
- A/C accumulator mounting bolts
- Left and right engine support insulators
- Lower ball joint
- Power steering oil cooler lines
- Lower radiator supports
- Bumper cover braces
5. Unbolt and lower the subframe to access the left control arm bushing bolts.
6. Remove the control arm.
   To install:

➡ **Replace all snaprings, split pins, and self-locking nuts.**

7. Install or connect the following:
   - Left control arm. Tighten the mounting bolts and nuts to 96 ft. lbs. (130 Nm).
   - Subframe
   - Special tool Subframe Alignment Pin Set T95P-2100-AH and the subframe bolts. Tighten the subframe bolts to 81–110 ft. lbs. (110–150 Nm). Remove the alignment pins.
   - A/C accumulator bolts
   - Power steering oil cooler lines
   - Special tool Powertrain Alignment Gauge T94P-6000-AH in place of the left engine support insulator. Tighten the 2 retaining bolts to 20 ft. lbs. (27 Nm) and snug the through-bolt.

➡ **The left and right support insulators must be aligned in the middle of the support insulator brackets.**

   - Right engine support insulator. Tighten the 2 subframe retaining bolts to 30–41 ft. lbs. (41–55 Nm) and the through-bolt to 75–102 ft. lbs. (103–137 Nm).
8. Remove the Powertrain Alignment Tool and install the left engine support insulator. Tighten the center bolt to 88 ft. lbs. (120 Nm), and the mounting bolts to 35 ft. lbs. (48 Nm).
   - Bumper cover braces
   - Lower radiator supports. Tighten the bolts to 71–97 inch lbs. (8–11 Nm).
   - Power steering oil cooler lines
   - Lower ball joint. Tighten the pinch bolt to 37–43 ft. lbs. (50–58 Nm) for 1997 vehicles or to 61 ft. lbs. (83 Nm) for 1998–01 vehicles.

- A/C accumulator mounting bolts
- Radiator air deflector
- VSS sensor
- Front wheel. Tighten the lug nuts to 63 ft. lbs. (86 Nm).
- Catalytic converter
- Exhaust crossover pipe (2.5L engine)
- Left, right and center splash shields
- Steering column pinch bolt. Tighten the bolt to 15–20 ft. lbs. (20–27 Nm).
- Battery
9. Road test the vehicle and check for proper operation.

➡ **Whenever the vehicle subframe is removed or lowered, the wheel alignment should be checked.**

Rear

1. Before servicing the vehicle, refer to the precautions in the beginning of this section.
2. Remove or disconnect the following:
   - Rear wheels
   - Rear control arms
   - Stabilizer bar link
   - Exhaust system hangers
   - Wheel spindle tie bar
3. Support the rear crossmember and remove the 4 attaching bolts.
4. Lower the rear crossmember to access the front control arm bolts.
5. Remove the front control arm.
   To install:

➡ **The final tightening of the rear suspension components is carried out with the full weight of the vehicle on its wheels.**

6. Install or connect the following:
   - Front control arm. Tighten the bolts to 62 ft. lbs. (84 Nm).
   - Rear crossmember. Use special tools Subframe Alignment Pins T94P-2100-AH, and tighten the crossmember bolts to 88 ft. lbs. (120 Nm).
   - Wheel spindle tie bar. Tighten the bolt to 88 ft. lbs. (120 Nm).
   - Exhaust system hangers
   - Stabilizer bar link. Tighten the nuts to 26 ft. lbs. (35 Nm).
   - Rear control arms. Tighten the bolts to 62 ft. lbs. (84 Nm).
   - Rear wheels. Tighten the lug nuts to 63 ft. lbs. (86 Nm).
7. Complete the final tightening of the rear suspension components with the full weight of the vehicle resting on its wheels.

CONTROL ARM BUSHING REPLACEMENT

The control arm bushings are serviced with the control arm as an assembly

Wheel Bearings

ADJUSTMENT

Front and Rear

The wheel bearings are not adjustable. If the bearings make noise or become loose, they must be replaced.

REMOVAL & INSTALLATION

Front

1. Before servicing the vehicle, refer to the precautions in the beginning of this section.

2. Remove or disconnect the following:

- Negative battery cable
- Front wheel
- Brake caliper support and rotor
- Wheel speed sensor
- Outer tie rod end
- Wheel hub retaining nut
- Lower ball joint
- Steering knuckle pinch bolt
- Halfshaft from the wheel hub
- Steering knuckle from the vehicle

3. Install Front Hub Remover/Replacer T81P-1104-C or equivalent with the appropriate adapters and separate the hub from the steering knuckle.

- Inner and outer snaprings securing the wheel bearing
- Wheel bearing from the steering knuckle. Drive or press the old wheel bearing out as required.

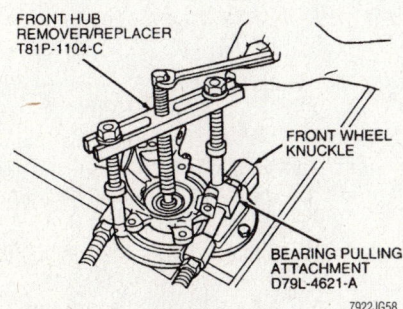

Use gear or bearing pulling tools to remove the hub from the steering knuckle

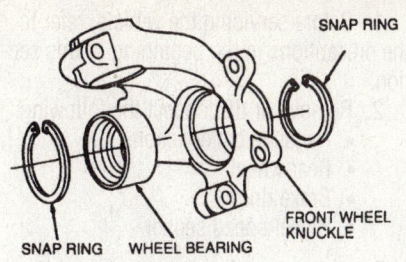

The wheel bearing is retained in the knuckle by 2 snaprings

To install:

➡**Replace all snaprings, split pins and self-locking nuts.**

4. Install or connect the following:

- Outer snapring into the steering knuckle
- Wheel bearing using a hydraulic press with Pinion Bearing Cup Replacer T80T-4000-E
- Inner snapring in the steering knuckle
- Hub to the steering knuckle using Threaded Drawbar T75T-1176-A or equivalent
- Steering knuckle. Tighten the strut pinch bolt to 40 ft. lbs. (54 Nm),

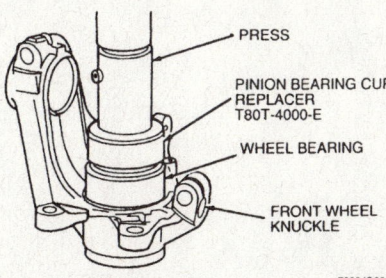

Using a press, install the new wheel bearing in the knuckle

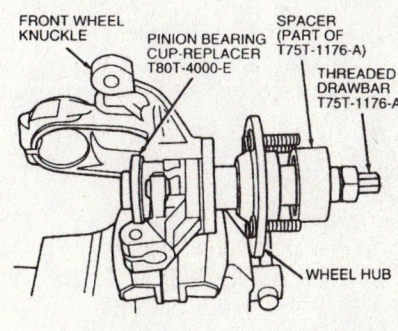

Use the special tools shown or a press to install the hub in the knuckle assembly

and the ball joint pinch bolt to 37–43 ft. lbs. (50–58 Nm) for 1997 vehicles or to 61 ft. lbs. (83 Nm) for 1998–01 vehicles.

- Wheel speed sensor
- Wheel hub retaining nut. Tighten the hub nut to 246 ft. lbs. (340 Nm).
- Outer tie rod end. Tighten the nut to 18–22 ft. lbs. (24–30 Nm).
- Wheel speed sensor
- Brake caliper support and rotor. Tighten the bolts to 88 ft. lbs. (120 Nm).
- Front wheel. Tighten the lug nuts to 63 ft. lbs. (86 Nm).
- Negative battery cable

5. Road test the vehicle and check for proper operation.

Rear

➡**The wheel bearings are contained within the wheel hub and must be replaced as an assembly.**

WITH REAR DISC BRAKES

1. Before servicing the vehicle, refer to the precautions in the beginning of this section.

2. Remove or disconnect the following:

- Negative battery cable
- Rear wheel
- Wheel speed sensor
- Brake caliper bracket and rotor

➡**Do not use an impact gun to remove the hub retainer nut.**

- Hub retainer nut

3. Slide the hub and wheel bearing assembly off of the spindle.

To install:

4. Install or connect the following:

- Hub and bearing assembly. Tighten the hub retainer nut to 170–192 ft. lbs. (230–260 Nm).
- Brake rotor and caliper bracket. Tighten the bracket bolts to 88 ft. lbs. (120 Nm).
- Wheel speed sensor
- Rear wheel. Tighten the lug nuts to 63 ft. lbs. (86 Nm).
- Negative battery cable

5. Road test the vehicle and check for proper operation.

WITH REAR DRUM BRAKES

➡**The wheel bearings are contained within the wheel hub and must be replaced as an assembly.**

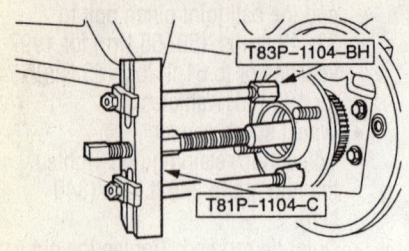

After removing the spindle nut, use the special tools or a puller to remove the rear hub/bearing assembly—Models equipped with rear drum brakes

7922JG62

1. Before servicing the vehicle, refer to the precautions in the beginning of this section.
2. Remove or disconnect the following:
   • Negative battery cable
   • Rear wheel
   • Brake drum
   • Wheel speed sensor

➡ **Do not use an impact gun to remove the hub retainer nut.**

   • Wheel hub retainer nut
3. Remove the hub from the spindle with a hub puller.

To install:
4. Install or connect the following:
   • Hub and bearing assembly. Tighten the hub retainer nut to 170–192 ft. lbs. (230–260 Nm).
   • Brake drum
   • Wheel speed sensor
   • Rear wheel. Tighten the lug nuts to 63 ft. lbs. (86 Nm).
   • Negative battery cable
5. Road test the vehicle and check for proper operation.

FORD MOTOR CO.

Ford-Taurus • Mercury-Sable

19

PRECAUTIONS

Before servicing any vehicle, please be sure to read all of the following precautions, which deal with personal safety, prevention of component damage, and important points to take into consideration when servicing a motor vehicle:

• Never open, service or drain the radiator or cooling system when the engine is hot; serious burns can occur from the steam and hot coolant.

• Observe all applicable safety precautions when working around fuel. Whenever servicing the fuel system, always work in a well-ventilated area. Do not allow fuel spray or vapors to come in contact with a spark, open flame, or excessive heat (a hot drop light, for example). Keep a dry chemical fire extinguisher near the work area. Always keep fuel in a container specifically designed for fuel storage; also, always properly seal fuel containers to avoid the possibility of fire or explosion. Refer to the additional fuel system precautions later in this section.

• Fuel injection systems often remain pressurized, even after the engine has been turned OFF. The fuel system pressure must be relieved before disconnecting any fuel lines. Failure to do so may result in fire and/or personal injury.

• Brake fluid often contains polyglycol ethers and polyglycols. Avoid contact with the eyes and wash your hands thoroughly after handling brake fluid. If you do get brake fluid in your eyes, flush your eyes with clean, running water for 15 minutes. If eye irritation persists, or if you have taken brake fluid internally, IMMEDIATELY seek medical assistance.

• The EPA warns that prolonged contact with used engine oil may cause a number of skin disorders, including cancer. You should make every effort to minimize your exposure to used engine oil. Protective gloves should be worn when changing oil. Wash your hands and any other exposed skin areas as soon as possible after exposure to used engine oil. Soap and water, or waterless hand cleaner should be used.

• All new vehicles are now equipped with an air bag system, often referred to as a Supplemental Restraint System (SRS) or Supplemental Inflatable Restraint (SIR) system. The system must be disabled before performing service on or around system components, steering column, instrument panel components, wiring and sensors. Failure to follow safety and disabling proce-

dures could result in accidental air bag deployment, possible personal injury and unnecessary system repairs.

• Always wear safety goggles when working with, or around, the air bag system. When carrying a non-deployed air bag, be sure the bag and trim cover are pointed away from your body. When placing a non-deployed air bag on a work surface, always face the bag and trim cover upward, away from the surface. This will reduce the motion of the module if it is accidentally deployed. Refer to the additional air bag system precautions later in this section.

• Clean, high quality brake fluid from a sealed container is essential to the safe and proper operation of the brake system. You should always buy the correct type of brake fluid for your vehicle. If the brake fluid becomes contaminated, completely flush the system with new fluid. Never reuse any brake fluid. Any brake fluid that is removed from the system should be discarded. Also, do not allow any brake fluid to come in contact with a painted surface; it will damage the paint.

• Never operate the engine without the proper amount and type of engine oil; doing so will result in severe engine damage.

• Timing belt maintenance is extremely important. Many models utilize an interference-type, non-freewheeling engine. If the timing belt breaks, the valves in the cylinder head may strike the pistons, causing potentially serious (also time-consuming and expensive) engine damage. Refer to the maintenance interval charts in the front of this manual for the recommended replacement interval for the timing belt, and to the timing belt section for belt replacement and inspection.

• Disconnecting the negative battery cable on some vehicles may interfere with the functions of the on-board computer system(s) and may require the computer to undergo a relearning process once the negative battery cable is reconnected.

• When servicing drum brakes, only disassemble and assemble one side at a time, leaving the remaining side intact for reference.

ENGINE REPAIR

➡**Disconnecting the negative battery cable on some vehicles may interfere with the functions of the on board computer system. The computer may**

undergo a relearning process once the negative battery cable is reconnected.

Alternator

REMOVAL

3.0L (VIN U) Engine

1. Before servicing the vehicle, refer to the precautions at the beginning of this section.
2. Remove or disconnect the following:
   • Negative battery cable
   • Accessory drive belt
   • Alternator wiring connectors
   • Alternator brace
   • Alternator

3.0L (VIN S) Engine

1. Before servicing the vehicle, refer to the precautions at the beginning of this section.
2. Remove or disconnect the following:
   • Negative battery cable
   • Accessory drive belt
   • Power steering line and heater hose bracket
   • Upper alternator bolts
   • Right front wheel
   • Right splash shield
   • Alternator splash shield
   • Alternator electrical connectors
   • Lower alternator bolt
3. Lower the right side of the subframe for clearance and remove the alternator.

3.4L (VIN N) Engine

1. Before servicing the vehicle, refer to the precautions at the beginning of this section.
2. Remove or disconnect the following:
   • Negative battery cable
   • Right cowl vent screen
   • Right front wheel
   • Right outer tie rod end
   • Accessory drive belt
   • Alternator electrical connectors
   • Engine control sensor wiring
   • Alternator

INSTALLATION

3.0L (VIN U) Engine

➡**Do not tighten the alternator pivot and bracket bolts until the accessory drive belt is installed.**

1. Install or connect the following:
   • Alternator
   • Alternator brace. Tighten the bolts to

76–97 inch lbs. (8–11 Nm), and the nut to 15–22 ft. lbs. (20–30 Nm).
- Alternator wiring connectors
- Accessory drive belt

2. Tighten the alternator pivot bolt to 30–40 ft. lbs. (40–55 Nm), and the bracket bolt to 15–22 ft. lbs. (20–30 Nm).

3. Install the negative battery cable. Start the engine and check for proper operation.

3.0L (VIN S) Engine

1. Install or connect the following:
- Alternator. Tighten the bolts to 18 ft. lbs. (25 Nm).
- Right subframe bolts. Tighten to 66 ft. lbs. (90 Nm).
- Alternator electrical connectors
- Alternator splash shield
- Right splash shield
- Right front wheel
- Power steering line and heater hose bracket
- Accessory drive belt
- Negative battery cable

2. Start the engine and check for proper operation.

3.4L (VIN N) Engine

1. Install or connect the following:
- Alternator. Tighten the bolts to 15–22 ft. lbs. (20–30 Nm).
- Engine control sensor wiring
- Alternator electrical connectors
- Accessory drive belt
- Right outer tie rod end
- Right front wheel
- Right cowl vent screen
- Negative battery cable

2. Start the engine and check for proper operation.

Ignition Timing

ADJUSTMENT

The base ignition timing is set at 10 degrees Before Top Dead Center (BTDC) and is not adjustable.

Engine Assembly

REMOVAL & INSTALLATION

1. Before servicing the vehicle, refer to the precautions at the beginning of this section.
2. Disconnect the negative battery cable.
3. Drain the engine oil.
4. Drain the cooling system.

5. Recover the A/C refrigerant.
6. On the 3.0L (VIN S) engine, remove or disconnect the following:
- Windshield wipers
- Cowl extension
- Emission vacuum control connector at the right side of the dash panel

7. On the 3.4L (VIN N) engine, remove or disconnect the following:
- Battery and tray
- Engine appearance cover
- Cowl top extension
- Windshield wiper module

8. For all vehicles, remove or disconnect the following:
- Hood
- Steering column pinch bolt
- Mass Airflow (MAF) sensor connector
- Intake Air Temperature (IAT) sensor
- Air cleaner assembly
- Fuel lines
- Intake manifold vacuum hoses
- Ground straps
- Powertrain Control Module (PCM) connector
- Engine control sensor wiring harness connectors from the bracket located at the top of the transaxle
- Evaporative emission canister purge valve connector
- Crankcase vent hose
- Accelerator cable
- Cruise control actuator
- Shift cable and lever
- Secondary air injection pump relay connector
- Main emission vacuum control connector near the fan shroud
- Radiator hoses
- Heater hoses
- Transaxle oil cooler lines
- Power steering return hose
- Alternator wiring harness connectors
- A/C compressor lines
- A/C pressure cutoff switch, if equipped
- Front wheels
- Stabilizer bar links
- Lower ball joints
- Outer tie rod ends
- Halfshafts
- Radiator splash shield
- Heated Oxygen (HO2S) sensors
- Dual converter Y-pipe
- Power steering pressure switch connector
- Power steering pressure hose

9. Support the powertrain from below and remove the subframe bolts.

10. Raise the vehicle away from the powertrain.

11. Attach an engine hoist to the powertrain.

12. Remove the left, right, and rear powertrain support insulators and lift the powertrain away from the subframe.

13. Support the transaxle from below.

14. Remove or disconnect the following:
- Starter
- Torque converter
- Transaxle flange bolts

15. Separate the engine from the transaxle.

To install:

16. Install the transaxle. For 1999–01 3.0L (VIN S) engines, tighten the flange bolts to 25–33 ft. lbs. (33–46 Nm). For all other engines, tighten the flange bolts to 30–44 ft. lbs. (40–60 Nm). Tighten the torque converter nuts to 20–34 ft. lbs. (27–46 Nm).

17. Install or connect the following:
- Starter. Tighten the fasteners to 21 ft. lbs. (29 Nm).
- Powertrain support insulators. Tighten the bracket bolts to 65 ft. lbs. (88 Nm), and the subframe bolts to 90 ft. lbs. (122 Nm).

18. Lower the vehicle on to the powertrain assembly. Use 2 pieces of ¾ inch outside diameter pipe in the alignment holes behind the front subframe mounts to align the subframe to the body. Tighten the subframe mounting bolts to 57–76 ft. lbs. (77–103 Nm).

19. Install or connect the following:
- Power steering pressure hose
- Power steering pressure switch connector
- Dual converter Y-pipe
- HO2S sensors
- Radiator splash shield
- Halfshafts. Tighten the hub retainer nuts to 170–202 ft. lbs. (230–275 Nm).
- Outer tie rod ends. Tighten the nuts to 35–46 ft. lbs. (47–63 Nm).
- Lower ball joints. Tighten the nuts to 50–68 ft. lbs. (68–92 Nm).
- Stabilizer bar links. Tighten the nuts to 30–40 ft. lbs. (40–55 Nm).
- Front wheels
- A/C pressure cutoff switch, if equipped
- A/C compressor lines
- Alternator wiring harness connectors
- Power steering return hose
- Transaxle oil cooler lines
- Heater hoses
- Radiator hoses
- Main emission vacuum control connector near the fan shroud

- Secondary air injection pump relay connector
- Shift cable and lever
- Cruise control actuator
- Accelerator cable
- Crankcase vent hose
- Evaporative emission canister purge valve connector
- Engine control sensor wiring harness connectors from the bracket located at the top of the transaxle
- PCM connector
- Ground straps
- Intake manifold vacuum hoses
- Fuel lines
- Air cleaner assembly
- IAT sensor

- MAF sensor connector
- Steering column pinch bolt
- Hood

19. On the 3.0L (VIN S) engine, install or connect the following:
- Windshield wipers
- Cowl extension
- Emission vacuum control connector at the right side of the dash panel

20. On the 3.4L (VIN N) engine, install or connect the following:
- Battery and tray
- Engine appearance cover
- Cowl top extension
- Windshield wiper module

21. Fill the cooling system, fill the crankcase, and recharge the A/C system.

22. Connect the negative battery cable.
23. Start the engine. Check for leaks and proper operation.

➡ **Whenever the vehicle's subframe is removed or lowered, the wheel alignment should be checked.**

Water Pump

REMOVAL & INSTALLATION

3.0L (VIN U) Engine

1. Before servicing the vehicle, refer to the precautions at the beginning of this section.

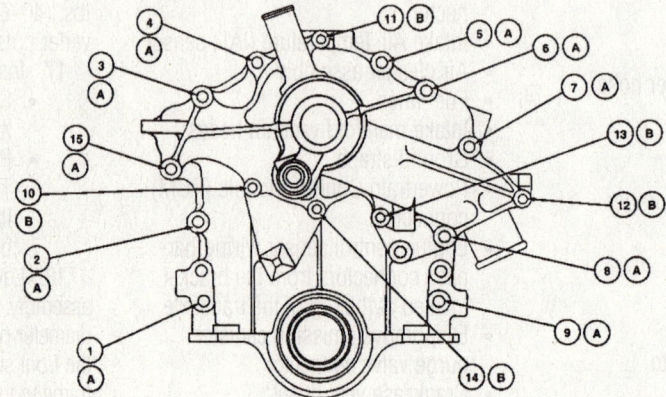

Fasteners			Torque Specifications	
Fastener And Hole No.	Size	Fastener Application	Nm	Lb-Ft
1A	M8 x 1.25 x 43.5	F/C TO BLOCK	20-30	15-22
2A	M8 x 1.25 x 73	W/P & F/C TO BLOCK	20-30	15-22
3A	M8 x 1.25 x 104.3	W/P & F/C TO BLOCK	20-30	15-22
4A	M8 x 1.25 x 71.3	F/C TO BLOCK	20-30	15-22
5A	M8 x 1.25 x 71.3	W/P & F/C TO BLOCK	20-30	15-22
6A	M8 x 1.25 x 71.3	W/P & F/C TO BLOCK	20-30	15-22
7A	M8 x 1.25 x 104.3	W/P & F/C TO BLOCK	20-30	15-22
8A	M8 x 1.25 x 104.3	W/P & F/C TO BLOCK	20-30	15-22
9A	M8 x 1.25 x 52	F/C TO BLOCK	20-30	15-22
10B	M6 x 1 x 28.5	W/P TO F/C	8-12	71-106 (lb-in)
11B	M6 x 1 x 28.5	W/P TO F/C	8-12	71-106 (lb-in)
12B	M6 x 1 x 28.5	W/P TO F/C	8-12	71-106 (lb-in)
13B	M6 x 1 x 28.5	W/P TO F/C	8-12	71-106 (lb-in)
14B	M6 x 1 x 28.5	W/P TO F/C	8-12	71-106 (lb-in)
15A	M8 x 1.25 x 71.3	W/P & F/C TO BLOCK	20-30	15-22

W/P—Water Pump
F/C—Engine Front Cover

9300KG01

Exploded view of the water pump and timing front cover bolt locations—3.0L (VIN U) engine

2. Drain the cooling system.
3. Remove or disconnect the following:
- Negative battery cable
- Accessory drive belt and tensioner
- Water pump pulley
- Heater hose
- Engine control sensor wiring
- Water pump

To install:

➡**The bolts are of different lengths and must be installed in the correct locations.**

4. Install the water pump. Tighten bolts No's. 1, 2, 3, 4, 5, 6, 7, 8, 9 and 15 to 15–22 ft. lbs. (20–30 Nm). Tighten bolts Nos. 10, 11, 12, 13 and 14 to 72–106 inch lbs. (8–12 Nm). Refer to the accompanying illustration for the bolt locations.
5. Install or connect the following:
- Engine control sensor wiring
- Heater hose
- Water pump pulley. Tighten the bolts to 15–22 ft. lbs. (20–30 Nm).
- Accessory drive belt and tensioner
- Negative battery cable

6. Fill the cooling system and check for leaks.

3.0L (VIN S) Engine

1. Before servicing the vehicle, refer to the precautions at the beginning of this section.
2. Drain the cooling system.
3. Remove or disconnect the following:
- Negative battery cable
- Water pump drive belt
- Radiator and heater hoses
- A/C compressor brace
- Water pump

To install:

4. Install or connect the following:
- Water pump. Tighten the nuts to 15–22 ft. lbs. (20–30 Nm).
- A/C compressor brace. Tighten the nuts to 15–22 ft. lbs. (20–30 Nm).
- Radiator and heater hoses
- Water pump drive belt
- Negative battery cable

5. Fill the cooling system and check for leaks.

3.4L (VIN N) Engine

1. Before servicing the vehicle, refer to the precautions at the beginning of this section.
2. Drain the cooling system.
3. Remove or disconnect the following:
- Engine appearance cover

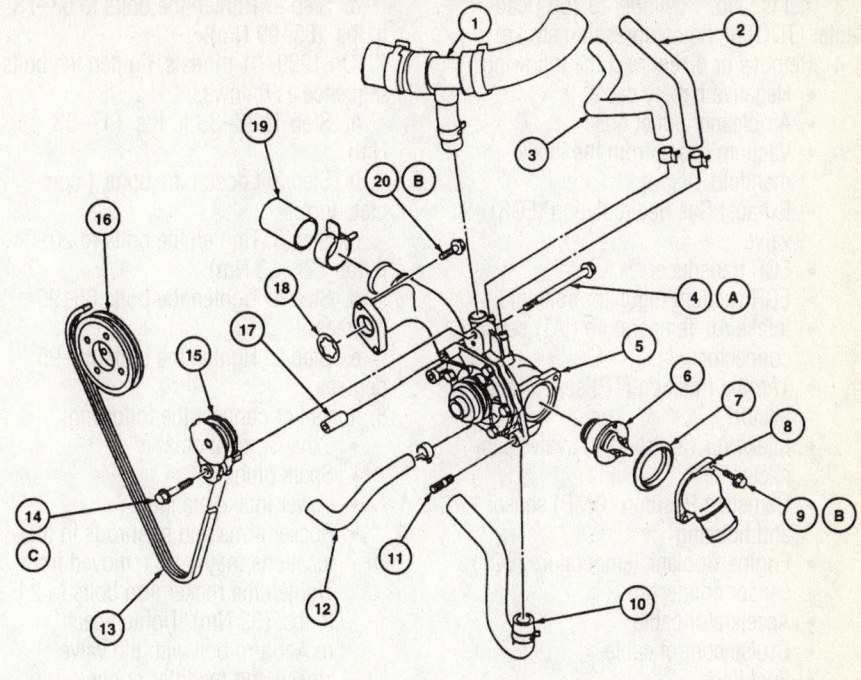

1	Water Outlet Hose		12	Oil Cooler to Water Pump Return Hose
2	Throttle Body to Water Pump Return Hose		13	Drive Belt
3	Water Pump to Throttle Body Supply Hose		14	Bolt
4	Bolt (2 Req'd)		15	Belt Idler Pulley
5	Water Pump		16	Water Pump Drive Pulley
6	Water Thermostat		17	Collar
7	Oil Cooler Return Tube Gasket		18	O-Ring
8	Water Hose Connection		19	Water Inlet Hose
9	Bolt (2 Req'd)		20	Bolt
10	Heater Core to Water Pump Return Hose		A	Tighten to 18-28 N·m (14-20 Lb-Ft)
11	Stud		B	Tighten to 10-16 N·m (89-141 Lb-In)
			C	Tighten to 8-12 N·m (71-106 Lb-In)

7922KG03

Exploded view of the water pump and related components—3.4L (VIN N) engine

- Battery and tray
- Water pump drive belt
- Coolant hoses
- Thermostat
- Water pump

To install:

4. If replacing the water pump, transfer the idler pulley and tighten the bolt to 89–141 inch lbs. (10–16 Nm).
5. Install or connect the following:
- Water pump. Tighten the 2 water inlet bolts to 71–106 inch lbs. (8–12 Nm). Tighten the 2 remaining bolts to 14–20 ft. lbs. (18–28 Nm).
- Thermostat. Tighten the bolts to 71–106 inch lbs. (8–12 Nm).

- Coolant hoses
- Water pump drive belt
- Battery and tray
- Engine appearance cover

6. Fill the cooling system and check for leaks.

Cylinder Head

REMOVAL & INSTALLATION

3.0L (VIN U) Engine

1. Before servicing the vehicle, refer to the precautions at the beginning of this section.
2. Drain the cooling system.

Timing belt service is covered in Section 4 of this manual

3. Set the No. 1 cylinder to Top Dead Center (TDC) of the compression stroke.

4. Remove or disconnect the following:
- Negative battery cable
- Air cleaner outlet hose
- Vacuum hoses from the intake manifold
- Exhaust Gas Recirculation (EGR) valve
- EGR transducer
- EGR vacuum regulator solenoid
- Intake Air Temperature (IAT) sensor connector
- Throttle Position (TP) sensor connector
- Intake Air Control (IAC) valve connector
- Camshaft Position (CMP) sensor and housing
- Engine Coolant Temperature (ECT) sensor connector
- Accelerator cable
- Cruise control cable
- Fuel lines
- Upper intake manifold
- Fuel injector wiring harness
- Coolant hoses
- Ignition coil and bracket
- Spark plug wires
- Accessory drive belt and tensioner
- Alternator
- Power steering pump
- Oil dipstick tube
- Heater supply tube brackets
- Valve covers
- Rocker arms and pushrods. Keep the rocker arms and pushrods in order for installation.
- Lower intake manifold
- Spark plugs
- Exhaust manifolds
- Cylinder heads

To install:

→The cylinder head bolts are a torque-to-yield design and cannot be reused.

→Refer to Section 1 of this manual for the cylinder head torque sequence illustration. The illustration is located after the Torque Specification Chart.

5. Install the cylinder heads with new gaskets.

6. On 1997–98 models, tighten the bolts in sequence as follows:

   a. Step 1: 53–66 ft. lbs. (70–90 Nm).

   b. Step 2: Loosen the bolts 1 complete turn.

   c. Step 3: Tighten the bolts to 34–40 ft. lbs. (45–55 Nm).

   d. Step 4: Tighten the bolts to 63–73 ft. lbs. (85–99 Nm).

7. On 1999–01 models, tighten the bolts in sequence as follows:

   a. Step 1: 36–39 ft. lbs. (47–53 Nm).

   b. Step 2: Loosen the bolts 1 complete turn.

   c. Step 3: Tighten the bolts to 20–24 ft. lbs. (27–33 Nm).

   d. Step 4: Tighten the bolts 85–95 degrees.

   e. Step 5: Tighten the bolts 85–95 degrees.

8. Install or connect the following:
- Exhaust manifolds
- Spark plugs
- Lower intake manifold
- Rocker arms and pushrods in the locations they were removed from. Tighten the rocker arm bolts to 24 ft. lbs. (32 Nm). Tighten each rocker arm bolt with the valve closed and the lifter on the camshaft lobe base circle. Rotate the crankshaft as necessary.
- Valve covers
- Heater supply tube brackets
- Oil dipstick tube. Tighten the nut to 13 ft. lbs. (18 Nm).
- Power steering pump
- Alternator
- Accessory drive belt and tensioner
- Spark plug wires

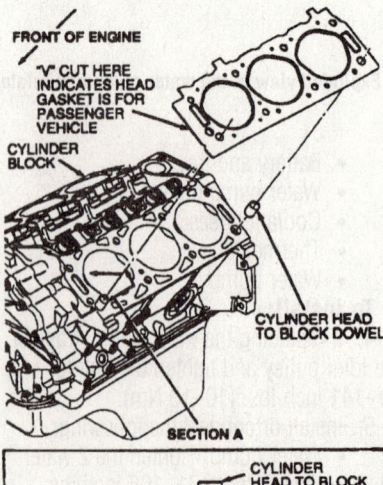

Install the cylinder head gasket with the "UP" designation on gasket facing the cylinder head—3.0L (VIN U) engines

- Ignition coil and bracket. Tighten the fasteners to 30–39 ft. lbs. (40–55 Nm).
- Coolant hoses
- Fuel injector wiring harness
- Upper intake manifold
- Fuel lines
- Cruise control cable
- Accelerator cable
- ECT sensor connector
- CMP sensor and housing
- IAC valve connector
- TP sensor connector
- IAT sensor connector
- EGR vacuum regulator solenoid
- EGR transducer
- EGR valve
- Vacuum hoses from the intake manifold
- Air cleaner outlet hose
- Negative battery cable

9. Fill the cooling system and check for leaks.

3.0L (VIN S) Engine

1. Before servicing the vehicle, refer to the precautions at the beginning of this section.

2. Remove the engine from the vehicle and position on a suitable workstand.

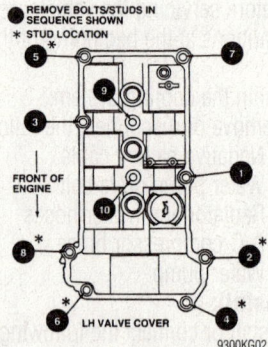

Left side valve cover bolt removal sequence—3.0L (VIN S) engine

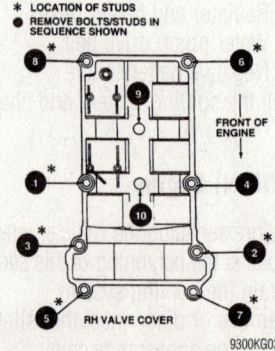

Right side valve cover bolt removal sequence—3.0L (VIN S) engine

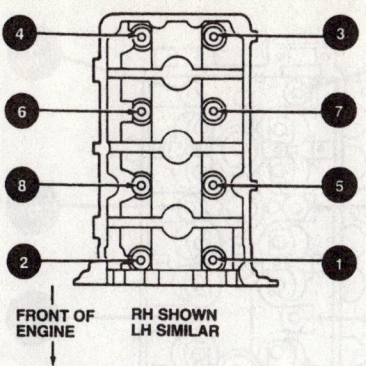

● REMOVE BOLTS IN SEQUENCE SHOWN

FRONT OF ENGINE

RH SHOWN LH SIMILAR

9300KG04

Cylinder head bolt removal sequence–right side head shown, left side similar—3.0L (VIN S) engine

3. Remove or disconnect the following:
- Upper intake manifold
- Lower intake manifold
- Exhaust manifolds
- Valve covers
- Radiator hose tube and bracket
- Accessory drive belt
- Crankcase ventilation tube
- Heater hose bypass tube
- Power steering pump
- A/C compressor and bracket
- Water pump

➡**The crankshaft accessory drive pulley shaft has left-hand threads. Rotate the pulley shaft clockwise to remove.**

- Crankshaft pulley
- Oil pan
- Front cover
- Timing chains
- Camshafts
- Valve lash adjusters

➡**Keep the lash adjusters in order for installation.**

4. Remove the cylinder head bolts from the cylinder heads in sequence and remove the cylinder heads.

To install:

➡**The cylinder head bolts are a torque-to-yield design and cannot be reused.**

➡**Left and right cylinder head gaskets are not interchangeable.**

➡**Refer to Section 1 of this manual for the cylinder head torque sequence illustration. The illustration is located after the Torque Specification Chart.**

5. Install new gaskets and install the cylinder heads. Use new bolts and tighten as follows:

a. Step 1: Tighten the bolts in sequence to 28–31 ft. lbs. (37–43 Nm).

b. Step 2: Plus 85–95 degrees.

c. Step 3: Loosen the bolts in reverse sequence 1 full turn.

d. Step 4: Tighten the bolts in sequence to 28–31 ft. lbs. (37–43 Nm).

e. Step 5: Tighten the bolts in sequence 85–95 degrees.

f. Step 6: Tighten the bolts in sequence 85–95 degrees.

➡ **Install the lash adjusters in the same positions they were removed from.**

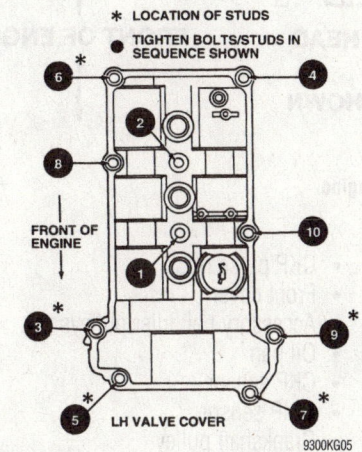

※ LOCATION OF STUDS
● TIGHTEN BOLTS/STUDS IN SEQUENCE SHOWN

FRONT OF ENGINE

LH VALVE COVER

9300KG05

Left side valve cover bolt tightening sequence—3.0L (VIN S) engine

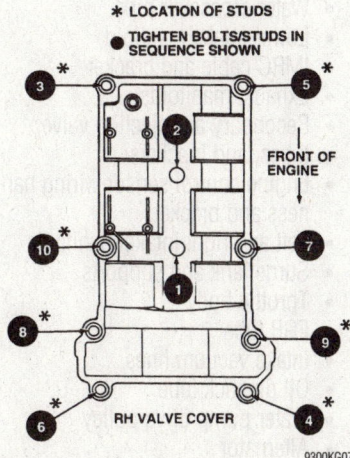

※ LOCATION OF STUDS
● TIGHTEN BOLTS/STUDS IN SEQUENCE SHOWN

FRONT OF ENGINE

RH VALVE COVER

9300KG07

Right side valve cover bolt tightening sequence—3.0L (VIN S) engine

6. Install or connect the following:
- Valve lash adjusters
- Camshafts
- Timing chains
- Front cover
- Oil pan
- Crankshaft pulley
- Water pump
- A/C compressor and bracket
- Power steering pump
- Heater hose bypass tube
- Crankcase ventilation tube
- Accessory drive belt
- Radiator hose tube and bracket
- Valve covers
- Exhaust manifolds
- Lower intake manifold
- Upper intake manifold
- Engine assembly into the vehicle

8. Run the engine and check for leaks.

3.4L (VIN N) Engine

1. Before servicing the vehicle, refer to the precautions at the beginning of this section.

2. Remove the engine from the vehicle and mount it on an engine stand.

3. Set the crankshaft at Top Dead Center of the compression stroke for the No. 1 cylinder.

4. Remove or disconnect the following:

- Accessory drive belts
- A/C compressor
- Alternator
- Water pump drive pulley
- Oil dipstick tube
- Intake vacuum lines
- Exhaust Gas Recirculation (EGR) tube
- Throttle body
- Surge tank and supports
- Left and right intake manifolds
- Engine control sensor wiring harness and brackets
- Secondary air injection valve, tubes and brackets
- Exhaust manifolds
- Intake Manifold Runner Control (IMRC) cable and bracket
- Lower intake manifold
- Water crossover pipe
- Water pump
- Left and right valve covers
- Spark plugs
- Power steering pump
- Crankshaft pulley
- Camshaft Position (CMP) sensor

Removal Sequence

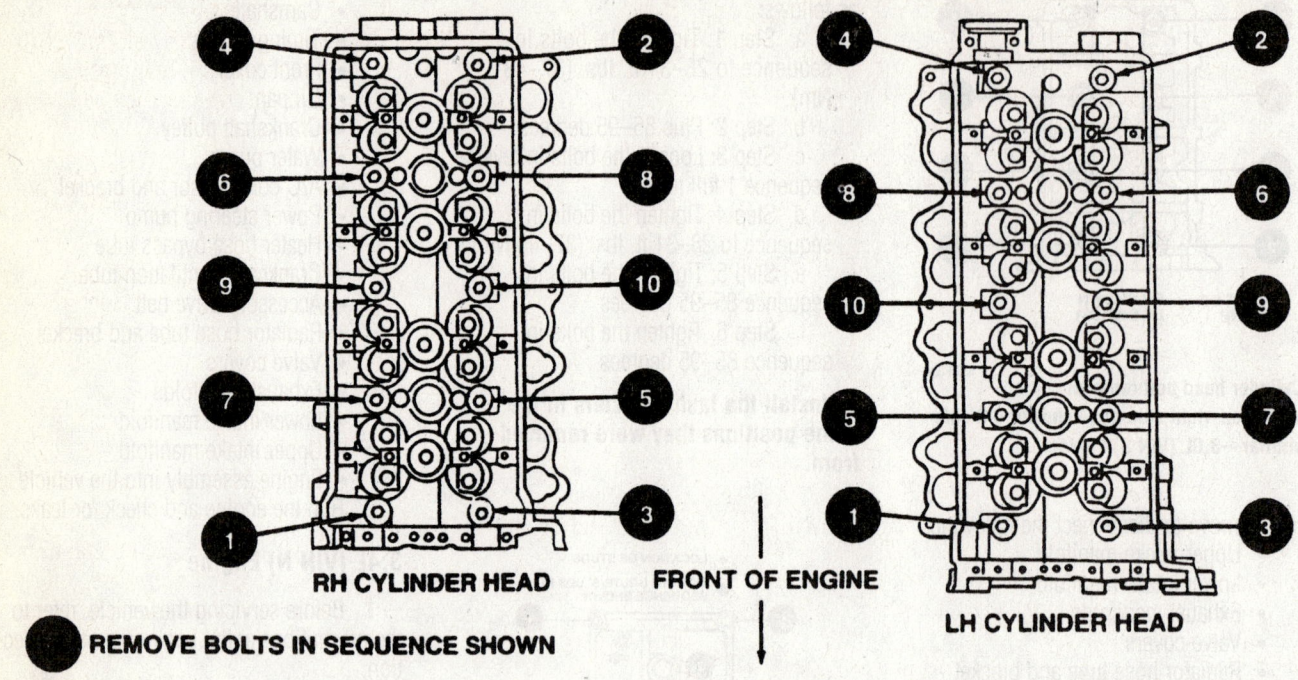

RH CYLINDER HEAD   FRONT OF ENGINE   LH CYLINDER HEAD

● REMOVE BOLTS IN SEQUENCE SHOWN

9300KG06

Cylinder head bolt removal sequence—3.4L (VIN N) engine

- Crankshaft Position (CKP) sensor
- Oil pan
- Accessory belt idler pulleys
- Front cover
- CKP pulse ring
- Timing chain
- Camshafts
- Cylinder heads

To install:

➡The cylinder head bolts are a torque-to-yield design and cannot be reused.

➡Left and right cylinder head gaskets are not interchangeable.

➡Refer to Section 1 of this manual for the cylinder head torque sequence illustration. The illustration is located after the Torque Specification Chart.

5. Install new gaskets and install the cylinder heads. Use new bolts and tighten as follows:

    a. Step 1: Tighten the bolts in sequence to 20–23 ft. lbs. (27–32 Nm).

    b. Step 2: Tighten the bolts in sequence 85–95 degrees.

6. Install or connect the following:
- Camshafts
- Timing chain

- CKP pulse ring
- Front cover
- Accessory belt idler pulleys
- Oil pan
- CKP sensor
- CMP sensor
- Crankshaft pulley
- Power steering pump
- Spark plugs
- Left and right valve covers
- Water pump
- Water crossover pipe
- Lower intake manifold
- IMRC cable and bracket
- Exhaust manifolds
- Secondary air injection valve, tubes, and brackets
- Engine control sensor wiring harness and brackets
- Left and right intake manifolds
- Surge tank and supports
- Throttle body
- EGR tube
- Intake vacuum lines
- Oil dipstick tube
- Water pump drive pulley
- Alternator
- A/C compressor
- Accessory drive belts
- Engine assembly into the vehicle.

7. Run the engine and check for leaks.

Rocker Arms/Shafts

REMOVAL & INSTALLATION

3.0L (VIN U) Engine

1. Before servicing the vehicle, refer to the precautions at the beginning of this section.

2. Remove or disconnect the following:
- Negative battery cable
- Upper intake manifold
- Valve covers
- Rocker arms

➡Keep the rocker arms in order for installation.

To install:

➡The rocker arm bolts are tightened with the valves closed. Rotate the crankshaft as necessary to position the lifter on the base circle of the camshaft lobe before tightening the corresponding rocker arm bolt.

3. Install the rocker arms. The rocker arm bolts are tightened in two steps as follows:

    a. Step 1: 96 inch lbs. (11 Nm).

    b. Step 2: 24 ft. lbs. (32 Nm).

4. Install or connect the following:
- Valve covers

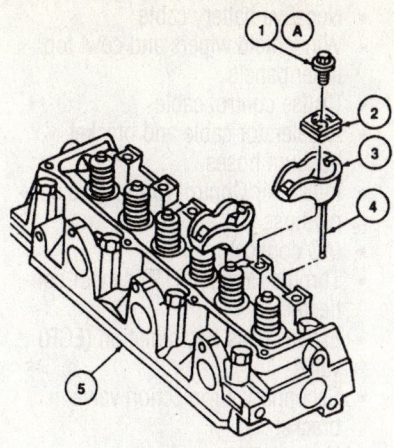

1 Bolt (12 Req'd)
2 Rocker Arm Seat (12 Req'd)
3 Rocker Arm (12 Req'd)
4 Push Rod (12 Req'd)
5 Cylinder Head (2 Req'd)
6 2.15-4.69 mm (0.085-0.185 inch)
A Tighten in Two Steps:
    7-15 N·m (5-11 Lb-Ft)
    26-38 N·m (19-28 Lb-Ft)

7922KG22

Exploded view of the rocker arms and related components—3.0L (VIN U) engines

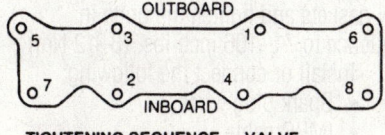

OUTBOARD

5   3   1   6

7   2   4   8

INBOARD

TIGHTENING SEQUENCE — VALVE COVER

9300KG08

Valve cover tightening sequence—3.0L (VIN U) engine

- Upper intake manifold
- Negative battery cable

5. Start the engine and check for proper operation.

3.0L (VIN S) Engine

1. Before servicing the vehicle, refer to the precautions at the beginning of this section.
2. Remove or disconnect the following:
    - Negative battery cable
    - Upper intake manifold
    - Valve covers
    - Spark plugs
3. Rotate the crankshaft so that the piston on the cylinder to be serviced is at bottom dead center with the valves closed.
4. Install an adapter in the spark plug hole and connect a compressed air supply at 102–144 psi.

5. Install special tool Valve Spring Compressor T94P-6565-BH.
6. Compress the valve spring and remove the rocker arm. Repeat for each arm to be removed.

➡ **If the rocker arms are to be reused, ensure that they are installed in the same position that they were removed from.**

To install:

7. Compress the valve spring and install the rocker arm. Repeat for each arm to be installed.
8. Install or connect the following:
    - Spark plugs
    - Valve covers
    - Upper intake manifold
    - Negative battery cable
9. Start the engine and check for proper operation.

3.4L (VIN N) Engine

The 3.4L (VIN N) engine does not have rocker arms. The camshaft lobes work directly on the valves.

Intake Manifold

REMOVAL & INSTALLATION

3.0L (VIN U) Engine

1. Before servicing the vehicle, refer to the precautions at the beginning of this section.
2. Drain the cooling system.
3. Remove or disconnect the following:
    - Negative battery cable
    - Air cleaner and outlet tube
    - Cruise control cable
    - Accelerator cable and bracket
    - Fuel lines
    - Vacuum lines
    - Exhaust Gas Recirculation (EGR) valve
    - EGR transducer
    - EGR vacuum solenoid
    - Throttle Position (TP) sensor connector
    - Intake Air Control (IAC) valve connector
    - Camshaft Position (CMP) sensor connector
    - Engine Coolant Temperature (ECT) sensor connector
    - Coolant temperature indicator sender connector
    - Coolant hoses
    - Upper alternator bracket

- Engine control sensor wiring harness and bracket
- Upper intake manifold

➡ **Note the position of the CMP sensor electrical connector. Installation requires that the connector be located in the same location.**

➡ **Before removing the CMP sensor, position No. 1 cylinder to TDC of its compression stroke.**

4. Remove or disconnect the following:
    - CMP sensor and housing
    - Spark plug wires
    - Ignition coil
    - Valve covers
    - No. 3 cylinder intake valve rocker arm and pushrod
    - Lower intake manifold

To install:

➡ **Refer to Section 1 of this manual for the intake manifold torque sequence illustration. The illustration is located after the Torque Specification Chart.**

5. Install the lower intake manifold. Use new gaskets and tighten the bolts as follows:
    a. Step 1: Tighten the bolts in sequence to 15–22 lbs. (20–30 Nm).
    b. Step 2: Tighten the bolts in sequence to 19–24 ft. lbs. (26–32 Nm).

➡ **A special Synchro Positioning tool T95T-12200-A must be used when installing the CMP sensor housing.**

6. Attach the Synchro Position tool T95T-12200-A as follows:
    a. Engage the CMP sensor housing vane into the radial slot of the tool.
    b. Rotate the tool on the CMP sensor housing until the tool boss engages the notch in the CMP sensor housing.
    c. Install the CMP sensor housing so the drive gear engagement occurs when the arrow on the locator tool is pointed about 75 degrees counterclockwise from the rear face of the cylinder block. This step will locate the CMP sensor electrical connector in the same position as was noted on removal.
    d. Install the hold-down clamp and tighten the bolt to 14–22 ft. lbs. (19–30 Nm).
7. Install or connect the following:
    - CMP sensor
    - No. 3 cylinder intake valve rocker arm and pushrod
    - Valve covers

Refer to Section 1 for engine rebuilding specifications

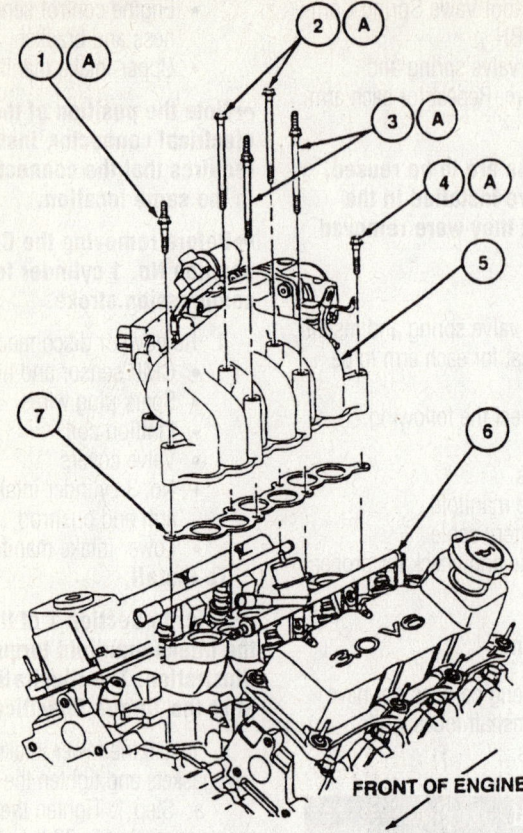

Item	Description
1	Stud Bolt
2	Bolt (2 Req'd)
3	Stud Bolt (2 Req'd)
4	Bolt
5	Upper Intake Manifold
6	Lower Intake Manifold
7	Intake Manifold Upper Gasket
A	Tighten to 20-30 N·m (15-22 Lb-Ft)

9300KG09

Exploded view of the upper intake manifold mounting—3.0L (VIN U) engine

- Ignition coil. Tighten the bolts to 30–40 ft. lbs. (40–55 Nm).
- Spark plug wires
- Upper intake manifold. Tighten the bolts to 15–22 ft. lbs. (20–30 Nm).
- Engine control sensor wiring harness and bracket
- Upper alternator bracket
- Coolant hoses
- Coolant temperature indicator sender connector
- ECT sensor connector
- CMP sensor connector
- IAC valve connector
- TP sensor connector
- EGR vacuum solenoid

- EGR transducer
- EGR valve
- Vacuum lines
- Fuel lines
- Accelerator cable and bracket
- Cruise control cable
- Air cleaner and outlet tube
- Negative battery cable
8. Fill the cooling system.
9. Start the engine and check for leaks and proper operation.

3.0L (VIN S) Engine

1. Before servicing the vehicle, refer to the precautions at the beginning of this section.
2. Remove or disconnect the following:

- Negative battery cable
- Windshield wipers and cowl top inner panels
- Cruise control cable
- Accelerator cable and bracket
- Vacuum hoses
- Intake Air Control (IAC) valve supply hose
- IAC connector
- Throttle Position (TP) sensor connector
- Exhaust Gas Recirculation (EGR) valve
- Secondary air injection valve bracket
- Upper intake manifold
- Fuel lines
- Fuel injector wiring harness
- Intake Manifold Runner Control (IMRC) cable
- Spark plug wires
- Lower intake manifold

To install:

➡ Refer to Section 1 of this manual for the intake manifold torque sequence illustration. The illustration is located after the Torque Specification Chart.

3. Install the lower intake manifold. Use new gaskets and tighten the bolts in sequence to 71–106 inch lbs. (8–12 Nm)
4. Install or connect the following:

- Spark plug wires
- IMRC cable
- Fuel injector wiring harness
- Fuel lines

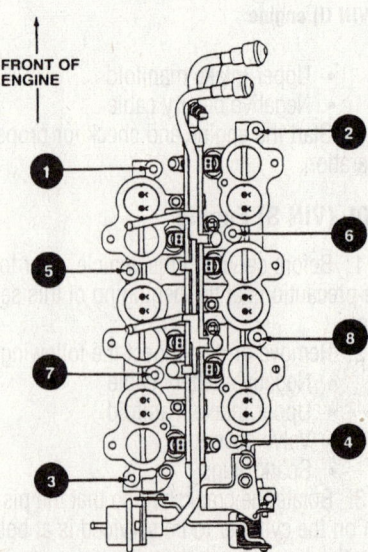

● REMOVE IN SEQUENCE SHOWN

LOWER INTAKE MANIFOLD

9300KG11

Lower intake manifold bolt removal sequence—3.0L (VIN S) engine

5. Install the upper intake manifold. Use new gaskets and tighten the bolts in sequence to 71–106 inch lbs. (8–12 Nm).

6. Install or connect the following:
- Secondary air injection valve bracket
- EGR valve
- TP sensor connector
- IAC connector
- IAC valve supply hose
- Vacuum hoses
- Accelerator cable and bracket
- Cruise control cable
- Windshield wipers and cowl top inner panels
- Negative battery cable

7. Run the engine and check for leaks and proper engine operation.

3.4L (VIN N) Engine

1. Before servicing the vehicle, refer to the precautions at the beginning of this section.

2. Remove or disconnect the following:
- Negative battery cable
- Engine appearance cover
- Right cowl vent screen
- Throttle body
- Vacuum lines
- Exhaust Gas Recirculation (EGR) valve
- EGR transducer and bracket
- Surge tank supports
- Surge tank
- Left and right intake manifold runners
- Fuel lines
- Intake Manifold Runner Control (IMRC) cable
- Engine control sensor wiring harness
- Lower intake manifold

To install:

3. Install or connect the following:

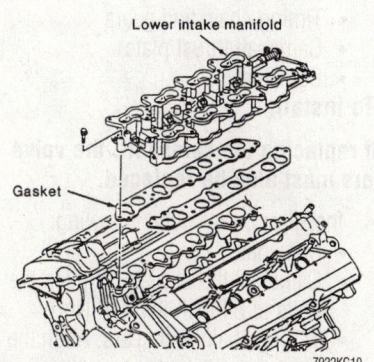

Exploded view of the lower intake manifold mounting—3.4L (VIN N) engine

- Lower intake manifold. Use new gaskets and tighten the bolts to 14–20 ft. lbs. (18–28 Nm).
- Engine control sensor wiring harness
- IMRC cable

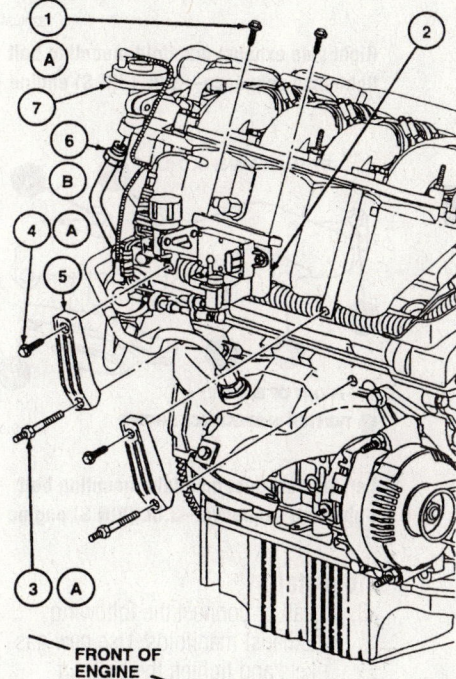

Item	Description
1	Bolt (2 Req'd)
2	Transducer Mounting Bracket
3	Stud Bolt (2 Req'd)
4	Bolt (2 Req'd)
5	Intake Manifold Support (2 Req'd)
6	EGR Valve to Exhaust Manifold Tube
7	EGR Valve
A	Tighten to 18-28 N·m (14-20 Lb-Ft)
B	Tighten to 25-35 N·m (19-25 Lb-Ft)

Exploded view of transducer mounting bracket and intake manifold support with torque specification—3.4L (VIN N) engine

- Fuel lines
- Left and right intake manifold runners. Tighten the bolts to 14–20 ft. lbs. (18–28 Nm).
- Surge tank

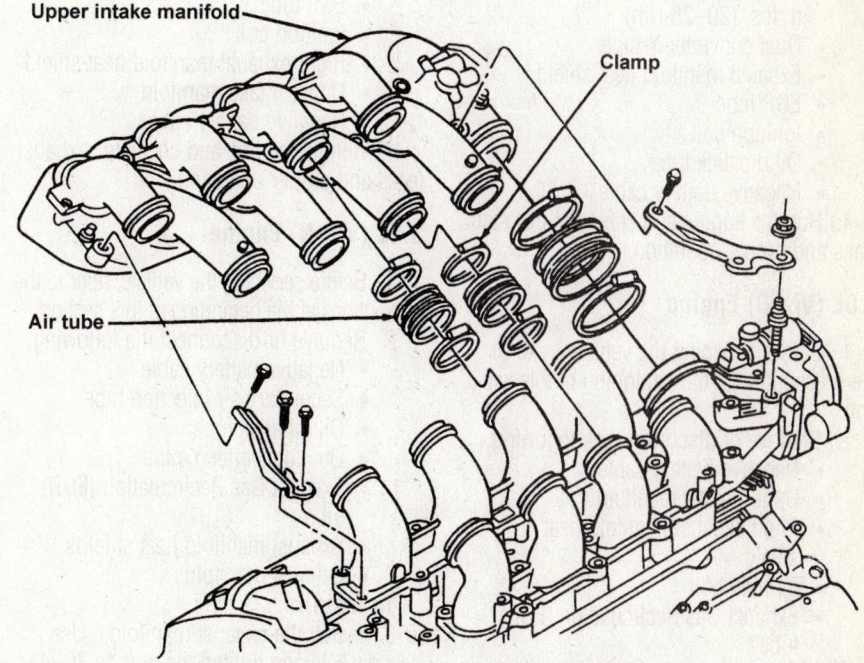

Exploded view of the upper intake manifold mounting—3.4L (VIN N) engine

For engine torque specifications, refer to Section 1 of this manual

- Surge tank supports. Tighten the fasteners to 14–20 ft. lbs. (18–28 Nm).
- EGR transducer and bracket
- EGR valve
- Vacuum lines
- Throttle body
- Right cowl vent screen
- Engine appearance cover
- Negative battery cable

4. Run the engine and check for leaks and proper engine operation.

Exhaust Manifold

REMOVAL & INSTALLATION

3.0L (VIN U) Engine

1. Before servicing the vehicle, refer to the precautions at the beginning of this section.
2. Remove or disconnect the following:
   - Negative battery cable
   - Oil dipstick tube
   - Ignition coil
   - Exhaust Gas Recirculation (EGR) tube
   - Exhaust manifold heat shield
   - Dual converter Y-pipe
   - Exhaust manifolds

To install:

3. Install or connect the following:
   - Exhaust manifolds. Use new gaskets and tighten the bolts to 15–18 ft. lbs. (20–25 Nm).
   - Dual converter Y-pipe
   - Exhaust manifold heat shield
   - EGR tube
   - Ignition coil
   - Oil dipstick tube
   - Negative battery cable

4. Run the engine and check for exhaust leaks and proper operation.

3.0L (VIN S) Engine

1. Before servicing the vehicle, refer to the precautions at the beginning of this section.
2. Remove or disconnect the following:
   - Negative battery cable
   - Upper intake manifold
   - Right exhaust manifold heat shield
   - Ignition coil
   - Exhaust Gas Recirculation (EGR) tube
   - Heated Oxygen (HO2S) sensor
   - Secondary air injection tube
   - Dual converter Y-pipe
   - Exhaust manifolds

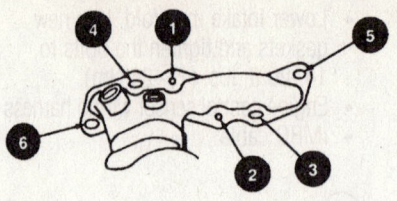

Right side exhaust manifold mounting bolt tightening sequence—3.0L (VIN S) engine

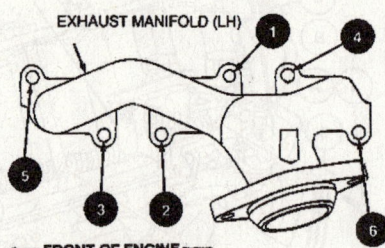

Left side exhaust manifold mounting bolt tightening sequence—3.0L (VIN S) engine

To install:

3. Install or connect the following:
   - Exhaust manifolds. Use new gaskets and tighten the bolts in sequence to 13–16 ft. lbs. (18–22 Nm).
   - Dual converter Y-pipe
   - Secondary air injection tube
   - HO2S sensor
   - EGR tube
   - Ignition coil
   - Right exhaust manifold heat shield
   - Upper intake manifold
   - Negative battery cable

4. Run the engine and check for exhaust leaks and proper operation.

3.4L (VIN N) Engine

1. Before servicing the vehicle, refer to the precautions at the beginning of this section.
2. Remove or disconnect the following:
   - Negative battery cable
   - Secondary air injection tube
   - Oil dipstick tube
   - Dual converter Y-pipe
   - Exhaust Gas Recirculation (EGR) tube
   - Exhaust manifold heat shields
   - Exhaust manifolds

To install:

3. Install the exhaust manifolds. Use new gaskets and tighten the nuts to 30–44 ft. lbs. (40–60 Nm).
4. Install or connect the following:
   - Exhaust manifold heat shields

- EGR tube
- Dual converter Y-pipe
- Oil dipstick tube
- Secondary air injection tube
- Negative battery cable

5. Run the engine and check for exhaust leaks and proper operation.

Front Crankshaft Seal

REMOVAL & INSTALLATION

➡**The front crankshaft oil seal procedure is only for timing belt-equipped engines. For engines equipped with timing chains or gears, refer to the Timing Chain, Sprockets, Front Cover and Seal procedure in this section.**

Camshaft and Valve Lifters

REMOVAL & INSTALLATION

3.0L (VIN U) Engine

➡**If the rocker arms, pushrods or lifters are to be reused, they must be installed in the same positions they were removed from.**

1. Before servicing the vehicle, refer to the precautions at the beginning of this section.
2. Remove the engine from the vehicle and mount it on an engine stand.
3. Remove or disconnect the following:
   - Valve covers
   - Rocker arms and pushrods
   - Accessory drive belt and tensioner
   - Alternator and brackets
   - Intake manifold
   - Valve lifter guide plate
   - Valve lifters
   - Crankshaft damper
   - Oil pan
   - Front cover
   - Timing chain and gears
   - Camshaft thrust plate
   - Camshaft

To install:

➡**If replacing the camshaft, the valve lifters must also be replaced.**

4. Install or connect the following:
   - Camshaft
   - Camshaft thrust plate. Tighten the bolts to 84 inch lbs. (10 Nm).
   - Timing chain and gears. Align the timing marks on the sprockets.
   - Front cover
   - Oil pan
   - Crankshaft damper

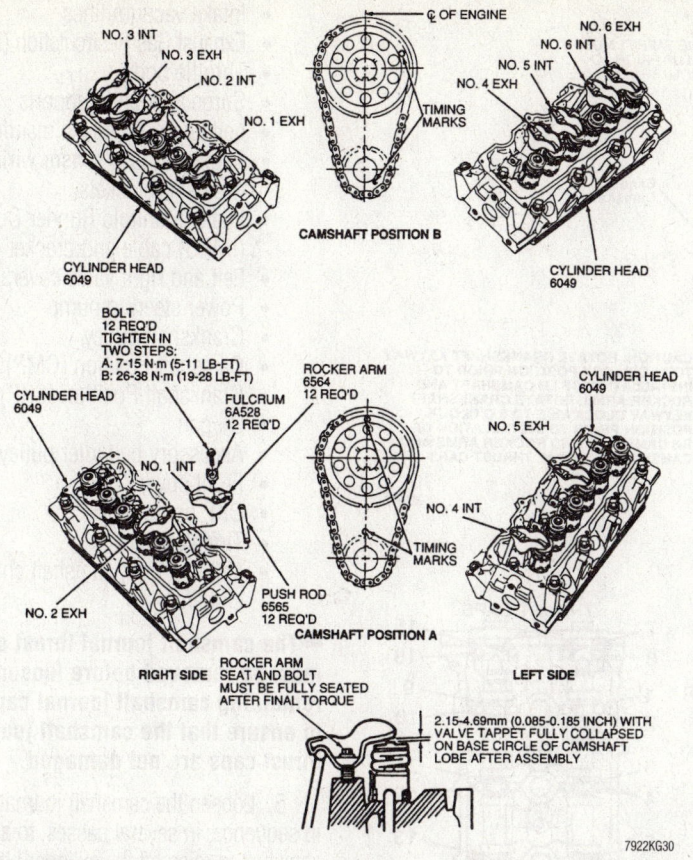

Tighten the rocker arm nuts according to the position of the camshaft—3.0L (VIN U) engine

- Valve lifters
- Valve lifter guide plate
- Intake manifold
- Alternator and brackets
- Accessory drive belt and tensioner
- Rocker arms and pushrods
- Valve covers

5. Install the engine assembly into the vehicle.

6. Start the engine and check for leaks and proper engine operation.

3.0L (VIN S) Engine

1. Before servicing the vehicle, refer to the precautions at the beginning of this section.

2. Remove the engine from the vehicle and mount it on an engine stand.

3. Remove or disconnect the following:
- Upper intake manifold
- Valve covers

➡**If the rocker arms are to be reused, they must be kept in order so that they can be installed in their original positions.**

- Rocker arms
- Accessory drive belt

- Power steering pump
- Water pump
- A/C compressor and bracket

➡**The crankshaft accessory drive pulley shaft has left-hand threads. Rotate the pulley shaft clockwise to remove.**

- Crankshaft pulley
- Oil pan
- Front cover
- Timing chains

➡The camshaft journal thrust caps must be removed first, before loosening the remaining camshaft journal cap bolts, to ensure that the camshaft journal thrust caps are not damaged.

4. Loosen the camshaft journal cap bolts in sequence and in several passes to allow the camshaft to raise off the cylinder head evenly.

5. Remove the journal caps and the camshafts.

➡**The camshaft journal caps and cylinder heads are numbered to ensure that they are assembled in their original positions.**

➡**If the hydraulic lifters are to be reused, they must be kept in order so that they can be installed in their original positions.**

6. Remove the hydraulic lifters.

To install:

7. Rotate the crankshaft so the keyway is at the 11 o'clock position for installation of the camshafts.

8. Install or connect the following:
- Hydraulic lifters in their original positions
- Camshafts with the timing marks (marked RFF) on the back of the camshaft sprockets aligned

➡**Do not install the camshaft journal thrust caps until the rocker arms and timing chains have been installed and the camshaft journal caps are tightened into position.**

- Camshaft journal caps in their original positions
- Timing chains

9. Tighten the camshaft journal cap bolts, in sequence, to 71–106 inch lbs.

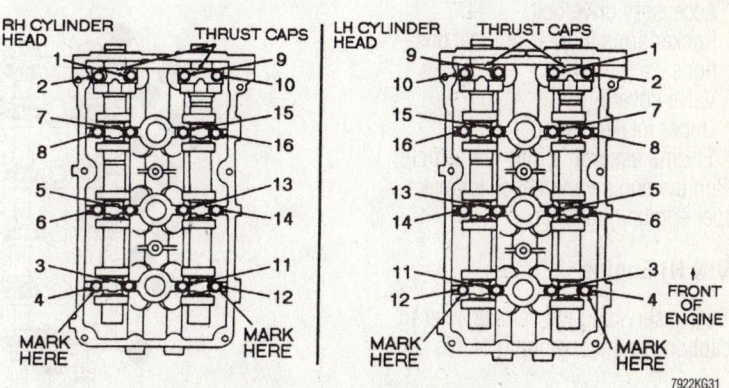

Camshaft journal bolt removal sequence—3.0L (VIN S) engine

For complete mechanical specifications, refer to Section 1 of this manual

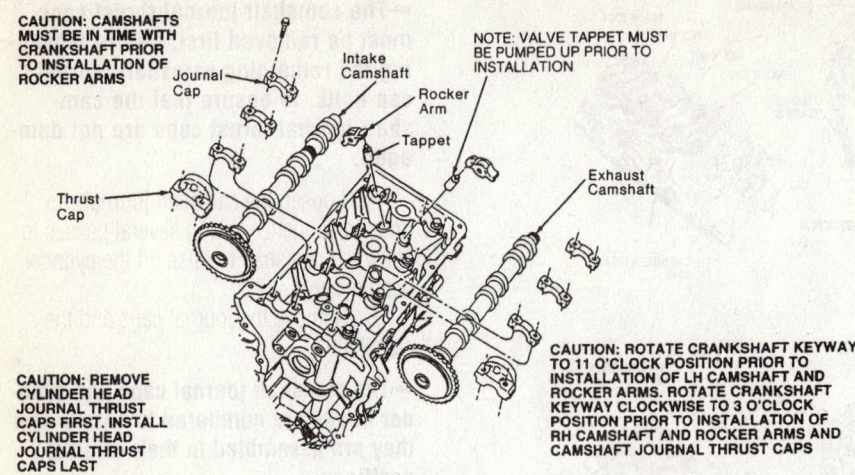

CAUTION: CAMSHAFTS MUST BE IN TIME WITH CRANKSHAFT PRIOR TO INSTALLATION OF ROCKER ARMS

Journal Cap

Intake Camshaft

Rocker Arm

Tappet

Thrust Cap

Exhaust Camshaft

NOTE: VALVE TAPPET MUST BE PUMPED UP PRIOR TO INSTALLATION

CAUTION: REMOVE CYLINDER HEAD JOURNAL THRUST CAPS FIRST. INSTALL CYLINDER HEAD JOURNAL THRUST CAPS LAST

CAUTION: ROTATE CRANKSHAFT KEYWAY TO 11 O'CLOCK POSITION PRIOR TO INSTALLATION OF LH CAMSHAFT AND ROCKER ARMS. ROTATE CRANKSHAFT KEYWAY CLOCKWISE TO 3 O'CLOCK POSITION PRIOR TO INSTALLATION OF RH CAMSHAFT AND ROCKER ARMS AND CAMSHAFT JOURNAL THRUST CAPS

7922KG10

Exploded view of camshaft mounting—3.0L (VIN S) engine

- Intake vacuum lines
- Exhaust Gas Recirculation (EGR) tube
- Throttle body
- Surge tank and supports
- Left and right intake manifolds
- Engine control sensor wiring harness and brackets
- Intake Manifold Runner Control (IMRC) cable and bracket
- Left and right valve covers
- Power steering pump
- Crankshaft pulley
- Camshaft Position (CMP) sensor
- Crankshaft Position (CKP) sensor
- Oil pan
- Accessory belt idler pulleys
- Front cover
- CKP pulse ring
- Timing chain
- Left and right camshaft chain tensioners

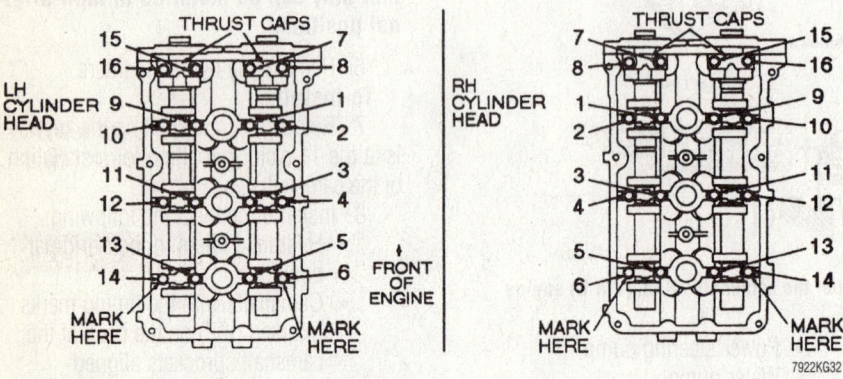

Camshaft journal bolt tightening sequence—3.0L (VIN S) engine

➡The camshaft journal thrust caps must be removed before loosening the remaining camshaft journal cap bolts to ensure that the camshaft journal thrust caps are not damaged.

5. Loosen the camshaft journal cap bolts in sequence, in several passes, to allow the camshaft to raise off the cylinder head evenly. Remove the journal caps and the camshafts

➡The camshaft journal caps and cylinder heads are numbered to ensure that they are assembled in their original positions.

➡If the hydraulic lifters are to be reused, they must be kept in order so that they can be installed in their original positions.

6. Remove the hydraulic lifters
To install:
7. Rotate the crankshaft so the keyway is aligned with the mark on the oil pump at

(8–12 Nm). Install the thrust caps and tighten the bolts to 71–106 inch lbs. (8–12 Nm).

10. Install or connect the following:
- Front cover
- Oil pan
- Crankshaft pulley
- A/C compressor and bracket
- Water pump
- Power steering pump
- Accessory drive belt
- Rocker arms in their original positions
- Valve covers
- Upper intake manifold
- Engine assembly into the vehicle

11. Run the engine and check for leaks and proper engine operation.

3.4L (VIN N) Engine

1. Before servicing the vehicle, refer to the precautions at the beginning of this section.

2. Remove the engine from the vehicle and mount it on an engine stand.

3. Set the crankshaft at Top Dead Center (TDC) of the compression stroke for the No. 1 cylinder.

4. Remove or disconnect the following:
- Accessory drive belts
- A/C compressor
- Alternator
- Water pump drive pulley

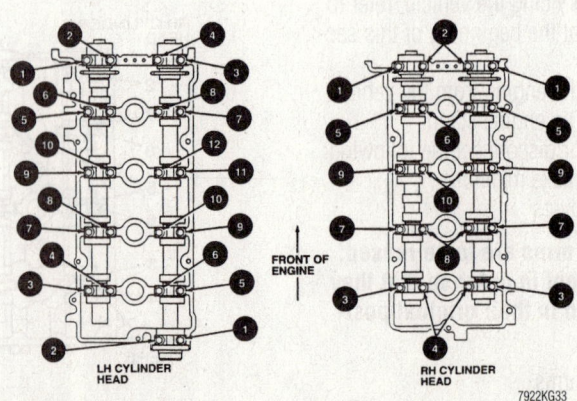

Camshaft journal cap bolt removal sequence—3.4L (VIN N) engine

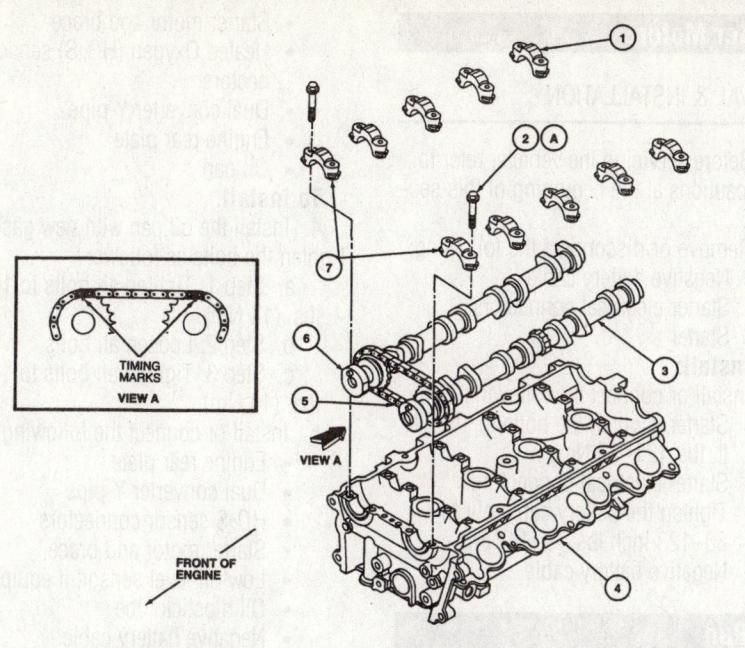

TIMING MARKS
VIEW A

VIEW A

FRONT OF ENGINE

Item	Part Number	Description
1	—	Camshaft Journal Cap (Part of 6049) (8 Req'd)
2	6L293	Hex Bolt with Washer (20 Req'd)
3	6250	Camshaft , RH Intake
4	6010	Cylinder Block , RH
5	6268	Timing Chain / Belt

Item	Part Number	Description
6	6250	Camshaft , RH Exhaust
7	—	Camshaft Journal Thrust Cap (Part of 6049) (2 Req'd)
A	—	Tighten in sequence in two steps: 7-12 N·m (62-106 Lb-In) and 16-21 N·m (12-15 Lb-Ft)

9306KG01

Camshaft installation—3.4L (VIN N) engine—Right head shown, left head similar

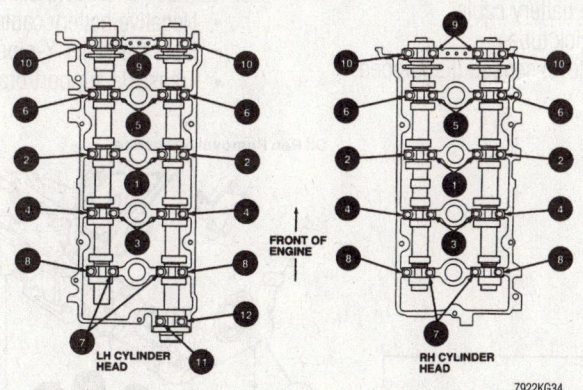

LH CYLINDER HEAD

FRONT OF ENGINE

RH CYLINDER HEAD

7922KG34

Camshaft journal cap bolt tightening sequence—3.4L (VIN N) engine

the 11 o'clock position for installation of the camshafts.

8. Install the hydraulic lifters in their original positions.

9. Install the camshafts. Match the camshaft and chain timing marks as shown, and install the camshafts with the timing marks facing up.

10. Apply a 0.08–0.11 inch (2–3mm) bead of silicone gasket and sealant to the left side cylinder head intake camshaft journal thrust cap.

11. Install the camshaft journal caps in their original positions.

12. Tighten the cylinder head camshaft journal cap bolts in sequence and in 2 steps:
   a. Step 1: Tighten the bolts to 62–106 inch lbs. (7–12 Nm).
   b. Step 2: Tighten the bolts to 12–15 ft. lbs. (16–21 Nm).

13. Install a new camshaft seal with a Cam Seal expander T89P-6256-B and Cam Seal Replacer T89-6256-A.

14. Install or connect the following:

- Left and right camshaft chain tensioners
- Timing chain
- CKP pulse ring
- Front cover
- Accessory belt idler pulleys
- Oil pan
- CKP sensor
- CMP sensor
- Crankshaft pulley
- Power steering pump
- Left and right valve covers
- IMRC cable and bracket
- Engine control sensor wiring harness and brackets
- Left and right intake manifolds
- Surge tank and supports
- Throttle body
- EGR tube
- Intake vacuum lines
- Water pump drive pulley
- Alternator
- A/C compressor
- Accessory drive belts
- Engine assembly into the vehicle

15. Run the engine and check for leaks and proper engine operation.

Valve Lash

ADJUSTMENT

3.0L (VIN U) Engine

The lash adjusters (valve tappets), are hydraulic and are not adjustable.

3.0L (VIN S) Engine

The lash adjusters (valve tappets), are hydraulic and are not adjustable.

3.4L (VIN N) Engine

➡**The valve clearance is checked with the engine COLD.**

1. Before servicing the vehicle, refer to the precautions at the beginning of this section.

2. Remove or disconnect the following:
- Negative battery cable
- Upper intake manifold
- Valve covers

3. Rotate the crankshaft so that the camshaft lobe is directed away from the valve tappet to be measured.

4. Insert a feeler gauge under the camshaft lobe at a 90 degree angle to the camshaft. Clearance for the intake valves should be 0.006–0.010 inch (0.15–0.25mm).

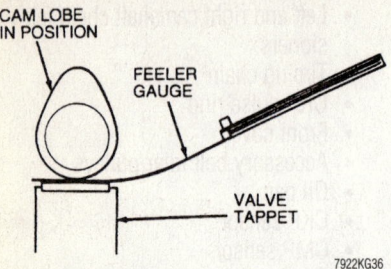

To measure the valve clearance, slide the feeler gauge between the base circle of the cam and the tappet—3.4L (VIN N) engine

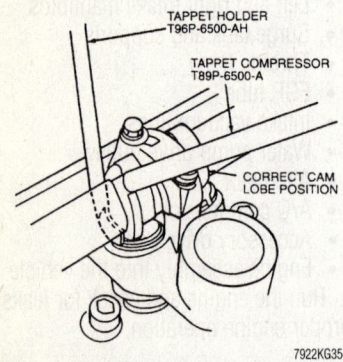

Correct positioning of the tappet compressor and holder tools—3.4L (VIN N) engine

Clearance for the exhaust valves should be 0.010–0.014 inch (0.25-0.35mm).

5. If adjustment is required, install Tappet Compressor T89P-6500-A under the camshaft next to the lobe and depress the valve tappet.

6. Install Tappet Holder T96P-6500-AH and remove the compressor tool.

7. Direct a jet of compressed air toward the hole in the face of the valve adjusting spacer to lift the valve adjusting spacer off of the valve tappet.

8. Determine the size of the adjusting spacer by the numbers on the bottom face of the spacer or by measuring with a micrometer.

9. Install the replacement adjusting spacer with the numbers down. Be sure the spacer is properly seated.

10. Release the tappet holder by installing the tappet compressor, then remove the tappet compressor.

11. Repeat the procedure for each valve requiring adjustment.

12. Install or connect the following:
- Valve covers
- Upper intake manifold
- Negative battery cable

13. Run the engine and check for leaks and proper engine operation.

Starter Motor

REMOVAL & INSTALLATION

1. Before servicing the vehicle, refer to the precautions at the beginning of this section.

2. Remove or disconnect the following:
- Negative battery cable
- Starter electrical connectors
- Starter

To install:

3. Install or connect the following:
- Starter. Tighten the bolts to 16–21 ft. lbs. (21–29 Nm).
- Starter electrical connectors. Tighten the battery cable nut to 80–123 inch lbs. (9–14 Nm).
- Negative battery cable

Oil Pan

REMOVAL & INSTALLATION

3.0L (VIN U) Engine

1. Before servicing the vehicle, refer to the precautions at the beginning of this section.

2. Drain the engine oil.

3. Remove or disconnect the following:
- Negative battery cable
- Oil dipstick tube
- Low oil level sensor, if equipped

Item	Description
1	Upper Cylinder Block
2	Lower Cylinder Block (Part of 6010)
3	Oil Pan
4	Stud Bolt (5 Req'd)
5	Bolt (10 Req'd)
6	Oil Pan Gasket
7	Engine Front Cover

- Starter motor and brace
- Heated Oxygen (HO2S) sensor connectors
- Dual converter Y-pipe
- Engine rear plate
- Oil pan

To install:

4. Install the oil pan with new gaskets. Tighten the bolts as follows:
   a. Step 1: Tighten all bolts to 10 ft. lbs. (14 Nm).
   b. Step 2: Loosen all bolts.
   c. Step 3: Tighten all bolts to 10 ft. lbs. (14 Nm).

5. Install or connect the following:
- Engine rear plate
- Dual converter Y-pipe
- HO2S sensor connectors
- Starter motor and brace
- Low oil level sensor, if equipped
- Oil dipstick tube
- Negative battery cable

6. Fill the crankcase.

7. Start the engine and check for leaks and proper operation.

3.0L (VIN S) Engine

1. Before servicing the vehicle, refer to the precautions at the beginning of this section.

2. Drain the engine oil.

3. Remove or disconnect the following:
- Negative battery cable
- Dual converter Y-pipe
- Transaxle support bracket

Oil Pan Removal Sequence

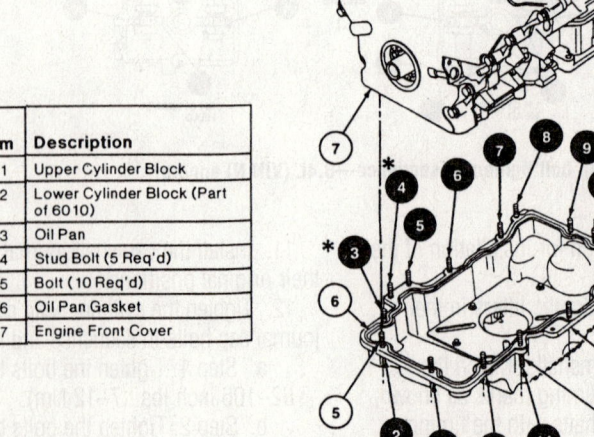

★ LOCATION OF STUDS

● REMOVE BOLTS/STUDS IN SEQUENCE SHOWN

FRONT OF ENGINE

Oil pan bolt removal sequence—3.0L (VIN S) engine

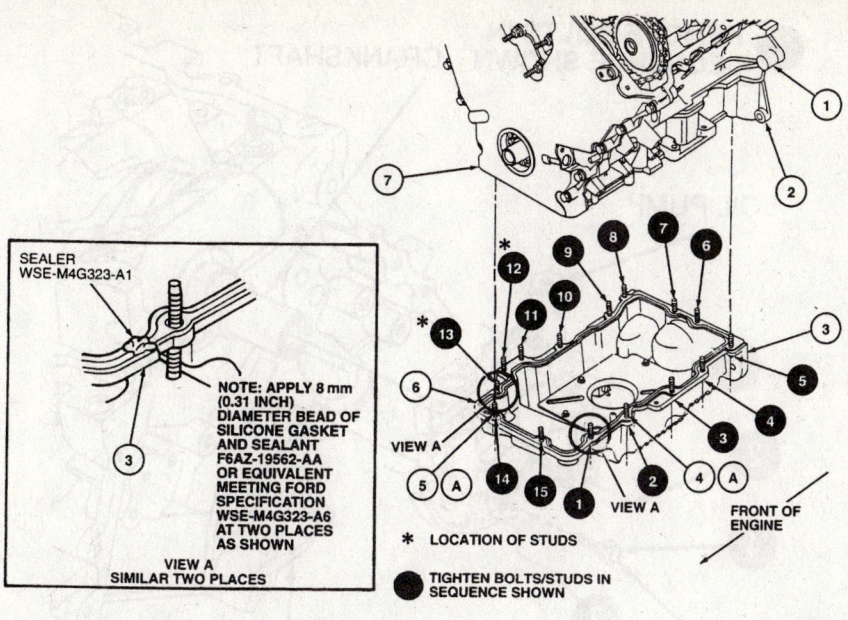

Oil pan bolt tightening sequence—3.0L (VIN S) engine

- Oil pan. Follow the bolt removal sequence shown.

To install:

4. Install or connect the following:
- Oil pan. Use a new gasket and tighten the bolts in sequence to 15–22 ft. lbs. (20–30 Nm).
- Transaxle support bracket. Tighten the nuts to 71–106 inch lbs. (8–12 Nm). Tighten the bolts to 15–22 ft. lbs. (20–30 Nm).
- Dual converter Y-pipe
- Negative battery cable

5. Fill the crankcase.

6. Start the engine and check for leaks and proper operation.

3.4L (VIN N) Engine

1. Before servicing the vehicle, refer to the precautions at the beginning of this section.

2. Drain the engine oil.

3. Remove or disconnect the following:
- Negative battery cable
- Dual converter Y-pipe
- Oil pan

To install:

4. Apply a 0.16 inch (4mm) bead of silicone sealer on the entire oil pan sealing surface.

5. Install the oil pan. Tighten the oil pan bolts and studs in sequence to 15–22 ft. lbs. (20–30 Nm). Tighten the oil pan-to-transaxle case bolts to 25–34 ft. lbs. (34–46 Nm).

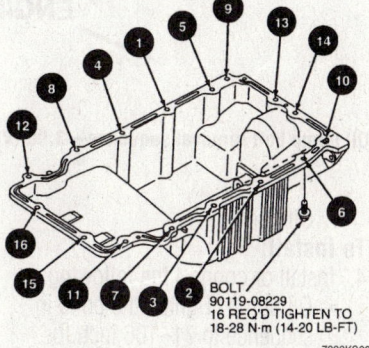

Oil pan bolt tightening sequence—3.4L (VIN N) engine

6. Install or connect the following:
- Dual converter Y-pipe
- Negative battery cable

7. Fill the crankcase.

8. Start the engine and check for leaks and proper operation.

Oil Pump

REMOVAL & INSTALLATION

3.0L (VIN U) Engine

1. Before servicing the vehicle, refer to the precautions at the beginning of this section.

2. Drain the engine oil.

3. Remove or disconnect the following:
- Negative battery cable
- Oil dipstick tube
- Low oil level sensor, if equipped
- Starter motor and brace
- Heated Oxygen (HO2S) sensor connectors
- Dual converter Y-pipe
- Engine rear plate
- Oil pan
- Oil pump

4. Separate the intermediate shaft from the oil pump.

To install:

5. Insert the intermediate shaft into the oil pump until the snapring seats.

6. Install or connect the following:
- Oil pump. Tighten the bolt to 30–40 ft. lbs. (40–55 Nm).
- Oil pan
- Engine rear plate
- Dual converter Y-pipe

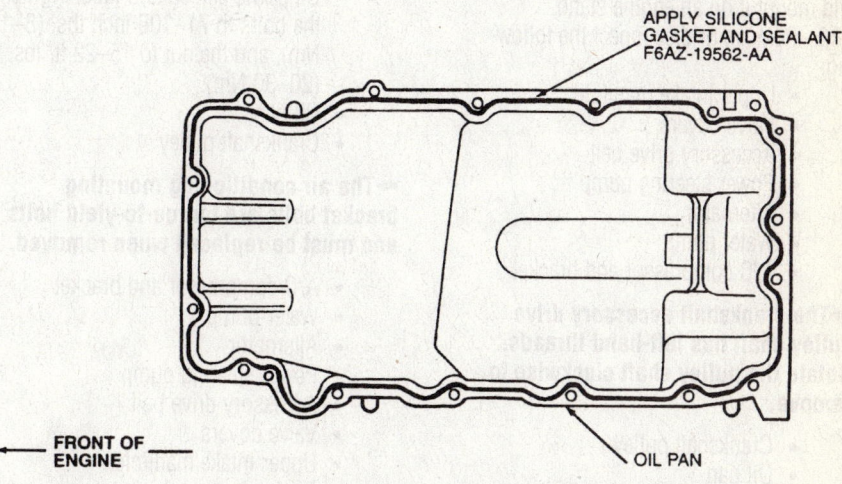

Apply silicone sealant to the entire sealing surface of the oil pan—3.4L (VIN N) engine

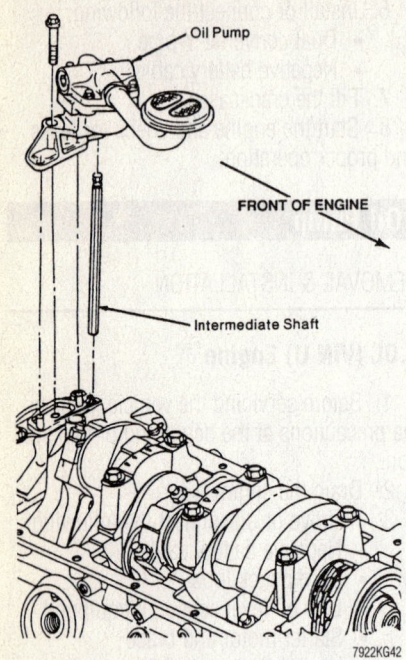

Exploded view of the oil pump mounting—3.0L (VIN U) engine

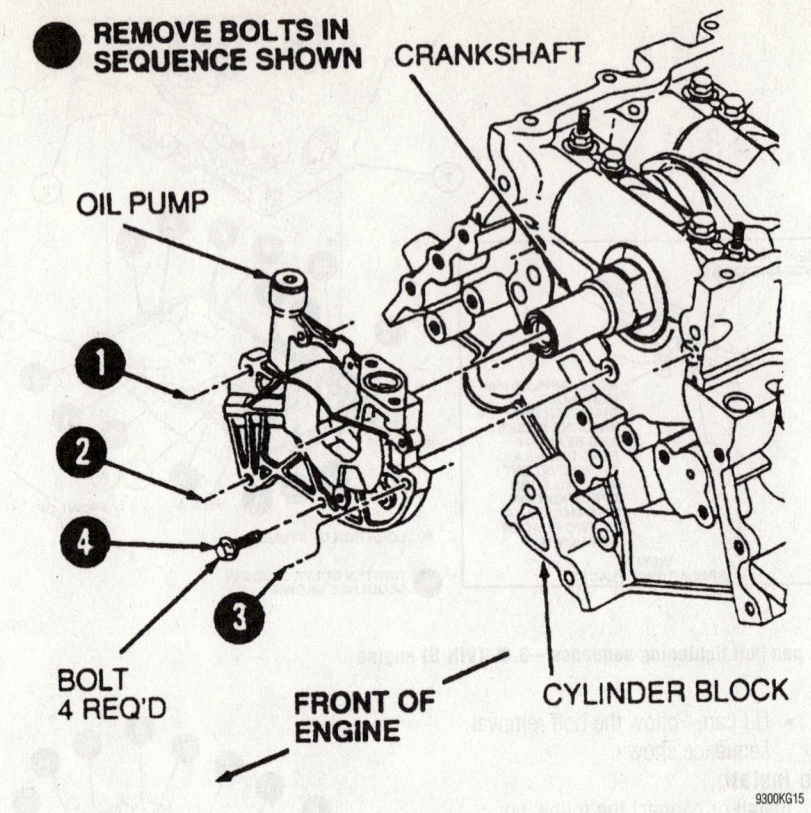

Oil pump bolt removal sequence—3.0L (VIN S) engine—3.4L (VIN N) engine is similar

- HO$_2$S sensor connectors
- Starter motor and brace
- Low oil level sensor, if equipped
- Oil dipstick tube
- Negative battery cable
7. Fill the crankcase.
8. Start the engine and check for leaks and proper operation.

3.0L (VIN S) Engine

1. Before servicing the vehicle, refer to the precautions at the beginning of this section.

2. Remove the engine from the vehicle and mount it on an engine stand.

3. Remove or disconnect the following:

- Upper intake manifold
- Valve covers
- Accessory drive belt
- Power steering pump
- Alternator
- Water pump
- A/C compressor and bracket

➡The crankshaft accessory drive pulley shaft has left-hand threads. Rotate the pulley shaft clockwise to remove.

- Crankshaft pulley
- Oil pan
- Oil pump screen and tube
- Front cover
- Timing chains
- Crankshaft timing gears

- Oil pump

To install:
4. Install or connect the following:
- Oil pump. Tighten the bolts in sequence to 71–106 inch lbs. (8–12 Nm).
- Crankshaft timing gears
- Timing chains
- Front cover
- Oil pump screen and tube. Tighten the bolts to 71–106 inch lbs. (8–12 Nm), and the nut to 15–22 ft. lbs. (20–30 Nm).
- Oil pan
- Crankshaft pulley

➡The air conditioning mounting bracket bolts are torque-to-yield bolts and must be replaced when removed.

- A/C compressor and bracket
- Water pump
- Alternator
- Power steering pump
- Accessory drive belt
- Valve covers
- Upper intake manifold
- Engine in the vehicle
5. Fill the crankcase.
6. Start the engine and check for leaks and proper operation.

3.4L (VIN N) Engine

1. Before servicing the vehicle, refer to the precautions at the beginning of this section.

2. Remove the engine from the vehicle and mount it on an engine stand.

3. Remove or disconnect the following:

- Accessory drive belts
- A/C compressor
- Alternator
- Water pump drive pulley
- Intake vacuum lines
- Exhaust Gas Recirculation (EGR) tube
- Throttle body
- Surge tank and supports
- Left and right valve covers
- Power steering pump
- Crankshaft pulley
- Camshaft Position (CMP) sensor
- Crankshaft Position (CKP) sensor
- Oil pan
- Oil pump screen and tube
- Accessory belt idler pulleys
- Front cover
- CKP pulse ring
- Timing chain
- Crankshaft timing sprocket
- Oil pump

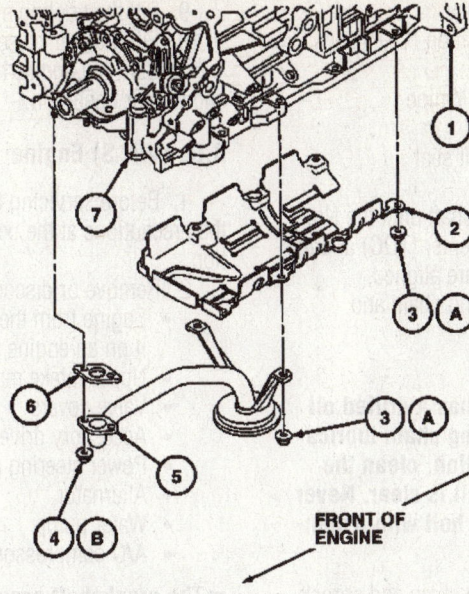

Item	Description
1	Cylinder Block
2	Oil Pan Baffle
3	Nut (5 Req'd)
4	Nut (2 Req'd)
5	Oil Pump Screen Cover and Tube
6	Oil Pump Inlet Tube Gasket
7	Oil Pump
A	Tighten to 14-25 Nm (11-18 Lb-Ft)
B	Tighten to 8-14 Nm (71-123 Lb-In)

9300KG16

Exploded view of the oil pump pickup tube and screen mounting—3.4L (VIN N) engine—3.0L (VIN S) engine is similar

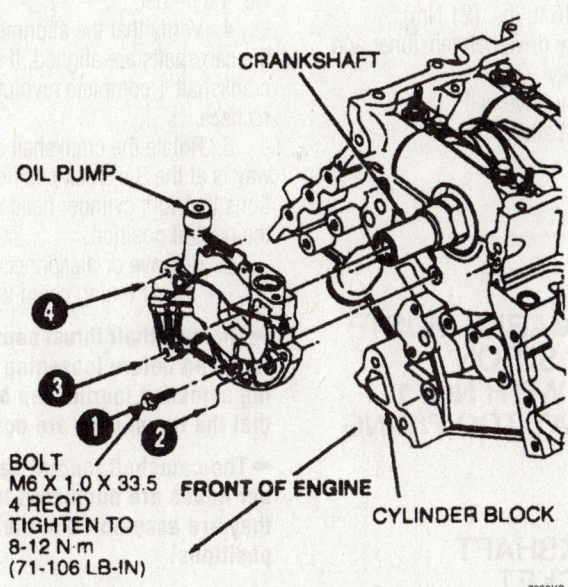

7922KG43

Oil pump bolt tightening sequence—3.0L (VIN S) engine—3.4L (VIN N) engine is similar

To install:

4. Install or connect the following:
- Oil pump. Tighten the bolts in sequence to 80–115 inch lbs. (9–13 Nm).
- Crankshaft timing sprocket
- Timing chain
- CKP pulse ring
- Front cover
- Accessory belt idler pulleys
- Oil pump screen and tube. Tighten the tube nuts to 71–123 inch lbs. (8–14 Nm) and the bracket nuts to 11–18 ft. lbs. (14–25 Nm).
- Oil pan
- CKP sensor
- CMP sensor
- Crankshaft pulley
- Power steering pump
- Left and right valve covers
- Surge tank and supports
- Throttle body
- EGR tube
- Intake vacuum lines
- Water pump drive pulley
- Alternator
- A/C compressor
- Accessory drive belts
- Engine in the vehicle

5. Fill the crankcase.

6. Start the engine and check for leaks and proper operation.

Rear Main Seal

REMOVAL & INSTALLATION

3.0L (VIN U) Engine

1. Before servicing the vehicle, refer to the precautions at the beginning of this section.

2. Attach an engine support fixture to the engine lifting eyes.

3. Remove or disconnect the following:
- Negative battery cable
- Transaxle
- Flexplate
- Rear main seal

To install:

4. Install or connect the following:
- Rear main seal flush with the cylinder block surface.
- Flexplate. Tighten the bolts to 54–64 ft. lbs. (73–87 Nm).
- Transaxle
- Negative battery cable

5. Run the engine and check for leaks.

Timing belt service is covered in Section 4 of this manual

3.0L (VIN S) and 3.4L (VIN N) Engines

1. Before servicing the vehicle, refer to the precautions at the beginning of this section.

2. Attach an engine support fixture to the engine lifting eyes.

3. Remove or disconnect the following:
   - Negative battery cable
   - Transaxle
   - Flexplate

4. Use Seal Remover T92C-6700-CH (3.0L) or T95P-6700-EH (3.4L) to remove the rear crankshaft seal.

To install:

5. Install or connect the following:
   - Rear main seal flush with the cylinder block surface
   - Flexplate. Tighten the bolts to 54–64 ft. lbs. (73–87 Nm).
   - Transaxle
   - Negative battery cable

6. Run the engine and check for leaks.

Timing Chain, Sprockets and Front Cover and Seal

REMOVAL & INSTALLATION

3.0L (VIN U) Engine

1. Before servicing the vehicle, refer to the precautions at the beginning of this section.

2. Drain the engine oil and the cooling system.

3. Remove or disconnect the following:
   - Negative battery cable
   - Accessory drive belt
   - Accessory drive belt tensioner and idler pulley
   - Water pump pulley

   - Crankshaft pulley
   - Crankshaft Position (CKP) sensor
   - Coolant hoses
   - Dual converter Y-pipe
   - Oil pan
   - Front crankshaft seal
   - Front cover

4. Rotate the crankshaft until the No. 1 piston is at Top Dead Center (TDC) and the timing sprocket marks are aligned.

5. Remove the timing chain and sprockets.

To install:

➡ **The camshaft bolt has a drilled oil passage in it for timing chain lubrication. Prior to installation, clean the passage and be sure it is clear. Never replace the camshaft bolt with a standard bolt.**

6. Install the timing chain and sprockets with the timing marks aligned. Tighten the camshaft sprocket bolt to 46 ft. lbs. (63 Nm).

7. Use a new gasket and install the front cover. Apply sealant to bolts 1, 2 and 3. Tighten bolts 1–10 to 19 ft. lbs. (25 Nm) and bolts 11–15 to 84 inch lbs. (10 Nm).

8. Install or connect the following:
   - Front crankshaft seal
   - Oil pan
   - Dual converter Y-pipe
   - Coolant hoses
   - CKP sensor
   - Crankshaft pulley. Tighten the damper bolt to 107 ft. lbs. (145 Nm).
   - Water pump pulley. Tighten the bolts to 16 ft. lbs. (21 Nm).
   - Accessory drive belt tensioner and idler pulley
   - Accessory drive belt
   - Negative battery cable

9. Fill the cooling system.
10. Fill the crankcase.
11. Start the engine and check for leaks and proper operation.

3.0L (VIN S) Engine

1. Before servicing the vehicle, refer to the precautions at the beginning of this section.

2. Remove or disconnect the following:
   - Engine from the vehicle and mount it on an engine stand
   - Upper intake manifold
   - Valve covers
   - Accessory drive belt
   - Power steering pump
   - Alternator
   - Water pump
   - A/C compressor and bracket

➡ **The crankshaft accessory drive pulley shaft has left-hand threads. Rotate the pulley shaft clockwise to remove.**

   - Crankshaft pulley
   - Crankshaft damper
   - Oil pan
   - Oil pump screen and tube
   - Crankshaft Position (CKP) sensor connector
   - Camshaft Position (CMP) sensor connector
   - Front cover
   - CKP sensor pulse ring

3. Rotate the crankshaft so that the keyway is at the 11 o'clock position to locate the crankshaft at Top Dead Center (TDC) for No. 1 cylinder.

4. Verify that the alignment arrows on the camshafts are aligned. If not, rotate the crankshaft 1 complete revolution and recheck.

5. Rotate the crankshaft so that the keyway is at the 3 o'clock position. This positions the right cylinder head camshafts to the neutral position.

6. Remove or disconnect the following:
   - Right timing chain tensioner.

➡ **The camshaft thrust caps must be removed before loosening the remaining camshaft journal cap bolts to ensure that the thrust caps are not damaged.**

➡ **The camshaft journal caps and cylinder heads are numbered to ensure that they are assembled in their original positions.**

   - Camshaft thrust caps
   - Camshaft journal caps. Loosen the bolts in sequence and in several passes to allow the camshaft to be

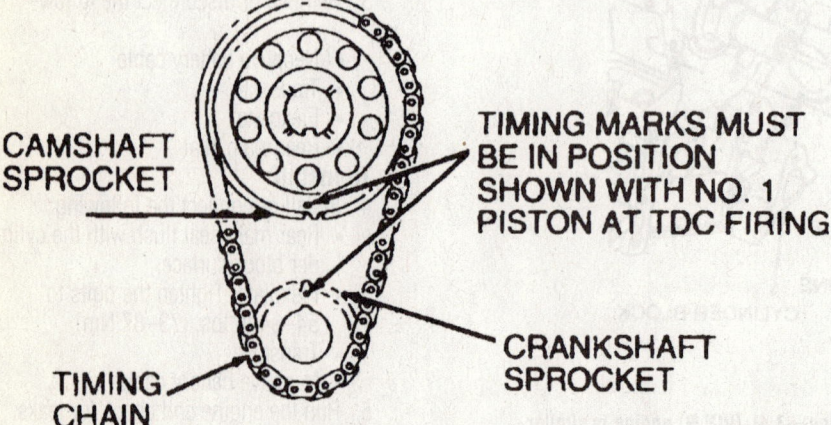

CAMSHAFT SPROCKET

TIMING MARKS MUST BE IN POSITION SHOWN WITH NO. 1 PISTON AT TDC FIRING

TIMING CHAIN

CRANKSHAFT SPROCKET

Timing chain alignment marks—3.0L (VIN U) engine

7922KG47

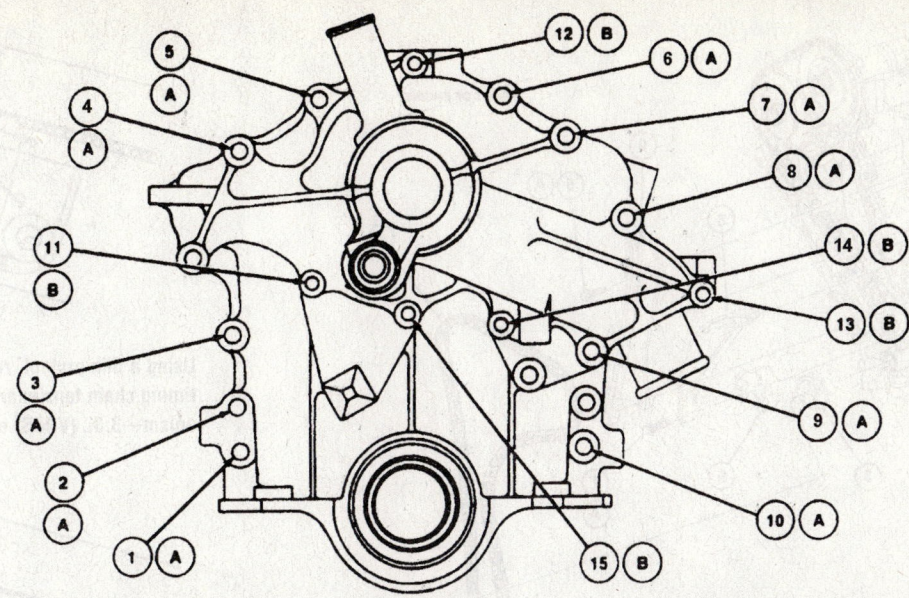

Fastener And Hole No.	Fasteners		Torque Specifications	
	Size	Fastener Application	N·m	LB-FT
1A	M8 x 1.25 x 43.5	F/C TO BLOCK	20-30	15-22
2A	M8 x 1.25 x 43.5	F/C TO BLOCK	20-30	15-22
3A	M8 x 1.25 x 73	W/P & F/C TO BLOCK	20-30	15-22
4A	M8 x 1.25 x 104.3	W/P & F/C TO BLOCK	20-30	15-22
5A	M8 x 1.25 x 73	F/C TO BLOCK	20-30	15-22
6A	M8 x 1.25 x 73	W/P & F/C TO BLOCK	20-30	15-22
7A	M8 x 1.25 x 73	W/P & F/C TO BLOCK	20-30	15-22
8A	M8 x 1.25 x 104.3	W/P & F/C TO BLOCK	20-30	15-22
9A	M8 x 1.25 x 104.3	W/P & F/C TO BLOCK	20-30	15-22
10A	M8 x 1.25 x 52	F/C TO BLOCK	20-30	15-22
11B	M6 x 1 x 28.5	W/P TO F/C	8-12	71-106 (lb-in)
12B	M6 x 1 x 28.5	W/P TO F/C	8-12	71-106 (lb-in)
13B	M6 x 1 x 28.5	W/P TO F/C	8-12	71-106 (lb-in)
14B	M6 x 1 x 28.5	W/P TO F/C	8-12	71-106 (lb-in)
15B	M6 x 1 x 28.5	W/P TO F/C	8-12	71-106 (lb-in)

W/P—Water Pump
F/C—Engine Front Cover

7922KG48

Timing chain front cover bolt location and identification—3.0L (VIN U) engine

raised from the cylinder head evenly.
- Rocker arms. Keep the rocker arms in order for installation.
- Right timing chain tensioner arm
- Right timing chain and crankshaft sprocket

7. Rotate the crankshaft 2 revolutions and locate the crankshaft keyway at the 11 o'clock position. This will position the left cylinder head camshafts to their neutral position.

8. Verify that the alignment arrows on the camshafts are aligned.

9. Remove the left cylinder head timing chain tensioner retaining bolts and the timing chain tensioner.

➡**The camshaft thrust caps must be removed before loosening the remaining camshaft journal cap bolts to ensure that the thrust caps are not damaged.**

➡**The camshaft journal caps and cylinder heads are numbered to ensure that**

they are assembled in their original positions.

10. Remove or disconnect the following:
- Camshaft thrust caps
- Camshaft journal caps. Loosen the bolts in sequence and in several passes to allow the camshaft to be raised from the cylinder head evenly.
- Rocker arms. Keep the rocker arms in order for installation.
- Left timing chain tensioner arm

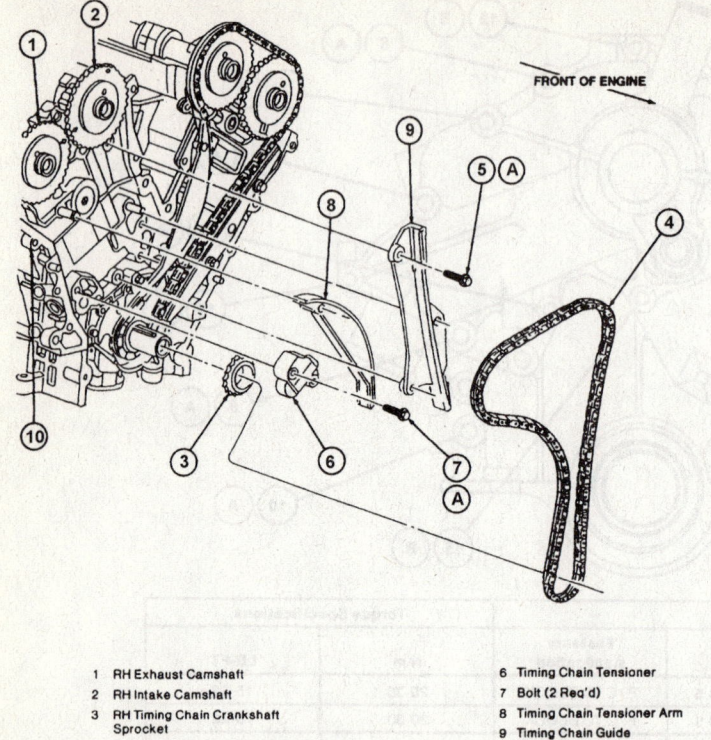

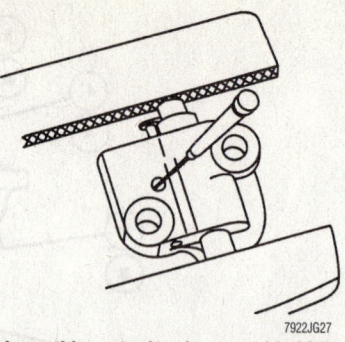

Using a thin prytool, release and hold the timing chain tensioner ratchet/pawl mechanism—3.0L (VIN S) engine

1 RH Exhaust Camshaft
2 RH Intake Camshaft
3 RH Timing Chain Crankshaft Sprocket
4 RH Timing Chain
5 Bolt (2 Req'd)

6 Timing Chain Tensioner
7 Bolt (2 Req'd)
8 Timing Chain Tensioner Arm
9 Timing Chain Guide
10 RH Cylinder Head
A Tighten to 20-30 N-m (15-22 Lb-Ft)

Exploded view of the right cylinder head timing chain and related components—3.0L (VIN S) engine—left side similar

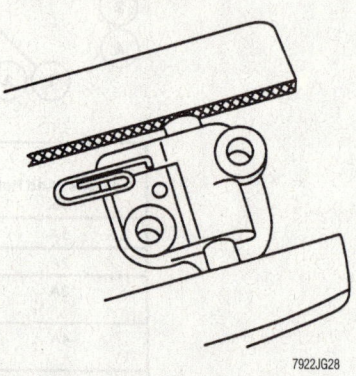

Retain the piston with a 1.5mm wire or paperclip—3.0L (VIN S) engine

- Left timing chain and crankshaft sprocket

To install:

11. Prepare the timing chain tensioners for installation as follows:

a. Place the left chain tensioner in a vise.

b. Using a small prytool, release and hold the timing chain tensioner ratchet/pawl mechanism through the access hole in the timing chain tensioner.

c. Slowly compress the tensioner.

d. Lock the piston with a 1.5mm wire or paperclip.

e. Repeat for the right chain tensioner.

➡ **Be sure that the crankshaft keyway is still at the 11 o'clock position.**

12. Install or connect the following:

- Left timing chain and crankshaft sprocket. Align the colored links with the index marks on the camshaft and crankshaft sprockets.
- Left timing chain tensioner arm
- Left timing chain tensioner. Tighten the retaining bolts to 15–22 ft. lbs. (20–30 Nm).
- Right timing chain and crankshaft sprocket. Align the colored links

with the index marks on the camshaft and crankshaft sprockets.

- Right timing chain tensioner arm
- Right timing chain tensioner. Tighten the retaining bolts to 15–22 ft. lbs. (20–30 Nm).

➡ **The crankshaft keyway must be in the 11 o'clock position to install the left cylinder head rocker arms.**

13. Install the left cylinder head rocker arms in their original positions.

➡ **Do not install the camshaft journal thrust caps until the other journal caps have been installed and tightened.**

14. Tighten the left camshaft journal caps in the order shown and in several passes to 71–106 inch lbs. (8–12 Nm).

15. Install the left camshaft journal thrust caps and tighten the bolts to 71–106 inch lbs. (8–12 Nm).

16. Remove the retaining wire from the left timing chain tensioner.

➡ **The crankshaft keyway must be in the 3 o'clock position to install the right cylinder head rocker arms.**

17. Rotate the crankshaft so that the keyway is in the 3 o'clock position.

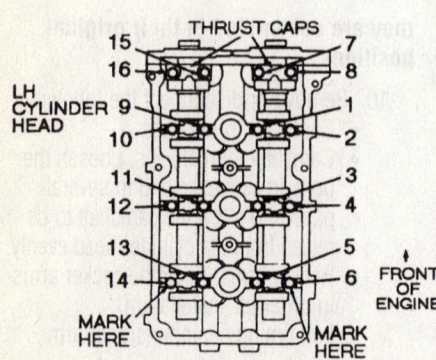

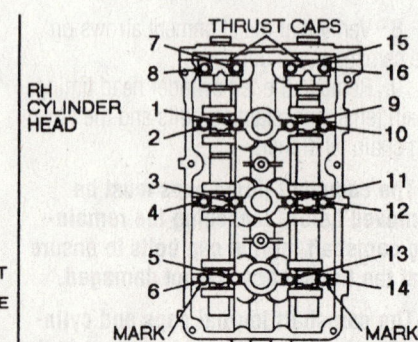

Camshaft journal bolt tightening sequence—3.0L (VIN S) engine

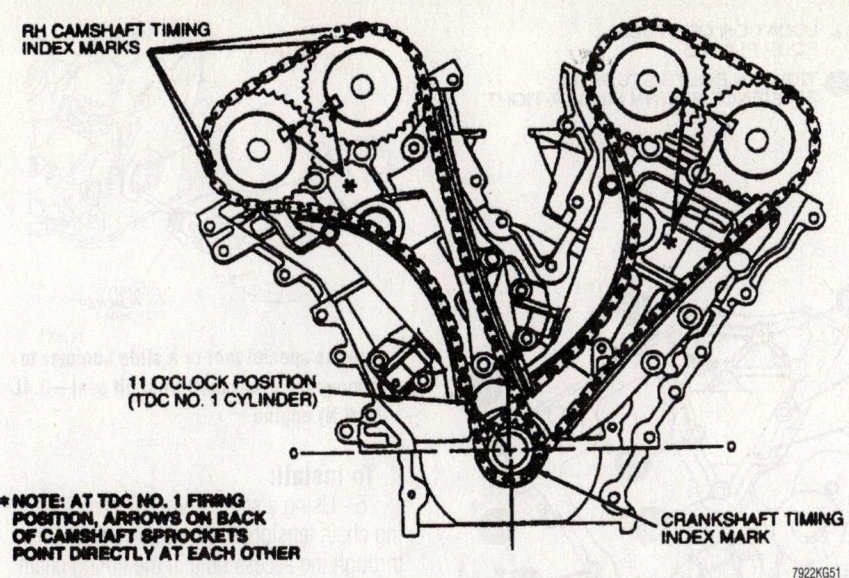

RH CAMSHAFT TIMING INDEX MARKS

11 O'CLOCK POSITION (TDC NO. 1 CYLINDER)

✱NOTE: AT TDC NO. 1 FIRING POSITION, ARROWS ON BACK OF CAMSHAFT SPROCKETS POINT DIRECTLY AT EACH OTHER

CRANKSHAFT TIMING INDEX MARK

7922KG51

Be sure the timing marks are as shown after the chain has been installed—3.0L (VIN S) engine

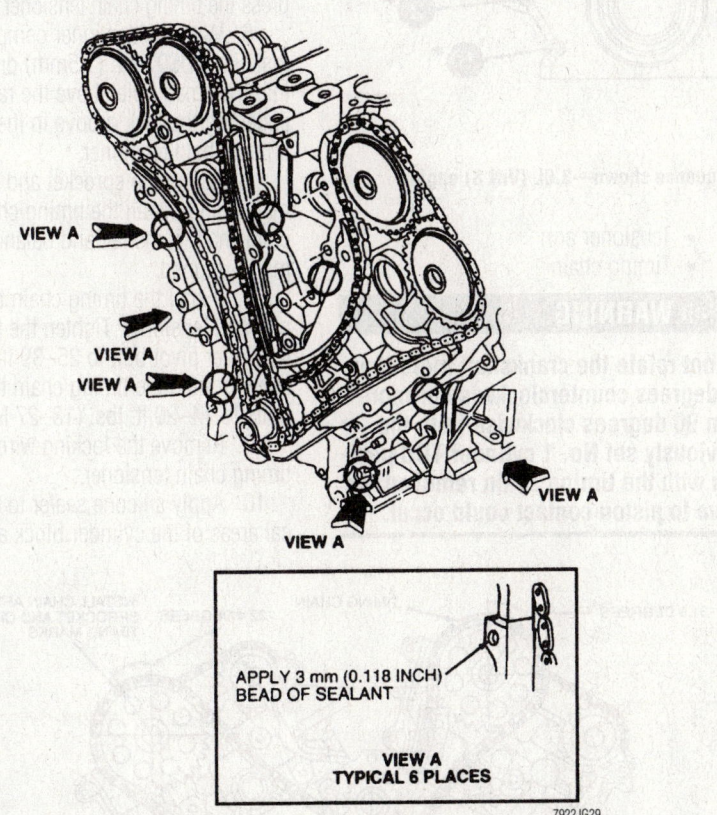

VIEW A
VIEW A
VIEW A
VIEW A
VIEW A

APPLY 3 mm (0.118 INCH) BEAD OF SEALANT

VIEW A
TYPICAL 6 PLACES

7922JG29

To prevent oil leakage, apply sealant to the places indicated—3.0L (VIN S) engine

18. Install the right cylinder head rocker arms in their original positions.

➡ **Do not install the camshaft journal thrust caps until the other journal caps have been installed and tightened.**

19. Tighten the right camshaft journal caps in the order shown and in several passes to 71–106 inch lbs. (8–12 Nm).

20. Install the right camshaft journal thrust caps and tighten the bolts to 71–106 inch lbs. (8–12 Nm).

21. Remove the retaining wire from the right timing chain tensioner.

22. Install the CKP sensor pulse ring using the keyway.

23. Replace the crankshaft seal in the front cover with a new one. Apply clean engine oil to the seal lip.

24. Apply silicone sealer to the 6 critical areas shown in View **A**, to the cylinder block to prevent oil seepage.

25. Place new front cover gaskets onto the dowel pins on the cylinder block and heads.

26. Place the front cover into position.

27. Install the 6 front cover retaining bolts and stud bolts where the silicone sealer was applied.

28. Tighten the bolts and stud bolts until the front cover contacts the cylinder block and heads an, then turn the bolts and stud bolts an additional ¼ turn.

29. Install the remaining front cover retaining bolts and stud bolts.

30. Tighten all of the front cover retaining bolts and stud bolts in sequence to 15–22 ft. lbs. (20–30 Nm).

➡ **The air conditioning mounting bracket bolts are torque-to-yield bolts and must be replaced.**

31. Install or connect the following:
- CMP sensor connector
- CKP sensor connector
- Oil pump screen and tube
- Oil pan

32. Install the crankshaft damper and tighten the bolt as follows:
  a. Step 1: Tighten the bolt to 78–99 ft. lbs. (105–135 Nm).
  b. Step 2: Loosen the bolt one full turn.
  c. Step 3: Tighten the bolt to 35–39 ft. lbs. (47–53 Nm).
  d. Step 4: Tighten the bolt 85–95 degrees.

33. Install or connect the following:
- Crankshaft pulley. Tighten counter-clockwise to 70–77 ft. lbs. (95–105 Nm).
- A/C compressor and bracket
- Water pump
- Alternator
- Power steering pump
- Accessory drive belt
- Valve covers
- Upper intake manifold
- Engine assembly into the vehicle

34. Run the engine and check for leaks and proper operation.

Refer to Section 1 for engine rebuilding specifications

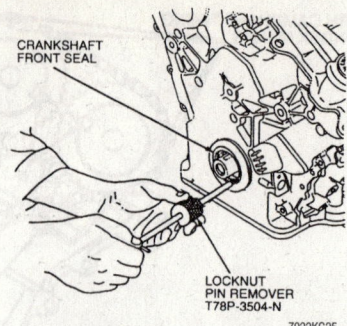

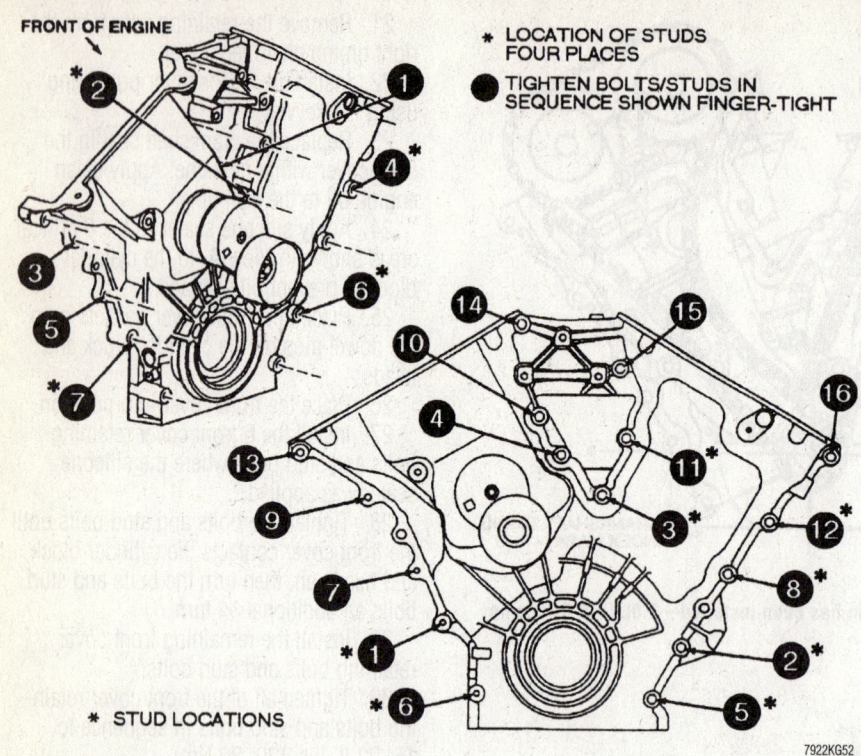

* LOCATION OF STUDS FOUR PLACES

● TIGHTEN BOLTS/STUDS IN SEQUENCE SHOWN FINGER-TIGHT

* STUD LOCATIONS

To prevent leaks, tighten the front cover bolts in the sequence shown—3.0L (VIN S) engine

CRANKSHAFT FRONT SEAL

LOCKNUT PIN REMOVER T78P-3504-N

Use the special tool or a slide hammer to remove the crankshaft front oil seal—3.4L (VIN N) engine

To install:

5. Using a small prybar, release the timing chain tensioner ratchet/pawl mechanism through the access hole in the timing chain tensioner. Insert a small wire into the top of the piston and unseat the oil check ball. Compress the timing chain tensioner by hand.

6. With the tensioner compressed, install a 0.060 inch (1.5mm) drill bit or wire into the small hole above the ratchet, engaging the lock groove in the rack of the timing chain tensioner.

7. Match the sprocket and chain timing marks, and install the timing chain with the crankshaft, camshaft and balance shaft marks aligned.

8. Install the timing chain tensioner arm and tensioner. Tighten the timing chain tensioner pivot bolt to 25–39 ft. lbs. (34–53 Nm). Tighten the timing chain tensioner bolts to 14–20 ft. lbs. (18–27 Nm).

9. Remove the locking wire from the timing chain tensioner.

10. Apply silicone sealer to the 13 critical areas of the cylinder block as shown.

3.4L (VIN N) Engine

1. Before servicing the vehicle, refer to the precautions at the beginning of this section.

2. Remove or disconnect the following:
* Engine from the vehicle and mount it on an engine stand
* Accessory drive belts
* A/C compressor
* Alternator
* Intake vacuum lines
* Exhaust Gas Recirculation (EGR) tube
* Throttle body
* Surge tank and supports
* Left and right intake manifolds
* Engine control sensor wiring harness and brackets
* Left and right valve covers
* Power steering pump
* Crankshaft pulley
* Front crankshaft seal
* Crankshaft Position (CKP) sensor
* Oil pan
* Accessory belt idler pulleys
* Front cover
* CKP pulse ring

3. Set the crankshaft at Top Dead Center (TDC) of the compression stroke for the No. 1 cylinder.

4. Remove or disconnect the following:
* Timing chain tensioner
* Tensioner arm
* Timing chain

❊❊ WARNING

Do not rotate the crankshaft more than 45 degrees counterclockwise or more than 90 degrees clockwise from the previously set No. 1 cylinder TDC position with the timing chain removed, or valve to piston contact could occur.

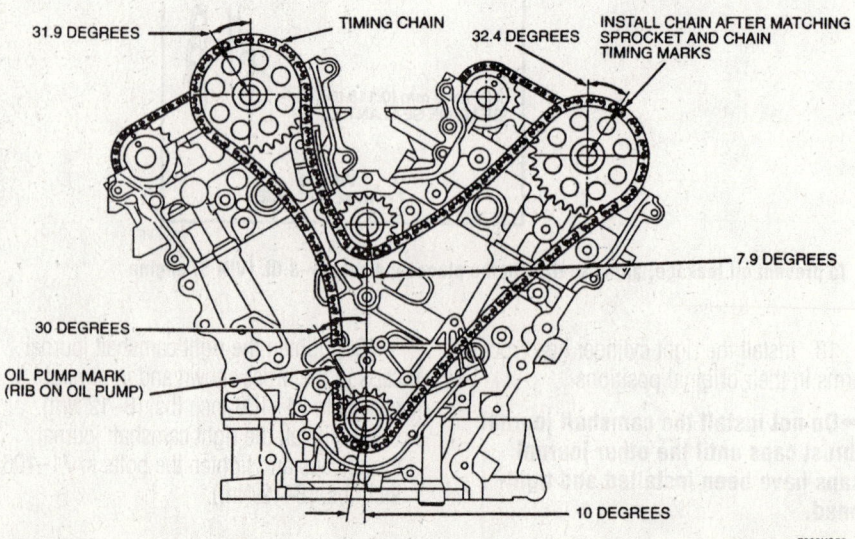

Timing chain alignment marks—3.4L (VIN N) engine

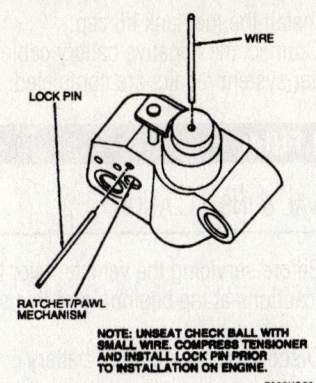

Timing chain tensioner—3.4L (VIN N) engine

11. Install or connect the following:
- CKP pulse ring
- Front cover. Tighten the bolts to 14–20 ft. lbs. (18–28 Nm).
- Accessory belt idler pulleys
- Oil pan
- CKP sensor
- Front crankshaft seal

12. Install the crankshaft pulley and tighten the bolt as follows:
   a. Step 1: Tighten the bolt to 78–99 ft. lbs. (105–135 Nm).
   b. Step 2: Loosen the bolt one full turn.

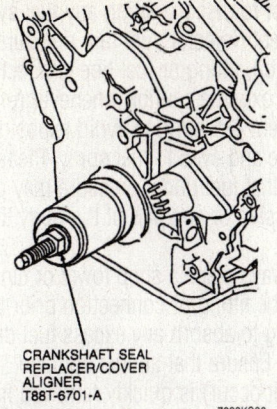

Install the new crankshaft front oil seal using a suitable seal driver or the special tool—3.4L (VIN N) engine

   c. Step 3: Tighten the bolt to 35–39 ft. lbs. (47–53 Nm).
   d. Step 4: Tighten the bolt 85–95 degrees.

13. Install or connect the following:
- Power steering pump
- Left and right valve covers
- Engine control sensor wiring harness and brackets
- Left and right intake manifolds
- Surge tank and supports
- Throttle body
- EGR tube
- Intake vacuum lines
- Alternator
- A/C compressor
- Accessory drive belts
- Engine assembly into the vehicle.

14. Run the engine and check for leaks and proper operation.

Piston and Ring

POSITIONING

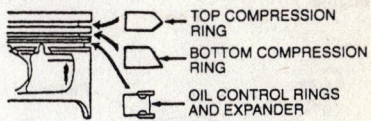

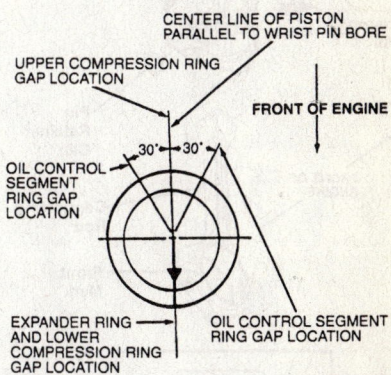

Ring end-gap spacing—3.0L (VIN S and U) engines

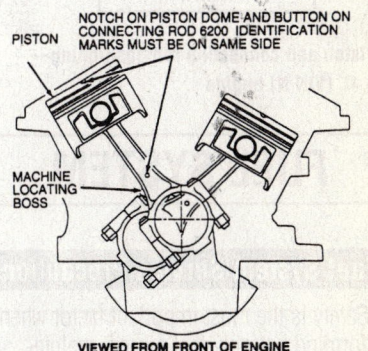

Piston and connecting rod positioning—3.0L (VIN S and U) engines

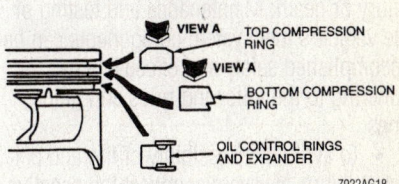

Piston ring positioning—3.4L (VIN N) engine

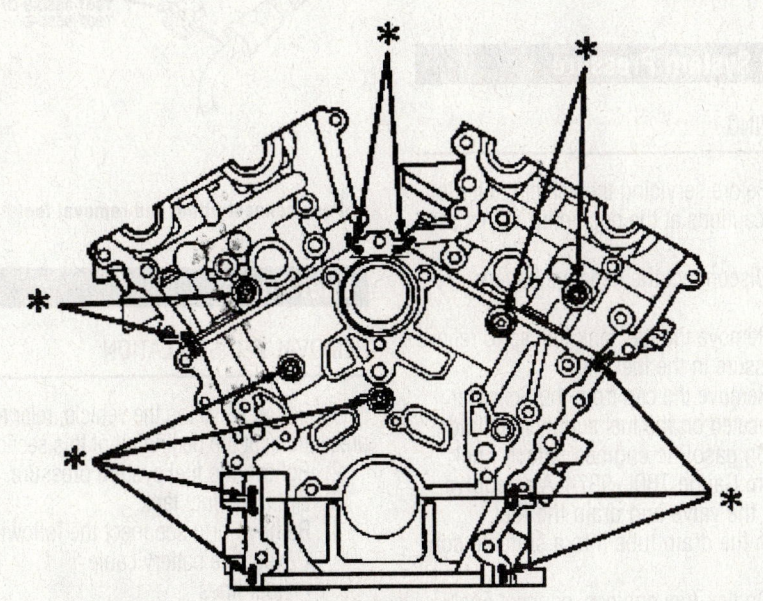

* APPLY 3 mm (0.118 INCH) BEAD OF SEALANT MEETING FORD SPECIFICATIONS (WSE-M4G323-A6) PRIOR TO INSTALLATION

Apply sealant to the cylinder block and heads—3.4L (VIN N) engine

For engine torque specifications, refer to Section 1 of this manual

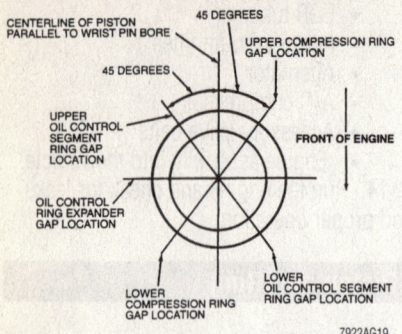

Ring end-gap positioning—3.4L (VIN N) engine

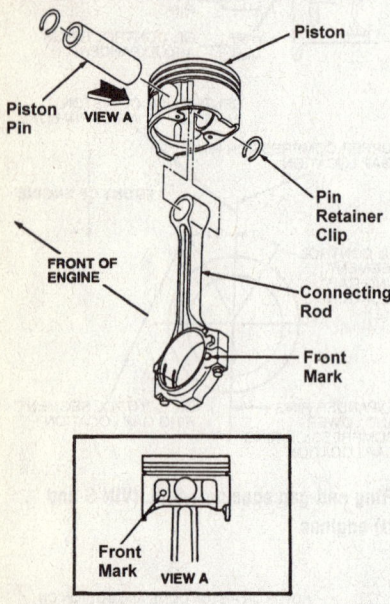

Piston and connecting rod positioning— 3.4L (VIN N) engine

FUEL SYSTEM

Fuel System Service Precautions

Safety is the most important factor when performing not only fuel system maintenance but any type of maintenance. Failure to conduct maintenance and repairs in a safe manner may result in serious personal injury or death. Maintenance and testing of the vehicle's fuel system components can be accomplished safely and effectively by adhering to the following rules and guidelines.

• To avoid the possibility of fire and personal injury, always disconnect the negative battery cable unless the repair or test procedure requires that battery voltage be applied.

• Always relieve the fuel system pressure prior to disconnecting any fuel system component (injector, fuel rail, pressure regulator, etc.), fitting or fuel line connection. Exercise extreme caution whenever relieving fuel system pressure, to avoid exposing skin, face and eyes to fuel spray. Please be advised that fuel under pressure may penetrate the skin or any part of the body that it contacts.

• Always place a shop towel or cloth around the fitting or connection prior to loosening to absorb any excess fuel due to spillage. Ensure that all fuel spillage (should it occur) is quickly removed from engine surfaces. Ensure that all fuel soaked cloths or towels are deposited into a suitable waste container.

• Always keep a dry chemical (Class B) fire extinguisher near the work area.

• Do not allow fuel spray or fuel vapors to come into contact with a spark or open flame.

• Always use a back-up wrench when loosening and tightening fuel line connection fittings. This will prevent unnecessary stress and torsion to fuel line piping. Always follow the proper torque specifications.

• Always replace worn fuel fitting O-rings with new. Do not substitute fuel hose or equivalent, where fuel pipe is installed.

Fuel System Pressure

RELIEVING

1. Before servicing the vehicle, refer to the precautions at the beginning of this section.

2. Disconnect the negative battery cable.

3. Remove the fuel tank fill cap to relieve the pressure in the fuel tank.

4. Remove the cap from the Schrader valve located on the fuel supply manifold.

5. On gasoline engines, attach Fuel Pressure Gauge T80L-9974-A or equivalent, to the valve and drain the fuel through the drain tube into a suitable container.

6. On flex-fuel engines, connect Fuel Pressure Gauge T80L-9974-A or equivalent and Fuel Pressure Test Kit 134-R0035 or equivalent, to the Schrader valve. Drain the fuel through the drain tube into a suitable container.

7. After the fuel system pressure is relieved, remove the fuel pressure gauge and install the cap on the Schrader valve.

8. Install the fuel tank fill cap.

9. Connect the negative battery cable only after system repairs are completed.

Fuel Filter

REMOVAL & INSTALLATION

1. Before servicing the vehicle, refer to the precautions at the beginning of this section.

2. Disconnect the negative battery cable.

3. Relieve the fuel system pressure.

4. Disconnect the fuel lines.

5. Loosen the filter retaining clamp and remove the fuel filter.

To install:

6. Install the fuel filter with the flow arrow facing the proper direction and tighten the filter retaining clamp.

7. Push the fuel lines on to the filter fittings until an audible click is heard.

8. Connect the negative battery cable.

9. Start the engine and check for fuel leaks and proper operation.

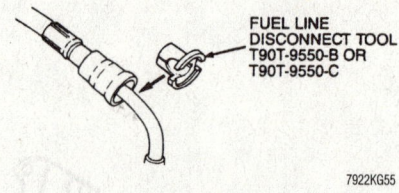

Push connect fitting and removal tool

Fuel Pump

REMOVAL & INSTALLATION

1. Before servicing the vehicle, refer to the precautions at the beginning of this section.

2. Relieve the fuel system pressure.

3. Drain the fuel tank.

4. Remove or disconnect the following:

• Negative battery cable
• Fuel lines
• Fuel pump module electrical connector
• Fuel tank
• Fuel pump module

To install:

5. Install the fuel pump module carefully to ensure the filter and hoses and float rod are not damaged. Use a new O-ring seal.

6. Align the fuel pump module and the fuel tank retainer and push the fuel pump

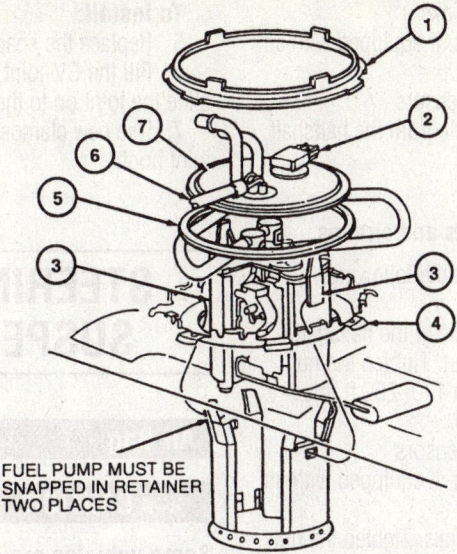

FUEL PUMP MUST BE
SNAPPED IN RETAINER
TWO PLACES

1	Fuel Pump Locking Retainer Ring
2	Fuel Tank Pressure / Vacuum Transducer
3	Locking Tab
4	Fuel Tank
5	O-Ring Seal
6	Connector
7	Fuel Pump Module

7922KG58

Exploded view of the fuel pump module mounting

module into the fuel tank retainer. When the fuel pump module is properly engaged, a definite click will be heard engaging 2 locking tabs on the outside of the fuel pump.

7. Install or connect the following:
- Fuel pump module locking ring
- Fuel tank
- Fuel pump module electrical connector
- Fuel lines
- Negative battery cable

8. Add a minimum of 10 gallons of clean fuel to the tank.

9. Start the engine and check for leaks.

Fuel Injector

REMOVAL & INSTALLATION

3.0L (VIN U and S) Engines

1. Before servicing the vehicle, refer to the precautions in the beginning of this section.

2. Relieve fuel system pressure.

3. Remove or disconnect the following:
- Negative battery cable
- Air cleaner outlet tube

- Fuel lines
- Upper intake manifold
- Fuel injector electrical connectors
- Fuel pressure regulator vacuum line
- Fuel supply manifold with the injectors attached
- Injectors from the supply manifold

To install:

4. Install or connect the following:
- Fuel injectors. Use new O-ring seals.
- Fuel supply manifold with the injectors attached. Tighten the bolts to 71–106 inch lbs. (8–12 Nm).
- Fuel pressure regulator vacuum line
- Fuel injector electrical connectors
- Upper intake manifold
- Fuel lines
- Air cleaner outlet tube
- Negative battery cable

5. Start the engine and check for leaks.

3.4L (VIN N) Engine

1. Before servicing the vehicle, refer to the precautions in the beginning of this section.

2. Relieve fuel system pressure.

3. Remove or disconnect the following:
- Negative battery cable

- Air cleaner outlet tube
- Fuel lines
- Throttle body
- Surge tank
- Left and right intake manifolds
- Fuel injector electrical connectors
- Fuel pressure regulator vacuum line
- Fuel supply manifold with the injectors attached
- Injectors from the supply manifold

To install:

4. Install or connect the following:
- Fuel injectors. Use new O-ring seals.
- Fuel supply manifold with the injectors attached. Tighten the bolts to 11–16 ft. lbs. (15–23 Nm).
- Fuel pressure regulator vacuum line
- Fuel injector electrical connectors
- Left and right intake manifolds
- Surge tank
- Throttle body
- Fuel lines
- Air cleaner outlet tube
- Negative battery cable

5. Start the engine and check for leaks.

DRIVE TRAIN

Transaxle

REMOVAL & INSTALLATION

1. Before servicing the vehicle, refer to the precautions at the beginning of this section.

2. Attach a powertrain support to the engine lifting eyes.

3. Remove or disconnect the following:
- Battery and tray
- Air cleaner assembly
- Transaxle electrical connectors
- Shift cable
- Transaxle cooler lines
- Front wheels
- Stabilizer bar links
- Lower ball joints
- Axle halfshafts
- Heated Oxygen (HO2S) sensor connectors
- Dual converter Y-pipe
- Starter
- Steering rack and pinion gear. Support the gear with safety wire.
- Powertrain support insulators
- Subframe
- Torque converter nuts

4. Support the transaxle with a transmission jack.

5. Remove the transaxle flange bolts and remove the transaxle.

To install:

6. Install the transaxle. For 1999–01 3.0L (VIN S) engines, tighten the flange bolts to 25–33 ft. lbs. (33–46 Nm). For all other engines, tighten the flange bolts to 30–44 ft. lbs. (40–60 Nm). Tighten the torque converter nuts to 20–34 ft. lbs. (27–46 Nm).

7. Install the subframe. Use 2 pieces of ¾ inch outside diameter pipe in the alignment holes behind the front subframe mounts to align the subframe to the body. Tighten the subframe mounting bolts to 57–76 ft. lbs. (77–103 Nm).

8. Install or connect the following:
- Powertrain support insulators. Tighten the bracket bolts to 65 ft. lbs. (88 Nm), and the subframe bolts to 90 ft. lbs. (122 Nm).
- Steering rack and pinion gear. Tighten the nuts to 84–113 ft. lbs. (113–133 Nm).
- Starter. Tighten the fasteners to 21 ft. lbs. (29 Nm).
- Dual converter Y-pipe
- HO2S sensor connectors
- Axle halfshafts. Tighten the hub retainer nuts to 170–202 ft. lbs. (230–275 Nm).
- Lower ball joints. Tighten the nuts to 51–67 ft. lbs. (68–92 Nm).
- Stabilizer bar links. Tighten the nuts to 35–46 ft. lbs. (47–63 Nm).
- Front wheels
- Transaxle cooler lines
- Shift cable
- Transaxle electrical connectors
- Air cleaner assembly
- Battery and tray

9. Start the engine. Check for leaks and proper operation.

➡ **Whenever the vehicles subframe is removed or lowered, the wheel alignment should be checked.**

Halfshaft

REMOVAL & INSTALLATION

1. Before servicing the vehicle, refer to the precautions at the beginning of this section.

2. Remove or disconnect the following:
- Front wheels
- Lower ball joints
- Outer tie rod ends
- Stabilizer bar links
- Height sensors, if equipped with air suspension
- Wheel speed sensors
- Steering knuckle from the halfshaft
- Halfshafts

To install:

➡ **Use new nuts, bolts and circlips.**

3. Install or connect the following:
- Halfshafts
- Steering knuckle to the halfshaft
- Hub retainer nut. Tighten the hub retainer nuts to 170–202 ft. lbs. (230–275 Nm).
- Wheel speed sensors
- Height sensors, if equipped with air suspension
- Stabilizer bar links. Tighten the nuts to 57–75 ft. lbs. (77–103 Nm).
- Outer tie rod ends. Tighten the nuts to 35–46 ft. lbs. (47–63 Nm).
- Lower ball joints. Tighten the fasteners to 50–68 ft. lbs. (68–92 Nm).
- Front wheels

CV-Joint

REMOVAL AND REPLACEMENT

Inner Tripod Joint

The inner CV-joint is serviced with the halfshaft as an assembly. The inner CV-joint boot can be serviced by removing the outer CV-joint.

Outer CV-Joint

1. Before servicing the vehicle, refer to the precautions in the beginning of this section.

2. Place the halfshaft in a vise.

3. Remove the CV-joint boot clamps and slide the boot away from the joint.

4. Drive the CV-joint off the halfshaft with a brass drift and a hammer.

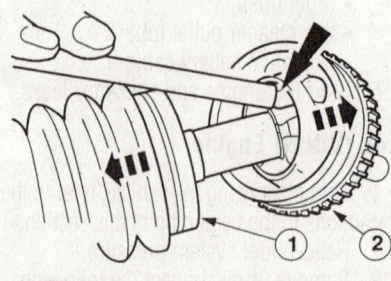

1. CV-Joint boot
2. CV-Joint

9306HG07

Removing the outer CV-joint

To install:

5. Replace the snapring.

6. Fill the CV-joint with fresh grease and slide the joint on to the halfshaft.

7. Use new clamps and install the CV-joint boot.

STEERING AND SUSPENSION

Air Bag

✳✳ CAUTION

Some vehicles are equipped with an air bag system. The system must be disarmed before performing service on, or around, system components, the steering column, instrument panel components, wiring and sensors. Failure to follow the safety precautions and the disarming procedure could result in accidental air bag deployment, possible injury and unnecessary system repairs.

PRECAUTIONS

Several precautions must be observed when handling the inflator module to avoid accidental deployment and possible personal injury.

- Never carry the inflator module by the wires or connector on the underside of the module.
- When carrying a live inflator module, hold securely with both hands, and ensure that the bag and trim cover are pointed away.
- Place the inflator module on a bench or other surface with the bag and trim cover facing up.
- With the inflator module on the bench, never place anything on or close to the module which may be thrown in the event of an accidental deployment.

Before servicing the vehicle, also be sure to refer to the precautions in the beginning of this section as well.

DISARMING

1. Before servicing the vehicle, refer to the precautions in the beginning of this section.

2. Position the vehicle with the front wheels in a straight-ahead position.

3. Disconnect the negative battery cable.

4. Disconnect the positive battery cable.

5. Wait at least 1 minute for the air bag back-up power supply to drain before continuing.

6. Proceed with the repair.

ARMING

1. After service is completed, connect the battery cables, negative cable last.

2. Check the functioning of the air bag system by turning the ignition key to the **RUN** position and visually monitoring the air bag indicator lamp in the instrument cluster. The indicator lamp should illuminate for approximately 6 seconds, then turn **OFF**. If the indicator lamp does not illuminate, stays **ON**, or flashes at any time, a fault has been detected by the air bag diagnostic monitor.

Power Rack and Pinion Steering Gear

REMOVAL & INSTALLATION

1. Before servicing the vehicle, refer to the precautions at the beginning of this section.

2. Remove or disconnect the following:
- Negative battery cable
- Intermediate steering shaft
- Front wheels
- Dual converter Y-pipe
- Outer tie rod ends
- Left stabilizer link
- Heat shield

- Power steering hose bracket
- Auxiliary actuator connector, if equipped
- Power steering pressure switch connector
- Rear subframe bolts and lower the rear of the subframe about 4 inches
- Steering gear mounting nuts. Move the steering gear to the left to access the power steering hoses.
- Power steering hoses and remove the steering gear through the left wheel opening.

To install:
3. Install or connect the following:
- Steering gear. Use new seals on the hydraulic fittings. Tighten the mounting nuts to 85–100 ft. lbs. (115–135 Nm).
- Rear subframe bolts and tighten them to 57–76 ft. lbs. (77–103 Nm).
- Power steering pressure switch connector
- Auxiliary actuator connector, if equipped
- Power steering hose bracket
- Heat shield
- Left stabilizer link

- Outer tie rod ends. Tighten the nuts to 35 ft. lbs. (48 Nm).
- Dual converter Y-pipe
- Front wheels
- Intermediate steering shaft
- Negative battery cable

4. Fill and bleed the power steering system. Check the system for leaks and proper operation. Adjust the toe setting as necessary.

Strut

REMOVAL & INSTALLATION

Front

1. Before servicing the vehicle, refer to the precautions at the beginning of this section.

2. Remove or disconnect the following:
- Negative battery cable
- Front wheels
- Height sensor and wiring, if equipped with air suspension
- Brake hose bracket
- Disc brake caliper and rotor
- Wheel speed sensor and wiring
- Outer tie rod end
- Stabilizer link

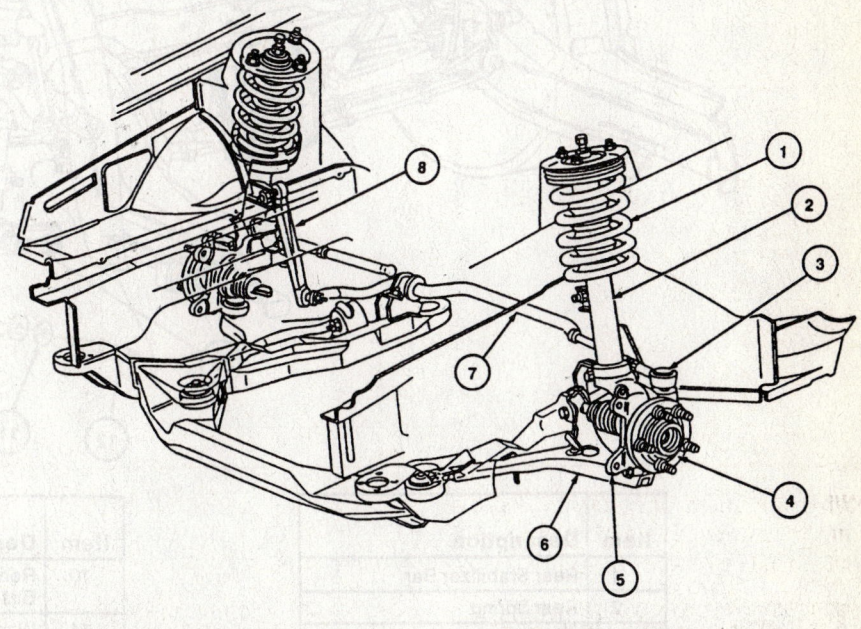

7922KG60

Support the rear of the subframe with 2 tall jackstands while removing the steering gear

JACK STANDS

Front suspension component identification

7922KG61

Item	Description
1	Front Coil Spring
2	Front Shock Absorber
3	Tie Rod End
4	Wheel Hub

Item	Description
5	Front Wheel Knuckle
6	Front Suspension Lower Arm
7	Front Stabilizer Bar
8	Stabilizer Bar Link

- Steering knuckle pinch bolt
- Strut assembly

To install:

3. Install or connect the following:
- Strut assembly. Tighten the upper nuts to 22–29 ft. lbs. (30–40 Nm), and the knuckle pinch bolt to 73–97 ft. lbs. (98–132 Nm).
- Stabilizer link. Tighten to 55–75 ft. lbs. (75–101 Nm).
- Outer tie rod end. Tighten the nut to 35 ft. lbs. (48 Nm).
- Wheel speed sensor and wiring
- Disc brake caliper and rotor. Tighten the caliper anchor bracket bolts to 65–87 ft. lbs. (88–118 Nm).
- Brake hose bracket
- Height sensor and wiring, if equipped with air suspension

- Front wheels
- Negative battery cable

4. Road test the vehicle and check for proper operation.

Rear

1. Before servicing the vehicle, refer to the precautions at the beginning of this section.

2. Remove or disconnect the following:
- Rear package tray trim panel
- Rear wheels
- Brake load sensor
- Brake hose
- Stabilizer bar bracket and link
- Tension strut
- Spindle pinch bolt
- Strut assembly

To install:

➡ **Use new mounting nuts and bolts.**

3. Install or connect the following:
- Strut assembly. Use a new pinch bolt and tighten to 50–67 ft. lbs. (68–92 Nm), and tighten the 3 upper mounting nuts to 19–25 ft. lbs. (25–34 Nm).
- Tension strut. Tighten the nut to 35–46 ft. lbs. (68–92 Nm).
- Stabilizer bar link. Tighten the nut to 60–81 inch lbs. (7–9 Nm).
- Stabilizer bar bracket. Tighten the bolts to 25 –33 ft. lbs. (34–46 Nm).
- Brake hose
- Brake load sensor
- Rear wheels
- Rear package tray trim panel

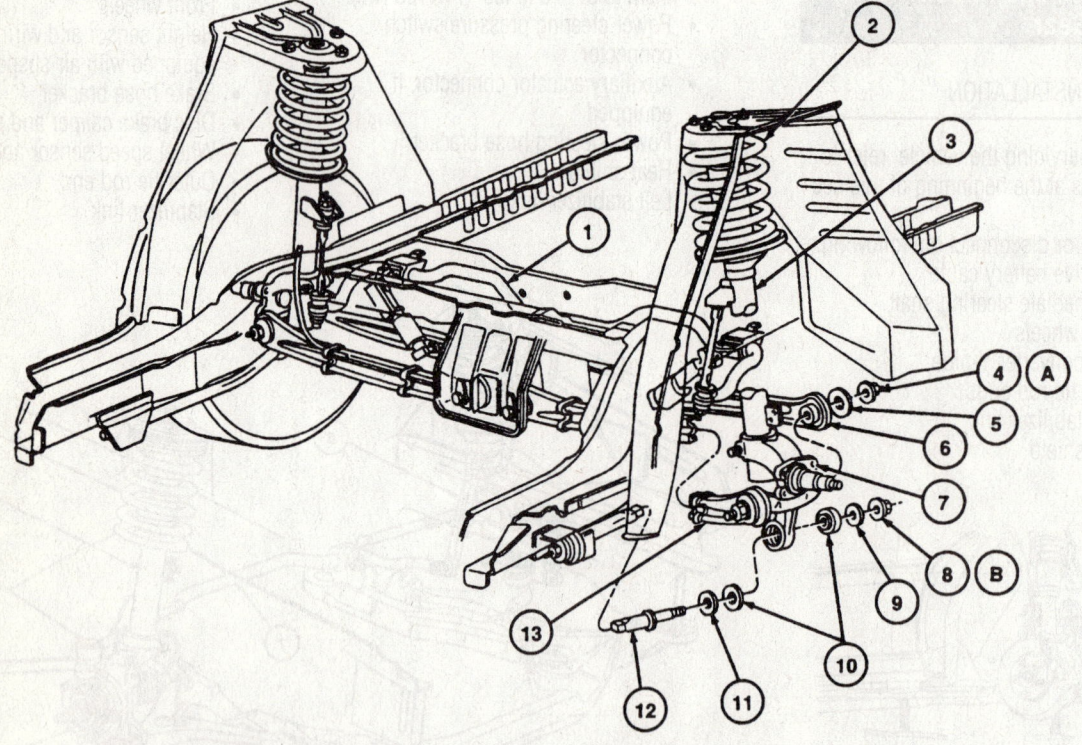

Item	Description
1	Rear Stabilizer Bar
2	Rear Spring
3	Shock Absorber
4	Nut
5	Washer
6	Lower Suspension Arm (Rear)
7	Rear Wheel Spindle
8	Nut (4 Req'd)
9	Washer (2 Req'd)

Item	Description
10	Rear Suspension Tie Rod Bushing (4 Req'd)
11	Washer (2 Req'd)
12	Rear Suspension Tension Strut and Bushing (2 Req'd)
13	Rear Suspension Lower Arm (Front)
A	Tighten to 68-92 N·m (50-67 Lb-Ft)
B	Tighten to 46.7-63.3 N·m (35-46 Lb-Ft)

Rear suspension component identification—sedan models

7922KG62

Shock Absorber

REMOVAL & INSTALLATION

Wagons

1. Before servicing the vehicle, refer to the precautions at the beginning of this section.
2. Remove the rear wheels and support the rear control arms on jackstands.
3. Remove or disconnect the following:
   - Rear compartment access panels
   - Upper shock mounting nuts and insulators
   - Lower shock mounting bolts
   - Shock absorbers

To install:

➡**Use new mounting fasteners and insulators.**

4. Install or connect the following:
   - Shock absorbers. Tighten the lower bolt to 50–68 ft. lbs. (68–92 Nm), and the upper nuts to19–25 ft. lbs. (26–34 Nm).
   - Rear compartment access panels
   - Rear wheels

Coil Spring

REMOVAL & INSTALLATION

Struts

1. Before servicing the vehicle, refer to the precautions at the beginning of this section.
2. Remove the strut from the vehicle.
3. Compress the coil spring using a suitable spring compressor until the spring comes away from the seat.
4. Remove the large center nut and slowly release the spring compressor.

To install:

5. Compress the spring and install it on the strut.

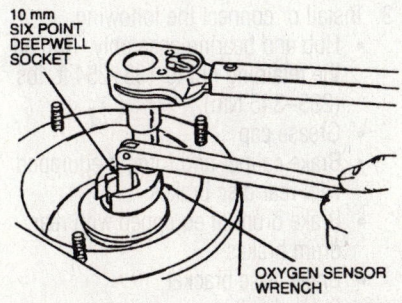

10 mm
SIX POINT
DEEPWELL
SOCKET

OXYGEN SENSOR
WRENCH

7922KG64

Hold the strut rod while loosening or tightening the nut

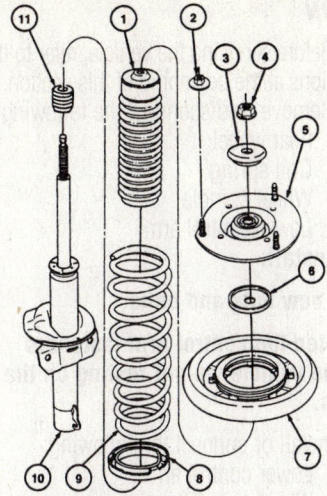

Item	Description
1	Dust Boot (Part of 18124)
2	Nut (3 Req'd)
3	Washer
4	Nut
5	Front Shock Absorber Mounting Bracket
6	Washer
7	Front Suspension Bearing and Seal
8	Front Spring Insulator (Part of 18124)
9	Front Coil Spring
10	Front Shock Absorber
11	Jounce Bumper (Part of 18124)

7922KG63

Exploded view of the front strut and coil spring assembly

6. Install the lower washer and mounting bracket.
7. Install the upper washer and a new nut. Tighten the nut to 39–53 ft. lbs. (53–72 Nm).
8. Install the strut assembly in the vehicle.

Wagons with Rear Shock Absorbers

1. Before servicing the vehicle, refer to the precautions at the beginning of this section.
2. Remove or disconnect the following:
   - Rear shock absorber
   - Stabilizer bar link and bracket
   - Brake hose bracket
   - Upper ball joint
3. Install spring keepers on the coil springs.
4. Slowly lower the lower control arm until the tension is relaxed on the coil spring. Remove the coil spring and the upper and lower spring insulators.

To install:

➡**Use new mounting nuts and bolts.**

5. Install or connect the following:
   - Coil spring with upper and lower spring insulators

   - Upper ball joint. Tighten the nut to 50–68 ft. lbs. (68–92 Nm).
   - Brake hose bracket
   - Stabilizer bar link and bracket
   - Rear shock absorber

Lower Ball Joints

REMOVAL & INSTALLATION

The lower ball joint is an integral part of the steering knuckle. If the lower ball joint is found to be defective, the entire steering knuckle must be replaced.

Upper Control Arm

REMOVAL & INSTALLATION

Rear

WAGON ONLY

1. Before servicing the vehicle, refer to the precautions at the beginning of this section.
2. Support the lower control arm on a jackstand.
3. Remove or disconnect the following:
   - Rear wheel
   - Brake hose bracket
   - Upper ball joint
   - Upper control arm

To install:

➡**Use new mounting nuts and bolts.**

4. Install the upper control arm. Tighten the ball joint nut to 50–67 ft. lbs. (68–92 Nm), then tighten the control arm mounting bolts to 73–97 ft. lbs. (98–132 Nm).
5. Install or connect the following:
   - Brake hose bracket
   - Rear wheel
6. Check the wheel alignment and adjust as necessary.

CONTROL ARM BUSHING REPLACEMENT

The control arm bushings are serviced with the control arm as an assembly.

Lower Control Arm

REMOVAL AND INSTALLATION

Front

1. Before servicing the vehicle, refer to the precautions at the beginning of this section.

2. Remove or disconnect the following:
- Front wheel
- Wheel speed sensor wiring harness
- Lower ball joint
- Lower control arm

To install:

3. Install or connect the following:
- Lower control arm. Tighten the front bolt to 57–75 ft. lbs. (77–103 Nm), and the rear bolt to 72–97 ft. lbs. (98–132 Nm).
- Lower ball joint. Use a new nut and tighten to 50–67 ft. lbs. (68–92 Nm).
- Wheel speed sensor wiring harness
- Front wheel

4. Check the wheel alignment and adjust as necessary.

Rear

SEDAN

1. Before servicing the vehicle, refer to the precautions at the beginning of this section.

2. Remove or disconnect the following:
- Rear wheel
- Parking brake cable
- Proportioning valve
- Lower control arm

To install:

➡ **Use new bolts and nuts.**

➡ **The rear suspension lower control arms are marked BOTTOM on the lower edge. The flange edge of the right side rear suspension arm and bushing stamping must face the front of the vehicle. The other three must face the rear of the vehicle.**

➡ **The rear suspension arms have two adjustment cams that fit inside the bushings at the arm-to-body attachment. Each adjustment cam is installed from the front on the rear suspension arm and bushing.**

3. Install or connect the following:
- Lower control arm. Tighten the bolts to 50–67 ft. lbs. (68–92 Nm).
- Proportioning valve
- Parking brake cable
- Rear wheel

4. Check the wheel alignment and adjust as necessary.

WAGON

1. Before servicing the vehicle, refer to the precautions at the beginning of this section.

2. Remove or disconnect the following:
- Rear wheel
- Coil spring
- Wheel spindle
- Lower control arm

To install:

➡ **Use new nuts and bolts.**

➡ **Tighten the control arm fasteners with the vehicle weight resting on the wheels.**

3. Install or connect the following:
- Lower control arm
- Wheel spindle
- Coil spring
- Rear wheel

4. Tighten the control arm-to-body bolt to 40–52 ft. lbs. (54–71 Nm), and the arm-to-spindle bolt to 50–67 ft. lbs. (68–92 Nm).

5. Check the wheel alignment and adjust as necessary.

CONTROL ARM BUSHING REPLACEMENT

The control arm bushings are serviced with the control arm as an assembly.

Wheel Bearings

ADJUSTMENT

There is no adjustment for the front or rear wheel bearings due to the nature of their design. These bearings are permanently lubricated and require no periodic maintenance.

REMOVAL & INSTALLATION

Front

1. Before servicing the vehicle, refer to the precautions at the beginning of this section.

2. Remove or disconnect the following:
- Front wheel
- Hub retainer nut
- Brake caliper and rotor
- Outer tie rod end
- Stabilizer bar link
- Wheel speed sensor
- Lower ball joint
- Steering knuckle

3. Unbolt and remove the hub and bearing assembly.

To install:

➡ **Use new nuts, bolts, and split pins.**

➡ **The knuckle must be clean enough to allow the wheel hub to be completely seated by hand. Do not press or draw the wheel hub into place.**

4. Install or connect the following:
- Hub and bearing assembly. Tighten the bolts to 61–78 ft. lbs. (83–107 Nm).
- Steering knuckle. Tighten the pinch bolt to 72–97 ft. lbs. (98–132 Nm).
- Lower ball joint. Tighten the nut to 50–67 ft. lbs. (68–92 Nm).
- Wheel speed sensor
- Stabilizer bar link. Tighten the nut to 57–75 ft. lbs. (77–103 Nm).
- Outer tie rod end. Tighten the nut to 35–46 ft. lbs. (47–63 Nm).
- Brake caliper and rotor. Tighten the caliper anchor bracket bolts to 65–87 ft. lbs. (88–118 Nm).
- Hub retainer nut. Tighten the nut to 170–202 ft. lbs. (230–275 Nm).
- Front wheel

Rear

1. Before servicing the vehicle, refer to the precautions at the beginning of this section.

2. Remove or disconnect the following:
- Rear wheel
- Brake hose bracket
- Brake caliper and rotor, if equipped with rear disc brakes
- Brake drum, if equipped with rear drum brakes
- Hub and bearing assembly grease cap and retaining nut
- Hub and bearing assembly

To install:

➡ **Use new retaining nuts and grease caps**

3. Install or connect the following:
- Hub and bearing assembly. Tighten the retaining nut to 188–254 ft. lbs. (255–345 Nm).
- Grease cap
- Brake caliper and rotor, if equipped with rear disc brakes
- Brake drum, if equipped with rear drum brakes
- Brake hose bracket
- Rear wheel

FORD MOTOR CO.

20

Lincoln-Continental

PRECAUTIONS

Before servicing any vehicle, please be sure to read all of the following precautions, which deal with personal safety, prevention of component damage, and important points to take into consideration when servicing a motor vehicle:

• Never open, service or drain the radiator or cooling system when the engine is hot; serious burns can occur from the steam and hot coolant.

• Observe all applicable safety precautions when working around fuel. Whenever servicing the fuel system, always work in a well-ventilated area. Do not allow fuel spray or vapors to come in contact with a spark, open flame, or excessive heat (a hot drop light, for example). Keep a dry chemical fire extinguisher near the work area. Always keep fuel in a container specifically designed for fuel storage; also, always properly seal fuel containers to avoid the possibility of fire or explosion. Refer to the additional fuel system precautions later in this section.

• Fuel injection systems often remain pressurized, even after the engine has been turned **OFF**. The fuel system pressure must be relieved before disconnecting any fuel lines. Failure to do so may result in fire and/or personal injury.

• Brake fluid often contains polyglycol ethers and polyglycols. Avoid contact with the eyes and wash your hands thoroughly after handling brake fluid. If you do get brake fluid in your eyes, flush your eyes with clean, running water for 15 minutes. If eye irritation persists, or if you have taken brake fluid internally, IMMEDIATELY seek medical assistance.

• The EPA warns that prolonged contact with used engine oil may cause a number of skin disorders, including cancer. You should make every effort to minimize your exposure to used engine oil. Protective gloves should be worn when changing oil. Wash your hands and any other exposed skin areas as soon as possible after exposure to used engine oil. Soap and water, or waterless hand cleaner should be used.

• All new vehicles are now equipped with an air bag system, often referred to as a Supplemental Restraint System (SRS) or Supplemental Inflatable Restraint (SIR) system. The system must be disabled before performing service on or around system components, steering column, instrument panel components, wiring and sensors.

Failure to follow safety and disabling procedures could result in accidental air bag deployment, possible personal injury and unnecessary system repairs.

• Always wear safety goggles when working with, or around, the air bag system. When carrying a non-deployed air bag, be sure the bag and trim cover are pointed away from your body. When placing a non-deployed air bag on a work surface, always face the bag and trim cover upward, away from the surface. This will reduce the motion of the module if it is accidentally deployed. Refer to the additional air bag system precautions later in this section.

• Clean, high quality brake fluid from a sealed container is essential to the safe and proper operation of the brake system. You should always buy the correct type of brake fluid for your vehicle. If the brake fluid becomes contaminated, completely flush the system with new fluid. Never reuse any brake fluid. Any brake fluid that is removed from the system should be discarded. Also, do not allow any brake fluid to come in contact with a painted surface; it will damage the paint.

• Never operate the engine without the proper amount and type of engine oil; doing so WILL result in severe engine damage.

• Timing belt maintenance is extremely important. Many models utilize an interference-type, non-freewheeling engine. If the timing belt breaks, the valves in the cylinder head may strike the pistons, causing potentially serious (also time-consuming and expensive) engine damage. Refer to the maintenance interval charts in the front of this manual for the recommended replacement interval for the timing belt, and to the timing belt section for belt replacement and inspection.

• Disconnecting the negative battery cable on some vehicles may interfere with the functions of the on-board computer system(s) and may require the computer to undergo a relearning process once the negative battery cable is reconnected.

• When servicing drum brakes, only disassemble and assemble one side at a time, leaving the remaining side intact for reference.

ENGINE REPAIR

➡**Disconnecting the negative battery cable on some vehicles may interfere with the functions of the on board com-**puter system. The computer may undergo a relearning process once the negative battery cable is reconnected.

Alternator

REMOVAL

1. Before servicing the vehicle, refer to the precautions in the beginning of this section.
2. Remove or disconnect the following:
   • Negative battery cable
   • Coolant recovery reservoir
   • Accessory drive belt
   • Alternator bracket
   • Alternator

INSTALLATION

Install or connect the following:
   • Alternator. Tighten the bolts to 15–22 ft. lbs. (20–30 Nm).
   • Alternator bracket. Tighten the nuts to 71–106 inch lbs. (8–12 Nm).
   • Accessory drive belt
   • Coolant recovery reservoir
   • Negative battery cable

Ignition Timing

ADJUSTMENT

The base ignition timing is set by the Powertrain Control Module (PCM) and is not adjustable.

Engine Assembly

REMOVAL & INSTALLATION

➡**Disable the air suspension before raising the vehicle. The switch is located in the left-hand side of the luggage compartment on 1997 models or on the right side kick panel for 1998–01 models.**

1. Before servicing the vehicle, refer to the precautions in the beginning of this section.
2. Turn the air suspension switch to the **OFF** position.
3. Recover the A/C refrigerant.
4. Drain the cooling system.
5. Remove or disconnect the following:
   • Negative battery cable
   • Hood
   • Steering column intermediate shaft

- Engine appearance cover
- Intake Air Temperature (IAT) sensor connector
- Air cleaner outlet tube
- Upper motor mount
- Fuel line
- Dash panel ground straps
- Powertrain Control Module (PCM) connector
- Mass Air Flow (MAF) sensor connector
- Traction control motor connector
- Throttle Position (TP) sensor connector
- Cruise control cable
- Accelerator cable and bracket
- Shift selector cable
- Engine control wiring harness (3 connectors) and bracket
- Intake manifold vacuum lines
- Transaxle cooler lines
- Power steering return hose at the fluid reservoir
- Alternator wiring harness
- Radiator splash shield
- Heater hoses
- Radiator hoses
- Front wheels
- Suspension height sensor links
- Lower ball joints
- Stabilizer bar links
- Outer tie rod ends
- Halfshafts
- Heated Oxygen (HO$_2$S) sensor connectors
- Dual converter Y-pipe
- Block heater connector
- Power steering cooler lines
- A/C compressor lines
- Starter
- Subframe brackets
- Torque converter shield and torque converter

6. Support the powertrain from below and remove the subframe bolts.

7. Raise the vehicle away from the powertrain.

8. Attach an engine hoist to the powertrain.

9. Remove or disconnect the following:
- Power steering sensor connector
- Power steering return line from the steering gear
- Turbine shaft speed sensor connector
- Transaxle range sensor connector
- Transaxle control harness connector
- Left and right engine support insulators

- Right engine support insulator bracket

10. Remove the transaxle flange bolts and separate the engine from the transaxle.

To install:

➡ **When installing suspension components and halfshafts, use new nuts, bolts, circlips and split pins.**

11. Install or connect the following:
- Transaxle. Tighten the flange bolts to 25–34 ft. lbs. (34–46 Nm).
- Right engine support insulator bracket. Tighten the bolts to 16–21 ft. lbs. (22–29 Nm).
- Left and right engine support insulators. Tighten the through-bolts to 64–88 ft. lbs. (87–119 Nm).
- Transaxle control harness connector
- Transaxle range sensor connector
- Turbine shaft speed sensor connector
- Power steering return line from the steering gear
- Power steering sensor connector

12. Lower the vehicle on to the powertrain assembly. Use 2 pieces of ¾ inch outside diameter pipe in the alignment holes behind the front subframe mounts to align the subframe to the body. Tighten the subframe mounting bolts to 57–76 ft. lbs. (77–103 Nm).

13. Install or connect the following:
- Torque converter shield and torque converter. Tighten the torque converter nuts to 20–34 ft. lbs. (27–46 Nm).
- Subframe brackets
- Starter
- A/C compressor lines
- Power steering cooler lines
- Block heater connector
- Dual converter Y-pipe
- HO$_2$S sensor connectors
- Halfshafts. Tighten the hub retainer nuts to 170–202 ft. lbs. (230–275 Nm).
- Outer tie rod ends. Tighten the nuts to 35–46 ft. lbs. (47–63 Nm).
- Stabilizer bar links. Tighten the nuts to 30–40 ft. lbs. (40–55 Nm).
- Lower ball joints. Tighten the nuts to 50–68 ft. lbs. (68–92 Nm).
- Suspension height sensor links
- Front wheels
- Radiator hoses
- Heater hoses
- Radiator splash shield
- Alternator wiring harness
- Power steering return hose at the fluid reservoir

- Transaxle cooler lines
- Intake manifold vacuum lines
- Engine control wiring harness (3 connectors) and bracket
- Shift selector cable
- Accelerator cable and bracket
- Cruise control cable
- TP sensor connector
- Traction control motor connector
- MAF sensor connector
- PCM connector
- Dash panel ground straps
- Fuel line
- Upper motor mount
- Air cleaner outlet tube
- IAT sensor connector
- Engine appearance cover
- Steering column intermediate shaft
- Hood
- Negative battery cable

14. Fill the cooling system.

15. Check and adjust fluid levels as necessary.

16. Recharge the A/C system.

17. Turn the air suspension switch to the **ON** position.

18. Run the engine and check for leaks.

➡ **Whenever the subframe is removed or lowered, the wheel alignment should be checked.**

Water Pump

REMOVAL & INSTALLATION

1. Before servicing the vehicle, refer to the precautions in the beginning of this section.

2. Drain the cooling system.

3. Remove or disconnect the following:
- Negative battery cable
- Coolant reservoir
- Accessory drive belt
- Alternator
- Water pump pulley
- Water pump

To install:

4. Install or connect the following:
- Water pump. Use a new O-ring seal and tighten the bolts to 15–22 ft. lbs. (20–30 Nm).
- Water pump pulley. Tighten the bolts to 15–22 ft. lbs. (20–30 Nm).
- Alternator
- Accessory drive belt
- Coolant reservoir
- Negative battery cable

5. Fill the cooling system.

6. Start the engine and check for leaks.

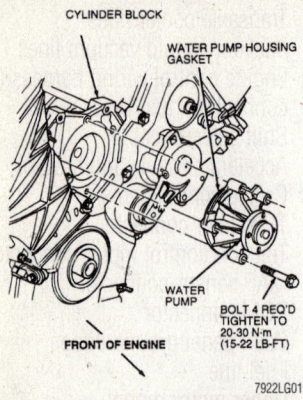

Exploded view of the water pump mounting

Cylinder Head

REMOVAL & INSTALLATION

1. Before servicing the vehicle, refer to the precautions in the beginning of this section.
2. Remove the engine from the vehicle and mount it on a suitable workstand.
3. Remove or disconnect the following:
   - Accessory drive belt and tensioner
   - Idler pulley
   - Engine Coolant Temperature (ECT) sensor connector
   - Water bypass tube
   - Alternator
   - Water pump
   - Power steering pump
   - Crankshaft pulley
   - Camshaft Position (CMP) sensor
   - Spark plug wires and coil packs (1997 engine)
   - Ignition coils (1998–01 engines)
   - Fuel pressure sensor connector and vacuum line
   - Valve covers
   - Rocker arms
   - Exhaust Gas Recirculation (EGR) vacuum regulator valve
   - EGR tube
   - Injector wiring connectors
   - Intake manifold
   - Left and right exhaust manifolds
   - Front cover
   - Crankshaft Position (CKP) sensor pulse wheel
   - Timing chains
   - Cylinder heads

To install:

➡ **The cylinder head bolts are a torque-to-yield design and cannot be reused.**

➡ **Refer to Section 1 of this manual for the cylinder head torque sequence illustration. The illustration is located after the Torque Specification Chart.**

4. Use new gaskets and install the cylinder heads.
5. For 1997 engines, tighten the cylinder head bolts in sequence as follows:
   a. Step 1: 27–32 ft. lbs. (37–43 Nm).
   b. Step 2: Tighten the bolts 85–95 degrees.
   c. Step 3: Tighten the bolts 85–95 degrees.
6. For 1998–01 engines, tighten the cylinder head bolts in sequence as follows:
   a. Step 1: 28–31 ft. lbs. (37–43 Nm).
   b. Step 2: Tighten the bolts 85–95 degrees.
   c. Step 3: Loosen all bolts 1 full turn.
   d. Step 4: Tighten all bolts to 28–31 ft. lbs. (37–43 Nm).
   e. Step 5: Tighten the bolts 85–95 degrees.
   f. Step 6: Tighten the bolts 85–95 degrees.
7. Install or connect the following:
   - Timing chains
   - CKP sensor pulse wheel
   - Front cover
   - Left and right exhaust manifolds
   - Intake manifold
   - Injector wiring connectors
   - EGR tube
   - EGR vacuum regulator valve
   - Rocker arms
   - Valve covers
   - Fuel pressure sensor connector and vacuum line
   - Spark plug wires and coil packs (1997 engine)
   - Ignition coils (1998–01 engines)
   - CMP sensor
   - Crankshaft pulley
   - Water pump
   - Power steering pump
   - Alternator
   - Water bypass tube
   - ECT sensor connector
   - Idler pulley
   - Accessory drive belt and tensioner

Rocker Arms

REMOVAL & INSTALLATION

1. Before servicing the vehicle, refer to the precautions at the beginning of this section.
2. Remove or disconnect the following:
   - Negative battery cable
   - Spark plug wires (1997 engine)
   - Ignition coils (1998–01 engines)
   - Valve covers
3. Rotate the crankshaft so that the piston on the cylinder to be serviced is at bottom dead center with the valves closed.

4. Install special tool Valve Spring Compressor T91P-6565-A for exhaust valves, and Valve Spring Compressor T93P-6565-A for intake valves.
5. Compress the valve spring and remove the rocker arm. Repeat for each arm to be removed.

➡ **If the rocker arms are to be reused, ensure that they are installed in the same position that they were removed from.**

To install:

6. Compress the valve spring and install the rocker arm. Repeat for each arm to be installed.
7. Install or connect the following:
   - Valve covers
   - Spark plug wires (1997 engine)
   - Ignition coils (1998–01 engines)
   - Negative battery cable
8. Start the engine and check for proper operation.

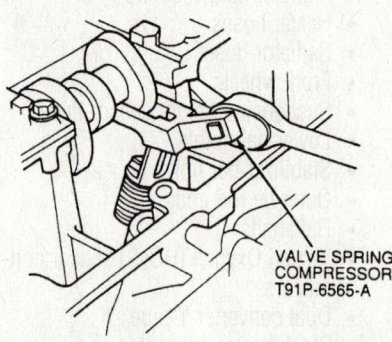

Rocker arm service tool—exhaust valve tool shown

Intake Manifold

REMOVAL & INSTALLATION

1. Before servicing the vehicle, refer to the precautions in the beginning of this section.
2. Drain the cooling system.
3. Remove or disconnect the following:
   - Negative battery cable
   - Engine appearance cover
   - Air cleaner outlet tube
   - Fuel lines
   - Fuel pressure regulator vacuum (1997 engine)
   - Fuel pressure sensor vacuum and wiring connectors (1998–01 engines)
   - Spark plug wires (1997 engine)
   - Upper radiator hose
   - Heater hose

- Engine Coolant Temperature (ECT) sensor connector
- Water bypass tube
- Cruise control cable
- Accelerator cable and bracket
- Crankcase vent hose
- Chassis vacuum supply line
- Secondary air injection vacuum lines
- Exhaust Gas Recirculation (EGR) vacuum regulator

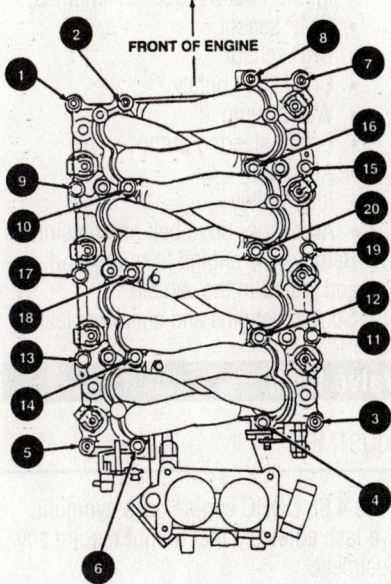

Intake manifold bolt removal sequence—1997 engine

- EGR valve
- Intake Manifold Runner Control (IMRC) cables and actuator
- Fuel injector connectors
- Throttle Position (TP) sensor connector
- Idle Air Control (IAC) connector
- Fuel temperature sensor connector
- Fuel injection supply manifold
- Intake manifold. Loosen the bolts in three steps in the sequence shown.
- IMRC housings

To install:

4. Install or connect the following:
- IMRC housings to the intake manifold
- Fuel supply manifold and tighten the bolts to 71–106 inch lbs. (8–12 Nm)

➡**Install the long bolts and studs in the outer holes. Install the short bolts and studs in the inner holes.**

➡**Refer to Section 1 of this manual for the intake manifold torque sequence illustration. The illustration is located after the Torque Specification Chart.**

5. Install the intake manifold assembly. Tighten the bolts in sequence as follows:
   a. Step 1: Tighten bolts 5, 7, 9, and 11 to 9–11 ft. lbs. (12–15 Nm).
   b. Step 2: Tighten all other bolts to 13–16 ft. lbs. (18–22 Nm).
   c. Step 3: Tighten all bolts in sequence 85–95 degrees.
6. Tighten the IMRC housing bolts as follows:
   a. Step 1: 71–89 inch lbs. (8–10 Nm).
   b. Step 2: Plus 85–95 degrees.
7. Install or connect the following:
- Fuel temperature sensor connector

- IAC connector
- TP sensor connector
- Fuel injector connectors
- IMRC cables and actuator
- EGR valve
- EGR vacuum regulator
- Secondary air injection vacuum lines
- Chassis vacuum supply line
- Crankcase vent hose
- Accelerator cable and bracket
- Cruise control cable
- Water bypass tube
- ECT sensor connector
- Heater hose
- Upper radiator hose
- Spark plug wires (1997 engine)
- Fuel pressure regulator vacuum (1997 engine)
- Fuel pressure sensor vacuum and wiring connectors (1998–01 engines)
- Fuel lines
- Air cleaner outlet tube
- Engine appearance cover
- Negative battery cable
8. Fill the cooling system.
9. Start the engine and check for leaks.

Exhaust Manifold

REMOVAL & INSTALLATION

➡**Disable the air suspension before raising the vehicle. The switch is located in the left-hand side of the luggage compartment on 1997 models or on the right side kick panel for 1998–01 models.**

1. Before servicing the vehicle, refer to the precautions in the beginning of this section.
2. Turn the air suspension switch to the **OFF** position.
3. Remove or disconnect the following:
- Negative battery cable
- Radiator splash shield
- Heated Oxygen (HO2S) sensor connectors
- Dual converter Y-pipe
- Exhaust Gas Recirculation (EGR) tube
- Secondary air injection tubes
- Exhaust manifolds

To install:

4. Install or connect the following:
- Exhaust manifolds. Tighten the nuts in sequence to 13–16 ft. lbs. (18–22 Nm).

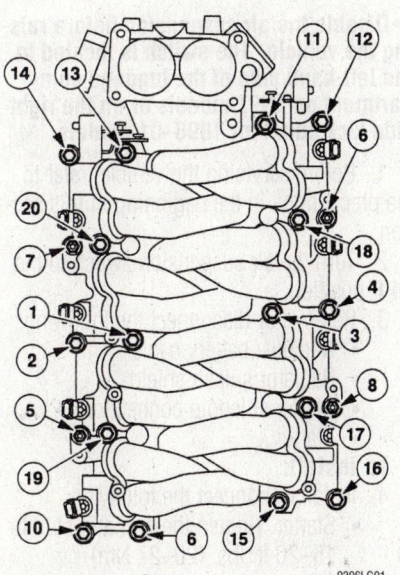

Intake manifold bolt removal sequence—1998–01 engines

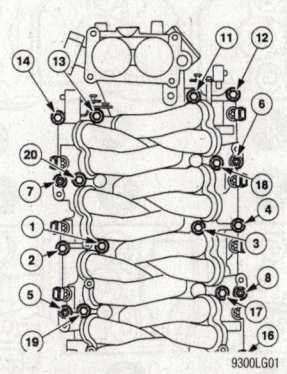

Exploded view of the crankcase vent hose and related components

Timing belt service is covered in Section 4 of this manual

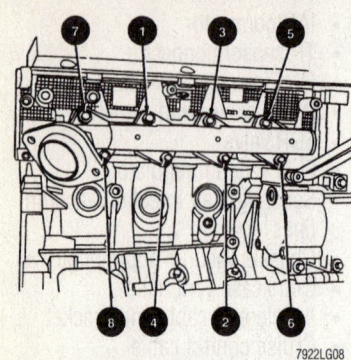

Exhaust manifold torque sequence—right side shown, left side similar

- Secondary air injection tubes. Tighten the nuts to 25–34 ft. lbs. (34–46 Nm).
- EGR tube. Tighten the nut to 30–33 ft. lbs. (40–45 Nm).
- Dual converter Y-pipe
- HO$_2$S sensor connectors
- Radiator splash shield
- Negative battery cable

5. Turn the air suspension switch to the **ON** position.

6. Start the engine and check for leaks.

Camshaft and Valve Lifters

REMOVAL & INSTALLATION

1. Before servicing the vehicle, refer to the precautions in the beginning of this section.

2. Remove the engine from the vehicle and mount it on a suitable workstand.

3. Remove or disconnect the following:

- Accessory drive belt and tensioner
- Idler pulley
- Alternator
- Power steering pump
- Water pump
- Crankshaft pulley
- Crankshaft Position (CKP) sensor
- Camshaft Position (CMP) sensor
- Spark plug wires and coil packs (1997 engine)
- Ignition coils (1998–01 engines)
- Valve covers

➡**If the rocker arms are to be reused, label them as they are removed so they can be reinstalled in their original locations.**

- Rocker arms
- Front cover
- Crankshaft Position (CKP) sensor pulse wheel
- Timing chains and sprockets
- Secondary chains and sprockets
- Secondary chain tensioners
- Camshaft cap assemblies
- Camshafts

To install:

➡**The exhaust camshaft cap assembly outboard bolts are shorter than the other cap assembly bolts.**

4. Install the camshafts and camshaft cap assemblies in their original positions.

5. Tighten the camshaft cap assembly bolts in sequence as follows:

a. Step 1: Tighten all bolts to 71–106 inch lbs. (8–12 Nm)

b. Step 2: Loosen all bolts 2 turns

c. Step 3: Tighten all bolts to 71–106 inch lbs. (8–12 Nm)

6. Install or connect the following:

- Secondary chain tensioners
- Secondary chains and sprockets
- Timing chains and sprockets
- CKP sensor pulse wheel
- Front cover
- Rocker arms in the original locations
- Valve covers
- Spark plug wires and coil packs (1997 engine)
- Ignition coils (1998–01 engines)
- CMP sensor
- CKP sensor
- Crankshaft pulley
- Water pump
- Power steering pump
- Alternator
- Idler pulley
- Accessory drive belt and tensioner

7. Remove the engine from the workstand and install in the vehicle.

8. Start the engine and check for leaks.

Valve Lash

ADJUSTMENT

The 4.6L DOHC engine uses hydraulic valve lash adjusters that do not require any adjustment.

Starter Motor

REMOVAL & INSTALLATION

➡**Disable the air suspension before raising the vehicle. The switch is located in the left-hand side of the luggage compartment on 1997 models or on the right side kick panel for 1998–01 models.**

1. Before servicing the vehicle, refer to the precautions in the beginning of this section.

2. Turn the air suspension switch to the **OFF** position.

3. Remove or disconnect the following:

- Negative battery cable
- Radiator splash shield
- Starter solenoid connections
- Starter

To install:

4. Install or connect the following:

- Starter. Tighten the bolt and stud to 15–20 ft. lbs. (20–27 Nm).
- Starter solenoid connections
- Radiator splash shield
- Negative battery cable

5. Turn the air suspension switch to the **ON** position.

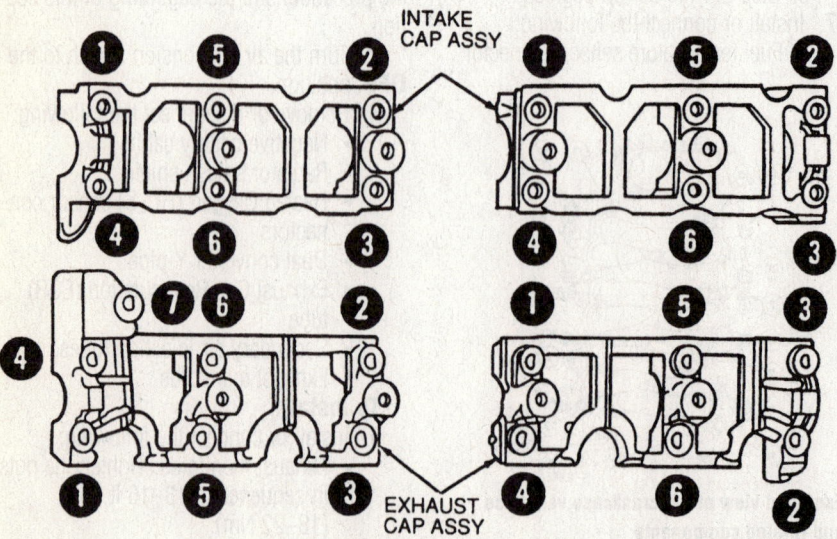

Camshaft cap assembly torque sequence

Oil Pan

REMOVAL & INSTALLATION

➡**Disable the air suspension before raising the vehicle. The switch is located in the left-hand side of the luggage compartment on 1997 models or on the right side kick panel for 1998–01 models.**

1. Before servicing the vehicle, refer to the precautions in the beginning of this section.
2. Turn the air suspension switch to the **OFF** position.
3. Remove or disconnect the following:
   - Negative battery cable
   - Oil level dipstick
   - Dual converter Y-pipe
   - Oil level sensor connector
   - Power steering pressure hose bracket
   - Oil pan

To install:

4. Apply a bead of silicone sealer to the oil pan flange. Also apply a bead of sealer to the front cover/cylinder block joint and fill the grooves on both sides of the rear main seal cap.
5. Use a new gasket and install the oil pan. Tighten the bolts in sequence as follows:
   a. Step 1: 14 ft. lbs. (20 Nm)
   b. Step 2: Plus 60 degrees
6. Install or connect the following:
   - Power steering pressure hose bracket
   - Oil level sensor connector
   - Dual converter Y-pipe
   - Oil level dipstick
   - Negative battery cable
7. Fill the crankcase with the correct type and quantity of engine oil.
8. Turn the air suspension switch to the **ON** position.
9. Start the engine and check for leaks.

Oil Pump

REMOVAL & INSTALLATION

1. Before servicing the vehicle, refer to the precautions in the beginning of this section.
2. Remove the engine from the vehicle and mount it on a suitable workstand.
3. Remove or disconnect the following:
   - Accessory drive belt and tensioner
   - Idler pulley
   - Alternator
   - Power steering pump
   - Water pump
   - Crankshaft pulley
   - Camshaft Position (CMP) sensor
   - Spark plug wires and coil packs (1997 engine)
   - Ignition coils (1998–01 engines)
   - Valve covers
   - Rocker arms
   - Front cover
   - Crankshaft Position (CKP) sensor pulse wheel
   - Timing chains and sprockets
   - Oil pan
   - Oil pump pickup screen and tube
   - Oil pump

To install:

4. Install or connect the following:
   - Oil pump. Tighten the bolts in sequence to 71–106 inch lbs. (8–12 Nm).
   - Oil pump pickup screen and tube. Use a new O-ring seal and tighten the mounting bolts to 71–106 inch lbs. (8–12 Nm). Tighten the bracket bolt to 15–22 ft. lbs. (20–30 Nm).
   - Oil pan
   - Timing chains and sprockets
   - CKP sensor pulse wheel
   - Front cover
   - Rocker arms
   - Valve covers
   - Ignition coils (1998–01 engines)
   - Spark plug wires and coil packs (1997 engine)

- CMP sensor
- Crankshaft pulley
- Water pump
- Power steering pump
- Alternator
- Idler pulley
- Accessory drive belt and tensioner

5. Remove the engine from the workstand and install in the vehicle.
6. Restore all fluid levels.
7. Run the engine and check for leaks and proper operation.

Rear Main Seal

REMOVAL & INSTALLATION

1. Before servicing the vehicle, refer to the precautions in the beginning of this section.
2. Remove or disconnect the following:
   - Transaxle
   - Flywheel
   - Oil seal retainer
   - Oil seal

To install:

3. Apply a 0.060 inch (1.5mm) continuous bead of silicone gasket sealer to the cylinder block.
4. Install or connect the following:

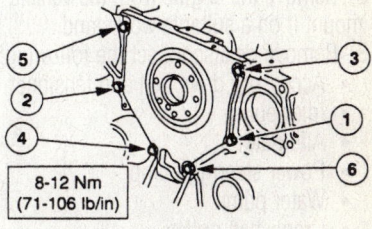

8-12 Nm
(71-106 lb/in)

7922LG12

Oil seal retainer torque sequence

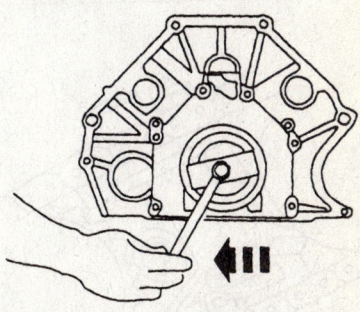

7922LG13

Use Seal Installer T82L-6701-A and adapter T91P-6701-A to press the seal into the retainer

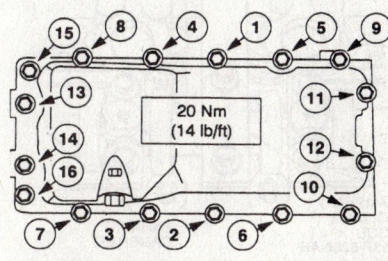

20 Nm
(14 lb/ft)

7922LG10

Oil pan bolt torque sequence

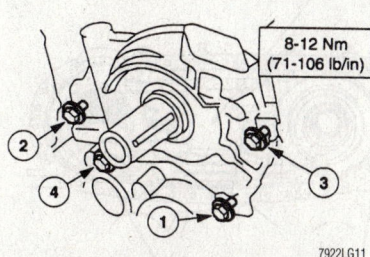

8-12 Nm
(71-106 lb/in)

7922LG11

Oil pump mounting bolt sequence

- Oil seal retainer. Tighten the bolts in sequence to 71–106 inch lbs. (8–12 Nm).
- Oil seal. Use special tool Seal Installer T82L-6701-A and adapter T91P-6701-A to press the seal into place.
- Flywheel. Tighten the bolts to 54–64 ft. lbs. (73–87 Nm).
- Transaxle

5. Check and adjust all fluid levels as necessary.

6. Start the engine and check for leaks.

Timing Chain, Sprockets, Front Cover and Seal

REMOVAL & INSTALLATION

✻✻ WARNING

This is an interference engine. When the timing chains are removed and the cylinder heads are installed, the crankshaft and/or camshafts must not be rotated unless as directed in this procedure. Failure to follow these instructions will result in valve and/or piston damage.

1. Before servicing the vehicle, refer to the precautions in the beginning of this section.

2. Remove the engine from the vehicle and mount it on a suitable workstand.

3. Remove or disconnect the following:
- Accessory drive belt and tensioner
- Idler pulley
- Alternator
- Power steering pump
- Water pump
- Crankshaft pulley
- Front crankshaft seal
- Crankshaft Position (CKP) sensor
- Camshaft Position (CMP) sensor

- Engine control sensor wiring harness
- Spark plug wires and coil packs (1997 engine)
- Ignition coils (1998–01 engines)
- Valve covers

➡️If the rocker arms are to be reused, label them as they are removed so they can be reinstalled in their original locations.

- Rocker arms
- Front cover

4. Rotate the crankshaft to place the piston for No. 1 cylinder at Top Dead Center (TDC) on its compression stroke.

5. Remove or disconnect the following:
- Right primary timing chain tensioner
- Right primary timing chain tensioner arm and chain guide
- Right primary timing chain and sprockets
- Left primary timing chain tensioner
- Left primary timing chain tensioner arm and chain guide
- Left primary timing chain and sprockets

6. Compress the secondary chain tensioners and install locking pins.

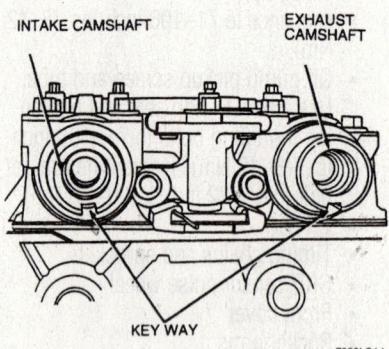

Position the camshafts for timing chain installation

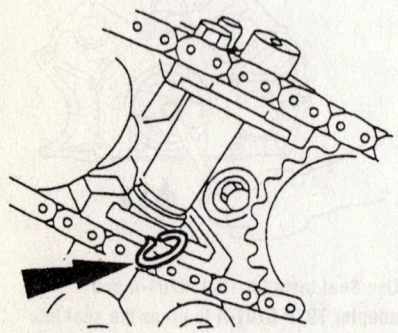

Secondary timing chain tensioner and locking pin

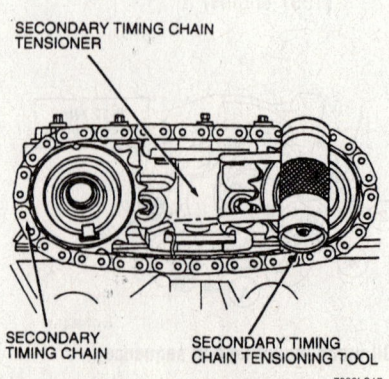

Secondary timing chain tensioning tool

7. Remove or disconnect the following:
- Left and right secondary timing chains and sprockets
- Camshaft Holding and Camshaft Positioning tools

To install:

8. Position the camshafts as shown for timing chain installation.

9. Install the secondary timing chains and sprockets. Do not tighten the sprocket bolts at this time.

10. Tension the secondary timing chains with the special tool Secondary Timing Chain Tensioning Tool T93P-6256-BH.

11. Install Camshaft Positioning tool T93P-6256-A in the rear D-slots of the camshaft.

12. Install Camshaft Holding tool T93P-6256-AH onto the camshafts to keep the camshafts from rotating and to prevent damaging the camshaft positioning tool.

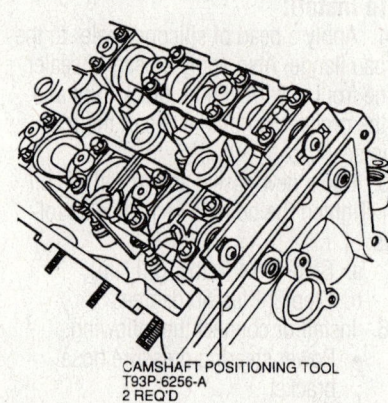

Install the Camshaft Positioning tool

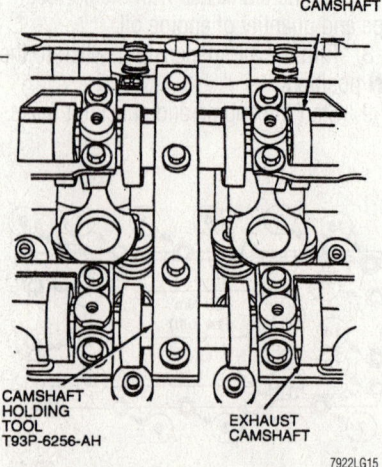

Install the Camshaft Holding tool to secure the camshafts and prevent damage to the Camshaft Positioning Tool

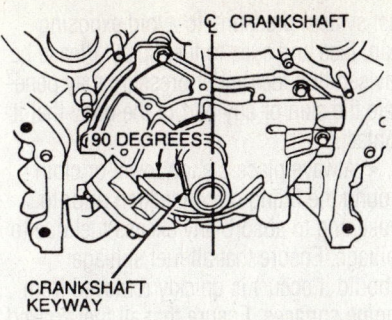

Turn the crankshaft to the 9 o'clock position for timing chain installation

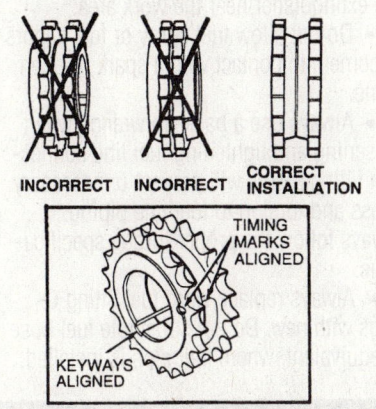

Crankshaft timing sprocket installation

13. Tighten the secondary timing chain sprocket bolts to 81–95 ft. lbs. (110–130 Nm).

14. Remove the secondary timing chain tensioner locking pins and remove the tensioner tool.

15. Position the crankshaft so that the keyway is at 9 o'clock as shown.

16. Compress the primary timing chain tensioners and install locking pins.

17. Install the crankshaft timing sprockets arranged as shown.

18. Align the copper colored primary timing chain links with the sprocket timing marks as shown.

19. Install or connect the following:
- Left primary timing chain and sprockets
- Left primary timing chain tensioner arm and chain guide
- Left primary timing chain tensioner
- Right primary timing chain and sprockets
- Right primary timing chain tensioner arm and chain guide
- Right primary timing chain tensioner

20. Tighten the camshaft sprocket bolts to 81–95 ft. lbs. (110–130 Nm).

21. Remove the primary timing chain tensioner locking pins.

22. Remove the Camshaft Holding and Camshaft Positioning tools.

23. Install or connect the following:
- Front cover. Tighten the bolts in sequence to 15–22 ft. lbs. (20–30 Nm).
- Rocker arms in their original positions
- Valve covers
- Spark plug wires and coil packs (1997 engine)
- Ignition coils (1998–01 engines)
- CMP sensor
- CKP sensor
- Engine control sensor wiring harness
- Front crankshaft seal

24. Install the crankshaft pulley and tighten the bolt as follows:
   a. Step 1: 89 ft. lbs. (120 Nm)
   b. Step 2: Loosen the bolt
   c. Step 3: 39 ft. lbs. (53 Nm)
   d. Step 4: Plus 90 degrees

25. Install or connect the following:
- Water pump
- Power steering pump
- Alternator

Sealer Location

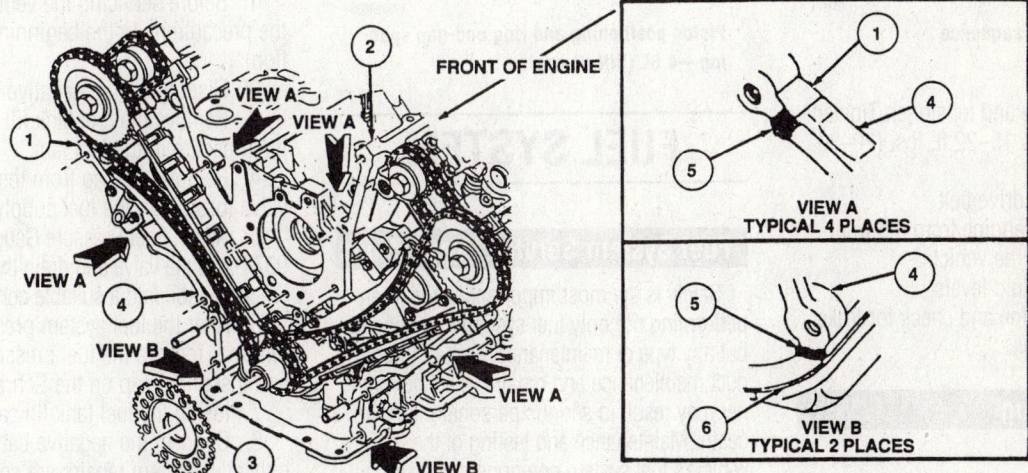

Item	Part Number	Description
1	6049	RH Cylinder Head
2	6049	LH Cylinder Head
3	12A227	Ignition Pulse Crankshaft Sensor Ring
4	6010	Cylinder Block
5	WSE-M4G320-A2	Sealer
6	6710	Oil Pan Gasket

Apply sealer to these locations

Refer to Section 1 for engine rebuilding specifications

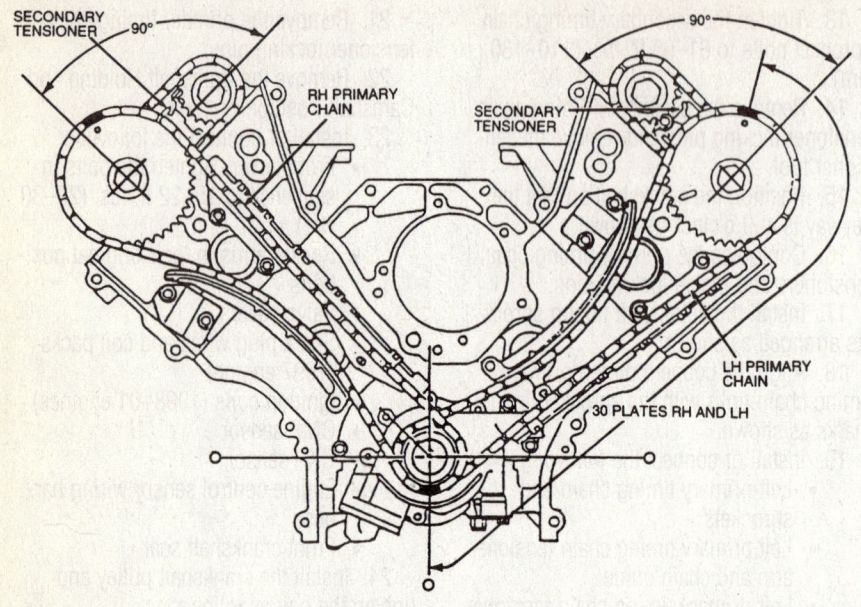

Correct alignment of the primary timing chains and sprockets

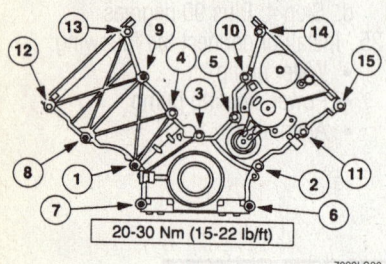

Front cover torque sequence

20-30 Nm (15-22 lb/ft)

- Idler pulley and tensioner. Tighten the bolts to 15–22 ft. lbs. (20–30 Nm).
- Accessory drive belt

26. Remove the engine from the workstand and install in the vehicle.
27. Restore all fluid levels.
28. Run the engine and check for leaks and proper operation.

Piston and Ring

POSITIONING

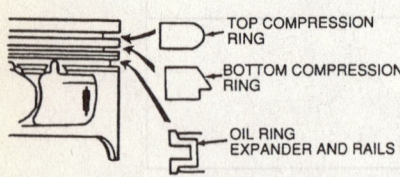

Piston ring positioning—4.6L (VIN V) engine

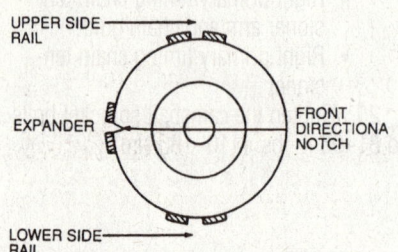

Piston positioning and ring end-gap spacing—4.6L (VIN V) engine

FUEL SYSTEM

Fuel System Service Precautions

Safety is the most important factor when performing not only fuel system maintenance but any type of maintenance. Failure to conduct maintenance and repairs in a safe manner may result in serious personal injury or death. Maintenance and testing of the vehicle's fuel system components can be accomplished safely and effectively by adhering to the following rules and guidelines.

- To avoid the possibility of fire and personal injury, always disconnect the negative battery cable unless the repair or test procedure requires that battery voltage be applied.
- Always relieve the fuel system pressure prior to disconnecting any fuel system component (injector, fuel rail, pressure regulator, etc.), fitting or fuel line connection. Exercise extreme caution whenever relieving fuel system pressure, to avoid exposing skin, face and eyes to fuel spray. Please be advised that fuel under pressure may penetrate the skin or any part of the body that it contacts.

- Always place a shop towel or cloth around the fitting or connection prior to loosening to absorb any excess fuel due to spillage. Ensure that all fuel spillage (should it occur) is quickly removed from engine surfaces. Ensure that all fuel soaked cloths or towels are deposited into a suitable waste container.
- Always keep a dry chemical (Class B) fire extinguisher near the work area.
- Do not allow fuel spray or fuel vapors to come into contact with a spark or open flame.
- Always use a back-up wrench when loosening and tightening fuel line connection fittings. This will prevent unnecessary stress and torsion to fuel line piping. Always follow the proper torque specifications.
- Always replace worn fuel fitting O-rings with new. Do not substitute fuel hose or equivalent, where fuel pipe is installed.

Fuel System Pressure

RELIEVING

1. Before servicing the vehicle, refer to the precautions in the beginning of this section.
2. Disconnect the negative battery cable.
3. Remove the fuel tank fill cap to relieve the pressure in the fuel tank.
4. Remove the cap from the Schrader valve located on the fuel supply manifold.
5. Attach Fuel Pressure Gauge T80L-9974-A to the valve and drain the fuel through the drain tube into a suitable container.
6. After the fuel system pressure is relieved, remove the fuel pressure gauge and install the cap on the Schrader valve.
7. Install the fuel tank fill cap.
8. Connect the negative battery cable only after system repairs are completed.

Fuel Filter

REMOVAL & INSTALLATION

1. Before servicing the vehicle, refer to the precautions in the beginning of this section.
2. Turn the air suspension service switch **OFF**.
3. Disconnect the negative battery cable.
4. Relieve the fuel system pressure.

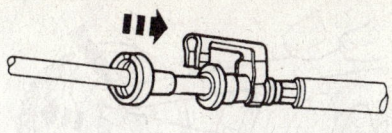

Slide the special tool into the fitting to disengage it

5. Disconnect the fuel lines.

6. Loosen the filter retaining clamp and remove the fuel filter.

To install:

7. Install the fuel filter with the flow arrow facing the proper direction and tighten the filter retaining clamp.

8. Push the fuel lines on to the filter fittings until an audible click is heard.

9. Connect the negative battery cable.

10. Start the engine and check for fuel leaks and proper operation.

11. Turn the air suspension switch to the **ON** position.

Fuel Pump

REMOVAL & INSTALLATION

➡**Disable the air suspension before raising the vehicle. The switch is located in the left-hand side of the luggage compartment on 1997 models or on the right side kick panel for 1998–01 models.**

1. Before servicing the vehicle, refer to the precautions in the beginning of this section.

2. Turn the air suspension switch to the **OFF** position.

3. Relieve the fuel system pressure.

4. Drain the fuel tank.

5. Remove or disconnect the following:
- Fuel fill and vent hoses
- Fuel supply line
- Fuel pump module wiring connector

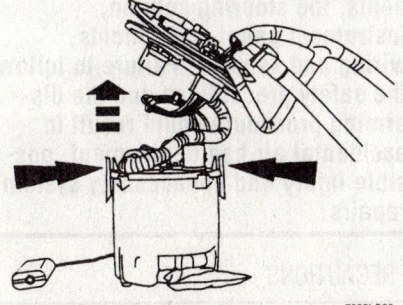

To remove the fuel pump, reach into the tank and press the locking tabs inward

- Fuel tank
- Fuel pump module locking ring

6. Pull the fuel pump module up and out of the fuel tank until the locking tabs for the fuel pump module are accessible. Squeeze both locking tabs together and remove the fuel pump module from the fuel tank.

To install:

7. Install or connect the following:
- Fuel pump module. Use a new O-ring seal and push the module into the tank so that the locking tabs engage.
- Fuel pump module lock ring
- Fuel tank. Tighten the tank strap bolts to 22–30 ft. lbs. (30–40 Nm).
- Fuel pump module wiring connector
- Fuel supply line
- Fuel fill and vent hoses

8. Add 10 gallons of clean fuel to the tank.

9. Turn the air suspension switch to the **ON** position.

10. Start the engine and check for leaks.

Fuel Injector

REMOVAL AND INSTALLATION

1. Before servicing the vehicle, refer to the precautions in the beginning of this section.

2. Relieve the fuel system pressure.

3. Remove or disconnect the following:
- Negative battery cable
- Fuel pressure regulator vacuum line (1997 vehicles)
- Fuel pressure sensor vacuum line and wiring connector (1998–01 vehicles)
- Fuel injector wiring connectors
- Fuel supply line
- Fuel return line (1997 vehicles)
- Fuel supply manifold with injectors attached

4. Remove the clips and the injectors from the fuel supply manifold.

To install:

5. Install the injectors with new O-ring seals.

6. Install the fuel supply manifold and tighten the bolts as follows:
   a. Step 1: 15 ft. lbs. (20 Nm)
   b. Step 2: Plus 85–95 degrees

7. Install or connect the following:
- Fuel supply line

- Fuel return line (1997 vehicles)
- Fuel injector wiring connectors
- Fuel pressure regulator vacuum line (1997 vehicles)
- Fuel pressure sensor vacuum line and wiring connector (1998–01 vehicles)
- Negative battery cable

8. Start the engine and check for leaks.

DRIVE TRAIN

Transaxle Assembly

REMOVAL & INSTALLATION

➡**Disable the air suspension before raising the vehicle. The switch is located in the left-hand side of the luggage compartment on 1997 models or on the right side kick panel for 1998–01 models.**

1. Before servicing the vehicle, refer to the precautions in the beginning of this section.

2. Turn the air suspension switch to the **OFF** position.

3. Attach a powertrain support fixture to the engine lifting eyes.

4. Drain the transaxle fluid.

5. Remove or disconnect the following:
- Battery and battery tray
- Intake Air Temperature (IAT) sensor connector
- Mass Air Flow (MAF) sensor connector
- Air cleaner assembly
- Transaxle control harness connector
- Transaxle range sensor
- Turbine shaft speed sensor connector
- Shift cable
- Transaxle oil cooler lines
- Front wheels
- Suspension height sensors
- Wheel speed sensors
- Outer tie rod ends
- Lower ball joints
- Stabilizer bar links
- Halfshafts
- Heated Oxygen (HO$_2$S) sensor connectors
- Dual converter Y-pipe
- Starter

- Left, right and rear engine support insulators
- Subframe
- Transaxle housing cover
- Torque converter
- Transaxle flange bolts

6. Separate the transaxle from the engine and lower it from the vehicle.

To install:

➡**When installing suspension components and halfshafts, use new nuts, bolts, circlips and split pins.**

7. Install or connect the following:
- Transaxle. Tighten the flange bolts to 25–34 ft. lbs. (34–46 Nm).
- Torque converter. Tighten the nuts to 20–34 ft. lbs. (27–46 Nm).
- Transaxle housing cover

8. Install the subframe. Use 2 pieces of ¾ inch outside diameter pipe in the alignment holes behind the front subframe mounts to align the subframe to the body. Tighten the subframe mounting bolts to 57–76 ft. lbs. (77–103 Nm).

9. Install or connect the following:
- Left, right and rear engine support insulators. Tighten the through-bolts to 64–88 ft. lbs. (87–119 Nm).
- Starter. Tighten the bolt and stud to 15–21 ft. lbs. (21–29 Nm).
- Dual converter Y-pipe
- HO2S sensor connectors
- Halfshafts
- Stabilizer bar links. Tighten the nuts to 30–40 ft. lbs. (40–55 Nm).
- Lower ball joints. Tighten the pinch bolts to 50–68 ft. lbs. (68–92 Nm).
- Outer tie rod ends. Tighten the nuts to 35–46 ft. lbs. (47–63 Nm).
- Wheel speed sensors
- Suspension height sensors
- Front wheels
- Transaxle oil cooler lines
- Shift cable
- Turbine shaft speed sensor connector
- Transaxle range sensor
- Transaxle control harness connector
- Air cleaner assembly
- MAF sensor connector
- IAT sensor connector
- Battery and battery tray

10. Fill the transaxle.
11. Check for leaks and proper operation.

➡**Whenever the subframe is removed or lowered, the wheel alignment should be checked.**

Halfshaft

REMOVAL & INSTALLATION

➡**Disable the air suspension before raising the vehicle. The switch is located in the left-hand side of the luggage compartment on 1997 models or on the right side kick panel for 1998–01 models.**

1. Before servicing the vehicle, refer to the precautions in the beginning of this section.
2. Turn the air suspension switch to the **OFF** position.
3. Remove or disconnect the following:
- Negative battery cable
- Front wheels
- Suspension height sensors
- Wheel speed sensors
- Outer tie rod ends
- Lower ball joints
- Stabilizer bar links

4. Separate the halfshaft from the wheel hubs and the transaxle and remove the halfshafts.

To install:

➡**When installing suspension components and halfshafts, use new nuts, bolts, circlips and split pins.**

5. Install or connect the following:
- Halfshafts. Tighten the hub retainer nuts to 180–200 ft. lbs. (245–270 Nm).
- Stabilizer bar links. Tighten the nuts to 30–40 ft. lbs. (40–55 Nm).
- Lower ball joints. Tighten the pinch bolts to 50–68 ft. lbs. (68–92 Nm).
- Outer tie rod ends. Tighten the nuts to 35–46 ft. lbs. (47–63 Nm).
- Wheel speed sensors
- Suspension height sensors
- Front wheels

6. Turn the air suspension switch to the **ON** position.
7. Road test the vehicle and check for proper operation.

CV-Joint

REMOVAL AND REPLACEMENT

Inner Tripod Joint

The inner CV-joint is serviced with the halfshaft as an assembly. The inner CV-joint boot can be serviced by removing the outer CV-joint.

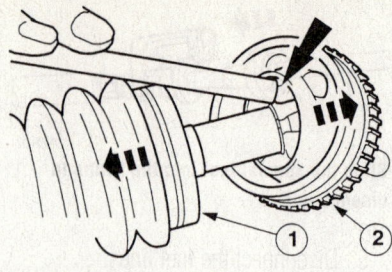

1. CV-Joint boot
2. CV-Joint

9306HG07

Removing the outer CV-joint

Outer CV-Joint

1. Before servicing the vehicle, refer to the precautions in the beginning of this section.
2. Place the halfshaft in a vise.
3. Remove the CV-joint boot clamps and slide the boot away from the joint.
4. Drive the CV-joint off the halfshaft with a brass drift and a hammer.

To install:

5. Replace the snapring.
6. Fill the CV-joint with fresh grease and slide the joint onto the halfshaft.
7. Use new clamps and install the CV-joint boot.

STEERING AND SUSPENSION

Air Bag

✳✳ CAUTION

Some vehicles are equipped with an air bag system. The system must be disarmed before performing service on, or around, system components, the steering column, instrument panel components, wiring and sensors. Failure to follow the safety precautions and the disarming procedure could result in accidental air bag deployment, possible injury and unnecessary system repairs.

PRECAUTIONS

Several precautions must be observed when handling the inflator module to avoid accidental deployment and possible personal injury.

• Never carry the inflator module by the wires or connector on the underside of the module.

• When carrying a live inflator module, hold securely with both hands, and ensure that the bag and trim cover are pointed away.

• Place the inflator module on a bench or other surface with the bag and trim cover facing up.

• With the inflator module on the bench, never place anything on or close to the module that may be thrown in the event of an accidental deployment.

DISARMING

1. Before servicing the vehicle, refer to the precautions in the beginning of this section.

2. Disconnect both battery cables from the battery, negative cable first.

3. Wait 1 minute before proceeding with the service procedure. This is the time required for the back-up power supply in the air bag diagnostic monitor to deplete its stored energy.

4. After service is completed, reconnect the battery cables, negative cable last.

5. Turn the ignition switch to the **RUN** position. The air bag indicator should light continuously for approximately 6 seconds, then turn **OFF**. If the indicator fails to light, flashes or remains lit continuously, there is a fault in the air bag system.

Power Rack and Pinion Steering Gear

REMOVAL & INSTALLATION

✳✳ CAUTION

Do not rotate the steering wheel when the intermediate shaft is disconnected. Damage to the air bag sliding contact will result.

➡**Disable the air suspension before raising the vehicle. The switch is located in the left-hand side of the luggage compartment on 1997 models or on the right side kick panel for 1998–01 models.**

1. Before servicing the vehicle, refer to the precautions in the beginning of this section.

2. Turn the air suspension switch to the **OFF** position.

3. Remove or disconnect the following:
   • Negative battery cable
   • Steering column intermediate shaft
   • Powertrain Control Module (PCM) harness connector and ground straps
   • Upper motor mount
   • Front wheels
   • Outer tie rod ends
   • Suspension height sensor
   • Heated Oxygen (HO2S) sensor connectors
   • Dual converter Y-pipe
   • Subframe brackets
   • Steering gear attachment nuts
   • Rear subframe bolts. Lower the rear of the subframe about 4 inches for access.
   • Steering gear heat shield and bracket
   • Steering gear harness connectors

4. Rotate the steering gear to clear the mounting bolts from the subframe, and pull the gear to the left to access the fluid lines.

5. Remove or disconnect the following:
   • Power steering pressure and return lines
   • Steering gear through the left fender opening

To install:

6. Install or connect the following:
   • Steering gear
   • Power steering pressure and return lines. Use new O-ring seals and tighten the fittings to 25–30 ft. lbs. (33–41 Nm).
   • Steering gear harness connectors
   • Steering gear heat shield and bracket
   • Rear subframe bolts. Tighten the bolts to 57–76 ft. lbs. (77–103 Nm).
   • Steering gear attachment nuts. Tighten the nuts to 84–112 ft. lbs. (113–153 Nm).
   • Subframe brackets
   • Dual converter Y-pipe
   • HO2S sensor connectors
   • Suspension height sensor
   • Outer tie rod ends. Use new nuts and tighten to 35–46 ft. lbs. (47–63 Nm).

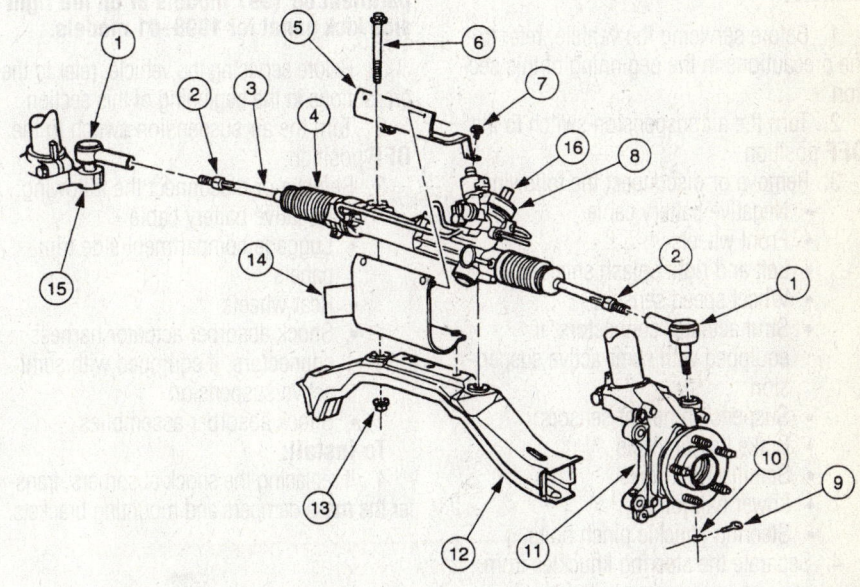

1 Tie Rod End	9 Screw (2 Req'd)
2 Nut	10 Nut (2 Req'd)
3 Front Wheel Spindle Tie Rod (2 Req'd)	11 Front Wheel Knuckle (LH)
4 Front Suspension Steering Ball Stud Dust Seal	12 Crossmember
5 Power Steering Hose Bracket	13 Nut (2 Req'd)
6 Bolt (2 Req'd)	14 Steering Shaft U-Joint Shield
7 Screw (2 Req'd)	15 Front Wheel Knuckle (RH)
8 Steering Gear	16 Power Steering Gear Input Shaft and Control

7922LG26

Exploded view of the power rack and pinion steering gear mounting

- Front wheels
- Upper motor mount
- PCM harness connector and ground straps
- Steering column intermediate shaft. Tighten the lower bolt to 30–38 ft. lbs. (41–51 Nm), and the upper bolt to 24–30 ft. lbs. (33–41 Nm).
- Negative battery cable

7. Fill the power steering system.

8. Turn the air suspension switch to the **ON** position.

9. Check the system for leaks and proper operation. Adjust the toe setting as necessary.

Strut

REMOVAL & INSTALLATION

Front

➡ **Disable the air suspension before raising the vehicle. The switch is located in the left-hand side of the luggage compartment on 1997 models or on the right side kick panel for 1998–01 models.**

1. Before servicing the vehicle, refer to the precautions in the beginning of this section.

2. Turn the air suspension switch to the **OFF** position.

3. Remove or disconnect the following:
- Negative battery cable
- Front wheels
- Left and right splash shields
- Wheel speed sensors
- Strut actuator connectors, if equipped with semi-active suspension
- Suspension height sensors
- Brake line brackets
- Stabilizer bar links
- Lower ball joints
- Steering knuckle pinch bolts

4. Separate the steering knuckles from the struts and remove the struts from the vehicle.

To install:

➡ **When installing suspension components, use new nuts, bolts, circlips and split pins.**

5. Install or connect the following:
- Struts. Tighten the shock tower nuts to 23–29 ft. lbs. (30–40 Nm), and the steering knuckle pinch bolts to 73–97 ft. lbs. (98–132 Nm).
- Stabilizer bar links. Tighten the nuts to 30–40 ft. lbs. (40–55 Nm).

- Lower ball joints. Tighten the pinch bolts to 50–68 ft. lbs. (68–92 Nm).
- Brake line brackets. Tighten the screws to 11 ft. lbs. (15 Nm).
- Suspension height sensors
- Strut actuator connectors, if equipped with semi-active suspension
- Wheel speed sensors
- Left and right splash shields
- Front wheels
- Negative battery cable

6. Turn the air suspension switch to the **ON** position.

7. Road test the vehicle and check for proper operation.

Shock Absorber

REMOVAL & INSTALLATION

Rear

➡ **Disable the air suspension before raising the vehicle. The switch is located in the left-hand side of the luggage compartment on 1997 models or on the right side kick panel for 1998–01 models.**

1. Before servicing the vehicle, refer to the precautions in the beginning of this section.

2. Turn the air suspension switch to the **OFF** position.

3. Remove or disconnect the following:
- Negative battery cable
- Luggage compartment side trim panels
- Rear wheels
- Shock absorber actuator harness connectors, if equipped with semi-active suspension
- Shock absorber assemblies

To install:

4. If replacing the shock absorbers, transfer the mass dampers and mounting brackets.

7922LG28

To bleed the air from the shock, turn it upside down, then compress and expand it several times

5. Turn the shock absorber upside down. Compress and expand the piston several times to remove the air from the working cylinder.

6. Install or connect the following:
- Shock absorber assemblies. Tighten the upper bolts to 25–34 ft. lbs. (34–46 Nm), and the lower bolts to 58–68 ft. lbs. (68–92 Nm).
- Shock absorber actuator harness connectors, if equipped with semi-active suspension
- Rear wheels
- Luggage compartment side trim panels
- Negative battery cable

7. Turn the air suspension system **ON**.

Coil Spring

REMOVAL & INSTALLATION

Front

1. Before servicing the vehicle, refer to the precautions in the beginning of this section.

2. Remove the strut assembly from the vehicle.

3. Install a spring compressor and

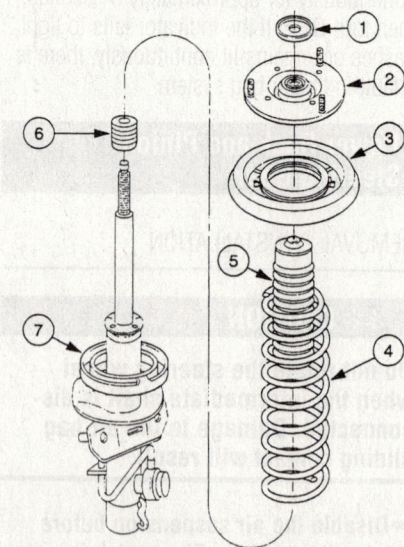

1. Washer
2. Strut mounting bracket
3. Bearing plate
4. Coil spring
5. Dust boot
6. Jounce bumper
7. Spring insulator

9306LG07

Exploded view of the front strut and coil spring assembly

retract the spring until the upper mount rotates freely.

4. Remove or disconnect the following:
- Flange nut
- Strut mounting bracket
- Strut bearing plate
- Coil spring

To install:

5. Install or connect the following:
- Coil spring
- Strut bearing plate
- Strut mounting bracket
- Flange nut. Tighten the nut to 63–70 ft. lbs. (85–95 Nm).

6. Remove the spring compressor and ensure that the spring seats correctly in the insulators.

7. Install the strut assembly to the vehicle.

Air Spring

REMOVAL & INSTALLATION

Rear

⁂ **CAUTION**

Do not attempt to service the rear suspension without first deflating the air springs.

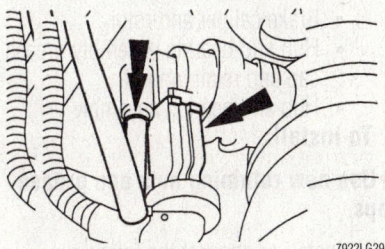

7922LG29

Air spring solenoid connectors

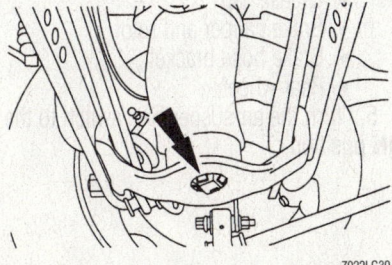

7922LG30

On 1998–01 models, depress the plastic locking tabs to disengage the air spring from the suspension

➡**Servicing the air suspension requires a scan tool with bi-directional capabilities to deflate the air springs.**

1. Properly deflate the air springs.
2. Turn the air suspension switch to the **OFF** position. The switch located in the luggage compartment on 1997 models or on the right kick panel for 1998–01 models.
3. Remove the rear wheels.
4. Disconnect the air spring solenoid wiring connector and air line.
5. For 1997 vehicles, unbolt the air spring from the lower control arm and remove the spring.
6. For 1998–01 vehicles, depress the locking tabs and remove the air spring from the vehicle.

To install:

7. Install or connect the following:
- Air spring. For 1997 vehicles, tighten the mounting bolts to 50–59 ft. lbs. (68–82 Nm). On 1998–00 models, press the plastic tab through the suspension until it clicks into place.
- Solenoid air line and electrical connectors
- Rear wheels
8. Turn the air suspension switch to the **ON** position and check for proper operation.

Lower Ball Joints

REMOVAL & INSTALLATION

The lower ball joint is an integral part of the steering knuckle. If the lower ball joint is found to be defective, the entire steering knuckle must be replaced.

Upper Control Arm

REMOVAL & INSTALLATION

Rear

⁂ **CAUTION**

Do not attempt to service the rear suspension without first deflating the air springs.

➡**Servicing the air suspension requires a scan tool with bi-directional capabilities to deflate the air springs.**

1. Properly deflate the air springs.
2. Turn the air suspension switch to the

OFF position. The switch located in the luggage compartment on 1997 models or on the right kick panel for 1998–01 models.

3. Support the lower control arm on a jackstand.
4. Remove or disconnect the following:
- Rear wheel
- Brake hose bracket
- Upper ball joint
- Upper control arm

To install:

➡**Use new mounting nuts and bolts.**

5. Install the upper control arm. Tighten the ball joint nut to 50–67 ft. lbs. (68–92 Nm), then tighten the control arm mounting bolts to 73–97 ft. lbs. (98–132 Nm).
6. Install or connect the following:
- Brake hose bracket
- Rear wheel
7. Turn the air suspension switch to the **ON** position and check for proper operation.
8. Check the wheel alignment and adjust as necessary.

CONTROL ARM BUSHING REPLACEMENT

The control arm bushings are serviced with the control arm as an assembly.

Lower Control Arm

REMOVAL & INSTALLATION

Front

➡**Disable the air suspension before raising the vehicle. The switch is located in the left-hand side of the luggage compartment on 1997 models or on the right side kick panel for 1998–01 models.**

1. Before servicing the vehicle, refer to the precautions in the beginning of this section.
2. Turn the air suspension switch to the **OFF** position.
3. Remove or disconnect the following:
- Front wheel
- Wheel speed sensor wiring harness
- Height sensor
- Lower ball joint
- Lower control arm strut
- Lower control arm

To install:

4. Install or connect the following:
- Lower control arm. Tighten the pivot bolt to 73–98 ft. lbs. (98–132 Nm).

- Lower control arm strut. Tighten the nut to 73–98 ft. lbs. (98–132 Nm).
- Lower ball joint. Use a new nut and tighten to 50–67 ft. lbs. (68–92 Nm).
- Wheel speed sensor wiring harness
- Height sensor
- Front wheel

5. Turn the air suspension switch to the **ON** position.

6. Check the wheel alignment and adjust as necessary.

Rear

✳ CAUTION

Do not attempt to service the rear suspension without first deflating the air springs.

➡ Disable the air suspension before raising the vehicle. The switch is located in the left-hand side of the luggage compartment on 1997 models or on the right side kick panel for 1998–01 models.

1. Before servicing the vehicle, refer to the precautions in the beginning of this section.

2. Turn the air suspension switch to the **OFF** position.

3. Remove or disconnect the following:
- Rear wheel
- Shock absorber actuator wiring, if equipped with semi-active suspension
- Air spring
- Stabilizer bar link
- Lower control arm

To install:

4. Install or connect the following:
- Lower control arm. Tighten the bolts to 50–68 ft. lbs. (68–92 Nm).
- Stabilizer bar link. Tighten the nut to 25–34 ft. lbs. (34–46 Nm).
- Air spring
- Shock absorber actuator wiring, if equipped with semi-active suspension
- Rear wheel

5. Turn the air suspension switch to the **ON** position.

CONTROL ARM BUSHING REPLACEMENT

The control arm bushings are serviced with the control arm as an assembly.

Wheel Bearings

ADJUSTMENT

There is no adjustment for the front or rear wheel bearings due to the nature of their design. These bearings are permanently lubricated and require no periodic maintenance.

REMOVAL & INSTALLATION

Front

➡ Disable the air suspension before raising the vehicle. The switch is located in the left-hand side of the luggage compartment on 1997 models or on the right side kick panel for 1998–01 models.

1. Before servicing the vehicle, refer to the precautions in the beginning of this section.

2. Turn the air suspension switch to the **OFF** position.

3. Remove or disconnect the following:

- Front wheel
- Hub retainer nut
- Brake caliper and rotor
- Outer tie rod end
- Stabilizer bar link
- Wheel speed sensor
- Lower ball joint
- Steering knuckle

4. Unbolt and remove the hub and bearing assembly.

To install:

➡ Use new nuts, bolts and split pins.

➡ The knuckle must be clean enough to allow the wheel hub to be completely seated by hand. Do not press or draw the wheel hub into place.

5. Install or connect the following:
- Hub and bearing assembly. Tighten the bolts to 61–78 ft. lbs. (83–107 Nm).
- Steering knuckle. Tighten the pinch bolt to 72–97 ft. lbs. (98–132 Nm).
- Lower ball joint. Tighten the nut to 50–67 ft. lbs. (68–92 Nm).
- Wheel speed sensor
- Stabilizer bar link. Tighten the nut to 57–75 ft. lbs. (77–103 Nm).
- Outer tie rod end. Tighten the nut to 35–46 ft. lbs. (47–63 Nm).
- Brake caliper and rotor. Tighten the caliper anchor bracket bolts to 65–87 ft. lbs. (88–118 Nm).
- Hub retainer nut. Tighten the nut to 170–202 ft. lbs. (230–275 Nm).
- Front wheel

6. Turn the air suspension switch to the **ON** position.

Rear

➡ Disable the air suspension before raising the vehicle. The switch is located in the left-hand side of the luggage compartment on 1997 models or on the right side kick panel for 1998–01 models.

1. Before servicing the vehicle, refer to the precautions in the beginning of this section.

2. Turn the air suspension switch to the **OFF** position.

3. Remove or disconnect the following:
- Rear wheel
- Brake hose bracket
- Brake caliper and rotor
- Hub and bearing assembly grease cap and retaining nut
- Hub and bearing assembly

To install:

➡ Use new retaining nuts and grease caps

4. Install or connect the following:
- Hub and bearing assembly. Tighten the retaining nut to 188–254 ft. lbs. (255–345 Nm).
- Grease cap
- Brake caliper and rotor
- Brake hose bracket
- Rear wheel

5. Turn the air suspension switch to the **ON** position.

FORD MOTOR CO.

Ford-Escort • Escort ZX2 • **Mercury**-Tracer

PRECAUTIONS

Before servicing any vehicle, please be sure to read all of the following precautions, which deal with personal safety, prevention of component damage, and important points to take into consideration when servicing a motor vehicle:

• Never open, service or drain the radiator or cooling system when the engine is hot; serious burns can occur from the steam and hot coolant.

• Observe all applicable safety precautions when working around fuel. Whenever servicing the fuel system, always work in a well-ventilated area. Do not allow fuel spray or vapors to come in contact with a spark, open flame, or excessive heat (a hot drop light, for example). Keep a dry chemical fire extinguisher near the work area. Always keep fuel in a container specifically designed for fuel storage; also, always properly seal fuel containers to avoid the possibility of fire or explosion. Refer to the additional fuel system precautions later in this section.

• Fuel injection systems often remain pressurized, even after the engine has been turned **OFF**. The fuel system pressure must be relieved before disconnecting any fuel lines. Failure to do so may result in fire and/or personal injury.

• Brake fluid often contains polyglycol ethers and polyglycols. Avoid contact with the eyes and wash your hands thoroughly after handling brake fluid. If you do get brake fluid in your eyes, flush your eyes with clean, running water for 15 minutes. If eye irritation persists, or if you have taken brake fluid internally, IMMEDIATELY seek medical assistance.

• The EPA warns that prolonged contact with used engine oil may cause a number of skin disorders, including cancer! You should make every effort to minimize your exposure to used engine oil. Protective gloves should be worn when changing oil. Wash your hands and any other exposed skin areas as soon as possible after exposure to used engine oil. Soap and water, or waterless hand cleaner should be used.

• All new vehicles are now equipped with an air bag system, often referred to as a Supplemental Restraint System (SRS) or Supplemental Inflatable Restraint (SIR) system. The system must be disabled before performing service on or around system components, steering column, instrument panel components, wiring and sensors. Failure to follow safety and disabling procedures could result in accidental air bag deployment, possible personal injury and unnecessary system repairs.

• Always wear safety goggles when working with, or around, the air bag system. When carrying a non-deployed air bag, be sure the bag and trim cover are pointed away from your body. When placing a non-deployed air bag on a work surface, always face the bag and trim cover upward, away from the surface. This will reduce the motion of the module if it is accidentally deployed. Refer to the additional air bag system precautions later in this section.

• Clean, high quality brake fluid from a sealed container is essential to the safe and proper operation of the brake system. You should always buy the correct type of brake fluid for your vehicle. If the brake fluid becomes contaminated, completely flush the system with new fluid. Never reuse any brake fluid. Any brake fluid that is removed from the system should be discarded. Also, do not allow any brake fluid to come in contact with a painted surface; it will damage the paint.

• Never operate the engine without the proper amount and type of engine oil; doing so WILL result in severe engine damage.

• Timing belt maintenance is extremely important! Many models utilize an interference-type, non-freewheeling engine. If the timing belt breaks, the valves in the cylinder head may strike the pistons, causing potentially serious (also time-consuming and expensive) engine damage. Refer to the maintenance interval charts in the front of this manual for the recommended replacement interval for the timing belt, and to the timing belt section for belt replacement and inspection.

• Disconnecting the negative battery cable on some vehicles may interfere with the functions of the on-board computer system(s) and may require the computer to undergo a relearning process once the negative battery cable is reconnected.

• When servicing drum brakes, only disassemble and assemble one side at a time, leaving the remaining side intact for reference.

• Only an MVAC-trained, EPA-certified automotive technician should service the air conditioning system or its components.

ENGINE REPAIR

Alternator

REMOVAL

Sedan and Wagon

➡ When the battery is disconnected it may cause some abnormal drive symptoms until the Powertrain Control Module (PCM) relearns its adaptive strategy. The vehicle may need to be driven 10 miles (16 km) or more for the PCM to relearn its strategy.

1. Before servicing the vehicle, refer to the precautions in the beginning of this section.
2. Remove or disconnect the following:

• Negative battery cable
• Drive belt
• Power steering hose bracket from the alternator bracket
• Alternator mounting bolts and position the assembly so that you can access the electrical connections
• Alternator electrical connectors
• Battery positive cable retaining nut, then the washer and cable
• Alternator from the vehicle

INSTALLATION

Sedan and Wagon

1. Before servicing the vehicle, refer to the precautions in the beginning of this section.
2. Install or connect the following:

• Battery positive cable, the nut and the washer. Tighten the nut to 7–9 ft. lbs. (9–12 Nm).
• Alternator electrical connections
• Alternator in position
• Alternator mounting bolts. Tighten the upper mounting bolt to 29–40 ft. lbs. (40–55 Nm) and the lower mounting bolt to 15–22 ft. lbs. (20–30 Nm).
• Power steering hose bracket to the alternator bracket
• Drive belt
• Negative battery cable

Location of the alternator upper and lower mounting bolts—sedan and wagon models

90982G23

Coupe

➡When the battery is disconnected it may cause some abnormal drive symptoms until the Powertrain Control Module (PCM) relearns its adaptive strategy. The vehicle may need to be driven 10 miles (16 km) or more for the PCM to relearn its strategy.

1. Before servicing the vehicle, refer to the precautions in the beginning of this section.

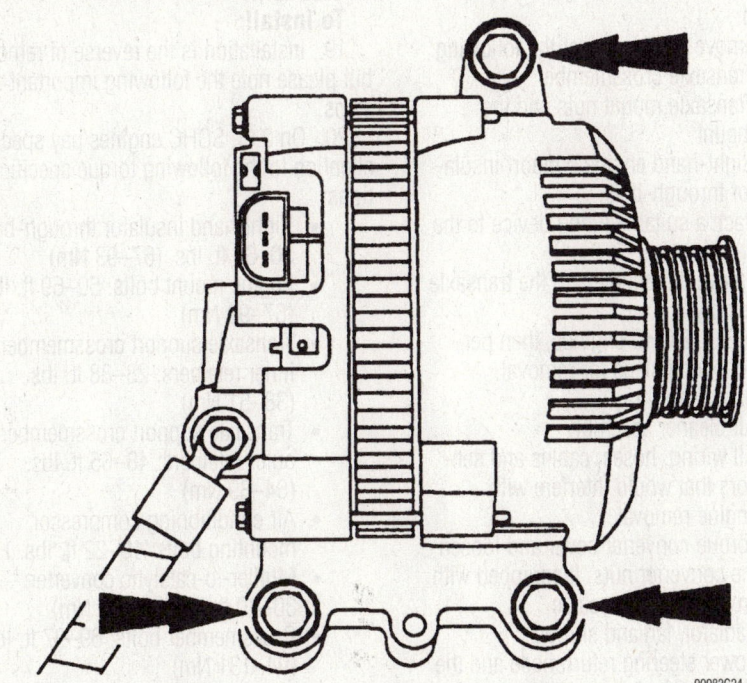

Location of the alternator upper and lower mounting bolts—coupe model

90982G24

2. Remove or disconnect the following:
   - Negative battery cable
   - Drive belt
   - Coolant tank reservoir
   - Alternator electrical connectors
   - Alternator mounting bolts and position the assembly so that you can access the battery positive cable-to-alternator retaining nut
   - Battery positive cable retaining nut, the washer and cable
   - Alternator from the vehicle

INSTALLATION

Coupe

1. Before servicing the vehicle, refer to the precautions in the beginning of this section.
2. Install or connect the following:
   - Battery positive cable, the washer and nut. Tighten the nut to 5–7 ft. lbs. (7–9 Nm).
   - Alternator in position
   - Alternator mounting bolts and tighten to 29–40 ft. lbs. (40–55 Nm)
   - Alternator electrical connections
   - Coolant tank reservoir
   - Drive belt
   - Negative battery cable

Ignition Timing

ADJUSTMENT

2.0L Engines

The Powertrain Control Module (PCM) controls ignition timing on these models. No adjustment is necessary or possible.

Engine Assembly

REMOVAL & INSTALLATION

1. Before servicing the vehicle, refer to the precautions in the beginning of this section.
2. Remove the hood from the vehicle.
3. Properly relieve the fuel system pressure.
4. Disconnect the negative battery cable.
5. If equipped with air conditioning, have the system discharged.
6. Remove or disconnect the following:

Properly support the engine as shown—2.0L SOHC engines

- All the wires and hoses that would interfere with engine removal
- All cables such as the accelerator and kickdown cables (etc.) that would interfere with engine removal
- Drive belt(s)

7. Drain the cooling system and the engine oil.

8. On 2.0L SOHC engines, then perform the following steps for removal.
- Battery and tray
- Air cleaner assembly
- All wiring, hoses, cables and sensors, etc., that would interfere with engine removal
- Power steering pressure hose bracket bolts and set the hose aside
- Exhaust manifold heat shield, exhaust manifold-to-catalytic converter nuts and 1 upper starter motor bolt. Position the starter motor bracket aside.
- Transaxle cooler lines from the transaxle, if equipped with an automatic transaxle
- Air conditioning manifold tube spring lock coupling at the accumulator/drier and the condenser
- Drive belt auto tensioner and, if equipped, the accessory drive belt tensioner

9. Drain the power steering fluid and disconnect the lines from the reservoir.

- Splash shield, crossmember and the catalytic converter
- Drive shafts and the air conditioning compressor with the lines still attached. Set the compressor aside.
- Radiator, fan and shroud

10. Attach a lifting bracket on the left rear side of the cylinder head.

11. Install a three-bar engine support as illustrated.

12. Remove or disconnect the following:
- Transaxle crossmember
- Transaxle mount nuts and the mount
- Right-hand engine support insulator through-bolt

13. Attach a suitable lifting device to the engine.

14. Remove the engine and the transaxle as an assembly.

15. On 2.0L DOHC engines, then perform the following steps for removal.
- Battery and tray
- Air cleaner assembly
- All wiring, hoses, cables and sensors that would interfere with engine removal
- Torque converter cover and loosen the converter nuts, if equipped with an automatic transaxle
- Radiator, fan and shroud
- Power steering return hose and the air conditioning compressor-to-condenser discharge line

- Catalytic converter and the front roll restrictor
- Halfshafts and disconnect the hydraulic clutch line.

16. Support the engine with a floor jack.

17. Unfasten all bolts that attach the engine to its compartment.

18. Remove the engine and transaxle as an assembly.

To install:

19. Installation is the reverse of removal, but please note the following important steps.

20. On 2.0L SOHC engines pay special attention to the following torque specifications:
- Right-hand insulator through-bolt: 50–69 ft. lbs. (67–93 Nm)
- Engine mount bolts: 50–69 ft. lbs. (67–93 Nm)
- Transaxle support crossmember inner retainers: 28–38 ft. lbs. (38–51 Nm)
- Transaxle support crossmember outer retainers: 48–65 ft. lbs. (64–89 Nm)
- Air conditioning compressor mounting bolts: 15–22 ft. lbs.)
- Muffler-to-catalytic converter: 30–40 ft. lbs. (40–55 Nm)
- Crossmember bolts: 69–97 ft. lbs. (94–131 Nm)
- Power steering pressure hose connection: 15–18 ft. lbs. (20–25 Nm)

- Air conditioning line bracket bolt: 15–18 ft. lbs. (20–25 Nm)
- Exhaust manifold-to-catalytic converter nuts: 26–34 ft. lbs. (34–47 Nm)

21. On 2.0L DOHC engines pay special attention to the following torque specifications:
  - Front isolator nuts and bolts: 50–68 ft. lbs. (67–93 Nm)

- Front engine support isolator through-bolt: 50–68 ft. lbs. (67–93 Nm)
- Front roll restrictor bolts: 48–65 ft. lbs. (64–89 Nm) and the nuts to 50–69 ft. lbs. (67–93 Nm)
- Rear roll restrictor nuts: 28–38 ft. lbs. (38–51 Nm)
- Torque converter nuts: 27 ft. lbs. (37 Nm)

REMOVAL & INSTALLATION

2.0L Engine

SOHC SPLIT PORT INJECTION (SPI)

1. Before servicing the vehicle, refer to the precautions in the beginning of this section.

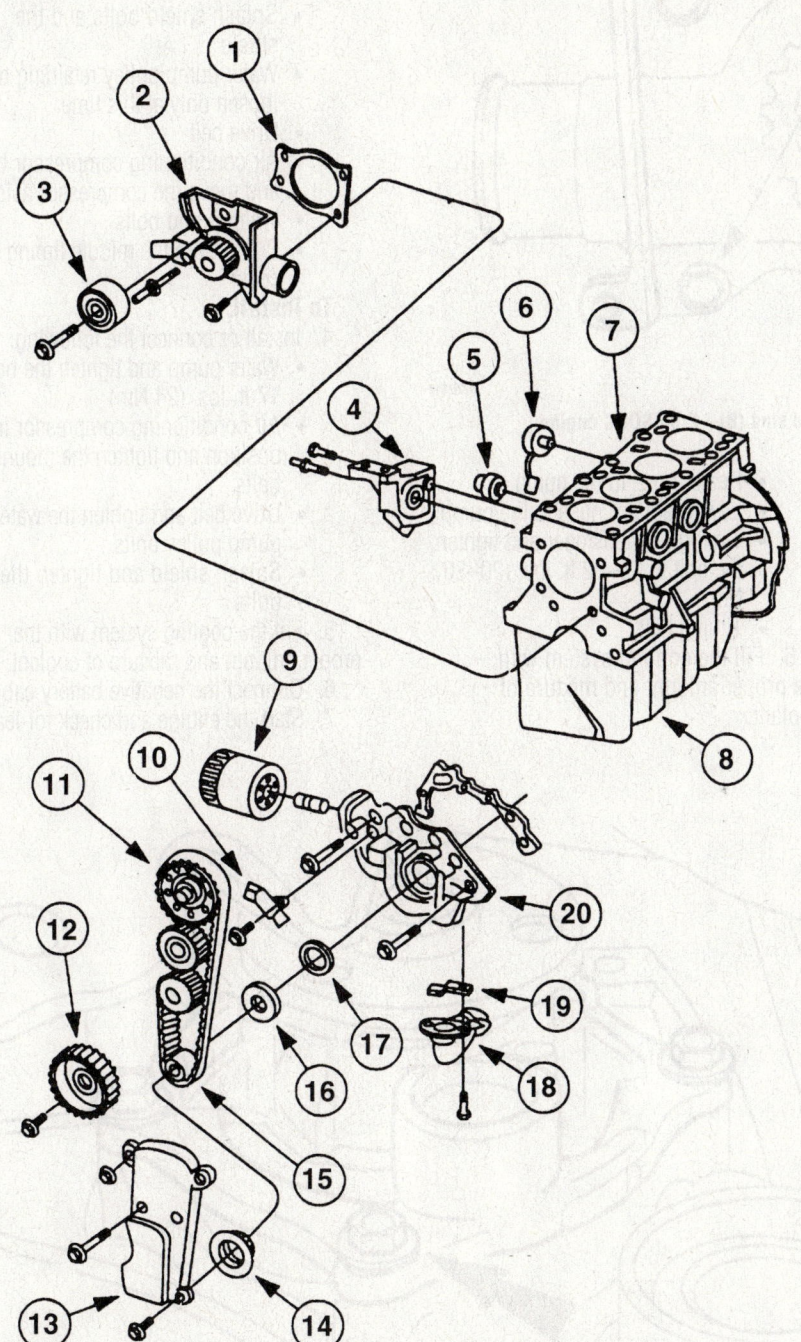

1. Water pump housing gasket
2. Water pump
3. Timing belt tensioner
4. Front engine support mounting bracket
5. Oil pressure sensor
6. Knock sensor
7. Engine block
8. Oil pan
9. Oil filter
10. Crankshaft Position (CKP) sensor
11. Camshaft sprocket
12. Crankshaft pulley
13. Outer engine front cover
14. Crankshaft sprocket
15. Timing belt
16. Timing belt guide
17. Crankshaft front seal
18. Oil pump screen cover and tube
19. Oil pump inlet tube gasket
20. Oil pump

9300MG11

Exploded view of the water pump, oil pump and timing belt mounting—2.0L SOHC SPI engine

Timing belt service is covered in Section 4 of this manual

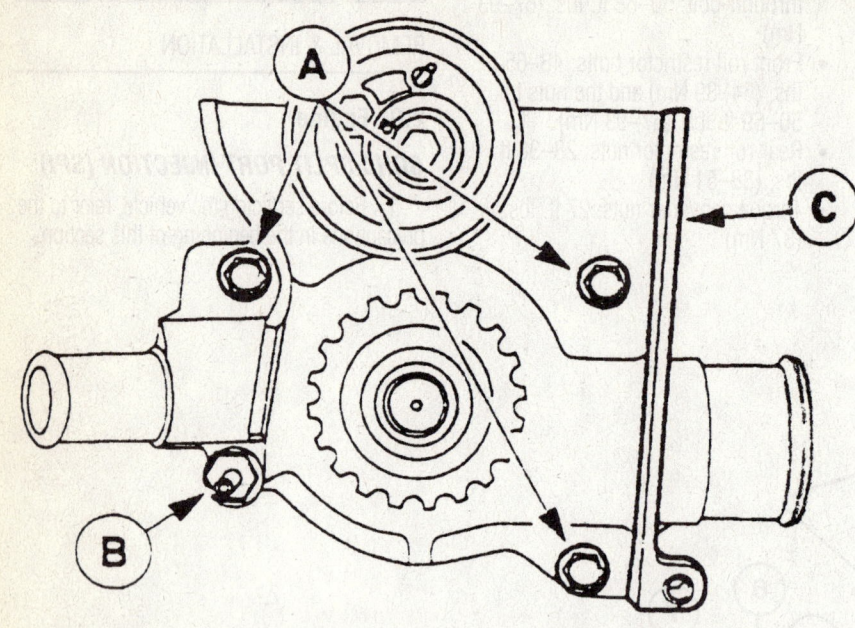

Location of the water pump (C) mounting bolts (A) and stud (B)—2.0L SOHC engine

7922MG18

2. Remove or disconnect the following:
  • Negative battery cable
3. Drain and recycle the engine coolant.
  • Timing belt
  • Timing belt tensioner bolt, unfasten only
  • Tensioner
  • Lower radiator hose from the water pump
  • Heater hose from the water pump
  • 3 bolts and 1 stud from the water pump
  • Water pump

To install:

> ❊❊ **WARNING**
>
> **Do not use any abrasive grinding discs to remove gasket material. Use a plastic manual gasket scraper to remove the gasket residue. Be careful not to scratch or gouge the aluminum sealing surfaces when cleaning them.**

4. Clean the gasket surfaces thoroughly until all traces of the old gasket residue are removed. Inspect the gasket mating surfaces, both must be clean and flat.
5. Install or connect the following:
  • New gasket and the water pump
  • Water pump bolts and stud. Tighten to 15–22 ft. lbs. (20–30 Nm).

  • Heater hose to the pump
  • Lower radiator hose to the pump
  • Timing belt tensioner and tighten the bolt to 15–22 ft. lbs. (20–30 Nm)
  • Timing belt
6. Fill the cooling system with the proper amount and mixture of coolant.

7. Start the engine and check for leaks.

DOHC ZETEC

1. Before servicing the vehicle, refer to the precautions in the beginning of this section.
2. Remove or disconnect the following:
  • Negative battery cable
3. Drain and recycle the engine coolant.
  • Splash shield bolts and the shield
  • Water pump pulley retaining bolts, loosen only at this time
  • Drive belt
  • Air conditioning compressor bolts and move the compressor aside
  • Water pump bolts
  • Pump from the middle timing belt cover

To install:
4. Install or connect the following:
  • Water pump and tighten the bolts to 17 ft. lbs. (24 Nm)
  • Air conditioning compressor in position and tighten the mounting bolts
  • Drive belt and tighten the water pump pulley bolts
  • Splash shield and tighten the bolts
5. Fill the cooling system with the proper amount and mixture of coolant.
6. Connect the negative battery cable.
7. Start the engine and check for leaks.

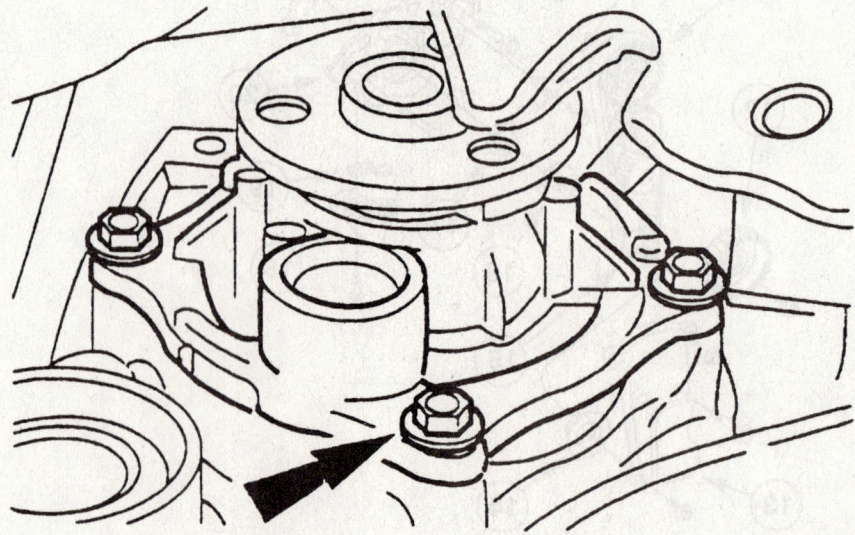

Remove the water pump mounting bolts—2.0L Zetec engine

7922MG19

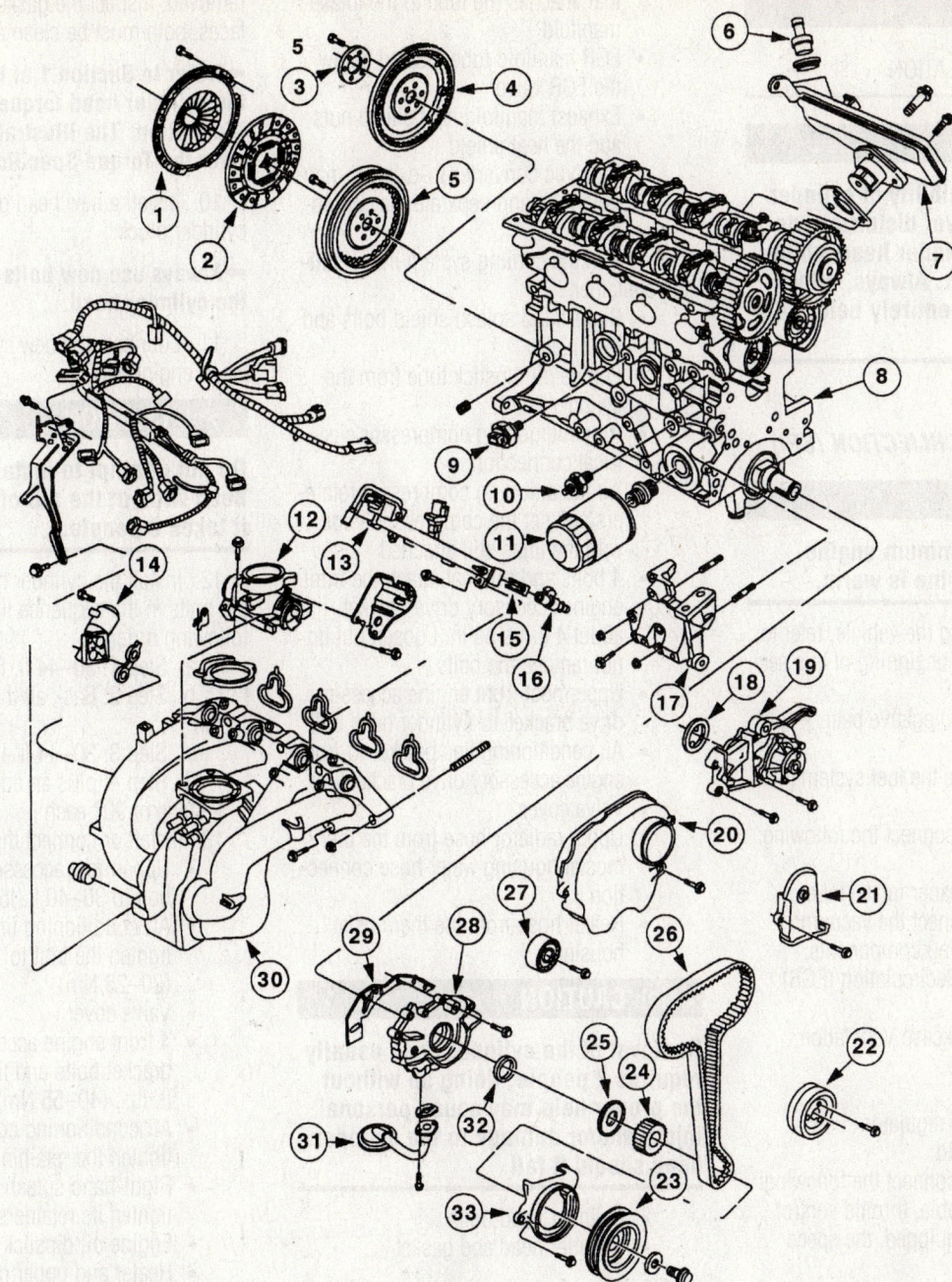

1. Clutch pressure plate
2. Clutch disc
3. Support
4. Flywheel (automatic trans.)
5. Flywheel (manual trans.)
6. PVC valve
7. Oil separator
8. Engine block
9. Knock sensor
10. Oil pressure sensor
11. Oil filter
12. Throttle body
13. Fuel injection supply manifold
14. Idle Air Control (IAC) valve
15. Retainer clip
16. Fuel injector
17. Bracket
18. Water pump housing gasket
19. Water pump
20. Upper timing belt cover
21. Center timing belt cover
22. Water pump pulley
23. Crankshaft pulley
24. Crankshaft sprocket
25. Timing belt guide
26. Timing belt
27. Timing belt idler pulley
28. Oil pump
29. Oil pump housing gasket
30. Intake manifold
31. Oil pump pick-up
32. Crankshaft front seal
33. Lower timing belt cover

9300MG10

Exploded view of peripheral engine component mounting, including water pump, oil pump and intake manifold—2.0L DOHC Zetec engine

Cylinder Head

REMOVAL & INSTALLATION

✳✳ WARNING

To reduce the possibility of cylinder head warpage and/or distortion, do not remove the cylinder head while the engine is warm. Always, allow the engine to cool entirely before disassembly.

2.0L Engine

SOHC SPLIT PORT INJECTION (SPI)

✳✳ WARNING

Never work on aluminum engine parts when the engine is warm.

1. Before servicing the vehicle, refer to the precautions in the beginning of this section.
2. Disconnect the negative battery cable.
3. Properly relieve the fuel system pressure.
4. Remove or disconnect the following:
   • Timing belt
   • Engine air cleaner intake tube
5. Tag and disconnect the vacuum hoses from the following components:
   • Exhaust gas Recirculation (EGR) valve
   • Positive Crankcase Ventilation (PCV) valve
   • Throttle body
   • Fuel pressure regulator
   • Intake manifold
6. Remove or disconnect the following:
   • Accelerator cable, throttle control lever and if equipped, the speed control cable
   • Speed control cable bracket bolt, if equipped
   • 2 fuel charging wiring electrical connections
   • Crankshaft Position (CKP) sensor and Heated Oxygen (HO2S) sensor electrical connections
   • Fuel supply line from the fuel rail, using tool D87L-9280-A
   • Power steering pressure hose bracket bolts, then position the bracket and hose aside
   • Alternator lower bolt, loosen only
   • Alternator upper bolt and pivot the alternator forward
   • engine oil dipstick tube bracket bolt

that attaches the tube to the intake manifold
   • EGR manifold tube located below the EGR valve
   • Exhaust manifold heat shield nuts and the heat shield
   • Catalytic converter-to-exhaust manifold nuts and separate the components
7. Drain the cooling system into a suitable container.
   • Right-hand splash shield bolts and the shield
   • Engine oil dipstick tube from the cylinder block
   • Air conditioning compressor electrical connection
   • Air conditioning compressor retainers and set the compressor aside with the lines still attached
   • 4 bolts and nut that attach the front engine accessory drive bracket about 4 turns ⅜ in. Loosen but do not remove the bolts.
   • Uppermost front engine accessory drive bracket-to-cylinder head bolt
   • Air conditioning line bracket-to-front engine accessory drive bracket bolt
   • Valve cover
   • Upper radiator hose from the thermostat housing water hose connection
   • Heater hose from the thermostat housing

✳✳ CAUTION

Removal of the cylinder head usually requires 2 people, doing so without the proper help may cause personal injury and/or damage to the cylinder head should it fall.

   • Cylinder head bolts
   • Cylinder head and gasket

➥**Maintain a balanced pressure when removing the cylinder head bolts.**

8. Discard the old bolts and the gasket.
To install:

✳✳ WARNING

Do not use any abrasive grinding discs to remove gasket material. Use a plastic manual gasket scraper to remove the gasket residue. Be careful not to scratch or gouge the aluminum sealing surfaces when cleaning them.

9. Clean the gasket surfaces thoroughly until all traces of the old gasket residue are

removed. Inspect the gasket mating surfaces, both must be clean and flat.

➥**Refer to Section 1 of this manual for the cylinder head torque sequence illustration. The illustration is located after the Torque Specification Chart.**

10. Install a new head gasket on the cylinder block.

➥**Always use new bolts when installing the cylinder head.**

11. Lubricate the new cylinder bolts when engine oil.

✳✳ CAUTION

Do not attempt to install the cylinder head without the aid of an assistant, it takes 2 people.

12. Install the cylinder head and tighten the bolts in the sequence illustrated in the following order:
   a. Step 1: 30–44 ft. lbs. (40–60 Nm).
   b. Step 2: Back all the bolts off ½ a turn.
   c. Step 3: 30–44 ft. lbs. (40–60 Nm).
   d. Step 4: plus an additional 180° in 2 steps of 90° each
13. Install or connect the following:
   • Uppermost accessory drive bracket bolt to 30–40 ft. lbs. (40–55 Nm)
   • Air conditioning line bracket and tighten the bolt to 15–18 ft. lbs. (20–25 Nm)
   • Valve cover
   • 4 front engine accessory drive bracket bolts and the nut to 30–40 ft. lbs. (40–55 Nm)
   • Air conditioning compressor and tighten the retaining bolts
   • Right-hand splash shield and tighten its retainers
   • Engine oil dipstick tube
   • Heater and upper radiator hoses
   • Timing belt and alternator
   • Power steering pressure hose
   • CKP sensor and 2 main fuel charging electrical connection
   • Engine oil dipstick tube bolt
   • EGR valve manifold tube connection
   • EGR valve manifold tube to the exhaust manifold
   • Fuel supply line to the fuel rail
   • Catalytic converter to the exhaust manifold using a new gasket and tighten the nuts
   • Heat shield and tighten the nuts
   • Speed control cable bracket, if equipped

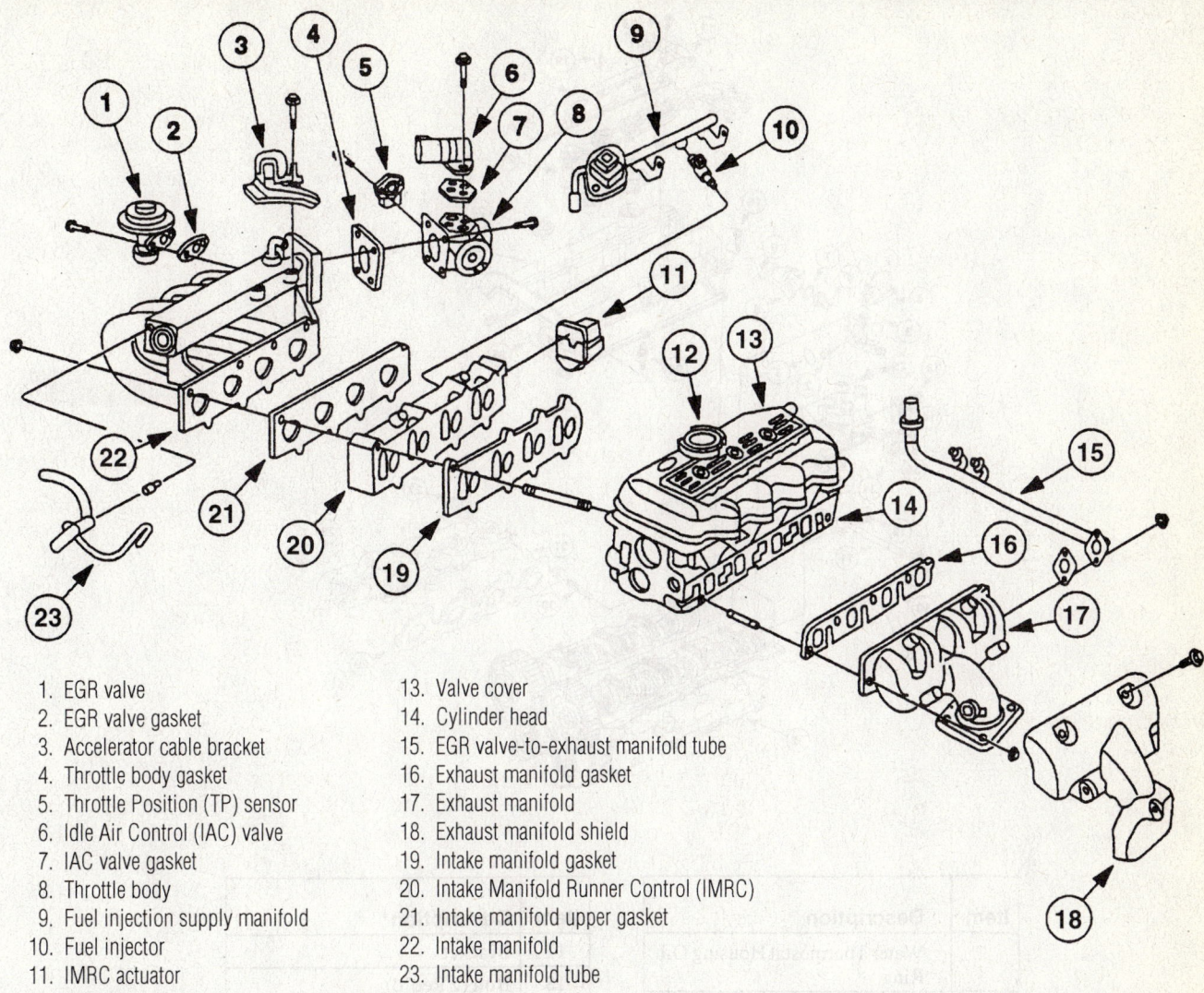

1. EGR valve
2. EGR valve gasket
3. Accelerator cable bracket
4. Throttle body gasket
5. Throttle Position (TP) sensor
6. Idle Air Control (IAC) valve
7. IAC valve gasket
8. Throttle body
9. Fuel injection supply manifold
10. Fuel injector
11. IMRC actuator
12. Oil filler cap
13. Valve cover
14. Cylinder head
15. EGR valve-to-exhaust manifold tube
16. Exhaust manifold gasket
17. Exhaust manifold
18. Exhaust manifold shield
19. Intake manifold gasket
20. Intake Manifold Runner Control (IMRC)
21. Intake manifold upper gasket
22. Intake manifold
23. Intake manifold tube

9300MG13

Exploded view of the cylinder head, exhaust manifold and intake manifold mounting—2.0L SOHC SPI engine

- Throttle control lever, accelerator cable and if equipped, the speed control cable

14. Connect the vacuum hoses tagged and removed to the following components:
- EGR valve
- PCV valve
- Throttle body
- Fuel pressure regulator
- Intake manifold

15. Install the air cleaner outlet tube.
16. Fill the cooling system.
17. Connect the negative battery cable.
18. Start the engine and check for leaks.

DOHC ZETEC

1. Before servicing the vehicle, refer to the precautions in the beginning of this section.

2. Disconnect the negative battery cable.
3. Properly relieve the fuel system pressure.
4. Remove or disconnect the following:
- Air cleaner assembly outlet tube
- Timing belt
5. Tag and disconnect the vacuum hoses from the following components:
- Positive Crankcase Ventilation Valve (PCV) valve
- Throttle body
- Fuel pressure sensor
- Intake manifold
6. Remove or disconnect the following:
- Speed control and accelerator cables from the control lever
- Fuel charging electrical connectors at the main engine connector

- Crankshaft Position (CKP) sensor and Heated Oxygen (HO2S) sensor electrical connections
- Fuel line
- Power steering pump and bracket, then set them aside with the lines still attached
- Alternator
- Engine oil dipstick tube
7. Drain the cooling system into a suitable container.
- Splash shield bolts and the shield
- Air conditioning compressor electrical connection
- Air conditioning compressor retainers and set the compressor aside with the lines still attached
- Spark plug wires and the plugs
- Valve cover

Refer to Section 1 for engine rebuilding specifications

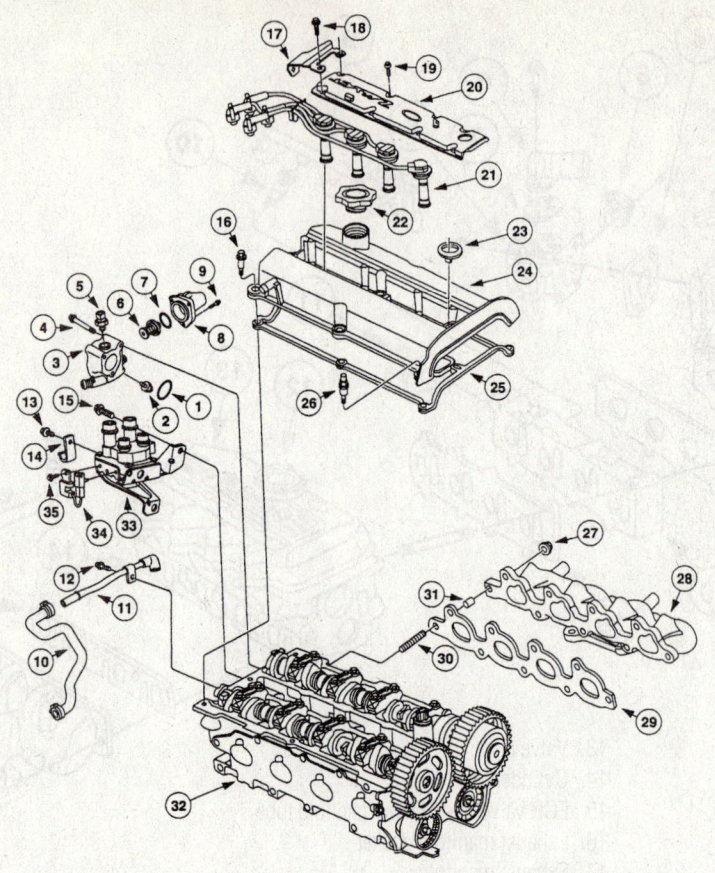

Item	Description
1	Water Thermostat Housing Oil Ring
2	Water Temperature Indicator Sender Unit
3	Water Thermostat Housing
4	Bolt (3 Req'd)
5	Engine Coolant Temperature Sensor
6	Water Thermostat
7	Water Thermostat Housing O-Ring
8	Water Outlet Connection
9	Bolt (3 Req'd)
10	Oil Separator Hose
11	Crankcase Ventilation Tube
12	Bolt
13	Bolt
14	Support Bracket
15	Bolt (3 Req'd)
16	Bolt (9 Req'd)

Item	Description
17	Bracket
18	Bolt (2 Req'd)
19	Bolt (6 Req'd)
20	Engine Appearance Cover
21	Ignition Wire (4 Req'd)
22	Oil Filler Cap
23	Grommet
24	Valve Cover
25	Valve Cover Gasket
26	Stud Bolt
27	Nut (9 Req'd)
28	Exhaust Manifold
29	Exhaust Manifold Gasket
30	Stud (9 Req'd)
31	Spacer
32	Cylinder Head
33	Ignition Coil Bracket
34	Radio Ignition Interference Capacitor
35	Bolt

9306MG77

Exploded view of the upper engine components—2.0L Zetec engine

- Upper radiator hose from the thermostat housing water hose connection
- Heater hose from the thermostat housing
- Camshafts
- Ignition coil
- Thermostat housing
- Cylinder head bolts
- Cylinder head and the gasket

To install:

※※ WARNING

Do not use any abrasive grinding discs to remove gasket material. Use a plastic manual gasket scraper to remove the gasket residue. Be careful not to scratch or gouge the aluminum sealing surfaces when cleaning them.

8. Clean the gasket surfaces thoroughly until all traces of the old gasket residue are removed. Inspect the gasket mating surfaces, both must be clean and flat.

➡**Refer to Section 1 of this manual for the cylinder head torque sequence illustration. The illustration is located after the Torque Specification Chart.**

9. Install a new head gasket on the cylinder block.

➡**Always use new bolts when installing the cylinder head.**

10. Lubricate the new cylinder bolts when engine oil.

※※ CAUTION

Do not attempt to install the cylinder head without the aid of an assistant, it takes 2 people.

11. Install the cylinder head and tighten the bolts in the sequence illustrated in the following steps:
   a. Step 1: 12–18 ft. lbs. (15–25 Nm).
   b. Step 2: 26–33 ft. lbs. (35–45 Nm).
   c. Step 3: plus an additional 90 degrees.
12. Install or connect the following:
   - Thermostat housing
   - Ignition coil and the camshafts
   - Heater and upper radiator hoses

- Valve cover
- Spark plugs
- Spark plug wires
- Air conditioning compressor and tighten the retaining bolts
- Air conditioning compressor electrical connection
- Splash shield and tighten its retainers
- Engine oil dipstick tube
- Alternator and the power steering reservoir and bracket
- Fuel line
- CKP sensor, HO2sensor, and 2 main fuel charging electrical connections
- accelerator cable and if equipped, the speed control cable to the control lever
13. Connect the vacuum hoses tagged and removed to the following components:
   - PCV valve
   - Throttle body
   - Fuel pressure sensor
   - Intake manifold
14. Install or connect the following:
   - Timing belt
   - Air cleaner outlet tube
15. Fill the cooling system.
16. Connect the negative battery cable.
17. Start the engine and check for leaks.

Rocker Arms

REMOVAL & INSTALLATION

The 2.0L SOHC Split Port Injection (SPI) engines are equipped with rocker arms. On the 2.0L DOHC ZETEC engines the camshafts acts directly on the valve, therefore, no rocker arms/shafts are used.

2.0L Engine

SOHC SPLIT PORT INJECTION (SPI)

➡**Refer to the illustration located in the camshaft procedure, earlier in this section, for a view of the rocker arms on this engine.**

1. Before servicing the vehicle, refer to the precautions in the beginning of this section.
2. Remove or disconnect the following:
   - Negative battery cable
   - Valve cover

3. Mark the location of the rocker arms.
   - Rocker arm bolts
   - Rocker arms and seats
To install:
4. Install or connect the following:
   - Seats and rocker arms in their original positions
   - Rocker arm bolts and tighten to 17–22 ft. lbs. (23–30 Nm)
   - Valve cover
   - Negative battery cable

Intake Manifold

REMOVAL & INSTALLATION

2.0L Engine

SOHC SPLIT PORT INJECTION (SPI)

➡**Refer to the illustration located in the cylinder head procedure, earlier in this section, for a view of the intake manifold mounting on this engine.**

1. Before servicing the vehicle, refer to the precautions in the beginning of this section.
2. Disconnect the negative battery cable.
3. Partially drain the cooling system.
4. Remove or disconnect the following:
   - Air cleaner outlet tube
5. Tag and disconnect the vacuum hoses from the following components:
   - Exhaust gas Recirculation (EGR) valve
   - Positive Crankcase Ventilation (PCV) valve
   - Throttle body
   - Fuel pressure regulator
   - Intake manifold
6. Remove or disconnect the following:
   - Accelerator cable, throttle control lever and if equipped, the speed control cable
   - Speed control cable bracket bolt, if equipped
   - Idle Air Control (IAC) valve and Throttle Position (TP) sensor electrical connections
   - Engine oil dipstick tube bracket bolt that attaches the tube to the intake manifold
   - EGR manifold tube located below the EGR valve
   - Engine oil dipstick tube from the block
   - Intake manifold lower nuts

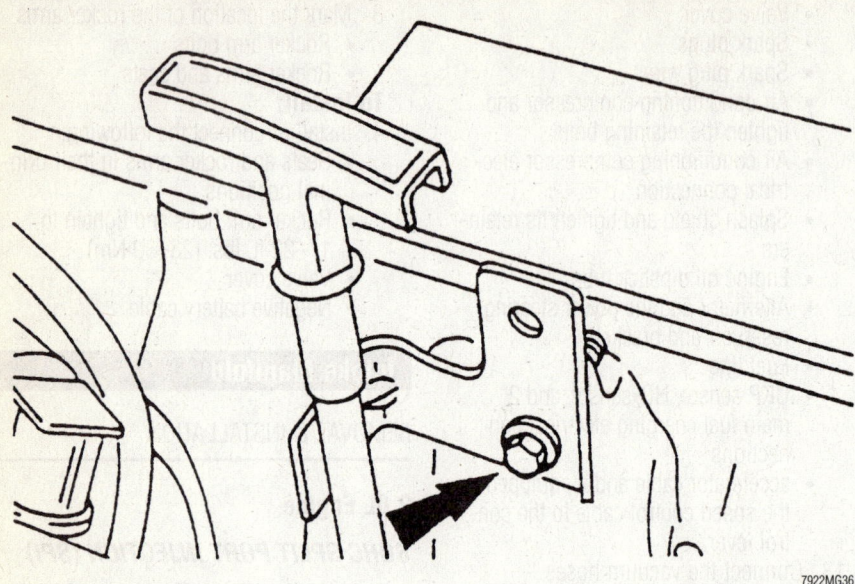

Remove the engine oil dipstick tube bracket bolt that attaches the tube to the intake manifold—2.0L SOHC engine

7922MG36

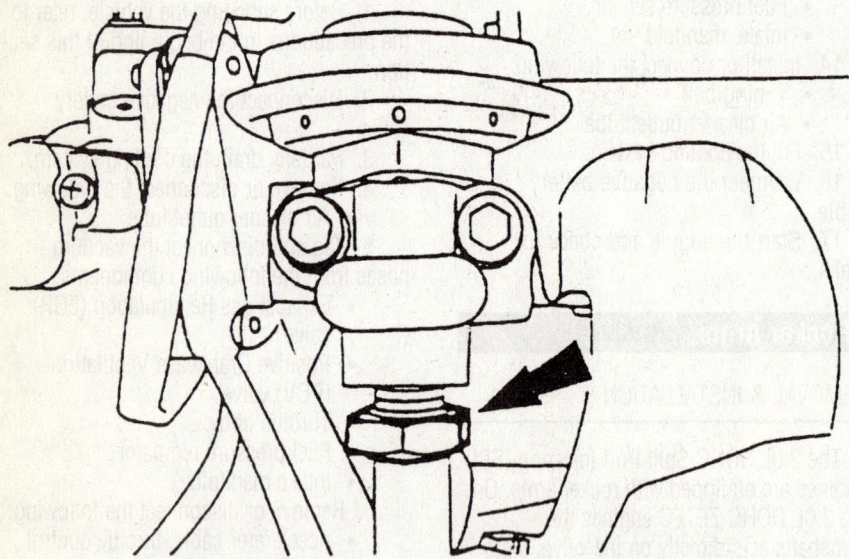

Disconnect the EGR manifold tube located below the EGR valve—2.0L SOHC engine

7922MG37

- Intake manifold upper nuts
- Manifold
- Manifold gasket

To install:

❄❄ WARNING

Do not use any abrasive grinding discs to remove gasket material. Use a plastic manual gasket scraper to remove the gasket residue. Be careful not to scratch or gouge the aluminum sealing surfaces when cleaning them.

7. Clean the gasket surfaces thoroughly until all traces of the old gasket residue are removed. Inspect the gasket mating surfaces, both must be clean and flat.

8. Clean and oil the intake manifold mounting studs.

9. Install or connect the following:
- Intake manifold and hand-tighten the upper nuts
- Lower manifold nuts and tighten them to 15–22 ft. lbs. (20–30 Nm)
- Engine oil dipstick tube to the block
- Manifold upper nuts and tighten to 15–22 ft. lbs. (20–30 Nm)

- EGR manifold tube and tighten it to 15–20 ft. lbs. (20–28 Nm)
- Engine oil dipstick tube bolt and tighten to 71–97 inch lbs. (8–11 Nm)
- IAC valve and TP sensor electrical connections
- Speed control cable bracket bolt, if equipped and tighten to 71–88 inch lbs. (8–10 Nm)
- Throttle control lever, accelerator cable and if equipped, the speed control cable

10. Connect the vacuum hoses tagged and removed to the following components:
- EGR valve
- PCV valve
- Throttle body
- Fuel pressure regulator.
- Intake manifold

11. Install the air cleaner outlet tube.

12. Fill the cooling system.

13. Connect the negative battery cable.

14. Start the engine and check for coolant leaks.

DOHC ZETEC

➡ **Refer to the illustration located in the water pump procedure, earlier in this section, for a view of the intake manifold on this engine.**

1. Before servicing the vehicle, refer to the precautions in the beginning of this section.

2. Properly relieve the fuel system pressure.

3. Remove or disconnect the following:
- Negative battery cable
- Air cleaner outlet tube
- Throttle Position (TP) sensor electrical connection

4. Drain the cooling system into a suitable container.
- Bolt that secures the pipe located by the crankshaft pulley
- Heater hoses from the core
- Main engine control sensor wiring
- Connectors from the mounting bracket
- Vacuum hoses from the intake manifold by squeezing the tabs, twisting the hoses and pulling them away from the manifold
- Crankcase ventilation hose from the valve cover
- Drive belt
- Alternator mounting bolts and move the alternator aside
- Fuel lines
- Intake manifold nuts and bolts in the sequence illustrated

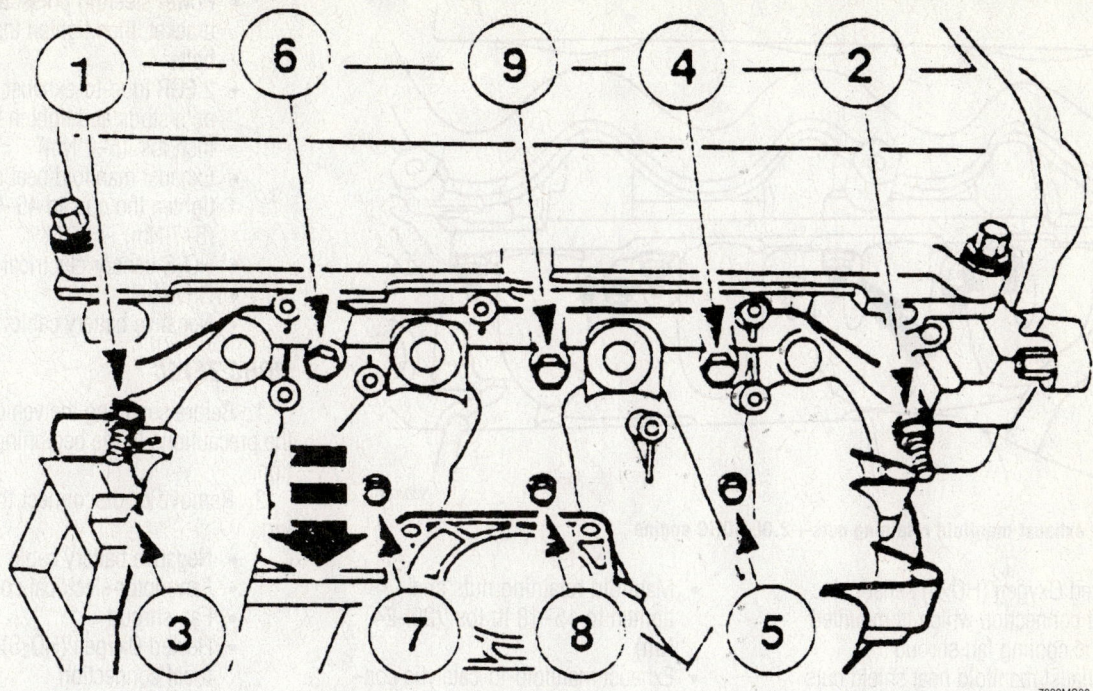

Remove the intake manifold bolts and nuts in this sequence—2.0L Zetec engine

- Intake manifold and gasket

To install:

➡ **Refer to Section 1 of this manual for the intake manifold torque sequence illustration. The illustration is located after the Torque Specification Chart.**

5. Clean all dirt and gasket residue from the intake manifold mating surfaces.

6. Install or connect the following:
- New gasket and place the manifold in position
- Manifold bolts and nuts. tighten in the sequence illustrated to 10–12 ft. lbs. (14–17 Nm).
- Fuel lines
- Alternator
- Drive belt
- Crankcase ventilation hose to the valve cover
- Vacuum hoses to the manifold making sure the tabs are firmly engaged
- Connectors in the mounting bracket
- Main engine control sensor wiring
- Heater hoses to the heater core
- Bolt that secures the pipe located by the crankshaft pulley. Tighten the bolt to 71–97 inch lbs. (8–11 Nm).
- TP sensor electrical connection
- Air cleaner outlet tube

7. Fill the cooling system.

8. Connect the negative battery cable.

Exhaust Manifold

REMOVAL & INSTALLATION

2.0L Engine

SOHC SPLIT PORT INJECTION (SPI)

➡ **Refer to the illustration located in the cylinder head procedure, earlier in this** section, for a view of the exhaust manifold on this engine.

1. Before servicing the vehicle, refer to the precautions in the beginning of this section.

2. Remove or disconnect the following:
- Negative battery cable
- Drive belt

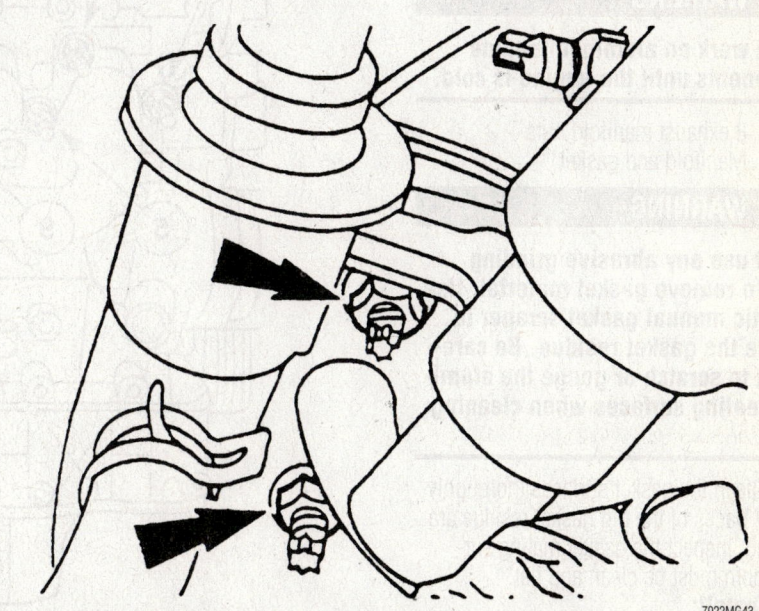

Remove the 2 EGR tube-to-exhaust manifold stud nuts—2.0L SOHC engine

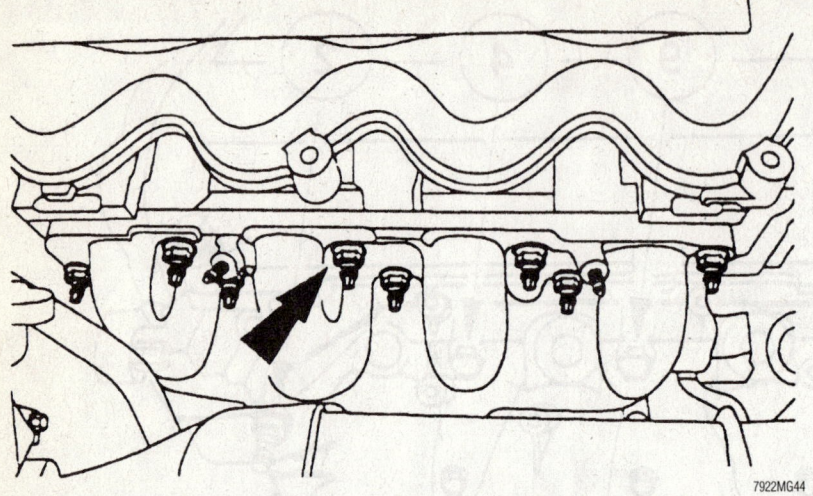

Remove the exhaust manifold retaining nuts—2.0L SOHC engine

7922MG44

- Heated Oxygen (HO2S) sensor electrical connection which is mounted on the cooling fan shroud
- 5 exhaust manifold heat shield nuts and the shield
- 2 Exhaust Gas Recirculation (EGR) tube-to-exhaust manifold nuts studs
- Power steering pressure hose bracket bolts, then position the bracket and hose aside
- Alternator lower bolt, loosen only
- Alternator upper bolt and pivot the alternator forward
- 4 exhaust manifold-to-catalytic converter nuts

❊❊ WARNING

Do not work on aluminum engine components until the engine is cold.

- 8 exhaust manifold nuts
- Manifold and gasket

❊❊ WARNING

Do not use any abrasive grinding discs to remove gasket material. Use a plastic manual gasket scraper to remove the gasket residue. Be careful not to scratch or gouge the aluminum sealing surfaces when cleaning them.

3. Clean the gasket surfaces thoroughly until all traces of the old gasket residue are removed. Inspect the gasket mating surfaces, both must be clean and flat.

To install:

4. Install or connect the following:
- New gasket and the exhaust manifold

- Manifold retaining nuts and tighten to 15–18 ft. lbs. (20–24 Nm)
- Exhaust manifold-to-catalytic converter nuts and tighten to 26–34 ft. lbs. (34–47 Nm)
- Alternator and tighten the upper and lower mounting bolts

- Power steering pressure hose and bracket, then tighten the retaining bolts
- 2 EGR tube-to-exhaust manifold nuts studs and tighten to 44.6–62 inch lbs. (5–7 Nm)
- Exhaust manifold heat shield and tighten the nuts to 45–61 inch lbs. (5–7 Nm)
- HO2S sensor electrical connec-tion
- Drive belt
- Negative battery cable

DOHC ZETEC

1. Before servicing the vehicle, refer to the precautions in the beginning of this section.

2. Remove or disconnect the following:

- Negative battery cable
- Fan motor electrical connection
- Fan shroud
- Heated Oxygen (HO2S) sensor electrical connection
- Catalytic converter-to-exhaust manifold bolt and nut, then disconnect the converter from the manifold

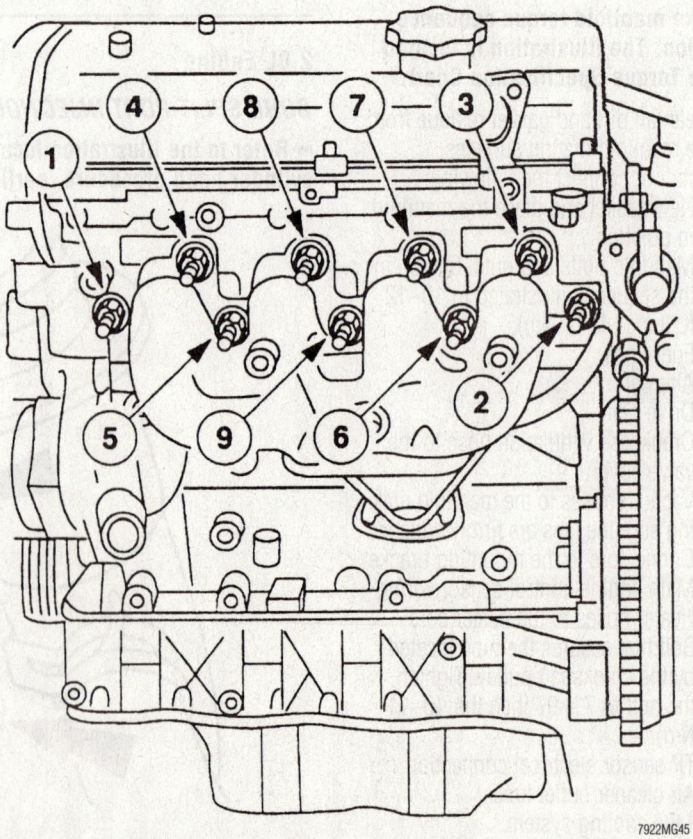

Remove the exhaust manifold nuts and bolts in the sequence illustrated—2.0L Zetec engine

7922MG45

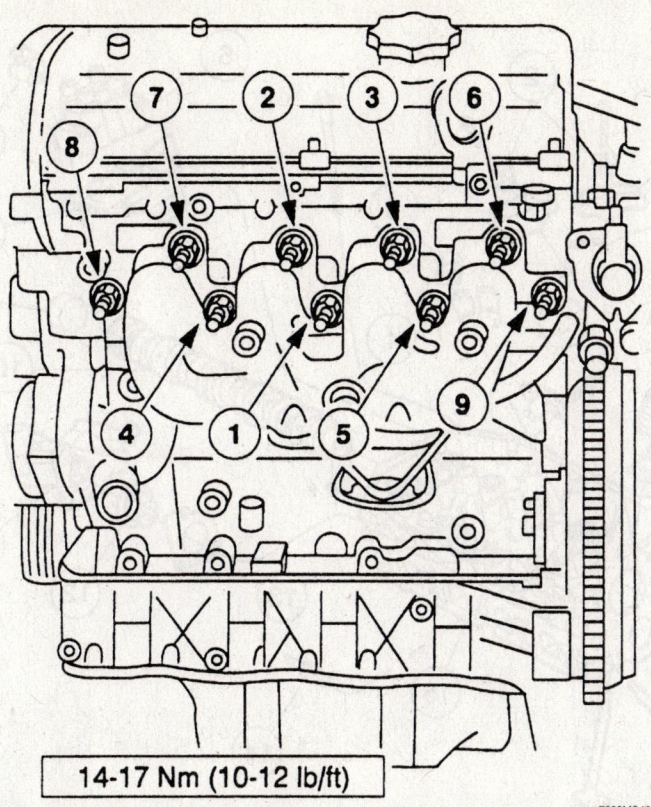

14-17 Nm (10-12 lb/ft)

7922MG46

Tighten the exhaust manifold nuts and bolts in the sequence illustrated to the proper specification—2.0L Zetec engine

❋❋ WARNING

Do not break the threadlock seal on the engine oil dipstick tube. If the seal is broken, relock it to prevent any oil leaks from the block.

- Engine oil dipstick tube bracket bolt
- Exhaust manifold heat shield bolts and nuts, then the shield

❋❋ WARNING

Do not work on aluminum engine components until the engine is cold.

- 7 exhaust manifold bolts and 2 studs
- Manifold and gasket

❋❋ WARNING

Do not use any abrasive grinding discs to remove gasket material. Use a plastic manual gasket scraper to remove the gasket residue. Be careful not to scratch or gouge the aluminum sealing surfaces when cleaning them.

3. Clean the gasket surfaces thoroughly until all traces of the old gasket residue are removed. Inspect the gasket mating surfaces, both must be clean and flat.

To install:

4. Install or connect the following:
- New gasket and the exhaust manifold
- Manifold retaining bolts and nuts and tighten to 13–16 ft. lbs. (14–17 Nm)
- Exhaust manifold heat shield and retainers. Tighten the retainers to 71–101 inch lbs. (8–11 Nm).
- Engine oil dipstick tube bracket bolt and tighten to 71–101 inch lbs. (8–11 Nm)
- Exhaust manifold-to-catalytic converter bolt and nut
- HO$_2$sensor electrical connection
- Fan shroud and the fan motor wiring
- Negative battery cable

Front Crankshaft Seal

REMOVAL & INSTALLATION

2.0L Engines

1. Before servicing the vehicle, refer to the precautions in the beginning of this section.
2. Remove the timing belt and crankshaft sprocket.

❋❋ WARNING

Be careful not to damage the crankshaft surface when removing the seal.

3. Using seal remover tool T92C-6700-CH, remove the crankshaft front oil seal.
To install:
4. Use seal replacer tool T81P-6700-A, install the new seal.
5. Install the crankshaft sprocket and the timing belt.

Camshaft(s) and Valve Lifters

All engines covered in this manual except the 2.0L Zetec engine, employ hydraulic (oil pressurized) valve lifters. These lifters operate more quietly and do not require periodic adjustments.

REMOVAL & INSTALLATION

2.0L Engine

SOHC SPLIT PORT INJECTION (SPI)

1. Before servicing the vehicle, refer to the precautions in the beginning of this section.
2. Disconnect the negative battery cable.
3. Remove the air cleaner and valve cover.
4. Remove the camshaft front seal as follows:
   a. Align the timing marks and remove the timing belt.
   b. Use cam sprocket holding/removing tool T74P-6256-B, and remove the camshaft sprocket.
   c. Unfasten the timing belt tensioner bolt and remove the tensioner.
   d. Remove the inner engine front cover.
   e. Use seal removal tool T92C-6700-CH, to remove the camshaft front seal.
5. Remove or disconnect the following:

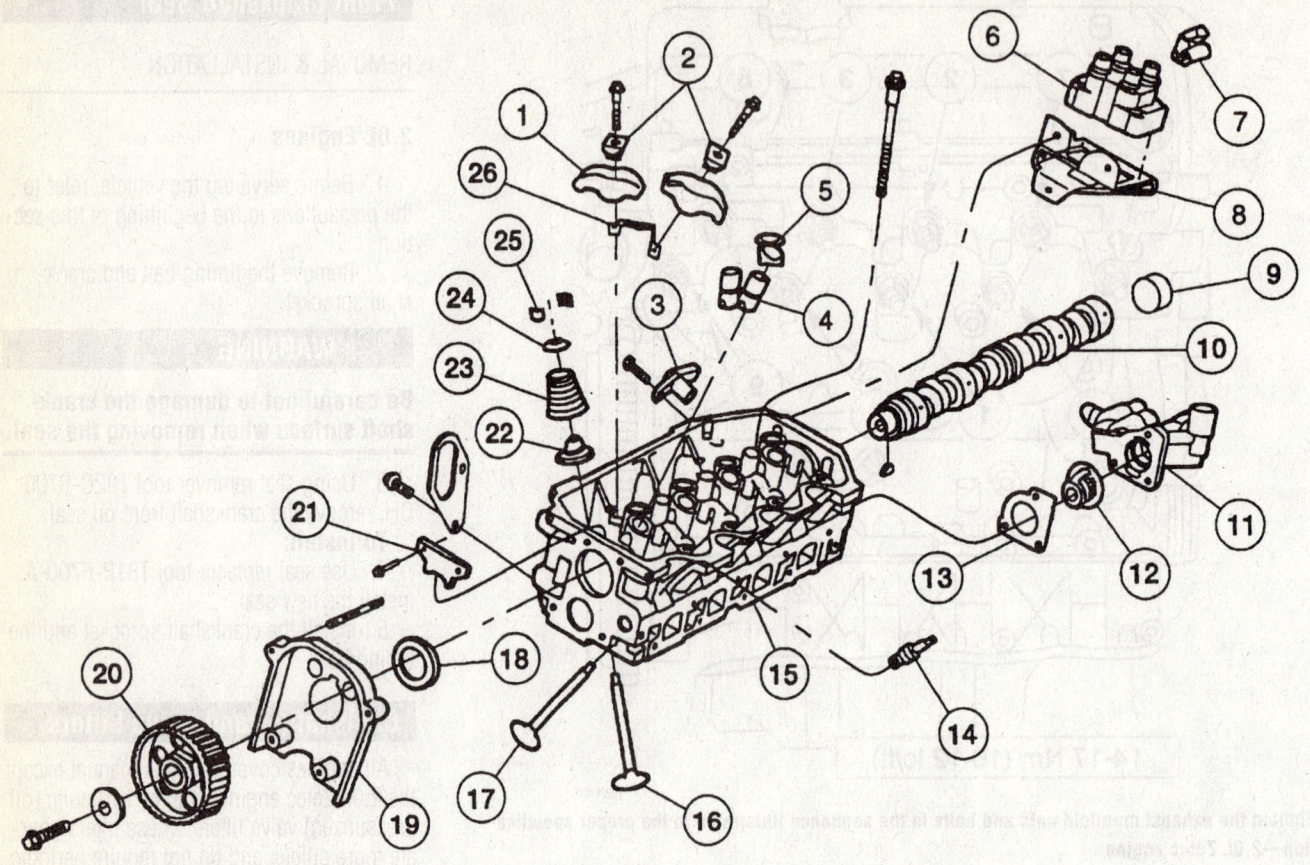

1. Rocker arm
2. Rocker arm seats
3. Camshaft Position (CMP) sensor
4. Valve tappet
5. Valve tappet guide plate
6. Ignition coil
7. Radio ignition interference capacitor
8. Ignition coil bracket
9. Cup plug
10. Camshaft
11. Water hose connection
12. Water thermostat
13. Water hose connection gasket

14. Spark plug
15. Cylinder head
16. Intake valve
17. Exhaust valve
18. Camshaft front seal
19. Engine front cover
20. Camshaft sprocket
21. Camshaft thrust plate
22. Valve stem seal
23. Valve spring
24. Valve spring retainer
25. Valve spring retainer key
26. Valve tappet guide plate retainer

9300MG12

Exploded view of the cylinder head—2.0L SOHC SPI engine

- Ignition coil and bracket
- Rocker arms and valve tappets
- Camshaft thrust plate bolts and the plate
- Cup plug from the rear of the cylinder head and discard
- Camshaft from the rear of the cylinder head, carefully

To install:

➡ **Liberally coat the cam bore in the cylinder with clean 5W30 motor oil.**

6. Install or connect the following:

- Camshaft through the rear of the cylinder head
- Camshaft thrust plate and the bolts. Tighten the bolts to 71–115 inch lbs. (8–13 Nm).
- New cup plug and the tappets
- Rocker arms
- Ignition coil bracket and coil

7. Install the camshaft front seal as follows:

a. Apply a thin film of 5W30 motor oil to the lip of the seal.

➡ **The seal depth should be 0.002–0.04 in. (0.05–1.0mm) below flush with the cylinder head front face.**

b. Use seal replacer T81P-6292-A, to install the camshaft front seal.

c. Install the inner engine front cover.

d. Install the timing belt tensioner. Tighten the tensioner bolt to 15–22 ft. lbs. (20–30 Nm).

e. Install the camshaft sprocket and the timing belt

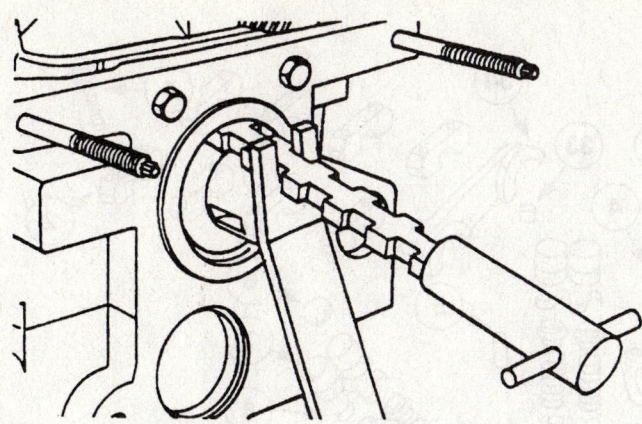

Removing the camshaft front seal—2.0L SOHC engine

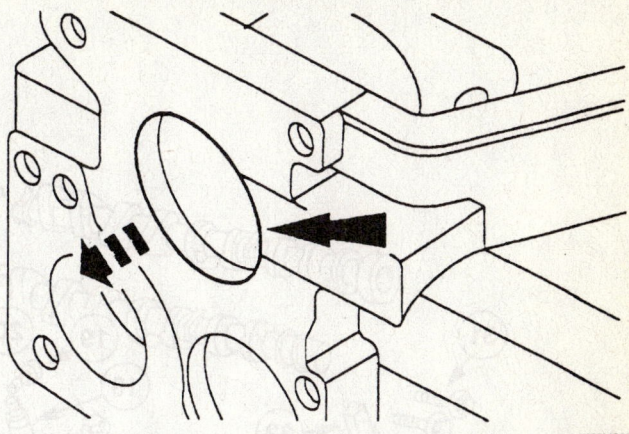

Remove and discard the cup plug located at the rear of the cylinder head—2.0L engine

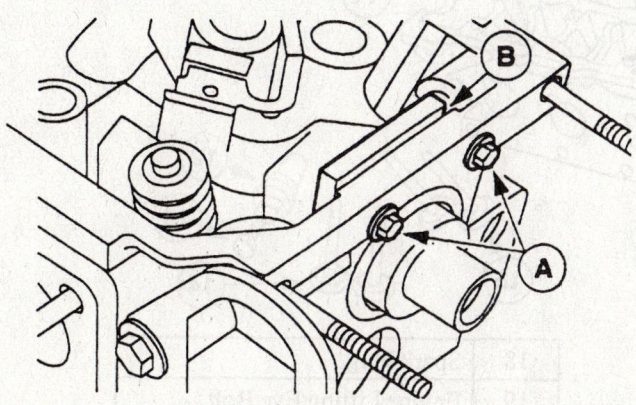

Remove the camshaft thrust plate retaining bolts (A) and the plate (B)—2.0L SOHC engine

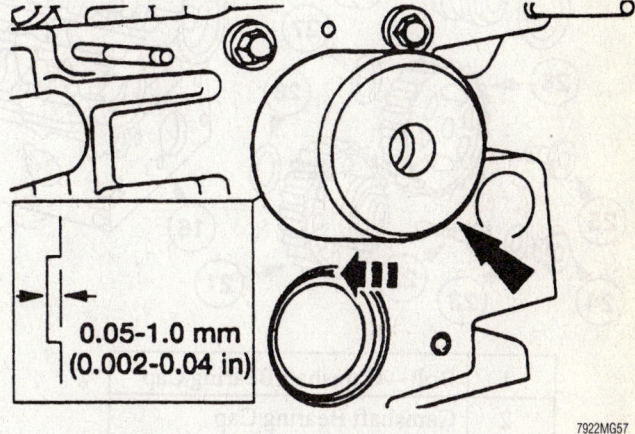

0.05–1.0 mm
(0.002–0.04 in)

Use seal Replacer T81P-6292-At, to install the camshaft front seal 0.002–0.04 in. (0.05–1.0mm) below flush with the cylinder head front face—2.0L SOHC engine

8. Install the valve cover and the air cleaner assembly.

9. Connect the negative battery cable.

DOHC ZETEC

1. Before servicing the vehicle, refer to the precautions in the beginning of this section.

2. Remove or disconnect the following:

- Timing belt
- Valve cover and camshaft sprockets

➡️**It may be necessary to rotate the oil control solenoid flange 90 degrees prior to removal.**

- Oil control solenoid flange bolts and the flange

➡️**Mark the camshaft journal caps with a number to identify their location, as they must be replaced in their original position.**

- Camshaft journal caps in several passes in the sequence illustrated, then remove the bolts and caps
- Camshafts from the cylinder head
- Oil control sensor and bushing

3. Inspect the camshafts for damage and wear.

To install:

4. Be sure the valve clearance is correct.

5. Install the oil control solenoid bushing and flange on the exhaust camshaft.

➡️**The front camshaft journal cap must be installed with the bolts tightened to**

specification within 4 minutes of applying the sealer.

6. Coat the surface of the front camshaft journal cap with gasket maker E2AZ-19562-B.

7. Place the camshafts in position and lubricate the bearing surfaces with engine assembly lubricant D9AZ-19579-D.

8. Install new camshaft front oil seals.

9. Apply a thin coat of silicone gasket and sealant F6AZ-19562-AA to the sealing surface of the of the front camshaft journal bearing cap.

10. Install or connect the following:

- Caps and tighten the bolts in several 2-turn passes in the sequence illustrated to 10–12 ft. lbs. (13–17 Nm)

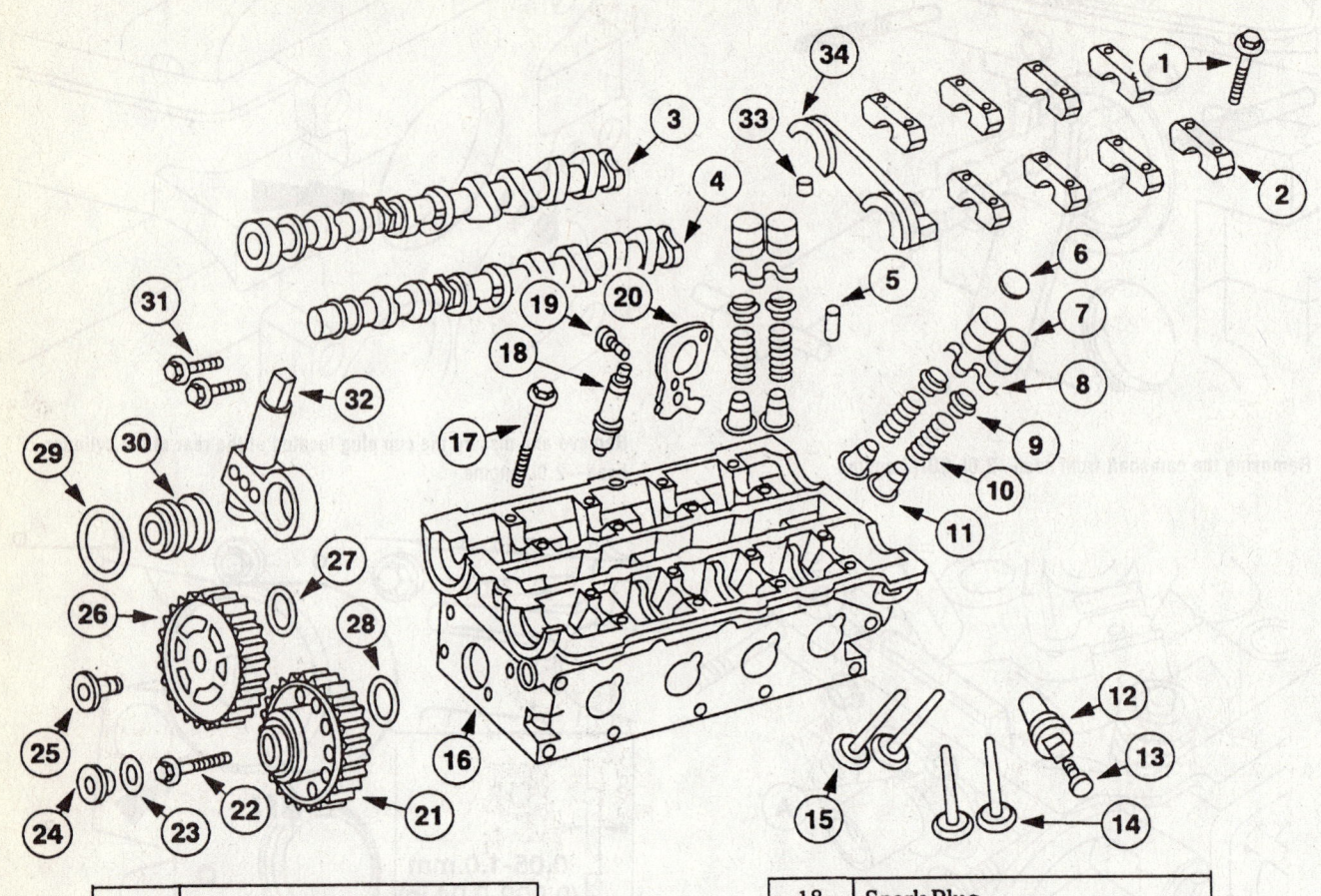

1	Bolt—Camshaft Bearing Cap		18	Spark Plug
2	Camshaft Bearing Cap		19	Engine Lifting Eye Bolt
3	Camshaft Intake		20	Engine Lifting Eye
4	Camshaft Exhaust		21	Camshaft Sprocket —Exhaust
5	Plug		22	Exhaust Camshaft Sprocket Bolt
6	Adjusting Shim—Valve Clearance		23	Blanking Plug O-Ring
7	Valve Tappets		24	Blanking Plug
8	Valve Spring Retainer Key		25	Bolt—Intake Camshaft
9	Valve Spring Retainers		26	Camshaft Sprocket Intake
10	Valve Spring (Color Coding: Exhaust – Blue, Intake – Red)		27	Camshaft Front Seal
			28	O-Ring
11	Valve Stem Seal		29	Camshaft Front Seal
12	Camshaft Position Sensor		30	Oil Feed Ring
13	CMP Sensor Bolt		31	Oil Feed Flange Bolts
14	Intake Valves		32	Oil Feed Flange
15	Exhaust Valves		33	Guide Sleeve—Front Camshaft Bearing Cap
16	Cylinder Head		34	Fifth Camshaft Bearing Cap
17	Cylinder Head Bolts			

Exploded view of the cylinder head, showing camshaft mounting—2.0L DOHC Zetec engine

9300MG06

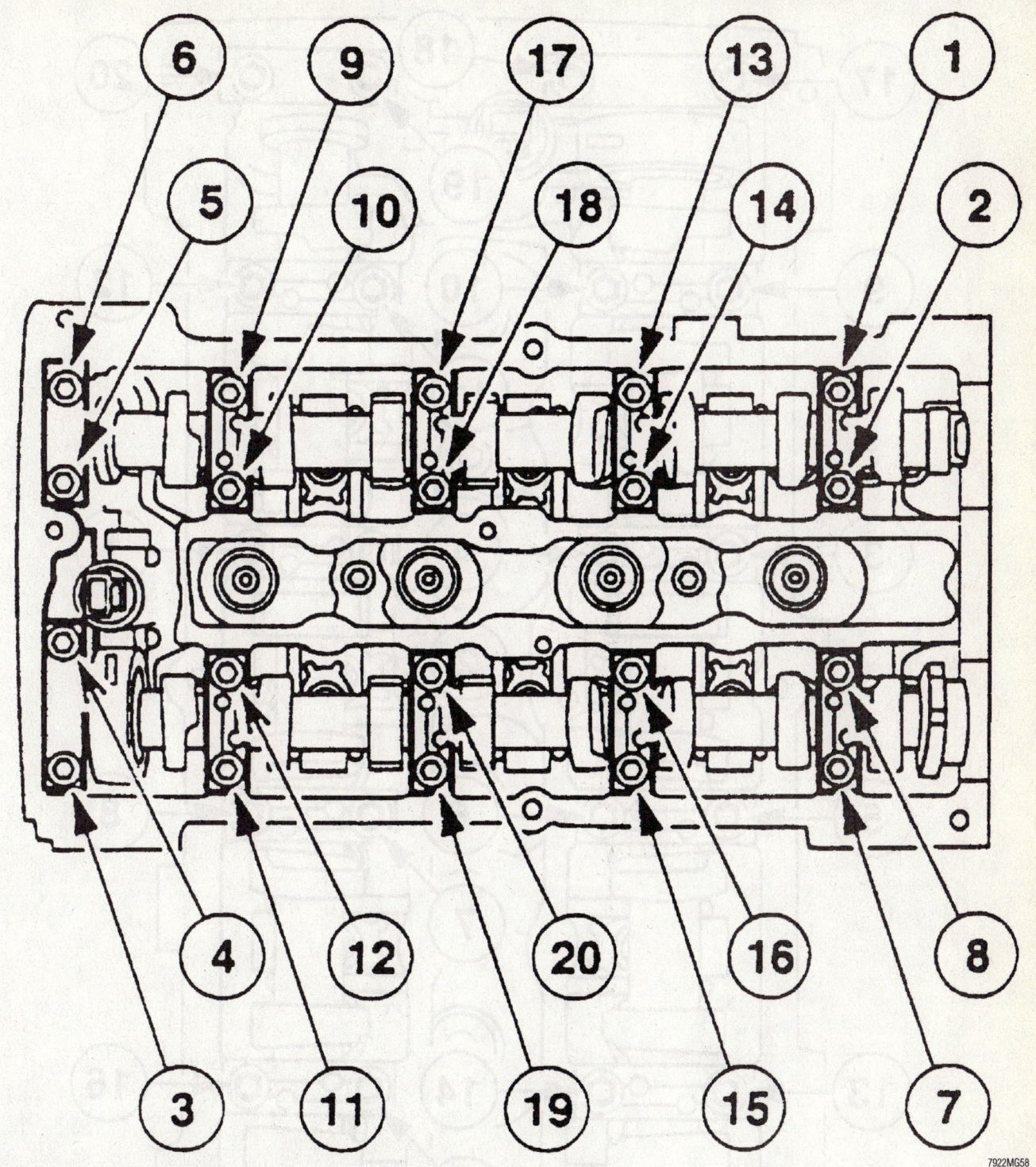

Loosen the camshaft journal caps in several passes in this sequence—2.0L Zetec engine

7922MG58

11. Inspect the oil control solenoid flange O-rings for damage or wear and replace as necessary.
- Oil control solenoid flange and tighten the bolts to 84–92 inch lbs. (9.5–10.5 Nm) in the sequence illustrated

12. Rotate the camshafts a full turn and check for binding.
- Camshaft sprockets and timing belt
- Valve cover

Timing belt service is covered in Section 4 of this manual

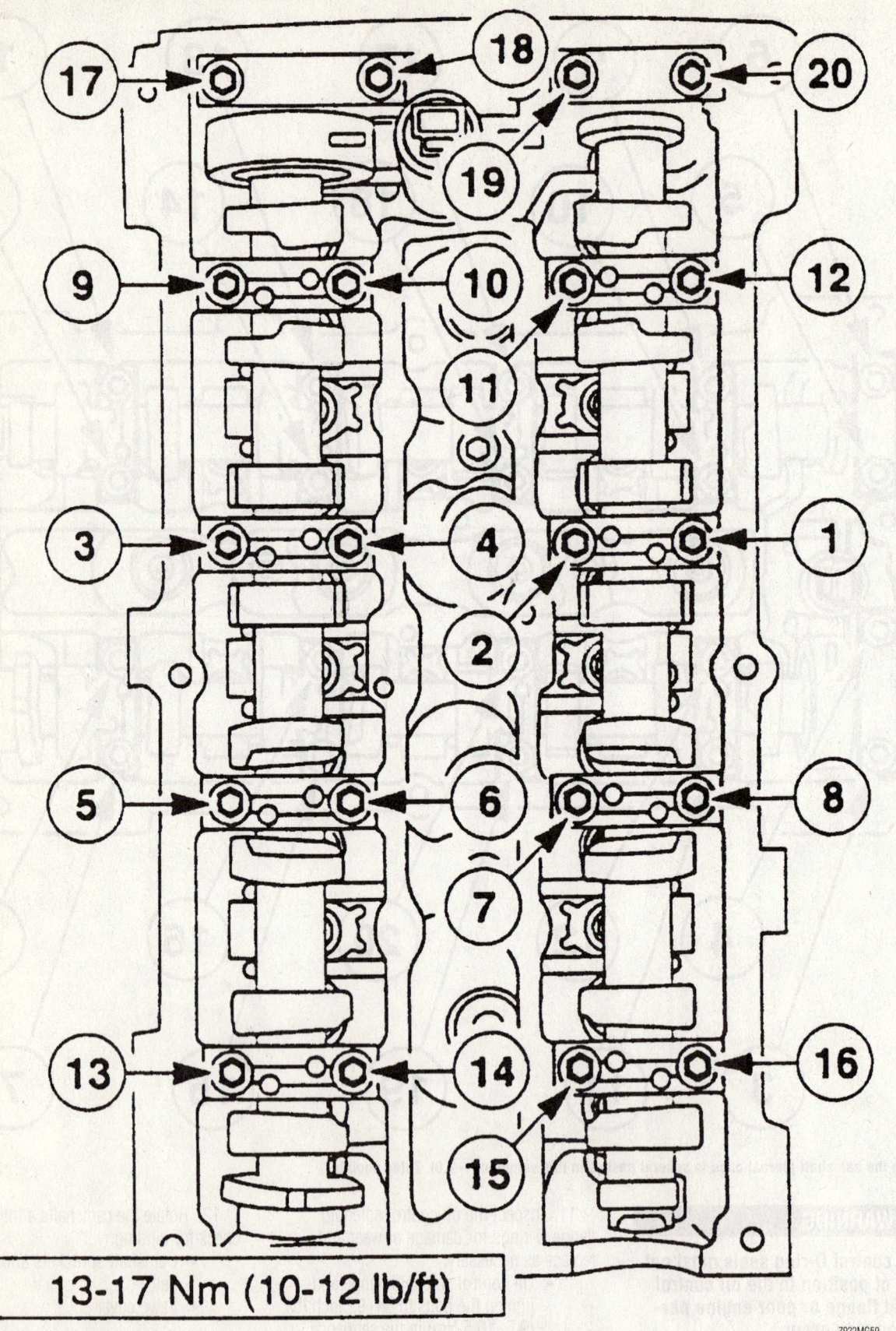

13-17 Nm (10-12 lb/ft)

7922MG59

Tighten the camshaft journal caps in the sequence illustrated to the proper specification—2.0L Zetec engine

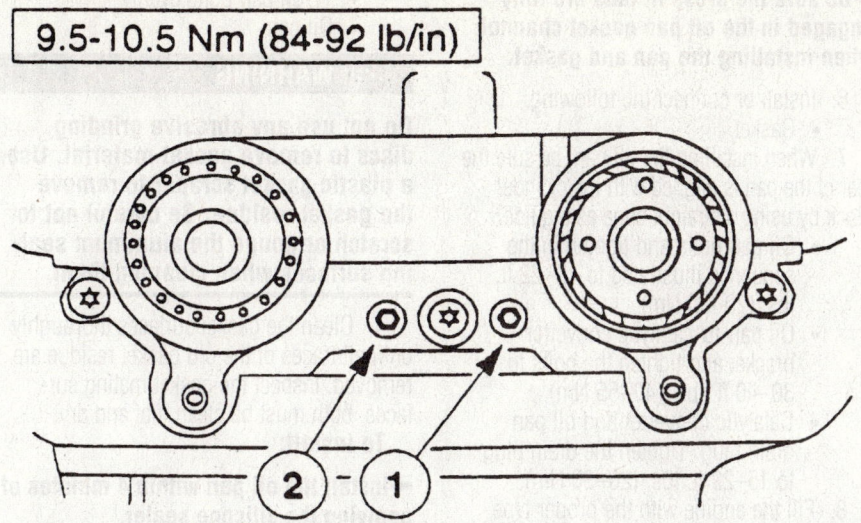

9.5-10.5 Nm (84-92 lb/in)

Tighten the oil control solenoid flange bolts in this sequence—2.0L Zetec engine

7922MG60

Valve Lash

ADJUSTMENT

2.0L DOHC Zetec Engine

1. Before servicing the vehicle, refer to the precautions in the beginning of this section.
2. Remove the valve cover.
3. Remove the timing belt.

➡**Measure each valve's clearance at the base circle before removing the camshafts. The shims are not serviceable with the camshafts in place. Failure to measure all valve clearances prior to removing the camshafts, will result in repeated camshaft removal and installation and a lot of wasted time.**

4. Measure the valve clearances, then remove the camshafts and shims.

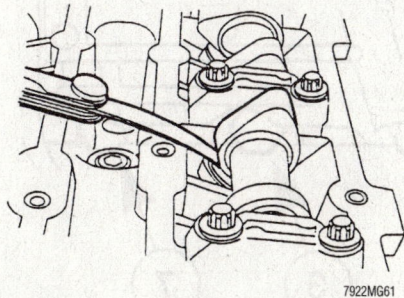

7922MG61

Measure each valve's clearance at the base circle before removing the camshafts—2.0L Zetec DOHC engine

➡**The shims are marked for thickness. For example: 2.2mm = 222 on shim.**

The correct shims allow the following valve clearances:
- Intake valve clearance: 0.0043–0.0071 in. (0.11–0.18mm)
- Exhaust valve clearance: 0.0106–0.0134 in. (0.27–0.34mm)

➡**A midrange clearance is the most desirable.**

The midrange clearances should be as follows:
- Intake valve clearance: 0.006 in. (0.15mm)
- Exhaust valve clearance: 0.012 in. (0.3mm)

5. Select the shims using the following

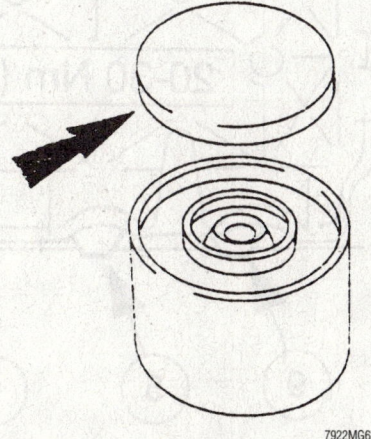

7922MG62

Example of a valve lifter shim (arrow)—2.0L Zetec DOHC engine

formula: shim thickness = measured clearance plus the base shim thickness minus the most desirable thickness.

6. Select the correct shims and mark their installation location (where they are going).
7. Replace the shims and install the camshafts.
8. Check the new valve clearances.
9. Install the timing belt and covers.
10. Install the valve cover.
11. Start the vehicle and check for proper operation.

Starter Motor

REMOVAL & INSTALLATION

2.0L Engines

SOHC ENGINES

1. Before servicing the vehicle, refer to the precautions in the beginning of this section.
2. Remove or disconnect the following:
- Negative battery cable
- Air cleaner outlet tube
- Two top starter motor bolts

➡**A protective cap is covering the B terminal and must be replaced after servicing the starter motor or solenoid.**

- S terminal wire and the B terminal nut and cable from the solenoid
- Lower starter motor bolt
- Starter

To install:
3. Install or connect the following:
- Starter motor assembly and tighten the lower mounting bolt to 18–20 ft. lbs. (25–27 Nm)
- S terminal wire, B terminal cable and nut. Tighten the nut to 80–120 inch lbs. (9–13.5 Nm).
- Top starter motor bolts. Tighten the bolts to 18–20 ft. lbs. (25–27 Nm).
- Air cleaner outlet tube
- Negative battery cable

DOHC ENGINES

1. Before servicing the vehicle, refer to the precautions in the beginning of this section.
2. Remove or disconnect the following:

- Negative battery cable
- Air cleaner outlet tube
- Lower starter motor bolt
- Two starter motor upper bolts

3. Slide the starter motor from its mounting until you can gain access to the wiring.
- Nuts and remove the integral connector
- Starter motor

To install:

4. Install or connect the following:
- Integral connector and tighten the retaining nuts to 61 inch lbs. (7 Nm)
- Starter motor to its mounting
- Two starter motor upper bolts and tighten to 15–20 ft. lbs. (20–27 Nm)
- Lower starter motor bolt and tighten to 15–20 ft. lbs. (20–27 Nm)
- Air cleaner outlet tube
- Negative battery cable

Oil Pan

REMOVAL & INSTALLATION

2.0L Engine

SOHC SPLIT PORT INJECTION (SPI)

1. Before servicing the vehicle, refer to the precautions in the beginning of this section.
2. Remove or disconnect the following:
- Catalytic converter
3. Drain the engine oil.
- Oil pan-to-catalytic converter bracket bolts and the bracket
- 10 oil pan bolts evenly
- Oil pan and gasket. Discard the old gasket.

✳✳ WARNING

Do not use any abrasive grinding discs to remove gasket material. Use a plastic manual gasket scraper to remove the gasket residue. Be careful not to scratch or gouge the aluminum sealing surfaces when cleaning them.

4. Clean the gasket surfaces thoroughly until all traces of the old gasket residue are removed. Inspect the gasket mating surfaces, both must be clean, flat and dry.

To install:

➡**Install the oil pan within 10 minutes of applying the silicone sealer.**

5. Apply a 0.125 in. (3.0mm) wide bead of silicone sealant F6AZ-19562-AA or its equivalent at the oil pump-to-cylinder block joints and the crankshaft rear oil seal retainer-to-cylinder block joints.

➡**Be sure the press fit tabs are fully engaged in the oil pan gasket channel when installing the pan and gasket.**

6. Install or connect the following:
- Gasket

7. When installing the oil pan, be sure the rear of the pan is aligned with the cylinder block by using a straight edge as a guide.
- Oil pan bolts and tighten in the sequence illustrated to 15–22 ft. lbs. (20–30 Nm)
- Oil pan-to-catalytic converter bracket and tighten the bolts to 30–40 ft. lbs. (40–55 Nm)
- Catalytic converter and oil pan drain plug. Tighten the drain plug to 15–22 ft. lbs. (20–30 Nm).

8. Fill the engine with the proper type and quantity of engine oil.

9. Start the vehicle and check for oil leaks.

DOHC ZETEC

1. Before servicing the vehicle, refer to the precautions in the beginning of this section.

2. Drain the engine oil.

3. Remove or disconnect the following:
- Catalytic converter

- 17 oil pan bolts evenly
- Oil pan

✳✳ WARNING

Do not use any abrasive grinding discs to remove gasket material. Use a plastic gasket scraper to remove the gasket residue. Be careful not to scratch or gouge the aluminum sealing surfaces when cleaning them.

4. Clean the gasket surfaces thoroughly until all traces of the old gasket residue are removed. Inspect the gasket mating surfaces, both must be clean, flat and dry.

To install:

➡**Install the oil pan within 4 minutes of applying the silicone sealer.**

5. Apply a 0.1 in. (3.0mm) wide bead of silicone sealant F6AZ-19562-AA or its equivalent to the oil pan.

6. Install or connect the following:
- Oil pan and the bolts. Tighten the oil pan bolts in the sequence illustrated to 15–22 ft. lbs. (20–30 Nm).
- Oil pan drain plug

7. Fill the engine with the proper type and quantity of engine oil.

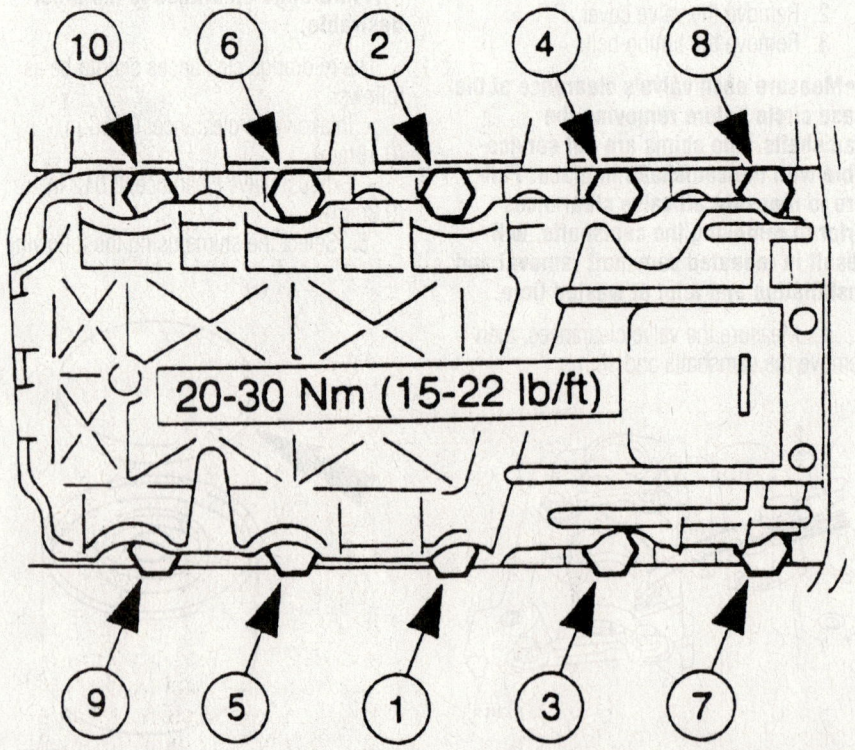

20-30 Nm (15-22 lb/ft)

Tighten the oil pan bolts in this sequence to the proper specification—2.0L SOHC engine

7922MG68

3. Clean the gasket surfaces thoroughly until all traces of the old gasket residue are removed. Inspect the gasket mating surfaces, both must be clean, flat and dry.

4. Lubricate the crankshaft front oil seal lip with clean engine oil.

➡ **When the oil pan bolts are tightened, the oil pump-to-cylinder block gasket must be below the cylinder block sealing surface.**

5. Install or connect the following:
   • Pump gasket and the pump
   • Oil pump and tighten the bolts to 10–12 ft. lbs. (13–16 Nm)
   • Oil pump screen cover and tube. Tighten the retaining bolts to 71–97 inch lbs. (8–11 Nm).
   • CKP sensor electrical connection
   • Oil pan
   • Timing belt

6. Fill the engine with the proper type and quantity of engine oil.

7. Start the vehicle and check for oil leaks.

DOHC ZETEC

➡ **Refer to the illustration located in the water pump procedure, earlier in this section, for a view of the oil pump on this engine.**

1. Before servicing the vehicle, refer to the precautions in the beginning of this section.

2. Remove or disconnect the following:
   • Timing covers and belt
   • Crankshaft pulley, sprocket and the timing chain guide
   • Oil pan
   • Oil pump cover and screen bolts
   • Cover and screen
   • Lower cylinder block shims, if necessary
   • Lower cylinder block, the gasket and the crankshaft front oil seal, if necessary
   • Oil pump retaining bolts
   • Oil pump and gasket

To install:

※※ **WARNING**

Do not use any abrasive grinding discs to remove gasket material. Use a plastic manual gasket scraper to remove the gasket residue. Be careful not to scratch or gouge the aluminum sealing surfaces when cleaning them.

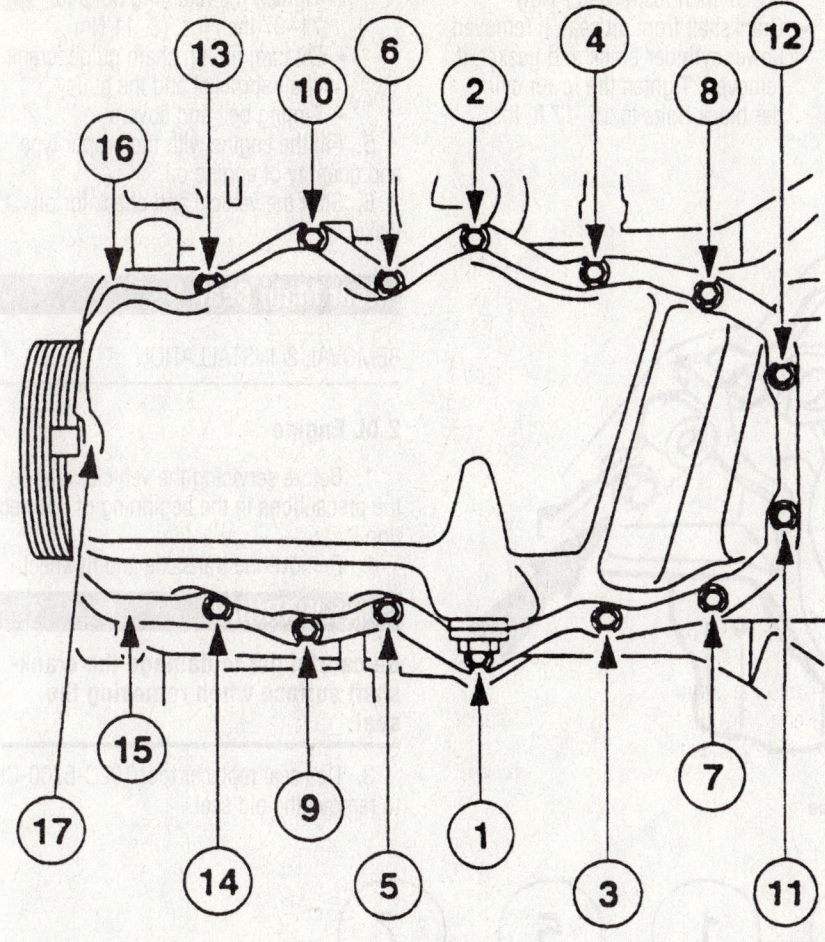

20-30 Nm (15-22 lb/ft)

7922MG69

Tighten the oil pan bolts in the proper sequence to the correct torque specification—2.0L Zetec engine

8. Start the vehicle and check for oil leaks.

Oil Pump

REMOVAL & INSTALLATION

2.0L Engine

SOHC SPLIT PORT INJECTION (SPI)

➡ Refer to the illustration located in the water pump procedure, earlier in this section, for a view of the oil pump on this engine.

1. Before servicing the vehicle, refer to the precautions in the beginning of this section.

2. Remove or disconnect the following:
   • Timing belt

   • Oil pan
   • Crankshaft Position (CKP) sensor electrical connection
   • Oil pump screen cover and tube bolts
   • Cover and tube
   • 6 oil pump retaining bolts
   • Oil pump and gasket. Discard the gasket.

To install:

※※ **WARNING**

Do not use any abrasive grinding discs to remove gasket material. Use a plastic manual gasket scraper to remove the gasket residue. Be careful not to scratch or gouge the aluminum sealing surfaces when cleaning them.

Refer to Section 1 for engine rebuilding specifications

3. Clean the gasket surfaces thoroughly until all traces of the old gasket residue are removed. Inspect the gasket mating surfaces, both must be clean, flat and dry.

➥**The clearance between the lower cylinder block sealing surfaces on the oil pump and the cylinder block cannot exceed 0.012–0.031 in. (0.3–0.8mm).**

4. Install or connect the following:
- New oil pump gasket and the pump
- Oil pump bolts and tighten to 88–97 inch lbs. (10–11 Nm)
- Crankshaft front oil seal, if removed
- Lower cylinder block and gasket, if removed. Tighten the lower cylinder block bolts to 15–17 ft. lbs.

(20–24 Nm) in the sequence illustrated.
- Oil pump screen cover and tube. Tighten the retaining bolts to 71–97 inch lbs. (8–11 Nm).
- Oil pan, timing chain guide, crankshaft sprocket and the pulley
- Timing belt and covers

5. Fill the engine with the proper type and quantity of engine oil.
6. Start the vehicle and check for oil leaks.

Rear Main Seal

REMOVAL & INSTALLATION

2.0L Engine

1. Before servicing the vehicle, refer to the precautions in the beginning of this section.
2. Remove the transaxle and flywheel.

✴✴ WARNING

Be careful not to damage the crankshaft surface when removing the seal.

3. Use seal replacer tool T92C-6700-Ch, to remove the old seal.

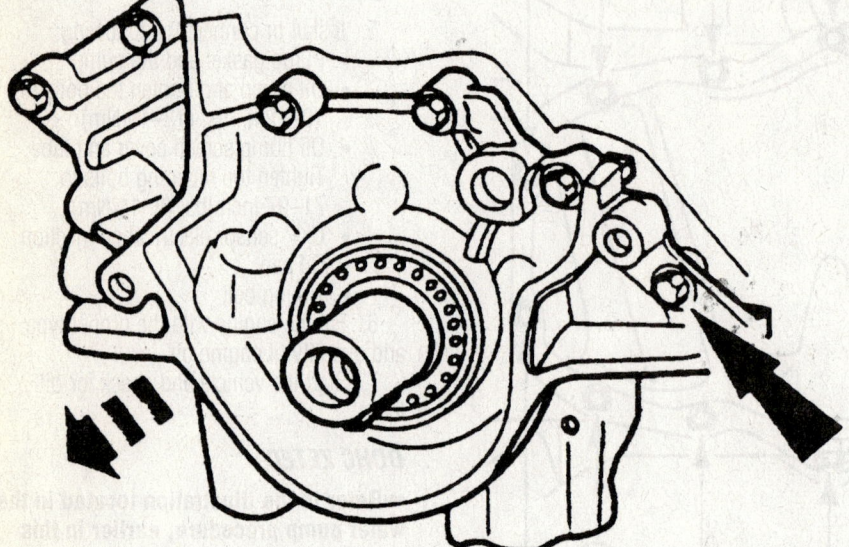

Remove the oil pump mounting bolts—2.0L Zetec engine

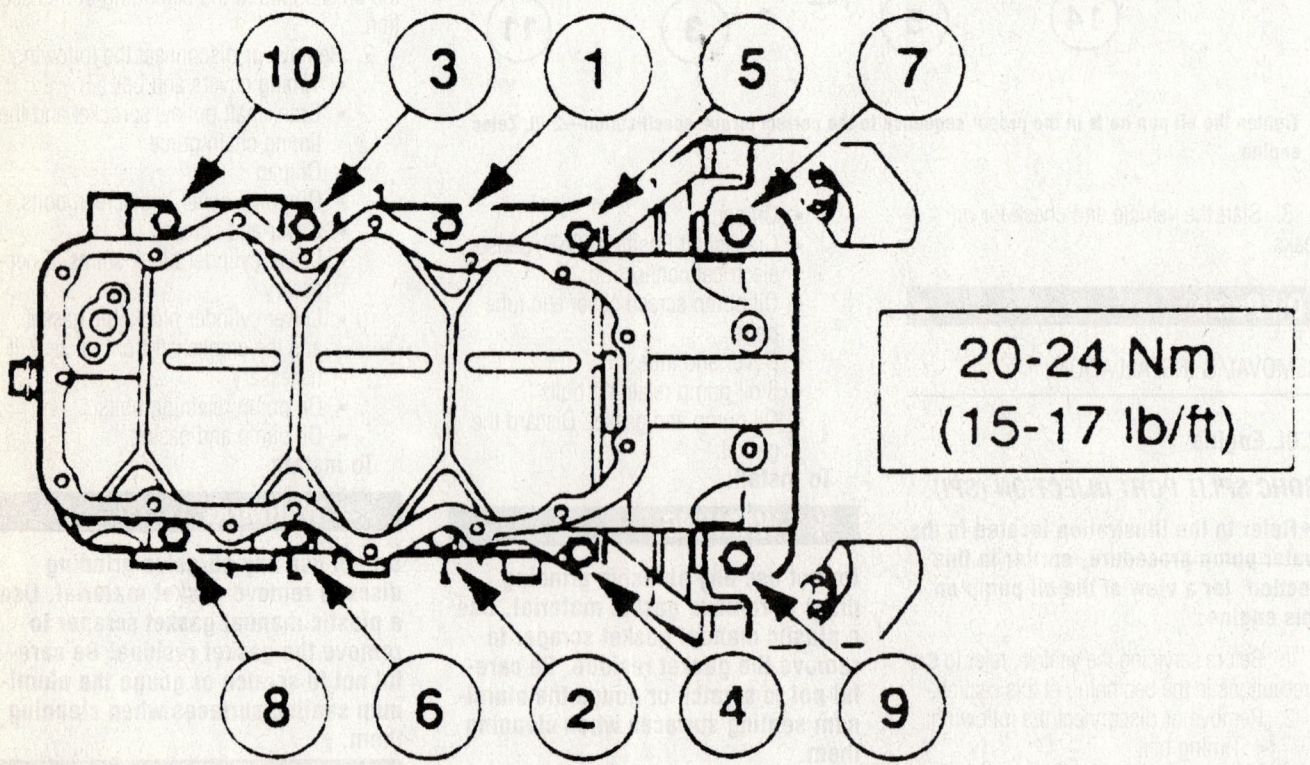

20-24 Nm
(15-17 lb/ft)

Tighten the lower cylinder block bolts in the sequence illustrated to the proper torque specification—2.0L Zetec engine

To install:

Coat the lip of the new seal with clean 5W30 engine oil.

➡ **Be sure the crankshaft rear oil seal is on correctly and that the edges are not rolled over.**

4. Install the new seal using crankshaft rear seal pilot tool T88P-6701-B2 and Rear seal replacer tool T88P-6701-B1.

5. Install the flywheel and the transaxle.

Piston and Ring

POSITIONING

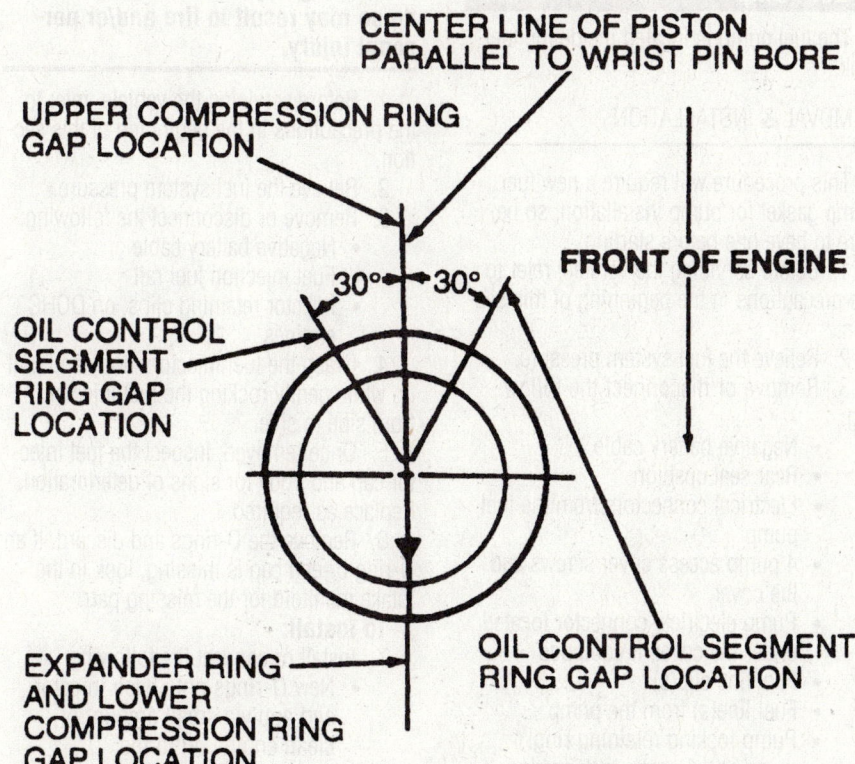

Ford 2.0L (VIN 3 and P) engines—piston ring positioning, end-gap spacing and piston positioning. The small directional arrow must face the front of the engine.

7922AG29

FUEL SYSTEM

Fuel System Service Precautions

Safety is the most important factor when performing not only fuel system maintenance but any type of maintenance. Failure to conduct maintenance and repairs in a safe manner may result in serious personal injury or death. Maintenance and testing of the vehicle's fuel system components can be accomplished safely and effectively by adhering to the following rules and guidelines.

• To avoid the possibility of fire and personal injury, always disconnect the negative battery cable unless the repair or test procedure requires that battery voltage be applied.

• Always relieve the fuel system pressure prior to disconnecting any fuel system component (injector, fuel rail, pressure regulator, etc.), fitting or fuel line connection. Exercise extreme caution whenever relieving fuel system pressure, to avoid exposing skin, face and eyes to fuel spray. Please be advised that fuel under pressure may penetrate the skin or any part of the body that it contacts.

• Always place a shop towel or cloth around the fitting or connection prior to loosening to absorb any excess fuel due to spillage. Ensure that all fuel spillage (should it occur) is quickly removed from engine surfaces. Ensure that all fuel soaked cloths or towels are deposited into a suitable waste container.

• Always keep a dry chemical (Class B) fire extinguisher near the work area.

• Do not allow fuel spray or fuel vapors to come into contact with a spark or open flame.

• Always use a back-up wrench when loosening and tightening fuel line connection fittings. This will prevent unnecessary stress and torsion to fuel line piping.

• Always replace worn fuel fitting O-rings with new. Do not substitute fuel hose or equivalent, where fuel pipe is installed.

Fuel System Pressure

RELIEVING

1. Before servicing the vehicle, refer to the precautions in the beginning of this section.

2. Remove the Schrader valve cap at the end of the fuel rail and attach a fuel pressure gauge.

3. Open the manual relief valve on the fuel pressure gauge slowly to relive the fuel pressure

Fuel Filter

REMOVAL & INSTALLATION

The inline fuel filter is located in the engine compartment between the fuel tank and the fuel rail.

1. Before servicing the vehicle, refer to the precautions in the beginning of this section.

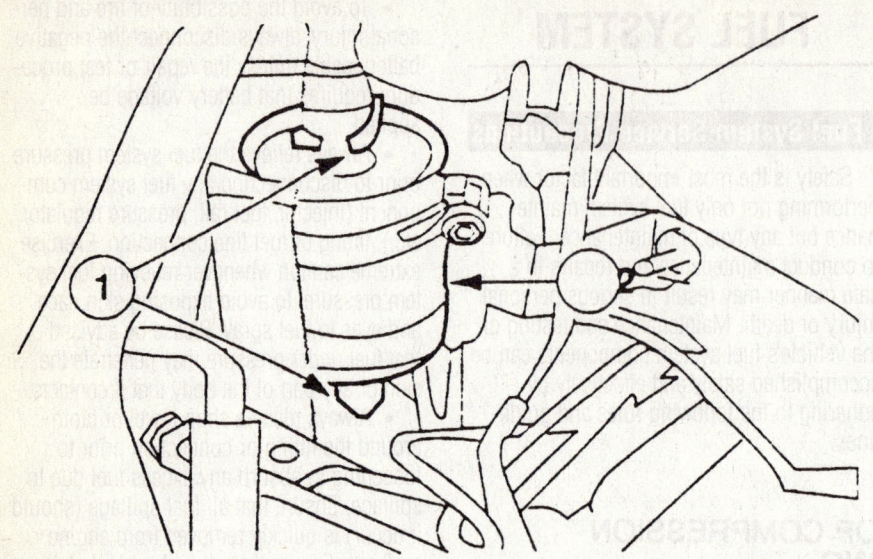

Detach the upper and lower hose clips before disconnecting hoses (1) from the fuel filter

2. Properly relieve the fuel system pressure.

3. Disconnect the negative battery cable.

4. Position a suitable container below the fuel filter to collect any excess fuel that may leak from the filter and lines.

5. Remove or disconnect the following:
- Fuel filter mounting clamp, loosen only
- Filter from the mounting bracket
- Retaining clips from the upper fuel filter hose
- Upper hose from the fuel filter and drain any excess fuel into the container. Plug the hose.
- Retaining clip from the fuel filter lower hose
- Lower hose from the fuel filter and drain any excess fuel into the container. Plug the hose.
- Fuel filter

To install:

6. Remove the plugs from the lower and upper hoses.

7. Install or connect the following:
- Lower hose to the filter
- Hose retaining clip
- Upper hose to the filter
- Hose retaining clip
- Fuel filter and tighten the filter mounting clamp
- negative battery cable

8. Start the engine and check for leaks.

➡**On newer model vehicles when the battery is disconnected it may cause some abnormal drive symptoms until** the Powertrain Control Module (PCM) **relearns its adaptive strategy. The vehicle may need to be driven 10 miles (16 km) or more for the PCM to relearn its strategy.**

Fuel Pump

The fuel pump is located inside the fuel tank.

REMOVAL & INSTALLATION

This procedure will require a new fuel pump gasket for pump installation, so be sure to have one before starting.

1. Before servicing the vehicle, refer to the precautions in the beginning of this section.

2. Relieve the fuel system pressure.

3. Remove or disconnect the following:

- Negative battery cable
- Rear seat cushion
- Electrical connectors from the fuel pump
- 4 pump access cover screws and the cover
- Pump electrical connector located under the cover, if equipped
- Fuel line clip(s)
- Fuel line(s) from the pump
- Pump locking retaining ring., using a fuel pump locking ring removal tool or a brass drift and a hammer
- Fuel pump and the gasket from the tank

To install:

4. Install or connect the following:
- New gasket and place the pump into position in the tank
- Pump locking retaining ring
- Fuel line(s) to the pump
-
- Line retaining clip(s)
- Fuel pump electrical connection(s), if equipped
- Access cover and tighten the retainers
- Pump electrical connector(s)
- Rear seat cushion
- Negative battery cable

5. Start the vehicle and check for proper operation.

Fuel Injector

REMOVAL & INSTALLATION

✳✳ CAUTION

Fuel injection systems remain under pressure, even after the engine has been turned OFF. The fuel system pressure must be relieved before disconnecting any fuel lines. Failure to do so may result in fire and/or personal injury.

1. Before servicing the vehicle, refer to the precautions in the beginning of this section.

2. Relieve the fuel system pressure.

3. Remove or disconnect the following:
- Negative battery cable
- Fuel injection fuel rail
- Injector retaining clips, on DOHC engines

4. Grasp the fuel injectors body and pull up while gently rocking the fuel injector from side to side.

5. Once removed, inspect the fuel injector cap and body for signs of deterioration. Replace as required.

6. Remove the O-rings and discard. If an O-ring or end cap is missing, look in the intake manifold for the missing part.

To install:

7. Install or connect the following:
- New O-rings onto each injector and apply a small amount of clean engine oil to the O-rings
- Injectors using a slight twisting downward motion
- Injector retaining clips, on DOHC engines

7922MG79

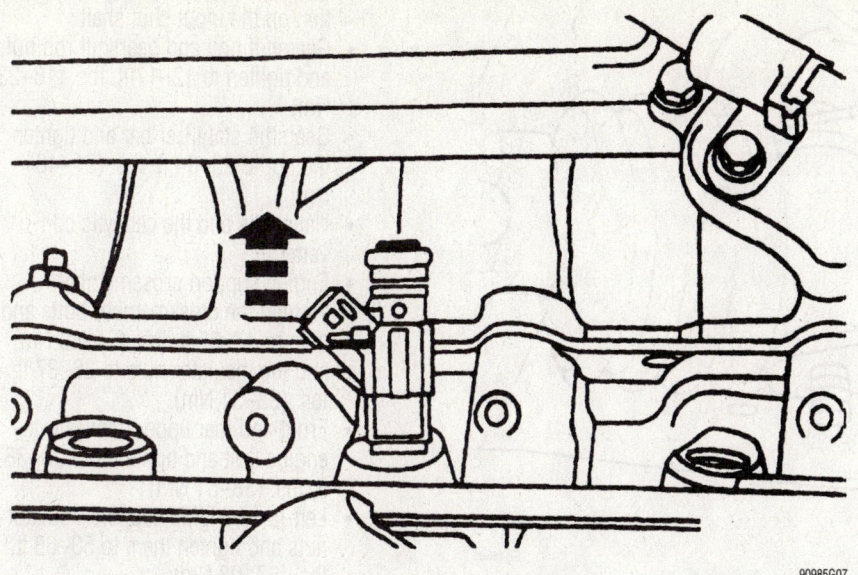

90985G07

Grasp the fuel injector's body and pull upward, while gently rocking the fuel injector from side to side

- Fuel injection fuel rail
- Negative battery cable

8. Run the engine at idle for 2 minutes, then turn the engine **OFF** and check for fuel leaks and proper operation.

DRIVE TRAIN

Transaxle Assembly

REMOVAL & INSTALLATION

Manual

1. Before servicing the vehicle, refer to the precautions in the beginning of this section.
2. Remove or disconnect the following:
   - Both battery cables, negative cable first
   - Battery and tray
   - Engine air cleaner outlet tube
   - Constant Control Relay Module (CCRM) electrical connection, loosen its retainers and remove the module and bracket as an assembly (if necessary)
   - Slave cylinder line from the slave cylinder hose and plug the hose

- Slave cylinder line retaining clip
- Slave cylinder line from the bracket
- Heated Oxygen (HO$_2$S) sensor electrical connection
- Back-up light electrical connection
- Electrical connector bracket bolt and the bracket
- Vehicle Speed Sensor (VSS) electrical connection

- Halfshafts

3. Install Engine Support Bar D88–6000A, and attach it to the engine lifting eyes with suitable chains or cables.
   - Insulator nuts from the left-hand engine support bracket
   - Front and rear upper transaxle-to-engine bolts

4. Drain the transaxle fluid and install the drain plug.
   - Air conditioning line from the retainer located on the engine support crossmember
   - Engine support crossmember bolts and nuts
   - Crossmember
   - Gearshift stabilizer bar-to-transaxle nut
   - Stabilizer bar and support from the transaxle
   - Transaxle gearshift rod nut
   - Transaxle gearshift bolt
   - Gearshift rod and clevis pin from the input shift shaft
   - Starter motor
   - Lower slave cylinder tube and the slave cylinder
   - Lower transaxle-to-engine bolts

5. Position and secure a suitable transaxle jack under the transaxle.
   - Catalytic converter
   - Middle transaxle-to-engine bolts
   - Transaxle from the vehicle

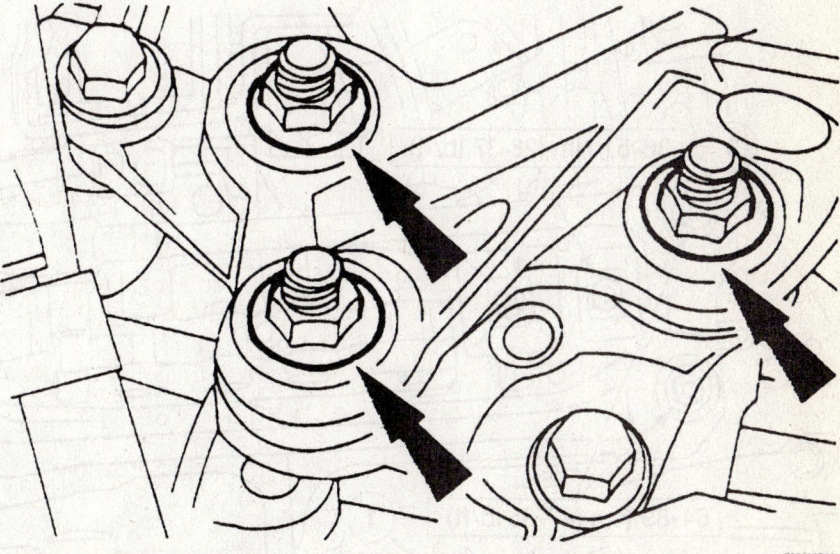

7922MG83

Location of the left-hand engine support bracket nuts—2.0L engines

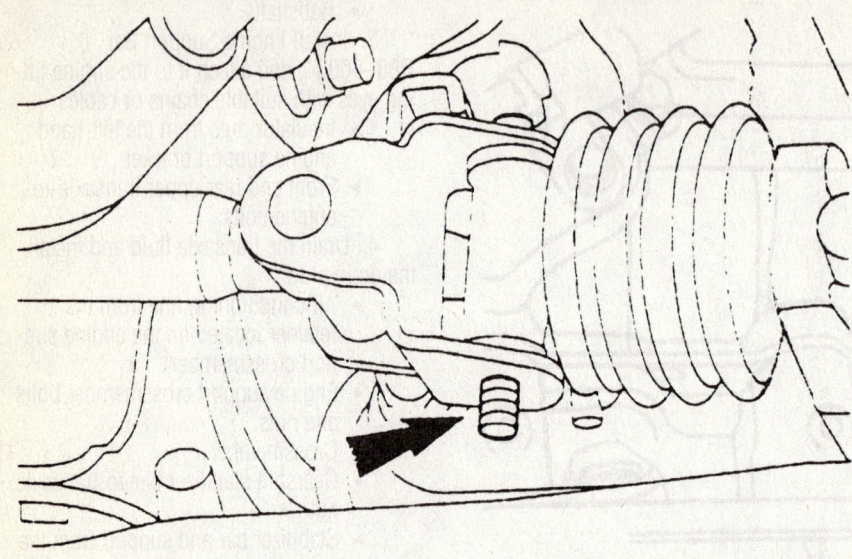

Loosen the transaxle gearshift bolt and remove the gearshift rod and clevis pin from the input shift shaft

To install:

6. Apply a thin coating of suitable grease to the spline of the input shaft.

7. Place the transaxle onto a suitable transaxle jack. Be sure the transaxle is secure.

8. Install or connect the following:

- Transaxle
- Middle transaxle-to-engine bolts and tighten them to 23–38 ft. lbs. (38–51 Nm)

- Lower engine-to-transaxle bolts and tighten them to 23–38 ft. lbs. (38–51 Nm)
- clutch slave cylinder and tighten the nuts to 12–17 ft. lbs. (16–23 Nm)
- Lower slave cylinder tube and tighten the fitting to 10–16 ft. lbs. (13–21 Nm)
- Starter motor

- Gearshift rod and clevis into position on the input shift shaft
- Gearshift bolt and gearshift rod nut and tighten to 12–17 ft. lbs. (16–23 Nm)
- Gearshift stabilizer bar and tighten the nut to 23–34 ft. lbs. (31–46 Nm)
- Halfshafts and the catalytic converter
- Engine support crossmember. Tighten the crossmember bolts and nuts to 47–65 ft. lbs. (64–89 Nm) and the insulator nuts to 28–37 ft. lbs. (38–51 Nm).
- Front and rear upper transaxle-to-engine bolt and tighten it to 28–38 ft. lbs. (38–51 Nm)
- Left-hand engine support insulator nuts and tighten them to 50–68 ft. lbs. (67–93 Nm)

9. Remove the engine support bar.

- Electrical connector support bracket
- all the electrical connector
- Slave cylinder line to the slave cylinder hose and attach the retaining clip. Tighten the fitting to 10–16 ft. lbs. (13–21 Nm).

10. Bleed the clutch hydraulic system.

11. Add the proper type and amount of fluid to the transaxle.

12. Install or connect the following:

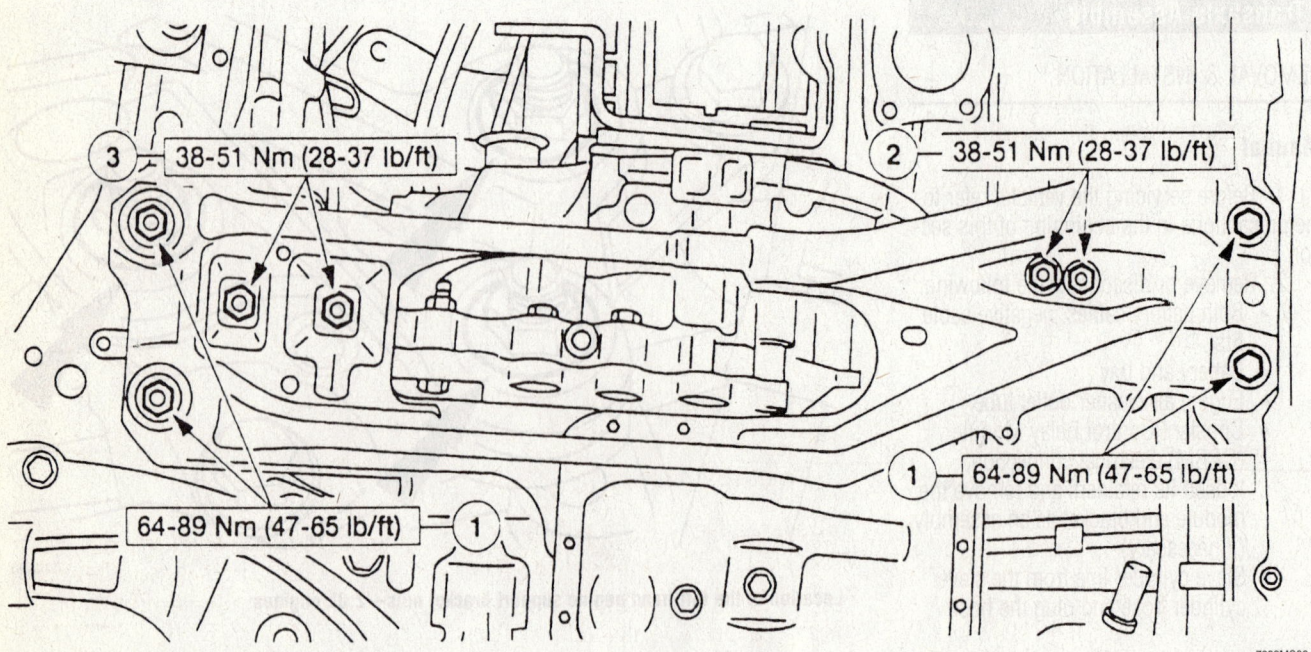

Install the engine support crossmember and tighten the retainers to specification

- CCRM and bracket assembly, if removed
- CCRM retainers and attach the electrical connection
- Engine air cleaner tube
- Battery tray and the batter
- Battery cables, negative cable last

13. Check for fluid leaks and proper clutch operation.

14. Road test the vehicle and check for proper transaxle operation.

Automatic

1. Before servicing the vehicle, refer to the precautions in the beginning of this section.

2. Remove or disconnect the following:

- Battery cables, negative cable first
- Battery and tray
- Engine air cleaner assembly
- Computer Control Relay Module (CCRM) electrical connections, relay retainers, the relay and bracket from the engine
- Shift control cable and bracket retaining nut from the manual shift lever
- Shift cable and bracket clip, then set the bracket and cable assembly aside
- All electrical connections from the transaxle
- Starter motor
- Throttle valve actuating cable bolts and disconnect the cable from the throttle cam, if equipped

3. Install Engine Support D88L-6000-A, to the engine. The engine must be properly supported for transaxle removal.

4. Place a suitable drain pan under the transaxle.

5. Remove or disconnect the following:

- Transaxle cooler lines at the transaxle
- Left-hand engine mount bolts and the mount
- Upper transaxle housing bolts
- Left-hand splash shields, if equipped
- Transaxle plug and drain the fluid
- Halfshafts. Install 2 transaxle plugs T88C-7025-AH, into the differential side gears

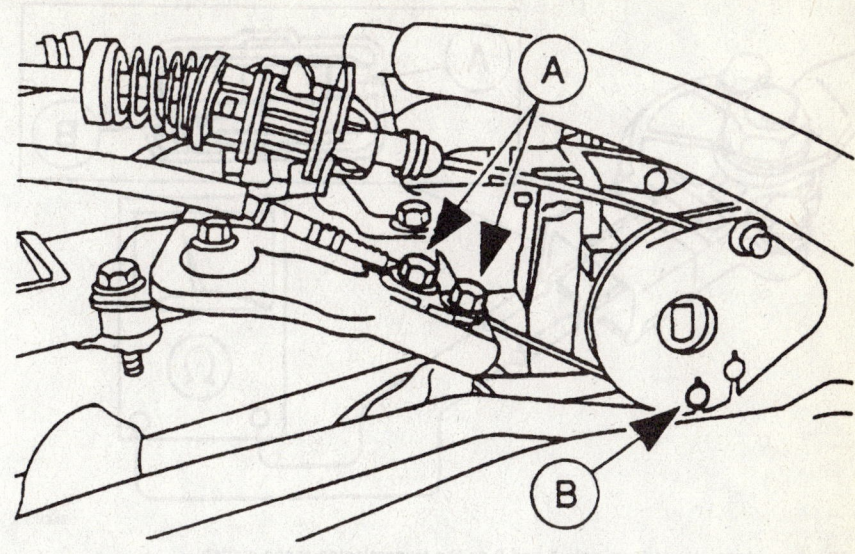

Connect the throttle valve cable at the throttle cam (B) and tighten the cable retaining bolts (A)

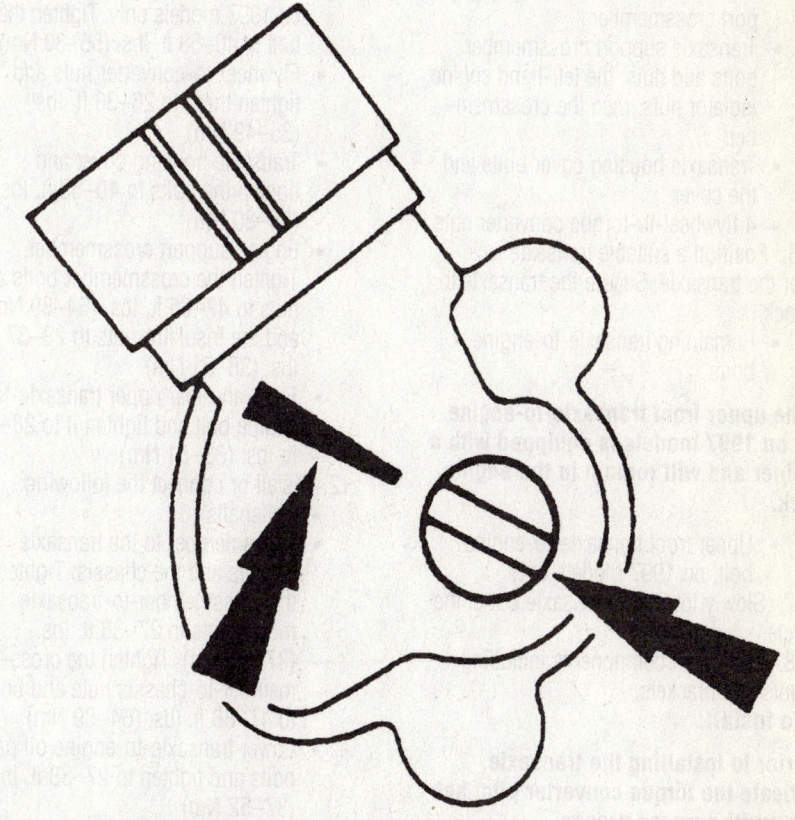

Align the marks on the MLP switch and the manual control lever as shown

⁂ WARNING

Failure to install the transaxle plugs may cause the differential side gears to become improperly positioned. If the gears become misaligned, the differential will have to be removed from the transaxle to align them.

- Engine support crossmember and the catalytic converter

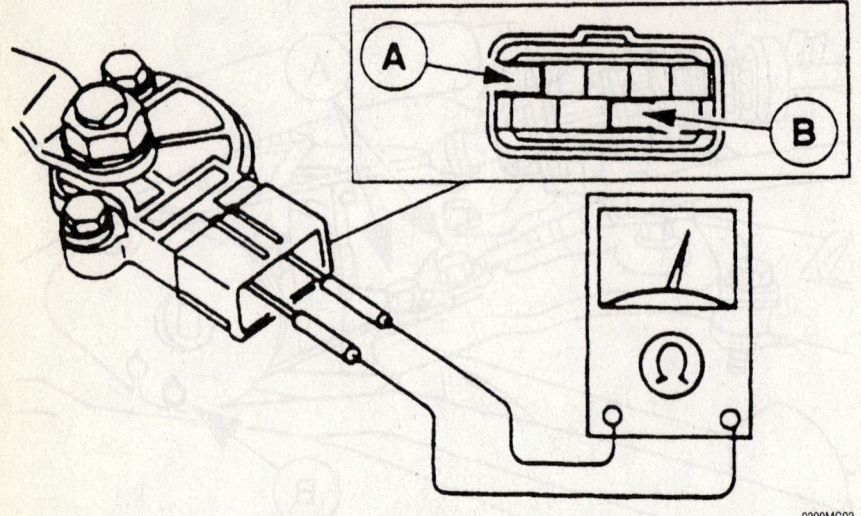

9300MG03

Attach an ohmmeter to terminals A and B on the transmission range switch

- Air conditioning line from the retainer located on the engine support crossmember
- Transaxle support crossmember bolts and nuts, the left-hand engine isolator nuts, then the crossmember
- Transaxle housing cover bolts and the cover
- 4 flywheel-to-torque converter nuts

6. Position a suitable transaxle jack under the transaxle. Secure the transaxle to the jack.

- Remaining transaxle-to-engine bolts

➡ **The upper front transaxle-to-engine bolt on 1997 models is equipped with a retainer and will remain in the engine block.**

- Upper front transaxle-to-engine bolt, on 1997 models only

7. Slowly lower the transaxle out of the vehicle.

8. Inspect all components including mounts and brackets.

To install:

➡ **Prior to installing the transaxle, lubricate the torque converter pilot hub with multi-purpose grease.**

9. Align the torque converter studs to the flywheel.

10. Secure the transaxle on the transaxle jack.

11. Install or connect the following:
- Transaxle into position
- Middle and lower transaxle-to-engine bolts. Tighten the bolts to 40–58 ft. lbs. (55–80 Nm).
- Upper front transaxle-to-engine bolt, on 1997 models only. Tighten the bolt to 40–58 ft. lbs. (55–80 Nm).
- Flywheel-to-converter nuts and tighten them to 26–36 ft. lbs. (35–49 Nm)
- Transaxle housing cover and tighten the bolts to 40–58 ft. lbs. (55–80 Nm)
- Engine support crossmember. Tighten the crossmember bolts and nuts to 47–65 ft. lbs. (64–89 Nm) and the insulator nuts to 28–37 ft. lbs. (38–51 Nm).
- Front and rear upper transaxle-to-engine bolt and tighten it to 28–38 ft. lbs. (38–51 Nm)

12. Install or connect the following:
- Halfshafts
- Crossmember to the transaxle mounts and the chassis. Tighten the crossmember-to-transaxle mount nuts to 27–38 ft. lbs. (37–52 Nm). Tighten the crossmember-to-chassis nuts and bolts to 47–66 ft. lbs. (64–89 Nm).
- Lower transaxle-to-engine oil pan bolts and tighten to 27–38 ft. lbs. (37–52 Nm)
- Engine/transaxle splash shields
- Starter motor
- All the electrical connections
- Upper transaxle-to-engine bolts and tighten to 40–58 ft. lbs. (55–80 Nm)
- Left-hand engine mount and tighten the nuts to 50–68 ft. lbs. (67–93 Nm)

- Throttle valve cable at the throttle cam, if equipped. Adjust the cable as necessary

13. Remove the engine support.
- Shift cable and bracket to the manual shift lever, the shift cable and bracket clip. Tighten the nut to 12–16 ft. lbs. (16–22 Nm).
- Engine air cleaner assembly. Adjust the cable as necessary.
- Battery tray and battery
- Both battery cables, negative cable last

14. Add the proper type and quantity of transaxle fluid.

15. Check the transaxle for leaks and for proper operation.

16. Check the MLP switch for proper adjustment, as follows:

   a. Shift the transaxle into NEUTRAL, then align the marks on the transmission range switch and the manual control lever.

   b. Install and finger-tighten the switch retaining bolts.

   c. Attach an ohmmeter between terminals **A** and **B** on the switch as shown in the accompanying illustration.

   d. Adjust the switch by rotating the switch housing on the manual control lever until there is no continuity between the terminals.

   e. Hold the switch in place, then tighten its retaining bolts to 70–95 inch lbs. (8–11 Nm).

   f. Remove the ohmmeter and attach the switch electrical connection.

   g. Place the manual control shift outer lever in position and tighten its retaining nut to 33–47 ft. lbs. (44–64 Nm).

17. Road test the vehicle and check for proper operation.

Clutch

ADJUSTMENT

Pedal Free-Play

1. Before servicing the vehicle, refer to the precautions in the beginning of this section.

2. Depress the clutch pedal until resistance can be felt, and measure the distance between the upper clutch height and where the resistance is felt. The free-play should be 0.0–0.40 in. (5.0–13.9mm).

3. If an adjustment is necessary, turn the locknut and equalizer bar-to-clutch release lever rod.

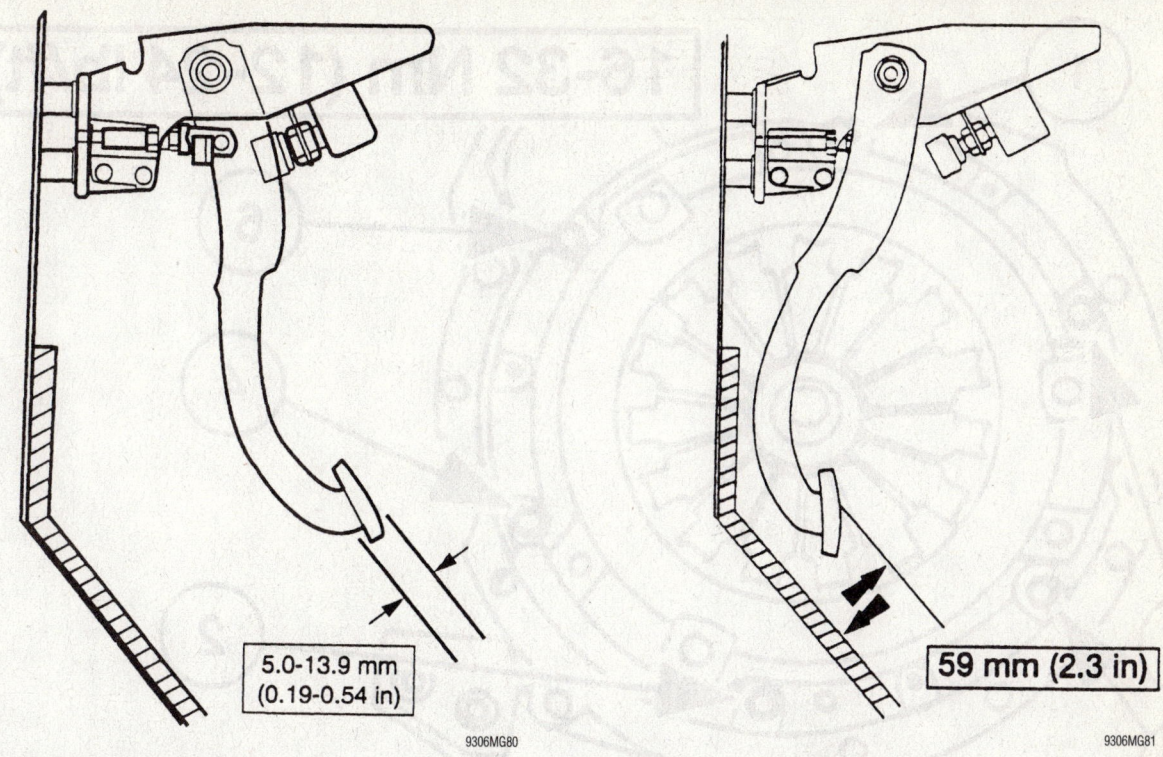

5.0-13.9 mm
(0.19-0.54 in)

9306MG80

Clutch pedal free play measurement

59 mm (2.3 in)

9306MG81

Clutch pedal free play adjustment

4. After adjustment, measure the disengagement height from the upper surface of the clutch pedal pad to the carpet. The distance should be 2.3 in. (59mm).

Pedal Height

1. Measure the distance from the upper surface of the pedal pad to the carpet. The measurement should be 8.35–8.54 in. (212–217mm).

2. If an adjustment is necessary, turn the locknut and the Clutch Pedal Position (CPP) switch until the pedal height is correct.

REMOVAL & INSTALLATION

1. Before servicing the vehicle, refer to the precautions in the beginning of this section.

2. Disconnect the negative battery cable.

3. Raise and safely support the vehicle.

4. Remove the transaxle assembly.

5. If the clutch assembly is to be reused, matchmark the pressure plate and the flywheel so they can be assembled in the same position.

6. Install a flywheel holding tool in a transaxle mounting hole on the engine and engage the tooth of the holding tool into the flywheel ring gear.

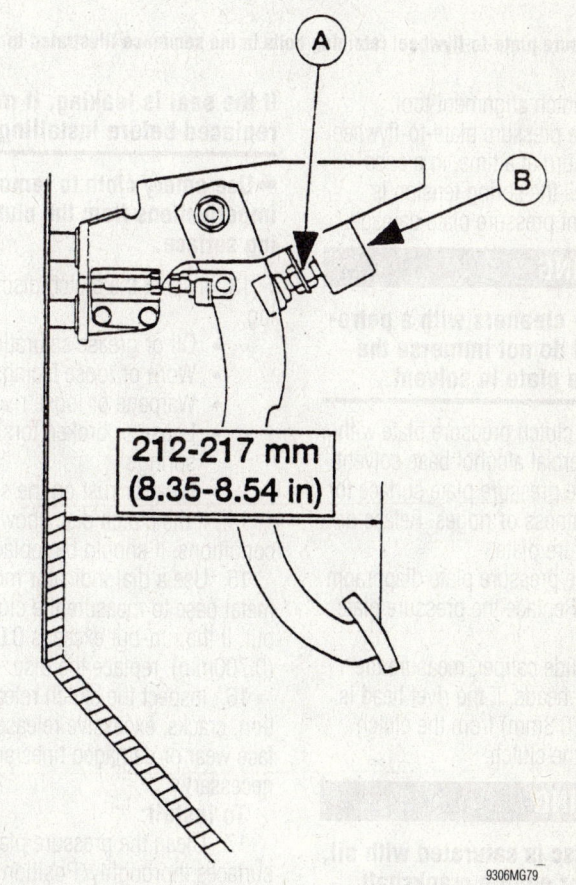

212-217 mm
(8.35-8.54 in)

9306MG79

Clutch pedal height adjustment

Turn to Section 5 for brake system applications

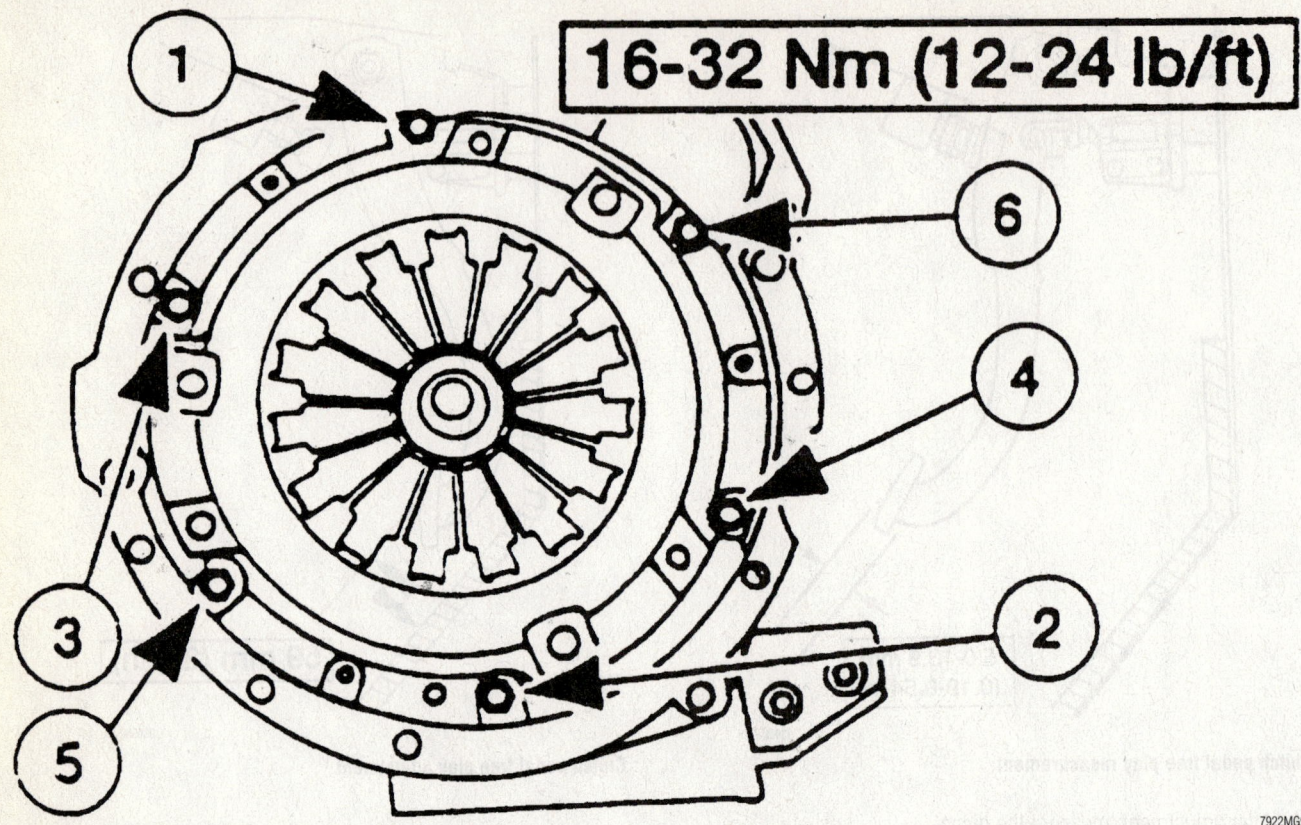

16-32 Nm (12-24 lb/ft)

Tighten the pressure plate-to-flywheel retaining bolts in the sequence illustrated to specification

7. Install a clutch alignment tool.

8. Loosen the pressure plate-to-flywheel retaining bolts 1 turn at a time, in a criss-cross pattern, until the spring tension is relieved, to prevent pressure plate damage.

❈❈ WARNING

Do not use any cleaners with a petroleum base and do not immerse the clutch pressure plate in solvent.

9. Clean the clutch pressure plate with a suitable commercial alcohol base solvent.

10. Inspect the pressure plate surface for burns, scores, flatness or ridges. Reface or replace the pressure plate.

11. Inspect the pressure plate diaphragm fingers for wear. Replace the pressure plate if necessary.

12. Using a slide caliper, measure the depth of the rivet heads. If the rivet head is within 0.012 in. (0.3mm) from the clutch surface, replace the clutch.

❈❈ WARNING

If the clutch disc is saturated with oil, inspect the rear engine crankshaft seal for leakage.

If the seal is leaking, it must be replaced before installing the clutch.

➡ **Use emery cloth to remove minor imperfections from the clutch disc lining surface.**

13. Inspect the clutch disc for the following:

- Oil or grease saturation
- Worn or loose facings
- Warpage or loose rivets at the hub
- Loose or broken torsion dampening springs
- Wear or rust on the splines.

14. If the clutch disc shows any of these conditions, it should be replaced.

15. Use a dial indicator mounted on a metal base to measure the clutch disc run-out. If the run-out exceeds 0.0276 in. (0.700mm), replace the disc.

16. Inspect the clutch release for distortion, cracks, excessive release bearing surface wear or damaged tines and replace as necessary.

To install:

17. Clean the pressure plate and flywheel surfaces thoroughly. Position the clutch disc and pressure plate into the installed position and support them with a clutch aligning

tool. If the clutch assembly is being reused, align the matchmarks that were made during the removal procedure.

18. Install the pressure plate-to-flywheel retaining bolts. Tighten the bolts in the correct sequence to 12–24 ft. lbs. (16–32 Nm). Remove the alignment tool.

19. Install the transaxle assembly.

20. Lower the vehicle.

21. Bleed the hydraulic clutch system.

22. Adjust the clutch pedal free-play.

23. Connect the negative battery cable.

24. Road test the vehicle and check the clutch for proper operation.

Hydraulic Clutch System

BLEEDING

1. Before servicing the vehicle, refer to the precautions in the beginning of this section.

2. Check that the brake master cylinder is at least ¾ full during the entire bleeding process.

3. Remove the bleeder screw cap from the clutch slave cylinder and attach a hose to the bleeder screw. Place the other end of the hose into a container to catch the fluid.

7922MG95

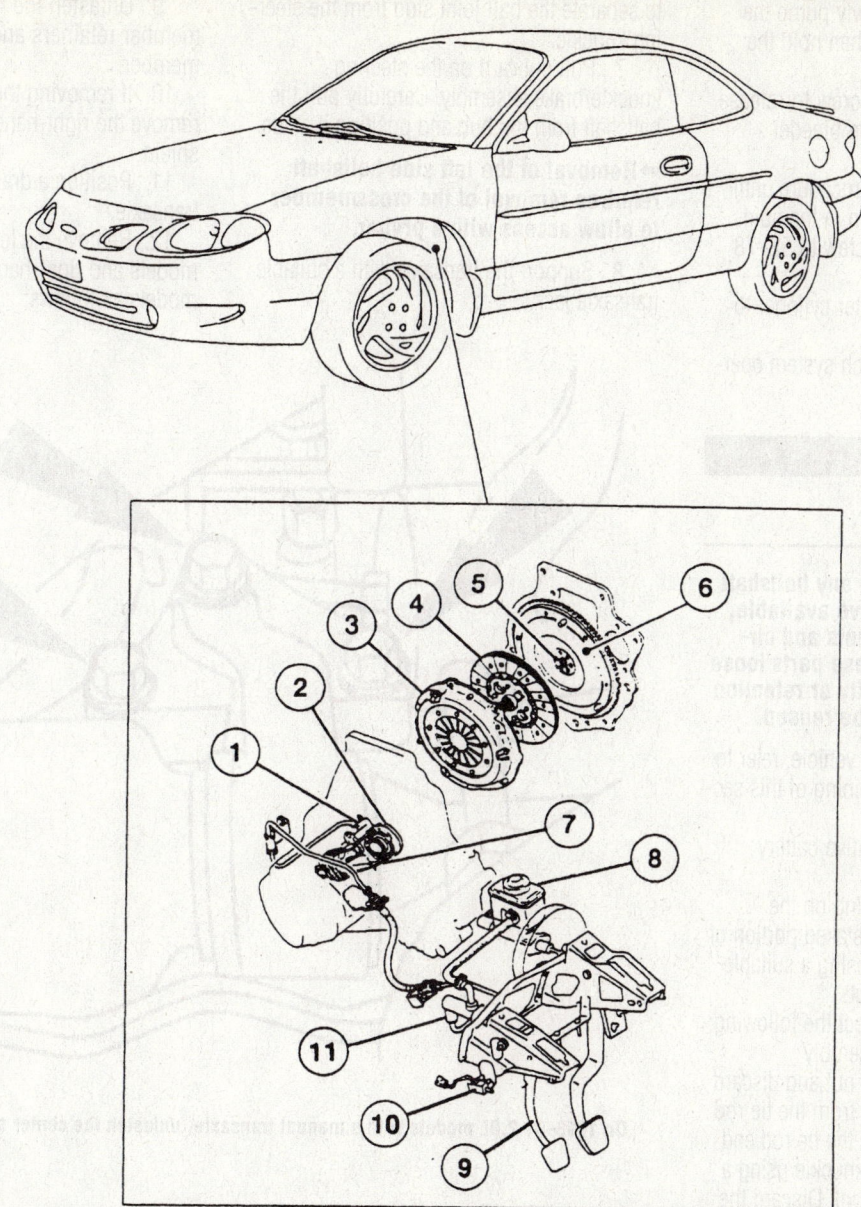

Exploded view of the clutch system components

Item	Description
1	Clutch Slave Cylinder
2	Clutch Release Hub and Bearing
3	Clutch Pressure Plate
4	Clutch Disc
5	Pilot Bearing
6	Flywheel

Item	Description
7	Clutch Release Fork
8	Brake Master Cylinder Reservoir
9	Clutch Pedal
10	Clutch Pedal Position (CPP) Switch
11	Clutch Master Cylinder

9306MG78

4. Have an assistant slowly pump the clutch pedal several times, then hold the clutch pedal down.

5. Loosen the bleeder screw to release the fluid and air. Tighten the bleeder screw.

6. Repeat the bleeding procedure until no more air bubbles are seen in the fluid.

7. Tighten the bleeder screw to 52–78 inch lbs. (6–9 Nm).

8. Top off the brake master cylinder to the full line.

9. Check for proper clutch system operation.

Halfshafts

REMOVAL & INSTALLATION

➡ **Before continuing with any halfshaft procedure, be sure to have available, new halfshaft retaining nuts and circlips. Once removed, these parts loose their torque holding ability or retention capability and must not be reused.**

1. Before servicing the vehicle, refer to the precautions in the beginning of this section.

2. Disconnect the negative battery cable.

3. With the vehicle sitting on the ground, carefully raise the staked portion of the halfshaft retaining nut using a suitable small chisel. Loosen the nut.

4. Remove or disconnect the following:
   • Wheel and tire assembly
   • Halfshaft retaining nut and discard
   • Cotter pin and nut from the tie rod end, then separate the tie rod end from the steering knuckle using a suitable removal tool. Discard the cotter pin.

5. On 1998–01 models, remove or disconnect the following components to remove the stabilizer bar link:
   • Stabilizer bar end nut (1) and bolt (2)
   • Stabilizer bar end retainer (3)
   • End bushing (4) above the stabilizer bar
   • End bushing (5) below the stabilizer bar
   • Stabilizer bar spacer (6)
   • Stabilizer bar end bushings from above (7) and below (8) the subframe
   • Lower stabilizer bar end retainer (9)
   • Stabilizer bar

6. remove the ball joint bolt and nut. Carefully pry down on the lower control arm

to separate the ball joint stud from the steering knuckle.

7. Pull outward on the steering knuckle/brake assembly. Carefully pull the halfshaft from the hub and position it aside.

➡ **Removal of the left side halfshaft requires removal of the crossmember to allow access with a prybar.**

8. Support the transaxle with a suitable transaxle jack.

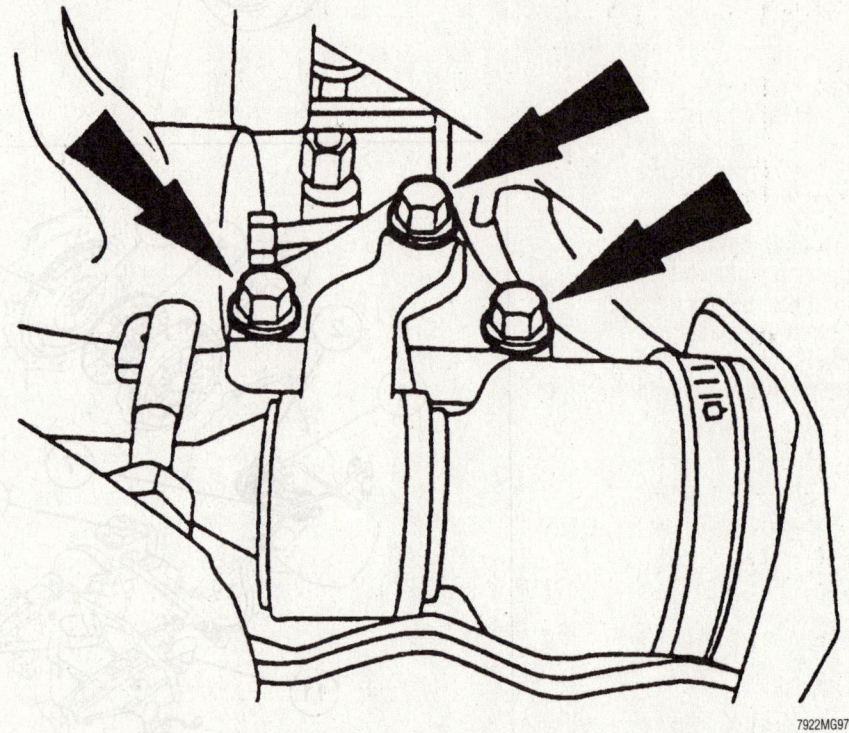

On 1998–01 2.0L models with a manual transaxle, unfasten the center support bearing bolts

9. Unfasten the 4 transaxle crossmember retainers and remove the crossmember.

10. If removing the right side halfshaft, remove the right-hand shield and splash shield.

11. Position a drain pan under the transaxle.

12. Remove the left-hand halfshaft on all models and right-hand halfshaft on 1997 models as follows:

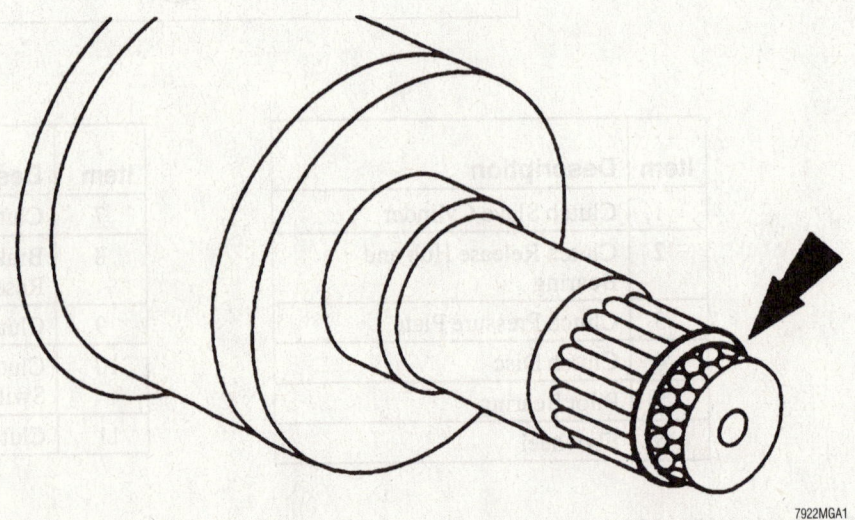

During assembly, be sure to install a new circlip on the inner CV-joint spline—2.0L engine

a. Insert a prybar between the half-shaft and the transaxle case. Gently pry outward to release the halfshaft from the differential side gear. Be careful not to damage the transaxle case, oil seal, CV-joint or CV-joint boot.

b. Remove the halfshaft.

13. On 1998–01 models, remove the right-hand halfshaft as follows:

a. On models with a manual transaxle, unfasten the center support bearing bolts.

b. Lower the halfshaft and remove it from the transaxle.

c. Separate the halfshaft from the center support bearing and remove the halfshaft from the vehicle.

d. Inspect the center support bearing for damage and replace as necessary.

➡Install suitable plugs after removing the halfshafts to prevent the differential side gears from moving out of place. Should the gears become misaligned, the differential will have to be removed from the transaxle to align the gears.

To install:

14. Position a new circlip on the inner CV-joint spline so the circlip gap is at the top. Lubricate the splines lightly with a suitable grease.

15. Remove the plugs that were installed in the differential side gears.

16. On all models except 1998–01 models wit a manual transaxle, position the halfshaft so the CV-joint splines are aligned with the differential side gear splines. Push the halfshaft into the differential.

➡When seated properly, the circlip can be felt snapping into the differential side gear groove.

17. Install the right-hand halfshaft on 1998–01 models with a manual transaxle as follows:

a. Position the halfshaft and joint so that the splines line up with the splines in the halfshaft, and push the halfshaft, joint and halfshaft together with the center support bearing.

b. Install the halfshaft in the transaxle.

18. Place the center support bearing into position and tighten it retaining bolts to 32–46 ft. lbs. (46–62 Nm).

a. Install the right-hand shield and splash shield.

19. Pull outward on the steering knuckle/brake assembly and insert the half-shaft into the hub.

20. Pry downward on the lower control arm and position the lower ball joint stud in the steering knuckle.

21. Install the crossmember and the crossmember-to-frame bolts. Tighten the bolts to 69–93 ft. lbs. (94–126 Nm).

22. Remove the transaxle jack.

23. Install or connect the following:

- Steering knuckle and ball joint nut and bolt. Tighten the nut and bolt to 32–43 ft. lbs. (43–59 Nm).
- Stabilizer bar link in reverse order of removal and tighten the bar end nut until the protruding bar end bolt length is 0.67–75 in. (17–19mm), on 1998–99 models
- Tie rod end to the steering knuckle
- Tie rod end nut and tighten to 25–33 ft. lbs. (34–46 Nm) on 1997 models and 32–41 ft. lbs. (43–56 Nm) on 1998–01 models. Install a new cotter pin.
- Wheel and tire assembly
- New halfshaft retaining nut and tighten to 174–235 ft. lbs. (235–319 Nm). Stake the halfshaft retaining nut using a suitable chisel with a rounded cutting edge.

➡If the nut splits or cracks after staking, replace it with a new nut.

24. Check and refill the transaxle with the proper type and quantity of fluid.

25. Connect the negative battery cable.

26. Road test the vehicle and check for proper operation.

CV-Joints

OVERHAUL

Outboard Side

1. Before servicing the vehicle, refer to the precautions in the beginning of this section.

2. Remove or disconnect the following:
- Halfshaft from the vehicle. Support the assembly in a vise with soft jaws.
- Front brake anti-lock sensor indicator off the halfshaft using a punch to drive it off
- Two halfshaft boot clamp and discard

3. Slide the boot back out of the way to access the outboard joint.

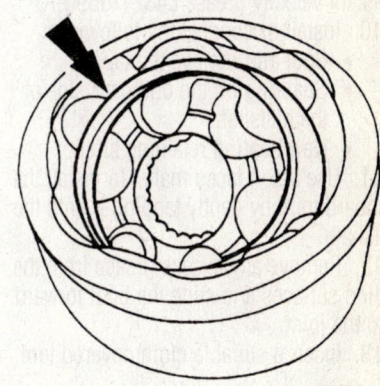

90987G15

Clean and inspect the outboard bearings for damage

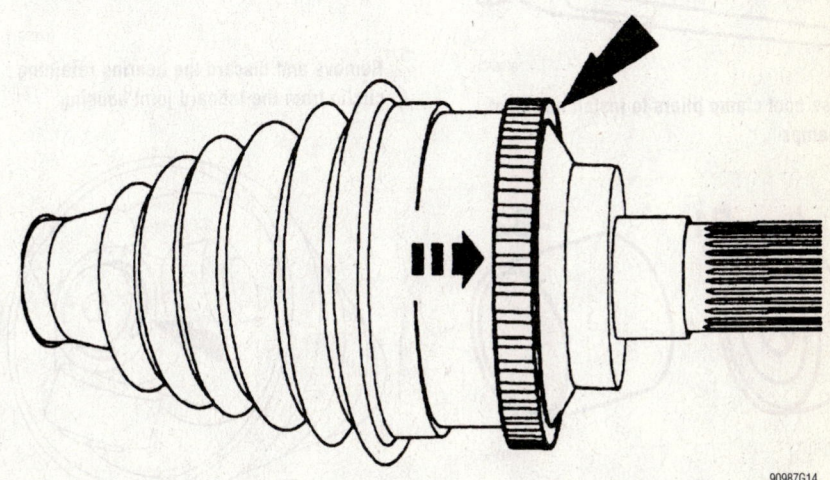

90987G14

If equipped with ABS, use a punch to drive the front brake anti-lock sensor indicator off the halfshaft

4. Matchmark the joint-to-halfshaft for reassembly.

5. Use a soft faced mallet to separate the outboard joint by gently tapping it off the halfshaft.

6. Remove or disconnect the following:

- Halfshaft bearing retaining circlip and discard
- snapring from the outboard side of the halfshaft

➡ **Do not remove the tape until after installation of the boot.**

7. Wrap the outboard halfshaft splines with tape and then slide the boot from the shaft.

8. Clean and inspect the outboard bearings for damage, grit in the grease, pitting or cracks and replace as necesary.

To install:

9. Lubricate the joint bearings with constant velocity grease E43Z-19590-A.

10. Install or connect the following:

- Boot and remove the tape
- Snapring on the outboard side of the halfshaft
- New bearing retaining circlip

11. Use a soft faced mallet to install the outboard joint by gently tapping it onto the halfshaft.

12. Remove any excess grease from the mating surfaces and slide the boot forward onto the joint.

13. Insert a suitable cloth covered tool

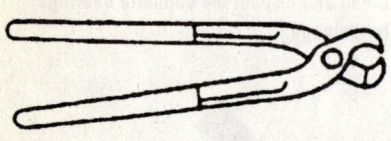

90987G16

Use boot clamp pliers to install new boot clamps

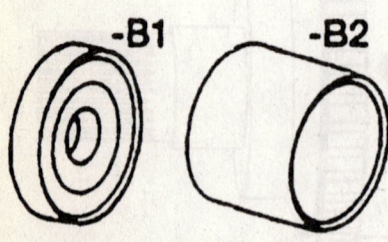

90987G17

Use sensing ring replacer tool T94P-20202-B to install the front brake anti-lock sensor indicator onto the halfshaft

between the boot and the outer bearing race to allow trapped air to escape from the boot.

14. Use boot clamp pliers to install two new boot clamps.

15. If equipped with anti-lock brakes, use sensing ring replacer tool T94P-20202-B, to install the front brake anti-lock sensor indicator onto the halfshaft.

16. Install the halfshaft.

INBOARD SIDE

1. Before servicing the vehicle, refer to the precautions in the beginning of this section.

2. Remove or disconnect the following:

- Halfshaft from the vehicle. Support the assembly in a vise with soft jaws.

➡ **The right-hand side halfshaft on models equipped with a manual transaxle do not have an inboard circlip.**

- Bearing retaining circlip from the inboard joint housing and discard
- Joint boot clamps and discard

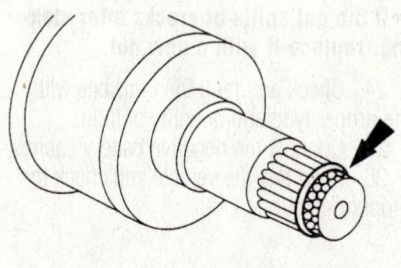

90987G18

Remove and discard the bearing retaining circlip from the inboard joint housing

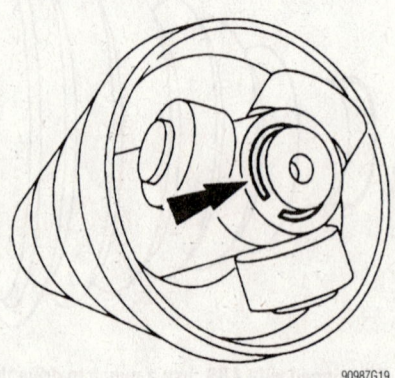

90987G19

Location of the tripot bearing snapring

- Joint boot from the joint housing
- Joint housing from the tripot bearing and halfshaft
- Tripot bearing snapring

3. Matchmark the tripot bearing-to-halfshaft for reassembly.

4. Remove the tripot bearing from the halfshaft.

➡ **Do not remove the tape until after installation of the boot.**

5. Wrap the halfshaft splines with tape and then slide the boot from the shaft.

6. Clean and inspect the tripot bearing assembly and outboard joint housing for damage, grit in the grease, pitting or cracks and replace as necessary.

To install:

7. Lubricate the tripot bearing and inboard joint housing with constant velocity grease E43Z-19590-A.

8. Install or connect the following:

- Boot and remove the tape
- Tripot bearing onto the halfshaft
- Tripot bearing snapring
- Inboard joint housing onto the tripot bearing

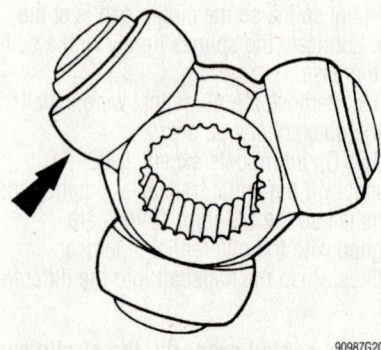

90987G20

Clean and inspect the tripot bearing assembly . . .

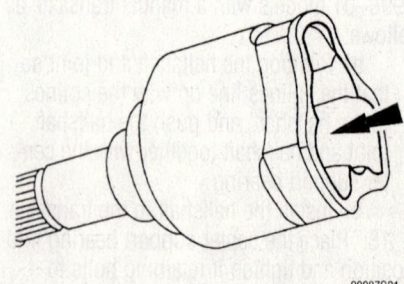

90987G21

. . . and outboard joint housing for damage, grit in the grease, pitting or cracks, and replace as necessary

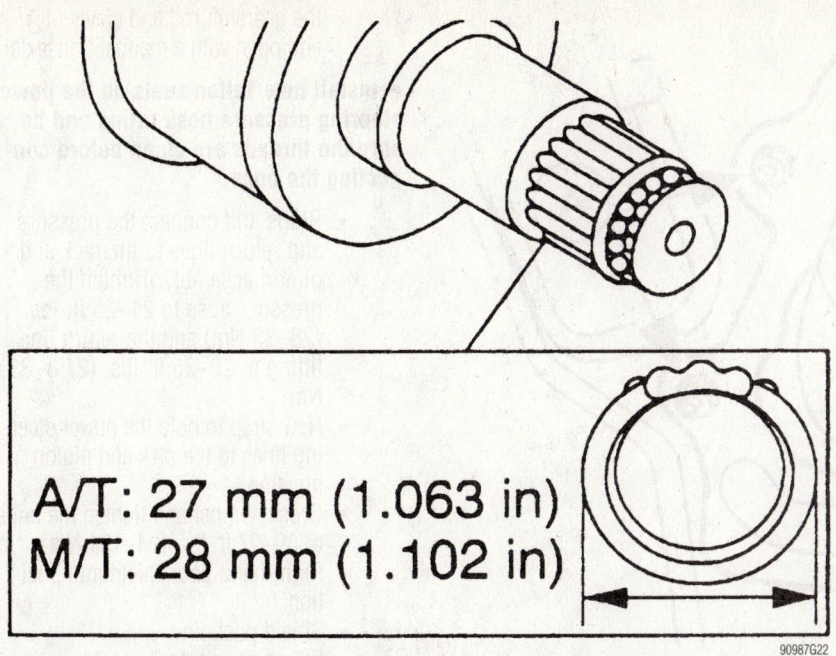

A/T: 27 mm (1.063 in)
M/T: 28 mm (1.102 in)

90987G22

Measure the relaxed state of the halfshaft bearing circlip installed on the shaft, and make sure it is within specification

- Boot onto the inboard joint housing

9. Insert a suitable cloth covered tool between the boot and the bearing to allow trapped air to escape from the boot.

10. Use boot clamp pliers to install two new boot clamps.

➡**Measure the relaxed state of the halfshaft bearing circlip installed on the shaft. Refer to the accompanying illustration. The wrong size clip will not retain the halfshaft properly.**

11. Install a new halfshaft bearing retainer circlip of the correct size onto the outboard halfshaft joint.

12. Install the halfshaft.

STEERING AND SUSPENSION

Air Bag

PRECAUTIONS

Several precautions must be observed when handling the inflator module to avoid accidental deployment and possible personal injury.

- Never carry the inflator module by the wires or connector on the underside of the module.
- When carrying a live inflator module, hold securely with both hands, and ensure that the bag and trim cover are pointed away.
- Place the inflator module on a bench or other surface with the bag and trim cover facing up.
- With the inflator module on the bench, never place anything on or close to the module that may be thrown in the event of an accidental deployment.

DISARMING

1. Before servicing the vehicle, refer to the precautions in the beginning of this section.

2. Disconnect both battery cables, negative cable first.

3. Wait at least 1 minute. This allows time for the back-up power supply to deplete its stored energy.

4. Remove the driver's side air bag module, then the passenger side if required.

5. Use caution when carrying live air bags. Always place the air bag with the cover up.

6. If the battery needs to be reconnected while one or both of the air bags are removed from the system, install Air Bag Simulator 105—00010, to the drivers side and/or passenger side air bag harness connectors as required. Before removing either air bag simulator, disconnect both battery cables and wait at least 1 minute before continuing.

ARMING

1. Once service is completed and the air bag modules are back in place, connect the negative battery cable and prove out the air bag system by turning the ignition key to the **RUN** position and visually monitoring the air bag indicator lamp in the instrument cluster. The indicator lamp should illuminate for approximately 6 seconds, then turn **OFF**. If the indicator lamp does not illuminate, stays **ON**, or flashes at any time, a fault has been detected by the air bag diagnostic monitor requiring immediate attention.

Rack and Pinion Steering Gear

REMOVAL & INSTALLATION

1. Before servicing the vehicle, refer to the precautions in the beginning of this section.

2. Turn the key to the **ACC** position.

3. Remove or disconnect the following:

- Steering column tube boot nuts at the base of the column and the tube boots, from inside the passenger compartment
- Steering column input shaft coupling-to-steering gear input shaft pinch bolt
- Front wheel and tire assemblies
- Separate the tie rod ends from the steering knuckles and discard the cotter pins
- Right-hand lower splash shield
- Crossmember
- Pressure and return lines from the rack and pinion assembly and plug the lines
- Strap holding the hoses to the steering gear and discard
- Gearshift rod and clevis from the transaxle, if equipped with a manual transaxle
- Extension bar nut and disconnect

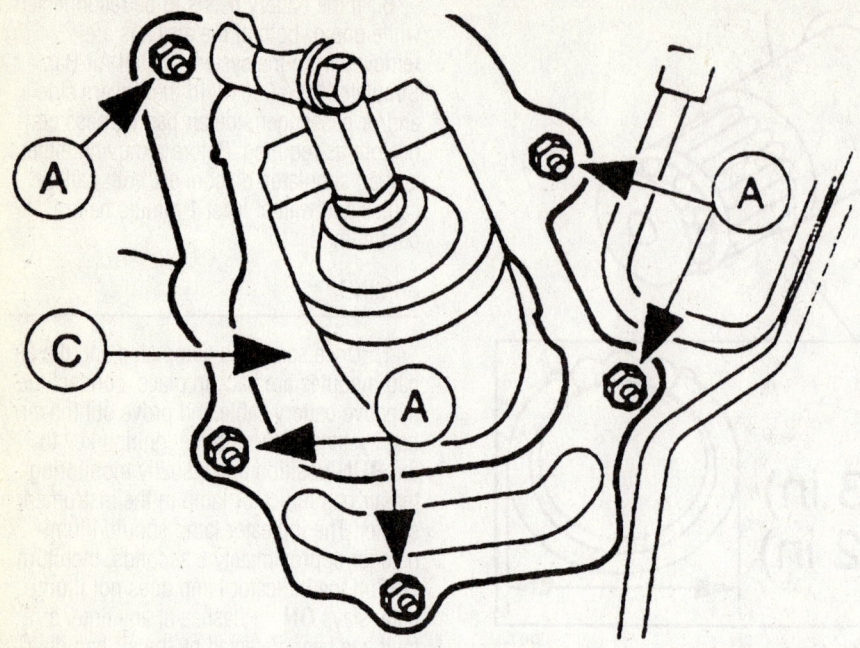

Unfasten the steering column tube boot nuts at the base of the column and remove the tube boots

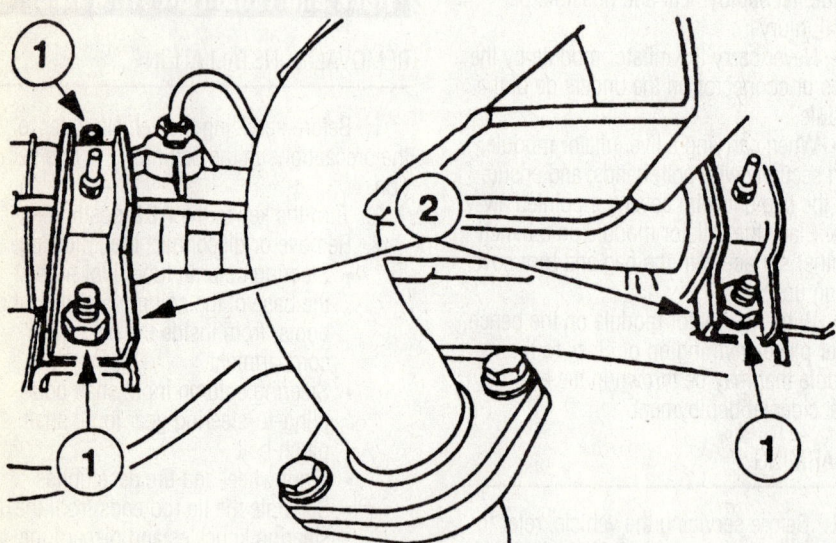

Unfasten the retaining nuts from the rack and pinion mounting brackets and remove the brackets

the gearshift lever stabilizer bar and support from the transaxle, if equipped with a manual transaxle
- Retaining nuts from the rack and pinion mounting brackets
- Pinion mounting brackets
- Pushpin and position the right-hand boot aside
- Rack and pinion assembly from the right-hand side of the vehicle

To install:

4. Install or connect the following:
- Rack and pinion assembly in its mounting location

5. Align the steering column input shaft coupling and the steering gear input shaft.
- Rack and pinion mounting brackets. Tighten the retaining nuts to 28–38 ft. lbs. (37–57 Nm).
- Gearshift stabilizer bar, support and

the gearshift rod and clevis, if equipped with a manual transaxle

→Install new Teflon seals on the power steering pressure hose fitting and be sure the threads are clean before connecting the hose.

- Plugs and connect the pressure and return lines to the rack and pinion assembly. Tighten the pressure hose to 21–25 ft. lbs. (28–33 Nm) and the return line fitting to 20–25 ft. lbs. (27.3–33.9 Nm).
- New strap to hold the power steering lines to the rack and pinion housing
- Crossmember and tighten the bolts to 69–97 ft. lbs. (94–131 Nm)
- Right-hand boot shield into position
- Shield pushpin
- Rright-hand splash shield
- Tie rod ends to the steering knuckles and the castellated nuts. Tighten to specification.
- New cotter pins
- Wheel and tire assemblies
- Steering column input shaft coupling-to-steering gear input shaft pinch bolt and tighten the bolt to 30–36 ft. lbs. (40–50 Nm)
- Steering column tube boots and the 5 retainers. Tighten the retainers to 18–52 inch lbs. (2–5.9 Nm).
- Negative battery cable

6. Fill and bleed the power steering system.

7. Check the alignment and adjust as required.

8. Start the engine and check for leaks.

9. Road test the vehicle and check for proper steering system operation.

Strut

REMOVAL & INSTALLATION

Front

1. Before servicing the vehicle, refer to the precautions in the beginning of this section.

2. Remove or disconnect the following:
- Negative battery cable
- Front wheel and tire assembly
- Clip securing the brake hose to the strut (spring and shock) assembly.
- Anti-lock brake harness cable and clip, if equipped with anti-lock brakes

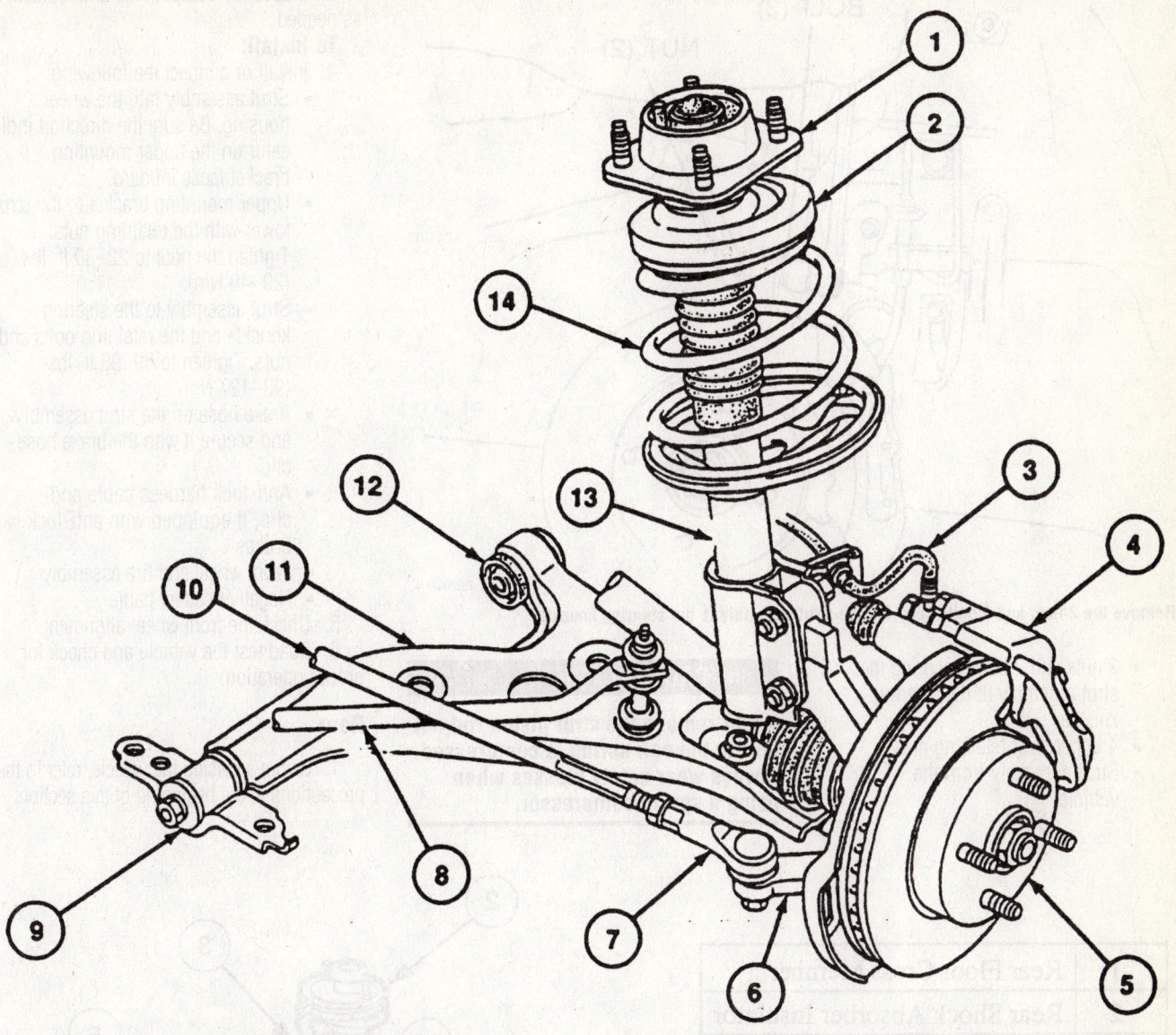

1	Front Shock Absorber Upper Mounting Bracket
2	Upper Spring Seat (Part of 18198)
3	Front Brake Hose
4	Disc Brake Caliper
5	Front Disc Brake Rotor
6	Front Wheel Knuckle
7	Tie Rod End
8	Front Stabilizer Bar

9	Front Suspension Lower Arm Mounting Bolt Bushing (Rear)
10	Front Wheel Spindle Tie Rod
11	Front Suspension Lower Arm
12	Front Suspension Lower Arm Mounting Bolt Bushing (Front)
13	Front Shock Absorber
14	Front Coil Spring

9300MG04

Identification of the front suspension components

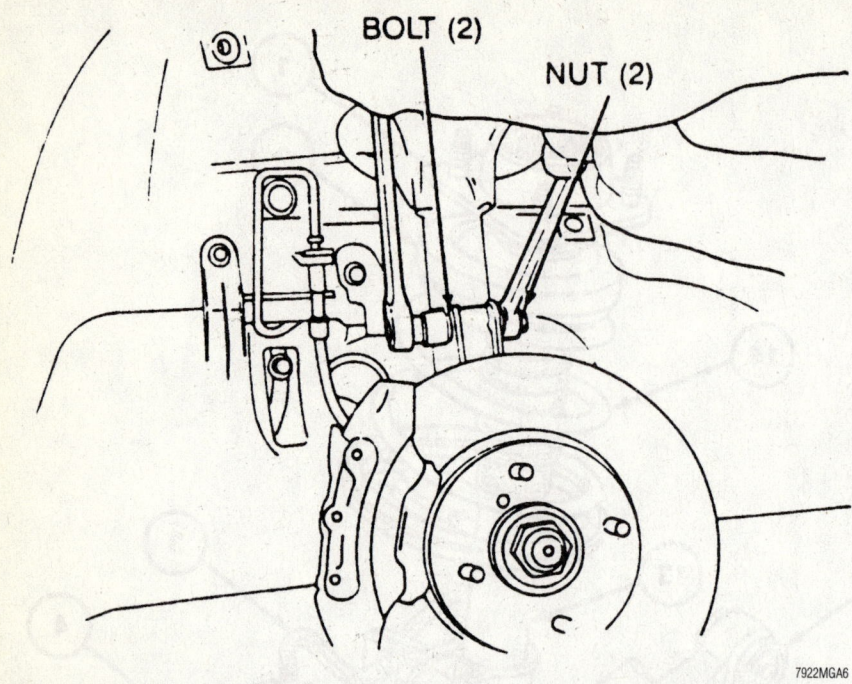

BOLT (2)

NUT (2)

7922MGA6

Remove the 2 nuts and 2 bolts securing the strut assembly to the steering knuckle

- 2 nuts and 2 bolts securing the strut assembly to the steering knuckle
- 4 upper strut retaining nuts
- Strut assembly from the vehicle

✳✳ CAUTION

Never remove the strut piston rod nut unless the coil spring is compressed. Always wear safety glasses when using a spring compressor.

3. Inspect all components and replace as needed.

To install:

4. Install or connect the following:
   - Strut assembly into the wheel housing. Be sure the direction indicator on the upper mounting bracket faces inboard.
   - Upper mounting bracket to the strut tower with the retaining nuts. Tighten the nuts to 22–30 ft. lbs. (29–40 Nm).
   - Strut assembly to the steering knuckle and the retaining bolts and nuts. Tighten to 69–93 ft. lbs. (93–127 Nm).
   - Brake hose on the strut assembly and secure it with the brake hose clip
   - Anti-lock harness cable and clip, if equipped with anti-lock brakes
   - Front wheel and tire assembly
   - Negative battery cable

5. Check the front wheel alignment.

6. Road test the vehicle and check for proper operation.

Rear

1. Before servicing the vehicle, refer to the precautions in the beginning of this section.

1	Rear Floor Cross Member
2	Rear Shock Absorber Insulator
3	Rear Spring
4	Rear Shock Absorber
5	Rear Wheel Spindle
6	Rear Suspension Tie Rod and Bushing
7	Rear Suspension Arm and Bushing (Rear)
8	Rear Stabilizer Bar
9	Rear Suspension Arm and Bushing (Front)
10	Rear Wheel Brake Hose

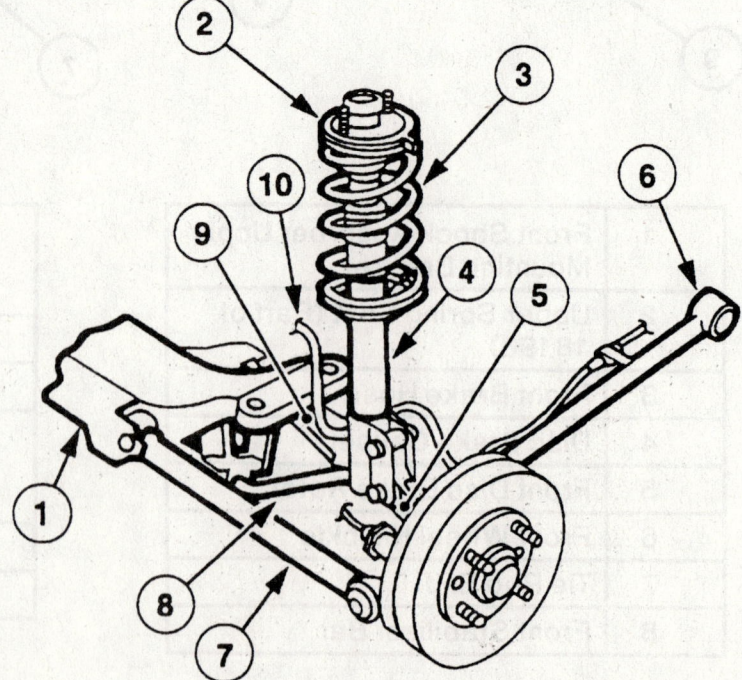

9300MG05

Identification of the rear suspension components

2. Remove or disconnect the follow-ing:
- Negative battery cable
- Package tray trim panel, on sedan and coupe models
- Quarter trim pane, on wagon models
- 2 upper strut retaining nuts
- Wheel and tire assembly
- Clip securing the brake hose to the rear strut assembly
- ABS sensor bolt, if equipped
- Nuts and bolts securing the rear strut assembly to the wheel spindle
- strut assembly from the vehicle

To install:

3. Install or connect the following:
- Strut assembly into the vehicle wheel housing
- Nuts and bolts securing the strut assembly to the rear wheel spindle assembly. Tighten the lower strut bolts and nuts to 76–100 ft. lbs. (103–136 Nm).
- ABS sensor bolt, if equipped
- Clip securing the flexible brake hose to the rear strut assembly
- Wheel and tire assembly
- 2 upper strut retaining nuts and tighten to 34–46 ft. lbs. (47–62 Nm)
- Trim panel
- Negative battery cable

4. Check the rear wheel alignment.

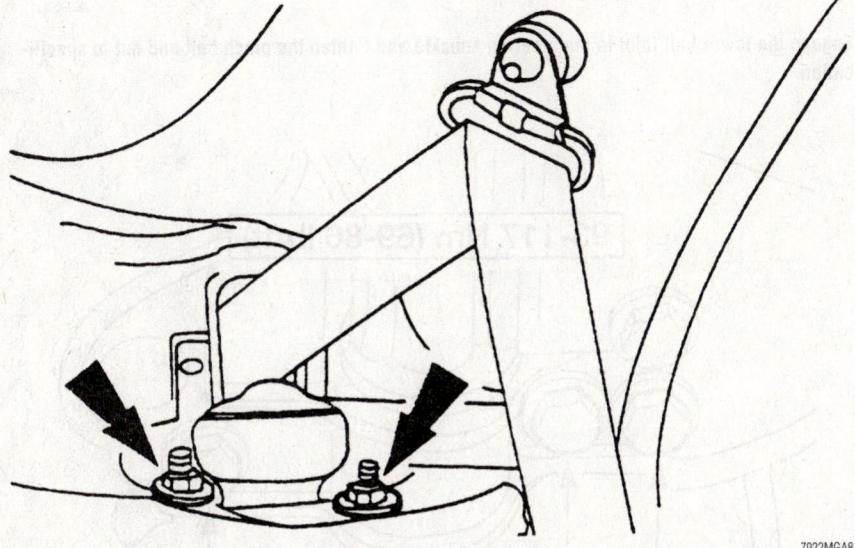

Location of the 2 rear strut upper retaining nuts (arrows) inside the vehicle

7922MGA8

5. Road test the vehicle and check for proper operation.

Coil Spring

REMOVAL & INSTALLATION

Front

1. Before servicing the vehicle, refer to the precautions in the beginning of this section.

2. Remove the strut assembly.

3. Place the strut assembly in a vise.

4. Install a suitable spring compressor tool onto the coil spring and compress the spring.

5. Unfasten the piston rod nut and remove the upper mounting bracket.

6. Remove the bound stopper, dust boot, rubber spring seat, spring, upper spring seat and thrust bearing.

To install:

7. Install the thrust bearing, upper spring seat, spring, rubber spring seat, dust boot and the bound stopper.

8. Install the piston rod nut and tighten it to 58–81 ft. lbs. (79–110 Nm).

9. After the piston rod nut has been tightened to specification, carefully remove the compressor tool from the spring while making sure the spring is properly seated in the upper and lower spring seats.

10. Install the strut assembly in the vehicle.

11. Have the vehicle alignment checked and if necessary, adjusted.

Rear

1. Remove the strut assembly.

2. Place the strut assembly in a vise.

✳✳ CAUTION

Always take the necessary precautions when using a spring compressor

3. Install a suitable spring compressor tool onto the coil spring and compress the spring.

4. Remove or disconnect the follow-ing:
- Rear strut assembly top mounting cover
- Piston rod nut and the retainer
- Strut insulator
- Spring compressor
- Rear strut dust boot and stopper seat
- Spring and the rear strut insulator

To install:

5. Place the strut assembly in a vise.

6. Install or connect the following:
- Strut insulator and spring
- Stopper seat and dust boot

7. Use the spring compressor tool to compress the strut spring.
- Strut insulator and the retainer
- Piston rod nut and tighten it to 41–49 ft. lbs. (55–67 Nm)
- Top mounting cover

8. Be sure the spring is properly aligned and carefully release the spring into the seats of the strut.

9. Remove the spring compressor from the coil spring.

10. Install the strut assembly.

Lower Ball Joint

REMOVAL & INSTALLATION

➡Refer to the illustration located in the strut procedure, earlier in this section, for a view of the front suspension.

1. Before servicing the vehicle, refer to the precautions in the beginning of this section.

2. Remove or disconnect the following:

Turn to Section 5 for brake system applications

- Wheel assembly
- Nut and bolt attaching the lower ball joint to the steering knuckle
- Ball joint from the steering knuckle
- Lower control arm ball joint nuts and bolt
- Ball joint

To install:

3. Install or connect the following:
- Ball joint into position on the lower control arm
- Ball joint-to-lower control arm retainers. Tighten the nuts and bolt to 69–86 ft. lbs. (93–117 Nm).

4. Apply Loctite® 290 thread locking compound to the ball joint nut and threads.

- Ball joint to the steering knuckle
- Ball joint nut and bolt. Tighten the nut and bolt to 32–43 ft. lbs. (43–59 Nm).
- Wheel assembly
- Check and adjust the wheel alignment as necessary

Control Arm

REMOVAL & INSTALLATION

Front

1. Before servicing the vehicle, refer to the precautions in the beginning of this section.

2. Remove or disconnect the following:
- Front wheel and tire assembly
- Stabilizer bar link nuts, retainers, bushings, bolts and sleeves
- Pinch bolt and nut securing the ball joint to the steering knuckle
- Lower ball joint from the steering knuckle by prying the lower control arm down with a prybar
- Front lower control arm pivot bolt
- Three lower control arm retaining bolts and the lower control arm

3. Inspect the lower control arm, lower control arm bushings and the lower ball joint. The ball joint and bushings can be replaced individually.

To install:

4. Install or connect the following:
- Lower control arm into position at the bushings
- Lower ball joint to the steering knuckle and tighten the pinch bolt and nut to 32–43 ft. lbs. (43–59 Nm)

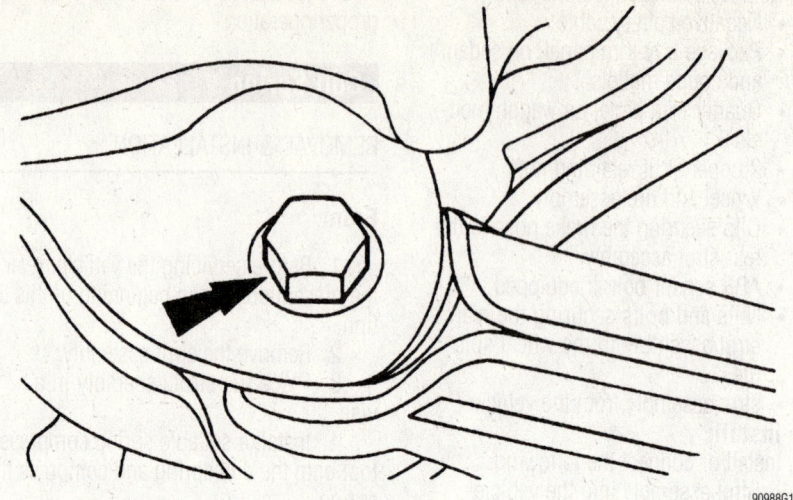

Unfasten of the lower control arm pivot bolt (arrow)

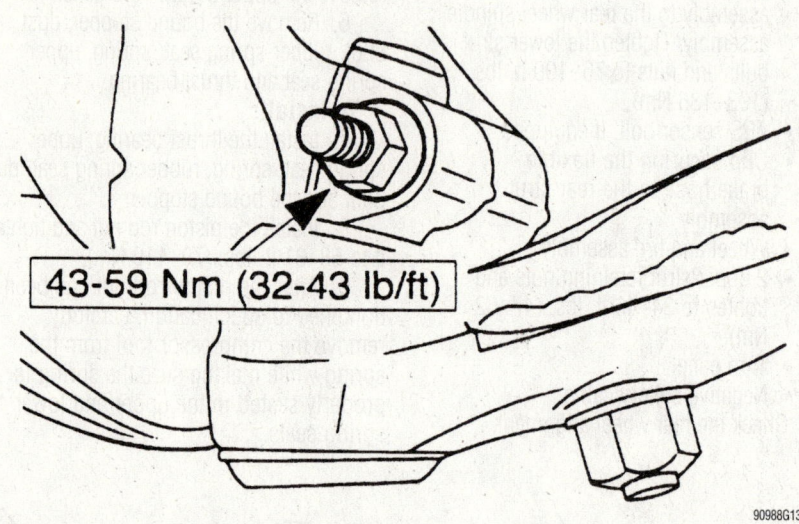

43-59 Nm (32-43 lb/ft)

Engage the lower ball joint to the steering knuckle and tighten the pinch bolt and nut to specification

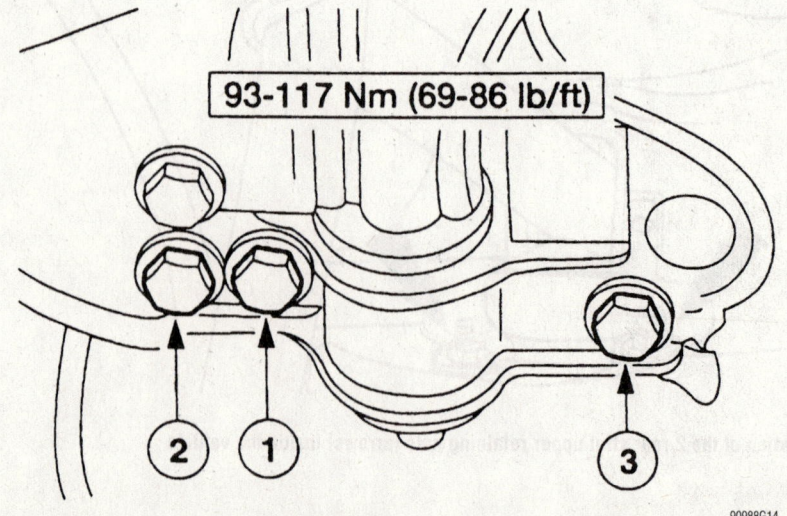

93-117 Nm (69-86 lb/ft)

Tighten the lower control arm retaining bolts in the sequence shown to the proper specification

5. Use a transmission jack to raise the lower control arm so that it is parallel with the ground.

- Control arm retaining bolts and tighten them to 69–86 ft. lbs. (93–117 Nm) in the order shown in the accompanying illustration
- Control arm pivot bolt and tighten to 69–86 ft. lbs. (93–117 Nm)
- Stabilizer bolts, washers, bushings, sleeves and nuts. Tighten the stabilizer nuts so 0.67–0.75 inches (17–19mm) of thread is exposed at the end of the bolt.
- Wheel and tire assembly

6. Check the front wheel alignment.

7. Road test the vehicle and check for proper operation.

CONTROL ARM BUSHING REPLACEMENT

1. Before servicing the vehicle, refer to the precautions in the beginning of this section.

2. Remove or disconnect the following:

- Control arm
- Nut and control arm mounting bushing (rear) and washer
- Front bushing from the arm using a suitable control arm bushing tool, C-frame and clamp assembly
- Front bushing into the arm using a suitable control arm bushing tool, C-frame and clamp assembly
- Washer, control arm mounting bushing (rear) and nut. Tighten the nut to 69 ft. lbs. (93 Nm).
- Control arm

Rear

1. Before servicing the vehicle, refer to the precautions in the beginning of this section.

2. Position a floor jackstand beneath the rear suspension crossmember.

3. Remove or disconnect the following:

- Wheel and tire assembly
- Stabilizer nuts, washers, bushings, sleeves and bolts
- Bolts securing the stabilizer bar brackets and grommets to the rear suspension crossmember
- Stabilizer bar
- Bolts securing the rear suspension crossmember to the vehicle frame

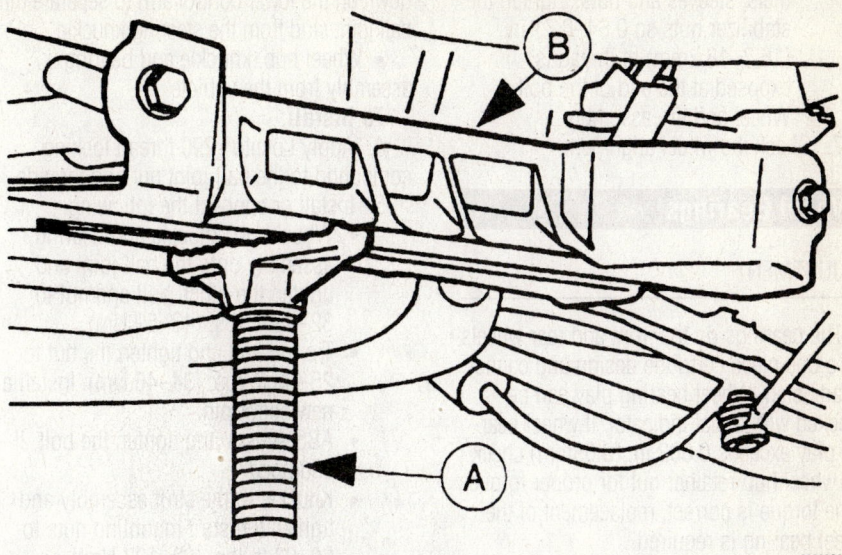

Support the rear suspension crossmember (B) with a floor jackstand (A)

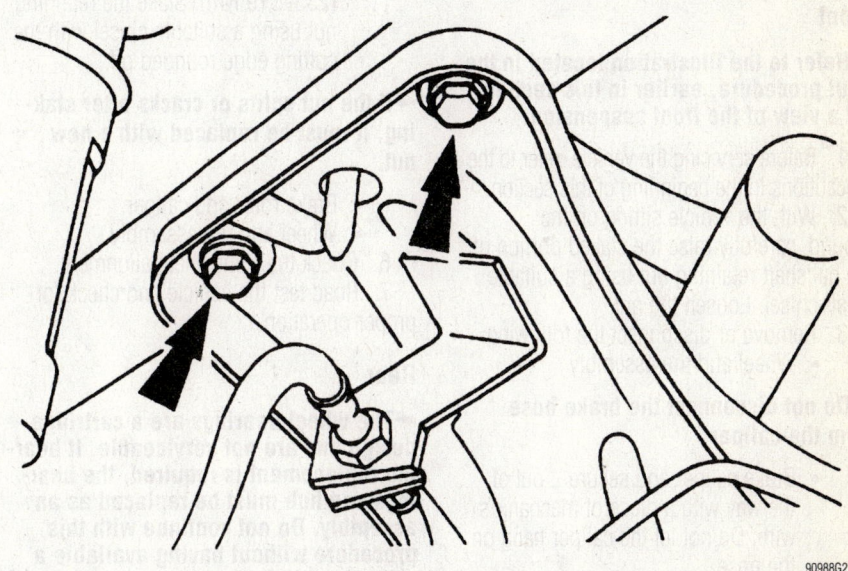

Unfasten the rear suspension crossmember bolts, then lower the floor jackstand and crossmember

4. Lower the floor jackstand to allow the rear suspension crossmember to be lowered from the vehicle frame.

- Control arm and bushing nut
- Control arm and bushing bolt
- Control arm

To install:

5. Install or connect the following:

- Control arm into position
- Retaining bolt and tighten it to 50–70 ft. lbs. (68–95 Nm)
- Control arm and bushing retaining nut, then tighten the nut to 64–86 ft. lbs. (87–116 Nm)

6. Raise the floor jack and place the crossmember into position.

- Crossmember bolts and tighten them to 34–46 ft. lbs. (47–62 Nm)
- Grommets onto the stabilizer bar and align the grommets to the positions painted on the bar
- Stabilizer bar to the rear suspension crossmember and secure it in place with the straps and bolts. Tighten the bolts to 32–43 ft. lbs. (43–59 Nm).
- Stabilizer bolts, washers, grom-

mets, sleeves and nuts. Tighten the stabilizer nuts so 0.64–0.71 in. (16.2–18.2mm) of thread is exposed at the end of the bolt.
  • Wheel and tire assembly
7. Check the wheel alignment.

Wheel Bearings

ADJUSTMENT

The bearings on the front and rear wheels are a one piece cartridge design and cannot be adjusted. Wheel bearing play can be checked with a dial indicator. If wheel bearing play exceeds 0.002 in. (0.05mm) check the wheel hub retainer nut for proper torque. If the torque is correct, replacement of the wheel bearing is required.

REMOVAL & INSTALLATION

Front

➡Refer to the illustration located in the strut procedure, earlier in this section, for a view of the front suspension.

1. Before servicing the vehicle, refer to the precautions in the beginning of this section.
2. With the vehicle sitting on the ground, carefully raise the staked portion of the halfshaft retaining nut using a suitable small chisel. Loosen the nut.
3. Remove or disconnect the following:
  • Wheel and tire assembly

➡Do not disconnect the brake hose from the caliper

  • Brake caliper and secure it out of the way with a piece of mechanic's wire. Do not let the caliper hang on the hose.
  • Brake rotor
  • Halfshaft retaining nut and discard it
  • Cotter pin and castellated nut from the tie rod end and separate the tie rod end from the steering knuckle using a suitable removal tool. Discard the cotter pin.
  • Separate the tie rod end from the wheel knuckle
  • ABS sensor bolt and the sensor, if equipped
  • Strut mounting nuts and the studs which attach the strut assembly to the steering knuckle
  • Strut from the steering knuckle
  • Lower ball joint pinch bolt. Carefully pry

down on the lower control arm to separate the ball joint stud from the steering knuckle.
  • Wheel hub, knuckle and bearing assembly from the vehicle

To install:

4. Apply Loctite® 290 thread locking compound to the ball joint nut and threads.
5. Install or connect the following:
  • Wheel hub, knuckle and bearing assembly onto the ball joint and tighten the pinch bolt and nut to 32–43 ft. lbs. (43–59 Nm)
  • Tie rod end and tighten the nut to 25–33 ft. lbs. (34–46 Nm). Install a new cotter pin.
  • ABS sensor and tighten the bolt, if equipped
  • Knuckle to the strut assembly and tighten the strut mounting nuts to 69–93 ft. lbs. (93–127 Nm)
  • New halfshaft retaining nut and tighten to 174–235 ft. lbs. (235–319 Nm). Stake the retaining nut using a suitable chisel with the cutting edge rounded off.

➡If the nut splits or cracks after staking, it must be replaced with a new nut.

  • Brake rotor and caliper
  • Wheel and tire assembly
6. Check the front wheel alignment.
7. Road test the vehicle and check for proper operation.

Rear

➡The wheel bearings are a cartridge design and are not serviceable. If bearing replacement is required, the bearings and hub must be replaced as an assembly. Do not continue with this procedure without having available a new wheel hub retainer nut. Once removed, the nut looses its torque holding ability or retention capability and must not be reused.

1. Before servicing the vehicle, refer to the precautions in the beginning of this section.
2. Remove or disconnect the following:
  • Wheel and tire assembly
  • Hub grease cap
  • Brake drum or disc brake caliper and rotor, as necessary
  • Wheel hub retainer nut securing the hub to the spindle, unstake the nut prior to loosening
  • Hub and bearing assembly. Discard the hub retainer nut.

  • Disc brake shield retaining bolts and the shield, if equipped with disc brakes
  • Backing plate, if equipped with drum brakes
  • Strut-to-spindle retaining bolts and nuts
  • Trailing arm bolt securing the trailing arm to the spindle
  • Stabilizer bar link nuts, retainers, bushings, sleeves and bolts
  • Control arm nut and bolt securing both control arms to the wheel spindle
  • Spindle from the vehicle
3. Inspect all components. If the wheel spindle is damaged, replace it. Wheel bearings are sealed and must be replaced if damaged with the wheel hub.

To install:

4. Install or connect the following:
  • Wheel spindle in position to the strut
  • Spindle retaining bolts and nuts. Tighten to 69–93 ft. lbs. (93–127 Nm).
  • Trailing arm to the spindle and tighten retaining bolt to 69–93 ft. lbs. (93–127 Nm)
  • Both control arms in position to the spindle and tighten the retaining bolt and nut to 63–86 ft. lbs. (85–117 Nm)
  • Stabilizer bar link nuts, retainers, bushings, sleeves and bolts
  • Brake backing plate, if equipped with drum brakes
  • Brake shield and the disc brake shield retaining bolts, if equipped with disc brakes
  • Wheel hub and bearing assembly to the wheel spindle
  • New wheel hub retainer nut and tighten to 130–174 ft. lbs. (177–235 Nm)
5. Stake the wheel hub retainer nut using a cape or round end chisel. Do not use a sharp chisel to stake the hub nut.
  • Brake drum or the disc brake rotor and caliper, as equipped
  • Hub grease cap
  • Wheel and tire assembly
6. Pump the brake pedal several times to position the brake lining before attempting to move the vehicle.
7. Road test the vehicle and check for proper operation.

FORD MOTOR CO.

Ford-Focus

DISTRIBUTORLESS IGNITION SYSTEM

PRECAUTIONS

Before servicing any vehicle, please be sure to read all of the following precautions, which deal with personal safety, prevention of component damage, and important points to take into consideration when servicing a motor vehicle:

• Never open, service or drain the radiator or cooling system when the engine is hot; serious burns can occur from the steam and hot coolant.

• Observe all applicable safety precautions when working around fuel. Whenever servicing the fuel system, always work in a well-ventilated area. Do not allow fuel spray or vapors to come in contact with a spark, open flame, or excessive heat (a hot drop light, for example). Keep a dry chemical fire extinguisher near the work area. Always keep fuel in a container specifically designed for fuel storage; also, always properly seal fuel containers to avoid the possibility of fire or explosion. Refer to the additional fuel system precautions later in this section.

• Fuel injection systems often remain pressurized, even after the engine has been turned **OFF**. The fuel system pressure must be relieved before disconnecting any fuel lines. Failure to do so may result in fire and/or personal injury.

• Brake fluid often contains polyglycol ethers and polyglycols. Avoid contact with the eyes and wash your hands thoroughly after handling brake fluid. If you do get brake fluid in your eyes, flush your eyes with clean, running water for 15 minutes. If eye irritation persists, or if you have taken brake fluid internally, IMMEDIATELY seek medical assistance.

• The EPA warns that prolonged contact with used engine oil may cause a number of skin disorders, including cancer. You should make every effort to minimize your exposure to used engine oil. Protective gloves should be worn when changing oil. Wash your hands and any other exposed skin areas as soon as possible after exposure to used engine oil. Soap and water, or waterless hand cleaner should be used.

• All new vehicles are now equipped with an air bag system, often referred to as a Supplemental Restraint System (SRS) or Supplemental Inflatable Restraint (SIR) system. The system must

be disabled before performing service on or around system components, steering column, instrument panel components, wiring and sensors. Failure to follow safety and disabling procedures could result in accidental air bag deployment, possible personal injury and unnecessary system repairs.

• Always wear safety goggles when working with, or around, the air bag system. When carrying a non-deployed air bag, be sure the bag and trim cover are pointed away from your body. When placing a non-deployed air bag on a work surface, always face the bag and trim cover upward, away from the surface. This will reduce the motion of the module if it is accidentally deployed. Refer to the additional air bag system precautions later in this section.

• Clean, high quality brake fluid from a sealed container is essential to the safe and proper operation of the brake system. You should always buy the correct type of brake fluid for your vehicle. If the brake fluid becomes contaminated, completely flush the system with new fluid. Never reuse any brake fluid. Any brake fluid that is removed from the system should be discarded. Also, do not allow any brake fluid to come in contact with a painted surface; it will damage the paint.

• Never operate the engine without the proper amount and type of engine oil; doing so WILL result in severe engine damage.

• Timing belt maintenance is extremely important. Many models utilize an interference-type, non-freewheeling engine. If the timing belt breaks, the valves in the cylinder head may strike the pistons, causing potentially serious (also time-consuming and expensive) engine damage. Refer to the maintenance interval charts in the front of this manual for the recommended replacement interval for the timing belt, and to the timing belt section for belt replacement and inspection.

• Disconnecting the negative battery cable on some vehicles may interfere with the functions of the on-board computer system(s) and may require the computer to undergo a relearning process once the negative battery cable is reconnected.

• When servicing drum brakes, only disassemble and assemble one side at a time, leaving the remaining side intact for reference.

ENGINE REPAIR

➡**Disconnecting the negative battery cable on some vehicles may interfere with the functions of the on board computer system. The computer may undergo a relearning process once the negative battery cable is reconnected.**

Alternator

REMOVAL

SOHC Engine

1. Before servicing the vehicle, refer to the precautions in the beginning of this section.

2. Remove or disconnect the following:
   • Negative battery cable
   • Accessory drive belt
   • Power steering pipe brackets
   • Exhaust manifold heat shield
   • Alternator harness connectors
   • Alternator

DOHC Engine

1. Before servicing the vehicle, refer to the precautions in the beginning of this section.

2. Remove or disconnect the following:
   • Negative battery cable
   • Accessory drive belt
   • Alternator harness connectors
   • Coolant expansion tank
   • Power steering reservoir
   • Engine wiring harness bracket
   • Ground cable
   • Evaporative Emissions (EVAP) canister purge valve
   • Alternator

INSTALLATION

SOHC Engine

Install or connect the following:
• Alternator. Tighten the bolts to 35 ft. lbs. (45 Nm).
• Alternator harness connectors
• Exhaust manifold heat shield
• Power steering pipe brackets
• Accessory drive belt
• Negative battery cable

DOHC Engine

Install or connect the following:
- Alternator. Tighten the bolts to 18 ft. lbs. (25 Nm).
- EVAP canister purge valve
- Ground cable
- Engine wiring harness bracket
- Power steering reservoir
- Coolant expansion tank
- Alternator harness connectors
- Accessory drive belt
- Negative battery cable

Ignition Timing

ADJUSTMENT

The engines are equipped with a Distributorless Ignition System (DIS). No adjustment is necessary.

Engine Assembly

REMOVAL & INSTALLATION

Manual Transaxle

1. Before servicing the vehicle, refer to the precautions in the beginning of this section.
2. Drain the cooling system.
3. Relieve the fuel system pressure.
4. Loosen the front strut center nuts 5 turns.
5. Remove or disconnect the following:
- Battery, tray and cables
- Mass Air Flow (MAF) sensor connector
- Air cleaner housing and tubes
- Accelerator cable
- Cruise control cable, if equipped
- Ignition coil connectors
- Power steering pump pressure switch connector
- Heated Oxygen (HO2S) sensor connectors
- Fuel injector harness connectors
- Powertrain Control Module (PCM) connectors
- Vehicle Speed (VSS) sensor connector
- Reverse lamp switch connector
- Clutch slave cylinder fluid pipe
- Evaporative Emissions (EVAP) canister vacuum lines
- Power brake booster vacuum line
- Delta Pressure Feedback Electronic (DPFE) system sensor vacuum line

- Exhaust Gas Recirculation (EGR) vacuum line
- Intake manifold vacuum line
- Fuel line
- Coolant bypass hoses
- Radiator hoses
- Coolant expansion tank
- Accessory drive belt
- Power steering pump and reservoir
- Power steering high pressure pipe
- Radiator cooling fan
- Catalytic converter
- Exhaust flex pipe
- Drive belt cover
- Shift cable cover
- Shift cables
- A/C compressor, if equipped
- Right engine mount
- Lower ball joints
- Axle halfshafts
6. Support the powertrain from below
7. Remove the front and rear engine mounts.
8. Raise the vehicle away from the powertrain.

To install:

9. Lower the vehicle over the powertrain.
10. Install or connect the following:
- Front engine mount. Tighten the nuts to 59 ft. lbs. (80 Nm) and the bolts to 35 ft. lbs. (47 Nm).
- Rear engine mount. Tighten the outer nuts to 35 ft. lbs. (48 Nm) and the center nut to 98 ft. lbs. (133 Nm).
- Axle halfshafts
- Lower ball joints. Tighten the pinch bolts to 37 ft. lbs. (50 Nm).
- Right engine mount. Tighten the bolts to 35 ft. lbs. (47 Nm).
- A/C compressor, if equipped
- Shift cables
- Shift cable cover
- Drive belt cover
- Exhaust flex pipe
- Catalytic converter
- Radiator cooling fan
- Power steering high pressure pipe
- Power steering pump and reservoir
- Accessory drive belt
- Coolant expansion tank
- Radiator hoses
- Coolant bypass hoses
- Fuel line
- Intake manifold vacuum line
- EGR vacuum line
- DPFE system sensor vacuum line
- Power brake booster vacuum line

- EVAP canister vacuum lines
- Clutch slave cylinder fluid pipe
- Reverse lamp switch connector
- VSS sensor connector
- PCM connectors
- Fuel injector harness connectors
- HO2S sensor connectors
- Power steering pump pressure switch connector
- Ignition coil connectors
- Cruise control cable, if equipped
- Accelerator cable
- Air cleaner housing and tubes
- MAF sensor connector
- Battery, tray and cables
11. Tighten the strut center nuts to 35 ft. lbs. (48 Nm).
12. Fill the cooling system.
13. Start the engine and check for leaks.

Automatic Transaxle

SOHC ENGINE

1. Before servicing the vehicle, refer to the precautions in the beginning of this section.
2. Drain the cooling system.
3. Relieve the fuel system pressure.
4. Loosen the front strut center nuts 5 turns.
5. Remove or disconnect the following:
- Battery, tray and cables
- Mass Air Flow (MAF) sensor connector
- Air cleaner housing and tubes
- Accelerator cable
- Cruise control cable, if equipped
- Ignition coil connectors
- Power steering pump pressure switch connector
- Heated Oxygen (HO2S) sensor connectors
- Fuel injection wiring harness connector
- Powertrain Control Module (PCM) connectors
- Radiator cooling fan
- Evaporative Emissions (EVAP) canister vacuum lines
- Power brake booster vacuum line
- Delta Pressure Feedback Electronic (DPFE) system sensor vacuum line
- Exhaust Gas Recirculation (EGR) vacuum line
- Intake manifold vacuum line
- Fuel line
- Coolant bypass hoses
- Radiator hoses
- Coolant expansion tank

- Accessory drive belt
- Power steering pump and reservoir
- Power steering high pressure pipe
- Alternator and bracket
- Drive belt cover
- A/C compressor, if equipped
- Lower ball joints
- Exhaust front pipe
- Torque converter cover
- Torque converter
- Transaxle fluid cooler lines
- Axle halfshafts
- Intermediate shaft bracket
- Starter motor
- Crankshaft pulley
- Right engine mount
- Transaxle flange bolts. Support the transaxle
- Engine front mount
- Crankshaft Position (CKP) sensor
- Engine

To install:

6. Install or connect the following:
- Engine
- CKP sensor
- Engine front mount. Tighten the nuts to 59 ft. lbs. (80 Nm) and the bolts to 35 ft. lbs. (47 Nm).
- Transaxle flange bolts. Tighten the large bolts to 35 ft. lbs. (47 Nm) and the small bolts to 16 ft. lbs. (22 Nm).
- Right engine mount. Tighten the bolts to 35 ft. lbs. (47 Nm).
- Crankshaft pulley. Tighten the bolt to 88 ft. lbs. (120 Nm).
- Starter motor
- Intermediate shaft bracket. Tighten the bolts to 35 ft. lbs. (47 Nm).
- Axle halfshafts
- Transaxle fluid cooler lines
- Torque converter. Tighten the nuts to 27 ft. lbs. (37 Nm).
- Torque converter cover
- Exhaust front pipe
- Lower ball joints. Tighten the pinch bolts to 37 ft. lbs. (50 Nm).
- A/C compressor, if equipped
- Drive belt cover
- Alternator and bracket
- Power steering high pressure pipe
- Power steering pump and reservoir
- Accessory drive belt
- Coolant expansion tank
- Radiator hoses
- Coolant bypass hoses
- Fuel line
- Intake manifold vacuum line
- EGR vacuum line
- DPFE system sensor vacuum line
- Power brake booster vacuum line
- EVAP canister vacuum lines

- Radiator cooling fan
- PCM connectors
- HO2S sensor connectors
- Fuel injection wiring harness connector
- Power steering pump pressure switch connector
- Ignition coil connectors
- Cruise control cable, if equipped
- Accelerator cable
- Air cleaner housing and tubes
- MAF sensor connector
- Battery, tray and cables

7. Tighten the strut center nuts to 35 ft. lbs. (48 Nm).
8. Fill the cooling system.
9. Start the engine and check for leaks.

DOHC ENGINE

1. Before servicing the vehicle, refer to the precautions in the beginning of this section.
2. Drain the cooling system.
3. Relieve the fuel system pressure.
4. Loosen the front strut center nuts 5 turns.
5. Remove or disconnect the following:
- Battery, tray and cables
- Mass Air Flow (MAF) sensor connector
- Positive Crankcase Ventilation (PCV) valve and hose
- Air cleaner assembly and tubes
- Accelerator cable
- Cruise control cable, if equipped
- Ignition coil connectors
- Heated Oxygen (HO2S) sensor connectors
- Fuel injector harness connectors
- Powertrain Control Module (PCM) connectors
- Radiator cooling fan
- Evaporative Emissions (EVAP) canister vacuum lines
- Power brake booster vacuum line
- Delta Pressure Feedback Electronic (DPFE) system sensor vacuum line
- Exhaust Gas Recirculation (EGR) vacuum line
- Intake manifold vacuum line
- Fuel line
- Coolant bypass hoses
- Radiator hoses
- Coolant expansion tank
- Shift select cable and bracket
- Transaxle fluid cooler lines
- Drive belt cover
- Power steering pressure switch connector
- Accessory drive belt
- A/C compressor, if equipped
- Power steering pump

- Power steering pressure pipe
- Exhaust flex pipe
- Right engine mount
- Lower ball joints
- Axle halfshafts and intermediate shaft

6. Support the powertrain from below
7. Remove the front and rear engine mounts.
8. Raise the vehicle away from the powertrain.

To install:

9. Lower the vehicle over the powertrain.
10. Install or connect the following:
- Front engine mount. Tighten the nuts to 59 ft. lbs. (80 Nm) and the bolts to 35 ft. lbs. (47 Nm).
- Rear engine mount. Tighten the outer nuts to 35 ft. lbs. (48 Nm) and the center nut to 98 ft. lbs. (133 Nm).
- Axle halfshafts and intermediate shaft
- Lower ball joints. Tighten the pinch bolts to 37 ft. lbs. (50 Nm).
- Right engine mount. Tighten the bolts to 35 ft. lbs. (47 Nm).
- Exhaust flex pipe
- Power steering pressure pipe
- Power steering pump
- A/C compressor, if equipped
- Accessory drive belt
- Power steering pressure switch connector
- Drive belt cover
- Transaxle fluid cooler lines
- Shift select cable and bracket
- Coolant expansion tank
- Radiator hoses
- Coolant bypass hoses
- Fuel line
- Intake manifold vacuum line
- EGR vacuum line
- DPFE system sensor vacuum line
- Power brake booster vacuum line
- EVAP canister vacuum lines
- Radiator cooling fan
- PCM connectors
- Fuel injector harness connectors
- HO2S sensor connectors
- Ignition coil connectors
- Cruise control cable, if equipped
- Accelerator cable
- Air cleaner assembly and tubes
- PCV valve and hose
- MAF sensor connector
- Battery, tray and cables

11. Tighten the strut center nuts to 35 ft. lbs. (48 Nm).
12. Fill the cooling system.
13. Start the engine and check for leaks.

Water Pump

REMOVAL & INSTALLATION

SOHC Engine

1. Before servicing the vehicle, refer to the precautions in the beginning of this section.
2. Drain the cooling system.
3. Remove or disconnect the following:

- Negative battery cable
- Accessory drive belt
- Front cover
- Timing belt. Refer to the Timing Belt unit repair section.
- Timing belt tensioner
- Water pump

To install:

4. Install or connect the following:

- Water pump. Tighten the bolts to 18 ft. lbs. (25 Nm).
- Timing belt tensioner
- Timing belt
- Accessory drive belt
- Negative battery cable

5. Fill the cooling system.
6. Start the engine and check for leaks.

DOHC Engine

1. Before servicing the vehicle, refer to the precautions in the beginning of this section.
2. Drain the cooling system.
3. Remove or disconnect the following:

- Negative battery cable
- Accessory drive belt
- Water pump pulley
- Front cover
- Timing belt. Refer to the Timing Belt unit repair section.
- Timing belt tensioner
- Water pump

To install:

4. Install or connect the following:

- Water pump. Tighten the bolts to 13 ft. lbs. (18 Nm).
- Timing belt tensioner
- Timing belt
- Front cover
- Water pump pulley
- Accessory drive belt
- Negative battery cable

5. Fill the cooling system.
6. Start the engine and check for leaks.

Cylinder Head

REMOVAL & INSTALLATION

SOHC Engine

1. Before servicing the vehicle, refer to the precautions in the beginning of this section.
2. Disconnect the negative battery cable.
3. Drain the cooling system.
4. Relieve the fuel system pressure.
5. Remove or disconnect the following:

- Timing belt. Refer to the Timing Belt unit repair section.
- Engine air cleaner intake tube

6. Tag and disconnect the vacuum hoses from the following components:

- Exhaust Gas Recirculation (EGR) valve
- Positive Crankcase Ventilation (PCV) valve
- Throttle body
- Fuel pressure regulator
- Intake manifold

7. Remove or disconnect the following:

- Accelerator cable, throttle control lever and if equipped, the speed control cable
- Speed control cable bracket bolt, if equipped
- 2 fuel charging wiring electrical connections
- Crankshaft Position (CKP) sensor and Heated Oxygen (HO$_2$S) sensor electrical connections
- Fuel supply line from the fuel rail, using tool D87L-9280-A
- Power steering pressure hose bracket bolts, then position the bracket and hose aside
- Alternator lower bolt, loosen only
- Alternator upper bolt and pivot the alternator forward
- Engine oil dipstick tube bracket bolt
- Exhaust Gas Recirculation (EGR) tube
- Exhaust manifold heat shield
- Catalytic converter
- Right-hand splash shield bolts and the shield
- Engine oil dipstick tube from the cylinder block
- Air conditioning compressor
- Engine accessory drive bracket
- Valve cover
- Upper radiator hose
- Heater hose
- Cylinder head bolts. Loosen the bolts in sequence.
- Cylinder head and gasket

To install:

➡ **Use new cylinder head bolts for assembly.**

➡ **Refer to Section 1 of this manual for the cylinder head torque sequence illustration. The illustration is located after the Torque Specification Chart.**

8. Install the cylinder head and tighten the bolts in sequence as follows:

   a. Step 1: 37 ft. lbs. (50 Nm)
   b. Step 2: Loosen all bolts ½ turn

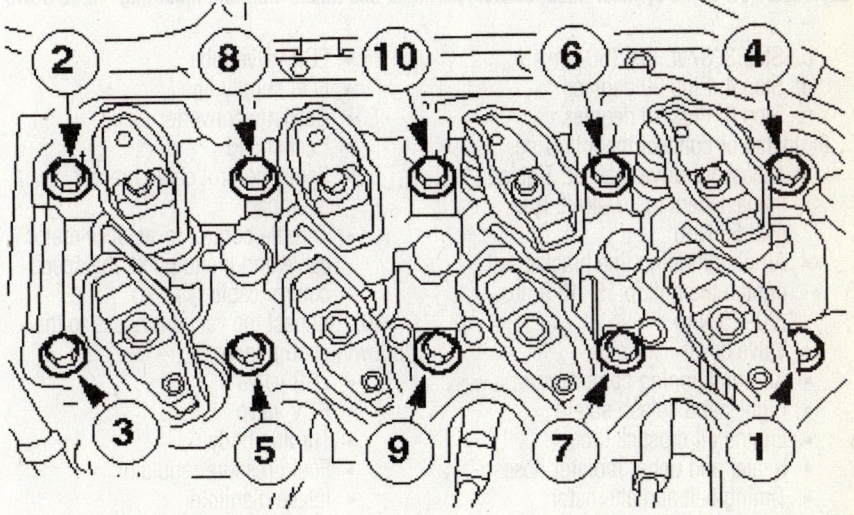

Cylinder head loosening sequence—SOHC engine

9306SG01

Timing belt service is covered in Section 4 of this manual

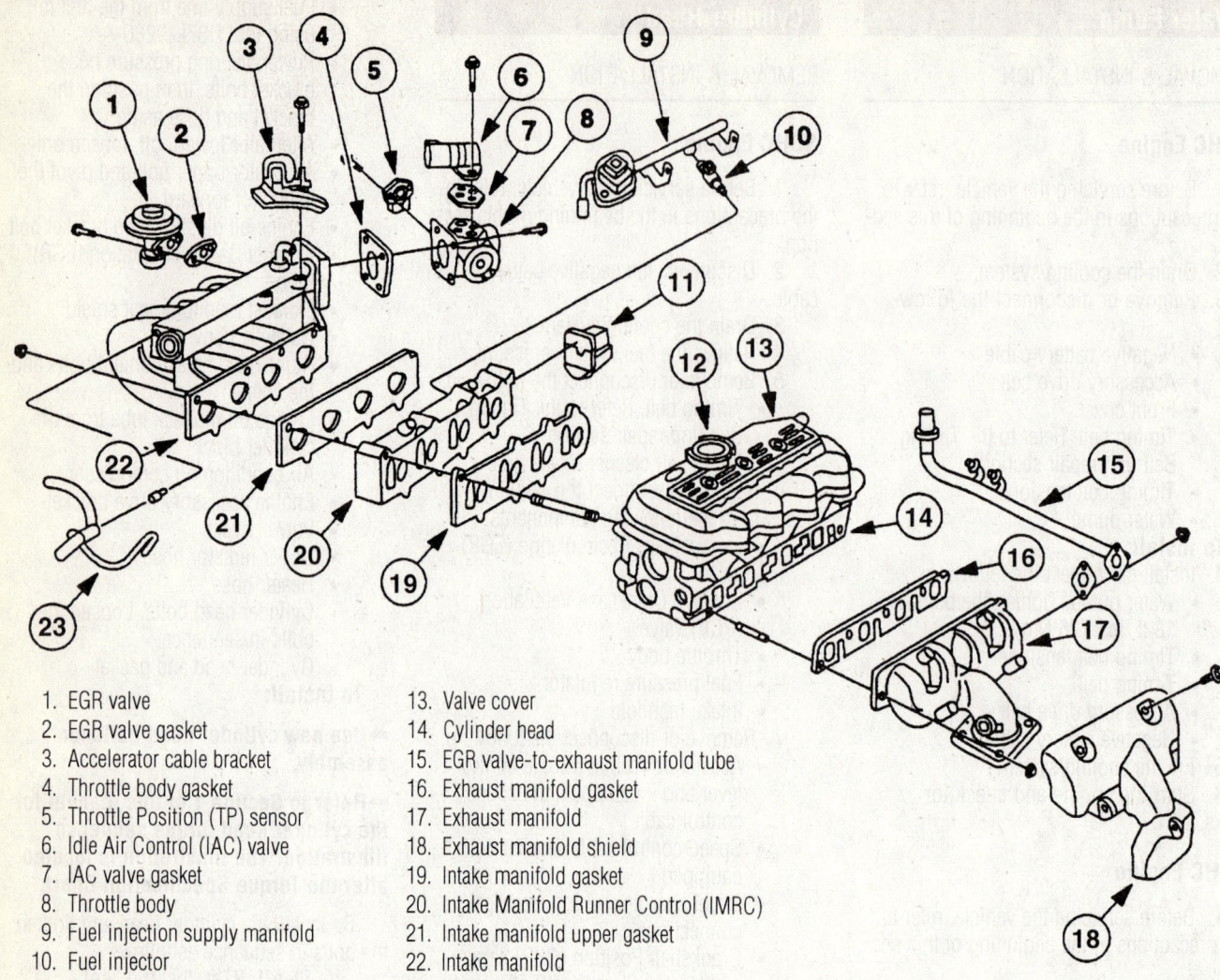

1. EGR valve
2. EGR valve gasket
3. Accelerator cable bracket
4. Throttle body gasket
5. Throttle Position (TP) sensor
6. Idle Air Control (IAC) valve
7. IAC valve gasket
8. Throttle body
9. Fuel injection supply manifold
10. Fuel injector
11. IMRC actuator
12. Oil filler cap
13. Valve cover
14. Cylinder head
15. EGR valve-to-exhaust manifold tube
16. Exhaust manifold gasket
17. Exhaust manifold
18. Exhaust manifold shield
19. Intake manifold gasket
20. Intake Manifold Runner Control (IMRC)
21. Intake manifold upper gasket
22. Intake manifold
23. Intake manifold tube

9300MG13

Exploded view of the cylinder head, exhaust manifold and intake manifold mounting—2.0L SOHC engine

c. Step 3: 37 ft. lbs. (50 Nm)
d. Step 4: Plus 90 degrees
e. Step 6: Plus 90 degrees
9. Install or connect the following:
   - Accessory drive bracket. Tighten the fasteners to 30–40 ft. lbs. (40–55 Nm)
   - Air conditioning line bracket and tighten the bolt to 15–18 ft. lbs. (20–25 Nm)
   - Valve cover
   - Air conditioning compressor
   - Right-hand splash shield
   - Engine oil dipstick tube
   - Heater and upper radiator hoses
   - Timing belt and alternator
   - Power steering pressure hose
   - CKP sensor and 2 main fuel charging electrical connections
   - Engine oil dipstick tube bolt

   - EGR valve tube
   - Fuel supply line
   - Catalytic converter
   - Heat shield
   - Speed control cable bracket, if equipped
   - Throttle control lever, accelerator cable and if equipped, the speed control cable
10. Connect the vacuum hoses to the following components:
   - EGR valve
   - PCV valve
   - Throttle body
   - Fuel pressure regulator
   - Intake manifold
   - Air cleaner outlet tube
   - Negative battery cable
11. Fill the cooling system.
12. Start the engine and check for leaks.

DOHC Engine

1. Before servicing the vehicle, refer to the precautions in the beginning of this section.

2. Disconnect the negative battery cable.

3. Properly relieve the fuel system pressure.

4. Remove or disconnect the following:
   - Air cleaner assembly outlet tube
   - Timing belt. Refer to the Timing Belt unit repair section.

5. Tag and disconnect the vacuum hoses from the following components:
   - Positive Crankcase Ventilation (PCV) valve
   - Throttle body
   - Fuel pressure sensor
   - Intake manifold

6. Remove or disconnect the following:

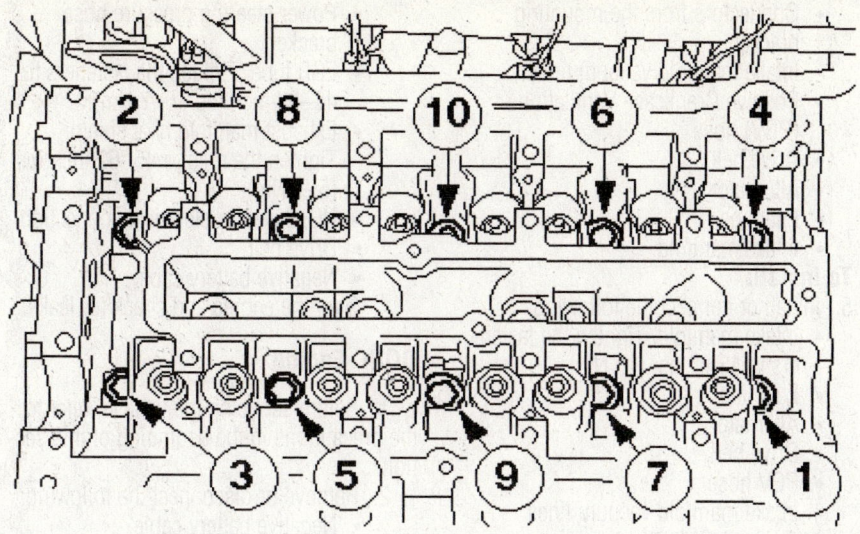

Cylinder head bolt loosening sequence—DOHC engine

- Speed control and accelerator cables from the control lever
- Fuel charging electrical connectors at the main engine connector
- Crankshaft Position (CKP) sensor and Heated Oxygen (HO₂S) sensor electrical connections
- Fuel line
- Power steering pump and bracket
- Alternator
- Engine oil dipstick tube

7. Drain the cooling system into a suitable container.

8. Remove or disconnect the following:

- Splash shield
- Air conditioning compressor
- Spark plug wires
- Valve cover
- Upper radiator hose
- Heater hose
- Camshafts
- Ignition coil
- Thermostat housing
- Cylinder head bolts. Mark each bolt with a punch and loosen them in the sequence shown.
- Cylinder head and the gasket

To install:

➡ **The cylinder head bolts may be reused twice. Only reuse bolts with one or two punch marks.**

➡ **Refer to Section 1 of this manual for the cylinder head torque sequence illustration. The illustration is located after the Torque Specification Chart.**

9. Lubricate the cylinder bolts when engine oil.

10. Install the cylinder head and tighten the bolts in sequence as follows:
   a. Step 1: 15 ft. lbs. (20 Nm)
   b. Step 2: 30 ft. lbs. (40 Nm)
   c. Step 3: Plus 90 degrees

11. Install or connect the following:

- Thermostat housing
- Ignition coil and the camshafts
- Heater and upper radiator hoses
- Valve cover
- Spark plugs
- Spark plug wires
- Air conditioning compressor
- Splash shield
- Engine oil dipstick tube
- Alternator and the power steering reservoir and bracket
- Fuel line
- CKP sensor, HO₂ sensor, and 2 main fuel charging electrical connections
- Accelerator cable and if equipped, the speed control cable to the control lever

12. Connect the vacuum hoses to the following components:

- PCV valve
- Throttle body
- Fuel pressure sensor
- Intake manifold

13. Install or connect the following:

- Timing belt
- Air cleaner outlet tube
- Negative battery cable

14. Fill the cooling system.

15. Start the engine and check for leaks.

REMOVAL & INSTALLATION

SOHC Engine

1. Before servicing the vehicle, refer to the precautions in the beginning of this section.

2. Remove or disconnect the following:

- Negative battery cable
- Valve cover

➡ **Keep all valvetrain components in order for assembly.**

- Rocker arm bolts
- Rocker arms and seats

To install:

3. Install or connect the following:

- Seats and rocker arms in their original positions
- Rocker arm bolts. Tighten to 17–22 ft. lbs. (23–30 Nm).
- Valve cover
- Negative battery cable

DOHC Engine

The DOHC engine is not equipped with rocker arms. The camshafts act directly on the valves.

Intake Manifold

REMOVAL & INSTALLATION

SOHC Engine

1. Before servicing the vehicle, refer to the precautions in the beginning of this section.

2. Drain the cooling system.

3. Relieve the fuel system pressure.

4. Remove or disconnect the following:

- Negative battery cable
- Air cleaner outlet tube

5. Tag and disconnect the vacuum hoses from the following components:

- Exhaust gas Recirculation (EGR) valve
- Positive Crankcase Ventilation (PCV) valve
- Throttle body
- Fuel pressure regulator
- Intake manifold

6. Remove or disconnect the following:

- Accelerator cable, throttle control lever and if equipped, the speed control cable

- Speed control cable bracket bolt, if equipped
- Idle Air Control (IAC) valve and Throttle Position (TP) sensor electrical connections
- Engine oil dipstick tube bracket bolt that attaches the tube to the intake manifold
- EGR manifold tube located below the EGR valve
- Engine oil dipstick tube from the block
- Intake manifold lower nuts
- Intake manifold upper nuts
- Manifold
- Manifold gasket

To install:

7. Clean and oil the intake manifold mounting studs.

8. Install or connect the following:
- Intake manifold. Tighten the nuts to 15–22 ft. lbs. (20–30 Nm).
- Engine oil dipstick tube
- EGR manifold tube. Tighten it to 15–20 ft. lbs. (20–28 Nm).
- IAC valve and TP sensor electrical connections
- Speed control cable bracket bolt, if equipped. Tighten to 71–88 inch lbs. (8–10 Nm).
- Throttle control lever, accelerator cable and if equipped, the speed control cable

9. Connect the vacuum hoses to the following components:
- EGR valve
- PCV valve
- Throttle body
- Fuel pressure regulator
- Intake manifold
- Air cleaner outlet tube
- Negative battery cable

10. Fill the cooling system.

11. Start the engine and check for coolant leaks.

DOHC Engine

1. Before servicing the vehicle, refer to the precautions in the beginning of this section.

2. Drain the cooling system.

3. Relieve the fuel system pressure.

4. Remove or disconnect the following:
- Negative battery cable
- Air cleaner outlet tube
- Throttle Position (TP) sensor connector
- Bolt that secures the pipe located by the crankshaft pulley
- Heater hoses
- Main engine control sensor wiring

- Connectors from the mounting bracket
- Intake manifold vacuum lines
- Positive Crankcase Ventilation (PCV) hose
- Drive belt
- Alternator
- Fuel line
- Intake manifold

To install:

5. Install or connect the following:
- Intake manifold. Tighten the fasteners to 13 ft. lbs. (18 Nm).
- Fuel line
- Alternator
- Drive belt
- PCV hose
- Intake manifold vacuum lines
- Connectors in the mounting bracket
- Main engine control sensor wiring
- Heater hoses
- Bolt that secures the pipe located by the crankshaft pulley. Tighten the bolt to 71–97 inch lbs. (8–11 Nm).
- TP sensor electrical connection
- Air cleaner outlet tube
- Negative battery cable

6. Fill the cooling system.

7. Start the engine and check for leaks.

Exhaust Manifold

REMOVAL & INSTALLATION

SOHC Engine

1. Before servicing the vehicle, refer to the precautions in the beginning of this section.

2. Remove or disconnect the following:
- Negative battery cable
- Drive belt
- Heated Oxygen (HO2S) sensor electrical connection
- Exhaust manifold heat shield
- Exhaust Gas Recirculation (EGR) tube
- Power steering pressure hose bracket
- Alternator
- Catalytic converter
- Exhaust manifold

To install:

3. Install or connect the following:
- Exhaust manifold. Tighten the nuts to 15–18 ft. lbs. (20–24 Nm).
- Catalytic converter. Tighten the nuts to 26–34 ft. lbs. (34–47 Nm).
- Alternator

- Power steering pressure hose bracket
- EGR tube. Tighten the fasteners to 45–62 inch lbs. (5–7 Nm).
- Exhaust manifold heat shield. Tighten the nuts to 45–62 inch lbs. (5–7 Nm).
- HO2S sensor electrical connection
- Drive belt
- Negative battery cable

4. Start the engine and check for leaks.

DOHC Engine

1. Before servicing the vehicle, refer to the precautions in the beginning of this section.

2. Remove or disconnect the following:
- Negative battery cable
- Fan motor electrical connection
- Fan shroud
- Heated Oxygen (HO2S) sensor electrical connection
- Catalytic converter
- Engine oil dipstick tube bracket bolt
- Exhaust manifold heat shield
- Exhaust manifold

To install:

3. Install or connect the following:
- Exhaust manifold. Tighten the fasteners to 13 ft. lbs. (18 Nm).
- Exhaust manifold heat shield. Tighten the retainers to 71–101 inch lbs. (8–11 Nm).
- Engine oil dipstick tube bracket. Tighten the bolt to 71–101 inch lbs. (8–11 Nm).
- Catalytic converter
- HO2S sensor electrical connection
- Fan shroud and the fan motor wiring
- Negative battery cable

4. Start the engine and check for leaks.

Front Crankshaft Seal

REMOVAL & INSTALLATION

1. Before servicing the vehicle, refer to the precautions in the beginning of this section.

2. Remove the timing belt and crankshaft sprocket.

✳✳ WARNING

Be careful not to damage the crankshaft surface when removing the seal.

3. Using seal remover tool T92C-6700-CH, remove the crankshaft front oil seal.

To install:

4. Use seal replacer tool T81P-6700-A, install the new seal.

5. Install the crankshaft sprocket and the timing belt.

Camshaft and Valve Lifters

REMOVAL & INSTALLATION

SOHC Engine

1. Before servicing the vehicle, refer to the precautions in the beginning of this section.

2. Disconnect the negative battery cable.

3. Remove the air cleaner and valve cover.

4. Remove the camshaft front seal as follows:

   a. Align the timing marks and remove the timing belt.

   b. Use cam sprocket holding/removing tool T74P-6256-B, and remove the camshaft sprocket.

   c. Unfasten the timing belt tensioner bolt and remove the tensioner.

   d. Remove the inner engine front cover.

   e. Use seal removal tool T92C-6700-CH, to remove the camshaft front seal.

5. Remove or disconnect the following:

   • Ignition coil and bracket
   • Rocker arms and valve tappets
   • Camshaft thrust plate bolts and the plate
   • Cup plug from the rear of the cylinder head and discard
   • Camshaft from the rear of the cylinder head

To install:

➡ Liberally coat the cam bore in the cylinder with clean 5W-30 motor oil.

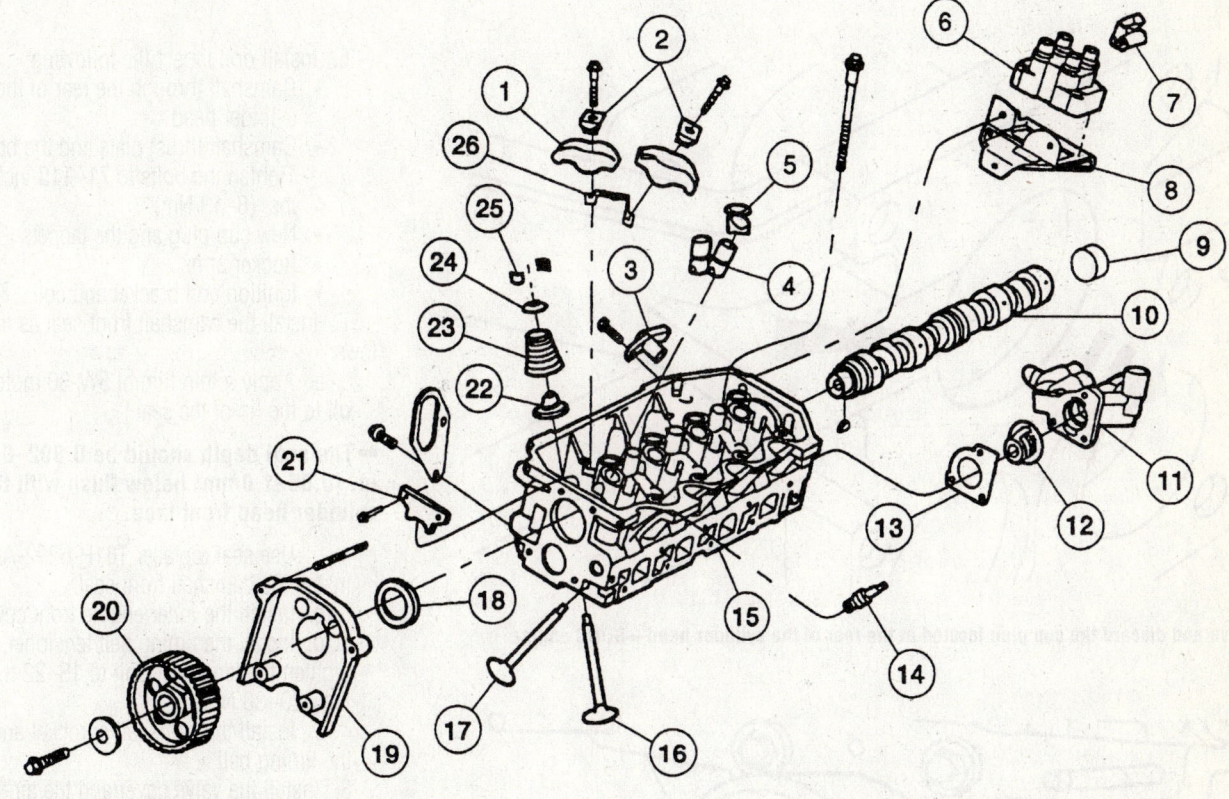

1. Rocker arm
2. Rocker arm seats
3. Camshaft Position (CMP) sensor
4. Valve tappet
5. Valve tappet guide plate
6. Ignition coil
7. Radio ignition interference capacitor
8. Ignition coil bracket
9. Cup plug
10. Camshaft
11. Water hose connection
12. Water thermostat
13. Water hose connection gasket
14. Spark plug
15. Cylinder head
16. Intake valve
17. Exhaust valve
18. Camshaft front seal
19. Engine front cover
20. Camshaft sprocket
21. Camshaft thrust plate
22. Valve stem seal
23. Valve spring
24. Valve spring retainer
25. Valve spring retainer key
26. Valve tappet guide plate retainer

9300MG12

Exploded view of the cylinder head—SOHC engine

Refer to Section 1 for engine rebuilding specifications

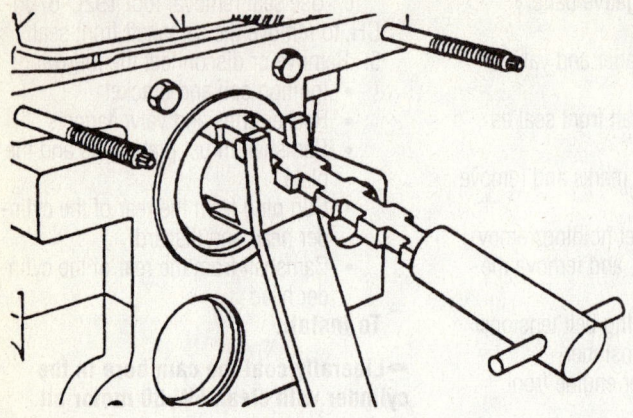

Removing the camshaft front seal—SOHC engine

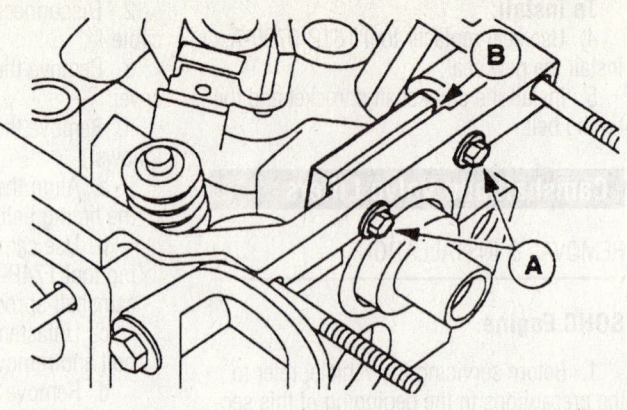

Remove the camshaft thrust plate retaining bolts (A) and the plate (B)—SOHC engine

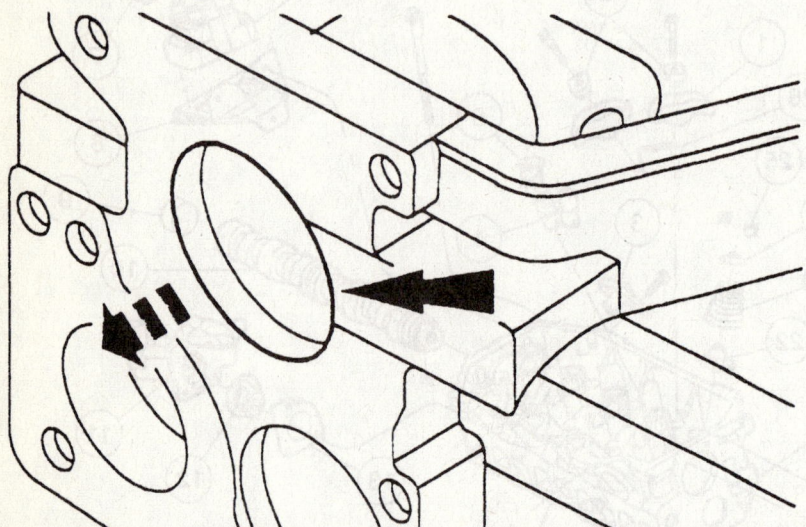

Remove and discard the cup plug located at the rear of the cylinder head—SOHC engine

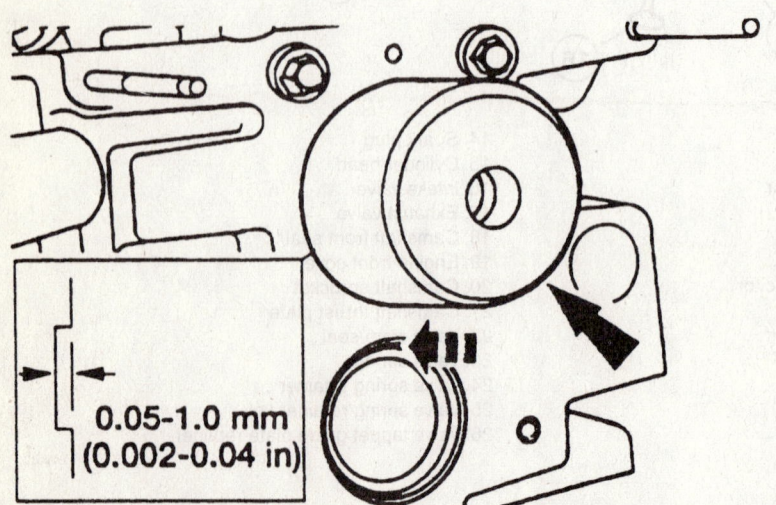

Use seal Replacer T81P-6292-A, to install the camshaft front seal 0.002–0.04 in. (0.05–1.0mm) below flush with the cylinder head front face—2.0L SOHC engine

6. Install or connect the following:
- Camshaft through the rear of the cylinder head
- Camshaft thrust plate and the bolts. Tighten the bolts to 71–115 inch lbs. (8–13 Nm).
- New cup plug and the tappets
- Rocker arms
- Ignition coil bracket and coil

7. Install the camshaft front seal as follows:

a. Apply a thin film of 5W-30 motor oil to the lip of the seal.

➡The seal depth should be 0.002–0.04 in. (0.05–1.0mm) below flush with the cylinder head front face.

b. Use seal replacer T81P-6292-A, to install the camshaft front seal.

c. Install the inner engine front cover.

d. Install the timing belt tensioner. Tighten the tensioner bolt to 15–22 ft. lbs. (20–30 Nm).

e. Install the camshaft sprocket and the timing belt

8. Install the valve cover and the air cleaner assembly.

9. Connect the negative battery cable.

DOHC Engine

1. Before servicing the vehicle, refer to the precautions in the beginning of this section.

2. Remove or disconnect the following:
- Timing belt. Refer to the Timing Belt unit repair section.
- Valve cover and camshaft sprockets
- Oil control solenoid flange

➡Mark the camshaft journal caps with a number to identify their location, as they must be replaced in their original position.

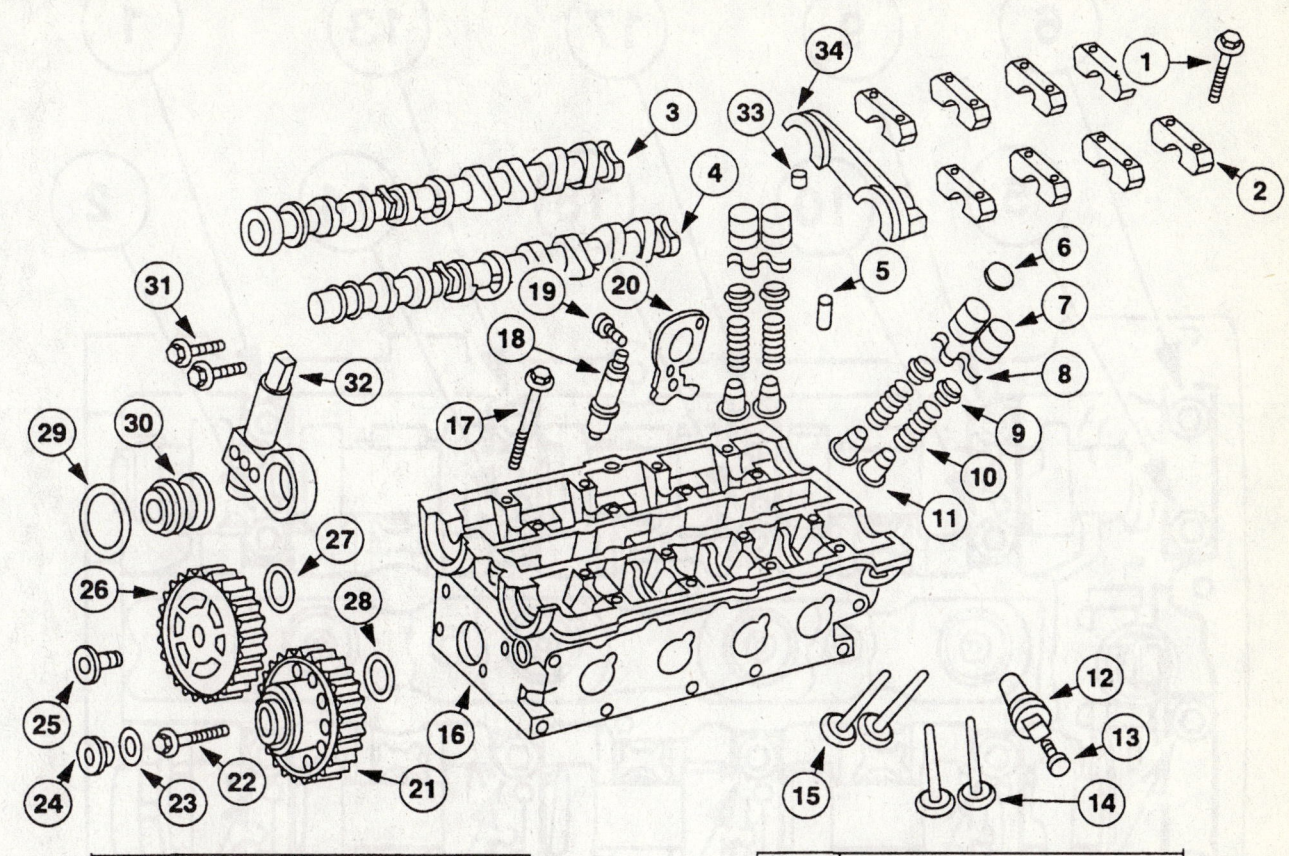

1	Bolt—Camshaft Bearing Cap		18	Spark Plug
2	Camshaft Bearing Cap		19	Engine Lifting Eye Bolt
3	Camshaft Intake		20	Engine Lifting Eye
4	Camshaft Exhaust		21	Camshaft Sprocket —Exhaust
5	Plug		22	Exhaust Camshaft Sprocket Bolt
6	Adjusting Shim—Valve Clearance		23	Blanking Plug O-Ring
7	Valve Tappets		24	Blanking Plug
8	Valve Spring Retainer Key		25	Bolt—Intake Camshaft
9	Valve Spring Retainers		26	Camshaft Sprocket Intake
10	Valve Spring (Color Coding: Exhaust = Blue, Intake = Red)		27	Camshaft Front Seal
			28	O-Ring
11	Valve Stem Seal		29	Camshaft Front Seal
12	Camshaft Position Sensor		30	Oil Feed Ring
13	CMP Sensor Bolt		31	Oil Feed Flange Bolts
14	Intake Valves		32	Oil Feed Flange
15	Exhaust Valves		33	Guide Sleeve—Front Camshaft Bearing Cap
16	Cylinder Head			
17	Cylinder Head Bolts		34	Fifth Camshaft Bearing Cap

9300MG06

Exploded view of the cylinder head and camshaft mounting—DOHC engine

For engine torque specifications, refer to Section 1 of this manual

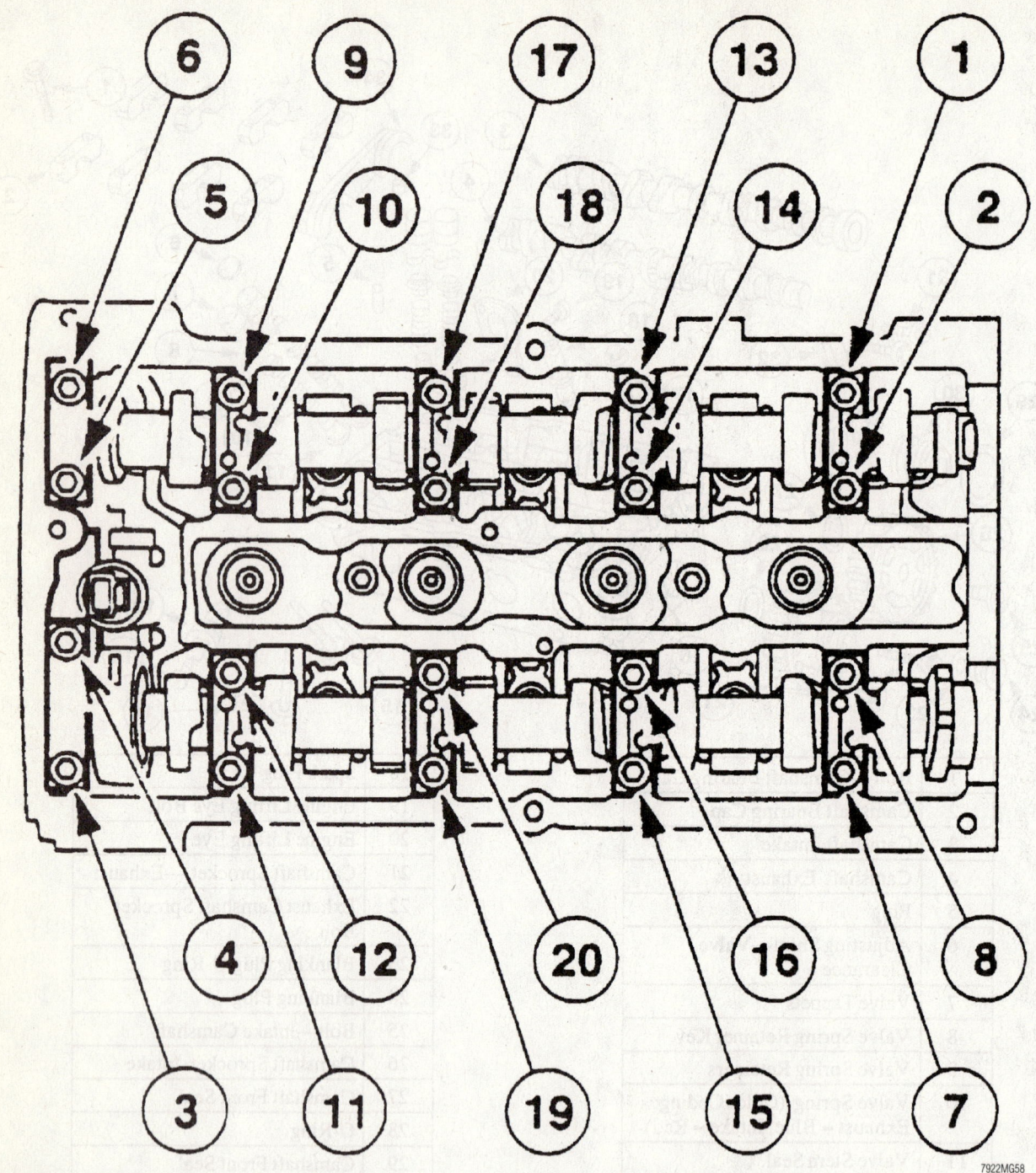

Camshaft journal cap loosening sequence—DOHC engine

- Camshaft journal caps. Loosen the bolts in sequence and in several passes.
- Camshafts
- Oil control sensor and bushing

To install:

3. Install the oil control solenoid bushing and flange on the exhaust camshaft.

4. Coat the surface of the front camshaft journal cap with gasket maker E2AZ-19562-B.

5. Place the camshafts in position and lubricate the bearing surfaces with engine assembly lubricant D9AZ-19579-D.

6. Install new camshaft front oil seals.

7. Apply a thin coat of silicone gasket and sealant F6AZ-19562-AA to the sealing surface of the of the front camshaft journal bearing cap.

8. Install the caps and tighten the bolts in several 2-turn passes in the

sequence illustrated to 10–12 ft. lbs. (13–17 Nm).

9. Inspect the oil control solenoid flange O-rings for damage or wear and replace, as necessary.

10. Install the oil control solenoid flange and tighten the bolts to 84–92 inch lbs. (9.5–10.5 Nm) in the sequence.

11. Rotate the camshafts a full turn and check for binding.

12. Install or connect the following:

- Camshaft sprockets and timing belt
- Valve cover

Valve Lash

ADJUSTMENT

SOHC Engine

The lash adjusters are hydraulic and are not adjustable.

DOHC Engine

1. Before servicing the vehicle, refer to the precautions in the beginning of this section.
2. Remove the valve cover.
3. Rotate the crankshaft so that the valve is closed and measure the clearance between the lifter shim and the camshaft base circle. Intake valve clearance should be 0.004–0.007 inches. Exhaust valve clearance should be 0.010–0.013 inches.
4. Measure each valve and note the clearance.
5. If adjustment is necessary, remove the camshafts and replace the shims. To obtain the correct shim size, measure the current shim, add the measured clearance, and subtract 0.006 inches for intake valves or 0.012 inches for exhaust valves.
6. Install or connect the following:
   - Camshafts
   - Valve cover

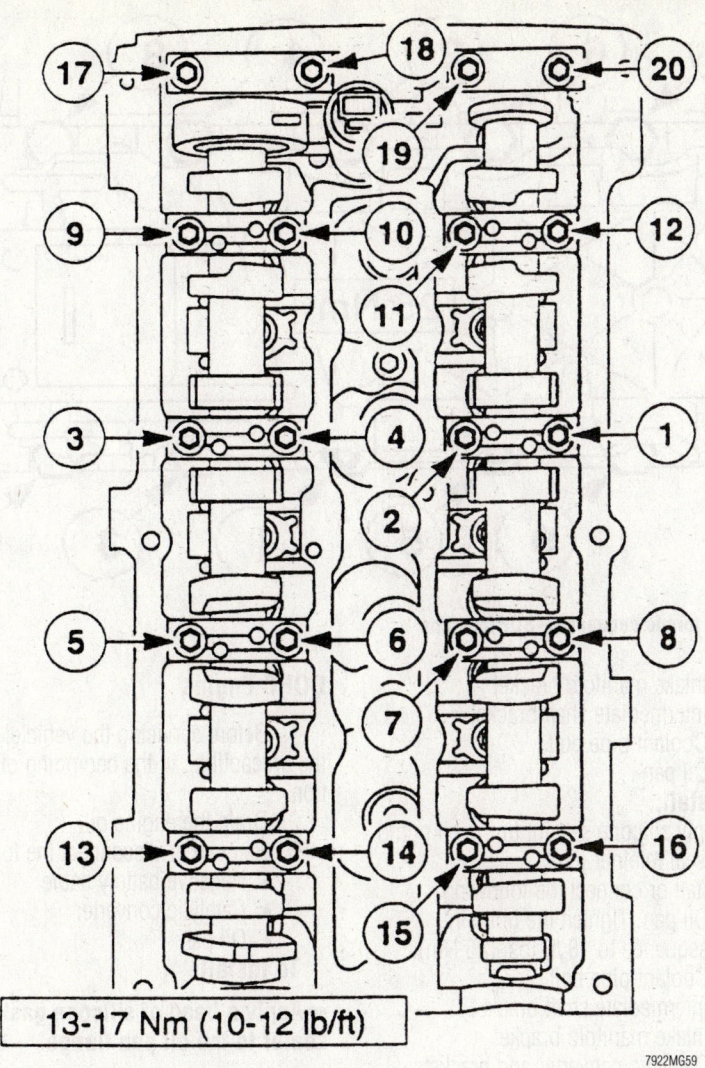

13-17 Nm (10-12 lb/ft)

7922MG59

Camshaft journal cap torque sequence—DOHC engine

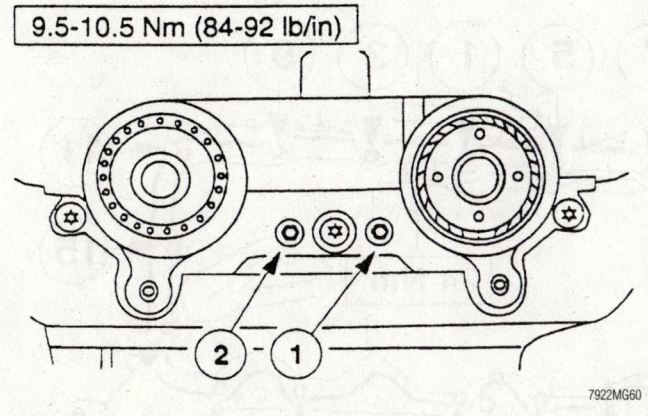

9.5-10.5 Nm (84-92 lb/in)

7922MG60

Tighten the oil control solenoid flange bolts in this sequence—DOHC engine

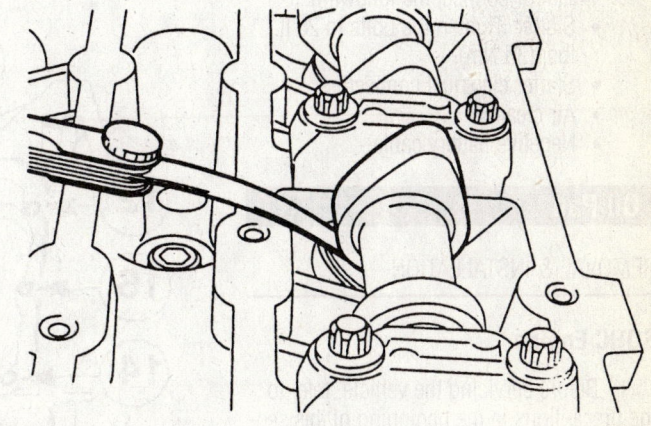

9306HG04

Checking valve clearance—2.0L engine

For complete mechanical specifications, refer to Section 1 of this manual

Starter Motor

REMOVAL & INSTALLATION

SOHC Engine

1. Before servicing the vehicle, refer to the precautions in the beginning of this section.
2. Remove or disconnect the following:
   - Negative battery cable
   - Air cleaner outlet tube
   - Two top starter motor bolts
   - **S** terminal wire and the **B** terminal nut and cable from the solenoid
   - Lower starter motor bolt
   - Starter

To install:

3. Install or connect the following:
   - Starter motor assembly and tighten the lower mounting bolt to 18–20 ft. lbs. (25–27 Nm)
   - **S** terminal wire, **B** terminal cable and nut. Tighten the nut to 80–120 inch lbs. (9–13.5 Nm).
   - Top starter motor bolts. Tighten the bolts to 18–20 ft. lbs. (25–27 Nm).
   - Air cleaner outlet tube
   - Negative battery cable

DOHC Engine

1. Before servicing the vehicle, refer to the precautions in the beginning of this section.
2. Remove or disconnect the following:
   - Negative battery cable
   - Air cleaner
   - Starter electrical connectors
   - Starter

To install:

3. Install or connect the following:
   - Starter. Tighten the bolts to 26 ft. lbs. (35 Nm).
   - Starter electrical connectors
   - Air cleaner
   - Negative battery cable

Oil Pan

REMOVAL & INSTALLATION

SOHC Engine

1. Before servicing the vehicle, refer to the precautions in the beginning of this section.
2. Drain the engine oil.
3. Remove or disconnect the following:
   - Negative battery cable
   - Catalytic converter and brackets

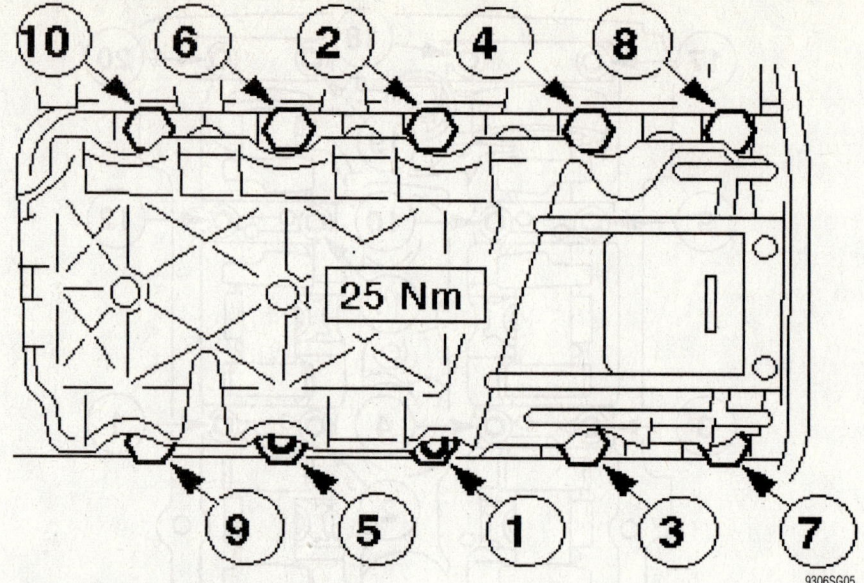

Oil pan torque sequence—SOHC engine

   - Intake manifold bracket
   - Intermediate shaft bracket
   - Coolant pipe bolt
   - Oil pan

To install:

4. Apply silicone sealant to the oil pump and rear seal retainer joints.
5. Install or connect the following:
   - Oil pan. Tighten the bolts in sequence to 18 ft. lbs. (25 Nm).
   - Coolant pipe bolt
   - Intermediate shaft bracket
   - Intake manifold bracket
   - Catalytic converter and brackets
   - Negative battery cable
6. Fill the crankcase to the correct level.
7. Start the engine and check for leaks.

DOHC Engine

1. Before servicing the vehicle, refer to the precautions in the beginning of this section.
2. Drain the engine oil.
3. Remove or disconnect the following:
   - Negative battery cable
   - Catalytic converter
   - Oil pan

To install:

➡ **Apply a bead of silicone gasket sealer to the oil pan flange.**

4. Install or connect the following:
   - Oil pan. Tighten the bolts in sequence and in several passes to 18 ft. lbs. (24 Nm).

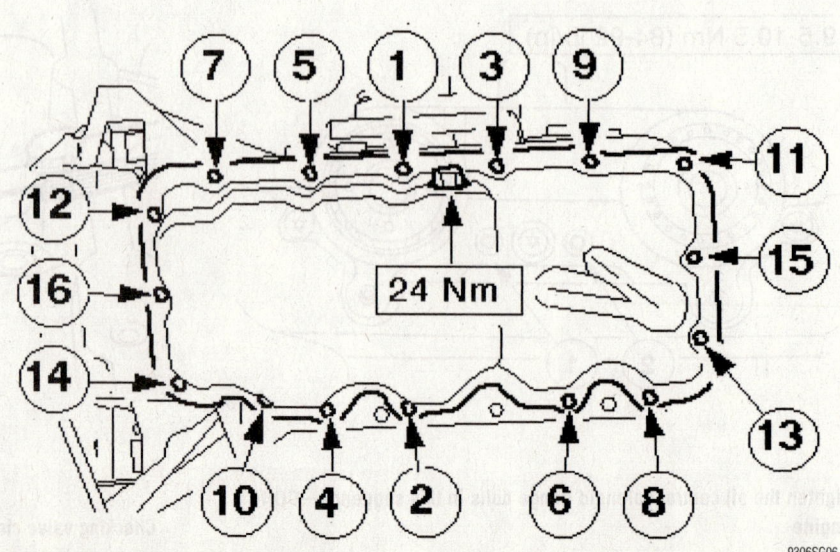

Oil pan torque sequence—DOHC engine

- Oil lever sensor connector
- Catalytic converter
- Negative battery cable

5. Fill the crankcase to the correct level.
6. Start the engine and check for leaks.

Oil Pump

REMOVAL & INSTALLATION

SOHC Engine

1. Before servicing the vehicle, refer to the precautions in the beginning of this section.
2. Remove or disconnect the following:
   - Timing belt
   - Oil pan
   - Crankshaft Position (CKP) sensor
   - Oil pump pickup tube
   - Oil pump

To install:

3. Lubricate the crankshaft front oil seal lip with clean engine oil.
4. Install or connect the following:
   - Oil pump. Tighten the bolts to 10–12 ft. lbs. (13–16 Nm).
   - Oil pump pickup tube. Tighten the retaining bolts to 71–97 inch lbs. (8–11 Nm).
   - CKP sensor
   - Oil pan
   - Timing belt

5. Fill the crankcase to the correct level.
6. Start the engine and check for leaks.

DOHC Engine

1. Before servicing the vehicle, refer to the precautions in the beginning of this section.
2. Drain the engine oil.
3. Remove or disconnect the following:
   - Negative battery cable
   - Timing belt. Refer to the Timing Belt unit repair section.
   - Oil pan
   - Oil pump pickup tube
   - Oil pump

To install:

4. Install or connect the following:
   - Oil pump. Tighten the bolts to 97 inch lbs. (11 Nm)
   - Oil pump pickup tube. Tighten the fasteners to 88 inch lbs. (10 Nm).
   - Oil pan
   - Timing belt
   - Negative battery cable

5. Fill the crankcase to the correct level.
6. Start the engine and check for leaks.

Rear Main Seal

REMOVAL & INSTALLATION

1. Before servicing the vehicle, refer to the precautions in the beginning of this section.
2. Remove or disconnect the following:
   - Negative battery cable
   - Transaxle
   - Clutch, if equipped
   - Flexplate/flywheel
   - Oil seal

To install:

3. Install or connect the following:
   - Oil seal. Seat the seal flush with the rear of the crankshaft oil seal retainer.
   - Flexplate/flywheel. Tighten the bolts to 82 ft. lbs. (112 Nm).
   - Clutch, if equipped
   - Transaxle
   - Negative battery cable

4. Start the engine and check for leaks.

Piston and Ring

POSITIONING

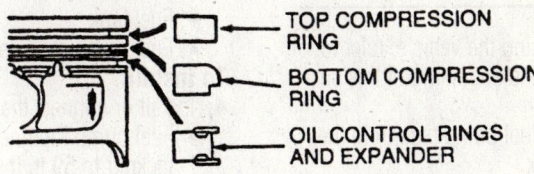

FUEL SYSTEM

Fuel System Service Precautions

Safety is the most important factor when performing not only fuel system maintenance but any type of maintenance. Failure to conduct maintenance and repairs in a safe manner may result in serious personal injury or death. Maintenance and testing of the vehicle's fuel system components can be accomplished safely and effectively by adhering to the following rules and guidelines.

- To avoid the possibility of fire and personal injury, always disconnect the negative battery cable unless the repair or test procedure requires that battery voltage be applied.

- Always relieve the fuel system pressure prior to disconnecting any fuel system component (injector, fuel rail, pressure regulator, etc.), fitting or fuel line connection. Exercise extreme caution whenever relieving fuel system pressure, to avoid exposing skin, face and eyes to fuel spray. Please be advised that fuel under pressure may pene-

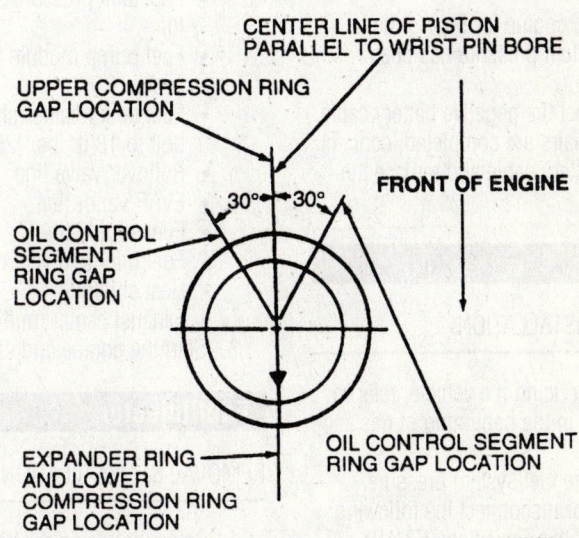

Ford 2.0L (VIN 3 and P) engines—piston ring positioning, end-gap spacing and piston positioning. The small directional arrow must face the front of the engine.

trate the skin or any part of the body that it contacts.

• Always place a shop towel or cloth around the fitting or connection prior to loosening to absorb any excess fuel due to spillage. Ensure that all fuel spillage (should it occur) is quickly removed from engine surfaces. Ensure that all fuel soaked cloths or towels are deposited into a suitable waste container.

• Always keep a dry chemical (Class B) fire extinguisher near the work area.

• Do not allow fuel spray or fuel vapors to come into contact with a spark or open flame.

• Always use a backup wrench when loosening and tightening fuel line connection fittings. This will prevent unnecessary stress and torsion to fuel line piping.

• Always replace worn fuel fitting O-rings with new. Do not substitute fuel hose or equivalent, where fuel pipe is installed.

Before servicing the vehicle, make sure to refer to the precautions in the beginning of this section as well.

Fuel System Pressure

RELIEVING

1. Before servicing the vehicle, refer to the precautions in the beginning of this section.

2. Remove the fuel pump fuse from the battery junction box.

3. Start the engine and allow it to idle until it stalls.

4. Crank the engine for 5 seconds to ensure that the fuel pressure has been relieved.

5. Disconnect the negative battery cable.

6. When repairs are completed, connect the negative battery cable and replace the fuel pump fuse.

Fuel Filter

REMOVAL & INSTALLATION

1. Before servicing the vehicle, refer to the precautions in the beginning of this section.

2. Relieve the fuel system pressure.

3. Remove or disconnect the following:
   • Evaporative Emissions (EVAP) vapor line
   • Fuel filter lines
   • Fuel filter and bracket assembly
   • Fuel filter

To install:

4. Install or connect the following:
   • Fuel filter
   • Fuel filter and bracket assembly
   • Fuel filter lines
   • EVAP vapor line

5. Start the engine and check for leaks.

Fuel Pump

REMOVAL & INSTALLATION

1. Before servicing the vehicle, refer to the precautions in the beginning of this section.

2. Relieve the fuel system pressure.

3. Remove or disconnect the following:
   • Exhaust center muffler
   • Heat shield
   • Fuel filler and vent hoses
   • Fuel supply line
   • Evaporative Emissions (EVAP) vapor line
   • Rollover valve line
   • Fuel tank retainer strap. Support the fuel tank.
   • Fuel pump module harness connector
   • Fuel tank pressure sensor connector
   • Fuel tank
   • Fuel pump module

To install:

4. Install or connect the following:
   • Fuel pump module. Tighten the locknut to 59 ft. lbs. (80 Nm).
   • Fuel tank
   • Fuel tank pressure sensor connector
   • Fuel pump module harness connector
   • Fuel tank retainer strap. Tighten the bolt to 18 ft. lbs. (25 Nm).
   • Rollover valve line
   • EVAP vapor line
   • Fuel supply line
   • Fuel filler and vent hoses
   • Heat shield
   • Exhaust center muffler

5. Start the engine and check for leaks.

Fuel Injector

REMOVAL & INSTALLATION

1. Before servicing the vehicle, refer to the precautions in the beginning of this section.

2. Relieve fuel system pressure.

3. Remove or disconnect the following:
   • Negative battery cable
   • Fuel line and retaining clip
   • Pressure regulator vacuum hose
   • Accelerator cable
   • Fuel injector electrical connectors
   • Fuel supply manifold with the injectors attached
   • Injectors from the supply manifold

To install:

4. Install or connect the following:
   • Fuel injectors using new O-ring seals
   • Fuel supply manifold with the injectors attached. Tighten the bolts to 88 inch lbs. (10 Nm).
   • Fuel injector electrical connectors
   • Accelerator cable
   • Pressure regulator vacuum hose
   • Fuel line and retaining clip
   • Negative battery cable

DRIVE TRAIN

Transaxle Assembly

REMOVAL & INSTALLATION

Manual

1. Before servicing the vehicle, refer to the precautions in the beginning of this section.

2. Attach a support fixture to the engine lifting eyes.

3. Loosen the front strut center nuts 5 turns.

4. Remove or disconnect the following:
   • Battery and tray
   • Mass Air Flow (MAF) sensor connector
   • Air cleaner assembly
   • Air intake pipe
   • Clutch slave cylinder fluid line
   • Shift cables
   • Exhaust flex pipe
   • Engine front mount
   • Lower ball joints
   • Axle halfshafts and intermediate shaft
   • Drive belt cover
   • Reverse light switch connector
   • Vehicle Speed (VSS) sensor connector
   • Rear engine mount and bracket
   • Starter motor
   • Transaxle flange bolts. Support the transaxle.
   • Transaxle

To install:

5. Install or connect the following:
- Transaxle. Tighten the flange bolts to 35 ft. lbs. (47 Nm).
- Starter motor
- Rear engine mount bracket. Tighten the fastener to 59 ft. lbs. (80 Nm).
- Rear engine mount. Tighten the outer nuts to 35 ft. lbs. (48 Nm) and the center nut to 98 ft. lbs. (133 Nm).
- VSS sensor connector
- Reverse light switch connector
- Drive belt cover
- Axle halfshafts and intermediate shaft
- Lower ball joints. Tighten the pinch bolts to 37 ft. lbs. (50 Nm).
- Right engine mount. Tighten the bolts to 35 ft. lbs. (47 Nm).
- Exhaust flex pipe
- Shift cables
- Clutch slave cylinder fluid line
- Air intake pipe
- Air cleaner assembly
- MAF sensor connector
- Battery and tray

6. Tighten the strut center nuts to 35 ft. lbs. (48 Nm).

Automatic

1. Before servicing the vehicle, refer to the precautions in the beginning of this section.

2. Attach a support fixture to the engine lifting eyes.

3. Loosen the front strut center nuts 5 turns.

4. Remove or disconnect the following:
- Battery and tray
- Mass Air Flow (MAF) sensor connector
- Positive Crankcase Ventilation (PCV) hose
- Air intake pipe and resonator
- Turbine Shaft Speed (TSS) sensor connector
- Transmission range sensor connector
- Transaxle harness connector
- Starter motor
- Shift cable and bracket
- Front wheels
- Exhaust front pipe
- Right engine support
- Outer tie rod ends
- Lower ball joints
- Axle halfshafts and intermediate shaft

- Output Shaft Speed (OSS) sensor connector
- Transaxle oil cooler lines
- Torque converter
- Transaxle oil dipstick tube
- Rear engine mount and bracket

➡ **The transaxle flange bolts vary in length. Note their locations for installation.**

- Transaxle flange bolts. Support the transaxle.
- Transaxle

To install:

5. Install or connect the following:
- Transaxle. Tighten the flange bolts to 35 ft. lbs. (48 Nm).
- Rear engine mount bracket. Tighten the fastener to 59 ft. lbs. (80 Nm).
- Rear engine mount. Tighten the outer nuts to 35 ft. lbs. (48 Nm) and the center nut to 98 ft. lbs. (133 Nm).
- Transaxle oil dipstick tube
- Torque converter. Tighten the nuts to 27 ft. lbs. (37 Nm).
- Transaxle oil cooler lines
- OSS sensor connector
- Axle halfshafts and intermediate shaft
- Lower ball joints. Tighten the pinch bolts to 37 ft. lbs. (50 Nm).
- Outer tie rod ends. Tighten the nuts to 35 ft. lbs. (47 Nm).
- Right engine support. Tighten the bolts to 35 ft. lbs. (48 Nm).
- Exhaust front pipe. Tighten the fasteners to 35 ft. lbs. (47 Nm).
- Front wheels
- Shift cable and bracket
- Starter motor
- Transaxle harness connector
- Transmission range sensor connector
- TSS sensor connector
- Air intake pipe and resonator
- PCV hose
- MAF sensor connector
- Battery and tray

6. Tighten the strut center nuts to 35 ft. lbs. (48 Nm).

Clutch

REMOVAL & INSTALLATION

1. Before servicing the vehicle, refer to the precautions in the beginning of this section.

2. Remove or disconnect the following:
- Negative battery cable
- Transaxle
- Pressure plate. Loosen the bolts evenly in ½ turn steps.
- Clutch disc

To install:

3. Install or connect the following:
- Clutch disc and pressure plate. Tighten the pressure plate bolts evenly in ½ turns to 21 ft. lbs. (29 Nm).
- Transaxle
- Negative battery cable

Hydraulic Clutch System

BLEEDING

1. Before servicing the vehicle, refer to the precautions in the beginning of this section.

2. Remove or disconnect the following:
- Air cleaner assembly
- Mass Air Flow (MAF) sensor connector
- Air intake pipe

3. Remove fluid from the brake fluid reservoir until the level reaches the **MIN** mark.

4. Fill the reservoir of Special Tool 416-D002 with DOT 4 brake fluid.

5. Attach the tool to the slave cylinder bleed nipple.

6. Open the bleed nipple and pump 80 ml brake fluid into the clutch control system.

7. Tighten the bleed nipple to 88 inch lbs. (10 Nm) and remove the tool.

8. Have an assistant depress the clutch pedal 4–5 times and hold the pedal at full travel.

9. Close the bleeder before releasing the clutch pedal.

10. Repeat the procedure until no more air bubbles are seen.

11. Check the clutch for proper operation.

12. Check the brake fluid reservoir level and fill with DOT 4 brake fluid, as necessary.

13. Install or connect the following:
- Air intake pipe
- MAF sensor connector
- Air cleaner assembly

Halfshaft

REMOVAL & INSTALLATION

Left

➡ **The IB5 manual transmission is used with the SOHC engine and the MTX75 manual transmission is used with the DOHC engine.**

➡ **The hub nut may be reused 4 times. Mark the nut at removal and only use hub nuts with 4 or fewer marks for assembly.**

1. Before servicing the vehicle, refer to the precautions in the beginning of this section.
2. Loosen the strut center nut 5 turns.

3. Remove or disconnect the following:
   - Front wheel
   - Hub retainer nut. Mark the nut.
   - Lower ball joint
4. Press the stub shaft out of the wheel hub.
5. Separate the inner CV-joint from the transaxle as follows:
   - If equipped with the IB5 manual transaxle, use Halfshaft remover 308-256
   - If equipped with the MTX75 manual transaxle or with an automatic transaxle, use Halfshaft remover 205-241 and a slide hammer

To install:

➡ **Replace the circlip for assembly.**

6. Install the halfshaft inner joint so that the circlip is felt to seat. Draw the stub shaft

into the wheel hub with Halfshaft installer 205-379.

7. Install or connect the following:
   - Lower ball joint. Tighten the pinch bolt to 37 ft. lbs. (50 Nm).
   - Hub retainer nut. Tighten the nut to 232 ft. lbs. (316 Nm).
   - Front wheel
8. Check the transaxle fluid and add, as necessary.
9. Tighten the strut center nuts to 35 ft. lbs. (48 Nm).

Right

➡ **The hub nut may be reused 4 times. Mark the nut at removal and only use hub nuts with 4 or fewer marks for assembly.**

1. Before servicing the vehicle, refer to the precautions in the beginning of this section.
2. Loosen the strut center nut 5 turns.
3. Remove or disconnect the following:
   - Front wheel
   - Hub retainer nut. Mark the nut.
   - Lower ball joint
   - Intermediate shaft retaining clip
4. Press the stub shaft out of the wheel hub.
5. Remove the right axle halfshaft and the intermediate shaft as an assembly.

To install:

➡ **Use a new retaining clip for assembly.**

6. Install or connect the following:
   - Axle halfshaft and intermediate shaft assembly. Tighten the nuts to 18 ft. lbs. (25 Nm).
   - Lower ball joint. Tighten the pinch bolt to 37 ft. lbs. (50 Nm).
   - Hub retainer nut. Tighten the nut to 232 ft. lbs. (316 Nm).
   - Front wheel
7. Check the transaxle fluid and add, as necessary.
8. Tighten the strut center nuts to 35 ft. lbs. (48 Nm).

CV-Joints

OVERHAUL

Inner Tri-Pot Joint

1. Before servicing the vehicle, refer to the precautions in the beginning of this section.
2. Remove the axle halfshaft from the vehicle and place it in a vise.

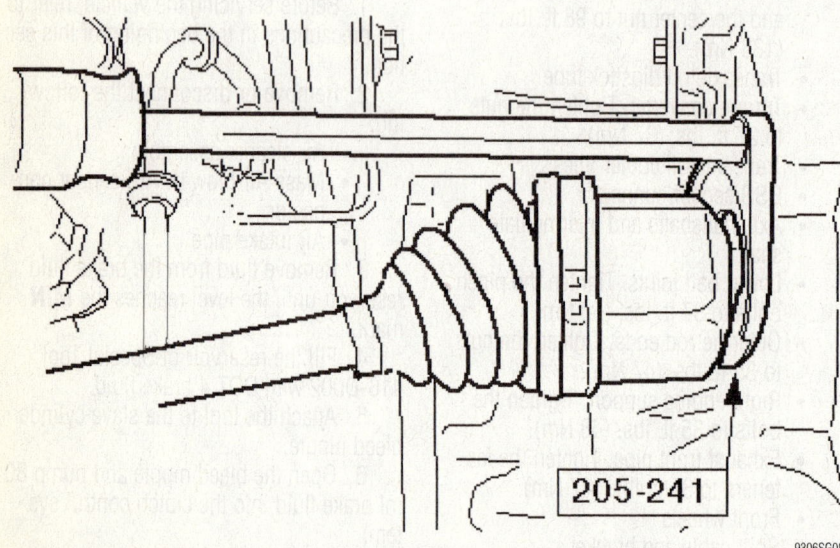

Left halfshaft removal—MTX75 manual transaxle and automatic transaxle

9306SG08

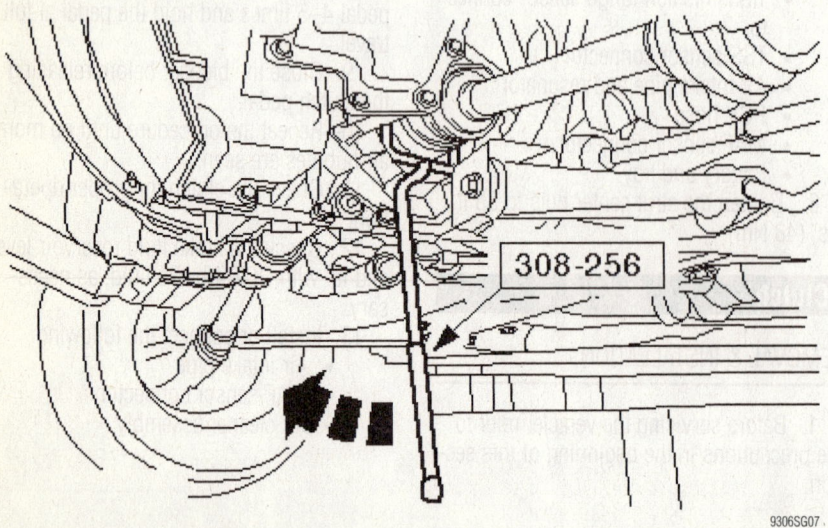

Left halfshaft removal—IB5 manual transaxle

9306SG07

3. Remove or disconnect the following:
- Tri-Pot joint boot clamps
- Tri-Pot joint boot
- Tri-Pot joint housing
- Snapring
- Tri-Pot joint

To install:

➡ **Use new snaprings and boot clamps for assembly.**

4. Install or connect the following:
- Tri-Pot joint
- Snapring
- Tri-Pot joint housing. Fill the joint housing with grease.
- Tri-Pot joint boot
- Tri-Pot joint boot clamps
5. Install the halfshaft.

Outer CV-Joint

The outer CV-joint is serviced with the halfshaft as an assembly. The outer CV-joint boot can be serviced by removing the inner Tri-Pot joint.

STEERING AND SUSPENSION

Air Bag

❋❋ CAUTION

These vehicles are equipped with an air bag system. The system must be disarmed before performing service on, or around, system components, the steering column, instrument panel components, wiring and sensors. Failure to follow the safety precautions and the disarming procedure could result in accidental air bag deployment, possible injury and unnecessary system repairs.

PRECAUTIONS

Several precautions must be observed when handling the inflator module to avoid accidental deployment and possible personal injury.
- Never carry the inflator module by the wires or connector on the underside of the module
- When carrying a live inflator module, hold securely with both hands, and ensure that the bag and trim cover are pointed away
- Place the inflator module on a bench or other surface with the bag and trim cover facing up
- With the inflator module on the bench, never place anything on or close to the module which may be thrown in the event of an accidental deployment

Before servicing the vehicle, also be sure to refer to the precautions in the beginning of this section as well

DISARMING

1. Before servicing the vehicle, refer to the precautions in the beginning of this section.
2. Position the vehicle with the front wheels in a straight-ahead position.
3. Disconnect the negative battery cable.
4. Disconnect the positive battery cable.
5. Wait at least 1 minute for the air bag backup power supply to drain before continuing.
6. Proceed with the repair.
7. Once complete, connect the battery cables, negative cable last.
8. Check the functioning of the air bag system by turning the ignition key to the **RUN** position and visually monitoring the air bag indicator lamp in the instrument cluster. The indicator lamp should illuminate for approximately 6 seconds, then turn **OFF**. If the indicator lamp does not illuminate, stays on, or flashes at any time, a fault has been detected by the air bag diagnostic monitor.

Power Rack & Pinion Steering Gear

REMOVAL & INSTALLATION

1. Before servicing the vehicle, refer to the precautions in the beginning of this section.
2. Center the steering wheel and turn the ignition to the **LOCK** position.
3. Remove or disconnect the following:
- Negative battery cable
- Lower instrument panel cover
- Steering shaft pinch bolt
- Front wheels
- Outer tie rod ends
- Stabilizer bar links
- Power steering fluid cooler hose
- Right engine mount

- Steering gear heat shield
- Power steering hose support clamp
- Power steering hoses
- 6 subframe bolts. Support the subframe.
- Floor seal
- Steering gear pinion extension
- Steering gear

To install:

4. Install or connect the following:
- Steering gear. Tighten the bolts to 59 ft. lbs. (80 Nm).
- Steering gear pinion extension. Tighten the pinch bolt to 26 ft. lbs. (35 Nm).
- Floor seal
5. Install Subframe Alignment Pins 502-002 and raise the subframe into position. Tighten the 4 rear bolts to 147 ft. lbs. (200 Nm) and the other bolts to 85 ft. lbs. (115 Nm).
6. Install or connect the following:
- Power steering hoses
- Power steering hose support clamp
- Steering gear heat shield
- Right engine mount. Tighten the bolt to 37 ft. lbs. (50 Nm).
- Power steering fluid cooler hose
- Stabilizer bar links. Tighten the nuts to 37 ft. lbs. (50 Nm).
- Outer tie rod ends. Tighten the nuts to 35 ft. lbs. (47 Nm).
- Front wheels
- Steering shaft pinch bolt. Tighten the bolt to 21 ft. lbs. (28 Nm).
- Lower instrument panel cover
- Negative battery cable
7. Check the wheel alignment and adjust, as necessary.

Strut

REMOVAL & INSTALLATION

1. Before servicing the vehicle, refer to the precautions in the beginning of this section.
2. Remove or disconnect the following:
- Front wheel
- Brake hose bracket
- Stabilizer bar link
- Wheel speed sensor, if equipped
- Brake caliper and rotor
- Outer tie rod end
- Lower ball joint
- Steering knuckle pinch bolt. Separate the knuckle from the strut.
- Upper strut mount nuts
- Strut assembly

To install:

3. Install or connect the following:
- Strut assembly. Tighten the upper mount nuts to 18 ft. lbs. (25 Nm).
- Steering knuckle. Tighten the pinch bolt to 66 ft. lbs. (90 Nm).
- Lower ball joint. Tighten the pinch bolt to 37 ft. lbs. (50 Nm).
- Outer tie rod end. Tighten the nut to 35 ft. lbs. (47 Nm).
- Brake caliper and rotor
- Wheel speed sensor, if equipped
- Stabilizer bar link. Tighten the nut to 37 ft. lbs. (50 Nm).
- Brake hose bracket
- Front wheel

4. Check the wheel alignment and adjust, as necessary.

Shock Absorber

REMOVAL & INSTALLATION

3 Door Model

1. Before servicing the vehicle, refer to the precautions in the beginning of this section.

2. Remove or disconnect the following:
- Luggage compartment interior trim panel
- Upper shock absorber mounting nut
- Lower shock absorber mounting bolt
- Shock absorber

To install:

➡Tighten the shock absorber mounting fasteners with the suspension at curb height and the vehicle weight supported by the wheels.

3. Install or connect the following:
- Shock absorber. Guide the rod into the locating hole.
- Lower shock absorber mounting bolt. Tighten the bolt to 85 ft. lbs. (115 Nm).
- Upper shock absorber mounting nut. Tighten the nut to 13 ft. lbs. (18 Nm).
- Luggage compartment interior trim panel

Wagon

1. Before servicing the vehicle, refer to the precautions in the beginning of this section.

2. Remove the upper and lower mounting bolts and remove the shock absorber.

To install:

➡Tighten the shock absorber mounting fasteners with the suspension at curb height and the vehicle weight supported by the wheels.

3. Install the shock absorber and tighten the mounting bolts to 85 ft. lbs. (115 Nm).

Coil spring

REMOVAL & INSTALLATION

Front

1. Before servicing the vehicle, refer to the precautions at the beginning of this section.

2. Remove the strut from the vehicle.

3. Compress the coil spring using a

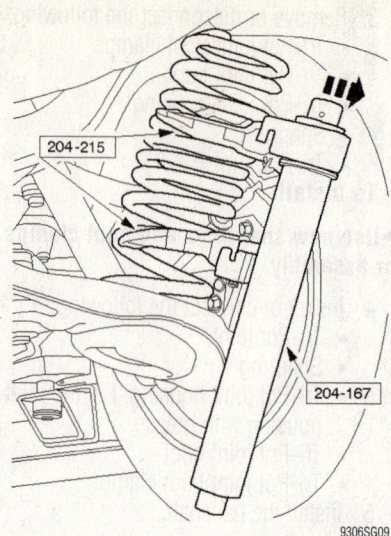

Coil spring compressor and adapters

9306SG09

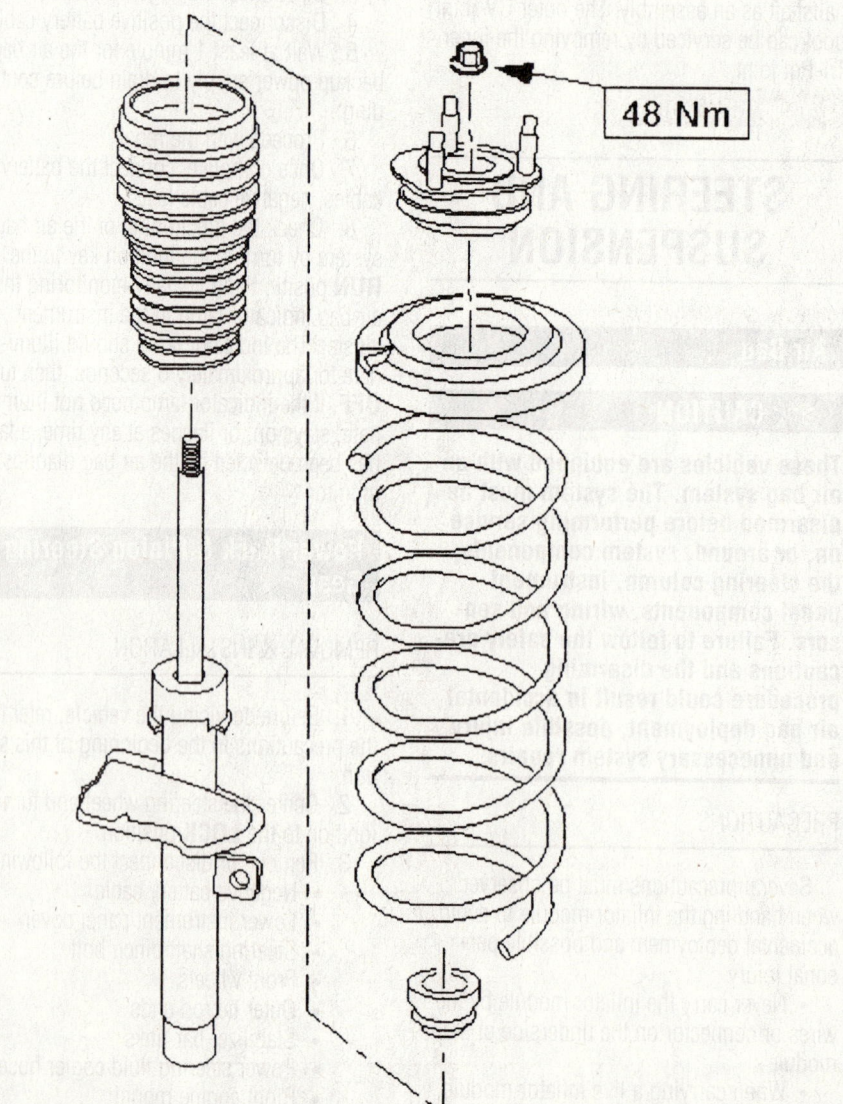

Front strut assembly exploded view

9306SG10

suitable spring compressor until the spring comes away from the seat.

4. Remove the large center nut and slowly release the spring compressor.

To install:

5. Compress the spring and install it on the strut.

6. Install the upper strut mount. Tighten the nut to 35 ft. lbs. (48 Nm).

7. Install the strut assembly in the vehicle.

Rear

1. Before servicing the vehicle, refer to the precautions in the beginning of this section.

2. Raise and support the vehicle.

3. Install spring compressor 204-167 with Adapters 204-215.

4. Compress the coil spring and remove it.

To install:

5. Install the coil spring and remove the compressor.

Lower Ball Joint

REMOVAL & INSTALLATION

The lower ball joint is replaced with the lower control arm as an assembly.

Lower Control Arm

REMOVAL & INSTALLATION

1. Before servicing the vehicle, refer to the precautions in the beginning of this section.

2. Remove or disconnect the following:
- Front wheel
- Lower ball joint
- Rear bracket bolts
- Front bolt
- Control arm

To install:

➡**Use new nuts, bolts and ball bearing washers for assembly.**

3. Install the control arm. Tighten the fasteners in sequence as follows:

a. Step 1: Tighten nut No. 1 to 74 ft. lbs. (100 Nm) plus 60 degrees

b. Step 2: Tighten nut No. 2 to 88 ft. lbs. (120 Nm)

c. Step 3: Tighten bolt No. 3 to 88 ft. lbs. (120 Nm) plus 90 degrees

d. Step 4: Check that bolt No. 3 is tightened to 125–169 ft. lbs. (170–230 Nm)

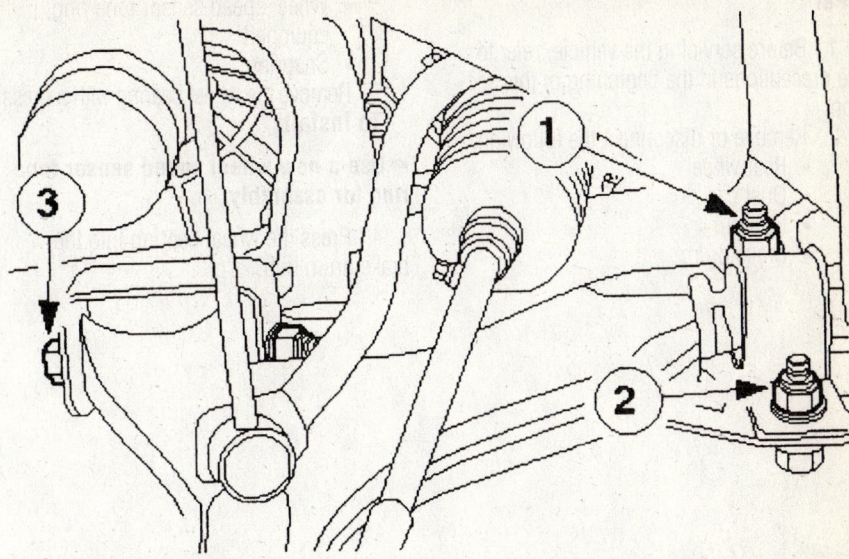

9306SG11

Control arm torque sequence

4. Install or connect the following:
- Lower ball joint. Tighten the pinch bolt to 37 ft. lbs. (50 Nm).
- Front wheel

5. Check the wheel alignment and adjust, as necessary.

CONTROL ARM BUSHING REPLACEMENT

The lower control arm bushings are replaced with the lower control arm as an assembly.

Wheel Bearings

ADJUSTMENT

The bearings on the front and rear wheels are a one piece cartridge design and cannot be adjusted. If wheel bearing play is excessive, check the wheel hub retainer nut for proper torque. If the torque is correct, replacement of the wheel bearing is required.

REMOVAL & REPLACEMENT

Front

➡**The hub nut may be reused 4 times. Mark the nut at removal and only use hub nuts with 4 or fewer marks for assembly.**

1. Before servicing the vehicle, refer to the precautions in the beginning of this section.

2. Loosen the strut center nut 5 turns.

3. Remove or disconnect the following:
- Front wheel
- Wheel speed sensor, if equipped
- Hub retainer nut. Mark the nut.
- Brake caliper and rotor
- Outer tie rod end
- Lower ball joint
- Steering knuckle pinch bolt

4. Press the stub shaft out of the wheel hub.

5. Press the hub out of the wheel bearing.

6. Remove the snapring.

7. Press the bearing out of the hub.

To install:

8. Press the bearing into the hub.

9. Install the snapring.

10. Press the hub into the wheel bearing.

11. Draw the stub shaft into the wheel hub with Halfshaft installer 205-379.

12. Install or connect the following:
- Steering knuckle. Tighten the pinch bolt to 66 ft. lbs. (90 Nm).
- Lower ball joint. Tighten the pinch bolt to 37 ft. lbs. (50 Nm).
- Outer tie rod end. Tighten the nut to 35 ft. lbs. (47 Nm).
- Brake caliper and rotor
- Hub retainer nut. Tighten the nut to 232 ft. lbs. (316 Nm).
- Wheel speed sensor, if equipped
- Front wheel

13. Tighten the strut center nuts to 35 ft. lbs. (48 Nm).

14. Check the wheel alignment and adjust, as necessary.

Rear

1. Before servicing the vehicle, refer to the precautions in the beginning of this section.

2. Remove or disconnect the following:
   - Rear wheel
   - Dust cap
   - Hub nut
   - Brake drum

- Wheel speed sensor tone ring, if equipped
- Snapring

3. Remove the wheel bearing with a press.

To install:

➡ **Use a new wheel speed sensor tone ring for assembly.**

4. Press the wheel bearing into the brake drum hub.

5. Install or connect the following:
   - Snapring
   - Wheel speed sensor tone ring, if equipped
   - Brake drum
   - Hub nut. Tighten the hub nut to 173 ft. lbs. (235 Nm).
   - Dust cap
   - Rear wheel

PRECAUTIONS

Before servicing any vehicle, please be sure to read all of the following precautions, which deal with personal safety, prevention of component damage, and important points to take into consideration when servicing a motor vehicle:

• Never open, service or drain the radiator or cooling system when the engine is hot; serious burns can occur from the steam and hot coolant.

• Observe all applicable safety precautions when working around fuel. Whenever servicing the fuel system, always work in a well-ventilated area. Do not allow fuel spray or vapors to come in contact with a spark, open flame, or excessive heat (a hot drop light, for example). Keep a dry chemical fire extinguisher near the work area. Always keep fuel in a container specifically designed for fuel storage; also, always properly seal fuel containers to avoid the possibility of fire or explosion. Refer to the additional fuel system precautions later in this section.

• Fuel injection systems often remain pressurized, even after the engine has been turned **OFF**. The fuel system pressure must be relieved before disconnecting any fuel lines. Failure to do so may result in fire and/or personal injury.

• Brake fluid often contains polyglycol ethers and polyglycols. Avoid contact with the eyes and wash your hands thoroughly after handling brake fluid. If you do get brake fluid in your eyes, flush your eyes with clean, running water for 15 minutes. If eye irritation persists, or if you have taken brake fluid internally, IMMEDIATELY seek medical assistance.

• The EPA warns that prolonged contact with used engine oil may cause a number of skin disorders, including cancer! You should make every effort to minimize your exposure to used engine oil. Protective gloves should be worn when changing oil. Wash your hands and any other exposed skin areas as soon as possible after exposure to used engine oil. Soap and water, or waterless hand cleaner should be used.

• All new vehicles are now equipped with an air bag system, often referred to as a Supplemental Restraint System (SRS) or Supplemental Inflatable Restraint (SIR) system. The system must be disabled before performing service on or around system components, steering column, instrument panel components, wiring and sensors.

Failure to follow safety and disabling procedures could result in accidental air bag deployment, possible personal injury and unnecessary system repairs.

• Always wear safety goggles when working with, or around, the air bag system. When carrying a non-deployed air bag, be sure the bag and trim cover are pointed away from your body. When placing a non-deployed air bag on a work surface, always face the bag and trim cover upward, away from the surface. This will reduce the motion of the module if it is accidentally deployed. Refer to the additional air bag system precautions later in this section.

• Clean, high quality brake fluid from a sealed container is essential to the safe and proper operation of the brake system. You should always buy the correct type of brake fluid for your vehicle. If the brake fluid becomes contaminated, completely flush the system with new fluid. Never reuse any brake fluid. Any brake fluid that is removed from the system should be discarded. Also, do not allow any brake fluid to come in contact with a painted surface; it will damage the paint.

• Never operate the engine without the proper amount and type of engine oil; doing so WILL result in severe engine damage.

• Timing belt maintenance is extremely important! Many models utilize an interference-type, non-freewheeling engine. If the timing belt breaks, the valves in the cylinder head may strike the pistons, causing potentially serious (also time-consuming and expensive) engine damage. Refer to the maintenance interval charts in the front of this manual for the recommended replacement interval for the timing belt, and to the timing belt section for belt replacement and inspection.

• Disconnecting the negative battery cable on some vehicles may interfere with the functions of the on-board computer system(s) and may require the computer to undergo a relearning process once the negative battery cable is reconnected.

• When servicing drum brakes, only disassemble and assemble one side at a time, leaving the remaining side intact for reference.

ENGINE REPAIR

➡**Disconnecting the negative battery cable on some vehicles may interfere with the functions of the on board com-**puter system. The computer may undergo a relearning process once the negative battery cable is reconnected.

Alternator

REMOVAL

3.0L Engine

1. Before servicing the vehicle, refer to the precautions in the beginning of this section.
2. Remove or disconnect the following:
   • Negative battery cable
   • Accessory drive belt
   • Lower splash shield
   • Alternator mounting bolts
   • Alternator harness connectors
   • Alternator

3.9L Engine

1. Before servicing the vehicle, refer to the precautions in the beginning of this section.
2. Remove or disconnect the following:
   • Negative battery cable
   • Air intake tube
   • Accessory drive belt
   • Lower splash shield
   • Alternator mounting bolts
   • Alternator harness connectors
   • Alternator

INSTALLATION

3.0L Engine

Install or connect the following:
   • Alternator
   • Alternator harness connectors. Tighten the battery cable terminal nut to 70 inch lbs. (8 Nm).
   • Alternator mounting bolts. Tighten the bolts to 35 ft. lbs. (48 Nm).
   • Lower splash shield
   • Accessory drive belt
   • Negative battery cable

3.9L Engine

1. Install the alternator harness connectors, then install the alternator. Tighten the bolts in sequence as follows:
   a. Step 1: Tighten bolt No. 1 to 35 ft. lbs. (48 Nm)
   b. Step 2: Tighten bolt No. 2 to 15 ft. lbs. (20 Nm) plus 90 degree turn
   c. Step 3: Tighten bolt No. 3 to 35 ft. lbs. (48 Nm)

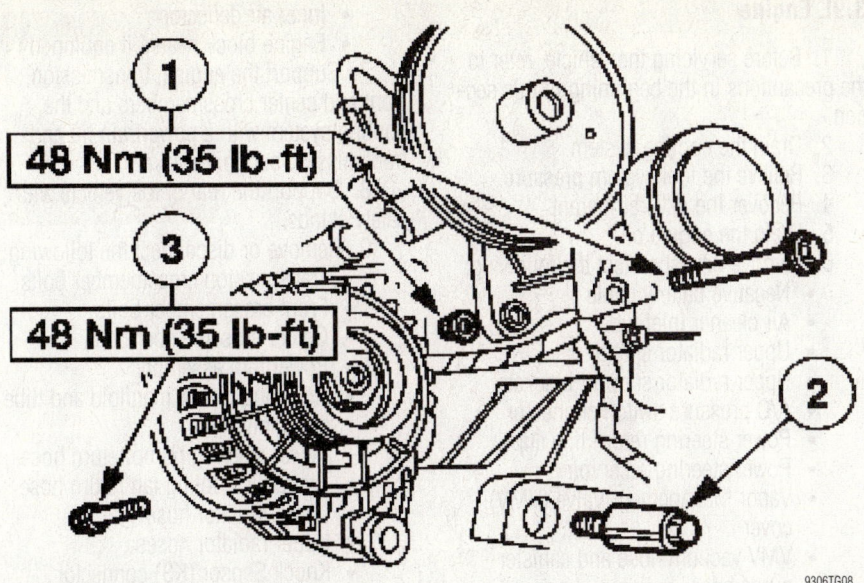

48 Nm (35 lb-ft)

48 Nm (35 lb-ft)

9306TG08

Alternator torque sequence—3.9L engine

2. Install or connect the following:
   • Lower splash shield
   • Accessory drive belt
   • Air intake tube
   • Negative battery cable

Ignition Timing

ADJUSTMENT

This vehicle is equipped with a Distributorless Ignition System (DIS). The ignition timing is not adjustable. It is controlled by the PCM.

Engine Assembly

REMOVAL & INSTALLATION

3.0L Engine

1. Before servicing the vehicle, refer to the precautions in the beginning of this section.
2. Drain the cooling system.
3. Relieve the fuel system pressure.
4. Recover the A/C refrigerant.
5. Drain the engine oil.
6. Remove or disconnect the following:
   • Negative battery cable
   • Air cleaner housing and outlet tube
   • Engine appearance cover
   • Upper radiator shield
   • Upper radiator support brackets
   • A/C pressure switch connector
   • Power steering reservoir
   • Fuel line
   • Vapor Management Valve (VMV) cover
   • VMV vacuum hose
   • Cowl leaf screens
   • Chassis vacuum lines
   • Cross vehicle support bar
   • Fresh air intake housing
   • Intake manifold rear main vacuum hose
   • Accelerator cable and cruise control cable
   • Cable bracket
   • Ground strap
   • Main engine wiring harness connector
   • Main transmission wiring harness connector
   • 2 fuel charging harness connectors
   • A/C line mounting bracket
   • Hydraulic cooling fan reservoir
   • Left, right and center splash shields
   • A/C compressor manifold and tube assembly
   • Coolant hoses
   • Exhaust front pipe and heat shields
   • Driveshaft
   • Shift cable and bracket
   • Front wheels
   • Front wheel speed sensor connectors
   • Front brake calipers
   • Lower stabilizer bar links
   • Upper ball joints
   • Lower strut mount bolts
   • Starter motor wiring harness connectors
   • Power Steering Pressure (PSP) switch connector
   • Steering shaft pinch bolt
   • Torque converter, if equipped
7. Support the engine, transmission, front and center crossmembers and the cooling system with a powertrain lift and transmission support bracket.
8. Support the rear of the vehicle with safety stands.
9. Remove or disconnect the following:
   • Transmission crossmember bolts
   • Subframe bolts
   • Crossmember bolts
   • Powertrain assembly
10. Attach a hoist to the engine.
11. Remove or disconnect the following:
   • Wire harness retainers
   • Starter motor
   • Heated Oxygen (HO2S) sensor bracket
   • Motor mount nuts
   • Accessory drive belt
   • Power steering pump
   • Hydraulic cooling fan pump
   • Upper radiator hose
   • Transmission oil cooler lines, if equipped
12. Lift the engine and transmission out of the subframe.
13. Remove or disconnect the following:
   • Oil cooler hoses
   • Transmission flange bolts
   • Transmission from the engine

To install:

14. Install or connect the following:
   • Transmission to the engine. Tighten the flange bolts to 35 ft. lbs. (48 Nm).
   • Powertrain on the subframe. Tighten the motor mount nuts to 46 ft. lbs. (63 Nm).
   • Oil cooler hoses
   • Transmission oil cooler lines, if equipped
   • Upper radiator hose
   • Hydraulic cooling fan pump. Tighten the bolts to 18 ft. lbs. (25 Nm).
   • Power steering pump. Tighten the bolts to 18 ft. lbs. (25 Nm).
   • Accessory drive belt
   • HO2S sensor bracket. Tighten the nut to 89 inch lbs. (10 Nm).
   • Starter motor. Tighten the bolts to 18 ft. lbs. (25 Nm).
   • Wire harness retainers
   • Powertrain assembly. Tighten the crossmember bolts to 76 ft. lbs. (103 Nm).

- Torque converter, if equipped.
- Steering shaft pinch bolt. Tighten the bolts to 18 ft. lbs. (25 Nm).
- PSP switch connector
- Starter motor wiring harness connectors
- Lower strut mount bolts. Tighten the bolts to 129 ft. lbs. (175 Nm).
- Upper ball joints. Tighten the nuts to 66 ft. lbs. (90 Nm).
- Lower stabilizer bar links. Tighten the nuts to 41 ft. lbs. (55 Nm).
- Front brake calipers
- Front wheel speed sensor connectors
- Front wheels
- Shift cable and bracket
- Driveshaft
- Exhaust front pipe and heat shields
- Coolant hoses
- A/C compressor manifold and tube assembly. Tighten the bolt to 15 ft. lbs. (21 Nm).
- Left, right and center splash shields
- Hydraulic cooling fan reservoir
- A/C line mounting bracket
- 2 fuel charging harness connectors
- Main transmission wiring harness connector. Tighten the bolt to 89 inch lbs. (10 Nm).
- Main engine wiring harness connector. Tighten the bolt to 89 inch lbs. (10 Nm).
- Ground strap. Tighten the bolt to 89 inch lbs. (10 Nm).
- Cable bracket. Tighten the bolts to 89 inch lbs. (10 Nm).
- Accelerator cable and cruise control cable
- Intake manifold rear main vacuum hose
- Fresh air intake housing
- Cross vehicle support bar. Tighten the bolts to 15 ft. lbs. (20 Nm).
- Chassis vacuum lines
- Cowl leaf screens
- VMV vacuum hose
- VMV cover
- Fuel line
- Power steering reservoir
- A/C pressure switch connector
- Upper radiator support brackets. Tighten the bolts to 89 inch lbs. (10 Nm).
- Upper radiator shield
- Engine appearance cover
- Air cleaner housing and outlet tube
- Negative battery cable

15. Fill the crankcase to the correct level.
16. Fill the cooling system.
17. Recharge the A/C system.
18. Start the engine and check for leaks.

3.9L Engine

1. Before servicing the vehicle, refer to the precautions in the beginning of this section.
2. Drain the cooling system.
3. Relieve the fuel system pressure.
4. Recover the A/C refrigerant.
5. Drain the engine oil.
6. Remove or disconnect the following:
   - Negative battery cable
   - Air cleaner inlet tube
   - Upper radiator shield
   - Upper radiator support brackets
   - A/C pressure switch connector
   - Power steering return line clip
   - Power steering reservoir
   - Vapor Management Valve (VMV) cover
   - VMV vacuum hose and canister purge hose
   - Main vacuum supply hose
   - Cowl vent screens
   - Cross vehicle support bar
   - Degas bottle hose
   - Accelerator cable
   - Cruise control cable
   - Ground strap
   - Fresh air filter and housing
   - Powertrain harness connectors at right strut tower
   - Fresh air filter panel
   - Main engine wiring harness connector
   - Main transmission wiring harness connector
   - Heater hoses at the water control valve. Note the locations for assembly.
   - Hydraulic cooling fan reservoir
   - Water control valve harness connector
   - Front wheels
   - Inner splash shields
   - Wheel speed sensor connectors and harness clips
   - Brake calipers
   - Lower stabilizer bar links
   - Upper ball joints
   - Lower strut mount bolts
   - Left, right and center splash shields
   - A/C suction and discharge lines
   - Shift cable and bracket
   - Power steering line frame rail clip
   - Rack and pinion harness connectors
   - Steering shaft bolt and coupling
   - Starter motor harness connectors and ground cable
   - Alternator harness connectors
   - Lower transmission flange bolts
   - Torque converter

- Inner air deflector
- Engine block heater, if equipped

7. Support the engine, transmission, front and center crossmembers and the cooling system with a powertrain lift and transmission support bracket.
8. Support the rear of the vehicle with safety stands.
9. Remove or disconnect the following:
   - Transmission crossmember bolts
   - Front crossmember bolts
   - Center crossmember bolts
   - Powertrain assembly
   - A/C compressor manifold and tube assembly
   - Power steering pump return hose
   - Hydraulic cooling fan return hose
   - Lower radiator hose
   - Upper radiator hoses
   - Knock Sensor (KS) connector
   - Heater hose
   - Transmission cooler lines and bracket
   - Power steering pressure line and bracket
   - Hydraulic cooling fan pressure line and bracket
10. Attach a hoist to the engine.
11. Remove the motor mount nuts and lift the powertrain out of the subframe.
12. Remove or disconnect the following:
   - Wiring harness retainers
   - Upper transmission flange bolts
   - Transmission from the engine

To install:
13. Install or connect the following:
   - Transmission to the engine. Tighten the upper flange bolts to 35 ft. lbs. (48 Nm).
   - Wiring harness retainers. Tighten the nuts to 89 inch lbs. (10 Nm).
   - Powertrain to the subframe. Tighten the mount nuts to 30 ft. lbs. (40 Nm).
   - Hydraulic cooling fan pressure line and bracket
   - Power steering pressure line and bracket
   - Transmission cooler lines and bracket
   - Heater hose
   - Knock sensor connector
   - Upper radiator hoses
   - Lower radiator hose
   - Hydraulic cooling fan return hose
   - Power steering pump return hose
   - A/C compressor manifold and tube assembly. Tighten the bolt to 15 ft. lbs. (21 Nm).
   - Powertrain assembly. Tighten the front and center crossmember bolts to 76 ft. lbs. (103 Nm) and the

transmission crossmember bolts to 30 ft. lbs. (40 Nm).
- Engine block heater, if equipped
- Inner air deflector
- Torque converter. Tighten the nuts to 28 ft. lbs. (38 Nm).
- Lower transmission flange bolts. Tighten the bolts to 35 ft. lbs. (47 Nm).
- Alternator harness connectors
- Starter motor harness connectors and ground cable
- Steering shaft bolt and coupling. Tighten the coupling pinch bolt to 26 ft. lbs. (35 Nm) and the shaft bolt to 22 ft. lbs. (30 Nm).
- Rack and pinion harness connectors
- Power steering line frame rail clip
- Shift cable and bracket
- A/C suction and discharge lines
- Left, right and center splash shields
- Lower strut mount bolts. Tighten the bolts to 129 ft. lbs. (175 Nm).
- Upper ball joints. Tighten the nuts to 66 ft. lbs. (90 Nm).
- Lower stabilizer bar links. Tighten the nuts to 41 ft. lbs. (55 Nm).
- Brake calipers
- Wheel speed sensor connectors and harness clips
- Inner splash shields
- Front wheels
- Water control valve harness connector
- Hydraulic cooling fan reservoir
- Heater hoses at the water control valve
- Main transmission wiring harness connector
- Main engine wiring harness connector
- Fresh air filter panel
- Powertrain harness connectors at right strut tower
- Fresh air filter and housing
- Ground strap
- Cruise control cable
- Accelerator cable
- Degas bottle hose
- Cross vehicle support bar. Tighten the bolts to 15 ft. lbs. (20 Nm).
- Cowl vent screens
- Main vacuum supply hose
- VMV vacuum hose and canister purge hose
- VMV cover
- Power steering reservoir
- Power steering return line clip

- A/C pressure switch connector
- Upper radiator support brackets
- Upper radiator shield
- Air cleaner inlet tube
- Negative battery cable

14. Fill the crankcase to the correct level.
15. Fill the cooling system.
16. Recharge the A/C system.
17. Start the engine and check for leaks.

Water Pump

REMOVAL & INSTALLATION

3.0L Engine

1. Before servicing the vehicle, refer to the precautions in the beginning of this section.
2. Drain the cooling system.
3. Remove or disconnect the following:
   - Negative battery cable
   - Air cleaner outlet tube
   - Engine vent hose
   - Upper radiator hose
   - Heater supply hose
   - Water pump hose
   - Lower radiator hose
   - Water crossover assembly
   - Water inlet hose
   - Accessory drive belt and idler pulley
   - Bracket assembly
   - Water pump
4. Install or connect the following:
   - Water pump. Tighten the bolts to 18 ft. lbs. (25 Nm).
   - Bracket assembly. Tighten the fasteners to 89 inch lbs. (10 Nm).
   - Accessory drive belt and idler pulley
   - Water inlet hose
   - Water crossover assembly
   - Lower radiator hose
   - Water pump hose
   - Heater supply hose
   - Upper radiator hose
   - Engine vent hose
   - Air cleaner outlet tube
   - Negative battery cable
5. Fill the cooling system.
6. Start the engine and check for leaks.

3.9L Engine

1. Before servicing the vehicle, refer to the precautions in the beginning of this section.
2. Drain the cooling system.
3. Remove or disconnect the following:

- Accessory drive belt
- Water pump pulley
- Water pump

To install:

4. Install or connect the following:
   - Water pump. Tighten the bolts to 71 inch lbs. (8 Nm) plus 90 degree turn.
   - Water pump pulley. Tighten the bolts to 89 inch lbs. (10 Nm) plus 45 degree turn.
   - Accessory drive belt
5. Fill the cooling system.
6. Start the engine and check for leaks.

Cylinder Head

REMOVAL & INSTALLATION

3.0L Engine

1. Before servicing the vehicle, refer to the precautions in the beginning of this section.
2. Drain the cooling system.
3. Relieve the fuel system pressure.
4. Drain the engine oil.
5. Remove or disconnect the following:
   - Negative battery cable
   - Upper and lower intake manifolds
   - Valve covers
   - Accessory drive belts
6. Install a support fixture to the engine lifting eyes.
7. Remove or disconnect the following:
   - Motor mount nuts
   - Subframe bolts
   - Oil pan
   - Front cover
   - Timing chains
   - Camshafts
   - Exhaust manifolds
   - Ground strap
   - Positive Crankcase Ventilation (PCV) tube
   - Ignition noise suppressor
   - Coolant outlet tube
   - Engine oil dipstick tube
8. Install the subframe bolts and remove the engine support fixture.
9. Remove the cylinder heads.

To install:

➡ **Refer to Section 1 of this manual for the cylinder head torque sequence illustration. The illustration is located after the Torque Specification Chart.**

10. Install the cylinder heads. Tighten the bolts in sequence as follows:

Timing belt service is covered in Section 4 of this manual

a. Step 1: 22 ft. lbs. (30 Nm)

b. Step 2: Plus 90 degree turn

c. Step 3: Loosen all bolts one full turn

d. Step 4: 22 ft. lbs. (30 Nm)

e. Step 5: Plus 90 degree turn

f. Step 6: Plus 90 degree turn

11. Install the engine support fixture and remove the subframe bolts.

12. Install or connect the following:
- Engine oil dipstick tube
- Coolant outlet tube
- Ignition noise suppressor
- PCV tube
- Ground strap
- Exhaust manifolds
- Camshafts
- Timing chains
- Front cover
- Oil pan
- Subframe bolts. Tighten the bolts to 76 ft. lbs. (103 Nm).
- Motor mount nuts. Tighten the nuts to 46 ft. lbs. (63 Nm).
- Accessory drive belts
- Valve covers
- Upper and lower intake manifolds
- Negative battery cable

13. Fill the crankcase to the correct level.
14. Fill the cooling system.
15. Start the engine and check for leaks.

3.9L Engine

1. Before servicing the vehicle, refer to the precautions in the beginning of this section.

2. Drain the cooling system.
3. Relieve the fuel system pressure.
4. Remove or disconnect the following:
- Negative battery cable
- Engine appearance cover
- Intake manifold
- Valve covers
- Accessory drive belts
- Front cover
- Timing chains
- Camshafts
- Water outlet pipe
- Cylinder head temperature sensor connector
- Exhaust front pipes
- Exhaust Gas Recirculation (EGR) tube
- Bolts and stud bolts at the rear of the cylinder heads
- Cylinder heads. Loosen the bolts in reverse of the tightening sequence.

To install:

➡ **Refer to Section 1 of this manual for the cylinder head torque sequence illustration. The illustration is located after the Torque Specification Chart.**

5. Install the cylinder heads. Tighten the bolts in sequence as follows:

a. Step 1: M10 bolts to 15 ft. lbs. (20 Nm)

b. Step 2: M10 bolts to 26 ft. lbs. (35 Nm)

c. Step 3: M10 bolts to 33 ft. lbs. (45 Nm)

d. Step 4: M10 bolts plus 90 degree turn

e. Step 5: M10 bolts plus 90 degree turn

f. Step 6: M8 bolts to 15 ft. lbs. (20 Nm)

g. Step 7: M8 bolts plus 90 degree turn

6. Install or connect the following:
- Bolts and stud bolts at the rear of the cylinder heads. Tighten the bolts to 37 ft. lbs. (50 Nm).
- EGR tube
- Exhaust front pipes
- Cylinder head temperature sensor connector
- Water outlet pipe
- Camshafts
- Timing chains
- Front cover
- Accessory drive belts
- Valve covers
- Intake manifold
- Engine appearance cover
- Negative battery cable

7. Fill the cooling system.
8. Start the engine and check for leaks.

Rocker Arms/Shafts

REMOVAL & INSTALLATION

The vehicles covered in this section are not equipped with rocker arms/shafts. The camshaft directly actuates the valves.

Intake Manifold

REMOVAL & INSTALLATION

3.0L Engine

1. Before servicing the vehicle, refer to the precautions in the beginning of this section.

2. Drain the cooling system.
3. Relieve the fuel system pressure.
4. Remove or disconnect the following:
- Negative battery cable
- Engine appearance cover
- Air cleaner outlet tube
- Throttle Position (TP) sensor connector

- Idle Air Control (IAC) valve connector
- Accelerator cable
- Cruise control cable
- Cable bracket
- Throttle body coolant bypass hose
- Positive Crankcase Ventilation (PCV) hose
- Evaporative Emissions (EVAP) canister purge hose
- Exhaust Gas Recirculation (EGR) vacuum line
- EGR tube
- Cowl vent screen
- Cross vehicle support bar
- Chassis vacuum supply hose
- EGR pressure transducer
- Fuel pressure sensor shield
- Upper intake manifold vacuum hose
- Intake Manifold Tuning Valve (IMTV) connector
- Exhaust Vacuum Regulator (EVR) valve connector and vacuum line
- Upper intake manifold support brackets
- Upper intake manifold
- Fuel line and bracket
- Fuel pressure sensor vacuum line
- Fuel injector harness connectors
- PCV tube
- Lower intake manifold assembly

To install:

➡ **Refer to Section 1 of this manual for the intake manifold torque sequence illustration. The illustration is located after the Torque Specification Chart.**

5. Install or connect the following:
- Lower intake manifold assembly. Tighten the bolts in sequence to 89 inch lbs. (10 Nm).
- PCV tube
- Fuel injector harness connectors
- Fuel pressure sensor vacuum line
- Fuel line and bracket. Tighten the bolt to 89 inch lbs. (10 Nm).
- Upper intake manifold. Tighten the bolts in sequence to 89 inch lbs. (10 Nm).
- Upper intake manifold support brackets. Tighten the bolts to 89 inch lbs. (10 Nm).
- EVR valve connector and vacuum line
- IMTV connector
- Upper intake manifold vacuum hose
- Fuel pressure sensor shield
- EGR pressure transducer
- Chassis vacuum supply hose
- Cross vehicle support bar. Tighten the bolts to 15 ft. lbs. (20 Nm).

- Cowl vent screen
- EGR tube
- EGR vacuum line
- EVAP canister purge hose
- PCV hose
- Throttle body coolant bypass hose
- Cable bracket
- Cruise control cable
- Accelerator cable
- IAC valve connector
- TP sensor connector
- Air cleaner outlet tube
- Engine appearance cover
- Negative battery cable
6. Fill the cooling system.
7. Start the engine and check for leaks.

3.9L Engine

1. Before servicing the vehicle, refer to the precautions in the beginning of this section.
2. Drain the cooling system.
3. Relieve the fuel system pressure.
4. Remove or disconnect the following:
   - Negative battery cable
   - Air cleaner outlet tube
   - Cowl vent screen
   - Cross vehicle support bar
   - Accelerator cable
   - Cruise control cable
   - Intake manifold vacuum hoses
   - Exhaust Gas Recirculation (EGR) valve
   - Camshaft Position (CMP) sensor connector
   - Evaporative Emissions (EVAP) canister purge valve line
   - Fuel pressure sensor connector and vacuum line
   - Fuel line
   - Knock Sensor (KS) connector
   - Cylinder head temperature sensor connector
   - Sensor connector bracket
   - Wiring harness and hose bracket
   - Left bank fuel injector connectors
   - Idle Air Control (IAC) valve connector
   - Throttle Position (TP) sensor connector
   - Positive Crankcase Ventilation (PCV) tube
   - Throttle body coolant hoses
   - Right bank fuel injector connectors
   - Delta Pressure Feedback Electronic (DPFE) system sensor
   - Intake manifold. Loosen the bolts in reverse of the tightening sequence.

To install:

➡ **Refer to Section 1 of this manual for the intake manifold torque sequence illustration. The illustration is located after the Torque Specification Chart.**

5. Install or connect the following:
   - Intake manifold. Tighten the bolts in sequence to 18 ft. lbs. (25 Nm).
   - DPFE system sensor
   - Right bank fuel injector connectors
   - Throttle body coolant hoses
   - PCV tube
   - TP sensor connector
   - IAC valve connector
   - Left bank fuel injector connectors
   - Wiring harness and hose bracket
   - Sensor connector bracket
   - Cylinder head temperature sensor connector
   - KS sensor connector
   - Fuel line
   - Fuel pressure sensor connector and vacuum line
   - EVAP canister purge valve line
   - CMP sensor connector
   - EGR valve
   - Intake manifold vacuum hoses
   - Cruise control cable
   - Accelerator cable
   - Cross vehicle support bar. Tighten the bolts to 15 ft. lbs. (20 Nm).
   - Cowl vent screen
   - Air cleaner outlet tube
   - Negative battery cable
6. Fill the cooling system.
7. Start the engine and check for leaks.

Exhaust Manifolds

REMOVAL & INSTALLATION

3.0L Engine

1. Before servicing the vehicle, refer to the precautions in the beginning of this section.
2. Remove or disconnect the following:
   - Negative battery cable
   - Heat shields
   - Lower splash shields
   - Exhaust front pipes
   - Secondary air tubes
   - Exhaust Gas Recirculation (EGR) tube
   - Exhaust manifolds

To install:
3. Install the exhaust manifolds. Tighten the fasteners in sequence as follows:

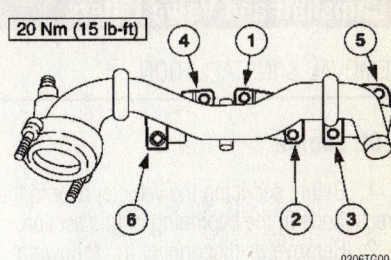

Right exhaust manifold torque sequence—3.0L engine

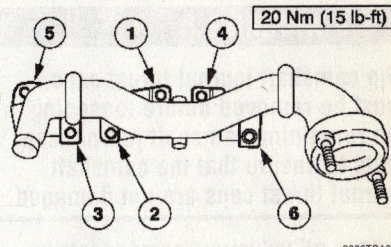

Left exhaust manifold torque sequence—3.0L engine

   a. Step 1: 15 ft. lbs. (20 Nm)
   b. Step 2: 15 ft. lbs. (20 Nm)
4. Install or connect the following:
   - Exhaust Gas Recirculation (EGR) tube
   - Secondary air tubes
   - Exhaust front pipes
   - Lower splash shields
   - Heat shields
   - Negative battery cable
5. Start the engine and check for leaks.

3.9L Engine

1. Before servicing the vehicle, refer to the precautions in the beginning of this section.
2. Remove or disconnect the following:
   - Negative battery cable
   - Power steering pump reservoir
   - Oil dipstick tube
   - Exhaust front pipes
   - Exhaust Gas Recirculation (EGR) tube
   - Exhaust manifolds

To install:
3. Install or connect the following:
   - Exhaust manifolds. Tighten the bolts to 18 ft. lbs. (25 Nm).
   - EGR tube
   - Exhaust front pipes
   - Oil dipstick tube
   - Power steering pump reservoir
   - Negative battery cable
4. Start the engine and check for leaks.

Camshaft and Valve Lifters

REMOVAL & INSTALLATION

3.0L Engine

1. Before servicing the vehicle, refer to the precautions in the beginning of this section.
2. Remove or disconnect the following:
   - Negative battery cable
   - Valve covers
   - Front cover
   - Timing chains

> ※※ **WARNING**
>
> **The camshaft journal thrust caps must be removed before loosening the remaining camshaft journal cap bolts to ensure that the camshaft journal thrust caps are not damaged.**

➡ **Keep all valvetrain components in order for assembly.**

   - Camshaft journal thrust caps
   - Remaining camshaft journal caps
   - Camshafts
   - Valve tappets and shims

To install:

3. Install or connect the following:
   - Valve tappets and shims in their original locations
   - Camshafts
   - Camshaft journal caps in their original positions. Install the thrust journal caps last. Tighten the bolts in sequence to 89 inch lbs. (10 Nm).
   - Timing chains

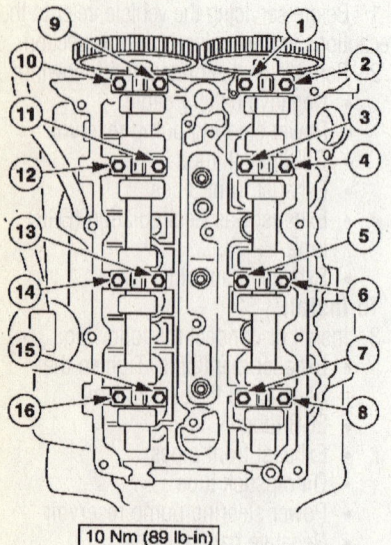

```
10 Nm (89 lb-in)
```
9306TG11

Camshaft journal cap torque sequence— 3.0L engine

   - Front cover
   - Valve covers
   - Negative battery cable
4. Start the engine and check for leaks.

3.9L Engine

1. Before servicing the vehicle, refer to the precautions in the beginning of this section.
2. Remove or disconnect the following:
   - Negative battery cable
   - Valve covers
   - Front cover
   - Timing chains

➡ **Keep all valvetrain components in order for assembly.**

   - Camshaft journal bearing caps
   - Camshafts
   - Valve tappets and shims

To install:

3. Install or connect the following:
   - Valve tappets and shims
   - Camshafts
4. Install the camshaft journal bearing caps in their original positions. Tighten the bolts in sequence as follows:
   a. Step 1: Finger tight
   b. Step 2: 53 inch lbs. (6 Nm)
   c. Step 3: Plus 90 degree turn
5. Install or connect the following:
   - Timing chains
   - Front cover
   - Valve covers
   - Negative battery cable
6. Start the engine and check for leaks.

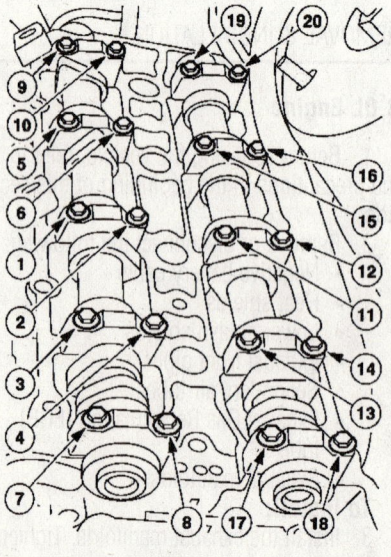

9306TG12

Camshaft journal bearing cap torque sequence—3.9L engine

Valve Lash

ADJUSTMENT

3.0L Engine

1. Before servicing the vehicle, refer to the precautions in the beginning of this section.
2. Remove or disconnect the following:
   - Negative battery cable
   - Engine appearance covers
   - Ignition coils
   - Valve covers
3. Measure the valve clearance while the camshaft lobe is pointed away from the valve shim. Rotate the crankshaft as necessary for each valve to be measured.

➡ **Keep all valvetrain components in order for assembly.**

4. Remove the camshaft thrust cap and the rear camshaft bearing journal cap from the camshaft that requires shim adjustment.
5. Install Service Tool set 303-659 in place of the bearing journal caps, with the taller tool in place of the rear bearing cap.
6. Remove the center camshaft bearing journal caps.
7. Remove the valve shims with compressed air and replace as required to achieve the correct adjustment.
8. Valve clearance should be 0.007–0.009 in. (0.18–0.23mm) for intake valves or 0.013–0.015 in. (0.33–0.38mm) for exhaust valves.
9. Install the center bearing journal caps.
10. Remove the service tools.
11. Install or connect the following:
    - Rear bearing journal cap and the thrust journal cap. Tighten the bearing journal caps in sequence to 89 inch lbs. (10 Nm).
    - Valve covers
    - Ignition coils
    - Engine appearance covers
    - Negative battery cable

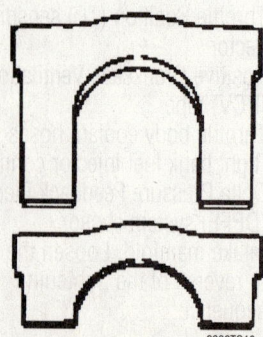

9306TG13

Camshaft lift tools 303-659—3.0L engine

3.9L Engine

1. Before servicing the vehicle, refer to the precautions in the beginning of this section.

2. Remove or disconnect the following:

- Negative battery cable
- Engine appearance covers
- Ignition coils
- Valve covers

3. Measure the valve clearance while the camshaft lobe is pointed away from the valve shim. Rotate the crankshaft as necessary for each valve to be measured.

4. Valve clearance should be 0.007–0.009 in. (0.18–0.23mm) for intake valves or 0.009–0.011 in. (0.23–0.28mm) for exhaust valves.

5. If adjustment is necessary, compress the valves with the special tools and remove the shim with compressed air. Repeat for each valve to be adjusted.

6. Install or connect the following:

- Valve covers
- Ignition coils
- Engine appearance covers
- Negative battery cable

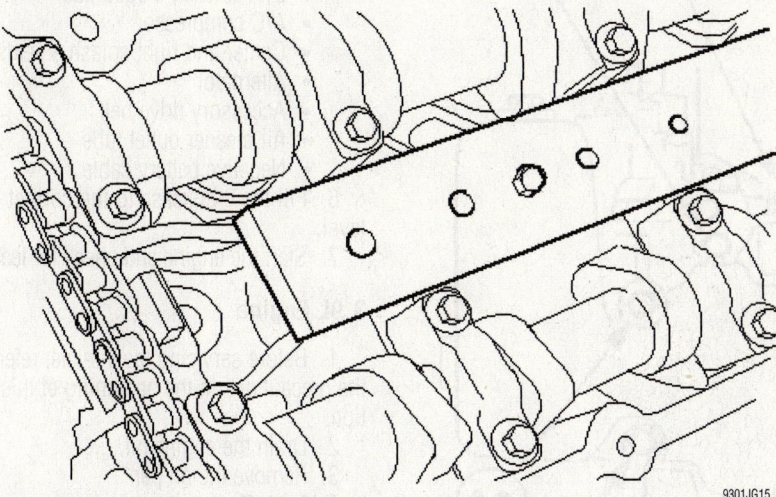

Valve adjustment tool base plate—3.9L engine

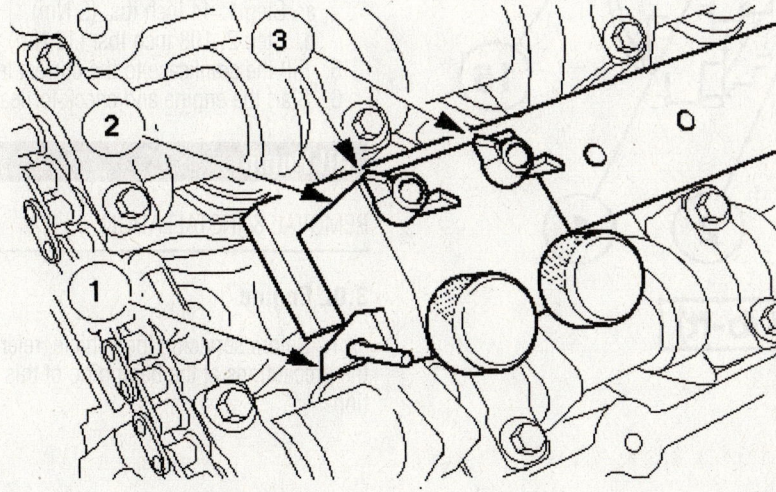

Valve adjustment tool attachment—3.9L engine

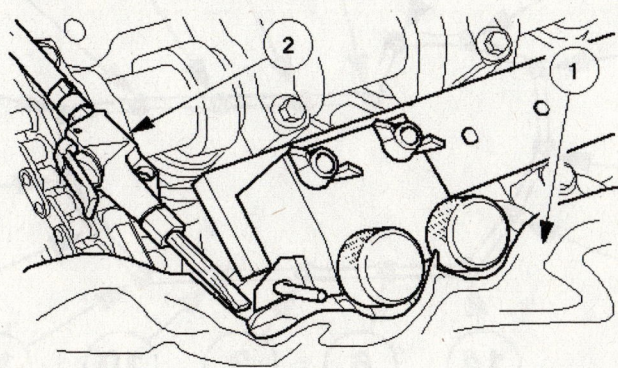

Remove the shims with compressed air—3.9L engine

Starter Motor

REMOVAL & INSTALLATION

1. Before servicing the vehicle, refer to the precautions in the beginning of this section.

2. Remove or disconnect the following:

- Negative battery cable
- Starter motor wiring connectors
- Starter motor

To install:

3. Install or connect the following:

- Starter motor. Tighten the bolts to 18 ft. lbs. (25 Nm).
- Starter motor wiring connectors
- Negative battery cable

Oil Pan

REMOVAL & INSTALLATION

3.0L Engine

1. Before servicing the vehicle, refer to the precautions in the beginning of this section.

2. Drain the engine oil.

3. Install a support fixture to the engine lifting eyes.

4. Remove or disconnect the following:

- Negative battery cable
- Air cleaner outlet tube
- Accessory drive belt
- Alternator
- Center and right splash shields
- A/C compressor
- Electronic Thermactor Air (ETA) bracket, if equipped
- Rack and pinion steering gear

Refer to Section 1 for engine rebuilding specifications

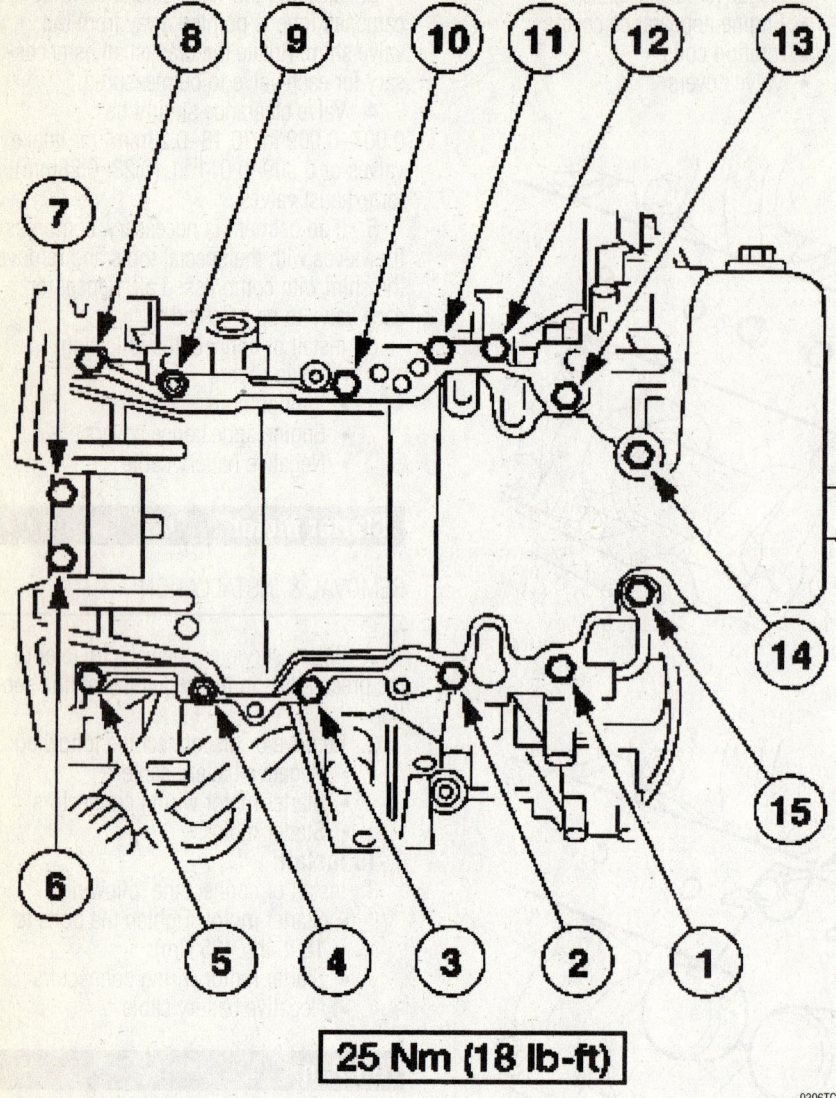

Oil pan torque sequence—3.0L engine

25 Nm (18 lb-ft)

9306TG14

- Lower control arm through bolts
- Transmission cooler line bracket
- Engine mount nuts
- Left and right subframe bolts. Pry the subframe down for clearance.
- Wiring harness bracket
- Oil pan

To install:

5. Install or connect the following:
- Oil pan. Tighten the pan bolts in sequence to 18 ft. lbs. (25 Nm) and the transmission bolts to 35 ft. lbs. (47 Nm).
- Wiring harness bracket
- Left and right subframe bolts. Tighten the bolts to 76 ft. lbs. (103 Nm).
- Engine mount nuts. Tighten the nuts to 46 ft. lbs. (63 Nm).
- Transmission cooler line bracket
- Lower control arm through bolts.

Tighten the bolts to 129 ft. lbs. (175 Nm).
- Rack and pinion steering gear. Tighten the nuts to 76 ft. lbs. (103 Nm).
- ETA bracket, if equipped
- A/C compressor
- Center and right splash shields
- Alternator
- Accessory drive belt
- Air cleaner outlet tube
- Negative battery cable
6. Fill the crankcase to the correct level.
7. Start the engine and check for leaks.

3.9L Engine

1. Before servicing the vehicle, refer to the precautions in the beginning of this section.
2. Drain the engine oil.
3. Remove the oil pan.

To install:

4. Install the oil pan. Tighten the bolts in sequence as follows:
   a. Step 1: 44 inch lbs. (5 Nm)
   b. Step 2: 108 inch lbs. (12 Nm)
5. Fill the crankcase to the correct level.
6. Start the engine and check for leaks.

Oil Pump

REMOVAL & INSTALLATION

3.0L Engine

1. Before servicing the vehicle, refer to the precautions at the beginning of this section.

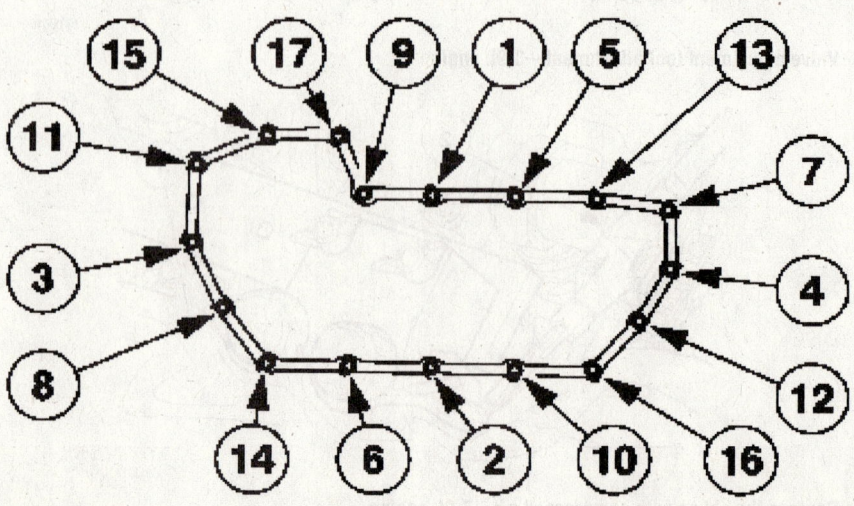

Oil pan torque sequence—3.9L engine

9306TG15

2. Remove or disconnect the following:
- Upper intake manifold
- Valve covers
- Accessory drive belt
- Power steering pump
- Alternator
- Water pump
- A/C compressor and bracket
- Crankshaft pulley
- Oil pan
- Oil pump screen and tube
- Front cover
- Timing chains
- Crankshaft timing gears
- Oil pump

To install:

3. Install or connect the following:
- Oil pump. Tighten the bolts to 89 inch lbs. (10 Nm).
- Crankshaft timing gears
- Timing chains
- Front cover
- Oil pump screen and tube. Tighten the bolts to 89 inch lbs. (10 Nm).
- Oil pan
- Crankshaft pulley
- A/C compressor and bracket
- Water pump
- Alternator
- Power steering pump
- Accessory drive belt
- Valve covers
- Upper intake manifold
4. Fill the crankcase.
5. Start the engine and check for leaks.

3.9L Engine

1. Before servicing the vehicle, refer to the precautions in the beginning of this section.
2. Remove or disconnect the following:
- Crankshaft pulley
- Front cover
- Primary timing chains
- Oil pump mounting bolts
- Oil pump

To install:

3. Install or connect the following:
- New gasket
- Oil pump. Tighten the bolts to 53 inch lbs. (6 Nm) plus 90 degree turn.
- Primary timing chains
- Front cover
- Crankshaft pulley

Rear Main Seal

REMOVAL & INSTALLATION

3.0L Engine

1. Before servicing the vehicle, refer to the precautions at the beginning of this section.
2. Attach an engine support fixture to the engine lifting eyes.
3. Remove or disconnect the following:

- Negative battery cable
- Transmission
- Clutch, if equipped
- Flywheel
- Rear crankshaft seal

To install:

4. Install or connect the following:
- Rear main seal flush with the cylinder block surface
- Flywheel. Tighten the bolts to 59 ft. lbs. (80 Nm).
- Clutch, if equipped
- Transmission
- Negative battery cable
5. Start the engine and check for leaks.

3.9L Engine

1. Before servicing the vehicle, refer to the precautions at the beginning of this section.
2. Attach an engine support fixture to the engine lifting eyes.
3. Remove or disconnect the following:

- Negative battery cable
- Transmission
- Flywheel
- Rear crankshaft seal

To install:

4. Install or connect the following:
- Rear main seal flush with the cylinder block surface
- Flywheel
5. Tighten the flywheel bolts in a crossing pattern as follows:
   a. Step 1: 11 ft. lbs. (15 Nm)
   b. Step 2: 81 ft. lbs. (110 Nm)
6. Install or connect the following:
- Transmission
- Negative battery cable
7. Start the engine and check for leaks.

Timing Chain, Sprockets, Front Cover and Seal

REMOVAL & INSTALLATION

3.0L Engine

1. Before servicing the vehicle, refer to the precautions at the beginning of this section.
2. Remove or disconnect the following:
- Upper intake manifold
- Valve covers
- Accessory drive belt
- Power steering pump
- Alternator
- Water pump
- A/C compressor and bracket
- Crankshaft pulley
- Oil pan
- Oil pump screen and tube

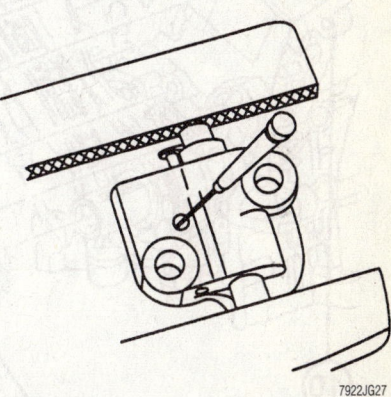

Using a thin prytool, release and hold the timing chain tensioner ratchet/pawl mechanism—3.0L engine

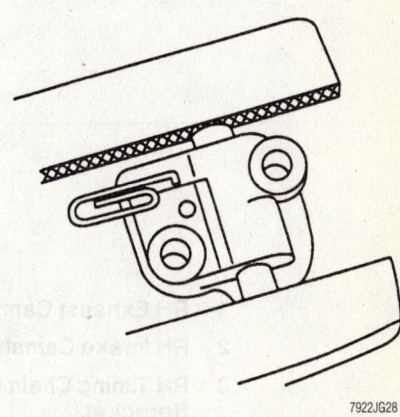

Retain the piston with a 1.5mm wire or paperclip—3.0L engine

- Crankshaft Position (CKP) sensor connector
- Camshaft Position (CMP) sensor connector
- Front cover
- CKP sensor pulse ring

3. Rotate the crankshaft so that the key-way is at the 11 o'clock position to locate the crankshaft at Top Dead Center (TDC) for No. 1 cylinder.

4. Verify that the alignment arrows on the camshafts are aligned. If not, rotate the crankshaft 1 complete revolution and recheck.

5. Rotate the crankshaft so that the key-way is at the 3 o'clock position. This positions the right cylinder head camshafts to the neutral position.

6. Remove or disconnect the follow-ing:

- Right timing chain tensioner

FRONT OF ENGINE

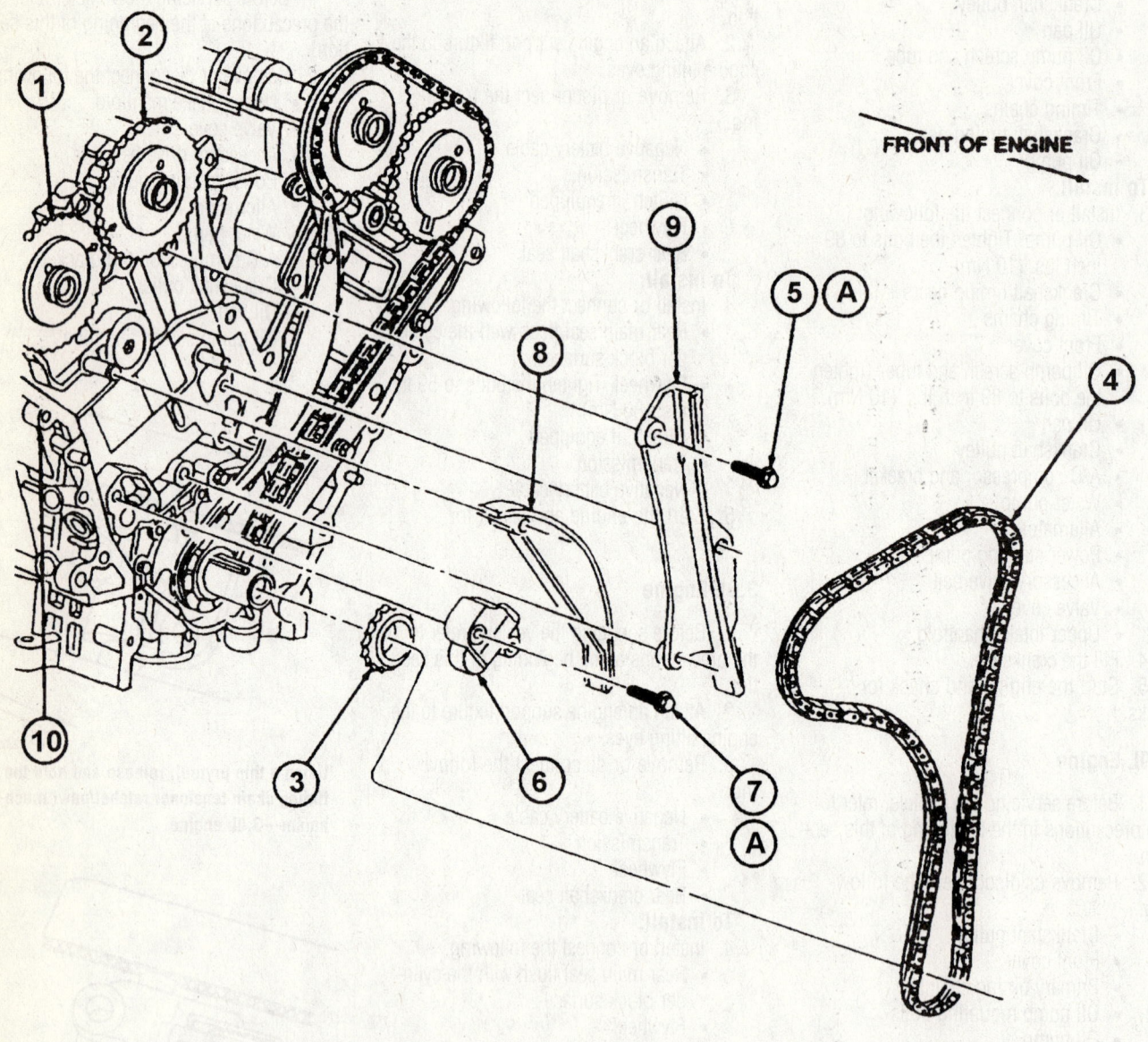

1	RH Exhaust Camshaft	6	Timing Chain Tensioner
2	RH Intake Camshaft	7	Bolt (2 Req'd)
3	RH Timing Chain Crankshaft Sprocket	8	Timing Chain Tensioner Arm
4	RH Timing Chain	9	Timing Chain Guide
5	Bolt (2 Req'd)	10	RH Cylinder Head
		A	Tighten to 20-30 N·m (15-22 Lb-Ft)

Exploded view of the right cylinder head timing chain and related components—3.0L engine—left side similar

7922KG49

- Right timing chain tensioner arm
- Right timing chain and crankshaft sprocket

❋❋ WARNING

The camshaft thrust caps must be removed before loosening the remaining camshaft journal cap bolts to ensure that the thrust caps are not damaged.

→The camshaft journal caps and cylinder heads are numbered to ensure that they are assembled in their original positions.

- Camshaft thrust caps
- Camshaft journal caps. Loosen the bolts in sequence and in several passes to allow the camshaft to be raised from the cylinder head evenly.
- Right bank camshafts

7. Rotate the crankshaft 2 revolutions and locate the crankshaft keyway at the 11 o'clock position. This will position the left cylinder head camshafts to their neutral position.

8. Verify that the alignment arrows on the camshafts are aligned.

9. Remove or disconnect the following:

- Left cylinder head timing chain tensioner
- Left timing chain tensioner arm
- Left timing chain and crankshaft sprocket

❋❋ WARNING

The camshaft thrust caps must be removed before loosening the remaining camshaft journal cap bolts to ensure that the thrust caps are not damaged.

→The camshaft journal caps and cylinder heads are numbered to ensure that they are assembled in their original positions.

10. Remove or disconnect the following:

- Camshaft thrust caps
- Camshaft journal caps. Loosen the bolts in sequence and in several passes to allow the camshaft to be raised from the cylinder head evenly.
- Left bank camshafts

To install:

11. Prepare the timing chain tensioners for installation as follows:

 a. Place the left chain tensioner in a vise.

 b. Using a small prytool, release and hold the timing chain tensioner ratchet/pawl mechanism through the access hole in the timing chain tensioner.

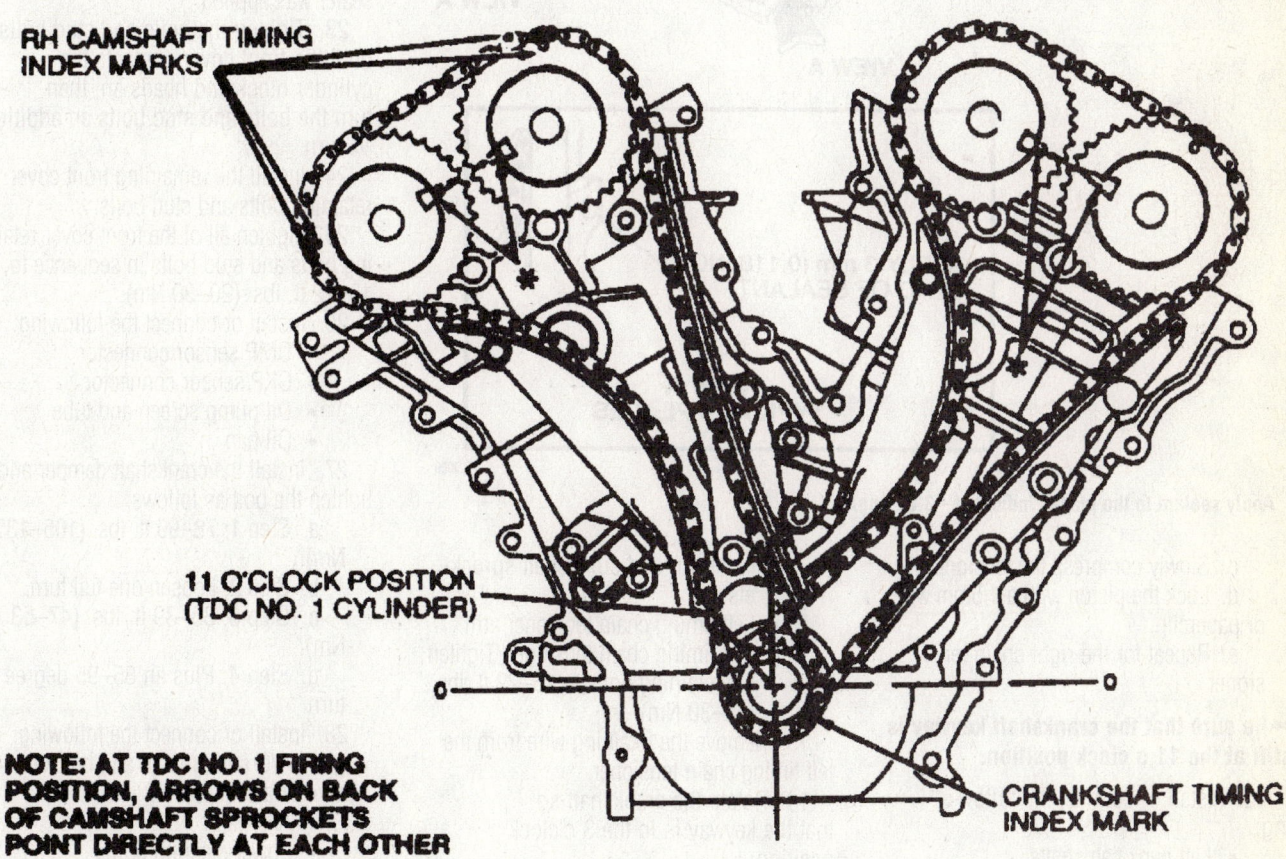

RH CAMSHAFT TIMING INDEX MARKS

11 O'CLOCK POSITION (TDC NO. 1 CYLINDER)

CRANKSHAFT TIMING INDEX MARK

*NOTE: AT TDC NO. 1 FIRING POSITION, ARROWS ON BACK OF CAMSHAFT SPROCKETS POINT DIRECTLY AT EACH OTHER

7922KG51

Timing mark alignment—3.0L engine

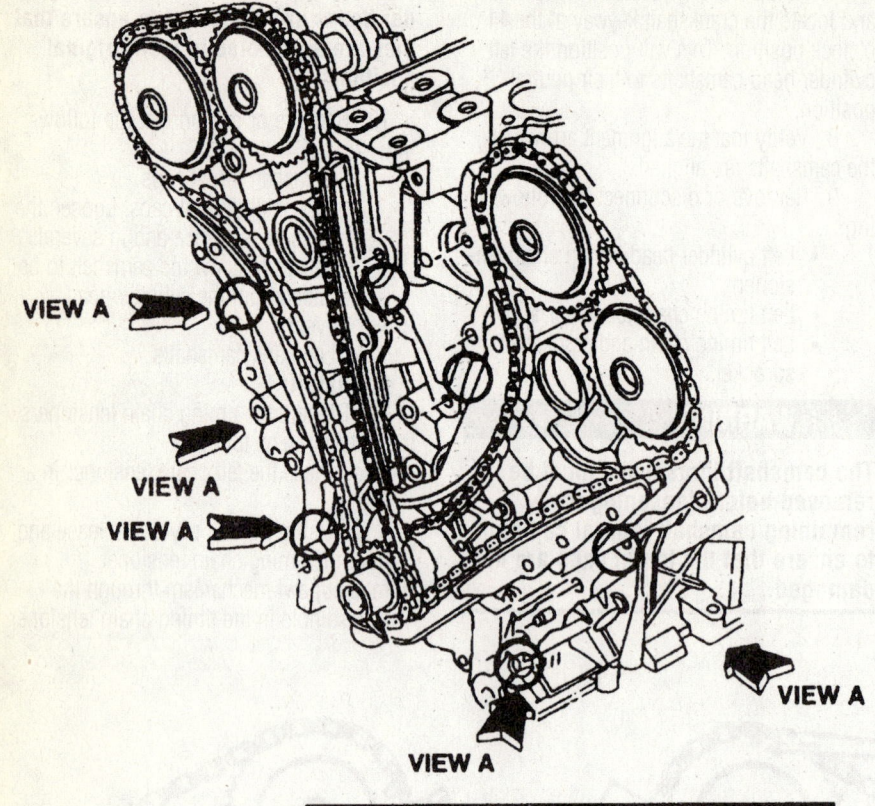

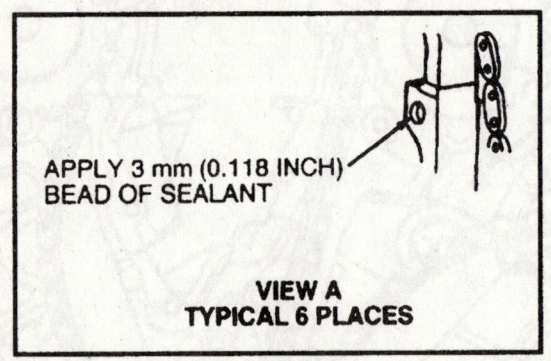

APPLY 3 mm (0.118 INCH)
BEAD OF SEALANT

**VIEW A
TYPICAL 6 PLACES**

7922JG29

Apply sealant to the places indicated—3.0L engine

c. Slowly compress the tensioner.

d. Lock the piston with a 1.5mm wire or paperclip.

e. Repeat for the right chain tensioner.

➡ **Be sure that the crankshaft keyway is still at the 11 o'clock position.**

12. Install or connect the following:

- Left bank camshafts
- Camshaft journal caps
- Camshaft thrust caps
- Left timing chain and crankshaft sprocket. Align the colored links with the index marks on the camshaft and crankshaft sprockets.
- Left timing chain tensioner arm
- Left timing chain tensioner. Tighten the retaining bolts to 15–22 ft. lbs. (20–30 Nm).

13. Remove the retaining wire from the left timing chain tensioner.

14. Rotate the crankshaft so that the keyway is in the 3 o'clock position.

15. Install or connect the following:

- Right bank camshafts
- Camshaft journal caps
- Camshaft thrust caps
- Right timing chain and crankshaft sprocket. Align the colored links with the index marks on the camshaft and crankshaft sprockets.
- Right timing chain tensioner arm
- Right timing chain tensioner. Tighten the retaining bolts to 15–22 ft. lbs. (20–30 Nm).

16. Remove the retaining wire from the right timing chain tensioner.

17. Install the CKP sensor pulse ring.

18. Replace the crankshaft seal in the front cover with a new one. Apply clean engine oil to the seal lip.

19. Apply silicone sealer to the 6 critical areas shown in View **A**, to the cylinder block.

20. Place new front cover gaskets onto the dowel pins on the cylinder block and heads.

21. Place the front cover into position.

22. Install the 6 front cover retaining bolts and stud bolts where the silicone sealer was applied.

23. Tighten the bolts and stud bolts until the front cover contacts the cylinder block and heads an, then turn the bolts and stud bolts an additional ¼ turn.

24. Install the remaining front cover retaining bolts and stud bolts.

25. Tighten all of the front cover retaining bolts and stud bolts in sequence to 15–22 ft. lbs. (20–30 Nm).

26. Install or connect the following:

- CMP sensor connector
- CKP sensor connector
- Oil pump screen and tube
- Oil pan

27. Install the crankshaft damper and tighten the bolt as follows:

a. Step 1: 78–99 ft. lbs. (105–135 Nm).

b. Step 2: Loosen one full turn.

c. Step 3: 35–39 ft. lbs. (47–53 Nm).

d. Step 4: Plus an 85–95 degree turn.

28. Install or connect the following:

- A/C compressor and bracket
- Water pump
- Alternator
- Power steering pump
- Accessory drive belt
- Valve covers
- Upper intake manifold

29. Start the engine and check for leaks.

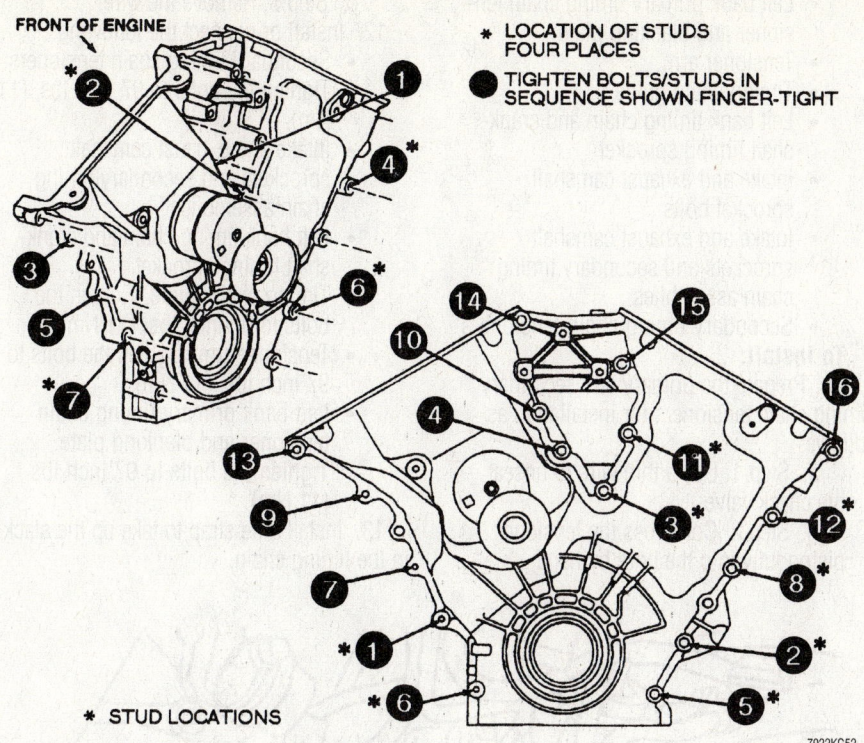

Front cover torque sequence—3.0L engine

3.9L Engine

1. Before servicing the vehicle, refer to the precautions in the beginning of this section.

2. Drain the cooling system.

3. Remove or disconnect the following:
   - Negative battery cable
   - Engine appearance cover and brackets
   - Valve covers
   - Engine cooling fan assembly
   - Accessory drive belt
   - Water pump pulley
   - Alternator
   - Lower radiator hose and pipe
   - Heater hose
   - Idler pulleys
   - Crankshaft pulley
   - Front crankshaft seal
   - Power steering reservoir hose
   - Power steering pump and bracket
   - Hydraulic cooling fan reservoir hose and bracket
   - Hydraulic cooling fan pump and bracket
   - Front cover wiring harness clips
   - Front cover. Loosen the bolts in sequence.
   - Torque converter access panel
   - Crankshaft Position (CKP) sensor

4. Rotate the crankshaft to 45 degrees After Top Dead Center (ATDC). The crankshaft keyway will be in the 6 o'clock position. Check that the camshaft lobes are facing upwards. If not, rotate the crankshaft 1 full turn.

5. Install Crankshaft Holding Tool 303-645 in place of the CKP sensor.

6. Install Camshaft Locking Tool 303-530 to the right bank camshafts.

7. Loosen the exhaust and intake camshaft sprocket bolts and slide the sprockets forward on the bolts.

8. Remove or disconnect the following:
   - Right bank primary timing chain tensioner and blanking plate
   - Tensioner arm
   - Timing chain guide
   - Right bank timing chain and crankshaft timing sprocket

9. Remove the locking tool from the right bank camshafts and install it on the left bank camshafts.

10. Remove or disconnect the following:

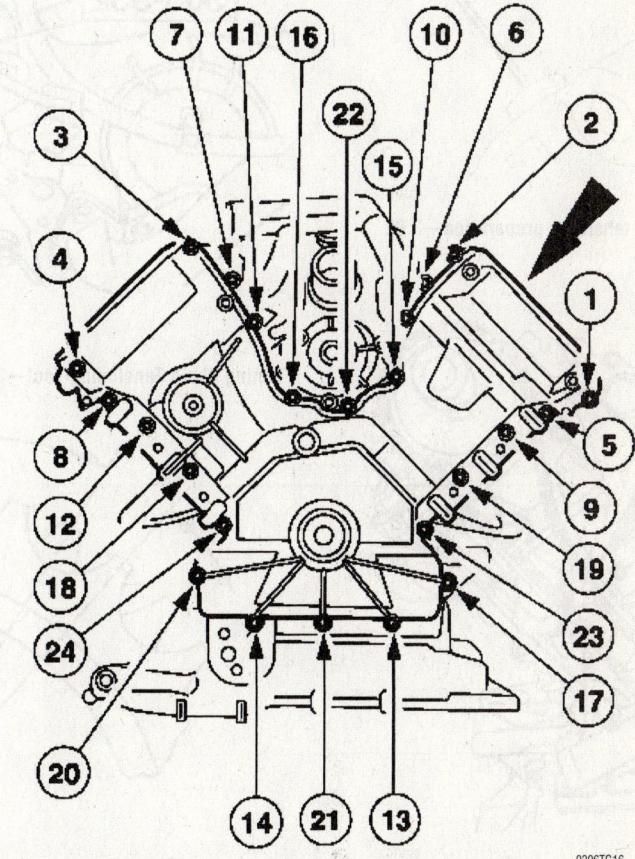

Front cover loosening sequence—3.9L engine

Please refer to Section 8 for electric cooling fan wiring schematics

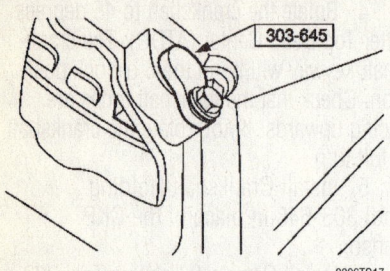

Crankshaft Holding Tool—3.9L engine

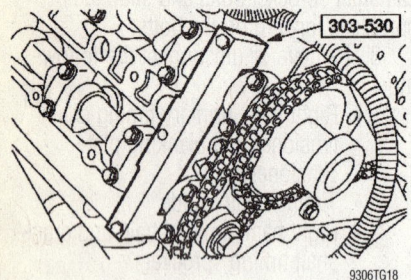

Camshaft Locking Tool—3.9L engine

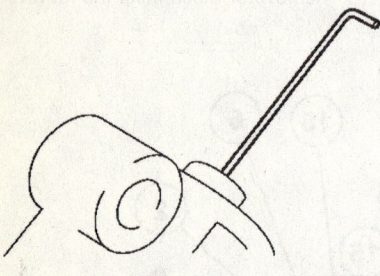

Timing chain tensioner preparation—3.9L engine

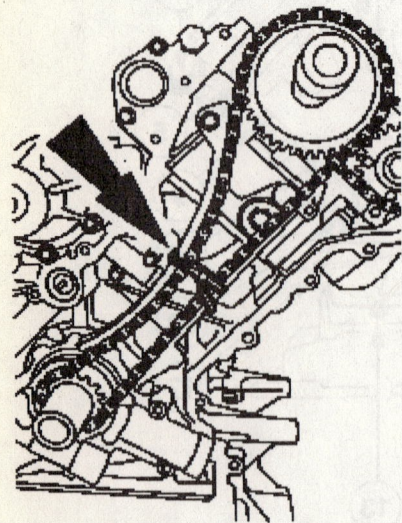

Use a tie strap to remove slack from the primary timing chain—3.9L engine

- Left bank primary timing chain tensioner and blanking plate
- Tensioner arm
- Timing chain guide
- Left bank timing chain and crankshaft timing sprocket
- Intake and exhaust camshaft sprocket bolts
- Intake and exhaust camshaft sprockets and secondary timing chain assemblies
- Secondary timing chain tensioners

To install:

11. Prepare the primary and secondary timing chain tensioners for installation as follows:

   a. Step 1: Use a thin wire to unseat the check valve

   b. Step 2: Compress the tensioner piston fully into the bore by hand

   c. Step 3: Remove the wire

12. Install or connect the following:
- Secondary timing chain tensioners. Tighten the bolts to 97 inch lbs. (11 Nm).
- Intake and exhaust camshaft sprockets and secondary timing chain assemblies
- Left bank timing chain and crankshaft timing sprocket
- Timing chain guide. Tighten the bolts to 97 inch lbs. (11 Nm).
- Tensioner arm. Tighten the bolts to 97 inch lbs. (11 Nm).
- Left bank primary timing chain tensioner and blanking plate. Tighten the bolts to 97 inch lbs. (11 Nm).

13. Install a tie strap to take up the slack in the timing chain.

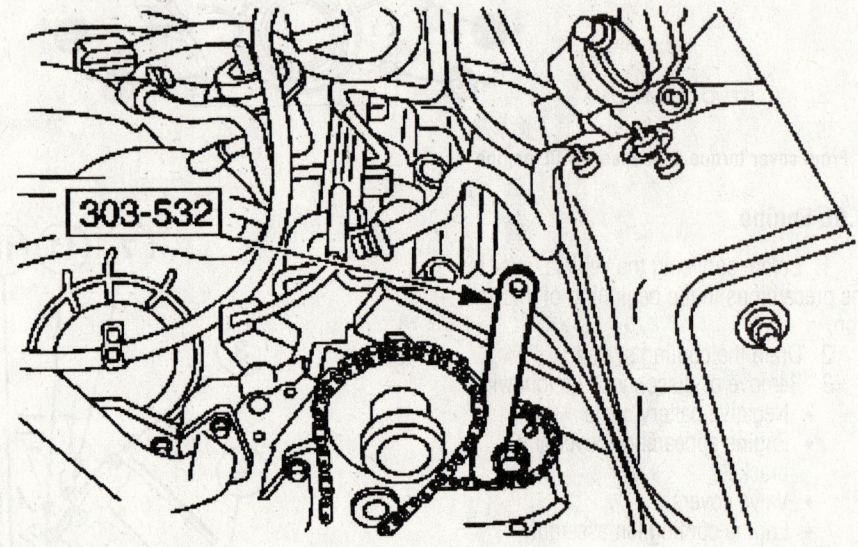

Timing Chain Tensioning Tool—3.9L engine

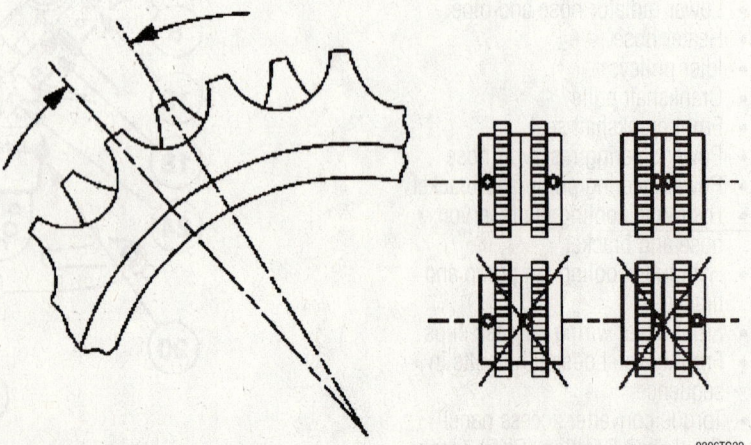

Crankshaft sprocket alignment—3.9L engine

14. Use Timing Chain Tensioning Tool 303-532 to apply tension to the left bank exhaust camshaft.

➡**Tighten the exhaust camshaft bolt first.**

15. Tighten the left bank camshaft sprocket bolts as follows:
   a. Step 1: 15 ft. lbs. (20 Nm)
   b. Step 2: Plus 90 degree turn

16. Remove the locking tool from the left bank camshafts and install it on the right bank camshafts.

17. Install or connect the following:
   • Right bank timing chain and crank-shaft timing sprocket. Ensure that the crankshaft sprocket is installed as shown.
   • Timing chain guide. Tighten the bolts to 97 inch lbs. (11 Nm).
   • Tensioner arm. Tighten the bolts to 97 inch lbs. (11 Nm).
   • Right bank primary timing chain tensioner and blanking plate. Tighten the bolts to 97 inch lbs. (11 Nm).

18. Install a tie strap to take up the slack in the timing chain.

19. Use Timing Chain Tensioning Tool 303-532 to apply tension to the right bank exhaust camshaft.

➡**Tighten the exhaust camshaft bolt first.**

20. Tighten the right bank camshaft sprocket bolts as follows:
   a. Step 1: 15 ft. lbs. (20 Nm)
   b. Step 2: Plus 90 degree turn

21. Remove the camshaft locking tool.

22. Apply silicone sealant to the areas indicated and install the front cover.

23. Tighten the front cover bolts in sequence as follows:
   a. Step 1: 44 inch lbs. (5 Nm)
   b. Step 2: 89 inch lbs. (10 Nm)

24. Remove the crankshaft locking tool.

25. Install or connect the following:
   • CKP sensor
   • Torque converter access panel
   • Front cover wiring harness clips
   • Hydraulic cooling fan pump and bracket. Tighten the bolts to 18 ft. lbs. (25 Nm).
   • Hydraulic cooling fan reservoir hose and bracket
   • Power steering pump and bracket. Tighten the bolts to 18 ft. lbs. (25 Nm).
   • Power steering reservoir hose

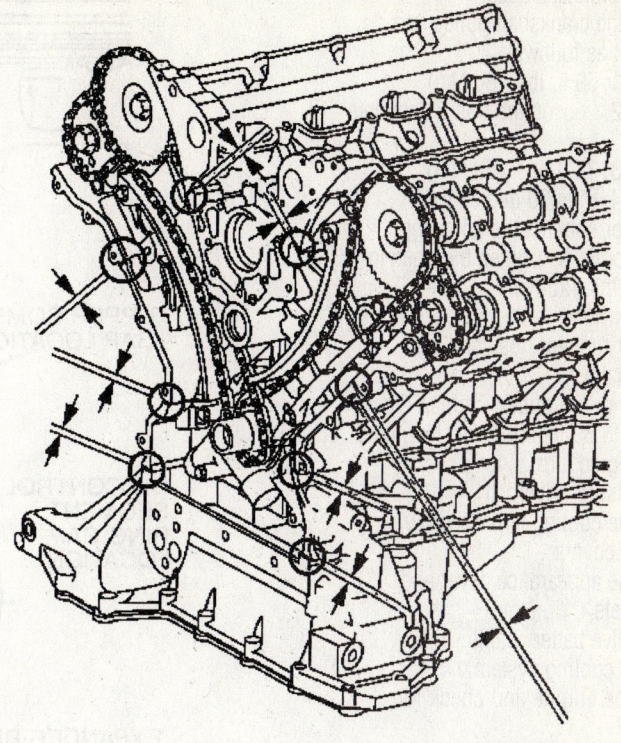

3 mm (0.12 in)

9306TG23

Apply silicone sealant to the areas indicated—3.9L engine

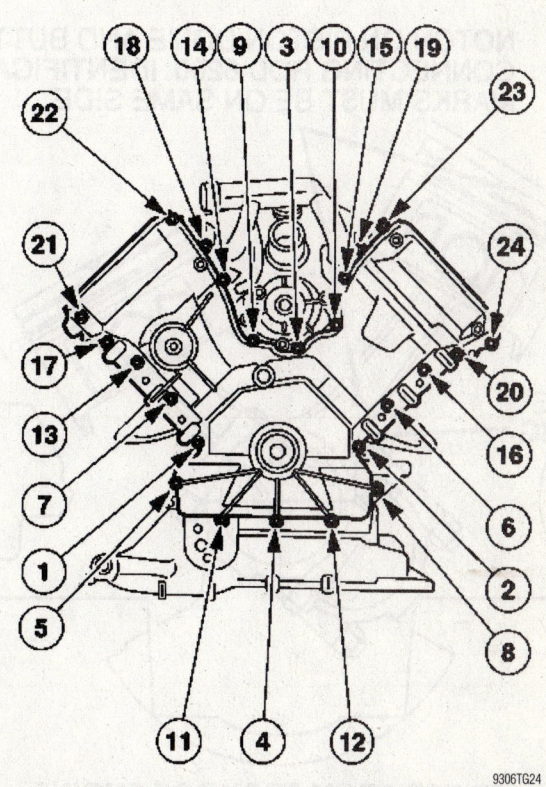

9306TG24

Front cover torque sequence—3.9L engine

For complete service labor times order Nichols' Chilton Labor Guide Manual

- Front crankshaft seal

26. Install the crankshaft pulley and tighten the bolt as follows:

    a. Step 1: 59 ft. lbs. (80 Nm)

    b. Step 2: Loosen the bolt 2 complete turns

    c. Step 3: 37 ft. lbs. (50 Nm)

    d. Step 4: Plus 90 degree turn

27. Install or connect the following:

- Idler pulleys. Tighten the bolts to 18 ft. lbs. (25 Nm).
- Heater hose
- Lower radiator hose and pipe
- Alternator
- Water pump pulley. Tighten the bolts to 89 inch lbs. (10 Nm) plus 45 degree turn.
- Accessory drive belt
- Engine cooling fan assembly
- Valve covers
- Engine appearance cover and brackets
- Negative battery cable

28. Fill the cooling system.

29. Start the engine and check for leaks.

Piston and Ring

POSITIONING

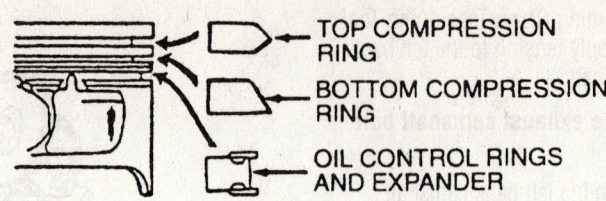

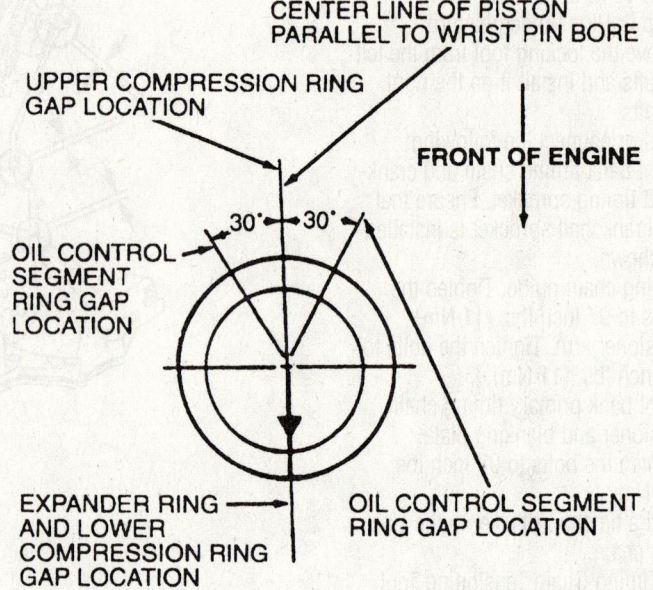

Piston ring end-gap spacing—3.0L (VIN S) engine

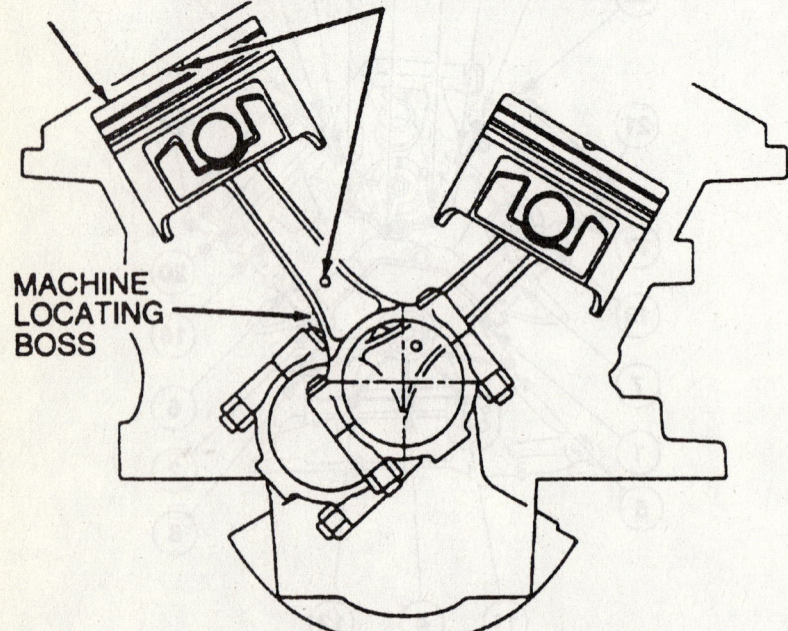

VIEWED FROM FRONT OF ENGINE

Piston ring end-gap spacing—3.0L (VIN S) engine

FUEL SYSTEM

Fuel System Service Precautions

Safety is the most important factor when performing not only fuel system maintenance but any type of maintenance. Failure to conduct maintenance and repairs in a safe manner may result in serious personal injury or death. Maintenance and testing of the vehicle's fuel system components can be accomplished safely and effectively by adhering to the following rules and guidelines.

- To avoid the possibility of fire and personal injury, always disconnect the negative battery cable unless the repair or test procedure requires that battery voltage be applied.

- Always relieve the fuel system pressure prior to disconnecting any fuel system component (injector, fuel rail, pressure regulator, etc.), fitting or fuel line connection. Exercise extreme caution whenever relieving fuel system pressure, to avoid exposing skin, face and eyes to fuel spray. Please be advised that fuel under pressure may penetrate the skin or any part of the body that it contacts.

• Always place a shop towel or cloth around the fitting or connection prior to loosening to absorb any excess fuel due to spillage. Ensure that all fuel spillage (should it occur) is quickly removed from engine surfaces. Ensure that all fuel soaked cloths or towels are deposited into a suitable waste container.

• Always keep a dry chemical (Class B) fire extinguisher near the work area.

• Do not allow fuel spray or fuel vapors to come into contact with a spark or open flame.

• Always use a back-up wrench when loosening and tightening fuel line connection fittings. This will prevent unnecessary stress and torsion to fuel line piping.

• Always replace worn fuel fitting O-rings with new. Do not substitute fuel hose or equivalent where fuel pipe is installed.

Fuel System Pressure

RELIEVING

1. Before servicing the vehicle, refer to the precautions in the beginning of this section.
2. Disconnect the negative battery cable.
3. Connect the fuel injection pressure test equipment JD 209 to the valve on the fuel supply manifold.
4. Insert the drain/bleed tube into the fuel container.
5. Follow the manufacturer's instructions and depressurize the fuel system.

Fuel Filter

REMOVAL & INSTALLATION

1. Before servicing the vehicle, refer to the precautions in the beginning of this section.
2. Relieve the fuel system pressure.
3. Remove or disconnect the following:
   • Negative battery cable
   • Fuel filter bracket cover
   • Fuel lines
   • Fuel filter
To install:
4. Install or connect the following:
   • Fuel filter into the bracket making sure the flow direction is correct. Tighten the clamp to 15–25 inch lbs. (2–3 Nm).
   • Fuel lines. Tighten the fittings to 22 ft. lbs. (30 Nm).
5. Start the engine and check for leaks.

Fuel Pump

REMOVAL & INSTALLATION

1. Before servicing the vehicle, refer to the precautions in the beginning of this section.
2. Relieve the fuel system pressure.
3. Drain the fuel tank.
4. Remove or disconnect the following:
   • Negative battery cable
   • Trunk liner
   • Trunk seal retainer
   • Rear lamp assembly interior trim finisher
   • Left and right side liners
   • Fuel feed and return lines
   • Fuel filler and vent hoses
   • Fuel tank wiring connectors
   • Fuel filler cap
   • Fuel tank retaining straps
   • Fuel tank
   • Fuel pump module
To install:
5. Install or connect the following:
   • Fuel pump module
   • Fuel tank
   • Fuel tank retaining straps
   • Fuel filler cap
   • Fuel tank wiring connectors
   • Fuel filler and vent hoses
   • Fuel feed and return lines
   • Left and right side liners
   • Rear lamp assembly interior trim finisher
   • Trunk seal retainer
   • Trunk liner
   • Negative battery cable
6. Fill the fuel tank with at least 10 gallons (38L) of fuel.
7. Start the engine and check for leaks.

Fuel Injector

REMOVAL & INSTALLATION

1. Before servicing the vehicle, refer to the precautions in the beginning of this section.
2. Relieve fuel system pressure.
3. Remove or disconnect the following:
   • Negative battery cable
   • Engine appearance covers
   • Fuel lines
   • Fuel pressure regulator
   • Fuel cross over elbow
   • Fuel injector connectors
   • Fuel injector clamping plates
   • Fuel injectors

To install:
4. Install or connect the following:
   • Fuel injectors. Use new O-ring seals.
   • Fuel injector clamping plates
   • Fuel injector connectors
   • Fuel cross over elbow
   • Fuel pressure regulator
   • Fuel lines
   • Engine appearance covers
   • Negative battery cable
5. Start the engine and check for leaks.

DRIVE TRAIN

Transmission Assembly

REMOVAL & INSTALLATION

Automatic

1. Before servicing the vehicle, refer to the precautions in the beginning of this section.
2. Install a support fixture to the engine lifting eyes.
3. Drain the transmission fluid.
4. Remove or disconnect the following:
   • Negative battery cable
   • Engine appearance covers
   • Mass Air Flow (MAF) meter
   • Air intake assembly
   • Coolant recovery tank
   • Exhaust front pipes
   • Driveshaft
   • Shift selector cable
   • Transmission electrical connectors
   • Transmission oil cooler lines
   • Torque converter
   • Transmission mount and bracket
   • Transmission flange bolts
   • Transmission
To install:
5. Install or connect the following:
   • Transmission to the engine. Tighten the flange bolts to 32–42 ft. lbs. (43–57 Nm).
   • Transmission mount and bracket. Tighten the mount bolts to 22–30 ft. lbs. (30–40 Nm) and the bracket bolts to 16–21 ft. lbs. (22–28 Nm).
   • Torque converter. Tighten the bolts to 32–42 ft. lbs. (43–57 Nm).
   • Transmission oil cooler lines
   • Transmission electrical connectors

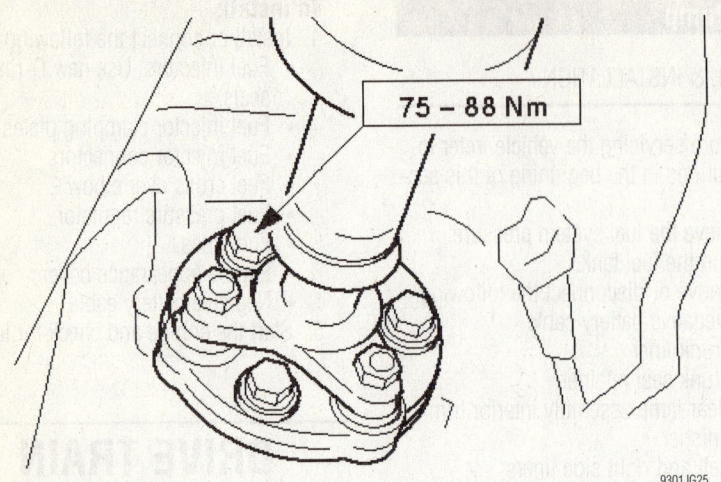

75 – 88 Nm

9301JG25

Driveshaft flange bolts

- Shift selector cable
- Driveshaft. Tighten the bolts to 55–65 ft. lbs. (75–88 Nm).
- Exhaust front pipes
- Coolant recovery tank
- Air intake assembly
- MAF meter
- Engine appearance covers
- Negative battery cable

6. Fill the transmission to the correct level with the proper fluid. Do not over-fill.

7. Start the engine and check for leaks.

Manual

1. Before servicing the vehicle, refer to the precautions in the beginning of this section.

2. Remove or disconnect the following:
- Negative battery cable
- Shift linkage
- Exhaust center section

➡The driveshaft flange may have additional nuts added for balance. These nuts must be replaced in the same position to maintain the driveshaft balance.

- Driveshaft. Matchmark the flange and note the location of the fasteners for assembly.
- Heated Oxygen (HO$_2$S) sensor connectors and harness
- Vehicle Speed (VSS) sensor connector
- Reverse light switch connector and harness
- Transmission mount and crossmember. Support the transmission.
- Clutch slave cylinder fluid line
- Starter motor
- Transmission flange bolts
- Transmission

To install:

3. Install or connect the following:

- Transmission. Tighten the flange bolts to 35 ft. lbs. (47 Nm).
- Starter motor
- Clutch slave cylinder fluid line
- Transmission mount and crossmember. Tighten the bolts to 41 ft. lbs. (55 Nm) and the nut to 30 ft. lbs. (40 Nm).
- Reverse light switch connector and harness
- VSS sensor connector
- HO$_2$S sensor connectors and harness
- Driveshaft. Align the matchmarks and tighten the retainers to 63 ft. lbs. (85 Nm). Tighten any balance nuts to 18 ft. lbs. (24 Nm).
- Exhaust center section
- Shift linkage
- Negative battery cable

Clutch

ADJUSTMENTS

Because the clutch system is hydraulic, the clutch pedal free-play is self-adjusting and requires no additional maintenance.

REMOVAL & INSTALLATION

1. Before servicing the vehicle, refer to the precautions in the beginning of this section.

2. Remove or disconnect the following:
- Transaxle
- Clutch pressure plate
- Clutch disk

To install:

3. Install or connect the following:
- Clutch disk and pressure plate.

Tighten the pressure plate bolts evenly in several passes to 17 ft. lbs. (23 Nm).
- Transmission

4. Bleed the hydraulic clutch system, if required.

5. Check the clutch system for proper operation.

Hydraulic Clutch System

BLEEDING

1. Before servicing the vehicle, refer to the precautions in the beginning of this section.

2. Remove the inspection cover.

3. Connect a hose to the bleeder valve fitting on the clutch slave cylinder. Submerge the other end of the hose into a container of clean brake fluid.

4. Open the bleeder valve and have an assistant depress the clutch pedal.

5. Close the bleeder before releasing the clutch pedal.

6. Repeat the procedure until no more air bubbles are seen.

7. Install the inspection cover to the bell housing.

8. Top off the clutch master cylinder fluid reservoir and install the diaphragm and cap.

Halfshaft

REMOVAL & INSTALLATION

1. Before servicing the vehicle, refer to the precautions in the beginning of this section.

2. Remove or disconnect the following:
- Negative battery cable
- Rear wheel
- Brake caliper
- Wheel speed sensor
- Hub carrier pivot bolt
- Hub retaining nut

3. Press the stub shaft out of the hub and pry the inner joint out of the differential.

To install:

4. Install or connect the following:
- Halfshaft inner joint to the differential
- Halfshaft in the wheel hub by applying Loctite® 270 thread locking compound to the splines
- Hub carrier pivot bolt by aligning the bolt head matchmarks. Tighten it to 66–81 ft. lbs. (90–110 Nm).
- Hub retaining nut. Tighten the new nut to 221 ft. lbs. (300 Nm).
- Wheel speed sensor

- Brake caliper
- Rear wheel
- Negative battery cable

5. Check the wheel alignment and adjust as necessary.

➡ If the hub is removed for any reason, a new bearing assembly must be installed. Never attempt to re-use a bearing.

CV-Joint

OVERHAUL

The CV-joints are serviced with the axle halfshaft as an assembly.

STEERING AND SUSPENSION

Air Bag

❊❊ CAUTION

Some vehicles are equipped with an air bag system. The system must be disarmed before performing service on, or around, system components, the steering column, instrument panel components, wiring and sensors. Failure to follow the safety precautions and the disarming procedure could result in accidental air bag deployment, possible injury and unnecessary system repairs.

PRECAUTIONS

Several precautions must be observed when handling the inflator module to avoid accidental deployment and possible personal injury.

- Never carry the inflator module by the wires or connector on the underside of the module.
- When carrying a live inflator module, hold securely with both hands, and ensure that the bag and trim cover are pointed away.
- Place the inflator module on a bench or other surface with the bag and trim cover facing up.
- With the inflator module on the bench, never place anything on or close to the

module that may be thrown in the event of an accidental deployment.

DISARMING

Proper SRS disarming can be obtained by disconnecting and isolating the negative battery cable. Allow the air bag system capacitor at least 2 minutes to discharge before removing any air bag system components.

Power Rack and Pinion Steering Gear

REMOVAL & INSTALLATION

1. Before servicing the vehicle, refer to the precautions in the beginning of this section.
2. Lock the steering wheel in the straight-ahead position.
3. Remove or disconnect the following:
   - Negative battery cable
   - Front wheels
   - Steering column intermediate shaft
   - Outer tie rod ends
   - Power steering lines
   - Steering rack and pinion gear

To install:
4. Install or connect the following:
   - Steering rack and pinion gear. Tighten the bolts to 76 ft. lbs. (103 Nm).
   - Power steering lines
   - Outer tie rod ends. Tighten the nuts to 52–63 ft. lbs. (71–85 Nm).
   - Steering column intermediate shaft
   - Front wheels
   - Negative battery cable

5. Fill the power steering fluid reservoir.
6. Start the engine and check for leaks.
7. Check the wheel alignment and adjust, as necessary.

Strut

REMOVAL & INSTALLATION

Front

1. Before servicing the vehicle, refer to the precautions in the beginning of this section.
2. Remove or disconnect the following:
   - Front wheel
   - Stabilizer bar link

- Lower strut mounting bolt
- Upper strut mount cover and fasteners
- Strut and spring assembly

To install:

➡ Use new fasteners for assembly.

3. Install or connect the following:
   - Strut and spring assembly. Tighten the upper mount nuts to 21 ft. lbs. (28 Nm).
   - Upper strut mount cover
   - Lower strut mounting bolt. Tighten the bolts to 129 ft. lbs. (175 Nm).
   - Stabilizer bar link. Tighten the nut to 41 ft. lbs. (55 Nm).
   - Front wheel

Rear

1. Before servicing the vehicle, refer to the precautions in the beginning of this section.
2. Remove or disconnect the following:
   - Trunk trim covers
   - Upper strut mount nuts
   - Lower strut mount bolt
   - Strut and spring assembly

To install:

➡ Use new fasteners for assembly.

3. Install or connect the following:
   - Strut and spring assembly. Tighten the lower bolt to 98 ft. lbs. (133 Nm) and the upper nuts to 21 ft. lbs. (28 Nm).
   - Trunk trim covers

Coil Spring

REMOVAL & INSTALLATION

1. Before servicing the vehicle, refer to the precautions in the beginning of this section.
2. Remove the strut assembly from the vehicle.
3. Compress the coil spring and remove the piston rod nut.
4. Remove or disconnect the following:
   - Upper strut mount
   - Spring upper seat
   - Coil spring

To install:
5. Install or connect the following:
   - Coil spring
   - Spring upper seat
   - Upper strut mount. Tighten the piston rod nut to 37 ft. lbs. (50 Nm).

6. Remove the spring compressor and install the strut assembly to the vehicle.

Upper Ball Joint

REMOVAL & INSTALLATION

The upper ball joint is serviced with the upper control arm as an assembly.

Lower Ball Joint

REMOVAL & INSTALLATION

The lower ball joint is serviced with the lower control arm as an assembly.

Upper Control Arm

REMOVAL & INSTALLATION

1. Before servicing the vehicle, refer to the precautions in the beginning of this section.
2. Remove or disconnect the following:
   - Front wheel
   - Strut and spring assembly
   - Upper ball joint and tapered washer
   - Inner control arm fasteners
   - Upper control arm

To install:

➡ Use new fasteners for assembly.

3. Install or connect the following:
   - Upper control arm. Tighten the inner fasteners to 35 ft. lbs. (48 Nm).
   - Upper ball joint and tapered washer. Tighten the nut to 66 ft. lbs. (90 Nm).
   - Strut and spring assembly
   - Front wheel

CONTROL ARM BUSHING REPLACEMENT

The control arm bushings are serviced with the control arm as an assembly.

Lower Control Arm

REMOVAL & INSTALLATION

1. Before servicing the vehicle, refer to the precautions in the beginning of this section.

2. Remove or disconnect the following:
   - Front wheel
   - Splash shield
   - Stabilizer bar link
   - Lower strut mounting bolt
   - Lower ball joint
   - Rack and pinion steering gear
   - Inner control arm mounting bolts
   - Lower control arm

To install:

➡ Use new fasteners for assembly.

3. Install or connect the following:
   - Lower control arm. Tighten the inner mounting bolts to 129 ft. lbs. (175 Nm).
   - Rack and pinion steering gear
   - Lower ball joint. Tighten the nut to 111 ft. lbs. (150 Nm).
   - Lower strut mounting bolt. Tighten the bolt to 129 ft. lbs. (175 Nm).
   - Stabilizer bar link. Tighten the nut to 41 ft. lbs. (55 Nm).
   - Splash shield
   - Front wheel

4. Check the wheel alignment and adjust as necessary.

CONTROL ARM BUSHING REPLACEMENT

The control arm bushings are serviced with the control arm as an assembly.

Wheel Bearings

ADJUSTMENT

The wheel bearings are not adjustable.

REMOVAL & REPLACEMENT

Front

1. Before servicing the vehicle, refer to the precautions in the beginning of this section.

2. Remove or disconnect the following:
   - Front wheel
   - Brake caliper and rotor
   - Wheel speed sensor connector
   - Hub and bearing assembly

➡ The hub and bearing assembly is not pressed into the knuckle. Do not use a slide hammer or press to remove the hub and bearing assembly. Damage to the hub and bearing assembly may result.

To install:

➡ Do not remove the wheel speed sensor from the hub and bearing assembly unless it is being replaced. If installing a new hub and bearing assembly, a new wheel speed sensor must be installed.

➡ Use new fasteners for assembly.

3. Install or connect the following:
   - Hub and bearing assembly. Tighten the bolts to 66 ft. lbs. (90 Nm).
   - Wheel speed sensor connector
   - Brake caliper and rotor
   - Front wheel

Rear

1. Before servicing the vehicle, refer to the precautions in the beginning of this section.

2. Remove or disconnect the following:
   - Rear wheel
   - Wheel speed sensor
   - Brake caliper and rotor
   - Hub, bearing and knuckle assembly
   - Disc brake dust shield

3. Press the hub from the knuckle and bearing assembly.

4. Remove the snapring and press the bearing assembly out of the knuckle.

To install:

5. Press the bearing assembly into the knuckle.

6. Install the snapring and press the hub into the knuckle and bearing assembly.

7. Install or connect the following:
   - Disc brake dust shield. Use aluminum rivets.
   - Hub, bearing and knuckle assembly
   - Brake caliper and rotor
   - Wheel speed sensor
   - Rear wheel

8. Check the wheel alignment and adjust as necessary.

FORD MOTOR CO.

Ford-Mustang

PRECAUTIONS

Before servicing any vehicle, please be sure to read all of the following precautions, which deal with personal safety, prevention of component damage, and important points to take into consideration when servicing a motor vehicle:

• Never open, service or drain the radiator or cooling system when the engine is hot; serious burns can occur from the steam and hot coolant.

• Observe all applicable safety precautions when working around fuel. Whenever servicing the fuel system, always work in a well-ventilated area. Do not allow fuel spray or vapors to come in contact with a spark, open flame, or excessive heat (a hot drop light, for example). Keep a dry chemical fire extinguisher near the work area. Always keep fuel in a container specifically designed for fuel storage; also, always properly seal fuel containers to avoid the possibility of fire or explosion. Refer to the additional fuel system precautions later in this section.

• Fuel injection systems often remain pressurized, even after the engine has been turned **OFF**. The fuel system pressure must be relieved before disconnecting any fuel lines. Failure to do so may result in fire and/or personal injury.

• Brake fluid often contains polyglycol ethers and polyglycols. Avoid contact with the eyes and wash your hands thoroughly after handling brake fluid. If you do get brake fluid in your eyes, flush your eyes with clean, running water for 15 minutes. If eye irritation persists, or if you have taken brake fluid internally, IMMEDIATELY seek medical assistance.

• The EPA warns that prolonged contact with used engine oil may cause a number of skin disorders, including cancer. You should make every effort to minimize your exposure to used engine oil. Protective gloves should be worn when changing oil. Wash your hands and any other exposed skin areas as soon as possible after exposure to used engine oil. Soap and water, or waterless hand cleaner should be used.

• All new vehicles are now equipped with an air bag system, often referred to as a Supplemental Restraint System (SRS) or Supplemental Inflatable Restraint (SIR) system. The system must be disabled before performing service on or around system components, steering column, instrument panel components, wiring and sensors. Failure to follow safety and disabling procedures could result in accidental air bag deployment, possible personal injury and unnecessary system repairs.

• Always wear safety goggles when working with, or around, the air bag system. When carrying a non-deployed air bag, be sure the bag and trim cover are pointed away from your body. When placing a non-deployed air bag on a work surface, always face the bag and trim cover upward, away from the surface. This will reduce the motion of the module if it is accidentally deployed. Refer to the additional air bag system precautions later in this section.

• Clean, high quality brake fluid from a sealed container is essential to the safe and proper operation of the brake system. You should always buy the correct type of brake fluid for your vehicle. If the brake fluid becomes contaminated, completely flush the system with new fluid. Never reuse any brake fluid. Any brake fluid that is removed from the system should be discarded. Also, do not allow any brake fluid to come in contact with a painted surface; it will damage the paint.

• Never operate the engine without the proper amount and type of engine oil; doing so WILL result in severe engine damage.

• Timing belt maintenance is extremely important. Many models utilize an interference-type, non-freewheeling engine. If the timing belt breaks, the valves in the cylinder head may strike the pistons, causing potentially serious (also time-consuming and expensive) engine damage. Refer to the maintenance interval charts in the front of this manual for the recommended replacement interval for the timing belt, and to the timing belt section for belt replacement and inspection.

• Disconnecting the negative battery cable on some vehicles may interfere with the functions of the on-board computer system(s) and may require the computer to undergo a relearning process once the negative battery cable is reconnected.

• When servicing drum brakes, only disassemble and assemble one side at a time, leaving the remaining side intact for reference.

• Only an MVAC-trained, EPA-certified automotive technician should service the air conditioning system or its components.

ENGINE REPAIR

➡ Disconnecting the negative battery cable on some vehicles may interfere with the functions of the on board computer system. The computer may undergo a relearning process once the negative battery cable is reconnected.

Distributor

The 3.8L and 4.6L engines use Distributorless Ignition Systems (DIS).

Alternator

REMOVAL

3.8L Engine

1. Before servicing the vehicle, refer to the precautions in the beginning of this section.
2. Remove or disconnect the following:
   • Negative battery cable
   • Accessory drive belt
   • Alternator electrical connectors
   • Alternator bolts
   • Alternator

4.6L Engines

1. Before servicing the vehicle, refer to the precautions in the beginning of this section.
2. Remove or disconnect the following:
   • Negative battery cable
   • Accessory drive belt
   • Upper alternator bracket
   • Alternator electrical connectors
   • Alternator bolts
   • Alternator

INSTALLATION

3.8L Engine

Install or connect the following:
   • Alternator. Tighten the lower bolt to 35 ft. lbs. (47 Nm) and the upper bolt to 18 ft. lbs. (25 Nm).
   • Alternator electrical connectors
   • Accessory drive belt
   • Negative battery cable

4.6L Engines

Install or connect the following:
   • Alternator. Tighten the mounting bolts to 18 ft. lbs. (25 Nm).

- Alternator electrical connectors
- Upper alternator bracket. Tighten the bolts to 89 inch lbs. (10 Nm).
- Accessory drive belt
- Negative battery cable

Ignition Timing

ADJUSTMENT

The ignition timing is controlled by the Powertrain Control Module (PCM). No adjustment is necessary.

Engine Assembly

REMOVAL & INSTALLATION

3.8L Engine

1. Before servicing the vehicle, refer to the precautions in the beginning of this section.
2. Discharge the air conditioning system.
3. Drain the engine cooling system.
4. Drain the engine oil and remove the oil filter.
5. Remove or disconnect the following:
   - Negative battery cable
   - Hood
   - Cooling fan
   - Radiator and hoses
   - Heater hoses
   - Intake Air Temperature (IAT) sensor connector
   - Air intake duct
   - Accessory drive belt
   - Alternator wiring connectors
   - Coolant recovery tank
   - Power steering pump and bracket
   - Power steering pressure switch connector
   - A/C compressor and bracket
   - Cruise control cable
   - Accelerator cable and bracket
   - Fuel supply line
   - Fuel return line, on 1997–98 engines
   - Fuel charging wiring harness connectors
   - Main vacuum source hose
   - Evaporative emissions hose
   - Heated Oxygen (HO2S) sensor connectors
   - Dual converter Y-pipe
   - Starter
   - Starter wiring harness retainers
   - Transmission flange bolts

- Torque converter, automatic transmission models only
- Transmission oil cooler lines, automatic transmission models only
- Left and right engine support insulators

6. Attach an engine hoist and remove the engine from the vehicle.

To install:

7. Lower the engine into the vehicle.
8. Install or connect the following:
   - Left and right engine support insulators. Tighten the through bolts to 35–50 ft. lbs. (47–68 Nm).
   - Transmission flange bolts. Tighten the bolts to 25–33 ft. lbs. (34–46 Nm).
   - Torque converter, automatic transmission models only. Tighten the nuts to 20–33 ft. lbs. (27–46 Nm).
   - Transmission oil cooler lines, automatic transmission models only
   - Starter wiring harness retainers
   - Starter
   - Dual converter Y-pipe
   - HO2S sensor connectors
   - Evaporative emissions hose
   - Main vacuum source hose
   - Fuel charging wiring harness connectors
   - Fuel supply line

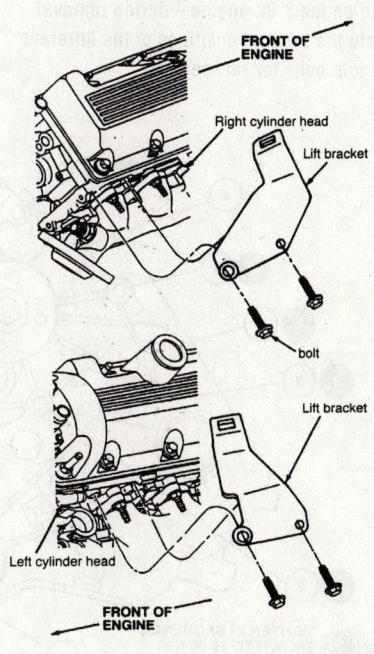

Install the engine lifting brackets on both sides of the engine—4.6L SOHC engine shown, other engines similar

7922NG02

- Fuel return line, on 1997–98 engines
- Accelerator cable and bracket
- Cruise control cable
- A/C compressor and bracket
- Power steering pressure switch connector
- Power steering pump and bracket
- Coolant recovery tank
- Alternator wiring connectors
- Accessory drive belt
- Air intake duct
- IAT sensor connector
- Heater hoses
- Radiator and hoses
- Cooling fan
- Hood
- Oil and oil filter
- Negative battery cable

9. Fill the cooling system.
10. Recharge the air conditioning.
11. Start the engine and check for leaks.

4.6L Engines

1. Before servicing the vehicle, refer to the precautions in the beginning of this section.
2. Discharge the air conditioning system.
3. Drain the engine cooling system.
4. Drain the engine oil and remove the oil filter.
5. Remove the transmission. Refer to the transmission procedure in this section.
6. Remove or disconnect the following:
   - Negative battery cable
   - Hood
   - Engine compartment brace
   - Cooling fan
   - Radiator hoses
   - Heater hoses
   - Intake Air Temperature (IAT) sensor connector
   - Air intake duct
   - Accessory drive belt
   - Alternator wiring connectors
   - Coolant recovery tank
   - A/C compressor suction and discharge lines
   - Cruise control cable
   - Accelerator cable
   - Fuel supply line
   - Fuel return line, on 1997–98 engines
   - Fuel charging wiring harness connectors
   - Main vacuum source hose

- Evaporative emissions hose
- Canister purge valve hose
- Secondary air injection switching valve, on DOHC engines
- Power steering reservoir
- Power distribution box
- Heated Oxygen (HO2S) sensor connectors
- Dual converter H-pipe
- Power steering fluid cooler hoses
- Power steering pressure and return hoses
- Starter
- Left and right engine support insulators

7. Attach an engine hoist and remove the engine from the vehicle.

To install:

8. Lower the engine into the vehicle.
9. Install or connect the following:
- Left and right engine support insulators. Tighten the through bolts to 15–22 ft. lbs. (20–30 Nm).
- Starter
- Power steering pressure and return hoses
- Power steering fluid cooler hoses
- Dual converter H-pipe
- HO2S sensor connectors
- Power distribution box
- Power steering reservoir
- Secondary air injection switching valve, on DOHC engines
- Canister purge valve hose
- Evaporative emissions hose
- Main vacuum source hose
- Fuel charging wiring harness connectors
- Fuel supply line
- Fuel return line, on 1997–98 engines
- Accelerator cable
- Cruise control cable
- A/C compressor suction and discharge lines
- Coolant recovery tank
- Alternator wiring connectors
- Accessory drive belt
- Air intake duct
- IAT sensor connector
- Heater hoses
- Radiator hoses
- Cooling fan
- Engine compartment brace
- Hood
- Transmission
- Oil and oil filter
- Negative battery cable

10. Fill the cooling system.
11. Recharge the air conditioning.
12. Start the engine and check for leaks.

Water Pump

REMOVAL & INSTALLATION

3.8L Engine

1. Before servicing the vehicle, refer to the precautions in the beginning of this section.
2. Drain the engine cooling system.
3. Remove or disconnect the following:

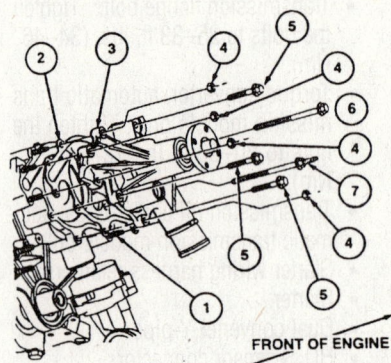

FRONT OF ENGINE

1. Mounting stud
2. Water pump housing gasket
3. Water pump
4. Mounting nuts
5. Short mounting bolts
6. Long mounting bolt
7. Mounting stud bolt

7922NG03

Exploded view of the water pump mounting on the 3.8L engine—during removal, note the original positions of the different length bolts for reassembly

- Electric cooling fan
- Accessory drive belt
- Water pump pulley
- Ignition coil and bracket
- Power steering pump pulley
- Power steering pump brace
- Heater water outlet tube
- Lower radiator hose
- Water pump

To install:

➡ **The threads of the No. 1 water pump retaining bolt must be coated with a Teflon® sealant prior to installation.**

4. Install or connect the following:
- Water pump. Use a new gasket and tighten the bolts and studs to 15–22 ft. lbs. (20–30 Nm). Tighten the nuts to 71–106 inch lbs. (8–12 Nm).
- Lower radiator hose
- Heater water outlet tube. Use a new O-ring seal and tighten the bolts to 71–106 inch lbs. (8–12 Nm).
- Power steering pump brace
- Power steering pump pulley
- Ignition coil and bracket
- Water pump pulley. Tighten the bolts to 15–21 ft. lbs. (21–29 Nm).
- Accessory drive belt
- Electric cooling fan

5. Fill the cooling system.
6. Start the engine and check for coolant leaks.

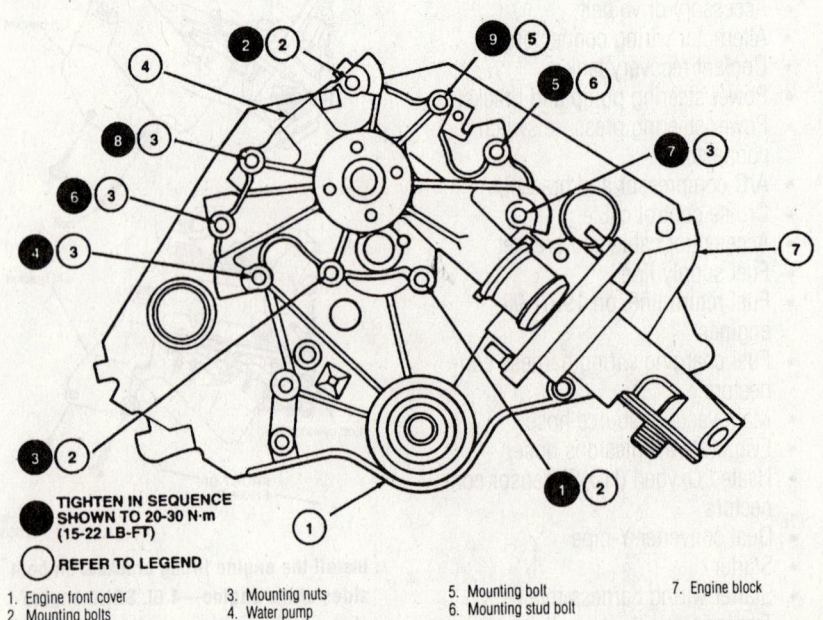

TIGHTEN IN SEQUENCE SHOWN TO 20-30 N·m (15-22 LB-FT)

⚪ **REFER TO LEGEND**

1. Engine front cover
2. Mounting bolts
3. Mounting nuts
4. Water pump
5. Mounting bolt
6. Mounting stud bolt
7. Engine block

Water pump torque sequence—3.8L engine

7922NG04

4.6L Engines

1. Before servicing the vehicle, refer to the precautions in the beginning of this section.
2. Drain the engine cooling system.
3. Remove or disconnect the following:
   - Electric cooling fan
   - Accessory drive belt
   - Water pump pulley
   - Water pump

To install:

4. Install or connect the following:
   - Water pump. Use a new O-ring seal and tighten the bolts in a crossing pattern to 15–22 ft. lbs. (20–30 Nm).
   - Water pump pulley. Tighten the bolts to 15–21 ft. lbs. (21–29 Nm).
   - Accessory drive belt
   - Electric cooling fan
5. Fill the cooling system.
6. Start the engine and check for coolant leaks.

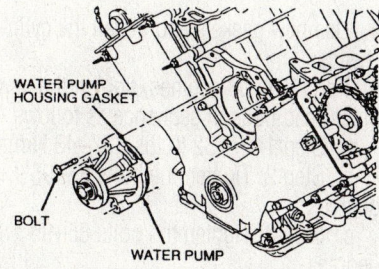

WATER PUMP
HOUSING GASKET

BOLT

WATER PUMP

7922NG05

Exploded view of the water pump mounting—4.6L engines

Cylinder Head

REMOVAL & INSTALLATION

3.8L Engine

1. Before servicing the vehicle, refer to the precautions in the beginning of this section.
2. Drain the cooling system.
3. Remove or disconnect the following:
   - Negative battery cable
   - Intake Air Temperature (IAT) sensor connector
   - Air intake tube
   - Accessory drive belt
   - Alternator and bracket
   - Power steering pump and bracket
   - A/C compressor and bracket

- Positive Crankcase Ventilation (PCV) valve
- Upper intake manifold
- Spark plug wires
- Valve covers
- Fuel supply line
- Fuel return line, on 1997–98 engines
- Fuel injector wiring connectors
- Fuel injection supply manifold
- Lower intake manifold
- Exhaust manifolds

➡ **Keep rocker arms and pushrods in order for installation.**

- Rocker arms
- Pushrods
- Cylinder heads

To install:

➡ **The cylinder head bolts are a torque-to-yield design and cannot be reused.**

➡ **Left and right cylinder head gaskets are not interchangeable.**

➡ **Refer to Section 1 of this manual for the cylinder head torque sequence illustration. The illustration is located after the Torque Specification Chart.**

4. Install the cylinder heads. Lubricate the new cylinder head bolt threads with clean oil and tighten them in sequence as follows:
   a. Step 1: 15 ft. lbs. (20 Nm).
   b. Step 2: 29 ft. lbs. (40 Nm).
   c. Step 3: 36 ft. lbs. (50 Nm).

➡ **Loosen and tighten each bolt individually for the remainder of the procedure. Do not loosen or tighten all the bolts at the same time.**

   d. Step 4: Loosen each bolt, one at a time, 2–3 turns. Tighten the long cylinder head bolts to 29–37 ft. lbs. (40–50 Nm) plus 180 degrees. Tighten the short cylinder head bolts to 15–22 ft. lbs. (20–30 Nm) plus 180 degrees.
   e. Step 5: Repeat step 4 for the next bolt in the tightening sequence.
5. Install or connect the following:
   - Pushrods and rocker arms in their original locations
   - Exhaust manifolds
   - Lower intake manifold
   - Fuel injection supply manifold
   - Fuel injector wiring connectors
   - Fuel supply line
   - Fuel return line, on 1997–98 engines
   - Valve covers
   - Spark plug wires

- Upper intake manifold
- PCV valve
- A/C compressor and bracket
- Power steering pump and bracket
- Alternator and bracket
- Accessory drive belt
- Air intake tube
- IAT sensor connector
- Negative battery cable
6. Fill the cooling system.
7. Start the engine and check for leaks.

4.6L SOHC Engine

1. Before servicing the vehicle, refer to the precautions in the beginning of this section.
2. Drain the cooling system.
3. Remove or disconnect the following:
   - Negative battery cable
   - Electric cooling fan
   - Fuel supply line
   - Fuel return line, on 1997–98 engines
   - Air intake tube
   - Windshield wiper governor
   - Accessory drive belt
   - Spark plug wires, on 1997–98 engines
   - Ignition coils
   - Camshaft Position (CMP) sensor connector
   - Power steering reservoir
   - Alternator and bracket
   - Water pump pulley
   - Mass Air Flow (MAF) sensor connector
   - Fuel injector wiring connectors
   - Crankshaft Position (CKP) sensor connector
   - A/C compressor clutch connector
   - Cruise control cable
   - Accelerator cable and bracket
   - Canister purge valve connector
   - Power steering pump
   - Oil pan
   - Crankshaft pulley
   - Oil pressure sensor connector
   - Exhaust Gas Recirculation (EGR) tube
   - Heated Oxygen (HO$_2$S) sensor connectors
   - Dual converter H-pipe
   - Starter motor wiring harness retainer
   - Valve covers
   - Throttle body vacuum adapter
   - Heater hoses
   - Upper radiator hose and adapter
   - Intake manifold

Timing belt service is covered in Section 4 of this manual

- Front cover
- Timing chains
- Heater water tube
- Cylinder heads

To install:

➡ The cylinder head bolts are a torque-to-yield design and cannot be reused.

➡ Refer to Section 1 of this manual for the cylinder head torque sequence illustration. The illustration is located after the Torque Specification Chart.

4. Rotate the crankshaft so that the keyway is at the 9 o'clock position.

5. Rotate each camshaft to a stable position where the valves do not extend below the cylinder head face.

6. Install the cylinder heads. Lubricate the new cylinder head bolt threads with clean oil and tighten them in sequence as follows:
   a. Step 1: 28–31 ft. lbs. (37–43 Nm).
   b. Step 2: Plus 85–95 degrees.
   c. Step 3: Loosen all bolts one full turn.
   d. Step 4: 28–31 ft. lbs. (37–43 Nm).
   e. Step 5: Plus 85–95 degrees.
   f. Step 6: Plus 85–95 degrees.

7. Install or connect the following:
   - Heater water tube
   - Timing chains
   - Front cover
   - Intake manifold
   - Upper radiator hose and adapter
   - Heater hoses
   - Throttle body vacuum adapter
   - Valve covers
   - Starter motor wiring harness retainer
   - Dual converter H-pipe
   - HO2S sensor connectors
   - EGR tube
   - Oil pressure sensor connector
   - Crankshaft pulley
   - Oil pan
   - Power steering pump
   - Canister purge valve connector

- Accelerator cable and bracket
- Cruise control cable
- A/C compressor clutch connector
- CKP sensor connector
- Fuel injector wiring connectors
- MAF sensor connector
- Water pump pulley
- Alternator and bracket
- Power steering reservoir
- CMP sensor connector
- Ignition coils
- Spark plug wires, on 1997–98 engines
- Accessory drive belt
- Windshield wiper governor
- Air intake tube
- Fuel supply line
- Fuel return line, on 1997–98 engines
- Electric cooling fan
- Negative battery cable

8. Fill the cooling system.
9. Start the engine and check for leaks.

4.6L DOHC Engine

1. Before servicing the vehicle, refer to the precautions in the beginning of this section.

2. Remove the engine from the vehicle and mount it on a suitable workstand.

3. Remove or disconnect the following:
   - Accessory drive belt and tensioner
   - Idler pulley
   - Engine Coolant Temperature (ECT) sensor connector
   - Water bypass tube
   - Alternator
   - Water pump
   - Power steering pump
   - Crankshaft pulley
   - Camshaft Position (CMP) sensor

- Spark plug wires, 1997–98 engines
- Ignition coils
- Fuel pressure sensor connector and vacuum line
- Valve covers
- Rocker arms
- Exhaust Gas Recirculation (EGR) vacuum regulator valve
- EGR tube
- Injector wiring connectors
- Intake manifold
- Left and right exhaust manifolds
- Front cover
- Crankshaft Position (CKP) sensor pulse wheel
- Timing chains
- Cylinder heads

To install:

➡ The cylinder head bolts are a torque-to-yield design and cannot be reused.

➡ Refer to Section 1 of this manual for the cylinder head torque sequence illustration. The illustration is located after the Torque Specification Chart.

4. Use new gaskets and install the cylinder heads.

5. For 1997–98 engines, tighten the new cylinder head bolts in sequence as follows:
   a. Step 1: 27–32 ft. lbs. (37–43 Nm).
   b. Step 2: Tighten the bolts 85–95 degrees.
   c. Step 3: Tighten the bolts 85–95 degrees.

6. For 1999–01 engines, tighten the cylinder head bolts in sequence as follows:
   a. Step 1: 28–31 ft. lbs. (37–43 Nm).
   b. Step 2: Tighten the bolts 85–95 degrees.
   c. Step 3: Loosen all bolts 1 full turn.

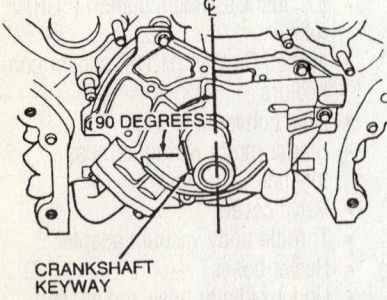

9306NG01

Place the crankshaft keyway at 9 o'clock for cylinder head installation—4.6L SOHC engine

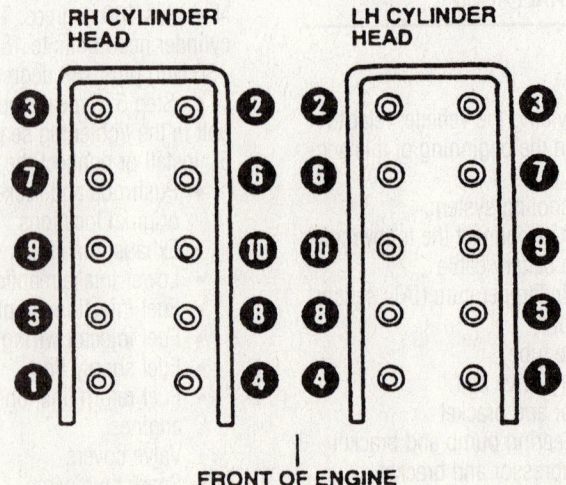

7922NG10

Cylinder head loosening sequence—4.6L DOHC engine

d. Step 4: Tighten all bolts to 28–31 ft. lbs. (37–43 Nm).

e. Step 5: Tighten the bolts 85–95 degrees.

f. Step 6: Tighten the bolts 85–95 degrees.

7. Install or connect the following:
- Timing chains
- CKP sensor pulse wheel
- Front cover
- Left and right exhaust manifolds
- Intake manifold
- Injector wiring connectors
- EGR tube
- EGR vacuum regulator valve
- Rocker arms
- Valve covers
- Fuel pressure sensor connector and vacuum line
- Ignition coils
- Spark plug wires, on 1997–98 engines
- CMP sensor
- Crankshaft pulley
- Water pump
- Power steering pump
- Alternator
- Water bypass tube
- ECT sensor connector
- Idler pulley
- Accessory drive belt and tensioner

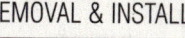

Rocker Arms

REMOVAL & INSTALLATION

3.8L Engine

1. Before servicing the vehicle, refer to the precautions in the beginning of this section.

2. Remove or disconnect the following:
- Negative battery cable
- Positive Crankcase Ventilation (PCV) valve and hose
- Valve covers
- Rocker arms

➡ Keep rocker arms in order for installation.

To install:

➡ The rocker arm bolts are tightened with the valves closed. Rotate the crankshaft as necessary to position the lifter on the base circle of the camshaft lobe before tightening the corresponding rocker arm bolt.

3. Install the rocker arms. The rocker arm bolts are tightened in two steps as follows:

a. Step 1: 44 inch lbs. (5 Nm).

b. Step 2: 23–29 ft. lbs. (30–40 Nm).

4. Install or connect the following:
- Valve covers
- PCV valve and hose
- Negative battery cable

5. Start the engine and check for proper operation.

4.6L Engines

1. Before servicing the vehicle, refer to the precautions at the beginning of this section.

2. Remove or disconnect the following:
- Negative battery cable
- Spark plug wires, on 1997–98 engines
- Ignition coils, on 1999–01 engines
- Valve covers

➡ The 4.6L DOHC engine requires special tool Valve Spring Compressor T91P-6565-A for exhaust valves, and Valve Spring Compressor T93P-6565-A for intake valves. The 4.6L SOHC engine requires special tool Valve Spring Compressor T91P-6565-A and Valve Spring Spacer T91P-6565-AH.

3. Rotate the crankshaft so that the piston on the cylinder to be serviced is at bottom dead center with the valves closed.

4. Compress the valve spring and remove the rocker arm. Repeat for each arm to be removed.

➡ If the rocker arms are to be reused, ensure that they are installed in the same position that they were removed from.

To install:

5. Compress the valve spring and install the rocker arm. Repeat for each arm to be installed.

6. Install or connect the following:
- Valve covers
- Spark plug wires, on 1997–98 engines
- Ignition coils, on 1999–01 engines
- Negative battery cable

7. Start the engine and check for proper operation.

Intake Manifold

REMOVAL & INSTALLATION

3.8L Engine

1. Before servicing the vehicle, refer to the precautions in the beginning of this section.

2. Drain the cooling system.

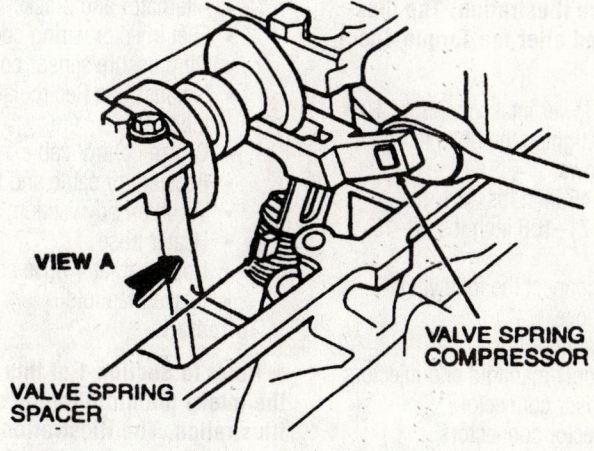

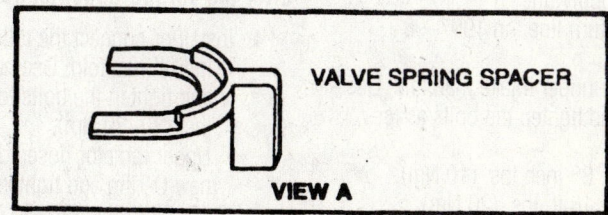

Valve spring compression tool and spacer—4.6L SOHC engine

3. Remove or disconnect the following:
- Negative battery cable
- Intake Air Temperature (IAT) sensor
- Air intake tube
- Cruise control cable
- Accelerator cable and bracket
- Spark plug wires and ignition coil assembly
- Upper intake vacuum lines
- Positive Crankcase Ventilation (PCV) valve and hose
- Throttle Position (TP) sensor connector
- Idle Air Control (IAC) valve connector
- Exhaust Gas Recirculation (EGR) valve
- Engine control sensor wiring harness retainer bracket
- Upper intake manifold
- Fuel supply line
- Fuel return line, on 1997–98 engines
- Fuel injector connectors
- Engine Coolant Temperature (ECT) sensor connector
- Fuel supply manifold and injectors
- Upper radiator hose
- Heater hose
- Lower intake manifold

To install:

➡ **Refer to Section 1 of this manual for the upper and lower intake manifold torque sequence illustration. The illustration is located after the Torque Specification Chart.**

4. Install the lower intake manifold. Use new gaskets and tighten the bolts in sequence as follows:
   a. Step 1: 45 inch lbs. (5 Nm).
   b. Step 2: 71–106 inch lbs. (8–12 Nm).

5. Install or connect the following:
- Heater hose
- Upper radiator hose
- Fuel supply manifold and injectors
- ECT sensor connector
- Fuel injector connectors
- Fuel supply line
- Fuel return line, on 1997–98 engines

6. Install the upper intake manifold. Use a new gasket and tighten the bolts as follows:
   a. Step 1: 88 inch lbs. (10 Nm).
   b. Step 2: 15 ft. lbs. (20 Nm).
   c. Step 3: 24 ft. lbs. (32 Nm).

7. Install or connect the following:
- Engine control sensor wiring harness retainer bracket
- EGR valve

- IAC valve connector
- TP sensor connector
- PCV valve and hose
- Upper intake vacuum lines
- Spark plug wires and ignition coil assembly
- Accelerator cable and bracket
- Cruise control cable
- Air intake tube
- IAT sensor connector
- Negative battery cable

8. Fill the cooling system.
9. Start the engine and check for leaks.

4.6L SOHC Engine

1. Before servicing the vehicle, refer to the precautions in the beginning of this section.

2. Drain the cooling system.
3. Remove or disconnect the following:
- Negative battery cable
- Fuel supply line
- Fuel return line, on 1997–98 engines
- Intake Air Temperature (IAT) sensor connector
- Air intake tube
- Accessory drive belt
- Spark plug wires, on 1997–98 engines
- Ignition coils, on 1997–98 engines
- Camshaft Position (CMP) sensor connector
- Alternator and bracket
- Fuel injector wiring connectors
- Oil pressure sensor connector
- Exhaust Gas Recirculation (EGR) tube
- Cruise control cable
- Accelerator cable and bracket
- Throttle body vacuum adapter hose
- Heater hose
- Upper radiator hose adapter
- Intake manifold

To install:

➡ **Refer to Section 1 of this manual for the intake manifold torque sequence illustration. The illustration is located after the Torque Specification Chart.**

4. Install or connect the following:
- Intake manifold. Use new gaskets and tighten the bolts to 15–22 ft. lbs. (20–30 Nm).
- Upper radiator hose adapter. Use a new O-ring and tighten the bolts to 15–22 ft. lbs. (20–30 Nm).
- Heater hose
- Throttle body vacuum adapter hose
- Accelerator cable and bracket
- Cruise control cable

- EGR tube. Tighten the nut to 26–33 ft. lbs. (35–45 Nm).
- Oil pressure sensor connector
- Fuel injector wiring connectors
- Alternator and bracket
- CMP sensor connector
- Ignition coils, on 1997–98 engines
- Spark plug wires, on 1997–98 engines
- Accessory drive belt
- Air intake tube
- IAT sensor connector
- Fuel supply line
- Fuel return line, on 1997–98 engines
- Negative battery cable

5. Fill the engine cooling system.
6. Start the engine and check for leaks.

4.6L DOHC Engine

1. Before servicing the vehicle, refer to the precautions in the beginning of this section.

2. Drain the cooling system.
3. Remove or disconnect the following:
- Negative battery cable
- Engine compartment brace
- Air intake tube
- Cruise control cable
- Accelerator cable and bracket
- Positive Crankcase Ventilation (PCV) valve and hose
- Exhaust Gas Recirculation (EGR) valve
- Upper intake manifold
- Fuel supply line
- Fuel return line, on 1997–98 engines
- Accessory drive belt

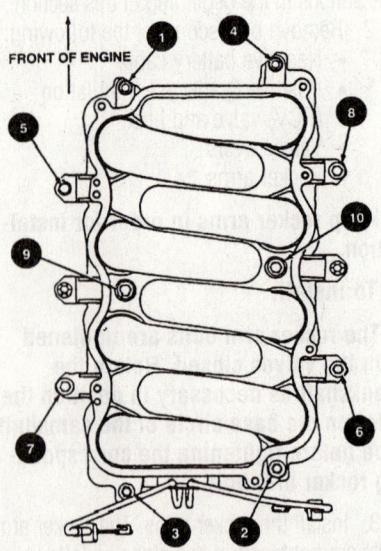

Lower intake manifold loosening sequence—1997–98 4.6L DOHC engines

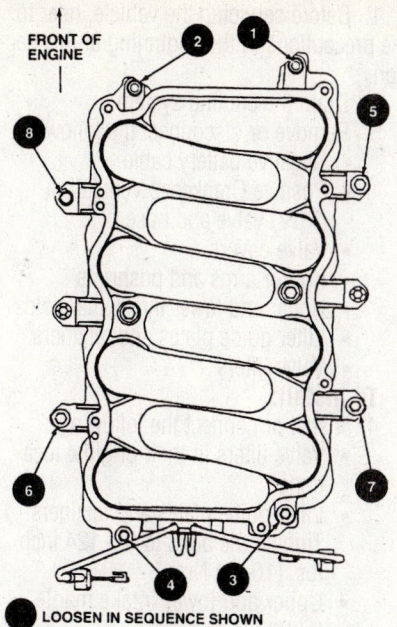

LOOSEN IN SEQUENCE SHOWN

9300NG01

Lower intake manifold loosening sequence—1999–01 4.6L DOHC engine

- Spark plug wires, on 1997–98 engines
- Alternator bracket
- Upper radiator hose
- Throttle Position (TP) sensor connector
- Engine Coolant Temperature (ECT) sensor connector
- Idle Air Control (IAC) valve connector
- Coolant temperature gauge sender connector
- Water bypass tube
- Alternator
- Fuel injector wiring connectors
- Fuel pressure regulator vacuum line, 1997–98 engines
- Fuel pressure sensor vacuum and wiring connectors, 1999–01 engines
- Lower intake manifold

To install:

➡ Refer to Section 1 of this manual for the upper and lower intake manifold torque sequence illustration. The illustration is located after the Torque Specification Chart.

4. Install or connect the following:
- Lower intake manifold. Tighten the bolts in sequence to 89 inch lbs. (10 Nm).
- Fuel pressure regulator vacuum line, on 1997–98 engines

- Fuel pressure sensor vacuum and wiring connectors, on 1999–01 engines
- Fuel injector wiring connectors
- Alternator. Tighten the bolts to 15–22 ft. lbs. (20–30 Nm).
- Water bypass tube
- Coolant temperature gauge sender connector
- IAC valve connector
- ECT sensor connector
- TP sensor connector
- Upper radiator hose
- Alternator bracket. Tighten the bolts to 71–106 inch lbs. (8–12 Nm).
- Spark plug wires, on 1997–98 engines
- Accessory drive belt
- Fuel supply line
- Fuel return line, on 1997–98 engines
- Upper intake manifold. Tighten the bolts to 71–106 inch lbs. (8–12 Nm).
- EGR valve
- PCV valve and hose
- Accelerator cable and bracket
- Cruise control cable
- Air intake tube
- Engine compartment brace
- Negative battery cable
5. Fill the engine cooling system.
6. Start the engine and check for leaks.

Exhaust Manifold

REMOVAL & INSTALLATION

3.8L Engine

1. Before servicing the vehicle, refer to the precautions in the beginning of this section.

2. Remove or disconnect the following:
- Negative battery cable
- Spark plug wires
- Secondary air injection diverter valve, if equipped
- Secondary air injection tubes, if equipped
- Exhaust Gas Recirculation (EGR) tube
- Oil dipstick tube
- Heated Oxygen (HO$_2$S) sensors
- Dual converter Y-pipe
- Exhaust manifolds. Note the locations of the studs and bolts for reassembly.

To install:

3. Install or connect the following:
- Exhaust manifolds. Tighten the bolts in sequence to 22–26 ft. lbs. (30–36 Nm).
- Dual converter Y-pipe
- HO$_2$S sensors. Tighten the sensors to 28–33 ft. lbs. (37–45 Nm).
- Oil dipstick tube
- EGR tube
- Secondary air injection tubes, if equipped
- Secondary air injection diverter valve, if equipped
- Spark plug wires
- Negative battery cable

4.6L Engines

1. Before servicing the vehicle, refer to the precautions in the beginning of this section.

2. Remove or disconnect the following:
- Negative battery cable
- Engine compartment brace
- Dual converter H-pipe
- Starter
- Steering column intermediate shaft
- Secondary air injection tubes, if equipped

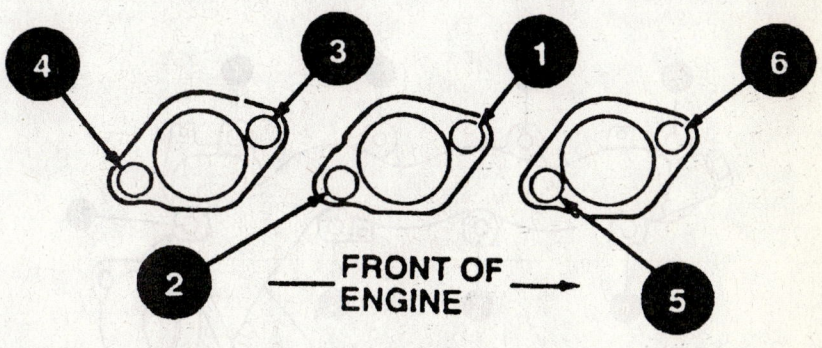

Exhaust manifold torque sequence—3.8L engine

Refer to Section 1 for engine rebuilding specifications

7922NG24

- Exhaust Gas Recirculation (EGR) tube
- Oil filter
- Left and right motor mounts

3. Raise the engine about 1.5 inches for clearance and remove the exhaust manifolds.

To install:

4. Install or connect the following:
   - Exhaust manifolds. Use new gaskets and tighten the nuts in sequence to 15 ft. lbs. (20 Nm).
   - Left and right motor mounts
   - Oil filter
   - EGR tube
   - Secondary air injection tubes, if equipped

- Steering column intermediate shaft
- Starter
- Dual converter H-pipe
- Engine compartment brace
- Negative battery cable

Camshaft and Valve Lifters

REMOVAL & INSTALLATION

3.8L Engine

VALVE LIFTERS

➡**Keep all valvetrain parts in order for installation.**

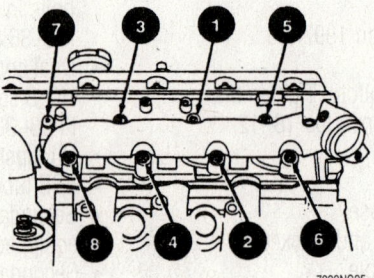

Exhaust manifold torque sequence—4.6L SOHC engine

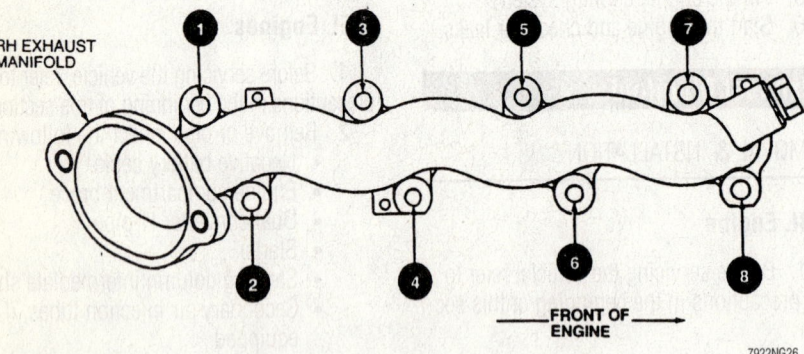

Left exhaust manifold torque sequence —4.6L DOHC engine

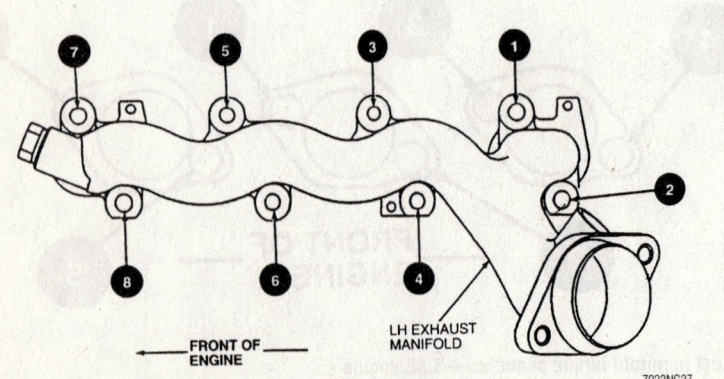

Right exhaust manifold torque sequence—4.6L DOHC engine

1. Before servicing the vehicle, refer to the precautions in the beginning of this section.
2. Drain the cooling system
3. Remove or disconnect the following:
   - Negative battery cable
   - Positive Crankcase Ventilation (PCV) valve and hose
   - Valve covers
   - Rocker arms and pushrods
   - Upper and lower intake manifolds
   - Lifter guide plates and retainers
   - Valve lifters

To install:

4. Install or connect the following:
   - Valve lifters in their original locations
   - Lifter guide plates and retainers. Tighten the bolts to 88–124 inch lbs. (10–14 Nm).
   - Upper and lower intake manifolds
   - Rocker arms and pushrods in their original locations
   - Valve covers
   - PCV valve and hose
   - Negative battery cable
5. Fill the cooling system.
6. Start the engine and check for leaks.

CAMSHAFT

1. Before servicing the vehicle, refer to the precautions in the beginning of this section.
2. Drain the cooling system.
3. Recover the A/C refrigerant.
4. Remove or disconnect the following:
   - Radiator and cooling fan
   - A/C condenser
   - Upper and lower intake manifolds
   - Valve lifters
   - Front cover
   - Timing chain and gears
   - Camshaft thrust plate
   - Camshaft

To install:

5. Install or connect the following:
   - Camshaft
   - Camshaft thrust plate. Tighten the bolts to 71–124 inch lbs. (8–14 Nm).
   - Timing chain and gears
   - Front cover
   - Valve lifters
   - Upper and lower intake manifolds
   - A/C condenser
   - Radiator and cooling fan
6. Fill the cooling system.
7. Recharge the A/C system.
8. Run the engine and check for leaks.

4.6L Engines

VALVE LIFTERS

➡ **Keep all valvetrain parts in order for installation.**

1. Before servicing the vehicle, refer to the precautions in the beginning of this section.

2. Remove or disconnect the following:
   - Valve covers
   - Rocker arms
   - Hydraulic lifters

To install:

3. Inspect each lifter. If the plunger travel exceeds 0.059 inches (1.5 mm), replace the lifter.

4. Install or connect the following:
   - Hydraulic lifters in their original positions
   - Rocker arms
   - Valve covers

CAMSHAFTS

1. Before servicing the vehicle, refer to the precautions in the beginning of this section.

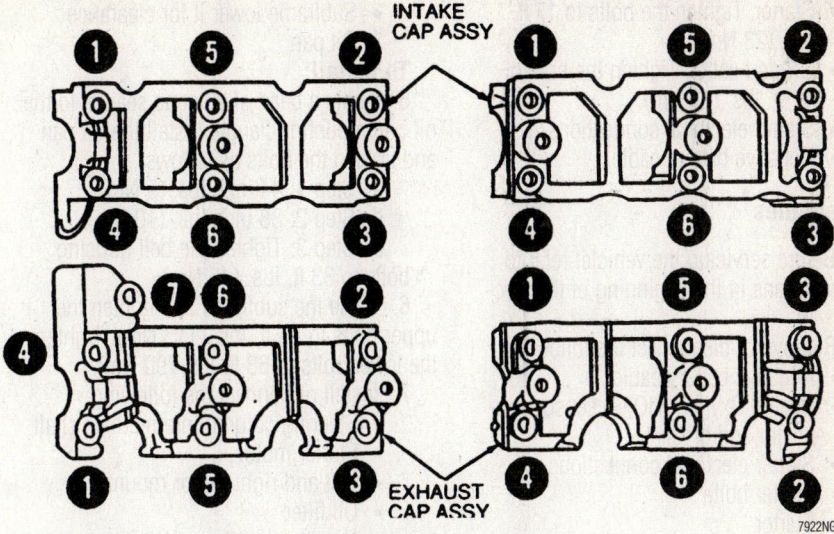

Camshaft bearing cap torque sequence—4.6L DOHC engine

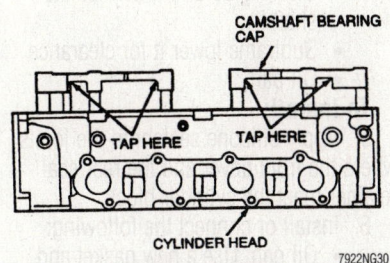

To remove the camshaft bearing caps, tap the caps with a rubber or leather mallet where shown—4.6L engines

2. Remove or disconnect the following:
   - Valve covers
   - Rocker arms
   - Oil pan (SOHC engine)
   - Front cover
   - Timing chains and sprockets
   - Camshaft bearing caps
   - Camshafts

To install:

➡ **On 4.6L DOHC engines, the outboard exhaust camshaft bearing cap bolts are shorter than the other bearing cap bolts.**

3. Install the camshafts. Tighten the bearing cap bolts in sequence as follows:
   a. Step 1: 71–106 inch lbs. (8–12 Nm).

   b. Step 2: Loosen all bolts 2 turns.
   c. Step 3: 71–106 inch lbs. (8–12 Nm).

4. Install or connect the following:
   - Timing chains and sprockets
   - Front cover
   - Oil pan (SOHC engine)
   - Rocker arms
   - Valve covers

5. Start the engine and check for leaks.

Valve lash

ADJUSTMENT

The 3.8L and 4.6L engines are equipped with hydraulic lash adjusters. Valve clearance is not adjustable.

Starter Motor

REMOVAL & INSTALLATION

3.8L engine

1. Before servicing the vehicle, refer to the precautions in the beginning of this section.

2. Remove or disconnect the following:
   - Negative battery cable
   - Starter electrical connections
   - Ground cable
   - Starter bolts
   - Starter

To install:

3. Install or connect the following:

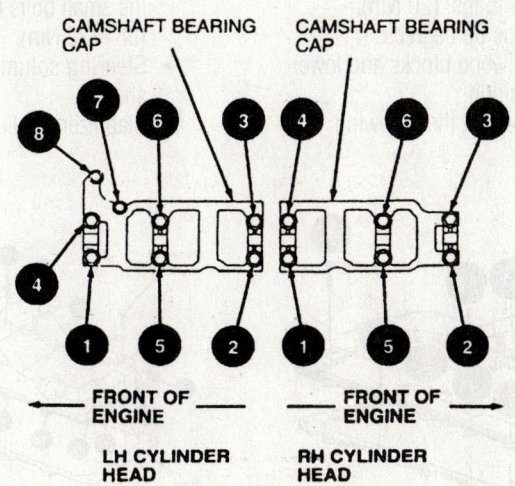

Camshaft bearing cap torque sequence—4.6L SOHC engine

For engine torque specifications, refer to Section 1 of this manual

- Starter. Tighten the bolts to 17 ft. lbs. (23 Nm).
- Ground cable. Tighten the bolt to 17 ft. lbs. (23 Nm).
- Starter electrical connections
- Negative battery cable

4.6L engines

1. Before servicing the vehicle, refer to the precautions in the beginning of this section.
2. Remove or disconnect the following:
   - Negative battery cable
   - Heated Oxygen (HO$_2$S) sensor connector and bracket
   - Starter electrical connections
   - Starter bolts
   - Starter

To install:

3. Install or connect the following:
   - Starter. Tighten the bolts to 17 ft. lbs. (23 Nm).
   - Starter electrical connections
   - HO$_2$S sensor connector and bracket
   - Negative battery cable

Oil Pan

REMOVAL & INSTALLATION

3.8L Engine

1. Before servicing the vehicle, refer to the precautions in the beginning of this section.
2. Drain the engine oil.
3. Install engine lifting brackets and attach an engine support fixture.
4. Remove or disconnect the following:
   - Negative battery cable
   - Oil filter
   - Left and right motor mounts
   - Starter motor
   - Steering column intermediate shaft

- Subframe lower it for clearance
- Oil pan

To install:

5. Apply a bead of silicone sealant to the oil pan mounting flange. Install the oil pan and tighten the bolts as follows:
   a. Step 1: 44 inch lbs. (5 Nm).
   b. Step 2: 88 inch lbs. (10 Nm).
   c. Step 3: Tighten the bell housing bolts to 33 ft. lbs. (45 Nm).
6. Raise the subframe and tighten the upper bolts to 85 ft. lbs. (115 Nm). Tighten the lower bolts to 68 ft. lbs. (90 Nm).
7. Install or connect the following:
   - Steering column intermediate shaft
   - Starter motor
   - Left and right motor mounts
   - Oil filter
   - Negative battery cable
8. Fill the engine with oil.
9. Run the engine and check for leaks.

4.6L SOHC Engine

1. Before servicing the vehicle, refer to the precautions in the beginning of this section.
2. Drain the engine oil.
3. Remove or disconnect the following:
   - Negative battery cable
   - Engine compartment brace
   - Front subframe crossmember brace
   - Left and right motor mounts
   - Transmission housing cover
4. Raise the engine about 4 inches and support with wood blocks under each motor mount.
5. Remove the oil pan.

To install:

6. Install the oil pan. Use a new gasket and tighten the bolts in sequence as follows:
   a. Step 1: 15 ft. lbs. (20 Nm).
   b. Step 2: Plus 60 degrees.
7. Remove the wood blocks and lower the engine into position.
8. Install or connect the following:

- Transmission housing cover
- Left and right motor mounts. Tighten the nuts to 95–126 ft. lbs. (128–172 Nm).
- Front subframe crossmember brace. Tighten the bolts to 30–40 ft. lbs. (40–55 Nm).
- Engine compartment brace
- Negative battery cable
9. Fill the engine with oil.
10. Start the engine and check for leaks.

4.6L DOHC Engine

1. Before servicing the vehicle, refer to the precautions in the beginning of this section.
2. Drain the engine oil.
3. Install engine lifting brackets and attach an engine support fixture.
4. Remove or disconnect the following:

   - Negative battery cable
   - Transmission
   - Oil filter
   - Left and right motor mounts
   - Stabilizer bar links
   - Steering column intermediate shaft
   - Subframe lower it for clearance
   - Oil pan

To install:

5. Apply silicone sealant to the joints where the front cover and the rear seal retainer meet the cylinder block.
6. Install or connect the following:
   - Oil pan. Use a new gasket and tighten the bolts in sequence to 15–22 ft. lbs. (20–30 Nm).
   - Subframe. Tighten the large bolts to 83–113 ft. lbs. (113–153 Nm) and the small bolts to 72–97 ft. lbs. (98–132 Nm).
   - Steering column intermediate shaft
   - Stabilizer bar links

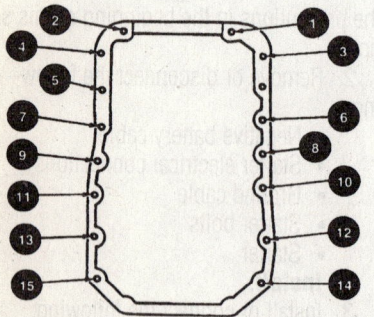

Oil pan torque sequence—3.8L engine

7922NG34

Oil pan torque sequence—4.6L SOHC engine

7922NG35

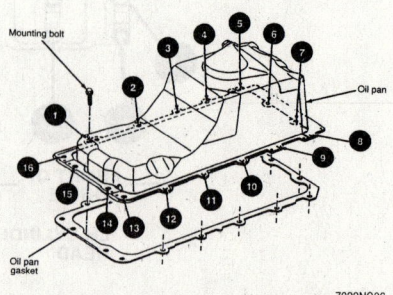

Oil pan torque sequence—4.6L DOHC engine

7922NG36

- Left and right motor mounts. Tighten the nuts to 95–126 ft. lbs. (128–172 Nm).
- Oil filter
- Transmission
- Negative battery cable
7. Fill the engine with oil.
8. Start the engine and check for oil leaks.

Oil Pump

REMOVAL & INSTALLATION

3.8L Engine

1. Before servicing the vehicle, refer to the precautions in the beginning of this section.
2. Remove or disconnect the following:
   - Oil filter
   - Oil pump body and gears

To install:

3. Install or connect the following:
   - Oil pump. Use a new O-ring seal. Tighten the large bolts to 18 ft. lbs. (25 Nm) and the small bolts to 88 inch lbs. (10 Nm).
   - Oil filter
4. Check for leaks and proper operation.

4.6L Engines

1. Before servicing the vehicle, refer to the precautions in the beginning of this section.
2. Remove or disconnect the following:
   - Valve covers
   - Oil pan
   - Front cover
   - Timing chains and sprockets
   - Oil pump

To install:

3. Install or connect the following:
   - Oil pump. Tighten the bolts to 71–106 inch lbs. (8–12 Nm).
   - Timing chains and sprockets

- Front cover
- Oil pan
- Valve covers
4. Check for leaks and proper operation.

Rear Main Seal

REMOVAL & INSTALLATION

3.8L Engine

1. Before servicing the vehicle, refer to the precautions in the beginning of this section.
2. Remove or disconnect the following:
   - Negative battery cable
   - Transmission
   - Clutch pressure plate and disc, if equipped
   - Flywheel
   - Engine rear plate
   - Rear main seal

To install:

3. Install or connect the following:
   - Rear main seal
   - Engine rear plate
   - Flywheel. Tighten the bolts to 54–64 ft. lbs. (73–87 Nm).
   - Clutch pressure plate and disc, if equipped
   - Transmission
   - Negative battery cable

4.6L Engines

1. Before servicing the vehicle, refer to the precautions in the beginning of this section.

2. Remove or disconnect the following:
   - Negative battery cable
   - Transmission
   - Clutch pressure plate and disc, if equipped
   - Flywheel
   - Oil slinger. Use Rear Crankshaft Oil Slinger Remover T95P-6701-AH.
   - Rear oil seal retainer
   - Rear oil seal

To install:

3. Install the rear oil seal retainer. Apply silicone sealant as shown. Tighten the bolts in sequence to 71–106 inch lbs. (8–12 Nm).
4. Install or connect the following:
   - Rear oil seal. Use Rear Crankshaft Seal Replacer T95P-6701-BH.
   - Oil slinger. Use Rear Crankshaft Oil Slinger Replacer T95P-6701-CH.
   - Flywheel. Tighten the bolts in a crossing pattern to 54–64 ft. lbs. (73–87 Nm).
   - Clutch pressure plate and disc, if equipped
   - Transmission
   - Negative battery cable
5. Run the engine and check for leaks.

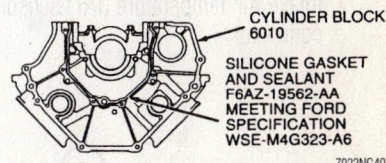

CYLINDER BLOCK 6010

SILICONE GASKET AND SEALANT F6AZ-19562-AA MEETING FORD SPECIFICATION WSE-M4G323-A6

7922NG40

Apply silicone sealant to the engine block when installing the oil seal retainer—4.6L engines

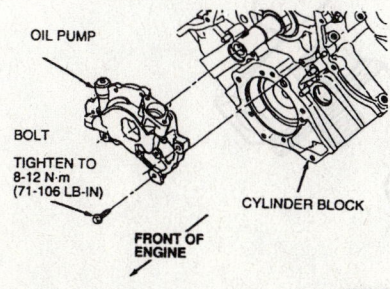

OIL PUMP

BOLT
TIGHTEN TO 8–12 N·m (71–106 LB-IN)

CYLINDER BLOCK

FRONT OF ENGINE

7922NG37

Exploded view of the oil pump mounting— 4.6L engines

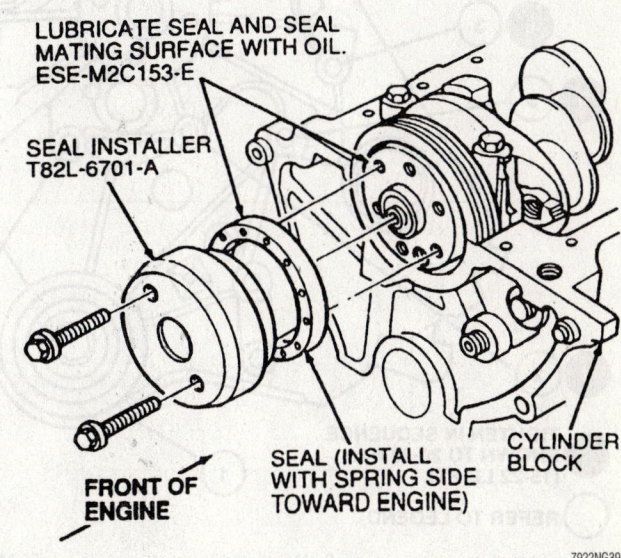

LUBRICATE SEAL AND SEAL MATING SURFACE WITH OIL. ESE-M2C153-E

SEAL INSTALLER T82L-6701-A

SEAL (INSTALL WITH SPRING SIDE TOWARD ENGINE)

CYLINDER BLOCK

FRONT OF ENGINE

7922NG39

Installing the rear main seal—3.8L engine

For complete mechanical specifications, refer to Section 1 of this manual

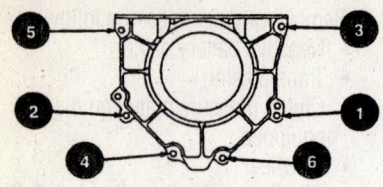

Oil seal retainer torque sequence—4.6L engines

Timing Chain, Sprockets, Front Cover and Seal

REMOVAL & INSTALLATION

3.8L Engine

1. Before servicing the vehicle, refer to the precautions in the beginning of this section.
2. Drain the cooling system and the engine oil.
3. Rotate the crankshaft so that the No. 1 cylinder is at Top Dead Center (TDC) of the compression stroke.
4. Remove or disconnect the following:
   - Negative battery cable
   - Intake Air Temperature (IAT) sensor connector

- Air cleaner and air intake tube
- Cooling fan and shroud
- Accessory drive belt
- Power steering pump and bracket
- A/C compressor front bracket, if equipped
- Oil filter
- Radiator hoses
- Heater water outlet tube
- Crankshaft pulley and damper
- Front crankshaft seal

➡Note the position of the Camshaft Position (CMP) sensor connector. The installation procedure requires that the connector be located in the same position.

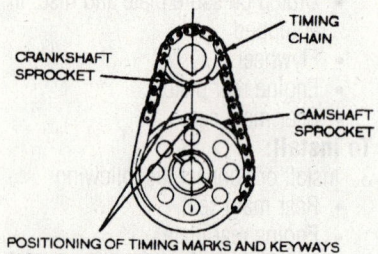

Camshaft timing marks—3.8L engine

- Camshaft Position (CMP) sensor housing
- Crankshaft Position (CKP) sensor
- Oil pan
- Front cover
- Distributor drive gear
- Timing chain and sprockets

To install:

5. Compress the timing chain vibration damper and install a retaining pin.
6. Install or connect the following:
   - Timing chain and sprockets with the timing marks aligned as shown
   - Distributor drive gear. Tighten the bolt to 30–36 ft. lbs. (40–50 Nm) and remove the vibration damper retaining pin.
   - Front cover. Tighten the bolts in sequence to 15–22 ft. lbs. (20–30 Nm).
   - Oil pan
   - CKP sensor
   - Front crankshaft seal
   - Crankshaft pulley and damper. Tighten the bolt to 103–132 ft. lbs. (140–180 Nm).
   - Heater water outlet tube
   - Radiator hoses
   - Oil filter
   - A/C compressor front bracket, if

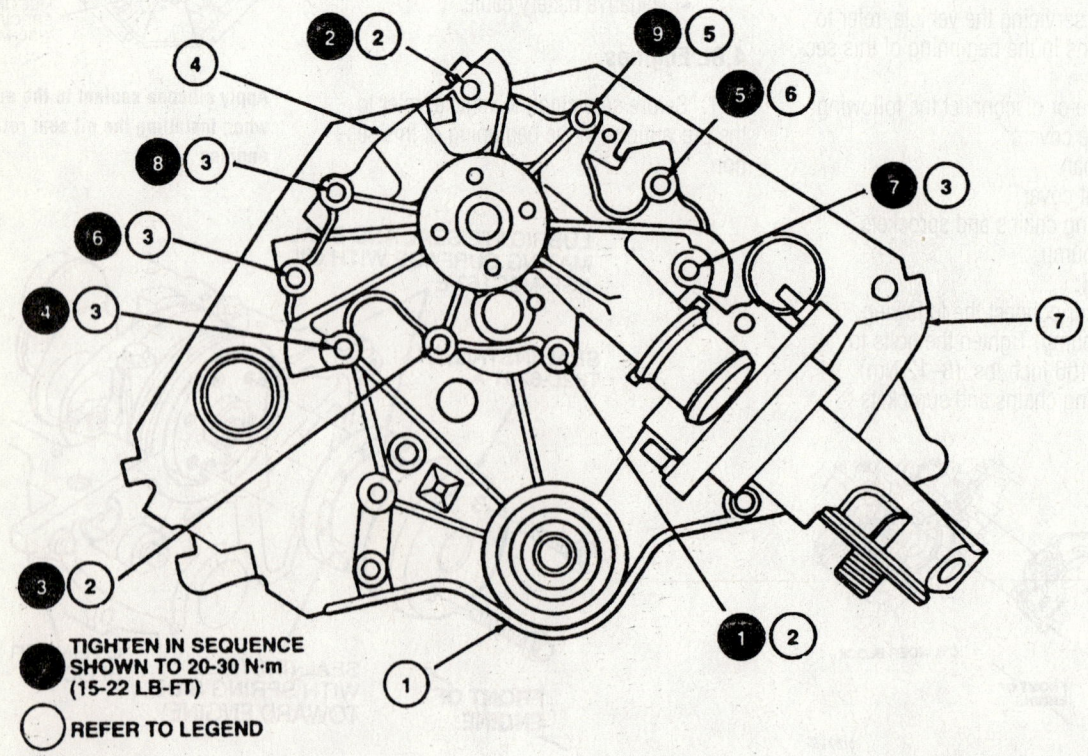

● TIGHTEN IN SEQUENCE SHOWN TO 20-30 N·m (15-22 LB-FT)

○ REFER TO LEGEND

1. Engine front cover
2. Mounting bolts
3. Mounting nuts
4. Water pump
5. Mounting bolt
6. Mounting stud bolt
7. Engine block

Front cover torque sequence—3.8L engine

Camshaft Position Sensor

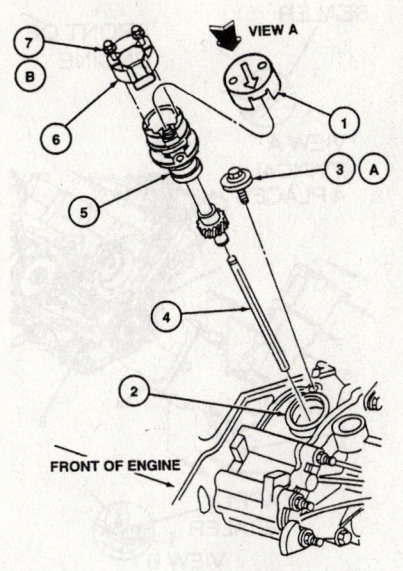

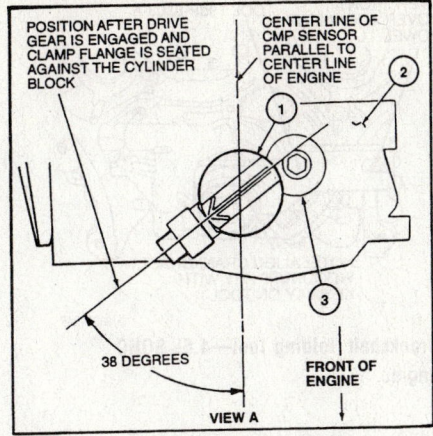

1 Syncro Positioning Tool
2 Engine front cover
3 Hold down clamp
4 Oil pump intermediate shaft
5 Camshaft Position Sensor housing
6 Camshaft Position Sensor
7 Sensor attaching screws
A Tighten to 15-22 ft. lbs.
B Tighten to 40-69 inch lbs.

9306NG03

Camshaft Position Sensor housing installation—3.8L engine

equipped. Tighten the bolts to 30–45 ft. lbs. (41–61 Nm).

• Power steering pump and bracket. Tighten the bolts to 30–45 ft. lbs. (41–61 Nm).

7. Install Synchro Positioning Tool T96T-12200-A to the CMP sensor housing and turn it clockwise until the tool boss engages the notch in the housing assembly.

8. Install the CMP sensor housing so that the CMP sensor connector is in the position noted earlier. Tighten the hold down bolt to 15–22 ft. lbs. (20–30 Nm).

9. Install or connect the following:
• Accessory drive belt
• Cooling fan and shroud
• Air cleaner and air intake tube
• IAT sensor connector
• Negative battery cable

10. Fill the cooling system.

11. Fill the crankcase with clean engine oil.

12. Run the engine. Check for leaks and proper operation.

4.6L SOHC Engine

➡This is not a free wheeling engine. Do not rotate the crankshaft or camshafts with the timing chains removed.

1. Before servicing the vehicle, refer to the precautions in the beginning of this section.

2. Remove or disconnect the following:
• Negative battery cable
• Cooling fan and shroud
• Accessory drive belt
• Water pump pulley
• Power steering pump and reservoir
• Oil pan
• Crankshaft pulley
• Front crankshaft seal
• Valve covers
• Ignition coils and brackets, on 1997–98 engines

• Idler pulley
• Camshaft Position (CMP) sensor connector
• Crankshaft Position (CKP) sensor connector
• Front cover
• CKP sensor pulse wheel

3. Rotate the crankshaft so that the No. 1 cylinder is at Top Dead Center (TDC) of the compression stroke.

4. Install Camshaft Positioning Tool Adapters T92P-6256-A and Camshaft Positioning Tool T91P-6256-A on the flats of the camshafts.

5. Remove or disconnect the following:
• Right timing chain tensioner
• Right timing chain tensioner arm
• Right timing chain guides
• Right timing chain and sprockets
• Left timing chain tensioner
• Left timing chain tensioner arm
• Left timing chain guides
• Left timing chain and sprockets

To install:

6. Install or connect the following:
• Timing chain guides. Tighten the bolts to 71–106 inch lbs. (8–12 Nm).

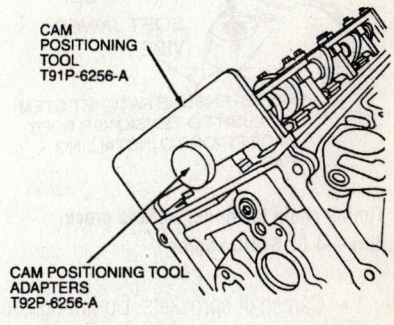

9306NG04

Camshaft Positioning Tool and Adapter— 4.6L SOHC engine

Crankshaft sprocket positioning—4.6L SOHC engine

7922NG55

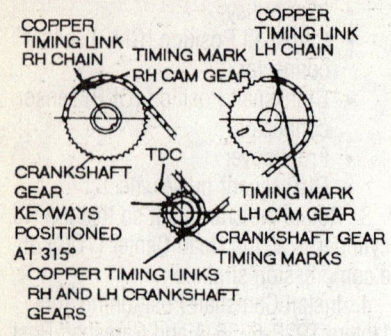

Timing chain and sprocket alignment—4.6L SOHC engine

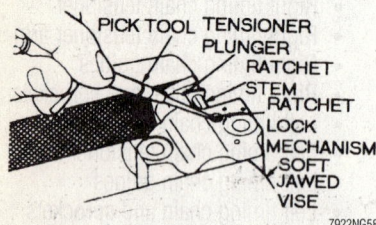

Timing chain tensioner bleeding procedure—4.6L SOHC engine

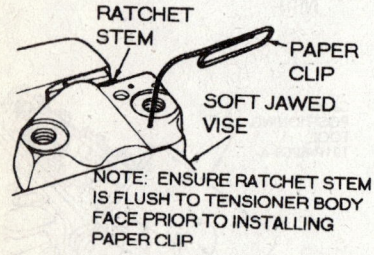

NOTE: ENSURE RATCHET STEM IS FLUSH TO TENSIONER BODY FACE PRIOR TO INSTALLING PAPER CLIP

Timing chain tensioner locking procedure—4.6L SOHC engine

- Camshaft sprockets. Do not tighten the bolts at this time.
- Crankshaft sprockets
- Left timing chain with the copper links aligned with the timing marks on the crankshaft and camshaft sprockets
- Right timing chain with the copper links aligned with the timing marks on the crankshaft and camshaft sprockets

7. Compress the timing chain tensioners as shown. Install locking pins.

8. Install or connect the following:
- Tensioner arms and tensioners. Tighten the tensioner mounting bolts to 15–22 ft. lbs. (20–30 Nm).
- Crankshaft Holding Tool T93P-6303-A as shown

9. Use a C-clamp on the tensioner arm and chain guide to remove slack from the timing chain.

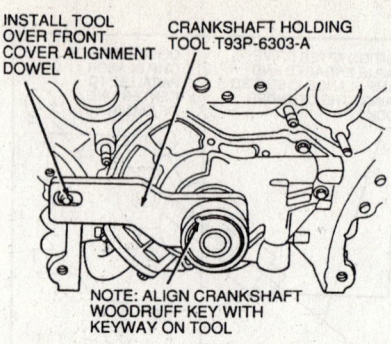

Crankshaft Holding Tool—4.6L SOHC engine

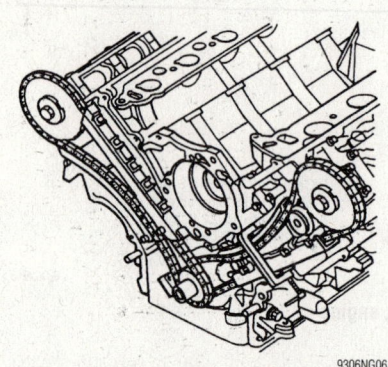

Remove slack from the timing chains with a C-clamp—4.6L SOHC engine

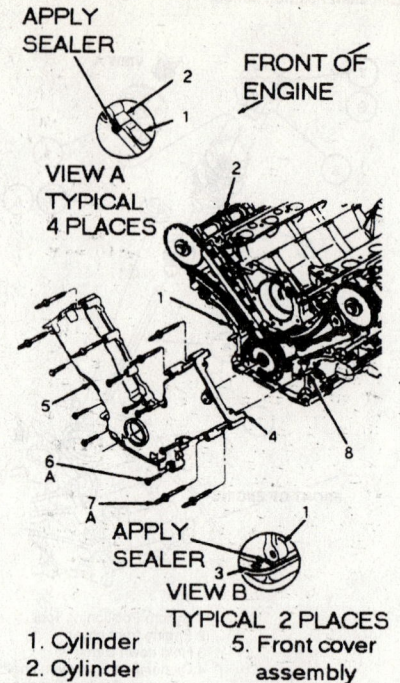

1. Cylinder
2. Cylinder
3. Oil pan gasket
4. Gasket
5. Front cover assembly
6a. Bolts
7a. Studs
8. Dowel

Apply sealer when installing the front cover—4.6L SOHC engine

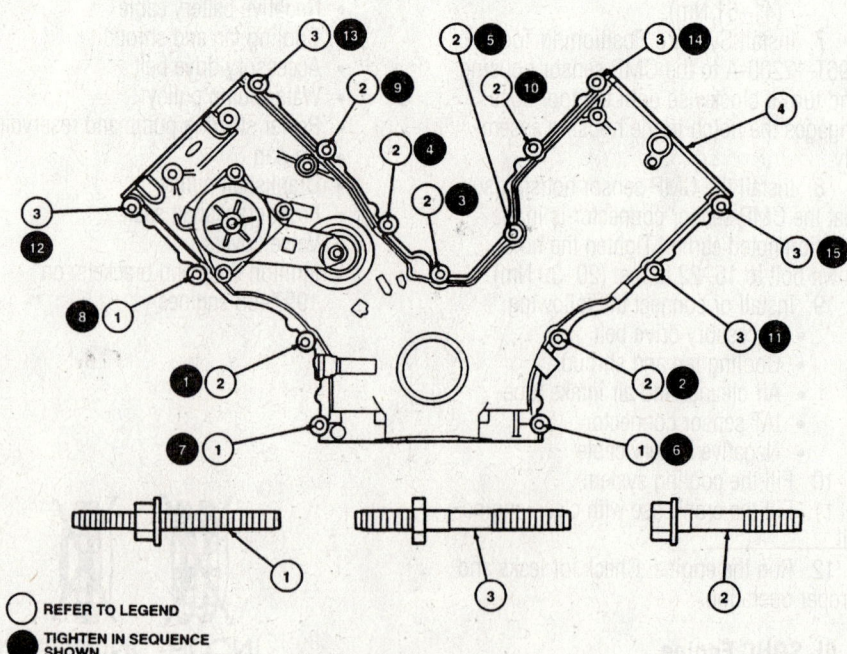

REFER TO LEGEND

TIGHTEN IN SEQUENCE SHOWN

1. Stud bolt (4 req'd)
2. Bolt (6 req'd)
3. Stud bolt (5 req'd)
4. Engine front cover

Front cover torque sequence and bolt identification—4.6L SOHC engine

10. Remove the tensioner locking pins.

11. Tighten the camshaft sprocket bolts to 81–95 ft. lbs. (110–130 Nm).

12. Remove the C-clamps, Camshaft Positioning Tools and Adapters, and the Crankshaft Holding Tool.

13. Install or connect the following:

- CKP sensor pulse wheel
- Front cover. Tighten the bolts in sequence to 15–22 ft. lbs. (20–30 Nm).
- CKP sensor connector
- CMP sensor connector
- Idler pulley
- Ignition coils and brackets, on 1997–98 engines
- Valve covers
- Front crankshaft seal
- Oil pan

14. Install the crankshaft pulley and tighten the bolt as follows:

a. Step 1: 66 ft. lbs. (90 Nm).

b. Step 2: Loosen one complete turn.

c. Step 3: 36 ft. lbs. (50 Nm).

d. Step 4: Plus 90 degrees.

15. Install or connect the following:

- Power steering pump and reservoir
- Water pump pulley
- Accessory drive belt
- Cooling fan and shroud
- Negative battery cable

16. Fill the crankcase with clean engine oil.

17. Start the engine. Check for leaks and proper operation.

4.6L DOHC Engine

➡**This is not a free wheeling engine. Do not rotate the crankshaft or camshafts with the timing chains removed.**

1. Before servicing the vehicle, refer to the precautions in the beginning of this section.

2. Drain the cooling system.

3. Remove or disconnect the following:

- Negative battery cable
- Engine compartment brace
- Air intake tube
- Upper radiator hose and bypass tube
- Cooling fan and shroud
- Engine control sensor wiring support bracket
- Fuel charging wiring retainer
- Accessory drive belt
- Water pump pulley
- Power steering pump reservoir
- Ignition coils
- Ignition coil brackets, on 1997–98 engines
- Power steering pump
- Crankshaft pulley
- Front crankshaft seal
- Valve covers

➡**Keep rocker arms in order for installation.**

- Rocker arms
- Camshaft Position (CMP) sensor connector
- Crankshaft Position (CKP) sensor connector
- Idler pulley
- Front cover
- CMP sensor pulse wheel

4. Rotate the crankshaft so that the No. 1 cylinder is at Top Dead Center (TDC) of the compression stroke.

5. Remove or disconnect the following:

- Right primary timing chain tensioner

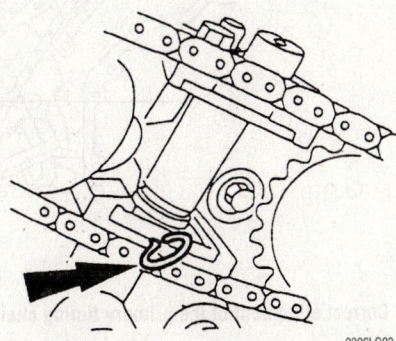

Secondary timing chain tensioner and locking pin—4.6L DOHC engine

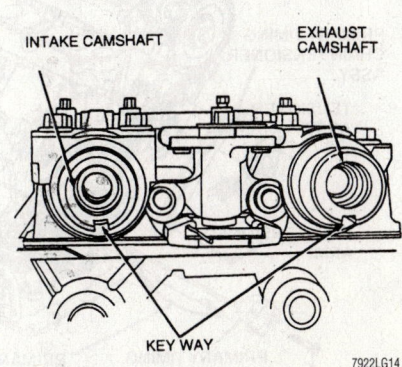

Position the camshafts for timing chain installation—4.6L DOHC engine

- Right primary timing chain tensioner arm and chain guide
- Right primary timing chain and sprockets
- Left primary timing chain tensioner

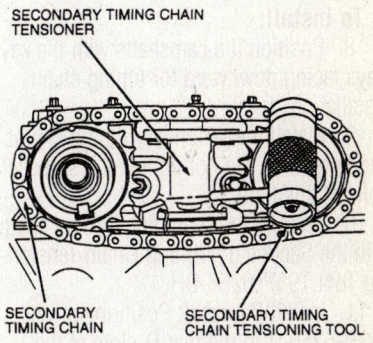

Secondary timing chain tensioning tool—4.6L DOHC engine

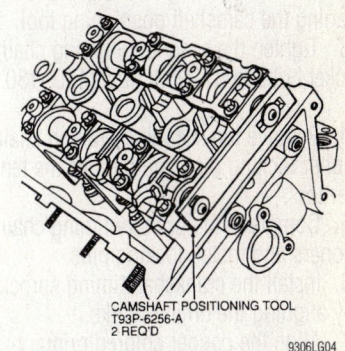

Install the camshaft positioning tool—4.6L DOHC engine

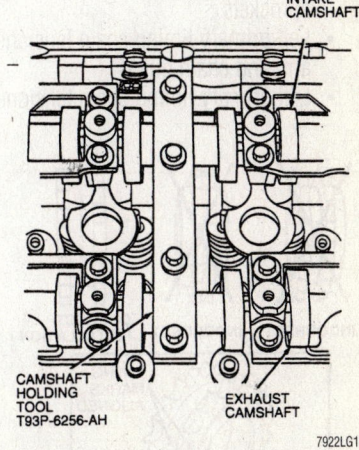

Install the Camshaft Holding tool to secure the camshafts and prevent damage to the camshaft positioning tool—4.6L DOHC engine

- Left primary timing chain tensioner arm and chain guide
- Left primary timing chain and sprockets

6. Compress the secondary chain tensioners and install locking pins.

7. Remove the left and right secondary timing chains and sprockets.

To install:

8. Position the camshafts with the keyways facing downward for timing chain installation.

9. Install the secondary timing chains and sprockets. Do not tighten the sprocket bolts at this time.

10. Tension the secondary timing chains with the Secondary Timing Chain Tensioning Tool T93P-6256-BH.

11. Install Camshaft Positioning tool T93P-6256-A in the rear D-slots of the camshaft.

12. Install Camshaft Holding tool T93P-6256-AH onto the camshafts to keep the camshafts from rotating and to prevent damaging the camshaft positioning tool.

13. Tighten the secondary timing chain sprocket bolts to 81–95 ft. lbs. (110–130 Nm).

14. Remove the secondary timing chain tensioner locking pins and remove the tensioner tool.

15. Compress the primary timing chain tensioners and install locking pins.

16. Install the crankshaft timing sprockets by aligning the timing marks.

17. Align the copper colored primary timing chain links with the sprocket timing marks by aligning the timing marks.

18. Install or connect the following:
- Left primary timing chain and sprockets
- Left primary timing chain tensioner arm and chain guide
- Left primary timing chain tensioner

- Right primary timing chain and sprockets
- Right primary timing chain tensioner arm and chain guide
- Right primary timing chain tensioner

19. Tighten the camshaft sprocket bolts to 81–95 ft. lbs. (110–130 Nm).

20. Remove the primary timing chain tensioner locking pins.

21. Remove the Camshaft Holding and Camshaft Positioning tools.

22. Install the CMP pulse wheel

23. Install the front cover. Tighten the bolts in sequence as follows:

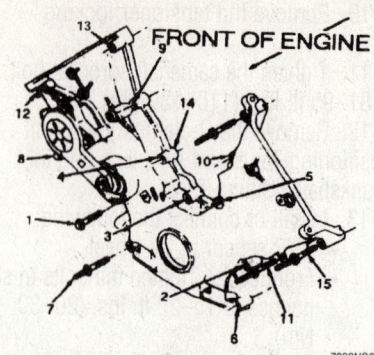

Front cover torque sequence—4.6L DOHC engines

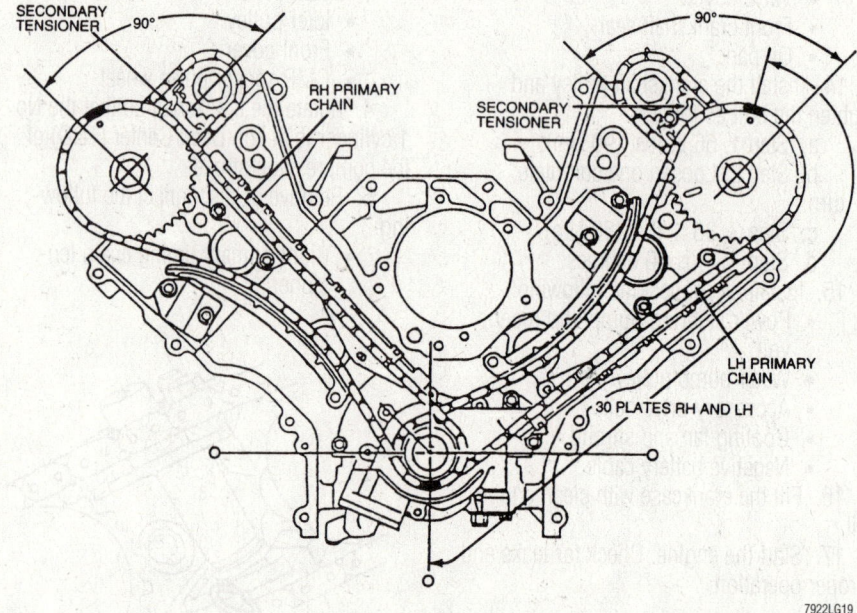

Correct alignment of the primary timing chains and sprockets—4.6L DOHC engines

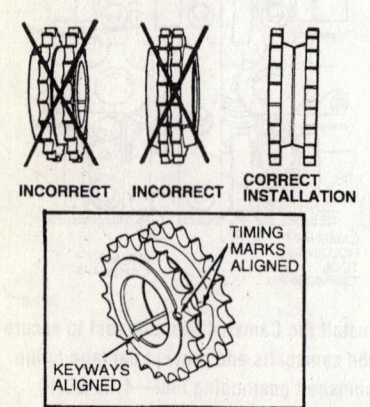

Crankshaft timing sprocket installation—4.6L DOHC engines

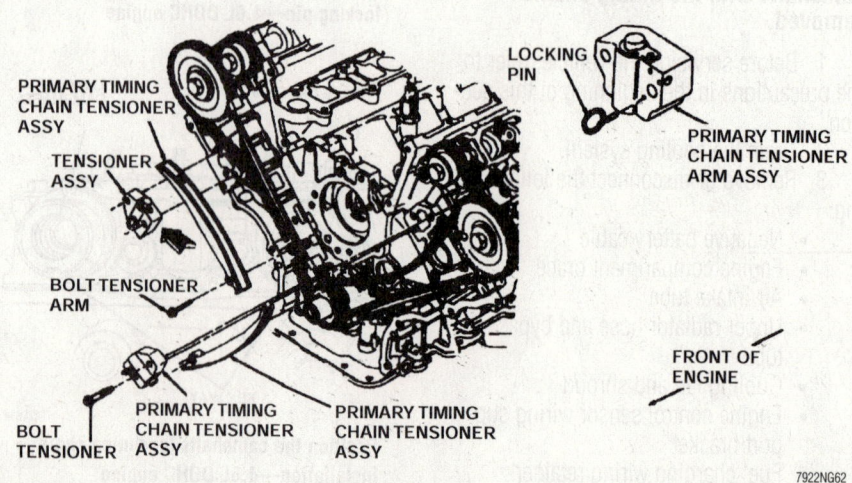

Timing chain tensioner installation—4.6L DOHC engine

Sealer Location

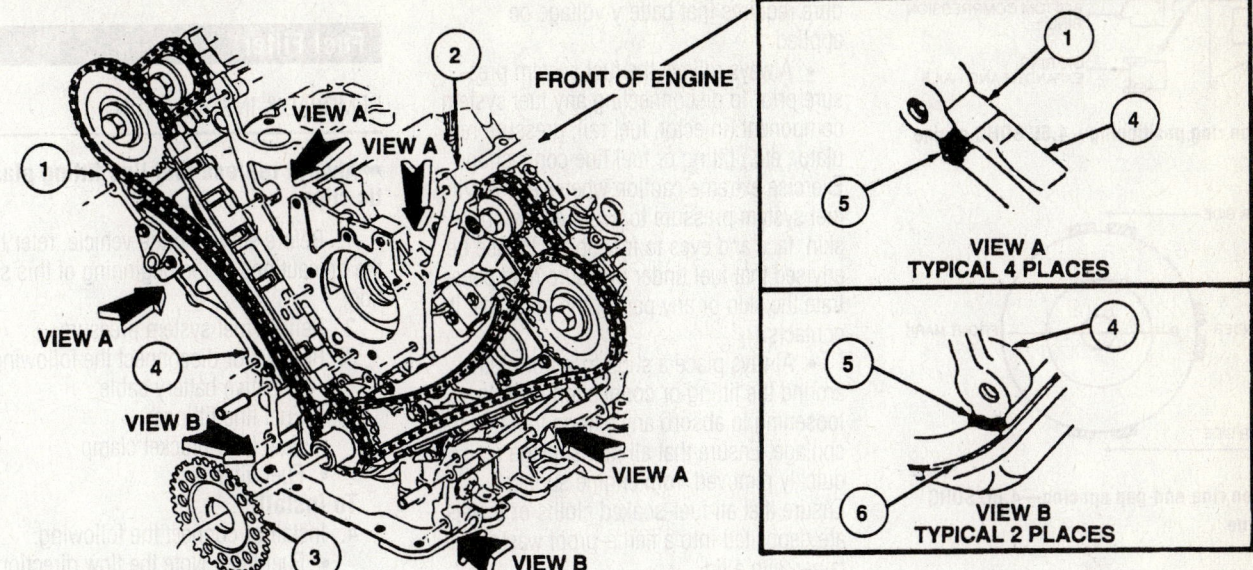

FRONT OF ENGINE

VIEW A

VIEW A

VIEW A

VIEW A

VIEW B

VIEW A

VIEW B

VIEW A
TYPICAL 4 PLACES

VIEW B
TYPICAL 2 PLACES

9306LG06

1 RH Cylinder Head
2 LH Cylinder Head
3 Ignition Pulse Crankshaft Sensor Ring
4 Cylinder Block
5 Sealer
6 Oil Pan Gasket

Apply sealer to these locations—4.6L DOHC engines

   a. Step 1: 14 ft. lbs. (20 Nm).
   b. Step 2: Plus 60 degrees.
24. Install or connect the following:
- Idler pulley
- Rocker arms in their original positions
- Valve covers
- Front crankshaft seal
- CKP sensor connector
- CMP sensor connector
- Crankshaft pulley
- Power steering pump
- Ignition coil brackets on 1997–98 engines
- Ignition coils
- Power steering pump reservoir
- Water pump pulley
- Accessory drive belt
- Fuel charging wiring retainer
- Engine control sensor wiring support bracket
- Cooling fan and shroud
- Upper radiator hose and bypass tube
- Air intake tube
- Engine compartment brace

- Negative battery cable
25. Fill the cooling system.
26. Start the engine. Check for leaks and proper operation.

Piston and Ring

POSITIONING

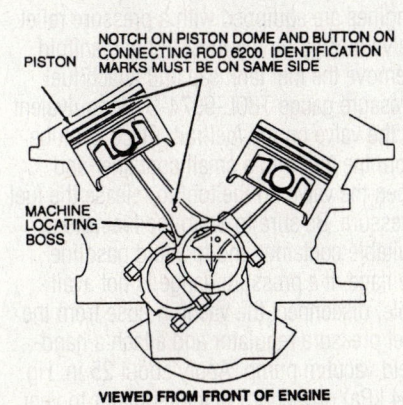

PISTON

NOTCH ON PISTON DOME AND BUTTON ON CONNECTING ROD 6200 IDENTIFICATION MARKS MUST BE ON SAME SIDE

MACHINE LOCATING BOSS

VIEWED FROM FRONT OF ENGINE

7922AG15

Piston and connecting rod positioning—3.8L engine

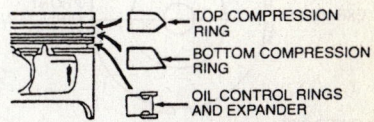

TOP COMPRESSION RING

BOTTOM COMPRESSION RING

OIL CONTROL RINGS AND EXPANDER

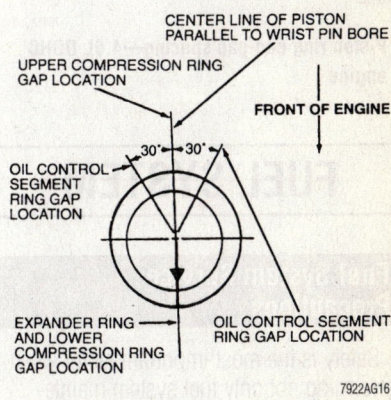

CENTER LINE OF PISTON PARALLEL TO WRIST PIN BORE

UPPER COMPRESSION RING GAP LOCATION

FRONT OF ENGINE

OIL CONTROL SEGMENT RING GAP LOCATION

30°   30°

EXPANDER RING AND LOWER COMPRESSION RING GAP LOCATION

OIL CONTROL SEGMENT RING GAP LOCATION

7922AG16

Piston ring end-gap spacing—3.8L engine

Timing belt service is covered in Section 4 of this manual

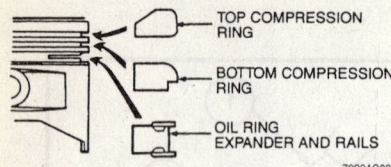

Piston ring positioning—4.6L SOHC engine

7922AG32

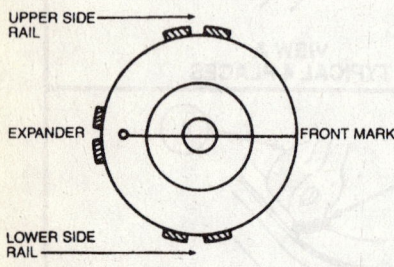

Piston ring end-gap spacing—4.6L SOHC engine

7922AG22

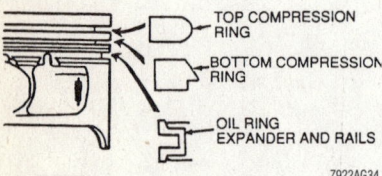

Piston ring positioning—4.6L DOHC engine

7922AG34

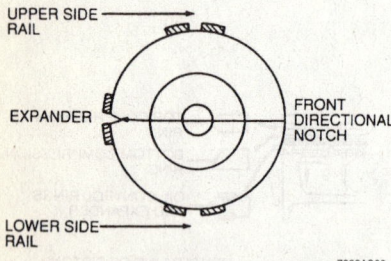

Piston ring end-gap spacing—4.6L DOHC engine

7922AG33

FUEL SYSTEM

Fuel System Service Precautions

Safety is the most important factor when performing not only fuel system maintenance, but any type of maintenance. Failure to conduct maintenance and repairs in a safe manner may result in serious personal injury or death. Work on a vehicle's fuel system components can be accomplished safely and effectively by adhering to the following rules and guidelines.

- To avoid the possibility of fire and personal injury, always disconnect the negative battery cable unless the repair or test procedure requires that battery voltage be applied.
- Always relieve the fuel system pressure prior to disconnecting any fuel system component (injector, fuel rail, pressure regulator, etc.) fitting or fuel line connection. Exercise extreme caution whenever relieving fuel system pressure to avoid exposing skin, face and eyes to fuel spray. Please be advised that fuel under pressure may penetrate the skin or any part of the body that it contacts.
- Always place a shop towel or cloth around the fitting or connection prior to loosening to absorb any excess fuel due to spillage. Ensure that all fuel spillage is quickly removed from engine surfaces. Ensure that all fuel-soaked cloths or towels are deposited into a flame-proof waste container with a lid.
- Always keep a dry chemical (Class B) fire extinguisher near the work area.
- Do not allow fuel spray or fuel vapors to come into contact with a spark or open flame.
- Always use a second wrench when loosening or tightening fuel line connection fittings. This will prevent unnecessary stress and torsion on fuel piping. Always follow the proper torque specifications.
- Always replace worn fuel fitting O-rings with new ones. Do not substitute fuel hose where rigid pipe is installed.

Fuel System Pressure

RELIEVING

All Sequential Fuel Injection (SFI) engines are equipped with a pressure relief valve located on the fuel supply manifold. Remove the fuel tank cap and attach fuel pressure gauge T80L-9974-B, or equivalent, to the valve on the fuel rail. Place the tube from the tool into a small container and open the valve on the tool to release the fuel pressure. Be sure to drain the fuel into a suitable container and to avoid gasoline spillage. If a pressure gauge is not available, disconnect the vacuum hose from the fuel pressure regulator and attach a hand-held vacuum pump. Apply about 25 in. Hg (84 kPa) of vacuum to the regulator to vent the fuel system pressure into the fuel tank through the fuel return hose.

➡ This procedure will remove the fuel pressure from the lines, but not the fuel. Take precautions to avoid the risk of fire and use clean rags to soak up any spilled fuel when the lines are disconnected.

Fuel Filter

REMOVAL & INSTALLATION

➡ Always replace fuel line fitting plastic clips.

1. Before servicing the vehicle, refer to the precautions in the beginning of this section.
2. Relieve fuel system pressure
3. Remove or disconnect the following:
   - Negative battery cable
   - Fuel line fittings
   - Fuel filter bracket clamp
   - Fuel filter

To install:

4. Install or connect the following:
   - Fuel filter. Note the flow direction arrow.
   - Fuel filter bracket clamp
   - Fuel line fittings
   - Negative battery cable
5. Start the engine and check for leaks.

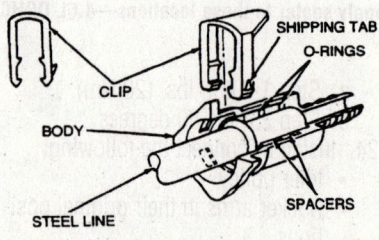

Hairpin clip fuel fitting

7922NG43

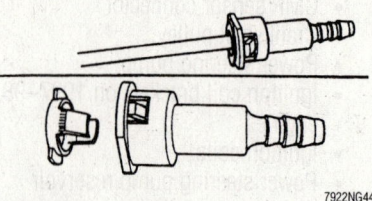

Duckbill clip fuel fitting

7922NG44

Fuel Pump

REMOVAL & INSTALLATION

1. Before servicing the vehicle, refer to the precautions in the beginning of this section.
2. Relieve fuel system pressure.
3. Drain the fuel tank.
4. Remove or disconnect the following:

- Negative battery cable
- Fuel tank filler pipe retainer
- Fuel tank vent hose
- Fuel tank support straps
- Fuel lines
- Fuel pump module electrical connector
- Fuel pump module locking ring, on 1997 vehicles
- Fuel pump module retaining bolts, on 1998–01 vehicles

5. Raise the fuel pump module until the locking tabs are accessible. Squeeze the locking tabs together and remove the fuel pump module from the fuel tank.

To install:

6. Install the fuel pump module into the retainer. Use a new O-ring seal and push the module into the retainer until both locking tabs engage.

7. Install or connect the following:

- Fuel pump module locking ring, on 1997 vehicles
- Fuel pump module retaining bolts, on 1998–01 vehicles. Tighten the bolts to 80–106 inch lbs. (9–12 Nm).
- Fuel pump module electrical connector

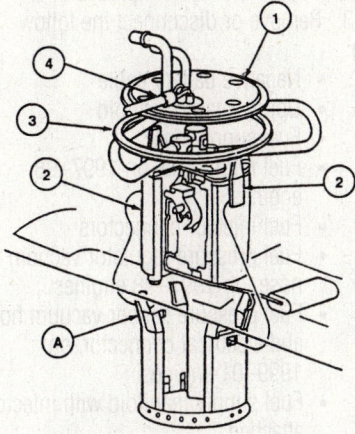

1 Fuel Pump Module
2 Locking Tab (Part of 9H307)
3 O-Ring Seal
4 Connector (Part of 14405 Wiring Assy)
A Fuel Pump Must Be Snapped Into Retainer (2 Places)

9306NG08

Fuel pump module assembly—1998–01 vehicles

- Fuel lines
- Fuel tank support straps. Tighten the bolts to 22–29 ft. lbs. (30–40 Nm).

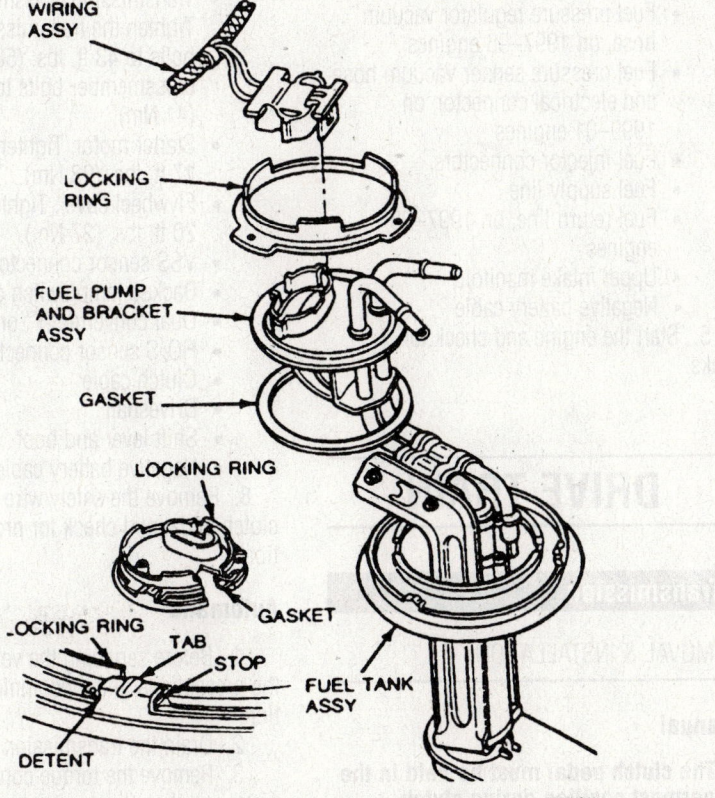

WIRING ASSY

LOCKING RING

FUEL PUMP AND BRACKET ASSY

GASKET

LOCKING RING

LOCKING RING
TAB
STOP

DETENT

GASKET

FUEL TANK ASSY

7922NG42

Exploded view of the electric fuel pump assembly—1997 vehicles

- Fuel tank vent hose
- Fuel tank filler pipe retainer
- Negative battery cable

8. Add fuel (10 gallons minimum) to the tank.

9. Start the engine and check for leaks.

Fuel Injector

REMOVAL & INSTALLATION

3.8L engine

1. Before servicing the vehicle, refer to the precautions in the beginning of this section.

2. Relieve fuel system pressure.

3. Remove or disconnect the following:

- Negative battery cable
- Upper intake manifold
- Fuel supply line
- Fuel return line, on 1997–98 engines
- Fuel injector connectors
- Fuel pressure regulator vacuum hose, on 1997–98 engines
- Fuel pressure sensor vacuum hose and electrical connector, on 1999–01 engines
- Fuel supply manifold with injectors attached
- Fuel injectors from the supply manifold

To install:

4. Install or connect the following:

- New O-rings
- Fuel injectors to the supply manifold
- Fuel supply manifold with injectors. Tighten the bolts to 80 inch lbs. (9 Nm).
- Fuel pressure regulator vacuum hose, on 1997–98 engines
- Fuel pressure sensor vacuum hose and electrical connector, on 1999–01 engines
- Fuel injector connectors
- Fuel supply line
- Fuel return line, on 1997–98 engines
- Upper intake manifold
- Negative battery cable

5. Start the engine and check for leaks.

4.6L SOHC engine

1. Before servicing the vehicle, refer to the precautions in the beginning of this section.

2. Relieve fuel system pressure.
3. Remove or disconnect the following:
   - Negative battery cable
   - Air intake tube
   - Fuel supply line
   - Fuel return line, on 1997–98 engines
   - Accelerator cable
   - Cruise control cable
   - Throttle body
   - Idle Air Control (IAC) valve connector and hose
   - Positive Crankcase Ventilation (PCV) hose
   - Main chassis vacuum supply hose
   - Fuel injector connectors
   - Fuel pressure regulator vacuum hose, on 1997–98 engines
   - Fuel pressure sensor vacuum hose and electrical connector, on 1999–01 engines
   - Exhaust Vacuum Regulator (EVR) solenoid vacuum lines
   - Exhaust Gas Recirculation (EGR) pressure transducer bracket
   - EGR tube and vacuum line
   - Fuel supply manifold with injectors attached
   - Fuel injectors from the supply manifold

To install:
4. Install or connect the following:
   - New O-rings
   - Fuel injectors to the supply manifold
   - Fuel supply manifold with injectors attached. Tighten the bolts to 80 inch lbs. (9 Nm).
   - EGR tube and vacuum line
   - EGR pressure transducer bracket
   - EVR solenoid vacuum lines
   - Fuel pressure regulator vacuum hose, on 1997–98 engines
   - Fuel pressure sensor vacuum hose and electrical connector, on 1999–01 engines
   - Fuel injector connectors
   - Main chassis vacuum supply hose
   - PCV hose
   - IAC valve connector and hose
   - Throttle body
   - Cruise control cable
   - Accelerator cable
   - Fuel supply line
   - Fuel return line, on 1997–98 engines
   - Air intake tube
   - Negative battery cable
5. Start the engine and check for leaks.

4.6L DOHC engine

1. Before servicing the vehicle, refer to the precautions in the beginning of this section.
2. Relieve fuel system pressure.
3. Remove or disconnect the following:
   - Negative battery cable
   - Upper intake manifold
   - Fuel supply line
   - Fuel return line, on 1997–98 engines
   - Fuel injector connectors
   - Fuel pressure regulator vacuum hose, on 1997–98 engines
   - Fuel pressure sensor vacuum hose and electrical connector, on 1999–01 engines
   - Fuel supply manifold with injectors attached
   - Fuel injectors from the supply manifold

To install:
4. Install or connect the following:
   - New O-rings
   - Fuel injectors to the supply manifold
   - Fuel supply manifold with injectors attached. Tighten the bolts to 80 inch lbs. (9 Nm).
   - Fuel pressure regulator vacuum hose, on 1997–98 engines
   - Fuel pressure sensor vacuum hose and electrical connector, on 1999–01 engines
   - Fuel injector connectors
   - Fuel supply line
   - Fuel return line, on 1997–98 engines
   - Upper intake manifold
   - Negative battery cable
5. Start the engine and check for leaks.

DRIVE TRAIN

Transmission

REMOVAL & INSTALLATION

Manual

➡The clutch pedal must be held in the uppermost position during clutch release cable removal and installation. Failure to properly position and support the clutch pedal can result in damage to the self-adjusting mechanism.

1. Before servicing the vehicle, refer to the precautions in the beginning of this section.
2. Lift the clutch pedal and secure in place with safety wire.
3. Remove or disconnect the following:
   - Negative battery cable
   - Shift lever and boot
   - Driveshaft
   - Clutch cable
   - Heated Oxygen (HO2S) sensor connectors
   - Dual converter "Y" or "H" pipe
   - Backup lamp switch connector
   - Vehicle Speed (VSS) sensor connector
   - Flywheel cover
   - Starter motor
4. Support the transmission with a jack and remove the rear transmission support crossmember.
5. Lower the transmission jack and remove the transmission flange bolts.
6. Slide the transmission input shaft out of the clutch and lower the transmission from the vehicle.

To install:
7. Install or connect the following:
   - Transmission. Tighten the flange bolts to 55 ft. lbs. (75 Nm).
   - Transmission crossmember. Tighten the transmission mount bolts to 43 ft. lbs. (58 Nm) and the crossmember bolts to 30 ft. lbs. (41 Nm).
   - Starter motor. Tighten the bolts to 17 ft. lbs. (23 Nm).
   - Flywheel cover. Tighten the bolts to 20 ft. lbs. (27 Nm).
   - VSS sensor connector
   - Backup lamp switch connector
   - Dual converter "Y" or "H" pipe
   - HO2S sensor connectors
   - Clutch cable
   - Driveshaft
   - Shift lever and boot
   - Negative battery cable
8. Remove the safety wire from the clutch pedal and check for proper operation.

Automatic

1. Before servicing the vehicle, refer to the precautions in the beginning of this section.
2. Drain the transmission fluid.
3. Remove the torque converter access cover and drain the torque converter.
4. Remove or disconnect the following:
   - Negative battery cable

- Heated Oxygen (HO2S) sensor connectors
- Dual converter "Y" or "H" pipe
- Torque converter
- Driveshaft
- Shift cable
- Transmission wiring connectors
- Transmission fluid cooler lines
- Starter motor

5. Support the transmission with a jack and remove the rear transmission support crossmember.

6. Lower the transmission jack and remove the transmission flange bolts.

7. Lower the transmission from the vehicle.

To install:

8. Install or connect the following:
- Transmission. Tighten the flange bolts to 41–50 ft. lbs. (55–68 Nm).
- Transmission crossmember. Tighten the transmission mount bolts to 72 ft. lbs. (98 Nm) and the crossmember bolts to 41 ft. lbs. (55 Nm).
- Starter motor. Tighten the bolts to 18 ft. lbs. (25 Nm).

- Transmission fluid cooler lines
- Transmission wiring connectors
- Shift cable
- Driveshaft
- Torque converter. Tighten the nuts to 20–33 ft. lbs. (27–46 Nm).
- Torque converter access cover. Tighten the bolts to 12–16 ft. lbs. (16–22 Nm).
- Dual converter "Y" or "H" pipe
- HO2S sensor connectors
- Negative battery cable

9. Fill the transmission with fluid.

10. Start the engine. Check for leaks and proper operation.

Clutch

ADJUSTMENTS

The clutch is equipped with a self-adjusting mechanism. Pull the clutch pedal up to activate the adjuster.

REMOVAL & INSTALLATION

➡The clutch pedal must be held in the uppermost position during clutch

release cable removal and installation. Failure to properly position and support the clutch pedal can result in damage to the self-adjusting mechanism.

1. Before servicing the vehicle, refer to the precautions in the beginning of this section.

2. Lift the clutch pedal and secure in place with safety wire.

3. Remove or disconnect the following:

- Transmission
- Pressure plate, loosen the bolts evenly in several passes to avoid distortion of the pressure plate.
- Pressure plate and clutch disk

To install:

- Clutch disk and pressure plate. Tighten the pressure plate bolts evenly in several passes to 20–28 ft. lbs. (27–39 Nm) for 3.8L engines, or to 19–24 ft. lbs. (25–33 Nm) for 4.6L engines.
- Transmission

4. Remove the clutch pedal safety wire and check for proper operation.

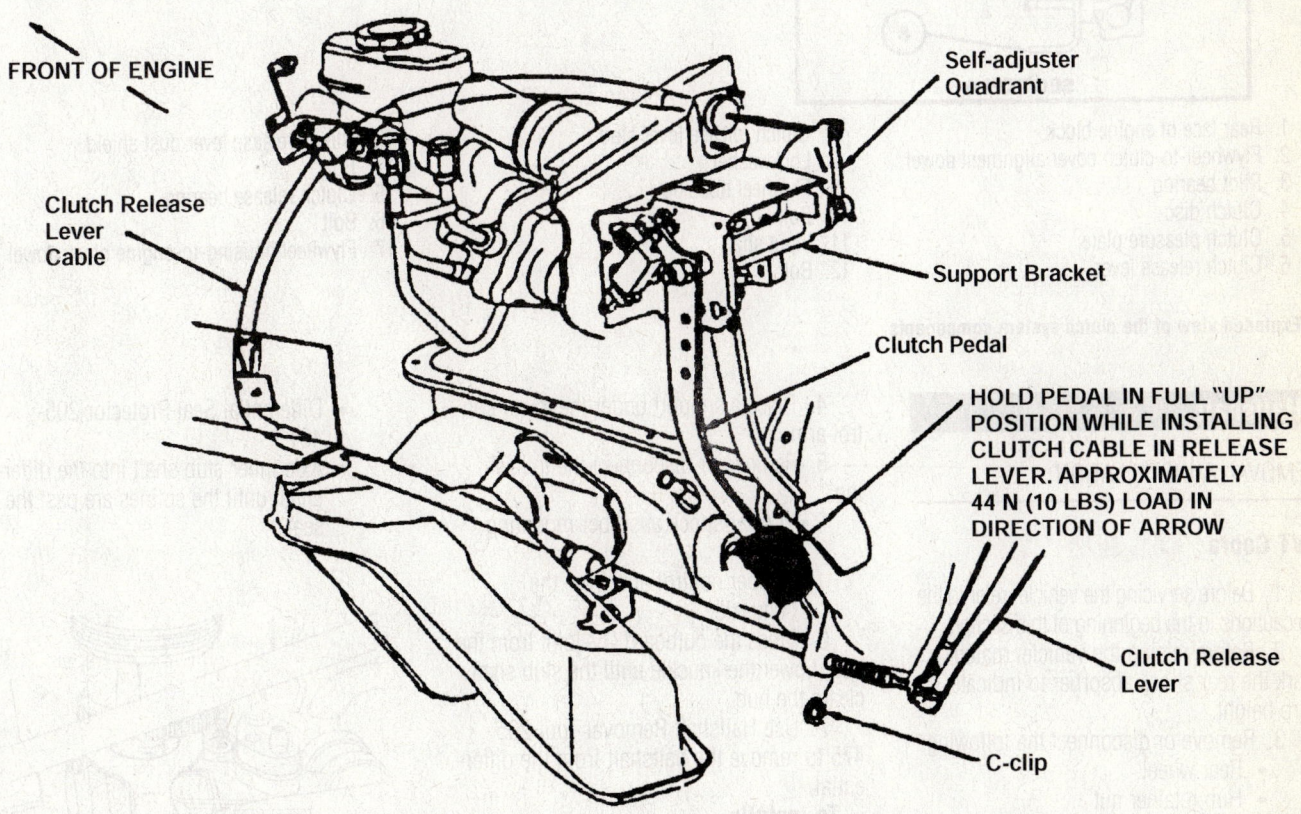

FRONT OF ENGINE

Clutch Release Lever Cable

Self-adjuster Quadrant

Support Bracket

Clutch Pedal

HOLD PEDAL IN FULL "UP" POSITION WHILE INSTALLING CLUTCH CABLE IN RELEASE LEVER. APPROXIMATELY 44 N (10 LBS) LOAD IN DIRECTION OF ARROW

Clutch Release Lever

C-clip

7922NG45

Clutch self-adjusting system component identification—4.6L engine shown—3.8L engine is similar

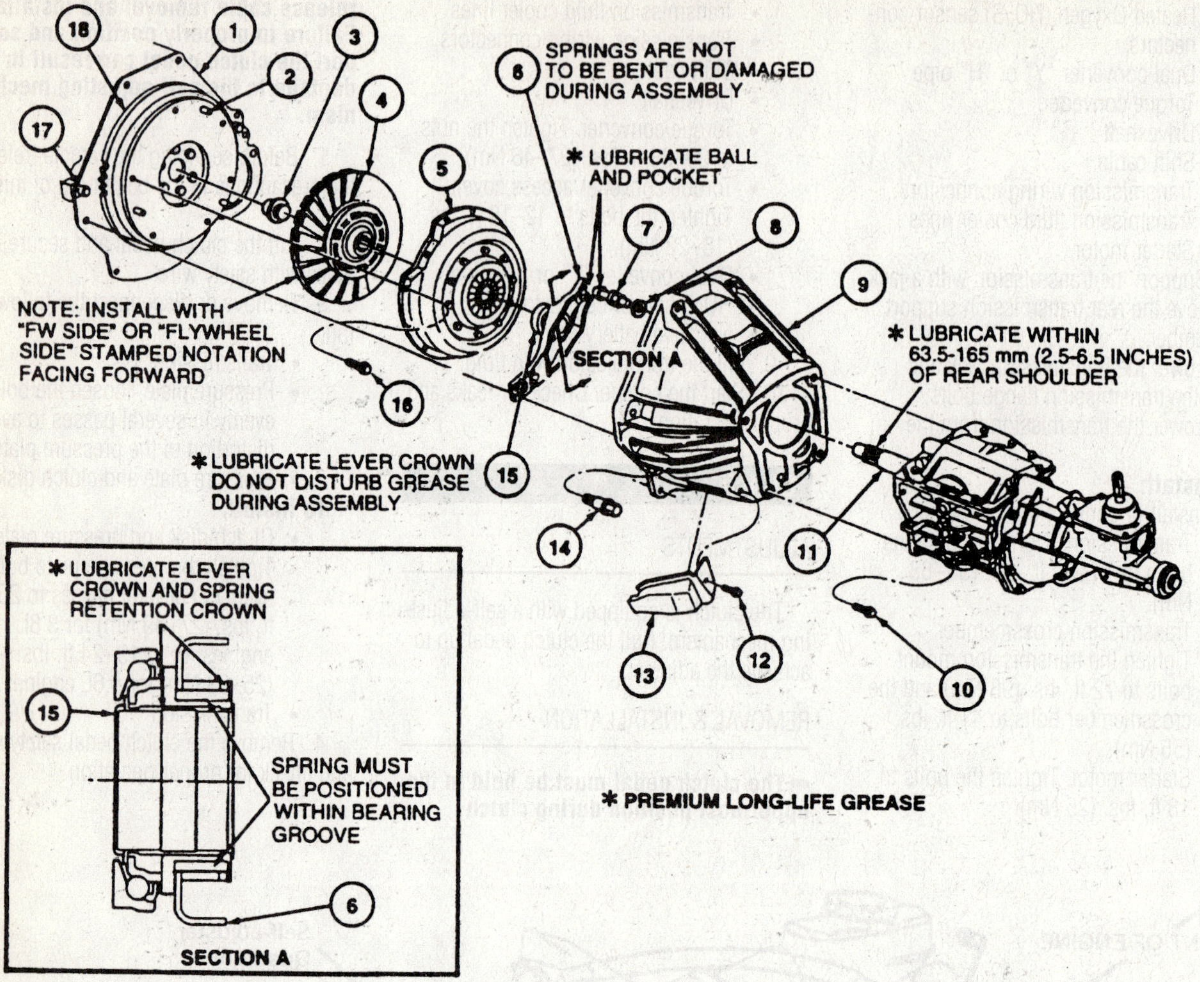

SPRINGS ARE NOT TO BE BENT OR DAMAGED DURING ASSEMBLY

✱ LUBRICATE BALL AND POCKET

SECTION A

✱ LUBRICATE WITHIN 63.5-165 mm (2.5-6.5 INCHES) OF REAR SHOULDER

NOTE: INSTALL WITH "FW SIDE" OR "FLYWHEEL SIDE" STAMPED NOTATION FACING FORWARD

✱ LUBRICATE LEVER CROWN DO NOT DISTURB GREASE DURING ASSEMBLY

✱ LUBRICATE LEVER CROWN AND SPRING RETENTION CROWN

SPRING MUST BE POSITIONED WITHIN BEARING GROOVE

SECTION A

✱ PREMIUM LONG-LIFE GREASE

1. Rear face of engine block
2. Flywheel-to-clutch cover alignment dowel
3. Pilot bearing
4. Clutch disc
5. Clutch pleasure plate
6. Clutch release lever
7. Clutch release lever stud
8. Lockwasher
9. Flywheel housing
10. Bolt
11. Input shaft
12. Bolt
13. Clutch release lever dust shield
14. Bolt
15. Clutch release bearing
16. Bolt
17. Flywheel housing-to-engine block dowel

7922NG46

Exploded view of the clutch system components

Halfshaft

REMOVAL & INSTALLATION

SVT Cobra

1. Before servicing the vehicle, refer to the precautions in the beginning of this section.
2. Before raising the vehicle, match-mark the rear shock absorber to indicate curb height.
3. Remove or disconnect the following:
   - Rear wheel
   - Hub retainer nut
   - Disc brake caliper and rotor
   - Wheel speed sensor
   - Tie rod link

4. Place a support under the lower control arm.
5. Remove or disconnect the following:
   - Lower shock absorber mounting bolt
   - Upper control arm from the knuckle
6. Press the outboard CV-joint from the hub. Lower the knuckle until the stub shaft clears the hub.
7. Use Halfshaft Removal Tool 205-475 to remove the halfshaft from the differential.

To install:

➡ Use new nuts, bolts, circlips, and split pins for assembly.

- Differential Seal Protector 205-461.
- Axle inner stub shaft into the differential until the splines are past the seal.

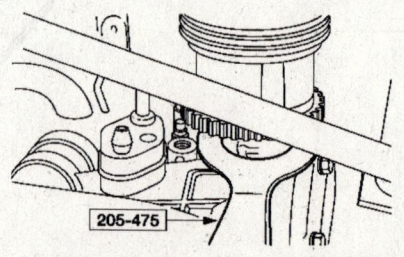

205-475

9306NG09

Halfshaft Removal Tool—SVT Cobra

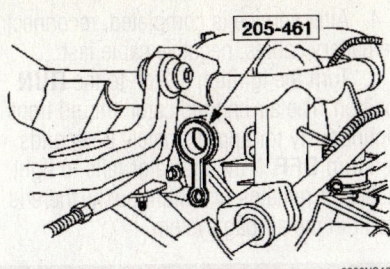

Differential Seal Protector—SVT Cobra

9306NG10

8. Remove the Differential Seal Protector.

9. Install or connect the following:
- Inner stub shaft into the differential until the circlip seats.
- Outer stub shaft into the knuckle.
- Upper control arm to the knuckle and install the lower shock absorber bolt.
- Lower control arm to align the matchmark on the shock absorber.
- Lower shock absorber mounting bolt. Torque it to 98 ft. lbs. (133 Nm).
- Upper control arm bolt. Torque it to 66 ft. lbs. (90 Nm).

10. Remove the lower control arm support.

11. Install or connect the following:
- Tie rod link. Tighten the nut to 35 ft. lbs. (47 Nm).
- Wheel speed sensor
- Disc brake rotor and caliper. Tighten the caliper support bolts to 76 ft. lbs. (103 Nm).

➡The hub retainer nut must be tightened with the brakes applied and the wheels off the ground to ensure correct bearing seating.

- Hub nut. Tighten it to 240 ft. lbs. (325 Nm)
- Wheel

12. Check the rear wheel alignment and adjust as necessary.

CV-Joints

REMOVAL & REPLACEMENT

Inner CV-Joint

1. Before servicing the vehicle, refer to the precautions in the beginning of this section.

2. Remove the inner CV-joint boot clamps and slide the boot away from the joint.

3. Release the snapring and remove the inner CV-joint from the axle shaft.

To install:

4. Fill the CV-joint with fresh grease and slide the joint on to the axle.

5. Install a new snapring.

6. Use new clamps and install the CV-joint boot.

Outer CV-Joint

The outer CV-joint is serviced with the axle shaft as an assembly. The outer CV-joint boot can be serviced by removing the inner CV-joint.

Axle Shaft, Bearing and Seal

REMOVAL & INSTALLATION

1. Before servicing the vehicle, refer to the precautions in the beginning of this section.

2. Remove or disconnect the following:
- Rear wheel
- Disc brake caliper and rotor
- Wheel speed sensor
- Axle housing cover
- Differential pinion shaft
- Axle retaining U-washer
- Axle shaft
- Bearing and seal, using a slide hammer

To install:

3. Install or connect the following:
- Bearing, so that it is fully seated in the axle tube
- Axle seal
- Axle shaft
- Axle retaining U-washer
- Differential pinion shaft. Tighten the lockbolt to 15–30 ft. lbs. (20–41 Nm).
- Axle housing cover. Tighten the

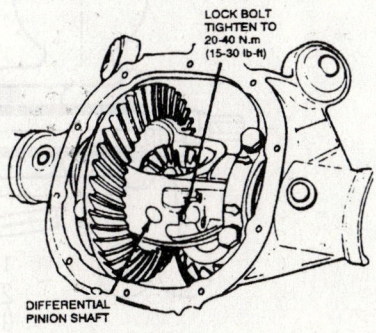

LOCK BOLT
TIGHTEN TO
20–40 N.m
(15–30 lb-ft)

DIFFERENTIAL
PINION SHAFT

Differential pinion shaft and lockbolt

7922NG65

cover bolts to 18–28 ft. lbs. (24–38 Nm).
- Wheel speed sensor
- Disc brake rotor and caliper. Tighten the caliper mounting bolts to 65–87 ft. lbs. (87–119 Nm).
- Rear wheel

4. Fill the differential with gear lubricant. Tighten the filler plug to 15–30 ft. lbs. (20–41 Nm).

Pinion Seal

REMOVAL & INSTALLATION

1. Before servicing the vehicle, refer to the precautions in the beginning of this section.

2. Remove or disconnect the following:
- Driveshaft
- Rear wheels
- Rear brake calipers

➡The rear brake calipers must be removed so that there is no additional drag when measuring pinion bearing preload.

3. Use an inch lb. torque wrench and measure the amount of torque required to maintain pinion rotation through several revolutions.

4. Remove the pinion flange and remove the seal.

To install:

5. Install or connect the following:
- Pinion seal
- Pinion flange
- New pinion flange nut

6. Rotate the pinion flange occasionally while tightening the flange nut to make sure the pinion bearings seat correctly.

7. Take frequent bearing preload torque readings.

8. If the preload recorded prior to disassembly is **lower** than the specification for used bearings, then tighten the pinion flange nut to specification. If the preload recorder prior to disassembly is **higher** than the specification for used bearings, then tighten the pinion flange nut to the original reading as recorded.

9. The pinion bearing preload specifications are as follows:
   a. Used bearings: 8–14 inch lbs. (0.9–1.6 Nm).
   b. New bearings: 16–29 inch lbs. (1.8–3.2 Nm).

✱✱ CAUTION

Never loosen the pinion nut to reduce bearing preload. If it is necessary to

reduce bearing preload, install a new collapsible spacer and pinion nut.

10. Install or connect the following:
- Driveshaft
- Brake calipers
- Rear wheels

11. Fill the differential with gear lubricant and check for leaks.

Axle Housing Assembly

REMOVAL & INSTALLATION

1. Before servicing the vehicle, refer to the precautions in the beginning of this section.
2. Support the axle with a jack or hoist.
3. Remove or disconnect the following:
- Driveshaft
- Rear wheels
- Rear disc brake calipers and rotors
- Rear brake hose
- Wheel speed sensors
- Axle housing vent
- Shock absorbers
- Upper control arms

4. Lower the axle housing until the coil springs are released.
5. Remove or disconnect the following:
- Coil springs.
- Lower control arms
- Axle from the vehicle.

To install:
6. Install or connect the following:
- Lower control arms
- Coil springs
- Upper control arms. Tighten all control arm bolts to 70–99 ft. lbs. (95–135 Nm).
- Shock absorbers
- Axle housing vent
- Wheel speed sensors
- Rear brake hose
- Rear disc brake calipers and rotors
- Driveshaft
- Rear wheels

STEERING AND SUSPENSION

Air Bag

✳✳ CAUTION

Some vehicles are equipped with an air bag system. The system must be disarmed before performing service on, or around, system components, the steering column, instrument panel components, wiring and sensors. Failure to follow the safety precautions and the disarming procedure could result in accidental air bag deployment, possible injury and unnecessary system repairs.

PRECAUTIONS

Several precautions must be observed when handling the inflator module to avoid accidental deployment and possible personal injury.

- Never carry the inflator module by the wires or connector on the underside of the module.
- When carrying a live inflator module, hold securely with both hands, and ensure that the bag and trim cover are pointed away.
- Place the inflator module on a bench or other surface with the bag and trim cover facing up.
- With the inflator module on the bench, never place anything on or close to the module that may be thrown in the event of an accidental deployment.

DISARMING

1. Before servicing the vehicle, refer to the precautions in the beginning of this section.
2. Disconnect both battery cables from the battery, negative cable first.
3. Wait 1 minute before proceeding with the service procedure. This is the time required for the back-up power supply in the air bag diagnostic monitor to deplete its stored energy.

4. After service is completed, reconnect the battery cables, negative cable last.
5. Turn the ignition switch to the **RUN** position. The air bag indicator should light continuously for approximately 6 seconds, then turn **OFF**. If the indicator fails to light, flashes or remains lit continuously, there is a fault in the air bag system.

Power Rack and Pinion Steering Gear

REMOVAL & INSTALLATION

1. Before servicing the vehicle, refer to the precautions in the beginning of this section.
2. Remove or disconnect the following:
- Negative battery cable
- Front wheels
- Steering column intermediate shaft coupling
- Outer tie rod ends
- Steering gear retaining bolts
- Power steering pressure and return lines
- Steering gear

To install:
3. Attach the pressure and return lines to the steering gear before attaching the steering gear to the subframe. Use new plastic seals and tighten the line fittings to 20–25 ft. lbs. (27–34 Nm).

➡ **The power steering fluid lines are designed to swivel when properly tightened. Do not overtighten the fittings.**

4. Install or connect the following:
- Steering gear. Tighten the bolts to 31–39 ft. lbs. (41–54 Nm).

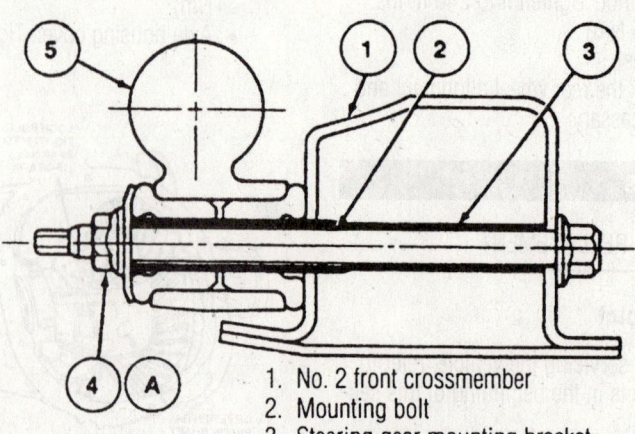

1. No. 2 front crossmember
2. Mounting bolt
3. Steering gear mounting bracket
4. Retaining nut
5. Power steering rack and pinion

7922NG47

Power rack and pinion steering gear mounting on the No. 2 crossmember

- Outer tie rod ends. Tighten the nuts to 36–46 ft. lbs. (48–63 Nm).
- Steering column intermediate shaft coupling. Tighten the pinch bolt to 21–29 ft. lbs. (28–40 Nm).
- Front wheels
- Negative battery cable

5. Fill the power steering system with the proper type and quantity of fluid.

6. Check the front end alignment and adjust as necessary.

Strut

REMOVAL & INSTALLATION

Front

1. Before servicing the vehicle, refer to the precautions in the beginning of this section.

2. Support the front of the vehicle on jackstands placed under the control arms.

3. Remove or disconnect the following:
- Front wheel
- Disc brake caliper
- Wheel speed sensor and bracket
- Upper strut retaining fasteners
- Wheel spindle attachment bolts

4. Compress the strut assembly and remove it from the vehicle.

To install:

5. If replacing the strut, transfer the upper mounting bracket.

6. Install or connect the following:
- Strut assembly. Tighten the spindle

bolts to 141–191 ft. lbs. (191–259 Nm).
- Upper strut retaining fasteners. Tighten to 25–34 ft. lbs. (34–46 Nm).
- Wheel speed sensor and bracket
- Disc brake caliper. Tighten the caliper mounting bolts to 96 ft. lbs. (130 Nm).
- Front wheel

7. Remove the jackstands and check the alignment. Adjust as necessary.

Shock Absorber

REMOVAL & INSTALLATION

Rear

1. Before servicing the vehicle, refer to the precautions in the beginning of this section.

2. Remove or disconnect the following:
- Rear compartment trim panels
- Upper shock absorber retaining nut
- Lower shock absorber bolt
- Shock absorber

To install:

3. Prime the new shock absorber as follows:

a. Step 1: With the shock absorber right side up, extend it fully.

b. Step 2: Turn the shock absorber upside down and fully compress it.

c. Step 3: Repeat for 3 cycles.

4. Install the shock absorber and tighten the lower bolt as follows:

a. SVT Cobra: 98 ft. lbs. (133 Nm).

b. All others: 57–75 ft. lbs. (76–103 Nm).

5. Install or connect the following:
- Upper shock absorber retaining nut. Tighten to 25–33 ft. lbs. (34–46 Nm).
- Rear compartment trim panels.

Coil Spring

REMOVAL & INSTALLATION

Front

1. Before servicing the vehicle, refer to the precautions in the beginning of this section.

2. Install an internal spring compressor to the spring to be serviced. Tighten the compressor to relieve spring pressure on the lower control arm.

3. Remove or disconnect the following:

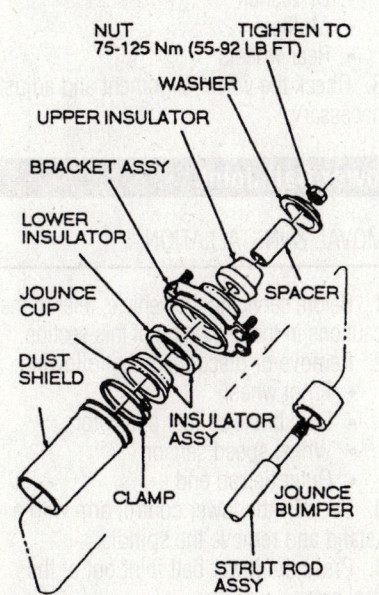

Exploded view of the front strut upper mounting

NUT — TIGHTEN TO 75–125 Nm (55–92 LB FT)
WASHER
UPPER INSULATOR
BRACKET ASSY
LOWER INSULATOR
JOUNCE CUP
SPACER
DUST SHIELD
INSULATOR ASSY
CLAMP
JOUNCE BUMPER
STRUT ROD ASSY

7922NG48

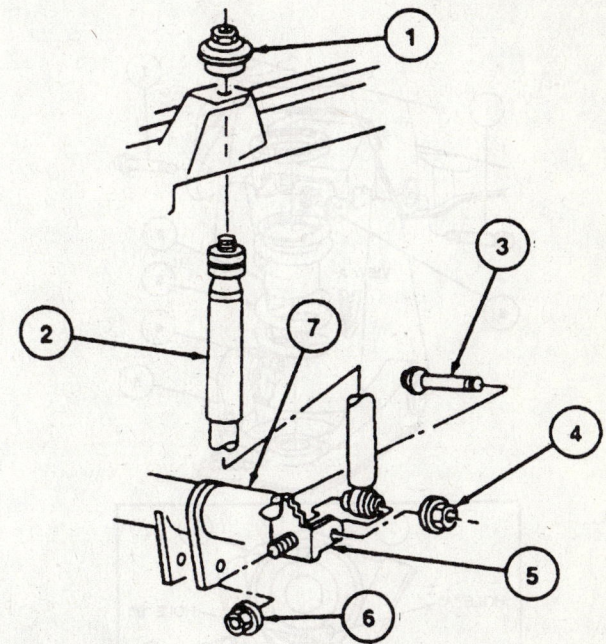

1. Insulator nut
2. Shock absorber
3. Mounting bolt
4. Mounting nut
5. Shock absorber lower mount bracket
6. Mounting nut
7. Rear axle housing

7922NG49

Exploded view of the rear shock absorber mounting

- Front wheel
- Disc brake caliper
- Outer tie rod end
- Stabilizer bar link
- Power steering gear
- Lower control arm mounting bolts
- Coil spring

To install:

4. If replacing the coil spring, transfer the spring compressor to the new spring.

5. Install or connect the following:
- Coil spring
- Lower control arm mounting bolts. Use a jack to raise the control arm to a normal position and tighten the bolts to 141–191 ft. lbs. (191–259 Nm).
- Power steering gear
- Stabilizer bar link. Tighten the nut to 11–16 ft. lbs. (16–22 Nm).
- Outer tie rod end. Tighten the nut to 36–46 ft. lbs. (48–63 Nm).
- Disc brake caliper. Tighten the caliper mounting bolts to 96 ft. lbs. (130 Nm).
- Front wheel

6. Position the coil spring and remove the spring compressor.

Rear

EXCEPT SVT COBRA

1. Before servicing the vehicle, refer to the precautions in the beginning of this section.

2. Raise and support the vehicle safely under the frame. Support the body at the rear body crossmember.

3. If equipped, remove the stabilizer bar.

4. Support the axle with a jack.

5. Place another jack under the lower arm axle pivot bolt. Remove and discard the bolt and nut. Lower the jack slowly until the coil spring load is relieved.

6. Remove the coil spring and insulator from the vehicle.

To install:

7. Place the upper spring insulator on top of the spring. Place the lower spring insulator on the lower arm.

8. Position the coil spring on the lower arm spring seat with the pigtail on the lower arm at the rear of the vehicle and pointing toward the left side of the vehicle.

9. Slowly raise the jack until the arm is in position. Insert a new rear pivot bolt and nut.

10. Raise the axle to curb height. Tighten the pivot bolt to 71–97 ft. lbs. (97–132 Nm).

11. If equipped, install the stabilizer bar.

12. Remove the crossmember supports and lower the vehicle.

SVT COBRA

1. Before servicing the vehicle, refer to the precautions in the beginning of this section.

2. Support the rear subframe with a jack.

3. Remove or disconnect the following:
- Rear wheels
- Mufflers
- Driveshaft
- Parking brake cables and brackets
- Brake fluid lines
- Wheel speed sensors
- Tie rod links
- Shock absorbers
- Lower control arms

4. Loosen the front subframe bolts and remove the rear subframe bolts.

5. Lower the rear subframe and remove the coil springs

To install:

➡ **Use new nuts, bolts and split pins for assembly.**

6. Install the coil springs and raise the rear subframe. Install new subframe bolts and tighten them to 76 ft. lbs. (103 Nm).

7. Install or connect the following:
- Lower control arms
- Shock absorbers. Tighten the bolts to 98 ft. lbs. (133 Nm).
- Tie rod links
- Wheel speed sensors
- Brake fluid lines
- Parking brake cables and brackets
- Driveshaft
- Mufflers
- Rear wheels

8. Check the wheel alignment and adjust as necessary.

Lower Ball Joint

REMOVAL & INSTALLATION

1. Before servicing the vehicle, refer to the precautions in the beginning of this section.

2. Remove or disconnect the following:
- Front wheel
- Disc brake caliper and rotor
- Wheel speed sensor
- Outer tie rod end

3. Support the lower control arm with a jackstand and remove the spindle.

4. Press the lower ball joint out of the control arm.

To install:

5. Press the lower ball joint into the control arm so that the joint is fully seated in the control arm.

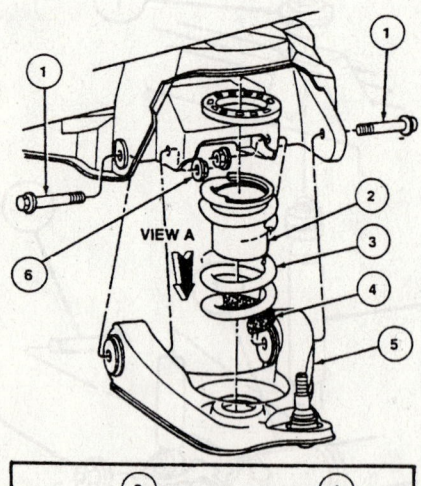

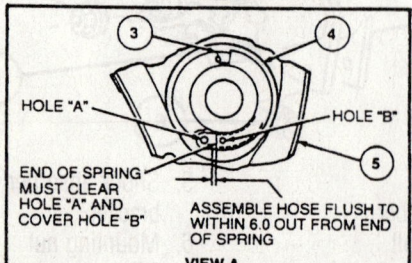

VIEW A

HOLE "A"　　HOLE "B"

END OF SPRING MUST CLEAR HOLE "A" AND COVER HOLE "B"

ASSEMBLE HOSE FLUSH TO WITHIN 6.0 OUT FROM END OF SPRING

VIEW A

1. Mounting bolt
2. Damper
3. Front coil spring
4. Insulator
5. Front suspension lower arm
6. Nuts

7922NG50

Exploded view of the front coil spring mounting

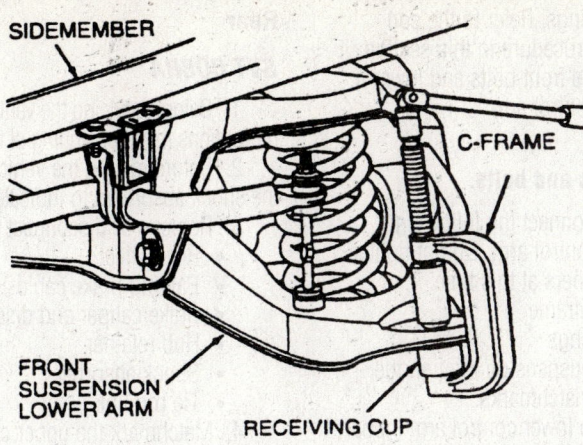

Use the C-clamp, cup and adapters to press the ball joint out of the lower control arm

6. Install or connect the following:
   - Spindle. Tighten the ball joint nut to 109–149 ft. lbs. (148–202 Nm). Tighten the strut bolts to 141–191 ft. lbs. (190–259 Nm).
   - Outer tie rod end. Tighten the nut to 36–46 ft. lbs. (48–63 Nm).
   - Disc brake rotor and caliper. Tighten the caliper mounting bolts to 96 ft. lbs. (130 Nm).
   - Wheel speed sensor
   - Front wheel

Upper Control Arm

REMOVAL & INSTALLATION

Rear

EXCEPT SVT COBRA

1. Before servicing the vehicle, refer to the precautions in the beginning of this section.
2. Before raising the vehicle, matchmark the shock absorbers to indicate curb height.
3. Support the axle housing with a jack.
4. Remove the upper control arms.

To install:

➡ Use new nuts and bolts.

5. Install the upper control arms.
6. Align the matchmarks on the shock absorbers and tighten the control arm bolts as follows:
   a. Step 1: Tighten the mounting bracket bolt to 76 ft. lbs. (103 Nm).
   b. Step 2: Tighten the axle housing bolt to 66 ft. lbs. (90 Nm).

SVT COBRA

1. Before servicing the vehicle, refer to the precautions in the beginning of this section.
2. Before raising the vehicle, matchmark the shock absorbers to indicate curb height.
3. Remove the coil springs.
4. Remove the subframe front bolts and lower the subframe from the vehicle.
5. Matchmark the upper control arm cam bolt to the knuckle.
6. Remove the upper control arm.

To install:

➡ Use new nuts and bolts.

7. Transfer the cam bolt matchmark to the new cam bolt.
8. Install the upper control arm. Do not tighten the fasteners at this time.
9. Install the coil springs.
10. Raise the suspension to align the shock absorber matchmarks and tighten the upper control arm inner bolts to 66 ft. lbs. (90 Nm).
11. Align the cam bolt matchmark and tighten the nut to 66 ft. lbs. (90 Nm).
12. Check the wheel alignment and adjust as necessary.

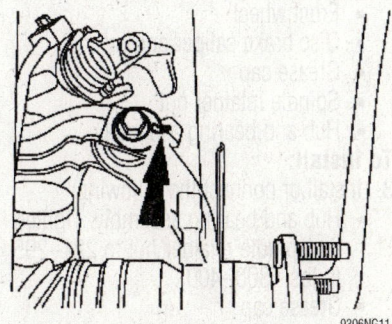

Cam bolt matchmark—SVT Cobra

CONTROL ARM BUSHING REPLACEMENT

Rear

EXCEPT SVT COBRA

The inboard control arm bushing is serviced with the control arm as an assembly.

1. Before servicing the vehicle, refer to the precautions in the beginning of this section.
2. Remove the upper control arm.
3. Press the bushing out of the axle housing.
4. Press a new bushing into the axle housing and install the upper control arm.

SVT COBRA

The upper control arm bushing are serviced with the control arm as an assembly.

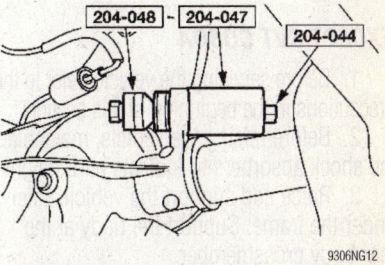

Axle bushing removal

Lower Control Arm

REMOVAL & INSTALLATION

Front

1. Before servicing the vehicle, refer to the precautions in the beginning of this section.
2. Install an internal spring compressor to the coil spring. Tighten the compressor to relieve spring pressure on the lower control arm.
3. Remove or disconnect the following:
   - Front wheel
   - Disc brake caliper
   - Outer tie rod end
   - Stabilizer bar link
   - Power steering gear
   - Lower control arm mounting bolts
   - Coil spring
   - Lower ball joint
   - Lower control arm

To install:

4. Connect the lower ball joint to the spindle and install the nut hand tight.
5. Install or connect the following:
   - Coil spring

- Lower control arm mounting bolts. Use a jack to raise the control arm to curb height and tighten the bolts to 141–191 ft. lbs. (191–259 Nm). Tighten the ball joint nut to 109–149 ft. lbs. (148–202 Nm).
- Power steering gear
- Stabilizer bar link. Tighten the nut to 11–16 ft. lbs. (16–22 Nm).
- Outer tie rod end. Tighten the nut to 36–46 ft. lbs. (48–63 Nm).
- Disc brake caliper. Tighten the caliper mounting bolts to 96 ft. lbs. (130 Nm).
- Front wheel

6. Position the coil spring and remove the spring compressor. Refer to the coil spring procedure illustration.

7. Check the front end alignment.

Rear

EXCEPT SVT COBRA

1. Before servicing the vehicle, refer to the precautions in the beginning of this section.

2. Before raising the vehicle, matchmark the shock absorbers to indicate curb height.

3. Raise and support the vehicle safely under the frame. Support the body at the rear body crossmember.

4. If equipped, remove the stabilizer bar.

5. Support the axle with a jack.

6. Place another jack under the lower arm axle pivot bolt. Remove and discard the bolt and nut. Lower the jack slowly until the coil spring load is relieved.

7. Remove or disconnect the following:
- Coil spring
- Lower control arm

To install:

➡Use new nuts and bolts.

8. Install or connect the following:
- Lower control arm to the axle housing
- Coil spring

9. Raise the control arm and install the pivot bolt.

10. Raise the axle to align the matchmarks on the shock absorbers and tighten the lower control arm bolts to 71–97 ft. lbs. (97–132 Nm).

11. install the stabilizer bar, if equipped.

SVT COBRA

1. Before servicing the vehicle, refer to the precautions in the beginning of this section.

2. Before raising the vehicle, matchmark the shock absorbers to indicate curb height.

3. Remove or disconnect the following:

- Coil springs. Refer to the coil spring procedure in this section.
- Subframe front bolts and lower it
- Lower control arm

To install:

➡Use new nuts and bolts.

4. Install or connect the following:
- Lower control arm. Do not tighten the fasteners at this time.
- Rear subframe
- Coil springs

5. Raise the suspension to align the shock absorber matchmarks.

6. Tighten the lower control arm inboard bolts to 184 ft. lbs. (250 Nm) and the knuckle bolt to 85 ft. lbs. (115 Nm).

7. Check the wheel alignment and adjust as necessary.

CONTROL ARM BUSHING REPLACEMENT

Front and Rear

ALL MODELS

The lower control arm bushings are serviced with the lower control arm as an assembly.

Wheel Bearings

ADJUSTMENT

The front wheel bearings are an integral part of the hub assembly. They require no periodic maintenance or adjustment. If the bearings are found to be defective, they must be replaced along with the hub assembly.

The rear wheel bearings are not adjustable.

REMOVAL & INSTALLATION

Front

1. Before servicing the vehicle, refer to the precautions in the beginning of this section.

2. Remove or disconnect the following:
- Front wheel
- Disc brake caliper and rotor
- Grease cap
- Spindle retainer nut
- Hub and bearing assembly

To install:

3. Install or connect the following:
- Hub and bearing assembly. Tighten the spindle retainer nut to 221–295 ft. lbs. (300–400).
- Grease cap
- Disc brake caliper and rotor. Tighten the mounting bolts to 96 ft. lbs. (130 Nm).
- Front wheel

Rear

SVT COBRA

1. Before servicing the vehicle, refer to the precautions in the beginning of this section.

2. Before raising the vehicle, matchmark the shock absorbers to indicate curb height.

3. Remove or disconnect the following:
- Rear wheel
- Parking brake cable
- Brake caliper and disc
- Hub retainer
- Shock absorber
- Tie rod link

4. Matchmark the upper control arm cam bolt to the knuckle.

5. Remove or disconnect the following:
- Knuckle from the vehicle.
- Dust shield and press the hub out of the bearing.
- Snapring and press the bearing out of the knuckle.

To install:

➡Use new nuts, bolts, snaprings, and split pins for assembly.

6. Install or connect the following:
- Bearing so that it is fully seated in the knuckle bore
- Snapring

7. Support the bearing inner race and press the hub into the bearing.

8. Install the dust shield and tighten the bolts to 88 inch lbs. (10 Nm).

9. Transfer the cam bolt matchmark to a new cam bolt.

10. Install or connect the following:
- Knuckle. Do not tighten the fasteners at this time.
- Tie rod link. Tighten the nut to 35 ft. lbs. (47 Nm).
- Shock absorber. Tighten the bolt to 98 ft. lbs. (133 Nm).
- Hub retainer. Do not tighten the nut at this time.

11. Raise the suspension to align the shock absorber matchmarks and tighten the lower control arm bolt to 85 ft. lbs. (115 Nm).

12. Align the cam bolt matchmarks and tighten the nut to 66 ft. lbs. (90 Nm).

13. Install the brake disc and caliper. Install the parking brake cable.

➡**The hub retainer nut must be tightened with the brakes applied and the wheels off the ground to ensure correct bearing seating.**

14. Tighten the hub retainer to 184 ft. lbs. (250 Nm) and install the wheel.

15. Check the wheel alignment and adjust as necessary.

PRECAUTIONS

Before servicing any vehicle, please be sure to read all of the following precautions, which deal with personal safety, prevention of component damage, and important points to take into consideration when servicing a motor vehicle:

• Never open, service or drain the radiator or cooling system when the engine is hot; serious burns can occur from the steam and hot coolant.

• Observe all applicable safety precautions when working around fuel. Whenever servicing the fuel system, always work in a well-ventilated area. Do not allow fuel spray or vapors to come in contact with a spark, open flame, or excessive heat (a hot drop light, for example). Keep a dry chemical fire extinguisher near the work area. Always keep fuel in a container specifically designed for fuel storage; also, always properly seal fuel containers to avoid the possibility of fire or explosion. Refer to the additional fuel system precautions later in this section.

• Fuel injection systems often remain pressurized, even after the engine has been turned **OFF**. The fuel system pressure must be relieved before disconnecting any fuel lines. Failure to do so may result in fire and/or personal injury.

• Brake fluid often contains polyglycol ethers and polyglycols. Avoid contact with the eyes and wash your hands thoroughly after handling brake fluid. If you do get brake fluid in your eyes, flush your eyes with clean, running water for 15 minutes. If eye irritation persists, or if you have taken brake fluid internally, IMMEDIATELY seek medical assistance.

• The EPA warns that prolonged contact with used engine oil may cause a number of skin disorders, including cancer! You should make every effort to minimize your exposure to used engine oil. Protective gloves should be worn when changing oil. Wash your hands and any other exposed skin areas as soon as possible after exposure to used engine oil. Soap and water, or waterless hand cleaner should be used.

• All new vehicles are now equipped with an air bag system, often referred to as a Supplemental Restraint System (SRS) or Supplemental Inflatable Restraint (SIR) system. The system must be dis-abled before performing service on or around system components, steering column, instrument panel components, wiring and sensors. Failure to follow safety and disabling procedures could result in accidental air bag deployment, possible personal injury and unnecessary system repairs.

• Always wear safety goggles when working with, or around, the air bag system. When carrying a non-deployed air bag, be sure the bag and trim cover are pointed away from your body. When placing a non-deployed air bag on a work surface, always face the bag and trim cover upward, away from the surface. This will reduce the motion of the module if it is accidentally deployed. Refer to the additional air bag system precautions later in this section.

• Clean, high quality brake fluid from a sealed container is essential to the safe and proper operation of the brake system. You should always buy the correct type of brake fluid for your vehicle. If the brake fluid becomes contaminated, completely flush the system with new fluid. Never reuse any brake fluid. Any brake fluid that is removed from the system should be discarded. Also, do not allow any brake fluid to come in contact with a painted surface; it will damage the paint.

• Never operate the engine without the proper amount and type of engine oil; doing so WILL result in severe engine damage.

• Timing belt maintenance is extremely important! Many models utilize an interference-type, non-freewheeling engine. If the timing belt breaks, the valves in the cylinder head may strike the pistons, causing potentially serious (also time-consuming and expensive) engine damage. Refer to the maintenance interval charts in the front of this manual for the recommended replacement interval for the timing belt, and to the timing belt section for belt replacement and inspection.

• Disconnecting the negative battery cable on some vehicles may interfere with the functions of the on-board computer system(s) and may require the computer to undergo a relearning process once the negative battery cable is reconnected.

• When servicing drum brakes, only disassemble and assemble one side at a time, leaving the remaining side intact for reference.

ENGINE REPAIR

Alternator

REMOVAL

1. Before servicing the vehicle, refer to the precautions in the beginning of this section.
2. Remove or disconnect the following:
   • Negative battery cable
   • Engine cover by unfastening the screw and pushing the cover to disengage the front clips, on 1998–01 models
   • Pushpins and wiring harness
   • Belt tension and belt
   • Mounting bolts
   • Bracket bolts
   • Accessory drive belt
   • Alternator

INSTALLATION

Install or connect the following:
   • Alternator
   • Mounting bolts and tighten to 15–22 ft. lbs. (20–30 Nm)
   • Bracket bolts and tighten to 71–106 inch lbs. (8–12 Nm)
   • Accessory drive belt
   • Pushpins and wiring harness
   • Engine cover, on 1998–01 models
   • Negative battery cable

Ignition Timing

ADJUSTMENT

The 4.6L engine used in the Mk. III utilizes a Distributorless Ignition System (DIS).

The Crankshaft Position (CKP) sensor is a variable reluctance-type sensor triggered by a 36-minus-1 tooth trigger wheel located inside the front cover.

Engine Assembly

REMOVAL & INSTALLATION

1. Before servicing the vehicle, refer to the precautions in the beginning of this section.
2. Drain the engine cooling system.

3. Recover the refrigerant from the air conditioning system.

4. Properly relieve the fuel system pressure.

5. Remove or disconnect the following:
- Both battery cables
- Hood
- Engine cooling fan, shroud and radiator
- Windshield wiper governor (module) and support bracket
- Engine air cleaner outlet tube
- Engine/transmission harness connector from the retaining bracket on the power brake booster and move aside
- Accelerator and cruise control cables at the throttle body
- Electrical connector and vacuum hose from the evaporative emission canister purge valve
- Positive battery cable from the power distribution box and harness
- Vacuum supply hose from the throttle body adapter vacuum port
- Both heater hoses
- Alternator harness from the front fender apron and the power distribution box
- Air conditioning hoses from the air conditioning compressor using the appropriate spring-lock disconnect tools
- Power steering control valve harness connector
- Body ground strap from the dash panel
- Exhaust system from the exhaust manifolds and support with wire hung from the crossmember
- Retaining nut from the transmission line bracket
- 3 bolts and 1 stud retaining the engine to the transmission knee braces
- Starter motor
- 4 bolts retaining the power steering pump to the cylinder block and position aside

6. Transmission housing cover from the cylinder block to access the torque converter nuts. Rotate the crankshaft until each of the 4 nuts is accessible and remove the nuts

7. Remove or disconnect the following:
- 6 transmission-to-engine retaining bolts
- Engine support insulator (mount) through-bolts

8. Support the transmission with a floor jack and a block of wood.

9. Remove the bolt retaining the right-hand front engine support insulator to the front engine mount insulator support bracket.

10. Install engine lifting bracket to the front of the left-hand cylinder head and to the rear of the right-hand cylinder head. Connect engine lifting equipment to the lifting brackets

11. Raise the engine slightly using a floor crane and carefully separate the engine from the transmission. Do not let the torque converter fall out of the transmission.

12. Carefully lift the engine out of the engine compartment and position on a workstand. Remove the engine lifting equipment.

To install:

13. Engine lifting brackets. Support the engine using a floor crane installed to the lifting equipment and remove the engine from the workstand.

14. Lower the engine into the engine compartment. Start the converter pilot into the flywheel and align the paint marks on the flywheel and torque converter. Be sure the studs on the torque converter align with the holes in the flywheel.

15. Fully engage the engine to the transmission and lower onto front engine support insulators.

16. Install or connect the following:
- Engine lifting equipment and brackets
- Bolt retaining the right-hand front engine support insulator to the front engine mount insulator support bracket
- 6 engine-to-transmission retaining bolts and tighten to 30–44 ft. lbs. (40–60 Nm)
- Front engine support insulator through-bolts and tighten to 15–22 ft. lbs. (20–30 Nm)
- 4 torque converter retaining nuts and tighten to 22–25 ft. lbs. (20–30 Nm)
- Transmission housing cover to the cylinder block
- Power steering pump on the cylinder block and the 4 retaining nuts. Tighten to 15–22 ft. lbs. (20–30 Nm).
- Starter motor
- Engine-to-transmission brace and the 3 bolts and 1 stud. Tighten the bolts and stud to 18–31 ft. lbs. (25–43 Nm).

- Transmission line bracket to the brace stud and 1 retaining nut. Tighten to 15–22 ft. lbs. (20–30 Nm).
- Exhaust system to the exhaust manifolds. Tighten the 4 nuts to 20–30 ft. lbs. (27–41 Nm). Be sure the exhaust system clears the No. 3 crossmember. Adjust as necessary.
- Power steering valve harness connector
- Ground strap to the dash panel
- Air conditioning lines to the air conditioning compressor
- Alternator harness at the front fender apron and the power distribution box
- Both heater hoses
- Vacuum supply hose to the throttle body adapter vacuum port
- Positive battery cable to the power distribution box and harness
- Electrical connector and vacuum hose to the evaporative emission canister purge valve
- Accelerator and cruise control cables at the throttle body
- Engine/transmission harness connector to the retaining bracket on the power brake booster
- Windshield wiper governor and support bracket
- Fuel supply and return lines
- Radiator, cooling fan and shroud
- Engine air cleaner outlet tube
- Hood
- Both battery cables

17. If needed, fill the crankcase.

18. Fill the cooling system.

19. Start the engine and allow it to reach normal operating temperature.

20. Check for leaks and proper fluid levels.

21. Evacuate and recharge the air conditioning system.

22. Road test the vehicle and check the engine and transmission for proper operation.

Water Pump

REMOVAL & INSTALLATION

1. Before servicing the vehicle, refer to the precautions in the beginning of this section.

2. Drain the cooling system.

3. Remove or disconnect the following:
- Negative battery cable

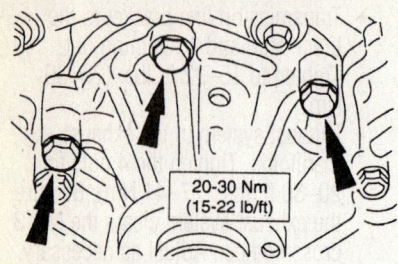

Be sure to tighten the water pump mounting bolts to the specification

20-30 Nm (15-22 lb/ft)

- Cooling fan and the shroud
- Accessory drive belt
- 4 water pump pulley-to-water pump bolts
- Pulley
- 4 water pump-to-engine bolts
- Water pump

To install:

4. Clean the sealing surfaces of the water pump and block.

5. Install or connect the following:
- New O-ring, lubricate it with clean antifreeze prior to installation
- Water pump. Tighten the bolts to 15–22 ft. lbs. (20–30 Nm).
- Water pump pulley. Tighten the bolts to 15–22 ft. lbs. (20–30 Nm).
- Accessory drive belt

6. Fill the cooling system.

7. Operate the engine to normal operating temperatures and check for leaks.

Cylinder Head

REMOVAL & INSTALLATION

➡The cylinder head bolts are a torque-to-yield design and cannot be reused. Before beginning this procedure, be sure new cylinder head bolts are available.

1. Before servicing the vehicle, refer to the precautions in the beginning of this section.

2. If equipped with air suspension, the air suspension switch, located on the right-hand side of the luggage compartment, must be turned to the **OFF** position before raising the vehicle.

3. Drain the engine cooling system.

4. Properly relieve the fuel system pressure.

5. Remove or disconnect the following:
- Negative battery cable
- Cooling fan and shroud assembly
- Engine air cleaner outlet tube
- Windshield wiper governor (module)

- Accessory drive belt
- Ignition wires from the spark plugs
- Ignition wire brackets from the cylinder head cover studs
- 2 ignition wire tray-to-ignition coil brackets bolts
- Bolt retaining the air conditioning pressure line to the right-hand ignition coil bracket
- Wiring to both ignition coils and the Camshaft Position (CMP) sensor
- Ignition coil brackets-to-engine front cover nuts. Slide the ignition coil brackets and ignition wire assemblies off the mounting studs and from the vehicle
- Water pump pulley
- Alternator wiring harness from the junction block, fender apron and alternator
- Alternator
- Positive battery cable at the power distribution box
- Retaining bolt from the positive battery cable bracket located on the side of the right-hand cylinder head
- Vent hose from the canister purge solenoid and position the positive battery cable aside
- Positive Crankcase Ventilation (PCV) valve from the cylinder head cover

- Engine/transmission harness connector from the retaining bracket on the power brake booster
- Crankshaft Position (CKP) sensor, air conditioning compressor clutch and canister purge solenoid electrical connectors

6. Remove the bolts retaining the power steering pump to the cylinder block and engine front cover. The front lower bolt on the power steering pump will not come all the way out. Wire the power steering pump aside.

7. Remove or disconnect the following:
- Engine oil pan and oil pan gasket
- Crankshaft pulley retaining bolt
- Pulley
- Power steering control valve actuator and oil pressure sensor wiring connectors and position aside.
- Exhaust Gas Recirculation (EGR) tube from the right-hand exhaust manifold
- Exhaust pipes from the exhaust manifolds. Lower the exhaust pipes and hang with wire from the crossmember.
- Bolts retaining the starter wiring harness to the rear of the right-hand cylinder head
- Cylinder head covers to the cylinder heads

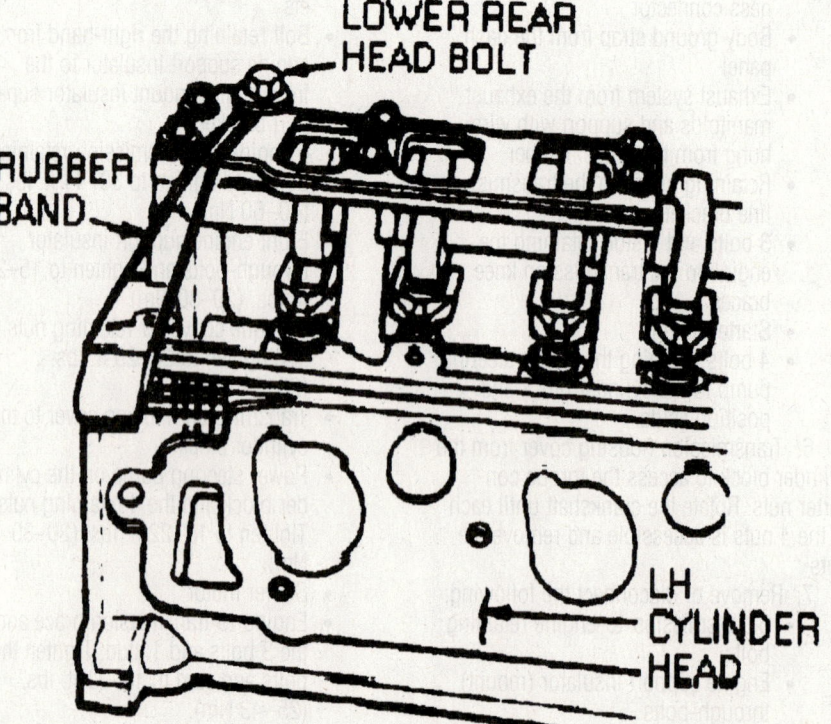

LOWER REAR HEAD BOLT

RUBBER BAND

LH CYLINDER HEAD

Use a rubber band to support the rear cylinder head bolt to ease removal of the head

- Accelerator and cruise control cables
- Accelerator cable bracket from the intake manifold and position aside
- Vacuum hose from the throttle body elbow vacuum port
- Heated Oxygen (HO$_2$S) sensors and the heater water hose
- 2 bolts retaining the thermostat housing to the intake manifold and position the upper hose and thermostat housing aside

➡ **The 2 thermostat housing bolts also retain the intake manifold.**

- 9 intake manifold-to-cylinder heads bolts
- Intake manifold and gaskets
- 7 stud bolts and the 4 bolts attaching the engine front cover to the engine
- Front cover
- Both timing chains

✲✲ WARNING

This is an interference engine. Camshaft Positioning Tools T92P-6256-A must be installed on the camshafts to prevent the camshafts from rotating.

- 10 left-hand cylinder head-to-cylinder block bolts

8. Remove the cylinder head. The lower rear cylinder head bolt must stay in the cylinder head until the cylinder head is removed due to lack of clearance for removal in the vehicle. Use a rubber band to secure the cylinder head bolt in the cylinder head during removal and installation of the cylinder head and to prevent the bolt from damaging the cylinder block or head gasket

➡ **The lower rear cylinder head bolt cannot be removed due to interference with the power brake booster. Use a rubber band to hold the bolt away from the cylinder block.**

9. Remove or disconnect the following:
- Ground strap, 1 stud and 1 bolt retaining the heater return line to the right-hand cylinder head
- 10 right-hand cylinder head-to-cylinder block bolts

10. Remove the cylinder head. The lower rear cylinder head bolt must stay in the cylinder head until the cylinder head is removed due to lack of clearance for removal in the vehicle. Use a rubber band to secure the cylinder head bolt in the cylinder

head during removal and installation of the cylinder head and to prevent the bolt from damaging the cylinder block or head gasket.

➡ **The lower rear cylinder head bolt cannot be removed due to interference with the evaporator housing. Use a rubber band to hold the bolt away from the cylinder block.**

11. Clean all gaskets mating surfaces. Check the cylinder heads and cylinder block for flatness. Check the cylinder heads for scratches near the coolant passages and combustion chambers that could provide leak paths.

To install:

12. Rotate the crankshaft counterclockwise 45 degrees. The crankshaft keyway should be at the 9 o'clock position viewed from the front of the engine. This ensures that all pistons are below the top of the engine block deck face.

13. Rotate the camshaft to a stable position where the valves do not extend below the head face.

14. Install or connect the following:
- New head gaskets on the cylinder block
- New bolts in the lower rear bolt holes on both cylinder heads and retain with rubber bands as explained during the removal procedure

➡ **New cylinder head bolts must be used whenever the cylinder head is removed and reinstalled. The cylinder head bolts are a torque-to-yield design and cannot be reused.**

15. Position the cylinder heads on the cylinder block dowels, being careful not to score the surface of the head face. Apply clean oil to the new cylinder head bolts, remove the rubber bands from the lower rear bolts and install all bolts hand-tight.

➡ **Refer to Section 1 of this manual for the cylinder head torque sequence illustration. The illustration is located after the Torque Specification Chart.**

16. Tighten the new cylinder head bolts, in sequence, as follows:
  a. Step 1: 28–31 ft. lbs. (37–43 Nm).
  b. Step 2: plus 85–95 degrees.
  c. Step 3: loosen all bolts at least 1 full turn.
  d. Step 4: 27–32 ft. lbs. (37–43 Nm).
  e. Step 5: plus 85–95 degrees.
  f. Step 6: again, plus 85–95 degrees.

17. Position the heater return hose and install the 2 retaining bolts.

18. Rotate the camshafts using the flats matched at the center of the camshaft until both are in time. Install Camshaft Positioning Tools T91P-6256-A, on the flats of the camshafts to keep them from rotating.

19. Rotate the crankshaft clockwise 45 degrees to position the crankshaft at Top Dead Center (TDC) for the No. 1 cylinder.

➡ **The crankshaft must only be rotated in the clockwise direction and only as far as TDC.**

20. Install or connect the following:
- Both timing chains
- New engine front cover seal and gasket. Apply silicone sealer to the lower corners of the cover where it meets the junction of the engine oil pan and cylinder block and to the points where the cover contacts the junction of the cylinder block and the cylinder heads.
- Engine front cover and the bolts. Tighten to 15–22 ft. lbs. (20–30 Nm).
- New intake manifold gaskets on the cylinder heads. Be sure the alignment tabs on the gaskets are aligned with the holes in the cylinder heads.

➡ **Before installing the intake manifold, inspect it for nicks and cuts that could provide leak paths.**

- Intake manifold on the cylinder heads and the retaining bolts. Tighten the bolts in sequence, to 15–22 ft. lbs. (20–30 Nm).
- Thermostat, O-ring, thermostat housing and upper hose. Tighten the 2 retaining bolts to 15–22 ft. lbs. (20–30 Nm).
- Heater water hose and both HO$_2$S sensors
- Vacuum hose to the throttle body adapter vacuum port
- Accelerator cable bracket on the intake manifold
- Accelerator and cruise control cables to the throttle body

21. Apply silicone sealer to both places where the engine front cover meets the cylinder heads.

22. Install or connect the following:
- Cylinder head covers with new gasket on the cylinder heads. Tighten the bolts and stud bolts to 71–106 inch lbs. (8–12 Nm).

Timing belt service is covered in Section 4 of this manual

- Starter motor wiring harness to the right-hand cylinder head and tighten the retaining bolt
- Exhaust pipes to the exhaust manifolds. Tighten the 4 nuts to 20–30 ft. lbs. (27–41 Nm).

➡ **Be sure the exhaust system clears the No. 3 crossmember. Adjust as necessary.**

- EGR tube to the right-hand exhaust manifold and tighten the line nut to 26–33 ft. lbs. (35–45 Nm).
- Power steering control valve actuator and oil pressure sensor electrical connectors

23. Apply a small amount of silicone sealer in the rear of the keyway on the crankshaft pulley.

24. Install pulley on the crankshaft, making sure the crankshaft key and keyway are aligned.

25. Install the crankshaft pulley and tighten the bolt as follows:

   a. Step 1: Tighten to 66 ft. lbs. (90 Nm).

   b. Step 2: Loosen one complete turn.

   c. Step 3: Tighten to 35–39 ft. lbs. (47–53 Nm).

   d. Step 4: Tighten an additional 85–95 degrees.

26. Install or connect the following:

- Engine oil pan and a new gasket
- Power steering pump in position on the cylinder block
- 4 retaining bolts. Tighten the bolts to 15–22 ft. lbs. (20–30 Nm).
- Air conditioning compressor, CKP sensor and canister purge solenoid electrical connectors
- Engine/transmission harness connector on the power brake booster
- PCV valve in the right-hand cylinder head cover and connect the canister purge solenoid vent hose
- Positive battery cable harness on the right-hand cylinder head
- Bolt retaining the cable bracket to the cylinder head
- Positive battery cable at the power distribution box and battery
- Alternator and the 2 retaining bolts. Tighten the bolts to 15–22 ft. lbs. (20–30 Nm).
- 2 bolts retaining the alternator brace to the intake manifold. Tighten to 72–96 inch lbs. (8–12 Nm).
- Water pump pulley. Tighten the bolts to 15–22 ft. lbs. (20–30 Nm).
- Ignition coil brackets and ignition wire assemblies onto the mounting studs

- 7 nuts retaining the ignition coil brackets to the engine front cover and tighten to 15–22 ft. lbs. (20–30 Nm)
- 2 bolts retaining the ignition wire tray to the ignition coil bracket and tighten to 71–106 inch lbs. (8–12 Nm)
- Ignition coil and CMP sensor harness connectors
- Air conditioning pressure line on the right-hand ignition coil bracket and tighten the retaining bolt
- Ignition wires to the spark plugs and the bracket onto the cylinder head cover studs
- Accessory drive belt and the windshield wiper governor
- Fuel supply and return lines
- Cooling fan and shroud
- Engine air cleaner outlet tube
- Negative battery cable

27. Fill the cooling system.

28. If equipped with air suspension, turn the air suspension switch to the **ON** position.

29. Refill the engine with the correct amount of oil and replace the filter.

30. Start the engine and bring to normal operating temperature while checking for leaks.

31. Road test the vehicle and check for proper engine operation.

Rocker Arms

REMOVAL & INSTALLATION

1. Before servicing the vehicle, refer to the precautions in the beginning of this section.

2. Relieve the fuel system pressure.

3. Disconnect the negative battery cable.

4. Remove the right camshaft cover by removing or disconnecting the following:

- Positive battery cable at the battery and at the power distribution box
- Retaining bolt from the positive battery cable bracket located on the side of the right cylinder head
- Crankshaft Position (CKP) sensor, air conditioning compressor clutch and canister purge solenoid connectors. Position the harness aside.
- Vent hose from the purge solenoid and position the positive battery cable aside
- Ignition wires from the spark plugs
- Ignition wire brackets from the camshaft cover studs and position the wires aside
- PCV valve from the camshaft cover grommet and position aside
- Bolts and stud bolts and remove the camshaft cover.

5. Remove the left camshaft cover by removing or disconnecting the following:

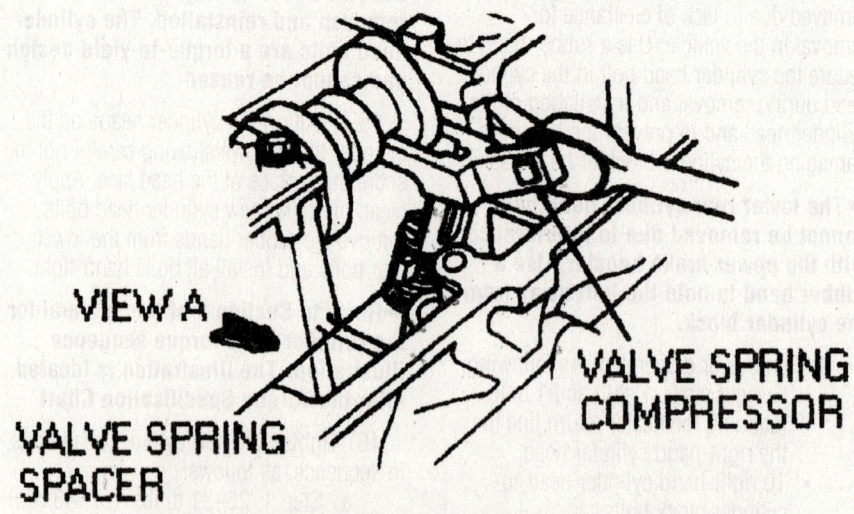

VIEW A

VALVE SPRING SPACER

VALVE SPRING COMPRESSOR

VALVE SPRING SPACER

After installing the spring spacer, compress the valve spring and remove the rocker arm

7922RG04

- Air inlet tube
- Fuel lines
- PSP switch and oil pressure sending unit and position the harness aside
- 42-pin engine harness connector from the retaining bracket on the brake vacuum booster and position aside
- Windshield wiper module
- Ignition wires from the spark plugs
- Ignition wire brackets from the studs and position the wires aside
- Camshaft cover

6. Position the piston of the cylinder being serviced at the bottom of its stroke and position the camshaft lobe on the base circle.

7. Install valve spring spacer tool T91P-6565-AH between the spring coils to prevent valve seal damage.

➡️**If the Valve Spring Spacer tool is not used, the retainer will hit the valve stem seal and damage the seal.**

8. Install a valve spring compressor under the camshaft and on top of the valve spring retainer.

9. Compress the valve spring and remove the roller follower. Remove the valve spring compressor and spacer.

To install:

10. Apply engine oil to the valve stem and tip and roller follower contact surfaces.

11. Install valve spring spacer tool T91P-6565-AH between the spring coils. Compress the valve spring, and install the roller follower.

➡️**The piston must be at the bottom of its stroke and the camshaft at the base circle.**

12. Remove the valve spring compressor and spacer.

13. Clean the sealing surfaces of the camshaft covers and cylinder heads. Apply silicone sealer to the places where the front cover meets the cylinder head.

14. Position new gaskets onto the camshaft covers and install the covers. Install the bolts and stud bolts and tighten to 72–106 inch lbs. (8–12 Nm).

15. When installing the right camshaft cover, install or connect the following:

- PCV into the camshaft cover grommet
- Ignition wire brackets on the studs
- Wires to the spark plugs
- Canister purge solenoid, air conditioning compressor clutch and CKP sensor

- Positive battery cable harness on the right cylinder head
- Bolt retaining the cable bracket to the cylinder head
- Positive battery cable at the power distribution box and the battery

16. When installing the left camshaft cover, install or connect the following:

- Ignition wire brackets on the studs
- Wires to the spark plugs
- Windshield wiper module
- 42-pin and transmission harness connectors
- Retaining bracket
- PSP switch and oil pressure sending unit harness.
- Fuel lines
- Negative battery cable

17. Start the engine and check for leaks.

Intake Manifold

REMOVAL & INSTALLATION

1. Before servicing the vehicle, refer to the precautions in the beginning of this section.

2. If equipped with air suspension, the air suspension switch, located on the right-hand side of the luggage compartment, must be turned to the **OFF** position before raising the vehicle.

3. Disconnect negative battery cable.

4. Drain the engine cooling system.

5. Properly relieve the fuel system pressure.

6. Remove or disconnect the following:

- Fuel supply and return lines
- Windshield wiper governor (module)
- Engine air cleaner outlet tube
- Accessory drive belt
- Ignition wires from the spark plugs
- Ignition wire brackets from the cylinder head cover studs
- Ignition coils and the Camshaft Position (CMP) sensor
- Ignition wires from both ignition coils
- 2 bolts retaining the ignition wire bracket to the ignition coil brackets
- Ignition wire assembly
- Alternator wiring harness from the junction block at the fender apron and alternator
- Bolts retaining the alternator brace to the intake manifold and the alternator to the cylinder block

- Alternator
- Oil pressure sensor and power steering control valve actuator wiring and position the wiring harness aside
- Exhaust Gas Recirculation (EGR) valve-to-exhaust manifold tube from the right-hand exhaust manifold
- Engine/transmission harness connector from the retaining bracket on the power brake booster
- Air conditioning compressor clutch, Crankshaft position (CKP) sensor and the canister purge solenoid wiring connectors
- Positive Crankcase Ventilation (PCV) valve from the cylinder head cover
- Canister purge vent hose from the PCV valve
- Accelerator and cruise control cables from the throttle body
- Accelerator cable bracket from the intake manifold and position aside
- Vacuum hose from the throttle body adapter port
- Heated Oxygen (HO$_2$S) sensor and the heater water hose
- 2 bolts retaining the thermostat housing to the intake manifold and position the upper hose and thermostat housing aside

➡️**The 2 thermostat housing bolts are also used to retain the intake manifold.**

- 9 bolts retaining the intake manifold to the cylinder heads
- Intake manifold and gaskets

7. If replacing the intake manifold, swap over the necessary parts.

To install:

8. Clean all gaskets mating surfaces.

9. Position new intake manifold gaskets on the cylinder heads. Be sure the alignment tabs on the gaskets are aligned with the holes in the cylinder heads.

➡️**Refer to Section 1 of this manual for the intake manifold torque sequence illustration. The illustration is located after the Torque Specification Chart.**

10. Install the intake manifold and the 9 retaining bolts. Hand-tighten the right-rear bolt (viewed from the front of the engine) before final tightening, then tighten the bolts, in sequence, to 15–22 ft. lbs. (20–30 Nm).

11. Inspect and if necessary, replace the O-ring seal on the thermostat housing.

Position the housing and upper hose and install the 2 retaining bolts. Tighten to 15–22 ft. lbs. (20–30 Nm).

12. Install or connect the following:
   - Heater water hose
   - HO2S sensor
   - Vacuum hose to the throttle body adapter vacuum port
   - Accelerator cable bracket on the intake manifold
   - Accelerator and cruise control cables to the throttle body
   - PCV valve in the cylinder head cover
   - Canister purge solenoid vent hose
   - Air conditioning compressor clutch, CKP sensor and canister purge solenoid wiring connectors
   - Engine/transmission harness connector the retaining bracket on the power brake booster
   - EGR valve-to-exhaust manifold tube to the right-hand exhaust manifold. Tighten the tube nut to 26–33 ft. lbs. (35–45 Nm).
   - Power steering control valve actuator
   - Oil pressure sensor wiring connectors
   - Alternator. Tighten the bolts to 15–22 ft. lbs. (20–30 Nm).
   - 2 bolts retaining the alternator brace to the intake manifold and tighten to 71–106 inch lbs. (8–12 Nm)
   - Alternator wiring harness to the alternator, right-hand fender apron and junction block
   - Ignition wire assembly on the engine
   - 2 bolts retaining the ignition wire bracket to the ignition coil brackets. Tighten the bolts to 71–106 inch lbs. (8–12 Nm).
   - Ignition wires to the ignition coils
   - Ignition wires to the spark plugs
   - Ignition wire brackets on the cylinder head cover studs
   - Wiring connectors to both ignition coils and the CMP sensor
   - Accessory drive belt
   - Air cleaner outlet tube
   - Windshield wiper governor
   - Fuel supply and return lines
   - Negative battery cable

13. Fill the engine cooling system.
14. If equipped with air suspension, turn the air suspension switch to the **ON** position.
15. Start the engine and check for leaks.
16. Road test the vehicle and check for proper operation.

Exhaust Manifold

REMOVAL & INSTALLATION

1. Before servicing the vehicle, refer to the precautions in the beginning of this section.
2. Drain the engine cooling system.
3. Relieve the fuel system pressure.
4. Discharge the air conditioning system
5. Remove or disconnect the following:
   - Battery cables
   - Engine air inlet tube
   - Cooling fan and shroud assembly
   - Fuel supply and return lines
   - Upper radiator hose
   - Windshield wiper governor and support bracket
   - Compressor outlet hose at the compressor and the hose assembly-to-right-hand ignition coil bracket bolt. Plug both openings.
   - Engine/transmission harness connector from the retaining bracket on the power brake booster
   - Heater hose
   - Ground strap-to-right-hand cylinder head nut
   - Upper stud and lower bolt retaining the heater hose to the right cylinder head and position aside
   - Heater blower motor switch resistor
   - Bolt retaining the right-hand front engine support insulator to the sub-frame
   - Both Heated Oxygen (HO2S) sensors
   - Engine support insulator through-bolts
   - Exhaust Gas Recirculation (EGR) valve-to-exhaust manifold tube nut from the right-hand exhaust manifold.
   - Catalytic converter pipes from both exhaust manifolds. Lower the exhaust system and hang it from the crossmember with wire.
   - Left-hand exhaust manifold
   - Front engine support insulator from the cylinder block and the 8 nuts retaining the exhaust manifold
   - Left-hand exhaust manifold and the 2 manifold gaskets

6. Position an adjustable jackstand and a block of wood under the engine oil pan, rearward of the oil drain hole. Raise the engine approximately 4 inches (100mm).
7. Install or connect the following:
   - 8 exhaust manifold retaining nuts and right-hand exhaust manifold
   - Manifold and gasket

To install:
8. If the exhaust manifolds are being replaced, transfer the heated O2 sensors and tighten to 27–33 ft. lbs. (37–45 Nm). On the right-hand exhaust manifold, transfer the EGR tube connector and tighten to 33–48 ft. lbs. (45–65 Nm).
9. Clean the mating surfaces of the exhaust manifolds and cylinder heads.
10. Install or connect the following:
   - Exhaust manifolds, using new gaskets. Tighten the bolts in sequence to 15–22 ft. lbs. (20–30 Nm).
   - EGR valve and tube assembly to the exhaust manifold. Tighten the line nut to 26–33 ft. lbs. (35–45 Nm).

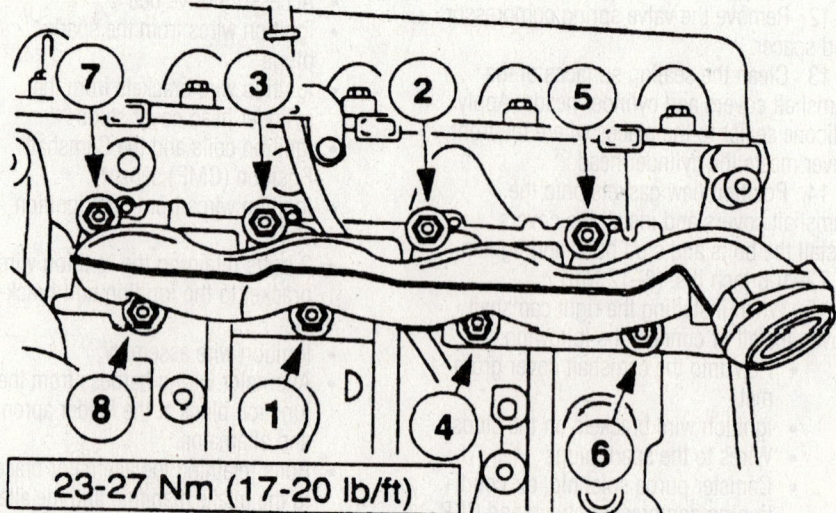

23-27 Nm (17-20 lb/ft)

To prevent warpage, be sure to tighten the exhaust manifold bolts according to the sequence shown—1997–01 models (left side)

7922RG08

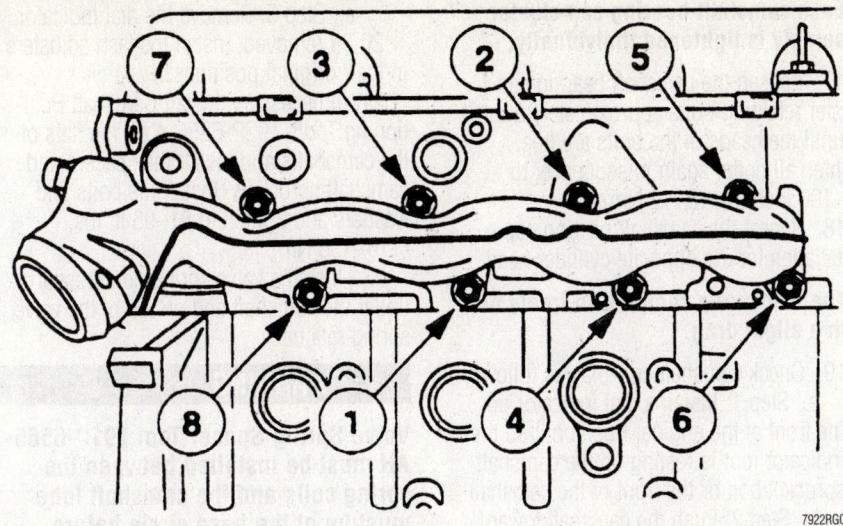

To prevent warpage, be sure to tighten the exhaust manifold bolts according to the sequence shown—1997–01 models (right side)

- Left-hand front engine support insulator to the cylinder block and tighten the bolts to 15–22 ft. lbs. (20–30 Nm)
11. Lower the engine onto the front engine support insulator and remove the jack.
12. Install or connect the following:
- Left-hand and right-hand engine support insulator through-bolts and tighten to 15–22 ft. lbs. (20–30 Nm).
- Catalytic converter pipes to both exhaust manifolds. Tighten he nuts to 20–30 ft. lbs. (27–41 Nm).

➡ **Be sure the exhaust system clears the No. 3 crossmember. Adjust as necessary.**

- Both HO2S sensors
- Bolt retaining the right-hand front engine support insulator to the sub-frame. Tighten to 15–22 ft. lbs. (20–30 Nm)
- Heater blower motor switch resistor using the 2 retaining screws
- Heater hose in position
- Upper stud and lower bolt and tighten to 15–22 ft. lbs. (20–30 Nm)
- Ground strap onto the stud and tighten the nut to 15–22 ft. lbs. (20–30 Nm)
- Heater hose
- Engine/transmission harness connector
- Retaining bracket on the power brake booster

- Air conditioning compressor outlet hose to the compressor
- Bolt retaining the hose assembly to the right-hand ignition coil bracket
- Upper radiator hose
- Fuel supply and return lines
- Windshield wiper governor and retaining bracket
- Engine cooling fan blade and fan shroud
- Engine air inlet tube
- Battery cables
13. Fill the cooling system.
14. Start the engine and check for leaks.
15. Properly evacuate and charge the air conditioning system.
16. Road test the vehicle and check for proper operation.

Camshaft and Valve Lifters

REMOVAL & INSTALLATION

1. Before servicing the vehicle, refer to the precautions in the beginning of this section.
2. If equipped with air suspension, the air suspension switch, must be turned to the **OFF** position before raising the vehicle.
3. Properly relieve the fuel system pressure.
4. Drain the engine oil
5. Remove or disconnect the following:
- Negative battery cable
- Fan blade and fan shroud assembly
- Fuel supply and return lines from the fuel injection supply manifold

- Windshield wiper governor (module) assembly from the vehicle
- Engine air cleaner outlet tube
- Accessory drive belt
- Ignition wires from the spark plugs
- Ignition wire brackets from the cylinder head cover studs
- 2 bolts retaining the ignition wire separator to the ignition coil brackets and the bolt retaining the air conditioning pressure line to the right-hand ignition coil bracket.
- Connectors from both ignition coils and the Crankshaft Position (CMP) sensor
- Ignition coils with brackets attached
- Electrical connector from the alternator and at the power distribution box
- Water pump pulley
- Positive battery cable at the power distribution box
- Bolt from the positive battery cable bracket located on the right-hand cylinder head
- Fuel vapor hose from the EVAP canister purge valve and position the positive battery cable aside
- Positive Crankcase Ventilation (PCV) valve from the cylinder head cover and position aside
- Engine/transmission harness connector from the bracket on the power brake booster
- Crankshaft Position (CKP) sensor and air conditioning clutch harness connectors
- Bolts retaining the power steering pump to the cylinder block and wire the pump aside

➡ **The front lower bolt on the power steering pump will not come all the way out.**

- Oil pan
- Crankshaft pulley bolt and washer and crankshaft pulley
- Engine oil filter
- Power steering control valve actuator and oil pressure sensor
- Oil filter adapter
- Cylinder head covers
- Engine front cover
- Timing chains
6. Rotate the crankshaft counterclockwise no more than 45 degrees from Top Dead Center (TDC) to ensure that all pistons are below the top of the engine block deck face.

Refer to Section 1 for engine rebuilding specifications

❊❊ WARNING

The crankshaft must be in this position prior to rotating the camshafts or damage to the pistons and/or valve train will result.

7. Install a valve spring compressor under the camshaft and on top of one of the valve spring retainers.

❊❊ WARNING

Valve Spring Spacer Tool T91P-6565-AH must be installed between the spring coils and the camshaft lobe must be at the base circle before compressing the valve spring for each valve to prevent damage.

8. Install Valve Spring Spacer T91P-6565-AH between the valve spring coils. Be sure that the valve being compressed is on its base circle. Compress the valve spring and remove the rocker arm. Repeat the procedure until all rocker arms are removed.

9. If required, pull the lash adjusters out of their bores in the cylinder head. Note their locations, they must be installed in the same bore they were removed from.

➡ **Do not mix the camshaft bearing caps. Note the camshaft bearing cap locations for installation.**

10. To remove each camshaft, unfasten the 14 bolts retaining the camshaft bearing caps (cluster assemblies) to the cylinder head. Tap upward on the camshaft bearing caps at points near the upper bearing halves and gradually lift the camshaft bearing cap clusters from the cylinder head.

11. Repeat the removal procedure for the opposite cylinder head.

12. Remove the camshaft straight upward to avoid bearing damage.

13. Clean and inspect the camshafts and related components for unusual wear or damage.

To install:

14. Clean and inspect the cylinder head covers, engine front cover and cylinder head sealing surfaces.

15. Apply clean engine oil to the camshaft journals and lobes. Position the camshafts on the cylinder heads.

16. Install and seat the camshaft bearing cap cluster assemblies. Install and hand start the retaining bolts. Tighten the camshaft cluster retaining bolts in sequence to 71–106 inch lbs. (8–12 Nm). Be sure to tighten each camshaft bearing cap cluster individually.

➡ **Each camshaft bearing cap cluster assembly is tightened individually.**

17. Loosen the camshaft bearing cap cluster retaining bolts approximately 2 turns or until the heads of the bolts are free. Tighten all bolts, again in sequence, to 71–106 inch lbs. (8–12 Nm).

18. Repeat the camshaft bearing cap installation for the opposite cylinder head.

➡ **The camshafts should turn freely but with a slight drag.**

19. Check camshaft end-play as follows:
   a. Step 1: Install a dial indicator on the front of the engine. Position it so the indicator foot is resting on the camshaft sprocket bolt or the front of the camshaft.
   b. Step 2: Push the camshaft toward the rear of the engine and zero the dial indicator.
   c. Step 3: Pull the camshaft forward and release it. Specified end-play is 0.0901–0.006 inch (0.025–0.190mm).
   d. Step 4: If end-play is too tight, check for binding or foreign material in the camshaft thrust bearing. If end-play is excessive, check for worn camshaft thrust plate and replace the cylinder head, as required.
   e. Step 5: Remove the dial indicator.

20. If removed, install the lash adjusters in their original positions.

21. If necessary, install Camshaft Positioning Tools T92P-6256-A on the flats of the camshafts and install the spacers and camshaft sprockets. Install the bolts and washers and tighten to 81–95 ft. lbs. (110–130 Nm).

22. Install a valve spring compressor under the camshaft and on top of the valve spring retainer.

❊❊ WARNING

Valve Spring Spacer Tool T91P-6565-AH must be installed between the spring coils and the camshaft lobe must be at the base circle before compressing the valve spring for each valve to prevent damage.

23. Install Valve Spring Spacer T91P-6565-AH between the valve spring coils. Be sure that the valve being compressed is on its base circle. Compress the valve spring and install the rocker arm. Repeat the procedure until all rocker arms are installed.

24. Rotate the crankshaft clockwise 45

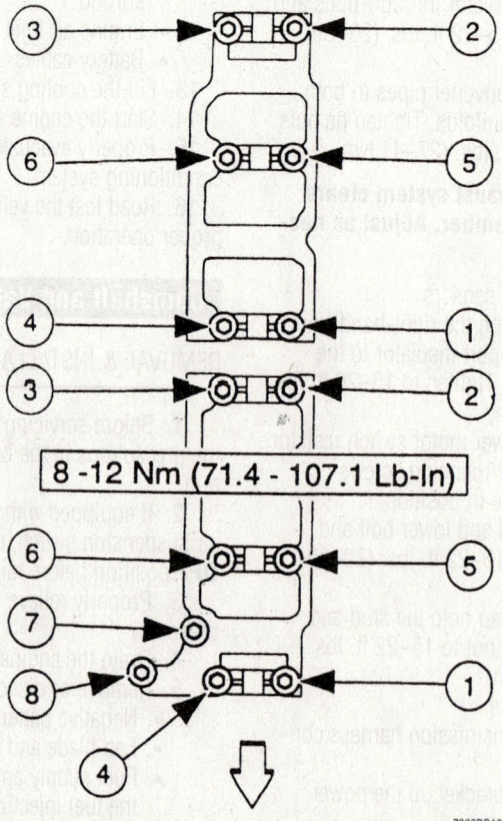

8 - 12 Nm (71.4 - 107.1 Lb-In)

7922RG10

Tighten the camshaft bearing cap cluster bolts in the sequence to avoid damage to the camshaft or bearings

degrees to position the crankshaft at Top Dead Center (TDC).

➡ **The crankshaft must only be rotated in the clockwise direction and only as far as TDC.**

25. Install or connect the following:
- Timing chains
- Engine front cover
- Cylinder head covers. Tighten the cylinder head cover bolts to 71–106 inch lbs. (8–12 Nm).
- Power steering control valve actuator connector
- Oil pressure sensor harness connector

26. Apply silicone sealer to the crankshaft keyway

27. Install the crankshaft pulley and tighten the bolt as follows:
   a. Step 1: Tighten to 66 ft. lbs. (90 Nm).
   b. Step 2: Loosen one complete turn.
   c. Step 3: Tighten to 35–39 ft. lbs. (47–53 Nm).
   d. Step 4: Tighten an additional 85–95 degrees.

28. Install or connect the following:
- Engine oil pan
- Power steering pump on the engine and the 4 retaining bolts. Tighten the bolts to 15–22 ft. lbs. (20–30 Nm).
- Air conditioning clutch and CKP sensor
- Evaporative emission canister purge valve harness connector
- Engine/transmission harness connectors on the power brake booster retaining bracket
- PCV valve to the right-hand cylinder head cover
- Positive battery cable harness on the right-hand cylinder head
- Bolt retaining the battery cable bracket to the cylinder head
- Evaporative emission hose to the canister purge valve
- Positive battery cable at the power distribution box
- Water pump pulley and tighten the bolts to 15–22 ft. lbs. (20–30 Nm)
- Ignition coil brackets and ignition wires to the engine front cover. Tighten the retaining nuts to 15–22 ft. lbs. (20–30 Nm).
- Harness connectors to the ignition coils and the CMP sensor
- Air conditioning pressure line on

the right-hand ignition coil bracket and the retaining bolt
- Ignition wires to the spark plugs and the brackets onto the cylinder head cover studs
- Accessory drive belt
- Windshield wiper governor
- Fuel supply and return lines
- Fan and shroud assembly
- Negative battery cable

29. Fill the engine cooling system.

30. Fill the crankcase.

31. If equipped with air suspension, turn the air suspension switch to the **ON** position.

32. Start the engine and check for leaks.

33. Road test the vehicle and check for proper engine operation.

Valve Lash

ADJUSTMENT

The valve lash is not adjustable. If the collapsed lash adjuster clearance is incorrect, check the camshaft, roller follower and valve for wear or damage.

1. Before servicing the vehicle, refer to the precautions in the beginning of this section.

2. Disconnect the negative battery cable.

3. Remove the camshaft covers.

4. Rotate the crankshaft until the camshaft base circle is contacting the roller follower.

5. Use a suitable tool to bleed down the lash adjuster. Slowly compress the lash adjuster until the plunger is bottomed.

6. Use a feeler gauge to check the clearance between the camshaft and the roller follower. The clearance should be 0.018–0.033 inch (0.45–0.85mm).

Starter Motor

REMOVAL & INSTALLATION

1. Before servicing the vehicle, refer to the precautions in the beginning of this section.

2. Remove or disconnect the following:
- Negative battery cable
- Red solenoid safety cap
- Wires from solenoid
- 2 upper bolts
- 1 lower bolt and starter

To install:

3. Install or connect the following:
- Starter and lower mounting bolt
- 2 upper mounting bolts. Tighten all 3 bolts to 15–20 ft. lbs. (20–27 Nm).
- Wires from solenoid and tighten the nut to 40–50 inch lbs.
- Red solenoid safety cap
- Negative battery cable

Oil Pan

REMOVAL & INSTALLATION

1. Before servicing the vehicle, refer to the precautions in the beginning of this section.

2. Drain the engine cooling system

3. Properly discharge the air conditioning system.

4. Relieve the fuel system pressure.

5. Remove or disconnect the following:
- Negative battery cable
- Engine air cleaner outlet tube
- Fuel supply and return lines at the fuel injection supply manifold
- Cooling fan and fan shroud
- Upper radiator hose
- Wiper governor and support bracket

➡ **Plug the compressor outlet hose at the compressor**

- Bolt retaining the hose assembly to the right-hand ignition coil bracket. Cap the compressor outlet.
- Engine/transmission electrical harness connector from the retaining bracket on the power brake booster
- Heater water hose
- Nut retaining the ground strap to the right-hand cylinder head
- Upper stud and loosen the lower bolt retaining the heater outlet hose to the right-hand cylinder head and position aside
- Heater blower motor switch resistor

6. Drain the engine oil and reinstall the oil pan drain plug with a new gasket. Tighten the plug to 10–12 ft. lbs. (13–16 Nm).

7. Remove or disconnect the following:
- Bolt retaining the right-hand engine support insulator to the lower front sub-frame

- Bolts retaining the left-hand and right-hand front engine support insulators to the engine mount supports
- Catalytic converter pipes from both exhaust manifolds. Lower the exhaust system and support it with wire from the transmission cross-member.

8. Position a jack and a block of wood under the oil pan, rearward of the oil drain hole. Raise the engine approximately 4 inches (100mm) and insert 2 wood blocks approximately 2½–2¾ inch (60–70mm) thick under each front engine support insulator. Lower the engine onto the wood blocks and remove the jack.

9. Remove the oil pan.

➡**It may be necessary to loosen, but not remove, the 2 nuts on the transmission support insulator and with a jack, raise the transmission extension housing slightly to allow enough clearance to remove the engine oil pan.**

10. If necessary, remove the 2 bolts retaining the oil pick-up tube to the oil pump and remove the bolt retaining the pick-up tube to the main bearing stud spacer. Remove the pick-up tube.

To install:

11. Clean the engine oil pan and inspect for damage. Clean the sealing surfaces of the front cover and cylinder block. Clean and inspect the oil pick-up tube and replace the O-ring.

12. If removed, position the oil pick-up tube on the oil pump and hand start the 2 retaining bolts. Install the bolt retaining the pick-up tube on the main bearing stud spacer, hand tight.

13. Tighten the pick-up tube-to-oil pump bolts to 72–108 inch lbs. (8–12 Nm), then tighten the pick-up tube-to-main bearing stud spacer bolt to 15–22 ft. lbs. (20–30 Nm).

14. Position a new gasket on the oil pan. Apply silicone sealer to where the front cover meets the cylinder block and the crankshaft rear oil seal and retainer meets the cylinder block. Position the oil pan to the engine and install the retaining bolts. Tighten the bolts in sequence, to 14 ft. lbs. (20 Nm), then rotate the oil pan retaining bolts, in sequence an additional 60 degrees within 4 minutes of applying the silicone sealer.

15. Position the jack and wood block under the engine oil pan, rearward of the oil drain hole, and raise the engine enough to

remove the wood blocks. Lower the engine and remove the jack.

16. Install or connect the following:
- Left-hand and right-hand engine support insulator through-bolts and tighten to 15–22 ft. lbs. (20–30 Nm)
- Bolt retaining the right-hand engine support insulator to the lower front sub-frame. Tighten the bolt to 15–22 ft. lbs. (20–30 Nm).
- Exhaust system to the exhaust manifolds and tighten the 4 retaining nuts to 20–30 ft. lbs. (27–41 Nm). Be sure the exhaust system clears the crossmember. Adjust as necessary.
- New engine oil filter
- Heater blower motor switch resistor using the 2 retaining screws
- Heater water hose
- Upper stud and tighten the upper and lower bolts to 15–22 ft. lbs. (20–30 Nm)
- Ground strap on the stud and tighten to 15–22 ft. lbs. (20–30 Nm)
- Heater water hose
- Throttle valve cable, if equipped
- Engine/transmission electrical harness connector
- Harness connector on the power brake booster bracket
- Air conditioning compressor outlet hose to the compressor
- Bolt retaining the hose to the right-hand ignition coil bracket
- Upper radiator hose
- Fuel supply and return lines
- Wiper governor and retaining bracket
- Engine cooling fan and fan shroud
- Engine air cleaner outlet tube
- Negative battery cable

17. Fill the cooling system.

18. Fill the engine crankcase with engine oil.

19. Start the engine and check for leaks.

20. Properly evacuate and recharge the air conditioning system.

21. Road test the vehicle and check for proper engine operation.

Oil Pump

REMOVAL & INSTALLATION

1. Before servicing the vehicle, refer to the precautions in the beginning of this section.

To prevent oil leaks, tighten the oil pan bolts in the sequence shown

7922RG11

2. Remove or disconnect the following:

- Negative battery cable
- Cylinder head covers
- Engine front cover
- Engine oil pan
- Timing chains
- 2 bolts retaining the oil pick-up tube to the oil pump and the bolt attaching the oil pick-up tube to the main bearing stud spacer
- Pick-up tube
- 4 bolts retaining the oil pump to the cylinder block
- Oil pump

To install:

3. Rotate the inner rotor of the oil pump to align with the flats on the crankshaft and install the oil pump flush with the cylinder block. Install the 4 retaining bolts and tighten to 72–106 inch lbs. (8–12 Nm).

4. Clean the oil pick-up tube and replace the O-ring.

5. Place the pick-up tube on the oil pump and hand start the 2 retaining bolts. Install the bolt retaining the pick-up tube to the main bearing stud spacer hand tight. Tighten the pick-up tube-to-oil pump bolts

to 72–106 inch lbs. (8–12 Nm). Tighten the pick-up tube to main bearing stud spacer bolt to 15–22 ft. lbs. (20–30 Nm).

6. Install or connect the following:
- New engine oil filter
- Timing chains
- Engine oil pan
- Engine front cover
- Cylinder head covers
- Negative battery cable
7. Fill the crankcase.
8. Start the engine and check for leaks and proper engine oil pressure.
9. Road test the vehicle and check for proper engine operation.

Rear Main Seal

REMOVAL & INSTALLATION

➡ **Special tools are available for installing rear main oil seals. In most cases, the seals can be installed using a common seal and bearing driver set.**

1. Before servicing the vehicle, refer to the precautions in the beginning of this section.

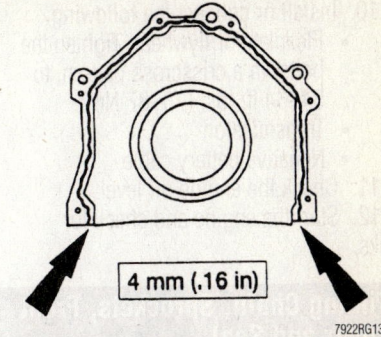

4 mm (.16 in)

7922RG13

Apply a continuos bead of silicone sealant to the back of the seal retainer before installing it on the engine

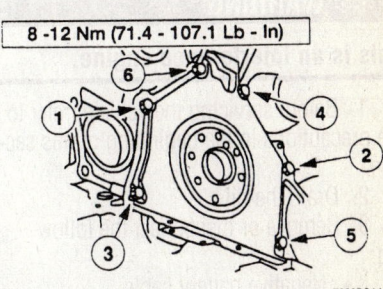

8 -12 Nm (71.4 - 107.1 Lb - In)

7922RG14

To avoid leakage, be sure to tighten the crankshaft rear oil seal retainer bolts in the correct sequence

2. Remove or disconnect the following:
- Transmission
- Flexplate or flywheel

3. With a sharp awl, carefully punch a small hole in the metal portion of the seal.

4. Remove the seal using a slide hammer with a sheet metal screw attached.

➡ **If the oil leak is coming from around the seal retainer, the retainer must also be removed and resealed.**

To install:

5. If the seal retainer was removed, carefully clean the sealant from the retainer and engine block using a plastic scraper. Remove any oil or grease residue from the sealing surfaces with a solvent.

6. Apply silicone sealant to the back of the retainer and immediately install it on the engine block. Tighten the bolts in sequence to 71–107 inch lbs. (8–12 Nm).

7. Lubricate the seal and the crankshaft with clean engine oil.

8. Install the seal with the spring side toward the engine.

9. Remove the installation tool.

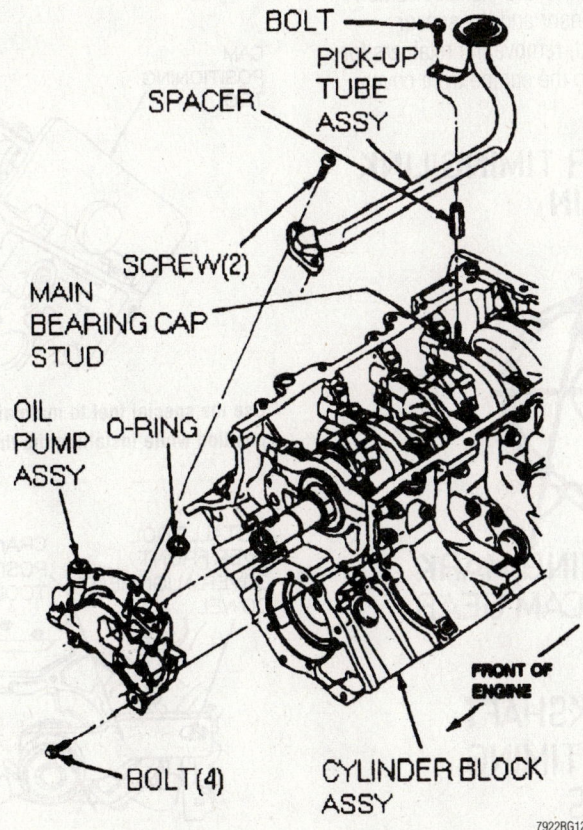

BOLT
PICK-UP TUBE ASSY
SPACER
SCREW(2)
MAIN BEARING CAP STUD
OIL PUMP ASSY
O-RING
BOLT(4)
CYLINDER BLOCK ASSY
FRONT OF ENGINE

7922RG12

The oil pump is mounted on the crankshaft at the front of the engine

For complete mechanical specifications, refer to Section 1 of this manual

10. Install or connect the following:
 • Flexplate or flywheel. Tighten the bolts, in a crisscross pattern, to 54–64 ft. lbs. (73–87 Nm).
 • Transmission
 • Negative battery cable
11. Check the engine oil level.
12. Start the engine and check for leaks.

Timing Chain, Sprockets, Front Cover and Seal

REMOVAL & INSTALLATION

✳✳ WARNING

This is an interference engine.

1. Before servicing the vehicle, refer to the precautions in the beginning of this section.
2. Drain the oil
3. Remove or disconnect the following:
 • Negative battery cable
 • Cooling fan and shroud

➡**Loosen water pump pulley bolts.**

 • Accessory drive belt
 • Water pump pulley
 • Bolts attaching the power steering pump to the cylinder block and

engine front cover. The lower front bolt on the power steering pump will not come all the way out. Wire the power steering pump aside.
 • Oil pan
 • Crankshaft pulley retaining bolt and washer
 • Crankshaft pulley
 • Bolt retaining the air conditioning pressure line to the right-hand ignition coil bracket
 • Cylinder head covers
 • Wiring at both ignition coils and the Crankshaft Position (CMP) sensor
 • 3 bolts retaining the right-hand ignition coil bracket to the engine front cover. Position the power steering hose aside.
 • 3 nuts retaining the left-hand ignition coil bracket to the engine front cover. Slide both ignition coil brackets and ignition wires off the mounting studs and lay the assembly on top of the engine.
 • Bolts retaining the drive belt idler pulley and the pulley
 • Wiring to the Crankshaft Position (CKP) sensor and the sensor
4. If equipped, remove the retainers for the oil cooler from the engine front cover

retaining stud bolts and position the oil cooler aside.
5. Remove or disconnect the following:
 • 9 stud bolts and the 6 standard engine front cover bolts and the cover
 • Crankshaft oil seal from the cover using a seal driver
 • CKP sensor pulse wheel
6. Rotate the engine to set the piston for No. 1 to Top Dead Center (TDC) on its compression stroke.

➡**Camshaft Positioning Adapters T92P-6256-A must be installed on the camshafts to prevent the camshafts from rotating.**

7. Install Camshaft Positioning Adapters T92P-6256-A on the flats of both camshafts. This will prevent accidental rotation of the camshafts.
8. Remove or disconnect the following:
 • 2 bolts retaining the tensioner to the right-hand cylinder head and the tensioner
 • Right-hand timing chain tensioner arm
 • 2 bolts retaining the right-hand timing chain guide to the cylinder

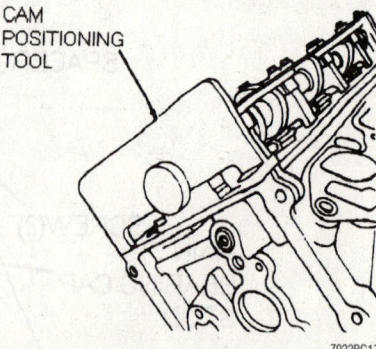

Use the special tool to maintain camshaft position while installing the timing chains

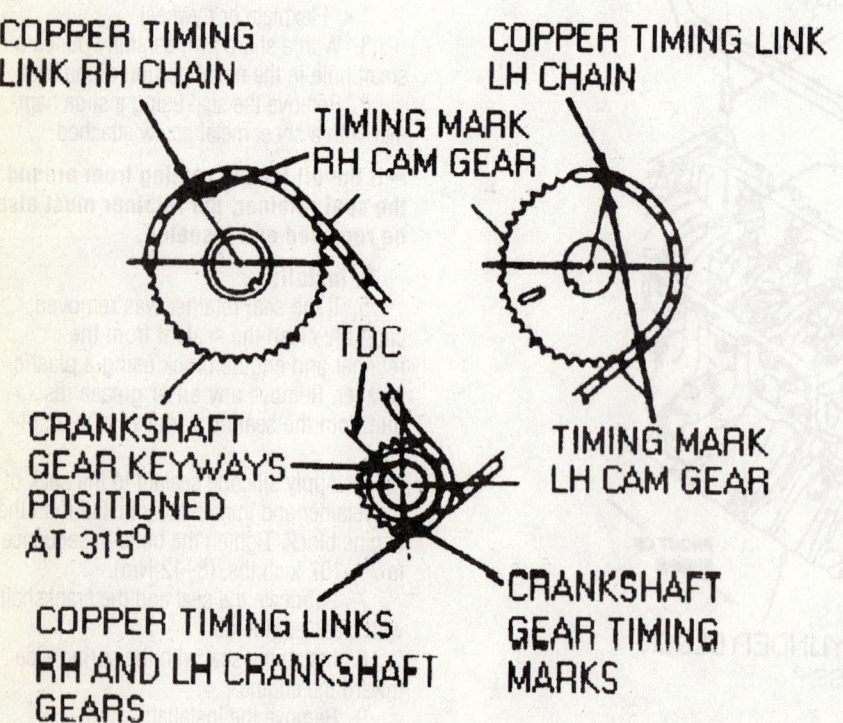

Be sure that the timing marks are aligned when the No. 1 piston is at TDC on compression

Install the crankshaft positioning tool to be sure the crankshaft does not turn while installing the timing chains

head and remove the timing chain guide.

- Right-hand timing chain from the camshaft and crankshaft sprockets
- Right-hand camshaft sprocket retaining bolt, washer, sprocket and spacer, if necessary
- 2 bolts retaining the timing chain tensioner to the left-hand cylinder head
- Timing chain tensioner
- Left-hand timing chain tensioner arm
- 2 bolts retaining the timing chain guide to the left-hand cylinder head
- Timing chain guide
- Left-hand timing chain from the camshaft and crankshaft sprockets
- Left-hand camshaft sprocket retaining bolt, washer, sprocket and spacer, if necessary

9. If necessary, note the position of the crankshaft sprockets and remove the crankshaft sprockets by sliding them off the front of the crankshaft.

10. Inspect the plastic running face on the tensioner arms and chain guides. If worn or damaged, inspect the engine oil pan for contamination and thoroughly clean the oil pan. Replace the oil pick-up tube.

To install:

11. Examine the timing chains, looking for the copper links. If the copper links are

not visible, lay the chain on a flat surface and pull the chain taught until the opposite sides of the chain contact one another. Mark the links at each end of the chain and use these marks in place of the copper links.

➡ **If the engine jumped time, damage has been done to valves and possibly pistons and/or connecting rods. Any damage must be corrected before installing the timing chains.**

12. Be sure Camshaft Positioning Adapters T92P-6256-A are installed on the flats of the camshafts to prevent them from rotating.

13. Install or connect the following:

- Left-hand and right-hand timing chain guides and retaining bolts. Tighten the retaining bolts to 71–106 inch lbs. (8–12 Nm).
- Left-hand and right-hand camshaft spacers and sprockets, (if removed) on the camshafts, the washers and retaining bolts but do not tighten at this time.
- Left-hand crankshaft sprocket with the tapered part of the sprocket facing away from the engine block

➡ **The crankshaft sprockets are identical. They may only be installed one way, with the tapered part of the sprockets facing each other. Ensure that the keyway and timing marks on the crankshaft sprockets are aligned.**

- Left-hand timing chain on the camshaft and crankshaft sprockets.

Be sure the copper links of the timing chain line up with the timing marks on both sprockets.

- Right-hand crankshaft sprocket with the tapered part of the sprocket facing the left-hand crankshaft sprocket, if removed
- Right-hand timing chain on the camshaft and crankshaft sprockets. Be sure the copper links of the timing chain line up with the timing marks on both sprockets.

14. It is necessary to bleed the timing chain tensioners before installation. Proceed as follows:

a. Step 1: position the timing chain tensioner in a soft-jawed vise.

b. Step 2: using a small pick or similar tool, hold the ratchet lock mechanism away from the ratchet stem and slowly compress the tensioner plunger by rotating the vise handle.

※※ WARNING

The tensioner must be compressed slowly or damage to the internal seals will result.

c. Step 3: once the tensioner plunger bottoms in the tensioner bore, continue

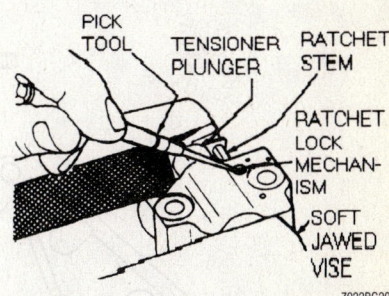

Slowly compress the timing chain tensioner while holding the ratchet lock away from the stem with a suitable tool

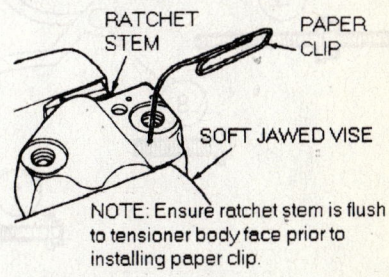

Install a paper clip or wire into the tensioner to hold the plunger in during assembly

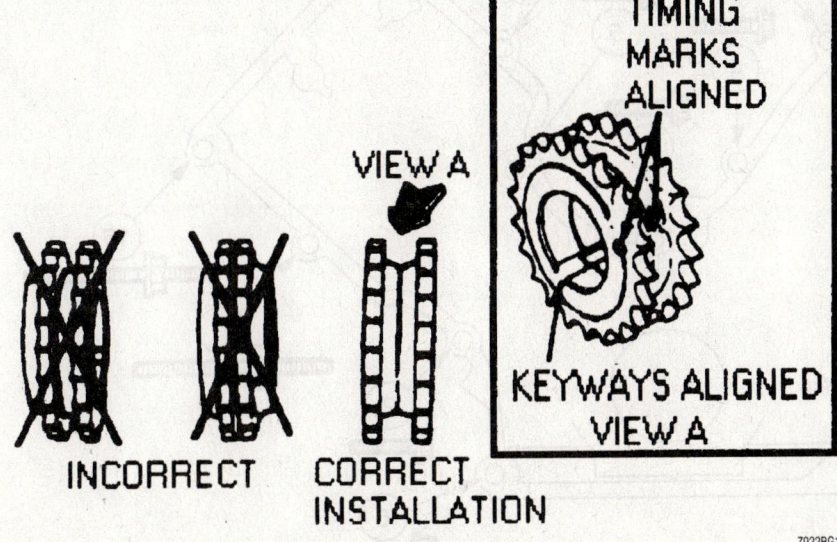

Install the crankshaft sprockets with the tapered sides facing each other

to hold the ratchet lock mechanism and push down on the ratchet stem until flush with the tensioner face.

d. Step 4: while holding the ratchet stem flush with the tensioner face, release the ratchet lock mechanism and install a paper clip or similar tool in the tensioner body to lock the tensioner in the collapsed position.

e. Step 5: the paper clip must not be removed until the timing chain, tensioner, tensioner arm and timing chain guide are completely installed on the engine.

15. Install the right-hand and left-hand timing chain tensioners and 2 bolts on each. Tighten the bolts to 15–22 ft. lbs. (20–30 Nm).

16. Crankshaft Positioning Tool T93P-6265-A over the crankshaft and the engine front cover alignment dowel to position the crankshaft.

17. Lubricate the timing chain tensioner arm contact surfaces with clean engine oil and install the right-hand and left-hand tensioner arms on their dowel pins.

18. Position a C-clamp around the timing chain tensioner arm and timing chain guide to remove all slack from the timing chain. Use care not to bend the timing chain guide.

19. Remove the locking pins or paper clips from the timing chain tensioners and be sure that all timing marks are aligned.

20. Using Camshaft Positioning Adapters T92P-6265-A to align and hold the camshafts, tighten the camshaft sprocket retaining bolts to 81–95 ft. lbs. (110–130 Nm).

21. Position a dial indicator in the No. 1 cylinder spark plug hole to measure intake valve lift. The intake valve should be at maximum lift when the crankshaft is at 114 degrees after TDC. If the intake valve lift is not at maximum lift, loosen the camshaft sprocket bolt and repeat the steps detailing the installation of the timing chain tensioners to the tightening of the camshaft sprockets.

22. Remove the camshaft and crankshaft positioning tools.

23. Install a new crankshaft seal in the front cover. Apply engine oil to the lip of the seal.

24. Thoroughly clean the sealing surfaces of the front cover, cylinder block and oil pan. Apply silicone sealer to the points where the cylinder head meets the cylinder block.

25. Install or connect the following:
• Front cover in position using new gaskets

• Retaining bolts and studs in their proper locations. Tighten in sequence to 15–22 ft. lbs. (20–30 Nm) within 4 minutes of applying the silicone sealer.
• Oil cooler to the front cover retaining stud bolts, if equipped
• CKP sensor and attach the harness connector
• Drive belt idler pulley
• Ignition coil brackets and ignition wires as an assembly onto the mounting studs
• Power steering hose and the nuts retaining the coil brackets to the front cover. Tighten the nuts to 15–22 ft. lbs. (20–30 Nm).
• Wiring to both ignition coils and the CMP sensor
• Cylinder head covers
• Air conditioning pressure line on the right-hand ignition coil bracket and tighten the retaining bolt

26. Apply a small amount of silicone sealer in the rear of the keyway in the crankshaft pulley.

27. Install or connect the following:
• Pulley on the crankshaft
• Crankshaft pulley bolt and washer

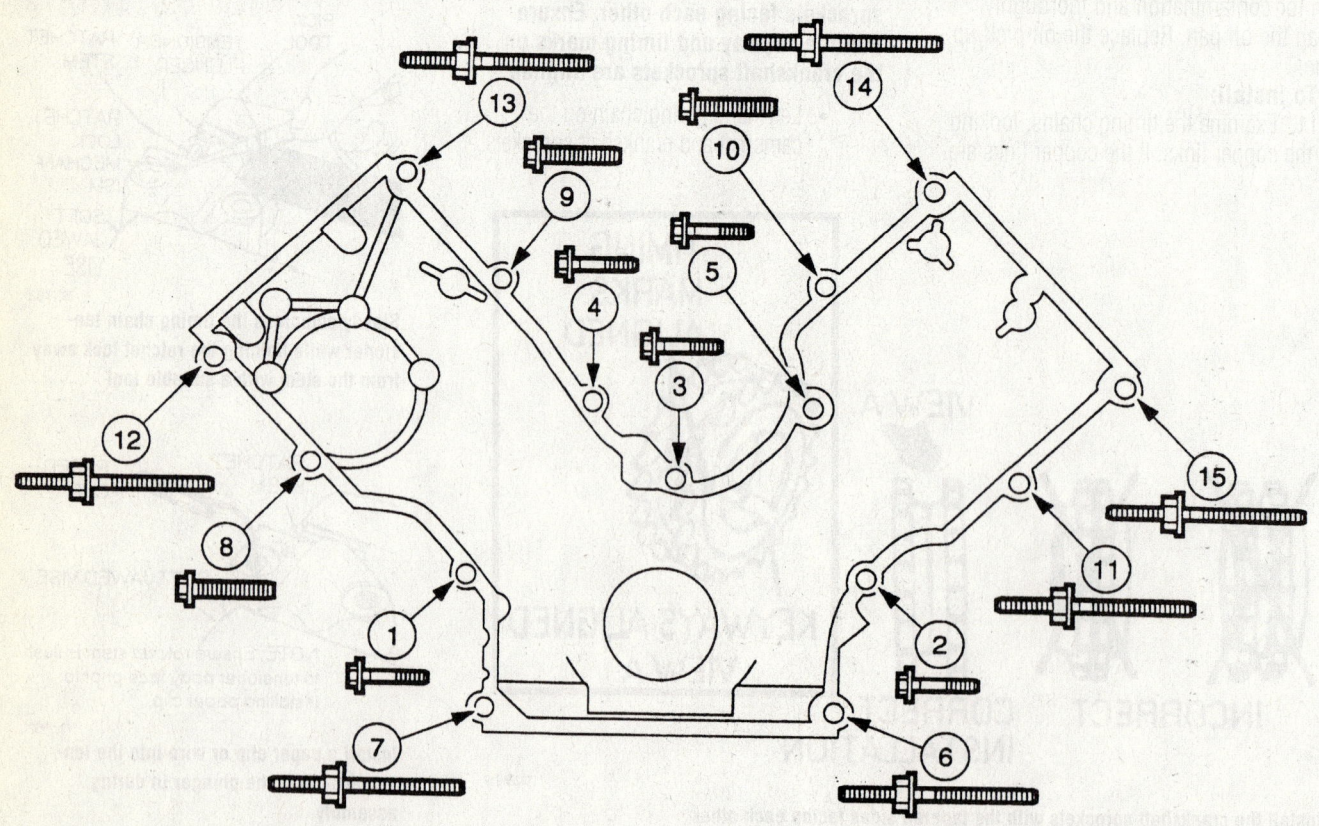

Timing chain front cover bolt tightening sequence

7922RG15

and tighten to 114–121 ft. lbs. (155–165 Nm)

- Oil pan
- Power steering pump on the engine. Tighten the bolts to 15–22 ft. lbs. (20–30 Nm).
- Water pump pulley. Tighten the bolts to 15–22 ft. lbs. (20–30 Nm).
- Accessory drive belt
- Engine cooling fan and shroud
- Negative battery cable

28. Fill the engine.

29. Start the engine and check for leaks.

30. Road test the vehicle and check for proper engine operation.

Piston and Ring

POSITIONING

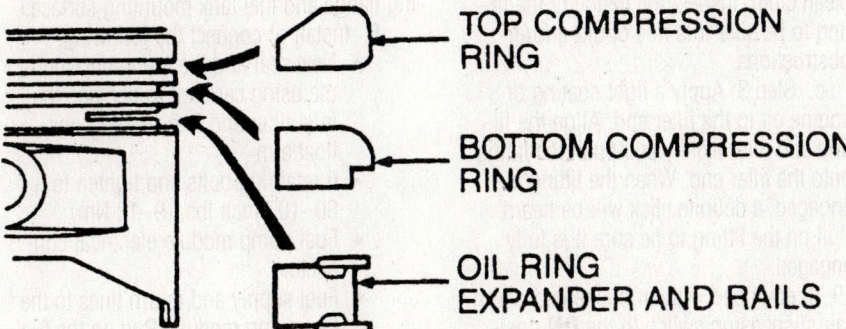

Ford 4.6L (VIN W and X) engines—piston ring positioning

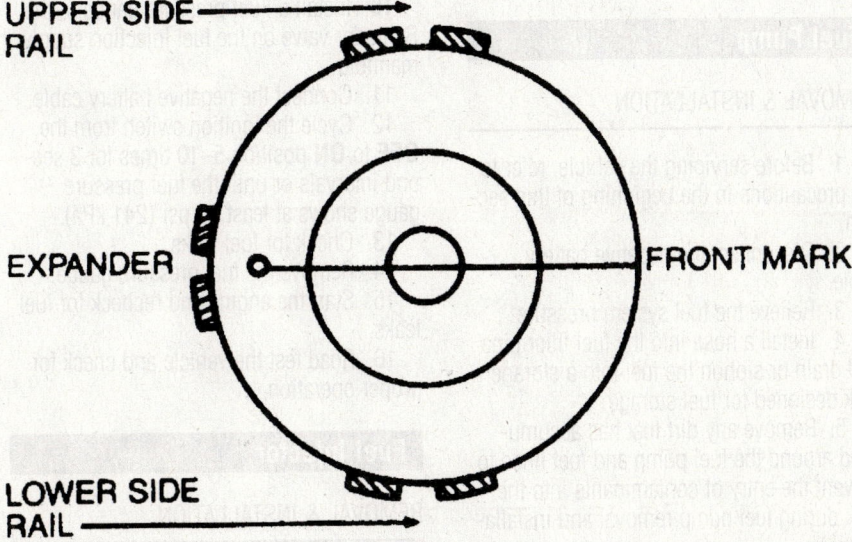

Ford 4.6L (VIN W and X) engines—piston ring end-gap spacing and piston positioning

FUEL SYSTEM

Fuel System Service Precautions

Safety is the most important factor when performing not only fuel system maintenance but any type of maintenance. Failure to conduct maintenance and repairs in a safe manner may result in serious personal injury or death. Maintenance and testing of the vehicle's fuel system components can be accomplished safely and effectively by adhering to the following rules and guidelines.

- To avoid the possibility of fire and personal injury, always disconnect the negative battery cable unless the repair or test procedure requires that battery voltage be applied.
- Always relieve the fuel system pressure prior to disconnecting any fuel system component (injector, fuel rail, pressure regulator, etc.), fitting or fuel line connection. Exercise extreme caution whenever relieving fuel system pressure, to avoid exposing skin, face and eyes to fuel spray. Please be advised that fuel under pressure may penetrate the skin or any part of the body that it contacts.
- Always place a shop towel or cloth around the fitting or connection prior to loosening to absorb any excess fuel due to spillage. Ensure that all fuel spillage (should it occur) is quickly removed from engine surfaces. Ensure that all fuel soaked cloths or towels are deposited into a waste container.
- Always keep a dry chemical (Class B) fire extinguisher near the work area.
- Do not allow fuel spray or fuel vapors to come into contact with a spark or open flame.
- Always use a back-up wrench when loosening and tightening fuel line connection fittings. This will prevent unnecessary stress and torsion to fuel line piping. Always follow the proper torque specifications.
- Always replace worn fuel fitting O-rings with new. Do not substitute fuel hose or equivalent, where fuel pipe is installed.

Fuel System Pressure

RELIEVING

Fuel supply lines on all fuel injected engines will remain pressurized for some period of time after the engine is shut **OFF**. This pressure must be relieved before servicing the fuel system. Pressure is relieved through the fuel pressure relief valve, located on the fuel rail.

To relieve the fuel system pressure, first remove the fuel tank cap to relieve pressure in the tank, then remove the cap on the fuel pressure relief valve. Attach a fuel pressure gauge and drain the system through the drain tube into a container. Remove the fuel pressure gauge and replace the cap on the relief valve.

Fuel Filter

REMOVAL & INSTALLATION

1. Before servicing the vehicle, refer to the precautions in the beginning of this section.

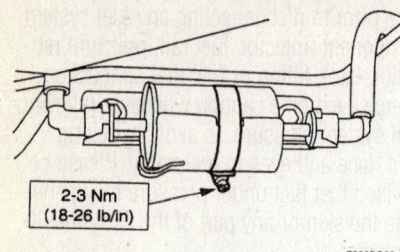

2-3 Nm
(18-26 lb/in)

7922RG22

The fuel filter is located near the center of the vehicle on the frame rail

2. Disconnect the negative battery cable.

3. Relieve the fuel system pressure.

4. If equipped with air suspension, turn the air suspension switch to the **OFF** position.

5. Remove the hairpin clip push connect fittings from both ends of the fuel filter as follows:

a. Step 1: Inspect the visible internal portion of the fitting for dirt accumulation. If more than a light coating of dust is present, clean the fitting before disassembly.

b. Step 2: Some adhesion between the seals in the fitting and the filter will occur with time. To separate, twist the fitting on the filter, then push and pull the fitting until it moves freely on the filter.

c. Step 3: Remove the hairpin clip from the fitting by first bending and breaking the shipping tab. Next, spread the 2 clip legs by hand about ⅛ inch each, to disengage the body and push the legs into the fitting. Lightly pull the triangular end of the clip and work it clear of the filter and fitting.

➡**Do not use hand tools to complete this operation.**

d. Step 4: Grasp the fitting and pull in an axial direction to remove the fitting from the filter. Be careful on 90 degree elbow connectors, as excessive side loading could break the connector body.

e. Step 5: After disassembly, inspect the inside of the fitting for any internal parts such as O-rings and spacers that may have been dislodged from the fitting. Replace any damaged connector.

6. Remove the filter retaining clamp and remove the fuel filter. Note the direction of the flow arrow on the filter, so the replacement filter can be reinstalled in the same position.

To install:

7. Install or connect the following:

• Fuel filter with the flow arrow facing the proper direction and tighten the filter retaining clamp

• Rubber insulator rings on the new filter. Replace the insulator rings if the filter moves freely after the retainer is installed.

• Filter into the retainer with the flow arrow pointing out the open end of the retainer

• Retainer on the bracket and tighten the mounting bolts to 27–44 inch lbs. (3–5 Nm)

8. Install the hairpin clip push connect fittings at both ends of the fuel filter as follows:

a. Step 1: Install a new connector if damage was found. Insert a new clip into any 2 adjacent openings with the triangular portion pointing away from the fitting opening. Install the clip until the legs of the clip are locked on the outside of the body. Piloting with an index finger is necessary.

b. Step 2: Before installing the fitting on the filter, wipe the filter end with a clean cloth. Inspect the inside of the fitting to be sure it is free of dirt and/or obstructions.

c. Step 3: Apply a light coating of engine oil to the filter end. Align the fitting and filter axially and push the fitting onto the filter end. When the fitting is engaged, a definite click will be heard. Pull on the fitting to be sure it is fully engaged.

9. If equipped with air suspension, turn the air suspension switch to the **ON** position.

10. Reconnect the negative battery cable.

11. Start the engine and check for fuel leaks and proper operation.

Fuel Pump

REMOVAL & INSTALLATION

1. Before servicing the vehicle, refer to the precautions in the beginning of this section.

2. Disconnect the negative battery cable.

3. Relieve the fuel system pressure.

4. Install a hose into the fuel filler pipe and drain or siphon the fuel into a storage tank designed for fuel storage.

5. Remove any dirt that has accumulated around the fuel pump and fuel lines to prevent the entry of contaminants into the tank during fuel pump removal and installation.

6. Remove or disconnect the following:

• Fuel supply and return line fittings

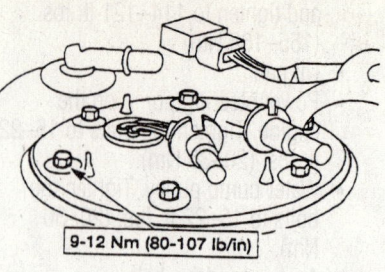

9-12 Nm (80-107 lb/in)

7922RG23

Tighten the fuel pump mounting bolts to 80–107 inch lbs. (9–12 Nm)

at the fuel pump using fuel line disconnect tools

• Fuel pump module electrical connector

• 6 retaining bolts around the perimeter of the fuel pump module

• Fuel pump module and seal from the fuel tank

To install:

7. Clean the fuel pump module mounting flange and fuel tank mounting surface.

8. Install or connect the following:

• New seal and the fuel pump module using care not to damage the inlet filter and fuel sending unit float arm

• 6 retaining bolts and tighten to 80–107 inch lbs. (9–12 Nm)

• Fuel pump module electrical connector

• Fuel supply and return lines to the fuel pump module. Pull on the fuel line fittings to verify engagement.

9. Minimum of 10 gallons (38L) of clean fuel to the fuel tank and check for leaks.

10. Install a Fuel pressure gauge to the Schrader valve on the fuel injection supply manifold.

11. Connect the negative battery cable.

12. Cycle the ignition switch from the **OFF** to **ON** position 5–10 times for 3 second intervals or until the fuel pressure gauge shows at least 35 psi (241 kPa).

13. Check for fuel leaks.

14. Remove the fuel pressure gauge.

15. Start the engine and recheck for fuel leaks.

16. Road test the vehicle and check for proper operation.

Fuel Injector

REMOVAL & INSTALLATION

1. Before servicing the vehicle, refer to the precautions in the beginning of this section.

The fuel system is pressurized and must be relieved before service.

2. Remove or disconnect the following:
- Injector supply manifold
- Wiring
- Injector by pulling it up and gently rocking it side to side
- O-rings and discard

To install:

3. Lubricate new O-rings with clean engine oil.

4. Install or connect the following:
- O-rings
- Fuel injector using a light, twisting and pushing motion
- Injector supply manifold
- Wiring

DRIVE TRAIN

Transmission Assembly

REMOVAL & INSTALLATION

1. Before servicing the vehicle, refer to the precautions in the beginning of this section.

2. Drain the transmission.

3. If equipped with air suspension, the air suspension switch, located on the right-hand side of the luggage compartment, must be turned to the **OFF** position before raising the vehicle.

4. Remove or disconnect the following:
- Negative battery cable
- Exhaust system as necessary for transmission removal
- Converter bottom access cover and adapter plate bolts
- Torque converter drain plug, to allow the converter to drain into a container, if equipped. After the converter has drained, reinstall the drain plug and tighten.
- 4 torque converter-to-flywheel retaining nuts

➡ **Crank the engine over with a wrench on the crankshaft pulley retaining bolt to gain access to each torque converter-to-flywheel retaining bolt. Never**

turn the crankshaft in a counterclockwise direction, as viewed from the front of the vehicle.

- Driveshaft (mark for installation), plug the transmission extension housing to prevent fluid leakage
- Vehicle Speed Sensor (VSS) or if equipped, the speedometer cable from the transmission extension housing
- Shift cable from the transmission manual control lever the throttle valve cable from the transmission throttle valve lever, if equipped
- Transmission wiring harness connectors.
- Starter motor retaining bolts and place the starter motor aside

5. Position a transmission jack under the transmission and raise it enough to allow crossmember removal.

6. Remove or disconnect the following:
- Engine rear support-to-crossmember bolts and the crossmember-to-frame side support retaining bolts
- Crossmember and transmission support insulator

7. Lower the transmission jack and allow the transmission to hang.

8. Place a jack to the front of the engine and raise the engine enough to gain access to the 2 upper transmission-to-cylinder block retaining bolts. Do not remove the bolts at this time.

9. Remove or disconnect the following:
- Transmission cooler lines at the transmission. Plug all openings to keep dirt out.
- Lower transmission-to-cylinder block retaining bolts

- Transmission fluid fill tube and plug the opening in the transmission

10. Secure the transmission to the transmission jack with a safety strap or chain.

11. Remove the 2 upper transmission-to-cylinder block bolts.

12. Carefully move the transmission rearward to disengage it from the dowel pins and the torque converter studs from the flywheel.

13. Remove or disconnect the following:
- Transmission
- Torque converter to prevent the converter from dropping out of the transmission causing possible damage or personal injury

➡ **If the transmission is to be removed for more than a speedy repair, support the rear of the engine with a safety stand and a block of wood.**

To install:

➡ **Verify the transmission cooler lines are thoroughly cleaned before installing the transmission assembly.**

14. Remove the safety stand and block of wood supporting the rear of the engine, if installed.

15. Install or connect the following:
- Torque converter drain plug to 21–23 ft. lbs. (28–30 Nm), if equipped
- Torque converter on the transmission and rotate into position to be sure the drive flats are fully engaged in the pump gear. When fully seated, the center of the torque converter should be about 7/16–9/16 inch (10.2–14.4mm) below the transmission mounting surface

DIMENSION A TO BE 10.23-14.43 mm (7/16-9/16 INCH) APPROXIMATELY

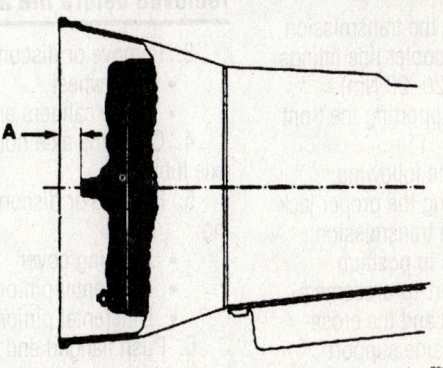

7922RG24

To prevent transmission damage, be sure that the torque converter is fully seated in the front pump of the transmission

16. Mount the transmission on a transmission jack and secure with a safely strap or chain. Raise the transmission and align with the cylinder block dowel pins.

➡ **Do not allow the transmission to get in a nose-down position causing possible torque converter disengagement from the pump gear.**

17. Rotate the converter until the studs and drain plug are in alignment with the holes in the flywheel. Align the orange balancing marks on the converter stud and flywheel bolt hole, if balancing marks are present.

18. Slide the transmission assembly forward into position, being careful not to damage the flywheel and converter pilot.

➡ **The converter face must rest squarely against the flywheel. This indicates that the converter pilot is not binding in the engine crankshaft. To ensure the converter is properly seated, grasp a converter stud. It should move freely back and forth in the flywheel hole. If the converter will not move, the transmission must be removed and the converter repositioned so the impeller hub is properly engaged in the pump gear.**

19. Install or connect the following:
- 2 transmission housing-to-cylinder block bolts at the engine dowel pin locations. Tighten the bolts to 41–50 ft. lbs. (55–68 Nm).
- Transmission housing-to-cylinder block bolts. Tighten the bolts to 41–50 ft. lbs. (55–68 Nm).

20. Remove the safety strap or chain from around the transmission.

21. Install or connect the following:
- Transmission fluid fill tube. Tighten the bolt to 28–38 ft. lbs. (38–51 Nm).
- Oil cooler lines to the transmission case. Tighten the cooler line fittings to 15–19 ft. lbs. (20–26 Nm).

22. Remove the jack supporting the front of the engine.

23. Install or connect the following:
- Crossmember using the proper jack
- Crossmember and transmission support insulators in position
- Engine rear support-to-crossmember retaining bolts and the crossmember-to-frame side support retaining bolts

24. Remove the transmission jack.

25. Install or connect the following:
- Transmission wiring harness connectors

- Starter motor and wiring
- 4 torque converter-to-flywheel retaining nuts. Tighten to 20–33 ft. lbs. (27–46 Nm).
- Torque converter access cover and cover plate bolts. Tighten the bolts to 12–16 ft. lbs. (16–22 Nm).
- Exhaust system
- VSS and the wiring, or if equipped, the speedometer cable to the transmission extension housing
- Driveshaft, aligning the marks that were made during removal
- Shift cable to the transmission manual control lever
- Throttle valve cable to the transmission throttle valve lever, if equipped

26. If equipped with air suspension, turn the air suspension switch to the **ON** position.

27. Fill the transmission.

28. Start the engine and check the transmission for leakage.

29. Road test the vehicle and check for proper transmission operation.

Axle Shaft

REMOVAL & INSTALLATION

1. Before servicing the vehicle, refer to the precautions in the beginning of this section.

2. If equipped with air suspension, the air suspension switch, located on the right-hand side of the luggage compartment, must be turned to the **OFF** position before raising the vehicle.

✸✸ WARNING

The rear anti-lock sensor must be removed before the axle shaft.

3. Remove or disconnect the following:
- Rear wheel
- Brake calipers and brake rotors

4. Clean the axle housing and drain the axle lubricant.

5. Remove or disconnect the following:
- Housing cover
- Differential pinion shaft lockpin
- Differential pinion shaft

6. Push flanged end of the axle shaft toward the center of the vehicle.

7. Remove or disconnect the following:
- U-washer
- Axle shaft

To install:

✸✸ WARNING

Be careful that the splines on the axle shaft do not damage the oil seal or bearing assembly

8. Install or connect the following:
- Axle shaft
- U-washer

9. Pull the shaft until the washer seats.

10. Install differential pinion shaft though the case and gears

11. Align the hole in the shaft with lockbolt hole.

12. Install the differential pinion shaft lockpin and tighten to 15–30 ft. lbs. (20–41 Nm).

➡ **Make sure that both the axle housing and the cover are clean before installing the new silicone seal.**

13. Install or connect the following:
- Axle housing cover with a 1/8–3/16 inch (3.18–4.76mm) wide bead of silicone on it
- Axle housing cover bolts and tighten to 28–38 ft. lbs. (38–52 Nm)
- Axle lubricant
- Rear anti-lock sensor and tighten bolt to 44–62 inch lbs. (5–7 Nm)
- Rotor and brake caliper
- Rear wheel

Bearing and Seal

REMOVAL & INSTALLATION

1. Before servicing the vehicle, refer to the precautions in the beginning of this section.

2. If equipped with air suspension, the air suspension switch, located on the right-hand side of the luggage compartment, must be turned to the **OFF** position before raising the vehicle.

3. Raise and safely support the vehicle.

✸✸ WARNING

The rear anti-lock sensor must be removed before the axle shaft.

4. Remove or disconnect the following:
- Axle shafts
- Oil seal and bearing

To install:

5. Lubricate with rear axle lubricant.

6. Install or connect the following:
- Bearing
- Oil seal
- Axle shafts

7. Lower the vehicle.

Axle Housing Assembly

REMOVAL & INSTALLATION

1. Before servicing the vehicle, refer to the precautions in the beginning of this section.

2. If equipped with air suspension, the air suspension switch, located on the right-hand side of the luggage compartment, must be turned to the **OFF** position before raising the vehicle.

3. Remove or disconnect the following:
   - Rear wheel
   - Brake calipers and support aside with a length of wire
   - Rotors
   - Parking brake cables and move aside
   - Anti-lock sensor
   - Rear stabilizer bar and bracket
   - Air suspension height sensor from the watts linkage arm
   - Driveshaft, matchmark it before removal
   - Watts linkage retaining nut and separate from axle housing

4. Support rear axle with jack

5. Remove or disconnect the following:
   - Shock absorber lower nut
   - Rear suspension lower arms nuts and bolts
   - Rear suspension upper arms nuts and bolts
   - Unseat rear springs
   - Axle housing

To install:

6. Transfer all old components to new housing, if necessary

7. Install or connect the following:
   - Axle housing
   - Bearings and oil seals
   - Rear springs
   - Rear suspension upper arms and nuts and bolts. Tighten to 64–87 ft. lbs. (87–119 Nm).
   - Shock absorber and nuts. Tighten to 57–75 ft. lbs. (76–103 Nm).
   - Watts linkage-to-bellcrank stud. Tighten to 157–212 ft. lbs. (212 –288 Nm).
   - Air suspension height sensor
   - Rear stabilizer bar and brackets and tighten the bracket nuts to 16–21 ft. lbs. (21–29 Nm)
   - Driveshaft. Make sure to align the matchmarks.
   - Rear stabilizer bar link and bushing

to bar. Tighten nuts to 13–16 ft. lbs. (17–23 Nm).
   - Anti-lock sensor and wires. Tighten to 45–53 inch lbs. (5–6 Nm).
   - Parking brake cable and restore tension
   - Rotor
   - Rear wheel
   - Axle lubricant

8. If equipped with air suspension, the air suspension switch, located on the right-hand side of the luggage compartment, must be turned to the **ON** position before raising the vehicle.

9. Road test the vehicle.

STEERING AND SUSPENSION

Air Bag

PRECAUTIONS

Several precautions must be observed when handling the inflator module to avoid accidental deployment and possible personal injury.
   - Never carry the inflator module by the wires or connector on the underside of the module.
   - When carrying a live inflator module, hold securely with both hands, and ensure that the bag and trim cover are pointed away.
   - Place the inflator module on a bench or other surface with the bag and trim cover facing up.
   - With the inflator module on the bench, never place anything on or close to the module which may be thrown in the event of an accidental deployment.

DISARMING

1. Before servicing the vehicle, refer to the precautions in the beginning of this section.

2. Position the vehicle with the front wheels in a straight-ahead position.

3. Disconnect both battery cables.

4. Wait at least 1 minute for the air bag back-up power supply to deplete its stored energy before continuing.

5. Proceed with the repair.

6. Once the repair is complete.

7. Reconnect both battery cables.

8. Prove out the air bag system by turning the ignition key to the **RUN** position and visually monitoring the air bag indicator lamp in the instrument cluster. The indicator lamp should illuminate for approximately 6 seconds, then turn **OFF**. If the indicator lamp does not illuminate, stays on, or flashes at any time, a fault has been detected by the air bag diagnostic monitor.

Power Steering Gear

REMOVAL & INSTALLATION

1. Before servicing the vehicle, refer to the precautions in the beginning of this section.

2. If equipped with air suspension, the air suspension switch must be turned to the **OFF** position before raising the vehicle.

3. Center the steering wheel and turn the key to the locked position.

4. Remove or disconnect the following:
   - Negative battery cable
   - Bolt and the intermediate shaft from the steering gear

5. Tag the power steering pressure and return lines so they may be reassembled in their original positions.

6. Place a drain pan under the steering gear

7. Remove or disconnect the following:
   - Pressure and return lines. Plug the lines and ports in the gear to prevent the entry of dirt.
   - Pitman arm from the center link using a puller. It is not necessary to remove the Pitman arm from the steering gear.

8. Support the steering gear

9. Remove or disconnect the following:
   - Steering gear-to-frame rail retaining bolts
   - Steering gear

To install:

10. Install or connect the following:
   - Steering gear on the frame rail. Tighten the steering gear-to-frame retaining bolts to 50–67 ft. lbs. (66–90 Nm).
   - Pitman arm to the center link. Tighten the retaining nut to 52–60 ft. lbs. (70–81 Nm).
   - Power steering pressure and return lines to the steering gear and tighten the lines to 12–18 ft. lbs. (16–24 Nm)

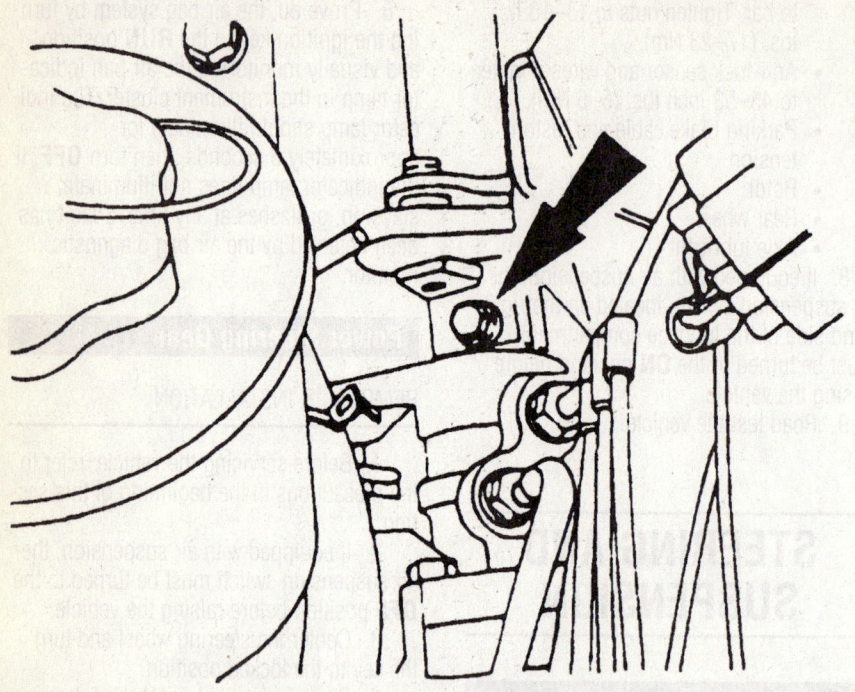

7922RG25

Remove the bolt and separate the intermediate shaft from the steering gear input shaft

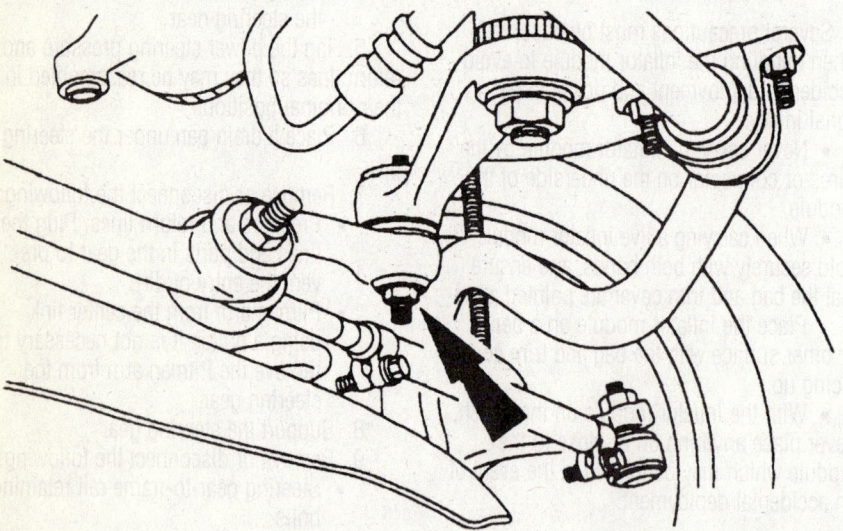

7922RG26

Remove the locknut and separate the Pitman arm from the center link using the appropriate puller

- Intermediate shaft to the steering gear. Tighten the bolt to 31–41 ft. lbs. (41–55 Nm).
- Negative battery cable

11. If equipped with air suspension, turn the air suspension switch to the **ON** position.

12. Fill the reservoir with the correct power steering fluid and turn the steering wheel from stop-to-stop to distribute the fluid. Check the fluid level and add fluid, if necessary.

13. Start the engine and turn the steering wheel from left to right. Check for leaks.

Shock Absorber

REMOVAL & INSTALLATION

Front

1. Before servicing the vehicle, refer to the precautions in the beginning of this section.

2. If equipped with air suspension, the air suspension switch, located on the right-hand side of the luggage compartment, must be turned to the **OFF** position before raising the vehicle.

3. Remove or disconnect the following:
- Nut, washer and bushing from the upper end of the shock absorber
- 2 bolts retaining the shock absorber to the lower control arm
- Shock absorber

To install:

4. Prior to installation, prime the new shock absorber. Fully extend the shock absorber while in the right side up (installed) position. Turn the shock absorber upside down and fully compress it. Repeat the procedure at least 3 times to purge any air trapped in the shock absorber.

5. Install or connect the following:
- New bushing and washer on the stud on the top of the new shock absorber and position the unit inside the front coil spring
- 2 lower retaining bolts and tighten them to 10–12 ft lbs. (13–17 Nm).
- New bushing and washer on the shock absorber top stud
- New retaining nut. Tighten the retaining nut to 25–34 ft. lbs. (34–46 Nm).

6. If equipped with air suspension, turn the air suspension switch to the **ON** position.

Rear

> ※※ **WARNING**
>
> When removing and installing rear shock absorbers on vehicles with air springs, it is very important that this procedure be followed exactly. Failure to do so may result in damaged shock absorbers.

1. Before servicing the vehicle, refer to the precautions in the beginning of this section.

2. If equipped with air suspension, turn the air suspension service switch **OFF**.

3. Be sure the ignition switch is in the **OFF** position.

4. Support the rear axle assembly with a jack.

➡ **To assist in removing the upper retainer on shock absorbers using a plastic dust tube, place an open end wrench on the hex stamped into the dust tube's metal cap. For shock absorbers with a steel dust tube, sim-**

ply grasp the tube to prevent stud rotation when loosening the retaining nut.

5. Remove or disconnect the following:
   - Top retaining nut, washer and bushing
   - Bottom retaining nut and washer
   - Shock absorber

To install:

6. Install or connect the following:
   - Shock absorber so the upper stud enters the hole in the frame
   - Top bushing, washer and retaining nut. Tighten to 26–34 ft. lbs. (34–46 Nm).

7. Extend the shock absorber and place the lower stud through the hole in the bracket

8. Bottom retaining washer and nut. Tighten to 57–75 ft. lbs. (76–103 Nm).

9. Remove the jack from the axle assembly.

10. Turn the air suspension service switch to the **ON** position.

Coil Spring

REMOVAL & INSTALLATION

Front

1. Before servicing the vehicle, refer to the precautions in the beginning of this section.

2. If equipped with air suspension, turn the air suspension service switch to the **OFF** position before raising the vehicle.

3. Remove or disconnect the following:
   - Wheel
   - Shock absorber
   - Center link from the Pitman arm

4. Using a spring compressor perform the following steps:

   a. Step 1: install 1 plate with the pivot ball seat facing downward into the coils of the spring. Rotate the plate so it is flush with the upper surface of the lower arm.

   b. Step 2: Install the other plate with the pivot ball seat facing upward into the coils of the spring. Insert the upper ball nut through the coils of the spring, so the nut rests in the upper plate.

   c. Step 3: Insert the compression rod into the opening in the lower arm, through the upper and lower plate and upper ball nut. Insert the securing pin through the upper ball nut and compression rod.

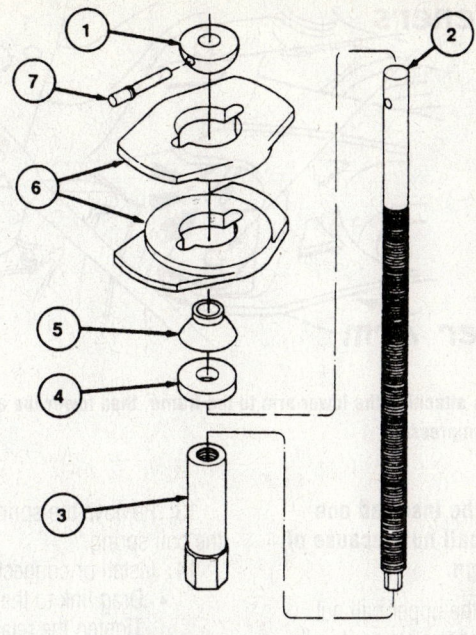

1 Upper Ball
2 Compression Rod
3 Forcing Nut
4 Thrust Washer
5 Lower Ball Nut
6 Plate
7 Pin

7922RG27

Exploded view of Spring Compressor D78P-5310-A—similar compressors are commercially available that will do the same job

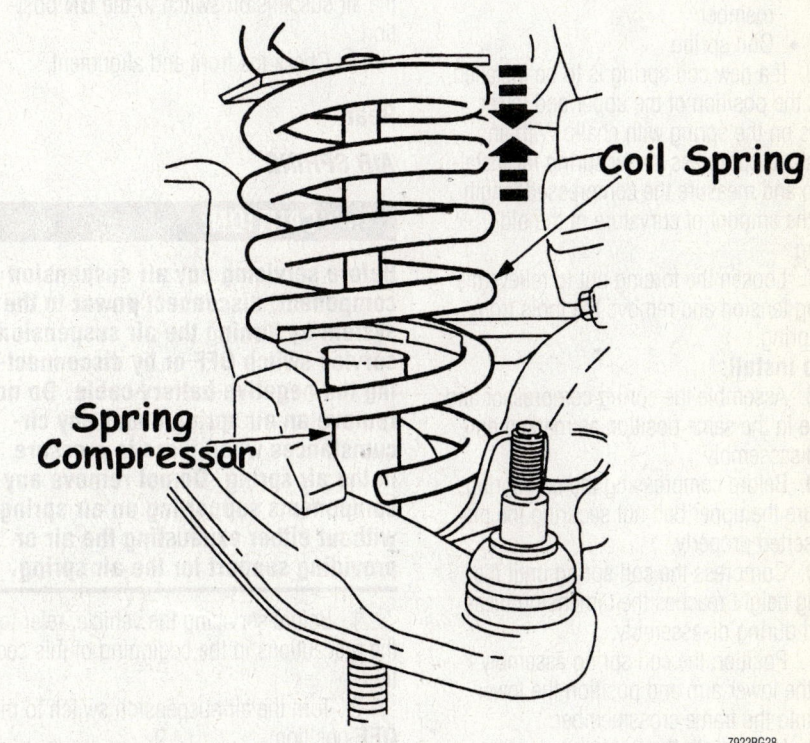

7922RG28

Compress the coil spring until it moves away from its seat

Fasteners

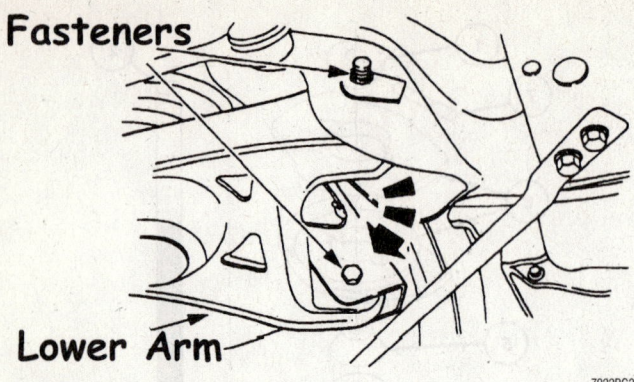

7922RG29

Remove the fasteners attaching the lower arm to the frame, then lower the arm and remove the spring with the compressor

➡ **This pin can only be inserted one way into the upper ball nut because of a stepped hole design.**

   d. Step 4: With the upper ball nut secured, turn the upper plate so it walks up the coil until it contacts the upper spring seat. Then, back off ½ turn.

   e. Step 5: Install the lower ball nut and thrust washer on the compression rod and screw on the forcing nut. Tighten the forcing nut until the spring is compressed enough so it is free in its seat.

  5. Remove or disconnect the following:
- 2 lower control arm pivot bolts
- Lower arm from the frame cross-member
- Coil spring

  6. If a new coil spring is to be installed, mark the position of the upper and lower plates on the spring with chalk. With an assistant, compress a new spring for installation and measure the compressed length and the amount of curvature of the old spring.

  7. Loosen the forcing nut to relieve the spring tension and remove the tools from the spring.

To install:

  8. Assemble the spring compressor and locate in the same position as marked during disassembly.

  9. Before compressing the coil spring, be sure the upper ball nut securing the pin is inserted properly.

  10. Compress the coil spring until the spring height reaches the dimension measured during disassembly.

  11. Position the coil spring assembly into the lower arm and position the lower arm into the frame crossmember.

  12. Install both the front and rear lower control arm pivot bolts through the frame and lower arm bushings. Tighten the bolts and nuts to 109–148 ft. lbs. (148–201 Nm).

  13. Remove the spring compressor from the coil spring.

  14. Install or connect the following:
- Drag link to the Pitman arm. Tighten the retaining nut to 60 ft. lbs. (80 Nm).
- Shock absorber inside the coil spring
- Retaining bolts
- Wheel. Tighten the lug nuts to 85–105 ft. lbs. (115–142 Nm).

  15. Place a washer and retaining nut on the shock absorber top stud. Tighten the nut to 25–34 ft. lbs. (34–46 Nm).

  16. If equipped with air suspension, turn the air suspension switch to the **ON** position.

  17. Check the front end alignment.

Rear

AIR SPRING

✳✳ CAUTION

Before servicing any air suspension component, disconnect power to the system by turning the air suspension service switch OFF or by disconnecting the negative battery cable. Do not remove an air spring under any circumstances when there is pressure in the air spring. Do not remove any components supporting an air spring without either exhausting the air or providing support for the air spring.

  1. Before servicing the vehicle, refer to the precautions in the beginning of this section.

  2. Turn the air suspension switch to the **OFF** position.

  3. Raise and safely support the vehicle so the suspension is fully down with no load.

  4. Remove or disconnect the following:
- Heat shield, as required
- Spring retainer clip
- Air spring solenoid valve electrical connector
- Air line
- Air spring solenoid retainer

  5. Rotate the solenoid valve counter-clockwise to the first stop.

  6. Pull the solenoid valve straight out slowly to the second stop to bleed air from the system.

✳✳ CAUTION

Do not fully release the solenoid until the air is completely bled from the air spring or personal injury may result.

  7. After the air is fully bled from the system, rotate the solenoid valve counter-clockwise to the third stop and remove the solenoid valve from the solenoid housing. Remove the large O-ring from the solenoid housing.

  8. On 1997 models, insert Air Spring Removal Tool T90P-5310-A or equivalent, between the axle tube and the spring seat on the forward side of the axle. Position the tool so its flat end rests on the piston knob. Push downward, forcing the piston and retainer clip off the axle spring seat.

  9. On 1998–01 models, lift the air spring off the rear axle.

  10. Remove the air spring.

To install:

  11. Check the solenoid valve O-rings for cuts or abrasions. Replace the O-rings as required. Lightly grease the O-ring area of the solenoid valve and the larger solenoid housing O-ring with silicone dielectric compound.

  12. Insert the solenoid into the air spring end cap and rotate clockwise to the third stop, push in to the second stop, then rotate clockwise to the first stop.

  13. Install or connect the following:
- Air spring solenoid retainer. Inspect the wiring harness connector and ensure the rubber gasket is in place at the bottom of the connector cavity
- Air spring into the frame (upper) spring seat, taking care to keep the solenoid air and electrical connections clean and free of damage
- Push-on ring spring retainer clip to the knob of the spring cap from the top side of the frame spring seat
- Air line and electrical connector to the solenoid

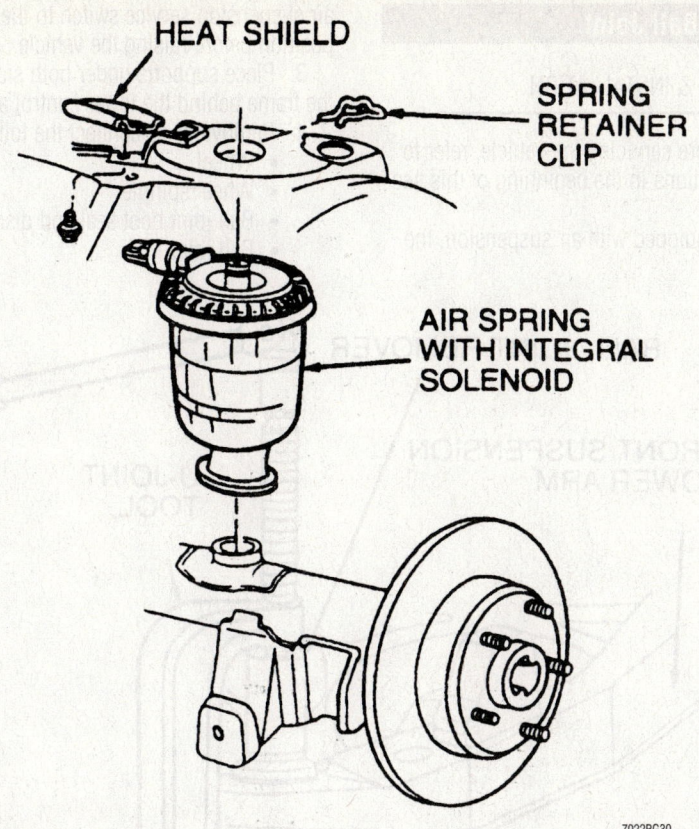

HEAT SHIELD

SPRING
RETAINER
CLIP

AIR SPRING
WITH INTEGRAL
SOLENOID

7922RG30

Exploded view of the air spring mounting

- Heat shield to the frame spring seat, if removed
- Align the air spring piston-to-axle (lower) seat. Squeeze to increase pressure and push downward on the piston, snapping the piston to the axle seat at rebound and supported by the shock absorber.
- Negative battery cable.

✳✳ WARNING

The air springs may be damaged if the suspension is allowed to compress before the spring is inflated.

14. Refill the air spring as follows:
   a. Step 1: Turn the air suspension switch to the **ON** position. The ignition switch must be **ON** and the engine running or a battery charger must be connected to the battery to reduce battery drain.
   b. Step 2: Fold back or remove the right-hand luggage compartment trim panel and connect Super Star II Tester 007–0041-A to the air suspension DLC, which is located near the air suspension switch.

   c. Step 3: Set the tester to EEC-IV/MCU mode. Also set the tester to FAST mode. Release the tester button to the HOLD (up) position and turn the tester **ON**.
   d. Step 4: Depress the tester button to TEST (down) position. A Code 10 will be displayed. Within 2 minutes a Code 13 will be displayed. After Code 13 is displayed, release the tester button to the HOLD (up) position, wait 5 seconds and depress the tester button to TEST (down) position. Ignore any codes displayed.
   e. Step 5: Release the tester button to the HOLD (up) position. Wait at least 20 seconds, then depress the tester button to TEST (down) position. Within 10 seconds, the codes will be displayed in the order shown.
   f. Step 6: Within 4 seconds after Code 26 is displayed, release the tester button to the HOLD (up) position. Waiting longer than 4 seconds may result in Functional Test 31 being entered. The compressor will fill the air springs with air as long as the tester button is in the HOLD (up) position. To stop filling the air springs, depress the tester button to the TEST (down) position.

➡ It is possible to overheat the compressor during this operation. If the compressor overheats, the self-resetting circuit breaker in the compressor will open and remain open for about 15 minutes. This allows the compressor to cool down.

   g. Step 7: To exit Functional Test 26, disconnect the tester and turn the ignition switch to the **OFF** position.
15. Luggage trim panel, if removed

COIL SPRING

1. Before servicing the vehicle, refer to the precautions in the beginning of this section.
2. Place a hoist under the rear axle housing and raise and safely support the vehicle.
3. Support the frame side rails with 2 jackstands.

➡ If the vehicle is raised by the frame rails, place a jack under the rear axle housing.

4. Remove or disconnect the following:
   - Rear sway bar
   - Lower studs of both rear shock absorbers from the mounting brackets on the axle tube
   - Parking brake cable from the upper arm retainer before lowering the axle housing
5. Lower the axle housing until the coil springs are released. If the axle housing is supported by the hoist, lower the hoist allowing the rear of the vehicle to rest on the jackstands. If the vehicle's axle housing is supported by the jackstands, leave the hoist stationary and lower the jackstands or raise the hoist to release the tension on the coil springs.
6. Remove the coil springs and insulators.

To install:
7. Install or connect the following:
   - Coil spring in the upper and lower seats with an insulator between the upper end of the spring and frame seat
   - Axle housing and connect the lower studs of the shock absorbers to the mounting brackets
   - Parking cable into the upper arm retainer
   - Sway bar
8. Road test the vehicle and check for proper operation.

Turn to Section 5 for brake system applications

Upper Ball Joint

REMOVAL & INSTALLATION

1. Before servicing the vehicle, refer to the precautions in the beginning of this section.

2. If equipped with air suspension, the air suspension switch to the **OFF** position before raising the vehicle.

3. Place supports under both sides of the frame just behind the lower control arms.

4. Remove the wheel.

5. Place a floor jack under the lower control arm at the lower ball joint area. The floor jack will support the spring load on the lower control arm.

6. Remove the retaining nut and pinch bolt from the upper ball joint stud.

7. Mark the position of the alignment cams. When replacing the upper ball joint this will approximate the current alignment.

8. Remove or disconnect the following:

   • 2 nuts retaining the upper ball joint to the upper control arm

   • Upper ball joint from the upper control arm and spread the slot in the wheel spindle with a prybar to remove the ball joint stud from the wheel spindle.

To install:

9. Install or connect the following:

   • Upper ball joint to the upper control arm

   • Ball stud into the wheel spindle

   • Upper ball joint pinch bolt and retaining nut. Tighten to 56–77 ft. lbs. (76–104 Nm).

   • Alignment cams to the approximate position at removal. If not marked, install in the neutral positions.

   • 2 nuts retaining the upper ball joint to the upper control arm. Hold the cams and tighten the nuts to 107–129 ft. lbs. (145–175 Nm).

   • Wheel and tire assembly. Tighten the lug nuts in a star pattern to 85–105 ft. lbs. (115–142 Nm).

10. Remove the floor jack from under the lower control arm.

11. If equipped with air suspension, turn the air suspension switch to the **ON** position.

12. Check and adjust the front wheel alignment.

Lower Ball Joint

REMOVAL & INSTALLATION

1. Before servicing the vehicle, refer to the precautions in the beginning of this section.

2. If equipped with air suspension, the air suspension service switch to the **OFF** position before raising the vehicle.

3. Place supports under both sides of the frame behind the lower control arms.

4. Remove or disconnect the following:

   • Wheel

   • Wheel spindle

   • Ball joint boot seal and discard

   • Ball joint

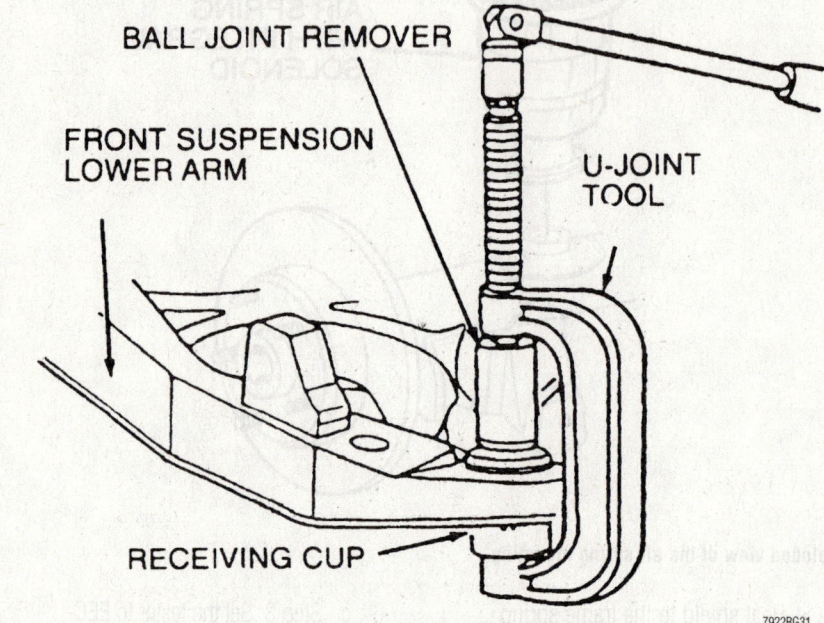

Use a ball joint press to remove the ball joint from the lower control arm

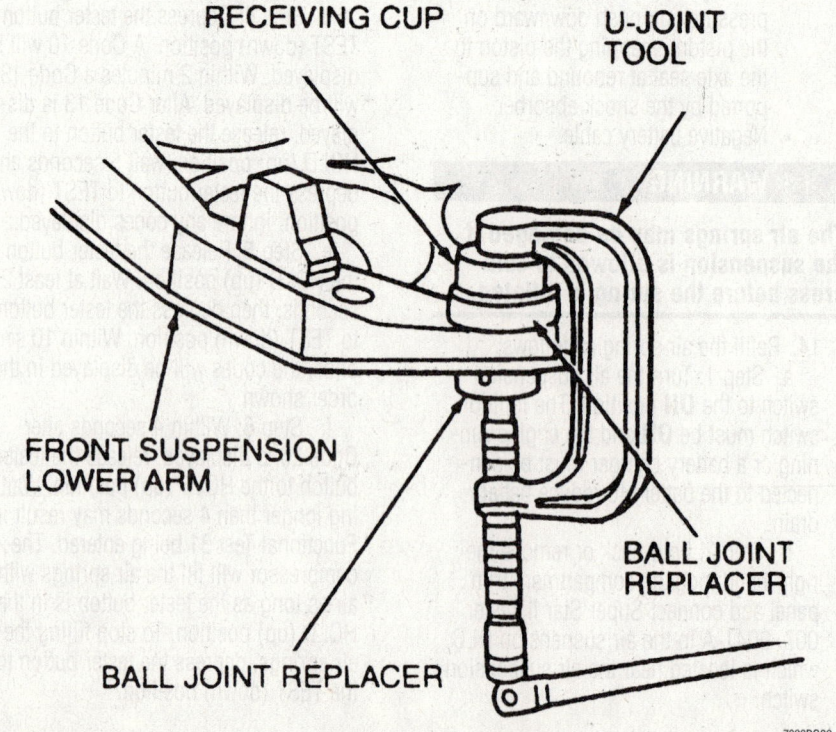

Use a ball joint press to install the new ball joint into the lower control arm

To install:

➡When installing a new ball joint, the protective cover should be left on to protect the ball joint seal during installation. It may be necessary to trim the cover so it can pass through the installation tool.

5. Install the ball joint.

6. Discard the protective cover and be sure the new ball joint is fully seated in the lower control arm. Ensure that the ball joint seal is not damaged.

7. Install or connect the following:
- Wheel spindle
- Wheel. Tighten the lug nuts to 85–105 ft. lbs. (115–142 Nm).

8. If equipped with air suspension, turn the air suspension service switch to the **ON** position.

9. Check the front end alignment.

Wheel Bearings

ADJUSTMENT

The front wheel bearings are of a hub unit design and are pre-greased, sealed and require no maintenance. The bearings are preset and cannot be adjusted. No adjustment is possible for the rear axle bearing. If either the front or rear bearings make noise or become loose, replacement is necessary.

REMOVAL & INSTALLATION

Front

➡Before continuing with this procedure, be sure that 2 new caliper mounting bolts, one sway bar link nut, one lower ball joint stud nut and one hub grease cap are available, per side. Once removed, these parts lose their torque holding ability or retention capability and must not be reused.

1. Before servicing the vehicle, refer to the precautions in the beginning of this section.

2. If equipped, turn the air suspension service switch to the **OFF** position before raising the vehicle.

3. Remove or disconnect the following
- Front wheel
- Grease cap from the hub
- Disc brake caliper. Suspend the caliper with a length of wire. Do not let it hang from the brake hose. Discard the disc brake caliper mounting bolts.
- Disc brake rotor. If the factory

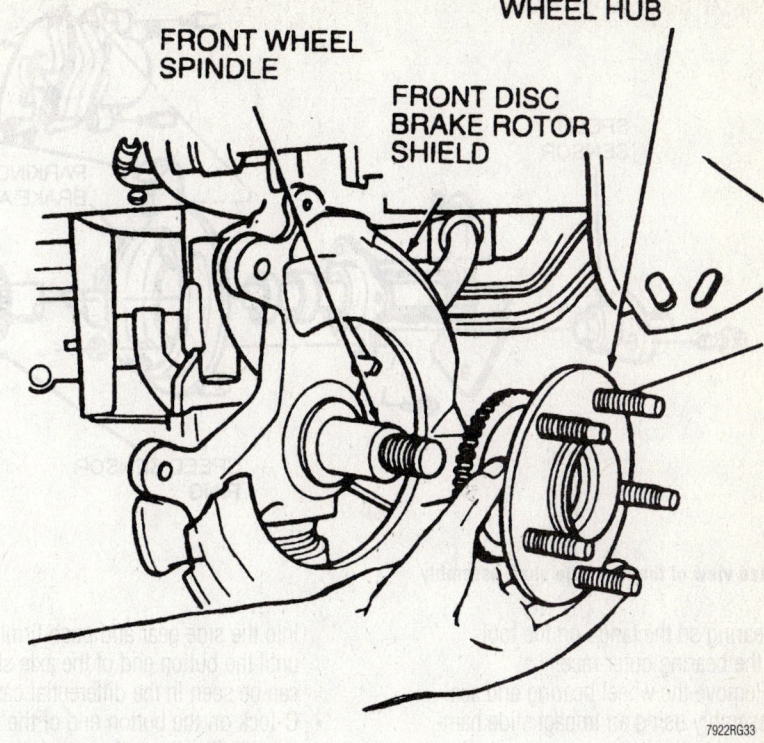

FRONT WHEEL SPINDLE

FRONT DISC BRAKE ROTOR SHIELD

WHEEL HUB

7922RG33

Front hub and bearing assembly

installed push on nuts are installed, remove them first.
- Wheel hub retainer nut and discard
- Hub and bearing assembly

➡The wheel bearings are permanently greased and sealed. If replacement is necessary, the wheel hub and bearings must be replaced as an assembly.

To install:

4. Install or connect the following:
- Hub and bearing assembly
- New wheel hub retainer nut and tighten to 189–254 ft. lbs. (255–345 Nm)
- Disc brake rotor and push on nuts, if equipped
- New grease cap seal
- Disc brake caliper using the 2 new disc brake caliper mounting bolts. Tighten the bolts to 125–170 ft. lbs. (170–230 Nm).
- Wheel. Tighten the lug nuts to 85–104 ft. lbs. (115–142 Nm).

5. If equipped with air suspension, turn the air suspension switch to the **ON** position.

6. Pump the brake pedal several times to position the brake pads prior to moving the vehicle.

7. Check the front end alignment.

Rear

1. Before servicing the vehicle, refer to the precautions in the beginning of this section.

2. Remove or disconnect the following
- Wheel
- Brake drum or brake rotor
- Anti-lock brake speed sensor, if equipped

3. Clean all dirt from the area of the axle housing cover.

4. Place a drain pan under the axle housing.

5. Remove or disconnect the following:
- Axle housing cover retaining bolts and the cover, draining the axle lubricant from the housing
- Differential pinion shaft lockbolt and the differential pinion shaft

6. Push the flanged end of the axle shaft being removed toward the center of the vehicle

7. Remove or disconnect the following:
- C-lock from the button end of the axle shaft
- Axle shaft from the housing, being careful not to damage the oil seal and anti-lock brake sensor ring, if equipped.

8. Insert an axle bearing remover in the axle housing bore and position it behind the

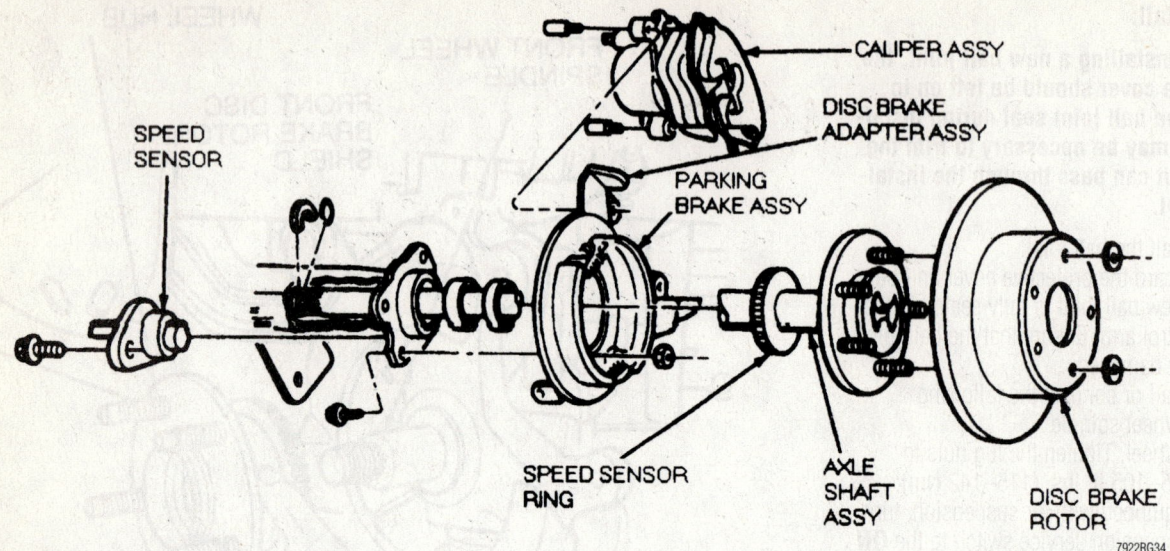

Exploded view of the rear axle shaft assembly

7922RG34

wheel bearing so the tangs on the tool engage the bearing outer race.

9. Remove the wheel bearing and seal as an assembly using an impact slide hammer attached to the bearing remover tool

To install:

10. Lubricate the new wheel bearing with rear axle lubricant.

11. Install the wheel bearing into the axle housing bore using a bearing replacer.

12. Lubricate the lips of a new wheel bearing oil seal with wheel bearing grease.

13. Install or connect the following:
- New wheel bearing seal using a seal replacer

➡**Check for the presence of an axle shaft O-ring on the spline end of the shaft and install, if not present.**

- Axle shaft into the axle housing without damaging the bearing/seal assembly or anti-lock brake sensor ring, if equipped. Start the splines

into the side gear and push firmly until the button end of the axle shaft can be seen in the differential case.

- C-lock on the button end of the axle shaft splines, then push the shaft outboard until the shaft splines engage and the C-lock seats in the counterbore of the differential side gear.
- Differential pinion shaft through the case and pinion gears, aligning the hole in the shaft with the lockbolt hole
- Apply a thread locking compound to the lockbolt threads and place in the case and pinion shaft. Tighten to 15–30 ft. lbs. (20–41 Nm).

14. Cover the inside of the differential case with a shop rag and clean the sealing surface of the axle housing and the axle housing cover. Remove the shop rag.

15. Apply a ⅛–³⁄₁₆ inch (3.18–4.76mm) wide bead of silicone sealer to the cover.

16. Install the axle housing and bolts and tighten in a crisscross pattern. Final torque the cover retaining bolts to 28–38 ft. lbs. (38–52 Nm).

➡**The axle housing cover must be installed and tightened within 15 minutes of applying the silicone sealer to prevent leakage.**

17. Add the appropriate rear axle lubricant to the axle housing to a level ¼–⁹⁄₁₆ inch (6–14mm) below the bottom of the fill hole. If equipped with a limited slip differential, add 4 oz. (118.3 ml) of the appropriate friction modifier.

18. Install or connect the following:
- Axle housing fill plug and tighten to 15–30 ft. lbs. (20–41 Nm)
- Anti-lock brake speed sensor, if equipped. Tighten the retaining bolt to 40–60 inch lbs. (4.5–6.8 Nm).
- Brake calipers and rotors or the brake drums, as required
- Wheel

19. Road test the vehicle and check for proper operation.

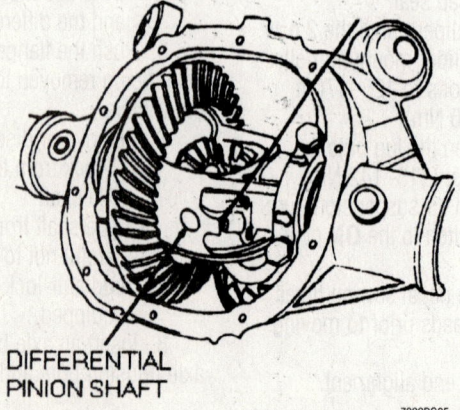

DIFFERENTIAL PINION SHAFT

7922RG35

Removal of differential pinion shaft

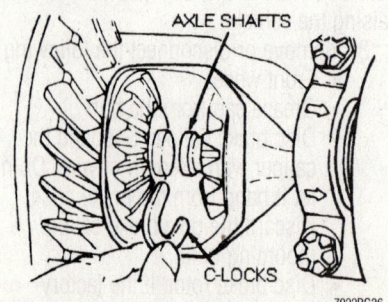

Removing axle shaft C-lock clips

7922RG36

FORD MOTOR CO.

Ford-Thunderbird • Mercury-1997 Cougar

26

PRECAUTIONS

Before servicing any vehicle, please be sure to read all of the following precautions. The following precautions deal with personal safety, prevention of component damage, and important points to take into consideration when servicing a motor vehicle:

• Never open, service or drain the radiator or cooling system when the engine is hot; serious burns can occur from the steam and hot coolant.

• Observe all applicable safety precautions when working around fuel. Whenever servicing the fuel system, always work in a well-ventilated area. Do not allow fuel spray or vapors to come in contact with a spark, open flame, or excessive heat (a hot drop light, for example). Keep a dry chemical fire extinguisher near the work area. Always keep fuel in a container specifically designed for fuel storage; also, always properly seal fuel containers to avoid the possibility of fire or explosion. Refer to the additional fuel system precautions later in this section.

• Fuel injection systems often remain pressurized, even after the engine has been turned **OFF**. The fuel system pressure must be relieved before disconnecting any fuel lines. Failure to do so may result in fire and/or personal injury.

• Brake fluid often contains polyglycol ethers and polyglycols. Avoid contact with the eyes and wash your hands thoroughly after handling brake fluid. If you do get brake fluid in your eyes, flush your eyes with clean, running water for 15 minutes. If eye irritation persists, or if you have taken brake fluid internally, IMMEDIATELY seek medical assistance.

• The EPA warns that prolonged contact with used engine oil may cause a number of skin disorders, including cancer! You should make every effort to minimize your exposure to used engine oil. Protective gloves should be worn when changing the oil. Wash your hands and any other exposed skin areas as soon as possible after exposure to used engine oil. Soap and water, or waterless hand cleaner should be used.

• All vehicles are equipped with an air bag system, often referred to as a Supplemental Restraint System (SRS) or as a Supplemental Inflatable Restraint (SIR) system. The system must be disabled before performing service on or around system components, steering column, instrument panel components, wiring and sensors. Failure to follow safety and disabling procedures could result in accidental air bag deployment, possible personal injury and unnecessary system repairs.

• Always wear safety goggles when working with, or around, the air bag system. When carrying a non-deployed air bag, be sure the bag and trim cover are pointed away from your body. When placing a non-deployed air bag on a work surface, always face the bag and trim cover upward, away from the surface. This will reduce the motion of the module if it is accidentally deployed. Refer to the additional air bag system precautions later in this section.

• Clean, high quality brake fluid from a sealed container is essential to the safe and proper operation of the brake system. You should always buy the correct type of brake fluid for your vehicle. If the brake fluid becomes contaminated, completely flush the system with new fluid. Never reuse any brake fluid. Any brake fluid that is removed from the system should be discarded. Also, do not allow any brake fluid to come in contact with a painted surface; it will damage the paint.

• Never operate the engine without the proper amount and type of engine oil; doing so WILL result in severe engine damage.

• Timing belt maintenance is extremely important! Many models may utilize an interference-type, non-free-wheeling engine. If the timing belt breaks, the valves in the cylinder head may strike the pistons, causing potentially serious (also time-consuming and expensive) engine damage. Refer to the maintenance interval charts in the front of this manual for the recommended replacement interval for the timing belt, and to the timing belt section for belt replacement and inspection.

• Disconnecting the negative battery cable on some vehicles may interfere with the functions of the on board computer system(s) and may require the computer to undergo a relearning process once the negative battery cable is reconnected.

• When servicing drum brakes, only disassemble and assemble one side at a time, leaving the remaining side intact for reference.

• Only an MVAC-trained, EPA-certified, automotive technician should service the air conditioning system or its components.

ENGINE REPAIR

Alternator

REMOVAL

3.8L Engine

1. Before servicing the vehicle, refer to the precautions in the beginning of this section.
2. Remove or disconnect the following:
   • Negative battery cable
   • Wire harness at the voltage regulator and wires attached to the alternator
3. Rotate drive belt tensioner away from drive belt by lifting drive belt tensioner pulley by applying counterclockwise torque to pulley bolt with a wrench and socket.
4. Remove or disconnect the following:
   • Drive belt
   • Alternator pivot and mounting bolts
   • Alternator

4.6L Engine

1. Before servicing the vehicle, refer to the precautions in the beginning of this section.
2. Remove or disconnect the following:
   • Negative battery cable
   • Wire harness at the voltage regulator and wires attached to the alternator
3. Rotate drive belt tensioner away from drive belt by lifting drive belt tensioner pulley by applying clockwise torque square slot with ½ in. drive breaker bar.
4. Remove or disconnect the following:
   • Drive belt
   • Alternator mounting bracket and mounting bolts
   • Alternator mounting bolts
   • Alternator

INSTALLATION

3.8L Engine

1. Install or connect the following:
   • Pivot bolt. Torque to 30–40 ft. lbs. (40–50 Nm).
   • Mounting bolts. Torque to 15–22 ft. lbs. (20–30 Nm).
   • Drive belt
   • Wire harness to voltage regulator

- Engine control wiring
- Alternator output nut. Torque to 62–79 inch lbs. (7–9 Nm).
- Negative battery cable

4.6L Engine

1. Install or connect the following:
   - Alternator bolts. Torque to 15–22 ft. lbs. (20–30 Nm).
   - Mounting bracket. Torque the bolts to 62–79 inch lbs. (7–9 Nm).
   - Drive belt
   - Wire harness to voltage regulator
   - Engine control wiring. Torque the alternator output nut to 62–79 inch lbs. (7–9 Nm).
   - Negative battery cable

Ignition Timing

ADJUSTMENT

➡ **Always refer to the Vehicle Emission Control Information (VECI) label to verify the timing adjustment procedure.**

The 3.8L and 4.6L engines are equipped with Distributorless Ignition Systems (DIS), and, therefore, the base timing for these engines is set from the factory at 10 degrees BTDC and is not adjustable.

Engine Assembly

REMOVAL & INSTALLATION

3.8L Engine

1. Before servicing the vehicle, refer to the precautions in the beginning of this section.
2. Drain the crankcase and the cooling system.
3. Relieve the fuel system pressure and discharge the air conditioning system.
4. Remove or disconnect the following:
   - Hood
   - Negative battery cable
   - Electrical connector from the underhood lamp
   - Left cowl vent screen and wiper module
   - Alternator-to-voltage regulator wiring assembly
   - Radiator upper sight shield
   - Drive and accessory belts (After releasing the belt tension)
   - Air cleaner-to-throttle body tube
   - Fan and shroud

- Upper radiator hose
- Heater hoses
- Oil cooler lines at radiator, if equipped with an automatic transmission
- Lower radiator hose at water pump
- Radiator
- Power steering pressure hose assembly
- Power steering pump and bracket assembly. Position the lines aside
- Compressor

➡ **Plug refrigerant lines after disconnecting.**

- Coolant recovery reservoir and wiring shield
- Accelerator cable mounting bracket and position aside
- Fuel lines from the fuel rail
- Engine Control Module (ECM) wiring, engine feed harnesses, and vacuum hoses. Tag all wiring or hoses before disconnecting them
- Ground and coil wires
- Canister purge line
- Oil filter element
- Exhaust pipe-to-manifold nuts
- Left exhaust shield
- Oxygen (O$_2$S) sensors
- Automatic transmission inspection plug and torque converter bolts, if equipped with an automatic transmission
- Engine-to-transmission bolts and engine mount through-bolts
- Crankshaft pulley assembly

➡ **If the crankshaft pulley and vibration damper have to be separated, mark the damper and pulley so they may be reassembled in the same relative position. This is important as the damper and pulley are initially balanced as a unit. If the crankshaft damper is being replaced, check if the original damper has balance pins installed. If so, new balance pins must be installed on the new damper in the same position as the original damper.**

- Starter, ground cable, and both (left and right) starter harness retainers
- Oil level indicator sensor
- Oil pressure sending unit gauge assembly

5. Position a floor jack under the transmission and install suitable engine lifting equipment.
6. Remove the engine from the vehicle and position it on a workstand.

To install:

➡ **Lightly oil all bolt and stud threads before installation except those specifying special sealant.**

7. Remove the engine assembly from the workstand and install the engine lifting equipment.
8. Position the engine in the vehicle and install the 2 engine-to-transmission bolts. Lower the engine onto the mounting seats, left side first, and remove the lifting equipment. Remove the jacks.
9. Torque the 2 engine-to-transmission bolts to 40–50 ft. lbs. (55–68 Nm) and connect the oil pressure sending unit gauge assembly.
10. Install or connect the following:
    - All remaining engine-to-transmission bolts. Torque to 25–33 ft. lbs. (34–46 Nm).
    - Torque converter bolts. Torque to 20–34 ft. lbs. (27–46 Nm).
    - Inspection plug
    - Engine mount through-bolts. Torque to 35–50 ft. lbs. (47–68 Nm).
    - Starter, starter harness retainer and ground cable
    - Transmission oil cooler line bracket
    - Exhaust pipe-to-manifold nuts
    - Crankshaft pulley assembly. Torque the bolts to 20–28 ft. lbs. (26–38 Nm).
    - O$_2$S sensors and the oil level indicator sensor
    - New oil filter
    - Canister purge line
    - Coolant recovery reservoir
    - Alternator-to-voltage regulator wiring, the ECM wiring assembly, engine feed harnesses and the vacuum hoses
    - Wiring assembly ground and coil wire
    - Fuel lines to the fuel rail
    - Accelerator cable mounting bracket and wiring shield
    - Air conditioning compressor. Torque the bolts to 16–21 ft. lbs. (21–29 Nm).
    - Air conditioner compressor lines and compressor clutch wire
    - Power steering pump bracket assembly and power steering hoses
    - Radiator
    - Lower radiator hose to the water pump
    - Heater hoses
    - Oil cooler lines to the radiator, if

equipped with an automatic transmission

- Upper radiator hose, fan, and fan shroud
- Drive belts and the accessory belts
- Radiator sight shield
- Cowl vent screen and wiper module
- Hood
- Underhood lamp wiring
- Negative battery cable

11. Refill the crankcase. Refill and bleed the cooling system.

12. Start the engine and bring to normal operating temperature. Check for leaks. Check all fluid levels.

13. Leak test, evacuate and charge the air conditioning system.

4.6L Engine

1. Before servicing the vehicle, refer to the precautions in the beginning of this section.

2. Relieve the fuel system pressure.

3. Drain the cooling system and discharge the air conditioning system.

4. Drain engine oil

5. Remove or disconnect the following:
- Negative battery cable
- Air cleaner outlet tube and air cleaner assembly
- Fan blade and shroud
- 42-pin and 8-pin connectors, move them aside
- Accelerator cable
- Speed control actuator
- Throttle valve control cable
- Canister purge electrical connector and vacuum lines
- Power supply from the power distribution box and starter relay
- Transmission oil cooler tubes from the transmission
- Upper radiator hose and heater hoses
- Front wheels
- Right and left front anti-lock sensor and brackets
- Right and left brake caliper bolts, support them with a wire
- Right and left front suspension upper arms from the spindles
- Front springs and shocks from the lower arms
- Dual converter Y-pipe from the manifolds
- Transmission shift cable and bracket

➡ **Matchmark the driveshaft centering socket yoke to the rear axle universal joint flange.**

- 4 bolts connecting the driveshaft centering socket yoke to the rear axle universal joint flange

➡ **Support the rear axle assembly.**

- Rear axle assembly to rear sub-frame bolts

➡ **Loosen the rear differential bracket-to-body bolts and lower.**

6. Slide the driveshaft rearward until it is free of the extension housing.

7. Remove or disconnect the following:
- Lower radiator hose, power steering lines and steering oil cooler
- Wiring connector at the bulkhead

➡ **Support the front sub-frame**

- Rear engine support insulator bolt
- Steering coupling at the pinch bolt joint
- 8 sub-frame bolts

8. Lower the engine/transmission assembly.

9. Remove or disconnect the following:
- All needed components
- Engine from the transmission and place the engine on a workstand

To install:

10. Install or connect the following:
- Engine brackets
- Transmission to the engine

11. Be sure the torque converter studs align with the holes in the flexplate. Torque the bell housing bolts to 30–44 ft. lbs. (40–60 Nm). Torque the torque converter-to-flexplate bolts to 23–25 ft. lbs. (30–35 Nm).

12. Install or connect the following:
- Transmission housing cover
- Starter motor
- Transmission-to-engine block brackets. Torque the retainers to 19–31 ft. lbs. (21–43 Nm).
- Transmission oil cooler tube bracket on the transmission case
- Engine/transmission assembly onto the front sub-frame
- Right and left front engine support insulator through-bolts. Torque the bolts to 15–22 ft. lbs. (20–30 Nm)
- Power steering lines

13. Remove engine lift brackets from the cylinder heads.

14. Install or connect the following:
- Engine/transmission/sub-frame assembly into the vehicle. Torque the bolts to 70–96 ft. lbs. (95–130 Nm).
- Steering shaft pinch joint and driveshaft.

- Rear axle assembly. Torque the rear sub-frame bolts to 73–88 ft. lbs. (98–120 Nm). Torque the 2 rear axle differential insulator nuts to 76–93 ft. lbs. (102–127 Nm).
- Driveshaft centering socket yoke to the rear axle universal joint flange. Torque the 4 bolts to 70–95 ft. lbs. (95–130 Nm).
- Transmission shift linkage, front suspension arms and lower radiator hose

15. Adjust the transmission shift linkage as follows:

a. Position the transmission range selector into the OVERDRIVE position.

b. Loosen the shift cable and bracket-to-cable bracket retaining nut.

c. Move the transmission manual control lever to the OVERDRIVE position (the third detent position from the full clockwise position).

d. Torque the nut to 10–18 ft. lbs. (13–25 Nm).

e. Check the operation of the transmission in each range.

16. Install or connect the following:
- Power steering hoses to steering cooler, ground straps and dual converter Y-pipe
- Front suspension upper arms to the spindles. Torque to 51–67 ft. lbs. (68–92 Nm).
- Anti-lock sensor and calipers
- Front wheels
- Air conditioning lines, transmission cooler lines and radiator hoses
- All remaining hoses, lines, electrical connectors and cables
- Fan, fan shroud and air cleaner
- Negative battery cable

17. Refill the cooling system.

18. Evacuate and recharge the air conditioning system.

19. Refill the crankcase.

20. Start the engine and check for leaks.

Water Pump

REMOVAL & INSTALLATION

3.8L Engine

1. Before servicing the vehicle, refer to the precautions in the beginning of this section.

2. Drain the cooling system.

3. Remove or disconnect the following:
- Negative battery cable
- Fan/clutch assembly and shroud
- Main accessory drive belt tensioner

- Main drive belt and water pump pulley
- Power steering pump pulley
- Water pump-to-power steering pump brace
- Coolant bypass hose(s) and the heater hose at the water pump
- Lower radiator hose
- Water pump retaining bolts and the pump

➡ **If a prybar is used to assist removal, be careful not to damage the mating surfaces.**

To install:

4. Clean the gasket mating surfaces.

➡ **The threads of the No. 1 water pump retaining stud/bolt must be coated with pipe sealant before installing.**

5. Install or connect the following:
   - Water pump. Torque the bolts to 16–21 ft. lbs. (21–29 Nm).
   - Lower radiator hose
   - Coolant bypass hose(s) and the heater hose at the water pump
   - Water pump-to-power steering pump brace
   - Power steering pump pulley
   - Main drive belt and water pump pulley
   - Main accessory drive belt tensioner
   - Fan/clutch assembly and shroud
   - Negative battery cable
6. Refill and bleed the cooling system.
7. Operate the engine to normal operating temperatures and check for leaks.

4.6L Engine

1. Before servicing the vehicle, refer to the precautions in the beginning of this section.
2. Drain cooling system.
3. Remove or disconnect the following:
   - Negative battery cable
   - Drive belt
   - Water pump pulley bolts and pulley
   - Water pump

To install:

4. Clean the gasket mating surfaces.
5. Install or connect the following:
   - Water pump. Torque the bolts to 15–22 ft. lbs. (20–30 Nm).
   - Water pump pulley. Torque the bolts to 15–22 ft. lbs. (20–30 Nm).
   - Drive belt
   - Negative battery cable
6. Refill and bleed the cooling system.

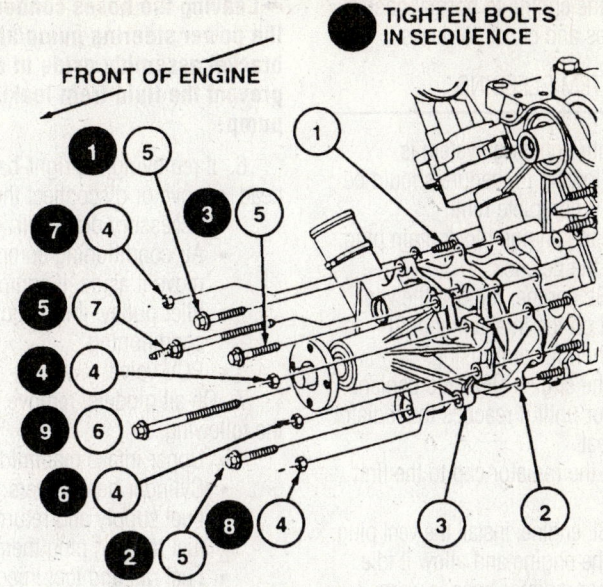

TIGHTEN BOLTS IN SEQUENCE

FRONT OF ENGINE

Item	Description
1	Stud (4 Req'd)
2	Water Pump Housing Gasket
3	Water Pump
4	Nut (4 Req'd)
5	Bolt (3 Req'd)
6	Bolt
7	Stud Bolt

93000QG01

Exploded view of the water pump—3.8L engine

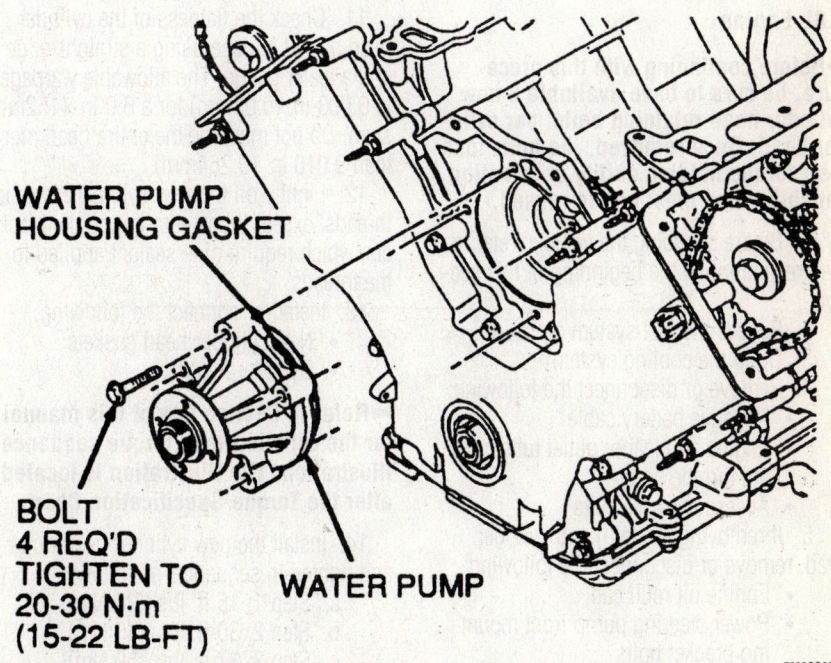

WATER PUMP HOUSING GASKET

BOLT 4 REQ'D TIGHTEN TO 20-30 N·m (15-22 LB-FT)

WATER PUMP

7922QG02

Exploded view of the water pump—4.6L engine

Timing belt service is covered in Section 4 of this manual

7. Operate the engine to normal operating temperatures and check for leaks.

COOLING SYSTEM BLEEDING

When the entire cooling system is drained, the following procedure should be used to ensure a complete refill:

   a. Install the engine block drain plug.

   b. Close the petcock.

   c. On 3.8L engine, remove the vent plug located on the intake manifold behind the thermostat housing.

   d. With the engine OFF, add coolant to the radiator until it reaches the radiator filler neck seat.

   e. Install the radiator cap to the first notch.

   f. On 3.8L engine, install the vent plug.

   g. Start the engine and allow it idle until the upper radiator hose is warm.

➡**This indicates that the thermostat is open and coolant is flowing through the entire system.**

   h. Remove the radiator cap and top off the cooling system.

   i. Install the radiator cap.

   j. Refill the coolant recovery reservoir to the FULL HOT mark.

Cylinder Head

REMOVAL & INSTALLATION

3.8L Engine

➡**Before continuing with this procedure, be sure to have available 8 new cylinder head retaining bolts, per cylinder head. Once removed, the bolts lose their torque holding ability or retention capability and must not be reused.**

1. Before servicing the vehicle, refer to the precautions in the beginning of this section.

2. Relieve the fuel system pressure.

3. Drain the cooling system

4. Remove or disconnect the following:
- Negative battery cable
- Engine air cleaner outlet tube from the throttle body
- Accessory drive belts

5. If removing the left-hand cylinder head, remove or disconnect the following:
- Engine oil refill cap
- Power steering pump front mounting bracket bolts
- Alternator and drive belt idler pulley
- Alternator/power steering pump bracket bolts

➡**Leaving the hoses connected, place the power steering pump/alternator bracket assembly aside in a position to prevent the fluid from leaking out of the pump.**

6. If removing the right-hand cylinder head, remove or disconnect the following:
- Accessory drive belt
- Air conditioning compressor and move it aside, if equipped
- Idler pulley, if not equipped with air conditioning
- PCV valve

7. On all models, remove or disconnect the following:
- Upper intake manifold
- Cylinder head covers
- Fuel supply and return lines at the fuel rail and plug them
- Fuel rail and fuel injectors
- Lower intake manifold
- Exhaust manifolds

8. Loosen the rocker arm seat retaining bolts enough to allow the rocker arms to be lifted off the pushrods and rotated aside.

9. Remove or disconnect the following:
- Pushrods. Identify the position of each rod so that they can be installed in their original positions.
- Cylinder head bolts and discard them
- Cylinder heads and discard the gaskets

To install:

10. Clean the gasket sealing surfaces.

11. Check the flatness of the cylinder head gasket surface using a straight-edge and a feeler gauge. The allowable warpage is 0.003 in. (0.08mm) for a 6.0 in. (152mm) span. Do not machine the entire head more than 0.010 in. (0.254mm).

12. Lightly oil the new cylinder head bolt threads, except those entering coolant jackets, which require pipe sealant applied to the threads.

13. Install or connect the following:
- New cylinder head gaskets
- Cylinder heads

➡**Refer to Section one of this manual for the cylinder head torque sequence illustration. The illustration is located after the Torque Specification Chart.**

14. Install the new cylinder head bolts and tighten in sequence, as follows:

   a. Step 1: 15 ft. lbs. (20 Nm).

   b. Step 2: 30 ft. lbs. (40 Nm).

   c. Step 3: 37 ft. lbs. (50 Nm).

15. Loosen each cylinder head bolt, one at a time, 2–3 turns, then retorque as follows:

   a. Long bolts: 30–37 ft. lbs. (40–50 Nm), plus a 175–185 degree turn.

   b. Short bolts: 15–22 ft. lbs. (20–30 Nm), plus a 175–185 degree turn.

16. Lubricate each pushrod tip with engine assembly lubricant.

17. Install the pushrods in their original positions and rotate the rocker arms into position.

18. For each valve, rotate the crankshaft until the valve lifter rests on the heel (base circle) of the camshaft lobe (pushrod all the way down). Torque the rocker arm fulcrum bolt to 44 inch lbs. (5 Nm). The fulcrum must be fully seated and the pushrod must be seated in the rocker arm socket before final tightening.

19. Lubricate the rocker arm assemblies with engine assembly lubricant. Torque the rocker arm fulcrum bolts to 22–29 ft. lbs. (30–40 Nm). Final tightening can be done with the camshaft in any position.

➡**If the original valve train components are being installed, valve lash adjustment is not required. If a component has been replaced, adjust the valve clearance.**

20. Install or connect the following:
- Exhaust manifolds
- Lower intake manifold, using new gaskets
- Fuel injection supply manifold
- Fuel supply and return lines

➡**Note the ignition wire routing clip stud bolt locations.**

- Cylinder head covers, using new gaskets. Torque the bolts to 71–106 inch lbs. (8–12 Nm).
- Upper intake manifold
- Spark plugs, if removed
- Ignition wires to the spark plugs

21. For the left-hand cylinder head, install or connect the following:
- Engine oil filler cap
- Alternator/power steering pump bracket
- Alternator assembly
- Accessory drive belt tensioner
- Power steering pump
- Power steering pump support bracket. Torque the bolts to 30–45 ft. lbs. (40–62 Nm).

22. For the right-hand cylinder head, install or connect the following:
- PCV valve
- Air conditioning compressor and brackets, if equipped
- Idler pulley, if not equipped with air conditioning
- Accessory drive belt

- Engine air cleaner outlet tube
- Negative battery cable

23. Refill and bleed the engine cooling system.

24. Start the engine and check for coolant, fuel and oil leaks.

25. Road test the vehicle and check for proper operation.

4.6L Engine

1. Before servicing the vehicle, refer to the precautions in the beginning of this section.

2. Relieve the fuel system pressure.

3. Drain the cooling system.

4. Remove or disconnect the following:
- Negative battery cable
- Cooling fan and shroud
- Fuel lines.
- Air inlet tube
- Wiper module
- Accessory drive belt
- Ignition wires from the spark plugs.
- Ignition wire brackets from the camshaft cover studs
- Both ignition wire tray to coil brackets bolts
- Air conditioner high pressure line to the right coil bracket bolt
- Both ignition coils and CID sensor
- Coil brackets to the front cover nuts
- Ignition coil brackets and ignition wire assembly from the mounting studs
- Water pump pulley
- Alternator wiring harness from the junction block, fender apron and alternator
- Alternator
- Positive battery cable at the power distribution box
- Positive battery cable bracket bolt from the side of the right cylinder head
- Vent hose from the canister purge solenoid; then, move the positive battery cable aside
- Canister purge solenoid vent hose from the Positive Crankcase Ventilation (PCV) valve
- PCV valve from the camshaft cover
- 42-pin engine harness connector from the brake vacuum booster bracket
- Crank Position (CKP) sensor electrical connector
- Air conditioning compressor electrical connector

- Canister purge solenoid electrical connector
- Power steering pump bolts from the engine block and front cover

➡ **The power steering pump's lower front bolt will not come all the way out. Wire the power steering pump aside.**

- 4 oil pan-to-front cover bolts
- Crankshaft damper, using a puller
- Oil pressure sending unit, move it aside
- Exhaust Gas Recirculation (EGR) tube from the right exhaust manifold
- Exhaust pipes from the exhaust manifolds and support them with wire from the crossmember
- Starter wiring harness bolt from the rear of the right cylinder head
- Camshaft covers
- Accelerator, cruise control and throttle valve cables
- Accelerator cable bracket from the intake manifold and move it aside
- Vacuum hose from the throttle body elbow vacuum port
- Both Oxygen (O_2) sensors and the heater supply hose

➡ **2 thermostat housing bolts also retain the intake manifold.**

- 2 thermostat housing-to-intake manifold bolts, move the upper hose and thermostat housing aside
- Intake manifold and discard the gaskets
- Front cover
- Timing chains
- Left cylinder head and discard the gasket

➡ **The lower rear bolt cannot be removed due to interference with the brake vacuum booster. Use a rubber band to hold the bolt away from the engine block.**

- Ground strap, 1 stud and 1 bolt retaining the heater return line to the right cylinder head
- Right cylinder head and discard the gasket

➡ **The lower rear bolt cannot be removed due to interference with the evaporator housing. Use a rubber band to hold the bolt away from the engine block.**

To install:

5. Clean all gasket mating surfaces. Check the cylinder head and engine block

for flatness. Check the cylinder head for scratches near the coolant passage and combustion chamber that could provide leak paths. Machine as necessary.

6. Rotate the crankshaft counterclockwise 45 degrees. The crankshaft keyway should be at the 9 o'clock position viewed from the front of the engine. This ensures that all pistons are below the top of the engine block deck face.

7. Rotate the camshaft to a stable position where the valves do not extend below the head face.

8. Install or connect the following:
- New head gaskets on the engine block
- Lower rear bolts on both cylinder heads and retain with rubber bands

➡ **Refer to Section one of this manual for the cylinder head torque sequence illustration. The illustration is located after the Torque Specification Chart.**

- Cylinder heads

➡ **Apply clean oil to the head bolts and remove the rubber band from the lower rear bolt.**

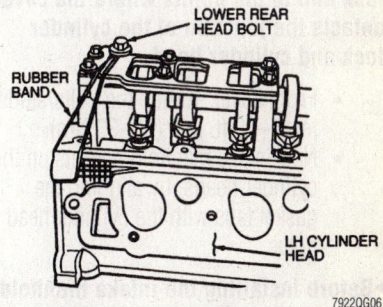

A rubber band should be used to secure the lower rear bolt in the up position—4.6L engine

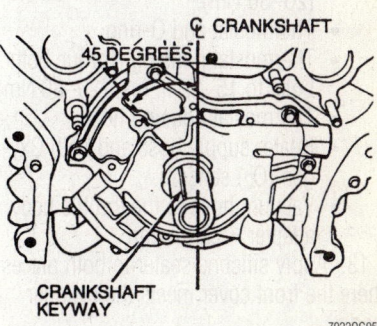

Rotate the crankshaft clockwise 45 degrees, then install the timing chains—4.6L engine

9. Torque the head bolts, in sequence, as follows:

   a. Step 1: 28–31 ft. lbs. (37–43 Nm).

   b. Step 2: Rotate, in sequence, an additional 85–95 degree turn.

   c. Step 3: Loosen, in sequence, 360 degrees.

   d. Step 4: 28–31 ft. lbs. (37–43 Nm).

10. Install the heater return hose and torque both bolts to 15–22 ft. lbs. (20–30 Nm). Rotate the camshafts using the flats matched at the center of the camshaft until both are in time. Install cam positioning tools T91P-6256-A or equivalent, on the flats of the camshafts to keep them from rotating.

11. Rotate the crankshaft clockwise 45 degrees to position the crankshaft at Top Dead Center (TDC) on No. 1 cylinder.

➡**The crankshaft must only be rotated in the clockwise direction and only as far as TDC.**

12. Install or connect the following:
- Timing chains
- New front cover seal and gasket

➡**Apply silicone sealer to the lower corners of the cover where it meets the junction of the oil pan and cylinder block and to the points where the cover contacts the junction of the cylinder block and cylinder head.**

- Front cover. Torque the bolts/studs to 15–22 ft. lbs. (20–30 Nm).
- New intake manifold gaskets on the cylinder heads, by aligning the gasket tabs with the cylinder head holes

➡**Before installing the intake manifold, inspect it for nicks and cuts that could provide leak paths.**

- Intake manifold. Torque the bolts, in sequence, to 15–22 ft. lbs. (20–30 Nm).
- Thermostat and O-ring
- Thermostat housing. Torque both bolts to 15–22 ft. lbs. (20–30 Nm).
- Thermostat housing hose
- Heater supply hose and both Oxygen (O2) sensors.
- Vacuum hose to the throttle body adapter vacuum port

13. Apply silicone sealer to both places where the front cover meets the cylinder head.

14. Install or connect the following:
- New camshaft cover gaskets.
- Camshaft covers. Torque the bolts/studs to 72–106 inch lbs. (8–12 Nm).

- Throttle valve cable, adjust it, if necessary
- Accelerator cable bracket on the intake manifold
- Accelerator and cruise control cables to the throttle body.
- Starter wiring harness to the right cylinder head
- Exhaust pipes to the exhaust manifolds. Torque the nuts to 20–30 ft. lbs. (27–41 Nm).

➡**Be sure the exhaust system clears the No. 3 crossmember. Adjust as necessary.**

- EGR tube to the right exhaust manifold. Torque the line nut to 26–33 ft. lbs. (35–45 Nm).
- Oil sending unit
- Fuel charging wire to the electronic variable orifice sensor

➡**When installing the crankshaft damper, apply a small amount of silicone sealer in the rear of the keyway on the damper.**

- Damper on the crankshaft using an installer, by aligning the crankshaft key

15. Install the damper bolt and washer and torque as follows:

   a. Torque to 67 ft. lbs. (90 Nm).

   b. Loosen 360 degrees

   c. Torque to 37 ft. lbs.

   d. Torque an additional 90 degree turn.

16. Install or connect the following:
- Oil pan to the front cover. Torque the 4 bolts to 15–22 ft. lbs. (20–30 Nm).
- Power steering pump. Torque the bolts to 15–22 ft. lbs. (20–30 Nm).
- Air conditioning compressor electrical connector
- Crankshaft position sensor electrical connector
- Canister purge solenoid electrical connector
- 42-pin engine harness connector
- 8 pin transmission harness connector
- PCV valve in the right camshaft cover
- Canister purge solenoid vent hose
- Positive battery cable at the power distribution box
- Positive battery cable harness on the right cylinder head
- Alternator. Torque the bolts to 15–22 ft. lbs. (20–30 Nm).
- Alternator brace to the intake manifold. Torque both bolts to 71–106 inch lbs. (6–12 Nm).

- Water pump pulley. Torque the bolts to 15–22 ft. lbs. (20–30 Nm).
- Ignition coil brackets and ignition wire assembly. Torque 7 the coil brackets-to-front cover nuts to 15–22 ft. lbs. (20–30 Nm) and ignition wire tray-to-coil bracket bolts to 72–106 inch lbs. (8–12 Nm).
- Both ignition coils and CID sensor
- Air conditioner high pressure line on the right coil bracket
- Ignition wires to the spark plugs and the bracket onto the camshaft cover studs
- Accessory drive belt
- Wiper module
- Fuel lines
- Cooling fan and shroud
- Air inlet tube
- Negative battery cable

17. Refill and bleed the cooling system.

18. Start the engine and bring to normal operating temperature.

19. Check for leaks. Check all fluid levels.

Rocker Arms

REMOVAL & INSTALLATION

3.8L Engine

1. Before servicing the vehicle, refer to the precautions in the beginning of this section.

2. Remove or disconnect the following:
- Negative battery cable
- Spark plug wires from the spark plugs
- Spark plug wire routing clips from the rocker arm cover
- Oil fill cap and crankcase vent tube, if removing the left rocker arm cover
- Positive Crankcase Ventilation (PCV) valve and position the air cleaner assembly aside, if removing the right rocker arm cover
- Rocker arm covers
- Rocker arm, fulcrum and bolt assemblies

➡**Keep each assembly together and identify the assemblies so they may be reinstalled in their original positions.**

To install:

3. Clean the gasket mating surfaces. Clean the rocker arms and fulcrums and inspect for wear or damage. Replace as necessary.

4. Apply grease to the pushrod tips and

valve stem tips. Lubricate the fulcrums and rocker arms with heavy engine oil and install them over the pushrods and valve stems.

5. For each valve, rotate the crankshaft until the lifter is on the base circle of the camshaft, not on the camshaft lobe. Install the fulcrum bolt and torque to 44 inch lbs. (5 Nm). Be sure the pushrod and fulcrum are fully seated prior to tightening the fulcrum bolt.

6. Lubricate all rocker arm assemblies with engine oil. Final torque the fulcrum bolts to 22–29 ft. lbs. (30–40 Nm). When final tightening, the camshaft may be in any position. Be sure the pushrod and fulcrum are fully seated before tightening.

7. Install or connect the following:
- Rocker arms. Torque the bolts to 71–106 inch lbs. (8–12 Nm).
- Rocker arm covers, using new gaskets
- Oil fill cap and crankcase vent tube, after installing the left rocker arm cover
- PCV valve and air cleaner assembly, after installing the right rocker arm cover
- Spark plug wire routing clips
- Spark plug wires
- Negative battery cable

8. Start the engine and check for leaks.

4.6L Engine

1. Before servicing the vehicle, refer to the precautions in the beginning of this section.

2. Remove or disconnect the following:
- Negative battery cable
- Valve covers, after disconnecting all necessary hoses

3. Rotate the camshaft so piston being serviced is at the bottom of its stroke.

4. In order to prevent valve stem seal damage, insert a valve spring spacer between valve spring coils.

5. Install a valve spring compressor between the camshaft and top of valve spring retainer.

6. Compress valve spring.

7. Remove or disconnect the following:
- Rocker arm
- Valve spring compressor and spacer

8. Repeat the previous steps for each rocker arms being removed.

To install:

➡**Before installation, lubricate rocker arm contact surfaces, valve tappet, valve stem and tip with fresh engine oil.**

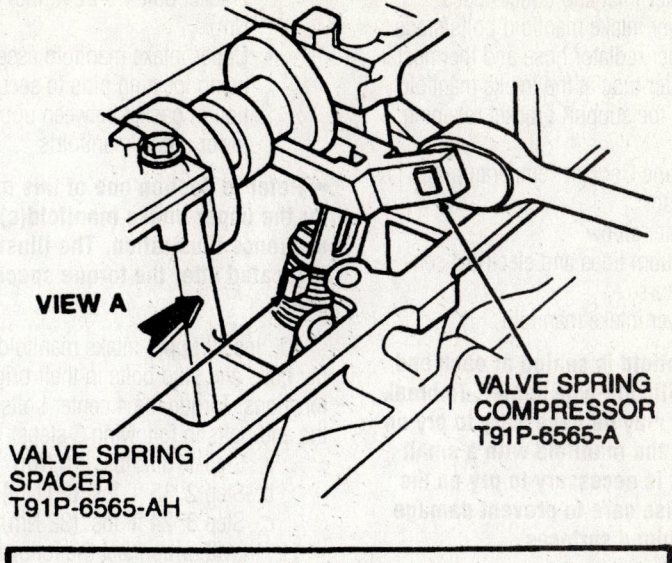

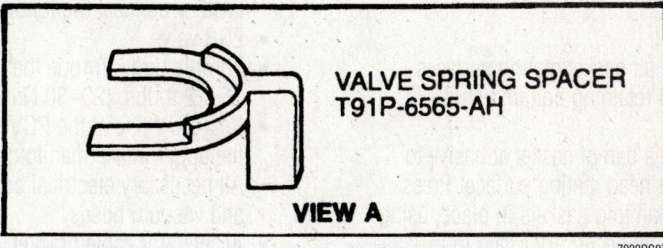

With the valve spring spacer installed, compress the valve spring and remove the rocker arm (cam follower)—4.6L engine

9. Rotate the camshaft so that piston being serviced is at the bottom of its stroke.

10. In order to prevent valve stem seal damage, insert a valve spring spacer between valve spring coils.

11. Install a valve spring compressor between the camshaft and top of valve spring retainer and install rocker arm.

12. Remove valve spring compressor and spacer.

13. Repeat the preceding steps for all rocker arms being replaced.

14. Install or connect the following:
- Rocker arm covers and necessary hoses
- Negative battery cable

15. Start the engine and check for leaks.

Intake Manifold

REMOVAL & INSTALLATION

3.8L Engine

1. Before servicing the vehicle, refer to the precautions in the beginning of this section.
- Relieve fuel system pressure

2. Drain cooling system
3. Remove or disconnect the following:
- Negative battery cable
- Air cleaner assembly or air inlet tube
- Accelerator cable at the throttle body
- Cruise control cable, if equipped
- Accelerator cable mounting bracket, move the cables aside
- Vacuum lines at upper intake manifold
- All necessary electrical connectors
- Positive Crankcase Ventilation (PCV) line at the upper intake manifold and at the valve
- Throttle body assembly
- Exhaust Gas Recirculation (EGR) valve assembly from the upper manifold
- Wiring retainer nut/bracket located at the left front of the intake manifold and set aside with the spark plug wires
- Intake manifold retaining bolts/studs
- Upper intake manifold and discard the gasket
- Injectors and fuel rail assembly

Refer to Section 1 for engine rebuilding specifications

- Heater inlet and outlet hoses
- Lower intake manifold bolts/studs
- Upper radiator hose and thermostat
- Heater tube at the intake manifold and the support bracket retaining nut
- Engine Coolant Temperature (ECT) sensor
- Heater elbow
- Vacuum lines and electrical connectors
- Lower intake manifold

➡**This manifold is sealed at each end with RTV silicone-type sealer. To break the seal, it may be necessary to pry on the front of the manifold with a small prybar. If it is necessary to pry on the manifold, use care to prevent damage to the machined surfaces.**

To install:

4. Clean all gasket mating surfaces. Lightly oil all retaining bolt and stud threads.

5. Apply a dab of gasket adhesive to each cylinder head mating surface. Press new intake manifold gaskets in place, using location pins as necessary to aid in installation.

6. Apply a ⅛ in. (3mm) bead of silicone sealer at each corner where the cylinder head joins the cylinder block. Install the front and rear intake manifold end seals. Also apply pipe sealant to all necessary connections.

7. Install or connect the following:
   - New intake manifold gaskets
   - Intake manifold

➡**Refer to Section one of this manual for the intake manifold(s) torque sequence illustration. The illustration is located after the torque specification chart.**

8. Install bolts and studs in their original locations and tighten, in sequence, using the following two steps:
   a. Step 1: 44 inch lbs. (5 Nm).
   b. Step 2: 71–106 inch lbs. (8–12 Nm).

9. Install or connect the following:
   - Front PCV line to the upper intake tube. Install the front PCV tube so the mounting bracket sits over the lower intake manifold stud. Torque the stud nut to 15–22 ft. lbs. (20–30 Nm).
   - Fuel injectors and fuel injection supply manifold. Torque the fuel injection supply manifold-to-lower intake manifold bolts to 71–97 inch lbs. (8-11 Nm) and fuel pressure

bracket bolt 15–22 ft. lbs. (20–30 Nm).
   - Upper intake manifold assembly, using locating pins to secure position of gasket between upper and lower intake manifolds.

➡**Refer to Section one of this manual for the upper intake manifold(s) torque sequence illustration. The illustration is located after the torque specification chart.**

10. Install upper intake manifold assembly bolts and stud bolts in their original locations. Torque the 4 center bolts, then the end bolts in following 3 steps:
   a. Step 1: 8 ft. lbs. (10 Nm).
   b. Step 2: 15 ft. lbs. (20 Nm).
   c. Step 3: 24 ft. lbs. (32 Nm).

11. Install or connect the following:
   - EGR valve
   - Throttle body. Torque the nuts to 15–22 ft. lbs. (20–30 Nm).
   - Rear PCV line at the PCV valve on the upper intake manifold
   - All necessary electrical connectors and vacuum hoses
   - Accelerator cable bracket. Torque the bolts to 11–14 ft. lbs. (14–20 Nm).
   - Accelerator cable. Check the cable and adjust, if necessary
   - Cruise control cable, if equipped. Check the cable and adjust, if necessary
   - Air cleaner outlet tube
   - Negative battery cable

12. Refill and bleed the cooling system.
13. Start the engine and check for leaks.

➡**Check engine idle air flow and adjust, if necessary.**

4.6L Engine

1. Before servicing the vehicle, refer to the precautions in the beginning of this section.

2. If equipped with air suspension, the air suspension switch, located on the right-hand side of the luggage compartment, must be turned to the **OFF** position before raising the vehicle.

3. Drain the cooling system.
4. Relieve the fuel system pressure.
5. Remove or disconnect the following:
   - Negative battery cable
   - Fuel supply and return lines
   - Windshield wiper governor (module)
   - Engine air cleaner outlet tube
   - Accessory drive belt
   - Ignition wires from the spark plugs

❊❊ WARNING

Take precaution not to pull on ignition wires, as this may cause the wire to separate from the connector in the boot.

   - Ignition wire brackets from the cylinder head cover
   - Ignition coils and the Camshaft Position (CMP) sensor electrical connectors
   - 4 ignition wire bracket-to-ignition coil brackets bolts
   - Alternator wiring harness from the junction block at the fender apron
   - Alternator
   - 4 alternator brace-to-intake manifold bolts
   - Alternator
   - Fuel charging-to-oil pressure sensor electrical connector
   - Power steering control valve actuator wiring.
   - Exhaust Gas Recirculation (EGR) valve-to-exhaust manifold tube from the right-hand exhaust manifold
   - Accelerator and cruise control cables from throttle body
   - Accelerator cable bracket from intake manifold
   - Vacuum hose from the throttle body adapter port
   - Heater coolant hose
   - Both thermostat housing-to-intake manifold bolts

➡**The 2 thermostat housing bolts are also used to retain the intake manifold.**

6. Position the upper radiator hose and thermostat housing aside

7. Remove or disconnect the following:
   - Intake manifold and discard the gaskets

8. If replacing the intake manifold, swap over the necessary parts.

To install:

9. Clean all gasket mating surfaces.
10. Install or connect the following:
   - New intake manifold gaskets, by aligning gasket tabs with the cylinder head holes

➡**Refer to Section one of this manual for the intake manifold(s) torque sequence illustration. The illustration is located after the torque specification chart.**

   - Intake manifold. Hand-tighten the right-rear bolt (viewed from the front of the engine) before final

tightening; then, torque the bolts, in sequence, to 15–22 ft. lbs. (20–30 Nm).
- New O-ring seal on the thermostat housing
- Thermostat housing and upper hose. Torque both bolts to 15–22 ft. lbs. (20–30 Nm).
- Heater coolant hose
- Vacuum hose to the throttle body adapter vacuum port
- Accelerator cable bracket on the intake manifold
- Accelerator and cruise control cables to the throttle body
- EGR valve-to-exhaust manifold tube to the right-hand exhaust manifold. Torque the tube nut to 26–33 ft. lbs. (35–45 Nm).
- Fuel charging wiring to the electronic variable orifice sensor
- Alternator. Torque the bolts to 15–22 ft. lbs. (20–30 Nm).
- Alternator brace to the intake manifold. Torque both bolts to 71–106 inch lbs. (8–12 Nm).
- Alternator wiring harness to the alternator, right-hand fender apron and junction block
- Ignition wire bracket to the ignition coil brackets. Torque both bolts to 71–106 inch lbs. (8–12 Nm).
- Spark plug wires
- Ignition wire separators on valve cover studs
- Fuel charging wiring to the ignition coils
- Engine air cleaner outlet tube
- Accessory drive belt
- Fuel supply and return lines
- Negative battery cable
11. Refill the crankcase.
12. Refill and bleed cooling system.
13. Start the engine and check for leaks.
14. Road test the vehicle and check for proper operation.

Exhaust Manifold

REMOVAL & INSTALLATION

3.8L Engine

LEFT SIDE

1. Before servicing the vehicle, refer to the precautions in the beginning of this section.
2. Remove or disconnect the following:
- Negative battery cable

- Oil level dipstick tube support bracket.
- Ignition wires from the spark plugs
- Exhaust pipe from the exhaust manifold
- Exhaust manifold

To install:

3. Install or connect the following:
- Exhaust manifold. Torque the nuts to 16–23 ft. lbs. (21–32 Nm) and bolts to 23–26 ft. lbs. (30–36 Nm).

✳✳ **WARNING**

A slight warpage in the exhaust manifold may cause a misalignment between the bolt holes in the cylinder head and the exhaust manifold. Elongate the holes in the exhaust manifold as necessary to correct a misalignment. DO NOT elongate the pilot hole (lower rear bolt hole on No. 5 cylinder).

- Exhaust pipe to the exhaust manifold
- Ignition wires to the spark plugs
- Oil level dipstick tube support bracket.
- Negative battery cable

RIGHT SIDE

1. Before servicing the vehicle, refer to the precautions in the beginning of this section.
2. Remove or disconnect the following:
- Negative battery cable
- Coil wire at coil
- Ignition wires at spark plugs
- Exhaust Gas Recirculation (EGR) valve-to-exhaust manifold tube at the exhaust manifold
- Heater inlet tube and hose
- Exhaust pipe from the exhaust manifold
- Exhaust manifold
- Exhaust Gar Recirculation (EGR) valve tube, if a new RH exhaust manifold is being installed
3. Clean the gasket mating surfaces.
4. Install or connect the following:
- EGR valve-to-exhaust manifold tube. Torque the tube to 34–47 ft. lbs. (46–65 Nm).
- New exhaust manifold gasket
- Exhaust manifold, loosely attach two bolts to hold it in place
- EGR valve, loosely to the exhaust manifold tube

✳✳ **WARNING**

A slight warpage in the exhaust manifold may cause a misalignment between the bolt holes in the cylinder head and the exhaust manifold. Elongate the holes in the exhaust manifold as necessary to correct a misalignment. DO NOT elongate the pilot hole (lower rear bolt hole on No. 2 cylinder).

5. Install or connect the following:
- Torque the bolts and studs to 16–23 ft. lbs. (21–32 Nm).
- Heater inlet tube and hose
- Spark plug wires
- Coil wire to coil
- Torque the EGR valve to 15–22 ft. lbs. (20–30 Nm).
- Negative battery cable
6. Start engine and check for leaks.

4.6L Engine

LEFT SIDE

1. Before servicing the vehicle, refer to the precautions in the beginning of this section.
2. Remove or disconnect the following:
- Negative battery cable
- Oil level indicator tube bolt
- Heated Oxygen (O_2) sensors electrical connector
- Catalytic converters from the exhaust manifolds and secure with wires to No. 3 crossmember
- Steering shaft and move it aside
- Exhaust manifold and discard the gaskets

To install:

3. Clean the gasket mating surfaces.
4. Install or connect the following:
- New exhaust manifold gaskets

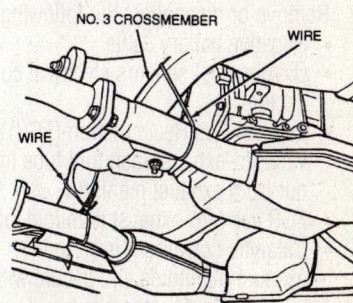

NOTE: WIRE BOTH RH AND LH PIPE TO NO. 3 CROSSMEMBER

9306QG01

Wire both RH and LH exhaust pipes to No. 3 crossmember

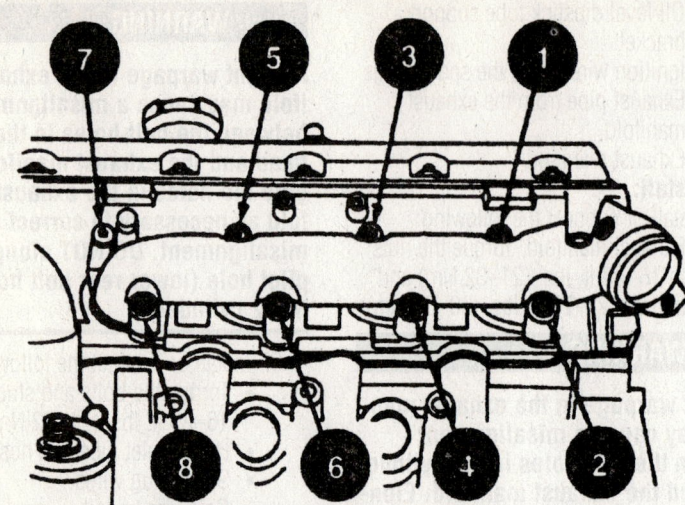

NOTE: ENGINE SHOWN REMOVED FOR CLARITY

NOTE: LH EXHAUST MANIFOLD SHOWN RH EXHAUST MANIFOLD SIMILAR

7922QG15

Exhaust manifold bolt tightening sequence—4.6L engine, left side shown, right side is similar

- Exhaust manifold. Torque the nuts to 14–16 ft. lbs. (18–22 Nm).
- Steering shaft

5. In order to allow enough movement to align EGR valve retaining bolts, loosen the line nut at EGR valve before installing exhaust manifold. Torque line nut to 26–33 ft. lbs. (35–45 Nm).

6. Install or connect the following:
- Catalytic converters. Torque the nuts to 20–30 ft. lbs. (27–41 Nm).
- O₂ sensors electrical connectors
- Negative battery cable

7. Start engine and check for exhaust leaks.

RIGHT SIDE

1. Before servicing the vehicle, refer to the precautions in the beginning of this section.

2. Remove or disconnect the following:
- Negative battery cable
- Oxygen (O₂) sensors electrical connectors
- Exhaust Gas Recirculation (EGR) valve-to-exhaust manifold tube line nut from exhaust manifold
- EGR valve-to-exhaust manifold tube
- Catalytic converters from the exhaust manifolds and secure with wires to No. 3 crossmember
- Exhaust manifold and discard the gasket

To install:

3. Clean all gasket mating surfaces.
4. Install or connect the following:
- EGR valve tube to manifold con-

nector. Torque to 34–47 ft. lbs. (45–65 Nm).

5. In order to allow enough movement to align EGR valve retaining bolts, loosen line nut at EGR valve before installing exhaust manifold. Torque line nut to 26–33 ft. lbs. (35–45 Nm).

6. Install or connect the following:
- Catalytic converters. Torque the nuts to 20–30 ft. lbs. (27–41 Nm).
- O₂ sensors electrical connectors
- Negative battery cable

7. Start engine and check for exhaust leaks.

Camshaft and Valve Lifters

REMOVAL & INSTALLATION

3.8L Engine

1. Before servicing the vehicle, refer to the precautions in the beginning of this section.
2. Relieve the fuel system pressure.
3. Evacuate the air conditioning system.
4. Drain the cooling system.
5. Drain the engine oil.
6. Remove or disconnect the following:
- Negative battery cable
- Radiator
- Condenser, if equipped with air conditioning
- Grille
- Camshaft Position (CMP) sensor

- Upper intake manifold
- Lower intake manifold
- Valve covers
- Pushrods

➡ Keep them in order so they can be returned to their original positions.

- Lifter guide plates
- Valve lifters

➡If necessary, use a magnet to remove lifters. Keep them in order so they can be returned to their original positions.

- Engine front cover
- Timing chain
- Camshaft sprocket spacer
- Oil pan
- Camshaft thrust plate
- Camshaft

➡Be careful not to damage the camshaft bearing surfaces.

➡ Inspect the camshaft rear bearing cover for damage and leaks. Replace cover, if necessary.

To install:

7. Lubricate the cam lobes and journals with heavy engine oil.

8. Install or connect the following:
- Camshaft, being careful not to damage the bearing surfaces while sliding into position
- Thrust plate. Torque the bolts to 71–123 inch lbs. (8–14 Nm).
- Timing chain
- Sprocket spacer
- Engine front cover
- Oil pan
- Lifters, guide plate and retainers
- Lower intake manifold
- Pushrods. Tighten the rocker arms to specifications
- Valve cover
- Upper intake manifold
- CMP sensor
- Grille
- Condenser, if equipped with air conditioning
- Radiator
- Negative battery cable

9. Refill and bleed the cooling system.
10. Refill the crankcase.
11. Evacuate and charge the air conditioning system.
12. Start the engine and check for leaks.

4.6L Engine

1. Before servicing the vehicle, refer to the precautions in the beginning of this section.

2. Drain the cooling system.
3. Relieve the fuel system pressure.
4. Remove or disconnect the following:
   - Negative battery cable
   - Cooling fan assembly and shroud
   - Air cleaner outlet tube
   - Accessory drive belt
   - Ignition wires from the spark plugs

✷✷ WARNING

Take precaution not to pull on ignition wires, as this may cause the wire to separate from the connector in the boot.

   - Ignition wire brackets from the cylinder head cover studs
   - Wiring from both ignition coils and the Camshaft Position (CMP) sensor
   - 3 right-side ignition coil bracket-to-engine front cover nuts
   - Ignition wire assembly, coil and coil bracket as an assembly
   - Power steering fluid reservoir from the left-side coil bracket and move it aside
   - Left-side ignition coil with spark plug wires
   - Left-side coil bracket from front cover
   - Water pump pulley
   - Positive Crankcase Ventilation (PCV) valve and move it aside
   - 42 pin wiring harness
   - 8 pin wiring harness
   - Air conditioning line-to-right-side front fender apron nut

5. Feed the 42 pin connector under the A/C line and move it aside.
6. Remove or disconnect the following:
   - Wiring from crankshaft position sensor, A/C clutch and evaporative emission canister purge valves
   - Power steering pump and move it aside
   - Oil pan and gasket
   - Crankshaft pulley from crankshaft, using a damper remover
   - Oil bypass filter, after positioning drain pan underneath
   - Oil pressure sensor and electronic variable orifice sensor wiring
   - Oil filter adapter and move the wiring aside
   - Right-side valve cover
   - Left-side valve cover
   - Timing chain front cover
   - Timing chains

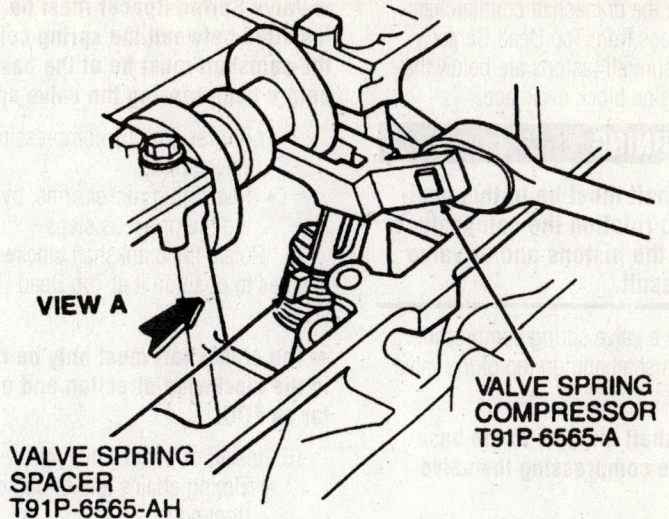

VIEW A

VALVE SPRING SPACER
T91P-6565-AH

VALVE SPRING COMPRESSOR
T91P-6565-A

VALVE SPRING SPACER
T91P-6565-AH

VIEW A

79220G07

To remove the rocker arm, install the spacer and compress the valve spring using the special tools—4.6L engine

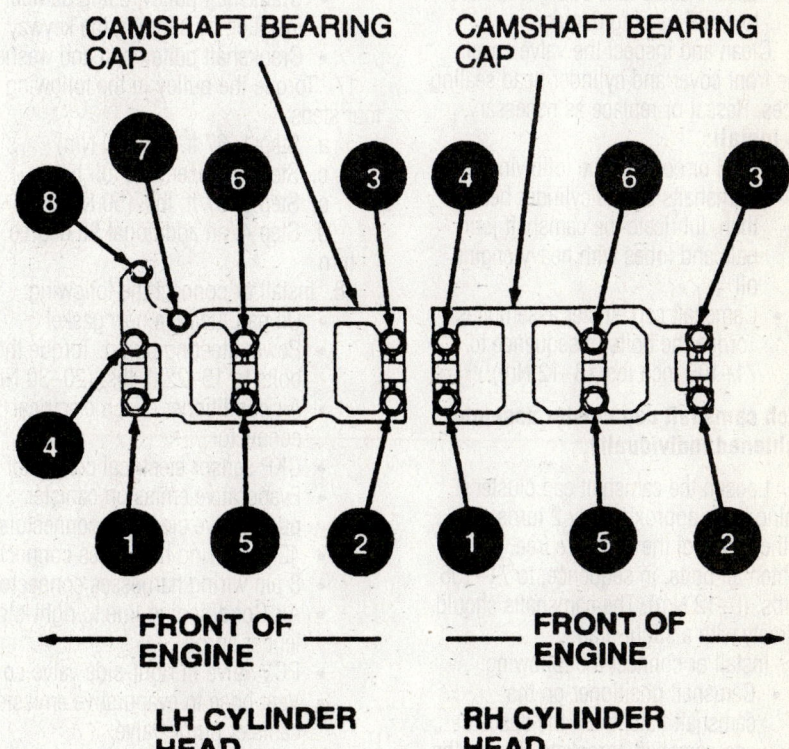

CAMSHAFT BEARING CAP

CAMSHAFT BEARING CAP

FRONT OF ENGINE

FRONT OF ENGINE

LH CYLINDER HEAD

RH CYLINDER HEAD

79220G16

To avoid damage to the camshaft and related components, tighten the cap cluster bolts in the order shown—4.6L engine

For complete mechanical specifications, refer to Section 1 of this manual

7. Rotate the crankshaft counterclockwise 45 degrees from Top Dead Center (TDC) to be sure all pistons are below the top of the engine block deck face.

✳✳ WARNING

The crankshaft must be in this position prior to rotating the camshafts or damage to the pistons and/or valve train will result.

8. Install a valve spring compressor under the camshaft and on top of the valve spring retainer.

➡ **The camshaft must be at the base circle before compressing the valve spring.**

9. Compress the valve spring far enough to remove the roller follower. Repeat the above steps until all rocker arms are removed.

10. Remove or disconnect the following:
- Camshaft cap cluster assemblies from the cylinder heads

➡ **Tap upward on the camshaft caps at points near the upper bearing halves and gradually lift the camshaft clusters from the cylinder heads**

- Lift the camshafts straight upward to avoid bearing damage

11. Clean and inspect the valve cover, engine front cover and cylinder head sealing surfaces. Reseal or replace as necessary.

To install:

12. Install or connect the following:
- Camshafts on the cylinder heads; then, lubricate the camshaft journals and lobes with heavy engine oil
- Camshaft cap cluster assemblies. Torque the bolts in sequence to 71–106 inch lbs. (8–12 Nm).

➡ **Each camshaft cap cluster assembly is tightened individually.**

13. Loosen the camshaft cap cluster retaining bolts approximately 2 turns or until the heads of the bolts are free. Retighten all bolts, in sequence, to 71–106 inch lbs. (8–12 Nm). The camshafts should turn freely with a slight drag.

14. Install or connect the following:
- Camshaft positioner on the camshaft flats; then, the spacers and camshaft sprockets. Torque the bolts to 82–95 ft. lbs. (110–130 Nm).
- Valve Spring Compressor under the camshaft and on top of the valve spring retainer

➡ **Valve Spring Spacer must be installed between the spring coils and the camshaft must be at the base circle before compressing the valve spring.**

- Rocker arm, by compressing the valve spring
- Remaining rocker arms, by repeating the previous steps

15. Rotate the crankshaft clockwise 45 degrees to position it at Top Dead Center (TDC).

➡ **The crankshaft must only be rotated in the clockwise direction and only as far as TDC.**

16. Install or connect the following:
- Timing chains and timing chain front cover
- Camshaft covers
- Crankshaft front seal and front cover

➡ **Inspect crankshaft front seal and engine front cover for cracks and replace, as necessary.**

- Valve covers, using new gaskets. Torque the retainers to 71–106 inch lbs. (8–12 Nm).
- Oil pressure sensor and electronic variable orifice sensor
- Crankshaft pulley, using damper installer, by aligning the keyway
- Crankshaft pulley bolt and washer

17. Torque the pulley in the following four steps:
a. Step 1: 67 ft. lbs. (90 Nm).
b. Step 2: loosen one full turn.
c. Step 3: 37 ft. lbs. (50 Nm).
d. Step 4: an additional 90 degree turn

18. Install or connect the following:
- Oil pan, using a new gasket
- Power steering pump. Torque the bolts to 15–22 ft. lbs. (20–30 Nm).
- Air conditioner clutch electrical connector
- CKP sensor electrical connector
- Evaporative emission canister purge valve electrical connectors
- 42 pin wiring harnesses connector
- 8 pin wiring harnesses connector
- Air Conditioning line to right-side fender apron
- PCV valve in right-side valve cover
- Vent hose to evaporative emission canister purge valve
- Water pump pulley. Torque the bolts to 15–22 ft. lbs. (20–30 Nm).
- Right-side coil bracket, spark plug wires and wire separators onto mounting studs

- Right-side coil bracket to the front cover. Torque the nuts to 15–22 ft. lbs. (20–30 Nm).
- Left-side coil bracket. Torque the nuts to 15–22 ft. lbs. (20–30 Nm).
- Left-side coil and wires as a unit
- Power steering fluid reservoir
- Both ignition coils and CMP sensor
- Spark plug wires to spark plugs and brackets onto valve cover studs
- Drive belt
- Fuel lines
- Cooling fan assembly and shroud
- Air cleaner outlet tube
- Negative battery cable

19. Refill the cooling system.
20. Start the engine and check for leaks.
21. Check the oil and add as needed.

Valve Lash

ADJUSTMENT

3.8L Engine

The valve lash is not adjustable. If the collapsed lifter clearance is found to be incorrect, there are replacement pushrods available to compensate for excessive or insufficient clearance. To check the lifter clearance, perform the following:

a. Before servicing the vehicle, refer to the precautions in the beginning of this section.

b. Disconnect the negative battery cable.

c. Remove the valve cover assembly on the side to be checked.

d. Turn the engine until the No. 1 piston is at Top Dead Center (TDC) on the compression stroke.

1. The following valves can be checked with the engine in this position:
- No. 1 intake
- No. 1 exhaust
- No. 2 exhaust
- No. 3 intake
- No. 4 exhaust
- No. 6 intake

2. Rotate the engine 360 degrees and check the following valves:
- No. 2 intake
- No. 3 exhaust
- No. 4 intake
- No. 5 exhaust
- No. 5 intake
- No. 6 exhaust

3. Check each of the lifters by placing a lifter compressor on the rocker arm and slowly applying pressure to the lifter, until the lifter is collapsed.

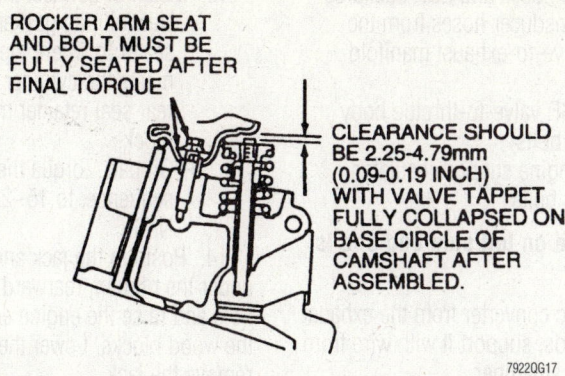

ROCKER ARM SEAT
AND BOLT MUST BE
FULLY SEATED AFTER
FINAL TORQUE

CLEARANCE SHOULD
BE 2.25-4.79mm
(0.09-0.19 INCH)
WITH VALVE TAPPET
FULLY COLLAPSED ON
BASE CIRCLE OF
CAMSHAFT AFTER
ASSEMBLED.

7922QG17

Collapse the valve lifter before measuring the valve clearance—3.8L engines

4. Hold the lifter in this position and check the clearance between the rocker arm and the valve stem tip. The clearance should be 0.09–0.19 in. (2.25–4.79mm).

5. Repeat this operation for each valve to be checked.

6. If the clearance is greater than specification, replace the pushrod with a longer one. If the clearance is less than specified, replace the pushrod with a shorter one.

4.6L Engine

The 4.6L SOHC engine requires no periodic valve adjustment. Hydraulic Lash Adjusters (HLA)'s are used in the valve train to compensate for excessive valve lash.

Starter Motor

REMOVAL & INSTALLATION

1. Before servicing the vehicle, refer to the precautions in the beginning of this section.

✹✹ WARNING

The heavy gauge input lead connected to the starter solenoid is hot at all times. Make sure that the protective cap is installed over the terminal and is replaced after service is the performed.

2. Remove or disconnect the following:
   • Negative battery cable
   • Starter electrical connectors
   • Starter
To install:
3. Install or connect the following:
   • Starter motor. Torque the bolts to 15–20 ft. lbs. (20–27 Nm).
   • Starter electrical connectors.

Torque the "B" terminal nut to 60–123 inch lbs. (9–14 Nm).
   • Red starter solenoid safety cap
   • Negative battery cable

Oil Pan

REMOVAL & INSTALLATION

3.8L Engine

1. Before servicing the vehicle, refer to the precautions in the beginning of this section.

2. Drain the crankcase.

3. Remove or disconnect the following:
   • Negative battery cable
   • Air cleaner outlet tube
   • Upper sight shield and move it aside
   • Hood weather seal
   • Windsheild wipers
   • Left cowl vent screen
   • Windsheild wiper module
   • Engine lifting brackets
   • Engine mount through-bolts

4. Partially, raise the engine with a support fixture.

5. Remove or disconnect the following:
   • Starter motor
   • Oil filter
   • Starter wire loom and ground strap
   • Automatic transmission oil cooler lines, if equipped
   • Oil pan-to-bell housing bolts
   • Crankshaft Position (CKP) sensor shield bolts, if equipped
   • All remaining oil pan retaining bolts
   • Steering shaft pinch bolts and separate the steering shaft

6. Position a jack under the front of the sub-frame.

7. Remove or disconnect the following:
   • 6 rear bolts at the front of the sub-frame
   • Both 2 front sub-frame bolts, loosen them
   • Lower strut-to-control arm bolts and nuts
   • Sub-frame, lower it
   • Oil pan
To install:
8. Clean the gasket mating surfaces and the oil pan. Apply silicone sealer to the oil pan.

9. Install or connect the following:
   • Oil pan

➡**Be sure enough clearance has been provided to allow the oil pan to be installed without sealer being scraped off under the cylinder block.**

   • Oil pan bolts at the cylinder block and bell housing
   • Lower CKP sensor shield, if equipped

10. Torque the bolts in the following two steps:
    a. Step 1: 36–44 inch lbs. (4–5 Nm).
    b. Step 2: 80–106 inch lbs. (9–12 Nm).

11. Raise the sub-frame into position.

12. Install or connect the following:
    • Lower strut mount to the control arm. Torque the bolts to 103–144 ft. lbs. (140–195 Nm).
    • 2 front sub-frame bolts and the 6 rear of the front sub-frame member bolts, loosely

13. Install a ¾ in. (19mm) outside diameter pipe, into both front left and right sub-frame and body alignment holes. Tighten 1 bolt at each corner. Remove the alignment tools and torque the bolts to 72–97 ft. lbs. (97–132 Nm).

14. Install or connect the following:
    • Steering shaft. Torque the pinch bolt to 31–42 ft. lbs. (41–57 Nm).
    • Transmission cooler lines, if equipped
    • Starter wire loom and ground strap
    • New oil filter
    • Starter

15. Partially lower the vehicle.

16. Lower the engine with the support fixture. Seat the left side locating pin before the right. Partially raise the vehicle and support safely.

17. Install or connect the following:
    • Engine mount. Torque the through-bolts to 35–50 ft. lbs. (47–68 Nm).

18. Remove the engine support fixture.

Please refer to Section 8 for electric cooling fan wiring schematics

19. Install or connect the following:
   - Windshield wiper module and the left cowl vent screen
   - Windsheild wipers and hood weather seal
   - Upper sight shield
   - Air cleaner outlet tube
   - Negative battery cable
20. Refill the crankcase.
21. Start the engine and check for leaks.

4.6L Engine

1. Before servicing the vehicle, refer to the precautions in the beginning of this section.
2. Drain the crankcase.
3. Drain the cooling system.
4. Relieve the fuel system pressure.
5. Evacuate the air conditioning system.
6. Remove or disconnect the following:
   - Negative battery cable
   - Air cleaner outlet tube
   - Cooling fan and shroud
   - Fuel lines
   - Upper radiator hose
   - Windshield wiper module and support bracket
   - Compressor outlet hose at the compressor; then, cap the compressor outlet and compressor.
   - Hose assembly to the right coil bracket bolt
   - 42-pin harness connector from the brake vacuum booster bracket
   - 8-pin transmission harness connector
   - Heater outlet hose
   - Exhaust Gas Recirculation (EGR) backpressure transducer
   - Heater hose/pipe assembly to the right cylinder head stud and move it aside
   - Blower motor resistor
   - Right front engine support insulator to subframe bolt

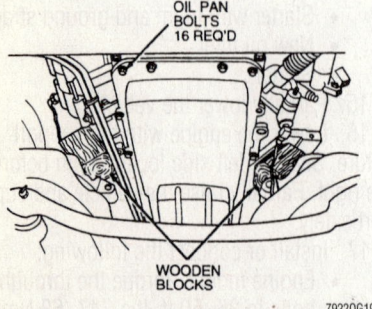

OIL PAN BOLTS 16 REQ'D

WOODEN BLOCKS

7922QG19

Place wooden blocks between the engine mounts and the frame to allow access to the oil pan—4.6L engine

   - Vacuum hoses and EGR backpressure transducer hoses from the EGR valve-to-exhaust manifold tube
   - Both EGR valve-to-throttle body adapter bolts
   - Front engine support insulator through bolts

➡ **Two bolts are on left side and one is on right side.**

   - Catalytic converter from the exhaust manifolds, support it with wire from the crossmember.

7. Position a jackstand under the oil pan with a block of wood between the pan and the jack. Position jack to the rear of the drain.
8. Raise the engine approximately 4 inches (100mm).
9. Slide two 2.5–2.75 inch (60–70mm) wood blocks and lower engine onto the blocks and remove jack from under the oil pan.
10. Raise the transmission extension housing slightly to remove the oil pan.
11. Remove the oil pan.

To install:
12. Clean the oil pan and the gasket mating surfaces.

13. Install or connect the following:
   - New oil pan gasket. Apply silicone sealer to where the front cover meets the cylinder block and the rear seal retainer meets the cylinder block.
   - Oil pan. Torque the bolts, in sequence, to 15–22 ft. lbs. (20–30 Nm).
14. Position the jack and wood block under the oil pan, rearward of the oil drain hole and raise the engine enough to remove the wood blocks. Lower the engine and remove the jack.
15. Install or connect the following:
   - Engine mount through-bolts. Torque the bolts to 15–22 ft. lbs. (20–30 Nm).
   - EGR valve/tube assembly to the exhaust manifold. Torque the line nut to 26–33 ft. lbs. (35–45 Nm).

➡ **Loosen the line nut at the EGR valve prior to installing the assembly. This will allow enough movement to align the EGR valve retaining bolts.**

16. Install or connect the following:
   - Exhaust system to the manifolds. Torque the 4 nuts to 20–30 ft. lbs. (27–41 Nm).

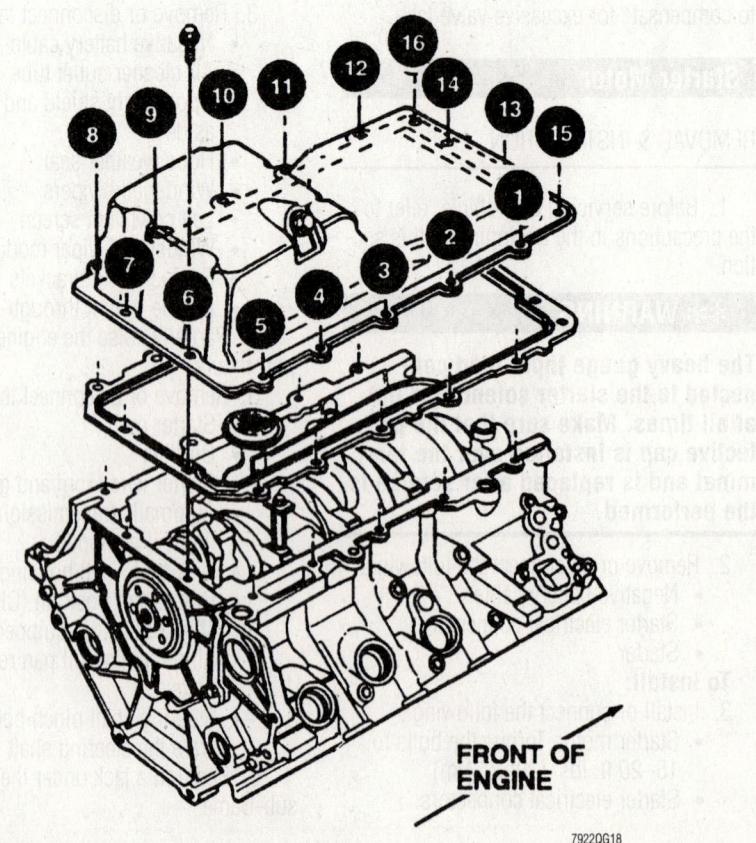

FRONT OF ENGINE

7922QG18

Oil pan bolt torquing sequence—4.6L engine

➡ **Be sure the exhaust system clears the crossmember. Adjust as necessary**

- New oil filter
- Right engine mount-to-lower engine bracket bolt. Torque the bolt to 15–22 ft. lbs. (20–30 Nm).
- New EGR valve gasket
- EGR valve to the intake manifold. Torque the bolts to 15–22 ft. lbs. (20–30 Nm).
- EGR tube line nut at the EGR valve. Torque it to 26–33 ft. lbs. (35–45 Nm).
- Vacuum hoses to the EGR valve and tube
- Blower motor resistor
- EGR backpressure transducer and all EGR valve vacuum hoses
- Heater outlet hose
- Upper stud. Torque the upper and lower bolts to 15–22 ft. lbs. (20–30 Nm).
- Ground strap on the stud. Torque it to 15–22 ft. lbs. (20–30 Nm).
- Heater inlet hose
- 42-pin connector and 8-pin transmission harness connectors
- Harness connector on the brake vacuum booster
- Air conditioning compressor hose to the compressor and the right coil bracket
- Upper radiator hose
- Fuel lines

- Wiper module and bracket
- Cooling fan and shroud
- Air cleaner outlet tube
- Negative battery cable

17. Refill the cooling system.
18. Refill the crankcase.
19. Start the engine and check engine for leaks.
20. Evacuate and recharge the air conditioning system.

Oil Pump

REMOVAL & INSTALLATION

3.8L Engine

➡ **The timing chain front cover houses the oil pump. If the oil pump housing is scored, worn or grooved, replace the front cover.**

1. Before servicing the vehicle, refer to the precautions in the beginning of this section.
2. Remove or disconnect the following:
   - Negative battery cable
   - Oil filter
   - Cover/filter mount assembly
   - Pump gears from the front cover pocket
3. Clean all gasket mounting surfaces.
4. Inspect the mounting pocket for wear. If excessive wear is present, replace the front cover.

5. Inspect the cover/filter mount gasket-to-timing cover surface for flatness. Place a straight-edge across the flat and check clearance with a feeler gauge. If the measured clearance exceeds 0.0016 in. (0.04mm), replace the cover/filter mount.

To install:

6. Install or connect the following:
   - Oil pump and filter body to engine front cover. Torque the 2 small bolts to 71–97 inch lbs. (8–11 Nm) and the 4 large bolts to 17–23 ft. lbs. (23–32 Nm).
   - New oil filter
   - Negative battery cable
7. Refill the crankcase.
8. Start the engine. Check for leaks and proper oil pressure.

4.6L Engine

1. Before servicing the vehicle, refer to the precautions in the beginning of this section.
2. Remove or disconnect the following:
   - Negative battery cable
   - Valve covers
   - Front cover
   - Oil pan and pickup tube
   - Timing chains
   - Oil pump
3. Clean the mating surfaces and inspect for damage.

To install:

4. Install or connect the following:
   - Oil pump, by aligning the inner oil pump rotor with the crankshaft flats. Torque the bolts to 71–106 inch lbs. (8–12 Nm).
   - Oil filter
   - Timing chains
   - Pickup tube and oil pan
   - Front cover
   - Negative battery cable
5. Refill the crankcase.
6. Start the engine. Check for leaks and proper oil pressure.

Rear Main Seal

REMOVAL & INSTALLATION

3.8L Engine

➡ **Special tools are available for installing rear main oil seals. In most cases, the seals can be installed using a common seal and bearing driver set.**

1. Before servicing the vehicle, refer to the precautions in the beginning of this section.

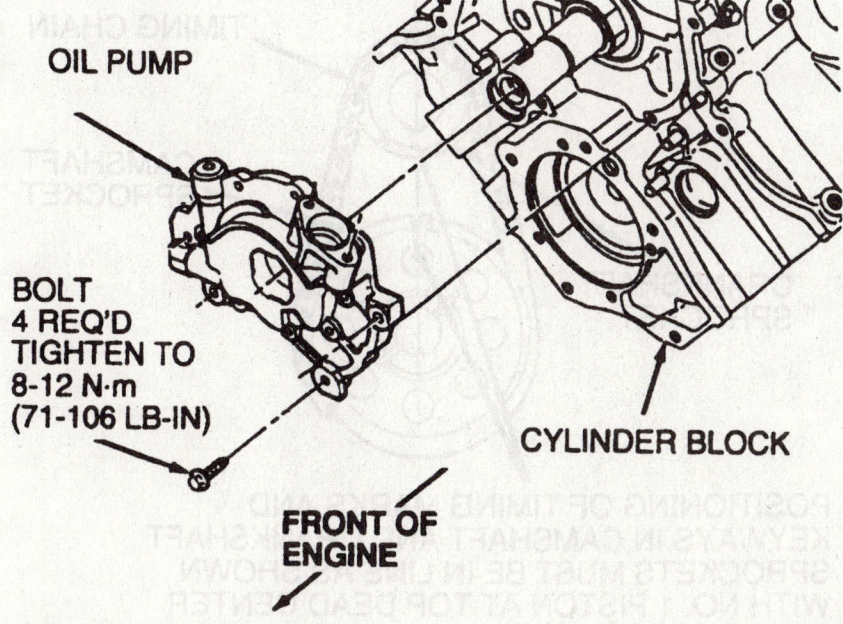

OIL PUMP

BOLT 4 REQ'D TIGHTEN TO 8-12 N·m (71-106 LB-IN)

CYLINDER BLOCK

FRONT OF ENGINE

7922QG20

Exploded view of the oil pump mounting—4.6L engine

2. Remove or disconnect the following:
- Negative battery cable
- Transmission
- Flexplate or flywheel

3. With a sharp awl, carefully punch a small hole in the metal portion of the seal.

4. Install or connect the following:
- Rear main oil seal, using a slide hammer with a sheet metal screw attached

To install:

5. Lubricate the seal and the crankshaft with clean engine oil.

6. Install the seal with the spring side toward the engine.

7. Remove the installation tool

8. Install or connect the following:
- Flexplate or flywheel
- Transmission
- Negative battery cable

4.6L Engine

1. Before servicing the vehicle, refer to the precautions in the beginning of this section.

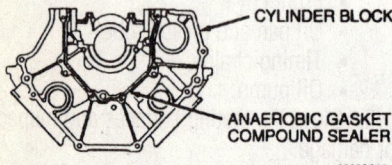

Apply a bead of sealant to the block as shown—4.6L engine

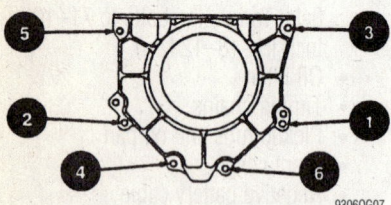

Torque the rear oil seal retainer bolts in the sequence shown—4.6L engine

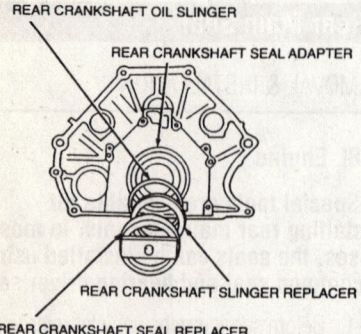

Install the crankshaft oil slinger using a replacer tool—4.6L engine

2. Remove or disconnect the following:
- Transmission
- Flywheel
- Crankshaft oil slinger, using a slinger removal tool and a slide hammer
- Rear main oil seal, using a seal removal tool and a slide hammer
- Rear oil seal retainer, if necessary.

3. Clean and inspect the oil retainer and the retainer-to-block mating surfaces.

To install:

4. Clean the sealing surface with a suitable metal surface cleaner before applying any sealer.

➡ **The crankshaft oil seal retainer must be installed and the bolts tightened to specification within 5 minutes of sealer application.**

5. Apply a 0.08 inch (2.0mm) bead of anaerobic gasket compound sealer to the cylinder block.

6. Install or connect the following:
- Rear main oil seal retainer. Torque the bolts, in sequence, to 71–106 inch lbs. (8–12 Nm).
- Rear main oil seal, using a seal driver/installer tool
- Cranshaft oil slinger, using a replacer tool
- Flywheel
- Transmission

Timing Chain, Sprockets, Front Cover and Seal

REMOVAL & INSTALLATION

3.8L Engine

1. Before servicing the vehicle, refer to the precautions in the beginning of this section.

2. Remove or disconnect the following:
- Negative battery cable
- Fan blade, clutch and shroud
- Front cover

➡ **If replacing the front cover, remove water pump and oil pump gears from old cover and install onto the new cover.**

- Camshaft sprocket bolt and washer from the end of the camshaft
- Distributor drive gear
- Camshaft sprocket, crankshaft sprocket and timing chain simultaneously

➡ **If the crankshaft sprocket is difficult to remove, use two approved prybars and pry simultaneously on both sides of the sprocket. Take necessary precautions when prying.**

- Timing chain vibration damper

➡ **In order to remove vibration damper, pull back on ratcheting mechanism and**

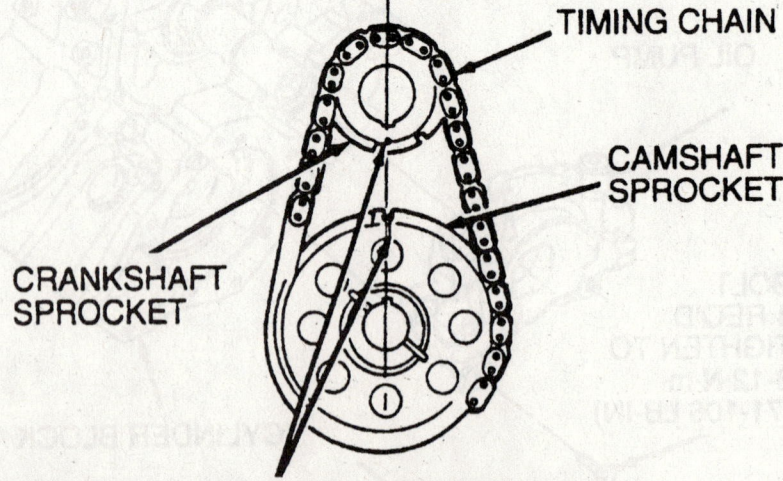

POSITIONING OF TIMING MARKS AND KEYWAYS IN CAMSHAFT AND CRANKSHAFT SPROCKETS MUST BE IN LINE AS SHOWN WITH NO. 1 PISTON AT TOP DEAD CENTER FIRING

The timing marks should be facing each other, when the timing chain is installed correctly—3.8L engines

then install pin through hole in bracket to relieve tension.

To install:

3. Clean all gasket mating surfaces.

➡ If reusing the front cover, replace the front cover oil seal.

4. Install or connect the following:
   • Timing chain vibration damper while the damper is in the compressed position. Torque the bolts to 71–123 inch lbs. (8–14 Nm).

5. Rotate the crankshaft to position the No. 1 piston at Top Dead Center (TDC) and the crankshaft keyway at the 12 o'clock position.

6. Lubricate the timing chain with fresh engine oil.

7. Install or connect the following:
   • Camshaft sprocket, crankshaft sprocket and timing chain as a unit, by aligning the timing marks
   • Distributor drive gear
   • Camshaft bolt and washer assembly. Torque the bolt to 30–37 ft. lbs. (40–50 Nm).

8. Remove timing chain vibration damper retaining pin.

9. Install or connect the following:
   • Engine front cover
   • Negative battery cable

10. Start engine. Check for leaks and proper operation.

4.6L Engine

1. Before servicing the vehicle, refer to the precautions in the beginning of this section.

➡ This is not a free-wheeling engine. Therefore, if it jumps time, damage to the valves and/or pistons will occur.

➡ The camshaft sprockets should only be taken off the camshafts when a component needs to be replaced.

❋❋ WARNING

Crankshaft and camshafts are not to be rotated while the timing chains are removed and the cylinder heads are installed, as this will result in damage to the valves and/or pistons.

2. Remove or disconnect the following:
   • Negative battery cable
   • Crankshaft Position (CKP) sensor pulse wheel
   • Valve covers

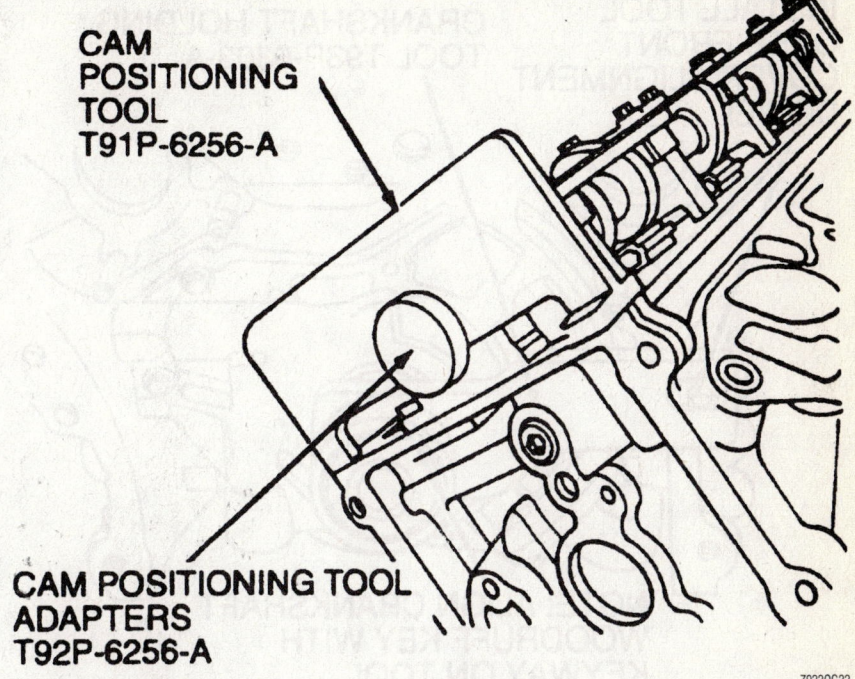

CAM POSITIONING TOOL T91P-6256-A

CAM POSITIONING TOOL ADAPTERS T92P-6256-A

7922QG22

Install the Camshaft Positioning tools in order to keep the camshaft in the correct position—4.6L engine

   • Front cover
   • Oil pan
3. Rotate engine to No. 1 Top Dead Center (TDC).
4. Install a camshaft positioning tool in order to prevent camshaft from turning and damaging valves and/or pistons. It is very important that the camshafts **DO NOT** turn.

5. Remove or disconnect the following:
   • Both right-side timing chain tensioner to cylinder head bolts

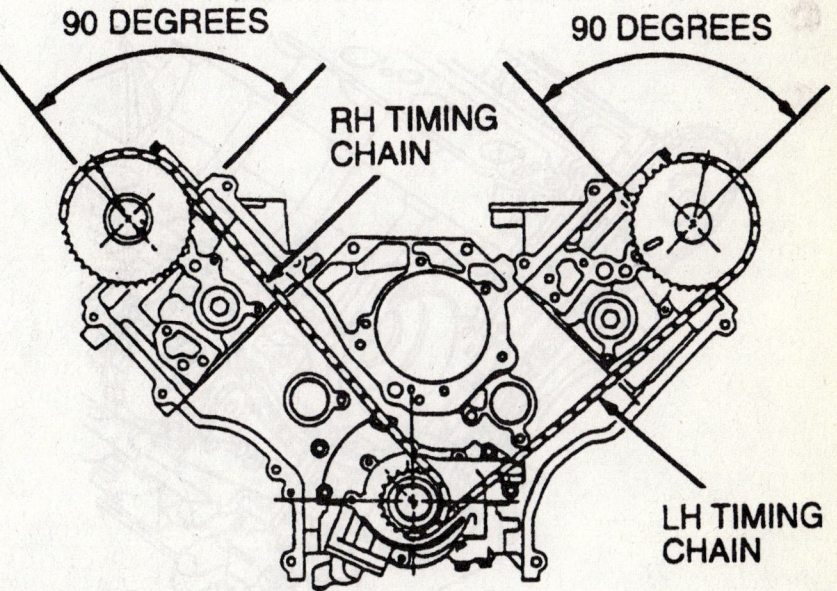

90 DEGREES   90 DEGREES

RH TIMING CHAIN

LH TIMING CHAIN

7922QG23

Be sure the sprocket marks align with the chain copper colored links —4.6L engine

Timing belt service is covered in Section 4 of this manual

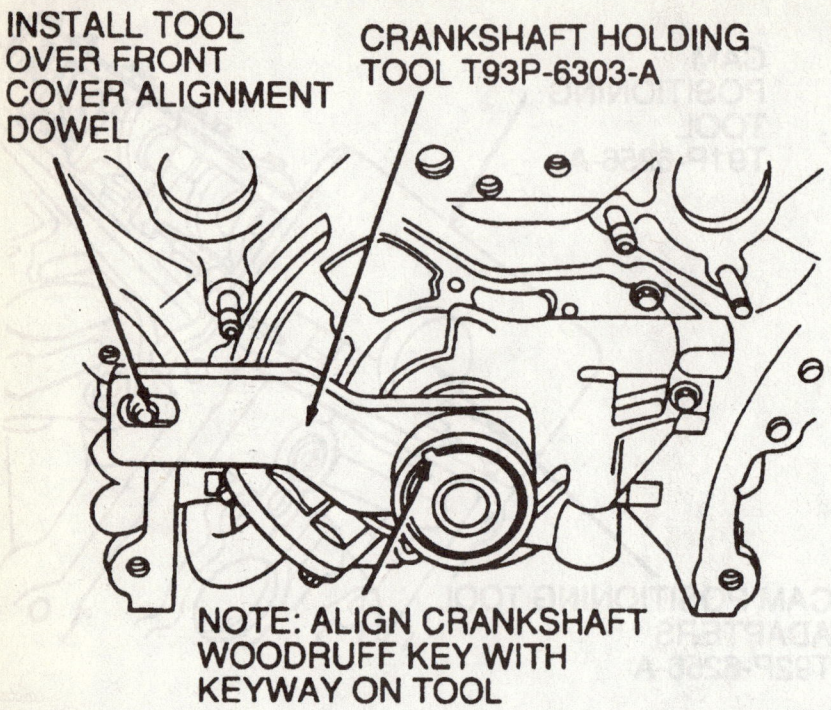

INSTALL TOOL OVER FRONT COVER ALIGNMENT DOWEL

CRANKSHAFT HOLDING TOOL T93P-6303-A

NOTE: ALIGN CRANKSHAFT WOODRUFF KEY WITH KEYWAY ON TOOL

7922QG25

Install the Crankshaft Holding tool to maintain crankshaft position while removing the slack from the timing chain—4.6L engine

- Right-side timing chain tensioner and arm
- Both right-side timing chain guide to cylinder head bolts
- Right-side timing chain guide
- Right-side timing chain from camshaft sprocket and crankshaft sprockets
- both left-side timing chain tensioner to cylinder head bolts

NOTE: USE C-CLAMP TO REMOVE SLACK FROM CAMSHAFT TIMING CHAIN

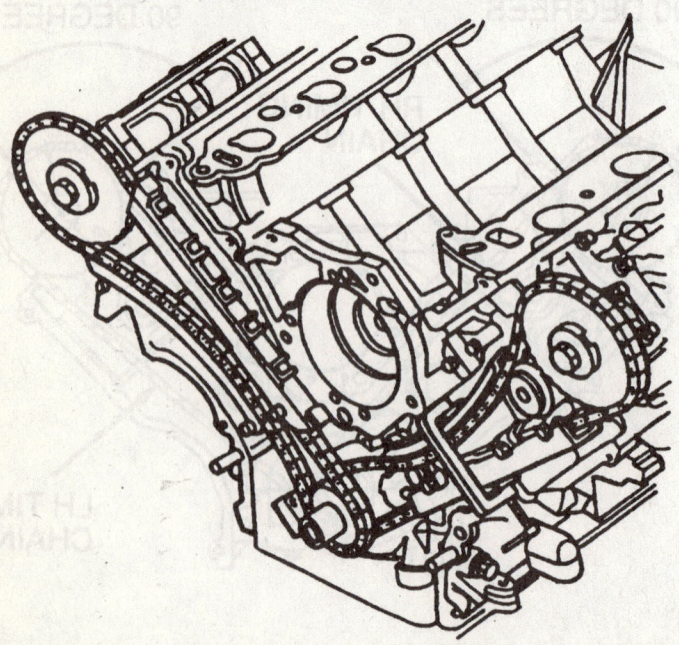

7922QG26

Remove the slack from the timing chain with a C-clamp before removing the pin from the tensioner—4.6L engine

- Left-side timing chain tensioner and arm
- Both left-side timing chain guide to cylinder head bolts
- Left-side timing chain guide
- Left-side timing chain from camshaft and crankshaft sprockets

6. Inspect plastic running face on timing chain guides and timing chain tensioner arms. If worn or damaged, remove and clean oil pan and oil pump screen cover and tube.

To install:

7. Be sure the camshaft positioners are installed on the camshafts to prevent them from rotating.

8. Before proceeding, make sure that any necessary component repairs have been made to an engine that has jumped time.

9. Install or connect the following:
- Left and right-side timing chain guides. Torque the bolts to 71–106 inch lbs. (8–12 Nm).
- Left-side camshaft sprocket spacer and sprocket onto camshaft
- Camshaft sprocket washer and bolt, finger-tighten
- Right-side camshaft sprocket spacer and sprocket onto camshaft
- Camshaft sprocket washer and bolt, finger-tighten

➡The crankshaft sprockets are identical. They may only be installed one way, with the tapered part of the sprocket facing each other.

- Left crankshaft sprocket with the tapered section facing outward
- Left timing chain on the camshaft and crankshaft sprockets. Be sure the chain copper links align with the sprockets timing marks.

➡If the timing chain copper links are not visible, pull the chain taught until the opposite sides of the chain contact one another and lay it on a flat surface. Mark the links at each end of the chain and use them in place of the copper links.

- Right crankshaft sprocket with the tapered part of the sprocket facing away from the engine block
- Right timing chain on the camshaft and crankshaft sprockets. Be sure the copper links of the chain line up with the timing marks of the sprockets.

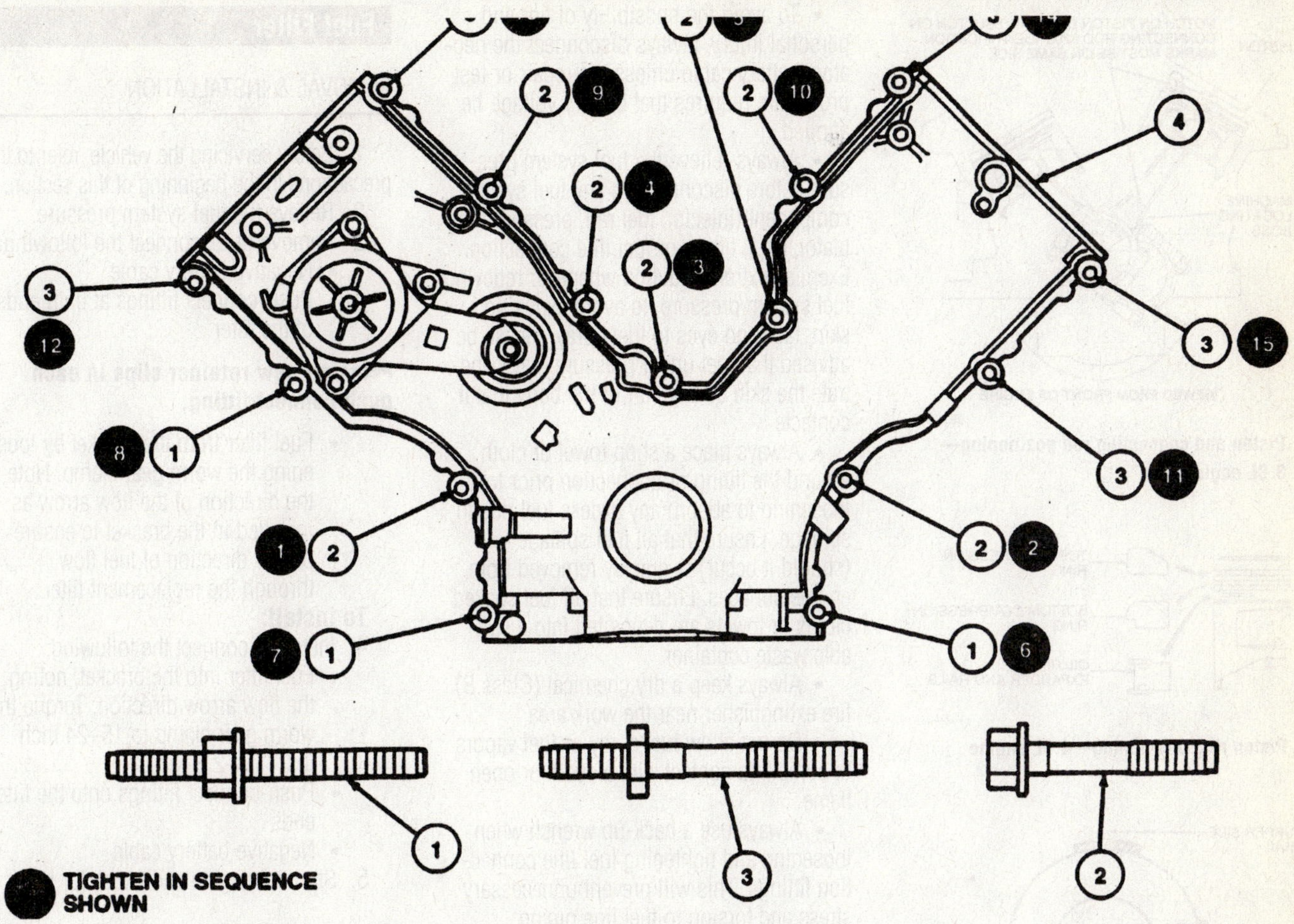

TIGHTEN IN SEQUENCE SHOWN

Be sure to install the fasteners in the correct position and tighten them in the sequence shown—4.6L engine

➡️**If the copper links of the timing chain are not visible, pull the chain taught until the opposite sides of the chain contact one another and lay it on a flat surface. Mark the links at each end of the chain and use them in place of the copper links.**

- Both timing chain tensioners. Torque the bolts to 15–22 ft. lbs. (20–30 Nm).
- Crankshaft holding tool to the crankshaft.
- Alignment dowel on the front cover to position crankshaft

10. Lubricate timing chain tensioner arm contact surfaces, using engine oil.
11. Install or connect the following:
    - Left and right timing chain tensioner arms on their dowels
12. Remove all slack from the timing chain by using a C-clamp around the timing chain tensioner arm and timing chain guide. Do not bend the timing chain.

13. Remove lock pins from timing chain tensioners and align all timing marks.
14. Align camshaft and torque the camshaft sprocket bolt to 81–95 ft. lbs. (110–130 Nm).
15. Check that camshaft is at maximum lift for the intake valve at 114 degrees after Top Dead Center (TDC).

➡️**If not at maximum lift, loosen camshaft sprocket bolt and repeat tightening procedures.**

16. Remove crankshaft holding tool, cam positioning tool and adapters
17. Install or connect the following:
    - Oil pan
    - Engine front cover
    - Valve covers
    - Crankshaft position (CKP) sensor pulse wheel
    - Negative battery cable
18. Refill the crankcase.
19. Start the engine. Check for leaks and proper operation.

Piston And Ring

POSITIONING

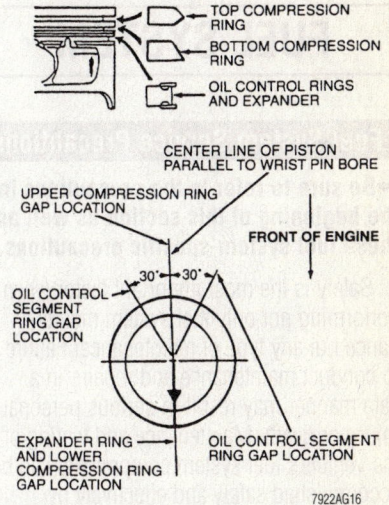

Piston ring end-gap spacing—3.8L engine

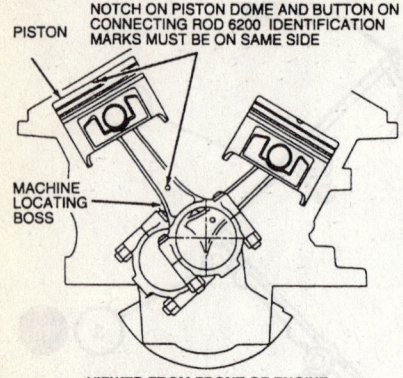

Piston and connecting rod positioning—3.8L engine

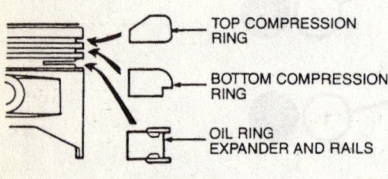

Piston ring positioning—4.6L engine

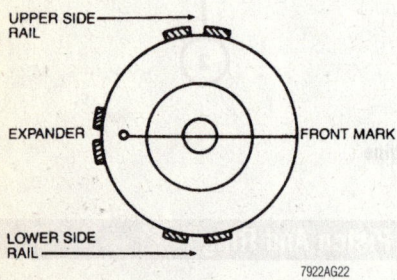

Piston ring end-gap spacing and piston positioning—4.6L engine

FUEL SYSTEM

Fuel System Service Precautions

➡ **Be sure to refer to the precautions in the beginning of this section as well as these fuel system-specific precautions.**

Safety is the most important factor when performing not only fuel system maintenance but any type of maintenance. Failure to conduct maintenance and repairs in a safe manner may result in serious personal injury or death. Maintenance and testing of the vehicle's fuel system components can be accomplished safely and effectively by adhering to the following rules and guidelines:

• To avoid the possibility of fire and personal injury, always disconnect the negative battery cable unless the repair or test procedure requires that battery voltage be applied

• Always relieve the fuel system pressure before disconnecting any fuel system component (injector, fuel rail, pressure regulator, etc.), fitting or fuel line connection. Exercise extreme caution whenever relieving fuel system pressure, to avoid exposing skin, face and eyes to fuel spray. Please be advised that fuel under pressure may penetrate the skin or any part of the body that it contacts

• Always place a shop towel or cloth around the fitting or connection prior to loosening to absorb any excess fuel due to spillage. Ensure that all fuel spillage (should it occur) is quickly removed from engine surfaces. Ensure that all fuel soaked cloths or towels are deposited into a suitable waste container.

• Always keep a dry chemical (Class B) fire extinguisher near the work area

• Do not allow fuel spray or fuel vapors to come into contact with a spark or open flame.

• Always use a back-up wrench when loosening and tightening fuel line connection fittings. This will prevent unnecessary stress and torsion to fuel line piping

• Always replace worn fuel fitting O-rings with new. Do not substitute fuel hose or equivalent, where fuel pipe is installed

Fuel System Pressure

RELIEVING

Fuel supply lines on all fuel injected engines will remain pressurized for some period of time after the engine is shut **OFF**. This pressure must be relieved before servicing the fuel system. Pressure is relieved through the fuel pressure relief valve.

1. Relieve the fuel system pressure as follows:

   a. Remove the fuel tank cap to relieve pressure in the tank.

   b. Remove the cap on the fuel pressure relief valve, located on the fuel injection supply manifold.

   c. Attach a fuel pressure gauge and open the manual valve on the pressure gauge to release the pressure and drain the system through the drain tube into a suitable container.

   d. Remove the fuel pressure gauge and replace the cap on the relief valve.

Fuel Filter

REMOVAL & INSTALLATION

1. Before servicing the vehicle, refer to the precautions in the beginning of this section.
2. Relieve the fuel system pressure.
3. Remove or disconnect the following:
   • Negative battery cable
   • Push-connect fittings at both ends of the filter

➡ **Install new retainer clips in each push-connect fitting.**

   • Fuel filter from the bracket by loosening the worm gear clamp. Note the direction of the flow arrow as installed in the bracket to ensure proper direction of fuel flow through the replacement filter.

To install:
4. Install or connect the following:
   • Fuel filter into the bracket, noting the flow arrow direction. Torque the worm gear clamp to 15–24 inch lbs. (1.7–2.8 Nm).
   • Push-connect fittings onto the filter ends
   • Negative battery cable
5. Start the engine and check for leaks.

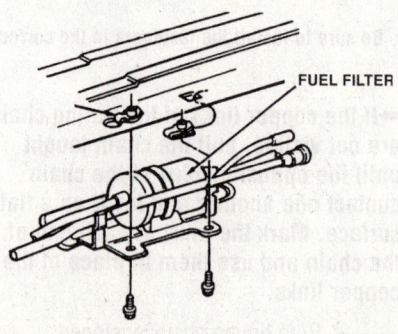

Exploded view of the fuel filter mounting

Fuel Pump

REMOVAL & INSTALLATION

1. Before servicing the vehicle, refer to the precautions in the beginning of this section.
2. Relieve the fuel system pressure.
3. Drain the fuel tank through the filler neck.
4. Remove or disconnect the following:
   • Negative battery cable
   • Exhaust system

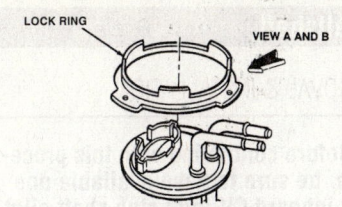

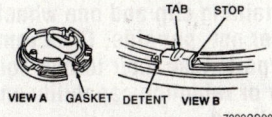

7922QG28

To remove the fuel pump, turn the locking ring counter clockwise

- Vent and fluid hoses from fuel tank
5. Safely support the fuel tank, partially lower the tank.
6. Remove or disconnect the following:
- Fuel level sensor and pump electrical connector and any remaining hoses.
- Fuel tank
7. Remove any dirt from around the fuel pump flange to prevent contamination.
8. Remove or disconnect the following:
- Locking ring, by turning it counterclockwise
- Fuel pump and bracket assembly
- Seal ring, discard it.

To install:
9. Clean the fuel pump mounting flange, fuel tank mounting surface and seal ring groove.
10. Apply a light coating of grease on a new seal ring to hold it in place during assembly and install in the seal ring groove.
11. Install or connect the following:
- Fuel pump and bracket assembly

➡**Be sure that the locating keys are in the keyways and the seal ring remains in the groove.**

- Locking ring, by rotating it clockwise

➡**Be sure all the locking tabs are under the tank lock ring tabs.**

- Fuel tank. Torque the support bracket bolts to 22–30 ft. lbs. (29–41 Nm).
12. Add a minimum of 10 gallons (40 liters) of fuel to the tank and check for leaks.
13. Install a fuel pressure gauge on the fuel rail valve.
14. Turn the ignition switch from **OFF** to **ON** for 3 seconds. Repeat this procedure 5–10 times until the pressure gauge shows at least 35 psi (241 kPa). Check for fuel leaks.

15. Remove the pressure gauge.
16. Start the engine and check for leaks.

Fuel Injector

REMOVAL & INSTALLATION

1. Before servicing the vehicle, refer to the precautions in the beginning of this section.
2. Relieve the fuel system pressure.
3. Remove or disconnect the following:
- Negative battery cable
- Air cleaner outlet tube
- Fuel pressure regulator vacuum line
- Spring lock coupling retainer clips from fuel inlet and outlet fittings
- Fuel supply and return lines from the fuel rail, using a spring lock disconnection tool
- Fuel injector electrical connectors
- Fuel rail
- Fuel injectors from fuel rail and discard the O-rings

To install:
4. Install or connect the following:
- New fuel injector O-rings
- Fuel injectors into fuel rail
5. Make sure that all fuel injector O-rings are properly seated in the fuel injection supply manifold cups and intake manifold pockets.
6. Install or connect the following:
- Fuel rail. Torque the bolts to 71–106 inch lbs. (8–12 Nm).
- Fuel supply and return line spring lock fittings
- Vacuum line to fuel pressure regulator
- Fuel injector electrical connectors
- Air cleaner outlet tube
- Negative battery cable
7. Start engine and road test.

DRIVE TRAIN

Transmission Assembly

REMOVAL & INSTALLATION

1. Before servicing the vehicle, refer to the precautions in the beginning of this section.
2. Drain the transmission fluid.

3. Remove or disconnect the following:
- Negative battery cable
- Exhaust system as required for transmission removal
- Converter inspection cover and adapter plate bolts from oil pan

✳✳ WARNING

Be careful not to damage transmission cooler lines.

- 4 torque converter-to-flywheel nuts
- Speedometer cable or Vehicle Speed Sensor (VSS), as equipped, from the extension housing.

➡**Rotate the engine using the crankshaft pulley bolt to access the converter-to-flywheel nuts.**

✳✳ WARNING

To prevent possible engine damage, never rotate the crankshaft pulley in a counterclockwise direction as viewed from the front of the engine.

4. Remove the driveshaft assembly as follows:
   a. Loosen the rear differential assembly nuts approximately ¼ in. (6mm).
   b. Position a support under the front of the differential housing; then, remove the forward nuts and bushings. Pull the vent tube from the sub-frame hole.
   c. Lower the front of the differential and slide the driveshaft from the transmission.

➡**Allow the driveshaft rest on the front driveshaft support and axle assembly.**

5. Drain the torque converter, using the drain plug.
6. Remove or disconnect the following:
- Shift cable from the manual control lever
- Starter cable
- Starter motor
- Electrical wires and vacuum lines from the transmission
7. Slightly, raise the transmission, using a jack.
- Transmission support insulator (mount)-to-crossmember bolts
- Crossmember-to-frame side rail bolts
- Crossmember and transmission support insulator
- Engine and transmission support
- Engine damper-to-body bracket

8. Lower the transmission and allow it to hang.

9. Place a jack under the front of the engine and raise it slightly to gain access to the upper bell housing-to-engine bolts. Do not remove the bolts at this time.

10. Remove or disconnect the following:
   • Oil cooler lines from the transmission, plug them
   • Lower bell housing-to-engine bolts
   • Transmission fluid fill tube

11. Secure the transmission to the transmission jack with a safely chain or strap.

12. Remove or disconnect the following:
   • 2 upper bell housing-to-engine bolts
   • Transmission
   • Torque converter

➡ Support engine using a safety stand and a wood block if it is to remain disassembled for an extended period of time.

To install:

➡ Thoroughly, flush the transmission oil cooler and cooler lines of any contaminates.

13. Install or connect the following:
   • Torque converter drain plug. Torque it to 21–22 ft. lbs. (28–30 Nm).
   • Torque converter onto the transmission, by aligning the drive flats with the pump gear
   • Transmission, secure it to a transmission jack with a safety chain or strap
   • Converter/transmission assembly, align the studs and drain plug with the flywheel or align the orange balancing marks on the converter stud and flywheel bolt hole, if balancing marks are present.

➡ The torque converter face must rest squarely against the flywheel. This indicates that the converter pilot is not binding in the engine crankshaft. To ensure the converter is properly seated, grasp a converter stud. It should move freely back and forth in the flywheel hole. If the converter will not move, the transmission must be removed and the converter repositioned so the impeller hub is properly engaged in the pump gear.

14. Install or connect the following:
   • Bell housing-to-engine bolts. Torque the bolts to 41–50 ft. lbs. (55–68 Nm).

15. Remove the transmission motor safety

chain or strap.

16. Install or connect the following:
   • New O-ring on the transmission fill tube
   • Transmission fluid fill tube. Torque the bolt to 28–37 ft. lbs. (38–51 Nm).
   • Oil cooler lines
   • Crossmember on the side supports, by raising the transmission
   • Engine and transmission support bolts
   • Engine damper bracket.
   • Transmission support insulator on the crossmember

17. Remove the transmission jack

18. Install or connect the following:
   • Torque converter-to-flywheel nuts. Torque the nuts to 20–33 ft. lbs. (27–46 Nm).
   • Converter access cover and cover plate bolts on engine oil pan, Torque the bolts to 12–16 ft. lbs. (16–22 Nm).
   • Exhaust system components
   • Speedometer or VSS cable to the transmission extension housing
   • Starter motor and wiring
   • Shift cable to the manual control lever
   • Transmission electrical connectors
   • Differential housing, by raising it. Torque the nuts to 70–95 ft. lbs. (95–130 Nm).
   • Vent tube in the sub-frame hole
   • Driveshaft yoke and companion flange, by aligning them. Torque the bolts to 70–95 ft. lbs. (95–129 Nm).
   • Negative battery cable

19. Remove all supports, if applicable.

20. Refill the transmission with the proper type and quantity of fluid.

21. Start the engine and check the transmission for leakage.

22. Adjust the transmission shift linkage as follows:

   a. Position the transmission range selector into the OVERDRIVE position.

   b. Loosen the shift cable and bracket-to-cable bracket nut.

   c. Move the transmission manual control lever to the OVERDRIVE position (the 3rd detent position from the full clockwise position).

   d. Torque the nut to 10–18 ft. lbs. (13–25 Nm).

   e. Check the operation of the transmission in each range.

23. Road test the vehicle and check transmission for proper operation.

Halfshaft

REMOVAL & INSTALLATION

➡ **Before continuing with this procedure, be sure to have available one new inboard CV-joint stub shaft pilot bearing housing seal, one shaft bearing retaining clip and one wheel hub retainer nut, per side. Once removed, these parts lose their torque holding ability or retention capability and must be replaced.**

1. Before servicing the vehicle, refer to the precautions in the beginning of this section.

2. Remove or disconnect the following:
   • Wheel hub nut
   • Rear wheel
   • Anti-lock brake speed sensor

3. Use needle-nose pliers or equivalent, to slide the parking brake cable adjusting clip downward until the cable is free.

4. Remove or disconnect the following:
   • Parking brake cable from the rear disc brake caliper
   • Rear caliper

➡ Support the caliper with wire. Do not allow it to hang from the brake hose.

   • Brake rotor
   • Upper control arm, support the upper control arm with a wire.

5. Matchmark the lower control arm to the knuckle with the lower bushings in the relaxed position.

➡ Failure to matchmark this relationship will result in bushing wind-up on assembly and incorrect ride height, causing misalignment and premature tire wear.

6. Remove or disconnect the following:
   • Halfshaft from the hub, using a puller.
   • Lower control arm-to-knuckle nuts

7. Push the halfshaft through the hub while positioning the CV-joint and knuckle to allow the front lower bolt to clear the CV-joint, then remove the bolt. Remove and save the washers.

✳✳ WARNING

Be careful not to damage the inboard CV-joint stub shaft pilot bearing housing seal, anti-lock brake sensor indicator, rear axle housing, CV-joint or boot.

8. Remove or disconnect the following:
- Rear bolt, washer, and knuckle assembly
- Halfshaft, plug the differential housing to prevent fluid loss

To install:

9. Install or connect the following:
- New differential oil seal
- New circlip on the halfshaft.
- Halfshaft into the differential housing until the clip seats
- Halfshaft into the hub
- Lower control arm, by aligning the paint marks. Torque the nuts/bolts to 118–147 ft. lbs. (160–200 Nm).
- New wheel hub nut
- Upper control arm. Torque the nut/bolt to 118–147 ft. lbs. (160–200 Nm).
- Brake caliper. Torque the bolts to 80–99 ft. lbs. (108–135 Nm).
- Parking brake cable and adjustment clip
- Anti-lock brake speed sensor. Torque the bolts to 14–20 ft. lbs. (19–27 Nm).
- Rear wheel. Torque the lug nuts to 85–105 ft. lbs. (115–142 Nm).
- Torque the wheel hub nut to 250 ft. lbs. (340 Nm).

10. Check the inboard CV-joint circlip engagement by attempting to pull the inboard CV-joint from the axle. If the CV-joint circlip is not seated, push the CV-joint in until the circlip is fully engaged in the side gear.

11. Refill the differential housing.

12. Check and/or adjust the rear wheel alignment.

13. Road test the vehicle and check for proper operation.

CV-Joints

REMOVAL & REPLACEMENT

Inner CV-Joint

1. Before servicing the vehicle, refer to the precautions in the beginning of this section.

2. Remove or disconnect the following:
- Halfshaft
- Inner CV-joint boot clamps
- CV-joint boot, slide it away from the joint
- Snapring, release it
- Inner CV-joint from the halfshaft.

To install:

3. CV-joint, fill it with fresh grease and slide it onto the halfshaft.

4. Install or connect the following:
- New snapring
- New CV-joint clamps
- CV-joint boot
- Halfshaft

Outer CV-Joint

The outer CV-joint is serviced with the halfshaft as an assembly. The outer CV-joint boot can be serviced by removing the inner CV-joint.

Pinion Seal

REMOVAL & INSTALLATION

1. Before servicing the vehicle, refer to the precautions in the beginning of this section.

2. Place a support under the rear of the differential housing

3. Remove or disconnect the following:
- Rear axle differential rear insulator-to-differential housing cover bolts and nuts

➡ **This procedure will allow the rear axle housing to pivot forward.**

4. Install rear axle differential rear insulator bolt in lower bolt hole.

5. Matchmark driveshaft centering socket yoke to the rear axle U-joint flange.

6. Remove or disconnect the following:
- Driveshaft-to-pinion flange bolts; then, slide the driveshaft forward to rest against reinforcement

✳✳ **WARNING**

Do not remove the differential housing support.

- Rear axle differential front lower insulator nuts

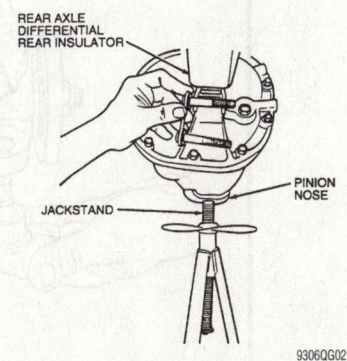

Install rear axle differential rear insulator bolt in lower bolt hole

7. Lower the differential housing to access rear axle universal joint flange.

8. Using a torque wrench on the pinion nut, record the torque (in ft. lbs.) required to maintain the rotation of the pinion through several revolutions.

9. Matchmark the rear axle U-joint flange to the pinion stem so the flange can be reinstalled correctly.

➡ **This step is unnecessary, if installing a new rear axle U-joint.**

10. Remove or disconnect the following:
- Pinion nut, by holding the rear axle U-joint flange with a flange holding tool
- Rear axle U-joint flange

✳✳ **WARNING**

Do not hammer or use air tools to remove rear axle U-joint flange, as these will damage components.

11. Place a drain pan under the rear axle housing.

12. Position a prybar under the pinion seal flange; then, strike the wedge with a hammer to wedge the prybar between the pinion seal and the rear axle housing.

13. Remove or disconnect the following:
- Pinion seal, using a prybar and pliers
- Pinion shaft oil slinger

To install:

➡ **Check drive pinion stem splines and rear U-joint for burrs before installation.**

14. Lubricat the flange splines with SAE 80W-90 gear oil.

✳✳ **WARNING**

Do not hammer or use air tools to install rear axle U-joint flange, as these will damage components.

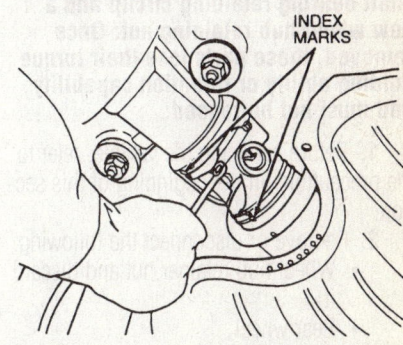

Mark the driveshaft centering socket yoke relative to rear axle U-joint flange

15. Install or connect the following:
   - Rear axle U-joint flange, by aligning the pinion stem matchmarks
   - Pinion nut. Tighten it while holding the rear U-joint with the flange holding tool. Rotate pinion to verify proper seating of the differential pinion bearing.

16. Take frequent differential pinion bearing torque preload readings until the original reading is obtained.

➡**Never back off the pinion nut to reduce preload. If reduced preload is required, a new differential drive pinion collapsible spacer and pinion nut must be installed.**

17. Raise the rear axle housing and locate front lower insulator bolts. Torque them to 68–100 ft. lbs. (92–136 Nm).

18. Remove rear insulator bolt from pivot position

19. Install or connect the following:
   - Rear insulator bolts in axle housing cover mount. Torque the bolts to 80–100 ft. lbs. (108–136 Nm).
   - Rear U-joint to centering socket yoke, by aligning the matchmarks. Torque the bolts to 70–95 ft. lbs. (95–130 Nm).

20. Add new SAE 80W-90 gear oil to ¼ in. (6mm) below bottom of filler hole.

21. Install the filler plug. Torque it to 15–30 ft. lbs. (20–40 Nm).

22. Lower vehicle and check for leaks.

Axle Housing Assembly

REMOVAL & INSTALLATION

7.5 Inch Ring Gear

➡**Before continuing with this procedure, be sure to have available one new inboard CV-joint stub shaft driveshaft bearing retaining circlip and a new wheel hub retaining nut. Once removed, these parts lose their torque holding ability or retention capability and must not be reused.**

1. Before servicing the vehicle, refer to the precautions in the beginning of this section.

2. Remove or disconnect the following:
   - Wheel hub retainer nut and discard it
   - Rear wheel
   - Brake drums
   - Rear Anti-Lock Brake (ABS) sensors
   - Lower control arm and bushing bolt

3. Wire the upper control arm to the top of shock absorber to protect the CV-boot when the halfshaft is removed.

4. Matchmark the lower control arm-to-knuckle location with the lower bushings in the relaxed position.

➡**Failure to matchmark this relationship will result in bushing wind-up on assembly and incorrect ride height, causing misalignment and premature tire wear.**

5. Remove or disconnect the following:
   - Halfshaft from the hub, using a puller
   - Lower control arm and bushing
   - Rear wheel knuckle assembly from halfshaft and joint assembly

6. Position the halfshaft on lower control arm and bushing. Wire rear wheel knuckle to top of rear shock.

✳✳ WARNING

Do not stretch, twist or kink brake hoses

7. Remove or disconnect the following:
   - Right halfshaft from axle housing

➡**Inboard CV-joint stub shaft pilot bearing housing seal must be replaced whenever the halfshaft is removed.**

   - Halfshaft from vehicle
8. Install a plug into the axle housing
9. Matchmark driveshaft centering socket yoke in relation to rear axle U-joint flange.
10. Remove or disconnect the following:
   - Driveshaft bolts; then, slide it forward to rest on center bridge support reinforcement
   - Rear axle differential rear insulator-to-crossmember nuts while supporting the axle housing with a transmission jack
   - Rear axle differential rear insulator from axle housing cover
   - Front axle housing-to-chassis nuts, bolts, bushings and washers
   - Left halfshaft from rear axle housing
11. Partially, lower rear axle housing.

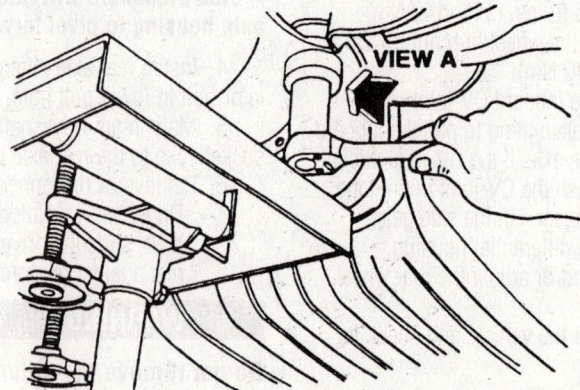

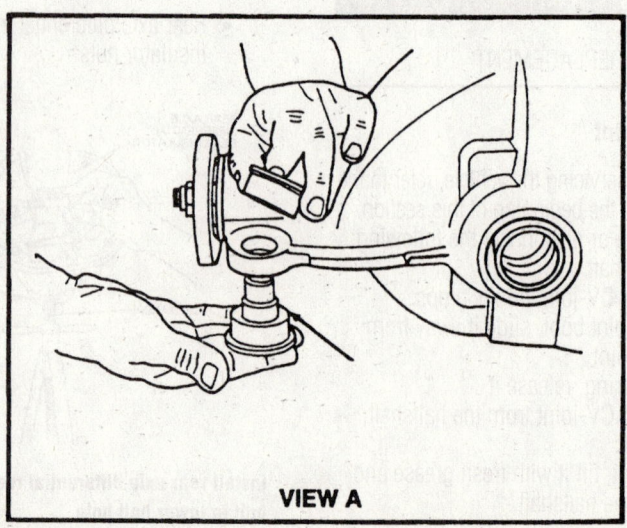

93060G04

Install bushings as shown—7.5 inch ring gear

Simultaneously, disengage the axle housing from left halfshaft.

12. Plug left side of axle housing and lower it from vehicle.

To install:

13. Install or connect the following:
   • New left halfshaft seal into the axle housing
   • Left halfshaft into the rear wheel knuckle
   • New circlip to left halfshaft

14. Position the axle housing on a transmission jack.

15. Raise the axle housing to align the left halfshaft, lubricated with gear oil.

16. Install or connect the following:
   • Front differential front lower insulator bushings, washers and nuts. Torque the nuts to 68–100 ft. lbs. (92–136 Nm).
   • Rear axle differential rear insulator to axle housing cover. Torque the nuts/bolts to 80–100 ft. lbs. (108–136 Nm).
   • Rear axle differential rear insulator-to-crossmember. Torque the nuts/bolts to 122–155 ft. lbs. (165–211 Nm).
   • Driveshaft centering socket yoke-to-rear axle U-joint. Torque the bolts to 70–95 ft. lbs. (95–130 Nm).
   • Circlip on right halfshaft and lubricate the splines
   • New halfshaft seal into the axle housing
   • Right halfshaft into the axle housing until circlip engages the side gear

➡ **If it is necessary to use a mallet, use only non-metallic variety and tap only on the outboard CV-joint stub shaft.**

17. Install or connect the following:
   • Right halfshaft to the rear wheel knuckle
   • Upper control arm and bushing, by aligning the paint marks. Torque the bolts to 119–147 ft. lbs. (160–200 Nm).
   • New hub nut
   • Lower control arm and bushing. Torque the bolts to 119–147 ft. lbs. (160–200 Nm).
   • Brake drum and new pushnuts

18. Refill the axle housing with SAE 80W-90 gear oil.

19. Install or connect the following:
   • Fill plug. Torque it to 14–20 ft. lbs. (19–27 Nm).
   • Rear wheel. Torque the lug nuts to 85–104 ft. lbs. (115–142 Nm).

   • Hub nut. Torque it to 250 ft. lbs. (340 Nm).

8.8 Inch Ring Gear

➡ **Before continuing with this procedure, be sure to have available two new inboard CV-joint stub shaft pilot bearing housing seals and two new driveshaft bearing retaining clips. Once removed, these parts lose their torque holding ability or retention capability and must not be reused.**

1. Before servicing the vehicle, refer to the precautions in the beginning of this section.

2. Slide parking brake cable adjusting clip downward until parking brake rear cable and conduit are released.

3. Remove or disconnect the following:
   • Anti-lock Brake System (ABS) sensors, if equipped
   • Parking brake cable and conduit from right caliper
   • Brake calipers and suspend them on a wire
   • Brake rotors
   • Right upper control arm bolt and

suspend it on a wire to upper shock absorber

4. Matchmark the lower control arm to knuckle location with the lower bushings in the relaxed position.

➡ **Failure to matchmark this relationship will result in bushing wind-up on assembly and incorrect ride height, causing misalignment and premature tire wear.**

5. Remove or disconnect the following:
   • Right-side lower control arm and bushing from the knuckle
   • Right halfshaft from the differential housing, using a suitable CV-joint remover tool

➡ **Differential oil seals must be replaced when halfshaft has been removed.**

6. Plug the axle housing to prevent fluid loss.

7. Matchmark the driveshaft to rear U-joint and remove the bolts; then, slide the driveshaft forward and rest on center bridge support reinforcement.

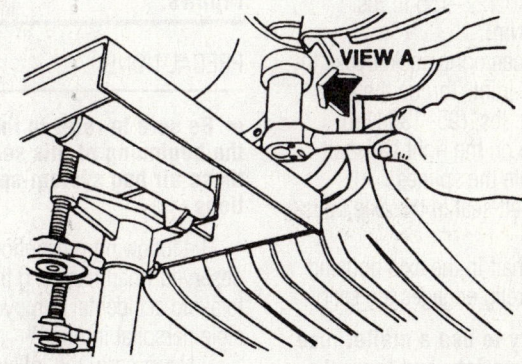

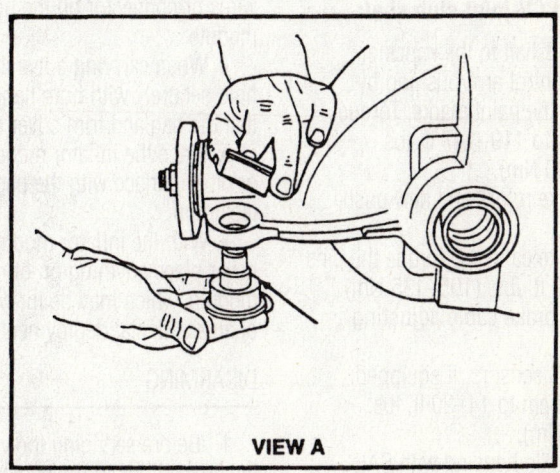

Install bushings—8.8 inch ring gear

9306QG04

Turn to Section 5 for brake system applications

8. Remove or disconnect the following:
- Rear axle differential rear insulator nuts, while supporting the axle housing with a transmission jack
- Rear axle differential rear insulator from axle housing cover
- Front axle housing nuts, bolts, bushings and washers
- Left halfshaft from axle housing and plug the opening
- Axle housing

To install:

9. Install or connect the following:
- New halfshaft seal in the axle housing
- Rear axle differential front lower insulator bushings
- Axle housing. Torque the nuts to 68–100 ft. lbs. (92–136 Nm).
- New circlip on the left halfshaft
- Left halfshaft in the axle housing until the circlip engages the seat
- Rear axle differential rear insulator to axle housing cover. Torque the nuts/bolts to 80–100 ft. lbs. (108–136 Nm).
- Rear axle differential rear insulator to crossmember. Torque the nuts/bolts to 122–155 ft. lbs. (165–211 Nm).
- Driveshaft centering socket yoke to rear axle U-joint. Torque the bolts to 70–95 ft. lbs. (95–130 Nm).
- New circlip on the right halfshaft and lubricate the splines
- New halfshaft seal in the axle housing
- Right halfshaft in the axle housing until the circlip engages the seat

➡ **If it is necessary to use a mallet, use only non-metallic variety and tap only on the outboard CV-joint stub shaft.**

- Right halfshaft to the knuckle
- Upper control arm/bushing by aligning the paint marks. Torque the bolts to 119–147 ft. lbs. (160–200 Nm).
- Rear brake rotors and new push-nuts
- Rear brake calipers. Torque the pins to 78–99 ft. lbs. (105–135 Nm).
- Parking brake cable adjusting clip.
- Rear ABS sensors, if equipped. Torque them to 14–20 ft. lbs. (19–27 Nm).

10. Refill the axle housing with SAE 80W-90 gear oil.
11. Fill plug. Torque it to 21–29 ft. lbs. (28–40 Nm).

➡ **If equipped with traction-lock axles, add 4 oz. (118 ml) of additive friction modifier.**

- Rear wheels. Torque the lug nuts to 85–104 ft. lbs. (115–142 Nm).

STEERING AND SUSPENSION

Air Bag

✳✳ CAUTION

Some vehicles are equipped with an air bag system. The system must be disabled before performing service on or around system components, steering column, instrument panel components, wiring and sensors. Failure to follow safety and disabling procedures could result in accidental air bag deployment, possible personal injury and unnecessary system repairs.

PRECAUTIONS

➡ **Be sure to refer to the precautions in the beginning of this section as well as these air bag system-specific precautions.**

The following precautions must be observed when handling the inflator module to avoid accidental deployment and possible personal injury:

- Never carry the inflator module by the wires or connector on the underside of the module
- When carrying a live inflator module, hold securely with both hands, and ensure that the bag and trim cover are pointed away
- Place the inflator module on a bench or other surface with the bag and trim cover facing up
- With the inflator module on the bench, never place anything on or close to the module, which may be thrown in the event of an accidental deployment

DISARMING

1. Before servicing the vehicle, refer to the precautions in the beginning of this section.
2. Disconnect the negative, then the positive, battery cables. Wait 1 minute for

the backup power supply in the diagnostic monitor to deplete its stored energy.

3. Remove the 4 nut and washer assemblies retaining the driver air bag module to the steering wheel.

✳✳ CAUTION

When carrying a live air bag, be sure the bag and trim cover are pointed away from the body. In the unlikely event of an accidental deployment, the bag will, then deploy with minimal chance of injury. When placing a live air bag on a bench or other surface, always face the bag and trim cover up, away from the surface. This will reduce the motion of the module if it is accidentally deployed.

4. Detach the driver air bag connector. Connect Air Bag Simulator 105–00008 or equivalent, to the vehicle harness at the top of the steering wheel.

After the applicable service is accomplished, re-enable the air bag system as follows:

5. Remove the air bag simulator from the air bag connector.
6. Attach the connector and install the air bag.
7. Connect the positive, then the negative, battery cables.
8. Turn the ignition key **ON** and be sure the air bag light does not stay **ON**.

Power Rack and Pinion Steering Gear

REMOVAL & INSTALLATION

1. Before servicing the vehicle, refer to the precautions in the beginning of this section.
2. Remove or disconnect the following:
- Negative battery cable
- Both front wheels
- Both tie rod ends and discard the cotter pins
3. Place a drain pan under the rack and pinion assembly.
4. Remove or disconnect the following:
- Pressure hose at intermediate fitting and move it aside
- Steering shaft retaining bolt
- Rack-to-sub-frame bolts and nuts

➡ **Access the nuts through hole in crossmember.**

5. Move the rack and pinion assembly to gain access to the pressure line inlet tube and discard the plastic seal on tube

Steering Gear

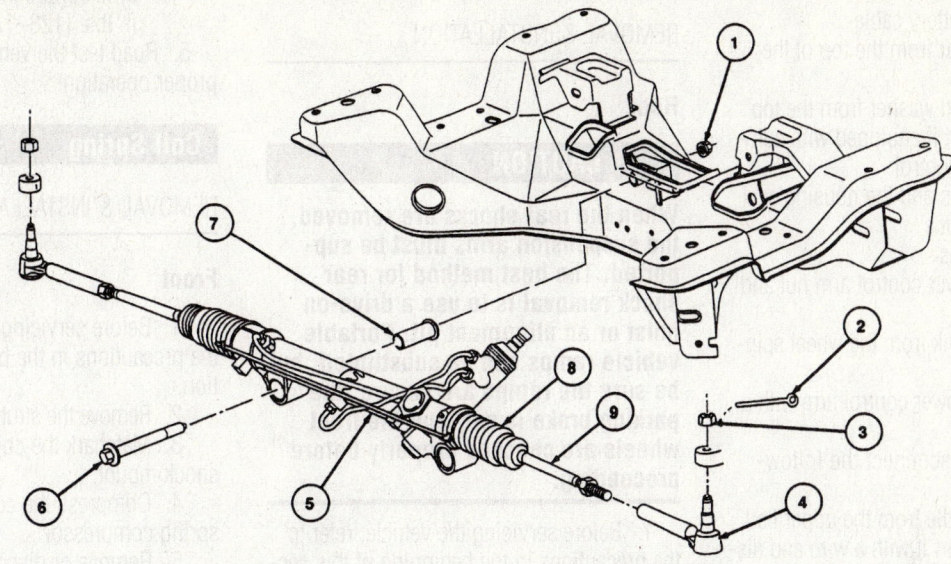

Item	Description
1	Nut (2 Req'd)
2	Pin (2 Req'd)
3	Nut (2 Req'd)
4	Tie Rod End (2 Req'd)
5	Steering Gear
6	Bolt and Washer Assy (2 Req'd)

Item	Description
7	Steering Gear Insulator (2 Req'd)
8	Front Suspension Steering Ball Stud Dust Seal
9	Front Wheel Spindle Tie Rod (2 Req'd)

7922QG30

Exploded view of the power rack and pinion steering gear mounting

6. Remove or disconnect the following:
   - Pressure hose to each tube strap, cut them
   - Rack and pinion assembly

To install:

7. Install or connect the following:
   - New plastic seals on the power steering pressure line
   - Rear steering gear housing insulator, seat it

➡**Use rubber lubricant to ease installation.**

   - Power rack and pinion steering gear to the front crossmember
   - Pressure line at the intermediate fitting

8. Align steering gear input shaft to allow power rack and pinion steering gear to properly seat on crossmember.
   - Steering gear. Torque the bolts to 100–143 ft. lbs. (135–195 Nm).
   - Steering shaft flex coupling. Torque the bolt to 31–42 ft. lbs. (41–57 Nm).

   - Pressure hose to tube with a new tie strap
   - Pressure hose
   - Return hose. Torque the clamp to 9–17 inch lbs. (1–2 Nm).
   - Tie rod ends. Torque the nuts to 36–50 ft. lbs. (48–68 Nm); then, tighten until a new cotter pin can be installed.
   - New cotter pins
   - Front wheels. Torque the lug nuts to 85–104 ft. lbs. (115–142 Nm).

9. Refill the power steering reservoir.
10. Check and adjust front end alignment.

Strut

REMOVAL & INSTALLATION

Front

1. Before servicing the vehicle, refer to the precautions in the beginning of this section.

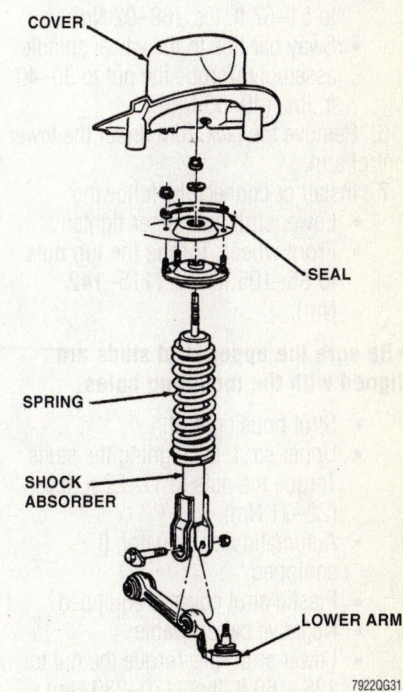

COVER

SEAL

SPRING

SHOCK ABSORBER

LOWER ARM

7922QG31

Exploded view of the front strut

2. Remove or disconnect the following:

- Negative battery cable
- Plastic cover from the top of the strut
- Actuator and washer from the top strut mount, if equipped with automatic ride control
- 3 upper nuts and the housing seal from the studs
- Front wheels
- Strut-to-lower control arm nut and bolt
- Sway bar link from the wheel spindle

3. Support the lower control arm with a jack.

4. Remove or disconnect the following:

- Wheel spindle from the upper ball joint, support it with a wire and discard the bolt and nut
- Jack from under the lower control arm
- Strut

To install:

5. Install or connect the following:

- Strut over the lower control arm, finger-tighten the nut and bolt
- Strut-to-chassis nuts, by raising and aligning the lower control arm/strut assembly with a jack
- Wheel spindle to the upper ball joint stud. Torque the new nut/bolt to 51–67 ft. lbs. (68–92 Nm).
- Sway bar link to the wheel spindle assembly. Torque the nut to 30–40 ft. lbs. (40–55 Nm).

6. Remove the jack from under the lower control arm.

7. Install or connect the following:

- Lower strut nut, finger-tighten
- Front wheel. Torque the lug nuts to 85–105 ft. lbs. (115–142 Nm).

➡Be sure the upper strut studs are aligned with the mounting holes.

- Strut housing seal.
- Upper strut, by aligning the studs. Torque the nuts to 17–22 ft. lbs. (22–31 Nm).
- Automatic ride actuator, if equipped
- Plastic strut cover, if equipped
- Negative battery cable
- Lower strut nut. Torque the nut to 126–169 ft. lbs. (170–230 Nm).

8. Check and/or adjust the front wheel alignment.

9. Road test the vehicle and check for proper operation.

Shock Absorber

REMOVAL & INSTALLATION

Rear

❊❊ CAUTION

When the rear shocks are removed, the suspension arms must be supported. The best method for rear shock removal is to use a drive-on hoist or an alignment pit. Portable vehicle ramps can be substituted, but be sure the ramps are secure, the parking brake is set, and the front wheels are chocked properly before proceeding.

1. Before servicing the vehicle, refer to the precautions in the beginning of this section.

2. Remove or disconnect the following:

- Upper shock absorber-to-chassis nut/washer from inside the luggage compartment
- Lower shock absorber-to-lower control arm retaining bolt, washer and nut
- Shock absorber

To install:

3. Properly prime the new shock absorber by inverting and compressing, then releasing the shock absorber to its fully extended position. Repeat this procedure several times.

4. Install or connect the following:

- Shock absorber-to-chassis. Torque the upper shock absorber nut to 27–40 ft. lbs. (37–54 Nm).

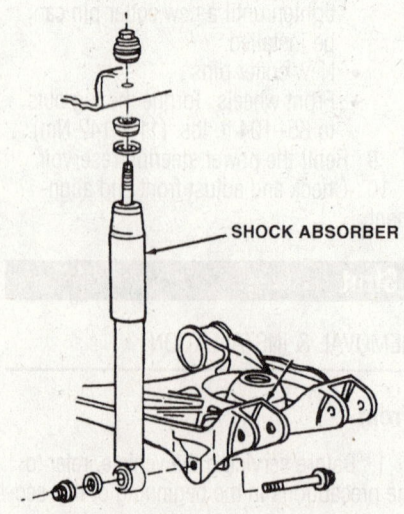

SHOCK ABSORBER

7922QG34

Exploded view of the rear shock absorber mounting

- Shock absorber-to-lower control arm. Torque the nut/bolt to 95–126 ft. lbs. (128–172 Nm)

5. Road test the vehicle and check for proper operation.

Coil Spring

REMOVAL & INSTALLATION

Front

1. Before servicing the vehicle, refer to the precautions in the beginning of this section.

2. Remove the strut and place it in a vise.

3. Matchark the coil spring to the upper shock mount.

4. Compress the coil spring, using a spring compressor

5. Remove or disconnect the following:

- Shock nut, washer and upper bracket

6. Coil spring, by slowly releasing the spring compressor

7. Inspect all components for damage or wear and replace parts, as necessary.

To install:

➡When installing a new coil spring or upper mount, transfer the reference marks from the old part to the new part. Always work on one shock/coil spring assembly at a time to avoid pos-

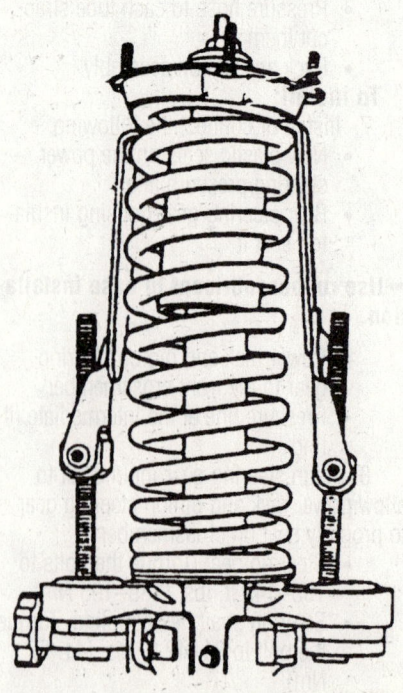

7922QG32

Safely compress the front coil spring in a spring compressor

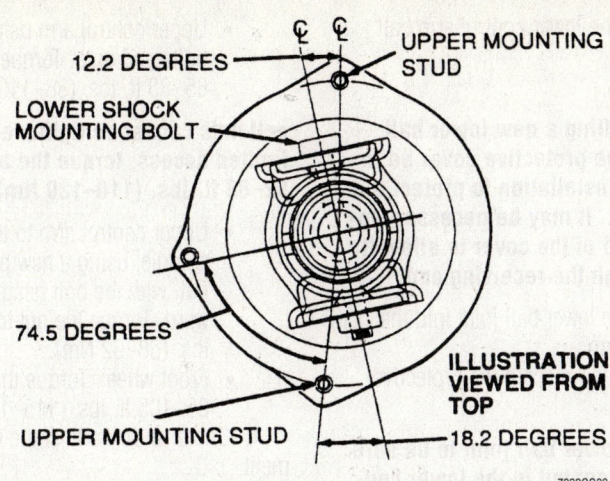

12.2 DEGREES

UPPER MOUNTING STUD

LOWER SHOCK MOUNTING BOLT

74.5 DEGREES

UPPER MOUNTING STUD

ILLUSTRATION VIEWED FROM TOP

18.2 DEGREES

7922QG33

Be sure to install the mounting bracket in the correct orientation—front coil spring

sible mixing of parts. Also, if the reference marks are missing, the opposite assembly may be used as reference for aligning the coil spring to the upper mount. The right-hand and left-hand upper mount orientations are identical.

8. Place the coil spring on the strut.

➡**If the coil spring is not positioned properly, the assembly will not mount correctly in the vehicle.**

9. Compress the coil spring and install the upper bracket/washer, by aligning the matchmarks. Torque the nut to 37–52 ft. lbs. (50–71 Nm).

10. Release the spring compressor and remove it.

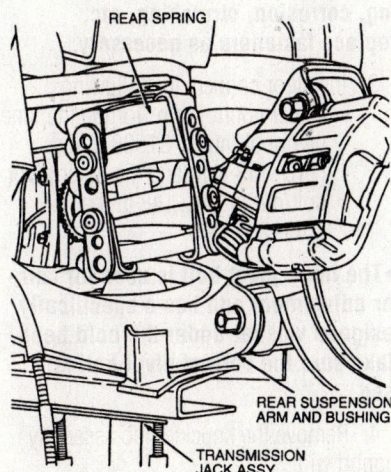

REAR SPRING

REAR SUSPENSION ARM AND BUSHING

TRANSMISSION JACK ASSY

7922QG35

Be sure the spring compressor is installed correctly before lowering the control arm—rear coil spring

11. Verify that the coil spring is seated properly at the top and bottom of the shock assembly.

12. Install the strut.

Rear

1. Before servicing the vehicle, refer to the precautions in the beginning of this section.

2. Remove or disconnect the following:
   • Rear wheel
   • Sway bar link nuts at both ends of the sway bar

3. Rotate the sway bar up and out of the way.
   • Parking brake cable at the disc brake caliper, if equipped with rear disc brakes

4. Install 3 Spring Cages 086-00031 or equivalent, as follows:
   a. Install one spring cage without an adjuster link, to the inboard side (the innermost bend of the spring) of the coil spring.
   b. Install the 2 more spring cages with adjusters, at 120 degree angles to the previously installed cage.

5. Place a jack, under the lower control arm.

6. Remove or disconnect the following:
   • Upper control arm from the chassis, secure it with a wire
   • Lower shock absorber bolt, washer and nut

➡**The lower control arm must not be lowered until the pivot bolts are loose. Do not attempt to remove the plastic cap on the front pivot nut.**

7. Matchmark the toe adjustment cam positioning with the sub-frame.

8. Remove or disconnect the following:
   • Inboard pivot bolts on the lower control arm, loosen them
   • Lower control arm to knuckle nuts/bolts; then, carefully lower the control arm

✶✶ CAUTION

Be sure the spring cages are securely holding the coil spring as the control arm is lowered.

   • Coil spring with the cages in place
   • Coil spring insulators if necessary

9. Remove the spring cages as follows:
   a. Measure the length of the coil spring with the cages installed. This dimension is needed for installation.
   b. Compress the spring.
   c. Remove the cages, then the spring compressor.

To install:

10. If the spring cages were removed, perform the following:
   a. Compress the spring, using a spring compressor, to the dimension measured during removal.
   b. If the original dimension is not available, compress the spring to a length of 10.5 in. (267mm) not including the mounting insulators.
   c. Install the spring cages.
   d. Remove the spring compressor.

11. Install or connect the following:
   • Spring mount insulators, if removed.
   • Caged coil spring onto the upper and lower control arm seats.

➡**The cage with no adjuster must face inward and the cages must be closer to the bottom of spring. The spring pigtails can be in any position.**

   • 2 jackstands under the front bumper reinforcement

➡**This will prevent the rear of the vehicle from lifting off of the hoist.**

   • Lower control arm, raise it with a jack to align the knuckle, ensuring that the coil spring is properly seated. Torque the nuts/bolts to 110–148 ft. lbs. (149–201 Nm).

12. Remove the wire supporting the upper control arm assembly.

13. Install the lower shock absorber bolt, washer and nut. Torque the nut to 83–113 ft. lbs. (113–153 Nm).

14. Remove the jack, from under the lower control arm.

15. Remove the jackstands from under the front bumper reinforcement.

16. Remove the spring cages from the coil spring.

17. Install or connect the following:
- Parking brake cable to the disc brake caliper, if equipped with rear disc brakes
- Sway bar. Torque the nuts to 35–47 ft. lbs. (47–63 Nm).
- Rear wheel. Torque the lug nuts to 85–105 ft. lbs. (115–142 Nm).

18. Align the toe adjustment cam matchmark. Torque the front lower control arm pivot nut at the sub-frame to 166–202 ft. lbs. (225–275 Nm) and the rear lower control arm pivot nut at the sub-frame to 142–191 ft. lbs. (192–259 Nm).

19. Check and/or adjust the alignment.

20. Road test the vehicle and check for proper operation.

Upper Ball Joint

REMOVAL & INSTALLATION

The ball joint is an integral part of the upper control arm. If the ball joint is defective, the entire upper control arm must be replaced.

Lower Ball Joint

REMOVAL & INSTALLATION

Front

1. Before servicing the vehicle, refer to the precautions in the beginning of this section.

2. Remove or disconnect the following:
- Front wheel
- Lower control arm assembly
- Lower ball joint boot seal and discard

3. Place the lower control arm in a vise

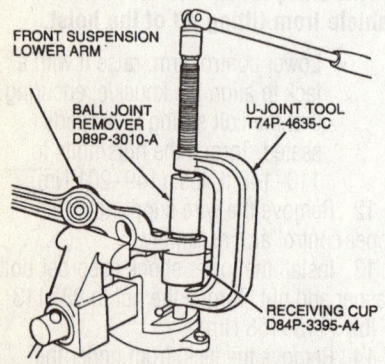

FRONT SUSPENSION
LOWER ARM

BALL JOINT
REMOVER
D89P-3010-A

U-JOINT TOOL
T74P-4635-C

RECEIVING CUP
D84P-3395-A4

79220G36

Use a ball joint press and adapters to remove the ball joint from the control arm

and press out the lower control arm ball joint.

To install:

➡ **When installing a new lower ball joint, leave the protective cover be in place during installation to protect the ball joint seal. It may be necessary to cut off the end of the cover to allow it to pass through the receiving cup.**

4. Install the lower ball joint into the lower control arm

5. Remove and discard the protective cover.

➡ **Check the lower ball joint to be sure that it is fully seated in the lower control arm.**

6. Inspect the ball joint seal and ensure that it is free of cuts or tears.

7. Install or connect the following:
- Lower control arm assembly
- Front wheel. Torque the lug nuts to 85–105 ft. lbs. (115–142 Nm).

8. Check and/or adjust the alignment.

9. Road test the vehicle and check for proper operation.

Rear

The ball joint is an integral part of the lower control arm. If the ball joint is defective, the entire lower control arm must be replaced.

Upper Control Arm

REMOVAL & INSTALLATION

Front

The following procedure is the same for both the right-hand and left-hand upper control arm assemblies.

1. Remove or disconnect the following:
- Front wheel
- Upper ball joint from the wheel spindle and discard the nut/bolt

➡ **A 6-point socket must be used on the bolt due to the fact that the corners of the heads have been shaved off. Replacement bolts do not require metal flags.**

- Upper control arm pivot bolt heads, break of the small metal flags
- Upper control arm

2. Inspect the upper control arm ball joint. If worn the entire upper control arm assembly must be replaced.

To install:

3. Install or connect the following:

- Upper control arm using new pivot bolts and nuts. Torque the nuts to 65–88 ft. lbs. (88–119 Nm).

➡ **If nuts cannot be tightened due to limited access, torque the bolts to 82–88 ft. lbs. (110–120 Nm).**

- Upper control arm to the wheel spindle, using a new pinch bolt and nut, with the bolt head facing forward. Torque the nut to 51–67 ft. lbs. (68–92 Nm).
- Front wheel. Torque the lug nuts to 85–105 ft. lbs. (115–142 Nm).

4. Check and/or adjust the wheel alignment.

5. Road test the vehicle and check for proper operation.

Rear

1. Before servicing the vehicle, refer to the precautions in the beginning of this section.

2. Remove or disconnect the following:
- Rear wheel
- Upper control arm from the knuckle/hub assembly and support it on a wire
- Upper control arm pivot bolts and nuts

➡ **Matchmark the position of the inner pivot bolt washer, relative to the frame mount, to ensure proper camber alignment upon installation.**

- Upper control arm

To install:

➡ **Inspect all fasteners for damage, pitting, corrosion, stretching, etc. Replace fasteners as necessary.**

3. Install or connect the following:
- Upper control arm. Torque the inner pivot bolt/nut to 81–98 ft. lbs. (110–133 Nm) and the outer pivot bolt/nut to 110–148 ft. lbs. (149–201 Nm).

➡ **The inner pivot bolt is used for camber adjustment and has a specifically designed washer under the bold head. Make sure the correct pivot bolt is used.**

4. Remove the knuckle/hub assembly support wire.

5. Install or connect the following:
- Rear wheel. Torque the lug nuts to 85–105 ft. lbs. (115–142 Nm).

6. Check and/or adjust the alignment.

7. Road test the vehicle and check for proper operation.

CONTROL ARM BUSHING REPLACEMENT

Front

The bushing is an integral part of the upper control arm. If the bushing is worn, the entire upper control arm must be replaced.

Rear

The bushing is an integral part of the upper control arm. If the bushing is worn, the entire upper control arm must be replaced.

Lower Control Arm

REMOVAL & INSTALLATION

Front

1. Before servicing the vehicle, refer to the precautions in the beginning of this section.
2. Remove or disconnect the following:
   - Lower ball joint nut, loosen it 3–4 turns
   - Lower control arm, separate it from wheel spindle with the nut attached
   - Wheel spindle, support it on a wire
3. Matchmark the camber adjustment cam position.

✷✷ CAUTION

Do not hold arm or damage surface in highlighted area.

4. Remove or disconnect the following:
   - Lower control arm nut, by holding the flats with wrench
   - Lower shock bolt and nut
   - Camber bolt and nut. Mark location before removal
   - Ball joint nut
   - Lower control arm

To install:

5. Install or connect the following:
   - Lower control arm, using a new ball joint nut, loosely install the fasteners
   - Lower shock absorber nut/bolt, loosely
   - Lower control arm strut-to-lower control arm nut. Torque it to 84–112 ft. lbs. (113–153 Nm).
6. Remove wheel spindle support wire.
   - Front wheel. Torque the lug nuts to 85–104 ft. lbs. (115–142 Nm).
   - Neutralize the suspension by pushing down on front of vehicle.
   - Lower shock absorber bolts. Torque

them to 126–169 ft. lbs. (170–230 Nm).
7. Align camber-to-pivot bolt marks. Torque the bolt to 84–112 ft. lbs. (113–153 Nm).
8. Check and/or adjust the front alignment.

Rear

1. Before servicing the vehicle, refer to the precautions in the beginning of this section.
2. Remove or disconnect the following:
   - Rear wheel
   - Sway bar link nuts at both ends of the sway bar, rotate it aside
   - Parking brake cable from the disc brake caliper, if equipped with rear disc brakes
3. Install 3 Spring Cages 086-00031 or equivalent, as follows:
   a. Install 1 spring cage without an adjuster link, to the inboard side (the inner-most bend of the spring) of the coil spring.
   b. Install 2 more spring cages with adjusters, at 120 degree angles to the previously installed cage.
4. Place a jack, under the lower control arm.
5. Upper control arm, support it with a wire.

➡ **The upper control arm must remain in place when the lower control arm is disconnected from the wheel knuckle.**

6. Remove the lower shock absorber bolt, washer and nut.

➡ **The lower control arm must not be lowered until the pivot bolts are loose. Do not attempt to remove the plastic cap on the front pivot nut.**

7. Matchmark the toe adjustment cam positioning to the sub-frame with a suitable marker. Loosen both inboard pivot bolts on the lower control arm.
8. Remove or disconnect the following:
   - Lower control arm to the wheel knuckle nuts/bolts
   - Lower the control arm with the jack

➡ **Make sure the spring cages are securely holding the coil spring as the control arm is lowered.**

- Jack once the coil spring pressure is relieved
- Coil spring with the cages in place from the lower control arm
- Lower control arm-to-sub-frame pivot bolts and nuts

- Lower control arm
- Compensator link from the lower control arm

To install:

9. Inspect the large nut used at the inner front arm attachment for the condition of the plastic cap. Use a new nut if the cap is cracked, loose or missing.
10. Install or connect the following:
    - Compensator link on the lower control arm
    - Lower control arm to the sub-frame brackets, loosely install the pivot bolts and nuts
    - Torque the compensator link nut to 110–148 ft. lbs. (149–201 Nm)
    - Coil spring onto the upper and lower control arm seats

➡ **The cage with no adjuster must face inward and cages must be closer to the bottom of spring. The spring pigtails can be in any position.**

- 2 jackstands under the front bumper reinforcement to prevent the rear of the vehicle from lifting off the hoist
- Lower control arm, raise it with a jack to align the knuckle

➡ **Ensure that the coil spring is properly seated.**

- Lower control arm to the knuckle. Torque the bolts to 110–148 ft. lbs. (149–201 Nm).
11. Remove the upper control arm support wire.
12. Install or connect the following:
    - Lower shock absorber bolt, washer and nut. Torque the nut to 83–113 ft. lbs. (113–153 Nm).
13. Remove the jack from under the lower control arm.
14. Remove the jackstands from under the front bumper reinforcement.
15. Remove the spring cages from the coil spring.
16. Install or connect the following:
    - Parking brake cable to the disc

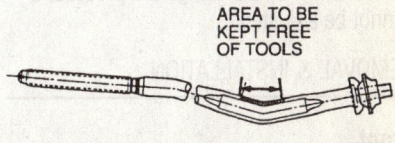

AREA TO BE KEPT FREE OF TOOLS

93060QG05

Do not hold arm or damage surface in highlighted area

Turn to Section 5 for brake system applications

brake caliper, if equipped with rear disc brakes
- Sway bar. Torque the nuts to 35–47 ft. lbs. (47–63 Nm).
- Rear wheel. Torque the lug nuts to 85–105 ft. lbs. (115–142 Nm).
- Toe adjustment cam, by aligning the matchmarks
- Torque the front lower control arm pivot nut to 166–202 ft. lbs. (225–275 Nm) and rear lower control arm pivot nut to 142–191 ft. lbs. (192–259 Nm).

17. Check and/or adjust the wheel alignment.

18. Road test the vehicle and check for proper operation.

CONTROL ARM BUSHING REPLACEMENT

Front

1. Before servicing the vehicle, refer to the precautions in the beginning of this section.
2. Remove lower control arm.
3. Press lower control arm mounting bolt bushing with appropriate bushing remover, receiving cup and forcing screw.

To install:

4. Install new lower control arm mounting bolt bushing to the front using appropriate bushing replacer, pivot bushing replacer, forcing screw and forcing screw washer.
5. Turn forcing screw until it bottoms.
6. Replace lower control arm.
7. Check and/or adjust the wheel alignment.

Rear

The bushing is an integral part of the lower control arm. If the bushing is worn, the entire lower control arm must be replaced.

Wheel Hub and Bearings

ADJUSTMENT

The front and rear wheel bearings are pre-greased, sealed and require no periodic maintenance. The bearings are preset and cannot be adjusted.

REMOVAL & INSTALLATION

Front

1. Before servicing the vehicle, refer to the precautions in the beginning of this section.
2. Remove or disconnect the following:

- Front wheel
- Hubcap grease seal and discard it
- Brake caliper, suspend it on a wire

3. Matchmark the rotor to the wheel stud.
4. Remove or disconnect the following:

- Hub retainer nut and discard it
- Hub/bearing assembly

To install:

5. Install or connect the following:

- Hub/bearing assembly
- New hub retainer nut. Torque it to 188–254 ft. lbs. (255–345 Nm).
- Brake rotor and push-on nuts after aligning the rotor with the stud
- New front hubcap grease seal
- Brake caliper. Torque the bolts to 97 ft. lbs. (132 Nm).
- Front wheel. Torque lug nuts to 85–105 ft. lbs. (115–142 Nm).

Rear

➥Before continuing with this procedure, be sure to have available, one new wheel hub retainer. Once removed, it will lose its torque holding ability or retention capability and must be replaced.

1. Be sure to observe all precautions in the beginning of this section.
2. Remove or disconnect the following:

- Halfshaft hub nut and discard it
- Rear wheel
- Parking brake cable adjusting clip, slide it downward until the cable is free
- Parking brake cable from the brake caliper, if equipped with rear disc brakes
- Brake caliper from the brake rotor, suspend the caliper on a wire
- Brake rotor or brake drum, as equipped
- Brake dust shield, if equipped with disc brakes
- Parking brake cable.
- Brake line at the wheel cylinder and plug it, if equipped with drum brakes
- Upper control arm from the knuckle, suspend it on a wire.
- Halfshaft from the hub, using a puller
- Lower control arm-to-knuckle location with the lower bushings in the relaxed position

➥Failure to matchmark this relationship will result in bushing wind-up on assembly and incorrect ride height, causing misalignment and premature tire wear.

- Lower control arm-to-knuckle bolts/nuts
- Knuckle/hub assembly

➥If replacing knuckle, note the approximate angle of it in the relaxed position by measuring the distance from the upper bushing to any convenient point on the vehicle body.

To install:

3. Install or connect the following:

- Knuckle to the lower control arm, by aligning the knuckle/hub assembly to the halfshaft splines

➥Align marks on bushings made during disassembly. If installing a new wheel knuckle, refer to the approximate angle noted during disassembly.

- Push wheel knuckle/hub assembly firmly onto halfshaft
- Upper control arm to the knuckle. Torque the nut/bolt to 110–148 ft. lbs. (149–201 Nm).
- New halfshaft nut. Torque it to 85–104 ft. lbs. (115–142 Nm).
- Disc brake backing plate on the knuckle, if equipped with rear disc brakes. Torque the bolts to 22–37 ft. lbs. (30–50 Nm).
- Brake backing plate to the wheel knuckle, if equipped with drum brakes. Torque the bolts to 44–59 ft. lbs. (59–80 Nm).
- Rear parking brake cable
- Brake line to the wheel cylinder, if equipped with drum brakes
- Brake rotor or brake drum, as equipped
- Upper control arm. Torque the nut to 117–142 ft. lbs. (158–193 Nm).
- Disc brake caliper. Torque the bolts to 64–88 ft. lbs. (87–119 Nm).
- Parking brake rear cable to the disc brake caliper and the adjustment clip
- Rear wheel. Torque the lug nuts to 85–105 ft. lbs. (115–142 Nm).

4. Apply the parking brake several times and adjust, if necessary.
5. Install or connect the following:

- Torque the hub nut to 188–254 ft. lbs. (255–345 Nm).
- Hubcap grease seal

6. Pump the brake pedal several times to position the brake pads before moving the vehicle.
7. Check and/or adjust the wheel alignment.
8. Road test the vehicle and check for proper operation.

FORD MOTOR CO.

Ford-Crown Victoria • **Lincoln**-Town Car • **Mercury**-Grand Marquis

PRECAUTIONS

Before servicing any vehicle, please be sure to read all of the following precautions, which deal with personal safety, prevention of component damage, and important points to take into consideration when servicing a motor vehicle:

• Never open, service or drain the radiator or cooling system when the engine is hot; serious burns can occur from the steam and hot coolant.

• Observe all applicable safety precautions when working around fuel. Whenever servicing the fuel system, always work in a well-ventilated area. Do not allow fuel spray or vapors to come in contact with a spark, open flame, or excessive heat (a hot drop light, for example). Keep a dry chemical fire extinguisher near the work area. Always keep fuel in a container specifically designed for fuel storage; also, always properly seal fuel containers to avoid the possibility of fire or explosion. Refer to the additional fuel system precautions later in this section.

• Fuel injection systems often remain pressurized, even after the engine has been turned **OFF**. The fuel system pressure must be relieved before disconnecting any fuel lines. Failure to do so may result in fire and/or personal injury.

• Brake fluid often contains polyglycol ethers and polyglycols. Avoid contact with the eyes and wash your hands thoroughly after handling brake fluid. If you do get brake fluid in your eyes, flush your eyes with clean, running water for 15 minutes. If eye irritation persists, or if you have taken brake fluid internally, IMMEDIATELY seek medical assistance.

• The EPA warns that prolonged contact with used engine oil may cause a number of skin disorders, including cancer! You should make every effort to minimize your exposure to used engine oil. Protective gloves should be worn when changing oil. Wash your hands and any other exposed skin areas as soon as possible after exposure to used engine oil. Soap and water, or waterless hand cleaner should be used.

• All new vehicles are now equipped with an air bag system, often referred to as a Supplemental Restraint System (SRS) or Supplemental Inflatable Restraint (SIR) system. The system must be disabled before performing service on or around system components, steering column, instrument panel components, wiring and sensors. Failure to follow safety and disabling procedures could result in accidental air bag deployment, possible personal injury and unnecessary system repairs.

• Always wear safety goggles when working with, or around, the air bag system. When carrying a non-deployed air bag, be sure the bag and trim cover are pointed away from your body. When placing a non-deployed air bag on a work surface, always face the bag and trim cover upward, away from the surface. This will reduce the motion of the module if it is accidentally deployed. Refer to the additional air bag system precautions later in this section.

• Clean, high quality brake fluid from a sealed container is essential to the safe and proper operation of the brake system. You should always buy the correct type of brake fluid for your vehicle. If the brake fluid becomes contaminated, completely flush the system with new fluid. Never reuse any brake fluid. Any brake fluid that is removed from the system should be discarded. Also, do not allow any brake fluid to come in contact with a painted surface; it will damage the paint.

• Never operate the engine without the proper amount and type of engine oil; doing so WILL result in severe engine damage.

• Timing belt maintenance is extremely important! Many models utilize an interference-type, non-freewheeling engine. If the timing belt breaks, the valves in the cylinder head may strike the pistons, causing potentially serious (also time-consuming and expensive) engine damage. Refer to the maintenance interval charts in the front of this manual for the recommended replacement interval for the timing belt, and to the timing belt section for belt replacement and inspection.

• Disconnecting the negative battery cable on some vehicles may interfere with the functions of the on-board computer system(s) and may require the computer to undergo a relearning process once the negative battery cable is reconnected.

• When servicing drum brakes, only disassemble and assemble one side at a time, leaving the remaining side intact for reference.

ENGINE REPAIR

Alternator

REMOVAL

1. Before servicing the vehicle, refer to the precautions in the beginning of this section.
2. Remove or disconnect the following:
   • Negative battery cable
   • Engine cover by unfastening the screw and pushing the cover to disengage the front clips, on 1998–01 models
   • Pushpins and wiring harness
   • Belt tension and belt
   • Mounting bolts
   • Bracket bolts
   • Accessory drive belt
   • Alternator

INSTALLATION

Install or connect the following:
   • Alternator
   • Mounting bolts and tighten to 15–22 ft. lbs. (20–30 Nm)
   • Bracket bolts and tighten to 71–106 inch lbs. (8–12 Nm)
   • Accessory drive belt
   • Pushpins and wiring harness
   • Engine cover, on 1998–01 models
   • Negative battery cable

Ignition Timing

ADJUSTMENT

The 4.6L engine used in the Ford Crown Victoria, Lincoln Town Car and Mercury Grand Marquis utilizes a Distributorless Ignition System (DIS).

The Crankshaft Position (CKP) sensor is a variable reluctance-type sensor triggered by a 36-minus-1 tooth trigger wheel located inside the front cover.

Engine Assembly

REMOVAL & INSTALLATION

1. Before servicing the vehicle, refer to the precautions in the beginning of this section.

2   Drain the engine cooling system.

3.   Recover the refrigerant from the air conditioning system using approved recovery equipment.

4.   Properly relieve the fuel system pressure.

5.   Remove or disconnect the following:

- Both battery cables
- Hood
- Engine cooling fan, shroud and radiator
- Windshield wiper governor (module) and support bracket
- Engine air cleaner outlet tube
- Engine/transmission harness connector from the retaining bracket on the power brake booster and move aside
- Accelerator and cruise control cables at the throttle body
- Electrical connector and vacuum hose from the evaporative emission canister purge valve
- Positive battery cable from the power distribution box and harness
- Vacuum supply hose from the throttle body adapter vacuum port
- Both heater hoses
- Alternator harness from the front fender apron and the power distribution box
- Air conditioning hoses from the air conditioning compressor using the appropriate spring-lock disconnect tools
- Power steering control valve harness connector
- Body ground strap from the dash panel
- Exhaust system from the exhaust manifolds and support with wire hung from the crossmember
- Retaining nut from the transmission line bracket
- 3 bolts and 1 stud retaining the engine to the transmission knee braces
- Starter motor
- 4 bolts retaining the power steering pump to the cylinder block and position aside

6.   Transmission housing cover from the cylinder block to access the torque converter nuts. Rotate the crankshaft until each of the 4 nuts is accessible and remove the nuts

7.   Remove or disconnect the following:

- 6 transmission-to-engine retaining bolts
- Engine support insulator (mount) through-bolts

8.   Support the transmission with a suitable floor jack and a block of wood.

- Bolt retaining the right-hand front engine support insulator to the front engine mount insulator support bracket

9.   Install engine lifting bracket to the front of the left-hand cylinder head and to the rear of the right-hand cylinder head. Connect engine lifting equipment to the lifting brackets

10.   Raise the engine slightly using a floor crane and carefully separate the engine from the transmission. Do not let the torque converter fall out of the transmission.

11.   Carefully lift the engine out of the engine compartment and position on a workstand. Remove the engine lifting equipment.

To install:

12.   Engine lifting brackets. Support the engine using a floor crane installed to the lifting equipment and remove the engine from the workstand

13.   Lower the engine into the engine compartment. Start the converter pilot into the flywheel and align the paint marks on the flywheel and torque converter. Be sure the studs on the torque converter align with the holes in the flywheel.

14.   Fully engage the engine to the transmission and lower onto front engine support insulators.

15.   Install or connect the following:

- Engine lifting equipment and brackets
- Bolt retaining the right-hand front engine support insulator to the front engine mount insulator support bracket
- 6 engine-to-transmission bolts and tighten to 30–44 ft. lbs. (40–60 Nm)
- Front engine support insulator through-bolts and tighten to 15–22 ft. lbs. (20–30 Nm)
- 4 torque converter retaining nuts and tighten to 22–25 ft. lbs. (20–30 Nm)
- Transmission housing cover to the cylinder block

- Power steering pump on the cylinder block and the 4 retaining nuts. Tighten to 15–22 ft. lbs. (20–30 Nm).
- Starter motor
- Engine-to-transmission brace and the 3 bolts and 1 stud. Tighten the bolts and stud to 18–31 ft. lbs. (25–43 Nm).
- Tansmission line bracket to the brace stud and 1 retaining nut. Tighten to 15–22 ft. lbs. (20–30 Nm).
- Exhaust system to the exhaust manifolds. Tighten the 4 nuts to 20–30 ft. lbs. (27–41 Nm). Be sure the exhaust system clears the No. 3 crossmember. Adjust as necessary.
- Power steering valve harness connector
- Ground strap to the dash panel
- Air conditioning lines to the air conditioning compressor
- Alternator harness at the front fender apron and the power distribution box
- Both heater hoses
- Vacuum supply hose to the throttle body adapter vacuum port
- Positive battery cable to the power distribution box and harness
- Electrical connector and vacuum hose to the evaporative emission canister purge valve
- Accelerator and cruise control cables at the throttle body
- Engine/transmission harness connector to the retaining bracket on the power brake booster
- Windshield wiper governor and support bracket
- Fuel supply and return lines
- Radiator, cooling fan and shroud
- Engine air cleaner outlet tube
- Both battery cables
- Hood, aligning the marks that were made during removal

16.   If needed, fill the crankcase.

17.   Fill the cooling system.

18.   Start the engine and allow it to reach normal operating temperature.

19.   Check for leaks and proper fluid levels.

20.   Evacuate and recharge the air conditioning system.

21.   Road test the vehicle and check the engine and transmission for proper operation.

Water Pump

REMOVAL & INSTALLATION

1. Before servicing the vehicle, refer to the precautions in the beginning of this section.

2. Drain the cooling system.

3. Remove or disconnect the following:

- Negative battery cable
- Cooling fan and the shroud
- Accessory drive belt
- Water pump pulley to the water pump bolts
- Pulley
- Water pump to the engine assembly bolts
- Water pump

To install:

4. Installation is the reverse of the removal procedure. Be sure to clean the sealing surfaces of the water pump and block and use a new O-ring. Lubricate the O-ring with clean antifreeze prior to installation.

5. Tighten the water pump-to-engine bolts and the pulley-to-water pump bolts to 15–22 ft. lbs. (20–30 Nm). Fill the cooling system. Operate the engine until normal operating temperatures have been reached and check for leaks.

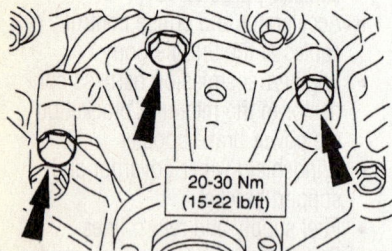

20-30 Nm
(15-22 lb/ft)

7922RG01

Be sure to tighten the water pump mounting bolts to the specification

Cylinder Head

REMOVAL & INSTALLATION

➡**The cylinder head bolts are a torque-to-yield design and cannot be reused. Before beginning this procedure, be sure new cylinder head bolts are available.**

1. Before servicing the vehicle, refer to the precautions in the beginning of this section.

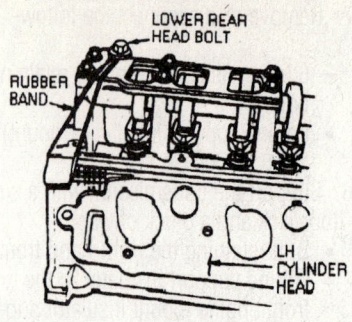

LOWER REAR
HEAD BOLT

RUBBER
BAND

LH
CYLINDER
HEAD

7922RG02

Use a rubber band to support the rear cylinder head bolt to ease removal of the head

2. If equipped with air suspension, the air suspension switch, located on the right-hand side of the luggage compartment, must be turned to the **OFF** position before raising the vehicle.

3. Drain the engine cooling system.

4. Properly relieve the fuel system pressure.

5. Remove or disconnect the following:

- Negative battery cable
- Cooling fan and shroud assembly
- Engine air cleaner outlet tube
- Windshield wiper governor (module)
- Accessory drive belt
- Ignition wires from the spark plugs
- Ignition wire brackets from the cylinder head cover studs
- Ignition wire tray to the ignition coil brackets bolts
- Bolt retaining the air conditioning pressure line to the right-hand ignition coil bracket
- Wiring to both ignition coils and the Camshaft Position (CMP) sensor
- Ignition coil brackets to the engine front cover nuts. Slide the ignition coil brackets and ignition wire assemblies off the mounting studs and from the vehicle
- Water pump pulley
- Alternator wiring harness from the junction block, fender apron and alternator
- Alternator
- Positive battery cable at the power distribution box
- Retaining bolt from the positive battery cable bracket located on the side of the right-hand cylinder head
- Vent hose from the canister purge

solenoid and position the positive battery cable aside

- Positive Crankcase Ventilation (PCV) valve from the cylinder head cover
- Engine/transmission harness connector from the retaining bracket on the power brake booster
- Crankshaft Position (CKP) sensor, air conditioning compressor clutch and canister purge solenoid electrical connectors

6. Remove the bolts retaining the power steering pump to the cylinder block and engine front cover. The front lower bolt on the power steering pump will not come all the way out. Wire the power steering pump out of the way.

7. Remove or disconnect the following:

- Engine oil pan and oil pan gasket
- Crankshaft pulley retaining bolt
- Pulley
- Power steering control valve actuator and oil pressure sensor wiring connectors and position aside
- Exhaust Gas Recirculation (EGR) tube from the right-hand exhaust manifold
- Exhaust pipes from the exhaust manifolds. Lower the exhaust pipes and hang with wire from the crossmember.
- Bolts retaining the starter wiring harness to the rear of the right-hand cylinder head
- Cylinder head covers to the cylinder heads
- Accelerator and cruise control cables
- Accelerator cable bracket from the intake manifold and position aside
- Vacuum hose from the throttle body elbow vacuum port
- Heated Oxygen (HO2S) sensors and the heater water hose
- 2 bolts retaining the thermostat housing to the intake manifold and position the upper hose and thermostat housing aside

➡**The 2 thermostat housing bolts also retain the intake manifold.**

- Intake manifold to cylinder heads bolts
- Intake manifold and gaskets
- 7 stud bolts and the 4 bolts attaching the engine front cover to the engine
- Front cover
- Both timing chains

✳✳ WARNING

This is an interference engine. Camshaft Positioning Tools T92P-6256-A must be installed on the camshafts to prevent the camshafts from rotating.

- Left-hand cylinder head to the cylinder block bolts

8. Remove the cylinder head. The lower rear cylinder head bolt must stay in the cylinder head until the cylinder head is removed due to lack of clearance for removal in the vehicle. Use a rubber band to secure the cylinder head bolt in the cylinder head during removal and installation of the cylinder head and to prevent the bolt from damaging the cylinder block or head gasket

➡ **The lower rear cylinder head bolt cannot be removed due to interference with the power brake booster. Use a rubber band to hold the bolt away from the cylinder block.**

9. Remove or disconnect the following:
- Ground strap, 1 stud and 1 bolt retaining the heater return line to the right-hand cylinder head
- Right-hand cylinder head to the cylinder block bolts

10. Remove the cylinder head. The lower rear cylinder head bolt must stay in the cylinder head until the cylinder head is removed due to lack of clearance for removal in the vehicle. Use a rubber band to secure the cylinder head bolt in the cylinder head during removal and installation of the cylinder head and to prevent the bolt from damaging the cylinder block or head gasket.

➡ **The lower rear cylinder head bolt cannot be removed due to interference with the evaporator housing. Use a rubber band to hold the bolt away from the cylinder block.**

11. Clean all gaskets mating surfaces. Check the cylinder heads and cylinder block for flatness. Check the cylinder heads for scratches near the coolant passages and combustion chambers that could provide leak paths.

To install:

12. Rotate the crankshaft counterclockwise 45 degrees. The crankshaft keyway should be at the 9 o'clock position viewed from the front of the engine. This ensures that all pistons are below the top of the engine block deck face.

13. Rotate the camshaft to a stable position where the valves do not extend below the head face.

14. Install or connect the following:
- New head gaskets on the cylinder block
- New bolts in the lower rear bolt holes on both cylinder heads and retain with rubber bands as explained during the removal procedure

➡ **New cylinder head bolts must be used whenever the cylinder head is removed and reinstalled. The cylinder head bolts are a torque-to-yield design and cannot be reused.**

15. Position the cylinder heads on the cylinder block dowels, being careful not to score the surface of the head face. Apply clean oil to the new cylinder head bolts, remove the rubber bands from the lower rear bolts and install all bolts hand-tight.

➡ **Refer to Section 1 of this manual for the cylinder head torque sequence illustration. The illustration is located after the Torque Specification Chart.**

16. Tighten the new cylinder head bolts, in sequence, as follows:
   a. Step 1: 28–31 ft. lbs. (37–43 Nm).
   b. Step 2: plus 85–95 degrees.
   c. Step 3: loosen all bolts at least 1 full turn.
   d. Step 4: 27–32 ft. lbs. (37–43 Nm).
   e. Step 5: plus 85–95 degrees.
   f. Step 6: again, plus 85–95 degrees.

17. Position the heater return hose and install the 2 retaining bolts.

18. Rotate the camshafts using the flats matched at the center of the camshaft until both are in time. Install Camshaft Positioning Tools T91P-6256-A on the flats of the camshafts to keep them from rotating.

19. Rotate the crankshaft clockwise 45 degrees to position the crankshaft at Top Dead Center (TDC) for the No. 1 cylinder.

➡ **The crankshaft must only be rotated in the clockwise direction and only as far as TDC.**

20. Install or connect the following:
- Both timing chains
- New engine front cover seal and gasket. Apply silicone sealer to the lower corners of the cover where it meets the junction of the engine oil pan and cylinder block and to the points where the cover contacts the junction of the cylinder block and the cylinder heads.
- Engine front cover and the bolts. Tighten to 15–22 ft. lbs. (20–30 Nm).
- New intake manifold gaskets on the cylinder heads. Be sure the alignment tabs on the gaskets are aligned with the holes in the cylinder heads.

➡ **Before installing the intake manifold, inspect it for nicks and cuts that could provide leak paths.**

- Intake manifold on the cylinder heads and the retaining bolts. Tighten the bolts in sequence, to 15–22 ft. lbs. (20–30 Nm).
- Thermostat, O-ring, thermostat housing and upper hose. Tighten the 2 retaining bolts to 15–22 ft. lbs. (20–30 Nm).
- Heater water hose and both HO2S sensors
- Vacuum hose to the throttle body adapter vacuum port
- Accelerator cable bracket on the intake manifold
- Accelerator and cruise control cables to the throttle body

21. Apply silicone sealer to both places where the engine front cover meets the cylinder heads.
- Cylinder head covers with new gasket on the cylinder heads. Tighten the bolts and stud bolts to 71–106 inch lbs. (8–12 Nm).
- Starter motor wiring harness to the right-hand cylinder head and tighten the retaining bolt
- Exhaust pipes to the exhaust manifolds. Tighten the 4 nuts to 20–30 ft. lbs. (27–41 Nm).

➡ **Be sure the exhaust system clears the No. 3 crossmember. Adjust as necessary.**

- EGR tube to the right-hand exhaust manifold and tighten the line nut to 26–33 ft. lbs. (35–45 Nm).
- Power steering control valve actuator and oil pressure sensor electrical connectors

22. Apply a small amount of silicone sealer in the rear of the keyway on the crankshaft pulley.
- Pulley on the crankshaft, making sure the crankshaft key and keyway are aligned.

Timing belt service is covered in Section 4 of this manual

23. Install the crankshaft pulley and tighten the bolt as follows:

    a. Step 1: Tighten to 66 ft. lbs. (90 Nm).

    b. Step 2: Loosen one complete turn.

    c. Step 3: Tighten to 35–39 ft. lbs. (47–53 Nm)

    d. Step 4: Tighten an additional 85–95 degrees.

24. Install or connect the following:

- Engine oil pan and a new gasket
- Power steering pump in position on the cylinder block
- 4 retaining bolts. Tighten the bolts to 15–22 ft. lbs. (20–30 Nm).
- Air conditioning compressor, CKP sensor and canister purge solenoid electrical connectors
- Engine/transmission harness connector on the power brake booster
- PCV valve in the right-hand cylinder head cover and connect the canister purge solenoid vent hose
- Positive battery cable harness on the right-hand cylinder head
- Bolt retaining the cable bracket to the cylinder head
- Positive battery cable at the power distribution box and battery
- Alternator and the 2 retaining bolts. Tighten the bolts to 15–22 ft. lbs. (20–30 Nm).
- 2 bolts retaining the alternator brace to the intake manifold. Tighten to 72–96 inch lbs. (8–12 Nm).
- Water pump pulley. Tighten the bolts to 15–22 ft. lbs. (20–30 Nm).
- Ignition coil brackets and ignition wire assemblies onto the mounting studs
- 7 nuts retaining the ignition coil brackets to the engine front cover and tighten to 15–22 ft. lbs. (20–30 Nm)
- 2 bolts retaining the ignition wire tray to the ignition coil bracket and tighten to 71–106 inch lbs. (8–12 Nm)
- Ignition coil and CMP sensor harness connectors
- Air conditioning pressure line on the right-hand ignition coil bracket and tighten the retaining bolt
- Ignition wires to the spark plugs and the bracket onto the cylinder head cover studs
- Accessory drive belt and the windshield wiper governor
- Fuel supply and return lines
- Cooling fan and shroud
- Engine air cleaner outlet tube
- Negative battery cable

25. Fill the cooling system.

26. If equipped with air suspension, turn the air suspension switch to the **ON** position.

27. Refill the engine with the correct amount of oil and replace the filter.

28. Start the engine and bring to normal operating temperature while checking for leaks.

29. Road test the vehicle and check for proper engine operation.

Rocker Arms

REMOVAL & INSTALLATION

1. Before servicing the vehicle, refer to the precautions in the beginning of this section.

2. Relieve the fuel system pressure.

3. Disconnect the negative battery cable.

4. Remove the right camshaft cover by removing or disconnecting the following:

- Positive battery cable at the battery and at the power distribution box
- Retaining bolt from the positive battery cable bracket located on the side of the right cylinder head
- Crankshaft Position (CKP) sensor, air conditioning compressor clutch and canister purge solenoid connectors. Position the harness out of the way.
- Vent hose from the purge solenoid and position the positive battery cable aside
- Ignition wires from the spark plugs
- Ignition wire brackets from the camshaft cover studs and position the wires aside
- PCV valve from the camshaft cover grommet and position aside
- Bolts and stud bolts and remove the camshaft cover.

5. Remove the left camshaft cover by removing or disconnecting the following:

- Air inlet tube
- Fuel lines
- Power Steering Pressure switch (PSP) and oil pressure sending unit and position the harness aside
- 42-pin engine harness connector from the retaining bracket on the brake vacuum booster and position aside

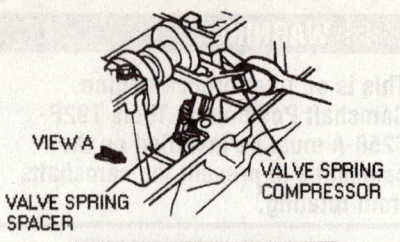

7922RG04

After installing the spring spacer, compress the valve spring and remove the rocker arm

- Windshield wiper module
- Ignition wires from the spark plugs
- Ignition wire brackets from the studs and position the wires aside
- Camshaft cover

6. Position the piston of the cylinder being serviced at the bottom of its stroke and position the camshaft lobe on the base circle.

7. Install Valve Spring Spacer tool T91P-6565-AH between the spring coils to prevent valve seal damage.

➡ **If the valve spring spacer tool is not used, the retainer will hit the valve stem seal and damage the seal.**

8. Install a valve spring compressor under the camshaft and on top of the valve spring retainer.

9. Compress the valve spring and remove the roller follower. Remove the valve spring compressor and spacer.

To install:

10. Apply engine oil to the valve stem and tip and roller follower contact surfaces.

11. Install valve spring spacer tool T91P-6565-AH between the spring coils. Compress the valve spring, and install the roller follower.

➡ **The piston must be at the bottom of its stroke and the camshaft at the base circle.**

12. Remove the valve spring compressor and spacer.

13. Clean the sealing surfaces of the camshaft covers and cylinder heads. Apply silicone sealer to the places where the front cover meets the cylinder head.

14. Position new gaskets onto the camshaft covers and install the covers. Install the bolts and stud bolts and tighten to 72–106 inch lbs. (8–12 Nm).

15. When installing the right camshaft cover, install or connect the following:

- PCV into the camshaft cover grommet
- Ignition wire brackets on the studs
- Wires to the spark plugs
- Canister purge solenoid, air conditioning compressor clutch and CKP sensor
- Positive battery cable harness on the right cylinder head
- Bolt retaining the cable bracket to the cylinder head
- Positive battery cable at the power distribution box and the battery

16. When installing the left camshaft cover, install or connect the following:

- Ignition wire brackets on the studs
- Wires to the spark plugs
- Windshield wiper module
- 42-pin and transmission harness connectors
- Retaining bracket
- PSP switch and oil pressure sending unit harness
- Fuel lines
- Negative battery cable

17. Start the engine and check for leaks.

Intake Manifold

REMOVAL & INSTALLATION

1. Before servicing the vehicle, refer to the precautions in the beginning of this section.

2. If equipped with air suspension, the air suspension switch, located on the right-hand side of the luggage compartment, must be turned to the **OFF** position before raising the vehicle.

3. Disconnect negative battery cable.

4. Drain the engine cooling system.

5. Properly relieve the fuel system pressure.

6. Remove or disconnect the following:

- Fuel supply and return lines
- Windshield wiper governor (module)
- Engine air cleaner outlet tube
- Accessory drive belt
- Ignition wires from the spark plugs
- Ignition wire brackets from the cylinder head cover studs
- Ignition coils and the Camshaft Position (CMP) sensor

- Ignition wires from both ignition coils
- 2 bolts retaining the ignition wire bracket to the ignition coil brackets
- Ignition wire assembly
- Alternator wiring harness from the junction block at the fender apron and alternator
- Bolts retaining the alternator brace to the intake manifold and the alternator to the cylinder block
- Alternator
- Oil pressure sensor and power steering control valve actuator wiring and position the wiring harness aside
- Exhaust Gas Recirculation (EGR) valve-to-exhaust manifold tube from the right-hand exhaust manifold
- Engine/transmission harness connector from the retaining bracket on the power brake booster
- Air conditioning compressor clutch, Crankshaft position (CKP) sensor and the canister purge solenoid wiring connectors
- Positive Crankcase Ventilation (PCV) valve from the cylinder head cover
- Canister purge vent hose from the PCV valve
- Accelerator and cruise control cables from the throttle body
- Accelerator cable bracket from the intake manifold and position aside
- Vacuum hose from the throttle body adapter port
- Heated Oxygen (HO$_2$S) sensor and the heater water hose
- 2 bolts retaining the thermostat housing to the intake manifold and position the upper hose and thermostat housing aside

➡The 2 thermostat housing bolts are also used to retain the intake manifold.

- 9 bolts retaining the intake manifold to the cylinder heads
- Intake manifold and gaskets

7. If replacing the intake manifold, swap over the necessary parts.

To install:

8. Clean all gaskets mating surfaces.

9. Position new intake manifold gaskets on the cylinder heads. Be sure the alignment tabs on the gaskets are aligned with the holes in the cylinder heads.

➡Refer to Section 1 of this manual for the intake manifold torque sequence illustration. The illustration is located after the Torque Specification Chart.

10. Install the intake manifold and the 9 retaining bolts. Hand-tighten the right-rear bolt (viewed from the front of the engine) before final tightening, then tighten the bolts, in sequence, to 15–22 ft. lbs. (20–30 Nm).

11. Inspect and if necessary, replace the O-ring seal on the thermostat housing. Position the housing and upper hose and install the 2 retaining bolts. Tighten to 15–22 ft. lbs. (20–30 Nm).

12. Install or connect the following:

- Heater water hose
- HO$_2$S sensor
- Vacuum hose to the throttle body adapter vacuum port
- Accelerator cable bracket on the intake manifold
- Accelerator and cruise control cables to the throttle body
- PCV valve in the cylinder head cover
- Canister purge solenoid vent hose
- Air conditioning compressor clutch, CKP sensor and canister purge solenoid wiring connectors
- Engine/transmission harness connector the retaining bracket on the power brake booster
- EGR valve-to-exhaust manifold tube to the right-hand exhaust manifold. Tighten the tube nut to 26–33 ft. lbs. (35–45 Nm).
- Power steering control valve actuator
- Oil pressure sensor wiring connectors
- Alternator. Tighten bolts to 15–22 ft. lbs. (20–30 Nm).
- 2 bolts retaining the alternator brace to the intake manifold and tighten to 71–106 inch lbs. (8–12 Nm)
- Alternator wiring harness to the alternator, right-hand fender apron and junction block
- Ignition wire assembly on the engine
- 2 bolts retaining the ignition wire bracket to the ignition coil brackets. Tighten the bolts to 71–106 inch lbs. (8–12 Nm).

- Ignition wires to the ignition coils
- Ignition wires to the spark plugs
- Ignition wire brackets on the cylinder head cover studs
- Wiring connectors to both ignition coils and the CMP sensor
- Accessory drive belt
- Air cleaner outlet tube
- Windshield wiper governor
- Fuel supply and return lines
- Negative battery cable

13. Fill the engine cooling system.

14. If equipped with air suspension, turn the air suspension switch to the **ON** position.

15. Start the engine and check for leaks.

16. Road test the vehicle and check for proper operation.

Exhaust Manifold

REMOVAL & INSTALLATION

1. Before servicing the vehicle, refer to the precautions in the beginning of this section.

2. Drain the engine cooling system.

3. Relieve the fuel system pressure.

4. Discharge the air conditioning system

5. Remove or disconnect the following:

- Battery cables
- Engine air inlet tube
- Cooling fan and shroud assembly
- Fuel supply and return lines
- Upper radiator hose
- Windshield wiper governor and support bracket
- Compressor outlet hose at the compressor and the hose assembly to the right-hand ignition coil bracket bolt. Plug both openings.

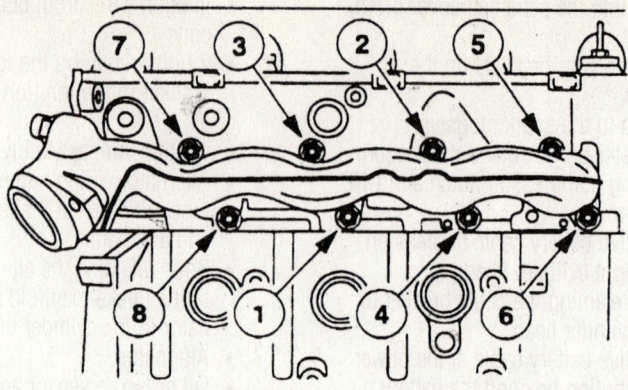

To prevent warpage, be sure to tighten the exhaust manifold bolts in sequence—1997–01 models (right side)

- Engine/transmission harness connector from the retaining bracket on the power brake booster
- Heater hose
- Ground strap to right-hand cylinder head nut
- Upper stud and lower bolt retaining the heater hose to the right cylinder head and position aside
- Heater blower motor switch resistor
- Bolt retaining the right-hand front engine support insulator to the sub-frame
- Both Heated Oxygen (HO2S) sensors
- Engine support insulator through-bolts
- Exhaust Gas Recirculation (EGR) valve-to-exhaust manifold tube nut from the right-hand exhaust manifold.
- Catalytic converter pipes from both exhaust manifolds. Lower the exhaust system and hang it from the crossmember with wire.
- Left-hand exhaust manifold
- Front engine support insulator from

the cylinder block and the 8 nuts retaining the exhaust manifold
- Left-hand exhaust manifold and the 2 manifold gaskets

6. Position an adjustable jackstand and a block of wood under the engine oil pan, rearward of the oil drain hole. Raise the engine approximately 4 inches (100mm).

7. Remove or disconnect the following:

- 8 exhaust manifold retaining nuts and right-hand exhaust manifold
- Manifold and gasket

To install:

8. If the exhaust manifolds are being replaced, transfer the heated O_2 sensors and tighten to 27–33 ft. lbs. (37–45 Nm). On the right-hand exhaust manifold, transfer the EGR tube connector and tighten to 33–48 ft. lbs. (45–65 Nm).

9. Clean the mating surfaces of the exhaust manifolds and cylinder heads.

10. Install or connect the following:

- Exhaust manifolds, using new gaskets. Tighten the bolts in sequence to 15–22 ft. lbs. (20–30 Nm).
- EGR valve and tube assembly to the exhaust manifold. Tighten the line nut to 26–33 ft. lbs. (35–45 Nm).
- Left-hand front engine support insulator to the cylinder block and tighten the bolts to 15–22 ft. lbs. (20–30 Nm)

11. Lower the engine onto the front engine support insulator and remove the jack.

12. Install or connect the following:

- Left-hand and right-hand engine support insulator through-bolts and tighten to 15–22 ft. lbs. (20–30 Nm).
- Catalytic converter pipes to both exhaust manifolds. Tighten the nuts to 20–30 ft. lbs. (27–41 Nm).

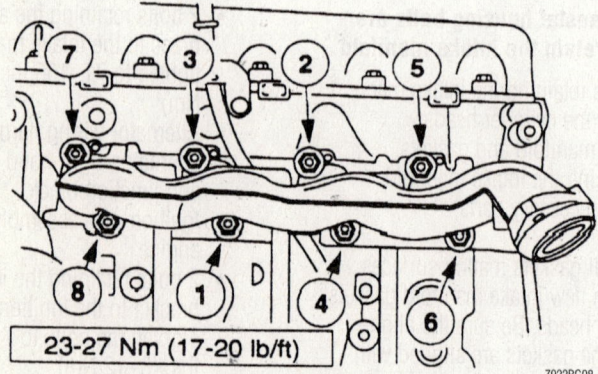

23-27 Nm (17-20 lb/ft)

To prevent warpage, be sure to tighten the exhaust manifold bolts in sequence —1997–01 models (left side)

➡ **Be sure the exhaust system clears the No. 3 crossmember. Adjust as necessary.**

- Both HO₂S sensors
- Bolt retaining the right-hand front engine support insulator to the sub-frame. Tighten to 15–22 ft. lbs. (20–30 Nm)
- Heater blower motor switch resistor using the 2 retaining screws
- Heater hose in position
- Upper stud and lower bolt and tighten to 15–22 ft. lbs. (20–30 Nm)
- Ground strap onto the stud and tighten the nut to 15–22 ft. lbs. (20–30 Nm)
- Heater hose
- Engine/transmission harness connector
- Retaining bracket on the power brake booster
- Air conditioning compressor outlet hose to the compressor
- Bolt retaining the hose assembly to the right-hand ignition coil bracket
- Upper radiator hose
- Fuel supply and return lines
- Windshield wiper governor and retaining bracket
- Engine cooling fan blade and fan shroud
- Engine air inlet tube
- Battery cables

13. Fill the cooling system.

14. Start the engine and check for leaks.

15. Properly evacuate and charge the air conditioning system.

16. Road test the vehicle and check for proper operation.

Camshaft and Valve Lifters

REMOVAL & INSTALLATION

1. Before servicing the vehicle, refer to the precautions in the beginning of this section.

2. Drain the engine oil.

3. Properly relieve the fuel system pressure.

4. If equipped with air suspension, the air suspension switch, must be turned to the **OFF** position before raising the vehicle.

5. Remove or disconnect the following:
- Negative battery cable
- Fan blade and fan shroud assembly
- Fuel supply and return lines from the fuel injection supply manifold
- Windshield wiper governor (module) assembly from the vehicle
- Engine air cleaner outlet tube
- Accessory drive belt
- Ignition wires from the spark plugs
- Ignition wire brackets from the cylinder head cover studs
- 2 bolts retaining the ignition wire separator to the ignition coil brackets and the bolt retaining the air conditioning pressure line to the right-hand ignition coil bracket.
- Connectors from both ignition coils and the Crankshaft Position (CMP) sensor
- Ignition coils with brackets attached
- Electrical connector from the alternator and at the power distribution box
- Water pump pulley
- Positive battery cable at the power distribution box
- Bolt from the positive battery cable bracket located on the right-hand cylinder head
- Fuel vapor hose from the EVAP canister purge valve and position the positive battery cable aside
- Positive Crankcase Ventilation (PCV) valve from the cylinder head cover and position aside
- Engine/transmission harness connector from the bracket on the power brake booster
- Crankshaft Position (CKP) sensor and air conditioning clutch harness connectors
- Bolts retaining the power steering pump to the cylinder block and wire the pump aside

➡ **The front lower bolt on the power steering pump will not come all the way out.**

- Oil pan
- Crankshaft pulley bolt and washer and crankshaft pulley
- Engine oil filter
- Power steering control valve actuator and oil pressure sensor
- Oil filter adapter
- Cylinder head covers
- Engine front cover
- Timing chains

6. Rotate the crankshaft counterclockwise no more than 45 degrees from Top Dead Center (TDC) to ensure that all pistons are below the top of the engine block deck face.

✱✱ **WARNING**

The crankshaft must be in this position prior to rotating the camshafts or damage to the pistons and/or valve train will result.

7. Install a valve spring compressor under the camshaft and on top of one of the valve spring retainers.

✱✱ **WARNING**

Valve Spring Spacer Tool T91P-6565-AH must be installed between the spring coils and the camshaft lobe must be at the base circle before compressing the valve spring for each valve to prevent damage.

8. Install Valve Spring Spacer T91P-6565-AH between the valve spring coils. Be sure that the valve being compressed is on its base circle. Compress the valve spring and remove the rocker arm. Repeat the procedure until all rocker arms are removed.

9. If required, pull the lash adjusters out of their bores in the cylinder head. Note their locations, they must be installed in the same bore they were removed from.

➡ **Do not mix the camshaft bearing caps. Note the camshaft bearing cap locations for installation.**

10. To remove each camshaft, unfasten the 14 bolts retaining the camshaft bearing caps (cluster assemblies) to the cylinder head. Tap upward on the camshaft bearing caps at points near the upper bearing halves and gradually lift the camshaft bearing cap clusters from the cylinder head.

11. Repeat the removal procedure for the opposite cylinder head.

12. Remove the camshaft straight upward to avoid bearing damage.

13. Clean and inspect the camshafts and related components for unusual wear or damage.

To install:

14. Clean and inspect the cylinder head covers, engine front cover and cylinder head sealing surfaces.

15. Apply clean engine oil to the camshaft journals and lobes. Position the camshafts on the cylinder heads.

16. Install and seat the camshaft bearing

Refer to Section 1 for engine rebuilding specifications

cap cluster assemblies. Install and hand start the retaining bolts. Tighten the camshaft cluster retaining bolts in sequence to 71–106 inch lbs. (8–12 Nm). Be sure to tighten each camshaft bearing cap cluster individually.

➡**Each camshaft bearing cap cluster assembly is tightened individually.**

17. Loosen the camshaft bearing cap cluster retaining bolts approximately 2 turns or until the heads of the bolts are free. Tighten all bolts, again in sequence, to 71–106 inch lbs. (8–12 Nm).

18. Repeat the camshaft bearing cap installation for the opposite cylinder head.

➡**The camshafts should turn freely but with a slight drag.**

19. Check camshaft end-play as follows:

  a. Step 1: install a dial indicator on the front of the engine. Position it so the indicator foot is resting on the camshaft sprocket bolt or the front of the camshaft.

  b. Step 2: push the camshaft toward the rear of the engine and zero the dial indicator.

  c. Step 3: pull the camshaft forward and release it. Specified end-play is 0.0901–0.006 inch (0.025–0.190mm).

  d. Step 4: if end-play is too tight, check for binding or foreign material in the camshaft thrust bearing. If end-play is excessive, check for worn camshaft thrust plate and replace the cylinder head, as required.

  e. Step 5: remove the dial indicator.

20. If removed, install the lash adjusters in their original positions.

21. If necessary, install Camshaft Positioning Tools T92P-6256-A on the flats of the camshafts and install the spacers and camshaft sprockets. Install the bolts and washers and tighten to 81–95 ft. lbs. (110–130 Nm).

22. Install a valve spring compressor under the camshaft and on top of the valve spring retainer.

✳✳ WARNING

Valve Spring Spacer Tool T91P-6565-AH must be installed between the spring coils and the camshaft lobe must be at the base circle before compressing the valve spring for each valve to prevent damage.

23. Install Valve Spring Spacer T91P-6565-AH between the valve spring coils. Be sure that the valve being compressed is on

its base circle. Compress the valve spring and install the rocker arm. Repeat the procedure until all rocker arms are installed.

24. Rotate the crankshaft clockwise 45 degrees to position the crankshaft at Top Dead Center (TDC).

➡**The crankshaft must only be rotated in the clockwise direction and only as far as TDC.**

25. Install or connect the following:
  • Timing chains
  • Engine front cover
  • Cylinder head covers. Tighten the cylinder head cover bolts to 71–106 inch lbs. (8–12 Nm).
  • Power steering control valve actuator connector
  • Oil pressure sensor harness connector

26. Apply silicone sealer to the crankshaft keyway

27. Install the crankshaft pulley and tighten the bolt as follows:
  a. Step 1: tighten to 66 ft. lbs. (90 Nm).
  b. Step 2: loosen one complete turn.
  c. Step 3: tighten to 35–39 ft. lbs. (47–53 Nm).

d. Step 4: tighten an additional 85–95 degrees.

28. Install or connect the following:
  • Engine oil pan
  • Power steering pump on the engine and the 4 retaining bolts. Tighten the bolts to 15–22 ft. lbs. (20–30 Nm).
  • Air conditioning clutch and CKP sensor
  • Evaporative emission canister purge valve harness connector
  • Engine/transmission harness connectors on the power brake booster retaining bracket
  • PCV valve to the right-hand cylinder head cover
  • Positive battery cable harness on the right-hand cylinder head
  • Bolt retaining the battery cable bracket to the cylinder head
  • Evaporative emission hose to the canister purge valve
  • Positive battery cable at the power distribution box
  • Water pump pulley and tighten the bolts to 15–22 ft. lbs. (20–30 Nm)
  • Ignition coil brackets and ignition

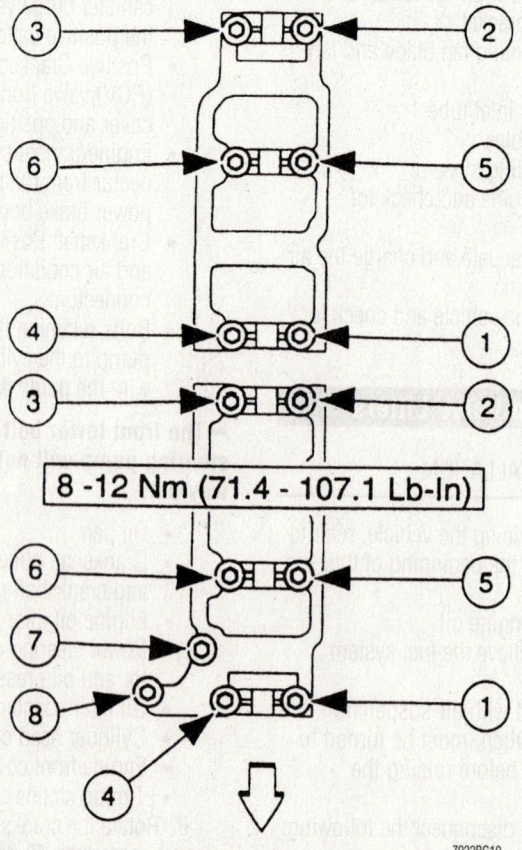

8 -12 Nm (71.4 - 107.1 Lb-In)

7922RG10

Tighten the camshaft bearing cap cluster bolts in the sequence to avoid damage to the camshaft or bearings

wires to the engine front cover. Tighten the retaining nuts to 15–22 ft. lbs. (20–30 Nm).

- Harness connectors to the ignition coils and the CMP sensor
- Air conditioning pressure line on the right-hand ignition coil bracket and the retaining bolt
- Ignition wires to the spark plugs and the brackets onto the cylinder head cover studs
- Accessory drive belt
- Windshield wiper governor
- Fuel supply and return lines
- Fan and shroud assembly
- Negative battery cable

29. Fill the engine cooling system.

30. Fill the crankcase.

31. If equipped with air suspension, turn the air suspension switch to the **ON** position.

32. Start the engine and check for leaks.

33. Road test the vehicle and check for proper engine operation.

Valve Lash

ADJUSTMENT

The valve lash is not adjustable. If the collapsed lash adjuster clearance is incorrect, check the camshaft, roller follower and valve for wear or damage.

1. Before servicing the vehicle, refer to the precautions in the beginning of this section.

2. Disconnect the negative battery cable.

3. Remove the camshaft covers.

4. Rotate the crankshaft until the camshaft base circle is contacting the roller follower.

5. Use a suitable tool to bleed down the lash adjuster. Slowly compress the lash adjuster until the plunger is bottomed.

6. Use a feeler gauge to check the clearance between the camshaft and the roller follower. The clearance should be 0.018–0.033 inch (0.45–0.85mm).

Starter Motor

REMOVAL & INSTALLATION

1. Before servicing the vehicle, refer to the precautions in the beginning of this section.

2. Remove or disconnect the following:

- Negative battery cable
- Red solenoid safety cap
- Wires from solenoid
- 2 upper bolts
- 1 lower bolt and starter

To install:

3. Install or connect the following:

- Starter and lower mounting bolt
- 2 upper mounting bolts. Tighten all 3 bolts to 15–20 ft. lbs. (20–27 Nm).
- Wires from solenoid and tighten the nut to 40–50 inch lbs.
- Red solenoid safety cap
- Negative battery cable

Oil Pan

REMOVAL & INSTALLATION

1. Before servicing the vehicle, refer to the precautions in the beginning of this section.

2. Relieve the fuel system pressure.

3. Drain the engine cooling system

4. Properly discharge the air conditioning system.

5. Remove or disconnect the following:

- Negative battery cable
- Engine air cleaner outlet tube
- Fuel supply and return lines at the fuel injection supply manifold
- Cooling fan and fan shroud
- Upper radiator hose
- Wiper governor and support bracket

➡ **Plug the compressor outlet hose at the compressor**

- Bolt retaining the hose assembly to the right-hand ignition coil bracket. Cap the compressor outlet.
- Engine/transmission electrical harness connector from the retaining bracket on the power brake booster
- Heater water hose
- Nut retaining the ground strap to the right-hand cylinder head
- Upper stud and loosen the lower bolt retaining the heater outlet hose to the right-hand cylinder head and position aside
- Heater blower motor switch resistor

6. Drain the engine oil and reinstall the oil pan drain plug with a new gasket.

Tighten the plug to 10–12 ft. lbs. (13–16 Nm).

7. Remove or disconnect the following:

- Bolt retaining the right-hand engine support insulator to the lower front sub-frame
- Bolts retaining the left-hand and right-hand front engine support insulators to the engine mount supports
- Catalytic converter pipes from both exhaust manifolds. Lower the exhaust system and support it with wire from the transmission cross-member.

8. Position a jack and a block of wood under the oil pan, rearward of the oil drain hole. Raise the engine approximately 4 inches (100mm) and insert 2 wood blocks approximately 2½–2¾ inch (60–70mm) thick under each front engine support insulator. Lower the engine onto the wood blocks and remove the jack.

9. Remove the oil pan.

➡ **It may be necessary to loosen, but not remove, the 2 nuts on the transmission support insulator and with a suitable jack, raise the transmission extension housing slightly to allow enough clearance to remove the engine oil pan.**

10. If necessary, remove the 2 bolts retaining the oil pick-up tube to the oil pump and remove the bolt retaining the pick-up tube to the main bearing stud spacer. Remove the pick-up tube.

To install:

11. Clean the engine oil pan and inspect for damage. Clean the sealing surfaces of the front cover and cylinder block. Clean and inspect the oil pick-up tube and replace the O-ring.

12. If removed, position the oil pick-up tube on the oil pump and hand start the 2 retaining bolts. Install the bolt retaining the pick-up tube on the main bearing stud spacer, hand tight.

13. Tighten the pick-up tube-to-oil pump bolts to 72–108 inch lbs. (8–12 Nm), then tighten the pick-up tube-to-main bearing stud spacer bolt to 15–22 ft. lbs. (20–30 Nm).

14. Position a new gasket on the oil pan. Apply silicone sealer to where the front cover meets the cylinder block and the crankshaft rear oil seal and retainer meets the cylinder block. Position the oil pan to

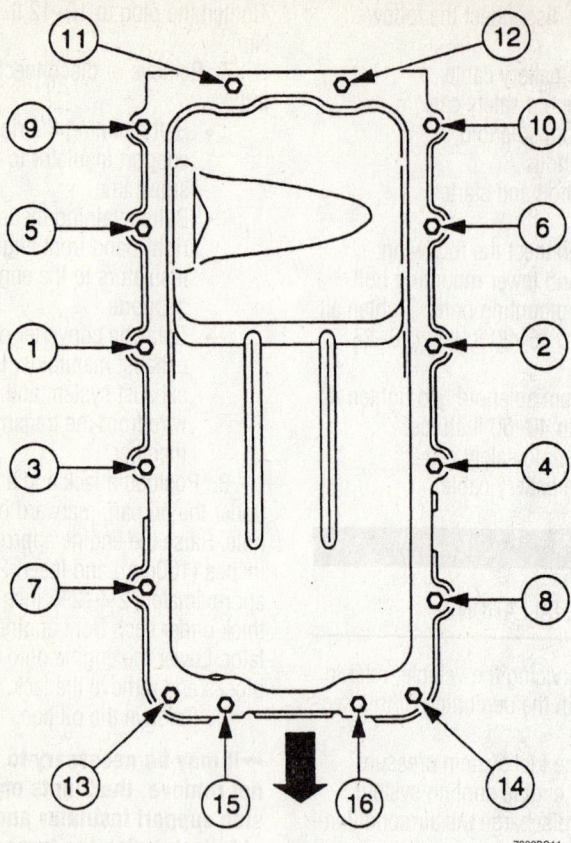

7922RG11

To prevent oil leaks, tighten the oil pan bolts in the sequence shown

the engine and install the retaining bolts. Tighten the bolts in sequence, to 14 ft. lbs. (20 Nm), then rotate the oil pan retaining bolts, in sequence an additional 60 degrees within 4 minutes of applying the silicone sealer.

15. Position the jack and wood block under the engine oil pan, rearward of the oil drain hole, and raise the engine enough to remove the wood blocks. Lower the engine and remove the jack.

16. Install or connect the following:
- Left-hand and right-hand engine support insulator through-bolts and tighten to 15–22 ft. lbs. (20–30 Nm)
- Bolt retaining the right-hand engine support insulator to the lower front sub-frame. Tighten the bolt to 15–22 ft. lbs. (20–30 Nm).
- Exhaust system to the exhaust manifolds and tighten the 4 retaining nuts to 20–30 ft. lbs. (27–41 Nm). Be sure the exhaust system clears the crossmember. Adjust as necessary.
- New engine oil filter
- Heater blower motor switch resistor using the 2 retaining screws
- Heater water hose

- Upper stud and tighten the upper and lower bolts to 15–22 ft. lbs. (20–30 Nm)
- Ground strap on the stud and tighten to 15–22 ft. lbs. (20–30 Nm)
- Heater water hose
- Throttle valve cable, if equipped
- Engine/transmission electrical harness connector
- Harness connector on the power brake booster bracket
- Air conditioning compressor outlet hose to the compressor
- Bolt retaining the hose to the right-hand ignition coil bracket
- Upper radiator hose
- Fuel supply and return lines
- Wiper governor and retaining bracket
- Engine cooling fan and fan shroud
- Engine air cleaner outlet tube
- Negative battery cable
17. Fill the cooling system.
18. Fill the engine crankcase.
19. Start the engine and check for leaks.
20. Properly evacuate and recharge the air conditioning system.

21. Road test the vehicle and check for proper engine operation.

Oil Pump

REMOVAL & INSTALLATION

1. Before servicing the vehicle, refer to the precautions in the beginning of this section.
2. Remove or disconnect the following:
- Negative battery cable
- Cylinder head covers
- Engine front cover
- Engine oil pan
- Timing chains
- 2 bolts retaining the oil pick-up tube to the oil pump and the bolt attaching the oil pick-up tube to the main bearing stud spacer
- Pick-up tube
- 4 bolts retaining the oil pump to the cylinder block
- Oil pump

To install:

3. Rotate the inner rotor of the oil pump to align with the flats on the crankshaft and install the oil pump flush with the cylinder block. Install the 4 retaining bolts and tighten to 72–106 inch lbs. (8–12 Nm).
4. Clean the oil pick-up tube and replace the O-ring.
5. Place the pick-up tube on the oil pump and hand start the 2 retaining bolts. Install the bolt retaining the pick-up tube to the main bearing stud spacer hand tight.

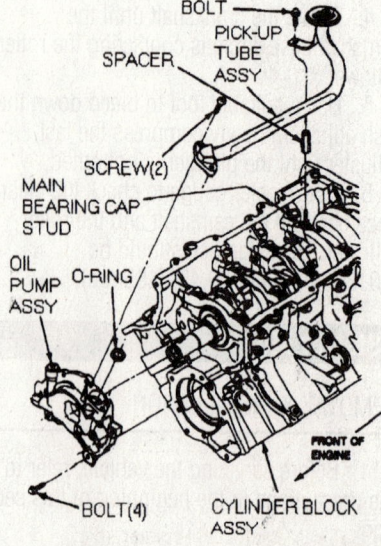

7922RG12

The oil pump is mounted on the crankshaft at the front of the engine

Tighten the pick-up tube-to-oil pump bolts to 72–106 inch lbs. (8–12 Nm). Tighten the pick-up tube to main bearing stud spacer bolt to 15–22 ft. lbs. (20–30 Nm).

6. Install or connect the following:
- New engine oil filter
- Timing chains
- Engine oil pan
- Engine front cover
- Cylinder head covers
- Negative battery cable

7. Fill the crankcase.

8. Start the engine and check for leaks and proper engine oil pressure.

9. Road test the vehicle and check for proper engine operation.

Rear Main Seal

REMOVAL & INSTALLATION

➡ **Special tools are available for installing rear main oil seals. In most cases, the seals can be installed using a common seal and bearing driver set.**

1. Before servicing the vehicle, refer to the precautions in the beginning of this section.

2. Remove the transmission assembly.

3. Remove the flexplate or flywheel.

4. With a sharp awl, carefully punch a small hole in the metal portion of the seal.

5. Remove the seal using a slide hammer with a sheet metal screw attached.

➡ **If the oil leak is coming from around the seal retainer, the retainer must also be removed and resealed.**

To install:

6. If the seal retainer was removed, carefully clean the sealant from the retainer

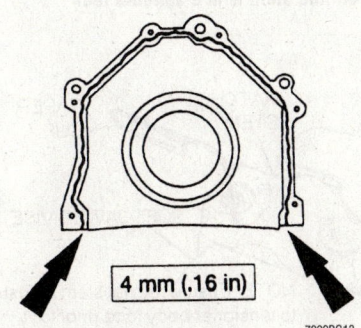

4 mm (.16 in)

7922RG13

Apply a continuos bead of silicone sealant to the back of the seal retainer before installing it on the engine

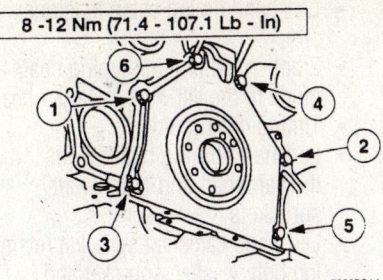

8 -12 Nm (71.4 - 107.1 Lb - In)

7922RG14

To avoid leakage, be sure to tighten the crankshaft rear oil seal retainer bolts in the correct sequence

and engine block using a plastic scraper. Remove any oil or grease residue from the sealing surfaces with a solvent.

7. Apply silicone sealant to the back of the retainer and immediately install it on the engine block. Tighten the bolts in sequence to 71–107 inch lbs. (8–12 Nm).

8. Lubricate the seal and the crankshaft with clean engine oil.

9. Install the seal with the spring side toward the engine.

10. Remove the installation tool.

11. Install or connect the following:
- Flexplate or flywheel. Tighten the bolts, in a crisscross pattern, to 54–64 ft. lbs. (73–87 Nm).
- Transmission
- Negative battery cable

12. Check the engine oil level.

13. Start the engine and check for leaks.

Timing Chain, Sprockets, Front Cover and Seal

REMOVAL & INSTALLATION

✳✳ **WARNING**

This is an interference engine.

1. Before servicing the vehicle, refer to the precautions in the beginning of this section.

2. Drain the oil.

3. Remove or disconnect the following:
- Negative battery cable
- Cooling fan and shroud

➡ **Loosen water pump pulley bolts.**

- Accessory drive belt
- Water pump pulley
- Bolts attaching the power steering pump to the cylinder block and

engine front cover. The lower front bolt on the power steering pump will not come all the way out. Wire the power steering pump out of the way.
- Oil pan
- Crankshaft pulley retaining bolt and washer
- Crankshaft pulley
- Bolt retaining the air conditioning pressure line to the right-hand ignition coil bracket
- Cylinder head covers
- Wiring at both ignition coils and the Crankshaft Position (CMP) sensor
- 3 bolts retaining the right-hand ignition coil bracket to the engine front cover. Position the power steering hose aside.
- 3 nuts retaining the left-hand ignition coil bracket to the engine front cover. Slide both ignition coil brackets and ignition wires off the mounting studs and lay the assembly on top of the engine.
- Bolts retaining the drive belt idler pulley and the pulley
- Wiring to the Crankshaft Position (CKP) sensor and the sensor

4. If equipped, remove the retainers for the oil cooler from the engine front cover retaining stud bolts and position the oil cooler aside.
- 9 stud bolts and the 6 standard engine front cover bolts and the cover
- Crankshaft oil seal from the cover using a suitable seal driver
- CKP sensor pulse wheel

5. Rotate the engine to set the piston for No. 1 to Top Dead Center (TDC) on its compression stroke.

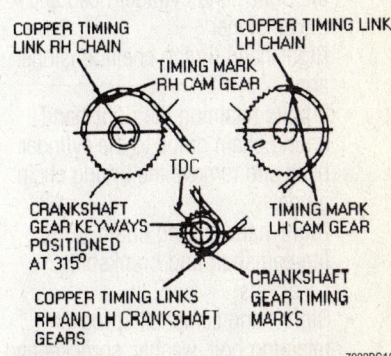

COPPER TIMING LINK RH CHAIN
COPPER TIMING LINK LH CHAIN
TIMING MARK RH CAM GEAR
CRANKSHAFT GEAR KEYWAYS POSITIONED AT 315°
TDC
TIMING MARK LH CAM GEAR
COPPER TIMING LINKS RH AND LH CRANKSHAFT GEARS
CRANKSHAFT GEAR TIMING MARKS

7922RG16

Be sure that the timing marks are aligned when the No. 1 piston is at TDC on compression

For complete mechanical specifications, refer to Section 1 of this manual

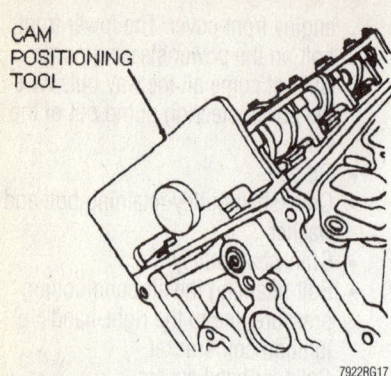

Use the special tool to maintain camshaft position while installing the timing chains

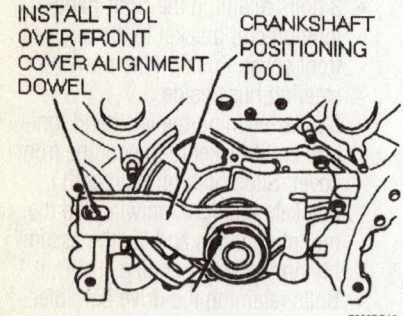

Install the crankshaft positioning tool to be sure the crankshaft does not turn while installing the timing chains

➡️**Camshaft Positioning Adapters T92P-6256-A, must be installed on the camshafts to prevent the camshafts from rotating.**

6. Install Camshaft Positioning Adapters T92P-6256-A on the flats of both camshafts. This will prevent accidental rotation of the camshafts.

7. Remove or disconnect the following:

- 2 bolts retaining the tensioner to the right-hand cylinder head and the tensioner
- Right-hand timing chain tensioner arm
- 2 bolts retaining the right-hand timing chain guide to the cylinder head and remove the timing chain guide.
- Right-hand timing chain from the camshaft and crankshaft sprockets
- Right-hand camshaft sprocket retaining bolt, washer, sprocket and spacer, if necessary
- 2 bolts retaining the timing chain tensioner to the left-hand cylinder head
- Timing chain tensioner

- Left-hand timing chain tensioner arm
- 2 bolts retaining the timing chain guide to the left-hand cylinder head
- Timing chain guide
- Left-hand timing chain from the camshaft and crankshaft sprockets
- Left-hand camshaft sprocket retaining bolt, washer, sprocket and spacer, if necessary

8. If necessary, note the position of the crankshaft sprockets and remove the crankshaft sprockets by sliding them off the front of the crankshaft.

9. Inspect the plastic running face on the tensioner arms and chain guides. If worn or damaged, inspect the engine oil pan for contamination and thoroughly clean the oil pan. Replace the oil pick-up tube.

To install:

10. Examine the timing chains, looking for the copper links. If the copper links are not visible, lay the chain on a flat surface and pull the chain taught until the opposite sides of the chain contact one another. Mark the links at each end of the chain and use these marks in place of the copper links.

➡️**If the engine jumped time, damage has been done to valves and possibly pistons and/or connecting rods. Any damage must be corrected before installing the timing chains.**

11. Be sure Camshaft Positioning Adapters T92P-6256-A are installed on the flats of the camshafts to prevent them from rotating.

12. Install or connect the following:

- Left-hand and right-hand timing chain guides and retaining bolts. Tighten the retaining bolts to 71–106 inch lbs. (8–12 Nm).
- Left-hand and right-hand camshaft spacers and sprockets, (if removed)

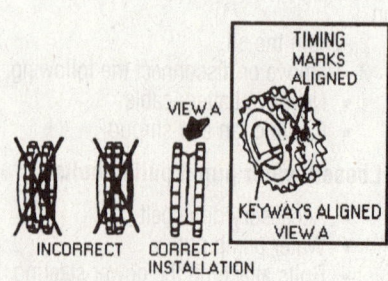

Install the crankshaft sprockets with the tapered sides facing each other

on the camshafts, the washers and retaining bolts but do not tighten at this time.

- Left-hand crankshaft sprocket with the tapered part of the sprocket facing away from the engine block

➡️**The crankshaft sprockets are identical. They may only be installed one way, with the tapered part of the sprockets facing each other. Ensure that the keyway and timing marks on the crankshaft sprockets are aligned.**

- Left-hand timing chain on the camshaft and crankshaft sprockets. Be sure the copper links of the timing chain line up with the timing marks on both sprockets.
- Right-hand crankshaft sprocket with the tapered part of the sprocket facing the left-hand crankshaft sprocket, if removed
- Right-hand timing chain on the camshaft and crankshaft sprockets. Be sure the copper links of the timing chain line up with the timing marks on both sprockets.

13. It is necessary to bleed the timing

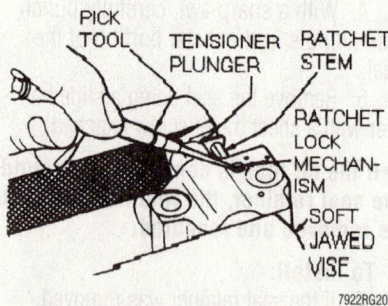

Slowly compress the timing chain tensioner while holding the ratchet lock away from the stem with a suitable tool

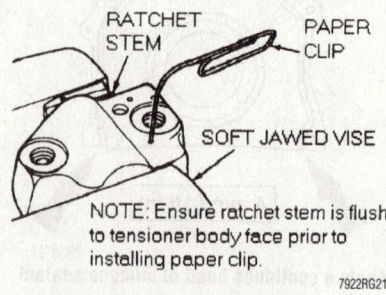

NOTE: Ensure ratchet stem is flush to tensioner body face prior to installing paper clip.

Install a paper clip or wire into the tensioner to hold the plunger in during assembly

chain tensioners before installation. Proceed as follows:

a. Step 1: position the timing chain tensioner in a soft-jawed vise.

b. Step 2: using a small pick or similar tool, hold the ratchet lock mechanism away from the ratchet stem and slowly compress the tensioner plunger by rotating the vise handle.

※※ WARNING

The tensioner must be compressed slowly or damage to the internal seals will result.

c. Step 3: once the tensioner plunger bottoms in the tensioner bore, continue to hold the ratchet lock mechanism and push down on the ratchet stem until flush with the tensioner face.

d. Step 4: while holding the ratchet stem flush with the tensioner face, release the ratchet lock mechanism and install a paper clip or similar tool in the tensioner body to lock the tensioner in the collapsed position.

e. Step 5: the paper clip must not be removed until the timing chain, tensioner, tensioner arm and timing chain guide are completely installed on the engine.

14. Install the right-hand and left-hand timing chain tensioners and 2 bolts on each. Tighten the bolts to 15–22 ft. lbs. (20–30 Nm).

15. Crankshaft Positioning Tool T93P-6265-A over the crankshaft and the engine front cover alignment dowel to position the crankshaft.

16. Lubricate the timing chain tensioner arm contact surfaces with clean engine oil and install the right-hand and left-hand tensioner arms on their dowel pins.

17. Position a suitable C-clamp around the timing chain tensioner arm and timing chain guide to remove all slack from the timing chain. Use care not to bend the timing chain guide.

18. Remove the locking pins or paper clips from the timing chain tensioners and be sure that all timing marks are aligned.

19. Using Camshaft Positioning Adapters T92P-6265-A to align and hold the camshafts, tighten the camshaft sprocket retaining bolts to 81–95 ft. lbs. (110–130 Nm).

20. Position a suitable dial indicator in the No. 1 cylinder spark plug hole to measure intake valve lift. The intake valve should be at maximum lift when the crankshaft is at 114 degrees after TDC. If the intake valve lift is not at maximum lift,

loosen the camshaft sprocket bolt and repeat the steps detailing the installation of the timing chain tensioners to the tightening of the camshaft sprockets.

21. Remove the camshaft and crankshaft positioning tools.

22. Install a new crankshaft seal in the front cover. Apply engine oil to the lip of the seal.

23. Thoroughly clean the sealing surfaces of the front cover, cylinder block and oil pan. Apply silicone sealer to the points where the cylinder head meets the cylinder block.

24. Install or connect the following:

- Front cover in position using new gaskets
- Retaining bolts and studs in their proper locations. Tighten in sequence to 15–22 ft. lbs. (20–30 Nm) within 4 minutes of applying the silicone sealer.
- Oil cooler to the front cover retaining stud bolts, if equipped
- CKP sensor and attach the harness connector
- Drive belt idler pulley
- Ignition coil brackets and ignition wires as an assembly onto the mounting studs
- Power steering hose and the nuts retaining the coil brackets to the

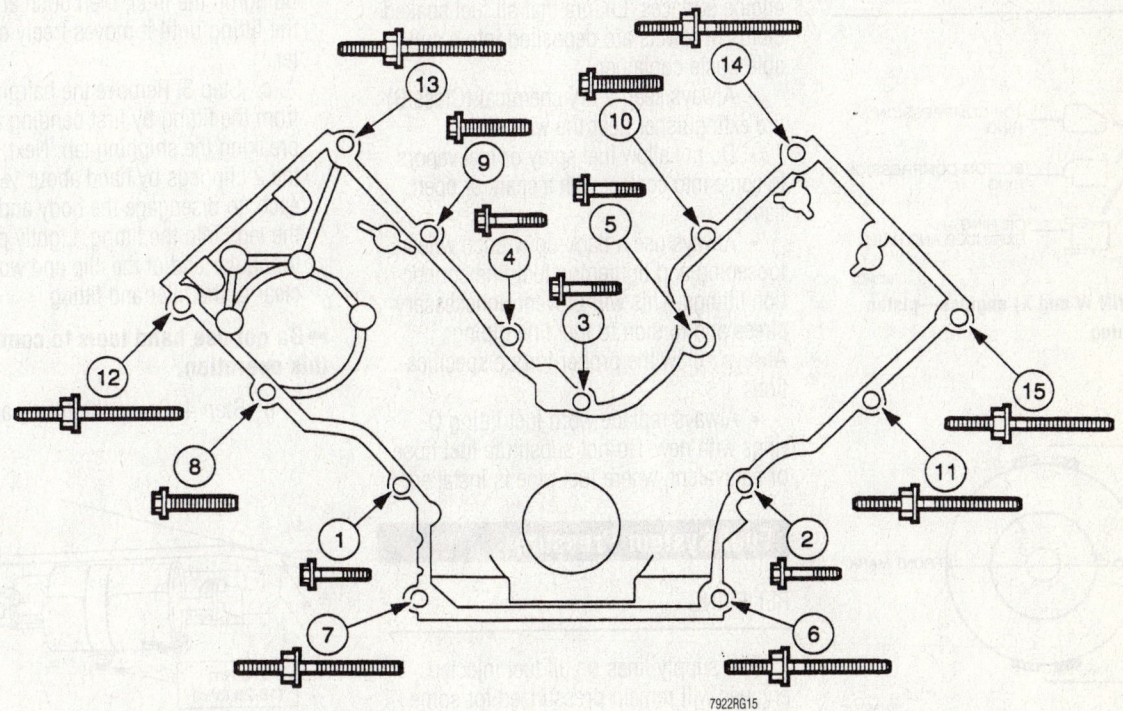

Timing chain front cover bolt tightening sequence

7922RG15

Please refer to Section 8 for electric cooling fan wiring schematics

front cover. Tighten the nuts to 15–22 ft. lbs. (20–30 Nm).

- Wiring to both ignition coils and the CMP sensor
- Cylinder head covers
- Air conditioning pressure line on the right-hand ignition coil bracket and tighten the retaining bolt

25. Apply a small amount of silicone sealer in the rear of the keyway in the crankshaft pulley.

26. Install or connect the following:

- Pulley on the crankshaft
- Crankshaft pulley bolt and washer and tighten to 114–121 ft. lbs. (155–165 Nm)
- Oil pan
- Power steering pump on the engine. Tighten bolts to 15–22 ft. lbs. (20–30 Nm).
- Water pump pulley. Tighten bolts to 15–22 ft. lbs. (20–30 Nm).
- Accessory drive belt
- Engine cooling fan and shroud
- Negative battery cable

27. Fill the engine.

28. Start the engine and check for leaks.

29. Road test the vehicle and check for proper engine operation.

Piston and Ring

POSITIONING

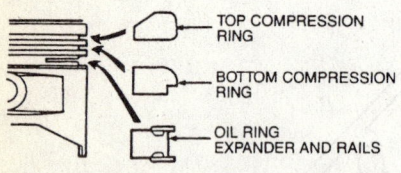

Ford 4.6L (VIN W and X) engines—piston ring positioning

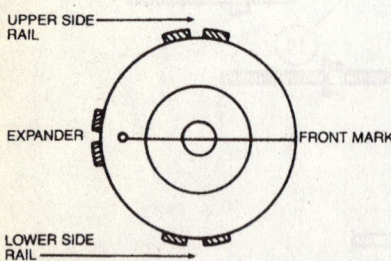

Ford 4.6L (VIN W and X) engines—piston ring end-gap spacing and piston positioning

FUEL SYSTEM

Fuel System Service Precautions

Safety is the most important factor when performing not only fuel system maintenance but any type of maintenance. Failure to conduct maintenance and repairs in a safe manner may result in serious personal injury or death. Maintenance and testing of the vehicle's fuel system components can be accomplished safely and effectively by adhering to the following rules and guidelines.

- To avoid the possibility of fire and personal injury, always disconnect the negative battery cable unless the repair or test procedure requires that battery voltage be applied.
- Always relieve the fuel system pressure prior to disconnecting any fuel system component (injector, fuel rail, pressure regulator, etc.), fitting or fuel line connection. Exercise extreme caution whenever relieving fuel system pressure, to avoid exposing skin, face and eyes to fuel spray. Please be advised that fuel under pressure may penetrate the skin or any part of the body that it contacts.
- Always place a shop towel or cloth around the fitting or connection prior to loosening to absorb any excess fuel due to spillage. Ensure that all fuel spillage (should it occur) is quickly removed from engine surfaces. Ensure that all fuel soaked cloths or towels are deposited into a suitable waste container.
- Always keep a dry chemical (Class B) fire extinguisher near the work area.
- Do not allow fuel spray or fuel vapors to come into contact with a spark or open flame.
- Always use a back-up wrench when loosening and tightening fuel line connection fittings. This will prevent unnecessary stress and torsion to fuel line piping. Always follow the proper torque specifications.
- Always replace worn fuel fitting O-rings with new. Do not substitute fuel hose or equivalent, where fuel pipe is installed.

Fuel System Pressure

RELIEVING

Fuel supply lines on all fuel injected engines will remain pressurized for some period of time after the engine is shut **OFF**. This pressure must be relieved before servicing the fuel system. Pressure is relieved through the fuel pressure relief valve, located on the fuel rail.

To relieve the fuel system pressure, first remove the fuel tank cap to relieve pressure in the tank, then remove the cap on the fuel pressure relief valve. Attach a fuel pressure gauge and drain the system through the drain tube into a suitable container. Remove the fuel pressure gauge and replace the cap on the relief valve.

Fuel Filter

REMOVAL & INSTALLATION

1. Before servicing the vehicle, refer to the precautions in the beginning of this section.

2. Disconnect the negative battery cable.

3. Relieve the fuel system pressure.

4. If equipped with air suspension, turn the air suspension switch to the **OFF** position.

5. Remove the hairpin clip push connect fittings from both ends of the fuel filter as follows:

a. Step 1: Inspect the visible internal portion of the fitting for dirt accumulation. If more than a light coating of dust is present, clean the fitting before disassembly.

b. Step 2: Some adhesion between the seals in the fitting and the filter will occur with time. To separate, twist the fitting on the filter, then push and pull the fitting until it moves freely on the filter.

c. Step 3: Remove the hairpin clip from the fitting by first bending and breaking the shipping tab. Next, spread the 2 clip legs by hand about ⅛ inch each, to disengage the body and push the legs into the fitting. Lightly pull the triangular end of the clip and work it clear of the filter and fitting.

➡**Do not use hand tools to complete this operation.**

d. Step 4: Grasp the fitting and pull

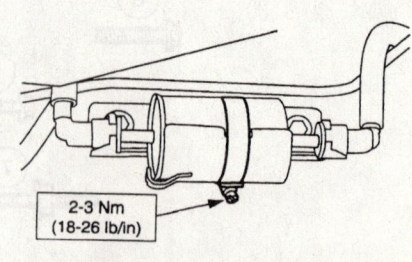

The fuel filter is located near the center of the vehicle on the frame rail

in an axial direction to remove the fitting from the filter. Be careful on 90 degree elbow connectors, as excessive side loading could break the connector body.

e. Step 5: After disassembly, inspect the inside of the fitting for any internal parts such as O-rings and spacers that may have been dislodged from the fitting. Replace any damaged connector.

6. Remove the filter retaining clamp and remove the fuel filter. Note the direction of the flow arrow on the filter, so the replacement filter can be reinstalled in the same position.

To install:

7. Install or connect the following:
- Fuel filter with the flow arrow facing the proper direction and tighten the filter retaining clamp
- Rubber insulator rings on the new filter. Replace the insulator rings if the filter moves freely after the retainer is installed.
- Filter into the retainer with the flow arrow pointing out the open end of the retainer
- Retainer on the bracket and tighten the mounting bolts to 27–44 inch lbs. (3–5 Nm)

8. Install the hairpin clip push connect fittings at both ends of the fuel filter as follows:

a. Step 1: Install a new connector if damage was found. Insert a new clip into any 2 adjacent openings with the triangular portion pointing away from the fitting opening. Install the clip until the legs of the clip are locked on the outside of the body. Piloting with an index finger is necessary.

b. Step 2: Before installing the fitting on the filter, wipe the filter end with a clean cloth. Inspect the inside of the fitting to be sure it is free of dirt and/or obstructions.

c. Step 3: Apply a light coating of engine oil to the filter end. Align the fitting and filter axially and push the fitting onto the filter end. When the fitting is engaged, a definite click will be heard. Pull on the fitting to be sure it is fully engaged.

9. If equipped with air suspension, turn the air suspension switch to the **ON** position.

10. Reconnect the negative battery cable.

11. Start the engine and check for fuel leaks and proper operation.

Fuel Pump

REMOVAL & INSTALLATION

1. Before servicing the vehicle, refer to the precautions in the beginning of this section.

2. Disconnect the negative battery cable.

3. Relieve the fuel system pressure.

4. Install a hose into the fuel filler pipe and drain or siphon the fuel into a suitable storage tank designed for fuel storage.

5. Remove any dirt that has accumulated around the fuel pump and fuel lines to prevent the entry of contaminants into the tank during fuel pump removal and installation.

6. Remove or disconnect the following:
- Fuel supply and return line fittings at the fuel pump using fuel line disconnect tools
- Fuel pump module electrical connector
- 6 retaining bolts around the perimeter of the fuel pump module
- Fuel pump module and seal from the fuel tank

To install:

7. Clean the fuel pump module mounting flange and fuel tank mounting surface.

8. Install or connect the following:
- New seal and the fuel pump module using care not to damage the inlet filter and fuel sending unit float arm
- 6 retaining bolts and tighten to 80–107 inch lbs. (9–12 Nm)
- Fuel pump module electrical connector
- Fuel supply and return lines to the fuel pump module. Pull on the fuel line fittings to verify engagement.

9. Minimum of 10 gallons (38L) of clean fuel to the fuel tank and check for leaks.

10. Install a Fuel pressure gauge to the

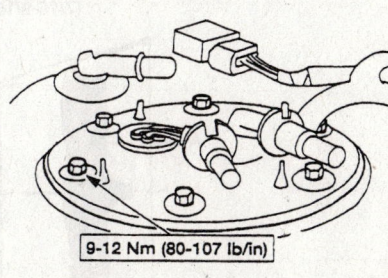

Tighten the fuel pump mounting bolts to 80–107 inch lbs. (9–12 Nm)

Schrader valve on the fuel injection supply manifold.

11. Connect the negative battery cable.

12. Cycle the ignition switch from the **OFF** to **ON** position 5–10 times for 3 second intervals or until the fuel pressure gauge shows at least 35 psi (241 kPa).

13. Check for fuel leaks.

14. Remove the fuel pressure gauge.

15. Start the engine and recheck for fuel leaks.

16. Road test the vehicle and check for proper operation.

Fuel Injector

REMOVAL & INSTALLATION

1. Before servicing the vehicle, refer to the precautions in the beginning of this section.

✳✳ WARNING

The fuel system is pressurized and must be relieved before service.

2. Remove or disconnect the following:
- Injector supply manifold
- Wiring
- Injector by pulling it up and gently rocking it side to side
- O-rings and discard

To install:

3. Lubricate new O-rings with clean engine oil.

4. Install or connect the following:
- O-rings
- Fuel injector using a light, twisting and pushing motion
- Injector supply manifold
- Wiring

DRIVE TRAIN

Transmission Assembly

REMOVAL & INSTALLATION

1. Before servicing the vehicle, refer to the precautions in the beginning of this section.

2. If equipped with air suspension, the air suspension switch, located on the right-hand side of the luggage compartment, must be turned to the **OFF** position before raising the vehicle.

3. Drain the transmission Fluid.

4. Remove or disconnect the following:

- Negative battery cable
- Exhaust system as necessary for transmission removal
- Converter bottom access cover and adapter plate bolts
- Torque converter drain plug, to allow the converter to drain into a suitable container, if equipped. After the converter has drained, reinstall the drain plug and tighten.
- 4 torque converter-to-flywheel retaining nuts

➡ **Crank the engine over with a wrench on the crankshaft pulley retaining bolt to gain access to each torque converter-to-flywheel retaining bolt. Never turn the crankshaft in a counterclockwise direction, as viewed from the front of the vehicle.**

- Driveshaft (mark for installation), put a suitable plug in the transmission extension housing to prevent fluid leakage
- Vehicle Speed Sensor (VSS) or if equipped, the speedometer cable from the transmission extension housing
- Shift cable from the transmission manual control lever the throttle valve cable from the transmission throttle valve lever, if equipped
- Transmission wiring harness connectors.
- Starter motor retaining bolts and place the starter motor aside

5. Position a transmission jack under the transmission and raise it enough to allow crossmember removal.

6. Remove or disconnect the following:

- Engine rear support-to-crossmember bolts and the crossmember-to-frame side support retaining bolts
- Crossmember and transmission support insulator

7. Lower the transmission jack and allow the transmission to hang.

8. Place a jack to the front of the engine and raise the engine enough to gain access to the 2 upper transmission-to-cylinder block retaining bolts. Do not remove the bolts at this time.

9. Remove or disconnect the following:

- Transmission cooler lines at the transmission. Plug all openings to keep dirt out.
- Lower transmission-to-cylinder block retaining bolts

- Transmission fluid fill tube and plug the opening in the transmission

10. Secure the transmission to the transmission jack with a safety strap or chain.

11. Remove the 2 upper transmission-to-cylinder block retaining bolts.

12. Carefully move the transmission rearward to disengage it from the dowel pins and the torque converter studs from the flywheel.

13. Remove or disconnect the following:

- Transmission
- Torque converter to prevent the converter from dropping out of the transmission causing possible damage or personal injury

➡ **If the transmission is to be removed for more than a speedy repair, support the rear of the engine with a safety stand and a block of wood.**

To install:

➡ **Verify the transmission cooler lines are thoroughly cleaned before installing the transmission assembly.**

14. Remove the safety stand and block of wood supporting the rear of the engine, if installed.

15. Install or connect the following:

- Torque converter drain plug to 21–23 ft. lbs. (28–30 Nm), if equipped
- Torque converter on the transmission and rotate into position to be sure the drive flats are fully engaged in the pump gear. When fully seated, the center of the torque converter should be about 7/16–9/16 inch (10.2–14.4mm) below the transmission mounting surface

16. Mount the transmission on a trans-

mission jack and secure with a safely strap or chain. Raise the transmission and align with the cylinder block dowel pins.

➡ **Do not allow the transmission to get in a nose-down position causing possible torque converter disengagement from the pump gear.**

17. Rotate the converter until the studs and drain plug are in alignment with the holes in the flywheel. Align the orange balancing marks on the converter stud and flywheel bolt hole, if balancing marks are present.

18. Slide the transmission assembly forward into position, being careful not to damage the flywheel and converter pilot.

➡ **The converter face must rest squarely against the flywheel. This indicates that the converter pilot is not binding in the engine crankshaft. To ensure the converter is properly seated, grasp a converter stud. It should move freely back and forth in the flywheel hole. If the converter will not move, the transmission must be removed and the converter repositioned so the impeller hub is properly engaged in the pump gear.**

19. Install or connect the following:

- 2 transmission housing-to-cylinder block bolts at the engine dowel pin locations. Tighten the bolts to 41–50 ft. lbs. (55–68 Nm).
- Transmission housing-to-cylinder block bolts. Tighten the bolts to 41–50 ft. lbs. (55–68 Nm).

20. Remove the safety strap or chain from around the transmission.

21. Install or connect the following:

- Transmission fluid fill tube. Tighten the bolt to 28–38 ft. lbs. (38–51 Nm).
- Oil cooler lines to the transmission

DIMENSION A TO BE 10.23-14.43 mm (7/16-9/16 INCH) APPROXIMATELY

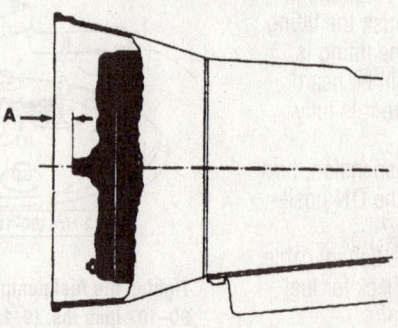

7922RG24

To prevent transmission damage, be sure that the torque converter is fully seated in the front pump of the transmission case. Tighten the cooler line fittings to 15–19 ft. lbs. (20–26 Nm).

22. Remove the jack supporting the front of the engine.

23. Install or connect the following:
- Crossmember using the proper jack
- Crossmember and transmission support insulators in position
- Engine rear support-to-crossmember retaining bolts and the crossmember-to-frame side support retaining bolts

24. Remove the transmission jack.

25. Install or connect the following:
- Transmission wiring harness connectors
- Starter motor and wiring
- 4 torque converter-to-flywheel retaining nuts. Tighten to 20–33 ft. lbs. (27–46 Nm).
- Torque converter access cover and cover plate bolts. Tighten the bolts to 12–16 ft. lbs. (16–22 Nm).
- Exhaust system
- VSS and the wiring, or if equipped, the speedometer cable to the transmission extension housing
- Driveshaft, aligning the marks that were made during removal
- Shift cable to the transmission manual control lever
- Throttle valve cable to the transmission throttle valve lever, if equipped

26. If equipped with air suspension, turn the air suspension switch to the **ON** position.

27. Fill the transmission.

28. Start the engine and check the transmission for leakage.

29. Road test the vehicle and check for proper transmission operation.

Axle Shaft

REMOVAL & INSTALLATION

1. Before servicing the vehicle, refer to the precautions in the beginning of this section.

2. If equipped with air suspension, the air suspension switch, located on the right-hand side of the luggage compartment, must be turned to the **OFF** position before raising the vehicle.

❋❋ WARNING

The rear anti-lock sensor must be removed before the axle shaft.

3. Remove or disconnect the following:
- Wheels
- Brake calipers and brake rotors

4. Clean the axle housing and drain the axle lubricant.

5. Remove or disconnect the following:
- Housing cover
- Differential pinion shaft lock pin
- Differential pinion shaft

6. Push flanged end of the axle shaft toward the center of the vehicle.

7. Remove or disconnect the following:
- U-washer
- Axle shaft

To install:

❋❋ WARNING

Be careful that the splines on the axle shaft do not damage the oil seal or bearing assembly

8. Install or connect the following:
- Axle shaft
- U-washer

9. Pull the shaft until the washer seats.

10. Install differential pinion shaft though the case and gears

11. Align the hole in the shaft with lock bolt hole.

12. Install or connect the following:
- Differential pinion shaft lock pin and tighten to 15–30 ft. lbs. (20–41 Nm)

➡**Make sure that both the axle housing and the cover are clean before installing the new silicone seal.**

- Axle housing cover with a ⅛–³⁄₁₆ inch (3.18–4.76mm) wide bead of silicone on it
- Axle housing cover bolts and tighten to 28–38 ft. lbs. (38–52 Nm)
- Axle lubricant
- Rear anti-lock sensor and tighten bolt to 44–62 inch lbs. (5–7 Nm)
- Rotor and brake caliper
- Wheel assembly

Bearing and Seal

REMOVAL & INSTALLATION

1. Before servicing the vehicle, refer to the precautions in the beginning of this section.

2. If equipped with air suspension, the air suspension switch, located on the right-

hand side of the luggage compartment, must be turned to the **OFF** position before raising the vehicle.

❋❋ WARNING

The rear anti-lock sensor must be removed before the axle shaft.

3. Remove or disconnect the following:
- Axle shafts
- Oil seal and bearing

To install:

4. Lubricate with rear axle lubricant.

5. Install or connect the following:
- Bearing
- Oil seal
- Axle shafts

Axle Housing Assembly

REMOVAL & INSTALLATION

1. Before servicing the vehicle, refer to the precautions in the beginning of this section.

2. If equipped with air suspension, the air suspension switch, located on the right-hand side of the luggage compartment, must be turned to the **OFF** position before raising the vehicle.

3. Remove or disconnect the following:
- Wheel assembly
- Brake calipers and support out of the way with a length of wire
- Rotors
- Parking brake cables and move aside
- Anti-lock sensor
- Rear stabilizer bar and bracket
- Air suspension height sensor from the watts linkage arm
- Driveshaft, matchmark it before removal
- Watts linkage retaining nut and separate from axle housing

4. Support rear axle with jack

5. Remove or disconnect the following:
- Shock absorber lower nut
- Rear suspension lower arms nuts and bolts
- Rear suspension upper arms nuts and bolts
- Unseat rear springs
- Axle housing

To install:

6. Transfer all old components to new housing, if necessary

7. Install or connect the following:
- Axle housing

- Bearings and oil seals
- Rear springs
- Rear suspension upper arms and nuts and bolts. Tighten to 64–87 ft lbs. (87–119 Nm).
- Shock absorber and nuts. Tighten to 57–75 ft. lbs. (76–103 Nm).
- Watts linkage-to-bellcrank stud. Tighten to 157–212 ft. lbs. (212 –288 Nm).
- Air suspension height sensor
- Rear stabilizer bar and brackets and tighten the bracket nuts to 16–21 ft. lbs. (21–29 Nm)
- Driveshaft. Make sure to align the matchmarks.
- Rear stabilizer bar link and bushing to bar. Tighten nuts to 13–16 ft. lbs. (17–23 Nm).
- Anti-lock sensor and wires. Tighten to 45–53 inch lbs. (5–6 Nm).
- Parking brake cable and restore tension
- Rotor
- Wheel assembly
- Axle lubricant

8. If equipped with air suspension, the air suspension switch, located on the right-hand side of the luggage compartment, must be turned to the **ON** position before raising the vehicle.

9. Road test the vehicle.

STEERING AND SUSPENSION

Air Bag

PRECAUTIONS

Several precautions must be observed when handling the inflator module to avoid accidental deployment and possible personal injury.

- Never carry the inflator module by the wires or connector on the underside of the module.
- When carrying a live inflator module, hold securely with both hands, and ensure that the bag and trim cover are pointed away.
- Place the inflator module on a bench or other surface with the bag and trim cover facing up.
- With the inflator module on the bench, never place anything on or close to the module which may be thrown in the event of an accidental deployment.

DISARMING

1. Before servicing the vehicle, refer to the precautions in the beginning of this section.
2. Position the vehicle with the front wheels in a straight-ahead position.
3. Disconnect both battery cables.
4. Wait at least 1 minute for the air bag back-up power supply to deplete its stored energy before continuing.
5. Proceed with the repair.
6. Once the repair is complete.
7. Reconnect both battery cables.
8. Prove out the air bag system by turning the ignition key to the **RUN** position and visually monitoring the air bag indicator lamp in the instrument cluster. The indicator lamp should illuminate for approximately 6 seconds, then turn **OFF**. If the indicator lamp does not illuminate, stays on, or flashes at any time, a fault has been detected by the air bag diagnostic monitor.

Power Steering Gear

REMOVAL & INSTALLATION

1. Before servicing the vehicle, refer to the precautions in the beginning of this section.
2. If equipped with air suspension, the air suspension switch must be turned to the **OFF** position before raising the vehicle.
3. Center the steering wheel and turn the key to the locked position.
4. Remove or disconnect the following:
   - Negative battery cable
   - Bolt and the intermediate shaft from the steering gear
5. On the Town Car, separate the 2 halves and remove the steering gear cover.
6. Tag the power steering pressure and return lines so they may be reassembled in their original positions.

7. Place a drain pan under the steering gear
8. Remove or disconnect the following:
   - Pressure and return lines. Plug the lines and ports in the gear to prevent the entry of dirt.
   - Pitman arm from the center link using a suitable puller. It is not necessary to remove the Pitman arm from the steering gear.
9. Support the steering gear
10. Remove or disconnect the following:
    - Steering gear-to-frame rail retaining bolts
    - Steering gear

To install:

11. Install or connect the following:
    - Steering gear on the frame rail. Tighten the steering gear-to-frame retaining bolts to 50–67 ft. lbs. (66–90 Nm).
    - Pitman arm to the center link. Tighten the retaining nut to 52–60 ft. lbs. (70–81 Nm).
    - Power steering pressure and return lines to the steering gear and tighten the lines to 12–18 ft. lbs. (16–24 Nm)

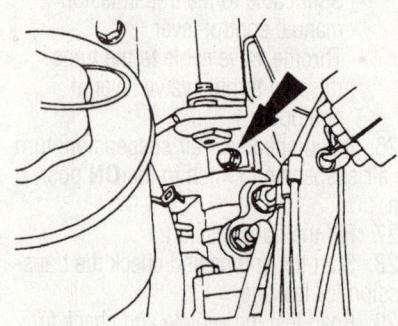

7922RG25

Remove the bolt and separate the intermediate shaft from the steering gear input shaft

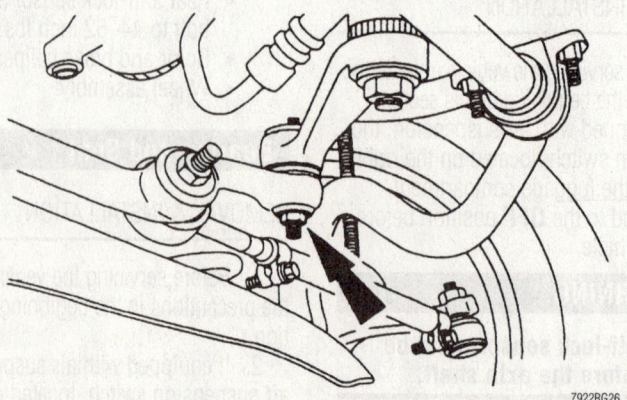

7922RG26

Remove the locknut and separate the Pitman arm from the center link using the appropriate puller

- Intermediate shaft to the steering gear. Tighten the bolt to 31–41 ft. lbs. (41–55 Nm).
- Negative battery cable

12. If equipped with air suspension, turn the air suspension switch to the **ON** position.

13. Fill the reservoir with the correct power steering fluid and turn the steering wheel from stop-to-stop to distribute the fluid. Check the fluid level and add fluid, if necessary.

14. Start the engine and turn the steering wheel from left to right. Check for leaks.

15. On the Town Car, install the steering gear cover.

Shock Absorber

REMOVAL & INSTALLATION

Front

1. Before servicing the vehicle, refer to the precautions in the beginning of this section.

2. If equipped with air suspension, the air suspension switch, located on the right-hand side of the luggage compartment, must be turned to the **OFF** position before raising the vehicle.

3. Remove or disconnect the following:

- Nut, washer and bushing from the upper end of the shock absorber
- 2 bolts retaining the shock absorber to the lower control arm
- Shock absorber

To install:

4. Prior to installation, prime the new shock absorber. Fully extend the shock absorber while in the right side up (installed) position. Turn the shock absorber upside down and fully compress it. Repeat the procedure at least 3 times to purge any air trapped in the shock absorber.

5. Install or connect the following:

- New bushing and washer on the stud on the top of the new shock absorber and position the unit inside the front coil spring
- 2 lower retaining bolts and tighten them to 10–12 ft lbs. (13–17 Nm).
- New bushing and washer on the shock absorber top stud

- New retaining nut. Tighten the retaining nut to 25–34 ft. lbs. (34–46 Nm).

6. If equipped with air suspension, turn the air suspension switch to the **ON** position.

Rear

> ✳✳ **WARNING**

When removing and installing rear shock absorbers on vehicles with air springs, it is very important that this procedure be followed exactly. Failure to do so may result in damaged shock absorbers.

1. Before servicing the vehicle, refer to the precautions in the beginning of this section.

2. If equipped with air suspension, turn the air suspension service switch **OFF**.

3. Be sure the ignition switch is in the **OFF** position.

4. Support the rear axle assembly with a jack.

➡ **To assist in removing the upper retainer on shock absorbers using a plastic dust tube, place an open end wrench on the hex stamped into the dust tube's metal cap. For shock absorbers with a steel dust tube, simply grasp the tube to prevent stud rotation when loosening the retaining nut.**

5. Remove or disconnect the following:

- Top retaining nut, washer and bushing
- Bottom retaining nut and washer
- Shock absorber

To install:

6. Install or connect the following:

- Shock absorber so the upper stud enters the hole in the frame
- Top bushing, washer and retaining nut. Tighten to 26–34 ft. lbs. (34–46 Nm).

7. Extend the shock absorber and place the lower stud through the hole in the bracket

8. Bottom retaining washer and nut. Tighten to 57–75 ft. lbs. (76–103 Nm).

9. Remove the jack from the axle assembly.

10. Turn the air suspension service switch to the **ON** position.

Coil Spring

REMOVAL & INSTALLATION

Front

1. Before servicing the vehicle, refer to the precautions in the beginning of this section.

2. If equipped with air suspension, turn the air suspension service switch to the **OFF** position before raising the vehicle.

3. Remove or disconnect the following:

- Wheel
- Shock absorber
- Center link from the Pitman arm

4. Using a spring compressor perform the following steps:

a. Step 1: Install 1 plate with the pivot ball seat facing downward into the coils of the spring. Rotate the plate so it is flush with the upper surface of the lower arm.

b. Step 2: Install the other plate with the pivot ball seat facing upward into the coils of the spring. Insert the upper ball nut through the coils of the spring, so the nut rests in the upper plate.

c. Step 3: Insert the compression rod

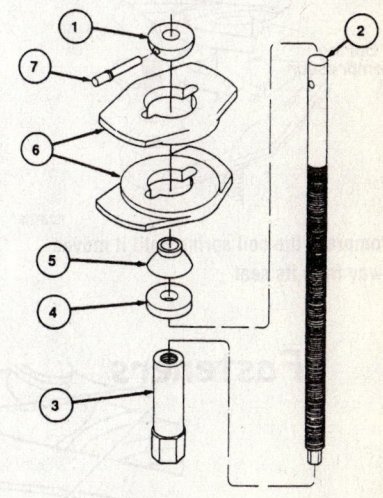

1	Upper Ball
2	Compression Rod
3	Forcing Nut
4	Thrust Washer
5	Lower Ball Nut
6	Plate
7	Pin

7922RG27

Exploded view of Spring Compressor D78P-5310-A—similar compressors are commercially available that will do the same job

into the opening in the lower arm, through the upper and lower plate and upper ball nut. Insert the securing pin through the upper ball nut and compression rod.

➡ **This pin can only be inserted one way into the upper ball nut because of a stepped hole design.**

d. Step 4: With the upper ball nut secured, turn the upper plate so it walks up the coil until it contacts the upper spring seat. Then, back off ½ turn.

e. Step 5: Install the lower ball nut and thrust washer on the compression rod and screw on the forcing nut. Tighten the forcing nut until the spring is compressed enough so it is free in its seat.

5. Remove or disconnect the following:

- 2 lower control arm pivot bolts
- Lower arm from the frame crossmember
- Coil spring

6. If a new coil spring is to be installed, mark the position of the upper and lower

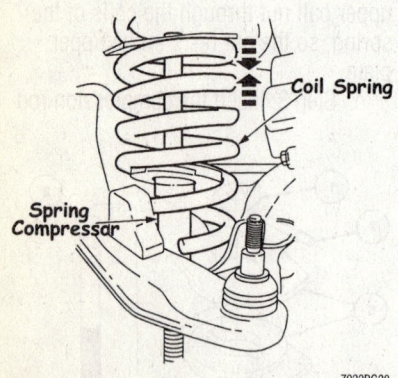

Compress the coil spring until it moves away from its seat

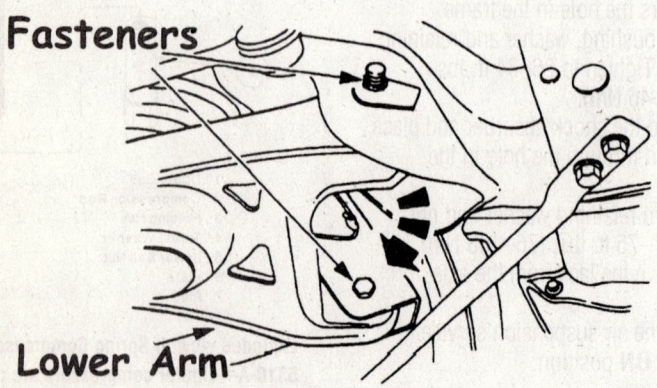

Remove the fasteners attaching the lower arm to the frame, then lower the arm and remove the spring with the compressor

plates on the spring with chalk. With an assistant, compress a new spring for installation and measure the compressed length and the amount of curvature of the old spring.

7. Loosen the forcing nut to relieve the spring tension and remove the tools from the spring.

To install:

8. Assemble the spring compressor and locate in the same position as marked during disassembly.

9. Before compressing the coil spring, be sure the upper ball nut securing the pin is inserted properly.

10. Compress the coil spring until the spring height reaches the dimension measured during disassembly.

11. Position the coil spring assembly into the lower arm and position the lower arm into the frame crossmember.

12. Install both the front and rear lower control arm pivot bolts through the frame and lower arm bushings. Tighten the bolts and nuts to 109–148 ft. lbs. (148–201 Nm).

13. Remove the spring compressor from the coil spring.

14. Install or connect the following:

- Drag link to the Pitman arm. Tighten the retaining nut to 60 ft. lbs. (80 Nm).
- Shock absorber inside the coil spring
- Retaining bolts
- Wheel. Tighten the lug nuts to 85–105 ft. lbs. (115–142 Nm).

15. Place a washer and retaining nut on the shock absorber top stud. Tighten the nut to 25–34 ft. lbs. (34–46 Nm).

16. If equipped with air suspension, turn the air suspension switch to the **ON** position.

17. Check the front end alignment.

Rear

AIR SPRING

❈❈ CAUTION

Before servicing any air suspension component, disconnect power to the system by turning the air suspension service switch OFF or by disconnecting the negative battery cable. Do not remove an air spring under any circumstances when there is pressure in the air spring. Do not remove any components supporting an air spring without either exhausting the air or providing support for the air spring.

1. Before servicing the vehicle, refer to the precautions in the beginning of this section.

2. Turn the air suspension switch to the **OFF** position.

3. Raise and safely support the vehicle so the suspension is fully down with no load.

4. Remove or disconnect the following:

- Heat shield, as required
- Spring retainer clip
- Air spring solenoid valve electrical connector
- Air line
- Air spring solenoid retainer

5. Rotate the solenoid valve counterclockwise to the first stop.

6. Pull the solenoid valve straight out slowly to the second stop to bleed air from the system.

❈❈ CAUTION

Do not fully release the solenoid until the air is completely bled from the

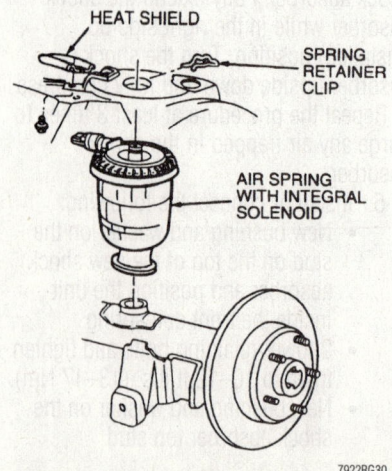

Exploded view of the air spring mounting

air spring or personal injury may result.

7. After the air is fully bled from the system, rotate the solenoid valve counter-clockwise to the third stop and remove the solenoid valve from the solenoid housing. Remove the large O-ring from the solenoid housing.

8. On 1997 models, insert Air Spring Removal Tool T90P-5310-A or equivalent, between the axle tube and the spring seat on the forward side of the axle. Position the tool so its flat end rests on the piston knob. Push downward, forcing the piston and retainer clip off the axle spring seat.

9. On 1998–01 models, lift the air spring off the rear axle.

10. Remove the air spring.

To install:

11. Check the solenoid valve O-rings for cuts or abrasions. Replace the O-rings as required. Lightly grease the O-ring area of the solenoid valve and the larger solenoid housing O-ring with silicone dielectric compound.

12. Insert the solenoid into the air spring end cap and rotate clockwise to the third stop, push in to the second stop, then rotate clockwise to the first stop.

13. Install or connect the following:

- Air spring solenoid retainer. Inspect the wiring harness connector and ensure the rubber gasket is in place at the bottom of the connector cavity
- Air spring into the frame (upper) spring seat, taking care to keep the solenoid air and electrical connections clean and free of damage
- Push-on ring spring retainer clip to the knob of the spring cap from the top side of the frame spring seat
- Air line and electrical connector to the solenoid
- Heat shield to the frame spring seat, if removed
- Align the air spring piston-to-axle (lower) seat. Squeeze to increase pressure and push downward on the piston, snapping the piston to the axle seat at rebound and supported by the shock absorber.
- Negative battery cable.

✳✳ WARNING

The air springs may be damaged if the suspension is allowed to compress before the spring is inflated.

14. Refill the air spring as follows:

a. Step 1: Turn the air suspension switch to the **ON** position. The ignition switch must be **ON** and the engine running or a battery charger must be connected to the battery to reduce battery drain.

b. Step 2: Fold back or remove the right-hand luggage compartment trim panel and connect Super Star II Tester 007–0041-A, or equivalent, to the air suspension DLC, which is located near the air suspension switch.

c. Step 3: Set the tester to EEC-IV/MCU mode. Also set the tester to FAST mode. Release the tester button to the HOLD (up) position and turn the tester **ON**.

d. Step 4: Depress the tester button to TEST (down) position. A Code 10 will be displayed. Within 2 minutes a Code 13 will be displayed. After Code 13 is displayed, release the tester button to the HOLD (up) position, wait 5 seconds and depress the tester button to TEST (down) position. Ignore any codes displayed.

e. Step 5: Release the tester button to the HOLD (up) position. Wait at least 20 seconds, then depress the tester button to TEST (down) position. Within 10 seconds, the codes will be displayed in the order shown.

f. Step 6: Within 4 seconds after Code 26 is displayed, release the tester button to the HOLD (up) position. Waiting longer than 4 seconds may result in Functional Test 31 being entered. The compressor will fill the air springs with air as long as the tester button is in the HOLD (up) position. To stop filling the air springs, depress the tester button to the TEST (down) position.

➡**It is possible to overheat the compressor during this operation. If the compressor overheats, the self-resetting circuit breaker in the compressor will open and remain open for about 15 minutes. This allows the compressor to cool down.**

---

g. Step 7: To exit Functional Test 26, disconnect the tester and turn the ignition switch to the **OFF** position.

15. Luggage trim panel, if removed

COIL SPRING

1. Before servicing the vehicle, refer to the precautions in the beginning of this section.

2. Place a hoist under the rear axle housing and raise and safely support the vehicle.

3. Support the frame side rails with 2 jackstands.

➡**If the vehicle is raised by the frame rails, place a jack under the rear axle housing.**

4. Remove or disconnect the following:

- Rear sway bar
- Lower studs of both rear shock absorbers from the mounting brackets on the axle tube
- Parking brake cable from the upper arm retainer before lowering the axle housing

5. Lower the axle housing until the coil springs are released. If the axle housing is supported by the hoist, lower the hoist allowing the rear of the vehicle to rest on the jackstands. If the vehicle's axle housing is supported by the jackstands, leave the hoist stationary and lower the jackstands or raise the hoist to release the tension on the coil springs.

6. Remove the coil springs and insulators.

To install:

7. Install or connect the following:

- Coil spring in the upper and lower seats with an insulator between the upper end of the spring and frame seat
- Axle housing and connect the lower studs of the shock absorbers to the mounting brackets
- Parking cable into the upper arm retainer
- Sway bar

8. Road test the vehicle and check for proper operation.

Upper Ball Joint

REMOVAL & INSTALLATION

1. Before servicing the vehicle, refer to the precautions in the beginning of this section.

2. If equipped with air suspension, the air suspension switch to the **OFF** position before raising the vehicle.

3. Place supports under both sides of the frame just behind the lower control arms.

4. Remove the wheel

5. Place a floor jack under the lower control arm at the lower ball joint area. The floor jack will support the spring load on the lower control arm.

6. Remove retaining nut and pinch bolt from the upper ball joint stud

7. Mark the position of the alignment cams. When replacing the upper ball joint this will approximate the current alignment.

8. Remove or disconnect the following:
- 2 nuts retaining the upper ball joint to the upper control arm
- Upper ball joint from the upper control arm and spread the slot in the wheel spindle with a suitable prybar to remove the ball joint stud from the wheel spindle.

To install:

9. Install or connect the following:
- Upper ball joint to the upper control arm
- Ball stud into the wheel spindle
- Upper ball joint pinch bolt and retaining nut. Tighten to 56–77 ft. lbs. (76–104 Nm).
- Alignment cams to the approximate position at removal. If not marked, install in the neutral positions.
- 2 nuts retaining the upper ball joint to the upper control arm. Hold the cams and tighten the nuts to 107–129 ft. lbs. (145–175 Nm).
- Wheel. Tighten the lug nuts to 85–105 ft. lbs. (115–142 Nm).

10. Remove the floor jack from under the lower control arm.

11. If equipped with air suspension, turn the air suspension switch to the **ON** position.

12. Check and adjust the front wheel alignment.

Lower Ball Joint

REMOVAL & INSTALLATION

1. Before servicing the vehicle, refer to the precautions in the beginning of this section.

2. If equipped with air suspension, the air suspension service switch to the **OFF** position before raising the vehicle.

3. Place supports under both sides of the frame behind the lower control arms.

4. Remove or disconnect the following:
- Wheel
- Wheel spindle
- Ball joint boot seal and discard
- Ball joint

To install:

➡ **When installing a new ball joint, the protective cover should be left on to protect the ball joint seal during installation. It may be necessary to trim the cover so it can pass through the installation tool.**

5. Install the ball joint

6. Discard the protective cover and be sure the new ball joint is fully seated in the lower control arm. Ensure that the ball joint seal is not damaged.

7. Install or connect the following:
- Wheel spindle
- Wheel. Tighten the lug nuts to 85–105 ft. lbs. (115–142 Nm).

8. If equipped with air suspension, turn the air suspension service switch to the **ON** position.

9. Check the front end alignment.

Wheel Bearings

ADJUSTMENT

The front wheel bearings are of a hub unit design and are pre-greased, sealed

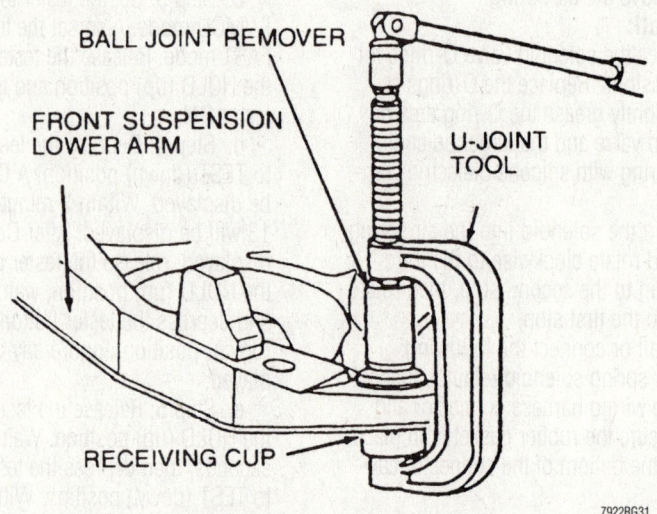

Use a ball joint press remove the ball joint from the lower control arm

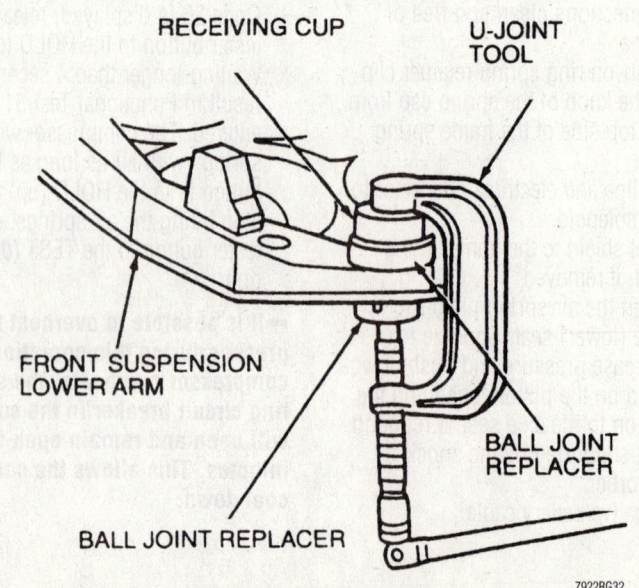

Use a ball joint press to install the new ball joint into the lower control arm

and require no maintenance. The bearings are preset and cannot be adjusted. No adjustment is possible for the rear axle bearing. If either the front or rear bearings make noise or become loose, replacement is necessary.

REMOVAL & INSTALLATION

Front

➡**Before continuing with this procedure, be sure that 2 new caliper mounting bolts, one sway bar link nut, one lower ball joint stud nut and one hub grease cap are available, per side. Once removed, these parts lose their torque holding ability or retention capability and must not be reused.**

1. Before servicing the vehicle, refer to the precautions in the beginning of this section.

2. If equipped, turn the air suspension service switch to the **OFF** position before raising the vehicle.

3. Remove or disconnect the following
   - Front wheel
   - Grease cap from the hub
   - Disc brake caliper. Suspend the caliper with a length of wire. Do not let it hang from the brake hose. Discard the disc brake caliper mounting bolts.
   - Disc brake rotor. If the factory installed push on nuts are installed, remove them first.

- Wheel hub retainer nut and discard
- Hub and bearing assembly

➡**The wheel bearings are permanently greased and sealed. If replacement is necessary, the wheel hub and bearings must be replaced as an assembly.**

To install:

4. Install or connect the following:
   - Hub and bearing assembly
   - New wheel hub retainer nut and tighten to 189–254 ft. lbs. (255–345 Nm)
   - Disc brake rotor and push on nuts, if equipped
   - New grease cap seal
   - Disc brake caliper using the 2 new disc brake caliper mounting bolts. Tighten the bolts to 125–170 ft. lbs. (170–230 Nm).
   - Wheel. Tighten the lug nuts to 85–104 ft. lbs. (115–142 Nm).

5. If equipped with air suspension, turn the air suspension switch to the **ON** position.

6. Pump the brake pedal several times to position the brake pads prior to moving the vehicle.

7. Check the front end alignment.

Rear

1. Before servicing the vehicle, refer to the precautions in the beginning of this section.

2. Remove or disconnect the following
   - Wheel
   - Brake drum or brake rotor
   - Anti-lock brake speed sensor, if equipped

3. Clean all dirt from the area of the axle housing cover.

4. Place a drain pan under the axle housing.

5. Remove or disconnect the following:
   - Axle housing cover retaining bolts and the cover, draining the axle lubricant from the housing
   - Differential pinion shaft lock bolt and the differential pinion shaft

6. Push the flanged end of the axle shaft being removed toward the center of the vehicle

7. Remove or disconnect the following:
   - C-lock from the button end of the axle shaft
   - Axle shaft from the housing, being careful not to damage the oil seal and anti-lock brake sensor ring, if equipped.

8. Insert an axle bearing remover in the axle housing bore and position it behind the wheel bearing so the tangs on the tool engage the bearing outer race.

9. Remove the wheel bearing and seal as an assembly using a impact slide hammer attached to the bearing remover tool

To install:

10. Lubricate the new wheel bearing with rear axle lubricant.

11. Install the wheel bearing into the axle housing bore using a bearing replacer

12. Lubricate the lips of a new wheel bearing oil seal with wheel bearing grease.

13. Install or connect the following:
   - New wheel bearing seal using a seal replacer

➡**Check for the presence of an axle shaft O-ring on the spline end of the shaft and install, if not present.**

   - Axle shaft into the axle housing without damaging the bearing/seal assembly or anti-lock brake sensor ring, if equipped. Start the splines into the side gear and push firmly until the button end of the axle shaft can be seen in the differential case.

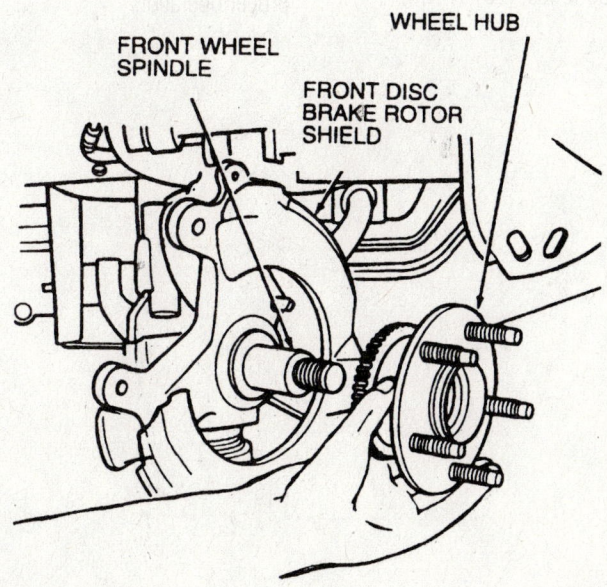

FRONT WHEEL SPINDLE

WHEEL HUB

FRONT DISC BRAKE ROTOR SHIELD

7922RG33

Front hub and bearing assembly

Turn to Section 5 for brake system applications

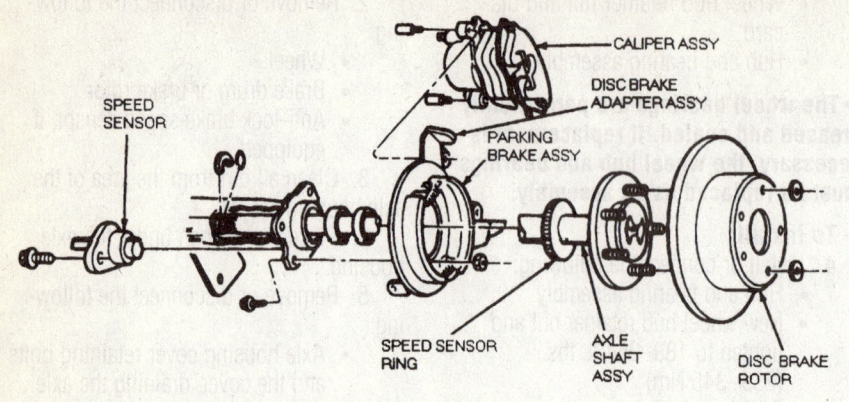

Exploded view of the rear axle shaft assembly

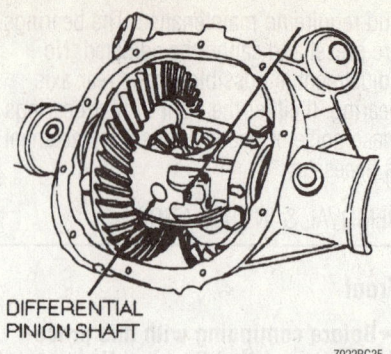

Removal of differential pinion shaft

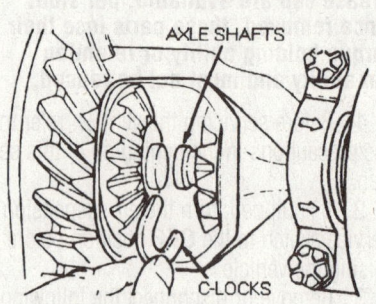

Removing axle shaft C-lock clips

- C-lock on the button end of the axle shaft splines, then push the shaft outboard until the shaft splines engage and the C-lock seats in the counterbore of the differential side gear.
- Differential pinion shaft through the case and pinion gears, aligning the hole in the shaft with the lock bolt hole
- Apply a suitable thread locking compound to the lock bolt threads and place in the case and pinion shaft. Tighten to 15–30 ft. lbs. (20–41 Nm).

14. Cover the inside of the differential case with a shop rag and clean the sealing surface of the axle housing and the axle housing cover. Remove the shop rag.

15. Apply a ⅛–³⁄₁₆ inch (3.18– 4.76mm) wide bead of silicone sealer to the cover.

16. Install the axle housing and bolts and tighten in a crisscross pattern. Final torque the cover retaining bolts to 28–38 ft. lbs. (38–52 Nm).

➡ **The axle housing cover must be installed and tightened within 15 minutes of applying the silicone sealer to prevent leakage.**

17. Add the appropriate rear axle lubricant to the axle housing to a level ¼–⁹⁄₁₆ inch (6–14mm) below the bottom of the fill hole. If equipped with a limited slip differential, add 4 oz. (118.3 ml) of the appropriate friction modifier.

18. Install or connect the following:
- Axle housing fill plug and tighten to 15–30 ft. lbs. (20–41 Nm)

- Anti-lock brake speed sensor, if equipped. Tighten the retaining bolt to 40–60 inch lbs. (4.5–6.8 Nm).
- Brake calipers and rotors or the brake drums, as required
- Wheel

19. Road test the vehicle and check for proper operation.

GENERAL MOTORS
CORPORATION—C & H-BODIES

28

Buick-Le Sabre • Park Ave. • **Oldsmobile-**Eighty Eight •
LSS • Regency • **Pontiac-**Bonneville

PRECAUTIONS

Before servicing any vehicle, please be sure to read all of the following precautions, which deal with personal safety, prevention of component damage, and important points to take into consideration when servicing a motor vehicle:

• Never open, service or drain the radiator or cooling system when the engine is hot; serious burns can occur from the steam and hot coolant.

• Observe all applicable safety precautions when working around fuel. Whenever servicing the fuel system, always work in a well-ventilated area. Do not allow fuel spray or vapors to come in contact with a spark, open flame, or excessive heat (a hot drop light, for example). Keep a dry chemical fire extinguisher near the work area. Always keep fuel in a container specifically designed for fuel storage; also, always properly seal fuel containers to avoid the possibility of fire or explosion. Refer to the additional fuel system precautions later in this section.

• Fuel injection systems often remain pressurized, even after the engine has been turned **OFF**. The fuel system pressure must be relieved before disconnecting any fuel lines. Failure to do so may result in fire and/or personal injury.

• Brake fluid often contains polyglycol ethers and polyglycols. Avoid contact with the eyes and wash your hands thoroughly after handling brake fluid. If you do get brake fluid in your eyes, flush your eyes with clean, running water for 15 minutes. If eye irritation persists, or if you have taken brake fluid internally, IMMEDIATELY seek medical assistance.

• The EPA warns that prolonged contact with used engine oil may cause a number of skin disorders, including cancer! You should make every effort to minimize your exposure to used engine oil. Protective gloves should be worn when changing oil. Wash your hands and any other exposed skin areas as soon as possible after exposure to used engine oil. Soap and water, or waterless hand cleaner should be used.

• All new vehicles are now equipped with an air bag system, often referred to as a Supplemental Restraint System (SRS) or Supplemental Inflatable Restraint (SIR) system. The system must be disabled before performing service on or around system components, steering column, instrument panel components, wiring and sensors.

Failure to follow safety and disabling procedures could result in accidental air bag deployment, possible personal injury and unnecessary system repairs.

• Always wear safety goggles when working with, or around, the air bag system. When carrying a non-deployed air bag, be sure the bag and trim cover are pointed away from your body. When placing a non-deployed air bag on a work surface, always face the bag and trim cover upward, away from the surface. This will reduce the motion of the module if it is accidentally deployed. Refer to the additional air bag system precautions later in this section.

• Clean, high quality brake fluid from a sealed container is essential to the safe and proper operation of the brake system. You should always buy the correct type of brake fluid for your vehicle. If the brake fluid becomes contaminated, completely flush the system with new fluid. Never reuse any brake fluid. Any brake fluid that is removed from the system should be discarded. Also, do not allow any brake fluid to come in contact with a painted surface; it will damage the paint.

• Never operate the engine without the proper amount and type of engine oil; doing so WILL result in severe engine damage.

• Timing belt maintenance is extremely important! Many models utilize an interference-type, non-freewheeling engine. If the timing belt breaks, the valves in the cylinder head may strike the pistons, causing potentially serious (also time-consuming and expensive) engine damage. Refer to the maintenance interval charts in the front of this manual for the recommended replacement interval for the timing belt, and to the timing belt section for belt replacement and inspection.

• Disconnecting the negative battery cable on some vehicles may interfere with the functions of the on-board computer system(s) and may require the computer to undergo a relearning process once the negative battery cable is reconnected.

• When servicing drum brakes, only disassemble and assemble one side at a time, leaving the remaining side intact for reference.

• Only an MVAC-trained, EPA-certified automotive technician should service the air conditioning system or its components.

ENGINE REPAIR

Alternator

REMOVAL

1. Before servicing the vehicle, refer to the precautions in the beginning of this section.

2. Remove or disconnect the following:

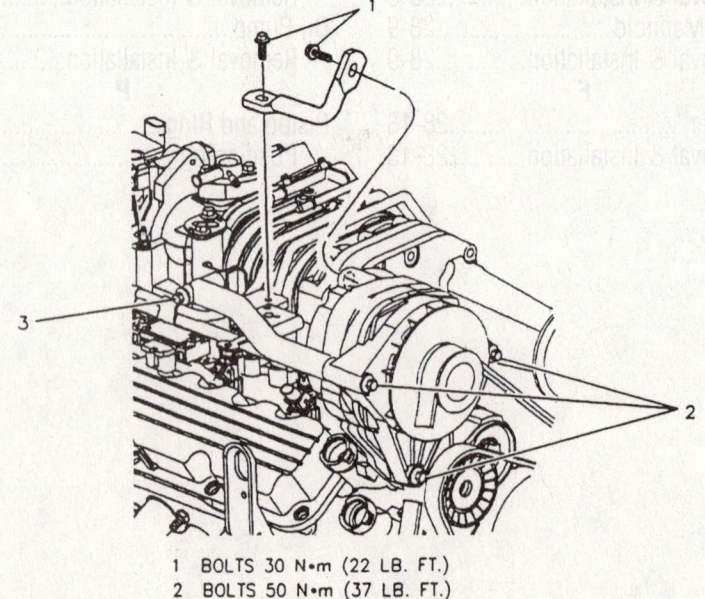

1	BOLTS 30 N·m (22 LB. FT.)
2	BOLTS 50 N·m (37 LB. FT.)
3	BOLTS 30 N·m (22 LB. FT.)

9306UG03

Exploded view of the alternator mounting

- Negative battery cable
- Accessory drive belt
- Engine cover
- Electrical connections
- Support bracket(s)
- Alternator

INSTALLATION

Install or connect the following:
- Alternator. Torque the bolts to 37 ft. lbs. (50 Nm).
- Electrical connections. Torque the nut to 15 ft. lbs. (20 Nm).
- Support bracket(s). Torque the front bracket retainers to 37 ft. lbs. (50 Nm) and the rear to 22 ft. lbs. (30 Nm).
- Engine cover
- Accessory drive belt
- Negative battery cable

Ignition Timing

The 3.8L (VIN K and 1) engines utilizes a Distributorless Ignition System (DIS). This system uses 3 twin tower coils which fire 2 spark plugs simultaneously.

ADJUSTMENT

The ignition timing is not adjustable, and is set according to engine demand electronically. The Powertrain Control Module (PCM) controls the ignition timing for all driving conditions.

Engine Assembly

REMOVAL & INSTALLATION

1. Before servicing the vehicle, refer to the precautions in the beginning of this section.
2. Relieve the fuel system pressure.
3. Drain the coolant system and crankcase.
4. Remove or disconnect the following:
- Negative battery cable
- Radiator and heater supply hoses
- Negative battery cable from the engine
- Engine harness at the bulkhead
- Drive belts
- Power steering pump, move it aside
- Air flow duct
- Throttle cable and other necessary cables

- Manifold Air Temperature (MAT) sensor
- Throttle Position (TP) sensor
- Idle Air Control (IAC)
- Oxygen (O2S) sensor
- Oil pressure switch
- Power Steering cutoff switch
- Vehicle Speed Sensor (VSS)
- Low oil level sensor
- Ignition assembly ground strap from the fender inner panel
- Fuel feed and return lines from the fuel rail and fuel pressure regulator
- Emission control canister hoses from the throttle body
- Brake booster and heater control hoses from the engine vacuum connections
- Vacuum hoses at the cruise control servo assembly
- Exhaust pipe from the right manifold
- Air conditioning compressor, move it aside, do not disconnect the refrigerant lines
- Right front engine-to-transaxle bracket
- Flexplate cover
- Starter
- Torque converter-to-flexplate bolts

➡ **Matchmark the flexplate-to-torque converter relationship for reassembly.**

5. Lower the vehicle.
6. Attach a suitable lifting hook and chain to the engine lifting brackets. Raise the engine slightly to take the weight off the engine mounts.
7. Support the transaxle
8. Remove or disconnect the following:
- Engine torque axis engine mount
- Engine from the transaxle
- Engine from the vehicle

To install:
9. Install or connect the following:
- Engine. Torque the engine-to-transaxle bolts to 55 ft. lbs. (75 Nm).
- Torque axis engine mount bolts. Torque them to 52 ft. lbs. (87 Nm).
10. Align the torque converter-to-flexplate matchmark
11. Install or connect the following:
- Converter-to-flexplate bolts. Torque them to 46 ft. lbs. (62 Nm).
- Starter
- Flexplate cover
- Engine-to-transaxle bracket
- Air conditioning compressor

- Exhaust pipe to the manifold
- Brake booster and heater control hoses to the engine vacuum connections
- Vacuum hoses to the cruise control servo assembly
- Emission control canister hoses to the throttle body
- Fuel feed and return lines to the fuel rail and fuel pressure regulator
- Ignition assembly ground strap to the fender inner panel
- MAT sensor
- TP sensor
- IAC valve
- O2S
- Oil pressure switch
- Power Steering cutoff switch
- VSS
- Low oil level sensor
- Throttle cable and other necessary cables
- Air flow duct
- Power steering pump
- Drive belts
- Engine harness at the bulkhead
- Negative battery cable to the engine
- Radiator and heater supply hoses
- Hood
- Negative battery cable
12. Refill the crankcase
13. Refill and bleed the engine cooling system
14. Start the engine and check for leaks.
15. Road test the vehicle and check operation.

Water Pump

REMOVAL & INSTALLATION

3.8L (VIN K) Engine

1. Before servicing the vehicle, refer to the precautions in the beginning of this section.
2. Drain the cooling system.
3. Remove or disconnect the following:
- Negative battery cable
- Accessory drive belt
- Coolant hoses from the water pump
- Water pump pulley bolts

➡ **The long bolt can be removed by aligning the bolt head up with the hole in the frame rail.**

- Pulley
- Water pump

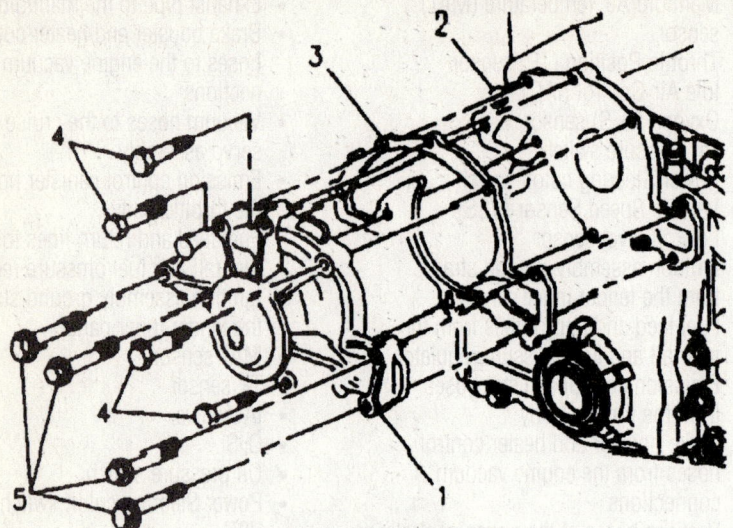

1. **Coolant pump**
2. **Engine front cover**
3. **Gasket**
4. **11 ft. lb. (15 Nm)**
5. **22 ft. lb. (30 Nm)**

7922UG01

Exploded view of the water pump—3.8L (VIN K and 1) engines

To install:

4. Clean all the sealing surfaces.
5. Apply a thin bead of sealer around the outside edge of the water pump
6. Install or connect the following:
   - New gasket
   - Water pump. Torque the water pump-to-engine block bolts to 22 ft. lbs. (30 Nm) and the water pump-to-front cover bolts to 11 ft. lbs. (15 Nm) plus an additional 80 degree turn.
   - Water pump pulley. Torque the bolts to 115 inch lbs. (13 Nm).
   - Coolant hoses to the water pump
   - Drive belt
7. Refill and bleed the cooling system.
8. Run the engine and check for leaks.
9. Recheck the coolant level when the engine has cooled.

3.8L (VIN 1) Engine

1. Before servicing the vehicle, refer to the precautions in the beginning of this section.
2. Drain the cooling system.
3. Remove or disconnect the following:
   - Negative battery cable
   - Air conditioning compressor splash shield

- Supercharger and accessory drive belts
- Coil pack, move it aside
- Supercharger belt tensioner
4. Support the engine using an engine support fixture
   - Front engine mount
   - Power steering pump
   - Engine mount bracket and idler pulley
   - Water pump pulley
   - Water pump

To install:

5. Clean all sealing surfaces.
6. Apply a thin bead of sealer around the outside edge of the water pump
7. Install or connect the following:
   - New gasket on the pump
   - Water pump. Torque the short bolts to 11 ft. lbs. (15 Nm) and the long bolts to 22 ft. lbs. (30 Nm).
   - Water pump pulley. Torque bolts to 115 inch lbs. (13 Nm).
   - Engine mount bracket
   - Idler pulley
   - Power steering pump
   - Front engine mount
   - Supercharger belt tensioner
   - Ignition coil pack assembly
   - Supercharger
   - Accessory drive belts

- Air conditioning compressor splash shield
- Negative battery cable
8. Refill and bleed the cooling system.
9. Run the engine and check for leaks.
10. Recheck the coolant level when the engine has cooled.

Cylinder Head

REMOVAL & INSTALLATION

1. Before servicing the vehicle, refer to the precautions in the beginning of this section.
2. Disconnect the negative battery cable.
3. Relieve the fuel system pressure.
4. Drain the cooling system.
5. Remove or disconnect the following:

- Supercharger assembly (VIN 1 engine)
- Intake manifold (VIN K engine)
- Valve covers
- Ignition wires and ignition coil/module assembly
- Alternator front mounting bracket
- air conditioning bracket-to-cylinder head bolt
- Power steering pump, move it aside

➡**Complete removal of the steering pump is not needed.**

- Accessory drive belt tensioner and supercharger belt tensioner (VIN 1 engine)
- Fuel pipe heat shield
- Rocker arm assemblies, note their original position
- Pushrods
- Cylinder head bolts and discard them
- Cylinder head gaskets and discard them
6. Clean all sealing surfaces and the cylinder head bolt holes in the block.

To install:

➡**Refer to Section 1 of this manual for the cylinder head torque sequence illustration. The illustration is located after the Torque Specification Chart.**

7. Place the new cylinder head gasket on the engine block dowels with the note **THIS SIDE UP** facing the cylinder head and the arrow facing the front of the engine. Position the cylinder head on the engine block.

✳✳ WARNING

In order to prevent damage to the gasket when installing the cylinder head, do not slide the cylinder head on the gasket. Head gaskets are not interchangeable. Failure to install with arrow pointing to the front will cause gasket failure and possible engine damage. Gaskets are identified by either an L or an R stamped on it next to the arrow.

➡**This engine uses special torque-to-yield head bolts. The procedure must be followed carefully and new bolts must be used whenever the head is removed. Total bolt torque should not exceed 60 ft. lbs. (81 Nm).**

8. Install new cylinder head bolts and torque them in sequence as follows:
   a. Step 1: 37 ft. lbs. (50 Nm).
   b. Step 2: plus 130 degrees, in sequence.
   c. Step 3: Rotate the center 4 bolts an additional 30 degrees.

9. Install or connect the following:
   • Pushrods and guide plate
   • Rocker arm assemblies into their original location

➡**Apply a thread lock compound to the rocker arm pedestal bolts before assembly**

   • Valve covers
   • Fuel pipe heat shield

   • Accessory drive belt tensioner
   • Supercharger belt tensioner (VIN 1 engine)
   • Power steering pump
   • Air conditioning compressor bracket bolt. Torque it to 52 ft. lbs. (70 Nm).
   • Alternator front mounting bracket
   • Ignition coil/module assembly and spark plug wires
   • Supercharger assembly (VIN 1 engine)
   • Intake manifold (VIN K engine)
   • Negative battery cable

10. Refill and bleed the cooling system following the proper procedure.

11. Start the engine and check for leaks and proper operation.

Rocker Arms

REMOVAL & INSTALLATION

➡**When removing valvetrain components, it is very important that they are marked for installation reference, so that they can be reinstalled in their original location**

1. Before servicing the vehicle, refer to the precautions in the beginning of this section.

2. Remove or disconnect the following:
   • Negative battery cable
   • Spark plug wires from the spark plugs and move them aside

   • Rocker arm cover(s)
   • Rocker arm pedestal bolts and assembly
   • Pushrods, keep them in order so they can be reinstalled in their original locations

➡**Keep all parts in order so they can be reinstalled in their original locations.**

3. Inspect the rocker arms and pedestals for wear and/or damage; replace as necessary.

4. Inspect the pushrod tips for wear and/or damage. Roll the pushrods on a flat surface to check for a bent condition. Replace any pushrod that is bent and/or damaged.

5. Clean all parts and all sealing surfaces. Be sure all thread adhesive is removed from the rocker arm pedestal and cover bolts.

To install:

6. Lubricate the pushrod tips and put them in their proper locations.

7. Lubricate the rocker arms and pedestals and install them. Be sure the pushrod tips are properly seated in the rocker arms.

8. Apply thread locking compound to the rocker arm pedestal bolt threads. Torque the bolts to 11 ft. lbs. (15 Nm) plus an additional 90 degree turn.

9. Apply suitable thread locking compound to the rocker arm cover bolts.

10. Install or connect the following:
   • Rocker arm cover using a new gasket. Torque the bolts to 89 inch lbs. (10 Nm).
   • Spark plug wires and to the spark plugs
   • Power steering pump and/or alternator brace, as required
   • Accessory drive belt(s)
   • Negative battery cable

11. Run the engine and check for leaks and proper engine operation.

Supercharger

REMOVAL & INSTALLATION

➡**A small amount of oil seepage through the front seal, behind the pulley, of the supercharger is normal.**

This seepage is caused by minute traces of oil escaping around the seal due to normal pressure build up in the oil cavity within the supercharger. A build up of dust can stick to the thin oil film, which causes

1. Dowel pin
2. Head gasket
3. Valve lifter
4. Pivot retainer
5. Rocker arm
6. Pushrod
7. Lifter guide
8. Bolt
9. Bolt
10. Head bolt

Exploded view of the rocker arms and related components mounting—3.8L engines

7922UG03

Timing belt service is covered in Section 4 of this manual

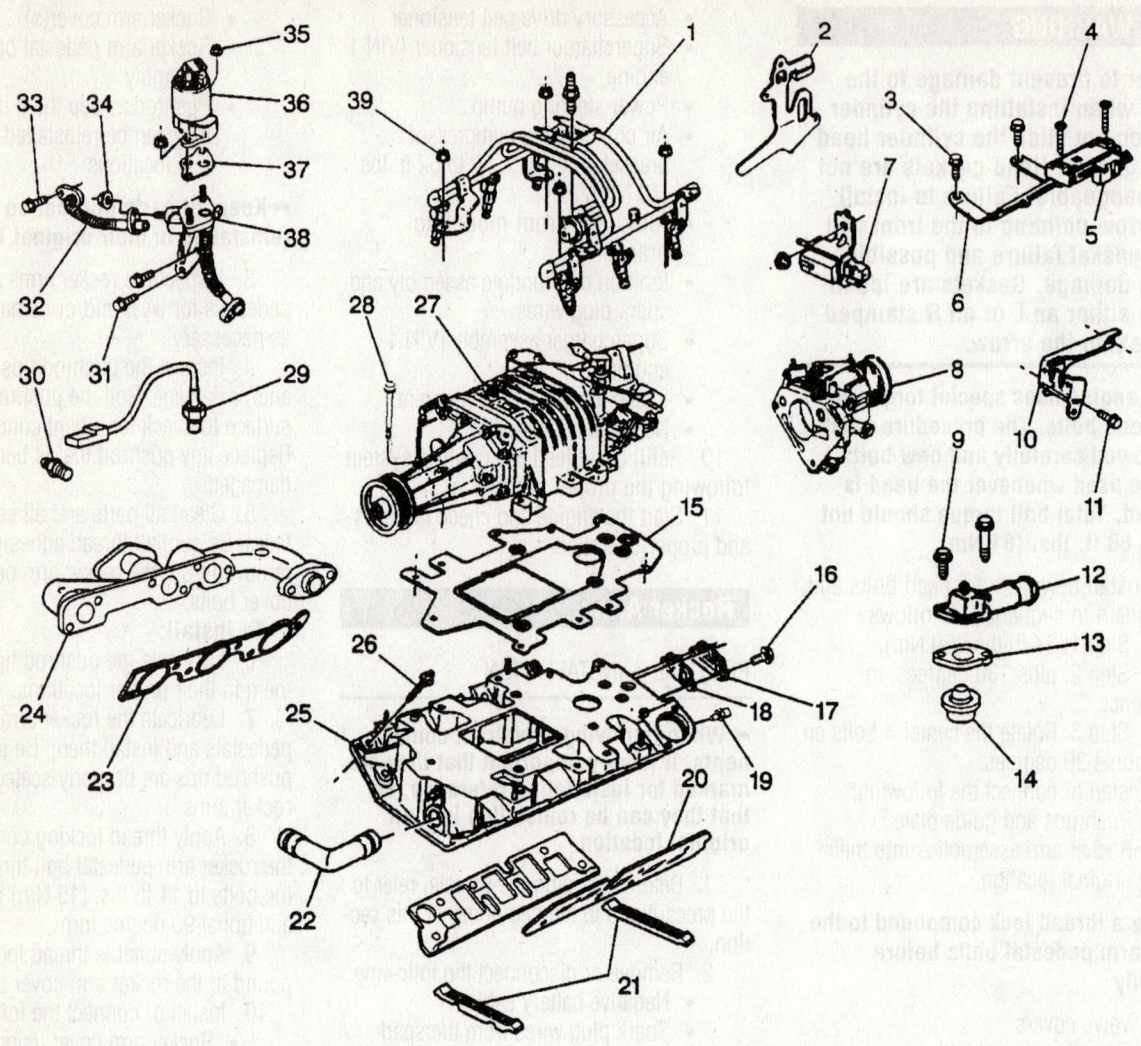

1	Fuel Injection Rail	
2	Fuel Injector Sight Shield Bracket	
3	MAP Sensor Bracket Bolt	
4	MAP Sensor Bolt	
5	MAP Sensor	
6	MAP Sensor Bracket	
7	Bypass Valve	
8	Throttle Body	
9	Water Outlet Bolt	
10	Accelerator Cable Control Bracket	
11	Accelerator Cable Control Bracket Bolt	
12	Water Outlet	
13	Water Outlet Gasket	
14	Thermostat	
15	Supercharger Gasket	
16	Engine Coolant Manifold Bolt	
17	Engine Coolant Manifold	
18	Engine Coolant Manifold Gasket	
19	Coolant Temperature Sensor	
20	Lower Intake Manifold Gasket	
21	Lower Intake Manifold Seal	
22	Heater Inlet Pipe With Seal	
23	Exhaust Manifold Gasket	
24	Exhaust Manifold (Right)	
25	Lower Intake Manifold	
26	Lower Intake Manifold Bolt	
27	Supercharger	
28	Supercharger Bolt	
29	Heated Oxygen Sensor	
30	Exhaust Manifold Bolt/Stud (Right)	
31	EGR Valve Adapter Bolt	
32	EGR Valve Outlet Pipe	
33	EGR Valve Outlet Pipe Bolt	
34	EGR Valve Outlet Pipe Nut	
35	EGR Valve Nut	
36	EGR Valve	
37	EGR Valve Gasket	
38	EGR Valve Adapter	
39	Fuel Injection Rail Nut	

Exploded view of the supercharger and related components—3.8L (VIN 1) engine

9300UG01

the oil seepage to appear worse than it really is. The supercharger should not be replaced for this seepage. However, if supercharger oil is visually dripping from the supercharger front seal, the supercharger will need to be replaced. The supercharger oil level should be checked every 30,000 miles or every 36 months.

1. Before servicing the vehicle, refer to the precautions in the beginning of this section.
2. Disconnect the negative battery cable.
3. Relieve the fuel system pressure.
4. Drain the cooling system.
5. Remove or disconnect the following:
   - Drive belt from the supercharger pulley
   - Engine cover
   - Air duct from the throttle body
   - Right side spark plug wires from the ignition module and move them aside
   - Alternator brace with purge solenoid
   - Exhaust Gas Recirculation (EGR) wiring harness and shield
   - Fuel injectors
   - Manifold Absolute Pressure (MAP) sensor bracket
   - Fuel lines from the fuel rail and cap them
   - Fuel rail
   - Boost control solenoid
   - Throttle body
   - Supercharger assembly

To install:
6. Thoroughly clean the supercharger and intake manifold sealing surfaces.
7. Install or connect the following:
   - New supercharger-to-intake manifold gasket, do not use any sealant on this gasket.
   - Supercharger. Torque the bolts, gradually and evenly, to 17 ft. lbs. (23 Nm).
   - MAP sensor bracket
   - Throttle body to the supercharger. Torque the nuts to 89 inch lbs. (10 Nm).
   - Boost control solenoid. Torque the nut to 72 inch lbs. (8 Nm).
   - Fuel rail and fuel lines
   - Electrical connectors to the fuel injectors
   - Alternator brace with purge solenoid
   - EGR wiring harness and shield
   - Right side spark plug wires to the ignition module

- Supercharger drive belt
- Air duct to the throttle body
- Engine dress up cover
- Negative battery cable
8. Refill and bleed the cooling system.
9. Run the engine and check for leaks and proper engine operation.

Intake Manifold

REMOVAL & INSTALLATION

3.8L (VIN K) Engine

1. Before servicing the vehicle, refer to the precautions in the beginning of this section.
2. Disconnect the negative battery cable.
3. Drain the cooling system.
4. Relieve the fuel system pressure.
5. Remove or disconnect the following:
   - Fuel injector sight shield
   - Air inlet duct
   - Spark plug wires from the right side spark plugs and move the aside
   - Vacuum lines from the intake manifold (label for reinstallation)
   - Fuel lines, vacuum lines and electrical connectors from the fuel rail
   - Fuel rail from the intake manifold
   - Exhaust Gas Recirculation (EGR) heat shield
   - Throttle cable bracket from the cylinder head mounting bracket and the cables from the throttle body lever
   - Throttle body support bracket
   - Upper intake plenum and gasket
   - Upper radiator hose from the thermostat housing
   - Serpentine belt and the alternator
   - Drive belt tensioner assembly
   - EGR valve outlet pipe, if necessary
   - Lower intake manifold and gaskets

To install:
6. Thoroughly clean all of the sealing surfaces.

➡**Refer to Section 1 of this manual for the intake manifold torque sequence illustration. The illustration is located after the Torque Specification Chart.**

7. Install or connect the following:
   - Intake manifold using new manifold gaskets. Torque the bolts in sequence to 11 ft. lbs. (15 Nm); then, retorque to 11 ft. lbs. (15 Nm).

- EGR valve outlet pipe, if necessary
- Drive belt tensioner assembly. Torque the tensioner bolts to 37 ft. lbs. (50 Nm).
- Alternator
- Serpentine belt
- Upper radiator hose to the thermostat housing
- Upper intake plenum. Torque the intake plenum bolts to 11 ft. lbs. (15 Nm).
- Throttle body support bracket
- Throttle cable bracket to the cylinder head mounting bracket and the cables to the throttle body lever
- EGR heat shield
- Fuel rail. Torque the fuel rail bolts to 88 inch. lbs. (10 Nm).
- Fuel lines, vacuum lines and electrical connectors to the fuel rail
- Vacuum lines to the intake manifold
- Spark plug wires to the right side spark plugs
- Fuel injector sight shield and air inlet duct
- Negative battery cable
8. Turn the ignition **ON**, to pressurize the fuel system and check for leaks.
9. Refill and bleed the cooling system.
10. Run the engine and check for leaks and proper engine operation.

3.8L (VIN 1) Engine

1. Before servicing the vehicle, refer to the precautions in the beginning of this section.
2. Relieve the fuel system pressure.
3. Drain the cooling system.
4. Remove or disconnect the following:
   - Negative battery cable
   - Supercharger
   - Thermostat housing
   - Exhaust Gas Recirculation (EGR) tube at the intake manifold
   - Engine Control Temperature (ECT) sensor
   - Intake manifold

To install:
5. Thoroughly clean all sealing surfaces.
6. Clean all old sealant from the intake manifold bolts and bolt holes.
7. Install or connect the following:
   - New gaskets and manifold seals
   - Sealant to the ends of the manifold seals
   - Intake manifold. Torque the bolts, in sequence, to 11 ft. lbs. (15 Nm).
   - Electrical connector to the ECT sensor

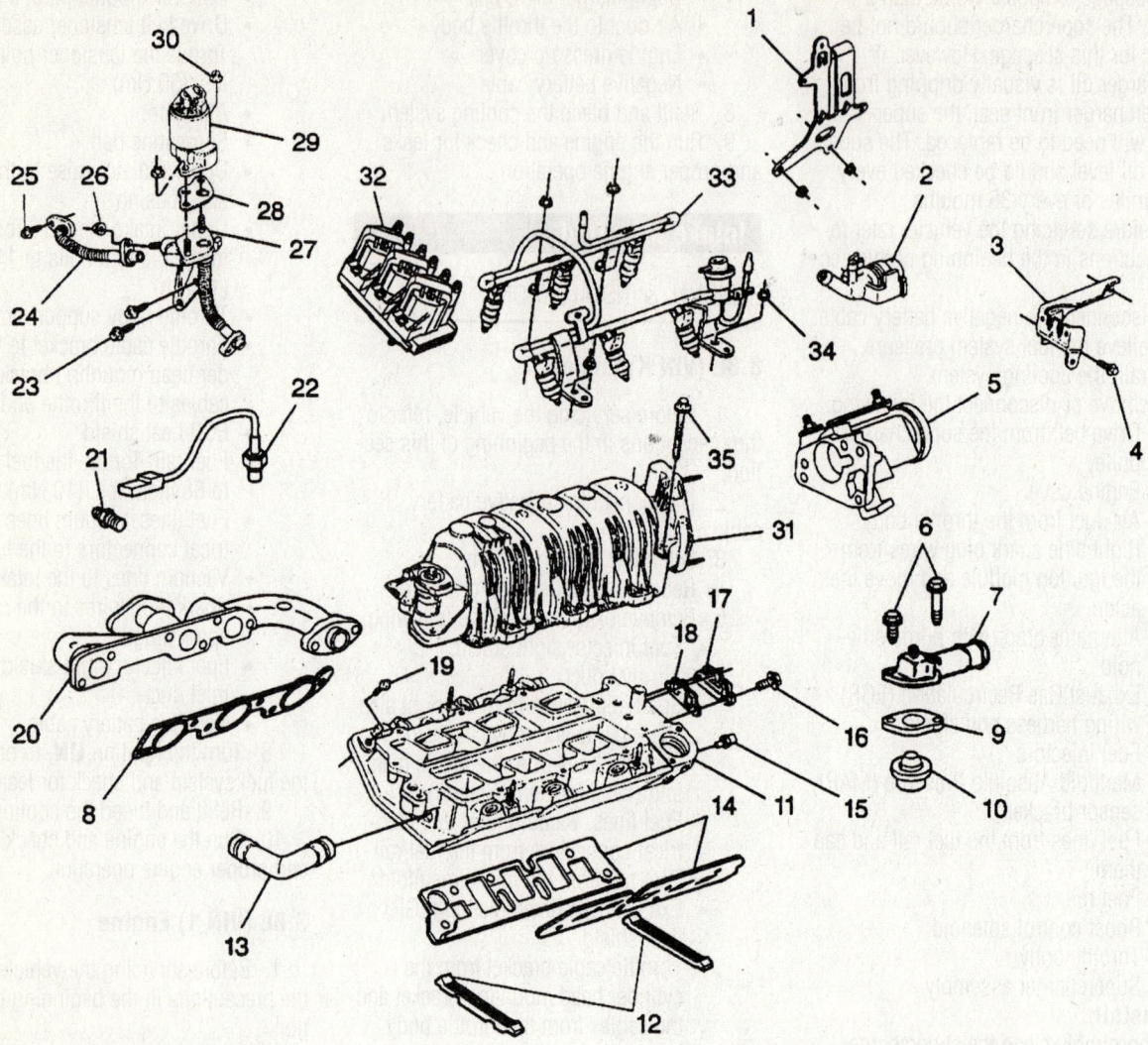

1 Fuel Injector Sight Shield Bracket	19 Lower Intake Manifold Bolt
2 Vacuum Source Manifold	20 Exhaust Manifold (Right)
3 Accelerator Cable Control Bracket	21 Exhaust Manifold Bolt/Stud
4 Throttle Body Support Bolt	22 Exhaust Oxygen Sensor
5 Throttle Body	23 EGR Valve Adapter Bolt
6 Water Outlet Bolt	24 EGR Valve Outlet Pipe
7 Water Outlet	25 EGR Valve Outlet Pipe Bolt
8 Exhaust Manifold Gasket	26 EGR Valve Outlet Pipe Nut
9 Water Outlet Gasket	27 EGR Valve Adapter
10 Thermostat	28 EGR Valve Gasket
11 Lower Intake Manifold	29 EGR Valve
12 Intake Manifold Seal	30 EGR Valve Nut
13 Heater Water Inlet Pipe	31 Upper Intake Manifold
14 Lower Intake Manifold Gasket	32 ICM
15 Coolant Temperature Sensor	33 Fuel Injection Rail
16 Engine Coolant Manifold Bolt	34 Fuel Injector Rail Nut
17 Engine Coolant Manifold	35 Upper Intake Manifold Bolt
18 Engine Coolant Manifold Gasket	

Exploded view of the intake manifold and related components—3.8L (VIN K) engine

9300UG02

- EGR tube to the intake manifold
- Thermostat housing
- Supercharger
- Negative battery cable

8. Refill and bleed the cooling system.

9. Run the engine and check for leaks and proper engine operation.

Exhaust Manifold

REMOVAL & INSTALLATION

Left Side (Front) Manifold

1. Before servicing the vehicle, refer to the precautions in the beginning of this section.

2. Remove or disconnect the following:
   - Negative battery cable
   - 2 bolts attaching the left exhaust manifold to the crossover pipe
   - Spark plug wires from the spark plugs and move them aside
   - Engine oil dipstick and tube
   - Exhaust manifold

To install:

3. Be sure that the manifold and cylinder head sealing surfaces are clean and free of any debris that might cause an exhaust leak.

4. Install or connect the following:
   - New gasket
   - Exhaust manifold. Torque the studs and bolts gradually and evenly to 22 ft. lbs. (30 Nm).
   - Engine oil dipstick and tube
   - Spark plug wires to the spark plugs
   - 2 bolts attaching the left exhaust manifold to the crossover pipe. Torque the bolts to 15 ft. lbs. (20 Nm).
   - Negative battery cable

5. Run the engine and check for exhaust leaks.

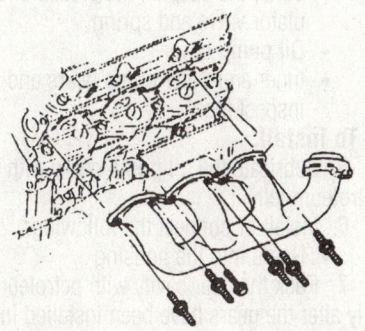

7922UG31

Exploded view of the left exhaust manifold mounting

Right Side (Rear) Manifold

1. Before servicing the vehicle, refer to the precautions in the beginning of this section.

2. Remove or disconnect the following:
   - Negative battery cable
   - Spark plug wires from the spark plugs
   - Transaxle fluid dipstick and tube
   - Oxygen (O$_2$S) sensor
   - 2 bolts right exhaust manifold to the crossover pipe bolts
   - Front exhaust pipe-to-exhaust manifold nuts and the exhaust pipe from the manifold
   - Engine lift bracket
   - Exhaust manifold
   - Manifold-to-crossover pipe gasket and manifold-to-front exhaust pipe gasket and discard them

To install:

3. Be sure the manifold, cylinder head and crossover pipe sealing surfaces are clean and free of any debris that might cause an exhaust leak.

4. Install or connect the following:
   - Manifold to the cylinder head and crossover pipe using a new gaskets
   - Manifold mounting studs. Torque the studs and bolts to 22 ft. lbs. (30 Nm), beginning at the center and working outwards
   - Engine lift bracket
   - Exhaust pipe to the manifold
   - Front exhaust pipe-to-manifold nuts. Torque the nuts to 18 ft. lbs. (25 Nm).
   - Both right exhaust manifold to the crossover pipe bolts. Torque the manifold-to-crossover pipe bolts to 15 ft. lbs. (20 Nm).
   - O$_2$S electrical connector
   - Transaxle fluid dipstick and tube
   - Spark plug wires to the spark plugs
   - Negative battery cable

5. Run the engine and check for exhaust leaks.

Camshaft and Valve Lifters

REMOVAL & INSTALLATION

1. Before servicing the vehicle, refer to the precautions in the beginning of this section.

2. Relieve the fuel system pressure.

3. Remove or disconnect the following:
   - Negative battery cable

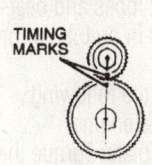 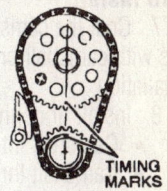

TIMING MARKS

BALANCE SHAFT GEAR TO BALANCE SHAFT DRIVE GEAR

TIMING MARKS

CAMSHAFT SPROCKET TO CRANKSHAFT SPROCKET

7922UG09

The timing marks should face each other when the chain and gears are installed properly

   - Engine and mount it on a engine stand
   - Supercharger, if equipped
   - Intake manifold
   - Rocker arm covers
   - Rocker arm assemblies, pushrods and lifters

➡ **A magnet may be helpful when pulling the lifters out of their bores. Identify all parts as they are removed, so they can be reinstalled in their original locations.**

   - Crankshaft balancer using a puller
   - Timing chain front cover

4. Set the engine to Top Dead Center (TDC) No. 1 cylinder (firing position) to align the timing marks, before disassembling the timing chain and sprockets.

✶✶ WARNING

Align the timing marks of the camshaft and crankshaft sprockets to avoid burring the camshaft journals by the crankshaft.

5. Remove or disconnect the following:
   - Camshaft sprocket and timing chain
   - Camshaft thrust
   - Camshaft

6. Inspect the camshaft lobes and journals for wear and/or damage, replace as necessary.

✶✶ WARNING

If the camshaft was replaced the lifters must also be replaced. The old lifters have developed a wear pattern and will cause the new camshaft to wear prematurely.

Refer to Section 1 for engine rebuilding specifications

To install:

7. Coat the camshaft lobes and bearings with camshaft break-in prelube prior to installation.

8. Install or connect the following:
- Camshaft into the engine
- Camshaft thrust plate. Torque the bolts to 10 ft. lbs. (14 Nm).
- Camshaft sprocket and timing chain, by aligning the timing marks. Torque the camshaft sprocket bolt to 74 ft. lbs. (100 Nm) plus an additional 90 degree (¼) turn.
- Timing chain front cover
- Crankshaft balancer. Torque the mounting bolt to 111 ft. lbs. (150 Nm). plus an additional 76 degree turn.

9. Coat the valve lifters with camshaft break-in prelube.

10. Remove or disconnect the following:
- Valve lifters
- Lifter guides and lifter guide retainer. Torque the retainer mounting bolts to 22 ft. lbs. (30 Nm).
- Pushrods and rocker arms. Torque the rocker arm bolts to 11 ft. lbs. (15 Nm) plus an additional 90 degree turn.
- Rocker arm covers
- Intake manifold
- Supercharger, if equipped
- Engine
- Negative battery cable

11. Verify that all fluid levels are full and correct.

12. Start the engine and check for leaks. Check engine operation.

Valve Lash

ADJUSTMENT

The valve clearance cannot be adjusted on these engines.

Starter Motor

REMOVAL & INSTALLATION

1. Before servicing the vehicle, refer to the precautions in the beginning of this section.

2. Remove or disconnect the following:
- Negative battery cable
- Splash shield
- Wiring
- Flywheel inspection cover
- Starter

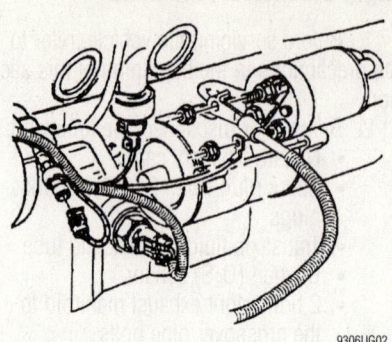

Starter in place with wiring

To install:

3. Install or connect the following:
- Starter. Torque the bolts to 22 ft. lbs. (30 Nm).
- Wiring. Torque the "B" terminal nut to 71 inch lbs. (8 Nm) and the "S" terminal nut to 26 inch lbs. (3 Nm).
- Flywheel inspection cover. Torque the bolts to 62 inch lbs. (7 Nm).
- Spash shield
- Negative battery cable

Oil Pan

REMOVAL & INSTALLATION

✳✳ WARNING

The oil level sensor, located in the oil pan, must be removed prior to removal of the oil pan. If the oil pan is removed first, damage to the oil level sensor may occur.

1. Before servicing the vehicle, refer to the precautions in the beginning of this section.

2. Remove or disconnect the following:
- Negative battery cable
- Flexplate cover
- Oil level sensor
- Oil filter
- Oil pan

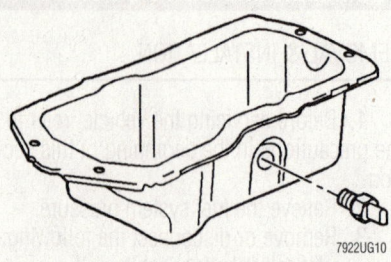

If equipped, be sure to remove the oil level sensor before removing the pan

To install:

✳✳ WARNING

The oil level sensor, located in the oil pan, must be installed after the oil pan has been installed. If the oil level sensor is installed first, damage to the sensor may occur.

3. Clean all sealing surfaces completely. Thoroughly clean the inside of the oil pan.

4. Install or connect the following:
- New gasket
- Oil pan. Torque to 125 inch lbs. (14 Nm).
- New oil filter
- Flexplate cover
- Oil level sensor
- Oil drain. Torque to 30 ft. lbs. (40 Nm).
- Negative battery cable

5. Refill the crankcase.

6. Run the engine and check for leaks.

Oil Pump

REMOVAL & INSTALLATION

1. Before servicing the vehicle, refer to the precautions in the beginning of this section.

2. Remove or disconnect the following:
- Negative battery cable
- Engine drive belts and tensioner assembly
- Drive belt idler pulley and bracket, if necessary

3. Support the engine using an engine support fixture.

4. Remove or disconnect the following:
- Torque axis mount and the bracket assembly
- Engine front cover assembly
- 4 oil filter adapter to the front cover bolts, the adapter, the pressure regulator valve and spring
- Oil pump cover
- Inner and outer pump gears and inspect them

To install:

5. Lubricate the oil pump gears with petroleum jelly

6. Install or connect the following:
- Gears into the housing

7. Pack the gear cavity with petroleum jelly after the gears have been installed in the housing.

8. Install or connect the following:
- Oil pump cover. Torque the screws to 97 inch lbs. (11 Nm).
- Oil filter adapter with new gasket

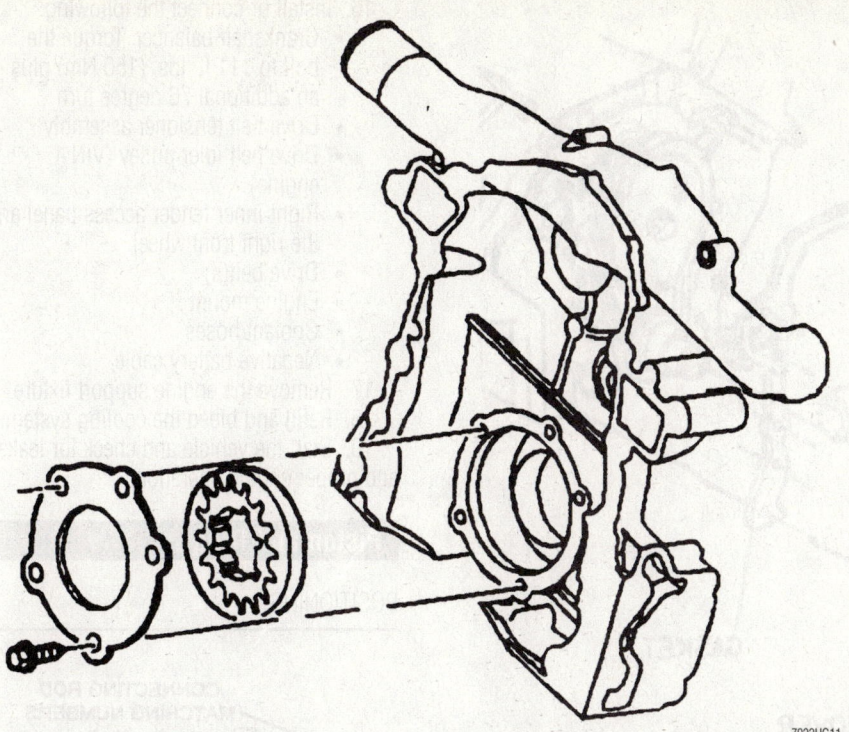

The oil pump is located inside the front engine cover—3.8L (VIN K and 1) engines

and pressure regulator valve and spring

9. Apply sealant to the bolt threads. Torque the mounting bolts to 24 ft. lbs. (33 Nm).

10. Install or connect the following:
- Front cover assembly
- Tensioner assembly
- Drive belt idler pulley and bracket, if removed
- Drive belts
- Torque axis mount assembly.
- Negative battery cable

11. Remove the engine support fixture.

12. Verify the correct engine oil level, a new oil filter is recommended.

13. Start the vehicle and verify no leaks and proper oil pressure.

Rear Main Seal

REMOVAL & INSTALLATION

1. Before servicing the vehicle, refer to the precautions in the beginning of this section.

2. Remove or disconnect the following:
- Transaxle assembly
- Flexplate from the crankshaft
- Rear main seal from engine block, pry it out

✳✳ WARNING

Do not damage or scratch the sealing surface of the crankshaft or the seal bore.

To install:

3. New rear main seal, lubricate with clean engine oil.

4. Slide the oil seal on the mandrel until the back of the seal is seated squarely against the collar of the tool.

5. Attach Seal Installer J-38196 to the rear of the crankshaft with the 2 mounting bolts, then turn the T-handle until the oil seal is fully seated into the rear of the engine.

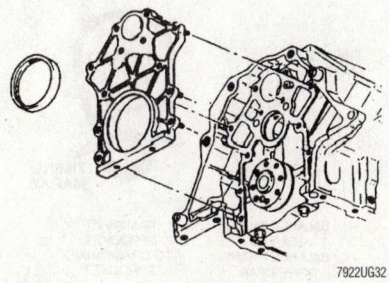

Rear main oil seal and rear cover

6. Loosen the T-handle of the tool completely.

7. Remove both bolts and the tool.

8. Install or connect the following:
- Flexplate. Torque the bolts to 11 ft. lbs. (15 Nm), plus an additional 50 degrees.
- Transaxle.

Timing Chain, Sprockets, Front Cover and Seal

REMOVAL & INSTALLATION

1. Before servicing the vehicle, refer to the precautions in the beginning of this section.

2. Drain the cooling system.

3. Support the engine.

4. Remove or disconnect the following:
- Negative battery cable
- Coolant hoses from the timing chain front cover
- Engine mount
- Drive belt(s)
- Right front wheel
- Right inner fender access panel
- Drive belt idler pulley and bracket (VIN 1 engine)
- Drive belt tensioner

5. Keep the flexplate from turning using holder tool J 37096 or equivalent.

6. Remove or disconnect the following:
- Crankshaft balancer from the crankshaft
- Crankshaft Position (CKP) sensor shield and the CKP sensor
- Oil pan-to-front cover bolts
- Timing chain front cover

7. Align the timing marks on the camshaft and crankshaft sprockets so they are as close together as possible.

8. Remove or disconnect the following:
- Timing chain damper
- Camshaft sprocket bolt, the camshaft sprocket and timing chain
- Crankshaft sprocket

➡ **Do not rotate the camshaft or crankshaft while the timing chain and sprockets are removed.**

9. Thoroughly clean all sealing surfaces.

To install:

10. Install or connect the following:
- Timing chain and sprockets, with the timing marks aligned, to the crankshaft first, then to the camshaft

For engine torque specifications, refer to Section 1 of this manual

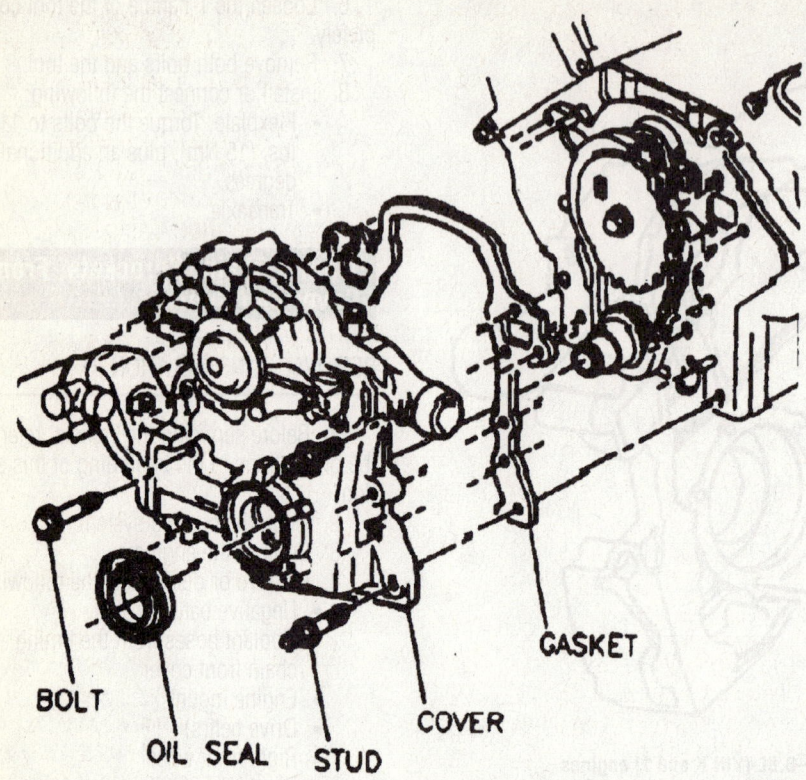

Timing chain front cover—3.8L (VIN K and 1) engines

- Camshaft sprocket bolt. Torque the bolt to 74 ft. lbs. (100 Nm) plus an additional 90 degree turn.

11. Recheck the camshaft and crankshaft sprocket timing marks to be sure they are still aligned.

12. Install or connect the following:
- Timing chain damper. Torque the bolts to 16 ft. lbs. (22 Nm).

✷✷ WARNING

The oil pump is built into the front cover. When the cover is removed, oil drains from the pump. Since the pump "loses its prime" it may not establish oil pressure as soon as the engine starts. Therefore, it is important to remove the oil pump cover from the back of the timing chain front cover and pack the space around the oil pump gears completely full of petroleum jelly. If this is not done, the oil pump may not pump engine oil when the engine is started, resulting in severe engine damage.

13. Remove the screws and the oil pump cover from the back of the timing chain front cover. Pack the space around the oil pump gears completely full of petroleum jelly. There must be no air space left inside the pump.

14. Install or connect the following:
- Pump cover. Torque the screws to 97 inch lbs. (11 Nm).
- New front cover gaskets
- Timing chain front cover. Torque the front cover-to-engine bolts to 11 ft. lbs. (15 Nm) plus an additional 40 degrees.
- Oil pan-to-front cover bolts. Torque the bolts to 125 inch lbs. (14 Nm).
- Crankshaft Position (CKP) sensor. Torque the bolts to 14–28 ft. lbs. (20–40 Nm).
- CKP sensor shield

15. Secure the flexplate using holder tool J 37096 or equivalent.

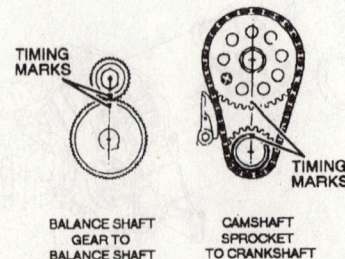

Timing chain sprocket and balance shaft gear alignment—3.8L (VIN K and 1) engines

16. Install or connect the following:
- Crankshaft balancer. Torque the bolt to 111 ft. lbs. (150 Nm) plus an additional 76 degree turn.
- Drive belt tensioner assembly
- Drive belt idler pulley (VIN 1 engine)
- Right inner fender access panel and the right front wheel
- Drive belt(s)
- Engine mount
- Coolant hoses
- Negative battery cable

17. Remove the engine support fixture.

18. Refill and bleed the cooling system.

19. Start the vehicle and check for leaks and proper engine operation.

Piston and Ring

POSITIONING

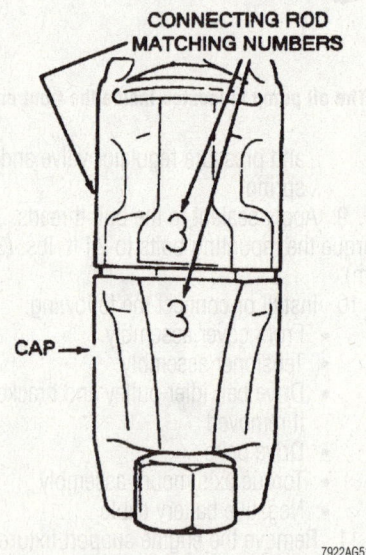

Engine connecting rod and cap installation. Be sure to matchmark the cap and rod prior to disassembly, as shown.

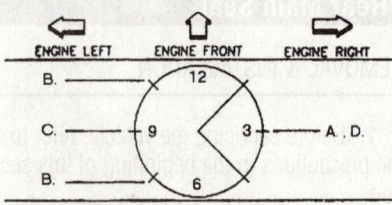

A. OIL RING SPACER GAP (TANG IN HOLE OR SLOT WITH ARC)

B. OIL RING RAIL GAPS

C. 2ND COMPRESSION RING GAP

D. TOP COMPRESSION RING GAP

Piston ring end–gap spacing—3.8L engines

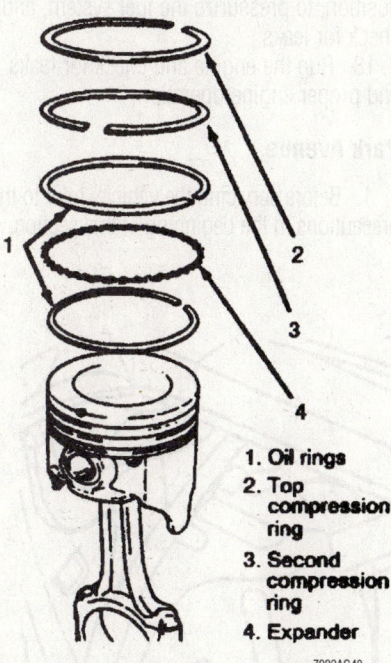

ARROW TOWARDS
FRONT OF ENGINE

FRT

7922AG47

Piston positioning. Often the arrow is replaced by a notch, switch also must face the toward the front of the engine—3.8L engines

1. Oil rings
2. Top compression ring
3. Second compression ring
4. Expander

7922AG48

Piston ring positioning—3.8L engines

FUEL SYSTEM

Fuel System Service Precautions

Safety is the most important factor when performing not only fuel system maintenance but any type of maintenance. Failure to conduct maintenance and repairs in a safe manner may result in serious personal injury or death. Maintenance and testing of the vehicle's fuel system components can be accomplished safely and effectively by adhering to the following rules and guidelines.

• To avoid the possibility of fire and personal injury, always disconnect the negative battery cable unless the repair or test procedure requires that battery voltage be applied.

• Always relieve the fuel system pressure prior to disconnecting any fuel system component (injector, fuel rail, pressure regulator, etc.), fitting or fuel line connection. Exercise extreme caution whenever relieving fuel system pressure, to avoid exposing skin, face and eyes to fuel spray. Please be advised that fuel under pressure may penetrate the skin or any part of the body that it contacts.

• Always place a shop towel or cloth around the fitting or connection prior to loosening to absorb any excess fuel due to spillage. Ensure that all fuel spillage (should it occur) is quickly removed from engine surfaces. Ensure that all fuel soaked cloths or towels are deposited into a suitable waste container.

• Always keep a dry chemical (Class B) fire extinguisher near the work area.

• Do not allow fuel spray or fuel vapors to come into contact with a spark or open flame.

• Always use a back-up wrench when loosening and Torqueing the fuel line connection fittings. This will prevent unnecessary stress and torsion to fuel line piping.

• Always replace worn fuel fitting O-rings with new. Do not substitute fuel hose or equivalent, where fuel pipe is installed.

Fuel System Pressure

RELIEVING

1. Disconnect the negative battery cable to avoid possible fuel discharge if an accidental attempt is made to start the engine.

2. Remove the fuel tank cap to relieve tank pressure. Do not Torque until service procedure has been completed.

3. Connect a fuel pressure gauge with bleed valve to the fuel pressure test port. Wrap a shop towel around the fitting while connecting the gauge to catch any spilled fuel.

4. Install the bleed hose into an approved container and open the valve to bleed off the fuel system pressure.

5. Drain any fuel remaining in the gauge into an approved container.

✳✳ CAUTION

There may still be residual fuel in the system, and a small amount of fuel may be released when servicing fuel lines or connections. In order to reduce the chance of personal injury, cover the fuel line fittings with a shop towel before disconnecting to catch any fuel that may leak out.

Fuel Filter

REMOVAL & INSTALLATION

1. Before servicing the vehicle, refer to the precautions in the beginning of this section.

2. Disconnect the negative battery cable.

3. Relieve the fuel system pressure.

4. Detach the quick connect fuel line from the filter as following steps:

a. Step 1: Twist quick connector ¼ turn in each direction to loosen any dirt that may have accumulated in the connector.

b. Step 2: Use compressed air to remove any dirt in the connector.

c. Step 3: Squeeze the plastic tabs of the male connector and pull apart.

5. Remove or disconnect the following:

• Threaded connection from the filter inlet
• Filter

To install:

6. Position the fuel filter, making sure it is facing in the proper direction.

7. Attach the outlet quick connect line to the fuel filter following these steps:

a. Step 1: Be sure the connector is clean and that a new plastic retainer is used on the filter.

b. Step 2: Apply a couple of drops of engine oil to the male pipe end of filter.

c. Step 3: Push the fuel line onto the fuel filter until the plastic retainer snaps into place.

d. Step 4: Check that the connector is locked into place by trying to pull the connector from the filter.

8. Install the threaded connection to the inlet side of filter.

9. Connect the negative battery cable.

10. Pressurize the fuel system by turning the ignition switch to the **ON** position, then check for leaks.

Fuel Pump

REMOVAL & INSTALLATION

Except Park Avenue

1. Before servicing the vehicle, refer to the precautions in the beginning of this section.
2. Relieve the fuel system pressure.
3. Remove or disconnect the following:
   • Negative battery cable
4. Drain the fuel tank.
5. Remove or disconnect the following:
   • Fuel tank filler pipe and the Evaporative Emissions (EVAP) pipe from the tank
   • Quick connect fuel lines from the fuel tank
   • Rear rubber exhaust hangers
6. Support the fuel tank with a transmission jack.
7. Remove or disconnect the following:
   • Fuel tank strap bolts, let the straps hang freely
   • Fuel tank to remove fuel sender connector
   • Fuel tank
8. Clean the fuel tank in the area of the fuel sender assembly, to prevent dirt and debris from entering the tank when the fuel sender is removed.
9. Rotate the lockring on top of the tank counterclockwise using a fuel sender spanner wrench and remove the fuel sender assembly from the tank.

➡ **Note the direction the strainer is pointing and remove the strainer from the pump by pulling it down and twisting.**

10. Remove or disconnect the following:
    • Pump electrical wires connectors and hoses
    • Pump assembly, pull it out of the rubber connectors

To install:

11. Transfer any insulators and grommets from the old pump to the new one.
12. Connect the pump to the fuel hose and tilt the bottom of the pump into the mounting bracket.
13. Install or connect the following:
    • New strainer on the pump so it points in the same direction as noted during removal
    • Electrical connectors and fuel lines to the pump
    • New O-ring on top of the fuel tank
    • Fuel sender assembly into the tank

    • Lockring, rotate it clockwise until the tabs are against the stops
    • Fuel tank
    • Fuel sender electrical connector
    • Fuel tank straps. Torque the bolts to 25 ft. lbs. (34 Nm).
14. Remove the support.
15. Install or connect the following:
    • Rubber exhaust hangers to rear exhaust
    • Quick connect fuel lines onto the fuel tank
    • Fuel tank EVAP pipe to the tank. Torque the hose clamp to 25 inch lbs. (2.8 Nm).
    • Fuel tank filler pipe to the tank. Torque the hose clamp to 25 inch lbs. (2.8 Nm).
    • Negative battery cable
16. Refill the fuel tank.
17. Turn the ignition switch to the **ON** position, to pressurize the fuel system, and check for leaks.
18. Run the engine and check for leaks and proper engine operation.

Park Avenue

1. Before servicing the vehicle, refer to the precautions in the beginning of this section.

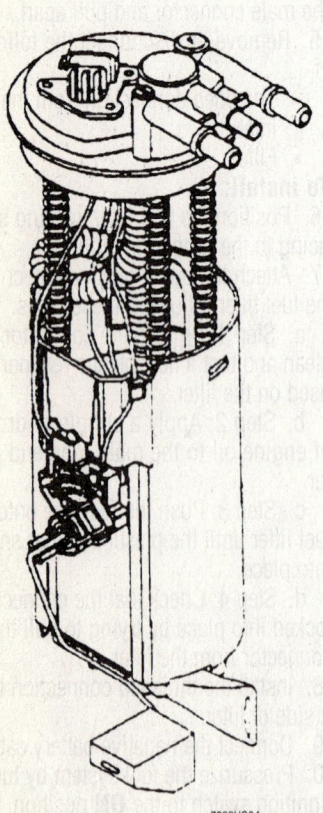

Fuel pump and level sender assembly

7922UG34

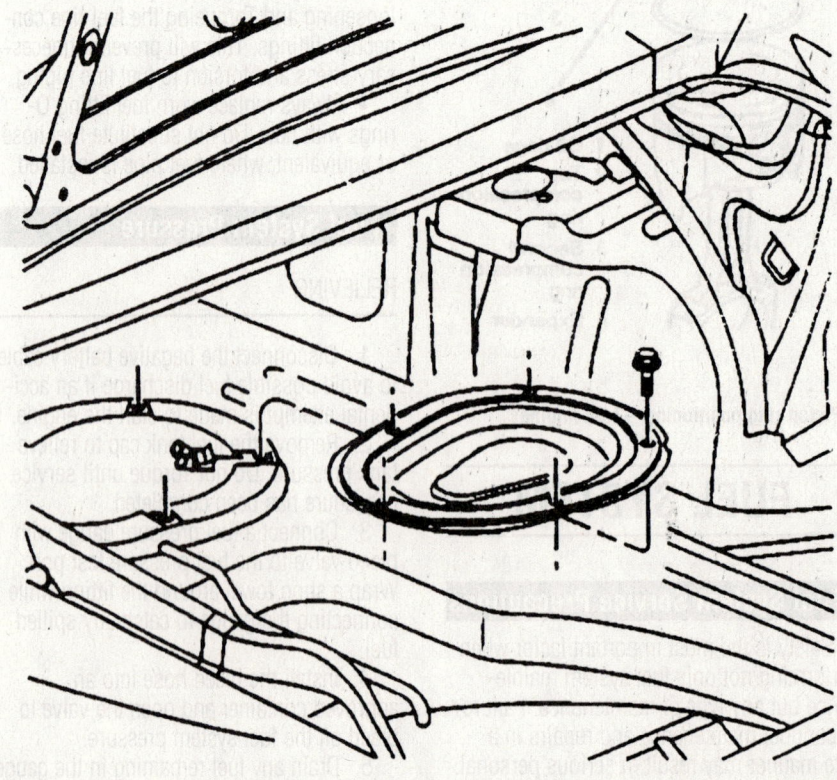

The fuel pump service cover is located in the luggage compartment under the spare tire—Park Avenue

7922UG13

2. Relieve the fuel system pressure.
3. Drain the fuel tank.
4. Remove or disconnect the following:
   - Negative battery cable
   - Spare tire and jack
   - Trunk lining, pull it back to access the fuel sender access panel
   - Retaining screws in the sender access panel. Clean the area around the connection.
   - Sender and quick connect fittings from the sender
   - Electrical connector from the sender and position harness and hoses aside

✳✳ CAUTION

When removing the fuel sender from the tank, the reservoir bucket is full of fuel. Use caution in containing the fuel.

   - Sender retaining ring with a fuel sender spanner wrench
   - Sender and take note of its position
   - Fuel sender O-ring and discard it

➡**Note the direction the strainer is pointing.**

   - Strainer from the pump by pulling it down and twisting.
   - Pump electrical wires and hoses
   - Pump assembly out of the rubber connectors

To install:
5. Transfer any insulators and grommets from the old pump to the new one.
6. Connect the pump to the fuel hose and tilt the bottom of the pump into the mounting bracket.
7. Install or connect the following:
   - New strainer on the pump so it points in the same direction as noted during removal
   - Electrical connectors and fuel lines to the pump
   - New O-ring on top of the fuel tank
   - Fuel sender assembly into the tank
   - Lockring, rotate it clockwise until the tabs are against the stops
   - Fuel line quick connectors
   - Sender electrical connector
   - Fuel sender access cover
   - Trunk liner and the spare tire, jack and spare tire cover
8. Refill with fuel and check for leaks.

Fuel Injectors

REMOVAL & INSTALLATION

1. Relieve pressure in fuel system
2. Remove or disconnect the following:
   - Negative battery cable
   - Fuel rail
   - Injector retaining clips
   - Fuel injector
   - Both O-rings and discard them

To install:
3. Install or connect the following:
   - New upper and lower O-rings
   - Fuel injector
   - Injector retaining clips
   - Fuel rail
   - Negative battery cable

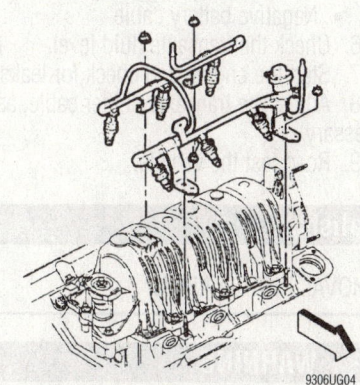

9306UG04

Exploded view of the fuel rail assembly

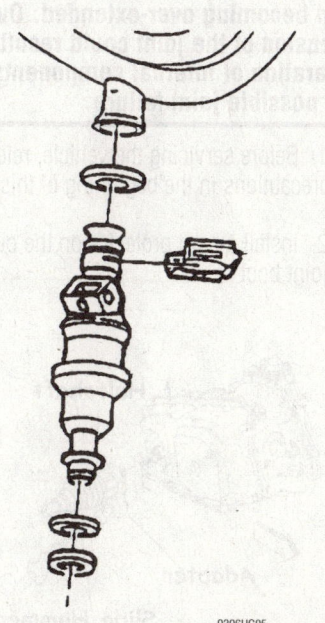

9306UG05

Exploded view of the fuel injector assembly

DRIVE TRAIN

Transaxle Assembly

REMOVAL & INSTALLATION

1. Before servicing the vehicle, refer to the precautions in the beginning of this section.
2. Remove or disconnect the following:
   - Negative battery cable
   - Crossbrace assembly, loosen the through-bolts
   - Inboard strut nuts
   - Crossbrace
3. Reinstall the inboard strut retaining nuts.
4. Remove or disconnect the following:
   - Air intake duct
   - Cruise control cable at throttle body
   - Shift control linkage and bracket at the transaxle
   - Electrical Connections
   - Transaxle electrical connector
   - Vehicle Speed Sensor (VSS)
   - Fuel pipe retainers
   - 3 upper transaxle-to-engine bolts
5. Install Engine Support Fixture tool J-28467-A. Load the engine support fixture by tightening the wing nuts several turns to relieve tension on the frame and mounts.
6. Turn the steering wheel to the full left position.

✳✳ CAUTION

To help avoid personal injury when a vehicle is on a hoist, provide additional support to the rear of the vehicle while removing the transaxle. The center of gravity will shift when the transaxle is removed.

7. Remove or disconnect the following:
   - Front wheels
   - Right and left front ball joint nuts
   - Right and left control arms from the steering knuckle
   - Right halfshaft from the transaxle only; do not remove it from the steering knuckle
   - Left halfshaft from the transaxle and steering knuckle
8. Support the transaxle with a jack.
9. Remove or disconnect the following:
   - Left front transaxle mount

- Torque strut bracket from the transaxle
- Left rear transaxle mount-to-transaxle bolts
- Transaxle brace from the engine bracket
- Stabilizer shaft link-to-control arm bolt
- Flexplate cover

10. Matchmark the flexplate to the torque converter.

11. Remove or disconnect the following:
- Flexplate-to-converter bolts
- Rear frame member to the front frame bolts
- Left frame-to-body bolts
- Frame assembly, swing it aside and support with a jackstand
- Oil cooler lines from the transaxle and plug the lines
- Lower transaxle-to-engine bolts

➡ **One transaxle bolt is located between the transaxle case and the engine block and is installed in the opposite direction.**

- Transaxle

To install:

12. Install or connect the following:
- Transaxle, support it with a jack
- Lower transaxle-to-engine bolts. Torque the bolts to 55 ft. lbs. (76 Nm).
- Cooler lines at the transaxle
- Frame assembly. Torque the frame-to-body bolts to 83 ft. lbs. (112 Nm).
- Front frame mount-to-right frame member and the left frame-to-body bolts. Torque the bolts to 83 ft. lbs. (112 Nm).
- Flexplate-to-converter bolts, by aligning the matchmarks. Torque the bolts to 46 ft. lbs. (62 Nm).
- Oil cooler lines to the transaxle
- Flexplate cover
- Stabilizer shaft link-to-control arm bolt
- Transaxle brace to the engine bracket. Torque the bolts to 70 ft. lbs. (95 Nm).
- Left rear transaxle mount-to-transaxle bolts
- Torque strut bracket to the transaxle
- Left front transaxle mount
- Halfshafts
- Control arms to the steering knuckle
- Front wheels

13. Turn the steering wheel to the straight-ahead position.

14. Remove the support fixture from the engine.

15. Install or connect the following:
- 3 top transaxle-to-engine bolts. Torque the bolts to 55 ft. lbs. (76 Nm).
- Fuel pipe retainers
- Transaxle park/neutral position switch
- Back-up light switch
- Transaxle electrical connector
- Vehicle Speed Sensor (VSS)
- Shift control linkage and mounting bracket at the transaxle
- Cruise control cable at throttle body
- Air intake duct
- Inboard strut retaining nuts
- Crossbrace
- Crossbrace assembly through-bolts and the inboard strut nuts. Torque the fasteners to 18 ft. lbs. (24 Nm).
- Negative battery cable

16. Check the transaxle fluid level.

17. Start the engine and check for leaks.

18. Adjust the transaxle shifter cable, as necessary.

19. Road test the vehicle.

Halfshaft

REMOVAL INSTALLATION

❊❊ **WARNING**

Use care when removing the half-shaft to prevent the inner CV-joint from becoming over-extended. Over-extension of the joint could result in separation of internal components and possible joint failure.

1. Before servicing the vehicle, refer to the precautions in the beginning of this section.

2. Install a boot protector on the outer CV-joint boot

3. Remove or disconnect the following:
- Front wheel
- Stabilizer shaft link assembly bolt, if necessary
- Ball joint cotter pin (discard it) and nut. Loosen the joint

➡ **The grease fitting may have to be removed from ball joint for tool access.**

4. Turn wheel as needed to remove right or left halfshaft.

5. Separate the lower control arm from the joint.

6. Remove or disconnect the following:
- Hub nut and discard it

➡ **A large amount of torque is required to loosen the hub nut. Insert a drift pin or punch through the opening in the caliper into the ventilation openings in the brake rotor to keep the rotor from turning as the nut is loosened.**

- Halfshaft from the hub
- Strut and knuckle, move it rearward
- Halfshaft from the transaxle

❊❊ **WARNING**

If equipped with anti-lock brakes, care must be used to prevent damage to the toothed sensor ring on the halfshaft and the wheel speed sensor on the steering knuckle.

To install:

7. If installing the right halfshaft, install a seal protector, so that it can be pulled out after the halfshaft is installed.

8. Install or connect the following:
- Halfshaft into the transaxle, by placing a drift pin or punch into the groove on the joint housing and tapping lightly until seated. Verify that the halfshaft is seated by grasping the inner joint housing and pulling, DO NOT pull on the halfshaft.

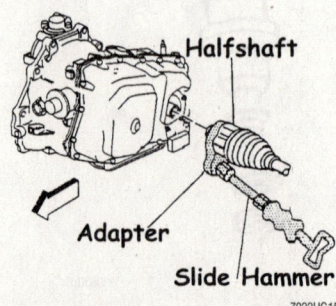

Use a slide hammer with the special adapter J-3308, to remove the halfshaft from the transaxle

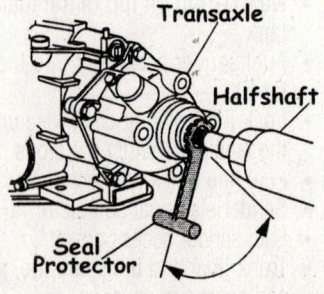

Insert the seal protector in the transaxle to prevent seal damage while the halfshaft is being installed

- Halfshaft into the hub/bearing assembly and hub nut loosely
- Ball joint into the steering knuckle. Torque the nut to 88 inch lbs. (10 Nm), plus an additional 120 degree (⅓) turn during which a torque of 41 ft. lbs. (55 Nm) must be obtained.

➡ **If necessary. Torque the nut up to 20 degrees additional. NEVER loosen the castle nut to install the new cotter pin.**

9. Insert a drift in the brake rotor cooling fins to keep the rotor from turning, then Torque the hub nut to 107 ft. lbs. (145 Nm), without J55 brake or to 130 ft. lbs. (177 Nm) with J55 brake

10. Install or connect the following:
- Stabilizer shaft link assembly. Torque the nut to 14 ft. lbs. (17 Nm).
- Front wheel

11. If a seal protector was installed, remove it by pulling in line with the handle.

12. Road test for proper operation.

CV-Joints

OVERHAUL

Inner (Tri-Pot) Joint

1. Before servicing the vehicle, refer to the precautions in the beginning of this section.
2. Raise and safely support the vehicle.
3. Remove or disconnect the following:
- Front wheel
- Halfshaft and place it in a vise
- Small CV-joint boot clamp, cut and discard it
- Large CV-joint boot clamp, cut and discard it
- CV-joint boot by sliding it away from the tri-pot joint
- Tri-pot housing from the tri-pot spider
- Inboard spacer ring slide it rearward on the shaft using Snapring Pliers tool J-8059
- Outboard retaining ring using Snapring Pliers tool J-8059 and discard it
- Tri-pot joint spider assembly
- Inboard spacer ring and discard it
- Tri-pot joint spider assembly by tapping it from the halfshaft with a brass drift

- Tri-pot spider retaining ring and discard it
- Trilobal tri-pot bushing from the housing
- CV-joint boot
4. Thoroughly clean and inspect all parts.

To install:

5. Install or connect the following:
- Small boot clamp
- CV-joint boot
- New inboard spacer ring slide it rearward on the shaft using

Snapring Pliers tool J-8059, past the 2nd groove
- Tri-pot joint spider assembly onto the shaft until it passes the 2nd groove

6. Assemble the tri-pot spider assembly onto the halfshaft as follows:
   a. Position the tri-pot spider assembly onto the shop press plate.
   b. Position the halfshaft onto the tri-pot spider assembly, in the shop press.
   c. Press the halfshaft into the tri-pot spider assembly until the spider assembly passes the 2nd groove.

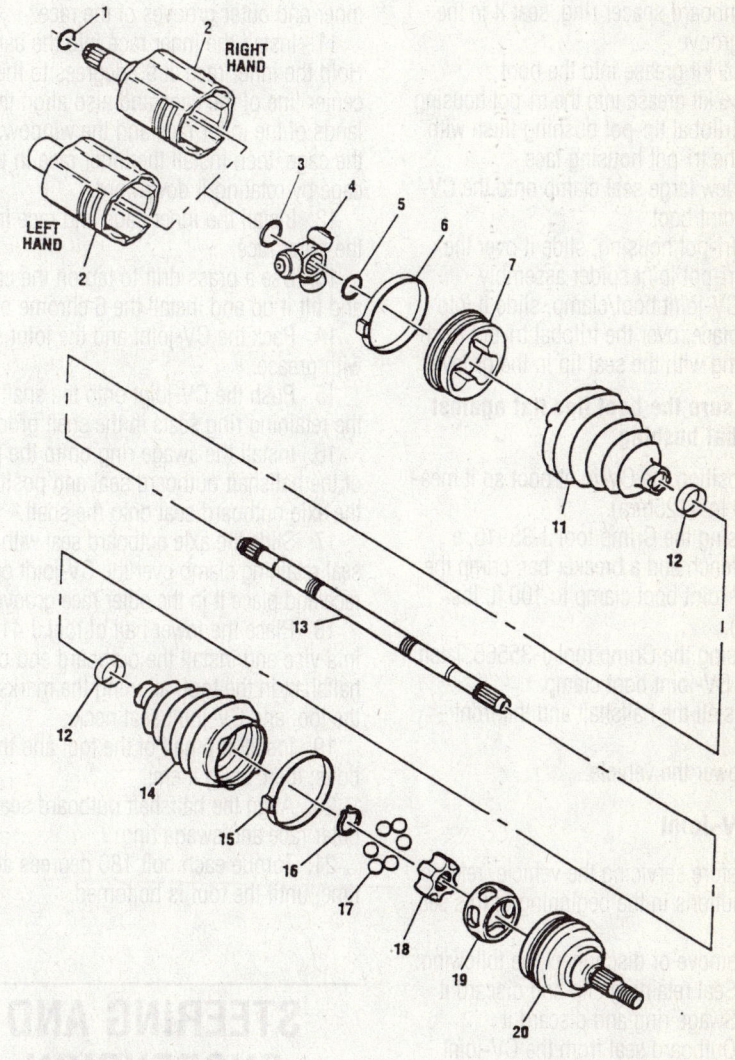

1 - RING, RETAINING
2 - HOUSING ASM, RETAINER &
3 - RING, SHAFT RETAINING
4 - SPIDER, TRIPOT JOINT
5 - RING, SPACER
6 - CLAMP, SEAL RETAINING
7 - BUSHING, TRILOBAL TRIPOT
11 - SEAL, DRIVE AXLE INBOARD
12 - RING, SWAGE

13 - SHAFT, AXLE (RH SHOWN, LH SIMILAR)
14 - SEAL, DRIVE AXLE OUTBOARD
15 - CLAMP, SEAL RETAINING
16 - RING, RACE RETAINING
17 - BALL, CHROME ALLOY
18 - RACE, C/V JOINT INNER
19 - CAGE, C/V JOINT
20 - RACE, C/V JOINT OUTER

9306UG06

Exploded view of the halfshaft assembly

✳✳ WARNING

When assembling the tri-pot assembly onto the halfshaft, do not exceed 4,000 lbs. pressure.

7. Remove the halfshaft from the shop press and place it in vise.
8. Install or connect the following:
   - New outboard retaining ring into the axle shaft groove using Snapring Pliers tool J-8039-A
   - Tri-pot joint spider assembly, slide it against the outboard retaining ring using a brass drift
   - Inboard spacer ring, seat it in the groove
   - ½ kit grease into the boot
   - ½ kit grease into the tri-pot housing
   - Trilobal tip-pot bushing flush with the tri-pot housing face
   - New large seal clamp onto the CV-joint boot
   - Tri-pot housing, slide it over the tri-pot joint spider assembly
   - CV-joint boot/clamp, slide it into place, over the trilobal tri-pot bushing with the seal lip in the groove

➥**Make sure the boot lies flat against the trilobal bushing.**

9. Position the CV-joint boot so it measures 4.9 in. (125mm).
10. Using the Crimp tool J-35910, a torque wrench and a breaker bar, crimp the small CV-joint boot clamp to 100 ft. lbs. (136 Nm).
11. Using the Crimp tool J-35566, latch the large CV-joint boot clamp.
12. Install the halfshaft and the front wheel.
13. Lower the vehicle.

Outer CV-Joint

1. Before servicing the vehicle, refer to the precautions in the beginning of this section.
2. Remove or disconnect the following:
   - Seal retaining clip and discard it
   - Swage ring and discard it
   - Outboard seal from the CV-joint outer race
3. Slide the boot down the shaft and wipe the grease from the face of the inner race.
4. Remove or disconnect the following:
   - Retaining ring using snapring pliers
   - CV-joint assembly from halfshaft
   - Halfshaft outboard seal and discard it

5. Place a brass drift on the CV-joint cage and tap it gently with a hammer to tilt the cage and remove the chrome alloy ball.
6. Repeat this to remove all 6 chrome alloy balls from race and cage.
7. Pivot the cage and the inner race 90 degrees to the center line of the outer race. At the same time align the lands of the outer race and lift out the cage and race.
8. Clean inner and outer race assembles, cage, chrome alloy balls and halfshaft.
9. Check all components for wear and replace, if damaged.

To install:

10. Put a light coat of grease on the inner and outer grooves of the race.
11. Install the inner race into the cage. Hold the inner race at 90 degrees to the center line of the cage and also align the lands of the inner race and the windows of the cage, then install the inner race in the cage by rotating it downward.
12. Install the inner cage and race into the outer race.
13. Use a brass drift to tap on the cage and tilt it up and install the 6 chrome balls.
14. Pack the CV-joint and the joint seal with grease.
15. Push the CV-joint onto the shaft until the retaining ring seats in the shaft groove.
16. Install the swage ring on to the neck of the halfshaft outboard seal and position the axle outboard seal onto the shaft.
17. Slide the axle outboard seal with large seal retaining clamp over the CV-joint outer race and place it in the outer race groove.
18. Place the lower half of tool J 41048 in a vise and install the outboard end of the halfshaft in the tool, aligning the marks in the tool and CV-joint seal neck.
19. Install top half of the tool and the bolts; then, snug them.
20. Align the halfshaft outboard seal, outer race and swage ring.
21. Torque each bolt 180 degrees at a time, until the tool is bottomed.

STEERING AND SUSPENSION

Air Bag

✳✳ CAUTION

Some vehicles are equipped with an air bag system. The system must be disabled before performing service on or around system components, steering column, instrument panel components, wiring and sensors. Failure to follow safety and disabling procedures could result in accidental air bag deployment, possible personal injury and unnecessary system repairs.

PRECAUTIONS

Several precautions must be observed when handling the inflator module to avoid accidental deployment and possible personal injury.
- Never carry the inflator module by the wires or connector on the underside of the module.
- When carrying a live inflator module, hold securely with both hands, and ensure that the bag and trim cover are pointed away
- Place the inflator module on a bench or other surface with the bag and trim cover facing up
- With the inflator module on the bench, never place anything on or close to the module which may be thrown in the event of an accidental deployment.

DISARMING

✳✳ CAUTION

The Supplemental Restraint System (SRS) must be disarmed before performing service around the air bag or SRS wiring. Failure to do so may cause accidental deployment of the air bag, resulting in unnecessary SRS repairs and/or personal injury.

1. Turn the steering wheel so the front wheels are in the straight-ahead position.
2. Turn the ignition switch to the **LOCK** position.
3. Remove or disconnect the following:
   - Negative battery cable
   - Air Bag fuse from the fuse panel

➥**The position of the fuse on the panel varies according to model and year. Consult the vehicle owner's manual for fuse location.**

- Left-hand sound insulator, trim panel under the instrument panel
- Connector Position Assurance (CPA) clip and the yellow 2-way connector at the base of the steering column
- CPA and detach the passenger side yellow 2-way connector, if equipped

➡Positions for the connector vary from behind the glove box to removing the right side sound insulator and finding the yellow connector.

ARMING

After the necessary repairs have been made, re-enable the air bag system as follows:

1. Turn the steering wheel so the front wheels are in the straight-ahead position.
2. Turn the ignition switch to the **LOCK** position.
3. Disconnect the negative battery cable.
4. Install or connect the following:
   - Yellow 2-way connector at the base of the steering column and the CPA
   - Left-hand sound insulator
   - Yellow 2-way connector on the right side and the CPA, if equipped
   - Sound insulator and/or glove box
   - Air bag fuse
   - Negative battery cable
5. Turn the ignition switch to the **RUN** position. Verify that the INFLATABLE RESTRAINT indicator lamp flashes 7–9 times, then remains OFF. If the lamp does not function as specified, there is a malfunction in the air bag system.

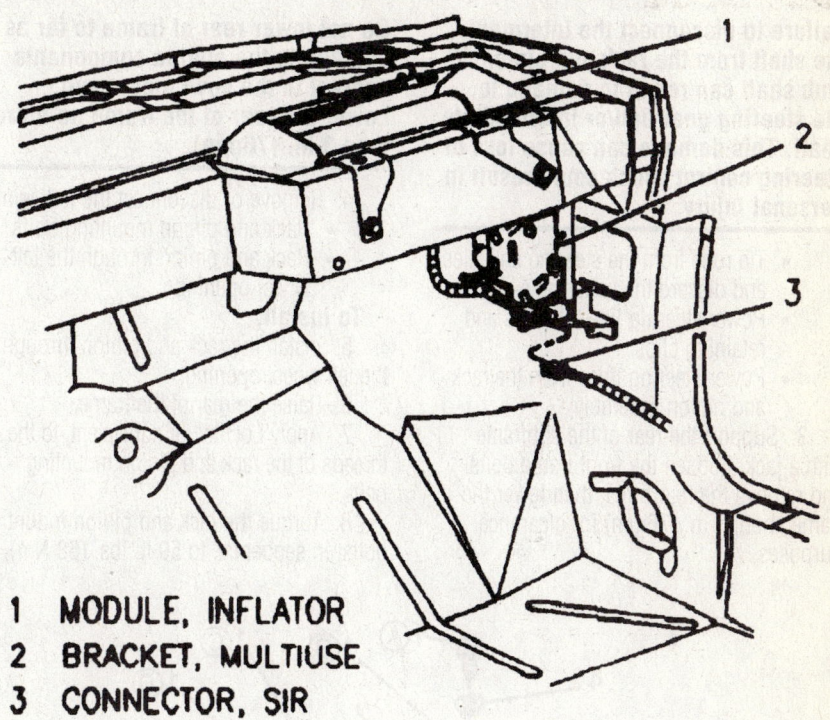

1 **MODULE, INFLATOR**
2 **BRACKET, MULTIUSE**
3 **CONNECTOR, SIR**

Passenger's side air bag connector

7922UG36

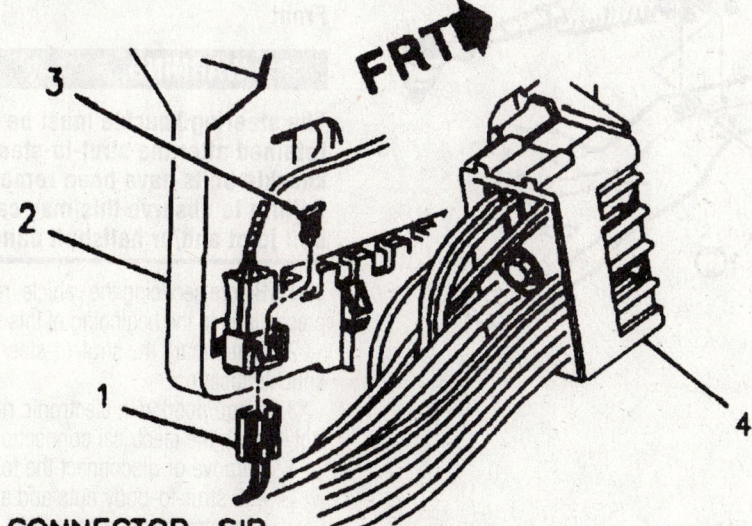

1 **CONNECTOR, SIR**
2 **BRACKET, MULTIUSE MODULE**
3 **CONNECTOR POSITION ASSURANCE (CPA)**
4 **CONNECTOR, STEERING COLUMN WIRING HARNESS**

7922UG35

Drivers side air bag connector

Power Rack and Pinion Steering Gear

REMOVAL & INSTALLATION

✳✳ WARNING

The wheels of the vehicle must be straight-ahead and the steering column in the LOCK position before disconnecting the steering column or intermediate shaft from the steering gear. Failure to do so will cause the Supplemental Inflatable Restraint (SIR) coil assembly in the steering column to become off-center, which will cause damage to the coil assembly.

1. Before servicing the vehicle, refer to the precautions in the beginning of this section.
2. Remove or disconnect the following:
   - Negative battery cable
   - Both front wheels
   - Intermediate shaft-to-rack/pinion assembly pinch bolt shaft

Turn to Section 5 for brake system applications

✳✳ CAUTION

Failure to disconnect the intermediate shaft from the rack and pinion stub shaft can result in damage to the steering gear and/or intermediate shaft. This damage can cause loss of steering control which could result in personal injury.

- Tie rods from the steering knuckles and discard the cotter pins
- Power steering line retainers and retaining clips
- Power steering lines from the rack and pinion assembly

3. Support the rear of the subframe with a jack. Loosen the front frame bolts and remove the rear bolts, then lower the frame about 3 in. (76mm) for clearance purposes.

✳✳ WARNING

Do not lower rear of frame to far as damage to the engine components nearest to the cowl may result. Lower the rear of the frame no more than 3 in. (76mm).

4. Remove or disconnect the following:
- Rack and pinion mounting bolts
- Rack and pinion through the left wheel opening

To install:

5. Install the rack and pinion through the left wheel opening.
6. Raise the rear of the frame.
7. Apply Loctite® or equivalent, to the threads of the rack and pinion mounting bolts.
8. Torque the rack and pinion mounting bolts, in sequence, to 50 ft. lbs. (68 Nm).

9. Raise the subframe into position. Torque the bolts to 76 ft. lbs. (103 Nm).
10. Remove the jack.
11. Install or connect the following:
- Power steering hoses. Torque the fittings to 20 ft. lbs. (27 Nm).
- Power steering lines to the retainers
- Tie rod ends to the steering knuckles. Torque the nuts to 35 ft. lbs. (47 Nm).

➡If necessary to align the holes for the new cotter pin, Torque the nuts up to 60 degrees additional. NEVER loosen the castle nuts to align the holes.

- Intermediate shaft to the rack and pinion. Torque the pinch bolt to 35 ft. lbs. (47 Nm).
- Front wheels. Torque the lug nuts to 100 ft. lbs. (140 Nm).
- Negative battery cable
12. Lower the vehicle.
13. Refill the reservoir with fluid and bleed the air from the system.
14. Start the engine, check for leaks and proper steering operation.
15. Check the wheel alignment.

Strut

REMOVAL & INSTALLATION

Front

✳✳ WARNING

The steering knuckle must be retained after the strut-to-steering knuckle bolts have been removed. Failure to observe this may cause ball joint and/or halfshaft damage.

1. Before servicing the vehicle, refer to the precautions in the beginning of this section.
2. Matchmark the strut-to-steering knuckle location.
3. If equipped with electronic ride control, detach the electrical connection.
4. Remove or disconnect the following:
- 3 strut-to-body nuts and allow the control arms to hang free
- Anti-lock Brakes System (ABS) front wheel speed sensor
- Wheel speed sensor bracket from the strut
- Brake line bracket from the strut
- Strut-to-steering knuckle bolts and the strut
5. Disassemble the strut as follows:
   a. Step 1: Place the strut assembly into compressor tool J 34013-B or equivalent, to compress the coil spring

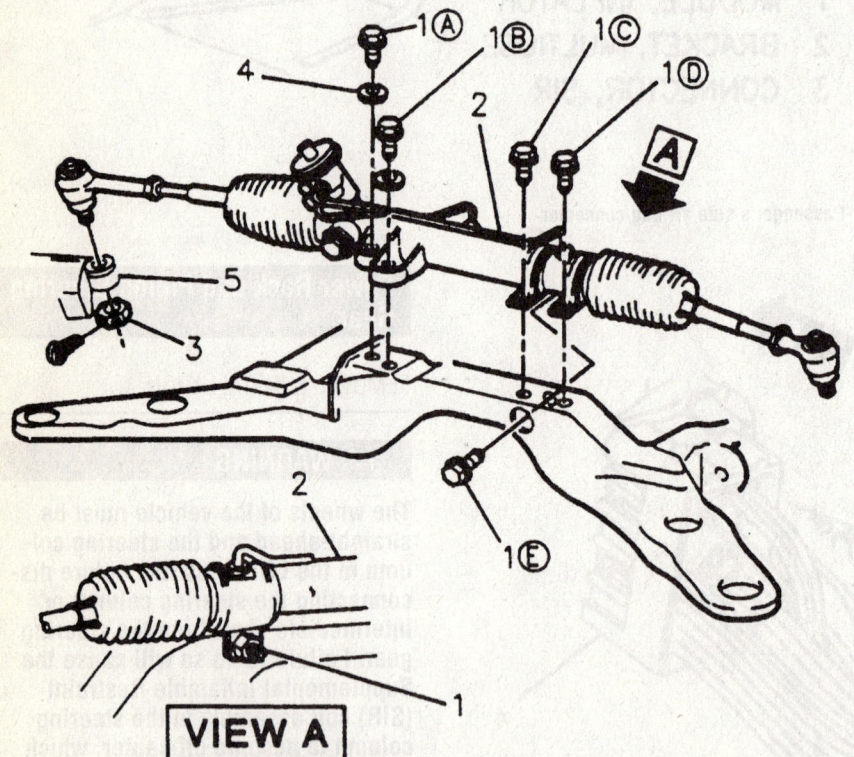

VIEW A

1 BOLT; 68 N•m (50 LB. FT.).
   TIGHTEN IN SEQUENCE A THRU E.
2 STEERING GEAR
3 NUT; 47 N•m (35 LB. FT.). MAXIMUM
   PERMISSIBLE TORQUE TO ALIGN COTTER
   PIN SLOT IS 70 N•m (52 LB. FT.).
4 WASHER
5 STEERING KNUCKLE

Torque the steering gear mounting bolts in the sequence shown

7922UG16

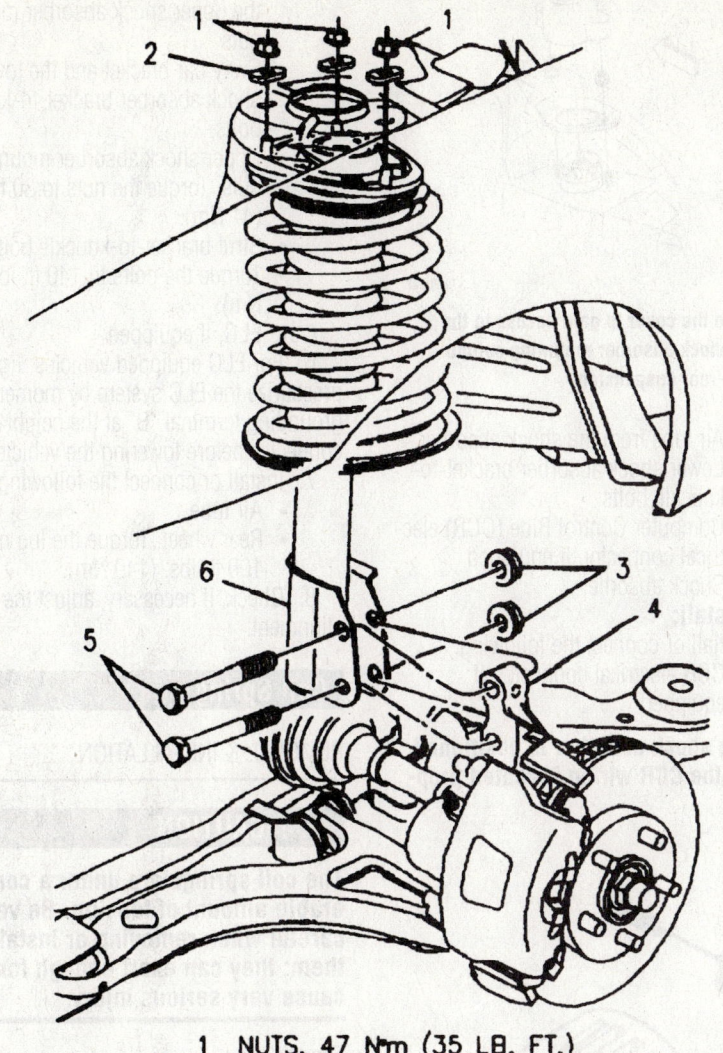

1 NUTS, 47 N·m (35 LB. FT.)
2 WASHER
3 NUTS, 185 N·m (136 LB. FT.)
4 KNUCKLE
5 BOLT
6 STRUT

7922UG17

The strut assembly is mounted between the steering knuckle and the body—front strut shown

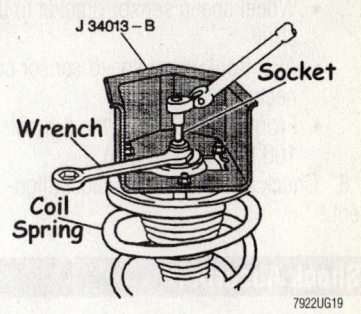

7922UG19

Use a Torx® socket to keep the piston rod from turning while removing the upper nut—front strut shown

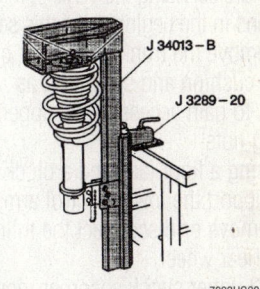

7922UG20

Install the strut assembly into a suitable compressor such as compressor tool J 34013-B to safely remove the strut from the coil spring—front strut shown

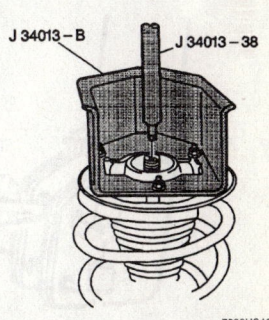

7922UG18

Install Rod J 34013-38 or equivalent, to help guide the strut shaft from the upper mount assembly—front strut shown

b. Step 2: Compress the spring slightly.

c. Step 3: Hold the strut shaft from turning using a No. 50 Torx® socket and remove the 24mm nut on the top end of the strut.

d. Step 4: Install Rod tool J 34013-38 or equivalent, to help guide the strut shaft from the upper mount assembly.

e. Step 5: Loosen the spring compressor tool until the coil spring and mount can be removed as an assembly.

Remove the lower spring insulator, if equipped.

To install:

6. Assemble the strut as follows:

a. Step 1: Strut into a spring compressor.

b. Step 2: Lower insulator, coil spring and upper mount.

c. Step 3: Compress the coil spring while guiding the strut shaft through the upper mount, using tool J 34013-38 or equivalent.

d. Step 4: Upper nut. Torque the nut

to 55 ft. lbs. (75 Nm) while holding the strut shaft with a socket.

e. Step 5: Strut assembly from the spring compressor

7. Install or connect the following:

• Strut. Torque the 3 nuts to 18 ft. lbs. (24 Nm).

• Electronic ride control electrical connector, if removed

• Strut-to-knuckle bolts. Torque the bolts to 140 ft. lbs. (190 Nm).

• Brake line bracket to the strut

- Wheel speed sensor bracket to the strut
- ABS front wheel speed sensor connector
- Front wheel. Torque the lug nuts to 100 ft. lbs. (140 Nm).

8. Check and adjust the wheel alignment.

Shock Absorber

REMOVAL & INSTALLATION

Rear

1. Before servicing the vehicle, refer to the precautions in the beginning of this section.

2. Remove the trunk side cover or the rear seat cushion and seat back, as required, to gain access to the upper strut mounting nuts.

3. Using a floor jack and a block of wood, support the lower control arm.

4. Remove or disconnect the following:
- Rear wheel
- 2 upper shock absorber mounting nuts
- Electronic Leveling Control (ELC), if equipped

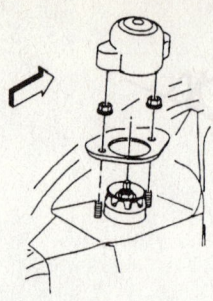

7922UG21

Remove the cover to gain access to the upper shock absorber mounting components—rear suspension

- Air tube from the shock absorber
- Lower shock absorber bracket-to-knuckle bolts
- Computer Control Ride (CCR) electrical connector, if equipped
- Shock absorber

To install:

5. Install or connect the following:
- CCR electrical connector, if equipped

➡ **As the shock absorber is positioned, be sure the CCR wiring is routed properly.**

- Shock absorber and loosely thread the upper shock absorber mounting nuts
- Sway bar bracket and the lower shock absorber bracket-to-knuckle bolts
- Upper shock absorber mounting nuts. Torque the nuts to 30 ft. lbs. (41 Nm).
- Strut bracket-to-knuckle bolts. Torque the bolts to 140 ft. lbs. (190 Nm).
- ELC, if equipped

6. For ELC equipped vehicles, lightly pressurize the ELC system by momentarily grounding terminal "B" at the height sensor connector before lowering the vehicle.

7. Install or connect the following:
- Air tube
- Rear wheel. Torque the lug nuts to 100 ft. lbs. (140 Nm).

8. Check, if necessary, adjust the wheel alignment.

Coil Spring

REMOVAL & INSTALLATION

❋❋ CAUTION

The coil springs are under a considerable amount of tension. Be very careful when removing or installing them; they can exert enough force to cause very serious injury.

Front

For front coil spring service, please refer to the front strut procedure.

Rear

1. Before servicing the vehicle, refer to the precautions in the beginning of this section.

2. Remove or disconnect the following:
- Rear wheel
- Height sensor link from the right control arm, if equipped with Electronic Leveling Control (ELC), if removing the right side coil spring
- Parking brake cable retaining clip from the left control arm, if removing the left side coil spring
- Rear sway bar link from the bracket on the knuckle, if equipped

3. Mount a Control Arm Support Adapter tool J-23028-01 or equivalent, on a transmission jack and position to cradle the control arm bushings.

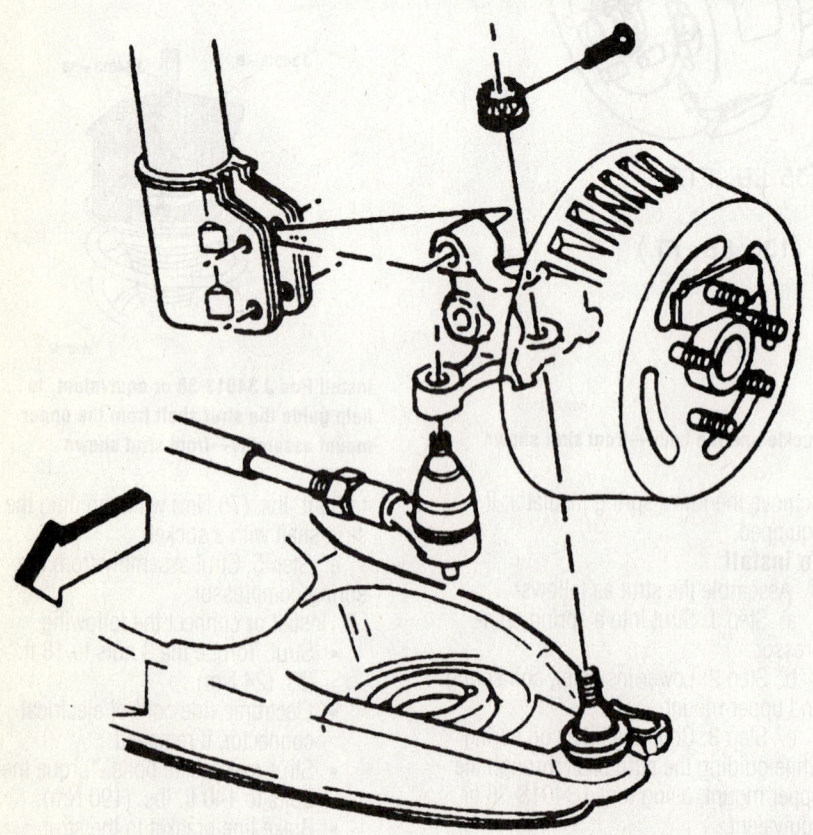

7922UG22

Exploded view of the lower shock absorber mounting to the knuckle assembly—rear suspension

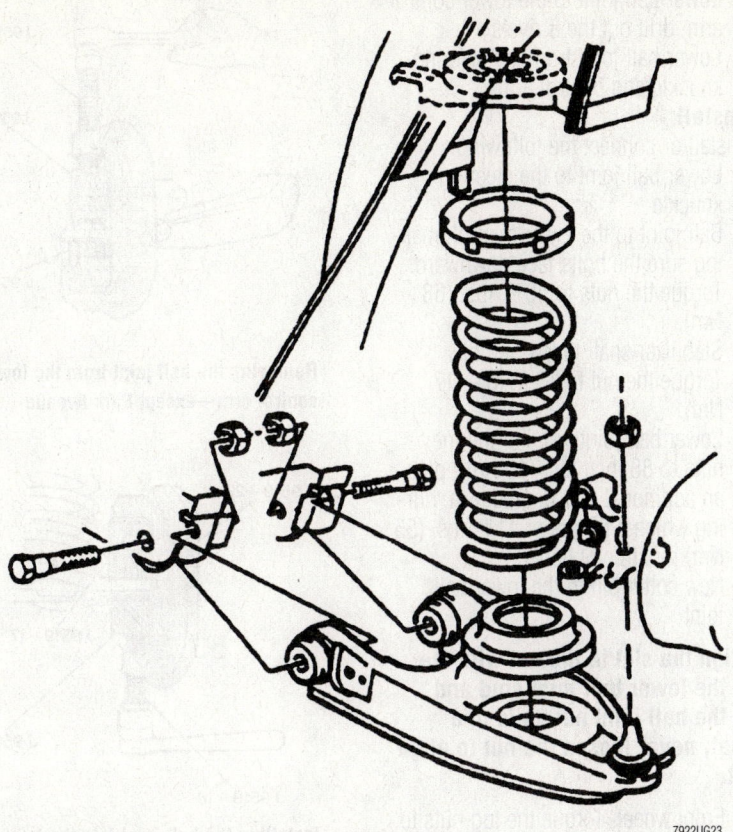

7922UG23

Exploded view of the rear coil spring mounting—H body

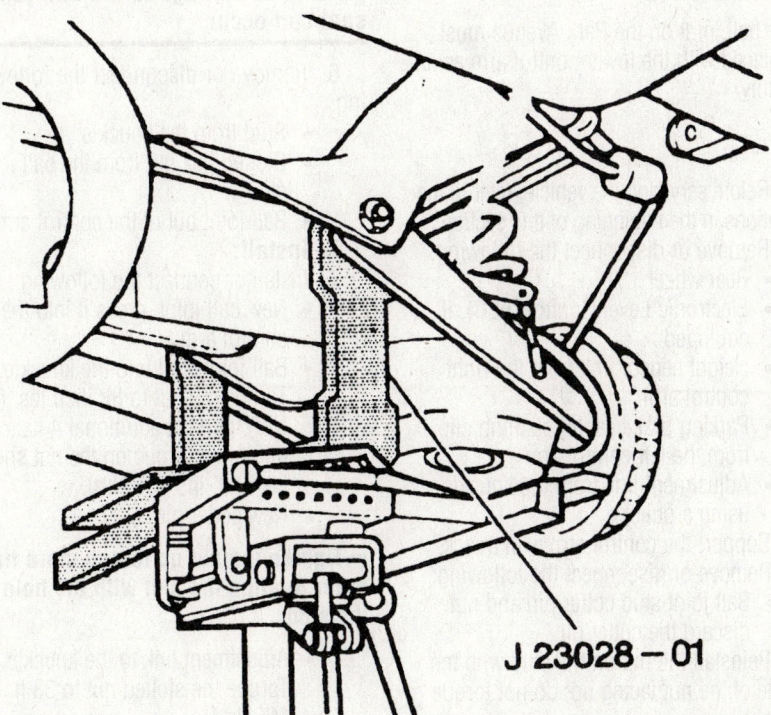

J 23028 — 01

7922UG24

Use a support bracket such as tool J-23028-01 mounted on a jack to support the rear lower control arm—H body

⁂ CAUTION

Tool J-23028-01 or equivalent, must be secured to the jack or personal injury could result.

4. Place a chain around the spring and through the control arm as a safety measure.

5. Raise the jack to remove tension from the control arm pivot bolts.

6. Remove the rear nut and through-bolt.

7. Slowly maneuver the jack to relieve tension from the front control arm bolt.

8. Remove the front nut and through-bolt.

➡**Do not apply force to the control arm and/or ball joint to remove the spring. Proper maneuvering of the spring will allow for easy removal.`**

9. Lower the jack to pivot the control arm downward. When all compression is removed from the spring, remove the safety chain, spring and insulators.

10. Inspect the spring insulators and replace them if they are cut or torn. If the vehicle has been driven more than 50,000 miles, replace them regardless of condition.

To install:

11. Snap the upper insulator onto the spring.

12. Position the lower insulator and spring in the vehicle.

13. Using the jack and tool J-23028-01 or equivalent, raise the control arm into place.

14. Maneuver the jack to permit installation of the control arm bolts and nuts.

➡**DO NOT torque the nuts until the weight of the vehicle is on the suspension.**

15. Install or connect the following:
- Rear sway bar to the knuckle bracket with the link assembly if equipped, do not torque the link bolt
- Height sensor link to the right control arm or connect the parking brake cable retaining clip to the left control arm, as required
- Rear wheel. Torque the lug nuts to 100 ft. lbs. (140 Nm).

16. With the vehicle resting on its wheels, torque the control arm through-bolt nuts to 85 ft. lbs. (115 Nm).

17. Torque the sway bar link bolt to 13 ft. lbs. (17 Nm).

18. Check, if necessary, adjust the rear wheel alignment.

19. Road test the vehicle for proper operation.

Lower Ball Joint

REMOVAL & INSTALLATION

Front

EXCEPT PARK AVENUE

✳✳ WARNING

If the ball joint is separated for related suspension/drive line service, the ball joint seal should be inspected for damage. A damaged seal will cause ball joint failure. The ball joint should be replaced if seal damage is found.

1. Before servicing the vehicle, refer to the precautions in the beginning of this section.
2. Allow the control arms to hang free.
3. Remove or disconnect the following:
   - Front wheel
   - Cotter pin from the lower ball joint and loosen the nut
   - Ball joint from the steering knuckle, using Separator tool J 36226
   - Stabilizer shaft link assembly

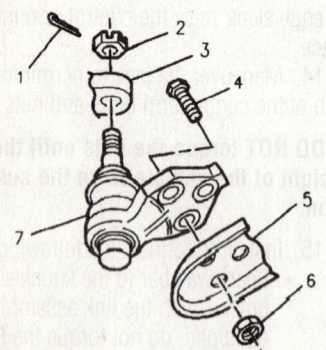

1 PIN
2 NUT, BALL JOINT TO KNUCKLE; TIGHTEN TO 10 Nm (88 LB. IN.) THEN TIGHTEN 2 FLATS TO 55 Nm (41 LB. FT.), MIN.
3 KNUCKLE
4 BALL JOINT MOUNTING BOLTS MUST FACE DOWN
5 CONTROL ARM
6 BALL JOINT MOUNTING NUTS 68 Nm (59 LB. FT.)
7 SERVICE BALL JOINT

7922UG25

The replacement ball joint should be attached to the control arm using 3 bolts and nuts—except Park Avenue

- Lower ball joint to the lower control arm, drill out the 3 rivets
- Lower ball joint from the steering knuckle and control arm

To install:

4. Install or connect the following:
   - Lower ball joint to the steering knuckle
   - Ball joint to the lower control, making sure the bolts face downward. Torque the nuts to 50 ft. lbs. (68 Nm).
   - Stabilizer shaft link assembly. Torque the nut to 13 ft. lbs. (17 Nm).
   - Lower ball joint nut. Torque the nuts to 88 inch lbs. (10 Nm); plus an additional 120 degree turn, during which a torque of 41 ft. lbs. (55 Nm) must be obtained.
   - New cotter pin to the lower ball joint

➡**To align the slot in the nut with the hole in the lower ball joint stud and tighten the ball joint nut up to one more flat, never loosen the nut to align the slot.**

   - Front wheel. Torque the lug nuts to 100 ft. lbs. (140 Nm).
5. Check and adjust the wheel alignment.

PARK AVENUE

The ball joint on the Park Avenue must be replaced with the lower control arm as an assembly.

Rear

1. Before servicing the vehicle, refer to the precautions in the beginning of this section.
2. Remove or disconnect the following:
   - Rear wheel
   - Electronic Level Control (ELC), if equipped
   - Height sensor link from the right control arm
   - Parking brake cable retaining clip from the left control arm
   - Adjustment link from the knuckle, using a puller
3. Support the control arm with a jack.
4. Remove or disconnect the following:
   - Ball joint stud cotter pin and nut, discard the cotter pin
5. Reinstall the nut on the stud with the flat side of the nut facing up; do not torque the nut.

✳✳ WARNING

Use only the recommended tools to remove the ball joint stud from the

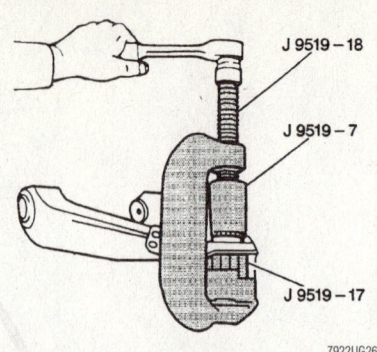

Removing the ball joint from the lower control arm—except Park Avenue

7922UG26

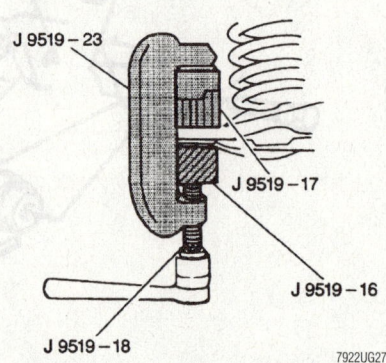

Installing the ball joint into the lower control arm—except Park Avenue

7922UG27

knuckle or damage to the ball joint or seal can occur.

6. Remove or disconnect the following:
   - Stud from the knuckle
   - Slotted hex nut from the ball joint stud
   - Ball joint out of the control arm

To install:

7. Install or connect the following:
   - New ball joint, press it into the control arm
   - Ball joint stud into the knuckle. Torque the nut to 88 inch lbs. (10 Nm), plus an additional 4 flats. The minimum torque on the nut should be 40 ft. lbs. (55 Nm).
   - New cotter pin

➡**Tighten the nut up to one more flat in order to align the slot with the hole in the stud.**

   - Adjustment link to the knuckle. Torque the slotted nut to 33 ft. lbs. (45 Nm).
   - New cotter pin.

➡**Tighten the nut up to one more flat in order to align the slot with the hole in the stud.**

- ELC, if equipped
- Height sensor link to the right control arm
- Parking brake cable retainer to the left control arm
- Rear wheel

Lower Control Arm

REMOVAL & INSTALLATION

Front

✳✳ WARNING

If the ball joint is separated for related suspension/drive line service, the ball joint seal should be inspected for damage. A damaged seal will cause ball joint failure. The ball joint should be replaced if seal damage is found.

1. Before servicing the vehicle, refer to the precautions in the beginning of this section.
2. Allow the control arms to hang free.
3. Remove or disconnect the following:
   - Front wheel
   - Stabilizer shaft link assembly from the control arm
   - Cotter pin from the lower ball joint and remove the nut

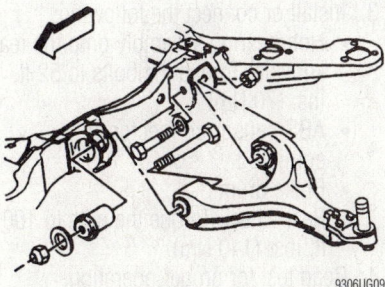

Lower control arm assembly—except Park Avenue

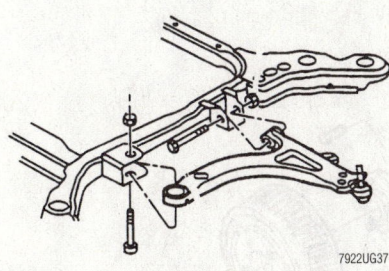

Lower control arm mounting—Park Avenue

- Ball joint from the steering knuckle
- Lower control arm from the frame

To install:

4. Install or connect the following:
   - Lower control arm to the frame

➡ **Do not Torque the lower control arm nuts at this time. The weight of the vehicle must be supported by the control arms, since the vehicle design trim heights are obtained before torque the lower control arm mounting nuts.**

- Ball joint stud to the steering knuckle. Torque the lower ball joint nut to 88 inch lbs. (10 Nm), then an additional 120 degree turn, during which a torque of 41 ft. lbs. (55 Nm) must be obtained.
- New cotter pin

➡ **Align the slot in the nut with the hole in the lower ball joint stud. Torque the ball joint nut up to one more flat, never loosen the nut to align the slot.**

- Stabilizer shaft link assembly. Torque the nuts to 13 ft. lbs. (17 Nm).
- Front wheel. Torque the lug nuts to 100 ft. lbs. (140 Nm).

5. Torque the front lower control arm mounting nut to 140 ft. lbs. (190 Nm) and the rear lower control arm nut to 91 ft. lbs. (123 Nm).
6. Check and adjust wheel alignment.

Rear

1. Before servicing the vehicle, refer to the precautions in the beginning of this section.
2. Remove or disconnect the following:
   - Rear wheel
   - Height sensor
   - Stabilizer link assembly from the control arm
   - Cotter pin from the lower ball joint and the nut, if equipped
   - Ball joint from the steering knuckle, if equipped
   - Lower control arm from the frame bolts

To install:

3. Install or connect the following:
   - Lower control arm to the frame
   - Ball joint from the steering knuckle, if equipped
   - New cotter pin from the lower ball joint and the nut, if equipped
   - Stabilizer link assembly from the control arm
   - Height sensor
   - Rear wheel

CONTROL ARM BUSHING REPLACEMENT

Except Park Avenue

1. Before servicing the vehicle, refer to the precautions in the beginning of this section
2. Remove or disconnect the following:
   - Front wheel
   - Lower control arm and place it in a vise
3. Assemble bolt, washer and bearing of the Remover/Installer tool J21474-19 through Bushing Driver tool J21474-13 with small end facing bushing.
4. Assemble the Bushing Receiver tool J21474-5 on the front of the bushing.
5. Thread tool J21474-18 onto bolt of the Remover/Installer tool J21474-19, after installed into control arm bushing.
6. Tighten until the bushing is removed
7. Remove the bushing and the tool.

To install:

8. Lubricate the outer case of the new bushing.
9. Insert the new bushing into control arm.
10. Assemble bolt, washer and bearing of Remover/Installer tool J21474-19 through Bushing Driver tool J21474-5 with large end facing bushing.
11. Assemble the larger end of tool J21474-13 facing the bushing.

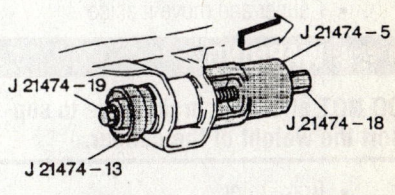

Removing the bushing from the control arm, using tools J 21474-5, J 21474-13, J 21474-18, J 21474-19

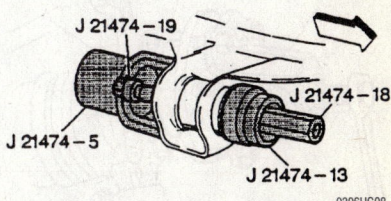

Installing the bushing into the control arm, using tools J21474-5, J 21474-13, J 21474-18, J 21474-19

Turn to Section 5 for brake system applications

12. Connect tool J21474-18 to the threads of the Remover/Installer tool J21474-19.

13. Tighten bolt of Remover/Installer tool J21474-19 until bushing is fully seated.

14. Install the lower control arm.

15. Front wheel

Park Avenue

The lower control arm is replaced as a unit.

Wheel Bearings

ADJUSTMENT

The wheel bearings are not adjustable. If a wheel bearing is out of specifications, it must be replaced. Using a dial indicator, check for looseness. If play exceeds 0.005 inch (0.127mm), the bearing wear is excessive and the hub/bearing should be replaced.

REMOVAL & INSTALLATION

Front

1. Before servicing the vehicle, refer to the precautions in the beginning of this section.

2. Remove or disconnect the following:
   • Front wheel

➡ **Insert a drift punch through the caliper and into the rotor cooling fins to prevent the rotor from turning.**

   • Halfshaft nut and washer
   • Caliper and move it aside

✻✻ WARNING

DO NOT allow the brake hose to support the weight of the caliper.

   • Brake rotor
   • Anti-Lock Brake Systems (ABS) speed sensor
   • 3 hub/bearing assembly bolts
   • Dust shield

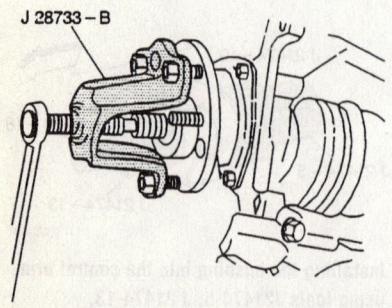
J 28733 – B

7922UG29

Use a puller such as J 2873-B to press the halfshaft from the hub assembly

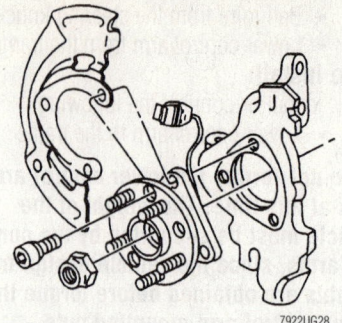
7922UG28

Exploded view of the front hub and wheel bearing assembly

3. Place the transaxle selector in the **P** detent.

4. Remove or disconnect the following:
   • Hub/bearing assembly from the halfshaft, using a puller
   • Hub/bearing assembly from the steering knuckle

To install:

➡ **The hub/bearing assembly is replaced only as an assembly.**

5. Install the hub/bearing assembly over the halfshaft splines. Be sure the splines engage smoothly.

6. Apply a light coating of grease to the steering knuckle bore.

7. Slide the hub assembly onto the halfshaft as far as possible. If the hub will not bottom out on the halfaxle, install the hub mounting bolts and use the halfshaft nut to draw the hub onto the halfshaft.

8. Once the hub is flush with the steering knuckle, remove the mounting bolts and install the dust shield.

9. Install or connect the following:
   • Mounting bolts. Torque to 70 ft. lbs. (95 Nm).

10. Place the transaxle in **N**.

11. Install or connect the following:
   • ABS front wheel speed sensor connector and clip to the dust shield

   • Brake rotor
   • Caliper. Torque the bolts to 38 ft. lbs. (51 Nm).

12. Insert a drift punch through the rotor to prevent the halfshaft from turning.

13. Torque the halfshaft nut to 107 ft. lbs. (145 Nm).

14. Remove the drift punch.

15. Install the front wheels. Torque the lug nuts to 100 ft. lbs. (140 Nm).

16. Road test the vehicle.

Rear

1. Before servicing the vehicle, refer to the precautions in the beginning of this section.

2. Remove or disconnect the following:
   • Rear wheel
   • Brake drum
   • Anti-Lock Brake Systems (ABS) sensor wire, if equipped

✻✻ WARNING

The hub assembly mounting bolts also secure the backing plate assembly. Once the bolts are removed, the backing plate must be supported with wire or other means. Do not allow the brake line or ABS electrical wire support the brake assembly.

   • 4 hub/bearing assembly bolts and the hub assembly

To install:

3. Install or connect the following:
   • Hub/bearing assembly onto the rear knuckle. Torque the bolts to 52 ft. lbs. (70 Nm).
   • ABS sensor connector, if equipped
   • Brake drum
   • Rear wheel. Torque the nuts to 100 ft. lbs. (140 Nm).

4. Road test for proper operation.

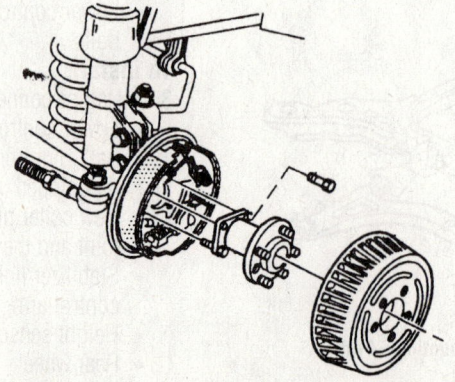
7922UG30

Exploded view of the rear hub/wheel bearing assembly

GENERAL MOTORS CORPORATION—E & K-BODIES

29

Cadillac-Deville • Concours • Eldorado • Seville

PRECAUTIONS

Before servicing any vehicle, please be sure to read all of the following precautions, which deal with personal safety, prevention of component damage, and important points to take into consideration when servicing a motor vehicle:

• Never open, service or drain the radiator or cooling system when the engine is hot; serious burns can occur from the steam and hot coolant.

• Observe all applicable safety precautions when working around fuel. Whenever servicing the fuel system, always work in a well-ventilated area. Do not allow fuel spray or vapors to come in contact with a spark, open flame, or excessive heat (a hot drop light, for example). Keep a dry chemical fire extinguisher near the work area. Always keep fuel in a container specifically designed for fuel storage; also, always properly seal fuel containers to avoid the possibility of fire or explosion. Refer to the additional fuel system precautions later in this section.

• Fuel injection systems often remain pressurized, even after the engine has been turned **OFF**. The fuel system pressure must be relieved before disconnecting any fuel lines. Failure to do so may result in fire and/or personal injury.

• Brake fluid often contains polyglycol ethers and polyglycols. Avoid contact with the eyes and wash your hands thoroughly after handling brake fluid. If you do get brake fluid in your eyes, flush your eyes with clean, running water for 15 minutes. If eye irritation persists, or if you have taken brake fluid internally, IMMEDIATELY seek medical assistance.

• The EPA warns that prolonged contact with used engine oil may cause a number of skin disorders, including cancer! You should make every effort to minimize your exposure to used engine oil. Protective gloves should be worn when changing oil. Wash your hands and any other exposed skin areas as soon as possible after exposure to used engine oil. Soap and water, or waterless hand cleaner should be used.

• All new vehicles are now equipped with an air bag system, often referred to as a Supplemental Restraint System (SRS) or Supplemental Inflatable Restraint (SIR) system. The system must be disabled before performing service on or around system components, steering column, instrument panel components, wiring and sensors. Failure to follow safety and disabling procedures could result in accidental air bag deployment, possible personal injury and unnecessary system repairs.

• Always wear safety goggles when working with, or around, the air bag system. When carrying a non-deployed air bag, be sure the bag and trim cover are pointed away from your body. When placing a non-deployed air bag on a work surface, always face the bag and trim cover upward, away from the surface. This will reduce the motion of the module if it is accidentally deployed. Refer to the additional air bag system precautions later in this section.

• Clean, high quality brake fluid from a sealed container is essential to the safe and proper operation of the brake system. You should always buy the correct type of brake fluid for your vehicle. If the brake fluid becomes contaminated, completely flush the system with new fluid. Never reuse any brake fluid. Any brake fluid that is removed from the system should be discarded. Also, do not allow any brake fluid to come in contact with a painted surface; it will damage the paint.

• Never operate the engine without the proper amount and type of engine oil; doing so WILL result in severe engine damage.

• Timing belt maintenance is extremely important! Many models utilize an interference-type, non-freewheeling engine. If the timing belt breaks, the valves in the cylinder head may strike the pistons, causing potentially serious (also time-consuming and expensive) engine damage. Refer to the maintenance interval charts in the front of this manual for the recommended replacement interval for the timing belt, and to the timing belt section for belt replacement and inspection.

• Disconnecting the negative battery cable on some vehicles may interfere with the functions of the on-board computer system(s) and may require the computer to undergo a relearning process once the negative battery cable is reconnected.

• When servicing drum brakes, only disassemble and assemble one side at a time, leaving the remaining side intact for reference.

• Only an MVAC-trained, EPA-certified automotive technician should service the air conditioning system or its components.

ENGINE REPAIR

Alternator

REMOVAL

Eldorado, 1997–99 Deville, 1997 Seville

1. Before servicing the vehicle, refer to the precautions in the beginning of this section.
2. Drain cooling system.
3. Remove or disconnect the following:
   • Negative battery cable
   • Accessory drive belt
   • Upper mounting bolt
   • Engine slash shield
   • Radiator support access panel
   • Rear alternator bracket from engine
   • Mounting bolts
   • Duct on back of alternator
   • Wires
   • Bracket
   • Alternator

1998 Seville, 2000–01 Deville

1. Before servicing the vehicle, refer to the precautions in the beginning of this section.
2. Drain cooling system.
3. Remove or disconnect the following:
   • Negative battery cable
   • Accessory drive belt
   • Radiator
   • Alternator cooler outlet hose retaining bolt
   • Alternator cooler inlet hose
   • Wires
   • Mounting bolts
   • Alternator

1999–01 Seville

1. Before servicing the vehicle, refer to the precautions in the beginning of this section.
2. Drain cooling system.
3. Remove or disconnect the following:
   • Negative battery cable
   • Accessory drive belt
   • Cooling fans
   • Alternator cooler outlet hose retaining bolt
   • Alternator cooler inlet hose
   • Wires

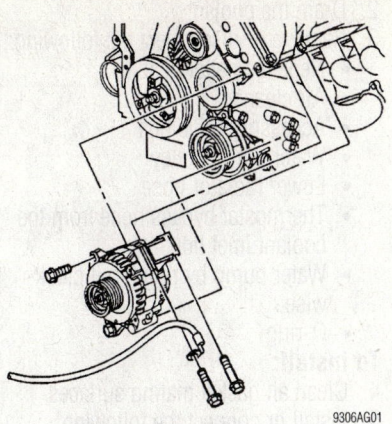

9306AG01

Alternator mounting and wires

- Mounting bolts
- Alternator

INSTALLATION

Eldorado, 1997–99 Deville, 1997 Seville

1. Install or connect the following:
   - Alternator
   - Bracket. Torque the bolt to 35 ft. lbs. (47 Nm).
   - Wires. Torque the nut to 15 ft. lbs. (20 Nm).
   - Duct on the back of the alternator
   - Mounting bolts. Torque the bolt to 35 ft. lbs. (47 Nm).
   - Upper front bolt. Torque the upper bolt to 35 ft. lbs. (47 Nm).
   - Rear bracket. Torque the bolt to 35 ft. lbs. (47 Nm).
   - Radiator support access panel
   - Engine splash shield
   - Accessory belt drive
   - Negative battery cable
2. Refill the cooling system

1998 Seville, 2000–01 Deville

1. Install or connect the following:
   - Alternator
   - Mounting bolts. Torque the bolt to 37 ft. lbs. (50 Nm).
   - Wires. Torque the nut to115 inch lbs. (13 Nm).
   - Alternator cooler inlet hose
   - Alternator cooler outlet hose. Torque the bolt to 80 inch lbs. (9 Nm).
   - Radiator
   - Accessory drive belt
   - Negative battery cable
2. Refill cooling system

1999–01 Seville

1. Install or connect the following:
   - Alternator. Torque the bolt to 37 ft. lbs. (50 Nm).
   - Wires. Torque the nut to 115 inch lbs. (13 Nm).
   - Alternator cooler inlet hose
   - Alternator cooler outlet hose. Torque the bolt to 80 inch lbs. (9 Nm).
   - Cooling fans
   - Accessory drive belt
   - Negative battery cable
2. Refill the cooling system

Ignition Timing

ADJUSTMENT

The 4.6L Northstar engine is equipped with a Distributorless Ignition System (DIS). The system consists of 2 Crankshaft Position (CKP) sensors, crankshaft reluctor ring, Camshaft Position (CMP) sensor, ignition control module, 4 ignition coils, 8 plug wires and spark plugs, knock sensor and the Powertrain Control Module (PCM).

The base ignition timing is determined by the relationship of the CKP sensors to the crankshaft reluctor ring. This relationship is not adjustable. Base ignition timing is 10 degrees Before Top Dead Center (BTDC).

The PCM controls spark advance under all driving conditions. The PCM incorporates a permanent spark control override, which electronically lowers the base timing if spark knock (detonation) is encountered during normal operation due to the use of low octane fuel.

Engine Assembly

REMOVAL & INSTALLATION

1. Before servicing the vehicle, refer to the precautions in the beginning of this section.
2. Drain the cooling system.
3. Discharge refrigerant from the air conditioning system.
4. Relieve fuel pressure.
5. Drain the crankcase.
6. Remove or disconnect the following:
   - Negative battery cable
   - Air cleaner assembly
   - Left and right torque struts and place the left front strut bolt back into the bracket
   - Radiator hoses at the water crossover
   - Cooling fans from the engine
   - Cruise control servo connections
   - Idle Speed Control (ISC) motor connectors
   - Throttle cable from the throttle body cam
   - Shift cable from the park/neutral switch
   - Cable bracket at the transaxle
   - Park/neutral switch connector and the power brake vacuum hose
   - Fuel inlet and return lines
   - Fuel line retainer at the transaxle case
   - Coolant reservoir
   - Heater hoses from the front of the right cylinder head
   - Temperature switch
   - Starter
   - Power steering pump pressure and return lines at the cooler
   - Power steering line retainer from the right front of the crankcase
   - Engine harness connectors from the Power Control Module (PCM)
   - Wiring harness retainer screws at the cowl and pull the engine harness through
   - Refrigerant high temperature switch
   - Engine harness on the left wheel housing

➡ **The engine portion of the harness will be removed with the engine.**

   - Serpentine drive belt
   - Front wheels
   - Oil cooler lines at the oil filter adapter
   - Exhaust Y-pipe
   - Coupling between the steering rack and the column
   - Speed sensitive steering solenoid and the knock sensor
   - Power steering switch
   - Lower ball joints and stabilizer links (the struts will stay in the vehicle)
   - Air conditioning hoses from the accumulator and the condenser
7. Move Powertrain Dolly into position and support for removal.
8. Remove or disconnect the following:
   - 6 engine cradle mounting bolts and the powertrain assembly by lifting the vehicle or lowering the table
   - Torque converter splash shield and the 4 converter-to-flywheel bolts
   - Engine from the transaxle

To install:

9. Install or connect the following:
   - Engine to the transaxle. Torque the bolts to 55 ft. lbs. (75 Nm).
   - Torque converter splash shield and the 4 converter-to-flywheel bolts
   - Exhaust manifolds. Torque the bolts to 18 ft. lbs. (25 Nm).
   - Transaxle to oil pan brace
10. With the powertrain on the dolly, move the assembly into position and lower the vehicle over the powertrain.
11. Install or connect the following:
   - Engine cradle-to-body bolts. Torque them to 75 ft. lbs. (100 Nm).
   - Oil cooler lines at the oil filter adapter
   - Exhaust Y-pipe
   - Steering rack to column coupling
   - Speed sensitive steering solenoid and the knock sensor
   - Power steering switch
   - Air conditioning hoses to the accumulator and the condenser
   - Lower ball joint and the stabilizer shaft link
   - Anti-Lock Brake System/ Traction Control Switch (ABS/TCS) assembly to the engine cradle
   - Engine harness connectors at the Power Control Module (PCM)
   - Refrigerant high temperature switch
   - Engine harness connector on the left wheel housing
   - Power steering line retainer to the right front of the crankcase
   - Power steering pump pressure and return lines at the cooler
   - Starter
   - Temperature switch
   - Engine harness connector on the left wheel housing
   - Coolant reservoir and the reservoir hoses
   - Fuel line retainer at the transaxle case
   - Fuel inlet and return lines
   - Park/neutral switch connector and the power brake vacuum hose
   - Cable bracket at the transaxle
   - Shift cable to the park/neutral switch
   - Throttle cable to the throttle body cam
   - Idle Speed Control (ISC) motor connectors
   - Cruise control servo connections
   - Cooling fans to the engine
   - Radiator hoses at the water crossover
   - Right and left torque struts. Torque the retainer bolts as follows:

➡**It is important during installation that the engine torque struts are not pre-loaded in their installed position. Adjustment is provided at the point the strut fastens to the core support bracket. Be sure this bolt is loose during assembly.**

12. Tighten the engine torque struts as follows:
   a. Step 1: Torque the strut bracket-to-cylinder head (M10) bolt: 35 ft. lbs. (50 Nm).
   b. Step 2: Torque the strut bracket-to-water manifold (M8) bolts: 20 ft. lbs. (25 Nm).
   c. Step 3: Torque to 45 ft. lbs. (60 Nm).
   d. Step 4: Torque the strut-to-core support bracket bolt: 45 ft. lbs. (60 Nm).
13. Install or connect the following:
   - Air cleaner
   - Negative battery cable
14. Evacuate and recharge the air conditioning system.
15. Refill the cooling system and engine crankcase.
16. Run the engine and check for leaks.

➡**A wheel alignment is recommended after the removal of the sub-frame assembly.**

Water Pump

REMOVAL & INSTALLATION

1. Before servicing the vehicle, refer to the precautions in the beginning of this section.

2. Drain the coolant.
3. Remove or disconnect the following:
   - Negative battery cable
   - Air cleaner
   - Accessory drive belt
   - Water pump pulley
   - Lower radiator hose
   - Thermostat bypass hose from the coolant inlet housing
   - Water pump by rotating it clockwise
   - O-ring

To install:

4. Clean all gasket mating surfaces.
5. Install or connect the following:
   - New O-ring seal
   - Water pump by turning it counterclockwise until it stops. Torque the bolts to 88 inch lbs. (10 Nm).
   - Water pump pulley, tighten the bolts finger-tight
   - Lower radiator hose
   - Thermostat bypass hose to the coolant inlet housing
   - Accessory drive belt
   - Water pump pulley. Torque the bolts to 115 inch lbs. (13 Nm).
   - Air cleaner
   - Negative battery cable
6. Refill and bleed the cooling system.
7. Run the engine and check for leaks.

Cylinder Head

REMOVAL & INSTALLATION

➡**The manufacturer recommends that the entire powertrain be removed from**

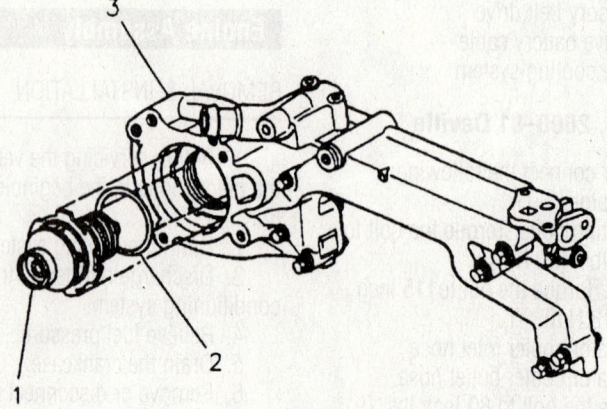

1	WATER PUMP ASSEMBLY
2	O-RING SEAL
3	WATER PUMP HOUSING ASSEMBLY

7922VG01

To ensure proper operation, be sure to install a new O-ring

the vehicle before removing the cylinder heads.

1. Before servicing the vehicle, refer to the precautions in the beginning of this section.

2. Drain the cooling system.

3. Properly relieve the fuel system pressure.

4. Remove or disconnect the following:
- Negative battery cable
- Powertrain assembly
- Intake manifold
- Cam covers
- Harmonic balancer
- Timing chain front cover
- Oil pump

❉❉ WARNING

Align all timing marks before performing the next step.

- Chain tensioner from the timing chain
- Cam sprockets

➡ **The timing chain remains in the chain case.**

- Timing chain guides, access for the retaining screws is through the plugs at the front of the cylinder head
- Water crossover
- Exhaust manifold
- Cylinder head bolts by reversing the torque sequence
- Cylinder head and discard the gasket

❉❉ WARNING

With the camshafts remaining in the cylinder head some valves will be open at all times. Do not rest the cylinder head on a flat service with the cylinder face down, or valve damage will result.

➡ **Clean all gasket mating surfaces. Clean the head bolt holes in the crankcase.**

❉❉ WARNING

Be careful when cleaning aluminum gasket surfaces to prevent damage to the sealing surfaces.

5. Check the cylinder head for warpage; it must be less than 0.002 in. (0.05mm). If the cylinder head was resurfaced, the dimension between the combustion chamber gauge pad and the deck surface must be at least 10.5mm.

To install:

➡ **Refer to Section 1 of this manual for the cylinder head torque sequence illustration. The illustration is located after the Torque Specification Chart.**

6. Install or connect the following:
- New cylinder head gasket
- Cylinder head, lubricate the bolts with engine oil

7. Torque the M11 bolts, in sequence, as follows:
   a. Step 1: 22 ft. lbs. (30 Nm).
   b. Step 2: Turn an additional 60 degrees.
   c. Step 3: Turn an additional 60 degrees (total 180 degrees).

8. Torque the M6 bolts to 106 inch lbs. (12 Nm).

9. Set the camshaft timing

10. Camshaft guide bolt access hole plugs in the cylinder heads. The plugs should be seated and snug

11. Install or connect the following:
- Intake cam covers
- Oil pump
- Timing chain front cover
- Harmonic balancer
- Cam sprockets
- Chain tensioner to the timing chain
- Timing chain guides
- Intake manifold
- Water crossover
- Exhaust manifold. Torque the nuts to 22 ft. lbs. (30 Nm) or the bolts to 18 ft. lbs. (25 Nm).
- Powertrain assembly
- Negative battery cable

12. Fill the cooling system.

13. Evacuate and charge the air conditioning system.

14. Run the engine and check for leaks.

Intake Manifold

REMOVAL & INSTALLATION

1. Before servicing the vehicle, refer to the precautions in the beginning of this section.

➡ **Refer to Section 1 of this manual for the intake manifold torque sequence illustration. The illustration is located after the Torque Specification Chart.**

2. Relieve the fuel system pressure.

3. Drain the cooling system.

4. Remove or disconnect the following:
- Negative battery cable
- Engine cover by removing the 4 nuts
- Inlet duct from the throttle body
- Transaxle vent hose and the transaxle shift cable at the bracket
- Throttle Position (TP) sensor and the Idle Air Control (IAC) valve connectors
- Throttle cable and the cruise control cable from the throttle body
- Throttle body coolant hoses and the surge tank pipe
- Exhaust Gas Recirculation (EGR) pipe and the crankcase ventilation pipe from the throttle body
- Brake booster vacuum hose from the intake manifold
- Fuel rail ground wire from the rear cylinder head
- Quick-disconnect fuel rail fittings using tool J-37088-A, insert the tool J-37088-A into the female connector and push inward to release the locking tabs and pull the connection apart
- Fuel rail bracket from the EGR valve
- Positive Crankcase Ventilation

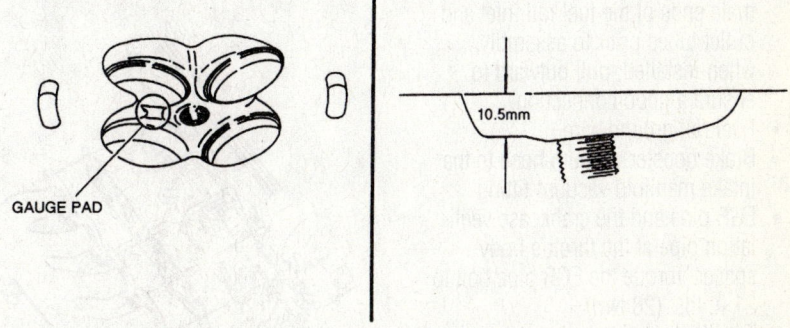

GAUGE PAD

10.5mm

7922VG04

Minimum head resurface dimension

Timing belt service is covered in Section 4 of this manual

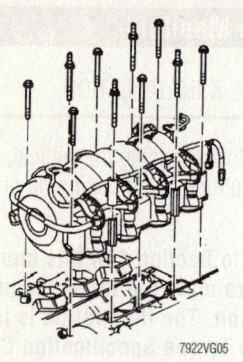

7922VG05

Exploded view of the intake manifold mounting—4.6L engine

(PCV) hose from the intake manifold
- Fuel injector harness connector
- Intake manifold

➡ **The intake manifold carrier gaskets are attached to the intake manifold through a snap-lock feature. When removing the intake manifold, the carrier gaskets will remain attached to the intake manifold. DO NOT replace the intake manifold gaskets after intake manifold removal. The gaskets are reusable. The gaskets should be replaced if the plastic housing or the rubber seals are damaged.**

To install:

5. Install or connect the following:
- Intake manifold. Torque the bolts and studs to 89 inch lbs. (10 Nm). Start at the center of the manifold and work outward in a circular pattern. DO NOT torque the intake manifold bolts when the engine is HOT or at operating temperature.
- Fuel injector harness connector
- PCV hose to the intake manifold
- Fuel bracket at the EGR valve
- Fuel lines to the fuel rail, apply a few drops of clean engine oil to the male ends of the fuel rail inlet and outlet tubes prior to assembly, when installed, pull outward to ensure a good connection.
- Fuel rail ground wire
- Brake booster vacuum hose to the intake manifold vacuum fitting
- EGR pipe and the crankcase ventilation pipe at the throttle body spacer. Torque the EGR pipe bolt to 21 ft. lbs. (28 Nm).
- Throttle body coolant hoses and the surge tank pipe
- Throttle cable and the cruise control cable to the throttle body

- TP sensor and the IAC valve connectors
- Transaxle vent hose and the transaxle shift cable at the bracket
- Inlet duct to the throttle body
- Negative battery cable

6. Turn the ignition switch to **RUN** and inspect for fuel leaks.

7. Install the engine cover. Torque the cover nuts to 89 inch lbs. (10 Nm).

8. Fill and bleed the cooling system.

9. Road test the vehicle.

Exhaust Manifold

REMOVAL & INSTALLATION

Left Side

1. Before servicing the vehicle, refer to the precautions in the beginning of this section.

2. Remove or disconnect the following:
- Negative battery cable
- Radiator cover panel
- Air cleaner assembly
- Left and right engine torque struts and position aside
- Engine cooling fans

3. Support the engine using Engine Support Fixture J-28467-A.

4. Remove or disconnect the following:
- Engine mount-to-engine cradle nuts
- Engine mount bracket-to-crankcase bolts
- Engine mount bracket-to-cylinder head bolts
- Engine mount-to-mount bracket nuts
- Y-pipe from the front of the catalytic converter

5. Raise the engine using the engine support fixture.

6. Remove or disconnect the following:

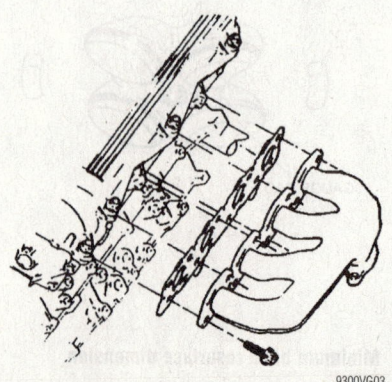

9300VG03

Exploded view of the left exhaust manifold

- Engine mount and bracket
- Rear alternator bracket
- Manifold outlet flange bolts
- Oxygen (O$_2$S) sensor
- Exhaust manifold and discard the gasket

7. Thoroughly clean the gasket mating surfaces.

To install:

8. Install or connect the following:
- New gasket to the manifold
- Exhaust manifold by inserting the outlet pipe partially into the exhaust crossover pipe. Torque all the bolts to 18 ft. lbs. (25 Nm).
- O$_2$S sensor by coating the threads with high temperature anti-seize compound. Torque the sensor to 30 ft. lbs. (40 Nm).
- O$_2$S sensor harness
- Rear alternator bracket. Torque the bolts to 40 ft. lbs. (60 Nm).
- Alternator bolts. Torque them to 25 ft. lbs. (30 Nm).
- New bolts manifold outlet flange. Torque them to 25 ft. lbs. (30 Nm).
- Engine mount and bracket

9. Lower the engine into position guiding the engine mount studs in the cradle holes and loosely install the fasteners.

10. Install or connect the following:
- Engine mount-to-engine cradle nuts. Torque the bolts to 22 ft. lbs. (30 Nm).
- Engine mount bracket-to-crankcase bolts. Torque the bolts to 22 ft. lbs. (30 Nm).
- Engine mount bracket-to-cylinder head bolts. Torque the bolts to 22 ft. lbs. (30 Nm).
- Engine mount-to-mount bracket nuts. Torque the bolts to 22 ft. lbs. (30 Nm).
- Converter-to-exhaust Y-pipe. Torque the bolts to 20 ft. lbs. (25 Nm).

11. Remove the engine support fixture.

12. Install or connect the following:
- Engine cooling fans
- Air cleaner assembly
- Left and right engine torque struts. Torque them to 44 ft. lbs. (60 Nm).

➡ **Be sure to Torque the bolts that attach the struts to the core support bracket last.**

- Radiator cover panel
- Negative battery cable

13. Run the engine and check for exhaust leaks.

Right Side

1. Before servicing the vehicle, refer to the precautions in the beginning of this section.

2. Remove or disconnect the following:
- Negative battery cable
- Oxygen (O2S) sensor at the rear of the right cam cover and harness clip
- Y-pipe from the front of the catalytic converter
- Suspension position sensor from the lower control arm at both sides
- Intermediate shaft from the steering gear

3. Place a support below the rear crossmember of the engine cradle and remove the 4 cradle to body bolts.

4. Lower the rear of the engine cradle.

5. Remove or disconnect the following:
- Y-pipe from the exhaust crossover and manifold
- Manifold
- Gasket

6. Thoroughly, clean all the gasket surfaces.

To install:

7. Install or connect the following:
- O2S sensor by coating the threads with hi-temperature anti-seize compound. Torque the sensor to 30 ft. lbs. (40 Nm).
- New gasket
- Exhaust manifold. Torque the nuts to 25 ft. lbs. (30 Nm).
- Y-pipe using 4 new bolts. Torque the M10 bolts to 35 ft. lbs. (50 Nm) and the M8 bolts to 25 ft. lbs. (30 Nm).
- Engine cradle, raise it into position. Torque the bolts to 75 ft. lbs. (100 Nm).
- Intermediate shaft to the steering

gear. Torque the bolts to 35 ft. lbs. (50 Nm).
- Y-pipe to the catalytic converter. Torque the bolts to 35 ft. lbs. (50 Nm).
- Suspension position sensors to the lower control arms
- O2S sensor harness clip
- Negative battery cable

8. Run the engine and check for exhaust leaks.

Camshaft and Valve Lifters

REMOVAL & INSTALLATION

Left Side

1. Before servicing the vehicle, refer to the precautions in the beginning of this section.

2. Drain the coolant.

3. Remove or disconnect the following:
- Negative battery cable
- Upper radiator hose at the water crossover
- Spark plug wires
- Right-side fan
- Battery cable at the alternator and

the cable harness at the cam cover and move aside
- Positive Crankcase ventilation (PCV) fresh air tube from the cam cover
- Right and left torque struts
- Water pump drive belt and pulley
- Camshaft seal retainer screws and discard the seal if damaged
- Cam cover by moving the cam drive end of the cover up, then pivot the entire cover around the water pump driveshaft. Continue moving the cover upward and pivoting so that the edge of the cover closely follows the left edge of the intake manifold cover.

➡**The spark plug seals may be reused if undamaged.**

4. Secure the cam sprocket to the timing chain by installing tie-wraps through the cam sprocket holes. Use 4 tie-wraps per sprocket.

➡**The sprocket/chain relationship must be maintained throughout this procedure or camshaft timing will be lost and require further engine disassembly to retime.**

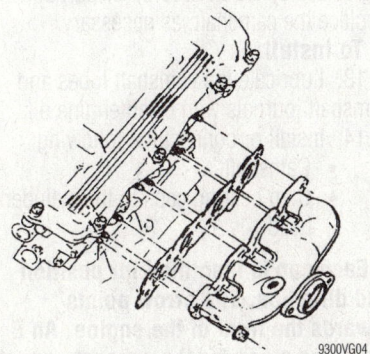

Exploded view of the right exhaust manifold

9300VG04

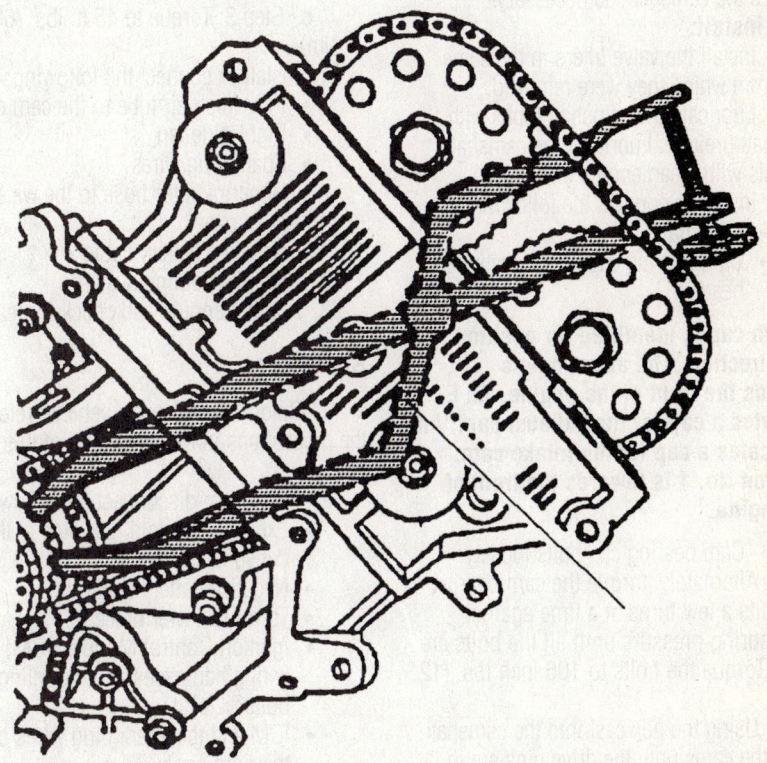

Use the Camshaft Chain Holder tool J-38822 to keep the chain in position while removing the camshafts

9300VG01

5. Working from behind the sprockets, install Camshaft Chain Holder J-38222 so that it is positioned between the chain tensioner and chain guide. Apply tension to the tool by tightening the tension adjusting screw.

6. Remove or disconnect the following:
- Cam sprocket bolts, note the relative location of the cam drive pins in the end of the camshafts
- Sprockets off the cams using play in the chain

➡**Alternately loosen the cam bearing cap screws a few turns at a time until all valve spring pressure has been released.**

- Camshaft bolts and caps
- Camshaft
- Valve lifters and store the lifters on their camshaft face so that the residual oil is retained

➡**Retain the valve lifters in order so that they can be installed in the same bores.**

7. Inspect the lifters for wear and/or damage; replace as necessary.

8. Inspect the camshaft for excessive lobe wear. Check the bearing journals, making sure they are not scored or burned. Replace the camshaft, as necessary.

To install:

9. Install the valve lifters in the same bore from which they were removed.

10. Lubricate the camshaft lobes with camshaft prelube. Lubricate the camshaft journals with clean engine oil.

11. Install or connect the following:
- Camshaft
- Cam bearing caps to the cylinder head

➡**Each cap is identified for position and direction. The arrow points towards the front of the engine. An E indicates a cap for the exhaust cam. An I indicates a cap for the intake cam. Position No. 1 is towards the front of the engine.**

- Cam bearing cap bolts loosely

12. Alternately, torque the cam bearing cap bolts a few turns at a time against valve spring pressure until all the bolts are snug. Torque the bolts to 106 inch lbs. (12 Nm).

13. Using the hex cast into the camshaft, rotate the cams until the drive pins are in position to engage the cam sprockets over the cams, and install the retaining bolts.

14. Install the cam sprockets. Torque the bolts to 90 ft. lbs. (120 Nm).

15. Remove the Chain Holder tool J-38222

16. Remove the tie-wraps from the cam sprockets

17. Install or connect the following:
- Cam cover. Torque the screws to 89 inch lbs. (10 Nm).
- Battery cable retainer to the front of the cam cover
- Battery cable at the alternator

18. Lubricate the seal lips and install the camshaft seal to the end of the intake cam. Seal the screw threads with sealer.

19. Install or connect the following:
- Water pump pulley with tool J-38825
- Drive belt

20. Install the right and left torque struts and torque the retaining bolts as follows:

➡**It is important during installation that the engine torque struts are not preloaded in their installed position. Adjustment is provided at the point the strut fastens to the core support bracket. Be sure this bolt is loose during assembly.**

   a. Step 1: Strut bracket to cylinder head (M10) bolt: 35 ft. lbs. (50 Nm).

   b. Step 2: Strut bracket to water manifold (M8) bolts: 20 ft. lbs. (25 Nm).

   c. Step 3: Torque to 45 ft. lbs. (60 Nm)

21. Install or connect the following:
- PCV fresh air tube to the cam cover
- Right-side fan
- Spark plug wires
- Upper radiator hose to the water crossover
- Negative battery cable

22. Refill the cooling system.

23. Run the engine and check for leaks.

Right Side

1. Before servicing the vehicle, refer to the precautions in the beginning of this section.

2. Remove or disconnect the following:
- Exhaust manifold rear pipe at the converter
- Negative battery cable
- Tower-to-tower brace
- Ignition Control Module (ICM) wiring harnesses and mounting bolts
- ICM and the spark plug wires on the right bank
- Positive Crankcase Ventilation (PCV) valve
- Purge canister solenoid from the rear of the camshaft cover

- Wiring harness from the camshaft cover
- Cam cover screws

3. Support the front of the engine cradle

4. Remove or disconnect the following:
- Mounting screws at the front of the cradle
- Right and left torque struts

5. Lower the engine cradle or raise the vehicle to provide clearance at the rear of the engine compartment.

6. Remove the camshaft cover and discard if damaged

➡**The spark plug seals may be reused if undamaged.**

7. Secure the cam sprocket to the timing chain by installing tie-wraps through the cam sprocket holes. Use 4 tie-wraps per sprocket.

➡**The sprocket/chain relationship must be maintained throughout this procedure or camshaft timing will be lost and require further engine disassembly to retime.**

8. Working from behind the sprockets, install Camshaft Chain Holder J-38222 so that it is positioned between the chain tensioner and chain guide. Apply tension to the tool by tightening the tension adjusting screw.

9. Remove or disconnect the following:
- Both cam sprocket bolts. Note the relative location of the cam drive pins in the end of the camshafts.
- Sprockets off the camshafts

10. Alternately loosen the cam bearing cap screws a few turns at a time until all valve spring pressure has been released. Remove the bolts and caps.

11. Remove or disconnect the following:
- Camshaft bolts and caps
- Camshaft

12. Inspect the camshaft for excessive lobe wear. Check the bearing journals, making sure they are not scored or burned. Replace the camshaft, as necessary.

To install:

13. Lubricate the camshaft lobes and camshaft journals with clean engine oil.

14. Install or connect the following:
- Camshaft
- Cam bearing caps to the cylinder head

➡**Each cap is identified for position and direction. The arrow points towards the front of the engine. An E indicates a cap for the exhaust cam. An I indicates a cap for the intake cam. Position No. 1 is towards the front of the engine.**

- Cam bearing cap bolts loosely

15. Alternately, torque the cam bearing cap bolts a few turns at a time against valve spring pressure until all the bolts are snug. Torque the bolts to 106 inch lbs. (12 Nm).

16. Using the hex cast into the camshaft, rotate the cams until the drive pins are in position to engage the cam sprockets over the cams and install the retaining bolts.

17. Install the camshaft sprockets. Torque the bolts to 90 ft. lbs. (120 Nm).

18. Remove the Chain Holder tool J-38222

19. Remove the tie-wraps from the cam sprockets

20. Install or connect the following:
- Spark plug and cam cover seals, as required
- Cam cover. Torque the screws to 84 inch lbs. (10 Nm).
- Engine cradle, raise it into position. Torque both bolts to 75 ft. lbs. (100 Nm).

21. Install the right and left torque struts and torque the bolts as follows:

➥It is important during installation that the engine torque struts are not pre-loaded in their installed position. Adjustment is provided at the point the strut fastens to the core support bracket. Be sure this bolt is loose during assembly.

   a. Step 1: Strut bracket to cylinder head (M10) bolt: 35 ft. lbs. (50 Nm).
   b. Step 2: Strut bracket to cylinder head (M10) stud: 35 ft. lbs. (50 Nm).
   c. Step 3: Strut to core support bracket bolt: 45 ft. lbs. (60 Nm) (see note above).

22. Install or connect the following:
- Wiring harness to cover
- Purge canister solenoid
- PCV valve
- ICM and the spark plug wires on the right bank
- ICM wiring harnesses
- Tower-to-tower brace
- Negative battery cable
- Exhaust manifold rear pipe to the converter

23. Run the engine and check for leaks.

Valve Lash

ADJUSTMENT

The valve clearance cannot be adjusted.

Starter Motor

REMOVAL & INSTALLATION

1. Before servicing the vehicle, refer to the precautions in the beginning of this section.

2. Remove or disconnect the following:
- Both battery cables
- Intake manifold
- Knock sensor and wire
- Starter electrical connectors
- Starter

To install:

3. Install or connect the following:
- "S" terminal. Torque the nut to 26 inch lbs. (3 Nm).
- Battery cables. Torque the nut to 70 inch lbs. (8 Nm).
- Starter and mounting. Torque the bolts to 22 ft. lbs. (30 Nm).
- Knock sensor and wire

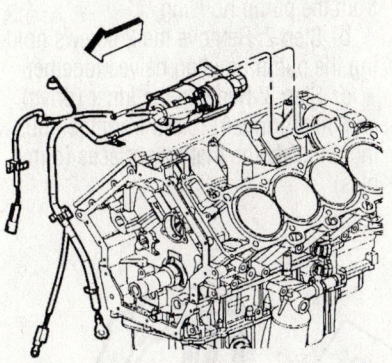

9306AG02

View of starter motor removal and wires

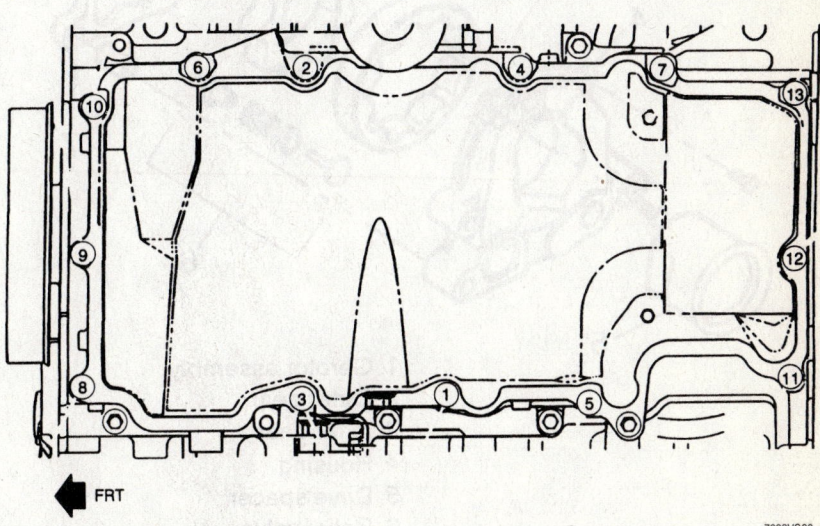

Oil pan bolt torque sequence

- Intake manifold
- Both battery cables. Torque them to 11 ft. lbs. (15 Nm).

Oil Pan

REMOVAL & INSTALLATION

1. Before servicing the vehicle, refer to the precautions in the beginning of this section.

2. Drain the crankcase.

3. Remove or disconnect the following:
- Negative battery cable
- Oil level indicator harness connector, if equipped
- Exhaust Y-pipe, if needed
- Transaxle assembly from the vehicle.
- Oil pan bolts and the oil pan

To install:

➥The oil pan gasket is reusable unless it is damaged. Do not remove the gasket from the oil pan groove unless gasket replacement is required.

4. Thoroughly clean the inside of the oil pan and the cylinder block contact surface. If the oil pan gasket is being reused, be careful not to damage it. Do not expose the gasket to cleaning solvents.

5. If a new gasket is being installed, start the gasket into the oil pan groove and work the gasket into the groove in both directions. Once the gasket is exposed to oil, it will expand and no longer stay in the groove without wrinkles. If this condition exists, replace the gasket.

7922VG08

6. Install or connect the following:
- Oil pan. Torque the bolts, in sequence, to 89 inch lbs. (10 Nm).
- Oil level indicator connector, if removed
- Transaxle assembly, if removed
- Y-pipe, if removed
- Flywheel cover, if removed
- Oil pan drain plug. Torque it to 15 ft. lbs. (20 Nm).
- Negative battery cable

7. Refill the crankcase.

8. Run the engine and check for leaks.

Oil Pump

REMOVAL & INSTALLATION

1. Before servicing the vehicle, refer to the precautions in the beginning of this section.

2. Remove or disconnect the following:
- Negative battery cable
- Drive belt
- Power steering hose retainer
- Right front wheel
- Wheel well splash shields
- Oil pan-to-transaxle brace

3. Install a flywheel holder to keep the crankshaft from turning.

4. Support the engine cradle with a jack.

5. Remove or disconnect the following:
- 3 right-side engine cradle bolts
- Crankshaft balancer bolt
- Road Sensing Suspension (RSS) sensor from the right lower control arm

6. Lower the cradle to gain access for the crankshaft balancer puller.

7. Remove or disconnect the following:
- Crankshaft balancer
- Accessory drive belt tensioner and idler pulley
- Front cover and gasket

➡The front cover gasket is reusable as long as it is not damaged.

- Oil pump mounting bolts
- Oil pump
- Drive spacer

8. If necessary, disassemble and inspect the pump as follows:

a. Step 1: Remove the drive spacer from the pump housing.

b. Step 2: Remove the 2 screws holding the pump housing halves together.

c. Step 3: Remove the inner (drive) and outer (driven) rotors from the housing. Indicate the mating surfaces (dimples).

d. Step 4: Remove the pressure relief valve.

e. Step 5: Inspect the pump housing for nicks, burrs, chips or debris that might cause a leak or binding condition in the rotor pocket.

f. Step 6: Inspect the drive and driven rotors for nicks or burrs.

g. Step 7: Check the pump cover and interior surface for excessive wear or score marks. Check for flatness.

h. Step 8: If any components show signs of excessive wear or damage, replace the pump assembly.

To install:

9. If the pump was disassembled, reassemble it, as follows:

a. Step 1: Install the inner and outer rotors to the pump cover in the same orientation as removed.

b. Step 2: Install the pressure relief valve seat, spring and pilot in the pump housing.

c. Step 3: Pack the pump housing halves with Amojell® or white petroleum grease to ensure pump priming.

d. Step 4: Assemble the housing and cover over the locating dowel.

e. Step 5: Insert a 9mm drill in the pump mounting hole on the opposite side to aid alignment of the housing and cover. Install the 2 screws and torque to 108 inch lbs. (12 Nm).

10. Install or connect the following:
- Oil pump drive spacer into the oil pump from the rear so the drive flat engages the pump rotor
- Oil pump over the crankshaft and the mounting bolts loosely

11. Hold the pump in its furthest up position. Torque the mounting bolts (1, 2 and 3), in sequence, to 89 inch lbs. (10 Nm); then, to 20 ft. lbs. (26 Nm).

12. Place a small amount of RTV sealant at the split line of the upper and lower crankcases.

13. Install or connect the following:
- Front cover gasket on the dowel pins on the block
- Front cover. Torque the bolts to 89 inch lbs. (10 Nm).
- Drive belt idler pulley. Torque the bolt to 37 ft. lbs. (50 Nm).
- Drive belt tensioner. Torque the bolt to 37 ft. lbs. (50 Nm).
- Crankshaft balancer by lubricating the bolt threads and using tool J-39344. Torque the bolt to 37 ft. lbs. (50 Nm) plus an additional 120 degree turn.
- Engine cradle, raise it into position.

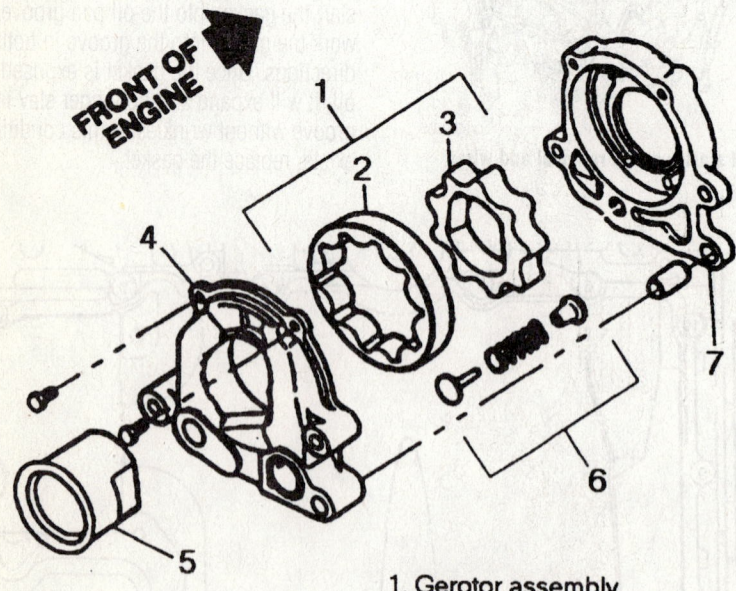

FRONT OF ENGINE

1. Gerotor assembly
2. Outer gear
3. Inner gear
4. Housing
5. Drive spacer
6. Relief valve
7. Cover

7922VG09

Exploded view of the oil pump

Torque the 3 bolts to 75 ft. lbs. (100 Nm).

14. Remove the flywheel holding tool

15. Install or connect the following:
   • RSS sensor
   • Oil pan-to-transaxle brace. Torque the bolts to 37 ft. lbs. (50 Nm).
   • Wheel well splash shields and the front wheel
   • Power steering hose retainer
   • Accessory drive belt
   • Negative battery cable

16. Run the engine and check for proper engine oil pressure. Check for leaks.

Rear Main Seal

REMOVAL & INSTALLATION

1. Before servicing the vehicle, refer to the precautions in the beginning of this section.

2. Remove or disconnect the following:
   • Transaxle
   • Flywheel
   • Rear main seal using a pry tool

✳✳ WARNING

Use care not to damage the crankshaft seal surface with a pry tool.

To install:

3. Before installing, lubricate the seal bore to seal surface with clean engine oil.

4. Install the new seal.

5. Slide the new seal over the mandrel until the dust lip bottoms squarely against the tool collar.

6. Thread the tool into the crankshaft flange and install the seal by turning the T-handle until the tool bottoms against the crankcase.

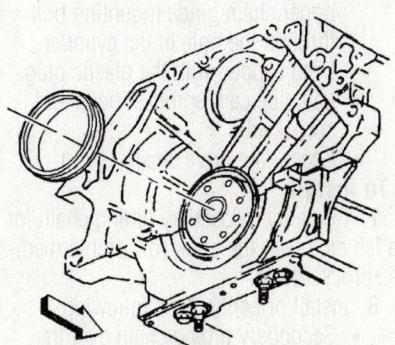

Exploded view of the rear main oil seal

7. Loosen and remove the tool from the crankshaft.

➡**Check to see that the seal is squarely seated in the bore.**

8. Install or connect the following:
   • Flywheel. Torque the bolts to 11 ft. lbs. (15 Nm) plus an additional 50 degree turn.
   • Transaxle

9. Start the engine and check for leaks.

Timing Chain, Sprockets, Front Cover And Seal

REMOVAL & INSTALLATION

The left and right-side secondary timing chains can be removed with the engine in the vehicle. If the primary timing chain or intermediate shaft sprocket need to be replaced, the engine must be removed from the vehicle and supported on an engine stand.

➡**Setting the camshaft timing is necessary whenever the cam drive system has been disturbed, meaning the relationship between any chain and**

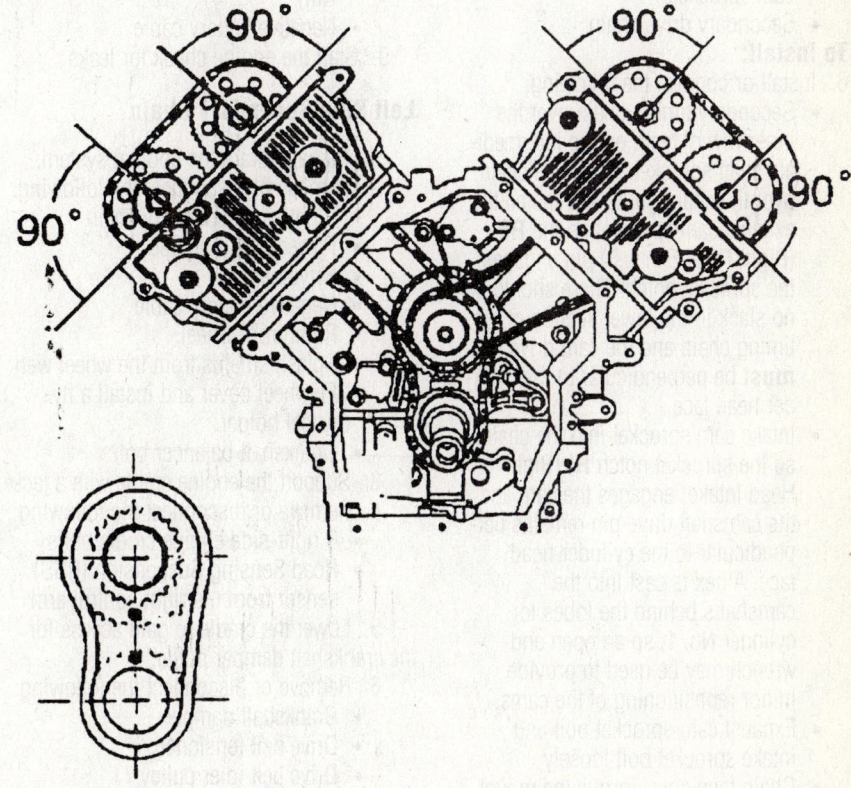

Correct timing chain alignment

sprocket has been lost. Correct timing exists when the crankshaft and intermediate shaft sprocket timing marks are in alignment and all 4 camshaft drive pins are perpendicular (90 degrees) to the cylinder head surface.

Right Side Secondary Chain

1. Before servicing the vehicle, refer to the precautions in the beginning of this section.

2. Remove or disconnect the following:
   • Exhaust Y-pipe at the converter
   • Tower-to-tower brace
   • Ignition Control Module (ICM) wiring connectors and mounting bolts
   • ICM and the plug wires on the right bank
   • Positive Crankcase Ventilation (PCV) valve
   • Purge canister solenoid from the rear of the cover
   • Cam cover screws
   • Right and left torque struts

3. Safely support the front of the engine cradle and remove the 2 mounting bolts at the front of the cradle.

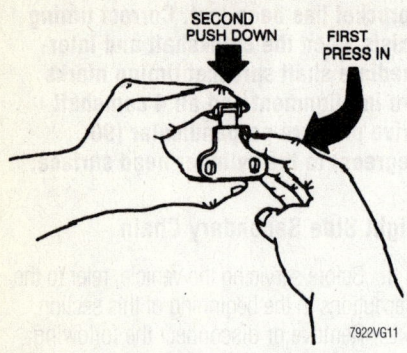

SECOND PUSH DOWN

FIRST PRESS IN

7922VG11

Rotating tensioner release lever

4. Lower the engine cradle or raise the vehicle to provide clearance at the rear of the engine compartment.

5. Remove or disconnect the following:
- Cam cover

➡**The cam cover gasket is reusable as long as it is not damaged.**

- Right side secondary chain tensioner
- Right side chain guide. Access the upper chain guide mounting bolt through the hole in the cylinder head capped with the plastic plug.
- Right side cam sprocket bolts and cam sprockets
- Secondary drive chain

To install:

6. Install or connect the following:
- Secondary timing chain over the inner row of teeth on the intermediate shaft sprocket. Route the chain over the chain guide and install the exhaust cam sprocket so the **RE** (Right Head Exhaust) pin engages the sprocket notch. There should be no slack in the lower section of the timing chain and the cam drive pin **must** be perpendicular to the cylinder head face.
- Intake cam sprocket into the chain so the sprocket notch **RI** (Right Head Intake) engages the cam and the camshaft drive pin remains perpendicular to the cylinder head face. A hex is cast into the camshafts behind the lobes for cylinder No. 1, so an open end wrench may be used to provide minor repositioning of the cams.
- Exhaust cam sprocket bolt and intake sprocket bolt loosely
- Chain tensioner. Torque the mounting bolts to 20 ft. lbs. (27 Nm).
- Camshaft sprocket bolts. Torque them to 90 ft. lbs. (120 Nm).
- Spark plug and camshaft cover seals

- Camshaft cover. Torque the screws to 84 inch lbs. (10 Nm).
- Engine cradle by raising it. Torque both bolts to 75 ft. lbs. (100 Nm).

7. Install the right and left torque struts. Torque the retaining bolts as follows:

➡**It is important during installation that the engine torque struts are not pre-loaded in their installed position. Adjustment is provided at the point the strut fastens to the core support bracket. Be sure this bolt is loose during assembly.**

a. Step 1: Strut bracket-to-cylinder head (M10) bolt: 35 ft. lbs. (50 Nm).
b. Step 2: Strut bracket-to-water manifold (M8) bolts: 20 ft. lbs. (25 Nm).
c. Step 3: Torque to 45 ft. lbs. (60 Nm).

8. Install or connect the following:
- Strut-to-core support bracket bolt. Torque it to 45 ft. lbs. (60 Nm).
- Wiring harness to the cover
- Purge canister solenoid to the rear of the cover
- PCV valve
- ICM and the wiring connectors.
- Spark plug wires on the right-bank
- Tower-to-tower brace
- Exhaust Y-pipe to the converter. Torque the bolts to 20 ft. lbs. (25 Nm).
- Negative battery cable

9. Start the engine check for leaks

Left Side Secondary Chain

1. Partially drain the coolant system.
2. Remove or disconnect the following:
- Right side secondary chain
- Power steering hose
- Drive belt
- Negative battery cable
- Right front wheel
- Splash shields from the wheel well
- Flywheel cover and install a flywheel holder
- Crankshaft balancer bolt
3. Support the engine cradle with a jack.
4. Remove or disconnect the following:
- 3 right-side engine cradle bolts
- Road Sensing Suspension (RSS) sensor from the right control arm
5. Lower the cradle to gain access for the crankshaft damper puller.
6. Remove or disconnect the following:
- Crankshaft damper
- Drive belt tensioner
- Drive belt idler pulley
- Front cover bolts
- Front cover and gasket

➡**The front cover gasket is reusable as long as it is not damaged.**

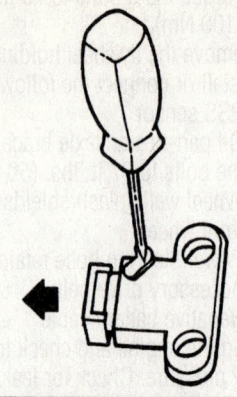

1 RELEASE TO FIRST CLICK
2 INSTALL LOCK PIN

7922VG12

Locking the tensioner in the collapsed position

- Upper radiator hose at the water crossover
- Spark plug wires and label
- Right side fan
- Battery cable at the alternator and the cable harness at the cam cover
- Positive Crankcase Ventilation (PCV) fresh air tube from the cam cover
- Right and left torque struts
- Water pump pulley
- Camshaft seal retainer screws and the seal
- Battery cable retainer at the front of the cam cover
- Cam cover by pivoting the entire cover around the water pump driveshaft. Continue moving the cover upward and pivoting so that the edge of the cover closely follows the left edge of the intake manifold cover.

➡**The cam cover gasket is reusable as long as it is not damaged.**

- Left side secondary chain tensioner
- Left side chain guide. Access the upper chain guide mounting bolt through the hole in the cylinder head capped with the plastic plug.
- Left side cam sprocket bolts and sprockets.
- Secondary drive chain

To install:

7. Route the secondary timing chain for the left side over the outer row of intermediate sprocket teeth.

8. Install or connect the following:
- Secondary timing chain over the inner row of teeth on the intermediate shaft sprocket. Route the chain over the chain guide and install the exhaust cam sprocket so the **LE**

(Left Head Exhaust) pin engages the sprocket notch. There should be no slack in the lower section of the timing chain and the cam drive pin **must** be perpendicular to the cylinder head face.

- Intake cam sprocket into the chain so the sprocket notch **LI** (Left Head Intake) engages the cam and the camshaft drive pin remains perpendicular to the cylinder head face. A hex is cast into the camshafts behind the lobes for cylinder No. 2, so an open-end wrench may be used to provide minor repositioning of the cams.
- Exhaust cam sprocket bolt and intake sprocket bolt loosely
- Chain tensioner. Torque the mounting bolts to 20 ft. lbs. (27 Nm).
- Camshaft sprocket bolts. Torque them to 90 ft. lbs. (120 Nm).

➡ **The RE cam sprocket must contain the CMP sensor pick-up.**

- Front cover gasket on the dowel pins on the block
- Front cover. Torque the bolts to 89 inch lbs. (10 Nm). Apply a dab of RTV to the split line between the upper and lower crankcase assemblies.
- Drive belt idler pulley. Torque the bolt to 35 ft. lbs. (47 Nm).
- Drive belt tensioner. Torque the nut to 35 ft. lbs. (47 Nm).
- Crankshaft balancer using tool J-39344. Torque the bolt to 44 ft. lbs. (60 Nm) plus an additional 120 degree turn.
- Engine cradle, raise it into position. Torque the bolts to 75 ft. lbs. (102 Nm).
- RSS sensor
- Wheel well splash shields

9. Remove the flywheel holding tool and install the flywheel cover.
10. Install or connect the following:
- Spark plug and camshaft cover seals
- Intake cam through the hole in the cam cover and using fingers, guide the cam cover up over the edge of the cylinder head

✳✳ WARNING

Use care to prevent the exposed section of the cam cover seal from being damaged by the edge of the cylinder head casting.

Camshaft cover into position by allowing the top edge of the cover to follow the left side edge of the intake manifold.
- Camshaft cover screws. Torque them to 84 inch lbs. (10 Nm).
- Battery cable retainer to the front of the camshaft cover
- Battery cable at the alternator
- Camshaft seal to the end of the intake camshaft. Seal the screw threads with sealer.
- Water pump pulley
- PCV fresh air tube to the cam cover
- Right side fan
- Spark plug wires
- Upper radiator hose to the water crossover

11. Refill the cooling system.

Primary Chain/Intermediate Sprocket

1. Remove or disconnect the following:
- Engine
- Accessory belt pulley and tensioner
- Front cover
- Right and left cam covers, align all marks before removal
- Timing chain tensioners
- Camshaft sprocket bolts
- Right and left secondary chains
- Intermediate shaft sprocket-to-intermediate shaft bolt and the sprocket
- Primary timing sprockets and primary chain off the engine

To install:

➡ **The following procedure must be followed to set the camshaft timing on the vehicle.**

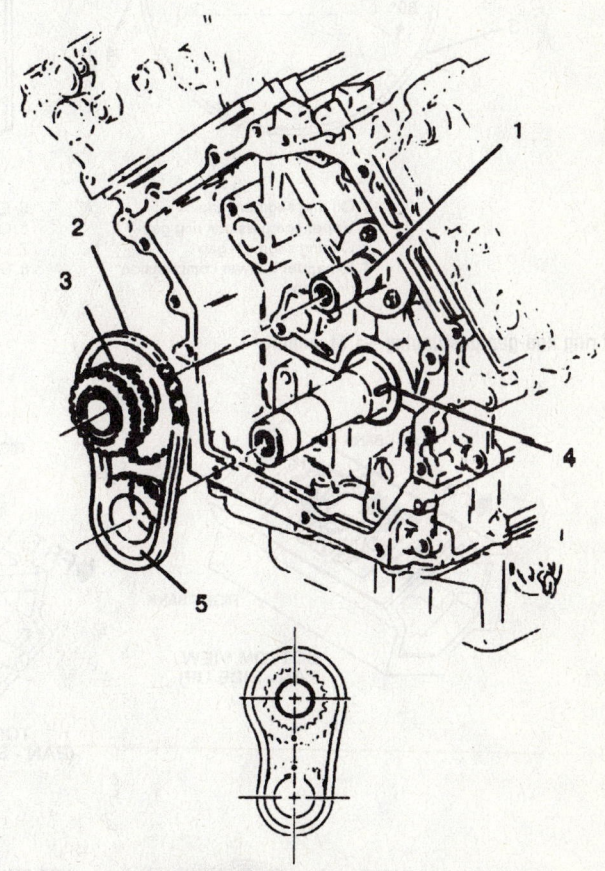

1	INTERMEDIATE SHAFT
2	PRIMARY CHAIN
3	INTERMEDIATE SHAFT SPROCKET
4	CRANKSHAFT SPROCKET KEY
5	SPROCKET

7922VG10

Primary drive chain components

For complete mechanical specifications, refer to Section 1 of this manual

2. Primary and secondary chain guide
3. Rotate the crankshaft until the sprocket drive key is at the 1 o'clock position.
4. Install or connect the following:
   - Crankshaft sprocket and intermediate shaft sprocket in the primary timing chain so the timing marks are aligned.
   - Assembly in position on the engine

➡ The crankshaft sprocket keyway will have to slide over the key on the crankshaft. If it is necessary to turn the crankshaft sprocket, the intermediate shaft sprocket will also have to be turned so the timing mark remains aligned with the crankshaft sprocket.

- Intermediate shaft sprocket-to-intermediate shaft bolt. Torque the bolt to 45 ft. lbs. (61 Nm).

- Primary timing chain tensioner. Torque the tensioner mounting bolts to 20 ft. lbs. (27 Nm).
- Flywheel holder to lock the crankshaft in position

Piston and Ring

POSITIONING

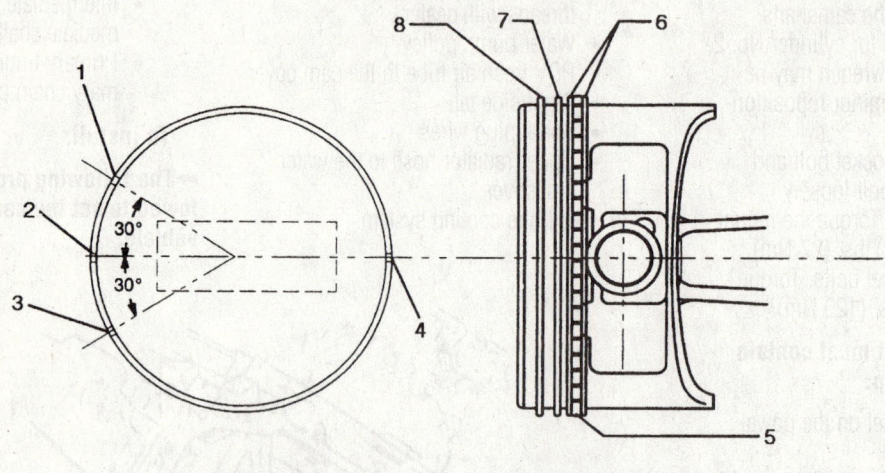

1. Oil ring segment gap
2. Upper compression ring gap
3. Oil ring segment gap
4. Expander & lower compression ring gaps

5. Expander ring
6. Oil segment rings
7. Lower compression ring
8. Upper compression ring

7922AG52

Piston ring and ring end-gap positioning—4.6L engine

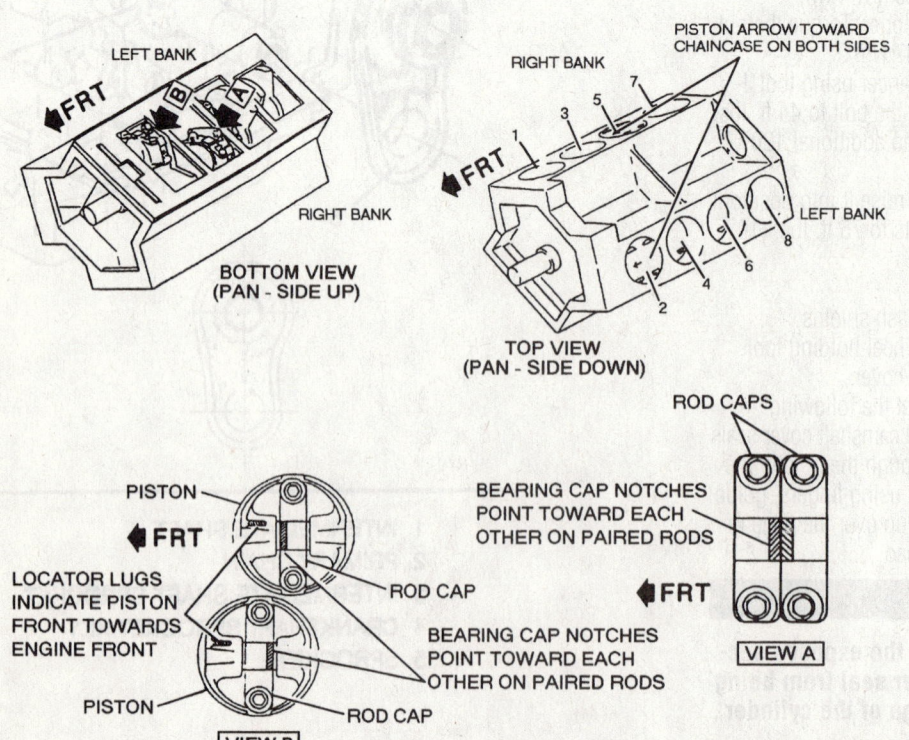

7922AG53

Piston and connecting rod assembly positioning—4.6L engine

FUEL SYSTEM

Fuel System Service Precautions

Safety is the most important factor when performing not only fuel system maintenance but also any type of maintenance. Failure to conduct maintenance and repairs in a safe manner may result in serious personal injury or death. Maintenance and testing of the vehicle's fuel system components can be accomplished safely and effectively by adhering to the following rules and guidelines.

• To avoid the possibility of fire and personal injury, always disconnect the negative battery cable unless the repair or test procedure requires that battery voltage be applied.

• Always relieve the fuel system pressure prior to disconnecting any fuel system component (injector, fuel rail, pressure regulator, etc.), fitting or fuel line connection. Exercise extreme caution whenever relieving fuel system pressure, to avoid exposing skin, face and eyes to fuel spray. Please be advised that fuel under pressure may penetrate the skin or any part of the body that it contacts.

• Always place a shop towel or cloth around the fitting or connection prior to loosening to absorb any excess fuel due to spillage. Ensure that all fuel spillage (should it occur) is quickly removed from engine surfaces. Ensure that all fuel soaked cloths or towels are deposited into a suitable waste container.

• Always keep a dry chemical (Class B) fire extinguisher near the work area.

• Do not allow fuel spray or fuel vapors to come into contact with a spark or open flame.

• Always use a back-up wrench when loosening. Torque the fuel line connection fittings. This will prevent unnecessary stress and torsion to fuel line piping.

• Always replace worn fuel fitting O-rings with new. Do not substitute fuel hose or equivalent, where fuel pipe is installed.

Fuel System Pressure

RELIEVING

✳✳ CAUTION

The fuel injection system remains under pressure, even when the engine has been turned OFF. The fuel system pressure must be relieved before disconnecting any fuel lines. Failure to do so may result in fire and/or personal injury.

1. Loosen the fuel filler cap to relieve tank vapor pressure.

✳✳ CAUTION

Observe all applicable safety precautions when working around fuel. Whenever servicing the fuel system, always work in a well-ventilated area. Do not allow fuel spray or vapors to come in contact with a spark or open flame. Keep a dry chemical fire extinguisher near the work area. Always keep fuel in a container specifically designed for fuel storage; also, always properly seal fuel containers to avoid the possibility of fire or explosion.

2. Be sure the ignition switch is in the **OFF** position.
3. Disconnect the negative battery cable.
4. Remove the engine cover.

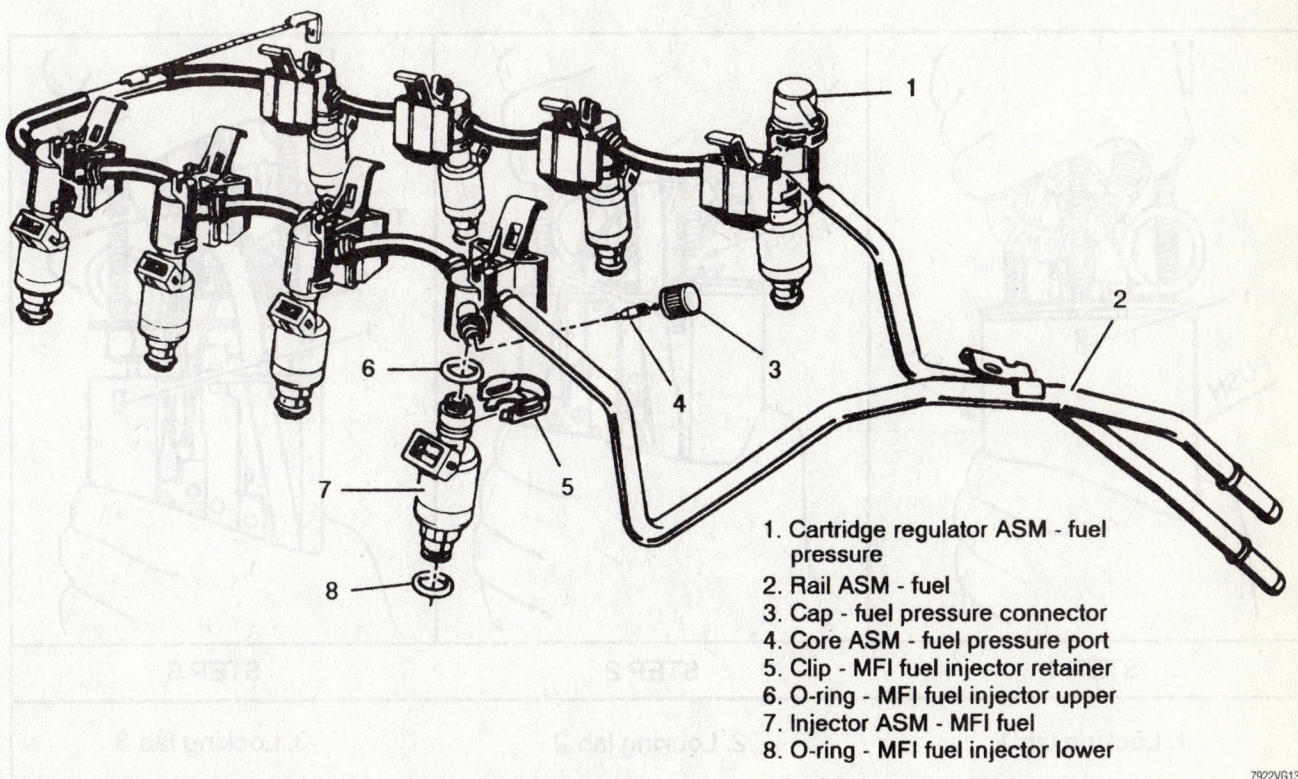

1. Cartridge regulator ASM - fuel pressure
2. Rail ASM - fuel
3. Cap - fuel pressure connector
4. Core ASM - fuel pressure port
5. Clip - MFI fuel injector retainer
6. O-ring - MFI fuel injector upper
7. Injector ASM - MFI fuel
8. O-ring - MFI fuel injector lower

View of the fuel rail assembly showing fuel system service port location

✳✳ CAUTION

There may still be residual fuel in the system, and a small amount of fuel may be released when servicing fuel lines or connections. In order to reduce the chance of personal injury, cover the fuel line fittings with a shop towel before disconnecting to catch any fuel that may leak out.

5. Install a fuel pressure gauge with a drain hose attached, J-34730–1, or equivalent. Wrap a shop towel around the fitting while connecting the gauge to avoid spillage.

6. Install the drain hose into an approved container and open the valve to drain the system pressure. Fuel connections are now safe for servicing.

7. Drain any remaining fuel from inside the gauge into the approved container.

Fuel Filter

REMOVAL & INSTALLATION

1. Before servicing the vehicle, refer to the precautions in the beginning of this section.

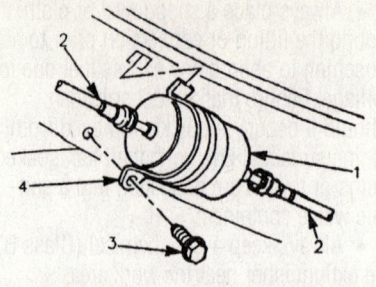

1.FUEL FILTER	3.BOLT/SCREW
2.QUICK CONNECTOR	4.FUEL FILTER BRACKET

7922VG14

Exploded view of the fuel filter mounting

2. Properly relieve the fuel system pressure.

3. Remove or disconnect the following:
- Negative battery cable
- Fuel filter retainer locking tabs
- Fuel lines from the fuel filter by releasing the locking tabs on the fuel filter quick-connects.
- Fuel filter

To install:

4. Apply a few drops of engine oil to the tips of the fuel filter.

5. Install or connect the following:
- Fuel filter in the bracket
- Fuel lines to the fuel filter and snap

the quick-connects into place. Be sure the tabs on the quick-connects lock into place.
- Locking tabs on the fuel filter retainer
- Negative battery cable

6. Turn the ignition key **ON** for 2 seconds, then **OFF** for 5 seconds. Again turn the ignition key **ON** and check for fuel leaks.

Fuel Pump

REMOVAL & INSTALLATION

➡**The modular fuel sender assembly must be disassembled in the exact order described.**

1. Before servicing the vehicle, refer to the precautions in the beginning of this section.

2. Relieve the fuel system pressure.

3. Drain the fuel tank.

4. Clean the fuel tank in the area of the modular fuel sender assembly.

5. Remove or disconnect the following:
- Fuel tank from the vehicle
- Negative battery cable
- Locking nut by turning it counter-clockwise

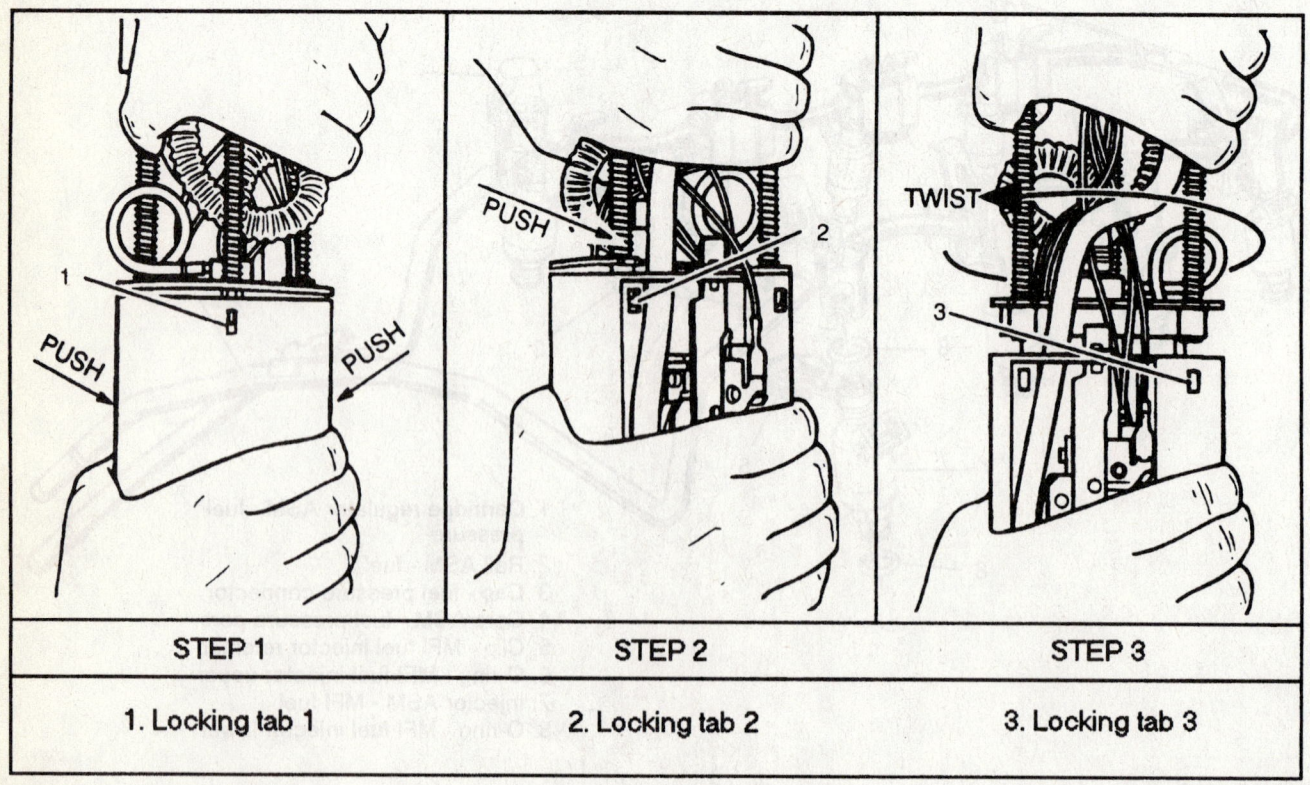

STEP 1	STEP 2	STEP 3
1. Locking tab 1	2. Locking tab 2	3. Locking tab 3

Modular fuel sender disassembly

7922VG15

- Modular fuel sender assembly from the fuel tank

❊❊ CAUTION

The modular fuel sender assembly may spring up from its position. When removing the assembly, be aware that the reservoir bucket is full of fuel. Tip the assembly slightly during removal to avoid damaging the float. Have a shop towel ready to absorb any leakage.

6. Slide the fuel sender seal downward, past the reservoir and carefully over the float arm assembly. Discard the seal.

7. Disconnect the Connector Position Assurance (CPA) clip from the wiring harness under the modular fuel sender assembly cover. Depress the black connector tabs to remove the electrical connector from the cover.

8. Locate the curved side of the modular unit's reservoir. Beginning at locking tab 1, squeeze the reservoir to release the first locking tab.

9. Moving clockwise to locking tab 2, apply gentle pressure to the guide rod to release the second locking tab.

10. At locking tab 3, gently twist and squeeze to release the reservoir from the retainer.

11. Remove or disconnect the following:
- Cover and the retainer from the reservoir. Be careful not to damage the crossover tube. The unit will still be attached by the fuel pipe and the crossover tube.
- External strainer by prying the strainer ferrule off the reservoir. Excessive force may dislodge the jet pump. Note the position of the strainer for installation reference. Discard the strainer.
- Rubber bumper pad and discard. The fuel pump and the sleeve assembly are attached to the retainer when pulled from the reservoir. Depress the flex member on the pump sleeve and rotate the sleeve counterclockwise to remove the fuel pump from the retainer. Note the orientation of the pump to the retainer.

12. Slide the lower connector assembly out of the retainer to remove the fuel pulse damper from the lower connector. Note the orientation of the seal (the modular unit is now held together by the crossover tube only). Discard the fuel pulse damper.

To install:

13. Install the fuel pulse damper

➡**Always use a new damper when installing a new fuel pump.**

14. Slide the lower connector into the retainer.

15. Push the pump outlet tube into the fuel pulse damper and rotate the flex member back to its original position. Align the pump outlet tube into the retainer opening. All 3 sleeve tabs should protrude through the retainer before rotating. Rotate the pump clockwise until a click is heard, be sure fit is snug before rotating. Place the fuel pump back into its reservoir. The crossover tube must be placed in its proper slot.

16. Install or connect the following:
- New rubber bumper pad. Insert the drain tube into the proper retainer and bumper pad slots.
- New strainer, being careful not to dislodge the jet pump
- Fuel pump wire connector, the undercover wiring harness connector and the CPA clip
- New lip seal on the modular fuel sender assembly

➡**Always use a new seal when servicing the modular fuel sender assembly. Lightly lubricate the inside diameter of the lip seal with clean engine oil. The lip seal should be positioned over the float arm assembly, moved up over the reservoir and half-way up the guide posts.**

- Modular fuel assembly into the tank. Seat the lip seal into the tank opening by aligning the arrows on top of the fuel tank to the arrow on the modular assembly.

17. Slowly apply pressure to the top of the spring-loaded sender until the lip seal is flush between the fuel tank and the modular cover.

18. Install or connect the following:
- Locking nut. Torque to 37 ft. lbs. (50 Nm).
- Fuel tank
- Negative battery cable

19. Pressurize the fuel system and verify there are no fuel leaks.

Fuel Injectors

REMOVAL & INSTALLATION

1. Before servicing the vehicle, refer to the precautions in the beginning of this section.

2. Remove or disconnect the following:
- Negative battery cable
- Fuel pressure
- Intake manifold top cover
- Fuel injector electrical connector
- Fuel rail from intake manifold
- Fuel injector
- Upper and lower O-rings and discard them

To install:

3. Install or connect the following:
- New O-rings and lubricate with clean engine oil
- Fuel injector into fuel rail
- Fuel rail into intake manifold
- Fuel injector electrical connector
- Negative battery cable

4. Inspect for fuel leaks as follows:
a. Step 1: Turn ignition switch to the ON position for 2 seconds.
b. Step 2: Turn ignition switch OFF for 10 seconds.
c. Step 3: Turn ignition switch ON.
d. Step 4: Check for leaks.

5. Install the intake manifold cover. Torque the nuts to 27 inch lbs. (3 Nm).

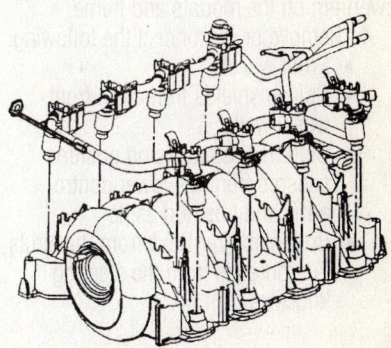

9306AG03

Exploded view of the fuel rail

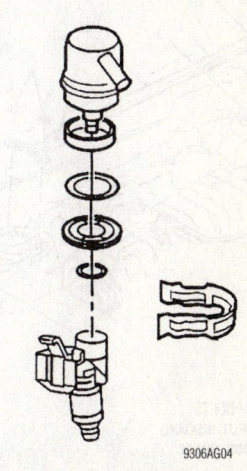

9306AG04

Exploded view of the fuel injector

DRIVE TRAIN

Transaxle Assembly

REMOVAL & INSTALLATION

1. Before servicing the vehicle, refer to the precautions in the beginning of this section.

2. Remove or disconnect the following:
   - Negative battery cable
   - Headlight housing upper filler panel and diagonal brace
   - Air cleaner assembly
   - Shift control cable and bracket at the transaxle
   - Torque struts
   - Oil cooler lines at the cooler and the oil sending line at the transaxle
   - 2 upper transaxle-to-engine bolts
   - Power steering return hose at the auxiliary cooler. Plug the cooler and return hose to prevent leakage.

3. Support the engine. Tighten the wing nuts several turns to take the weight of the powertrain off the mounts and frame.

4. Remove or disconnect the following:
   - Front wheels
   - Splash shields from both front wheel wells
   - Both front suspension position sensors from the lower control arms and position aside
   - Both stabilizer links from the struts
   - Tie rod ends from the steering knuckles
   - Lower ball joints from the steering knuckles
   - Halfshafts
   - Power steering filter at the cradle and the air conditioning splash shield from the frame
   - Anti-lock Brake System (ABS) modulator from the bracket and support
   - Engine oil pan-to-transaxle bracket
   - Torque converter cover
   - Torque converter-to-flexplate bolts by matchmarking it first.
   - Powertrain mount nuts from the cradle

5. Rotate the intermediate steering shaft until the steering gear stub shaft clamp bolt is accessible at the left wheel well. Remove the clamp bolt and disconnect the intermediate steering shaft from the steering gear.

✷✷ CAUTION

If the intermediate steering shaft is not disconnected from the steering gear stub shaft, damage to the steering gear and/or intermediate shaft may result. This damage can cause loss of steering control, which could result in personal injury.

✷✷ WARNING

Do not turn the steering wheel or move the position of the steering gear once the intermediate steering shaft is disconnected as this will off-center the air bag coil in the steering column. If the air bag coil becomes off-centered, it may be damaged during vehicle operation.

6. Disconnect the electrical harness and connector from the engine cradle.

7. Support the rear of the cradle with a jack, then remove the 4 rear cradle bolts.

8. Lower the jack a few inches to gain access to the power steering gear heat shield and return line fitting.

9. Remove or disconnect the following:
   - Heat shield
   - Return line. Plug the line and the opening in the gear to prevent fluid leakage.
   - Power steering electrical connector

10. Raise the jack and reinstall 1 rear cradle bolt on each side finger-tight to support the cradle. Remove the jack.

11. Support the frame with a jack and remove the 6 frame mount bolts. Lower the frame and/or raise the vehicle with the steering gear attached.

12. Remove or disconnect the following:
   - Electrical connectors to the transaxle
   - Vehicle Speed Sensor (VSS)
   - Transaxle harness from the transaxle clip
   - Fuel line bundle from the transaxle
   - Left and right transaxle mount and bracket from the transaxle

13. Support the transaxle with a jack.

14. Remove or disconnect the following:
   - Engine-to-transaxle heat shield and bracket
   - Remaining transaxle-to-engine bolts
   - Manual shaft linkage
   - Neutral safety switch
   - Vehicle Speed Sensor (VSS) and oil return line

To install:

15. Install or connect the following:

1 75 N•m (55 LB. FT.)
2 LOCATING PIN (NO BOLT AT THIS POSITION)
3 TIGHTEN BOLTS TWICE IN SEQUENCE TO 62 N•m (46 LB. FT.)

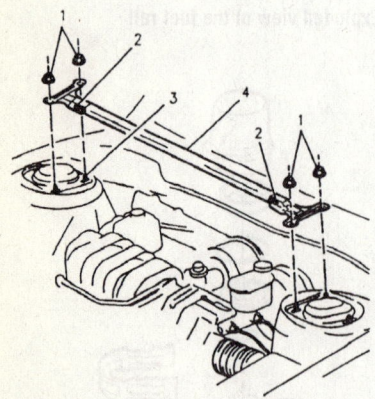

1 NUT
2 THROUGH-BOLTS
3 STUD, STRUT INBOARD
4 BAR, CROSS BRACE

7922VG16

Exploded view of the crossbrace-to-strut towers mounting

LOCATING PIN

Exploded view of the engine-to-transaxle attachments

VIEW A

7922VG17

- Oil return line and the VSS
- Neutral safety switch. Torque the bolts to 106 inch lbs. (12 Nm).
- Manual shaft linkage. Torque the manual shaft nut to 15 ft. lbs. (20 Nm).
- Transaxle. Torque the 2 lower transaxle-to-engine bolts to 35 ft. lbs. (47 Nm).
- Engine-to-transaxle bracket and heat shield. Torque the bolts to 35 ft. lbs. (47 Nm).

16. Remove the transaxle jack.
17. Install or connect the following:
- Right and left transaxle bracket and mount to the transaxle. Torque the nuts/bolts to 35 ft. lbs. (47 Nm).
- Fuel line bundle to the transaxle
- Electrical connectors to the transaxle and VSS
- Transaxle harness to the transaxle clip

18. Raise the frame and/or lower the vehicle while locating the engine and transaxle mount studs into the frame, harnesses at the cradle, and frame mount bolt holes to the underbody.
19. Install the 2 front and 2 rear cradle bolts finger-tight to support the cradle, then the cradle support.
20. Support the rear of the cradle with a jack and remove the 2 rear cradle bolts.
21. Lower the jack a few inches to gain access to the power steering gear.
22. Install or connect the following:
- Hose at the steering gear. Torque the fitting to 20 ft. lbs. (27 Nm).
- Power steering gear electrical connector
- Steering gear heat shield
- Engine cradle, raise it into position. Torque the bolts to 74 ft. lbs. (100 Nm).

➡**When tightening the engine cradle bolts, begin with the No. 2 mount-to-body bolts, followed by the No. 1 mount-to-body bolts and finally the remaining frame mount bolts.**

- Electrical harness to the front of the cradle
- Intermediate steering shaft to the steering gear and the clamp bolt. Torque the bolt to 35 ft. lbs. (47 Nm).

✳✳ WARNING

Do not turn the steering wheel or move the position of the steering

gear while the intermediate steering shaft is disconnected as this will off-center the air bag coil in the steering column. If the air bag coil becomes off-centered, it may be damaged during vehicle operation.

- Left and right transaxle mount nuts and right engine mount nuts at the frame. Torque the nuts to 35 ft. lbs. (47 Nm).
- Flexplate to the torque converter by aligning the matchmarks. Torque the bolts to 35 ft. lbs. (47 Nm).
- Torque converter cover. Torque the bolts to 106 inch lbs. (12 Nm).
- Engine oil pan-to-transaxle bracket. Torque the bolts to 35 ft. lbs. (47 Nm).
- ABS modulator to the bracket and the air conditioning splash shield at the frame
- Halfshafts. Torque the halfshaft nuts to 110 ft. lbs. (145 Nm).
- Lower ball joints into the steering knuckles, use new cotter pins
- Tie rod ends into the steering knuckles, use new cotter pins
- Stabilizer links to the struts. Torque the nuts to 49 ft. lbs. (65 Nm).
- Front suspension position sensors to the lower control arms
- Power steering filter to the cradle
- Splash shields in the wheel wells
- Wheels
- Engine support fixture
- Power steering hose at the auxiliary cooler
- Remaining transaxle-to-engine bolts. Torque to 35 ft. lbs. (47 Nm).

23. Flush the transaxle oil cooler. The transaxle oil cooler and lines should be flushed before the oil cooler lines are connected to the transaxle.
24. Install or connect the following:
- Oil cooler lines to the transaxle. Torque the fittings to 16 ft. lbs. (22 Nm).
- Torque struts
- Neutral safety switch, adjust it
- Shift control cable and bracket to the transaxle. Torque the bracket bolts to 106 inch lbs. (12 Nm). Adjust the shift control cable.
- Air cleaner assembly
- Headlight housing upper filler panel and diagonal brace
- Negative battery cable

25. Fill the transaxle. Bleed the power steering system.
26. Check and/or adjust the front alignment.
27. The PCM maintains 3 types of transaxle adapt parameters which are used to modify transaxle line pressure. The line pressure is modified to maintain shift quality regardless of wear or tolerance variations within the transaxle. Whenever the transaxle is replaced, the transaxle adapts must be reset as follows:
  a. Step 1: Turn the ignition key **ON**. Enter the self-diagnostic system.
  b. Step 2: Select PCM override PS13 (TP SENSOR LEARN).
  c. Step 3: Press the WARMER button. The Driver Information Center (DIC) should display 09, indicating that the Garage Shift Adapt value has been reset.
  d. Step 4: Select PCM override PS14 (TRAN ADAPT).
  e. Step 5: Press the COOLER button. The DIC should display 90, indicating the Upshift Adapt (UA) value has been reset.
  f. Step 6: Press the WARMER button. The DIC should display 09, indicating the Steady State Adapt (SSA) value has been reset.
28. The PCM maintains a value for transaxle oil life. This value indicates the percentage of oil life remaining and is calculated based on transaxle temperature and speed. When the vehicle is new, the transaxle oil life value is 100. As the vehicle operates, the percentage will decrease. Whenever the transaxle is replaced, the transaxle oil life indicator should be reset to 100 as follows:
  a. Step 1: Turn the ignition key ON, but leave the engine OFF.
  b. Step 2: Press and hold the OFF and REAR DEFOG buttons on the DIC until the message TRANSAXLE OIL LIFE RESET is displayed on the DIC.

Halfshaft

REMOVAL & INSTALLATION

✳✳ WARNING

Use care when removing the halfshaft to prevent the inner CV-joint from becoming over-extended. Over-extension of the joint could result in separation of internal components and possible joint failure.

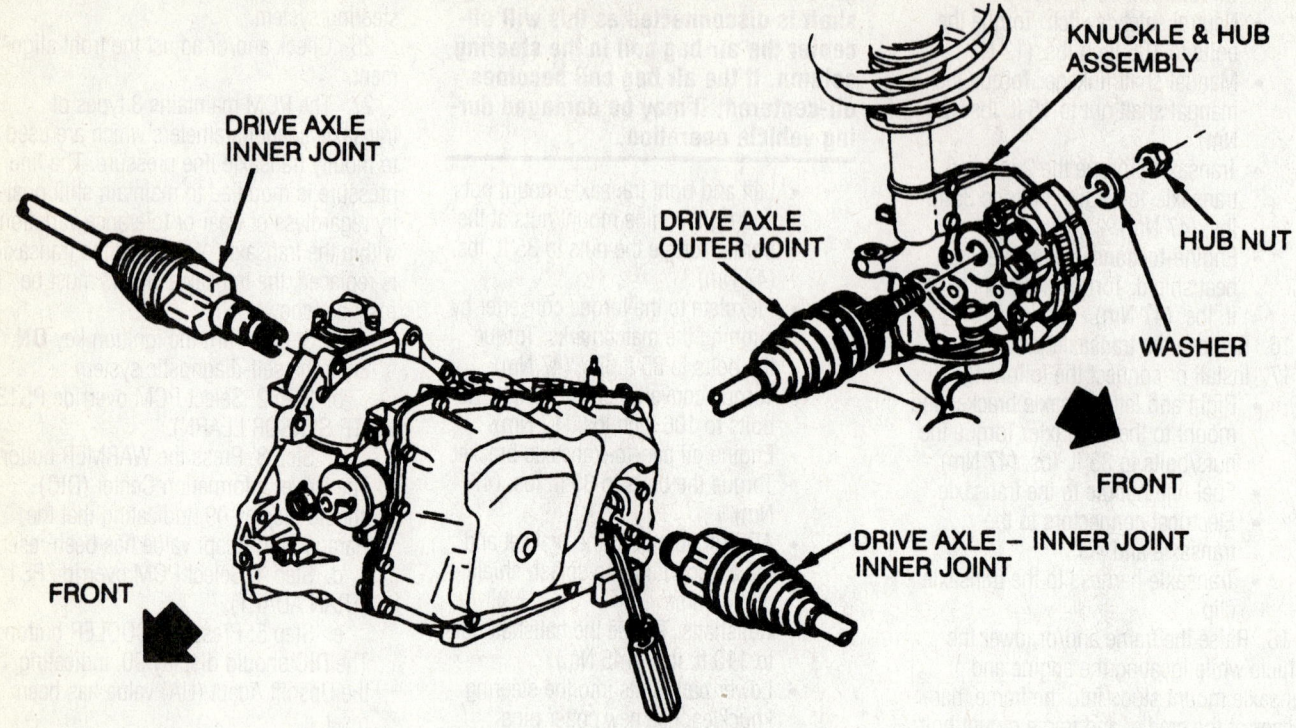

DRIVE AXLE INNER JOINT

DRIVE AXLE OUTER JOINT

DRIVE AXLE – INNER JOINT INNER JOINT

FRONT

KNUCKLE & HUB ASSEMBLY

HUB NUT

WASHER

FRONT

7922VG18

Removing the halfshaft from the transaxle

1. Before servicing the vehicle, refer to the precautions in the beginning of this section.
2. Remove the front wheel.
3. Install a boot protector on the outer CV-joint boot.
4. Remove or disconnect the following:
   • Hub nut and discard it
   • Stabilizer link, if necessary
   • Ball joint cotter pin and nut
   • Ball joint from the steering knuckle
5. Partially install the hub nut to protect the threads, then remove the halfshaft from the hub.
6. Move the strut and knuckle rearward.
7. Remove the halfshaft from the transaxle.

➡ **If equipped with anti-lock brakes, care must be used to prevent damage to the toothed sensor ring on the halfshaft and the wheel speed sensor on the steering knuckle.**

To install:

8. If installing the right-side halfshaft, install tool J-37292-B, so it can be pulled out after the halfshaft is installed.
9. Install or connect the following:
   • Halfshaft into the transaxle

➡ **To verify the halfshaft is properly seated, grasp the inner CV-joint housing and pull it outward. DO NOT pull on**

the halfshaft. If the CV-joint is properly seated, the halfshaft will not pull back out.

   • Halfshaft into the hub/bearing assembly
   • New hub nut loosely
   • Ball joint into the steering knuckle
   • Castle nut. Torque to 84 inch lbs. plus an additional 120 degrees (⅓) turn. A minimum of 37 ft. lbs. (51 Nm) of torque must be attained.

➡ **If necessary to install the cotter pin, the nut can be tightened up to 20 degrees additional. NEVER loosen the castle nut to install the cotter pin.**

   • Torque the nut to 110 ft. lbs. (149 Nm) on all models, except DeVille

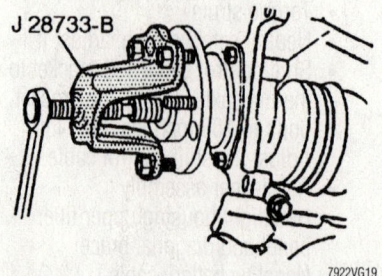

J 28733-B

7922VG19

Removing the halfshaft from the hub

with J55 brake option, in which case the torque is 130 ft. lbs. (177 Nm).
   • Stabilizer link, if removed
10. Remove the boot protector.
11. If tool J-37292-B was installed, remove it by pulling in line with the handle.
12. Install the wheel.
13. Road test and check vehicle operation.

CV-Joints

OVERHAUL

Inner (Tri-Pot) Joint

1. Before servicing the vehicle, refer to the precautions in the beginning of this section.
2. Remove or disconnect the following:
   • Front wheel
   • Halfshaft and place it in a vise
   • Snapring from the stub shaft and discard it
   • Small CV-joint boot clamp, cut and discard it
   • Large CV-joint boot clamp, cut and discard it
   • CV-joint boot by sliding it away from the tri-pot joint

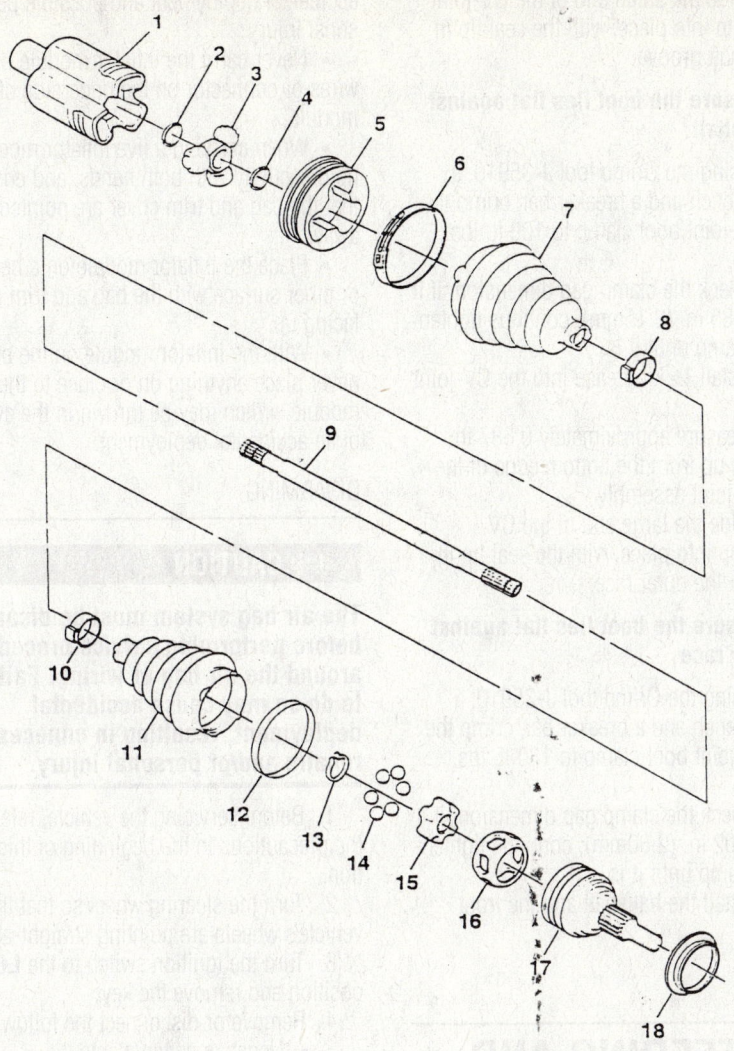

1. Assembly, Tripot Housing
2. Ring, Spacer
3. Spider Assembly, Tripot Joint
4. Ring, Spacer
5. Bushing, Tripot
6. Clamp, Seal Retaining
7. Seal, Tripot Joint
8. Clamp, Small Seal Retaining
9. Shaft, Axle
10. Clamp, Small Seal Retaining
11. Seal, CV Joint
12. Ring, Swage
13. Ring, Race Retaining
14. Ball
15. Race, CV Joint Inner
16. Cage, CV Joint
17. Race, CV Joint Outer
18. Ring, Deflector

9306AG08

Exploded view of CV-joints

3. Install a Stub Shaft Removal tool J-38868-A to the stub shaft snapring groove.

4. Using a slide hammer puller, press the stub shaft from the tri-pot housing.
- Tri-pot housing from the tri-pot spider
- Inboard spacer ring slide it rearward on the shaft using Snapring Pliers tool J-8059
- Outboard retaining ring using Snapring Pliers tool J-8059 and discard it
- Tri-pot joint spider assembly

- Inboard spacer ring and discard it
- CV-joint boot
- Trilobal tri-pot bushing from the housing

5. Thoroughly clean and inspect all parts.

To install:

6. Install or connect the following:
- New snapring onto the stub shaft
- Small boot clamp
- CV-joint boot

7. Using the Crimp tool J-35910, a torque wrench and a breaker bar, crimp the

small CV-joint boot clamp to 130 ft. lbs. (176 Nm).

8. Install or connect the following:
- Inboard spacer ring slide it rearward on the shaft using Snapring Pliers tool J-8059, past the 2nd groove
- Tri-pot joint spider assembly onto the shaft until it passes the 2nd groove
- Outboard retaining ring into the axle shaft groove using Snapring Pliers tool J-8059
- Tri-pot joint spider assembly, slide it against the outboard retaining ring
- Inboard spacer ring, seat it in the groove
- ½ kit grease into the boot
- ½ kit grease into the tri-pot housing
- Trilobal tip-pot bushing flush with the tri-pot housing face
- New large seal clamp onto the CV-joint boot
- Tri-pot housing, slide it over the tri-pot joint spider assembly
- CV-joint boot/clamp, slide it into place, over the trilobal tri-pot bushing with the seal lip in the groove

➡ **Make sure the boot lies flat against the trilobal bushing.**

9. Position the CV-joint boot so it measures 4.9 in. (125mm).

10. Using the Crimp tool J-35910, latch the large CV-joint boot clamp.

11. Install the halfshaft and the front wheel.

Outer CV-Joint

1. Before servicing the vehicle, refer to the precautions in the beginning of this section.

2. Remove or disconnect the following:
- Front wheel
- Halfshaft, position it in a vise
- Large CV-joint boot clamp and discard it
- Small CV-joint boot clamp and discard it
- CV-joint boot and slide it back on the shaft
- Outer race from the halfshaft by spreading the outer race-to-halfshaft retaining ring using Snapring Pliers J-8059
- Retaining ring from the halfshaft and discard it
- CV-joint boot from the halfshaft and discard it if damaged

3. Disassemble the chrome alloy balls from the CV-joint cage as follows:

  a. Step 1: Position a brass drift against the CV-joint cage and tap it with a hammer to tilt the cage.

  b. Step 2: Remove the 1st chrome alloy ball from the cage.

  c. Step 3: Tilt the cage in the opposite direction.

  d. Step 4: Remove the opposite chrome alloy ball.

  e. Step 5: Repeat the procedure until all 6 balls are removed.

4. Disassemble the CV-joint cage and inner race as follows:

  a. Step 1: Pivot the cage and race 90 degrees to the center line of the outer race.

  b. Step 2: Align the cage windows with outer race lands.

  c. Step 3: Remove the cage from the outer race.

  d. Step 4: Rotate the inner race upward and remove it from the cage.

5. Thoroughly clean and inspect all parts.

To install:

6. Lubricate the parts with a light coat of grease.

7. Assemble the CV-joint cage and inner race, as follows:

  a. Step 1: Rotate the inner race 90 degrees to the cage centerline.

  b. Step 2: Align the cage windows with inner race lands.

  c. Step 3: Insert the inner race into the cage by rotating the inner race downward.

  d. Step 4: Insert the cage/inner race into the outer race.

8. Assemble the chrome alloy balls into the CV-joint cage, as follows:

  a. Step 1: Position a brass drift against the CV-joint cage and tap it with a hammer to tilt the cage.

  b. Step 2: Insert the 1st chrome alloy ball into the cage.

  c. Step 3: Tilt the cage in the opposite direction.

  d. Step 4: Insert the opposite chrome alloy ball.

  e. Step 5: Repeat the procedure until all 6 balls are inserted.

9. Install ½ kit grease into the CV-joint.

10. Install or connect the following:

- Small ring clamp on the CV boot
- New retaining ring on the halfshaft
- Large ring clamp on the CV boot
- Outer race assembly onto the halfshaft until the ring engages the halfshaft groove

11. Slide the small end of the CV-joint boot/clamp into place, with the seal lip in the halfshaft groove

➡**Make sure the boot lies flat against the halfshaft.**

12. Using the Crimp tool J-35910, a torque wrench and a breaker bar, crimp the small CV-joint boot clamp to 100 ft. lbs. (136 Nm).

13. Check the clamp gap dimension; if it is not 0.085 in. (2.15mm), continue tightening the clamp until it is.

14. Install ½ kit grease into the CV-joint boot.

15. Measure approximately 0.687 in. (17.5mm) up from the bottom edge of the outer CV-joint assembly.

16. Slide the large end of the CV boot/clamp into place, with the seal lip in place over the outer race.

➡**Make sure the boot lies flat against the outer race.**

17. Using the Crimp tool J-35910, a torque wrench and a breaker bar, crimp the large CV-joint boot clamp to 130 ft. lbs. (176 Nm).

18. Check the clamp gap dimension; if it is not 0.102 in. (2.60mm), continue tightening the clamp until it is.

19. Install the halfshaft and the front wheel.

STEERING AND SUSPENSION

Air Bag

✳✳ CAUTION

Some vehicles are equipped with an air bag system. The system must be disabled before performing service on or round system components, steering column, instrument panel components, wiring and sensors. Failure to follow safety and disabling procedures could result in accidental air bag deployment, possible personal injury and unnecessary system repairs.

PRECAUTIONS

Several precautions must be observed when handling the inflator module to avoid accidental deployment and possible personal injury.

- Never carry the inflator module by the wires or connector on the underside of the module.
- When carrying a live inflator module, hold securely with both hands, and ensure that the bag and trim cover are pointed away.
- Place the inflator module on a bench or other surface with the bag and trim cover facing up.
- With the inflator module on the bench, never place anything on or close to the module, which may be thrown in the event of an accidental deployment.

DISARMING

✳✳ CAUTION

The air bag system must be disarmed before performing service procedures around the air bag or wiring. Failure to do so may cause accidental deployment, resulting in unnecessary repairs and/or personal injury.

1. Before servicing the vehicle, refer to the precautions in the beginning of this section.

2. Turn the steering wheel so that the vehicle's wheels are pointing straight-ahead.

3. Turn the ignition switch to the **LOCK** position and remove the key.

4. Remove or disconnect the following:

- Negative battery cable
- **AIR BAG** fuse from the fuse block
- Left sound insulator
- Connector Position Assurance (CPA) clip from the yellow 2-way connector at the base of the steering column, and detach the harness. If equipped with a passenger's side air bag, remove the CPA and detach the yellow 2-

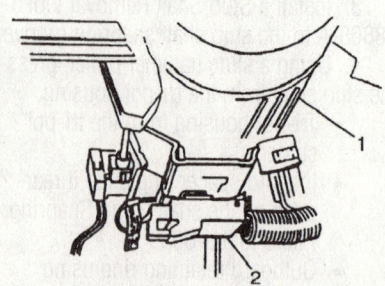

1. Steering column
2. Connector, SRS (yellow)

7922VG20

Detach the SRS yellow 2-way connector

way connector from the passenger air bag lead.

ARMING

After the applicable service is concluded, enable the air bag system as follows:

1. Turn the ignition switch to the **LOCK** position and remove the key.
2. Install or connect the following:
   - Yellow 2-way connector at the base of steering column and secure it with the CPA clip. If equipped with a passenger's side air bag, attach the yellow 2-way connector at the passenger air bag lead and secure it with the CPA clip.
   - Left sound insulator
   - **AIR BAG** fuse in the fuse block
3. Turn the ignition switch to the **RUN** position and verify that the **AIR BAG** warning lamp flashes 7 times, then turns **OFF**.
4. Connect the negative battery cable.

Power Rack and Pinion Steering Gear

REMOVAL & INSTALLATION

✳✳ CAUTION

Failure to disconnect the intermediate shaft from the rack and pinion stub shaft can result in damage to the steering gear and/or intermediate shaft. This damage can cause loss of steering control, which could result in personal injury.

✳✳ WARNING

The wheels of the vehicle must be straight-ahead and the steering column in the LOCK position before disconnecting the steering column or intermediate shaft from the steering gear. Failure to do so will cause the coil assembly in the steering column to become off-centered, which will cause damage to the coil assembly.

1. Before servicing the vehicle, refer to the precautions in the beginning of this section.
2. Remove or disconnect the following:
   - Negative battery cable
   - Front wheels
   - Bolt holding the intermediate shaft to the steering shaft and the intermediate shaft lower coupling.
   - Road Sensing Suspension (RSS) sensor from the lower control arm.
   - Outer tie rod ends from the steering knuckles
   - Y-pipe from the catalytic converter
3. Support the rear of the subframe with a jack.
4. Remove the rear subframe bolts
5. Slowly lower the subframe to gain access.
6. Remove or disconnect the following:
   - Heat shield
   - Power steering line retainer
7. Place a catch pan under the power steering rack and the line fittings.
8. Remove or disconnect the following:
   - Power steering pressure and return lines from the rack and pinion unit.

- Speed Sensitive Steering (SSS) solenoid valve connector
- 5 power steering rack-to-subframe bolts
- Rack and pinion unit out the left wheel well

To install:

9. Install or connect the following:
   - Rack and pinion through the left wheel well. Torque the bolts to 50 ft. lbs. (68 Nm).
   - Speed Sensitive Steering (SSS) solenoid valve connector
   - Power steering pressure and return hoses. Torque the fittings to 20 ft. lbs. (27 Nm).
   - Power steering line retainer
   - Heat shield
   - Subframe, raise it into position. Torque the bolts to 76 ft. lbs. (103 Nm).
   - Y-pipe to the catalytic converter
   - Outer tie rod ends to the steering knuckle using new cotter pins
   - RSS sensor to the lower control arm
   - Intermediate shaft to the steering shaft. Torque the bolt to 30 ft. lbs. (41 Nm).
   - Front wheels
   - Negative battery cable
10. Refill and bleed the power steering system.
11. Check the wheel alignment.
12. Road test the vehicle.

Strut

REMOVAL & INSTALLATION

Front

✳✳ WARNING

When working near the halfshafts, use care to prevent the inner Tripot CV-joint from being overextended. If the joint is overextended, the internal joint components could separate, resulting in CV-joint failure.

1. Before servicing the vehicle, refer to the precautions in the beginning of this section.
2. Remove or disconnect the following:
   - Negative battery cable
   - Front wheel
   - Electrical connector from the top of the strut, if equipped

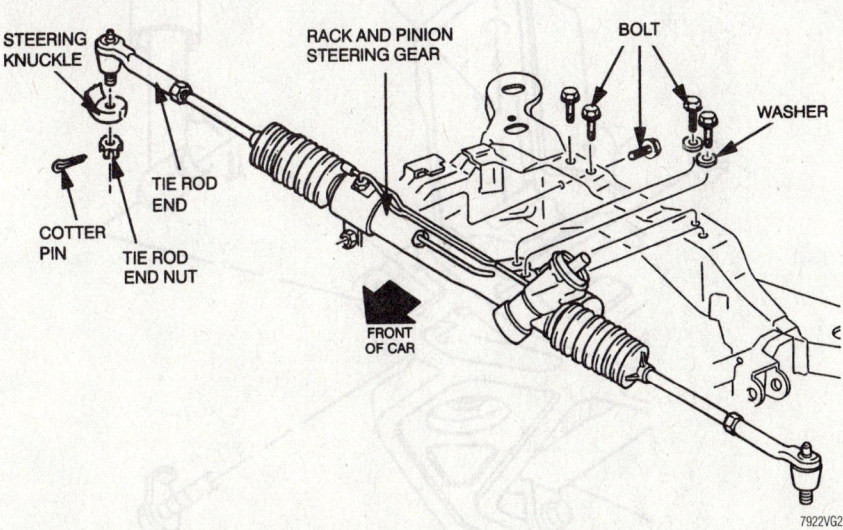

7922VG21

Exploded view of the power steering rack components

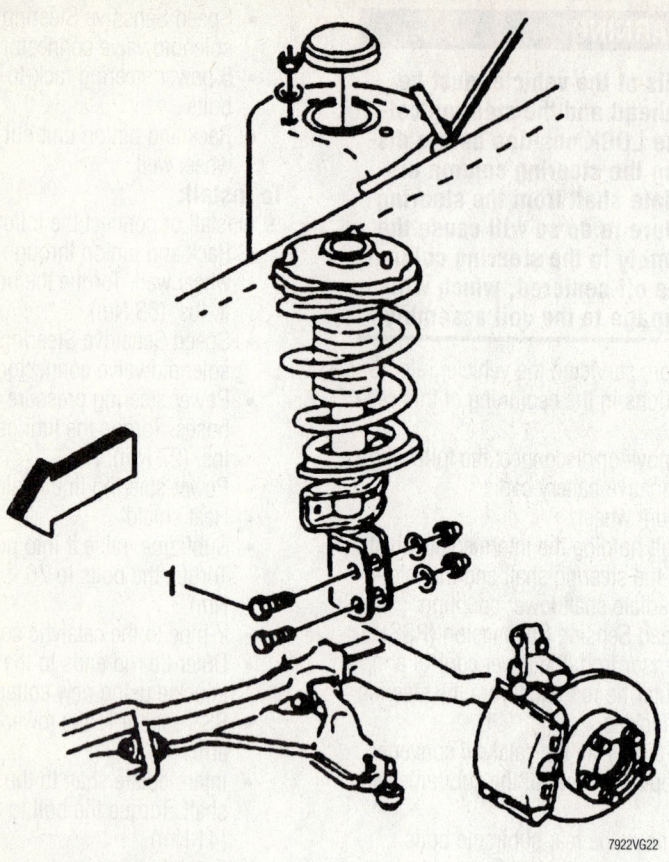

Exploded view of the strut mounting

- Upper strut mounting nuts
- Road Sensing Suspension (RSS) position sensor from the lower control arm, if equipped.
- Anti-lock Brake System (ABS) wheel speed sensor, if equipped
- Wheel speed sensor from the strut bracket, if equipped
- Brake line bracket from the strut
- Stabilizer link from the strut

3. Scribe a mark on the strut referencing the lower strut bracket to the steering knuckle.

4. Remove the strut from the steering knuckle.

To install:

5. Install or connect the following:
- Strut assembly into the vehicle
- Strut-to-knuckle bolts and nuts, but do not torque yet
- Stabilizer link to the strut assembly, but do not torque the nuts yet
- Brake line bracket to the strut
- Speed sensor bracket on the strut, if equipped
- ABS sensor, if equipped
- RSS sensor to the lower control arm, if equipped.
- Electrical connector to the top of the strut, if equipped

- Upper strut mounting nuts. Torque to 18 ft. lbs. (24 Nm).
- Stabilizer link nuts. Torque to 48 ft. lbs. (65 Nm).
- Torque the strut-to-knuckle bolt nuts to 140 ft. lbs. (190 Nm).
- Front wheel

Shock Absorber

REMOVAL & INSTALLATION

Rear

1. Before servicing the vehicle, refer to the precautions in the beginning of this section.

2. Remove or disconnect the following:
- Rear wheel
- Negative battery cable
- Shock absorber electrical connector from the rear suspension support, If equipped

3. Support the lower control arm with a jack to relieve the tension on the shock absorber.

4. Remove or disconnect the following:
- Lower shock absorber mounting bolt and nut

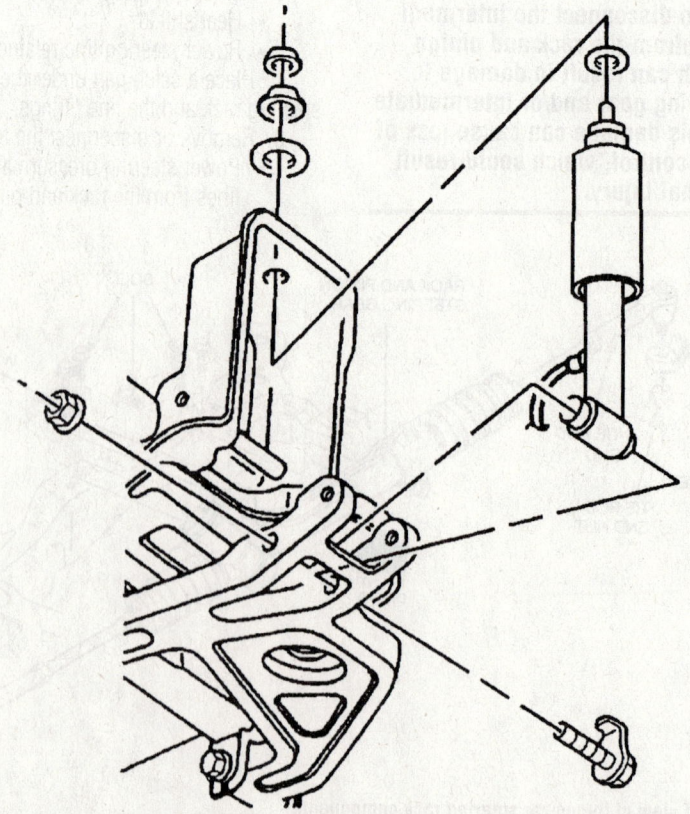

Exploded view of the rear shock absorber mounting

- Upper mounting nut, retainer, and insulator
- Shock absorber compress by hand and remove through the upper control arm

To install:

5. Position the top of the shock absorber with the insulator attached into the suspension support.

6. Install or connect the following:

- Upper shock insulator, retainer and nut. Torque the nut to 55 ft. lbs. (74 Nm).
- Shock absorber lower mounting nut/bolt. Torque the nut to 75 ft. lbs. (102 Nm).
- Shock absorber electrical connector to the rear suspension support, if equipped
- Rear wheel
- Negative battery cable

Coil Spring

REMOVAL & INSTALLATION

Front

1. Before servicing the vehicle, refer to the precautions in the beginning of this section.

2. Remove the strut from the vehicle.

3. Mount the strut assembly in a strut compressor.

4. Turn the compressor forcing screw until the spring compresses slightly.

5. Use a T-50 Torx® bit to keep the strut shaft from turning and remove the nut on the top of the strut shaft.

6. Loosen the compressor screw while guiding the strut shaft out of the assembly. Continue loosening the compressor screw until the spring can be removed.

To install:

7. Mount the strut in the compressor tool. Use the clamping tool to hold the strut shaft in place.

8. Install the spring over the strut. The flat on the upper spring seat must face out from the centerline of the vehicle or when mounted in the strut compressor, the spring seat must face the same direction as the steering knuckle mounting flange.

➡ **If the bearing was removed from the upper spring seat, it must be reinstalled in the spring seat in the same position before attaching to the strut mount.**

9. Turn the compressor screw to compress the spring, while guiding the strut shaft through the top of the strut assembly.

10. When the strut shaft threads are visible through the top of the strut assembly, install the nut.

11. Remove the clamping tool from the strut shaft.

12. Torque the strut shaft nut to 55 ft. lbs. (75 Nm) while holding the strut shaft with a T-50 Torx® bit.

13. Remove the strut assembly from the compressor tool, then install the strut into the vehicle.

Rear

1. Before servicing the vehicle, refer to the precautions in the beginning of this section.

2. Support the inboard end of the lower control arm with a jack.

3. Remove or disconnect the following:

- Rear wheel
- Sway bar link lower mounting bolt
- Shock absorber lower mounting bolt and push the shock up and out of the way

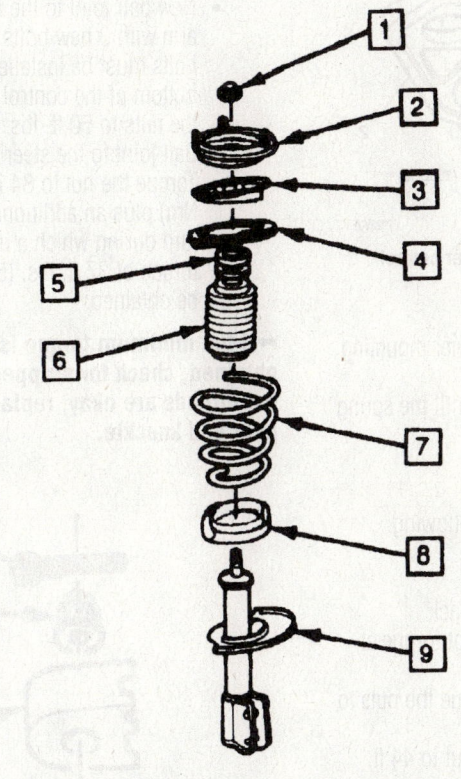

1	NUT, STRUT TO MOUNT
2	STRUT MOUNT
3	FRONT SPRING SEAT
4	FRONT SPRING UPPER INSULATOR
5	JOUNCE BUMPER
6	DUST SHIELD
7	SPRING
8	FRONT SPRING LOWER INSULATOR
9	FRONT STRUT

7922VG23

Disassembled view of strut

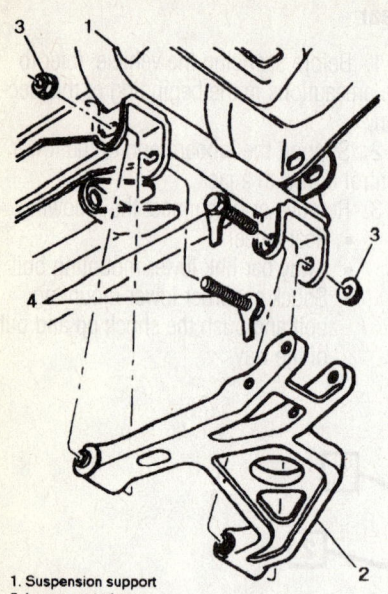

1. Suspension support
2. Lower control arm
3. Lower control arm inner nut - 102 Nm (75 lb. ft.)
4. Lower control arm inner bolt

7922VG24

Exploded view of the rear lower control arm mounting

- Lower control arm inner mounting nuts and bolts

4. Slowly lower the jack until the spring tension has been released.

5. Remove the coil spring.

To install:

6. Install or connect the following:
- Coil spring
- Spring insulators
- Control arm using a jack
- Mounting nuts. Do not torque at this time.
- Shock absorber. Torque the nuts to 75 ft. lbs. (102 Nm).
- Link kit. Torque the nut to 44 ft. lbs. (60 Nm).
- Rear wheel
- Lower control arm inner bolts. Torque the bolts to 75 ft. lbs. (102 Nm).

7. Check the alignment and adjust, as necessary.

Lower Ball Joint

REMOVAL & INSTALLATION

Except Commercial Chassis

1. Before servicing the vehicle, refer to the precautions in the beginning of this section.

2. Allow the front suspension to hang free.

3. Remove or disconnect the following:
- Front wheel

※※ CAUTION

Be careful when working in the area of the CV-boot. Damage to the boot could result in eventual joint failure. Install a boot protector.

- Road Sensing Suspension (RSS) position sensor from the lower control arm if equipped
- Ball joint from the steering knuckle
- Ball joint by drilling out the 3 ball joint-to-lower control arm rivets

To install:

4. Install or connect the following:
- New ball joint to the lower control arm with 3 new bolts and nuts. The bolts must be installed from the bottom of the control arm. Torque the nuts to 50 ft. lbs. (68 Nm).
- Ball joint to the steering knuckle. Torque the nut to 84 inch lbs. (10 Nm) plus an additional 120 degree turn during which a minimum torque of 37 ft. lbs. (50 Nm) must be obtained.

➡If the minimum torque is not obtained, check for stripped threads. If the threads are okay, replace the ball joint and knuckle.

- New cotter pin. If the cotter pin cannot be installed because the hole in the stud does not align with a nut slot, torque the nut an additional 60 degrees to allow for installation. NEVER loosen the nut to provide for cotter pin installation.
- RSS position sensor to the lower control arm if equipped

5. If used, remove the CV-Joint boot protector tool.

6. Install the front wheel

Commercial Chassis

1. Before servicing the vehicle, refer to the precautions in the beginning of this section.

2. Support the control arm with jack.

※※ CAUTION

Be careful when working in the area of the CV-boot. Damage to the boot could result in eventual joint failure. Install a boot protector.

3. Remove or disconnect the following:
- Rear wheel
- Cotter pin and nut

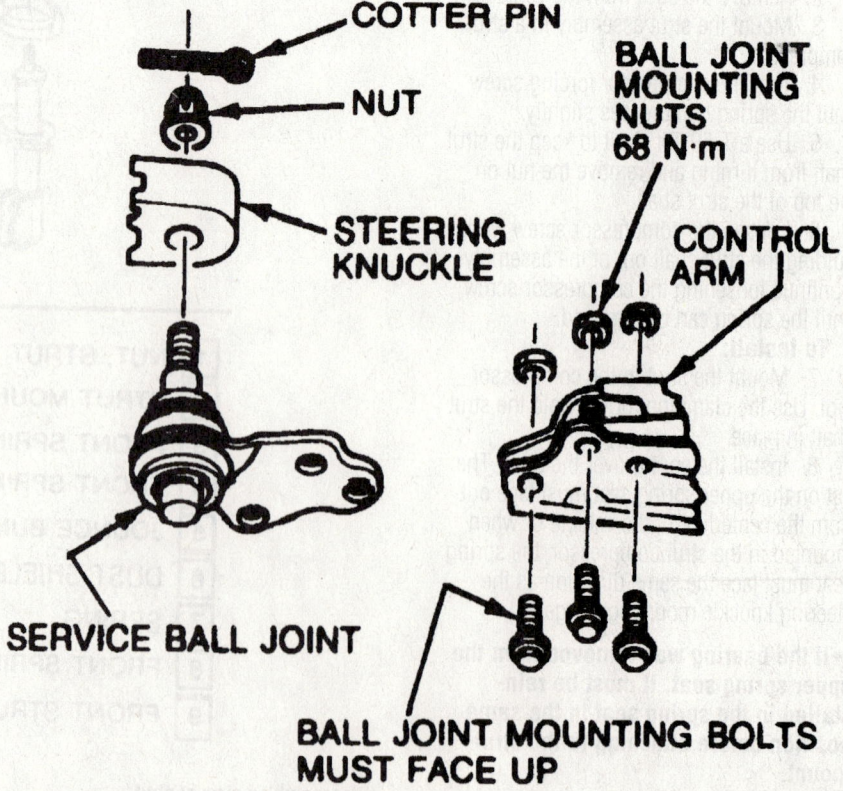

Exploded view of the lower ball joint mounting

7922VG25

- Ball joint from the lower control arm by using Lower Ball Joint Remove/Installer tool J-9519-E

To install:

4. Install or connect the following:
   - Ball joint
   - Hex nut. Torque the nut to 129 ft. lbs. (175 Nm).
   - New cotter pin

➡ **If the cotter pin cannot be installed because the hole in the stud does not align with a nut slot, torque the nut an additional 60 degrees to allow for installation. NEVER loosen the nut to provide for cotter pin installation.**

   - Rear wheel

Lower Control Arm

REMOVAL & INSTALATION

Front

1. Before servicing the vehicle, refer to the precautions in the beginning of this section.
2. Remove or disconnect the following:
   - Wheel Assembly
   - Road Sensing Suspension (RSS) sensor
   - Ball joint from lower control arm
   - Mounting bolts
   - Lower control arm

To install:

3. Install or connect the following:
   - Lower control arm. Torque the front nut to 93 ft. lbs. (126 Nm) and the rear nut to 116 ft. lbs. (157 Nm).
   - Ball joint to lower control arm. Torque the nut to 84 inch lbs. (10 Nm) plus an additional 120 degree turn.
   - New cotter pin
   - RSS sensor
   - Wheel Assembly

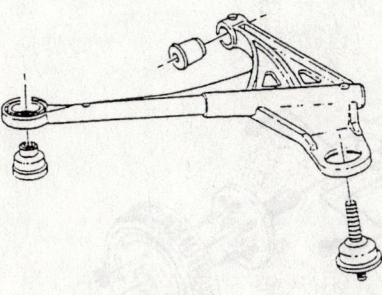

9306AG05

Exploded view of the lower control arm

Rear

1. Before servicing the vehicle, refer to the precautions in the beginning of this section.
2. Remove or disconnect the following:
   - Wheel Assembly
   - Stabalizer link
   - Shock Absorber
   - Ball joint from lower control arm
   - Mounting bolts
   - Lower control arm

To install:

3. Install or connect the following:
   - Lower control arm
   - Mounting nuts. Torque the nut to 75 ft. lbs. (102 Nm)
   - Shock Absorber
   - Ball joint to lower control arm
   - Stabalizer link
   - Wheel Assembly

CONTROL ARM BUSHING REPLACEMENT

Front

1. Before servicing the vehicle, refer to the precautions in the beginning of this section.
2. Remove or disconnect the following:
   - Wheel Assembly
   - Lower control arm and place in a vise
3. Assemble the bolt, washer and bearing of Remover/Installer tool J 21474-27 with the Remover/Installer tool J 41014-1 over bushing in control arm.
4. Place Remover/Installer tools J 41014-2 and J 41014-4 on other side of bushing.

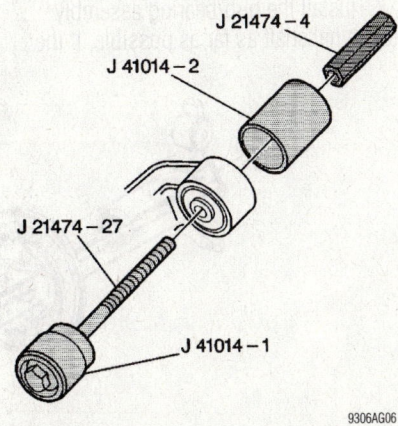

9306AG06

Removing the bushing from control arm using tools J 21474-27, J 41014-1, J 41014-2 and J 41014-4

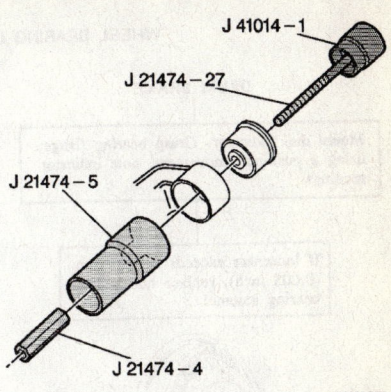

9306AG07

Installing the bushing into control arm using tools J 21474-27, J 41014-1, J 41014-2 and J 41014-4

5. Tighten nut until bushing is pressed out.

To install:

6. Install or connect the following:
   - Lubricate the outer case of the new bushing
   - New bushing into control arm
7. Assemble the bolt, washer and bearing of Remover/Installer tool J21474-27 with Remover/Installer tool J41014-1 over bushing in control arm
8. Place Remover/Installer tools J41014-2 and J41014-4 on other side of bushing.
9. Tighten nut until bushing is seated in the control arm.
10. Install or connect the following:
    - Lower control arm
    - Wheel

Wheel Bearings

ADJUSTMENT

The wheel bearings are not adjustable. If a wheel bearing is out of specifications, it must be replaced. Using a dial indicator, check for looseness. If play exceeds 0.005 in. (0.127mm), the bearing wear is excessive and the hub and bearing should be replaced.

REMOVAL & INSTALLATION

Front

1. Before servicing the vehicle, refer to the precautions in the beginning of this section.
2. Remove or disconnect the following:

Turn to Section 5 for brake system applications

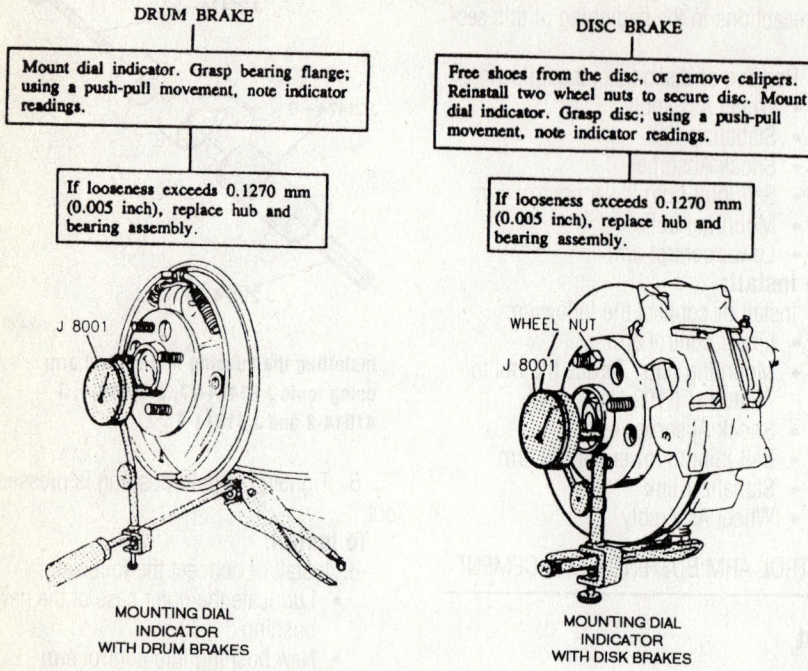

WHEEL BEARING LOOSENESS DIAGNOSIS

DRUM BRAKE

Mount dial indicator. Grasp bearing flange; using a push-pull movement, note indicator readings.

If looseness exceeds 0.1270 mm (0.005 inch), replace hub and bearing assembly.

J 8001

MOUNTING DIAL INDICATOR WITH DRUM BRAKES

DISC BRAKE

Free shoes from the disc, or remove calipers. Reinstall two wheel nuts to secure disc. Mount dial indicator. Grasp disc; using a push-pull movement, note indicator readings.

If looseness exceeds 0.1270 mm (0.005 inch), replace hub and bearing assembly.

WHEEL NUT

J 8001

MOUNTING DIAL INDICATOR WITH DISK BRAKES

7922VG33

Inspect the wheel bearings for play with a dial indicator

- Front wheel
- Halfshaft nut and washer
- Caliper from the steering knuckle and support it on a wire.

⁂ WARNING

DO NOT allow the brake hose to support the weight of the caliper.

- Brake rotor
- Anti-lock Brake System (ABS) speed sensor electrical connector
- 3 hub/bearing assembly to steering knuckle bolts
- Dust shield

3. Place the transaxle selector in the **P** detent.

4. Remove or disconnect the following:
- Hub/bearing assembly from the halfshaft using a puller
- Hub/bearing assembly from the steering knuckle

To install:

5. Install the hub/bearing assembly over the halfshaft splines

➡**Be sure the splines engage smoothly.**

6. Apply a light coating of grease to the steering knuckle bore.

7. Install the hub/bearing assembly onto the halfshaft as far as possible. If the hub will not bottom out on the halfshaft, install the hub bolts and use the hub nut to draw the hub onto the halfshaft.

8. Once the hub is flush with the steering knuckle, remove the mounting bolts and install the dust shield. Reinstall the mounting bolts and torque to 70 ft. lbs. (95 Nm).

9. Place the transaxle in **N**.

10. Install or connect the following:
- ABS speed sensor electrical connector
- Brake rotor
- Caliper. Torque the bolts to 38 ft. lbs. (51 Nm).
- Halfshaft nut. Torque it to 107 ft. lbs. (145 Nm).
- Wheel

11. Road test for proper operation.

Rear

➡**The wheel bearing and hub are serviced as an assembly. The individual components are not serviceable separately.**

1. Before servicing the vehicle, refer to the precautions in the beginning of this section.

2. Remove or disconnect the following:
- Rear wheel
- Caliper bracket from the knuckle and support it on a wire
- Brake rotor
- Hub/bearing assembly bolts
- Hub/bearing assembly

To install:

3. Install or connect the following:
- Hub/bearing assembly. Torque the bolts to 52 ft. lbs. (70 Nm).
- Brake rotor
- Caliper. Torque the new bolts to 83 ft. lbs. (113 Nm).
- Wheel

4. Road test the vehicle.

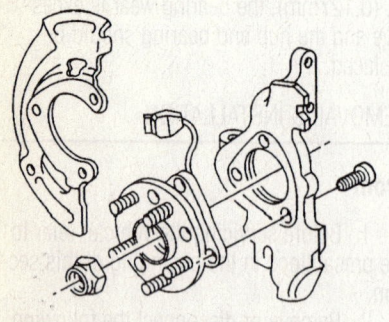

Exploded view of the front wheel bearing mounting

7922VG26

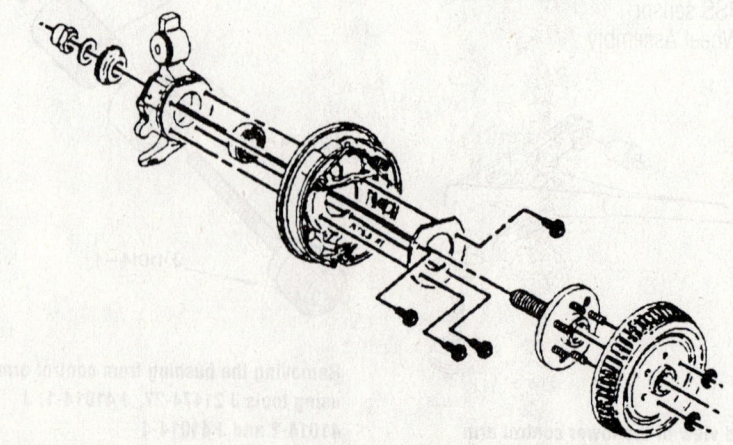

Exploded view of the rear wheel bearing hub mounting

GENERAL MOTORS CORPORATION—F-BODY

Chevrolet-Camaro • Z28 • Pontiac-Firebird • Trans Am

PRECAUTIONS

Before servicing any vehicle, please be sure to read all of the following precautions, which deal with personal safety, prevention of component damage, and important points to take into consideration when servicing a motor vehicle:

• Never open, service or drain the radiator or cooling system when the engine is hot; serious burns can occur from the steam and hot coolant.

• Observe all applicable safety precautions when working around fuel. Whenever servicing the fuel system, always work in a well-ventilated area. Do not allow fuel spray or vapors to come in contact with a spark, open flame or excessive heat (a hot drop light, for example). Keep a dry chemical fire extinguisher near the work area. Always keep fuel in a container specifically designed for fuel storage; also, always properly seal fuel containers to avoid the possibility of fire or explosion. Refer to the additional fuel system precautions later in this section.

• Fuel injection systems often remain pressurized, even after the engine has been turned **OFF**. The fuel system pressure must be relieved before disconnecting any fuel lines. Failure to do so may result in fire and/or personal injury.

• Brake fluid often contains polyglycol ethers and polyglycols. Avoid contact with the eyes and wash your hands thoroughly after handling brake fluid. If you do get brake fluid in your eyes, flush your eyes with clean, running water for 15 minutes. If eye irritation persists, or if you have taken brake fluid internally, IMMEDIATELY seek medical assistance.

• The EPA warns that prolonged contact with used engine oil may cause a number of skin disorders, including cancer! You should make every effort to minimize your exposure to used engine oil. Protective gloves should be worn when changing oil. Wash your hands and any other exposed skin areas as soon as possible after exposure to used engine oil. Soap and water, or waterless hand cleaner should be used.

• All new vehicles are now equipped with an air bag system. The system must be disabled before performing service on or around system components, steering column, instrument panel components, wiring and sensors. Failure to follow safety and disabling procedures could result in accidental air bag deployment, possible personal injury and unnecessary system repairs.

• Always wear safety goggles when working with, or around, the air bag system. When carrying a non-deployed air bag, be sure the bag and trim cover are pointed away from your body. When placing a non-deployed air bag on a work surface, always face the bag and trim cover upward, away from the surface. This will reduce the motion of the module if it is accidentally deployed. Refer to the additional air bag system precautions later in this section.

• Clean, high quality brake fluid from a sealed container is essential to the safe and proper operation of the brake system. You should always buy the correct type of brake fluid for your vehicle. If the brake fluid becomes contaminated, completely flush the system with new fluid. Never reuse any brake fluid. Any brake fluid that is removed from the system should be discarded. Also, do not allow any brake fluid to come in contact with a painted surface; it will damage the paint.

• Never operate the engine without the proper amount and type of engine oil; doing so WILL result in severe engine damage.

• Timing belt maintenance is extremely important! Many models utilize an interference-type, non-freewheeling engine. If the timing belt breaks, the valves in the cylinder head may strike the pistons, causing potentially serious (also time-consuming and expensive) engine damage. Refer to the maintenance interval charts in the front of this manual for the recommended replacement interval for the timing belt, and to the timing belt section for belt replacement and inspection.

• Disconnecting the negative battery cable on some vehicles may interfere with the functions of the on-board computer system(s) and may require the computer to undergo a relearning process once the negative battery cable is reconnected.

• When servicing drum brakes, only disassemble and assemble one side at a time, leaving the remaining side intact for reference.

• Only an MVAC-trained, EPA-certified automotive technician should service the air conditioning system or its components.

ENGINE REPAIR

Distributor

All 1998–00 5.7L (VIN G) engines use a Direct Ignition System (DIS).

REMOVAL

5.7L (VIN P) Engine

1. Before servicing the vehicle, refer to the precautions in the beginning of this section.

2. Be sure the ignition is in the **OFF** or **LOCK** position.

3. Remove or disconnect the following:

• Negative battery cable
• Water pump and crankshaft balancer

✸✸ WARNING

To prevent wire damage, the spark plug wire boots should be twisted ½ turn in each direction while removing. Do not pull on the wires to remove them from the spark plugs. Pull on the boots or use a tool specifically designed for this purpose.

• Power steering pump
• Spark plug wiring harness from the wiring harness clips
• Spark plug wiring harness from the distributor
• 4-terminal electrical connector from the distributor
• Distributor vacuum harness from the distributor, if equipped
• Distributor bolts
• Distributor. Pull it forward until the

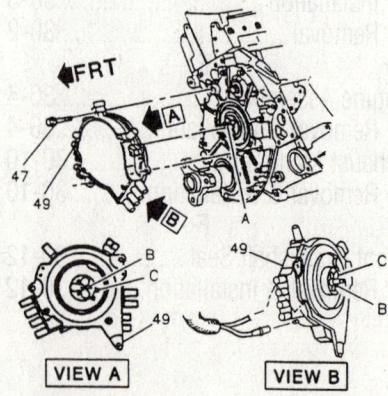

A CAMSHAFT PIN
B CAMSHAFT PIN SLOT
C DISTRIBUTOR BASE TIMING MARK
24 DISTRIBUTOR VACUUM HARNESS
47 BOLT/SCREW DISTRIBUTOR
49 DISTRIBUTOR

7922WG01

Exploded view of the distributor assembly mounting (located under the water pump)—5.7L (VIN P) engine

driveshaft disengages from the end of the camshaft.

4. Mark the top surface of the driveshaft for proper alignment during installation.

INSTALLATION

Timing Not Disturbed

➡Replace the O-rings on the coupling shaft, otherwise ignition system performance may suffer. Lubricate the O-rings and the end of the camshaft.

❊❊ WARNING

Don't try to fully seat the distributor using the distributor retainers. If the distributor will not seat by hand, it's not properly aligned with the camshaft. Rotate the crankshaft until the engine is at the No. 1 cylinder Top Dead Center (TDC) and the camshaft sprocket pin is at the 9 o'clock position. Rotate the distributor coupling until the camshaft sprocket pin slot aligns with the distributor base timing mark. Install the distributor using hand pressure to fully seat the distributor.

Install or connect the following:
- Distributor. Torque the bolts to 97–106 inch lbs. (11–12 Nm).
- All electrical connectors and/or vacuum hoses onto the distributor
- Crankshaft balancer and water pump
- Negative battery cable

Timing Disturbed

➡Replace the O-rings on the coupling shaft, otherwise ignition system performance may suffer. Lubricate the O-rings and the end of the camshaft.

❊❊ WARNING

Don't try to fully seat the distributor using the distributor retainers. If the distributor will not seat by hand, it's not properly aligned with the camshaft. Rotate the crankshaft until the engine is at the No. 1 cylinder Top Dead Center (TDC) and the camshaft sprocket pin is at the 9 o'clock position. Rotate the distributor coupling until the camshaft sprocket pin slot aligns with the distributor base timing mark. Install the distributor using hand pressure to fully seat the distributor.

1. Rotate the crankshaft until the No. 1 piston is at Top Dead Center (TDC) of the compression stroke.

2. Align the rotor with the No. 1 cylinder position on the distributor cap.

3. Install or connect the following:
- Distributor. Torque the bolts to 97–106 inch lbs. (11–12 Nm).
- All electrical connectors and/or vacuum hoses onto the distributor
- Crankshaft balancer and water pump
- Negative battery cable

Alternator

REMOVAL

3.8L Engine

1. Before servicing the vehicle, refer to the precautions in the beginning of this section.

2. Remove or disconnect the following:
- Negative battery cable
- Accessory drive belt
- Alternator electrical connectors
- Evaporative Emissions (EVAP) canister purge solenoid
- Rear alternator brace-to-alternator bolt

- Both front alternator bolts
- Alternator

5.7L (VIN P) Engine

1. Before servicing the vehicle, refer to the precautions in the beginning of this section.

2. Remove or disconnect the following:
- Negative battery cable
- Serpentine drive belt
- Alternator electrical connectors
- Alternator nuts/bolts
- Alternator rear inner brace
- Alternator

5.7L (VIN G) Engine

1. Before servicing the vehicle, refer to the precautions in the beginning of this section.

2. Remove or disconnect the following:
- Negative battery cable
- Accessory drive belt
- Alternator electrical connectors
- Rear alternator bracket bolt
- Transmission cooler lines from the oil cooler clip
- Front alternator bolts and oil cooler clip
- Alternator

INSTALLATION

3.8L Engine

Install or connect the following:
- Alternator. Torque the upper (drive belt tensioner) bolt to 22 ft. lbs. (30

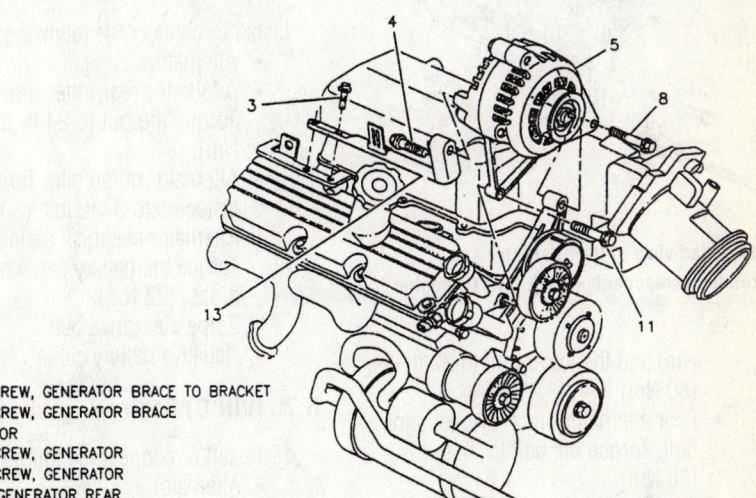

3 BOLT/SCREW, GENERATOR BRACE TO BRACKET
4 BOLT/SCREW, GENERATOR BRACE
5 GENERATOR
8 BOLT/SCREW, GENERATOR
11 BOLT/SCREW, GENERATOR
13 BRACE, GENERATOR REAR

9306WG01

Exploded view of the alternator and related components—3.8L engine

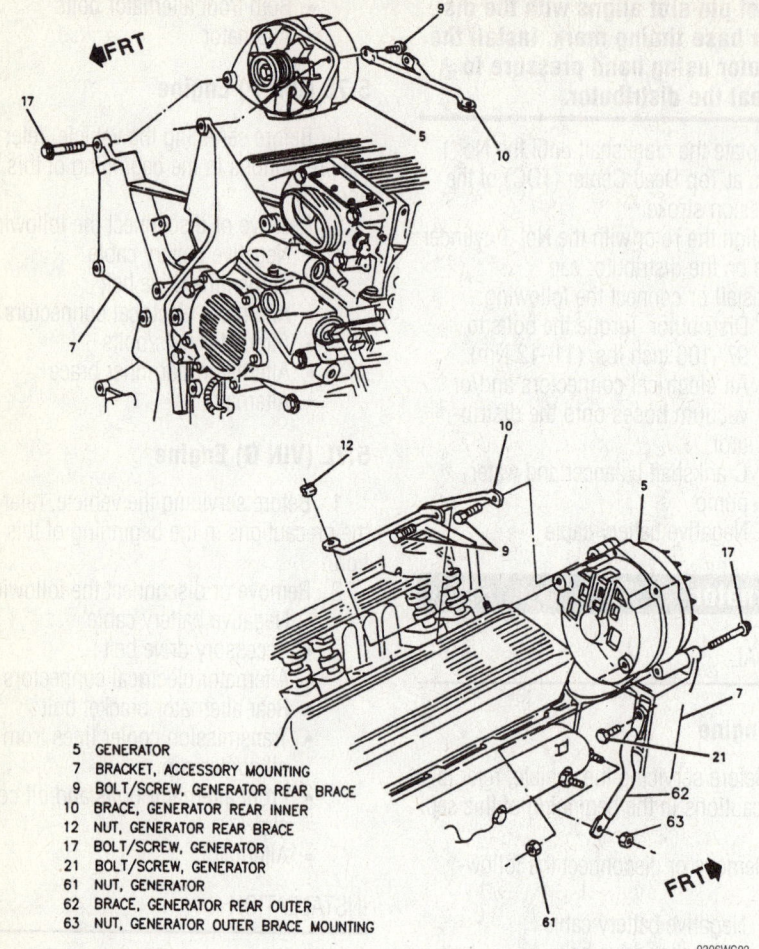

5	GENERATOR
7	BRACKET, ACCESSORY MOUNTING
9	BOLT/SCREW, GENERATOR REAR BRACE
10	BRACE, GENERATOR REAR INNER
12	NUT, GENERATOR REAR BRACE
17	BOLT/SCREW, GENERATOR
21	BOLT/SCREW, GENERATOR
61	NUT, GENERATOR
62	BRACE, GENERATOR REAR OUTER
63	NUT, GENERATOR OUTER BRACE MOUNTING

9306WG02

Exploded view of the alternator and related components—5.7L (VIN P) engine

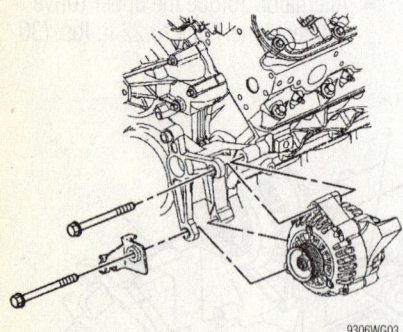

9306WG03

Exploded view of the alternator and related components—5.7L (VIN G) engine

Nm) and the lower bolt to 37 ft. lbs. (50 Nm).
- Rear alternator brace-to-alternator bolt. Torque the bolt to 22 ft. lbs. (30 Nm).
- Evaporative Emissions (EVAP) canister purge solenoid
- Alternator electrical connectors. Torque the battery cable nut to 16 ft. lbs. (22 Nm).

- Accessory drive belt
- Negative battery cable

5.7L (VIN P) Engine

Install or connect the following:
- Alternator
- Alternator rear inner brace. Torque the nut to 24 ft. lbs. (33 Nm).
- Alternator nuts/bolts. Torque the fasteners to 37 ft. lbs. (50 Nm).
- Alternator electrical connectors. Torque the battery cable nut to 16 ft. lbs. (22 Nm).
- Serpentine drive belt
- Negative battery cable

5.7L (VIN G) Engine

1. Install or connect the following:
- Alternator
- Front alternator bolts and oil cooler clip. Torque the bolts to 37 ft. lbs. (50 Nm).
- Transmission cooler lines to the oil cooler clip

- Rear alternator bracket bolt. Torque the bolt to 18 ft. lbs. (25 Nm).
- Alternator electrical connectors. Torque the battery cable nut to 16 ft. lbs. (22 Nm).
- Accessory drive belt
- Negative battery cable

Ignition Timing

ADJUSTMENT

When checking ignition timing NEVER pierce a secondary ignition wire.

➡ Some engines incorporate a magnetic timing probe hole for use with electronic timing equipment. Be sure to consult the tool manufacture's instructions for the use of this equipment.

On these vehicles, base timing is preset when the engine is manufactured. All timing changes are, then controlled directly by the Power Control Module (PCM) based on information from the ignition and knock sensor systems. No adjustments are necessary or possible.

Engine Assembly

REMOVAL & INSTALLATION

➡ The engine, transmission and suspension assembly is removed from the bottom of the vehicle. After the assembly is removed, separate the engine from the transmission and frame.

1. Before servicing the vehicle, refer to the precautions in the beginning of this section.
2. Discharge the air conditioning system.
3. Relieve the fuel system pressure.
4. Drain the cooling system and crankcase.
5. Remove or disconnect the following:
- Both battery cables
- Front wheels
- Exhaust pipes from the exhaust manifolds
- Front fascia lower deflectors
- Stabilizer bar
- Drive belt
- Transmission cooler lines from the radiator, if equipped
- Radiator and heater hoses
- Electrical connections from the engine and wheel speed sensors
- Right front brake line from the caliper brake hose
- Electrical connectors from the transmission

- Shift linkage from the transmission
- Driveshaft. Matchmark the driveshaft prior to removal.
- Torque arm from the transmission
- Intermediate steering shaft from the rack and pinion assembly
- Ground straps from the left side frame rail
- Air intake duct
- Fuel pipes from the engine
- Throttle and cruise control cables from the throttle body
- Radiator fan electrical connectors
- Radiator fan
- Brake booster vacuum hose
- "Y" brace from the right side exhaust manifold
- Alternator and air conditioning compressor bracket, move is aside
- Brake master cylinder and move it aside
- Both upper strut assemblies from the chassis
- Right front brake line from the modulator valve assembly and clips

6. Position a lift table under the engine and engine frame assembly.

7. Remove the engine frame and transmission support screws

8. Raise the vehicle from the engine, transmission and engine frame assemblies.

9. Secure the strut assemblies to the engine frame.

10. Remove the transmission assembly from the engine

To install:

11. Install or connect the following:

- Engine onto the frame. Tighten the through-bolt to 70 ft. lbs. (95 Nm).
- Transmission
- Engine, transmission and frame assembly
- Frame and transmission support bolts

12. Remove the engine lift table.

13. Remove or disconnect the following:

- Upper strut nuts and bolts
- Right front brake line to the modulator valve assembly and clips
- Brake master cylinder
- Engine wiring harness connectors
- Alternator and compressor bracket
- "Y" brace to the right exhaust manifold assembly, if removed
- Brake booster vacuum line

- Radiator fan assembly
- Radiator hoses
- Cruise control and accelerator cables to the throttle body
- Engine fuel pipes
- Intermediate steering shaft to the rack and pinion assembly
- Torque arm to the transmission
- Driveshaft
- Wiring and shift linkage to the transmission
- Right front brake line to the caliper brake hose
- All electrical connectors
- Heater hoses
- Transmission fluid cooler lines to the radiator, if equipped
- Drive belt
- Stabilizer bar
- Front fascia lower deflectors
- Catalytic converter, if equipped with an automatic transmission
- Front exhaust pipes
- Front wheels
- Negative battery cable
- Air intake duct

14. Refill the crankcase and cooling system

15. Refill and bleed the brake and power steering systems

16. Check and/or align the front wheels.

Water Pump

REMOVAL & INSTALLATION

3.8L Engine

1. Before servicing the vehicle, refer to the precautions in the beginning of this section.

2. Drain the cooling system.

3. Remove or disconnect the following:

- Negative battery cable
- Serpentine belt
- Radiator inlet hose from the water pump
- Water pump pulley
- Water pump. Discard the gasket and thoroughly clean the gasket mating surfaces.

To install:

4. Install or connect the following:

- Water pump using a new gasket. Torque the water pump bolts to 11 ft. lbs. (15 Nm), plus an additional 80 degree rotation.
- Water pump pulley. Torque the bolts to 115 inch lbs. (13 Nm).
- Serpentine drive belt
- Radiator inlet hose to the water pump
- Negative battery cable

5. Refill the cooling system. Start the engine and check for leaks.

5.7L Engines

1. Before servicing the vehicle, refer to the precautions in the beginning of this section.

2. Drain the cooling system by removing the block coolant drain plug and the knock sensor.

3. Remove or disconnect the following:

- Electrical connector from the cooling fan
- Both cooling fan assemblies
- Air intake duct and air cleaner
- Upper and lower radiator hoses from the water pump
- Heater hoses from the water pump and throttle body
- Electrical connector from the Engine Coolant Temperature (ECT) sensor

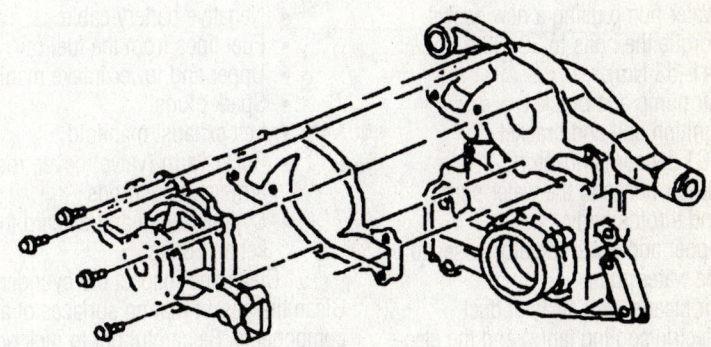

7922WG03

Exploded view of the water pump mounting—3.8L engine

Timing belt service is covered in Section 4 of this manual

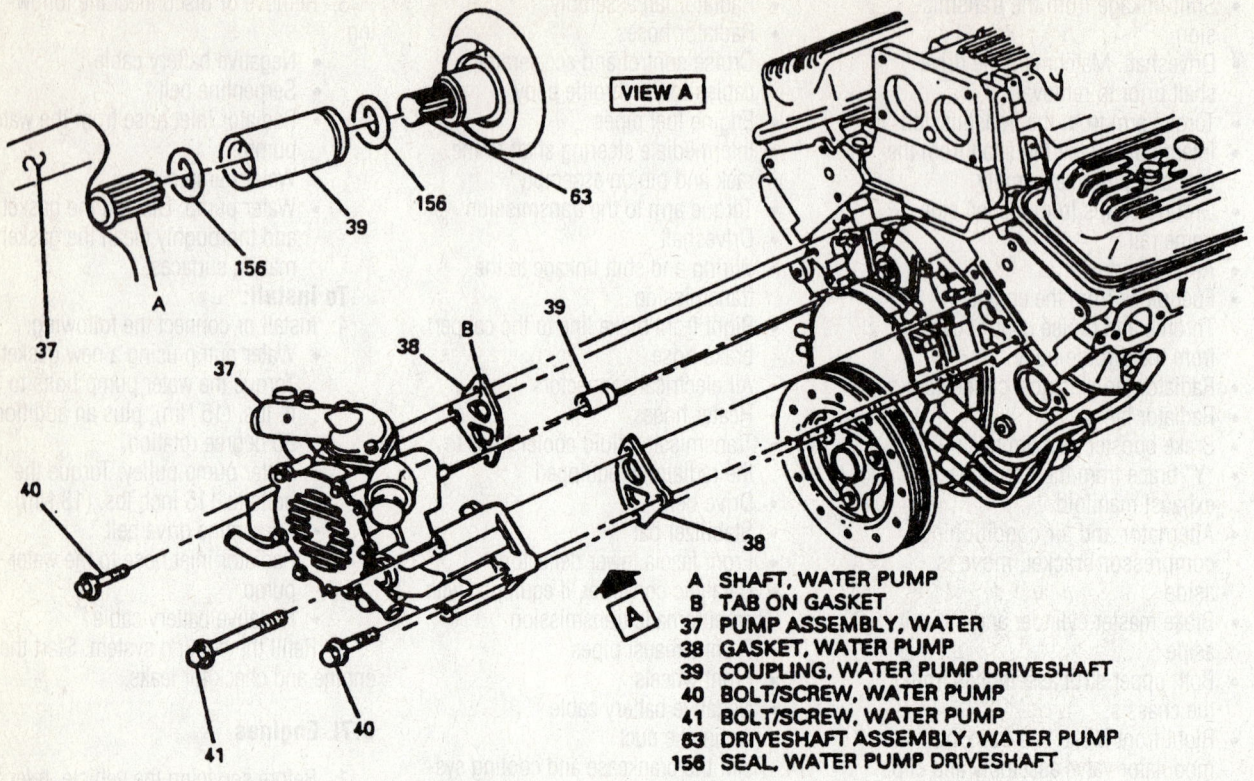

VIEW A

A SHAFT, WATER PUMP
B TAB ON GASKET
37 PUMP ASSEMBLY, WATER
38 GASKET, WATER PUMP
39 COUPLING, WATER PUMP DRIVESHAFT
40 BOLT/SCREW, WATER PUMP
41 BOLT/SCREW, WATER PUMP
63 DRIVESHAFT ASSEMBLY, WATER PUMP
156 SEAL, WATER PUMP DRIVESHAFT

7922WG04

Exploded view of the water pump mounting and related components—5.7L engines

- Ignition coil and bracket, move them aside
- Air pump and bracket, if equipped
- Water pump and discard the gasket
- Shaft coupling and water pump driveshaft seals, if necessary

4. Thoroughly, clean the gasket mating surfaces

To install:

5. Install or connect the following:
- Drain plug and knock sensor
- Shaft coupling and water pump driveshaft, using a Water Pump Driveshaft O-ring Installer tool J 39089
- Water pump using a new gasket. Torque the bolts to 30–32 ft. lbs. (41–43 Nm).
- Air pump and bracket
- Ignition coil and bracket
- ECT sensor connector
- Heater hoses to the water pump and throttle body
- Upper and lower radiator hoses to the water pump
- Air cleaner and air inlet duct
- Electric cooling fan(s) and the electrical connector
- Negative battery cable

6. Refill the cooling system.
7. Start the engine and check for leaks.

Cylinder Head

REMOVAL & INSTALLATION

3.8L Engine

LEFT SIDE

1. Before servicing the vehicle, refer to the precautions in the beginning of this section.
2. Relieve the fuel system pressure.
3. Drain the cooling system.
4. Remove or disconnect the following:

- Negative battery cable
- Fuel lines from the fuel rail
- Upper and lower intake manifolds
- Spark plugs
- Left exhaust manifold
- Rocker arm (valve) cover, rocker arms and pushrods
- Cylinder head and discard the gasket and bolts

5. Clean and inspect the cylinder head. Clean the gasket mating surfaces of all components. Be careful not to nick or scratch any surfaces as this will allow leak paths. Clean the bolt threads in the cylinder block and on the head bolts. Dirt will affect bolt torque.

To install:

➡ Refer to Section 1 of this manual for the cylinder head torque sequence illustration. The illustration is located after the Torque Specification Chart.

6. Install the new cylinder head with the arrow pointing to the front of the engine.
7. New cylinder head bolts. Torque the bolts in sequence, as follows:
   a. Step 1: 37 ft. lbs. (50 Nm).
   b. Step 2: Plus 130 degree turn.
   c. Step 3: Rotate the 4 center bolts an additional 30 degrees.
8. Install or connect the following:
- Rocker arms and pushrods
- Valve cover
- Left exhaust manifold
- Spark plugs and tighten to 20 ft. lbs. (27 Nm)
- Lower and upper intake manifolds
- Negative battery cable

9. Refill the cooling system.
10. Start the engine and check for leaks.

RIGHT SIDE

1. Before servicing the vehicle, refer to the precautions in the beginning of this section.
2. Relieve the fuel system pressure.
3. Drain the cooling system.

4. Remove or disconnect the following:
- Negative battery cable
- Fuel lines from the fuel rail
- Upper and lower intake manifolds
- Spark plugs
- Right exhaust manifold
- Rocker arm (valve) cover, rocker arms and pushrods
- Serpentine drive belt tensioner
- Rear alternator brace
- Cylinder head and discard the gasket and bolts

5. Clean and inspect the cylinder head. Clean the gasket mating surfaces of all components. Be careful not to nick or scratch any surfaces. Clean the bolt threads in the cylinder block and on the head bolts.

To install:

➡Refer to Section 1 of this manual for the cylinder head torque sequence illustration. The illustration is located after the Torque Specification Chart.

6. Install a new cylinder head gasket with the arrow pointing to the front of the engine.

7. Install the cylinder head and secure with NEW head bolts. Torque the bolts, in sequence, as follows:
- a. Step 1: 37 ft. lbs. (50 Nm).
- b. Step 2: Plus a 130 degree turn.
- c. Step 3: Rotate the 4 center bolts an additional 30 degrees.

8. Install or connect the following:
- Rocker arms and pushrods
- Valve cover
- Right exhaust manifold
- Spark plugs. Torque them to 20 ft. lbs. (27 Nm).
- Lower and upper intake manifolds
- Negative battery cable

9. Refill the cooling system.

10. Start the engine and check for leaks.

5.7L Engines

LEFT SIDE

1. Before servicing the vehicle, refer to the precautions in the beginning of this section.

2. Drain the cooling system.

3. Remove the catalytic converter.

4. Remove or disconnect the following:
- Negative battery cable
- Intake manifold
- Secondary air injection hose from the check valve

- Engine coolant bleed pipe bolt from the left cylinder head
- Ignition coil
- Left exhaust manifold
- Spark plugs
- Engine Coolant Temperature (ECT) sensor electrical connector
- Rocker arm cover
- Rocker arm nuts, rocker arms and pushrods
- Cylinder head and discard the gasket

5. Clean and inspect the cylinder. Clean the gasket mating surfaces of all components. Be careful not to nick or scratch any surfaces as this will allow leak paths. Clean the bolt threads in the cylinder block and on the head bolts. Dirt will affect bolt torque.

To install:

➡Refer to Section 1 of this manual for the cylinder head torque sequence illustration. The illustration is located after the Torque Specification Chart.

6. Install or connect the following:
- New cylinder head gasket with the yellow tab facing up
- Cylinder head

➡Before installing the head bolts, be sure to mark the short bolts so the correct tightening specifications are used.

7. Lubricate the head bolt threads with GM 1052080 or equivalent, then install them.

8. Torque the cylinder head bolts in sequence as follows:
- a. Step 1: 22 ft. lbs. (30 Nm).
- b. Step 2: Long and medium length bolts an additional 80 degrees.
- c. Step 3: Short bolts an additional 67 degrees.

9. Install or connect the following:
- Pushrods and rocker arms
- Rocker arm (valve) cover. Torque the bolts to 106 inch lbs. (12 Nm).
- ECT sensor electrical connector.
- Spark plugs. Torque the plugs to 15 ft. lbs. (20 Nm).
- Left exhaust manifold
- Ignition coil. Torque the fasteners to 30 ft. lbs. (40 Nm).
- Engine coolant air bleed pipe to the left cylinder head. Torque the bolts to 30 ft. lbs. (40 Nm).
- Secondary air injection hose to the check valve
- Intake manifold

- Catalytic converter
- Negative battery cable

10. Refill the cooling system.

11. Start the engine and check for leaks.

RIGHT SIDE

1. Before servicing the vehicle, refer to the precautions in the beginning of this section.

2. Drain the cooling system.

3. Remove or disconnect the following:
- Negative battery cable
- Serpentine drive belt and belt tensioner
- Automatic transmission fluid level indicator tube bracket, if equipped
- Air conditioning compressor rear brace bolt from the engine block, if equipped
- Compressor electrical connector
- Air conditioning compressor and move it aside

➡DO NOT disconnect the refrigerant lines.

- Right exhaust manifold
- Alternator
- Right side rocker arm cover
- Intake manifold
- Engine coolant bleed pipe bolt from the left cylinder head using a back-up wrench on the pipe fitting
- Lower radiator hose and heater hose from the water pump
- Engine coolant air bleed pipe hose from the radiator
- Power steering pump and move it aside without disconnecting the lines
- Alternator, air conditioning compressor and power steering pump brackets
- Spark plugs
- Rrocker arms and pushrods
- Cylinder head and discard the gasket
- Engine coolant air bleed pipe bolt, nut and fitting from the cylinder head

To install:

➡Refer to Section 1 of this manual for the cylinder head torque sequence illustration. The illustration is located after the Torque Specification Chart.

4. Install or connect the following:
- Engine coolant air bleed pipe, nut and bolt to the cylinder head hand-tight

- New cylinder head gasket with the yellow tab facing up

➡**When installing the head bolts, be sure the mark the short bolts to ensure the correct tightening specifications are achieved.**

5. Lubricate head bolt threads with GM 1052080 or equivalent, then install them.

6. Torque the cylinder head bolts, in sequence, as follows:

   a. Step 1: 22 ft. lbs. (30 Nm).

   b. Step 2: Long and medium length bolts an additional 80 degrees.

   c. Step 3: Short bolts an additional 67 degrees.

7. Install or connect the following:

- Engine coolant air bleed pipe. Torque the bolt to 30 ft. lbs. (40 Nm) and the nut to 13 ft. lbs. (17 Nm).
- Pushrods and rocker arms
- Spark plugs. Torque them to 15 ft. lbs. (20 Nm).
- Alternator, air conditioning compressor and power steering pump bracket(s). Torque the bolts to 30 ft. lbs. (40 Nm).
- Valve cover
- Alternator and power steering pump
- Engine coolant air bleed pipe hose to the radiator
- Heater and lower radiator hoses to the water pump
- Air bleed pipe to the left cylinder head. Torque the bolt to 30 ft. lbs. (40 Nm).
- Intake manifold
- Right exhaust manifold
- Air conditioning compressor. Torque the bolts to 24 ft. lbs. (33 Nm).
- Compressor electrical connector
- Automatic transmission fluid level indicator tube bracket, if equipped
- Serpentine drive belt and tensioner
- Negative battery cable

8. Refill the cooling system.

9. Start the engine and check for leaks.

Rocker Arms

REMOVAL & INSTALLATION

Be sure to keep all the components in the exact order of removal so they may be installed in their original locations; adjust the valve lash after replacing the rocker arms. Coat the replacement rocker arm and

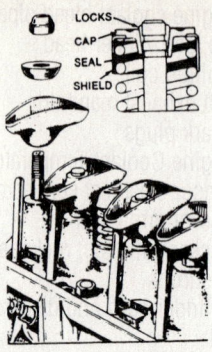

7922WG08

Exploded view of common rocker arm components and valve spring retainer

ball with engine oil before installation. Rocker arm studs that have damaged threads or are loose in the cylinder heads should be replaced. Available oversizes are 0.003 in. (0.076mm) and 0.013 in. (0.33mm). The bore may also be tapped, and screw-in studs installed. Several aftermarket companies produce complete rocker arm stud kits with installation tools.

➡**The 5.7L engines use press-fit studs.**

1. Before servicing the vehicle, refer to the precautions in the beginning of this section.

2. Remove or disconnect the following:

- Negative battery cable
- Rocker arm cover
- Rocker arm nuts, balls and rocker arms

➡**Place the components in a rack so they can be reinstalled in the same locations.**

To install:

3. Lubricate the bearing surfaces with a thin coating of Molykote® or equivalent lube.

4. Install or connect the following:

- Pushrods
- Rocker arm, balls and nut. Tighten the nut until all lash is eliminated.

5. The engine must be on the No. 1 firing position before proceeding.

6. For the 3.8L engine, adjust the valves as follows:

   a. Place the engine on Top Dead Center (TDC) of the No. 1 firing position.

   b. Tighten exhaust valves No. 1, 2 and 3; then, intake valves No. 1, 5 and 6.

   c. Loosen the adjusting nut until lash is felt at the pushrod.

   d. Tighten the adjusting nut until all lash is removed, then tighten the nut an additional 1½ turns to center the lifter plunger.

   e. Rotate the crankshaft 1 revolution until the "0" timing mark is once again aligned.

   f. Adjust exhaust valves No. 4, 5 and 6 and intake valves No. 2, 3 and 4.

7. For the 5.7L engines, adjust the valves as follows:

8. Place the engine on TDC of the No. 1 firing position.

   a. Tighten the exhaust valves No. 1, 3, 4 and 8; then, intake valves No. 1, 2, 5 and 7.

   b. Loosen the adjusting nut until lash is felt at the pushrod.

   c. Tighten the adjusting nut until all lash is removed; then, tighten an additional 1 turn to center the lifter plunger.

   d. Rotate the crankshaft 1 revolution until the "0" timing mark is once again aligned.

   e. Adjust exhaust valves No. 2, 5, 6 and 7; then, intake valves 3, 4, 6 and 8.

9. Install rocker arm cover and connect the negative battery cable.

Intake Manifold

REMOVAL & INSTALLATION

3.8L Engine

UPPER MANIFOLD

1. Before servicing the vehicle, refer to the precautions in the beginning of this section.

2. Relieve the fuel system pressure.

3. Drain the cooling system.

4. Remove or disconnect the following:

- Negative battery cable
- Serpentine drive belt
- Transmission fluid level indicator, if equipped
- Alternator and serpentine drive belt tensioner
- Manifold Absolute Pressure (MAP) sensor and vacuum source from the upper intake manifold
- Evaporative emission canister purge solenoid valve
- Fuel pressure regulator and canister purge harness
- Idle Air Control (IAC) valve from the upper intake manifold
- Fuel lines from the fuel rail
- Accelerator control cable bracket and control cables from the throttle body
- Ignition coil pack/control module assembly
- Brake booster hose from the upper manifold
- Alternator brace from the upper manifold

- Electrical connectors from the IAC, Throttle Position (TP), Mass Air Flow (MAF) and Intake Air Temperature (IAT) sensors
- Wiring harness from the fuel rail rosebud clips
- Air cleaner, outlet rear duct and resonator duct
- Throttle body from the upper intake manifold, if necessary
- Exhaust Gas Recirculation (EGR) valve outlet pipe

➡ **The thermostat must be removed to get to the "hidden" bolt located under the housing: this bolt retains the upper and lower manifolds.**

- Thermostat and thermostat housing
- Electrical connectors from the fuel injectors
- Fuel rail
- Upper intake manifold, discard the gasket

5. Clean the mating surfaces and bolt threads.

To install:

➡ **Refer to Section 1 of this manual for the upper intake manifold torque sequence illustration. The illustration is located after the Torque Specification Chart.**

6. Install the upper intake manifold using a new gasket. Torque the bolts as follows:

   a. Bolts 1–10, in sequence: 11 ft. lbs. (15 Nm).

   b. Coolant outlet bolts: 20 ft. lbs. (27 Nm).

   c. Side bolts: 22 ft. lbs. (30 Nm).

7. Install the fuel rail as follows:

- Fuel injector O-rings lubricated with engine oil
- Fuel injectors into the manifold bores
- Fuel rail until the injectors are properly seated. Torque the nuts to 89 inch lbs. (10 Nm).

8. Install or connect the following:

- Fuel injector electrical connectors
- Thermostat and thermostat housing
- EGR valve outlet pipe
- Throttle body to the intake manifold
- Air cleaner, resonator duct and air cleaner outlet duct
- Wiring harness to the furl rail rose-bud clips
- Electrical connectors to the IAC, TP, MAF and IAT sensors
- Alternator brace

- Brake booster hose to the upper intake manifold
- Ignition control module
- Accelerator cable bracket and control cables to the throttle body. Torque the bracket bolts to 89 inch lbs. (10 Nm).
- Fuel lines to the fuel rail
- IAC valve to the upper intake manifold
- Fuel pressure regulator and the canister purge harness
- Evaporative emissions canister purge solenoid valve
- MAP sensor and vacuum source to the upper intake manifold
- Serpentine drive belt tensioner
- Alternator
- Transmission level indicator, if equipped
- Serpentine drive belt
- Negative battery cable

9. Refill the coolant system.

10. Start the engine and check for leaks.

LOWER MANIFOLD

1. Before servicing the vehicle, refer to the precautions in the beginning of this section.

➡ **There are 2 bolts that are hidden under the upper manifold. They are located in the front and left rear corners of the lower manifold. It is necessary to remove the upper manifold to service the lower manifold.**

2. Remove or disconnect the following:

- Negative battery cable
- Upper intake manifold
- Rocker arm (valve) covers
- Engine Coolant Temperature (ECT) sensor
- Lower intake manifold, discard the gaskets and seals

3. Thoroughly, clean the gasket mating surfaces.

To install:

➡ **Refer to Section 1 of this manual for the lower intake manifold torque sequence illustration. The illustration is located after the Torque Specification Chart.**

➡ **Apply the manifold seals with GM part No. 12345336 and the bolt threads with GM part No. 12345493.**

4. Install or connect the following:

- New gaskets and seals

- Lower manifold. Torque the manifold bolts, in sequence, to 11 ft. lbs. (15 Nm).

➡ **The 2 lower intake manifold bolts are located under the upper intake manifold (right front and left rear corners) and must be installed before upper manifold installation.**

- ECT sensor
- Valve covers and upper intake manifold
- Negative battery cable

5.7L Engines

1. Before servicing the vehicle, refer to the precautions in the beginning of this section.

2. Relieve the fuel system pressure.

3. Drain the coolant system.

4. Remove or disconnect the following:

- Negative battery cable
- Air duct
- Fuel injectors and move wiring harnesses aside
- Control cables from the throttle body
- Secondary air injection diverter valve hoses
- Fuel pipe connectors from the fuel rail
- Fuel pressure regulator vacuum tube
- Fuel rail
- Vacuum and crankcase vent hoses
- Exhaust Gas Recirculation (EGR) control valve relay
- Emission canister purge solenoid
- EGR valve
- EGR valve pipe
- Secondary air injection pipe from the intake and right exhaust manifold
- Alternator rear brace
- Hoses and electrical connectors from the throttle body
- Throttle body and discard the gasket
- Intake manifold and discard the gaskets

5. Thoroughly, clean the gasket mating surfaces, bolt and stud threads.

To install:

➡ **Refer to Section 1 of this manual for the intake manifold torque sequence illustration. The illustration is located after the Torque Specification Chart.**

6. Be sure the sealing surfaces are clean.

7. Apply a 3/16 in. (5mm) bead of RTV sealant on the front and rear ridge of the cylinder block.

Refer to Section 1 for engine rebuilding specifications

8. Install or connect the following:
- New gaskets. Secure the gaskets by extending the RTV bead up onto the gasket ends.
- Intake manifold. Torque the bolts, in sequence, to 71 inch lbs. (8 Nm) for 1st pass and 35 ft. lbs. (48 Nm) for 2nd pass.
- Throttle body. Torque the bolts to 18 ft. lbs. (26 Nm).
- All cable, hose and wiring connections to the throttle body
- Alternator rear brace
- Accelerator control/cruise control servo cable adjuster
- Accelerator cable bracket and cables. Torque the screws to 90 inch lbs. (10 Nm).

- Secondary air injection pipe. Torque the fitting to 41 ft. lbs. (55 Nm).

9. Install the EGR valve pipe, EGR valve and the control valve relay; then, torque as follows:

a. EGR valve pipe studs: 53 inch lbs. (6 Nm).

b. EGR valve pipe nuts, valve nuts and control valve relay nut: 18 ft. lbs. (25 Nm).

10. Install or connect the following:
- Emission canister purge solenoid. Tighten the bracket bolt to 53 inch lbs. (6 Nm).
- Vacuum and crankcase vent hoses
- Fuel rail and fuel pressure regulator vacuum tube. Tighten the bolt to 15 ft. lbs. (20 Nm).
- Fuel pipe to the fuel rail.

- Secondary air injection diverter valve hoses
- Wiring harnesses
- Air duct
- Ngative battery cable

11. Refill the cooling system.

Exhaust Manifold

REMOVAL & INSTALLATION

3.8L Engine

LEFT SIDE

1. Before servicing the vehicle, refer to the precautions in the beginning of this section.

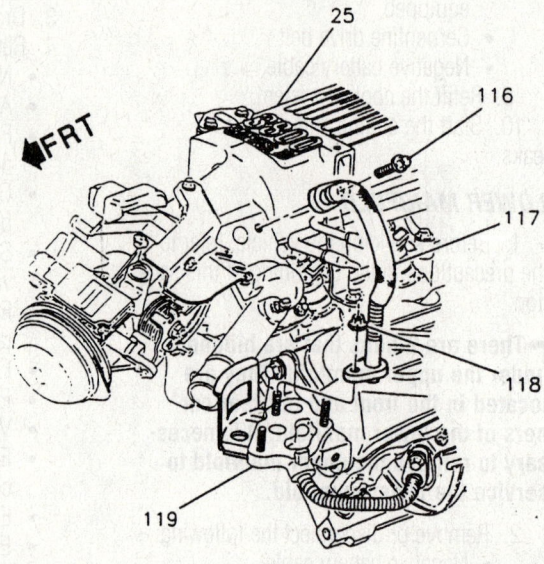

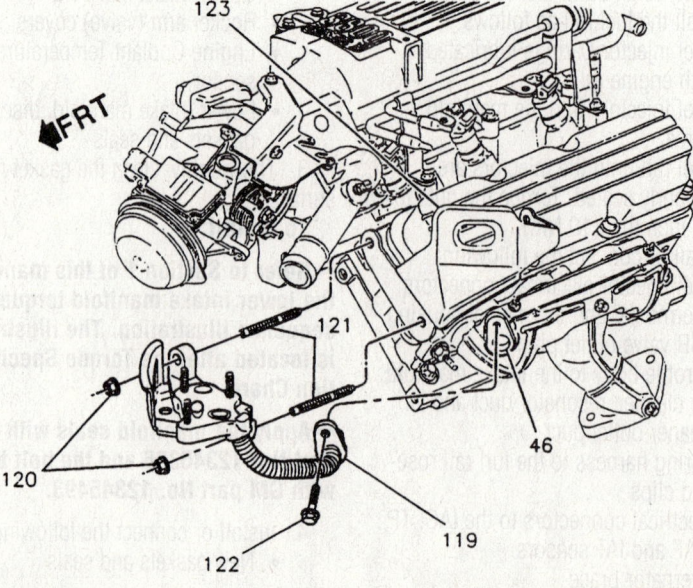

25	MANIFOLD, UPPER INTAKE
46	MANIFOLD, LEFT EXHAUST
116	BOLT/SCREW, EGR VALVE OUTLET PIPE
117	PIPE, EGR VALVE OUTLET
118	NUT, EGR VALVE OUTLET PIPE
119	ADAPTER, EGR VALVE
120	NUT, EGR VALVE ADAPTER
121	STUD, EGR VALVE ADAPTER
122	BOLT/SCREW, EGR VALVE ADAPTER
123	BRACKET, ENGINE LIFT

9300WG01

Exploded view of the EGR valve adapter and outlet pipe—3.8L engine

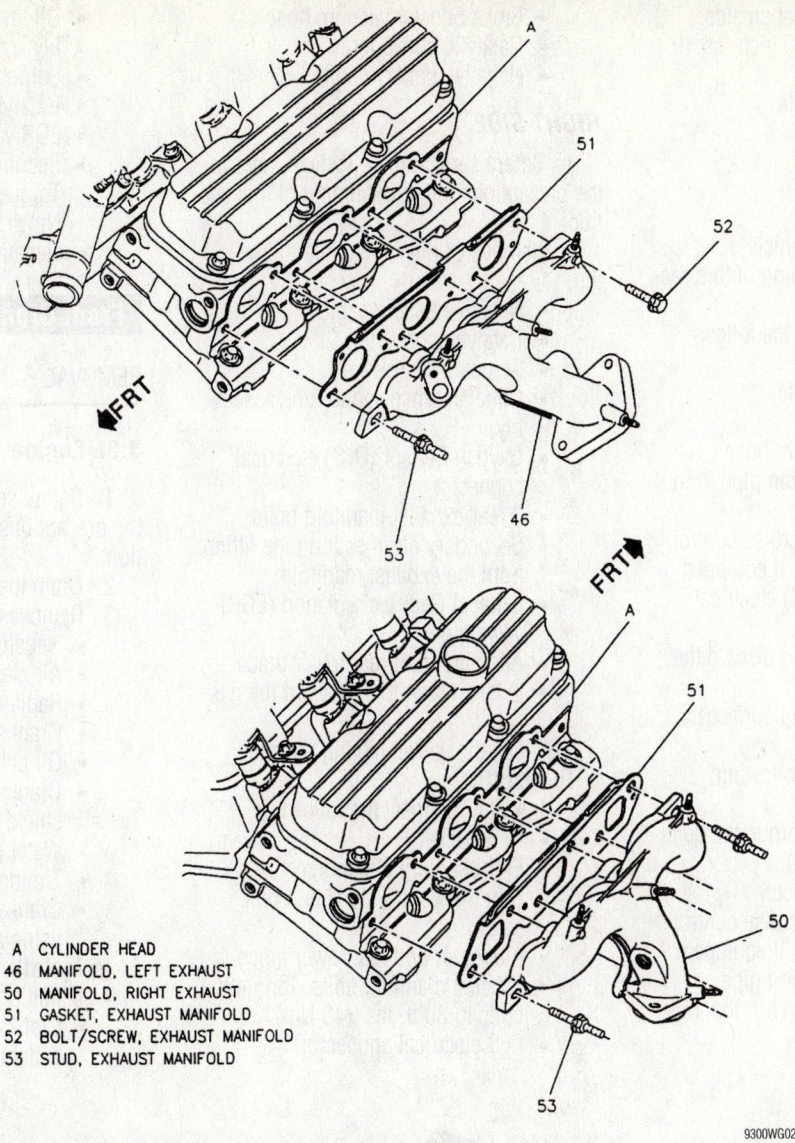

A CYLINDER HEAD
46 MANIFOLD, LEFT EXHAUST
50 MANIFOLD, RIGHT EXHAUST
51 GASKET, EXHAUST MANIFOLD
52 BOLT/SCREW, EXHAUST MANIFOLD
53 STUD, EXHAUST MANIFOLD

9300WG02

Exploded view of the right and left exhaust manifold mounting—3.8L engine

2. Remove or disconnect the following:
- Negative battery cable
- Exhaust Gas Recirculation (EGR) valve adapter from the exhaust manifold
- Oil level dipstick and tube
- Exhaust manifold heat shields
- Catalytic converter pipe
- Oxygen Sensor (O_2S) electrical connector
- Spark plug cables from the plugs
- Exhaust manifold and discard the gasket

3. Clean the exhaust manifold and cylinder head mating surfaces.

To install:

4. Install or connect the following:
- New gasket

- Exhaust manifold. Torque the fasteners to 106 inch lbs. (12 Nm).
- O_2S electrical connector
- Catalytic converter pipe
- Spark plug cables
- Exhaust manifold heat shields. Torque the nuts to 80 inch lbs. (9 Nm).
- Oil level dipstick and tube
- EGR valve adapter. Torque the bolt to 18 ft. lbs. (25 Nm).
- Negative battery cable

RIGHT SIDE

1. Before servicing the vehicle, refer to the precautions in the beginning of this section.

2. Remove or disconnect the following:

- Negative battery cable
- Exhaust manifold heat shields
- Exhaust catalytic converter pipe
- Oxygen Sensor (O_2S) electrical connector
- Spark plug cables from the plugs
- Exhaust manifold and discard the gasket

3. Clean the gasket mating surfaces.

To install:

4. Install or connect the following:
- New gasket
- Exhaust manifold. Torque the fasteners to 106 inch lbs. (12 Nm).
- O_2S electrical connector
- Catalytic converter pipe
- Spark plugs cables

For engine torque specifications, refer to Section 1 of this manual

- Exhaust manifold heat shields. Torque the nuts to 80 inch lbs. (9 Nm).
- Negative battery cable

5.7L Engines

LEFT SIDE

1. Before servicing the vehicle, refer to the precautions in the beginning of this section.
2. Remove or disconnect the following:

- Negative battery cable
- Catalytic converter
- Brake booster vacuum hose
- Secondary air injection pipe from the exhaust manifold
- Accelerator control/cruise control servo cable adjuster, if equipped
- Oxygen Sensor (O2S) electrical connector
- Exhaust manifold and discard the gasket

3. Clean the gasket mating surfaces.

To install:

4. Install or connect the following:
- New gasket
- Exhaust manifold. Torque the bolts to 30 ft. lbs. (40 Nm).
- O2S electrical connector
- Accelerator control/cruise control servo cable adjuster, if equipped
- Secondary air injection pipe. Torque the fitting to 41 ft. lbs. (55 Nm).

- Brake booster vacuum hose
- Catalytic converter
- Negative battery cable

RIGHT SIDE

1. Before servicing the vehicle, refer to the precautions in the beginning of this section.
2. Remove or disconnect the following:

- Negative battery cable
- Catalytic converter
- Serpentine drive belt
- Oil level dipstick and tube assembly
- Oxygen Sensor (O2S) electrical connector
- 3 rear exhaust manifold bolts
- Secondary air injection pipe fitting from the exhaust manifold
- Exhaust Gas Recirculation (EGR) valve pipe
- Alternator and rear lower brace
- Exhaust manifold, discard the gasket

3. Clean the gasket mating surfaces.

To install:

4. Install or connect the following:
- New gasket
- Exhaust manifold and secure with the front 3 studs and bolt screw
- Alternator and rear lower brace
- Exhaust manifold bolts. Torque the bolts to 30 ft. lbs. (40 Nm).
- O2S electrical connector

- Oil level dipstick and tube assembly
- Serpentine drive belt
- Catalytic converter
- EGR valve pipe
- Secondary air injection pipe fitting. Torque the fitting to 41 ft. lbs. (55 Nm).
- Negative battery cable

Front Crankshaft Seal

REMOVAL & INSTALLATION

3.8L Engine

1. Before servicing the vehicle, refer to the precautions in the beginning of this section.
2. Drain the cooling system.
3. Remove or disconnect the following:
- Negative battery cable
- Air cleaner and intake air duct
- Radiator hose from the front cover
- Crankshaft balancer
- Oil pan-to-front cover bolts
- Crankshaft Position (CKP) sensor shield
- Water pump
- Timing chain (front) cover
- Crankshaft seal from the cover using a suitable seal driver

To install:

4. Install or connect the following:
- Crankshaft seal to the cover using a suitable seal driver

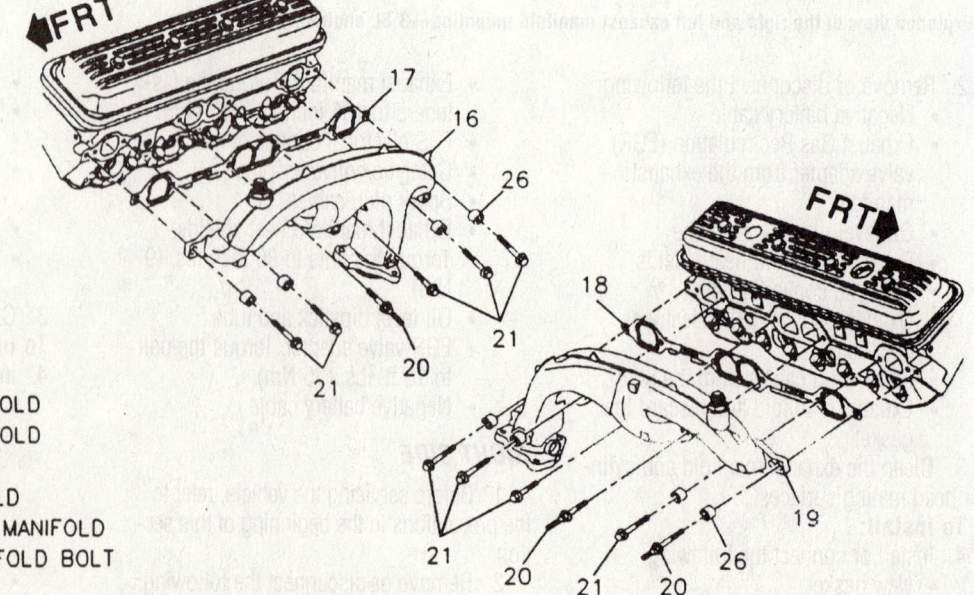

16	MANIFOLD, EXHAUST
17	GASKET, EXHAUST MANIFOLD
18	GASKET, EXHAUST MANIFOLD
19	MANIFOLD, EXHAUST
20	STUD, EXHAUST MANIFOLD
21	BOLT/SCREW, EXHAUST MANIFOLD
26	SPACER, EXHAUST MANIFOLD BOLT

Exploded view of right and left exhaust manifold mounting—5.7L engines

7922WG36

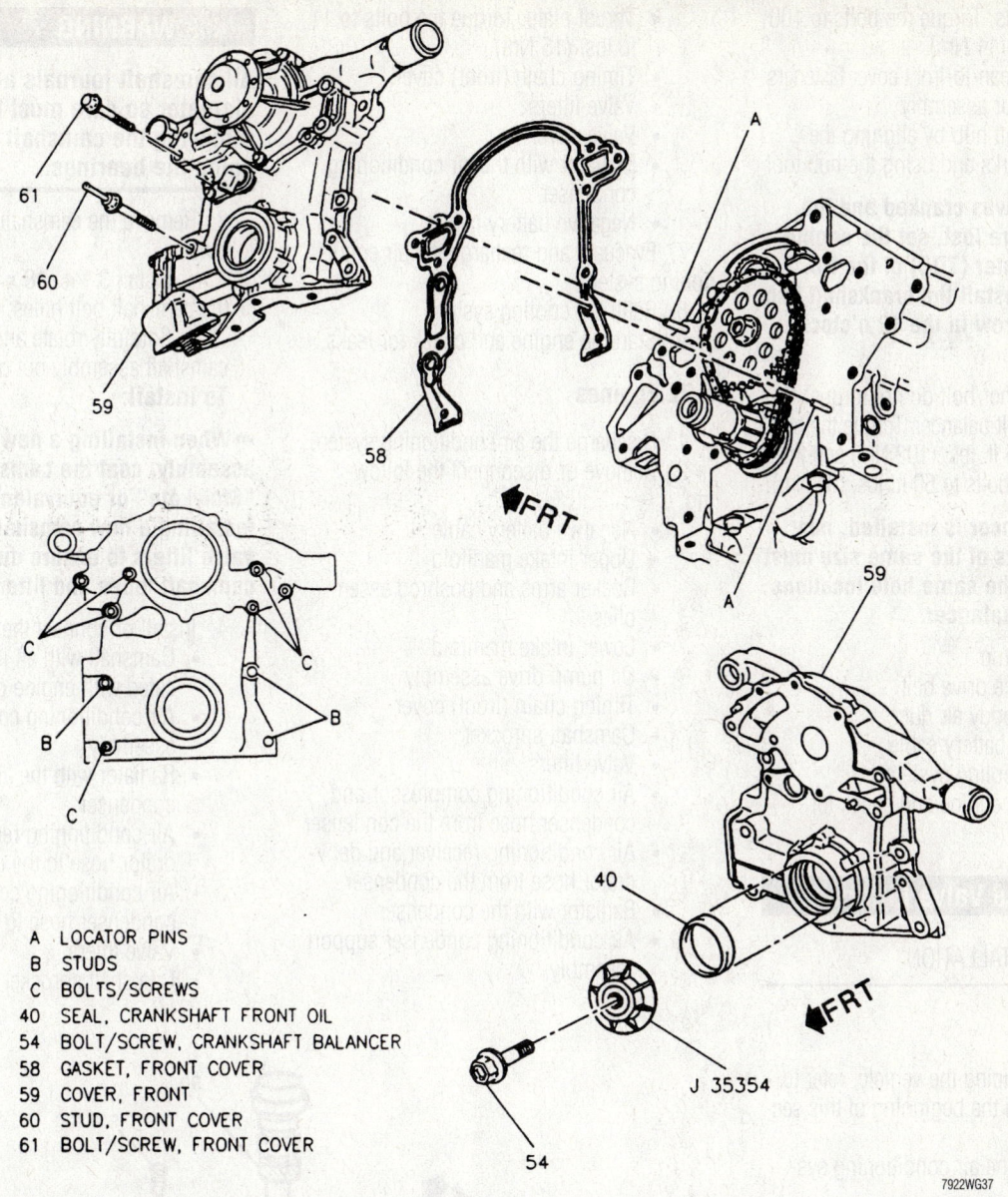

A	LOCATOR PINS
B	STUDS
C	BOLTS/SCREWS
40	SEAL, CRANKSHAFT FRONT OIL
54	BOLT/SCREW, CRANKSHAFT BALANCER
58	GASKET, FRONT COVER
59	COVER, FRONT
60	STUD, FRONT COVER
61	BOLT/SCREW, FRONT COVER

Exploded view of the front cover mounting and bolt locations—3.8L engine

- Timing chain (front) cover. Torque the fasteners to 11 ft. lbs. (15 Nm) plus 40 degrees using a torque angle meter.
- Water pump
- CKP sensor shield
- Oil pan-to-front cover bolts. Torque the bolts to 10 ft. lbs. (14 Nm).
- Crankshaft balancer
- Radiator hose to the front cover
- Serpentine belt and air cleaner assembly
- Negative battery cable

5. Refill the cooling system.
6. Start the engine and check for leaks.

5.7L Engines

1. Before servicing the vehicle, refer to the precautions in the beginning of this section.
2. Drain the cooling system.
3. Remove or disconnect the following:
   - Negative battery cable
   - Throttle body air intake duct
   - Serpentine drive belt
   - Water pump assembly
   - Crankshaft balancer

➥**Matchmark the crankshaft hub to the engine front cover.**

   - Crankshaft hub
   - Distributor assembly

   - Oil pan-to-front cover fasteners
   - Engine front cover, discard the gasket
   - Crankshaft seal from the front cover using a suitable seal driver

To install:

4. Thoroughly, clean the gasket mating surfaces. Inspect the engine front cover for damage. Replace as necessary.
5. Install or connect the following:
   - New crankshaft seal into the front cover
   - Front cover seal protector on the water pump driveshaft
   - New gasket
   - Front cover over the shafts and

For complete mechanical specifications, refer to Section 1 of this manual

guide pins. Torque the bolts to 100 inch lbs. (11 Nm).
- Front oil pan-to-front cover fasteners
- Distributor assembly
- Crankshaft hub by aligning the matchmarks and using the hub tool

➡ **If the engine was cranked and the matchmarks were lost, set the engine to Top Dead Center (TDC) of the No. 1 cylinder, then install the crankshaft hub with the cast arrow in the 12 o'clock position.**

- Hub washer/bolt do not torque
- Crankshaft balancer. Torque the hub bolt to 75 ft. lbs. (102 Nm) and the balancer bolts to 60 ft. lbs. (81 Nm).

➡ **If a new balancer is installed, new balancer weights of the same size must be installed in the same hole locations as the original balancer.**

- Water pump
- Serpentine drive belt
- Throttle body air duct
- Negative battery cable
6. Refill the cooling system.
7. Operate the engine and check for leaks.

Camshaft and Valve Lifters

REMOVAL & INSTALLATION

3.8L Engine

1. Before servicing the vehicle, refer to the precautions in the beginning of this section.
2. Discharge the air conditioning system.
3. Remove or disconnect the following:
- Negative battery cable
- Radiator with the air conditioning condenser assembly
- Valve cover
- Valve lifters
- Timing chain (engine) front cover
- Camshaft sprocket and timing chain
- Camshaft thrust plate
4. Remove the camshaft assembly, as follows:
    a. Install 3 ⁵⁄₁₆–18 x 4-inch bolts in the camshaft bolt holes.
    b. Carefully rotate and pull the camshaft assembly out of the bearings.
5. Inspect the camshaft for damage and replace if necessary.
To install:
6. Install or connect the following:
- Camshaft lubricated with prelube

- Thrust plate. Torque the bolts to 11 ft. lbs. (15 Nm).
- Timing chain (front) cover
- Valve lifters
- Valve cover
- Radiator with the air conditioning condenser
- Negative battery cable
7. Evacuate and recharge the air conditioning system.
8. Refill the cooling system.
9. Start the engine and check for leaks.

5.7L Engines

1. Discharge the air conditioning system.
2. Remove or disconnect the following:

- Negative battery cable
- Upper intake manifold
- Rocker arms and pushrod assemblies
- Lower intake manifold
- Oil pump drive assembly
- Timing chain (front) cover
- Camshaft sprocket
- Valve lifters
- Air conditioning compressor and condenser hose from the condenser
- Air conditioning receiver and dehydrator hose from the condenser
- Radiator with the condenser
- Air conditioning condenser support assembly

⁂ WARNING

All camshaft journals are the same diameter so care must be used when removing the camshaft to avoid damaging the bearings.

3. Remove the camshaft assembly, as follows:
    a. Install 3 ⁵⁄₁₆–18 x 4-inch bolts in the camshaft bolt holes.
    b. Carefully rotate and pull the camshaft assembly out of the bearings.
To install:

➡ **When installing a new camshaft assembly, coat the camshaft lobes with "Molykote" or equivalent. When installing a new camshaft, replace all valve lifters to ensure durability of the camshaft lobes and lifters.**

4. Install or connect the following:
- Camshaft with all journals lubricated with engine oil
- Air conditioning condenser support assembly
- Radiator with the air conditioning condenser
- Air conditioning receiver and dehydrator hose to the condenser
- Air conditioning compressor and condenser hose to the condenser
- Valve lifters
- Camshaft sprocket

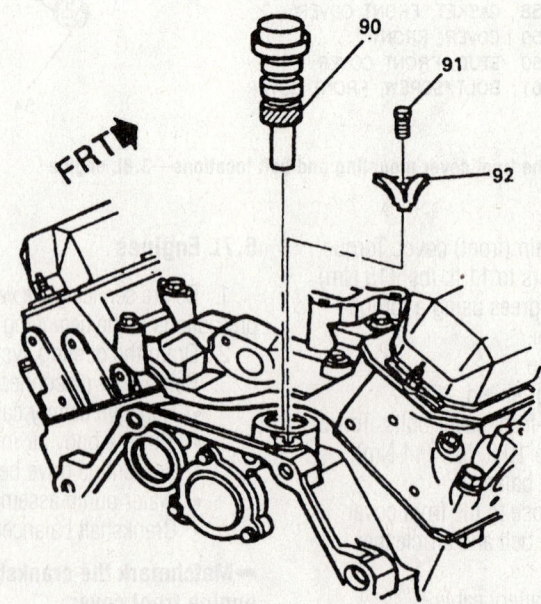

90 DRIVE ASSEMBLY, OIL PUMP
91 BOLT/SCREW, OIL PUMP DRIVE CLAMP
92 CLAMP, OIL PUMP DRIVE

7922WG12

Unfasten the retaining bolt and clamp, then remove the oil pump drive—5.7L Engines

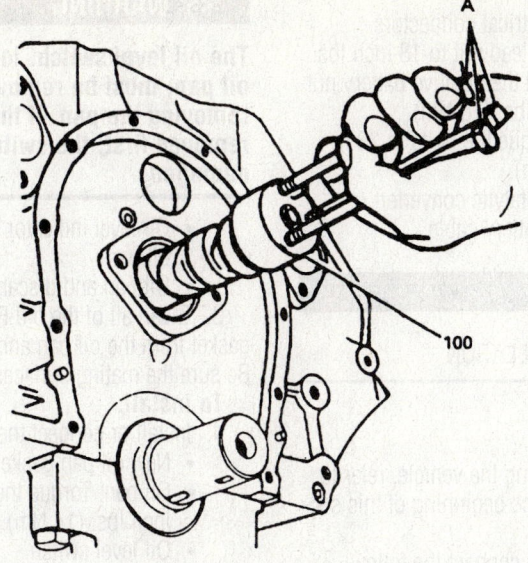

A BOLTS
100 CAMSHAFT ASSEMBLY

7922WG11

Thread 3 bolts into the camshaft to facilitate removal and installation—5.7L Engines

- Timing chain (front) cover
- Oil pump drive assembly with the oil pump drive gear lubricated with prelube. Torque the bolt to 25 ft. lbs. (34 Nm).
- Lower intake manifold
- Pushrods and rocker arms
- Upper intake manifold
- Negative battery cable
5. Recharge the air conditioning system.

Valve Lash

ADJUSTMENT

➥The engines in this section utilize hydraulic valve lifters. Use the following procedure for initial adjustment.

1. Remove or disconnect the following:
   - Negative battery cable
   - Valve covers
2. Loosen the rocker arm nuts, if necessary.

➥Make sure the pushrods is seated in the lifter seat.

3. Tighten the rocker arm nut until all lash is eliminated.
4. The engine must be on the No. 1 firing position before proceeding.
5. For the 3.8L engine, adjust the valves as follows:
   a. Place the engine on Top Dead Center (TDC) of the No. 1 firing position.

   b. Tighten exhaust valves No. 1, 2 and 3; then, intake valves No. 1, 5 and 6.

   c. Loosen the adjusting nut until lash is felt at the pushrod.

   d. Tighten the adjusting nut until all lash is removed, then tighten the nut an additional 1½ turns to center the lifter plunger.

   e. Rotate the crankshaft 1 revolution until the "0" timing mark is once again aligned.

   f. Adjust exhaust valves No. 4, 5 and 6 and intake valves No. 2, 3 and 4.
6. For the 5.7L engines, adjust the valves as follows:
7. Place the engine on TDC of the No. 1 firing position.

   a. Tighten the exhaust valves No. 1, 3, 4 and 8; then, intake valves No. 1, 2, 5 and 7.

   b. Loosen the adjusting nut until lash is felt at the pushrod.

   c. Tighten the adjusting nut until all lash is removed; then, tighten an additional 1 turn to center the lifter plunger.

   d. Rotate the crankshaft 1 revolution until the "0" timing mark is once again aligned.

   e. Adjust exhaust valves No. 2, 5, 6 and 7; then, intake valves 3, 4, 6 and 8.
8. Install or connect the following:
   - Rocker arm cover
   - Negative battery cable

Starter

REMOVAL & INSTALLATION

3.8L Engine

1. Before servicing the vehicle, refer to the precautions in the beginning of this section.
2. Remove or disconnect the following:

   - Negative battery cable
   - Starter shield
   - Starter bolt and stud
   - Starter and lower it
   - Starter electrical connectors
   - Starter

To install:

3. Install or connect the following:
   - Starter
   - Starter electrical connectors. Torque the lead nut to 17 inch lbs. (2 Nm) and the positive battery nut to 89 inch lbs. (10 Nm).
   - Starter. Torque the bolt to 35 ft. lbs. (47 Nm) and the stud to 33 ft. lbs. (45 Nm).
   - Starter shield
   - Negative battery cable

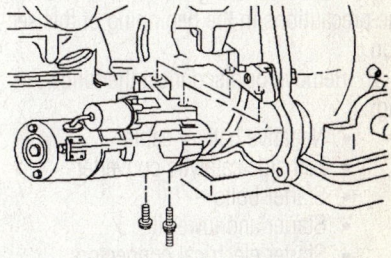

9306WG04

View of the starter—3.8L engine

5.7L (VIN P) Engine

1. Before servicing the vehicle, refer to the precautions in the beginning of this section.
2. Remove or disconnect the following:

   - Negative battery cable
   - Catalytic converter
   - Starter bolts
   - Starter and lower it
   - Starter electrical connectors
   - Starter

To install:

3. Install or connect the following:
   - Starter
   - Starter electrical connectors.

Please refer to Section 8 for electric cooling fan wiring schematics

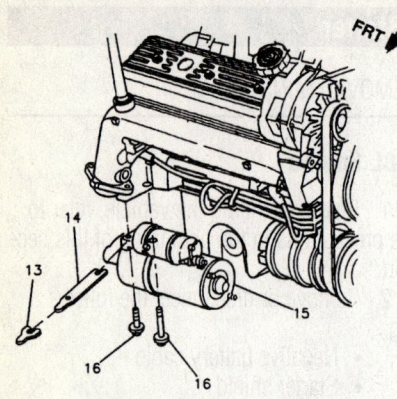

13 SHIM, STARTER MOTOR SINGLE
14 SHIM, STARTER MOTOR DOUBLE
15 MOTOR, STARTER
16 BOLT/SCREW, STARTER MOTOR
21 STUD, STARTER MOTOR

9306WG06

View of the starter—5.7L (VIN P) engine

Torque the lead nut to 18 inch lbs. (2 Nm) and the positive battery nut to 89 inch lbs. (10 Nm).
- Starter. Torque the bolts to 33 ft. lbs. (45 Nm).
- Catalytic converter
- Negative battery cable

5.7L (VIN G) Engine

1. Before servicing the vehicle, refer to the precautions in the beginning of this section.
2. Remove or disconnect the following:

- Negative battery cable
- Left side catalytic converter
- Starter bolts
- Starter and lower it
- Starter electrical connectors
- Starter
- Starter shield, if necessary

To install:
3. Install or connect the following:
- Starter shield, if removed

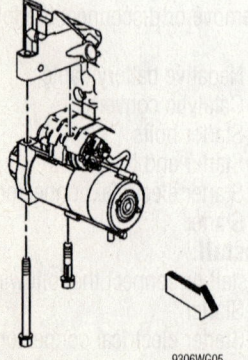

9306WG05

View of the starter—5.7L (VIN G) engine

- Starter
- Starter electrical connectors. Torque the lead nut to 18 inch lbs. (2 Nm) and the positive battery nut to 89 inch lbs. (10 Nm).
- Starter. Torque the bolts to 33 ft. lbs. (45 Nm).
- Left side catalytic converter
- Negative battery cable

Oil Pan

REMOVAL & INSTALLATION

3.8L Engine

1. Before servicing the vehicle, refer to the precautions in the beginning of this section.
2. Remove or disconnect the following:

- Negative battery cable
- Alternator
- Ignition coil
- Catalytic converter pipe
- Converter cover, if equipped with an automatic transmission
- Engine mount through-bolts and nuts

✳✳ WARNING

The oil level switch, located in the oil pan, must be removed before removing the pan. If the pan is removed first, the switch may be damaged.

- Oil level indicator switch from the oil pan
- Oil pan and discard the gasket

3. Clean all of the old RTV sealant or gasket from the oil pan and engine block. Be sure the mating surfaces are clean.

To install:
4. Install or connect the following:
- New oil pan gasket
- Oil pan. Torque the bolts to 125 inch lbs. (14 Nm).
- Oil level switch
- Engine mount through-bolts
- Converter cover, if equipped with an automatic transmission
- Catalytic converter pipe
- Ignition coil
- Alternator
- Negative battery cable
5. Refill the crankcase.
6. Start the engine and check for leaks.

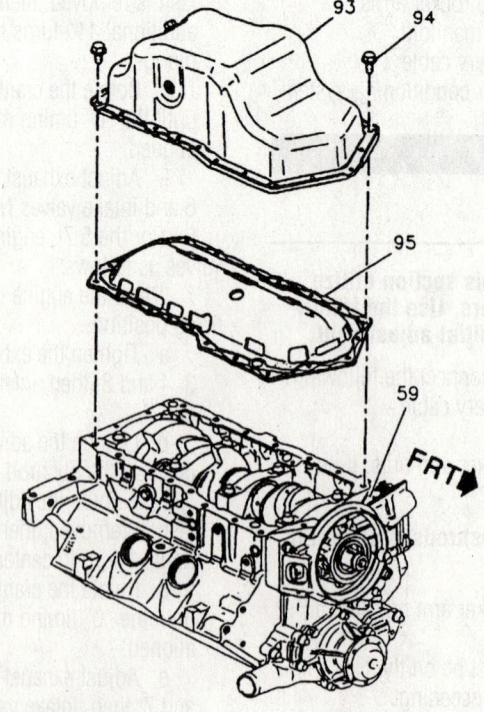

59 COVER, FRONT
93 PAN, OIL
94 BOLT/SCREW, OIL PAN
95 GASKET, OIL PAN

7922WG14

Exploded view of the oil pan and gasket—3.8L engine

5.7L Engines

1. Before servicing the vehicle, refer to the precautions in the beginning of this section.
2. Drain the crankcase.
3. Remove or disconnect the following:
   • Negative battery cable
   • Air intake duct
   • Oil level sensor

✳✳ CAUTION

Be sure that the exhaust system is cool before proceeding.

   • Catalytic converter
   • Exhaust pipe hanger bolt, reposition the pipe
   • Cooler lines from the oil pan clip, if equipped with an automatic transmission
   • Starter
   • Converter cover, if equipped with an automatic transmission
   • Engine mount through-bolts
4. Using a jack, raise the engine enough to provide sufficient clearance for oil pan removal.

➡**If the front crankshaft counterweight prohibits removal of the pan, turn the crankshaft to position it horizontally.**

5. Remove the oil pan and discard the gasket.
6. Clean all of the old RTV sealant or gasket from the mating surfaces.

To install:

7. Apply a small amount of RTV sealer to the front cover and engine block junction and to the rear oil seal housing and engine block junction. Apply sealer 1 in. (25mm) in either direction of the radius cavity of these junctions.
8. Install or connect the following:
   • New oil pan gasket

   • Oil pan. Torque the corner fasteners to 15 ft. lbs. (20 Nm) and the remaining fasteners to 106 inch lbs. (12 Nm).
   • Engine mount through-bolts. Torque the bolts to 70 ft. lbs. (95 Nm).
   • Oil level sensor. Torque it to 16 ft. lbs. (22 Nm).
   • Converter cover, if equipped with an automatic transmission. Torque the bolts to 89 inch lbs. (10 Nm).
   • Starter
   • Transmission fluid cooler lines, if equipped, to the oil pan clip
   • Exhaust pipe hanger bolt
   • Catalytic converter
   • Oil level sensor electrical connector
   • Air cleaner duct
   • Negative battery cable
9. Refill the crankcase.
10. Start the engine and check for leaks.

Oil Pump

REMOVAL & INSTALLATION

3.8L Engine

1. Before servicing the vehicle, refer to the precautions in the beginning of this section.
2. Remove or disconnect the following:
   • Negative battery cable
   • Engine front cover
   • Oil filter adapter, pressure valve and spring
   • Oil pump cover
   • Oil pump gear set

To install:

3. Lubricate the gear set with petroleum jelly.
4. Install the oil pump gear set into the front cover.
5. Pack the gear cavity with petroleum jelly after the gear set has been installed.

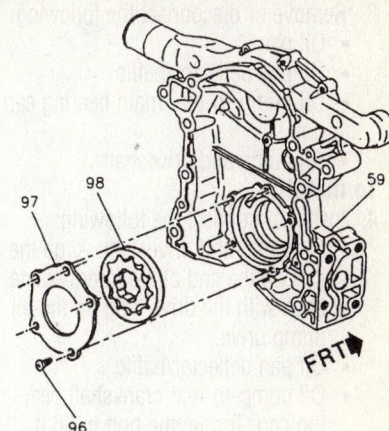

59   COVER, FRONT
96   BOLT/SCREW, OIL PUMP COVER
97   COVER, OIL PUMP
98   GEAR SET, OIL PUMP

7922WG16

Exploded view of the oil pump gear set— 3.8L engine

6. Install or connect the following:
   • Oil pump cover
   • Oil filter adapter, pressure valve and spring
   • Engine front cover
   • Negative battery cable

5.7L Engines

1. Before servicing the vehicle, refer to the precautions in the beginning of this section.
2. Drain the crankcase.

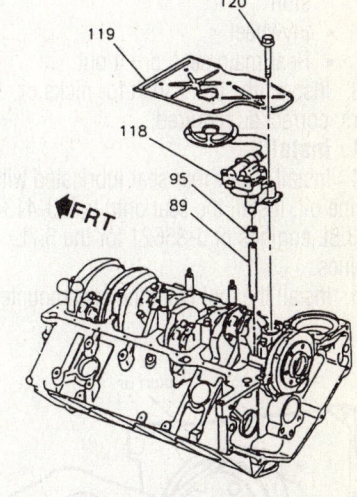

89   DRIVESHAFT, OIL PUMP
95   RETAINER, OIL PUMP DRIVESHAFT
118 PUMP, OIL
119 DEFLECTOR, CRANKSHAFT OIL
120 BOLT/SCREW, OIL PUMP

7922WG17

Exploded view of the oil pump and drive-shaft mounting—5.7L engine

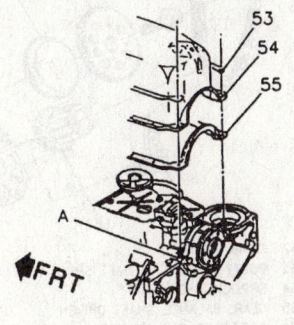

A   SEALER
53   REINFORCEMENT, OIL PAN
54   PAN, OIL
55   GASKET, OIL PAN

Oil pan sealer and gasket location—5.7L engines

7922WG13

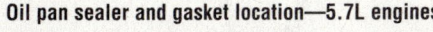

3. Remove or disconnect the following:
- Oil pan
- Oil pan deflector/baffle
- Oil pump-to-rear main bearing cap bolt
- Oil pump and driveshaft

To install:

4. Install or connect the following:
- Oil pump and driveshaft. Align the slot on the end of the intermediate shaft with the drive tang on the oil pump drive.
- Oil pan deflector/baffle
- Oil pump-to-rear crankshaft bearing cap. Torque the bolt to 66 ft. lbs. (90 Nm) and the oil pan baffle nuts to 30 ft. lbs. (40 Nm).
- Oil pan

5. Refill the crankcase.

Rear Main Seal

REMOVAL & INSTALLATION

➡**The rear main seal is a 1-piece unit. It can be removed or installed without removing the oil pan or crankshaft.**

1. Before servicing the vehicle, refer to the precautions in the beginning of this section.

2. Remove or disconnect the following:
- Transmission.
- Clutch and pressure plate, if equipped with a manual transmission
- Flywheel
- Rear main seal, pry it out

3. Inspect the crankshaft for nicks or burrs, correct as required.

To install:

4. Install a new rear seal lubricated with engine oil. Install the seal onto tool J-41349 for 3.8L engines or J-35621 for the 5.7L engines.

5. Install the tool (with the seal mounted

to it) onto the rear of the crankshaft. Tighten the screws snugly to be sure the seal will be installed squarely over the crankshaft.

6. Tighten the wing nut on the installation tool until it bottoms out.

7. Remove the tool from the crankshaft or rear oil seal housing, as applicable.

8. Install or connect the following:
- Flywheel
- Clutch and pressure plate, ,if equipped with a manual transmission
- Transmission

9. Check the fluid levels, start the engine and check for leaks.

Timing Chain, Sprockets, Front Cover and Seal

REMOVAL & INSTALLATION

3.8L Engine

1. Before servicing the vehicle, refer to the precautions in the beginning of this section.

2. Drain the cooling system.

3. Remove or disconnect the following:
- Negative battery cable
- Air cleaner and intake air duct
- Radiator hose from the front cover
- Crankshaft balancer
- Oil pan-to-front cover bolts
- Crankshaft Position (CKP) sensor shield
- Water pump
- Timing chain (front) cover
- Crankshaft seal from the cover using a suitable seal driver

4. Align the timing marks on the

sprockets so they are as close together as possible.

5. Remove or disconnect the following:
- Timing chain damper
- Camshaft sprocket by pulling the timing chain and sprocket from the camshaft
- Crankshaft sprocket, if necessary

➡**If the sprocket does not come off easily, a light blow on the edge of the sprocket with a plastic mallet should dislodge it.**

6. Clean the chain and sprockets. Inspect all components for damage and replace as necessary.

To install:

7. If the crankshaft has been turned in the engine, perform the following:

a. Turn the crankshaft so the No. 1 piston is at top Dead Center (TDC) of its compression stroke.

b. Turn the camshaft so that, with the sprocket temporarily installed, the timing mark is straight down.

8. Install or connect the following:
- Timing chain on the sprockets with the timing marks aligned
- Timing chain and sprockets. Torque the bolt to 74 ft. lbs. (100 Nm) plus an additional 90 degrees using a Torque Angle Meter tool J-36660 or equivalent.
- Timing chain damper. Torque the bolt to 16 ft. lbs. (22 Nm).

9. Rotate the engine 2 revolutions, then check to be sure the timing marks are aligned.

➡**It may be necessary to loosen the oil pan bolts to provide clearance for the front cover.**

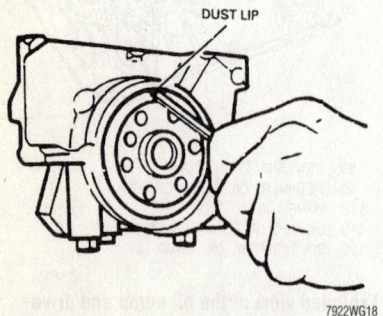

When prying the rear main seal out, be careful not to damage the crankshaft sealing surface or the seal bore

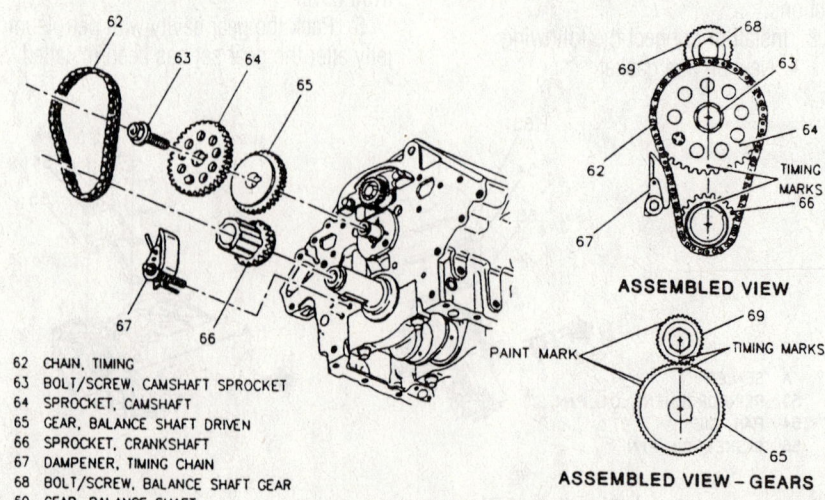

62 CHAIN, TIMING
63 BOLT/SCREW, CAMSHAFT SPROCKET
64 SPROCKET, CAMSHAFT
65 GEAR, BALANCE SHAFT DRIVEN
66 SPROCKET, CRANKSHAFT
67 DAMPENER, TIMING CHAIN
68 BOLT/SCREW, BALANCE SHAFT GEAR
69 GEAR, BALANCE SHAFT

Exploded view of the timing chain and sprockets and timing mark alignment—3.8L engine

10. Install or connect the following:
- Timing chain (front) cover. Torque the fasteners to 11 ft. lbs. (15 Nm) plus 40 degrees using a torque angle meter.
- Water pump
- CKP sensor shield
- Oil pan-to-front cover bolts. Torque the bolts to 125 inch lbs. (14 Nm).
- Crankshaft balancer
- Radiator hose to the front cover
- Serpentine belt and air cleaner assembly
- Negative battery cable

11. Refill the cooling system.
12. Start the engine and check for leaks.

5.7L Engines

1. Before servicing the vehicle, refer to the precautions in the beginning of this section.

2. Drain the crankcase and cooling system.

3. Remove or disconnect the following:
- Negative battery cable
- Throttle body air intake duct
- Serpentine drive belt
- Water pump assembly
- Crankshaft balancer from the hub. Matchmark the balancer prior to removal.
- Crankshaft hub
- Distributor, if equipped
- Oil pan
- Engine front cover and discard the gasket
- Crankshaft seal from the front cover, using a seal driver

4. Rotate the crankshaft until the timing marks punched on the crankshaft and camshaft sprockets are aligned.

5. Remove or disconnect the following:
- Camshaft sprocket and timing chain

✳✳ WARNING

Do not turn the crankshaft after the timing chain has been removed to prevent damage to the pistons or valves.

- Water pump
- Water pump driveshaft assembly using Driven Gear Remover tool J-39243
- Driveshaft O-ring and discard it
- Crankshaft sprocket
- Crankshaft sprocket key, if necessary

6. Clean the chain and sprockets.

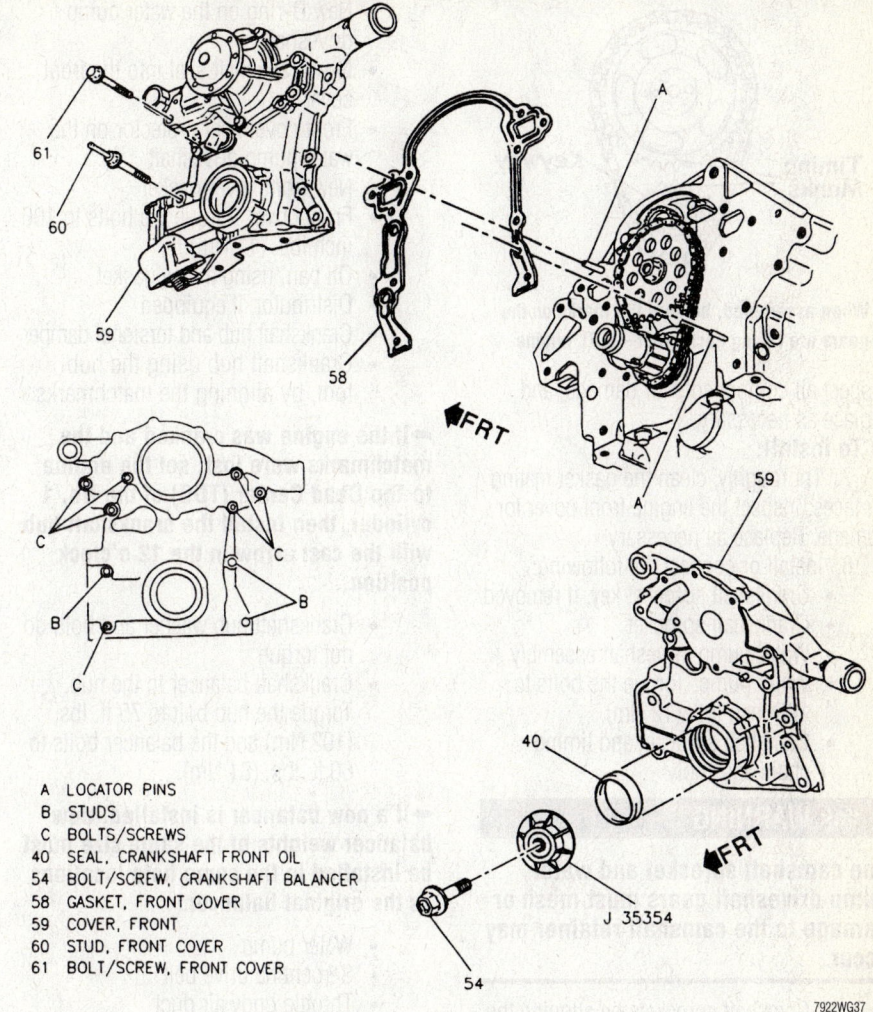

A LOCATOR PINS
B STUDS
C BOLTS/SCREWS
40 SEAL, CRANKSHAFT FRONT OIL
54 BOLT/SCREW, CRANKSHAFT BALANCER
58 GASKET, FRONT COVER
59 COVER, FRONT
60 STUD, FRONT COVER
61 BOLT/SCREW, FRONT COVER

Exploded view of the front cover mounting and bolt locations—3.8L engine

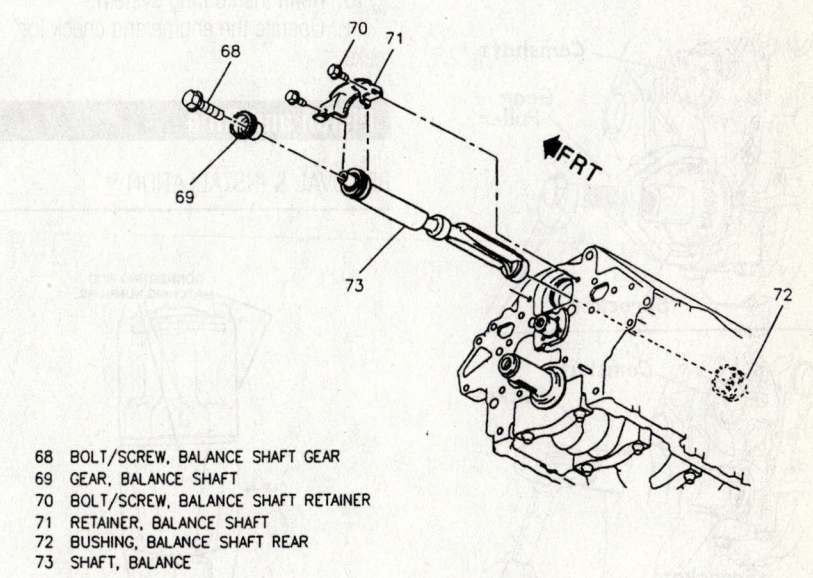

68 BOLT/SCREW, BALANCE SHAFT GEAR
69 GEAR, BALANCE SHAFT
70 BOLT/SCREW, BALANCE SHAFT RETAINER
71 RETAINER, BALANCE SHAFT
72 BUSHING, BALANCE SHAFT REAR
73 SHAFT, BALANCE

Exploded view of the balance shaft assembly—3.8L engine

Timing belt service is covered in Section 4 of this manual

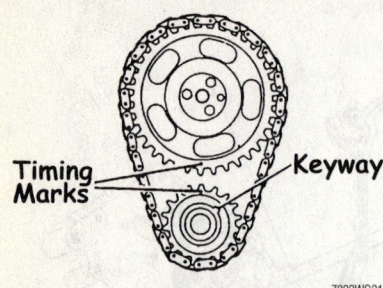

When assembled, be sure the marks are facing each other—5.7L engine

Inspect all components for damage, and replace as necessary.

To install:

7. Thoroughly, clean the gasket mating surfaces. Inspect the engine front cover for damage. Replace as necessary.

8. Install or connect the following:
- Crankshaft sprocket key, if removed
- Crankshaft sprocket
- Water pump driveshaft assembly
- Water pump. Torque the bolts to 105 inch lbs. (12 Nm).
- Camshaft sprocket and timing chain assembly

✱✱ WARNING

The camshaft sprocket and water pump driveshaft gears must mesh or damage to the camshaft retainer may occur.

- Camshaft sprockets by aligning the timing marks. Torque the bolts to 18 ft. lbs. (25 Nm).

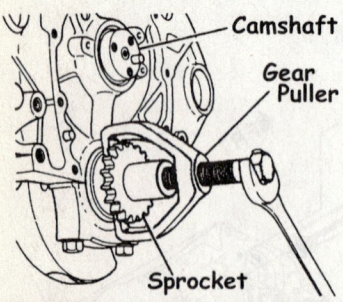

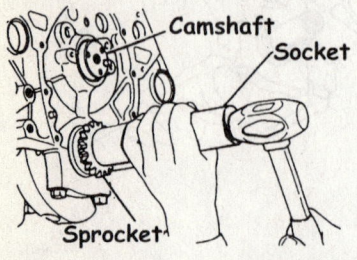

Use a gear puller to remove, and a large socket to install, the crankshaft sprocket—5.7L engine shown

- New O-ring on the water pump driveshaft
- New crankshaft seal into the front cover
- Front cover seal protector on the water pump driveshaft
- New front cover gasket
- Front cover. Torque the bolts to 100 inch lbs. (11 Nm).
- Oil pan, using a new gasket
- Distributor, if equipped
- Crankshaft hub and torsional damper
- Crankshaft hub using the hub tool, by aligning the matchmarks

➡ **If the engine was cranked and the matchmarks were lost, set the engine to Top Dead Center (TDC) of the No. 1 cylinder, then install the crankshaft hub with the cast arrow in the 12 o'clock position.**

- Crankshaft hub washer and bolt, do not torque
- Crankshaft balancer to the hub. Torque the hub bolt to 75 ft. lbs. (102 Nm) and the balancer bolts to 60 ft. lbs. (81 Nm).

➡ **If a new balancer is installed, new balancer weights of the same size must be installed in the same hole locations as the original balancer.**

- Water pump
- Serpentine drive belt
- Throttle body air duct
- Negative battery cable

9. Refill the engine crankcase.
10. Refill the cooling system.
11. Operate the engine and check for leaks.

Piston and Ring

REMOVAL & INSTALLATION

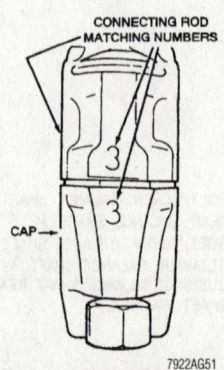

Engine connecting rod and cap installation. Be sure to matchmark the cap and rod prior to disassembly, as shown

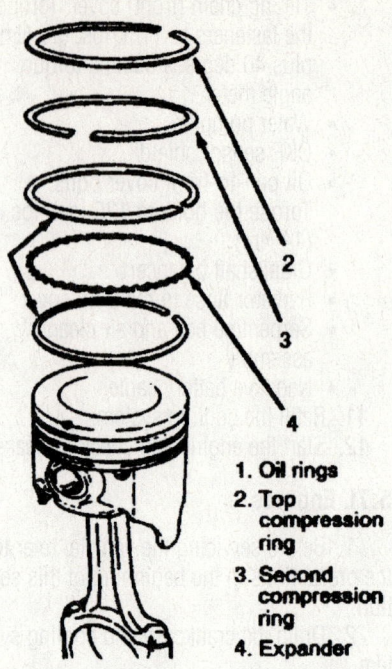

1. Oil rings
2. Top compression ring
3. Second compression ring
4. Expander

Piston ring positioning—3.8L engine

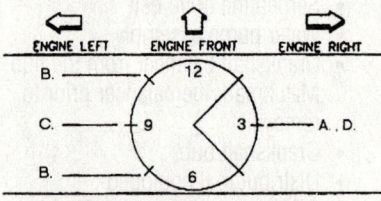

A. OIL RING SPACER GAP (TANG IN HOLE OR SLOT WITH ARC)
B. OIL RING RAIL GAPS
C. 2ND COMPRESSION RING GAP
D. TOP COMPRESSION RING GAP

Piston ring end-gap spacing—3.8L engine

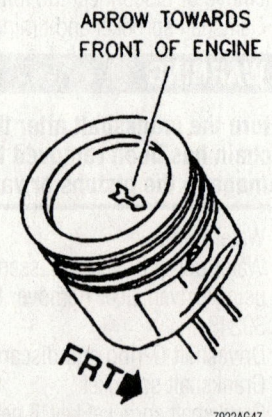

ARROW TOWARDS FRONT OF ENGINE

Piston positioning. Often the arrow is replaced by a notch, which also must face the front of the engine—3.8L engine

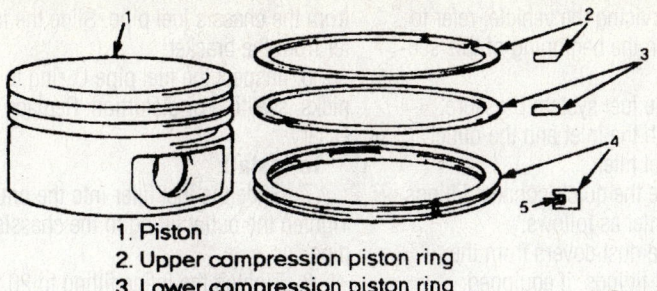

1. Piston
2. Upper compression piston ring
3. Lower compression piston ring
4. Oil control piston ring
5. Oil control ring spring w/spacer

7922AG43

Piston ring positioning—5.7L engine

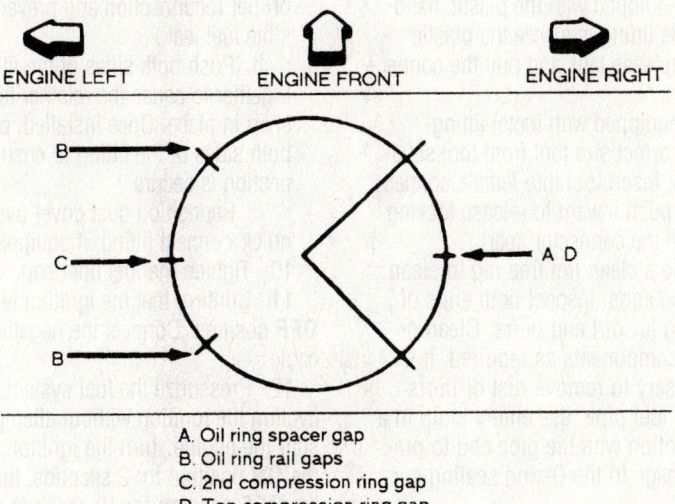

ENGINE LEFT ENGINE FRONT ENGINE RIGHT

A. Oil ring spacer gap
B. Oil ring rail gaps
C. 2nd compression ring gap
D. Top compression ring gap

7922AG42

Piston ring end-gap spacing—5.7L engine

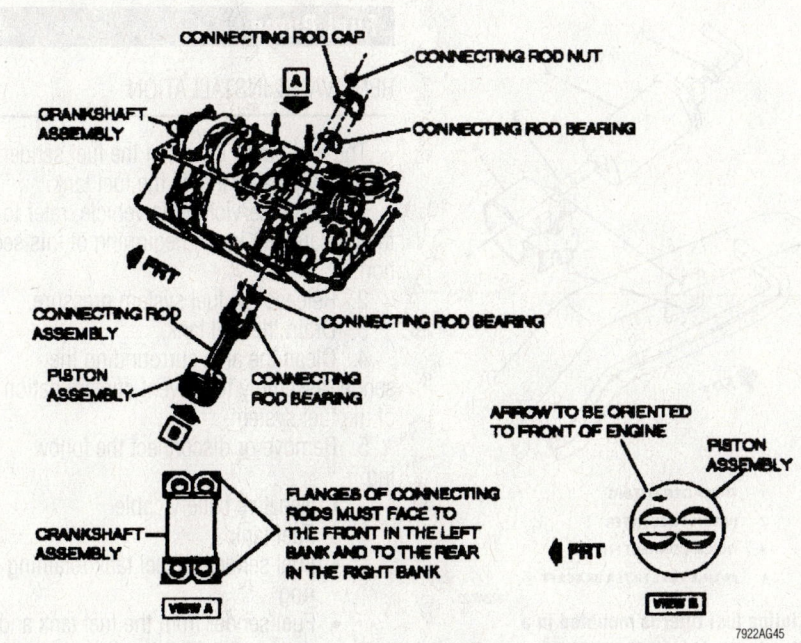

CONNECTING ROD CAP
CONNECTING ROD NUT
CRANKSHAFT ASSEMBLY
CONNECTING ROD BEARING
CONNECTING ROD ASSEMBLY
CONNECTING ROD BEARING
PISTON ASSEMBLY
CONNECTING ROD BEARING

ARROW TO BE ORIENTED TO FRONT OF ENGINE
PISTON ASSEMBLY

FLANGES OF CONNECTING RODS MUST FACE TO THE FRONT IN THE LEFT BANK AND TO THE REAR IN THE RIGHT BANK

CRANKSHAFT ASSEMBLY

VIEW A

VIEW B

7922AG45

Piston and connecting rod assembly positioning—5.7L (VIN P) engine

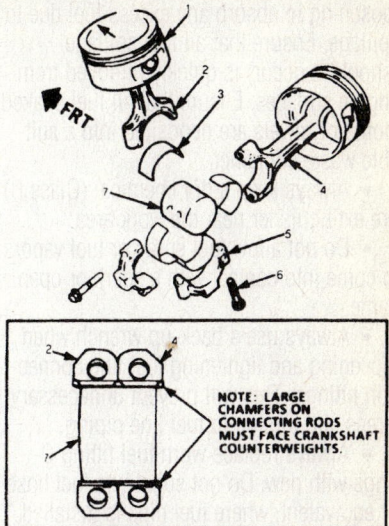

FRT

NOTE: LARGE CHAMFERS ON CONNECTING RODS MUST FACE CRANKSHAFT COUNTERWEIGHTS.

1. Piston
2. Connecting rod LH
3. Connecting rod bearing
4. Connecting rod RH
5. Connecting rod bearing cap
6. Connecting rod bearing cap bolt
7. Crankshaft

7922AG44

Piston and connecting rod assembly positioning—5.7L (VIN G) engine

FUEL SYSTEM

Fuel System Service Precautions

Safety is the most important factor when performing not only fuel system maintenance but any type of maintenance. Failure to conduct maintenance and repairs in a safe manner may result in serious personal injury or death. Maintenance and testing of the vehicle's fuel system components can be accomplished safely and effectively by adhering to the following rules and guidelines.

• To avoid the possibility of fire and personal injury, always disconnect the negative battery cable unless the repair or test procedure requires that battery voltage be applied.

• Always relieve the fuel system pressure prior to disconnecting any fuel system component (injector, fuel rail, pressure regulator, etc.), fitting or fuel line connection. Exercise extreme caution whenever relieving fuel system pressure, to avoid exposing skin, face and eyes to fuel spray. Please be advised that fuel under pressure may penetrate the skin or any part of the body that it contacts.

• Always place a shop towel or cloth around the fitting or connection prior to loosening to absorb any excess fuel due to spillage. Ensure that all fuel spillage (should it occur) is quickly removed from engine surfaces. Ensure that all fuel soaked cloths or towels are deposited into a suitable waste container.

• Always keep a dry chemical (Class B) fire extinguisher near the work area.

• Do not allow fuel spray or fuel vapors to come into contact with a spark or open flame.

• Always use a back-up wrench when loosening and tightening fuel line connection fittings. This will prevent unnecessary stress and torsion to fuel line piping.

• Always replace worn fuel fitting O-rings with new. Do not substitute fuel hose or equivalent, where fuel pipe is installed.

Fuel System Pressure

RELIEVING

1. Before servicing the vehicle, refer to the precautions in the beginning of this section.

2. Disconnect the negative battery cable to prevent fuel discharge if the key is accidentally turned to the **RUN** position.

3. Loosen the fuel filler cap to relieve the tank pressure and do not tighten until service has been completed.

4. Connect J-34730–1 fuel pressure gauge or equivalent, to the fuel pressure valve. Wrap a shop cloth around the fitting while connecting the gauge to avoid spillage.

5. Place the end of the bleed hose into a suitable container and open the valve to relieve the fuel system pressure.

Fuel Filter

REMOVAL & INSTALLATION

The inline fuel filter is located on the fuel feed pipe before the fuel injection system and mounted directly in front of the rear axle. The filter housing is constructed of steel with quick-connect inlet and threaded outlet fittings. The threaded fitting is sealed with an O-ring. In order to disengage quick-connect fittings, a fuel line quick-connect separator tool set, such as J-37088-A or equivalent, is required. There is no service interval for fuel filter replacement. We suggest replacing the filter every 30–40 thousand miles.

1. Before servicing the vehicle, refer to the precautions in the beginning of this section.

2. Relieve the fuel system pressure.

3. Clean both the inlet and the outlet fittings on the fuel filter.

4. Disengage the quick-connect fittings at the fuel filter inlet as follows:

a. Slide the dust covers from the quick-connect fittings, if equipped.

b. Grasp both sides of the fitting. Twist female connector ¼ turn in each direction to loosen any dirt within the fitting. Using compressed air and safety glasses, blow dirt out of fitting.

c. If equipped with the plastic hand releasable fitting, squeeze the plastic retainer release tabs and pull the connection apart.

d. If equipped with metal fitting, choose correct size tool from tool set J-37088-A. Insert tool into female connector, then push inward to release locking tabs. Pull the connector apart.

e. Use a clean lint free rag to clean male pipe ends. Inspect both ends of the fitting for dirt and burrs. Clean or replace components as required. If it is necessary to remove rust or burrs from the fuel pipe, use emery cloth in a radial motion with the pipe end to prevent damage to the O-ring sealing surface.

5. Remove the threaded outlet fitting

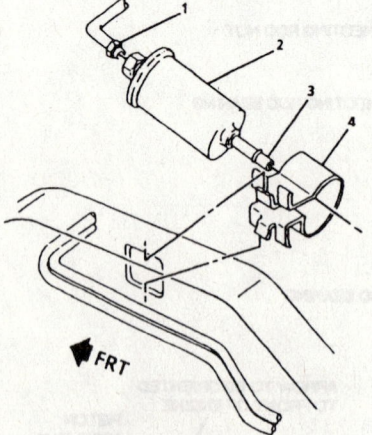

1	THREADED FITTING
2	IN-LINE FUEL FILTER
3	QUICK-CONNECT FITTING
4	IN-LINE FUEL FILTER BRACKET

7922WG23

The inline fuel filter is mounted in a bracket located under the vehicle, directly in front of the rear axle

from the chassis fuel pipe. Slide the fuel filter from the bracket.

6. Inspect the fuel pipe O-ring for cuts, nicks, swelling or distortion. Replace if necessary.

To install:

7. Slide the fuel filter into the bracket. Tighten the outlet fitting to the chassis fuel pipe.

8. Tighten the inline fitting to 20 ft. lbs. (27 Nm).

9. Engage the quick-connect inlet fitting as follows:

a. Apply a few drops of clean engine oil to the male pipe end. This will ensure proper reconnection and prevent a possible fuel leak.

b. Push both sides of the fitting together to cause the retainer tabs to snap in place. Once installed, pull on both sides of the fitting to ensure connection is secure.

c. Reposition dust cover over the quick-connect fitting, if equipped.

10. Tighten the fuel filler cap.

11. Confirm that the ignition is in the **OFF** position. Connect the negative battery cable.

12. Pressurize the fuel system by cycling the ignition without attempting to start the engine. Turn the ignition switch to the **ON** position for 2 seconds, then turn to the **OFF** position for 10 seconds. Again, turn to the **ON** position and check for fuel leaks.

Fuel Pump

REMOVAL & INSTALLATION

The fuel pump is part of the fuel sender assembly located inside the fuel tank.

1. Before servicing the vehicle, refer to the precautions in the beginning of this section.

2. Release the fuel system pressure.

3. Drain the fuel tank.

4. Clean the area surrounding the sender assembly to prevent contamination of the fuel system.

5. Remove or disconnect the following:

• Negative battery cable
• Fuel tank
• Fuel sender-to-fuel tank retaining ring
• Fuel sender from the fuel tank and discard the O-rings
• Fuel pump from the sending unit

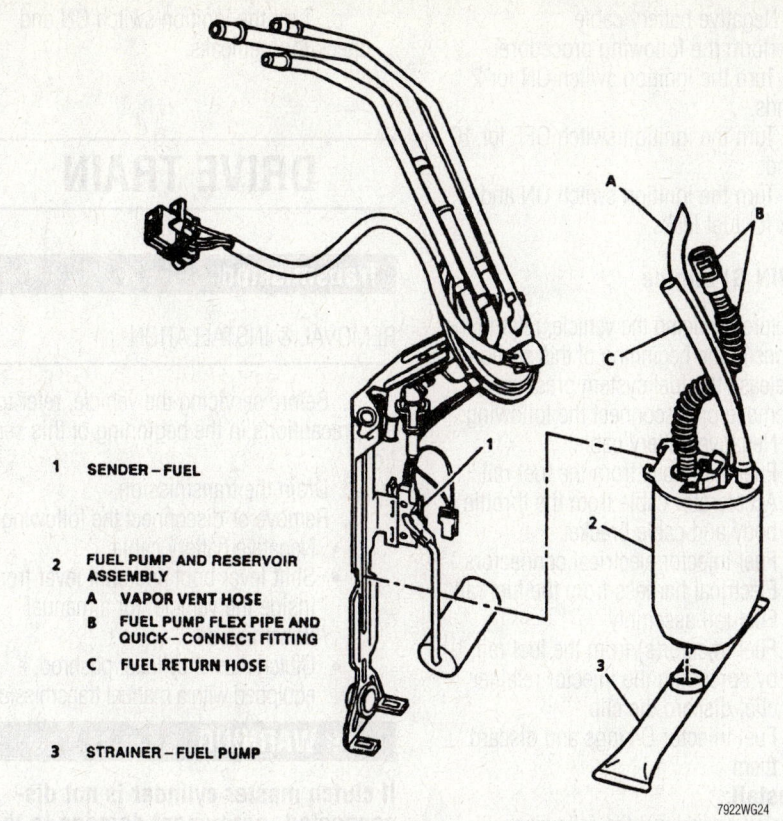

1 **SENDER – FUEL**

2 **FUEL PUMP AND RESERVOIR ASSEMBLY**
   A VAPOR VENT HOSE
   B FUEL PUMP FLEX PIPE AND QUICK – CONNECT FITTING
   C FUEL RETURN HOSE

3 **STRAINER – FUEL PUMP**

Fuel sender/pump assembly component identification

To install:
6. Install or connect the following:
   • Fuel pump onto the sending unit

➡ If the strainer was removed, it must be replaced with a new one.

   • New O-ring in the tank opening groove
   • New O-ring on the fuel sender feed tube, if applicable

7. Install the fuel sender assembly as follows:
   a. The fuel pump strainer must be in a horizontal position and must not block the float arm travel.
   b. Fold the strainer over itself and slowly position the sending assembly in the tank so the strainer is not damaged or trapped by the sump walls.

8. Install or connect the following:
   • Retaining ring. Torque the nuts to 63 inch lbs. (7 Nm).
   • Fuel tank
   • Fuel filler cap
   • Negative battery cable

9. Turn the ignition switch to the **ON** position for 2 seconds, **OFF** for 10 seconds, then back to the **ON** position. Check for fuel leaks.

Fuel Injector

REMOVAL & INSTALLATION

3.8L Engine

1. Before servicing the vehicle, refer to the precautions in the beginning of this section.
2. Release the fuel system pressure.
3. Remove or disconnect the following:
   • Negative battery cable
   • Fuel feed and return pipes from the fuel rail
   • Fuel injector electrical connectors
   • Vacuum line from the fuel pressure regulator
   • Manifold Absolute Pressure (MAP) electrical connector
   • Vacuum line from the vacuum switch at the fuel pipe bundle
   • Vacuum line from the intake manifold
   • Fuel injector harness fasteners
   • Fuel rail hold-down bolts
   • Fuel rail with fuel injectors
   • Fuel injector(s) by removing the retainer clip(s)
   • Fuel injector O-rings and discard them

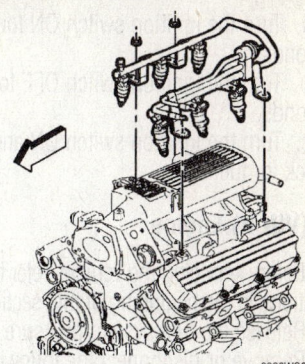

View of the fuel rail assembly—3.8L engine

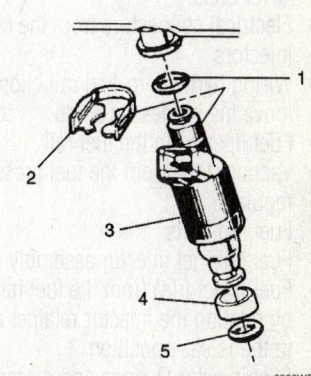

Exploded view of the fuel injector—3.8L engine

To install:

✱✱ WARNING

If the O-rings are different colors (black and brown), install the black one in the upper portion and the brown one in the lower portion of the fuel injector.

4. Install or connect the following:
   • New O-rings on the fuel injector(s) lubricated with engine oil
   • Fuel injector(s) by installing the retainer clip(s)
   • Fuel rail with fuel injectors. Torque the bolts to 89 inch lbs. (10 Nm).
   • Fuel injector harness fasteners
   • Vacuum line to the intake manifold
   • Vacuum line to the vacuum switch at the fuel pipe bundle
   • MAP electrical connector
   • Vacuum line to the fuel pressure regulator
   • Fuel injector electrical connectors
   • Fuel feed and return pipes to the fuel rail
   • Negative battery cable

5. Perform the following procedure:

a. Turn the ignition switch ON for 2 seconds.

b. Turn the ignition switch OFF for 10 seconds.

c. Turn the ignition switch ON and check for fuel leaks.

5.7L (VIN P) Engine

1. Before servicing the vehicle, refer to the precautions in the beginning of this section.
2. Release the fuel system pressure.
3. Remove or disconnect the following:
   - Negative battery cable
   - Fuel lines to throttle body linkage cover clips
   - Electrical connectors from the fuel injectors
   - Wiring harness-to-fuel rail clips, move the harnesses aside
   - Fuel lines from the fuel rail
   - Vacuum tube from the fuel pressure regulator
   - Fuel rail bolts
   - Fuel rail/fuel injector assembly
   - Fuel injector(s) from the fuel rail, by rotating the injector retainer clip to the release position
   - Fuel injector O-rings and discard them

To install:

4. Install or connect the following:
   - New O-rings on the fuel injectors, lubricate them with engine oil
   - Fuel injector(s) to the fuel rail by rotating the clips to the lock position
   - Fuel rail assembly. Torque the bolts to 89 inch lbs. (10 Nm).
   - Vacuum tube to the fuel pressure regulator
   - Fuel lines to the fuel rail
   - Wiring harness-to-fuel rail clips
   - Electrical connectors to the fuel injectors
   - Fuel lines to throttle body linkage cover clips

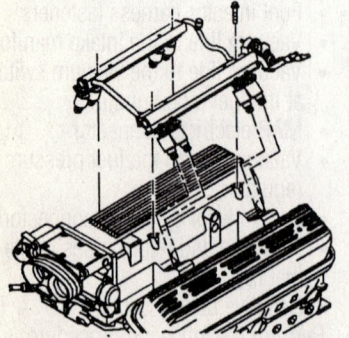

Exploded view of the fuel injector and fuel rail assembly—5.7L (VIN P) engine

9306WG10

- Negative battery cable
5. Perform the following procedure:
   a. Turn the ignition switch ON for 2 seconds.

   b. Turn the ignition switch OFF for 10 seconds.

   c. Turn the ignition switch ON and check for fuel leaks.

5.7L (VIN G) Engine

1. Before servicing the vehicle, refer to the precautions in the beginning of this section.
2. Release the fuel system pressure.
3. Remove or disconnect the following:
   - Negative battery cable
   - Fuel feed hose from the fuel rail
   - Accelerator cable from the throttle body and cable bracket
   - Fuel injector electrical connectors
   - Electrical harness from the fuel rail
   - Fuel rail assembly
   - Fuel injector(s) from the fuel rail, by spreading the injector retainer clip, discard the clip
   - Fuel injector O-rings and discard them

To install:

4. Install or connect the following:
   - New O-rings on the fuel injectors, lubricate them with engine oil
   - Fuel injector(s) to the fuel rail using new clips

➡ **Position the fuel injector electrical connector facing outward**

   - Fuel rail assembly. Torque the bolts to 89 inch lbs. (10 Nm).
   - Electrical harness to the fuel rail
   - Fuel injector electrical connectors
   - Accelerator cable to the throttle body and cable bracket
   - Fuel feed hose to the fuel rail
   - Fuel filler cap
   - Negative battery cable
5. Perform the following procedure:
   a. Turn the ignition switch ON for 2 seconds.

   b. Turn the ignition switch OFF for 10 seconds.

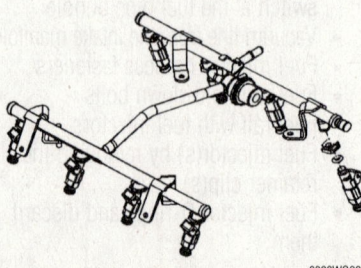

Exploded view of the fuel injector and fuel rail assembly—5.7L (VIN G) engine

9306WG09

c. Turn the ignition switch ON and check for fuel leaks.

DRIVE TRAIN

Transmission

REMOVAL & INSTALLATION

1. Before servicing the vehicle, refer to the precautions in the beginning of this section.
2. Drain the transmission.
3. Remove or disconnect the following:
   - Negative battery cable
   - Shift lever boot and shift lever from inside the vehicle, for a manual transmission
   - Clutch master cylinder pushrod, if equipped with a manual transmission

❈❈ WARNING

If clutch master cylinder is not disconnected, permanent damage to the actuator cylinder will occur if the clutch pedal is depressed while the actuator is disconnected.

   - Clutch actuator line from the actuator, if equipped with a manual transmission
   - Fluid cooler lines, throttle valve cable and dipstick tube, if equipped with a automatic transmission
4. Support the rear axle.
5. Remove or disconnect the following:
   - Driveshaft. Matchmark the driveshaft prior to removal.
   - Rear axle torque arm from the vehicle
   - Catalytic converter hanger
   - Electrical connectors from the transmission, move them aside
   - Clutch fork from the release bearing, if equipped with a manual transmission

❈❈ WARNING

The clutch fork MUST be detached from the release bearing to prevent damage to the clutch system.

   - Starter and the torque converter-to-flexplate bolts, if equipped with a automatic transmission

➡ **Push the torque converter into the transmission.**

6. Support the engine and the transmission.

7. Remove or disconnect the following:
- Transmission rear crossmember
- Transmission from the engine

To install:

8. Install the transmission and torque the following:
- 5-speed manual transmission-to-engine bolts: 55 ft. lbs. (75 Nm)
- 6-speed manual transmission-to-engine bolts: 26 ft. lbs. (35 Nm)
- 3.8L engine-to-automatic transmission bolts: 70 ft. lbs. (95 Nm)
- 5.7L engine-to-automatic transmission bolts: 35 ft. lbs. (47 Nm)
- Transmission rear crossmember. Torque the crossmember-to-chassis bolts to 42 ft. lbs. (57 Nm) except for 1998–01 automatic transmission or 66 ft. lbs. (90 Nm) for 1998–01 automatic transmission

9. Install or connect the following:
- Starter, if equipped with a automatic transmission
- Torque converter-to-flexplate bolts, for an automatic transmission. Torque the bolts to 44 ft. lbs. (60 Nm).
- Clutch fork to the release bearing, if equipped with a manual transmission
- Electrical connectors to the transmission
- Catalytic converter hanger
- Rear axle torque arm to the vehicle
- Driveshaft
- Fluid cooler lines, throttle valve cable and dipstick tube, if equipped with a automatic transmission
- Clutch actuator line to the actuator, if equipped with a manual transmission. Torque the actuator cylinder nuts to 15 ft. lbs. (25 Nm).

➡ **On manual transmissions, when connecting the actuator line, be sure it is not twisted or kinked and will not rub against any other components. Also, the quick-connect fitting must be pushed on, then pulled back to be sure of proper engagement.**

- Clutch master cylinder pushrod, if equipped with a manual transmission
- Shift lever boot and shift lever from inside the vehicle, if equipped with a manual transmission. Torque the bolts to 15 ft. lbs. (20 Nm).
- Negative battery cable

10. Refill the transmission.

11. Bleed the clutch system, if any hydraulic clutch components were removed.

Clutch

REMOVAL & INSTALLATION

1. Before servicing the vehicle, refer to the precautions in the beginning of this section.

2. Remove or disconnect the following:
- Negative battery cable
- Instrument panel knee bolster assembly
- Clutch master cylinder pushrod from the clutch pedal
- Transmission assembly
- Clutch actuator cylinder nuts

✷✷ WARNING

DO NOT allow the actuator cylinder hang by the fluid lines, as this could damage them.

- Clutch actuator cylinder, move it aside and suspended on a wire
- Transmission brace
- Flywheel housing cover
- Flywheel housing

3. Install a clutch disc alignment tool through the center of the disc and into the pilot bearing to prevent the disc from falling when the pressure plate is removed.

4. Remove or disconnect the following:

- Pressure plate retaining bolts
- Pressure plate with clutch disc

5. Inspect the pressure plate, clutch disc and flywheel for damage and replace, if necessary.

To install:

6. Install or connect the following:
- Clutch plate to the flywheel
- Pressure plate (with the cover) with the bolts finger-tight

7. Align the clutch plate with the pilot bearing and clutch pressure plate.

8. Tighten the clutch pressure plate and cover bolts, in a star pattern, as follows:
   a. 5-speed transmission: 15 ft. lbs. (20 Nm), plus 45 degree turn.
   b. 6-speed transmission: 22 ft. lbs. (30 Nm).

9. Install or connect the following:
- Transmission. Torque the bolts to 55 ft. lbs. (75 Nm) for 5-speed or 35 ft. lbs. (47 Nm) for 6-speed transmission.

➡ **Check for proper clutch fork-to-clutch release bearing engagement.**

- Flywheel housing cover. Torque the bolts to 75 inch lbs. (8.5 Nm).
- Transmission brace. Torque the nut/bolt to 37 ft. lbs. (50 Nm).
- Clutch actuator cylinder. Torque the nuts to 15 ft. lbs. (20 Nm).
- Clutch master cylinder pushrod to the clutch pedal
- Instrument panel knee bolster
- Negative battery cable

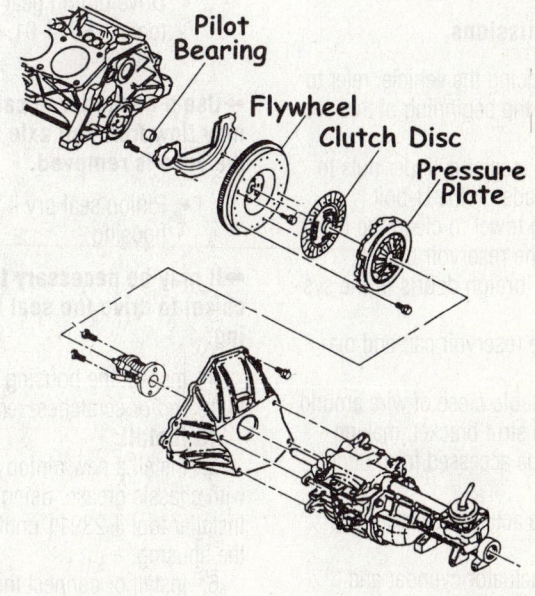

Exploded view of the clutch disc, pressure plate and related components—5-speed transmission

7922WG25

Hydraulic Clutch System

BLEEDING

Bleeding air from the hydraulic clutch system is necessary whenever any part of the system has been disconnected or the fluid level (in the reservoir) has been allowed to fall so low that air has been drawn into the master cylinder.

❈❈ WARNING

NEVER use fluid that has been bled from a clutch system to fill the master cylinder reservoir, as it may be aerated, contain excessive moisture and/or be contaminated in some other way.

5-Speed Transmissions

1. Before servicing the vehicle, refer to the precautions in the beginning of this section.
2. Attach a hose to the bleeder on the clutch actuator and submerge the other end of the hose in a container of hydraulic clutch fluid.
3. Have an assistant slowly depress and hold the clutch pedal.
4. Loosen the bleeder to purge air.
5. Tighten the bleeder.
6. Repeat the above 2 steps until all air is completely purged from the system.
7. Refill the clutch master cylinder reservoir.

6-Speed Transmissions

1. Before servicing the vehicle, refer to the precautions in the beginning of this section.
2. Loosen the master cylinder nuts to the end of the threads on the U-bolt.
3. Use a shop towel to clean the dirt and grease from the reservoir cap to avoid getting and foreign debris in the system.
4. Remove the reservoir cap and diaphragm.
5. Wrap a suitable piece of wire around the left-hand hood strut bracket, making sure the wire can be accessed from under the vehicle.
6. Remove the actuator cylinder and support on a wire.
7. Grasp the actuator cylinder and depress the actuator cylinder pushrod about 0.0787 in. (20mm) into the cylinder bore and hold.
8. Have an assistant install the diaphragm and reservoir cap while holding the actuator pushrod in. Release the pushrod.
9. Hold the actuator cylinder lower than the master cylinder, vertically with the pushrod end facing down.
10. Press the pushrod into the actuator cylinder bore with short 0.0390 in. (10mm) strokes. Check the master cylinder reservoir for bubbles.
11. Continue until bubbles are not longer entering the reservoir.
12. Install the actuator cylinder and torque the fasteners to 15 ft. lbs. (20 Nm).
13. Remove the wire from the hood strut.
14. Refill the clutch master cylinder reservoir.

Pinion Seal

REMOVAL & INSTALLATION

1. Before servicing the vehicle, refer to the precautions in the beginning of this section.
2. Matchmark the driveshaft-to-drive pinion gear yoke, drive pinion gear and drive pinion yoke nut.
3. Remove or disconnect the following:

- Driveshaft. Matchmark the driveshaft prior to removal.
- Drive pinion gear yoke nut using a Pinion Flange Remover/Installer tool J-8614-01 to hold the yoke and a socket wrench
- Drive pinion gear yoke using tools J-8614-01, J-8614-2 and J-8614-3

➡**Use a container to catch the oil that may flow from the axle housing once the yoke is removed.**

- Pinion seal pry it from the axle housing

➡**It may be necessary to use a blunt chisel to drive the seal from the housing.**

4. Inspect the housing bore for nicks, burrs and/or scratches; remove them.
   To install:
5. Install a new pinion seal, lubricated with chassis grease, using a Pinion Oil Seal Installer tool J-23911 until it is flush with the housing.
6. Install or connect the following:
- Drive pinion gear yoke using tool J-8614-01 and a socket wrench
- Drive pinion gear nut, tighten to 1⁄16 in. (1.59mm) beyond the alignment mark

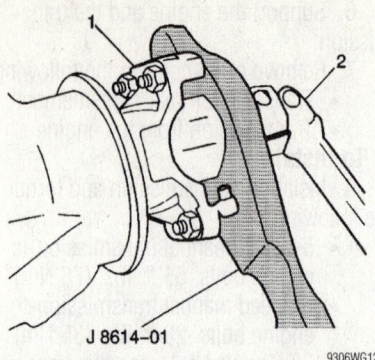

View of the drive pinion gear yoke nut removal tools

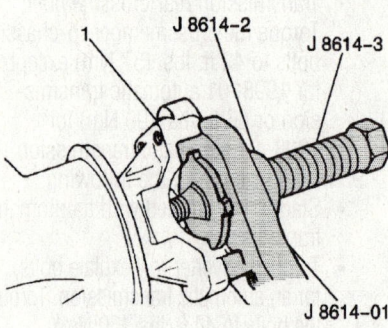

View of the drive pinion gear yoke removal tools

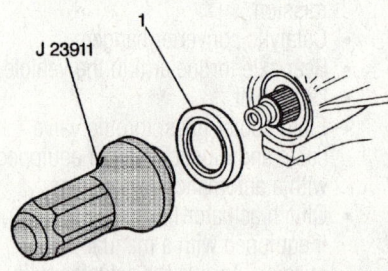

View of the pinion seal nut installer tool

- Driveshaft. Torque the driveshaft-to-pinion yoke bolts to 16 ft. lbs. (22 Nm) and the driveshaft-to-center support to 37 ft. lbs. (50 Nm) for 2-piece shaft.
7. Refill the axle housing.
8. Lower the vehicle.

Axle Housing

REMOVAL & INSTALLATION

1. Before servicing the vehicle, refer to the precautions in the beginning of this section.
2. Remove or disconnect the following:
- Rear wheels

- Driveshaft. Matchmark the drive-shaft prior to removal.
- Rear stabilizer shaft

3. Support the rear axle housing with a lifting device.

4. Remove or disconnect the following:
- Rear shock absorbers
- Rear axle track bar
- Center brake hose from the rear brake hose junction block
- Rear springs
- Parking brake cables from the rear axle housing
- Electrical connectors from the rear wheel sensors
- Rear axle torque arm
- Rear axle lower control arm
- Rear axle housing using an assistant

To install:

5. Install or connect the following:
- Rear axle housing using an assistant
- Rear axle lower control arm. Torque the lower control arm-to-axle housing bolts to 74 ft. lbs. (108 Nm) and the nuts to 60 ft. lbs. (82 Nm).
- Rear axle torque arm. Torque the torque arm-to-axle housing nuts/bolts to 97 ft. lbs. (132 Nm).

- Electrical connectors to the rear wheel sensors
- Parking brake cables to the rear axle housing
- Rear springs
- Center brake hose to the rear brake hose junction block
- Rear axle track bar. Torque the track bar-to-axle housing nut/bolt to 61 ft. lbs. (82 Nm).
- Rear shock absorbers. Torque the shock absorber-to-axle housing nut to 66 ft. lbs. (90 Nm).

6. Support the rear axle housing with a lifting device.

7. Install or connect the following:
- Rear stabilizer shaft. Torque the link nut to 16 ft. lbs. (22 Nm).
- Driveshaft. Torque the driveshaft-to-pinion yoke bolts to 16 ft. lbs. (22 Nm) and the driveshaft-to-center support to 37 ft. lbs. (50 Nm) for 2-piece shaft.
- Rear wheels. Torque the lug nuts to 100 ft. lbs.

8. Refill the rear axle.
9. Bleed the brake system.

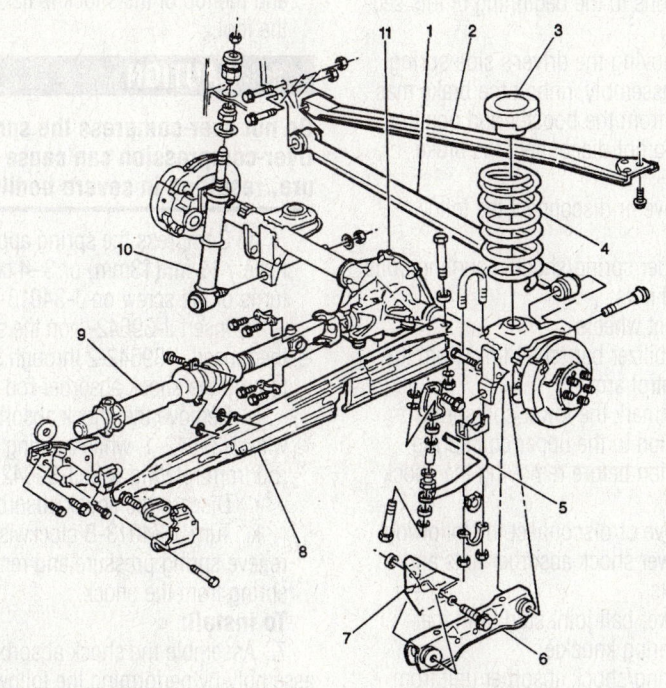

(1) Rear Axle Tie Rod
(2) Rear Axle Tie Rod Bracket Brace
(3) Rear Spring Upper Insulator
(4) Rear Spring
(5) Rear Stabilizer Shaft
(6) Rear Axle Lower Control Arm
(7) Floor Panel
(8) Rear Axle Torque Arm
(9) Propeller Shaft
(10) Rear Shock Absorber
(11) Rear Axle
(12) With Rear Disc Brakes

9306WG11

Exploded view of the rear axle assembly with a 2-piece driveshaft

STEERING AND SUSPENSION

Air Bag

✳✳ CAUTION

Some vehicles are equipped with an air bag system. The system must be disabled before performing service on or around system components, steering column, instrument panel components, wiring and sensors. Failure to follow safety and disabling procedures could result in accidental air bag deployment, possible personal injury and unnecessary system repairs.

PRECAUTIONS

Several precautions must be observed when handling the inflator module to avoid accidental deployment and possible personal injury.
- Never carry the inflator module by the wires or connector on the underside of the module.
- When carrying a live inflator module, hold securely with both hands, and ensure that the bag and trim cover are pointed away.
- Place the inflator module on a bench or other surface with the bag and trim cover facing up.
- With the inflator module on the bench, never place anything on or close to the module which may be thrown in the event of an accidental deployment.

DISARMING

1. Align the steering wheel so the vehicle wheels are pointing in the straight-ahead position.
2. Turn the ignition switch to the **LOCK** position.
3. Remove the SIR or AIR BAG fuse from the fuse block.
4. Remove the Connector Position Assurance (CPA) device, then disengage the yellow 2-way SIR wiring harness connector at the base of the steering column.

ARMING

1. Turn the ignition switch to the **LOCK** position.

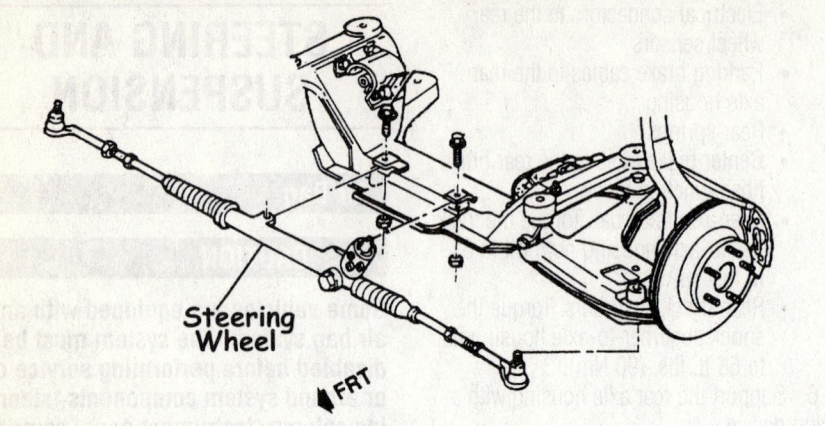

Steering Wheel

← FRT

7922WG26

Exploded view of the power steering gear mounting

2. Engage the yellow 2-way connector at the base of the steering column, then install the CPA device.

3. Reinstall the SIR or AIR BAG fuse.

4. Turn the ignition switch to the **RUN** position.

5. Verify the SIR indicator light flashes 7–9 times, if not, inspect system for malfunction.

Power Rack and Pinion Steering Gear

REMOVAL & INSTALLATION

1. Before servicing the vehicle, refer to the precautions in the beginning of this section.

2. Place a drain pan under the steering gear unit.

3. Remove or disconnect the following:
   - Front wheels
   - Inlet and outlet hoses from the steering gear
   - Outer tie rod ends from the knuckles
   - Steering gear coupling shaft from the steering gear
   - Steering gear from the vehicle

To install:

4. Install or connect the following:
   - Steering gear to the crossmember. Torque the bolts to 63 ft. lbs. (85 Nm).

➡**Adjust the steering gear so it aligns as straight as possible with the steering gear coupling shaft.**

   - Steering gear to the coupling shaft
   - Outer tie rod ends to the steering knuckle
   - Inlet and outlet hoses to the steering gear

   - Front wheels

5. Refill and bleed the power steering system.

Shock Absorber

REMOVAL & INSTALLATION

Front

1. Before servicing the vehicle, refer to the precautions in the beginning of this section.

2. If removing the driver's side spring and shock assembly, unbolt the brake master cylinder from the booster and position it aside, but do not disconnect the brake lines.

3. Remove or disconnect the following:
   - Upper spring/shock mounting bolts and nuts
   - Front wheels
   - Stabilizer bar (shaft link) from the control arm

4. Matchmark the lower coil spring mount location to the upper coil spring mount location before removing the shock absorber.

5. Remove or disconnect the following:
   - Lower shock absorber nuts and bolts
   - Lower ball joint stud from the steering knuckle
   - Spring/shock absorber unit from the vehicle

6. Remove the spring from the shock absorber assembly by performing the following steps:

➡**If using other than a GM spring compressor, follow the manufacturers instructions regarding the use of the specific tool you are using.**

   a. Assemble J-34013-B and J-34013-114 on the spring unit.

   b. Use the wing nuts to secure the tool to mounting holes **C-H** (lower left corner) and **P** (upper right corner) for the driver's side shock and to mounting holes **A-X-P** (upper left) and **C-H** (lower right) for the passenger's side shock.

   c. Install J-34013-114 and J 34013-88.

➡**Make certain that J-34013-114 and J-34013-88 are aligned so that they can open and close together. If not properly aligned, they will not function.**

   d. Attach the shock unit to the tools.

➡**Make certain that the top of the shock is flat against J-34013-114!**

   e. Close the tools and install the locking pin.

➡**Make certain that the mounting ears of the shock are facing downward toward the rear of J-34013-B, otherwise the shock will not align properly.**

   f. Turn the screw of J-34013-B counterclockwise to raise the shock up to J-34013-114. Be sure that the studs go through the guide holes in J-34013-114 and the top of the shock is flat against the tool.

✴✴ CAUTION

Do not over-compress the spring! Over-compression can cause tool failure, resulting in severe bodily injury!

   g. Compress the spring approximately ½ in. (13mm) or 3–4 complete turns of the screw on J-34013-114.

   h. Insert J-39642-1 on the shock nut, then insert J-39642-2 through J-39642-1 to hold the shock absorber rod in place.

   i. Remove the shock absorber nut with J-39642-1, while holding the shock rod from rotating with J-39642-2.

   j. Discard the shock absorber nut.

   k. Turn J-34013-B clockwise to fully relieve spring pressure and remove the spring from the shock.

To install:

7. Assemble the shock absorber/spring assembly by performing the following procedure:

   a. Assemble J-34013-B spring compressor and J-34013-114 adapter on the spring unit. Use wing nuts to secure the tool to mounting holes **C-H** (lower left corner and **P** (upper right corner) for the driver's side shock and to mounting holes **A-X-P** (upper left) and **C-H** (lower right) for the passenger's side shock.

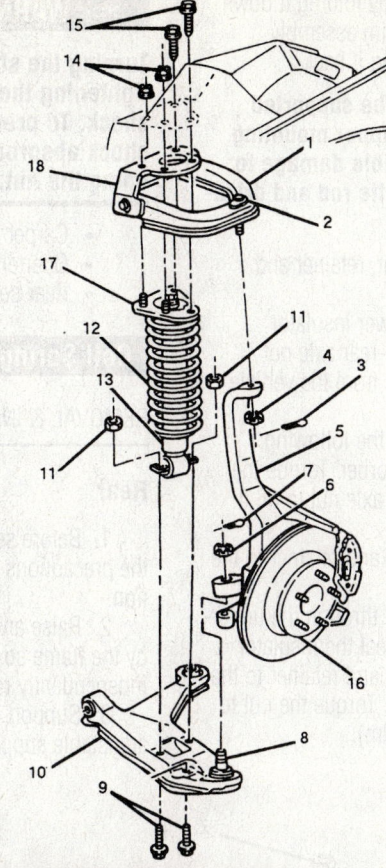

1. ARM ASSEMBLY, FRONT UPPER CONTROL
2. STUD ASSEMBLY, FRONT UPPER CONTROL ARM BALL
3. PIN, FRONT UPPER CONTROL ARM COTTER
4. NUT, FRONT UPPER CONTROL ARM, 53 N•m (39 LB. FT.)
5. KNUCKLE ASSEMBLY, STEERING
6. NUT, FRONT LOWER CONTROL ARM, 110 N•m (81 LB. FT.)
7. PIN, FRONT LOWER CONTROL ARM COTTER
8. STUD ASSEMBLY, FRONT LOWER CONTROL ARM BALL
9. BOLT/SCREW, FRONT SHOCK ABSORBER, 65 N•m (48 LB. FT.)
10. ARM ASSEMBLY, FRONT LOWER CONTROL
11. NUT, FRONT SHOCK ABSORBER LOWER BRACKET, 65 N•m (48 LB. FT.)
12. SPRING ASSEMBLY, FRONT
13. ABSORBER ASSEMBLY, FRONT SHOCK
14. NUT, FRONT SHOCK ABSORBER UPPER MOUNT, 43 N•m (32 LB. FT.)
15. BOLT/SCREW, FRONT SHOCK ABSORBER UPPER MOUNT, 50 N•m (37 LB. FT.)
16. HUB ASSEMBLY, FRONT WHEEL
17. MOUNT ASSEMBLY, FRONT UPPER SHOCK ABSORBER
18. SUPPORT, FRONT UPPER CONTROL ARM

7922WG27

Exploded view of the shock absorber unit and related suspension components

b. Install tools J-34013-114 and J-34013-88.

c. Attach the shock unit to the tools.

➡ **Make certain that the mounting ears of the shock are facing downward towards the rear of J 34013-B!**

d. Close the tools and install the locking pin.

e. Be sure that the spring seats are positioned properly.

➡ **Make certain that the top of the shock is flat against J-34013-114!**

f. Turn the screws of J-34013-B counterclockwise to raise the shock up to J-34013-114. Be sure that the studs go through the guide holes in J-34013-114 and the top of the shock is flat against the tool.

➡ **Turn the screw only enough to secure the shock. DO NOT compress the spring.**

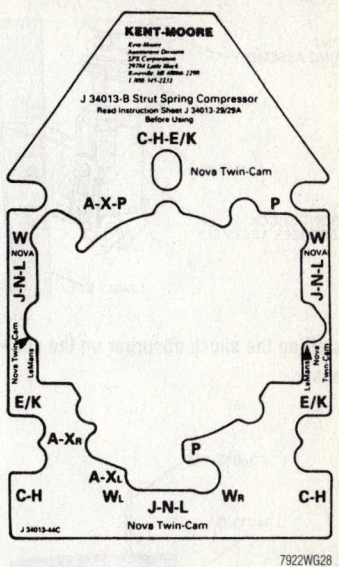

7922WG28

Shock absorber compressor mounting hole locations

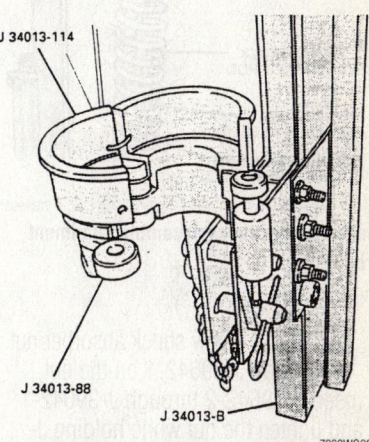

7922WG29

Install the strut compressor adapter on the spring compressor

g. Place J-34013-115 down through the top of J-34013-B, through the top of the shock absorber and onto the rod.

➡ **Make certain that J-34013-115 is straight with the shock.**

✳✳ CAUTION

Do not over-compress the spring! Over-compression can cause tool failure, resulting in severe bodily injury!

h. Turn the operating screw clockwise to compress the spring until the threaded portion of the rod is through the top of the shock. Remove J-34013-115.

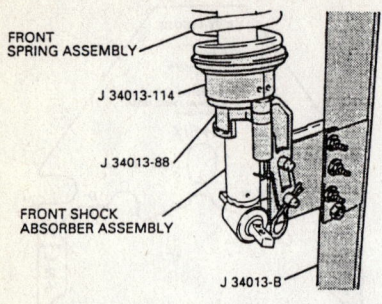

FRONT SPRING ASSEMBLY
J 34013-114
J 34013-88
FRONT SHOCK ABSORBER ASSEMBLY
J 34013-B

7922WG30

Installing the shock absorber on the compressor

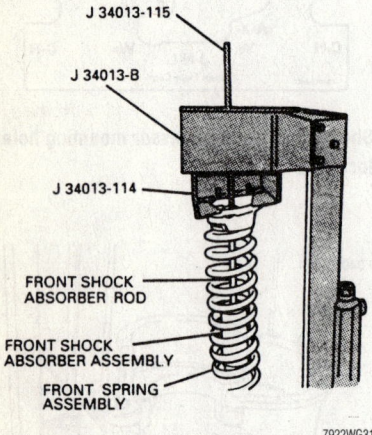

J 34013-115
J 34013-B
J 34013-114
FRONT SHOCK ABSORBER ROD
FRONT SHOCK ABSORBER ASSEMBLY
FRONT SPRING ASSEMBLY

7922WG31

Inserting the shock assembly alignment rod

i. Install a new shock absorber nut.

j. Install J-39642-1 on the nut, insert J-39642-2 through J-39642-1 and tighten the nut while holding J-39642-2.

8. Remove the shock/spring assembly from the tool.

9. Install or connect the following:
- Shock/spring assembly on the lower control arm. Torque the lower nuts to 48 ft. lbs. (65 Nm).
- Lower ball joint to the steering knuckle
- Stabilizer shaft link
- Front wheel
- Upper shock/spring assembly. Torque the bolts to 37 ft. lbs. (50 Nm) and the nuts to 32 ft. lbs. (43 Nm).
- Master cylinder

Rear

1. Before servicing the vehicle, refer to the precautions in the beginning of this section.

2. Place a support under the rear axle.

3. Remove or disconnect the following:

- Rear seat back by folding it down
- Quarter panel trim assembly
- Carpet by folding it back

➡The rear axle must be supported before removing the upper mounting nut to avoid any possible damage to the brake hose lines, tie rod and driveshaft.

- Upper shock nut, retainer and upper insulator
- Retainer and lower insulator
- Lower shock-to-rear axle nut
- Shock absorber from the vehicle

To install:

4. Install or connect the following:
- Rear shock absorber. Torque the lower shock-to-axle nut to 66 ft. lbs. (90 Nm).
- Lower insulator and retainer to the shock absorber
- Shock absorber through the underbody pan and seat the insulator
- Upper insulator and retainer to the shock absorber. Torque the nut to 13 ft. lbs. (17 Nm).

✱✱ WARNING

Turning the shock absorber while tightening the nut could damage the shock. To prevent damage, keep the shock absorber stationary when tightening the nut.

- Carpet
- Quarter panel trim assembly
- Rear seat back, raise it

Coil Spring

REMOVAL & INSTALLATION

Rear

1. Before servicing the vehicle, refer to the precautions in the beginning of this section.

2. Raise and safely support the vehicle by the frame so that the rear axle can be independently raised and lowered.

3. Support the rear axle with an adjustable support.

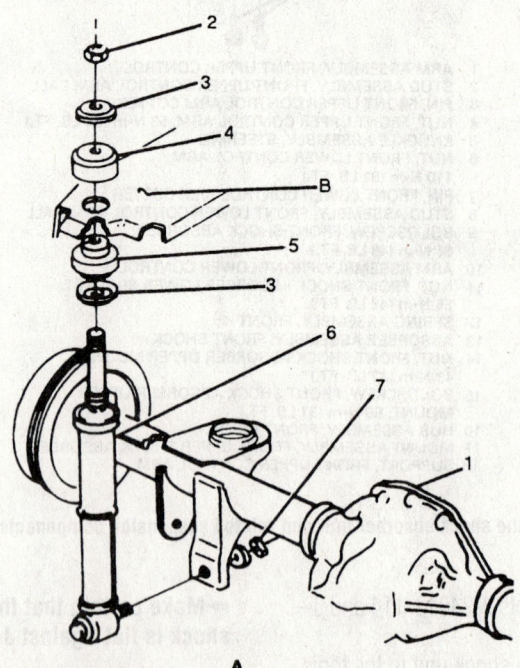

A

A Typical rear shock absorber assembly installation (right-hand shown)
B Underbody pan assembly
1 Rear axle assembly
2 Rear shock absorber nut 17 Nm (13 lb. ft.)
3 Rear shock absorber upper insulator retainer
4 Rear shock absorber upper insulator
5 Rear shock absorber lower insulator
6 Rear shock absorber assembly
7 Rear shock absorber nut 90 Nm (66 lb. ft.)

7922WG32

Exploded view of the rear shock absorber mounting

4. Remove or disconnect the following:
- Brake hose brackets, if equipped, allowing the hoses to hang free. Do not disconnect the hoses.

➡ **Perform the previous step only if the hoses would be stretched and damaged when the axle is lowered.**

- Lower shock absorber bolts
5. Lower the rear axle.

➡ **Be sure the axle is supported securely on the floor jack and that there is no chance of the axle slipping after the shock absorbers are disconnected.**

6. Remove or disconnect the following:
- Axle and lower it
- Upper insulator
- Spring

➡ **The springs are painted with a protective coating. Take care to avoid damaging this coating. If the coating is chipped or damaged, paint the exposed spring to prevent rust.**

To install:
7. Install or connect the following:
- Spring on the axle with the open lower end facing forward
- Upper insulator
8. Raise and safely support the rear axle
9. Install or connect the following:
- Lower shock absorber bolts
- Brake hose brackets, if removed
10. Remove the rear axle support.

Torsion Bars

REMOVAL & INSTALLATION

Rear Torque Arm

1. Before servicing the vehicle, refer to the precautions in the beginning of this section.
2. Support the rear axle with a lifting device.
3. Remove or disconnect the following:
- Both center support bearing-to-torque arm bolts, if equipped with a 2-piece driveshaft
- Both torque arm-to-rear axle bolts, washers and nuts
4. If equipped with an automatic transmission, remove the following:
- Torque arm inner bracket bolts and nuts
- Torque arm outer bracket
- Torque arm inner bracket

- Torque arm
5. If equipped with a manual transmission, remove the following:
- Torque arm outer bracket bolt, washer and nut
- Torque arm inner bracket bolt and nut
- Torque arm outer bracket
- Torque arm inner bracket
- Torque arm

To install:
6. If equipped with a manual transmission, install the following:
- Torque arm
- Torque arm inner bracket
- Torque arm outer bracket. Torque the large bolt to 37 ft. lbs. (50 Nm) and the small bolt to 20 ft. lbs. (27 Nm).
- Torque arm inner bracket bolt and nut. Torque the nut to 33 ft. lbs. (45 Nm).
- Torque arm outer bracket bolt, washer and nut. Torque the nut to 33 ft. lbs. (45 Nm).
7. If equipped with an automatic transmission, install the following:
- Torque arm
- Torque arm inner bracket

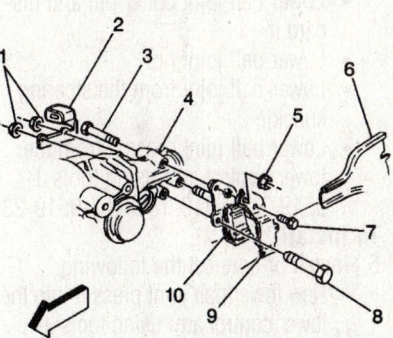

Exploded view of the torque arm bracket assembly—automatic transmission

9306WG15

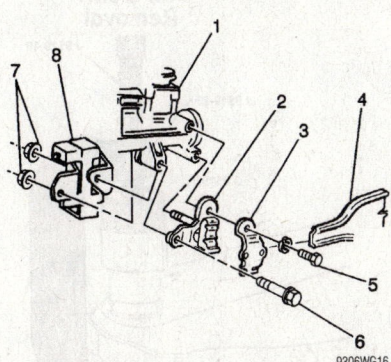

Exploded view of the torque arm bracket assembly—manual transmission

9306WG16

- Torque arm outer bracket
- Torque arm inner bracket bolts and nuts. Torque the bolts to 37 ft. lbs. (50 Nm) and the nuts to 33 ft. lbs. (45 Nm).
8. Install or connect the following:
- Both torque arm-to-rear axle bolts, washers and nuts. Torque the bolts to 96 ft. lbs. (130 Nm) and the nuts to 97 ft. lbs. (132 Nm).
- Both center support bearing-to-torque arm bolts, if equipped with a 2-piece driveshaft. Torque the bolts to 37 ft. lbs. (50 Nm).

Rear Track Bar/Bracket Brace

1. Before servicing the vehicle, refer to the precautions in the beginning of this section.
2. Support the rear axle housing with a lifting device.
3. Remove or disconnect the following:
- Track bar-to-spring seat nut and bolt
- Track bar bracket brace-to-chassis bracket bolts
- Track bar/bracket brace-to-chassis brace/bracket nuts/bolts
- Track bar and track bar bracket brace

To install:
4. Install or connect the following:
- Track bar and track bar bracket brace
- Track bar/bracket brace-to-chassis brace/bracket nuts/bolts. Torque the bolts to 87 ft. lbs. (118 Nm) or the nuts to 55 ft. lbs. (75 Nm).
- Track bar bracket brace-to-chassis bracket bolts. Torque the nuts/bolts to 35 ft. lbs. (47 Nm).
- Track bar-to-spring seat nut and bolt. Torque the bolts to 87 ft. lbs. (118 Nm) or the nuts to 55 ft. lbs. (75 Nm).
5. Remove the lifting device.

Upper Ball Joint

REMOVAL & INSTALLATION

1. Before servicing the vehicle, refer to the precautions in the beginning of this section.
2. Remove the front wheel.
3. Position a floor jack under the shock mount for support.

Turn to Section 5 for brake system applications

✷✷ WARNING

The jack must remain in place for the entire duration of the procedure to hold the spring and lower control arm in proper position.

4   Remove or disconnect the following:
- Cotter pin and discard it
- Ball stud nut

5. Support the steering knuckle with a stand.

6. Remove or disconnect the following:
- Ball joint from the upper control arm using Separator tool J-39549.
- 4 ball joint rivets by drilling them about 0.25 in. (6mm) deep using a ⅛ in. (3.175mm) bit
- Rivet heads by drilling them off using a ½ in. (12.7mm) bit
- Rivets by using a small drift to punch them out
- Upper ball joint from the control arm

To install:

7. Install or connect the following:
- New upper ball joint to the control arm. Torque the nuts/bolts follow the specifications given in the replacement kit.
- Ball joint to the steering knuckle. Torque the nut to 39 ft. lbs. (53 Nm).

➡**Advance the nut to align the nearest cotter pin hole; NEVER back off the nut to align a hole!**

- New cotter pin
- Front wheel

Lower Ball Joint

REMOVAL & INSTALLATION

➡**To prevent component damage, an on-car ball joint press should be used.**

1. Before servicing the vehicle, refer to the precautions in the beginning of this section.

2. Remove the front wheel.

3. Position a support under the shock mount for support.

✷✷ WARNING

The support must remain in place for the entire duration of the procedure to hold the spring and lower control arm in proper position.

4. Remove or disconnect the following:

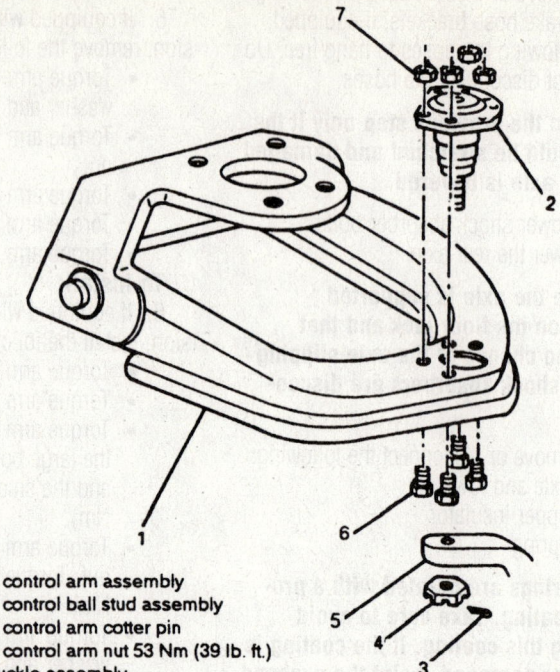

1 Front upper control arm assembly
2 Front upper control ball stud assembly
3 Front upper control arm cotter pin
4 Front upper control arm nut 53 Nm (39 lb. ft.)
5 Steering knuckle assembly
6 Service kit bolt/screw
7 Service kit nut

7922WG33

Position the new upper ball joint (stud) in the control arm and secure with the replacement nuts and bolts

- Lower ball joint cotter pin and discard it
- Lower ball joint nut
- Lower ball joint from the steering knuckle
- Lower ball joint press it from the lower control arm using tools J-9519-7, J-9519-18 and J-9519-23

To install:

5. Install or connect the following:
- New lower ball joint press it into the lower control arm using tools J-9519-9, J-9519-18 and J-9518-23

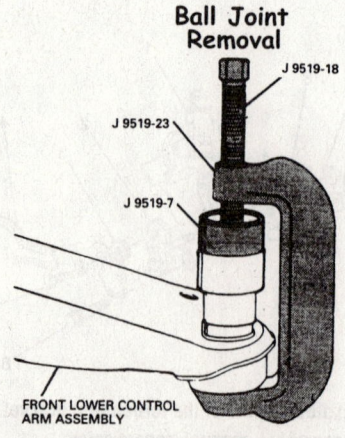

Ball Joint Removal

J 9519-18
J 9519-23
J 9519-7

FRONT LOWER CONTROL ARM ASSEMBLY

✷✷ WARNING

The ball joint must firmly press into the lower control arm; if it doesn't, replace the lower control arm.

- Ball joint to the steering knuckle. Torque the nut to 81 ft. lbs. (110 Nm).

➡**Continue to tighten the nut just until the cotter pin holes align; NEVER back off the nut to align the holes.**

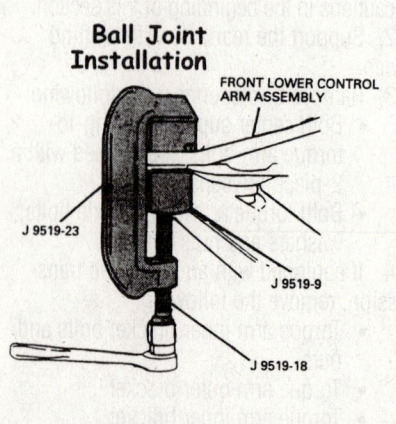

Ball Joint Installation

FRONT LOWER CONTROL ARM ASSEMBLY

J 9519-23
J 9519-9
J 9519-18

7922WG34

Lower ball joint replacement requires the use of special tools, such as the ones shown

- New cotter pin
- Front wheel
7. Check and/or adjust the alignment.

Upper Control Arm

REMOVAL & INSTALLATION

1. Before servicing the vehicle, refer to the precautions in the beginning of this section.
2. Remove or disconnect the following:
   - Brake master cylinder, move it aside, if removing the drivers side control arm
   - Upper shock absorber mount nuts/bolts
   - Front wheel
   - Stabilizer shaft link
   - Lower shock absorber nuts/bolts
   - Upper control arm cotter pin and discard it
   - Upper ball joint nut
3. Support the steering knuckle with a jackstand.
4. Remove or disconnect the following:
   - Upper ball joint from the steering knuckle using Separator tool J-39549
   - Upper control arm with the shock absorber
   - Upper control arm from the shock absorber
   To install:
5. Install or connect the following:
   - Upper control arm with the shock absorber. Torque the upper control arm-to-chassis nuts/bolts to 72 ft. lbs. (98 Nm).
   - Upper ball joint to the steering knuckle. Torque the upper ball joint nut to 39 ft. lbs. (53 Nm).

➡**Never loosen the ball joint nut to align the cotter pin; the nut can be overtorqued ⅙ of a turn MAX.**

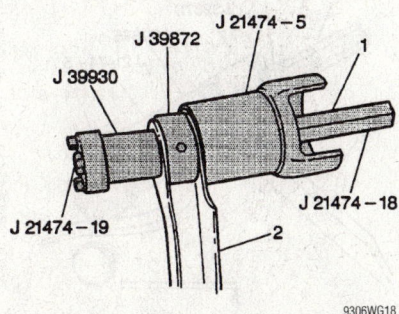

Removing the upper control arm bushing

- New cotter pin
6. Remove the steering knuckle jackstand.
7. Install or connect the following:
   - Lower shock absorber to the steering knuckle. Torque the nuts/bolts to 48 ft. lbs. (65 Nm).
   - Stabilizer shaft link
   - Front wheel
   - Upper shock absorber. Torque the nuts to 30 ft. lbs. (41 Nm) and the bolts to 37 ft. lbs. (50 Nm).
   - Brake master cylinder. Torque the nuts to 21 ft. lbs. (29 Nm).

CONTROL ARM BUSHING REPLACEMENT

1. Before servicing the vehicle, refer to the precautions in the beginning of this section.
2. Remove or disconnect the following:
   - Upper control arm
   - Upper control arm from the upper control arm support
3. Remove the bushing from the upper control arm by performing the following procedure:
   a. Thread the Upper Control Arm Screw tool J-21474-19 through the Upper Control Arm Bushing Receiver/Installer tool J-39930; the 3 tangs must be against the screw head.
   b. Thread the Upper Control Arm Screw tool J-21474-19 through the upper control arm bushing.
   c. Run the smaller end of the Control Arm Bushing Receiver tool J-21474-5 onto the Upper Control Arm Screw tool J-21474-19; then, place the thrust washer onto tool J-21474-19 with the seams facing tool J-21474-5.
   d. Position the Half Moon Spacer tool J-39872 around the outside of the bushing to prevent metal distortion during removal.
   e. Ensure that the tools are aligned; then, install the Upper Control Arm Nut

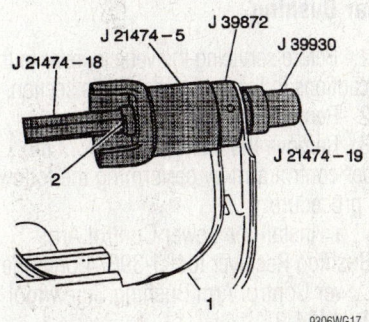

Installing the upper control arm bushing

tool J-21474-18 on the Upper Control Arm Screw tool J-21474-19.
   f. Tighen the Upper Control Arm Nut tool J-21474-18 and Upper Control Arm Screw tool J-21474-19 until the busing is pressed from the upper control arm.
To install:
4. Install the bushing to the upper control arm by performing the following procedure:
   a. Thread the Upper Control Arm Screw tool J-21474-19 through the Upper Control Arm Bushing Receiver/Installer tool J-39930; the 3 tangs must NOT be against the screw head.
   b. Install a new bushing onto the Upper Control Arm Screw tool J-21474-19 with the 3 indentations facing the 3 tangs on the Upper Control Arm Bushing Receiver/Installer tool J-39930.
   c. Install the threaded end of the Upper Control Arm Screw tool J-21474-19 to the upper control arm from the outside.
   d. Install the Control Arm Bushing Receiver tool J-21474-5 onto the Upper Control Arm Screw tool J-21474-19 from the inside.
   e. Place the thrust washer onto tool J-21474-19 with the seam facing the bushing.
   f. Position the Half Moon Spacer tool J-39872 around the outside of the bushing to prevent metal distortion during installation.
   g. Install the Upper Control Arm Nut tool J-21474-18 on the Upper Control Arm Screw tool J-21474-19; ensure that the 3 tangs on the Upper Control Arm Bushing Receiver/Installer tool J-39930 fit into the bushing indentations.
   h. Tighen the assembly until the busing is pressed into the upper control arm.
5. Install or connect the following:
   - Upper control arm to the upper control arm support. Torque the nuts/bolts to 72 ft. lbs. (98 Nm).
   - Upper control arm

Lower Control Arm

REMOVAL & INSTALLATION

1. Before servicing the vehicle, refer to the precautions in the beginning of this section.
2. Remove or disconnect the following:
   - Front wheel
   - Stabilizer shaft link
   - Outer tie rod end cotter pin and discard it

- Outer tie rod end nut
- Outer tie rod end from the steering knuckle
- Lower shock absorber nuts/bolts
- Lower ball joint cotter pin and discard it
- Lower control arm nut
- Lower control arm from the steering knuckle
- Lower control arm-to-crossmember nuts/bolts
- Lower control arm

To install:

3. Install or connect the following:

- Lower control arm. Torque the lower control arm-to-crossmember horizontal nut to 74 ft. lbs. (100 Nm) and the vertical nut to 85 ft. lbs. (115 Nm).
- Lower control arm to the steering knuckle. Torque the lower control arm nut to 81 ft. lbs. (110 Nm).
- New lower ball joint cotter pin
- Lower shock absorber. Torque the nuts/bolts to 48 ft. lbs. (65 Nm).
- Outer tie rod end to the steering knuckle. Torque the nut to 35 ft. lbs. (47 Nm).

➡**Never loosen the ball joint nut to align the cotter pin; the nut can be overtorqued ⅙ of a turn MAX.**

- New outer tie rod end cotter pin
- Stabilizer shaft link. Torque the nut to 17 ft. lbs. (23 Nm).
- Front wheel

CONTROL ARM BUSHING REPLACEMENT

Front Bushing

1. Before servicing the vehicle, refer to the precautions in the beginning of this section.
2. Remove the lower control arm.
3. Remove the front bushing from the upper control arm by performing the following procedure:

    a. Install the Lower Control Arm Bushing Screw tool J-21474-3 through the large end of the Control Arm Bushing Receiver tool J-21474-6.

    b. Install the Lower Control Arm Bushing Screw tool J-21474-3 through the front bushing and the open end of the Lower Control Arm Bushing Receiver tool J-39876.

    c. Place the thrust washer onto the Lower Control Arm Bushing Screw tool

J-21474-3 so the seam faces the front bushing.

    d. Install the Half Moon Spacer tool J-39875 around the outside of the bushing to avoid metal distortion during removal.

    e. Ensure that the tools align; then, install the Lower Control Arm Bushing Nut tool J-21474-4 and tighten the assembly until the bushing is pressed from the control arm.

To install:

4. Install the front bushing to the lower control arm by performing the following procedure:

    a. Thread the Lower Control Arm Bushing Screw tool J-21474-3 through the Control Arm Bushing Receiver tool J-21474-5.

    b. Install the Lower Control Arm Bushing Screw tool J-21474-3 through the new front bushing and the lower control arm.

    c. Thread the Lower Control Arm Bushing Screw tool J-21474-3 and accessories into the front lower control arm.

    d. Install the Lower Control Arm Bushing Receiver tool J-39876 onto the Lower Control Arm Bushing screw tool J-21474-3 with the open end facing the control arm.

    e. Install the Half Moon Spacer tool J-39875 around the outside of the bushing to avoid metal distortion during installation.

    f. Place the thrust washer onto the Lower Control Arm Bushing Screw tool J-21474-3 threaded end with the seam facing the control arm.

    g. Ensure that the tools align; then, install the Lower Control Arm Bushing Nut and the Lower Control Arm Bushing Screw tool J-21474-3.

    h. Tighten the assembly until the front bushing is flush with the lower control arm.

5. Install the lower control arm.

Rear Bushing

1. Before servicing the vehicle, refer to the precautions in the beginning of this section.
2. Remove the lower control arm.
3. Remove the rear bushing from the upper control arm by performing the following procedure:

    a. Install the Lower Control Arm Bushing Receiver tool J-39874 onto the Lower Control Arm Bushing Screw tool J-21474-3.

    b. Install the Lower Control Arm Bushing Screw tool J-21474-3 through

the rear bushing, the control arm and into the small end of the Lower Control Arm Bushing Receiver tool J-39931.

    c. Place the thrust washer onto the Lower Control Arm Bushing Screw tool J-21474-3 so the seam faces the control arm.

    d. Install the Lower Control Arm Bushing Nut tool J-21474-4 onto the Lower Control Arm Bushing Screw tool J-21474-3; then, ensure that the assembly aligns with the bushing.

    e. Tighten the assembly until the bushing is pressed from the control arm.

To install:

4. Install the rear bushing to the lower control arm by performing the following procedure:

    a. Thread the Lower Control Arm Bushing Screw tool J-21474-3 through the small end of the Lower Control Arm Bushing Receiver tool J-39931.

    b. Install the Lower Control Arm Bushing Screw tool J-21474-3 through the new rear bushing and the closed end of the lower control arm.

    c. Place the small end of the Control Arm Bushing Receiver tool J-21474-5

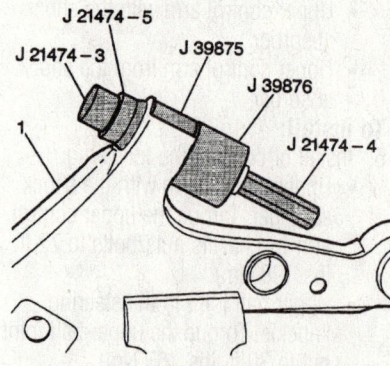

Removing the lower control arm front bushing

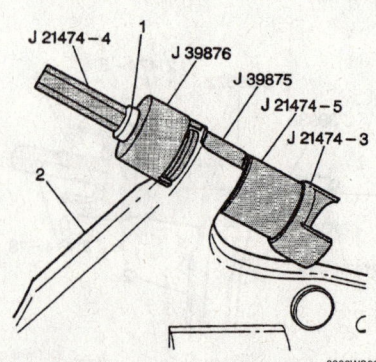

Installing the lower control arm front bushing

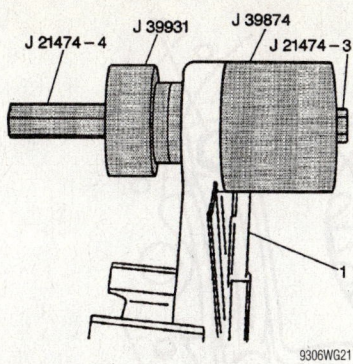

Removing the lower control arm rear bushing

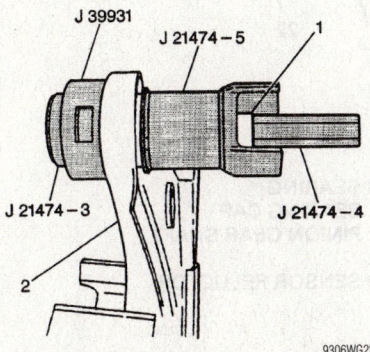

Installing the lower control arm rear bushing

onto the Lower Control Arm Bushing Screw tool J-21474-3.

d. Place the thrust washer onto the Lower Control Arm Bushing Screw tool J-21474-3 with the seam facing the control arm.

e. Ensure that the tools align and the window on the Lower Control Arm Bushing Receiver tool J-39931 faces straight up and is visible.

f. Install the Lower Control Arm Bushing Nut tool J-21474-4 onto the Lower Control Arm Bushing Screw tool J-21474-3; then, tighten the assembly until the rubber protrusion on the Lower Control Arm Bushing Receiver tool J-39931 side bottoms against tool J-39931.

5. Install the lower control arm.

Wheel Bearings

ADJUSTMENT

The front wheel bearing assembly used on these vehicles is a sealed, non-serviceable unit. No wheel bearing adjustments (front or rear bearings) are necessary or possible.

REMOVAL & INSTALLATION

Front

1. Before servicing the vehicle, refer to the precautions in the beginning of this section.

2. Remove or disconnect the following:
   - Front wheel
   - Brake caliper and rotor
   - Wheel speed sensor electrical connector
   - Hub bolts
   - Hub/bearing assembly by pulling it from the spindle

To install:

3. Install or connect the following:
   - Hub/bearing assembly on the spindle. Torque the bolts to 63 ft. lbs. (86 Nm).
   - Wheel speed sensor electrical connector

✳✳ WARNING

Be sure the wheel speed sensor electrical connector is reattached to the sensor wire bracket and sensor or the wires could be damaged.

- Brake rotor and caliper
- Front wheel

Rear

1. Before servicing the vehicle, refer to the precautions in the beginning of this section.

2. Remove or disconnect the following:
   - Rear wheel
   - Brake rotor or brake drum and components, as equipped.

3. Clean the carrier cover and surrounding area to prevent dirt or contamination from entering the housing.

4. Remove or disconnect the following:
   - Carrier cover and drain the gear oil

5. Install an Anti-lock Brake System (ABS) tone ring protector kit.

6. Remove or disconnect the following:
   - Rear axle pinion shaft lockscrew and pinion shaft

7. Push the flanged end of the axle shaft into the axle housing.

8. Remove or disconnect the following:

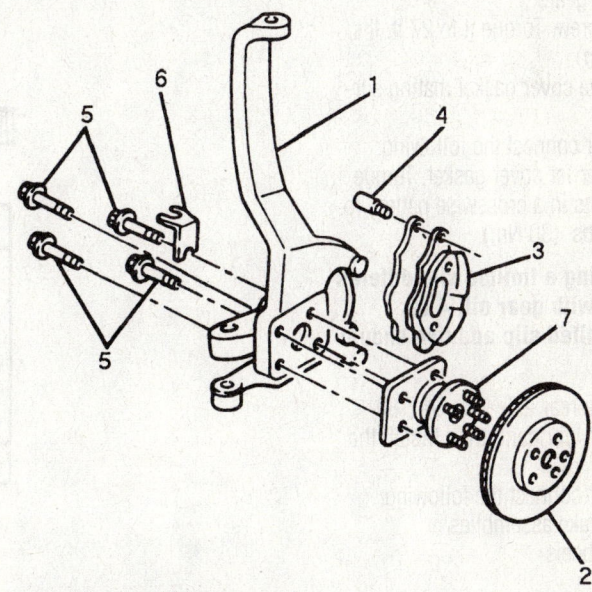

1 Steering knuckle assembly
2 Front brake rotor assembly
3 Front brake caliper assembly
4 Front brake caliper bolt/screw
5 Front wheel bolt/screw 86 Nm (63 lb. ft.)
6 Wheel speed sensor wire bracket
7 Front wheel hub assembly

Exploded view of the wheel hub/bearing unit mounting

- C-clip shaft lock from the differential case end of the shaft
- Axle shaft from the axle housing

9. If necessary to service the seal or bearing, use a small suitable prytool to remove the oil seal from the axle housing. Be careful not to score or damage the housing.

10. If necessary, install an axle bearing remover into the bore of the axle housing and position it behind the bearing, ensure the tangs of the tool engage the outer race. Remove the bearing using a slide hammer.

To install:

11. If removed, install a new bearing (lubricated with gear oil) with a suitable driver so the tool bottoms against the shoulder in axle housing.

12. If removed, position a new seal (lubricated with gear oil) on suitable seal installer, then insert the seal into the housing bore. Position the seal flush with the axle tube.

13. Install or connect the following:
- Axle shaft
- C-lock so it seats in the axle side gear counterbore
- Pinion gear shaft through the differential case, thrust washer and pinion gears.
- Lockscrew. Torque it to 27 ft. lbs. (36 Nm).

14. Clean the cover gasket mating surfaces.

15. Install or connect the following:
- New carrier cover gasket. Torque the bolts in a crosswise pattern to 22 ft. lbs. (30 Nm).

➡When refilling a limited slip differential rear axle with gear oil, 4 oz. (118ml) of limited slip additive should be added.

16. Refill the rear axle with SAE 80-90W GL-5 gear lubricant, then install the plug.

17. Install or connect the following:
- Rear brake assemblies
- Rear wheels

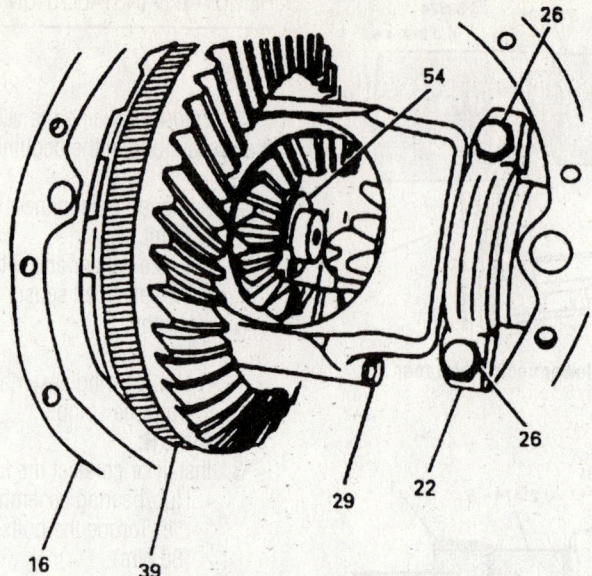

16 HOUSING, REAR AXLE
22 CAP, DIFFERENTIAL CARRIER BEARING
26 BOLT/SCREW, DIFFERENTIAL BEARING CAP
29 BOLT/SCREW, DIFFERENTIAL PINION GEAR SHAFT LOCK
39 WHEEL, REAR WHEEL SPEED SENSOR RELUCTOR
54 LOCK, REAR AXLE SHAFT

7922WG38

Differential component identification

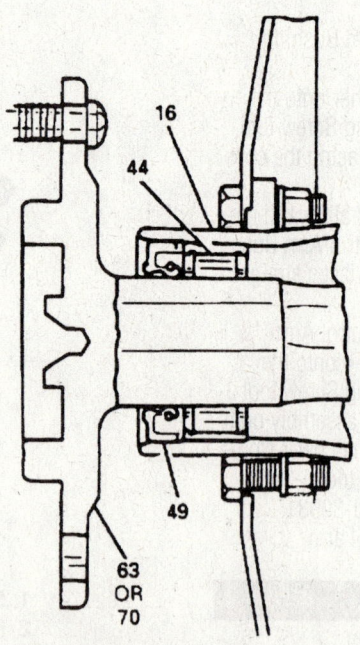

16 HOUSING, REAR AXLE
44 BEARING, REAR AXLE SHAFT
49 SEAL, REAR AXLE SHAFT BEARING
63 SHAFT, REAR AXLE (DRUM BRAKE ASSEMBLY)
70 SHAFT, REAR AXLE (DISC BRAKE ASSEMBLY)

7922WG39

Cut-away view of the rear axle bearing and seal

GENERAL MOTORS CORPORATION—G BODY

31

Buick-Riviera • **Oldsmobile**-Aurora

PRECAUTIONS

Before servicing any vehicle, please be sure to read all of the following precautions, which deal with personal safety, prevention of component damage, and important points to take into consideration when servicing a motor vehicle:

• Never open, service or drain the radiator or cooling system when the engine is hot; serious burns can occur from the steam and hot coolant.

• Observe all applicable safety precautions when working around fuel. Whenever servicing the fuel system, always work in a well-ventilated area. Do not allow fuel spray or vapors to come in contact with a spark, open flame, or excessive heat (a hot drop light, for example). Keep a dry chemical fire extinguisher near the work area. Always keep fuel in a container specifically designed for fuel storage; also, always properly seal fuel containers to avoid the possibility of fire or explosion. Refer to the additional fuel system precautions later in this section.

• Fuel injection systems often remain pressurized, even after the engine has been turned **OFF**. The fuel system pressure must be relieved before disconnecting any fuel lines. Failure to do so may result in fire and/or personal injury.

• Brake fluid often contains polyglycol ethers and polyglycols. Avoid contact with the eyes and wash your hands thoroughly after handling brake fluid. If you do get brake fluid in your eyes, flush your eyes with clean, running water for 15 minutes. If eye irritation persists, or if you have taken brake fluid internally, IMMEDIATELY seek medical assistance.

• The EPA warns that prolonged contact with used engine oil may cause a number of skin disorders, including cancer! You should make every effort to minimize your exposure to used engine oil. Protective gloves should be worn when changing oil. Wash your hands and any other exposed skin areas as soon as possible after exposure to used engine oil. Soap and water, or waterless hand cleaner should be used.

• All new vehicles are now equipped with an air bag system. The system must be disabled before performing service on or around system components, steering column, instrument panel components, wiring and sensors. Failure to follow safety and disabling procedures could result in accidental air bag deployment, possible personal injury and unnecessary system repairs.

• Always wear safety goggles when working with, or around, the air bag system. When carrying a non-deployed air bag, be sure the bag and trim cover are pointed away from your body. When placing a non-deployed air bag on a work surface, always face the bag and trim cover upward, away from the surface. This will reduce the motion of the module if it is accidentally deployed. Refer to the additional air bag system precautions later in this section.

• Clean, high quality brake fluid from a sealed container is essential to the safe and proper operation of the brake system. You should always buy the correct type of brake fluid for your vehicle. If the brake fluid becomes contaminated, completely flush the system with new fluid. Never reuse any brake fluid. Any brake fluid that is removed from the system should be discarded. Also, do not allow any brake fluid to come in contact with a painted surface; it will damage the paint.

• Never operate the engine without the proper amount and type of engine oil; doing so WILL result in severe engine damage.

• Timing belt maintenance is extremely important! Many models utilize an interference-type, non-freewheeling engine. If the timing belt breaks, the valves in the cylinder head may strike the pistons, causing potentially serious (also time-consuming and expensive) engine damage. Refer to the maintenance interval charts in the front of this manual for the recommended replacement interval for the timing belt, and to the timing belt section for belt replacement and inspection.

• Disconnecting the negative battery cable on some vehicles may interfere with the functions of the on-board computer system(s) and may require the computer to undergo a relearning process once the negative battery cable is reconnected.

• When servicing drum brakes, only disassemble and assemble one side at a time, leaving the remaining side intact for reference.

• Only an MVAC-trained, EPA-certified automotive technician should service the air conditioning system or its components.

ENGINE REPAIR

Alternator

REMOVAL

3.5L Engine

1. Before servicing the vehicle, refer to the precautions in the beginning of this section.
2. Drain the cooling system
3. Remove or disconnect the following:
   • Battery
   • Battery tray
   • Drive belt
   • Engine cooling fan assembly
   • Thermostat housing and radiator hose
   • Outboard alternator bolt
   • Inboard alternator bolt
   • Idler pulley bolt and pulley
   • Alternator electrical connectors
   • Alternator

3.8L Engine

1. Before servicing the vehicle, refer to the precautions in the beginning of this section.
2. Remove or disconnect the following:
   • Rear seat cushion
   • Negative battery cable
   • Accessory drive belt
   • Engine front cover
   • Rear alternator brace
   • Alternator electrical connectors
   • Alternator

4.0L Engine

1. Before servicing the vehicle, refer to the precautions in the beginning of this section.
2. Remove or disconnect the following:
   • Rear seat cushion
   • Negative battery cable
   • Both cooling fans
   • Accessory drive belts
   • Upper alternator bolts
   • Alternator electrical connectors
   • Ground strap
   • Power steering line bracket
   • Lower alternator bolts
3. Drain the cooling system.
   • Lower radiator hose
   • Air inlet duct
   • Alternator through the top left side of the engine compartment

INSTALLATION

3.5L Engine

1. Install or connect the following:
   - Alternator
   - Alternator electrical connectors. Torque the positive battery terminal to 15 ft. lbs. (20 Nm).
   - Idler pulley. Torque the bolt to 37 ft. lbs. (50 Nm).
   - Alternator bolts. Torque the bolts to 37 ft. lbs. (50 Nm).
   - Thermostat housing and radiator hose
   - Engine cooling fan assembly
   - Drive belt
   - Battery tray
   - Battery
2. Refill the cooling system.

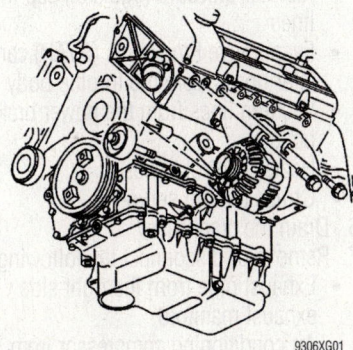

View of the alternator mounting—3.5L engine

9306XG01

3.8L Engine

Install or connect the following:
- Alternator. Torque the bolts to 37 ft. lbs. (50 Nm).
- Alternator electrical connectors. Torque the positive battery terminal to 15 ft. lbs. (20 Nm).
- Rear alternator brace. Torque the bolts to 22 ft. lbs. (30 Nm).
- Engine front cover
- Accessory drive belt
- Negative battery cable
- Rear seat cushion

4.0L Engine

1. Install or connect the following:
   - Alternator
   - Air inlet duct
   - Lower radiator hose
   - Lower alternator bolts. Torque the bolts to 28 ft. lbs. (38 Nm).

- Power steering line bracket
- Ground strap
- Alternator electrical connectors. Torque the positive battery terminal to 15 ft. lbs. (20 Nm).
- Upper alternator bolts. Torque the bolts to 35 ft. lbs. (47 Nm).
- Accessory drive belts
- Both cooling fans
- Negative battery cable
- Rear seat cushion
2. Refill the cooling system.

Ignition Timing

ADJUSTMENT

The engines are equipped with a Distributorless Ignition System (DIS). The system consists of 2 Crankshaft Position (CKP) sensors, crankshaft reluctor ring, Camshaft Position (CMP) sensor, Ignition Control Module (ICM), 4 ignition coils, 8 plug wires and spark plugs, Knock Sensor (KS) and the Powertrain Control Module (PCM).

The PCM controls spark advance under all driving conditions. The PCM incorporates a permanent spark control override, which electronically lowers the base timing if spark knock (detonation) is encountered during normal operation due to the use of low octane fuel.

Engine Assembly

REMOVAL & INSTALLATION

3.5L Engine

1. Before servicing the vehicle, refer to the precautions in the beginning of this section.
2. Remove or disconnect the following:
   - Negative battery cable
   - Sight shield from the fuel injectors
   - Air intake duct from the throttle body
   - Engine mount strut from the bracket
   - Fuel lines from the fuel supply rail
   - Fuel vapor line
   - Throttle and cruise control cables with the bracket from the throttle body
   - Range selector cable from the Park/Neutral Position (PNP) switch
   - Vacuum booster hose from the engine

- Air conditioning vacuum hose from the engine
- Wiring harness from the engine and transaxle
3. Drain the engine cooling system.
4. Remove or disconnect the following:
   - Radiator inlet hose from the engine
   - Transaxle fluid cooler lines from the radiator
   - Surge tank inlet hose
   - Heater hoses from the engine
5. Drain the crankcase.
   - Lower radiator air deflector
   - Secondary Air Injection (AIR) pipe from the AIR inlet valve
   - Battery cables from the retainers
   - Radiator outlet hose from the engine
   - Air conditioning compressor, move it aside without disconnecting the lines
   - Torque converter cover
   - Starter
   - Flexplate-to-torque converter bolts. Matchmark the bolts before removal.
   - Catalytic converter from the rear exhaust manifold
   - Lower transaxle-to-engine bolts
   - Front wheels and splash shields
   - Fog lamp electrical connectors
   - Halfshafts
   - Intermediate shaft from the steering rack

✸✸ WARNING

Secure the front of the vehicle to the lift. The vehicle may become unstable as the engine/transaxle assembly is removed from the vehicle.

6. Position a frame table under the vehicle.
7. Lower the vehicle so the frame is resting on the frame table.
8. Remove or disconnect the following:
   - Frame-to-chassis bolts

✸✸ WARNING

Do not damage the air conditioning compressor or lines when removing the frame from the vehicle.

- Lift the vehicle from the engine/transaxle assembly
- Transaxle from the engine

To install:
9. Install or connect the following:
   - Transaxle to the engine. Torque the bolts to 55 ft. lbs. (75 Nm).

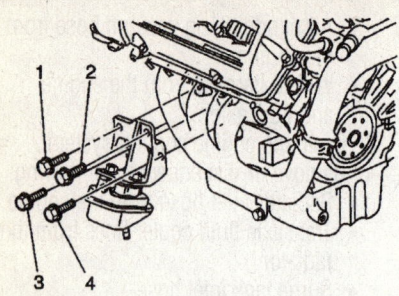

93002501

Engine mount bracket bolt tightening sequence—3.5L engine

- Transaxle brace. Torque the bolts to 32 ft. lbs. (43 Nm).
- Engine mount bracket to the front of the engine. Torque the bolts in sequence to 43 ft. lbs. (58 Nm).
- Engine/transaxle assembly under the vehicle

10. Coat the sub-frame bushings with rubber lubricant.

11. Lower the vehicle onto the assembly. Align the sub-frame on the vehicle using 2 bolts or drill bits, ¾ inches thick by 8 inches long through the alignment holes on the right side of the frame.

12. Install or connect the following:
- New frame-to-body bolts. Torque the bolts to 133 ft. lbs. (180 Nm) starting with the rear bolts and then the front bolts.

13. Raise the vehicle and remove the frame table.

14. Install or connect the following:
- Intermediate shaft to the steering rack. Torque the bolts to 35 ft. lbs. (48 Nm).

➡ **Be sure the shaft is fully seated on the stub before installing the pinch bolt.**

- Halfshafts and assemble the suspension
- Splash shields and front wheels
- Fog lamp electrical connectors
- Lower transaxle-to-engine bolts. Torque the bolts to 55 ft. lbs. (75 Nm).
- Catalytic converter to the rear exhaust manifold
- Flexplate-to-torque converter by aligning the matchmarks. Torque the bolts to 47 ft. lbs. (63 Nm).
- Starter and torque converter cover
- Air conditioning compressor. Torque the nuts/bolts to 37 ft. lbs. (50 Nm).
- Lower radiator hose to the engine
- Battery cables in the retainers
- AIR pipe
- Lower radiator air deflector
- Heater hoses

- Surge tank hose
- Transaxle fluid cooler lines to the radiator
- Upper radiator hose to the engine
- Wiring harness connectors to the engine/transaxle
- Air conditioning vacuum hose to the engine
- Brake booster hose to the engine
- Shifter cable to the transaxle PNP switch

➡ **Always us a new throttle cable when replacing the engine assembly.**

15. Remove the trim panel under the left instrument panel and detach the throttle cable from the top of the pedal then squeeze the retainer and push the cable through the bulkhead to remove it.

16. Install or connect the following:
- New throttle cable
- Cruise and throttle cables to the throttle body
- Fuel vapor line
- Fuel lines to the supply rail
- Engine mount strut
- Air duct to the throttle body
- Fuel injector shield
- Negative battery cable

17. Refill the cooling system.

18. Install a new oil filter and refill the crankcase.

19. Start the engine and check for leaks.

3.8L (VIN 1 and K) Engines

1. Before servicing the vehicle, refer to the precautions in the beginning of this section.

2. Relieve the fuel system pressure.

3. Remove or disconnect the following:
- Negative battery cable
- Hood. Matchmark the hood hinges before removal.

4. Drain the cooling system.

5. Remove or disconnect the following:
- Radiator hoses
- Heater hoses from the heater core
- Negative battery cable from the engine
- Engine harness connector at the bulkhead
- Serpentine belt(s)
- Power steering pump from the bracket and move it aside. DO NOT disconnect the power steering lines from the pump.
- Air inlet duct
- Throttle cables from the linkage bracket
- All cables from the throttle body lever

- Manifold Air Temperature (MAT) sensor electrical connector
- Throttle Position (TP) sensor electrical connector
- Idle Air Control (IAC) valve electrical connector
- Oxygen Sensor (O2S) electrical connector
- Air conditioning compressor electrical connector
- Oil pressure switch electrical connector
- Power steering cutout switch electrical connector
- Vehicle Speed Sensor (VSS) electrical connector
- Low oil level sensor electrical connector
- Ignition assembly ground strap from the inner fender panel
- Fuel feed and sender lines from the fuel rail/pressure regulator, cap the lines
- Evaporative Emissions (EVAP) canister hoses from the throttle body
- Vacuum lines from the power brake booster
- Heater control hoses
- Cruise control servo

6. Drain the crankcase.

7. Remove or disconnect the following:
- Exhaust pipe from the right side exhaust manifold
- Air conditioning compressor from the bracket and move it aside. DO NOT disconnect the refrigerant lines.
- Right front engine-to-transaxle brace
- Flywheel cover
- Starter
- Torque converter-to-flywheel bolts. Matchmark the bolts before removal.

8. Install an engine lifting device and slightly raise the engine to take the weight off the front engine mount.

9. Remove or disconnect the following:
- Torque axis mount

10. Support the transaxle with a floor jack.

11. Remove or disconnect the following:
- Engine-to-transaxle bolts
- Engine

✱✱ WARNING

Be sure all electrical or vacuum connections are disconnected.

To install:

12. Install or connect the following:
- Engine. Torque the engine-to-transaxle bolts to 55 ft. lbs. (75 Nm).

- Torque axis mount. Torque the mount-to-frame bolts to 64 ft. lbs. (87 Nm), the engine side through-bolt to 65 ft. lbs. (87 Nm) and the frame side through-bolt to 52 ft. lbs. (70 Nm).
13. Remove the engine lifting assembly and floor jack.
14. Install or connect the following:
- Torque converter-to-flywheel bolts, aligning the matchmarks made earlier. Torque the bolts to 46 ft. lbs. (62 Nm).
- Starter
- Flywheel cover. Torque the screws to 88 inch lbs. (10 Nm).
- Right side engine-to-transaxle bracket
- Air conditioning compressor to the bracket. Torque the front mounting bolts to 44 ft. lbs. (60 Nm), the rear mounting nut/bolts to 18 ft. lbs. (25 Nm).
- Exhaust pipe to the rear exhaust manifold. Torque the nuts to 18 ft. lbs. (25 Nm).
- Cruise control servo
- Power brake booster vacuum hoses
- Heater control hoses
- EVAP canister hoses to the throttle body
- Fuel feed and return lines to the fuel rail/pressure regulator
- Ignition assembly ground strap to the inner fender well
- MAT sensor electrical connector
- TP sensor electrical connector
- IAC valve electrical connector
- O2S electrical connector
- Air conditioning compressor electrical connector
- Oil pressure switch electrical connector
- Power steering cutout switch electrical connector
- VSS electrical connector
- Low oil level sensor electrical connector
- Control cables to the throttle body lever
- Throttle cable to the mounting bracket
- Air inlet duct
- Power steering pump in the bracket
- Serpentine belt(s)
- Main engine harness at the bulkhead connector
- Negative battery cable to the engine
- Heater hoses to the heater core
- Upper and lower radiator hoses

15. Refill the crankcase.
16. Install or connect the following:
- Negative battery cable
- Hood
17. Pressurize the fuel system and verify no leaks.
18. Refill and bleed the cooling system.

4.0L Engine

On this vehicle, some engine-related service procedures require that the entire Powertrain Assembly be removed from the vehicle.
1. Before servicing the vehicle, refer to the precautions in the beginning of this section.
2. Relieve the fuel system pressure using the recommended procedure.
3. Remove or disconnect the following:
- Negative battery cable
- Air inlet duct
4. Drain the cooling system and the crankcase.
5. Discharge and recover the air conditioning system refrigerant.
6. Remove or disconnect the following:
- Fuel feed and return lines from the fuel rail and cap them
- Vacuum harness from the rear of the intake manifold
- Throttle cables from the throttle body lever/bracket and move them aside
- Engine harness connector at the bulkhead
- Coolant hoses from the radiator surge tank
- Upper radiator hose from the coolant crossover
- Lower radiator hose from the thermostat housing
- Upper transaxle cooler line from the radiator and plug it
- Lower cooler line from the transaxle and plug it
- Heater hoses from the heater pipes
- Vacuum supply line from the power booster
- Shift lever from the transaxle manual shift lever
- Transaxle cable bracket and move the cable aside
- Vacuum reservoir
- Electrical connectors and vacuum lines from the cruise control servo
7. Install an engine support fixture.
8. Remove or disconnect the following:
- Positive battery cable at the junction block
- Torque axis mount through-bolt
- Front engine mount bolts from the

torque axis mount bracket, move the mount aside
- Negative battery cable from the engine
- Both front wheels
- Both inner fender well splash shields
- Power steering rack electrical connector
- Lower ball joints from the steering knuckles
- Outer tie rod ends from the steering knuckles
- Halfshafts from the wheel bearing/hub assemblies
- Power steering rack-to-intermediate shaft pinch bolt
- Exhaust system
- Engine oil cooler lines at the adapter
- Engine-to-transaxle brace located at the oil pan, right cylinder bank in the rear of the engine and the left bank on the front of the engine
- Flywheel cover
- Torque converter-to-flywheel bolts. Matchmark the bolts before removal.
- Oil cooler adapter from the engine
- Air conditioning hose and muffler from the rear of the air conditioning compressor
9. Position a frame support table under the powertrain assembly.
10. Remove or disconnect the following:
- Left transaxle mount
- Subframe bolts
11. Release the engine support fixture.
12. Raise the vehicle off the engine table and verify no electrical or vacuum connections are still hooked to the engine.
13. Remove or disconnect the following:
- Transaxle/engine assembly
- Engine from the transaxle and subframe assembly

To install:
14. Install or connect the following:
- Engine assembly onto the subframe. Torque the bolts to 55 ft. lbs. (75 Nm).
- Powertrain assembly under the vehicle
15. Lower the vehicle and align the subframe. Torque the bolts to 142 ft. lbs. (192 Nm).
16. Install or connect the following:
- Engine support fixture
17. Raise the vehicle and remove the engine dolly.
18. Install or connect the following:
- Left side transaxle mount

Timing belt service is covered in Section 4 of this manual

- Air conditioning hose and muffler to the air conditioning compressor
- Oil filter adapter to the engine. Torque the bolts to 12 ft. lbs. (16 Nm).
- Torque converter-to-flywheel aligning the matchmarks made earlier. Torque the bolts to 35 ft. lbs. (47 Nm).
- Rear engine-to-transaxle brace. Torque the bolts to 44 ft. lbs. (60 Nm).
- Front engine-to-transaxle brace. Torque the bolts to 44 ft. lbs. (60 Nm).
- Oil pan brace. Torque the bolts to 37 ft. lbs. (50 Nm).
- Flywheel cover
- Oil cooler hoses to the adapter. Torque the fittings to 12 ft. lbs. (18 Nm).
- Exhaust system
- Halfshafts to the hub/bearing assemblies. Torque the axle nuts to 107 ft. lbs. (148 Nm).
- Tie rod ends to the steering knuckle. Torque the castle nuts to 41 ft. lbs. (55 Nm).

➡If necessary, tighten the castle nuts up to 60 degrees additional to align the cotter pin holes. NEVER loosen the castle nut and DO NOT exceed 52 ft. lbs. (70 Nm) to make the holes align.

- New tie rod end cotter pins
- Ball joints to the steering knuckles. Torque the castle nuts to 88 inch lbs. (10 Nm) plus 120 degrees additional.

➡If necessary tighten the castle nuts up to 60 degrees additional to align the cotter pin holes. NEVER loosen the castle nuts to make the holes align.

- New ball joint cotter pins
- Intermediate shaft to the rack and pinion. Torque the pinch bolt to 35 ft. lbs. (47 Nm).
- Electrical connector to the rack and pinion assembly
- Both inner fender splash shields
- Front wheels. Torque nuts to 100 ft. lbs. (140 Nm).
- Negative battery cable to the engine
- Front engine mount bracket-to-torque axis mount bolts
- Torque axis mount through-bolt
- Positive battery cable to the junction block

19. Remove the engine support fixture.
20. Install or connect the following:
    - Electrical and vacuum connectors to the cruise control servo
    - Vacuum reservoir
    - Shift cable to the transaxle manual shift lever
    - Cable bracket
    - Vacuum hose to the power booster
    - Heater hoses at the rear of the engine
    - Transaxle cooler lines
    - Lower radiator hose to the thermostat housing
    - Upper radiator hose to the coolant crossover
    - Coolant surge tank hose
    - Main engine harness to the bulkhead connector
    - Throttle cables to the throttle body lever
    - Intake manifold bracket
    - Vacuum hoses to the rear of the intake manifold
    - Fuel feed and return lines
21. Refill the cooling system, engine crankcase and recharge the air conditioning system.
22. Install or connect the following:
    - Air inlet duct
    - Negative battery cable

⁂ WARNING

Operating the engine without the proper amount and type of engine oil will result in severe engine damage.

23. Start the vehicle and verify no leaks.

Water Pump

REMOVAL & INSTALLATION

3.5L Engine

1. Before servicing the vehicle, refer to the precautions in the beginning of this section.
2. Partially drain the cooling system.
3. Remove or disconnect the following:
    - Water pump pulley bolts, loosen but do not remove at this time
    - Drive belt
    - Idler pulley
    - Water pump pulley

➡The water pump is attached to the engine with both long and short bolts, be sure to note their locations.

- Water pump and discard the gasket

➡Note the locations of the 5 long bolts.

4. Clean the water pump mounting surface.

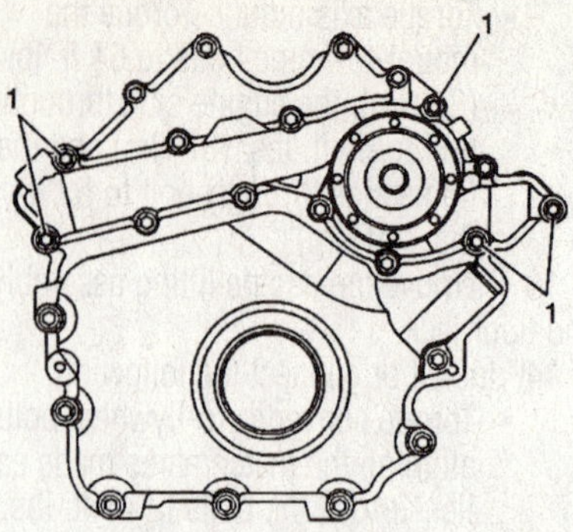

9300Z502

Be sure to install the 5 long water pump bolts in the correct locations—3.5L engine

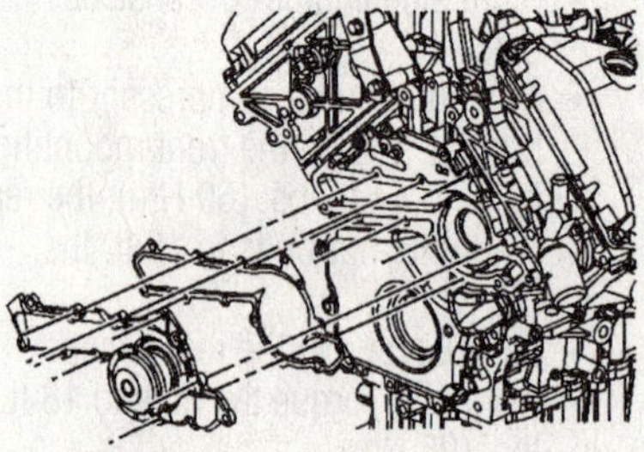

9300Z503

Water pump mounting—3.5L engine

To install:

➡Be sure to install the 5 long bolts in the proper locations.

5. Install or connect the following:
    - Water pump using a new gasket. Torque the bolts to 124 inch lbs. (14 Nm).
    - Water pump pulley
    - Idler pulley. Torque the bolt to 37 ft. lbs. (50 Nm).
    - Drive belt
6. Refill the cooling system.
7. Start the engine and check for leaks.

3.8L Engines

1. Before servicing the vehicle, refer to the precautions in the beginning of this section.
2. Disconnect the negative battery cable.
3. Drain the cooling system.
4. Remove or disconnect the following:
    - Serpentine belt
    - Heater and bypass hoses from the water pump
    - Water pump pulley

➡The long bolt can be removed by aligning the bolt head with the frame rail hole.

5. Install an engine support fixture.
6. Remove or disconnect the following:
    - Torque axis mount
    - Water pump and discard the gasket

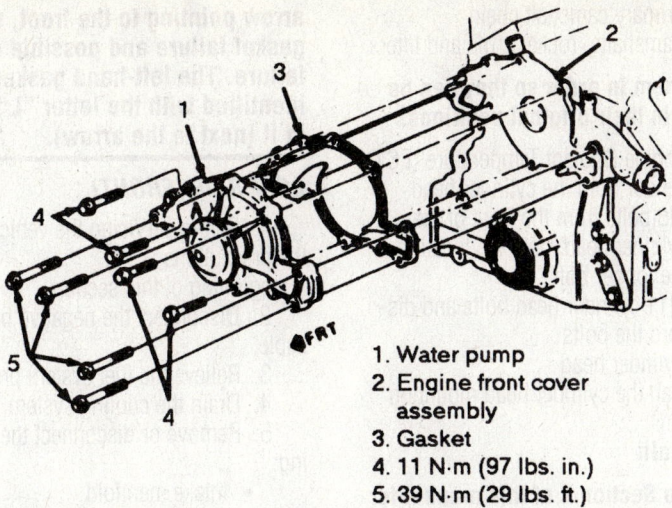

1. Water pump
2. Engine front cover assembly
3. Gasket
4. 11 N·m (97 lbs. in.)
5. 39 N·m (29 lbs. ft.)

7922XG01

Exploded view of the water pump and mounting bolt locations—3.8L engines

To install:

7. Thoroughly clean all the sealing surfaces.

8. Apply a thin bead of sealer around the outside edge of the water pump

9. Install or connect the following:
- New gasket
- Water pump. Torque the inlet and outlet side bolts to 29 ft. lbs. (39 Nm) and the remaining bolts to 97 inch lbs. (11 Nm).
- Torque axis mount

10. Remove the support fixture.

11. Install or connect the following:
- Water pump pulley
- Water pump hoses
- Serpentine belt
- Water pump pulley bolts. Torque the bolts to 115 inch lbs. (13 Nm).
- Negative battery cable

12. Refill the cooling system.

13. Start the vehicle and check for proper operation.

4.0L Engine

1. Before servicing the vehicle, refer to the precautions in the beginning of this section.

2. Disconnect the negative battery cable.

3. Drain the cooling system.

4. Remove or disconnect the following:
- Air inlet duct
- Water pump drive belt cover
- Water pump drive belt
- Lower radiator hose and bypass hose
- Thermostat housing from the water pump housing
- Water pump from the water pump housing, by turning the locking ring with a Water Pump Remover/Installer tool J-38816

To install:

5. Install or connect the following:
- Water pump, seat the locking ring
- Thermostat housing to the water pump housing

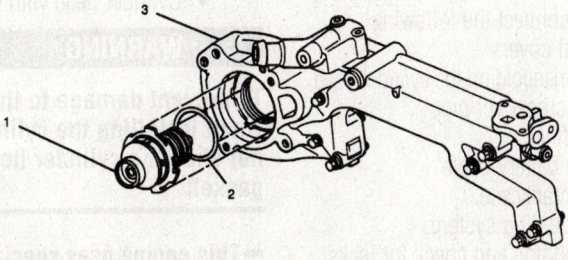

1 WATER PUMP ASM.
2 O-RING SEAL
3 WATER PUMP HOUSING ASM.

7922XG02

Exploded view of the water pump housing and water pump—4.0L engine

- Lower radiator hose and coolant bypass hose
- Drive belt and drive belt cover
- Air inlet duct
- Negative battery cable

6. Refill and bleed the cooling system.

Cylinder Head

REMOVAL & INSTALLATION

3.5L Engine

FRONT

1. Before servicing the vehicle, refer to the precautions in the beginning of this section.

2. Drain the crankcase and the cooling system.

3. Remove or disconnect the following:
- Negative battery cable
- Intake manifold
- Water outlet housing
- Engine mount strut bracket
- Coolant crossover pipe
- Front exhaust manifold
- Camshaft covers

4. Install a holding tool on the camshafts to hold them in position.

5. Remove or disconnect the following:
- Camshaft primary chain
- Camshafts from the front cylinder head
- Rocker arms and valve lifters

➡ **Be sure to keep the arms and lifters in order so they can be installed the their original locations.**

- M6 bolts from the front of the cylinder head, note the location of the longer bolt
- M11 cylinder head bolts, discard them
- Cylinder head

6. Clean the cylinder head mounting surfaces.

To install:

➡ **Refer to Section 1 of this manual for the cylinder head torque sequence illustration. The illustration is located after the Torque Specification Chart.**

7. Be sure the dowels are securely mounted in the engine block.

8. Install or connect the following:
- New gasket
- Cylinder head
- New M11 bolts
- M6 bolts in the front of the cylinder head

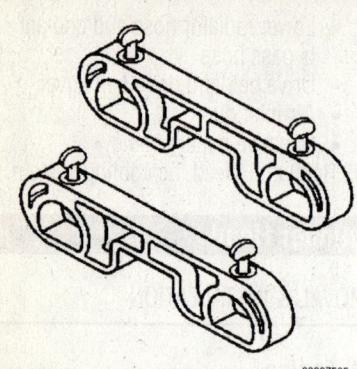

Camshaft holding fixture J-42038—3.5L engine

9300Z505

9. Torque the M11 bolts in sequence to:
 a. Step 1: 22 ft. lbs. (30 Nm).
 b. Step 2: 60 degree turn.
 c. Step 3: 60 degree turn.
 d. Step 4: 60 degree turn.
10. Torque the long M6 bolt to 22 ft. lbs. (30 Nm).
11. Torque both shorter M6 bolts to 106 inch lbs. (12 Nm).
12. Install or connect the following:
 • Lifters and rocker arms in their original positions
 • Camshafts, primary chain and covers
 • Exhaust manifold
 • Coolant crossover pipe
 • Engine mount strut bracket
 • Water outlet housing
 • Intake manifold
 • New oil filter
 • Negative battery cable
13. Refill the crankcase.
14. Refill the cooling system.
15. Start the engine and check for leaks.

REAR

1. Before servicing the vehicle, refer to the precautions in the beginning of this section.
2. Drain the crankcase and the cooling system.
3. Remove or disconnect the following:
 • Negative battery cable
 • Intake manifold
 • Coolant crossover pipe

➡ **Do not remove the rear exhaust manifold. Detach it from the cylinder head and the connection from the front manifold; then, move it aside.**

 • Rear exhaust manifold from the cylinder head and front manifold
 • Camshaft covers
4. Install a holding tool on the camshafts to hold them in position.
5. Remove or disconnect the following:

 • Primary camshaft chain
 • Camshafts, rocker arms and lifters

➡ **Keep them in order so they can be installed in their original positions.**

 • Engine Coolant Temperature (ECT) sensor from the cylinder head
 • M6 bolts from the front of the cylinder head, note the location of the longer bolt
 • M11 cylinder head bolts and discard the bolts
 • Cylinder head
6. Clean the cylinder head mounting surfaces.

To install:

➡ **Refer to Section 1 of this manual for the cylinder head torque sequence illustration. The illustration is located after the Torque Specification Chart.**

7. Be sure the dowels are securely mounted in the engine block.
8. Install or connect the following:
 • New gasket
 • Cylinder head
 • New M11 bolts
 • M6 bolts in the front of the cylinder head
9. Tighten the M11 bolts in sequence using the following sub-steps:
 a. Step 1: 22 ft. lbs. (30 Nm).
 b. Step 2: 60 degree turn.
 c. Step 3: 60 degree turn.
 d. Step 4: 60 degree turn.
10. Torque the long M6 bolt to 22 ft. lbs. (30 Nm).
11. Torque both short M6 bolts to 106 inch lbs. (12 Nm).
12. Install or connect the following:
 • ECT sensor. Torque the sensor to 15 ft. lbs. (20 Nm).
 • Lifters and rocker arms in their original positions
 • Camshafts and primary chain
13. Remove the camshaft holding fixture.
14. Install or connect the following:
 • Camshaft covers
 • Exhaust manifold on the cylinder head
 • Coolant crossover pipe
 • New oil filter
 • Negative battery cable
15. Refill the crankcase.
16. Refill the cooling system.
17. Start the engine and check for leaks.

3.8L Engines

Head gaskets are not interchangeable. Failure to install them with the

arrow pointing to the front, will cause gasket failure and possible engine failure. The left-hand gasket can be identified with the letter "L" punched in it (next to the arrow).

LEFT SIDE (FRONT)

1. Before servicing the vehicle, refer to the precautions in the beginning of this section.
2. Disconnect the negative battery cable.
3. Relieve the fuel system pressure.
4. Drain the cooling system.
5. Remove or disconnect the following:
 • Intake manifold
 • Left exhaust manifold
 • Valve covers, the rocker arm assemblies and pushrods, keep everything in order for reinstallation
 • Ignition wires
 • Spark plugs
 • Alternator front mounting bracket
 • Ignition module with bracket
 • Air conditioning bracket-to-cylinder head bolt
 • Power steering pump
 • Drive belt tensioner
 • Cylinder head. Discard the gasket and bolts.
6. Clean all sealing surfaces and the cylinder head bolt holes in the block.

To install:

➡ **Refer to Section 1 of this manual for the cylinder head torque sequence illustration. The illustration is located after the Torque Specification Chart.**

7. Install or connect the following:
 • New cylinder head gasket with the note **THIS SIDE UP** facing the cylinder head and the arrow facing the front of the engine
 • Cylinder head with new bolts

To prevent damage to the gasket when installing the cylinder head, do not slide the cylinder head on the gasket.

➡ **This engine uses special torque-to-yield head bolts. The procedure must be followed carefully and new bolts must be used whenever the head is removed. Total bolt torque should not exceed 60 ft. lbs. (81 Nm). All bolts should be tightened in sequence, as follows:**

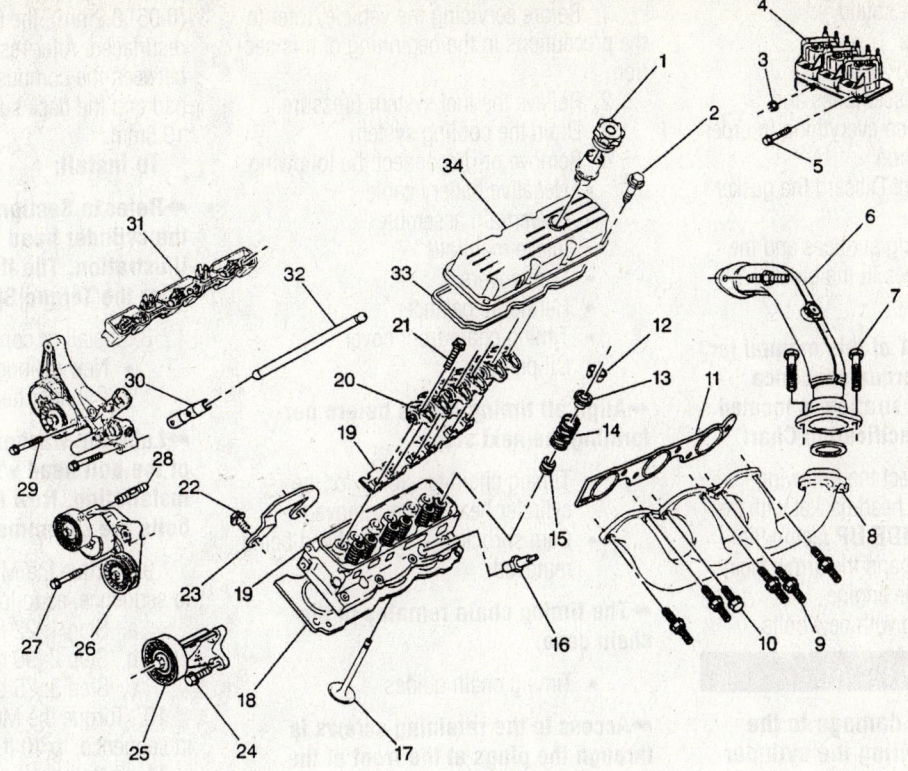

Legend

(1) Oil Fill Cap
(2) Valve Rocker Arm Cover Bolt
(3) ICM Bracket Nut
(4) ICM
(5) ICM Bracket Bolt
(6) Exhaust Crossover Pipe
(7) Exhaust Crossover Bolt
(8) Exhaust Manifold
(9) Exhaust Manifold Stud
(10) Exhaust Manifold Bolt
(11) Exhaust Manifold Gasket
(12) Valve Stem Key
(13) Valve Stem Cap
(14) Valve Spring
(15) Valve Seal
(16) Spark Plug
(17) Intake Valve
(18) Cylinder Head Gasket
(19) Cylinder Head
(20) Valve Rocker Arm
(21) Valve Rocker Arm Bolt
(22) Generator Brace Bolt
(23) Generator Brace
(24) Idler Pulley Bracket Bolt
(25) Idler Pulley
(26) Drive Belt Tensioner
(27) Drive Belt Tensioner Bracket Bolt
(28) Drive Belt Tensioner Bracket Stud
(29) Drive Belt Tensioner Bracket
(30) Valve Lifter
(31) Valve Lifter Guide
(32) Pushrod
(33) Valve Rocker Arm Cover Gasket
(34) Valve Rocker Arm Cover

9300XG03

Exploded view of the cylinder head and related components—3.8L (VIN 1) engine

8. Install the cylinder head bolts and tighten as follows:
   a. Step 1: 35 ft. lbs. (47 Nm).
   b. Step 2: 130 degree turn.
   c. Step 3: Rotate the 4 center bolts an additional 30 degrees.
9. Install or connect the following:
   • Pushrods, rocker arm assemblies and valve covers
   • Intake and exhaust manifolds
   • Alternator front mount bracket
   • Ignition module with bracket
   • Spark plugs and wires
   • Power steering pump
   • Drive belt tensioner
   • Air conditioning compressor bracket bolt. Torque the bolt to 52 ft. lbs. (70 Nm).
   • Negative battery cable
10. Refill the cooling system.

RIGHT SIDE (REAR)

1. Before servicing the vehicle, refer to the precautions in the beginning of this section.

2. Disconnect the negative battery cable.
3. Relieve the fuel system pressure.
4. Drain the cooling system.
5. Remove or disconnect the following:
   • Exhaust crossover pipe
   • Intake manifold
   • Right side exhaust manifold
   • Valve covers
   • Serpentine drive belt
   • Belt tensioner pulley
   • Power steering pump bracket, move it aside

Refer to Section 1 for engine rebuilding specifications

- Fuel line heat shield
- Ignition wires
- Spark plugs
- Rocker arm assemblies and pushrods, keep everything in order for reinstallation
- Cylinder head. Discard the gasket and bolts.

6. Clean all sealing surfaces and the cylinder head bolt holes in the block.

To install:

➡Refer to Section 1 of this manual for the cylinder head torque sequence illustration. The illustration is located after the Torque Specification Chart.

7. Install or connect the following:
- New cylinder head gasket with the note **THIS SIDE UP** facing the cylinder head and the arrow facing the front of the engine
- Cylinder head with new bolts

✳✳ WARNING

In order to prevent damage to the gasket, when installing the cylinder head, do not slide the cylinder head on the gasket.

➡**This engine uses special torque-to-yield head bolts. The procedure must be followed carefully and new bolts must be used whenever the head is removed. Total bolt torque should not exceed 60 ft. lbs. (81 Nm).**

8. Torque the cylinder head bolts, in sequence, as follows:
   a. Step 1: 35 ft. lbs. (47 Nm).
   b. Step 2: 130 degree turn.
   c. Step 3: Rotate 4 center bolts an additional 30 degree turn.
9. Install or connect the following:
- Exhaust manifold and intake manifold
- Pushrods and rocker arm assemblies
- Valve cover(s)
- Spark plugs and wires
- Power steering pump bracket. Torque the bolts to 35 ft. lbs. (47 Nm).
- Belt tensioner pulley and serpentine belt
- Exhaust crossover pipe
- Negative battery cable
10. Refill the cooling system.

4.0L Engine

➡**The manufacturer recommends that the entire powertrain be removed from the vehicle before removing the cylinder heads.**

1. Before servicing the vehicle, refer to the precautions in the beginning of this section.
2. Relieve the fuel system pressure.
3. Drain the cooling system.
4. Remove or disconnect the following:
- Negative battery cable
- Powertrain assembly
- Intake manifold
- Cam covers
- Harmonic balancer
- Timing chain front cover
- Oil pump

➡**Align all timing marks before performing the next step.**

- Timing chain tensioner for the cylinder head being removed
- Cam sprockets from the head being removed

➡**The timing chain remains in the chain case.**

- Timing chain guides

➡**Access to the retaining screws is through the plugs at the front of the cylinder head.**

- Water crossover
- Exhaust manifold
- Cylinder head bolts a little at a time, by reversing the torque sequence
- Cylinder head and discard the gasket

✳✳ WARNING

With the camshafts remaining in the cylinder head, some valves will be open at all times. Do not rest the cylinder head on a flat service with the cylinder face down or valve damage will result.

5. Clean all gasket sealing surfaces. Clean the head bolt holes in the crankcase with compressed air and clean the head bolt bosses in the cylinder head.

✳✳ WARNING

Be careful when cleaning aluminum gasket surfaces to prevent damage to the sealing surfaces. Use only plastic, wood or "dull" gasket scrapers.

6. Check the cylinder head for warpage using a straightedge and feeler gauge. Measure along each edge, at the center and across both ends.
7. If warpage is less than 0.002 in. (0.05mm), the cylinder head surface is usable. If warpage is 0.002–0.008 in.

(0.05–0.2mm), the cylinder head must be resurfaced. After resurfacing, the dimension between the combustion chamber gauge pad and the deck surface must be at least 10.5mm.

To install:

➡**Refer to Section 1 of this manual for the cylinder head torque sequence illustration. The illustration is located after the Torque Specification Chart.**

8. Install or connect the following:
- New cylinder head gasket
- Cylinder head

➡**Lube the washer and the underside of the bolt head with engine oil prior to installation. New replacement head bolts are recommended.**

9. Torque the M11 cylinder head bolts, in sequence, as follows:
   a. Step 1: 22 ft. lbs. (30 Nm).
   b. Step 2: 90 degree (¼) turn.
   c. Step 3: 75 degree turn.
10. Torque the M6 cylinder head bolts, in sequence, to 10 ft. lbs. (12 Nm).
11. Install or connect the following:
- Camshafts, set the camshaft timing
- Camshaft guide bolt access hole plugs, seat them in the cylinder heads
- Intake cam covers
- Oil pump
- Timing chain front cover
- Harmonic balancer
- Intake manifold
- Water crossover
- Exhaust manifold. Torque the nuts to 22 ft. lbs. (30 Nm) and bolts to 18 ft. lbs. (25 Nm).
- Powertrain assembly
- Negative battery cable
12. Refill the cooling system and check all fluid levels.
13. Properly charge the air conditioning system.
14. Run the engine and check for leaks and proper engine performance.

Rocker Arms

REMOVAL & INSTALLATION

➡**All valve train components should be kept in the order that they were removed, so that they can be reinstalled in the their original position.**

3.5L Engine

Refer to the camshaft removal and installation procedure for rocker arm service.

3.8L Engines

LEFT SIDE (FRONT)

1. Before servicing the vehicle, refer to the precautions in the beginning of this section.
2. Remove or disconnect the following:

- Negative battery cable
- Spark plug wires from the plugs and move them aside.
- Rocker arm cover
- Rocker arm bolt, pedestal and rocker arm
- Pushrod

To install:

3. Install or connect the following:

- Pushrod into the lifter
- Rocker arm and pedestal. Torque the bolt to 19 ft. lbs. (25 Nm) plus a 70 degree turn.
- Rocker arm cover with a new gasket. Torque the bolts to 88 ft. lbs. (10 Nm).
- Spark plug wires to the front plugs
- Negative battery cable

RIGHT SIDE (REAR)

1. Before servicing the vehicle, refer to the precautions in the beginning of this section.
2. Remove or disconnect the following:

- Negative battery cable
- Serpentine belt
- Alternator rear brace
- Spark plug wires from the plugs, move the aside
- Rocker arm cover
- Rocker arm bolt, pedestal and rocker arm
- Pushrod

To install:

3. Install or connect the following:

- Pushrod into the lifter
- Rocker arm and pedestal. Torque the bolt to 19 ft. lbs. (25 Nm) plus 70 degree turn.
- Rocker arm cover with a new gasket. Torque the bolts to 88 ft. lbs. (10 Nm).
- Spark plug wires to the front plugs
- Alternator rear brace
- Serpentine belt
- Negative battery cable

4.0L Engine

The 4.0L engine is not equipped with rocker arms. The camshaft directly actuates the valves.

Supercharger

REMOVAL & INSTALLATION

3.8L (VIN 1) Engine

1. Before servicing the vehicle, refer to the precautions in the beginning of this section.
2. Remove or disconnect the following:
   - Negative battery cable
   - Engine cover
3. Relieve the fuel system pressure.
4. Remove or disconnect the following:
   - Drive belt from the supercharger pulley

➡**It is not necessary to remove the drive belt from the remainder of the pulleys.**

- Right side spark plug wires from the ignition module and move them aside
- Alternator brace
- Fuel injector electrical connectors
- Manifold Absolute Pressure (MAP) sensor bracket
- Fuel rail with the injectors
- Boost control solenoid
- Throttle body nuts
- Supercharger

To install:

5. Clean all sealing surfaces.
6. Install or connect the following:

- Supercharger with a new intake gasket. Tighten the bolts to 17 ft. lbs. (23 Nm).
- MAP sensor bracket
- Throttle body to the supercharger
- Boost control solenoid
- Fuel rail
- Fuel lines
- Alternator brace
- Right side spark plug wires to the ignition module
- Supercharger belt
- Engine cover
- Negative battery cable

7. Start the engine and check for proper operation and no leaks.

Intake Manifold

REMOVAL & INSTALLATION

3.5L Engine

1. Before servicing the vehicle, refer to the precautions in the beginning of this section.
2. Remove or disconnect the following:

- Negative battery cable
- Air duct from the throttle body

3. Partially drain the engine coolant.
4. Remove or disconnect the following:

- Fuel injector cover
- Cruise control and accelerator cables from the throttle body and bracket
- Coolant hoses from the throttle body
- Fuel lines from the fuel supply rail
- Fuel vapor line from the Evaporative Emission (EVAP) canister purge solenoid
- Brake booster vacuum hose
- Air conditioning vacuum hose from the engine
- Surge tank inlet pipe retainer from the fuel supply rail
- Fuel injector electrical connectors
- Throttle Position Sensor (TPS) electrical connectors
- Idle Air Control (IAC) valve electrical connector
- Evaporative Emission (EVAP) canister purge solenoid connector
- Manifold Absolute Pressure (MAP) sensor connector
- Wiring harness channels from the camshaft covers and move them aside with harness
- Vacuum tube from the fuel pressure regulator and throttle body
- Positive Crankcase Ventilation (PCV) tubes from both camshaft covers and intake manifold
- Exhaust Gas Recirculation (EGR) valve outlet pipe
- Fuel supply rail with injectors

➡**Disengage the snap-lock retainers by pushing toward the camshaft covers and lifting.**

- Intake manifold

➡**The manifold-to-cylinder head seals are reusable unless cut or damaged.**

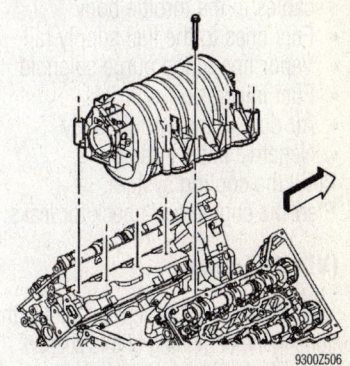

93002506

Intake manifold assembly—3.5L engine

For engine torque specifications, refer to Section 1 of this manual

5. Inspect the intake manifold-to-cylinder head seals for damage or cuts.

6. Clean the intake manifold and cylinder head mating surfaces.

To install:

7. Install or connect the following:

- Throttle body using a new gasket, if removed. Torque the nuts to 106 inch lbs. (12 Nm).
- New intake manifold-to-cylinder head seals
- Intake manifold. Torque the bolts, in a circular pattern, starting from the center to 62 inch lbs. (7 Nm).

✷✷ WARNING

Do not apply excessive pressure to the fuel supply rail assembly. If the assembly is hard to install, check for misalignment of a fuel injector(s).

- New O-rings on the fuel injectors
- Fuel supply rail with injectors by pressing the snap-lock retainers until they lock in place
- EGR pipe. Torque the intake manifold bolt to 89 inch lbs. (10 Nm) and the coolant crossover bolt to 18 ft. lbs. (24 Nm).
- PCV valve and related tubing
- Brake booster and fuel pressure regulator vacuum hoses
- Air conditioning vacuum hose to the intake manifold
- Engine wiring harness with channel to the camshaft covers. Torque the bolts to 89 inch lbs. (10 Nm).
- Surge tank pipe retainer to the fuel supply rail
- Wiring harness connectors to the TPS, IAC, EVAP solenoid and MAP sensor
- Fuel injector electrical connectors
- Coolant hoses to the throttle body
- Cruise control and accelerator cables to the throttle body
- Fuel lines to the fuel supply rail
- Vapor line to the purge solenoid
- Fuel injector cover
- Air duct to the throttle body
- Negative battery cable

8. Refill the cooling system.

9. Start the engine and check for leaks.

3.8L (VIN 1) Engine

1. Before servicing the vehicle, refer to the precautions in the beginning of this section.

2. Relieve the fuel system pressure.

3. Disconnect the negative battery cable.

4. Remove the front splash shield and drain the cooling system.

5. Close the drain cock, reinstall the splash shield and lower the vehicle.

6. Remove or disconnect the following:

- Supercharger
- Thermostat housing
- Exhaust Gas Recirculation (EGR) tube at the intake manifold
- Temperature sensor electrical connector
- Intake manifold and discard the gaskets

To install:

➡ **Refer to Section 1 of this manual for the intake manifold torque sequence illustration. The illustration is located after the Torque Specification Chart.**

7. Thoroughly clean all sealing surfaces.

8. Install or connect the following:

- New intake manifold gaskets
- Intake manifold. Torque the bolts, in sequence, to 11 ft. lbs. (15 Nm). Torque the bolts again in sequence to ensure a torque of 11 ft. lbs. (15 Nm) was achieved.
- Temperature sensor electrical connector
- EGR tube to the intake manifold
- Thermostat housing
- Supercharger
- Negative battery cable

9. Start the vehicle and check for proper operation.

10. Pressurize the fuel system, refill and bleed the cooling system.

3.8L (VIN K) Engine

➡ **There are 2 bolts hidden beneath the upper intake manifold. These bolts are located in the right front and left rear corners of the lower intake manifold. It is necessary to remove the upper intake manifold to service the lower intake manifold.**

1. Relieve the fuel system pressure.

2. Remove or disconnect the following:

- Negative battery cable
- Fuel injector sight shield and air inlet duct
- Air intake duct
- Spark plug wires from the right side of the engine, move them aside
- Manifold vacuum source
- Fuel rail and the Exhaust Gas Recirculation (EGR) heat shield
- Throttle cable bracket from the cylinder head bracket
- Throttle cables from the throttle body lever
- Throttle body support bracket
- Upper intake plenum and discard the gasket

3. Drain the cooling system.

4. Remove or disconnect the following:

- Upper radiator hose from the thermostat housing
- Alternator
- Drive belt tensioner
- EGR valve outlet pipe
- Lower intake manifold and discard the gaskets

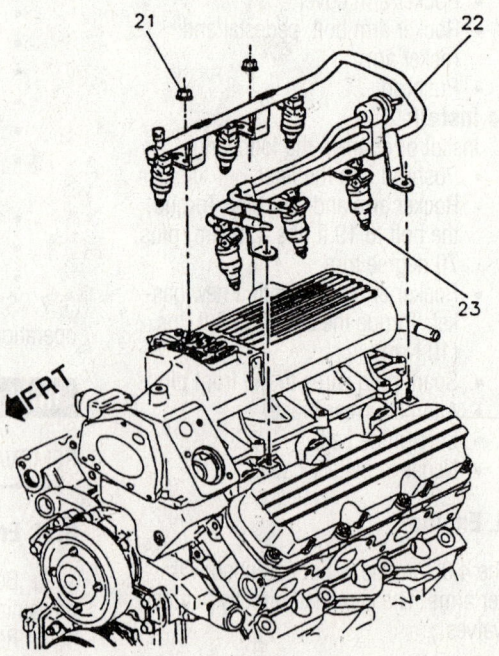

21 NUT, FUEL RAIL MOUNTING
22 RAIL, FUEL
23 INJECTOR, FUEL

Fuel supply rail mounting points—3.8L engine

9300XG02

To install:

➡ Refer to Section 1 of this manual for the intake manifold torque sequence illustration. The illustration is located after the Torque Specification Chart.

5. Thoroughly clean all sealing surfaces.

6. Install or connect the following:
- New intake manifold gaskets
- Intake manifold. Torque the bolts, in sequence, to 11 ft. lbs. (15 Nm). Torque the bolts again in sequence to ensure a torque of 11 ft. lbs. (15 Nm) was achieved.
- EGR valve outlet pipe
- Drive belt tensioner. Torque the bolts to 37 ft. lbs. (50 Nm).
- Alternator and serpentine belt
- Upper radiator hose to the thermostat housing
- Intake plenum using a new gasket. Torque the bolts, in sequence, to 89 inch lbs. (10 Nm).
- Throttle body support bracket
- Throttle cables to the throttle body lever
- EGR heat shield
- Fuel rail assembly. Torque the bolts to 84 inch lbs. (10 Nm).
- Vacuum lines, fuel lines and electrical connectors to the fuel injectors
- Vacuum lines to the intake manifold
- Spark plug wires to the rear bank spark plugs
- Air inlet duct and fuel injector sight shield
- Negative battery cable

7. Pressurize the fuel system and verify no leaks.

8. Refill and bleed the cooling system.

4.0L Engine

1. Before servicing the vehicle, refer to the precautions in the beginning of this section.

2. Relieve the fuel system pressure.

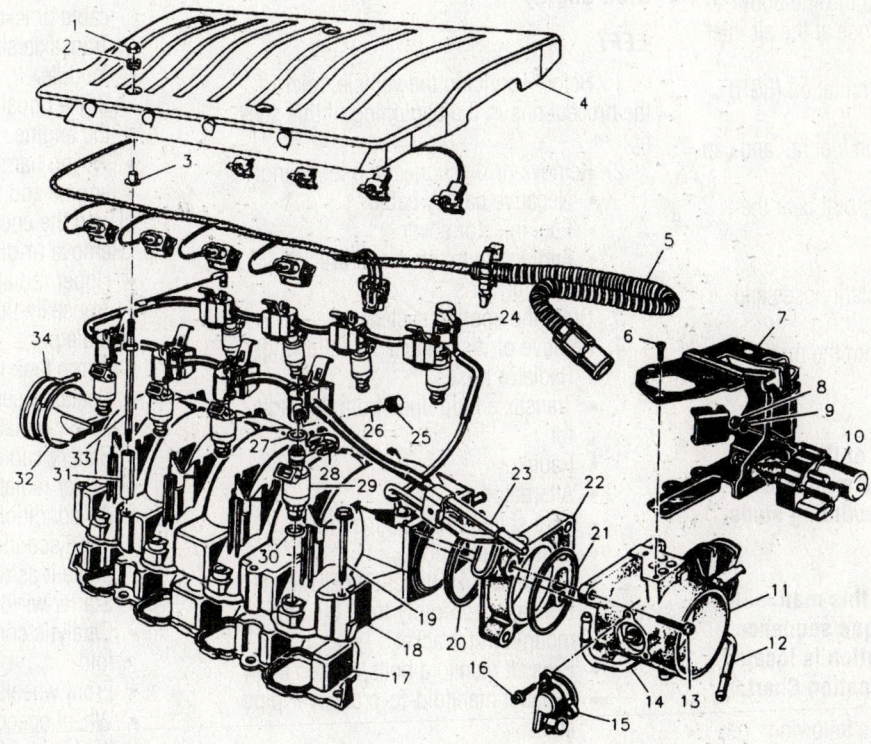

1   NUT, ATTACHING COVER
2   GROMMET, COVER
3   WASHER, COVER GROMMET
4   COVER, INTAKE MANIFOLD
5   WIRING HARNESS ASM
6   SCREW, ISC BRACKET ASM ATTACHING
7   BRACKET ASM, IDLE SPEED CONTROL (ISC)
8   NUT, HEX
9   WASHER, LOCK
10 ACTUATOR ASM, IDLE SPEED CONTROL (ISC)
11 BODY ASM, THROTTLE
12 TUBE, COOLANT OUTLET
13 BOLT, THROTTLE BODY ATTACHING
14 TUBE, COOLANT INLET
15 SENSOR, THROTTLE POSITION (TP)
16 SCREW ASM, TP SENSOR ATTACHING
17 GASKET, INTAKE MANIFOLD

18 HOUSING ASM, INTAKE MANIFOLD
19 BOLT, INTAKE MANIFOLD ATTACHING
20 SEAL, EGR TRANSFER SPACER TO INTAKE MANIFOLD
21 SEAL, THROTTLE BODY TO EGR TRANSFER SPACER
22 SPACER, EGR TRANSFER
23 RAIL ASM, FUEL
24 CARTRIDGE REGULATOR ASM, FUEL PRESSURE
25 CAP, FUEL PRESSURE CONNECTION
26 CORE ASM, FUEL PRESSURE CONNECTION VALVE
27 O-RING, MFI FUEL INJECTOR UPPER
28 CLIP, MFI FUEL INJECTOR RETAINER
29 INJECTOR ASM, MFI FUEL
30 O-RING, MFI FUEL INJECTOR LOWER
31 SPACER, INTAKE MANIFOLD
32 O-RING, PRESSURE RELIEF VALVE
33 STUD, INTAKE MANIFOLD/COVER ATTACHING
34 VALVE ASM, PRESSURE RELIEF

7922XG11

Exploded view of the intake manifold and related components—4.0L engine

For complete mechanical specifications, refer to Section 1 of this manual

3. Remove or disconnect the following:
- Negative battery cable
- Intake manifold sight shield
- Positive Crankcase Ventilation (PCV) hose from the intake manifold
- Front spark plug wires and move them aside
- Main fuel injector harness
- Idle Speed Control (ISC) motor electrical connector
- Throttle Position (TP) sensor electrical connector
- Manifold Absolute Pressure (MAP) sensor electrical connector
- Fuel rail ground wires from the right cylinder head
- Vacuum hoses from the power brake booster and throttle body
- Crankcase vent hose at the air inlet duct
- Exhaust Gas Recirculation (EGR) outlet tube
- Fuel lines from the fuel rail and cap them
- Fuel line retaining bolt near the throttle body
- Air inlet duct
- Throttle body coolant hoses and cap them
- Control cables from the throttle body lever
- Intake manifold

➡Note of the positions of the 4 studs and remove the 6 intake manifold mounting bolts and 4 mounting studs.

To install:

➡Refer to Section 1 of this manual for the intake manifold torque sequence illustration. The illustration is located after the Torque Specification Chart.

4. Install or connect the following:
- New intake manifold gasket
- Intake manifold. Torque bolts to 89 inch lbs. (10 Nm) starting in the center and working in a circular pattern.
- Control cables to the throttle body lever
- Throttle body coolant hoses
- Air inlet duct
- Fuel lines to the fuel rail
- Fuel line retaining bolt near the throttle body
- EGR outlet pipe
- Crankcase vent pipe to the air inlet duct
- Vacuum hoses to the power booster and throttle body
- Fuel rail ground wires to the right cylinder head

- Electrical connectors to the ISC motor, the TP sensor and the MAP sensor
- Main fuel injector harness
- Spark plug wires to the front plugs
- PCV hose to the intake manifold
- Negative battery cable
- Intake manifold sight shield

5. Pressurize the fuel system and verify no leaks.

6. Refill the cooling system.

Exhaust Manifold

REMOVAL & INSTALLATION

3.5L Engine

LEFT

1. Before servicing the vehicle, refer to the precautions in the beginning of this section.

2. Remove or disconnect the following:
- Negative battery cable
- Fuel injector cover
- Engine mount strut and bracket
- Cooling fans

3. Drain the cooling system.

4. Remove or disconnect the following:
- Radiator hoses
- Transaxle fluid lines from the radiator
- Radiator
- Alternator
- Heat shield from the manifold
- Dipstick and tube
- Secondary Air Injection (AIR) control valve assembly from the engine mount strut bracket
- Exhaust manifold bolts, loosen them
- Exhaust manifold-to-crossover pipe studs
- Exhaust manifold

To install:
5. Install or connect the following:
- Manifold to the crossover pipe using a new gasket. Torque the studs to 18 ft. lbs. (25 Nm).
- Exhaust manifold, using a new gasket. Torque the bolts to 18 ft. lbs. (25 Nm).
- AIR valve. Torque the pipe nut to 44 ft. lbs. (60 Nm) and the bolt to 80 inch lbs. (9 Nm).
- Dipstick and tube
- Heat shield
- Alternator and radiator
- Cooling fans
- Engine mount strut
- Fel injector cover
- Negative battery cable

RIGHT

1. Before servicing the vehicle, refer to the precautions in the beginning of this section.

2. Remove or disconnect the following:
- Negative battery cable
- Fuel injector cover
- Air intake duct
- Engine mount strut

3. Relieve the fuel system pressure.

4. Remove or disconnect the following:
- Fuel lines from the supply rail
- Cruise control and accelerator cables from the throttle body
- Transaxle selector range cable and cable brackets
- Transaxle shift cable from the shift module
- Brake booster vacuum hose from the engine
- Wiring harness connectors from the engine and transaxle

5. Drain the cooling system.

6. Remove or disconnect the following:
- Upper radiator hose
- Transaxle fluid cooler lines from the radiator
- Surge tank inlet hose
- Heater hoses from the engine
- Lower radiator air deflector
- Battery cables from the retainers
- Lower radiator hose
- Air conditioning compressor without disconnecting the lines and move it aside
- Starter wiring
- Catalytic converter from the manifold
- Front wheels and splash shields
- Wheel speed sensor wiring from the lower control arms
- Tie rod ends from the steering knuckles
- Lower ball joints from the knuckles

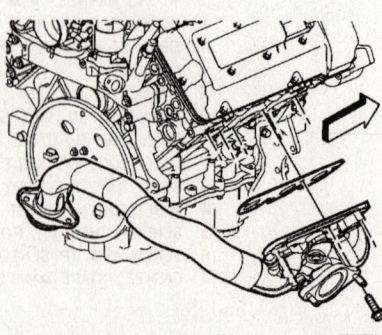

93002507

Exploded view of the right exhaust manifold—3.5L engine

- Halfshafts
- Intermediate shaft from the steering rack

7. Secure the vehicle to the lift in preparation for engine removal.

8. Position an engine/frame support table under the vehicle and lower the vehicle to meet the table.

9. Remove or disconnect the following:

- Frame-to-body bolts
- Crossover pipe from the front manifold
- Exhaust Gas Recirculation (EGR) pipe from the crossover pipe
- Right exhaust manifold from the engine

To install:

10. Install or connect the following:

- Right exhaust manifold using a new gasket. Torque the bolts to 18 ft. lbs. (25 Nm).
- Crossover pipe to the front exhaust manifold
- EGR pipe to the crossover pipe. Torque the pipe nut to 44 ft. lbs. (60 Nm).

11. Position the engine/transaxle assembly under the vehicle.

12. Coat the sub-frame bushings with rubber lubricant.

13. Lower the vehicle onto the assembly. Align the sub-frame on the vehicle using 2 bolts or drill bits, ¾ inches thick by 8 inches long through the alignment holes on the right side of the frame.

14. Install new frame-to-body bolts. Torque the bolts to 133 ft. lbs. (180 Nm) starting with the rear bolts and then the front bolts.

15. Raise the vehicle and remove the frame table.

16. Install or connect the following:

- Intermediate shaft to the steering rack. Torque the bolts to 35 ft. lbs. (48 Nm).

➡Be sure the shaft is fully seated on the stub before installing the pinch bolt.

- Halfshafts and assemble the suspension
- Splash shields and front wheels
- Catalytic converter. Torque the nuts to 53 inch lbs. (6 Nm).
- Starter wiring
- Air conditioning compressor
- Lower radiator hose
- Battery cables in their retainers
- Lower radiator air deflector

17. Remove the straps securing the vehicle to the lift.

18. Install or connect the following:

- Heater hoses
- Surge tank hose
- Transaxle cooler lines to the radiator
- Upper radiator hose
- Wiring harness connectors to the engine and transaxle
- Transaxle shift cable to the shift module and bracket
- Transaxle selector range cable
- Cruise control and accelerator cables to the throttle body
- Fuel lines to the supply rail
- Engine mount strut
- Intake air duct
- Fuel injector cover
- Negative battery cable

19. Refill the cooling system.

20. Start the engine and check for leaks.

3.8L Engines

LEFT SIDE (FRONT)

1. Before servicing the vehicle, refer to the precautions in the beginning of this section.

2. Remove or disconnect the following:

- Negative battery cable
- Both left exhaust manifold to the crossover pipe bolts
- Spark plug wires from the plugs and move them aside

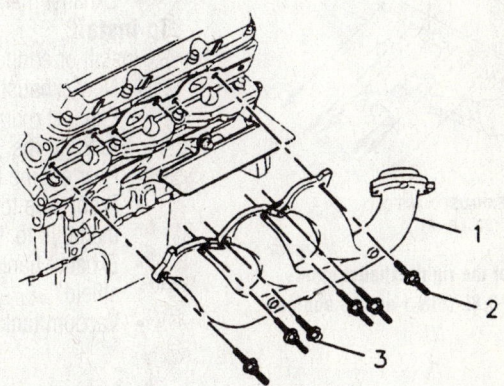

1 LEFT (FRONT) EXHAUST MANIFOLD
2 STUD 30 N•m (22 LB. FT.)
3 BOLT 30 N•m (22 LB. FT.)

7922XG30

Exploded view of the left exhaust manifold mounting—3.8L (VIN 1 and K) engines

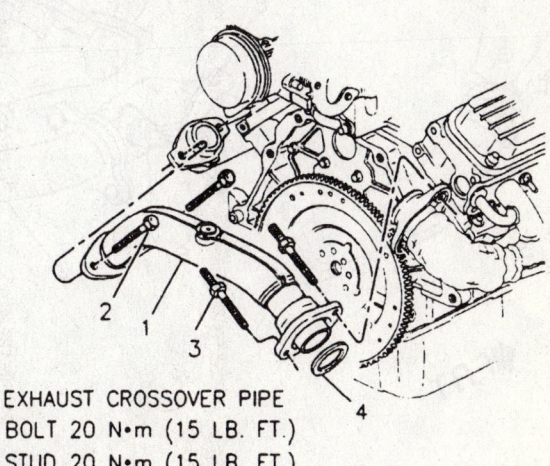

1 EXHAUST CROSSOVER PIPE
2 BOLT 20 N•m (15 LB. FT.)
3 STUD 20 N•m (15 LB. FT.)
4 SEAL

7922XG31

Exploded view of the crossover pipe mounting—3.8L (VIN 1 and K) engines

Please refer to Section 8 for electric cooling fan wiring schematics

- Oil level indicator tube
- Exhaust manifold

To install:

3. Install or connect the following:
- New exhaust manifold gasket
- Exhaust manifold. Torque the bolts to 22 ft. lbs. (30 Nm).
- Oil level indicator tube
- Spark plug wires to the plugs
- Left exhaust manifold-to-crossover pipe. Torque the bolts to 15 ft. lbs. (20 Nm).
- Negative battery cable

4. Start the vehicle and verify no leaks.

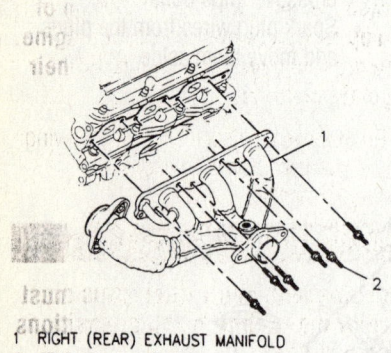

1 RIGHT (REAR) EXHAUST MANIFOLD
2 STUD 30 N•m (22 LB. FT.)

7922XG29

Exploded view of the right exhaust manifold mounting—3.8L (VIN 1 and K) engines

RIGHT SIDE (REAR)

1. Before servicing the vehicle, refer to the precautions in the beginning of this section.

2. Remove or disconnect the following:
- Negative battery cable
- Spark plug wires from the plugs and move them aside
- Transaxle level indicator tube
- Oxygen Sensor (O_2S) electrical connector
- Both right exhaust manifold to the crossover pipe bolts
- Plastic vacuum tank from the cowl
- Converter heat shield and pipe hanger
- Exhaust pipe from the manifold
- Rear engine lift bracket
- Exhaust manifold bolts
- Exhaust manifold

To install:

3. Install or connect the following:
- New exhaust manifold gasket
- Exhaust manifold. Torque the bolts to 22 ft. lbs. (30 Nm).
- Rear engine lift bracket
- Front pipe to the manifold. Torque the bolts to 15 ft. lbs. (20 Nm).
- Exhaust hanger and converter heat shield
- Vacuum tank on the cowl

- Right exhaust manifold-to-crossover pipe. Torque the bolts to 15 ft. lbs. (20 Nm).
- Transaxle level indicator tube
- O_2S sensor electrical connector
- Spark plug wires to the plugs
- Negative battery cable

4. Start the vehicle and verify no leaks.

4.0L Engine

LEFT SIDE (FRONT)

1. Before servicing the vehicle, refer to the precautions in the beginning of this section.

2. Remove or disconnect the following:
- Negative battery cable
- Serpentine belt
- Alternator upper mounting bolt
- Right inner fender well splash shield
- Lower center air deflector
- Alternator rear bracket
- Lower alternator bolt and move the alternator aside
- Exhaust manifold-to-exhaust crossover pipe bolts
- Oxygen Sensor (O_2S) electrical connector
- Power steering line retainer bolts
- Exhaust manifold

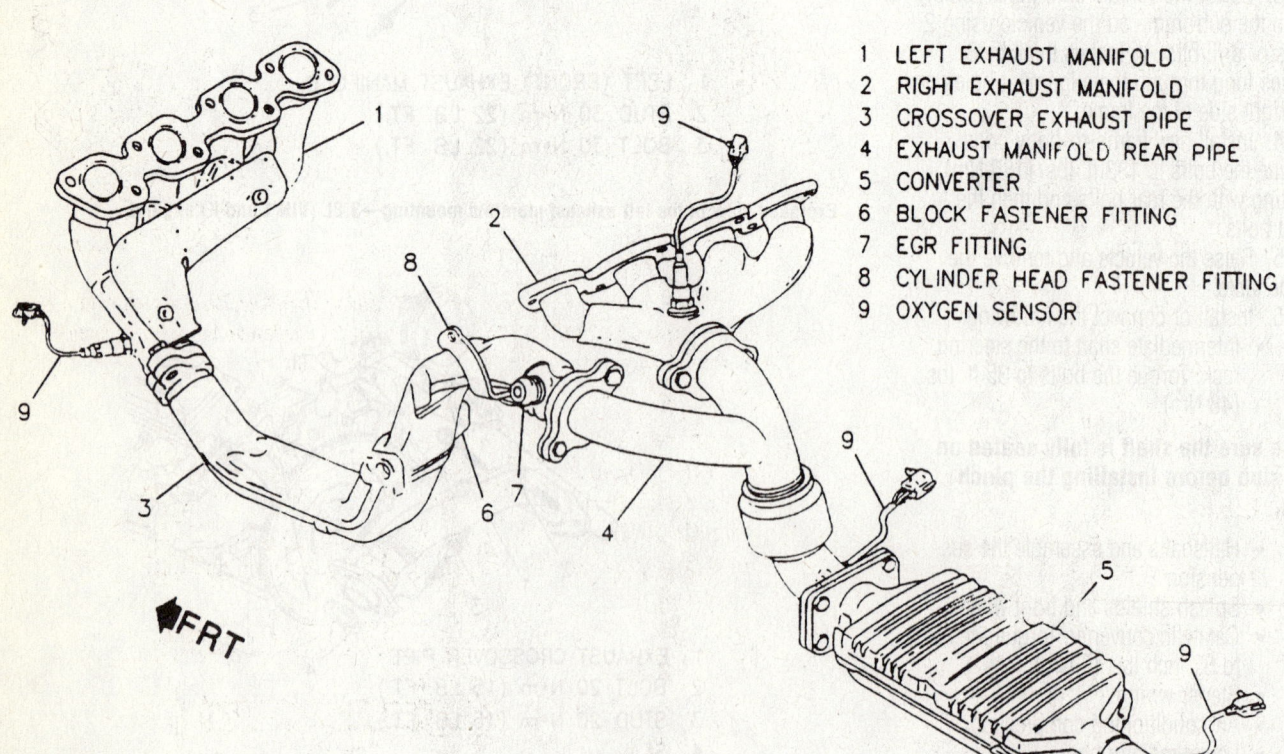

1 LEFT EXHAUST MANIFOLD
2 RIGHT EXHAUST MANIFOLD
3 CROSSOVER EXHAUST PIPE
4 EXHAUST MANIFOLD REAR PIPE
5 CONVERTER
6 BLOCK FASTENER FITTING
7 EGR FITTING
8 CYLINDER HEAD FASTENER FITTING
9 OXYGEN SENSOR

7922XG32

Exhaust system component identification—4.0L engine

3. If the manifold is being replaced, remove the O2 sensor.

To install:

4. Thoroughly clean all sealing surfaces.

5. Install or connect the following:
- O2S, coat the threads with high temperature anti-seize. Torque it to 30 ft. lbs. (40 Nm).
- New exhaust manifold gasket
- Outlet pipe on the manifold partially into the crossover pipe
- Exhaust manifold. Torque the nuts, starting in the center and working outward, to 18 ft. lbs. (24 Nm).
- O2S electrical connector
- Power steering line retainers. Torque the bolts to 10 ft. lbs. (14 Nm).
- Alternator. Torque the lower bolts to 35 ft. lbs. (47 Nm) and the nuts to 28 ft. lbs. (38 Nm).
- Crossover pipe bolts. Torque the bolts to 37 ft. lbs. (50 Nm).
- Lower center air deflector
- Right inner fender well splash shield
- Upper alternator bolt. Torque the bolt to 35 ft. lbs. (47 Nm).
- Serpentine belt
- Negative battery cable

6. Start the vehicle and verify no leaks.

RIGHT SIDE (REAR)

1. Before servicing the vehicle, refer to the precautions in the beginning of this section.

2. Remove or disconnect the following:
- Negative battery cable
- Exhaust system
- Crossover pipe
- Heat shield from the Knock Sensor (KS)
- Oxygen Sensor (O2) electrical connector
- Exhaust manifold

3. If the manifold is being replaced, remove the O2 sensor.

To install:

4. Thoroughly clean all sealing surfaces.

5. Install or connect the following:
- O2sensor coat the threads with high temperature anti-seize. Torque it to 30 ft. lbs. (40 Nm).
- New exhaust manifold gasket
- Exhaust manifold. Torque the nuts, starting in the center and working outward, to 18 ft. lbs. (24 Nm).
- KS heat shield

- O2 electrical connector
- Connector pipe. Torque the bolts to 30 ft. lbs. (40 Nm).
- Exhaust system. Torque the nuts to 18 ft. lbs. (25 Nm).
- Negative battery cable

6. Start the vehicle and verify no leaks.

Camshaft and Valve Lifters

REMOVAL & INSTALLATION

➡ **All valve train components should be kept in the order that they were removed, so that they can be reinstalled in the their original position.**

3.5L Engine

1. Before servicing the vehicle, refer to the precautions in the beginning of this section.

2. Disconnect the negative battery cable.

3. If removing the front (left) camshafts, perform the following:

   a. Partially drain the engine cooling system.

   b. Remove the thermostat housing for

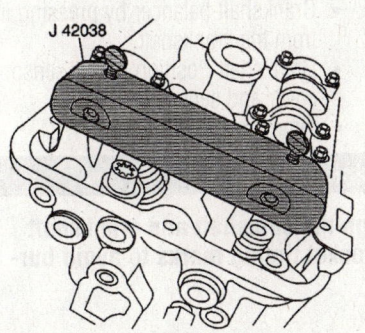

Camshaft holding fixture J-42038 installed on the camshafts—3.5L engine

clearance when installing the Camshaft Holding Fixture tool J-42038.

4. Remove the front camshaft cover.

5. Rotate the crankshaft so the camshaft flats are parallel to the camshaft's sealing surface, then install a camshaft holding fixture.

6. Remove the camshaft sprocket bolts.

7. Install a timing chain/sprocket holding fixture.

8. Evenly slide the camshaft sprocket and chain from the camshafts onto the holding tool.

➡ **The camshaft bearing caps are marked. Be sure the raised portion of the cap faces the outside of the engine. They must always be installed in their original positions.**

9. Remove or disconnect the following:
- Camshaft bearing caps
- Camshafts

❉❉ WARNING

The camshafts and rocker arms must be returned to their original positions when installed.

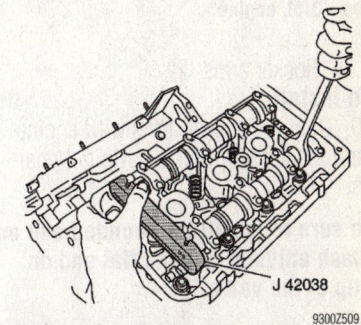

Timing chain/sprocket holding fixture J-42042 installed on the cylinder head—3.5L engine

1. Left intake
2. Left exhaust
3. Right intake
4. Right exhaust

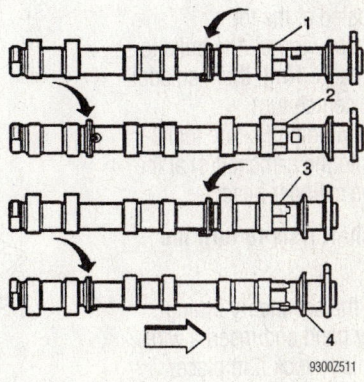

Camshaft identification—3.5L engine

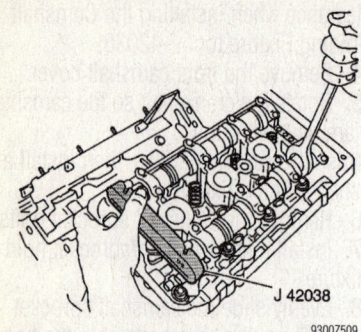

Use the flats on the camshaft if rotation is necessary for installation of the holding tool—3.5L engine

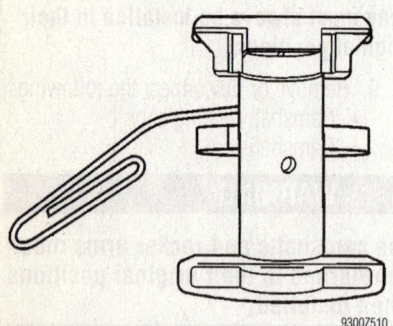

Before installation, compress the tensioner and lock it in place with a piece of wire—3.5L engine

• Rocker arms

To install:

10. Coat the rocker arms with engine oil and place them in their original positions.

➡**Be sure to install the rounded end on the lash adjuster and the flat end on the tip of the valve.**

11. Clean the camshaft carriers and journals with a lint free cloth.

12. Install or connect the following:
• Camshafts, lubricated with engine oil, with the sprocket drive pin notch located at the top.
• Bearing caps. Torque the bolts to 44 inch lbs. (5 Nm); then, an additional 30 degree turn
• Camshaft Holding Fixture tool J-42038 onto the camshaft(s) at the rear of the cylinder head

➡**Use the camshaft flats to turn the camshaft.**

13. Compress the secondary timing chain tensioner by hand and insert a wire into the access hole to lock it in place.

14. Slide the camshaft sprockets/timing chain off the tool and onto the camshafts. Be sure to align the drive pins.

15. Remove the timing chain/sprocket holder from the front of the cylinder head. Torque the sprocket bolts to 18 ft. lbs. (25 Nm); then, an additional 45 degree turn.

16. Remove the wire from the chain tensioner and allow the tensioner to apply pressure to the chain.

17. Remove the camshaft holding fixture.

18. Install or connect the following:
• Camshaft cover
• Thermostat housing, if removed
• Negative battery cable

19. Refill the cooling system.

3.8L Engines

1. Before servicing the vehicle, refer to the precautions in the beginning of this section.

2. Relieve the fuel system pressure.

3. Remove or disconnect the following:
• Negative battery cable
• Engine and mount it on an engine stand
• Intake manifold
• Rocker arm covers
• Rocker arm assemblies and pushrods
• Lifter guide retainer
• Lifter guides
• Lifters from their bores
• Crankshaft balancer by pressing it from the crankshaft
• Crankshaft Position (CKP) sensor cover and sensor
• Timing chain front cover

☀ WARNING

Align the camshaft and crankshaft sprocket timing marks to avoid burring the camshaft journals by the crankshaft.

• Camshaft sprocket and timing chain
• Camshaft thrust plate
• Camshaft

To install:

4. Coat the camshaft lobes and bearings with prelube prior to installation.

5. Install or connect the following:
• Camshaft
• Camshaft thrust plate. Torque the bolts to 10 ft. lbs. (14 Nm).
• Camshaft sprocket and timing chain
• Timing chain cover
• CKP sensor and cover
• Crankshaft balancer. Torque the bolt to 111 ft. lbs. (150 Nm); then, an additional 76 degree turn

☀ WARNING

If the camshaft was replaced the lifters must also be replaced. The old lifters have developed a wear pattern and will cause the new camshaft to wear prematurely. New lifters MUST be installed with a new camshaft.

• Valve lifters, lubricated with prelube
• Lifter guides and retainer. Torque the bolts to 27 ft. lbs. (37 Nm).
• Pushrods and rocker arms. Torque the bolts to 28 ft. lbs. (38 Nm).
• Rocker arm covers
• Intake manifold
• Engine
• Negative battery cable

6. Start the engine and check for leaks.

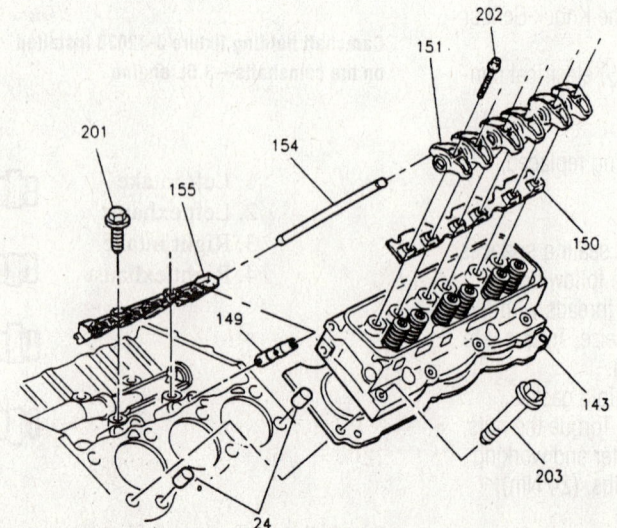

24	DOWEL PIN
143	HEAD GASKET
149	VALVE LIFTER
150	PIVOT RETAINER
151	ROCKER ARM
154	PUSHROD
155	LIFTER GUIDE
201	BOLT
202	BOLT
203	HEAD BOLT

Exploded view of the cylinder head and valve train components—3.8L (VIN 1 and K) engines

9.

4.0L Engine

LEFT SIDE (FRONT)

1. Before servicing the vehicle, refer to the precautions in the beginning of this section.

2. Remove or disconnect the following:

- Negative battery cable
- Intake manifold sight shield

3. Drain the cooling system to a level below the water pump assembly.

4. Remove or disconnect the following:

- Oil level indicator tube
- Upper radiator hose from the thermostat housing
- Spark plug wires from the front plugs and move them aside
- Upper radiator support assembly
- Positive Crankcase Ventilation (PCV) fresh air tube from the left side camshaft cover
- Air inlet duct
- Exhaust Gas Recirculation (EGR) outlet pipe
- Water pump drive belt shield
- Water pump drive belt and drive belt tensioner
- Coolant pump pulley
- Camshaft seal retainer and seal
- Camshaft cover bolts

5. Remove the camshaft cover by pivoting up the intake manifold side of the cover 10 inches. Lift up the exhaust manifold side of the cover 2 inches. Swing the oil fill cap end of the cover up over the intake manifold and slide the cover over the camshafts.

6. Secure the cam sprocket to the timing chain by installing tie-wraps through the cam sprocket holes. Use 4 tie-wraps per sprocket.

➡ **The sprocket/chain relationship must be maintained throughout this procedure or camshaft timing will be lost and require further engine disassembly to retime.**

7. Working behind the sprockets, install a chain holder so that it is positioned between the chain tensioner and chain guide. Apply tension to the tool by tightening the tension adjusting screw.

8. Remove or disconnect the following:

- Camshaft sprocket bolts. Note the relative location of the camshaft drive pins.
- Sprockets from camshafts
- Camshaft bearing caps

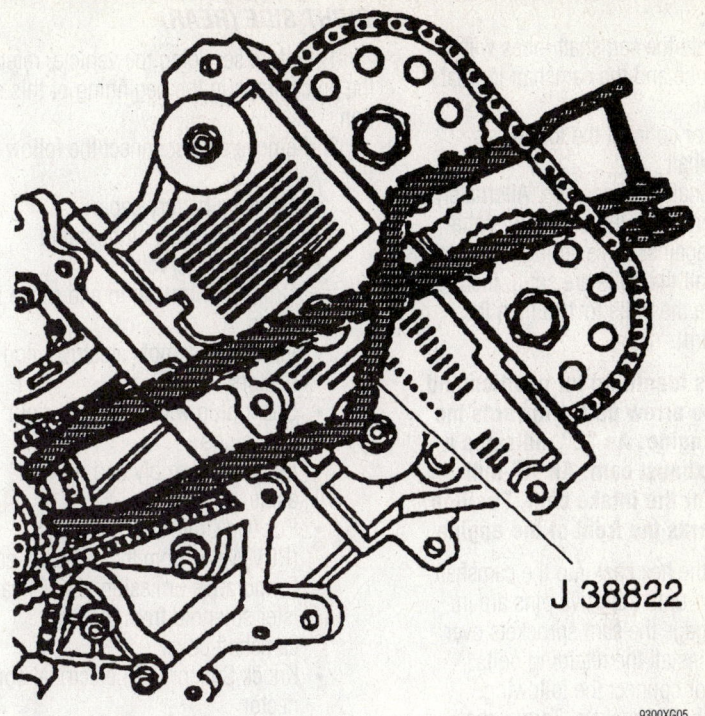

J 38822

9300XG05

Camshaft chain holding tool J-38822—4.0L engine

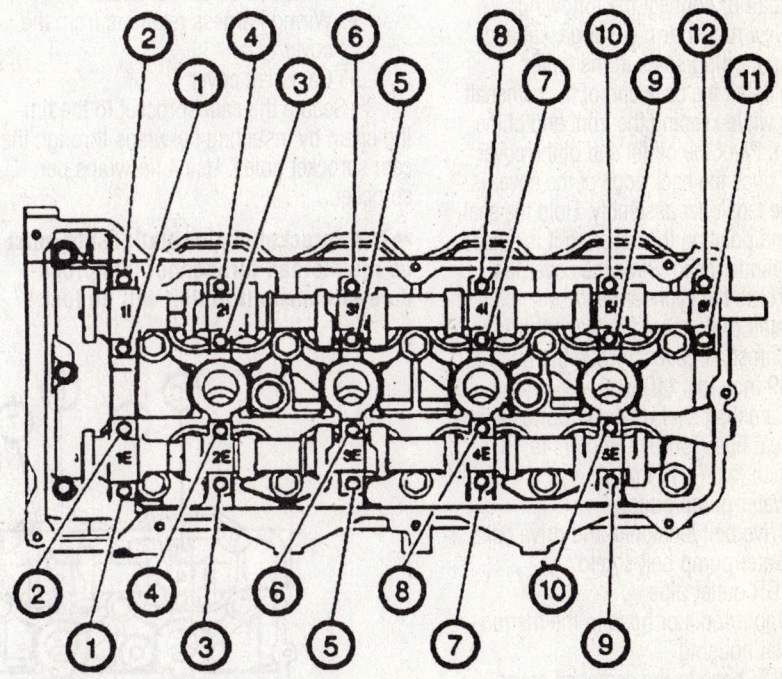

7922XG06

Left cylinder head camshaft bearing cap tightening sequence—4.0L (VIN C) engine

➡ **Alternately, loosen the cap bolts, a few turns at a time, until all valve spring pressure has been released.**

- Camshaft

Inspect the camshaft for excessive lobe wear such as the evidence of grooves, scoring or flaking. Check the bearing journals, making sure they are not scored or burned. Replace the camshaft, as necessary.

Timing belt service is covered in Section 4 of this manual

To install:

10. Lubricate the camshaft lobes with camshaft prelube and the camshaft journals with engine oil.

11. Install or connect the following:

- Camshaft
- Camshaft bearing caps. Alternately, tighten the bolts, a few turns at a time against valve spring pressure, until all the bolts are snug; then, torque the bolts to 108 inch lbs. (12 Nm).

➡**Each cap is identified for position and direction. The arrow points towards the front of the engine. An "E" indicates a cap for the exhaust cam. An "I" indicates a cap for the intake cam. Position No. 1 is towards the front of the engine.**

12. Using the hex cast into the camshaft, rotate the cams until the drive pins are in position to engage the cam sprockets over the cams and install the retaining bolts.

13. Install or connect the following:

- Camshaft sprockets. Torque the bolts to 90 ft. lbs. (120 Nm).

14. Remove the chain holder and the camshaft sprocket tie-wraps.

15. Install or connect the following:

- New rocker arm cover gasket and spark plug seals in the cover

16. Reinstall the back end of the camshaft cover first while keeping the front end of the cover high. Pivot the oil fill end of the cover into place once the back edge of the cover is clear of the tensioner assembly. Hold the seal in place and position the cover so it is square with the cylinder head. Slide the cover left and down onto the cylinder head.

17. Install or connect the following:

- Camshaft cover. Torque the bolts to 89 inch lbs. (10 Nm).
- Camshaft seal retainer, lubricate the seal lips. Torque the bolts to 10 inch lbs. (1.1 Nm).
- Water pump pulley
- Drive belt tensioner and drive belt
- Water pump belt shield
- EGR outlet pipe
- Upper radiator hose to the thermostat housing
- PCV hose to the camshaft cover
- Air inlet duct
- Spark plug wires to the front plugs
- Upper radiator support
- Oil level indicator tube

18. Refill the cooling system.

19. Install or connect the following:

- Intake manifold sight shield
- Negative battery cable

20. Run the engine and check for leaks and proper engine operation.

RIGHT SIDE (REAR)

1. Before servicing the vehicle, refer to the precautions in the beginning of this section.

2. Remove or disconnect the following:

- Negative battery cable
- Intake manifold sight shield
- Vacuum reservoir
- Cruise control servo and move it aside
- Ignition assembly electrical connectors
- Spark plug wires from the right side plugs
- Ignition assembly and move it aside
- Positive Crankcase Ventilation (PCV) valve from the camshaft cover
- Evaporative Emission (EVAP) canister solenoid from the right camshaft cover
- Knock Sensor (KS) electrical connector
- Vehicle Speed Sensor (VSS) electrical connector
- Power Steering (PS) pressure switch electrical connector
- Wiring harness retainers from the cover
- Camshaft cover

3. Secure the cam sprocket to the timing chain by installing tie-wraps through the cam sprocket holes. Use 4 tie-wraps per sprocket.

➡**The sprocket/chain relationship must be maintained throughout this procedure or camshaft timing will be lost**

and require further engine disassembly to retime.

4. Working from behind the sprockets, install a chain holder so that it is positioned between the chain tensioner and chain guide. Apply tension to the tool by tightening the tension adjusting screw.

5. Remove or disconnect the following:

- Camshaft sprocket bolts. Note the relative location of the camshaft drive pins.
- Sprockets from camshafts
- Camshaft bearing caps

➡**Alternately, loosen the cap bolts, a few turns at a time, until all valve spring pressure has been released.**

- Camshaft

6. Inspect the camshaft for excessive lobe wear such as the evidence of grooves, scoring or flaking. Check the bearing journals, making sure they are not scored or burned. Replace the camshaft, as necessary.

To install:

7. Lubricate the camshaft lobes with camshaft prelube. Lubricate the camshaft journals with clean engine oil.

8. Install or connect the following:

- Camshaft
- Cam bearing caps. Alternately, tighten the bolts, a few turns at a time against valve spring pressure, until all the bolts are snug; then, torque the bolts to 108 inch lbs. (12 Nm).

➡**Each cap is identified for position and direction. The arrow points towards the front of the engine. An "E"**

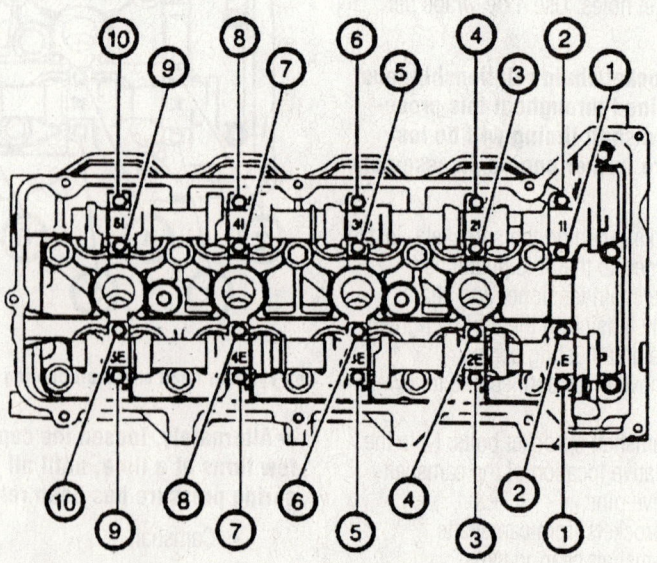

Right cylinder head camshaft bearing cap tightening sequence—4.0L engine

7922XG07

indicates a cap for the exhaust cam. An "I" indicates a cap for the intake cam. Position No. 1 is towards the front of the engine.

9. Using the hex cast into the camshaft, rotate the cams until the drive pins are in position to engage the cam sprockets over the cams and install the retaining bolts.

10. Install or connect the following:
- Camshaft sprockets. Torque the bolts to 90 ft. lbs. (120 Nm).

11. Remove the chain holder and the camshaft sprocket tie-wraps.

12. Install or connect the following:
- New rocker arm cover gasket and spark plug seals
- Rocker arm cover. Torque the bolts to 89 inch lbs. (10 Nm).
- Wiring harness retainers to the camshaft cover
- KS, VSS and power steering pressure switch electrical connectors
- EVAP canister solenoid on the right side camshaft cover
- PCV valve
- Ignition assembly on the right side cover
- Spark plugs wires to the plugs
- Electrical connector to the ignition assembly
- Cruise control servo
- Vacuum reservoir
- Intake manifold sight shield

13. Reconnect the negative battery cable.

14. Run the engine and check for leaks and proper engine operation.

Starter

REMOVAL & INSTALLATION

3.5L Engine

1. Before servicing the vehicle, refer to the precautions in the beginning of this section.
2. Disconnect the negative battery cable.
3. Remove or disconnect the following:
- Lower front air deflector
- Starter electrical connectors
- Torque converter cover
- Starter bolts and shims
- Starter

To install:

4. Install or connect the following:
- Starter. Torque the bolts to 37 ft. lbs. (50 Nm).
- Torque converter cover

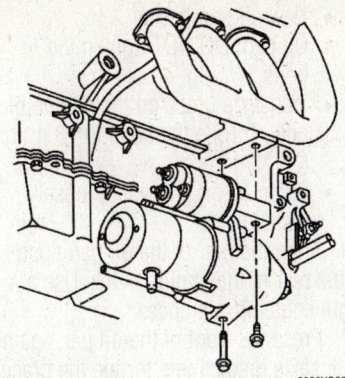
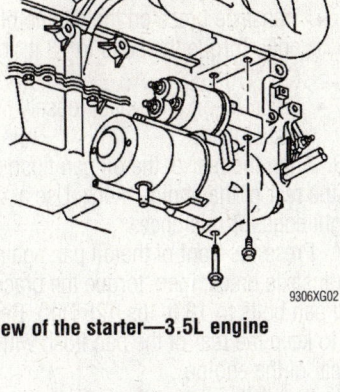

9306XG02

View of the starter—3.5L engine

- Starter electrical connectors. Torque the positive battery terminal nut to 84 inch lbs. (10 Nm) and the "S" terminal nut to 20 inch lbs. (2 Nm).
- Lower front air deflector
- Negative battery cable

3.8L Engine

1. Before servicing the vehicle, refer to the precautions in the beginning of this section.
2. Disconnect the negative battery cable.
3. Remove or disconnect the following:
- Splash shield
- Flywheel cover
- Starter electrical connectors
- Starter

To install:

4. Install or connect the following:
- Starter. Torque the bolts to 32 ft. lbs. (43 Nm).
- Flywheel cover. Torque the bolts to 22 inch lbs. (7 Nm).
- Starter electrical connectors. Torque the positive battery terminal

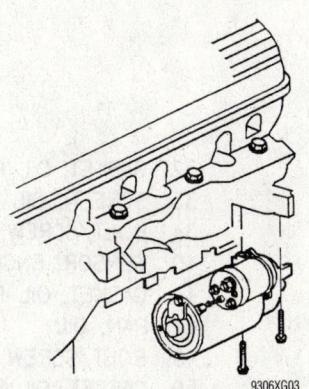

9306XG03

View of the starter—3.8L engine

nut to 12 ft. lbs. (16 Nm) and the "S" terminal nut to 22 inch lbs. (2.5 Nm).
- Splash shield
- Negative battery cable

4.0L Engine

1. Before servicing the vehicle, refer to the precautions in the beginning of this section.
2. Remove or disconnect the following:
- Negative battery cable
- Intake manifold
- Starter electrical connectors
- Starter

To install:

> ※※ **WARNING**

Before installing the starter, torque the inner solenoid and battery terminal nuts to 70 inch lbs. (8 Nm). If not properly tightened, the starter may fail due to terminal or cap damage.

- Starter. Torque the bolts to 22 ft. lbs. (30 Nm).
- Starter electrical connectors. Torque the positive battery terminal nut to 70 inch lbs. (8 Nm) and the "S" terminal nut to 26 inch lbs. (3 Nm).
- Intake manifold
- Negative battery cable

9306XG04

Exploded view of the starter—4.0L engine

Oil Pan

REMOVAL & INSTALLATION

3.5L Engine

1. Before servicing the vehicle, refer to the precautions in the beginning of this section.

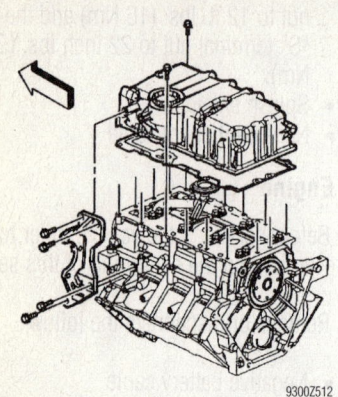

Exploded view of the oil pan—3.5L engine

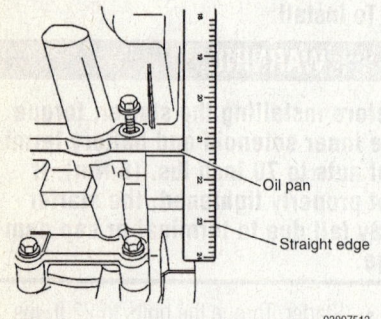

Oil pan

Straight edge

Use a straight edge to align the rear of the oil pan to the rear of the engine—3.5L engine

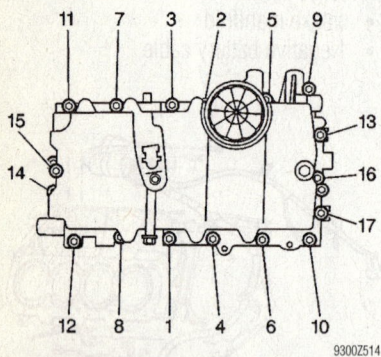

Oil pan mounting bolt tightening sequence—3.5L engine

2. Drain the crankcase.
3. Remove or disconnect the following:
- Oil filter cap and filter
- Oil level sensor harness connector
- Transaxle brace
- Oil pan and discard the gasket

4. Clean the gasket surface carefully to avoid gouging the aluminum.

To install:

5. Install or connect the following:
- Oil level sensor. Torque the bolt to 80 inch lbs. (9 Nm).

- New oil pan gasket
- Oil pan. DO NOT tighten the bolts
- Transaxle brace on the engine block only. Torque the bolts to 18 ft. lbs. (25 Nm).
- Brace-to-oil pan bolts, loosely install them

6. Align the rear of the oil pan flush with the rear of the engine block. Use a straight edge for reference.

7. Press the front of the oil pan against the transaxle brace; then, torque the brace-to-oil pan bolts to 18 ft. lbs. (25 Nm). Be sure to keep the rear of the pan flush with the rear of the engine.

8. Install or connect the following:
- Oil pan bolts. Torque them in sequence, to 18 ft. lbs. (25 Nm).
- Brace-to-transaxle bolts. Torque them to 32 ft. lbs. (43 Nm).
- Oil level sensor connector
- Drain plug. Torque it to 15 ft. lbs. (20 m).
- New oil filter. Torque the cap to 18 ft. lbs. (25 Nm).

9. Refill the crankcase.
10. Start the engine and inspect for leaks.
11. Stop the engine and verify the oil level.

3.8L Engines

1. Before servicing the vehicle, refer to the precautions in the beginning of this section.
2. Disconnect the negative battery cable.
3. Drain the crankcase.
4. Remove or disconnect the following:
- Oil level indicator connector
- Oil pan and discard the gasket

To install:

5. Clean all the gasket surfaces completely.
6. Install or connect the following:
- New oil pan gasket
- Oil pan. Torque the bolts to 10 ft. lbs. (14 Nm).
- Oil level indicator connector
- Negative battery cable

7. Refill the crankcase.
8. Start the vehicle and verify no oil leaks.

4.0L Engine

1. Before servicing the vehicle, refer to the precautions in the beginning of this section.
2. Raise the rear seat cushion to access the battery.

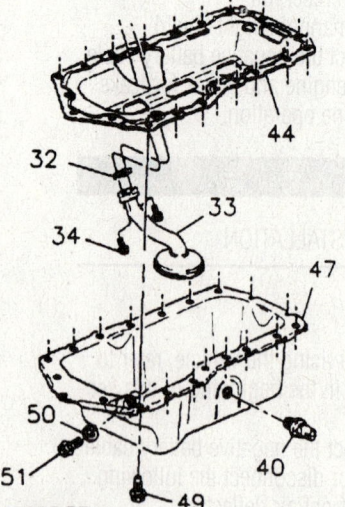

32	GASKET, OIL PAN SCREEN
33	SCREEN, OIL PAN
34	BOLT/SCREW, OIL PAN SCREEN
40	SENSOR, ENGINE OIL LEVEL
44	GASKET, OIL PAN (INCLUDES BAFFLE)
47	PAN, OIL
49	BOLT/SCREW, OIL PAN
50	GASKET, OIL PAN DRAIN PLUG
51	PLUG, OIL PAN DRAIN

Exploded view of the oil pan mounting and related components—3.8L (VIN 1 and K) engines

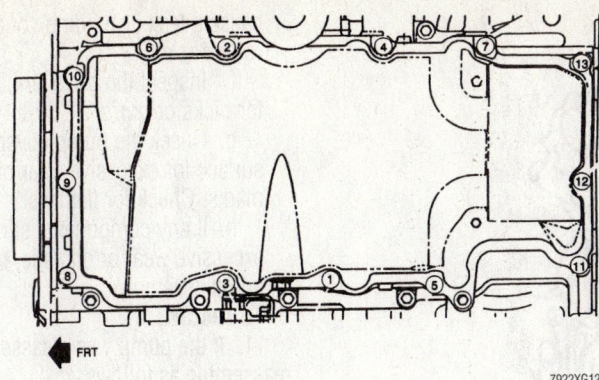

Oil pan bolt tightening sequence—4.0L engine

7922XG12

3. Disconnect the negative battery cable.

4. Drain the crankcase.

5. Remove or disconnect the following:
- Exhaust crossover pipe bolts (if necessary) from the left exhaust manifold flange and the exhaust manifold rear pipe
- Transaxle
- Oil pan

➡ **The oil pan gasket is reusable unless it is damaged. Do not remove the gasket from the oil pan groove unless gasket replacement is required.**

To install:

6. Install or connect the following:
- Oil pan and seal. Torque the bolts in sequence, to 108 inch. lbs. (13 Nm).
- Transaxle
- Exhaust crossover pipe bolts on the left exhaust manifold flange and the exhaust manifold rear pipe, if removed
- Oil pan drain plug. Torque it to 15 ft. lbs. (20 Nm).
- Negative battery cable

7. Refill the crankcase.

Oil Pump

REMOVAL & INSTALLATION

3.5L Engine

1. Before servicing the vehicle, refer to the precautions in the beginning of this section.

2. Remove or disconnect the following:
- Front cover
- Rocker arm covers

3. Install camshaft holding fixtures on both sets of camshafts. Turn the hex portion of the camshaft to align them for tool installation. When installed, the flats on the rear of the camshafts will be parallel with the camshaft cover sealing surface.

4. Remove or disconnect the following:
- Primary chain tensioner
- Primary chain from the drive sprocket
- Oil pump by sliding it off the crankshaft

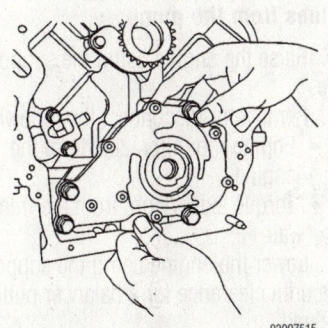

93002515

The oil pump is mounted on the front of the engine and driven by the crankshaft— 3.5L engine

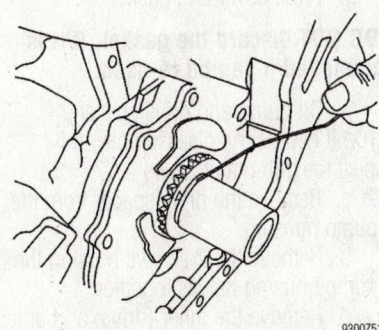

93002516

Correct position of the crankshaft sprocket when the oil pump is installed correctly— 3.5L engine

➡ **The internal parts of the oil pump are not serviced separately. The oil pump may be opened for inspection. If damage or wear is noted, replace the entire pump as an assembly.**

To install:

5. Pack the oil pump housing with white petroleum jelly to insure priming.

6. Install or connect the following:
- Oil pump housing cover. Torque the bolts to 97 inch lbs. (11 Nm).
- Sprocket in the oil pump by aligning the splines

7. Align the sprocket with the crankshaft and install the pump on the engine until a positive stop is felt. When installed properly, the sprocket will protrude slightly from the oil pump and the face of the sprocket will be behind the machined step in the crankshaft.

8. Install or connect the following:
- Oil pump. Torque the bolts to 18 ft. lbs. (25 Nm).
- Primary chain on the sprocket

➡ **Be sure to maintain correct timing.**

- Chain tensioner

9. Remove the camshaft holding tools.

10. Install or connect the following:
- Crankshaft covers
- Engine front cover and remaining components

3.8L Engines

1. Before servicing the vehicle, refer to the precautions in the beginning of this section.

2. Disconnect the negative battery cable.

3. Drain the crankcase.

4. Remove or disconnect the following:
- Front cover assembly
- Oil filter adapter, pressure regulator valve and spring
- Oil pump cover
- Inner and outer pump gears

5. Make the following measurements and replace any components not within specification:

6. Remove or disconnect the following:
- Gear pocket depth: 0.461–0.465 in. (11.71–11.75mm)
- Gear pocket diameter: 3.508–3.512 in. (89.10–89.20mm)
- Inner gear tip clearance: 0.006 in. (0.152mm)
- Outer gear diameter clearance: 0.008–0.015 in. (0.203– 0.381mm)

Refer to Section 1 for engine rebuilding specifications

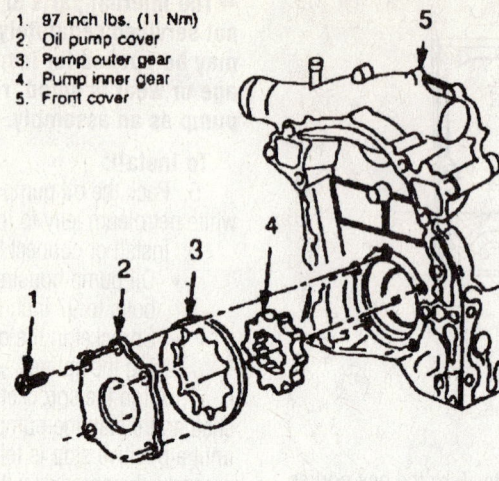

1. 97 inch lbs. (11 Nm)
2. Oil pump cover
3. Pump outer gear
4. Pump inner gear
5. Front cover

7922XG13

Exploded view of the oil pump assembly—3.8L (VIN 1 and K) engines

- Gear end clearance: 0.001–0.0035 in. (0.025–0.089mm)

To install:

7. Lubricate the gears with petroleum jelly and install the gears into the housing.

8. Pack the gear cavity with petroleum jelly after the gears have been installed in the housing.

9. Install or connect the following:
- Oil pump cover. Torque the screws to 97 inch lbs. (11 Nm).
- New oil filter adapter gasket
- Oil filter adapter, pressure regulator valve and spring. Torque the bolts to 24 ft. lbs. (33 Nm).
- Front cover assembly
- Negative battery cable

10. Refill the crankcase.

11. Start the vehicle and verify no leaks and proper oil pressure.

4.0L Engine

1. Before servicing the vehicle, refer to the precautions in the beginning of this section.

2. Disconnect the negative battery cable.

3. Install an engine support fixture.

4. Remove or disconnect the following:
- Engine mount-to-body through-bolt/nut
- Engine mount-to-engine through-bolt/nut
- Front wheel
- Right inner fender well splash shield
- Lower center air deflector
- Left transaxle mount-to-frame through-bolt
- Lower bolt/nut from the engine mount bracket
- Power steering line retainer from the bracket

- Upper nut/bolt from the engine mount bracket
- Serpentine belt from the power steering pump pulley
- Fuel plastic sight shield from the intake manifold
- Power steering pump from the mounting bracket, move it aside

➡ **DO NOT disconnect the power steering lines from the pump.**

6. Raise the engine using the support fixture.

7. Remove or disconnect the following:
- Engine mount bracket from the engine
- Torque axis mount from the frame rail

8. Lower the engine using the support fixture until clearance for a balancer puller is attained.

9. Remove or disconnect the following:
- Crankshaft balancer
- Serpentine belt tensioner
- Serpentine belt idler pulley
- Front cover and gasket

➡ **DO NOT discard the gasket, if it is undamaged it can be re-used.**

- Oil pump and drive spacer

10. If necessary, disassemble and inspect the pump as follows:

a. Remove the drive spacer from the pump housing.

b. Remove the 2 screws holding the pump housing halves together.

c. Remove the inner (drive) and outer (driven) rotors from the housing. Indicate the mating surfaces (dimples).

d. Remove the pressure relief valve.

e. Inspect the pump housing for nicks, burrs, chips or debris that might

cause a leak or binding condition in the rotor pocket.

f. Inspect the drive and driven rotors for nicks or burrs.

g. Check the pump cover and interior surface for excessive wear or score marks. Check for flatness.

h. If any components show signs of excessive wear or damage, replace the pump assembly.

To install:

11. If the pump was disassembled, reassemble as follows:

a. Install the inner and outer rotors to the pump cover in the same orientation as removed.

b. Install the pressure relief valve seat, spring and pilot in the pump housing.

c. Pack the pump housing halves with petroleum jelly to ensure pump priming.

d. Assemble the housing and cover over the locating dowel.

e. Insert a 9mm drill in the pump mounting hole on the opposite side to aid alignment of the housing and cover. Install the 2 screws and tighten to 108 inch lbs. (12 Nm).

12. Install or connect the following:
- Oil pump drive spacer into the oil pump from the rear so the drive flat engages the pump rotor
- Oil pump, by holding the pump in its highest position. Torque the bolts to 89 inch lbs. (10 Nm); then, an additional 35 degree turn

13. Place a small amount of RTV sealant at the split line of the upper and lower crankcases.

14. Install or connect the following:
- Front cover gasket over the engine dowel pins
- Front cover. Torque the bolts to 89 inch lbs. (10 Nm).
- Serpentine belt idler pulley. Torque the bolt to 37 ft. lbs. (50 Nm).
- Serpentine belt tensioner. Torque the bolt to 37 ft. lbs. (50 Nm).

15. Coat the seal contact area on the crankshaft balancer with engine oil.

16. Install or connect the following:
- Crankshaft balancer, press it onto the crankshaft with the notch aligned with the key, using tool J-39344. Torque the bolt to 44 ft. lbs. (60 Nm); then, an additional 120 degrees (⅔) turn.

17. Raise the engine with the support fixture.

18. Install or connect the following:
- Torque axis mount on the body
- Engine mount bracket on the

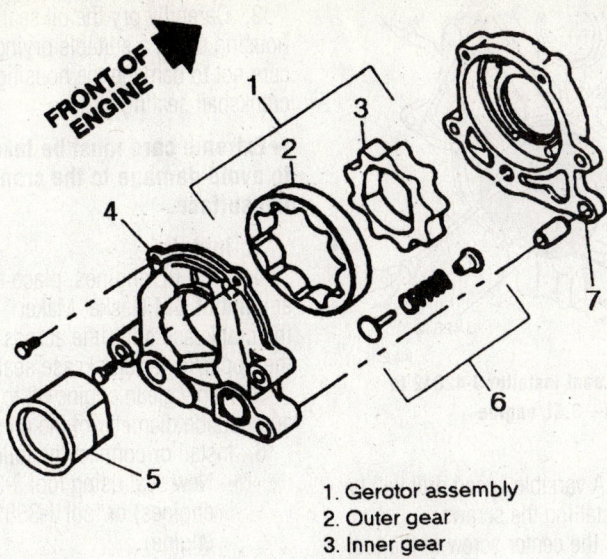

1. Gerotor assembly
2. Outer gear
3. Inner gear
4. Housing
5. Drive spacer
6. Relief valve
7. Cover

7922XG14

Exploded view of the oil pump—4.0L engine

engine. Torque the nuts to 30 ft. lbs. (40 Nm) and the bolts to 41 ft. lbs. (55 Nm).

19. Lower the engine support fixture until the engine is at its normal height.

20. Install or connect the following:
- Power steering pump to the bracket
- Serpentine belt
- Power steering line retainer to the engine mount bracket
- Left transaxle mount-to-frame through-bolt. Torque the bolt to 63 ft. lbs. (85 Nm).
- Lower center air deflector
- Right inner fender well splash shield
- Front wheel. Torque the nuts to 100 ft. lbs. (140 Nm).
- Torque axis mount-to-engine mount bracket. Torque the through-bolt/nut to 70 ft. lbs. (95 Nm).
- Torque axis mount-to-frame. Torque the through-bolt to 37 ft. lbs. (50 Nm).
- Negative battery cable

21. Remove the engine support fixture.

22. Run the engine and check for leaks and proper engine operation.

ENGINE LUBRICATION SYSTEM PRIMING PROCEDURE

➡️**After completing service on a 4.0L (VIN C) engine requiring engine oil**

pump removal, the following priming procedures MUST be performed before engine start-up.

The factory recommends a coat of GM Prelube No. 1052367 be applied to all bearing surfaces and crankshaft journals (cover completely) whenever servicing connecting rod and/or main crankshaft bearings. Also, perform the following when servicing the internal components. These steps will aid in priming the lubrication system:

- Store the valve lifters with the camshaft contact surface down, so engine oil will not drain from the lifters
- Apply liberal amounts of camshaft prelube to the camshaft lobes, bearing caps and lifter surfaces
- Piston rings and pistons should be completely covered with the proper specification motor oil during installation.

To perform the factory-required Engine Lubrication System Priming Procedure, use the following procedures.

1. Thoroughly pack the oil pump with petroleum jelly during reassembly and fill the oil filter with correct specification engine oil before installation.

2. Verify engine oil is at the proper level. System capacity is 7 quarts with the oil filter full. Fill to proper level if necessary.

3. Disconnect the right front connector (power lead) from the Distributorless Ignition System (DIS) module and crank the engine for 30 seconds.

4. Connect the power lead to the DIS and start the engine. Check the Driver Information Center (DIC) for **Low Oil Pressure** message and listen for any audible noise such as lifters "ticking".

5. If engine noises persist, stop the engine and remove the oil pressure switch from the oil filter adapter and install a mechanical oil pressure gauge. **Be careful not to damage the threads in the adapter.** It is made of soft magnesium and is easily damaged. Also note that the ports are sealed with O-rings which must be in

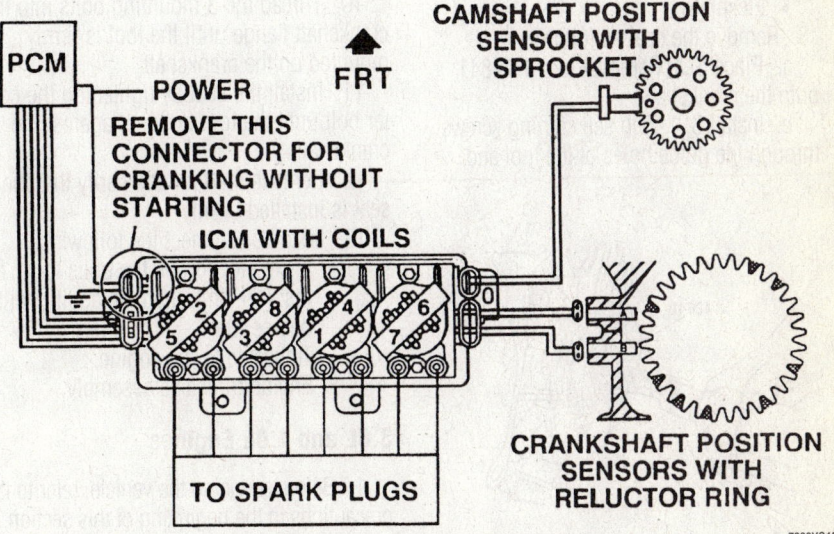

Remove the connector shown to disable the ignition system—4.0L engine

7922XG15

For engine torque specifications, refer to Section 1 of this manual

place and in good condition to seal properly. The bypass valves in the adapter are non-serviceable.

6. If oil is indicated on the gauge and no unusual sounds are heard, oil pressure is present and both the oil pump and engine lubrication system are primed. If no oil pressure is recorded, repeat Step 3 of this procedure, then proceed to Step 7.

7. If no oil pressure is recorded after repeating the process given above, remove the oil filter adapter and force engine oil under pressure (using shop air) in the engine block outlet port (the port closest to the front of the engine). Reinstall the oil filter adapter with the mechanical oil pressure gauge installed in the sender port and start the engine.

8. If oil pressure is obtained, stop the engine and reinstall the oil pressure switch in the oil filter adapter. Once connected, check the instrument display for no oil pressure or **Low Oil Pressure** message. If that message is present, check the switch connection or begin low oil pressure complaint troubleshooting.

Rear Main Seal

REMOVAL & INSTALLATION

3.5L Engine

1. Before servicing the vehicle, refer to the precautions in the beginning of this section.

2. Remove or disconnect the following:
   • Engine/transaxle assembly
   • Transaxle from the engine
   • Flexplate

3. Remove the seal as follows:
   a. Place Seal Removal tool J-42841 onto the crankshaft.
   b. Install 8, 1-inch self starting screws through the guide holes of the tool and

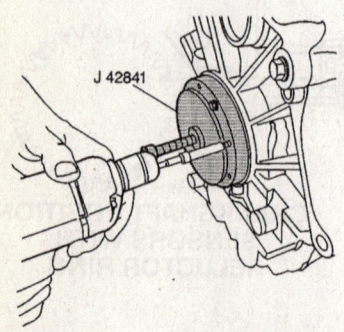

9300Z517

Use the guide holes in tool J-42841 to install the screws in the seal—3.5L engine

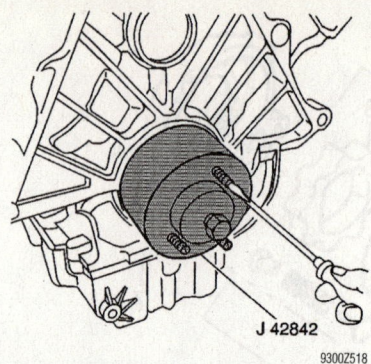

J 42842

9300Z518

Use rear main seal installer J-42842 to install the seal—3.5L engine

into the seal. A variable speed drill will be helpful for installing the screws.
   c. Tighten the center screw of the tool to remove the seal.

4. Clean out the drain at the bottom of the seal bore with a piece of wire or pipe cleaner.

To install:

5. Apply a small amount of RTV gasket maker at the crankcase split line across the end of the upper/lower crankcase seal.

6. Coat the outer diameter of the cylinder block rear crankshaft seal area with engine oil.

7. Wipe the outer diameter of the crankshaft flexplate flange with a lint-free cloth.

8. Lubricate the outer rubber surface of the seal with clean engine oil. DO NOT apply any oil to the green coating pre-applied to the inner diameter of the seal.

9. Loosen the center bolt of the seal installer until the center hub protrudes about ½ inch past the outer plate.

10. Thread the 3 mounting bolts into the crankshaft flange until the tool is firmly mounted on the crankshaft.

11. Install the seal by tightening the center bolt until the tool bottoms against the crankshaft.

12. Remove the tool and verify that the seal is installed evenly.

13. Install or connect the following:
   • Flexplate. Torque the bolts to 11 ft. lbs. (15 Nm); then, an additional 50 degree turn.
   • Transaxle to the engine
   • Engine/transaxle assembly

3.8L and 4.0L Engines

1. Before servicing the vehicle, refer to the precautions in the beginning of this section.

2. Remove or disconnect the following:
   • Negative battery cable
   • Transaxle
   • Flexplate

3. Carefully pry the oil seal from the housing using a suitable prying tool taking care not to damage the housing or the crankshaft sealing surface.

➡**Extreme care must be taken in order to avoid damage to the crankshaft sealing surface.**

To install:

4. On 4.0L engines, place a small amount of GM Gasket Maker® at the top of the crankcase split line across the end of the upper/lower crankcase seal.

5. Apply clean engine oil to the inside and outside diameter of the oil seal.

6. Install or connect the following:
   • New seal using tool J-38196 (3.8L engines) or tool J-38817 (4.0L engine)
   • Flexplate
   • Transaxle
   • Negative battery cable

7. Start the engine and check for leaks.

Timing Chain, Sprockets, Front Cover and Seal

REMOVAL & INSTALLATION

3.5L Engine

PRIMARY CHAIN

1. Before servicing the vehicle, refer to the precautions in the beginning of this section.

2. Remove or disconnect the following:
   • Negative battery cable
   • Camshaft covers

3. Rotate the crankshaft so the No. 1 piston is at Top Dead Center (TDC) and the flats on the rear of the camshafts are parallel with the camshaft cover sealing surface.

4. Install camshaft holding fixtures on both sets of camshafts. Turn the hex portion of the camshaft to align them for tool installation.

➡**When installed, the flats on the rear of the camshafts will be parallel with the camshaft cover sealing surface.**

5. Drain the cooling system.

6. Remove or disconnect the following:
   • Front diagonal brace
   • Battery and tray
   • Washer and coolant reservoirs
   • Underhood accessory wiring junction block and move it aside
   • Drive belt
   • Power steering pump pulley
   • Idler pulley and belt tensioner
   • Water pump and discard the gasket

7. Support the engine cradle

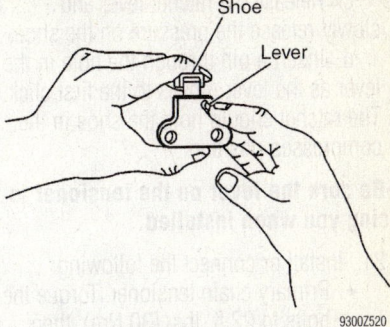

Compressing the primary chain tensioner—3.5L engine

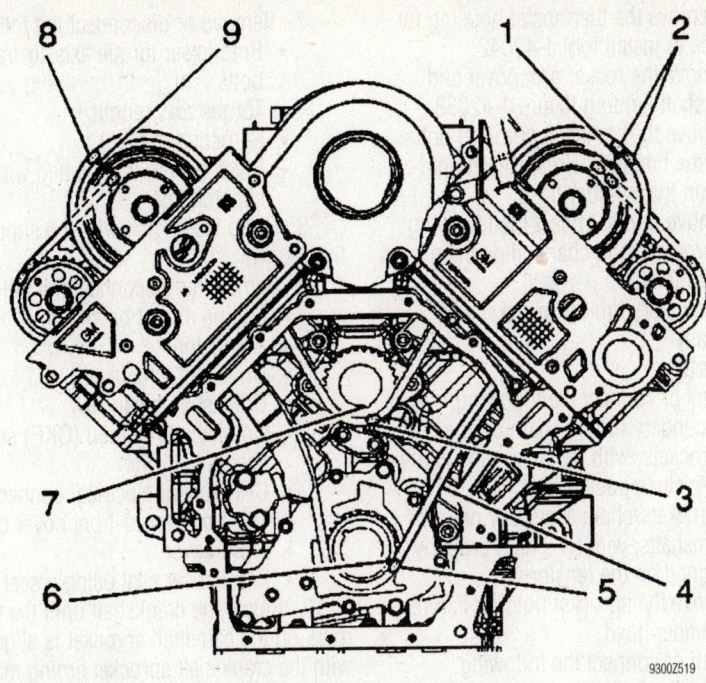

Primary timing chain alignment marks—3.5L engine

8. Remove or disconnect the following:
- Right side engine cradle bolts
9. Lower the cradle
10. Remove or disconnect the following:
- Crankshaft balancer
11. Drain the cooling system.
12. Remove or disconnect the following:
- Front cover and discard the gasket
- Lift bracket from the front of the engine
- Camshaft Position (CMP) sensor
- Sprocket bolt from the exhaust camshaft on the right cylinder head to allow for clearance of the chain guide
- 4 chain guide access plugs from the cylinder heads

➡Note that each plug has an O-ring.

- Primary chain tensioner

➡Remove the lower bolt allowing the tensioner to swing down and expand.

- Primary chain tensioner shoe by removing the bolt, pushing the guide downward slightly and pulling it up through the cylinder head
- Primary chain from the right camshaft, allowing it to fall into the oil pump area
- Primary chain

To install:
13. Rotate the crankshaft so the No. 1 piston is at TDC and the mark on the crankshaft is at the 4 o'clock position.

14. Rotate the balance shaft so the timing mark is at the 5 o'clock position.

➡Be sure the painted links are facing the front of the engine.

15. Install or connect the following:
- Timing chain on the sprockets

➡Turn the camshaft with a wrench on the hex when aligning the links with

the marks on the sprockets. Be sure the marks are aligned.

16. Center the mark on the left intake camshaft sprocket between the 2 painted links.

17. Make a wire hook to feed down through the right cylinder head and lift the chain onto the right intake camshaft sprocket. While doing this, align the marks on the balance shaft and crankshaft sprockets with the painted marks on the chain.

18. Verify that all of the timing marks are aligned.

19. Install or connect the following:
- Primary chain tensioner shoe. Torque the bolt to 22 ft. lbs. (30 Nm).

20. Compress the primary chain tensioner using the following sub-steps:

a. Rotate the ratchet release lever counterclockwise and hold it.

b. Press the tensioner shoe in and hold it.

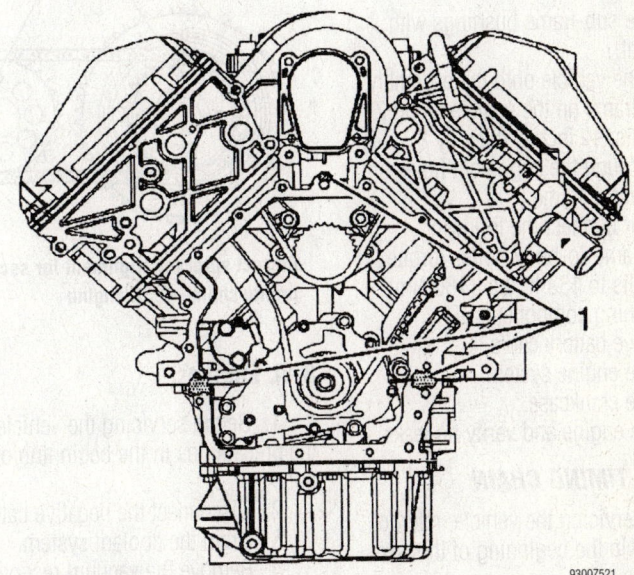

Apply RTV sealant to the 3 areas indicated before installing the front cover and gasket—3.5L engine

For complete mechanical specifications, refer to Section 1 of this manual

c. Release the ratchet lever and slowly release the pressure on the shoe.

d. Insert a pin through the hole in the lever as the lever moves to the first click. The ratchet should hold the shoe in the compressed position.

➡ **Be sure the lever on the tensioner is facing you when installed.**

21. Install or connect the following:
- Primary chain tensioner. Torque the bolts to 22 ft. lbs. (30 Nm); then, remove the chain tensioner pin.
- 4 chain guide access plugs. Torque the plugs to 44 inch lbs. (5 Nm).
- Front engine lift bracket. Torque the hex head bolt to 37 ft. lbs. (50 Nm) and the internal drive bolt to 18 ft. lbs. (25 Nm).
- CMP sensor. Torque the bolts to 80 inch lbs. (9 Nm).

22. Remove the camshaft holding tools

23. Install or connect the following:
- Rocker arm covers

24. Place a small bead of RTV sealant on the 3 areas indicated in the diagram.

25. Install or connect the following:
- New gasket on the front cover, use 2 cover bolts to hold it in position
- Front cover. Torque the bolts to 124 inch lbs. (14 Nm) and the coolant drain plug to 89 inch lbs. (10 Nm).
- Crankshaft balancer. Torque the bolt to 37 ft. lbs. (50 Nm); then, an additional 120 degree turn.

26. Raise the engine cradle and install the bolts.

27. Coat the sub-frame bushings with rubber lubricant.

28. Lower the vehicle onto the assembly. Align the sub-frame on the vehicle using 2 bolts or drill bits, ¾ inches thick by 8 inches long through the alignment holes on the right side of the frame.

29. Install or connect the following:
- New frame-to-body bolts. Torque the bolts to 133 ft. lbs. (180 Nm).
- Remaining components
- Negative battery cable

30. Refill the engine system.

31. Refill the crankcase.

32. Start the engine and verify no leaks.

SECONDARY TIMING CHAIN

1. Before servicing the vehicle, refer to the precautions in the beginning of this section.

2. Disconnect the negative battery cable.

3. For the front cylinder head, perform the following:
   a. Partially drain the cooling system.

b. Remove the thermostat housing for clearance to install tool J-42042.

4. Remove the rocker arm cover and install camshaft holding fixture J-42038.

5. Remove the camshaft sprocket bolts and install the timing chain/sprocket holding fixture on the cylinder head.

6. Remove or disconnect the following:
- Sprockets and chain, slide them onto the tool
- Secondary timing sprocket and chain

To install:

7. Install or connect the following:
- Secondary timing chain on the sprockets, with the drive pins at the 12 o'clock positions
- Sprockets/chain assembly onto the camshafts, with the chain properly aligned on the tensioner

8. Remove the sprocket holding fixture from the cylinder head.

9. Install or connect the following:
- Sprocket bolts. Torque the bolts to 18 ft. lbs. (25 Nm); then, an additional 45 degree turn.

10. Remove the camshaft holding fixture.

11. Install or connect the following:
- Rocker arm cover
- Thermostat housing, if removed
- Negative battery cable

12. Refill the cooling system.

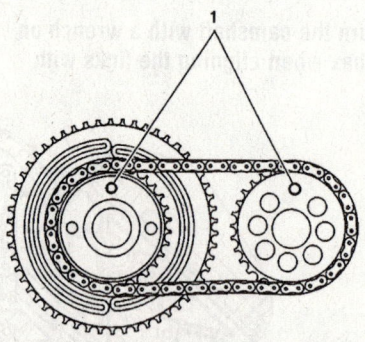

9300Z522

Correct sprocket alignment for secondary timing chain—3.5L engine

3.8L Engines

1. Before servicing the vehicle, refer to the precautions in the beginning of this section.

2. Disconnect the negative battery cable.

3. Drain the coolant system.

4. Remove the vacuum reservoir.

5. Install an Engine Support Fixture tool J-28467-A.

6. Raise the engine so that the weight is removed from the torque axis mount.

7. Remove or disconnect the following:
- Both lower torque axis-to-frame bolts
- Torque axis mount
- Serpentine belt(s)
- Water pump, if equipped with a supercharger

8. Raise the engine with the support fixture.

9. Remove or disconnect the following:
- Engine mount bracket
- Alternator
- Drive belt tensioner
- Crankshaft balancer
- Crankshaft Position (CKP) sensor shield
- CKP sensor electrical connector
- Front oil pan-to-front cover bolts
- Front cover
- Front cover seal using a seal driver

10. Rotate the crankshaft until the timing mark on the camshaft sprocket is aligned with the crankshaft sprocket timing mark.

11. Remove or disconnect the following:
- Timing chain damper assembly
- Camshaft sprocket bolt
- Camshaft sprocket with the timing chain
- Crankshaft sprocket using a gear puller

To install:

12. Install or connect the following:
- Crankshaft sprocket by aligning it with the crankshaft key

➡ **It may be necessary to use a gear installer to fully seat the gear. Be sure the timing mark on the crankshaft gear is pointing straight up.**

- Camshaft gear with the timing chain

➡ **Hold the sprocket with the timing mark facing downward and the chain hanging down off the sprocket; then, loop the chain under the crankshaft sprocket.**

- Camshaft sprocket by aligning the notch with the camshaft key

➡ **The camshaft and crankshaft timing marks should be aligned.**

13. If the marks are not in alignment perform the following:
   a. Remove the camshaft sprocket and timing chain.
   b. Install the camshaft sprocket onto the camshaft and rotate the camshaft until the camshaft and crankshaft marks are aligned.
   c. Remove the camshaft sprocket.
   d. Reinstall the assembly.

14. Install or connect the following:

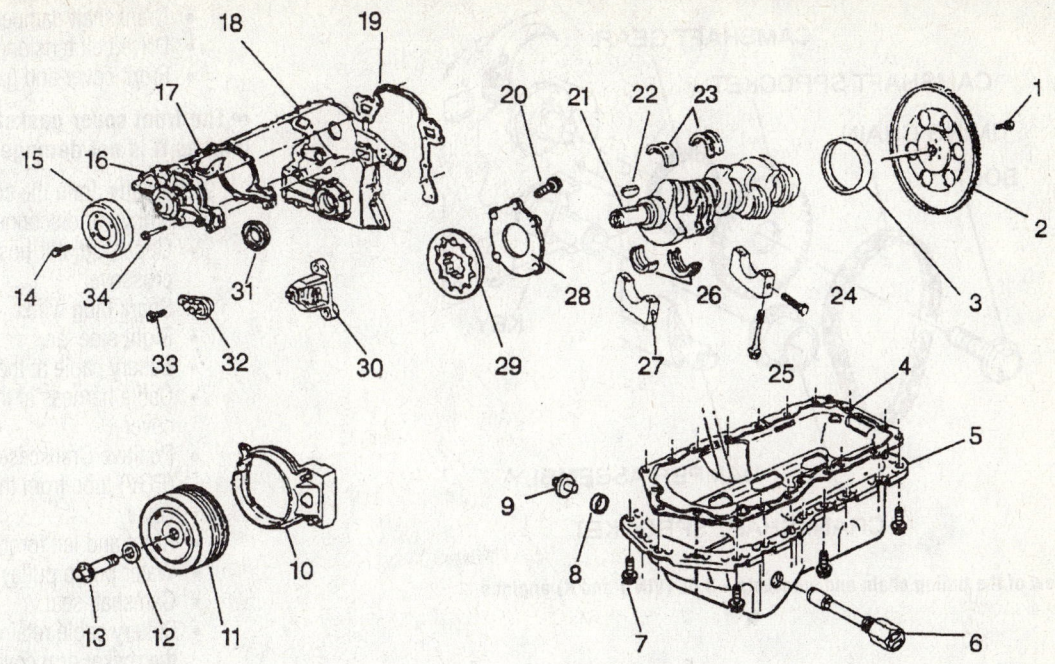

Legend

(1) Flywheel Bolt
(2) Flywheel
(3) Crankshaft Rear Oil Seal
(4) Oil Pan Gasket (Includes Baffle)
(5) Engine Oil Pan
(6) Oil Level Sensor
(7) Oil Pan Bolt
(8) Oil Pan Drain Plug
(9) Oil Pan Drain Gasket
(10) Crankshaft Position Sensor Shield
(11) Crankshaft Balancer
(12) Crankshaft Balancer Washer
(13) Crankshaft Balancer Bolt
(14) Water Pump Pulley Bolt
(15) Water Pump Pulley
(16) Water Pump
(17) Water Pump Gasket

(18) Engine Front Cover
(19) Engine Front Cover Gasket
(20) Oil Pump Cover Bolt
(21) Engine Crankshaft
(22) Crankshaft Balancer Key
(23) Crankshaft Upper Bearing
(24) Side Main Bolt
(25) Crankshaft Main Bearing Cap Bolt
(26) Crankshaft Lower Bearing
(27) Crankshaft Main Bearing Cap
(28) Oil Pump Cover
(29) Oil Pump Gear Set
(30) Crankshaft Position Sensor
(31) Crankshaft Front Oil Seal
(32) Camshaft Position Sensor
(33) Camshaft Position Sensor Bolt
(34) Water Pump Bolt

9300XG04

Exploded view of lower engine components—3.8L (VIN 1 and K) engines

- Camshaft sprocket bolt. Torque the bolt to 74 ft. lbs. (100 Nm); then, an additional 90 degree (¼) turn.
- Timing chain damper. Torque the mounting bolts to 16 ft. lbs. (22 Nm).
15. Thoroughly clean all sealing surfaces.
16. Install or connect the following:
  - Front cover seal lubricated with engine oil, using the appropriate seal driver
  - New front cover gasket

- Front cover. Torque the bolts to 22 ft. lbs. (30 Nm).
- Oil pan-to-front cover bolts. Torque the bolts to 125 inch lbs. (14 Nm).
- Belt tensioner. Torque the bolts to 37 ft. lbs. (50 Nm).
- Alternator
- CKP sensor electrical connector and shield
- Crankshaft balancer. Torque the bolt to 111 ft. lbs. (150 Nm); then, an additional 75 degree turn.

- Engine mount bracket. Torque the bolts to 65 ft. lbs. (87 Nm).
- Power steering pump and belt(s).
- Torque axis mount so the lower bracket slips around both frame bolts
- Both torque axis mount through-bolts/nuts. Torque the torque axis mount-to-frame bolts to 52 ft. lbs. (70 Nm) and the through-bolts to 65 ft. lbs. (87 Nm).
17. Remove the engine support fixture.

Please refer to Section 8 for electric cooling fan wiring schematics

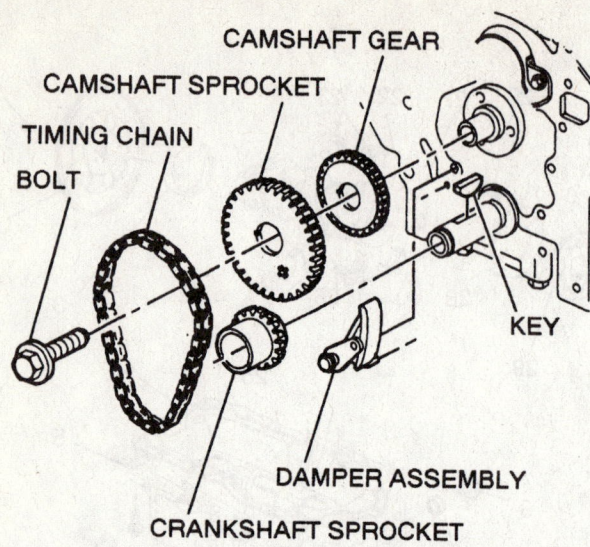

Exploded view of the timing chain and sprockets—3.8L (VIN 1 and K) engines

7922XG16

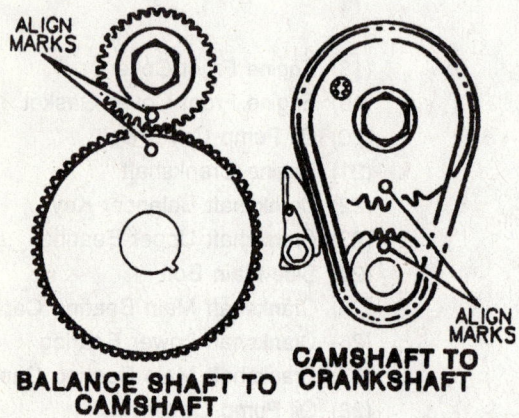

Balance shaft-to-camshaft and camshaft-to-crankshaft timing mark alignment—3.8L (VIN 1 and K) engines

7922XG17

18. Install or connect the following:
   • Vacuum reservoir
   • Negative battery cable
19. Refill the cooling system.
20. Start the vehicle and verify no leaks.
21. Road test the vehicle and ensure proper operation.

4.0L Engine

➡Correct timing exists when the crankshaft and intermediate shaft sprocket timing marks are in alignment and all 4 camshaft drive pins are perpendicular (90 degrees) to the cylinder head surface.

LEFT SIDE SECONDARY CHAIN

The left side secondary timing chain can be removed with the engine in the vehicle.

1. Before servicing the vehicle, refer to the precautions in the beginning of this section.
2. Remove or disconnect the following:
   • Negative battery cable
   • Drive belt
   • Power steering hose bolt
   • Right front wheel
   • Both wheel well splash shields
   • Flywheel cover
3. Install a flywheel holder.
4. Remove or disconnect the following:
   • Crankshaft balancer bolt
5. Support the engine cradle with a screw type jack.
6. Remove or disconnect the following:
   • 3 right-side engine cradle bolts
   • Vehicle Speed Sensor (VSS) from the right control arm
7. Lower the cradle to gain access for the crankshaft damper puller.
8. Remove or disconnect the following:

• Crankshaft damper
• Drive belt tensioner and idler pulley
• Front cover and gasket

➡The front cover gasket is reusable as long as it is not damaged.

9. Partially drain the cooling system.
10. Remove or disconnect the following:
   • Upper radiator hose at the water crossover
   • Spark plug wires
   • Right side fan
   • Battery cable at the alternator
   • Cable harness at the rocker arm cover
   • Positive Crankcase Ventilation (PCV) tube from the rocker arm cover
   • Right and left torque struts
   • Water pump pulley
   • Camshaft seal
   • Battery cable retainer at the front of the rocker arm cover
   • Rocker arm cover by pivoting it around the water pump drive shaft

➡Continue moving the cover upward and pivoting so that the edge of the cover closely follows the left edge of the intake manifold cover. The gasket is reusable as long as it is not damaged.

   • Left side secondary chain tensioner
   • Left side chain guide

➡Access the upper chain guide mounting bolt through the hole in the cylinder head capped with the plastic plug.

   • Left side cam sprocket bolts and sprockets
   • Secondary drive chain

To install:

11. Assemble the left side secondary timing chain as follows:
   a. Route the timing chain over the intermediate sprocket teeth outer row.
   b. Route the timing chain over the chain guide and install the exhaust cam sprocket so the **LE** (Left Head Exhaust) pin engages the sprocket notch.

➡There should be no slack in the lower section of the timing chain and the cam drive pin must be perpendicular to the cylinder head face.

   c. Install the intake cam sprocket into the chain so the sprocket notch **LI** (Left Head Intake) engages the cam and the camshaft drive pin remains perpendicular to the cylinder head face.

➡A hex is cast into the camshafts behind the lobes for cylinder No. 2, so

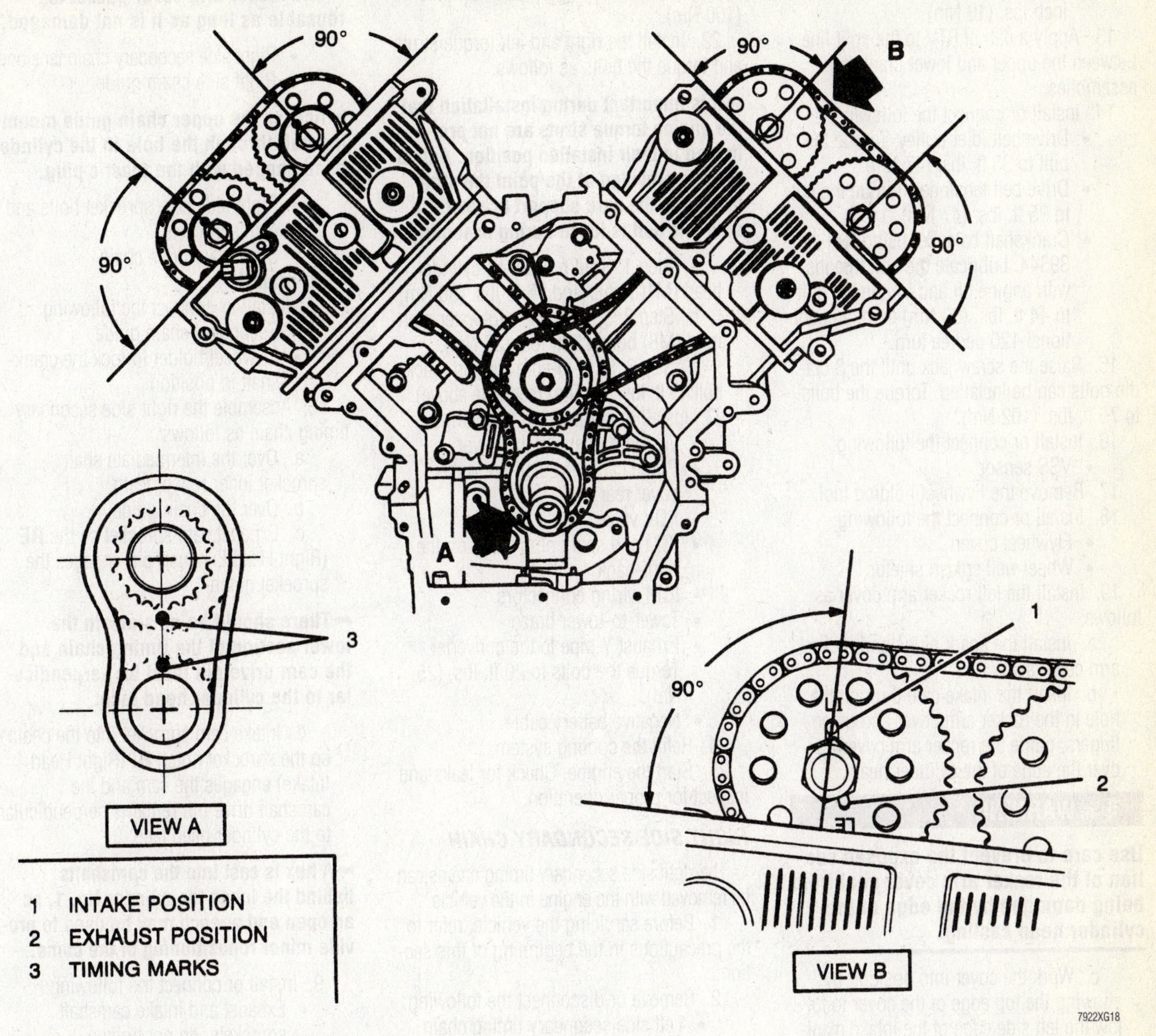

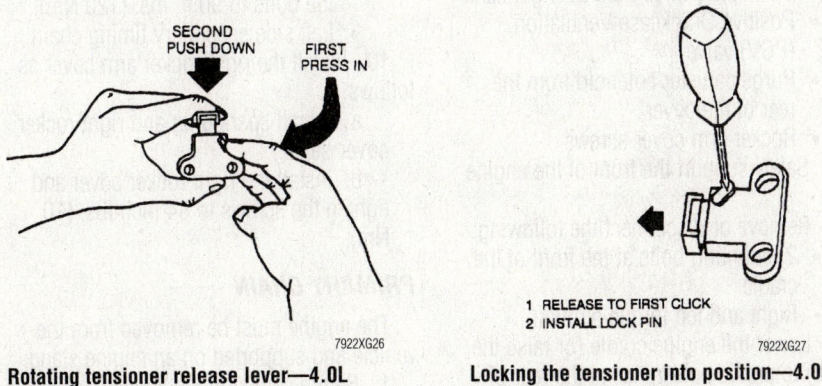

90° **90°** **90°** **90°** **90°** **B** **A**

VIEW A

1. **INTAKE POSITION**
2. **EXHAUST POSITION**
3. **TIMING MARKS**

Primary and secondary timing mark alignment—4.0L (VIN C) engine

90° **1** **2**

VIEW B

7922XG18

SECOND PUSH DOWN **FIRST PRESS IN**

7922XG26

Rotating tensioner release lever—4.0L (VIN C) engine

1 RELEASE TO FIRST CLICK
2 INSTALL LOCK PIN

7922XG27

Locking the tensioner into position—4.0L (VIN C) engine

an open end wrench may be used to provide minor repositioning of the cams.

12. Install or connect the following:
- Exhaust and intake camshaft sprockets, do not tighten the bolts
- Chain tensioner. Torque the bolts to 20 ft. lbs. (27 Nm).
- Camshaft sprocket bolts. Torque the bolts to 90 ft. lbs. (120 Nm).

➡ **The RE cam sprocket must contain the CMP sensor pick-up.**

- Front cover gasket on the engine

For complete service labor times order Nichols' Chilton Labor Guide Manual

- Front cover. Torque the bolts to 89 inch lbs. (10 Nm).

13. Apply a dab of RTV to the split line between the upper and lower crankcase assemblies.

14. Install or connect the following:
- Drive belt idler pulley. Torque the bolt to 35 ft. lbs. (47 Nm).
- Drive belt tensioner. Torque the nut to 35 ft. lbs. (47 Nm).
- Crankshaft balancer using tool J-39344. Lubricate the bolt threads with engine oil and torque the bolt to 44 ft. lbs. (60 Nm) then, an additional 120 degree turn.

15. Raise the screw jack until the 3 cradle bolts can be installed. Torque the bolts to 75 ft. lbs. (102 Nm).

16. Install or connect the following:
- VSS sensor

17. Remove the flywheel holding tool.

18. Install or connect the following:
- Flywheel cover
- Wheel well splash shields

19. Install the left rocker arm cover as follows:

a. Install the spark plugs and rocker arm cover seals.

b. Insert the intake cam through the hole in the rocker arm cover and using fingers, guide the rocker arm cover up over the edge of the cylinder head.

✳✳ WARNING

Use care to prevent the exposed section of the rocker arm cover seal from being damaged by the edge of the cylinder head casting.

c. Work the cover into position by allowing the top edge of the cover to follow the left side edge of the intake manifold.

d. Install the rocker arm cover screws. Torque the screws to 84 inch lbs. (10 Nm).

20. Install or connect the following:
- Battery cable retainer to the front of the rocker arm cover
- Battery cable at the alternator
- Camshaft seal to the intake cam end, lubricate the seal

➡ **Seal the screw threads with sealer.**

- Water pump pulley with tool J-38825
- PCV fresh air tube to the rocker arm cover
- Right side fan
- Spark plug wires
- Upper radiator hose to the water crossover

21. Raise the engine cradle into position.

Torque the 2 mounting bolts to 75 ft. lbs. (100 Nm).

22. Install the right and left torque struts and torque the bolts as follows:

➡ **It is important during installation that the engine torque struts are not pre-loaded in their installed position. Adjustment is provided at the point the strut fastens to the core support bracket. Be sure this bolt is loose during assembly.**

a. Step 1: Strut bracket-to-cylinder head (M10) bolt/stud:35 ft. lbs. (50 Nm).

b. Step 2: Strut bracket-to-water manifold (M8) bolts:20 ft. lbs. (25 Nm).

c. Step 3: Strut-to-core support bracket bolt:45 ft. lbs. (60 Nm) (see note above).

23. Install or connect the following:
- Wiring harness to the cover
- Purge canister solenoid to the cover rear
- PCV valve
- ICM and spark plug wires on the right-bank
- ICM wiring connectors
- Tower-to-tower brace
- Exhaust Y-pipe to the converter. Torque the bolts to 20 ft. lbs. (25 Nm).
- Negative battery cable

24. Refill the cooling system.

25. Start the engine. Check for leaks and inspect for proper operation.

RIGHT SIDE SECONDARY CHAIN

The right side secondary timing chains can be removed with the engine in the vehicle.

1. Before servicing the vehicle, refer to the precautions in the beginning of this section.

2. Remove or disconnect the following:
- Left side secondary timing chain
- Exhaust Y-pipe at the converter
- Tower-to-tower brace
- Ignition Control Module (ICM)
- Spark plug wires from the right bank
- Positive Crankcase Ventilation (PCV) valve
- Purge canister solenoid from the rear of the cover
- Rocker arm cover screws

3. Safely support the front of the engine cradle

4. Remove or disconnect the following:
- 2 mounting bolts at the front of the cradle
- Right and left torque struts

5. Lower the engine cradle (or raise the vehicle) to provide clearance at the rear of the engine compartment.

6. Remove or disconnect the following:
- Rocker arm cover

➡ **The rocker arm cover gasket is reusable as long as it is not damaged.**

- Right side secondary chain tensioner
- Right side chain guide

➡ **Access the upper chain guide mounting bolt through the hole in the cylinder head capped with the plastic plug.**

- Right side cam sprocket bolts and cam sprockets
- Secondary drive chain

To install:

7. Install or connect the following:
- Secondary chain guide
- Flywheel holder to lock the crankshaft in position

8. Assemble the right side secondary timing chain as follows:

a. Over the intermediate shaft sprocket inner row of teeth.

b. Over the chain guide.

c. Exhaust cam sprocket so the **RE** (Right Head Exhaust) pin engages the sprocket notch.

➡ **There should be no slack in the lower section of the timing chain and the cam drive pin must be perpendicular to the cylinder head face.**

d. Intake cam sprocket into the chain so the sprocket notch **RI** (Right Head Intake) engages the cam and the camshaft drive pin remains perpendicular to the cylinder head face.

➡ **A hex is cast into the camshafts behind the lobes for cylinder No. 1, so an open end wrench may be used to provide minor repositioning of the cams.**

9. Install or connect the following:
- Exhaust and intake camshaft sprockets, do not tighten
- Timing chain tensioner. Torque the bolts to 20 ft. lbs. (27 Nm).
- Camshaft sprocket bolts. Torque the bolts to 90 ft. lbs. (120 Nm).
- Left side secondary timing chain

10. Install the right rocker arm cover as follows:

a. Install spark plug and right rocker cover seals.

b. Install the right rocker cover and tighten the screws to 84 inch lbs. (10 Nm).

PRIMARY CHAIN

The engine must be removed from the vehicle and supported on an engine stand.

1. Before servicing the vehicle, refer to the precautions in the beginning of this section.

2. Remove or disconnect the following:

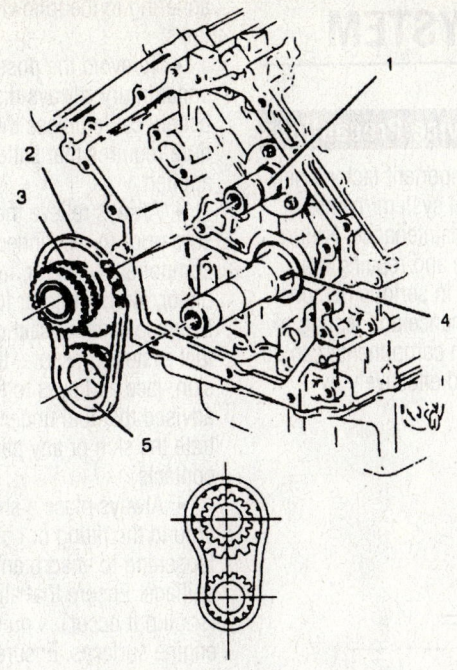

1 INTERMEDIATE SHAFT
2 PRIMARY CHAIN
3 INTERMEDIATE SHAFT SPROCKET
4 CRANKSHAFT SPROCKET KEY
5 SPROCKET

7922XG25

Primary drive chain components—4.0L (VIN C) engine

- Negative battery cable
- Engine and mount it on an engine stand
- Both secondary timing chains
- Intermediate shaft sprocket-to-intermediate shaft bolt
- Intermediate sprocket
- Primary chain/sprocket assembly by sliding it off the shafts

To install:
3. Install or connect the following:
- Primary guide
- Crankshaft sprocket key

➡**Rotate the crankshaft until the sprocket drive key is at the 1 o'clock position.**

- Crankshaft sprocket, intermediate shaft sprocket and primary timing chain assembly so the timing marks are aligned; then, slide the assembly onto the engine

➡**If it is necessary to turn the crankshaft sprocket, the intermediate shaft sprocket will also have to be turned so the timing mark aligns with the crankshaft sprocket.**

- Intermediate shaft sprocket bolt. Torque the bolt to 45 ft. lbs. (61 Nm).
- Primary timing chain tensioner bolts. Torque them to 20 ft. lbs. (27 Nm).
- Both secondary timing chains
- Engine

Piston and Ring

POSITIONING

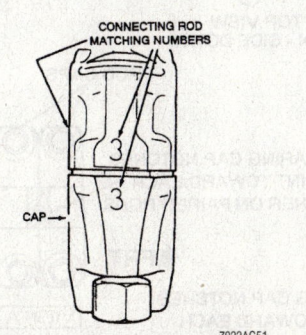

Connecting rod and cap installation. Be sure to matchmark the cap and rod prior to disassembly, as shown

7922AG51

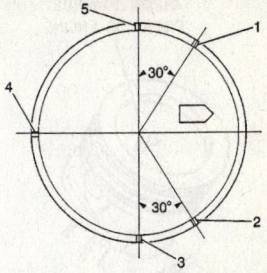

1. Lower oil control ring
2. Upper oil control ring
3. Top Ring
4. Oil control ring expander
5. Second ring

9306XG05

Piston ring end-gap positioning—3.5L engine

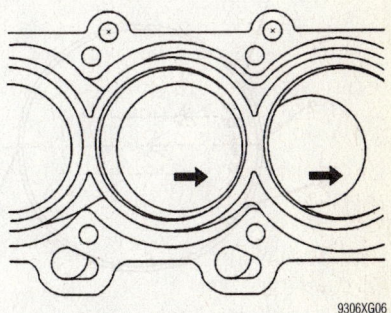

9306XG06

Piston positioning—3.5L engine

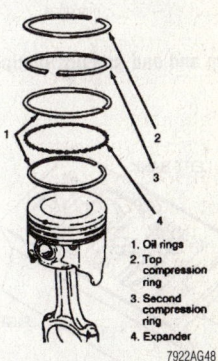

1. Oil rings
2. Top compression ring
3. Second compression ring
4. Expander

7922AG48

Piston ring positioning—3.5L and 3.8L engines

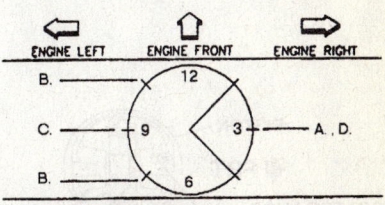

A. OIL RING SPACER GAP (TANG IN HOLE OR SLOT WITH ARC)
B. OIL RING RAIL GAPS
C. 2ND COMPRESSION RING GAP
D. TOP COMPRESSION RING GAP

7922AG46

Piston ring end-gap spacing—3.8L engine

Timing belt service is covered in Section 4 of this manual

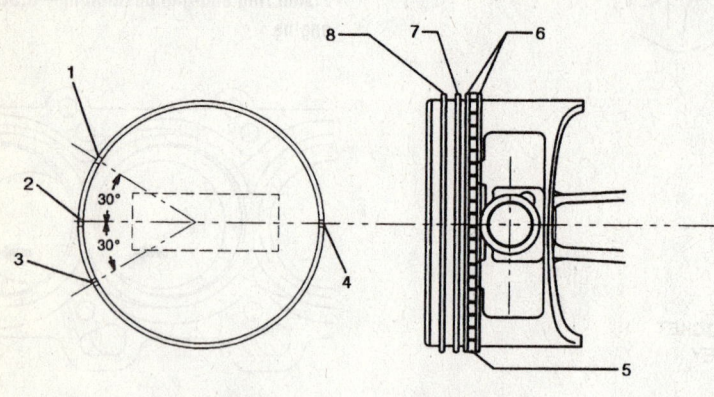

Piston positioning. Often the arrow is replaced by a notch, which also must face toward the front of the engine—3.8L engine

1. Oil ring segment gap
2. Upper compression ring gap
3. Oil ring segment gap
4. Expander & lower compression ring gaps
5. Expander ring
6. Oil segment rings
7. Lower compression ring
8. Upper compression ring

Piston ring and end-gap positioning—4.0L engine

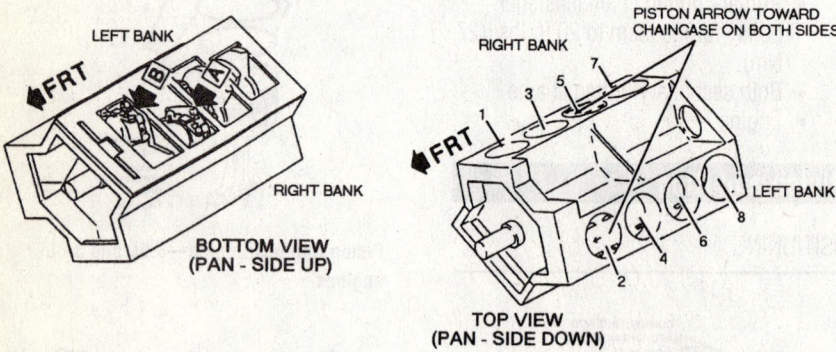

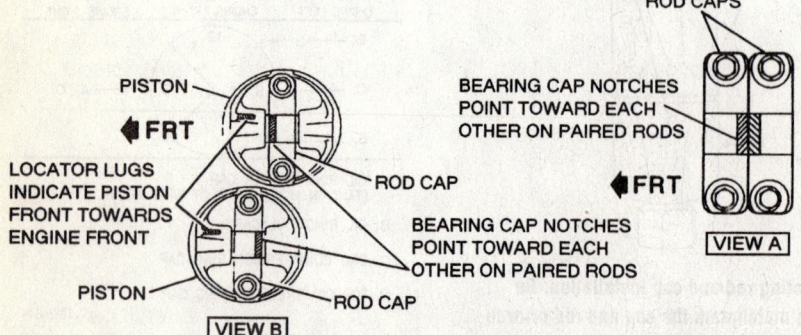

Piston and connecting rod assembly positioning—4.0L engine

FUEL SYSTEM

Fuel System Service Precautions

Safety is the most important factor when performing not only fuel system maintenance but any type of maintenance. Failure to conduct maintenance and repairs in a safe manner may result in serious personal injury or death. Maintenance and testing of the vehicle's fuel system components can be accomplished safely and effectively by adhering to the following rules and guidelines.

• To avoid the possibility of fire and personal injury, always disconnect the negative battery cable unless the repair or test procedure requires that battery voltage be applied.

• Always relieve the fuel system pressure prior to disconnecting any fuel system component (injector, fuel rail, pressure regulator, etc.), fitting or fuel line connection. Exercise extreme caution whenever relieving fuel system pressure, to avoid exposing skin, face and eyes to fuel spray. Please be advised that fuel under pressure may penetrate the skin or any part of the body that it contacts.

• Always place a shop towel or cloth around the fitting or connection prior to loosening to absorb any excess fuel due to spillage. Ensure that all fuel spillage (should it occur) is quickly removed from engine surfaces. Ensure that all fuel soaked cloths or towels are deposited into a suitable waste container.

• Always keep a dry chemical (Class B) fire extinguisher near the work area.

• Do not allow fuel spray or fuel vapors to come into contact with a spark or open flame.

• Always use a back-up wrench when loosening and tightening fuel line connection fittings. This will prevent un-necessary stress and torsion to fuel line piping.

• Always replace worn fuel fitting O-rings with new. Do not substitute fuel hose or equivalent, where fuel pipe is installed.

Fuel System Pressure

RELIEVING

1. Before servicing the vehicle, refer to the precautions in the beginning of this section.

2. Disconnect the negative battery cable.

3. Remove the fuel filler cap from the filler neck.

4. Connect J-34730-1 fuel pressure gauge to the fuel pressure test port. Wrap a shop towel around the fitting while connecting the gauge to prevent fuel spillage.

5. Install the gauge bleed hose into a suitable container and open the valve to bleed the system.

6. Drain any remaining fuel from the gauge into the container and remove the gauge from the test port.

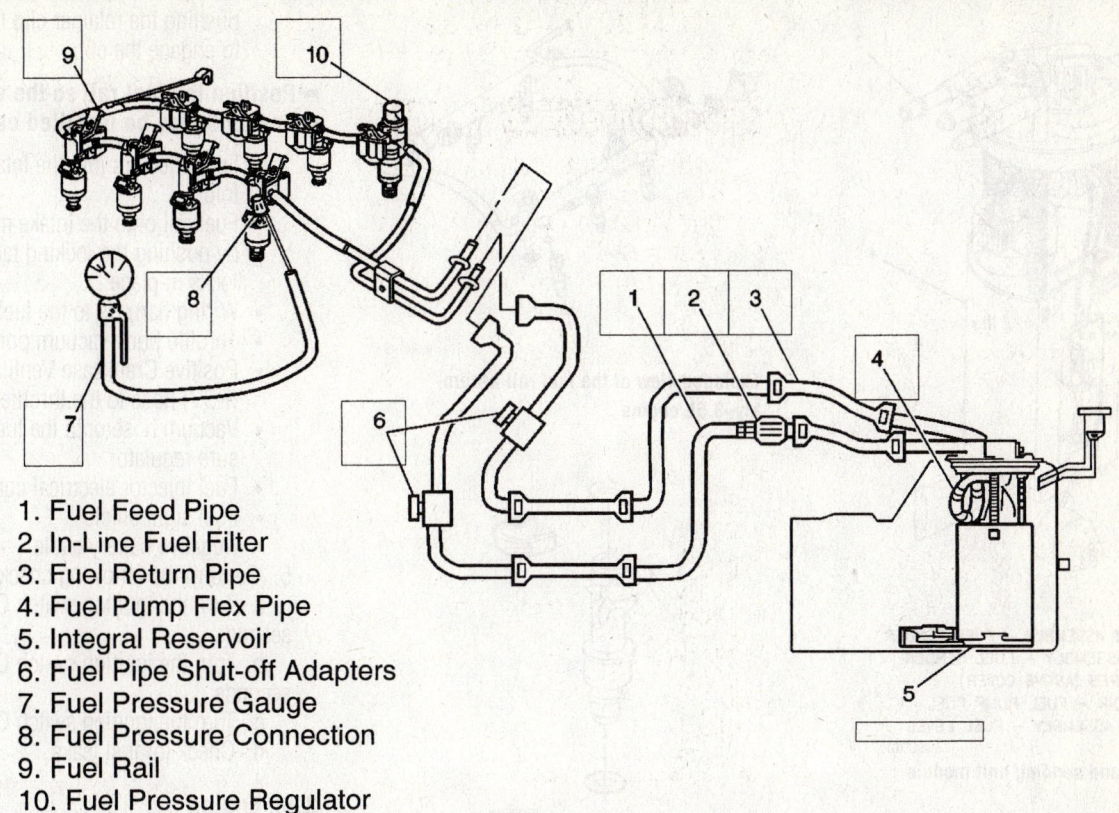

1. Fuel Feed Pipe
2. In-Line Fuel Filter
3. Fuel Return Pipe
4. Fuel Pump Flex Pipe
5. Integral Reservoir
6. Fuel Pipe Shut-off Adapters
7. Fuel Pressure Gauge
8. Fuel Pressure Connection
9. Fuel Rail
10. Fuel Pressure Regulator

9300XG07

Fuel system circuit showing the pressure test port on the supply rail—4.0L engine

Fuel Filter

REMOVAL & INSTALLATION

1. Before servicing the vehicle, refer to the precautions in the beginning of this section.
2. Relieve the fuel system pressure.
3. Disconnect the negative battery cable.
4. Remove or disconnect the following:
   - Quick connect fitting at the fuel filter inlet
   - Fuel filter outlet fitting from the fuel filter while holding the filter fitting with a back-up wrench
   - Fuel filter from the vehicle

To install:

5. Install a new plastic retainer on the fuel inlet line.
6. Apply a drop of oil on the fuel filter inlet fitting and snap the fitting onto the fuel filter.
7. Reconnect the fuel outlet line to the filter and while holding the filter with a back-up wrench tighten the line fitting to 22 ft. lbs. (30 Nm).
8. Pressurize the fuel system and verify no leaks.

Fuel Pump

REMOVAL & INSTALLATION

1. Before servicing the vehicle, refer to the precautions in the beginning of this section.
2. Relieve the fuel system pressure.
3. Disconnect the negative battery cable.
4. Drain the fuel tank with a hand held siphon until the level is less than ¼ full.
5. Remove or disconnect the following:
   - Spare tire and jack
   - Floor trunk liner by pulling it back
   - Fuel sender access cover
   - Fuel sender assembly quick connect fittings
   - Fuel sender assembly electrical connector

✳✳ WARNING

When the lock-ring is removed from the fuel sender, the sender assembly will spring up. Downward pressure should be kept on the assembly and slowly released to ensure the sender assembly does not get damaged.

- Lock-ring from the fuel sender using tool J-39765 or a spanner-wrench

6. Slowly release the spring pressure on the sender.

✳✳ CAUTION

The reservoir bucket on the fuel sender assembly will be full of fuel when it is removed from the tank. Be sure to have a catch pan nearby to drain the sender into.

7. Remove or disconnect the following:
   - Sender assembly from the tank

➡**It will have to be tilted slightly about half way out to be sure the fuel level float clears the side of the tank.**

To install:

8. Install or connect the following:
   - New O-ring on top of the tank
   - Sender assembly into the tank
   - Retainer on top of the fuel tank, compress the sender until the retainer can be engaged; then, lock it in place with tool J-39765

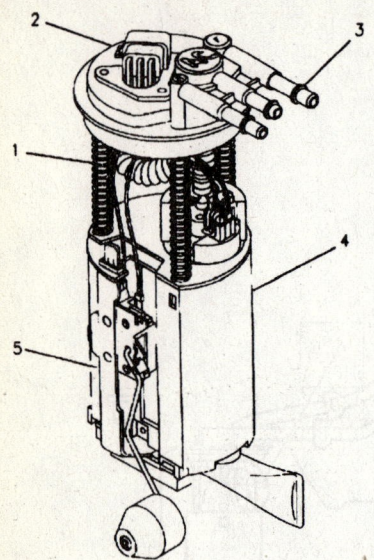

1 SUPPORT ASSEMBLY – FUEL SENDER
2 COVER ASSEMBLY – FUEL SENDER
3 FUEL PIPES (ABOVE COVER)
4 RESERVOIR – FUEL PUMP FUEL
5 SENSOR ASSEMBLY – FUEL LEVEL

7922XG19

Fuel pump and sending unit module assembly

- Quick connect fittings to the fuel sender assembly
- Sender assembly electrical connector
- Negative battery cable

9. Pressurize the fuel system and verify no leaks.

10. Install or connect the following:
- Fuel sender access panel
- Trunk liner
- Spare tire, jack and spare tire cover

11. Refill the fuel tank.

Fuel Injector

REMOVAL & INSTALLATION

3.5L Engine

1. Before servicing the vehicle, refer to the precautions in the beginning of this section.

2. Relieve the fuel system pressure.

3. Remove or disconnect the following:
- Negative battery cable
- Fuel sight shield
- Fuel injector electrical connectors
- Vacuum hose from the fuel pressure regulator
- Positive Crankcase Ventilation (PCV) hose from the throttle body

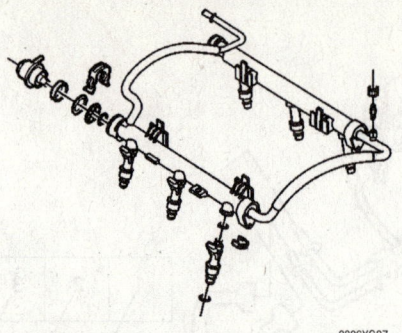

9306XG07

Exploded view of the fuel rail assembly–3.5L engine

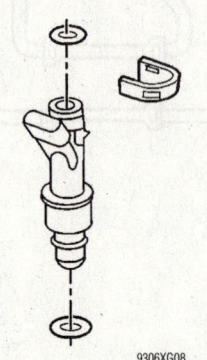

9306XG08

Exploded view of the fuel injector–3.5L engine

- Throttle body vacuum port hose
- Wiring harness from the fuel rail
- Fuel rail from the intake manifold by pushing the locking tab away from the center of the intake manifold
- Fuel injectors out of the intake manifold

➡**Remove the fuel injector by positioning the Fuel Injector Removal tool J-43013 between the bottom of the fuel injector and the intake manifold and lifting it.**

- Fuel injector from the fuel rail and by spreading the retainer clip to release it
- O-rings from the fuel injectors and discard them

To install:

✳✳ WARNING

If the O-rings are different colors, install the black O-ring in the upper position and the brown O-ring in the lower position.

4. Install or connect the following:
- New O-rings on the fuel injectors, lubricated with engine oil
- Fuel injector on the fuel rail by

pushing the retainer clip far enough to engage the clip

➡**Position the fuel rail so the electrical connectors may be installed easily**

- Fuel injectors into the intake manifold
- Fuel rail onto the intake manifold by pushing the locking tab until it locks in place
- Wiring harness to the fuel rail
- Throttle body vacuum port hose
- Positive Crankcase Ventilation (PCV) hose to the throttle body
- Vacuum hose onto the fuel pressure regulator
- Fuel injector electrical connectors
- Fuel sight shield
- Negative battery cable

5. Perform the following check:
a. Turn the ignition switch ON for 2 seconds.
b. Turn the ignition switch OFF for 10 seconds.
c. Turn the ignition switch ON.
d. Check for fuel leaks.

3.8L Engine

1. Before servicing the vehicle, refer to the precautions in the beginning of this section.

2. Relieve the fuel system pressure.

3. Remove or disconnect the following:
- Rear seat cushion
- Negative battery cable
- Fuel sight shield
- Fuel feed and return lines from the fuel rail by squeezing the tabs
- Vacuum line from the pressure regulator
- Vacuum line from the throttle body
- Ignition coil wires
- Retainer clips from the top of the supercharger, for VIN 1 engine
- Alternator and rear mount bracket, for VIN 1 engine

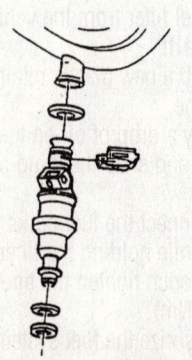

9306XG09

Exploded view of the fuel injector—3.8L engine

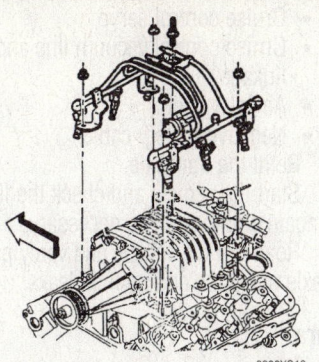

Exploded view of the fuel rail assembly—3.8L (VIN 1) engine

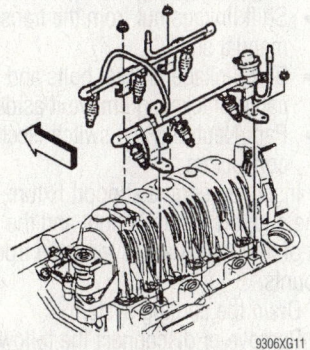

Exploded view of the fuel rail assembly—3.8L (VIN K) engine

- Fuel injector electrical connectors
- Fuel rail hold-down bolts
- Fuel Rail by applying equal force on both sides
- Fuel injector-to-fuel rail retainer clips
- Fuel injector and discard the O-rings
- Fuel injector backup O-ring

To install:

> ※※ **WARNING**
>
> If the O-rings are different colors, install the black O-ring in the upper position and the brown O-ring in the lower position.

> ※※ **WARNING**
>
> The backup O-ring is made of nylon, it prevents the lower O-ring from moving on the injector and causing a possible vacuum leak.

4. Install or connect the following:
  - Backup O-ring on the Fuel injector
  - New O-rings on the fuel injectors, lubricated with engine oil

- Fuel injectors onto the fuel rail and secure with the retainer
- Fuel rail. Torque the bolts to 7 ft. lbs. (10 Nm).
- Alternator and rear mount bracket, for VIN 1 engine
- Fuel injector electrical connectors
- Ignition coil wires
- Retainer clips to the top of the supercharger, for VIN 1 engine
- Vacuum line to the pressure regulator
- Vacuum line to the throttle body
- Fuel feed and return lines to the fuel rail by squeezing the tabs and pulling the lines apart
- Fuel sight shield. Torque the bolts to 18 inch lbs. (2 Nm).
- Negative battery cable
- Rear seat cushion

5. Perform the following check:
  a. Turn the ignition switch ON for 2 seconds.
  b. Turn the ignition switch OFF for 10 seconds.
  c. Turn the ignition switch ON.
  d. Check for fuel leaks.

4.0L Engine

1. Before servicing the vehicle, refer to the precautions in the beginning of this section.
2. Relieve the fuel system pressure.
3. Remove or disconnect the following:
  - Rear seat cushion
  - Negative battery cable
  - Intake manifold cover
  - Fuel injector electrical connector
  - Fuel rail-to-intake manifold locking tab, release it by pushing it toward the center of the intake manifold
  - Fuel injector from the intake manifold by prying it with the Injector Remover tool J-41081
  - Fuel injector from the fuel rail by spreading the retainer clip

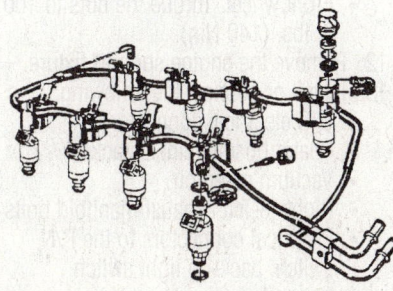

Exploded view of the fuel rail and fuel injector—4.0L engine

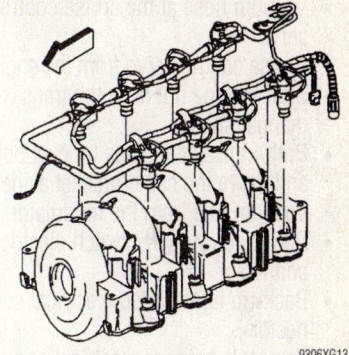

Exploded view of the fuel rail and intake manifold—4.0L engine

➡ It may be necessary to remove the adjacent fuel injector(s) to provide increased fuel rail movement.

- Fuel injector
- O-rings and discard them

To install:

4. Install or connect the following:
  - New O-rings, lubricated with engine oil
  - Fuel injector using a new retainer clip
  - Fuel injector to the fuel rail, push the injector in far enough to engage the retainer clip in the socket slots
  - Fuel rail onto the intake manifold until the locks latch
  - Fuel injector electrical connector
  - Fuel filler cap and tighten it
  - Intake manifold cover. Torque the nuts to 18 inch lbs. (2 Nm).
  - Negative battery cable
  - Rear seat cushion

DRIVE TRAIN

Transaxle Assembly

REMOVAL & INSTALLATION

Riviera

1. Before servicing the vehicle, refer to the precautions in the beginning of this section.
2. Remove or disconnect the following:
  - Negative battery cable
  - Air intake duct
  - Cruise control cable from the throttle body lever

- Vacuum hose at the cruise control servo
- Cruise control servo from the engine
- Shift linkage nut from the transaxle manual shaft
- Both transaxle linkage bracket bolts and move the cable/bracket aside
- Vacuum line from the modulator
- Park/Neutral (P/N) switch electrical connector
- Back-up light switch electrical connector
- Transaxle harness electrical connector
- Vehicle Speed Sensor (VSS) electrical connector
- Left-to-right exhaust manifold bolts
- Vacuum reservoir
- Heater hose retainer bracket
- Oxygen Sensor (O2S) electrical connector

3. Install an engine support fixture. Be sure the support fixture is tight and the weight of the powertrain is removed from the mounts.

4. Remove or disconnect the following:
- Upper transaxle-to-engine bolts
- Front wheels
- Left side power steering rack bolts
- Left front splash shield
- Lower ball joints from the steering knuckles using a ball joint separator tool and discard the cotter pins
- Front lower air deflector
- Power steering line clamp from the frame
- Remaining rack bolt; then, raise the rack and support it
- Left and right transaxle mount through-bolts
- Exhaust system

5. Support the subframe assembly.
6. Remove or disconnect the following:
- Subframe assembly
- Torque converter cover
- Torque converter-to-flywheel bolts. Matchmark the bolts before removal.
- Starter
- Halfshafts

7. Support the transaxle with a jack.
8. Remove or disconnect the following:
- Rear transaxle mount
- Rear spark plug wires from the plugs and move them aside
- Transaxle filler tube
- Right side exhaust manifold
- Lower transaxle-to-engine mounting bolts
- Oil cooler lines from the transaxle and cap them
- Transaxle

To install:

9. Install or connect the following:
- Transaxle. Torque the bolts to 55 ft. lbs. (75 Nm).
- Oil cooler lines to the transaxle
- Right side exhaust manifold. Torque the bolts to 38 ft. lbs. (52 Nm).
- Oil filler tube
- Spark plug wires to the rear plugs
- Rear transaxle mount. Torque the transaxle-to-chassis bolts to 37 ft. lbs. (50 Nm), the mount-to-transaxle bolts to 55 ft. lbs. (75 Nm) and the mount-to-transaxle bracket nuts to 29 ft. lbs. (40 Nm).

10. Remove the transaxle jack.
11. Install or connect the following:
- Halfshafts
- Starter
- Torque converter-to-flywheel aligning the matchmarks made before removal. Torque the bolts to 44 ft. lbs. (60 Nm).
- Flywheel cover
- Subframe. Torque the bolts to 142 ft. lbs. (192 Nm).
- Exhaust system
- Left transaxle mount-to-frame. Torque the bolts to 63 ft. lbs. (85 Nm).
- Right transaxle mount-to-transaxle. Torque the bolts to 75 ft. lbs. (102 Nm).
- Steering rack and right-side through-bolt, do not tighten
- Power steering line bracket to the subframe
- Ball joints to the steering knuckles. Torque the castle nuts to 41 ft. lbs. (55 Nm).

➡ **If necessary, tighten the nuts up to an additional 60 degree (⅙) turn to align the cotter pin holes. NEVER loosen the nuts to make the holes align.**

- Left side splash shield
- Left side rack and pinion bolts
- Front wheel. Torque the nuts to 100 ft. lbs. (140 Nm).

12. Remove the engine support fixture.
13. Install or connect the following:
- O2S electrical connector
- Heater hose retainer bracket
- Vacuum reservoir
- Right-to-left exhaust manifold bolts
- Electrical connectors to the P/N switch, back-up light switch, transaxle harness and VSS
- Vacuum line to the modulator
- Shift cable to the manual shaft and cable bracket. Torque the manual shaft nut to 15 ft. lbs. (20 Nm).

- Cruise control servo
- Cruise control vacuum line and linkage
- Air inlet duct
- Negative battery cable

14. Refill the transaxle.
15. Start the vehicle and check the fluid level again and top off, as necessary.
16. Road test the vehicle and verify proper transaxle operation and no fluid leaks.

Aurora

1. Before servicing the vehicle, refer to the precautions in the beginning of this section.
2. Remove or disconnect the following:
- Negative battery cable
- Shift linkage nut from the transaxle manual shaft
- Both linkage bracket bolts and cable/bracket and move it aside
- Park/Neutral (P/N) switch electrical connectors

3. Install an engine support fixture. Be sure the support fixture is tight and the weight of the powertrain is removed from the mounts.

4. Drain the cooling system.
5. Remove or disconnect the following:
- Vacuum line at the brake booster
- Transaxle vent hose
- Vehicle Speed Sensor (VSS) electrical connector
- Power steering gear electrical connector
- Upper transaxle oil cooler line from the radiator and cap it
- Lower transaxle oil cooler line from the transaxle and cap it
- Oil cooler bracket nut at the transaxle
- Coolant bypass pipe from the thermostat housing and move it aside
- Left and right transaxle mount bolts
- Left front wheel
- Left front splash shield
- Outer tie rod end from the steering knuckles using a ball joint separator tool and discard the cotter pins
- Lower ball joints from the steering knuckles using a ball joint separator tool and discard the cotter pins
- Halfshafts
- Engine oil pan-to-transaxle bracket
- Torque converter cover
- Torque converter from the flywheel. Matchmark the bolts before removal.
- Exhaust system
- Exhaust manifold rear pipe
- Steering rack-to-right transaxle mount bolts

- Right transaxle mount
- Power steering line clamp from the frame
- Remaining rack bolt; then, raise the rack and support it

6. Support the subframe assembly.
7. Remove or disconnect the following:
   - Knock Sensor (KS) shield
   - Engine-to-transaxle brace
   - Rear transaxle mount bracket
   - Right and left lower transaxle-to-engine bolts
   - Subframe assembly

8. Support the transaxle with a suitable jack.
9. Remove or disconnect the following:
   - Remaining transaxle-to-engine bolts
   - Transaxle

To install:

10. Install or connect the following:
    - Transaxle. Torque the transaxle-to-engine bolts to 55 ft. lbs. (75 Nm), the rear transaxle mount-to-chassis bolts to 37 ft. lbs. (50 Nm), rear transaxle mount bracket-to-transaxle bolts to 43 ft. lbs. (58 Nm), the engine-to-transaxle brace bolts to 35 ft. lbs. (47 Nm).
    - KS shield
    - VSS and KS electrical connectors
    - Torque converter to the flywheel aligning the matchmarks made before removal. Torque the bolts to 44 ft. lbs. (60 Nm).
    - Flywheel cover
    - Transaxle-to-oil pan brace
    - Subframe. Torque the bolts to 142 ft. lbs. (192 Nm).
    - Left transaxle mount-to-frame. Torque the bolt to 63 ft. lbs. (85 Nm).
    - Steering rack and the right-side through-bolt
    - Power steering line bracket to the subframe
    - Right transaxle mount to the frame. Torque the bolts to 54 ft. lbs. (73 Nm).
    - Right transaxle mount-to-transaxle Torque the bolts to 81 ft. lbs. (110 Nm).
    - Rear exhaust manifold pipe
    - Exhaust system
    - Halfshafts
    - Ball joints to the steering knuckles. Torque the castle nuts to 41 ft. lbs. (55 Nm).

➡**If necessary, tighten the nuts up to an additional 60 degree (⅙) turn to align the cotter pin holes. NEVER loosen the nuts to make the holes align.**

- Tie rod ends to the steering knuckles. Torque the castle nuts to 52 ft. lbs. (70 Nm).

➡**If necessary, tighten the nuts up to an additional 60 degree (⅙) turn to align the cotter pin holes. NEVER loosen the nuts to make the holes align.**

- Left side splash shield
- Front wheels. Torque the nuts to 100 ft. lbs. (140 Nm).

11. Remove the engine support fixture.
12. Install or connect the following:
    - Coolant bypass pipe to the thermostat housing
    - Transaxle oil cooler line bracket
    - Upper and lower transaxle oil cooler lines
    - Shift cable to the manual shaft and cable bracket. Torque the manual shaft nut to 15 ft. lbs. (20 Nm).
    - Vacuum line to the brake booster
    - Transaxle vent
    - Negative battery cable

13. Refill the cooling system.
14. Refill the transaxle with fluid.
15. Start the vehicle and check the fluid level again and top off as necessary.

➡**Service the vehicle with DEXRON®II or DEXRON®IIE automatic transmission fluid.**

16. Road test the vehicle and verify proper transaxle operation and no fluid leaks.

Halfshaft

REMOVAL & INSTALLATION

1. Before servicing the vehicle, refer to the precautions in the beginning of this section.
2. Remove or disconnect the following:
   - Front wheel
   - Sway bar link kit
   - Lower ball joint pry it from the steering knuckle and discard the cotter pin

➡**If removing the right halfshaft, turn the wheel to the left or if removing the left halfshaft, turn the wheel to the right.**

3. Insert a drift punch through the caliper and into the rotor cooling fins.
4. Remove or disconnect the following:
   - Halfshaft hub nut
   - Halfshaft from the hub using a puller

➡**Once the halfshaft is clear of the knuckle, swing the strut assembly rearward.**

- Halfshaft from the transaxle using a slide hammer and adapter
- Halfshaft

To install:

5. If installing the right side halfshaft, install a tear away axle seal protector over the seal.
6. Install or connect the following:
   - Halfshaft into the transaxle, seat it by inserting a prybar in the inboard joint groove and tapping the joint in place

➡**Be sure the joint is properly seated, by grasping the inboard joint and making sure it won't pull out of the transaxle. DO NOT pull on the shaft itself or the inboard joint can become damaged.**

- Halfshaft through the hub. Torque the nut to 107 ft. lbs. (145 Nm).
- Ball joint to the steering knuckle. Torque the castle nut to 41 ft. lbs. (55 Nm).

➡**If necessary to align the cotter pin holes, rotate the nut up to an additional 60 degree (⅙) turn. NEVER loosen the nut to align the holes.**

- New cotter pin
- Sway bar link kit. Torque the bolt to 13 ft. lbs. (17 Nm).

7. Remove the tear away seal protector. Be sure no pieces of the tool remain in the transaxle.
8. Install or connect the following:
   - Front wheel. Torque the nuts to 100 ft. lbs. (140 Nm).

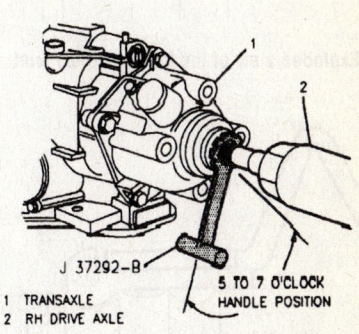

1 TRANSAXLE
2 RH DRIVE AXLE

5 TO 7 O'CLOCK HANDLE POSITION

J 37292-B

7922XG20

Installing the right side axle with the tear away seal protector

CV-Joint

REMOVAL & INSTALLATION

Inner (Tri-Pot) Joint

1. Before servicing the vehicle, refer to the precautions in the beginning of this section.

2. Remove or disconnect the following:

- Front wheel
- Halfshaft
- Swage ring using a hand grinder
- Large CV-joint boot clamp, cut and discard it
- CV-joint boot by sliding it away from the tri-pot joint
- Tri-pot housing from the tri-pot spider
- Trilobal tri-pot bushing from the housing
- Inboard spacer ring slide it rearward on the shaft using Snapring Pliers tool J-8059
- Outboard retaining ring using Snapring Pliers tool J-8059
- Tri-pot joint spider assembly
- Inboard spacer ring and CV-joint boot

3. Throughly clean and inspect all parts.

To install:

4. Install or connect the following:

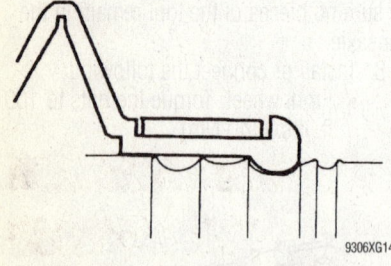

Exploded view of the inner (tri-pot) joint

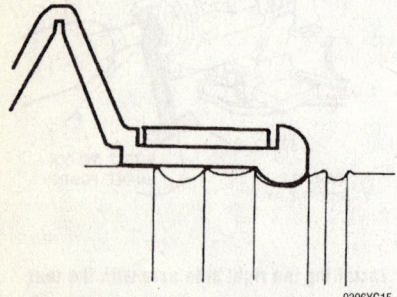

Positioning the inner CV-joint boot seal and swage ring—Inner (tri-pot) joint

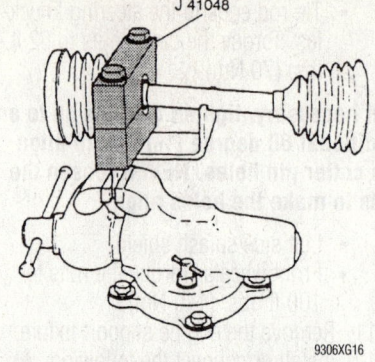

View of the swage ring crimping tool—Inner (tri-pot) joint

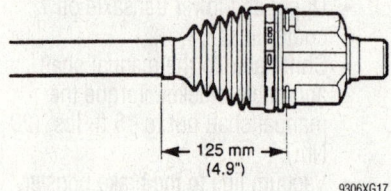

Boot measurement—Inner (tri-pot) joint

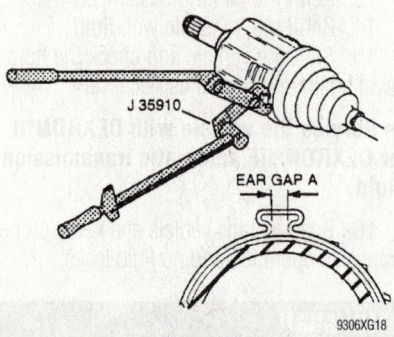

Crimping the large CV-joint boot ring—Inner (tri-pot) joint

- Swage ring clamp
- CV-joint boot

5. Position the CV-joint boot seal into the axle shaft's joint seal groove and align the swage ring clamp on the boot.

6. Secure the swage ring clamp as follows:

   a. Mount the lower half of tool J-41048 in a vise.

   b. Position the outboard of the halfshaft in the tool.

   c. Position the upper end of tool J-41048 onto the lower half.

❊❊ WARNING

Make sure that there are no pinch points on the inboard seal.

   d. Insert both bolts and tighten by hand until snug.

   e. Tighten each bolt 180 degree (½) turn at a time, alternating between the bolts, until both sides are bottomed.

   f. Remove the tool.

7. Install or connect the following:

- Inboard spacer ring slide it rearward on the shaft using Snapring Pliers tool J-8059
- Tri-pot joint spider assembly onto the shaft
- Outboard retaining ring into the axle shaft groove using Snapring Pliers tool J-8059
- Tri-pot joint spider assembly, slide it against the outboard retaining ring
- Inboard spacer ring, seat it in the groove
- ½ kit grease into the boot
- ½ kit grease into the tri-pot housing
- Trilobal tip-pot bushing flush with the tri-pot housing face
- New large seal clamp onto the CV-joint boot
- Tri-pot housing, slide it over the tri-pot joint spider assembly
- CV-joint boot/clamp, slide it into place, over the trilobal tri-pot bushing with the seal lip in the groove

➡ Make sure the boot lies flat against the trilobal bushing.

8. Position the CV-joint boot so it measures 4.9 in. (125mm).

9. Using the Crimp tool J-35910, a torque wrench and a breaker bar, crimp the large CV-joint boot clamp to 130 ft. lbs. (176 Nm).

10. Install or connect the following:

- Halfshaft
- Front wheel

Outer Joint

1. Before servicing the vehicle, refer to the precautions in the beginning of this section.

2. Remove or disconnect the following:

- Front wheel
- Halfshaft
- Swage ring using a hand grinder
- Large boot clamp, cut and discard it
- CV-joint boot, slide it away from the CV-joint
- CV-joint assembly by spreading the inner race-to-axle shaft retaining ring ears using Snapring Pliers tool J-8059
- CV-joint boot from the axle shaft and discard it

3. Disassemble the chrome alloy balls from the CV-joint cage as follows:

    a. Position a brass drift against the CV-joint cage and tap it with a hammer to tilt the cage.

    b. Remove the 1st chrome alloy ball from the cage.

    c. Tilt the cage in the opposite direction.

    d. Remove the opposite chrome alloy ball.

    e. Repeat the procedure until all 6 balls are removed.

4. Disassemble the CV-joint cage and inner race as follows:

    a. Pivot the cage and race 90 degrees to the center line of the outer race.

    b. Align the cage windows with outer race lands.

    c. Remove the cage from the outer race.

    d. Rotate the inner race upward and remove it from the cage.

5. Throughly clean and inspect all parts.

To install:

6. Lubricate the parts with a light coat of grease.

7. Assemble the CV-joint cage and inner race, as follows:

    a. Rotate the inner race 90 degrees to the cage centerline.

    b. Align the cage windows with inner race lands.

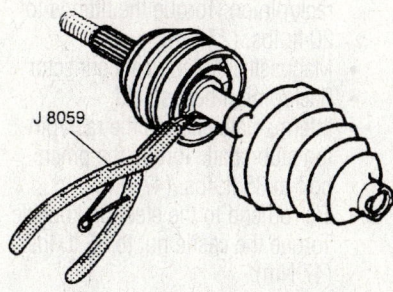

Disconnecting the outer CV-joint from the axle shaft

J 8059

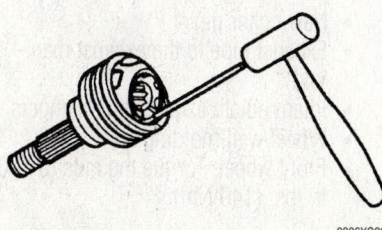

Tilting the cage—Outer CV-joint

9306XG20

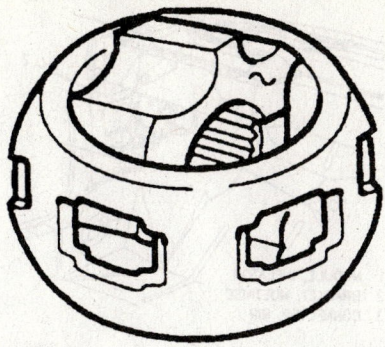

9306XG21

View the cage and inner race—Outer CV-joint

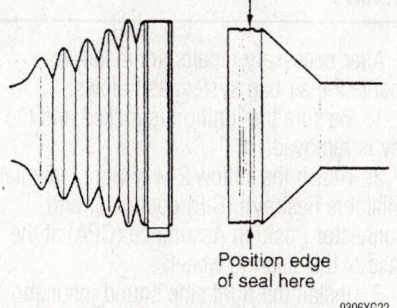

Position edge of seal here

9306XG22

Positioning the boot—Outer CV-joint

    c. Insert the inner race into the cage by rotating the inner race downward.

    d. Insert the cage/inner race into the outer race.

8. Assemble the chrome alloy balls into the CV-joint cage, as follows:

    a. Position a brass drift against the CV-joint cage and tap it with a hammer to tilt the cage.

    b. Insert the 1st chrome alloy ball into the cage.

    c. Tilt the cage in the opposite direction.

    d. Insert the opposite chrome alloy ball.

    e. Repeat the procedure until all 6 balls are inserted.

9. Install or connect the following:
- ½ kit grease into the CV-joint boot
- ½ kit grease into the CV-joint
- Swage ring clamp
- CV-joint boot
- CV-joint onto the axle shaft until the retaining ring seats into the groove

10. Position the CV-joint boot seal into the axle shaft's joint seal groove and align the swage ring clamp on the boot.

11. Secure the swage ring clamp as follows:

    a. Mount the lower half of tool J-41048 in a vise.

    b. Position the outboard of the half-shaft in the tool.

    c. Position the upper end of tool J-41048 onto the lower half.

✳✳ WARNING

Make sure that there are no pinch points on the inboard seal.

    d. Insert both bolts and tighten by hand until snug.

    e. Tighten each bolt 180 degree (½) turn at a time, alternating between the bolts, until both sides are bottomed.

    f. Remove the tool.

12. Install or connect the following:
- New large seal clamp onto the CV-joint boot
- CV-joint boot/clamp, slide it into place, over the outer race with the seal lip in the groove

➡ **Make sure the boot lies flat against the outer race.**

13. Using the Crimp tool J-35910, a torque wrench and a breaker bar, crimp the large CV-joint boot clamp to 130 ft. lbs. (176 Nm).

14. Install or connect the following:
- Halfshaft
- Front wheel

STEERING AND SUSPENSION

Air Bag

✳✳ CAUTION

The vehicles are equipped with the Supplemental Inflatable Restraint (SIR) or air bag system. The SIR system must be disabled before performing service on or around SIR system components, steering column, instrument panel components, wiring and sensors. Failure to follow safety and disabling procedures could result in accidental air bag deployment, possible personal injury and unnecessary SIR system repairs.

PRECAUTIONS

Several precautions must be observed when handling the inflator module to avoid accidental deployment and possible personal injury.

• Never carry the inflator module by the wires or connector on the underside of the module.

• When carrying a live inflator module, hold securely with both hands, and ensure that the bag and trim cover are pointed away.

• Place the inflator module on a bench or other surface with the bag and trim cover facing up.

• With the inflator module on the bench, never place anything on or close to the module which may be thrown in the event of an accidental deployment.

DISARMING

1. Turn the steering wheel so the vehicle wheels are pointing straight-ahead.

2. Turn the ignition key to the **LOCK** position and remove the key.

3. Remove the AIR BAG fuse from the fuse block.

4. Remove the left side sound insulator.

5. Detach the Connector Position Assurance (CPA) and yellow 2-way Supplemental Inflatable Restraint (SIR) connector at the multi-use bracket near the base of the steering column. The driver's side air bag is now disabled.

6. Remove the right side sound insulator.

7. Detach the Connector Position Assurance (CPA) and yellow 2-way SIR connector at the base of the steering wheel. The passenger's side air bag is now disabled.

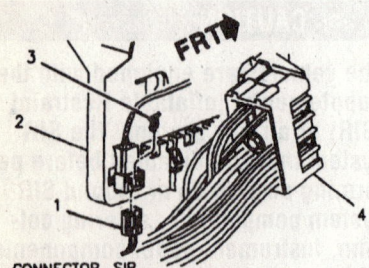

1 CONNECTOR, SIR
2 BRACKET, MULTIUSE MODULE
3 CONNECTOR POSITION ASSURANCE (CPA)
4 CONNECTOR, STEERING COLUMN
  WIRING HARNESS

7922XG21

SRS 2-way connector location—driver's side

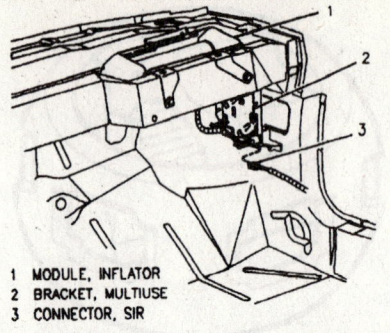

1 MODULE, INFLATOR
2 BRACKET, MULTIUSE
3 CONNECTOR, SIR

7922XG22

SRS 2-way connector location—passenger's side

ARMING

After necessary repairs are made, re-enable the air bag system as follows:

1. Be sure the ignition is locked and the key is removed.

2. Attach the yellow 2-way Supplemental Inflatable Restraint (SIR) connector and Connector Position Assurance (CPA) at the base of the steering wheel.

3. Install the right side sound insulator.

4. Attach the yellow 2-way SIR connector and Connector Position Assurance (CPA) at the multi-use bracket at the base of the column.

5. Install the left side sound insulator.

6. Install the AIR BAG fuse.

7. Turn the ignition switch to the **RUN** position and verify the AIR BAG light flashes 7 times, then shuts off.

Power Rack and Pinion Steering Gear

REMOVAL & INSTALLATION

1. Before servicing the vehicle, refer to the precautions in the beginning of this section.

2. Lock the steering wheel in the straight-ahead position.

3. Remove or disconnect the following:
• Front wheel
• Outer tie rod end ball stud nut and discard the cotter pin
• Inner tie rod jam nut, back it off ½ turn
• Outer tie rod end from the steering knuckle
• Exhaust pipe from the rear manifold
• Intermediate exhaust pipe hangers
• Wheel well fasteners and fold the inner panel back

• Intermediate shaft pinch bolt at the rack and pinion unit
• Intermediate shaft from the rack/pinion stub shaft
• Power steering unit heat shield
• Magnasteer® electrical connector
• Power steering lines from the rack/pinion and cap them
• Rack/pinion-to-chassis bolts

4. Support the rear of the subframe.

5. Remove or disconnect the following:
• Both rear subframe-to-chassis bolts

6. Lower the frame enough to remove the rack and pinion assembly.

7. Remove or disconnect the following:
• Rack/pinion assembly through the right side wheel well

To install:

8. Install or connect the following:
• Rack/pinion through the right side wheel well
• 3 rack/pinion-to-chassis bolts, do not tighten
• Subframe. Torque the bolts to 142 ft. lbs. (192 Nm).

9. Remove the subframe support.

10. Install or connect the following:
• Rack/pinion. Torque the bolts in sequence to 48 ft. lbs. (65 Nm).

➡ **Start with the vertically installed bolt closest to the pinion housing and work toward the passenger side of the vehicle.**

• Power steering hoses to the rack/pinion. Torque the fittings to 20 ft. lbs. (27 Nm).
• Magnasteer® electrical connector
• Rack/pinion heat shield
• Intermediate shaft to the rack/pinion stub shaft. Torque the pinch bolt to 35 ft. lbs. (47 Nm).
• Tie rod end to the steering knuckle. Torque the castle nut to 35 ft. lbs. (47 Nm).

➡ **If necessary to align the cotter pin holes, tighten the nut up to an additional 60 degree turn. NEVER loosen the castle nut to align the cotter pin holes.**

• New cotter pin
• Exhaust pipe to the exhaust manifold
• Intermediate exhaust pipe hangers
• Wheel well molding
• Front wheel. Torque the nuts to 100 ft. lbs. (140 Nm).

➡ **Whenever the vehicle sub-frame is removed or lowered, the front wheel alignment should be checked.**

11. Refill and bleed the power steering system. Check for leaks.

12. Check the front end alignment and adjust as necessary.

Strut

REMOVAL & INSTALLATION

Front

1. Before servicing the vehicle, refer to the precautions in the beginning of this section.

2. Remove or disconnect the following:
- Negative battery cable
- Front wheel
- Anti-lock Brake System (ABS) wheel speed sensor electrical connector
- ABS speed sensor bracket from the strut
- Brake line bracket, if removing the left strut

3. Matchmark the lower strut bracket to the steering knuckle.

4. Support the steering knuckle.

5. Remove or disconnect the following:
- Lower strut bracket nut and through-bolts

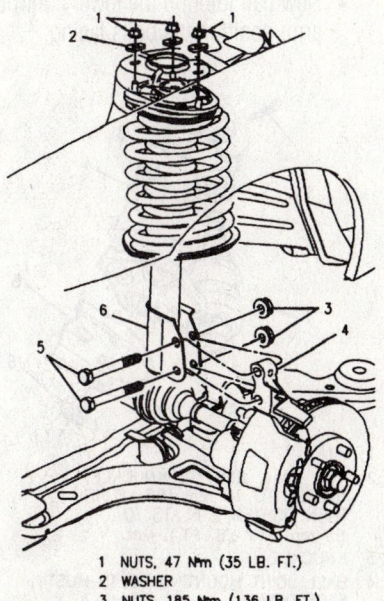

1 NUTS, 47 N•m (35 LB. FT.)
2 WASHER
3 NUTS, 185 N•m (136 LB. FT.)
4 KNUCKLE
5 BOLT
6 STRUT

7922XG23

Exploded view of the upper and lower strut mounting components

- 3 upper strut plate mounting nuts and washers
- Strut from the vehicle

6. Disassemble the strut as follows:

a. Place the strut in an approved fixture.

b. With the spring compressed, hold the strut shaft from turning using a socket and remove the 24mm strut shaft nut.

c. Relieve the pressure on the spring.

d. Separate the front coil spring from the strut.

To install:

7. If the spring and strut were disassembled, assemble using an approved fixture.

8. Install or connect the following:
- Strut, do not tighten the upper strut plate-to-body nuts
- Lower strut through-bolts by aligning the matchmarks. Torque the nuts to 136 ft. lbs. (185 Nm)

9. Remove the steering knuckle support.

10. Install or connect the following:
- Brake line to the strut, if removed
- Speed sensor bracket on the strut
- ABS sensor electrical connector
- Front wheel. Torque the nuts to 100 ft. lbs. (140 Nm).
- Upper strut plate nuts. Torque the nuts to 35 ft. lbs. (47 Nm).
- Negative battery cable

11. Check the front end alignment and adjust, as necessary.

Shock Absorber

REMOVAL & INSTALLATION

Rear

1. Before servicing the vehicle, refer to the precautions in the beginning of this section.

2. Support the lower control arm at such a height that the upper shock bolts will still be accessible.

3. Remove or disconnect the following:
- Rear wheel
- Electronic Level Control (ELC) air tube from the shock
- Both lower shock mount bolts
- Trunk trim panel to access the upper shock mount bolts

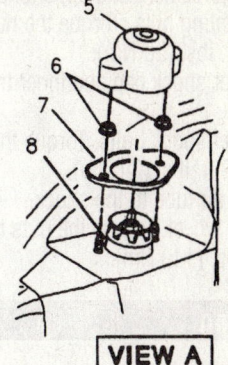

VIEW A

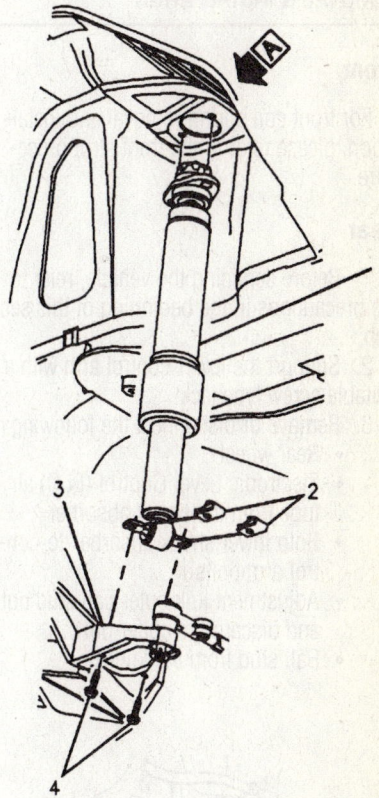

1 SHOCK
2 U-NUTS
3 CONTROL ARM
4 BOLTS 24 N•m (18 LB. FT.)
5 COVER
6 NUTS 20 N•m (15 LB. FT.)
7 REINFORCEMENT
8 MOUNT, UPPER

7922XG34

Exploded view of the rear shock mounting

- Upper shock cap
- Both upper shock mount nuts and reinforcement
- Shock

To install:

4. Install or connect the following:
- Shock

- Reinforcement and upper shock mounting nuts. Torque the nuts to 15 ft. lbs. (20 Nm).
- Upper shock cap and inner trunk trim
- Lower shock bolts. Torque the bolts to 18 ft. lbs. (24 Nm).
- ELC air tube to the shock
- Rear wheel. Torque the nuts to 100 ft. lbs. (140 Nm).

Coil Spring

REMOVAL & INSTALLATION

Front

For front coil spring removal and installation, please refer to the front strut procedure.

Rear

1. Before servicing the vehicle, refer to the precautions in the beginning of this section.
2. Support the lower control arm with a suitable screw type jack.
3. Remove or disconnect the following:
   - Rear wheel
   - Electronic Level Control (ELC) air tube from the shock absorber
   - Both lower shock absorber-to-control arm bolts
   - Adjustment link outer ball stud nut and discard the cotter pin
   - Ball stud from the knuckle

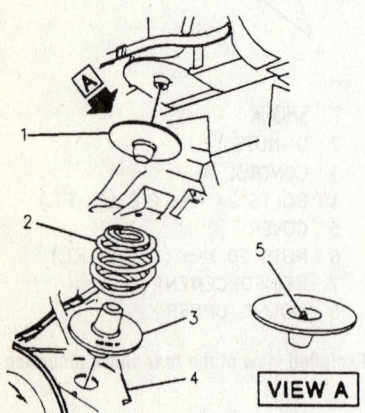

1 JOUNCE BUMPER
2 SPRING
3 LOWER SPRING INSULATOR
4 CONTROL ARM
5 RETAINER

7922XG35

Exploded view of the rear coil spring and related components

4. Lower the control arm until the arm bottoms out on the rear suspension support.
5. Using a suitable prying tool, pry under the lower spring insulator to unseat it from the control arm
6. Remove or disconnect the following:
   - Insulator and coil spring
   - Upper spring insulator, if necessary

To install:

7. Install or connect the following:
   - Upper spring insulator, if removed

➡**Engage the retainer on the back of the insulator in the upper mount hole.**

   - Coil spring and lower insulator

➡**Be sure to seat the lower insulator in the control arm hole.**

   - Lower shock absorber-to-control arm bolts. Torque both bolts to 18 ft. lbs. (24 Nm).
8. Remove the jack.
9. Install or connect the following:
   - Adjustment link ball stud to the knuckle. Torque the castle nut to 88 inch lbs. (10 Nm) plus an additional 180 degree (½) turn.

➡**If necessary to align the cotter pin holes, tighten the nut up to an additional 60 degree (⅙) turn. NEVER loosen the castle nut to align the cotter pin holes.**

   - New cotter pin
   - ELC air tube to the shock absorber
   - Rear wheel. Torque the nuts to 100 ft. lbs. (140 Nm).

Lower Ball Joint

REMOVAL & INSTALLATION

Ball joints must be replaced if any looseness is detected in the joint or if the ball joint seal is cut. To inspect the ball joints, raise the front of the vehicle allowing the suspension to hang free. Grasp the tire at the top and bottom and move the top of the tire in an in-and-out motion. Check for any horizontal movement of the knuckle relative to the control arm. If movement is in the wheel bearing, the bearing and hub must be replaced. If the ball joint stud is disconnected from the knuckle and looseness can be detected or if the ball stud can be twisted in its socket using finger pressure, replace the ball joint.

Ball joint tightness in the knuckle boss

should also be checked. This may be done by shaking the wheel and feeling for movement of the stud end or nut at the knuckle boss. Worn or damaged ball joints and knuckles must be replaced.

1. Before servicing the vehicle, refer to the precautions in the beginning of this section.
2. Remove or disconnect the following:
   - Front wheel
   - Sway bar link kit

➡**Take note of the positions of the washers and insulators for installation purposes.**

   - Lower ball joint from the steering knuckle using the Ball Joint Separator tool J-36226 and discard the cotter pin

✳✳ WARNING

Be careful not to overextend the half-shaft tri-pot joint.

   - Ball joint-to-lower control arm rivets by drilling off the heads using a ½ in. drill bit
   - Ball joint rivets from the lower control arm and drive them out using a punch.
   - Ball joint

To install:

3. Install or connect the following:
   - New ball joint on the lower control arm, position the bolts facing

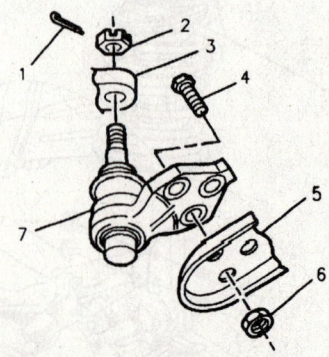

1 PIN
2 NUT, BALL JOINT TO KNUCKLE; TIGHTEN TO 10 N·m (88 LB. IN.) THEN TIGHTEN 2 FLATS TO 55 N·m (41 LB. FT.), MIN.
3 KNUCKLE
4 BALL JOINT MOUNTING BOLTS MUST FACE DOWN
5 CONTROL ARM
6 BALL JOINT MOUNTING NUTS 68 N·m (50 LB. FT.)
7 SERVICE BALL JOINT

7922XG24

Exploded view the lower ball joint and replacement mounting bolts and nuts

down. Torque the nuts/bolts to 50 ft. lbs. (68 Nm).

- Lower ball joint to the steering knuckle. Torque the castle nut to 41 ft. lbs. (55 Nm).

➡ **If necessary, tighten the castle nut up to an additional 60 degree (⅙ turn to align the cotter pin holes. NEVER loosen the nut to make the alignment.**

- New cotter pin
- Sway bar link kit. Torque the nut to 13 ft. lbs. (17 Nm).
- Front wheel. Torque the nuts to 100 ft. lbs. (140 Nm).

Lower Control Arm

REMOVAL & INSTALLATION

Front

1. Before servicing the vehicle, refer to the precautions in the beginning of this section.
2. Remove or disconnect the following:
   - Front wheel
   - Sway bar link kit

➡ **Take note of the positions of the washers and insulators for installation purposes.**

- Lower ball joint from the steering knuckle, using the Ball Joint Separator tool J-36226, discard the cotter pin

✳✳ WARNING

Be careful not to overextend the half-shaft tri-pot joint.

- Lower control arm-to-engine frame nuts/bolts
- Lower control arm

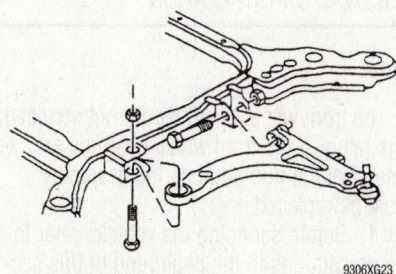

Exploded view of the lower control arm—Front suspension

9306XG23

To install:

3. Install or connect the following:
   - Lower control arm, do not tighten the nuts/bolts
   - Lower ball joint to the steering knuckle. Torque the castle nut to 41 ft. lbs. (55 Nm).

➡ **If necessary, tighten the castle nut up to an additional 60 degree (⅙ turn to align the cotter pin holes. NEVER loosen the nut to make the alignment.**

- New cotter pin
- Sway bar link kit. Torque the nut to 13 ft. lbs. (17 Nm).
- Front wheel. Torque the nuts to 100 ft. lbs. (140 Nm).

4. Inspect the trim height.
5. Torque the lower control arm-to-frame rear bolt to 117 ft. lbs. (158 Nm) and the lower control arm-to-frame front nut to 93 ft. lbs. (126 Nm).

Rear

1. Remove or disconnect the following:
   - Rear wheels
   - Exhaust system
   - Coil springs
   - Brake calipers from the control arms
   - Parking brake cable from the brake calipers
   - Praking brake cable from the rear suspension support assembly
   - Support assembly electrical connectors
   - Electronic Level Control (ELC) electrical connector and vent hose
   - Electronic Level Control (ELC) air tube from the air compressor
2. Support the rear suspension support assembly with a transmission jack

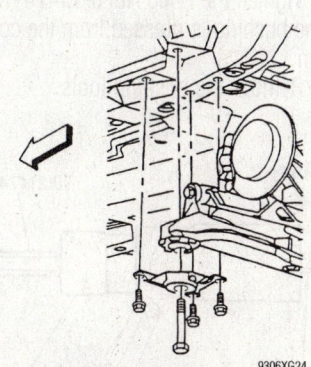

Exploded view of the support assembly—Rear suspension

9306XG24

3. Remove or disconnect the following:
   - 3 support bracket-to-chassis bolts at each side
   - Both front and both rear support assembly bolts
   - Support assembly
   - ELC height sensor link from the left control arm
   - Stabilizer link bolt and nut
   - Anti-lock Brake System (ABS) electrical connector
   - Rear wheel hub/bearing assembly, if necessary
   - Lower control arm-to-rear suspension support assembly nuts/bolts
   - Lower control arm

To install:

4. Install or connect the following:
   - Lower control arm
   - Lower control arm-to-rear suspension support assembly nuts/bolts, do not tighten
   - Rear wheel hub/bearing assembly, if necessary
   - Anti-lock Brake System (ABS) electrical connector
   - Stabilizer link nut/bolt. Torque the nut/bolt to 13 ft. lbs. (17 Nm).
   - ELC height sensor link to the left control arm
   - Support assembly
   - Both front and both rear support assembly bolts. Torque the front support assembly bolts to 141 ft. lbs. (191 Nm) and the rear support assembly bolts to 122 ft. lbs. (165 Nm).
   - 3 support bracket-to-chassis bolts at each side. Torque the bolts to 63 ft. lbs. (86 Nm).
   - ELC air tube from the air compressor
   - ELC electrical connector and vent hose
   - Support assembly electrical connectors
   - Praking brake cable to the rear suspension support assembly
   - Parking brake cable to the brake calipers
   - Brake calipers to the control arms
   - Coil springs
   - Exhaust system
   - Rear wheels. Torque the nuts to 100 ft. lbs. (140 Nm).

5. Inspect the trim height.
6. Torque the lower control arm nuts to 78 ft. lbs. (106 Nm).

Turn to Section 5 for brake system applications

CONTROL ARM BUSHING REPLACEMENT

Front

The rear (horizontal) control bushing is replaced with the control arm and cannot be replace separately.

1. Before servicing the vehicle, refer to the precautions in the beginning of this section.

2. Remove or disconnect the following:
- Front wheel
- Lower control arm

3. Assemble the bushing tools as follows:

a. Position the Bolt Assembly tool J-21474-27 with a washer, through the Bushing Receiver tool J-21474-5 with the larger diameter end over the bushing against the control arm.

b. Lubricate the bolt threads with high pressure lubricant.

c. Install the Bushing Remover tool J-41014-1 (large end facing the bushing), the thrust bearing and Nut J-21474-4 onto the Bolt Assembly J-21474-27.

4. Tighten the nut until the bushing is driven from the control arm.

5. Remove the tools.

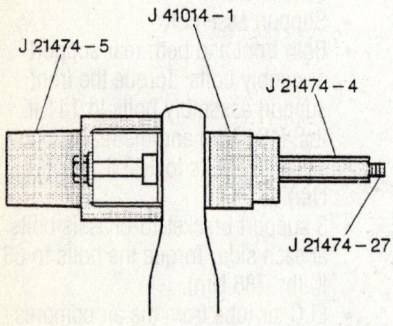

Removing the bushing from the lower control arm—Front suspension

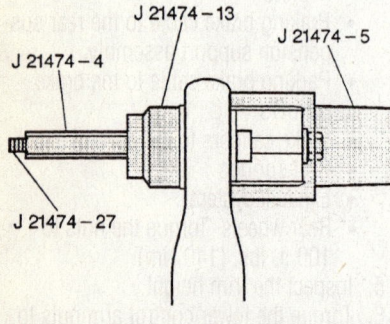

Installing the bushing to the lower control arm—Front suspension

To install:

6. Start the new busing into the control arm.

7. Assemble the bushing tools as follows:

a. Position the Bolt Assembly tool J-21474-27 with a washer, through the Bushing Receiver tool J-21474-5 with the larger diameter end over the bushing against the control arm.

b. Lubricate the bolt threads with high pressure lubricant.

c. Install the Bushing Installer tool J-21474-13 (large end facing the bushing), the thrust bearing and Nut J-21474-4 onto the Bolt Assembly J-21474-27.

8. Tighten the nut until the bushing is fully seated in the control arm.

9. Remove the tools.

10. Install or connect the following:
- Lower control arm
- Front wheel

Rear

1. Before servicing the vehicle, refer to the precautions in the beginning of this section.

2. Remove or disconnect the following:
- Rear wheel
- Lower control arm

3. Assemble the bushing tools as follows:

a. Assemble the Puller Bolt/Thrust Bearing tool J-21474-19 through the Bushing Receiver tool J-14014-2 over the bushing against the control arm.

b. Lubricate the bolt threads with high pressure lubricant.

c. Install the Bushing tool J-22222-2 (with the small end facing the bushing) and the Long Nut J-21474-18 onto the Puller Bolt/Thrust Bearing tool J-21474-19.

4. Tighten the Long Nut J-21474-18 until the bushing is pressed from the control arm.

5. Remove the bushing tools.

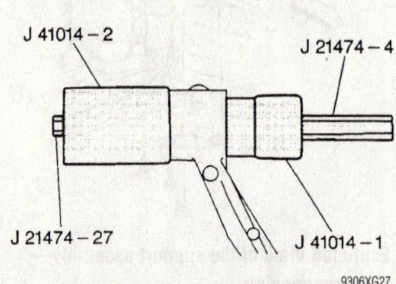
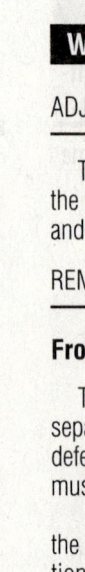

Removing the bushing from the lower control arm—Rear suspension

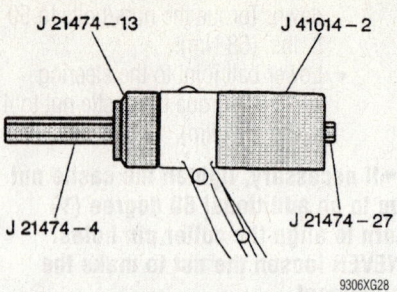

Installing the bushing to the lower control arm—Rear suspension

To install:

6. Start the bushing onto the control arm.

➡ **Position the bushing flat vertical and rearward.**

7. Assemble the bushing tools as follows:

a. Position the Puller Bolt/Thrust Bearing tool J-21474-19 through the Bushing Receiver tool J-14014-2 over the bushing against the control arm.

b. Lubricate the bolt threads with high pressure lubricant.

c. Install the Bushing Installer tool J-28685 (large end facing the bushing) and Long Nut J-21474-18 onto the Puller Bolt/Thrust Bearing tool J-21474-19.

8. Tighten the Puller Bolt/Thrust Bearing tool J-21474-19 until the bushing is fully seated in the control arm.

9. Remove the tools.

10. Install or connect the following:
- Lower control arm
- Front wheel

Wheel Bearings

ADJUSTMENT

The wheel bearings are not adjustable. If the wheel bearings are defective, the hub and bearing assembly must be replaced.

REMOVAL & INSTALLATION

Front

The front wheel bearings are not serviced separately. If the front wheel bearings are defective, the hub and bearing assembly must be replaced.

1. Before servicing the vehicle, refer to the precautions in the beginning of this section.

2. Remove or disconnect the following:
- Negative battery cable
- Front wheel

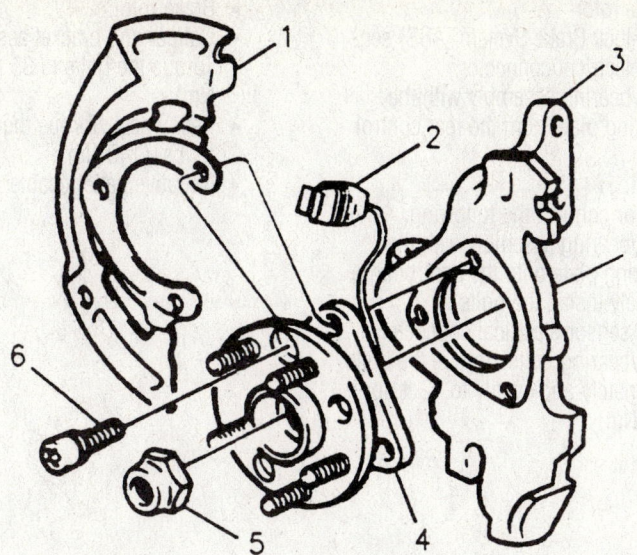

1   DUST SHIELD

2   WHEEL SPEED
    SENSOR CONNECTOR

3   STEERING KNUCKLE

4   HUB AND BEARING

5   NUT, DRIVE AXLE,
    145 N•m (107 LB. FT.)

6   RETAINING BOLT,
    95 N•m (75 LB. FT.)

7922XG36

Exploded view of the front hub mounting and related components

3. Lubricate the threads on the halfshaft with clean engine oil.

4. Install a drift punch through the caliper and into the brake rotor cooling fins. This keeps the hub from turning when removing the hub nut.

5. Remove or disconnect the following:

- Halfshaft hub nut
- Caliper from the steering knuckle and support it aside

❊❊ WARNING

DO NOT allow the brake hose to support the weight of the caliper.

- Brake rotor
- Anti-lock Brake System (ABS) sensor from the backing plate
- Hub/bearing assembly from the backing plate
- Hub/bearing assembly from the halfshaft using Axle Puller tool J-28733
- Hub/bearing assembly

To install:

6. Install or connect the following:

- Hub/bearing assembly slide it onto the halfshaft

- New halfshaft nut to draw the hub/bearing assembly into place
- Backing plate. Torque the 3 bolts alternately and evenly to 70 ft. lbs. (95 Nm).
- ABS sensor and attach the wiring harness connector
- Brake rotor
- Caliper on the steering knuckle. Torque the bolts to 38 ft. lbs. (51 Nm).

7. Insert a drift punch through the caliper and into the brake rotor cooling fins.

8. Install or connect the following:

- Halfshaft nut. Torque it to 107 ft. lbs. (145 Nm).
- Front wheel. Torque the nuts to 100 ft. lbs. (140 Nm).
- Negative battery cable

9. Lower the vehicle.

10. Pump the brakes to obtain a firm pedal before attempting to move the vehicle.

11. Check the front end alignment and adjust, as necessary.

Rear

The rear wheel bearings are not serviced separately. If the rear wheel bearings are

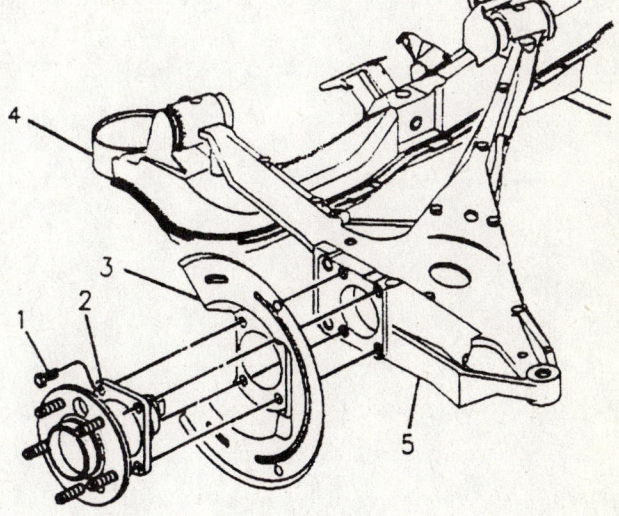

1   BOLT

2   HUB & BEARING

3   BRAKE SHIELD

4   REAR SUSPENSION SUPPORT
    ASSEMBLY

5   CONTROL ARM

7922XG37

Exploded view of the rear hub mounting and related components

defective, the hub/bearing assembly must be replaced.

1. Before servicing the vehicle, refer to the precautions in the beginning of this section.

2. Remove or disconnect the following:
   - Negative battery cable
   - Rear wheel
   - Caliper/bracket assembly from the brake rotor and support it aside

✳✳ WARNING

DO NOT allow the brake hose to support the weight of the caliper and bracket.

- Brake rotor
- Anti-lock Brake System (ABS) sensor electrical connector
- Hub/bearing assembly with the backing plate from the rear control arm

To install:

3. Install or connect the following:
   - Hub/bearing assembly with the backing plate onto the control arm, loosely install the bolts
   - ABS sensor electrical connector
   - Hub/bearing bolts. Torque the bolts alternately and evenly to 52 ft. lbs. (70 Nm)

- Brake rotor
- Caliper and bracket assembly. Torque the bolts to 35 ft. lbs. (48 Nm).
- Rear wheel. Torque the nuts to 100 ft. lbs. (140 Nm).
- Negative battery cable

GENERAL MOTORS CORPORATION—J-BODY

Chevrolet-Cavalier • **Pontiac**-Sunfire

PRECAUTIONS

Before servicing any vehicle, please be sure to read all of the following precautions, which deal with personal safety, prevention of component damage, and important points to take into consideration when servicing a motor vehicle:

• Never open, service or drain the radiator or cooling system when the engine is hot; serious burns can occur from the steam and hot coolant.

• Observe all applicable safety precautions when working around fuel. Whenever servicing the fuel system, always work in a well-ventilated area. Do not allow fuel spray or vapors to come in contact with a spark, open flame, or excessive heat (a hot drop light, for example). Keep a dry chemical fire extinguisher near the work area. Always keep fuel in a container specifically designed for fuel storage; also, always properly seal fuel containers to avoid the possibility of fire or explosion. Refer to the additional fuel system precautions later in this section.

• Fuel injection systems often remain pressurized, even after the engine has been turned **OFF**. The fuel system pressure must be relieved before disconnecting any fuel lines. Failure to do so may result in fire and/or personal injury.

• Brake fluid often contains polyglycol ethers and polyglycols. Avoid contact with the eyes and wash your hands thoroughly after handling brake fluid. If you do get brake fluid in your eyes, flush your eyes with clean, running water for 15 minutes. If eye irritation persists, or if you have taken brake fluid internally, IMMEDIATELY seek medical assistance.

• The EPA warns that prolonged contact with used engine oil may cause a number of skin disorders, including cancer! You should make every effort to minimize your exposure to used engine oil. Protective gloves should be worn when changing oil. Wash your hands and any other exposed skin areas as soon as possible after exposure to used engine oil. Soap and water, or waterless hand cleaner should be used.

• All new vehicles are now equipped with an air bag system, often referred to as a Supplemental Restraint System (SRS) or Supplemental Inflatable Restraint (SIR) system. The system must be disabled before performing service on or around system components, steering column, instrument panel components, wiring and sensors. Failure to follow safety and disabling procedures could result in accidental air bag deployment, possible personal injury and unnecessary system repairs.

• Always wear safety goggles when working with, or around, the air bag system. When carrying a non-deployed air bag, be sure the bag and trim cover are pointed away from your body. When placing a non-deployed air bag on a work surface, always face the bag and trim cover upward, away from the surface. This will reduce the motion of the module if it is accidentally deployed. Refer to the additional air bag system precautions later in this section.

• Clean, high quality brake fluid from a sealed container is essential to the safe and proper operation of the brake system. You should always buy the correct type of brake fluid for your vehicle. If the brake fluid becomes contaminated, completely flush the system with new fluid. Never reuse any brake fluid. Any brake fluid that is removed from the system should be discarded. Also, do not allow any brake fluid to come in contact with a painted surface; it will damage the paint.

• Never operate the engine without the proper amount and type of engine oil; doing so WILL result in severe engine damage.

• Timing belt maintenance is extremely important! Many models utilize an interference-type, non-freewheeling engine. If the timing belt breaks, the valves in the cylinder head may strike the pistons, causing potentially serious (also time-consuming and expensive) engine damage. Refer to the maintenance interval charts in the front of this manual for the recommended replacement interval for the timing belt, and to the timing belt section for belt replacement and inspection.

• Disconnecting the negative battery cable on some vehicles may interfere with the functions of the on-board computer system(s) and may require the computer to undergo a relearning process once the negative battery cable is reconnected.

• When servicing drum brakes, only disassemble and assemble one side at a time, leaving the remaining side intact for reference.

• Only an MVAC-trained, EPA-certified automotive technician should service the air conditioning system or its components.

ENGINE REPAIR

Alternator

REMOVAL

2.2L Engine

1997—99 MODELS

1. Before servicing the vehicle, refer to the precautions in the beginning of this section.

2. Remove or disconnect the following:
   • Negative battery cable
   • Alternator electrical connectors
   • Alternator drive belt
   • Alternator through bolts
   • Alternator

2000—01 MODELS

1. Before servicing the vehicle, refer to the precautions in the beginning of this section.

2. Remove or disconnect the following:
   • Negative battery cable
   • Serpentine drive belt
   • Alternator electrical connectors
   • Power steering line clip
   • Alternator rear brace
   • Alternator bolts
   • Alternator

2.4L Engine

1. Before servicing the vehicle, refer to the precautions in the beginning of this section.

2. Remove or disconnect the following:
   • Negative battery cable
   • Serpentine drive belt
   • Alternator electrical connectors
   • Alternator through bolts
   • Alternator

INSTALLATION

2.2L Engine

1997—99 MODELS

Install or connect the following:
   • Alternator. Torque the nuts to 32 ft. lbs. (43 Nm), the lower bolt to 37 ft. lbs. (50 Nm) and the upper/rear bolts to 22 ft. lbs. (30 Nm).
   • Alternator drive belt

- Alternator electrical connectors
- Negative battery cable

2000—01 MODELS

Install or connect the following:
- Alternator. Torque the nut to 37 ft. lbs. (50 Nm).
- Alternator rear brace
- Power steering line clip
- Alternator electrical connectors
- Serpentine drive belt
- Negative battery cable

2.4L Engine

Install or connect the following:
- Alternator. Torque the bolts to 37 ft. lbs. (50 Nm).
- Alternator electrical connectors
- Serpentine drive belt
- Negative battery cable

Ignition Timing

ADJUSTMENT

Ignition timing is controlled by the Powertrain Control Module (PCM). No adjustment is necessary or possible.

Engine Assembly

REMOVAL & INSTALLATION

2.2L Engine

1. Before servicing the vehicle, refer to the precautions in the beginning of this section.
2. Relieve the fuel system pressure.
3. Drain the cooling system.
4. Remove or disconnect the following:
- Both battery cables
- Throttle body air inlet duct
- Battery
- Air cleaner assembly
- Upper radiator hose
- Vacuum hose from the power brake booster
- Alternator upper brace
- Alternator electrical connectors
- Oxygen (O_2S) sensor
- Fuel injector electrical harness
- Idle Air Control (IAC)
- Throttle Position (TP) sensor
- Engine Coolant Temperature (ECT) sender
- Park/Neutral (P/N) switch

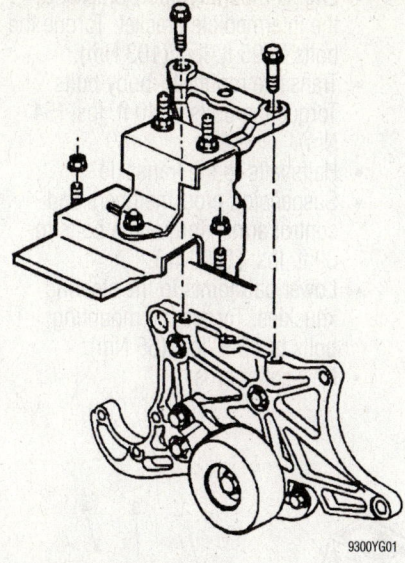

9300YG01

Exploded view of the upper engine mount—2.2L engine

- Torque Converter Clutch (TCC) solenoid
- Transaxle shift solenoid
- Transaxle ground
- Manifold Absolute Pressure (MAP) sensor
- Exhaust Gas Recirculation (EGR) valve
- Cooling fan

5. Discharge and recover the air conditioning refrigerant.
6. Remove or disconnect the following:

- Refrigerant lines from air conditioner compressor, if equipped
- Slave cylinder from the transaxle, if equipped with a manual transaxle
- Fuel lines and cap them
- Shift linkage from the transaxle bracket
- Control cables from the throttle body lever
- Cable bracket from the rocker arm cover and intake manifold
- Power steering lines and plug them

7. Install an engine support fixture.
8. Raise and safely support the vehicle.
9. Drain the crankcase.
10. Remove or disconnect the following:
- Front wheels
- Both inner fender splash shields
- Exhaust pipe
- Ignition assembly
- Starter
- Vehicle Speed Sensor (VSS)
- Transaxle ground wire

- Flywheel cover
- Lower radiator hose
- Heater hoses from the heater core pipes
- Transaxle cooler lines from the radiator and plug them
- Lower engine strut-to-suspension crossmember bolt
- Both front Anti-lock Brake System (ABS) wheel sensor connectors
- ABS harnesses from the suspension crossmember
- Lower ball joints from the steering knuckles and discard the cotter pins
- Suspension crossmembers
- Halfshafts from the transaxle and support them aside

11. Position a suitable table under the engine and transaxle assembly; then, lower the vehicle until the powertrain assembly is on the table.
- Transaxle-to-frame mount bolts
- Intermediate bracket from the right engine mount support bracket
- Engine support fixture

12. Raise the vehicle, leaving the powertrain assembly on the table.

❋❋ WARNING

When raising the vehicle, take it up slowly and verify that no lines are still connected to the powertrain assembly.

13. Remove or disconnect the following:
- Torque converter-to-flywheel bolts. Matchmark the bolts before removal.
- Transaxle-to-engine bolts
- Transaxle

To install:

14. Install or connect the following:
- Transaxle on the engine. Torque the bolts to 68 ft. lbs. (93 Nm).

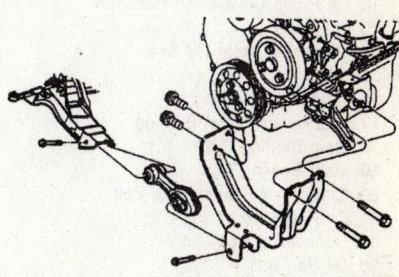

9300YG02

Exploded view of the lower engine mount and strut—2.2L engine

- Flywheel-to-converter bolts aligning the matchmarks made earlier. Torque the bolts to 46 ft. lbs. (62 Nm).
- Engine on the table; then, lower the vehicle over the engine
- Engine support fixture

15. Raise and safely support the vehicle and remove the engine table.
- Transaxle cooler lines to the radiator
- Heater hoses to the heater core outlet pipes
- Lower radiator hose

- Engine mount support bracket to the intermediate bracket. Torque the bolts to 96 ft. lbs. (103 Nm).
- Transaxle mount-to-body bolts. Torque the bolts to 40 ft. lbs. (54 Nm).
- Halfshafts to the transaxle
- Suspension crossmembers and control arms. Torque the bolts to 89 ft. lbs. (120 Nm).
- Lower ball joints to the steering knuckles. Torque the mounting bolts to 48 ft. lbs. (65 Nm).
- New cotter pins

- Front ABS wheel speed sensors electrical connectors
- Engine strut to the suspension support. Torque the bolt to 89 ft. lbs. (120 Nm).
- Transaxle cover
- Ignition assembly
- Starter
- VSS
- Transaxle ground wire
- Exhaust pipe. Torque the pipe-to-manifold bolts to 22 ft. lbs. (30 Nm).
- Both inner fender splash shields
- Front wheels. Torque the nuts to 100 ft. lbs. (140 Nm).

16. Lower the vehicle.
- Power steering lines to the pump
- Control cables to the throttle body lever and bracket
- Shift linkage to the transaxle and bracket
- Fuel lines
- Clutch slave cylinder, if equipped
- Air conditioning compressor-to-accumulator and condenser lines

17. Evacuate and charge the air conditioning system.
- O_2S sensor
- Fuel injector harness
- IAC
- TP sensor
- ECT sender
- P/N switch
- TCC solenoid
- Transaxle shift solenoid
- Transaxle ground
- MAP sensor
- EGR valve
- Cooling fan
- Alternator upper bracket
- Alternator electrical connectors
- Vacuum hose to the power brake booster
- Upper radiator hoses
- Air cleaner
- Battery
- Throttle body air inlet duct
- Negative battery cable

18. Refill the cooling system and crankcase.

19. Refill and bleed the power steering system.

20. Start the vehicle and verify no leaks.

21. Check and/or adjust the wheel alignment.

2.4L Engine

1. Before servicing the vehicle, refer to the precautions in the beginning of this section.

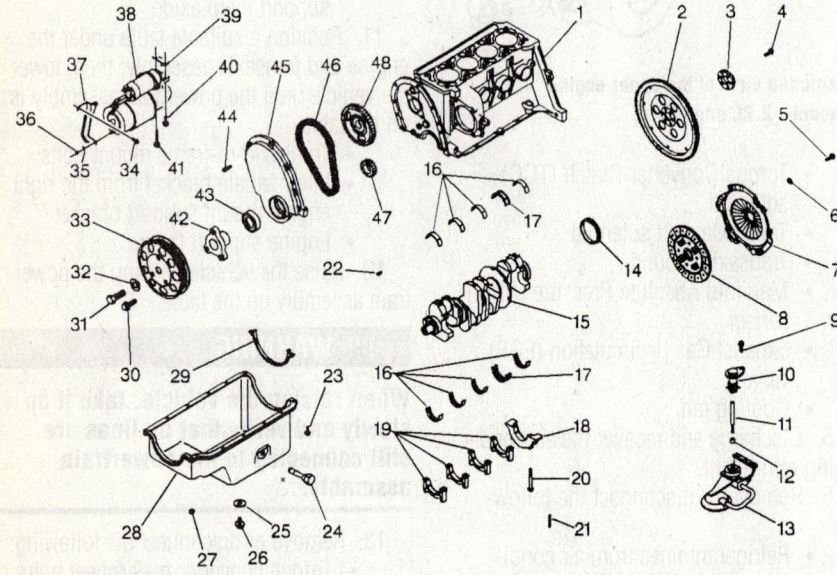

1 Cylinder Block
2 Flywheel
3 Flywheel Retainer
4 Flywheel Bolt
5 Clutch Pressure Plate Bolt
6 Clutch Pressure Plate Washer
7 Clutch Pressure Plate
8 Clutch Disc
9 Oil Pump Drive Bolt
10 Oil Pump Drive
11 Oil Pump Drive Shaft
12 Oil Pump Drive Shaft Retainer
13 Oil Pump
14 Crankshaft Rear Oil Seal
15 Crankshaft
16 Crankshaft Bearing
17 Crankshaft Thrust Bearing
18 Main Bearing Cap
19 Main Bearing Cap
20 Crankshaft Bearing Cap Bolt
21 Oil Pan Stud
22 Connecting Rod Nut
23 Oil Pan Bolt
24 Connecting Rod Nut

25 Oil Pan Drain Plug Gasket
26 Oil Pan Drain Plug
27 Oil Pan Nut
28 Oil Pan
29 Oil Pan Rear Seal
30 Crankshaft Pulley Bolt
31 Crankshaft Pulley Hub Bolt
32 Crankshaft Pulley Hub Bolt Washer
33 Crankshaft Pulley
34 Bracket Bolt
35 Starter Motor Bracket Nut
36 Starter Motor Bracket Nut
37 Starter Motor Bracket
38 Starter Motor
39 Starter Motor Shim
40 Starter Motor Bolt
41 Starter Motor Bolt
42 Crankshaft Pulley Hub
43 Crankshaft Front Oil Seal
44 Crankcase Front Cover Bolt
45 Crankcase Front Cover
46 Timing Chain
47 Crankshaft Sprocket
48 Camshaft Sprocket

9300YG06

Exploded view of the crankshaft and related components—2.2L engine

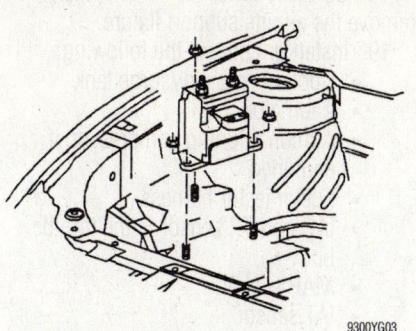

Exploded view of the upper engine mount—2.4L engine

2. Discharge and recover the air conditioning refrigerant.

3. Properly drain the cooling system into an approved container.

4. Relieve the fuel system pressure.

5. Remove or disconnect the following:
- Negative battery
- Left sound insulator
- Clutch pushrod from the pedal assembly
- Heater hose at the thermostat assembly
- Radiator inlet (upper) hose
- Air cleaner assembly and coolant fan
- Refrigerant hose assembly at the compressor and discard the O-rings, if equipped with air conditioning
- Both vacuum hoses from the front of the engine
- Alternator
- Air conditioning compressor, if equipped
- Fuel injector harness
- Idle Air Control (IAC) at the throttle body
- Throttle Position (TP) sensor at the throttle body
- Manifold Absolute Pressure (MAP) sensor
- Intake Air Temperature (IAT) sensor
- Evaporative Emissions (EVAP) canister purge solenoid
- Starter solenoid
- Ground connections
- Negative battery cable from the transaxle
- Electronic ignition coil and module assembly
- Engine Coolant Temperature (ECT) sensor(s)
- Oil pressure sensor/switch
- Oxygen (O2S) sensor

- Crankshaft Position (CKP) sensor
- Back-up lamp switch, move the harness aside
- Power brake vacuum hose from the throttle body
- Power brake vacuum tube-to-check valve hose from the tube
- Throttle cable and bracket
- Power steering pump rear bracket/vacuum tube assembly
- Power steering pump and move it aside with the lines attached
- Fuel lines
- Shift cables
- Clutch actuator line
- Exhaust manifold and heat shield
- Radiator outlet (lower) hose from the radiator

6. Install an engine support fixture.

7. Remove or disconnect the following:
- Coolant recovery/surge tank, move it aside with the hoses attached
- Engine mount assembly
- Front wheels
- Right splash shield

8. Drain the crankcase.

9. Remove or disconnect the following:
- Radiator air deflector
- Vehicle Speed Sensor (VSS)
- Knock Sensor (KS)
- Starter solenoid
- Both front Anti-lock Brake System (ABS) wheel speed sensors, if equipped
- Engine mount strut and transaxle mount
- Ball joints from the steering knuckles

- Suspension supports, crossmember and stabilizer shaft as an assembly
- Heater outlet hose from the radiator outlet pipe
- Halfshaft from the transaxle and intermediate shaft and move them aside
- Air conditioning lines from the oil pan, if equipped with air conditioning
- Flywheel housing cover

10. Position a suitable support below the engine, then carefully lower the vehicle onto the support.

11. Matchmark the threads on the support fixture hooks, so the setting can be duplicated when reinstalling the engine.

12. Remove the engine support fixture J-hooks.

13. Raise the vehicle slowly off the engine/transaxle assembly.

➡**It may be necessary to move the engine/transaxle assembly rearward to clear the intake manifold.**

14. Remove the engine from the transaxle.

To install:

❄❄ WARNING

Be sure the retaining bolts are in their correct locations. If not, engine damage may occur.

15. Install or connect the following:
- Engine to the transaxle
- Engine/transaxle assembly under

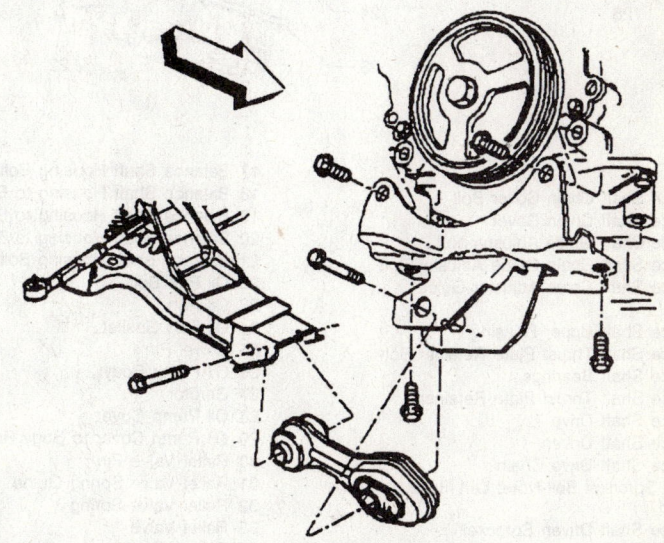

Exploded view of the lower engine mount and strut—2.4L engine

Timing belt service is covered in Section 4 of this manual

the vehicle, then lower the vehicle over the assembly
- Engine support fixture, making sure to adjust it to the previous setting
- Engine mount assembly and transaxle mount

16. Carefully raise the vehicle off the support.

17. Install or connect the following:
- Halfshafts to the transaxle
- Heater outlet hose to the radiator outlet pipe
- Suspension supports, crossmember and stabilizer shaft assembly
- Ball joints to the steering knuckles
- Engine strut mount
- Air conditioning line to the oil pan, if equipped
- VSS
- KS
- Starter solenoid
- Both front ABS wheel speed sensors, if equipped
- Flywheel housing cover
- Radiator air deflector
- Lower radiator hose
- Right splash shield
- Front wheels

18. Carefully lower the vehicle, then remove the engine support fixture.

19. Install or connect the following:
- Coolant recovery/surge tank
- Alternator
- Air conditioning compressor, if equipped
- Fuel injector harness
- IAC and TP sensor at the throttle body
- MAP sensor
- IAT sensor
- EVAP canister purge solenoid
- Starter solenoid
- Ground connections
- Negative battery cable to the transaxle
- Electronic ignition coil and module assembly
- ECT sensor(s)
- Oil pressure sensor/switch
- O$_2$S
- CKP sensor
- Back-up lamp switch
- Vacuum hoses
- Refrigerant hose assembly to the compressor, if equipped with air conditioning
- Clutch actuator line
- Exhaust manifold and heat shield
- Fuel lines
- Power steering pump, rear bracket and tension belt
- Vacuum hoses to the intake manifold and the brake booster
- Throttle cable and bracket
- Coolant fan and air cleaner assembly
- Upper radiator outlet hose. Refill the cooling system.
- Clutch pushrod to the pedal assembly
- Left sound insulator
- Heater hose at the thermostat housing
- Negative battery cable

20. Refill the transaxle and the crankcase.

21. Evacuate and recharge the air conditioning system, if equipped.

22. Start the engine and check for leaks.

Water Pump

REMOVAL & INSTALLATION

2.2L Engine

✳✳ WARNING

When adding coolant, it is important to use GM Goodwrench DEX-COOL®

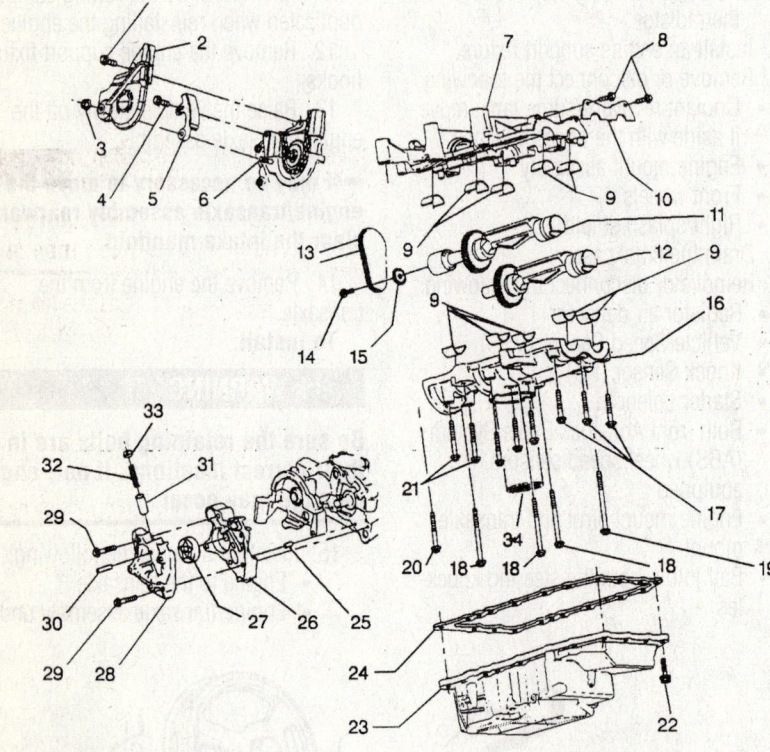

1. Balance Shaft Chain Cover Bolt
2. Balance Shaft Chain Cover
3. Balance Shaft Guide Adjuster Nut
4. Balance Shaft Chain Guide Adjuster Bolt
5. Balance Shaft Chain Adjuster Guide
6. Stud
7. Balance Shaft Upper Housing
8. Balance Shaft Thrust Plate Retainer Bolt
9. Balance Shaft Bearings
10. Balance Shaft Thrust Plate Retainer
11. Balance Shaft Drive
12. Balance Shaft Driven
13. Balance Shaft Drive Chain
14. Driven Sprocket Bolt-Note: Left Hand Thread
15. Balance Shaft Driven Sprocket
16. Balance Shaft Lower Housing
17. Balance Shaft Housing Bolt
18. Balance Shaft Housing to Block Bolt
19. Balance Shaft Housing to Block Bolt
20. Balance Shaft Housing to Block Bolt
21. Balance Shaft Housing Bolt
22. Oil Pan Bolt
23. Oil Pan
24. Oil Pan Gasket
25. Dowel Pin
26. Oil Pump Body
27. Gerotor
28. Oil Pump Cover
29. Oil Pump Cover to Body Bolt
30. Relief Valve Pin
31. Relief Valve Spring Guide
32. Relief Valve Spring
33. Relief Valve
34. Pickup Screen

Exploded view of the balance shafts and related components—2.4L engine

9300YG09

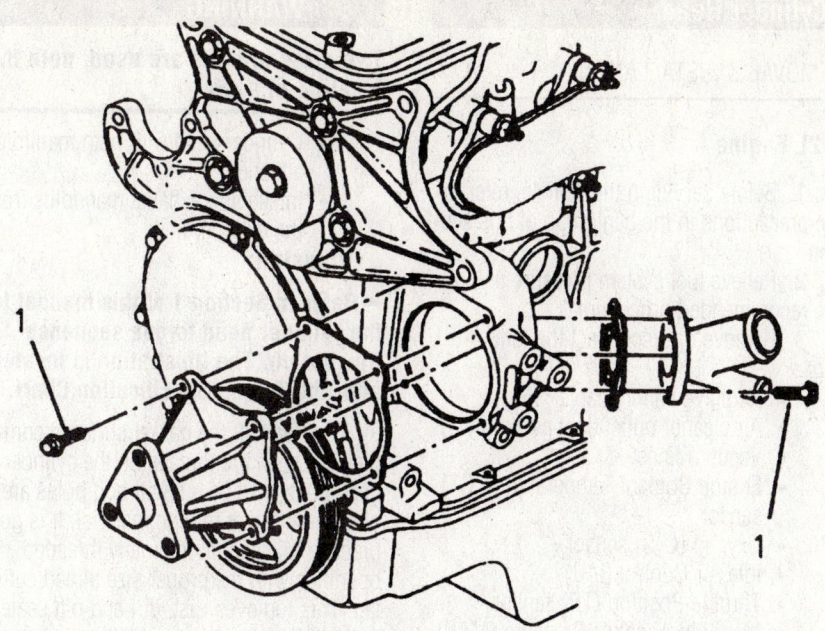

1 BOLT – 25 N·m (18 LBS. FT.)

7922YG01

Exploded view of the water pump mounting—2.2L engine

coolant meeting GM Specification 6277M.

1. Before servicing the vehicle, refer to the precautions in the beginning of this section.
2. Drain the cooling system.
3. Remove or disconnect the following:
   - Negative battery cable
   - Water pump pulley bolts, loosen them
   - Serpentine belt
   - Alternator
   - Water pump pulley
   - Water pump

To install:

4. Clean all the gasket surfaces completely.
5. Apply a thin bead of sealer around the outer edge of the water pump gasket seating area and place the gasket on the pump.
6. Install or connect the following:
   - Water pump. Torque the bolts to 18 ft. lbs. (25 Nm).
   - Water pump pulley and tighten the bolts finger-tight
   - Alternator in the mounting bracket
   - Serpentine belt
   - Water pump pulley. Torque the bolts to 22 ft. lbs. (30 Nm).
   - Negative battery cable
7. Refill and bleed the cooling system.

2.4L Engine

1. Before servicing the vehicle, refer to the precautions in the beginning of this section.
2. Remove or disconnect the following:
   - Negative battery cable
   - Oxygen (O_2S) sensor electrical connector
3. Drain the cooling system.
4. Remove or disconnect the following:
   - Heater hose from the thermostat housing
   - Upper exhaust manifold heat shield
   - Exhaust manifold brace-to-manifold bolt
   - Lower exhaust manifold heat shield

- Manifold-to-exhaust pipe spring loaded bolts, break the loose using a 13mm box wrench

✳✳ WARNING

It is necessary to relieve the spring pressure from 1 bolt prior to removing the 2nd bolt. If the spring pressure is not relieved, the exhaust pipe will twist and bind the bolt during removal.

- Both radiator outlet pipe-to-water pump cover bolts

5. Remove the manifold to exhaust pipe bolts from the exhaust pipe flange as follows:
   a. Unscrew either bolt clockwise 4 turns.
   b. Remove the other bolt.
   c. Remove the first bolt.

✳✳ WARNING

DO NOT rotate the flex coupling more than 4 degrees or damage may occur.

6. Remove or disconnect the following:
   - Exhaust pipe from the exhaust manifold by pulling it downward
   - Radiator outlet pipe from the oil pan and transaxle
   - Exhaust manifold brace, if equipped with a manual transaxle
   - Outlet pipe by pulling it downward from the water pump leaving the lower radiator hose attached

➡ **Allow the radiator outlet pipe hang.**

   - Exhaust manifold from the cylinder head, discard the seals and gaskets
   - Timing chain cover and tensioner
   - Water pump and timing chain housing as an assembly, then separate them

1 TIMING CHAIN HOUSING
2 GASKET, TIMING CHAIN HOUSING TO WATER PUMP COVER
3 NUT (3)
4 WATER PUMP BODY ASM.
5 GASKET, WATER PUMP BODY TO WATER PUMP COVER
6 WATER PUMP COVER
7 BOLT (M6 X 1 X 65) – 3 LOWER POSITIONS
8 BOLT (M6 X 1 X 25)
9 BOLT (M6 X 1 X 90)
10 GASKET, WATER PUMP COVER TO BLOCK
11 BOLTS, WATER PUMP COVER TO BLOCK (2)

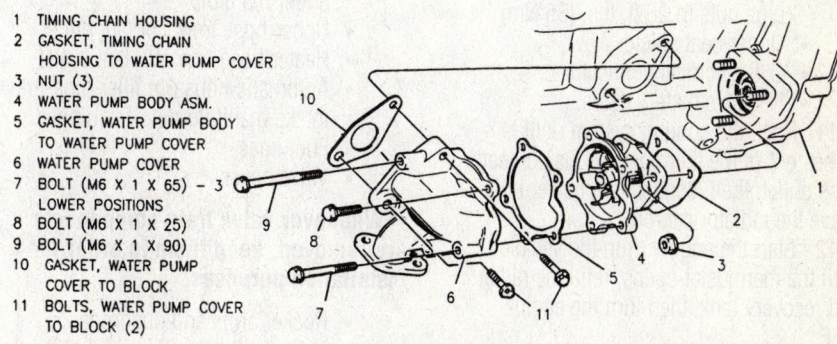

7922YG02

Exploded view of the water pump mounting and related components—2.4L engine

To install:

7. Thoroughly clean and dry all mounting surfaces.

8. Install or connect the following:
- New gasket
- Water pump to the cover and tighten the bolts finger-tight

➡ **Lubricate the splines with clean grease**

- Water pump using new gaskets and tighten the bolts and nuts finger-tight
- Radiator outlet pipe O-ring, lubricated with antifreeze
- Radiator outlet pipe onto the water pump cover and tighten the bolts finger-tight

9. With all gaps closed, torque the bolts, in the following sequence, to the proper values:
- Pump assembly-to-chain housing nuts: 19 ft. lbs. (26 Nm).
- Pump cover-to-pump assembly: 106 inch lbs. (12 Nm).
- Cover-to-block, bottom bolt first: 19 ft. lbs. (26 Nm).
- Radiator outlet pipe assembly-to-pump cover: 125 inch lbs. (14 Nm).

10. Install or connect the following:
- New gaskets
- Exhaust manifold
- Exhaust pipe to the manifold. Tighten the exhaust pipe flange bolts evenly and gradually to avoid binding, until fully seated.
- Radiator outlet pipe to the transaxle and oil pan
- Exhaust manifold brace, if removed
- Timing chain tensioner and front cover
- Lower heat shield
- Exhaust manifold brace to the manifold
- Torque the manifold-to-exhaust pipe nuts to 26 ft. lbs. (35 Nm)
- Upper heat shield
- O₂S electrical connector
- Negative battery cable

11. Refill the cooling system until it comes out of the thermostat housing heater hose outlet; then, connect the heater hose. Leave the radiator cap off.

12. Start the engine. Run the vehicle until the thermostat opens, refill the radiator and recovery tank, then turn the engine **OFF**.

13. Once the vehicle has cooled, recheck the coolant level.

Cylinder Head

REMOVAL & INSTALLATION

2.2L Engine

1. Before servicing the vehicle, refer to the precautions in the beginning of this section.

2. Relieve fuel system pressure using the recommended procedure.

3. Remove or disconnect the following:
- Negative battery cable
- Air cleaner outlet duct assembly
- Vacuum lines
- Engine Coolant Temperature (ECT) sensor
- Oxygen (O₂S) sensor
- Idle Air Control (IAC)
- Throttle Position (TP) sensor
- Manifold Absolute Pressure (MAP) sensor
- Evaporative Emission (EVAP) canister purge solenoid
- Fuel injector harness
- Accelerator control, cruise and Throttle Valve (TV) cables from accelerator control bracket
- Accelerator control cable bracket
- Exhaust pipe from exhaust manifold

4. Drain cooling system.

5. Remove or disconnect the following:
- Serpentine drive belt
- Alternator
- Power steering pump and move it aside with lines attached
- Power steering pump bracket

6. Install an engine support fixture.

7. Remove or disconnect the following:
- Serpentine drive belt tensioner bracket
- Spark plug wires
- EVAP canister purge line from under manifold
- Upper hose from coolant outlet
- Heater hose from coolant outlet
- Automatic transaxle filler tube-to-intake manifold nut, if equipped
- Fuel lines
- Valve cover

➡ **Whenever valve train components are removed, keep them in order for installation purposes.**

- Rocker arms and pushrods
- Cylinder head bolts and discard them

✳✳ WARNING

Two sizes of bolts are used; note the location of each.

- Cylinder head with both manifolds attached
- Intake and exhaust manifolds from the cylinder head

To install:

➡ **Refer to Section 1 of this manual for the cylinder head torque sequence illustration. The illustration is located after the Torque Specification Chart.**

8. Clean all the gasket surfaces completely. Clean the threads on the cylinder head bolts, and be sure all bolt holes are clean and free of foreign material. It is good practice to clean all internally threaded openings with the proper size thread cutting tap. This removes rust, dirt and old sealer build-up that can prevent getting a proper torque reading when tightening bolts.

9. Inspect cylinder head and block surface for cracks, nicks, heavy scratches and flatness.

10. Install or connect the following:
- Exhaust and intake manifolds on cylinder head using new gaskets
- New cylinder head gasket
- Cylinder head using new cylinder head bolts. Torque the long bolts, in sequence, bolts to 46 ft. lbs. (63 Nm) plus an additional 90 degree turn and the short bolts to 43 ft. lbs. (58 Nm) plus an additional 90 degree turn.
- Pushrods and rocker arms. Torque nuts to 22 ft. lbs. (30 Nm).
- Valve cover. Torque the bolts to 89 inch lbs. (10 Nm).
- Fuel lines
- Transaxle filler tube. Torque the nut to 20 ft. lbs. (27 Nm).
- Heater hose to the coolant outlet
- Upper radiator hose
- EVAP canister purge line
- Spark plugs wires
- Serpentine drive belt tensioner bracket. Tighten the bolts to 37 ft. lbs. (27 Nm).

11. Remove engine support fixture.

12. Install or connect the following:
- Power steering pump and bracket
- Alternator and brace
- Serpentine drive belt
- Exhaust pipe to the exhaust manifold
- Accelerator control cable bracket

Torque the bolts to 18 inch lbs. (25 Nm).
- Accelerator control, cruise and TV cables to control bracket
- Electrical connections to the sensors
- Vacuum lines
- Air cleaner outlet duct assembly
- Negative battery cable

13. Refill the coolant system.
14. Start vehicle and inspect for leaks.
15. Bleed air from coolant system as follows:

   a. Loosen the engine coolant air bleed screw, (located on the top side of the engine coolant outlet) and add coolant until all of the air is evacuated through the air bleed.

   b. Tighten the air bleed screw.

2.4L Engine

1. Before servicing the vehicle, refer to the precautions in the beginning of this section.
2. Relieve the fuel system pressure.
3. Drain the cooling system.
4. Remove or disconnect the following:
   - Negative battery cable
   - Heater inlet and throttle body heater hoses from water outlet
   - Exhaust manifold

- Intake camshaft housing and lifters
- Exhaust camshaft housing and lifters
- Oil fill tube
- Throttle body-to-air cleaner duct
- Power brake vacuum hose from throttle body
- Throttle cable bracket
- Throttle body from intake manifold, move it aside with electrical harness and throttle cable attached
- Manifold Absolute Pressure (MAP) sensor vacuum hose from intake manifold
- Intake manifold brace
- MAP sensor electrical connector
- Intake Air Temperature (IAT) sensor electrical connector
- Evaporative Emission (EVAP) canister purge solenoid
- Upper radiator hose from water outlet
- Engine Coolant Temperature (ECT) sensors electrical connectors
- Cylinder head and discard the gasket

To install:

➡ **Refer to Section 1 of this manual for the cylinder head torque sequence illustration. The illustration is located after the Torque Specification Chart.**

5. This is an aluminum cylinder head and must be treated with care. Do not use abrasive pads to clean the cylinder head or block surfaces. An abrasive pad may damage the cylinder head and block. GM says that abrasive pads should not be used for the following reasons:

   a. Abrasive pads will produce a fine grit that the oil filter will not be able to remove from the oil. This grit is abrasive and has been known to cause internal engine damage.

   b. Abrasive pads can easily remove enough metal to round cylinder head edges. This has been known to affect the gasket's ability to seal, especially in the narrow areas between the combustion chambers and coolant jackets. The cylinder head gasket is likely to leak if these edges are rounded.

   c. Abrasive pads can also remove enough metal to affect cylinder head flatness. It takes only about 15 seconds to remove 0.008 in. (0.20mm) of metal from the cylinder head with an abrasive pad. If the cylinder head flatness is out of specification, the gasket will not be able to seal and the gasket will leak.

6. Use a razor blade gasket scraper to clean the cylinder head and cylinder block gasket surfaces. Be careful not to gouge or scratch the gasket surfaces. Do not gouge or scrape the combustion chamber surfaces. Use a new razor blade for each cylinder head. Hold the scraper so the razor blade is as parallel to the gasket surface as possible. Do not use any other method or technique to clean these gasket surfaces. In addition, GM warns not to use a tap to clean cylinder head bolt holes.

7. When working on an aluminum head, do not remove spark plugs from an aluminum cylinder head until the cylinder head has cooled. Always clean all dirt and debris from the spark plug recess area. If the spark plug opening threads are damaged and NOT restorable with a Thread Chaser, replace the cylinder head. GM **DOES NOT** approve of the installation of thread inserts into the spark plug openings on this engine. If threads are installed into the spark plug openings, severe engine damage will occur.

8. Clean all gasket surfaces completely. Clean the threads on cylinder head bolts and be sure all bolt holes are clean and free of debris.

9. Inspect the cylinder head and block surface for cracks, nicks, heavy scratches and flatness.

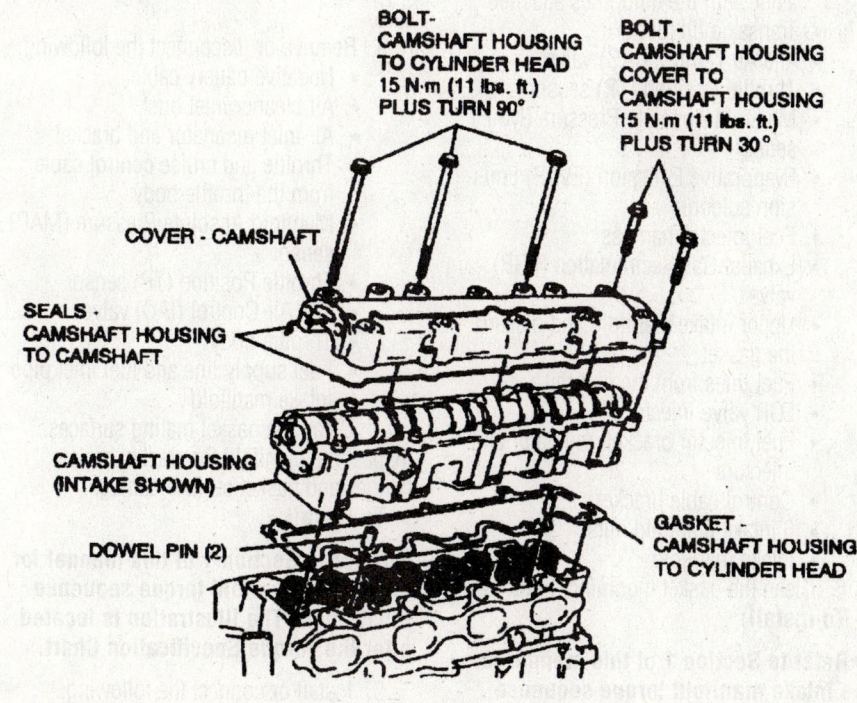

BOLT-
CAMSHAFT HOUSING
TO CYLINDER HEAD
15 N·m (11 lbs. ft.)
PLUS TURN 90°

BOLT -
CAMSHAFT HOUSING
COVER TO
CAMSHAFT HOUSING
15 N·m (11 lbs. ft.)
PLUS TURN 30°

COVER - CAMSHAFT

SEALS -
CAMSHAFT HOUSING
TO CAMSHAFT

CAMSHAFT HOUSING
(INTAKE SHOWN)

DOWEL PIN (2)

GASKET -
CAMSHAFT HOUSING
TO CYLINDER HEAD

7922YG05

Exploded view of the camshaft housing cover mounting—2.4L engine

Refer to Section 1 for engine rebuilding specifications

10. Install or connect the following:
- New cylinder head gasket
- Cylinder head. Torque the new bolts 1-8 to 40 ft. lbs. (65 Nm) and bolts 9-10 to 30 ft. lbs. (40 Nm); then, turn all bolts an additional 90 degrees (¼ turn) in sequence.
- ECT sensor connections
- Upper radiator hose to coolant outlet
- Manifold brace. Torque to 19 ft. lbs. (26 Nm).
- All sensor connections
- MAP sensor vacuum hose to intake manifold
- Throttle body onto the intake manifold using a new gasket
- Accelerator control cable bracket to the throttle body. Torque the bolts to 106 inch lbs. (12 Nm) and the nut to 19 ft. lbs. (26 Nm).
- Throttle body-to-air cleaner duct
- Oil filler tube. Torque the bolt to 71 inch lbs. (8 Nm).
- Lifters and camshaft housing
- Exhaust manifold. Torque the exhaust nuts to 26 ft. lbs. (35 Nm).
- Negative battery cable

11. Refill and bleed the cooling system. An oil and filter change is recommended.

12. Check and verify that vehicle has no coolant or vacuum leaks.

Rocker Arms

REMOVAL & INSTALLATION

➡**Place the components in a rack in order to be sure they are installed at the same location and with the same mating surface as when removed.**

1. Before servicing the vehicle, refer to the precautions in the beginning of this section.

2. Remove or disconnect the following:
- Negative battery cable
- Rocker (valve) arm cover(s)
- Rocker arm nuts
- Rocker arm pivot ball(s)
- Rocker arm(s)
- Pushrods

To install:

3. Install the pushrods.

➡**Be sure to install the pushrods in the correct positions and be sure they seat properly in the lifters.**

4. Coat the bearing surfaces of the rocker arms and pivot balls with camshaft and lifter prelube.
Install the rocker arm(s).

5. Install or connect the following:
- Rocker arms. Torque the nuts to 22 ft. lbs. (30 Nm).
- Rocker arm covers
- Negative battery cable

Intake Manifold

REMOVAL & INSTALLATION

2.2L Engine

1997 MODELS

These vehicles use a 2-piece intake manifold.

1. Before servicing the vehicle, refer to the precautions in the beginning of this section.

2. Properly relieve the fuel system pressure.

3. Remove or disconnect the following:
- Negative battery cable
- Throttle body air intake duct

4. Drain the cooling system.

5. Remove or disconnect the following:
- Necessary vacuum lines
- Control cables from the throttle body lever
- Control cable bracket from the intake manifold
- Serpentine belt
- Power steering pump and move it aside with the fluid lines attached
- Transaxle fill tube
- Idle Air Control (IAC) valve
- Throttle Position (TP) sensor
- Manifold Absolute Pressure (MAP) sensor
- Evaporative Emission (EVAP) Emission solenoid
- Fuel injector harness
- Exhaust Gas Recirculation (EGR) valve
- Upper intake manifold and discard the gasket
- Fuel lines from the fuel rail
- EGR valve injector
- Fuel injector bracket, regulator and injectors
- Control cable bracket
- 6 intake manifold nuts
- Intake manifold

6. Clean the gasket mounting surfaces.

To install:

➡**Refer to Section 1 of this manual for the intake manifold torque sequence illustration. The illustration is located after the Torque Specification Chart.**

7. Install or connect the following:

- New gasket
- Lower intake manifold. Torque the nuts in the proper sequence to 24 ft. lbs. (33 Nm).
- Control cables and bracket
- EGR valve
- Fuel lines to the fuel rail
- Fuel injectors, regulator and injector bracket. Torque the bolts to 22 inch lbs. (3.5 Nm).
- EGR valve injector with the port is facing the throttle body
- Upper intake manifold assembly. Torque the nuts in sequence to 22 ft. lbs. (30 Nm).
- MAP sensor
- EGR solenoid valve
- IAC valve
- TP sensor
- Fuel injectors
- Transaxle filler tube
- Power steering pump
- Serpentine belt
- Vacuum lines
- Air intake duct
- Negative battery cable

8. Refill the cooling system.

9. Start the engine and check for leaks.

1998–01 MODELS

1. Before servicing the vehicle, refer to the precautions in the beginning of this section.

2. Properly relieve the fuel system pressure.

3. Remove or disconnect the following:
- Negative battery cable
- Air cleaner inlet duct
- Air inlet resonator and bracket
- Throttle and cruise control cable from the throttle body
- Manifold Absolute Pressure (MAP) sensor
- Throttle Position (TP) sensor
- Idle Air Control (IAC) valve
- Throttle body
- Fuel supply line and fuel inlet pipe
- Intake manifold

4. Clean the gasket mating surfaces. Inspect the manifold for cracks, broken flanges and gasket surface damage.

To install:

➡**Refer to Section 1 of this manual for the intake manifold torque sequence illustration. The illustration is located after the Torque Specification Chart.**

5. Install or connect the following:
- New gasket
- Intake manifold. Torque the bolts/nuts, in sequence, to 17 ft. lbs. (24 Nm).

- Throttle body. Torque the bolts to 89 inch lbs. (10 Nm).
- Fuel pipe and fuel supply line.
- MAP sensor
- TP sensor
- IAC valve
- Cruise control and throttle cables to the throttle body
- Air inlet resonator bracket and resonator
- Air cleaner inlet duct
- Negative battery cable

2.4L Engine

1. Before servicing the vehicle, refer to the precautions in the beginning of this section.

2. Properly relieve the fuel system pressure.

3. Drain the cooling system.

4. Remove or disconnect the following:
- Negative battery cable
- Manifold Absolute Pressure (MAP) sensor
- Intake Air Temperature (IAT) sensor
- Evaporative Emission (EVAP) canister purge solenoid
- Fuel injector harness
- Fuel regulator vacuum hose
- EVAP canister purge solenoid to canister vacuum hose
- Air cleaner duct
- Accelerator control cable bracket
- Stud-ended alternator mount bolt
- Exhaust Gas Recirculation (EGR) pipe from the EGR adapter
- Oil fill tube out the top, rotating it to gain clearance for the oil/air separator nipple between the intake tubes and fuel rail electrical harness
- Intake manifold support brace
- Intake manifold and discard the gasket

➡ **If installing a new intake manifold, transfer all necessary parts from the old manifold to the new one.**

5. Using a suitable scraping tool, clean the old gasket material from the intake manifold mating surfaces.

✳✳ WARNING

Do not allow any debris to fall into the engine!

To install:

➡ **Refer to Section 1 of this manual for the intake manifold torque sequence**

illustration. The illustration is located after the Torque Specification Chart.

6. Install or connect the following:
- New gasket
- Intake manifold. Torque the bolts/nuts, in sequence, to 18 ft. lbs. (24 Nm).

➡ **Be sure the numbers stamped on the gasket are facing the manifold surface.**

- Intake manifold brace and retainers
- Oil fill tube, seat the O-ring
- Oil/air separator hose to the oil fill tube

➡ **Lubricate the hose to ease the installation.**

- EGR pipe to the adapter. Torque the fasteners to 19 ft. lbs. (26 Nm).
- Stud-ended alternator bolt
- Accelerator control cable bracket
- Vacuum hoses to the fuel regulator and EVAP canister purge solenoid
- All electrical connectors
- Air cleaner duct
- Negative battery cable

7. Refill the cooling system.
8. Start the engine and inspect for leaks.

Exhaust Manifold

REMOVAL & INSTALLATION

2.2L Engine

1. Before servicing the vehicle, refer to the precautions in the beginning of this section.

2. Remove or disconnect the following:
- Negative battery cable
- Oxygen (O_2S) sensor
- Serpentine belt
- Alternator and support it aside with the wires attached
- Exhaust pipe-to-exhaust manifold bolts
- Oil filler tube, if necessary
- Heater outlet hose assembly-to-exhaust manifold nut
- Exhaust manifold-to-cylinder head bolts
- Exhaust manifold from the exhaust pipe flange
- Exhaust manifold, discard the gasket(s)

To install:
3. Using a gasket scraper, carefully clean the gasket mounting surfaces.

4. Install or connect the following:
- New gaskets
- Exhaust manifold. Torque the nuts to 10–12 ft. lbs. (13–16 Nm) and the bolts to 10–13 ft. lbs. (13–18 Nm).
- Heater outlet hose assembly-to-exhaust manifold nut
- Oil filler tube, if necessary
- Exhaust pipe-to-exhaust manifold bolts
- Alternator
- Serpentine belt
- O_2S sensor
- Negative battery cable

5. Start the engine and check for exhaust leaks.

2.4L Engine

1. Before servicing the vehicle, refer to the precautions in the beginning of this section.

2. Remove or disconnect the following:
- Negative battery cable
- Oxygen (O_2S) sensor
- Exhaust manifold brace-to-manifold bolt
- Oil pan nuts, if necessary

➡ **Do not bend the exhaust flex coupler more than necessary to remove it. Excessive movement will damage the flex coupler.**

- Manifold-to-exhaust flex coupler fasteners

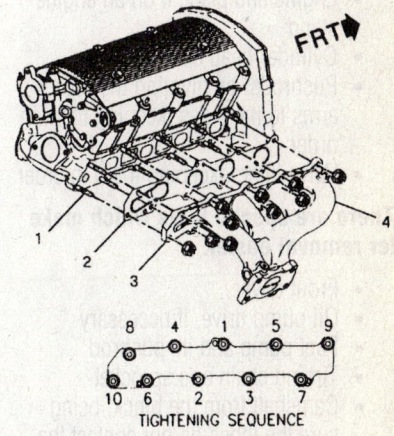

FRT➤

TIGHTENING SEQUENCE

1. STUD, EXHAUST MANIFOLD
2. GASKET, EXHAUST MANIFOLD
3. MANIFOLD, EXHAUST
4. NUT, EXHAUST MANIFOLD, MUST BE TIGHTENED IN SEQUENCE SHOWN TO 12.5 N•m (110 LB. IN.)

7922YG11

Exploded view of the exhaust manifold, showing the torque sequence—2.4L

For engine torque specifications, refer to Section 1 of this manual

- Exhaust pipe from the exhaust manifold by pulling it downward
- Exhaust manifold, discard the gaskets and/or seals

3. Clean the mating surfaces.

To install:

4. Install or connect the following:
- New gaskets
- Exhaust manifold. Torque the nuts to 110 inch lbs. (12.5 Nm), in sequence.
- Heat shield. Torque the bolts to 124 inch lbs. (14 Nm).
- Exhaust manifold brace-to-manifold bolt and oil pan nuts. Torque the bolts to 41 ft. lbs. (56 Nm) and nuts to 19 ft. lbs. (26 Nm).
- Manifold-to-flex coupler fasteners. Torque the bolts to 26 ft. lbs. (35 Nm).
- O$_2$S sensor, coat the threads with anti-seize compound 5613695 or equivalent
- Negative battery cable

5. Check for leaks.

Camshaft and Valve Lifters

REMOVAL & INSTALLATION

2.2L Engine

1. Before servicing the vehicle, refer to the precautions in the beginning of this section.

2. Remove or disconnect the following:
- Engine and place it on an engine stand
- Cylinder head cover
- Pushrods, by pivoting the rocker arms to the sides, keeping them in order
- Valve lifters, keeping them in order

➡ **There are special tools which make lifter removal easier.**

- Front cover
- Oil pump drive, if necessary
- Fuel pump and its pushrod
- Timing chain and sprocket
- Camshaft from the block, being sure the lobes do not contact the bearings

To install:

3. Lubricate the camshaft with clean engine oil and the lobes with Molykote® or the equivalent.

4. Install or connect the following:
- Camshaft, being careful not to contact the bearings with the cam lobes

---

- Timing chain and sprocket
- Fuel pump and pushrod
- Timing cover
- Valve lifters

✳ WARNING

If a new camshaft has been installed, new lifters should be used to ensure durability of the cam lobes.

- Pushrods
- Rocker arms

5. Adjust the valve lash after installing the engine.

6. Install the cylinder head cover.

2.4L Engine

INTAKE CAMSHAFT

➡ **Any time the camshaft housing-to-cylinder head bolts are loosened or removed, the camshaft housing to cylinder head gasket must be replaced.**

1. Before servicing the vehicle, refer to the precautions in the beginning of this section.

2. Relieve the fuel system pressure.

3. Remove or disconnect the following:
- Negative battery cable
- Ignition coil and module assembly, by pulling it straight up.

➡ **Use a special spark plug boot wire remover tool to remove connector assemblies, if they have stuck to the spark plugs.**

- Idle speed power steering pressure switch connector, if equipped
- 3 power steering pump pivot bolts, loosen them
- Drive belt
- Both rear power steering pump bracket-to-transaxle bolts
- Front power steering pump bracket to cylinder block bolt
- Power steering pump assembly, move it aside
- Power steering pump drive pulley from the intake camshaft, using a special tool
- Oil/air separator assembly

➡ **Leave the hoses attached to the separator but disconnect them from the oil fill, chain housing and intake manifold.**

- Vacuum line from fuel pressure regulator
- Fuel injector harness connector
- Fuel line clamp from the bracket at top of intake camshaft housing
- Fuel rail from the cylinder head

---

with the lines attached, cover or plug injector openings
- Timing chain and housing, DO NOT remove from the engine
- Intake camshaft housing cover
- Intake camshaft housing, by reversing the torquing sequence

➡ **Leave 2 of the bolts loosely in place to hold the camshaft housing while separating the camshaft cover from housing.**

4. Press the cover off the housing by threading 4 housing-to-head bolts into the cam housing cover tapped holes. Tighten the bolts evenly so the cover does not bind on the dowel pins.

5. Remove or disconnect the following:
- Camshaft housing, discard the gaskets

➡ **Note the position of the chain sprocket dowel pin for reassembly.**

- Intake camshaft oil seal from camshaft and discard the seal

➡ **The seal must be replaced any time the housing and cover are separated.**

- Camshaft carrier from the cylinder head and discard the gasket

To install:

6. Thoroughly, clean the mating surfaces.

7. Install or connect the following:
- New gasket
- Lifters into their bores

➡ **If the camshaft is being replaced, the lifters must also be replaced. Lubricate camshaft lobes, journals and lifters with camshaft and lifter prelube.**

✳ WARNING

The camshaft lobes and journals must be adequately lubricated or engine damage could occur upon start up.

- Camshaft

➡ **The timing chain sprocket dowel pin should be straight up and align with the centerline of the lifter bores.**

- New camshaft housing cover seals; do not use sealer. Be sure the correct color seal is placed in each groove.

➡ **Apply thread locking compound to the camshaft housing cover bolt threads.**

- Camshaft housing cover to the housing. Torque the bolts, in sequence, to 11 ft. lbs. (15 Nm) plus an additional 75 degree turn (except for the 2 rear fuel pipe to the camshaft housing bolts). Torque the 2 rear bolts to 16 ft. lbs. (15 Nm), plus an additional 25 degree turn.
- Timing chain housing and timing chain
- New fuel injector O-ring seals

- lubricated with engine oil
- Fuel the fuel rail
- Fuel line clamp/bracket on top of the intake camshaft housing
- Vacuum line to the fuel pressure regulator
- Fuel injector harness connectors
- Oil/air separator assembly
- New intake camshaft seal lubricated with engine oil
- Power steering pump pulley onto the intake camshaft

- Power steering pump and drive belt
- Idle speed power steering pressure switch connector

8. Clean and apply Loctite® 592 or equivalent, onto the ignition coil/module assembly to camshaft housing bolts. Torque the bolts to 13 ft. lbs. (18 Nm).

9. Install or connect the following:
- Ignition coil/module assembly electrical connectors
- Negative battery cable

10. Start the engine and check for leaks.

EXHAUST CAMSHAFT

➡ **Any time the camshaft housing-to-cylinder head bolts are loosened or removed, the camshaft housing to cylinder head gasket must be replaced.**

1. Before servicing the vehicle, refer to the precautions in the beginning of this section.

2. Relieve the fuel system pressure.

3. Remove or disconnect the following:
- Negative battery cable
- Ignition coil/module assembly electrical connectors
- Ignition coil/module assembly by pulling it straight up

➡ **Use a special tool to remove connector assemblies if they are stuck to the spark plugs.**

- Idle speed power steering pressure switch connector, if equipped
- Transaxle fluid level indicator tube assembly, (if equipped) from exhaust camshaft cover, move it aside
- Exhaust camshaft cover and discard the gasket
- Timing chain and housing; do not remove from the engine
- Exhaust camshaft housing by reversing of the torquing sequence

4. Press the cover off the housing by threading 4 housing-to-head bolts into the cam housing cover tapped holes. Tighten the bolts evenly so the cover does not bind on the dowel pins.

5. Remove the camshaft housing cover and discard the gaskets.

6. Loosely install a camshaft housing-to-cylinder head bolt to retain the housing during camshaft and lifter removal.

➡ **Note the position of the chain sprocket dowel pin for reassembly.**

7. Remove or disconnect the following:
- Camshaft

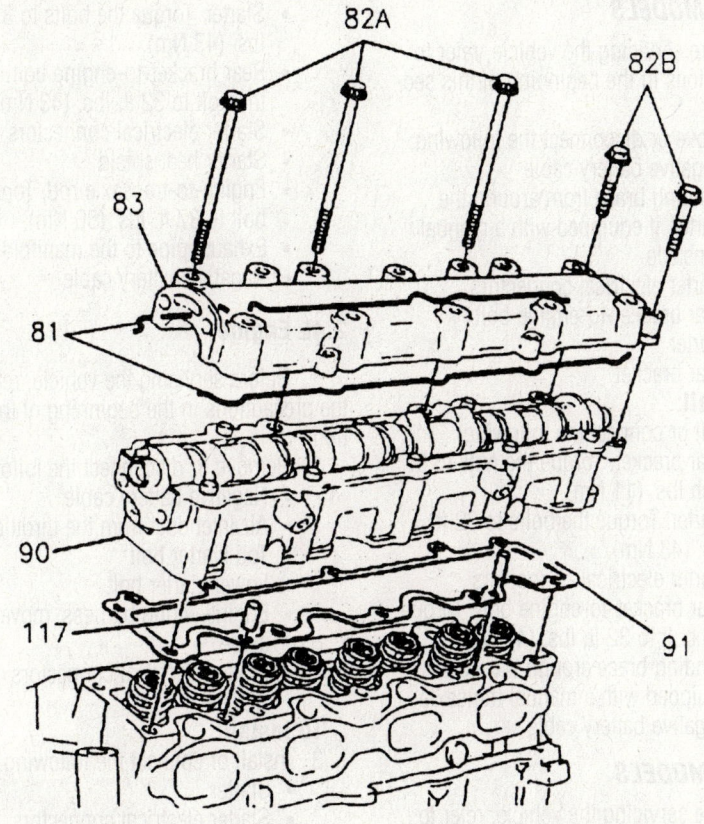

81 SEALS – CAMSHAFT HOUSING TO CAMSHAFT

82A BOLT – CAMSHAFT HOUSING TO CYLINDER HEAD – 15 N·m (11 LBS. FT.) PLUS TURN 90°

82B BOLT – CAMSHAFT HOUSING COVER TO CAMSHAFT HOUSING – 15 N·m (11 LBS. FT.) PLUS TURN 30°

83 COVER – CAMSHAFT

90 CAMSHAFT HOUSING (INTAKE SHOWN)

91 GASKET – CAMSHAFT HOUSING TO CYLINDER HEAD

117 DOWEL PIN (2)

7922YG31

Exploded view of the camshaft housing, cover and gaskets—2.4L engine

For complete mechanical specifications, refer to Section 1 of this manual

- Camshaft carrier from the cylinder head and discard the gasket

To install:

8. Thoroughly, clean the mating surfaces.

9. Install or connect the following:
- New gasket
- Camshaft carrier on the cylinder head with 1 bolt loosely to hold it in place
- Lifters in their bores

➡ **If the camshaft is being replaced, the lifters must also be replaced.**

✳✳ WARNING

Lubricate camshaft lobes, journals and lifters with camshaft and lifter prelube. The camshaft lobes and journals must be adequately lubricated or engine damage could occur upon start up.

- Camshaft

➡ **The timing chain sprocket dowel pin should be straight up and align with the centerline of the lifter bores.**

- New camshaft housing cover seals; do not use sealer.

✳✳ WARNING

Be sure the correct color seal is placed in each groove.

➡ **Apply thread locking compound to the camshaft housing cover bolt threads.**

- Camshaft housing cover. Torque the bolts, in sequence, to 11 ft. lbs. (15 Nm), plus an additional 75 degree turn.
- Timing chain housing and timing chain
- Transaxle fluid level indicator tube assembly to the exhaust camshaft cover
- Idle speed power steering pressure switch connector

10. Clean and apply Loctite® 592 or equivalent, to the ignition coil/module assembly bolts.

11. Install or connect the following:
- Ignition coil/module assembly. Torque bolts to 13 ft. lbs. (18 Nm).
- Ignition coil/module assembly electrical connectors
- Negative battery cable

12. Start the engine and check for leaks.

Valve Lash

ADJUSTMENT

All of the engines are equipped with hydraulic valve lifters.

Starter

REMOVAL & INSTALLATION

2.2L Engine

1997–99 MODELS

1. Before servicing the vehicle, refer to the precautions in the beginning of this section.

2. Remove or disconnect the following:
- Negative battery cable
- Bending brace from around the starter, if equipped with a manual transaxle
- Starter electrical connectors
- Rear bracket-to-engine bolt
- Starter
- Rear bracket

To install:

3. Install or connect the following:
- Rear bracket. Torque the nuts to 97 inch lbs. (11 Nm).
- Starter. Torque the bolts to 32 ft. lbs. (43 Nm).
- Starter electrical connectors
- Rear bracket-to-engine bolt. Torque the bolt to 32 ft. lbs. (43 Nm).
- Bending brace around the starter, if equipped with a manual transaxle
- Negative battery cable

2000–01 MODELS

1. Before servicing the vehicle, refer to the precautions in the beginning of this section.

2. Remove or disconnect the following:
- Negative battery cable
- Exhaust pipe from the manifold
- Engine-to-transaxle rod
- Starter heat shield
- Starter electrical connectors
- Rear bracket-to-engine bolt
- Starter
- Rear bracket

To install:

3. Install or connect the following:
- Rear bracket. Torque the nuts to 97 inch lbs. (11 Nm).
- Starter. Torque the bolts to 32 ft. lbs. (43 Nm).
- Rear bracket-to-engine bolt. Torque the bolt to 32 ft. lbs. (43 Nm).
- Starter electrical connectors
- Starter heat shield
- Engine-to-transaxle rod. Torque the bolt to 37 ft. lbs. (50 Nm).
- Exhaust pipe to the manifold
- Negative battery cable

2.4L Engine

1. Before servicing the vehicle, refer to the precautions in the beginning of this section.

2. Remove or disconnect the following:
- Negative battery cable
- Air inlet duct from the throttle body
- Top starter bolt
- Lower starter bolt
- Engine wiring harness, move it aside
- Starter electrical connectors
- Starter

To install:

3. Install or connect the following:
- Starter
- Starter electrical connectors
- Engine wiring harness
- Lower starter bolt.

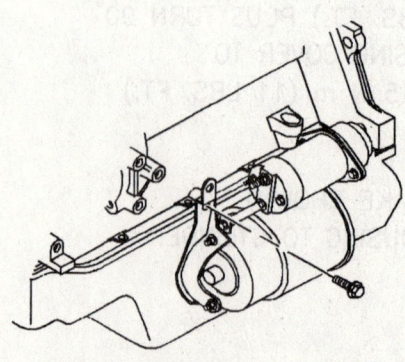

Exploded view of the starter—2.2L engine

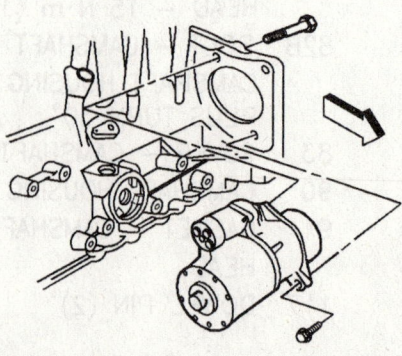

Exploded view of the starter—2.4L engine

- Top starter bolt. Torque the bolt to 66 ft. lbs. (90 Nm).
- Air inlet duct to the throttle body
- Negative battery cable

Oil Pan

REMOVAL & INSTALLATION

2.2L Engine

1. Before servicing the vehicle, refer to the precautions in the beginning of this section.
2. Drain the engine oil.
3. Remove or disconnect the following:
   - Negative battery cable
   - Right front wheel
   - Right inner fender splash shield
   - Starter and bracket
   - Flywheel cover
   - Engine support strut and bracket
   - Oil level sensor
   - Oil pan and discard the gasket

To install:

4. Clean all the gasket surfaces completely.
5. Place a 2mm bead of RTV sealer to the oil pan sealing surface except at the rear seal mounting surface. Using a new oil pan rear seal, apply a thin coat RTV sealer on the end down to the ears.
6. Install or connect the following:
   - New gasket

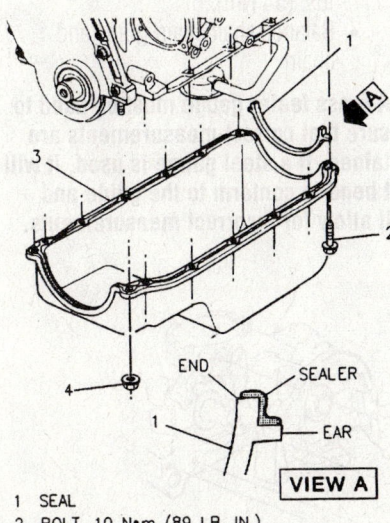

1 SEAL
2 BOLT, 10 N•m (89 LB. IN.)
3 OIL PAN
4 NUT, OIL PAN 10 N•m (89 LB. IN.)

7922YG32

Exploded view of the oil pan mounting and related components—2.2L engine

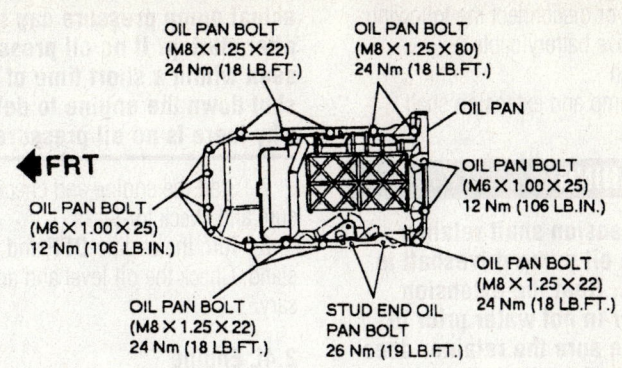

OIL PAN BOLT (M8 X 1.25 X 22) 24 Nm (18 LB.FT.)
OIL PAN BOLT (M8 X 1.25 X 80) 24 Nm (18 LB.FT.)
OIL PAN
◄FRT
OIL PAN BOLT (M6 X 1.00 X 25) 12 Nm (106 LB.IN.)
OIL PAN BOLT (M6 X 1.00 X 25) 12 Nm (106 LB.IN.)
OIL PAN BOLT (M8 X 1.25 X 22) 24 Nm (18 LB.FT.)
OIL PAN BOLT (M8 X 1.25 X 22) 24 Nm (18 LB.FT.)
STUD END OIL PAN BOLT 26 Nm (19 LB.FT.)

7922YG12

Oil pan fastener torque specifications—2.4L engine

- Oil pan. Torque the nuts and bolts to 89 inch lbs. (10 Nm).
- Oil level sensor
- Engine mount strut and bracket
- Starter and bracket
- Flywheel cover
- Right fender splash shield
- Right front wheel. Torque the nuts to 100 ft. lbs. (140 Nm).
- Negative battery cable

7. Refill the crankcase.
8. Start the vehicle and verify no leaks.

2.4L Engine

➡The oil pan is die cast aluminum and must be handled with care to avoid damage. The oil pan includes an attachment to the transaxle to provide additional structural support.

1. Before servicing the vehicle, refer to the precautions in the beginning of this section.
2. Drain the engine oil.
3. Drain the cooling system.
4. Remove or disconnect the following:
   - Negative battery cable
   - Flywheel/converter cover
   - Right wheel
   - Serpentine drive belt
   - Air conditioning compressor and move it aside without disconnecting the hoses
   - Engine mount strut bracket
   - Radiator outlet pipe bolts
   - Air conditioning and radiator outlet pipes from the oil pan
   - Exhaust manifold brace
   - Oil pan-to-flywheel cover bolt and nut
   - Flywheel cover stud for clearance
   - Radiator outlet pipe from the lower radiator hose and oil pan
   - Oil level sensor connector

- Oil pan

To install:

5. Inspect the oil pan gasket; it is reusable, if not damaged.
6. Install or connect the following:
   - Oil pan with the gasket. Torque the M8 bolts to 18 ft. lbs. (24 Nm) and the M6 bolts to 106 inch lbs. (12 Nm).
   - Flywheel cover stud, spacer and nut. Torque the nut to 19 ft. lbs. (26 Nm).
   - Oil level sensor connector
   - Radiator outlet pipe to lower radiator hose and oil pan
   - Exhaust manifold brace
   - Air conditioning and radiator outlet pipes to the oil pan
   - Radiator outlet pipe. Torque the bolts to 124 inch lbs. (14 Nm).
   - Engine mount strut bracket. Torque the bolts to 55 ft. lbs. (75 Nm).
   - Air conditioning compressor
   - Serpentine drive belt
   - Right splash shield
   - Right front wheel
   - Flywheel/converter cover
   - Negative battery cable

7. Refill the crankcase.
8. Refill the cooling system.
9. Start the vehicle and verify no leaks.

Oil Pump

REMOVAL & INSTALLATION

2.2L Engine

1. Before servicing the vehicle, refer to the precautions in the beginning of this section.
2. Drain the crankcase.

Please refer to Section 8 for electric cooling fan wiring schematics

3. Remove or disconnect the following:
- Negative battery cable
- Oil pan
- Oil pump and extension shaft

To install:

❋❋ WARNING

A plastic extension shaft retainer connects the oil pump driveshaft to the oil pump. Heat the extension shaft retainer in hot water prior to assemble. Be sure the retainer does not crack upon installation.

4. Fill the oil pump cavities with petroleum jelly before installing the gears into the pump body.
5. Install or connect the following:
- Extension shaft and oil pump. Torque the oil pump-to-bearing cap bolt to 32 ft. lbs. (43 Nm) and the upper oil pump drive bolt to 18 ft. lbs. (25 Nm).
- Oil pan
- Negative battery cable
6. Refill the crankcase.

❋❋ WARNING

It is good practice to install a reliable mechanical oil pressure gauge so actual pump pressure can be read after startup. If no oil pressure is seen within a short time of start-up, shut down the engine to determine why there is no oil pressure.

7. Start the engine and check oil pressure and check for leaks.
8. Turn the engine **OFF** and allow to stand. Check the oil level and add as necessary.

2.4L Engine

➡ **The transaxle must be removed to service the oil pump.**

1. Before servicing the vehicle, refer to the precautions in the beginning of this section.
2. Disconnect the negative battery cable.
3. Install an engine support fixture.
4. Drain the crankcase.
5. Remove or disconnect the following:
- Oil pan
- Transaxle
- Flywheel
- Balance shaft chain cover and guide

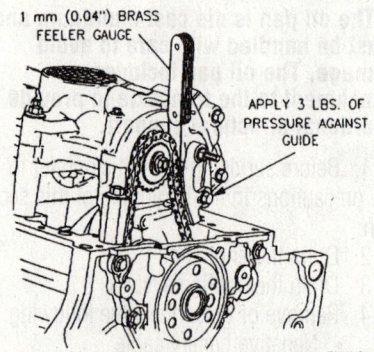

Using a feeler gauge to check the chain tension—2.4L engine

- Oil pump
6. Disassemble the oil pump as follows:
- Oil pump cover
- Pump gear, pull the housing to disconnect it from the balance shaft
- Sub-assembly from the balance shaft assembly
- Gerotor from the oil pump housing
- Oil pump from the balance shaft housing
- Pressure relief valve
- Roll pin by driving it out with a small punch

To install:

7. Clean all of the parts in suitable cleaning solvent. Remove all varnish, sludge and dirt.
8. Inspect the pump cover and housing for cracks and excessive wear, replace as necessary.
9. Lubricate the gears with clean engine oil.
10. Assemble the oil pump as follows:
- Gerotor gear into the housing
- Fill oil pump cavities with petroleum jelly
- Pressure relief valve, use a 9/16 in. deep well socket to seat the valve
- Roll pin
- Pump housing to the balance shaft assembly
- Pump cover to the oil pump housing
11. Install or connect the following:
- Oil pump. Torque the bolts to 40 ft. lbs. (54 Nm).
- Balance shaft chain guide and chain

➡ **A brass feeler gauge must be used to ensure that correct measurements are obtained. If a steel gauge is used, it will not bend to conform to the guide and will allow for incorrect measurements.**

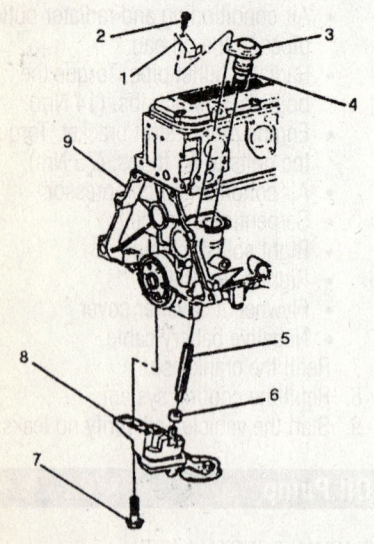

1 Bracket
2 Bolt
3 Oil pump drive assembly
4 O-ring
5 Shaft
6 Retainer; Heat and water soak prior to installation
7 Bolt
8 Oil pump
9 Cylinder block

Exploded view of the oil pump mounting to engine block—2.2L engine

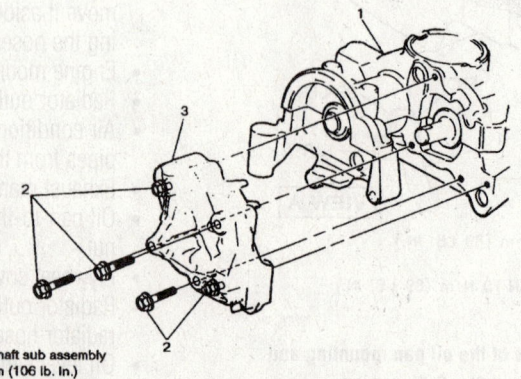

1 Balance shaft sub assembly
2 Bolt 12 Nm (106 lb. In.)
3 Oil pump sub assembly

Exploded view of the oil pump assembly mounting—2.4L engine

12. Adjust the chain tension as follows:
   a. Insert a 0.40 in. (1mm) brass feeler between the chain guide and the chain.
   b. Press the guide against the chain using about 3 pounds of force.
   c. Torque the chain tensioner fastener to 115 inch lbs. (13 Nm).
13. Install or connect the following:
   • Balance shaft chain cover. Torque the nut and bolt to 115 inch lbs. (13 Nm).
   • Fywheel. Torque the bolts to 22 ft. lbs. (30 Nm) plus an additional 45 degree turn.
   • Transaxle
   • Oil pan
   • Negative battery cable
14. Refill the crankcase.
15. Remove the engine support fixture.
16. Start the vehicle and verify oil pressure and no leaks.

Rear Main Seal

REMOVAL & INSTALLATION

2.2L Engine

1. Before servicing the vehicle, refer to the precautions in the beginning of this section.
2. Remove or disconnect the following:
   • Negative battery cable
   • Transaxle
   • Clutch/pressure plate assembly, if equipped with a manual transmission
   • Flywheel
   • Rear main bearing seal by prying it from the engine

➡**Be careful not to damage or scratch the seal mounting surfaces**

To install:
3. Lubricate the new rear main bearing seal with engine oil.
4. Install or connect the following:
   • New rear main bearing seal using the Rear Main Bearing Oil Seal Installer tool J-34686 until it is flush with the block
   • Flywheel
   • Clutch/pressure plate assembly, if equipped with a manual transmission
   • Transaxle
   • Negative battery cable
5. Start the engine and check for leaks.

2.4L Engine

1. Before servicing the vehicle, refer to the precautions in the beginning of this section.
2. Remove or disconnect the following:
   • Negative battery cable
   • Transaxle
   • Clutch/pressure plate assembly, if equipped with a manual transmission
   • Flywheel and discard the bolts
   • Oil pan-to-crankshaft seal housing bolts
   • Seal housing and discard the gasket
   • Oil seal from the transaxle side of the seal housing

To install:
3. Clean and inspect the gasket mounting surfaces.
4. If necessary, add the silicone sealer along the oil pan-to-cylinder block mating surface.
5. Lubricate the new rear main bearing seal with engine oil.
6. Install or connect the following:
   • New rear main bearing seal into the seal housing using the Rear Crankshaft Seal Installer tool J-36005 until it is flush with the housing
   • New oil seal housing gasket
   • Oil seal housing. Torque the bolts to 10 ft. lbs. (12 Nm).
7. Secure the flywheel with the Crankshaft Balancer Holder tool J-38122 to keep the flywheel from turning.
8. Install or connect the following:
   • Flywheel, using new bolts. Torque the bolts to 22 ft. lbs. (30 Nm) plus an additional 45 degree turn.
   • Clutch/pressure plate assembly, if equipped with a manual transmission
   • Transaxle
   • Negative battery cable
9. Start the engine and check for leaks.

Timing Chain, Sprockets, Front Cover and Seal

REMOVAL & INSTALLATION

2.2L Engine

➡**The following procedure requires the use of a Centering tool J-23042.**

1. Before servicing the vehicle, refer to the precautions in the beginning of this section.

2. Remove or disconnect the following:
   • Negative battery cable
   • Serpentine belt and tensioner

➡**Although not absolutely necessary, removal of the right front inner fender splash shield will facilitate access to the front cover.**

3. Install an engine support fixture.
4. Remove or disconnect the following:
   • Engine mount assembly
   • Alternator rear brace and alternator
   • Power steering pump and move it aside with the lines attached
   • Oil pan
   • Crankshaft pulley/hub from the crankshaft
   • Front cover

➡**If the cover is difficult to remove, use a plastic mallet to carefully loosen it.**

   • Oil seal from the front cover by tapping it with a seal driver
5. Position the No. 1 piston at Top Dead Center (TDC) of the compression stroke so the camshaft and crankshaft sprockets timing marks are aligned.
6. Remove or disconnect the following:
   • Timing chain tensioner nut, loosen it
   • Camshaft sprocket bolts
   • Camshaft sprocket and chain as an assembly

➡**If the sprocket does not slide from the camshaft easily, a light blow with a soft mallet at the lower edge of the sprocket will dislodge it.**

   • Crankshaft sprocket, using a puller
To install:
7. Clean and inspect the gasket mounting surfaces.
8. Lubricate the timing chain with clean engine oil.

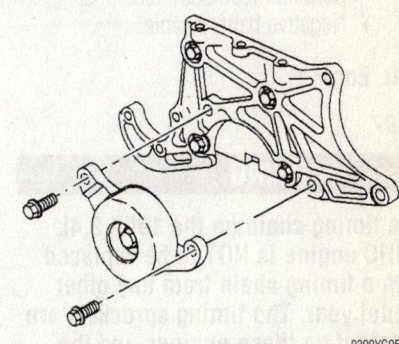

9300YG05

Exploded view of the serpentine belt tensioner mounting—2.2L engine

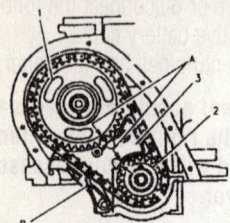

1. Camshaft sprocket
2. Crankshaft sprocket
3. Timing chain tensioner
A. Line up timing marks on sprockets with tabs on timing chain tensioner
B. Remove pin after timing chain is installed

7922YG16

Align the sprocket timing marks with the alignment tabs on the tensioner during timing chain installation—2.2L engine

9. Install the crankshaft sprocket, press it onto the crankshaft.

10. Install the timing chain over the camshaft sprocket, then around the crankshaft sprocket. Be sure the marks on the 2 sprockets are in alignment. Lubricate the thrust surface with Molykote® or equivalent.

11. Install or connect the following:
- Camshaft sprocket. Torque the bolts to 66–68 ft. lbs. (89–92 Nm).
- Chain tensioner, tighten it
- New seal into the front cover, using a seal installer tool

12. Lubricate the seal lip with engine oil.

13. Install or connect the following:
- New gasket
- Front cover on the block using Centering tool J-23042. Torque the bolts to 72–108 inch lbs. (8–12 Nm).
- Crankshaft pulley/hub to the crankshaft
- Oil pan
- Power steering pump
- Alternator rear brace and alternator
- Engine mount assembly

14. Remove the engine support fixture.

15. Install or connect the following:
- Serpentine belt and tensioner
- Negative battery cable

2.4L Engine

1997

✳✳ **WARNING**

The timing chain on the 1997 2.4L DOHC engine is NOT to be replaced with a timing chain from any other model year. The timing sprockets are different on these engines and the shape of the links matches the sprockets. Engine damage may result if the wrong timing chain is used.

1. Before servicing the vehicle, refer to the precautions in the beginning of this section.

2. Remove or disconnect the following:
- Negative battery cable
- Coolant recovery reservoir
- Serpentine belt, using a 13mm wrench that is at least 24 in. (61cm) long

3. Install tool J-28467-400 onto the alternator stud-ended bolt and attach the fixture.

4. Remove or disconnect the following:
- Upper cover fasteners
- Cover vent hose
- Right engine mount, bracket or bracket adapter and discard the bolts
- Right front wheel and splash shield
- Crankshaft balancer assembly

➡**Do not install an automatic transaxle engine balancer on a manual transaxle engine or vice-versa.**

- Lower cover fasteners
- Front cover, discard the gasket, if necessary
- Oil seal from the front cover using a seal driver

5. Rotate the crankshaft clockwise, as viewed from the front of engine/normal rotation, until the camshaft sprocket timing dowel pin holes align with the holes in the timing chain housing. The crankshaft sprocket keyway should point upwards and align with the centerline of the cylinder bores; this is the "timed" position.

6. Remove or disconnect the following:
- Timing chain guides
- Tensioner, when the slack in the timing chain is above the tensioner assembly

➡**The timing chain must be disengaged from any wear grooves in the tensioner shoe in order to remove the shoe. Slide a suitable prytool under the timing chain while pulling the shoe outward.**

✳✳ **WARNING**

DO NOT attempt to pry the socket off the camshaft or damage to the sprocket and/or chain housing could occur.

7. If difficulty is encountered in removing the chain tensioner shoe, remove the intake camshaft sprocket as follows:

a. Secure the intake camshaft sprocket and remove the sprocket bolt and washer.

b. Remove the washer from the bolts and thread the bolt back into the camshaft by hand. The bolt provides a surface to push against.

c. Remove the camshaft sprocket using a 3-jaw puller in the 3 sprocket relief holes.

8. Remove or disconnect the following:
- Tensioner assembly bolts
- Tensioner

✳✳ **WARNING**

The timing chain and crankshaft sprocket MUST be marked before removal. If the chain or sprocket is installed with the wear pattern in the opposite direction, noise and increased wear may occur.

- Timing chain. Matchmark the crankshaft sprocket and timing chain before removal.

9. Clean the old sealant off the bolt with a wire brush. Clean the threaded hole in the camshaft with a round nylon brush. Inspect the parts for wear and replace as necessary. Note that some scoring of the chain shoe and guides is normal.

To install:

✳✳ **WARNING**

Failure to follow this procedure may result in severe engine damage.

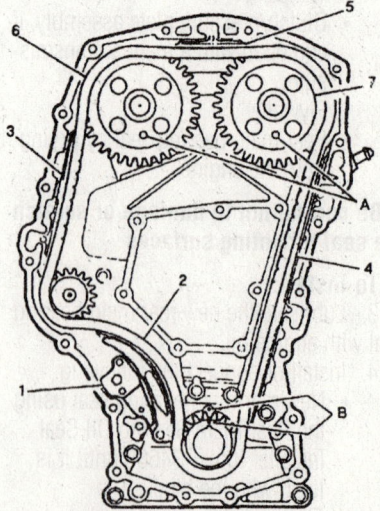

A Camshaft timing alignment pin location
B Crankshaft gear timing mark
1 Shoe assembly timing chain tensioner
2 Timing chain
3 R.H. timing chain guide
4 L.H. timing chain guide
5 Upper timing chain guide
6 Exhaust camshaft sprocket
7 Intake camshaft sprocket

7922YG17

After installation the chain must be in the "timed" position—2.4L engine

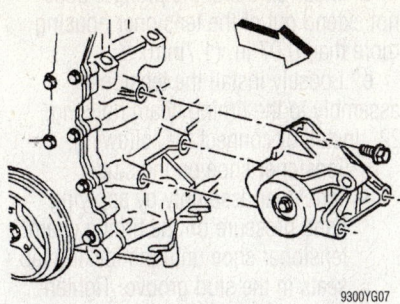

Exploded view of the serpentine belt tensioner mounting—2.4L engine

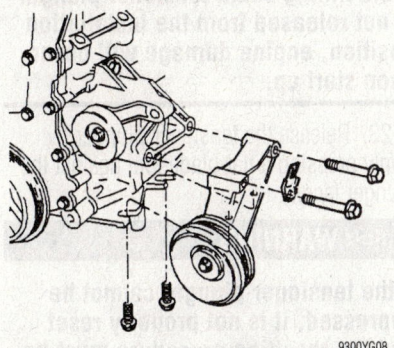

Exploded view of the serpentine belt idler pulley mounting—2.4L engine

10. Install or connect the following:
- Intake camshaft sprocket onto the camshaft with the matchmarked surface showing
- Intake camshaft sprocket bolt. Torque the sprocket bolt to 52 ft. lbs. (70 Nm) while holding the sprocket. Use sealant on the camshaft sprocket bolt.

11. Place camshaft aligning pins through the holes in the camshaft sprockets into the holes in the timing chain housing. This positions the cams for correct timing.

12. If the camshafts are out of position and must be rotated more than ⅛ turn in order to install the alignment dowel pins, proceed as follows:
  a. The crankshaft MUST be rotated 90 degrees clockwise off Top Dead Center (TDC) in order to give the valves adequate clearance to open.
  b. Once the camshafts are in position and the dowels installed, rotate the crankshaft counterclockwise back to TDC.

✳✳ WARNING

Do not rotate the crankshaft clockwise to TDC; valve or piston damage could result.

13. Place the timing chain over the exhaust camshaft sprocket, around the idler sprocket and the crankshaft sprocket.

14. Install the timing chain as follows:
  a. Set the camshafts at the timed position.
  b. Remove the alignment dowel pin from the intake camshaft.
  c. Using the Camshaft Sprocket Wrench J-39579, rotate the intake camshaft sprocket counterclockwise enough to slide the timing chain over the intake camshaft sprocket.
  d. Release the Camshaft Sprocket Wrench J-39579. The length of the chain between the 2 camshaft sprockets will tighten.
  e. If properly timed, the intake camshaft alignment dowel pin should slide in easily. If the dowel pin does not fully index, the camshafts are NOT timed correctly and the procedure must be repeated.

15. Leave the alignment dowel pins installed. Raise and safely support the vehicle.

16. With the slack removed from the chain between the intake camshaft and crankshaft sprockets, the timing marks on the crankshaft and cylinder block should be aligned. If the marks are not aligned, move the chain 1 tooth forward or rearward, remove the slack and recheck the marks.

17. Reload the timing chain tensioner assembly to it "zero" position as follows:
  a. Form a keeper from a piece of heavy gauge wire.
  b. Apply slight force on the tensioner blade to compress the plunger.
  c. Insert a small prytool into the reset access hole, and pry the ratchet pawl away from the ratchet teeth while forcing the plunger completely in the hole.
  d. Install the keeper between the access hole and the blade.

18. Install the tensioner assembly to the timing chain housing. Recheck the plunger assembly installation, it is correctly installed when the long end is toward the crankshaft. Torque the tensioner bolts to 89 inch lbs. (10 Nm).

19. Lower the vehicle enough to remove the alignment dowel pins.

✳✳ WARNING

Severe engine damage could result if the engine is not properly timed.

20. Rotate the crankshaft clockwise (normal rotation) 2 full rotations. Align the

crankshaft keyway with the mark on the cylinder block and reinstall the alignment dowel pins. The pins will slide in easily if the engine is correctly timed.

21. Install or connect the following:
- New seal into the front cover by tapping it with a seal driver, lubricate the seal lip before installation
- Timing chain guides
- Lower front cover. Torque the fasteners to 106 inch lbs. (12 Nm).
- Crankshaft balancer. Torque the bolt to 74 ft. lbs. (100 Nm).
- Right front wheel and splash shield
- Right engine mount, bracket or bracket adapter, using new bolts
- Cover vent hose
- Upper cover. Torque the fasteners to 106 inch lbs. (12 Nm).

22. Remove the fixture.

23. Install or connect the following:
- Serpentine belt using a 13mm wrench that is at least 24 in. (61cm) long
- Coolant recovery reservoir
- Negative battery cable

1998–01

➡ **It is recommended that the entire procedure be reviewed before attempting to service the timing chain.**

1. Before servicing the vehicle, refer to the precautions in the beginning of this section.

2. Disconnect the negative battery cable.

3. Drain the cooling system.

4. Remove or disconnect the following:
- Coolant surge tank
- Serpentine drive belt using a 13mm wrench that is at least 24 in. (61cm) long
- Alternator

5. Install an engine support.

6. Remove or disconnect the following:
- Upper cover fasteners
- Upper cover vent hose
- Right engine mount and bracket.
- Right front wheel
- Lower splash shield from the right wheel house
- Crankshaft balancer using a puller
- Lower cover fasteners
- Front cover and gaskets
- Crankshaft oil slinger

7. Using a seal driver, tap the seal from the front cover

8. Rotate the crankshaft clockwise, as viewed from front of engine (normal rota-

Timing belt service is covered in Section 4 of this manual

tion), until the camshaft sprocket's timing dowel pin holes align with the holes in the timing chain housing. The mark on the crankshaft sprocket should align with the mark on the cylinder block. The crankshaft sprocket keyway should point upwards and align with the center line of the cylinder bores. This is the normal timed position.

9. Remove or disconnect the following:
   • Timing chain guides
   • Timing chain tensioner spring retainer by prying it off
   • Tensioner spring
   • Timing chain tensioner shoe retainer

10. Be sure all the slack in the timing chain is above the tensioner assembly; remove the chain tensioner shoe. The timing chain must be disengaged from the wear grooves in the tensioner shoe in order to remove the shoe. Slide a prybar under the timing chain while pulling shoe outward.

11. If difficulty is encountered removing chain tensioner shoe, proceed as follows:
   a. Hold the intake camshaft sprocket with a holding tool and remove the sprocket bolt and washer.
   b. Remove the washer from the bolt and partially install the bolt back into the camshaft, the bolt provides a surface to push against.
   c. Remove intake camshaft sprocket using a 3-jaw puller placed in the 3 sprocket relief holes.

❈❈ WARNING

Do not attempt to pry the sprocket off the camshaft or damage to the sprocket or chain housing could occur.

12. Remove or disconnect the following:
   • Tensioner assembly bolts and the tensioner

❈❈ CAUTION

The tensioner piston is spring loaded and could fly out causing personal injury.

   • Chain housing-to-block stud, which is actually the timing chain tensioner shoe pivot
   • Timing chain

To install:

13. Coat the camshaft bolts with Sealant GM 1234593.

14. Install the intake camshaft sprocket, if removed. Tighten the bolt to 52 ft. lbs. (70 Nm), while holding the sprocket with a Camshaft Sprocket Wrench J-39579.

➡**Install the Special tool J 36008-A through holes in camshaft sprockets into holes in timing chain housing. This positions the camshafts for correct timing.**

15. If the camshafts are out of position and must be rotated more than ⅛ turn in order to install the alignment dowel pins, perform the following:
   a. Rotate the crankshaft 90 degrees clockwise off Top Dead Center (TDC) in order to give the valves adequate clearance to open.
   b. Once the camshafts are in position and the dowels installed, rotate the crankshaft counterclockwise back to TDC.

❈❈ WARNING

Do not rotate the crankshaft clockwise to TDC or valve and piston damage may occur.

16. Install the timing chain over the exhaust camshaft sprocket, around the coolant pump sprocket and around the crankshaft sprocket.

17. Remove the alignment dowel pin from the intake camshaft. Using tool J 39579, rotate the intake camshaft sprocket counterclockwise enough to slide the timing chain over the intake camshaft sprocket. Release the camshaft sprocket wrench. The length of chain between the 2 camshaft sprockets will tighten. If properly timed, the intake camshaft alignment dowel pin should slide in easily. If the dowel pin does not fully index, the camshafts are not timed correctly and the procedure must be repeated.

18. Leave the alignment dowel pins installed.

19. With slack removed from chain between intake camshaft sprocket and crankshaft sprocket, the crankshaft keyway and the cylinder block mark should be aligned. If not aligned, move the chain 1 tooth forward or rearward. Remove slack and recheck marks.

20. Tighten the chain housing-to-block stud. The stud is installed under the timing chain. Tighten to 19 ft. lbs. (26 Nm).

21. Reload timing chain tensioner assembly to its **0** position as follows:
   a. Insert the tensioner plunger assembly into the tensioner housing.
   b. With the tensioner plunger fully extended, turn the complete assembly upside down on a flat surface.
   c. Press the bottom of the tensioner housing to compress the plunger into the housing until it is seated.

   d. Make sure that the plunger does not extend out of the tensioner housing more than 0.07 in. (1.7mm).
   e. Loosely install the tensioner assembly to the timing chain housing.

22. Install or connect the following:
   • Tensioner shoe on the stud.
   • Tensioner assembly by applying hand pressure on the timing chain tensioner shoe until the locking tab seats in the stud groove. Tighten the bolts to 89 inch lbs. (10 Nm).

❈❈ WARNING

If the timing chain tensioner plunger is not released from the installation position, engine damage will occur upon start up.

23. Release the tensioner plunger by firmly pressing a flat blade tool against the plunger face.

❈❈ WARNING

If the tensioner plunger cannot be depressed, it is not properly reset and the resetting procedure must be repeated.

24. Remove tool J 36008-A from the camshaft sprockets.
   a. Rotate crankshaft clockwise 2 full rotations. Align crankshaft keyway with mark on cylinder block and reinstall alignment dowel pins. Alignment dowel pins will slide in easily if engine is timed correctly.

25. Install or connect the following:
   • Timing chain guides and crankshaft oil slinger
   • New seal lubricated with engine oil
   • Front cover using new gaskets. Tighten the nuts and bolts to 106 inch lbs. (12 Nm).

26. Install the torsional damper as follows:
   a. Coat the seal contact area on the crankshaft damper with clean engine oil.
   b. Align the damper on the crankshaft so the notch in the damper aligns with the crankshaft key.
   c. Tap the balancer into place using a rubber mallet.
   d. Install the damper bolt/washer. Tighten the bolt to 129 ft. lbs. (175 Nm) plus a 90 degree turn.

27. Install or connect the following:
   • Right front lower splash shield
   • Wheel
   • Right engine mount bracket
   • Right engine mount

- Upper cover vent hose
28. Remove the engine support.
29. Install or connect the following:
- Alternator
- Serpentine belt
- Coolant surge tank
- Negative battery cable
30. Refill the cooling system and check for leaks.

Piston and Ring

POSITIONING

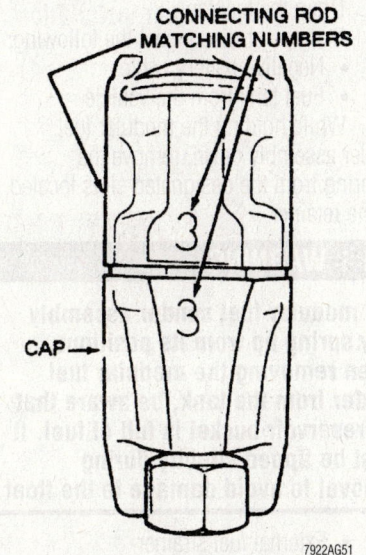

Connecting rod and cap installation. Be sure to matchmark the cap and rod prior to disassembly—2.2L and 2.4L engines

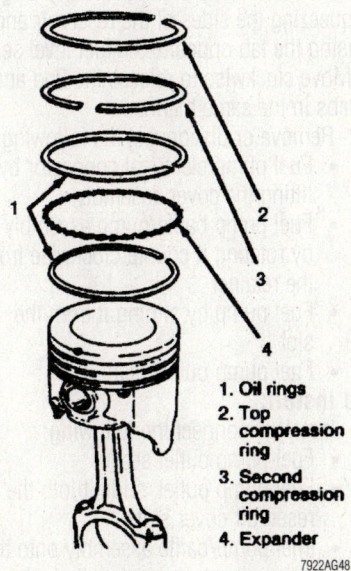

1. Oil rings
2. Top compression ring
3. Second compression ring
4. Expander

Piston ring positioning—2.2L engine

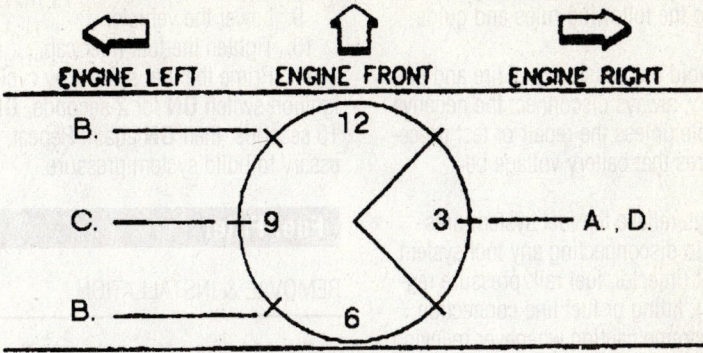

ENGINE LEFT   ENGINE FRONT   ENGINE RIGHT

A. OIL RING SPACER GAP (TANG IN HOLE OR SLOT WITH ARC)
B. OIL RING RAIL GAPS
C. 2ND COMPRESSION RING GAP
D. TOP COMPRESSION RING GAP

Piston ring end-gap spacing—2.2L engine

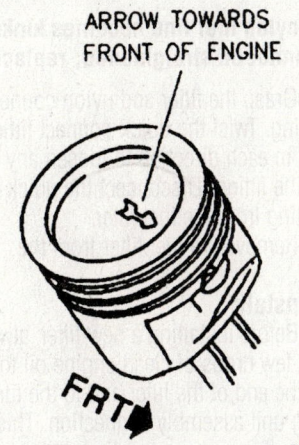

ARROW TOWARDS FRONT OF ENGINE

FRT

Piston positioning. Often the arrow is replaced by a notch, which also must face toward the front of the engine—2.2L engine

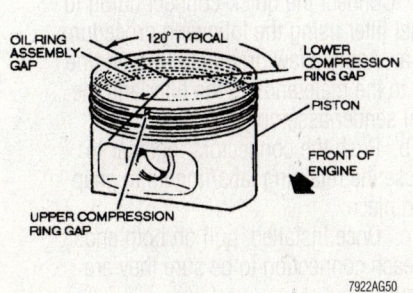

OIL RING ASSEMBLY GAP   120° TYPICAL   LOWER COMPRESSION RING GAP
PISTON
FRONT OF ENGINE
UPPER COMPRESSION RING GAP

Piston ring end-gap spacing—2.4L engine

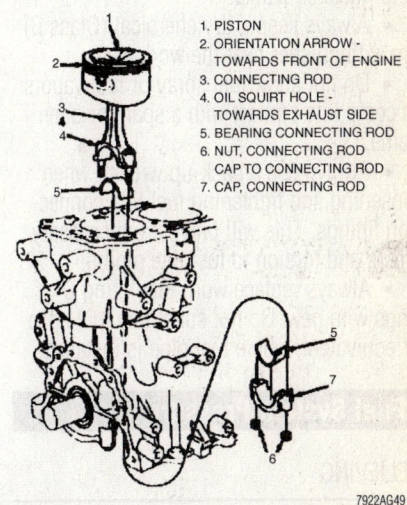

1. PISTON
2. ORIENTATION ARROW - TOWARDS FRONT OF ENGINE
3. CONNECTING ROD
4. OIL SQUIRT HOLE - TOWARDS EXHAUST SIDE
5. BEARING CONNECTING ROD
6. NUT, CONNECTING ROD CAP TO CONNECTING ROD
7. CAP, CONNECTING ROD

Piston and connecting rod assembly positioning—2.4L engine

FUEL SYSTEM

Fuel System Service Precautions

Safety is the most important factor when performing not only fuel system maintenance but any type of maintenance. Failure to conduct maintenance and repairs in a safe manner may result in serious personal injury or death. Maintenance and testing of the vehicle's fuel system components can be accomplished safely and effectively by adhering to the following rules and guidelines.

• To avoid the possibility of fire and personal injury, always disconnect the negative battery cable unless the repair or test procedure requires that battery voltage be applied.

• Always relieve the fuel system pressure prior to disconnecting any fuel system component (injector, fuel rail, pressure regulator, etc.), fitting or fuel line connection. Exercise extreme caution whenever relieving fuel system pressure, to avoid exposing skin, face and eyes to fuel spray. Please be advised that fuel under pressure may penetrate the skin or any part of the body that it contacts.

• Always place a shop towel or cloth around the fitting or connection prior to loosening to absorb any excess fuel due to spillage. Ensure that all fuel spillage (should it occur) is quickly removed from engine surfaces. Ensure that all fuel soaked cloths or towels are deposited into a suitable waste container.

• Always keep a dry chemical (Class B) fire extinguisher near the work area.

• Do not allow fuel spray or fuel vapors to come into contact with a spark or open flame.

• Always use a back-up wrench when loosening and tightening fuel line connection fittings. This will prevent unnecessary stress and torsion to fuel line piping.

• Always replace worn fuel fitting O-rings with new. Do not substitute fuel hose or equivalent, where fuel pipe is installed.

Fuel System Pressure

RELIEVING

1. Before servicing the vehicle, refer to the precautions in the beginning of this section.

2. Loosen the fuel filler cap in order to relieve the pressure in the tank (do not tighten at this time).

3. Raise and safely support the vehicle.

4. Detach the fuel pump electrical connector.

5. Start and run the vehicle until it stalls, the engage the starter for an additional 3 seconds to ensure the relief of any remaining pressure.

6. Disconnect the negative battery cable.

7. Once the tests or repairs are completed, reattach the fuel pump electrical connector.

8. Connect the negative battery cable.

9. Lower the vehicle.

10. Tighten the fuel filler cap.

11. Prime the fuel system by cycling the ignition switch **ON** for 2 seconds, **OFF** for 10 seconds, then **ON** again. Repeat, if necessary to build system pressure.

Fuel Filter

REMOVAL & INSTALLATION

The fuel filter is located under the rear of the vehicle, rearward of the fuel tank. Note that there is an additional filter/strainer inside the fuel tank attached to the fuel pump/sending unit assembly.

1. Before servicing the vehicle, refer to the precautions in the beginning of this section.

2. Relieve the fuel system pressure.

3. Remove or disconnect the following:
   • Negative battery cable
   • Fuel filter from the fuel line using a back-up wrench

➡ **If a nylon fuel line becomes kinked and cannot be straightened, replace it.**

4. Grasp the filter and nylon connection line fitting. Twist the quick-connect fitting ¼ turn in each direction to loosen any dirt within the fitting. Disconnect the quick-connect fitting from the fuel filter.

5. Remove the fuel filter from the bracket.

To install:

6. Before installing a new filter, always apply a few drops of clean engine oil to the male tube end of the filter and to the fuel sending unit assembly connection. This will help ensure proper connection and prevent possible fuel leaks. During normal operation, the O-rings located in the female connector will swell and may prevent proper connection if not lubricated.

7. Install the fuel filter in the mounting bracket.

8. Connect the quick-connect fitting to the fuel filter using the following procedure:
   a. Apply a few drops of clean engine oil to the male ends of the filter and the fuel sender assembly.
   b. Push the connectors together to cause the retaining tabs/fingers to snap into place.
   c. Once installed, pull on both ends of each connection to be sure they are secure.

9. Install or connect the following:
   • New O-ring
   • Fuel filter using a back-up wrench.

Torque the fitting to 20 ft. lbs. (27 Nm).
   • Negative battery cable

10. Pressurize the fuel system and verify no leaks.

Fuel Pump

REMOVAL & INSTALLATION

1. Before servicing the vehicle, refer to the precautions in the beginning of this section.

2. Relieve the fuel system pressure.

3. Drain the fuel tank.

4. Remove or disconnect the following:
   • Negative battery cable
   • Fuel tank from the vehicle

5. While holding the modular fuel sender assembly down, remove the snapring from the designated slots located on the retainer.

✳✳ WARNING

The modular fuel sender assembly may spring up from its position. When removing the modular fuel sender from the tank, be aware that the reservoir bucket is full of fuel. It must be tipped slightly during removal to avoid damage to the float.

   • External fuel strainer
   • Connector Position Assurance (CPA) piece from the fuel pump electrical connector

6. Gently release the tabs on the sides of the fuel sender at the cover assembly. Begin by squeezing the sides of the reservoir and releasing the tab opposite the fuel level sensor. Move clockwise to release the 2nd and 3rd tabs in the same manner.

7. Remove or disconnect the following:
   • Fuel pump electrical connector by lifting the cover assembly
   • Fuel pump baffle/pump assembly by rotating it counterclockwise from the retainer
   • Fuel pump by sliding it from the slot
   • Fuel pump outlet seal

To install:

8. Install or connect the following:
   • Fuel pump outlet seal
   • Fuel pump outlet, slide it into the reservoir cover slots
   • Fuel pump/baffle assembly onto the reservoir retainer; rotate it clockwise until seated
   • Lower retainer assembly partially into the reservoir; align the 3 tabs

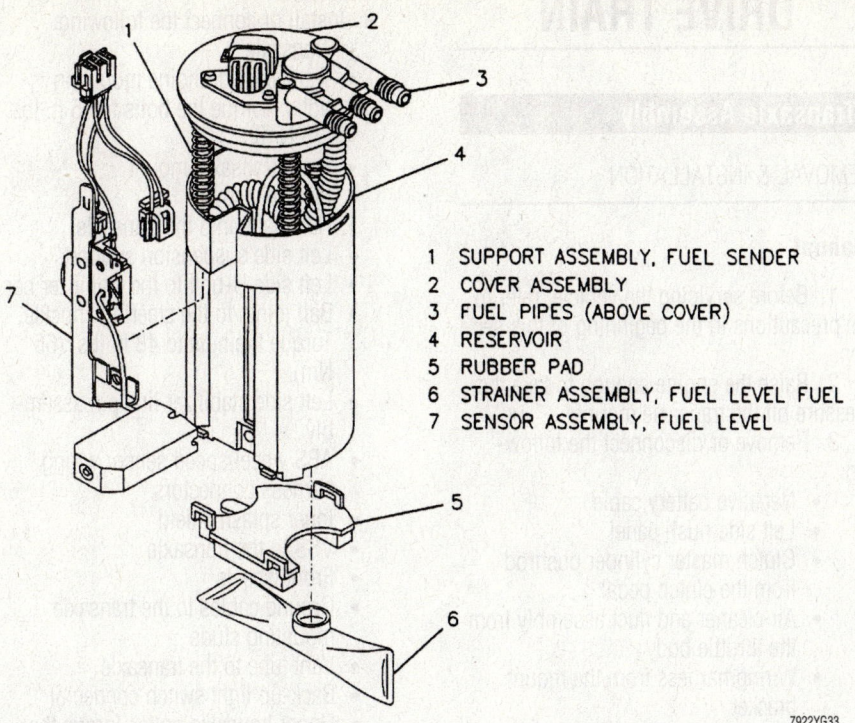

1 SUPPORT ASSEMBLY, FUEL SENDER
2 COVER ASSEMBLY
3 FUEL PIPES (ABOVE COVER)
4 RESERVOIR
5 RUBBER PAD
6 STRAINER ASSEMBLY, FUEL LEVEL FUEL
7 SENSOR ASSEMBLY, FUEL LEVEL

7922YG33

Modular fuel pump component identification

and press the retainer onto the reservoir making sure all 3 tabs are firmly seated

➡️**Gently, pull on the fuel pump reservoir to assure it is secure to the retainer. If not secure, replace the entire fuel sender.**

- Fuel pump connector
- CPA connector to the fuel sender cover
- New external fuel strainer
- Modular fuel sender
- Fuel tank in the vehicle
- Negative battery cable

9. Pressurize the fuel system and verify no leaks.

Fuel Injector

REMOVAL & INSTALLATION

2.2L Engine

1. Before servicing the vehicle, refer to the precautions in the beginning of this section.
2. Relieve the fuel system pressure.
3. Remove or disconnect the following:
   - Negative battery cable
   - Air cleaner resonator and bracket

- Fuel injector electrical connectors by pushing in the connector clip and pulling the connector away
- Fuel feed inlet pipe
- Fuel return pipe from the pressure regulator
- Fuel Rail
- Fuel injector-to-fuel rail retaining clip
- Fuel injector and discard the O-rings

To install:

4. Install or connect the following:
   - New O-rings, lubricated with engine oil

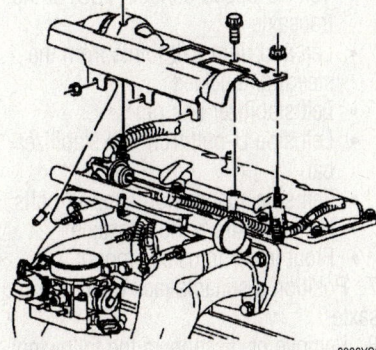

View of the fuel rail assembly—2.2L engine

9306YG03

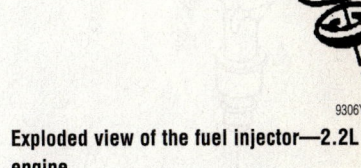

9306YG04

Exploded view of the fuel injector—2.2L engine

- Fuel injector(s) to the fuel rail
- Fuel injector-to-fuel rail retaining clip
- Fuel Rail. Torque the bolts to 18 ft. lbs. (24 Nm).
- Fuel return pipe to the pressure regulator. Torque the nut to 22 ft. lbs. (30 Nm).
- Fuel feed inlet pipe
- Fuel injector electrical connectors
- Air cleaner resonator and bracket
- Negative battery cable

5. Perform the following:
   a. Turn the ignition switch ON for 2 seconds.
   b. Turn the ignition switch OFF for 10 seconds.
   c. Turn the ignition switch ON.
   d. Inspect for fuel leaks.

2.4L Engine

1. Before servicing the vehicle, refer to the precautions in the beginning of this section.
2. Relieve the fuel system pressure.
3. Remove or disconnect the following:
   - Negative battery cable
   - Fuel injector electrical connectors
   - Fuel line from the fuel pressure regulator
   - Fuel rail
   - Fuel pressure regulator screw

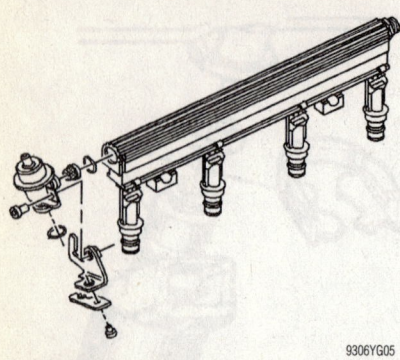

Exploded view of the fuel rail assembly—2.4L engine

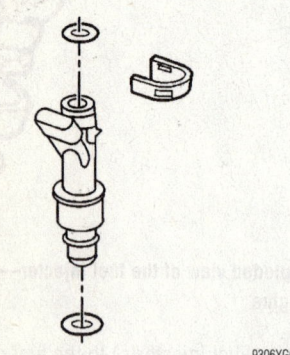

Exploded view of the fuel injector—2.4L engine

- Fuel pressure regulator from the fuel rail, twist it back and forth
- Fuel injector-to-fuel rail retaining clip
- Fuel injector and discard the O-rings

To install:

4. Install or connect the following:
- New fuel injector O-rings, lubricated with engine oil
- Fuel injector(s) to the fuel rail
- Fuel injector-to-fuel rail retaining clip
- New fuel pressure regulator O-ring, lubricated with engine oil
- Fuel pressure regulator to the fuel rail. Torque the screw to 97 inch lbs. (11 Nm).
- Fuel rail
- Fuel line to the fuel pressure regulator
- Fuel injector electrical connectors
- Negative battery cable

5. Perform the following:
  a. Turn the ignition switch ON for 2 seconds.
  b. Turn the ignition switch OFF for 10 seconds.
  c. Turn the ignition switch ON.
  d. Inspect for fuel leaks.

DRIVE TRAIN

Transaxle Assembly

REMOVAL & INSTALLATION

Manual

1. Before servicing the vehicle, refer to the precautions in the beginning of this section.

2. Raise the engine enough to take the pressure off the transaxle mounts.

3. Remove or disconnect the following:
- Negative battery cable
- Left side hush panel
- Clutch master cylinder pushrod from the clutch pedal
- Air cleaner and duct assembly from the throttle body
- Wiring harness from the mount bracket
- Upper transaxle mount-to-transaxle bolts
- Clutch master cylinder from the clutch actuator
- Ground cables from the transaxle mounting studs
- Back-up light switch connector
- Transaxle vent tube
- Rear transaxle-to-engine bolts

4. Lower the engine support fixture enough to ease removal of the transaxle.

5. Drain the transaxle.

6. Remove or disconnect the following:
- Front wheels
- Left side splash shield
- Both front Anti-lock Brake System (ABS) wheel speed sensor harness and move it aside
- Flywheel cover
- Vehicle Speed Sensor (VSS) at the transaxle
- Left and right ball joints from the steering knuckles
- Left stabilizer link pin
- Left side U-bolt from the stabilizer bar
- Left side suspension support bolts
- Halfshafts from the transaxle
- Front lower transaxle mount

7. Position a suitable jack under the transaxle.

8. Remove or disconnect the following:
- Transaxle-to-engine mounting bolts (noting their location)
- Transaxle from the engine by lowering the jack

To install:

9. Install or connect the following:
- Transaxle
- Transaxle-to-engine mounting bolts. Torque the bolts to 55 ft. lbs. (75 Nm).
- Front transaxle mount
- Flywheel cover
- Halfshafts into the transaxle
- Left side suspension support
- Left side U-bolt to the stabilizer bar
- Ball joints to the steering knuckle. Torque the nuts to 48 ft. lbs. (65 Nm).
- Left side stabilizer link pin assembly
- ABS wheel speed sensor wiring harness connectors
- Inner splash shield
- VSS to the transaxle
- Front wheels
- Ground cables to the transaxle mounting studs
- Vent tube to the transaxle
- Back-up light switch connector
- Upper transaxle bolts. Torque the bolts to 55 ft. lbs. (75 Nm).
- Clutch master cylinder to clutch actuator cylinder
- Rear transaxle mount. Torque the bolts to 55 ft. lbs. (75 Nm).
- Wiring harness to the mount bracket

10. Remove the engine support fixture.

11. Install or connect the following:
- Shift cables clamp. Torque the nut to 89 inch lbs. (10 Nm).
- Air cleaner and duct assembly to the throttle body
- Pushrod to the clutch pedal
- Left side hush panel
- Negative battery cable

12. Refill the transaxle.

13. Road test the vehicle and verify proper operation.

Automatic

1. Before servicing the vehicle, refer to the precautions in the beginning of this section.

2. Remove or disconnect the following:
- Negative battery cable
- Air intake duct
- Throttle Valve (TV) cable, shift cable and bracket
- Vacuum lines
- All necessary electrical connectors
- Power steering pump and move it aside with the hoses attached
- Filler tube

3. Attach an engine support fixture.

4. Remove or disconnect the following:
• Upper engine-to-transaxle bolts
• Front wheels
• Left side splash shield
• Both front Anti-lock Brake System (ABS) wheel speed sensors and harness from left suspension support
• Both lower ball joints
• Stabilizer shaft links
• Front air deflector
• Left suspension support
• Both halfshafts
• Engine-to-transaxle brace
• Torque converter cover
• Starter
• Torque converter bolts
• Transaxle oil cooler lines and brace
• Ground wires from the transaxle
• Exhaust brace
• Engine and transaxle mount bolts

5. Support transaxle with a jack
6. Remove or disconnect the following:
• Transaxle mount-to-body bolts
• Heater core hose brace from transaxle
• Engine-to-transaxle bolts
• Transaxle

To install:
7. Be sure to properly seat the torque converter in the oil pump.
8. Install or connect the following:
• Transaxle while installing right half-shaft
• Lower engine-to-transaxle bolts. Torque the bolts to 71 ft. lbs. (96 Nm).
• Transaxle mount-to-body bolts
• Engine and transaxle mount bolts
• Exhaust brace
• Oil cooler line brace
• Ground wires to transaxle bolt
• Oil cooler lines
• Torque converter. Torque the bolts to 46 ft. lbs. (62 Nm).
• Transaxle converter cover
• Starter
• Engine-to-transaxle brace. Torque the bolts to 32 ft. lbs. (43 Nm).
• Halfshafts
• Left suspension support
• Front air deflector
• Stabilizer links
• Lower ball joints
• Both ABS wheel speed sensors
• Left splash shield
• Heater core pipe brace nut and bolt
• Front wheels
• Upper engine-to-transaxle bolts.

Torque the bolts to 71 ft. lbs. (96 Nm).
9. Remove the engine support fixture.
10. Install or connect the following:
• Filler tube
• Power steering pump assembly
• Electrical connectors
• Vacuum lines
• Shift cable and bracket
• TV cable and adjust, as necessary
• Intake air duct
• Negative battery cable

11. Refill transaxle, start the vehicle and verify that there are no leaks.
12. Road test the vehicle.

Clutch

REMOVAL & INSTALLATION

The manual transaxle assembly must be removed from the vehicle to service the clutch assembly.

➡️**Prior to any vehicle service that requires the removal of the actuator cylinder, the master cylinder pushrod must be disconnected from the clutch pedal. If not disconnected, permanent damage to the actuator cylinder will occur if the clutch pedal is depressed while the actuator cylinder is disconnected.**

1. Before servicing the vehicle, refer to the precautions in the beginning of this section.
2. Remove or disconnect the following:
• Negative battery cable
• Clutch master cylinder pushrod from the clutch pedal
• Transaxle

3. If any of the parts are to be reused, mark the pressure plate assembly and the flywheel so they can be assembled in the

same position; they are balanced as an assembly.
4. Loosen the attaching bolts 1 turn at a time until spring tension is relieved.
5. Support the pressure plate and remove the bolts. Remove the pressure plate and clutch disc. Do not disassemble the pressure plate assembly. Replace it if defective.
6. Inspect the flywheel, clutch disc, pressure plate, throwout bearing and the clutch fork and pivot shaft assembly for wear. Replace the parts as required. If the flywheel shows any signs of overheating or if it is badly grooved or scored, it should be resurfaced or replaced.
7. Clean the pressure plate and flywheel mating surfaces thoroughly.

To install:
8. Clean all parts. Apply a small amount of high temperature grease to the pilot bearing inside the end of the crankshaft.
9. Install or connect the following:
• Clutch disc, support it with a clutch aligning tool
• Pressure plate

➡️**The clutch plate is assembled with the damper springs offset toward the transaxle. One side of the factory supplied clutch disc should be stamped "Flywheel Side".**

10. Torque the pressure plate-to-flywheel bolts, gradually, in a cross pattern, as follows:
a. Step 1: Lightly seat all bolts.
b. Step 2: Bolts 1, 2, 3: 12 ft. lbs. (16 Nm).
c. Step 3: Bolts 4, 5, 6: 12 ft. lbs. (16 Nm).
d. Step 4: Bolts 1, 2, 3: 15 ft. lbs. (20 Nm).
e. Step 5: Bolts 4, 5, 6: 15 ft. lbs. (20 Nm).

11. Lubricate the outside groove and the inside recess of the release bearing with high temperature grease. Wipe off any excess. Install the release bearing.
a. On the M86/M94 Getrag transaxle, lubricate the inside diameter of the bearing with clutch bearing lubricant.
b. On the Isuzu transaxle, pack the inside recess of the release bearing completely full of chassis grease.

➡️**On the Isuzu transaxle, be sure the bearing pads are located on the fork ends and both spring ends are in the fork holes with the spring completely seated in bearing groove.**

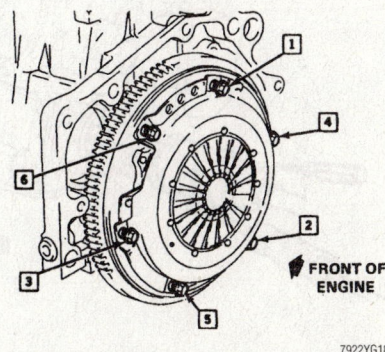

7922YG18

Clutch cover bolt tightening sequence

12. Install or connect the following:
- Transaxle
- Clutch master cylinder pushrod to the clutch pedal and secure with the retaining clip
- Cruise control switch adjustment at clutch pedal bracket, if equipped
- Negative battery cable

✴✴ WARNING

When adjusting the cruise control switch, do not exert an upward force on the clutch pedal pad of more than 20 ft. lbs. (27 Nm) or damage to the master cylinder pushrod retaining ring can result.

13. Bleed clutch system as necessary and road test vehicle.

Hydraulic Clutch System

BLEEDING

1. Before servicing the vehicle, refer to the precautions in the beginning of this section.
2. Attach a hose to the bleeder screw on the clutch actuator assembly and submerge the other end of the hose in a container of hydraulic clutch fluid.
3. Depress the clutch pedal slowly and hold.
4. Loosen the bleeder screw to purge air.
5. Tighten the bleeder screw to 18 inch lbs. (2 Nm).
6. Release the clutch pedal.
7. Repeat Steps 3 through 6 until all air is purged from the system.
8. Refill the reservoir to the top step with hydraulic clutch fluid.
9. Repeat this bleeding procedure if there is a grinding noise during the clutch spin down procedure.

Halfshaft

REMOVAL & INSTALLATION

Some manual transaxle applications may also use an intermediate shaft.

1. Before servicing the vehicle, refer to the precautions in the beginning of this section.
2. Remove or disconnect the following:
- Negative battery cable
- Front hub nut, loosen it
- Front wheel
- Hub nut and washer

3. Install an axle boot seal protector on the right-hand inner boot, if equipped.
4. Remove or disconnect the following:
- Brake caliper and support it on a wire
- Brake rotor
- Lower ball joint, loosen it and discard the cotter pin

5. If removing the right halfshaft, turn the wheel to the left; if removing the left halfshaft, turn the wheel to the right.
6. Remove or disconnect the following:
- Anti-lock Brake System (ABS) sensor, if equipped
- Stabilizer bar link
- Lower ball joint and separate it from the steering knuckle
- Halfshaft, press it from wheel bearing/hub assembly
- Halfshaft from the transaxle

✴✴ WARNING

Do not pull the halfshaft by the CV-joint boot or on the joint itself.

To install:

7. Cover all sharp edges in the area of the halfshaft with shop towels so the CV-joint boots will be protected from damage. When a halfshaft is removed for any reason, the transaxle (the halfshaft male and female shank) and knuckle sealing surfaces should be inspected for debris and corrosion. If debris or corrosion are present, clean with 320 grit crocus cloth or equivalent. Transmission fluid may be used to clean off any remaining debris. The surface should be wiped clean and dry before attempting to install the halfshaft.

8. Install the halfshaft into the transaxle (or intermediate shaft, if equipped) by placing a brass drift pin into the groove on the joint housing and tapping until seated. Be careful not to damage the axle seal or dislodge the seal garter spring when installing the axle.

➡ **Be sure the halfshaft is fully engaged in the transaxle. Verify that the halfshaft is seated by grasping the inner joint housing and pulling outward. Do not pull on the shaft or the boot, but on the inner joint housing only.**

9. Install or connect the following:
- Halfshaft into the hub/bearing assembly
- Lower ball joint to the steering knuckle. Torque the nut to 41–48 ft. lbs. (55–65 Nm).
- New cotter pin
- Washer and a new hub nut. Torque the nut to 185 ft. lbs. (260 Nm).

➡ **To keep the hub from turning while the hub nut is being torqued, insert a drift pin through the caliper opening into one of the ventilation openings in the brake rotor.**

- Front wheel
- Negative battery cable

10. Test drive vehicle to verify no front drive noise.

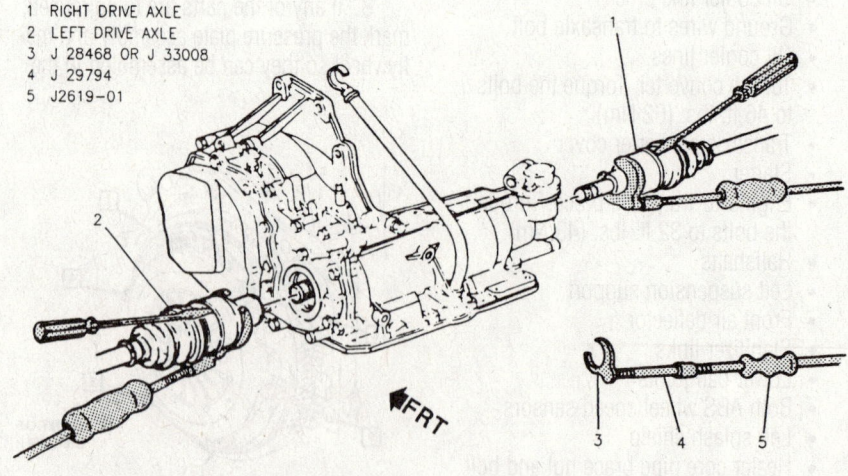

1 RIGHT DRIVE AXLE
2 LEFT DRIVE AXLE
3 J 28468 OR J 33008
4 J 29794
5 J2619-01

To prevent damaging the transaxle or halfshaft, use the tools as shown to remove the halfshafts

7922YG34

CV-Joints

OVERHAUL

Outer CV-Joint

1997 2.4L ENGINE WITH AUTOMATIC TRANSAXLE

1. Before servicing the vehicle, refer to the precautions in the beginning of this section.

2. Remove or disconnect the following:
   - Front wheel
   - Halfshaft, position it in a vise
   - Large CV-joint boot clamp and discard it
   - Small CV-joint boot clamp and discard it
   - CV-joint boot and slide it back on the shaft
   - Outer race from the halfshaft, by spreading the outer race-to-halfshaft retaining ring, using Snapring Pliers J-8059
   - Retaining ring from the halfshaft and discard it
   - CV-joint boot from the halfshaft and discard it if damaged

3. Disassemble the chrome alloy balls from the CV-joint cage as follows:

   a. Position a brass drift against the CV-joint cage and tap it with a hammer to tilt the cage.

   b. Remove the 1st chrome alloy ball from the cage.

   c. Tilt the cage in the opposite direction.

   d. Remove the opposite chrome alloy ball.

   e. Repeat the procedure until all 6 balls are removed.

4. Disassemble the CV-joint cage and inner race as follows:

   a. Pivot the cage and race 90 degrees to the center line of the outer race.

   b. Align the cage windows with outer race lands.

   c. Remove the cage from the outer race.

   d. Rotate the inner race upward and remove it from the cage.

5. Throughly clean and inspect all parts.

   To install:

6. Lubricate the parts with a light coat of grease.

7. Assemble the CV-joint cage and inner race, as follows:

2 - HOUSING ASM, RETAINER &
3 - RING, SHAFT RETAINING
4 - SPIDER ASM, TRIPOT JOINT
9 - RING, SPACER
10 - CLAMP, SEAL RETAINING
11 - BUSHING, TRILOBAL TRIPOT
12 - SEAL, DRIVE AXLE INBOARD
13 - CLAMP, SEAL RETAINING
14 - SHAFT, AXLE (RH SHOWN, LH SIMILAR)
15 - SEAL, DRIVE AXLE OUTBOARD
16 - CLAMP, SEAL RETAINING
17 - RING, RACE RETAINING
18 - BALL, CHROME ALLOY
19 - RACE, C/V JOINT INNER
20 - CAGE, C/V JOINT
21 - RACE, C/V JOINT OUTER

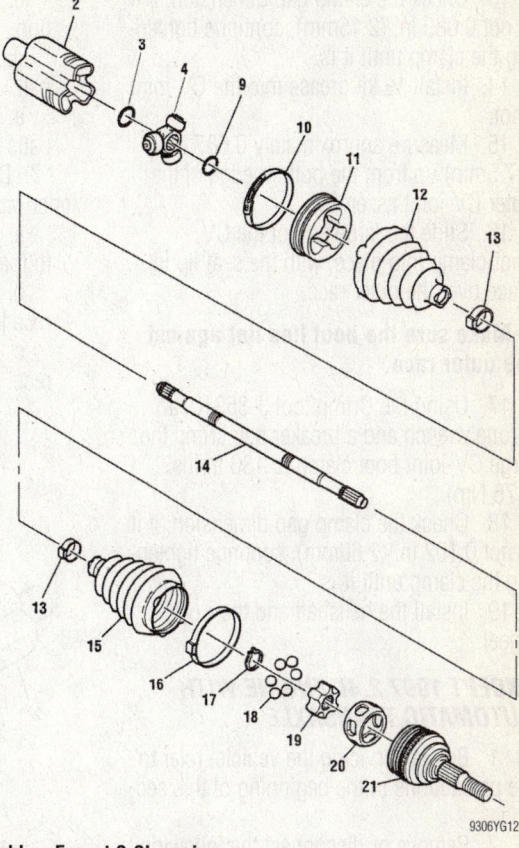

Exploded view of the halfshaft assembly—Except 2.2L engine

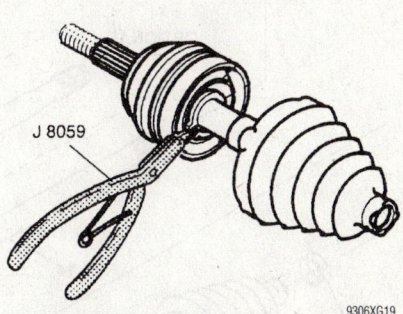

Disconnecting the outer CV-joint from the axle shaft—1997 2.4L engine with automatic transaxle

   a. Rotate the inner race 90 degrees to the cage centerline.

   b. Align the cage windows with inner race lands.

   c. Insert the inner race into the cage by rotating the inner race downward.

   d. Insert the cage/inner race into the outer race.

8. Assemble the chrome alloy balls into the CV-joint cage, as follows:

   a. Position a brass drift against the CV-joint cage and tap it with a hammer to tilt the cage.

   b. Insert the 1st chrome alloy ball into the cage.

   c. Tilt the cage in the opposite direction.

   d. Insert the opposite chrome alloy ball.

   e. Repeat the procedure until all 6 balls are inserted.

9. Install ½ of the kit grease into the CV-joint.

10. Install or connect the following:
    - Small ring clamp on the CV boot
    - New retaining ring on the halfshaft
    - Large ring clamp on the CV boot
    - Outer race assembly onto the halfshaft until the ring engages the halfshaft groove

11. Slide the small end of the CV-joint boot/clamp into place, with the seal lip in the halfshaft groove

➡**Make sure the boot lies flat against the halfshaft.**

12. Using the Crimp tool J-35910, a torque wrench and a breaker bar, crimp the small CV-joint boot clamp to 100 ft. lbs. (136 Nm).

13. Check the clamp gap dimension; if it is not 0.085 in. (2.15mm), continue tightening the clamp until it is.

14. Install ½ kit grease into the CV-joint boot.

15. Measure approximately 0.687 in. (17.5mm) up from the bottom edge of the outer CV-joint assembly.

16. Slide the large end of the CV boot/clamp into place, with the seal lip in place over the outer race.

➡ **Make sure the boot lies flat against the outer race.**

17. Using the Crimp tool J-35910, a torque wrench and a breaker bar, crimp the large CV-joint boot clamp to 130 ft. lbs. (176 Nm).

18. Check the clamp gap dimension; if it is not 0.102 in. (2.60mm), continue tightening the clamp until it is.

19. Install the halfshaft and the front wheel.

EXCEPT 1997 2.4L ENGINE WITH AUTOMATIC TRANSAXLE

1. Before servicing the vehicle, refer to the precautions in the beginning of this section.

2. Remove or disconnect the following:
- Front wheel
- Halfshaft and position it in a vise
- Large CV-joint boot clamp and discard it
- Small CV-joint boot clamp and discard it
- CV-joint boot and slide it back on the shaft

3. Perform the following:
   a. Choose a reference mark on the halfshaft.
   b. Measure the distance between the reference mark and the CV-joint inner race face; retain this measurement.

4. Attach CV Puller tool J-41398 to the outer race threaded area.

5. Remove or disconnect the following:
- CV-joint outer race from the halfshaft using a slide hammer puller
- CV Puller tool J-41398 and slide hammer puller from the outer race
- Retaining ring from the halfshaft and discard it
- CV-joint boot from the halfshaft and discard it if damaged

6. Disassemble the chrome alloy balls from the CV-joint cage as follows:
   a. Position a brass drift against the CV-joint cage and tap it with a hammer to tilt the cage.
   b. Remove the 1st chrome alloy ball from the cage.

c. Tilt the cage in the opposite direction.

d. Remove the opposite chrome alloy ball.

e. Repeat the procedure until all 6 balls are removed.

7. Disassemble the CV-joint cage and inner race as follows:
   a. Pivot the cage and race 90 degrees to the center line of the outer race.
   b. Align the cage windows with outer race lands.
   c. Remove the cage from the outer race.

d. Rotate the inner race upward and remove it from the cage.

8. Throughly clean and inspect all parts.

To install:

9. Lubricate the parts with a light coat of grease.

10. Assemble the CV-joint cage and inner race, as follows:
   a. Rotate the inner race 90 degrees to the cage centerline.
   b. Align the cage windows with inner race lands.
   c. Insert the inner race into the cage by rotating the inner race downward.

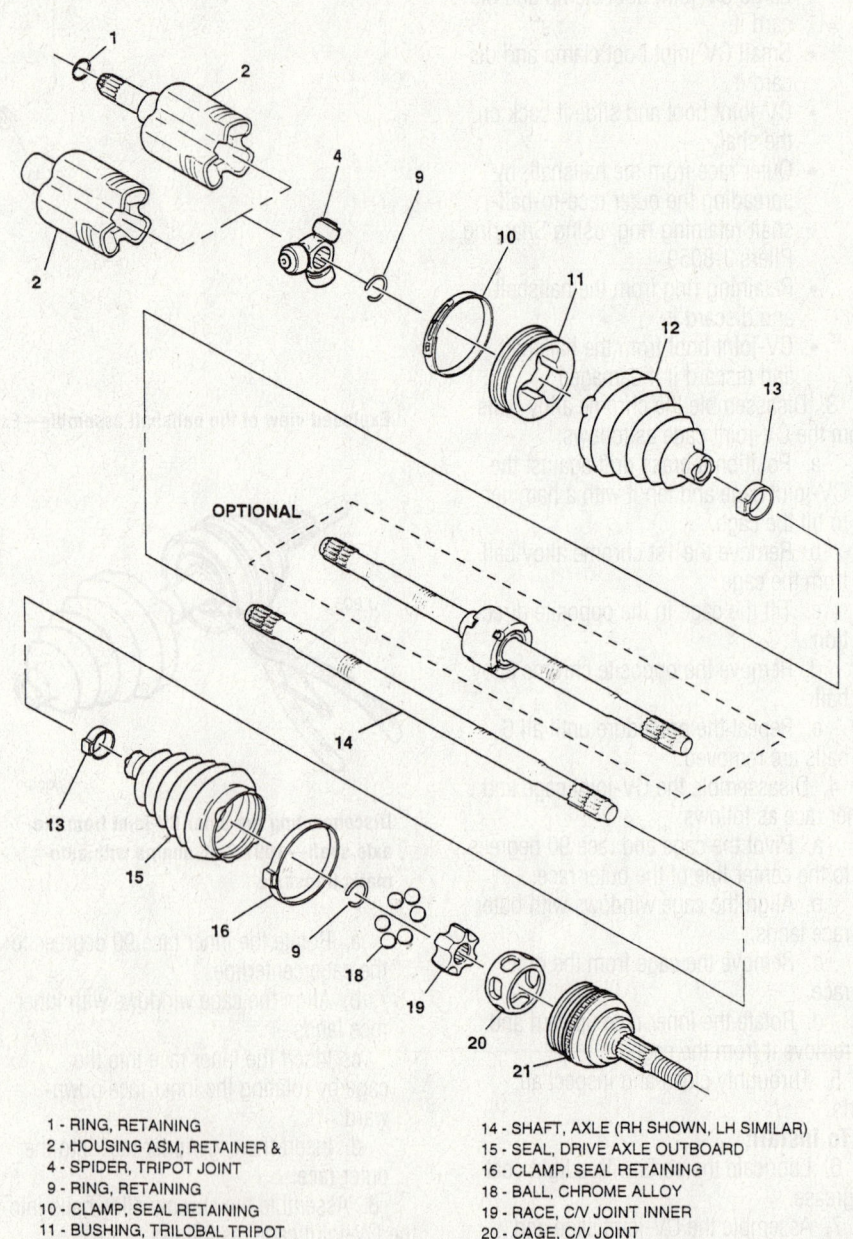

OPTIONAL

1 - RING, RETAINING
2 - HOUSING ASM, RETAINER &
4 - SPIDER, TRIPOT JOINT
9 - RING, RETAINING
10 - CLAMP, SEAL RETAINING
11 - BUSHING, TRILOBAL TRIPOT
12 - SEAL, DRIVE AXLE INBOARD
13 - CLAMP, SEAL RETAINING

14 - SHAFT, AXLE (RH SHOWN, LH SIMILAR)
15 - SEAL, DRIVE AXLE OUTBOARD
16 - CLAMP, SEAL RETAINING
18 - BALL, CHROME ALLOY
19 - RACE, C/V JOINT INNER
20 - CAGE, C/V JOINT
21 - RACE, C/V JOINT OUTER

Exploded view of the halfshaft assembly—1997 2.2L engine

9306YG13

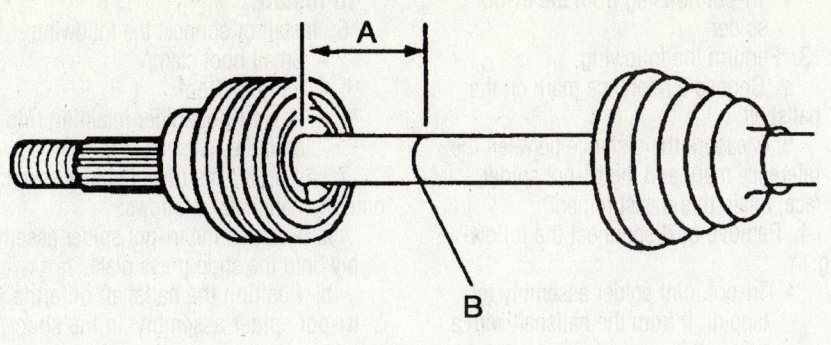

Measuring the halfshaft-to-inner race reference distance—Outer CV-joint—Except 1997 2.4L engine with automatic transaxle

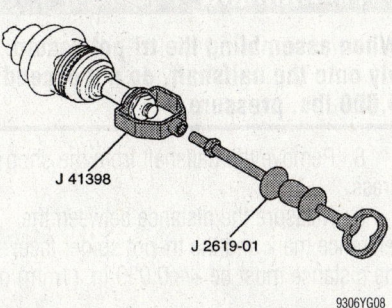

Removing the outer race from the halfshaft—Outer CV-joint—Except 1997 2.4L engine with automatic transaxle

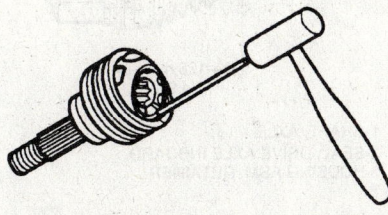

Tilting the cage—Outer CV-joint

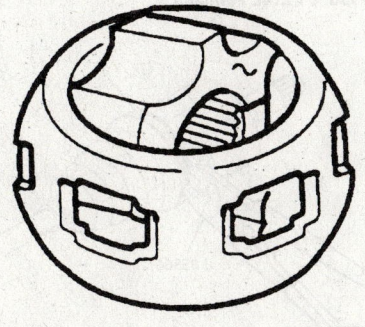

View the cage and inner race—Outer CV-joint

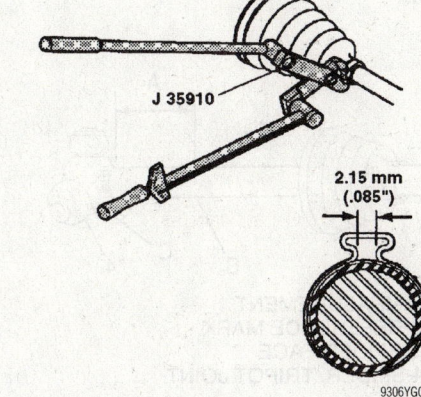

Crimping the small boot clamp—Outer CV-joint

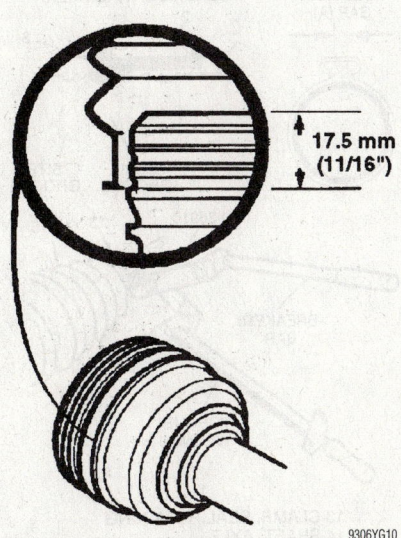

Positioning the CV boot onto the outer race—Outer CV-joint

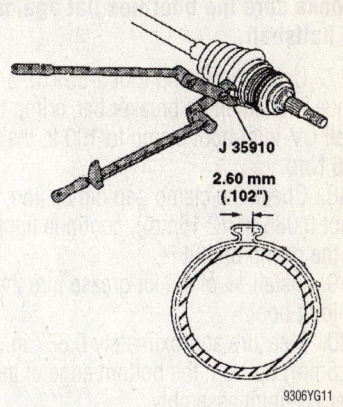

Crimping the large boot clamp—Outer CV-joint

   d. Insert the cage/inner race into the outer race.

11. Assemble the chrome alloy balls into the CV-joint cage, as follows:

   a. Position a brass drift against the CV-joint cage and tap it with a hammer to tilt the cage.

   b. Insert the 1st chrome alloy ball into the cage.

   c. Tilt the cage in the opposite direction.

   d. Insert the opposite chrome alloy ball.

   e. Repeat the procedure until all 6 balls are inserted.

12. Install ½ of the kit grease into the CV-joint.

13. Install or connect the following:
- Small ring clamp on the CV boot
- CV-joint boot and slide it up the shaft to expose the reference mark
- New retaining ring on the halfshaft
- Large ring clamp on the CV boot
- Outer race assembly by pressing it onto the halfshaft until the ring engages, using a shop press

❄❄ WARNING

When installing the outer race assembly onto the halfshaft, do not exceed 4,000 lbs. pressure.

14. Remove the halfshaft from the shop press.

15. Measure the distance between the reference mark and the CV-joint inner race face; the distance must be +/- 0.039 in. (1mm) of the original measurement. If the measurement is not correct, repress the outer race assembly and recheck it.

16. Slide the small end of the CV-joint boot/clamp into place, with the seal lip in the halfshaft groove

Turn to Section 5 for brake system applications

➡**Make sure the boot lies flat against the halfshaft.**

17. Using the Crimp tool J-35910, a torque wrench and a breaker bar, crimp the small CV-joint boot clamp to 100 ft. lbs. (136 Nm).

18. Check the clamp gap dimension; if it is not 0.085 in. (2.15mm), continue tightening the clamp until it is.

19. Install ½ of the kit grease into the CV-joint boot.

20. Measure approximately 0.687 in. (17.5mm) up from the bottom edge of the outer CV-joint assembly.

21. Slide the large end of the CV boot/clamp into place, with the seal lip in place over the outer race.

➡**Make sure the boot lies flat against the outer race.**

22. Using the Crimp tool J-35910, a torque wrench and a breaker bar, crimp the large CV-joint boot clamp to 130 ft. lbs. (176 Nm).

23. Check the clamp gap dimension; if it is not 0.102 in. (2.60mm), continue tightening the clamp until it is.

24. Install the halfshaft and the front wheel.

Inner (Tri-Pot) Joint

1997 2.2L ENGINE

1. Before servicing the vehicle, refer to the precautions in the beginning of this section.

2. Remove or disconnect the following:
- Front wheel
- Halfshaft and place it in a vise
- Small CV-joint boot clamp, cut and discard it
- Large CV-joint boot clamp, cut and discard it
- CV-joint boot by sliding it away from the tri-pot joint

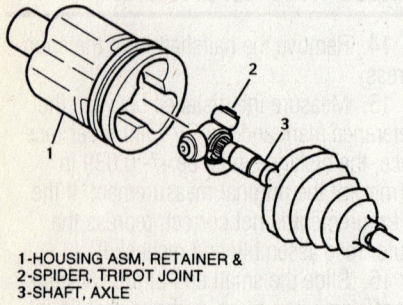

1-HOUSING ASM, RETAINER &
2-SPIDER, TRIPOT JOINT
3-SHAFT, AXLE

9306YG14

Exploded view of the inner (tri-pot) joint— 1997 2.2L engine

- Tri-pot housing from the tri-pot spider

3. Perform the following:
  a. Choose a reference mark on the halfshaft.
  b. Measure the distance between the reference mark and the tri-pot spider face; retain this measurement.

4. Remove or disconnect the following:
- Tri-pot joint spider assembly by tapping it from the halfshaft with a brass drift
- Tri-pot spider retaining ring and discard it
- Trilobal tri-pot bushing from the housing
- CV-joint boot

5. Throughly clean and inspect all parts.

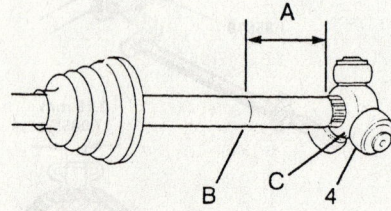

A-MEASUREMENT
B-REFERENCE MARK
C-SPIDER FACE
4-SPIDER, TRIPOT JOINT

9306YG15

View of the reference mark—Inner (tri-pot) joint—1997 2.2L engine

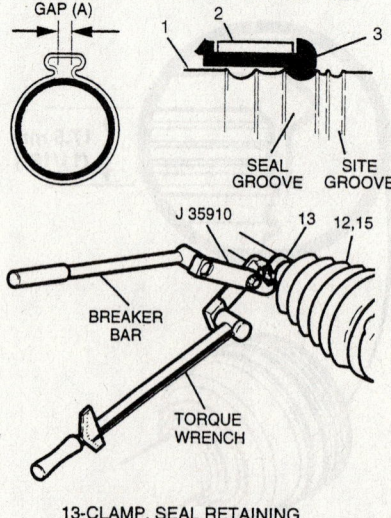

1-SHAFT, AXLE
13-CLAMP, SEAL RETAINING
14-SHAFT, AXLE
12,15-SEAL, DRIVE AXLE OUTBOARD

9306YG16

Crimping the small CV-joint boot ring— Inner (tri-pot) joint

To install:

6. Install or connect the following:
- Small boot clamp
- CV-joint boot
- New tri-pot spider retaining ring onto the halfshaft

7. Assemble the tri-pot spider assembly onto the halfshaft as follows:
  a. Position the tri-pot spider assembly onto the shop press plate.
  b. Position the halfshaft onto the tri-pot spider assembly, in the shop press.
  c. Press the halfshaft into the tri-pot spider assembly until the ring engages the spider

✳✳ WARNING

When assembling the tri-pot assembly onto the halfshaft, do not exceed 4,000 lbs. pressure.

8. Remove the halfshaft from the shop press.

9. Measure the distance between the reference mark and the tri-pot spider face; the distance must be +/- 0.039 in. (1mm) of

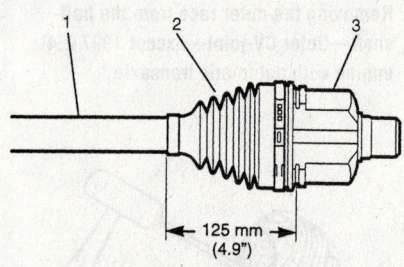

1-SHAFT, AXLE
2-SEAL, DRIVE AXLE INBOARD
3-HOUSING ASM, RETAINER

9306YG17

CV-joint boot measurement—Inner (tri-pot) joint—1997 2.2L engine, 1997 2.4L engine with automatic transaxle and all 1998–01 2.4L vehicles

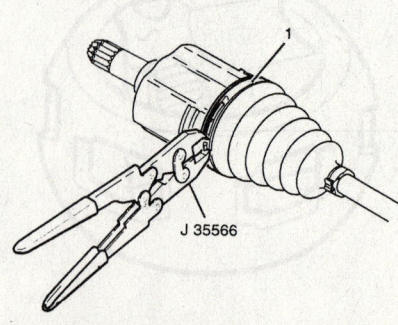

1-CLAMP, SEAL RETAINING

9306YG18

Latching the large CV-joint boot ring— Inner (tri-pot) joint

the original measurement. If the measurement is not correct, repress the outer race assembly and recheck it.

10. Install or connect the following:
- ½ of the kit grease into the boot
- ½ kit grease into the tri-pot housing
- Trilobal tip-pot bushing flush with the tri-pot housing face
- New large seal clamp onto the CV-joint boot
- Tri-pot housing, slide it over the tri-pot joint spider assembly
- CV-joint boot/clamp, slide it into place, over the trilobal tri-pot bushing with the seal lip in the groove

➡ **Make sure the boot lies flat against the trilobal bushing.**

11. Position the CV-joint boot so it measures 4.9 in. (125mm).

12. Using the Crimp tool J-35910, a torque wrench and a breaker bar, crimp the small CV-joint boot clamp to 100 ft. lbs. (136 Nm).

13. Using the Crimp tool J-35566, latch the large CV-joint boot clamp.

14. Install the halfshaft and the front wheel.

1998–01 2.2L ENGINE

1. Before servicing the vehicle, refer to the precautions in the beginning of this section.

2. Remove or disconnect the following:
- Front wheel
- Halfshaft and place it in a vise
- Small CV-joint boot clamp, cut and discard it
- Large CV-joint boot clamp, cut and discard it
- CV-joint boot by sliding it away from the tri-pot joint
- Tri-pot housing from the tri-pot spider
- Inboard spacer ring slide it rearward on the shaft using Snapring Pliers tool J-8059

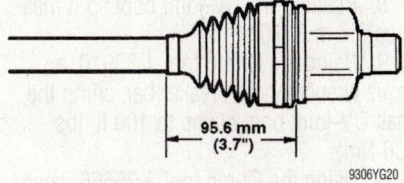

95.6 mm (3.7")

9306YG20

CV-joint boot measurement—Inner (tri-pot) joint—1998–01 2.2L engine

- Outboard retaining ring using Snapring Pliers tool J-8059 and discard it
- Tri-pot joint spider assembly
- Inboard spacer ring and discard it
- Tri-pot joint spider assembly by tapping it from the halfshaft with a brass drift
- Tri-pot spider retaining ring and discard it
- Trilobal tri-pot bushing from the housing
- CV-joint boot

3. Throughly clean and inspect all parts.

To install:

4. Install or connect the following:
- Small boot clamp
- CV-joint boot
- New inboard spacer ring slide it rearward on the shaft using Snapring Pliers tool J-8039-A, past the 2nd groove
- Tri-pot joint spider assembly onto the shaft until it passes the 2nd groove

5. Assemble the tri-pot spider assembly onto the halfshaft as follows:

a. Position the tri-pot spider assembly onto the shop press plate.

b. Position the halfshaft onto the tri-pot spider assembly, in the shop press.

c. Press the halfshaft into the tri-pot spider assembly until the spider assembly passes the 2nd groove.

✳✳ WARNING

When assembling the tri-pot assembly onto the halfshaft, do not exceed 4,000 lbs. pressure.

6. Remove the halfshaft from the shop press and place it in vise.

7. Install or connect the following:
- New outboard retaining ring into the axle shaft groove using Snapring Pliers tool J-8039-A
- Tri-pot joint spider assembly, slide it against the outboard retaining ring using a brass drift
- Inboard spacer ring, seat it in the groove
- ½ of the kit grease into the boot
- ½ of the kit grease into the tri-pot housing
- Trilobal tip-pot bushing flush with the tri-pot housing face
- New large seal clamp onto the CV-joint boot
- Tri-pot housing, slide it over the tri-pot joint spider assembly
- CV-joint boot/clamp, slide it into place, over the trilobal tri-pot bushing with the seal lip in the groove

➡ **Make sure the boot lies flat against the trilobal bushing.**

8. Position the CV-joint boot so it measures 4.9 in. (125mm) for 1998–99 or 3.7 in. (95.7) for 2000–01.

9. Using the Crimp tool J-35910, a torque wrench and a breaker bar, crimp the small CV-joint boot clamp to 100 ft. lbs. (136 Nm).

10. Using the Crimp tool J-35566, latch the large CV-joint boot clamp.

11. Install the halfshaft and the front wheel.

1997 2.4L ENGINE WITH AUTOMATIC TRANSAXLE

1998–01 2.4L ENGINES

1. Before servicing the vehicle, refer to the precautions in the beginning of this section.

2. Remove or disconnect the following:
- Front wheel
- Halfshaft and place it in a vise
- Snapring from the stub shaft and discard it
- Small CV-joint boot clamp, cut and discard it
- Large CV-joint boot clamp, cut and discard it
- CV-joint boot by sliding it away from the tri-pot joint

3. Install a Stub Shaft Removal tool J-38868-A to the stub shaft snapring groove.

4. Using a slide hammer puller, press the stub shaft from the tri-pot housing.

5. Remove or disconnect the following:
- Tri-pot housing from the tri-pot spider
- Inboard spacer ring slide it rearward on the shaft using Snapring Pliers tool J-8059
- Outboard retaining ring using Snapring Pliers tool J-8059 and discard it
- Tri-pot joint spider assembly
- Inboard spacer ring and discard it
- CV-joint boot
- Trilobal tri-pot bushing from the housing

6. Throughly clean and inspect all parts.

To install:

7. Install or connect the following:
- New snapring onto the stub shaft
- Small boot clamp
- CV-joint boot

8. Using the Crimp tool J-35910, a torque wrench and a breaker bar, crimp the small CV-joint boot clamp to 100 ft. lbs. (136 Nm).

9. Install or connect the following:
- Inboard spacer ring slide it rearward on the shaft using Snapring Pliers tool J-8059, past the 2nd groove
- Tri-pot joint spider assembly onto the shaft until it passes the 2nd groove
- Outboard retaining ring into the axle shaft groove using Snapring Pliers tool J-8059
- Tri-pot joint spider assembly, slide it against the outboard retaining ring
- Inboard spacer ring, seat it in the groove
- ½ kit grease into the boot
- ½ kit grease into the tri-pot housing
- Trilobal tip-pot bushing flush with the tri-pot housing face
- New large seal clamp onto the CV-joint boot
- Tri-pot housing, slide it over the tri-pot joint spider assembly
- CV-joint boot/clamp, slide it into place, over the trilobal tri-pot bushing with the seal lip in the groove

➡**Make sure the boot lies flat against the trilobal bushing.**

10. Position the CV-joint boot so it measures 4.9 in. (125mm).

11. Using the Crimp tool J-35566, latch the large CV-joint boot clamp.

12. Install the halfshaft and the front wheel.

1997 2.4L ENGINE WITH MANUAL TRANSAXLE

1. Before servicing the vehicle, refer to the precautions in the beginning of this section.

2. Remove or disconnect the following:
- Front wheel
- Halfshaft and place it in a vise
- Small CV-joint boot clamp, cut and discard it
- Large CV-joint boot clamp, cut and discard it
- CV-joint boot by sliding it away from the tri-pot joint

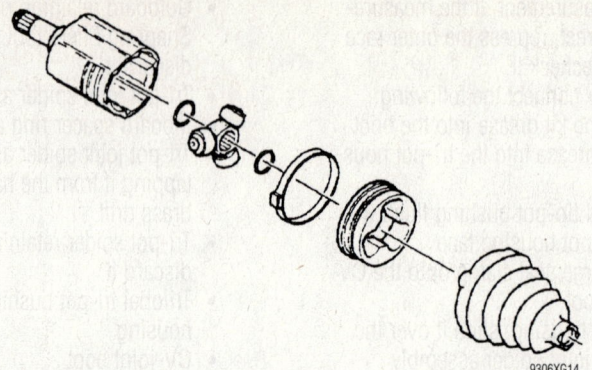

9306XG14

Exploded view of the inner (tri-pot) joint—1997 2.4L engine and all 1998–01 vehicles

- Tri-pot housing from the tri-pot spider
- Inboard spacer ring and slide it rearward on the shaft, using Snapring Pliers tool J-8059
- Outboard retaining ring, using Snapring Pliers tool J-8059, discard it
- Tri-pot joint spider assembly by tapping it from the halfshaft with a brass drift
- Inboard tri-pot spider retaining ring and discard it
- Trilobal tri-pot bushing from the housing
- CV-joint boot

3. Throughly clean and inspect all parts.

To install:

4. Install or connect the following:
- Small boot clamp
- CV-joint boot
- New tri-pot spider retaining ring onto the halfshaft, slide it past the 2nd ring groove

5. Assemble the tri-pot spider assembly onto the halfshaft as follows:
   a. Position the tri-pot spider assembly onto the shop press plate.
   b. Position the halfshaft onto the tri-pot spider assembly, in the shop press.
   c. Press the halfshaft into the tri-pot spider assembly until it passes the 2nd ring groove

6. Remove the halfshaft from the shop press.

7. Install or connect the following:
- Outboard retaining ring into the axle shaft groove using Snapring Pliers tool J-8059
- Tri-pot joint spider assembly, slide it against the outboard retaining ring
- Inboard spacer ring, seat it in the groove

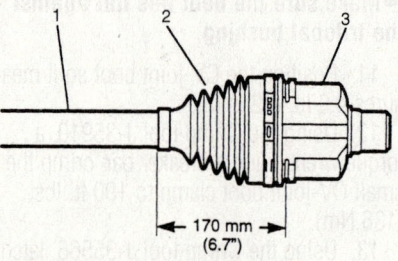

1-SHAFT, AXLE
2-SEAL, DRIVE AXLE INBOARD
3-HOUSING ASM, RETAINER

9306YG19

CV-joint boot measurement—Inner (tri-pot) joint—1997 2.4L engine with manual transaxle

- ½ of the kit grease into the boot
- ½ of the kit grease into the tri-pot housing
- Trilobal tip-pot bushing flush with the tri-pot housing face
- New large seal clamp onto the CV-joint boot
- Tri-pot housing, slide it over the tri-pot joint spider assembly
- CV-joint boot/clamp, slide it into place, over the trilobal tri-pot bushing with the seal lip in the groove

➡**Make sure the boot lies flat against the trilobal bushing.**

8. Position the CV-joint boot so it measures 6.7 in. (170mm).

9. Using the Crimp tool J-35910, a torque wrench and a breaker bar, crimp the small CV-joint boot clamp to 100 ft. lbs. (136 Nm).

10. Using the Crimp tool J-35566, latch the large CV-joint boot clamp.

11. Install the halfshaft and the front wheel.

STEERING AND SUSPENSION

Air Bag

✳✳ CAUTION

Some vehicles are equipped with an air bag system. The system must be disabled before performing service

on or around system components, steering column, instrument panel components, wiring and sensors. Failure to follow safety and disabling procedures could result in accidental air bag deployment, possible personal injury and unnecessary system repairs.

PRECAUTIONS

Several precautions must be observed when handling the inflator module to avoid

accidental deployment and possible personal injury.

• Never carry the inflator module by the wires or connector on the underside of the module.

• When carrying a live inflator module, hold securely with both hands, and ensure that the bag and trim cover are pointed away.

• Place the inflator module on a bench or other surface with the bag and trim cover facing up.

• With the inflator module on the bench,

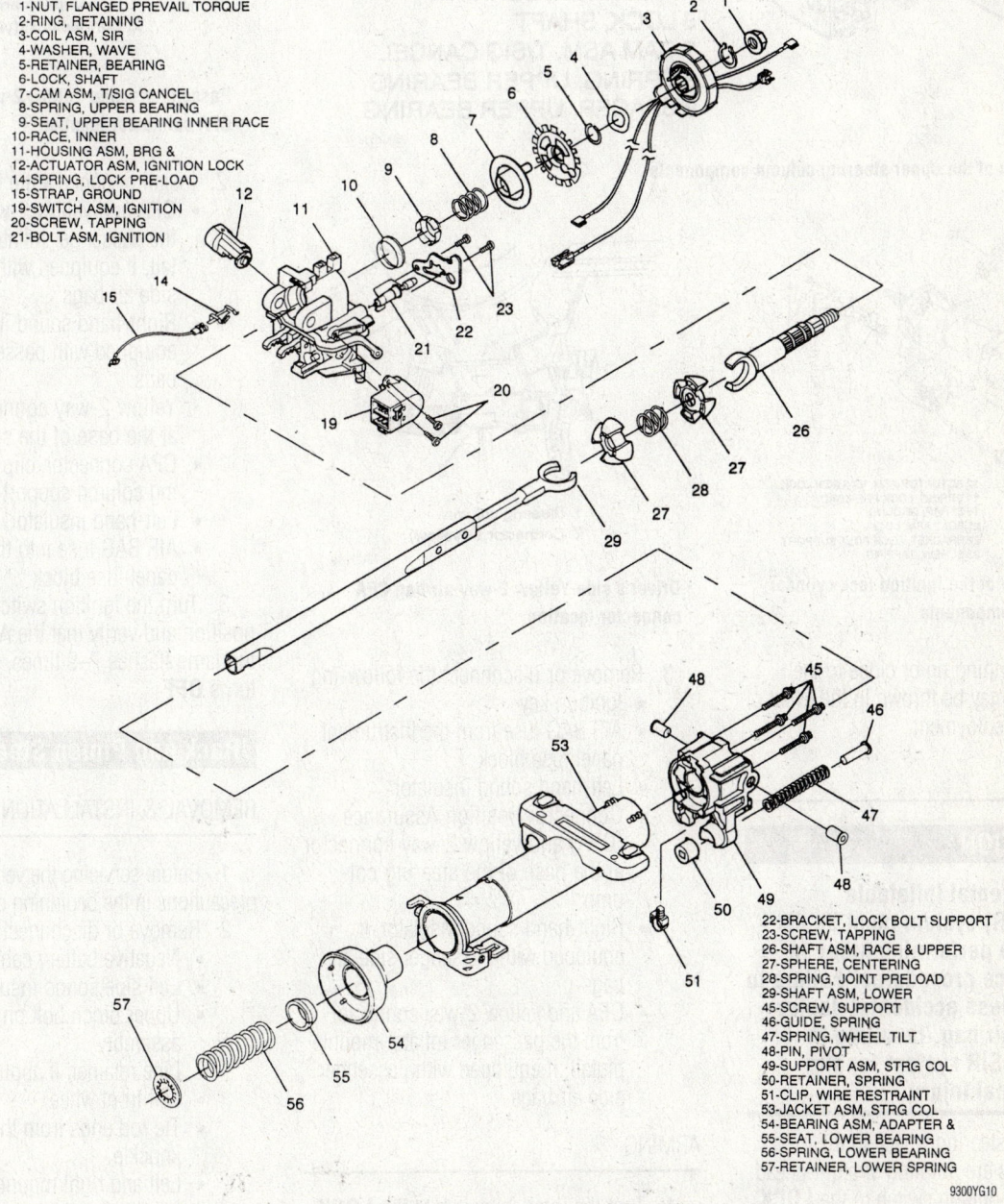

1-NUT, FLANGED PREVAIL TORQUE
2-RING, RETAINING
3-COIL ASM, SIR
4-WASHER, WAVE
5-RETAINER, BEARING
6-LOCK, SHAFT
7-CAM ASM, T/SIG CANCEL
8-SPRING, UPPER BEARING
9-SEAT, UPPER BEARING INNER RACE
10-RACE, INNER
11-HOUSING ASM, BRG &
12-ACTUATOR ASM, IGNITION LOCK
14-SPRING, LOCK PRE-LOAD
15-STRAP, GROUND
19-SWITCH ASM, IGNITION
20-SCREW, TAPPING
21-BOLT ASM, IGNITION

22-BRACKET, LOCK BOLT SUPPORT
23-SCREW, TAPPING
26-SHAFT ASM, RACE & UPPER
27-SPHERE, CENTERING
28-SPRING, JOINT PRELOAD
29-SHAFT ASM, LOWER
45-SCREW, SUPPORT
46-GUIDE, SPRING
47-SPRING, WHEEL TILT
48-PIN, PIVOT
49-SUPPORT ASM, STRG COL
50-RETAINER, SPRING
51-CLIP, WIRE RESTRAINT
53-JACKET ASM, STRG COL
54-BEARING ASM, ADAPTER &
55-SEAT, LOWER BEARING
56-SPRING, LOWER BEARING
57-RETAINER, LOWER SPRING

9300YG10

Exploded view of the steering column with tilt wheel

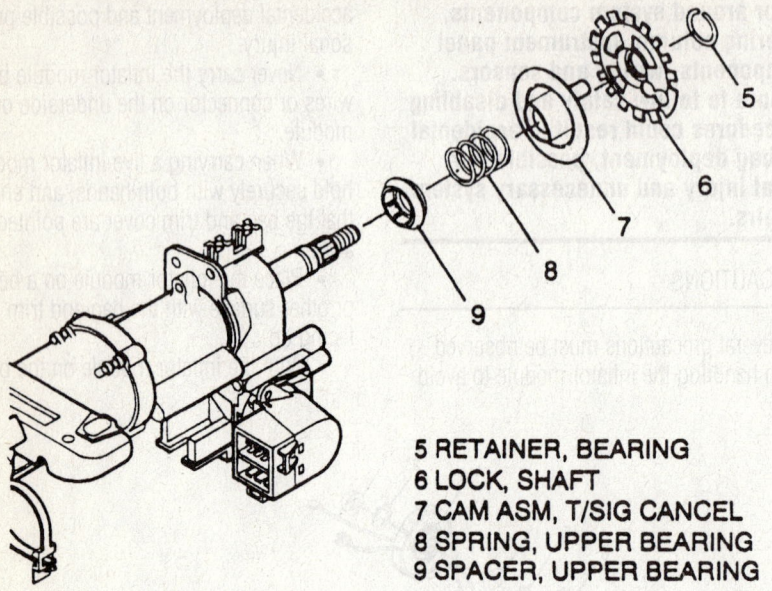

5 RETAINER, BEARING
6 LOCK, SHAFT
7 CAM ASM, T/SIG CANCEL
8 SPRING, UPPER BEARING
9 SPACER, UPPER BEARING

9300YG12

Exploded view of the upper steering column components

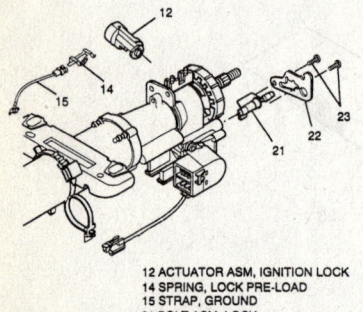

12 ACTUATOR ASM, IGNITION LOCK
14 SPRING, LOCK PRE-LOAD
15 STRAP, GROUND
21 BOLT ASM, LOCK
22 BRACKET, LOCK BOLT SUPPORT
23 SCREW, TAPPING

9300YG11

Exploded view of the ignition lock cylinder and related components

never place anything on or close to the module which may be thrown in the event of an accidental deployment.

DISARMING

✳✳ CAUTION

The Supplemental Inflatable Restraint (SIR) system must be disarmed before performing many in-vehicle service procedures. Failure to do so may cause accidental deployment of the air bag, resulting in unnecessary SIR system repairs and/or personal injury.

1. Turn the steering wheel so the vehicle's wheels are pointing straight-ahead.
2. Turn the ignition switch to the **LOCK** position.

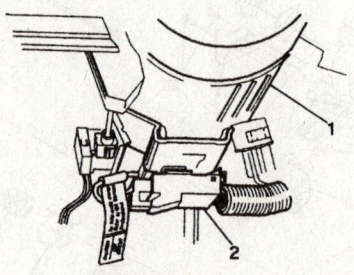

1. Steering column
2. Connector, sir(yellow)

7922YG19

Driver's side Yellow 2-way air bag CPA connector location

3. Remove or disconnect the follow-ing:
   - Ignition key
   - AIR BAG fuse from the instrument panel fuse block
   - Left-hand sound insulator
   - Connector Position Assurance (CPA) and yellow 2-way connector at the base of the steering column.
   - Right-hand sound insulator, if equipped with passenger side air bags
   - CPA and yellow 2-way connector from the passenger inflator module pigtail, if equipped with passenger side air bags

ARMING

1. Turn the ignition switch to the **LOCK** position and remove the key.

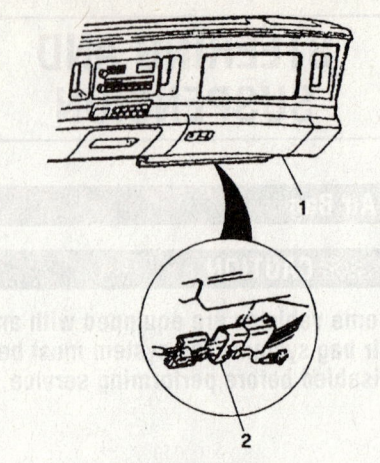

1. I/P compartment
2. Connector, sir(yellow)

7922YG20

Passenger's side Yellow 2-way air bag CPA connector location

2. Install or connect the following:
   - CPA and yellow 2-way connector to the passenger inflator module pigtail, if equipped with passenger side air bags
   - Right-hand sound insulator, if equipped with passenger side air bags
   - Yellow 2-way connector and CPA at the base of the steering column
   - CPA connector, clip it to the steering column support flange
   - Left-hand insulator
   - AIR BAG fuse into the instrument panel fuse block
3. Turn the ignition switch to the **RUN** position and verify that the AIR BAG warning lamp flashes 7–9 times, then the light turns **OFF**.

Rack and Pinion Steering Gear

REMOVAL & INSTALLATION

1. Before servicing the vehicle, refer to the precautions in the beginning of this section.
2. Remove or disconnect the following:
   - Negative battery cable
   - Left side sound insulator
   - Upper pinch bolt on the inter-shaft assembly
   - Line retainer, if applicable
   - Left front wheel
   - Tie rod ends from the steering knuckle
   - Left and right mounting bolts
   - Inlet and outlet hose assemblies from the rack and pinion

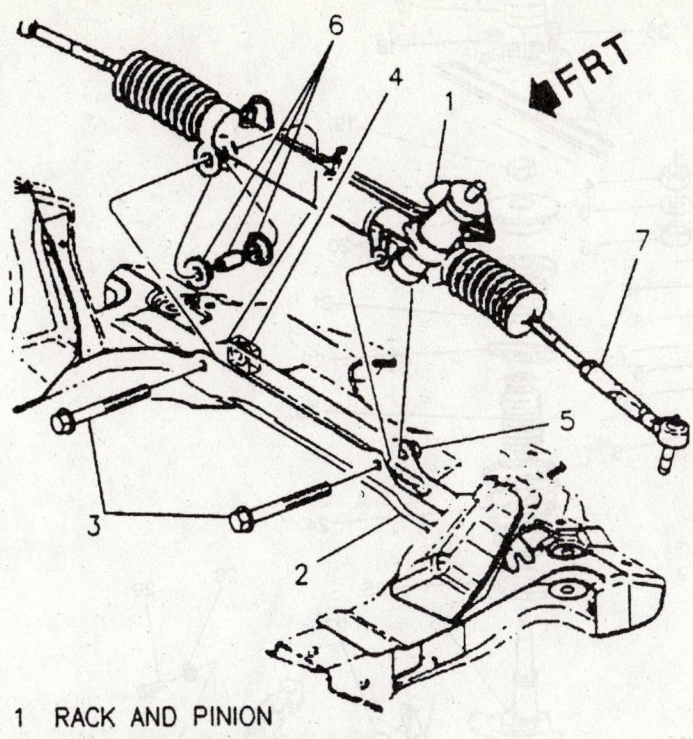

1 RACK AND PINION
2 CROSSMEMBER, SUSPENSION
3 BOLTS, STEERING GEAR
4 CAGE NUT
5 WELD NUTS
6 BUSHING AND SLEEVE
7 TIE ROD

7922YG21

Exploded view of the rack and pinion steering gear mounting

- Lower pinch bolt from the flange inter-shaft assembly
- Inter-shaft assembly
- Crossmember bolts, loosen them to gain additional clearance
- Rack and pinion through the wheel opening

To install:

3. Install or connect the following:
   - Rack and pinion through the left wheel opening
4. Install the crossmember bolts in the following order:
   a. Step 1: Left rear outboard to 96 ft. lbs. (130 Nm).
   b. Step 2: Right rear outboard 2nd to 96 ft. lbs. (130 Nm).
   c. Step 3: Front upper bolts to 96 ft. lbs. (130 Nm).
   d. Step 4: Rear inboard bolts to 96 ft. lbs. (130 Nm).
5. Install or connect the following:
   - Lower pinch bolt (flange to inter-shaft bolt). Torque it to 30 ft. lbs. (41 Nm).
   - Inlet and outlet pipes to the rack and pinion. Torque the fittings to 20 ft. lbs. (27 Nm).
   - Rack and pinion bolts and nuts. Torque left side to 89 ft. lbs. (120 Nm); then, right side to 89 ft. lbs. (120 Nm).
   - Tie rod ends to the struts. Torque the nuts to 44 ft. lbs. (60 Nm), use new cotter pins.
   - Left wheel
   - Line retainer, if applicable
   - Upper pinch bolt. Torque it to 30 ft. lbs. (41 Nm).
   - Left side sound insulator
   - Negative battery cable
6. Refill with fluid and bleed air from system.
7. Check and/or the toe setting
8. Road test vehicle and verify no leaks.

Strut

REMOVAL & INSTALLATION

Front

1. Before servicing the vehicle, refer to the precautions in the beginning of this section.
2. Remove or disconnect the following:
   - Strut tower cover, if equipped
   - Upper strut-to-body nuts and/or bolts
3. Support the front crossmember with jackstands.
4. Lower the vehicle so the weight of the vehicle rests on the jackstands and NOT the control arms.
5. Before removing front suspension components, their positions should be marked so they may assemble correctly.

❄❄ WARNING

Whenever working near the halfshaft, use care to prevent damage from over-extension of the halfshaft joints. When either end of the shaft is disconnected, over-extension of the joint could result in separation of the internal components and possible joint failure.

6. Install a drive axle joint protective cover.
7. Remove or disconnect the following:
   - Front wheel
   - Brake line bracket, if necessary
   - Tie rod end from the steering knuckle, discard the cotter pin
   - Strut from the steering knuckle. Matchmark the assembly before removal.

❄❄ WARNING

The steering knuckle MUST be supported to prevent axle joint over-extension.

   - Strut

To install:

8. Install or connect the following:
   - Strut to the steering knuckle, aligning the matchmarks made during removal. Torque the bolts and nuts to 133 ft. lbs. (180 Nm).
   - Tie rod end to the steering knuckle. Torque the bolt to 44 ft. lbs. (60 Nm), use a new cotter pin

Turn to Section 5 for brake system applications

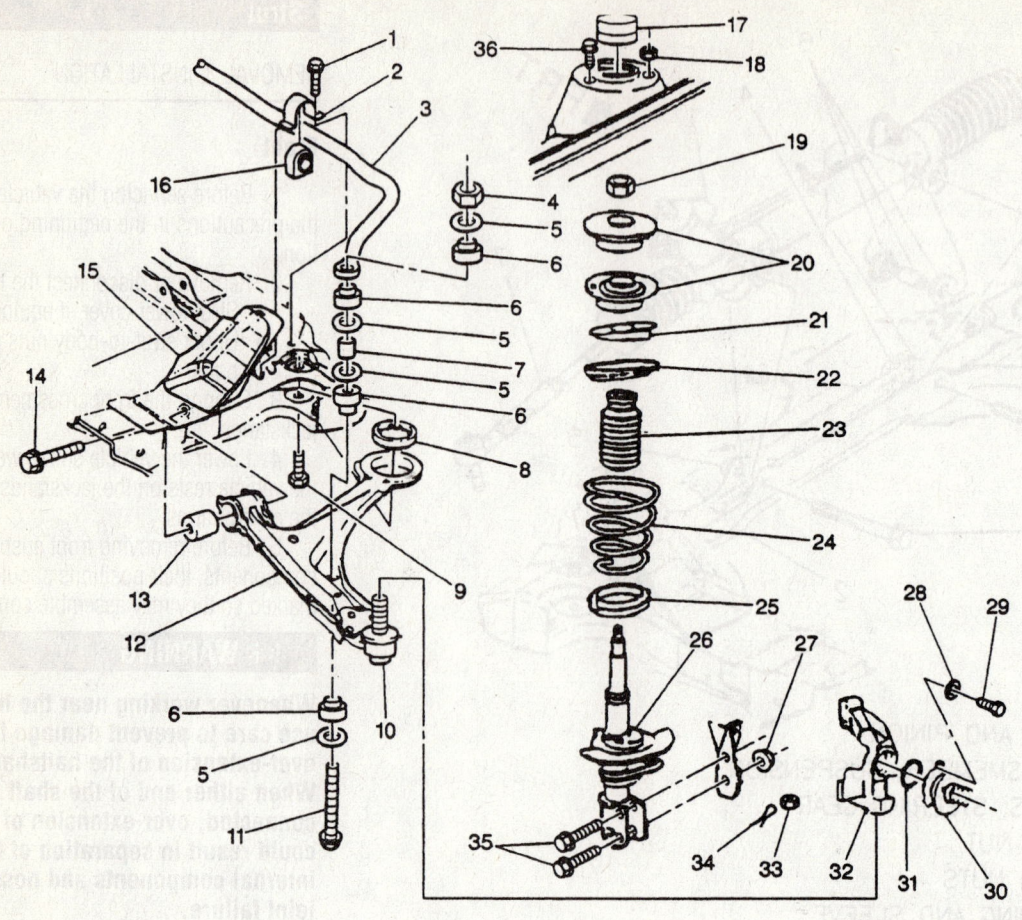

1 Bolt
2 Clamp, Stabilizer Shaft
3 Stabilizer Shaft
4 Nut, Stabilizer Link
5 Washer
6 Insulator, Stabilizer Link
7 Spacer Stabilizer Link
8 Bushing, Vertical
9 Bolt, Vertical Bushing
10 Ball Joint
11 Bolt, Stabilizer Link

12 Control Arm
13 Bushing, Control Arm
14 Lower Spring Insulator
15 Suspension Support
16 Insulator, Stabilizer Shaft
17 Cover, Strut Mount
18 Nut
19 Nut, Strut Dampener Shaft
20 Strut Mount and Rate Washer Assembly
21 Spring Seat
22 Upper Spring Insulator
23 Strut Bumper and Shield

24 Spring
25 Lower Spring Insulator
26 Strut
27 Nut
28 Washer
29 Bolt
30 Hub and Bearing Assembly
31 Seal (Part of 5)
32 Steering Knuckle
33 Nut, Ball Joint
34 Cotter Pin
35 Bolt
36 Bolt

7922YG22

Exploded view of the front suspension

- Upper strut to the body, Torque the nuts/bolts to 18–20 ft. lbs. (25–27 Nm).
- Brake line bracket

9. Remove the jackstands from under the crossmember.

10. Install the front wheel. Torque the lug nuts to 100 ft. lbs. (140 Nm).

Rear

1. Before servicing the vehicle, refer to the precautions in the beginning of this section.

⁂ WARNING

Do not remove both struts at one time. Suspending the rear axle at full length could result in damage to brake lines and/or hoses.

2. Open the deck lid.
3. Remove or disconnect the following:
   - Lower strut nut
4. Raise and safely support the rear axle with jackstands.
5. Remove or disconnect the follow-ing:

- Strut upper mount nuts/bolts
- Strut

To install:

6. Install or connect the following:
   - Strut
   - Strut fasteners, finger tight
   - Lower strut bolt. Torque it to 125 ft. lbs. (170 Nm).
   - Upper strut-to-body bolts. Torque them to 21 ft. lbs. (28 Nm).
   - Upper strut nuts. Torque them to 15 ft. lbs. (20 Nm).

7. Road test the vehicle.

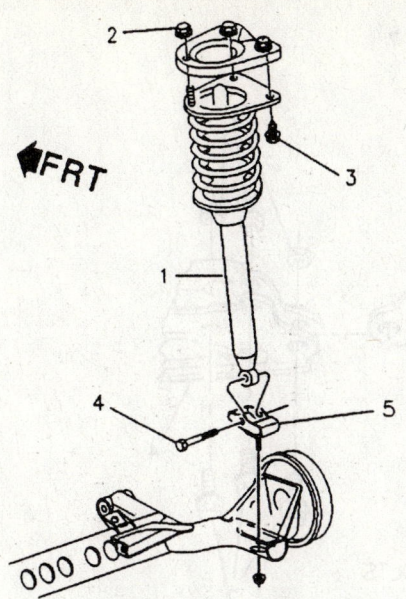

1 SHOCK, COIL-OVER
2 NUT
3 BOLT, UPPER STRUT (2)
4 BOLT, AXLE
5 ADAPTER

7922YG23

Exploded view of the rear strut mounting

Coil Spring

REMOVAL & INSTALLATION

Front and Rear

1. Before servicing the vehicle, refer to the precautions in the beginning of this section.
2. Remove the strut from the vehicle.
3. Mount the strut compressor in a holding fixture.
4. Mount the strut assembly into the compressor. Note that the strut compressor has strut mounting holes drilled for specific vehicle lines.
5. Compress the strut approximately ½ its height after initial contact with the top cap.

✳✳ WARNING

Never bottom the spring or damper rod!

6. Remove the nut from the strut damper shaft and place alignment/guiding rod J-34013-27 on top of the damper shaft. Use the rod to guide the damper shaft

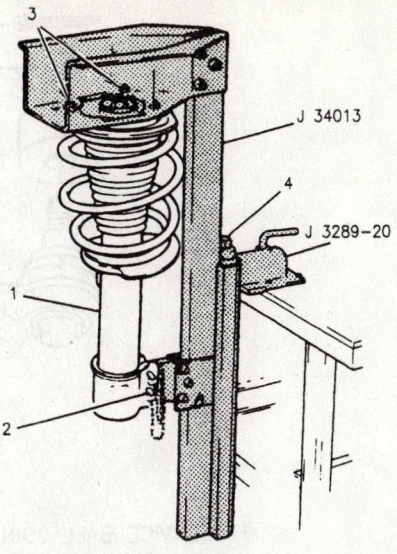

1 STRUT ASSEMBLY
2 INSTALL LOCKING PINS THROUGH STRUT ASSEMBLY
3 TIGHTEN NUTS UNTIL FLUSH WITH STRUT COMPRESSOR
4 COMPRESSOR FORCING SCREW

7922YG24

View of a typical strut assembly mounted in a compressor

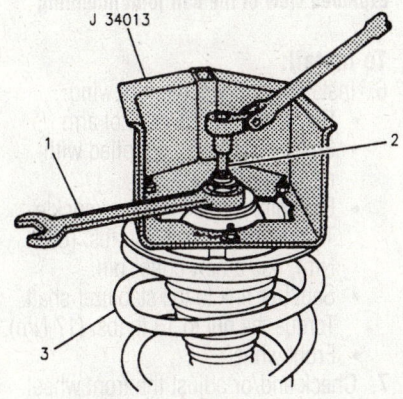

1 WRENCH
2 SOCKET
3 STRUT ASSEMBLY

7922YG25

Use a socket and a wrench to remove the damper shaft nut spring cap while compressing the spring

straight down through the spring cap while compressing the spring. Remove the components.

To install:

7. Install the bearing cap into the strut compressor, if removed.
8. Mount the strut assembly in strut compressor, using bottom locking pin only.

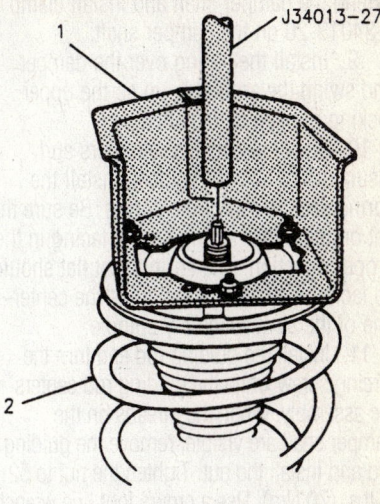

1 STRUT COMPRESSOR
2 STRUT ASSEMBLY

7922YG26

Install the rod to guide the damper shaft straight down through the spring cap while compressing the spring

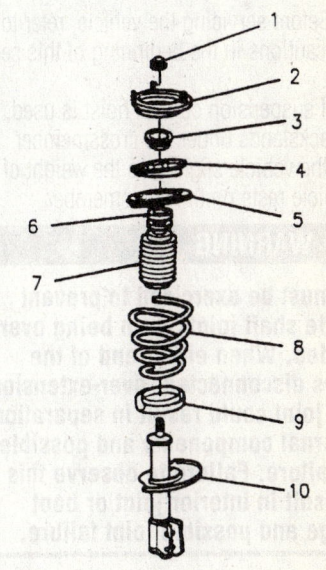

1 STRUT MOUNT NUT
2 STRUT MOUNT
3 RATE WASHER
4 SPRING SEAT
5 SPRING UPPER INSULATOR
6 JOUNCE BUMPER
7 STRUT DUST SHIELD
8 SPRING
9 SPRING LOWER INSULATOR
10 STRUT

7922YG27

Exploded view of the front strut assembly

Extend the damper shaft and install clamp J-34013-20 on the damper shaft.

9. Install the spring over the damper and swing the assembly up so the upper locking pin can be installed.

10. Install all shields, bumpers and insulators on the spring seat. Install the spring seat on top of the spring. Be sure the flat on the upper spring seat is facing in the proper direction. The spring seat flat should be facing the same direction as the center-line of the strut assembly spindle.

11. Install the guiding rod and turn the forcing screw while the guiding rod centers the assembly. When the threads on the damper shaft are visible, remove the guiding rod and install the nut. Tighten the nut to 52 ft. lbs. (70 Nm). Use a crow's foot line wrench while holding the damper shaft with a socket.

12. Remove the clamp.

13. Install the strut.

Lower Ball Joint

REMOVAL & INSTALLATION

1. Before servicing the vehicle, refer to the precautions in the beginning of this section.

2. If suspension contact hoist is used, place jackstands under the crossmember. Lower the vehicle slightly so the weight of the vehicle rests on the crossmember.

※※ WARNING

Care must be exercised to prevent the axle shaft joints from being over-extended. When either end of the shaft is disconnected, over-extension of the joint could result in separation of internal components and possible joint failure. Failure to observe this can result in interior joint or boot damage and possible joint failure.

3. Remove or disconnect the following:
- Front wheel
- Stabilizer shaft link nut
- Lower ball joint from the steering knuckle, using tool J-38892, discard the cotter pin

4. Drill out the 3 ball joint-to-lower control arm rivets as follows:
   a. Use an 1/8 in. (3mm) drill bit to make a pilot hole through the rivets.
   b. Finish drilling rivets with a 1/2 in. (13mm) drill bit.
   c. Remove the rivets with a punch, if necessary.

5. Remove the ball joint from the steering knuckle.

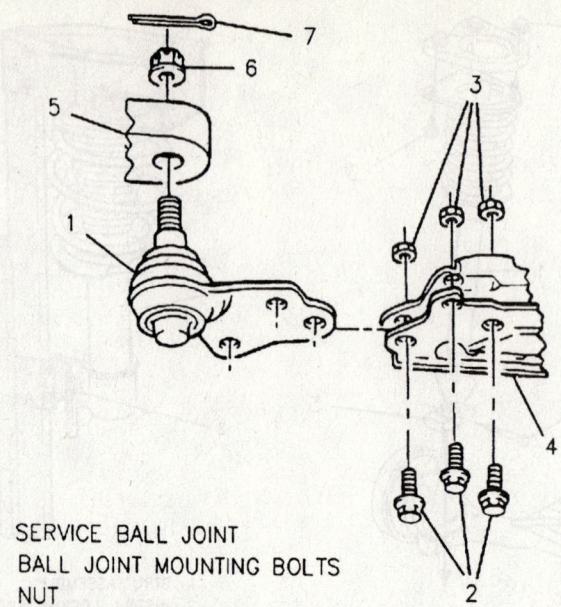

1   SERVICE BALL JOINT
2   BALL JOINT MOUNTING BOLTS
3   NUT
4   LOWER CONTROL ARM
5   STEERING KNUCKLE
6   NUT — 55 N·m (41 LBS. FT.) MINIMUM TORQUE
        65 N·m (48 LBS. FT.) MAXIMUM TORQUE
        TO INSTALL PIN
7   PIN

7922YG28

Exploded view of the ball joint mounting

To install:
6. Install or connect the following:
- Ball joint into the control arm
- 3 new nuts/bolts, supplied with new ball joint
- Ball joint to the steering knuckle. Torque the nut to 50 ft. lbs. (65 Nm), use a new cotter pin.
- Sabilizer link to the stabilizer shaft. Torque the nut to 13 ft. lbs. (17 Nm).
- Front wheel

7. Check and/or adjust the front wheel alignment.

Lower Control Arm

REMOVAL & INSTALLATION

1. Before servicing the vehicle, refer to the precautions in the beginning of this section.

2. Remove or disconnect the following:
- Front wheel
- Stabilizer shaft link
- Ball joint from the steering knuckle
- Wiring harness from the lower control arm
- Lower control arm-to-crossmember nut/bolts

- Lower control arm

To install:
3. Install or connect the following:
- Lower control arm
- Lower control arm to the cross-member. Torque the front bolt to 79 ft. lbs. (107 Nm) and the rear nut/bolt to 81 ft. lbs. (110 Nm).
- Wiring harness to the lower control arm
- Ball joint to the steering knuckle. Torque the nut to 50 ft. lbs. (65 Nm), use a new cotter pin.

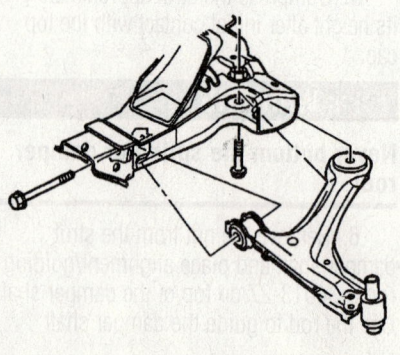

9306YG21

View of the lower control arm

- Stabilizer shaft link. Torque the nut to 13 ft. lbs. (17 Nm).
- Front wheel

4. Check and/or adjust the front wheel alignment.

CONTROL ARM BUSHING REPLACEMENT

Front Bushing

1. Before servicing the vehicle, refer to the precautions in the beginning of this section.
2. Remove or disconnect the following:
   - Front wheel
   - Lower control arm and place it in a vise
3. Lubricate the threads of tool J-21474-19 with High Pressure Lubricant J-23444-A.
4. Assemble ⅜ in. Bolt J-21474-19, Remover/Installer tool J-41397-1A, Remover/Installer tool J-41397-2A and ⅜ in. Nut J-21474-18 onto the lower control arm bushing.
5. Tighten the ⅜ in. Nut J-21474-18 to press the front bushing from the lower control arm.

6. Disassemble the tools.

To install:

7. Lubricate the outer case of the new front bushing.
8. Insert the new front bushing into the lower control arm.
9. Assemble ⅜ in. Bolt J-21474-19, Remover/Installer tool J-41397-1A, Remover/Installer tool J-41397-2A and ⅜ in. Nut J-21474-18 onto the lower control arm.
10. Tighten the ⅜ in. Nut J-21474-18 to press the bushing into the lower control arm.
11. Disassemble the tools.

Rear Bushing

1. Before servicing the vehicle, refer to the precautions in the beginning of this section.
2. Remove or disconnect the following:
   - Front wheel
   - Lower control arm and place it in a vise
3. Lubricate the threads of tool J-21474-27 with High Pressure Lubricant J-23444-A.
4. Assemble bolt J-21474-27,

Remover/Installer tool J-41211-1, Remover/Installer tool J-41211-3 and ½ in. Nut J-21474-4.
5. Tighten the Bolt J-21474-27 to press the rear bushing from the lower control arm.
6. Disassemble the tools.

To install:

7. Insert the rear lower control arm bushing.
8. Assemble bolt J-21474-27, Remover/Installer tool J-41211-1, Remover/Installer tool J-41211-3 and ½ in. Nut J-21474-4.
9. Tighten the Nut J-21474-4 to press the rear bushing into the lower control arm.
10. Disassemble the tools.

Wheel Bearings

ADJUSTMENT

These vehicles are equipped with sealed hub and bearing assemblies. The hub and bearing assemblies are non-serviceable. If the assembly is damaged, the complete unit must be replaced.

REMOVAL & INSTALLATION

Front

1. Before servicing the vehicle, refer to the precautions in the beginning of this section.
2. Remove or disconnect the following:
   - Front wheel
   - Halfshaft nut
   - Brake caliper and support it aside without disconnecting the fluid line
   - Brake rotor
   - 3 hub/bearing assembly-to-steering knuckle bolts

➡ **Rust buildup may require a generous application of penetrating oil where the hub fits into the knuckle.**

   - Hub/bearing assembly from the steering knuckle

To install:

3. Install or connect the following:
   - Hub/bearing assembly to the steering knuckle. Torque the bolts to 70 ft. lbs. (95 Nm).
   - Brake rotor
   - Brake caliper
   - Halfshaft through hub/knuckle

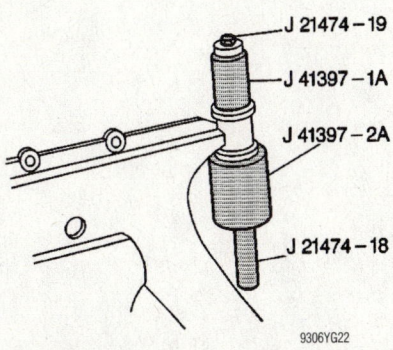

Removing the lower control arm front bushing

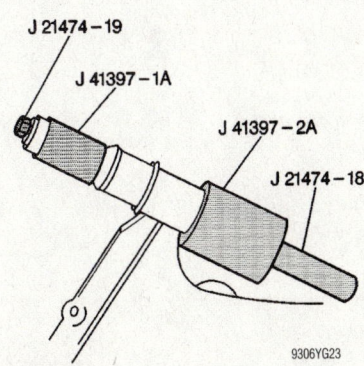

Installing the lower control arm front bushing

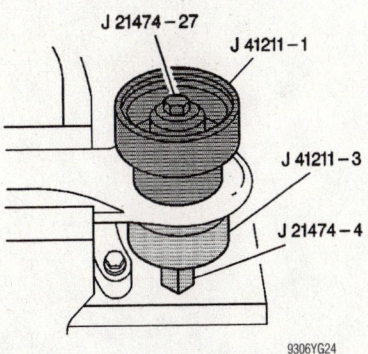

Removing the lower control arm rear bushing

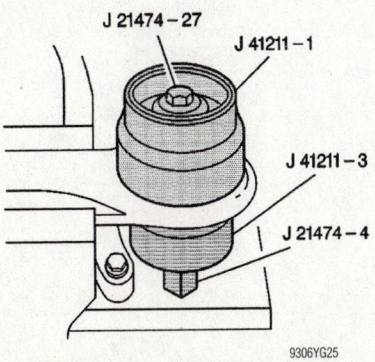

Installing the lower control arm rear bushing

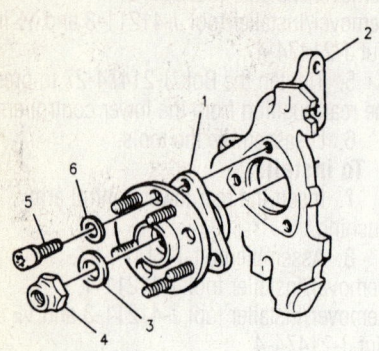

1 HUB AND BEARING ASSEMBLY
2 STEERING KNUCKLE
3 WASHER
4 DRIVE AXLE NUT – 260 N·m (192 LBS. FT.)
5 HUB AND BEARING RETAINING BOLT
6 WASHER

7922YG29

Exploded view of the front hub and bearing assembly

assembly. Torque the nut to 192 ft. lbs. (260 Nm).
  • Front wheel
4. Road test the vehicle and verify proper operation.

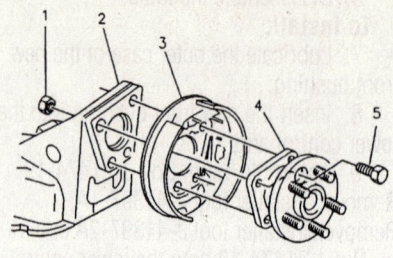

1 NUT
2 REAR AXLE ASSEMBLY
3 BACKING PLATE
4 HUB AND BEARING ASSEMBLY
5 BOLT

7922YG30

Exploded view of the rear hub and bearing assembly

Rear

A single-unit hub/bearing assembly is bolted to both ends of the rear axle assembly or rear knuckle assembly. The hub/bearing assembly is a sealed unit.

1. Before servicing the vehicle, refer to the precautions in the beginning of this section.

2. Remove or disconnect the following:
  • Rear wheel
  • Brake drum
  • Hub/bearing assembly-to-rear axle assembly nuts/bolts

➡ **The top rear mounting bolt will not clear the brake shoe when removing the hub and bearing assembly. Partially remove the hub and bearing assembly prior to removing this bolt.**

  • Anti-lock Brake System (ABS) wheel speed sensor electrical connector
  • Hub/bearing assembly from the rear axle

To install:

3. Install or connect the following:
  • Hub/bearing assembly. Torque the nuts/bolts to 44 ft. lbs. (60 Nm).

➡ **Position the top rear mounting bolt in the hub and bearing assembly prior to installation to the axle housing.**

  • Rear ABS wheel speed sensor wire connector
  • Brake drum
  • Rear wheel
4. Road test the vehicle.

GENERAL MOTORS CORPORATION—L/N BODY

33

Chevrolet-Malibu • Oldsmobile-Cutlass

PRECAUTIONS

Before servicing any vehicle, please be sure to read all of the following precautions, which deal with personal safety, prevention of component damage, and important points to take into consideration when servicing a motor vehicle:

- Never open, service or drain the radiator or cooling system when the engine is hot; serious burns can occur from the steam and hot coolant.

- Observe all applicable safety precautions when working around fuel. Whenever servicing the fuel system, always work in a well-ventilated area. Do not allow fuel spray or vapors to come in contact with a spark, open flame or excessive heat (a hot drop light, for example). Keep a dry chemical fire extinguisher near the work area. Always keep fuel in a container specifically designed for fuel storage; also, always properly seal fuel containers to avoid the possibility of fire or explosion. Refer to the additional fuel system precautions later in this section.

- Fuel injection systems often remain pressurized, even after the engine has been turned OFF. The fuel system pressure must be relieved before disconnecting any fuel lines. Failure to do so may result in fire and/or personal injury.

- Brake fluid often contains polyglycol ethers and polyglycols. Avoid contact with the eyes and wash your hands thoroughly after handling brake fluid. If you do get brake fluid in your eyes, flush your eyes with clean, running water for 15 minutes. If eye irritation persists, or if you have taken brake fluid internally, IMMEDIATELY seek medical assistance.

- The EPA warns that prolonged contact with used engine oil may cause a number of skin disorders, including cancer! You should make every effort to minimize your exposure to used engine oil. Protective gloves should be worn when changing oil. Wash your hands and any other exposed skin areas as soon as possible after exposure to used engine oil. Soap and water, or waterless hand cleaner should be used.

- All new vehicles are now equipped with an air bag system, often referred to as a Supplemental Restraint System (SRS) or Supplemental Inflatable Restraint (SIR) system. The system must be disabled before performing service on or around system components, steering column, instrument panel components, wiring and sensors. Failure to follow safety and disabling procedures could result in accidental air bag deployment, possible personal injury and unnecessary system repairs.

- Always wear safety goggles when working with, or around, the air bag system. When carrying a non-deployed air bag, be sure the bag and trim cover are pointed away from your body. When placing a non-deployed air bag on a work surface, always face the bag and trim cover upward, away from the surface. This will reduce the motion of the module if it is accidentally deployed. Refer to the additional air bag system precautions later in this section.

- Clean, high quality brake fluid from a sealed container is essential to the safe and proper operation of the brake system. You should always buy the correct type of brake fluid for your vehicle. If the brake fluid becomes contaminated, completely flush the system with new fluid. Never reuse any brake fluid. Any brake fluid that is removed from the system should be discarded. Also, do not allow any brake fluid to come in contact with a painted surface; it will damage the paint.

- Never operate the engine without the proper amount and type of engine oil; doing so WILL result in severe engine damage.

- Timing belt maintenance is extremely important! Many models utilize an interference-type, non-freewheeling engine. If the timing belt breaks, the valves in the cylinder head may strike the pistons, causing potentially serious (also time-consuming and expensive) engine damage. Refer to the maintenance interval charts in the front of this manual for the recommended replacement interval for the timing belt, and to the timing belt section for belt replacement and inspection.

- Disconnecting the negative battery cable on some vehicles may interfere with the functions of the on-board computer system(s) and may require the computer to undergo a relearning process once the negative battery cable is reconnected.

- When servicing drum brakes, only disassemble and assemble one side at a time, leaving the remaining side intact for reference.

ENGINE REPAIR

Alternator

REMOVAL

2.4L Engine

1. Before servicing the vehicle, refer to the precautions in the beginning of this section.
2. Remove or disconnect the following:
- Negative battery cable
- Serpentine belt
- Alternator electrical connectors
- Alternator

3.1L Engine

1. Before servicing the vehicle, refer to the precautions in the beginning of this section.
2. Remove or disconnect the following:
- Negative battery cable
- Serpentine belt
- Alternator electrical connectors
- Power steering line clip
- Alternator

INSTALLATION

2.4L Engine

Install or connect the following:
- Alternator electrical connectors
- Alternator. Tighten nuts/bolts to 37 ft. lbs. (50 Nm).
- Serpentine belt
- Negative battery cable

3.1L Engine

Install or connect the following:
- Alternator output terminal. Tighten the nut to 15 ft. lbs. (20 Nm).
- Alternator. Tighten nuts/bolts to 37 ft. lbs. (50 Nm).
- Power steering line clip. Tighten the nut to 22 ft. lbs. (30 Nm).
- Alternator electrical connector
- Serpentine belt
- Negative battery cable

Ignition Timing

ADJUSTMENT

Ignition timing is controlled by the Powertrain Control Module (PCM). No adjustment is necessary or possible.

Engine Assembly

REMOVAL & INSTALLATION

2.4L Engine

1. Before servicing the vehicle, refer to the precautions in the beginning of this section.
2. If equipped with air conditioning, discharge and recover the refrigerant.
3. Properly drain the cooling system.
4. Relieve the fuel system pressure.
5. Remove or disconnect the following:
   - Left sound insulator
   - Heater hose at the thermostat assembly
   - Radiator upper hose
   - Air cleaner assembly
   - Coolant fan
   - Compressor/condenser hose assembly at the compressor and discard the O-rings, if equipped with A/C
   - Both vacuum hoses from the front of the engine
6. Label and disconnect the following electrical connectors:
   - Alternator
   - Air conditioning compressor, if equipped
   - Fuel injector harness
   - Idle Air Control (IAC) and Throttle Position (TP) sensor at the throttle body
   - Manifold Absolute Pressure (MAP) sensor
   - Intake Air Temperature (IAT) sensor
   - Evaporative Emissions (EVAP) canister purge solenoid
   - Starter solenoid
   - Ground connections
   - Negative battery cable from the transaxle
   - Electronic ignition coil and module assembly
   - Engine Coolant Temperature (ECT) sensor(s)
   - Oil pressure sensor/switch
   - Oxygen (O$_2$S) sensor
   - Crankshaft Position (CKP) sensor
   - Back-up lamp switch and move the harness aside
7. Remove or disconnect the following:
   - Power brake vacuum hose from the throttle body
   - Power brake vacuum tube-to-check valve hose from the tube
   - Throttle cable and bracket
   - Power steering pump rear bracket and vacuum tube as an assembly
   - Power steering pump drive belt
   - Power steering pump and move it aside with the lines attached
   - Fuel lines
   - Shift cables
   - Exhaust manifold and heat shield
   - Radiator lower hose from the radiator
8. Install an engine support fixture.
9. Remove or disconnect the following:
   - Coolant recovery/surge tank and position the tank aside with the hoses connected
   - Engine mount assembly
   - Front wheel
   - Right splash shield
10. Drain the engine oil.
11. Remove or disconnect the following:
    - Radiator air deflector
    - Vehicle Speed Sensor (VSS)
    - Knock (KS) sensor
    - Starter solenoid
    - Both front Anti-lock Brake System (ABS) wheel speed sensors, if equipped
    - Engine mount strut
    - Transaxle mount
    - Ball joints and separate them from the steering knuckles
    - Suspension supports, crossmember and stabilizer shaft as an assembly
    - Heater outlet hose from the radiator outlet pipe
    - Halfshaft from the transaxle and intermediate shaft, move it aside
    - Air conditioning lines from the oil pan, if equipped
    - Flywheel housing cover
12. Position a support under the engine and lower the vehicle onto the support.
13. Matchmark the threads on the support fixture hooks so the setting can be duplicated when reinstalling the engine. Remove the engine support fixture J-hooks.
14. Raise the vehicle slowly off the engine and transaxle assembly. If may be necessary to move the engine/transaxle assembly rearward to clear the intake manifold.
15. Noting the position of the bolts, separate the engine from the transaxle.

To install:

16. Assemble the engine to the transaxle.
17. Position the engine and transaxle assembly under the engine compartment, then slowly lower the vehicle over the assembly until the transaxle mount is indexed and install the retaining bolt.
18. Install or connect the following:
    - Engine support fixture by adjusting it to the previous setting
    - Engine mount assembly
    - Transaxle mount
19. Raise the vehicle off the support.
20. Install or connect the following:
    - Halfshafts to the transaxle
    - Heater outlet hose to the radiator outlet pipe
    - Suspension supports, crossmember and stabilizer shaft assembly
    - Ball joints to the steering knuckles and secure with the nuts
    - Engine strut mount
    - Air conditioning line to the oil pan, if equipped
    - VSS
    - KS sensor
    - Starter solenoid
    - Both front ABS wheel speed sensors, if equipped
    - Flywheel housing cover
    - Radiator air deflector
    - Lower radiator hose
    - Right splash shield
    - Front wheels
    - Engine support fixture
    - Coolant recovery/surge tank
    - Alternator
    - Air conditioning compressor, if equipped
    - Fuel injector harness
    - IAC and TP sensors
    - MAP sensor
    - IAT sensor
    - EVAP canister purge solenoid
    - Starter solenoid
    - Ground connections
    - Negative battery cable to the transaxle
    - Electronic ignition coil and module assembly
    - ECT sensor(s)
    - Oil pressure sensor/switch
    - O$_2$S sensor
    - CKP sensor
    - Back-up lamp switch
    - Vacuum hoses
    - Compressor/condenser hose assembly to the compressor, if equipped

- Exhaust manifold and heat shield
- Fuel lines
- Positive battery cable
- Power steering pump and tension the belt
- Vacuum hoses to the intake manifold
- Tube to the brake booster
- Throttle cable and bracket
- Coolant fan and air cleaner assembly
- Upper radiator hose
- Left sound insulator
- Heater hose at the thermostat housing
- Negative battery cable

21. Refill the cooling system.
22. Refill the transaxle and the crankcase.
23. If equipped with air conditioning, evacuate, charge and leak test the system.
24. Start the engine and check the fluid levels, proper operation of the engine and/or fluid leakage.

3.1L Engine

Please note that the engine and transaxle are removed as an assembly from under the vehicle.

1. Before servicing the vehicle, refer to the precautions in the beginning of this section.
2. Relieve the fuel system pressure.
3. Remove or disconnect the following:
   - Upper half of the air cleaner assembly
   - Throttle body inlet duct
4. Drain the cooling system.
5. Remove or disconnect the following:
   - Upper and lower radiator hoses
   - Coolant inlet line from the coolant surge tank
   - Vacuum hoses from the Evaporative Emissions (EVAP) canister purge valve, vacuum modulator and power brake booster
   - Heater outlet hose from the water pump
   - Serpentine drive belt
   - Control cables from the throttle body lever and intake manifold bracket; then, move them aside
   - All necessary electrical connectors
   - Alternator
   - Power steering lines from the power steering pump and plug them
   - Fuel lines from the fuel rail and plug them
   - Cooling fan assembly
   - Shift control cable from the transaxle shift lever and cable bracket
   - Vent tube from the transaxle
   - Vacuum hose from the vacuum reservoir
6. Install an Engine Support Fixture tool J-28467-A.
7. Remove or disconnect the following:
   - Both upper air conditioning compressor mounting bolts, loosen them
   - Front wheels
   - Both inner fender splash shields
8. Drain the engine oil.
9. Remove or disconnect the following:
   - Engine mount strut
   - Anti-lock Brake System (ABS) sensor wires from the wheel sensors and suspension member supports, if equipped
   - Lower ball joints from the steering knuckles and discard the cotter pins
   - Lower suspension support assemblies with the lower control arms attached
   - Halfshafts from the transaxle and support aside
   - Oil filter and oil filter adapter
   - Flywheel cover
   - Starter
   - Heater hoses from the heater core
   - A/C compressor and move it aside without disconnecting the refrigerant lines
   - Vacuum reservoir tank
   - Exhaust pipe from the exhaust manifold and move it aside
   - Engine mount strut bracket from the engine
   - Transaxle cooler lines from the radiator
   - Transaxle oil fill tube
10. Lower the vehicle until the power train assembly is resting on an engine table.
11. Remove or disconnect the following:
    - Transaxle mount-to-body bolts
    - Intermediate bracket from the right engine mount
    - Engine support fixture
12. Raise the vehicle leaving the powertrain assembly on the engine table.
13. Separate the engine and transaxle assemblies.

To install:

14. Install or connect the following:
    - Transaxle to the engine. Torque the bolts to 55 ft. lbs. (75 Nm).
    - Powertrain assembly under the vehicle; then, lower the vehicle into position.
    - Serpentine belt, loosely install it

- Engine Support Fixture tool J-28467-A
- Intermediate bracket to the right engine mount
- Transaxle mount to the body
- Transaxle oil fill tube
- Transaxle cooler lines to the radiator
- Engine mount strut bracket to the engine. Torque the bolts to 44 ft. lbs. (60 Nm).
- Exhaust pipe to the exhaust manifold. Torque the bolts to 18 ft. lbs. (25 Nm).
- Vacuum reservoir tank
- A/C compressor
- Heater hoses to the heater core
- Starter
- Flywheel cover
- Oil filter and oil filter adapter
- Halfshafts to the transaxle
- Lower suspension support assemblies with the lower control arms attached
- Lower ball joints to the steering knuckles using new cotter pins. Torque the nuts to 41 ft. lbs. (55 Nm).
- ABS sensor wires to the wheel sensors and suspension member supports, if equipped
- Engine mount strut
- Both inner fender splash shields
- Front wheels
- Both upper air conditioning compressor mounting bolts

15. Remove the engine support fixture.
16. Install or connect the following:
    - Vacuum hose to the vacuum reservoir
    - Vent tube to the transaxle
    - Shift control cable to the transaxle shift lever and cable bracket
    - Cooling fan assembly
    - Fuel lines to the fuel rail
    - Power steering lines to the power steering pump
    - Alternator
    - All necessary electrical connectors
    - Control cables to the throttle body lever and intake manifold bracket
    - Serpentine drive belt
    - Heater outlet hose to the water pump
    - Vacuum hoses to the EVAP canister purge valve, vacuum modulator and power brake booster
    - Coolant inlet line to the coolant surge tank
    - Upper and lower radiator hoses
    - Throttle body inlet duct
    - Upper half of the air cleaner assembly
    - Negative battery cable

17. Check and fill all the engine fluids as necessary.

18. Start the vehicle and bleed the power steering system.

Water Pump

REMOVAL & INSTALLATION

2.4L Engine

1. Before servicing the vehicle, refer to the precautions in the beginning of this section.

2. Remove or disconnect the following:
- Negative battery cable
- Oxygen Sensor (O2S) electrical connector

3. Drain the cooling system.

4. Remove or disconnect the following:
- Heater hose from the thermostat housing
- Upper exhaust manifold heat shield
- Exhaust manifold brace-to-manifold bolt
- Lower exhaust manifold heat shield
- Manifold-to-exhaust pipe spring loaded bolts, break the loose using a 13mm box wrench

※ WARNING

It is necessary to relieve the spring pressure from 1 bolt prior to removing the 2nd bolt. If the spring pressure is not relieved, the exhaust pipe will twist and bind the bolt during removal.

- Both radiator outlet pipe-to-water pump cover bolts

5. Remove the manifold to exhaust pipe bolts from the exhaust pipe flange by removing or disconnecting the following:
- Either bolt clockwise 4 turns
- Other bolt
- First bolt

※ WARNING

DO NOT rotate the flex coupling more than 4 degrees or damage may occur.

6. Remove or disconnect the following:
- Exhaust pipe from the exhaust manifold by pulling it downward
- Radiator outlet pipe from the oil pan and transaxle
- Outlet pipe by pulling it downward from the water pump leaving the lower radiator hose attached

➡**Allow the radiator outlet pipe hang.**

- Exhaust manifold from the cylinder head, discard the seals and gaskets
- Timing chain cover and tensioner
- Water pump and timing chain housing as an assembly, then separate them

To install:

7. Thoroughly clean and dry all mounting surfaces.

8. Install or connect the following:
- New gasket
- Water pump to the cover and tighten the bolts finger-tight

➡**Lubricate the splines with clean grease.**

- Water pump using new gaskets and tighten the bolts and nuts finger-tight
- Radiator outlet pipe O-ring, lubricated with antifreeze
- Radiator outlet pipe onto the water pump cover and tighten the bolts finger-tight

9. With all gaps closed, torque the bolts, in the following sequence, to the proper values:
- Pump assembly-to-chain housing nuts to 19 ft. lbs. (26 Nm).
- Pump cover-to-pump bolts to 106 inch lbs. (12 Nm).
- Cover-to-block, bottom bolt first to 19 ft. lbs. (26 Nm).
- Radiator outlet pipe assembly-to-

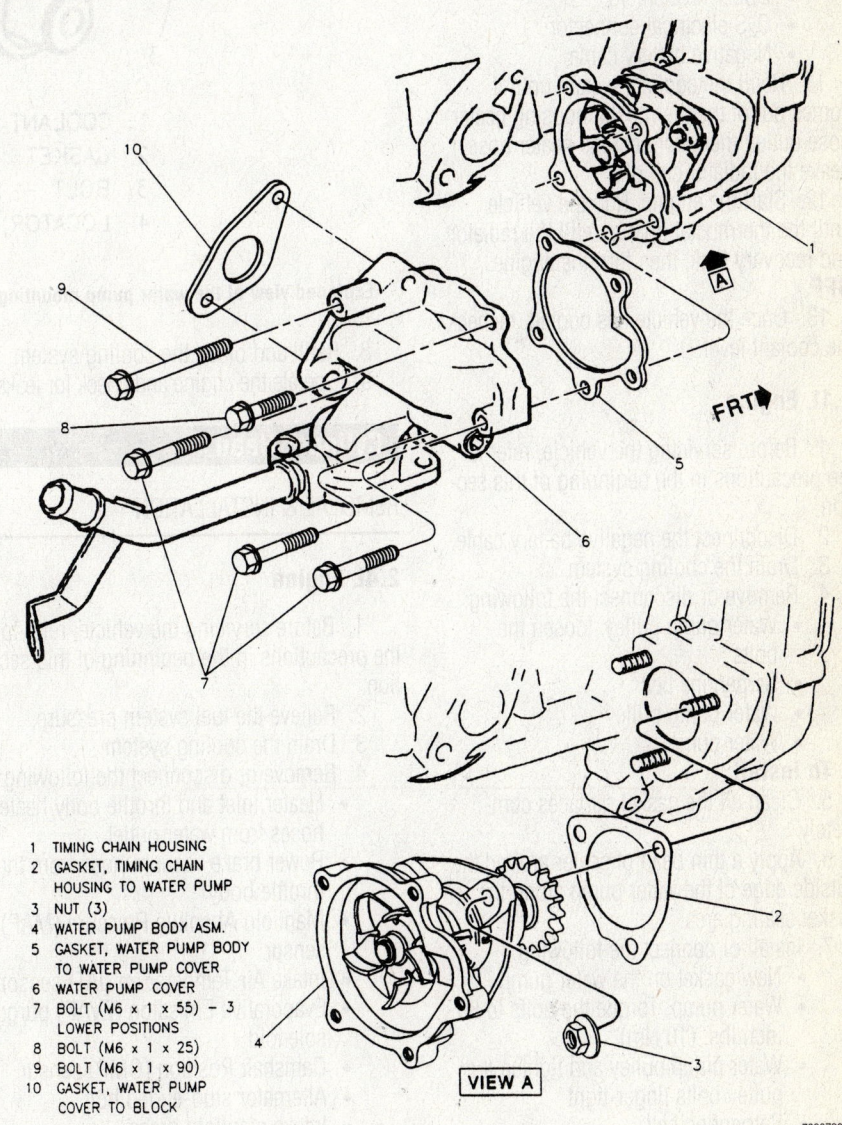

1 TIMING CHAIN HOUSING
2 GASKET, TIMING CHAIN HOUSING TO WATER PUMP
3 NUT (3)
4 WATER PUMP BODY ASM.
5 GASKET, WATER PUMP BODY TO WATER PUMP COVER
6 WATER PUMP COVER
7 BOLT (M6 x 1 x 55) – 3 LOWER POSITIONS
8 BOLT (M6 x 1 x 25)
9 BOLT (M6 x 1 x 90)
10 GASKET, WATER PUMP COVER TO BLOCK

VIEW A

79222Z201

Exploded view of the water pump mounting—2.4L engine

Timing belt service is covered in Section 4 of this manual

pump cover boltto 125 inch lbs. (14 Nm).

10. Install or connect the following:
- New gaskets
- Exhaust manifold
- Exhaust pipe to the manifold. Tighten the exhaust pipe flange bolts evenly and gradually to avoid binding, until fully seated.
- Radiator outlet pipe to the transaxle and oil pan
- Exhaust manifold brace, if removed
- Timing chain tensioner and front cover
- Lower heat shield
- Exhaust manifold brace to the manifold
- Torque the manifold-to-exhaust pipe nuts to 26 ft. lbs. (35 Nm)
- Upper heat shield
- O_2S electrical connector
- Negative battery cable

11. Refill the cooling system until it comes out of the thermostat housing heater hose outlet; then, connect the heater hose. Leave the radiator cap off.

12. Start the engine. Run the vehicle until the thermostat opens, refill the radiator and recovery tank, then turn the engine **OFF**.

13. Once the vehicle has cooled, recheck the coolant level.

3.1L Engine

1. Before servicing the vehicle, refer to the precautions in the beginning of this section.

2. Disconnect the negative battery cable.

3. Drain the cooling system.

4. Remove or disconnect the following:
- Water pump pulley, loosen the bolts
- Serpentine belt
- Water pump pulley
- Water pump

To install:

5. Clean all the gasket surfaces completely.

6. Apply a thin bead of sealer around the outside edge of the water pump along the gasket sealing area.

7. Install or connect the following:
- New gasket on the water pump
- Water pump. Torque the bolts to 89 inch lbs. (10 Nm).
- Water pump pulley and tighten the pulley bolts finger-tight
- Serpentine belt
- Water pump pulley bolts. Torque them to 18 ft. lbs. (25 Nm).
- Negative battery cable

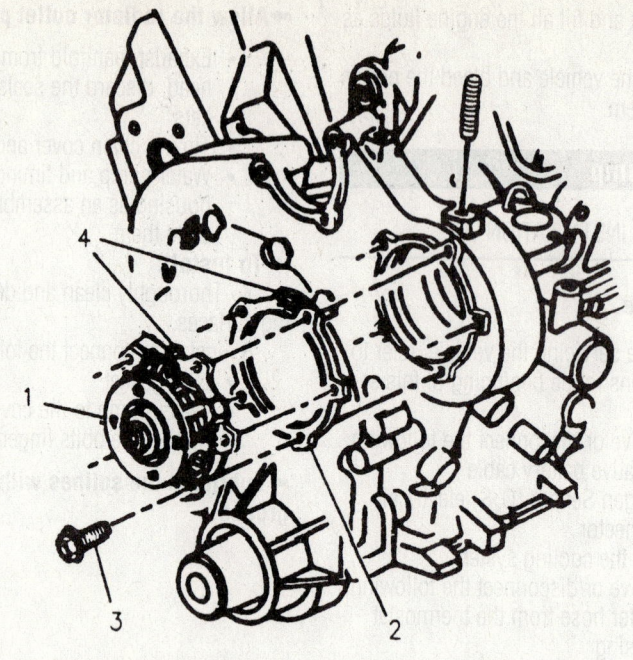

1 COOLANT PUMP
2 GASKET
3 BOLT – 10 N·m (89 LBS. IN.)
4 LOCATOR (MUST BE VERTICAL)

7922Z202

Exploded view of the water pump mounting—3.1L engine

8. Refill and bleed the cooling system.

9. Operate the engine and check for leaks.

Cylinder Head

REMOVAL & INSTALLATION

2.4L Engine

1. Before servicing the vehicle, refer to the precautions in the beginning of this section.

2. Relieve the fuel system pressure.

3. Drain the cooling system.

4. Remove or disconnect the following:
- Heater inlet and throttle body heater hoses from water outlet
- Power brake vacuum hose from the throttle body
- Manifold Absolute Pressure (MAP) sensor
- Intake Air Temperature (IAT) sensor
- Evaporative Emission (EVAP) purge solenoid
- Camshaft Position (CMP) sensor
- Alternator stud-ended bolt
- Intake manifold brace
- Intake manifold

5. Install the stud-ended alternator bolt back onto the engine.

6. Install Engine Support Fixtures J-28467-400 and J-28467-A.

7. Remove or disconnect the following:
- Exhaust manifold
- Ignition coil and module assembly
- Camshaft Position (CMP) sensor
- Power steering pump and move it aside without disconnecting the lines
- Vacuum line from the fuel pressure regulator
- Fuel injector and fuel injector wiring harness
- Fuel line clamp from the bracket located on top of the intake camshaft housing
- Fuel line rail and move it aside with the fuel lines attached
- Timing chain housing at the intake camshaft housing, but do not remove from the vehicle
- Oil switch electrical connector
- Transaxle fluid level indicator tube assembly from the exhaust camshaft cover and move it aside

➡️ **Any time the camshaft housing-to-cylinder head bolts are loosened or removed, the camshaft housing-to-cylinder head gasket must be replaced.**

- Intake camshaft the housing and gasket

❄❄ WARNING

Invert the camshaft housing once it is removed from the cylinder head. The lifters may fall out of the camshaft housing if it is not turned upside down. The lifters may be damaged if they fall out and hit a hard surface.

- Exhaust camshaft housing by reversing the bolts torque sequence
- Radiator inlet (upper) hose from the coolant outlet
- Coolant temperature sensor electrical connectors
- Cylinder head by reversing the bolt torque sequence and discard the gasket

❄❄ WARNING

Do not use abrasive pads to clean the cylinder head or block surfaces. An abrasive pad may damage the cylinder head and block. Use a razor or scraper to clean the gasket surfaces.

To install:

➡ **Refer to Section 1 of this manual for the cylinder head torque sequence illustration. The illustration is located after the Torque Specification Chart.**

8. Clean all gasket surfaces completely. Be sure the threaded holes in the engine block for the cylinder head bolts are clean.
9. Install or connect the following:
   - New cylinder head gasket
   - Cylinder head

➡ **New replacement head bolts should be used. Do not use the old bolts. Coat the new cylinder head bolt threads with clean engine oil before installation.**

10. Install the new cylinder head bolts and tighten, in sequence, as follows:
   a. Step 1: Bolts 1 through 8: 40 ft. lbs. (65 Nm)
   b. Step 2: Bolts 9 and 10: 30 ft. lbs. (40 Nm)
   c. Step 3: All 10 bolts: an additional 90 degree (¼) turn
11. Install or connect the following:
   - Intake and exhaust camshaft housings. Tighten the long bolts to 11 ft. lbs. (15 Nm) plus an additional 90 degree (¼) turn and the short bolts to 11 ft. lbs. (15 Nm) plus an additional 30 degree (⅙) turn.

- Timing chain
- Timing chain housing
- Upper radiator hose to the water outlet
- Both coolant sensor connectors
- Fuel rail on the intake manifold
- Intake manifold brace
- MAP sensor
- IAT sensor
- EVAP purge solenoid
- CMP sensor
- MAP sensor vacuum hose to the intake manifold
- Power steering pump
- Throttle body and throttle cable bracket
- Throttle body air intake duct
- Oil fill tube. Lubricate the O-ring with engine oil before installation.
- Ignition coil and module assembly
- Fuel injector harness electrical connector

12. Remove the engine support fixture.
13. Install or connect the following:
   - Exhaust manifold
   - Negative battery cable
14. Fill all fluids to their proper levels.

➡ **An oil and filter change is recommended.**

15. Start the vehicle and verify no leaks.

3.1L Engine

LEFT (FRONT)

1. Before servicing the vehicle, refer to the precautions in the beginning of this section.
2. Relieve the fuel system pressure.
3. Drain the cooling system.
4. Remove or disconnect the following:
   - Upper half of the air cleaner assembly
   - Throttle body air inlet duct
   - Exhaust crossover pipe heat shield and the crossover pipe
   - Spark plug wires from the spark plugs and move them aside
   - Rocker arm covers
   - Intake plenum and lower intake manifold
   - Left side exhaust manifold
   - Oil level indicator tube

➡ **When removing the valvetrain components, keep them in order for installation in the same locations they were removed from.**

   - Rocker arms nut, rocker arms, balls and pushrods

- Cylinder head bolts, evenly, by reversing the torque sequence
- Cylinder head

To install:

5. Clean all the gasket surfaces completely. Clean the threads on the cylinder head bolts and block threads.
6. Install the new cylinder head gasket with the words **THIS SIDE UP** showing.
7. Coat the bolt threads with sealer and install finger-tight.

➡ **Refer to Section 1 of this manual for the cylinder head torque sequence illustration. The illustration is located after the Torque Specification Chart.**

8. On 1997 models, tighten the cylinder head bolts in sequence to:
   a. Step 1: 33 ft. lbs. (45 Nm).
   b. Step 2: an additional 90 degree (¼) turn.
9. On 1998–01 models, tighten the cylinder head bolts in sequence to:
   a. Step 1: 37 ft. lbs. (50 Nm).
   b. Step 2: an additional 90 degree (¼) turn.
10. Install or connect the following:
   - Pushrods, rocker arms and balls. Tighten the rocker arm nuts to 18 ft. lbs. (25 Nm).
   - Lower intake manifold
   - Intake plenum
   - Rocker arm covers
   - Oil level indicator tube
   - Spark plug wires to spark plugs
   - Left side exhaust manifold
   - Exhaust crossover pipe and crossover pipe heat shield
   - Upper half of the air cleaner assembly
   - Throttle body air inlet duct
   - Negative battery cable
11. Refill the cooling system.
12. Drain the engine oil and refill. A filter change is recommended.
13. Start the engine and verify no leaks.

RIGHT (REAR)

1. Before servicing the vehicle, refer to the precautions in the beginning of this section.
2. Relieve the fuel system pressure.
3. Drain the cooling system.
4. Remove or disconnect the following:
   - Upper half of the air cleaner assembly
   - Throttle body air inlet duct
   - Exhaust crossover pipe heat shield and the crossover pipe
   - Oxygen (O_2S) sensor

- Exhaust pipe from the exhaust manifold
- Right side exhaust manifold
- Spark plug wires from spark plugs and move them aside
- Rocker arm covers
- Upper intake plenum
- Lower intake manifold

➡ **When removing the valvetrain components, keep them in order for installation in the same locations they were removed from.**

- Rocker arms nut, rocker arms, balls and pushrods
- Cylinder head bolts, evenly, by reversing the torque sequence
- Cylinder head

To install:

5. Clean all the gasket surfaces completely. Clean the threads on the cylinder head bolts and block threads.

6. Install the new cylinder head gasket so the words **THIS SIDE UP** showing.

7. Coat the bolt threads with sealer and install finger-tight.

➡ **Refer to Section 1 of this manual for the cylinder head torque sequence illustration. The illustration is located after the Torque Specification Chart.**

8. On 1997 models, tighten the cylinder head bolts in sequence to:
   a. Step 1: 33 ft. lbs. (45 Nm).
   b. Step 2: an additional 90 degree (¼) turn.

9. On 1998–01 models, tighten the cylinder head bolts in sequence to:
   a. Step 1: 37 ft. lbs. (50 Nm).
   b. Step 2: an additional 90 degree (¼) turn.

10. Install or connect the following:
- Pushrods, rocker arms and balls. Tighten the rocker arm nuts to 18 ft. lbs. (25 Nm).
- Lower intake manifold and upper intake plenum
- Rocker arm covers
- Spark plug wires to spark plugs
- Exhaust manifold
- Exhaust pipe to the exhaust manifold
- O₂S sensor
- Exhaust crossover pipe and heat shield.
- Upper half of the air cleaner assembly
- Throttle body air inlet duct
- Negative battery cable

11. Refill the cooling system.

12. Drain the engine oil and refill. A filter change is recommended.

13. Start the engine and verify no leaks.

Rocker Arms

REMOVAL & INSTALLATION

2.4L Engine

The 2.4L engine is not equipped with rocker arms. The camshafts directly actuate the valves.

3.1L Engine

1. Before servicing the vehicle, refer to the precautions in the beginning of this section.

2. Disconnect the negative battery cable.

3. Partially drain the cooling system to a level below the coolant pipe.

4. For the left side (front), remove or disconnect the following:
- Coolant bypass hose clamp at the coolant tube
- Coolant tube from the cylinder head and move it aside
- Positive Crankcase Ventilation (PCV) valve from the rocker arm cover

5. For the right side (rear), remove or disconnect the following:
- Spark plug wires from the spark plugs and upper intake plenum wire retainer and move them aside
- Power brake booster vacuum pipe from the intake plenum
- Serpentine belt
- Alternator
- Ignition assembly and Evaporative Emission (EVAP) canister purge solenoid as an assembly

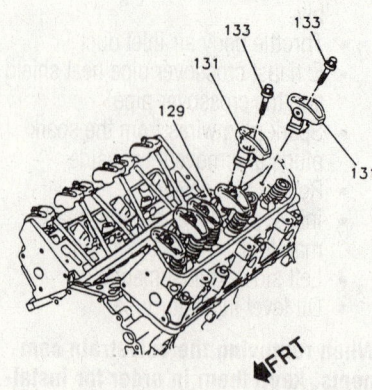

129 PUSHROD
131 ARM, ROLLER ROCKER
133 BOLT

79222205

Rocker arm components—3.1L engine

- Rocker arm cover
- Rocker arm bolts, balls, rocker arms and pushrods

To install:

6. Clean all gasket surfaces completely.

7. Coat all valvetrain components with engine oil.

8. Install or connect the following:
- Pushrods, rocker arms, balls and bolts. Tighten the rocker arm bolts to 89 inch lbs. (10 Nm) plus an additional 30 degree turn.
- Rocker arm cover using a new gasket. Tighten the bolts to 90 inch lbs. (10 Nm).

9. For the left side (front), install or connect the following:
- PCV valve to the rocker arm cover
- Coolant tube and thermostat bypass hose. Tighten the screw at the water pump to 106 inch lbs. (12 Nm) and the nut/bolt at the cylinder head corner to 18 ft. lbs. (25 Nm).

10. For the right side (rear), install or connect following:
- Ignition assembly and EVAP canister purge solenoid as an assembly
- Alternator
- Serpentine belt
- Power brake booster vacuum pipe to the plenum
- EVAP solenoid and ignition assembly
- Spark plug wires to the plenum and the spark plugs
- Negative battery cable

11. Refill the cooling system.

12. Start the vehicle and verify no leaks.

Intake Manifold

REMOVAL & INSTALLATION

2.4L Engine

1. Before servicing the vehicle, refer to the precautions in the beginning of this section.

2. Relieve the fuel system pressure.

3. Drain the cooling system to a level below the intake manifold.

4. Disconnect the electrical connectors from the following:
- Manifold Absolute Pressure (MAP) sensor
- Intake Air Temperature (IAT) sensor
- Evaporative Emissions (EVAP) canister purge solenoid
- Fuel injectors

5. Disconnect the vacuum hoses from the following:

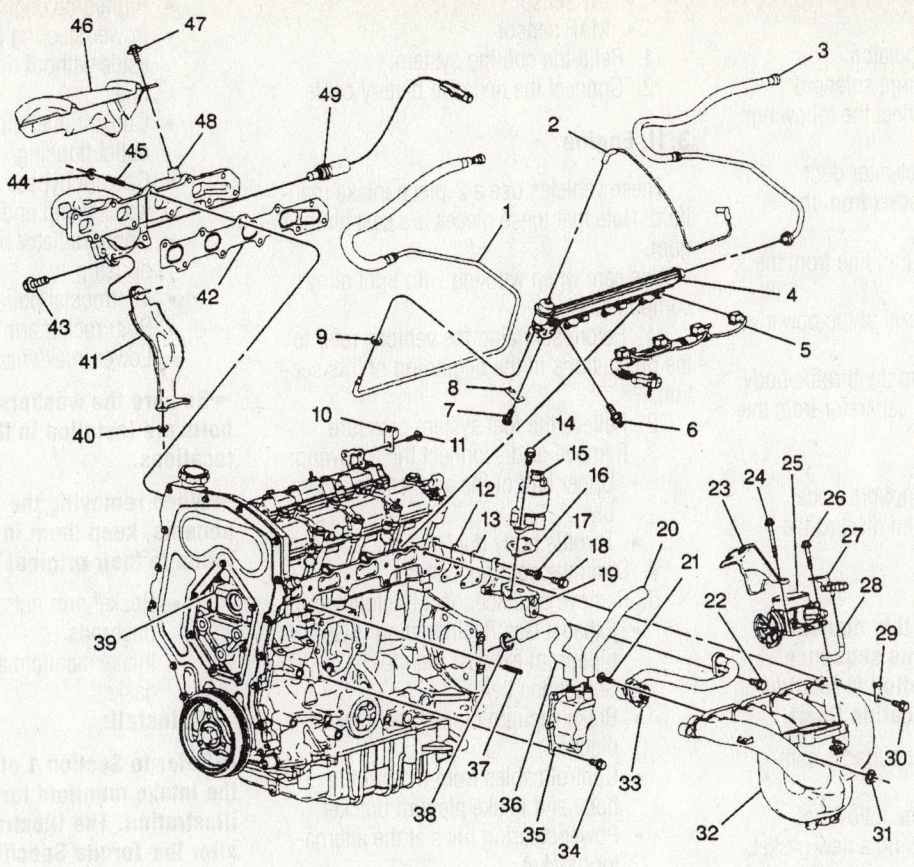

(1) Fuel Return Line
(2) Fuel Pressure Regulator Vacuum Harness
(3) Fuel Line
(4) Fuel Rail (with Injectors)
(5) Fuel Injector Harness
(6) Bolt, Fuel Rail to Cylinder Head
(7) Bolt, Fuel Line Retainer
(8) Fuel Line Retainer
(9) Fuel Line Seal
(10) Fuel Line Retainer
(11) Bolt, Fuel Line Retainer
(12) Gasket, EGR Adapter
(13) EGR Passage Cover (Export Only)
(14) Bolt, EGR Valve
(15) EGR Valve
(16) Gasket, EGR Valve
(17) Bolt, EGR Valve Adapter to Cylinder Head
(18) Bolt, EGR Passage Cover (Export Only)
(19) EGR Adapter
(20) Oil/Air Separator Fresh Air Tube
(21) Bolt, EGR Tube to Intake Manifold
(22) Bolt, EGR Tube to EGR Adapter
(23) Throttle Cable Bracket
(24) Bolt, Throttle Body to Intake Manifold
(25) Throttle Body
(26) Bolt, Throttle Body to Intake Manifold

(27) Manifold Absolute Pressure Sensor
(28) MAP Sensor Vacuum Line
(29) Fuel Rail Bracket
(30) Bolt, Intake Manifold to Cylinder Head
(31) Nut, Intake Manifold to Cylinder Head
(32) Intake Manifold
(33) EGR Pipe
(34) Bolt, Oil/Air Separator to Engine Block
(35) Oil/Air Separator
(36) Oil/Air Separator Foul Air Tube
(37) Stud, Intake Manifold to Cylinder Head
(38) Clamp, Oil/Air Separator Tube
(39) Cylinder Head
(40) Nut, Exhaust Manifold Brace to Oil Pan Stud
(41) Exhaust Manifold Brace
(42) Gasket, Exhaust Manifold
(43) Bolt, Exhaust Manifold Brace to Exhaust Manifold
(44) Nut, Exhaust Manifold to Cylinder Head
(45) Stud, Exhaust Manifold to Cylinder Head
(46) Exhaust Manifold Heat Shield
(47) Bolt, Exhaust Manifold Heat Shield to Exhaust Manifold
(48) Exhaust Manifold
(49) Oxygen Sensor

7922Z206

Exploded view of the intake and exhaust manifolds—2.4L engine

Refer to Section 1 for engine rebuilding specifications

- MAP sensor
- Intake manifold
- Fuel pressure regulator
- EVAP canister purge solenoid

6. Remove or disconnect the following:
- Air cleaner duct
- Vent tube-to-air cleaner duct
- Control cable bracket from the intake manifold
- Power brake vacuum line from the intake manifold
- Vacuum line bracket at the power steering pump
- Coolant lines from the throttle body
- Crankcase air/oil separator from the intake manifold
- Oil fill tube
- Intake manifold support brace
- Intake manifold and discard the gasket

To install:

➡ **Refer to Section 1 of this manual for the intake manfold torque sequence illustration. The illustration is located after the Torque Specification Chart.**

7. Clean all the gasket surfaces completely.

8. Install or connect the following:
- Intake manifold using a new gasket. Tighten the fasteners, in sequence, to 18 ft. lbs. (25 Nm).
- Intake manifold brace. Tighten the bolts to 19 ft. lbs. (26 Nm).

➡ **Tighten the brace-to-block bolts first, then the brace-to-manifold bolt.**

- Oil fill tube using a new O-ring lubricated with engine oil; then, rotate it to gain clearance for the oil/air separator nipple on fill tube.
- Crankcase air/oil separator to the intake manifold
- Coolant lines to the throttle body
- Vacuum line bracket at the power steering pump
- Power brake vacuum line to the intake manifold
- Control cable bracket to the intake manifold
- Vent tube-to-air cleaner duct
- Air cleaner duct

9. Connect the vacuum hoses to the following:
- EVAP canister purge solenoid
- Fuel pressure regulator
- Intake manifold
- MAP sensor

10. Connect the electrical connectors to the following:
- Fuel injectors
- EVAP canister purge solenoid

- IAT sensor
- MAP sensor

11. Refill the cooling system.
12. Connect the negative battery cable.

3.1L Engine

These vehicles use a 2-piece intake manifold. Note that these pieces are cast aluminum.

Use care when working with light alloy components.

1. Before servicing the vehicle, refer to the precautions in the beginning of this section.

2. Relieve the fuel system pressure.
3. Remove or disconnect the following:
- Upper half of the air cleaner assembly
- Throttle body duct

4. Drain the cooling system.
5. Remove or disconnect the following:
- Exhaust Gas Recirculation (EGR) pipe from exhaust manifold
- Serpentine belt
- Brake vacuum pipe at the intake plenum
- Control cables from the throttle body and intake plenum bracket
- Power steering lines at the alternator bracket
- Alternator
- Spark plug wires from the spark plugs and the intake plenum retainers
- Ignition assembly and Evaporative Emission (EVAP) canister purge solenoid as an assembly

6. Disconnect the electrical connectors from the following:
- Throttle Position (TP) sensor
- Idle Air Control (IAC) valve
- Fuel Injectors
- Engine Coolant Temperature (ECT) sensor
- Manifold Absolute Pressure (MAP) sensor
- Camshaft Position (CMP) sensor

7. Disconnect the vacuum lines from the following:
- Vacuum modulator
- Fuel pressure regulator
- Positive Crankcase Ventilation (PCV) valve

8. Remove or disconnect the following:
- MAP sensor from upper intake manifold
- Upper intake manifold
- Fuel lines from the fuel rail and bracket

9. Install an engine support fixture.
10. Remove or disconnect the following:

- Right side engine mount
- Power steering pump and move it aside without disconnecting the lines
- Coolant inlet pipe from coolant outlet housing
- Coolant bypass hose from the water pump and cylinder head
- Upper radiator hose at thermostat housing
- Thermostat housing
- Both rocker arm covers
- Lower intake manifold bolts

➡ **Be sure the washers on the 4 center bolts are installed in their original locations.**

➡ **When removing the valvetrain components, keep them in order for installation to their original locations.**

- Rocker arm nuts, rocker arms and pushrods
- Intake manifold and discard the gasket

To install:

➡ **Refer to Section 1 of this manual for the intake manifold torque sequence illustration. The illustration is located after the Torque Specification Chart.**

11. Clean the gasket material from all mating surfaces. Remove all excess RTV sealant from front and rear ridges of cylinder block.

12. Place a 3mm bead of RTV on each ridge, where the front and rear of the intake manifold contact the block.

13. Install or connect the following:
- Lower intake manifold using a new gasket
- Pushrods and rocker arms

➡ **Be sure the pushrods are properly seated in the valve lifters and rocker arms.**

- Rocker arm nuts. Tighten them to 18 ft. lbs. (24 Nm).
- Lower intake manifold bolts, lubricated with sealant. Tighten the bolts to 115 inch lbs. (13 Nm).
- Both rocker arm covers
- Thermostat housing
- Upper radiator hose at thermostat housing
- Coolant bypass hose to the water pump and cylinder head
- Coolant inlet pipe to coolant outlet housing
- Power steering pump
- Right side engine mount

14. Remove the engine support fixture.

15. Install or connect the following:
- Fuel lines to the fuel rail and bracket
- Upper intake manifold. Tighten the mounting bolts to 18 ft. lbs. (25 Nm).

- MAP sensor to upper intake manifold

16. Connect the vacuum lines to the following:
- PCV valve
- Fuel pressure regulator

- Vacuum modulator

17. Connect the electrical connectors to the following:
- CMP sensor
- MAP sensor
- ECT sensor

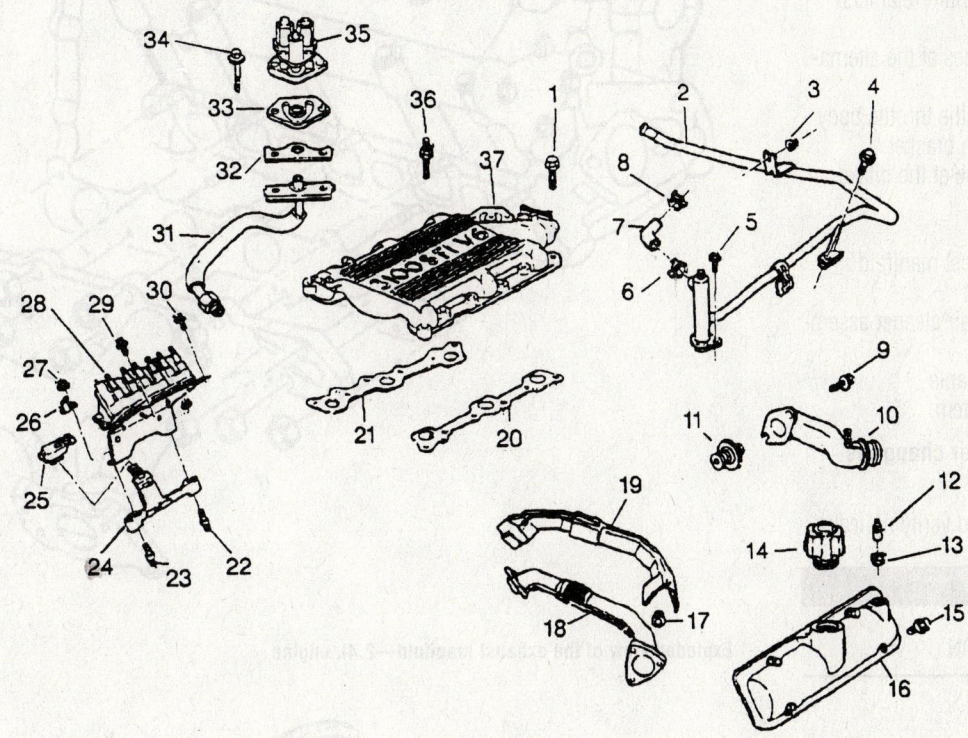

(1) Upper Intake Manifold Bolt
(2) Thermostat Bypass Pipe
(3) Thermostat Bypass Pipe Nut
(4) Thermostat Bypass Pipe Bolt
(5) Thermostat Bypass Pipe Screw
(6) Thermostat Bypass Hose Clamp
(7) Thermostat Bypass Hose
(8) Thermostat Bypass Hose Clamp
(9) Coolant Outlet Bolt
(10) Coolant Outlet Assembly
(11) Thermostat
(12) PCV Valve
(13) PCV Valve Grommet
(14) Oil Fill Cap
(15) Rocker Arm Cover Bolt
(16) Rocker Arm Cover
(17) Exhaust Crossover Nut
(18) Exhaust Crossover Pipe

(19) Exhaust Crossover Upper Heat Shield
(20) Upper Intake Manifold Gasket
(21) Upper Intake Manifold Gasket
(22) EVAP Canister Purge Valve Bracket Stud
(23) EVAP Canister Purge Valve Bracket Stud
(24) EVAP Canister Purge Valve Bracket
(25) EVAP Canister Purge Valve
(26) Spark Plug Wire Support
(27) Electronic Ignition System Nut
(28) Electronic Ignition System
(29) Electronic Ignition System Bolt
(30) Electronic Ignition System Bolt
(31) EGR Valve Pipe Assembly
(32) EGR Valve Pipe Gasket
(33) EGR Valve Gasket
(34) EGR Valve Assembly Bolt
(35) EGR Valve Assembly
(36) Upper Intake Manifold Stud
(37) Upper Intake Manifold

Exploded view of the upper intake and related components—3.1L engine

79222207

For engine torque specifications, refer to Section 1 of this manual

- Fuel injectors
- IAC valve
- TP sensor

18. Install or connect the following:
- Ignition assembly and EVAP canister purge solenoid as an assembly
- Spark plug wires to the spark plugs and the intake plenum retainers
- Alternator
- Power steering lines at the alternator bracket
- Control cables to the throttle body and intake plenum bracket
- Brake vacuum pipe at the intake plenum
- Serpentine belt
- EGR pipe to exhaust manifold
- Throttle body duct
- Upper half of the air cleaner assembly
- Negative battery cable

19. Fill the cooling system.

➡**An engine oil and filter change is recommended.**

20. Start the vehicle and verify no leaks.

Exhaust Manifold

REMOVAL & INSTALLATION

2.4L Engine

1. Before servicing the vehicle, refer to the precautions in the beginning of this section.
2. Remove or disconnect the following:
- Negative battery cable
- Oxygen (O$_2$S) sensor
- Exhaust manifold brace-to-manifold bolt
- Heat shield
- Exhaust manifold-to-exhaust pipe spring loaded bolts

➡**The nuts should be loosened alternately and evenly to prevent the pipe from binding the nuts.**

➡**Pull down and back on the exhaust pipe to disengage it from the exhaust manifold bolts.**

✱✱ WARNING

Do not bend the exhaust flex coupler more than 3 degrees in any direction. Movement of more than 3 degrees will damage the flex coupler.

3. Remove the exhaust manifold.
To install:
4. Clean all gasket surfaces.

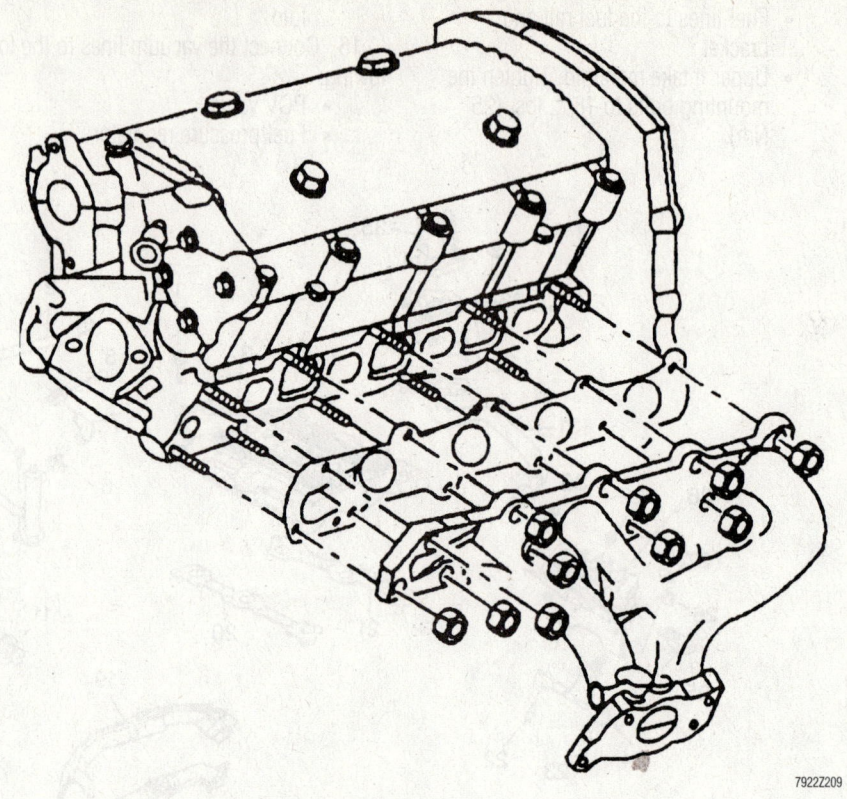

79222Z209

Exploded view of the exhaust manifold—2.4L engine

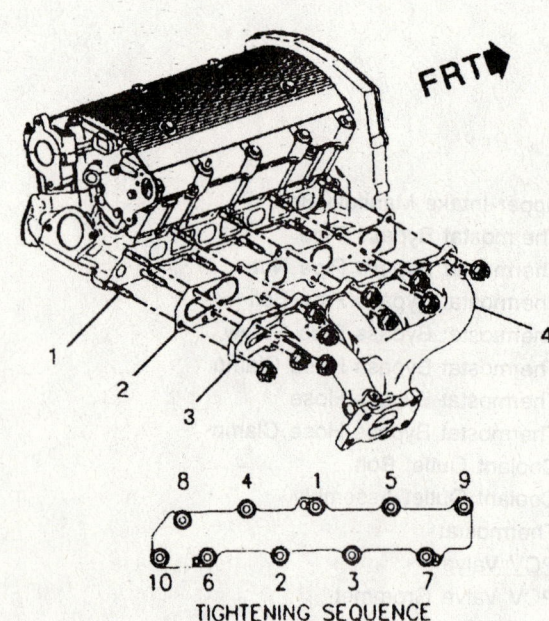

TIGHTENING SEQUENCE

1. STUD, EXHAUST MANIFOLD
2. GASKET, EXHAUST MANIFOLD
3. MANIFOLD, EXHAUST
4. NUT, EXHAUST MANIFOLD, MUST BE TIGHTENED IN SEQUENCE SHOWN TO 12.5 N•m (110 LB. IN.)

7922YG11

Exhaust manifold torque sequence—2.4L engine

5. Install or connect the following:
- Exhaust manifold using a new gasket. Tighten the nuts, in sequence, to 110 inch lbs. (13 Nm).
- Heat shield
- Exhaust manifold brace-to-manifold bolt
- Exhaust manifold-to-exhaust pipe nuts. Tighten the nuts evenly to 26 ft. lbs. (35 Nm).
- O_2S sensor
- Negative battery cable

6. Start the vehicle and verify no exhaust leaks.

3.1L Engine

1. Before servicing the vehicle, refer to the precautions in the beginning of this section.

2. Partially drain the cooling system.

3. Remove or disconnect the following:
- Negative battery cable
- Upper half of the air cleaner assembly
- Throttle cable duct

4. On the left side (front), remove the following:
- Radiator hose from the thermostat housing

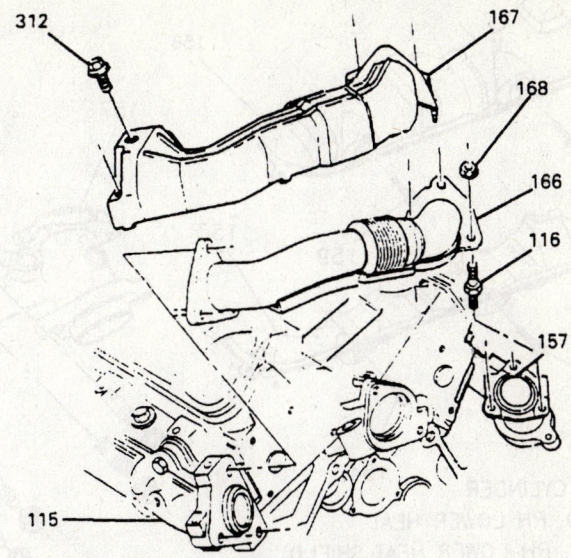

115	MANIFOLD, LEFT HAND EXHAUST
116	STUD, EXHAUST CROSSOVER
157	MANIFOLD, RIGHT HAND EXHAUST
166	CROSSOVER PIPE, EXHAUST
167	SHIELD, EXHAUST CROSSOVER UPPER HEAT
168	NUT, EXHAUST CROSSOVER
312	BOLT/SCREW, EXHAUST CROSSOVER UPPER HEAT SHIELD

Exploded view of the exhaust crossover pipe—3.1L engine

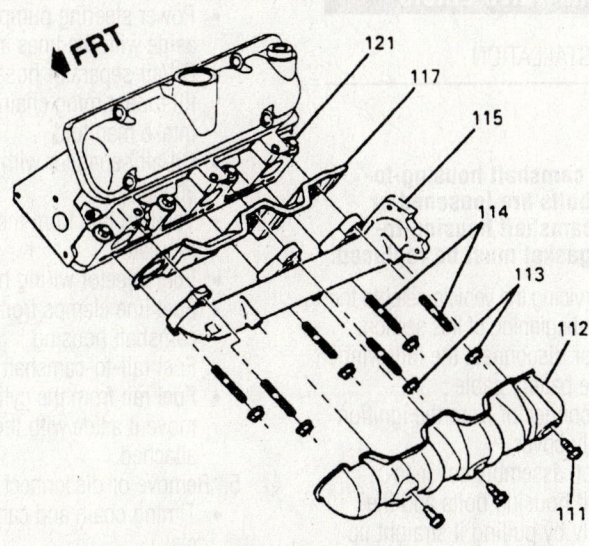

111	SCREW, LH EXHAUST MANIFOLD HEAT SHIELD
112	SHIELD LH EXHAUST MANIFOLD
113	NUT, LH EXHAUST MANIFOLD
114	STUD, LH EXHAUST MANIFOLD
115	MANIFOLD, LH EXHAUST
117	GASKET, LH EXHAUST MANIFOLD
121	HEAD, LH CYLINDER

Exploded view of the left-hand exhaust manifold—3.1L engine

- Coolant bypass hose from the coolant pump and exhaust manifold

5. Remove or disconnect the following:
- Exhaust crossover heat shield
- Exhaust crossover pipe from the manifold

6. On the right side (rear), remove or disconnect the following:
- Heated Oxygen (HO_2S) sensor
- Exhaust Gas Recirculation (EGR) pipe from the exhaust manifold
- Transaxle oil fill tube
- Lever indicator assembly
- Front exhaust pipe from the exhaust manifold
- Exhaust pipe from the converter flange and support the converter
- Converter heat shield from the body

7. Remove or disconnect the following:
- Secondary ignition wires from the spark plugs
- Exhaust manifold heat shield
- Exhaust manifold

To install:

8. Clean mating surfaces.

For complete mechanical specifications, refer to Section 1 of this manual

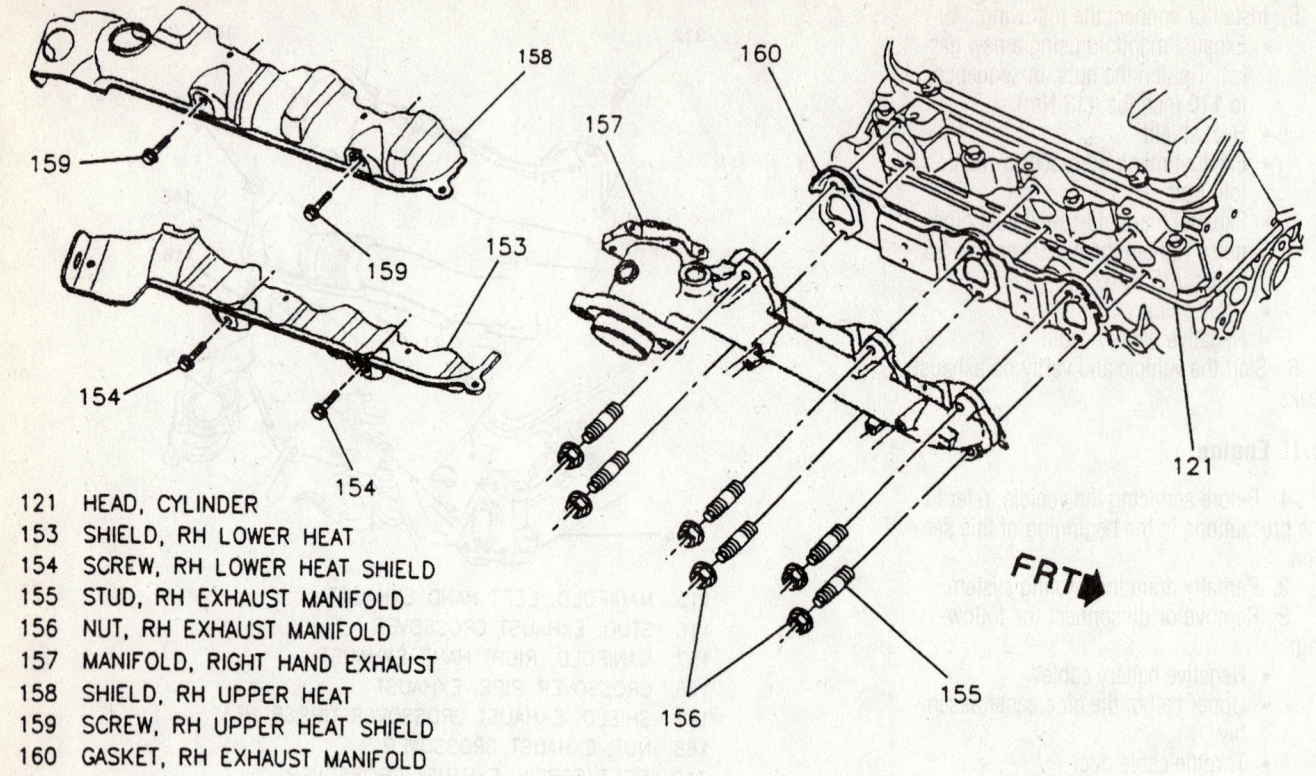

121 HEAD, CYLINDER
153 SHIELD, RH LOWER HEAT
154 SCREW, RH LOWER HEAT SHIELD
155 STUD, RH EXHAUST MANIFOLD
156 NUT, RH EXHAUST MANIFOLD
157 MANIFOLD, RIGHT HAND EXHAUST
158 SHIELD, RH UPPER HEAT
159 SCREW, RH UPPER HEAT SHIELD
160 GASKET, RH EXHAUST MANIFOLD

Exploded view of the right-hand exhaust manifold—3.1L engine

9. Install or connect the following:
- Exhaust manifold using a new gasket. Tighten the nuts to 12 ft. lbs. (16 Nm).
- Exhaust manifold heat shield
- Secondary ignition wires to the spark plugs

10. On the right side (rear), install or connect the following:
- Converter heat shield to the body
- Exhaust pipe to the exhaust manifold
- Transaxle oil level indicator and fill tube assembly
- HO2S sensor
- EGR pipe to exhaust manifold

11. Install or connect the following:
- Exhaust crossover pipe to the manifold
- Exhaust crossover pipe heat shield

12. On the left side (front), install or connect the following:
- Coolant bypass pipe to the coolant pump and exhaust manifold
- Radiator hose to the coolant outlet housing

13. Install or connect the following:
- Throttle body duct
- Upper half of the air cleaner
- Negative battery cable

Camshaft and Valve Lifters

REMOVAL & INSTALLATION

2.4L Engine

➡**Anytime the camshaft housing-to-cylinder head bolts are loosened or removed, the camshaft housing-to-cylinder head gasket must be replaced.**

1. Before servicing the vehicle, refer to the precautions in the beginning of this section.
2. Remove or disconnect the following:
- Negative battery cable
- 11-pin connector from the ignition assembly cover
- 4 ignition assembly cover-to-camshaft housing bolts and the assembly by pulling it straight up
- Connector assemblies using a spark plug boot wire remover
3. On the exhaust camshaft side, remove or disconnect the following:
- Transaxle fill tube
- Oil pressure switch
4. On the intake camshaft side, remove or disconnect the following:
- Camshaft Position (CMP) sensor and power steering pressure switch connector

- Drive belt
- Power steering pump and move it aside with the lines attached
- Oil/air separator hoses from the oil fill tube, timing chain housing and intake manifold
- Oil/air separator with the hoses attached
- Vacuum line from the fuel pressure regulator
- Fuel injector wiring harness
- Fuel line clamps from the intake camshaft housing
- Fuel rail-to-camshaft housing bolts
- Fuel rail from the cylinder head and move it aside with the fuel lines attached.
5. Remove or disconnect the following:
- Timing chain and camshaft sprockets
- Timing chain housing bolts but do not the housing
- Camshaft housing cover-to-camshaft housing bolts
- Camshaft housing-to-cylinder head bolts by reversing the tightening sequence

➡**Leave 2 bolts loosely in place to hold the camshaft housing while separating camshaft cover from housing.**

6. Push the cover off the housing by threading 4 of the housing-to-cylinder head bolts into the tapped holes in the cam housing cover. Tighten the bolts evenly so the cover does not bind on the dowel pins.

7. Remove or disconnect the following:
- Both loosely installed camshaft housing-to-cylinder head bolts
- Camshaft housing cover and discard the gaskets

➡**Note the position of the chain sprocket dowel pin for reassembly.**

- Camshaft, be careful do not damage the camshaft oil seal
- Camshaft oil seal from camshaft and discard it

➡**The oil seal must be replaced any time the housing and cover are separated.**

➡**The valve lifters must be kept in order for installation in the same locations they were removed.**

- Valve lifters from the camshaft housing
- Camshaft carrier from the cylinder head and discard the gasket

To install:

8. Clean all gasket surfaces.
9. Install or connect the following:
- New gasket on the cylinder head
- Camshaft housing using 1 bolt loosely to hold it in place

➡**If the camshaft is replaced, the valve lifters must also be replaced.**

- Valve lifters in their original bores

➡**Lubricate the camshaft lobes, journals and lifters with camshaft and lifter prelube.**

❊❊ WARNING

The camshaft lobes and journals must be adequately lubricated or engine damage could occur upon start up.

- Camshaft, so the timing chain sprocket dowel pin faces upward and aligns with the lifter bores centerline
- New camshaft seals in the cover

➡**The seals for the intake and exhaust covers are different; be sure the correct seals are used.**

10. Remove the camshaft housing securing bolt

11. Lubricate the camshaft housing-to-cover bolts with thread locking compound.

12. Install or connect the following:
- Camshaft housing cover. Tighten the bolts, in sequence, to 11 ft. lbs. (15 Nm) plus 75 degrees additional rotation (Long bolts) and to 16 ft. lbs. (21 Nm) plus 25 degrees additional rotation (Short bolts).
- Timing chain housing bolts
- Timing chain and sprockets
- New O-rings on the fuel injectors, lubricated with engine oil
- Fuel rail. Tighten the bolts to 19 ft. lbs. (26 Nm).

13. On the intake camshaft side, install or connect the following:
- Fuel line clamp bolts on top of the intake camshaft housing
- Vacuum line to the fuel pressure regulator
- Fuel injector harness connector
- Oil/air separator
- Oil/air separator hoses to the oil fill tube, timing chain housing and intake manifold
- New oil seal into the intake camshaft housing, lubricated with oil
- Power steering pump pulley onto the intake camshaft
- Power steering pump
- Drive belt
- CMP sensor and power steering pressure switch connectors

14. On the exhaust camshaft side, install or connect the following:
- Transaxle fill tube
- Oil pressure switch

15. Install or connect the following:
- Ignition assembly on the camshaft housing. Tighten the bolts to 13 ft. lbs. (18 Nm).

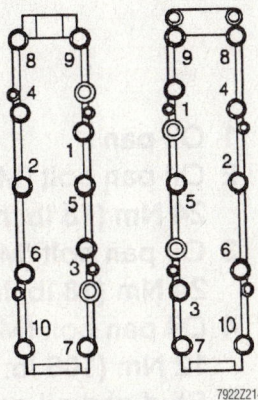

7922Z214

Camshaft housing bolt tightening sequence—2.4L engine

- 11-pin connector to ignition assembly
- Negative battery cable

16. Start the vehicle and verify proper operation and no leaks.

3.1L Engine

1. Before servicing the vehicle, refer to the precautions in the beginning of this section.

2. Relieve the fuel system pressure.

3. Remove or disconnect the following:
- Engine assembly

➡**When removing valvetrain components, marked them for installation in the same location they are removed from. When the camshaft is being replaced, the valve lifters should also be replaced.**

- Rocker arm covers
- Intake manifold
- Rocker arm, rocker arm balls, rocker arms and pushrods
- Lifter guide bolts and the guide
- Valve lifter(s) from the lifter bores
- Crankshaft balancer and front cover
- Timing chain and sprockets
- Oil pump driven gear bolt and gear
- Camshaft thrust plate
- Camshaft

➡**Avoid marring the camshaft bearing surfaces.**

To install:

4. Install or connect the following:
- Camshaft, lubricated with prelube
- Camshaft thrust plate. Tighten bolts to 89 inch lbs. (10 Nm).
- Oil pump driven gear. Tighten bolt to 27 ft. lbs. (36 Nm).
- Timing chain and sprocket
- Camshaft thrust button and front cover
- Crankshaft balancer

5. Lubricate the bearing surfaces with Molykote®.

➡**Installation of a new camshaft or a wear pattern on the old valve lifter will require the replacement of the camshaft and lifters together. If camshaft replacement is not necessary, be sure to install the used valve lifters in their original position upon reinstallation.**

6. Install or connect the following:
- Valve lifters in their original locations

Please refer to Section 8 for electric cooling fan wiring schematics

- Lifter guide. Tighten the bolts to 89 inch lbs. (10 Nm).
- Pushrods, rocker arms, rocker balls and rocker arm nuts. Tighten the rocker arm nuts to 89 inch lbs. (10 Nm) plus an additional 30 degrees.
- Intake manifold and rocker arm covers
- Engine assembly
- Negative battery cable

7. Adjust the valves, as required.

8. Start the engine and verify no oil leaks.

Valve Lash

ADJUSTMENT

The 2.4L and 3.1L engines are equipped with hydraulic valve lifters; no adjustment is necessary.

Starter

REMOVAL & INSTALLATION

2.4L Engine

1. Before servicing the vehicle, refer to the precautions in the beginning of this section.

2. Remove or disconnect the following:
- Negative battery cable
- Air inlet duct from the throttle body
- Oil filter
- Starter bolts
- Starter electrical connectors
- Starter

To install:

3. Install or connect the following:
- Starter
- Starter electrical connectors
- Starter. Tighten the bolts to 66 ft. lbs. (90 Nm).
- Oil filter
- Air inlet duct to the throttle body
- Negative battery cable

4. Check the oil level.

5. Start the engine.

3.1L Engine

1. Before servicing the vehicle, refer to the precautions in the beginning of this section.

2. Remove or disconnect the following:
- Negative battery cable
- Lower closeout panel
- Sarter electrical connectors
- Starter bolts
- Starter

To install:

3. Install or connect the following:
- Starter
- Starter electrical connectors. Tighten the solenoid cable to 106 inch lbs. (12 Nm).
- Starter. Tighten the bolts to 37 ft. lbs. (50 Nm).
- Lower closeout panel
- Negative battery cable

Oil Pan

REMOVAL & INSTALLATION

2.4L Engine

1. Before servicing the vehicle, refer to the precautions in the beginning of this section.

2. Disconnect the negative battery cable.

3. Drain the engine oil and cooling system.

4. Remove or disconnect the following:
- Flywheel inspection cover
- Right front wheel
- Right inner fender splash shield
- Serpentine belt
- Engine mount strut from the engine mount strut bracket
- Air conditioning compressor and support it aside with the lines attached
- Engine mount strut bracket
- Radiator outlet pipe bolts
- Radiator and air conditioning outlet pipes from the suspension supports
- Exhaust manifold brace
- Oil pan-to-flywheel cover bolt and nut
- Flywheel cover stud and spacer
- Radiator outlet pipe from the lower radiator hose and oil pan
- Oil level sensor wire, if equipped
- Oil pan

To install:

5. Install or connect the following:
- Oil pan using a new gasket. Tighten the chain housing/carrier seal bolts to 106 inch lbs. (12 Nm) and the oil pan-to-block bolts to 17 ft. lbs. (23 Nm).
- Oil level sensor wire, if equipped
- Radiator outlet pipe to the lower radiator hose and oil pan
- Flywheel cover spacer stud, nut and bolt. Tighten the nut to 41 ft. lbs. (56 Nm), the stud to 115 inch lbs. (13 Nm) and the bolt to 41 ft. lbs. (56 Nm).
- Oil pan-to-transaxle nut. Tighten the nut to 41 ft. lbs. (56 Nm).
- Exhaust manifold brace
- Radiator and air conditioning outlet pipes to the suspension supports

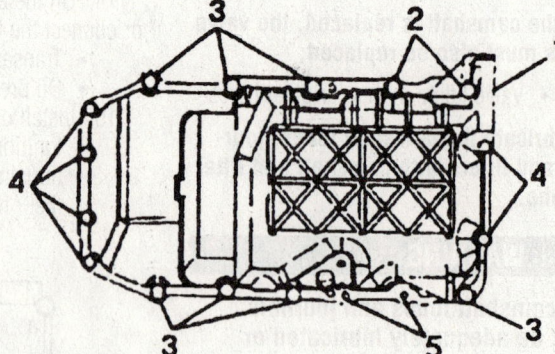

1 Oil pan
2 Oil pan bolt (M8 x 1.25 x 80) 24 Nm (18 lb. ft.)
3 Oil pan bolt (M8 x 1.25 x 22) 24 Nm (18 lb. ft.)
4 Oil pan bolt (M6 x 1.00 x 25) 12 Nm (106 lb. in.)
5 Stud end oil pan bolt 26 Nm (19 lb. ft.)

Oil pan mounting bolt locations—2.4L engine

7922Z215

- Radiator outlet pipe bolts
- Air conditioning compressor
- Serpentine belt
- Right inner fender splash shield
- Right front wheel
- Engine mount strut bracket. Tighten the bolts to 49 ft. lbs. (66 Nm).
- Negative battery cable

6. Fill the crankcase with oil.

➡ **A filter change is recommended.**

7. Fill the cooling system.
8. Start the engine and check for leaks.

3.1L Engine

1. Before servicing the vehicle, refer to the precautions in the beginning of this section.
2. Remove or disconnect the following:
   - Negative battery cable
   - Serpentine belt
   - Upper air conditioning compressor bolts, if equipped
3. Properly drain the engine oil.
4. Remove or disconnect the following:
   - Right front wheel
   - Engine mount strut from the suspension support
   - Ball joint from the steering knuckle and discard the cotter pin
   - Right side sway bar link
   - Anti-lock Brake System (ABS) sensor from the right subframe
   - Right side subframe and control arm as an assembly
   - Lower A/C compressor bolts and move it aside

❋❋ WARNING

DO NOT disconnect the refrigerant lines or allow the compressor to hang unsupported.

   - Engine mount strut bracket from the engine
   - Oil filter
   - Starter
   - Flywheel cover
   - Oil pan

To install:

5. Clean the gasket mating surfaces.
6. Install or connect the following:
   - Oil pan using a new gasket

➡ **Apply silicone sealer to the portion of the pan that contacts the rear of the block.**

   - Oil pan bolts. Tighten the flange bolts to 18 ft. lbs. (25 Nm) and the side bolts to 34 ft. lbs. (50 Nm).

- Starter
- Oil filter
- Engine mount strut bracket to the engine. Tighten the bracket-to-engine fastener to 85 ft. lbs. (115 Nm) and the engine-to-transaxle brace fastener to 68 ft. lbs. (93 Nm)
- Lower A/C compressor bolts.
- Right side subframe and control arm as an assembly. Tighten the fasteners to 89 ft. lbs. (120 Nm).
- Anti-lock Brake System (ABS) sensor to the right subframe
- Right side sway bar link. Tighten it to 22 ft. lbs. (30 Nm).
- Ball joint to the steering knuckle using a new cotter pin. Tighten the nut 48 ft. lbs. (60 Nm).
- Engine mount strut to the suspension support. Tighten the fasteners to 89 ft. lbs. (120 Nm).
- Right front wheel
- Upper air conditioning compressor bolts, if equipped
- Serpentine belt
- Negative battery cable

7. Refill the crankcase.

➡ **A filter change is recommended.**

8. Start the engine and check for leaks.

➡ **Whenever the vehicle subframe is removed or lowered, the wheel alignment should be checked.**

9. Check the front end alignment and adjust as required.

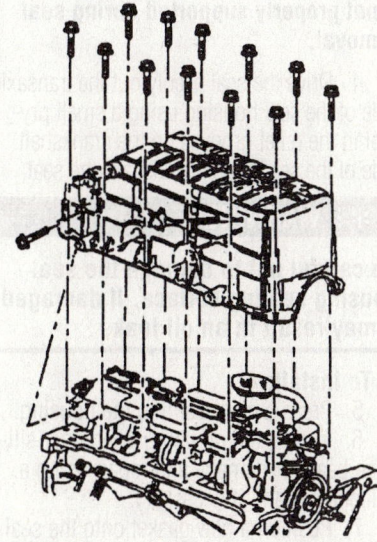

79222216

Exploded view of the oil pan mounting—3.1L engine

Oil Pump

REMOVAL & INSTALLATION

2.4L Engine

➡ **Please note that the transaxle must be removed from the vehicle to service the oil pump.**

1. Before servicing the vehicle, refer to the precautions in the beginning of this section.
2. Disconnect the negative battery cable.
3. Install an engine support fixture.
4. Drain the engine oil.
5. Remove or disconnect the following:
   - Oil pan
   - Transaxle
   - Flywheel
   - Balance shaft chain cover and chain guide
   - Oil pump cover bolts and the cover
   - Pump gear from the balance shaft by pulling the housing
   - Oil pump housing from the balance shaft

To install:

6. Clean all of the parts in suitable cleaning solvent. Remove all varnish sludge and dirt.
7. Lubricate the gears with clean engine oil.
8. Install or connect the following:
   - Gerotor gear into the housing; then, fill the oil pump cavities with petroleum jelly
   - Oil pump housing to the balance shaft
   - Oil pump cover to the housing. Tighten the bolts to 40 ft. lbs. (54 Nm).
   - Balance shaft chain guide and chain

9. Adjust the chain tension by performing the following procedure:

   a. Insert a 0.40 in. (1mm) brass feeler between the chain guide and chain.

➡ **A brass feeler gauge must be used to ensure that correct measurements are obtained. If a steel gauge is used, it will not bend to conform to the guide and will allow for incorrect measurements.**

   b. Press the guide against the chain using about 3 lbs. (13.3 N) of force.
   c. Tighten the chain tensioner fastener to 115 inch lbs. (13 Nm).

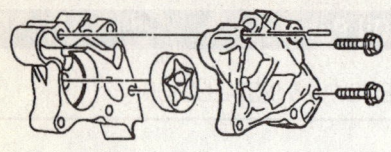

Exploded view of the oil pump components—2.4L engine

10. Install or connect the following:
- Balance shaft chain cover. Tighten the nut and bolt to 115 inch lbs. (13 Nm).
- Flywheel
- Transaxle
- Oil pan
- Negative battery cable

11. Refill the crankcase.

➡ **A filter change is recommended.**

12. Remove the engine support fixture.
13. Start the engine and verify oil pressure and no leaks.

3.1L Engine

1. Before servicing the vehicle, refer to the precautions in the beginning of this section.
2. Disconnect the negative battery cable.
3. Drain the engine oil.
4. Remove or disconnect the following:
- Oil pan
- Crankshaft oil deflector
- Oil pump and pump driveshaft

To install:

5. Install or connect the following:

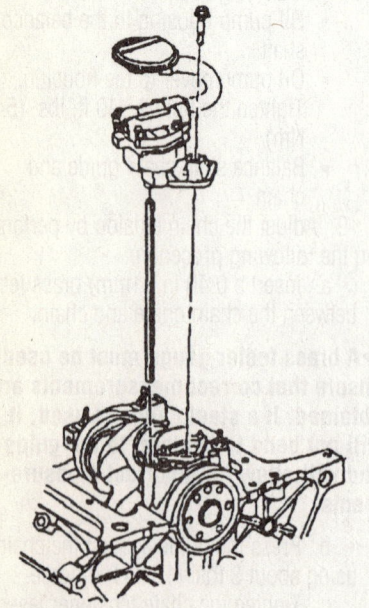

Exploded view of the oil pump mounting— 3.1L engine

- Oil pump and pump driveshaft. Tighten the bolts to 30 ft. lbs. (41 Nm).
- Crankshaft oil deflector. Tighten the nuts to 18 ft. lbs. (25 Nm).
- Oil pan
- Negative battery cable

6. Refill the crankcase.

➡ **A filter change is recommended.**

7. Start the engine, check the oil pressure and check for leaks.

Rear Main Seal

REMOVAL & INSTALLATION

2.4L Engine

1. Before servicing the vehicle, refer to the precautions in the beginning of this section.
2. Remove or disconnect the following:
- Negative battery cable
- Transaxle
- Flywheel
- Oil pan-to-seal housing bolts
- Seal housing-to-block bolts
- Seal housing and discard the gasket

3. To support the seal housing for seal removal, place 2 blocks of wood or metal of equal thickness on a flat surface. Position the seal housing and blocks so the transaxle side of the seal housing is supported across the dowel pin and center bolt holes on both sides of the seal opening.

➡ **The seal housing could be damaged if not properly supported during seal removal.**

4. Drive the seal evenly out the transaxle side of the seal housing using a small prytool in the relief grooves on the crankshaft side of the seal housing. Discard the seal.

✷✷ WARNING

Be careful not to damage the seal housing sealing surface. If damaged, it may result in an oil leak.

To install:

5. Press a new seal into the housing.
6. Inspect the oil pan gasket inner silicone bead for damage and repair using a silicone sealant, if necessary.
7. Position a new gasket onto the seal housing.
8. Lubricate the seal lip with clean engine oil.
9. Install or connect the following:
- Seal housing. Tighten the housing-

to-engine bolts to 106 inch lbs. (12 Nm) and the oil pan-to-seal housing bolts to 106 inch lbs. (12 Nm).
- Flywheel
- Transaxle
- Negative battery cable

10. Start the engine and check for leaks.

3.1L Engine

1. Before servicing the vehicle, refer to the precautions in the beginning of this section.
2. Support the engine.
3. Remove or disconnect the following:
- Transaxle
- Flywheel
- Rear main seal by prying it from the housing

✷✷ WARNING

Use care not to damage the crankshaft seal surface with a prytool.

To install:

4. Lubricate the seal bore and new seal with engine oil.
5. Install the new seal by performing the following procedure:

a. Slide the new seal over the mandrel until the dust lip bottoms squarely against the tool collar.

b. Align the dowel pin of the tool with the dowel pin hole in the crankshaft and attach the tool to the crankshaft. Tighten the attaching screws to 24–60 inch lbs. (2.7–6.8 Nm).

c. Tighten the T-handle of the tool to push the seal into the bore. Continue until the tool collar is flush against the block.

d. Loosen the T-handle completely. Remove the attaching screws and the tool.

➡ **Check to see that the seal is squarely seated in the bore.**

6. Install or connect the following:
- Flywheel
- Transaxle

7. Start the engine and check for leaks.

Timing Chain, Sprockets, Front Cover and Seal

REMOVAL & INSTALLATION

2.4L Engine

1997

➡ **It is recommended that the entire procedure be reviewed before attempting to service the timing chain.**

1. Before servicing the vehicle, refer to the precautions in the beginning of this section.

2. Disconnect the negative battery cable.

3. Drain the cooling system.

4. Remove or disconnect the following:
- Coolant surge tank
- Serpentine drive belt using a 13mm wrench that is at least 24 in. (61cm) long
- Alternator

5. Install an engine support.

6. Remove or disconnect the following:
- Upper cover fasteners
- Upper cover vent hose
- Right engine mount and bracket.
- Right front wheel
- Lower splash shield from the right wheel house
- Crankshaft balancer using a puller
- Lower cover fasteners
- Front cover and gaskets
- Crankshaft oil slinger

7. Using a seal driver, tap the seal from the front cover

8. Rotate the crankshaft clockwise, as viewed from front of engine (normal rotation), until the camshaft sprocket's timing dowel pin holes align with the holes in the timing chain housing. The mark on the crankshaft sprocket should align with the mark on the cylinder block. The crankshaft sprocket keyway should point upwards and align with the center line of the cylinder bores. This is the normal timed position.

9. Remove or disconnect the following:
- Timing chain guides
- Timing chain tensioner spring retainer by prying it off
- Tensioner spring
- Timing chain tensioner shoe retainer

10. Be sure all the slack in the timing chain is above the tensioner assembly; remove the chain tensioner shoe. The timing chain must be disengaged from the wear grooves in the tensioner shoe in order to remove the shoe. Slide a prybar under the timing chain while pulling shoe outward.

11. If difficulty is encountered removing chain tensioner shoe, proceed as follows:

a. Hold the intake camshaft sprocket with a holding tool and remove the sprocket bolt and washer.

b. Remove the washer from the bolt and partially install the bolt back into the camshaft, the bolt provides a surface to push against.

c. Remove intake camshaft sprocket using a 3-jaw puller placed in the 3 sprocket relief holes.

⁜ WARNING

Do not attempt to pry the sprocket off the camshaft or damage to the sprocket or chain housing could occur.

12. Remove or disconnect the following:
- Tensioner assembly bolts and the tensioner

⁜ CAUTION

The tensioner piston is spring loaded and could fly out causing personal injury.

- Chain housing-to-block stud, which is actually the timing chain tensioner shoe pivot
- Timing chain

To install:

⁜ WARNING

Failure to follow this procedure may result in severe engine damage.

13. Install or connect the following:
- Intake camshaft sprocket onto the camshaft with the matchmarked surface showing
- Intake camshaft sprocket bolt. Torque the sprocket bolt to 52 ft. lbs. (70 Nm) while holding the sprocket. Use sealant on the camshaft sprocket bolt.

14. Place camshaft aligning pins through the holes in the camshaft sprockets into the holes in the timing chain housing. This positions the cams for correct timing.

15. If the camshafts are out of position and must be rotated more than ⅛ turn in order to install the alignment dowel pins, proceed as follows:

a. The crankshaft MUST be rotated 90 degrees clockwise off Top Dead Center (TDC) in order to give the valves adequate clearance to open.

b. Once the camshafts are in position and the dowels installed, rotate the crankshaft counterclockwise back to TDC.

⁜ WARNING

Do not rotate the crankshaft clockwise to TDC; valve or piston damage could result.

16. Place the timing chain over the exhaust camshaft sprocket, around the idler sprocket and the crankshaft sprocket.

17. Install the timing chain as follows:

a. Set the camshafts at the timed position.

b. Remove the alignment dowel pin from the intake camshaft.

c. Using the Camshaft Sprocket Wrench J-39579, rotate the intake camshaft sprocket counterclockwise enough to slide the timing chain over the intake camshaft sprocket.

d. Release the Camshaft Sprocket Wrench J-39579. The length of the chain between the 2 camshaft sprockets will tighten.

e. If properly timed, the intake camshaft alignment dowel pin should slide in easily. If the dowel pin does not fully index, the camshafts are NOT timed correctly and the procedure must be repeated.

18. Leave the alignment dowel pins installed. Raise and safely support the vehicle.

19. With the slack removed from the chain between the intake camshaft and crankshaft sprockets, the timing marks on the crankshaft and cylinder block should be aligned. If the marks are not aligned, move the chain 1 tooth forward or rearward, remove the slack and recheck the marks.

20. Reload the timing chain tensioner assembly to it "zero" position as follows:

a. Form a keeper from a piece of heavy gauge wire.

b. Apply slight force on the tensioner blade to compress the plunger.

c. Insert a small prytool into the reset access hole, and pry the ratchet pawl away from the ratchet teeth while forcing the plunger completely in the hole.

d. Install the keeper between the access hole and the blade.

21. Install the tensioner assembly to the timing chain housing. Recheck the plunger assembly installation, it is correctly installed when the long end is toward the crankshaft. Torque the tensioner bolts to 89 inch lbs. (10 Nm).

22. Lower the vehicle enough to remove the alignment dowel pins.

⁜ WARNING

Severe engine damage could result if the engine is not properly timed.

23. Rotate the crankshaft clockwise (normal rotation) 2 full rotations. Align the

Timing belt service is covered in Section 4 of this manual

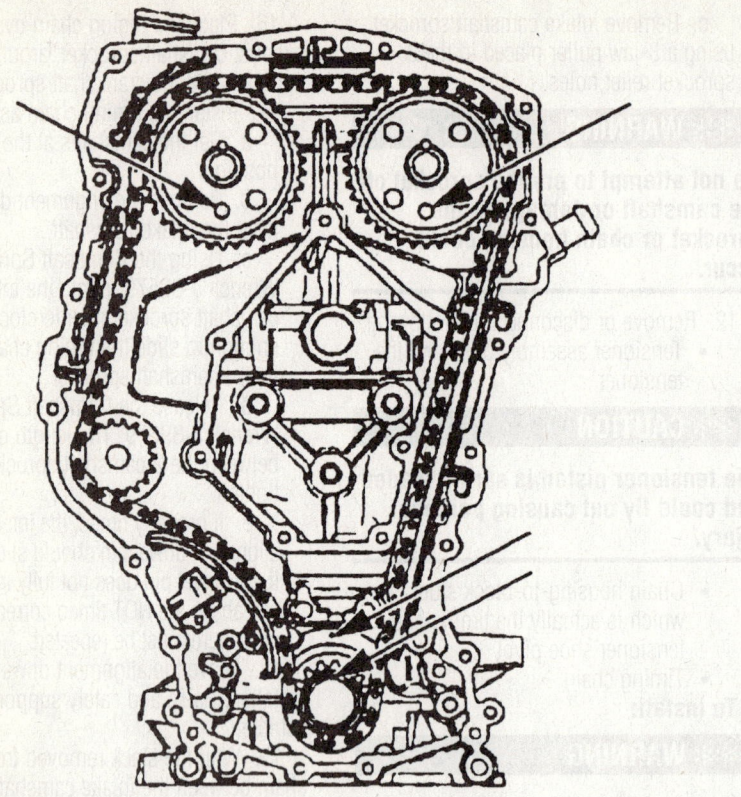

Timing chain and sprocket alignment positions—2.4L DOHC engine

crankshaft keyway with the mark on the cylinder block and reinstall the alignment dowel pins. The pins will slide in easily if the engine is correctly timed.

24. Install or connect the following:
- New seal into the front cover by tapping it with a seal driver, lubricate the seal lip before installation
- Timing chain guides
- Lower front cover. Torque the fasteners to 106 inch lbs. (12 Nm).
- Crankshaft balancer. Torque the bolt to 74 ft. lbs. (100 Nm).
- Right front wheel and splash shield
- Right engine mount, bracket or bracket adapter, using new bolts
- Cover vent hose
- Upper cover. Torque the fasteners to 106 inch lbs. (12 Nm).

25. Remove the fixture.

26. Install or connect the following:
- Serpentine belt using a 13mm wrench that is at least 24 in. (61cm) long
- Coolant recovery reservoir
- Negative battery cable

1998–01

➡ It is recommended that the entire procedure be reviewed before attempting to service the timing chain.

1. Before servicing the vehicle, refer to the precautions in the beginning of this section.

2. Disconnect the negative battery cable.

3. Drain the cooling system.

4. Remove or disconnect the following:
- Coolant surge tank
- Serpentine drive belt using a 13mm wrench that is at least 24 in. (61cm) long
- Alternator

5. Install an engine support.

6. Remove or disconnect the following:
- Upper cover fasteners
- Upper cover vent hose
- Right engine mount and bracket.
- Right front wheel
- Lower splash shield from the right wheel house
- Crankshaft balancer using a puller
- Lower cover fasteners
- Front cover and gaskets
- Crankshaft oil slinger

7. Using a seal driver, tap the seal from the front cover

8. Rotate the crankshaft clockwise, as viewed from front of engine (normal rotation), until the camshaft sprocket's timing dowel pin holes align with the holes in the timing chain housing. The mark on the

crankshaft sprocket should align with the mark on the cylinder block. The crankshaft sprocket keyway should point upwards and align with the center line of the cylinder bores. This is the normal timed position.

9. Remove or disconnect the following:
- Timing chain guides
- Timing chain tensioner spring retainer by prying it off
- Tensioner spring
- Timing chain tensioner shoe retainer

10. Be sure all the slack in the timing chain is above the tensioner assembly; remove the chain tensioner shoe. The timing chain must be disengaged from the wear grooves in the tensioner shoe in order to remove the shoe. Slide a prybar under the timing chain while pulling shoe outward.

11. If difficulty is encountered removing chain tensioner shoe, proceed as follows:
   a. Hold the intake camshaft sprocket with a holding tool and remove the sprocket bolt and washer.
   b. Remove the washer from the bolt and partially install the bolt back into the camshaft, the bolt provides a surface to push against.
   c. Remove intake camshaft sprocket using a 3-jaw puller placed in the 3 sprocket relief holes.

✳✳ WARNING

Do not attempt to pry the sprocket off the camshaft or damage to the sprocket or chain housing could occur.

12. Remove or disconnect the following:
- Tensioner assembly bolts and the tensioner

✳✳ CAUTION

The tensioner piston is spring loaded and could fly out causing personal injury.

- Chain housing-to-block stud, which is actually the timing chain tensioner shoe pivot
- Timing chain

To install:

13. Coat the camshaft bolts with Sealant GM 1234593.

14. Install the intake camshaft sprocket, if removed. Tighten the bolt to 52 ft. lbs. (70 Nm), while holding the sprocket with a Camshaft Sprocket Wrench J-39579.

➡ Install the Special tool J 36008-A through holes in camshaft sprockets into holes in timing chain housing. This positions the camshafts for correct timing.

15. If the camshafts are out of position and must be rotated more than 1/8 turn in order to install the alignment dowel pins, perform the following:

   a. Rotate the crankshaft 90 degrees clockwise off Top Dead Center (TDC) in order to give the valves adequate clearance to open.

   b. Once the camshafts are in position and the dowels installed, rotate the crankshaft counterclockwise back to TDC.

✳✳ WARNING

Do not rotate the crankshaft clockwise to TDC or valve and piston damage may occur.

16. Install the timing chain over the exhaust camshaft sprocket, around the coolant pump sprocket and around the crankshaft sprocket.

17. Remove the alignment dowel pin from the intake camshaft. Using tool J 39579, rotate the intake camshaft sprocket counterclockwise enough to slide the timing chain over the intake camshaft sprocket. Release the camshaft sprocket wrench. The length of chain between the 2 camshaft sprockets will tighten. If properly timed, the intake camshaft alignment dowel pin should slide in easily. If the dowel pin does not fully index, the camshafts are not timed correctly and the procedure must be repeated.

18. Leave the alignment dowel pins installed.

19. With slack removed from chain between intake camshaft sprocket and crankshaft sprocket, the crankshaft keyway and the cylinder block mark should be aligned. If not aligned, move the chain 1 tooth forward or rearward. Remove slack and recheck marks.

20. Tighten the chain housing-to-block stud. The stud is installed under the timing chain. Tighten to 19 ft. lbs. (26 Nm).

21. Reload timing chain tensioner assembly to its **0** position as follows:

   a. Insert the tensioner plunger assembly into the tensioner housing.

   b. With the tensioner plunger fully extended, turn the complete assembly upside down on a flat surface.

   c. Press the bottom of the tensioner housing to compress the plunger into the housing until it is seated.

   d. Make sure that the plunger does not extend out of the tensioner housing more than 0.07 in. (1.7mm).

   e. Loosely install the tensioner assembly to the timing chain housing.

22. Install or connect the following:
   • Tensioner shoe on the stud.
   • Tensioner assembly by applying hand pressure on the timing chain tensioner shoe until the locking tab seats in the stud groove. Tighten the bolts to 89 inch lbs. (10 Nm).

✳✳ WARNING

If the timing chain tensioner plunger is not released from the installation position, engine damage will occur upon start up.

23. Release the tensioner plunger by firmly pressing a flat blade tool against the plunger face.

✳✳ WARNING

If the tensioner plunger cannot be depressed, it is not properly reset and the resetting procedure must be repeated.

24. Remove tool J 36008-A from the camshaft sprockets.

   a. Rotate crankshaft clockwise 2 full rotations. Align crankshaft keyway with mark on cylinder block and reinstall alignment dowel pins. Alignment dowel pins will slide in easily if engine is timed correctly.

25. Install or connect the following:
   • Timing chain guides and crankshaft oil slinger
   • New seal lubricated with engine oil
   • Front cover using new gaskets. Tighten the nuts and bolts to 106 inch lbs. (12 Nm).

26. Install the torsional damper as follows:

   a. Coat the seal contact area on the crankshaft damper with clean engine oil.

   b. Align the damper on the crankshaft so the notch in the damper aligns with the crankshaft key.

   c. Tap the balancer into place using a rubber mallet.

   d. Install the damper bolt/washer. Tighten the bolt to 129 ft. lbs. (175 Nm) plus a 90 degree turn.

27. Install or connect the following:
   • Right front lower splash shield
   • Wheel

   • Right engine mount bracket
   • Right engine mount
   • Upper cover vent hose

28. Remove the engine support.

29. Install or connect the following:
   • Alternator
   • Serpentine belt
   • Coolant surge tank
   • Negative battery cable

30. Refill the cooling system and check for leaks.

3.1L Engine

1. Before servicing the vehicle, refer to the precautions in the beginning of this section.

2. Disconnect the negative battery cable.

3. Drain the cooling system.

4. Remove or disconnect the following:
   • Right engine mount bracket
   • Serpentine belt
   • Right front wheel
   • Right inner fender well splash shield
   • Flywheel cover

5. Install a flywheel holding tool

6. Remove or disconnect the following:
   • Crankshaft balancer
   • Serpentine belt tensioner
   • Oil pan
   • Coolant bypass pipe from the water pump and the intake manifold
   • Lower radiator hose from the front cover outlet
   • Front cover
   • Oil seal from the front cover using a seal driver

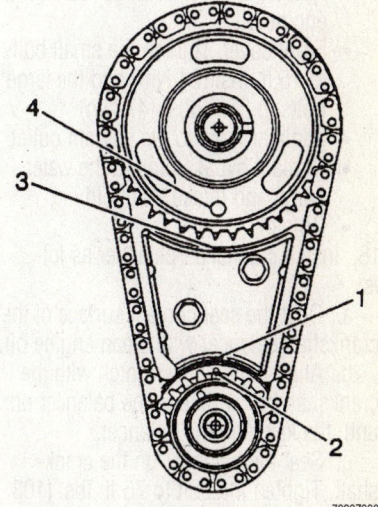

Timing chain and sprocket timing mark alignment—3.1L engine

7. Rotate the crankshaft until the timing marks on the camshaft and crankshaft sprockets are in alignment at their closest approach.

8. Remove or disconnect the following:
- Camshaft sprocket bolt, sprocket and timing chain
- Crankshaft sprocket
- Timing chain damper

To install:

9. Install or connect the following:
- Timing chain damper. Tighten the bolts to 15 ft. lbs. (21 Nm).
- Crankshaft sprocket

10. Be sure the crankshaft sprocket timing mark is pointing straight up.

11. Install the timing chain over the camshaft sprocket and hold the sprocket in such a way, that the timing mark is pointing down, and the timing chain is hanging down off the sprocket.

12. Loop the timing chain under the crankshaft sprocket and install the camshaft sprocket on the camshaft. The sprocket will only fit on the camshaft if the dowel on the camshaft aligns with the hole in the sprocket.

13. Verify that the marks are aligned (the camshaft sprocket will be at the 6 o'clock position and the crankshaft sprocket will be in the 12 o'clock position).

14. Tighten the camshaft sprocket mounting bolt to 81 ft. lbs. (110 Nm).

15. Lubricate the timing chain components with engine oil. Clean all gasket surfaces completely.

16. Apply a thin bead of sealer around the gasket sealing area of the front cover.

17. Install or connect the following:
- New front cover seal lubricated with engine oil
- Front cover. Tighten the small bolts to 15 ft. lbs. (21 Nm) and the large bolts to 35 ft. lbs. (47 Nm).
- Radiator hose to the coolant outlet
- Coolant bypass pipe to the water pump and intake manifold
- Oil pan

18. Install crankshaft balancer as follows:

    a. Coat the seal contact surface of the crankshaft balancer with clean engine oil.

    b. Align the balancer notch with the crankshaft key and slide the balancer on until the key is in the balancer.

    c. Seat the balancer on the crankshaft. Tighten the bolt to 76 ft. lbs. (103 Nm).

19. Install or connect the following:
- Serpentine belt tensioner. Tighten the bolt to 40 ft. lbs. (54 Nm).
- Serpentine belt

- Right engine mount bracket. Tighten the bolts to 96 ft. lbs. (130 Nm).
- Flywheel cover
- Right inner fender well splash shield
- Wheel
- Negative battery cable

20. Refill the cooling system.

21. Check the engine oil level.

➡ **An oil and filter change is recommended.**

22. Start the engine and verify that there are no leaks.

Piston and Ring

POSITIONING

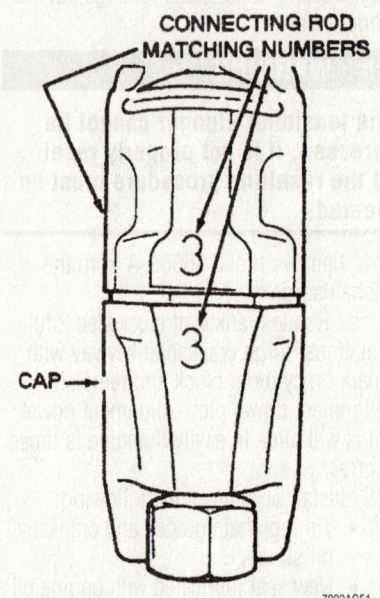

Connecting rod and cap installation. Be sure to matchmark the cap and rod prior to disassembly, as shown

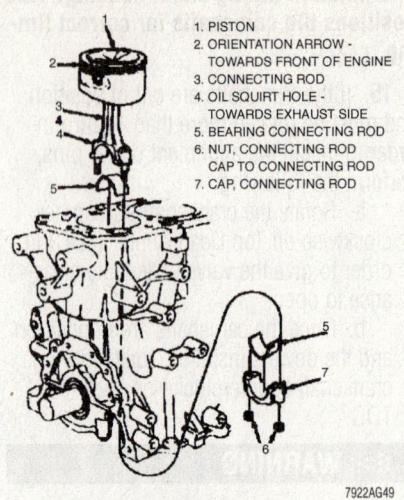

1. PISTON
2. ORIENTATION ARROW - TOWARDS FRONT OF ENGINE
3. CONNECTING ROD
4. OIL SQUIRT HOLE - TOWARDS EXHAUST SIDE
5. BEARING CONNECTING ROD
6. NUT, CONNECTING ROD CAP TO CONNECTING ROD
7. CAP, CONNECTING ROD

Piston and connecting rod assembly positioning—2.4L engine

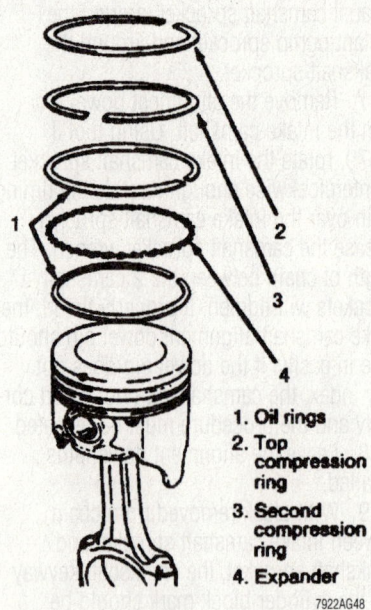

1. Oil rings
2. Top compression ring
3. Second compression ring
4. Expander

Piston ring positioning—3.1L engine

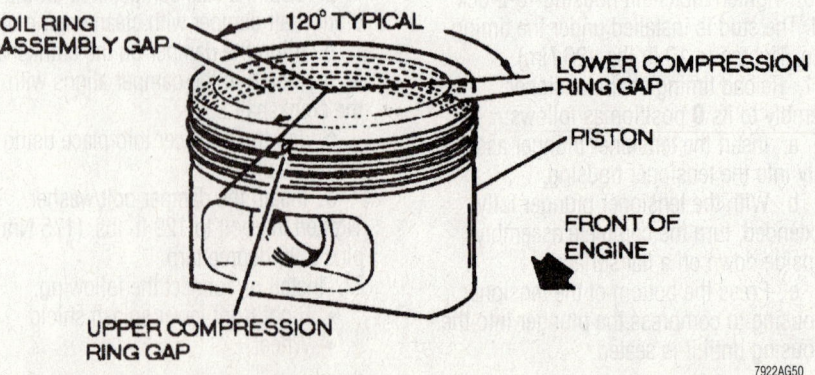

Piston ring end-gap spacing—2.4L engine

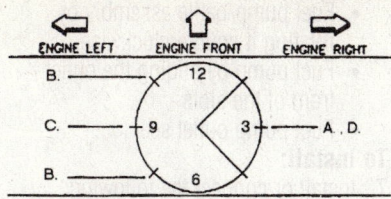

A. OIL RING SPACER GAP
   (TANG IN HOLE OR SLOT WITH ARC)
B. OIL RING RAIL GAPS
C. 2ND COMPRESSION RING GAP
D. TOP COMPRESSION RING GAP

7922AG46

Piston ring end-gap spacing—3.1L engine

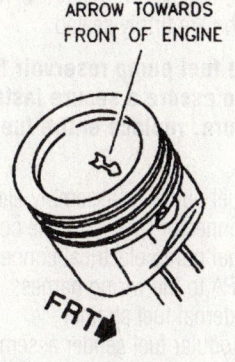

ARROW TOWARDS
FRONT OF ENGINE

FRT

7922AG47

Piston positioning. Often the arrow is replaced by a notch, which also must face toward the front of the engine—3.1L engine

FUEL SYSTEM

Fuel System Service Precautions

Safety is the most important factor when performing not only fuel system maintenance but any type of maintenance. Failure to conduct maintenance and repairs in a safe manner may result in serious personal injury or death. Maintenance and testing of the vehicle's fuel system components can be accomplished safely and effectively by adhering to the following rules and guidelines.

• To avoid the possibility of fire and personal injury, always disconnect the negative battery cable unless the repair or test procedure requires that battery voltage be applied.

• Always relieve the fuel system pressure prior to disconnecting any fuel system component (injector, fuel rail, pressure regulator, etc.), fitting or fuel line connection. Exercise extreme caution whenever relieving fuel system pressure, to avoid exposing

skin, face and eyes to fuel spray. Please be advised that fuel under pressure may penetrate the skin or any part of the body that it contacts.

• Always place a shop towel or cloth around the fitting or connection prior to loosening to absorb any excess fuel due to spillage. Ensure that all fuel spillage (should it occur) is quickly removed from engine surfaces. Ensure that all fuel soaked cloths or towels are deposited into a suitable waste container.

• Always keep a dry chemical (Class B) fire extinguisher near the work area.

• Do not allow fuel spray or fuel vapors to come into contact with a spark or open flame.

• Always use a back-up wrench when loosening and tightening fuel line connection fittings. This will prevent unnecessary stress and torsion to fuel line piping. Always follow the proper torque specifications.

• Always replace worn fuel fitting O-rings with new. Do not substitute fuel hose, where fuel pipe is installed.

Fuel System Pressure

RELIEVING

2.4L Engine

1. Before servicing the vehicle, refer to the precautions in the beginning of this section.

2. Loosen the fuel filler cap in order to relieve the pressure in the tank (do not tighten at this time).

3. Detach the fuel pump electrical connector.

4. Start and run the vehicle until it stalls, then engage the starter for an additional 3 seconds to ensure the relief of any remaining pressure.

5. Disconnect the negative battery cable.

6. Once the tests or repairs are completed, reattach the fuel pump electrical connector.

7. Connect the negative battery cable.

8. Tighten the fuel filler cap.

9. Prime the fuel system by cycling the ignition switch **ON** for 2 seconds, **OFF** for 10 seconds, then **ON** again. Repeat, if necessary to build system pressure.

3.1L Engine

1. Before servicing the vehicle, refer to the precautions in the beginning of this section.

2. Disconnect the negative battery cable in order to avoid possible fuel discharge if an accidental attempt is made to start the engine.

3. Loosen the fuel tank filler cap in order to relieve fuel tank pressure.

4. Connect a fuel pressure gauge to the fuel pressure test port connection. Wrap a towel around the fuel pressure connection when installing the fuel pressure gauge in order to avoid fuel spillage.

5. Install the bleed hose into an approved container and open the valve in order to bleed the fuel system pressure. The fuel pipe connections are now safe for servicing.

6. Drain any fuel remaining in the fuel pressure gauge into an approved container.

Fuel Filter

REMOVAL & INSTALLATION

1. Before servicing the vehicle, refer to the precautions in the beginning of this section.

2. Relieve the fuel system pressure.

3. Remove or disconnect the following:

• Fuel line from the filter using a back-up wrench

• Quick-connect fitting from the fuel filter by compressing the tabs while pulling the line outward

• Fuel filter from the mounting bracket

To install:

4. Install or connect the following:

• Fuel filter. Tighten the fuel line fitting to 20 ft. lbs. (27 Nm).

• Quick-connect fitting to the fuel filter

• Negative battery cable

5. Pressurize the fuel system and verify no leaks.

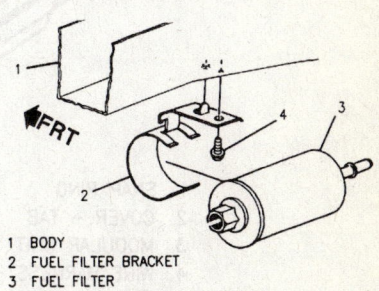

1 BODY
2 FUEL FILTER BRACKET
3 FUEL FILTER
4 SCREW – FULLY DRIVEN, SEATED AND NOT STRIPPED

7922Z221

Exploded view of the fuel filter mounting

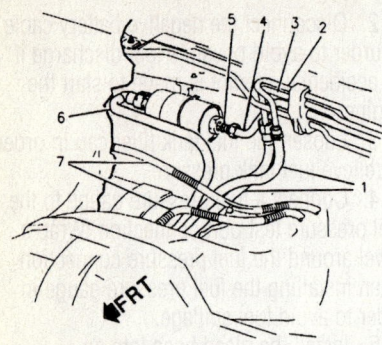

1 HOSE, PART OF FUEL SENDER
2 FUEL VAPOR PIPE
3 FUEL RETURN PIPE
4 FUEL FEED PIPE
5 FUEL FEED PIPE NUT
  27 N•m (20 LBS. FT.)
6 HOSE, PART OF FUEL SENDER
7 ABS AND FUEL SENDER HARNESS

79222222

Fuel filter mounting location and component identification

Fuel Pump

REMOVAL & INSTALLATION

1. Before servicing the vehicle, refer to the precautions in the beginning of this section.
2. Relieve the fuel system pressure.

3. Drain fuel tank.
4. Remove or disconnect the following:
   • Fuel tank
   • Modular fuel sender assembly-to-fuel tank snapring by pressing the assembly downward

➡ **When removing the modular fuel sender from the tank, be aware that it may spring upward.**

   • Modular fuel sender assembly

※ CAUTION

When removing the modular fuel sender from the tank, be aware that the reservoir bucket is full of fuel.

   • External fuel strainer
   • Connector Position Assurance (CPA) from the wiring harness
   • Fuel pump electrical connector
5. Gently release the tabs on the sides of the fuel sender at the cover assembly. Begin by squeezing the sides of the reservoir and releasing the tab opposite the fuel level sensor. Move clockwise to release the second and third tab in the same manner.
6. Remove or disconnect the following:
   • Fuel pump-to-assembly electrical connector by raising the cover

   • Fuel pump/baffle assembly by rotating it counterclockwise
   • Fuel pump by sliding the outlet from of the slots
   • Fuel pump outlet seal

To install:
7. Install or connect the following:
   • Fuel pump outlet seal
   • Fuel pump outlet by sliding it into the reservoir cover slots
   • Fuel pump/baffle assembly onto the reservoir retainer by rotating it clockwise until seated
   • Lower retainer assembly by aligning the 3 sleeve tabs and pressing the retainer onto the reservoir until tabs are firmly seated

➡ **Pull the fuel pump reservoir from the retainer to assure a secure fastening. If not secure, replace entire fuel sender.**

   • Fuel pump-to-assembly electrical connector by raising the cover
   • Fuel pump electrical connector
   • CPA to the wiring harness
   • External fuel strainer
   • Modular fuel sender assembly
   • Modular fuel sender assembly-to-fuel tank snapring by pressing the assembly downward

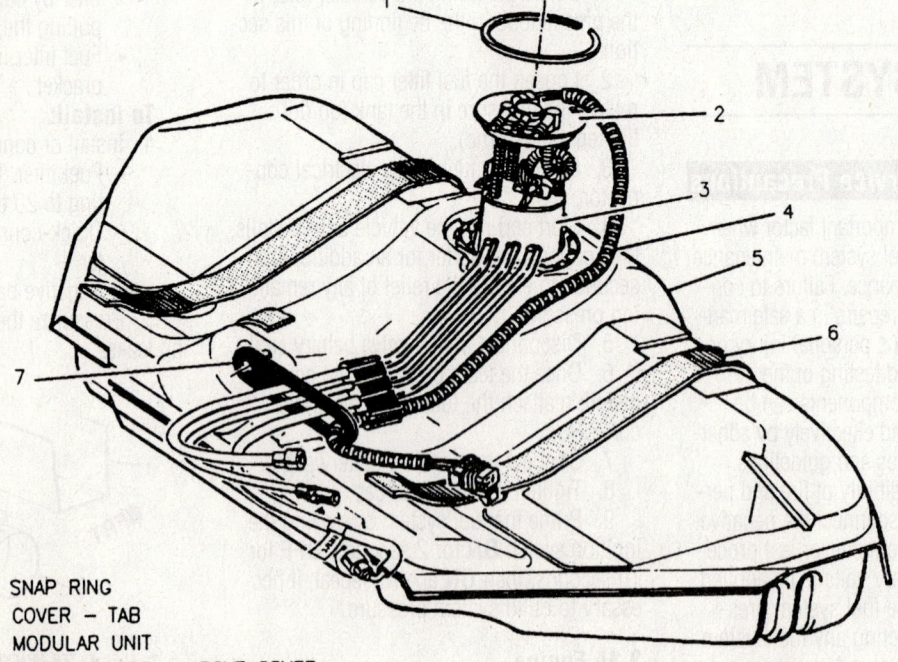

1 SNAP RING
2 COVER – TAB
3 MODULAR UNIT
4 WIRE HARNESS – ABOVE COVER
5 FUEL TANK
6 TANK ISOLATION STRIPS (3)
7 RUBBER ISOLATOR

79222223

Exploded view of the fuel sender assembly mounting to the tank

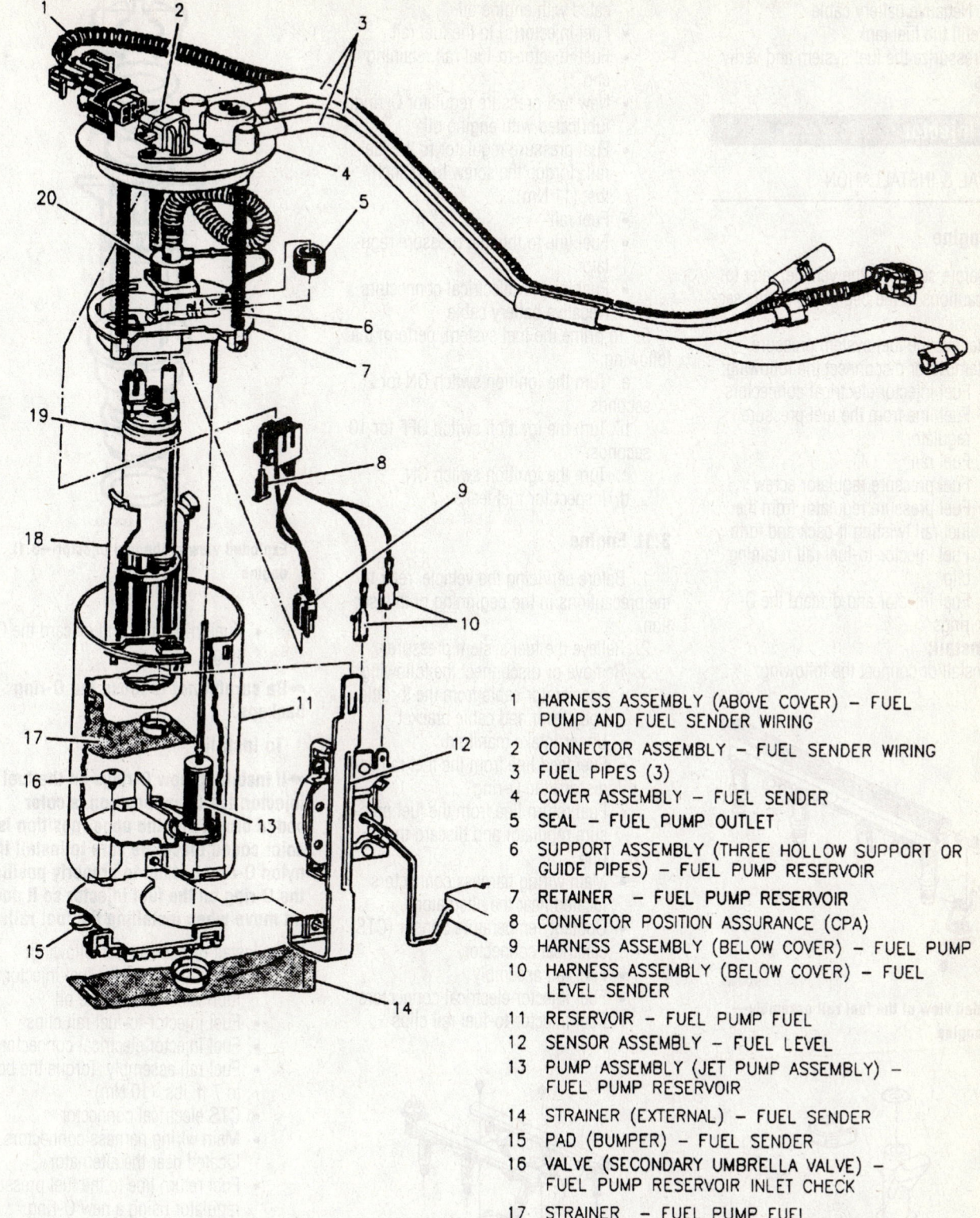

1 HARNESS ASSEMBLY (ABOVE COVER) – FUEL
   PUMP AND FUEL SENDER WIRING
2 CONNECTOR ASSEMBLY – FUEL SENDER WIRING
3 FUEL PIPES (3)
4 COVER ASSEMBLY – FUEL SENDER
5 SEAL – FUEL PUMP OUTLET
6 SUPPORT ASSEMBLY (THREE HOLLOW SUPPORT OR
   GUIDE PIPES) – FUEL PUMP RESERVOIR
7 RETAINER – FUEL PUMP RESERVOIR
8 CONNECTOR POSITION ASSURANCE (CPA)
9 HARNESS ASSEMBLY (BELOW COVER) – FUEL PUMP
10 HARNESS ASSEMBLY (BELOW COVER) – FUEL
    LEVEL SENDER
11 RESERVOIR – FUEL PUMP FUEL
12 SENSOR ASSEMBLY – FUEL LEVEL
13 PUMP ASSEMBLY (JET PUMP ASSEMBLY) –
    FUEL PUMP RESERVOIR
14 STRAINER (EXTERNAL) – FUEL SENDER
15 PAD (BUMPER) – FUEL SENDER
16 VALVE (SECONDARY UMBRELLA VALVE) –
    FUEL PUMP RESERVOIR INLET CHECK
17 STRAINER – FUEL PUMP FUEL
18 BAFFLE (ISOLATOR CUP) – FUEL PUMP
19 PUMP ASSEMBLY (ROLLERVANE) – FUEL
20 OUTLET – FUEL PUMP

79222224

Exploded view of the fuel pump assembly

- Fuel tank
- Negative battery cable

8. Refill the fuel tank.

9. Pressurize the fuel system and verify no leaks.

Fuel Injector

REMOVAL & INSTALLATION

2.4L Engine

1. Before servicing the vehicle, refer to the precautions in the beginning of this section.

2. Relieve the fuel system pressure.

3. Remove or disconnect the following:
   - Fuel injector electrical connectors
   - Fuel line from the fuel pressure regulator
   - Fuel rail
   - Fuel pressure regulator screw
   - Fuel pressure regulator from the fuel rail twisting it back and forth
   - Fuel injector-to-fuel rail retaining clip
   - Fuel injector and discard the O-rings

To install:

4. Install or connect the following:

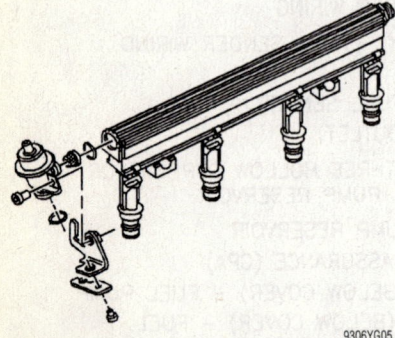

Exploded view of the fuel rail assembly—2.4L engine

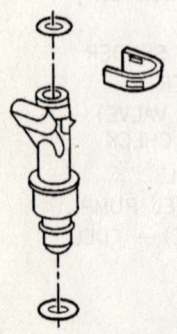

Exploded view of the fuel injector—2.4L engine

- New fuel injector O-rings, lubricated with engine oil
- Fuel injector(s) to the fuel rail
- Fuel injector-to-fuel rail retaining clip
- New fuel pressure regulator O-ring, lubricated with engine oil
- Fuel pressure regulator to the fuel rail. Torque the screw to 97 inch lbs. (11 Nm).
- Fuel rail
- Fuel line to the fuel pressure regulator
- Fuel injector electrical connectors
- Negative battery cable

5. To prime the fuel system, perform the following:

   a. Turn the ignition switch ON for 2 seconds.

   b. Turn the ignition switch OFF for 10 seconds.

   c. Turn the ignition switch ON.

   d. Inspect for fuel leaks.

3.1L Engine

1. Before servicing the vehicle, refer to the precautions in the beginning of this section.

2. Relieve the fuel system pressure.

3. Remove or disconnect the following:
   - Accelerator cable from the throttle body lever and cable bracket
   - Upper intake manifold
   - Fuel feed line from the fuel rail and discard the O-ring
   - Fuel return line from the fuel pressure regulator and discard the O-ring
   - Main wiring harness connectors located near the alternator
   - Coolant Temperature Sensor (CTS) electrical connector
   - Fuel rail assembly
   - Fuel injector electrical connectors
   - Fuel injector-to-fuel rail clips

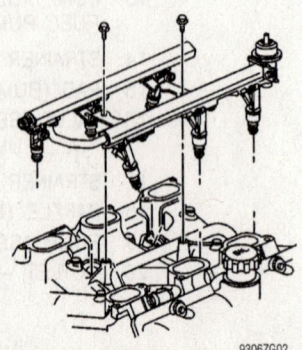

Exploded view of the fuel rail assembly—3.1L engine

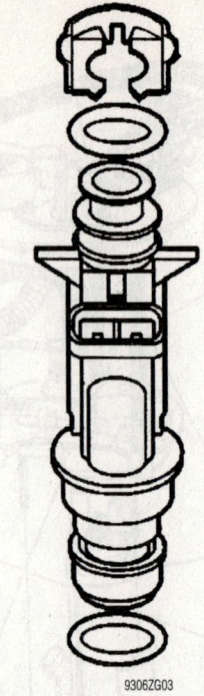

Exploded view of the fuel injector—3.1L engine

- Fuel injector(s) and discard the O-rings

➥Be careful not to loose the O-ring backups.

To install:

➥If installing new O-rings on the fuel injector, the lower position is color coded brown and the upper position is color coded black. Be sure to install the nylon O-ring backup to properly position the O-ring on the fuel injector so it doesn't move when installing the fuel rail.

4. Install or connect the following:
   - New O-rings on the fuel injector, lubricated with engine oil
   - Fuel injector-to-fuel rail clips
   - Fuel injector electrical connectors
   - Fuel rail assembly. Torque the bolts to 7 ft. lbs. (10 Nm).
   - CTS electrical connector
   - Main wiring harness connectors located near the alternator
   - Fuel return line to the fuel pressure regulator using a new O-ring. Tighten the fitting to 13 ft. lbs. (17 Nm).
   - Fuel feed line to the fuel rail using a new O-ring. Tighten the fitting to 13 ft. lbs. (17 Nm).
   - Upper intake manifold
   - Accelerator cable to the throttle body lever and cable bracket

• Fuel cap and tighten it
• Negative battery cable

5. To prime the fuel system, perform the following:

   a. Turn the ignition switch ON for 2 seconds.

   b. Turn the ignition switch OFF for 10 seconds.

   c. Turn the ignition switch ON.

   d. Inspect for fuel leaks.

DRIVE TRAIN

Transaxle

REMOVAL & INSTALLATION

1. Before servicing the vehicle, refer to the precautions in the beginning of this section.

2. Remove or disconnect the following:
• Negative battery cable
• Air cleaner assembly
• Shift linkage from the transaxle
• Wiring harness connection from the transaxle

3. Install an Engine Support Fixture J 28467-360.

4. Remove or disconnect the following:
• Upper transaxle-to-engine bolts
• Front wheels
• Left and right splash shields
• Anti-lock Brake System (ABS) wheel speed sensors and electrical harnesses from the suspension supports
• Outer tie rod ends and ball joints from the steering knuckle
• Front suspension support brace
• Suspension support assembly by first supporting it; then, lowering it enough to disconnect the steering coupling and the power steering fluid lines
• Halfshafts from the transaxle
• Engine-to-transaxle brace
• Shift cable bracket.
• Starter
• Torque converter cover
• Torque converter-to-flywheel bolts, after matchmarking the assembly
• Transaxle fluid cooling lines and plug the lines
• Brake hose bracket from the body
• Transaxle mount pipe expansion bolt

• Transaxle-to-body mount bolts

5. Lower the transaxle/engine, utilizing the engine support fixture, enough to access the transaxle.

6. Support the transaxle with a jack.

7. Remove or disconnect the following:
• Transaxle mount-to-body bolts
• Transaxle from the engine

✼✼ WARNING

Transaxle cooler lines should be flushed whenever the transaxle has been removed.

To install:

8. Apply a thin film of grease on the torque converter pilot hub.

✼✼ WARNING

Be sure to properly seat the torque converter in the pump.

9. Install or connect the following:
• Transaxle. Tighten the lower transaxle-to-engine bolts to 66 ft. lbs. (90 Nm).
• Transaxle-to-body mounting bolts
• Brake hose bracket to the body
• Transaxle fluid cooling lines
• Torque converter to the flywheel by aligning the matchmarks. Tighten the bolts to 46 ft. lbs. (62 Nm).
• Torque converter cover
• Starter
• Shift cable bracket. Tighten the bolt to 18 ft. lbs. (24 Nm) and the nut to 37 ft. lbs. (50 Nm).
• Engine-to-transaxle support brace
• Halfshafts to the transaxle
• Steering coupling and the power steering fluid lines; then, raise the suspension support assembly
• Suspension support assembly. Tighten the bolts to 71 ft. lbs. (110 Nm), plus an additional 90 degree turn.
• Front suspension support brace
• Ball joints and outer tie rod ends to the steering knuckle
• Front ABS wheel speed sensors and harnesses to the suspension support
• Left and right splash shields
• Front wheels
• Upper transaxle-to-engine bolts. Tighten them to 66 ft. lbs. (90 Nm).

10. Remove the engine support fixture.

11. Install or connect the following:
• Wiring harness to the transaxle

• Shift linkage to the transaxle
• Air cleaner assembly
• Transaxle mount pipe expansion bolt
• Negative battery cable

12. Refill the transaxle.

13. Apply the brakes and start the engine.

14. Shift the transaxle from **R** to **D**.

15. Recheck the fluid level.

Halfshaft

REMOVAL & INSTALLATION

1. Before servicing the vehicle, refer to the precautions in the beginning of this section.

2. Remove or disconnect the following:
• Wheel
• Tie rod from the steering knuckle
• Halfshaft hub nut and washer
• Stabilizer link
• Lower ball joint from the steering knuckle and discard the cotter pin
• Halfshaft from the hub/bearing assembly using a puller
• Halfshaft from the hub/bearing assembly and move the strut/knuckle assembly rearward
• Halfshaft from the transaxle using Axle Remover tool J-28468 or J-33008 attached to Axle Shaft Remover Extension J-29794 and Slide Hammer J-2619-01

To install:

3. Install the halfshaft into the transaxle by placing a tool in the joint housing groove and tapping until seated.

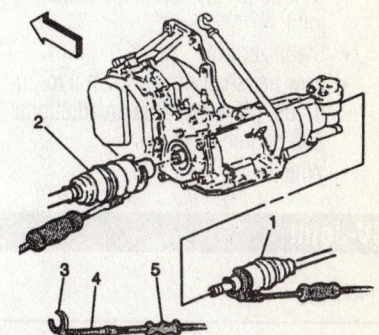

(1) Drive Axle, Right Side
(2) Drive Axle, Left Side
(3) J 28468 or J 33008
(4) J 29794
(5) J 2619-01

7922Z225

Removing the left and right halfshafts

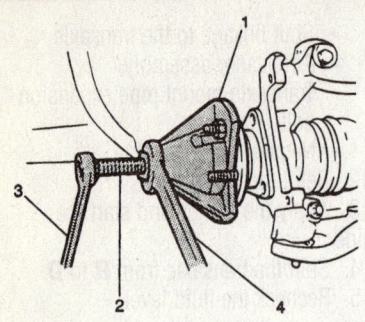

(1) J 28733A
(2) Forcing Screw
(3) Turn Box Wrench
(4) Hold Wrench

7922Z226

Removing the halfshaft from the hub utilizing the appropriate tools

4. Verify that the halfshaft is seated in the transaxle by grasping on the housing and pulling outward.

5. Install or connect the following:

- Tie rod to the steering knuckle. Tighten the nut to 89 inch lbs. (10 Nm), plus an additional 210 degree turn.
- Halfshaft into the hub/bearing assembly
- Lower ball joint to the steering knuckle. Tighten the nut to 89 inch lbs. (10 Nm), plus an additional 180 degree turn
- New cotter pin to the lower ball joint
- Stabilizer link
- New halfshaft nut. Tighten it to 30 ft. lbs. (40 Nm), plus an additional 235 degree turn.
- Wheel

CV-Joint

OVERHAUL

Outer CV-Joint

1. Before servicing the vehicle, refer to the precautions in the beginning of this section.

2. Remove or disconnect the following:
- Front wheel
- Halfshaft and position it in a vise

- Large CV-joint boot clamp and discard it
- Small CV-joint boot clamp and discard it
- CV-joint boot and slide it back on the shaft
- Outer race from the halfshaft by spreading the outer race-to-halfshaft retaining ring using Snapring Pliers J-8059
- Retaining ring from the halfshaft and discard it
- CV-joint boot from the halfshaft and discard it if damaged

3. Disassemble the chrome alloy balls from the CV-joint cage as follows:

a. Position a brass drift against the CV-joint cage and tap it with a hammer to tilt the cage.

b. Remove the 1st chrome alloy ball from the cage.

c. Tilt the cage in the opposite direction.

d. Remove the opposite chrome alloy ball.

e. Repeat the procedure until all 6 balls are removed.

4. Disassemble the CV-joint cage and inner race as follows:

a. Pivot the cage and race 90 degrees to the center line of the outer race.

b. Align the cage windows with outer race lands.

c. Remove the cage from the outer race.

d. Rotate the inner race upward and remove it from the cage.

5. Throughly clean and inspect all parts.

To install:

6. Lubricate the parts with a light coat of grease.

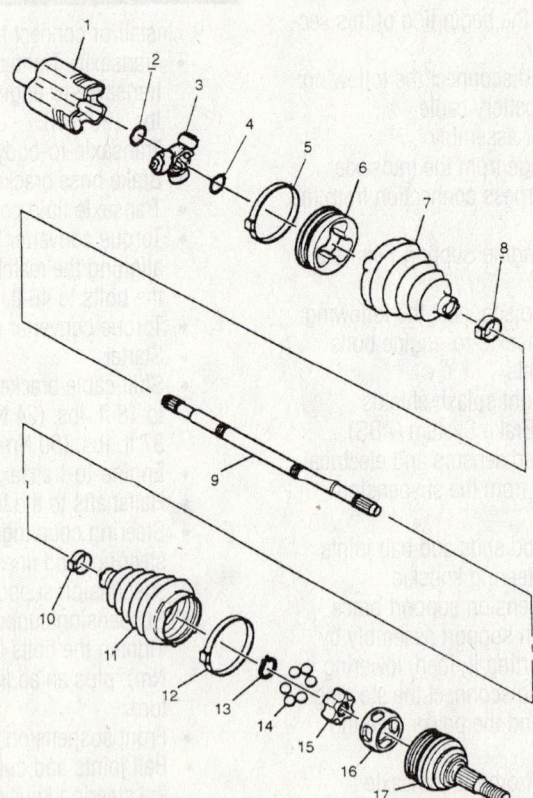

1 Retainer and Housing Assembly	10	Seal Retaining Clamp
2 Shaft Retaining Ring	11	Drive Axle Outboard Seal
3 Tripot Joint Spider Assembly	12	Seal Retaining Clamp
4 Spacer Ring	13	Race Retaining Ring
5 Seal Retaining Clamp	14	Chrome Alloy Ball
6 Tripot Trilobal Bushing	15	CV Joint Inner Race
7 Drive Axle Inboard Seal	16	CV Joint Cage
8 Seal Retaining Clamp	17	CV Joint Outer Race
9 Axle Shaft		

9306ZG01

Exploded view of the halfshaft assembly

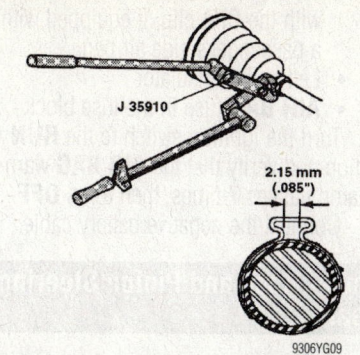

J 35910

2.15 mm (.085")

9306YG09

Crimping the small boot clamp—Outer CV-joint

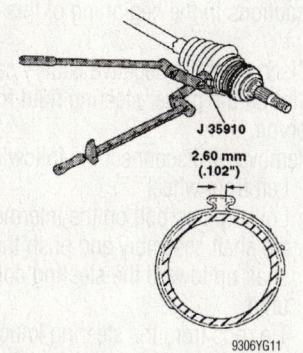

J 35910

2.60 mm (.102")

9306YG11

Crimping the large boot clamp—Outer CV-joint

7. Assemble the CV-joint cage and inner race, as follows:

a. Rotate the inner race 90 degrees to the cage centerline.

b. Align the cage windows with inner race lands.

c. Insert the inner race into the cage by rotating the inner race downward.

d. Insert the cage/inner race into the outer race.

8. Assemble the chrome alloy balls into the CV-joint cage, as follows:

a. Position a brass drift against the CV-joint cage and tap it with a hammer to tilt the cage.

b. Insert the 1st chrome alloy ball into the cage.

c. Tilt the cage in the opposite direction.

d. Insert the opposite chrome alloy ball.

e. Repeat the procedure until all 6 balls are inserted.

9. Install ½ of the kit grease into the CV-joint.

10. Install or connect the following:
- Small ring clamp on the CV boot
- New retaining ring on the halfshaft
- Large ring clamp on the CV boot

- Outer race assembly onto the half-shaft until the ring engages the halfshaft groove

11. Slide the small end of the CV-joint boot/clamp into place, with the seal lip in the halfshaft groove

➡**Make sure the boot lies flat against the halfshaft.**

12. Using the Crimp tool J-35910, a torque wrench and a breaker bar, crimp the small CV-joint boot clamp to 100 ft. lbs. (136 Nm).

13. Check the clamp gap dimension; if it is not 0.085 in. (2.15mm), continue tightening the clamp until it is.

14. Install ½ of the kit grease into the CV-joint boot.

15. Slide the large end of the CV boot/clamp into place, with the seal lip in place over the outer race.

➡**Make sure the boot lies flat against the outer race.**

16. Using the Crimp tool J-35910, a torque wrench and a breaker bar, crimp the large CV-joint boot clamp to 130 ft. lbs. (176 Nm).

17. Check the clamp gap dimension; if it is not 0.102 in. (2.60mm), continue tightening the clamp until it is.

18. Install the halfshaft and the front wheel.

Inner (Tri-Pot) Joint

1. Before servicing the vehicle, refer to the precautions in the beginning of this section.

2. Remove or disconnect the following:
- Front wheel
- Halfshaft and place it in a vise
- Snapring from the stub shaft and discard it
- Small CV-joint boot clamp, cut and discard it
- Large CV-joint boot clamp, cut and discard it
- CV-joint boot by sliding it away from the tri-pot joint

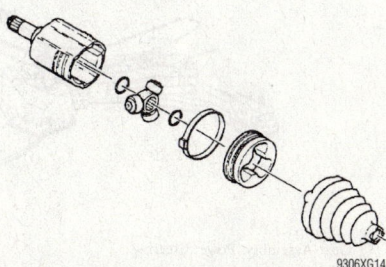

9306XG14

Exploded view of the inner (tri-pot) joint

3. Install a Stub Shaft Removal tool J-38868-A to the stub shaft snapring groove.

4. Using a slide hammer puller, press the stub shaft from the tri-pot housing.

5. Remove or disconnect the following:
- Tri-pot housing from the tri-pot spider
- Inboard spacer ring slide it rearward on the shaft using Snapring Pliers tool J-8059
- Outboard retaining ring using Snapring Pliers tool J-8059 and discard it
- Tri-pot joint spider assembly
- Inboard spacer ring and discard it
- CV-joint boot
- Trilobal tri-pot bushing from the housing

6. Throughly clean and inspect all parts.

To install:

7. Install or connect the following:
- New snapring onto the stub shaft
- Small boot clamp
- CV-joint boot

8. Using the Crimp tool J-35910, a torque wrench and a breaker bar, crimp the small CV-joint boot clamp to 100 ft. lbs. (136 Nm).

9. Install or connect the following:
- Inboard spacer ring slide it rearward on the shaft using Snapring Pliers tool J-8059, past the 2nd groove
- Tri-pot joint spider assembly onto the shaft until it passes the 2nd groove
- Outboard retaining ring into the axle shaft groove using Snapring Pliers tool J-8059
- Tri-pot joint spider assembly, slide it against the outboard retaining ring
- Inboard spacer ring, seat it in the groove
- ½ of the kit grease into the boot
- ½ of the kit grease into the tri-pot housing
- Trilobal tip-pot bushing flush with the tri-pot housing face
- New large seal clamp onto the CV-joint boot
- Tri-pot housing, slide it over the tri-pot joint spider assembly
- CV-joint boot/clamp, slide it into place, over the trilobal tri-pot bushing with the seal lip in the groove

➡**Make sure the boot lies flat against the trilobal bushing.**

10. Using the Crimp tool J-35910, a torque wrench and a breaker bar, crimp the large CV-joint boot clamp to 130 ft. lbs. (176 Nm).

11. Check the clamp gap dimension; if it is not 0.102 in. (2.60mm), continue tightening the clamp until it is.

12. Install the halfshaft and the front wheel.

STEERING AND SUSPENSION

Air Bag

✳✳ CAUTION

Some vehicles are equipped with an air bag system, also known as the Supplemental Inflatable Restraint (SIR) or Supplemental Restraint System (SRS). The system must be disabled before performing service on or around system components, steering column, instrument panel components, wiring and sensors. Failure to follow safety and disabling procedures could result in accidental air bag deployment, possible personal injury and unnecessary system repairs.

PRECAUTIONS

Several precautions must be observed when handling the inflator module to avoid accidental deployment and possible personal injury.

• Never carry the inflator module by the wires or connector on the underside of the module.

• When carrying a live inflator module, hold securely with both hands, and ensure that the bag and trim cover are pointed away.

• Place the inflator module on a bench or other surface with the bag and trim cover facing up.

• With the inflator module on the bench, never place anything on or close to the module which may be thrown in the event of an accidental deployment.

DISARMING

✳✳ CAUTION

The Supplemental Restraint System (SRS) must be disarmed before per-

forming service procedures around the air bag or SRS wiring. Failure to do so may cause accidental deployment of the air bag, resulting in unnecessary SRS repairs and/or personal injury.

1. Disconnect the negative battery cable.
2. Turn the steering wheel so the vehicle's wheels are pointing straight-ahead.
3. Turn the ignition switch to the **LOCK** position.
4. Remove or disconnect the following:
   • Key
   • **AIR BAG** fuse from the fuse block
   • Left sound insulator
   • Connector Position Assurance (CPA) clip from the yellow 2-way connector at the base of the steering column
   • CPA clip and the yellow 2-way connector from the passenger air bag lead, if equipped with a passenger's side air bag

ARMING

1. Turn the ignition switch to the **LOCK** position and remove the key.
2. Install or connect the following:
   • Yellow 2-way connector at the base of steering column and the Connector Position Assurance (CPA) clip
   • Yellow 2-way connector at the passenger air bag lead and secure it

with the CPA clip, if equipped with a passenger's side air bag
   • Left sound insulator
   • **AIR BAG** fuse in the fuse block

3. Turn the ignition switch to the **RUN** position and verify that the **AIR BAG** warning lamp flashes 7 times, then turns **OFF**.
4. Connect the negative battery cable.

Power Rack and Pinion Steering Gear

REMOVAL & INSTALLATION

1. Before servicing the vehicle, refer to the precautions in the beginning of this section.
2. Disconnect the negative battery cable.
3. Siphon the power steering fluid from the reservoir.
4. Remove or disconnect the following:
   • Left front wheel
   • Lower pinch bolt on the intermediate shaft assembly and push the shaft up toward the steering column
   • Tie rods from the steering knuckle
   • Steering gear mounting bolts
   • Transaxle-to-crossmember mounting bolt
   • Rear crossmember-to-body bolts
   • Front crossmember bolts, loosen them
   • Power steering pipes from the steering gear

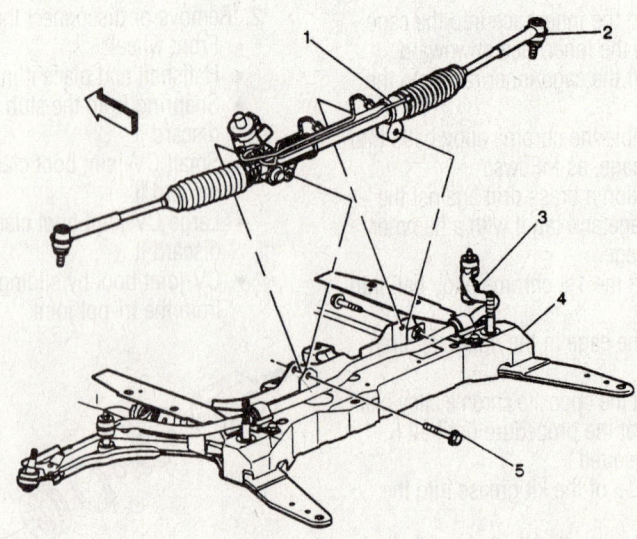

(1) Gear Assembly, Power Steering
(2) Tie Rod
(3) Shaft, Front Stabilizer
(4) Frame Assembly, Drivetrain and Front Crossmember
(5) Bolt, Power Steering Gear Assembly

79222227

Exploded view of the power rack and pinion steering gear mounting

- Steering gear through the left wheel opening

To install:

5. Install or connect the following:
- Steering gear through the left wheel opening
- Power steering pipes to the steering gear
- Front crossmember bolts. Tighten them to 71 ft. lbs. (110 Nm) plus an additional 90 degree turn.
- Rear crossmember-to-body bolts. Tighten them to 71 ft. lbs. (110 Nm) plus an additional 90 degree turn.
- Transaxle mount-to-crossmember bolt. Tighten it to 49 ft. lbs. (66 Nm).
- Steering gear bolts. Tighten them to 89 ft. lbs. (120 Nm).
- Tie rod ends to the steering knuckle. Tighten the nut to 15 ft. lbs. (20 Nm) plus an additional 180 degree turn.
- Lower pinch bolt on the intermediate shaft. Tighten it to 16 ft. lbs. (22 Nm).
- Left front wheel
- Negative battery cable

6. Refill and bleed the power steering system.
7. Check and/or adjust the front end alignment.

Strut

REMOVAL & INSTALLATION

Front

1. Before servicing the vehicle, refer to the precautions in the beginning of this section.
2. Remove or disconnect the following:
- Front wheel
- Outer tie rod end from the steering knuckle
- Brake line bracket from the strut
- Matchmark the front strut-to-steering knuckle location
- Strut lower mounting bracket nut and through-bolts

3. Support the lower control arm.
4. Remove or disconnect the following:
- Upper strut-to-chassis nuts and bolt
- Strut

※※ CAUTION

If the strut is being replaced, a spring compressor must be used to remove the coil spring from the strut assembly. Failure to use a spring compressor can result in personal injury.

To install:

5. Install or connect the following:
- Strut and finger-tighten the upper strut-to-chassis nuts
- Strut to the steering knuckle. Tighten the through-bolts/nuts to 133 ft. lbs. (180 Nm) with the reference marks aligned.
- Tie rod end to the steering knuckle. Tighten the nut to 15 ft. lbs. (20 Nm) plus an additional 90 degree turn.
- Brake line bracket to the strut. Tighten the bolt to 10 ft. lbs. (14 Nm).
- Wheel

- Upper strut plate-to-chassis nuts/bolt. Tighten them to 18 ft. lbs. (25 Nm).

6. Check and/or adjust the front end alignment.

Rear

1. Matchmark the strut-to-knuckle position.
2. Remove or disconnect the following:
- Rear wheels
- Upper strut-to-chassis nuts/bolts
- Strut-to-knuckle bolts
- Strut

To install:

3. Install or connect the following:
- Strut and finger-tighten the strut-to-knuckle bolts
- Upper strut-to-chassis nuts/bolts

➡**Align the matchmarks to ensure proper alignment.**

- Strut-to-knuckle bolts. Tighten them to 89 ft. lbs. (120 Nm).
- Rear wheels

4. Check and/or adjust the alignment.

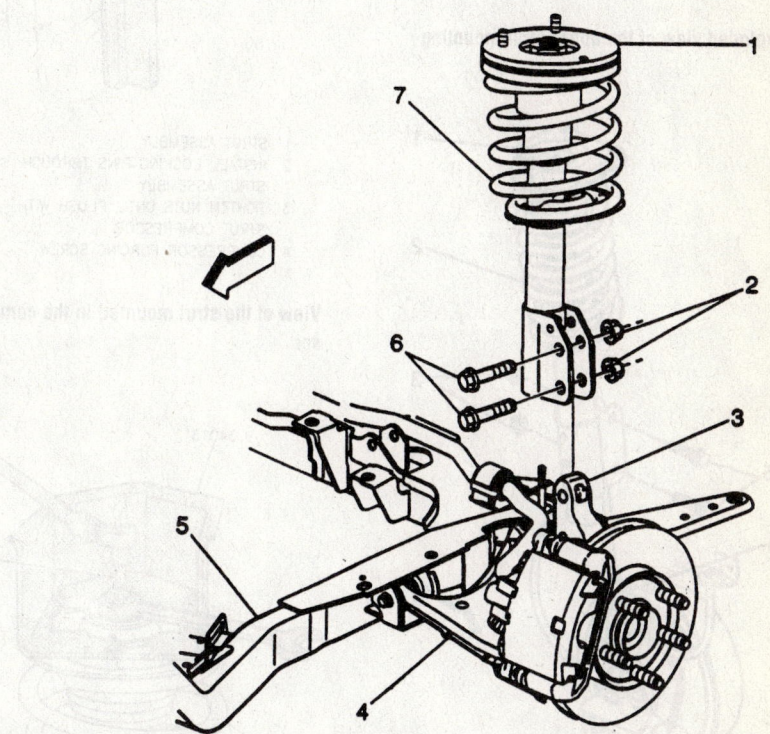

(1) Bearing, Strut Mount
(2) Nuts, Strut Mount
(3) Knuckle
(4) Arm, Control
(5) Crossmember
(6) Bolts, Strut Mount
(7) Spring, Strut Coil

7922Z228

Exploded view and component identification of the front strut

Turn to Section 5 for brake system applications

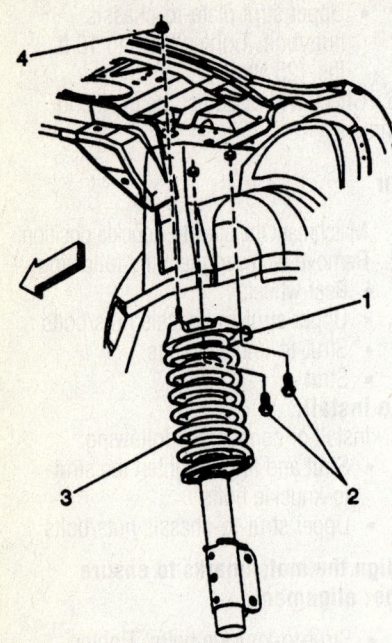

(1) Mount, Strut Upper
(2) Bolt, Strut Mount
(3) Spring, Coil
(4) Nut

7922Z229

Exploded view of the upper strut mounting

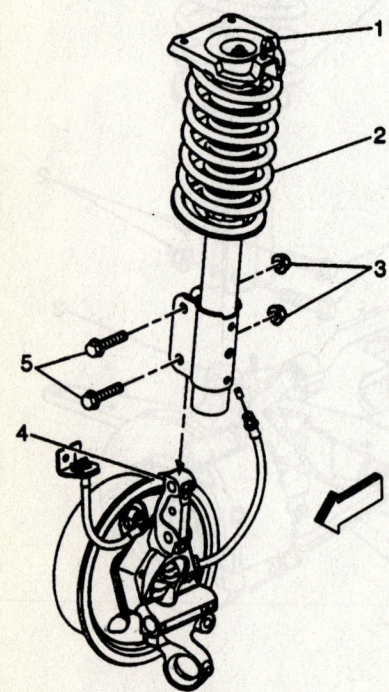

(1) Mount, Strut Upper
(2) Spring, Coil
(3) Nuts, Strut Bolt
(4) Knuckle
(5) Bolt, Strut Mount

7922Z230

Exploded view of the lower strut mounting

Coil Spring

REMOVAL & INSTALLATION

Front and Rear

1. Remove the strut
2. Mount the strut compressor J-34013 in holding fixture J-3289-20.
3. Mount the strut in the compressor.

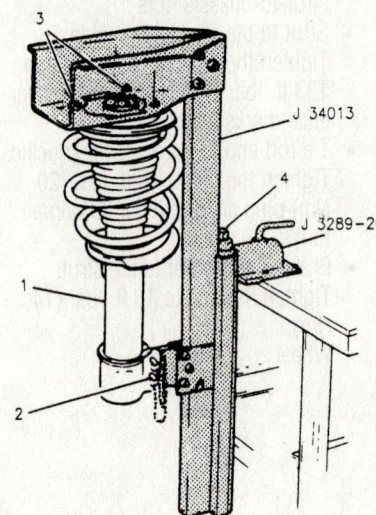

1 STRUT ASSEMBLY
2 INSTALL LOCKING PINS THROUGH STRUT ASSEMBLY
3 TIGHTEN NUTS UNTIL FLUSH WITH STRUT COMPRESSOR
4 COMPRESSOR FORCING SCREW

7922Z231

View of the strut mounted in the compressor

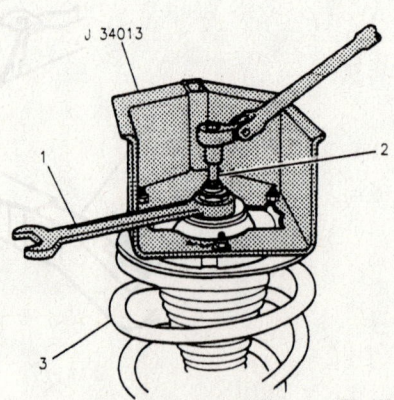

1 WRENCH
2 SOCKET
3 STRUT ASSEMBLY

7922Z232

Use a socket and a wrench to remove the damper shaft nut spring cap while compressing the spring

➡ The strut compressor has strut mounting holes drilled for specific vehicle lines.

4. Compress the strut approximately ½ of its height after initial contact with the top cap.

❊❊ WARNING

Never bottom the spring or damper rod.

5. Remove the strut damper shaft nut and place alignment/guiding rod J-34013-27 on top of the damper shaft. Use the rod to guide the damper shaft straight down through the spring cap while compressing the spring. Remove the components.

To install:

6. Install the bearing cap onto the strut compressor, if removed.
7. Mount the strut in strut compressor using bottom locking pin only. Extend the

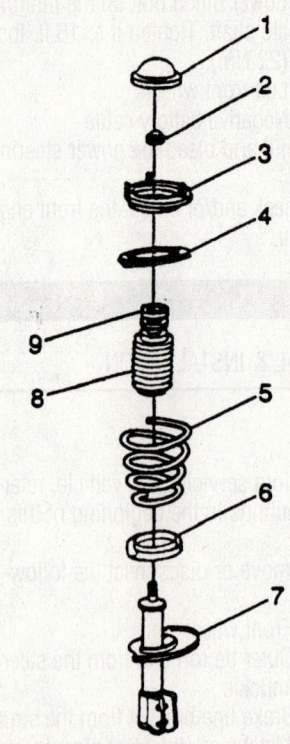

(1) Cap
(2) Nut, Strut Mount
(3) Bearing, Strut Mount
(4) Insulator, Spring (Upper)
(5) Spring, Strut Coil
(6) Insulator, Spring (Lower)
(7) Strut
(8) Bumper, Jounce
(9) Shield, Strut Dust

7922Z233

Exploded view of the front strut

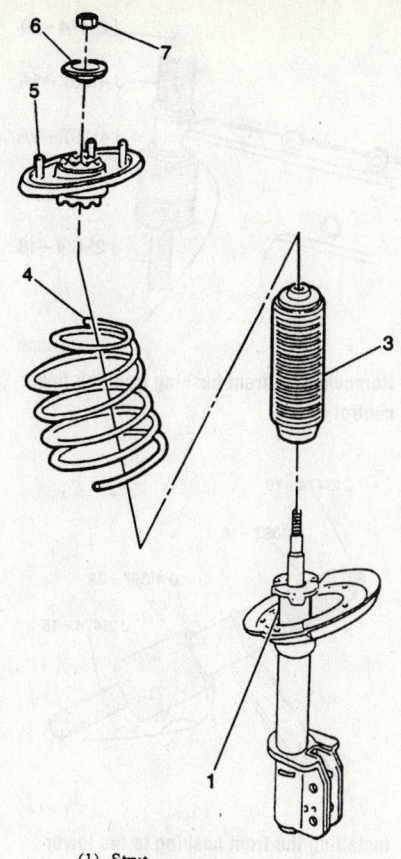

(1) Strut
(2) Dust Shield, Strut
(3) Spring, Strut Coil
(4) Mount, Strut Upper
(5) Washer
(6) Nut

7922Z234

Exploded view of the rear strut

damper shaft and install clamp J-34013-20 on the damper shaft.

8. Install the spring over the damper and swing the assembly up so the upper locking pin can be installed.

9. Install all shields, bumpers and insulators on the spring seat. Install the spring seat on top of the spring. Be sure the flat on the upper spring seat is facing in the proper direction. The spring seat flat should be facing the same direction as the centerline of the strut assembly spindle.

10. Install the guiding rod and turn the forcing screw while the guiding rod centers the assembly. When the threads on the damper shaft are visible, remove the guiding rod and install the nut. Tighten the nut to 52 ft. lbs. (70 Nm). Use a crow's foot line wrench while holding the damper shaft with a socket.

11. Remove the clamp.

Lower Ball Joint

REMOVAL & INSTALLATION

1. Before servicing the vehicle, refer to the precautions in the beginning of this section.

2. Remove the wheel.

➡ **Care must be exercised to prevent the halfshaft joints from being over-extended. When either end of the shaft is disconnected, over-extension of the joint could result in separation of internal components and possible joint failure. Failure to observe this can result in interior joint or boot damage and possible joint failure.**

3. Separate the ball joint from the steering knuckle and discard the cotter pin.

4. Drill out the 3 ball joint-to-lower control arm rivets. Use an ⅛ in. (3mm) drill bit to make a pilot hole through the rivets; then, finish drilling the rivets with a ½ in. (13mm) drill bit.

5. Remove or disconnect the following:
   • Link to the stabilizer shaft nut
   • Ball joint from the control arm

To install:

6. Install or connect the following:
   • Ball joint to the control arm. Tighten the 3 new nuts/bolts (supplied with new ball joint).
   • Ball joint to the steering knuckle. Tighten nut to 48 ft. lbs. (65 Nm) and install a new cotter pin.
   • Stabilizer link to the stabilizer shaft. Tighten the nut to 13 ft. lbs. (17 Nm).
   • Wheel

7. Check and/or adjust the front wheel alignment.

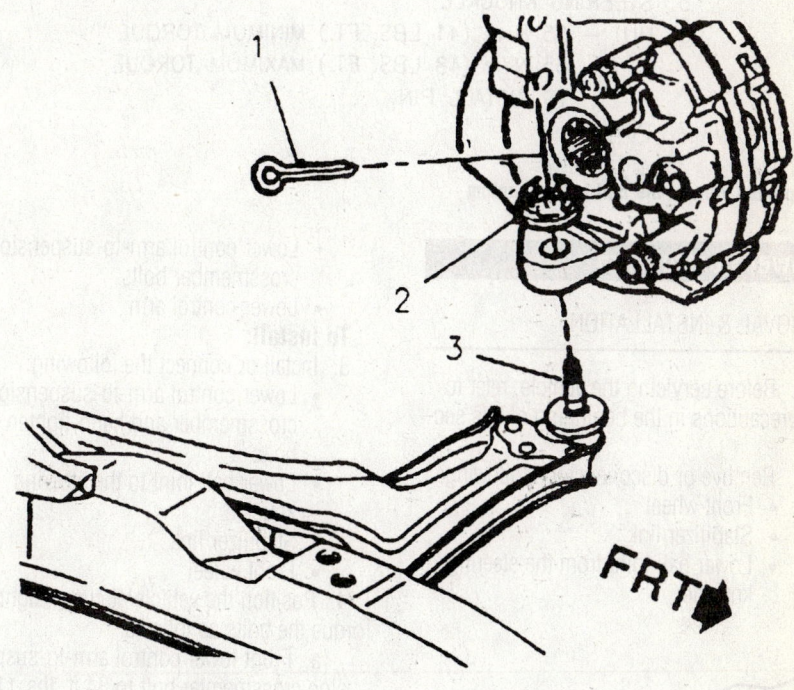

1   PIN
2   NUT – 55 N·m (41 LBS. FT.) MINIMUM TORQUE 65 N·m (48 LBS. FT.) MAXIMUM TORQUE TO INSTALL PIN
3   LOWER BALL JOINT

7922Z235

Exploded view of the ball joint-to-knuckle mounting

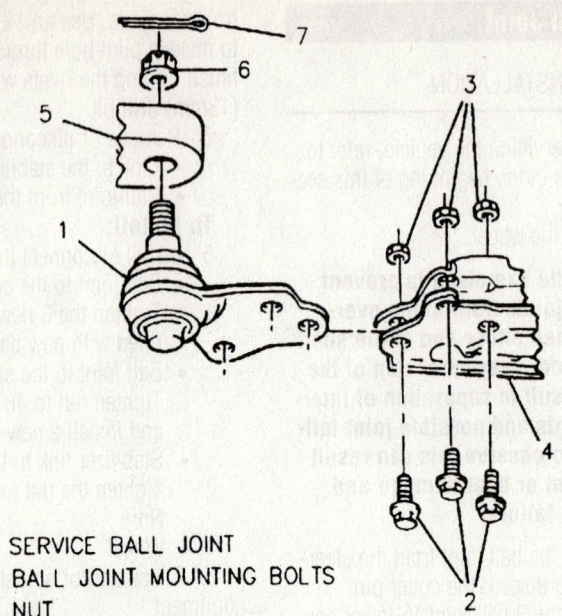

1 SERVICE BALL JOINT
2 BALL JOINT MOUNTING BOLTS
3 NUT
4 LOWER CONTROL ARM
5 STEERING KNUCKLE
6 NUT — 55 N·m (41 LBS. FT.) MINIMUM TORQUE
65 N·m (48 LBS. FT.) MAXIMUM TORQUE
TO INSTALL PIN
7 PIN

7922Z236

Exploded view of the ball joint mounting

Lower Control Arm

REMOVAL & INSTALLATION

1. Before servicing the vehicle, refer to the precautions in the beginning of this section.

2. Remove or disconnect the following:
- Front wheel
- Stabilizer link
- Lower ball joint from the steering knuckle

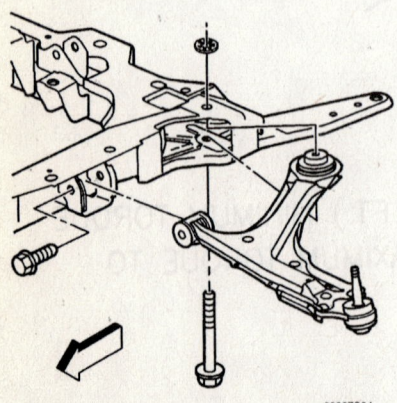

9306ZG04

Exploded view of the lower control arm and related components

- Lower control arm-to-suspension crossmember bolts
- Lower control arm

To install:

3. Install or connect the following:
- Lower control arm-to-suspension crossmember and hand-tighten the bolts
- Lower ball joint to the steering knuckle
- Stabilizer link
- Front wheel

4. Position the vehicle at curb height. Torque the bolts as follows:

   a. Front lower control arm-to-suspension crossmemter bolt to 84 ft. lbs. (115 Nm), plus an additional 120 degree turn.

   b. Rear lower control arm-to-suspension crossmemter bolt to 180 ft. lbs. (245 Nm), plus an additional 180 degree turn.

5. Check and/or adjust the front alignment.

CONTROL ARM BUSHING REPLACEMENT

Front Bushing

1. Before servicing the vehicle, refer to the precautions in the beginning of this section.

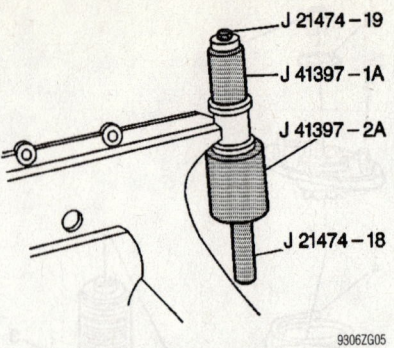

9306ZG05

Removing the front bushing from the lower control arm

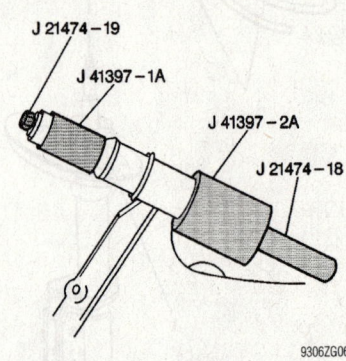

9306ZG06

Installing the front bushing to the lower control arm

2. Remove the lower control arm and place it in a vise.

3. Lubricate the threads of Screw J-21474-19 with high pressure lubricant.

4. Assemble tools Screw J-21474-19, Remover/Installer J-41397-1A, Receiver J-41397-2A and J-21474-18 onto the front control arm bushing.

5. Tighten tool J-21474-18 until the front bushing is pressed from the control arm.

6. Disassemble the tools.

To install:

7. Lubricate the new front bushing outer casing.

8. Insert the new bushing into the control arm.

9. Assemble tools Screw J-21474-19, Remover/Installer J-41397-1A, Receiver J-41397-2A and J-21474-18 onto the front control arm bushing.

10. Tighten Screw J-21474-19 until the front bushing is pressed into the control arm.

11. Disassemble the tools.

12. Install the lower control arm.

Rear Bushing

1. Before servicing the vehicle, refer to the precautions in the beginning of this section.

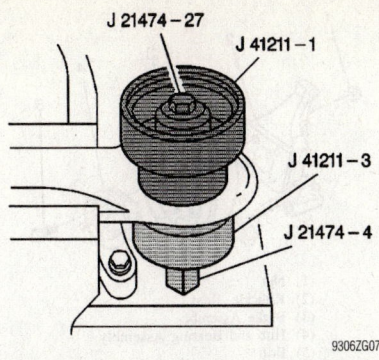

Removing the rear bushing from the lower control arm

9306ZG07

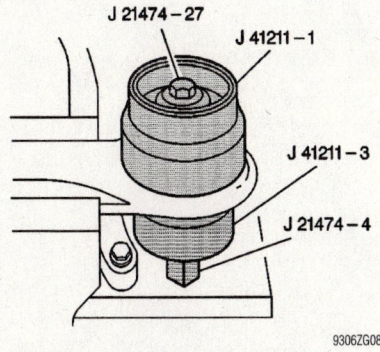

Installing the rear bushing to the lower control arm

9306ZG08

2. Remove the lower control arm and place it in a vise.

3. Assemble tools Screw J-21474-27, Remover/Installer J-41211-1, Receiver J-41211-3 and J-21474-4 onto the rear control arm bushing.

4. Tighten tool J-21474-27 until the rear bushing is pressed from the control arm.

5. Disassemble the tools.

To install:

6. Insert the new bushing into the control arm.

7. Assemble tools Screw J-21474-27, Remover/Installer J-41211-1, Receiver J-41211-3 and J-21474-4 onto the rear control arm bushing.

8. Tighten Screw J-21474-4 until the rear bushing is pressed into the control arm.

9. Disassemble the tools.

10. Install the lower control arm.

Wheel Bearings

ADJUSTMENT

These vehicles are equipped with sealed hub and bearing assemblies. The hub and bearing assemblies are non-serviceable. If the assembly is damaged, the complete unit must be replaced.

REMOVAL & INSTALLATION

Front

1. Before servicing the vehicle, refer to the precautions in the beginning of this section.

2. Remove the front wheel.

3. Insert a drift punch through the caliper and into the rotor cooling fins; this keeps the assembly from turning while the halfshaft nut is being loosened.

4. Remove or disconnect the following:
- Halfshaft nut and the punch
- Caliper from the steering knuckle and support it aside.

✳✳ WARNING

DO NOT allow the caliper to hang unsupported from the brake hose.

- Brake rotor
- 3 hub bearing-to-steering knuckle bolts
- Backing plate

- Halfshaft from the hub/bearing assembly
- Hub/bearing assembly

To install:

5. Install or connect the following:
- Hub/bearing assembly on the halfshaft, make sure the splines engage smoothly
- Backing plate
- 3 hub/bearing-to-steering knuckle bolts. Tighten the bolts to 70 ft. lbs. (95 Nm).
- Brake rotor
- Caliper onto the steering knuckle. Tighten the bolts to 38 ft. lbs. (51 Nm).
- Halfshaft nut. Tighten it to 192 ft. lbs. (260 Nm).
- Front wheel. Tighten the nuts to 100 ft. lbs. (140 Nm).

Rear

1. Before servicing the vehicle, refer to the precautions in the beginning of this section.

2. Remove or disconnect the following:
- Wheel

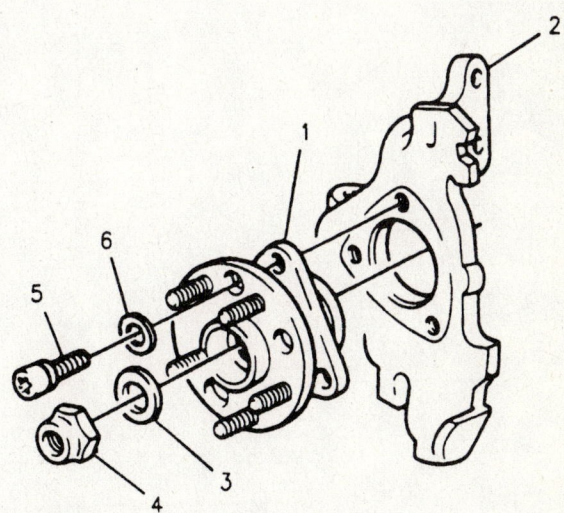

1 HUB AND BEARING ASSEMBLY
2 STEERING KNUCKLE
3 WASHER
4 DRIVE AXLE NUT – 260 N·m (192 LBS. FT.)
5 HUB AND BEARING RETAINING BOLT
6 WASHER

7922Z237

Exploded view of the front hub and bearing assembly

- Brake drum
- 4 hub/bearing assembly-to-knuckle nuts

➡ **The top rear bolt will not clear the brake shoes and must be removed with the bearing assembly.**

- Anti-lock Brake System (ABS) speed sensor wire from the hub/bearing assembly
- Hub/bearing assembly

To install:
3. Install or connect the following:
   - Hub/bearing assembly
   - ABS wheel speed sensor, if equipped
   - Hub/bearing-to-knuckle nuts. Tighten the nuts to 38 ft. lbs. (52 Nm).
   - Brake drum
   - Wheel. Tighten the bolts to 100 ft. lbs. (140 Nm).

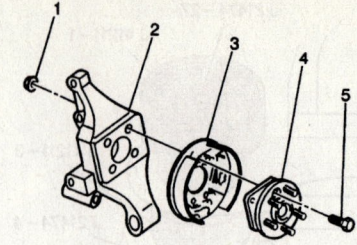

(1) Nut
(2) Knuckle, Rear
(3) Brake Assembly
(4) Hub and Bearing Assembly
(5) Bolt

7922Z238

Hub and bearing components

GENERAL MOTORS CORPORATION—N-BODY

34

Buick-Skylark • **Oldsmobile**-Achieva • **Alero** • **Pontiac**-Grand Am

PRECAUTIONS

Before servicing any vehicle, please be sure to read all of the following precautions, which deal with personal safety, prevention of component damage, and important points to take into consideration when servicing a motor vehicle:

• Never open, service or drain the radiator or cooling system when the engine is hot; serious burns can occur from the steam and hot coolant.

• Observe all applicable safety precautions when working around fuel. Whenever servicing the fuel system, always work in a well-ventilated area. Do not allow fuel spray or vapors to come in contact with a spark, open flame or excessive heat (a hot drop light, for example). Keep a dry chemical fire extinguisher near the work area. Always keep fuel in a container specifically designed for fuel storage; also, always properly seal fuel containers to avoid the possibility of fire or explosion. Refer to the additional fuel system precautions later in this section.

• Fuel injection systems often remain pressurized, even after the engine has been turned **OFF**. The fuel system pressure must be relieved before disconnecting any fuel lines. Failure to do so may result in fire and/or personal injury.

• Brake fluid often contains polyglycol ethers and polyglycols. Avoid contact with the eyes and wash your hands thoroughly after handling brake fluid. If you do get brake fluid in your eyes, flush your eyes with clean, running water for 15 minutes. If eye irritation persists, or if you have taken brake fluid internally, IMMEDIATELY seek medical assistance.

• The EPA warns that prolonged contact with used engine oil may cause a number of skin disorders, including cancer! You should make every effort to minimize your exposure to used engine oil. Protective gloves should be worn when changing oil. Wash your hands and any other exposed skin areas as soon as possible after exposure to used engine oil. Soap and water, or waterless hand cleaner should be used.

• All new vehicles are now equipped with an air bag system. The system must be disabled before performing service on or around system components, steering col-

umn, instrument panel components, wiring and sensors. Failure to follow safety and disabling procedures could result in accidental air bag deployment, possible personal injury and unnecessary system repairs.

• Always wear safety goggles when working with, or around, the air bag system. When carrying a non-deployed air bag, be sure the bag and trim cover are pointed away from your body. When placing a non-deployed air bag on a work surface, always face the bag and trim cover upward, away from the surface. This will reduce the motion of the module if it is accidentally deployed. Refer to the additional air bag system precautions later in this section.

• Clean, high quality brake fluid from a sealed container is essential to the safe and proper operation of the brake system. You should always buy the correct type of brake fluid for your vehicle. If the brake fluid becomes contaminated, completely flush the system with new fluid. Never reuse any brake fluid. Any brake fluid that is removed from the system should be discarded. Also, do not allow any brake fluid to come in contact with a painted surface; it will damage the paint.

• Never operate the engine without the proper amount and type of engine oil; doing so WILL result in severe engine damage.

• Timing belt maintenance is extremely important! Many models utilize an interference-type, non-freewheeling engine. If the timing belt breaks, the valves in the cylinder head may strike the pistons, causing potentially serious (also time-consuming and expensive) engine damage. Refer to the maintenance interval charts in the front of this manual for the recommended replacement interval for the timing belt, and to the timing belt section for belt replacement and inspection.

• Disconnecting the negative battery cable on some vehicles may interfere with the functions of the on-board computer system(s) and may require the computer to undergo a relearning process once the negative battery cable is reconnected.

• When servicing drum brakes, only disassemble and assemble one side at a time, leaving the remaining side intact for reference.

ENGINE REPAIR

Alternator

REMOVAL

2.4L Engine

1. Before servicing the vehicle, refer to the precautions in the beginning of this section.
2. Remove or disconnect the following:
   • Negative battery cable
   • Serpentine drive belt

✲✲ CAUTION

To avoid personal injury when rotating the serpentine belt tensioner, use a tight fitting 13mm wrench with a handle of at least 24 in. (51cm) length.

   • Alternator mounting studs and bolts
   • Alternator electrical connectors
   • Alternator

3.1L Engine

1. Before servicing the vehicle, refer to the precautions in the beginning of this section.
2. Remove or disconnect the following:
   • Negative battery cable
   • Drive belt
   • Alternator electrical connectors
   • Power steering-to-alternator line clip
   • Rear alternator brace
   • Alternator air intake connector
   • Alternator-to-bracket nut/bolt
   • Alternator

3.4L Engine

1. Before servicing the vehicle, refer to the precautions in the beginning of this section.
2. Remove or disconnect the following:
   • Negative battery cable
   • Drive belt
   • Alternator electrical connectors
   • Power steering-to-alternator line clip
   • Alternator mounting nuts and bolts
   • Alternator

INSTALLATION

2.4L Engine

Install or connect the following:

- Alternator
- Alternator electrical connectors
- Alternator mounting studs and bolts. Tighten the studs/bolts to 37 ft. lbs. (50 Nm).
- Serpentine drive belt
- Negative battery cable

3.1L Engine

Install or connect the following:

- Alternator
- Alternator-to-bracket nut/bolts. Tighten the nut to 37 ft. lbs. (50 Nm) and the bolt to 18 ft. lbs. (25 Nm).
- Alternator air intake connector
- Rear alternator brace. Tighten the nut/bolt to 18 ft. lbs. (25 Nm).
- Power steering-to-alternator line clip
- Alternator electrical connectors
- Drive belt
- Negative battery cable

3.4L Engine

Install or connect the following:

- Alternator
- Alternator mounting nuts and bolts. Tighten the nuts to 22 ft. lbs. (30 Nm) and the bolts to 37 ft. lbs. (50 Nm).
- Power steering-to-alternator line clip
- Alternator electrical connectors
- Drive belt
- Negative battery cable

Ignition Timing

ADJUSTMENT

The ignition timing is not adjustable, and is set electronically according to engine demand.

Engine Assembly

REMOVAL & INSTALLATION

2.4L Engine

The engine and transaxle are removed as a unit from under the vehicle.

1. Before servicing the vehicle, refer to the precautions in the beginning of this section.
2. Relieve the fuel system pressure.
3. Disconnect the negative battery cable.
4. Drain the cooling system.
5. Discharge and recover the refrigerant, if equipped with air conditioning.
6. Remove or disconnect the following:
   - Left sound insulator
   - Clutch pushrod from the pedal assembly, manual transaxle only
   - Heater and upper radiator hoses from the thermostat housing
   - Air cleaner-to-throttle body duct
   - Upper radiator support
   - Cooling fan assembly
   - Refrigerant line and discard the O-rings, if equipped with air conditioning
   - Vacuum hoses from the front of the engine
   - Electrical connectors from the necessary components
   - Power brake booster vacuum lines
   - Throttle cables and the cable bracket
   - Power steering pump and rear bracket; move the pump aside with the lines attached
   - Fuel lines from the fuel rail, cap the lines
   - Shift cable from the transaxle and the Throttle Valve (TV) cable, on automatic transaxle
   - Exhaust manifold and heat shield
   - Lower radiator hose
   - Coolant recovery tank and move it aside with the hoses attached
7. Install an Engine Support Fixture J-28467-A.
8. Remove the right engine mount.
9. Drain the crankcase.
10. Remove or disconnect the following:
    - Front wheel and the right lower splash shield
    - Electrical connections from the Anti-lock Brake System (ABS) wheel speed sensors
    - Ground connections from the transaxle
    - Lower ball joints from the steering knuckles and discard the cotter pins
11. Support the suspension crossmembers.
12. Remove or disconnect the following:
    - Crossmember mounting bolts
    - Heater outlet hose from the radiator outlet pipe
    - Halfshafts from the transaxle
    - Intermediate shaft, if equipped with a manual transaxle
13. Position an engine table under the powertrain and lower the vehicle until the powertrain is resting on the table.
14. Remove or disconnect the following:
    - Engine strut
    - Transaxle mount bolts
    - Engine support fixture
15. Raise the vehicle until it is clear of the engine.
16. Separate the transaxle from the engine.

To install:

17. Install or connect the following:
    - Transaxle onto the engine. Tighten the bolts to 55 ft. lbs. (75 Nm).
    - Powertrain assembly and the engine table under the vehicle
    - Engine Support Fixture J-28467-A
    - Engine strut and transaxle mounts
18. Raise the vehicle and remove the engine table.
19. Install or connect the following:
    - Halfshafts and intermediate shaft to the transaxle
    - Heater outlet hose to the radiator outlet pipe
    - Suspension crossmember
    - Lower ball joints to the steering knuckles. Tighten the ball joint-to-steering knuckle nuts to 41 ft. lbs. (55 Nm). Install new cotter pins.
    - Ground connections to the transaxle
    - Electrical connections to the ABS wheel speed sensors
    - Front wheel and the right lower splash shield
    - Right engine mount
    - Coolant recovery tank
    - Lower radiator hose
    - Exhaust manifold and heat shield
    - Shift cable to the transaxle and the TV cable, on automatic transaxle
    - Fuel lines to the fuel rail
    - Power steering pump and rear bracket
    - Throttle cables and the cable bracket
    - Power brake booster vacuum lines
    - Electrical connectors to the necessary components
    - Vacuum hoses to the front of the engine
    - Refrigerant line, using new O-rings, if equipped with air conditioning

- Cooling fan assembly
- Upper radiator support
- Air cleaner-to-throttle body duct
- Heater and upper radiator hoses to the thermostat housing
- Clutch pushrod to the pedal assembly, manual transaxle only
- Left sound insulator
- Negative battery cable

20. Refill the cooling system
21. Refill the crankcase.
22. Recharge the air conditioning system.
23. Start the vehicle and verify no leaks.
24. Check and/or adjust the wheel alignment.

3.1L Engine

Please note that the engine and transaxle are removed as an assembly from under the vehicle.

1. Before servicing the vehicle, refer to the precautions in the beginning of this section.
2. Relieve the fuel system pressure.
3. Remove or disconnect the following:
   - Negative battery cable
   - Upper half of the air cleaner assembly
   - Throttle body inlet duct
4. Drain the cooling system.
5. Remove or disconnect the following:
   - Upper and lower radiator hoses
   - Coolant inlet line from the coolant surge tank
   - Vacuum hoses from the Evaporative Emissions (EVAP) canister purge valve, vacuum modulator and power brake booster
   - Heater outlet hose from the water pump
   - Serpentine drive belt
   - Control cables from the throttle body lever and intake manifold bracket; then
   - Electrical connectors from the necessary components
   - Alternator
   - Power steering lines from the power steering pump and cap the lines
   - Fuel lines from the fuel rail and cap them
   - Cooling fan assembly
   - Shift control cable from the transaxle shift lever and cable bracket
   - Transaxle vent tube from the transaxle
   - Vacuum hose from the vacuum reservoir

6. Install an engine support fixture
7. Loosen, but do not remove the top 2 air conditioning compressor mounting bolts.
8. Drain the engine crankcase.
9. Remove or disconnect the following:
   - Front wheel
   - Right and left inner fender splash shields
   - Engine mount strut
   - Anti-lock Brake System (ABS) sensor wires from the wheel sensors
   - Lower ball joints from the steering knuckles and discard the cotter pins
   - Lower suspension support assemblies with the lower control arms attached
   - Halfshafts from the transaxle and support aside
   - Oil filter and oil filter adapter
   - Flywheel cover
   - Starter
   - Heater hoses from the heater core
   - Air conditioning compressor and move it aside with the refrigerant lines connected
   - Vacuum reservoir tank
   - Exhaust pipe from the exhaust manifold
   - Engine mount strut bracket from the engine
   - Transaxle cooler lines from the radiator
   - Transaxle oil fill tube
10. Lower the vehicle until the powertrain assembly is resting on an engine table.
11. Remove or disconnect the following:
    - Transaxle mount-to-body bolts
    - Intermediate bracket from the right engine mount
    - Engine support fixture
12. Raise the vehicle leaving the powertrain assembly on the engine table.
13. Separate the engine from the transaxle.

To install:

14. Install or connect the following:
    - Transaxle to the engine. Tighten the bolts to 55 ft. lbs. (75 Nm).
    - Powertrain assembly under the vehicle
    - Serpentine belt, loosely install it
15. Lower the vehicle over the powertrain assembly.
16. Install or connect the following:
    - Engine support fixture
    - Intermediate bracket to the right engine mount
    - Transaxle mount-to-body bolts
17. Remove the engine table.
18. Install or connect the following:

- Transaxle oil fill tube
- Transaxle cooler lines to the radiator
- Engine mount strut bracket to the engine. Tighten the bolts to 44 ft. lbs. (60 Nm).
- Exhaust pipe to the exhaust manifold. Tighten the bolts to 18 ft. lbs. (25 Nm).
- Vacuum reservoir tank
- Air conditioning compressor
- Heater hoses to the heater core
- Starter
- Flywheel cover
- Oil filter and oil filter adapter
- Halfshafts to the transaxle and support aside
- Lower suspension support assemblies with the lower control arms attached
- Lower ball joints to the steering knuckles, using new cotter pins. Tighten the nuts to 41 ft. lbs. (55 Nm).
- ABS sensor wires to the wheel sensors
- Engine mount strut
- Right and left inner fender splash shields
- Front wheel
- Top 2 air conditioning compressor mounting bolts.

19. Remove the engine support fixture
20. Install or connect the following:
    - Vacuum hose to the vacuum reservoir
    - Transaxle vent tube to the transaxle
    - Shift control cable to the transaxle shift lever and cable bracket
    - Cooling fan assembly
    - Fuel lines to the fuel rail
    - Power steering lines to the power steering pump
    - Alternator
    - Electrical connectors to the necessary components
    - Control cables to the throttle body lever and intake manifold bracket
    - Serpentine drive belt
    - Heater outlet hose to the water pump
    - Vacuum hoses to the EVAP canister purge valve, vacuum modulator and power brake booster
    - Coolant inlet line to the coolant surge tank
    - Upper and lower radiator hoses
    - Throttle body inlet duct
    - Upper half of the air cleaner assembly
    - Negative battery cable
21. Check and fill all the engine fluids as necessary.

22. Start the vehicle and bleed the power steering system.

3.4L Engine

1. Before servicing the vehicle, refer to the precautions in the beginning of this section.
2. Disconnect the negative battery cable.
3. Drain the engine coolant.
4. Remove or disconnect the following:
   - Air cleaner assembly
   - Hood
   - Drive belt
   - Hoses from the surge tank
   - Cruise control module
   - Upper wiring harness from the components on the top of the engine
   - Throttle and cruise control cables
   - Starter
   - Air conditioning compressor and move it aside with the lines attached
   - Lower wiring harness from the engine components
   - Catalytic converter from the rear exhaust manifold
   - Torque converter cover
   - Flexplate-to-torque converter bolts, after matchmarking the assembly
   - Engine splash shields
   - Transaxle-to-engine brace and the 2 outer transaxle mounting bolts
   - Upper and lower radiator hoses
   - Fuel lines from the engine
   - Vacuum hose from the power brake booster
   - Heater hoses

5. Install an engine hoist and raise the engine slightly.
6. Remove or disconnect the following:
   - Engine mount and adapter
   - Power steering pump
   - Transaxle-to-engine bolts
   - Engine from the vehicle

To install:

7. Install or connect the following:
   - Engine. Tighten the upper transaxle-to-engine bolts to 66 ft. lbs. (90 Nm).
   - Engine support fixture and remove the engine hoist
   - Power steering pump
   - Engine mount bracket and mount. Tighten the bracket bolts to 43 ft. lbs. (58 Nm).
   - Power steering lines to the pump
   - Upper and lower radiator hoses

- Both outer transaxle to engine bolts. Tighten the bolts to 66 ft. lbs. (90 Nm).
- Transaxle to the engine brace. Tighten the bolts to 32 ft. lbs. (43 Nm).
- Right splash shield
- Flexplate to the torque converter. Tighten the bolts to 46 ft. lbs. (62 Nm).
- Torque converter cover
- Air conditioning compressor
- Starter
- Engine mount. Tighten the nuts to 35 ft. lbs. (47 Nm).
- Catalytic converter to the exhaust manifold
- New oil filter
- Lower and upper wiring harnesses to the correct components.
- Vacuum hoses

⁕⁕ CAUTION

To avoid personal injury and/or damage to the vehicle, replace the throttle cable with a new one any time the engine has been removed from the vehicle.

- Cruise control and throttle cables
- Cruise control module
- Fuel lines
- Drive belt
- Hoses to the surge tank
- Hood
- Air cleaner assembly

8. Refill the cooling system.
9. Refill the crankcase.

10. Start the engine and inspect for coolant and/or oil leaks.
11. Stop the engine and recheck the fluid levels after the engine has cooled.

Water Pump

REMOVAL & INSTALLATION

2.4L Engine

1. Before servicing the vehicle, refer to the precautions in the beginning of this section.
2. Disconnect the negative battery cable.
3. Drain the cooling system.
4. Remove or disconnect the following:
   - Oxygen (O₂S) sensor electrical connector
   - Exhaust manifold heat shield
   - Heater hose heat wrap
   - Coolant inlet housing bolt through the exhaust manifold
   - Exhaust manifold brace-to-manifold bolt
   - Manifold-to-exhaust pipe studs
   - Heater outlet pipe bracket-to-transaxle bolt
   - Coolant inlet housing-to-water pump cover bolt
   - Exhaust pipe from the exhaust manifold by pulling it downward

⁕⁕ WARNING

Do not rotate the flex coupling more than 4 degrees for damage may occur.

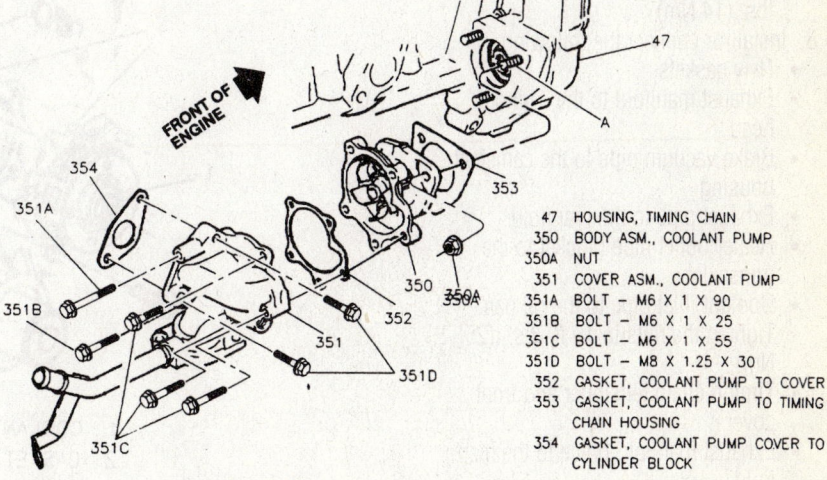

47	HOUSING, TIMING CHAIN
350	BODY ASM., COOLANT PUMP
350A	NUT
351	COVER ASM., COOLANT PUMP
351A	BOLT — M6 X 1 X 90
351B	BOLT — M6 X 1 X 25
351C	BOLT — M6 X 1 X 55
351D	BOLT — M8 X 1.25 X 30
352	GASKET, COOLANT PUMP TO COVER
353	GASKET, COOLANT PUMP TO TIMING CHAIN HOUSING
354	GASKET, COOLANT PUMP COVER TO CYLINDER BLOCK

79222302

Exploded view of the water pump mounting—2.4L engine

Timing belt service is covered in Section 4 of this manual

- Coolant inlet pipe from the oil pan
- Brake vacuum pipe from the camshaft housing
- Exhaust manifold from the cylinder head, discard the seals and gaskets
- Heater hose from the heater outlet pipe
- Timing chain cover and tensioner
- Water pump cover-to-engine bolts
- 3 water pump-to-timing chain housing nuts
- Water pump and cover assembly
- Water pump cover from the pump

To install:

5. Thoroughly clean and dry all mounting surfaces.

6. Install or connect the following:
- New gasket
- Water pump to the cover and tighten the bolts finger-tight
- Water pump cover-to-engine bolts and tighten finger-tight
- Water pump-to-timing chain housing nuts and tighten finger-tight
- Coolant inlet pipe O-ring lubricated with antifreeze
- Coolant inlet pipe into the water pump cover and tighten the bolts finger-tight

7. With all gaps closed, torque the bolts, in the following sequence, to the proper values:
- Pump assembly-to-chain housing nuts to 19 ft. lbs. (26 Nm)
- Pump cover-to-pump assembly to 124 inch lbs. (14 Nm)
- Water pump cover-to-engine bolts, bottom bolt first to 19 ft. lbs. (26 Nm)
- Coolant inlet pipe assembly-to-water pump cover bolts to 124 inch lbs. (14 Nm)

8. Install or connect the following:
- New gaskets
- Exhaust manifold to the cylinder head
- Brake vacuum pipe to the camshaft housing
- Exhaust pipe to the manifold
- Heater outlet pipe bracket to the transaxle
- Coolant inlet pipe to the oil pan. Tighten the nuts to 19 ft. lbs. ((25 Nm).
- Timing chain tensioner and front cover
- Exhaust manifold brace to the manifold
- Exhaust manifold to the exhaust pipe. Tighten nuts to 26 ft. lbs. (35 Nm).
- Heater hose to the heater pipe

- Exhaust manifold heat shield
- O₂S electrical connector
- Negative battery cable

9. Refill the cooling system

10. Start the engine and check for leaks.

3.1L and 3.4L Engines

1. Before servicing the vehicle, refer to the precautions in the beginning of this section.

2. Disconnect the negative battery cable.

3. Drain the cooling system.

4. Remove or disconnect the following:
- Water pump pulley bolts, loosen them
- Serpentine belt
- Water pump pulley bolts and the pulley
- Water pump bolts and the pump

To install:

5. Clean all the gasket mounting surfaces.

6. Apply a thin bead of sealer around the outside edge of the water pump along the gasket sealing area

7. Install or connect the following:
- New water pump gasket
- Water pump. Tighten the bolts to 89 inch lbs. (10 Nm).
- Water pump pulley and tighten the pulley bolts finger-tight
- Serpentine belt

- Water pump pulley bolts. Tighten the bolts to 18 ft. lbs. (25 Nm).
- Negative battery cable

8. Refill and bleed the cooling system.

9. Test run the engine and check for leaks.

Cylinder Head

REMOVAL & INSTALLATION

2.4L Engine

1. Before servicing the vehicle, refer to the precautions in the beginning of this section.

2. Disconnect the negative battery cable.

3. Drain the cooling system.

4. Remove or disconnect the following:
- Heater inlet and throttle body heater hoses from water outlet
- Power brake vacuum hose from the throttle body
- Manifold Absolute Pressure (MAP) sensor
- Intake Air Temperature (IAT) sensor
- Evaporative Emissions (EVAP) purge solenoid
- Camshaft Position (CMP) sensor
- Stud-ended bolt from the alternator
- Intake manifold brace
- Intake manifold

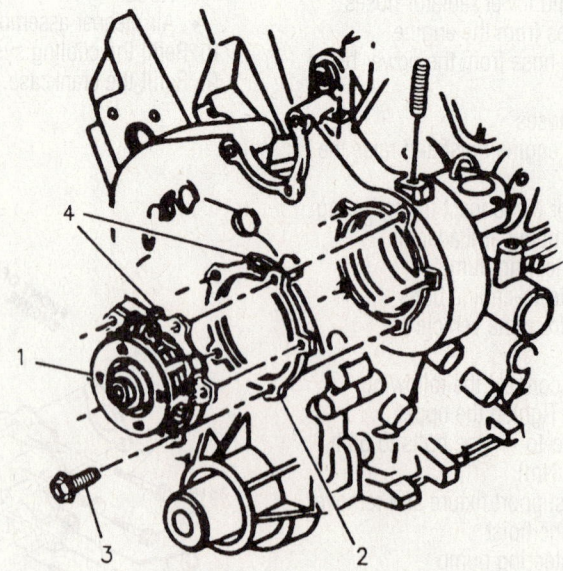

1 COOLANT PUMP
2 GASKET
3 BOLT - 10 N·m (89 LBS. IN.)
4 LOCATOR (MUST BE VERTICAL)

7922Z303

Exploded view of the water pump mounting—3.1L and 3.4L engines

5. Install the stud-ended alternator bolt back into the engine.

6. Install an engine support fixture.

7. Remove or disconnect the following:
- Exhaust manifold
- Ignition coil and module assembly
- Power steering pump
- Vacuum line from the fuel pressure regulator, fuel injector and fuel injector wiring harness
- Fuel line clamp from the intake camshaft housing bracket
- Fuel line rail and move it aside with the fuel lines attached
- Timing chain housing at the intake camshaft housing but do not remove it
- Electrical connection from the oil switch
- Transaxle fluid level indicator tube assembly from the exhaust camshaft cover and move it aside, if equipped with an automatic transaxle

➡ **Any time the camshaft housing-to-cylinder head bolts are loosened or removed, the camshaft housing-to-cylinder head gasket must be replaced.**

- Intake camshaft housing and discard the gasket

➡ **Turn the camshaft housing upside down as soon as it is removed from the cylinder head; otherwise, the lifters may will fall out.**

- Exhaust camshaft housing and discard the gasket
- Upper radiator hose from the coolant outlet
- Engine Coolant Temperature (ECT) sensor electrical connector
- Cylinder head bolts by reversing of the tightening sequence
- Cylinder head and discard the gasket

To install:

8. Clean all gasket mounting surfaces.

➡ **Be sure the threaded holes in the engine block for the cylinder head bolts are clean.**

➡ **Refer to Section 1 of this manual for the cylinder head torque sequence illustration. The illustration is located after the Torque Specification Chart.**

9. Install or connect the following:
- New cylinder head gasket
- New cylinder head bolts lubricated with clean engine oil

10. Tighten the cylinder head bolts, in sequence, as follows:
   a. Step 1: Bolts 1 through 8 to 40 ft. lbs. (65 Nm).
   b. Step 2: Bolts 9 and 10 to 30 ft. lbs. (40 Nm).
   c. Step 3: All bolts an additional 90 degrees (¼) turn.

11. Install the intake and exhaust camshaft housings. Tighten the bolts to:
   a. Long bolts: 11 ft. lbs. (15 Nm) plus an additional 90 degree turn.
   b. Short bolts: 11 ft. lbs. (15 Nm) plus an additional 30 degree turn.

12. Install or connect the following:
- Timing chain and timing chain housing
- Upper radiator hose to the water outlet
- Both ECT sensor connectors
- Fuel rail on the intake manifold and the intake manifold brace
- MAP sensor
- IAT sensor
- EVAP purge solenoid
- CMP sensor
- Power steering pump
- Throttle body and the throttle cable bracket
- Throttle body air intake duct
- Lubricate the O-ring on the oil fill tube with engine oil
- Oil fill tube into the engine
- Ignition coil and module assembly. Attach the injector harness electrical connector.

13. Remove the engine support fixture. Install the exhaust manifold.

14. Fill all fluids to their proper levels. An oil and filter change is recommended.

15. Connect the negative battery cable. Start the vehicle and verify no leaks.

3.1L and 3.4L Engines

LEFT (FRONT) CYLINDER HEAD

1. Before servicing the vehicle, refer to the precautions in the beginning of this section.

2. Relieve the fuel system pressure.

3. Drain the crankcase.

4. Drain the cooling system.

5. Remove or disconnect the following:
- Upper half of the air cleaner assembly
- Throttle body air inlet duct
- Exhaust crossover pipe heat shield
- Crossover pipe
- Spark plug wires from the spark plugs

- Rocker arm covers
- Upper intake plenum and lower intake manifold
- Left side exhaust manifold
- Oil level indicator tube

➡ **When removing the valvetrain components, keep them in order for installation purposes.**

- Rocker arm bolt, rocker arms, balls and pushrods
- Cylinder head bolts evenly
- Cylinder head and discard the gasket

To install:

6. Clean all the gasket mounting surfaces. Clean the threads on the cylinder head bolts and block threads.

➡ **Refer to Section 1 of this manual for the cylinder head torque sequence illustration. The illustration is located after the Torque Specification Chart.**

7. Install or connect the following:
- New cylinder head gasket in position with the words **THIS SIDE UP** showing
- Cylinder head and lubricate the bolt threads with sealer

8. On 1997 models, tighten the cylinder head bolts, in sequence, to:
   a. Step 1: 33 ft. lbs. (45 Nm)
   b. Step 2: Plus an additional 90 degree (¼) turn

9. On 1998–99 3.1L engines, tighten the cylinder head bolts, in sequence, to:
   a. Step 1: 37 ft. lbs. (50 Nm)
   b. Step 2: Plus an additional 90 degree (¼) turn

10. On the 3.4L engines, tighten the cylinder head bolts, in sequence, to:
   a. Step 1: 33 ft. lbs. (45 Nm)
   b. Step 2: Plus an additional 90 degree (¼) turn

11. Install or connect the following:
- Pushrods, rocker arms, balls and bolts. Tighten the bolts to 89 inch lbs. (10 Nm) plus an additional 30 degree turn.
- Lower intake manifold
- Upper intake plenum
- Rocker arm covers
- Oil level indicator tube
- Spark the plug wires
- Left side exhaust manifold
- Exhaust crossover pipe
- Crossover pipe heat shield
- Upper half of the air cleaner assembly

- Throttle body air inlet duct
- Negative battery cable

12. Refill the cooling system.
13. Refill the crankcase.

→**A filter change is recommended.**

14. Start the engine and verify no leaks.

RIGHT (REAR) CYLINDER HEAD

1. Before servicing the vehicle, refer to the precautions in the beginning of this section.
2. Relieve the fuel system pressure.
3. Drain the crankcase.
4. Drain the cooling system.
5. Remove or disconnect the following:
   - Upper half of the air cleaner assembly
   - Throttle body air inlet duct
   - Exhaust crossover pipe heat shield
   - Crossover pipe
   - Oxygen (O₂S) sensor
   - Exhaust pipe from the exhaust manifold
   - Right side exhaust manifold
   - Spark plug wires from the spark plugs
   - Rocker arm covers
   - Upper intake plenum
   - Lower intake manifold

→**When removing the valvetrain components keep them in order for installation purposes.**

   - Rocker arms bolt, rocker arms, balls and pushrods
   - Cylinder head bolts evenly
   - Cylinder head and discard the gasket

To install:

6. Clean all the gasket mounting surfaces. Clean the threads on the cylinder head bolts and block threads.

→**Refer to Section 1 of this manual for the cylinder head torque sequence illustration. The illustration is located after the Torque Specification Chart.**

7. Install or connect the following:
   - New cylinder head gasket in position with the words **THIS SIDE UP** showing
   - Cylinder head and lubricate the bolt threads with sealer

8. On 1997 models, tighten the cylinder head bolts, in sequence, to:
   a. Step 1: 33 ft. lbs. (45 Nm)
   b. Step 2: Plus an additional 90 degree (¼) turn

9. On 1998–99 3.1L engines, tighten the cylinder head bolts, in sequence, to:
   a. Step 1: 37 ft. lbs. (50 Nm)

   b. Step 2: Plus an additional 90 degree (¼) turn

10. On the 3.4L engines, tighten the cylinder head bolts, in sequence, to:
   a. Step 1: 33 ft. lbs. (45 Nm)
   b. Step 2: Plus an additional 90 degree (¼) turn

11. Install or connect the following:
   - Pushrods, rocker arms, balls and rocker arm bolts. Tighten the bolts to 89 inch lbs. (10 Nm) plus an additional 30 degree turn.
   - Lower intake manifold
   - Upper intake plenum
   - Rocker arm covers
   - Spark plug wires
   - Exhaust manifold
   - Exhaust pipe to the exhaust manifold
   - O₂S sensor
   - Exhaust crossover pipe
   - Heat shield
   - Upper half of the air cleaner assembly
   - Throttle body air inlet duct
   - Negative battery cable

12. Refill the cooling system.
13. Refill the crankcase.

→**An oil filter change is recommended.**

14. Start the engine and verify no leaks.

Rocker Arms

REMOVAL & INSTALLATION

2.4L Engine

The 2.4L engine is not equipped with rocker arms. The camshafts directly actuate the valves.

3.1L and 3.4L Engines

LEFT SIDE

1. Before servicing the vehicle, refer to the precautions in the beginning of this section.
2. Disconnect the negative battery cable
3. Drain the cooling system to a level below the coolant pipe on the front of the engine.
4. Remove or disconnect the following:
   - Coolant bypass hose clamp at the coolant tube
   - Coolant tube at the cylinder head and move it aside
   - Positive Crankcase Ventilation (PCV) valve from the rocker arm cover
   - Rocker arm cover

→**Keep the pushrods in order. Intake pushrods are 5¾ inches long and exhaust pushrods are 6 inches long.**

   - Rocker arm bolts, balls, rocker arms and pushrods

To install:

5. Clean all the gasket mounting surfaces.
6. Lubricate all the valvetrain components with engine oil.
7. Install or connect the following:
   - Pushrods and the rocker arms. Tighten the bolts to 89 inch lbs. (10 Nm) plus an additional 30 degree turn.
   - Rocker arm cover using a new gasket. Tighten the rocker cover bolts to 90 inch lbs. (10 Nm).
   - PCV valve to the rocker arm cover
   - Coolant tube and the thermostat bypass hose. Tighten the screw at the water pump to 106 inch lbs. (12 Nm), the bolt at the cylinder head corner to 18 ft. lbs. (25 Nm) and the nut to 18 ft. lbs. (25 Nm).
   - Negative battery cable

8. Refill the cooling system.
9. Start the vehicle and verify no leaks.

RIGHT SIDE

1. Before servicing the vehicle, refer to the precautions in the beginning of this section.
2. Remove or disconnect the following:
   - Negative battery cable
   - Spark plug wires from the spark plugs and the upper intake plenum wire retainer
   - Power brake booster vacuum pipe from the intake plenum
   - Serpentine belt
   - Alternator
   - Ignition assembly and Evaporative Emissions (EVAP) canister purge solenoid as an assembly
   - Rocker arm cover

→**Keep the pushrods in order. Intake pushrods are 5¾ inches long and exhaust pushrods are 6 inches long.**

   - Rocker arm bolts, balls, rocker arms and pushrods

To install:

3. Clean all the gasket mounting surfaces.
4. Lubricate all the valvetrain components with engine oil.
5. Install or connect the following:
   - Pushrods and the rocker arms. Tighten the bolts to 89 inch lbs. (10 Nm) plus an additional 30 degree turn.

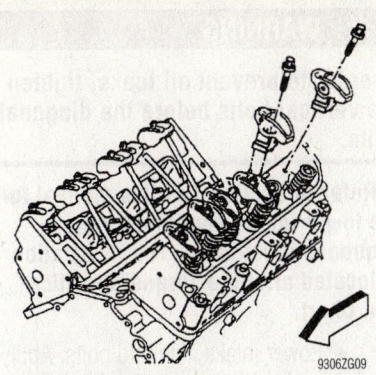

Rocker arm components—3.1L and 3.4L engines

- Rocker arm cover using a new gasket. Tighten the rocker cover bolts to 90 inch lbs. (10 Nm).
- Alternator
- Serpentine belt
- Power brake booster vacuum pipe to the plenum
- EVAP solenoid and ignition assembly
- Spark plug wires
- Negative battery cable
6. Start the vehicle and verify no leaks.

Intake Manifold

REMOVAL & INSTALLATION

These vehicles were filled at the factory with an antifreeze/coolant called GM Goodwrench DEX-COOL®. When adding coolant to vehicles, it is important that you use GM Goodwrench DEX-COOL (orange-colored, silicate-free) coolant. **Propylene glycol is not recommended for use in GM vehicles**. A 50/50 mixture of DEX-COOL and clean water will provide all the recommended protection. **DO NOT mix DEX-COOL with any other type of antifreeze.**

2.4L Engine

1. Before servicing the vehicle, refer to the precautions in the beginning of this section.
2. Relieve the fuel system pressure.
3. Disconnect the negative battery cable.
4. Drain the cooling system to a level below the intake manifold.
5. Remove or disconnect the following:
- Vacuum hose from the Manifold Absolute Pressure (MAP) sensor
- Electrical connectors from the MAP sensor, Intake Air Temperature (IAT) sensor, Evaporative Emissions (EVAP) canister purge solenoid
- Electrical connectors from the fuel injectors
- Vacuum hoses from the intake manifold, fuel pressure regulator and EVAP canister purge solenoid to the canister
- Air cleaner duct
- Vent tube-to-air cleaner duct
- Control cable mounting bracket from the intake manifold
- Power brake vacuum line from the intake manifold
- Vacuum line mounting bracket at the power steering pump
- Coolant lines from the throttle body
- Crankcase air/oil separator
- Oil fill tube
- Intake manifold support brace
- Intake manifold and discard the gasket

To install:
6. Clean the gasket surfaces.

➡**Refer to Section 1 of this manual for the intake manifold torque sequence illustration. The illustration is located after the Torque Specification Chart.**

7. Install or connect the following:
- New intake manifold gasket
- Intake manifold. Tighten the intake manifold fasteners, in sequence, to 18 ft. lbs. (25 Nm).
- Intake manifold brace. Tighten the bolts to 19 ft. lbs. (26 Nm).

➡**The brace-to-block bolts must be tightened first, then the brace-to-manifold bolt.**

- Oil fill tube
- Crankcase air/oil separator
- Coolant lines to the throttle body

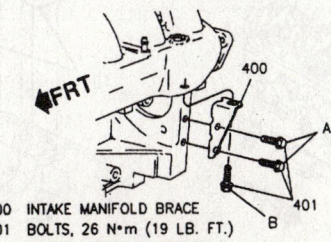

400 INTAKE MANIFOLD BRACE
401 BOLTS, 26 N•m (19 LB. FT.)
A FINGER START ALL BOLTS
B PUSH BRACE AGAINST MANIFOLD WITH FINGERS
C TIGHTEN BOLTS "A" TO SPECIFICATION
D TIGHTEN BOLTS "B" TO SPECIFICATION

Exploded view of the intake manifold brace mounting—2.4L engine

- Vacuum line mounting bracket at the power steering pump
- Power brake vacuum line to the intake manifold
- Control cable mounting bracket to the intake manifold
- Vent tube-to-air cleaner duct
- Air cleaner duct
- Vacuum hoses to the intake manifold, fuel pressure regulator and EVAP canister purge solenoid to the canister
- Electrical connectors to the fuel injectors
- Electrical connectors to the MAP sensor, IAT sensor, EVAP canister purge solenoid
- Vacuum hose to the MAP sensor

8. Lubricate a new oil fill tube O-ring seal with engine oil and install the tube between No. 1 and 2 intake tubes. Rotate as necessary to gain clearance for the oil/air separator nipple on the fill tube.
9. Refill the cooling system.
10. Connect the negative battery cable.

3.1L and 3.4L Engines

These vehicles use a 2-piece intake manifold. Note that these pieces are cast aluminum. Use care when working with light alloy components.
1. Before servicing the vehicle, refer to the precautions in the beginning of this section.
2. Relieve the fuel system pressure.
3. Remove or disconnect the following:
- Upper half of the air cleaner assembly
- Throttle body duct
4. Drain the cooling system.
5. Remove or disconnect the following:
- Exhaust Gas Recirculation (EGR) pipe from exhaust manifold
- Serpentine belt
- Brake vacuum pipe at the intake plenum
- Control cables from the throttle body and intake plenum bracket
- Power steering lines at the alternator bracket
- Alternator
- Spark plug wires from the spark plugs and the intake plenum retainers
- Ignition assembly and the Evaporative Emissions (EVAP) canister purge solenoid as an assembly
- Electrical connectors from the Throttle Position Sensor (TPS), Idle

Air Control (IAC), fuel Injectors, Engine Coolant Temperature (ECT) sensor, Manifold Absolute Pressure (MAP) sensor and Camshaft Position (CMP) sensor.

- Vacuum lines from the vacuum modulator, fuel pressure regulator and Positive Crankcase Ventilation (PCV) valve
- MAP sensor from upper intake manifold
- Upper intake plenum
- Fuel lines from the fuel rail and fuel line bracket

6. Install an engine support fixture.
7. Remove or disconnect the following:
- Right side engine mount
- Power steering pump and move it aside without disconnecting the lines
- Coolant inlet pipe from coolant outlet housing
- Coolant bypass hose from the water pump and the cylinder head
- Upper radiator hose at thermostat housing
- Thermostat housing
- Both rocker arm covers
- Lower intake manifold bolts. Be

sure the washers on the 4 center bolts are installed in their original locations.

➡ When removing the valvetrain components, keep them in order for installation purposes.

- Rocker arm bolts, rocker arms and pushrods
- Intake manifold and discard the gasket

To install:
8. Clean the gasket mating surfaces and the excess RTV sealant from front and rear ridges of engine block.
9. Place a 3mm bead of RTV, on each ridge, where the front and rear of the intake manifold contact the block.
10. Install or connect the following:
- New intake manifold gasket
- Intake manifold
- Pushrods, rocker arms and bolts

➡ Be sure the pushrods are properly seated in the valve lifters and rocker arms.

- Rocker arm bolts. Tighten the them to 89 inch lbs. (10 Nm) plus an additional 30 degree turn.

➡ Refer to Section 1 of this manual for the lower intake manifold torque sequence illustration. The illustration is located after the Torque Specification Chart.

- Lower intake manifold bolts. Apply sealant to the threads of bolts and tighten the bolts to 115 inch lbs. (13 Nm).
- Both rocker arm covers
- Thermostat housing
- Upper radiator hose at thermostat housing
- Coolant bypass hose to the water pump and the cylinder head
- Coolant inlet pipe to coolant outlet housing
- Power steering pump
- Right side engine mount

11. Remove the engine support fixture.
12. Install or connect the following:

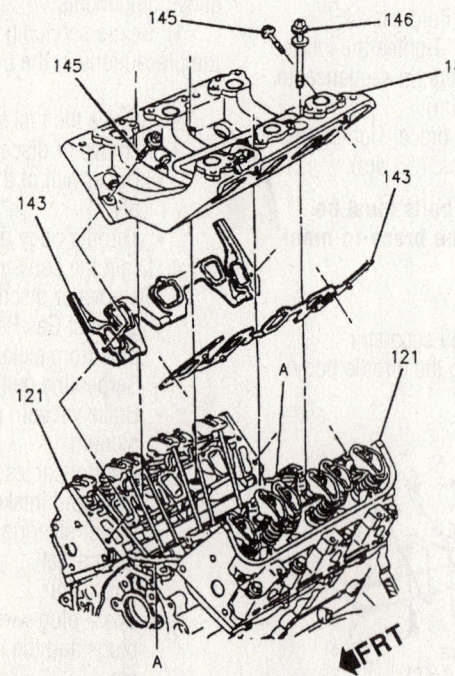

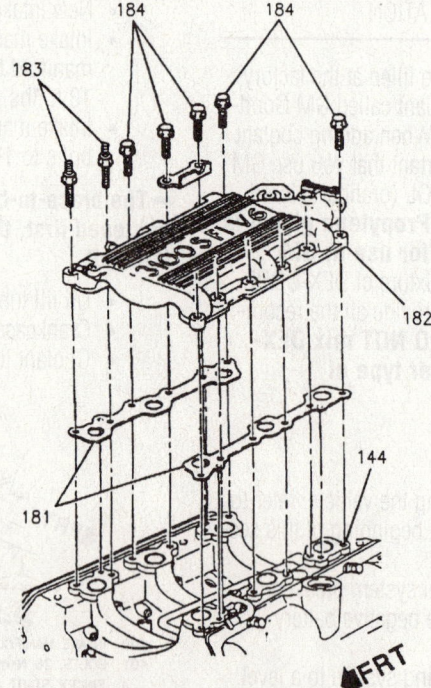

A	APPLY SEALANT
121	HEAD ASSEMBLY, CYLINDER
143	GASKET, LOWER INTAKE MANIFOLD
144	BOLT, LOWER INTAKE
145	BOLT, LOWER INTAKE MANIFOLD
146	BOLT, LOWER INTAKE MANIFOLD
144	MANIFOLD, LOWER INTAKE
181	GASKET, UPPER INTAKE MANIFOLD
182	MANIFOLD, UPPER INTAKE
183	STUD, UPPER INTAKE MANIFOLD
184	BOLT, UPPER INTAKE MANIFOLD

Exploded view of the upper and lower intake—3.1L and 3.4L engines

7922Z310

- Fuel lines to the fuel rail and fuel line bracket
- Upper intake manifold. Tighten the bolts to 18 ft. lbs. (25 Nm).
- MAP sensor to upper intake manifold
- Vacuum lines to the vacuum modulator, fuel pressure regulator and PCV valve
- Electrical connectors to the TPS, IAC, fuel Injectors, ECT sensor, MAP sensor and CMP sensor.
- Ignition assembly and the EVAP canister purge solenoid as an assembly
- Spark plug wires to the spark plugs and the intake plenum retainers
- Alternator
- Power steering lines at the alternator bracket
- Control cables to the throttle body and intake plenum bracket
- Brake vacuum pipe at the intake plenum
- Serpentine belt
- EGR pipe to exhaust manifold
- Throttle body duct
- Upper half of the air cleaner assembly
- Negative battery cable
13. Refill the cooling system.

➡**An engine oil and filter change is recommended.**

14. Start the vehicle and verify no leaks.

Exhaust Manifold

REMOVAL & INSTALLATION

2.4L Engine

➡**There are 2 different exhaust manifolds used on the Quad 4 engine. While the manifolds vary greatly in appearance, the removal and installation procedures are the same. The cast iron manifold is a single outlet design and the sheet metal manifold is a tubular construction with a dual outlet flange.**

1. Before servicing the vehicle, refer to the precautions in the beginning of this section.
2. Remove or disconnect the following:
- Negative battery cable
- Oxygen (O_2S) sensor
- Exhaust manifold brace-to-manifold bolt
- Exhaust manifold-to-exhaust pipe spring loaded bolts

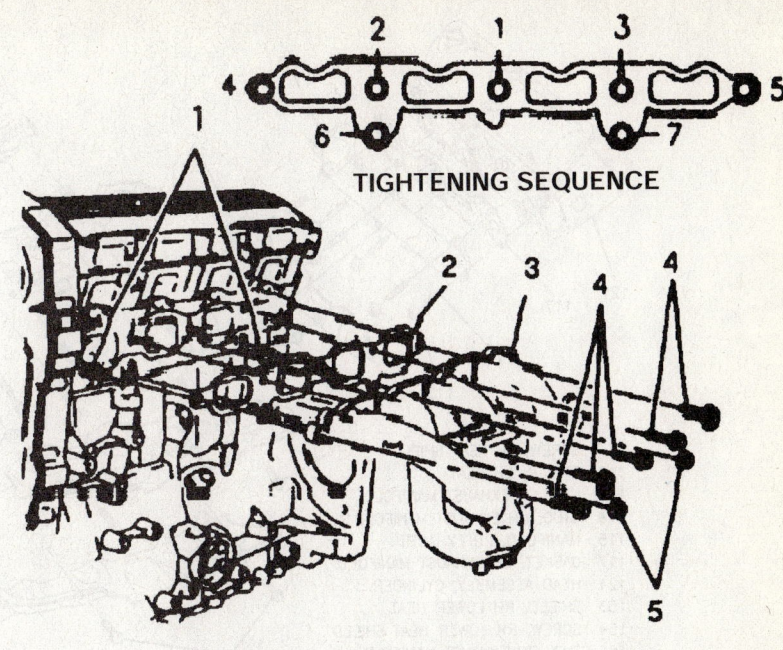

TIGHTENING SEQUENCE

1. Stud - 100 in. lbs. (12Nm)
2. Intake manifold gasket
3. Intake manifold
4. Bolt - 17 ft. lbs. (24 Nm)
5. Nut - 17 ft. lbs. (24 Nm)

7922Z313

Exploded view of the exhaust manifold assembly mounting—2.4L engine

➡**The nuts should be loosened alternately and evenly to prevent the pipe from binding the nuts.**

- Exhaust pipe by pulling it down and back from the exhaust manifold

➡**Do not bend the exhaust flex coupler more than 3 degrees in any direction, for it may damage the flex coupler.**

3. Remove the exhaust manifold.
To install:
4. Clean all gasket mounting surfaces.
5. Install or connect the following:
- New gaskets
- Exhaust manifold. Tighten the nuts, in sequence, to 110 inch lbs. (13 Nm).
- Heat shields
- Exhaust manifold brace-to-manifold bolt
- Exhaust manifold-to-exhaust pipe nuts. Tighten them evenly to 26 ft. lbs. (35 Nm).
- O_2S sensor
- Negative battery cable
6. Start the vehicle and verify no exhaust leaks.

3.1L and 3.4L Engines

LEFT SIDE

1. Before servicing the vehicle, refer to the precautions in the beginning of this section.
2. Remove or disconnect the following:
- Negative battery cable
- Upper half of the air cleaner assembly
- Throttle cable duct
3. Partially drain the cooling system.
4. Remove or disconnect the following:
- Radiator hose from the thermostat housing
- Coolant bypass hose at the coolant pump and the exhaust manifold
- Exhaust crossover heat shield
- Exhaust crossover pipe from the manifold
- Wires from the spark plugs
- Exhaust manifold heat shield
- Exhaust manifold
To install:
5. Clean the mating surfaces.
6. Install or connect the following:
- New gasket
- Exhaust manifold. Tighten the nuts to 12 ft. lbs. (16 Nm).

For engine torque specifications, refer to Section 1 of this manual

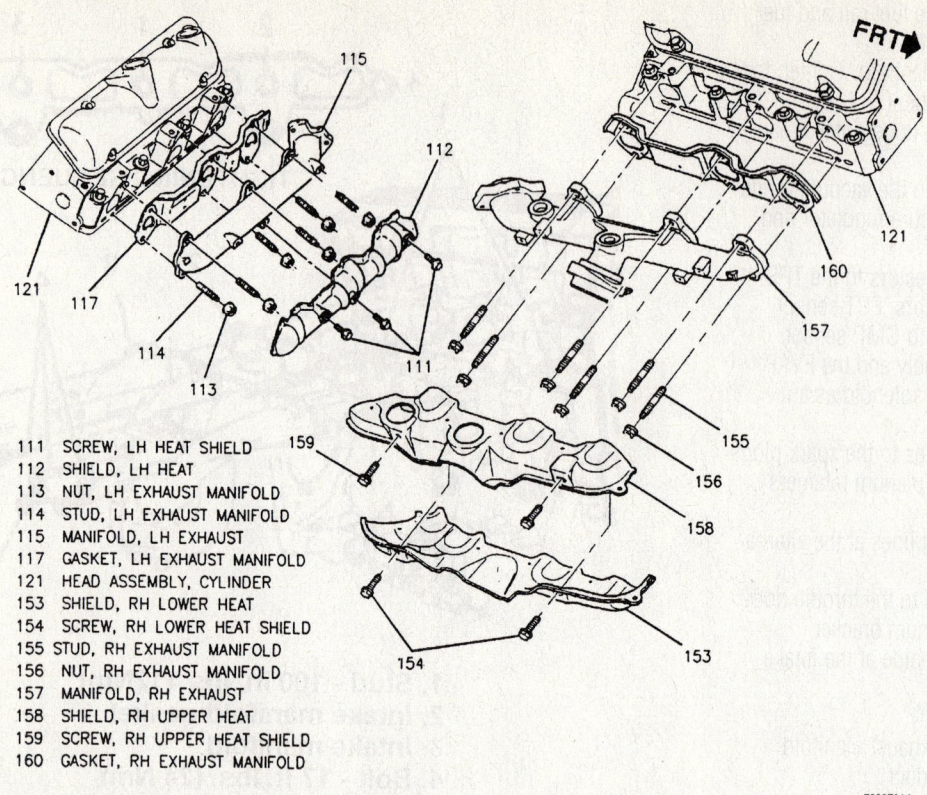

111 SCREW, LH HEAT SHIELD
112 SHIELD, LH HEAT
113 NUT, LH EXHAUST MANIFOLD
114 STUD, LH EXHAUST MANIFOLD
115 MANIFOLD, LH EXHAUST
117 GASKET, LH EXHAUST MANIFOLD
121 HEAD ASSEMBLY, CYLINDER
153 SHIELD, RH LOWER HEAT
154 SCREW, RH LOWER HEAT SHIELD
155 STUD, RH EXHAUST MANIFOLD
156 NUT, RH EXHAUST MANIFOLD
157 MANIFOLD, RH EXHAUST
158 SHIELD, RH UPPER HEAT
159 SCREW, RH UPPER HEAT SHIELD
160 GASKET, RH EXHAUST MANIFOLD

Exploded view of the exhaust manifold mounting—3.1L and 3.4L engines

- Exhaust manifold heat shield
- Exhaust crossover pipe to the manifold
- Spark plug wires
- Coolant bypass pipe to the coolant pump and exhaust manifold
- Radiator hose to the coolant outlet housing
- Upper half of the air cleaner
- Throttle body duct
- Negative battery cable

RIGHT SIDE

1. Before servicing the vehicle, refer to the precautions in the beginning of this section.
2. Remove or disconnect the following:
   - Negative battery cable
   - Upper half of the air cleaner assembly
   - Heated Oxygen (HO2S) sensor
   - Exhaust Gas Recirculation (EGR) pipe from the exhaust manifold
   - Transaxle oil fill tube
   - Lever indicator assembly
   - Front exhaust pipe from the exhaust manifold
   - Exhaust pipe from the converter flange
   - Converter heat shield from the body
   - Wires from the spark plugs
   - Exhaust manifold heat shield
   - Exhaust manifold

To install:

3. Clean the mating surfaces.
4. Install or connect the following:
   - New gasket
   - Exhaust manifold. Tighten the nuts to 12 ft. lbs. (16 Nm).
   - Exhaust manifold heat shield
   - Exhaust crossover pipe to the manifold
   - Converter heat shield to the body
   - Exhaust crossover pipe heat shield
   - Exhaust pipe to the exhaust manifold
   - Transaxle oil level indicator and fill tube assembly
   - HO2S sensor
   - EGR pipe to the exhaust manifold
   - Upper half of the air cleaner
   - Throttle body duct
   - Negative battery cable

Camshaft and Valve Lifters

REMOVAL & INSTALLATION

2.4L Engine

INTAKE SIDE

➡ Anytime the camshaft housing-to-cylinder head bolts are loosened or removed, the camshaft housing-to-cylinder head gasket must be replaced.

1. Before servicing the vehicle, refer to the precautions in the beginning of this section.
2. Remove or disconnect the following:
   - Negative battery cable
   - Ignition assembly electrical connector
   - 4 ignition assembly-to-camshaft housing bolts and the assembly by pulling it straight up

➡ Use a spark plug boot wire remover to remove connector assemblies.

   - Camshaft Position (CMP) sensor electrical connector
   - Power steering pump and move it aside without disconnecting the lines
   - Vacuum line from fuel pressure regulator
   - Fuel injector wiring harness
   - Both fuel line-to-intake camshaft housing clamps
   - Fuel rail-to-camshaft housing bolts
   - Fuel rail from the cylinder head and move it aside with the fuel lines attached
   - Timing chain and camshaft sprockets
   - Timing chain housing bolts but do not remove from the engine
   - Camshaft housing cover-to-camshaft housing bolts

- Camshaft housing-to-cylinder head bolts by reversing of the tightening sequence

➡**Leave 2 bolts loosely in place to hold the camshaft housing while separating the camshaft cover from housing.**

3. Press the cover off the housing by threading 4 of the housing-to-cylinder head bolts into the tapped camshaft housing cover holes. Tighten the bolts in evenly so the cover does not bind on the dowel pins.

4. Remove the camshaft housing cover and discard the gaskets.

5. Note the position of the chain sprocket dowel pin for reassembly.

6. Remove or disconnect the following:
- Camshaft
- Camshaft oil seal from camshaft and discard it

➡**The camshaft seal must be replaced any time the housing and cover are separated.**

➡**Store the valve lifters in order so that they may be installed in the their locations.**

- Valve lifters from the camshaft housing
- Camshaft carrier from the cylinder head and discard the gasket

To install:

7. Clean all the gasket surfaces completely.

8. Install or connect the following:
- New camshaft housing gasket
- Camshaft housing

➡**Install 1 bolt loosely to hold the housing in place.**

➡**If the camshaft was replaced the valve lifters must also be replaced.**

9. Install the lifters into their original bores.

10. Lubricate the camshaft lobes, journals and lifters with camshaft and lifter pre-lube. The camshaft lobes and journals must be adequately lubricated or engine damage could occur upon start up.

11. Install or connect the following:
- Camshaft in its original position with the timing chain sprocket dowel pin straight up and aligned with the centerline of the lifter bores.
- New Green camshaft housing cover seal

➡**The seals for the intake and exhaust covers are different and the correct seals must be used.**

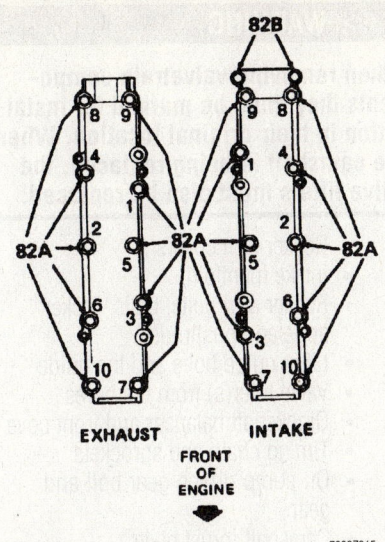

7922Z315

Camshaft housing bolt tightening sequence—2.4L engine

12. Remove the bolt holding the housing in place.

13. Apply thread locking compound to the camshaft housing and cover bolt threads.

14. Install or connect the following:
- Camshaft housing cover. Tighten the bolts, in sequence, to 11 ft. lbs. (15 Nm) plus an additional 90 degree turn (long bolts) and 11 ft. lbs. (15 Nm) plus an additional 30 degree turn (short bolts).
- Timing chain housing bolts
- Timing chain and sprockets
- New fuel injector O-ring seals lubricated with engine oil
- Fuel rail. Tighten the bolts to 19 ft. lbs. (26 Nm).
- Ignition assembly on the camshaft housing. Tighten the bolts to 11 ft. lbs. (15 Nm), plus an additional 30 degree turn.
- Ignition assembly electrical connector
- Negative battery cable

15. Start the vehicle and verify proper operation and no leaks.

EXHAUST SIDE

➡**Anytime the camshaft housing-to-cylinder head bolts are loosened or removed, the camshaft housing-to-cylinder head gasket must be replaced.**

1. Before servicing the vehicle, refer to the precautions in the beginning of this section.

2. Remove or disconnect the following:
- Negative battery cable
- Ignition assembly electrical connector
- 4 ignition assembly-to-camshaft housing bolts and the assembly by pulling it straight up

➡**Use a spark plug boot wire remover to remove connector assemblies.**

- Oil pressure switch electrical connector
- Transaxle fill tube
- Timing chain and camshaft sprockets
- Timing chain housing bolts but do not remove from the engine
- Camshaft housing cover-to-camshaft housing bolts
- Camshaft housing-to-cylinder head bolts by reversing of the tightening sequence

➡**Leave 2 bolts loosely in place to hold the camshaft housing while separating the camshaft cover from housing.**

3. Press the cover off the housing by threading 4 of the housing-to-cylinder head bolts into the tapped camshaft housing cover holes. Tighten the bolts in evenly so the cover does not bind on the dowel pins.

4. Remove the camshaft housing cover and discard the gaskets.

5. Note the position of the chain sprocket dowel pin for reassembly.

6. Remove or disconnect the following:
- Camshaft
- Camshaft oil seal from camshaft and discard it

➡**The camshaft seal must be replaced any time the housing and cover are separated.**

➡**Store the valve lifters in order so that they may be installed in the their locations.**

- Valve lifters from the camshaft housing
- Camshaft carrier from the cylinder head and discard the gasket

To install:

7. Clean all the gasket surfaces completely.

8. Install or connect the following:
- New camshaft housing gasket
- Camshaft housing

➡**Install 1 bolt loosely to hold the housing in place.**

For complete mechanical specifications, refer to Section 1 of this manual

➡️If the camshaft was replaced the valve lifters must also be replaced.

9. Install the lifters into their original bores.

10. Lubricate the camshaft lobes, journals and lifters with camshaft and lifter prelube. The camshaft lobes and journals must be adequately lubricated or engine damage could occur upon start up.

11. Install or connect the following:
- Camshaft in it original position with the timing chain sprocket dowel pin straight up and aligned with the centerline of the lifter bores.
- New Orange camshaft housing cover seal

➡️The seals for the intake and exhaust covers are different and the correct seals must be used.

12. Remove the bolt holding the housing in place.

13. Apply thread locking compound to the camshaft housing and cover bolt threads.

14. Install or connect the following:
- Camshaft housing cover. Tighten the bolts, in sequence, to 11 ft. lbs. (15 Nm) plus an additional 90 degree turn (long bolts) and 11 ft. lbs. (15 Nm) plus an additional 30 degree turn (short bolts).
- Timing chain housing mounting bolts
- Timing chain and sprockets
- New fuel injector O-ring seals lubricated with engine oil
- Fuel rail. Tighten the bolts to 19 ft. lbs. (26 Nm).
- Transaxle fill tube
- Oil pressure switch electrical connector
- Ignition assembly on the camshaft housing. Tighten the bolts to 11 ft. lbs. (15 Nm), plus an additional 30 degree turn.
- Ignition assembly electrical connector
- Negative battery cable

15. Start the vehicle and verify proper operation and no leaks.

3.1L and 3.4L Engines

1. Before servicing the vehicle, refer to the precautions in the beginning of this section.

2. Relieve the fuel system pressure.

3. Remove or disconnect the following:
- Engine assembly

✳✳ WARNING

When removing valvetrain components they must be marked for installation in their original location. When the camshaft is being replaced, the valve lifters must also be replaced.

- Rocker arm covers
- Intake manifold
- Rocker arm bolts, balls, rocker arms and pushrods
- Lifter guide bolts and the guide
- Valve lifter(s) from the bores
- Crankshaft balancer and front cove
- Timing chain and sprockets
- Oil pump driven gear bolt and gear
- Camshaft thrust plate
- Camshaft

✳✳ WARNING

Avoid damaging the camshaft bearing surfaces.

To install:

4. Coat the camshaft with Prelube.

5. Install or connect the following:
- Camshaft
- Camshaft thrust plate. Tighten the bolts to 89 inch lbs. (10 Nm).
- Oil pump driven gear. Tighten the bolt to 27 ft. lbs. (36 Nm).
- Timing chain and sprocket
- Camshaft thrust button and front cover
- Crankshaft balancer

6. Lubricate the bearing surfaces with Molykote®.

➡️Installation of a new camshaft or a wear pattern on the old valve lifter will require the replacement of the camshaft and lifters together. If camshaft replacement is not necessary, be sure to install the used valve lifters in their original position.

7. Install or connect the following:
- Lifters in their original locations
- Lifter guide. Tighten the guide bolts to 89 inch lbs. (10 Nm).
- Pushrods, rocker arms, balls and bolts. Tighten the nuts to 89 inch lbs. (10 Nm) plus an additional 30 degree turn.
- Intake manifold
- Rocker arm covers
- Engine assembly
- Negative battery cable

8. Adjust the valves, as required. Start the engine and verify no oil leaks.

Valve Lash

ADJUSTMENT

The engines are equipped with hydraulic valve lifters that do not require periodic valve lash adjustment. Adjustment to zero lash is maintained automatically by hydraulic pressure in the lifters.

Starter Motor

REMOVAL & INSTALLATION

2.4L Engine

1. Before servicing the vehicle, refer to the precautions in the beginning of this section.

2. Remove or disconnect the following:
- Negative battery cable
- Air inlet duct from the throttle body
- Upper starter bolt
- Lower closeout panel
- Lower starter bolt
- Engine wiring harness and move it aside
- Starter electrical connectors
- Starter

To install:

3. Install or connect the following:
- Starter
- Starter electrical connectors
- Engine wiring harness
- Lower starter bolt. Tighten the bolt to 106 inch lbs. (12 Nm).
- Lower closeout panel
- Upper starter bolt. Tighten the bolt to 106 inch lbs. (12 Nm).
- Air inlet duct from the throttle body
- Negative battery cable

3.1L Engine

1. Before servicing the vehicle, refer to the precautions in the beginning of this section.

2. Remove or disconnect the following:
- Negative battery cable
- Starter electrical connectors
- Starter

To install:

3. Install or connect the following:
- Starter. Tighten the bolts to 32 ft. lbs. (43 Nm).
- Starter electrical connectors
- Negative battery cable

3.4L Engine

1. Before servicing the vehicle, refer to the precautions in the beginning of this section.
2. Remove or disconnect the following:
   - Negative battery cable
   - Flywheel inspection cover
   - Starter electrical connectors
   - Starter

To install:

3. Install or connect the following:
   - Starter. Tighten the bolts to 32 ft. lbs. (43 Nm).
   - Starter electrical connectors
   - Flywheel inspection cover. Tighten the bolts to 89 inch lbs. (10 Nm).
   - Negative battery cable

Oil Pan

REMOVAL & INSTALLATION

2.4L Engine

1. Before servicing the vehicle, refer to the precautions in the beginning of this section.
2. Disconnect the negative battery cable.
3. Drain the engine oil and cooling system.
4. Remove or disconnect the following:
   - Flywheel inspection cover
   - Right front wheel
   - Right inner fender splash shield
   - Serpentine belt
   - Engine mount strut from the bracket
   - Air conditioning compressor and support it aside without disconnecting the refrigerant lines
   - Engine mount strut bracket
   - Radiator and air conditioning outlet pipes from the suspension supports
   - Exhaust manifold brace
   - Oil pan-to-flywheel cover bolt/nut
   - Flywheel cover stud/spacer
   - Radiator outlet pipe from the lower radiator hose and oil pan
   - Oil level sensor wire, if equipped
   - Oil pan

To install:

5. Install or connect the following:
   - New gasket
   - Oil pan. Tighten the chain housing and carrier seal bolts to 106 inch lbs. (12 Nm) and the oil pan-to-block bolts to 17 ft. lbs. (23 Nm).
   - Oil level sensor wire, if equipped

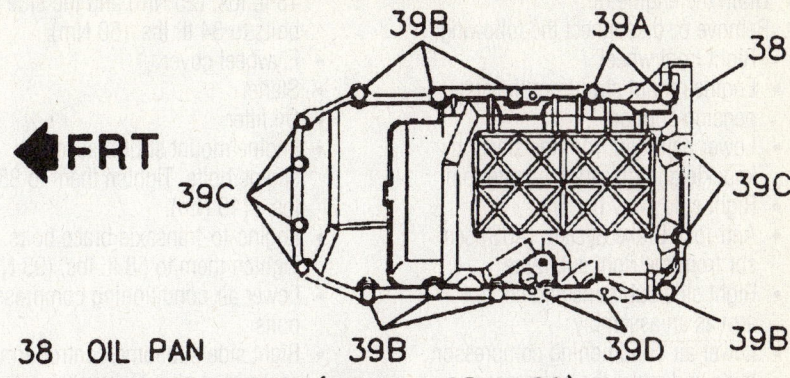

◀FRT

38	OIL PAN	
39A	BOLT, OIL PAN (M8 X 1.25 X 80) 24 N•m (18 LB. FT.)	
39B	BOLT, OIL PAN (M8 X 1.25 X 22) 24 N•m (18 LB. FT.)	
39C	BOLT, OIL PAN (M6 X 1.00 X 25) 12 N•m (106 LB. IN.)	
39D	BOLT, STUD END OIL PAN 26 N•m (19 LB. FT.)	

7922Z316

Oil pan mounting bolt locations—2.4L engine

- Radiator outlet pipe to the lower radiator hose and oil pan
- Flywheel cover spacer, stud nut and bolt. Tighten the nut to 41 ft. lbs. (56 Nm), the stud to 115 inch lbs. (13 Nm) and the bolt to 41 ft. lbs. (56 Nm).
- Oil pan-to-flywheel cover bolt/nut. Tighten to 41 ft. lbs. (56 Nm).
- Exhaust manifold brace
- Radiator and air conditioning outlet pipes to the suspension supports
- Engine mount strut bracket
- Air conditioning compressor
- Engine mount strut bracket. Tighten bolts to 49 ft. lbs. (66 Nm).
- Serpentine belt
- Right inner fender splash shield
- Right front wheel
- Flywheel inspection cover
- Negative battery cable

6. Fill the crankcase with oil.

➡**An oil filter change is recommended.**

7. Fill the cooling system.
8. Start the engine and check for leaks.

3.1L and 3.4L Engine

1. Before servicing the vehicle, refer to the precautions in the beginning of this section.

2. Remove or disconnect the following:
   - Negative battery cable
   - Serpentine belt
   - Upper air conditioning compressor bolts, if equipped

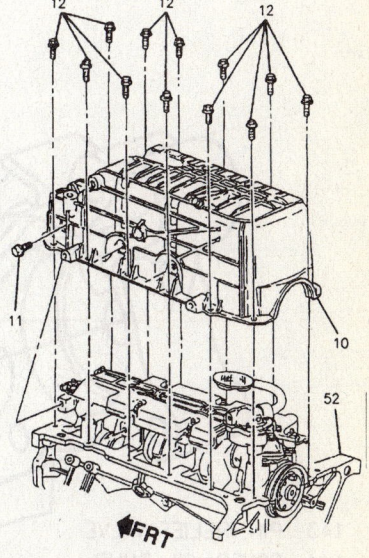

10 PAN, OIL
11 BOLT, OIL PAN SIDE
12 BOLT, OIL PAN RETAINING
52 BLOCK, ENGINE

7922Z317

Exploded view of the oil pan mounting— 3.1L engine

Please refer to Section 8 for electric cooling fan wiring schematics

3. Drain the engine oil.
4. Remove or disconnect the following:
- Right front wheel
- Engine mount strut from the suspension support
- Lower ball joint from the steering knuckle and discard the cotter pin
- Right side sway bar link
- Anti-lock Brake System (ABS) sensor from the right subframe
- Right side subframe and control arm as an assembly
- Lower air conditioning compressor bolts and move the compressor aside without disconnecting the lines
- Engine mount strut bracket from the engine
- Oil filter
- Starter
- Flywheel cover
- Oil pan

To install:
5. Clean the gasket mating surfaces. I
6. Install or connect the following:
- New oil pan gasket by applying silicone sealer to the portion of the pan that contacts the rear of the block.
- Oil pan. Tighten the flange bolts to 18 ft. lbs. (25 Nm) and the side bolts to 34 ft. lbs. (50 Nm).
- Flywheel cover
- Starter
- Oil filter
- Engine mount strut bracket-to-engine bolts. Tighten them to 85 ft. lbs. (115 Nm).
- Engine-to-transaxle brace bolts. Tighten them to 68 ft. lbs. (93 Nm).
- Lower air conditioning compressor bolts
- Right side subframe/control arm assembly bolts. Tighten them to 89 ft. lbs. (120 Nm).
- Anti-lock Brake System (ABS) sensor to the right subframe
- Right side sway bar line bolt. Tighten it to 22 ft. lbs. (30 Nm).
- Ball joint-to-steering knuckle nut: 48 ft. lbs. (60 Nm). Install a new cotter pin.
- Engine mount strut bracket bolt-to-frame bolt. Tighten it to 89 ft. lbs. (120 Nm)
- Right front wheel
7. Drain the engine oil.
8. Install or connect the following:
- Upper air conditioning compressor bolts, if equipped
- Serpentine belt
- Negative battery cable
9. Fill the crankcase to the correct level.
10. Start the engine and check for leaks.

➡**Whenever the vehicle subframe is removed or lowered, the wheel alignment should be checked.**

11. Check and/or adjust the front end alignment.

Oil Pump

REMOVAL & INSTALLATION

2.4L Engine

➡**Please note that the transaxle must be removed from the vehicle to service the oil pump.**

1. Before servicing the vehicle, refer to the precautions in the beginning of this section.
2. Disconnect the negative battery cable.
3. Install an engine support fixture.
4. Properly drain the engine oil.
5. Remove or disconnect the following:
- Oil pan
- Transaxle and the flywheel

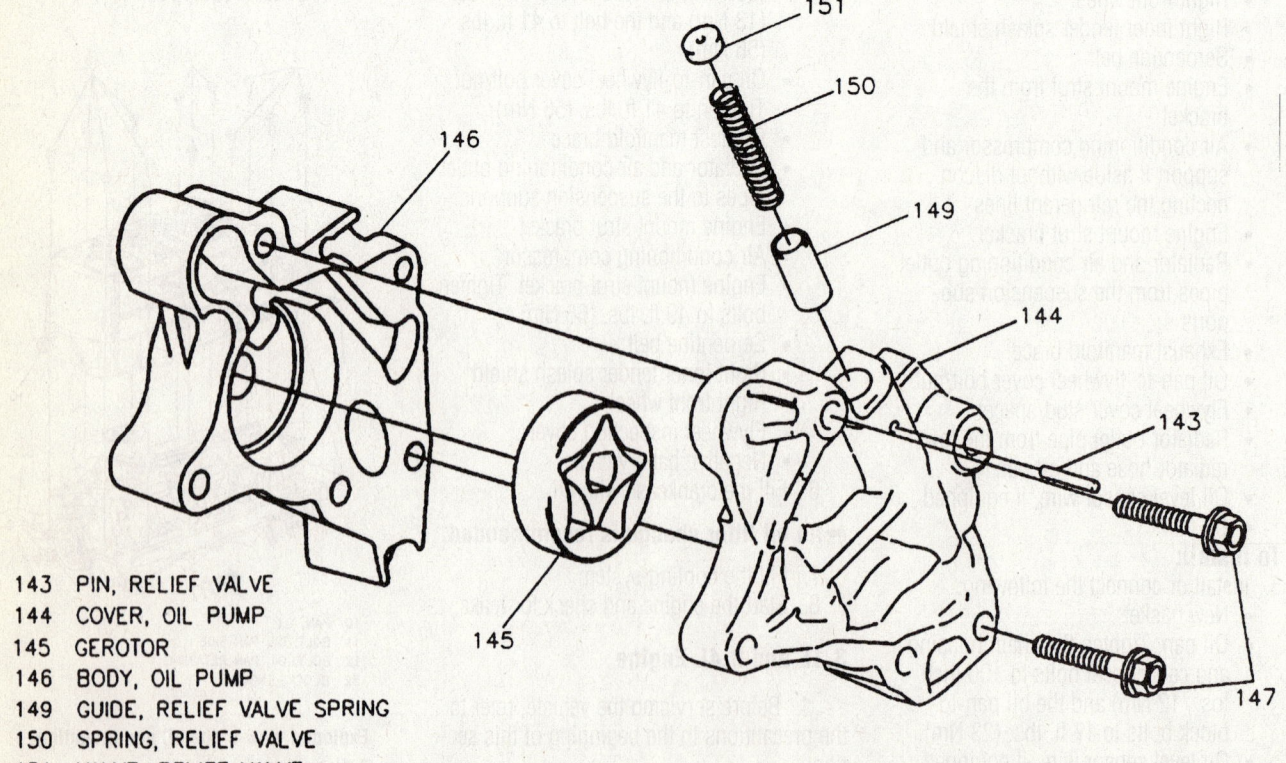

143 PIN, RELIEF VALVE
144 COVER, OIL PUMP
145 GEROTOR
146 BODY, OIL PUMP
149 GUIDE, RELIEF VALVE SPRING
150 SPRING, RELIEF VALVE
151 VALVE, RELIEF VALVE

Exploded view of the oil pump components—2.4L engine

- Balance shaft chain cover and chain guide
- Oil pump bolts and the oil pump cover
- Oil pump housing assembly from the balance shaft assembly, by pulling the housing to disconnect the pump gear from the balance shaft

To install:

6. Clean all of the parts. Remove all varnish sludge and dirt.

7. Lubricate the gears with clean engine oil.

8. Assemble the geroter gear into the housing.

➡**Fill oil pump cavities with petroleum jelly prior to installation. This seals the pump and acts like a "prime" so the pump will draw oil as soon as the engine begins to turn. This will ensure that there is oil pressure immediately on start-up and will prevent engine damage.**

9. Install or connect the following:
- Oil pump housing to the balance shaft assembly
- Oil pump cover to the oil pump housing. Tighten the oil pump-to-block bolts to 40 ft. lbs. (54 Nm).
- Balance shaft chain guide and chain

10. Adjust the chain tension inserting a 0.40 in. (1mm) brass feeler, between the chain guide and the chain.

➡**A brass feeler gauge must be used to ensure that correct measurements are obtained. If a steel gauge is used, it will not bend to conform to the guide and will allow for incorrect measurements.**

11. Press the guide against the chain using about 3 lbs. of force. Tighten the chain tensioner fastener to 115 inch lbs. (13 Nm).

12. Install or connect the following:
- Balance shaft chain cover. Tighten the nut/bolt to 115 inch lbs. (13 Nm).
- Flywheel
- Transaxle
- Oil pan
- Negative battery cable

13. Fill the crankcase.

➡**An oil filter change is recommended.**

14. Remove the engine support fixture.

15. Start the engine and verify oil pressure and no leaks.

3.1L and 3.4L Engines

1. Before servicing the vehicle, refer to the precautions in the beginning of this section.

2. Disconnect the negative battery cable.

3. Drain the engine oil.

4. Remove or disconnect the following:

- Oil pan
- Crankshaft oil deflector bolts and deflector
- Oil pump and pump driveshaft

To install:

5. Install or connect the following:
- Oil pump by engaging the oil pump driveshaft. Tighten the oil pump bolts to 30 ft. lbs. (41 Nm).
- Crankshaft oil deflector. Tighten the nuts to 18 ft. lbs. (25 Nm).
- Oil pan
- Negative battery cable

6. Fill the crankcase.

➡**An oil filter change is recommended.**

7. Start the engine, check the oil pressure and check for leaks.

Rear Main Seal

REMOVAL & INSTALLATION

2.4L Engine

1. Before servicing the vehicle, refer to the precautions in the beginning of this section.

2. Remove or disconnect the following:
- Negative battery cable
- Transaxle
- Pressure plate and clutch disc, if equipped
- Flywheel
- Oil pan-to-seal housing bolts
- Seal housing-to-block bolts, the seal housing and discard the gasket
- Rear main seal from the housing and discard it

✱✱ WARNING

Be careful not to damage the seal housing sealing surface; damage may result in an oil leak.

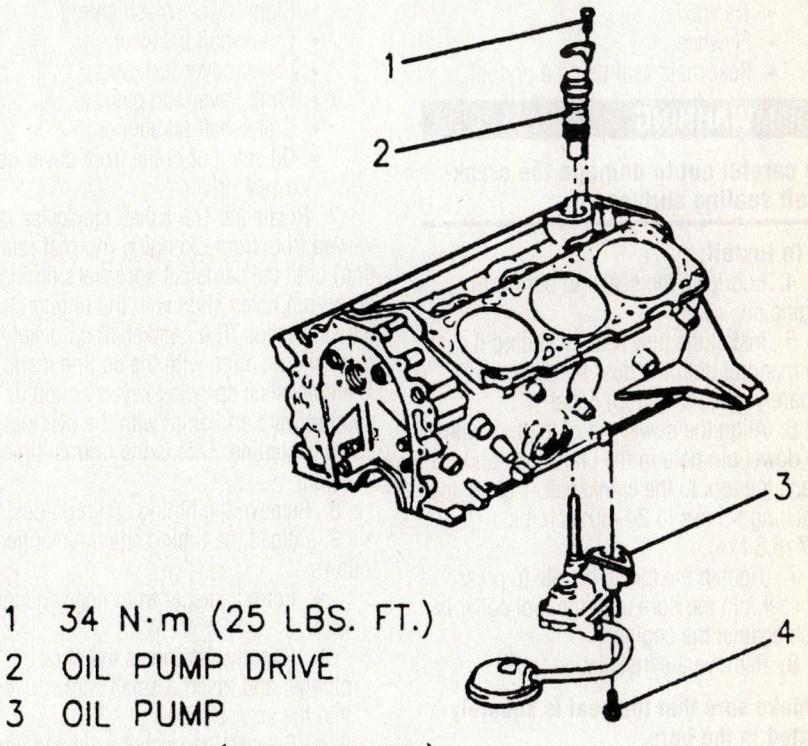

1	34 N·m (25 LBS. FT.)
2	OIL PUMP DRIVE
3	OIL PUMP
4	41 N·m (30 LBS. FT.)

Exploded view of the oil pump mounting—3.1L and 3.4L engines

7922Z319

To install:

3. Install the new rear main seal into the housing.

4. Inspect the oil pan gasket inner silicone bead for damage and repair using a silicone sealant, if necessary.

5. Lubricate the lip of the seal with clean engine oil.

6. Install or connect the following:
- New seal housing-to-engine gasket.
- Seal housing. Tighten the housing-to-engine and the oil pan-to-seal housing bolts to 106 inch lbs. (12 Nm).
- Flywheel
- Clutch, pressure plate and clutch cover assembly, if equipped with a manual transaxle
- Transaxle
- Negative battery cable

7. Start the engine and check for leaks.

3.1L and 3.4L Engines

1. Before servicing the vehicle, refer to the precautions in the beginning of this section.

2. Support the engine.

3. Remove or disconnect the following:
- Transaxle
- Flywheel
- Rear main seal using a prytool

❋❋ WARNING

Be careful not to damage the crankshaft sealing surface.

To install:

4. Lubricate the seal and bore with engine oil.

5. Install the new seal by sliding it over the mandrel until the dust lip bottoms squarely against the tool collar.

6. Align the dowel pin of the tool with the dowel pin hole in the crankshaft and attach the tool to the crankshaft. Tighten the attaching screws to 24–60 inch lbs. (2.7–6.8 Nm).

7. Tighten the tool T-handle to press the seal into the bore until the tool collar is flush against the engine.

8. Remove the installation tool.

➡**Make sure that the seal is squarely seated in the bore.**

9. Install or connect the following:
- Flywheel. Tighten the flywheel-to-crankshaft bolts to 52 ft. lbs. (71 Nm).
- Transaxle

10. Start the engine and check for leaks.

Timing Chain, Sprockets, Front Cover and Seal

REMOVAL & INSTALLATION

2.4L Engine

➡**It is recommended that the entire procedure be reviewed before attempting to service the timing chain.**

1. Before servicing the vehicle, refer to the precautions in the beginning of this section.

2. Disconnect the negative battery cable.

3. Drain the cooling system.

4. Remove or disconnect the following:
- Coolant surge tank
- Serpentine drive belt using a 13mm wrench that is at least 24 in. (61cm) long
- Alternator

5. Install an engine support.

6. Remove or disconnect the following:
- Upper cover fasteners
- Upper cover vent hose
- Right engine mount and bracket
- Right front wheel
- Right lower splash shield
- Crankshaft balancer
- Lower cover fasteners
- Front cover and gaskets
- Crankshaft oil slinger
- Oil seal out of the front cover using a seal driver

7. Rotate the crankshaft clockwise, as viewed from front of engine (normal rotation) until the camshaft sprocket's timing dowel pin holes align with the timing chain housing holes. The crankshaft sprocket mark should align with the engine mark. The crankshaft sprocket keyway should point upward and align with the cylinder bores centerline. This is the normal timed position.

8. Remove the timing chain guides.

9. Reload the timing chain tensioner as follows:

a. Form a keeper from heavy gauge wire.

b. Slightly, compress the shoe plunger and insert a small screwdriver into the access hole.

c. Release the ratchet pawl and compress the plunger completely into the hole.

d. Insert the keeper between the access hole and the blade.

10. Remove the timing chain tensioner.

➡**Be sure all the slack in the timing**

chain is above the tensioner assembly when removing it.

❋❋ CAUTION

The tensioner plunger is spring loaded and could fly out causing personal injury.

11. Remove or disconnect the following:
- Timing chain
- Camshaft sprockets bolts
- Camshaft sprockets using a 3-jawed puller, if necessary

To install:

12. Install or connect the following:
- Intake camshaft sprocket. Tighten the bolt to 52 ft. lbs. (70 Nm) while holding the sprocket.
- Camshaft sprocket alignment pin through the camshaft sprockets holes into the timing chain housing holes to position the camshafts for timing.

13. If the camshafts are out of position and must be rotated more than ⅛ turn in order to install the alignment dowel pins, perform the following:

a. Rotated the crankshaft 90 degrees clockwise off Top Dead Center (TDC) in order to give the valves adequate clearance to open.

b. Once the camshafts are positioned and the dowels installed, rotate the crankshaft counterclockwise back to TDC.

❋❋ WARNING

Do not rotate the crankshaft clockwise to TDC or valve and piston damage may occur.

14. Install the timing chain over the exhaust camshaft sprocket, around the idler sprocket and around the crankshaft sprocket.

15. Remove the alignment dowel pin from the intake camshaft. Using a dowel pin remover tool, rotate the intake camshaft sprocket counterclockwise enough to slide the timing chain over the intake camshaft sprocket. Release the camshaft sprocket wrench. The length of chain between the 2 camshaft sprockets will tighten.

➡**If properly timed, the intake camshaft alignment dowel pin should slide in easily. If the dowel pin does not fully index, the camshafts are not timed correctly and the procedure must be repeated.**

16. Leave the alignment dowel pins installed.

17. With slack removed from chain between intake camshaft sprocket and crankshaft sprocket, the timing marks on the crankshaft and the cylinder block should be aligned. If marks are not aligned, move the chain 1 tooth forward or rearward, remove slack and recheck marks.

18. Tighten the chain housing to engine stud. The stud is installed under the timing chain. Tighten it to 19 ft. lbs. (26 Nm).

19. Reload the timing chain tensioner as follows:

   a. Form a keeper from heavy gauge wire.

   b. Slightly, compress the shoe plunger and insert a small screwdriver into the access hole.

   c. Release the ratchet pawl and compress the plunger completely into the hole.

   d. Insert the keeper between the access hole and the blade.

20. Remove the timing chain tensioner.

➡ **Be sure all the slack in the timing chain is above the tensioner assembly when removing it.**

✳✳ CAUTION

The tensioner plunger is spring loaded and could fly out causing personal injury.

21. Install or connect the following:
- Tensioner assembly to the chain housing. Tighten the bolts to 89 inch lbs. (10 Nm).

➡ **Recheck plunger assembly installation. It is correctly installed when the long end is toward the crankshaft.**

- Tensioner shoe and retainer. Remove tool J36589 and squeeze plunger assembly into the tensioner body to unload it.

22. Remove the alignment dowel pins. Rotate crankshaft clockwise 2 full rotations. Align the crankshaft timing mark with mark on cylinder block and reinstall alignment dowel pins. Alignment dowel pins will slide in easily if engine is timed correctly.

✳✳ WARNING

If the engine is not correctly timed, severe engine damage could occur.

23. Install or connect the following:
- Timing chain guides and crankshaft oil slinger

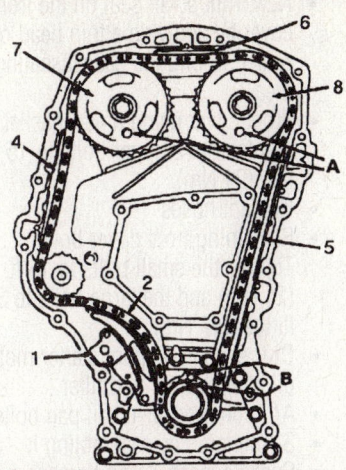

A. Camshaft timing alignment pin locations
B. Crankshaft gear timing marks
1. Shoe asm. timing chain tensioner
2. Timing chain
3. Timing chain tensioner
4. R.H. timing chain guide
5. L.H. timing chain guide
6. Upper timing chain guide
7. Exhaust camshaft sprocket
8. Intake camshaft sprocket

7922Z321

Timing chain and sprocket alignment positions—2.4L DOHC engine

- New seal into the front cover by lubricating the seal lip and tapping it into place with an seal installer
- Front cover and gaskets. Tighten the nuts and bolts to 106 inch lbs. (12 Nm).

24. Install the torsional damper as follows:

   a. Coat the seal contact area on the crankshaft damper with clean engine oil.

   b. Align the crankshaft damper so the notch in the damper aligns with the crankshaft key.

   c. Tap the balancer into place using a rubber mallet.

   d. Tighten the damper bolt to 129 ft. lbs. (175 Nm) plus an additional 90 degree turn.

25. Install or connect the following:
- Right front lower splash shield
- Front wheel. Tighten the nuts to 100 ft. lbs. (140 Nm).
- Right engine mount bracket
- Right engine mount
- Upper cover vent hose

26. Remove the engine support.

27. Install or connect the following:
- Alternator and the electrical connectors
- Serpentine belt
- Coolant surge tank

- Negative battery cable

28. Refill the cooling system.

29. Start the engine and check for leaks.

3.1L and 3.4L Engines

1. Before servicing the vehicle, refer to the precautions in the beginning of this section.

2. Disconnect the negative battery cable.

3. Drain the cooling system.

4. Discharge and recover the A/C refrigerant.

5. Install an engine support fixture.

6. Remove or disconnect the following:
- Front engine mount and bracket
- Serpentine belt
- Air cleaner assembly
- Air intake duct
- Power steering pump
- 2 upper air conditioning compressor mounting bolts, loosen them.
- Alternator and bracket
- Right front wheel and splash shield
- Flywheel inspection cover so the ring gear can be held while removing the crankshaft balancer bolt
- Crankshaft balancer
- Drive belt tensioner
- Right wheel speed sensor harness at the suspension support
- Ball joint
- Stabilizer bar from the control arm and suspension support

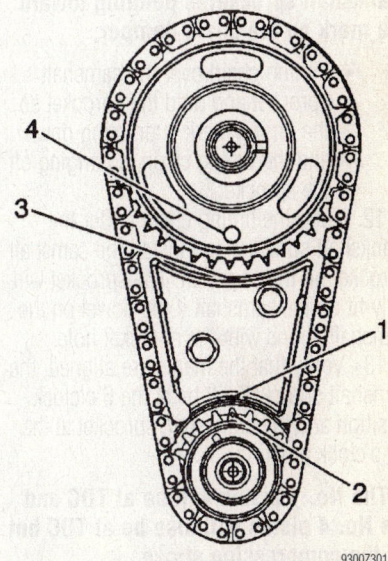

9300Z301

Be sure to align the damper mark (1) with the crankshaft mark (2) and the damper mark (3) with the camshaft sprocket mark (4)—3.1L and 3.4L engines

Timing belt service is covered in Section 4 of this manual

- Suspension support
- A/C compressor-to-oil pan bolts
- Oil filter and adapter
7. Drain the oil.
8. Remove or disconnect the following:
   - Starter and the oil pan
   - Crankshaft Position (CKP) sensor
   - Lower front cover bolts
   - Coolant hoses and the remaining front cover bolts
   - Engine front cover
   - Oil seal from the front cover using a seal driver
9. Using the flywheel and a flywheel turning tool, rotate the crankshaft until the timing marks on the camshaft and crankshaft sprockets are in alignment (facing each other).
10. Remove or disconnect the following:
    - Camshaft sprocket bolt, sprocket and timing chain
    - Crankshaft sprocket
    - Timing chain damper bolts and damper, if necessary

To install:

11. Install or connect the following:
    - Timing chain damper, if removed. Tighten the bolts to 15 ft. lbs. (21 Nm).
    - Crankshaft sprocket onto the crankshaft making sure the notch in the sprocket fits over the crankshaft key. Fully seat the sprocket on the crankshaft.

➡ **Be sure the timing mark on the crankshaft sprocket is pointing toward the mark on the chain damper.**

   - Timing chain over the camshaft sprocket and hold the sprocket so the timing mark is pointing down and the timing chain is hanging off the sprocket.
12. Loop the timing chain under the crankshaft sprocket and install the camshaft sprocket on the camshaft. The sprocket will only fit on the camshaft if the dowel on the camshaft aligns with the sprocket hole.
13. Verify that the marks are aligned; the camshaft sprocket will be at the 6 o'clock position and the crankshaft sprocket at the 12 o'clock position.

➡ **The No. 1 piston will be at TDC and the No. 4 piston will also be at TDC but on the compression stroke.**

14. Tighten the camshaft sprocket bolt to 103 ft. lbs. (140 Nm).
15. Lubricate the timing chain components with engine oil. Clean all gasket surfaces completely.
16. Install or connect the following:

- New front cover seal on the front cover by applying a thin bead of sealer around the gasket sealing area.
- Front cover using a new gasket. Tighten the 2 upper bolts to 15 ft. lbs. (21 Nm).
- Coolant hoses
- Remaining front cover bolts. Tighten the small bolts to 15 ft. lbs. (21 Nm) and the large bolts to 35 ft. lbs. (47 Nm).
- CKP sensor, oil pan, starter motor, oil filter adapter and filter
- A/C compressor-to-oil pan bolts
- Suspension by assembling it
- Speed sensor wiring harness
- Drive belt tensioner
- Crankshaft balancer using a balancer installer

✳ WARNING

Do not hammer the balancer on the crankshaft.

- Flywheel inspection cover
- Right front wheel and splash shield
- Alternator and bracket
- 2 upper air conditioning compressor mounting bolts
- Power steering pump
- Air intake duct
- Air cleaner assembly
- Serpentine belt
- Front engine mount and bracket. Tighten the 8mm bolts to 15 ft. lbs. (20 Nm) and the 12mm bolts to 30 ft. lbs. (40 Nm).
- Negative battery cable
17. Refill the fluids.
18. Start the engine and check for leaks.

Piston and Ring

POSITIONING

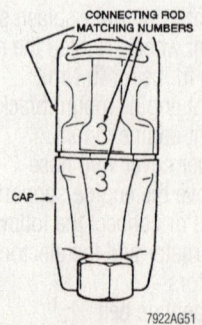

Connecting rod and cap installation. Be sure to matchmark the cap and rod prior to disassembly, as shown—All engines

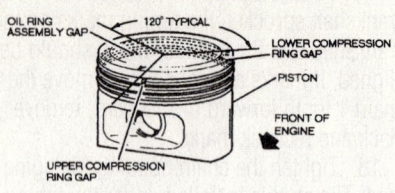

Piston ring end-gap spacing—2.4L engine

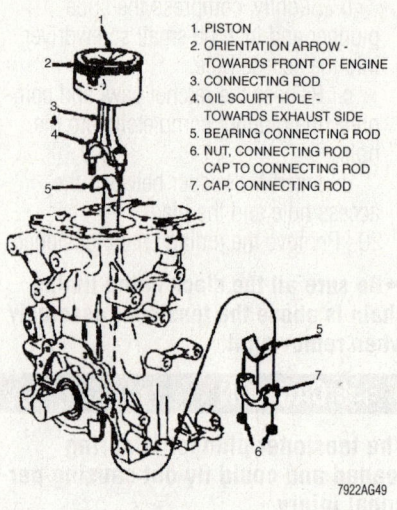

1. PISTON
2. ORIENTATION ARROW - TOWARDS FRONT OF ENGINE
3. CONNECTING ROD
4. OIL SQUIRT HOLE - TOWARDS EXHAUST SIDE
5. BEARING CONNECTING ROD
6. NUT, CONNECTING ROD CAP TO CONNECTING ROD
7. CAP, CONNECTING ROD

Piston and connecting rod assembly positioning—2.4L engine

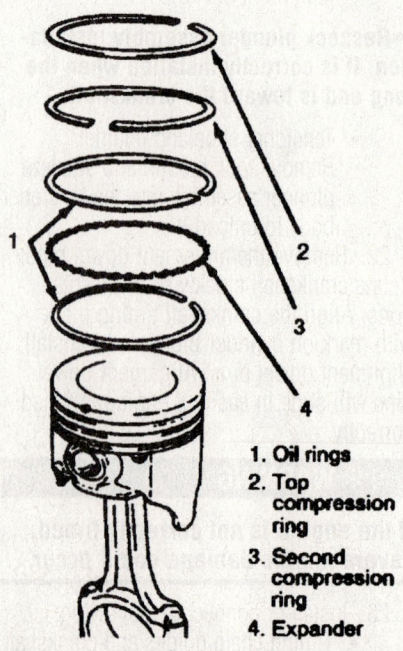

1. Oil rings
2. Top compression ring
3. Second compression ring
4. Expander

Piston ring positioning—3.1 and 3.4L engines

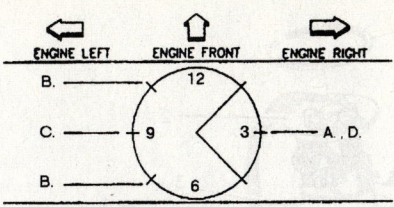

A. OIL RING SPACER GAP
(TANG IN HOLE OR SLOT WITH ARC)
B. OIL RING RAIL GAPS
C. 2ND COMPRESSION RING GAP
D. TOP COMPRESSION RING GAP

7922AG46

Piston ring end-gap spacing—3.1 and 3.4L engines

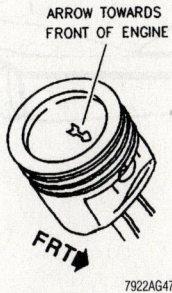

ARROW TOWARDS FRONT OF ENGINE

FRT

7922AG47

Piston positioning. Often the arrow is replaced by a notch, which also must face the front of the engine—3.1 and 3.4L engines

FUEL SYSTEM

Fuel System Service Precautions

Safety is the most important factor when performing not only fuel system maintenance but any type of maintenance. Failure to conduct maintenance and repairs in a safe manner may result in serious personal injury or death. Maintenance and testing of the vehicle's fuel system components can be accomplished safely and effectively by adhering to the following rules and guidelines.

• To avoid the possibility of fire and personal injury, always disconnect the negative battery cable unless the repair or test procedure requires that battery voltage be applied.

• Always relieve the fuel system pressure prior to disconnecting any fuel system component (injector, fuel rail, pressure regulator, etc.), fitting or fuel line connection. Exercise extreme caution whenever relieving fuel system pressure, to avoid exposing skin, face and eyes to fuel spray. Please be advised that fuel under pressure may penetrate the skin or any part of the body that it contacts.

• Always place a shop towel or cloth around the fitting or connection prior to loosening to absorb any excess fuel due to spillage. Ensure that all fuel spillage (should it occur) is quickly removed from engine surfaces. Ensure that all fuel soaked cloths or towels are deposited into a waste container.

• Always keep a dry chemical (Class B) fire extinguisher near the work area.

• Do not allow fuel spray or fuel vapors to come into contact with a spark or open flame.

• Always use a backup wrench when loosening and tightening fuel line connection fittings. This will prevent unnecessary stress and torsion to fuel line piping. Always follow the proper torque specifications.

• Always replace worn fuel fitting O-rings with new. Do not substitute fuel hose or equivalent, where fuel pipe is installed.

Fuel System Pressure

RELIEVING

2.4L Engine

1. Before servicing the vehicle, refer to the precautions in the beginning of this section.

2. Loosen the fuel filler cap in order to relieve the pressure in the tank (do not tighten at this time).

3. Detach the fuel pump electrical connector.

4. Start and run the vehicle until it stalls, then engage the starter for an additional 3 seconds to ensure the relief of any remaining pressure.

5. Disconnect the negative battery cable.

6. Once the tests or repairs are completed, reattach the fuel pump electrical connector.

7. Connect the negative battery cable.

8. Tighten the fuel filler cap.

9. Prime the fuel system by cycling the ignition switch **ON** for 2 seconds, **OFF** for 10 seconds, then **ON** again. Repeat, if necessary to build system pressure.

3.1L and 3.4L Engines

1. Before servicing the vehicle, refer to the precautions in the beginning of this section.

2. Disconnect the negative battery cable in order to avoid possible fuel discharge if an accidental attempt is made to start the engine.

3. Loosen the fuel tank filler cap in order to relieve fuel tank pressure.

4. Connect a fuel pressure gauge (with bleed hose) to the fuel pressure test port connection. Wrap a towel around the fuel pressure connection when installing the fuel pressure gauge in order to avoid fuel spillage.

5. Install the bleed hose into an approved container and open the valve in order to bleed the fuel system pressure. The fuel pipe connections are now safe for servicing.

6. Drain any fuel remaining in the fuel pressure gauge into an approved container.

Fuel Filter

REMOVAL & INSTALLATION

All Engines

1. Before servicing the vehicle, refer to the precautions in the beginning of this section.

2. Relieve the fuel system pressure.

3. Remove or disconnect the following:
   • Negative battery cable
   • Fuel line from the filter, using a backup wrench
   • Quick-connect fitting from the fuel filter by compressing the tabs while pulling outward on the line
   • Fuel filter from the mounting bracket

To install:

4. Install or connect the following:
   • Fuel filter to the mounting bracket
   • Fuel filter using a backup wrench.

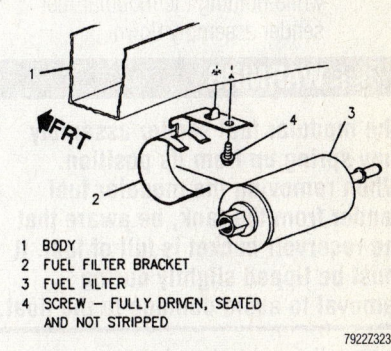

1 BODY
2 FUEL FILTER BRACKET
3 FUEL FILTER
4 SCREW – FULLY DRIVEN, SEATED AND NOT STRIPPED

7922Z323

Exploded view of the fuel filter mounting

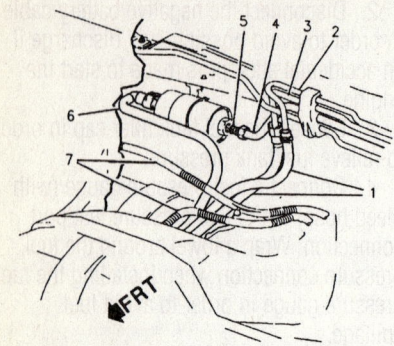

1 HOSE, PART OF FUEL SENDER
2 FUEL VAPOR PIPE
3 FUEL RETURN PIPE
4 FUEL FEED PIPE
5 FUEL FEED PIPE NUT
    27 N•m (20 LBS. FT.)
6 HOSE, PART OF FUEL SENDER
7 ABS AND FUEL SENDER HARNESS

7922Z324

Fuel filter mounting location and component identification

Tighten the fitting to 20 ft. lbs. (27 Nm).
- Quick-connect fitting to the fuel filter
- Negative battery cable

5. Pressurize the fuel system and verify no leaks.

Fuel Pump

REMOVAL & INSTALLATION

All Engines

1. Before servicing the vehicle, refer to the precautions in the beginning of this section.
2. Relieve the fuel system pressure.
3. Disconnect the negative battery cable.
4. Drain fuel tank.
5. Remove or disconnect the following:
- Fuel tank
- Snapring from the retainer slots while holding the modular fuel sender assembly down

❊❊ WARNING

The modular fuel sender assembly may spring up from its position. When removing the modular fuel sender from the tank, be aware that the reservoir bucket is full of fuel. It must be tipped slightly during removal to avoid damage to the float.

- External fuel strainer
- Connector Position Assurance (CPA) piece from the wiring harness and the fuel pump

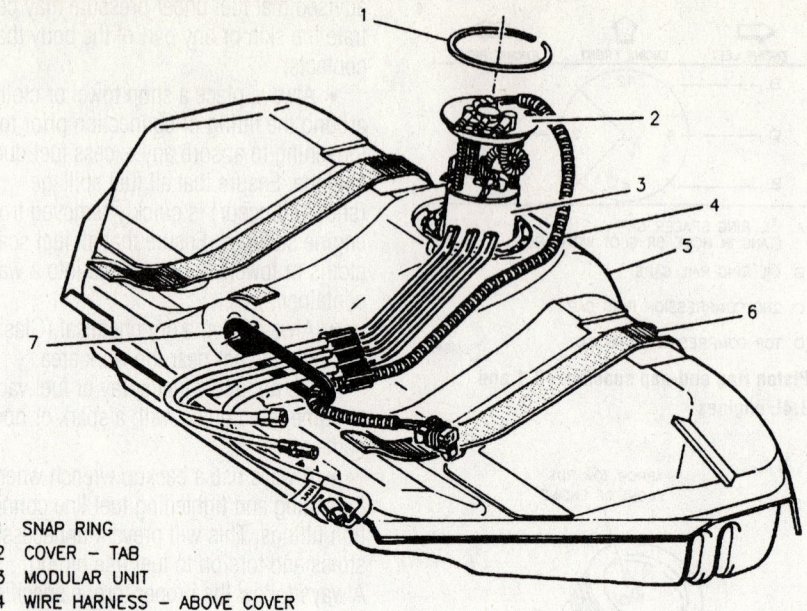

1 SNAP RING
2 COVER – TAB
3 MODULAR UNIT
4 WIRE HARNESS – ABOVE COVER
5 FUEL TANK
6 TANK ISOLATION STRIPS (3)
7 RUBBER ISOLATOR

7922Z325

Exploded view of the fuel sender assembly mounting to the tank

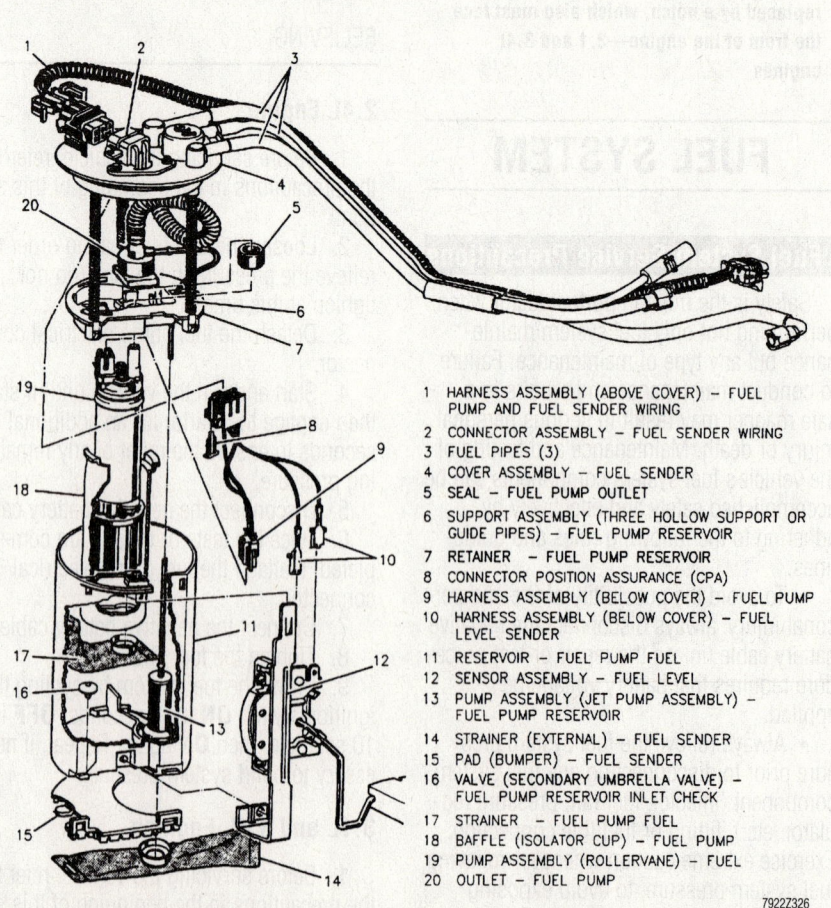

1   HARNESS ASSEMBLY (ABOVE COVER) – FUEL PUMP AND FUEL SENDER WIRING
2   CONNECTOR ASSEMBLY – FUEL SENDER WIRING
3   FUEL PIPES (3)
4   COVER ASSEMBLY – FUEL SENDER
5   SEAL – FUEL PUMP OUTLET
6   SUPPORT ASSEMBLY (THREE HOLLOW SUPPORT OR GUIDE PIPES) – FUEL PUMP RESERVOIR
7   RETAINER – FUEL PUMP RESERVOIR
8   CONNECTOR POSITION ASSURANCE (CPA)
9   HARNESS ASSEMBLY (BELOW COVER) – FUEL PUMP
10 HARNESS ASSEMBLY (BELOW COVER) – FUEL LEVEL SENDER
11 RESERVOIR – FUEL PUMP FUEL
12 SENSOR ASSEMBLY – FUEL LEVEL
13 PUMP ASSEMBLY (JET PUMP ASSEMBLY) – FUEL PUMP RESERVOIR
14 STRAINER (EXTERNAL) – FUEL SENDER
15 PAD (BUMPER) – FUEL SENDER
16 VALVE (SECONDARY UMBRELLA VALVE) – FUEL PUMP RESERVOIR INLET CHECK
17 STRAINER – FUEL PUMP FUEL
18 BAFFLE (ISOLATOR CUP) – FUEL PUMP
19 PUMP ASSEMBLY (ROLLERVANE) – FUEL
20 OUTLET – FUEL PUMP

7922Z326

Exploded view of the fuel pump assembly

6. Gently release the tabs on the sides of the fuel sender at the cover assembly. Begin by squeezing the sides of the reservoir and releasing the tab opposite the fuel level sensor. Move clockwise to release the second and third tab in the same manner.

7. Remove or disconnect the following:
- Fuel pump electrical connection by lifting the cover assembly
- Baffle and pump assembly from the retainer by rotating the fuel pump baffle counterclockwise
- Fuel pump outlet by sliding it out of slot
- Fuel pump outlet seal

To install:

8. Install or connect the following:
- Fuel pump outlet seal
- Fuel pump outlet by sliding it in the reservoir cover slots
- Fuel pump and baffle assembly onto the reservoir retainer by rotating it clockwise until seated
- Lower retainer assembly partially into the reservoir by aligning all 3 sleeve tabs and pressing the retainer onto the reservoir making sure all 3 tabs are firmly seated

➡ **Gently pull on the fuel pump reservoir from retainer to assure it is secure. If not secure, replace the entire fuel sender.**

- Connector Position Assurance (CPA) piece to the wiring harness and the fuel pump
- External fuel strainer
- Snapring to the retainer slots while holding the modular fuel sender assembly down
- Fuel tank
- Negative battery cable

9. Pressurize the fuel system and verify no leaks.

Fuel Injector

REMOVAL & INSTALLATION

2.4L Engine

1. Before servicing the vehicle, refer to the precautions in the beginning of this section.
2. Relieve the fuel system pressure.
3. Remove or disconnect the following:
- Negative battery cable
- Air cleaner outlet resonator
- Vacuum hose at the fuel pressure regulator

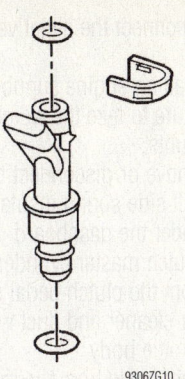

9306ZG10

Exploded view of the fuel injector—2.4L engine

- Camshaft Position (CMP) sensor electrical connector, if equipped
- Fuel injector electrical connectors
- Fuel inlet at the fuel rail
- Fuel pipe retainer clip nut, if equipped
- Fuel pipe retainer clip bolt
- Fuel rail-to-cylinder head bolts
- Fuel rail from the cylinder head
- Fuel return pipe bracket screw, bracket and separate the fuel pipe from the pressure regulator
- Fuel inlet pipe
- Fuel pipe O-rings and discard them
- Fuel rail assembly
- Fuel injector-to-fuel rail clip
- Fuel injector

To install:

4. Install or connect the following:
- Fuel injector by lubricating the new O-rings with engine oil
- Fuel injector-to-fuel rail clip
- Fuel rail assembly
- New fuel pipe O-rings lubricated with engine oil
- Fuel inlet pipe
- Fuel return pipe to the pressure regulator, the bracket and screw. Tighten the screw to 53 inch lbs. (6 Nm).
- Fuel rail assembly to the cylinder head. Tighten the bolts to 19 ft. lbs. (26 Nm).
- Fuel pipe retainer clip bolt. Tighten the bolt to 106 inch lbs. (12 Nm).
- Fuel pipe retainer clip nut, if equipped. Tighten the nut to 106 inch lbs. (12 Nm).
- Fuel inlet at the fuel rail. Tighten the fitting to 22 ft. lbs. (30 Nm).
- Fuel injector electrical connectors
- Camshaft Position (CMP) sensor electrical connector, if equipped

- Vacuum hose at the fuel pressure regulator
- Air cleaner outlet resonator
- Negative battery cable

5. Pressurize the fuel system by performing the following procedure:
   a. Step 1: Turn the ignition switch ON with the engine OFF for 2 seconds.
   b. Step 2: Turn the ignition switch OFF for 10 seconds.
   c. Step 3: Turn the ignition switch ON with the engine OFF.
   d. Step 4: Inspect for fuel leaks.

3.1L and 3.4L Engines

An 8 digit identification number is stamped on the left hand fuel rail which fuel the even numbered cylinders: 2, 4, 6.

1. Before servicing the vehicle, refer to the precautions in the beginning of this section.
2. Relieve the fuel system pressure.
3. Remove or disconnect the following:
- Upper intake manifold
- Fuel feed pipe at the fuel rail
- Fuel return pipe from the pressure regulator

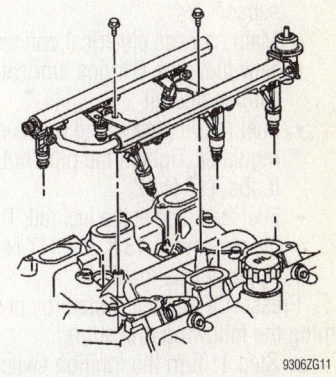

9306ZG11

Exploded view of the fuel rail assembly—3.4L engine—3.1L engine is similar

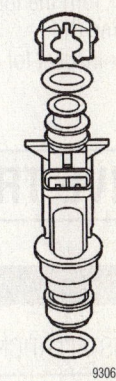

9306ZG12

Exploded view of the fuel injector—3.4L engine—3.1L engine is similar

- Fuel pipe O-rings and discard them
- Main harness electrical connector
- Engine Coolant Temperature (ECT) sensor
- Fuel rail assembly
- Fuel injector electrical connectors
- Fuel injector-to-fuel rail clip
- Fuel injector
- Fuel injector O-rings and discard them

To install:

✸✸ WARNING

If the fuel injector O-rings are color coded, install the black O-ring in the upper position and the brown O-ring in the lower position.

4. Install or connect the following:
- New fuel injector O-rings lubricated with engine oil
- Fuel injector
- Fuel injector-to-fuel rail clip
- Fuel injector electrical connectors
- Fuel rail assembly. Tighten the bolts to 7 ft. lbs. (10 Nm).
- Engine Coolant Temperature (ECT) sensor
- Main harness electrical connector
- New fuel pipe O-rings lubricated with engine oil
- Fuel return pipe to the pressure regulator. Tighten the pipe nut to 13 ft. lbs. (17 Nm).
- Fuel feed pipe at the fuel rail. Tighten the pipe nut to 13 ft. lbs. (17 Nm).
- Upper intake manifold

5. Pressurize the fuel system by performing the following procedure:
  a. Step 1: Turn the ignition switch ON with the engine OFF for 2 seconds.
  b. Step 2: Turn the ignition switch OFF for 10 seconds.
  c. Step 3: Turn the ignition switch ON with the engine OFF.
  d. Step 4: Inspect for fuel leaks.

DRIVE TRAIN

Transaxle

REMOVAL & INSTALLATION

Manual

1. Before servicing the vehicle, refer to the precautions in the beginning of this section.

2. Disconnect the negative battery cable.

3. Install an engine support fixture and use the fixture to take the weight off the engine mounts.

4. Remove or disconnect the following:
- Left side sound insulator from under the dashboard
- Clutch master cylinder pushrod from the clutch pedal stud
- Air cleaner and duct work from the throttle body
- Shift cable from the manual shift lever on the transaxle
- Wiring harness from the transaxle mount bracket
- Upper transaxle mount-to-transaxle bolts
- Clutch master cylinder from the slave cylinder
- Ground wires from the transaxle mounting studs
- Backup light switch connector
- Transaxle vent tube
- Upper transaxle-to-engine bolts

5. Lower the powertrain assembly with the support fixture.

6. Drain the transaxle fluid.

7. Remove or disconnect the following:
- Front wheels
- Left inner fender well splash shield
- Anti-lock Brake System (ABS) sensor connectors
- Flywheel housing cover bolts
- Vehicle Speed Sensor (VSS) from the transaxle
- Ball joints from the steering knuckles
- Left side link kit
- Left side U-bolt from the sway bar
- Left side suspension support
- Halfshafts from the transaxle
- Front lower transaxle mount

8. Support the transaxle with a jack.

9. Remove or disconnect the following:
- Remaining engine-to-transaxle bolts
- Transaxle

To install:

10. Install or connect the following:
- Transaxle. Tighten the lower bolts to 55 ft. lbs. (75 Nm).
- Front transaxle mount. Tighten the bolts to 55 ft. lbs. (75 Nm).
- Halfshafts to the transaxle
- Left side suspension support
- Left side U-bolt to the sway bar
- Left side link kit
- Ball joints to the steering knuckles
- Vehicle Speed Sensor (VSS) to the transaxle
- Flywheel housing cover bolts

- Anti-lock Brake System (ABS) sensor connectors
- Left inner fender well splash shield
- Front wheels

11. Raise the powertrain assembly with the support fixture.

12. Install or connect the following:
- Upper transaxle-to-engine bolts. Tighten the bolts to 55 ft. lbs. (75 Nm).
- Transaxle vent tube
- Backup light switch connector
- Ground wires to the transaxle mounting studs
- Clutch master cylinder to the slave cylinder
- Upper transaxle mount-to-transaxle bolts. Tighten the bolts to 55 ft. lbs. (75 Nm) on Isuzu transaxle or 96 ft. lbs. (130 Nm) on NVG transaxle.
- Wiring harness to the transaxle mount bracket
- Shift cable to the manual shift lever on the transaxle
- Air cleaner and duct work to the throttle body
- Clutch master cylinder pushrod to the clutch pedal stud
- Left side sound insulator to under the dashboard
- Negative battery cable

13. Refill the transaxle.

Automatic

1997–98 MODELS

1. Before servicing the vehicle, refer to the precautions in the beginning of this section.

2. Remove or disconnect the following:
- Negative battery cable
- Air intake duct
- Cable control cover, for the 3T40 transaxle
- Shift linkage from the transaxle, for the 4T60-E transaxle
- Vacuum modulator line from the modulator
- Throttle cable from the throttle body, for the 3T40 transaxle
- Electrical connectors from the Torque Converter Clutch (TCC), Park/Neutral position switch and shift solenoid.
- Power steering pump, for the 3T40 transaxle and move it aside with the hoses attached

✸✸ CAUTION

When servicing requires that the "T" latch type wiring connector be detached from the switch, use care to

ensure proper reassembly of both the connector and the "T" latch. Failure to do so may result in intermittent loss of switch functions.

- Oil fill tube, for the 3T40 transaxle
3. Install engine support fixture J-28467-A.
4. Remove or disconnect the following:
- Upper (2) transaxle-to-engine bolts
- Rubber hose from the transaxle vent pipe, for the 4T60-E transaxle
- Remaining upper transaxle-to-engine bolts
- Both front tires
- Right and left engine splash shields
- Anti-lock Brake System (ABS) Wheel Speed Sensor (WSS) connectors and the harness from the left side suspension support
- Both ball joints from the control arms
- Left side stabilizer shaft link pin bolt
- Left side stabilizer shaft frame bushing clamp nuts
- Left side suspension support assembly
- Both halfshafts
- Engine-to-transaxle brace
- Starter motor
- Transaxle converter cover
- Heater core hose pipe brace-to-transaxle nut and bolt
- Torque converter-to-flywheel bolts

➡ Using a scribe mark the flywheel-to-torque converter relationship to assure proper reassembly.

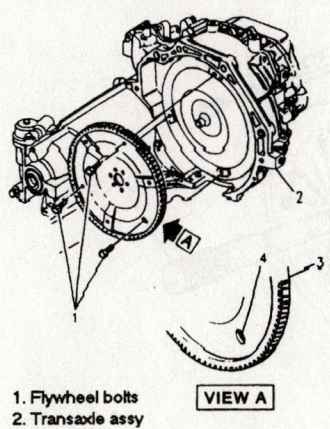

1. Flywheel bolts
2. Transaxle assy
3. Flywheel
4. Net slot

VIEW A

79222Z327

Flywheel net slot view—vehicles with the 4T60-E transaxle

- Oil level indicator and fill tube, for the 4T60-E transaxle
- Transaxle cooler lines and plug the openings
- VSS and the vacuum reservoir tank, for the 4T60-E transaxle
5. Position jack under transaxle.
6. Remove or disconnect the following:
- Transaxle mount-to-body bolts
- Remaining engine-to-transaxle bolts
- Transaxle

➡ Transaxle cooler and lines should be flushed whenever the transaxle has been removed for overhaul or replacement.

To install:
7. Apply a thin film of grease on the torque converter pilot hub.

➡ Be sure to properly seat the torque converter in the pump.

8. Install or connect the following:
- Transaxle
- Lower transaxle-to-engine bolts
- Transaxle mount-to-body bolts. Tighten the bolts to 66 ft. lbs. (90 Nm).
- Transaxle cooler lines
- Torque converter-to-flywheel bolts. Tighten the bolts to 46 ft. (62 Nm).

➡ For 4T60-E transaxle, note that the flywheel has 1 oval shaped bolt opening. This is for the so-called "net slot bolt." Hand-start and tighten the net slot bolt first, then tighten the remaining bolts.

- Oil level indicator and fill tube
- Vacuum reserve tank, for the 4T60-E transaxle
- Starter
- Transaxle converter cover
- Electrical connector to the VSS, for the 4T60-E transaxle
- Halfshafts
- Left side suspension support assembly
- Left stabilizer shaft frame bushing nuts
- Stabilizer shaft link pin bolt
- Engine-to-transaxle brace
- Ball joints to the control arms
- ABS WSS harness and connectors
- Right and left side splash shields
- Heater core pipe brace-to-transaxle nut and bolt
- Wheels
- Upper transaxle-to-engine bolts.

Tighten the bolts to 66 ft. lbs. (90 Nm).
- Shift linkage to the transaxle
- Electrical connector to the torque converter clutch
- Electrical connector to the park/neutral and backup lamp switch
- Wiring harness to the transaxle, for the 4T60-E transaxle
- Throttle cable to the throttle body, for the 3T40 transaxle
9. Remove the engine support fixture.
10. Install or connect the following:
- Rubber hose to the vent pipe, for the 4T60-E transaxle
- Vacuum line to the modulator
- Air intake duct
- Negative battery cable
11. Refill the transaxle.
12. Verify proper shift linkage adjustment. Start the engine and check for leaks.
13. Road test the vehicle verify proper operation and check the transaxle fluid level.
14. Check and/or adjust the wheel alignment.

1999–01 MODELS

1. Before servicing the vehicle, refer to the precautions in the beginning of this section.
2. Use a scan tool to perform the Anti-lock Brake System (ABS) brake modulator gear tension relief procedure.
3. Disconnect the negative battery cable.
4. Install an engine support fixture.
5. Remove or disconnect the following:
- Front transmission mount bolts
- Splash shield
- Air cleaner and duct assembly
- Wiring harness from the upper transaxle mount bracket
- Upper transaxle mount
- Shifter cable from the transaxle
6. Secure the radiator and condenser to the upper radiator support.
7. Remove or disconnect the following:
- Ground cables from the engine
- Park/Neutral Position (PNP) switch connectors from the transaxle
8. Drain the transaxle fluid.
9. Remove or disconnect the following:
- Front wheels and splash shields
- Lower radiator and condenser support
- Front transaxle mount and bracket
- Both front ABS Wheel Speed Sensors (WSS)

- Speed sensor wiring harness from the body clips
- Battery and tray
- Radiator inlet hose
- Wiring from the ABS modulator assembly
- 2 ABS modulator hydraulic lines from the master cylinder
- 3 hydraulic lines at the ABS modulator that go out to the wheels
- Modulator
- Vehicle Speed Sensor (VSS) electrical connector on the transaxle
- Torque converter bolts
- Ball joints from the control arms
- Halfshafts
- Front transaxle mount
- ABS brake control module
- Tie rod ends from the steering knuckles
- Power steering pressure line from the steering rack
- Brake lines from the retainer under the steering rack
- Steering column intermediate shaft from the steering gear

10. Place a jack under the transaxle.

✳✳ CAUTION

The torque converter may fall out of the transaxle if it is tilted downward.

11. Remove or disconnect the following:
- Transaxle-to-engine bolts
- Transaxle

To install:

12. Install the transaxle onto the engine and tighten the bolts to 66 ft. lbs. (90 Nm).
13. Remove the jack from the transaxle.
14. Install or connect the following:
- Intermediate shaft to the steering gear
- Brake lines in the retainer under the steering gear
- Power steering pressure line to the steering gear
- Tie rod ends to the steering knuckles
- ABS control module
- Front transaxle mount
- Halfshafts
- Suspension by assembling it
- Torque converter bolts. Tighten them to 46 ft. lbs. (62 Nm).
- VSS wiring
- ABS modulator assembly. Tighten the nut to 22 ft. lbs. (30 Nm) and the fluid lines to 18 ft. lbs. (24 Nm).
- WSS electrical connector
- Front transaxle mount bracket
- Lower radiator and condenser support

- Transaxle fluid pan
- Splash shields and the front wheels
- PNP switch wiring at the transaxle
- Ground wiring on the engine
- Shifter cable and the upper transaxle mount
- Wiring harness to the mount bracket
- Air cleaner and duct assembly
- Splash shield and front transaxle mount bolts

15. Remove the engine support fixture.
16. Connect the negative battery cable.
17. Refill the transaxle with fluid and bleed the brakes.

Clutch

REMOVAL & INSTALLATION

1. Before servicing the vehicle, refer to the precautions in the beginning of this section.
2. Remove or disconnect the following:
- Negative battery cable
- Hydraulic line from the clutch actuator (slave cylinder), if necessary
- Transaxle from the vehicle

3. If any clutch components are to be reused, use the following procedure:
  a. Matchmark the clutch pressure

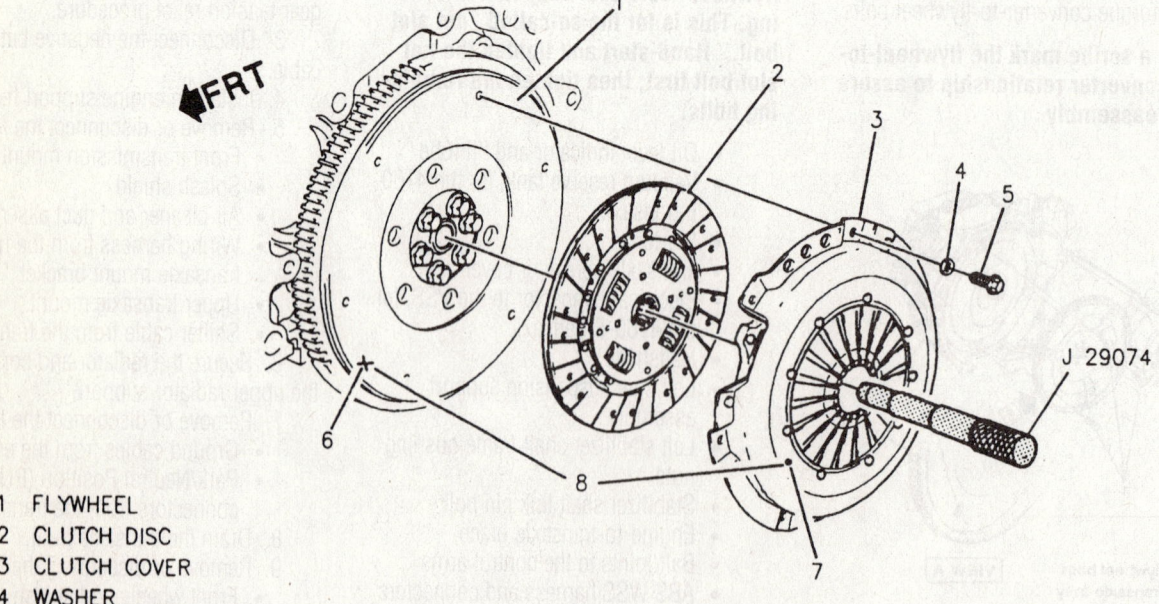

1 FLYWHEEL
2 CLUTCH DISC
3 CLUTCH COVER
4 WASHER
5 BOLT
6 FLYWHEEL "HEAVY SIDE" IDENTIFICATION
7 CLUTCH COVER "LIGHT SIDE" IDENTIFICATION
8 ALIGN IDENTIFICATION MARKS ON ASSEMBLY

J 29074

Exploded view of the clutch components—showing the clutch disk alignment tool

7922Z328

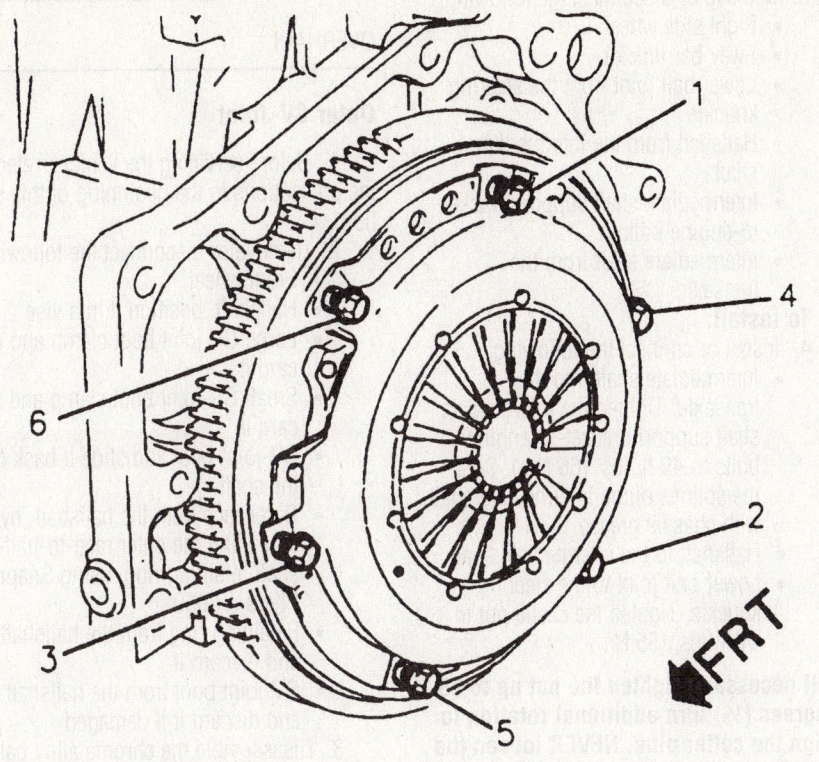

79222Z329

Clutch cover tightening sequence

plate to the flywheel. This is to retain the balance of the original parts. If all parts are to be replaced with new, this step is not necessary.

b. If the pressure plate is to be reused, loosen the pressure plate mounting bolts by turning each bolt 1 full turn until all the spring pressure is removed. This helps avoid warping the pressure plate.

c. Remove the clutch disc and pressure plate.

To install:

4. Apply a small amount of high-temperature grease to the pilot bearing as well as the tip of the transaxle input shaft and the clutch splines.

5. Install or connect the following:
- Clutch alignment tool into the flywheel
- Clutch disc onto the tool
- Pressure plate

➡**New pressure plate-to-flywheel replacement bolts are recommended.**

6. Torque the pressure plate-to-flywheel bolts, in sequence, as follows:
a. Step 1: 12 ft. lbs. (16 Nm).

b. Step 2: 15 ft. lbs. (20 Nm).

c. Step 3: Plus an additional 30 degree turn if equipped with a 3.1L engine or 45 degree turn if equipped with the 2.4L engine.

7. Remove the clutch alignment tool.

8. Lubricate the inside diameter of the actuator (slave cylinder/throwout bearing) with clutch bearing lubricant.

9. Install or connect the following:
- Transaxle
- Clutch master cylinder hydraulic line to the actuator (slave cylinder), if disconnected
- Negative battery cable

10. Bleed the clutch hydraulic system.

11. Road test the vehicle to verify correct operation and easy shifting.

Hydraulic Clutch System

BLEEDING

With Bleeder Screw

1. Before servicing the vehicle, refer to the precautions in the beginning of this section.

2. Be sure the reservoir and is kept topped off throughout this procedure.

3. Loosen the bleed screw, located on the actuator cylinder body next to the inlet connection.

4. When a steady stream of fluid comes out the bleeder, tighten it to 17 inch lbs. (2 Nm).

5. Refill the fluid reservoir.

6. To check the system, start the engine and wait 10 seconds.

7. Depress the clutch pedal and shift into **R**. If there is any gear clash, air may still be present.

Without Bleeder Screw

1. Before servicing the vehicle, refer to the precautions in the beginning of this section.

2. Remove or disconnect the following:
- Actuator cylinder from the transaxle
- Loosen the master cylinder attaching nuts to the ends of the studs
- Reservoir cap and diaphragm

3. Depress the actuator cylinder pushrod about ¾ in. into its bore and hold the position.

4. Install the reservoir diaphragm and cap while holding the actuator pushrod.

5. Release the pushrod when the diaphragm and cap are properly installed.

6. With the actuator lower than the master cylinder, hold the actuator vertically with the pushrod end facing the ground.

7. Press the actuator pushrod into its bore with ½ in. strokes. Check the reservoir for bubbles. Continue until no bubbles enter the reservoir.

8. Install the master cylinder and actuator. Refill the fluid reservoir.

9. To check the system, start the engine and wait 10 seconds.

10. Depress the clutch pedal and shift into reverse. If there is any gear clash, air may still be present.

Halfshaft

REMOVAL & INSTALLATION

Left and Right Halfshafts

1. Before servicing the vehicle, refer to the precautions in the beginning of this section.

2. Remove or disconnect the following:
- Negative battery cable
- Wheel

3. Insert a drift or a punch through the caliper and into the rotor cooling fins to keep the axle from turning.

4. Remove or disconnect the following:
- Hub nut and washer and the drift
- Lower ball joint from the steering knuckle
- Anti-lock Brake System (ABS) sensor wire
- Sway bar link kit
- Halfshaft press it from the hub/bearing assembly using Hub Spindle Remover J-28733-A
- Left halfshaft from the transaxle using Axle Remover J-28468, an extension and a slide hammer
- Right halfshaft from the intermediate shaft using Axle Remover J-33008, an extension and a slide hammer

To install:

5. Install or connect the following:
- Halfshaft into the transaxle or intermediate shaft using a brass drift positioned in the inboard joint groove and tap the joint in until it is seated

➡️**Verify the joint is seated properly by grasping the inboard joint and pulling on it firmly.**

✳️ WARNING

DO NOT pull on the halfshaft or damage to the inner joint may result.

- Halfshaft into the hub assembly
- Lower ball joint to the steering knuckle. Tighten the nut to 41 ft. lbs. (55 Nm).

➡️**If necessary, tighten the nut up to 60 degree (⅙) turn additional rotation to align the cotter pins. NEVER loosen the nut to make the holes align.**

- New cotter pin
- Washer and hub nut. Tighten the hub nut to 185 ft. lbs. (260 Nm), for 1997–98 or to 284 ft. lbs. (385 Nm), for 1999–01.
- Link kit. Tighten the nut to 13 ft. lbs. (17 Nm).
- Wheel. Tighten the nuts to 100 ft. lbs. (140 Nm).
- Negative battery cable

6. Check the transaxle fluid level and top off as necessary.

Intermediate Shaft

1. Before servicing the vehicle, refer to the precautions in the beginning of this section.

2. Install an engine support fixture.
3. Remove or disconnect the following:
- Right side wheel
- Sway bar link kit
- Lower ball joint from the steering knuckle
- Halfshaft from the intermediate shaft
- Intermediate shaft support bracket-to-engine bolts
- Intermediate shaft from the transaxle

To install:

4. Install or connect the following:
- Intermediate shaft into the transaxle. Tighten the intermediate shaft support bracket-to-engine bolts to 49 ft. lbs. (66 Nm). Coat the splines of the intermediate shaft with chassis grease.
- Halfshaft to the intermediate shaft
- Lower ball joint to the steering knuckle. Tighten the castle nut to 41 ft. lbs. (55 Nm).

➡️**If necessary, tighten the nut up to 60 degrees (⅙) turn additional rotation to align the cotter pins. NEVER loosen the nut to make the holes align.**

- New cotter pin
- Link kit. Tighten the nut to 13 ft. lbs. (17 Nm).
- Wheel. Tighten the nuts to 100 ft. lbs. (140 Nm).

5. Remove the engine support fixture.
6. Connect the negative battery cable.
7. Check the transaxle fluid level and top off as necessary.

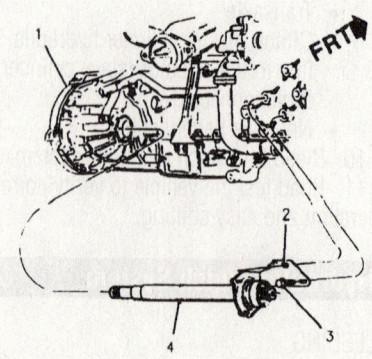

1 TRANSAXLE
2 INTERMEDIATE SHAFT SUPPORT BRACKET
3 BOLT
4 INTERMEDIATE SHAFT

79222Z330

Intermediate shaft components

CV-Joints

OVERHAUL

Outer CV-Joint

1. Before servicing the vehicle, refer to the precautions in the beginning of this section.

2. Remove or disconnect the following:
- Front wheel
- Halfshaft, position it in a vise
- Large CV-joint boot clamp and discard it
- Small CV-joint boot clamp and discard it
- CV-joint boot and slide it back on the shaft
- Outer race from the halfshaft, by spreading the outer race-to-halfshaft retaining ring, using Snapring Pliers J-8059
- Retaining ring from the halfshaft and discard it
- CV-joint boot from the halfshaft and discard it if damaged

3. Disassemble the chrome alloy balls from the CV-joint cage as follows:
   a. Position a brass drift against the CV-joint cage and tap it with a hammer to tilt the cage.
   b. Remove the 1st chrome alloy ball from the cage.
   c. Tilt the cage in the opposite direction.
   d. Remove the opposite chrome alloy ball.
   e. Repeat the procedure until all 6 balls are removed.

4. Disassemble the CV-joint cage and inner race as follows:
   a. Pivot the cage and race 90 degrees to the center line of the outer race.
   b. Align the cage windows with outer race lands.
   c. Remove the cage from the outer race.
   d. Rotate the inner race upward and remove it from the cage.

5. Thoroughly clean and inspect all parts.

To install:

6. Lubricate the parts with a light coat of grease.

7. Assemble the CV-joint cage and inner race, as follows:
   a. Rotate the inner race 90 degrees to the cage centerline.
   b. Align the cage windows with inner race lands.
   c. Insert the inner race into the cage

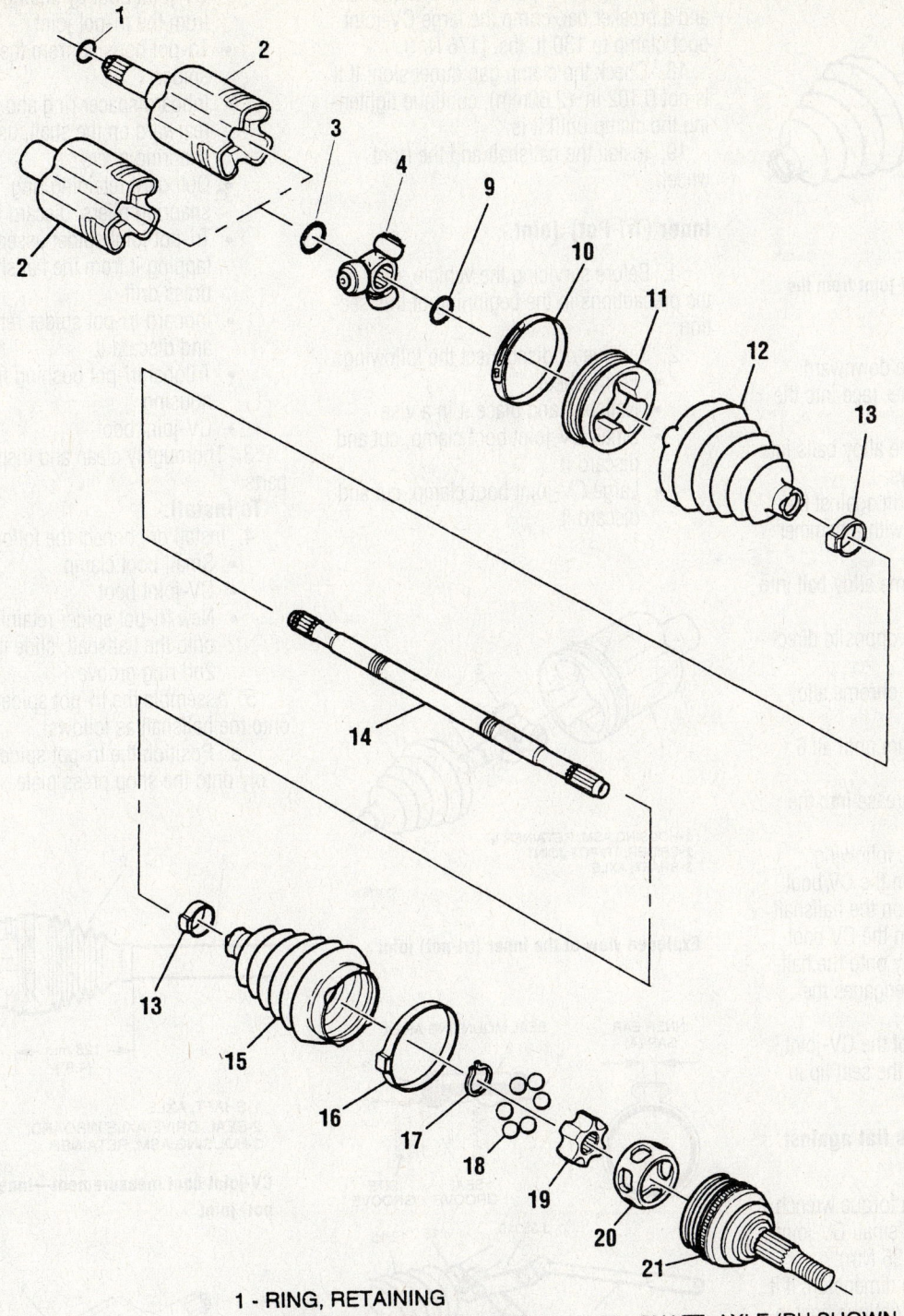

Exploded view of the halfshaft assembly

1 - RING, RETAINING
2 - HOUSING ASM, RETAINER &
3 - RING, SHAFT RETAINING
4 - SPIDER, TRIPOT JOINT
9 - RING, SPACER
10 - CLAMP, SEAL RETAINING
11 - BUSHING, TRILOBAL TRIPOT
12 - SEAL, DRIVE AXLE INBOARD
13 - CLAMP, SEAL RETAINING

14 - SHAFT, AXLE (RH SHOWN, LH SIMILAR)
15 - SEAL, DRIVE AXLE OUTBOARD
16 - CLAMP, SEAL RETAINING
17 - RING, RACE RETAINING
18 - BALL, CHROME ALLOY
19 - RACE, C/V JOINT INNER
20 - CAGE, C/V JOINT
21 - RACE, C/V JOINT OUTER

9306ZG13

Turn to Section 5 for brake system applications

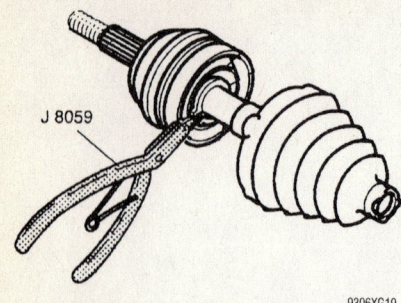

J 8059

9306XG19

Disconnecting the outer CV-joint from the axle shaft

by rotating the inner race downward.

   d. Insert the cage/inner race into the outer race.

8. Assemble the chrome alloy balls into the CV-joint cage, as follows:

   a. Position a brass drift against the CV-joint cage and tap it with a hammer to tilt the cage.

   b. Insert the 1st chrome alloy ball into the cage.

   c. Tilt the cage in the opposite direction.

   d. Insert the opposite chrome alloy ball.

   e. Repeat the procedure until all 6 balls are inserted.

9. Install ½ of the kit grease into the CV-joint.

10. Install or connect the following:
- Small ring clamp on the CV boot
- New retaining ring on the halfshaft
- Large ring clamp on the CV boot
- Outer race assembly onto the halfshaft until the ring engages the halfshaft groove

11. Slide the small end of the CV-joint boot/clamp into place, with the seal lip in the halfshaft groove

➡**Make sure the boot lies flat against the halfshaft.**

12. Using a crimp tool, a torque wrench and a breaker bar, crimp the small CV-joint boot clamp to 100 ft. lbs. (136 Nm).

13. Check the clamp gap dimension; if it is not 0.085 in. (2.15mm), continue tightening the clamp until it is.

14. Install ½ kit grease into the CV-joint boot.

15. Measure approximately 0.687 in. (17.5mm) up from the bottom edge of the outer CV-joint assembly.

16. Slide the large end of the CV boot/clamp into place, with the seal lip in place over the outer race.

➡**Make sure the boot lies flat against the outer race.**

17. Using a crimp tool, a torque wrench and a breaker bar, crimp the large CV-joint boot clamp to 130 ft. lbs. (176 Nm).

18. Check the clamp gap dimension; if it is not 0.102 in. (2.60mm), continue tightening the clamp until it is.

19. Install the halfshaft and the front wheel.

Inner (Tri-Pot) Joint

1. Before servicing the vehicle, refer to the precautions in the beginning of this section.

2. Remove or disconnect the following:
- Front wheel
- Halfshaft and place it in a vise
- Small CV-joint boot clamp, cut and discard it
- Large CV-joint boot clamp, cut and discard it

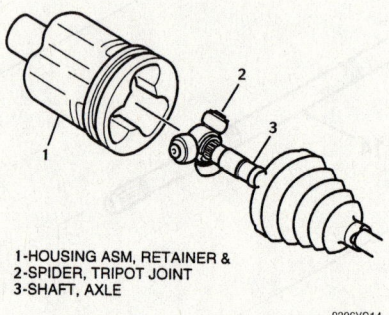

1-HOUSING ASM, RETAINER &
2-SPIDER, TRIPOT JOINT
3-SHAFT, AXLE

9306YG14

Exploded view of the inner (tri-pot) joint

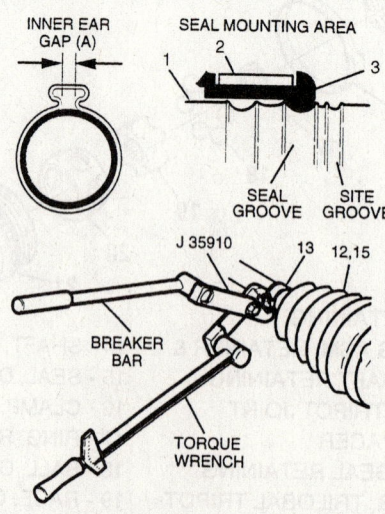

INNER EAR GAP (A)

SEAL MOUNTING AREA

SEAL GROOVE   SITE GROOVE

J 35910   13   12,15

BREAKER BAR

TORQUE WRENCH

13-CLAMP, SEAL RETAINING
14-SHAFT, AXLE
12,15-SEAL, DRIVE AXLE OUTBOARD

9306YG16

Crimping the small CV-joint boot ring— Inner (tri-pot) joint

- CV-joint boot by sliding it away from the tri-pot joint
- Tri-pot housing from the tri-pot spider
- Inboard spacer ring and slide it rearward on the shaft, using snapring pliers
- Outboard retaining ring, using snapring pliers, discard it
- Tri-pot joint spider assembly by tapping it from the halfshaft with a brass drift
- Inboard tri-pot spider retaining ring and discard it
- Trilobal tri-pot bushing from the housing
- CV-joint boot

3. Thoroughly clean and inspect all parts.

To install:

4. Install or connect the following:
- Small boot clamp
- CV-joint boot
- New tri-pot spider retaining ring onto the halfshaft, slide it past the 2nd ring groove

5. Assemble the tri-pot spider assembly onto the halfshaft as follows:

   a. Position the tri-pot spider assembly onto the shop press plate.

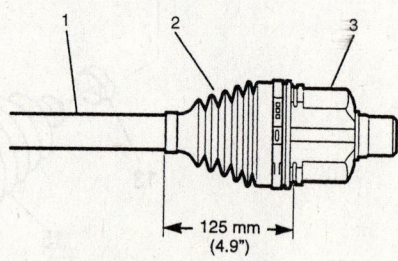

1   2   3

125 mm (4.9")

1-SHAFT, AXLE
2-SEAL, DRIVE AXLE INBOARD
3-HOUSING ASM, RETAINER

9306YG17

CV-joint boot measurement—Inner (tri-pot) joint

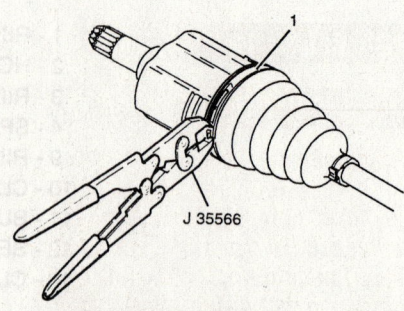

1

J 35566

1-CLAMP, SEAL RETAINING

9306YG18

Latching the large CV-joint boot ring— Inner (tri-pot) joint

b. Position the halfshaft onto the tri-pot spider assembly, in the shop press.

c. Press the halfshaft into the tri-pot spider assembly until it passes the 2nd ring groove

6. Remove the halfshaft from the shop press.

7. Install or connect the following:
- Outboard retaining ring into the axle shaft groove using snapring pliers
- Tri-pot joint spider assembly, slide it against the outboard retaining ring
- Inboard spacer ring, seat it in the groove
- ½ of the kit grease into the boot
- ½ of the kit grease into the tri-pot housing
- Trilobal tip-pot bushing flush with the tri-pot housing face
- New large seal clamp onto the CV-joint boot
- Tri-pot housing, slide it over the tri-pot joint spider assembly
- CV-joint boot/clamp, slide it into place, over the trilobal tri-pot bushing with the seal lip in the groove

➡Make sure the boot lies flat against the trilobal bushing.

8. Position the CV-joint boot so it measures 4.9 in. (125mm).

9. Using a crimp tool, a torque wrench and a breaker bar, crimp the small CV-joint boot clamp to 100 ft. lbs. (136 Nm).

10. Using a crimp tool, latch the large CV-joint boot clamp.

11. Install the halfshaft and the front wheel.

STEERING AND SUSPENSION

Air Bag

✳✳ CAUTION

Some vehicles are equipped with an air bag system. The system must be disabled before performing service on or around system components, steering column, instrument panel components, wiring and sensors. Failure to follow safety and disabling procedures could result in accidental air bag deployment, possible personal injury and unnecessary system repairs.

PRECAUTIONS

Several precautions must be observed when handling the inflator module to avoid accidental deployment and possible personal injury.
- Never carry the inflator module by the wires or connector on the underside of the module.
- When carrying a live inflator module, hold securely with both hands, and ensure that the bag and trim cover are pointed away.
- Place the inflator module on a bench or other surface with the bag and trim cover facing up.
- With the inflator module on the bench, never place anything on or close to the module which may be thrown in the event of an accidental deployment.

DISARMING

✳✳ CAUTION

The SRS must be disarmed before performing service procedures around the air bag or SRS wiring. Failure to do so may cause accidental deployment of the air bag, resulting in unnecessary SRS repairs and/or personal injury.

1. Disconnect the negative battery cable.
2. Turn the steering wheel so the vehicle's wheels are pointing straight ahead.
3. Turn the ignition switch to the **LOCK** position and remove the key.
4. Remove the **AIR BAG** fuse from the fuse block.
5. Remove the left sound insulator.
6. Remove the Connector Position Assurance (CPA) clip from the yellow 2-way connector at the base of the steering column, and detach the connector. If equipped with a passenger's side air bag, remove the CPA and detach the yellow 2-way connector from the passenger air bag lead.

REARMING

1. Turn the ignition switch to the **LOCK** position and remove the key.
2. Attach the yellow 2-way connector at the base of steering column and secure it with the Connector Position Assurance (CPA) clip. If equipped with a passenger's side air bag, attach the yellow 2-way connector at the passenger air bag lead and secure it with the CPA clip.
3. Install the left sound insulator.
4. Install the **AIR BAG** fuse in the fuse block.
5. Turn the ignition switch to the **RUN** position and verify that the **AIR BAG** warning lamp flashes 7 times, then turns **OFF**.
6. Connect the negative battery cable.

Power Rack and Pinion Steering Gear

REMOVAL & INSTALLATION

1997–98 Models

1. Before servicing the vehicle, refer to the precautions in the beginning of this section.
2. Remove or disconnect the following:
- Left sound insulator from under the dashboard
- Upper pinch bolt from the steering shaft coupling assembly
- Power steering line retainer, if equipped.
- Master cylinder from the Power brake booster
- Power brake booster from the cowl
- Brake pedal pushrod from the pedal clip

3. Pull the booster away from the firewall and position away from the rack and pinion mounting clamp. DO NOT remove the master cylinder or allow the brake lines to kink.
4. Remove or disconnect the following:
- Inner tie rod bolts, lock plates and washers
- Left and right mounting clamps
- Power steering lines from the rack and pinion unit and cap them

5. Pull the rack away from the firewall and remove the lower steering shaft pinch bolt and separate the steering shaft from the rack and pinion stub shaft.
6. Remove or disconnect the following:
- Dash seal from the rack and pinion housing
- Rack and pinion unit

7. If when removing the rack and pinion mounting clamp nuts the studs came out,

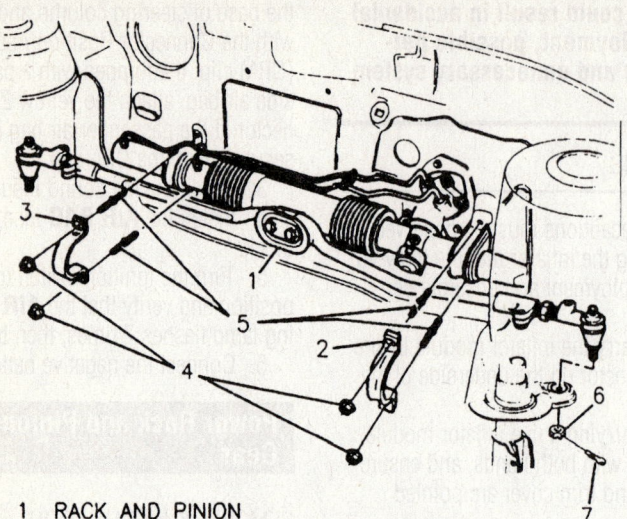

1 RACK AND PINION
2 L.H. CLAMP – HORIZONTAL SLOT AT TOP
3 R.H. CLAMP – HORIZONTAL SLOT AT TOP
4 NUT – 30 N·m (22 LBS.FT.) – HAND START ALL
NUTS. TIGHTEN LEFT HAND SIDE CLAMP NUTS
FIRST, THEN TIGHTEN RIGHT SIDE NUTS.
5 STUD – 18 N·m (13 LBS. FT.) – AFTER SECOND
REUSE OF STUD, THREAD LOCKING KIT NO.
1052624 MUST BE USED.
6 NUT – 60 N·m (44 LBS. FT.)
7 COTTER PIN

79227331

Rack and pinion mounting components–1997–98 models

remove the nuts from the studs and install the studs back into the firewall. Tighten the studs to 15 ft. lbs. (20 Nm).

To install:

8. Install or connect the following:
   • Rack and pinion assembly
   • Dash seal on the firewall
   • Steering shaft coupling to the stub shaft. Tighten the pinch bolt to 30 ft. lbs. (41 Nm).
   • Power steering lines to the rack and pinion assembly. Tighten the fittings to 20 ft. lbs. (27 Nm).
   • Rack and pinion clamps. Tighten the left side clamps first, then the right to 22 ft. lbs. (30 Nm).
   • Inner tie rods. Tighten the bolts to 65 ft. lbs. (90 Nm).
   • Power booster on the firewall
   • Brake pedal pushrod clip
   • Master cylinder to the brake booster
   • Steering column upper pinch bolt. Tighten the bolt to 30 ft. lbs. (41 Nm).
   • Left side sound insulator
9. Refill and bleed the power steering system.
10. Check and/or adjust the front end alignment.

1999–01 Models

1. Before servicing the vehicle, refer to the precautions in the beginning of this section.
2. Remove or disconnect the following:
   • Negative battery cable
   • Both front wheels
   • Stabilizer shaft links from the control arms
   • Tie rod ends from the steering knuckles
   • Intermediate shaft lower pinch bolt from the power steering gear
   • Through-bolt from the rear transmission mount
   • Power steering line bracket from the crossmember
   • Stabilizer shaft brackets from the crossmember.
3. Support the rear of the sub-frame with jacks.
4. Remove the rear sub-frame mounting bolts and loosen the front ones.
5. Lower the sub-frame about 3 inches using the jacks.
6. Remove or disconnect the following:
   • Stabilizer bar
   • Hoses from the steering gear

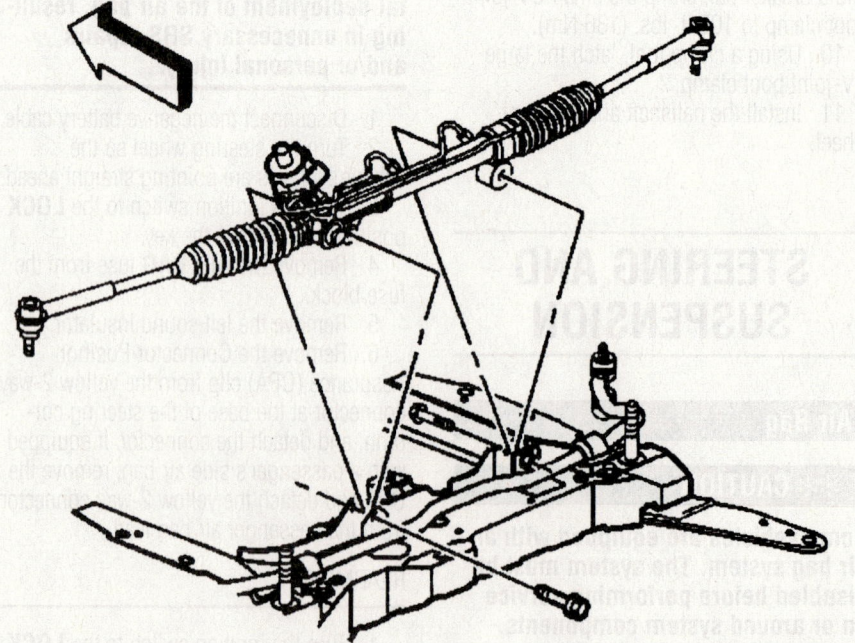

9300Z303

Power steering gear mounting—1999–01 models

- Steering gear through the left wheel opening

To install:

7. Install or connect the following:
   - Steering gear. Tighten the bolts to 89 ft. lbs. (120 Nm).
   - Hoses to the steering gear
   - Stabilizer bar
   - Sub-frame. Tighten the bolts in the following order: left rear, right rear, left front, right front to 71 ft. lbs. (110 Nm).
   - Stabilizer bar bracket. Tighten the bolts to 49 ft. lbs. (66 Nm).
   - Intermediate shaft pinch bolt. Tighten the bolt to 16 ft. lbs. (22 Nm).
   - Tie rod ends and the stabilizer bar links

8. Verify all steering hose fittings are tight.

9. Install the front wheels.

10. Fill the steering reservoir.

11. Install an adapter cap on the fluid reservoir with a vacuum pump attached to it.

12. Apply about 20 inches of vacuum to the system and wait 5 minutes. Typical vacuum drop is 2–3 inches. If the vacuum drop is greater, there may be a leak in the system allowing air to enter.

13. Remove the tools and install the reservoir cap.

14. Start the engine and allow it to idle.

15. Turn the engine **OFF** and check the fluid level. Do this until the fluid level stabilizes.

16. Start the engine and allow it to idle.

17. Turn the steering wheel in both directions 180–360 degrees 5 times.

18. Turn the engine **OFF** and check the fluid level.

19. Install an adapter cap on the fluid reservoir with a vacuum pump attached to it once again.

20. Apply about 20 inches of vacuum to the system and wait 5 minutes.

21. Remove the tools and check the fluid level. Install the cap.

Strut

REMOVAL & INSTALLATION

Front

1. Before servicing the vehicle, refer to the precautions in the beginning of this section.

2. Remove or disconnect the following:

- Front wheel
- Outer tie rod end from the strut arm or steering knuckle
- Brake line bracket from the strut

3. Scribe reference marks on the front strut and steering knuckle for installation purposes.

4. Remove the strut lower mounting bracket nut and through-bolts.

5. Lower the vehicle until the upper strut plate mounting bolts are accessible.

6. Support the lower control arm.

7. Hold the strut and remove the strut plate mounting nuts and bolt. Remove the strut from the vehicle.

✳✳ WARNING

If the strut is being replaced, a strut compressor tool must be used to remove the coil spring from the strut assembly. Failure to use a spring compressing tool can result in personal injury and/or part damage.

To install:

8. Install or connect the following:
   - Strut assembly
   - Upper strut plate mounting nuts
   - Lower strut bracket to the steering

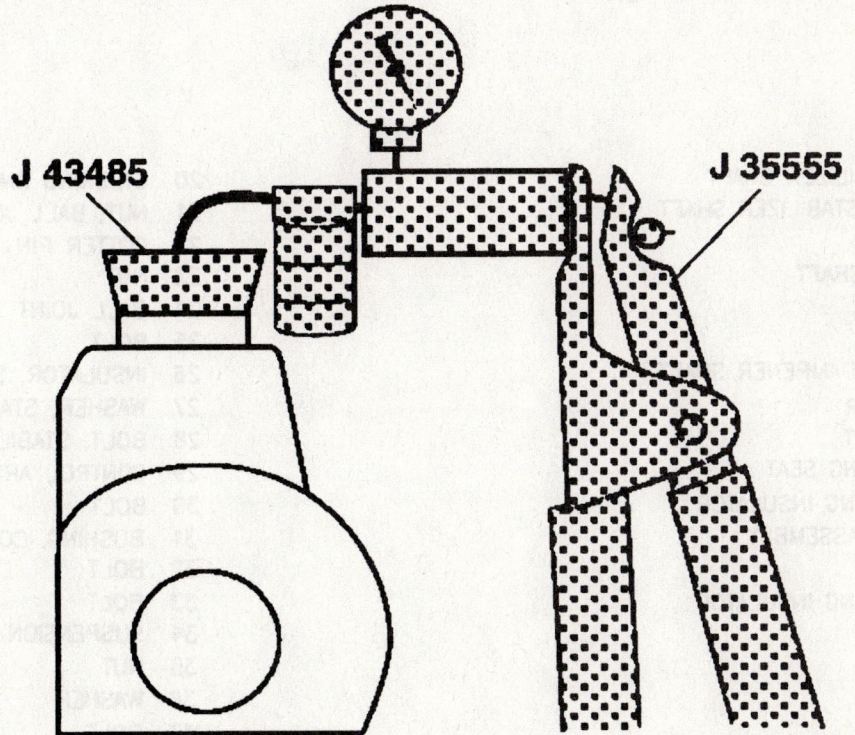

J 43485   **J 35555**

9300Z302

Install the special tools as shown on the steering fluid reservoir when bleeding the system

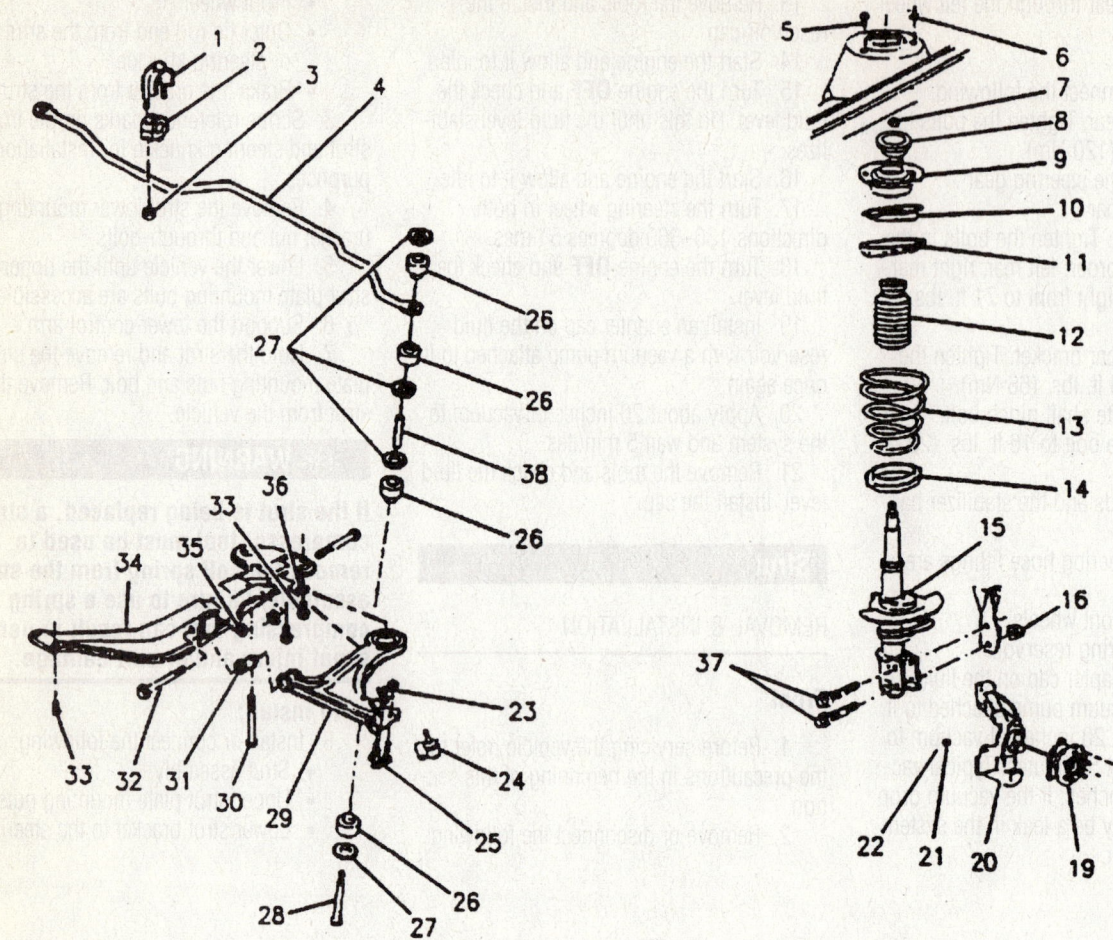

1	CLAMP, STABILIZER SHAFT	20	STEERING KNUCKLE
2	INSULATOR, STABILIZER SHAFT	21	NUT, BALL JOINT
3	NUT	22	COTTER PIN
4	STABILIZER SHAFT	23	NUT
5	BOLT	24	BALL JOINT
6	NUT	25	BOLT
7	NUT, STRUT DAMPENER SHAFT	26	INSULATOR, STABILIZER LINK
8	RATE WASHER	27	WASHER, STABILIZER LINK
9	STRUT MOUNT	28	BOLT, STABILIZER LINK
10	UPPER SPRING SEAT	29	CONTROL ARM
11	UPPER SPRING INSULATOR	30	BOLT
12	DUST TUBE ASSEMBLY	31	BUSHING, CONTROL ARM
13	SPRING	32	BOLT
14	LOWER SPRING INSULATOR	33	BOLT
15	STRUT	34	SUSPENSION SUPPORT
16	NUT	35	NUT
17	WASHER	36	WASHER
18	BOLT	37	BOLT
19	HUB AND BEARING ASSEMBLY	38	SPACER, STABILIZER LINK

Exploded view of the front suspension

7922Z332

knuckle. Tighten the through-bolt/nuts to 133 ft. lbs. (180 Nm) with the reference marks in alignment.

- Tie rod end to the strut arm. Tighten the castle nut to 44 ft. lbs. (60 Nm).

➡️ **If necessary tighten the nut up to 60 degree (⅙) turn additional to align the cotter pin holes. NEVER loosen the nut to make the holes align.**

9. Install or connect the following:
- New cotter pin
- Brake line bracket to the strut. Tighten the bolt to 10 ft. lbs. (14 Nm).
- Wheel
- Tighten the upper strut plate mounting nuts/bolt to 18 ft. lbs. (25 Nm).

10. Check and/or adjust the front end alignment.

Rear

1999–01

1. Before servicing the vehicle, refer to the precautions in the beginning of this section.

2. Remove the rear wheel.
3. Scribe a mark indicating the position of the strut on the knuckle.
4. Remove or disconnect the following:
- Strut nuts from inside the trunk
- Strut bolts from the wheel well area
- Strut-to-knuckle bolts
- Strut from the vehicle

✳✳ WARNING

If the strut is being replaced, a spring compressor tool must be used to remove the coil spring from the strut assembly. Failure to use a spring compressing tool can result in personal injury and/or part damage.

To install:

5. Install or connect the following:
- Strut. Tighten the upper bolts and nuts to 18 ft. lbs. (25 Nm).
- Strut on the knuckle by aligning the scribe marks made earlier. Tighten the bolts to 89 ft. lbs. (120 Nm).
- Wheel

6. Check and/or adjust the wheel alignment.

Shock Absorber

REMOVAL & INSTALLATION

1997–98

✳✳ WARNING

When doing this procedure, if both shocks are to be replaced, only remove one shock at a time or damage can occur to the axle assembly and/or personal injury.

1. Before servicing the vehicle, refer to the precautions in the beginning of this section.
2. Support the rear axle assembly.
3. Remove or disconnect the following:
- Upper shock cap and the 2 shock plate mounting nuts from inside the trunk
- Shock tower reinforcement
- Lower shock mounting nut from under the suspension
- Shock by compressing it
- Upper shock insulator, washer and mount, if the shock is being replaced

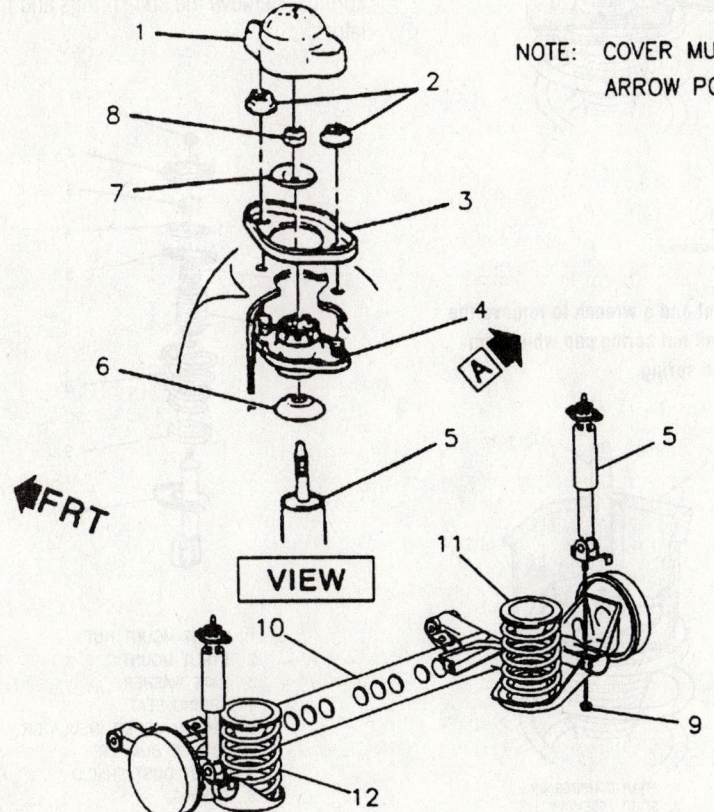

NOTE: COVER MUST BE INSTALLED SO THAT ARROW POINTS TO LEFT SIDE OF VEHICLE

1 COVER (MUST BE INSTALLED WITH ARROW POINTING TO LEFT OF VEHICLE)
2 NUT
3 REINFORCEMENT
4 UPPER SHOCK ABSORBER MOUNT
5 SHOCK ABSORBER
6 WASHER
7 WASHER
8 NUT
9 NUT
10 REAR AXLE; SPRING-ON-CENTER TYPE
11 INSULATOR, COIL SPRING
12 COIL SPRING

Exploded view of the rear suspension—1997–98 models

Turn to Section 5 for brake system applications

To install:

4. Install or connect the following:
- Mount, washer and insulator on the shock, if removed. Tighten the mounting nut to 21 ft. lbs. (29 Nm).
- Shock assembly with the alignment tab on the lower mount is pointing rearward
- Tighten the shock mounting nut to 35 ft. lbs. (47 Nm).
- Reinforcement and upper shock plate mounting nuts. Tighten the nuts to 18 ft. lbs. (24 Nm).
- Cap over the mounting plate

5. Remove the axle support.

Coil Spring

REMOVAL & INSTALLATION

Rear

EXCEPT 1997–98 MODELS

1. Before servicing the vehicle, refer to the precautions in the beginning of this section.

2. Remove the strut assembly from the vehicle.

3. Mount the strut compressor in a holding fixture.

4. Mount the strut assembly into the compressor. Note that the strut compressor has strut mounting holes drilled for specific vehicle lines.

5. Compress the strut approximately ½

its height after initial contact with the top cap.

✳✳ WARNING

Never bottom the spring or damper rod.

6. Remove the nut from the strut damper shaft and place alignment/guiding rod J-34013-27 on top of the damper shaft. Use the rod to guide the damper shaft straight down through the spring cap while compressing the spring. Remove the components.

To install:

7. Install the bearing cap into the strut compressor, if removed.

8. Mount the strut assembly in strut compressor, using bottom locking pin only. Extend the damper shaft and install clamp J-34013-20 on the damper shaft.

9. Install the spring over the damper

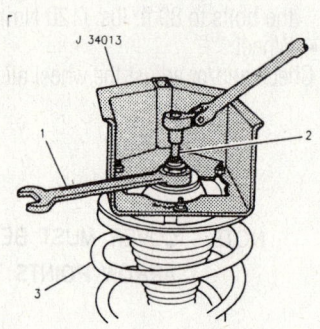

1 WRENCH
2 SOCKET
3 STRUT ASSEMBLY

7922Z335

Use a socket and a wrench to remove the damper shaft nut spring cap while compressing the spring

and swing the assembly up so the upper locking pin can be installed.

10. Install all shields, bumpers and insulators on the spring seat. Install the spring seat on top of the spring. Be sure the flat on the upper spring seat is facing in the proper direction. The spring seat flat should be facing the same direction as the centerline of the strut assembly spindle.

11. Install the guiding rod and turn the forcing screw while the guiding rod centers the assembly. When the threads on the damper shaft are visible, remove the guiding rod and install the nut. Tighten the nut to 52 ft. lbs. (70 Nm). Use a crow's foot line wrench while holding the damper shaft with a socket.

12. Remove the clamp.

1997–98 MODELS

1. Before servicing the vehicle, refer to the precautions in the beginning of this section.

2. Support the rear axle with a jack.

3. Remove the lower shock absorber mounting nuts. Remove the right and left brake line mounting bolts from the floor of the vehicle.

4. Slowly lower the rear axle assembly until the tension is removed from the coil springs. Remove the coil springs and insulators.

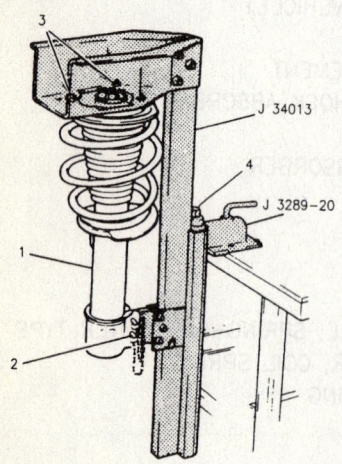

1 STRUT ASSEMBLY
2 INSTALL LOCKING PINS THROUGH STRUT ASSEMBLY
3 TIGHTEN NUTS UNTIL FLUSH WITH STRUT COMPRESSOR
4 COMPRESSOR FORCING SCREW

7922Z334

View of the strut assembly mounted in a compressor

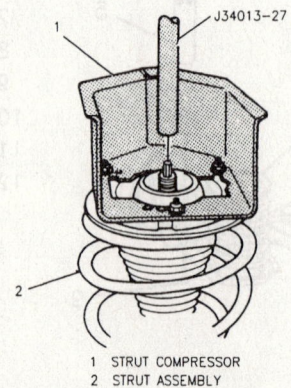

1 STRUT COMPRESSOR
2 STRUT ASSEMBLY

7922Z336

Install the rod to guide the damper shaft straight down through the spring cap while compressing the spring

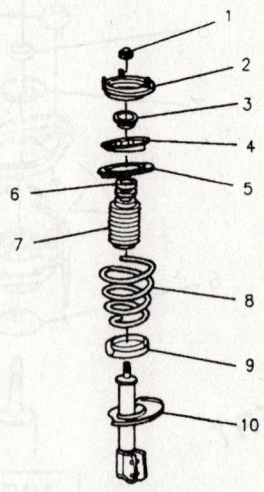

1 STRUT MOUNT NUT
2 STRUT MOUNT
3 RATE WASHER
4 SPRING SEAT
5 SPRING UPPER INSULATOR
6 JOUNCE BUMPER
7 STRUT DUST SHIELD
8 SPRING
9 SPRING LOWER INSULATOR
10 STRUT

7922Z337

Exploded view of the front strut assembly

To install:

5. Install the springs and insulator into the vehicle. The ends of the lowest coil must be within ⁄₁₆ of the spring stop.

6. Raise the rear axle assembly until the lower shock nuts can be installed. Tighten the nuts to 35 ft. lbs. (47 Nm).

7. Connect the brake line brackets to the frame and tighten the mounting bolts to 97 inch lbs. (11 Nm).

8. Remove the jack.

Torsion Bars

REMOVAL & INSTALLATION

1. Before servicing the vehicle, refer to the precautions in the beginning of this section.

2. Remove or disconnect the following:
   - Torsion bar-to-knuckle bolt, washer and bushing
   - Torsion bar-to-chassis bolt
   - Torsion bar from the chassis

To install:

3. Install or connect the following:
   - Torsion bar to the chassis. Tighten the nut/bolt to 48 ft. lbs. (65 Nm) plus an additional 120 degree turn.
   - Torsion bar to the knuckle. Tighten the bolt to 51 ft. lbs. (69 Nm).

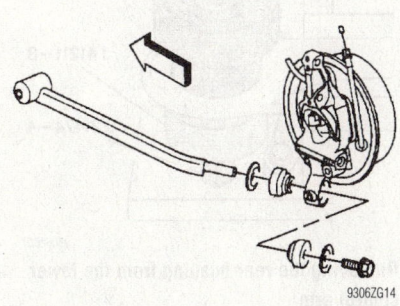

Exploded view of the torsion bar

Lower Ball Joint

REMOVAL & INSTALLATION

1. Before servicing the vehicle, refer to the precautions in the beginning of this section.

2. Remove or disconnect the following:
   - Wheel

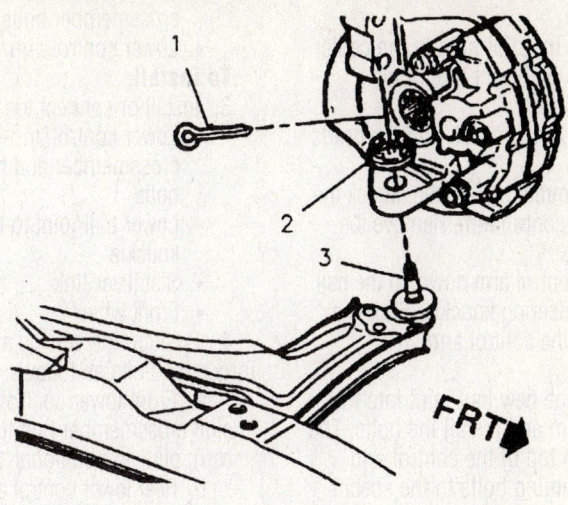

1   PIN
2   NUT – 55 N·m (41 LBS. FT.) MINIMUM TORQUE
     65 N·m (48 LBS. FT.) MAXIMUM TORQUE TO
     INSTALL PIN
3   LOWER BALL JOINT

Exploded view of the ball joint-to-knuckle mounting

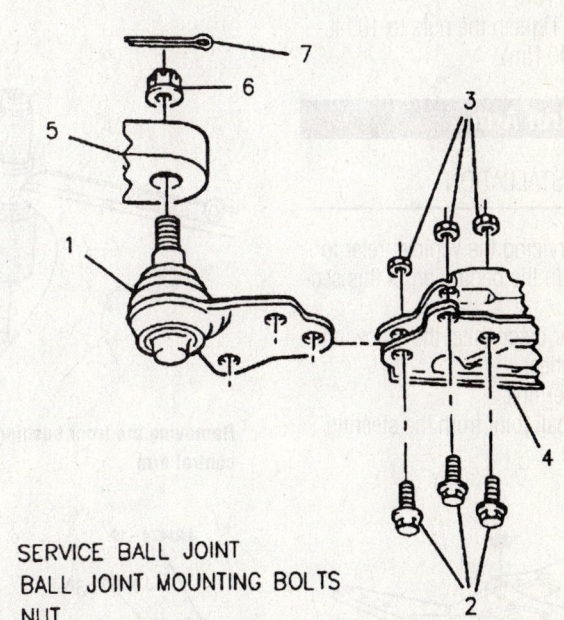

1   SERVICE BALL JOINT
2   BALL JOINT MOUNTING BOLTS
3   NUT
4   LOWER CONTROL ARM
5   STEERING KNUCKLE
6   NUT – 55 N·m (41 LBS. FT.) MINIMUM TORQUE
     65 N·m (48 LBS. FT.) MAXIMUM TORQUE
     TO INSTALL PIN
7   PIN

Exploded view of the replacement ball joint mounting

- Lower ball joint from the steering knuckle

3. Drill a ⅛ in. pilot hole in the center of each of the 3 ball joint mounting rivets.

4. Using a ½ in. drill bit, drill the heads off the rivets.

5. With a hammer and punch, knock the rivets out of the control arm. Remove the sway bar link kit.

6. Pull the control arm down so the ball stud clears the steering knuckle. Slide the ball joint out of the control arm.

To install:

7. Position the new ball joint into the lower control arm and install the bolts. The nuts must be on top of the control arm. Tighten the mounting bolts to the specification provided with the ball joint service kit.

8. Connect the ball joint to the steering knuckle and tighten the castle nut to 41 ft. lbs. (55 Nm). If necessary to align the cotter pin holes tighten the nut up to 60 degree (⅙) turn additional rotation. NEVER loosen the nut to make the holes align.

9. Install or connect the following:
- New cotter pin
- Link kit. Tighten the nut to 22 ft. lbs. (30 Nm).
- Wheel. Tighten the nuts to 100 ft. lbs. (140 Nm).

Lower Control Arm

REMOVAL & INSTALLATION

1. Before servicing the vehicle, refer to the precautions in the beginning of this section.

2. Remove or disconnect the following:
- Front wheel
- Stabilizer link
- Lower ball joint from the steering knuckle

- Lower control arm-to-suspension crossmember bolts
- Lower control arm

To install:

3. Install or connect the following:
- Lower control arm-to-suspension crossmember and hand-tighten the bolts
- Lower ball joint to the steering knuckle
- Stabilizer link
- Front wheel

4. Position the vehicle at curb height. Torque the bolts as follows:

   a. Front lower control arm-to-suspension crossmember bolt to 84 ft. lbs. (115 Nm), plus an additional 120 degree turn.

   b. Rear lower control arm-to-suspension crossmember bolt to 180 ft. lbs. (245 Nm), plus an additional 180 degree turn.

5. Check and/or adjust the front alignment.

CONTROL ARM BUSHING REPLACEMENT

Front Bushing

1. Before servicing the vehicle, refer to the precautions in the beginning of this section.

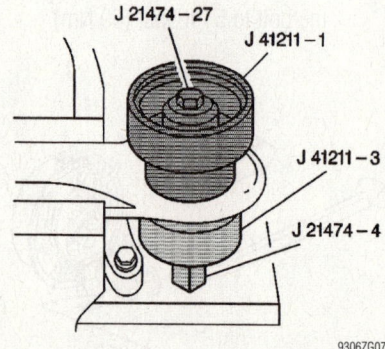

9306ZG05
Removing the front bushing from the lower control arm

2. Remove the lower control arm and place it in a vise.

3. Lubricate the threads of a bushing driver with high pressure lubricant.

4. Assemble the tool onto the front control arm bushing.

5. Tighten the tool until the front bushing is pressed from the control arm.

6. Disassemble the tools.

To install:

7. Lubricate the new front bushing outer casing.

8. Insert the new bushing into the control arm.

9. Assemble a bushing driver/installer set onto the front control.

10. Tighten the screw until the front bushing is pressed into the control arm.

11. Disassemble the tools.

12. Install the lower control arm.

Rear Bushing

1. Before servicing the vehicle, refer to the precautions in the beginning of this section.

2. Remove the lower control arm and place it in a vise.

3. Assemble a bushing driver set onto the rear control.

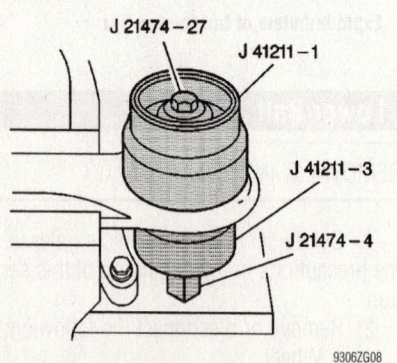

9306ZG07
Removing the rear bushing from the lower control arm

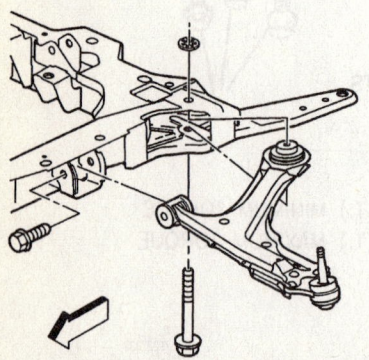

9306ZG04
Exploded view of the lower control arm and related components

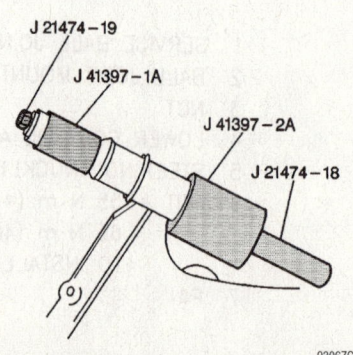

9306ZG06
Installing the front bushing to the lower control arm

9306ZG08
Installing the rear bushing to the lower control arm

4. Tighten the tool until the rear bushing is pressed from the control arm.

5. Disassemble the tools.

To install:

6. Insert the new bushing into the control arm.

7. Assemble the driver/installer set onto the rear control arm bushing.

8. Tighten the screw until the rear bushing is pressed into the control arm.

9. Disassemble the tools.

10. Install the lower control arm.

Wheel Bearings

ADJUSTMENT

These vehicles are equipped with sealed hub and bearing assemblies. The hub and bearing assemblies are non-serviceable. If the assembly is damaged, the complete unit must be replaced.

REMOVAL & INSTALLATION

Front

1. Before servicing the vehicle, refer to the precautions in the beginning of this section.

2. Remove or disconnect the following:
   - Front wheel
   - Halfshaft nut and washer.
   - Caliper from the steering knuckle and support it aside.

> **※ WARNING**
>
> **DO NOT allow the caliper to hang unsupported from the brake hose.**

   - Brake rotor
   - 3 hub/bearing assembly to the steering knuckle bolts
   - Backing plate
   - Halfshaft from the hub/bearing assembly

   - Hub/bearing assembly

To install:

3. Install or connect the following:
   - Hub/bearing assembly onto the halfshaft making sure the splines engage smoothly
   - Backing plate
   - Hub/bearing assembly to steering knuckle. Tighten the bolts to 70 ft. lbs. (95 Nm).
   - Brake rotor
   - Caliper onto the steering knuckle. Tighten the bolts to 38 ft. lbs. (51 Nm).
   - Tighten the halfshaft nut to 192 ft. lbs. (260 Nm).
   - Front wheel. Tighten the nuts to 100 ft. lbs. (140 Nm).

Rear

DRUM BRAKE

1. Before servicing the vehicle, refer to the precautions in the beginning of this section.

2. Remove or disconnect the following:
   - Wheel
   - Brake drum
   - 4 hub/bearing assembly to knuckle nuts

➡ **The top rear bolt will not clear the brake shoes and must be removed with the bearing assembly.**

   - Anti-lock Brake System (ABS) speed sensor wire from the hub/bearing assembly
   - Hub/bearing assembly

To install:

3. Install or connect the following:

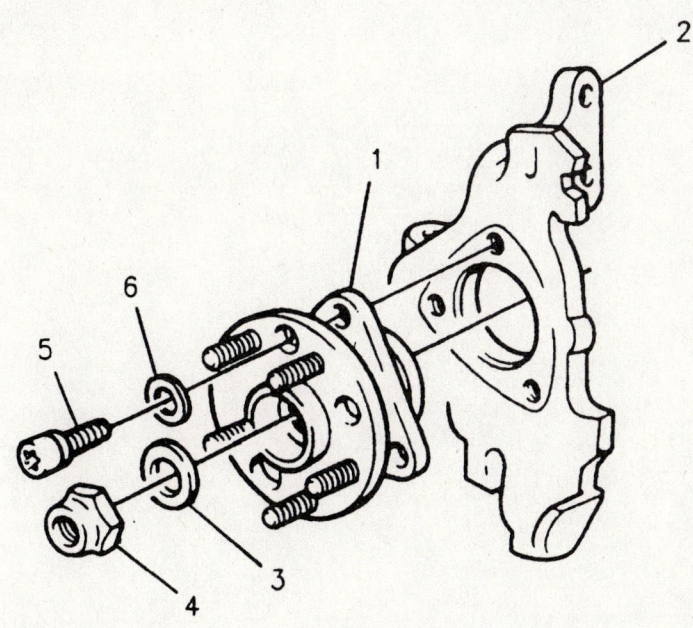

1   HUB AND BEARING ASSEMBLY
2   STEERING KNUCKLE
3   WASHER
4   DRIVE AXLE NUT — 260 N·m (192 LBS. FT.)
5   HUB AND BEARING RETAINING BOLT
6   WASHER

7922Z340

Exploded view of the front hub/bearing assembly

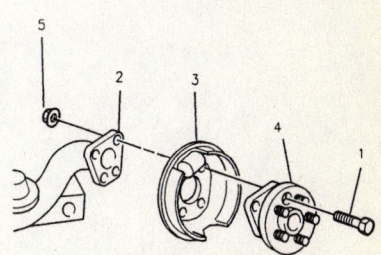

1   BOLT
2   REAR AXLE ASSEMBLY
3   BACKING PLATE
4   HUB AND BEARING ASSEMBLY
5   LOCKNUT

7922Z341

Hub and bearing components

- Hub/bearing assembly on the knuckle
- ABS wheel speed sensor, if equipped.
- Hub/bearing nuts. Tighten the nuts to 38 ft. lbs. (52 Nm).
- Brake drum
- Wheel. Tighten the nuts to 100 ft. lbs. (140 Nm).

DISC BRAKE

1. Before servicing the vehicle, refer to the precautions in the beginning of this section.

2. Remove or disconnect the following:
   - Wheel
   - Brake rotor

- Parking brake cable from the lever
- Wheel Speed Sensor (WSS)
- Hub/bearing assembly bolts from the knuckle
- Torx® bolts from the rear of the hub/bearing assembly
- Hub/bearing assembly from the backing plate

To install:

3. Install or connect the following:
   - Hub/bearing assembly to the backing plate. Tighten the Torx® bolts to 90 inch lbs. (10 Nm).
   - Hub/bearing assembly on the knuckle. Tighten the bolts to 70 ft. lbs. (95 Nm).
   - WSS and the parking brake cable

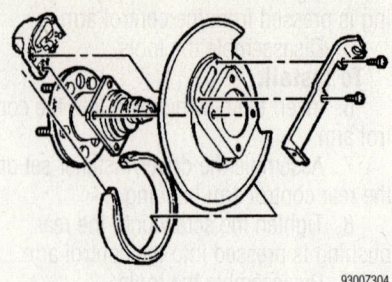

Rear wheel bearing assembly with disc brakes—1999–01 models

- Brake rotor
- Wheel assembly

GENERAL MOTORS CORPRATION—V-BODY

35

Cadillac-Catera

PRECAUTIONS

Before servicing any vehicle, please be sure to read all of the following precautions, which deal with personal safety, prevention of component damage, and important points to take into consideration when servicing a motor vehicle:

• Never open, service or drain the radiator or cooling system when the engine is hot, serious burns can occur from the steam and hot coolant.

• Observe all applicable safety precautions when working around fuel. Whenever servicing the fuel system, always work in a well-ventilated area. Do not allow fuel spray or vapors to come in contact with a spark, open flame or excessive heat (a hot drop light, for example). Keep a dry chemical fire extinguisher near the work area. Always keep fuel in a container specifically designed for fuel storage; also, always properly seal fuel containers to avoid the possibility of fire or explosion. Refer to the additional fuel system precautions later in this section.

• Fuel injection systems often remain pressurized, even after the engine has been turned **OFF**. The fuel system pressure must be relieved before disconnecting any fuel lines. Failure to do so may result in fire and/or personal injury.

• Brake fluid often contains polyglycol ethers and polyglycols. Avoid contact with the eyes and wash your hands thoroughly after handling brake fluid. If you do get brake fluid in your eyes, flush your eyes with clean, running water for 15 minutes. If eye irritation persists, or if you have taken brake fluid internally, seek medical assistance IMMEDIATELY.

• The EPA warns that prolonged contact with used engine oil may cause a number of skin disorders, including cancer! You should make every effort to minimize your exposure to used engine oil. Protective gloves should be worn when changing oil. Wash your hands and any other exposed skin areas as soon as possible after exposure to used engine oil. Soap and water, or waterless hand cleaner should be used.

• All new vehicles are now equipped with an air bag system. The system must be disabled before performing service on or around system components, steering column, instrument panel components, wiring and sensors. Failure to follow safety and disabling procedures could result in accidental air bag deployment, possible personal injury and unnecessary system repairs.

• Always wear safety goggles when working with, or around, the air bag system. When carrying a non-deployed air bag, be sure the bag and trim cover are pointed away from your body. When placing a non-deployed air bag on a work surface, always face the bag and trim cover upward, away from the surface. This will reduce the motion of the module if it is accidentally deployed. Refer to the additional air bag system precautions later in this section.

• Clean, high quality brake fluid from a sealed container is essential to the safe and proper operation of the brake system. You should always buy the correct type of brake fluid for your vehicle. If the brake fluid becomes contaminated, completely flush the system with new fluid. Never reuse any brake fluid. Any brake fluid that is removed from the system should be discarded. Also, do not allow any brake fluid to come in contact with a painted surface; it will damage the paint.

• Never operate the engine without the proper amount and type of engine oil; doing so WILL result in severe engine damage.

• Timing belt maintenance is extremely important! Many models utilize an interference-type, non-freewheeling engine. If the timing belt breaks, the valves in the cylinder head may strike the pistons, causing potentially serious (also time-consuming and expensive) engine damage. Refer to the maintenance interval charts in the front of this manual for the recommended replacement interval for the timing belt, and to the timing belt section for belt replacement and inspection.

• Disconnecting the negative battery cable on some vehicles may interfere with the functions of the on-board computer system(s) and may require the computer to undergo a relearning process once the negative battery cable is reconnected.

• When servicing drum brakes, only disassemble and assemble one side at a time, leaving the remaining side intact for reference.

ENGINE REPAIR

➡**Disconnecting the negative battery cable on some vehicles may interfere with the operation of the on board computer system. The computer may undergo a relearning process once the negative battery cable is reconnected.**

Ignition Timing

ADJUSTMENT

➡**The 3.0L DOHC engine used in the Catera utilizes a Distributorless Ignition System (DIS). No ignition timing adjustment is possible.**

Alternator

REMOVAL

1. Before servicing the vehicle, refer to the precautions in the beginning of this section.

2. Remove or disconnect the following:
   • Negative battery cable
   • Intake air resonator
   • Drive belt
   • Coolant heater, if equipped
   • Alternator cooling duct
   • Field coil terminal lead
   • Battery terminal lead
   • Upper mounting nut
   • Lower mounting nut
   • Lower mounting bolt
   • Upper mounting bolt by pushing the bolt through the alternator and bracket
   • Alternator

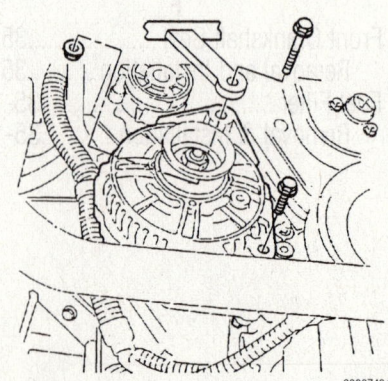

9306Z404

Alternator mounting hardware

INSTALLATION

1. Install or connect the following:
   • Alternator. Torque the lower nut to 26 ft. lbs. (35 Nm) and the upper nut to 30 ft. lbs. (40 Nm).
   • Cooling duct

- Field coil terminal. Torque the nut to 31 inch lbs. (4 Nm).
- Battery terminal lead. Torque the nut 71 inch lbs. (8 Nm).
- Cooling heater, if equipped
- Drive belt
- Intake air resonator
- Negative battery cable

2. Perform a charging system test and verify that the system is operating properly.

Engine Assembly

REMOVAL & INSTALLATION

1. Before servicing the vehicle, refer to the precautions in the beginning of this section.
2. Drain the cooling system.
3. Recover the A/C refrigerant.
4. Relieve the fuel system pressure.
5. Install a support fixture to the engine lifting eyes.

➡**Support the engine whenever the transmission is removed. The motor mounts are silicone filled and do not provide sufficient rigidity to support the engine with the transmission removed.**

6. Remove or disconnect the following:
- Battery
- Wiper arms
- Left and right air inlet grilles
- Hood
- Red, white and black wiring harness connectors
- Body ground cable
- Power supply wires at the battery cable end
- Power steering hoses
- Brake booster vacuum lines
- Intake plenum switchover valve
- Powertrain Control Module (PCM)

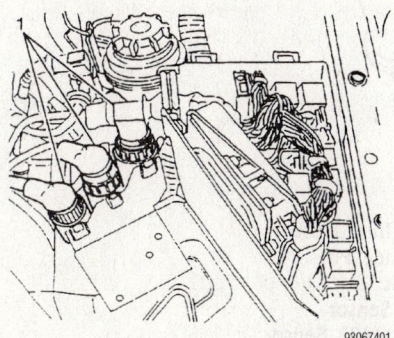

9306Z401

Red, white and black harness connectors (1)

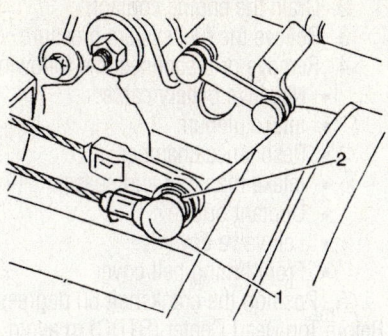

9306Z402

Accelerator (1) and cruise control (2) cables

- Relays and wiring harness from electrical center box
- Accelerator and cruise control cables from the throttle body
- Fuel lines from the fuel rail. Use a backup wrench to prevent damage to the fuel rail
- Fuel return hose
- Coolant hose from the throttle body
- Vacuum hose from the purge valve on the engine ventilation chamber
- Vacuum hose from the heater control valve
- Coolant reservoir hose from the coolant inlet pipe
- Coolant hoses from the heater core
- Heater hose quick-disconnects
- Intake air resonator
- Radiator
- Quick connects near the high pressure and low pressure fittings
- Refrigerant line from the A/C compressor and compressor bracket
- Splash shield
- A/C compressor electrical connector

➡**Support the engine whenever the transmission is removed. The motor mounts are silicone filled and do not provide sufficient rigidity to support the engine with the transmission removed.**

- Transmission

7. Attach a hoist to the engine lifting eyes. Raise the engine slightly and remove the engine support fixture.

8. Remove the engine mount nuts and lift the engine out of the vehicle. Raise the engine slowly after being certain all wiring, cables and hoses have been removed.

To install:

9. Install or connect the following:
- Engine by lowering it into the vehicle

- Engine mount. Torque the nuts to 41 ft. lbs. (55 Nm).
- Engine support fixture

10. Remove the chain hoist.

11. Install or connect the following:
- Transmission
- A/C compressor electrical connector
- Splash shield and tighten securely
- A/C compressor bracket. Torque the bolts to 71 inch lbs. (8 Nm).
- Refrigerant line to the compressor.
- Quick connects for the high and low pressure fittings
- Radiator
- Intake air resonator
- Heater hose quick connects
- Coolant hoses to the heater core
- Coolant reservoir hose to the coolant inlet pipe
- Vacuum hose to the heater control valve
- Vacuum hose for the purge valve on the engine ventilation chamber
- Coolant hose to the throttle body
- Fuel return and supply lines. Torque the lines to 11 ft. lbs. (15 Nm).
- Cruise control and accelerator cables to the throttle body
- Relays and wiring harness to the electrical center box
- PCM
- Brake booster vacuum lines
- Switchover valve on the intake plenum. Torque the fasteners to 71 inch lbs. (8 Nm).
- Power steering hoses to the steering pump. Torque the discharge hose fasteners to 21 ft. lbs. (28 Nm).
- Power supply wires at the battery cable ends
- Body ground cable
- Red, white and black wiring harness connectors
- Hood
- Left and right air inlet grilles
- Wiper arms
- Negative battery cable

12. Fill and bleed the power steering system.

13. Fill and bleed the coolant system.

➡**When refilling the coolant system add 2 crushed engine coolant supplement sealant pellets PN 3634621 into the reservoir.**

14. Recharge the A/C system and check for leaks.

15. Start the vehicle and inspect for leaks.

Water Pump

REMOVAL & INSTALLATION

1. Before servicing the vehicle, refer to the precautions in the beginning of this section.
2. Drain the coolant.
3. Remove or disconnect the following:
   - Negative battery cables
   - Resonance chamber
   - Front timing belt cover
   - Water pump

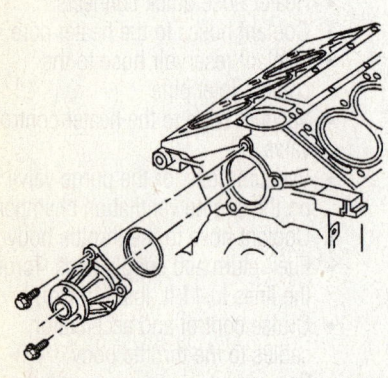

9300Z401

Exploded view of the water pump mounting

To install:

4. Clean the water pump mounting surface.
5. Install or connect the following:
   - New O-ring lubricated with coolant
   - Water pump. Torque the bolts to 18 ft. lbs. (21 Nm).
   - Front timing belt cover
   - Resonance chamber
   - Negative battery cable
6. Fill the cooling system through the reservoir tank.

➡**When refilling the cooling system, add 2 crushed engine coolant supplement sealant pellets PN 3634621 into the coolant reservoir.**

7. Start the vehicle and inspect the coolant systems for leaks and top off the reservoir as needed.

Cylinder Head

REMOVAL & INSTALLATION

1. Before servicing the vehicle, refer to the precautions in the beginning of this section.

2. Drain the engine coolant.
3. Relieve the fuel system pressure.
4. Remove or disconnect the following:
   - Negative battery cable
   - Intake plenum
   - Resonance chamber
   - Intake manifold and spacer
   - Coolant bridge
   - Left valve cover
   - Front timing belt cover
5. Position the crankshaft 60 degrees Before Top Dead Center (BTDC) to avoid contact between the valves and the pistons.
6. Remove or disconnect the following:

- Timing belt
- Timing belt tensioner bracket
7. Install the Camshaft Gear Holding tools Nos. J 42069-1 and J42069-2 on the camshaft sprockets.
8. Remove or disconnect the following:
   - Sprocket mounting bolts and sprockets
   - Water pump
   - Rear timing belt cover
   - Camshaft Position Sensor (CMP)
   - Drivers side exhaust camshaft
   - Coolant pipe/engine lift bracket to the cylinder head

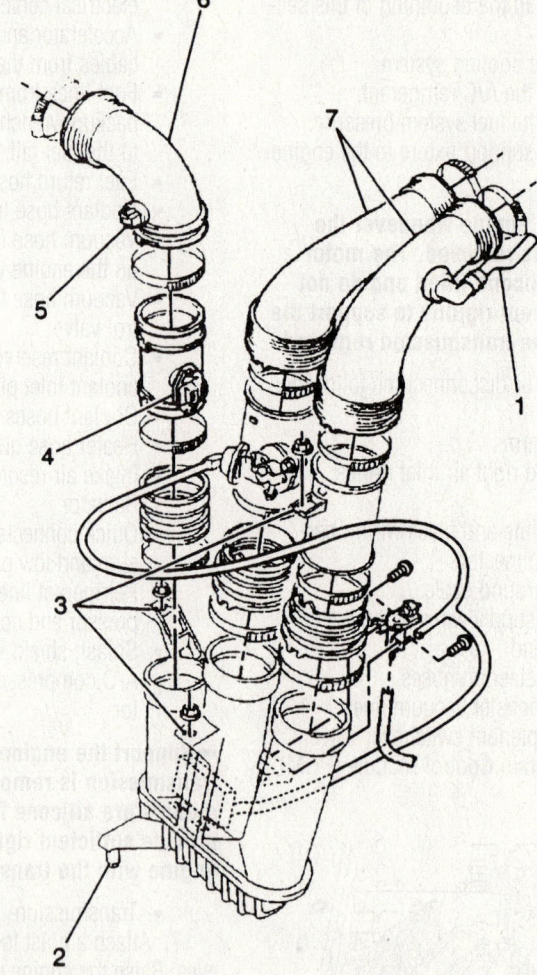

(1) Idle Air Control (IAC) Inlet Hose
(2) Resonance Chamber Guide Pin
(3) Resonance Chamber Nut
(4) Mass Air Flow (MAF) Sensor
(5) Intake Air Temperature (IAT) Sensor
(6) Resonance Chamber Air Intake Hose
(7) Intake Plenum Air Inlet Hose

79222Z406

Resonance chamber and related components

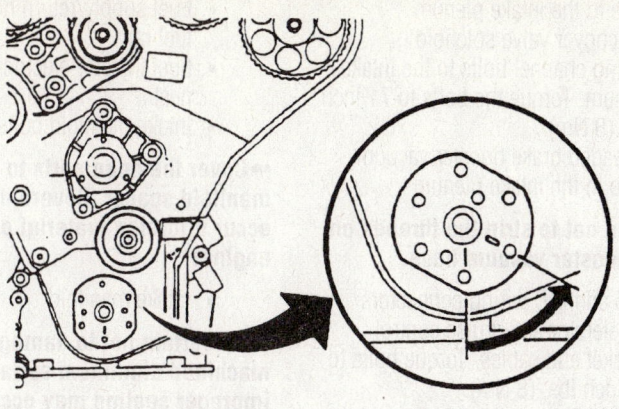

Before removing the timing belt, be sure to turn the crankshaft 60 degrees BTDC to avoid valve-to-piston contact and subsequent engine damage.

- Dipstick tube
- Upper radiator hose from the coolant pipe
- Coolant intake pipe
- Exhaust manifold from the cylinder head
- Wiring from the ignition coil pack if working on the left cylinder head
- Ignition coil pack and bracket if working on the left cylinder head
- Cylinder head bolts
- Cylinder head and discard the gasket

To install:

9. Clean and inspect the mating surface of the engine block and cylinder head.

10. Install or connect the following:
- New gasket with "OBEN/TOP" facing up and towards the front for the left side or towards the rear for the right side of the engine
- Cylinder head to the engine block

➡**Refer to Section 1 of this manual for the cylinder head torque sequence illustration. The illustration is located after the Torque Specification Chart.**

Proper head gasket installation position— left cylinder head

Proper head gasket installation position— right cylinder head

➡**Be sure to use new cylinder head bolts when installing the cylinder head. The old bolts have been stretched and are not reusable.**

- New cylinder head bolts. Tighten the bolts, in sequence, to 18 ft. lbs. (25 Nm).

11. Using a torque angle meter, tighten the cylinder head bolts, in sequence, using 4 steps:
  a. Step 1: 90 degrees
  b. Step 2: 90 degrees
  c. Step 3: 90 degrees
  d. Step 4: 15 degrees

12. Install or connect the following:
- Ignition coil pack and bracket to the cylinder head
- Ignition coil pack electrical connector
- Exhaust manifold using a new gasket
- Coolant pipe with new O-rings
- Upper radiator hose to the coolant pipe
- Dipstick tube and engine lift bracket
- Engine lift bracket. Torque the bolt to 15 ft. lbs. (20 Nm).

➡**Make certain that the engine lift bracket bolt passes through all attaching components.**

13. Install or connect the following:
- Drivers side exhaust camshaft
- CMP sensor and electrical connector
- Rear timing belt cover
- Water pump. Torque the bolts to 18 ft. lbs. (21 Nm).
- Camshaft gears
- Timing belt tensioner bracket
- Timing belt
- Front timing belt cover
- Left valve cover with new O-rings and gaskets. Torque the fasteners to 71 inch lbs. (8 Nm).
- Coolant bridge
- Intake manifold spacer. Torque the bolts in a spiral direction, starting from the inside and working outward, to 15 ft. lbs. (20 Nm).
- Intake manifold
- Resonance chamber
- Intake plenum
- New oil filter
- Negative battery cable

14. Drain and refill the engine oil.
15. Refill the cooling system.
16. Start the engine and inspect for leakage. Repair as needed.
17. Inspect all fluid levels and top off, if necessary.

Intake Manifold Assembly

REMOVAL & INSTALLATION

Intake Plenum

1. Before servicing the vehicle, refer to the precautions in the beginning of this section.

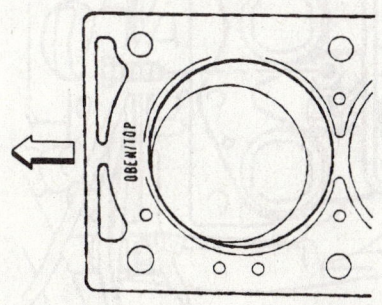

Proper head gasket installation position— left cylinder head

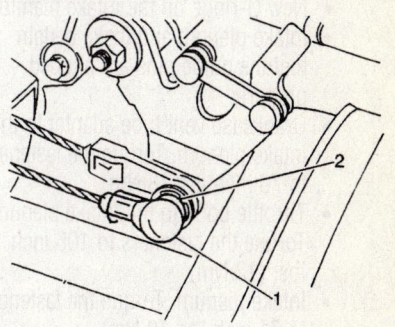

Disconnect the accelerator and cruise control cables

Timing belt service is covered in Section 4 of this manual

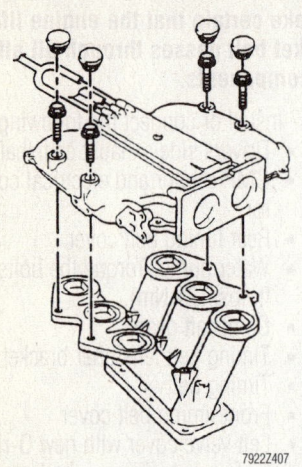

Intake plenum mounting bolt locations

2. Remove or disconnect the following:
   - Negative battery cable
   - Idle Air Control (IAC) inlet hose
   - Intake plenum air inlet hoses from the throttle body
   - Accelerator and cruise control cables from the throttle body with the bracket
   - Throttle Position Sensor (TPS) and IAC electrical connections
   - Threaded brake booster vacuum hose from the intake plenum
   - Wiring channel bolts from the intake plenum
   - Electrical connection and vacuum hose from the intake plenum switchover valve solenoid
   - Vacuum hose from the fuel pressure regulator
   - Four intake plenum caps and bolts
   - Throttle body from the intake plenum
   - Crankcase vent tube adapter and cover from the intake plenum
   - Intake plenum and O-rings

To install:

3. Install or connect the following:
   - New O-rings on the intake manifold
   - Intake plenum and make certain that the guide pins are aligned properly
   - Crankcase vent tube adapter to the intake plenum. Torque the fastener to 70 inch lbs. (8 Nm).
   - Throttle body to the intake plenum. Torque the fasteners to 106 inch lbs. (12 Nm).
   - Intake plenum. Torque the fasteners to 71 inch lbs. (8 Nm).
   - Caps on the bolts
   - Vacuum hose to the fuel pressure regulator
   - Electrical connector and vacuum

hose to the intake plenum switchover valve solenoid
   - Wiring channel bolts to the intake plenum. Torque the bolts to 71 inch lbs. (8 Nm).
   - Threaded brake booster vacuum hose to the intake plenum

➡ **Be certain not to strip the threads on the brake booster vacuum hose.**

   - TPS and IAC wiring connectors
   - Accelerator and cruise control bracket and cables. Torque bolts to 71 inch lbs. (8 Nm).
   - Intake plenum air inlet hoses to the throttle body
   - Negative battery cable.

4. Start the engine and check for proper performance.

Intake Manifold

➡ **The fuel injector connectors are numbered. Be sure to attach the correct connector to the proper fuel injector when installing the intake manifold.**

1. Before servicing the vehicle, refer to the precautions in the beginning of this section.
2. Remove or disconnect the following:
   - Negative battery cable
   - Intake plenum
   - Relieve the fuel system pressure

   - Fuel supply/return hoses from the fuel rail
   - Fuel injector electrical harness connector
   - Intake manifold bolts

➡ **Cover the open ports to the intake manifold spacer. Severe damage may occur if foreign material enters the engine.**

   - Intake manifold

➡ **Be certain not to damage the machined aluminum surfaces or improper sealing may occur during installation.**

   - Clean the intake manifold mating surface with a non abrasive solvent
3. Fill the cooling system.
4. Start the engine and check for leaks.

To install:

5. Install or connect the following:
   - New gaskets (if equipped) on the intake manifold spacer
   - Intake manifold. Torque the bolts to 15 ft. lbs. (20 Nm).
   - Fuel injector electrical harness connector
   - Fuel supply/return hoses. Torque the hoses to 11 ft. lbs. (15 Nm).
   - Intake plenum
   - Negative battery cable.
6. Start the vehicle and inspect for leaks.

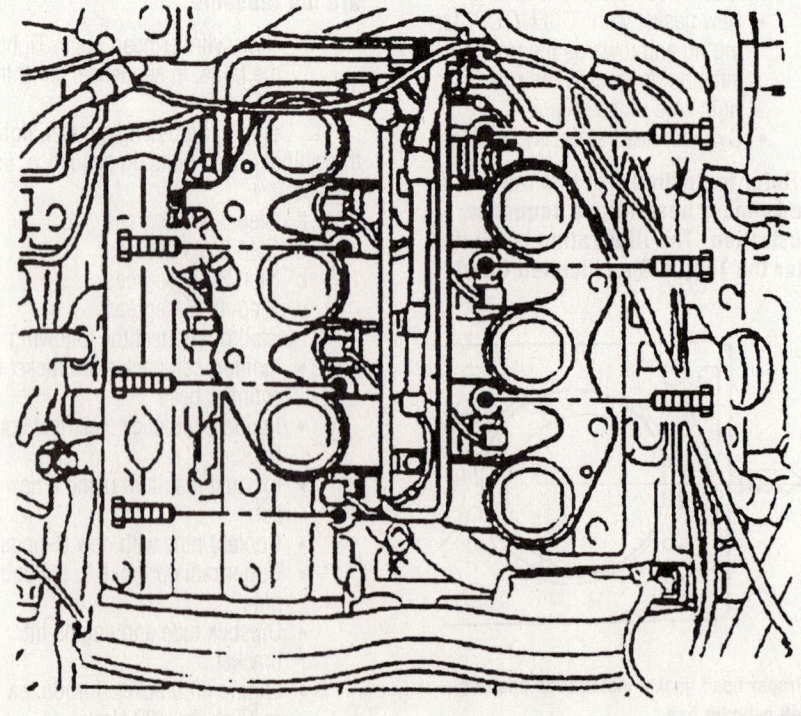

Intake manifold mounting bolt locations

Exhaust Manifold

REMOVAL & INSTALLATION

Left Side

1. Before servicing the vehicle, refer to the precautions in the beginning of this section.
2. Remove or disconnect the following:
   - Engine assembly
   - Exhaust manifold lower/upper heat shields
   - Secondary Air Injection (AIR) pipe from the exhaust manifold
   - Coolant pipe and engine lift bracket from the cylinder head
   - Oil level indicator tube
   - Exhaust manifold
3. Clean the gasket mating surfaces.

To install:

4. Install or connect the following:
   - New gasket
   - Exhaust manifold. Torque the nuts to 15 ft. lbs. (20 Nm).
   - Oil level indicator tube. Torque the bolt to 15 ft. lbs. (20 Nm).
   - Engine lifting bracket and coolant pipe. Torque the bolt to 15 ft. lbs. (20 Nm).
   - Air injection pipe to the exhaust manifold. Lubricate the pipe bolts with a high temperature anti-seize compound
   - AIR pipe bolts. Torque the bolts to 15 ft. lbs. (20 Nm).
   - Exhaust manifold upper/lower heat shields. Torque the bolts to 71 inch lbs. (8 Nm) lubricated with high temperature anti-seize compound
   - Engine assembly
5. Start the vehicle and inspect for any leaks.
6. Check and top off any fluid levels as needed.

Right Side

1. Before servicing the vehicle, refer to the precautions in the beginning of this section.
2. Remove or disconnect the following:
   - Transmission assembly
   - Coolant intake pipe
3. Remove or disconnect the following:
   - Exhaust manifold lower heat shield bolts
   - Exhaust manifold lower rear bolts

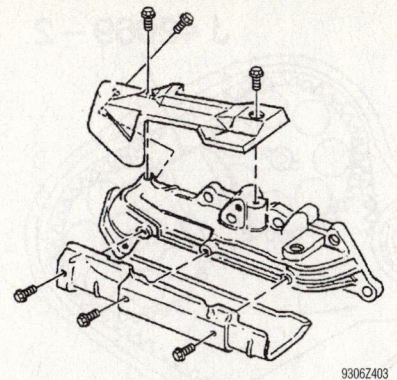

93062403

Exhaust manifold heat shield bolts

   - Exhaust manifold upper rear heat shield bolt
   - Catalytic converter nuts from the exhaust manifold
   - Drive belt tensioner
   - Exhaust manifold front two nuts
   - Exhaust manifold upper heat shield bolts

➡**It is not necessary to remove the upper heat shield.**

   - Secondary Air Injection (AIR) injection pipe from the exhaust manifold
   - Exhaust manifold
4. Clean the gasket mating surfaces.

To install:

5. Install or connect the following:
   - Exhaust manifold and the 3 upper nuts. Torque the nuts to 15 ft. lbs. (20 Nm).
   - AIR injection pipe to the exhaust manifold. Torque the bolts to 15 ft. lbs. (20 Nm) lubricated with high temperature anti-seize compound.
   - Upper heat shield bolts. Torque the bolts to 71 inch lbs. (8 Nm) lubricated with high temperature anti-seize compound.
   - Exhaust manifold upper heat shield bolts. Torque the bolts to 71 inch lbs. (8 Nm).
   - Exhaust manifold lower front nuts. Torque the nuts to 15 ft. lbs. (20 Nm).
   - Drive belt tensioner
   - Catalytic converter nuts. Torque the nuts to 15 ft. lbs. (20 Nm)
   - Exhaust manifold lower heat shield. Torque the bolts to 71 inch lbs. (8 Nm) lubricated with high temperature anti-seize compound.
   - Coolant intake pipe
   - Transmission assembly
6. Start the vehicle and inspect for leaks.

7. Inspect and top off any fluid levels as needed.

Front Crankshaft Seal

REMOVAL AND INSTALLATION

1. Before servicing the vehicle, refer to the precautions in the beginning of this section.
2. Remove or disconnect the following:
   - Timing belt
   - Crankshaft gear
3. Drill a small shallow hole into the steel ring of the seal.

➡**Use caution so as not to damage the area around and behind the seal.**

4. Insert a self-tapping screw.
5. Using pliers, pull the front crankshaft seal out.

To install:

6. Install or connect the following:
   - New seal coated with grease using a Seal Installer tool.
   - Crankshaft gear
   - Timing belt

Camshaft

REMOVAL & INSTALLATION

1. Before servicing the vehicle, refer to the precautions in the beginning of this section.
2. Remove or disconnect the following:
   - Negative battery cable
   - Intake plenum
   - Resonance chamber
   - Valve cover
   - Front timing belt cover
   - Timing belt
3. Rotate the crankshaft 60 degrees counterclockwise Before Top Dead Center (BTDC) to prevent valve/piston contact.
4. Use a Camshaft Locking tool to hold the camshaft gears in place and loosen the camshaft gear bolt.
5. Remove or disconnect the following:
   - Locking tool from the gears
   - Camshaft gear bolt
   - Camshaft gear. Be certain that the camshaft is not under load from the lifters.
6. Gradually loosen the camshaft bearing cap bolts sequentially, starting in the center and working outward in a spiral. Note the identification marks on the caps.

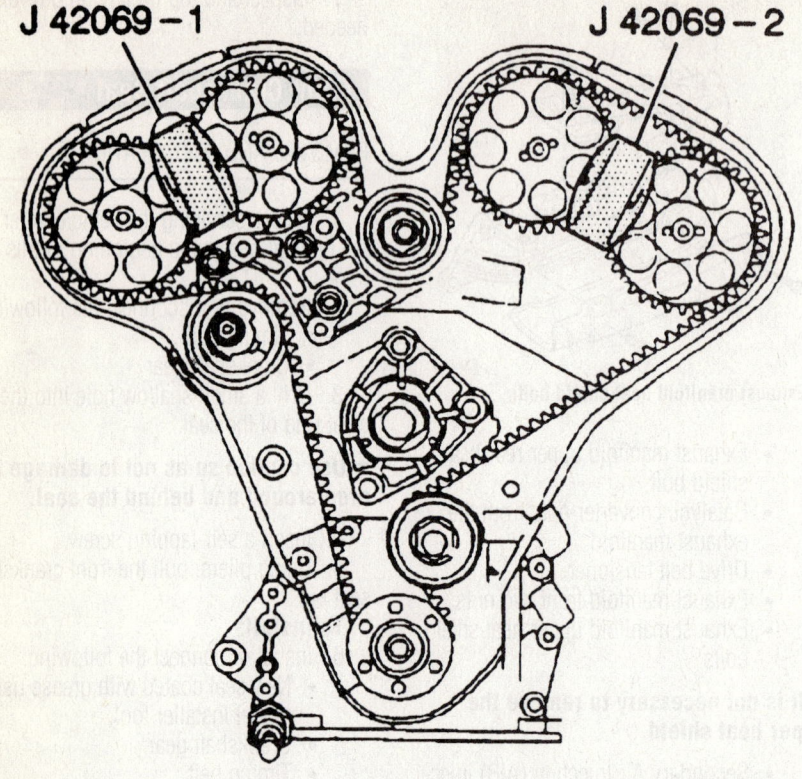

7922Z409

Camshaft gear holding tools must be installed before attempting to remove the gears from the camshafts

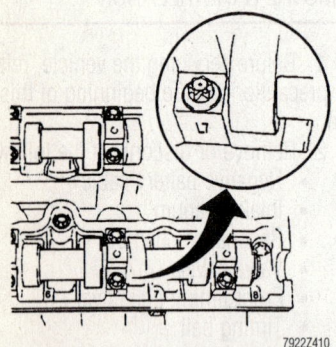

79222410

The camshaft bearing caps have identification marks stamped on the side

7. Remove the camshaft from the cylinder head.

To install:

8. Lubricate the camshaft lobes, lifters and bearing journals with pre-lube.

9. Install the camshaft to the cylinder head.

10. To reduce the lifter load, position the pin on the front of the camshaft as follows:
- 1 o'clock position: right exhaust camshaft
- 11 o'clock position: right intake camshaft

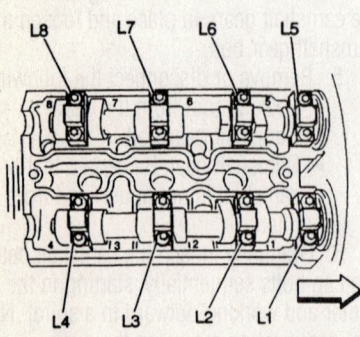

7922Z411

Camshaft bearing cap locations-right cylinder head

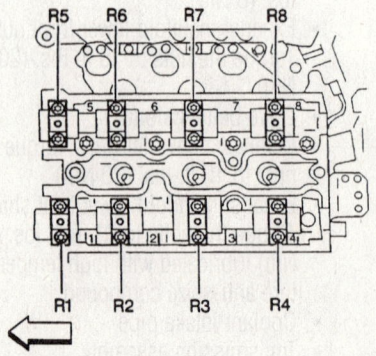

7922Z412

Camshaft bearing cap locations—left cylinder head

- 12 o'clock position: left exhaust camshaft
- 7 o'clock position: left intake camshaft

11. Place a small amount of Locktite® on the edge of the front bearing cap to ensure a good seal between the cap and surface of the cylinder head. Do not allow the sealer to get into the oil journal of the cap.

✳✳ WARNING

The bearing caps must be installed in their original positions.

12. Install or connect the following:
- Camshaft bearing caps. Torque the bolts in sequence starting in the center and working outwards to 71 inch lbs. (8 Nm).
- Camshaft seal lubricated with engine oil

➡**Make certain that the camshaft seal is fully seated.**

- Camshaft gear. Tighten the new bolt to 37 ft. lbs. (50 Nm), plus a 60 degree turn, plus a 15 degree turn using a torque angle meter.

✳✳ WARNING

A new camshaft gear bolt must be installed. The required tightening method will stretch the bolt making the original bolt unusable.

➡**Use a camshaft gear locking tool to secure the camshaft and gear while tightening the bolt.**

- Timing belt and adjust as needed
- Front timing belt cover
- Valve cover
- Intake plenum
- Negative battery cable

13. Start the vehicle and verify the engine is running properly.

Valve Lash

ADJUSTMENT

➡**No adjustment is possible.**

Starter Motor

REMOVAL & INSTALLATION

1. Before servicing the vehicle, refer to the precautions in the beginning of this section.

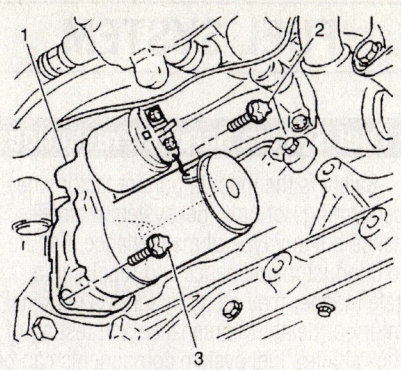

Remove the starter motor and bolts

2. Remove or disconnect the following:
   - Negative battery cable
   - Starter terminal nuts
   - Washers
   - Battery cable terminal lead
   - Starter solenoid terminal lead
   - Right hand catalytic converter
   - Right side engine mount nuts
   - Resonance chamber to the throttle body ducts

3. Install a Engine Support Fixture J 28467-A and an Adapter J 28467-450 to the right side of the engine.

4. Raise the engine approximately 1.5 inches (38mm) to gain access to the starter motor bolts.

5. Remove or disconnect the following:
   - Engine mount from the bracket and cradle
   - Engine mount bracket bolts and reposition the bracket
   - Starter bolts
   - Starter motor

To install:

6. Install or connect the following:
   - Starter motor. Torque the bolts to 44 ft. lbs. (60 Nm).
   - Engine mount to the bracket and front crossmember

7. Lower the engine into position and make certain that the mount locator tap is fully seated in the front crossmember slot.

8. Remove the special tools from the engine.

9. Install or connect the following:
   - Engine mount. Torque the upper nut to 30 ft. lbs. (40 Nm) and the lower nut to 41 ft. lbs. (55 Nm).
   - Resonance chamber to the throttle body ducts
   - Catalytic converter. Torque the bolt to 25 ft. lbs. (34 Nm).
   - Battery cable terminal lead
   - Starter solenoid terminal lead

   - Washers and nuts. Torque the battery cable nut to 115 inch lbs. (13 Nm) and the starter solenoid nut to 35 inch lbs. (4 Nm).
   - Negative battery cable

10. Perform a charging system test and verify the system is working properly.

Oil Pan

REMOVAL & INSTALLATION

1. Before servicing the vehicle, refer to the precautions in the beginning of this section.

2. Drain the engine oil.

3. Remove or disconnect the following:
   - Negative battery cable
   - Splash shield
   - Oil level sensor wiring C-clip from the oil pan housing
   - Oil pan from the oil pan housing
   - Oil level sensor from the oil pan.

To install:

4. Clean the oil pan and housing sealing surfaces with a non-abrasive cleaner.

5. Install or connect the following:
   - Oil level sensor on the oil pan. Tighten the bolts just until fully seated.
   - New oil pan gasket
   - New O-ring on the oil level sensor wire connector
   - Oil level sensor wire connector to the oil pan housing C-clip
   - Oil pan to the housing. Torque the bolts 71 inch lbs. (8 Nm).
   - Oil level sensor electrical connector
   - Splash shield. Torque the bolts until they are fully seated.
   - Negative battery cable

6. Refill the engine oil.

7. Start the vehicle and check for leaks.

Oil Pump

REMOVAL & INSTALLATION

1. Before servicing the vehicle, refer to the precautions in the beginning of this section.

2. Drain the engine oil.

3. Drain the engine coolant.

4. Discharge and recover the A/C system.

5. Remove or disconnect the following:
   - Negative battery cable
   - Resonance chamber

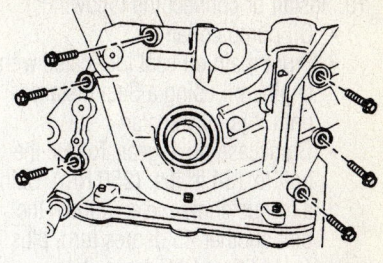

Oil pump mounting bolt locations

   - Front timing belt cover
   - Timing belt
   - Rear timing belt cover
   - A/C compressor
   - A/C compressor and power steering pump bracket and position it out of the way of the oil pump housing
   - Lower alternator mounting bolt and loosen the upper mounting bolt- then, position the alternator aside.
   - Oil pan
   - Upper oil pan housing
   - Crankcase drive gear by securing the gear with a Crank Hub Holding tool J 42065 and Hub Torx Socket J 42098.
   - Oil pump
   - Front main oil seal and collar

To install:

6. Clean the oil pump, oil pan and engine block mounting surface with a non-abrasive cleaner and be sure to remove all old gasket material.

7. Coat the pump side of the oil pump gasket with a thin layer of sealant. Do not cover or restrict the gasket openings with sealant.

8. Install or connect the following:
   - New oil pump gasket
   - Oil pump by aligning the guide pins and coating the bolts with sealant. Torque the bolts to 71 inch lbs. (8 Nm).
   - Timing belt idler pulley and washer for camshafts No. 3 and 4. Torque the pulley bolt to 30 ft. lbs. (40 Nm) to ensure compression of the of the oil pump gasket.

➡**Do not install the timing belt at this time.**

   - Alternator. Torque the upper and lower bolts to 30 ft. lbs. (40 Nm).
   - Oil pump bolts. Torque the bolts, in sequence, to 80 inch lbs. (9 Nm).

9. Remove the timing belt idler pulley and washer from camshafts No. 3 and 4

Refer to Section 1 for engine rebuilding specifications

10. Install or connect the following:
- Oil pump collar
- Front main oil seal lubricated with engine oil using a Seal Installer until it is fully seated
- Crankcase drive gear. Torque the bolt to 184 ft. lbs. (250 Nm). Using a torque angle meter, tighten the bolt another 45 degree turn, plus an additional 15 degree turn.

➡**Make certain that the crankshaft drive gear does not turn during the tightening procedure.**

- Upper oil pan housing
- Oil pan
- A/C compressor and power steering pump bracket. Torque the fasteners to 30 ft. lbs. (40 Nm).
- A/C compressor
- Rear timing belt cover
- Timing belt
- Front timing belt cover
- Resonance chamber
- Negative battery cable

11. Fill the engine oil.
12. Fill the coolant.
13. Recharge the A/C system.
14. Start the vehicle and checks for leaks.
15. Check all fluid levels and top off, if necessary.

Rear Main Seal

REMOVAL & INSTALLATION

1. Before servicing the vehicle, refer to the precautions in the beginning of this section.
2. Remove or disconnect the following:
- Negative battery cable.
- Flywheel
3. Center punch the steel ring of the rear main seal.
4. Drill a small hole into the steel ring.

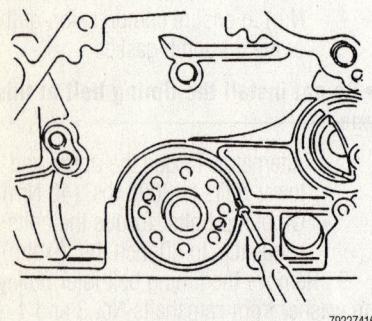

7922Z416

Thread a self-tapping screw into the metal part of the seal and remove the seal

➡**Make certain not to damage any engine components on the opposite side of the seal.**

5. Install a small self tapping screw.
6. Remove the rear main oil seal.
To install:
7. Clean all sealing surfaces with a non-abrasive cleaner.
8. Install or connect the following:
- New seal lubricated with chassis grease
- Rear main oil seal using an Oil Seal Installer tool J 42067
- Flexplate. Torque the new bolts to 48 ft. lbs. (65 Nm), plus a 30 degree turn, plus a 15 degree turn.
- Negative battery cable

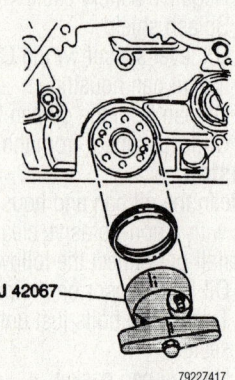

J 42067

7922Z417

Press the rear main seal into position using a threaded seal installer like J 42067

Piston and Ring

POSITIONING

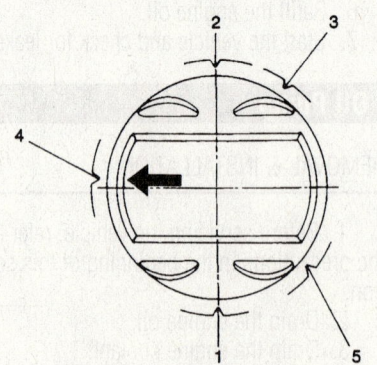

(1) 1st Compression Ring End Gap Location
(2) 2nd Compression Ring End Gap Location
(3) Oil Control Ring Upper Ring End Gap Location
(4) Oil Control Ring Spacer End Gap Location
(5) Oil Control Ring Lower Ring End Gap Location

7922AG55

Piston ring end-gap spacing—GM 3.0L engine

FUEL SYSTEM

Fuel System Service Precautions

Safety is the most important factor when performing not only fuel system maintenance but any type of maintenance. Failure to conduct maintenance and repairs in a safe manner may result in serious personal injury or death. Maintenance and testing of the vehicle's fuel system components can be accomplished safely and effectively by adhering to the following rules and guidelines.

- To avoid the possibility of fire and personal injury, always disconnect the negative battery cable unless the repair or test procedure requires that battery voltage be applied.
- Always relieve the fuel system pressure prior to disconnecting any fuel system component (injector, fuel rail, pressure regulator, etc.), fitting or fuel line connection. Exercise extreme caution whenever relieving fuel system pressure, to avoid exposing skin, face and eyes to fuel spray. Please be advised that fuel under pressure may penetrate the skin or any part of the body that it contacts.
- Always place a shop towel or cloth around the fitting or connection prior to loosening to absorb any excess fuel due to spillage. Ensure that all fuel spillage (should it occur) is quickly removed from engine surfaces. Ensure that all fuel soaked cloths or towels are deposited into a suitable waste container.
- Always keep a dry chemical (Class B) fire extinguisher near the work area.
- Do not allow fuel spray or fuel vapors to come into contact with a spark or open flame.
- Always use a backup wrench when loosening and tightening fuel line connection fittings. This will prevent unnecessary stress and torsion to fuel line piping. Always follow the proper torque specifications.
- Always replace worn fuel fitting O-rings with new. Do not substitute fuel hose or equivalent, where fuel pipe is installed.

Fuel System Pressure

RELIEVING

1. Before servicing the vehicle, refer to the precautions in the beginning of this section.

2. Loosen the fuel filler cap to relieve the tank pressure.

3. Remove or disconnect the following:
- Negative battery cable
- Intake manifold top cover

4. Install a Fuel Pressure Gauge to the fuel pressure fitting. Wrap a shop towel around the fitting while installing the gauge.

5. Connect a bleed hose into an approved container and open the valve to bleed the system.

6. Close the valve and disconnect the gauge.

7. Drain any remaining fuel from the gauge into the approved container.

Fuel Filter

REMOVAL & INSTALLATION

1. Before servicing the vehicle, refer to the precautions in the beginning of this section.

2. Loosen the fuel filler cap to relieve pressure in the tank.

3. Relieve the fuel system pressure.

4. Remove or disconnect the following:
- Fuel line attaching bolts and loosen the filter retaining strap
- Fuel filter from the bracket

To install:

5. Clean the bolts and fittings on bolt fuel lines.

6. Install or connect the following:
- Filter in the retaining strap making certain that the flow is in the proper direction as indicated on the filter
- Bolts to the fuel line fittings
- Fuel filter bracket mounting bolt
- Fuel filler cap

7. Crank the engine for a few seconds and check for leakage. If the engine starts, turn it off and repair the leak.

Fuel Pump

REMOVAL & INSTALLATION

1. Before servicing the vehicle, refer to the precautions in the beginning of this section.

2. Relieve the fuel system pressure.

3. Drain the fuel tank.

4. Remove or disconnect the following:
- Negative battery cable
- Fuel tank
- Spring loaded clamp around the tank boot

- Fuel tank sending unit wiring harness

➡**The fuel pump assembly may spring up from its position. The reservoir bucket on the assembly is full of fuel. Tip the assembly slightly so the float is not damaged during removal.**

- Fuel pump from the tank using a Fuel Tank Sender Wrench J 42219
- Lip seal from the cover by sliding it downward, past the reservoir and over the float arm and discard it

5. Drain the remaining fuel from the reservoir into an approved container.

To install:

6. Install or connect the following:
- New lip seal lubricated with engine oil
- Lip seal over the float arm
- Lip seal over the reservoir and onto the cover
- Fuel pump assembly into the fuel tank

7. Seat the lip seal properly into the fuel tank opening.

➡**Be sure to align the hole on the module with the mark on the fuel tank.**

8. Install or connect the following:
- Spring loaded clamp. Tighten the locknut by using a Fuel Tank Sender Wrench J 42219 to 37 ft. lbs. (50 Nm).
- Fuel tank to the vehicle
- Fuel tank sending unit wiring harness
- Negative battery cable

9. Refill the fuel tank.

10. Start the vehicle and inspect for leaks.

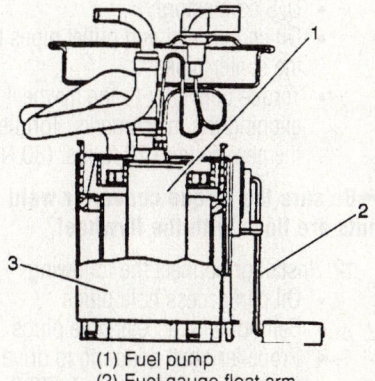

(1) Fuel pump
(2) Fuel gauge float arm
(3) Fuel reservoir

79222419

Fuel pump module components

Fuel Injector

REMOVAL & INSTALLATION

✳✳ CAUTION

Remove the fuel rail assembly carefully to prevent damage to the injector electrical connector terminals and spray tips. Support the fuel rail after it is removed in order to avoid damaging the fuel rail components. Cap the fittings and plug the holes when servicing the fuel system to prevent debris from entering open ports.

Fuel injection systems often remain pressurized, even after the engine has been turned **OFF**. The fuel system pressure must be relieved before disconnecting any fuel lines. Failure to do so may result in fire and/or personal injury.

1. Before servicing the vehicle, refer to the precautions in the beginning of this section.

2. Relieve fuel system pressure.

3. Remove or disconnect the following:
- Negative battery cable
- Intake plenum
- Fuel rail supply and return lines and move them away from the fuel rail
- Fuel injector electrical connectors
- Harness from the fuel rail
- Fuel rail attaching bolts from the intake manifold
- Fuel pressure regulator vacuum lines
- Locking tabs on the fuel rail
- Injector out of the intake manifold
- Fuel rail assembly
- Injectors from the fuel rail and discard the O-rings

To install:

4. Install or connect the following:
- New O-rings lubricated with engine oil
- Injectors to the fuel rail with new retainer clips.

➡**Make certain that the injectors are aligned properly by orientating the electrical connector perpendicular to the center line of the crankshaft.**

- Fuel rail to the intake manifold. Torque the bolt to 89 inch lbs. (10 Nm).
- Fuel pressure regulator vacuum line

- Fuel injector electrical connectors
- Harness to the fuel rail
- Fuel supply/return lines to the fuel rail. Torque the fasteners to 13 ft. lbs. (17 Nm).
- Fuel line bracket. Torque the bolts to 37 ft. lbs. (50 Nm).
- Intake plenum. Torque the bolts to 71 inch lbs. (8 Nm).
- Negative battery cable

5. Crank the engine several times to pressurize the system.

6. Check for leaks and repair, if necessary.

DRIVE TRAIN

Transmission Assembly

REMOVAL & INSTALLATION

1. Before servicing the vehicle, refer to the precautions in the beginning of this section.

2. Remove or disconnect the following:

- Negative battery cable
- Shift lever rod from the transmission
- Propeller shaft coupling bolts
- Propeller shaft coupling from the drive flange using a prybar.
- Access holes plugs from the oil pan and bell housing

➡ Mark the flywheel to the torque converter to ease the installation procedure.

- Flywheel to torque converter bolts
- Oil cooler inlet and outlet pipes
- Oxygen (O2S) sensor connections
- Catalytic converters
- Transmission housing to oil pan bolts

3. Support the transmission.

4. Remove or disconnect the following:

- Transmission crossmember to mount nuts
- Transmission to crossmember to body bolts and the crossmember

5. Lower the transmission to gain access to the upper housing bolts.

6. Remove or disconnect the following:

- Vent hose
- Electrical connector from the transmission control selector switch
- Electrical connector from the adapter case

- Electrical connector from the main case
- Electrical connector from the transmission speed sensor
- Upper housing bolts by properly supporting the front of the engine
- Transmission

To install:

The transmission fluid cooler and lines must be flushed out prior to installing a new or reconditioned transmission.

7. Clean the bolt holes in the engine block with a 12 x 1.75mm tap.

8. Apply thread locking compound to the transmission-to-engine mounting bolts.

9. Install or connect the following:

- Transmission. Torque the transmission to engine bolts to 44 ft. lbs. (60 Nm).
- Electrical connector to the transmission control selector switch
- Electrical connector to the adapter case
- Electrical connector to the main case
- Electrical connector to the speed sensor
- Vent hose
- Crossmember. Torque the bolts to 33 ft. lbs. (45 Nm).
- Crossmember to mount. Torque the nuts to 15 ft. lbs. (20 Nm).

10. Remove the transmission support.

11. Install or connect the following:

- Transmission housing to oil pan bolts. Torque the bolts to 15 ft. lbs. (20 Nm).
- Catalytic converters
- O2S connectors
- Oil cooler inlet and outlet pipes to the center pipes
- Torque converter to the flywheel by aligning the matchmarks. Torque the new bolts to 22 ft. lbs. (30 Nm).

➡ Be sure the torque converter weld nuts are flush with the flywheel.

12. Install or connect the following:

- Oil pan access hole plugs
- Bell housing access hole plugs
- Propeller shaft coupling to drive flange. Torque the bolts to 70 ft. lbs. (90 Nm).
- Shift lever rod to the transmission
- Negative battery cable

13. Adjust the shift lever rod as follows:
    a. Place the shift control lever in the **P**.

b. Loosen the adjusting bolt on the rod.

c. Hold the selector lever on the transmission toward the rear stop to eliminate any free-play.

d. Tighten the adjusting bolt to 71 inch lbs. (8 Nm).

14. Refill the transmission. Tighten the plug to 33 ft. lbs. (45 Nm).

15. Start the vehicle and check for leaks. Be sure the vehicle will only start in the **P** and **N** positions.

Halfshaft

REMOVAL & INSTALLATION

1. Before servicing the vehicle, refer to the precautions in the beginning of this section.

2. Place the gear selector in **N**.

3. Remove or disconnect the following:

- Rear wheel
- Drive axle flange bolts. To prevent the outer hub from turning, install a Wheel Hub Flange Holding Adapter J42066 to the hub.
- Outer end of the drive axle from the wheel bearing hub inner flange by using a Drive Axle Separator tool J 42071.

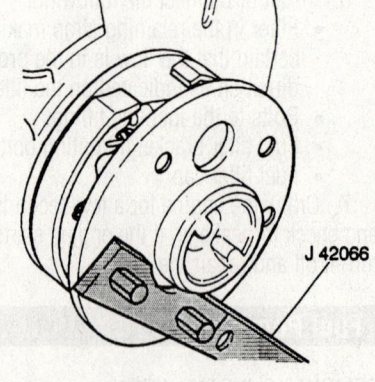

79222420

Prevent the outer hub from turning by installing a tool such as Hub Holding tool J 42066

➡ **Make certain that the drive axle separator tool is properly aligned to the differential and drive axle. The tool is clearly marked "Differential Side". If installed incorrectly, damage to the Anti-lock Brake System (ABS) sensor reluctor ring is possible.**

- Halfshaft

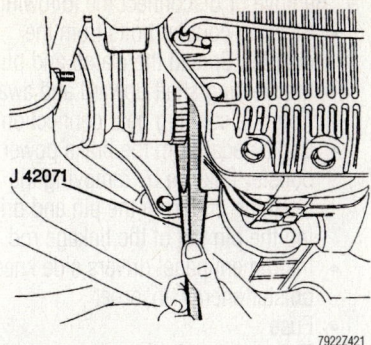

Pry the halfshaft out of the differential using tool J 42071

To install:

4. Lubricate the splined portion of the halfshaft and the sealing surfaces with differential oil.

5. Install or connect the following:
- Outer end of the halfshaft into the differential bore by aligning the splines.

➡ **If necessary use a soft faced tool, such as a rubber mallet, to seat the halfshaft fully in the differential bore.**

- Opposite end of the halfshaft into the wheel bearing hub inner flange
- Bolts to the drive axle flange. Torque the bolts to 37 ft. lbs. (50 Nm). Use a Wheel Hub Adapter tool J 42066 to hold the outer hub from turning.
- Rear wheel

6. Road test the vehicle.

Pinion Seal

REMOVAL & INSTALLATION

1. Before servicing the vehicle, refer to the precautions in the beginning of this section.

2. Place the transmission in **N**.

3. Remove or disconnect the following:
- Underbody heat shields
- Bolts from the propeller shaft center bearing bracket
- Propeller shaft from the front propeller shaft coupling
- Hardware and slide the front section of the shaft rearward to clear the coupling
- Shaft
- Propeller shaft from the rear propeller shaft coupling

- Hardware and slide the propeller shaft away from the coupling

4. Mark the position of the gear yoke, gear and nut for correct bearing preload.

5. Remove the pinion seal from the rear axle housing by using a blunt chisel to drive the seal out.

6. Inspect the pinion seal surface of the yoke for damage.

7. Inspect the housing bore for burrs.

To install:

8. Apply lubricant to the outer diameter of the gear yoke and the outer lip of the new seal.

9. Install or connect the following:
- New seal lubricated with chassis grease using an Oil Seal Installer tool J 23911
- Drive pinion gear yoke
- Drive pinion gear nut and hand-tighten

10. Using a Pinion Flange tool J 8614-01 and tighten the nut to the position marked in the removal procedure. Tighten the nut an additional 0.062 inch (1.59mm).

11. Install or connect the following:
- Propeller shaft center bearing bracket. Torque the bolts to 15 ft. lbs. (20 Nm).
- Propeller shaft to the rear coupling. Torque the bolts to 70 ft. lbs. (90 Nm).
- Propeller shaft to the front coupling. Torque the bolts to 70 ft. lbs. (90 Nm).
- Underbody heat shields. Torque the bolts to 18 inch lbs. (2 Nm).

12. Road test the vehicle.

STEERING AND SUSPENSION

Air Bag

✳✳ CAUTION

These vehicles are equipped with an air bag system, known as a Supplemental Inflatable Restraint (SIR) system. The system must be disabled before performing service on or around system components, steering column, instrument panel components, wiring and sensors. Failure to follow safety and disabling proce-

dures could result in accidental air bag deployment, possible personal injury and unnecessary system repairs.

PRECAUTIONS

Several precautions must be observed when handling the inflator module to avoid accidental deployment and possible personal injury.
- Never carry the inflator module by the wires or connector on the underside of the module.
- When carrying a live inflator module, hold securely with both hands, and ensure that the bag and trim cover are pointed away.
- Place the inflator module on a bench or other surface with the bag and trim cover facing up.
- With the inflator module on the bench, never place anything on or close to the module which may be thrown in the event of an accidental deployment.

DISARMING

1. Turn the steering wheel to align the wheels in the straight-ahead position.

2. Turn the ignition switch to the **LOCK** position and remove the key.

3. Wait 1 minute until the capacitors in the Sensing and Diagnostic Module (SDM) discharge.

4. Disconnect the negative battery cable.

✳✳ WARNING

If major electrical or mechanical repairs are being performed on the vehicle, including painting, body part replacement or welding, the SDM module must first be disarmed.

REARMING

1. Turn the steering wheel so that the wheels are pointing straight ahead.

2. Turn the ignition switch to the **LOCK** position and remove the key.

3. Reconnect the negative battery cable.

4. Wait at least 1 minute for the capacitors to recharge.

5. While staying away from the inflator modules, turn the key to the **RUN** position. The air bag warning lamp should turn ON for 3–4 seconds, then turn OFF.

Recirculating Ball Power Steering Gear

REMOVAL & INSTALLATION

1. Before servicing the vehicle, refer to the precautions in the beginning of this section.

2. Center the front wheels, then turn the ignition key to the **LOCK** position.

3. Drain the coolant.

4. Evacuate the A/C system.

5. Siphon the power steering fluid from the reservoir.

6. Siphon the brake fluid from the reservoir.

7. Remove or disconnect the following:
- Negative battery cable
- Windshield wiper assembly
- 3 body harness electrical connectors
- Electronic Control Module (ECM) from the electrical box
- Upper radiator hose
- Evaporative line extension bolt
- Power steering fluid reservoir and bracket
- Brake booster vacuum connection from the intake plenum

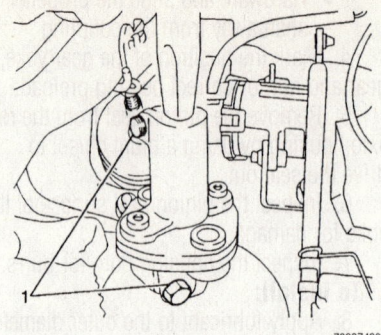

Matchmark the coupler to the steering gear before removing the coupler bolts (1)

- Brake pipes from the master cylinder
- Electrical connector from the master cylinder reservoir cap
- Sound insulator

8. Matchmark the steering coupler and input shaft of the steering gear.

✴✴ WARNING

Do not allow the steering wheel to rotate when the steering gear coupler is disconnected. Use a locking devise to secure the steering wheel in place. Damage to the SIR coil in the steering column may occur.

9. Remove or disconnect the following:
- Steering coupler bolts from the coupler. Spread the clamp and pull the steering shaft upward and away from the steering gear connection.
- Brake pedal from the brake power booster link rod by removing the retaining clip from the pin and driving the pin out of the linkage rod
- Instrument panel drivers side knee bolster energy absorber
- Fuse
- Relay panel. Move the fuse and relay panel away from the brake booster.
- Brake booster nuts from the inward side of the cowling
- Brake booster and master cylinder as one unit
- A/C evaporator line quick connect fitting
- Power steering hoses from the steering gear
- Electronic Brake Traction Control (EBTCM) Module/Brake Pressure Modulator Valve (BPMV)
- Heat shield upper fastening bolt
- Pitman arm washer and nut. Mark the alignment of the pitman arm to the steering gear for ease of installation.
- Pitman arm using a suitable puller
- Lower heat shield mounting nuts
- Steering gear lower washers, bolts and nuts
- Heat Shield
- Electrical connector from the power steering fluid flow control valve actuator
- Upper steering gear shims and bolt
- Steering gear

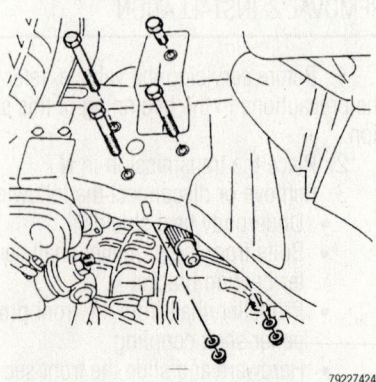

Steering gear mounting bolt locations

To install:

10. Find the center of travel of the steering gear by turning the stubshaft and counting the number of turns from lock-to-lock. Divide the total number in half and turn the

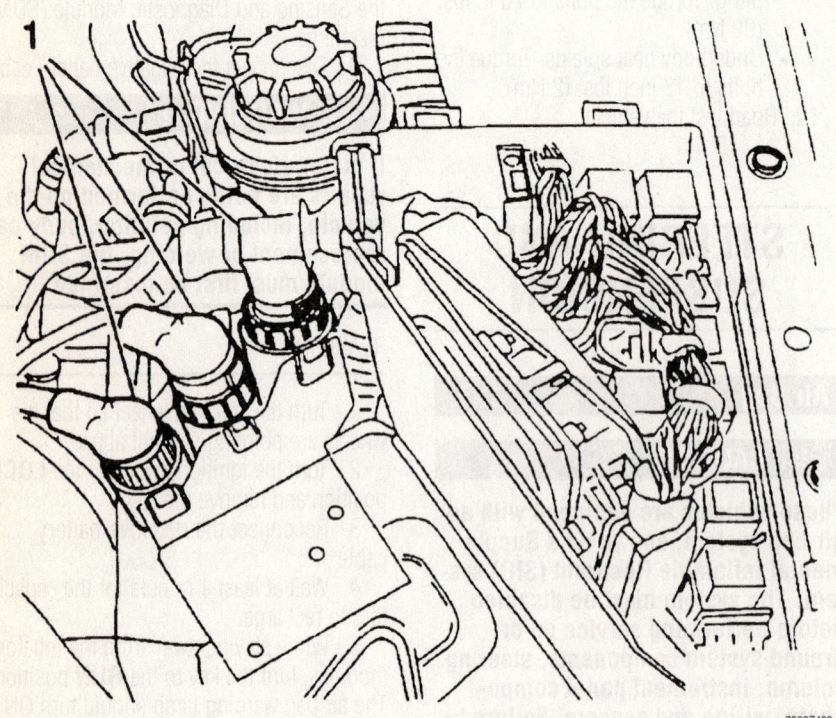

Body harness electrical connector locations (1)

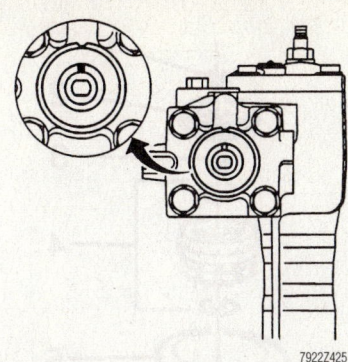

Align the mark on the stub shaft with the "V" mark on the steering gear mounting bolt locations

stub shaft from either lock position by this amount. Finally align the mark on the stub shaft to the "V" mark on the steering gear.

11. Install or connect the following:
- Steering gear
- Steering gear shims and bolt. Torque the bolt snugly at this time. Do not tighten the bolt to proper specification at this time.
- Electrical connector to the power steering flow control valve actuator
- Heat shield with the upper mounting bolt. Torque the bolt to 71 inch lbs. (8 Nm).
- Lower steering gear washers, bolts and nuts. Torque the bolts to 30 ft. lbs. (40 Nm).
- Heat shield lower mounting bolt. Torque the bolt to 11 ft. lbs. (15 Nm).
- Pitman arm to the splines steering gear. Make certain that the steering gear shaft protector is in place.
- Pitman arm washer and nut. Torque the fastener to 118 ft. lbs. (160 Nm).
- EBTCM/BPMV assembly
- Inlet and outlet hoses to the steering gear. Torque the hoses to 21 ft. lbs. (28 Nm).
- A/C evaporator line quick connect with a new O-ring lubricated with mineral oil
- Vacuum booster/master cylinder assembly. Make certain the vacuum booster nuts are facing the inward side of the cowl. Torque the fasteners to 15 ft. lbs. (20 Nm).
- Fuse and relay panels and tighten the fasteners securely
- Drivers side instrument panel knee bolster energy absorber
- Brake pedal to the power booster

by driving the pin into the linkage rod
- Retaining clip to the pin
- Steering coupler to the gear by aligning the matchmarks
- Coupler bolts. Torque the bolts to 16 ft. lbs. (22 Nm).
- Sound insulator
- Brake pipes to the master cylinder. Torque the fasteners to 12 ft. lbs. (16 Nm).
- Electrical connector to the master cylinder reservoir cap
- Brake booster vacuum connection to the intake plenum
- Power steering fluid reservoir and clamp. Torque the clamp to 62 inch lbs. (6 Nm).
- New O-ring lubricated with mineral oil to the A/C evaporator line extension
- Evaporator line to the cowl. Torque the bolt to 15 ft. lbs. (20 Nm).
- Upper radiator hose
- ECM to the electrical box
- Body harness electrical connectors
- Wiper assembly
- Negative battery cable

12. Fill and bleed the brake fluid.
13. Fill and bleed the power steering system.
14. Fill the coolant system.
15. Recharge the A/C system.
16. Start the vehicle and check all fluid system for leaks.
17. Check all fluid levels and top off, if necessary.
18. Road test the vehicle.
19. Bleed the systems again, if necessary.

Strut

REMOVAL & INSTALLATION

Front

1. Before servicing the vehicle, refer to the precautions in the beginning of this section.
2. Remove or disconnect the following:
- Front wheel
- Speed sensor wiring from the strut
- Brake wear indicator wires from the strut
- Brake flex hose clip from the strut
- Caliper bolts from the steering knuckle
- Caliper from the steering knuckle.

DO not open the brake hydraulic system.
- Stabilizer shaft link
- Lower strut mounting bolts from the steering knuckle
- Upper support plate protective cap and nut
- Upper support plate
- Strut from the wheel well

To install:
3. Install or connect the following:
- Strut into the strut tower
- Upper support plate and nut. Torque the nut to 41 ft. lbs. (55 Nm).
- Cap to the upper support nut
- Steering knuckle to the strut
- New bolts for the steering knuckle. Tighten the bolts snugly from the front of the vehicle towards the rear.
- Stabilizer shaft link to the strut
- Stabilizer shaft nut and torque to 48 ft. lbs. (65 Nm).

➡ **Before installing the bolts for the caliper, run an M12 x 1.5 tap through the holes and coat the new bolts with a thread locking compound.**

- Brake caliper to the steering knuckle. Using a Torque/Angle Meter J36660, torque the bolts to 70 ft. lbs. (95 Nm) plus a 37 degree turn.
- Flex hose to the strut and retain it with the clip
- Speed sensor wiring to the strut
- Wear indicator wires to the strut
- Front wheel

4. Road test the vehicle.
5. Check and/or adjust the front end alignment.

Shock Absorber

REMOVAL & INSTALLATION

Rear

1. Before servicing the vehicle, refer to the precautions in the beginning of this section.
2. Position the rear seat backs forward to allow access to the upper shock absorber mounting.
3. Remove or disconnect the following:
- Protective cap and nut from shock tower
- Upper mounting washer and grommet

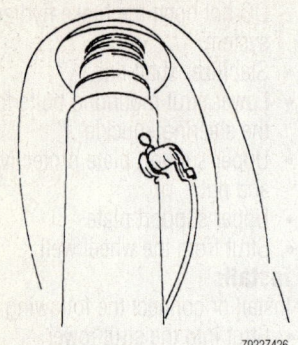

Air line connection to the shock absorber for Automatic Level Control (ALC)

- Automatic Level Control (ALC) air line connection from the shock
- Lower shock mounting bolt
- Shock absorber

To install:

4. Install or connect the following:
- Lower rubber mounting grommet and washer
- Shock into the tower and the upper mounting washer and grommet
- Upper shock mounting nut. Torque the nut 15 ft. lbs. (20 Nm).
- Protective cap to the shock tower
- Lower shock mounting bolt. Torque the bolt 81 ft. lbs. (110 Nm).

➡ **It may be necessary to support the lower control arm for ease of installation of the lower nut.**

- ACL air line connection to the shock

5. Position the rear seats in their proper position.

6. Road test the vehicle and verify a smooth ride.

Coil Spring

REMOVAL & INSTALLATION

Front

1. Before servicing the vehicle, refer to the precautions in the beginning of this section.

2. Remove the strut from the vehicle.

3. Using a Strut Compressor Holding tool J 3289-20 place the strut in a Compressor tool J 34013-A along with an Adapter J 3413-88

4. Remove or disconnect the following:
- Compress the spring
- Upper bearing support nut
- Bearing and plate assembly

5. Decompress the spring.

6. Remove or disconnect the following:

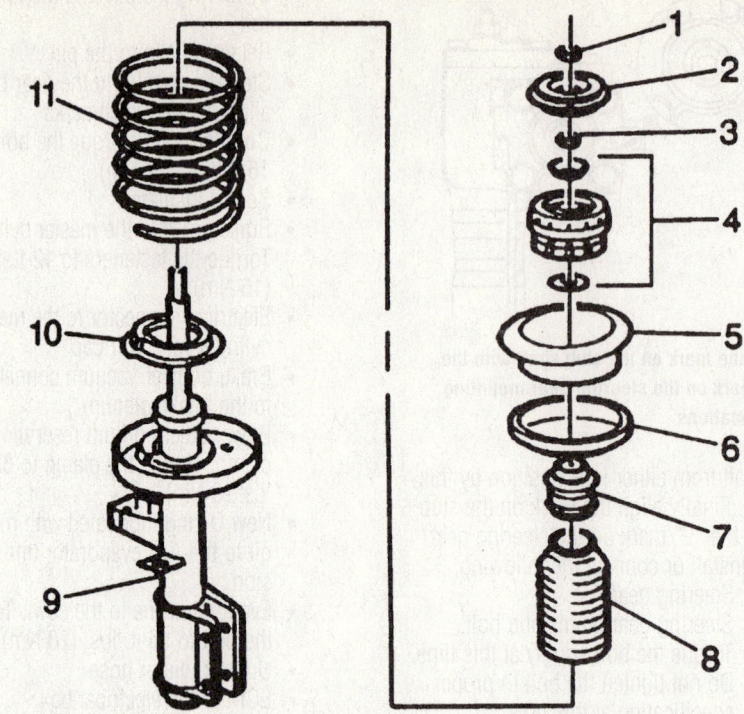

(1) Upper Support Plate Nut
(2) Upper Support Plate
(3) Upper Bearing Support Nut
(4) Bearing and Bearing Plate Assembly
(5) Upper Spring Support Plate
(6) Upper Insulator
(7) Strut Bumper
(8) Strut Cover
(9) Strut
(10) Lower Insulator
(11) Spring

Exploded view of the strut assembly

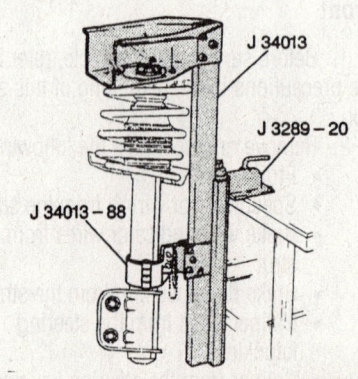

J 34013
J 3289 – 20
J 34013 – 88

Be sure to compress the coil spring before removing the upper bearing support nut

- Upper spring support plate
- Upper insulator
- Strut bumper
- Cover from the strut
- Spring from the strut
- Lower insulator from the strut

To install:

7. Before servicing the vehicle, refer to the precautions in the beginning of this section.

- Lower insulator to the strut
- Spring on the strut
- Upper spring support plate
- Upper insulator
- Strut bumper
- Cover

8. Align the spring between the upper and lower rubber isolation rings.

9. Compress the spring.

10. Install or connect the following:
- Bearing and plate assembly
- Upper bearing support nut. Torque the nut to 52 ft. lbs. (70 Nm).

11. Release the tension from the spring.

12. Remove the strut compressor tools from the strut.

13. Install the strut to the vehicle.

14. Road test the vehicle and verify a smooth ride and no abnormal noises from the strut and spring.

Rear

1. Before servicing the vehicle, refer to the precautions in the beginning of this section.

2. Remove or disconnect the following:
- Retainers from the lower control arms
- Brake pipes from the lower control arms without disconnect the brake fitting
- Stabilizer shaft link bolts
- Stabilizer shaft link from the lower control arms
- Rubber exhaust insulators from the hangers. Support the exhaust system so no damage occurs to the pipes or gaskets.
- Rear wheel speed sensor electrical connections
- Shock lower mounting bolt after properly supporting the lower control arms
- Support from the lower control arms and place on the rear differential
- Rear axle cradle mounts to the body bolts

3. Lower the rear differential so that coil spring can be removed.

4. Remove or disconnect the following:
- Rear springs with the seats on the spring
- Seats from the spring

To install:

5. Install or connect the following:
- Seats to the spring
- Rear springs to the lower control arm and body. Make certain that the spring leg is aligned properly.
- Protective shields
- Rear differential with the cradle mounting bolts. Torque the bolts to 48 ft. lbs. (65 Nm).
- Shock absorber. Torque the bolt to 81 ft. lbs. (110 Nm).

- Rear wheel speed sensor electrical connections
- Rubber exhaust insulators to the hangers
- Stabilizer shaft link to the lower control arm. Torque the bolts to 15 ft. lbs. (20 Nm).
- Brake pipes to the lower control arm and secure with the retainers

6. Check and/or adjust the rear toe.

Lower Ball Joint

REMOVAL & INSTALLATION

1. Before servicing the vehicle, refer to the precautions in the beginning of this section.

2. Remove or disconnect the following:
- Front wheel
- Lower control arm

3. Using a 0.5 inch (13mm) drill, drill out the 3 rivet heads that attach the ball stud to the lower control arm.

4. Remove the ball stud from the lower control arm

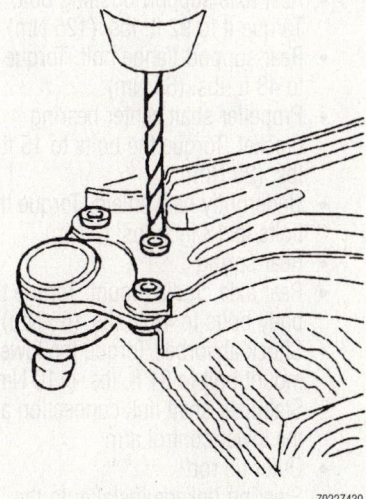

79227430

Drill out the rivets to remove the ball joint from the lower control arm

To install:

5. Install or connect the following:
- Ball stud to the lower control arm
- Upper side of the lower control arm. Torque the new bolts to 26 ft. lbs. (35 Nm).
- Lower control arm
- Front wheel

6. Check and/or adjust the front end alignment.

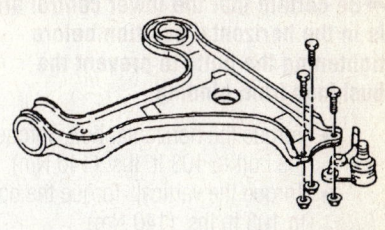

79222431

The replacement ball joint will be bolted to the lower control arm with the bolts supplied in the kit

Lower Control Arm

REMOVAL & INSTALLATION

Front

1. Before servicing the vehicle, refer to the precautions in the beginning of this section.

2. Remove or disconnect the following:
- Front wheel
- Brake pad wear indicator rubber sleeve
- Wheel speed sensor
- Brake hose from the strut bracket
- Brake caliper from the steering knuckle

➡ **Do not open the hydraulic brake system**

- Outer tie rod from the steering knuckle by using a Tie Rod Remover
- Stabilizer shaft nut from the shaft
- Steering knuckle from the strut
- Lower control arm ball stud pinch bolt
- Steering knuckle from the lower control arm ball stud. The rotor and wheel hub will remain attached.

3. Loosen the lower control arm horizontal/vertical bolts.

4. Remove or disconnect the following:
- Horizontal bolts by rotating the lower control arm from the support bracket
- Vertical bolts and lower control arm

To install:

5. Install or connect the following:
- Lower control arm into the support bracket
- Vertical bolt and hand-tighten at this time
- Horizontal bolt by inserting it from the rear side of the vehicle

Turn to Section 5 for brake system applications

➡**Be certain that the lower control arm is in the horizontal position before tightening the bolts to prevent the bushings from binding.**

- Torque the horizontal bolt. Torque the bolt to 103 ft. lbs. (140 Nm).
- Torque the vertical. Torque the bolt to 103 ft. lbs. (140 Nm).
- Steering knuckle to the lower control arm ball stud
- New ball stud pinch bolt to the rear of the vehicle. Torque the bolt to 74 ft. lbs. (100 Nm).
- Steering knuckle to the strut with new bolts from the front of the vehicle. Hand tighten the bolts at this time
- Stabilizer shaft link to the shaft
- Stabilizer shaft link nut. Torque the nut to 48 ft. lbs. (65 Nm).
- Outer tie rod to the steering knuckle
- Linkage Installer tool J 42089 to the tie rod ball stud. Tighten the tool to 22 ft. lbs. (30 Nm) to allow the ball stud taper to seat.
- New outer tie rod nut after removing the linkage installer tool. Torque the nut 44 ft. lbs. (60 Nm).

➡**Clean the bolt holes for the brake caliper by running a M12 x 105 tap through the holes. Use new bolts for the caliper to steering knuckle connection after applying a thread locking compound.**

- Caliper to the steering knuckle. Using the Linkage Installer tool, torque the new bolts to 70 ft. lbs. (95 Nm) plus a 37 degree turn.
- Brake hose to the strut bracket with a new clip
- Wheel sped sensor. Torque the bolt to 71 inch lbs. (8 Nm).
- Brake pad wear indicator sleeve to the strut
- Front wheel

6. Road test the vehicle.
7. Check and/or adjust the wheel alignment.

Rear

1. Before servicing the vehicle, refer to the precautions in the beginning of this section.
2. Remove or disconnect the following:
   - Wheel
   - Driveshaft from the rear wheel hub flange while counter holding the rear hub with a Rear Hub Holding tool J 42066

- Brake pipe from the lower control arm
- Brake caliper
- Brake rotor
- Parking brake cable from the actuator bracket
- Rear hub and flange
- Wheel bearing
- Brake backing plate
- Exhaust system from the rubber mounts
- Rear outer tie rod from the rear control arm with a tie rod puller
- Stabilizer shaft link connection at the lower control arm
- Lower rear cradle

➡**Make certain that the rear differential is properly supported.**

- Rear spring
- Underbody heat shield
- Lower control arm

To install:

3. Install or connect the following:
   - Lower control arm
   - Inboard/outboard lower control arm bolts. Torque them to 74 ft. lbs. (100 Nm).
   - Rear axle support bushing bolt. Torque it to 92 ft. lbs. (125 Nm).
   - Rear support flange bolt. Torque it to 48 ft. lbs. (65 Nm).
   - Propeller shaft center bearing bracket. Torque the bolts to 15 ft. lbs. (20 Nm).
   - Underbody heat shield. Torque the bolts to 18 inch lbs. (2 Nm).
   - Rear spring
   - Rear axle cradle mount. Torque the body bolts to 48 ft. lbs. (65 Nm).
   - Shock absorber. Torque the lower mount bolt to 81 ft. lbs. (110 Nm).
   - Stabilizer shaft link connection at the lower control arm
   - Outer tie rod
   - Steering linkage installer to the outer tie rod ball stud. Torque it to 22 ft. lbs. (30 Nm).
   - New self locking outer tie rod nut. Torque it to 44 ft. lbs. (60 Nm).
   - Exhaust system to the rubber mounts
   - Brake backing plate
   - Wheel bearing
   - Hub and flange
   - Parking brake cable and route it through the bracket in the rear lower control arm
   - Brake rotor and setscrew. Torque the screw to 35 ft. lbs. (45 Nm).
   - Brake caliper and adjust the parking brake

- Brake pipe and clip to the lower control arm
- Driveshaft while counter holding the wheel hub with tool J 42066. Torque the bolts to 37 ft. lbs. (50 Nm) plus an additional 70 degree turn.
- Wheel

4. Check and/or adjust the rear toe.

CONTROL ARM BUSHING REPLACEMENT

Front

1. Before servicing the vehicle, refer to the precautions in the beginning of this section.
2. Remove or disconnect the following:
   - Lower control arm
   - Horizontal bushing with a Horizontal Bushing Remover tool J 42092-2
   - Vertical bushing with a Bushing Receiver tool J 21474-5, a Rear Differential Remover tool J 42112-4, a ⅜ inch bolt and nut

To install:

3. Install or connect the following:
   - Vertical bushing into the lower control arm until flush with a Bushing Receiver tool J 21474-5, a Rear Differential Remover tool J 42112-4, a ⅜ inch bolt and nut
   - Horizontal bushing into the lower control arm until flush with a Horizontal Bushing Remover tool J 42092-2
   - Lower control arm

Rear

1. Before servicing the vehicle, refer to the precautions in the beginning of this section.
2. Remove or disconnect the following:
   - Wheel
   - Rear axle lower control arm
   - Collar for the inboard and outboard lower control arm bushings by cutting it off
   - Bushing using a Universal Bushing Kit J 21474-01 and a 30mm socket

To install:

3. Install or connect the following:
   - Inboard side bushing, lubricated with soapy water, by pressing it with a Bushing Receiver tool J 21474-5 with the collar facing the rear differential
   - Outboard side bushing, lubricated with soapy water, by pressing it

into position with a Bushing Receiver tool J 21474-5
- Lower control arm
- Wheel

Wheel Bearings

ADJUSTMENT

The wheel bearings used by the Catera are not adjustable.

REMOVAL & INSTALLATION

Front

1. Before servicing the vehicle, refer to the precautions in the beginning of this section.
2. Remove or disconnect the following:
   - Front wheel
   - Brake pad wear indicator wire from the strut bracket
   - Brake hose from the strut bracket
   - Caliper bolts from the steering knuckle
   - Brake caliper. The brake system should remain closed.
   - Brake rotor and setscrew
   - Dust cap from the hub
   - Hub with the bearing
   - Bearing by pressing it from the hub

To install:
3. Install or connect the following:
   - Bearing onto the spindle and press the outer bearing ring into the hub
   - Hub nut. Torque the nut to 236 ft. lbs. (320 Nm).
   - Dust cap to the hub
   - Brake rotor and setscrew. Torque the screw to 35 inch lbs. (4 Nm).
   - Brake caliper to the steering knuckle after cleaning the bolt holes with an M12 x 1.5 tap and

coating the new bolts with a thread locking compound. Torque the bolts to 70 ft. lbs. (95 Nm), plus a 37 degree turn.
   - Brake hose to the strut bracket with a retaining clip
   - Brake pad wear indicator wire to the strut
   - Front wheel
4. Road test the vehicle.
5. Check and/or adjust the front end alignment.

Rear

➡**Several special tools are necessary to remove the rear wheel bearing from the knuckle. The tools required are as follows:**

   - J 36660 Torque angle meter
   - J 42066 Holding tool
   - J 42094-1 Holding Fixture
   - J 42094-2 Spacer
   - J 42094-3 Threaded Driver
   - J 42094-4 Threaded Arbor
   - J 42094-5 Ball Head
   - J 42094-6 Bearing Remover
   - J 42094-7 Threaded spacer pin
   - J 42094-8 Bearing Installer
   - J 42094-9 Hub Installer
   - J 42094-10 Thrust Bearing
   - J 42072 Triple Hex Head (10mm) deep socket

The tool numbers mentioned are Kent-Moore tools used by GM. Equivalent tools may be available from other sources.

1. Before servicing the vehicle, refer to the precautions in the beginning of this section.
2. Remove the rear wheel.
3. Use a Holding tool J 42066 and a 0.5 inch breaker bar to counter hold the rear wheel hub.
4. Remove or disconnect the following:
   - Driveshaft and bolts from the rear hub

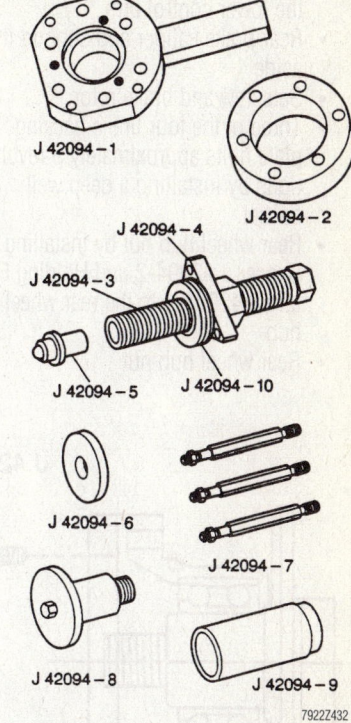

J 42094-1
J 42094-2
J 42094-4
J 42094-3
J 42094-5 · J 42094-10
J 42094-6
J 42094-7
J 42094-8 · J 42094-9

7922Z432

Several tools make up the J 42094 tool kit for rear wheel bearing removal and installation

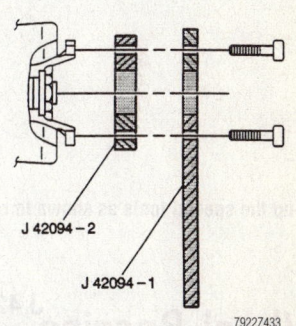

J 42094-2
J 42094-1

7922Z433

Attach the spacer and holding fixture to the flange before removing the hub retaining nut

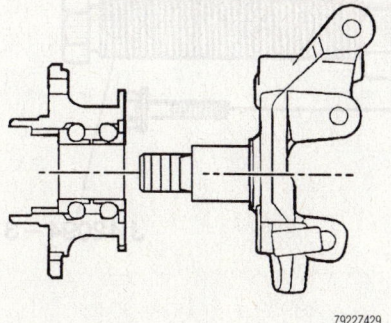

7922Z429

Cut-away view of the hub/wheel bearing assembly and steering knuckle

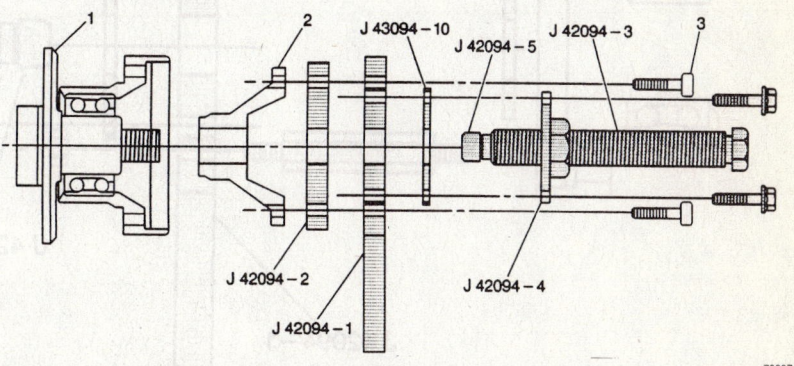

7922Z434

Set up the special tools as shown to remove the flange

- Brake pipe and retaining clip from the lower control arm
- Rear brake caliper and support it aside
- Setscrew and brake rotor
- Three of the four brake backing plate bolts approximately 9 revolutions by installing a deep well socket.
- Rear wheel hub nut by installing a Spacer J 42094-2 and Holding Fixture J 42094-1 to the rear wheel hub
- Rear wheel hub nut

5. Use a Thrust Bearing J 42094-10 as a spacer to attach a Threaded Arbor J42094-4 to the holding Fixture J 42094-7 with 3 bolts.

6. Attach a Threaded Driver into the threaded arbor.

7. Screw the bolts to into the backing plate and attach the holding fixture with the stem upward.

8. Press out the rear wheel hub.

➡ **Damage to the wheel bearing seal is possible while pressing out the rear wheel hub. Inspect the seal and replace if needed.**

9. Remove the wheel bearing retainer with snaping pliers.

10. Attach a Bearing Remover J 42094-6 to the end of the threaded driver.

11. Turn the driver in a clockwise manner to press out the wheel bearing.

To install:

12. Install or connect the following:
- Wheel Bearing Installer tool J 42094-8 through the wheel bearing and on to the threaded driver
- Wheel bearing until fully seated by turning the threaded driver
- Wheel bearing retaining ring

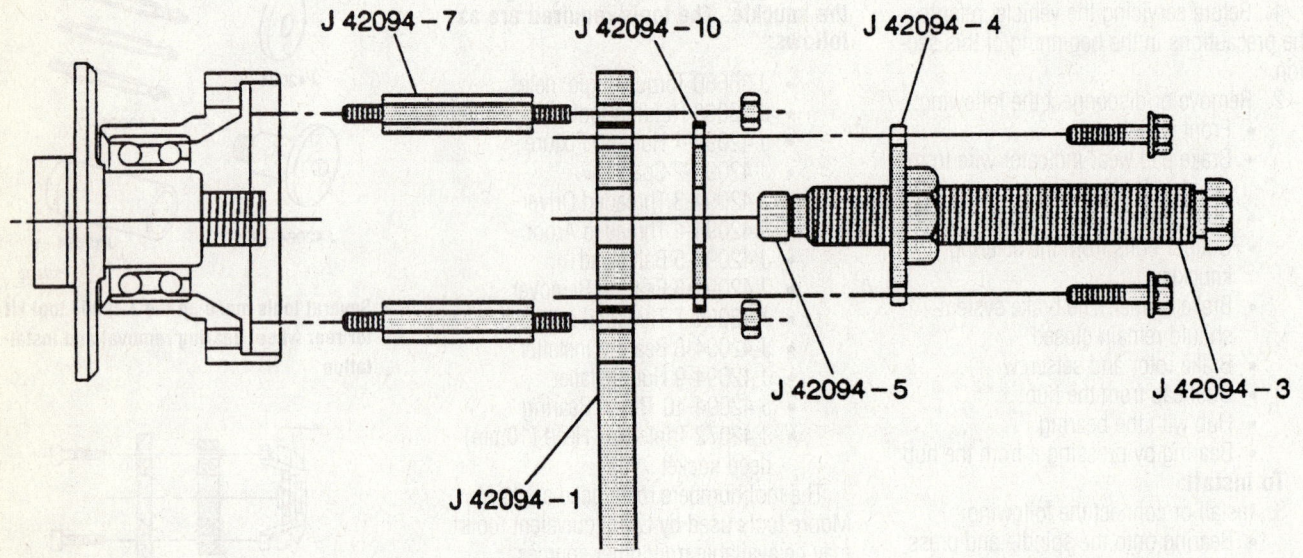

Set up the special tools as shown to remove the hub

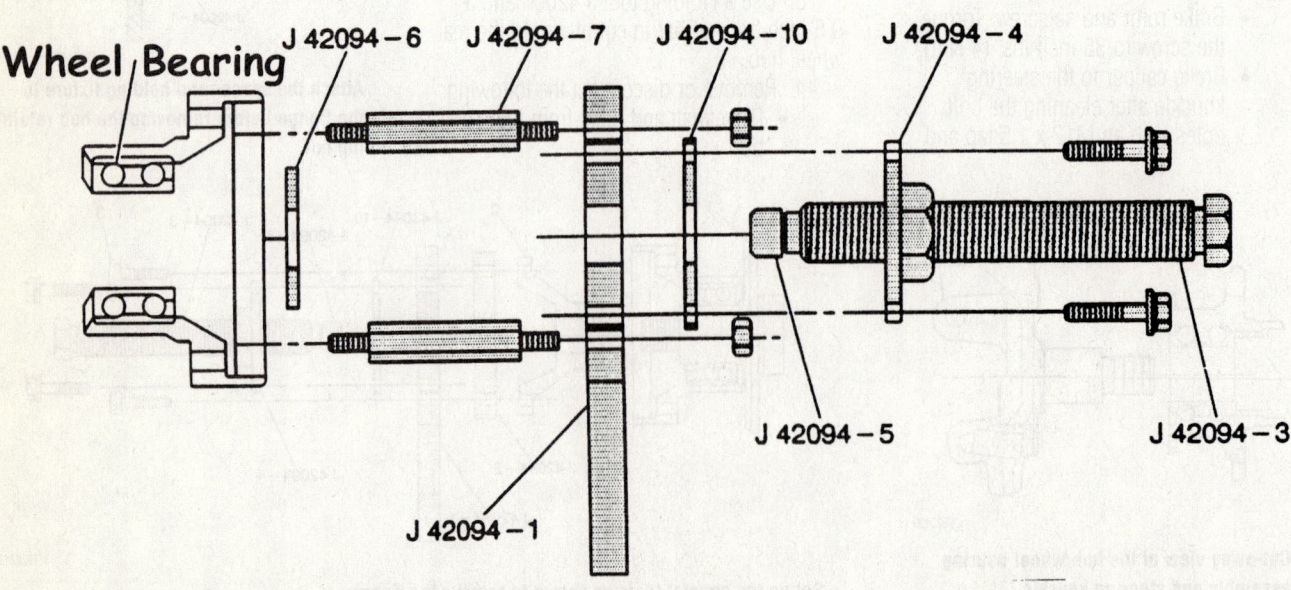

Set up the special tools as shown to remove the bearing assembly

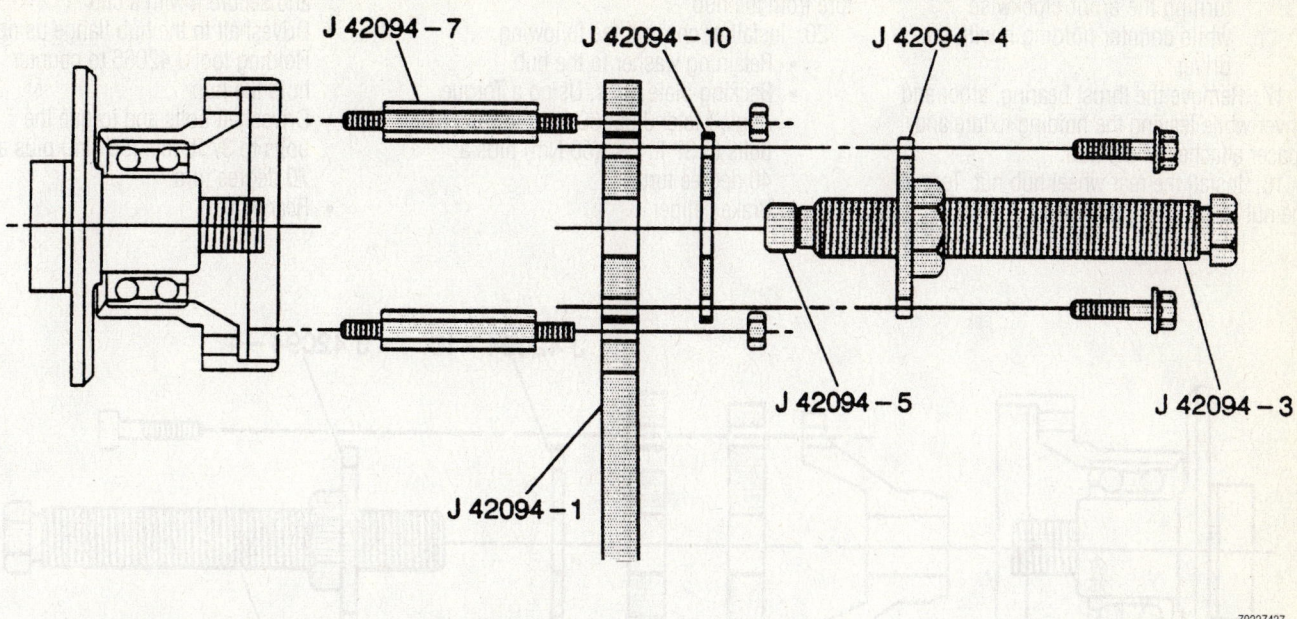

Set up the special tools as shown to install the bearing assembly

Wheel Bearing

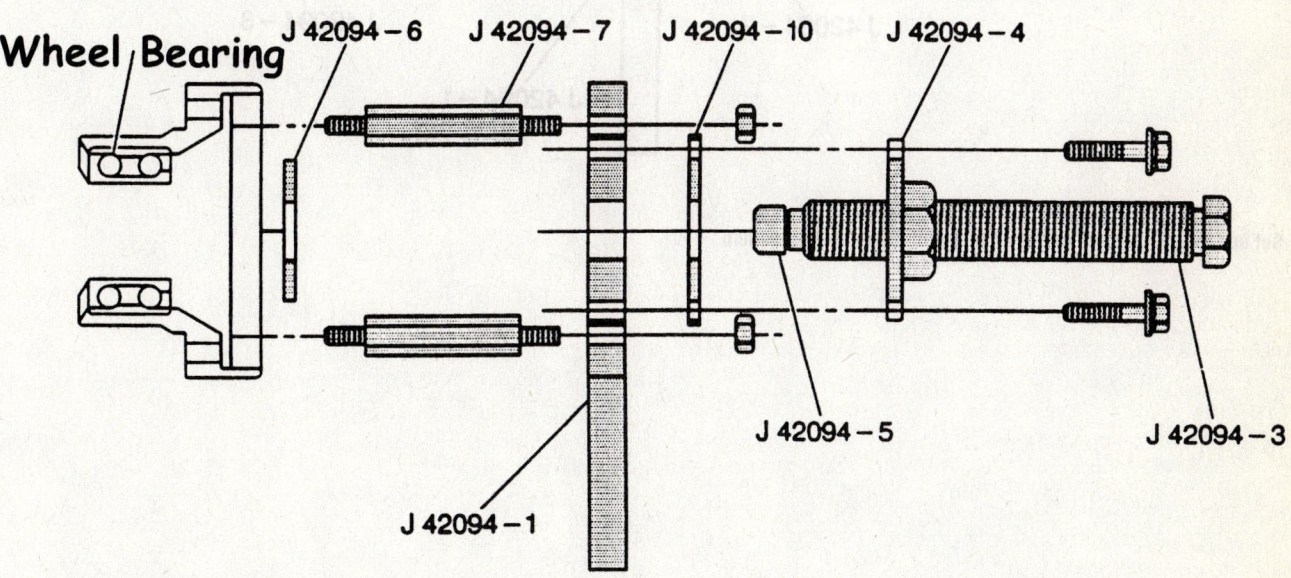

Set up the special tools as shown to pull the hub into the bearing assembly

- Hub Installer tool J 42094-9 on the shaft of the threaded driver. Make certain that the rear wheel hub installer is on the inner ring of the wheel bearing

13. Attach the Holding Fixture to a Threaded Spacer Pin J 42094-7 and remove the anchoring bolts from the threaded arbor.

14. Install or connect the following:

- Rear wheel hub into the driver and make certain the driver is seated properly on the wheel bearing. If not centered properly, it may cause the hub to bind
- Wheel hub into the wheel bearing by holding the driver and turning the arbor clockwise. When fully seated, remove the tools

15. Connect the Threaded Arbor J 42094-4, Threaded Driver J 42094-3, Holding Fixture J 42094-1, Spacer J 42094-2, and Thrust Bearing J 42094-10 to the wheel flange with the halfshaft mounting bolts.

16. Install or connect the following:

- Hub to the flange and make certain that the splines are aligned properly

- Flange fully onto the hub by turning the arbor clockwise while counter holding it with the driver

17. Remove the thrust bearing, arbor and driver while leaving the holding fixture and spacer attached to the hub.

18. Install the rear wheel hub nut. Torque the nut 221 ft. lbs. (300 Nm).

19. Remove the spacer and holding fixture from the hub

20. Install or connect the following:
- Retaining washer to the hub
- Backing plate bolts. Using a Torque Angle Meter J 36660, torque the bolts to 37 ft. lbs. (50 Nm) plus a 40 degree turn.
- Brake caliper

- Brake pipe to the lower control arm and secure it with a clip
- Driveshaft to the hub flange using a Holding tool J 42066 to counter hold the hub
- Driveshaft bolts and torque the bolts to 37 ft. lbs. (50 Nm) plus a 70 degree turn.
- Rear wheel

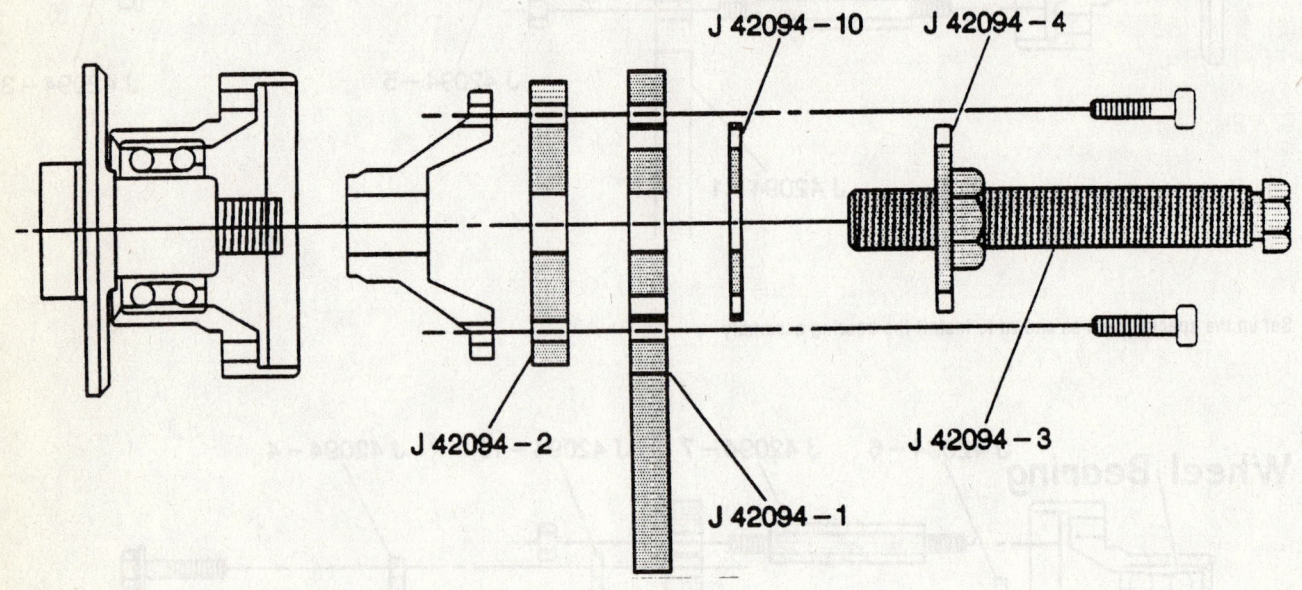

Set up the special tools as shown to install the flange on the hub

GENERAL MOTORS CORPORATION—W-BODY

36

Buick-Century • Regal • **Chevrolet**-Impala • Lumina • Monte Carlo • **Oldsmobile**-Cutlass Supreme • Intrigue • **Pontiac**-Grand Prix

PRECAUTIONS

Before servicing any vehicle, please be sure to read all of the following precautions, which deal with personal safety, prevention of component damage, and important points to take into consideration when servicing a motor vehicle:

• Never open, service or drain the radiator or cooling system when the engine is hot; serious burns can occur from the steam and hot coolant.

• Observe all applicable safety precautions when working around fuel. Whenever servicing the fuel system, always work in a well-ventilated area. Do not allow fuel spray or vapors to come in contact with a spark, open flame or excessive heat (a hot drop light, for example). Keep a dry chemical fire extinguisher near the work area. Always keep fuel in a container specifically designed for fuel storage; also, always properly seal fuel containers to avoid the possibility of fire or explosion. Refer to the additional fuel system precautions later in this section.

• Fuel injection systems often remain pressurized, even after the engine has been turned **OFF**. The fuel system pressure must be relieved before disconnecting any fuel lines. Failure to do so may result in fire and/or personal injury.

• Brake fluid often contains polyglycol ethers and polyglycols. Avoid contact with the eyes and wash your hands thoroughly after handling brake fluid. If you do get brake fluid in your eyes, flush your eyes with clean, running water for 15 minutes. If eye irritation persists, or if you have taken brake fluid internally, seek medical assistance IMMEDIATELY.

• The EPA warns that prolonged contact with used engine oil may cause a number of skin disorders, including cancer! You should make every effort to minimize your exposure to used engine oil. Protective gloves should be worn when changing oil. Wash your hands and any other exposed skin areas as soon as possible after exposure to used engine oil. Soap and water, or waterless hand cleaner should be used.

• All new vehicles are now equipped with an air bag system. The system must be disabled before performing service on or around system components, steering column, instrument panel components, wiring and sensors. Failure to follow safety and disabling procedures could result in accidental air bag deployment, possible personal injury and unnecessary system repairs.

• Always wear safety goggles when working with, or around, the air bag system. When carrying a non-deployed air bag, be sure the bag and trim cover are pointed away from your body. When placing a non-deployed air bag on a work surface, always face the bag and trim cover upward, away from the surface. This will reduce the motion of the module if it is accidentally deployed. Refer to the additional air bag system precautions later in this section.

• Clean, high quality brake fluid from a sealed container is essential to the safe and proper operation of the brake system. You should always buy the correct type of brake fluid for your vehicle. If the brake fluid becomes contaminated, completely flush the system with new fluid. Never reuse any brake fluid. Any brake fluid that is removed from the system should be discarded. Also, do not allow any brake fluid to come in contact with a painted surface; it will damage the paint.

• Never operate the engine without the proper amount and type of engine oil; doing so WILL result in severe engine damage.

• Timing belt maintenance is extremely important! Many models utilize an interference-type, non-freewheeling engine. If the timing belt breaks, the valves in the cylinder head may strike the pistons, causing potentially serious (also time-consuming and expensive) engine damage. Refer to the maintenance interval charts in the front of this manual for the recommended replacement interval for the timing belt, and to the timing belt section for belt replacement and inspection.

• Disconnecting the negative battery cable on some vehicles may interfere with the functions of the on-board computer system(s) and may require the computer to undergo a relearning process once the negative battery cable is reconnected.

• When servicing drum brakes, only disassemble and assemble one side at a time, leaving the remaining side intact for reference.

ENGINE REPAIR

The 3.1L, 3.4L, 3.5L and 3.8L engines all utilize a Distributorless Ignition System (DIS).

REMOVAL

3.1L Engine

1. Before servicing the vehicle, refer to the precautions in the beginning of this section.
2. Remove or disconnect the following:

• Negative battery cable
• Drive belt from the alternator
• Coolant recovery reservoir and place it away from the alternator
• Electrical connector
• Protective boot for the output BAT terminal
• Alternator

3.4L Engine

1. Before servicing the vehicle, refer to the precautions in the beginning of this section.
2. Remove or disconnect the following:

• Negative battery cable
• Wiper system module cover
• Fuel injector sight shield
3. Rotate the engine forward.
4. Remove or disconnect the following:

• Alternator terminal nut, lead and electrical connector
• Serpentine belt
• Front bolts and two rear bolts
• Alternator from the bracket
• Serpentine belt tensioner
• Bracket
• Power steering pipes from the retainer
• Fuel pressure test port cap from the injector rail

➡ **Do not disconnect the power steering pipes from the pump**

• Power steering pump and reposition it to gain access to the alternator
• Alternator

3.5L Engine

1. Before servicing the vehicle, refer to the precautions in the beginning of this section.
2. Drain the cooling system.
3. Remove or disconnect the following:

• Battery and tray
• Drive belt
• Engine cooling fan assembly

- Thermostat housing and radiator hose
- Outboard/inboard alternator bolts
- Idler pulley bolt and pulley
- Alternator electrical connectors
- Alternator

3.8L Engine

1. Before servicing the vehicle, refer to the precautions in the beginning of this section.
2. Remove or disconnect the following:
   - Negative battery cable
   - Drive belt
   - Rear alternator brace
   - Alternator electrical connectors
   - Alternator

INSTALLATION

3.1L Engine

1. Install or connect the following:
   - Alternator
   - Alternator output BAT terminal. Torque the nut to 15 ft. lbs. (20 Nm).
   - Protective boot from the output terminal
   - Electrical connector
2. Tighten the alternator bolts in the order described:
   - Alternator pivot bolt. Torque it to 37 ft. lbs. (50 Nm).
   - Alternator bolt. Torque it to 37 ft. lbs. (50 Nm).
   - Alternator bracket bolt. Torque it to 37 ft. lbs. (50 Nm).
3. Install or connect the following:
   - Coolant recovery reservoir
   - Drive belt
   - Negative battery cable

3.4L Engine

1. Install or connect the following:
   - Alternator
   - Power steering pump. Torque the bolt to 25 ft. lbs. (34 Nm).
   - Fuel pressure test port cap to the fuel rail
   - Power steering pipes to the retainer. Torque the fastener to 54 inch lbs. (6 Nm).
   - Alternator bracket. Torque the bolt to 37 ft. lbs. (50 Nm).
   - Serpentine belt tensioner
   - Alternator to the bracket. Torque the bolts to 37 ft. lbs. (50 Nm).
   - Serpentine belt

- Alternator electrical connector, lead and nut. Torque the nut to 115 inch lbs. (13 Nm).
2. Rotate the engine to its original position.
3. Install or connect the following:
   - Fuel injector sight shield. Torque the nut to 54 inch lbs. (6 Nm).
   - Wiper system module cover
   - Negative battery cable
4. Perform a charging system test and verify the proper operation of the system.

3.5L Engine

1. Install or connect the following:
   - Alternator
   - Alternator electrical connectors. Torque the positive (+) battery terminal to 15 ft. lbs. (20 Nm).
   - Idler pulley. Torque the bolt to 37 ft. lbs. (50 Nm).
   - Alternator bolts. Torque the bolts to 37 ft. lbs. (50 Nm).
   - Thermostat housing and radiator hose
   - Engine cooling fan assembly
   - Drive belt
   - Battery tray
   - Battery
2. Refill the cooling system.

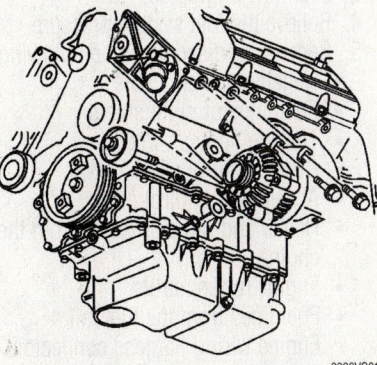

View of the alternator—3.5L engine

3.8L Engine

Install or connect the following:
- Alternator. Torque the bolts to 37 ft. lbs. (50 Nm).
- Alternator electrical connectors. Torque the positive (+) battery terminal to 15 ft. lbs. (20 Nm).
- Rear alternator brace. Torque the bolts to 22 ft. lbs. (30 Nm).
- Accessory drive belt
- Negative battery cable

Ignition Timing

ADJUSTMENT

The ignition timing is not adjustable.

Engine Assembly

REMOVAL & INSTALLATION

3.1L Engine

1. Before servicing the vehicle, refer to the precautions in the beginning of this section.
2. Drain the engine coolant.
3. Drain the oil.
4. Relieve fuel system pressure.
5. Remove or disconnect the following:
   - Negative battery cable
   - Hood
   - Throttle body air inlet duct
   - Air cleaner
   - Engine mount struts
   - Drive belt
   - Knock Sensor (KS)
   - Heated Oxygen (HO$_2$) sensor
   - Camshaft Position (CMP) sensor
   - Crankshaft Position (CKP) sensor
   - Manifold Air Pressure (MAP) sensor
   - Exhaust Gas Recirculation (EGR) valve
   - Evaporative (EVAP) emissions canister purge solenoid valve
   - Throttle Position (TP) sensor
   - Idle Air Control (IAC) valve
   - Starter
   - A/C compressor
   - Alternator
   - Ignition coil
   - Wiring harness grounds
   - Two body wiring harness to engine harness connectors
   - Oil filter
   - Catalytic converter pipe from the rear exhaust manifold
   - Engine mount lower nuts
   - Torque converter cover and bolts
   - Right side splash shield
   - Transaxle brace
   - Radiator outlet hose from the engine
   - Lower transmission to axle bolt
   - Accelerator and cruise control cables
   - Vacuum hoses from the upper intake manifold

- Fuel feed and return hoses
- Power steering lines from the pump
- Power steering pump
- Heater inlet and outlet hoses
- Radiator inlet and outlet hoses

6. Attach an engine lifting device
7. Remove or disconnect the following:
- Upper transmission to engine bolts
- Engine and place it on an approved stand
- Alternator and bracket
- Flywheel
- Engine mount bracket
- Drive belt tensioner
- Ignition control module

To install:

8. Install or connect the following:
- Ignition control module
- Drive belt tensioner
- Engine mount bracket
- Alternator and bracket
- Engine
- Transmission to engine bolts. Torque the bolts to 55 ft. lbs. (75 Nm).

9. Remove the engine lifting device.
10. Install or connect the following:
- Power steering pump. Torque the bolt to 25 ft. lbs. (34 Nm).
- Power steering lines to the pump. Torque the fasteners to 20 ft. lbs. (27 Nm).
- Radiator inlet hose
- Heater inlet and outlet hoses
- Fuel feed and return hoses
- Brake booster vacuum hose to the upper intake manifold
- New accelerator cable
- Cruise control cable
- Radiator outlet hose
- Lower transmission to engine bolt. Torque it to 55 ft. lbs. (75 Nm).
- Transmission brace. Torque the bolts to 32 ft. lbs. (43 Nm).
- Right side splash shield. Torque the fastener to 44 inch lbs. (5 Nm).
- A/C compressor. Torque the bolts 37 ft. lbs. (50 Nm).
- Starter. Torque the bolt to 32 ft. lbs. (43 Nm).
- Torque converter cover. Torque the bolts to 89 inch lbs. (10 Nm).
- Engine mount lower nuts. Torque the nuts to 32 ft. lbs. (43 Nm).
- Catalytic converter pipe to the rear exhaust manifold. Torque the fastener to 24 ft. lbs. (32 Nm).
- Oil Filter
- Two body wiring to engine harness
- Wiring harness grounds
- Ignition coil
- Alternator

- A/C compressor
- Starter
- IAC valve
- TP sensor
- EVAP canister purge solenoid valve
- EGR valve
- MAP sensor
- CKP sensor
- CMP sensor
- Heated Oxygen (HO_2) sensor
- KS sensor
- Drive belt
- Engine mount struts. Torque the fasteners to 35 ft. lbs. (48 Nm).
- Hood. Torque the bolts to 18 ft. lbs. (25 Nm). Adjust the hood as necessary
- Throttle body air inlet duct
- Air cleaner
- Negative battery cable

11. Fill the engine with clean oil.
12. Fill the coolant system.
13. Fill the power steering system.
14. Start the vehicle and check for leaks, repair if necessary.

3.4L Engine

1. Before servicing the vehicle, refer to the precautions in the beginning of this section.
2. Drain the cooling system.
3. Drain the engine oil.
4. Relieve the fuel system pressure.
5. Remove or disconnect the following:
- Negative battery cable
- Fuel injector sight shield
- Throttle body air inlet duct
- Cruise control cable
- Accelerator control cable
- Heater and radiator hoses from the engine
- Engine mount struts
- Fuel lines from the fuel rail
- Engine wiring harness connectors
- Vacuum hoses
- Brake booster vacuum hose
- Automatic transaxle range selector cable
- Wiring harness grounds
- Catalytic converter three-way pipe from the right side exhaust manifold
- Front wheels
- Splash shields
- Stabilizer shaft links from the lower control arms
- Tie rod ends from the steering knuckles
- lower ball joints from the steering knuckles
- Cooler lines and bracket from the transmission

- Axles from the transaxle and secure them to the steering knuckle/struts

✱✱ CAUTION

Failure to remove the intermediate shaft from the steering gear may result in damage to the gear or intermediate shaft and may cause a loss of steering control

- Intermediate shaft from the steering gear
- Frame bolts and make certain that an engine stand (such as J 39580) is aligned below the engine
- Engine to transaxle bolts and studs
- Engine flywheel to torque converter bolts
- Engine from the transaxle and place it on the engine stand

To install:

6. Install or connect the following:
- Engine to the transaxle/frame and install the bolts. Torque the bolts to 133 ft. lbs. (180 Nm) on 1997 models and 55 ft. lbs. (75 Nm) for 1998–01 models.
- Torque converter to flywheel bolts. Torque the bolts to 47 ft. lbs. (63 Nm).
- New frame to body bolts. Torque them to 118 ft. lbs. (160 Nm).
- Interdemiate shaft to the steering gear

✱✱ CAUTION

When installing the intermediate shaft make certain that the shaft is seated properly before installing the pinch bolt. If the pinch bolt is inserted into the coupling before the shaft, the mating surfaces disengage. Disengagement of the two shafts may lead to a loss of steering control.

- Pinch bolt at the intermediate shaft. Torque the bolt 35 ft. lbs. (48 Nm).
- Drive axles to the transaxle.
- Cooler lines and bracket to the transaxle. Torque the fasteners to 17 ft. lbs. (23 Nm).
- Lower ball joints to the steering knuckles. Torque to 40 ft. lbs. (55 Nm).
- Tie rod ends to the steering knuckles
- Stabilizer shaft links to the lower control arms. Torque the bolts 17 ft. lbs. (23 Nm).
- Inner fender splash shield. Torque the fasteners to 18 inch lbs. (2 Nm).

- Front wheels
- catalytic converter pipe to the right side exhaust manifold. Torque the nuts to 25 ft. lbs. (34 Nm).
- Wiring harness grounds
- Brake booster vacuum hose
- Vacuum hoses to the engine
- Range selector cable. Torque the screw to 14 ft. lbs. (20 Nm).
- Engine wiring harness connectors
- Fuel lines to the fuel rail. Torque the fasteners to 13 ft. lbs. (17 Nm).
- Throttle body brackets and cables. Torque the fasteners to 18 ft. lbs. (25 Nm).
- Engine mount strut. Torque the bolt to 35 ft. lbs. (48 Nm).
- Heater and radiator hoses

✱✱ CAUTION

Whenever the engine has been removed from the vehicle it is necessary to install a new accelerator control cable to avoid damage.

- New accelerator control cable
- Cruise control cable
- Throttle body air inlet duct
- Fuel injector sight shield
- Negative battery cable

7. Fill the engine with oil.
8. Fill the engine with coolant.
9. Inspect the transmission fluid level and top off if necessary.
10. Turn the ignition to the **ON** position several times to pressurize the fuel system. Start the engine and inspect for any leaks, repair if necessary. Check and top off the fluid levels if required.

3.5L Engine

1. Before servicing the vehicle, refer to the precautions in the beginning of this section.
2. Relieve the fuel system pressure.
3. Drain the engine oil.
4. Drain the engine cooling system.
5. Remove or disconnect the following:
- Negative battery cable
- Sight shield from the fuel injectors
- Power steering pump and move it aside
- Air intake duct from the throttle body
- Engine mount strut from the bracket
- Fuel lines from the fuel supply rail
- Fuel vapor line
- Throttle and cruise control cables

with the bracket from the throttle body
- Range selector cable from the Park/Neutral Position (PNP) switch
- Vacuum booster hose from the engine
- Air conditioning vacuum hose from the engine
- Wiring harness from the engine and transaxle
- Radiator inlet hose from the engine
- Transaxle fluid cooler lines from the radiator
- Thermostat housing
- Surge tank inlet hose
- Heater hoses from the engine
- Lower radiator air deflector
- Secondary Air Injection (AIR) pipe from the AIR inlet valve
- Battery cables from the retainers
- Radiator outlet hose from the engine
- Alternator
- A/C compressor, move it aside without disconnecting the lines
- Torque converter cover
- Starter
- Flexplate-to-torque converter bolts by matchmarking them
- Catalytic converter from the rear exhaust manifold
- Lower transaxle-to-engine bolts
- Front wheels and splash shields
- Fog lamp electrical connectors
- Halfshafts
- Intermediate shaft from the steering rack

✱✱ WARNING

Secure the front of the vehicle to the lift. The vehicle may become unstable as the engine/transaxle assembly is removed from the vehicle.

6. Position a frame table under the vehicle.
7. Lower the vehicle so the frame is resting on the frame table.
8. Remove or disconnect the following:
- Frame-to-chassis bolts

✱✱ WARNING

Do not damage the air conditioning compressor or lines when removing the frame from the vehicle.

- Lift the vehicle from the engine/transaxle assembly
- Engine from the transaxle

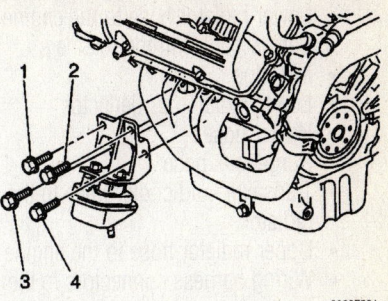

Engine mount bracket bolt tightening sequence—3.5L engine

9300Z501

To install:

9. Install or connect the following:
- Transaxle to the engine. Torque the bolts to 55 ft. lbs. (75 Nm).
- Transaxle brace. Torque the bolts to 32 ft. lbs. (43 Nm).
- Engine mount bracket to the front of the engine. Torque the bolts in sequence to 43 ft. lbs. (58 Nm).
- Engine/transaxle assembly under the vehicle

10. Coat the sub-frame bushings with rubber lubricant.
11. Lower the vehicle onto the assembly. Align the sub-frame on the vehicle using 2 bolts or drill bits, ¾ inches thick by 8 inches long through the alignment holes on the right side of the frame.
12. Install new frame-to-body bolts. Torque the bolts to 133 ft. lbs. (180 Nm) starting with the rear bolts and then the front bolts.
13. Raise the vehicle and remove the frame table.
14. Install or connect the following:
- Intermediate shaft to the steering rack. Torque the bolts to 35 ft. lbs. (48 Nm).

➡ **Be sure the shaft is fully seated on the stub before installing the pinch bolt.**

- Halfshafts and assemble the suspension
- Splash shields and front wheels
- Fog lamp electrical connectors
- Lower transaxle-to-engine bolts. Torque the bolts to 55 ft. lbs. (75 Nm).
- Catalytic converter to the rear exhaust manifold
- Flexplate-to-torque converter by aligning the matchmarks. Torque the bolts to 47 ft. lbs. (63 Nm).
- Starter and torque converter cover
- A/C compressor. Torque the bolts to 37 ft. lbs. (50 Nm).

Timing belt service is covered in Section 4 of this manual

- Lower radiator hose to the engine
- Battery cables in the retainers
- AIR pipe
- Lower radiator air deflector
- Heater hoses
- Surge tank hose
- Transaxle fluid cooler lines to the radiator
- Upper radiator hose to the engine
- Wiring harness connectors to the engine/transaxle
- A/C vacuum hose to the engine
- Brake booster hose to the engine
- Shifter cable to the transaxle PNP switch

➡ **Always use a new accelerator cable when replacing the engine assembly.**

15. Remove the trim panel under the left instrument panel and detach the throttle cable from the top of the pedal then squeeze the retainer and push the cable through the bulkhead to remove it.

16. Install or connect the following:
- New throttle cable
- Cruise and throttle cables to the throttle body
- Fuel vapor line
- Fuel lines to the supply rail
- Engine mount strut
- Air duct to the throttle body
- Fuel injector shield
- Negative battery cable

17. Refill the cooling system.

18. Install a new oil filter and refill the engine with new oil.

19. Start the engine and check for leaks, repair if necessary.

3.8L Engine

➡ **The engine, transmission and suspension assembly is removed from the bottom of the vehicle. After the assembly is removed, separate the engine from the transmission and frame.**

1. Before servicing the vehicle, refer to the precautions in the beginning of this section.

2. Discharge the A/C system.

3. Relieve the fuel system pressure.

4. Drain the cooling system.

5. Drain the engine oil.

6. Remove or disconnect the following:
- Negative battery cable
- Front fascia lower deflectors
- Engine mount struts from the brackets
- Throttle body air inlet duct
- Air cleaner
- Underhood wiring junction block
- Washer reservoir

- Hood
- Radiator inlet/outlet hoses
- A/C compressor
- Starter wiring harness
- Accelerator and cruise control cables
- Wiring harness from the top of the engine
- Fuel lines from the fuel rail
- Vacuum lines
- Heater hoses
- Engine mount strut bracket from the upper radiator support
- Power steering pump and move it aside
- Starter
- Torque converter cover
- Engine mounts
- Transaxle brace
- Catalytic converter pipe from the rear exhaust manifold
- Lower transaxle to engine bolts and place a suitable engine lifting device
- Upper transaxle to engine bolts
- Engine
- Alternator
- Ignition control module
- Drive belt tensioner
- Engine mount brackets

To install:

7. Install or connect the following:
- Engine mount brackets. Torque the bolts to 37 ft. lbs. (50 Nm).
- Drive belt tensioner
- Ignition control module
- Alternator. Torque the brace bolt to 37 ft. lbs. (50 Nm).
- Flywheel. Torque the new bolt to 47 ft. lbs. (63 Nm).
- Engine
- Upper transaxle to engine bolts. Torque the bolts 55 ft. lbs. (75 Nm).
- Remove the engine lifting device
- Lower transaxle to engine bolts. Torque the bolts to 55 ft. lbs. (75 Nm).
- Catalytic converter pipe to the rear exhaust manifold. Torque the fastener to 22 ft. lbs. (30 Nm).
- Transaxle brace. Torque the bolts to 32 ft. lbs. (43 Nm).
- Lower engine mount. Torque the bolts to 32 ft. lbs. (43 Nm).
- Torque converter cover. Torque the bolts to 89 inch lbs. (10 Nm).
- Starter. Torque the bolt to 22 inch lbs. (30 Nm).
- Power steering pump. Torque the bolt to 25 ft. lbs. (34 Nm).
- Engine mount strut brackets to the

upper radiator support. Torque the bolt to 21 ft. lbs. (28 Nm).
- Heater hoses
- Vacuum lines
- Wiring harness to the top of the engine

➡ **Whenever the engine is removed from the engine a new accelerator cable must be installed to avoid possibly injury or vehicle damage.**

- New accelerator cable and cruise control cable to the bracket. Torque the bolt to 89 inch lbs. (10 Nm).
- Starter motor wiring harness
- A/C compressor. Torque the two upper mounting bolts and the lower bolt to 37 ft. lbs. (50 Nm).
- Inlet and outlet radiator hoses
- Throttle body air inlet duct
- Air cleaner
- Hood and adjust as necessary
- Washer reservoir
- Underhood accessory wiring junction block
- Front fascia lower deflectors. Torque the fasteners to 53 inch lbs. (6 Nm).
- Fuel injector sight shield
- Negative battery cable

8. Fill the engine with new oil.

9. Fill the cooling system.

10. Charge the A/C system.

11. Start the engine and check for leaks, repair if necessary.

Water Pump

REMOVAL & INSTALLATION

3.1L and 3.4L Engines

1. Before servicing the vehicle, refer to the precautions in the beginning of this section.

2. Drain the coolant from the engine.

3. Remove or disconnect the following:

- Negative battery cable
- Serpentine drive belt guard
- Loosen the water pump pulley bolts
- Serpentine drive belt
- Water pump pulley
- Water pump
- Water pump gasket

To install:

4. Clean the gasket mating surface.

5. Install or connect the following:
- Gasket
- Water pump. Torque the bolts to 89 inch lbs. (10 Nm).

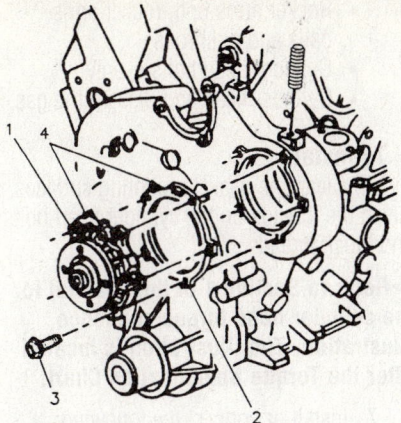

1 WATER PUMP
2 GASKET
3 10 N•m (89 LB. IN.)
4 LOCATOR – MUST BE VERTICAL

7924LG01

Water pump assembly mounting—3.1L and 3.4L engines

- Water pump pulley and hand tighten the bolts at this time.
- Serpentine drive belt
- Torque the water pump pulley bolts to 18 inch lbs. (25 Nm)
- Serpentine drive belt guard
6. Fill the cooling system.
7. Start the engine and check for leaks, repair if necessary. Roadtest the vehicle and verify there is no air in the cooling system.

3.5L Engine

1. Before servicing the vehicle, refer to the precautions in the beginning of this section.
2. Partially drain the cooling system.
3. Remove or disconnect the following:
- Water pump pulley bolts, loosen them
- Drive belt
- Idler pulley
- Water pump pulley

➡**The water pump is attached to the engine with both long and short bolts, be sure to note their locations.**

- Water pump and discard the gasket
4. Clean the water pump mounting surface.

To install:

➡**Be sure to install the 5 long bolts in the proper locations.**

5. Install or connect the following:
- Water pump using a new gasket. Torque the bolts to 124 inch lbs. (14 Nm).

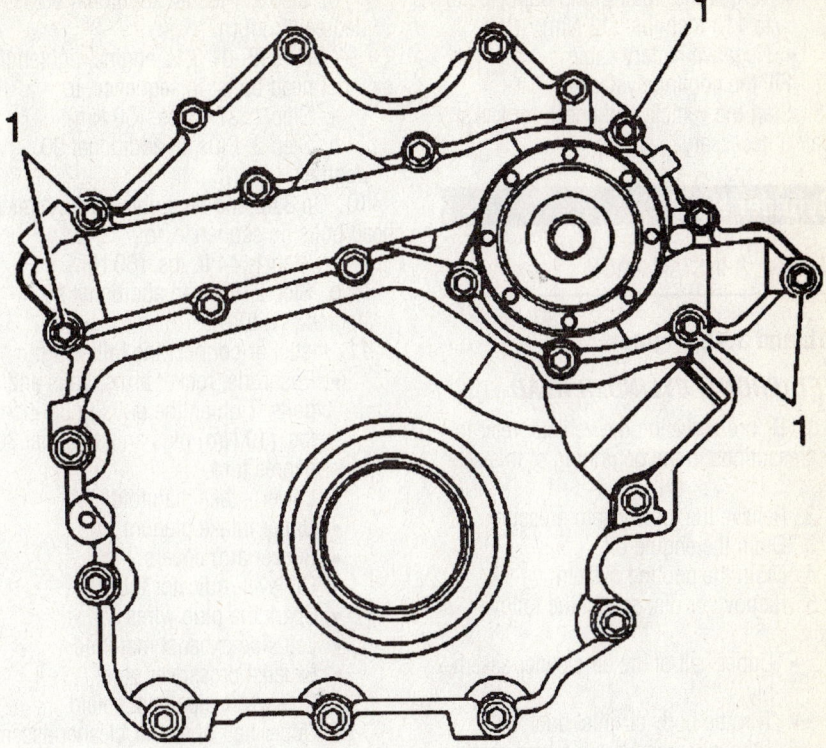

9300Z502

Be sure to install the 5 long water pump bolts in the correct locations—3.5L engine

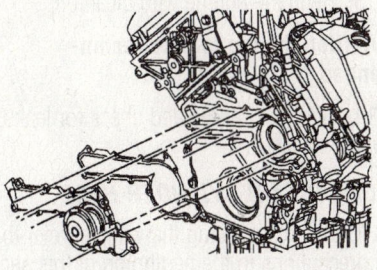

9300Z503

Water pump mounting—3.5L engine

- Water pump pulley
- Idler pulley. Torque the bolt to 37 ft. lbs. (50 Nm).
- Drive belt
6. Refill the cooling system.
7. Start the engine and check for leaks.

3.8L Engines

1. Before servicing the vehicle, refer to the precautions in the beginning of this section.
2. Negative battery cable.
3. Drain the engine coolant.
4. Remove or disconnect the following:
- Drive belt
- Water pump pulley

- Power steering pump and move it aside
- Water pump
- Water pump gasket
5. Clean the gasket mating surface.

To install:

6. Install or connect the following:
- Water pump gasket
- Water pump and using a torque angle meter torque the long water pump bolts to 15 ft. lbs. (20 Nm).
- Short water pump bolts. Torque the bolts to 11 ft. lbs. (15 Nm).
- Water pump pulley and hand tighten the bolts
- Power steering pump. Torque the bolts to 25 ft. lbs. (34 Nm).
- Drive belt

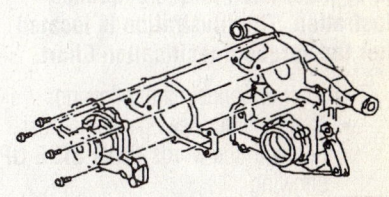

7922Z504

Exploded view of the water pump assembly mounting—3.8L engine

- Torque the water pump pulley bolts to 115 inch lbs. (13 Nm).
- Negative battery cable
7. Fill the cooling system.
8. Start the vehicle and check for leaks, repair if necessary.

Cylinder Head

REMOVAL & INSTALLATION

3.1L and 3.4L Engines

LEFT (FRONT) CYLINDER HEAD

1. Before servicing the vehicle, refer to the precautions in the beginning of this section.
2. Relieve the fuel system pressure.
3. Drain the engine oil.
4. Drain the cooling system.
5. Remove or disconnect the following:

- Upper half of the air cleaner assembly
- Throttle body air inlet duct
- Exhaust crossover pipe heat shield
- Crossover pipe
- Spark plug wires from the spark plugs
- Rocker arm covers
- Upper intake plenum and lower intake manifold
- Left side exhaust manifold
- Oil level indicator tube

➡ **When removing the valve train components, keep them in order for installation purposes.**

- Rocker arm bolt, rocker arms, balls and pushrods
- Cylinder head bolts evenly
- Cylinder head and discard the gasket

To install:

6. Clean all the gasket mounting surfaces. Clean the threads on the cylinder head bolts and block threads.

➡ **Refer to Section 1 of this manual for the cylinder head torque sequence illustration. The illustration is located after the Torque Specification Chart.**

7. Install or connect the following:
- New cylinder head gasket in position with the words **THIS SIDE UP** showing
- Cylinder head and lubricate the bolt threads with sealer
8. On 1997 3.1L engine, tighten the cylinder head bolts, in sequence, to:
   a. Step 1: 33 ft. lbs. (45 Nm).

b. Step 2: Plus an additional 90 degree (¼) turn.
9. On 1998–01 3.1L engine, tighten the cylinder head bolts, in sequence, to:
   a. Step 1: 37 ft. lbs. (50 Nm).
   b. Step 2: Plus an additional 90 degree (¼) turn.
10. On 3.4L engine, tighten the cylinder head bolts, in sequence, to:
   a. Step 1: 44 ft. lbs. (60 Nm).
   b. Step 2: Plus an additional 90 degree (¼) turn.
11. Install or connect the following:
- Pushrods, rocker arms, balls and bolts. Tighten the bolts to 89 inch lbs. (10 Nm) plus an additional 30 degree turn.
- Lower intake manifold
- Upper intake plenum
- Rocker arm covers
- Oil level indicator tube
- Spark the plug wires
- Left side exhaust manifold
- Exhaust crossover pipe
- Crossover pipe heat shield
- Upper half of the air cleaner assembly
- Throttle body air inlet duct
- Negative battery cable
12. Refill the cooling system.
13. Refill the engine with clean oil.

➡ **A filter change is also recommended.**

14. Start the engine and check for leaks, repair if necessary.

RIGHT (REAR) CYLINDER HEAD

1. Before servicing the vehicle, refer to the precautions in the beginning of this section.
2. Relieve the fuel system pressure.
3. Drain the engine oil.
4. Drain the cooling system.
5. Remove or disconnect the following:
- Upper half of the air cleaner
- Throttle body air inlet duct
- Exhaust crossover pipe heat shield
- Crossover pipe
- Oxygen (O₂S) sensor
- Exhaust pipe from the exhaust manifold
- Right side exhaust manifold
- Spark plug wires from the spark plugs
- Rocker arm covers
- Upper intake plenum
- Lower intake manifold

➡ **When removing the valve train components keep them in order for installation purposes.**

- Rocker arms bolt, rocker arms, balls and pushrods
- Cylinder head bolts evenly
- Cylinder head and discard the gasket

To install:

6. Clean the gasket mounting surfaces. Clean the threads on the cylinder head bolts and block threads.

➡ **Refer to Section 1 of this manual for the cylinder head torque sequence illustration. The illustration is located after the Torque Specification Chart.**

7. Install or connect the following:
- New cylinder head gasket in position with the words **THIS SIDE UP** showing
- Cylinder head and lubricate the bolt threads with sealer
8. On 1997 3.1L engine, tighten the cylinder head bolts, in sequence, to:
   a. Step 1: 33 ft. lbs. (45 Nm).
   b. Step 2: Plus an additional 90 degree (¼) turn.
9. On 1998–01 3.1L engine, tighten the cylinder head bolts, in sequence, to:
   a. Step 1: 37 ft. lbs. (50 Nm).
   b. Step 2: Plus an additional 90 degree (¼) turn.
10. On 3.4L engine, tighten the cylinder head bolts, in sequence, to:
   a. Step 1: 44 ft. lbs. (60 Nm).
   b. Step 2: Plus an additional 90 degree (¼) turn.
11. Install or connect the following:
- Pushrods, rocker arms, balls and rocker arm bolts. Tighten the bolts to 89 inch lbs. (10 Nm) plus an additional 30 degrees.
- Lower intake manifold
- Upper intake plenum
- Rocker arm covers
- Spark plug wires
- Exhaust manifold
- Exhaust pipe to the exhaust manifold
- O₂S sensor
- Exhaust crossover pipe
- Heat shield
- Upper half of the air cleaner assembly
- Throttle body air inlet duct
- Negative battery cable
12. Refill the cooling system.
13. Refill the engine with clean oil.

➡ **An oil filter change is recommended.**

14. Start the engine and check for leaks, repair if necessary.

3.5L Engine

FRONT

1. Before servicing the vehicle, refer to the precautions in the beginning of this section.
2. Drain the engine oil.
3. Drain the cooling system.
4. Remove or disconnect the following:
   - Negative battery cable
   - Intake manifold
   - Water outlet housing
   - Engine mount strut bracket
   - Coolant crossover pipe
   - Front exhaust manifold
   - Camshaft covers
5. Install a holding tool on the camshafts to hold them in position.
6. Remove or disconnect the following:
   - Camshaft primary chain
   - Camshafts from the front cylinder head
   - Rocker arms and valve lifters

➡**Be sure to keep the arms and lifters in order so they can be installed the their original locations.**

   - M6 bolts from the front of the cylinder head
   - M11 cylinder head bolts, discard them. Note the location of the longer bolt
   - Cylinder head
7. Clean the cylinder head mounting surfaces.

To install:

➡**Refer to Section 1 of this manual for the cylinder head torque sequence illustration. The illustration is located after the Torque Specification Chart.**

8. Be sure the dowels are securely mounted in the engine block.
9. Install or connect the following:
   - New gasket
   - Cylinder head
   - New M11 bolts
   - M6 bolts in the front of the cylinder head
10. Torque the M11 bolts in sequence to:
    a. Step 1: 22 ft. lbs. (30 Nm).
    b. Step 2: 60 degree turn.
    c. Step 3: 60 degree turn.
    d. Step 4: 60 degree turn.
11. Torque the long M6 bolt to 22 ft. lbs. (30 Nm).
12. Torque both shorter M6 bolts to 106 inch lbs. (12 Nm).
13. Install or connect the following:

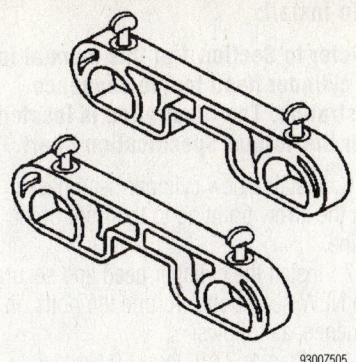

Camshaft holding fixture J-42038—3.5L engine

   - Lifters and rocker arms in their original positions
   - Camshafts, primary chain and covers
   - Exhaust manifold
   - Coolant crossover pipe
   - Engine mount strut bracket
   - Water outlet housing
   - Intake manifold
   - New oil filter
   - Negative battery cable
14. Refill the engine with clean oil.
15. Refill the cooling system.
16. Start the engine and check for leaks, repair if necessary.

REAR

1. Before servicing the vehicle, refer to the precautions in the beginning of this section.
2. Drain the engine oil.
3. Drain the cooling system.
4. Remove or disconnect the following:
   - Negative battery cable
   - Intake manifold
   - Coolant crossover pipe

➡**Do not remove the rear exhaust manifold. Detach it from the cylinder head and the connection from the front manifold; then, move it aside.**

   - Camshaft covers. Install a holding tool on the camshafts to hold them in position
   - Primary camshaft chain
   - Camshafts, rocker arms and lifters

➡**Keep them in order so they can be installed in their original positions.**

   - Engine Coolant Temperature (ECT) sensor from the cylinder head
   - M6 bolts from the front of the cylinder head, note the location of the longer bolt

   - M11 cylinder head bolts and discard the bolts
   - Cylinder head
5. Clean the cylinder head mounting surfaces.

To install:

➡**Refer to Section 1 of this manual for the cylinder head torque sequence illustration. The illustration is located after the Torque Specification Chart.**

6. Be sure the dowels are securely mounted in the engine block.
7. Install or connect the following:
   - New gasket
   - Cylinder head
   - New M11 bolts
   - M6 bolts in the front of the cylinder head
8. Torque the M11 bolts in sequence using the following steps:
   a. Step 1: 22 ft. lbs. (30 Nm).
   b. Step 2: 60 degree turn.
   c. Step 3: 60 degree turn.
   d. Step 4: 60 degree turn.
9. Torque the long M6 bolt to 22 ft. lbs. (30 Nm).
10. Torque both short M6 bolts to 106 inch lbs. (12 Nm).
11. Install or connect the following:
    - ECT sensor. Torque the sensor to 15 ft. lbs. (20 Nm).
    - Lifters and rocker arms in their original positions
    - Camshafts and primary chain
12. Remove the camshaft holding fixture.
13. Install or connect the following:
    - Camshaft covers
    - Exhaust manifold on the cylinder head
    - Coolant crossover pipe
    - New oil filter
    - Negative battery cable
14. Refill the engine with clean oil.
15. Refill the cooling system.
16. Start the engine and check for leaks, repair if necessary.

3.8L Engine

LEFT SIDE

1. Before servicing the vehicle, refer to the precautions in the beginning of this section.
2. Relieve the fuel system pressure.
3. Drain the cooling system.
4. Remove or disconnect the following:
   - Negative battery cable
   - Fuel lines from the fuel rail

Refer to Section 1 for engine rebuilding specifications

- Upper and lower intake manifolds
- Spark plugs
- Left exhaust manifold
- Rocker arm (valve) cover, rocker arms and pushrods
- Cylinder head and discard the gasket and bolts

5. Clean and inspect the cylinder head. Clean the gasket mating surfaces of all components. Be careful not to nick or scratch any surfaces as this will allow leak paths. Clean the bolt threads in the cylinder block and on the head bolts. Dirt will affect bolt torque.

To install:

➡ **Refer to Section 1 of this manual for the cylinder head torque sequence illustration. The illustration is located after the Torque Specification Chart.**

6. Install the new cylinder head gasket with the arrow pointing to the front of the engine.

7. New cylinder head bolts. Torque the bolts in sequence, as follows:
   a. Step 1: 37 ft. lbs. (50 Nm).
   b. Step 2: Plus 130 degree turn.
   c. Step 3: Rotate the 4 center bolts an additional 30 degrees.

8. Install or connect the following:
   - Rocker arms and pushrods
   - Valve cover
   - Left exhaust manifold
   - Spark plugs. Tighten to 20 ft. lbs. (27 Nm).
   - Lower and upper intake manifolds
   - Negative battery cable

9. Refill the cooling system.

10. Start the engine and check for leaks.

RIGHT SIDE

1. Before servicing the vehicle, refer to the precautions in the beginning of this section.

2. Relieve the fuel system pressure.

3. Drain the cooling system.

4. Remove or disconnect the following:
   - Negative battery cable
   - Fuel lines from the fuel rail
   - Upper and lower intake manifolds
   - Spark plugs
   - Right exhaust manifold
   - Rocker arm (valve) cover, rocker arms and pushrods
   - Serpentine drive belt tensioner
   - Rear alternator brace
   - Cylinder head and discard the gasket and bolts

5. Clean and inspect the cylinder head. Clean the gasket mating surfaces of all components. Be careful not to nick or scratch any surfaces. Clean the bolt threads in the cylinder block and on the head bolts.

To install:

➡ **Refer to Section 1 of this manual for the cylinder head torque sequence illustration. The illustration is located after the Torque Specification Chart.**

6. Install a new cylinder head gasket with the arrow pointing to the front of the engine.

7. Install the cylinder head and secure with NEW head bolts. Torque the bolts, in sequence, as follows:
   a. Step 1: 37 ft. lbs. (50 Nm)
   b. Step 2: Plus a 130 degree turn
   c. Step 3: Rotate the 4 center bolts an additional 30 degrees

8. Install or connect the following:
   - Rocker arms and pushrods
   - Valve cover
   - Right exhaust manifold
   - Spark plugs. Torque them to 20 ft. lbs. (27 Nm).
   - Lower and upper intake manifolds
   - Negative battery cable

9. Refill the cooling system.

10. Start the engine and check for leaks.

Rocker Arms

REMOVAL & INSTALLATION

3.1L and 3.4L Engines

LEFT SIDE

1. Before servicing the vehicle, refer to the precautions in the beginning of this section.

2. Disconnect the negative battery cable

3. Drain the cooling system to a level below the coolant pipe on the front of the engine.

4. Remove or disconnect the following:
   - Coolant bypass hose clamp at the coolant tube
   - Coolant tube at the cylinder head and move it aside
   - Positive Crankcase Ventilation (PCV) valve from the rocker arm cover
   - Rocker arm cover

➡ **Keep the pushrods in order. Intake pushrods are 5¾ inches long and exhaust pushrods are 6 inches long.**

   - Rocker arm bolts, balls, rocker arms and pushrods

To install:

5. Clean all the gasket mounting surfaces.

6. Lubricate all the valvetrain components with engine oil.

7. Install or connect the following:
   - Pushrods and the rocker arms. Tighten the bolts to 89 inch lbs. (10 Nm) plus an additional 30 degree turn.
   - Rocker arm cover using a new gasket. Tighten the rocker cover bolts to 90 inch lbs. (10 Nm).
   - PCV valve to the rocker arm cover
   - Coolant tube and the thermostat bypass hose. Tighten the screw at the water pump to 106 inch lbs. (12 Nm), the bolt at the cylinder head corner to 18 ft. lbs. (25 Nm) and the nut to 18 ft. lbs. (25 Nm).
   - Negative battery cable

8. Refill the cooling system.

9. Start the vehicle and verify no leaks.

RIGHT SIDE

1. Before servicing the vehicle, refer to the precautions in the beginning of this section.

2. Remove or disconnect the following:
   - Negative battery cable
   - Spark plug wires from the spark plugs and the upper intake plenum wire retainer
   - Power brake booster vacuum pipe from the intake plenum
   - Serpentine belt
   - Alternator
   - Ignition assembly and Evaporative Emissions (EVAP) canister purge solenoid as an assembly
   - Rocker arm cover

➡ **Keep the pushrods in order. Intake pushrods are 5¾ inches long and exhaust pushrods are 6 inches long.**

   - Rocker arm bolts, balls, rocker arms and pushrods

To install:

3. Clean the gasket mounting surfaces.

4. Lubricate all the valve train components with engine oil.

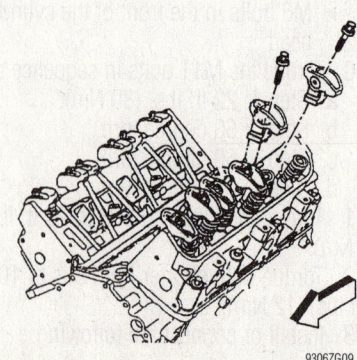

Rocker arm components—3.1L and 3.4L engines

Rocker arm mounting—3.1L engine

5. Install or connect the following:
   - Pushrods and the rocker arms. Tighten the bolts to 89 inch lbs. (10 Nm) plus an additional 30 degree turn.
   - Rocker arm cover using a new gasket. Tighten the rocker cover bolts to 90 inch lbs. (10 Nm).
   - Alternator
   - Serpentine belt
   - Power brake booster vacuum pipe to the plenum
   - EVAP solenoid and ignition assembly
   - Spark plug wires
   - Negative battery cable
6. Start the vehicle and verify no leaks.

3.5L Engine

Refer to the camshaft removal and installation procedure for rocker arm service.

3.8L Engine

✷✷ WARNING

The rocker arm bolts have been permanently stretched during installation. New bolts must be used each time the rocker arm assemblies have been removed for any reason.

LEFT SIDE (FRONT) ROCKER ARMS

1. Before servicing the vehicle, refer to the precautions in the beginning of this section.
2. Remove or disconnect the following:
   - Negative battery cable
   - Engine lift bracket from the exhaust manifold studs
   - Fuel injector sight shield
   - Engine mount strut bracket
   - Left side spark plug wires
   - Left side spark plug cover from the valve rocker arm cover
   - Left valve rocker arm cover

➡The rocker arms, pushrods, pedestals and bolts must be kept in

order for installation in the same locations they were removed from.

3. Remove the rocker arm bolt(s), pedestal(s), rocker arm(s) and pushrod(s).
   To install:
4. Clean all gasket surfaces completely.
5. Apply thread locking compound to the rocker arm bolt(s).
6. Install or connect the following:
   - Seat the pushrod in the lifter and install the rocker arm, pedestal and mounting bolt. Tighten the mounting bolt to 19 ft. lbs. (25 Nm), then using a torque angle meter, tighten the bolts an additional 70 degrees.
   - Rocker arm cover with a new gasket. Torque the mounting bolts to 89 inch lbs. (10 Nm).
   - Spark plug wire cover to the rocker arm cover
   - Spark plug wires
   - Engine mount strut bracket. Torque the bolt to 75 ft. lbs. (102 Nm).
   - Fuel injector sight shield
   - Engine lift bracket to the exhaust manifold. Torque the bolt to 22 ft. lbs. (30 Nm).
   - Negative battery cable
7. Start the vehicle and check for leaks, repair if necessary.

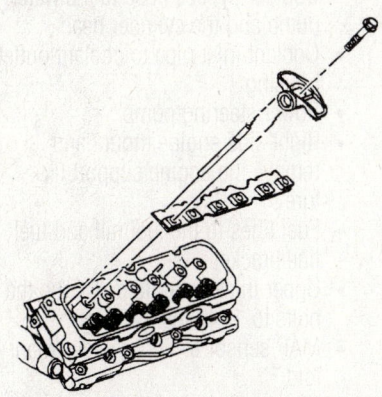

Exploded view of the rocker arm, pushrod and pushrod guide plate assembly—3.8L engine

RIGHT SIDE (REAR) ROCKER ARMS

1. Before servicing the vehicle, refer to the precautions in the beginning of this section.
2. Remove or disconnect the following:
   - Negative battery cable
   - Alternator
   - Engine mount struts
3. Rotate the engine for proper access.

4. Remove or disconnect the following:
   - Evaporative (EVAP) emissions purge solenoid and brace
   - Right side spark plug wires
   - Rocker arm cover and gasket

➡**The rocker arms, pushrods, pedestals and bolts must be kept in order for installation in the same locations they were removed from.**

   - Rocker arm bolt(s), pedestal(s), rocker arm(s) and pushrod(s)
   To install:
5. Clean all gasket surfaces completely.
6. Apply thread locking compound to the rocker arm bolt(s).
7. Seat the pushrod in the lifter and install the rocker arm, pedestal and mounting bolt. Tighten the mounting bolt to 11 ft. lbs. (15 Nm), then using a torque angle meter, tighten the bolts an additional 90 degrees.
8. Install or connect the following:
   - Rocker arm cover. Torque the bolts to 89 inch lbs. (10 Nm).
   - EVAP purge solenoid and brace
   - Right side spark plug wires and rotate the engine back to the original position
   - Engine mount struts. Torque the bolt to 37 ft. lbs. (50 Nm).
   - Alternator. Torque the bolt to 37 ft. lbs. (50 Nm).
   - Fuel injector sight shield
   - Negative battery cable
9. Start the vehicle and check for leaks, repair if necessary.

Intake Manifold

REMOVAL & INSTALLATION

3.1L and 3.4L Engines

These vehicles use a 2-piece intake manifold. Note that these pieces are cast aluminum. Use care when working with light alloy components.

1. Before servicing the vehicle, refer to the precautions in the beginning of this section.
2. Relieve the fuel system pressure.
3. Drain the cooling system.
4. Remove or disconnect the following:
   - Upper half of the air cleaner
   - Throttle body duct
5. Drain the cooling system.
6. Remove or disconnect the following:
   - Exhaust Gas Recirculation (EGR) pipe from exhaust manifold

- Serpentine belt
- Brake vacuum pipe at the intake plenum
- Control cables from the throttle body and intake plenum bracket
- Power steering lines at the alternator bracket
- Alternator
- Spark plug wires from the spark plugs and the intake plenum retainers
- Ignition assembly
- Evaporative Emissions (EVAP) canister purge solenoid as an assembly
- Electrical connectors from the Throttle Position Sensor (TPS), Idle Air Control (IAC), fuel Injectors, Engine Coolant Temperature (ECT) sensor, Manifold Absolute Pressure (MAP) sensor and Camshaft Position (CMP) sensor.
- Vacuum lines from the vacuum modulator, fuel pressure regulator and Positive Crankcase Ventilation (PCV) valve
- MAP sensor
- Upper intake plenum
- Fuel lines from the fuel rail and fuel line bracket

7. Install an engine support fixture.
8. Remove or disconnect the following:
- Right side engine mount
- Power steering pump and move it aside without disconnecting the lines
- Coolant inlet pipe from coolant outlet housing
- Coolant bypass hose from the water pump and the cylinder head
- Upper radiator hose at thermostat housing
- Thermostat housing
- Both rocker arm covers
- Lower intake manifold bolts. Be sure the washers on the 4 center bolts are installed in their original locations

➡**When removing the valvetrain components, keep them in order for installation purposes.**

- Rocker arm bolts, rocker arms and pushrods
- Intake manifold and discard the gasket

To install:

9. Clean the gasket mating surfaces and the excess RTV sealant from front and rear ridges of engine block.
10. Place a 3mm bead of RTV, on each ridge, where the front and rear of the intake manifold contact the block.

11. Install or connect the following:
- New intake manifold gasket
- Intake manifold
- Pushrods, rocker arms and bolts

➡**Be sure the pushrods are properly seated in the valve lifters and rocker arms.**

- Rocker arm bolts. Torque the bolts to 89 inch lbs. (10 Nm) plus an additional 30 degree turn.

✳✳ WARNING

In order to prevent oil leaks, tighten the vertical bolts before the diagonal bolts.

➡**Refer to Section 1 of this manual for the lower intake manifold torque sequence illustration. The illustration is located after the Torque Specification Chart.**

- Lower intake manifold bolts. Apply sealant to the threads of bolts. Torque the bolts to 115 inch lbs. (13 Nm).
- Both rocker arm covers
- Thermostat housing
- Upper radiator hose at thermostat housing
- Coolant bypass hose to the water pump and the cylinder head
- Coolant inlet pipe to coolant outlet housing
- Power steering pump
- Right side engine mount and remove the engine support fixture
- Fuel lines to the fuel rail and fuel line bracket
- Upper intake manifold. Torque the bolts to 18 ft. lbs. (25 Nm).
- MAP sensor to upper intake manifold
- Vacuum lines to the vacuum modulator, fuel pressure regulator and PCV valve
- Electrical connectors to the TPS, IAC, fuel Injectors, ECT sensor, MAP sensor and CMP sensor
- Ignition assembly and the EVAP canister purge solenoid as an assembly
- Spark plug wires to the spark plugs and the intake plenum retainers
- Alternator
- Power steering lines at the alternator bracket
- Control cables to the throttle body and intake plenum bracket

- Brake vacuum pipe at the intake plenum
- Serpentine belt
- EGR pipe to exhaust manifold
- Throttle body duct
- Upper half of the air cleaner assembly
- Negative battery cable

13. Refill the cooling system.

➡**An engine oil and filter change is recommended.**

14. Start the vehicle and check for leaks, repair if necessary.

3.5L Engine

1. Before servicing the vehicle, refer to the precautions in the beginning of this section.
2. Remove or disconnect the following:
- Negative battery cable
- Air duct from the throttle body
3. Partially drain the engine coolant.
4. Remove or disconnect the following:
- Fuel injector cover
- Cruise control and accelerator cables from the throttle body and bracket
- Coolant hoses from the throttle body
- Fuel lines from the fuel supply rail
- Fuel vapor line from the Evaporative Emission (EVAP) canister purge solenoid
- Brake booster vacuum hose
- Air conditioning vacuum hose from the engine
- Surge tank inlet pipe retainer from the fuel supply rail
- Fuel injector electrical connectors
- Throttle Position Sensor (TPS) electrical connectors
- Idle Air Control (IAC) valve electrical connector
- Evaporative Emission (EVAP) canister purge solenoid connector

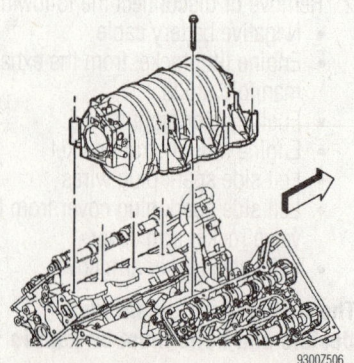

93002506

Intake manifold assembly—3.5L engine

- Manifold Absolute Pressure (MAP) sensor connector
- Wiring harness channels from the camshaft covers and move them aside with harness
- Vacuum tube from the fuel pressure regulator and throttle body
- Positive Crankcase Ventilation (PCV) tubes from both camshaft covers and intake manifold
- Exhaust Gas Recirculation (EGR) valve outlet pipe
- Fuel supply rail with injectors

➡ **Disengage the snap-lock retainers by pushing toward the camshaft covers and lifting.**

- Intake manifold

➡ **The manifold-to-cylinder head seals are reusable unless cut or damaged.**

5. Inspect the intake manifold-to-cylinder head seals for damage or cuts.
6. Clean the intake manifold and cylinder head mating surfaces.

To install:

➡ **Refer to Section 1 of this manual for the intake manifold torque sequence illustration. The illustration is located after the Torque Specification Chart.**

7. Install or connect the following:
- Throttle body using a new gasket. Torque the nuts to 106 inch lbs. (12 Nm).
- New intake manifold-to-cylinder head seals
- Intake manifold. Torque the bolts, in a circular pattern, starting from the center to 62 inch lbs. (7 Nm).

✳✳ WARNING

Do not apply excessive pressure to the fuel supply rail assembly. If the assembly is hard to install, check for misalignment of a fuel injector(s).

- New O-rings on the fuel injectors
- Fuel supply rail with injectors by pressing the snap-lock retainers until they lock in place
- EGR pipe. Torque the intake manifold bolt to 89 inch lbs. (10 Nm) and the coolant crossover bolt to 18 ft. lbs. (24 Nm).
- PCV valve and related tubing
- Brake booster and fuel pressure regulator vacuum hoses
- Air conditioning vacuum hose to the intake manifold

- Engine wiring harness with channel to the camshaft covers. Torque the bolts to 89 inch lbs. (10 Nm).
- Surge tank pipe retainer to the fuel supply rail
- Wiring harness connectors to the TPS, IAC, EVAP solenoid and MAP sensor
- Fuel injector electrical connectors
- Coolant hoses to the throttle body
- Cruise control and accelerator cables to the throttle body
- Fuel lines to the fuel supply rail
- Vapor line to the purge solenoid
- Fuel injector cover
- Air duct to the throttle body
- Negative battery cable

8. Refill the cooling system.
9. Start the engine and check for leaks, repair if necessary.

3.8L Engine

➡ **There are 2 bolts hidden beneath the upper intake manifold. These bolts are located in the right front and left rear corners of the lower intake manifold. It is necessary to remove the upper intake manifold to service the lower intake manifold.**

1. Relieve the fuel system pressure.
2. Drain the cooling system.
3. Remove or disconnect the following:
- Negative battery cable
- Fuel injector sight shield and air inlet duct
- Air intake duct
- Spark plug wires from the right side of the engine, move them aside
- Manifold vacuum source
- Fuel rail and the Exhaust Gas Recirculation (EGR) heat shield
- Throttle cable bracket from the cylinder head bracket
- Throttle cables from the throttle body lever
- Throttle body support bracket
- Upper intake plenum and discard the gasket
- Upper radiator hose from the thermostat housing
- Alternator
- Drive belt tensioner
- EGR valve outlet pipe
- Lower intake manifold and discard the gaskets

To install:

➡ **Refer to Section 1 of this manual for the intake manifold torque sequence**

illustration. The illustration is located after the Torque Specification Chart.

4. Thoroughly clean all sealing surfaces.
5. Install or connect the following:
- New intake manifold gaskets
- Intake manifold. Torque the bolts, in sequence, to 11 ft. lbs. (15 Nm). Torque the bolts again in sequence to ensure a torque of 11 ft. lbs. (15 Nm) was achieved.
- EGR valve outlet pipe
- Drive belt tensioner. Torque the bolts to 37 ft. lbs. (50 Nm).
- Alternator and serpentine belt
- Upper radiator hose to the thermostat housing
- Intake plenum using a new gasket. Torque the bolts, in sequence, to 89 inch lbs. (10 Nm).
- Throttle body support bracket
- Throttle cables to the throttle body lever
- EGR heat shield
- Fuel rail assembly. Torque the bolts to 84 inch lbs. (10 Nm).
- Vacuum lines, fuel lines and electrical connectors to the fuel injectors
- Vacuum lines to the intake manifold
- Spark plug wires to the rear bank spark plugs
- Air inlet duct and fuel injector sight shield
- Negative battery cable

6. Pressurize the fuel system.
7. Refill and bleed the cooling system.
8. Start the vehicle and check for leaks, repair if necessary.

Exhaust Manifold

REMOVAL & INSTALLATION

3.1L Engine

LEFT SIDE

1. Before servicing the vehicle, refer to the precautions in the beginning of this section.
2. Remove or disconnect the following:
- Negative battery cable
- Throttle body air inlet duct
- Right engine mount strut bracket
- Crossover pipe heat shield
- Crossover pipe bolts to the exhaust manifold
- Exhaust manifold heat shield
- Exhaust manifold

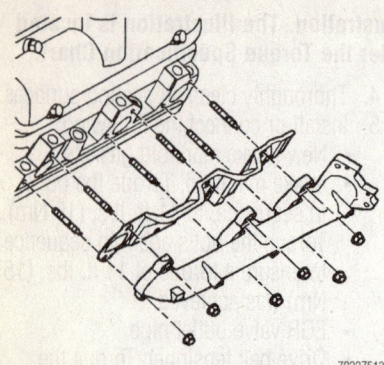

Exploded view of the left exhaust manifold mounting

To install:

3. Clean the mating surfaces.

4. Install or connect the following:
- New gasket
- Exhaust manifold. Torque the nuts to 12 ft. lbs. (16 Nm).
- Exhaust manifold heat shield. Torque the nuts to 89 inch lbs. (10 Nm).
- Exhaust crossover pipe to the manifold. Torque the bolt to 15 ft. lbs. (20 Nm).
- Crossover pipe heat shield. Torque the bolt to 15 ft. lbs. (20 Nm).
- Left side engine mount strut bracket. Torque the bolt to 37 ft. lbs. (50 Nm).
- Throttle body air inlet duct
- Negative battery cable

RIGHT SIDE

1. Before servicing the vehicle, refer to the precautions in the beginning of this section.

2. Remove or disconnect the following:
- Negative battery cable
- Throttle body air inlet duct
- Crossover pipe and heat shield

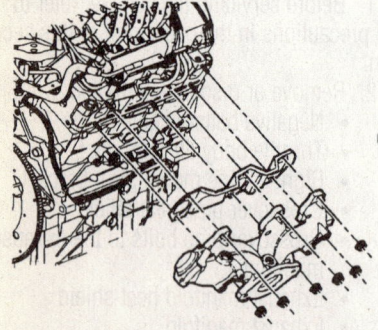

Exploded view of the right exhaust manifold mounting—3.1L engine

- Heated Oxygen (HO2S) sensor
- Catalytic converter pipe from the exhaust manifold
- Exhaust Gas Recirculation (EGR) pipe from the exhaust manifold
- Exhaust pipe from the converter flange
- Exhaust manifold heat shields
- Exhaust manifold

To install:

3. Clean the mating surfaces.

4. Install or connect the following:
- New gasket
- Exhaust manifold. Torque the nuts to 12 ft. lbs. (16 Nm).
- Exhaust manifold heat shield. Torque the bolts to 89 inch lbs. (10 Nm).
- Exhaust crossover pipe to the manifold
- Catalytic converter heat shield
- Exhaust crossover pipe heat shield
- Exhaust pipe to the exhaust manifold
- HO2S sensor
- EGR pipe to the exhaust manifold
- Throttle body air inlet duct
- Negative battery cable

3.4L Engine

LEFT SIDE (FRONT) MANIFOLD

1. Before servicing the vehicle, refer to the precautions in the beginning of this section.

2. Drain the cooling system

3. Remove or disconnect the following:
- Negative battery cable
- Air cleaner
- Throttle body air inlet duct
- Exhaust crossover heat shield
- Crossover pipe
- Upper radiator hose from the thermostat housing
- Ignition wires from the front spark plugs
- Exhaust manifold heat shield
- Exhaust manifold

To install:

4. Clean the mating surface for the exhaust manifold and the cylinder head.

5. Install or connect the following:
- New gasket
- Exhaust manifold. Torque the bolts to 12 ft. lbs. (16 Nm).
- Exhaust manifold heat shield. Torque the bolts to 89 inch lbs. (10 Nm).
- Crossover pipe. Torque the bolts to 18 ft. lbs. (25 Nm).

- Crossovere pipe heat shield. Torque the bolts to 89 inch lbs. (10 Nm).
- Upper radiator hose to the thermostat housing
- Ignition wires to the front spark plugs
- Negative battery cable

6. Fill the cooling system.

7. Start the vehicle and check for leaks, repair if necessary.

RIGHT SIDE (REAR) MANIFOLD

1. Before servicing the vehicle, refer to the precautions in the beginning of this section.

2. Remove or disconnect the following:
- Negative battery cable
- Air cleaner
- Throttle body air inlet duct
- Oxygen Sensor (O2S)
- Exhaust Gas Recirculation (EGR) pipe from the exhaust manifold
- Crossover pipe
- Exhaust manifold heat shield
- Exhaust manifold

To install:

3. Clean all gasket surfaces completely.

4. Install or connect the following:
- New gasket
- Exhaust manifold. Torque the nuts to 12 ft. lbs. (18 Nm).
- Exhaust manifold heat shield. Torque the bolts to 89 inch lbs. (10 Nm).
- Crossover pipe to the manifold. Torque the bolts to 18 ft. lbs. (25 Nm).
- Crossover pipe heat shield. Torque the bolts to 89 inch lbs. (10 Nm).
- Throttle body air inlet duct
- Air cleaner
- Negative battery cable

5. Start the vehicle and check for leaks, repair if necessary.

3.5L Engine

LEFT

1. Before servicing the vehicle, refer to the precautions in the beginning of this section.

2. Drain the cooling system.

3. Remove or disconnect the following:
- Negative battery cable
- Fuel injector cover
- Engine mount strut and bracket
- Cooling fans

- Radiator hoses
- Transaxle fluid lines from the radiator
- Radiator
- Alternator
- Heat shield from the manifold
- Dipstick and tube
- Secondary Air Injection (AIR) control valve assembly from the engine mount strut bracket
- Exhaust manifold bolts, loosen them
- Exhaust manifold-to-crossover pipe studs
- Exhaust manifold

To install:

4. Install or connect the following:
- Manifold to the crossover pipe using a new gasket. Torque the studs to 18 ft. lbs. (25 Nm).
- Exhaust manifold, using a new gasket. Torque the bolts to 18 ft. lbs. (25 Nm).
- AIR valve. Torque the pipe nut to 44 ft. lbs. (60 Nm) and the bolt to 80 inch lbs. (9 Nm).
- Dipstick and tube
- Heat shield
- Alternator and radiator
- Cooling fans
- Engine mount strut
- Fuel injector cover
- Negative battery cable

5. Fill the cooling system.

6. Start the vehicle and check for leaks, repair if necessary.

RIGHT

1. Before servicing the vehicle, refer to the precautions in the beginning of this section.

2. Relieve the fuel system pressure.

3. Drain the cooling system.

4. Remove or disconnect the following:
- Negative battery cable
- Fuel injector cover
- Air intake duct
- Engine mount strut
- Fuel lines from the supply rail
- Cruise control and accelerator cables from the throttle body
- Transaxle selector range cable and cable brackets
- Transaxle shift cable from the shift module
- Brake booster vacuum hose from the engine
- Wiring harness connectors from the engine and transaxle

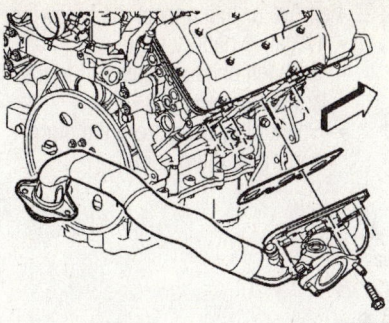

Exploded view of the right exhaust manifold—3.5L engine

- Upper radiator hose
- Transaxle fluid cooler lines from the radiator
- Surge tank inlet hose
- Heater hoses from the engine
- Lower radiator air deflector
- Battery cables from the retainers
- Lower radiator hose
- A/C compressor without disconnecting the lines and move it aside
- Starter wiring
- Catalytic converter from the manifold
- Front wheels and splash shields
- Wheel speed sensor wiring from the lower control arms
- Tie rod ends from the steering knuckles
- Lower ball joints from the knuckles
- Halfshafts
- Intermediate shaft from the steering rack

5. Secure the vehicle to the lift in preparation for engine removal.

6. Position an engine/frame support table under the vehicle and lower the vehicle to meet the table.

7. Remove or disconnect the following:
- Frame-to-body bolts
- Crossover pipe from the front manifold
- Exhaust Gas Recirculation (EGR) pipe from the crossover pipe
- Right exhaust manifold from the engine

To install:

8. Install or connect the following:
- Right exhaust manifold using a new gasket. Torque the bolts to 18 ft. lbs. (25 Nm).
- Crossover pipe to the front exhaust manifold

- EGR pipe to the crossover pipe. Torque the pipe nut to 44 ft. lbs. (60 Nm).

9. Position the engine/transaxle assembly under the vehicle.

10. Coat the sub-frame bushings with rubber lubricant.

11. Lower the vehicle onto the assembly. Align the sub-frame on the vehicle using 2 bolts or drill bits, ¾ inches thick by 8 inches long through the alignment holes on the right side of the frame.

12. Install new frame-to-body bolts. Torque the bolts to 133 ft. lbs. (180 Nm) starting with the rear bolts and then the front bolts.

13. Raise the vehicle and remove the frame table.

14. Install or connect the following:
- Intermediate shaft to the steering rack. Torque the bolts to 35 ft. lbs. (48 Nm).

➡ **Be sure the shaft is fully seated on the stub before installing the pinch bolt.**

- Halfshafts and assemble the suspension
- Splash shields and front wheels
- Catalytic converter. Torque the nuts to 53 inch lbs. (6 Nm).
- Starter wiring
- A/C compressor
- Lower radiator hose
- Battery cables in their retainers
- Lower radiator air deflector

15. Remove the straps securing the vehicle to the lift.

16. Install or connect the following:
- Heater hoses
- Surge tank hose
- Transaxle cooler lines to the radiator
- Upper radiator hose
- Wiring harness connectors to the engine and transaxle
- Transaxle shift cable to the shift module and bracket
- Transaxle selector range cable
- Cruise control and accelerator cables to the throttle body
- Fuel lines to the supply rail
- Engine mount strut
- Intake air duct
- Fuel injector cover
- Negative battery cable

17. Refill the cooling system.

18. Start the engine and check for leaks, repair if necessary.

Please refer to Section 8 for electric cooling fan wiring schematics

3.8L Engines

LEFT SIDE (FRONT)

1. Before servicing the vehicle, refer to the precautions in the beginning of this section.

2. Remove or disconnect the following:
- Negative battery cable
- Both left exhaust manifold to the crossover pipe bolts
- Spark plug wires from the plugs and move them aside

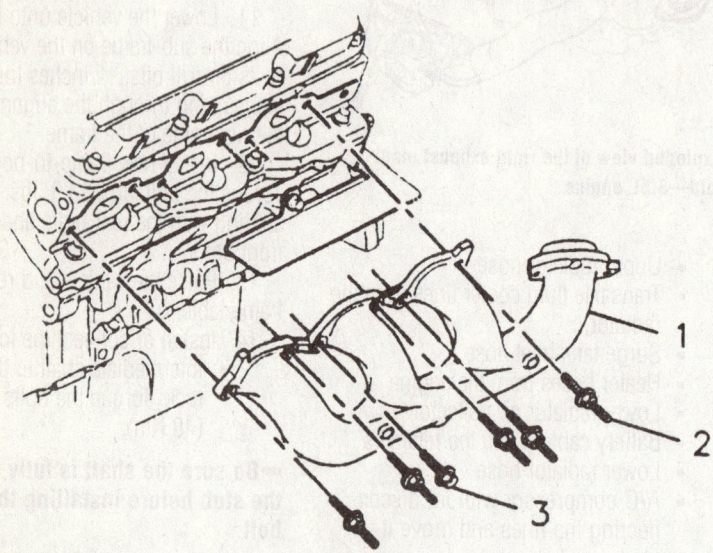

1   LEFT (FRONT) EXHAUST MANIFOLD
2   STUD 30 N•m (22 LB. FT.)
3   BOLT 30 N•m (22 LB. FT.)

7922XG30

Exploded view of the left exhaust manifold mounting—3.8L engine

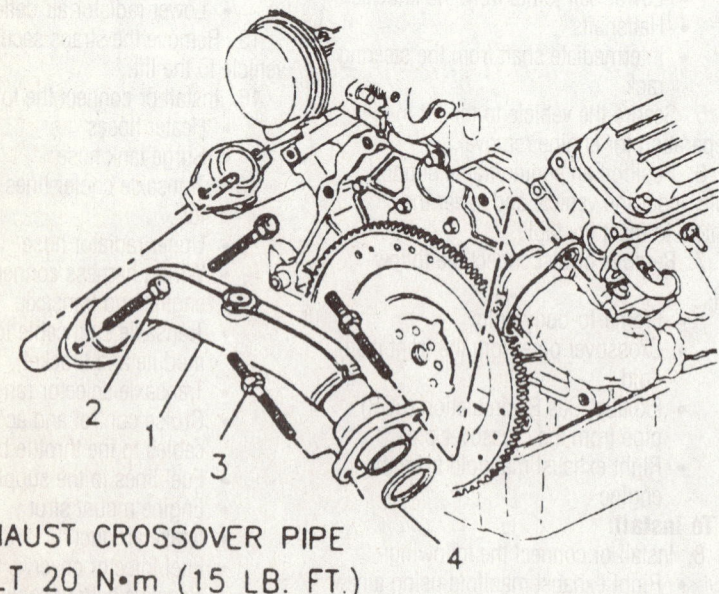

1   EXHAUST CROSSOVER PIPE
2   BOLT 20 N•m (15 LB. FT.)
3   STUD 20 N•m (15 LB. FT.)
4   SEAL

7922XG31

Exploded view of the crossover pipe mounting—3.8L engine

- Oil level indicator tube
- Exhaust manifold

To install:

3. Install or connect the following:
- New exhaust manifold gasket
- Exhaust manifold. Torque the bolts to 22 ft. lbs. (30 Nm).
- Oil level indicator tube
- Spark plug wires to the plugs
- Left exhaust manifold-to-crossover pipe. Torque the bolts to 15 ft. lbs. (20 Nm).
- Negative battery cable

4. Start the vehicle and check for leaks, repair if necessary.

RIGHT SIDE (REAR)

1. Before servicing the vehicle, refer to the precautions in the beginning of this section.

2. Remove or disconnect the following:
- Negative battery cable
- Spark plug wires from the plugs and move them aside
- Transaxle level indicator tube
- Oxygen Sensor (O2S) electrical connector
- Both right exhaust manifold to the crossover pipe bolts
- Plastic vacuum tank from the cowl
- Converter heat shield and pipe hanger
- Exhaust pipe from the manifold
- Rear engine lift bracket
- Exhaust manifold bolts
- Exhaust manifold

To install:

3. Install or connect the following:
- New exhaust manifold gasket
- Exhaust manifold. Torque the bolts to 22 ft. lbs. (30 Nm).
- Rear engine lift bracket
- Front pipe to the manifold. Torque the bolts to 15 ft. lbs. (20 Nm).
- Exhaust hanger and converter heat shield
- Vacuum tank on the cowl
- Right exhaust manifold-to-crossover pipe. Torque the bolts to 15 ft. lbs. (20 Nm).
- Transaxle level indicator tube
- O2S sensor electrical connector
- Spark plug wires to the plugs
- Negative battery cable

4. Start the vehicle and check for leaks, repair if necessary.

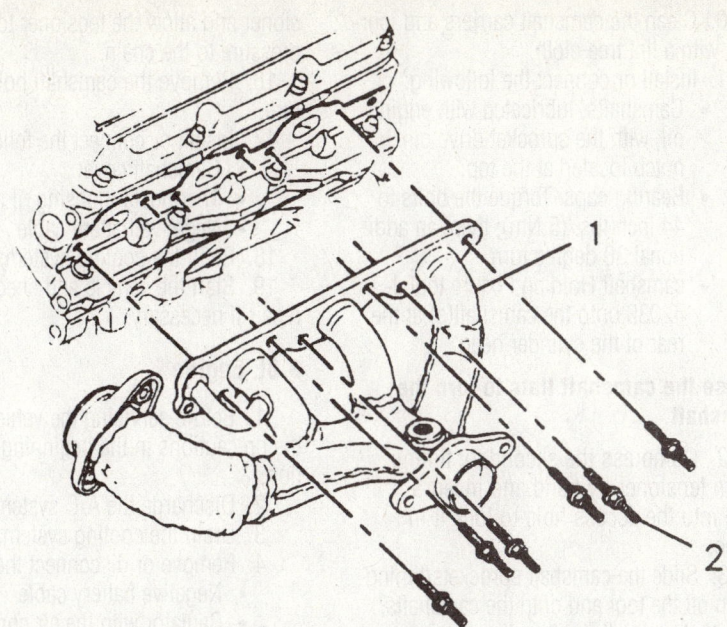

1 RIGHT (REAR) EXHAUST MANIFOLD
2 STUD 30 N•m (22 LB. FT.)

7922XG29

Exploded view of the right exhaust manifold mounting—3.8L engine

Camshaft And Valve Lifters

REMOVAL & INSTALLATION

3.1L and 3.4L Engines

1. Before servicing the vehicle, refer to the precautions in the beginning of this section.
2. Relieve the fuel system pressure.
3. Remove or disconnect the following:
   • Engine assembly

✳✳ WARNING

When removing valve train components they must be marked for installation in their original location. When the camshaft is being replaced, the valve lifters must also be replaced.

   • Rocker arm covers
   • Intake manifold
   • Rocker arm bolts, balls, rocker arms and pushrods
   • Lifter guide bolts and the guide
   • Valve lifter(s) from the bores
   • Crankshaft balancer and front cove
   • Timing chain and sprockets

   • Oil pump driven gear bolt and gear
   • Camshaft thrust plate
   • Camshaft

✳✳ WARNING

Avoid damaging the camshaft bearing surfaces.

To install:
4. Coat the camshaft with prelube.
5. Install or connect the following:
   • Camshaft
   • Camshaft thrust plate. Torque the bolts to 89 inch lbs. (10 Nm).
   • Oil pump driven gear. Torque the bolt to 27 ft. lbs. (36 Nm).
   • Timing chain and sprocket
   • Camshaft thrust button and front cover
   • Crankshaft balancer
6. Lubricate the bearing surfaces with Molykote®.

➡**Installation of a new camshaft or a wear pattern on the old valve lifter will require the replacement of the camshaft and lifters together. If camshaft replacement is not necessary, be sure to install the used valve lifters in their original position.**

7. Install or connect the following:
   • Lifters in their original locations
   • Lifter guide. Torque guide bolts to 89 inch lbs. (10 Nm).
   • Pushrods, rocker arms, balls and bolts. Torque the nuts to 89 inch lbs. (10 Nm) plus an additional 30 degree turn
   • Intake manifold
   • Rocker arm covers
   • Engine assembly
   • Negative battery cable

➡**The only time valve adjustment in needed is if there was a valve job performed or the rocker studs have been replaced with an adjustable rocker arm stud. The rocker arm stud installed from the factory should be shouldered and not need any adjustment.**

8. Adjust the valves, as required.
9. Start the engine and check for leaks, repair if necessary.

3.5L Engine

1. Before servicing the vehicle, refer to the precautions in the beginning of this section.
2. Drain the cooling system
3. Remove or disconnect the following:
   • Negative battery cable
   • Thermostat housing for clearance when installing the camshaft Holding Fixture tool J-42038
   • Front camshaft cover
4. Rotate the crankshaft so the camshaft flats are parallel to the camshaft's sealing surface, then install a camshaft holding fixture.
5. Remove the camshaft sprocket bolts.
6. Install a timing chain/sprocket holding fixture.
7. Evenly slide the camshaft sprocket and chain from the camshafts onto the holding tool.

➡**The camshaft bearing caps are marked. Be sure the raised portion of the cap faces the outside of the engine. They must always be installed in their original positions.**

8. Remove or disconnect the following:
   • Camshaft bearing caps
   • Camshafts

✳✳ WARNING

The camshafts and rocker arms must be returned to their original positions when installed.

• Camshafts from the cylinder head

To install:

9. Coat the rocker arms with engine oil and place them in their original positions.

➡ **Be sure to install the rounded end on the lash adjuster and the flat end on the tip of the valve.**

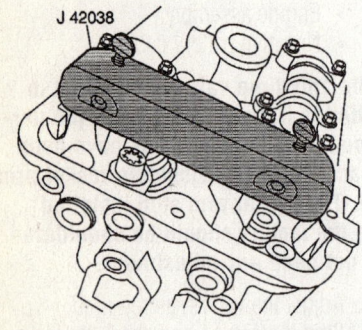

Camshaft holding fixture J-42038 installed on the camshafts—3.5L engine

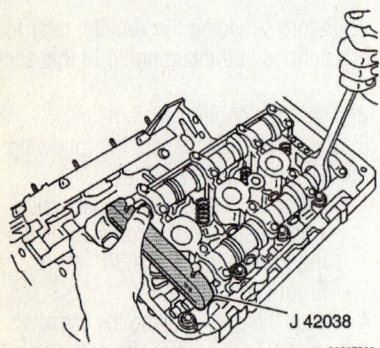

Timing chain/sprocket holding fixture J-42038 installed on the cylinder head; use the flats on the camshaft if rotation is necessary for installation of the holding tool—3.5L engine

1. Left intake
2. Left exhaust
3. Right intake
4. Right exhaust

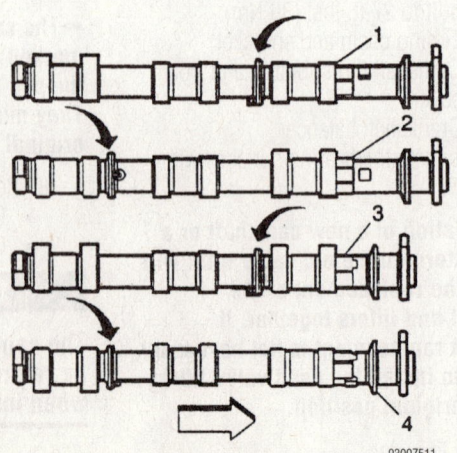

Camshaft identification—3.5L engine

10. Clean the camshaft carriers and journals with a lint free cloth.

11. Install or connect the following:

• Camshafts, lubricated with engine oil, with the sprocket drive pin notch located at the top.
• Bearing caps. Torque the bolts to 44 inch lbs. (5 Nm); then, an additional 30 degree turn
• camshaft Holding Fixture tool J-42038 onto the camshaft(s) at the rear of the cylinder head

➡ **Use the camshaft flats to turn the camshaft.**

12. Compress the secondary timing chain tensioner by hand and insert a wire into the access hole to lock it in place.

13. Slide the camshaft sprockets/timing chain off the tool and onto the camshafts. Be sure to align the drive pins.

14. Remove the timing chain/sprocket holder from the front of the cylinder head. Torque the sprocket bolts to 18 ft. lbs. (25 Nm); then, an additional 45 degree turn.

15. Remove the wire from the chain ten-

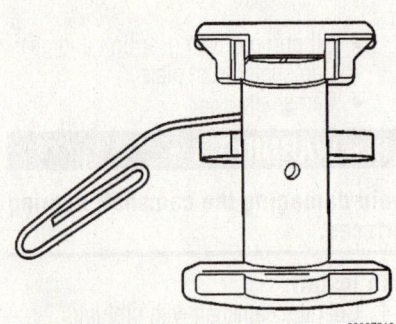

Before installation, compress the tensioner and lock it in place with a piece of wire—3.5L engine

sioner and allow the tensioner to apply pressure to the chain.

16. Remove the camshaft holding fixture.

17. Install or connect the following:

• Camshaft cover
• Thermostat housing, if removed
• Negative battery cable

18. Refill the cooling system.

19. Start the vehicle and check for leaks, repair if necessary.

3.8L Engine

1. Before servicing the vehicle, refer to the precautions in the beginning of this section.

2. Discharge the A/C system.

3. Drain the cooling system.

4. Remove or disconnect the following:

• Negative battery cable
• Radiator with the air conditioning condenser assembly
• Valve cover
• Valve lifters
• Timing chain (engine) front cover
• Camshaft sprocket and timing chain
• Camshaft thrust plate

5. Remove the camshaft assembly, as follows:

a. Install $3\frac{5}{16}$–18 x 4-inch bolts in the camshaft bolt holes.

b. Carefully rotate and pull the camshaft assembly out of the bearings.

6. Inspect the camshaft for damage and replace if necessary.

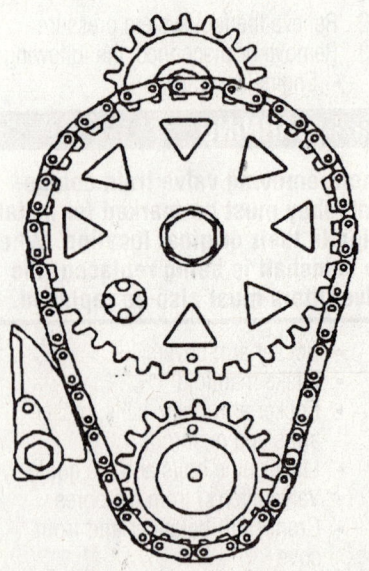

The timing marks should face each other if the chain and gears are installed properly—3.8L engine

To install:

7. Install or connect the following:
- Camshaft lubricated with prelube
- Thrust plate. Torque the bolts to 11 ft. lbs. (15 Nm).
- Timing chain (front) cover
- Valve lifters
- Valve cover
- Radiator with the air conditioning condenser
- Negative battery cable

8. Evacuate and recharge the A/C system.

9. Refill the cooling system.

10. Start the engine and check for leaks, repair if necessary.

Valve Lash

ADJUSTMENT

The valve clearance cannot be adjusted on these engines.

Starter

REMOVAL & INSTALLATION

All Engines

1. Before servicing the vehicle, refer to the precautions in the beginning of this section.

2. Remove or disconnect the following:
- Negative battery cable
- Electrical connections from the starter

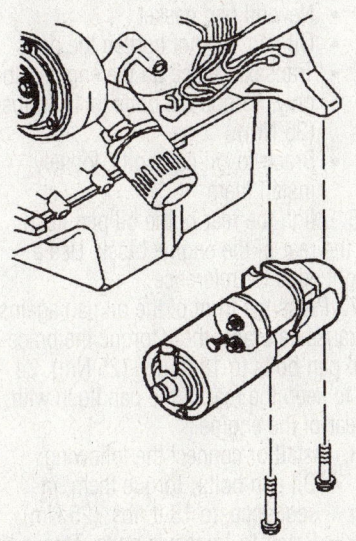

9306ZG15

Exploded view of the starter—3.1L and 3.4L engines

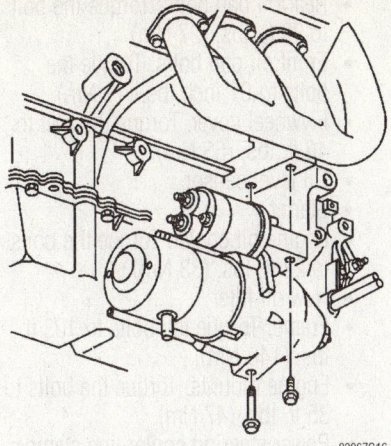

9306ZG16

Exploded view of the starter—3.5L engine

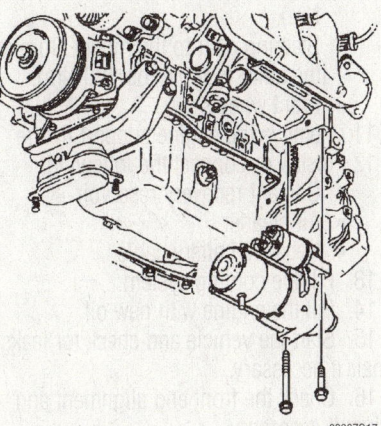

9306ZG17

Exploded view of the starter—3.8L engine

- Torque converter cover
- Starter

To install:

3. Install or connect the following:
- Starter. Torque the bolts to 32 ft. lbs. (43 Nm).
- Torque converter cover. Torque the bolts to 89 inch lbs. (10 Nm).
- Starter solenoid BAT terminal. Torque the fastener to 89 inch lbs. (10 Nm).
- Starter solenoid S terminal. Torque the fastener to 27 inch lbs. (3 Nm).
- Negative battery cable

Oil Pan

REMOVAL & INSTALLATION

3.1L Engine

1. Before servicing the vehicle, refer to the precautions in the beginning of this section.

2. Drain the engine oil.

3. Remove or disconnect the following:
- Negative battery cable
- Engine mount struts
- Drive belt
- A/C compressor mounting bolts and reposition the compressor

4. Install an engine support fixture.

5. Remove or disconnect the following:
- Exhaust manifold pipe from the right exhaust manifold
- Oil level sensor wiring
- Starter
- Transaxle brace from the oil pan
- Transaxle mount lower nuts
- Engine mount lower nuts and raise the engine to gain access to the oil pan
- Engine mount from the oil pan
- Rear oil pan side bolts
- Front oil pan side bolts
- Oil pan retaining bolts
- Oil pan and gasket

To install:

6. Clean the mating surface of the oil pan and engine block.

7. Apply a small amount of sealer on both sides of the rear main bearing cap between the gasket and the engine.

8. Install or connect the following:
- Gasket
- Oil pan
- Oil pan retaining bolts. Torque the bolts to 18 ft. lbs. (25 Nm).
- Front and rear oil pan bolts. Torque the bolts to 37 ft. lbs. (50 Nm).
- Engine mount and bracket to the oil pan. Torque the bolts to 43 ft. lbs. (58 Nm).

9. Lower the engine into position.

10. Install or connect the following:
- Engine mount lower nuts. Torque the nuts to 32 ft. lbs. (43 Nm).
- Transaxle mount lower nuts. Torque the nuts to 55 ft. lbs. (75 Nm).
- Transaxle brace to the oil pan. Torque the bolts to 46 ft. lbs. (63 Nm).
- Starter. Torque the bolts to 32 ft. lbs. (43 Nm).
- Oil level sensor wire connector
- Exhaust manifold pipe to the rear manifold. Torque the bolts to 18 ft. lbs. (25 Nm).

11. Remove the engine support fixture.

12. Install or connect the following:
- A/C compressor
- Drive belt

Timing belt service is covered in Section 4 of this manual

- Engine mount struts. Torque the bolts to 41 ft. lbs. (56 Nm).
- Negative battery cable

13. Fill the engine with new oil.

14. Start the vehicle and check for leaks, repair if necessary.

3.4L Engine

1. Before servicing the vehicle, refer to the precautions in the beginning of this section.

2. Drain the cooling system.

3. Drain the engine oil.

4. Remove or disconnect the following:
- Negative battery cable
- Air cleaner duct
- Coolant recovery reservoir

5. Install an engine support fixture.

6. Remove or disconnect the following:
- Both front wheels
- Steering gear retaining bolts
- Lower ball joint nuts and separate the ball joints from the control arms
- Power steering cooler line clamps at the frame
- Engine mount nuts at the frame

7. Properly support the frame and remove the frame mounting bolts.

8. Remove or disconnect the following:
- Frame
- Oil filter
- Oil cooler
- Oil level sensor
- Starter
- Flywheel cover
- Oil pan and gasket

To install:

9. Clean all the gasket surfaces completely. Apply sealer to the gasket near the rear main bearing cap.

10. Install or connect the following:
- Oil pan
- Oil pan mounting nuts. Torque the nuts to 97 inch lbs. (11 Nm).

- Rear oil pan bolts. Torque the bolts to 20 ft. lbs. (27 Nm).
- Front oil pan bolts. Torque the bolts to 97 inch lbs. (11 Nm).
- Flywheel cover. Torque the bolt to 46 ft. lbs. (63 Nm).
- Oil level sensor
- Starter
- Engine oil cooler. Torque the bolts to 24 ft. lbs. (33 Nm).
- New oil filter
- Frame. Torque the bolts to 103 ft. lbs. (140 Nm).
- Engine mounts. Torque the bolts to 35 ft. lbs. (47 Nm).
- Power steering cooler line clamps at the frame
- Ball joints to the control arms. Torque the bolts to 63 ft. lbs. (85 Nm).
- Steering gear to the mount. Torque the bolts to 59 ft. lbs. (80 Nm).
- Front wheels

11. Remove the engine support fixture

12. Install or connect the following:
- Coolant recovery reservoir
- Air cleaner
- Negative battery cable

13. Fill the cooling system.

14. Fill the engine with new oil.

15. Start the vehicle and check for leaks, repair if necessary.

16. Check the front end alignment and adjust if necessary.

3.5L Engine

1. Before servicing the vehicle, refer to the precautions in the beginning of this section.

2. Drain the oil.

3. Remove or disconnect the following:
- Negative battery cable
- Oil filter cap and filter
- Oil level sensor harness connector
- Transaxle brace
- Oil pan, discard the gasket

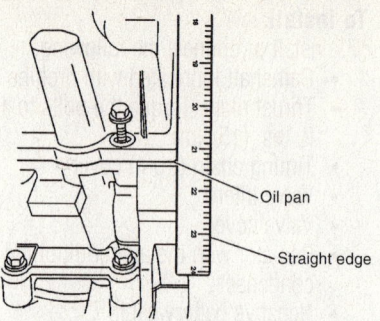

Use a straight-edge to align the rear of the oil pan to the rear of the engine—3.5L engine

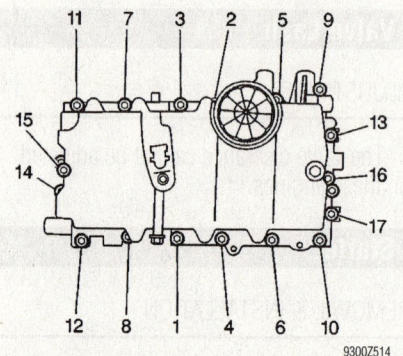

Oil pan mounting bolt tightening sequence—3.5L engine

4. Clean the gasket surface carefully to avoid gouging the aluminum.

To install:

5. Install or connect the following:
- Oil level sensor. Torque the bolt to 80 inch lbs. (9 Nm).
- New oil pan gasket
- Oil pan, Do not tighten the bolts
- Transaxle brace on the engine block only. Torque the bolts to 18 ft. lbs. (25 Nm).
- Brace-to-oil pan bolts, loosely install them

6. Align the rear of the oil pan flush with the rear of the engine block. Use a straight edge for reference.

7. Press the front of the oil pan against the transaxle brace; then, torque the brace-to-oil pan bolts to 18 ft. lbs. (25 Nm). Be sure to keep the rear of the pan flush with the rear of the engine.

8. Install or connect the following:
- Oil pan bolts. Torque them, in sequence, to 18 ft. lbs. (25 Nm).
- Brace-to-transaxle bolts. Torque the bolts to 32 ft. lbs. (43 Nm).
- Oil level sensor connector
- Drain plug. Torque it to 15 ft. lbs. (20 m).

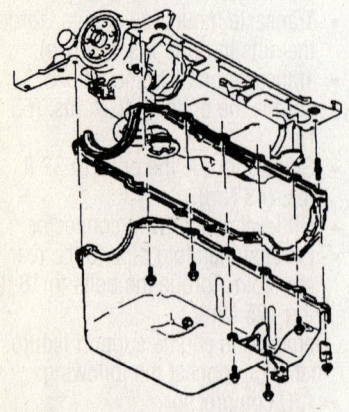

Exploded view of the oil pan mounting—3.4L engine

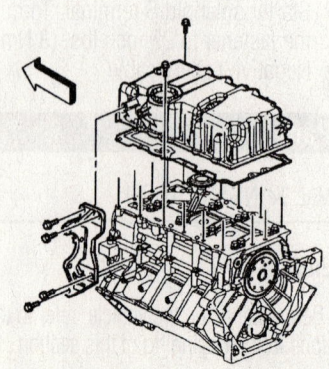

Exploded view of the oil pan—3.5L engine

- New oil filter. Torque the cap to 18 ft. lbs. (25 Nm).
- Negative battery cable

9. Refill the engine with clean oil.

10. Start the vehicle and check for leaks, repair if necessary.

3.8L Engine

1. Before servicing the vehicle, refer to the precautions in the beginning of this section.

2. Drain the engine oil.

3. Remove or disconnect the following:
- Negative battery cable
- Throttle body air inlet duct
- Engine mount struts
- Drive belt

4. Install an engine support fixture.

5. Remove or disconnect the following:
- Catalytic converter from the right exhaust manifold
- Right front wheel
- Right side splash shield
- Oil filter and discard
- A/C compressor bracket and reposition the compressor
- Engine mount bracket bolts
- Lower engine mount nuts
- Torque converter cover
- Oil level sensor wire connector
- Oil level sensor
- Right side frame bolts and loosen the left side bolt. Make certain the frame is properly supported
- Engine mount and bracket
- Oil pan
- Oil pump pipe and screen

To install:

6. Clean all parts well, especially the gasket sealing flanges on the engine block and the oil pan.

7. Clean the oil pan bolts and add a drop of thread locking compound to the threads.

8. Install or connect the following:
- New oil pan gasket and the oil pump pipe and screen assembly. Torque the oil pump bolts to 11 ft. lbs. (15 Nm).

➡ **Do not overtighten the oil pan bolts or damage to the pan may occur.**

- Oil pan. Torque the bolts to 125 inch lbs. (14 Nm).
- Engine mount and bracket. Torque the bolts to 50 ft. lbs. (68 Nm).
- New right side frame bolts. Torque all the bolts to 133 ft. lbs. (180 Nm).
- Lower engine mount. Torque the nuts to 50 ft. lbs. (68 Nm).
- Oil level sensor. Torque the fastener to 15 ft. lbs. (20 Nm).
- Oil level wire connector
- Torque converter cover. Torque the bolts to 46 ft. lbs. (63 Nm).
- Power steering oil cooler pipe brackets to the frame
- A/C compressor. Torque the bolts to 74 ft. lbs. (100 Nm).
- New oil filter

- Drain plug. Torque the plug to 22 ft. lbs. (30 Nm).
- Right front wheel
- Catalytic converter pipe to the right exhaust manifold. Torque the bolts to 22 ft. lbs. (30 Nm).

9. Remove the engine support fixture.

10. Install or connect the following:
- Drive belt
- Engine mount struts to the engine. Torque the bolts to 41 ft. lbs. (56 Nm).
- Throttle body air inlet duct
- Negative battery cable

11. Fill the engine with new oil.

12. Start the vehicle and check for leaks, repair if necessary.

13. Roadtest the vehicle, check the front end alignment and adjust if necessary.

Oil Pump

REMOVAL & INSTALLATION

3.1L Engine

1. Before servicing the vehicle, refer to the precautions in the beginning of this section.

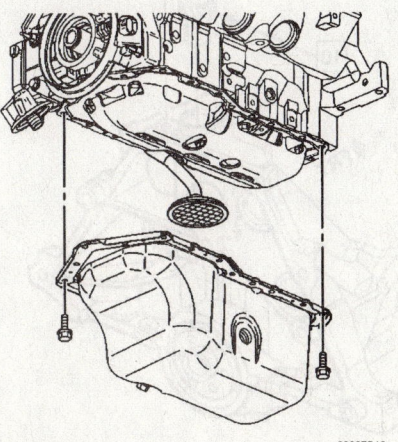

Exploded view of the oil pan mounting—3.8L engine

9306ZG18

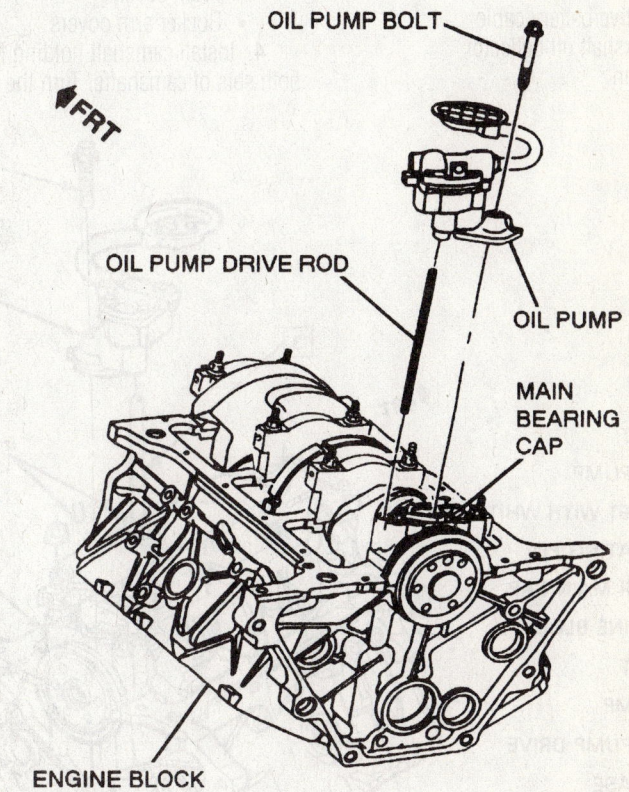

Oil pump and driveshaft components—3.1L engine

OIL PUMP BOLT

OIL PUMP DRIVE ROD

OIL PUMP

MAIN BEARING CAP

ENGINE BLOCK

FRT

7922Z519

2. Drain the engine oil.
3. Remove or disconnect the following:
  • Negative battery cable
  • Oil pan
  • Bolt attaching the oil pump to the rear crankshaft bearing cap
  • Oil pump and driveshaft

To install:

➡**Rotate the driveshaft as required to obtain the proper engagement with the oil pump drive unit.**

4. Install or connect the following:
  • Oil pump and driveshaft
  • Bolt attaching the oil pump to the rear crankshaft bearing cap. Torque the bolt to 30 ft. lbs. (41 Nm).
  • Oil pan.
  • Negative battery cable.
5. Fill the engine with new oil.
6. Start the vehicle and check for leaks, repair if necessary.

3.4L Engine

1. Before servicing the vehicle, refer to the precautions in the beginning of this section.
2. Drain the engine oil.
3. Remove or disconnect the following:
  • Negative battery cable
  • Crankshaft oil deflector
  • Oil pan

  • Oil pump retaining bolt
  • Oil pump drive

To install:

4. Clean all parts well. Clean the inside of the oil pan, the gasket flanges on the pan and gasket rail on the block.
5. Install or connect the following:
  • Oil pump with the driveshaft extension and pickup assembly onto the rear main bearing cap making sure the driveshaft extension engages in the oil pump drive
  • Oil pump retaining bolt. Torque the bolt to 40 ft. lbs. 54 (Nm).
  • Crankshaft oil deflector. Torque the bolts to 18 ft. lbs. (25 Nm).
  • Oil pan
  • Negative battery cable
6. Refill the engine with new oil.
7. Start the vehicle and check for leaks, repair if necessary.

3.5L Engine

1. Before servicing the vehicle, refer to the precautions in the beginning of this section.
2. Drain the engine oil.
3. Remove or disconnect the following:
  • Negative battery cable
  • Front cover
  • Rocker arm covers
4. Install camshaft holding fixtures on both sets of camshafts. Turn the hex portion

of the camshaft to align them for tool installation. When installed, the flats on the rear of the camshafts will be parallel with the camshaft cover sealing surface.
5. Remove or disconnect the following:
  • Primary chain tensioner
  • Primary chain from the drive sprocket
  • Oil pump by sliding it off the crankshaft

To install:

6. Pack the oil pump housing with white petroleum jelly to insure priming.

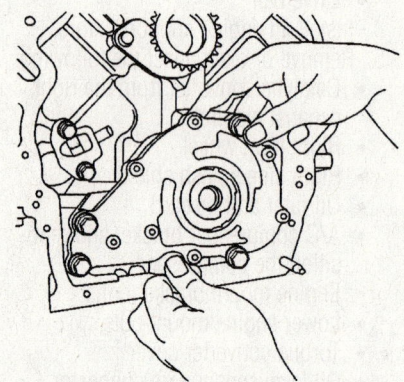

The oil pump is mounted on the front of the engine and driven by the crankshaft— 3.5L engine

9300Z515

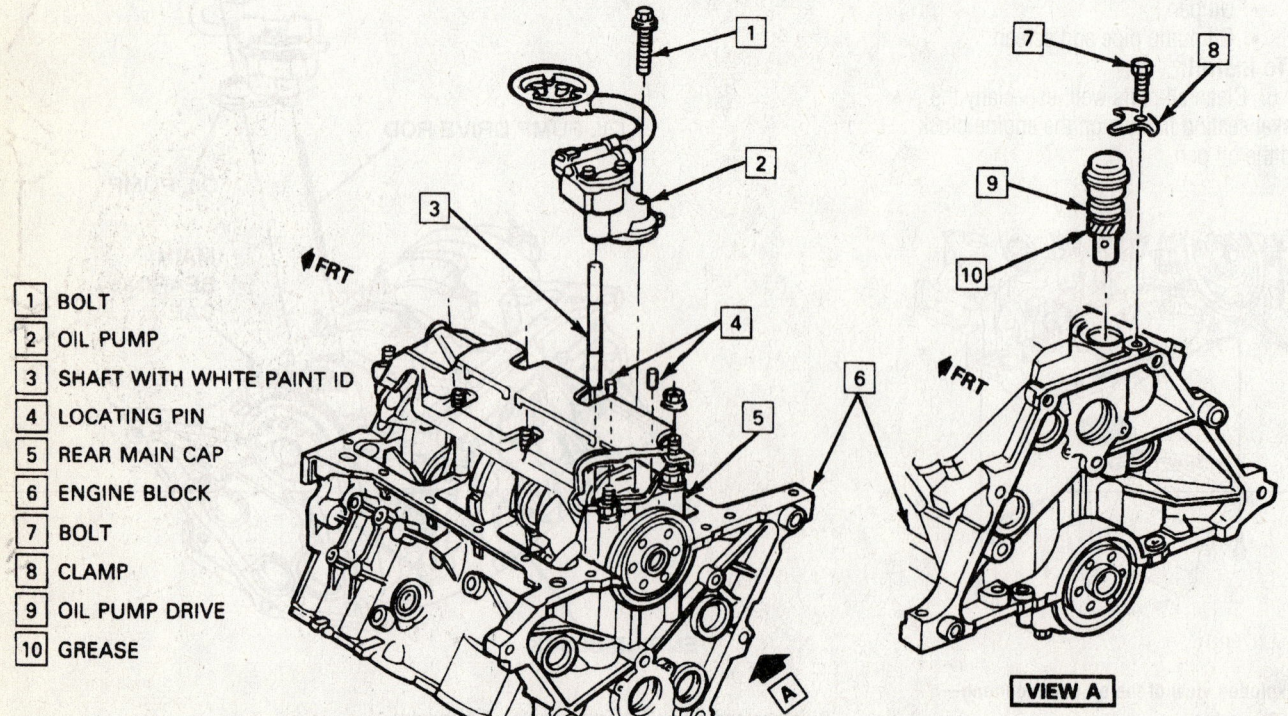

1	BOLT
2	OIL PUMP
3	SHAFT WITH WHITE PAINT ID
4	LOCATING PIN
5	REAR MAIN CAP
6	ENGINE BLOCK
7	BOLT
8	CLAMP
9	OIL PUMP DRIVE
10	GREASE

FRT

VIEW A

Oil pump and drive gear assembly—3.4L engine

79222Z520

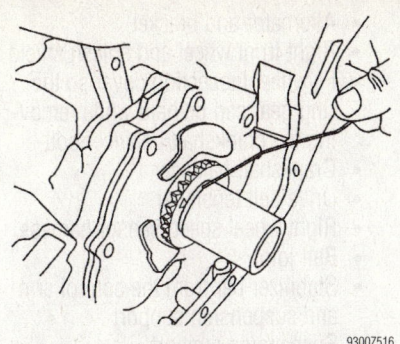

Correct position of the crankshaft sprocket when the oil pump is installed correctly—3.5L engine

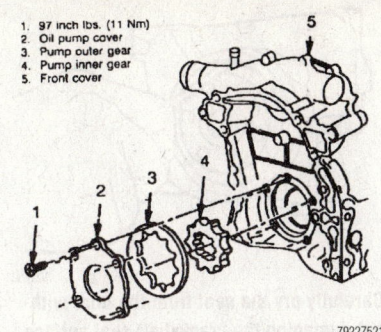

1. 97 inch lbs. (11 Nm)
2. Oil pump cover
3. Pump outer gear
4. Pump inner gear
5. Front cover

Oil pump assembly—3.8L engine

7. Install or connect the following:
   • Oil pump housing cover. Torque the bolts to 97 inch lbs. (11 Nm).
   • Sprocket in the oil pump by aligning the splines
8. Align the sprocket with the crankshaft and install the pump on the engine until a positive stop is felt. When installed properly, the sprocket will protrude slightly from the oil pump and the face of the sprocket will be behind the machined step in the crankshaft.
9. Install or connect the following:
   • Oil pump. Torque the bolts to 18 ft. lbs. (25 Nm).
   • Primary chain on the sprocket

➡ **Be sure to maintain correct timing.**

   • Chain tensioner
10. Remove the camshaft holding tools.
11. Install or connect the following:
   • Crankshaft covers
   • Engine front cover
   • Negative battery cable
12. Fill the engine with new oil.
13. Start the vehicle and check for leaks, repair if necessary.

3.8L Engines

1. Before servicing the vehicle, refer to the precautions in the beginning of this section.
2. Drain the engine oil.
3. Remove or disconnect the following:
   • Negative battery cable
   • Front cover
   • Oil pump cover
   • Oil pump gear set

To install:
4. Lubricate the oil pump gears with petroleum jelly and install the gears into the housing.

5. Pack the gear cavity with petroleum jelly after the gears have been installed in the housing.
6. Install or connect the following:
   • Oil pump cover. Torque the screws to 97 inch lbs. (11 Nm).
   • Front cover
   • Negative battery cable
7. Verify the correct engine oil level. A new oil filter is recommended.
8. Start the vehicle and check for leaks, repair if necessary.

Rear Main Seal

REMOVAL & INSTALLATION

3.5L Engine

1. Before servicing the vehicle, refer to the precautions in the beginning of this section.
2. Remove or disconnect the following:
   • Negative battery cable
   • Transaxle
   • Engine flywheel

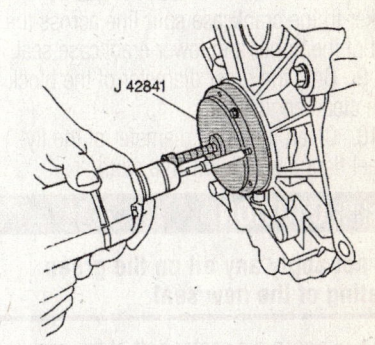

Use the guide holes in tool J 42841 to install the screws in the seal—3.5L engine

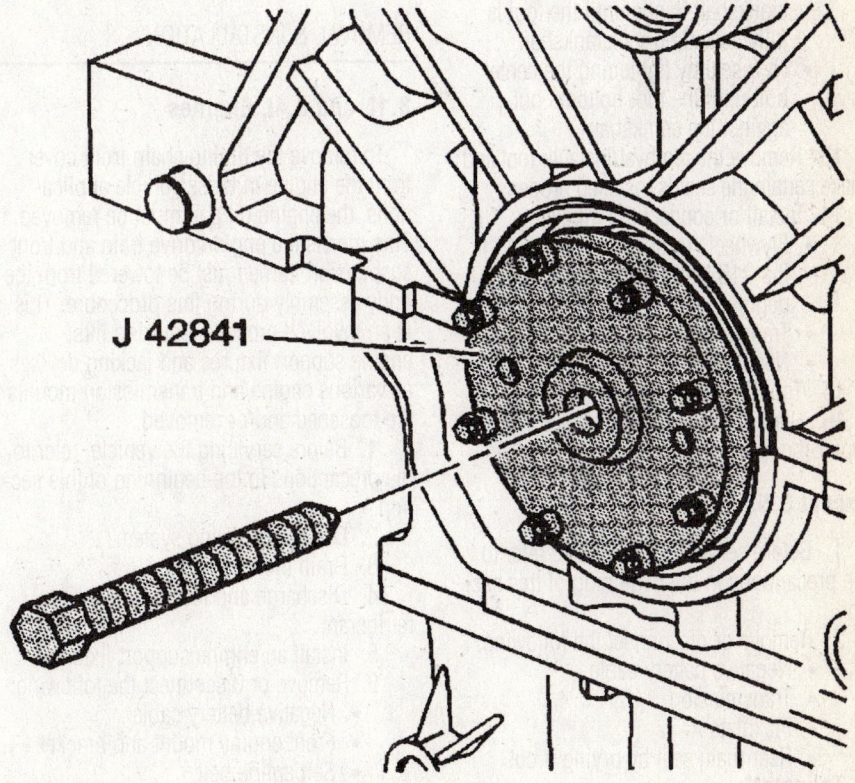

Install a center forcing screw into the removal tool—3.5L engine

Refer to Section 1 for engine rebuilding specifications

3. Place a rear seal remover tool on the crankshaft with retaining bolts.

4. Install eight one-inch self starting screws through the guide holes of the tool. Tighten the screws.

5. Install the two retaining bolts.

6. Install a center forcing screw into the removal tool and pull the seal off the end of the crankshaft.

To install:

7. Clean debris from the crankshaft rear seal drain. The seal may leak if the drain is not properly cleaned.

8. Place a small amount of gasket maker to the crankcase split line across the end of the upper and lower crankcase seal.

9. Coat the outer diameter of the block with clean engine oil.

10. Clean the outer diameter of the flywheel flange with a lint-free cloth.

※※ CAUTION

Do not apply any oil on the green coating of the new seal.

11. Loosen the center bolt of the seal installer tool until the hub protrudes past the outer plate (approximately inch).

12. Install or connect the following:
- Three mounting bolts into the crankshaft flange until the tool is fully seated on the crankshaft
- New seal by tightening the center bolt until the tool bottoms out against the crankshaft

13. Remove the removal/installer tool and make certain the seal is installed properly

14. Install or connect the following:
- Flywheel. Torque the bolts to 11 ft. lbs. (15 Nm) plus an additional 50 degrees with a torque angle meter.
- Transaxle
- Negative battery cable

15. Top off the engine oil if needed.

16. Start the vehicle and check for leaks, repair if necessary.

Except 3.5L Engine

1. Before servicing the vehicle, refer to the precautions in the beginning of this section.

2. Remove or disconnect the following:
- Negative battery cable
- Transmission
- Flexplate
- Rear main seal by prying it out

To install:

3. Lubricate the lip and the outer edge of the new seal with clean engine oil.

4. Install or connect the following:
- Position the new seal on the

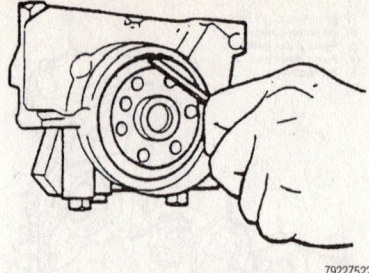

Carefully pry the seal from the bore without damaging the crankshaft seal surface

mandrel until the back of the seal is flush against the collar of the tool
- Seal installer tool to the rear of the crankshaft with the 2 mounting bolts. Turn the handle until the seal is seated in the rear of the engine. Remove the installer tool
- Flexplate
- Transmission
- Negative battery cable

5. Start the vehicle and check for leaks, repair if necessary.

Timing Chain, Sprockets, Front Cover and Seal

REMOVAL & INSTALLATION

3.1L and 3.4L Engines

To remove the timing chain front cover from the engine in these vehicle applications, the engine oil pan must be removed. This means the engine/drive train and front suspension frame must be lowered from the body assembly during this procedure. This is an involved process requiring lifts, engine support fixtures and jacking devices as various engine and transmission mounts are loosened and/or removed.

1. Before servicing the vehicle, refer to the precautions in the beginning of this section.

2. Drain the cooling system.

3. Drain the engine oil.

4. Discharge and recover the A/C refrigerant.

5. Install an engine support fixture.

6. Remove or disconnect the following:
- Negative battery cable
- Front engine mount and bracket
- Serpentine belt
- Air cleaner assembly
- Air intake duct
- Power steering pump
- 2 upper A/C compressor mounting bolts, loosen them

- Alternator and bracket
- Right front wheel and splash shield
- Flywheel inspection cover so the ring gear can be held while removing the crankshaft balancer bolt
- Crankshaft balancer
- Drive belt tensioner
- Right wheel speed sensor harness
- Ball joint
- Stabilizer bar from the control arm and suspension support
- Suspension support
- A/C compressor-to-oil pan bolts
- Oil filter and adapter
- Starter
- Oil pan
- Crankshaft Position (CKP) sensor
- Lower front cover bolts
- Coolant hoses and the remaining front cover bolts
- Engine front cover
- Oil seal from the front cover using a seal driver

7. Using the flywheel and a flywheel turning tool, rotate the crankshaft until the timing marks on the camshaft and crankshaft sprockets are in alignment (facing each other).

8. Remove or disconnect the following:
- Camshaft sprocket bolt, sprocket and timing chain
- Crankshaft sprocket
- Timing chain damper bolts and damper, if necessary

To install:

9. Install or connect the following:

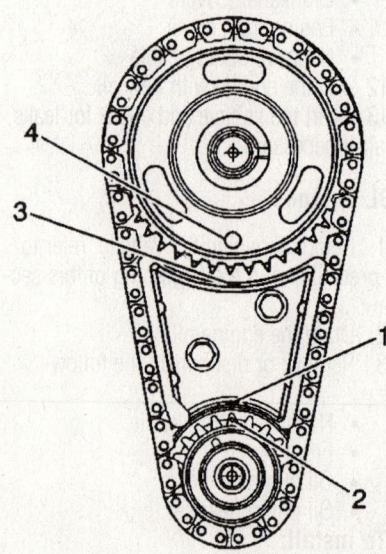

Be sure to align the damper mark (1) with the crankshaft mark (2) and the damper mark (3) with the camshaft sprocket mark (4)—3.1L and 3.4L engines

- Timing chain damper, if removed. Torque the bolts to 15 ft. lbs. (21 Nm).
- Crankshaft sprocket onto the crankshaft making sure the notch in the sprocket fits over the crankshaft key. Fully seat the sprocket on the crankshaft

➥**Be sure the timing mark on the crankshaft sprocket is pointing toward the mark on the chain damper.**

- Timing chain over the camshaft sprocket and hold the sprocket so the timing mark is pointing down and the timing chain is hanging off the sprocket

10. Loop the timing chain under the crankshaft sprocket and install the camshaft sprocket on the camshaft. The sprocket will only fit on the camshaft if the dowel on the camshaft aligns with the sprocket hole.

11. Verify that the marks are aligned; the camshaft sprocket will be at the 6 o'clock position and the crankshaft sprocket at the 12 o'clock position.

➥**The No. 1 piston will be at TDC and the No. 4 piston will also be at TDC but on the compression stroke.**

12. Tighten the camshaft sprocket bolt to 103 ft. lbs. (140 Nm).

13. Lubricate the timing chain components with engine oil. Clean all gasket surfaces completely.

14. Install or connect the following:
- New front cover seal on the front cover by applying a thin bead of sealer around the gasket sealing area
- Front cover using a new gasket. Torque the 2 upper bolts to 15 ft. lbs. (21 Nm).
- Coolant hoses
- Remaining front cover bolts. Torque the small bolts to 15 ft. lbs. (21 Nm) and the large bolts to 35 ft. lbs. (47 Nm).
- CKP sensor, oil pan, starter motor, oil filter adapter and filter
- A/C compressor-to-oil pan bolts
- Suspension
- Speed sensor wiring harness
- Drive belt tensioner
- Crankshaft balancer using a balancer installer

✳✳ WARNING

Do not hammer the balancer on the crankshaft.

- Flywheel inspection cover
- Right front wheel and splash shield
- Alternator and bracket
- 2 upper A/C compressor mounting bolts
- Power steering pump
- Air intake duct
- Air cleaner assembly
- Serpentine belt
- Front engine mount and bracket. Torque the 8mm bolts to 15 ft. lbs. (20 Nm) and the 12mm bolts to 30 ft. lbs. (40 Nm).
- Negative battery cable

15. Refill the fluids.

16. Start the engine and check for leaks, repair if necessary.

➥**Whenever the vehicle sub-frame is removed or lowered, the wheel alignment should be checked.**

3.5L Engine

PRIMARY CHAIN

1. Before servicing the vehicle, refer to the precautions in the beginning of this section.

2. Remove or disconnect the following:

3. Drain the engine oil.

4. Drain the cooling system.

5. Remove or disconnect the following:
- Negative battery cable
- Camshaft covers

6. Rotate the crankshaft so the No. 1 piston is at Top Dead Center (TDC) and the flats on the rear of the camshafts are parallel with the camshaft cover sealing surface.

7. Install camshaft holding fixtures on both sets of camshafts. Turn the hex portion of the camshaft to align them for tool installation.

➥**When installed, the flats on the rear of the camshafts will be parallel with the camshaft cover sealing surface.**

8. Remove or disconnect the following:
- Front diagonal brace
- Battery and tray
- Washer and coolant reservoir
- Underhood accessory wiring junction block, move it aside
- Drive belt
- Power steering pump pulley
- Idler pulley and belt tensioner
- Water pump, discard the gasket

9. Support the engine cradle.

10. Remove the right side engine cradle bolts.

11. Lower the cradle.

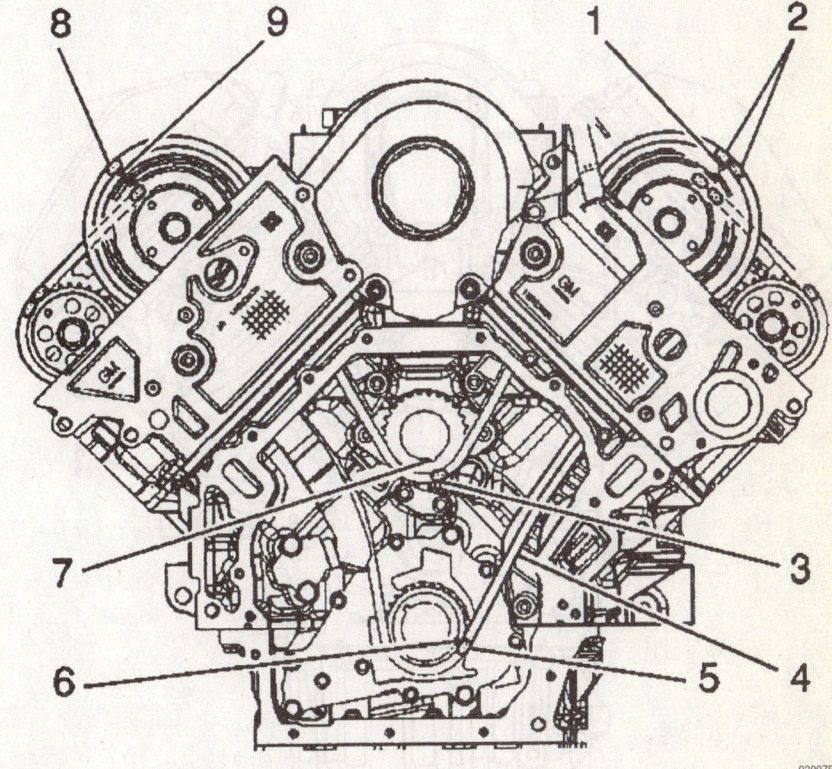

Primary timing chain alignment marks—3.5L engine

93002519

For engine torque specifications, refer to Section 1 of this manual

12. Remove or disconnect the following:
- Crankshaft balancer
- Front cover and discard the gasket
- Lift bracket from the front of the engine
- Camshaft Position (CMP) sensor
- Sprocket bolt from the exhaust camshaft on the right cylinder head to allow for clearance of the chain guide
- Four chain guide access plugs from the cylinder heads

➡ **Note that each plug has an O-ring.**

- Primary chain tensioner

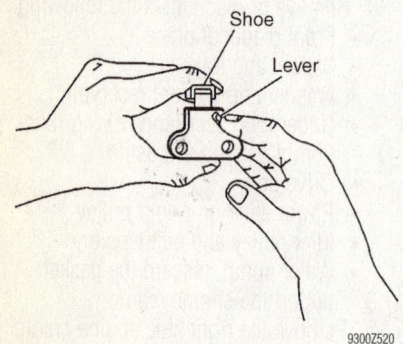

Compressing the primary chain tensioner—3.5L engine

➡**Remove the lower bolt allowing the tensioner to swing down and expand.**

- Primary chain tensioner shoe, by removing the bolt, pushing the guide downward slightly and pulling it up through the cylinder head
- Primary chain from the right camshaft, allowing it to fall into the oil pump area
- Primary chain

To install:

13. Rotate the crankshaft so the No. 1 piston is at Top Dead Center (TDC) and the mark on the crankshaft is at the 4 o'clock position.

14. Rotate the balance shaft so the timing mark is at the 5 o'clock position.

➡ **Be sure the painted links are facing the front of the engine.**

15. Install the timing chain on the sprockets.

➡ **Turn the camshaft with a wrench on the hex when aligning the links with the marks on the sprockets. Be sure the marks are aligned.**

16. Center the mark on the left intake camshaft sprocket between the 2 painted links.

17. Make a wire hook to feed down through the right cylinder head and lift the chain onto the right intake camshaft sprocket. While doing this, align the marks on the balance shaft and crankshaft sprockets with the painted marks on the chain.

18. Verify that all of the timing marks are aligned.

19. Install the primary chain tensioner shoe. Torque the bolt to 22 ft. lbs. (30 Nm).

20. Compress the primary chain tensioner using the following sub-steps:

   a. Rotate the ratchet release lever counterclockwise and hold it.

   b. Press the tensioner shoe in and hold it.

   c. Release the ratchet lever and slowly release the pressure on the shoe.

   d. Insert a pin through the hole in the lever as the lever moves to the first click. The ratchet should hold the shoe in the compressed position.

➡ **Be sure the lever on the tensioner is facing you when installed.**

21. Install or connect the following:
- Primary chain tensioner. Torque the bolts to 18 ft. lbs. (25 Nm); then, remove the chain tensioner pin.
- Four chain guide access plugs. Torque the plugs to 44 inch lbs. (5 Nm).
- Front engine lift bracket. Torque the hex head bolt to 37 ft. lbs. (50 Nm) and the internal drive bolt to 18 ft. lbs. (25 Nm).
- CMP sensor. Torque the bolts to 80 inch lbs. (9 Nm).

22. Remove the camshaft holding tools.

23. Install the rocker arm covers.

24. Place a small bead of RTV sealant on the 3 areas indicated in the diagram.

25. Install or connect the following:
- New gasket on the front cover, use 2 cover bolts to hold it in position
- Front cover. Torque the bolts to 124 inch lbs. (14 Nm) and the coolant drain plug to 89 inch lbs. (10 Nm).
- Crankshaft balancer. Torque the bolt to 37 ft. lbs. (50 Nm); then, an additional 120 degree turn.

26. Raise the engine cradle and install the bolts.

27. Coat the sub-frame bushings with rubber lubricant.

28. Lower the vehicle onto the assembly. Align the sub-frame on the vehicle using 2 bolts or drill bits, ¾ inches thick by 8 inches long through the alignment holes on the right side of the frame.

29. Install or connect the following:

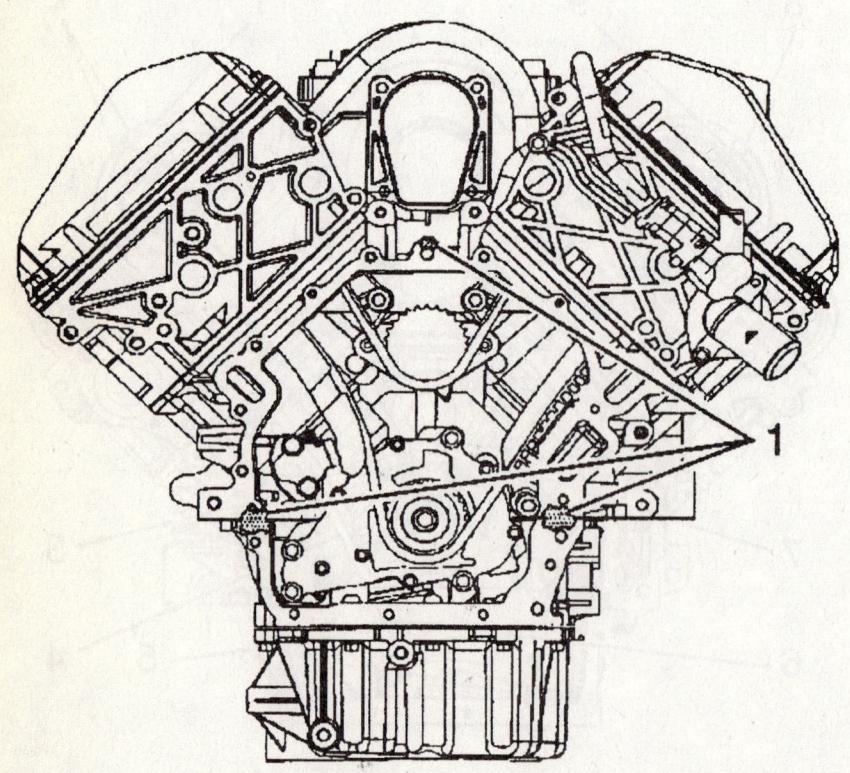

Apply RTV sealant to the 3 areas indicated before installing the front cover and gasket—3.5L engine

- New frame-to-body bolts. Torque the bolts to 133 ft. lbs. (180 Nm).
- Water pump
- Idler pulley and belt tensioner
- Power steering pump
- Drive belt
- Underhood accessories
- Battery and tray
- Front diagonal brace
- Camshaft covers
- Negative battery cable

30. Refill the engine cooling system.

31. Refill the engine with new oil.

32. Start the vehicle and check for leaks, repair if necessary.

SECONDARY TIMING CHAIN

1. Before servicing the vehicle, refer to the precautions in the beginning of this section.

2. Drain the cooling system.

3. Disconnect the negative battery cable.

4. For the front cylinder head, perform the following:

　a. Remove the thermostat housing for clearance to install tool J-42042 or equivalent.

　b. Remove the left rocker arm cover and install a Camshaft Holding Fixture J-42038.

5. For the rear cylinder head, perform the following:

　a. Remove the rear camshaft cover.

　b. Install a Camshaft Holding tool J 42038 to the rear camshafts.

　c. Remove the camshaft position sensor.

➡For either cylinder head, perform the following procecdure:

6. Remove or disconnect the following:
- Camshaft sprocket bolts and install the timing chain/sprocket holding fixture on the cylinder head.
- Sprockets and chain, slide them onto the tool
- Secondary timing sprocket and chain

To install:

7. Install or connect the following:
- Secondary timing chain on the sprockets, with the drive pins at the 12 o'clock positions
- Sprockets/chain assembly onto the camshafts, with the chain properly aligned on the tensioner

8. Remove the sprocket holding fixture from the cylinder head.

9. Install or connect the following:
- Sprocket bolts. Torque the bolts to

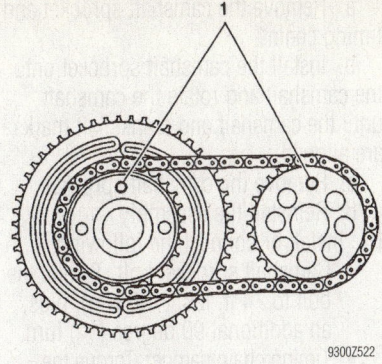

Correct sprocket alignment for secondary timing chain—3.5L engine

18 ft. lbs. (25 Nm), plus, an additional 45 degree turn.

10. Remove the camshaft holding fixture.

11. Install or connect the following:
- Rocker arm cover
- Thermostat housing for the front cylinder head
- Camshaft position sensor fore the rear cylinder head
- Negative battery cable

12. Refill the cooling system.

13. Start the vehicle and check for leaks, repair if necessary.

3.8L Engines

1. Before servicing the vehicle, refer to the precautions in the beginning of this section.

2. Drain the coolant system.

3. Install an Engine Support Fixture tool J-28467-A.

4. Raise the engine so that the weight is removed from the torque axis mount.

5. Remove or disconnect the following:
- Negative battery cable
- Vacuum reservoir
- Both lower torque axis-to-frame bolts
- Torque axis mount
- Serpentine belt(s)
- Engine mount bracket
- Alternator
- Drive belt tensioner
- Crankshaft balancer
- Crankshaft Position (CKP) sensor shield
- CKP sensor electrical connector
- Front oil pan-to-front cover bolts
- Front cover
- Front cover seal using a seal driver

6. Rotate the crankshaft until the timing mark on the camshaft sprocket is aligned with the crankshaft sprocket timing mark.

7. Remove or disconnect the following:
- Timing chain damper assembly
- Camshaft sprocket bolt
- Camshaft sprocket with the timing chain
- Crankshaft sprocket using a gear puller

To install:

8. Install or connect the following:
- Crankshaft sprocket by aligning it with the crankshaft key

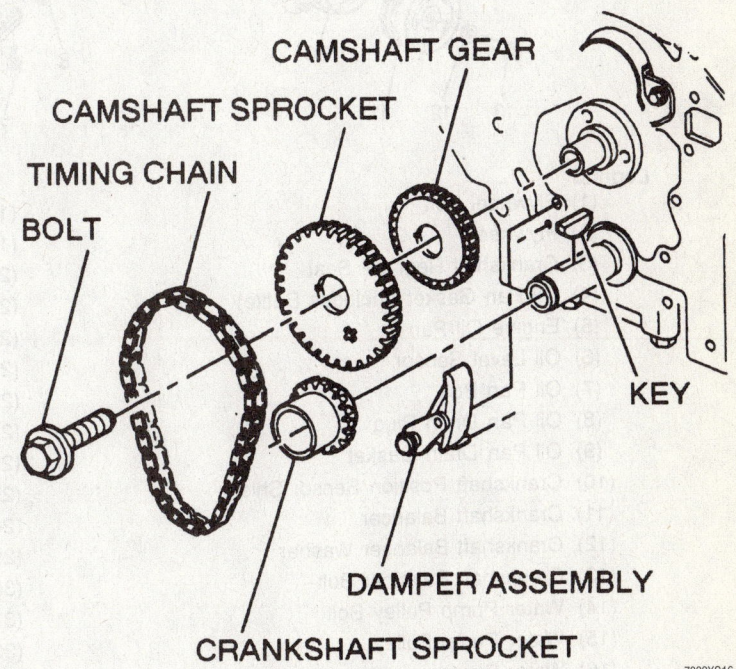

CAMSHAFT GEAR

CAMSHAFT SPROCKET

TIMING CHAIN

BOLT

KEY

DAMPER ASSEMBLY

CRANKSHAFT SPROCKET

Exploded view of the timing chain and sprockets—3.8L (VIN 1 and K) engines

For complete mechanical specifications, refer to Section 1 of this manual

➡It may be necessary to use a gear installer to fully seat the gear. Be sure the timing mark on the crankshaft gear is pointing straight up.

• Camshaft gear with the timing chain

➡Hold the sprocket with the timing mark facing downward and the chain hanging down off the sprocket; then, loop the chain under the crankshaft sprocket.

• Camshaft sprocket by aligning the notch with the camshaft key

➡The camshaft and crankshaft timing marks should be aligned.

9. If the marks are not in alignment perform the following:

a. Remove the camshaft sprocket and timing chain.

b. Install the camshaft sprocket onto the camshaft and rotate the camshaft until the camshaft and crankshaft marks are aligned.

c. Remove the camshaft sprocket.

d. Reinstall the assembly.

10. Install or connect the following:

• Camshaft sprocket bolt. Torque the bolt to 74 ft. lbs. (100 Nm), plus, an additional 90 degree (¼) turn.

• Timing chain damper. Torque the mounting bolts to 16 ft. lbs. (22 Nm).

11. Thoroughly clean all sealing surfaces.

12. Install or connect the following:

• Front cover seal lubricated with engine oil, using the appropriate seal driver

• New front cover gasket

• Front cover. Torque the bolts to 22 ft. lbs. (30 Nm).

• Oil pan-to-front cover bolts. Torque the bolts to 125 inch lbs. (14 Nm).

• Belt tensioner. Torque the bolts to 37 ft. lbs. (50 Nm).

• Alternator

• CKP sensor electrical connector and shield

• Crankshaft balancer. Torque the bolt to 111 ft. lbs. (150 Nm), plus, an additional 75 degree turn.

• Engine mount bracket. Torque the bolts to 65 ft. lbs. (87 Nm).

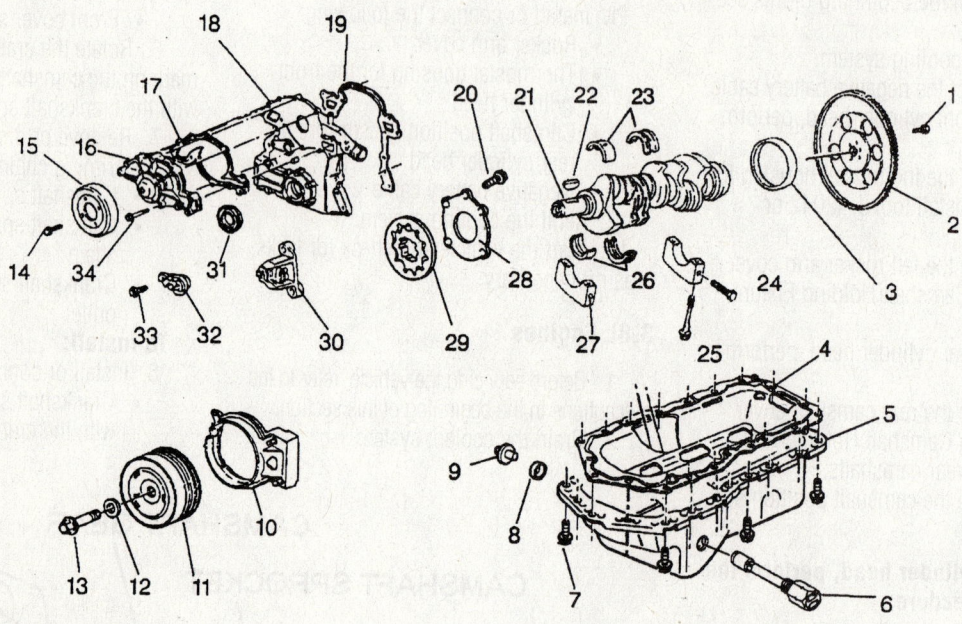

Legend

(1) Flywheel Bolt
(2) Flywheel
(3) Crankshaft Rear Oil Seal
(4) Oil Pan Gasket (Includes Baffle)
(5) Engine Oil Pan
(6) Oil Level Sensor
(7) Oil Pan Bolt
(8) Oil Pan Drain Plug
(9) Oil Pan Drain Gasket
(10) Crankshaft Position Sensor Shield
(11) Crankshaft Balancer
(12) Crankshaft Balancer Washer
(13) Crankshaft Balancer Bolt
(14) Water Pump Pulley Bolt
(15) Water Pump Pulley
(16) Water Pump
(17) Water Pump Gasket
(18) Engine Front Cover
(19) Engine Front Cover Gasket
(20) Oil Pump Cover Bolt
(21) Engine Crankshaft
(22) Crankshaft Balancer Key
(23) Crankshaft Upper Bearing
(24) Side Main Bolt
(25) Crankshaft Main Bearing Cap Bolt
(26) Crankshaft Lower Bearing
(27) Crankshaft Main Bearing Cap
(28) Oil Pump Cover
(29) Oil Pump Gear Set
(30) Crankshaft Position Sensor
(31) Crankshaft Front Oil Seal
(32) Camshaft Position Sensor
(33) Camshaft Position Sensor Bolt
(34) Water Pump Bolt

Exploded view of lower engine components—3.8L engine

9300XG04

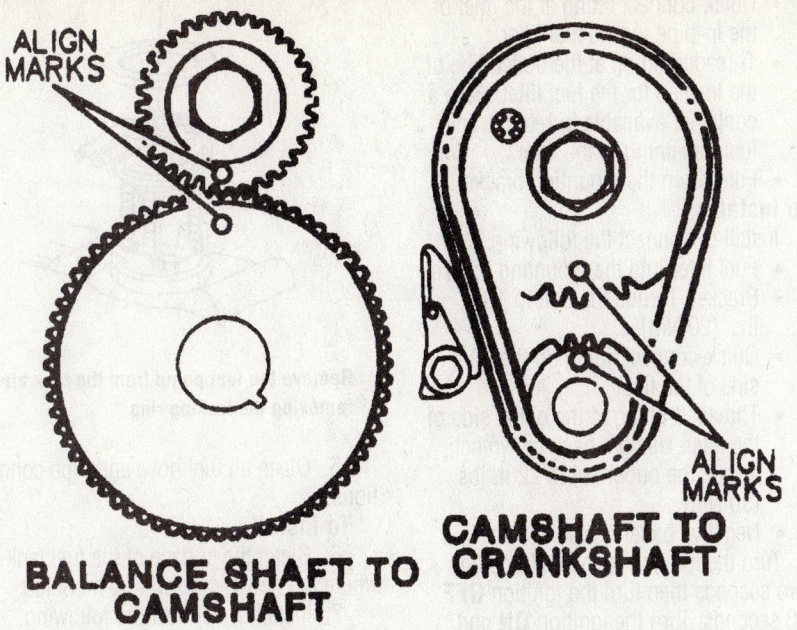

BALANCE SHAFT TO CAMSHAFT

CAMSHAFT TO CRANKSHAFT

ALIGN MARKS

ALIGN MARKS

7922XG17

Balance shaft-to-camshaft and camshaft-to-crankshaft timing mark alignment—3.8L engine

- Power steering pump and belt(s)
- Torque axis mount so the lower bracket slips around both frame bolts
- Both torque axis mount through-bolts/nuts. Torque the torque axis mount-to-frame bolts to 52 ft. lbs. (70 Nm) and the through-bolts to 65 ft. lbs. (87 Nm).

13. Remove the engine support fixture.
14. Install or connect the following:
   - Vacuum reservoir
   - Negative battery cable
15. Refill the cooling system.
16. Start the engine and check for leaks, repair if necessary.

Piston and Ring

POSITIONING

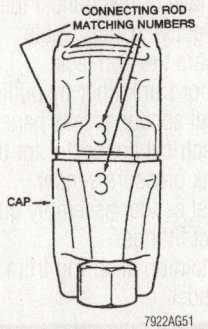

CONNECTING ROD MATCHING NUMBERS

CAP

7922AG51

Connecting rod and cap installation. Be sure to matchmark the cap and rod prior to disassembly, as shown

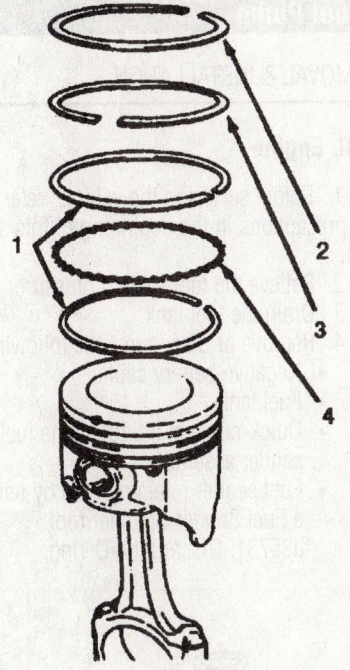

1. Oil rings
2. Top compression ring
3. Second compression ring
4. Expander

7922AG48

Piston ring positioning—3.1L, 3.4L, 3.5L and 3.8L engines

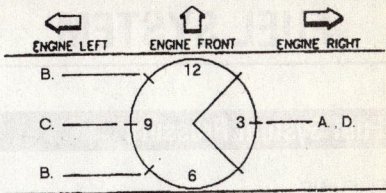

ENGINE LEFT   ENGINE FRONT   ENGINE RIGHT

B. — 12
C. — 9   3 — A. D.
B. — 6

A. OIL RING SPACER GAP (TANG IN HOLE OR SLOT WITH ARC)
B. OIL RING RAIL GAPS
C. 2ND COMPRESSION RING GAP
D. TOP COMPRESSION RING GAP

7922AG46

Piston ring end-gap spacing—3.1L, 3.4L, 3.8L engines

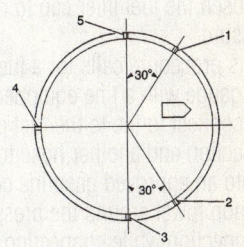

1. Lower oil control ring
2. Upper oil control ring
3. Top Ring
4. Oil control ring expander
5. Second ring

9306XG05

Piston ring end-gap positioning—3.5L engine

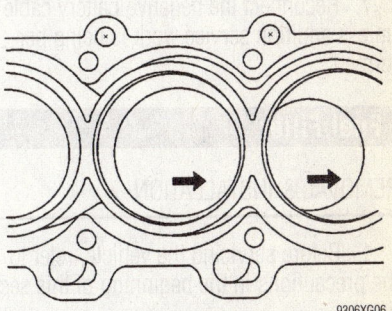

9306XG06

Piston positioning—3.5L engine

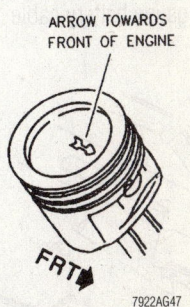

ARROW TOWARDS FRONT OF ENGINE

FRT

7922AG47

Piston positioning. Often the arrow is replaced by a notch, which also must face toward the front of the engine—3.1L, 3.4L and 3.8L engines

Please refer to Section 8 for electric cooling fan wiring schematics

FUEL SYSTEM

Fuel System Pressure

RELIEVING

1. Before servicing the vehicle, refer to the precautions in the beginning of this section.

2. Disconnect the negative battery cable to prevent possible discharge of fuel if an accidental attempt is made to start the engine.

3. Loosen the fuel filler cap to relieve tank pressure.

4. This procedure calls for a fuel pressure test gauge with a line equipped with a fitting to connect to the to the fuel pressure test connection and another hose to discharge into an approved gasoline container. Wrap a shop towel around the pressure test fitting connection while connecting gauge to avoid spillage.

5. Install the bleed hose into an approved container and open the valve to bleed fuel system pressure. The fuel connections are now safe for servicing.

6. Drain any fuel remaining in the gauge into an approved container.

7. Reconnect the negative battery cable unless addition service work is being performed.

Fuel Filter

REMOVAL & INSTALLATION

1. Before servicing the vehicle, refer to the precautions in the beginning of this section.

2. Relieve fuel system pressure.

3. Remove or disconnect the following:
   - Negative battery cable

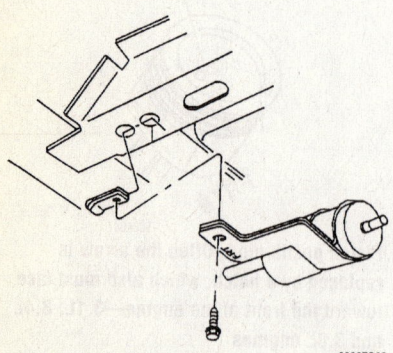

Common fuel filter mounting

9306ZG20

- Quick-connect fitting at the inlet of the in-pipe for the fuel filter
- Threaded fitting at the outlet side of the in-pipe for the fuel filter. Have a container available to retrieve any fuel remaining in the filter
- Filter from the mounting bracket

To install:

4. Install or connect the following:
   - Fuel filter into the mounting bracket
   - Bracket. Torque the bolt to 15 ft. lbs. (20 Nm).
   - Quick-connect fitting on the inlet side of the filter
   - Threaded fitting to the outlet side of the filter. Using a back up wrench, torque the outlet nut to 22 ft. lbs. (30 Nm).
   - Negative battery cable

5. Turn the ignition to the **ON** position for two seconds then turn the ignition **OFF** for 10 seconds. Turn the ignition **ON** and check for leaks.

6. Turn the ignition **OFF** if leaks are found and repair if necessary.

Fuel Pump

REMOVAL & INSTALLATION

3.4L Engine

1. Before servicing the vehicle, refer to the precautions in the beginning of this section.

2. Relieve the fuel system pressure.

3. Drain the fuel tank.

4. Remove or disconnect the following:
   - Negative battery cable
   - Fuel tank
   - Quick-connect fittings at the fuel sender assembly
   - Fuel sender retaining cam by using a Fuel Sender Spanner tool J35731. Discard the O-ring

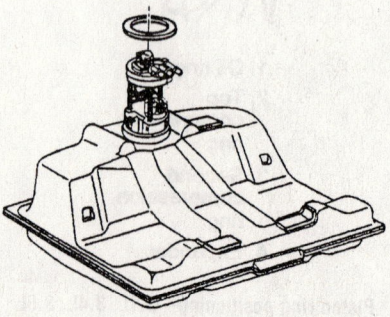

Exploded view of the fuel sender—3.4L engine

9306ZG21

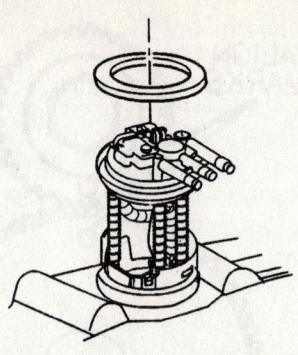

79222Z528

Remove the fuel pump from the tank after removing the locking ring

5. Clean all fuel hose and pipe connections.

To install:

6. Clean the surface of the fuel tank where the new O-ring will be mounted.

7. Install or connect the following:
   - New O-ring on the fuel tank
   - Fuel sender assembly and retainer cam by using a spanner tool
   - Quick-connect fittings at the fuel sender. Make certain the fittings are properly seated
   - Fuel tank
   - Negative battery cable

8. Fill the fuel tank.

9. Turn the ignition to the **ON** position for 2 seconds then turn the ignition **OFF** for 10 seconds. Turn the ignition **ON** and check for leaks.

10. Turn the ignition **OFF** if leaks are found and repair immediately.

3.1L and 3.5L Engines

1. Before servicing the vehicle, refer to the precautions in the beginning of this section.

2. Relieve the fuel system pressure.

3. Drain the fuel tank with a hand held siphon until the level is less than ¼ full.

4. Remove or disconnect the following:
   - Negative battery cable
   - Spare tire and jack
   - Floor trunk liner by pulling it back
   - Fuel sender access panel
   - Electrical connector for the fuel tank pressure sensor
   - Fuel sender assembly quick connect fittings
   - Retaining snapring from the fuel sender

✳✳ WARNING

When the lockring is removed from the fuel sender, the sender assembly will spring up. Downward pressure

should be kept on the assembly and slowly released to ensure the sender assembly does not get damaged.

- Modular fuel sender assembly and discard the O-ring

5. Clean the surface where the new O-ring will be installed on the fuel tank.

To install:

6. Install or connect the following:
- New O-ring on the fuel tank
- Fuel sender into the fuel tank
- Snapring on the fuel sender
- Electrical connectors to the fuel tank pressure sensor
- Quick connect fittings at the fuel sender. Make certain that the fittings are properly installed
- Negative battery cable

7. Add a small amount of fuel to the fuel tank

8. Turn the ignition to the **ON** position for 2 seconds then turn the ignition **OFF** for 10 seconds. Turn the ignition **ON** and check for leaks.

9. Turn the ignition **OFF** if leaks are found and repair immediately.

10. Install or connect the following:
- Fuel sender access panel. Torque the nuts to 89 inch lbs. (10 Nm).
- Trunk liner
- Spare tire, jack and spare tire cover

11. Refill the fuel tank.

3.8L Engine

1. Before servicing the vehicle, refer to the precautions in the beginning of this section.

2. Relieve the fuel system pressure.

3. Drain the fuel tank

4. Remove or disconnect the following:
- Negative battery cable
- Fuel tank
- Quick-connect fittings at the fuel sender assembly
- Fuel sender retaining cam by using a Fuel Sender Spanner tool J35731. Discard the O-ring

5. Clean all fuel hose and pipe connections.

To install:

6. Clean the surface of the fuel tank where the new O-ring will be mounted.

7. Install or connect the following:
- New O-ring on the fuel tank
- Fuel sender assembly and retainer cam by using a spanner tool
- Quick-connect fittings at the fuel

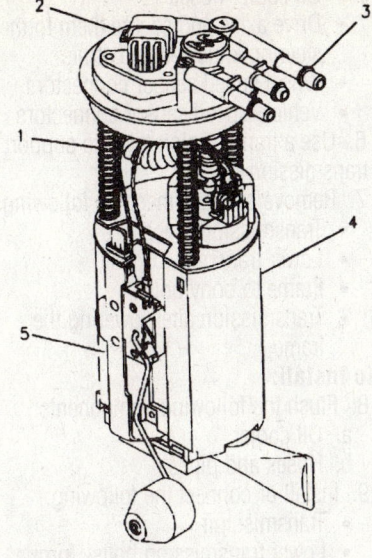

1 SUPPORT ASSEMBLY – FUEL SENDER
2 COVER ASSEMBLY – FUEL SENDER
3 FUEL PIPES (ABOVE COVER)
4 RESERVOIR – FUEL PUMP FUEL
5 SENSOR ASSEMBLY – FUEL LEVEL

7922XG19

Fuel pump and sending unit module assembly

sender. Make certain the fittings are properly seated
- Fuel tank
- Fill to the fuel tank
- Negative battery cable

8. Turn the ignition to the **ON** position for 2 seconds then turn the ignition **OFF** for 10 seconds. Turn the ignition **ON** and check for leaks.

9. Turn the ignition **OFF** if leaks are found and repair immediately.

Fuel Injector

REMOVAL & INSTALLATION

3.1L and 3.4L Engines

1. Before servicing the vehicle, refer to the precautions in the beginning of this section.

2. Relieve the fuel system pressure.

3. Remove or disconnect the following:
- Negative battery cable
- Upper intake manifold
- Fuel rail
- Fuel injector retaining clips
- Fuel injectors
- Upper, lower and lower backup O-rings and discard them

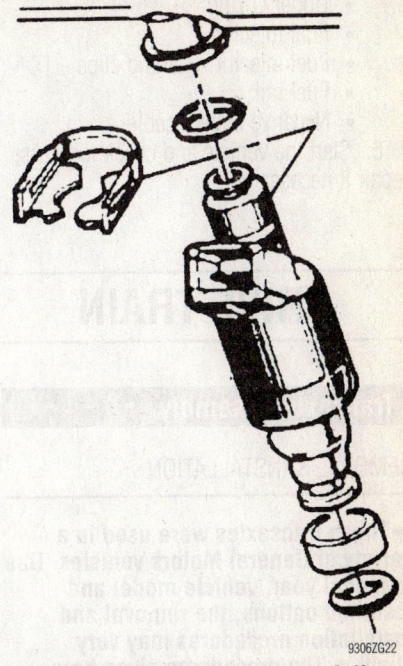

9306ZG22

Exploded view of the fuel injector—3.1L and 3.4L engines

To install:

4. Coat the new O-rings with clean engine oil.

5. Install or connect the following:
- Lower backup O-ring
- Lower O-ring
- Upper O-ring
- Fuel injector
- Fuel injector retaining clips
- Fuel rail
- Upper intake manifold
- Negative battery cable

6. Start the vehicle and check for leaks, repair if necessary.

3.5L and 3.8L Engines

1. Before servicing the vehicle, refer to the precautions in the beginning of this section.

2. Relieve the fuel system pressure.

3. Remove or disconnect the following:
- Negative battery cable
- Fuel rail
- Fuel injector retaining clips
- Fuel injectors
- Upper, lower and lower backup O-rings and discard them

To install:

4. Coat the new O-rings with clean engine oil.

5. Install or connect the following:
- Lower backup O-ring
- Lower O-ring

- Upper O-ring
- Fuel injector
- Fuel injector retaining clips
- Fuel rail
- Negative battery cable

6. Start the vehicle and check for leaks, repair if necessary.

DRIVE TRAIN

Transaxle Assembly

REMOVAL & INSTALLATION

➡These transaxles were used in a variety of General Motors vehicles. Due to model year, vehicle model and installed options, the removal and installation procedures may vary slightly. The procedures given here should suffice for most all vehicles using these transaxles.

4T60-E Transmission

1. Before servicing the vehicle, refer to the precautions in the beginning of this section.
2. Drain the transmission fluid.
3. Remove or disconnect the following:
   - Negative battery cable
   - Throttle body air inlet duct
4. Install an engine support fixture.
5. Remove or disconnect the following:
   - Engine mount struts
   - Wire harness connectors from the transmission
   - Vacuum hose and pipe from the modulator
   - Range selector cable from the Park/Neutral Position (PNP) switch
   - PNP switch
   - Fluid filler tube
   - Upper transmission bolts
   - Wire harness grounds
   - Both front wheels
   - Engine splash shields
   - Both tie rod ends from the steering knuckles
   - Power steering gear from the frame and secure it to the body of the vehicle
   - Power steering cooler line clamps
   - Engine mount lower nuts
   - Lower ball joints from the steering knuckles
   - Torque converter cover
   - Starter
   - Torque converter bolts

- Oil cooler hoses
- Drive axles and secure them to the steering knuckles and struts
- Wheel speed sensor connectors
- Vehicle speed sensor connectors

6. Use a transmission table to support the transmission
7. Remove or disconnect the following:
   - Transmission brace
   - Lower transmission bolt
   - Frame to body bolts
   - Transmission after lowering the frame

To install:
8. Flush the following components:
   a. Oil cooler
   b. Hoses and pipes
9. Install or connect the following:
   - Transmission
   - Lower transmission bolts. Torque the bolts to 55 ft. lbs. (75 Nm).
   - New frame to body bolts. Torque the bolts to 125 ft. lbs. (170 Nm).
   - Transmission brace. Torque the bolts to 35 ft. lbs. (47 Nm).
   - Vehicle speed sensor wire connector and remove the transmission table
   - Wheel speed sensor wire connectors
   - Drive axles to the transmission
   - Oil cooler hoses
   - Torque converter bolts. Torque the bolts to 46 ft. lbs. (63 Nm).
   - Starter
   - Torque converter cover. Torque the bolts to 89 inch lbs. (10 Nm).
   - Lower ball joints to the steering knuckle
   - Engine mount lower nuts. Torque the nuts to 32 ft. lbs. (43 Nm).
   - Power steering cooler line clamps to the frame
   - Power steering gear to the frame. Torque the bolts to 59 ft. lbs. (80 Nm).
   - Tie rod ends to the steering knuckles. Torque the nut to 63 ft. lbs. (85 Nm).
   - Engine splash shields
   - Front wheels
   - Fluid filler tube
   - Upper transaxle bolts. Torque the bolts to 55 ft. lbs. (75 Nm).
   - PNP switch. Torque the bolts to 18 ft. lbs. (25 Nm).
   - Range selector cable and bracket. Torque the nut to 15 ft. lbs. (20 Nm).
   - Range selector cable to the PNP switch
   - Wire harness connectors to the transmission

- Engine mount struts. Torque the bolts to 37 ft. lbs. (50 Nm).
10. Remove the engine support fixture.
11. Install or connect the following:
    - Throttle body air inlet duct
    - Negative battery cable
12. Fill the transmission with fluid.
13. Adjust the shift linkage and TV cables.
14. Start engine and check the engine and transaxle oil level. Add oil if necessary.

4T65-E Transmission

1. Before servicing the vehicle, refer to the precautions in the beginning of this section.
2. Drain the transmission fluid.
3. Remove or disconnect the following:
   - Negative battery cable
   - Throttle body air inlet duct
4. Install an engine support fixture.
5. Remove or disconnect the following:
   - Engine mount struts
   - Wire harness connectors from the transmission
   - Range selector cable from the Park Neutral Position (PNP) switch
   - Range selector cable and bracket
   - PNP switch
   - Fluid filler tube
   - Upper transmission bolts
   - Wire harness grounds
   - Both front wheels
   - Engine splash shields
   - Both tie rod ends from the steering knuckles
   - Power steering gear from the frame and secure it to the body of the vehicle
   - Power steering cooler line clamps
   - Engine mount lower nuts
   - Lower ball joints from the steering knuckles
   - Torque converter cover
   - Starter
   - Torque converter bolts
   - Oil cooler hoses
   - Drive axles and secure them to the steering knuckles and struts
   - Wheel speed sensor connectors
   - Vehicle speed sensor connectors
6. Use a transmission table to support the transmission
7. Remove or disconnect the following:
   - Rear engine mount and bracket
   - Transmission brace
   - Lower transmission bolts
   - Frame to body bolts
8. Separate the transmission from the engine.

9. Lower the transmission and frame from the vehicle.

10. Remove the transmission.

To install:

11. Install or connect the following:
- Transmission to the frame and raise the assembly into position
- New frame to body bolts. Torque the bolts to 125 ft. lbs. (170 Nm).
- Lower transmission to engine bolts. Torque the longer bolts to 55 ft. lbs. (75 Nm) and the shorter bolt to 36 ft. lbs. (50 Nm).
- Transmission brace. Torque the bolts to 35 ft. lbs. (47 Nm).
- Rear engine bracket and mount. Torque the bolts to 75 ft. lbs. (102 Nm).
- Vehicle speed sensor wire connector and remove the transmission table
- Wheel speed sensor wire connectors
- Drive axles to the transmission
- Oil cooler hoses
- Torque converter bolts. Torque the bolts to 46 ft. lbs. (63 Nm).
- Starter
- Torque converter cover. Torque the bolts to 89 inch lbs. (10 Nm).
- Lower ball joints to the steering knuckle
- Engine mount lower nuts. Torque the nuts to 32 ft. lbs. (43 Nm).
- Power steering cooler line clamps to the frame
- Power steering gear to the frame. Torque the bolts to 59 ft. lbs. (80 Nm).
- Tie rod ends to the steering knuckles. Torque the nut to 63 ft. lbs. (85 Nm).
- Engine splash shields
- Front wheels
- Fluid filler tube
- Upper transmission bolts. Torque the bolts to 55 ft. lbs. (75 Nm).
- PNP switch. Torque the bolts to 18 ft. lbs. (25 Nm).
- Range selector cable and bracket. Torque the nut to 15 ft. lbs. (20 Nm).
- Range selector cable to the PNP switch
- Wire harness connectors to the transmission
- Engine mount strut. Torque the bolts to 37 ft. lbs. (50 Nm).

12. Remove the engine support fixture.

13. Install or connect the following:
- Throttle body air inlet duct
- Negative battery cable

14. Fill the transmission with fluid.

15. Adjust the shift linkage and TV cables.

16. Start engine and check the engine and transaxle oil levels. Add oil if necessary.

Halfshaft

REMOVAL & INSTALLATION

Intrigue

1. Before servicing the vehicle, refer to the precautions in the beginning of this section.

2. Remove or disconnect the following:
- Front wheel
- Stabilizer shaft link
- Drive shaft nut by inserting a drift into the rotor to prevent it from turning.
- Outer tie rod end and the ball joint from the steering knuckle.

3. Press the axle shaft through the hub.

✳✳ WARNING

To prevent damage to the inner CV-joint, do not pull on the axle shaft to remove it from the transaxle.

4. Place a drain pan under the transaxle to catch any transaxle fluid that leaks out when the axle shaft is removed.

5. Remove the axle shaft from the transaxle by prying between the transaxle and the inner CV-joint housing.

To install:

6. Install or connect the following:
- Axle shaft in the transaxle. Verify that it is seated by pulling on the housing

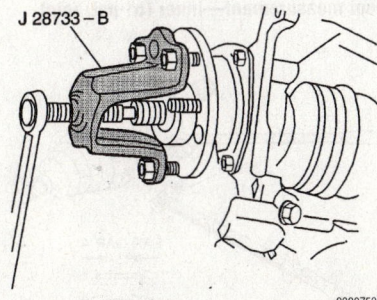

Use a puller to press the axle shaft through the hub/bearing assembly—Intrigue

- Axle shaft through the hub/bearing assembly
- Ball joint and the tie rod end to the steering knuckle
- New shaft nut. Torque the nut to 118 ft. lbs. (160 Nm).
- Stabilizer shaft link
- Front wheel

7. Check the transaxle fluid level.

8. Check the front alignment and adjust, if necessary.

Except Intrigue

➡️**If equipped with Antilock Brake System (ABS) brakes, use care to avoid damage to the ABS toothed ring. Damage to the ring may cause the self-diagnostic feature of the ABS system to set a system fault code.**

1. Before servicing the vehicle, refer to the precautions in the beginning of this section.

2. Remove or disconnect the following:
- Front wheel
- Front wheel drive axle nut
- Brake calipers bracket assemblies
- Brake rotors
- 4 hub/bearing retaining bolts and hub
- Front wheel speed sensor connector

3. Remove the halfshaft from the vehicle using the appropriate procedure for each side and transmission model:

a. To remove the right side halfshaft, use special tool J 33008, J 29794 and J 2619-01. Separate the halfshaft from the transaxle.

b. To remove the left side halfshaft, using the frame for leverage, separate the halfshaft from the transaxle with a suitable prying tool in the groove provided on the inner joint.

4. Remove the halfshaft/bearing assembly through the steering knuckle

To install:

5. Install or connect the following:
- Halfshaft/bearing assembly through the knuckle and into the transaxle
- ABS sensor and mounting bolt, if removed
- Bearing to the knuckle bolts
- Halfshaft into the transaxle, using a suitable prying tool in the groove provided on the inner joint. Carefully pry against the frame or the lower control arm to seat the half-shaft.

6. Verify that the snapring is seated properly by tapping on the inner groove with a prying tool. Grasp the inner housing of the axle shaft and pull outboard. Do not pull on the axle shaft. If the snapring is properly seated, the axle will remain in place.

7. Install or connect the following:
- Front wheel drive speed sensor connector
- Front wheel driveshaft bearing
- New driveshaft nut. Torque the nut to 60 ft. lbs. (80 Nm).
- Brake rotor
- Brake caliper and attaching bracket
- Front wheel
- Front wheel drive axle nut. Torque the nut to 150 ft. lbs. (205 Nm).
- Negative battery cable

8. Check the transaxle fluid level.

9. Check the front alignment and adjust if necessary.

CV-Joint

OVERHAUL

Inner (Tri-Pot) Joint

1. Before servicing the vehicle, refer to the precautions in the beginning of this section.

2. Remove or disconnect the following:
- Front wheel
- Halfshaft
- Swage ring using a hand grinder
- Large CV-joint boot clamp, cut and discard it
- CV-joint boot by sliding it away from the tri-pot joint
- Tri-pot housing from the tri-pot spider
- Trilobal tri-pot bushing from the housing
- Inboard spacer ring slide it rearward on the shaft using Snapring Pliers tool J-8059
- Outboard retaining ring using Snapring Pliers tool J-8059

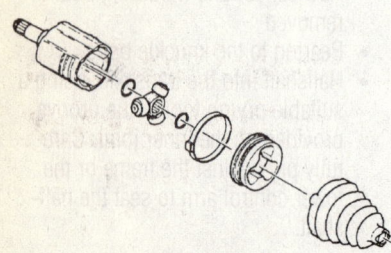
9306XG14

Exploded view of the inner (tri-pot) joint

- Tri-pot joint spider assembly
- Inboard spacer ring and CV-joint boot

3. Throughly clean and inspect all parts.

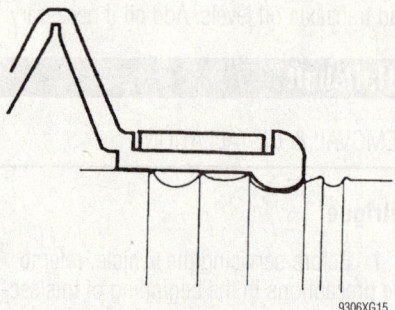
9306XG15

Positioning the inner CV-joint boot seal and swage ring—Inner (tri-pot) joint

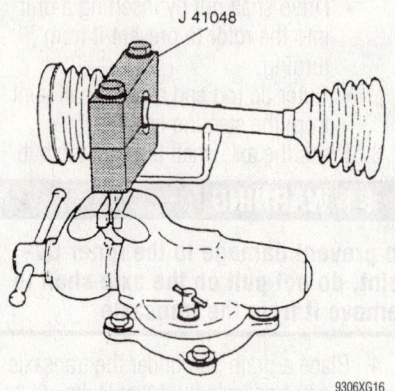
J 41048
9306XG16

View of the swage ring crimping tool— Inner (tri-pot) joint

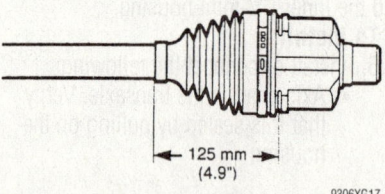
← 125 mm → (4.9")
9306XG17

Boot measurement—Inner (tri-pot) joint

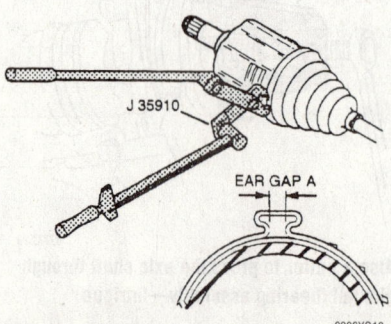
J 35910
EAR GAP A
9306XG18

Crimping the large CV-joint boot ring— Inner (tri-pot) joint

To install:

4. Install or connect the following:
- Swage ring clamp
- CV-joint boot

5. Position the CV-joint boot seal into the axle shaft's joint seal groove and align the swage ring clamp on the boot.

6. Secure the swage ring clamp as follows:

a. Mount the lower half of tool J-41048 in a vise.

b. Position the outboard of the half-shaft in the tool.

c. Position the upper end of tool J-41048 onto the lower half.

✳✳ WARNING

Make sure that there are no pinch points on the inboard seal.

d. Insert both bolts and tighten by hand until snug.

e. Tighten each bolt 180 degree (½ turn) at a time, alternating between the bolts, until both sides are bottomed.

f. Remove the tool.

7. Install or connect the following:
- Inboard spacer ring, slide it rearward on the shaft using Snapring Pliers tool J-8059
- Tri-pot joint spider assembly onto the shaft
- Outboard retaining ring into the axle shaft groove using Snapring Pliers tool J-8059
- Tri-pot joint spider assembly, slide it against the outboard retaining ring
- Inboard spacer ring, seat it in the groove
- ½ kit grease into the boot
- ½ kit grease into the tri-pot housing
- Trilobal tip-pot bushing flush with the tri-pot housing face
- New large seal clamp onto the CV-joint boot
- Tri-pot housing, slide it over the tri-pot joint spider assembly
- CV-joint boot/clamp, slide it into place, over the trilobal tri-pot bushing with the seal lip in the groove

➡️**Make sure the boot lies flat against the trilobal bushing.**

8. Position the CV-joint boot so it measures 4.9 in. (125mm).

9. Using the Crimp tool J-35910, a torque wrench and a breaker bar, crimp the large CV-joint boot clamp to 130 ft. lbs. (176 Nm).

10. Install or connect the following:
- Halfshaft
- Front wheel

Outer Joint

1. Before servicing the vehicle, refer to the precautions in the beginning of this section.

2. Remove or disconnect the following:
- Front wheel
- Halfshaft
- Swage ring using a hand grinder
- Large boot clamp, cut and discard it
- CV-joint boot, slide it away from the CV-joint
- CV-joint assembly by spreading the inner race-to-axle shaft retaining ring ears using Snapring Pliers tool J-8059
- CV-joint boot from the axle shaft and discard it

3. Disassemble the chrome alloy balls from the CV-joint cage as follows:

a. Position a brass drift against the CV-joint cage and tap it with a hammer to tilt the cage.

b. Chrome alloy ball from the cage.

c. Tilt the cage in the opposite direction.

d. Remove the opposite chrome alloy ball.

e. Repeat the procedure until all 6 balls are removed.

4. Disassemble the CV-joint cage and inner race as follows:

a. Pivot the cage and race 90 degrees to the center line of the outer race.

b. Align the cage windows with outer race lands.

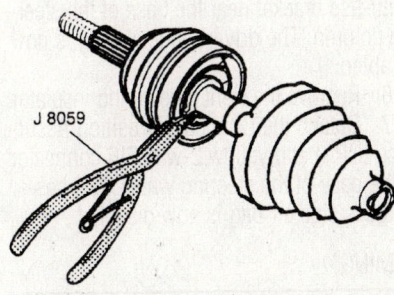

Disconnecting the outer CV-joint from the axle shaft

9306XG19

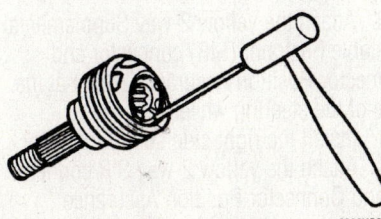

Tilting the cage—Outer CV-joint

9306XG20

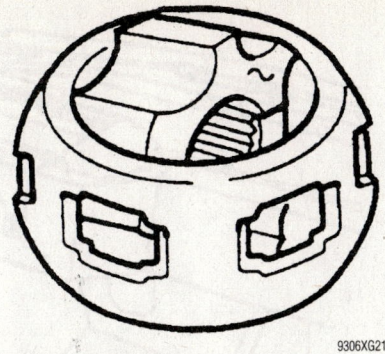

View the cage and inner race—Outer CV-joint

9306XG21

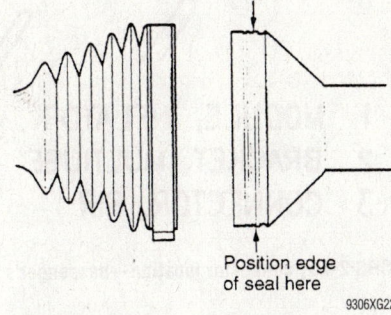

Position edge of seal here

9306XG22

Positioning the boot—Outer CV-joint

c. Remove the cage from the outer race.

d. Rotate the inner race upward and remove it from the cage.

5. Throughly clean and inspect all parts.

To install:

6. Lubricate the parts with a light coat of grease.

7. Assemble the CV-joint cage and inner race, as follows:

a. Rotate the inner race 90 degrees to the cage centerline.

b. Align the cage windows with inner race lands.

c. Insert the inner race into the cage by rotating the inner race downward.

d. Insert the cage/inner race into the outer race.

8. Assemble the chrome alloy balls into the CV-joint cage, as follows:

a. Position a brass drift against the CV-joint cage and tap it with a hammer to tilt the cage.

b. Insert the 1st chrome alloy ball into the cage.

c. Tilt the cage in the opposite direction.

d. Insert the opposite chrome alloy ball.

e. Repeat the procedure until all 6 balls are inserted.

9. Install or connect the following:
- ½ kit grease into the CV-joint boot
- ½ kit grease into the CV-joint
- Swage ring clamp
- CV-joint boot
- CV-joint onto the axle shaft until the retaining ring seats into the groove

10. Position the CV-joint boot seal into the axle shaft's joint seal groove and align the swage ring clamp on the boot.

11. Secure the swage ring clamp as follows:

a. Mount the lower half of tool J-41048 in a vise.

b. Position the outboard of the half-shaft in the tool.

c. Position the upper end of tool J-41048 onto the lower half.

✳✳ WARNING

Make sure that there are no pinch points on the inboard seal.

d. Insert both bolts and tighten by hand until snug.

e. Tighten each bolt 180 degree (½) turn at a time, alternating between the bolts, until both sides are bottomed.

f. Remove the tool.

12. Install or connect the following:
- New large seal clamp onto the CV-joint boot
- CV-joint boot/clamp, slide it into place, over the outer race with the seal lip in the groove

➡ **Make sure the boot lies flat against the outer race.**

13. Using the Crimp tool J-35910, a torque wrench and a breaker bar, crimp the large CV-joint boot clamp to 130 ft. lbs. (176 Nm).

14. Install or connect the following:
- Halfshaft
- Front wheel

STEERING AND SUSPENSION

Air Bag

✳✳ CAUTION

The vehicles are equipped with the Supplemental Inflatable Restraint (SIR) or air bag system. The SIR

system must be disabled before performing service on or around SIR system components, steering column, instrument panel components, wiring and sensors. Failure to follow safety and disabling procedures could result in accidental air bag deployment, possible personal injury and unnecessary SIR system repairs.

PRECAUTIONS

Several precautions must be observed when handling the inflator module to avoid accidental deployment and possible personal injury.

• Never carry the inflator module by the wires or connector on the underside of the module.

• When carrying a live inflator module, hold securely with both hands, and ensure that the bag and trim cover are pointed away.

• Place the inflator module on a bench or other surface with the bag and trim cover facing up.

• With the inflator module on the bench, never place anything on or close to the module which may be thrown in the event of an accidental deployment.

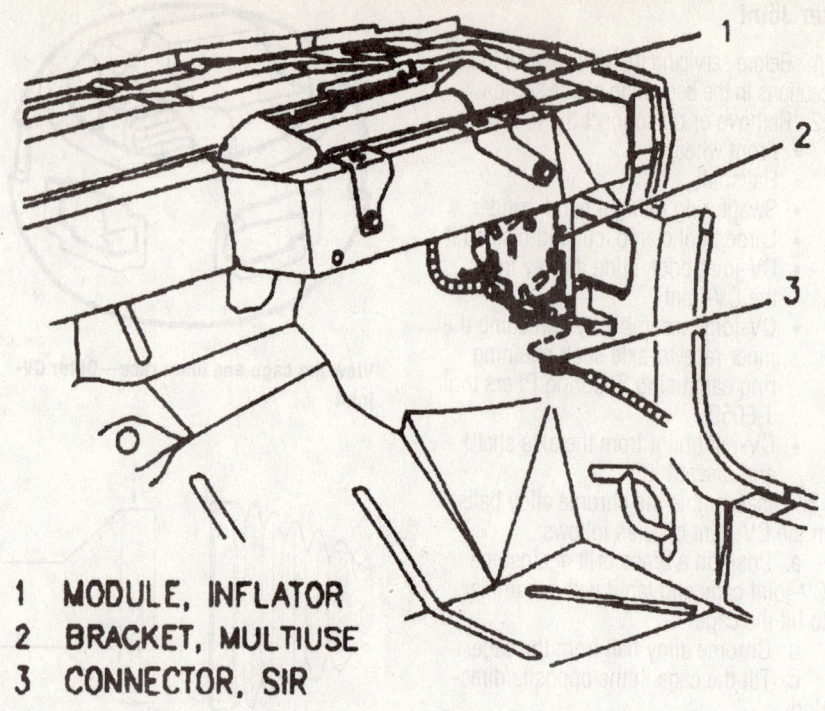

1 MODULE, INFLATOR
2 BRACKET, MULTIUSE
3 CONNECTOR, SIR

7922XG22

SRS 2-way connector location—passenger's side

DISARMING

1. Turn the steering wheel so the vehicle wheels are pointing straight-ahead.

2. Turn the ignition key to the **LOCK** position and remove the key.

3. Remove the AIR BAG fuse from the fuse block.

4. Remove the left side sound insulator.

5. Detach the Connector Position Assurance (CPA) and yellow 2-way Supplemental Inflatable Restraint (SIR) connector at the multi-use bracket near the base of the steering column. The driver's side air bag is now disabled.

6. Remove the right side sound insulator.

7. Detach the Connector Position Assurance (CPA) and yellow 2-way SIR connector at the base of the steering wheel. The passenger's side air bag is now disabled.

ARMING

After necessary repairs are made, re-enable the air bag system as follows:

1. Be sure the ignition is locked and the key is removed.

2. Attach the yellow 2-way Supplemental Inflatable Restraint (SIR) connector and Connector Position Assurance (CPA) at the base of the steering wheel.

3. Install the right side sound insulator.

4. Attach the yellow 2-way SIR connector and Connector Position Assurance (CPA) at the multi-use bracket at the base of the column.

5. Install the left side sound insulator.

6. Install the AIR BAG fuse.

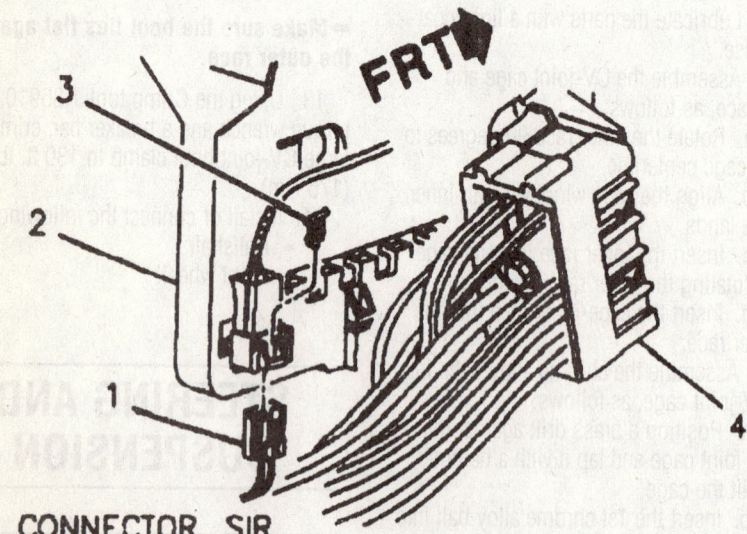

1 CONNECTOR, SIR
2 BRACKET, MULTIUSE MODULE
3 CONNECTOR POSITION ASSURANCE (CPA)
4 CONNECTOR, STEERING COLUMN
   WIRING HARNESS

7922XG21

SRS 2-way connector location—driver's side

7. Turn the ignition switch to the **RUN** position and verify the AIR BAG light flashes 7 times, then shuts off.

Power Rack and Pinion Steering Gear

REMOVAL & INSTALLATION

1. Before servicing the vehicle, refer to the precautions in the beginning of this section.

2. Remove or disconnect the following:
- Negative battery cable
- Front wheels

☀☀ CAUTION

Failure to disconnect the intermediate shaft from the rack and pinion stub shaft may result in damage to the steering gear. This damage may cause a loss of steering control and may cause personal injury.

➡Set the steering shaft so that the block tooth on the upper steering shaft is at the 12 o'clock position. The wheels should be straight ahead. Set the ignition key lock to the LOCK position. Failure to follow these procedures could result in damage to the SIR coil assembly.

3. Remove or disconnect the following:
- Intermediate steering shaft lower pinch bolt from the steering gear stub shaft

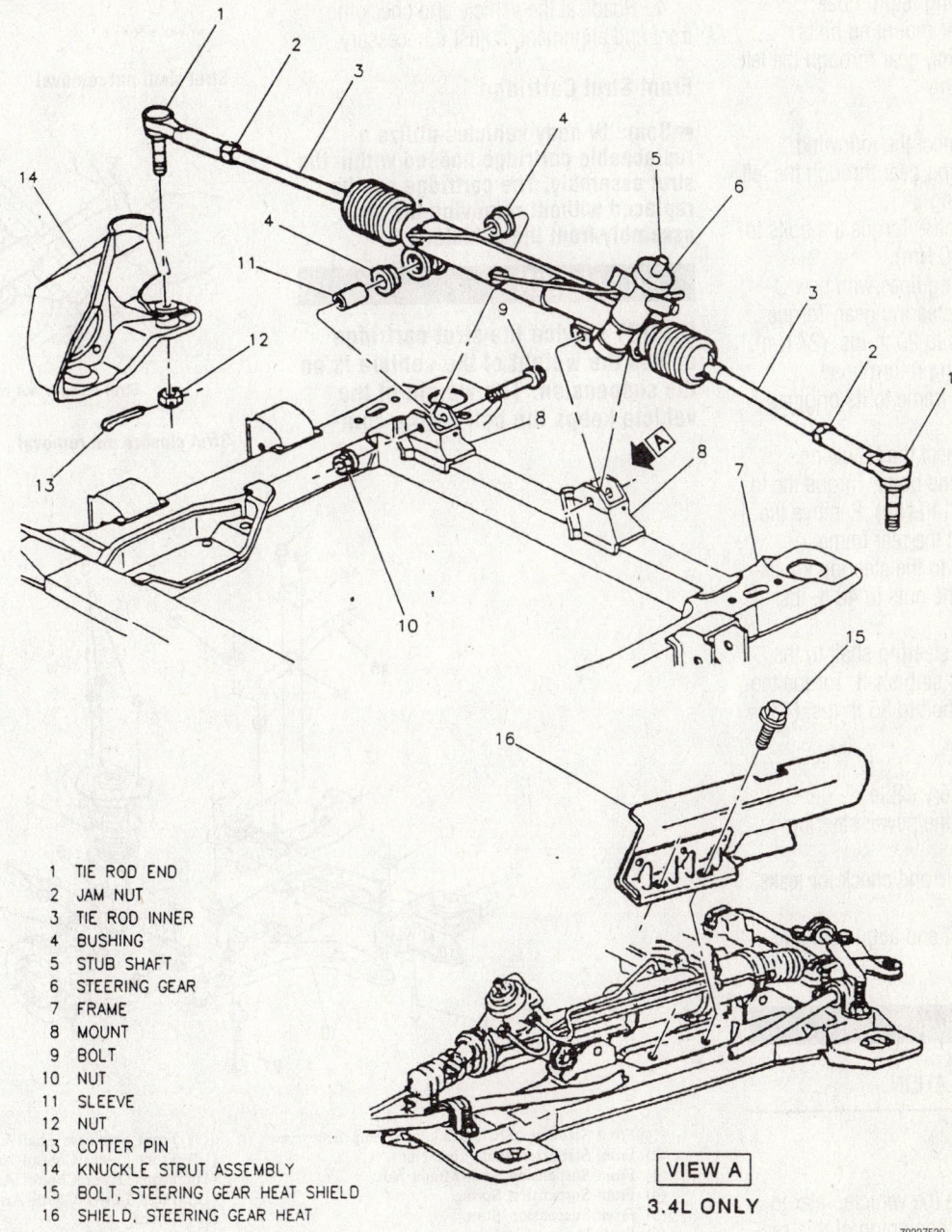

1 TIE ROD END
2 JAM NUT
3 TIE ROD INNER
4 BUSHING
5 STUB SHAFT
6 STEERING GEAR
7 FRAME
8 MOUNT
9 BOLT
10 NUT
11 SLEEVE
12 NUT
13 COTTER PIN
14 KNUCKLE STRUT ASSEMBLY
15 BOLT, STEERING GEAR HEAT SHIELD
16 SHIELD, STEERING GEAR HEAT

VIEW A
3.4L ONLY

79222529

Common rack and pinion steering gear mounting

- Intermediate steering shaft
- Both tie rod ends from the steering knuckles

4. Support the frame at the center rear using safety stands.

➡**DO NOT lower the frame too far. Engine components near the firewall may be damaged.**

5. Remove or disconnect the following:
- Frame bolts from the rear of the frame. Lower the frame slightly
- Power steering pressure line from the steering gear
- Power steering return hose
- Steering gear mounting bolts
- Power steering gear through the left wheel opening

To install:

6. Install or connect the following:
- Power steering gear through the left wheel opening
- Mounting bolts. Torque the bolts to 59 ft. lbs. (80 Nm).
- Power steering lines with new O-rings to the steering gear. Torque the fasteners to 20 ft. lbs. (27 Nm).
- Power steering return hose

7. Raise the rear frame to its original position.

8. Install or connect the following:
- New rear frame bolts. Torque the to 103 ft. lbs. (140 Nm). Remove the support from the rear frame
- Tie rod ends to the steering knuckles. Torque the nuts to 40 ft. lbs. (54 Nm).
- Intermediate steering shaft to the steering gear stub shaft. Torque the lower pinch bolt to 35 ft. lbs. (47 Nm).
- Front wheels
- Negative battery cable

9. Fill and bleed the power steering system.

10. Start the vehicle and check for leaks, repair if necessary.

11. Check the front end alignment and adjust as needed.

Strut

REMOVAL & INSTALLATION

Front Strut

1. Before servicing the vehicle, refer to the precautions in the beginning of this section.

2. Remove or disconnect the following:
- Front wheel

- Three upper strut nuts and scribe the strut to the steering knuckle
- Lower strut bolts
- Strut

To install:

3. Install or connect the following:
- Strut
- Three upper strut nuts. Torque the nuts to 30 ft. lbs. (41 Nm).
- Lower strut bolts
- Align the strut to the scribe on the steering knuckle. Torque the lower bolts to 90 ft. lbs. (123 Nm).
- Front wheel

4. Roadtest the vehicle and check the front end alignment, adjust if necessary.

Front Strut Cartridge

➡**Some W body vehicles utilize a replaceable cartridge housed within the strut assembly. The cartridge can be replaced without removing the strut assembly from the vehicle.**

❊❊ CAUTION

DO NOT service the strut cartridge unless the weight of the vehicle is on the suspension. The weight of the vehicle keeps the coil spring com- pressed. Otherwise the released coil spring could result in personal injury.

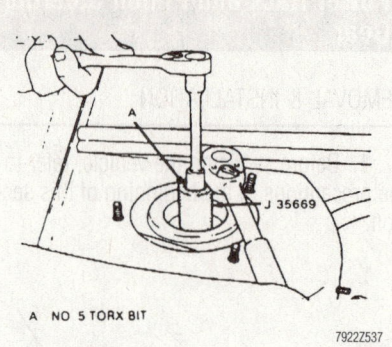

A   NO 5 TORX BIT

Strut shaft nut removal

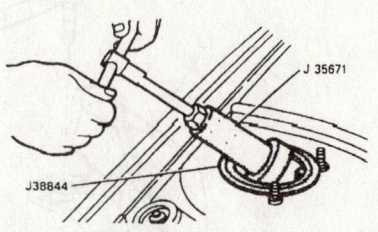

Strut closure nut removal

Strut closure nut removal

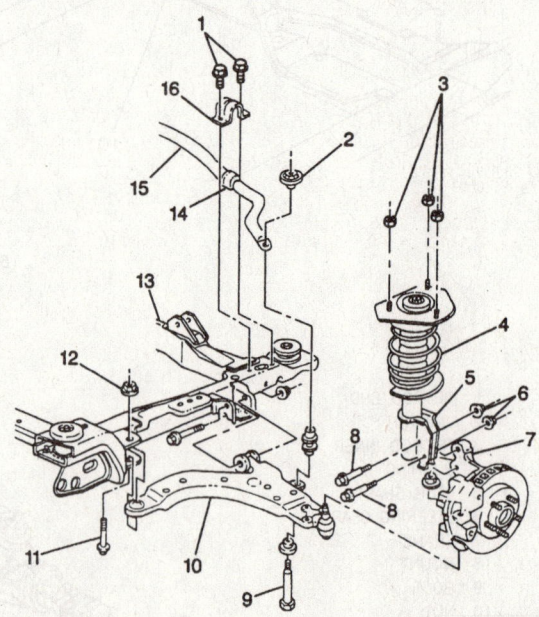

(1) Front Stabilizer Shaft Insulator Clamp Bolt/screw
(2) Front Stabilizer Shaft Link Nut
(3) Front Suspension Strut Mount Nut
(4) Front Suspension Spring
(5) Front Suspension Strut
(6) Strut To Knuckle Nut
(7) Front Steering Knuckle
(8) Strut To Knuckle Bolt/screw

(9) Front Stabilizer Shaft Link]
(10) Front Lower Control Arm
(11) Front Lower Control Arm Bolt/screw
(12) Front Lower Cotrol Arm Nut
(13) Frame
(14) Front Stabilizer Shaft Insulator
(15) Front Stabilizer Shaft
(16) Front Stabilizer Shaft Clamp

Exploded view of the front suspension without replaceable strut cartridge

1. Before servicing the vehicle, refer to the precautions in the beginning of this section.

2. Scribe the strut cover to body to assure proper camber adjustment.

3. Remove or disconnect the following:
- Strut cover by removing the three cover nuts
- Strut shaft nut by using a No. 50 Torx® bit and Strut Alignment Rod tool J 35668
- Strut mount insulator by prying with a flat bladed tool. Use J 35668 to apply pressure on the strut as necessary to relieve the side load (compression) on the bushing
- Strut bumper by attaching J 35668 to the strut and pulling out the bumper

4. Install a Strut Alignment tool J 38844 in the correct position and compress the strut into the cartridge.

5. Remove or disconnect the following:
- Strut closure nut by unscrewing the closure nut using a Strut Cap Nut wrench J 35671
- Cartridge and remove the oil in the strut housing using a suction pump

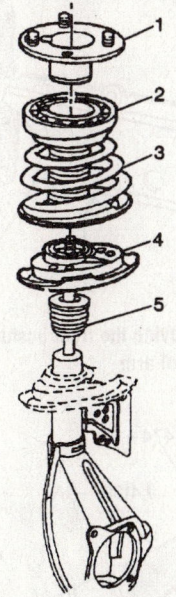

(1) Front Suspension Strut Mount Retainer
(2) Front Spring Upper Insulator
(3) Front Spring
(4) Front Spring Seat
(5) Front Suspension Strut Bumper

79222531

Knuckle and strut assembly with replaceable strut cartridge

To install:
6. Install or connect the following:
- Self-contained replacement cartridge into the strut housing
- Strut cartridge closure nut. Torque the nut to 82 ft. lbs. (110 Nm).
- Compress the shaft into the cartridge with a strut alignment tool
- Strut bumper after removing the strut alignment tool

7. Raise the strut and remove the alignment rod

8. Install the strut mount insulator as follows:
  a. Use a soap solution to lubricate the bushing for ease of installation.
  b. If necessary, install an alignment rod tool after the bushing is partially installed and position the strut as required to assist in the bushing installation.

9. Install or connect the following:
- Strut shaft nut using the No. 50 Torx® bit and a Strut Rod Nut socket, J 35669, and tighten the nut to 59 ft. lbs. (80 Nm).
- Strut cover mount and align the scribe marks. Torque the bolts to 24 ft. lbs. (33 Nm).

10. A 4-wheel alignment is recommended after any steering/suspension repairs are performed.

Rear Strut

1. Before servicing the vehicle, refer to the precautions in the beginning of this section.

2. Remove or disconnect the following:
- Negative battery cable
- Three strut to body nuts
- Rear tire and wheel
- Stabilizer shaft link from the strut

3. Scribe the strut to the knuckle.

➡**The knuckle must be retained after the strut to knuckle bolts have been removed. Damage may occur to the ball joint or drive axle if the knuckle is not retained.**

4. Remove or disconnect the following:
- Strut to knuckle bolts
- Strut

To install:
5. Install or connect the following:
- Strut
- Strut to knuckle bolts. Torque the bolts to 90 ft. lbs. (122 Nm).

- Stabilizer shaft link to the strut
- Rear tire and wheel
- Three strut to body mount nuts. Torque the nuts to 30 ft. lbs. (41 Nm).

6. Roadtest the vehicle and adjust the rear wheel alignment if needed.

Coil Spring

REMOVAL & INSTALLATION

1. Before servicing the vehicle, refer to the precautions in the beginning of this section.

2. Remove the strut assembly from the vehicle.

※※ CAUTION

Do not over compress the coil spring. Only compress the spring until it comes away from the seat.

3. Compress the coil spring approximately ½inch (13mm) using a spring compressor.

4. Remove or disconnect the following:
- Strut rod nut with the proper socket while not allowing the rod to rod to rotate. Discard the nut

5. Relieve the spring tension and remove the spring.

To install:
6. Install or connect the following:
- Spring to the strut and make certain that the upper and lower seats are positioned correctly
- Strut rod nut with the replaceable cartridge. Torque the nut to 81 ft. lbs. (110 Nm). On non replaceable cartridges, torque the nut to 63 ft. lbs. (85 Nm). Torque the nut on rear strut assemblies to 55 ft. lbs. (75 Nm).
- Strut

Lower Ball Joint

REMOVAL & INSTALLATION

1. Before servicing the vehicle, refer to the precautions in the beginning of this section.

2. Remove or disconnect the following:
- Wheel
- Ball joint heat shield
- Ball joint cotter pin and nut

Turn to Section 5 for brake system applications

3. Loosen, but do not remove, the stabilizer shaft bushing bolts.

4. Remove the ball joint from the lower control arm.

5. Drill out the 4 rivets retaining the ball joint to the steering knuckle. Use an ⅛ in. drill bit to make a pilot hole through the rivets. Finish drilling the rivets using a ½ in. drill bit.

➡ **Do not damage the drive axle boots when drilling out the ball joint rivets.**

6. Remove the ball joint.

To install:

7. Install or connect the following:
- Ball joint to the control arm
- Nuts with the heads facing down. Torque the nuts to 50 ft. lbs. (68 Nm).
- Torque the stabilizer shaft bushings bolts to 35 ft. lbs. (48 Nm).
- New cotter pin
- Heat shield. Torque the bolts to 62 inch lbs. (7 Nm).
- Wheel

➡ **A 4-wheel alignment is recommended after any steering/suspension repairs are performed.**

Lower Control Arm

REMOVAL & INSTALLATION

Lumina, Monte Carlo and Cutlass Supreme

1. Before servicing the vehicle, refer to the precautions in the beginning of this section.

2. Remove or disconnect the following:
- Front wheel
- Stabilizer shaft to lower control arm insulator clamp bolts
- Lower ball joint cotter pin and nut
- Ball joint from the lower control arm with a tie rod puller tool

3. Scribe the bolt location for proper alignment.

4. Remove or disconnect the following:
- Lower control arm to frame bolts
- Lower control arm

To install:

5. Install or connect the following:
- Lower control arm
- Lower control arm to frame bolts. Torque the bolts to 52 ft. lbs. (70 Nm).

6. Pivot the lower control arm up to the steering knuckle.

7. Install or connect the following:
- Ball joint stud and nut to the lower control arm. Tighten the castle nut to align the next slot in the nut with the cotter pin hole in the stud. Torque the nut to 63 ft. lbs. (85 Nm).
- New cotter pin
- Stabilizer shaft to the lower control arm insulator clamp. Torque the clamp bolts to 35 ft. lbs. (48 Nm).
- Front wheel

Century, Grand Prix, Intrigue and Regal

1. Before servicing the vehicle, refer to the precautions in the beginning of this section.

2. Remove or disconnect the following:
- Front wheel
- Antilock Brake System (ABS) wheel speed sensor connector and jumper harness from the retainer
- Stabilizer shaft link
- Cotter pin from the ball stud and loosen the nut

3. Install a ball joint removal tool over the ball joint and lower control arm. Rotate the ball stud nut counterclockwise to separate the ball stud from the steering knuckle.

4. Remove the lower control arm

To install:

5. Install or connect the following:
- Lower control arm and bolts

➡ **Align the all stud cotter pin hole parallel to the knuckle to ease the cotter pin installation.**

- Ball stud to the knuckle. Torque the nut to 40 ft. lbs. (55 Nm). Tighten the ball stud nut to align the slot to the cotter pin hole. Do Not loosen the nut to align the cotter pin hole.
- New cotter pin and bend the ends. Make certain the ends do not make contact with the ABS wheel speed sensor
- Stabilizer shaft link
- ABS wheel speed sensor wire harness to the retainer clips
- ABS wheel speed sensor connector
- Lower control arm nuts. Torque the nuts to 83 ft. lbs. (113 Nm).
- Front wheel

CONTROL ARM BUSHING REPLACEMENT

1. Before servicing the vehicle, refer to the precautions in the beginning of this section.

2. Remove or disconnect the following:
- Front wheel
- Lower control arm and place it in a vise

3. Lubricate the threads of a bushing driver with high pressure lubricant.

4. Assemble the tool onto the front control arm bushing.

5. Tighten the tool until the front bushing is pressed from the control arm.

6. Disassemble the tools.

To install:

7. Lubricate the new front bushing outer casing.

8. Install a new bushing into the control arm.

9. Assemble a bushing driver/installer set onto the front control arm.

10. Tighten the screw until the front bushing is pressed into the control arm.

11. Disassemble the tools.

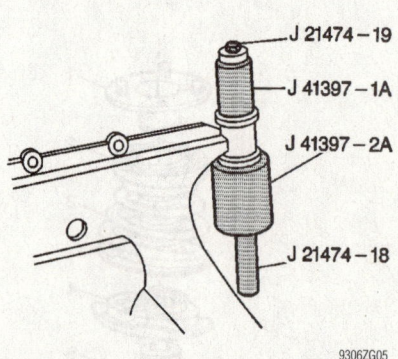

Removing the front bushing from the lower control arm

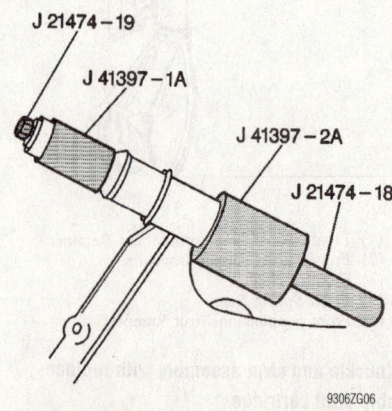

Installing the front bushing to the lower control arm

12. Install or connect the following:
- Lower control arm
- Front wheel

Wheel Bearings

ADJUSTMENT

The wheel bearings are not adjustable. If a wheel bearing is out of specification, it must be replaced. Using a dial indicator, check for looseness. If it exceeds 0.005 in. (0.127mm) on drum or disc brakes the bearing wear is excessive and the hub and bearing should be replaced.

REMOVAL & INSTALLATION

Front

➡**Do not remove the drive axle nut at this time. Failure to follow the proper sequence of removal steps may cause permanent bearing damage.**

1. Before servicing the vehicle, refer to the precautions in the beginning of this section.
2. Remove or disconnect the following:
- Front wheel
- Wheel speed sensor electrical connector
- Brake caliper
- Rotor
- Driveshaft nut
3. Install a front hub removal tool to the wheel bearing/hub assembly with three wheel nuts. Use the tool to push the driveshaft out of the wheel bearing/hub.
4. Remove the wheel bearing/hub assembly and discard the bolts.

To install:

5. Install or connect the following:
- Wheel bearing/hub assembly. Torque the bolts to 96 ft. lbs. (130 Nm).
- Driveshaft nut
- Brake rotor
- Front caliper. Torque the caliper mounting bolts to 79 ft. lbs. (107 Nm).
- Wheel speed sensor connector to the bracket and attach the electrical connectors
- Front wheel

Rear

The rear wheel bearing/hub is integrated into one unit. The unit is non-serviceable. If the hub or bearing is damaged, the com-

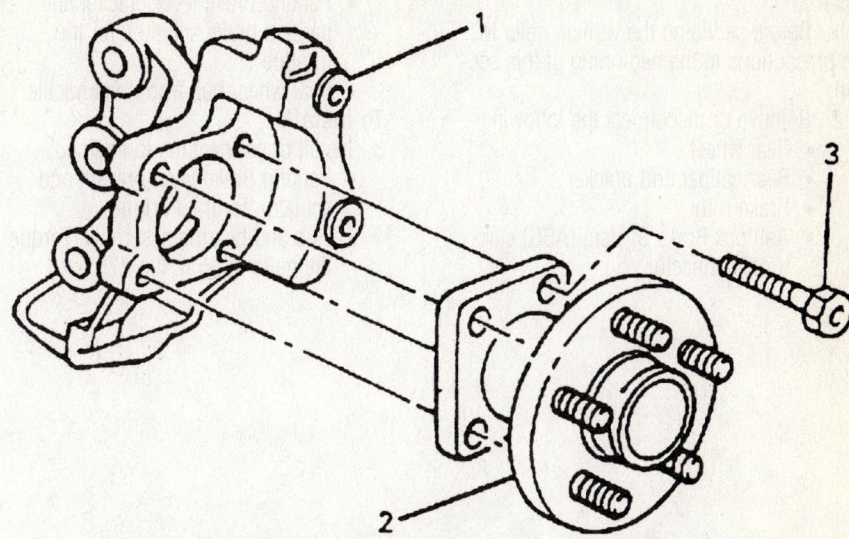

1 KNUCKLE ASSEMBLY, REAR SUSPENSION
2 HUB AND BEARING ASSEMBLY
3 BOLT/SCREW, WHEEL

79222535

The rear hub/bearing assembly is bolted to the knuckle

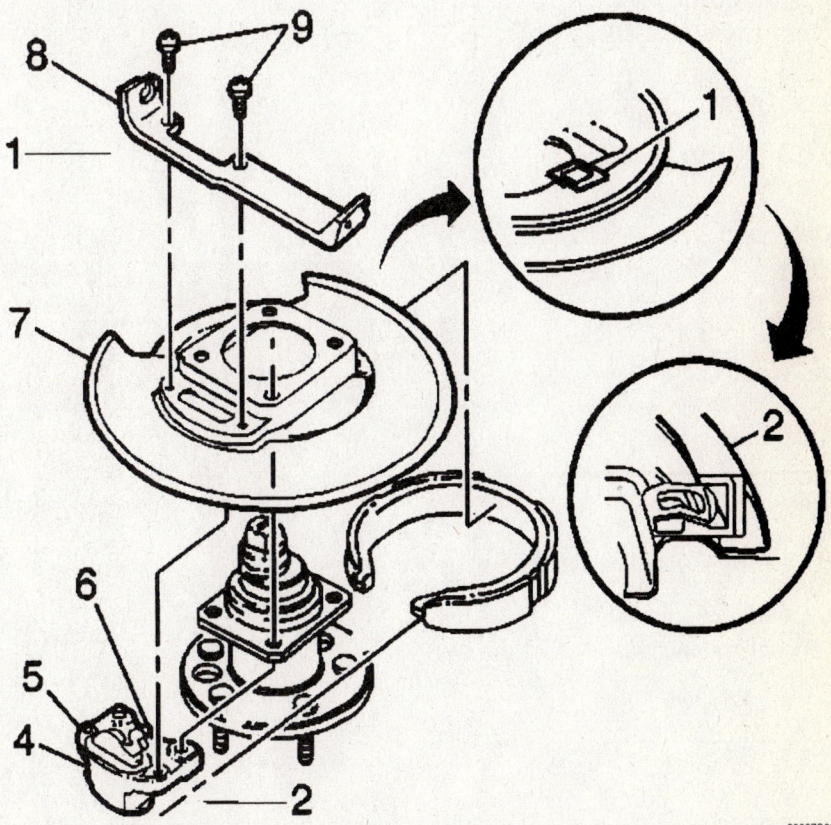

Parking brake lever bracket (1) and parking brake actuator (2)—Intrigue

9306ZG23

plete hub and bearing unit must be replaced.

1. Before servicing the vehicle, refer to the precautions in the beginning of this section.

2. Remove or disconnect the following:
   - Rear wheel
   - Rear caliper and bracket
   - Brake rotor
   - Antilock Brake System (ABS) electrical connector
   - Rear wheel hub to knuckle bolts
   - Parking brake lever bracket and parking brake actuator, for the Intrigue
   - Rear wheel hub from the knuckle

To install:

3. Install or connect the following:
   - Parking Brake lever bracket and actuator, for the Intrigue
   - Hub and bearing assembly. Torque the bolts to 55 ft. lbs. (75 Nm).
   - ABS harness and electrical connector.
   - Brake rotor
   - Brake caliper. Torque the mounting bolts to 81 ft. lbs. (110 Nm).
   - Rear wheel

4. A 4 wheel alignment is recommended after any steering/suspension repairs have been performed.

GENERAL MOTORS CORPORATION—Y-BODY

37

Chevrolet-Corvette

PRECAUTIONS

Before servicing any vehicle, please be sure to read all of the following precautions, which deal with personal safety, prevention of component damage, and important points to take into consideration when servicing a motor vehicle:

• Never open, service or drain the radiator or cooling system when the engine is hot; serious burns can occur from the steam and hot coolant.

• Observe all applicable safety precautions when working around fuel. Whenever servicing the fuel system, always work in a well-ventilated area. Do not allow fuel spray or vapors to come in contact with a spark, open flame or excessive heat (a hot drop light, for example). Keep a dry chemical fire extinguisher near the work area. Always keep fuel in a container specifically designed for fuel storage; also, always properly seal fuel containers to avoid the possibility of fire or explosion. Refer to the additional fuel system precautions later in this section.

• Fuel injection systems often remain pressurized, even after the engine has been turned **OFF**. The fuel system pressure must be relieved before disconnecting any fuel lines. Failure to do so may result in fire and/or personal injury.

• Brake fluid often contains polyglycol ethers and polyglycols. Avoid contact with the eyes and wash your hands thoroughly after handling brake fluid. If you do get brake fluid in your eyes, flush your eyes with clean, running water for 15 minutes. If eye irritation persists, or if you have taken brake fluid internally, seek medical assistance IMMEDIATELY.

• The EPA warns that prolonged contact with used engine oil may cause a number of skin disorders, including cancer! You should make every effort to minimize your exposure to used engine oil. Protective gloves should be worn when changing oil. Wash your hands and any other exposed skin areas as soon as possible after exposure to used engine oil. Soap and water, or waterless hand cleaner should be used.

• All new vehicles are now equipped with an air bag system. The system must be disabled before performing service on or around system components, steering column, instrument panel components, wiring and sensors. Failure to follow safety and disabling procedures could result in accidental air bag deployment, possible personal injury and unnecessary system repairs.

• Always wear safety goggles when working with, or around, the air bag system. When carrying a non-deployed air bag, be sure the bag and trim cover are pointed away from your body. When placing a non-deployed air bag on a work surface, always face the bag and trim cover upward, away from the surface. This will reduce the motion of the module if it is accidentally deployed. Refer to the additional air bag system precautions later in this section.

• Clean, high quality brake fluid from a sealed container is essential to the safe and proper operation of the brake system. You should always buy the correct type of brake fluid for your vehicle. If the brake fluid becomes contaminated, completely flush the system with new fluid. Never reuse any brake fluid. Any brake fluid that is removed from the system should be discarded. Also, do not allow any brake fluid to come in contact with a painted surface; it will damage the paint.

• Never operate the engine without the proper amount and type of engine oil; doing so WILL result in severe engine damage.

• Timing belt maintenance is extremely important! Many models utilize an interference-type, non-freewheeling engine. If the timing belt breaks, the valves in the cylinder head may strike the pistons, causing potentially serious (also time-consuming and expensive) engine damage. Refer to the maintenance interval charts in the front of this manual for the recommended replacement interval for the timing belt, and to the timing belt section for belt replacement and inspection.

• Disconnecting the negative battery cable on some vehicles may interfere with the functions of the on-board computer system(s) and may require the computer to undergo a relearning process once the negative battery cable is reconnected.

• When servicing drum brakes, only disassemble and assemble one side at a time, leaving the remaining side intact for reference.

ENGINE REPAIR

Distributor

All 5.7L (VIN G) engines use a direct ignition system.

Alternator

REMOVAL

1. Before servicing the vehicle, refer to the precautions in the beginning of this section.
2. Remove or disconnect the following:
   • Negative battery cable
   • Regulator connector and battery to alternator terminal from the rear of the alternator
   • Drive belt after releasing the tension
   • Rear mounting bracket
   • Alternator mounting bolts
   • Alternator

To install:
3. Install or connect the following:
   • Alternator
   • Alternator mounting bolts. Torque the bolts to 37 ft. lbs. (50 Nm).
   • Alternator rear mounting bracket. Torque the bolts to 37 ft. lbs. (50 Nm).
   • Drive belt

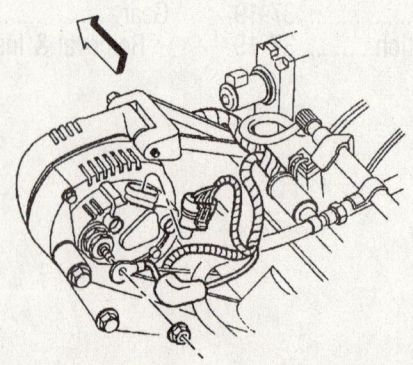

9306ZG24

Exploded view of the alternator—5.7L engine

- Regulator connector and battery to alternator terminals. Torque the alternator terminal nut to 10 inch lbs. (15 Nm).
- Negative battery cable

Engine Assembly

REMOVAL & INSTALLATION

1. Before servicing the vehicle, refer to the precautions in the beginning of this section.

The following tools will be required in addition to the basic hand tools:

- Transverse spring compressor and adapters
  - Ball joint separator
  - Engine support table
  - Driveshaft support strap
  - Fuel pressure gauge
2. Relieve the fuel system pressure.
3. Drain the cooling system.
4. Drain the engine oil.
5. Evacuate the A/C system.

6. Remove or disconnect the following:
- Negative battery cable
- Wiring connectors for the Intake Air Temperature (IAT) sensor and the Mass Air Flow (MAF) sensor
- Air intake duct and air cleaner
- Upper radiator support
- Radiator
- Electronic Brake Control Traction Module/Brake Pressure Modulator Valve (EBTCM/BPMV) and bracket
- Brake pipes

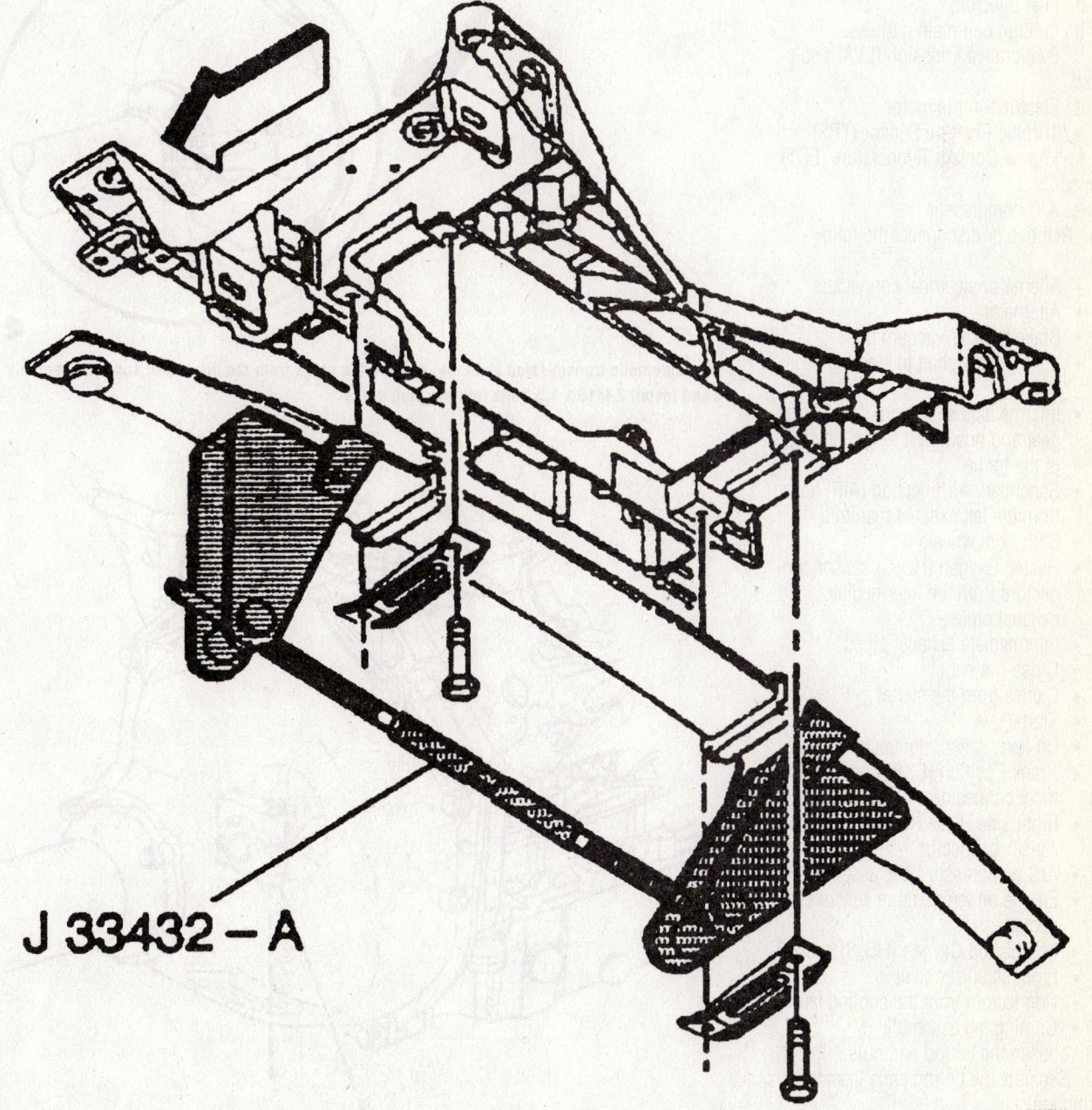

J 33432 – A

79222Z602

Use a compressor such as J 33432-A to compress the front transverse spring—5.7L (VIN G) engine

- Drive belt
- Fuel line from the connector at the front of the dash

➡ Cap and plug all openings for the fuel system to prevent contaminants from entering the system.

- Fuel rail covers
- Fuel line at the fuel rail
- Radiator hoses from the water pump
- Heater hoses from the water pump

7. Disconnect the electrical connectors on the top of the engine for the following components:

  a. Fuel injectors.
  b. Ignition coil main harness.
  c. Evaporative Emission (EVAP) solenoid.
  d. Electric throttle motor.
  e. Throttle Position Sensor (TPS).
  f. Engine Coolant Temperature (ECT) sensor.
  g. A/C compressor.

8. Remove or disconnect the following:

- Alternator electrical connectors
- Alternator
- Brake booster vacuum hose
- Intermediate shaft to steering gear bolt
- Intermediate shaft from the steering gear and position it to the left side of the frame
- Secondary Air Injection (AIR) hose from the left exhaust manifold
- Both front wheels
- Heated Oxygen (HO2S) sensor connectors from the intermediate exhaust pipes
- Intermediate exhaust pipes
- Close-out panel
- Cables from the starter
- Starter
- Oil level sensor connector
- Crank Position (CKP) sensor electrical connector
- Right side Heated Oxygen (HO2S) sensor connector
- A/C compressor hose assembly
- Engine oil temperature sensor connector
- Left Heated Oxygen (HO2S) sensor
- Front stabilizer shaft
- Connectors from the cooling fans
- Cooling fan assembly

9. Loosen the tie rod end nuts.
10. Separate the tie rod ends from the steering knuckles.
11. Remove or disconnect the following:

- Antilock Brake System (ABS) electrical connectors from the crossmember, if equipped.

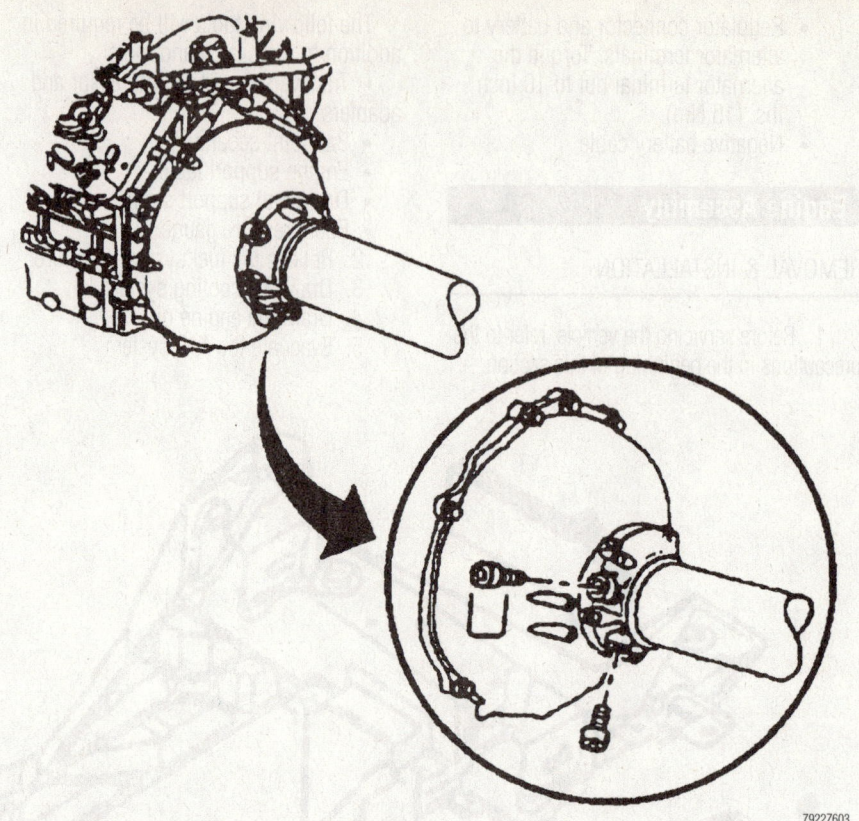

79222603

On automatic transmission vehicles, remove the plugs from the driveshaft support assembly and install 2 M10 x 1.5 bolts into the plug holes

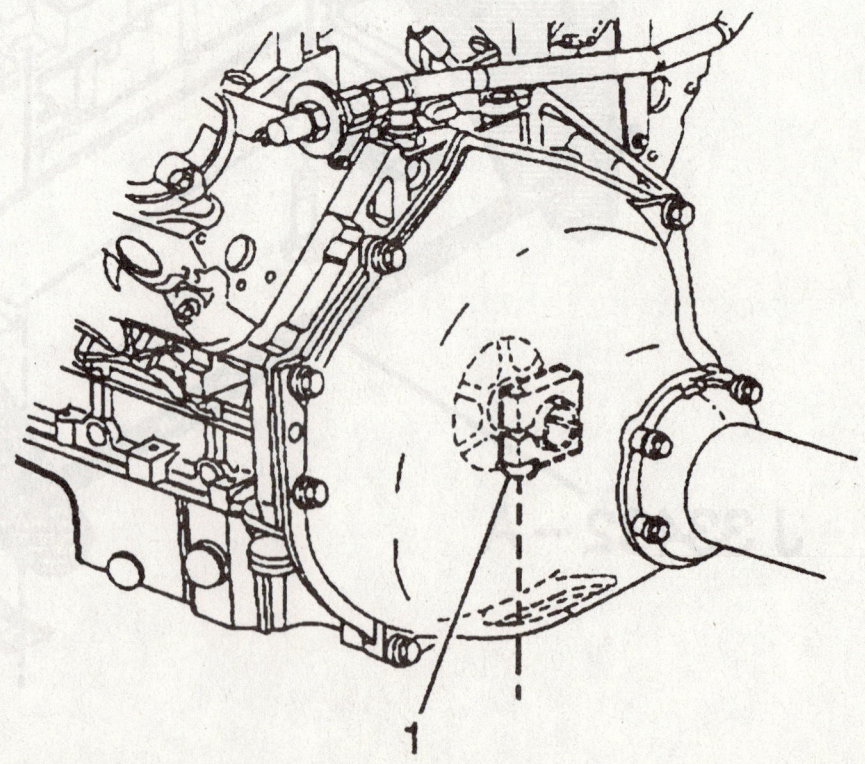

79222604

Loosen the bolt on the flywheel hub collar after turning it for access

- Electronic Variable Orifice (EVO) connector clips from the crossmember, if equipped.
- Real Time Damping (RTD) connector clips from the crossmember, if equipped.
- Shock absorber lower mounting bolts
- Front transverse leaf spring
- Automatic transmission cooler pipes at the flywheel housing junction, if equipped
- Automatic transmission cooler pipe clamps from the and rear of the engine oil pan, if equipped
- Automatic transmission cooler pipe from the radiator, if equipped

✳✳ CAUTION

Failure to use the minimum fastener length specified will prevent the proper retention of the propeller shaft during assembly.

12. For vehicles with an automatic transmission, perform the following steps:

a. Two plug bolts driveline support assembly.

b. Install an M10 x 55 bolt or longer, in each plug location. Torque the bearing support bolts to 26 ft. lbs. (35 Nm).

13. On vehicles with automatic transmission, remove the bell housing inspection cover, then turn the flywheel hub collar to access the bolt and loosen it.

14. Remove the engine flywheel housing access plug.

15. Orientate the automatic transmission collar so that the bolt is facing down.

16. Loosen the bolt and unclip the wire harness from the engine and reposition it to the driveline.

17. Install a driveline support tool to the close out panel flange.

✳✳ CAUTION

Never use a driveline support tool to support the weight of the engine assembly.

18. If equipped with a manual transmission, perform the following steps:

a. Unclip the clutch actuator hose from the engine flywheel housing clip.

b. Using a hydraulic clutch line separator tool, depress the white release ring on the actuator hose and pull lightly on the master cylinder hose.

c. Remove the flywheel bolts from the driveline support.

19. Remove or disconnect the following:

- Front crossmember nuts BY HAND and lower the engine assembly slightly
- Secondary Air Injection (AIR) tube bracket bolt and reposition the bracket to gain access to the ground strap
- Ground strap from the rear of the left cylinder head

20. Disconnect the wiring from the following components from the rear of the engine:

a. Engine oil pressure sensor.

b. Camshaft Position (CMP) sensor.

c. Manifold Absolute Pressure (MAP) sensor.

d. Knock Sensor (KS) and all other electrical connections.

21. Remove or disconnect the following:

- Front driveline support assembly bolts
- Engine from the driveline, by placing a flat blade tool between edge of the driveline and the flywheel housing

22. Pull the engine away from the propeller shaft.

23. Slide the engine and crossmember forward to clear the propeller shaft spline and remove the engine from the crossmember.

To install:

24. Install or connect the following:

- Engine on the crossmember. Torque the nuts to 40 ft. lbs. (54 Nm).
- Power steering pump and reservoir on the engine. Torque the bolts to 18 ft. lbs. (25 Nm).
- AIR pipe and mounting bolts to the exhaust manifolds. Torque the bolts to 15 ft. lbs. (20 Nm).
- Ground strap to the rear of the left cylinder head. Torque the bolt to 24 ft. lbs. (32 Nm).

25. Route the electrical harnesses and attach the connectors at the rear of the engine for the following components:

a. Engine oil pressure sensor.

b. CMP sensor.

c. MAP sensor.

d. KS and all other electrical connections.

26. If equipped with a manual transmission, slide the engine and crossmember rearward.

27. Install or connect the following:

- Propeller input shaft into the clutch driven plate hub. Do Not force the splines together. Rotate them into proper alignment

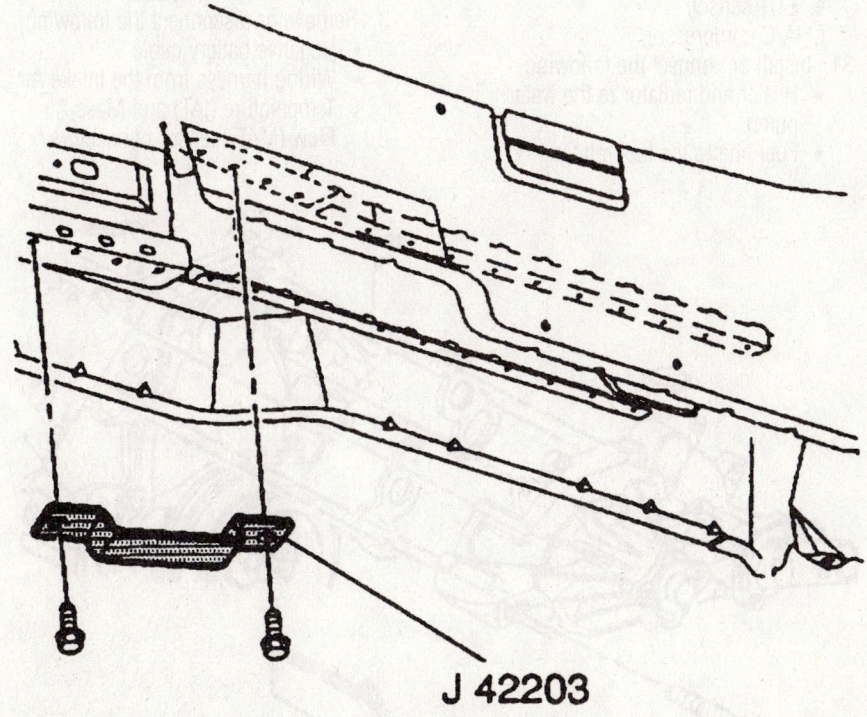

J 42203

7922Z605

Install a Driveline Support tool J 42203 to the under cover flange

Timing belt service is covered in Section 4 of this manual

- Engine flywheel housing to the driveline and install the bolts. Torque the bolts to 37 ft. lbs. (50 Nm).
- Clutch actuator hose clip to the flywheel housing clip
- Master cylinder hose to the clutch actuator hose

➡ **Do Not tighten the flywheel hub collar bolt at this time.**

28. If equipped with an automatic transmission, slide the engine assembly rearward and install the propeller input shaft and align the splines properly.

29. Install or connect the following:
- Front driveline support bolts. Torque the flywheel housing to driveline support bolts to 37 ft. lbs. (50 Nm).
- Flywheel hub collar bolt and hand tighten at this time
- Air tube and bracket. Torque the bolt to 37 ft. lbs. (50 Nm).
- New crossmember nuts. Torque the nuts to 81 ft. lbs. (110 Nm).
- Wire harness to the rear of the engine
- Two plugs in the driveline support assembly after removing the M10 x 55 bolts. Torque the plugs to 37 ft. lbs. (50 Nm).
- Automatic transmission cooler pipes at the flywheel housing junction. Torque the pipes to 20 ft. lbs. (27 Nm).
- Automatic transmission cooler pipes to the front and rear of the oil pan
- Front transverse spring
- Shock absorber lower mounting nuts. Torque the nuts to 21 ft. lbs. (28 Nm).
- ABS, EVO and RTD electrical connector clips to the crossmember
- Radiator
- Cooling fan assembly to the radiator and attach the electrical connectors and harness to the fans
- Front stabilizer shaft to the lower control arms
- Ground wires to the left side of the engine
- Left front Heated Oxygen (HO2S) sensor connector
- Engine oil temperature sensor connector
- A/C compressor hoses to the compressor
- A/C compressor line retaining bolt. Torque the bolt to 26 ft. lbs. (35 Nm).

- Right side Heated Oxygen (HO2S) sensor connector
- CKP sensor connector
- Oil level sensor connector
- Wire harness ground wires to the right side of the engine
- Starter
- Driveline close out panel. Torque the bolts to 106 inch lbs. (12 Nm).
- Intermediate exhaust pipe and hangers
- Heated Oxygen (HO2S) sensors and clip harness
- Front wheels
- Automatic transmission cooler pipes to the radiator
- AIR hose to the left exhaust manifold
- Intermediate steering shaft to the steering gear. Torque the bolt to 35 ft. lbs. (48 Nm).
- Brake booster vacuum hose to the brake booster
- Alternator and bracket. Torque the bolts to 37 ft. lbs. (50 Nm).
- Alternator connectors. Torque the nuts to 10 ft. lbs. (13 Nm).

30. Attach the electrical connectors for the following components:
a. Fuel injectors.
b. Ignition coil main connectors.
c. EVAP solenoid.
d. Electric throttle motor.
e. ECT sensor.
f. A/C compressor.

31. Install or connect the following:
- Heater and radiator to the water pump
- Fuel line to the fuel rail

- Fuel rail covers
- Drive belt
- EBTCM/BPMV and bracket
- Top radiator hose
- Upper radiator support
- Air cleaner and air intake duct
- IAT and MAF sensor connectors
- Negative battery cable

32. Fill the engine with new oil.

33. Fill the cooling system.

34. Evacuate and recharge the A/C system.

35. Check and top off any other fluid levels.

36. On vehicles with an automatic transmissions, start the engine and allow it to idle for 10 minutes. Torque the hub collar bolt to 96 ft. lbs. (130 Nm) and install the flywheel inspection plug.

37. A wheel alignment is recommended when the engine and crossmember have been removed from the vehicle.

38. Check the vehicle for leaks and repair if necessary.

Water Pump

REMOVAL & INSTALLATION

1. Before servicing the vehicle, refer to the precautions in the beginning of this section.

2. Drain the cooling system.

3. Remove or disconnect the following:
- Negative battery cable
- Wiring harness from the Intake Air Temperature (IAT) and Mass Air Flow (MAF) sensor connectors

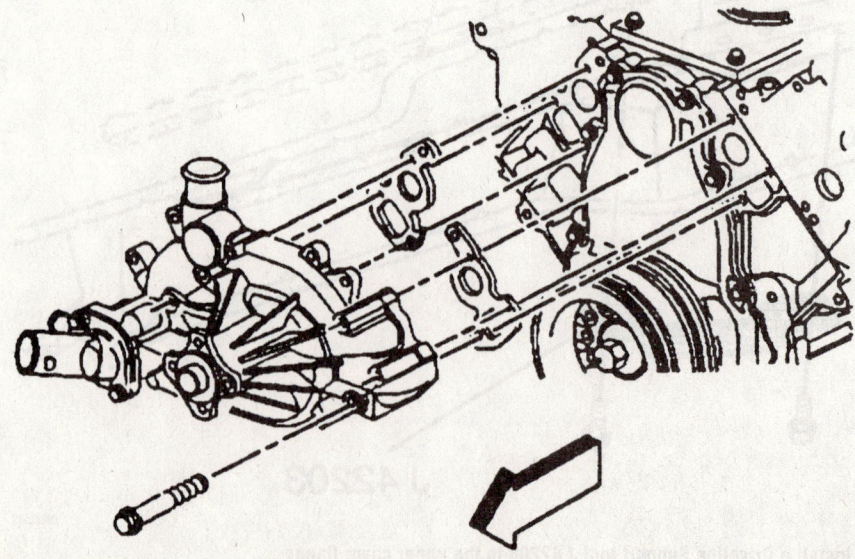

Exploded view of the water pump mounting assembly—5.7L engine

79222608

- Air intake duct
- Drive belt
- Inlet and outlet hoses from the water pump
- Heater hoses from the water pump
- Four water pump puller bolts
- Six water pump retaining bolts from the engine
- Water pump and gasket

To install:

4. Clean the sealing surfaces on the water pump and engine block.

5. Install or connect the following:
- New gasket with the tabs facing up
- Water pump. Torque the bolts to 11 ft. lbs. (15 Nm) and then to 22 ft. lbs. (30 Nm).
- Water pump pulley (if equipped). Torque the bolts to 89 inch lbs. (10 Nm) and then to 18 ft. lbs. (25 Nm).
- Heater hoses to the water pump
- Radiator inlet and outlet hoses to the water pump
- Drive belt
- Air intake duct
- MAF and IAT sensor connectors
- Negative battery cable

6. Fill the cooling system.

7. Start the vehicle and check for leaks, repair if necessary.

Cylinder Head

REMOVAL & INSTALLATION

1. Before servicing the vehicle, refer to the precautions in the beginning of this section.

2. Drain the engine coolant.

3. Relieve the fuel system pressure.

4. Remove or disconnect the following:
- Negative battery cable
- Valve rocker arm cover
- Left side exhaust manifold from the cylinder head
- Intake manifold
- Vapor vent pipe
- Power steering pump pulley
- Power steering pump and reposition the pump and reservoir
- Ground wire bolt from the rear of the cylinder head
- Cylinder head

To install:

➡**Refer to Section 1 of this manual for the cylinder head torque sequence illustration. The illustration is located after the Torque Specification Chart.**

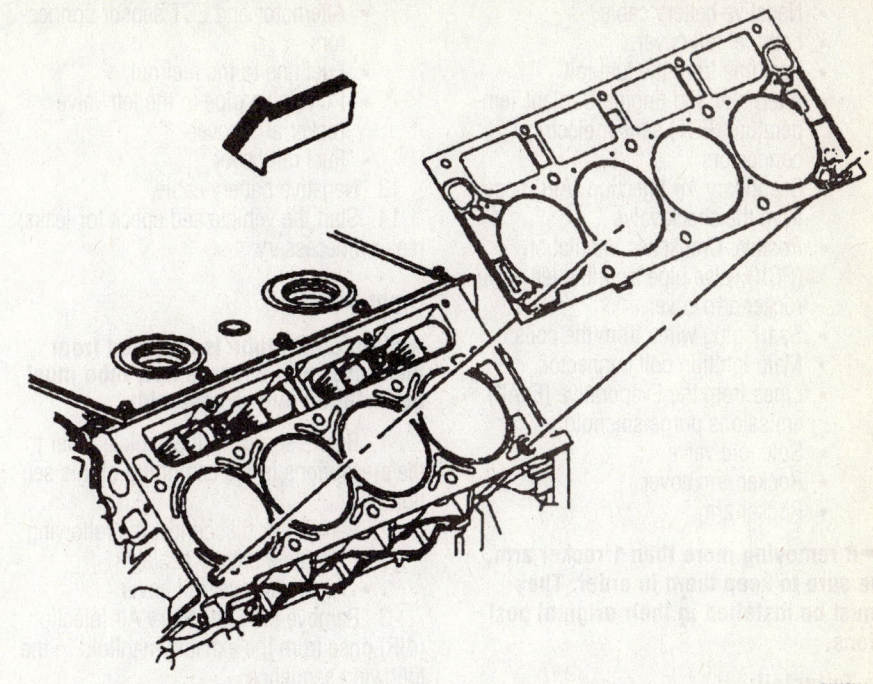

Be sure the tab on the edge of the gasket is closer to the front of the engine when installed

➡**New M11 cylinder head bolts must be used when installing the cylinder head assembly.**

5. Clean and degrease the deck of the engine block and the bottom of the cylinder head assembly. Clean the bolt holes with compressed air.

➡**The tab on the edge of the head gasket will be closer to the front of the engine when properly installed.**

6. Install the new cylinder head gasket onto the locating pins.

7. Place the cylinder head on the engine and install the bolts finger-tight. Tighten the bolts in sequence to:
  a. Step 1: M11 bolts: 22 ft. lbs. (30 Nm)
  b. Step 2: M11 bolts: plus 76 degrees
  c. Step 3: M11 bolts 1–8: plus 76 degrees
  d. Step 4: M11 bolts 9–10: plus 34 degrees
  e. Step 5: M8 bolts (11–15): 22 ft. lbs. (30 Nm)

8. Install or connect the following:
- Ground wire to the rear of the cylinder head. Torque the bolt to 24 ft. lbs. (32 Nm).
- Accessory mounting bracket and make certain it is aligned properly.

Torque the bolts to 37 ft. lbs. (50 Nm).
- Power steering pump to the accessory bracket. Torque the bolts to 18 ft. lbs. (25 Nm).
- Power steering reservoir to the accessory bracket. Torque the bolts to 37 ft. lbs. (50 Nm).
- Power steering pump pulley
- Exhaust manifold
- Valve rocker arm cover
- Intake manifold
- Vapor vent pipe
- Negative battery cable

9. Fill the cooling system.

10. Start the vehicle and check for leaks, repair if necessary.

Rocker Arms

REMOVAL & INSTALLATION

Left Side

➡**Always keep the rocker arms and pushrods in order so they can be installed in their original positions.**

1. Before servicing the vehicle, refer to the precautions in the beginning of this section.

2. Relieve the fuel system pressure.

3. Remove or disconnect the following:

- Negative battery cable
- Left fuel rail cover
- Fuel line from the fuel rail
- Alternator and Engine Coolant Temperature (ECT) sensor electrical connectors
- Secondary Air Injection (AIR) hose from the check valve
- Positive Crankcase Ventilation (PCV) valve pipe from the left valve rocker arm cover
- Spark plug wires from the coils
- Main ignition coil connector
- Lines from the Evaporative (EVAP) emissions purge solenoid
- Solenoid valve
- Rocker arm cover
- Rocker arm

➡**If removing more than 1 rocker arm, be sure to keep them in order. They must be installed in their original positions.**

To install:

4. If removed, install the rocker arm pivot support.

5. Lubricate the rocker arms and pushrods with clean engine oil.

6. Lubricate the flange and washer surface of the rocker arm mounting bolts.

7. Install or connect the following:

- Pushrod. Be sure it is seated in the lifter socket
- Rocker arms but do not tighten the bolts at this time

8. Rotate the crankshaft so the No. 1 piston is at Top Dead Center (TDC).

9. With the engine in this position, tighten the exhaust valve rocker arm bolts on cylinders No. 1, 2, 7 and 8. Then, tighten the intake valve rocker arm bolts on cylinders No. 1, 3, 4 and 5. Torque the bolts to 22 ft. lbs. 30 Nm).

10. Rotate the crankshaft 1 revolution (360 degrees).

11. With the engine in this position, tighten the exhaust valve rocker arm bolts on cylinders No. 3, 4, 5 and 6. Then, tighten the intake valve rocker arm bolts on cylinders No. 2, 6, 7 and 8. Tighten the bolts to 22 ft. lbs. 30 Nm).

12. Install or connect the following:

- Rocker arm Cover using a new gasket. Torque the bolts to 106 inch lbs. (12 Nm).
- EVAP purge solenoid
- Ignition coil connector
- AIR hose to the check valve
- Spark plug wires to the ignition coils
- Ignition coil main harness electrical connector

- Alternator and ECT sensor connectors
- Fuel line to the fuel rail
- PCV valve pipe to the left valve rocker arm cover
- Fuel rail cover

13. Negative battery cable.

14. Start the vehicle and check for leaks, repair if necessary.

Right Side

➡**If the oil fill tube is removed from the rocker arm cover, a new tube must be installed during assembly.**

1. Before servicing the vehicle, refer to the precautions in the beginning of this section.

2. Remove or disconnect the following:
- Negative battery cable
- Right side fuel rail cover

3. Remove the Secondary Air Injection (AIR) hose from the exhaust manifold in the following sequence:
   a. Bolts.
   b. Pipe.
   c. Gasket.

4. Remove or disconnect the following:

- Secondary Air Injection (AIR) hose from the check valve
- Positive Crankcase Ventilation (PCV) hoses from the breather pipes
- Spark plug wires from the ignition coils
- Ignition coil main wire harness connector
- Valve rocker arm cover

➡**Always keep the rocker arms and pushrods in order so they can be installed in their original positions.**

5. Remove the rocker arm. If removing more than 1 rocker arm, be sure to keep them in order. They must be installed in their original positions.

To install:

6. If removed, install the rocker arm pivot support.

7. Lubricate the rocker arms and pushrods with clean engine oil.

8. Lubricate the flange and washer surface of the bolt rocker arm mounting bolts.

9. Install or connect the following:

- Pushrod. Be sure it is seated in the lifter socket
- Rocker arms but do not tighten the bolts at this time

10. Rotate the crankshaft so the No. 1 piston is at Top Dead Center (TDC) on compression.

11. With the engine in this position,

tighten the exhaust valve rocker arm bolts on cylinders No. 2 and 8. Then, tighten the intake valve rocker arm bolts on cylinder No. 4. Torque the bolts to 22 ft. lbs. (30 Nm).

12. Rotate the crankshaft 1 revolution (360 degrees).

13. With the engine in this position, tighten the exhaust valve rocker arm bolts on cylinders No. 4 and 6. Then, tighten the intake valve rocker arm bolts on cylinders No. 2, 6 and 8. Tighten the bolts to 22 ft. lbs. (30 Nm).

14. Install or connect the following:

- Rocker arm cover using a new gasket. Tighten the bolts to 106 inch lbs. (12 Nm).
- Ignition coil main wire harness connector
- Spark plug wires to the ignition coils
- PCV hoses to the breather pipes
- AIR hose to the check valve
- AIR hose to the exhaust manifold
- Right side fuel rail cover
- Negative battery cable

15. Start the vehicle and check for leaks, repair if necessary.

Intake Manifold

REMOVAL & INSTALLATION

➡**The intake manifold, throttle body, fuel injectors and rail may be removed from the engine as an assembly.**

1. Before servicing the vehicle, refer to the precautions in the beginning of this section.

2. Drain the cooling system.

3. Relieve the fuel system pressure.

4. Remove or disconnect the following:

- Negative battery cable
- Intake Air Temperature (IAT) and Mass Air Flow (MAF) sensor connectors from air intake duct and the throttle body
- Air intake duct
- Fuel rail covers
- Fuel line from the fuel rail
- Vacuum ventilation hose
- Fuel injector wire harness connectors
- Throttle Position Sensor (TPS) connector
- Knock Sensor (KS) connector
- All other connections from the intake manifold
- KS jumper pigtail from the fuel rail stop bracket

- Positive Crankcase Ventilation (PCV) valve pipe from the left valve rocker arm cover
- PCV valve pipe from the right side valve rocker arm cover
- PCV tube from the throttle body
- Engine cooling air bleed hose from the throttle body
- Throttle body heater outlet hose
- Intake manifold

To install:

➡ **Refer to Section 1 of this manual for the intake manifold torque sequence illustration. The illustration is located after the Torque Specification Chart.**

5. Apply a 0.20 in. (5mm) bead of threadlock to the threads of the intake manifold bolts.

✳✳ CAUTION

The fuel rail stop bracket must be installed on the intake manifold in its original position. Failure to reinstall this part may result in fuel spray causing personal injury.

6. Install or connect the following:

- New gaskets on the cylinder heads and engine
- Intake manifold on the engine
- Fuel stop bracket
- Intake manifold bolts. Torque the bolts first to 44 inch lbs. (5 Nm) in the sequence shown. Then, make a second pass and tighten the bolts to 89 inch lbs. (8 Nm) using the same sequence.
- MAP sensor
- Throttle body heater outlet hose
- Engine bleed air bleed hose to the throttle body
- PCV tube to the throttle body
- PCV valve pipe to the right side rocker arm cover
- PCV pipe to the left side rocker arm cover
- KS sensor jumper pigtail to the fuel rail bracket
- KS connector
- TPS connector
- Fuel injector wire harness connector
- Vacuum vent hose
- Fuel line to the fuel rail
- Fuel rail cover

- Air intake duct
- IAT and MAF sensor connectors to the throttle body and the air intake duct
- Negative battery cable

7. Fill the cooling system.

8. Start the vehicle and check for leaks, repair if necessary.

Exhaust Manifold

REMOVAL & INSTALLATION

Left Side

1. Before servicing the vehicle, refer to the precautions in the beginning of this section.

2. Relieve the fuel system pressure.

3. Remove or disconnect the following:

- Negative battery cable
- Left hand intermediate pipe flange nuts from the exhaust manifold studs
- Heated Oxygen (HO2S) sensor
- Fuel rail cover
- Alternator and Engine Coolant Temperature (ECT) sensor electrical connectors
- Drive belt
- Alternator
- Seconday Air Injection (AIR) hose from the check valve
- Air pipe from the exhaust manifold and reposition it
- Air pipe retainer from the rear of the cylinder head and reposition it
- Spark plug wires from the coils
- Spark plugs
- Exhaust manifold and discard the gasket

To install:

4. Clean the bolt holes and the mounting surface of the cylinder head.

5. Apply threadlock to the threads of the bolts. Do not apply it to the first 3 threads.

6. Install or connect the following:

- New gasket
- Exhaust manifold and bolts

7. Beginning with the center 2 bolts, torque the bolts to 11 ft. inch lbs. (15 Nm) alternating from side-to-side until all the bolts are tight. Torque the bolts again in the same sequence to 18 ft. lbs. (25 Nm).

8. Bend over the exposed portion of the gasket at the rear of the cylinder head.

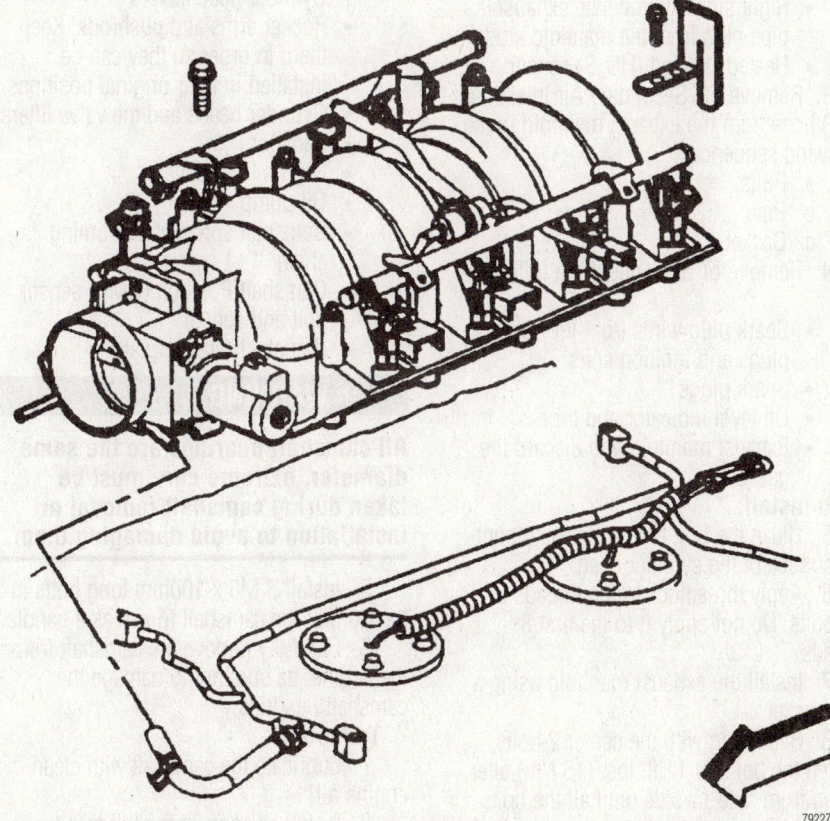

79222Z613

Be sure to reinstall the fuel stop bracket when installing the intake manifold

Refer to Section 1 for engine rebuilding specifications

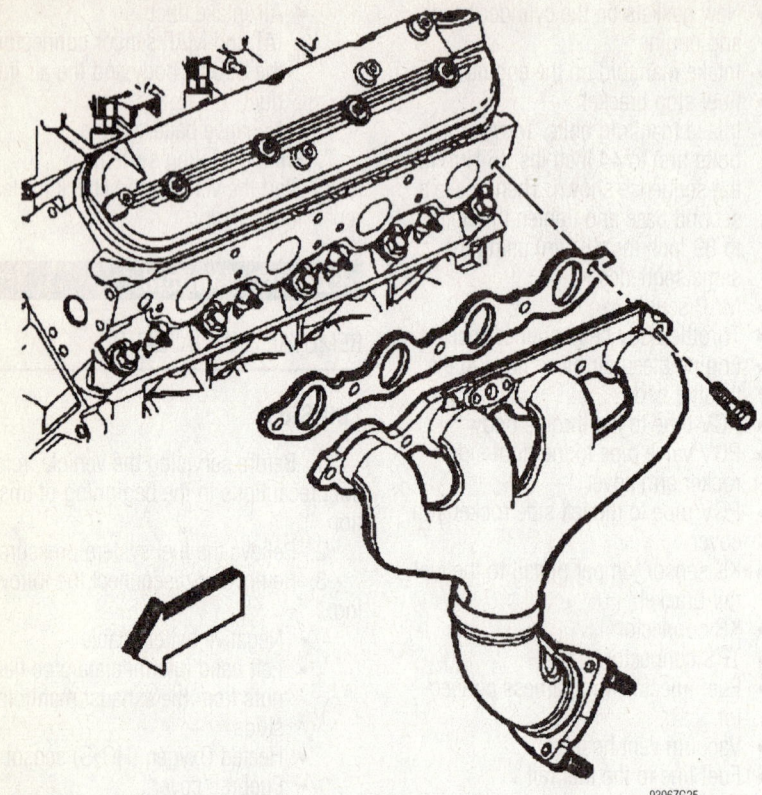

Exploded view of the exhaust manifold—5.7L engine

9. Install or connect the following:
- Spark plug wires to the spark plugs and the ignition coils
- AIR pipe and gasket to the exhaust manifold. Torque the bolts to 15 ft. lbs. (20 Nm).
- AIR pipe retainer bolt to the rear of the cylinder head. Torque the bolt to 15 ft. lbs. (20 Nm).
- AIR hose to the check valve. Torque the hose to 15 ft. lbs. (20 Nm).
- Alternator
- Drive belt
- Alternator and ECT sensor connectors
- Fuel rail cover
- Heated Oxygen (HO2S) sensor
- Fuel lines
- Intermediate pipe flange to exhaust manifold studs. Torque the nuts to 15 ft. lbs. (20 Nm).
- Negative battery cable

10. Start the vehicle and check for leaks, repair if necessary.

Right Side

1. Before servicing the vehicle, refer to the precautions in the beginning of this section.
2. Remove or disconnect the following:
- Negative battery cable

- Right side intermediate exhaust pipe nuts from the manifold studs
- Heated Oxygen (HO2S) sensor

3. Remove the Secondary Air Injection (AIR) hose from the exhaust manifold in the following sequence:
   a. Bolts.
   b. Pipe.
   c. Gasket.

4. Remove or disconnect the following:
- Spark plug wires from the spark plugs and ignition coils
- Spark plugs
- Oil level indicator and tube
- Exhaust manifold and discard the gasket

To install:

5. Clean the bolt holes and the mounting surface of the cylinder head.
6. Apply threadlock to the threads of the bolts. Do not apply it to the first 3 threads.
7. Install the exhaust manifold using a new gasket.
8. Beginning with the center 2 bolts, tighten the bolts to 11 ft. lbs. (15 Nm) alternating from side-to-side until all the bolts are tight. Then, tighten the bolts again in the same sequence to 18 ft. lbs. (25 Nm).
9. Bend over the exposed portion of the gasket at the rear of the cylinder head.

10. Install or connect the following:
- Oil level indicator tube. Torque the bolt to 12 ft. lbs. (16 Nm).
- AIR pipe using a new gasket. Torque the bolts to 15 ft. lbs. (20 Nm).
- Heated Oxygen (HO2S) sensor in the manifold. Torque it to 30 ft. lbs. (42 Nm).
- Spark plug wires to the plugs and the ignition coils
- Intermediate pipe flange to the exhaust manifold studs. Torque the nuts to 15 ft. lbs. (20 Nm).
- Negative battery cable

11. Start the vehicle and check for leaks, repair if necessary.

Camshaft

REMOVAL & INSTALLATION

1. Before servicing the vehicle, refer to the precautions in the beginning of this section.
2. Drain the cooling system.
3. Relieve the fuel system pressure.
4. Remove or disconnect the following:
- Negative battery cable
- Fuel lines from the fuel rail
- Cylinder head covers
- Rocker arms and pushrods. Keep them in order so they can be installed in their original positions
- Cylinder heads and the valve lifters
- Radiator
- Engine front cover
- Oil pump
- Camshaft sprocket and timing chain
- Camshaft Position (CMP) sensor bolt and sensor
- Camshaft retainer plate

✳✳ WARNING

All camshaft bearings are the same diameter, extreme care must be taken during camshaft removal or installation to avoid damaging them.

5. Install 3 M8 x 100mm long bolts in the front of the camshaft to use as a handle.
6. Carefully remove the camshaft from the engine, be sure not to damage the camshaft bearings.

To install:

7. Lubricate the camshaft with clean engine oil.
8. Install or connect the following:
- Three M8–1.25 x 100mm long bolts in the front of the camshaft to use as a handle

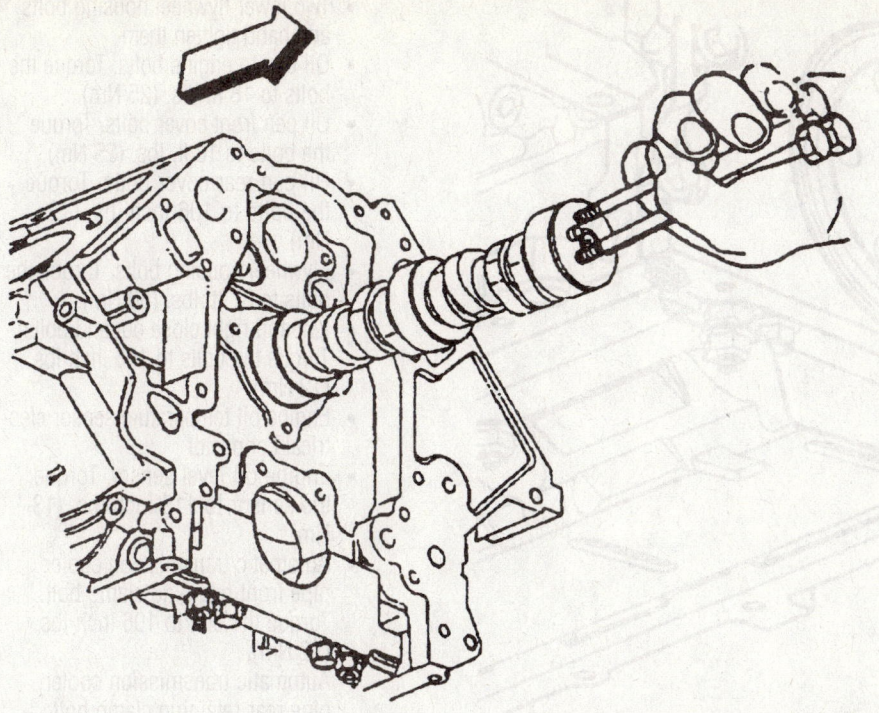

Install three M8–1.25 x 100mm long bolts into the camshaft to use as a handle

79222628

- Camshaft into the engine and remove the 3 bolts
- Camshaft retainer using a new gasket. Torque the bolts to 18 ft. lbs. (25 Nm).
- CMP sensor with a new O-ring. Torque the bolt to 18 ft. lbs. (25 Nm).
- Timing chain and make certain that the valve timing marks are facing each other
- Oil pump
- Front cover
- Radiator
- Pushrods and rocker arms. Make certain that they are installed in the original order
- Cylinder heads, valve lifters, pushrods and rocker arms
- Cylinder head covers
- Fuel lines to the fuel rail
- Negative battery cable
9. Refill the cooling system.
10. Start the engine and check for leaks, repair if necessary.

Valve Lash

ADJUSTMENT

The rocker arms on the 5.7L (VIN G) engine are bolted into position so that no initial adjustment is possible. If the valves are noisy, suspect low oil pressure or worn valve train components.

Starter

REMOVAL & INSTALLATION

1. Before servicing the vehicle, refer to the precautions in the beginning of this section.
2. Remove or disconnect the following:

- Negative battery cable
- Intermediate exhaust pipe
- Positive battery cable
- "S" terminal nut, wire and washer
- Starter bolts
- Starter

To install:
3. Install or connect the following:
- Starter. Torque the bolts to 37 ft. lbs. (50 Nm).
- "S" terminal washer, wire and nut. Torque the nut to 35 inch lbs. (4 Nm).
- Positive battery cable. Torque the nut to 89 inch lbs. (10 Nm).
- Intermediate exhaust pipe
- Negative battery cable

Exploded view of the starter assembly— 5.7L engine

9306ZG26

Oil Pan

REMOVAL & INSTALLATION

1. Before servicing the vehicle, refer to the precautions in the beginning of this section.
2. Drain the engine oil.
3. Remove or disconnect the following:

- Negative battery cable
- Front crossmember
- Oil filter
- Automatic transmission cooler line front and rear retaining clamp bolts
- Engine flywheel to oil pan bolts
- Engine flywheel close out bolts
- Engine oil level sensor
- Engine oil temperature sensor electrical connector
- Oil pan
- Oil pan gasket and discard it. Drill out the oil pan retaining rivets

To install:
4. Apply a 0.20 in. (5mm) bead of RTV sealant directly on the tabs of the front and rear cover gaskets that extend onto the oil pan mounting surface.
5. Install or connect the following:
- New gasket on the oil pan. It is not necessary to rivet the new gasket on the oil pan.
- Oil pan and hand tighten the bolts

For engine torque specifications, refer to Section 1 of this manual

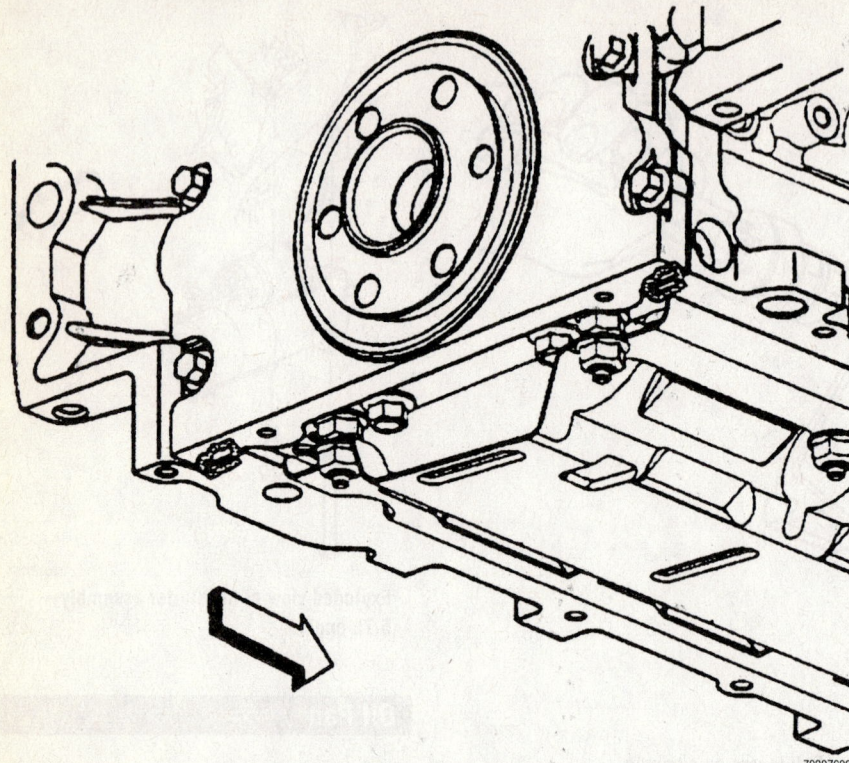

Apply sealant to the areas where the front and rear covers attach to the engine block—5.7L engine

- Two lower flywheel housing bolts and hand tighten them
- Oil pan to engine bolts. Torque the bolts to 18 ft. lbs. (25 Nm).
- Oil pan front cover bolts. Torque the bolts to 18 ft. lbs. (25 Nm).
- Oil pan rear cover bolts. Torque the bolts to 106 inch lbs. (12 Nm).
- Flywheel housing bolts. Torque the bolts to 37 ft. lbs. (50 Nm).
- Left and right close out and bolts. Torque the bolts to 106 inch lbs. (12 Nm).
- Engine oil temperature sensor electrical connector
- Engine oil level sensor. Torque the sensor to 115 inch lbs. (13 Nm).
- Automatic transmission cooler pipe front retaining clamp bolt. Torque the bolt to 106 inch lbs. (12 Nm).
- Automatic transmission cooler pipe rear retaining clamp bolt. Torque the bolt to 22 inch lbs. (3 Nm).
- Oil filter. Torque the filter to 22 ft. lbs. (30 Nm).
- Oil drain plug. Torque the plug to 18 ft. lbs. (25 Nm).
- Front crossmember
- Negative battery cable

6. Fill the engine with new oil.
7. Check and top off all fluids.
8. Start the vehicle and check for leaks, repair if necessary.
9. Check and adjust the front end alignment.

Oil Pump

REMOVAL & INSTALLATION

1. Before servicing the vehicle, refer to the precautions in the beginning of this section.
2. Drain the engine oil.
3. Drain the cooling system.
4. Remove or disconnect the following:

- Negative battery cable
- Engine front cover
- Oil pan
- Oil pump, pump screen and deflector

To install:

5. Inspect the oil passages in the pump and on the mounting surface. Be sure they are clean and free of debris.
6. Align the splined surface of the

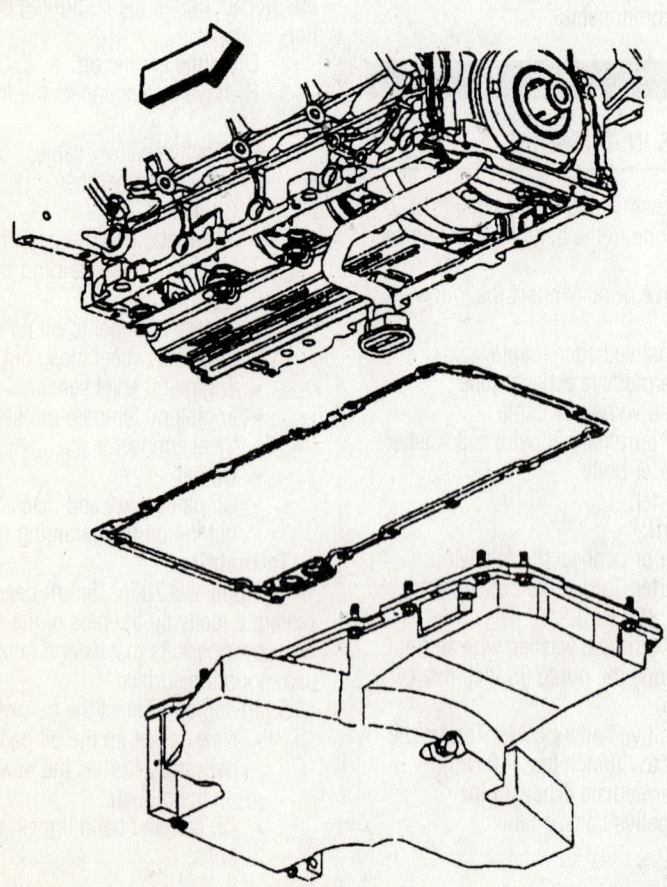

Exploded view of the oil pan mounting—5.7L engine

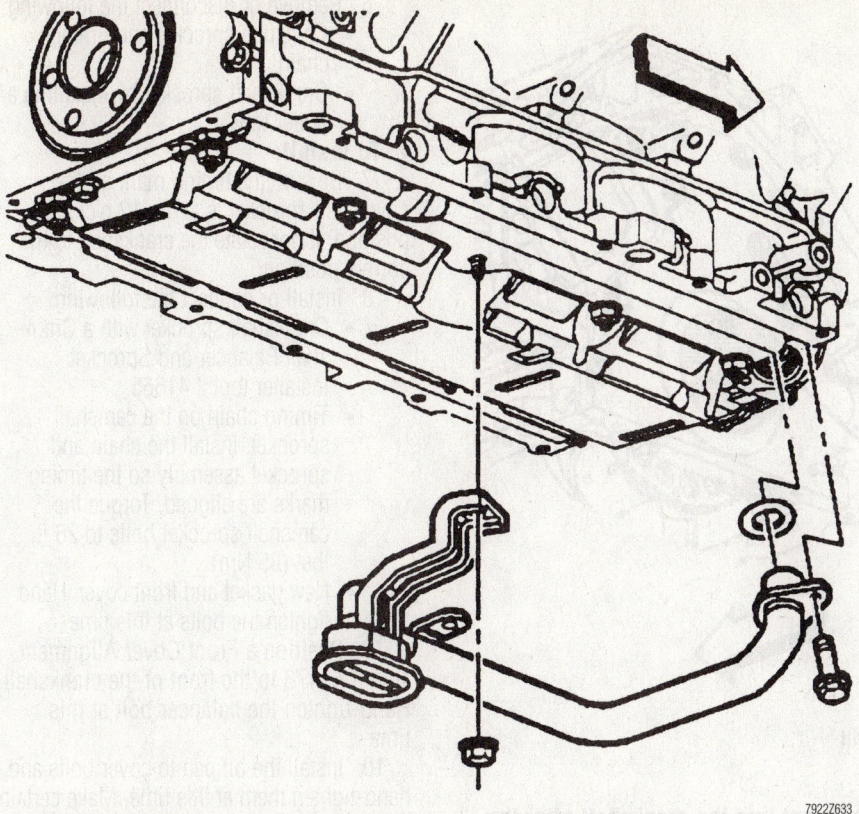

Be sure to seat the tube into the pump before installing the bolt

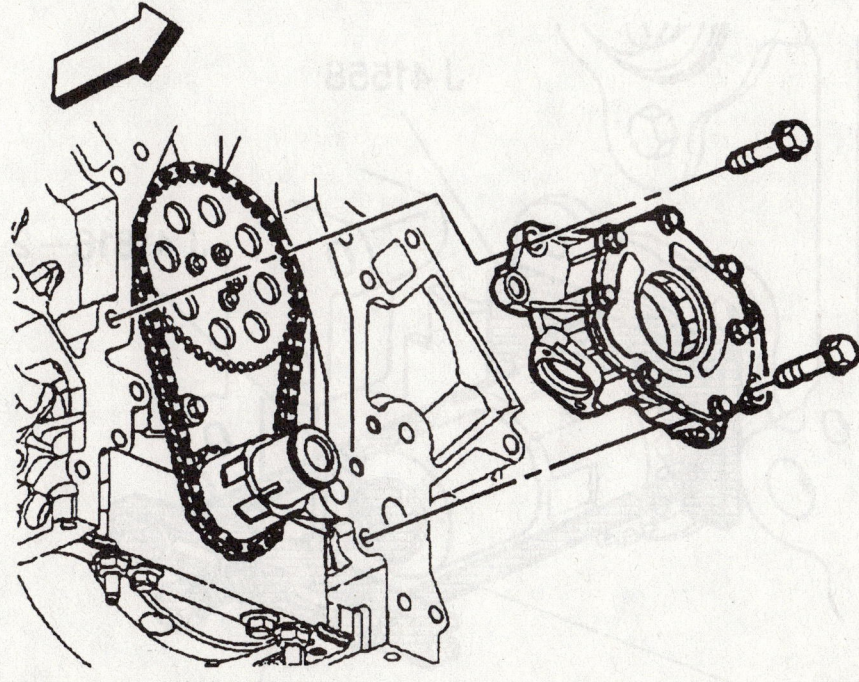

Oil pump assembly mounting—5.7L engine

crankshaft sprocket and the oil pump drive gear.

7. Install or connect the following:
   - Oil pump. Torque the bolts to 18 ft. lbs. (25 Nm).
   - New O-ring on the pickup tube and install it into the pump by hand. Don't use the bolt to force the tube into the pump. After the tube is seated torque the bolt to 106 inch lbs. (12 Nm). Torque the nut to 18 ft. lbs. (25 Nm).
   - Oil pan
   - Engine front cover.
   - Negative battery cable
8. Fill the engine with new oil.
9. Fill the cooling system.
10. Start the vehicle and check for leaks, repair if necessary.

Rear Main Seal

REMOVAL & INSTALLATION

➡**The rear main seal is a 1-piece unit. It can be removed or installed without removing the oil pan or crankshaft.**

1. Before servicing the vehicle, refer to the precautions in the beginning of this section.
2. Remove or disconnect the following:
   - Driveshaft support and bell housing
   - Clutch and pressure plate, if equipped with a manual transmission
   - Flywheel
3. Using a prytool, carefully pry the old seal out.

To install:

4. Inspect the crankshaft for nicks or burrs, correct as required.
5. Clean the area and coat the seal and crankshaft with engine oil.
6. Install or connect the following:
   - Seal, using a seal installer
   - Flywheel
   - Clutch and pressure plate if equipped with a manual transmission
   - Belling housing driveshaft support
7. Start the vehicle and check for leaks, repair if necessary.

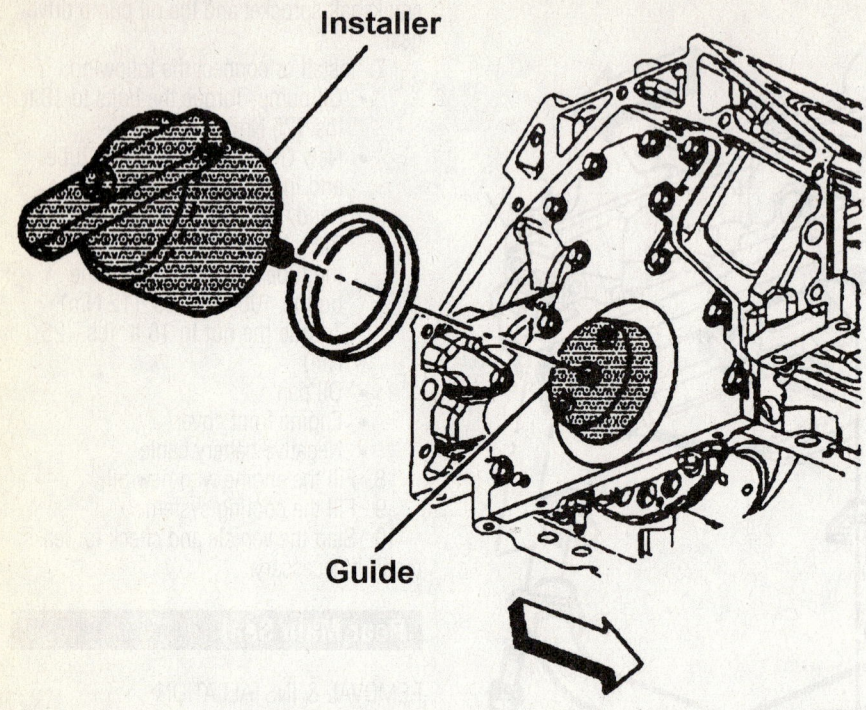

Installer

Guide

Use a seal installer to press the seal on the crankshaft

Timing Chain, Sprockets, Front Cover and Seal

REMOVAL & INSTALLATION

1. Before servicing the vehicle, refer to the precautions in the beginning of this section.
2. Drain the cooling system.
3. Drain the engine oil.
4. Remove or disconnect the following:
   - Negative battery cable
   - Air intake duct
   - Drive belt
   - Electronic Brake Traction Control Module (EBTCM) and reposition it
   - Power steering gear
   - Starter
   - Power steering gear cooler from the front crossmember
   - A/C belt
   - Radiator/heater hoses from the water pump
   - Water pump
   - Oil pan
   - Front cover and discard the gasket
   - Front oil seal from the front cover and discard it
5. Rotate the crankshaft until the timing marks are aligned. The marks should face each other. Remove the camshaft sprocket bolts.

➡ Do not turn the crankshaft after the timing chain has been removed. Damage to the pistons or valves may occur.

6. Remove or disconnect the following:
   - Camshaft sprocket and timing chain
   - Crankshaft sprocket by installing a puller tool

To install:

7. Be sure the timing mark on the crankshaft sprocket is at the 12 o'clock position. If not rotate the crankshaft to the correct position.
8. Install or connect the following:
   - Crankshaft sprocket with a Crankshaft Balancer and Sprocket Installer tool J 41665
   - Timing chain on the camshaft sprocket. Install the chain and sprocket assembly so the timing marks are aligned. Torque the camshaft sprocket bolts to 26 ft. lbs. (35 Nm).
   - New gasket and front cover. Hand tighten the bolts at this time
9. Position a Front Cover Alignment Tool J 41476 to the front of the crankshaft. Hand-tighten the balancer bolt at this time.
10. Install the oil pan to cover bolts and hand-tighten them at this time. Make certain that the front cover is properly aligned. Torque the oil pan-to-front cover bolts to 18 ft. lbs. (25 Nm).

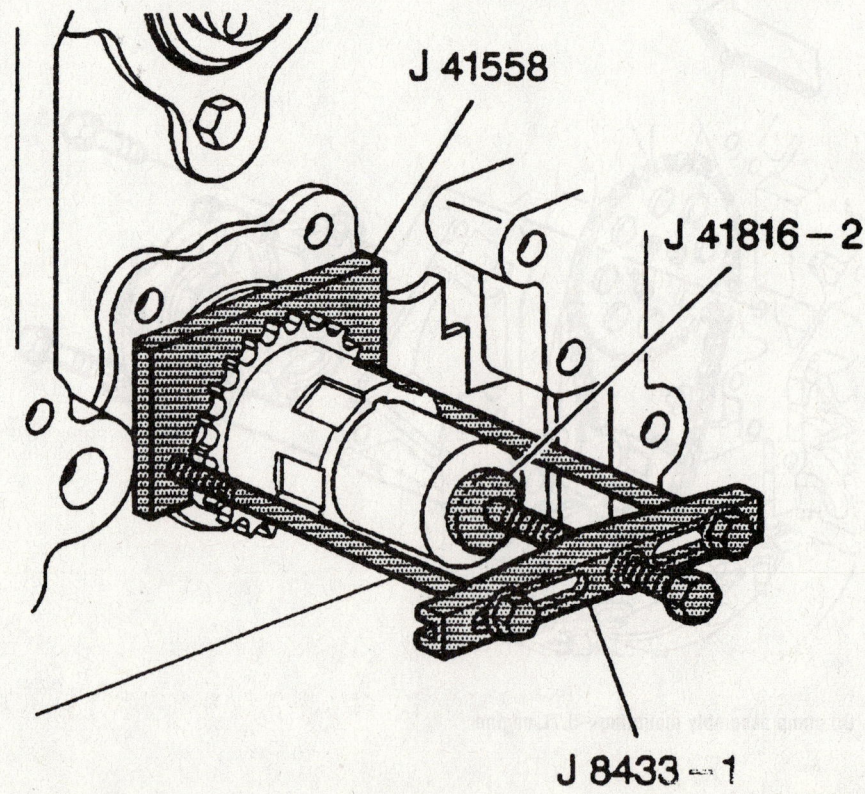

J 41558

J 41816 – 2

J 8433 – 1

A puller is needed to remove the crankshaft sprocket

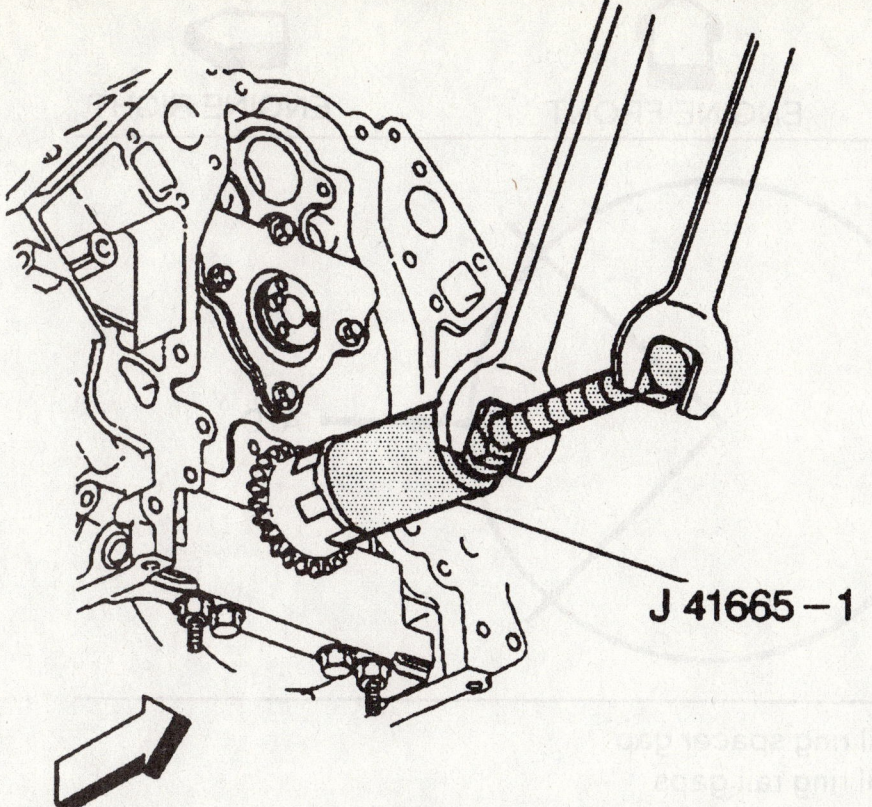

J 41665 – 1

Be sure to install the crankshaft sprocket properly

11. Remove the alignment tool.
12. Lubricate the front cover oil seal bore with clean oil.
13. Install or connect the following:
- New seal to a suitable installation tool and install the oil seal. Make certain that the new seal is fully seated in the front cover oil seal bore. Remove the tool.
- Water pump
- Radiator/heater hoses to the water pump
- A/C belt
- Power steering gear cooler to the front crossmember
- Starter
- Power steering gear
- EBTCM
- Drive belt
- Negative battery cable
14. Fill the cooling system.
15. Fill the engine with new oil.
16. Start the vehicle and check for leaks, repair if necessary.

Piston and Ring

POSITIONING

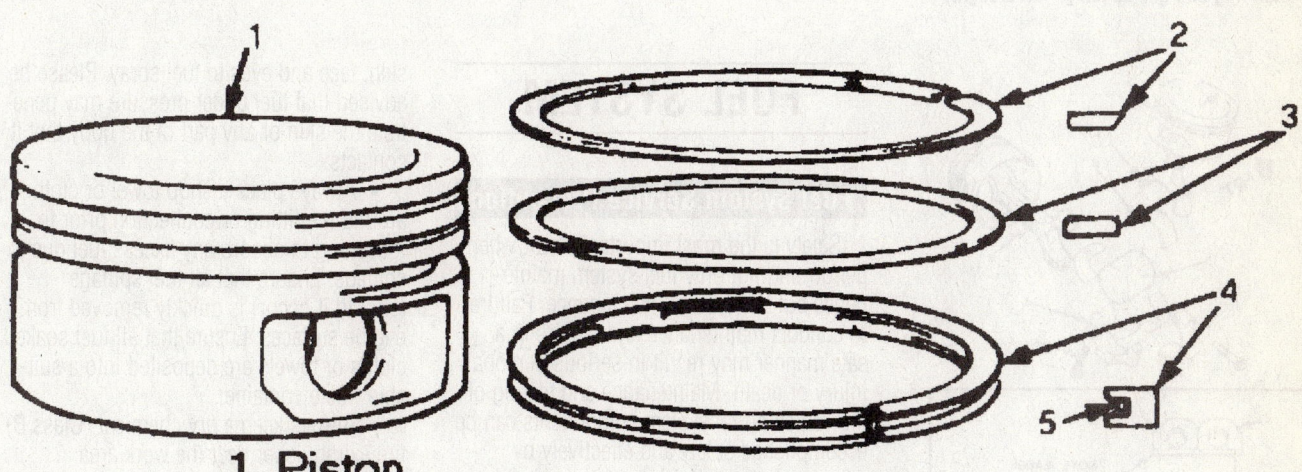

1. Piston
2. Upper compression piston ring
3. Lower compression piston ring
4. Oil control piston ring
5. Oil control ring spring w/spacer

Piston ring positioning—5.7L engine

Please refer to Section 8 for electric cooling fan wiring schematics

ENGINE LEFT

ENGINE FRONT

ENGINE RIGHT

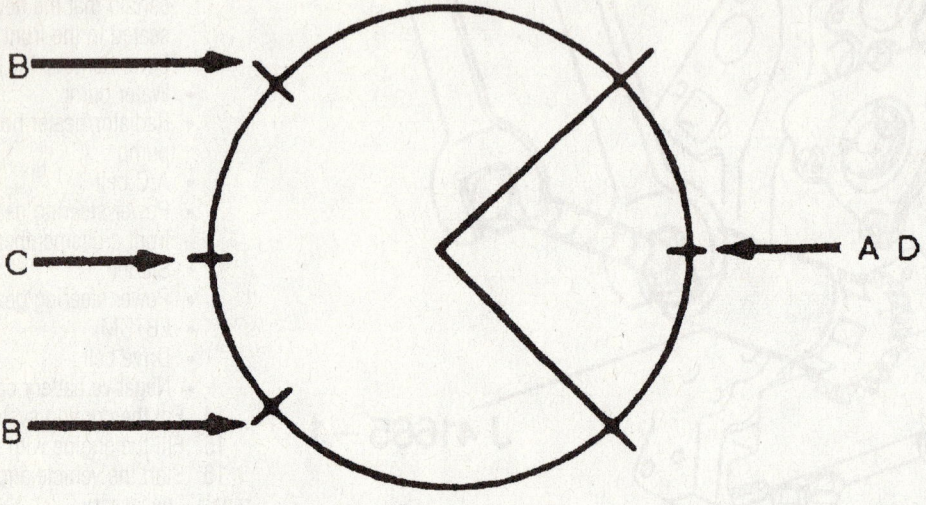

A. Oil ring spacer gap
B. Oil ring rail gaps
C. 2nd compression ring gap
D. Top compression ring gap

7922AG42

Piston ring end-gap spacing—5.7L engine

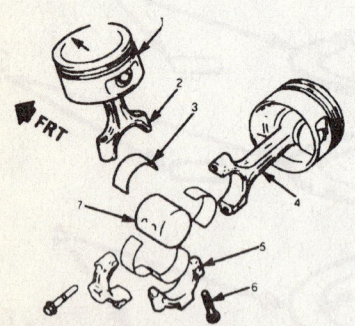

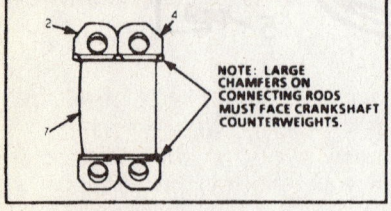

NOTE: LARGE CHAMFERS ON CONNECTING RODS MUST FACE CRANKSHAFT COUNTERWEIGHTS.

1. Piston
2. Connecting rod LH
3. Connecting rod bearing
4. Connecting rod RH
5. Connecting rod bearing cap
6. Connecting rod bearing cap bolt
7. Crankshaft

7922AG44

Piston and connecting rod positioning—5.7L engine

FUEL SYSTEM

Fuel System Service Precautions

Safety is the most important factor when performing not only fuel system maintenance but any type of maintenance. Failure to conduct maintenance and repairs in a safe manner may result in serious personal injury or death. Maintenance and testing of the vehicle's fuel system components can be accomplished safely and effectively by adhering to the following rules and guidelines.

• To avoid the possibility of fire and personal injury, always disconnect the negative battery cable unless the repair or test procedure requires that battery voltage be applied.

• Always relieve the fuel system pressure prior to disconnecting any fuel system component (injector, fuel rail, pressure regulator, etc.), fitting or fuel line connection. Exercise extreme caution whenever relieving fuel system pressure, to avoid exposing skin, face and eyes to fuel spray. Please be advised that fuel under pressure may penetrate the skin or any part of the body that it contacts.

• Always place a shop towel or cloth around the fitting or connection prior to loosening to absorb any excess fuel due to spillage. Ensure that all fuel spillage (should it occur) is quickly removed from engine surfaces. Ensure that all fuel soaked cloths or towels are deposited into a suitable waste container.

• Always keep a dry chemical (Class B) fire extinguisher near the work area.

• Do not allow fuel spray or fuel vapors to come into contact with a spark or open flame.

• Always use a back-up wrench when loosening and tightening fuel line connection fittings. This will prevent unnecessary stress and torsion to fuel line piping. Always follow the proper torque specifications.

• Always replace worn fuel fitting O-rings with new. Do not substitute fuel hose or equivalent, where fuel pipe is installed.

Fuel System Pressure

RELIEVING

1. Before servicing the vehicle, refer to the precautions in the beginning of this section.
2. Disconnect the negative battery cable.
3. Loosen the fuel filler cap to relieve the tank pressure.
4. Remove the left fuel rail cover.
5. Wrap a shop towel around the fuel pressure valve fitting (located on the side or end of the fuel rail assembly) to catch any fuel spray and connect a fuel pressure gauge.
6. Place the bleed hose into a suitable container, then open the valve to bleed the fuel system pressure.
7. Close the valve and disconnect the fuel gauge. Drain any remaining fuel from the gauge into the bleed container.

Fuel Filter

REMOVAL & INSTALLATION

1. Before servicing the vehicle, refer to the precautions in the beginning of this section.
2. Relieve the fuel system pressure.
3. Disconnect the negative battery cable.
4. Clean the filter connections, then depress the locking tabs and detach the quick-connect fittings from the filter.
5. On 1997–98 vehicles with an automatic transmission, disconnect the stabilizer bar from the rear cradle, remove the intermediate pipe to muffler bolts and lower the left muffler.
6. Remove or disconnect the following:
   - Fuel feed and return quick connect fittings from the fuel filter/pressure regulator
   - Fuel filter/pressure regulator bracket mount nut
   - Fuel system ground strap from the fuel filter/pressure regulator
   - Fuel feed pipe from the outlet side of the fuel filter/pressure regulator
   - Fuel filter/pressure regulator from the stud and cap all open lines
   - Fuel filter/pressure regulator from the bracket

To install:

7. Install or connect the following:

- New plastic quick connector retainers on the inlet and outlet tubes
- Fuel filter/pressure regulator into the bracket and remove the protective caps from the fuel pipes
- Fuel feed pipe to the outlet side of the fuel filter/pressure regulator
- Fuel filter/pressure regulator and bracket to the mounting stud

8. Engage the anti-rotation tab of the fuel filter/pressure regulator into the opening of the tunnel reinforcement.
9. Install or connect the following:

- Ground strap to the mounting stud
- Bracket nut. Torque the nut to 40 inch lbs. (4.5 Nm).
- Fuel return and feed quick connect fittings to the fuel filter/pressure regulator

10. On 1997–98 vehicles with automatic transmissions, connect the exhaust pipe to the muffler, install the stabilizer bar and raise the left muffler into position.
11. Connect the negative battery cable.
12. Turn the ignition switch **ON** for 2 seconds, then **OFF** for 10 seconds. Turn the ignition switch back **ON** and inspect for leaks.

Fuel Pump

REMOVAL & INSTALLATION

These models have 2 fuel tanks (right and left). The fuel pump is part of the fuel sender assembly in the left fuel tank. The right fuel tank contains a fuel sender assembly with a siphon jet pump which supplies fuel to the left tank through the fuel sender feed pipe.

Right Side

1. Before servicing the vehicle, refer to the precautions in the beginning of this section.
2. Properly relieve the fuel system pressure.
3. Drain the fuel tanks.
4. Remove or disconnect the following:
   - Negative battery cable
   - Both rear wheels
   - Fuel tank shield
5. Clean the area around the fuel sender assembly.
6. Mark each fuel line to help identify them during installation.
7. Remove or disconnect the following:
   - Quick connect fittings from the fuel sender

- Fuel sender electrical connector
- Fuel tank strap and properly support the fuel tank
- Fuel sender attaching bolts and discard them
- Float arm retaining clip and the float arm (left side sender only)
- Fuel sender and gasket. Discard the gasket

To install:

➡**Always install a new fuel strainer before installing the fuel sender assembly. A strainer that has been exposed to fuel will not unfold completely and may interfere with the full travel of the float arm.**

8. Install the new gasket on the fuel sender.

✳✳ WARNING

Do not damage the float arm during installation.

9. Fold the long strainer in half over itself and hold the strainer in this position.
10. Pinch both strainers upward toward each other.
11. Install the float arm through the fuel tank opening with the folded strainers. Release the strainers.

➡**It may be necessary to rotate the sender for proper installation.**

12. Look into the fuel tank opening and make certain that the long strainer is visible. If it is not visible, rotate the fuel sender until the strainer is free
13. Align the fuel sender gasket tab with the fuel sender cover mark and align the cover mark with the fuel tank mark.
14. Install the new break away head attaching bolts to the fuel sender and hand tighten them.

✳✳ CAUTION

The upper hex head portion of the fuel sender attaching bolts is designed to shear off the lower section of the bolt when the proper torque is reached. Do not tighten the bolts after the head is sheared off.

15. Tighten the new break away attaching bolts in sequence until the hex head shears off of the lower section.
16. Install or connect the following:
   - Fuel sender fuel feed pipe and rear crossover pipe

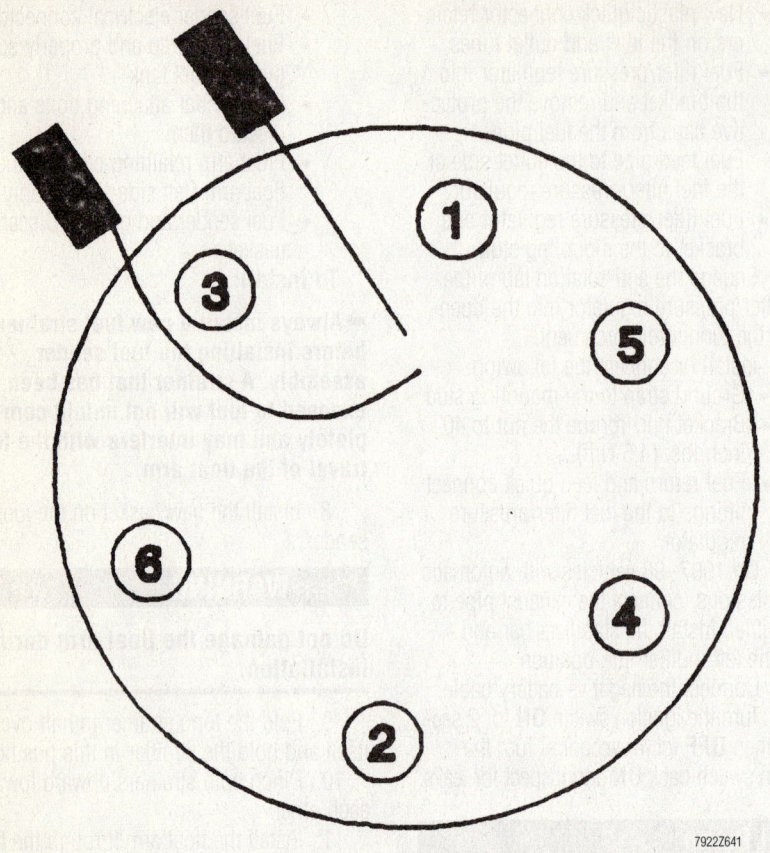

Tighten the fuel pump mounting bolts in the sequence shown—5.7L engine

- Fuel sender electrical connector
- Fuel tank strap. Torque the bolts to 18 ft. lbs. (25 Nm).
- Fuel tank shield. Torque the bolts to 18 ft. lbs. (25 Nm).
- Both rear wheels
- Negative battery cable

17. Fill the fuel tank and install the fuel filler cap.

18. Turn the ignition **ON** for 2 seconds, **OFF** for 10 seconds, then **ON** again and inspect the system for leaks.

Left Side

1. Before servicing the vehicle, refer to the precautions in the beginning of this section.

2. Properly relieve the fuel system pressure.

3. Drain the fuel tanks.

4. Remove or disconnect the following:
- Negative battery cable
- Both rear wheels
- Fuel tank shield

5. Clean the area around the fuel sender assembly.

6. Mark each fuel line to help identify them during installation.

7. Remove or disconnect the following:

- Quick connect fittings from the fuel sender
- Fuel sender electrical connector
- Fuel tank strap and properly support the fuel tank
- Fuel sender attaching bolts and discard them
- Float arm retaining clip and the float arm (left side sender only)
- Fuel sender and gasket. Discard the gasket

To install:

➡**Always install a new fuel strainer before installing the fuel sender. A** strainer that has been exposed to fuel will not unfold completely and may interfere with the full travel of the float arm.

8. Install or connect the following:
- New fuel strainer on the sender
- New gasket on the fuel sender

✳✳ WARNING

Do not damage the float arm during installation.

9. Fold the strainer 3 times so the strainer is about the same size as the opening in the tank. Insert the fuel sender in the tank. It may be necessary to turn the fuel sender to ease installation. Look into the opening to ensure that the long strainer is about 1 inch from the opening; if not, rotate the pump assembly back-and-forth until the strainer is visible. Install the float arm and retaining clip.

10. Align the fuel sender gasket tab with the fuel sender cover mark and align the cover mark with the fuel tank mark. Install new break away head attaching bolts to the fuel sender and hand-tighten them.

✳✳ CAUTION

The upper hex head portion of the fuel sender attaching bolts is designed to shear off the lower section of the bolt when the proper torque is reached. Do not tighten the bolts after the head is sheared off.

11. Tighten the new break away attaching bolts in sequence until the hex head shears off of the lower section.

12. Install or connect the following:
- Fuel sender fuel feed pipe, fuel return rear pipe and the fuel feed rear pipe
- Fuel sender electrical connector
- Fuel tank strap. Torque the bolts to 18 ft. lbs. (25 Nm).

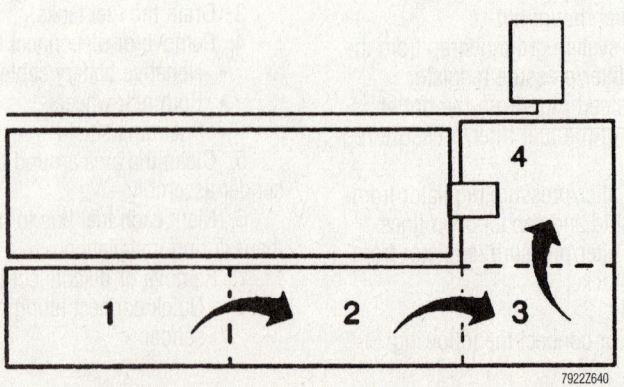

Fold the strainer on itself 3 times so it will fit into the opening in the fuel tank

- Fuel tank shield. Torque the bolts to 18 ft. lbs. (25 Nm).
- Both rear wheels
- Negative battery cable

13. Fill the fuel tank and install the fuel filler cap.

14. Turn the ignition **ON** for 2 seconds, **OFF** for 10 seconds, then **ON** again and inspect the system for leaks.

Fuel Injector

REMOVAL & INSTALLATION

1. Before servicing the vehicle, refer to the precautions in the beginning of this section.

2. Relieve the fuel system pressure.

3. Remove or disconnect the following:
- Negative battery cable
- Both fuel rail covers
- Fuel feed hose from the fuel rail
- Fuel injector electrical connectors and identify the connectors to ensure the proper sequential firing order during reassembly
- Fuel rail ground strap from the intake manifold
- Fuel rail
- Spread the injector clip to release the injector from the fuel rail
- Fuel injector and discard the retaining clip
- Injector O-ring seals from both ends and discard them

To install:

➡ **The fuel injector is stamped with a part number identification, manufacturing date, week code and plant number. Make certain the correct injector is ordered when replacing them.**

4. Lubricate the new injector seals with clean oil.

5. Install or connect the following:
- New O-ring seals to the injectors
- New retainer clip on the injector
- Fuel injector into the fuel rail socket facing outward

✳✳ CAUTION

The fuel rail stop bracket must be installed onto the engine. The bracket serves as protection for the fuel rail in the event of a frontal crash. If the bracket is not installed, fuel could spray possibly causing a fire and personal injury.

- Fuel rail and ground strap to the intake manifold. Torque the fuel rail; attaching bolts to 89 inch lbs. (10 Nm).
- Electrical connectors to the injectors
- Fuel feed hose to the fuel rail
- Negative battery cable
- Left and right fuel rail covers

6. Turn the ignition **ON** for 2 seconds, **OFF** for 10 seconds, then **ON** again and inspect the system for leaks.

DRIVE TRAIN

Automatic Transmission Assembly

REMOVAL & INSTALLATION

1. Before servicing the vehicle, refer to the precautions in the beginning of this section.

2. Disconnect the negative battery cable.

3. Shift the transmission into **N**.

4. Remove the rear wheels.

5. Remove or disconnect the following:
- Intermediate exhaust pipe
- Right side muffler and tie the left side muffler to the underbody
- Driveline tunnel closeout panel
- Rear bell housing access plug and matchmark the flexplate to the torque converter
- Flexplate to torque converter bolts
- 2 plug bolts from the front of the driveshaft support assembly. Install two M10 x 1.5 x 55mm or longer bolts into the bolt holes. Torque the bolts to 26 ft. lbs. (35 Nm). These bolts must remain installed until instructed to remove them in order to maintain the position of the input shaft bearing.
- Engine flywheel housing access plug and loosen the propeller shaft hub clamp bolt. It may be necessary to rotate the engine at the flywheel to gain access

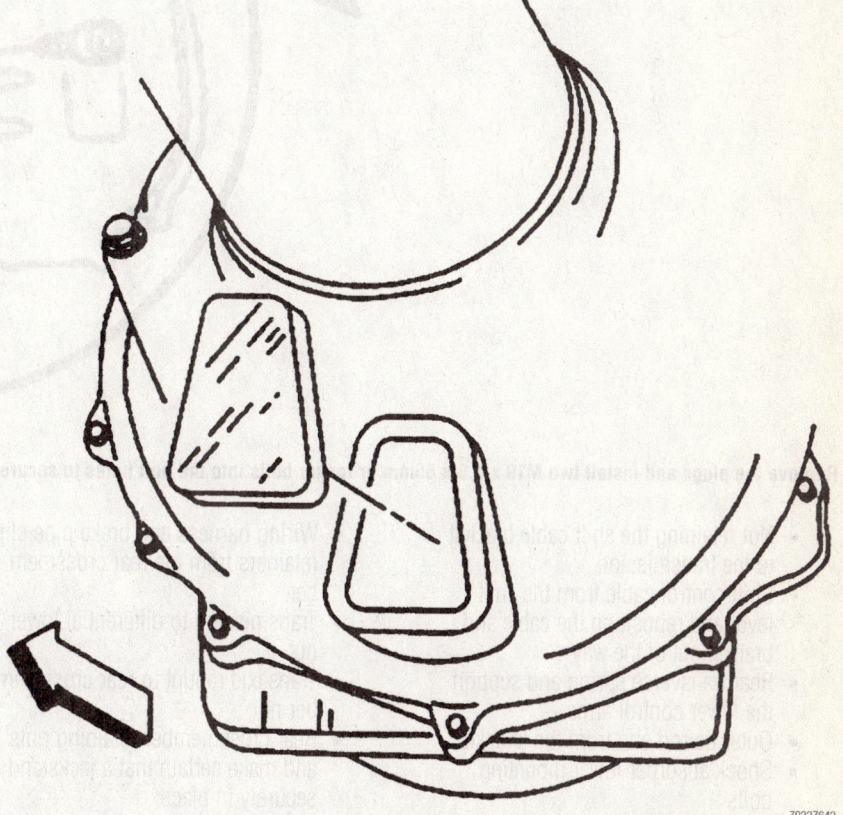

Remove the inspection plug, then remove the flexplate-to-torque converter bolts

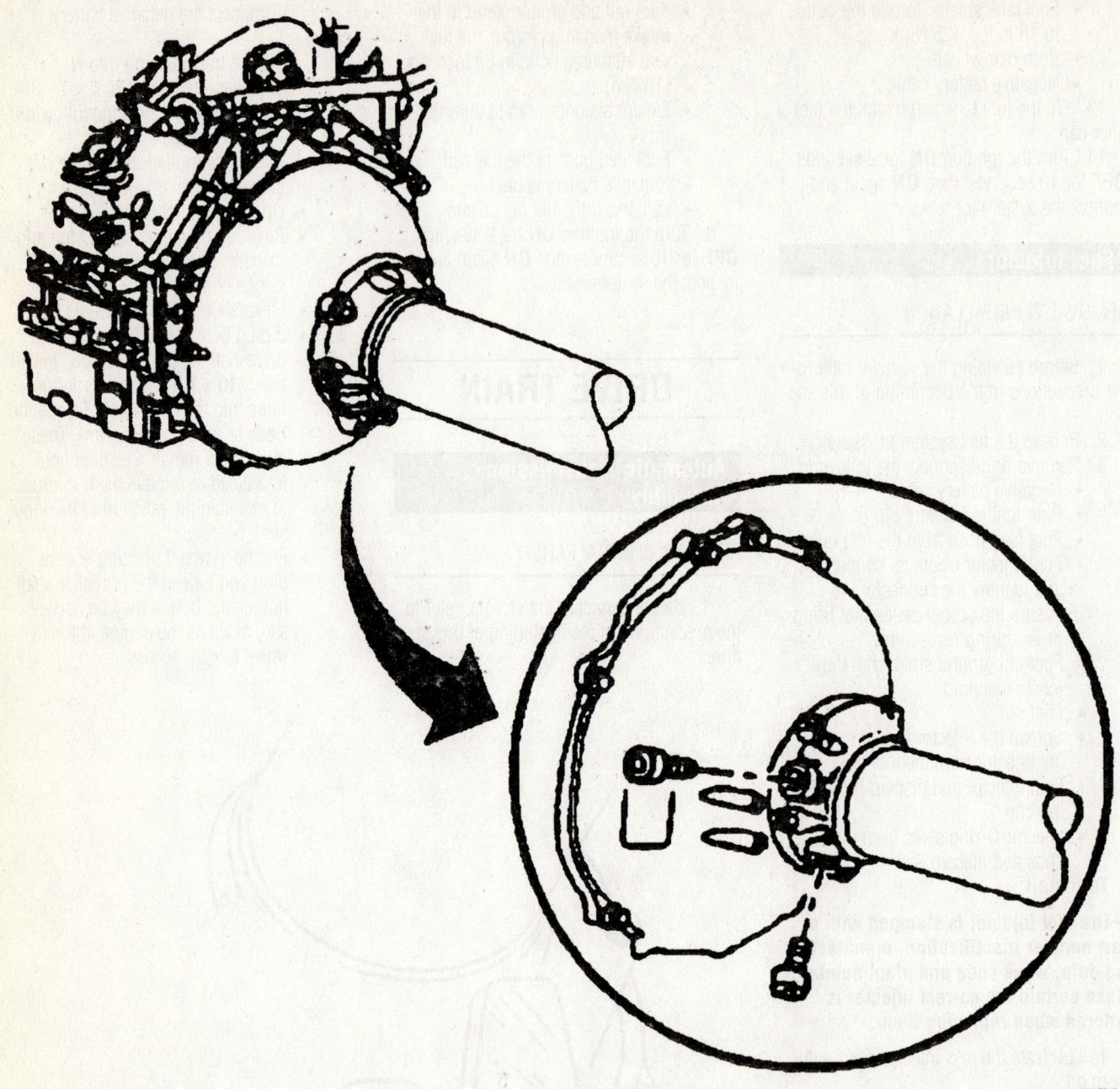

Remove the plugs and install two M10 x 1.5 x 55mm or longer bolts into the bolt holes to secure the bearing—5.7L engine

- Nut retaining the shift cable bracket to the transmission
- Shift control cable from the shift lever and reposition the cable and bracket out of the way
- Rear transverse spring and support the lower control arms
- Outer tie rod end from the knuckle
- Shock absorber lower mounting bolts
- Lower ball joints from the knuckles

6. Install a transmission support fixture to the transmission.

7. Remove or disconnect the following:

- Wiring harness and brake pipe clip retainers from the rear crossmember
- Transmission to differential lower nut
- Transaxle mount to rear crossmember nut
- Rear crossmember retaining nuts and make certain that a jackstand is securely in place
- Crossmember
- Transaxle mount bracket

8. Separate the axle shafts from the differential and tie them to the underbody.

9. Release the retainer securing the wiring harness from the "L" shaped brackets along the driveline support. Move the harness out of the way.

10. Lower the driveline slightly and tilt it to gain access to the electrical connectors.

11. Remove or disconnect the following:

- Vehicle Speed Sensor (VSS) electrical connector
- Electronic Brake Traction Control Module (EBTCM) electrical connectors
- Wire harness retainer from the differential rear cover stud

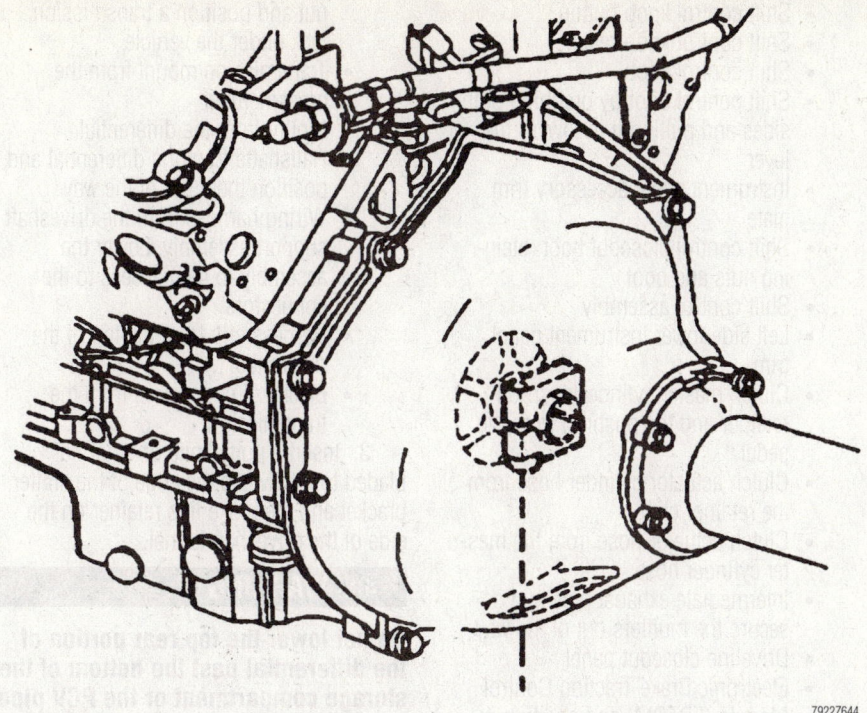

Rotate the flywheel to gain access to the clamp bolt, then loosen it—5.7L engine

- Wire harness retainer clip from the top of the differential
- Transmission harness 20 way connector
- Park Neutral Position (PNP) switch electrical connectors
- Bolt securing the wire harness to the left side of the case

12. Lower the driveline and angle it while observing the top rear of the differential and the lowest part of the rear compartment floor panel. The engine Positive Crankcase Ventilation (PCV) pipes will most likely contact the dash panel. Make certain not to damage the dash.

13. Remove or disconnect the following:
- Wire harness from the retainer along the top of transmission
- Transmission rear oil cooler pipes from the junction fittings at the flywheel housing
- 5 driveline to flywheel housing bolts after securing the rear of the oil pan

14. Bend the wiring harness bracket away from the driveline, toward the tunnel wall to have access to remove the driveline.

15. Separate the driveline from the engine by prying them apart with a flat blade tool.

16. Lower the driveline and tilt it away

from the engine until the input shaft clears the flywheel housing.

17. Remove or disconnect the following:
- Driveline
- Transmission oil cooler rear pipes from the fittings
- Transmission to driveline bolts
- Separate the transmission from the driveline with a flat blade tool
- Driveline from the transmission while supporting the torque converter
- Differential to transmission bolts. Use caution so the output shaft seal is not damaged
- Differential plate from the differential

To install:

18. Install or connect the following:
- Differential plate to the transmission. Use caution not to damage the output seal. Torque the bolts to 37 ft. lbs. (50 Nm).
- Transmission to driveline support. Torque the bolts to 37 ft. lbs. (50 Nm).

19. Using a chain hoist, place the assembly on a transmission jack.

20. Carefully raise the assembly into the vehicle while placing the wiring harness loosely into the harness retaining slots.

21. Align the assembly for installation into the engine. The driveshaft will slide into the rear of the engine as long as the angles are the same.

22. Install or connect the following:
- Driveshaft assembly in the engine. Reposition the wiring harness bracket to align with the appropriate hole in the driveshaft assembly. Torque the bolts to 37 ft. lbs. (50 Nm).
- Wiring harness on the top of the driveshaft assembly
- Oil cooler lines. Torque the fittings to 20 ft. lbs. (27 Nm).
- Wiring harness to the left side of the transmission. Reattach the connectors

23. Raise the transmission to installed height and remove the jack from the engine.

24. Install or connect the following:
- Suspension crossmember. Torque the nuts to 81 ft. lbs. (110 Nm).
- Transmission mount to the crossmember. Torque the nuts to 37 ft. lbs. (50 Nm).
- Transmission to differential lower nut. Torque the nut to 37 ft. lbs. (50 Nm).

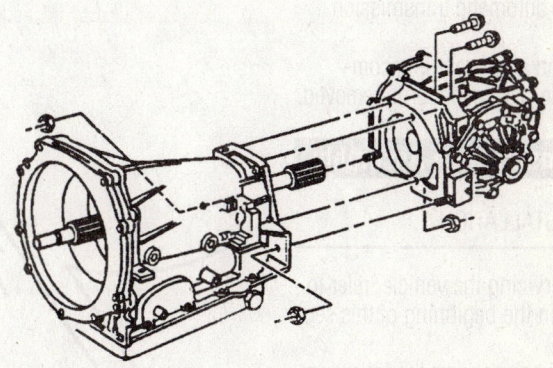

Transmission-to-differential mounting bolt locations—5.7L engine

- Lower ball joints to the suspension knuckles
- Shock absorber lower mounting bolts. Torque the bolts to 162 ft. lbs. (220 Nm).
- Outer tie rod ends to the suspension knuckle
- Rear transverse spring
- EBTCM and bracket. Torque the bolts to 37 ft. lbs. (50 Nm).
- Electrical connector for the VSS and the EBTCM
- EBTCM ground lead. Torque the nut 25 inch lbs. (3 Nm).
- Electrical connector for the PNP switch
- Transmission cable and bracket. Torque the nuts to 15 ft. lbs. (20 Nm).
- Transmission flexplate to the torque converter using the matchmarks made during removal. Torque the bolts to 47 ft. lbs. (63 Nm).
- Rear bell housing access plug
- Propeller shaft hub bolt until it is finger tight

25. Remove the two M10 x 55mm bolts from the input shaft front bearing.

26. Install or connect the following:
- 2 plug bolts to the driveline support assembly. Torque the bolts to 37 ft. lbs. (50 Nm).
- Driveline tunnel closeout panel
- Both mufflers and the intermediate pipe
- Both rear wheels
- Negative battery cable

27. Start the vehicle and allow it to reach normal operating temperature. Turn the engine **OFF**. Allow the engine to cool to ambient temperature, then tighten the flywheel hub collar bolt to 96 ft. lbs. (130 Nm).

28. Install the bell housing inspection plug.

29. Flush the automatic transmission fluid cooler.

30. A front end alignment is recommended when the crossmember is removed.

Manual Transmission Assembly

REMOVAL & INSTALLATION

1. Before servicing the vehicle, refer to the precautions in the beginning of this section.

2. Remove or disconnect the following:
- Negative battery cable
- Both rear wheels
- Console

- Shift control knob button
- Shift control knob retainer
- Shift control knob
- Shift control boot by grabbing both sides and pulling it in toward the lever
- Instrument panel accessory trim plate
- Shift control closeout boot retaining nuts and boot
- Shift control assembly
- Left side lower instrument panel trim
- Clutch master cylinder pushrod retainer and the pushrod from the pedal
- Clutch actuator cylinder hose from the retainer clip
- Clutch actuator hose from the master cylinder hose
- Intermediate exhaust pipe and secure the mufflers out of the way
- Driveline closeout panel
- Electronic Brake Traction Control Module (EBTCM) and position it out of the way
- Rear transverse spring
- Lower shock absorber, tie rod end and lower ball joint
- Wiring harness and brake lines from the suspension crossmember
- Transmission-to-differential lower nut and position a transmission jack under the vehicle
- Transmission mount from the crossmember
- Mount from the differential
- Halfshafts from the differential and position them out of the way
- Wiring harness from the driveshaft support assembly. Lower the assembly to gain access to the connectors
- Harness clip from the top of the differential
- Electrical connectors from the transmission

3. Insert a putty knife or other flat bladed tool between the edge of the shifter bracket and the brake line retainer on the side of the driveshaft tunnel.

❄❄ WARNING

Do not lower the top rear portion of the differential past the bottom of the storage compartment or the PCV pipe will hit the dash panel possibly causing damage.

4. Lower the transmission enough to remove the wiring harness from the top of the assembly.

5. Support the engine with a block of wood and a jack.

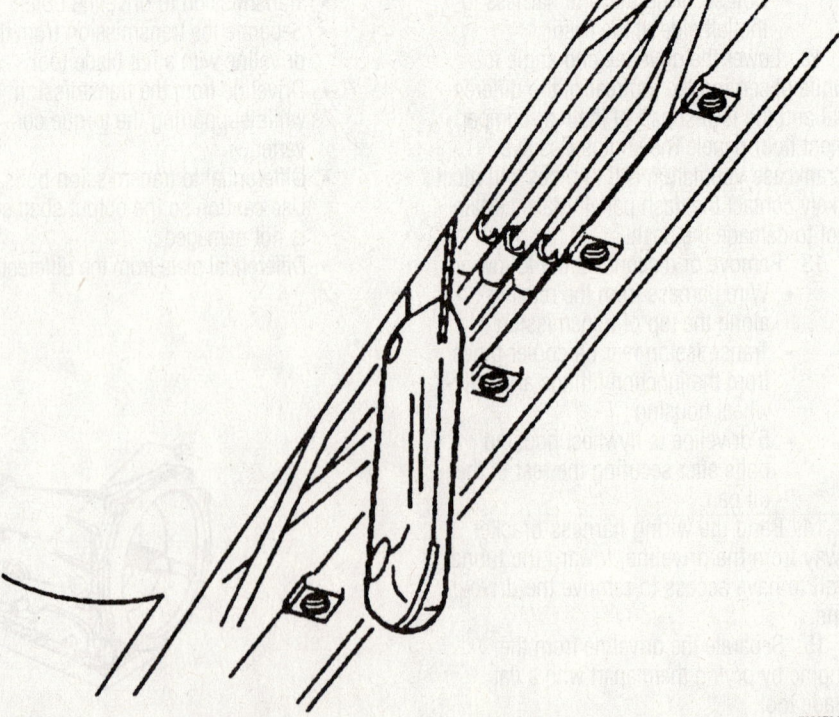

Insert a flat bladed tool between the shifter bracket and brake liner retainer before lowering the transmission assembly—5.7L engine

79222646

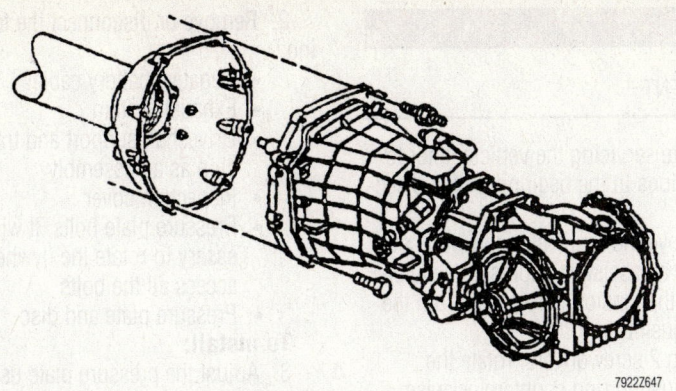

IDriveshaft support-to-transmission mounting—5.7L engine

6. Remove or disconnect the following:
   - Vehicle Speed Sensor (VSS) electrical connector
   - Gear select/skip shift solenoid electrical connector
   - Backup lamp switch electrical connector
   - Reverse lockout solenoid electrical connector
   - Transmission fluid temperature sensor electrical connector
   - Driveshaft support-to-bell housing bolts. It may be necessary to bend the wiring harness bracket toward the tunnel wall for greater clearance when removing the driveshaft assembly
   - Front driveshaft support out of the bell housing while an assistant moves the assembly rearward
7. Carefully lower the assembly away from the vehicle while simultaneously adjusting the angle.
8. Attach a chain hoist to the assembly, then remove it from the jack and place it on a workbench.
9. Remove or disconnect the following:
   - Driveshaft-to-transmission mounting bolts. Carefully pry the driveshaft assembly away from the transmission while guiding the shift rod through the opening in the driveshaft support
   - Roll pin to detach the shift rod from the transmission
   - Transmission-to-differential mounting bolts and separate the differential from the transmission

To install:
10. Install or connect the following:
    - Differential on the transmission. Torque the bolts to 37 ft. lbs. (50 Nm).
    - Driveshaft support to the transmis-

sion. Torque the bolts to 37 ft. lbs. (50 Nm).
11. To help connect the shift rod to the shift control assembly, place a rubber band on the shift rod just behind the clamp, then tape the rod to the driveshaft support.
12. Place the assembly on the transmission jack with a chain hoist.
13. Begin to raise the assembly into the vehicle while loosely installing the wiring harness along the driveshaft assembly retaining slots.

14. Have an assistant guide the front of the driveshaft to the bell housing.
15. Insert a flat blade tool between the edge of the shifter bracket and the brake line retainer on the side of the driveshaft tunnel.
16. Be sure the driveshaft assembly is at the same angle as the engine before trying to install it.
17. Install or connect the following:
    - Driveshaft splines into the clutch disc and turn the shaft to align the

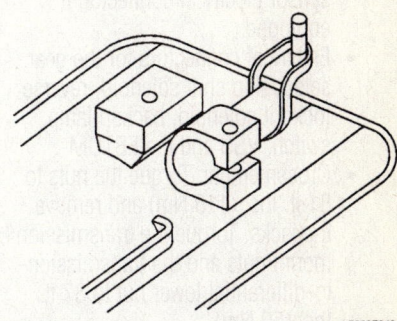

Pull the shift rod up to break the tape and hook the rubber band on the rear stud—5.7L engine

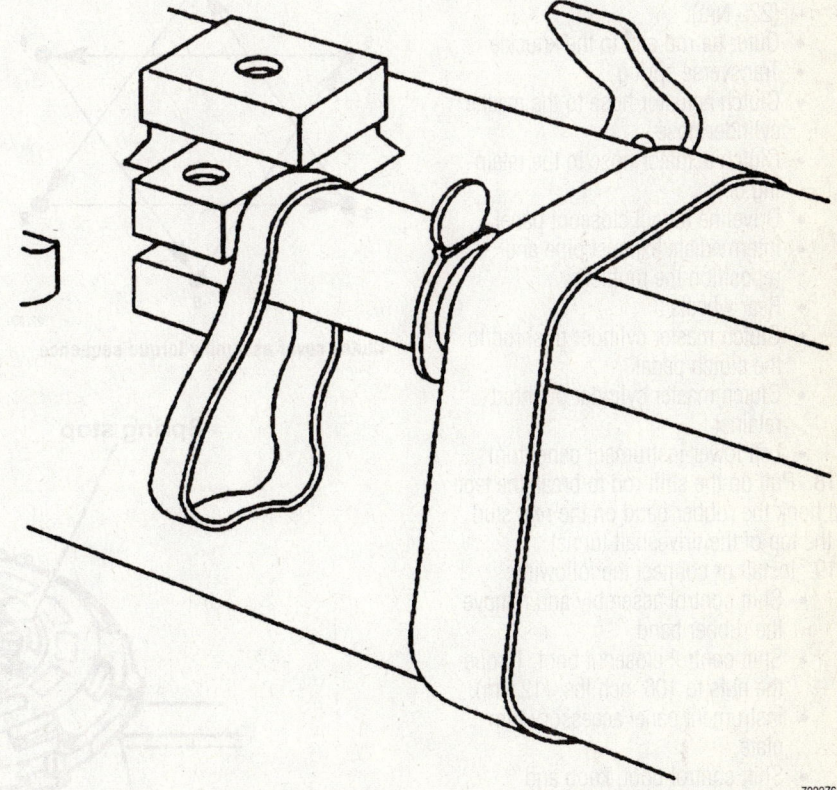

Place a rubber band on the shift rod, then tape the rod to the driveshaft support assembly—5.7L engine

Turn to Section 5 for brake system applications

splines. Torque the bolts to 37 ft. lbs. (50 Nm).

- Wiring harness bracket to align with the appropriate hole in the driveshaft assembly
- Wiring harness to the retainer on the top of the transmission and attach the connectors
- Halfshafts in the differential
- Transmission mount on the differential. Torque the bolts to 37 ft. lbs. (50 Nm).
- Transmission fluid temperature sensor electrical connector, if equipped
- Electrical connectors for the gear select/skip shift solenoid, reverse lockout solenoid, backup lamp switch, VSS and the EBTCM
- Crossmember. Torque the nuts to 81 ft. lbs. (110 Nm) and remove the jacks. Torque the transmission mount nuts and the transmission-to-differential lower nut to 37 ft. lbs. (50 Nm).
- Wiring harness and brake line retainers to the crossmember
- Lower ball joint to the knuckle
- Shock absorber lower mounting bolt. Torque the bolt 162 ft. lbs. (220 Nm).
- Outer tie rod end to the knuckle
- Transverse spring
- Clutch actuator hose to the master cylinder hose
- Clutch actuator hose to the retaining clip
- Driveline tunnel closeout panel
- Intermediate exhaust pipe and reposition the mufflers
- Rear wheels
- Clutch master cylinder pushrod to the clutch pedal
- Clutch master cylinder pushrod retainer
- Left lower instrument panel trim

18. Pull up the shift rod to break the tape and hook the rubber band on the rear stud on the top of the driveshaft tunnel.

19. Install or connect the following:
- Shift control assembly and remove the rubber band
- Shift control closeout boot. Torque the nuts to 106 inch lbs. (12 Nm).
- Instrument panel accessory trim plate
- Shift control boot, knob and retainer and button on the shift lever
- Console
- Negative battery cable

20. Bleed the clutch system.

Clutch

ADJUSTMENT

1. Before servicing the vehicle, refer to the precautions in the beginning of this section.

2. Remove the flywheel inspection cover.

3. Have an assistant depress the clutch pedal until the tension is released from the stepped adjusting ring.

4. Using 2 screwdrivers, rotate the stepped adjusting ring counterclockwise until fully adjusted out.

5. Continue to hold them in this position and have the assistant release the clutch pedal.

6. Remove the screwdrivers.

7. Install the inspection cover. Torque the bolts to 18 ft. lbs. (25 Nm).

REMOVAL & INSTALLATION

1. Before servicing the vehicle, refer to the precautions in the beginning of this section.

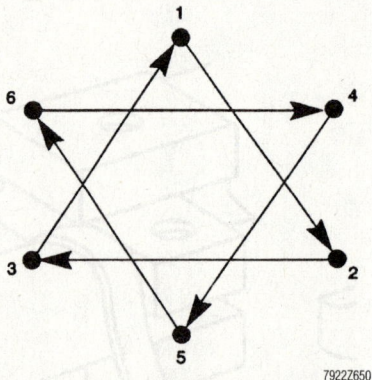

Clutch cover assembly torque sequence

2. Remove or disconnect the following:
- Negative battery cable
- Exhaust system
- Driveshaft support and transmission as an assembly
- Inspection cover
- Pressure plate bolts. It will be necessary to rotate the flywheel to access all the bolts
- Pressure plate and disc

To install:

3. Adjust the pressure plate using the following procedure:
- a. Step 1: Place the pressure plate assembly on a press.
- b. Step 2: Compress the diaphragm fingers until the tension is released from the stepped adjusting ring.
- c. Step 3: Using 2 screwdrivers, rotate the stepped adjusting ring counterclockwise until fully adjusted out.
- d. Step 4: Continue to hold them in this position and release the press.
- e. Step 5: Remove the screwdrivers.

4. Install or connect the following:
- Clutch disc and pressure plate on the flywheel
- Clutch disc alignment tool through the disc to keep it in place
- Pressure plate bolts finger-tight. Turn the flywheel to access all the bolt holes
- Torque the bolts evenly using 3 steps to 37 ft. lbs. (50 Nm).
- Inspection cover
- Driveshaft support and transmission assembly
- Exhaust system
- Negative battery cable

5. Bleed the clutch system.

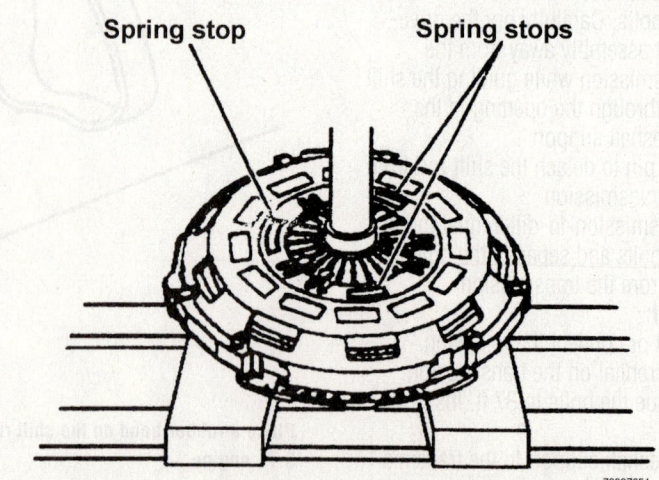

There are 3 stepped adjusting ring tension spring stops on the pressure plate assembly

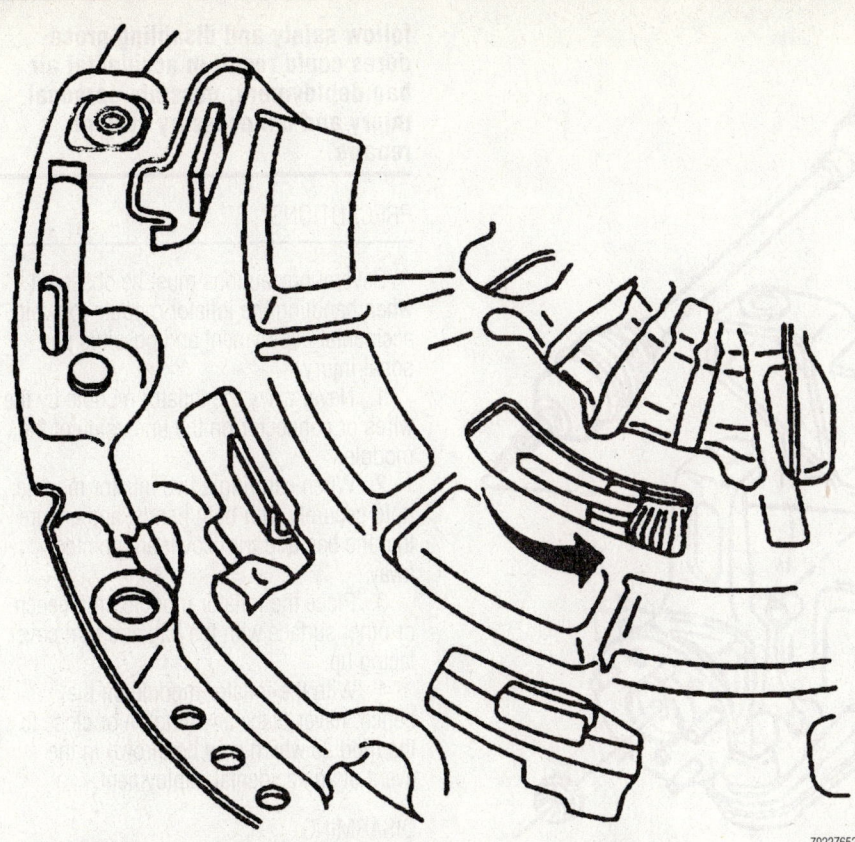

Rotate the stepped adjusting ring counterclockwise to compress the springs

Hydraulic Clutch System

BLEEDING

1. Before servicing the vehicle, refer to the precautions in the beginning of this section.

2. Fill the clutch master cylinder with clean clutch hydraulic fluid.

3. Raise and safely support the vehicle with an assistant in it.

4. Remove the intermediate exhaust pipe.

5. Remove the driveshaft tunnel undercover.

6. Have the assistant depress and hold the clutch pedal down.

7. Loosen the bleeder screw on the actuator cylinder to release the air, then tighten the screw. Do not allow the clutch pedal to be released until the bleeder screw is closed or air will be drawn into the system.

8. Repeat the prior two steps until the air has been purged from the system. Check the master cylinder fluid level and refill as needed.

9. Install the driveshaft tunnel undercover.

10. Install the intermediate exhaust pipe.
11. Lower the vehicle.

Halfshaft

REMOVAL & INSTALLATION

1. Before servicing the vehicle, refer to the precautions in the beginning of this section.

2. Shift the transmission into **P** for automatic transmissions or **neutral** for manual transmissions.

3. Apply the parking brake.

4. Remove or disconnect the following:
   - Wheel
   - Insert a large drift through the brake rotor cooling fins to prevent the hub assembly from turning
   - axle nut

5. Release the parking brake.

6. Remove or disconnect the following:
   - Rear spring
   - Outer tie rod end from the knuckle and position it to the rear
   - Antilock Brake System (ABS) wheel speed sensor
   - Park brake cable from the lever and bracket

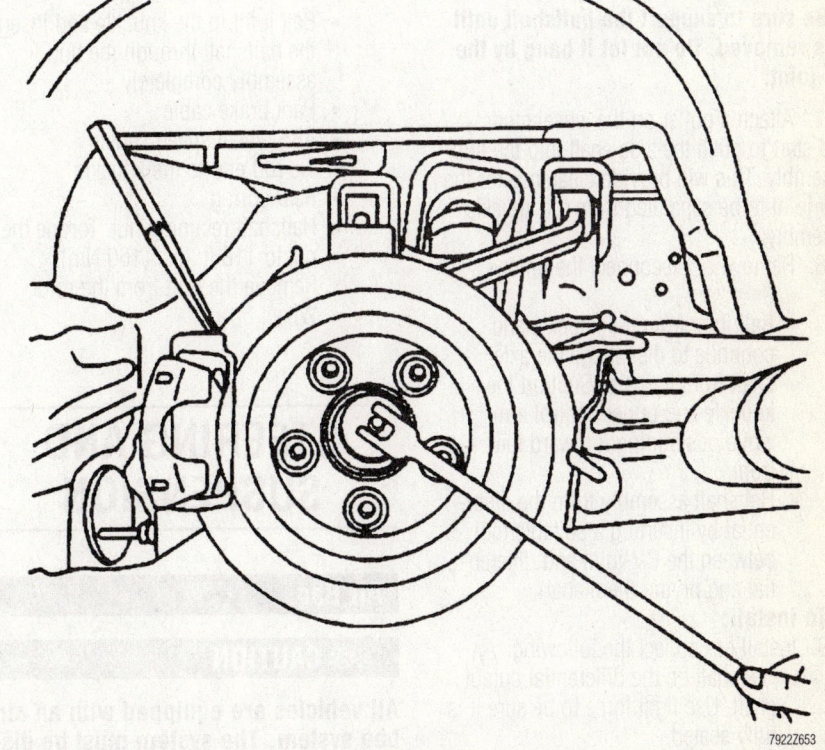

Insert a large drift through the cooling fins to keep the hub assembly from turning while removing the retaining nut—5.7L engine

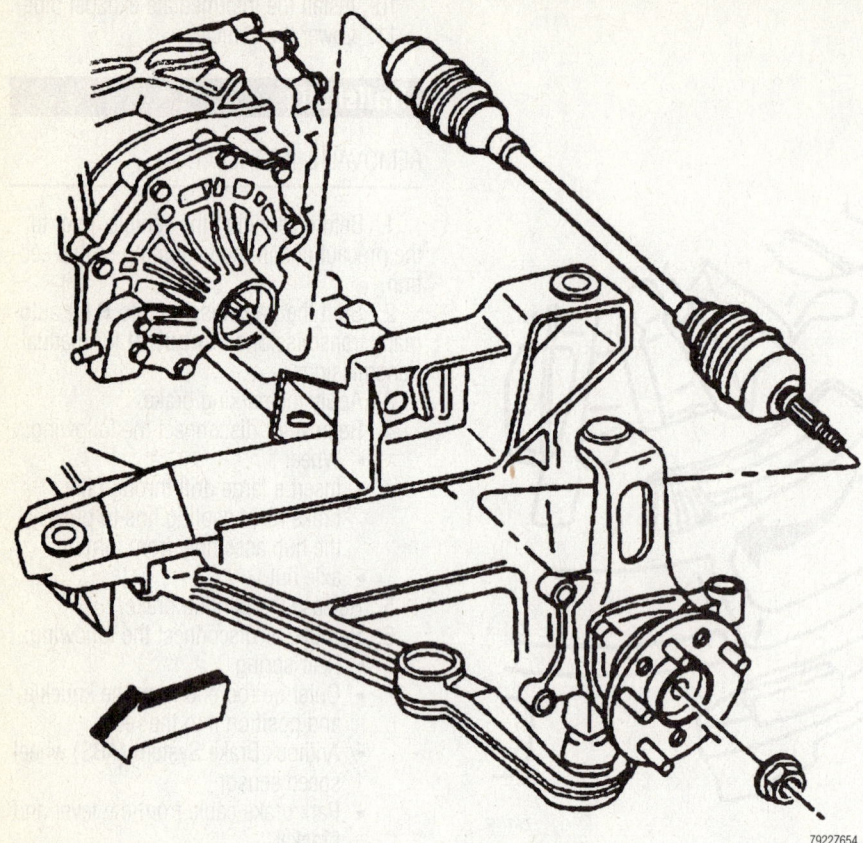

Exploded view of the halfshaft mounting—5.7L engine

➡**Be sure to support the halfshaft until it is removed. Do not let it hang by the CV-joint.**

7. Attach a puller on the wheel studs and start to push the axle shaft into the hub assembly. This will provide clearance for the ball joint to be separated from the knuckle assembly.

8. Remove or disconnect the following:

- Ball joint from the knuckle and continue to disengage the axle shaft from the hub. Support the knuckle and upper control arm while positioning it toward the front.
- Halfshaft assembly from the differential by inserting a suitable tool between the CV-joint and differential and prying them apart

To install:

9. Install or connect the following:

- Halfshaft on the differential output shaft. Use light force to be sure it is fully seated
- Halfshaft through the hub assembly but do not install completely. This will provide clearance for installing the ball joint

- Ball joint to the knuckle and insert the halfshaft through the hub assembly completely
- Park brake cable
- ABS wheel speed sensor
- Tie rod end to the knuckle
- Rear spring
- Halfshaft retaining nut. Torque the nut to 118 ft. lbs. (160 Nm). Remove the drift from the rotor
- Wheel

STEERING AND SUSPENSION

Air Bag

✳✳ CAUTION

All vehicles are equipped with an air bag system. The system must be disabled before performing service on or around system components, steering column, instrument panel components, wiring and sensors. Failure to follow safety and disabling procedures could result in accidental air bag deployment, possible personal injury and unnecessary system repairs.

PRECAUTIONS

Several precautions must be observed when handling the inflator module to avoid accidental deployment and possible personal injury.

1. Never carry the inflator module by the wires or connector on the underside of the module.

2. When carrying a live inflator module, hold securely with both hands, and ensure that the bag and trim cover are pointed away.

3. Place the inflator module on a bench or other surface with the bag and trim cover facing up.

4. With the inflator module on the bench, never place anything on or close to the module which may be thrown in the event of an accidental deployment.

DISARMING

1. Before servicing the vehicle, refer to the precautions in the beginning of this section.

2. Turn the steering wheel to align the wheels in the straight-ahead position.

3. Turn the ignition switch to the **LOCK** position.

4. Remove the AIR BAG fuse from the fuse block.

5. Remove the left side lower trim panel, then unplug the Connector Position Assurance (CPA) device and the yellow 2-way SIR harness wire connector at the base of the steering column.

ARMING

After the necessary repairs have been made, re-enable the air bag system as follows:

1. Turn the ignition switch to the **LOCK** position.

2. Engage the yellow 2-way connector and the CPA device at the base of the steering column.

3. Install the left side lower trim panel, then install the SIR fuse to the fuse block.

4. Turn the ignition switch to the **RUN** position.

5. Verify the SIR indicator light flashes 7–9 times, then turns OFF. If not, inspect system for malfunction.

Power Rack and Pinion Steering Gear

REMOVAL & INSTALLATION

1. Before servicing the vehicle, refer to the precautions in the beginning of this section.
2. Drain the power steering fluid.
3. Remove or disconnect the following:
   - Negative battery cable
   - Both front wheels
   - Intermediate shaft lower coupling from the power steering gear
   - Power steering inlet hose from the steering gear
   - Steering cooler pipe from the steering gear
   - Cooler
   - Both outer tie rod ends from the knuckles
   - Electrical connector for Magnasteer
   - Stabilizer shaft from the crossmember
   - Wire harness clips from the crossmember
   - Brake pipe from the crossmember
   - Steering gear mounting bolts and loosen the crossmember mounting nuts
   - Power steering gear through the left wheel opening

To install:

4. Install or connect the following:
   - Steering gear to the crossmember. Torque the nuts to 74 ft. lbs. (100 Nm).
   - Torque the crossmember mounting nuts 81 ft. lbs. (110 Nm).
   - Brake pipe to the crossmember
   - Stabilizer shaft
   - Both outer tie rod ends to the steering knuckle. Torque the nuts to 33 ft. lbs. (45 Nm).
   - Intermediate shaft lower steering coupling to the steering gear
   - Magnasteer electrical connector
   - Wire harness clips to the crossmember
   - Cooler to the crossmember
   - Cooler pipe to the steering gear. Torque the fitting to 20 ft. lbs. (27 Nm).
   - Inlet hose to the steering gear. Torque the fitting to 20 ft. lbs. (27 Nm).
   - Intermediate shaft shield. Torque the fitting to 32 inch lbs. (3.5 Nm).

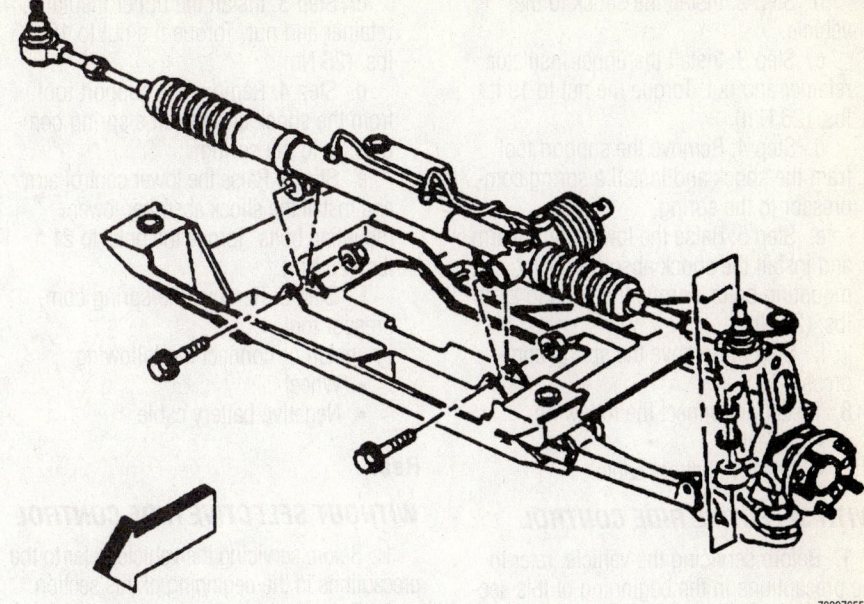

Exploded view of the power steering gear mounting—5.7L engine

- Both front wheels
- Negative battery cable
5. Refill and bleed the power steering system.
6. Check and adjust the front end alignment.

Shock Absorber

REMOVAL & INSTALLATION

Front

WITHOUT SELECTIVE RIDE CONTROL

1. Before servicing the vehicle, refer to the precautions in the beginning of this section.
2. Remove or disconnect the following:
   - Negative battery cable
   - Wheel
   - Shock absorber from the lower control arm and the shock tower. If necessary, remove the front wheel housing lower center panel to access the upper mount nut
   - Insulator and retainers from the shock absorber
3. If equipped with heavy duty shocks (FE3) perform the following steps:
   a. Step 1: Compress the shock absorber from the bottom upward.
   b. Step 2: Install a shock support tool to the shock while it is compressed.
   c. Step 3: Remove the shock from the vehicle.

   d. Step 4: Remove the tool from the shock.
4. Remove the shock absorber.

To install:

5. Install or connect the following:
   - Retainer and insulator to the shock absorber
   - Shock absorber to the upper shock tower
   - Upper insulator, retainer and nut. Torque the nut to 19 ft. lbs. (26 Nm).
   - Lower mounting bolt. Torque the bolt to 21 ft. lbs. (28 Nm).
6. If equipped with heavy duty shocks (FE3) perform the following steps:
   a. Step 1: Install a shock support tool to the shock absorber.

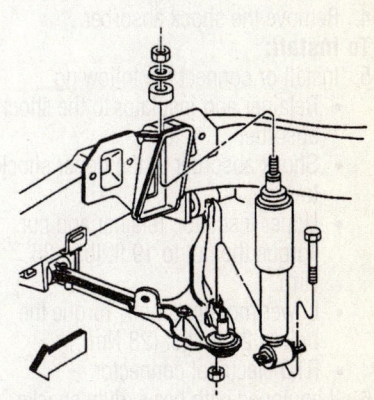

Exploded view of the front shock absorber mounting—5.7L engine

b. Step 2: Install the shock to the vehicle.

c. Step 3: Install the upper insulator, retainer and nut. Torque the nut to 19 ft. lbs. (26 Nm).

d. Step 4: Remove the support tool from the shock and install a spring compressor to the spring.

e. Step 5: Raise the lower control arm and install the shock absorber lower mounting bolts. Torque the bolts to 21 ft. lbs. (28 Nm).

f. Step 6: Remove the spring compressor tool.

8. Install or connect the following:
- Wheel
- Negative battery cable

WITH SELECTIVE RIDE CONTROL

1. Before servicing the vehicle, refer to the precautions in the beginning of this section.

2. Remove or disconnect the following:
- Negative battery cable
- Wheel
- Real Time Damper (RTD) electrical connector from the shock absorber
- Upper mounting nut retainer and insulator
- Shock absorber lower mounting bolts
- Shock absorber from the upper tower

3. If equipped with heavy duty shocks (FE3) perform the following steps:

a. Step 1: Compress the shock absorber from the bottom upward.

b. Step 2: Install a shock support tool to the shock while it is compressed.

c. Step 3: Remove the shock from the vehicle.

d. Step 4: Remove the tool from the shock.

4. Remove the shock absorber.

To install:

5. Install or connect the following:
- Retainer and insulator to the shock absorber
- Shock absorber to the upper shock tower
- Upper insulator, retainer and nut. Torque the nut to 19 ft. lbs. (26 Nm).
- Lower mounting bolt. Torque the bolt to 21 ft. lbs. (28 Nm).
- RTD electrical connector

6. If equipped with heavy duty shocks (FE3) perform the following steps:

a. Step 1: Install a shock support tool to the shock absorber.

b. Step 2: Install the shock to the vehicle.

c. Step 3: Install the upper insulator, retainer and nut. Torque the nut to 19 ft. lbs. (26 Nm).

d. Step 4: Remove the support tool from the shock and install a spring compressor to the spring.

e. Step 5: Raise the lower control arm and install the shock absorber lower mounting bolts. Torque the bolts to 21 ft. lbs. (28 Nm).

f. Step 6: Remove the spring compressor tool.

7. Install or connect the following:
- Wheel
- Negative battery cable

Rear

WITHOUT SELECTIVE RIDE CONTROL

1. Before servicing the vehicle, refer to the precautions in the beginning of this section.

2. Remove or disconnect the following:
- Negative battery cable
- Wheel
- Shock absorber lower mounting nut and washer
- Shock absorber upper bracket mounting bolt
- Shock absorber from the lower control arm and shock tower
- Upper insulator and retainer from the shock absorber
- Shock absorber

To install:

3. Install or connect the following:
- Upper insulator and retainer to the shock absorber
- Shock absorber to the shock tower and lower control arm
- Upper mounting bolts. Torque the bolts to 22 ft. lbs. (30 Nm).
- Lower shock absorber mounting bolts. Torque the bolts to 162 ft. lbs. (220 Nm).
- Wheel
- Negative battery cable

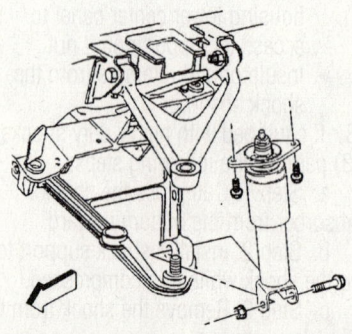

Exploded view of the rear shock absorber—5.7L engine

WITH SELECTIVE RIDE CONTROL

1. Before servicing the vehicle, refer to the precautions in the beginning of this section.

2. Remove or disconnect the following:
- Negative battery cable
- Wheel
- Rear position sensor electrical connector
- Shock absorber lower mounting nut and washer
- Shock absorber upper bracket mounting bolt
- Shock absorber from the lower control arm and shock tower
- Upper insulator and retainer from the shock absorber
- Shock absorber

To install:

3. Install or connect the following:
- Upper insulator and retainer to the shock absorber
- Shock absorber to the shock tower and lower control arm
- Upper mounting bolts. Torque the bolts to 22 ft. lbs. (30 Nm).
- Lower shock absorber mounting bolts. Torque the bolts to 162 ft. lbs. (220 Nm).
- Rear position sensor electrical connector
- Wheel
- Negative battery cable

Transverse Spring

REMOVAL & INSTALLATION

Front

1. Before servicing the vehicle, refer to the precautions in the beginning of this section.

2. Remove or disconnect the following:
- Negative battery cable
- Front wheel

3. Measure the front spring adjuster bolt gap to ease the installation procedure and setting the proper vehicle trim height.

4. Install a spring compressor tool to the spring and compress it.

5. Remove or disconnect the following:
- Lower shock absorber mounting bolts from the lower control arm
- Stabilizer shaft link from the lower control arm

6. Loosen, but do not remove, the lower ball joint nut on the lower control arm.

7. Separate the lower ball joint from the steering knuckle by using a separator tool.

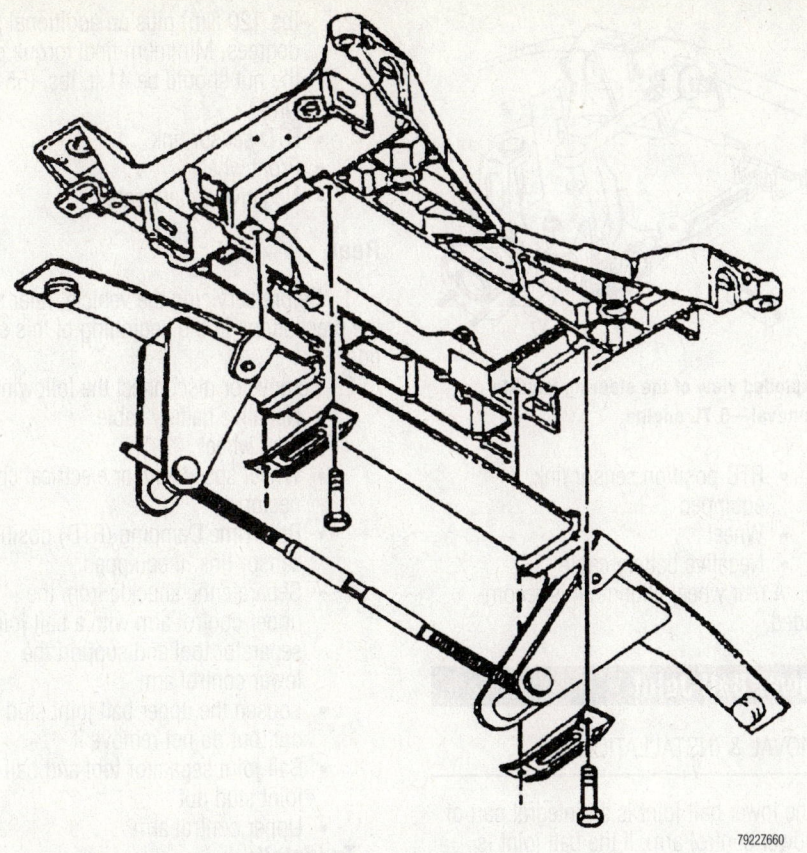

Exploded view of the front transverse spring—5.7L engine

8. Remove or disconnect the following:
- Lower ball joint nut and discard it. Support the lower control arm
- Cam bolts from the lower control arm after matchmarking them
- Lower control arm
- Transverse spring bolts and retainers
- Transverse spring and the compressor tool

To install:

9. Install or connect the following:
- Transverse spring compressor tool to the spring
- Spring to the crossmember
- New spring retainers and bolts to the crossmember. Torque the bolts to 46 ft. lbs. (62 Nm).
- Lower control arm to the crossmember
- Cam bolts to the matchmarks made during the removal procedure. Hand tighten the cam bolts at this time
- Lower control arm ball joint stud to the steering knuckle. Torque the nut to 15 ft. lbs. (20 Nm) plus an additional 210 degrees. Final torque on

the nut should be 41 ft. lbs. (55 Nm).
- Support the lower control arm and install shock absorber lower mounting bolts. Torque the bolts to 21 ft. lbs. (28 Nm).
- Stabilizer shaft link to the lower control arm. Torque the link nut to 53 ft. lbs. (72 Nm).

10. Remove the spring compressor tool from the transverse spring and move the lower control arm supports.

11. Install or connect the following:
- Front wheel
- Negative battery cable

12. Adjust the front trim height.

13. Perform a front end alignment. The cam bolts will be properly torqued during this procedure.

Rear

1. Before servicing the vehicle, refer to the precautions in the beginning of this section.

2. Remove or disconnect the following:
- Negative battery cable
- Rear wheel

3. Measure the transverse spring stud height to ease the installation procedure and setting the proper vehicle trim height.

4. Install a spring compressor tool to the spring and compress it.

5. Remove or disconnect the following:
- Spring mounting bolts, spacers and insulators from the crossmember
- Spring from the vehicle and remove the compressor tool

To install:

6. Install or connect the following:
- Spring compressor to the transverse spring
- Spring to the vehicle
- Spring spacers, insulators and mounting bolts to the crossmember. Torque the bolts to 46 ft. lbs. (62 Nm).
- Spring to the lower control arm
- Lower control arm to spring bolts and insulators and release the compressor tool
- Retainers to the lower control arm bolts and set the trim height
- Rear wheel
- Negative battery cable

7. Adjust the trim height.

8. Check and adjust the alignment, if needed.

Upper Ball Joint

REMOVAL & INSTALLATION

The upper ball joint is a part of the steering knuckle assembly and must be replaced as a complete unit. Refer to the steering knuckle procedure.

Steering Knuckle

REMOVAL & INSTALLATION

Front

1. Before servicing the vehicle, refer to the precautions in the beginning of this section.

2. Remove or disconnect the following:
- Negative battery cable
- Wheel
- Brake caliper and rotor
- Stabilizer shaft link from the lower control arm
- Wheel speed sensor electrical connector

- Separate the steering linkage outer tie rod ball stud from the knuckle
- Upper control arm ball joint stud from the knuckle
- Lower ball joint stud from the knuckle
- Knuckle

To install:

3. Install or connect the following:
- Knuckle to the upper control arm. Torque the nut 44 ft. lbs. (60 Nm).
- Knuckle to the lower control arm. Torque the nut to 55 ft. lbs. (75 Nm).
- Steering linkage outer tie rod ball stud to the knuckle. Torque the nut to 33 ft. lbs. (45 Nm).
- Stabilizer shaft link to the lower control arm. Torque the nut to 53 ft. lbs. (72 Nm).
- Wheel speed sensor electrical connector
- Brake rotor and caliper
- Wheel
- Negative battery cable

4. A front end alignment is recommended at this time.

Rear

1. Before servicing the vehicle, refer to the precautions in the beginning of this section.
2. Remove or disconnect the following:
- Negative battery cable
- Wheel
- Wheel speed sensor electrical connector
- Real Time Damping (RTD) position sensor link, if equipped
- Brake caliper and rotor
- Shock absorber solenoid electrical connector, if equipped
- Outer tie rod end
- Spindle nut retainer
- Suspension knuckle from the upper control arm
- Knuckle

To install:

3. Install or connect the following:
- Knuckle to the lower control arm ball joint stud
- Kuckle ball joint stud to the upper control arm
- Spindle nut, washer and retainer
- Outer tie rod end to the knuckle
- Brake rotor and caliper
- Wheel speed sensor electrical connector
- Shock absorber solenoid electrical connector, if equipped

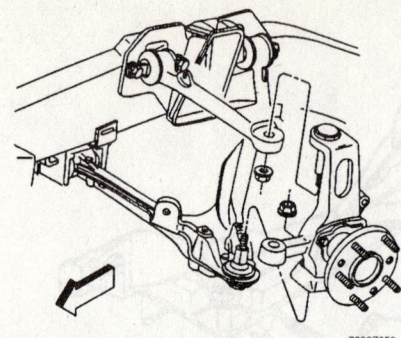

Exploded view of the steering knuckle removal—5.7L engine

- RTD position sensor link, if equipped
- Wheel
- Negative battery cable

4. A rear wheel alignment is recommended.

Lower Ball Joint

REMOVAL & INSTALLATION

The lower ball joint is an integral part of the lower control arm. If the ball joint is bad, a new lower control arm must be installed.

Upper Control Arm

REMOVAL & INSTALLATION

Front

1. Before servicing the vehicle, refer to the precautions in the beginning of this section.
2. Remove or disconnect the following:
- Negative battery cable
- Front wheel
- Real Time Damping (RTD) sensor link and support the lower control arm
- Loosen the ball joint stud nut but do not remove it
- Separate the upper ball joint from the upper control arm and remove the stud nut
- Upper control arm after noting the number and position of the shims

To install:

3. Install or connect the following:
- Upper control arm and shims. Torque the bolts to 48 ft. lbs. (65 Nm).
- Ball joint stud into the upper control arm. Torque the nut to 15 ft.

lbs. (20 Nm) plus an additional 250 degrees. Minimum final torque on the nut should be 41 ft. lbs. (55 Nm).
- RTD sensor link
- Front wheel
- Negative battery cable

Rear

1. Before servicing the vehicle, refer to the precautions in the beginning of this section.
2. Remove or disconnect the following:
- Negative battery cable
- Rear wheel
- Wheel speed sensor electrical connector
- Real Time Damping (RTD) position sensor link, if equipped
- Separate the knuckle from the upper control arm with a ball joint separator tool and support the lower control arm
- Loosen the upper ball joint stud nut, but do not remove it
- Ball joint separator tool and ball joint stud nut
- Upper control arm

To install:

3. Install or connect the following:
- Upper control arm. Torque the bolts to 81 ft. lbs. (110 Nm).
- Suspension knuckle ball joint stud nut into the upper control arm. Torque the nut to 15 ft. lbs. (20 Nm) plus an additional 250 degrees. Minimum final torque should be 41 ft. lbs. (55 Nm).
- Wheel speed sensor electrical connector
- RTD position sensor link, if equipped
- Rear wheel
- Negative battery cable

CONTROL ARM BUSHING REPLACEMENT

The manufacturer does not provide a bushing replacement procedure. The bushing is replaced when a new control arm is installed.

Lower Control Arm

REMOVAL & INSTALLATION

Front

1. Before servicing the vehicle, refer to the precautions in the beginning of this section.

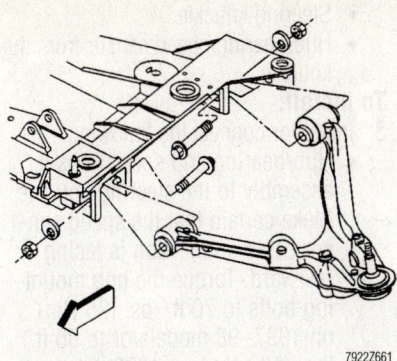

Lower control arm mounting bolts—5.7L engine

2. Remove or disconnect the following:

- Front wheel
- Front transverse spring and support the lower control arm
- Wheel speed sensor electrical connector
- Real Time Damping (RTD) electrical connector, if equipped
- Shock absorber from the lower control arm
- Stabilizer shaft link from the lower control arm
- Loosen the ball joint stud nut but do not remove the nut
- Separate the ball joint stud from the knuckle
- Cam bolts, washers and nuts after matchmarking them
- Lower control arm

To install:

3. Install or connect the following:

- Lower control arm
- Cam bolts to the position matchmarked during the removal procedure and hand tighten the bolts
- Lower ball joint stud to the knuckle after supporting the lower control arm
- Lower control arm ball joint stud to the steering knuckle. Torque the nut to 15 ft. lbs. (20 Nm) plus an additional 210 degrees. Final torque on the nut should be 41 ft. lbs. (55 Nm).
- Stabilizer shaft link to the lower control arm. Torque the link nut to 53 ft. lbs. (72 Nm).
- Transverse spring and remove the compressor tool
- Shock absorber lower mounting bolts. Torque the bolts to 21 ft. lbs. (28 Nm).

- RTD electrical connector, if equipped
- Wheel speed sensor electrical connector and remove the lower control arm support
- Front wheel
- Negative battery cable

4. Perform a front wheel alignment. Tighten the lower control arm nuts to 125 ft. lbs. (170 Nm).

Rear

1. Before servicing the vehicle, refer to the precautions in the beginning of this section.

2. Remove or disconnect the following:

- Negative battery cable
- Rear wheel
- Measure the spring stud height and remove the transverse spring mount bolt. Compress the transverse spring
- Insulators and bolts retaining the spring to the lower control arm
- Transverse spring and support the lower control arm
- Shock absorber from the lower control arm
- Loosen the ball joint stud nut but do not remove the nut
- Separate the ball joint stud from the knuckle
- Lower ball joint stud nut from the knuckle
- Stabilizer shaft link from the lower control arm
- Cam bolts, washers and nuts after matchmarking them
- Lower control arm

To install:

3. Install or connect the following:

- Lower control arm and properly support it
- Cam bolts to the position matchmarked during the removal procedure and hand tighten the bolts
- Lower ball joint stud to the knuckle
- Lower control arm ball joint stud to the steering knuckle. Torque the nut to 15 ft. lbs. (20 Nm) plus an additional 210 degrees. Final torque on the nut should be 41 ft. lbs. (55 Nm).
- Stabilizer shaft link to the lower control arm. Torque the link nut to 53 ft. lbs. (72 Nm).
- Shock absorber lower mounting bolts. Torque the bolts to 162 ft. lbs. (220 Nm).

- Transverse spring to the lower control arm and remove the compressor tool. Set the stud height to the height matchmarked during the removal procedure
- Rear wheel
- Negative battery cable

4. Perform a rear wheel alignment. Torque the lower control arm front cam bolt to 107 ft. lbs. (145 Nm) and the rear cam bolt to 70 ft. lbs. (95 Nm).

CONTROL ARM BUSHING REPLACEMENT

The manufacturer does not provide a bushing replacement procedure. The bushing is replaced when a new control arm is installed.

Wheel Bearings

ADJUSTMENT

No periodic wheel bearing adjustment is necessary. The wheel bearings are a sealed unit that must be replaced if loose or noisy.

REMOVAL & INSTALLATION

Front

1. Before servicing the vehicle, refer to the precautions in the beginning of this section.

2. Remove or disconnect the following:

- Negative battery cable
- Front wheel
- Wheel speed sensor electrical connector
- Brake caliper and rotor
- Stabilizer shaft link from the lower control arm and support the lower control arm

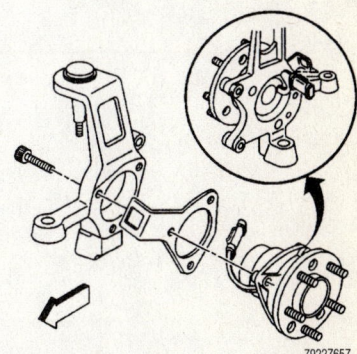

Exploded view of the front hub/wheel bearing and knuckle assembly—5.7L engine

Turn to Section 5 for brake system applications

- Separate the outer tie rod ball stud from the steering knuckle
- Lower ball joint stud from the steering knuckle
- Wheel hub/ bearing/speed sensor

To install:

3. Install or connect the following:
- Hub/bearing and speed sensor assembly to the steering knuckle. Make certain that the speed sensor cable connection is facing rearward. Torque the hub mounting bolts to 70 ft. lbs. (95 Nm) on 1997–98 models or to 96 ft. lbs. (130 Nm) on 1999–01 models.
- Lower control arm ball stud to the steering knuckle. Torque the nut to 55 ft. lbs. (75 Nm).
- Outer tie rod ball stud to the steering knuckle. Torque the nut to 33 ft. lbs. (45 Nm).
- Wheel speed sensor electrical connector
- Stabilizer shaft link to the lower control arm. Torque the nut to 55 ft. lbs. (75 Nm).
- Brake rotor and caliper
- Front wheel
- Negative battery cable

Rear

1. Before servicing the vehicle, refer to the precautions in the beginning of this section.

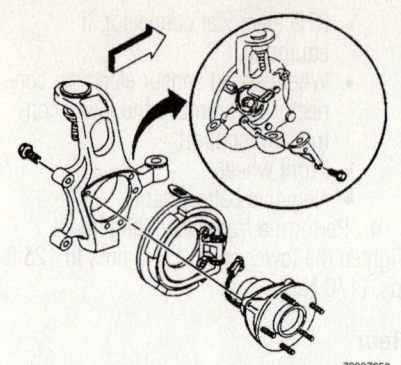

Exploded view of the rear hub/wheel bearing and knuckle assembly—5.7L engine

2. Remove or disconnect the following:
- Negative battery cable
- Rear wheel
- Wheel speed sensor electrical connector
- Real Time Damping (RTD) position sensor link, if equipped
- Brake caliper and rotor
- Shock absorber solenoid electrical connector, if equipped
- Outer tie rod end from the steering knuckle
- Spindle nut retainer, washer and nut
- Separate the upper control arm from the steering knuckle
- Steering knuckle from the lower control arm ball joint stud

- Steering knuckle
- Hub/bearing/speed sensor from the knuckle

To install:

3. Install or connect the following:
- Hub/bearing and speed sensor assembly to the steering knuckle. Make certain that the speed sensor cable connection is facing rearward. Torque the hub mounting bolts to 70 ft. lbs. (95 Nm) on 1997–98 models or to 96 ft. lbs. (130 Nm) on 1999–01 models.
- Lower control arm ball stud to the steering knuckle. Torque the nut to 55 ft. lbs. (75 Nm).
- Upper control arm to the steering knuckle. Torque the bolt to 49 ft. lbs. (65 Nm).
- Outer tie rod ball stud to the steering knuckle. Torque the nut to 33 ft. lbs. (45 Nm).
- Spindle retainer, washer and nut
- Outer tie rod ball stud to the steering knuckle. Torque the nut to 33 ft. lbs. (45 Nm).
- Brake rotor and caliper
- Electrical connectors for the wheel speed sensor, shock absorber solenoid and RTD position sensor link, if equipped
- Rear wheel
- Negative battery cable

GEO/CHEVROLET

Metro • Prizm

PRECAUTIONS

Before servicing any vehicle, please be sure to read all of the following precautions, which deal with personal safety, prevention of component damage, and important points to take into consideration when servicing a motor vehicle:

• Never open, service or drain the radiator or cooling system when the engine is hot; serious burns can occur from the steam and hot coolant.

• Observe all applicable safety precautions when working around fuel. Whenever servicing the fuel system, always work in a well-ventilated area. Do not allow fuel spray or vapors to come in contact with a spark, open flame or excessive heat (a hot drop light, for example). Keep a dry chemical fire extinguisher near the work area. Always keep fuel in a container specifically designed for fuel storage; also, always properly seal fuel containers to avoid the possibility of fire or explosion. Refer to the additional fuel system precautions later in this section.

• Fuel injection systems often remain pressurized, even after the engine has been turned **OFF**. The fuel system pressure must be relieved before disconnecting any fuel lines. Failure to do so may result in fire and/or personal injury.

• Brake fluid often contains polyglycol ethers and polyglycols. Avoid contact with the eyes and wash your hands thoroughly after handling brake fluid. If you do get brake fluid in your eyes, flush your eyes with clean, running water for 15 minutes. If eye irritation persists, or if you have taken brake fluid internally, IMMEDIATELY seek medical assistance.

• The EPA warns that prolonged contact with used engine oil may cause a number of skin disorders, including cancer! You should make every effort to minimize your exposure to used engine oil. Protective gloves should be worn when changing oil. Wash your hands and any other exposed skin areas as soon as possible after exposure to used engine oil. Soap and water, or waterless hand cleaner should be used.

• All new vehicles are now equipped with an air bag system. The system must be disabled before performing service on or around system components, steering col-

umn, instrument panel components, wiring and sensors. Failure to follow safety and disabling procedures could result in accidental air bag deployment, possible personal injury and unnecessary system repairs.

• Always wear safety goggles when working with, or around, the air bag system. When carrying a non-deployed air bag, be sure the bag and trim cover are pointed away from your body. When placing a non-deployed air bag on a work surface, always face the bag and trim cover upward, away from the surface. This will reduce the motion of the module if it is accidentally deployed. Refer to the additional air bag system precautions later in this section.

• Clean, high quality brake fluid from a sealed container is essential to the safe and proper operation of the brake system. You should always buy the correct type of brake fluid for your vehicle. If the brake fluid becomes contaminated, completely flush the system with new fluid. Never reuse any brake fluid. Any brake fluid that is removed from the system should be discarded. Also, do not allow any brake fluid to come in contact with a painted surface; it will damage the paint.

• Never operate the engine without the proper amount and type of engine oil; doing so WILL result in severe engine damage.

• Timing belt maintenance is extremely important! Many models utilize an interference-type, non-freewheeling engine. If the timing belt breaks, the valves in the cylinder head may strike the pistons, causing potentially serious (also time-consuming and expensive) engine damage. Refer to the maintenance interval charts in the front of this manual for the recommended replacement interval for the timing belt, and to the timing belt section for belt replacement and inspection.

• Disconnecting the negative battery cable on some vehicles may interfere with the functions of the on-board computer system(s) and may require the computer to undergo a relearning process once the negative battery cable is reconnected.

• When servicing drum brakes, only disassemble and assemble one side at a time, leaving the remaining side intact for reference.

ENGINE REPAIR

Distributor

REMOVAL

1. Before servicing the vehicle, refer to the precautions in the beginning of this section.

2. Remove or disconnect the following:
   • Negative battery cable
   • Spark plug wires, wiring harness and vacuum line at the distributor, if equipped
   • Distributor cap
   • Mark the position of the distributor rotor in relation to the distributor body and mark the position of the distributor body in relation to the cylinder head
   • Mark the distributor position on the housing and engine. Remove the hold-down bolt(s) and the distributor from the cylinder head. Do not rotate the engine after the distributor has been removed.
   • Distributor from the engine and the O-ring from the distributor shaft

3. Inspect all components of the assembly, including the cap and rotor, for cracks, terminal corrosion or wear and replace, if necessary.

INSTALLATION

Timing Not Disturbed

1. Install or connect the following:
   • Align the reference marks made during removal. Position carefully and be sure the drive gear engages properly within the slot.
   • Hold-down bolts but do not tighten
   • Wiring harness and spark plug wires
   • Vacuum hoses, if equipped
   • Distributor cap
   • Negative battery cable

2. Check and/or adjust the ignition timing

3. Tighten the distributor hold-down bolt(s).

Timing Disturbed

1. Remove the No. 1 spark plug

2. Place a thumb over the spark plug hole. Have someone rotate the engine by hand, using a wrench on the crankshaft pulley, until compression is felt.

3. Align the timing mark on the crankshaft pulley with the **0** degrees mark on the timing scale attached to the front of the engine. This places the engine at Top Dead Center (TDC) on the compression stroke.

4. Turn the distributor shaft until the rotor points to the No. 1 spark plug tower on the cap.

5. Install or connect the following:
   - Distributor, by aligning the distributor housing-to-cylinder head marks made during the removal procedure.
   - Spark plug wires and electrical wires
   - Vacuum advance hose, if equipped
   - Distributor cap
   - Negative battery cable

6. Check and/or adjust ignition timing.

7. Tighten the distributor hold-down bolt.

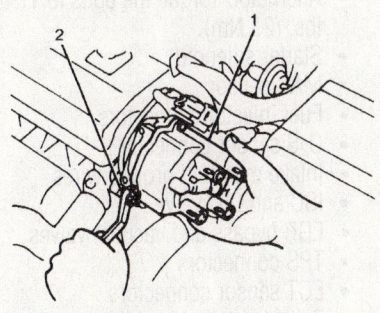

1. Distributor
2. Distributor mounting bolts

79227701

Be sure to tighten the distributor mounting bolts to prevent the timing from changing—Prizm

Ignition Timing

ADJUSTMENT

➡**The ignition timing on the Prizm is not adjustable.**

Metro

1. Before servicing the vehicle, refer to the precautions in the beginning of this section.

2. Run the engine until it reaches nor-

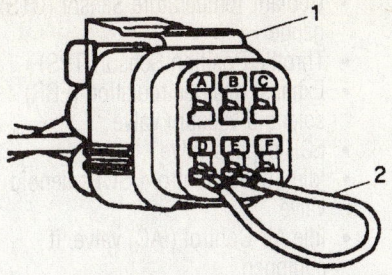

A. Blank (cavity 1)
B. Diagnostic request terminal (cavity 2)
C. Diagnostic output terminal (cavity 3)
D. Ground terminal(cavity 4)
E. Test switch terminal(cavity 5)
F. Duty check terminal(cavity 6)
1. Duty check DLC
2. Jumper

79222Z702

Jumping terminals in the 6 terminal DLC—Metro models

mal operating temperature. Stop the engine, but keep the ignition switch in the **ON** position for approximately 5 seconds. Start the engine again.

3. Run the engine at 2000 RPM for approximately 5 minutes. After 5 minutes, allow it to run at idle speed.

4. Be sure all accessories are turned **OFF**.

5. Fully engage the parking brake.

6. Be sure the shift lever is placed in the **NEUTRAL** or **PARK** depending on transaxle type.

7. Connect a tachometer to the negative terminal of the ignition coil. Connect a timing light to the No. 1 spark plug wire. Check the engine idle speed and adjust, if needed.

8. Refer to the underhood vehicle emission control information label for ignition timing specifications.

9. Remove the cap from the diagnostic check connector, located next to the ignition coil or left side strut tower and insert a fused jumper wire between appropriate the terminals.

10. On 4 terminal connectors, hold the connector with the locking tab at the top and jump the lower 2 terminals (**C** and **D**).

11. On 6 terminal connectors, hold the connector with the locking tab at the top and jump the 2 terminals at the lower left (**D** and **E**).

12. Loosen the distributor hold-down bolt and rotate the distributor until the correct timing marks are aligned.

13. Tighten the distributor hold-down bolt to 11–15 ft. lbs. (15–20 Nm) and recheck the timing. Be sure the timing advances according to engine speed.

14. Remove the diagnostic check jumper. Remove the timing light and tachometer.

Prizm

➡**If the ignition timing is out of specification, a possible engine electrical failure may have occurred. The following procedure may be used to check the timing:**

1. Before servicing the vehicle, refer to the precautions in the beginning of this section.

2. Warm the engine to normal operating temperature. Turn all electrical accessories OFF.

3. Connect a tachometer or engine scan tool and check the engine idle speed and be sure it is 650–750 rpm.

4. Connect a timing light. Remove the cap on the Data Link Connector (DLC). Using a fused jumper wire, connect terminals **E1** and **TE1**.

5. Start the engine and check timing. With the jumper wire connected, the timing should be at 10 degrees BTDC.

6. Remove the jumper wire from the DLC and reinstall the cap.

7. Shut the engine **OFF** and disconnect all test equipment.

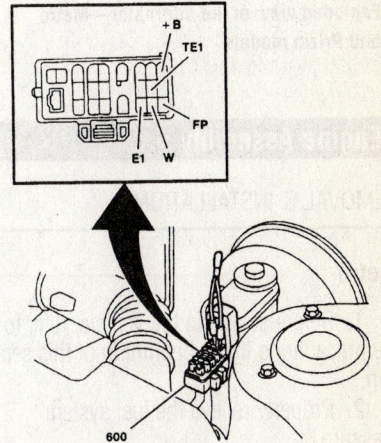

+B	SYSTEM VOLTAGE
E1	GROUND TERMINAL
FP	FUEL PUMP TERMINAL
TE1	DIAGNOSTIC REQUEST TERMINAL
W	MALFUNCTION INDICATOR LAMP (MIL) TERMINAL
600	DATA LINK CONNECTOR (DLC) (UNDER HOOD)

79222Z703

DLC pin locations—Prizm models

Alternator

REMOVAL

1. Before servicing the vehicle, refer to the precautions in the beginning of this section.
2. Remove or disconnect the following:
   - Negative battery cable
   - Drive belt. Loosen the tensioner by turning it clockwise
   - Wiring from the alternator
   - Alternator

To install:

3. Install or connect the following:
   - Alternator. Torque the bolts to 17 ft. lbs. (23 Nm).
   - Drive belt and adjust as needed. Torque the bolt to 17 ft. lbs. (23 Nm).
   - Electrical connector to the **B** terminal. Torque the nut to 71 inch lbs. (8 Nm).
   - Negative battery cable

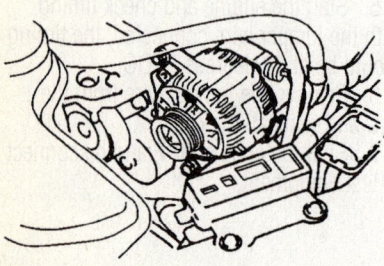

Exploded view of the alternator—Metro and Prizm models

Engine Assembly

REMOVAL & INSTALLATION

Metro

1. Before servicing the vehicle, refer to the precautions in the beginning of this section.
2. Properly relieve the fuel system pressure.
3. Drain the cooling system.
4. Drain the engine oil.
5. Remove or disconnect the following:
   - Negative battery cable
   - Hood after scribing the hood hinge to the hood
   - Air cleaner
   - Radiator and cooling fans
   - Fuel return and feed lines

- Coolant Temperature Sensor (CTS) gauge
- Throttle Position Sensor (TPS)
- Exhaust gas Recirculation (EGR) solenoid vacuum valve
- EGR bypass valve
- Idle Speed Control (ISC) solenoid valve
- Idle Air Control (IAC) valve, if equipped
- Early Fuel Evaporation (EFE) connector, if equipped
- A/C compressor switch, if equipped
- Intake manifold ground wires
- Oxygen (O$_2$S) sensor connector
- Fuel injector connector
- Manifold Absolute Pressure (MAP) sensor
- Starter solenoid connectors
- Alternator connectors
- Backup lamp switch
- Vehicle Speed Sensor (VSS) connector
- Direct clutch and second brake solenoid
- Engine vacuum lines
- Heater inlet and outlet hoses
- Accelerator cable from the throttle body
- Clutch cable, if equipped
- Gear select cable for automatic transmissions
- Oil pressure control cable for automatic transmissions
- Speedometer cable and properly support the engine assembly
- Exhaust pipe from the manifold
- Both front halfshafts

➡ **It is not necessary to disconnect the halfshaft from the knuckle.**

- Gearshift control shaft and extension, for a manual transmission
- A/C compressor and belt without disconnecting the hoses
- Power steering hoses from the pump, if equipped
- Rear torque rod bracket, for a automatic transmission

6. Attach a lifting device to the engine.
7. Remove or disconnect the following:
   - Lesf side transmission mount
   - Right side and rear engine mount
   - Engine/transmission assembly

To install:

8. Install or connect the following:
   - Engine/transmission assembly
   - Rear mount for automatic transmissions. Torque the nut to 41 ft. lbs. (55 Nm).
   - Right and left side mounts. Torque the bolts to 41 ft. lbs. (55 Nm).

9. Remove the engine lifting device and properly support the engine assembly.
10. Install or connect the following:
    - Rear torque rod bracket, if equipped. Torque the bolts to 41 ft. lbs. (55 Nm).
    - Halfshafts
    - Gearshift control shaft and extension, if equipped
    - Power steering hoses to the pump
    - A/C compressor and belt. Torque the bolts to 37 ft. lbs. (50 Nm).
    - Exhaust pipe to the manifold. Torque the bolts to 37 ft. lbs. (50 Nm).
    - Speedometer cable
    - Oil pressure control cable, if equipped
    - Gear select cable, if equipped
    - Clutch cable, if equipped
    - Accelerator cable
    - Heater inlet/outlet hoses
    - Engine vacuum lines
    - Direct clutch and second brake solenoid
    - VSS connector
    - Backup lamp switch
    - Alternator. Torque the bolts to 17 ft. lbs. (23 Nm).
    - Starter solenoid
    - MAP sensor
    - Fuel injector connectors
    - O$_2$S sensor connector
    - Intake manifold ground wires
    - ISC and IAC valve
    - EGR bypass and vacuum valves
    - TPS connectors
    - ECT sensor connectors
    - Fuel return and feed lines
    - Radiator and cooling fans. Torque the bolts to 89 inch lbs. (10 Nm).
    - Air cleaner assembly
    - Hood. Torque the bolts to 20 ft. lbs. (27 Nm).
    - Negative battery cable

11. Adjust the clutch pedal free-play, gear select cable and accelerator cable play, if equipped.
12. Fill the engine with clean oil.
13. Fill the cooling system.
14. Fill the transmission.
15. Fill the power steering reservoir.
16. Start the engine and check for leaks, repair if necessary.

Prizm

1. Before servicing the vehicle, refer to the precautions in the beginning of this section.
2. Properly relieve the fuel system pressure.

3. Drain the cooling system.
4. Drain the engine oil.
5. Drain the transmission fluid.
6. Evacuate the A/C system, if equipped.
7. Remove or disconnect the following:
   - Negative battery cable
   - Hood after scribing the hood hinge to the hood
   - Ignition coil and spark plug wires
   - Drive belt
   - Air cleaner
   - Radiator and cooling fans
   - Splash shields
   - Accelerator cable from the throttle lever, if equipped with an automatic transmission and disconnect the throttle cable from the bracket
   - Crankshaft pulley, alternator and drive belt tensioner, if equipped with manual transmission
   - Coolant reservoir support bracket
   - Windshield washer reservoir
8. If equipped with cruise control, remove of disconnect as follows:
   - Actuator cover
   - Accelerator cable from the actuator
   - 3 bolts and actuator
   - Actuator bracket
9. Remove or disconnect the following:
   - Manifold Absolute Pressure (MAP) sensor hose, brake booster hose and A/C solenoid vacuum valve hose
   - A/C solenoid vacuum valve, MAP sensor, Data Link Connector (DLC) and A/C pressure switch wiring harnesses
   - Ground wires from the intake manifold and fenders
   - Fuse and relay box
   - Evaporative Emissions (EVAP) canister
   - Heater hoses from the thermostat housing
   - Fuel feed and return hoses
   - Clutch slave cylinder, if equipped
   - Shift select cable
   - Side sill plates
   - Knee bolster, glove box and center console
   - Radio
   - Cruise control module, if equipped
   - Powertrain Control Module (PCM) wiring harness
   - A/C compressor and belt, if equipped

- Power steering pump and hose, if equipped
- Oxygen (O₂S) sensor harness
- Front exhaust pipe
- Both front halfshafts without removing them from the knuckles
10. Attach an engine hoist to the engine/transaxle assembly.
11. Remove or disconnect the following:
    - Front and rear transmission mounts
    - Left transmission mount
    - Engine/transaxle assembly
    - Starter

To install:
12. Install or connect the following:
    - Starter. Torque the bolts to 22 ft. lbs. (30 Nm).
    - Engine/transmission assembly
    - Left transmission mount. Torque the bracket bolts to 41 ft. lbs. (56 Nm), the through-bolt to 64 ft. lbs. (87 Nm) and the reinforcement bolts to 15 ft. lbs. (21 Nm).
    - Front and rear transmission mounts. Torque the front mount bolts to 47 ft. lbs. (64 Nm) and the through-bolt to 64 ft. lbs. (87 Nm). Torque the rear transmission nuts to 42 ft. lbs. (52 Nm) and the through-bolt to 64 ft. lbs. (87 Nm).
13. Remove the engine hoist and support the engine.
14. Install or connect the following:
    - Both halfshafts
    - Front exhaust pipe. Torque the bolts to 46 ft. lbs. (62 Nm).
    - O₂S sensor
    - Power steering pump and drive belt, if equipped. Torque the bolts to 27 ft. lbs. (37 Nm).
    - A/C compressor, if equipped. Torque the bolts to 18 ft. lbs. (25 Nm).
    - Wiring harness through the bulkhead into the passenger compartment and install the grommet to the bulkhead
    - PCM wiring
    - Cruise control module, if equipped. Torque the bolts to 44 inch lbs. (5 Nm).
    - Radio, knee bolster, glove box and center console
    - Left and right sill plates
    - Shift cable
    - Clutch slave cylinder, if equipped
    - Fuel return hose to the fuel pressure regulator

- Fuel feed pipe to the fuel rail, using new gaskets. Torque the bolt to 22 ft. lbs. (29 Nm).
- Heater hoses to the thermostat housing
- EVAP canister. Torque the bolt to 89 inch lbs. (10 Nm).
- Fuse and relay box. Connect the wiring and torque the bolts to 89 inch lbs. (10 Nm).
- Engine ground wires to the intake manifold and fenders
- A/C compressor switch, DLC and MAP sensor wire harness
- Hoses to the air conditioning solenoid vacuum valve (if equipped), brake booster and MAP sensor
15. If equipped with cruise control, install or connect as follows:
    - Actuator bracket. Torque the bolts to 18 ft. lbs. (25 Nm).
    - Actuator. Torque the bolts to 89 inch lbs. (10 Nm).
    - Accelerator cable
    - Actuator cover
16. Install or connect the following:
    - Windshield washer reservoir and connect the wiring harness and hose
    - Coolant reservoir. Torque the bolts to 11 ft. lbs. (15 Nm).
    - Radiator hoses
    - Air cleaner assembly. Torque the bolts to 89 inch lbs. (10 Nm).
    - EVAP canister. Torque the bolt to 89 inch lbs. (10 Nm).
    - Fuse and relay box. Torque the bolts to 89 inch lbs. (10 Nm).
    - IAC and ISC sensors
    - Radiator and cooling fans. Torque the bolts to 9 ft. lbs. (13 Nm).
    - Throttle cable
    - Accelerator cable to the throttle lever
    - Both splash shields. Torque the bolts to 89 inch lbs. (10 Nm).
    - Hood. Align and torque the bolts to 20 ft.lbs. (27 Nm).
    - Negative battery cable
17. Adjust the clutch pedal free-play, gear select cable and accelerator cable play, if equipped.
18. Recharge the A/C system.
19. Fill the engine with clean oil.
20. Fill the cooling system.
21. Fill the transmission.
22. Fill the power steering reservoir.
23. Start the engine and check for leaks, repair if necessary.

Timing belt service is covered in Section 4 of this manual

Water Pump

REMOVAL & INSTALLATION

Metro

1. Before servicing the vehicle, refer to the precautions in the beginning of this section.
2. Drain the cooling system.
3. Remove or disconnect the following:
   - Negative battery cable
   - Air cleaner
   - A/C compressor suction pipe bracket, if equipped
   - Loosen the water pump pulley bolts. Do not remove them at this time
   - Right side lower splash shield
   - A/C compressor drive belt
   - Lower alternator cover plate
   - Water pump/alternator drive belt
   - Crankshaft pulley
   - Water pump pulley
   - Timing belt
   - Dipstick tube
   - Upper alternator bracket from the water pump
   - Water pump and discard the gasket

To install:

4. Clean the gasket mating surfaces thoroughly.
5. Install or connect the following:
   - Water pump with new gasket. Torque the bolts to 115 inch lbs. (13 Nm).
   - New rubber seals
   - Upper alternator adjusting bracket
   - Oil dipstick tube
   - Timing belt
   - Water pump and crankshaft pulleys. Leave the water pump pulley bolts hand-tight
   - Alternator drive belt

- Lower alternator cover plate. Torque the bolts to 89 inch lbs. (10 Nm).
- A/C compressor drive belt, if equipped
- Right side lower splash shield.
- Torque the water pump pulley bolts to 18 ft. lbs. (24 Nm).

6. Adjust the water pump drive belt tension and torque the alternator adjustment bolt to 17 ft. lbs. (23 Nm).
7. Install or connect the following:
   - A/C compressor suction pipe bracket, if equipped
   - Air cleaner
   - Negative battery cable
8. Refill the cooling system.
9. Start the engine and check for leaks, repair if necessary.

Prizm

1.6L ENGINE

1. Before servicing the vehicle, refer to the precautions in the beginning of this section.
2. Drain the engine coolant.
3. Remove or disconnect the following:
   - Negative battery cable and properly support the engine
   - Right side engine mount and support
   - Upper and middle timing belt covers
4. If equipped with power steering remove the following components:
   - Front transmission mount
   - Radiator fan motor
   - Coolant reservoir
   - Upper radiator hose
5. Remove or disconnect the following:
   - Crankshaft Position (CKP) sensor electrical connector from the dipstick tube
   - Dipstick tube
   - Engine Coolant Temperature (ECT) sending unit
   - Coolant inlet pipe
   - Water pump and discard the O-ring

To install:

6. Install or connect the following:
   - New O-ring and Water pump. Torque the bolts to 10 ft. lbs. (14 Nm).
   - Coolant hose to the pump
   - Coolant inlet pipe. Torque the fastener to 11 ft. lbs. (15 Nm).
   - Dipstick tube. Torque the bolt to 89 inch lbs. (10 Nm).
   - ECT sending unit to the dipstick tube
   - Engine wire harness. Torque the bolt to 89 inch lbs. (10 Nm).
   - Radiator fan. Torque the bolts to 52 inch lbs. (6 Nm).
   - Upper radiator hose
   - Coolant reservoir
   - Front transmission mount. Torque the bolt to 47 ft. lbs. (64 Nm).
   - Upper and middle timing belt covers. Torque the bolts to 62 inch lbs. (7 Nm).
   - Right side transmission mount and insulator. Torque the bolt to 47 ft. lbs. (64 Nm).
   - Negative battery cable
7. Fill the cooling system.
8. Start the vehicle and check for leaks, repair if necessary.

1.8L ENGINE

1. Before servicing the vehicle, refer to the precautions in the beginning of this section.
2. Drain the engine coolant.
3. Remove or disconnect the following:
   - Negative battery cable
   - Drive belt
   - Right side lower splash shield
   - Water pump and discard the O-ring

To install:

4. Install or connect the following:
   - New O-ring and water pump. Torque the bolts to 8 ft. lbs. (11 Nm).
   - Right side lower splash shield
   - Drive belt
   - Negative battery cable
5. Fill the cooling system.
6. Start the vehicle and check for leaks, repair if necessary.

Cylinder Head

REMOVAL & INSTALLATION

Metro

1. Before servicing the vehicle, refer to the precautions in the beginning of this section.

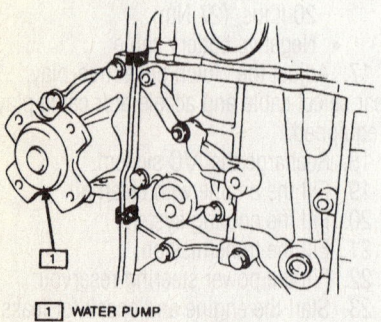

1 WATER PUMP

79222704

To ensure a tight seal, be sure gasket surfaces are properly prepared—Metro

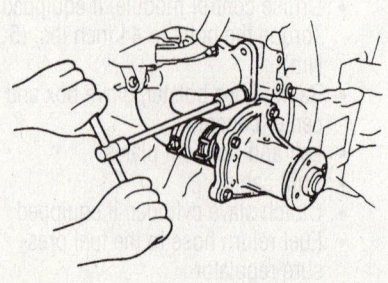

79222705

Remove the coolant inlet pipe from the block, then the pump—Prizm

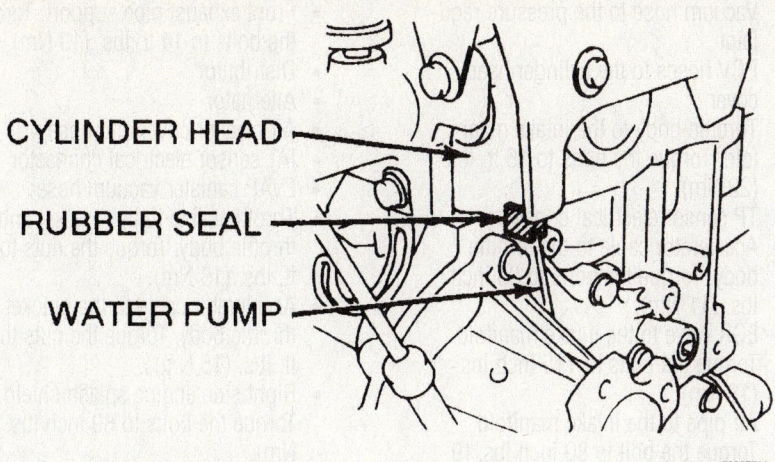

Install the rubber seal as shown—Metro

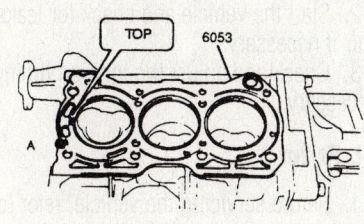

A CRANKSHAFT PULLEY SIDE
6053 CYLINDER HEAD GASKET

Cylinder head gasket positioning—1.0L engine

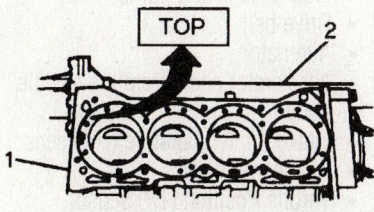

1. Cylinder head gasket
2. Cylinder block

Cylinder head gasket positioning—1.3L engine

2. Remove or disconnect the following:
   - Negative battery cable
   - Intake manifold and throttle body
   - Exhaust manifold
   - Timing belt and tensioner
   - Distributor
   - Cylinder head cover
   - Cylinder head, rubber seal and gasket
3. Clean the mating surfaces.

To install:

4. Install or connect the following:
   - New cylinder head gasket. Make certain that the "TOP" mark faces up and on the crankshaft pulley side
   - Cylinder head. Torque the bolts in 3 even stages, in sequence, to 54 ft. lbs. (73 Nm).
   - Rubber seal between the water pump and cylinder head
   - Cylinder head cover. Torque the bolts to 44 inch lbs. (5 Nm).
   - Timing belt and tensioner
   - Distributor
   - Intake manifold and throttle body. Torque the bolts to 17 ft. lbs. (23 Nm).
   - Exhaust manifold. Torque the bolts to 17 ft. lbs. (23 Nm).
   - Negative battery cable
5. Start the engine and allow it to reach normal operating temperature. Check for leaks and adjust the ignition timing, if necessary.

1.6L Prizm

1. Before servicing the vehicle, refer to the precautions in the beginning of this section.
2. Properly relieve the fuel system pressure.
3. Drain the engine coolant.
4. Drain the engine oil.
5. Remove or disconnect the following:
   - Negative battery cable
   - Right side engine splash shield
   - Accelerator cable from the throttle body
   - Throttle cable and bracket, if equipped

- Vacuum hoses from the Evaporative Emissions (EVAP) canister
- Intake Air Temperature (IAT) sensor
- Air cleaner hose
- Alternator
- Distributor
- Front exhaust pipe
- Oxygen (O₂S) sensor
- Exhaust manifold
- Thermostat housing
- Engine Coolant Temperature (ECT) sensor
- Idle Air Control (IAC) valve
- Lower radiator hose
- Engine coolant control valve and outlet hoses from the thermostat housing
- Coolant bypass hoses
- Ground strap connector
- Manifold Absolute Pressure (MAP) sensor
- A/C pressure switch electrical connector
- Exhaust Gas Recirculation (EGR) valve and vacuum modulator
- Fuel return hose from the pressure regulator
- Fuel inlet hose
- Throttle Position (TP) sensor
- Positive Crankcase Ventilation (PCV) hoses
- Cylinder head cover
- Fuel rail and injectors
- A/C compressor electrical connector, if equipped
- Oil pressure switch electrical connector
- Crankcase Position (CKP) sensor electrical connector
- Thermostat fan electrical connector
- Intake manifold
- Engine mount
- Timing belt
- Dipstick and tube
- Coolant inlet pipe
- Intake and exhaust camshafts
- Cylinder head bolts
- Cylinder head
6. Clean all mating surfaces.

To install:

7. Install or connect the following:
   - New gasket
   - Cylinder head

➡ The cylinder head bolts are in lengths of 3.54 in. (90mm) and 4.25 in. (108mm). The 3.54 in. (90mm) bolts are to be installed in the intake side of the cylinder head. The 4.25 in.

(108mm) bolts are to be installed in the exhaust manifold side of the cylinder head.

8. Torque the cylinder head bolts, in sequence, using 3 steps:
   - Step 1: 22 ft. lbs. (29 Nm).
   - Step 2: an additional 90 degrees.
   - Step 3: an additional 90 degrees.
9. Install or connect the following:
   - Intake and exhaust camshafts
   - Engine coolant inlet pipe. Torque the bolts to 11 ft. lbs. (15 Nm).
   - Coolant hose to the inlet pipe
   - Dipstick tube. Torque the bolt to 89 inch lbs. (10 Nm).
   - CKP sensor to the dipstick tube
   - Alternator mounting bracket. Torque the bolts to 19 ft. lbs. (26 Nm).
   - Front engine hanger. Torque the bolt to 20 ft. lbs. (27 Nm).
   - Engine mount. Torque bolt **A** to 47 ft. lbs. (64 Nm) and bolt **B** to 18 ft. lbs. (25 Nm).
   - Insulator to the mount. Torque the bolt to 18 ft. lbs. (25 Nm).
   - Engine mount reinforcement bracket. Torque the bolt to 18 ft. lbs. (25 Nm).
   - A/C pipe bracket, if equipped. Torque the bolt to 89 inch lbs. (10 Nm).
   - Engine mount studs. Torque the studs to 38 ft. lbs. (52 Nm).
   - Cruise control actuator, if equipped. Torque the bolts to 89 inch lbs. (10 Nm).
   - Intake manifold and new gaskets. Torque bolt **A**, in several passes, to 9 ft. lbs. (13 Nm) and bolt **B**, in several passes, to 14 ft. lbs. (19 Nm).
   - Engine wire harness retainer. Torque the bolts to 89 inch lbs. (10 Nm).
   - Engine ground strap. Torque the bolt to 89 inch lbs. (10 Nm).
   - Fan thermostat switch connector
   - Engine wire cover. Torque the bolts to 89 inch lbs. (10 Nm).
   - Oil pressure switch and A/C compressor switch electrical connectors
   - Fuel rail and injectors to the intake manifold. Torque the fuel rail bolts to 11 ft. lbs. (15 Nm).
   - Fuel injector electrical connectors
   - Fuel injector pipe to the fuel rail. Torque the union bolt to 22 ft. lbs. (29 Nm).
   - Intake chamber cover. Torque the bolts to 14 ft. lbs. (19 Nm).
   - Vacuum hose to the pressure regulator
   - PCV hoses to the cylinder head cover
   - Throttle body to the intake manifold. Torque the bolts to 16 ft. lbs. (22 Nm).
   - TP sensor electrical connector
   - Accelerator cable to the throttle body. Torque the bolts to 98 inch lbs. (11 Nm).
   - EGR valve to the intake manifold. Torque the bolts to 115 inch lbs. (13 Nm).
   - Air pipe to the intake manifold. Torque the bolt to 80 inch lbs. (9 Nm).
   - Fuel return hose to the pressure regulator
   - Intake manifold brace. Torque the 12mm bolt to 14 ft. lbs. (19 Nm) and the 14mm bolt to 29 ft. lbs. (39 Nm).
   - EGR valve and vacuum modulator. Torque the bolt to 115 inch lbs. (13 Nm).
   - EGR valve electrical connector and hose
   - Air hose to the air pipe
   - A/C vacuum hose, if equipped
   - Brake booster vacuum hose
   - Vacuum sensor hose to the fuel filter
   - Engine wire harness
   - A/C pressure switch, if equipped
   - MAP sensor electrical connector
   - Ground strap
   - Left side engine hanger. Torque the bolt to 21 ft. lbs. (28 Nm).
   - Thermostat housing. Torque the bolt to 14 ft. lbs. (20 Nm).
   - Engine coolant bypass hoses
   - EVAP valve vacuum hose
   - Inlet and outlet hoses to the thermostat housing
   - Lower radiator hose
   - IAC valve electrical connector
   - ECT sensor electrical connector
   - Engine coolant outlet housing. Torque the bolts to 14 ft. lbs. (20 Nm).
   - Upper radiator hose
   - Exhaust manifold. Torque the bolts, in several passes, to 25 ft. lbs. (34 Nm).
   - Exhaust manifold brace. Torque the bolts to 43 ft. lbs. (59 Nm).
   - Upper heat insulator. Torque the bolts to 12 ft. lbs. (17 Nm).
   - Front exhaust pipe. Torque the bolts to 46 ft. lbs. (62 Nm).
   - Front exhaust pipe support. Torque the bolts to 14 ft. lbs. (19 Nm).
   - Distributor
   - Alternator
   - Air cleaner cover and hose
   - IAT sensor electrical connector
   - EVAP canister vacuum hose
   - Throttle cable to the bracket and throttle body. Torque the nuts to 11 ft. lbs. (15 Nm).
   - Accelerator cable to the bracket and throttle body. Torque the nuts to 11 ft. lbs. (15 Nm).
   - Right side engine splash shield. Torque the bolts to 89 inch lbs. (10 Nm).
   - Negative battery cable
10. Fill the engine with new oil.
11. Fill the cooling system.
12. Start the vehicle and check for leaks, repair if necessary.
13. Check and adjust the ignition timing, if necessary.

1.8L Prizm

1. Before servicing the vehicle, refer to the precautions in the beginning of this section.
2. Properly relieve the fuel system pressure.
3. Drain the engine coolant.
4. Drain the engine oil.
5. Remove or disconnect the following:
   - Negative battery cable
   - Washer tank and pump
   - Drive belt
   - Alternator
   - Accelerator cable from the throttle body
   - Intake Air Temperature (IAT) sensor
   - Air cleaner hose
   - Throttle Position (TP) sensor
   - Idle Air Control (IAC) valve
   - Manifold Absolute Pressure (MAP) sensor
   - Coolant bypass hoses
   - Engine Coolant Temperature (ECT) sensor
   - Fuel injector connectors
   - Upper radiator hose
   - Fuel injector harness from the intake manifold
   - Oxygen (O₂S) sensor
   - Exhaust pipe
   - A/C receiver pinch clamp and move the receiver aside
   - Right side engine mount
   - Ignition coil connectors
   - Fuel line at the fuel rail
   - Secondary spark plug wires
   - Ignition coils and wires

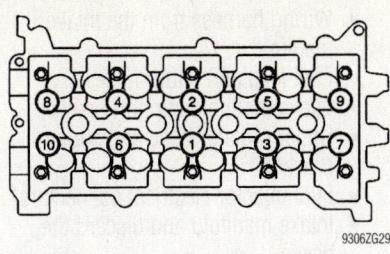

Cylinder head bolt torque sequence—1.8L Prizm

- Fuel rail
- Ground wires
- Positive Crankcase Ventilation (PCV) valve and hoses
- Cylinder head cover

6. Set the No. 1 piston to Top Dead Center (TDC) and align the camshaft timing sprockets

7. Remove or disconnect the following:
- Power steering oil pressure switch connector
- Right side lower engine splash shield
- Power steering pump
- Crankshaft pulley
- Crankcase Position (CKP) sensor
- Drive belt tensioner
- Engine mounting bracket
- Timing chain tensioner
- Timing chain cover
- Crank sensor reluctor
- Timing chain slipper
- Crankshaft sprocket
- Timing chain
- Camshaft sprockets
- Camshafts
- Intake manifold
- Cylinder head and discard the gasket

8. Clean the mating surfaces for the engine block and cylinder head.

To install:

9. Install or connect the following:
- New gasket
- Cylinder head

10. Torque the cylinder head bolts in the following sequence:
- a. Step 1: 18 ft. lbs. (25 Nm).
- b. Step 2: 36 ft. lbs. (49 Nm).
- c. Step 3: Plus an additional 90 degrees

11. Install or connect the following:
- Intake and exhaust camshafts
- Timing chain and housing
- Crankshaft pulley
- Cylinder head cover. Torque the bolts to 53 inch lbs. (6 Nm).

- ECT sensor
- Camshaft sensor. Torque the bolt to 11 ft. lbs. (15 Nm).
- Water bypass pipe. Torque the bolt to 11 ft. lbs. (15 Nm).
- Heater hoses
- Ground wires. Torque the bolts to 11 ft. lbs. (15 Nm).
- Fuel rail. Torque the bolts to 10 ft. lbs. (14 Nm).
- Fuel line to the rail
- Ignition coils. Torque the bolts to 10 ft. lbs. (14 Nm).
- Secondary spark plugs and connect the ignition coil connectors
- Right side engine mount. Torque the bolts to 40 ft. lbs. (54 Nm).
- Engine mount support bracket. Torque the bolt to 26 ft. lbs. (35 Nm).
- Exhaust pipe. Torque the bolts to 46 ft. lbs. (62 Nm).
- O_2 sensor. Torque the nuts to 30 ft. lbs. (41 Nm).
- Fuel injector harness brackets
- Vacuum hoses
- Intake manifold support bracket. Torque the bolts to 37 ft. lbs. (50 Nm).
- Fuel injector harness to the intake manifold. Torque the bolts to 106 inch lbs. (12 Nm).
- Upper radiator hose
- Fuel injector connectors
- Coolant bypass hoses
- MAP sensor connector
- IAC valve connector
- TP sensor connector
- Accelerator cable to the throttle body
- Alternator. Torque the bolts to 17 ft. lbs. (23 Nm).
- Washer pump. Torque the bolt to 89 inch lbs. (10 Nm).
- Negative battery cable

12. Fill the engine with new oil.

13. Fill and bleed the cooling system.

14. Start the vehicle and check for leaks, repair if necessary. Road test and check for proper operation.

Rocker Arms/Shafts

REMOVAL & INSTALLATION

All engines, except the 1.3L engine, do not use rocker arms/shafts, the camshaft directly actuates the valves.

1.3L Engine

1. Before servicing the vehicle, refer to the precautions in the beginning of this section.

2. Remove or disconnect the following:
- Negative battery cable
- A/C compressor and bracket, if equipped
- Cylinder head cover
- Distributor
- Rocker shaft retaining bolts. Lift out the exhaust and intake rocker arm shafts, with the springs and rocker arms attached
- If necessary, remove the rocker arms, washers and springs from the rocker shafts. Note the order in which the components are removed; they must be re-assembled in the same order and position

➡The intake and exhaust rocker arm shafts are NOT the same. Both can be distinguished by looking at the ends of the shafts, which are different. Install the intake rocker arm shaft with the stepped end toward the distributor side.

3. Inspect the rockers arms, shafts and lash adjusters for wear and/or damage; replace as necessary.

To install:

4. If disassembled earlier, assemble the springs, washers and rocker arms on to the rocker shafts.

5. Install or connect the following:
- Lubricate the rocker arms and shafts with clean engine oil. Position the intake and exhaust rocker arm shafts in their original positions. Torque the bolts, in the correct sequence, to 97 inch lbs. (11 Nm).
- Distributor
- Cylinder head cover. Torque the bolts to 44 inch lbs. (5 Nm).
- A/C compressor and bracket, if equipped
- Negative battery cable

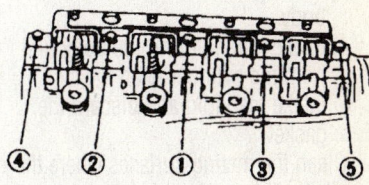

Rocker arm shaft retaining bolts tightening sequence—1.3L engines

Refer to Section 1 for engine rebuilding specifications

Intake Manifold

REMOVAL & INSTALLATION

Metro

1. Before servicing the vehicle, refer to the precautions in the beginning of this section.
2. Relieve the fuel system pressure.
3. Drain the cooling system.
4. Remove or disconnect the following:
   - Negative battery cable
   - Air cleaner
   - Engine Coolant Temperature (ECT) sensor connector
   - ECT sending unit connector
   - Throttle Position (TP) sensor connector
   - Exhaust Gas Recirculation (EGR) valve
   - Idle Air Control (IAC) valve
   - Ground wires from the intake manifold
   - Heated Oxygen (HO2S) sensor harness
   - Throttle body electrical connector
   - Manifold Absolute Pressure (MAP) sensor connector
   - Oil pressure switch electrical connector
   - Early Fuel Evaporative (EFE) heater electrical connector, if equipped
   - Alternator electrical connector
   - Starter solenoid electrical connectors
   - Fuel feed and return hoses from the throttle body
   - Coolant hoses from the throttle body
   - Evaporative Emissions (EVAP) canister vacuum hose
   - MAP sensor hose from the intake manifold
   - Brake booster vacuum hose
   - IAC valve vacuum hose
   - Positive Crankcase Ventilation (PCV) vacuum hose
   - Accelerator cable from the throttle body
   - Intake manifold/throttle body unit from the cylinder head
   - Intake manifold and discard the gasket
5. Clean the mating surfaces where the new gasket will be installed.

To install:
6. Install or connect the following:
   - New gasket to the cylinder head
   - Intake manifold. Torque the bolts to 17 ft. lbs. (23 Nm).
     - PCV hose to the cylinder head cover
   - EVAP canister vacuum hose
   - MAP sensor vacuum hose
   - Brake booster vacuum hose
   - IAC vacuum hose to the throttle body
   - Coolant hoses
   - Fuel feed/return hoses
   - ECT sensor electrical connector
   - EFE heater electrical connector, if equipped
   - ECT switch electrical connector
   - TP sensor electrical connector
   - EGR solenoid valve electrical connector
   - IAC valve/ISC motor electrical connectors
   - Ground wires to the intake manifold
   - HO2S sensor harness
   - Throttle body electrical connector
   - ECT sending unit connector
   - Oil pressure switch electrical connector
   - Alternator wires
   - Starter wires
   - Wiring harness to the retaining clamps
   - Accelerator cable to the throttle body and adjust as needed
   - Air cleaner
   - Negative battery cable
7. Fill the cooling system.
8. Start the vehicle and check for leaks, repair if necessary.

Prizm

1. Before servicing the vehicle, refer to the precautions in the beginning of this section.
2. Relieve the fuel system pressure.
3. Drain the cooling system.
4. Remove or disconnect the following:
   - Negative battery cable
   - Accelerator and throttle valve cables from the throttle body
   - Vacuum sensor hose from the fuel fitler
   - Brake booster vacuum hose
   - A/C vacuum hoses from the actuator, if equipped
   - Intake Air Temperature (IAT) sensor
   - Air cleaner hose from the throttle body
   - Air cleaner
   - Throttle Position (TP) sensor
   - Idle Air Control (IAC) valve
   - Manifold Absolute Pressure (MAP) sensor
   - Coolant bypass hoses
   - Wiring harness from the intake manifold
   - Fuel feed and return hoses
   - Intake manifold support bracket
   - Upper radiator hose and support bracket
   - Fuel injector electrical connectors
   - Intake manifold and discard the gasket
5. Clean all gasket mating surfaces.

To install:
6. Install or connect the following:
   - New gasket
   - Intake manifold. Torque the bolts to 13 ft. lbs. (18 Nm).
   - Engine wire harness to the intake manifold. Torque the bolt to 89 inch lbs. (10 Nm).
   - Upper radiator hose and support bracket. Torque the bolt to 13 ft. lbs. (18 Nm).
   - Intake manifold support bracket. Torque the bolts to 13 ft. lbs. (18 Nm).
   - Fuel injector wire harness. Torque the bolts to 10 ft. lbs. (14 Nm).
   - Fuel injector connectors to the fuel injectors
   - Fuel inlet pipe to the fuel rail. Torque the union bolt to 22 ft. lbs. (29 Nm).
   - Coolant bypass hoses
   - MAP sensor
   - IAC valve
   - TP sensor
   - Air cleaner and connect the hose to the throttle body
   - IAT sensor
   - A/C vacuum hoses to the actuator, if equipped
   - Brake booster vacuum hose
   - Vacuum sensor hose to the fuel filter
   - Accelerator cable. Torque the bolts to 98 inch lbs. (11 Nm).
   - Throttle valve cable. Torque the bolts to 11 ft. lbs. (15 Nm).
   - Negative battery cable
7. Fill the cooling system.
8. Start the vehicle and check for leaks, repair if necessary.

Exhaust Manifold

REMOVAL & INSTALLATION

Metro

1. Before servicing the vehicle, refer to the precautions in the beginning of this section.

2. Remove or disconnect the following:
- Negative battery cable
- Front pipe from the exhaust manifold
- Oxygen (O_2S) sensor electrical connector
- Exhaust manifold heat shield
- Spark plug wires
- Exhaust manifold and discard the gasket

3. Clean all gasket mating surfaces.

To install:

4. Install or connect the following:
- New gasket
- Exhaust manifold. Torque the bolts to 17 ft. lbs. (23 Nm).
- Exhaust manifold heat shield. Torque the bolts to 11 ft. lbs. (15 Nm).
- Front pipe to the exhaust manifold. Torque the bolts to 37 ft. lbs. (50 Nm).
- Spark plug wires to the spark plugs
- O_2S electrical connector
- Negative battery cable

5. Start the vehicle and check for exhaust leaks, repair if necessary.

Prizm

1. Before servicing the vehicle, refer to the precautions in the beginning of this section.

2. Remove or disconnect the following:
- Neagtive battery cable
- Oxygen (O_2S) sensor and sub-oxygen sensor connectors, if equipped
- Front exhaust pipe from the exhaust manifold
- Exhaust manifold support bracket
- Exhaust manifold heat shield
- Lower heat shield from the exhaust manifold
- Exhaust manifold and discard the gasket

3. Clean all gasket mating surfaces.

To install:

4. Install or connect the following:
- Lower heat shield. Torque the bolts to 11 ft. lbs. (15 Nm).
- New gasket to the cylinder head
- Exhaust manifold. Torque the bolts to 43 ft. lbs. (59 Nm).
- Upper exhaust manifold heat shield. Torque the bolts to 11 ft. lbs. (15 Nm).
- Exhaust manifold support bracket. Torque the bolts to 24 ft. lbs. (32 Nm).
- Front pipe to the exhaust manifold.

Torque the bolts to 46 ft. lbs. (62 Nm).
- O_2sensor. Torque the fasteners to 30 ft. lbs. (41 Nm).
- Negative battery cable

5. Start the vehicle and check for exhaust leaks, repair if necessary.

Front Crankshaft Seal

REMOVAL & INSTALLATION

Metro

1. Before servicing the vehicle, refer to the precautions in the beginning of this section.

2. Drain the engine oil.

3. Remove or disconnect the following:
- Negative battery cable
- Timing belt
- Crankshaft sprocket
- Oil pan
- Oil pump and identify the bolts to ease installation
- Crankshaft oil seal using a removal tool

To install:

4. Lubricate the lip of the new seal with clean engine oil.

5. Install or connect the following:
- New oil seal into the oil pump body. Make certain that the seal is properly seated
- Oil pump while using an oil seal protector to aid installation. Torque the bolts to 97 inch lbs. (11 Nm).

➡**Take care not to damage the front seal on the crankshaft snout.**

- Crankshaft sprocket. With the crankshaft locked, torque the bolt to 81 ft. lbs. (110 Nm).

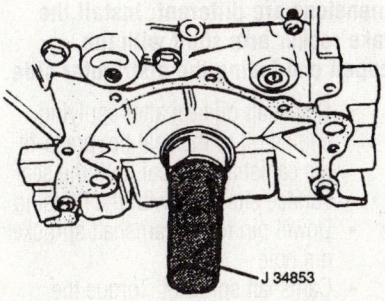

79222Z713

To prevent damage to the lip of the seal use an oil seal protector as shown—Metro

- Oil strainer and pan
- Timing belt
- Negative battery cable

6. Fill the engine with new oil.

7. Start the vehicle and check for leaks, repair if necessary.

Prizm

1. Before servicing the vehicle, refer to the precautions in the beginning of this section.

2. Remove or disconnect the following:
- Negative battery cable
- Drive belt
- Right side splash shield
- Timing belt
- Crankshaft pulley
- Crankshaft front seal

To install:

3. Apply clean engine oil to the new oil seal and lubricate the lip of the oil seal with multi-purpose grease.

4. Install or connect the following:
- New oil seal using a seal driver. Make certain that the seal is flush against the retainer edge
- Timing belt
- Crankshaft pulley. Torque the bolt to 105 ft. lbs. (140 Nm).
- Right side splash shield.
- Drive belt
- Negative battery cable

5. Start the vehicle and check for leaks, repair if necessary.

Camshaft

REMOVAL & INSTALLATION

Metro

1. Before servicing the vehicle, refer to the precautions in the beginning of this section.

2. Remove or disconnect the following:
- Negative battery cable
- A/C compressor and bracket, if equipped
- Cylinder head cover
- Distributor
- Timing belt and tensioner
- Camshaft timing belt sprocket. Lock the camshaft with a 0.39 in. (10mm) rod inserted into the hole in the camshaft, before loosening the sprocket retaining bolt.

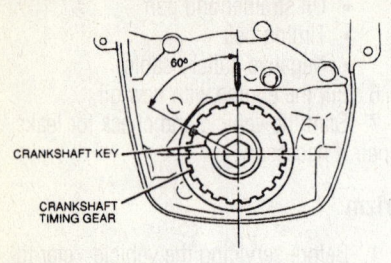

Position the crankshaft as shown before removing the camshaft—Metro with 1.0L engines

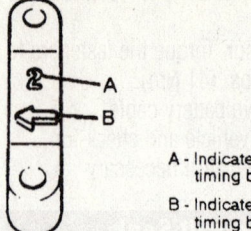

A - Indicates position from timing belt

B - Indicates direction to timing belt

Directional markings for the camshaft bearing caps—Metro with 1.0L engine

❋❋ WARNING

The mating surface of the cylinder head and cover must not be damaged during this procedure. Place a clean shop cloth between the rod and mating surfaces and use care not to bump the rod when loosening.

3. On 1.3L engines, remove the rocker arms and shafts from the cylinder head. Keep all parts in order so they can be reinstalled in their original locations. The intake and exhaust rocker arm shafts are different. Be sure to identify them as they are removed.

4. Turn the crankshaft until the crankshaft sprocket timing mark is 60 degrees to the left of the arrow mark on the oil pump case.

5. Remove or disconnect the following:
- Camshaft caps from the cylinder head
- Camshaft

6. On 1.3L engine, remove the camshaft from the cylinder head by removing it from the flywheel end.

To install:

7. Fill the oil passage in the cylinder head with clean engine oil. Pour engine oil through the camshaft journal oil holes and check that engine oil comes out from the oil holes in the lash adjuster bores.

8. Install the camshaft in the cylinder head. After applying engine oil to the camshaft journal and all around the cam, position the camshaft so the camshaft timing sprocket pin hole in the camshaft is at the lower position.

9. On 1.0L engines, install the camshaft bearing caps to the camshaft and the cylinder head as follows:

a. Apply clean engine oil to the sliding surface of each bearing cap against the camshaft journal

b. Apply silicone sealant to the mating surface of the No. 1 and No. 3 bear-

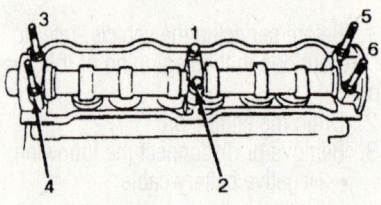

Torque sequence for the camshaft bearing cap bolts—Metro with 1.0L engine

ing cap which will mate with the cylinder head.

c. There are marks provided on each camshaft bearing cap indicating the position and direction for installation. Install the bearing cap as indicated by the marks.

d. Camshaft bearing cap No. 1 is installed first. It retains the camshaft in the proper position and thrust direction. Apply clean engine oil to the retaining bolts and install but do not tighten fully.

10. Install or connect the following:
- Camshaft bearing caps and bolts. Torque the bolts evenly, repeating the tightening sequence 3–4 times to 96 inch lbs. (11 Nm).

➡ **On 1.3L engines, the exhaust and intake rocker shafts are different. To distinguish between them, the end dimensions are different. Install the intake rocker arm shaft with the stepped end facing the distributor side.**

- Camshaft oil seal after applying engine oil to the seal lip, press-fit the camshaft oil seal until the seal surface sits flush with the housing
- Dowel pin to the camshaft sprocket pin hole
- Camshaft sprocket. Torque the retaining bolt to 44 ft. lbs. (60 Nm).
- New valve cover gasket and apply a small bead of silicone to the corners
- Valve cover. Torque the bolts to 44 inch lbs. (5 Nm).

- Timing belt
- Distributor to the cylinder head and connect the spark plug wires
- A/C compressor and bracket, if equipped
- Negative battery cable

11. Start the engine and check the ignition timing. Adjust the timing as necessary.

➡ **When the engine is started, if air is trapped in the Hydraulic Valve Lash (HVL) adjuster, the valve may make a tapping sound when the engine is operated after the HVL adjuster is installed. In such a case, run the engine at 2000 rpm until the air is purged and the tapping sound ceases.**

Prizm

1997

1. Before servicing the vehicle, refer to the precautions in the beginning of this section.

2. Remove or disconnect the following:
- Negative battery cable

❋❋ CAUTION

You must wait at least 90 seconds from the time the ignition switch is turned to the LOCK position and the negative battery cable is disconnected before starting work.

- Spark plug wires
- Valve cover
- Timing belt

3. Set the exhaust camshaft so the knock pin is slightly above the cylinder head (10 o'clock position). This angle allows the No. 1 and No. 3 cylinder cam lobes of the intake camshaft to push the lash adjusters evenly.

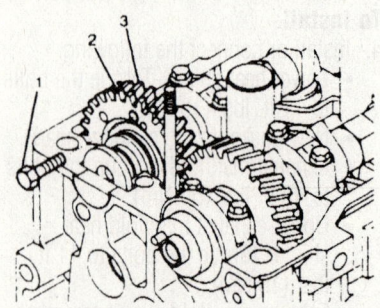

1. M6X1.0X 16 - 20 mm service bolt
2. Intake camshaft sub-gear
3. Intake camshaft main gear

Fastening the sub-gear to the main gear—Prizm

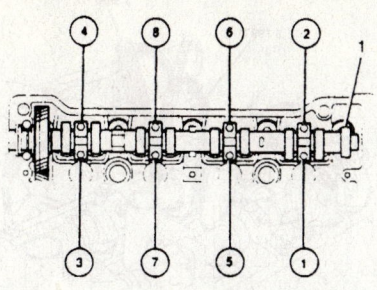

1. Intake camshaft

79222718

Intake camshaft bearing cap removal sequence—Prizm

4. Remove or disconnect the following:
- Bolts and the front bearing cap of the intake camshaft

5. Secure the intake camshaft end gear to the sub gear with a service bolt. The service bolt should match the following specifications:

    a. Thread diameter: 6.0mm

    b. Thread pitch: 1.0mm

    c. Bolt length: 16mm

    d. Uniformly loosen each intake camshaft bearing cap bolt in several passes in the proper sequence.

✺✺ WARNING

The camshaft must be held level while it is being removed. If not, the portion of the cylinder head receiving the thrust may become damaged. This could cause the camshaft to bind or break.

6. Remove or disconnect the following:
- Bearing caps and intake camshaft

➡️**If the camshaft cannot be removed straight and level, install and retighten the No. 3 bearing cap. Alternately loosen the bolts on the bearing cap a little at a time while pulling upwards on the camshaft gear. DO NOT attempt to pry or force the cam loose.**

7. Turn the exhaust camshaft approximately 105 degrees, so the guide pin is just past the 4 o'clock position. This angle allows the No. 1 and the No. 3 cylinder cam lobes of the exhaust camshaft to push the lash adjusters evenly.

8. Loosen the exhaust camshaft bearing cap bolts uniformly in several passes in sequence.

9. Remove the bearing caps and exhaust camshaft.

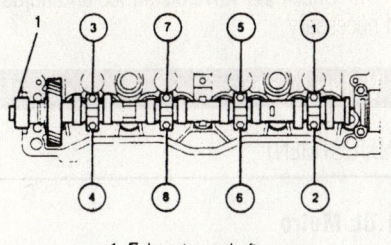

1. Exhaust camshaft

79222719

Exhaust camshaft bearing cap removal sequence—Prizm

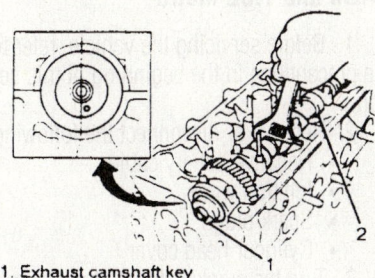

1. Exhaust camshaft key
2. Exhaust camshaft

79222720

Positioning the exhaust camshaft for removal—Prizm

To install:

10. Apply multi-purpose grease to the thrust portion of the camshaft.

11. Install or connect the following:
- Exhaust camshaft on the cylinder head so the cam lobes press evenly on the lash adjusters for cylinders Nos. 1 and 3. This will place the guide pin on the camshaft slightly counter clockwise at about 4 o'clock.
- 5 bearing caps in position, after lightly coating them with clean engine oil, according to the number cast in the cap. Torque the bearing cap bolts uniformly and in several passes in the proper sequence to 115 inch lbs. (13 Nm).

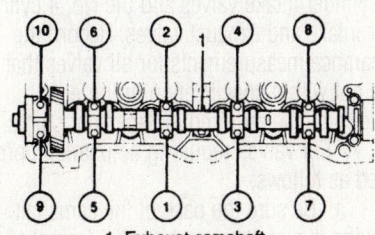

1. Exhaust camshaft

79222721

Exhaust camshaft bearing cap tightening sequence—Prizm

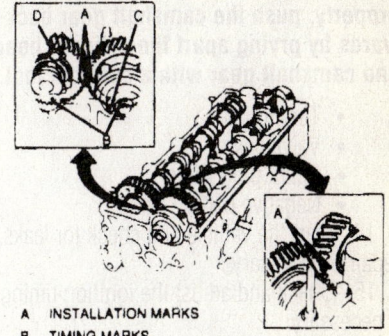

A   INSTALLATION MARKS
B   TIMING MARKS
C   EXHAUST CAMSHAFT KEY
D   INTAKE CAMSHAFT SERVICE BOLT

79222722

Engaging the intake camshaft with the exhaust camshaft—Prizm

- New camshaft oil seal after coating the lip with lithium
- Intake camshaft so the guide pin is slightly above the cylinder head and apply multi-purpose grease to the thrust portion of the intake camshaft

12. Hold the intake camshaft next to the exhaust camshaft and engage the gears by matching the alignment marks.

➡️**DO NOT use the Top Dead Center (TDC) timing marks for the timing belt.**

13. Install or connect the following:
- With the gears still engaged, roll the intake camshaft down and into the bearing journals. This angle allows the No. 1 and the No. 3 cylinder cam lobes of the camshaft to push the lash adjusters evenly.
- Install the bearing caps after coating the bolts with clean engine oil. Observe the numbers on each cap and make certain the arrows point to the pulley end of the motor. Torque the bolts in several passes in the proper sequence to 115 inch lbs. (13 Nm).

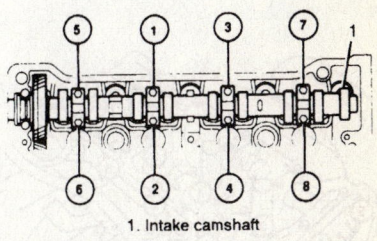

1. Intake camshaft

79222723

Intake camshaft bearing cap tightening sequence—Prizm

➡ If the No. 1 bearing cap does not fit properly, push the camshaft gear backwards by prying apart the cylinder head and camshaft gear with a suitable tool.

- Timing belt
- Valve cover
- Spark plug wires
- Negative battery cable

14. Start the vehicle and check for leaks, repair if necessary.

15. Check and adjust the ignition timing, if necessary.

Prizm

1998–01

➡ The procedure is the same for the exhaust camshaft and the intake camshaft.

1. Before servicing the vehicle, refer to the precautions in the beginning of this section.
2. Remove or disconnect the following:
- Negative battery cable
- Timing chain
- Camshaft sprocket bolt
- Camshaft sprocket
- Camshaft bearing cap bolts, in sequence, by starting at the ends and working towards the center of the camshaft
- Camshaft from the cylinder head

To install:

3. Install or connect the following:
- Camshaft to the cylinder head with the No. 1 cam lobes facing the proper direction
- Camshaft bearing caps in their proper location and direction. Each cap has a number and directional arrow marked on it. Torque the bolts in sequence to 10 ft. lbs. (13 Nm). Torque the front bearing cap bolts to 17 ft. lbs. (23 Nm).
- Sprocket to the camshaft. Torque the bolt to 33 ft. lbs. (44 Nm).
- Timing chain
- Negative battery cable

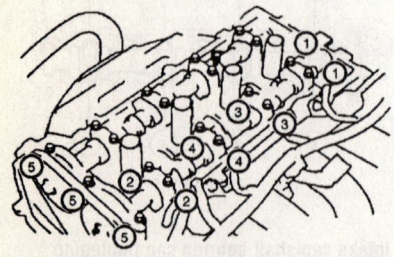

Camshaft bearing cap tightening sequence—1998–01 Prizm

4. Check the valve clearance and adjust if necessary.

Valve Lash

ADJUSTMENT

1.0L Metro

Lash adjusters, located between the camshaft and valve stems, are used to adjust the valve clearance to 0 lash automatically at all times. Adjustment is not required.

Prizm and 1.3L Metro

1. Before servicing the vehicle, refer to the precautions in the beginning of this section.
2. Remove or disconnect the following:
- Negative battery cable
- Ignition wires
- Spark plugs
- Cylinder head cover
3. Turn the crankshaft until the piston in No. 1 cylinder is at Top Dead Center (TDC) on the compression stroke. Align the groove in the crankshaft pulley with the **0** mark on the timing belt cover. Be sure No. 1 cylinder lash adjusters are loose and those on No. 4 are tight. If not, turn the crankshaft pulley 1 full revolution (360 degrees) and again align the mark on the crankshaft pulley.
4. The intake valve clearance should be 0.006–0.010 in. (0.15–0.25mm) and the exhaust valve clearance should be 0.010–0.014 in. (0.25–0.35mm).
5. Using a feeler gauge, measure the clearance between the camshaft and valve lifter shim at the No. 1 cylinder intake and exhaust valves, the No. 2 cylinder intake valves and the No. 3 cylinder exhaust valves. Record the clearance measurements for all valves that are not within specification, in order to determine the required replacement shims.
6. Rotate the crankshaft pulley 1 full turn (360 degrees) and check the clearance at the No. 2 cylinder exhaust valves, the No. 3 cylinder intake valves and the No. 4 cylinder intake and exhaust valves. Record the clearance measurements for all valves that are not within specification, in order to determine the required replacement shims.
7. For valves requiring adjustment, proceed as follows:
   a. Be sure the base of the camshaft lobe is directly over the valve (camshaft lobe pointing away from the valve).
   b. Insert tool J-3987-1 between the camshaft and lifter adjustment shim, to compress the valve spring and push the lifter down.

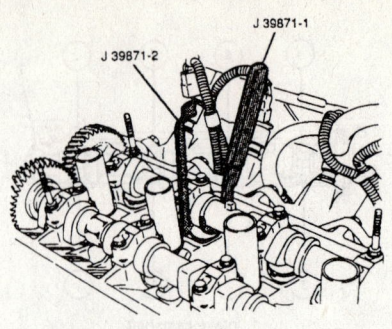

J 39871-1
J 39871-2

7922Z724

Using the valve clearance adjustment tool set to hold the lifter

   c. Insert tool J-39871-2 between the camshaft and the lifter, to hold the lifter away from the camshaft. Position the bottom edge of the tool on the lifter.
   d. Using a small screwdriver and a magnet, remove the adjustment shim from the top of the lifter.
   e. Use the micrometer to measure the thickness of the removed shim. Determine the thickness of the new shim using the formula below. For the purposes of the following formula, T = Thickness of the shim removed; A = Valve clearance measured; N = Thickness of the required new shim.
8. For the intake camshaft valves: N = T + A—0.008 in. (0.20mm)
9. For the exhaust camshaft valves: N = T + A—0.010 in. (0.25mm)
   a. Select a shim closest to the calculated thickness. Shims are available in 16 sizes, in increments of 0.002 in. (0.050mm), from 0.1004 in. (2.55mm) to 0.1299 in. (3.30mm).
   b. Install the shim on the valve lifter and remove tool J-39871-2. Recheck the valve clearance.
10. Install or connect the following:
- Cylinder head cover, using a new gasket. Tighten the nuts to 53 inch lbs. (6 Nm).
- Spark plugs
- Ignition wires
- Negative battery cable
11. Run the engine and check operation.

Starter

REMOVAL & INSTALLATION

Metro

1. Before servicing the vehicle, refer to the precautions in the beginning of this section.

2. Remove or disconnect the following:
- Negative battery cable
- Positive battery cable
- Starter solenoid electrical connector
- Starter

To install:
3. Install or connect the following:
- Starter. Torque the bolts to 17 ft. lbs. (23 Nm).
- Positive battery cable
- Negative battery cable

Prizm

1997

1. Before servicing the vehicle, refer to the precautions in the beginning of this section.
2. Remove or disconnect the following:
- Negative battery cable
- Intake Air Temperature (IAT) sensor from the air cleaner
- Air cleaner clips, hose and cap from the lower housing and throttle body
- Starter motor electrical connector
- Positive battery cable
- Starter

To install:
3. Install or connect the following:
- Starter. Torque the bolts to 27 ft. lbs. (37 Nm).
- Positive battery cable
- Starter motor electrical connector
- Air cleaner hose, cap and clips. Torque the hose fastener to 11 ft. lbs. (15 Nm).
- IAT sensor to the air cleaner
- Negative battery cable

1998–01

1. Before servicing the vehicle, refer to the precautions in the beginning of this section.
2. Remove or disconnect the following:
- Negative battery cable
- Upper mounting bolt
- Right side splash shield
- Starter motor electrical connector
- Positive battery cable
- Starter

To install:
3. Install or connect the following:
- Starter. Torque the bolts to 27 ft. lbs. (37 Nm).
- Starter motor electrical connector
- Positive battery cable
- Right side splash shield
- Negative battery cable

Oil Pan

REMOVAL & INSTALLATION

Metro

1. Before servicing the vehicle, refer to the precautions in the beginning of this section.
2. Drain the engine oil.
3. Remove or disconnect the following:
- Negative battery cable
- Front pipe from the exhaust manifold and separate it from the center/resonator pipe
- Catalytic converter
- Crankshaft Position (CKP) sensor
- Flywheel inspection cover
- Oil pan
- Oil pump strainer and bracket
4. Clean the mating surface of the oil pan and the cylinder block.
5. Clean the oil pan and oil pump strainer.

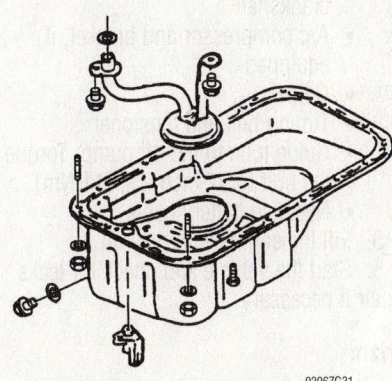

9306ZG31

Exploded view of the oil pan and strainer—Metro

To install:
6. Install or connect the following:
- New oil pump strainer seal
- Oil pump strainer to the cylinder block. Torque the bolts to 97 inch lbs. (11 Nm).
- Oil pan to the cylinder block after applying a continuous bead of sealant around the oil pan. Torque the bolts to 97 inch lbs. (11 Nm) starting in the center and working outward.
- CKP sensor
- Flywheel inspection cover
- Front pipe to the exhaust manifold
- Center pipe to the front pipe
- Catalytic converter
- Negative battery cable

7. Fill the engine with new oil.
8. Start the vehicle and check for leaks, repair if necessary.

Prizm

1. Before servicing the vehicle, refer to the precautions in the beginning of this section.
2. Drain the engine oil.
3. Remove or disconnect the following:
- Negative battery cable
- Oxygen (O_2S) sensor electrical connector
- Right side lower splash shield
- Front exhaust pipe from the exhaust manifold
- Front end center support
- Oil pan
- Oil pump strainer
4. Clean all gasket material from the mating surfaces.

To install:
5. Install or connect the following:
- Oil pump strainer with a new seal. Torque the bolt to 80 inch lbs. (9 Nm).
- Apply a continuous bead of RTV sealant to the engine oil pan. Torque the bolts to 97 inch lbs. (11 Nm) starting in the center and working outward.
- Exhaust pipe with a new seal to the manifold. Do not fully tighten the bolts.
- Apply a bead of RTV sealant to the powertrain reinforcement brace-to-

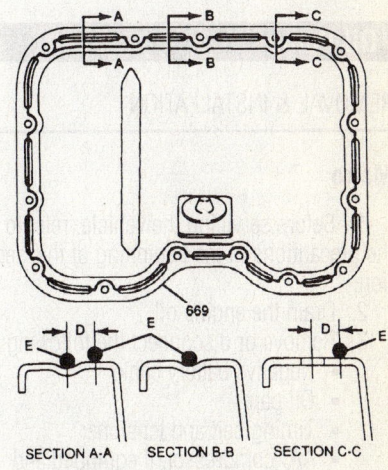

7922Z725

To ensure a leak-free seal, apply sealer as shown—Prizm 1.8L engine

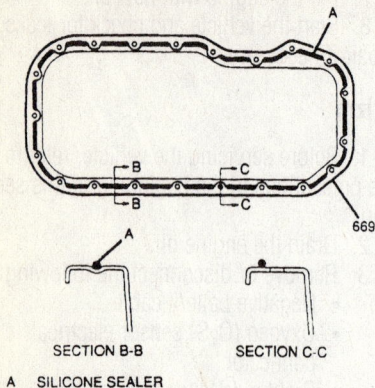

SECTION B-B   **SECTION C-C**

A   SILICONE SEALER
669   OIL PAN

7922Z726

To ensure a leak-free seal, apply sealer as shown—Prizm 1.6L engine

cylinder block mating surface and install tighten the Torx• bolts to 12 ft. lbs. (16 Nm) and remaining bolts to 69 inch lbs. (7.8 Nm). Torque the 3 brace-to-transaxle bolts to 17 ft. lbs. (23 Nm).
- Lower engine reinforcement brace. Torque the bolts to 47 ft. lbs. (64 Nm).
- Center support. Torque the bolts to 45 ft. lbs. (61 Nm).
- Front pipe to the resonator/muffler/tail pipe assembly. Torque the bolts to 32 ft. lbs. (43 Nm).
- O_2S electrical connector
- Negative battery cable

6. Start the vehicle and check for leaks, repair if necessary.

Oil Pump

REMOVAL & INSTALLATION

Metro

1. Before servicing the vehicle, refer to the precautions in the beginning of this section.
2. Drain the engine oil.
3. Remove or disconnect the following:
- Negative battery cable
- Oil pan
- Timing belt and tensioner
- A/C compressor, if equipped and lock the crankshaft
- Timing belt guide
- Oil pump and discard the gasket
- Rotor plate pins from the oil pump

To install:
4. Install or connect the following:
- Rotor plate pins to the oil pump
- Oil seal over the crankshaft and

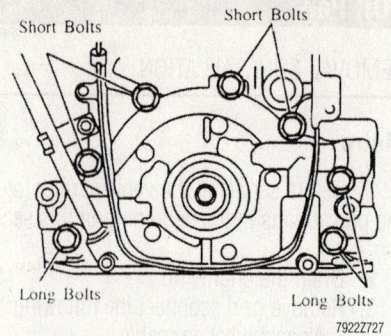

Short Bolts   Short Bolts

Long Bolts   Long Bolts

7922Z727

Oil pump mounting bolt identification—Metro

make certain that the lip is not turned out
- Apply Loctite®sealant to the threads of the short mounting bolts and install the oil pump. Torque the bolts to 97 inch lbs. (11 Nm).
- Rubber seal between the oil pump and the water pump
- Timing belt guide and lock the crankshaft
- A/c compressor and bracket, if equipped
- Oil pan
- Timing belt and tensioner
- Guide tube to the oil pump. Torque the bolt to 97 inch lbs. (11 Nm).
- Negative battery cable

5. Fill the engine with new oil.
6. Start the vehicle and check for leaks, repair if necessary.

Prizm

1997

1. Before servicing the vehicle, refer to the precautions in the beginning of this section.
2. Drain the engine oil.
3. Remove or disconnect the following:
- Negative battery cable
- Timing belt and tensioner
- Oil pan
- Crankshaft Position (CKP) sensor electrical connector from the guide tube
- Guide tube and O-ring from the oil pump
- Oil pump and seal

4. Clean the mating surface where the oil pump connects to the cylinder block.
To install:
5. Install or connect the following:
- New seal to the oil pump
- New gasket to the oil pump
- Oil pump and engage the splined teeth of the oil pump drive rotor with the large teeth on the crank-

shaft. Torque the bolts to 16 ft. lbs. (21 Nm).
- Guide tube with a new O-ring to the oil pump. Torque the bolt to 89 inch lbs. (10 Nm).
- CKP electrical connector to the guide tube
- Oil pan
- Timing belt and tensioner
- Negative battery cable

6. Fill the engine with new oil.
7. Start the vehicle and check for leaks, repair if necessary.

1998–01

1. Before servicing the vehicle, refer to the precautions in the beginning of this section.
2. Drain the engine oil.
3. Remove or disconnect the following:
- Negative battery cable
- Timing chain
- Oil pump and gasket

To install:
4. Install or connect the following:
- Oil pump with a new gasket. Torque the bolts to 97 inch lbs. (11 Nm).
- Timing chain
- Negative battery cable

5. Fill the engine with new oil.
6. Start the vehicle and check for leaks, repair if necessary.

Rear Main Seal

REMOVAL & INSTALLATION

Metro

1. Before servicing the vehicle, refer to the precautions in the beginning of this section.
2. Remove or disconnect the following:
- Negative battery cable
- Transmission from the vehicle
- Pressure plate and clutch disc, for manual transmission

3. Matchmark the flywheel-to-engine position.
4. Remove or disconnect the following:
- Flywheel from the crankshaft
- Rear crankshaft seal housing
- Rear crankshaft seal

To install:
5. Lubricate the inside and outside edges of the rear crankshaft seal.
6. Install or connect the following:
- Rear crankshaft seal in the housing
- Housing on the block. Torque the bolts to 108 inch lbs. (12 Nm).

7. Apply Loctite• sealant to the flywheel retaining bolt threads.

8. Install or connect the following:
- Flywheel. Torque the bolts to 56 ft. lbs. (78 Nm).
- Pressure plate and clutch disc, for manual transmission
- Transmission
- Negative battery cable

9. Check the oil level and top off if necessary.

10. Start the vehicle and check for leaks, repair if necessary.

Prizm

1997

1. Before servicing the vehicle, refer to the precautions in the beginning of this section.
2. Remove or disconnect the following:
- Negative battery cable
- Transmission
- Pressure plate and clutch disc, for manual transmission
3. Mark the flywheel-to-engine position.
4. Remove or disconnect the following:
- Flywheel and spacers from the crankshaft
- Rear end plate
- Rear main seal from the retainer

To install:
5. Lubricate the inside and outside edges of the rear crankshaft seal
6. Install or connect the following:
- Rear main seal to the retainer
- Retainer to the cylinder block. Torque the bolts to 82 inch lbs. (9 Nm).
- Rear end plate to the cylinder block. Torque the bolts to 50 inch lbs. (6 Nm).
- Flywheel and spacers. Torque the bolts to 47 ft. lbs. (64 Nm).
- Pressure plate and clutch disc, for manual transmission
- Transmission
- Negative battery cable
7. Check the oil level and top off, if necessary.
8. Start the vehicle and check for leaks, repair if necessary.

1998–01

1. Before servicing the vehicle, refer to the precautions in the beginning of this section.
2. Remove or disconnect the following:
- Negative battery cable
- Transmission
- Pressure plate and clutch disc, for manual transmission

3. Matchmark the flywheel-to-engine position.
4. Remove or disconnect the following:
- Flywheel from the crankshaft
- Rear crankshaft seal

To install:
5. Lubricate the lip of the new rear oil seal.
6. Install or connect the following:
- Rear oil seal and tap it into place until the surface is flush with the retainer edge
- Flywheel. Torque the bolts to 39 ft. lbs. (49 Nm).
- Pressure plate and clutch disc, for manual transmission
- Transmission
- Negative battery cable
7. Check the oil level and top off, if necessary.
8. Start the vehicle and check for leaks, repair if necessary.

Timing Chain, Sprockets, Front Cover & Seal

REMOVAL & INSTALLATION

1998–01 Prizm

1. Before servicing the vehicle, refer to the precautions in the beginning of this section.
2. Remove or disconnect the following:
3. Drain the cooling system.
- Negative battery cable
- Windshield washer reservoir
- Drive belt
- Alternator and install an engine support fixture
- Right side engine mount
- Cylinder head cover
4. Set the No. 1 piston to the Top Dead Center (TDC) position on the compression stroke and align the camshaft timing sprockets.
5. Remove or disconnect the following:
- Power steering oil pressure switch connector
- Power steering pump
- Crankshaft pulley
- Crankshaft Position (CKP) sensor
- Drive belt tensioner
- Timing chain cover
- Crankshaft sensor reluctor
- Timing chain damper and shoe
- Crankshaft sprocket

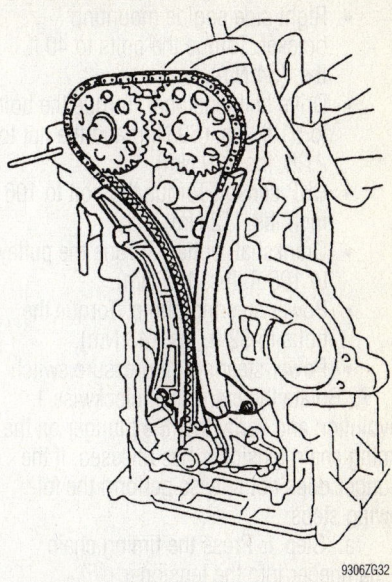

93062G32

Exploded view of the timing chain and sprockets–1.8L Prizm

- Timing chain
- Front seal
- Camshaft sprocket bolt
- Camshaft sprocket

To install:
6. Install or connect the following:
- Camshaft sprocket. Use a wrench to turn the camshafts to align the timing marks
- Crankshaft bolt and turn it until the keyway faces upward. When aligned properly, torque the sprocket bolts to 33 ft. lbs. (44 Nm).
- Front seal and tap it into position until the surface is flush against the retainer edge
- Timing chain
- Crankshaft timing sprocket
- Timing chain shoe. Torque the bolts to 89 inch lbs. (10 Nm).
- Timing chain damper. Torque the bolt to 14 ft. lbs. (18 Nm).
- Crankshaft sensor reluctor and make certain that the **F** is facing outward
- Timing chain cover after applying a sealant to the mating surface. Torque the 10mm bolts to 89 inch lbs. (10 Nm) and the 12mm bolts to 14 ft. lbs. (18 Nm).
- Install the timing chain tensioner by depressing the plunger and applying the hook to the pin. Torque the bolts to 89 inch lbs. (10 Nm).

- Right side engine mounting bracket. Torque the bolts to 40 ft. lbs. (54 Nm).
- Drive belt tensioner. Torque the bolt to 51 ft. lbs. (69 Nm) and the nut to 21 ft. lbs. (29 Nm).
- CKP sensor. Torque the bolt to 106 inch lbs. (12 Nm).
- Crankshaft pulley. Torque the pulley to 105 ft. lbs. 142 Nm).
- Power steering pump. Torque the bolts to 32 ft. lbs. (43 Nm).
- Power steering oil pressure switch

7. Rotate the crankshaft clockwise 1 revolution and verify that the plunger on the timing chain tensioner has released. If the plunger does not release perform the following steps:

   a. Step 1: Press the timing chain dampener into the tensioner.

   b. Step 2: Release the hook from the pin.

   c. Step 3: Verify proper timing chain alignment after the plunger is released.

8. Install or connect the following:
- Cylinder head cover
- Right side engine mount and insulator. Torque the bolts to 40 ft. lbs. (54 Nm).
- Alternator

9. Remove the engine support fixture.

10. Install or connect the following:
- Windshield washer reservoir
- Negative battery cable

11. Fill the cooling system.

12. Start the vehicle and check for leaks, repair if necessary.

Piston & Ring

POSITIONING

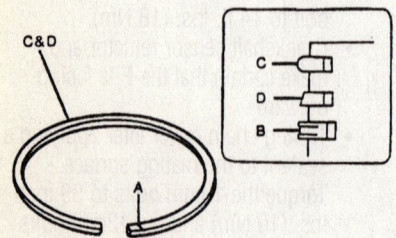

A "R" OR "T" MARK
B OIL RING
C UPPER COMPRESSION RING
D LOWER COMPRESSION RING

7922AG40

GEO/Chevrolet 1.0L, 1.3L, 1.6L and 1.8L engines—piston ring positioning

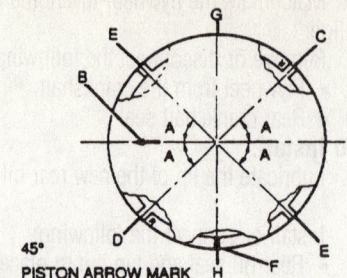

A 45°
B PISTON ARROW MARK
C FIRST RING END GAP
D SECOND RING END GAP
E OIL RING END GAPS
F OIL RING SPACER GAP
G INTAKE SIDE
H EXHAUST SIDE

7922AG39

GEO/Chevrolet 1.0L, 1.3L, 1.6L and 1.8L engines—piston ring end-gap spacing

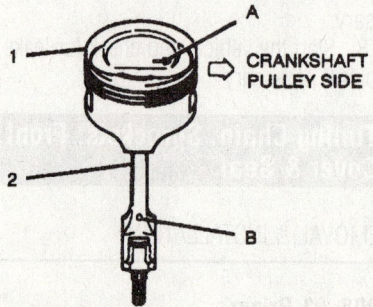

A. Arrow mark
B. Oil hole (oil hole should come on intake side)
1. Piston
2. Connecting rod

7922AG41

GEO/Chevrolet 1.0L, 1.3L, 1.6L and 1.8L engines—piston and connecting rod assembly positioning

FUEL SYSTEM

Fuel System Pressure

RELIEVING

1. Before servicing the vehicle, refer to the precautions in the beginning of this section.

2. Remove the fuel filler cap.

3. On Metro, perform the following:

   a. Remove the control relay box cover from the relay box.

   b. Disconnect the fuel pump relay from the relay box connector.

4. On 1997 Prizm, perform the following:

   a. Remove the center trim bezel from the center console by gently prying around the edges.

   b. Remove the radio from the center console.

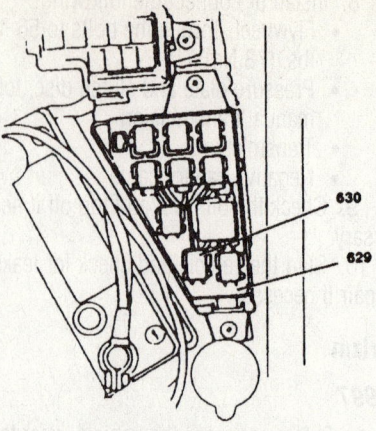

629 RELAY BOX
630 FUEL PUMP RELAY

7922Z728

View of the relay box showing the location of the fuel pump relay—Metro

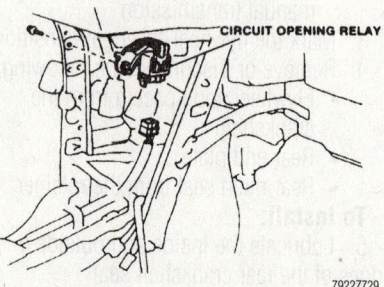

7922Z729

Leave the circuit opening relay unplugged during fuel system servicing—Prizm

   c. Disconnect the circuit opening relay, located in the center console.

5. On 1998–01 Prizm, remove the circuit opening relay above the lower left side kick panel.

6. Attempt to start the engine, if it starts, let it run until the engine stalls due to lack of fuel.

7. Engage the starter for a few seconds to assure relief of remaining fuel pressure.

8. Disconnect the negative battery cable.

9. Continue with the required service procedure(s).

Fuel Filter

REMOVAL & INSTALLATION

➡The 1998—01 Metro and Prizm have the fuel filter in the fuel tank and is part of the fuel pump assembly.

1997

METRO

1. Before servicing the vehicle, refer to the precautions in the beginning of this section.

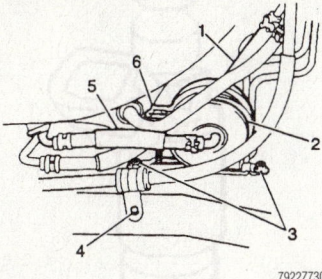

1. Fuel Feed Outlet Hose
2. Fuel Filter
3. Fuel Filter Mounting Bolts
4. Parking Brake Cable Bracket Bolt
5. Fuel Feed Inlet Hose
6. Fuel Filter Mounting Bracket to Fuel Filter Bolt

79222Z730

Component view of the fuel filter mounting—1997 Metro

2. Properly relieve the fuel system pressure.

3. Remove or disconnect the following:
- Negative battery cable
- Bolt securing the parking brake cable bracket to the underbody
- Fuel feed hose from the fuel filter
- Fuel filter mounting bracket and the fuel filter from the frame
- Outlet hose from the fuel filter
- Fuel filter from the bracket

To install:

4. Install or connect the following:
- Fuel filter on the bracket. Torque the bolt to 11 ft. lbs. (15 Nm).

➡**Be sure the matchmarks between the fuel filter and the mounting bracket are aligned before tightening the bolt.**

- Fuel feed outlet hose to the fuel filter and secure with a new clamp
- Fuel filter on the frame. Torque the bolts to 11 ft. lbs. (15 Nm).
- Fuel inlet hose to the fuel filter and secure with a new clamp
- Parking brake cable bracket. Torque the bolt to 11 ft. lbs. (15 Nm).
- Negative battery cable

5. Turn the ignition switch to **ON**, then back to **LOCK** to pressurize the fuel system.

6. Start the vehicle and check for leaks, repair if necessary.

PRIZM

1. Before servicing the vehicle, refer to the precautions in the beginning of this section.

2. Properly relieve the fuel system pressure.

3. Remove or disconnect the following:
- Negative battery cable
- Intake Air Temperature (IAT) sensor electrical connector
- Air cleaner clamp and release the 4 housing clips. Remove the hose and air cleaner cover
- Evaporative Emissions (EVAP) hoses from the canister
- EVAP canister and bracket
- Fuel feed outlet hose from the top of the fuel filter
- Fuel filter from the bracket
- Fuel inlet pipe from the bottom of the fuel filter

To install:

4. Install or connect the following:
- Fuel filter to the bracket. Torque the bolts to 43 inch lbs. (5 Nm).
- Fuel inlet pipe to the bottom of the fuel filter. Torque the nut to 22 ft. lbs. (30 Nm).
- Fuel outlet hose to the top of the fuel filter, using new gaskets. Torque the bolt to 21 ft. lbs. (29 Nm).
- EVAP canister to the bracket. Torque the bolt to 21 ft. lbs. (29 Nm).
- EVAP hoses to the canister
- Air cleaner cover and secure with the clips and connect the air cleaner hose
- IAT sensor electrical connector
- Negative battery cable

5. Turn the ignition switch **ON** to pressurize the fuel system. Check for fuel leaks and repair if necessary.

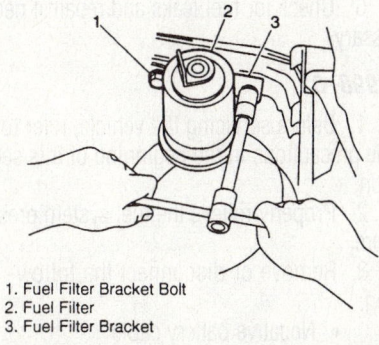

1. Fuel Filter Bracket Bolt
2. Fuel Filter
3. Fuel Filter Bracket

79222Z731

To remove the filter, detach the fuel lines and remove the 2 bracket bolts, then slide the filter out of the bracket—be sure to check for fuel leaks after replacing the filter—1997 Prizm

Fuel Pump

REMOVAL & INSTALLATION

Metro

1. Before servicing the vehicle, refer to the precautions in the beginning of this section.

2. Properly relieve the fuel system pressure.

3. Drain the fuel tank by pumping the fuel out through the filler neck into a suitable container.

4. Remove or disconnect the following:
- Negative battery cable
- Fuel tank and clean all dirt from the fuel pump area, to prevent fuel system contamination
- Fuel feed and return clamps and hoses from the pump
- Screws from the pump assembly and remove with the gasket from the fuel tank.
- Fuel pump electrical connectors
- Fuel pump

To install:

5. Install or connect the following:
- Fuel pump electrical connectors
- Pump motor on the pump
- Fuel pump with a new gasket on the fuel tank
- Fuel feed and return hoses and clamps on the fuel pump
- Fuel tank
- Negative battery cable

6. Refill the fuel tank.

7. Turn the ignition key **ON** and allow the fuel system to pressurize.

8. Start the engine and check for leaks, repair if necessary

Prizm

1. Before servicing the vehicle, refer to the precautions in the beginning of this section.

2. Properly relieve the fuel system pressure.

3. Drain the fuel tank into a suitable container.

4. Remove or disconnect the following:
- Negative battery cable
- Rear seat cushion to gain access to the service panel
- Access panel
- Fuel sender electrical connectors
- Fuel feed and return hoses from the fuel sender

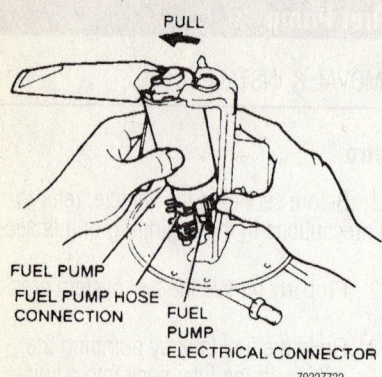

PULL

FUEL PUMP
FUEL PUMP HOSE
CONNECTION   FUEL
PUMP
ELECTRICAL CONNECTOR

7922Z732

Remove the fuel pump and the sender assembly from the fuel tank slowly to keep from splashing fuel—Prizm

- Fuel sender from the tank
- Fuel pump electrical connectors
- Rubber cushion from the fuel pump
- Fuel pump

To install:

5. Install or connect the following:
- New strainer to the fuel pump
- Rubber cushion to the pump
- Fuel pump to the bracket
- Fuel pump electrical connector
- Fuel sender assembly to the tank, using a new gasket. Torque the bolts to 35 inch lbs. (4 Nm).
- Fuel return hose to the sender
- Fuel feed hose to the sender. Torque the nut to 22 ft. lbs. (30 Nm).
- Negative battery cable

6. Refill the fuel tank.
7. Turn the ignition **ON** to pressurize the fuel system.
8. Check for fuel leaks and repair if necessary.
9. Install the service access panel and rear seat cushion.

Fuel Injector

REMOVAL & INSTALLATION

Metro

1997

1. Before servicing the vehicle, refer to the precautions in the beginning of this section.
2. Properly relieve the fuel system pressure.
3. Remove or disconnect the following:
- Negative battery cable
- Intake Air Temperature (IAT) sensor electrical connector

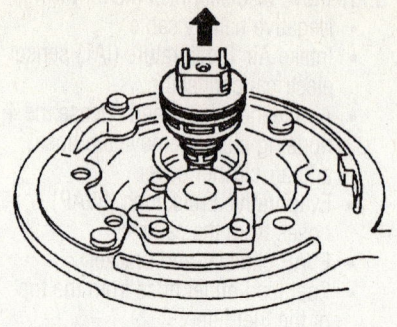

9306ZG33

Remove the fuel injector from the throttle body unit—1997 Metro

- Positive Crankcase Ventilation (PCV) hose from the air cleaner
- Air cleaner and bracket from the throttle body
- Fuel injector cover from the throttle body
- Fuel injector

To install:

4. Install or connect the following:
- New O-rings coated in clean oil to the fuel injector
- New lower fuel injector insulator into the injector cavity of the throttle body
- Fuel injector
- Fuel injector cover
- Air cleaner bracket to the throttle body. Torque the bolt to 7.5 ft. lbs. (10 Nm).
- PCV hose to the air cleaner
- IAT electrical connector
- Air cleaner to the throttle body
- Negative battery cable

5. Turn the ignition **ON** to pressurize the fuel system.
6. Check for fuel leaks and repair if necessary.

1998–01

1. Before servicing the vehicle, refer to the precautions in the beginning of this section.
2. Properly relieve the fuel system pressure.
3. Remove or disconnect the following:

- Negative battery cable
- Positive Crankcase Ventilation (PCV) valve and hose from the intake and valve cover
- Intake manifold brace
- Fuel injector electrical connectors
- Fuel pressure regulator hose
- Fuel feed and return hoses
- Fuel rail
- fuel injectors from the fuel rail

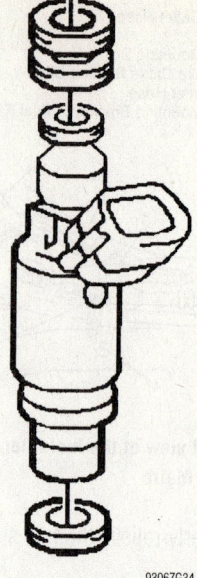

9306ZG34

Exploded view of the fuel injector—1998–01 Metro

To install:

4. Install or connect the following:
- New O-rings to the injectors
- Injectors into the fuel rail after coating the O-rings with clean fuel
- Fuel rail and insulators to the intake manifold. Torque the bolts to 20 ft. lbs. (28 Nm).

➡**Make certain that the fuel injectors rotate smoothly.**

- Fuel feed hose to the inlet pipe and secure with a new clamp
- Fuel return hose to the return pipe and secure with a new clamp
- Fuel pressure regulator vacuum hose
- Fuel injector electrical connectors
- Intake manifold brace. Torque the bolts to 25 ft. lbs. (35 Nm).
- Negative battery cable

5. Turn the ignition **ON** to pressurize the fuel system.
6. Check for fuel leaks and repair if necessary.

Prizm

1997

1. Before servicing the vehicle, refer to the precautions in the beginning of this section.
2. Properly relieve the fuel system pressure.
3. Remove or disconnect the following:
- Negative battery cable
- Accelerator and cruise control cable, if equipped

- Intake Air Temperature (IAT) sensor electrical connector
- Air cleaner hose clamp from the throttle body
- Cap clips from the air cleaner
- Exhaust Gas Recirculation (EGR) regulator vacuum valve electrical connector
- EGR vacuum hoses
- Fuel pressure regulator vacuum hose
- Positive Crankcase Ventilation (PCV) from the cylinder head cover
- Air intake chamber cover and set it aside
- Air intake cover gasket and discard it
- Fuel injector electrical connectors
- Fuel return/feed hoses
- Fuel rail
- Fuel injectors from the fuel rail
- O-rings and grommets from the injectors
- Insulators and spacers from the intake manifold

To install:

4. Install or connect the following:
- New O-rings and grommets to the injectors
- New insulators and spacers in the intake manifold
- Fuel injectors to the fuel rail with the connectors facing upward
- Fuel rail to the intake manifold and hand tighten the bolts
- Fuel feed hose. Torque the bolt to 22 ft. lbs. (29 Nm).
- Fuel return hose to the pressure regulator
- Fuel injector electrical connectors
- Air intake chamber cover to the throttle body. Torque the fasteners to 14 ft. lbs. (19 Nm).
- Fuel pressure regulator vacuum hose
- PCV hose to the valve and the cylinder head cover
- EGR vacuum regulator valve electrical connector
- EGR hoses
- Air cleaner hose and cap to the throttle body. Torque the bolt to 11 ft. lbs. (15 Nm).
- IAT sensor electrical connector
- Accelerator and cruise control cables, if equipped, to the air cleaner
- Negative battery cable

5. Turn the ignition **ON** to pressurize the fuel system.
6. Check for fuel leaks and repair, if necessary.

1998–01

1. Before servicing the vehicle, refer to the precautions in the beginning of this section.
2. Properly relieve the fuel system pressure.
3. Remove or disconnect the following:
- Negative battery cable
- Spark plug wires from the ignition coils
- Positive Crankcase Ventilation (PCV) and breather hoses from the valve cover
- Accelerator cable bracket from the cylinder head
- Wire harness cover plate
- Fuel injector electrical connectors
- Fuel feed hose quick connect coupling cover
- Fuel rail from the cylinder head
- O-rings and grommets from the injectors
- Spacers from the cylinder head

To install:

4. Install or connect the following:
- New spacers to the cylinder head
- Fuel injectors and grommets with new O-rings to the fuel rail
- Fuel rail to the cylinder head. Torque the bolts to 13 ft. lbs. (15 Nm).
- Fuel rail inlet pipe. Torque the bolt to 79 inch lbs. (9 Nm).
- Fuel feed hose quick connect fitting
- Fuel feed hose coupling cover
- Wire harness to the cylinder head. Torque the bolt to 71 inch lbs. (8 Nm).
- Fuel injector electrical connectors
- Wire harness cover plate. Torque the bolt to 71 inch lbs. (8 Nm).
- Accelerator cable bracket to the cylinder head. Torque the bolt to 71 inch lbs. (8 Nm).
- PCV and breather hoses to the valve cover
- Spark plug wires to the ignition coils
- Negative battery cable

5. Turn the ignition **ON** to pressurize the fuel system.
6. Check for fuel leaks and repair if necessary.

DRIVE TRAIN

Transaxle Assembly

REMOVAL & INSTALLATION

Manual

METRO

1. Before servicing the vehicle, refer to the precautions in the beginning of this section.
2. Drain the transmission fluid.
3. Remove or disconnect the following:
- Negative battery cable
- Both front wheels
- Backup lamp switch electrical connector
- Clutch release lever from the clutch release shaft
- Clutch cable bracket and move it aside
- Negative battery cable and hanger from the transmission
- Gearshift guide case bolts and set the engine wire harness and bracket aside
- Speedometer cable
- Two right side upper case to engine bolts and properly support the engine
- Both drive axles after properly supporting the transmission
- Flywheel cover
- Control joint shaft through bolt and separate the control shaft from the control joint
- Gearshift control lever guide plate and separate the extension rod from the lever guide plate
- Starter
- Bolts from the rear transmission mount, left side mounting bracket and right side case to engine mounting bolts
- Transmission through the left side of the engine compartment and make certain that the input shaft clears the clutch pressure plate

To install:

4. Install or connect the following:
- Transmission to the engine
- Right side lower case to engine bolts. Torque the bolts to 44 ft. lbs. (60 Nm).
- Left side mounting bracket. Torque the bolts to 44 ft. lbs. (60 Nm).

- Rear transmission through bolt. Torque the bolt to 44 ft. lbs. (60 Nm).
- Starter. Torque the bolts to 21 ft. lbs. (28 Nm).
- Starter electrical connectors
- Extension rod to the mounting stud on the transmission. Torque the nut to 29 ft. lbs. (40 Nm).
- Extension rod to the gearshift control lever guide plate. Torque the bolts to 89 inch lbs. (10 Nm).
- Gearshift control shaft and joint. Torque the joint through bolt to 15 ft. lbs. (20 Nm).
- Flywheel cover. Torque the bolts to 15 ft. lbs. (20 Nm).
- Both driveshafts
- Two upper right side case to engine block mounting bolts. Torque the bolts to 44 ft. lbs. (60 Nm).
- Speedometer cable to the speedometer driven gear case and secure it with a retaining clip
- Engine wire harness and bracket to the gearshift guide case. Torque the bolts to 106 inch lbs. (12 Nm).
- Transmission hanger. Torque the bolt to 106 inch lbs. (12 Nm).
- Clutch cable and bracket. Torque the bolts to 21 ft. lbs. (28 Nm).
- Clutch release shaft to the clutch release lever. When aligned properly, torque the bolt to 17 ft. lbs. (23 Nm).
- Backup lamp switch
- Both wheels
- Negative battery cable

5. Fill the transmission with clean fluid.
6. Start the vehicle and check for leaks, repair if necessary.

PRIZM

1. Before servicing the vehicle, refer to the precautions in the beginning of this section.
2. Drain the transmission fluid.
3. Remove or disconnect the following:
- Negative battery cable
- Battery and tray
- Both front wheels
- Air cleaner
- Backup switch electrical connector
- Vehicle Speed Sensor (VSS) connectors
- Ground strap
- Actuator line bracket
- Shift cables from the bracket and move them to the side
- Left side transmission mount cover and brace

- Upper transmission to engine bolts
- Upper starter bolt
- Splash shields
- Starter electrical connectors and starter
- Both driveshafts
- Crossmember
- Left side lower transmission mount
- Transmission from the engine

To install:

4. Install or connect the following:
- Transmission to the engine. It may be necessary to raise the left side of the engine to align them properly. Torque the transmission to engine bolts to 46 ft. lbs. (34 Nm) and the mount bolts to 17 ft. lbs. (23 Nm).
- Starter. Torque the bolts to 29 ft. lbs. (39 Nm).
- Starter electrical connectors
- Crossmember. Torque the bolts in the following sequence:

a. Main crossmember to underbody bolts to 152 ft. lbs. (206 Nm).

b. Lower "A" frame to underbody bolt to 161 ft. lbs. (218 Nm).

c. Lower "A" frame to underbody bolts to 109 ft. lbs. (147 Nm).

d. Radiator support bolts to 45 ft. lbs. (61 Nm).

5. Install or connect the following:
- Front mount. Torque the bolts to 47 ft. lbs. (64 Nm).
- Rear mount. Torque the bolts to 42 ft. lbs. (57 Nm).
- Front mount through bolt. Torque the bolt to 64 ft. lbs. (87 Nm).
- Heat insulator. Torque the bolts to 15 ft. lbs. (20 Nm).
- Both driveshafts
- Both splash shields
- Left side transmission mount and cover. Torque the bolt to 21 ft. lbs. (28 Nm).
- Upper transmission mount. Torque the bolts to 47 ft. lbs. (64 Nm).
- Shift cables to the bracket and align the bracket
- Ground strap
- VSS electrical connector
- Backup switch electrical connector
- Clutch release cylinder and line. Torque the bolts to 106 inch lbs. (12 Nm).
- Both front wheels
- Air cleaner
- Battery and cables

6. Fill the transmission with clean fluid.
7. Start the vehicle and check for leaks, repair if necessary.

Automatic

METRO

1. Before servicing the vehicle, refer to the precautions in the beginning of this section.
2. Drain the transmission fluid.
- Negative battery cable
- Throttle Valve (TV) cable
- Shift select cable from the manual select cable joint
- Retaining clip and shift select cable from the bracket on top of the transmission case
- Accelerator cable from the bracket on top of the transmission case
- Vehicle Speed Sensor (VSS) electrical connector
- Shift solenoid harness electrical connectors
- Transmission range switch electrical connectors
- Speedometer cable from the speedometer driven gear case
- Cooler hoses from the pipes
- Starter
- Both front wheels
- Splash shields
- Driveshafts after properly supporting the engine assembly
- Rear engine torque rod

➡**Make alignment marks on the torque converter and driveplate for assembly reference.**

- Flywheel cover. Lock the flywheel and remove the 6 flywheel to torque converter bolts
- Muffler mounting from the rear of the engine mount bracket hanger
- Rear engine mount
- Properly support the transmission and remove the left mount and bracket
- Engine to transmission bolts and the transmission

To install:

3. Use grease to lubricate the cup around the center of the torque converter.
4. Measure the distance between the torque converter and the edge of the transaxle housing; it should be at least 0.85 in. (21.4mm). If the distance is less than specified, the torque converter is improperly installed. Remove and reinstall it.
5. Install or connect the following:
- Transmission to the engine. Torque the lower transaxle-to-engine bolt to 40 ft. lbs. (55 Nm).
- Left transmission mount and bracket. Torque the bolts to 40 ft. lbs. (55 Nm).

- Rear engine mount bracket to the transmission. Torque the bolts to 40 ft. lbs. (55 Nm).
- Rear engine mount-to-bulkhead bolt. Torque the bolt to 40 ft. lbs. (55 Nm).
- Muffler mount to the rear exhaust hanger.
- Flywheel-to-torque converter bolts. Lock the flywheel in place and torque the bolts to 14 ft. lbs. (19 Nm).
- Flywheel inspection cover. Torque the bolts to 89 inch lbs. (10 Nm).
- Rear engine torque rod assembly. Torque the bolts to 40 ft. lbs. (55 Nm).
- Both driveshafts
- Ball joints to the steering knuckles. Torque the bolts 44 ft. lbs. (60 Nm).
- Splash shields and remove the engine support fixture
- Both front wheels
- Negative battery cable to the transmission. Torque the bolt to 11 ft. lbs. (15 Nm).
- Upper transmission-to-engine mounting bolts. Torque the bolts to 40 ft. lbs. (55 Nm).
- Through-bolt to the rear engine mount. Torque the bolt to 40 ft. lbs. (55 Nm).
- Starter. Torque the bolts to 17 ft. lbs. (23 Nm).
- Inlet and outlet fluid cooler lines with new hose clamps
- Speedometer cable into the gear case
- Engine wire harness bracket to the rear of the transmission. Torque the bolts 12 ft. lbs. (16 Nm).
- Accelerator and shift select cables into the bracket on top of the transmission
- Shift select cable end to the manual select cable joint and adjust as necessary
- TV cable to the accelerator cable
- Negative battery cable

6. Fill the transmission with new oil.

7. Flush the oil cooler lines.

8. Start the engine and verify the proper gear select range.

9. Check the fluid level and adjust, as needed.

PRIZM

1. Before servicing the vehicle, refer to the precautions in the beginning of this section.

2. Drain the transmission fluid.

3. Remove or disconnect the following:
- Both battery cables
- Battery and tray
- Intake Air Temperature (IAT) sensor electrical connector
- Air cleaner
- Park Neutral Position (PNP) switch electrical connector
- Solenoid wire harness
- Ground strap from the transmission
- Throttle Valve (TV) cable from the linkage and the bracket
- Vehicle Speed Sensor (VSS) electrical connector
- Shift select cable from the manual lever and the TV cable bracket guide
- Upper transmission to engine bolts
- Starter and install an engine/transmission support fixture
- Left transmission mounting bracket
- Both splash shields
- Cooler hoses from the pipes at the transmission
- Both front wheels
- Both driveshafts
- Exhaust pipe support
- Oxygen (O_2S) sensor harness
- Front transmission mount
- Rear transmission mount
- Front crossmember and lower the engine reinforcement brace
- Flywheel access cover
- Flywheel-to-torque converter bolts
- Lower transmission to engine bolts
- Transmission

To install:

4. Before installing the transmission assembly, perform the following:

a. Apply grease around the pilot shaft at the center of the torque converter.

b. Measure the distance between the outside edge of the torque converter housing and the torque converter lug. The distance should be more than 0.906 in. (23mm). If it is less than 0.906 in. (23mm), the torque converter is improperly installed. Remove and properly seat on the input shaft.

5. Install or connect the following:
- Transmission. Torque the two lower transmission-to-engine bolts to 47 ft. lbs. (64 Nm).
- Flywheel-to-torque converter bolts. Torque the bolts to 14 ft. lbs. (19 Nm).
- Flywheel access cover
- Lower engine reinforcement brace.

Torque the bolts to 47 ft. lbs. (64 Nm).

6. Remove the engine/transmission support fixture.

7. Install or connect the following:
- Front crossmember. Torque the 10 front bolts to 152 ft. lbs. (206 Nm) and the two center bolts to 45 ft. lbs. (61 Nm).
- Rear transmission mount. Torque the bolts to 42 ft. lbs. (57 Nm).
- Front transmission mount. Torque the bolts to 47 ft. lbs. (64 Nm).
- Center crossmember access cover
- Front exhaust pipe to the manifold. Torque the bolts to 46 ft. lbs. (62 Nm).
- Electrical connector for the O_2S sensor harness.
- Both driveshafts
- Both front wheels
- Left transmission brace. Torque the bolts to 35 ft. lbs. (48 Nm).
- Oil cooler hoses to the pipes and secure them with new clamps
- Both splash shields. Torque the bolts to 44 inch lbs. (5 Nm).
- Starter

✷✷ WARNING

The differential portion of the 3-speed transmission is separated from the rest of the transmission and must be drained and refilled separately. The differential cannot be drained or refilled through the transmission drain plug or filler tube.

8. On 3-speed transmission, refill the differential with 1½ qts. (1.4 L) of Dexron®III automatic transmission fluid, into the differential filler plug hole. The fluid level should be even with the bottom of the differential filler plug hole. Install the filler plug and tighten to 29 ft. lbs. (39 Nm).

9. Install or connect the following:
- Left side transmission mounting bracket. Torque the bolts to 41 ft. lbs. (56 Nm).
- Left transmission bracket reinforcement. Torque the bolts to 15 ft. lbs. (21 Nm).
- Upper transmission to engine bolts. Torque the bolts to 47 ft. lbs. (64 Nm).
- TV guide cable bracket onto the transmission. Torque the bolt to 71 inch lbs. (8 Nm).

- Shift select cable into the bracket at the transaxle and secure with clip
- Shift select cable to the manual lever and secure with the nut and lockwasher. Adjust the shift select cable as needed. Torque the nut to 106 inch lbs. (12 Nm).
- VSS electrical connector
- TV cable to the throttle linkage and bracket.

10. Adjust the TV cable as follows:

a. Be sure the throttle valve is fully closed.

b. Measure the distance between the end of the outer cable boot and the end of the TV cable stopper, it should be 0–0.04 in. (0–1mm).

c. If the distance is greater than specified, loosen the TV cable locknut and tighten the adjust nut until within specification.

d. If the distance is less than specified, loosen the TV cable adjust nut. Torque the locknut to 71 inch lbs. (8 Nm).

11. Install or connect the following:

- Ground strap. Torque the bolt to 115 inch lbs. (13 Nm).
- Solenoid wire harness connector
- PNP electrical connector
- IAT electrical connector
- Air cleaner. Torque the bolts to 106 inch lbs. (12 Nm).
- Battery
- Both battery cables

12. Fill the transmission with new oil.

13. Flush the oil cooler lines.

14. Start the engine and verify the proper gear select range.

15. Check the fluid level and adjust, as needed.

Clutch

ADJUSTMENT

Clutch Pedal Height

Inspect the clutch pedal height. If it is not within 5.45–5.84 in. (138.4–148.4mm), adjust the pedal height as follows:

1. Before servicing the vehicle, refer to the precautions in the beginning of this section.

2. Remove the lower instrument panel and air duct.

3. Loosen the locknut.

4. Turn the stopper bolt until the pedal height is within 5.12–5.51 in. (130–140mm).

5. Tighten the locknut and install the air duct and lower instrument panel.

Clutch Pedal Free Play

Inspect the clutch pedal free play. If it is not within 0.197–0.521 in. (5.0–15.0mm), adjust the pedal free-play as follows:

1. Before servicing the vehicle, refer to the precautions in the beginning of this section.

2. Remove the lower instrument panel and air duct.

3. Depress the pedal until resistance is felt.

4. Loosen the locknut.

5. Turn the pushrod until the free play is within 0.197–0.591 in. (5.0–15.0mm).

6. Tighten the locknut and install the air duct and lower instrument panel.

REMOVAL & INSTALLATION

1. Before servicing the vehicle, refer to the precautions in the beginning of this section.

2. Remove or disconnect the following:

- Negative battery cable
- Transmission assembly and match-mark the flywheel to the engine
- On Prizm, unfasten the release fork bearing clips and remove the release bearing, fork and boot
- Slowly and evenly loosen the clutch pressure plate cover bolts until the spring tension is released
- Clutch disc

To install:

3. Clean the flywheel mating surfaces of all oil, grease and metal deposits.

4. Check the diaphragm spring and pressure plate for wear or damage. If the spring or plate is excessively worn, replace the clutch cover assembly.

5. Check the pilot bearing for smooth operation. If the bearing does not spin freely, replace it.

6. Inspect the disc, pressure plate and flywheel for damage and wear using a caliper to measure depth and width and a dial indicator to measure run-out.

7. The minimum clutch disc rivet head depth: 0.02 in. (0.5mm).

8. The maximum clutch disc run-out: 0.031 in. (0.8mm).

9. The maximum pressure plate spring depth: 0.024 in. (0.6mm).

10. The maximum pressure plate spring width: 0.197 in. (5.0mm).

11. The maximum flywheel run-out: 0.004 in. (0.1mm).

12. When reassembling, apply a thin coating of multi-purpose grease to the release bearing hub and release fork contact points. Also, pack the groove inside the clutch hub with multi-purpose grease and lubricate the pivot points of the release fork.

13. Install or connect the following:

- Clutch disc and clutch cover with the matchmarks

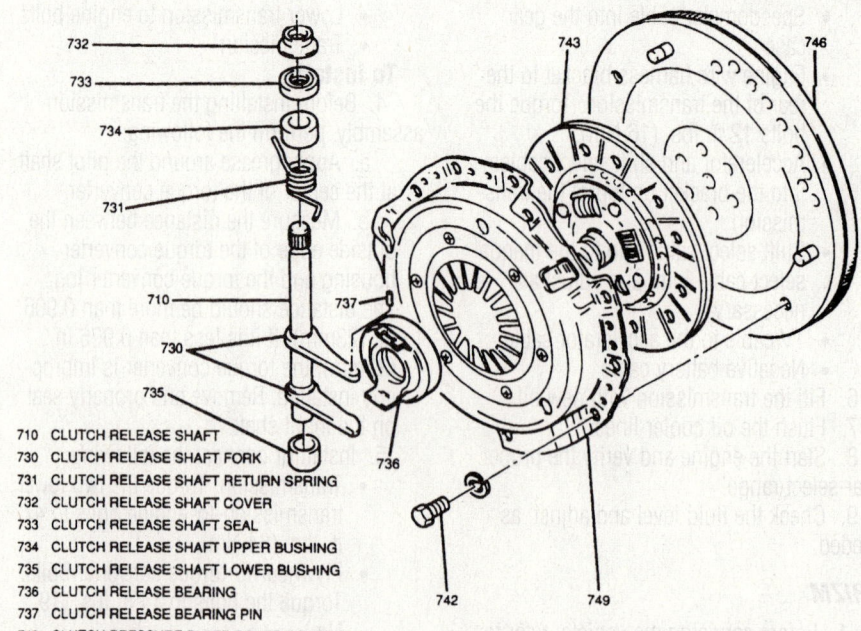

710 CLUTCH RELEASE SHAFT
730 CLUTCH RELEASE SHAFT FORK
731 CLUTCH RELEASE SHAFT RETURN SPRING
732 CLUTCH RELEASE SHAFT COVER
733 CLUTCH RELEASE SHAFT SEAL
734 CLUTCH RELEASE SHAFT UPPER BUSHING
735 CLUTCH RELEASE SHAFT LOWER BUSHING
736 CLUTCH RELEASE BEARING
737 CLUTCH RELEASE BEARING PIN
742 CLUTCH PRESSURE PLATE COVER BOLTS
743 CLUTCH DISC
746 FLYWHEEL
749 CLUTCH PRESSURE PLATE COVER

Exploded view of the clutch assembly—Metro

79227733

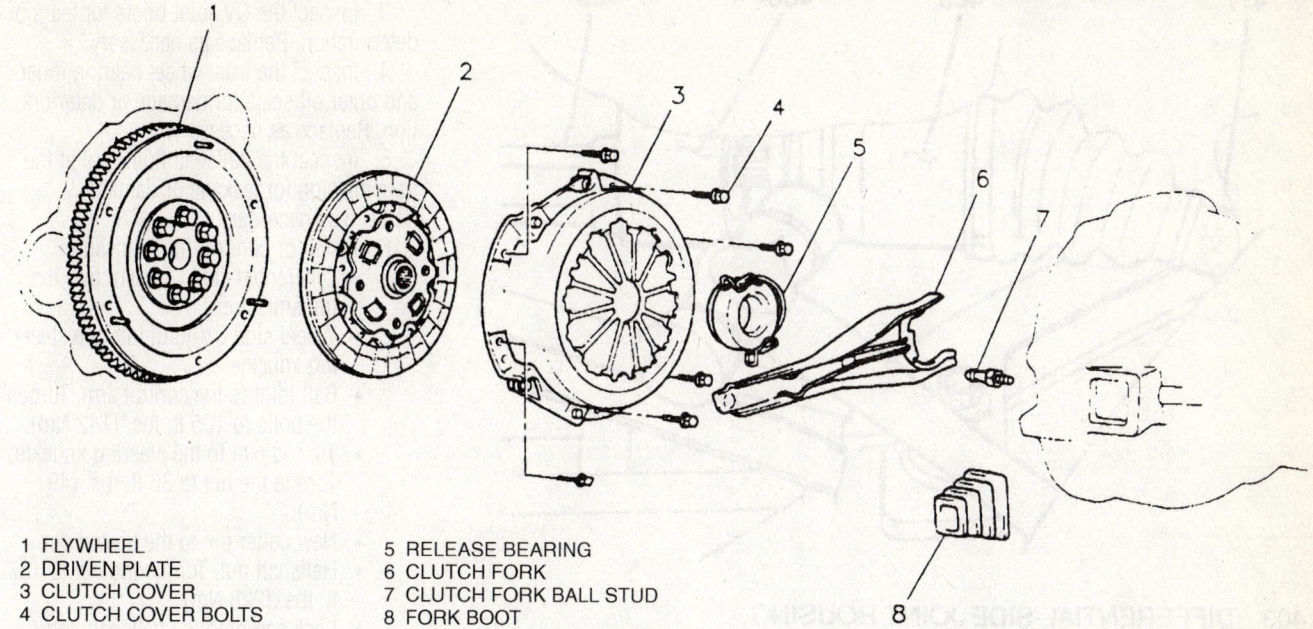

1 FLYWHEEL
2 DRIVEN PLATE
3 CLUTCH COVER
4 CLUTCH COVER BOLTS
5 RELEASE BEARING
6 CLUTCH FORK
7 CLUTCH FORK BALL STUD
8 FORK BOOT

7922Z734

Exploded view of the clutch assembly—Prizm

- Clutch cover bolts. Torque the bolts to 17 ft. lbs. (23 Nm).
- Release bearing, fork, and boot on the prizm
- Transmission
- Negative battery cable
14. Adjust the clutch cable, if needed.

Hydraulic Clutch System

BLEEDING

➡**If any maintenance on the clutch system was performed or the system is suspected of containing air, bleed the system as follows:**

Fill the clutch reservoir with brake fluid. Check the reservoir level frequently and add fluid as needed.

Connect one end of a vinyl tube to the bleeder plug on the slave cylinder and submerge the other end into a clear container half-filled with clean brake fluid.

Slowly pump the clutch pedal several times.

Repeat Steps 2 and 3 until all of the air bubbles are removed from the system.

Tighten the bleeder screw to 97 inch lbs. (11 Nm).

Refill the master cylinder to the proper level.

Check the system for leaks.

Halfshaft

REMOVAL & INSTALLATION

Metro

1. Before servicing the vehicle, refer to the precautions in the beginning of this section.
2. Drain the transmission fluid.
3. Remove or disconnect the following:

- Negative battery cable
- Anti-lock Brake System (ABS) speed sensor from the steering knuckle, if equipped
- Front wheel
- Unstake and remove the halfshaft nut with the vehicle's weight on the ground.
- Ball joint from the steering knuckle

➡**On 4-door sedan, the right side halfshaft is stabilized by a center support bearing between the transmission and the inner Tri-pod joint. It is not necessary to remove the right inner drive axle and center support bearing assembly. The right side halfshaft assembly can be separated from the center support bearing by lightly tapping with a plastic mallet.**

- Using a suitable prytool, pry on the inboard joints of the halfshaft to detach the snapring lock in the differential. On 4-door sedans, separate the right side halfshaft assembly from the center support bearing by tapping lightly with a plastic mallet.
- Stabilizer bar mounting bracket
4. Pull the halfshaft out of the transmission, then from the steering knuckle.

To install:
5. Inspect the CV-joint boots for tears or deterioration and replace, if necessary.
6. Install or connect the following:

- Halfshaft into the steering knuckle first, then into the transmission
- Control arm to the steering knuckle. Torque the ball stud bolt to 44 ft. lbs. (60 Nm).
- Stabilizer bar mounting bracket
- Halfshaft nut and washer. Torque the fastener to 129 ft. lbs. (175 Nm) and stake the nut
- ABS speed sensor electrical connector
- Front wheel
- Negative battery cable
7. Fill the transmission with clean fluid.
8. Road test the vehicle.

Turn to Section 5 for brake system applications

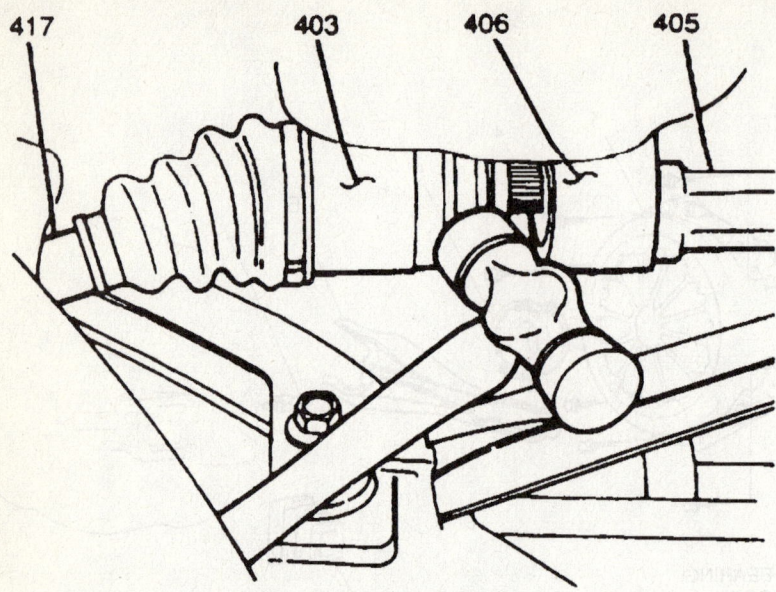

417   403   406   405

403 DIFFERENTIAL-SIDE JOINT HOUSING

405 RIGHT INNER DRIVE AXLE SHAFT

406 RIGHT INNER DRIVE AXLE SUPPORT ARBOR

417 RIGHT DRIVE AXLE ASSEMBLY

79222735

Tapping out the right inner halfshaft from the transaxle—4-door models

Prizm

✳✳ WARNING

Care must be exercised to prevent the differential-side CV-joint from being over-extended. Over-extension of the CV-joint could result in separation of internal components and possible joint failure. If the vehicle is to be lowered and moved, the front wheel bearings must be supported using a 9/16 in. bolt, 1¾ in. washer, 2 in. washer and a 9/16 in. nut, assembled through the shaft opening in the hub. Tighten the nut and bolt to 40 ft. lbs. (54 Nm). If equipped with Anti-lock Brake Systems (ABS), use caution not to damage the ABS speed sensor ring on the wheel-side CV-joint. DO NOT pry against the ring with metal tools. If the serrations on the speed sensor ring appear damaged, replace the wheel-side CV-joint.

1. Before servicing the vehicle, refer to the precautions in the beginning of this section.
2. Remove or disconnect the following:
   - Negative battery cable
   - Front wheel

- Splash shield
- ABS speed sensor, if equipped
- Cotter pin and lock cap from the halfshaft
- Tie rod end from the steering knuckle
- Ball joint from the control arm
- Wheel side CV-joint from the steering knuckle
- Differential side CV-joint from the transmission by gently prying the joint out
- Halfshaft

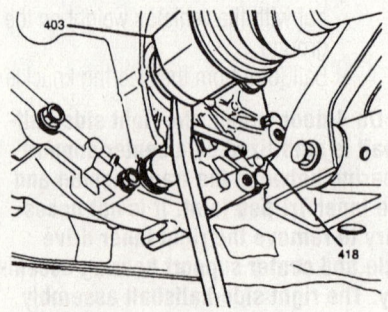

403

418

403 DIFFERENTIAL-SIDE JOINT HOUSING
418 TRANSAXLE ASSEMBLY

79222736

Prying out the inner halfshaft from the transaxle—Prizm

To install:

3. Inspect the CV-joint boots for tears or deterioration. Replace as necessary.
4. Inspect the front wheel bearing inner and outer oil seals for damage or deterioration. Replace as necessary.
5. Inspect the halfshaft fluid seal at the transmission for leakage or damage. Replace as necessary.
6. Install or connect the following:
   - Differential side CV-joint into the transmission
   - Wheel side CV-joint into the steering knuckle
   - Ball joint to the control arm. Torque the bolts to 105 ft. lbs. (142 Nm).
   - Tie rod end to the steering knuckle. Torque the nut to 36 ft. lbs. (49 Nm).
   - New cotter pin to the tie rod end
   - Halfshaft nut. Torque the nut to 167 ft. lbs. (228 Nm).
   - Lock cap onto the halfshaft and secure with a new cotter pin
   - ABS speed sensor electrical connector, if equipped
   - Splash shield. Torque the bolts to 71 inch lbs. (8 Nm).
   - Front wheel
   - Negative battery cable
7. Check the wheel alignment and adjust as needed.

CV-Joints

Do not disassemble the CV-Joint. If an abnormality is found, replace the assembly.

STEERING AND SUSPENSION

Air Bag

✳✳ CAUTION

All vehicles are equipped with an Air Bag system. The system must be disabled before performing service on or around system components, steering column, instrument panel components, wiring and sensors. Failure to follow safety and disabling procedures could result in accidental Air Bag deployment, possible personal injury and unnecessary system repairs.

PRECAUTIONS

Several precautions must be observed when handling the inflator module to avoid accidental deployment and possible personal injury.

• Never carry the inflator module by the wires or connector on the underside of the module.

• When carrying a live inflator module, hold securely with both hands, and ensure that the bag and trim cover are pointed away.

• Place the inflator module on a bench or other surface with the bag and trim cover facing up.

• With the inflator module on the bench, never place anything on or close to the module which may be thrown in the event of an accidental deployment.

DISARMING

Metro

1. Before servicing the vehicle, refer to the precautions in the beginning of this section.
2. Turn the steering wheel so the wheels are pointing straight-ahead.
3. Turn the ignition switch to the **LOCK** position and remove the key.
4. Remove or disconnect the following:
   • Negative battery cable
   • **AIR BAG-IG** fuse from the junction block near the base of the steering column
   • Steering wheel side cap, Connector Position Assurance (CPA) and yel-

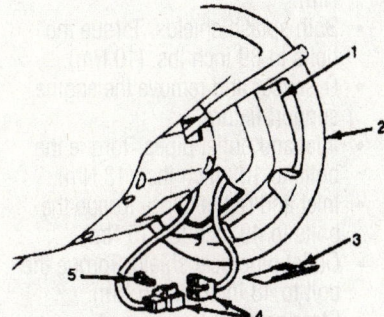

1 Inflator module housing
2 Steering wheel
3 Rear plastic access cover
4 SIR harness connector
5 Connector position assurance (CPA)

7922Z737

Location of the SIR harness connector—Metro

low 2-way connector for the driver's side Air Bag (inflator) module
• Glove box while pushing in on the stoppers from the left and the right sides. Disconnect the yellow connector for the passenger Air Bag (inflator) module.

To arm:
5. Install or connect the following:
   • Negative battery cable
   • Turn the ignition switch to the **LOCK** position and remove the key
   • Yellow connector for the passenger's side Air Bag (inflator) module and the yellow connector for the driver's air bag (inflator) module. Be sure to lock each connector with the lock lever
   • Glove box
   • Left side steering wheel side cap
   • **AIR BAG-IG** fuse to the junction block
6. Staying away from both air bags, turn the ignition switch to the **ON** position and verify that the **AIR BAG** warning lamp flashes 7 times, then turns OFF. If the system does not operate as described, diagnosis and repairs to the air bag system are necessary.

Prizm

➡ **The center sensor assembly can maintain sufficient voltage to cause deployment for up to 2 minutes after the ignition switch is turned to the LOCK position or the battery is disconnected.**

1. Before servicing the vehicle, refer to the precautions in the beginning of this section.
2. Turn the steering wheel so the front wheels are in the straight-ahead position.
3. Turn the ignition switch to **LOCK**.
4. Remove or disconnect the following:
   • Negative battery cable
   • Lower steering column trim cover
   • **IGN** fuse and **CIG** and **RADIO** fuse from junction block 1
   • Connector Position Assurance (CPA) and disconnect the yellow 2-way connector at the base of the steering column.
   • Inflatable restraint steering wheel module coil connector
   • Glove box
   • Unlock the passenger's side module connector and disconnect the pigtail
   • Unlock the left and right hand side seat module connectors and disconnect the seat modules

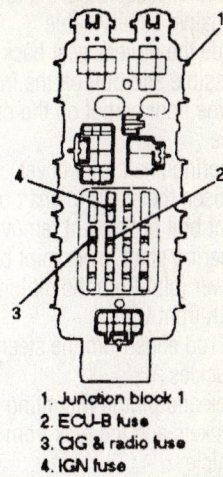

1. Junction block 1
2. ECU-B fuse
3. CIG & radio fuse
4. IGN fuse

7922Z738

Connector view and terminal identification of junction block 1—Prizm

To arm:
5. Turn the ignition switch to the **LOCK** position and remove the key.
6. Install or connect the following:
   • Negative battery cable
   • Yellow 2-way connectors for the driver's and passenger's seat modules
   • Connectors and lock them into place with the lock levers
   • Yellow 2-way connector to the passenger's side inflatable restraint pigtail. Connect the lock with the lever
   • Glove box
   • Yellow 2-way connector for the steering wheel module coil
   • Connectors and lock them into place with the lock levers
   • Lower steering column trim cover
   • **IGN** fuse and **CIG** and **RADIO** fuse to the junction block
7. Staying away from both air bags, turn the ignition **ON** and verify that the **AIR BAG** warning lamp flashes 7 times, then turns OFF. If the system does not operate as described, diagnosis and repairs to the air bag system are necessary.

Rack and Pinion Steering Gear

REMOVAL & INSTALLATION

Manual

METRO

1. Before servicing the vehicle, refer to the precautions in the beginning of this section.

2. Remove or disconnect the following:
- Negative battery cable
- Slide the driver's seat back as far as possible and pull off the front part of the floor carpet on the driver's side
- Steering shaft joint cover
- Loosen the steering shaft upper joint bolt but do not remove
- Steering shaft lower joint bolt
- Lower joint from the pinion
- Both front wheels
- Tie rod ends from the steering knuckles
- Rack and pinion mounting bolts, brackets and the rack from the vehicle

To install:

3. Install or connect the following:
- Steering gear through the front wheel opening and secure it to the bulkhead with mounting brackets. Torque the bolts to 18 ft. lbs. (25 Nm).
- Right and left tie rod ends to the steering knuckles
- Castle nuts to the tie rod ends. Torque the nuts to 32 ft. lbs. (43 Nm).
- New cotter pins
- Both front wheels
- Steering shaft to the steering gear. Torque the upper and lower steering shaft joint bolts to 18 ft. lbs. (25 Nm).
- Steering shaft joint cover
- Driver's side floor carpet
- Negative battery cable

4. Check and adjust the front wheel alignment.

Power

METRO

1. Before servicing the vehicle, refer to the precautions in the beginning of this section.

2. Remove or disconnect the following:
- Negative battery cable
- Slide the driver's seat back, pull off the front part of the floor carpet on the driver's side and remove the steering shaft joint cover
- Loosen the steering shaft upper joint bolt but do not remove
- Steering shaft lower joint bolt and disconnect the lower joint from the pinion
- Both front wheels
- Tie rod ends
- Exhaust pipe at the manifold
- Separate the shift linkage and

extension rod from the transmission, for manual transmission
- Engine rear torque rod with the bracket from the transmission, for automatic transmission
- Power steering lines from the rack and pinion assembly and plug the openings to prevent system contamination
- Rack and pinion from the vehicle

To install:

3. Install or connect the following:
- Steering rack, brackets and mounting bolts to the bulkhead. When aligned properly, torque the bolts to 18 ft. lbs. (25 Nm).
- Power steering lines to the rack and pinion. Torque the inlet and outlet fluid lines to 25 ft. lbs. (35 Nm) and the remaining lines to 18 ft. lbs. (25 Nm).
- Shift linkage and extension rod to the manual transmission
- Engine rear torque rod and bracket to the automatic transmission
- Front exhaust pipe to the manifold using a new seal. Torque the bolts to 37 ft. lbs. (50 Nm).
- Tie rod ends to the steering knuckles. Torque the castle nuts to 32 ft. lbs. (43 Nm).
- New cotter pins
- Both front wheels
- Lower steering shaft-to-steering gear. Torque the bolts to 18 ft. lbs. (25 Nm).
- Upper steering shaft. Torque the bolt to 18 ft. lbs. (25 Nm).
- Steering joint cover
- Negative battery cable

4. Place the driver's side floor carpet back into the original position.

5. Bleed the steering system and check for leaks, repair if necessary.

6. Check and adjust the front wheel alignment.

PRIZM

1. Before servicing the vehicle, refer to the precautions in the beginning of this section.

2. The front wheels must be straight and the steering column in the **LOCK** position before disconnecting the intermediate shaft from the steering gear.

3. Remove or disconnect the following:
- Negative battery cable
- Steering column upper cover
- Steering shaft lower coupling
- Inlet and outlet pipes from the steering gear

- Oxygen (O2S) sensor and install an engine support fixture
- Both splash shields
- Both front wheels
- Exhaust manifold heat shield
- Outer tie rods
- Front crossmember brace
- Front suspension crossmember, transmission support, both control arms and front stabilizer shaft as a complete unit
- Rear transmission mount and bracket
- Steering gear boot heat shield
- Steering gear

To install:

4. Install or connect the following:
- Steering gear and clamps. Torque the bolts to 52 ft. lbs. (71 Nm).
- Stedering gear boot heat shield. Torque the bolt to 48 inch lbs. (5 Nm).
- Exhaust manifold pipe. Torque the bolts to 46 ft. lbs. (62 Nm).
- Rear transmission mount bracket. Torque the bolts to 57 ft. lbs. (77 Nm).
- Rear transmission mount. Torque the bolt to 64 ft. lbs. (87 Nm).
- Front suspension crossmember, transmission support, control arms and stabilizer shaft
- Front crossmember. Torque the bolts to 51 ft. lbs. (69 Nm).
- Outer tie rods
- Front wheels
- Exhaust manifold heat shield. Torque the bolt to 48 inch lbs. (5 Nm).
- Both splash shields. Torque the bolts to 89 inch lbs. (10 Nm).
- O2 sensor and remove the engine support fixture
- Inlet and outlet pipes. Torque the bolts to 108 inch lbs. (13 Nm).
- Inlet and outlet clips. Torque the bolts to 48 inch lbs. (5 Nm).
- Outlet pipe heat shield. Torque the bolt to 48 inch lbs. (5 Nm).
- Steering shaft lower coupling. Torque the bolt to 26 ft. lbs. (35 Nm).
- Steering column upper cover. Torque the bolts to 48 inch lbs. (5 Nm).
- Negative battery cable

5. Refill and bleed the power steering system.

6. Check and adjust the front end alignment as needed.

Strut

REMOVAL & INSTALLATION

Front

METRO

1. Before servicing the vehicle, refer to the precautions in the beginning of this section.

2. Remove or disconnect the following:
   - Negative battery cable
   - Upper strut support nuts from the tower
   - Front wheel
   - Wheel speed sensor harness, if equipped with the Anti-lock Brake System (ABS)
   - Brake hose
   - Strut from the steering knuckle
   - Strut

To install:

3. Install or connect the following:
   - Strut to the vehicle. Torque the upper support nuts to 21 ft. lbs. (28 Nm).
   - Strut to steering knuckle. Torque the bolts to 59 ft. lbs. (80 Nm).
   - Brake hose to the strut bracket and secure with a new E-ring
   - Wheel speed sensor to the strut, if equipped. Torque the harness bolt to 89 inch lbs. (10 Nm).
   - Front wheel
   - Negative battery cable

4. Check the front alignment and adjust if necessary.

PRIZM

1. Before servicing the vehicle, refer to the precautions in the beginning of this section.

2. Properly support the front suspension crossmember.

3. Remove or disconnect the following:

   - Negative battery cable
   - Front wheel and make certain that the weight of the vehicle is resting on the crossmember and not the control arms
   - Wheel speed sensor, if equipped with Anti-lock Brakes System (ABS)
   - Brake hose from the strut
   - Loosen the fasteners on the lower side of the strut
   - Strut assembly from the strut tower
   - Strut

To install:

4. Install or connect the following:
   - Strut to the lower mount and hand-tighten the bolts
   - Strut to the strut tower. Torque the strut tower bolts to 29 ft. lbs. (39 Nm) and the lower bolts to 203 ft. lbs. (274 Nm).
   - Brake hose to the strut. Torque the bolt to 22 ft. lbs. (29 Nm).
   - Wheel speed sensor, if equipped. Torque the bolt to 71 inch lbs. (8 Nm).
   - Front wheel and remove the crossmember support.
   - Negative battery cable

5. Check and adjust the front end alignment.

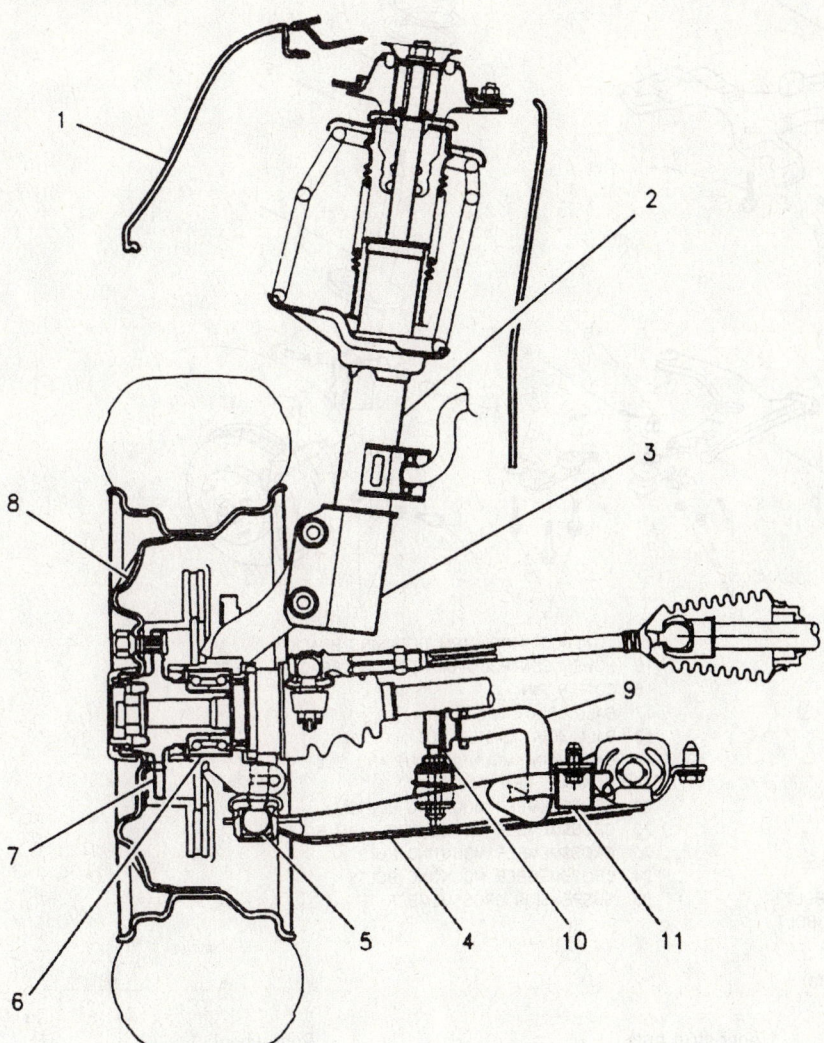

1	VEHICLE BODY	7	HUB
2	STRUT ASSEMBLY	8	WHEEL
3	STEERING KNUCKLE	9	SWAY BAR
4	CONTROL ARM	10	SWAY BAR LINK
5	BALL STUD	11	SWAY BAR BRACKET
6	WHEEL BEARING		

79222744

Cut-away view of the front suspension—Metro

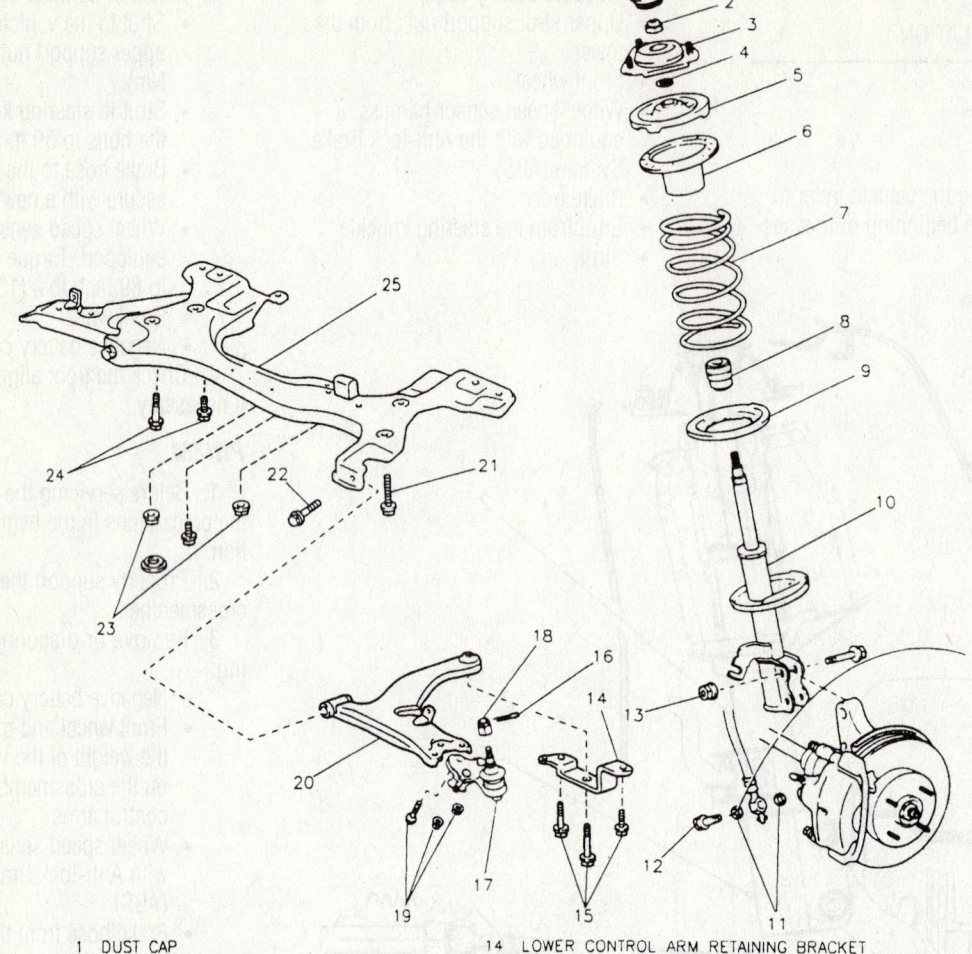

1 DUST CAP
2 STRUT ROD PISTON NUT
3 STRUT SUPPORT
4 DUST SEAL
5 SPRING SEAT
6 UPPER INSULATOR
7 COIL SPRING
8 SPRING BUMPER
9 LOWER INSULATOR
10 STRUT
11 BRAKE LINE GASKETS
12 BRAKE LINE-TO-CALIPER BOLT
13 STRUT MOUNTING NUT AND BOLT
14 LOWER CONTROL ARM RETAINING BRACKET
15 LOWER CONTROL ARM RETAINING BRACKET BOLTS
16 COTTER PIN
17 BALL JOINT
18 BALL JOINT CASTLE NUT
19 BALL JOINT MOUNTING NUT AND BOLT
20 CONTROL ARM
21 CROSSMEMBER MOUNTING BOLTS
22 CROSSMEMBER-TO-CONTROL ARM BOLT
23 CROSSMEMBER MOUNTING NUTS
24 CROSSMEMBER MOUNTING BOLTS
25 SUSPENSION CROSSMEMBER

79222Z739

Exploded view of the front suspension assembly—Prizm

Rear

METRO

1. Before servicing the vehicle, refer to the precautions in the beginning of this section.

2. Open the lift gate or trunk lid and reposition the trim cover from the strut tower.

3. Remove or disconnect the following:
   • Negative battery cable
   • Rear wheel and properly support the rear suspension
   • Strut from the knuckle
   • Upper strut nuts
   • Compress the strut and separate it from the steering knuckle
   • Strut

To install:

4. Compress the strut.
5. Install or connect the following:
   • Strut to the steering knuckle and position the alignment projection inside the opening in the knuckle. Torque the nuts to 24 ft. lbs. (30 Nm).
   • Steering knuckle. Torque the nut to 44 ft. lbs. (60 Nm).
   • Rear wheel
   • Negative battery cable
6. Reposition the rear trim cover.

PRIZM

1. Before servicing the vehicle, refer to the precautions in the beginning of this section.

2. Remove or disconnect the following:
   • Negative battery cable
   • Rear seat cushions
   • Rear wheel and properly support the rear suspension

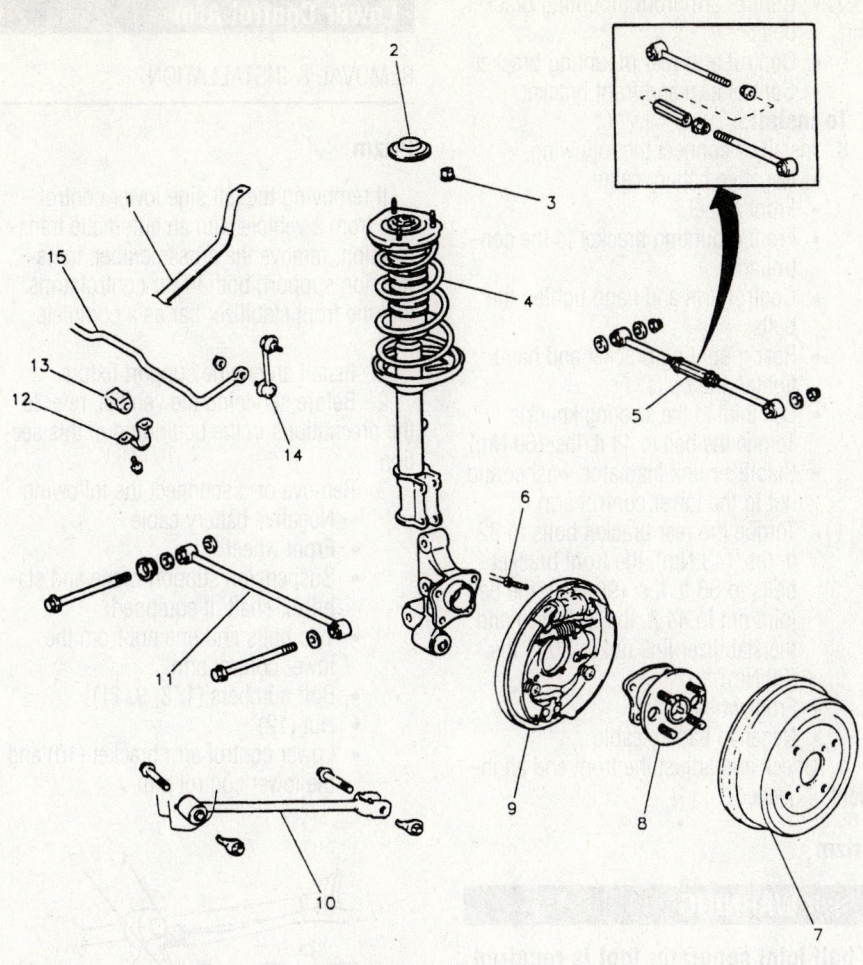

1 FUEL TANK BAND
2 STRUT TOWER COVER
3 STRUT ROD PISTON NUT
4 STRUT ASSEMBLY
5 REAR LATERAL LINK
6 BRAKE PIPE
7 BRAKE DRUM
8 HUB ASSEMBLY
9 BRAKE ASSEMBLY
10 TRAILING ARM
11 FRONT LATERAL LINK
12 STABILIZER SHAFT BRACKET
13 BUSHING
14 STABILIZER SHAFT JOINT
15 STABILIZER SHAFT

7922Z740

Exploded view of the rear strut assembly—Prizm

- Anti-lock Brake System (ABS) speed sensor, if equipped
- Flex hose from the strut
- Stabilizer shaft joint from the strut, if equipped
- Strut from the rear knuckle
- Cap from the strut support
- Strut mounting fasteners from the top strut support
- Strut from the vehicle

To install:
3. Install or connect the following:
- Strut to the rear knuckle and hand-tighten the nuts at this time
- Strut to the support. Torque the strut bolts to 29 ft. lbs. (39 Nm) and the knuckle bolts to 105 ft. lbs. (142 Nm).
- Cap to the strut support
- Stabilizer shaft joint, if equipped. Torque the fastener to 33 ft. lbs. (44 Nm).
- ABS speed sensor wire harness to the strut, if equipped
- Brake hose with a new clip
- Rear wheel and remove the support from the rear suspension
- Rear seat cushions
- Negative battery cable
4. Fill and bleed the brake system.

5. Check and adjust the rear wheel alignment as needed

Coil Spring

REMOVAL & INSTALLATION

Rear
METRO

1. Before servicing the vehicle, refer to the precautions in the beginning of this section.
2. Remove or disconnect the following:
- Negative battery cable
- Rear wheel
- Control rod from the knuckle
- Wheel speed sensor electrical connector from the control arm, if equipped
- Stabilizer link from the control arm and properly support the rear suspension
- Knuckle from the suspension arm
- Coil spring from the suspension arm and upper seat

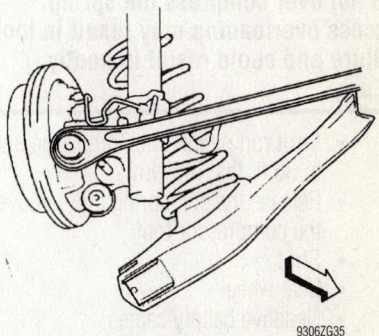

9306ZG35

Remove the coil spring from the rear suspension—Metro

To install:
3. Install or connect the following:
- Spring to the suspension arm with the larger diameter on the bottom
- Suspension arm to steering knuckle. Torque the bolt to 29 ft. lbs. (40 Nm).
- Wheel speed sensor to the control arm, if equipped
- Stabilizer link to the control arm. Torque the nut to 19 ft. lbs. (25 Nm).
- Control rod to the knuckle stud. Torque the nut to 59 ft. lbs. (80 Nm).
- Rear wheel
- Negative battery cable

Turn to Section 5 for brake system applications

PRIZM

1. Before servicing the vehicle, refer to the precautions in the beginning of this section.

2. Remove or disconnect the following:
   - Negative battery cable
   - Rear wheel
   - Strut

3. Mount a strut compressor tool into a holding fixture and install the strut using an adapter.

4. Compress the coil spring.

5. Remove or disconnect the following:
   - Strut rod piston nut and carefully release the compressed spring
   - Strut from the compressor tool
   - Strut cap, nuts, insulator and coil spring

To install:

6. Install or connect the following:
   - Coil spring, insulator nuts and strut cap
   - Mount the strut into a compressor tool and compress the coil spring.

✳✳ CAUTION

Do not over compress the spring. Excess overloading may result in tool failure and could result in bodily injury.

   - Strut rod piston nut. Torque the nut to 36 ft. lbs. (49 Nm).
   - Release the coil spring and remove the compressor tool
   - Strut
   - Rear wheel
   - Negative battery cable

Lower Ball Joint

REMOVAL & INSTALLATION

Metro

The lower ball joint is an integral part of the lower control arm assembly and is not serviceable as an individual component. If the lower ball joint is defective, the entire lower control arm must be replaced.

1. Before servicing the vehicle, refer to the precautions in the beginning of this section.

2. Remove or disconnect the following:
   - Negative battery cable
   - Stabilizer bar link nut, washer and insulator from the control arm
   - Ball joint nut
   - Separate the ball joint from the knuckle

   - Control arm front mounting bracket bolts
   - Control arm rear mounting bracket
   - Control arm and front bracket

To install:

3. Install or connect the following:
   - Negative battery cable
   - Front wheel
   - Front mounting bracket to the control arm
   - Control arm and hand tighten the bolts
   - Rear mounting bracket and hand tighten the bolts
   - Ball joint to the steering knuckle. Torque the bolt to 44 ft. lbs. (60 Nm).
   - Stabilizer link insulator, washer and nut to the lower control arm
   - Torque the rear bracket bolts to 32 ft. lbs. (43 Nm), the front bracket bolts to 66 ft. lbs. (90 Nm), the ball joint nut to 44 ft. lbs. (60 Nm) and the stabilizer link nut to 20 ft. lbs. (28 Nm).
   - Front wheel
   - Negative battery cable

4. Check and adjust the front end alignment, if needed.

Prizm

✳✳ WARNING

A ball joint separator tool is required to complete this procedure. It is a commonly available tool that prevents damage to the joint and knuckle. Do not attempt to separate the joint without it.

1. Before servicing the vehicle, refer to the precautions in the beginning of this section.

2. Remove or disconnect the following:
   - Negative battery cable
   - Front wheel and position a jack-stand under the crossmember
   - Cotter pin from the ball joint nut
   - Separate the ball joint from the steering knuckle
   - Ball joint from the steering knuckle

To install:

3. Install or connect the following:
   - Ball joint to the steering knuckle. Torque the new castle nut to 91 ft. lbs. (124 Nm).
   - New cotter pin
   - Steering knuckle
   - Front wheel
   - Negative battery cable

4. Check the front wheel alignment and adjust as needed.

Lower Control Arm

REMOVAL & INSTALLATION

Prizm

If removing the left side lower control arm from a vehicle with an automatic transmission, remove the crossmember, transmission support, both lower control arms and the front stabilizer bar as a complete unit.

1. Install an engine support fixture.

2. Before servicing the vehicle, refer to the precautions in the beginning of this section.

3. Remove or disconnect the following:
   - Negative battery cable
   - Front wheel
   - Suspension support brace and stabilizer shaft, if equipped
   - Two bolts and one nut from the lower control arm
   - Bolt numbers (1, 8, 9, 11)
   - Nut (12)
   - Lower control arm bracket (10) and the lower control arm

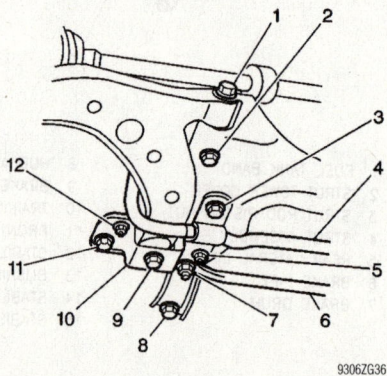

9306ZG36

Remove the hardware as shown–Prizm

To install:

4. Install or connect the following:
   - Lower control arm and hand-tighten the bolt
   - Stabilizer shaft and link, if equipped, to the lower control arm and hand-tighten the bolt
   - Lower control arm bracket. Torque the nut to 14 ft. lbs. (19 Nm).
   - Stabilizer shaft insulator clamp, if equipped. Torque the nut to 14 ft. lbs. (19 Nm).
   - Bolts (3, 8, 9, 11) and hand-tighten
   - Two bolts and one nut to the lower control arm. Torque the fasteners to 105 ft. lbs. (142 Nm).

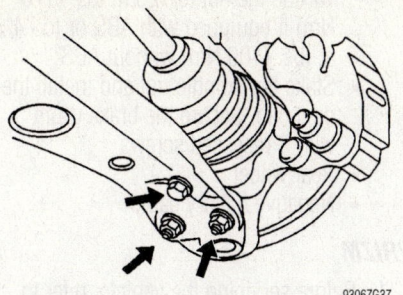

Install the two bolts and nut to the lower control arm–Prizm

- Suspension support brace. Torque the nuts to 51 ft. lbs. (69 Nm).
- Front wheel and stabilize the front suspension

5. Torque the bolts in the following sequence:
   a. Bolt No. 9: 129 ft. lbs. (175 Nm).
   b. Bolt No. 1: 158 ft. lbs. (215 Nm).
   c. Bolt No. 3: 167 ft. lbs. (225 Nm).
   d. Bolt No. 11: 109 ft. lbs. (147 Nm).
   e. Bolt No. 8: 91 ft. lbs. (123 Nm).
   f. Stabilizer shaft nut to 33 ft. lbs. (44 Nm).

6. Remove the engine support fixture and connect the negative battery cable.

7. Check and adjust the front end alignment, if needed.

CONTROL ARM BUSHING REPLACEMENT

Metro

1. Before servicing the vehicle, refer to the precautions in the beginning of this section.

2. Remove or disconnect the following:
- Negative battery cable
- Control arm
- Control arm rear bushing from the control arm with tool J 34865
- Control arm bracket
- Front bushing from the control arm with tool J 34865

To install:

3. Lubricate the circumference of the bushings with soapy water to ease installation.

4. Install or connect the following:
- Center the bushing in the control arm and using tool J 34865 install the front bushing to the control arm
- Rear bushing to the control arm with tool J 34865
- Control arm bracket. Torque the nut to 92 ft. lbs. (125 Nm).
- Control arm
- Negative battery cable

Prizm

➡ **The lower control arm bushings are service as part of the control arm and cannot be serviced separately.**

Wheel Bearings

ADJUSTMENT

The wheel bearings cannot be adjusted.

REMOVAL & INSTALLATION

Front

METRO

1. Before servicing the vehicle, refer to the precautions in the beginning of this section.

2. Remove or disconnect the following:
- Negative battery cable
- Front wheel
- Steering knuckle
- Inner/outer bearing oil seals from the steering knuckle
- Inner race and bearing from the knuckle
- Snapring from the outboard side of the knuckle
- Outer bearing from the knuckle
- Bearing from the knuckle

3. Inspect the wheel bearings for excessive wear, corrosion or contamination by dirt or water; replace as necessary.

To install:

4. Properly support the steering knuckle

5. Install or connect the following:
- Outer bearing to the knuckle
- Snapring to the outboard side of the knuckle
- Inner bearing and race to the knuckle
- Outer bearing race to the wheel hub

6. Lubricate the inner seal with wheel bearing grease.

7. If equipped with the Anti-lock Brakes System (ABS), align the hole in the seal with the hole in the knuckle for the wheel speed sensor

8. Install or connect the following:
- Inner seal to the inboard side of the knuckle
- Outer seal to the outboard side of the knuckle
- Knuckle
- Front wheel
- Negative battery cable

9. Check the wheel alignment and adjust, if necessary.

PRIZM

1. Before servicing the vehicle, refer to the precautions in the beginning of this section.

2. Remove or disconnect the following:
- Negative battery cable
- Front wheel
- Wheel speed sensor, if equipped
- Brake hose from the strut
- Brake caliper bracket
- Brake rotor
- Steering knuckle and clamp it in a soft face vise
- Inner seal shield from the knuckle
- Inner oil seal from the knuckle
- Wheel bearing retainer from the knuckle
- Hub and brake shield from the knuckle
- Outer seal
- Front wheel bearing outside inner race from the knuckle
- Wheel bearing

To install:

3. Clean and inspect the hub and knuckle for cracks, wear or other damage; replace as necessary.

4. Remove the inner and outer races from the new bearing.

5. Install or connect the following:
- Press a new bearing into the steering knuckle using Installation tool J-37777 and Driver Handle J-8092.
- New races into the bearing
- Drive the outer seal into the steering knuckle with a Hub Seal Installer tool J 35737-01 and lubricate the outer lip of the seal with a multi-purpose grease
- Brake shield to the knuckle. Torque the bolts to 75 ft. lbs. (9 Nm).
- Hub in a press with the wheel stud side down and install the knuckle to the hub
- Press the hub into the knuckle
- Front wheel bearing retainer to the knuckle
- Inner seal to the knuckle and apply a multi-purpose grease to the inner seal lip

6. If equipped with Anti-lock Brake System (ABS), align the holes for the speed sensor in the inner shield and the knuckle.

7. Install or connect the following:
- Inner seal shield to the knuckle and remove the knuckle from the vise
- Steering knuckle to the vehicle

- Brake rotor
- Brake caliper
- Brake hose to the strut. Torque the bolt to 22 ft. lbs. (29 Nm).
- ABS wheel speed sensor, if equipped. Torque the bolt to 70 inch lbs. (8 Nm).
- Front wheel
- Negative battery cable

8. Check the front wheel alignment and adjust if necessary.

Rear

METRO

1. Before servicing the vehicle, refer to the precautions in the beginning of this section.
2. Remove or disconnect the following:
   - Negative battery cable
   - Rear wheel
   - Spindle nut dust cap
   - Unstake the spindle nut and washer and discard the spindle nut
   - If not equipped with a wheel hub, tap on the brake drum/hub assembly to loosen and remove the assembly from the spindle
   - Inner bearing from the outboard side of the assembly, using a hammer and punch

➡It is be necessary to move the bearing spacer from side-to-side to work the punch around the perimeter of the inner bearing.

- Outer bearing from the inboard side of the assembly, using a hammer and punch.

➡It is be necessary to move the bearing spacer from side-to-side to work the punch around the perimeter of the outer bearing.

3. Inspect the wheel bearings for wear, corrosion or contamination and replace, as necessary.

To install:

➡The outer bearing is smaller in diameter than the inner one.

4. Install or connect the following:
   - Outer bearing in the drum/hub assembly using installation tools J-34842 and J-7079-2
   - Bearing spacer in the brake drum hub with the inner lip toward the outer bearing.

➡Be sure the bearing spacer is properly installed. The assembly will not fit on the spindle if the spacer lip is toward the inner bearing.

- Install the inner bearing in the drum/hub assembly using installation tools J-34842 and J-7079-2
- Brake drum/hub assembly to the spindle if not equipped with Anti-lock brake System (ABS) and install the wheel hub to the knuckle spindle if equipped with ABS.
- Washer and a new spindle nut.

Torque the nut to 120 ft. lbs. (170 Nm) if equipped with ABS or to 74 ft. lbs. (100 Nm) without ABS.
- Stake the spindle nut and install the dust cap. Secure the brake drum with 2 recessed screws
- Rear wheel
- Negative battery cable

PRIZM

1. Before servicing the vehicle, refer to the precautions in the beginning of this section.
2. Remove or disconnect the following:
   - Negative battery cable
   - Rear wheel
   - Brake drum or rotor
   - Anti-lock Brake System (ABS) wheel speed sensor, if equipped
   - Axle hub
   - O-ring from the backing plate

To install:

3. Install or connect the following:
   - New O-ring onto the backing plate
   - Hub to the knuckle. Torque the 4 mounting bolts to 59 ft. lbs. (80 Nm).
   - Wheel speed sensor, if equipped. Torque the bolt to 70 inch lbs. (8 Nm).
   - Brake drum
   - Rear wheel
   - Negative Battery cable

4. Check the rear wheel alignment and adjust, if necessary.

Saturn-LW • SC1 • SC2 • SL • SL1 • SL2 • SW1 • SW2l

PRECAUTIONS

Before servicing any vehicle, please be sure to read all of the following precautions, which deal with personal safety, prevention of component damage, and important points to take into consideration when servicing a motor vehicle:

• Never open, service or drain the radiator or cooling system when the engine is hot; serious burns can occur from the steam and hot coolant.

• Observe all applicable safety precautions when working around fuel. Whenever servicing the fuel system, always work in a well-ventilated area. Do not allow fuel spray or vapors to come in contact with a spark, open flame or excessive heat (a hot drop light, for example). Keep a dry chemical fire extinguisher near the work area. Always keep fuel in a container specifically designed for fuel storage; also, always properly seal fuel containers to avoid the possibility of fire or explosion. Refer to the additional fuel system precautions later in this section.

• Fuel injection systems often remain pressurized, even after the engine has been turned **OFF**. The fuel system pressure must be relieved before disconnecting any fuel lines. Failure to do so may result in fire and/or personal injury.

• Brake fluid often contains polyglycol ethers and polyglycols. Avoid contact with the eyes and wash your hands thoroughly after handling brake fluid. If you do get brake fluid in your eyes, flush your eyes with clean, running water for 15 minutes. If eye irritation persists, or if you have taken brake fluid internally, IMMEDIATELY seek medical assistance.

• The EPA warns that prolonged contact with used engine oil may cause a number of skin disorders, including cancer! You should make every effort to minimize your exposure to used engine oil. Protective gloves should be worn when changing oil. Wash your hands and any other exposed skin areas as soon as possible after exposure to used engine oil. Soap and water, or waterless hand cleaner should be used.

• All new vehicles are now equipped with an air bag system. The system must be disabled before performing service on or around system components, steering column, instrument panel components, wiring and sensors. Failure to follow safety and disabling procedures could result in accidental air bag deployment, possible personal injury and unnecessary system repairs.

• Always wear safety goggles when working with, or around, the air bag system. When carrying a non-deployed air bag, be sure the bag and trim cover are pointed away from your body. When placing a non-deployed air bag on a work surface, always face the bag and trim cover upward, away from the surface. This will reduce the motion of the module if it is accidentally deployed. Refer to the additional air bag system precautions later in this section.

• Clean, high quality brake fluid from a sealed container is essential to the safe and proper operation of the brake system. You should always buy the correct type of brake fluid for your vehicle. If the brake fluid becomes contaminated, completely flush the system with new fluid. Never reuse any brake fluid. Any brake fluid that is removed from the system should be discarded. Also, do not allow any brake fluid to come in contact with a painted surface; it will damage the paint.

• Never operate the engine without the proper amount and type of engine oil; doing so WILL result in severe engine damage.

• Timing belt maintenance is extremely important! Many models utilize an interference-type, non-freewheeling engine. If the timing belt breaks, the valves in the cylinder head may strike the pistons, causing potentially serious (also time-consuming and expensive) engine damage. Refer to the maintenance interval charts in the front of this manual for the recommended replacement interval for the timing belt, and to the timing belt section for belt replacement and inspection.

• Disconnecting the negative battery cable on some vehicles may interfere with the functions of the on-board computer system(s) and may require the computer to undergo a relearning process once the negative battery cable is reconnected.

• When servicing drum brakes, only disassemble and assemble one side at a time, leaving the remaining side intact for reference.

• Only an MVAC-trained, EPA-certified automotive technician should service the air conditioning system or its components.

ENGINE REPAIR

Ignition Timing

ADJUSTMENT

The 1.9L, 2.2L and 3.0L engines utilize a Distributorless Ignition System (DIS).

Alternator

REMOVAL

1.9L Engine

1. Before servicing the vehicle, refer to the precautions in the beginning of this section.

2. Remove or disconnect the following:
   • Negative battery cable
   • Drive belt
   • Right front wheel
   • Right front wheel well splash shield
   • Field wires from the alternator
   • Alternator through the wheel well opening

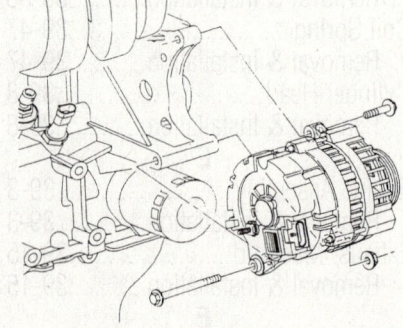

9306ZG39

Alternator mounting–1.9L engine

2.2L Engine

1. Before servicing the vehicle, refer to the precautions in the beginning of this section.

2. Remove or disconnect the following:
   • Negative battery cable
   • Throttle body air duct
   • Drive belt
   • Alternator wiring connectors
   • Alternator

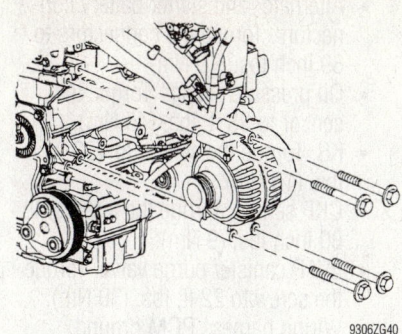

Alternator mounting–2.2L engine

9306ZG40

3.0L Engine

1. Before servicing the vehicle, refer to the precautions in the beginning of this section.

2. Remove or disconnect the following:

- Negative battery cable
- Drive belt and tensioner
- Upper alternator bolts and turn the steering wheel to the right side to gain access to the lower bolts
- Alternator lower bolts and separate the alternator from the engine
- Wiring connectors
- Alternator

INSTALLATION

1.9L Engine

Install or connect the following:

➡**Make certain the alternator shield is in place before installation.**

- Alternator to the cylinder block bracket. Torque the bolts to 24 ft. lbs. (32 Nm).
- Alternator regulator connector and fusible link. The link must be orientated between the 10–11 o'clock position
  - Splash shield
  - Right front wheel
  - Drive belt
  - Negative battery cable

2.2L Engine

Install or connect the following:

- Alternator. Torque the bolts to 15 ft. lbs. (20 Nm).
  - Alternator wiring connectors
  - Drive belt
  - Throttle body air duct
  - Negative battery cable

3.0L Engine

Install or connect the following:

- Alternator electrical connectors
- Alternator. Torque the bolts to 30 ft. lbs. (40 Nm).
- Drive belt tensioner. Torque the bolts to 30 ft lbs. (40 Nm).
- Drive belt
- Negative battery cable

Engine Assembly

REMOVAL & INSTALLATION

1.9L Engine

➡**The manufacturer recommends that the engine and transmission be removed as a complete unit. Disconnect the cradle and lower the entire assembly instead of lifting the assembly out of the vehicle. Both the SOHC and DOHC engines are removed or installed in the same manner. We have found that it is often possible, however, to remove the engine or transmission alone on some models with automatic transmissions by raising it up and out of the engine compartment.**

1. Before servicing the vehicle, refer to the precautions in the beginning of this section.

2. Properly disable the SIR system.

3. Properly relieve the fuel system pressure.

4. Drain the engine coolant.

5. Drain the engine oil.

6. Remove or disconnect the following:

- Both battery cables
- Air cleaner and intake duct assembly
- Engine Coolant Temperature (ECT) sensor electrical connector
- Oxygen (O_2S) sensor and clip
- Idle Air Control (IAC) valve
- Ignition coil connectors
- Throttle Position (TP) sensor
- Manifold Absolute Pressure (MAP) sensor
- Exhaust Gas Recirculation (EGR) solenoid
- Brake booster hose
- Ground connectors at the rear of the cylinder block
- Fuel injector connectors
- Neutral Safety Selector (NSS) switch
- Valve body actuator connector

- Transmission temperature sensor
- Turbine speed sensor
- Back-up light switch on manual transmissions
- Accelerator cable
- Fuel pressure and return lines
- Drive belt
- Upper radiator hose and de-aeration hose
- A/C compressor, if equipped. Do not discharge the system
- Transmission cooler lines
- Automatic transmission shifter cable, if equipped
- Manual transmission shifter cables and hydraulic clutch system, if equipped
- Tie the radiator, condenser and fan module to the crossbar
- Front wheels and fender shields
- Brake caliper brackets and secure the calipers to the shock tower
- Struts from the knuckles
- Lower radiator hose
- Heater inlet and outlet hoses
- Steering shaft and pressure switch electrical connectors
- Front exhaust pipe from the exhaust manifold
- Catalytic converter
- Powertrain stiffening bracket
- Flywheel cover and torque converter bolts, if equipped
- Starter
- Alternator
- Oil pressure sensor
- Knock Sensor (KS)
- Crankshaft Position (CKP) sensor
- Electronic Variable Orifice (EVO) solenoid, if equipped
- Vehicle Speed Sensor (VSS)
- Evaporative Emissions (EVAP) purge solenoid
- Powertrain Control Module (PCM)
- Oxygen (O_2S) sensor
- Antilock Brake System (ABS) connectors, if equipped
- Brake lines from the rear of the cradle
- Electrical harness from the engine and position it on top of the battery cover and junction block

7. Place a block of wood between the torque strut and cradle. Remove the 3 right side upper engine torque axis to front cover nuts and the 2 mount-to-midrail bracket nuts, allowing the powertrain to rest on the block of wood. Properly support the engine/transmission assembly.

8. Remove or disconnect the following:
- 2 right side front engine mount torque strut bracket to cradle nuts
- 4 cradle attaching bolts
- Powertrain assembly
- Spark plug wire ends from the ignition module
- Power steering pump and bracket, if equipped

9. Attach the 2 washers located between the cradle and body, to the cradle.

10. Install an engine lifting device to the service support brackets.

11. Remove or disconnect the following:
- Front mount assembly
- Motion restrictor bracket, if applicable and place a block of wood under the axle shaft
- Starter support bracket bolt, intake manifold support brace (DOHC engines) and 3 axle shaft bracket support bolts. Allow the bracket to rotate rearward. Lift the engine slightly for clearance, as necessary
- Engine strut bracket and torque strut from the engine
- Transmission attaching bolts
- Engine from the transmission

To install:

12. Install or connect the following:
- Engine to the transmission. Torque the lower transmission bolts to 96 ft. lbs. (130 Nm) and the upper transmission bolts to 66 ft. lbs. (90 Nm).
- Stiffening bracket. Torque the bolts to 40 ft. lbs. (54 Nm).
- Front engine mount. Torque the bolt to 41 ft. lbs. (55 Nm).
- Engine mount torque strut bracket and engine strut to engine bracket. Torque the bolts to 52 ft. lbs. (70 Nm).
- Axle shaft bracket. Torque the bolt to 41 ft. lbs. (55 Nm).
- Starter bracket. Torque the bolt to 80 inch lbs. (9 Nm).
- Engine/transmission assembly to the chassis. Torque the cradle to body bolts to 151 ft. lbs. (205 Nm).
- Brake lines to the cradle and steering shaft U-joint. Torque the bolts to 35 ft. lbs. (47 Nm).
- Starter. Torque the connector to 44 inch lbs. (5 Nm).
- Alternator. Torque the bolts to 24 ft. lbs. (32 Nm).

- Alternator and starter battery connectors. Torque the connectors to 89 inch lbs. (10 Nm).
- Oil pressure sensor. Torque the sensor to 33 ft. lbs. (45 Nm).
- KS. Torque the sensor to 133 inch lbs. (15 Nm).
- CKP sensor. Torque the fastener to 80 inch lbs. (9 Nm).
- EVAP canister purge valve. Torque the screw to 22 ft. lbs. (30 Nm).
- Wiring harness PCM ground. Torque the fastener to 89 inch lbs. (10 Nm).
- Wiring harness to the transmission/engine block. Torque the fasteners to 18 ft. lbs. (25 Nm).
- EVO solenoid, if equipped
- VSS
- ABS wheel sensors, if equipped
- Front exhaust pipe to the manifold. Torque the bolts to 23 ft. lbs. 31 Nm).
- Exhaust pipe to stiffening bracket. Torque the bolts to 35 ft. lbs. (47 Nm).
- Exhaust pipe to support bracket. Torque the bolts to 23 ft. lbs. (31 Nm).
- Exhaust pipe to catalytic converter. Torque the bolts to 35 ft. lbs. (48 Nm).
- Heater, lower radiator and coolant fill hoses
- Cylinder block drain plug. Torque the plug to 27 ft. lbs. (36 Nm).
- Steering knuckle to the strut. Torque the bolts to 148 ft. lbs. (20 Nm).
- Brake caliper. Torque the bolts to 81 ft. lbs. (110 Nm).
- Hydraulic clutch slave cylinder, if equipped. Torque the fasteners to 19 ft. lbs. (25 Nm).
- Shift cables
- Cooler lines, if equipped
- A/C compressor and drive belt. Torque the front bolt to 40 ft. lbs. (54 Nm) and the rear bolt to 22 ft. lbs. (30 Nm).
- Engine mount to midrail bracket and the engine mount to the front cover. Torque the bolts to 37 ft. lbs. (50 Nm).
- Torque converter to the flexplate bolts. Torque the bolts to 52 ft. lbs. (70 Nm).
- Dust cover. Torque the fasteners to 89 inch lbs. (10 Nm).
- Splash shields
- Both front wheels
- ECT sensor electrical connector

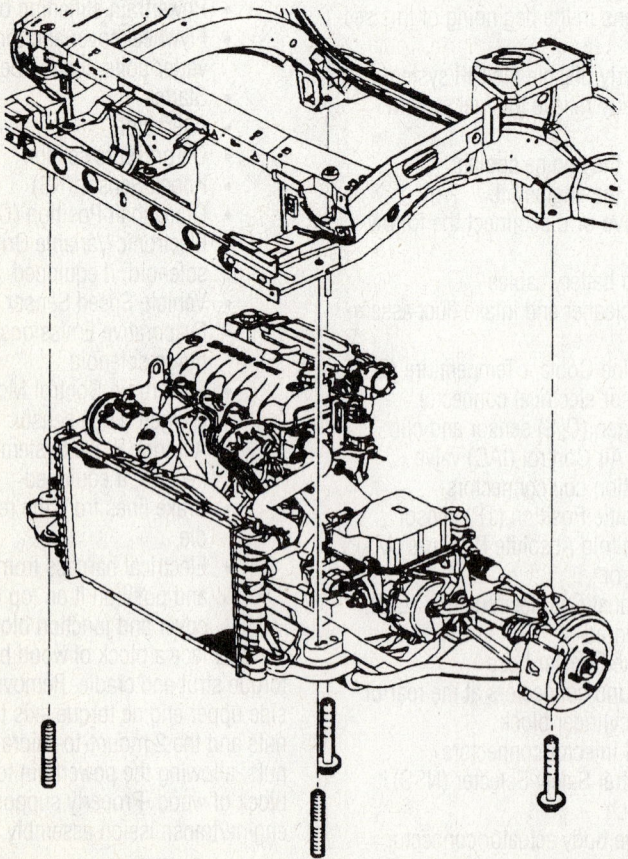

9306ZG41

Exploded view of the cradle to body bolts–1.9L engine

- Oxygen (O$_2$S) sensor electrical connector
- IAC valve electrical connector
- Fuel injector connectors
- TP sensor electrical connectors
- MAP sensor electrical connector
- EGR valve electrical connector
- A/C compressor electrical connector, if equipped
- Brake booster vacuum hose
- Ground connections
- NSS switch connectors
- PNP switch connectors
- Valve body actuator connector
- Transmission turbine speed sensor connector
- Back-up light switch connector, if equipped
- Temperature sensor electrical connector
- Accelerator cable
- Fuel feed and return line quick connectors
- Upper radiator and de-aeration hoses

➡**Check the upper cooling module grommets for misalignment. The cooling module must be able to move freely.**

- Air cleaner and intake duct assembly
- Both battery cables

13. Fill the engine with new oil.

14. Fill the coolant system.

15. Prime the fuel system by cycling the ignition **ON** for 5 seconds and **OFF** for 10 seconds a few times without cranking the engine. Start the engine and check for leaks.

16. Perform a short road test and check the engine again for leaks. Be sure the cooling system is filled to the surge tank FULL COLD line.

2.2L Engine

AUTOMATIC TRANSMISSION

1. Before servicing the vehicle, refer to the precautions in the beginning of this section.

2. Properly relieve the fuel system pressure.

3. Drain the engine coolant.

4. Drain the engine oil.

5. Drain the power steering fluid.

6. Remove or disconnect the following:
- Both battery cables
- Main wire feed to the fuse block
- Ground wire on the left fender well
- Intake Air Temperature (IAT) sensor electrical connector

- Air cleaner and intake duct assembly
- Purge hose from the throttle body
- Purge solenoid electrical connector
- Rear Heated Oxygen (HO$_2$S) sensor
- Back-up switch electrical connector, if equipped
- Main harness connector by the master cylinder
- Alternator electrical connector
- A/C pressure switch electrical connector
- Transmission electrical connectors
- Right front speed sensor electrical connector
- Cowl cover
- Powertrain Control Module (PCM) boot from the cowl
- PCM electrical connectors
- Engine harness connectors from the fuse block
- Battery, tray and fuse block tray
- Cruise control and throttle cables
- Brake assist vacuum line from the throttle body
- Fuel lines and position them away from the engine
- Evaporative Emissions (EVAP) purge hose at the solenoid
- Starter
- Torque converter
- Exhaust system from the catalytic converter to the exhaust manifold
- A/C compressor. It is not necessary to discharge the system
- Lower engine to the transmission bell housing bolts. Do not remove the upper bolts
- Heater hoses at the lower cowl
- Coolant reservoir hose
- Upper and lower radiator hoses
- Metal power steering line and attach a lifting hoist to the engine lifting eyes
- Right front engine mount while supporting the weight of the transmission with a jack
- Engine mount bracket and remove the upper bell housing bolts
- Engine

To install:

7. Lower the engine into the vehicle and align it on the pins on the transmission.

8. Install or connect the following:
- Upper bell housing bolts and hand-tighten them
- Engine mount bracket. Torque the bolts to 66 ft. lbs. (90 Nm).
- Engine mount. Torque the bolts to 41 ft. lbs. (55 Nm).

- Transmission nose bracket. Torque the bolts to 26 ft. lbs. (35 Nm).
- Metal power steering line and remove the engine lifting device
- Upper and lower radiator hoses
- Coolant reservoir hose
- Lower bell housing bolts. Torque the lower bolts to 48 ft. lbs. (65 Nm).
- Torque converter. Torque the bolts to 33 ft. lbs. (45 Nm).
- Starter
- Heater hoses
- A/C compressor. Torque the bolts to 18 ft. lbs. (25 Nm).
- Drive belt
- Exhaust from the catalytic converter to the exhaust manifold
- Torque the upper bell housing bolts to 48 ft. lbs. (65 Nm).
- EVAP purge solenoid and hose
- Fuel feed and return lines
- Brake assist vacuum hose
- Cruise control and throttle cables
- Fuse block and battery trays
- Engine harness to the fuse block
- Main engine harness under the fuse block panel
- PCM electrical connector
- PCM boot to the cowl
- Cowl cover
- Main harness connector near the master cylinder
- Rear (HO$_2$S) sensor
- Purge solenoid electrical connector
- Purge hose to the throttle body
- Air cleaner and intake duct assembly
- IAT electrical connector
- Ground wire to the left fender well
- Main wire feed to the fuse block
- Battery and both cables

9. Fill the engine with coolant.

10. Fill the engine with new oil.

11. Fill the power fluid reservoir.

12. Prime the fuel system by cycling the ignition **ON** for 5 seconds and **OFF** for 10 seconds a few times without cranking the engine.

13. Start the engine, check for leaks, and repair if necessary.

MANUAL TRANSMISSION

1. Before servicing the vehicle, refer to the precautions in the beginning of this section.

2. Properly relieve the fuel system pressure.

3. Drain the engine coolant.

4. Drain the engine oil.

5. Drain the power steering fluid.
6. Remove or disconnect the following:
- Both battery cables
- Steering gear pinch bolt to interme-diate shaft pinch bolt
- Main wire feed to the fuse block
- Ground wire on the left fender well
- Intake Air Temperature (IAT) sensor electrical connector
- Air cleaner and intake duct assem-bly
- Purge hose from the throttle body
- Purge solenoid electrical connector
- Rear Heated Oxygen (HO2S) sensor
- Back-up switch electrical connector
- Front dash cover
- Powertrain Control Module (PCM) boot from the front of the dash
- Main harness connector by the master cylinder
- PCM electrical connectors
- Engine harness connectors from the fuse block
- Battery, tray and fuse block tray
- Cruise control and throttle cables
- Brake assist vacuum line from the throttle body
- Pin retaining the control shaft lever to the shift control shaft
- Retaining clips connecting the con-trol shaft lever to the transmission
- Control shaft lever assembly
- Heater hoses at the lower cowl
- Upper and lower radiator hoses
- Fuel lines and position them away from the engine
- Secure the radiator to the upper radiator support
- Both front wheels and the right front splash shield
- Left front wheel liner push pin from the frame and install wood blocks between the transmission case and frame and the crank pulley and frame
- Right side engine mount
- Left side transmission mount
- Exhaust system from the catalytic converter to the exhaust manifold
- A/C compressor. It is not necessary to discharge the system
- Tie rod from the steering knuckle and discard the bolts
- Stabilizer bar links from the strut
- Lower ball joint stud and separate the ball joint from the steering knuckle
- Suspension support assemblies
- Suspension support cage nuts from the body and discard the nuts and properly support the powertrain and frame assembly

- Remaining frame to body attach-ment fasteners
- Lower the powertrain and frame assembly from the vehicle

To install:

7. Raise the powertrain into the vehicle.
8. Install or connect the following:
- New frame to body bolts and sus-pension supports. Torque the new bolts to 74 ft. lbs. (100 Nm) plus 45 degrees
- Ball stud to the steering knuckle. Torque the nuts to 74 ft. lbs. (100 Nm).
- Stabilizer to the strut. Torque the fasteners to 50 ft. lbs. (65 Nm).
- Tie rod to the steering knuckle. Torque the new nuts to 35 ft. lbs. (45 Nm).
- Exhaust system from the catalytic converter to the exhaust manifold
- A/C compressor. Torque the bolts to 18 ft. lbs. (25 Nm).
- Rear (HO2S) sensor
- Right side engine mount. Torque the bolts to 41 ft. lbs. (55 Nm).
- Left side transmission mount. Torque the bolts to 41 ft. lbs. (55 Nm).
- Left front wheel liner push pins
- Right front splash shield
- Both front wheels and remove the radiator from the upper radiator support
- Fuel feed and return lines
- Upper and lower radiator hoses
- Heater hoses
- Brake assist vacuum hose
- Shift control rod and adjust as fol-lows:

a. Rotate the transmission shift con-trol shaft clockwise and depress the spring loaded transmission shift linkage lock pin on the case.

b. Pull up the shift lever boot.

c. Move the shift lever to the 5 (reverse gate) and use a 3/8 inch punch to hold it in place.

d. Tighten the pinch bolt.

9. Install or connect the following:
- Cruise control and throttle cables
- Fuse block and battery trays
- Fuse block
- PCM electrical connector
- PCM boot to the cowl
- Cowl cover
- EVAP purge solenoid and hose
- Purge solenoid electrical connector
- Main harness connector near the master cylinder
- Transmission back-up switch elec-trical connector

- Purge hose to the throttle body
- Air cleaner and intake duct assem-bly
- IAT electrical connector
- Ground wire to the left fender well
- Main wire feed to the fuse block
- Battery and both cables
- Steering gear to the intermediate shaft pinch bolt

10. Fill the engine with coolant.
11. Fill the engine with new oil.
12. Fill the power fluid reservoir.
13. Prime the fuel system by cycling the ignition **ON** for 5 seconds and **OFF** for 10 seconds a few times without cranking the engine.
14. Start the engine, check for leaks, and repair if necessary.

3.0L Engine

1. Before servicing the vehicle, refer to the precautions in the beginning of this sec-tion.
2. Properly relieve the fuel system pressure.
3. Drain the engine coolant.
4. Drain the engine oil.
5. Drain the power steering fluid.
6. Remove or disconnect the following:
- Both battery cables
- Battery ground cable at the fuse block
- Transmission Control Module (TCM) main connector from under the cowl cover
- TCM inline connector by the brake master cylinder
- A/C pressure connector
- Black engine harness connector from under the fuse block panel
- Lower weather pack connector from inside the fuse block and secure the engine harness to the engine
- Fuse block
- Battery tray
- Evaporative Emissions (EVAP) purge connector
- Right front speed sensor connector
- Front Oxygen (O2S) sensor from the down pipe
- Transmission ground electrical connector
- Transmission main electrical con-nector
- Transmission shift control electrical connector
- Rear connector on the Engine Con-trol Module (ECM)
- Brake booster vacuum hose
- Fuel lines
- EVAP purge hose and solenoid

- Starter
- Torque converter
- Exhaust system from the catalytic converter to the exhaust manifold
- Transmission nose bracket
- A/C compressor. Do not discharge the system
- Heater hoses at the lower cowl
- Loosen the lower engine to bell housing bolts, but do not remove them
- Upper, lower and coolant reservoir hoses
- Metal power steering line
- Power steering reservoir from the radiator support and attach an engine lifting devise to the engine lifting eyes
- Right front engine mount and bracket
- Upper and lower bell housing bolts
- Engine from the vehicle

To install:

7. Lower the engine into the vehicle and align it on the pins on the transmission.

8. Install or connect the following:
- Upper bell housing bolts and hand-tighten them
- Engine mount bracket. Torque the bolt to 30 ft. lbs. (40 Nm).
- Engine mount. Torque the upper bolt to 30 ft. lbs. (40 Nm) and the lower bolt to 41 ft. lbs. (55 Nm).
- Transmission nose bracket. Torque the bolts to 30 ft. lbs. (40 Nm).
- Metal power steering line and remove the engine lifting devise
- Upper and lower radiator hoses
- Coolant reservoir hose
- Lower bell housing bolts. Torque the bolts to 48 ft. lbs. (65 Nm).
- Torque converter. Torque the bolts to 48 ft. lbs. (65 Nm).
- Starter
- Heater hoses at the lower cowl
- A/C compressor. Torque the bolts to 30 ft. lbs. (40 Nm).
- Exhaust from the catalytic converter to the exhaust manifold
- EVAP purge solenoid and hose
- Fuel feed and return lines
- Brake assist vacuum hose
- ECM rear connector
- Transmission shift control electrical connector
- Transmission ground connector
- Right front speed sensor electrical connector
- Front (HO$_2$S) sensor

- Right front speed sensor
- EVAP purge solenoid electrical connector
- Torque the upper bell housing bolts to 48 ft. lbs. (65 Nm).
- Battery tray
- Fuse block and route the engine harness to the block
- Lower weather pack connector
- Main wire feed to the fuse block
- A/C pressure connector
- TCM inline connector
- TCM main connector under the cowl cover and secure it to the engine
- Positive main feed cable at the fuse block
- Battery ground cable at the wheel housing
- Battery and both cables
- Air cleaner and intake duct assembly

9. Fill the engine with coolant.

10. Fill the engine with new oil.

11. Fill the power fluid reservoir.

12. Prime the fuel system by cycling the ignition **ON** for 5 seconds and **OFF** for 10 seconds a few times without cranking the engine.

13. Start the engine, check for leaks, and repair if necessary.

Water Pump

REMOVAL & INSTALLATION

1.9L Engine

1. Before servicing the vehicle, refer to the precautions in the beginning of this section.

2. Drain the coolant system.

3. Remove or disconnect the following:
- Negative battery cable
- Drive belt
- Right front wheel and inner wheel well splash shield
- A/C compressor and move it to the side. Do not discharge the system
- Water pump pulley bolts and allow the pulley to hang freely on the water pump hub
- Water pump flange bolts
- Water pump and pulley

To install:

4. Thoroughly clean the gasket mating surfaces of all old gasket material. Apply a small amount of gasket sealant at the outer edges of the bolt holes to hold the gasket in

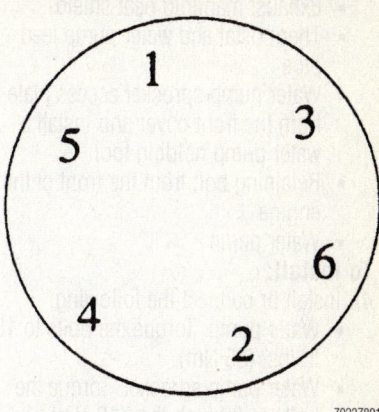

Water pump bolt torque sequence—1.9L engine

place. Install the gasket onto the water pump.

5. Install or connect the following:
- water pump with the small bump located next to one of the attaching bolts in the 11 o'clock position. Torque the bolts in a crisscross sequence to 22 ft. lbs. (30 Nm).
- Water pump pulley to the hub. Torque the bolts to 19 ft. lbs. (25 Nm).
- Drive belt
- Right front wheel well splash shield
- Right front wheel
- Negative battery cable

6. Fill the coolant system.

7. Start the vehicle and check for leaks, repair if necessary.

2.2L Engine

1. Before servicing the vehicle, refer to the precautions in the beginning of this section.

2. Drain the coolant system.

3. Remove or disconnect the following:
- Negative battery cable
- Air cleaner and intake duct

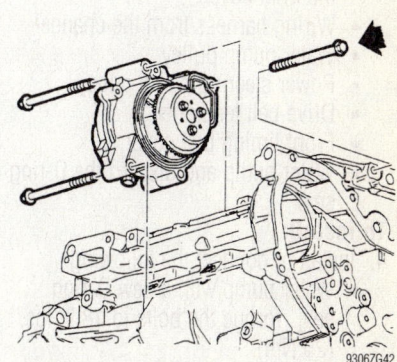

Exploded view of the water pump—2.2L engine

- Exhaust manifold heat shield
- Thermostat and water pump feed pipe
- Water pump sprocket access plate from the front cover and install a water pump holding tool
- Retaining bolt from the front of the engine
- Water pump

To install:

4. Install or connect the following:
- Water pump. Torque the bolts to 18 ft. lbs. (25 Nm).
- Water pump sprocket. Torque the bolts to 89 inch lbs. (10 Nm).
- Water pump sprocket access plate
- Water feed tube after lubricating the o-ring
- Thermostat housing. Torque the bolts to 89 inch lbs. (10 Nm).
- Exhaust manifold heat shield
- Air cleaner and intake duct
- Negative battery cable

5. Fill the coolant system.

6. Start the vehicle and check for leaks, repair if necessary.

3.0L Engine

1. Before servicing the vehicle, refer to the precautions in the beginning of this section.

2. Drain the coolant system.

3. Remove or disconnect the following:
- Negative battery cable
- Air cleaner and intake duct
- Left front wheel and splash shield
- Loosen the water pump pulley and power steering bolts, but do not remove them. Install an engine support fixture
- Right front engine mount
- Drive belt
- Release the retaining tabs on the wiring harness channel and remove the front cover
- Wiring harness from the channel
- Water pump pulley
- Power steering pump pulley
- Drive belt tensioner
- Front timing belt cover
- Water pump and discard the O-ring seal

To install:

4. Install or connect the following:
- Water pump with a new O-ring seal. Torque the bolts to 18 ft. lbs. (25 Nm).
- Front timing belt cover. Torque the bolts to 71 inch lbs. (8 Nm).
- Drive belt tensioner. Torque the bolts to 30 ft. lbs. (40 Nm).

- Power steering pump and water pump pulley's and hand-tighten the bolts
- Wiring harness into the channel
- Wiring harness channel front cover
- Drive belt. Torque the power steering pump pulley bolts to 71 inch lbs. (8 Nm) and the water pump pulley bolts to 15 ft. lbs. (20 Nm). Remove the engine support fixture
- Splash shield. Torque the bolts to 44 inch lbs. (5 Nm).
- Front wheel
- Air cleaner and intake duct
- Negative battery cable

5. Fill the coolant system.

6. Start the vehicle and check for leaks, repair if necessary.

Cylinder Head

REMOVAL & INSTALLATION

1.9L Engine

> ❄ **WARNING**
>
> **Only remove the cylinder head when the engine is cold. Warpage may result if the cylinder head is removed while the engine is hot.**

1. Before servicing the vehicle, refer to the precautions in the beginning of this section.

2. Drain the coolant system.

3. Drain the engine oil.

4. Properly relieve the fuel system pressure.

5. Remove or disconnect the following:
- Negative battery cable
- Air cleaner and intake duct
- Rocker cover fresh air hose
- Intake Air Temperature (IAT) sensor
- Accelerator cable from the throttle body and intake manifold bracket
- Coolant temperature gauge electrical connector
- Fuel injector connectors
- Idle Air Control (IAC) valve electrical connectors
- Throttle Position (TP) sensor electrical connectors
- A/C compressor electrical connectors
- Manifold Absolute Pressure (MAP) sensor electrical connectors
- Oxygen (O2S) sensor electrical connectors
- Exhaust Gas Recirculation (EGR)

solenoid and reposition the wire harness to the underhood junction block
- Evaporative Emissions (EVAP) purge valve vacuum hose
- Positive Crankcase Ventilation (PCV) vacuum hose
- Throttle body connector
- Brake booster vacuum hose
- Upper radiator hose from the cylinder head outlet
- Deaeration hose from the intake manifold
- Heater hose from the intake manifold
- Fuel supply line
- Engine torque axis mount
- Drive belt, tensioner and idler pulley
- Rocker cover
- Deaeration line from the cylinder head water outlet
- A/C compressor and front bracket. Do not discharge the system
- Right front wheel and splash shield
- Front crankshaft pulley
- Front exhaust pipe from the exhaust manifold
- Front cover and install a crankshaft gear retainer tool with the flat side toward the sprocket
- Front four oil pan bolts and cut the oil pan seal away from the front cover

➡ **Position the crankshaft 90 degrees off of Top Dead Center (TDC) to make certain that the pistons do not touch the valves during assembly.**

- Timing chain, tensioner, guides and camshaft sprocket
- Lossen and uniformly remove the 10 cylinder head bolts in several passes
- Cylinder head from the dowels on the engine block

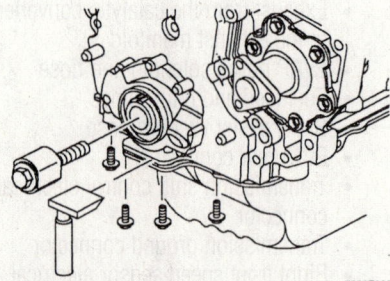

79222Z802

Crankshaft gear retaining and oil pan removal tool shown—be sure to install the crankshaft tool with the flat side toward the gear

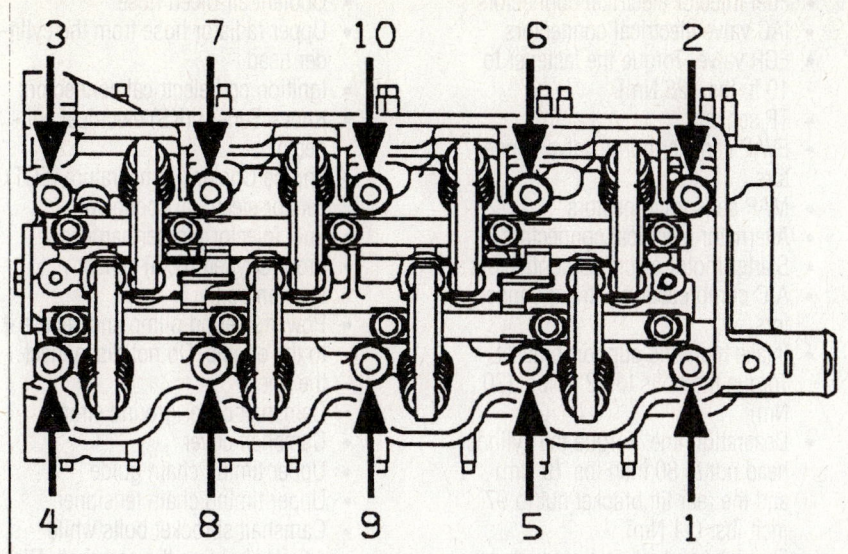

Gradually remove the cylinder head bolts in the sequence shown to prevent warping the head

79227803

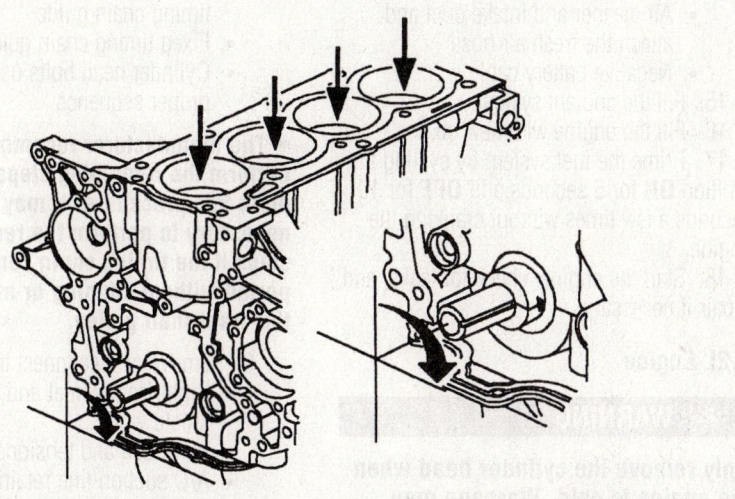

79227805

Rotate the crankshaft clockwise to 90 degrees past TDC (the crankshaft sprocket timing mark will be at 3 o'clock) to prevent valve damage during assembly

To install:

➡**Before installing the cylinder head, it should be cleaned and inspected for excessive wear or damage.**

6. Clean the gasket mating surfaces. Be careful not to damage the aluminum components and be sure the block bolt holes are clean of any residual sealer, oil or foreign matter.

7. Using a dial gauge, check that the cylinder liners are flush or do not deviate more than 0.0005 in. (0.013mm).

8. Be sure the crankshaft is still 90 degrees past TDC and that the camshaft(s) are properly positioned with the dowel

pin(s) at the 12 o'clock position to prevent valve damage.

9. Install the cylinder head gasket and carefully guide the head into place over the dowels.

➡**Refer to Section 1 of this manual for the cylinder head torque sequence illustration. The illustration is located after the Torque Specification chart.**

10. If the head bolts and/or the block were replaced, install the bolts and tighten in sequence to 48 ft. lbs. (65 Nm) to insure proper clamp load; then, remove the bolts.

11. Coat the cylinder head bolts with

clean engine oil and thread the bolts by hand until finger-tight.

12. Install the cylinder head bolts, in sequence, as follows:
- Step 1: Tighten the bolts to 22 ft. lbs. (30 Nm).
- Step 2: Tighten the bolts to 33 ft. lbs. (45 Nm) for SOHC engines or to 37 ft. lbs. (50 Nm) for DOHC engines.
- Step 3: Install a torque angle gauge tool and calibrate the tool to **0**.
- Step 4: Tighten each bolt an additional 90 degree turn.

13. Install the timing chain, sprockets, guides and tensioners, using the following procedure :

a. Verify that the crankshaft is positioned 90 degrees clockwise past TDC. The crankshaft key way sprocket timing mark must be aligned with the cylinder block main bearing cap split line to prevent piston and valve damage.

b. If required, rotate the camshaft up to No. 1 TDC position. Install the camshaft sprocket and bolt if the camshaft must be rotated more than a few degrees.

c. Rotate the crankshaft 90 degrees counterclockwise to No. 1 TDC position. The crankshaft sprocket timing mark must align with the cylinder block timing mark

14. Install or connect the following:
- Timing chain over the camshaft sprocket and under the crankshaft sprocket. Slide the camshaft sprocket onto the camshaft with the letters **FRT** facing away from the cylinder head
- Camshaft sprocket timing pin
- Camshaft washer and bolt. Torque the bolt to 74 ft. lbs. (100 Nm).
- Fixed chain guide and check for clearance between the guide to cylinder head. The guide must be installed with the word **FRONT** facing away from the engine block. Torque the fastener to 19 ft. lbs. (26 Nm). The timing chain should be snug against the fixed guide
- Pivoting chain guide making certain there is clearance between the block and head. Torque the bolts to 19 ft. lbs. (26 Nm).
- Retract the tensioner plunger and install the chain tensioner. Torque the bolts to 168 inch lbs. (19 Nm) and allow the tensioner plunger to extend

Refer to Section 1 for engine rebuilding specifications

- Oil pressure regulator and pump cover, if removed
- Crankshaft timing gear retainer tool to align the gerotor oil pump to the front cover
- Front cover. Torque the perimeter bolts to 22 ft. lbs. (30 Nm) and the lower center bolt to 89 inch lbs. (10 Nm).
- Oil pan. Torque the bolts to 80 inch lbs. (9 Nm).
- Water pump pulley. Torque the bolts to 19 ft. lbs. (25 Nm) and remove the crankshaft gear timing tool
- Crankshaft pulley. Torque the bolt to 159 ft. lbs. (215 Nm).
- Apply RTV across the cylinder head and front cover T-joints and install a new rocker cover gasket
- Rocker cover. Uniformly torque the bolts to 22 ft. lbs. (30 Nm).
- Belt tensioner. Torque the fastener to 22 ft. lbs. (30 Nm).
- Drive belt idler pulley. Torque the fastener to 20 ft. lbs. (27 Nm).
- Accelerator linkage bracket and the throttle cable. Make certain that the cable is routed properly and is not binding. Torque the bolts to 19 ft. lbs. (25 Nm).
- Alternator. Torque the bolts to 24 ft. lbs. (32 Nm).
- Starter. Torque the bolts to 27 ft. lbs. (37 Nm).
- Starter support bracket to the axle shaft bracket. Torque the bolts to 22 ft. lbs. (30 Nm).
- Power steering pump. Torque the bolts to 22 ft. lbs. (30 Nm).
- A/C compressor. Torque the rear bracket bolts to 19 ft. lbs. (25 Nm) and the front bracket bolts to 35 ft. lbs. (47 Nm).
- Drive belt
- Upper mount. Torque the midrail bracket nuts to 37 ft. lbs. (50 Nm) and then torque the mount to cover bolts to 37 ft. lbs. (50 Nm).
- Splash shield and wheel
- EVAP canister purge hose
- Throttle body vacuum harness hose
- PCV hose
- Brake booster vacuum hose
- MAP sensor
- Upper radiator hose
- Heater hose
- Ground wire electrical connectors
- Oxygen (O2S) sensor. Torque the fastener to 19 ft. lbs. (25 Nm).
- ECT sensor. Torque the fastener to 71 inch lbs. (8 Nm).

- Fuel injector electrical connectors
- IAC valve electrical connectors
- EGR valve. Torque the fastener to 19 ft. lbs. (25 Nm).
- TP sensor
- EVAP canister purge valve connectors
- MAP sensor connectors
- Alternator electrical connectors
- Starter motor electrical connectors
- A/C compressor electrical connectors
- Intake manifold support bracket. Torque the bolts to 22 ft. lbs. (30 Nm).
- Deaeration line. Torque the cylinder head nut to 80 inch lbs. (9 Nm) and the rear lift bracket nut to 97 inch lbs. (11 Nm).
- Fuel feed and return lines with new retainers. Torque the fastener to 53 inch lbs. (6 Nm).
- Right front splash shield and wheel
- Air cleaner and intake duct and attach the fresh air hose
- Negative battery cable

15. Fill the coolant system.
16. Fill the engine with new oil.
17. Prime the fuel system by cycling the ignition **ON** for 5 seconds and **OFF** for 10 seconds a few times without cranking the engine.
18. Start the engine, check for leaks, and repair if necessary.

2.2L Engine

✳✳ WARNING

Only remove the cylinder head when the engine is cold. Warpage may result if the cylinder head is removed while the engine is hot.

1. Before servicing the vehicle, refer to the precautions in the beginning of this section.
2. Drain the coolant system.
3. Drain the engine oil.
4. Properly relieve the fuel system pressure.
5. Remove or disconnect the following:
- Negative battery cable
- Intake manifold
- Exhaust manifold flange bolts
- Exhaust manifold down pipe to the catalytic converter
- Fuel lines
- A/C compressor switch electrical connector
- Crankcase vent hose from the camshaft cover

- Coolant air bleed hose
- Upper radiator hose from the cylinder head
- Ignition coil electrical connectors
- Knock Sensor (KS) electrical connector
- Engine Coolant Temperature (ECT) sensor electrical connector
- Fuel injector jumper harness
- Front Oxygen (O2S) sensor
- Ignition coil
- Power steering pump and secure it to the engine. Do not disconnect the lines
- Camshaft cover ground strap
- Camshaft cover
- Upper timing chain guide
- Upper timing chain tensioner
- Camshaft sprocket bolts while counter holding the camshaft. Discard the bolts
- Camshaft sprocket
- Plug to gain access to the fixed timing chain guide
- Fixed timing chain guide upper bolt
- Cylinder head bolts using the proper sequence

➡ **The manufacturer recommends to perform the remaining steps to complete this procedure. It may be not be necessary to perform the remaining steps if the timing chain can be supported without slipping or moving on the crankshaft pulley.**

6. Remove or disconnect the following:
- Right front wheel and splash shield
- Drive belt and tensioner
- A/C suction line retaining clips and move the line away to allow clearance to the crankshaft pulley bolt
7. Position the crankshaft 60 degrees Before Top Dead Center (BTDC) and install a crankshaft pulley holder tool
8. Remove or disconnect the following:
- Crankshaft pulley
- Front cover bolts except for the one blocked by the engine mount bracket
- Loosen water pump bolt but do not remove it
- Support the engine and remove the right side engine mount
- Engine mount bracket
- Upper front cover bolt which was blocked by the mount bracket
- Water pump bolt
- Front cover
- Adjustable timing chain guide
- Fixed timing chain guide lower bolt

To install:

➡ Refer to Section 1 of this manual for the cylinder head torque sequence illustration. The illustration is located after the Torque Specification Chart.

➡ Set the crankshaft to 60 degrees BTDC or after Top Dead Center (TDC) to prevent contact between the pistons and valves.

9. Install or connect the following:
- New cylinder head gasket with the side imprinted **OBEN** facing up
- Cylinder head and align it on the dowels
- Lubricate the new cylinder head bolts with clean engine oil. Torque the bolts in sequence to 22 ft. lbs. (30 Nm) plus 155 degrees.
- Coat the front 4 cylinder head bolts with Loctite® and install the front bolts. Torque the bolts to 18 ft. lbs. (22 Nm).

10. Position the exhaust camshaft with the offset slot in the 2 o'clock position and the intake camshaft with the offset slot in the 11 o'clock position

11. Install or connect the following:
- Timing chain around the intake camshaft sprocket with the copper link aligned with the **INT** diamond timing mark
- Sprocket to the camshaft and align it with the offset slot. Install a new camshaft sprocket bolt but do not tighten
- Timing chain around the crankshaft sprocket and align the silver link to the timing mark
- Adjustable timing chain guide through the opening on top of the

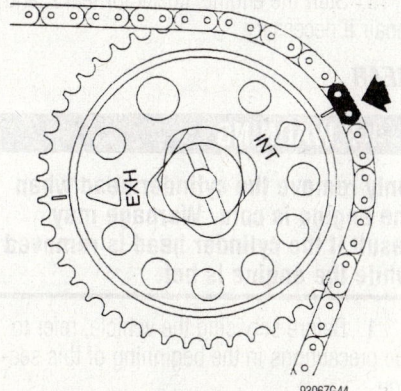

Align the copper link on the timing belt with the INT diamond timing mark

cylinder head. Torque the chain guide bolt to 89 inch lbs. (10 Nm).
- Timing chain around the exhaust camshaft sprocket with the silver link aligned with the offset slot. Install but do not tighten a new sprocket bolt

☀☀ CAUTION

Make certain that all timing marks and colored links are aligned properly before proceeding to the next step. If the timing chain is not aligned properly, severe engine damage may occur.

- Torque the intake and exhaust camshaft bolts to 63 ft. lbs. (85 Nm) plus a 30 degree turn
- Fixed timing guide. Torque the bolt to 89 inch lbs. (10 Nm).
- Fixed timing guide bolt access plug after applying Loctite® to the threads. Torque the plug to 30 ft. lbs. (40 Nm).
- Reset the timing chain tensioner by depressing the plunger and install a sealing ring
- Tensioner. Torque the bolts 44 ft. lbs. (60 Nm).
- Tap the top of the timing chain between the camshaft sprockets to engage the tensioner
- Upper timing chain guide. Torque the bolts to 89 inch lbs. (10 Nm).
- Front cover with a new gasket. Torque the bolts to 18 ft. lbs. (25 Nm).
- Water pump bolt. Torque the bolt to 18 ft. lbs. (25 Nm).
- Drive belt and tensioner
- Engine mount bracket. Torque the bolts to 66 ft. lbs. (90 Nm).
- Engine mount to the side rail. Torque the fasteners to 41 ft. lbs. (55 Nm).
- Engine mount align the mount bolts to the bracket bolts. Torque the mount to bracket bolts to 41 ft. lbs. (55 Nm).
- Crankshaft damper, making certain that the key way is aligned properly
- Lubricate the front oil seal and crankshaft balancer with clean oil and install the damper to the indexing key way
- Washer and crankshaft damper pulley bolt. Torque the bolt to 74 ft. lbs. (100 Nm).

- Drive belt
- A/C line clamps
- Right wheel splash shield and right front wheel
- Camshaft cover and make certain the seals are fully seated. Torque the bolts and ground strap nut to 89 inch lbs. (10 Nm).
- Power steering pump. Torque the bolts to 18 ft. lbs. (25 Nm).
- Ignition coil and module to the camshaft cover. Torque the bolts to 71 inch lbs. (8 Nm).
- Intake manifold with a new gasket. Torque the bolts to 89 inch lbs. (10 Nm).
- Wiring harness to the intake manifold bracket and install the oil indicator tube. Torque the bolts to 89 inch lbs. (10 Nm).
- Throttle body. Torque the bolts to 89 inch lbs. (10 Nm) and install the throttle cable
- Engine wiring harness and fasteners. Torque the fasteners to 89 inch lbs. (10 Nm).
- All component electrical connections and attach the camshaft cover ground strap. Torque the fastener to 89 inch lbs. (10 Nm).
- Upper radiator hose
- Crankcase ventilation hose
- Fuel pressure regulator hose
- Brake booster vacuum hose
- EVAP purge hose
- Fuel lines and clips and position the lines to the bracket. Torque the bracket bolt to 89 inch lbs. (10 Nm).
- Exhaust flange
- Exhaust down pipe to the flange. Torque the bolts to 25 ft. lbs. (30 Nm).
- Exhaust pipe to the resonator. Torque the bolts to 15 ft. lbs. (20 Nm).
- Exhaust manifold heat shield. Torque the bolts to 18 ft. lbs. (25 Nm).
- Air cleaner and intake duct
- Negative battery cable

12. Fill the engine with clean oil.
13. Fill the coolant system.
14. Prime the fuel system by cycling the ignition **ON** for 5 seconds and **OFF** for 10 seconds a few times without cranking the engine.
15. Start the engine, check for leaks, and repair if necessary.

3.0L Engine

FRONT

> ※ **WARNING**
>
> **Only remove the cylinder head when the engine is cold. Warpage may result if the cylinder head is removed while the engine is hot.**

1. Before servicing the vehicle, refer to the precautions in the beginning of this section.

2. Drain the coolant system.

3. Drain the engine oil.

4. Properly relieve the fuel system pressure.

5. Remove or disconnect the following:
- Negative battery cable
- Intake plenum
- Intake manifold
- Intake manifold spacer
- Coolant bridge
- Upper radiator hose from the coolant extension housing and properly support the powertrain assembly
- Front transmission mount through bolt
- Extension housing over the coolant module
- Oil level indicator tube
- Front camshaft cover
- Ground wires from the lift bracket
- Down pipe from the exhaust manifold
- Front timing belt cover
- Timing belt and tensioner bracket
- Rear timing belt cover
- Camshaft sensor electrical connector
- Exhaust camshaft
- Loosen the cylinder head bolts in stages as shown
- Cylinder head and discard the gasket
- Exhaust manifold

To install:

➡ **Refer to Section 1 of this manual for the cylinder head torque sequence illustration. The illustration is located after the Torque Specification Chart.**

6. Clean the mating surface for the cylinder head and engine.

7. Install or connect the following:
- Exhaust manifold and new gasket. Torque the bolts to 15 ft. lbs. (20 Nm).
- New cylinder head gasket with the part number imprint facing the top of the engine

8. Torque the new cylinder head bolts, in sequence, as follows:
- Step 1: 18 ft. lbs. (25 Nm)
- Step 2: Plus a 90 degree turn
- Step 3: Plus a 90 degree turn
- Step 4: Plus a 90 degree turn
- Step 5: Plus a 15 degree turn

9. Install or connect the following:
- Lubricate the sealing rings for the coolant pipe and install the pipe and engine lift bracket bolt to the cylinder head. Torque the bolt to 15 ft. lbs. (20 Nm).
- Upper radiator hose to the coolant pipe
- Front transmission mount through bolt
- Exhaust camshaft
- Exhaust camshaft electrical connector
- Rear timing belt cover and lubricate the bolts with Loctite®. Torque the bolts to 71 inch lbs. (8 Nm).
- Rear timing belt threaded pin. Torque the pin to 89 inch lbs. (10 Nm).
- Camshaft gears
- Timing belt tensioner bracket
- Timing belt
- Front timing belt cover
- Front camshaft cover
- Coolant bridge
- Intake manifold spacer. Torque the spacer bolts in a spiral direction from the inside and working out to 15 ft. lbs. (20 Nm).
- Intake manifold
- Intake plenum
- Negative battery cable

10. Fill the engine with clean oil.

11. Fill the coolant system.

12. Prime the fuel system by cycling the ignition **ON** for 5 seconds and **OFF** for 10 seconds a few times without cranking the engine.

13. Start the engine, check for leaks, and repair if necessary.

REAR

> ※ **WARNING**
>
> **Only remove the cylinder head when the engine is cold. Warpage may result if the cylinder head is removed while the engine is hot.**

1. Before servicing the vehicle, refer to the precautions in the beginning of this section.

2. Drain the coolant system.

3. Drain the engine oil.

4. Properly relieve the fuel system pressure.

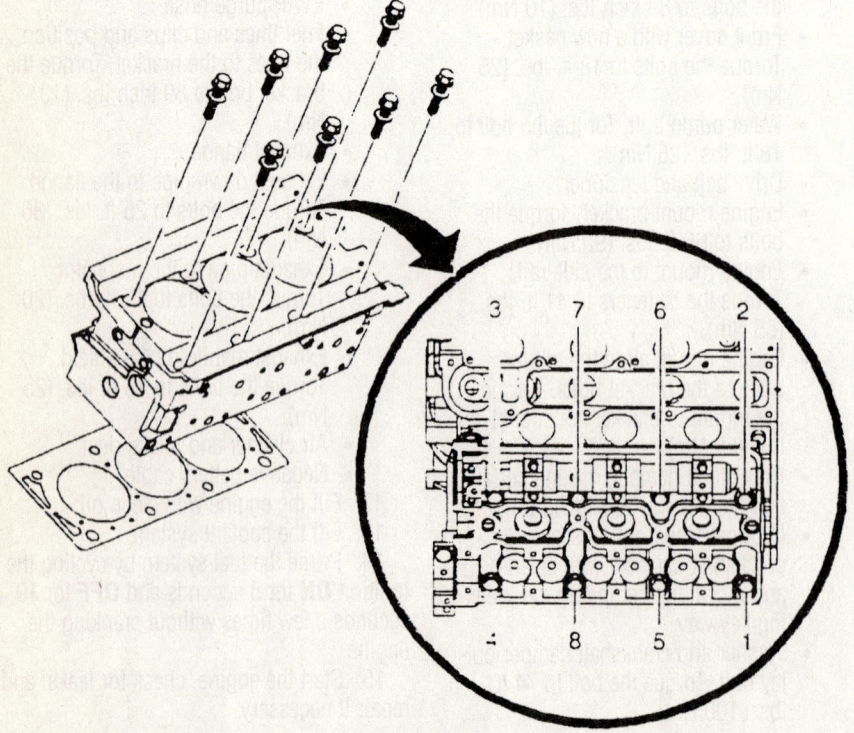

Cylinder head bolt removal for the front cylinder head–3.0L engine

9306ZG45

5. Remove or disconnect the following:
- Negative battery cable
- Intake plenum
- Intake manifold
- Intake manifold spacer
- Coolant bridge
- Engine ventilation chamber
- Rear camshaft cover
- Front timing belt cover
- Timing belt
- Timing belt tensioner bracket
- Camshaft gears
- Rear timing belt cover
- Exhaust manifold pipe heat shield
- Front exhaust manifold pipe to rear exhaust manifold pipe fasteners
- Rear exhaust manifold pipe nuts, pull the manifold pipe down and discard the gasket
- Exhaust Gas Recirculation (EGR) to the exhaust manifold
- Exhaust camshaft
- Cylinder head bolts in sequence
- Cylinder head gasket
- Exhaust manifold

To install:

➡**Refer to Section 1 of this manual for the cylinder head torque sequence illustration. The illustration is located after the Torque Specification Chart.**

6. Install or connect the following:
- Rear exhaust manifold to the cylinder head. Torque the bolts to 15 ft. lbs. (20 Nm).
- New cylinder head gasket with the part number imprint facing the top of the engine

7. Torque the new cylinder head bolts, in sequence, as follows:
- Step 1: 18 ft. lbs. (25 Nm)
- Step 2: Plus a 90 degree turn
- Step 3: Plus a 90 degree turn
- Step 4: Plus a 90 degree turn
- Step 5: Plus a 15 degree turn

8. Install or connect the following:
- Exhaust camshaft
- Exhaust manifold pipe gasket
- Exhaust manifold pipe to the manifold
- Exhaust manifold pipe heat shield
- EGR valve to the exhaust manifold
- Exhaust camshaft
- Rear timing belt cover
- Camshaft gears
- Timing belt tensioner bracket
- Timing belt
- Front timing belt cover
- Rear camshaft cover
- Coolant bridge

- Engine ventilation chamber
- Intake manifold spacer. Torque the bolts to 15 ft. lbs. (20 Nm).
- Intake manifold
- Intake plenum
- Negative battery cable

9. Fill the engine with clean oil.
10. Fill the coolant system.
11. Prime the fuel system by cycling the ignition **ON** for 5 seconds and **OFF** for 10 seconds a few times without cranking the engine.
12. Start the engine, check for leaks, and repair if necessary.

Rocker Arms/Shafts

REMOVAL & INSTALLATION

1.9L and 2.2L Engines

1. Before servicing the vehicle, refer to the precautions in the beginning of this section.
2. Remove or disconnect the following:
- Negative battery cable
- Spark plug wires
- Drive belt
- Fresh air hose
- Camshaft cover
- Fuel injector electrical connectors

3. Install a rocker arm removal tool to the cylinder head rail.
4. Position the crankshaft at Top Dead Center (TDC) with the pip marks on the camshaft sprockets at the 12 o'clock position.
5. Rotate the crankshaft 90 degrees past TDC and remove the following rocker arm assemblies:

a. No. 1 Intake.
b. No. 2 Intake.
c. No. 1 Exhaust.
d. No. 3 Exhaust.

6. Rotate the crankshaft 360 degrees to remove the following rocker arm assemblies:

a. No. 2 Exhaust.
b. No. 4 Intake.
c. No. 3 Intake.
d. No. 4 Exhaust.

7. Compress the valve springs.

To install:

8. Install or connect the following:
- Rocker arm assemblies with the removal tool attached to the cylinder head rail and the valves compressed. Remove the rocker arm tool
- Camshaft cover
- Fresh air hose
- Drive belt
- Fuel injector electrical connectors
- Spark plug wires
- Negative battery cable

Intake Manifold

REMOVAL & INSTALLATION

1.9L SOHC Engine

1. Before servicing the vehicle, refer to the precautions in the beginning of this section.
2. Properly relieve the fuel system pressure.
3. Drain the coolant system.
4. Remove or disconnect the following:

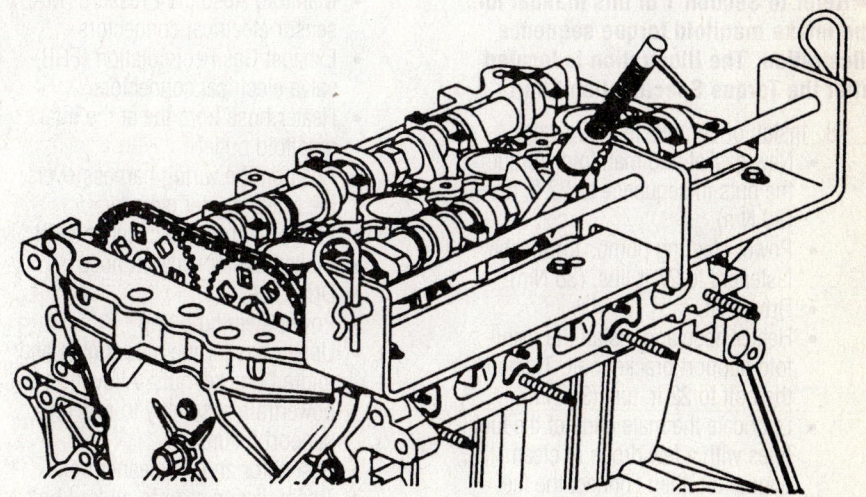

Valve spring compressor installed–1.9L DOHC

9306ZG47

- Negative battery cable
- Air cleaner fresh air hose
- Positive Crankcase Ventilation (PCV) valve hose
- Fuel line from the rail
- Throttle cable from the throttle body
- Throttle cable bracket nuts
- Fuel injector electrical connectors
- Throttle Position (TP) sensor electrical connectors
- Idle Air Control (IAC) valve electrical connectors
- Manifold Absolute Pressure (MAP) sensor electrical connectors
- Exhaust Gas Recirculation (EGR) valve electrical connectors
- Heater hose from the intake manifold outlet

5. Position the wiring harness over the brake master cylinder

6. Remove or disconnect the following:

- Intake manifold support bracket bolt
- Label the vacuum line for proper assembly
- Drive belt
- Power steering pump
- Upper intake manifold bolts
- Evaporative Emissions (EVAP) canister purge valve solenoid vacuum hose
- Brake booster vacuum hose
- Lower intake manifold bolts
- Intake manifold

To install:

7. Thoroughly clean all gasket mating surfaces. Be careful not to damage or score the aluminum surface. If replaced, use Loctite® 290, to seal the new PCV valve inlet tube into the manifold.

➡**Refer to Section 1 of this manual for the intake manifold torque sequence illustration. The illustration is located after the Torque Specification Chart.**

8. Install or connect the following:

- New gasket and manifold. Torque the nuts in sequence to 22 ft. lbs. (30 Nm).
- Power steering pump. Torque the fasteners to 27 ft. lbs. (38 Nm).
- Drive belt.
- Heater hose and install the manifold support bracket bolt. Tighten the bolt to 22 ft. lbs. (30 Nm).
- Lubricate the male ends of the fuel lines with a few drops of clean engine oil, then connect the fuel supply and return lines.
- Fuel line(s) in the retaining bracket. Torque the mounting screw to 36 inch lbs. (4 Nm).

- Throttle cable to the throttle body and attach the accelerator cable bracket. Torque the bolts to 22 ft. lbs. (30 Nm).
- Reposition the wiring harness and connect the wiring and vacuum hoses to their original locations. The harness leads to the TP sensor and EGR solenoid must be routed between the intake manifold runners.
- Negative battery cable

9. Fill the coolant system.

10. Prime the fuel system by cycling the ignition **ON** for 5 seconds and **OFF** for 10 seconds a few times without cranking the engine.

11. Start the engine, check for leaks, and repair if necessary.

1.9L DOHC Engine

1. Before servicing the vehicle, refer to the precautions in the beginning of this section.

2. Properly relieve the fuel system pressure.

3. Drain the coolant system.

4. Remove or disconnect the following:

- Negative battery cable
- Air cleaner fresh air hose
- Positive Crankcase Ventilation (PCV) valve hose
- Fuel line from the rail
- Throttle cable from the throttle body
- Throttle cable bracket nuts
- Fuel injector electrical connectors
- Throttle Position (TP) sensor electrical connectors
- Idle Air Control (IAC) valve electrical connectors
- Manifold Absolute Pressure (MAP) sensor electrical connectors
- Exhaust Gas Recirculation (EGR) valve electrical connectors
- Heater hose from the at the intake manifold outlet
- Position the wiring harness over the brake master cylinder
- EGR pipe from the cylinder head
- Brake booster vacuum hose
- Drive belt
- Power steering pump
- Upper axis torque mount nuts and midrail bracket nuts. Allow the powertrain assembly to rest on a support fixture
- Resonator and air cleaner box
- Transmission strut to midrail bolt and rotate the engine
- Intake manifold and discard the gasket

To install:

5. Thoroughly clean the gasket mating surfaces. Be careful not to score or damage the aluminum sealing surfaces.

➡**Refer to Section 1 of this manual for the intake manifold torque sequence illustration. The illustration is located after the Torque Specification Chart.**

- New gasket and intake manifold. Torque the nuts in sequence to 22 ft. lbs. (30 Nm) for 1997–99 or to 115 inch lbs. (13 Nm) for 2000–01.
- Power steering pump. Torque the bolts to 28 ft. lbs. (38 Nm).
- Drive belt
- Fuel supply line to the rail. Torque the bolt to 36 inch lbs. (4 Nm).
- Throttle cable to the throttle body and install the support bracket. Torque the bolts to 19 ft. lbs. (25 Nm).
- IAC valve electrical connector
- TP sensor electrical connector
- MAP sensor electrical connector
- Fuel injector electrical connector
- EGR valve electrical connector
- EVAP canister purge solenoid vacuum hose
- PCV valve hose
- Air cleaner
- Negative battery cable

6. Fill the coolant system.

7. Prime the fuel system by cycling the ignition **ON** for 5 seconds and **OFF** for 10 seconds a few times without cranking the engine.

8. Start the engine, check for leaks, and repair if necessary.

2.2L Engine

1. Before servicing the vehicle, refer to the precautions in the beginning of this section.

2. Remove or disconnect the following:

- Negative battery cable
- Air cleaner fresh air hose
- Intake Air Temperature (IAT) sensor electrical connector
- Throttle Position (TP) sensor electrical connectors
- Idle Air Control (IAC) valve electrical connectors
- Manifold Absolute Pressure (MAP) sensor electrical connectors
- Position the wiring harness over the brake master cylinder
- Fuel pressure regulator vacuum pipe

- Evaporative Emissions (EVAP) purge solenoid hose from the throttle body
- Throttle cable and automatic transmission downshift cable from the throttle body
- Throttle cable bracket nuts
- Brake booster vacuum hose
- Oil level indicator tube
- Throttle body
- Intake manifold and discard the gasket

To install:

3. Thoroughly clean the gasket mating surfaces. Be careful not to score or damage the aluminum sealing surfaces.

4. Install or connect the following:
- New gasket and the intake manifold. Torque the nuts to 89 inch lbs. (10 Nm).
- Throttle body to the intake manifold. Torque the bolts to 19 ft. lbs. (25 Nm).
- Throttle cable bracket to the throttle body studs
- Oil level indicator tube. Torque the fastener to 89 inch lbs. (10 Nm).
- Brake booster vacuum pipe
- Throttle cable to the throttle body and install the support bracket. Torque the bolts to 19 ft. lbs. (25 Nm).
- EVAP canister purge solenoid vacuum hose
- Fuel pressure regulator vacuum pipe to the throttle body
- Route the engine wiring harness on top of the engine and secure the harness under the intake manifold
- IAC valve electrical connector
- TP sensor electrical connector
- MAP sensor electrical connector
- Air inlet hose to the throttle body
- Crankcase vent hose to the camshaft cover
- IAT sensor electrical connector
- Air cleaner
- Negative battery cable

5. Start the engine, check for leaks, and repair if necessary.

3.0L Engine

1. Before servicing the vehicle, refer to the precautions in the beginning of this section.

2. Properly relieve the fuel system pressure.

3. Remove or disconnect the following:
- Negative battery cable

- Both intake runners
- Intake plenum
- Fuel supply and return hoses
- Fuel injector electrical connector
- Intake manifold spacer and O-ring gaskets
- Intake manifold

To install:

4. Thoroughly clean the gasket mating surfaces. Be careful not to score or damage the aluminum sealing surfaces.

5. Install or connect the following:
- Intake manifold spacer seal and spacer
- New gasket and intake manifold using the proper sequence. Torque the bolts to 15 ft. lbs. (25 Nm).
- Fuel injector electrical connectors
- Fuel supply and return hoses. Torque the fuel return fastener to 11 ft. lbs. (15 Nm).
- Intake plenum
- Intake manifold runners
- Negative battery cable

6. Prime the fuel system by cycling the ignition **ON** for 5 seconds and **OFF** for 10 seconds a few times without cranking the engine.

7. Start the engine, check for leaks, and repair if necessary.

Exhaust Manifold

REMOVAL & INSTALLATION

1.9L Engine

1. Before servicing the vehicle, refer to the precautions in the beginning of this section.

2. Remove or disconnect the following:
- Negative battery cable
- Front exhaust pipe-to-engine support bracket mounting fasteners
- Pipe-to-manifold nuts and lower the pipe
- Powertrain supports and lower the vehicle

➡**When performing the next step, DO NOT disconnect the refrigerant lines.**

- A/C compressor and bracket from the engine, which will first require the removal of the serpentine belt, then position them aside
- O₂S sensor connector. If necessary, use a 19mm, 6-point crow's foot wrench to remove the O₂S sensor from the manifold

- Manifold retaining nuts and remove the manifold from the cylinder head. Remove and discard the gasket

To install:

3. Thoroughly clean the gasket mating surfaces, being careful not to score or damage the aluminum surface.

4. Install or connect the following:
- New gasket with the smooth side facing the manifold
- Manifold and attaching nuts. Torque the nuts in sequence to 16 ft. lbs. (22 Nm) for the SOHC engine or to 105 inch lbs. (17 Nm) for the DOHC engine
- O₂S sensor, coat the threads with nickel-based anti-seize compound and torque to 33 ft. lbs. (45 Nm).
- O₂S sensor electrical connector
- A/C compressor and brackets. Torque all fasteners except the front bracket-to-compressor to 19 ft. lbs. (25 Nm) or to 40 ft. lbs. (54 Nm) for the front bracket-to-compressor.
- New gasket onto the studs between the pipe and manifold

Upper Side			
8	4	1	5
7	3	2	6
Lower Side			

79222810

Exhaust manifold bolt torque sequence—1.9L SOHC engine

Upper Side		
	2	3
4	1	5
Lower Side		

79222811

Exhaust manifold bolt torque sequence—1.9L DOHC engine

- Pipe and manifold. Torque the fasteners in a crosswise pattern to 23 ft. lbs. (31 Nm).
- Position the exhaust pipe-to-engine support bracket in place and install the 2 mounting fasteners. Torque both mounting fasteners to 23 ft. lbs. (31 Nm).
- Negative battery cable

5. Start the vehicle and check for leaks, repair if necessary.

2.2L Engine

1. Before servicing the vehicle, refer to the precautions in the beginning of this section.

2. Remove or disconnect the following:
- Negative battery cable
- Exhaust manifold heat shield
- Exhaust manifold and discard the gasket

To install:

3. Thoroughly clean the gasket mating surfaces, being careful not to score or damage the aluminum surface.

4. Install or connect the following:
- New exhaust manifold to cylinder head studs. Torque the studs to 89 inch lbs. (10 Nm).
- New gasket
- Exhaust manifold. Torque the bolts, starting from the center and working outward, to 13 ft. lbs. (18 Nm).
- Exhaust manifold heat shield. Torque the bolts to 18 ft. lbs. (25 Nm).
- Negative battery cable

5. Start the vehicle and check for leaks, repair if necessary.

3.0L Engine

FRONT MANIFOLD

1. Before servicing the vehicle, refer to the precautions in the beginning of this section.

2. Drain the coolant system.

3. Remove or disconnect the following:
- Negative battery cable
- Exhaust manifold Oxygen (O2S) sensor electrical connector
- Oxygen (O2S) sensor using J39194C
- Upper radiator hose from the coolant extension housing

4. Install and engine support fixture and support the powertrain.

5. Remove or disconnect the following:
- Front transmission through bolt and raise the powertrain assembly
- Oil level indicator tube and coolant extension tube bolt

- Twist the coolant extension housing
- Power steering pipe bracket bolt
- Upper exhaust manifold nuts
- Front exhaust manifold pipe Oxygen (O2S) sensor electrical connector
- Front exhaust manifold pipe from the manifold
- Oil filter housing
- Lower exhaust manifold nuts
- Exhaust manifold and discard the gasket

6. Clean the mating surfaces.

To install:

7. Install or connect the following:
- New gasket
- Exhaust manifold. Torque the bolts to 15 ft. lbs. (20 Nm).
- Oil filter housing. Torque the filter cartridge to 33 ft. lbs. (45 Nm).
- Front exhaust manifold pipe and gaskets. Hand-tighten the bolts
- Front exhaust pipe to the rear exhaust manifold. Torque the bolts to 25 ft. lbs. (30 Nm).
- Torque the front manifold pipe bolts to 15 ft. lbs. (20 Nm).
- Front exhaust manifold (O2S) sensor. Torque the sensor to 73 ft. lbs. (45 Nm).
- (O2S) sensor electrical connector
- Upper exhaust manifold. Torque the bolts to 15 ft. lbs. (20 Nm).
- Power steering pipe bracket. Torque the bolt to 71 inch lbs. (8 Nm).
- New O-rings to the coolant extension housing and install the housing
- Oil level indicator tube. Torque the bolts to 15 ft. lbs. (20 Nm). lower the powertrain assembly
- Front transmission mount through bolt. Torque the bolt to 41 ft. lbs. (55 Nm). Remove the engine support fixture
- Upper radiator hose
- Exhaust manifold (O2S) sensor. Torque the sensor to 37 ft. lbs. (50 Nm).
- (O2S) sensor electrical connector
- Negative battery cable

8. Fill the coolant system.

9. Start the vehicle and check for leaks, repair if necessary.

REAR MANIFOLD

1. Before servicing the vehicle, refer to the precautions in the beginning of this section.

2. Drain the coolant system.

3. Remove or disconnect the following:
- Negative battery cable
- Exhaust manifold Oxygen (O2S) sensor electrical connector

- Oxygen (O2S) sensor using J39194C
- Exhaust Gas Recirculation (EGR) pipe
- Rear exhaust manifold Oxygen (O2S) sensor electrical connector
- Exhaust manifold heat shield
- Rear Oxygen (O2S) sensor using J39194C
- Rear exhaust manifold pipe
- Exhaust manifold and discard the gasket

To install:

4. Install or connect the following:
- New gasket
- Exhaust manifold. Torque the bolts to 15 ft. lbs. (20 Nm).
- Rear exhaust manifold pipe and hand-tighten the bolts
- Exhaust manifold to the rear manifold pipe
- Front exhaust manifold pipe to the rear exhaust manifold pipe. Torque the bolts to 15 ft. lbs. (20 Nm).
- Rear exhaust manifold pipe to the resonator. Torque the bolts to 154 ft. lbs. (20 Nm).
- Torque the exhaust manifold to pipe bolts to 25 ft. lbs. (30 Nm).
- EGR pipe. Torque the fasteners to 19 ft. lbs. (25 Nm).
- Oxygen (O2S) sensor using J39194C and connect the electrical connector
- Exhaust manifold heat shield. Torque the bolts to 71 inch lbs. (8 Nm).
- Negative battery cable

5. Start the vehicle and check for leaks, repair if necessary.

Front Crankshaft Seal

REPLACEMENT

The front crankshaft seal is located in the timing chain front cover. Refer to the timing chain procedure for information about removing the front cover and replacing the seal.

Camshaft and Lifters

REMOVAL & INSTALLATION

1.9L (SOHC) Engine

1. Before servicing the vehicle, refer to the precautions in the beginning of this section.

2. Remove or disconnect the following:

- Both battery cables
- Battery and tray
- Timing chain front cover
- Timing chain and camshaft sprocket
- Rocker arm/shaft assemblies
- Lifters and label or position them for assembly in their original locations

3. Drive the camshaft plug inward, then remove it from the cylinder head with a magnet.

4. Carefully pull the camshaft from the rear of the cylinder head through the oversized camshaft plug hole. Turn the camshaft back and forth slowly while withdrawing to help prevent journal or bearing damage.

To install:

5. Clean and inspect all parts prior to installation. Lubricate the camshaft and carefully insert it through the hole at the rear of the cylinder head.

6. Install or connect the following:
- Coat a new rear cylinder head plug with Loctite® 242 and install the plug using a standard bushing driver
- Valve lifters into their original bores, or if the camshaft has been replaced, install new lifters
- Rocker arm/shaft assemblies
- Timing chain and camshaft sprocket
- Timing chain front cover
- Battery and tray. Torque the battery hold-down nut and screw to 80 inch lbs. (9 Nm).
- Both battery cables

7. Start the engine and check for leaks, repair if necessary.

1.9L (DOHC) Engine

➡ Be careful when working around the camshaft sprockets and timing chain cover during this procedure. If a bolt or washer is accidentally dropped between the front cover and engine assembly, the cover will have to be removed for retrieval.

1. Before servicing the vehicle, refer to the precautions in the beginning of this section.

2. Remove or disconnect the following:
- Negative battery cable
- Drive belt
- Spark plug wires
- Positive Crankcase Ventilation (PCV) fresh air hose
- Cam cover

3. Turn the crankshaft clockwise until the mark on the crankshaft pulley is in alignment with the pointer on the front cover and the No. 1 cylinder is at Top Dead Center (TDC) of the compression stroke. Both camshaft dowel pins will be at the 12 o'clock position and the timing pin holes will be aligned when the No. 1 cylinder is at TDC. If necessary, the right wheel and splash shield can be removed to help observe the timing marks.

4. Remove or disconnect the following:
- Camshaft sprocket's retaining bolt. Use a 7/8 in. (21mm) open-end wrench to hold the camshaft from turning while removing the bolts
- Position a front angled support fixture in front of the camshaft sprockets.

5. Attach the camshaft sprocket adapters to the end of each camshaft using the pilot bolts, but do not tighten the bolts. The front angled support should come between the sprocket adapters and camshaft sprockets.

6. Remove or disconnect the following:
- Upper timing chain guide
- Both front camshaft bearing caps

7. Secure the support fixture using 7/8 in. bolts/blocks and align the 2 holes in

each camshaft sprocket, adapter and the front support fixture. Install the 4 nuts, but do not tighten.

➡ The steel blocks should be installed against the rearward side of the camshaft sprocket.

8. Tighten the sprocket pilot bolts to 19 ft. lbs. (25 Nm) while holding the camshafts from turning with an open end wrench.

9. Move each camshaft sprocket off the end of the camshaft by rocking the sprocket forward or by carefully prying between the end of the camshaft and the sprocket. Then, tighten the 4 nuts and bolts with blocks from the side of the support fixture to 19 ft. lbs. (25 Nm).

10. Install the 2 bolts retaining the support fixture to the engine front cover and tighten the bolts to 89 inch lbs. (10 Nm). Then, remove each camshaft sprocket pilot bolt while holding the camshafts with a wrench.

11. Carefully pry between the sprocket and the end of the camshaft to move the camshaft rearward. Pry only enough to remove its end from inside the sprocket pilot otherwise camshaft or lifter damage may occur.

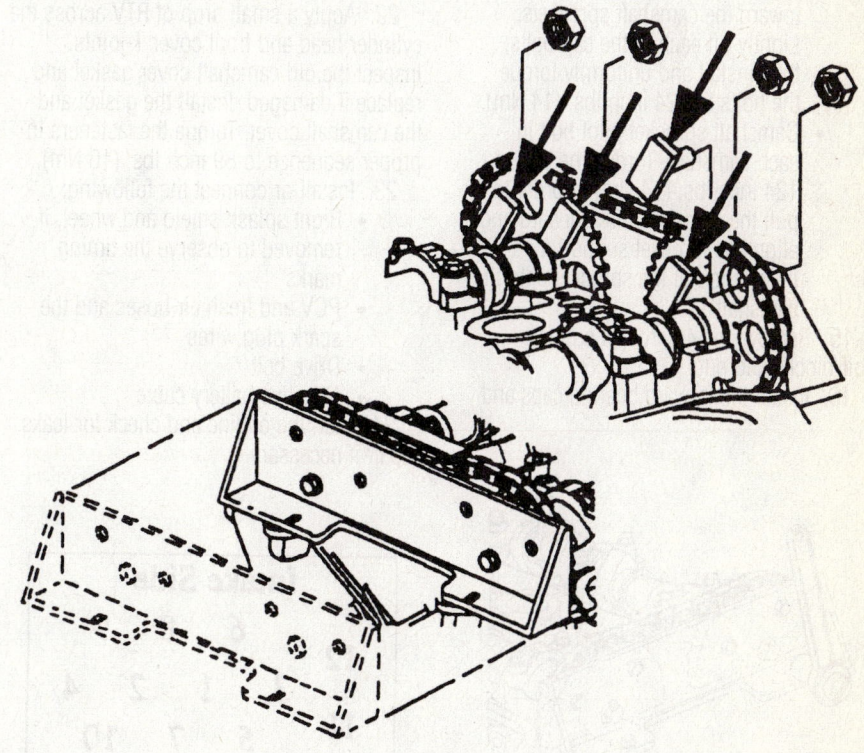

Install the camshaft support fixture to securely hold the camshafts in position—1.9L (DOHC) engine

12. Remove or disconnect the following:
- Uniformly loosen and remove the remaining camshaft bearing cap bolts. To prevent bolt/cap damage, do not use power tools and make several passes. Then, remove each camshaft. Position the bearing caps for installation in their original locations
- Pull the lifters out to remove them, always place them in the order in which they were removed and with the camshaft side facing down. Oil will drain out of the lifter if it is placed valve side down.

To install:

13. Clean and inspect all parts prior to installation. Oil the camshaft and install with the **IN** camshaft on the intake side and **EX** camshaft on the exhaust side.

➡**The dowel pin in each camshaft must be located at the 12 o'clock position during installation to prevent valve and piston damage.**

14. Install or connect the following:
- Lifters in their original locations
- Bearing caps, except for the forward pair, in their original positions, making sure the arrows on the caps are pointing forward toward the camshaft sprockets. Lightly oil each of the cap bolts, then install and uniformly torque the bolts to 124 inch lbs. (14 Nm).
- Camshaft sprocket pilot bolt in each camshaft. Torque the bolts to 124 inch lbs. (14 Nm) in order to pull the camshaft fully forward and align the sprocket support for installation of the sprocket onto the camshaft

15. Remove the 4 sprocket support bolt/blocks and nuts.

16. Install the forward bearing caps and the upper chain guide. Torque the cap bolts to 124 inch lbs. (14 Nm).

17. Be sure the camshaft dowel pin aligns with the slot in each camshaft sprocket. If necessary, rotate the camshaft slightly (1–2 degrees) and move each sprocket from the adapter onto the end of the camshaft. Fully seat each sprocket on the end of each camshaft.

18. Remove the 2 sprocket pilot bolts and adapters while using a wrench on the camshaft flats to assure the camshaft cannot move.

19. Remove the support angle fixture.

20. Install the camshaft sprocket retaining bolts and washers. Hold the camshafts and torque the bolts to 76 ft. lbs. (103 Nm).

21. Verify all visible timing marks and holes are in alignment. Turn the crankshaft clockwise until the mark on the crankshaft pulley aligns with the mark on the front cover. Check timing by inserting 3/16 in. drill bits through the camshaft sprocket alignment holes, into the cylinder head. If the alignment pins cannot be inserted, turn the crankshaft 360 degrees clockwise and repeat. If the pins cannot be inserted within 1–2 degrees of either TDC position, the camshafts are not properly timed. Do not start the engine until the camshafts are timed.

22. Apply a small drop of RTV across the cylinder head and front cover T-joints. Inspect the old camshaft cover gasket and replace if damaged. Install the gasket and the camshaft cover. Torque the fasteners in proper sequence to 89 inch lbs. (10 Nm).

23. Install or connect the following:
- Right splash shield and wheel, if removed to observe the timing marks
- PCV and fresh air hoses and the spark plug wires
- Drive belt
- Negative battery cable

24. Start the engine and check for leaks, repair if necessary.

2.2L Engine

➡**Be very careful when working around the camshaft sprockets and timing chain cover during this procedure. If a bolt or washer is accidentally dropped between the front cover and engine assembly, the cover will have to be removed for retrieval.**

1. Before servicing the vehicle, refer to the precautions in the beginning of this section.

2. Remove or disconnect the following:
- Negative battery cable
- Ignition coil
- Ground strap
- Positive Crankcase Ventilation (PCV) fresh air hose
- Cam cover
- Fuel line
- Wire harness bracket
- Power steering pump

➡**To avoid valve piston contact, the No. 1 cylinder piston must be positioned at 60 degrees Before Top Dead Center (BTDC). The pistons are properly aligned when the diamond shaped hole on the intake camshaft sprocket is located at 12 o'clock.**

3. Remove the upper timing chain guide and front camshaft caps

4. Install a camshaft sprocket holding tool J43655, through the sprocket holes from the timing chain side. Align the guide pins into the slot on the support head. Torque the pins to 89 inch lbs. (10 Nm).

5. Hold each camshaft in place with a 24mm open end wrench and remove the camshaft timing sprocket retaining bolts and washers. Discard the bolts.

6. Uniformly loosen and remove the remaining camshaft bearing caps.

7. Slide the camshaft sprockets away from the camshafts and remove the camshaft

To install:

8. Lubricate the camshaft bearing journals with clean engine oil.

9. Install or connect the following:
- Both camshafts and all bearing caps except for cap on each camshaft. Make certain that the camshaft slot faces up with the notches on the camshaft sprocket
- Torque the bearing caps uniformly, except for the front caps and the rear intake cap, to 89 inch lbs. (10 Nm).

➡**Make certain that the alignment notches are properly positioned with the notches in the camshaft sprockets**

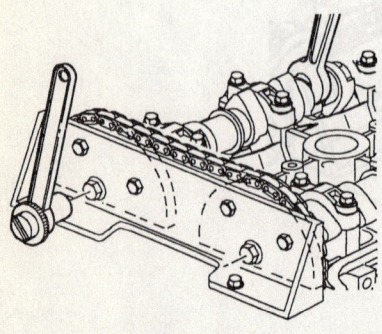

79222813

Hold the camshaft with a wrench while tightening the sprocket bolts—1.9L (DOHC) engine shown

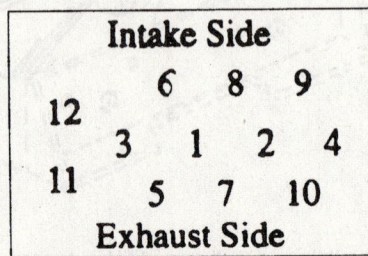

Intake Side		
	6　8　9	
12		
	3　1　2　4	
11		
	5　7　10	
Exhaust Side		

79222817

Camshaft cover bolt tightening sequence—DOHC engine

before final torque is applied. Also, be sure that the timing chain is properly aligned on the fixed guide.

- Slide the camshaft sprockets and timing chain on the guide pins toward the camshafts. Rotate the camshafts with a 24mm open end wrench to align the camshaft and sprocket
- New camshaft sprocket bolts. Torque the bolts to 63 ft. lbs. (85 Nm) plus 30 degrees. Remove the camshaft sprocket holding tool
- Front camshaft bearing caps. Torque the bolts to 89 inch lbs. (10 Nm).
- Upper timing chain guide and apply Loctite® to the bolts
- Rear intake camshaft bearing cap. Torque the bolts 19 ft. lbs. (25 Nm) and apply Loctite 518® to the cylinder
- Power steering pump. Torque the bolts to 19 ft. lbs. (25 Nm).
- Ignition coil
- PCV fresh air hose
- Ground strap
- Fuel line
- Wire harness bracket
- Cam cover
- Negative battery cable

10. Start the vehicle and check for leaks, repair if necessary.

3.0L Engine

This engine is equipped with front and rear camshafts.

The front camshaft bearing caps for the cylinder head are marked R1–R8 and the rear cylinder head bearing caps are marked L1–L8.

➡**Be very careful when working around the camshaft sprockets and timing chain cover during this procedure. If a bolt or washer is accidentally dropped between the front cover and engine assembly, the cover will have to be removed for retrieval.**

1. Before servicing the vehicle, refer to the precautions in the beginning of this section.
2. Remove or disconnect the following:
- Negative battery cable
- Intake plenum
- Air cleaner
- Front camshaft cover
- Front timing belt cover
- Timing belt

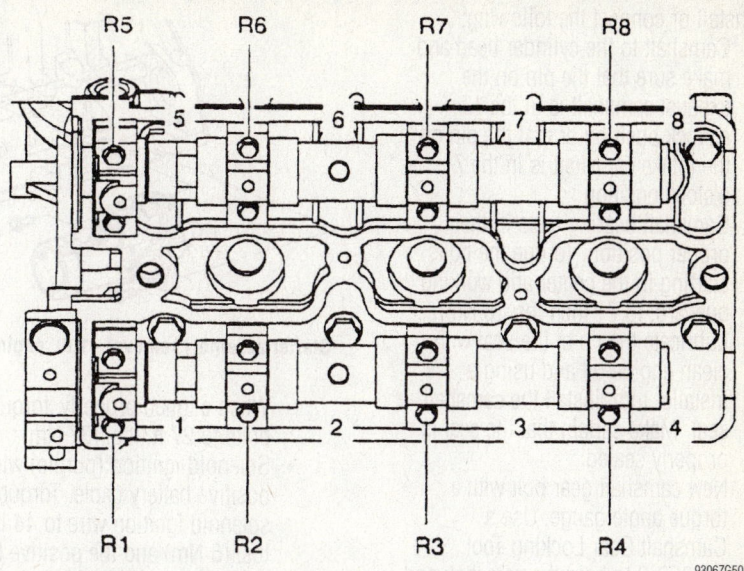

Front camshaft bearing cap removal sequence–3.0L engine

➡**Rotate the crankshaft counterclockwise to 60 degrees Before Top Dead Center (BTDC) to prevent valve to piston contact.**

3. Install a Camshaft Gear Locking Tool, J42069-2 into the camshaft gears.
4. Remove or disconnect the following:
- Loose the camshaft gear bolt, remove the holding tool
- Camshaft gear bolt and discard it
- Camshaft gear
- Loosen the camshaft bearing caps

sequentially starting in the center and working outward in a spiral direction
- Camshaft bearing caps. The caps are marked with an **R** followed by a number
- Camshaft and seal
- Camshaft seal and discard it

To install:

5. Clean all bearing and mating surfaces
6. Lubricate all bearing surfaces with clean engine oil.

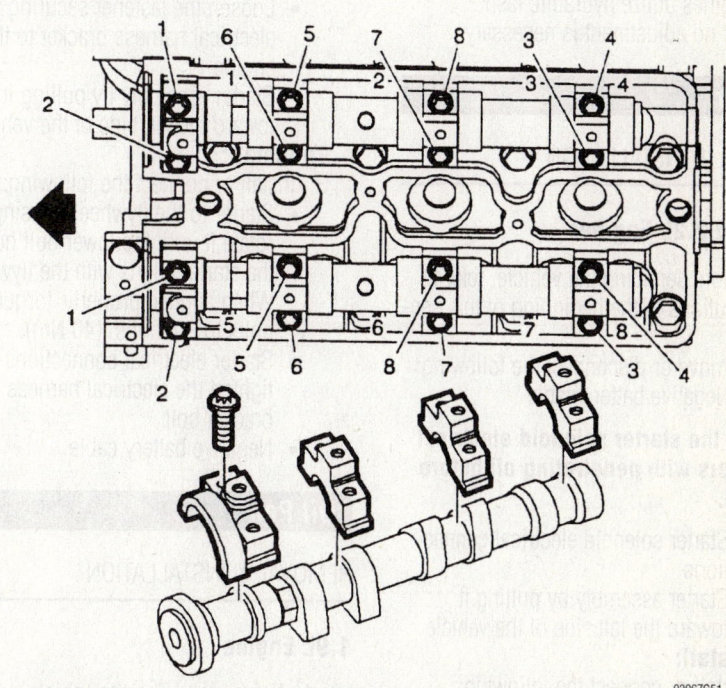

Front camshaft bearing cap installation sequence–3.0L engine

Timing belt service is covered in Section 4 of this manual

7. Install or connect the following:
- Camshaft to the cylinder head and make sure that the pin on the exhaust camshaft is in the 12 o'clock position or that the pin on the intake camshaft is in the 7 o'clock position
- Camshaft bearing caps in their proper position. Torque the bolts, starting in the center and working outward, to 71 inch lbs. (8 Nm).
- Lubricate the lip of the seal with clean engine oil and using a installer tool, install the camshaft seal. Make certain that the seal is properly seated
- New camshaft gear bolt with a torque angle gauge. Use a Camshaft Gear Locking Tool, J42069-2 to hold the camshaft and gear in place. Torque the bolt to 27 ft. lbs. (50 Nm) plus 60 degrees and an additional 15 degrees
- Timing belt and adjust as needed
- Timing belt cover
- Front camshaft cover
- Intake plenum
- Air cleaner
- Negative battery cable

Valve Lash

ADJUSTMENT

All engines utilize hydraulic lash adjusters; no adjustment is necessary.

Starter

REMOVAL & INSTALLATION

1.9L and 2.2L Engines

1. Before servicing the vehicle, refer to the precautions in the beginning of this section.
2. Remove or disconnect the following:
- Negative battery cable

➡ Spary the starter solenoid electrical connectors with penetrating oil before removal.

- Starter solenoid electrical connections
- Starter assembly by pulling it toward the left side of the vehicle

To install:
3. Install or connect the following:
- Starter to the flywheel housing and rotate it until the lower bolt hole in the starter aligns with the flywheel.

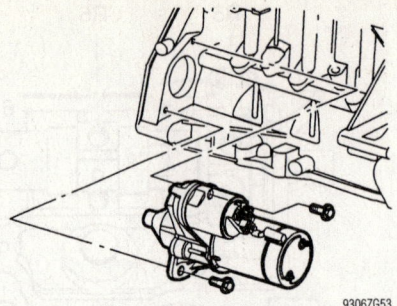
Starter assembly removal −1.9L engine

When aligned properly, torque the bolts to 27 ft. lbs. (37 Nm).
- Solenoid ignition (purple) wire and positive battery cable. Torque the solenoid ignition wire to 44 inch lbs. (5 Nm) and the positive battery cable to 89 inch lbs. (10 Nm).
- Negative battery cable

3.0L Engine

1. Before servicing the vehicle, refer to the precautions in the beginning of this section.
2. Remove or disconnect the following:
- Negative battery cable
- Right front wheel

➡ Spary the starter solenoid electrical connectors with penetrating oil before removal.

- Starter solenoid electrical connections
- Loosen the fastener securing the electrical harness bracket to the engine
- Starter assembly by pulling it toward the left side of the vehicle

To install:
3. Install or connect the following:
- Starter to the flywheel housing and rotate it until the lower bolt hole in the starter aligns with the flywheel. When aligned properly, torque the bolts to 30 ft. lbs. (40 Nm).
- Starter electrical connections and tighten the electrical harness bracket bolt
- Negative battery cable

Oil Pan

REMOVAL & INSTALLATION

1.9L Engine

1. Before servicing the vehicle, refer to the precautions in the beginning of this section.
2. Drain the oil from the engine.

3. Remove or disconnect the following:
- Negative battery cable
- Front exhaust pipe
- Front stiffening bracket and flywheel cover
- Right front wheel, splash shield and damper. Loosen the 4 front motor mount bolts approximately ½ in. (12mm).
- Oil pan bolts.

➡ If equipped with a manual transaxle, an 8mm flex socket may be used to access the rear oil pan bolts located next to the flywheel.

4. Using an RTV cutter tool, separate the oil pan from the engine. Drive the tool around the pan to shear the RTV seam, then tap the pan sideways with a rubber mallet to loosen.
5. Pry the engine mount away from the engine as necessary and remove the oil pan. Be careful not to damage or score component surfaces when prying.

To install:
6. Carefully clean the gasket mating surfaces with a scraper and solvent.
7. Apply a 0.16 in. (4mm) bead of RTV sealer to the pan flange. Be sure the RTV is applied to the inner side of the flange from the bolt holes.
8. Install or connect the following:
- Oil pan within 3 minutes of RTV application. Torque the bolts to 80 inch lbs. (9 Nm).
- Front mount bolts. Torque the bolts to 37 ft. lbs. (50 Nm).
- Right splash shield and wheel
- Engine stiffening bracket and the flywheel cover

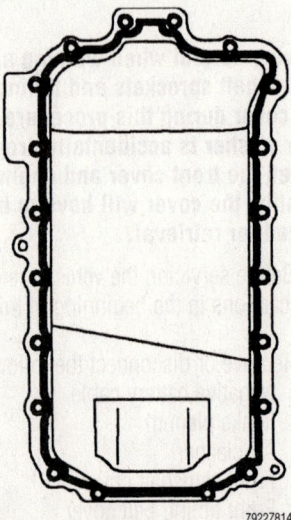
Apply a 0.16 in (4mm) bead of RTV to the oil pan flange to the inner side of the bolt holes.

- Exhaust pipe. Torque the pipe-to-manifold nuts in a crosswise pattern to 23 ft. lbs. (31 Nm) and the pipe to converter bolts to 33 ft. lbs. (45 Nm).
- Negative battery cable
9. Fill the engine with clean oil.
10. Start the vehicle and check for leaks, repair if necessary.

2.2L Engine

1. Before servicing the vehicle, refer to the precautions in the beginning of this section.
2. Drain the engine oil.
3. Remove or disconnect the following:
   - Negative battery cable
   - Oil pan bolts
4. Using a flat blade tool, pry the oil pan from the engine block.

To install:

5. Carefully clean the gasket mating surfaces with a scraper and solvent.
6. Apply a 0.16 in. (4mm) bead of RTV sealer to the pan flange. Be sure the RTV is applied to the inner side of the flange.
7. Install or connect the following:
   - Oil pan within 3 minutes of RTV application. Torque the bolts in the proper sequence to 18 ft. lbs. (25 Nm).
   - Negative battery cable
8. Fill the engine with clean oil.
9. Start the vehicle and check for leaks, repair if necessary.

3.0L Engine

1. Before servicing the vehicle, refer to the precautions in the beginning of this section.
2. Drain the engine oil.
3. Remove or disconnect the following:
   - Negative battery cable
   - Nose cone bracket from the oil pan
   - Lower transmission flange to oil pan bolts
   - Oil pan bolts
   - Separate the oil pan from the engine with an RTV cutter tool. Drive the tool around the pan to shear the RTV seam, then tap the pan sideways with a rubber mallet to loosen.
   - Oil pan

To install:

4. Carefully clean the gasket mating surfaces.
5. Apply a 0.10 in. (2mm) bead of RTV sealer to the pan flange. Be sure the RTV is applied to the inner side of the flange.
6. Install or connect the following:
   - Oil pan within 3 minutes of RTV application. Torque the bolts in the proper sequence to 18 ft. lbs. (25 Nm).
   - Transmission nose cone as a guide for fore/aft alignment
   - Transmission nose cone bolts and hand-tighten them
   - Transmission to oil pan bolts and hand-tighten them

- Oil pan bolts with Loctite® 242 on the threads. Torque all the bolts to 11 ft. lbs. (15 Nm).
- Negative battery cable
7. Fill the engine with clean oil.
8. Start the vehicle and check for leaks, repair if necessary.

Oil Pump

REMOVAL & INSTALLATION

1.9L Engine

1. Before servicing the vehicle, refer to the precautions in the beginning of this section.
2. Drain the engine oil
3. Remove or disconnect the following:
   - Negative battery cable
   - Right front wheel and splash shield
   - Drive belt
   - Timing chain front cover which contains the oil pump
   - Front crankshaft vibration damper/pulley
   - Drive belt idler pulley
   - Power steering pump, SOHC only
   - Belt tensioner and properly support the powertrain assembly
   - Camshaft cover, DOHC only
   - Right side engine mount to front cover nuts and the engine mount to midrail bracket nuts
   - Front cover and install a Crankcase Timing Gear Service tool, SA9104E, to hold the crankshaft timing gear in place
   - Front 4 oil pan and 14 front cover bolts
   - Oil gallery transfer seals and discard them
   - Remove the drive rotor and driven rotor
4. If necessary, remove the relief valve. Because the puller jaws will damage the relief valve sealing seat, the valve cannot be used again when removed.

To install:

5. Install or connect the following:
   - New relief valve into the cover bore, if removed. Coat the valve with clean engine oil and tap it into the bore.

➡**Whenever the oil pump is installed, the assembly must be packed with petroleum jelly in order to prime the pump.**

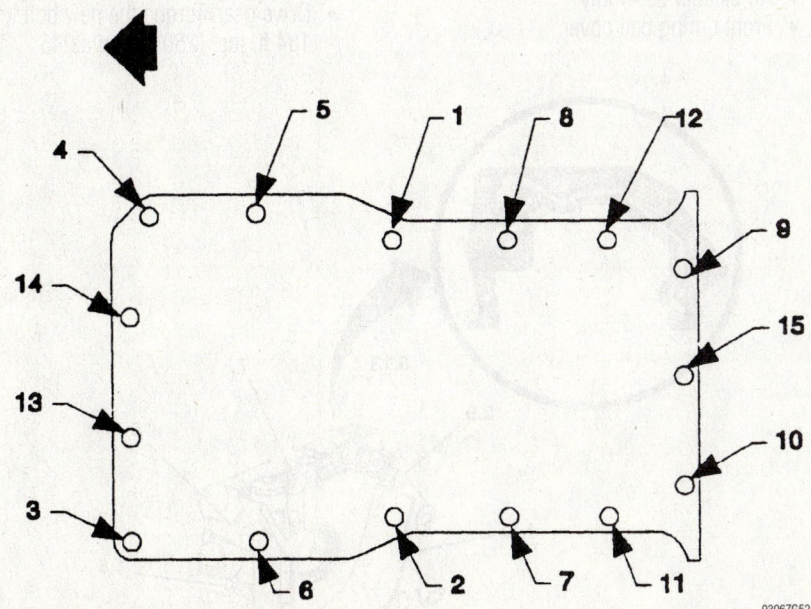

Oil pan bolts torque sequence–2.2L engine

9306ZG52

- Drive and driven rotors into the pump with the chamfer toward the front oil seal
- Oil pump body cover and secure using new bolts that are coated with sealant to prevent oil leakage. Torque the bolts to 97 inch lbs. (11 Nm).
- New oil pressure and suction seals in the cylinder block
- Front oil pan bolts. Torque the bolts to 80 inch lbs. (9 Nm).
- Front cover. Torque the perimeter and center bolts to 19 ft. lbs. (25 Nm) and the lower center bolt to 89 inch lbs. (10 Nm).
- Camshaft/rocker cover
- Drive belt tensioner. Torque the fastener to 26 ft. lbs. (35 Nm).
- Power steering pump, if removed
- Drive belt. Torque the pulley bolts to 33 ft. lbs. (45 Nm).
- Engine mount to midrail bracket nuts first and the engine mount to front cover nuts last. Torque all nuts to 37 ft. lbs. (50 Nm).
- Right front splash shield and wheel
- Negative battery cable

6. Fill the engine with clean oil and replace the oil filter.

7. Start the vehicle and check for leaks, repair if necessary.

2.2L Engine

1. Before servicing the vehicle, refer to the precautions in the beginning of this section.

2. Drain the engine oil

3. Remove or disconnect the following:
- Negative battery cable
- Air cleaner assembly
- Right front wheel and splash shield
- Drive belt
- Belt tensioner and properly support the powertrain assembly
- Right front engine mount
- Timing chain front cover bolts and the 13mm bolt under the water pump
- Oil pump cover plate
- Drive rotor and driven rotor
- Pressure relief valve

To install:

4. Install or connect the following:
- New relief valve into the cover bore, if removed. Coat the valve with clean engine oil and tap it into the bore. Torque the plug to 30 ft. lbs. (40 Nm).

➡ **Whenever the oil pump is installed, the assembly must be packed with petroleum jelly in order to prime the pump.**

- Drive and driven rotors into the pump with the chamfer toward the front oil seal
- Oil pump body cover and secure using new bolts that are coated with sealant to prevent oil leakage. Torque the bolts to 53 inch lbs. (6 Nm).
- Front cover. Torque the perimeter and center bolts to 19 ft. lbs. (25 Nm) and the lower center bolt to 89 inch lbs. (10 Nm).
- Right side engine mount. Torque the bolts to 41 ft. lbs. (55 Nm) and remove the engine support fixture
- Drive belt tensioner. Torque the bolt 37 ft. lbs. (50 Nm).
- Crankshaft damper pulley. Torque the bolt to 74 ft. lbs. (100 Nm) plus 75 degrees
- Drive belt
- Right front splash shield and wheel
- Air cleaner assembly
- Negative battery cable

5. Fill the engine with clean oil and replace the oil filter.

6. Start the vehicle and check for leaks, repair if necessary.

3.0L Engine

1. Before servicing the vehicle, refer to the precautions in the beginning of this section.

2. Drain the engine oil.

3. Drain the coolant system.

4. Remove or disconnect the following:
- Negative battery cable
- Air cleaner assembly
- Front timing belt cover

- Timing belt
- rear timing belt cover
- A/C compressor and power steering pump bracket and move them away from the oil pump housing
- Alternator bolts and move the alternator out of the way
- Oil pan

5. Mount a crank Hub Holding tool J42065, to the crankshaft drive gear and remove the drive gear

6. Remove or disconnect the following:
- Oil pump bolts
- Oil pan housing bolts that thread into the oil pump
- Oil pump
- Front main oil seal and collar
- Oil pump cover plate
- Drive rotor and driven rotor
- Pressure relief valve

To install:

7. Install the new relief valve into the cover bore, if removed. Coat the valve with clean engine oil and tap it into the bore. Torque the plug to 30 ft. lbs. (40 Nm).

➡ **Whenever the oil pump is installed, the new gasket must be coated with a thin bead of sealing Loctite 518®**

8. Install or connect the following:
- Drive and driven rotors into the pump with the chamfer toward the front oil seal
- Oil pump body cover and secure using new bolts that are coated with sealant to prevent oil leakage. Torque the bolts to 89 inch lbs. (10 Nm).
- Drive gear. Torque the new bolt to 184 ft. lbs. (250 Nm) plus 45

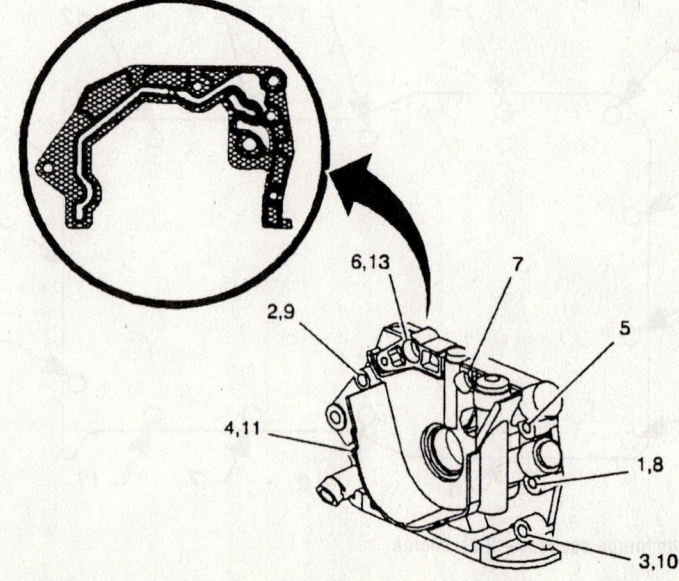

Oil pump bolt tightening sequence—3.0L engine

9306ZG54

degrees and an additional 15 degrees
- Oil pan
- Alternator. Torque the bolts to 30 ft. lbs. (40 Nm).
- A/C compressor and power steering pump bracket. Torque the bolts to 30 ft. lbs. (40 Nm).
- Rear timing belt cover
- Drive belt idler pulley. Torque the oil pump bolts an additional 80 inch lbs. (9 Nm) to compress the oil pump gasket. Torque the oil pump bolts in sequence
- Timing belt and front cover
- Air cleaner assembly
- Negative battery cable

9. Fill the engine with clean oil. An oil filter replacement is also recommended.

10. Fill the coolant system.

11. Start the vehicle and check for leaks, repair if necessary.

Rear Main Seal

REMOVAL & INSTALLATION

1.9L Engine

Both engines use a 1-piece round seal mounted in a seal carrier.

1. Before servicing the vehicle, refer to the precautions in the beginning of this section.

2. Drain the engine oil.

3. Remove or disconnect the following:
- Negative battery cable
- Oil pan

4. Use the prying tangs provided in the carrier to remove the seal with a small suitable prybar and hammer. Be careful not to damage the crankshaft oil seal lip contact surface.

To install:

5. Clean the carrier and crankshaft with solvent and a rag to prevent seal lip damage during installation. Check for scores or damage to the sealing surfaces.

6. Apply a light coat of clean engine oil to the seal lip and the carrier inner diameter.

7. Install or connect the following:
- New rear main seal, using a Seal Installer tool SA9121E. The tool is designed to prevent the seal lip from rolling during installation and will seat the seal 0.04 in. (1mm) lower than the factory seal. Never tap on the seal or seal installer with a hammer

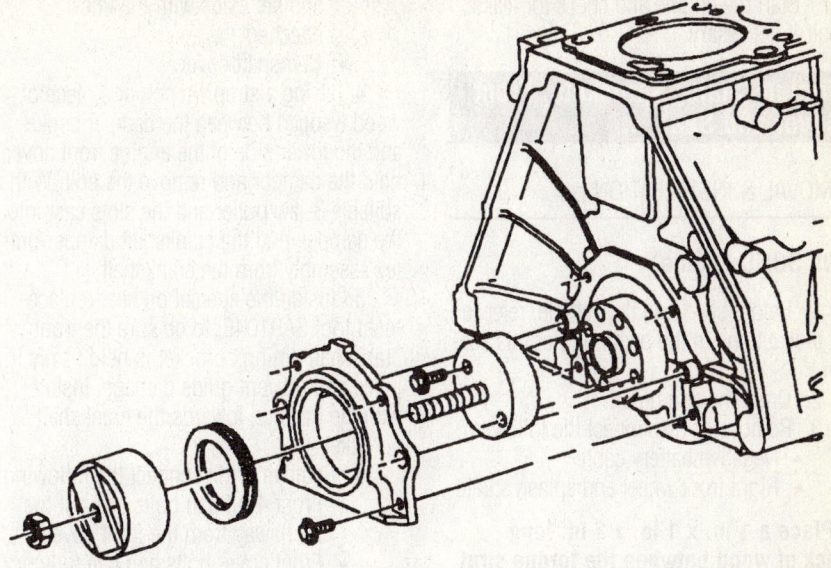

Exploded view of the rear main seal installation

- Oil pan
- Negative battery cable

8. Fill the engine with clean oil.

9. Start the vehicle and check for leaks, repair if necessary.

2.2L Engine

1. Before servicing the vehicle, refer to the precautions in the beginning of this section.

2. Remove or disconnect the following:
- Negative battery cable
- Transmission
- Clutch/pressure plate assembly, if equipped with a manual transmission
- Flywheel
- Rear main bearing seal by prying it from the engine

➡**Be careful not to damage or scratch the seal mounting surfaces.**

To install:

3. Lubricate the new rear main bearing seal with engine oil.

4. Install or connect the following:
- New rear main seal using the Rear Main Bearing Oil Seal Installer tool J-42067 until it is flush with the block
- Flywheel
- Clutch/pressure plate assembly, if equipped with a manual transmission
- Transmission
- Negative battery cable

5. Start the engine and check for leaks, repair if necessary.

3.0L Engine

1. Before servicing the vehicle, refer to the precautions in the beginning of this section.

2. Remove or disconnect the following:
- Negative battery cable
- Transmission
- Clutch/pressure plate assembly, if equipped with a manual transmission
- Flywheel

3. Center punch the steel ring of the oil seal.

4. Drill a small hole into the steel ring. Install a self-tapping screw and using pliers, pull out the rear main oil seal.

➡**Be careful not to damage or scratch the seal mounting surfaces.**

To install:

5. Lubricate the new rear main oil seal with engine oil.

6. Install or connect the following:
- New rear main seal using the Rear Main Bearing Oil Seal Installer tool J-42067 until it is flush with the block
- Flywheel
- Clutch/pressure plate assembly, if equipped with a manual transmission
- Transmission
- Negative battery cable

Refer to Section 1 for engine rebuilding specifications

7. Start the engine and check for leaks, repair if necessary.

Timing Chain, Sprockets, Front Cover and Seal

REMOVAL & INSTALLATION

1.9L SOHC Engine

1. Before servicing the vehicle, refer to the precautions in the beginning of this section.
2. Drain the engine oil.
3. Remove or disconnect the following:
   - Negative battery cable
   - Right front wheel and splash shield

➡ Place a 1 in. x 1 in. x 2 in. long block of wood between the torque strut and cradle to ease removal and installation of the torque engine mount.

   - 3 right side upper engine torque axis to front cover nuts and the 2 mount to midrail bracket nuts, allowing the powertrain to rest on the block of wood
   - Drive belt, tensioner and pulley
   - Power steering pump attaching bolts and set the pump to the side with the lines still attached
   - A/C compressor from the bracket

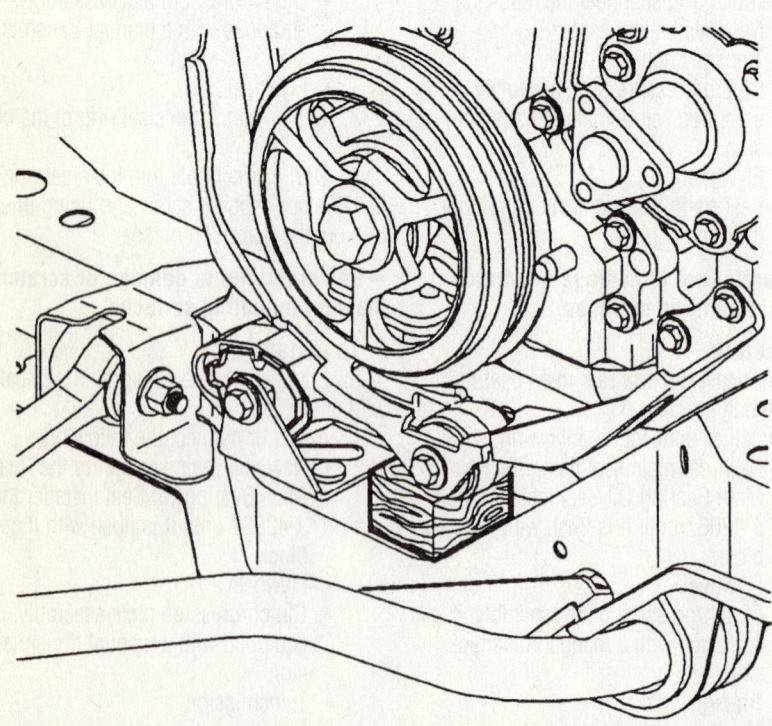

Place a 1 x 1 x 2 in. (25 x 25 x 51mm) piece of wood between the torque strut and cradle before removal of the torque engine mount—1.9L (SOHC) engine

and set aside with the lines attached
   - Camshaft cover

4. Using a strap wrench or a piece of wood wedged between the damper spoke and the lower side of the engine front cover, hold the damper and remove the bolt. With a suitable 3-jaw puller and the slots cast into the damper, pull the crankshaft damper/pulley assembly from the crankshaft.

5. Install the special oil seal replacement tool SA9104E, to be sure the front crankshaft timing sprocket is held firmly in place and prevent guide damage. Install with the flat side towards the crankshaft sprocket.

6. Remove or disconnect the following:
   - Front 4 oil pan bolts and cut the seal away from the front cover
   - Front cover bolts and carefully pry the cover away from the cylinder block at the pry location tabs, which are provided. Remove the cover from under the hood or through the wheel well
   - Front cover oil seal from the cover

➡ During timing chain and sprocket removal, position the crankshaft 90 degrees past Top Dead Center (TDC), to be sure the pistons will not contact the valves upon assembly.

7. Carefully rotate the crankshaft clockwise so the timing mark on the crankshaft sprocket and keyway align with the main bearing cap split line (90 degrees past TDC).

8. Remove or disconnect the following:
   - Timing guides and tensioner
   - Camshaft sprocket bolt, using a ⅞ in. (21mm) wrench to hold the camshaft. Then, remove the timing chain and camshaft sprocket
   - Crankshaft sprocket

To install:

9. Inspect the chain for wear and damage. Check the inside diameter of the chain, it should be no more than 16.77 in. (426mm). Inspect the chain guides for wear or cracks and the timing sprockets for teeth or key wear. Replace components as necessary.

10. Verify that the crankshaft keyway is positioned 90 degrees clockwise past TDC (keyway at 3 o'clock). The keyway should align with the split between the bearing cap and engine block.

11. Bring the camshaft up to No. 1 TDC by loosely installing the sprocket and rotating the sprocket until the timing pin can be inserted. The camshaft contains wrench flats to assist in turning the shaft. The dowel pin should be at 12 o'clock when the camshaft is at TDC.

12. Install the crankshaft sprocket, then rotate the crankshaft counterclockwise 90 degrees up to No. 1 TDC (keyway at 12 o'clock).

13. Position the chain under the crankshaft sprocket and over the camshaft sprocket. The timing chain should be positioned so that 1 silver link plate aligns with the reference mark on the camshaft sprocket and the other aligns with the downward tooth (at the 6 o'clock position) on the crankshaft sprocket. The letters FRT on the camshaft sprocket must face forward, away from the cylinder head and excess chain slack should be located on the tensioner side of the block.

14. Install or connect the following:
   - Timing pin to verify proper alignment of the camshaft and sprocket. Torque the sprocket bolt to 75 ft. lbs. (102 Nm).

➡ Do not allow the camshaft retaining bolt to torque against the timing pin or cylinder head damage will result.

   - Timing chain guides with the words FRONT facing out. Install the fixed guide first and verify the chain is snug against the guide, then install the pivot guide. Torque the bolts to 19 ft. lbs. (26 Nm) and verify that the pivot guide moves freely

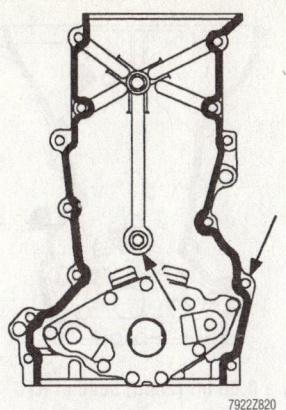

Apply a 0.08 in. (2mm) bead of RTV sealer along the vertical sealing surfaces of the front cover—1.9L (SOHC) engine

- Retract the tensioner plunger and pin the ratchet lever using a ⅛ in. No. 31 drill bit inserted in the alignment hole at the bottom front of the component
- Tensioner. Torque the bolts to 14 ft. lbs. (19 Nm), then remove the drill bit

15. Make one final check to verify all components are properly timed, then remove all timing pins.

16. Install or connect the following:
- Seat a new front cover oil seal using the installation tool with a press
- If the engine front cover casting or assembly is replaced, the 3 torque axis mount studs should also be replaced. Torque the new studs to 19 ft. lbs. (25 Nm).

➡Apply a 0.08 in. (2mm) bead of RTV sealer along the vertical sealing surfaces of the front cover to the inside of the bolt holes and to the front of the oil pan. Extra sealer is necessary at the oil pan and cylinder head joints. Be sure to assemble the front cover to the engine within 3 minutes of RTV application.

- Crankshaft sprocket retaining tool to align the oil pump and crankshaft during cover installation. Position the front cover to the engine. Torque the perimeter bolts starting at the center and working outwards on both sides to 19 ft. lbs. (25 Nm).
- Torque the front cover center or inner bolts to 89 inch lbs. (10 Nm), except for the upper inside bolt which should be tightened to 22 ft. lbs. (30 Nm).
- Tighten the 4 oil pan front bolts to 80 inch lbs. (9 Nm).

17. After front cover installation, spray 6–12 squirts of oil through the front oil seal drain back hole to verify that it is not plugged.

18. Apply a thin film of RTV between the damper/pulley assembly flange and washer only; the washer and bolt head flange are designed to prevent oil leakage.

19. Remove the crankshaft retaining tool.

20. Position the crankshaft damper/pulley assembly, then secure using the wood or strap wrench (as accomplished during removal). Torque the bolt to 159 ft. lbs. (215 Nm).

21. Apply a small drop of RTV across the cylinder head and front cover T-joints. Inspect the old camshaft cover gasket and replace if damaged. Install the gasket and the camshaft cover. Torque the fasteners uniformly to 22 ft. lbs. (30 Nm).

22. Install or connect the following:
- A/C compressor assembly and/or the power steering pump assembly
- Idler pulley, belt tensioner and drive belt

- 2 engine mount-to-midrail bracket nuts. Torque the nuts to 37 ft. lbs. (50 Nm).
- 3 mount-to-front cover nuts. Torque the nuts uniformly to 37 ft. lbs. (50 Nm) in order to prevent front cover damage

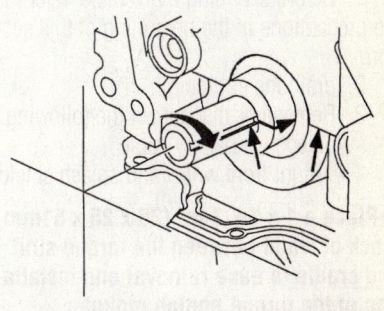

At 90 degrees past TDC, the crankshaft sprocket keyway will align with the main bearing cap split line—1.9L (SOHC) engine

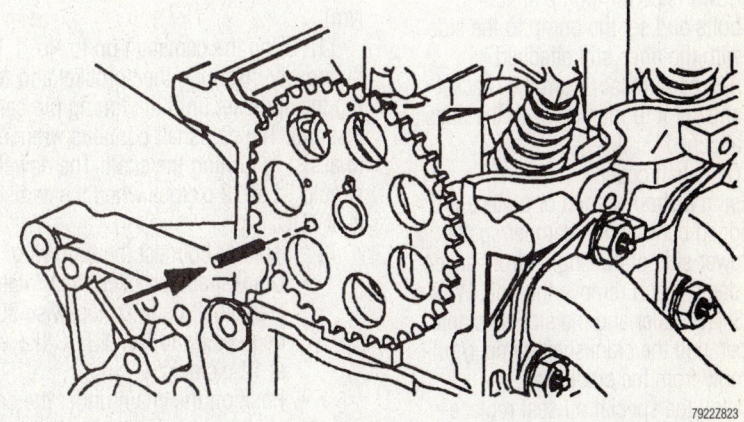

Insert a timing pin to ensure that the camshaft is at No. 1 TDC—1.9L (SOHC) engine

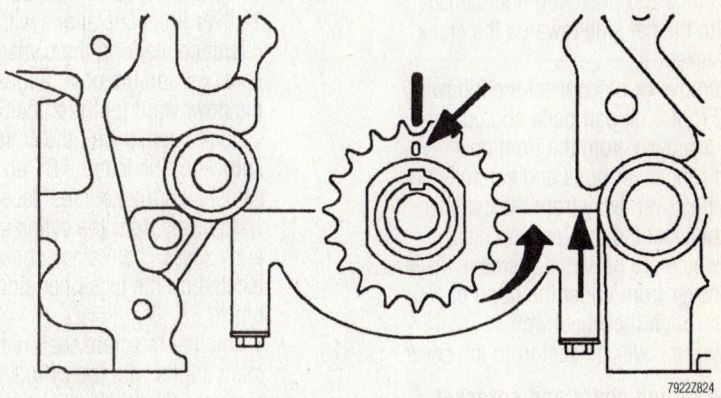

When the camshaft is at TDC, rotate the crankshaft counterclockwise 90 degrees to achieve TDC—1.9L (SOHC) engine

For engine torque specifications, refer to Section 1 of this manual

- Splash shield and the wheel assembly
- Negative battery cable
23. Fill the engine with clean oil.
24. Start the engine and check for leaks, repair if necessary.

1.9L (DOHC) Engine

1. Before servicing the vehicle, refer to the precautions in the beginning of this section.
2. drain the engine oil.
3. Remove or disconnect the following:
- Negative battery cable
- Right front wheel and splash shield

➡ **Place a 1 x 1 x 2 in. (25 x 25 x 51mm) block of wood between the torque strut and cradle to ease removal and installation of the torque engine mount.**

- 3 right side upper engine torque axis to front cover nuts and the 2 mount to midrail bracket nuts, allowing the powertrain to rest on the block of wood
- Drive belt, tensioner and pulley
- Power steering pump attaching bolts and set the pump to the side with the lines still attached
- A/C compressor from the bracket and set it to the side with the lines attached
- Camshaft cover
4. Using a strap wrench or a piece of wood wedged between the damper spoke and the lower side of the engine front cover, hold the damper and remove the bolt. With a suitable 3-jaw puller and the slots cast into the damper, pull the crankshaft damper/pulley assembly from the crankshaft.
5. Install the special oil seal replacement tool SA9104E or equivalent, to be sure the front crankshaft timing sprocket is held firmly in place and prevent guide damage. Install with the flat side towards the crankshaft sprocket.
6. Remove or disconnect the following:
- Front 4 oil pan bolts and cut the seal away from the front cover
- Front cover bolts and carefully pry the cover away from the cylinder block at the pry location tabs, which are provided. Remove the cover from under the hood or through the wheel well
- Front cover oil seal from the cover

➡ **During timing chain and sprocket removal, position the crankshaft 90 degrees past top Dead Center (TDC), to be sure the pistons will not contact the valves upon assembly.**

7. Carefully rotate the crankshaft clockwise so the timing mark on the crankshaft sprocket and keyway align with the main bearing cap split line (90 degrees past TDC).
- Timing guides and tensioner
- Camshaft sprocket bolt, using a ⅞ in. (21mm) wrench to hold the camshaft. Then, remove the timing chain and camshaft sprocket
- Crankshaft sprocket

To install:

8. Inspect the chain for wear and damage. Check the inside diameter of the chain, it should be no more than 23.15 in. (588mm). Inspect the chain guides for wear or cracks and the timing sprockets for teeth or key wear. Replace components as necessary.
9. Verify that the crankshaft keyway is positioned 90 degrees clockwise past TDC (keyway at 3 o'clock). The keyway should align with the split between the bearing cap and engine block.
10. Install the camshaft sprockets. Use the wrench flats on the camshafts to secure the shaft. Torque the bolts to 75 ft. lbs. (102 Nm).
11. Bring the camshaft up to No. 1 TDC by loosely installing the sprocket and rotating the sprocket until the timing pin can be inserted. The camshaft contains wrench flats to assist in turning the shaft. The dowel pin should be at 12 o'clock when the camshaft is at TDC.
12. Install or connect the following:
- Crankshaft sprocket, then rotate the crankshaft counterclockwise 90 degrees up to No. 1 TDC (keyway at 12 o'clock).
- Position the chain under the crankshaft sprocket and over the camshaft sprocket. The timing chain should be positioned so that 1 silver link plate aligns with the reference mark on the camshaft sprocket and the other aligns with the downward tooth (at the 6 o'clock position) on the crankshaft sprocket. The letters FRT on the camshaft sprocket must face forward, away from the cylinder head and excess chain slack should be located on the tensioner side of the block
- Verify that the crankshaft reference mark aligns with the cylinder block mark at 12 o'clock
- Timing chain fixed guide to the right of the block and facing the water pump. Torque the bolts to 21 ft. lbs. (28 Nm).

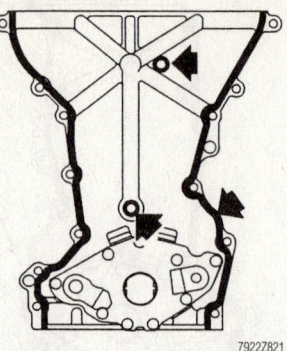

Apply a 0.08 in. (2mm) bead of RTV sealer along the vertical sealing surfaces of the front cover and the front of the oil pan—1.9L (DOHC) engine.

- Pivoting chain guide. Torque the bolt to 19 ft. lbs. (26 Nm) and make certain the guide moves freely
- Two forward bearing caps and the upper timing chain guide. Torque the retaining bolts to 124 inch lbs. (14 Nm).
- Retract the tensioner plunger and pin the ratchet lever using a ⅛ in. No. 31 drill bit inserted in the alignment hole at the bottom front of the component
- Tensioner. Torque the bolts to 14 ft. lbs. (19 Nm), then remove the drill bit
13. Make one final check to verify all components are properly timed, then remove all timing pins.
14. Install or connect the following:
- Seat a new front cover oil seal using the installation tool with a press
- If the engine front cover casting or assembly is replaced, the 3 torque axis mount studs should also be replaced. Torque the new studs to 19 ft. lbs. (25 Nm).

➡ **Apply a 0.08 in. (2mm) bead of RTV sealer along the vertical sealing surfaces of the front cover to the inside of the bolt holes and to the front of the oil pan. Extra sealer is necessary at the oil pan and cylinder head joints. Be sure to assemble the front cover to the engine within 3 minutes of RTV application.**

- Crankshaft sprocket retaining tool to align the oil pump and crankshaft during cover installation. Position the front cover to the engine. Torque the perimeter bolts starting at the center and working outwards on both sides to 22 ft. lbs. (30 Nm).

- Torque the front cover center or inner bolts to 89 inch lbs. (10 Nm) except for the upper inside bolt which should be tightened to 22 ft. lbs. (30 Nm).
- 4 oil pan front bolts and tighten to 80 inch lbs. (9 Nm).

15. After front cover installation, spray 6–12 squirts of oil through the front oil seal drain back hole to verify that it is not plugged.

16. Apply a thin film of RTV between the damper/pulley assembly flange and washer only; the washer and bolt head flange are designed to prevent oil leakage.

17. Position the crankshaft damper/pulley assembly, then secure using the wood or strap wrench (as accomplished during removal). Torque the bolt to 159 ft. lbs. (215 Nm).

18. Apply a small drop of RTV across the cylinder head and front cover T-joints. Inspect the old camshaft cover gasket and replace if damaged. Install the gasket and the camshaft cover. Torque the fasteners uniformly to 89 inch lbs. (10 Nm).

19. Remove the crankshaft retaining tool.

20. Install or connect the following:

- A/C compressor assembly and/or the power steering pump assembly
- Idler pulley, belt tensioner and drive belt

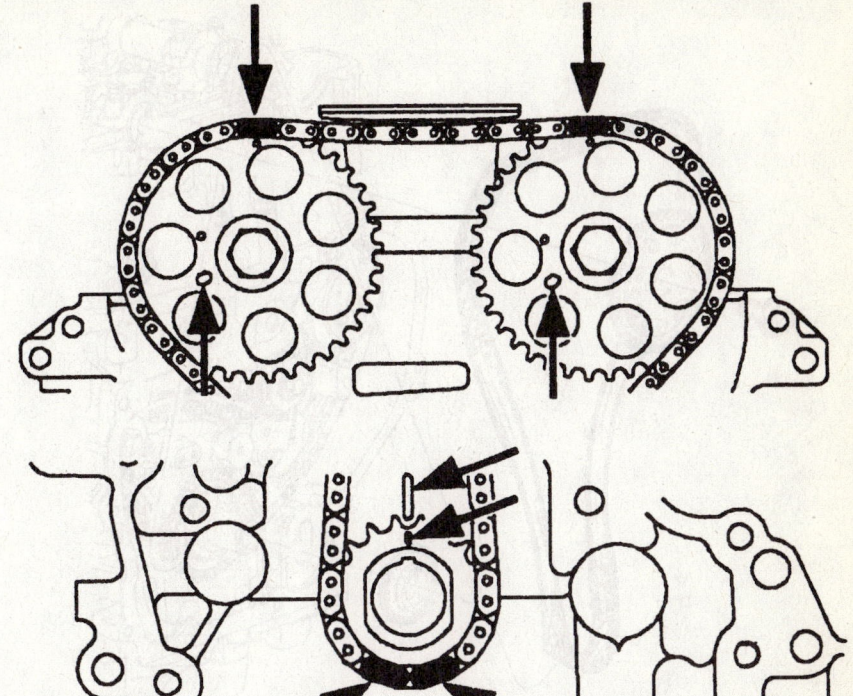

Be sure that the silver link plates and reference marks are all in alignment as shown—1.9L (DOHC) engine

- 2 engine mount-to-midrail bracket nuts. Torque the nuts to 37 ft. lbs. (50 Nm).
- 3 mount-to-front cover nuts. Torque the nuts uniformly to 37 ft. lbs. (50 Nm) in order to prevent front cover damage
- Splash shield and the wheel assembly
- Negative battery cable

21. Fill the engine with clean oil.

22. Start the engine and check for leaks, repair if necessary.

2.2L Engine

1. Before servicing the vehicle, refer to the precautions in the beginning of this section.

2. Drain the engine oil.

3. Remove or disconnect the following:

- Negative battery cable
- Front cover
- Camshaft cover
- Timing chain tensioner
- Upper timing chain guide
- Exhaust camshaft sprocket and discard the bolt
- Adjustable timing chain guide
- Fixed timing chain guide access plug and guide
- Inner camshaft sprocket and discard the bolt
- Timing chain through the top of the cylinder head

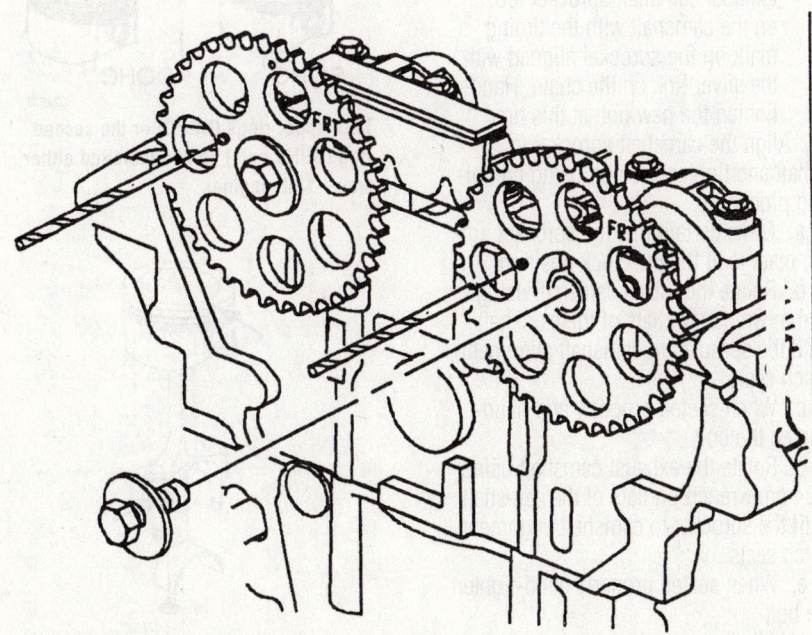

Use drill bits as timing pins to verify that the camshafts are at TDC—1.9L (DOHC) engine

For complete mechanical specifications, refer to Section 1 of this manual

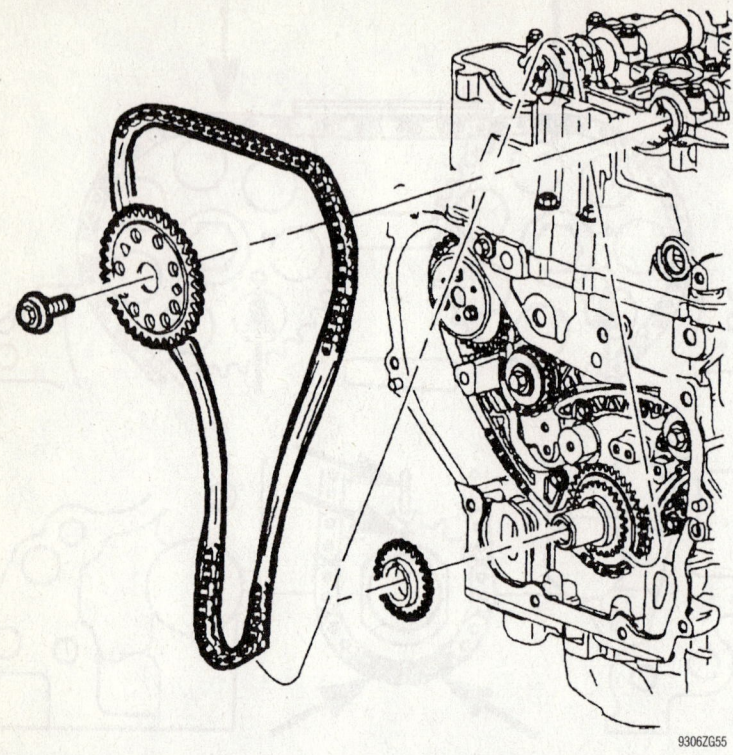

Remove the timing chain through the top of the cylinder head—2.2L engine

- Timing chain sprocket
- Timing chain oiling nozzle

To install:

4. Inspect the chain guides for wear and damage. Replace the guides if wear exceeds 0.045 inch (1.12mm). Inspect the timing chain shoe. Replace the shoe if wear exceeds 0.045 inch (1.12mm).

5. Install or connect the following:
- Timing chain sprocket to the crankshaft. Rotate the crankshaft so that the mark on the sprocket is at the 5 o'clock position
- Assemble the timing chain to the intake camshaft sprocket alignment copper link to the "INT" diamond timing mark on the camshaft sprocket

➥ When lowering the timing chain, rotate the assembly 90 degrees to allow the chain to fall between the cylinder block bosses. Rotate the chain back so that the camshaft sprocket is facing forward.

- Chain through the housing opening on top of the cylinder head. Make certain that the chain goes around both sides of the bosses
- Route the chain around the crankshaft sprocket and align the silver link to the timing mark. The crankshaft sprocket timing mark will be at the 5 o'clock position

- Intake camshaft sprocket loosely on the camshaft and hand-tighten the new bolt
- Adjustable timing chain guide through the opening on top of the cylinder head. Torque the bolt to 89 inch lbs. (10 Nm).
- Exhaust camshaft sprocket loosely on the camshaft with the timing mark on the sprocket aligned with the silver link on the chain. Hand-tighten the new bolt at this time

6. Align the camshaft sprocket to camshaft and tighten the bolt using the following procedure:

a. Make certain that the sprocket timing mark is at the 5 o'clock position.

b. Rotate the intake camshaft using a 24mm wrench on flats of the camshaft until the sprocket to camshaft alignment notch seats.

c. When seated properly and hand-tighten the bolt.

d. Rotate the exhaust camshaft using a 24mm wrench on flats of the camshaft until the sprocket to camshaft alignment notch seats.

e. When seated properly hand-tighten the bolt.

7. Verify that all colored links are aligned with the proper marks on the camshaft and crankshaft sprockets.

8. Install or connect the following:

- Torque the fixed timing chain guide bolt to 89 inch lbs. (10 Nm).
- Fixed timing chain guide bolt access plug. Torque the plug to 30 ft. lbs. (40 Nm).
- Upper timing chain guide. Torque the bolts to 89 inch lbs. (10 Nm).
- Intake and exhaust camshaft sprocket bolts. Torque the bolts to 63 ft. lbs. (85 Nm) plus 30 degrees
- Sealing ring and tensioner assembly. Torque the tensioner to 44 ft. lbs. (60 Nm).
- Timing chain oiling nozzle. Torque the bolt to 89 inch lbs. (10 Nm).
- Camshaft cover
- Front engine cover
- Negative battery cable

9. Fill the engine with clean oil.

10. Start the vehicle and check for leaks, repair if necessary.

Piston and Ring

POSITIONING

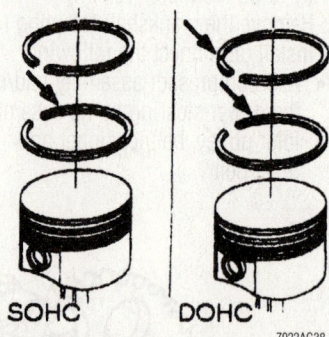

Both upper rings (DOHC) or the second ring (SOHC only) can be installed either way—1.9L engines

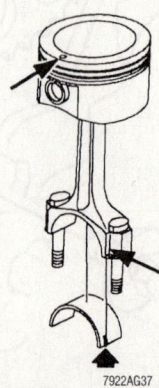

Piston and connecting rod assembly positioning mark locations. The mark on the piston and rod bearing tang slots must face the front of the engine—1.9L engines

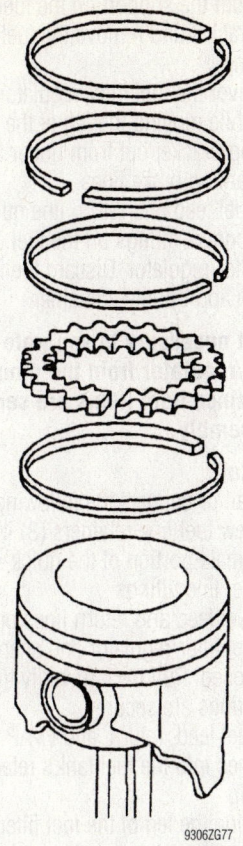

Piston ring positioning—2.2L engine

FUEL SYSTEM

Fuel System Service Precautions

Safety is the most important factor when performing not only fuel system maintenance but any type of maintenance. Failure to conduct maintenance and repairs in a safe manner may result in serious personal injury or death. Maintenance and testing of the vehicle's fuel system components can be accomplished safely and effectively by adhering to the following rules and guidelines.

• To avoid the possibility of fire and personal injury, always disconnect the negative battery cable unless the repair or test procedure requires that battery voltage be applied

• Always relieve the fuel system pressure prior to disconnecting any fuel system component (injector, fuel rail, pressure regulator, etc.), fitting or fuel line connection. Exercise extreme caution whenever relieving fuel system pressure, to avoid exposing skin, face and eyes to fuel spray. Please be advised that fuel under pressure may penetrate the skin or any part of the body that it contacts

• Always place a shop towel or cloth around the fitting or connection prior to loosening to absorb any excess fuel due to spillage. Ensure that all fuel spillage (should it occur) is quickly removed from engine surfaces. Ensure that all fuel soaked cloths or towels are deposited into a suitable waste container

• Always keep a dry chemical (Class B) fire extinguisher near the work area

• Do not allow fuel spray or fuel vapors to come into contact with a spark or open flame

• Always use a back-up wrench when loosening and tightening fuel line connection fittings. This will prevent unnecessary stress and torsion to fuel line piping

• Always replace worn fuel fitting O-rings with new. Do not substitute fuel hose or equivalent, where fuel pipe is installed

Fuel System Pressure

RELIEVING

1. Before servicing the vehicle, refer to the precautions in the beginning of this section.

2. Unless battery voltage is necessary for testing, disconnect the negative battery cable. This will prevent the fuel pump from running and causing a fuel spill through the disconnected components if the ignition key is accidentally turned **ON**.

3. Remove the air cleaner assembly, for access.

4. Wrap a shop rag around the fuel test port fitting, located at the lower rear of the engine, then remove the cap and connect a fuel pressure gauge.

5. Install the bleed hose from the pressure gauge into an approved container and open the valve to bleed the system pressure.

6. After the pressure is bled, remove the gauge from the test port and recap it.

7. Install the air cleaner assembly.

8. After servicing the vehicle, connect the negative battery cable and prime the fuel system as follows:

   a. Turn the ignition **ON** for 5 seconds, then **OFF** for 10 seconds.

   b. Repeat the **ON/OFF** cycle 2 more times.

   c. Crank the engine until it starts.

   d. If the engine does not readily start, repeat sub-steps A–C.

9. Run the engine and check for leaks.

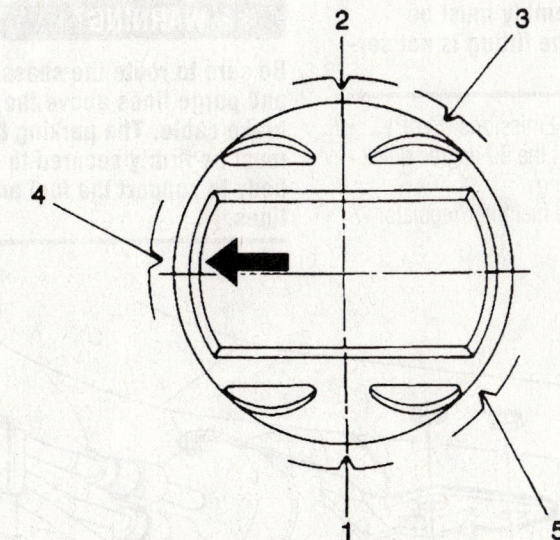

(1) 1st Compression Ring End Gap Location
(2) 2nd Compression Ring End Gap Location
(3) Oil Control Ring Upper Ring End Gap Location
(4) Oil Control Ring Spacer End Gap Location
(5) Oil Control Ring Lower Ring End Gap Location

Piston ring positioning—3.0L engine

Fuel Filter

On 1997 models, the fuel filter is attached to the vehicle's frame, in the lower left portion of the engine compartment. On 1998–01 models, the fuel filter and fuel pressure regulator are one integral component of the new anti-return fuel injection system, and is located underneath the vehicle at the forward edge of the left side of the fuel tank.

REMOVAL & INSTALLATION

1.9L Engines

1997

1. Before servicing the vehicle, refer to the precautions in the beginning of this section.
2. Properly relieve the fuel system pressure.
3. Remove or disconnect the following:
   - Negative battery cable
   - Fresh air intake hose from the camshaft cover
   - Fuel line connection near the intake manifold support brace
   - Quick connect fitting at the fuel filter inlet (rear of the filter) by pinching the plastic tabs together and pulling on the fuel supply line
   - Loosen the filter band clamp nut, but do not remove it
   - Filter from the band and discard it safely

To install:

4. If the band clamp was removed, clip the fuel return and vapor lines in place and install 2 new band clamp nuts. Be sure all lines are in place and will not interfere with, or be damaged by, filter installation, then tighten the bracket nuts to 27 inch lbs. (3 Nm).
5. Install or connect the following:
   - Insert a new snap-lock retainer into the female end of the filter inlet fitting
   - Route the nylon outlet line through the band clamp and insert the filter far enough into the band clamp to connect the outlet line to the engine's fuel line attachment. Snap the connector together and pull on the line to verify proper fitting
   - Position the filter in the band clamp assembly with the filter's forward edge located ¼ in. (6.35mm) from the front of the band clamp
   - Snap the fuel supply line into the fuel filter and pull back to verify that the fitting is secure. Torque the

band clamp nut to 89 inch lbs. (10 Nm).
   - Fresh air inlet hose
   - Negative battery cable
6. Prime the fuel system as follows:
   a. Turn the ignition **ON** for 5 seconds, then **OFF** for 10 seconds.
   b. Repeat the **ON/OFF** cycle 2 more times.
   c. Crank the engine until it starts.
   d. If it does not start, repeat sub-steps A–C.
7. Start the engine and check for leaks, repair if necessary.

1998–01

1. Before servicing the vehicle, refer to the precautions in the beginning of this section.
2. Properly relieve the fuel system pressure.
3. Remove or disconnect the following:
   - Negative battery cable
   - Fuel filter/pressure regulator bracket screws
   - Fuel line bundle retaining clip on the left side of the fuel tank

✳✳ WARNING

Exercise extreme care when opening the retaining clip. The fuel lines must be retained in this clip; if damaged, the fuel tank assembly must be replaced, since the fitting is not serviced separately.

   - Evaporative Emissions (EVAP) purge line at the 90 degree quick connect fitting
   - Outlet of the fuel filter/regulator

from the support on the fuel tank bracket and remove the fuel feed line
   - Pivot the fuel filter/regulator down while moving the leg of the mounting bracket out from under the parking brake lines.
   - Fuel feed and return line quick-connect fittings on the fuel filter/regulator. Discard the filter in an appropriate container.

➡**It is not necessary to separate the fuel filter/regulator from the mounting bracket, since both items are serviced as an assembly.**

To install:

4. Install or connect the following:
   - New fuel line retainers (3) into the female portion of the quick-connect fuel line fittings
   - Fuel feed and return lines onto the fuel filter/regulator and snap them closed. Pull back to verify that the fittings are secure
   - Fuel feed, return, and EVAP purge lines into the fuel tank's retaining clip
   - Slide the leg of the fuel filter/regulator mounting bracket under the parking brake lines and pivot upward

✳✳ WARNING

Be sure to route the chassis fuel feed and purge lines above the parking brake cable. The parking brake cable must be firmly secured to the underbody to support the fuel and purge lines.

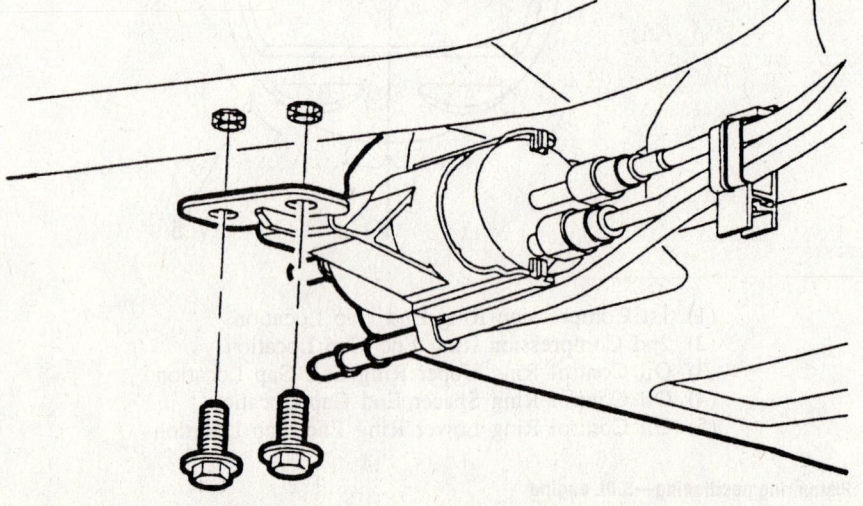

The fuel filter/regulator bracket is held to the frame with 2 bolts—1998–01 models

79222827

- 90 degree fuel feed line quick-connect fitting onto the fuel filter/regulator outlet and snap it closed. Pull back to verify that the fitting is secure
- 90 degree EVAP purge line quick-connect fitting to the purge line and snap it closed. Pull back to verify that the fitting is secure
- Fuel feed outlet pipe of the fuel filter/regulator into the retaining clip on the fuel tank bracket
- Fuel filter/regulator bracket mounting screws. Torque the screws to 71 inch lbs. (8 Nm).
- Negative battery cable

5. Prime the fuel system as follows:

a. Turn the ignition **ON** for 5 seconds, then **OFF** for 10 seconds.

b. Repeat the **ON/OFF** cycle 2 more times.

c. Crank the engine until it starts.

d. If it does not start, repeat the 3 above steps.

6. Start the engine and check for leaks, repair if necessary.

2.2L And 3.0L Engines

1. Before servicing the vehicle, refer to the precautions in the beginning of this section.

2. Properly relieve the fuel system pressure.

3. Remove or disconnect the following:

- Negative battery cable
- Fuel filter bracket screw
- Inlet and outlet fuel lines from the filter
- Fuel filter from the bracket

To install:

4. Install or connect the following:

- New fuel filter into the bracket
- New fuel line retainers to the female portion of the quick connect fittings
- Fuel feed lines
- Fuel filter bracket attaching screw. Torque the screw to 35 inch lbs. (4 Nm).
- Negative battery cable

5. Prime the fuel system as follows:

a. Turn the ignition **ON** for 5 seconds, then **OFF** for 10 seconds.

b. Repeat the **ON/OFF** cycle 2 more times.

c. Crank the engine until it starts.

d. If it does not start, repeat the 3 above steps.

6. Start the engine and check for leaks, repair if necessary.

Fuel Pump

REMOVAL & INSTALLATION

1.9L Engine

To prevent excessive fuel spillage, whenever the tank is removed from the vehicle it should be no more than ½ full. Removal of the fuel pump module assembly requires the removal of the fuel tank.

1. Before servicing the vehicle, refer to the precautions in the beginning of this section.

2. Properly relieve the fuel system pressure.

3. Remove or disconnect the following:

- Negative battery cable
- Fuel feed and return lines from the filter/pressure regulator
- Fuel pump vapor line from the fuel tank vent pipe
- Fuel pump module retaining ring with service tool SA9156E. A ½ inch breaker bar will loosen the lockring

➡ **To prevent bending of the sending unit float arm, lift the pump module up slightly to disengage the orientation tabs in the tank. Rotate the module 90 degrees clockwise until the fuel lines are facing the 1 o'clock position.**

- Fuel pump module from the fuel tank until the bottom of the pump module is close to the fuel tank opening
- Tilt the pump module approximately 45 degrees to the right hand side of the tank and lift the pump from the fuel tank
- Fuel pump to tank seal and discard it

To install:

4. Install or connect the following:

- Fuel pump module into the fuel tank by orientating the float to face the right side and tilting the module approximately 45 degrees
- Fuel pump into the tank and rotate the assembly 90 degrees counterclockwise to align the module tabs with the slots in the tank

➡ **The fuel pump retaining ring cannot be properly installed if the flange locator tabs are not aligned with the slots in the fuel tank.**

- Retaining lockring with tool SA9156E
- Vapor line to the fuel tank vent pipe
- Fuel feed and return lines to the filter/pressure regulator
- Fuel feed, return and EVAP canister purge line in the fuel tank retaining clip
- Fuel tank
- Negative battery cable

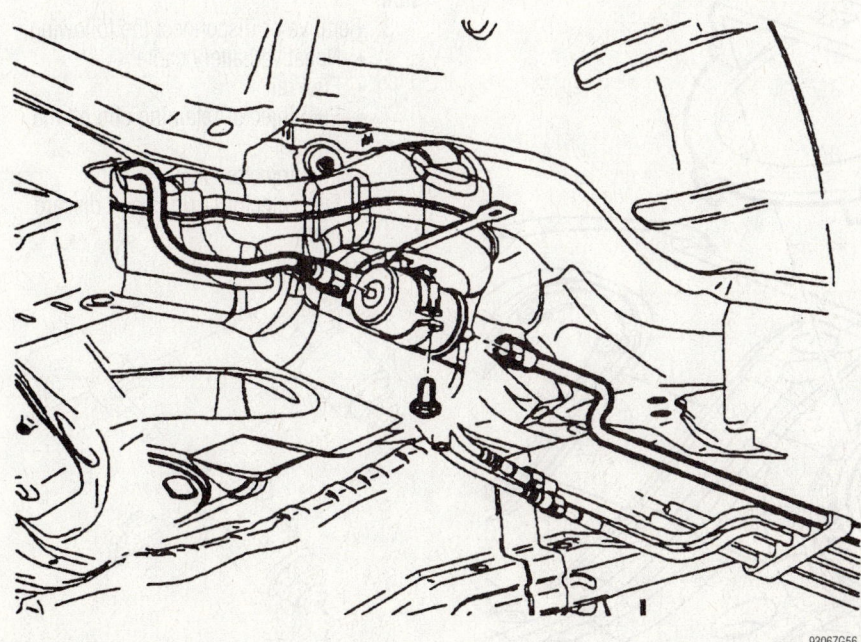

9306ZG56

Remove the fuel filter bracket attaching screw 2.2L and 3.0L engines

5. Start the vehicle and check for leaks, repair if necessary.

2.2L and 3.0L Engines

1. Before servicing the vehicle, refer to the precautions in the beginning of this section.

2. Properly relieve the fuel system pressure.

3. Remove or disconnect the following:
- Negative battery cable
- Fuel tank
- Fuel lines from the fuel pump module cover
- Fuel pump module retaining ring with a Sending Unit Wrench, J43827
- Pull the retaining clip toward the float arm and lift up
- Fuel pump straight up from the fuel tank
- Fuel pump tank seal and discard the seal
- Fuel feed line from the bottom of the fuel pump cover with Clamp Pliers J43914
- Fuel pump electrical connector

To install:

4. Install or connect the following:
- Fuel pump feed line to the cover
- Fuel pump electrical connector
- Fuel pump to the new seal

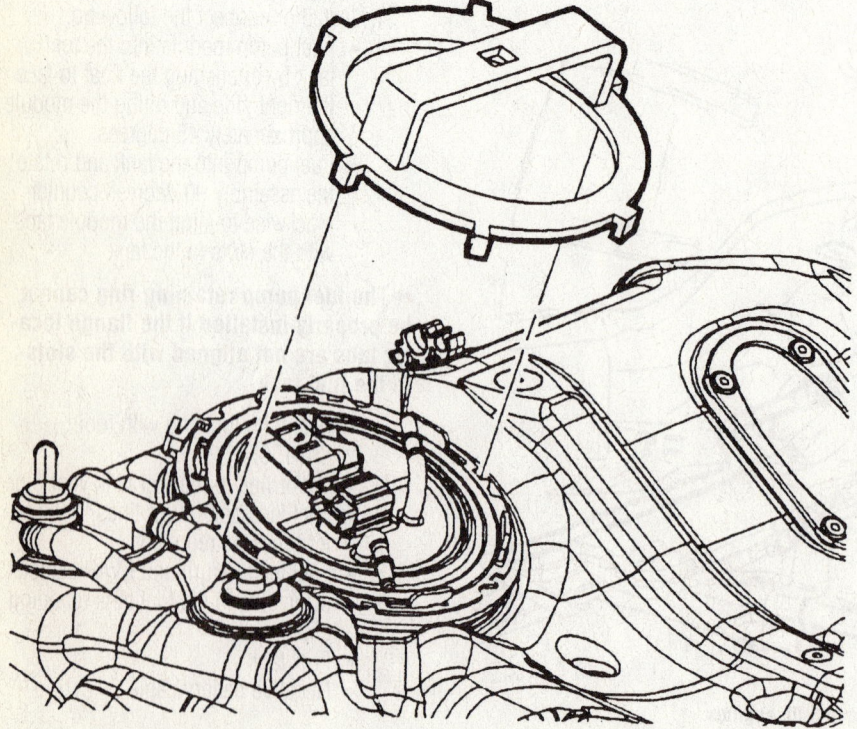

Remove the fuel pump cover lockring—2.2L and 3.0L engines
9306ZG57

- Fuel pump cover lockring with tool J-43827
- Fuel lines and wiring harness
- Fuel tank
- Negative battery cable

5. Start the vehicle and check for leaks, repair if necessary.

Fuel Injector

REMOVAL AND INSTALLATION

1.9L Engines

1. Before servicing the vehicle, refer to the precautions in the beginning of this section.

2. Properly relieve the fuel system pressure.

3. Remove or disconnect the following:
- Negative battery cable
- Fuel rail
- Fuel injector retaining clip off the injector
- Fuel injector
- Fuel injector O-rings and discard them

To install:

➡ **The SOHC and DOHC fuel injectors are not interchangeable. The injectors are identified by a color coded plastic ring near the bottom of the injector.**

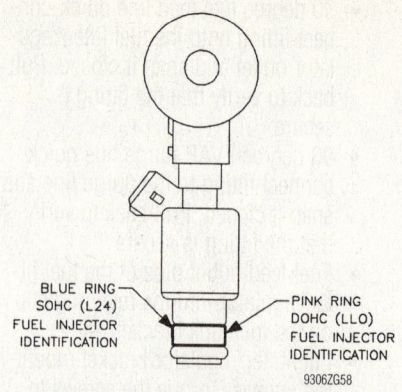

BLUE RING SOHC (L24) FUEL INJECTOR IDENTIFICATION

PINK RING DOHC (LLO) FUEL INJECTOR IDENTIFICATION

9306ZG58

Fuel injector identification—1.9L engine

The SOHC injector has a blue ring near the O-ring that mates to the intake manifold and the DOHC has a pink ring.

4. Lubricate the new fuel injector O-ring with clean engine oil.

5. Install or connect the following:
- New O-ring seals on the fuel injector
- Retaining clip to the fuel injector
- Fuel injector to the fuel rail
- Fuel rail
- Negative battery cable

6. Start the vehicle and check for leaks, repair if necessary.

2.2L and 3.0L Engines

1. Before servicing the vehicle, refer to the precautions in the beginning of this section.

2. Properly relieve the fuel system pressure.

3. Remove or disconnect the following:
- Negative battery cable
- Fuel rail
- Fuel injector retaining clip off the injector
- Fuel injector
- Fuel injector O-rings and discard them

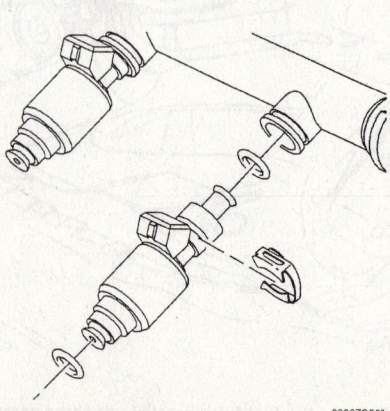

9306ZG59

Remove the retainer clip from the fuel injector—2.2L and 3.0L engines

To install:

4. Lubricate the new fuel injector O-ring with clean engine oil.

5. Install or connect the following:
- New O-ring seals on the fuel injector
- Retaining clip to the fuel injector
- Fuel injector to the fuel rail
- Fuel rail
- Negative battery cable

6. Start the vehicle and check for leaks, repair if necessary.

DRIVE TRAIN

Manual Transmission Assembly

REMOVAL & INSTALLATION

1.9L Engines

1. Before servicing the vehicle, refer to the precautions in the beginning of this section.

2. Drain the transmission fluid.

3. Remove or disconnect the following:
- Both battery cables
- Air cleaner assembly
- Battery and tray
- Powertrain Control Module (PCM) **J2** (black 28-way) harness connector. Do not disconnect the **J1** (80-way) connector
- PCM attaching bolts and move it aside
- Transmission strut to midrail bracket fastener and loosen the strut to transmission fastener and move the strut aside
- Back-up lamp electrical connector
- Vehicle Speed Sensor (VSS) electrical connector, if equipped
- Ground terminals from the clutch housing bolts
- Vent tube retaining clip
- Top 2 clutch housing to the engine bolts
- Spark plug wires from the coil towers
- Electronic ignition module electrical connectors
- Electronic ignition module
- Shifter cables from the arms and clutch housing
- Clutch slave cylinder by rotating it

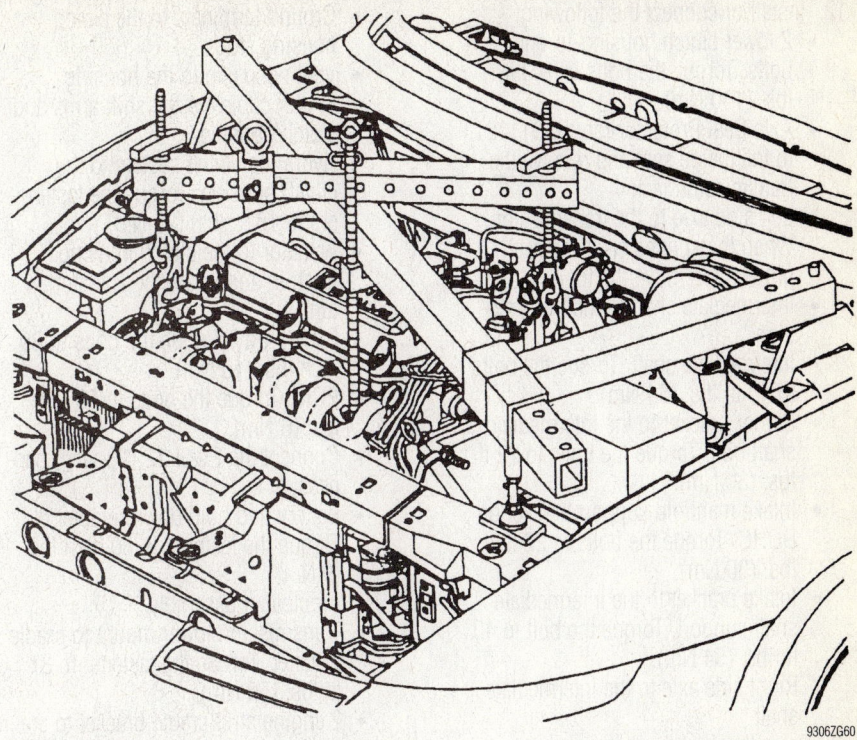

Install an Engine Support tool SA9105E

¼ turn counterclockwise and pushing it into the housing
- 2 clutch hydraulic damper to housing fasteners and wire the actuator cylinder and damper to the upper radiator hose

4. Wire the radiator to the upper support.

5. Install an engine support bar, SA9105E and place the feet on the outer edge of the shock tower.

6. Connect the bar hooks to the engine support bracket.

7. Position the stabilizer foot on the engine to the right of the dipstick tube.

8. Adjust the hooks and stabilizer to remove any looseness.

9. Remove or disconnect the following:
- Both front wheels and inner splash shields
- Engine splash shield
- Engine strut cradle bracket fasteners
- Transmission mount to cradle fasteners
- Front exhaust pipe to manifold and catalytic converter fasteners
- Front exhaust pipe
- Steering gear to cradle fasteners
- Brake pipe bracket push pin
- Engine to transmission stiffening brace
- Dust cover

- Cotter pin from the lower ball joints
- Ball joint from the lower control arm with Separator tool SA9132S
- Separate the left axle from the transmission and install an axle seal protector
- Separate the right axle from the intermediate shaft
- Intake bracket to intake manifold bolt on DOHC engines
- Intake bracket to intermediate shaft support bolt
- Support bracket
- Intermediate shaft from the transmission
- 4 cradle to body bolts and lower the cradle on a support dolly
- Bottom clutch housing bolts and install a guide bolt into the rear housing bolt hole
- Separate the transmission from the engine

To install:

10. Place the transmission assembly securely onto a jack and position under the vehicle. Install axle seal protectors into seals on both sides.

11. Raise the transmission into the vehicle to align the input shaft to the center of the clutch. Rotate the transmission back and forth to align the input shaft splines to the clutch disc.

For complete service labor times order Nichols' Chilton Labor Guide Manual

12. Install or connect the following:
- 2 lower clutch housing-to-engine bolts. Torque the bolts to 103 ft. lbs. (140 Nm).
- Axle Seal Protector tool SA91112T to the inside seal and remove the transmission jack
- Left side axle to the transmission. When the splines clear the seal protector, remove the tool
- Intermediate shaft to the transmission
- Intermediate shaft. Torque the bolts to 40 ft. lbs. (54 Nm).
- Starter bracket to the intermediate shaft bolt. Torque the bolts to 22 ft. lbs. (30 Nm).
- Intake manifold support bracket on DOHC. Torque the bolts to 22 ft. lbs. (30 Nm).
- Intake bracket to the intermediate shaft support. Torque the bolt to 40 ft. lbs. (54 Nm).
- Right side axle to the intermediate shaft

13. Raise the cradle up on a support dolly and place the ball joints into the knuckles. Verify the correct positioning of the lower control arm bar studs to the knuckles, the cooling module support bushings, the engine strut bracket and the transaxle mount.

14. Insert 9/16 in. round steel rods into the cradle-to-body alignment holes near the front cradle to body fastener holes. Guide the cradle into position making sure all mount studs are properly guided into their holes.

15. Be sure the washers are in place, then install the 2 rear cradle to body bolts. Verify proper cradle positioning and install the 2 front cradle bolts, then torque the 4 cradle bolts to 155 ft. lbs. (210 Nm).

16. Remove the support dolly and lower the vehicle sufficiently for underhood access. Remove the engine support bar assembly.

17. Install or connect the following:
- Transmission strut-to-cradle bracket through-bolt and nut. Torque the fasteners to 40 ft. lbs. (54 Nm).
- Strut cradle bracket-to-cradle bolt. Torque the bolt to 52 ft. lbs. (70 Nm). Remove the cooling module support wire
- Ignition module. Torque the bolts to 71 inch lbs. (8 Nm).
- 2 top transmission housing-to-engine studs. Torque the studs to 74 ft. lbs. (100 Nm).
- VSS electrical connector
- Back-up lamp electrical connector

- Ground terminals to the clutch housing studs
- Vent hose clip to the housing
- Shifter cables to the shift arms and clutch housing
- Hydraulic clutch system to the clutch housing. Torque the fasteners to 18 ft. lbs. (25 Nm).
- Actuator to the clutch housing. Push in and rotate the actuator ¼ turn
- Battery tray. Torque the bolts to 89 inch lbs. (10 Nm).
- PCM. Torque the bolts to 53 inch lbs. (6 Nm).
- Connect the PCM **J2** (28-way) harness
- Battery and hold down retainer. Torque the fastener to 80 inch lbs. (9 Nm).
- Air cleaner assembly
- Transmission lower mount to cradle fastener. Torque the fastener to 37 ft. lbs. (50 Nm).
- 2 engine strut cradle bracket to cradle fasteners. Torque the fasteners to 37 ft. lbs. (50 Nm).
- Steering gear to cradle fasteners. Torque the fasteners to 37 ft. lbs. (50 Nm).
- Brake pipe to cradle retainer
- Dust cover. Torque the bolts to 8 ft. lbs. (11 Nm).
- Engine to transmission stiffening brace. Torque the bolts to 40 ft. lbs. (54 Nm).
- Exhaust manifold pipe. Torque the bolts to 23 ft. lbs. (31 Nm).
- Intermediate exhaust pipe to the catalytic converter. Torque the bolts to 18 ft. lbs. (25 Nm).
- Front exhaust pipe support to the stiffening bracket. Torque the fasteners to 89 inch lbs. (10 Nm).
- Both front wheels
- Both battery cables

18. Fill the transmission to the proper level.

19. Warm the engine and check the transmission fluid. Check and adjust vehicle alignment, as necessary.

2.2L and 3.0L Engines

1. Before servicing the vehicle, refer to the precautions in the beginning of this section.

2. Drain the transmission fluid.

3. Remove or disconnect the following:
- Both battery cables
- Move the fan control module up and out of the way

- Battery feed to the underhood fuse block
- Coolant hose from the underhood fuse block
- Release the retaining tabs on the fuse block cover and remove it
- Engine 68-way electrical connector
- Forward lamp 68-way connector
- Forward lamp 2-way (white) connector
- Black, green and brown instrument panel 2-way connectors
- Fuse block from the case
- Engine, forward lamp and instrument panel harness from the fuse block case
- Case from the battery tray
- Battery tray and battery
- Loosen the pinch bolt securing the control assembly rod to the control shaft lever

➡ **The control shaft lever retaining pin has a spring loaded locking feature to keep the pin in place. The spring must be depressed before attempting to remove it.**

- Pin retaining the control shaft lever to shift control shaft
- Retaining clips holding the control shaft lever to the transmission and frame brackets
- Control shaft lever
- Back-up lamp switch electrical connector
- Wire harness from the transmission
- Spring loaded locking pin from the hole on top of the transmission, if equipped
- Clutch hydraulic fitting from the transmission
- Upper transmission to engine bolts and install and engine support bar, SA9105E, and adapter kit J43405
- Matchmark the position of the left transmission mount and remove the mount
- Frame assembly
- Front transmission mount
- Rear transmission mount
- Axle shafts from the transmission
- A/C line retaining clips and drop the A/C line down from the body

4. Lower the left side of the powertrain assembly to allow the transmission to clear the engine compartment rail

5. Remove or disconnect the following:
- Left side transmission mount bracket
- Control shaft lever assembly pivot pin bracket

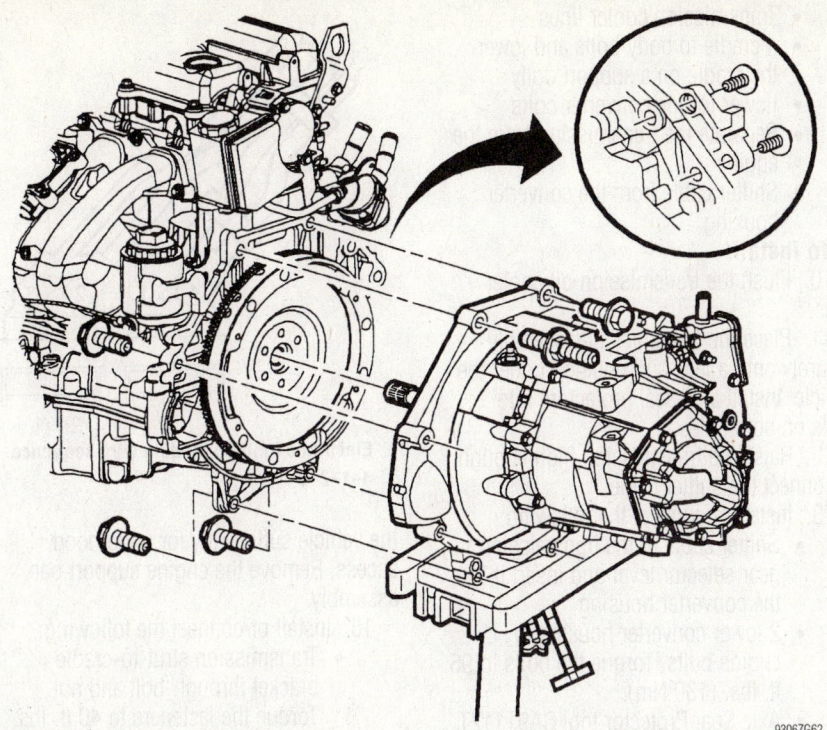

Remove the remaining engine to transmission bolts—2.2L and 3.0L engines

6. Properly support the powertrain assembly and remove the remaining engine to transmission bolts.

7. Separate the transmission from the engine

To install:

8. Raise the transmission into the vehicle and align the input shaft to the center of the clutch disc.

9. Install or connect the following:
- Lower transmission to engine bolts. Torque the bolts to 48 ft. lbs. (65 Nm). Remove the transmission jack
- Control shaft lever assembly pivot pin bracket. Torque the fastener to 18 ft. lbs. (24 Nm).
- Using a Seal Protector tool SA91112T, install the axle shafts to the transmission. After the splines clear the tool, remove the seal protector and snap the axle into place

10. Remove the transmission fill plug, fill the transmission with 2 quarts of manual fluid and install the plug. Torque the plug to 22 ft. lbs. (30 Nm).

11. Install or connect the following:
- Left side transmission mount bracket. Torque the bolts to 41 ft. lbs. (55 Nm). Raise the left side of the powertrain assembly
- Reposition the A/C line against the body and install the retaining clips

- Rear transmission mount. Torque the bolts to 41 ft. lbs. (55 Nm).
- Front transmission mount. Torque the bolts to 41 ft. lbs. (55 Nm).
- Frame assembly
- Upper transmission to engine bolts. Torque the bolts to 48 ft. lbs. (65 Nm).
- Left side transmission mount bolts using the matchmarks made during removal. Torque the bolts to 41 ft. lbs. (55 Nm).
- Back-up lamp switch electrical connector
- Control shaft lever assembly onto the pivot pin brackets
- Retaining clips holding the control shaft lever to the transmission and frame brackets
- Pin to retain the control shaft lever to the shift control shaft
- Rotate the shift control shaft clockwise and install the shift linkage lock pin
- Move the shift lever to the 5th gear/reverse gate and install a ⅜ inch punch
- Pinch bolt securing the control assembly rod to the control shaft lever. Torque the bolt to 9 ft. lbs. (12 Nm) plus 180 degrees
- Shift lever hole plug

- Clutch hydraulic fitting to the transmission and bleed the hydraulic system
- Battery tray. Torque the fasteners to 11 ft. lbs. (15 Nm).
- Underhood fuse block to the battery tray. Torque the fasteners to 80 inch lbs. (9 Nm).
- Wire harness to the fuse case. The wire harness grommets have retaining tabs that lock into the case
- Snap the fuse block onto the hinges
- Engine 68-way connectors
- Forward lamp 68-way connectors
- Instrument panel 68-way connectors
- Forward 2-way (white) connector
- Black, green and brown 2-way connectors
- Snap the fuse block to the case
- Coolant hose to the fuse block
- Battery feed to the fuse block. Torque the fastener to 12 inch lbs. (16 Nm).
- Battery tray and hold down bracket. Torque the fastener to 15 ft. lbs. (20 Nm).
- Battery
- Fan control module to the battery hold down bracket
- Both battery cables

12. Fill the transmission to the proper level.

13. Warm the engine and check the transmission fluid. Check and adjust vehicle alignment, as necessary.

Automatic Transmission Assembly

REMOVAL & INSTALLATION

1.9L Engines

1. Before servicing the vehicle, refer to the precautions in the beginning of this section.

2. Drain the transmission fluid.

3. Remove or disconnect the following:
- Both battery cables
- Air cleaner assembly
- Battery and tray
- Powertrain Control Module (PCM) **J2** (black 28-way) harness connector. Do not disconnect the **J1** (80-way) connector
- PCM attaching bolts and move aside

- Transmission strut to midrail bracket fastener and loosen the strut to transmission fastener and move the strut aside
- Transmission solenoid harness connector
- Vehicle speed and input sensor harness connectors
- Transmission fluid temperature sensor connector
- Range switch harness connector
- Ground terminals from the converter housing
- Ground wire from the range switch
- Spark plug wires from the coil towers
- Electronic ignition module electrical connectors
- Electronic ignition module

4. Wire the radiator to the upper support.

5. Install an engine support bar, SA9105E and place the feet on the outer edge of the shock tower

6. Connect the bar hooks to the engine support bracket

7. Position the stabilizer foot on the engine to the right of the dipstick tube.

8. Adjust the hooks and stabilizer to remove any looseness.

9. Remove or disconnect the following:
- Both front wheels and inner splash shields
- Engine splash shield
- Engine strut cradle bracket fasteners
- Transmission mount to cradle fasteners
- Front exhaust pipe to manifold and catalytic converter fasteners
- Front exhaust pipe
- Steering gear to cradle fasteners
- Brake pipe bracket push pin
- Engine to transmission stiffening brace
- Dust cover
- Torque converter to flywheel bolts
- Cotter pin from the lower ball joints
- Ball joint from the lower control arm with Separator tool SA9132S
- Separate the left axle from the transmission and install an axle seal protector
- Separate the right axle from the intermediate shaft
- Intake bracket to intake manifold bolt, on DOHC engines
- Intake bracket to intermediate shaft support bolt
- Support bracket
- Intermediate shaft from the transmission

- Transmission cooler lines
- 4 cradle to body bolts and lower the cradle on a support dolly
- Lower torque converter bolts
- Separate the transmission from the engine
- Shifter cable from the converter housing

To install:

10. Flush the transmission oil cooler lines.

11. Place the transmission assembly securely onto a jack and position under the vehicle. Install axle seal protectors into seals on both sides.

12. Raise the transmission high enough to connect the shifter cable.

13. Install or connect the following:
- Shifter cable to the transmission gear selector lever and insert it in the converter housing
- 2 lower converter housing to engine bolts. Torque the bolts to 96 ft. lbs. (130 Nm).
- Axle Seal Protector tool SA91112T, to the inside seal and remove the transmission jack
- Left side axle to the transmission. When the splines clear the seal protector, remove the tool
- Intermediate shaft to the transmission
- Intermediate shaft. Torque the bolts to 40 ft. lbs. (54 Nm).
- Intake manifold support bracket, on DOHC. Torque the bolts to 22 ft. lbs. (30 Nm).
- Intake bracket to the intermediate shaft support. Torque the bolt to 40 ft. lbs. (54 Nm).
- Right side axle to the intermediate shaft
- Cooler lines to the transmission

14. Raise the cradle up on a support dolly and place the ball joints into the knuckles. Verify the correct positioning of the lower control arm bar studs to the knuckles, the cooling module support bushings, the engine strut bracket and the transaxle mount.

15. Insert ⁹⁄₁₆ in. round steel rods into the cradle-to-body alignment holes near the front cradle to body fastener holes. Guide the cradle into position making sure all mount studs are properly guided into their holes.

16. Be sure the washers are in place, then install the 2 rear cradle to body bolts. Verify proper cradle positioning and install the 2 front cradle bolts, then torque the 4 cradle bolts to 155 ft. lbs. (210 Nm).

17. Remove the support dolly and lower

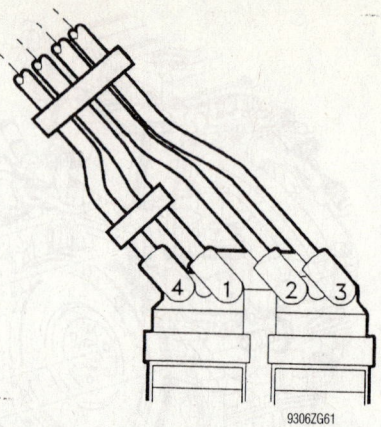

Electronic ignition module wire sequence 4–1–2–3

the vehicle sufficiently for underhood access. Remove the engine support bar assembly.

18. Install or connect the following:
- Transmission strut-to-cradle bracket through-bolt and nut. Torque the fasteners to 40 ft. lbs. (54 Nm).
- Strut midrail bracket. Torque the bolt to 52 ft. lbs. (70 Nm). Remove the cooling module support wire
- Ignition module. Torque the bolts to 71 inch lbs. (8 Nm).
- Ignition module wire connector
- Spark plug wires to the coil towers

➡Proper orientation of the ignition module is critical to the operation of the module and the on board diagnostic system. The proper sequence is 4–1–2–3 from left to right

- 2 top converter housing to engine studs. Torque the studs to 74 ft. lbs. (100 Nm).
- Transmission solenoid harness connector. Torque the fastener to 22 inch lbs. (2.5 Nm).
- Vehicle speed and input sensor connectors
- Transmission fluid temperature sensor connectors
- Transmission range switch harness connectors
- Ground terminals to the top 2 converter housing bolts. Torque the bolts to 19 ft. lbs. (25 Nm).
- Ground wire to the neutral selector switch
- Adjust the control cable
- Air cleaner assembly
- Battery tray. Torque the bolts to 89 inch lbs. (10 Nm).
- PCM. Torque the bolts to 53 inch lbs. (6 Nm).

- Connect the PCM **J2** (28-way) harness
- Battery and hold down retainer. Torque the fastener to 80 inch lbs. (9 Nm).
- Transmission lower mount to cradle fastener. Torque the fastener to 37 ft. lbs. (50 Nm).
- 2 engine strut cradle bracket to cradle fasteners. Torque the fasteners to 37 ft. lbs. (50 Nm).
- Steering gear to cradle fasteners. Torque the fasteners to 37 ft. lbs. (50 Nm).
- Brake pipe to cradle retainer
- Torque converter to flexplate. Torque the bolts to 52 ft. lbs. (70 Nm).
- Dust cover. Torque the bolts to 8 ft. lbs. (11 Nm).
- Engine to transmission stiffening brace. Torque the bolts to 40 ft. lbs. (54 Nm).
- Exhaust manifold pipe. Torque the bolts to 23 ft. lbs. (31 Nm).
- Intermediate exhaust pipe to the catalytic converter. Torque the bolts to 18 ft. lbs. (25 Nm).
- Front exhaust pipe support to the stiffening bracket. Torque the fasteners to 23 ft. lbs. (31 Nm).
- Lower ball joint nut. Torque the nut to 55 ft. lbs. (75 Nm).
- New cotter pins
- Splash shields
- Both front wheels
- Both battery cables

19. Fill the transmission to the proper level.

20. Warm the engine and check the transmission fluid. Check and adjust vehicle alignment, as necessary.

2.2L And 3.0L Engines

1. Before servicing the vehicle, refer to the precautions in the beginning of this section.

2. Drain the transmission fluid.

3. Remove or disconnect the following:
- Both battery cables
- Move the fan control module up and out of the way
- Battery feed to the underhood fuse block
- Coolant hose from the underhood fuse block
- Release the retaining tabs on the fuse block cover and remove it
- Engine 68-way electrical connector

- Forward lamp 68-way connector
- Forward lamp 2-way (white) connector
- Black, green and brown instrument panel 2-way connectors
- Fuse block from the case
- Engine, forward lamp and instrument panel harness from the fuse block case
- Case from the battery tray
- Battery tray and battery
- Control cable from the range switch lever
- Control cable bracket from the rear powertrain mount
- Transmission electrical connector and ground wire
- Remaining wire harness connectors from the transmission
- Transmission range switch electrical connector
- Upper engine to transmission bolts
- Drive belt from the alternator, for 3.0L engine
- Drive belt tensioner, for 3.0L engine
- Alternator, for 3.0L engine
- Output speed sensor electrical connector and install an Engine Support Fixture tool, SA9105E and Adapter kit, J43405
- Frame
- Axle shafts from the transmission
- Engine to transmission bracket
- Starter solenoid electrical connector
- Starter. The wire harness mounting bracket on the rear of the engine must be removed on the 3.0L
- Using a torque converter socket, remove the torque converter to flexplate bolts through the starter opening
- Transmission oil cooler lines
- 2 lower engine to transmission bolts
- Matchmark the left side transmission mount bolts and remove the bolts

4. Slide a hydraulic lifting table under the transmission and remove the remaining mounting bolts.

5. Separate the transmission from the engine.

To install:

6. With the transmission on a hydraulic lift, raise the transmission to the engine.

7. Install or connect the following:
- Rear wire harness bracket, for 3.0L engine

- Engine to transmission mounting bolts. Torque the bolts to 48 ft. lbs. (60 Nm).
- Using the reference marks made during removal, install the left side transmission mount bolts. Torque the bolts to 41 ft. lbs. (55 Nm).
- Bottom 2 engine to transmission mounting bolts. Torque the bolts to 48 ft. lbs. (65 Nm).
- Transmission oil cooler lines after lubricating them with automatic transmission fluid. Torque the fasteners to 71 inch lbs. (8 Nm).
- Loosely install the flex plate to torque converter bolts. When aligned properly, torque the bolts to 33 ft. lbs. (45 Nm).
- Starter. Torque the bolts to 30 ft. lbs. (40 Nm).
- Starter solenoid electrical connectors
- Engine to transmission bracket. Torque the bolts to 26 ft. lbs. (35 Nm).
- New axle shaft retaining rings on the end of the output shafts and install the axle shafts to the transmission
- Frame assembly
- Output speed sensor electrical connector and secure it to the mounting stud
- Alternator. Torque the bolts to 30 ft. lbs. (40 Nm), for 3.0L engine
- Drive belt tensioner. Torque the bolts to 30 ft. lbs. (40 Nm), for 3.0L engine
- Drive belt, for 3.0L engine
- Remaining transmission to engine mounting bolts. Torque the bolts to 48 ft. lbs. (65 Nm).
- Transmission electrical connector and ground wire. Torque the fasteners to 18 ft. lbs. (25 Nm).
- Wire harness attachments to the transmission side cover. Torque the fasteners to 15 ft. lbs. (20 Nm).
- Control cable mounting bracket. Torque the bolts to 15 ft. lbs. (20 Nm).
- Control cable to the range switch lever
- Battery tray. Torque the fasteners to 11 ft. lbs. (15 Nm).
- Underhood fuse block case to the battery tray. Torque the bolt to 80 inch lbs. (9 Nm) and snap the block onto the hinges

Turn to Section 5 for brake system applications

- Engine 68-way connectors
- Forward lamp 68-way connectors
- Instrument panel 68-way connectors
- Forward 2-way (white) connector
- Black, green and brown 2-way connectors
- Snap the fuse block to the case
- Coolant hose to the fuse block
- Battery feed to the fuse block. Torque the fastener to 12 inch lbs. (16 Nm).
- Battery tray and hold down bracket. Torque the fastener to 15 ft. lbs. (20 Nm).
- Battery
- Fan control module to the battery hold down bracket
- Both battery cables

8. Fill the transmission to the proper level.

9. Warm the engine and check the transmission fluid. Check and adjust vehicle alignment, as necessary.

Clutch

ADJUSTMENT

The hydraulic clutch system is self-adjusting.

REMOVAL & INSTALLATION

1.9L Engine

1. Before servicing the vehicle, refer to the precautions in the beginning of this section.

2. Remove the transmission from the vehicle

3. Unsnap the release fork from the ball stud, then remove the fork and bearing from the vehicle. Slide the bearing from the fork. The bearing should be checked for excessive play and for minimal bearing drag. It should be replaced if no/little drag or excessive play is found

➡**The release bearing is packed with grease and should not be washed with solvent.**

4. Using a feeler gauge, measure the distance between the pressure plate and flywheel surfaces in order to determine clutch face thickness. Replace the clutch disc if it is not within 0.205–0.287 in. (5.2–7.3mm) for 1997–00 or to 0.18 –0.28 in. (4.65mm–7.10mm) for 2001

5. Remove the pressure plate-to-flywheel bolts in a progressive crisscross pat-

tern to prevent warping the cover, then remove the pressure plate and clutch disc

6. Inspect the pressure plate, as follows:

a. Check for excessive wear, chatter marks, cracks or overheating (indicated by a blue discoloration). Black random spots on the friction surface of the pressure plate is normal.

b. Check the plate for warpage using a straightedge and a feeler gauge; the maximum allowable warpage is 0.006 in. (0.15mm).

c. Replace the plate, if necessary.

7. Inspect the clutch disc, as follows:

a. Check the disc face for oil or burnt spots.

b. Check the disc for loose damper springs, hub or rivets.

c. Replace the disc, if necessary.

8. Check the flywheel, as follows:

a. Check the ring gear for wear or damage.

b. Check the friction surface for excessive wear, chatter marks, cracks or overheating.

c. Check flywheel thickness; the minimum allowable is 1.102 in. (28mm).

d. Measure flywheel run-out using a dial indicator, positioned for at least 2

flywheel revolutions. Push the crankshaft forward to take up thrust bearing clearance. Maximum flywheel run-out is 0.006 in. (0.15mm).

e. Check the flywheel for warpage using a straight-edge and a feeler gauge; the maximum allowable warpage is 0.006 in. (0.15mm).

f. Replace the flywheel, if necessary.

9. If necessary, remove the flywheel retaining bolts and remove the flywheel from the crankshaft.

To install:

10. If removed, install the flywheel and torque the bolts in a crisscross sequence to 59 ft. lbs. (80 Nm).

11. Install or connect the following:

- Clutch disc and pressure plate with the yellow dot on the pressure plate aligned as close as possible to the mark on the flywheel. The clutch disc is labeled FLYWHEEL SIDE in order to help correctly position the disc. Start the pressure plate bolts
- Clutch alignment tool in the clutch disc temperature grease and install the release bearing to the fork. Do not lubricate the release bearing or bearing quill

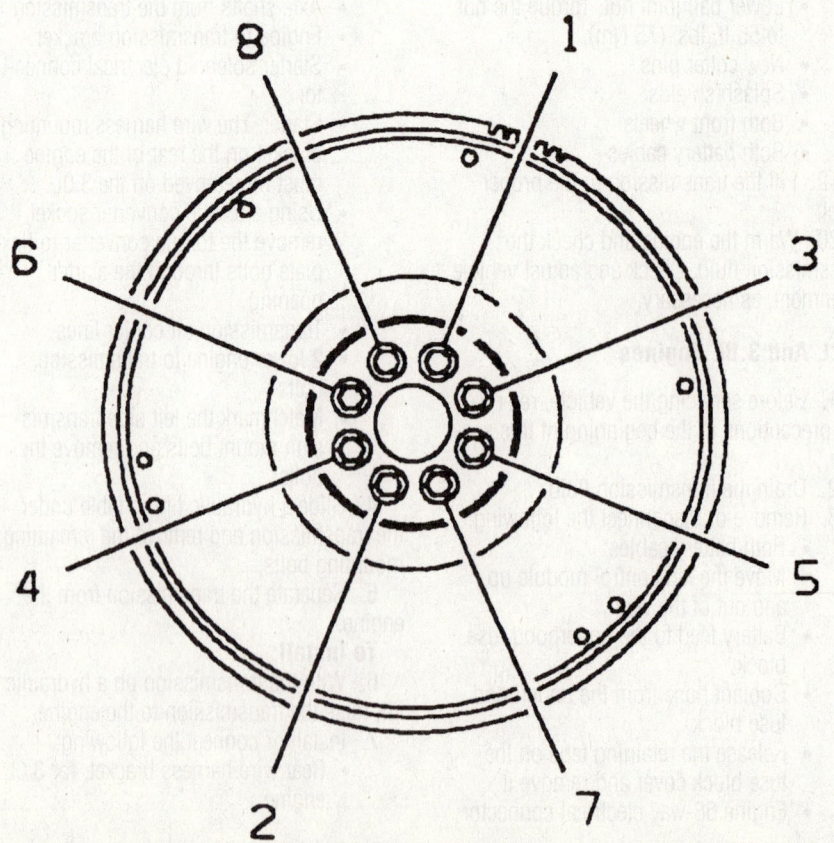

Flywheel mounting bolt tightening sequence—1.9L engine

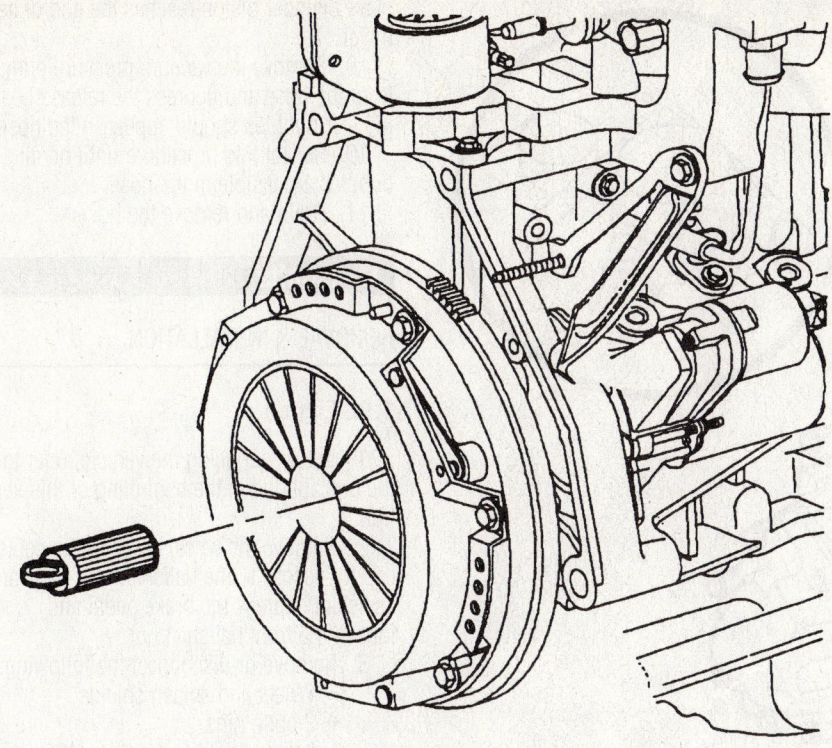

79222832

Use a proper clutch alignment tool before tightening the pressure plate retaining bolts—1.9L engine

- Snap the release bearing and fork onto the ball stud
- Lubricate the splines of the input shaft lightly with a high temperature grease
- Transmission assembly
- Negative battery cable

2.2L and 3.0L Engines

1. Before servicing the vehicle, refer to the precautions in the beginning of this section.

2. Remove the transmission from the vehicle

3. Check the slave cylinder release bearing minimal bearing drag. Replace the slave cylinder if little or drag is found.

4. Remove the pressure plate and clutch disc

5. Inspect the pressure plate, as follows:
   a. Check for excessive wear, chatter marks, cracks or overheating (indicated by a blue discoloration). Black random spots on the friction surface of the pressure plate is normal.
   b. Check the plate for warpage using a straightedge and a feeler gauge; the maximum allowable warpage is 0.006 in. (0.15mm).

c. Replace the plate, if necessary.

6. Inspect the clutch disc, as follows:
   a. Check the disc face for oil or burnt spots.
   b. Check the disc for loose damper springs, hub or rivets.
   c. Replace the disc, if necessary.

7. Check the flywheel, as follows:
   a. Check the ring gear for wear or damage.
   b. Check the friction surface for excessive wear, chatter marks, cracks or overheating.
   c. Check flywheel thickness; the minimum allowable is 1.102 in. (28mm).
   d. Measure flywheel run-out using a dial indicator, positioned for at least 2 flywheel revolutions. Push the crankshaft forward to take up thrust bearing clearance. Maximum flywheel run-out is 0.006 in. (0.15mm).
   e. Check the flywheel for warpage using a straight-edge and a feeler gauge; the maximum allowable warpage is 0.006 in. (0.15mm).
   f. Replace the flywheel, if necessary.

8. If necessary, remove the flywheel retaining bolts and remove the flywheel from the crankshaft.

To install:

9. Install or connect the following:
   - Flywheel. Torque the bolts in a crisscross pattern to 39 ft. lbs. (53 Nm) plus 25 degrees.
   - Clutch disc and pressure plate and loosely start the pressure plate bolts
   - Clutch alignment tool in the clutch disc, and push in until it bottoms out in the crankshaft
   - Tighten the pressure plate bolts using multiple passes of a crisscross sequence to 11 ft. lbs. (15 Nm) and remove the alignment tool
   - Lubricate the splines of the input shaft lightly with a high temperature grease
   - Transmission assembly
   - Negative battery cable

Hydraulic Clutch System

BLEEDING

1.9L Engine

The clutch hydraulic assembly has been filled with fluid and bled of air at the factory. Do not attempt to bleed the hydraulic system. While the unit does not require periodic checking, it must be serviced, when necessary, as a complete assembly. The system is full when the reservoir is half full.

Only DOT 3 brake fluid should be added to the system. If the fluid level drops, inspect the system, including the slave cylinder, for leakage. A slight wetting of the slave cylinder surface is normal. Fill the clutch master cylinder reservoir with brake fluid. Be careful not to spill brake fluid on the painted surface of the vehicle.

2.2L and 3.0L Engines

This procedure outlines how to bleed the hydraulic clutch with the transmission in the vehicle. Only **DOT 3** brake fluid should be added to the system.

1. Before servicing the vehicle, refer to the precautions in the beginning of this section.

2. Remove or disconnect the following:

3. Remove the reservoir cap and fill the reservoir with new brake fluid.

4. Install a Bleeder Adapter tool J43915, to the reservoir and connect a pressure bleeder to the adapter.

5. Charge the pressure bleeder to 20–25 psi (138–172 kPa).

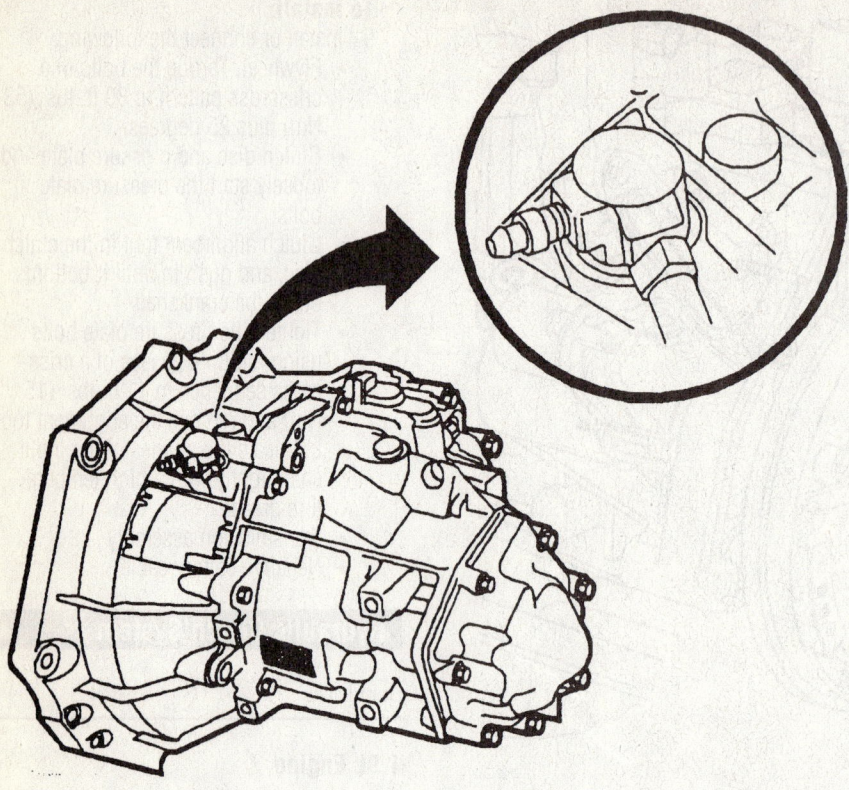

9306ZG63

Loosen the clutch bleeder screw on the hydraulic fitting

6. Attach a transparent hose over the clutch bleeder screw nipple and submerge the opposite end of the hose in a container of brake fluid.

7. Loosen the bleeder screw on the transmission hydraulic fitting.

8. Bleed the system until no air bubbles are seen in the hose.

9. Tighten the bleeder screw

10. Check the clutch pedal for a spongy feel. If the pedal feels soft, repeat the bleeding procedure.

11. Remove the bleeder tools and top off the fluid level if necessary.

REMOVAL & INSTALLATION

2.2L and 3.0L Engines

This procedure outlines how to bleed the clutch slave cylinder while the transmission is out of the vehicle. Only **DOT 3** brake fluid should be added to the system.

1. Before servicing the vehicle, refer to the precautions in the beginning of this section.

2. Remove or disconnect the following:

3. Connect a long piece of transparent hose to the slave cylinder fitting.

4. Depress the release bearing on the slave cylinder towards the clutch housing and release it.

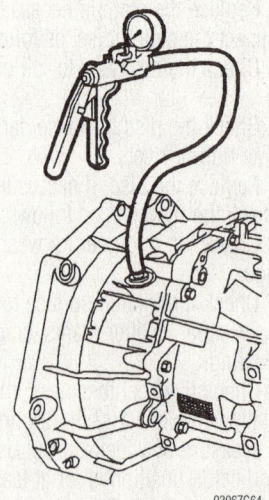

9306ZG64

Install a vacuum pump and pressure adapter to bleed the slave cylinder.

5. The release bearing will spring back, but the piston will remain depressed next to the clutch housing.

6. Fill the hose with 13.8 inches (350mm) of DOT 3 brake fluid.

7. Connect a Vacuum Pump SA9180NE with a Pressure Adapter J35555-92, to the top of the hose.

8. Apply pressure to the hose to force the brake fluid into the slave cylinder. Pressure in the gauge will increase when the

slave cylinder piston reaches the end of its travel.

9. Remove the vacuum pressure pump from the hose and depress the release bearing. Air bubbles should appear in the hose.

10. Repeat this procedure until no air bubbles are visible in the hose.

11. Drain and remove the hose.

Halfshafts

REMOVAL & INSTALLATION

1.9L Engine

1. Before servicing the vehicle, refer to the precautions in the beginning of this section.

2. Remove the wheel cover or the center cap for access to the halfshaft nut. Have an assistant depress the brake pedal and loosen the front halfshaft nut.

3. Remove or disconnect the following:

- Wheel and splash shields
- 2 push pins
- Lower shield to cradle molded-in fasteners at the cradle
- Drain the transmission fluid if replacing the left side halfshaft
- Drive axle nut and washer and discard them
- Lower control arm to steering knuckle cotter pin and discard it
- Loosen the lower control arm to steering knuckle castle nut so that the top of the nut is even with the top of the ball stud

✳✳ WARNING

The outer CV-joint, if equipped with Anti-lock Brake System (ABS), contains a speed sensor ring. Use of an incorrect tool to separate the control arm from the knuckle may result in damage and loss of the ABS system.

- Lower control arm from the steering knuckle by using a Lower Control arm Separator tool SA9132S
- Cotter pin and castle nut and discard them, if equipped
- Torque prevailing nut and discard it, if equipped
- Separate the tie rod end from the steering knuckle using a Tie Rod Separator tool, SA91100C
- Lower control arm to steering knuckle castle nut
- Position a pry bar at the proper cradle and front stabilizer and place a cloth over the ball stud boot

- Separate the lower control arm from the steering knuckle and pull the knuckle away from the ball stud
- While pulling the knuckle/strut away, pull the outer end of the halfshaft out of the wheel hub and properly support the halfshaft

4. For right side halfshafts, remove the halfshaft from the intermediate shaft by tapping the axle with a block of wood and hammer. Separate the halfshaft from the intermediate shaft.

5. For left side halfshafts, remove the halfshaft by installing a prybar and prying the halfshaft from the transmission.

To install:

➡ **Be careful not to damage the halfshaft oil seal when installing the halfshaft into the transmission.**

6. Install or connect the following:
- Transaxle Seal Protector tool SA91112T, when installing the left side halfshaft
- Halfshaft into the transmission. After the splines have safely passed the oil seal, remove the protector tool
- Insert the inner end of the halfshaft onto the outer end of the intermediate shaft for the right side halfshaft. Push on the axle firmly to engage the retaining ring
- Outer end of the halfshaft into the wheel hub. Do not install any hardware at this time
- Lower control arm ball stud into the steering knuckle. Hand-tighten the castle nut at this time
- Attach the tie rod end to the steering knuckle, if equipped. Torque the nut to 33 ft. lbs. (45 Nm) and install a new cotter pin
- If equipped with a torque prevailing nut, attach the tie rod to steering knuckle with a new nut. Do not allow the ball stud to turn while tightening the prevailing nut. Torque the nut to 41 ft. lbs. (55 Nm).
- Axle to hub washer and new nut. Torque the nut to 148 ft. lbs. (200 Nm).

➡ **When tightening the axle nut, have an assistant depress the brake pedal to prevent axle rotation.**

- Splash shields
- Align the molded in shield fasteners with the holes in the cradle and install push pins
- Wheel

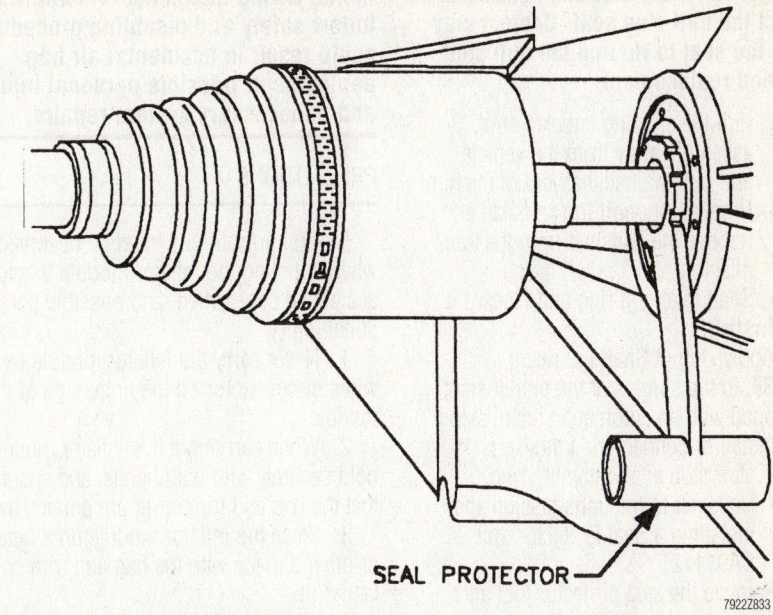

SEAL PROTECTOR

79222833

Failure to use a seal protector may allow the halfshaft splines to damage the transaxle seal

7. Top off the transmission with the proper fluid.

8. Check and adjust the front end alignment as necessary.

2.2L and 3.0L Engines

1. Before servicing the vehicle, refer to the precautions in the beginning of this section.

2. Remove the wheel cover or the center cap for access to the halfshaft nut. Have an assistant depress the brake pedal and loosen the front halfshaft nut.

3. Remove or disconnect the following:
- Wheel
- Tie rod end torque prevailing nut and discard it
- Tie rod end from the steering knuckle, using a Tie Rod Separator tool SA91100C
- Lower control arm to steering knuckle

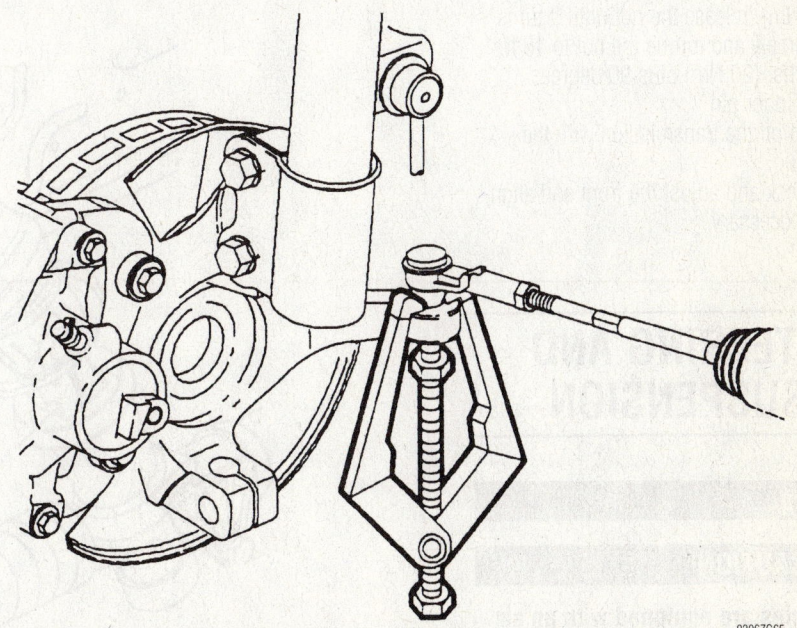

9306ZG65

Separate the tie rod end from the steering knuckle with a Tie Rod Separator tool

➡️Do not allow the steering knuckle to contact the ball stud seal. Contact may cause the seal to rip and the ball stud will need replacement.

- Pull the steering knuckle/strut assembly away from the vehicle and pull the halfshaft out of the hub
- Properly support the halfshaft and remove the halfshaft from the transmission
- Shaft retaining ring and discard it

To install:

4. Apply Output Shaft Lubricant 7847638, to the splines of the output shaft, if equipped with an automatic transmission.

5. Install or connect the following:
- New stub shaft retaining ring
- Halfshaft to the transmission after installing a Seal Protector tool SA91112T

6. Remove the seal protector tool after the splines have passed the oil seal.

7. Install or connect the following:
- Fully seat the halfshaft into the transmission
- Outer end of the halfshaft to the wheel hub with a new washer and nut
- Lower control arm ball stud to the steering knuckle. Torque the fastener to 75 ft. lbs. (100 Nm).
- Tie rod end to the steering knuckle. When seated properly, torque the fastener to 45 ft. lbs. (60 Nm).
- Wheel
- Halfshaft to wheel nut. Torque the nut to 74–118 ft. lbs. (100–160 Nm), release the nut until it turns freely and torque the nut to 15 ft. lbs. (20 Nm) plus 90 degrees
- Cotter pin

8. Top off the transmission with the proper fluid.

9. Check and adjust the front end alignment as necessary.

STEERING AND SUSPENSION

Air Bag

✱✱ CAUTION

All vehicles are equipped with an air bag system. The system must be disabled before performing service on or around system components, steering column, instrument panel compo- nents, wiring and sensors. Failure to follow safety and disabling procedures could result in accidental air bag deployment, possible personal injury and unnecessary system repairs.

PRECAUTIONS

Several precautions must be observed when handling the inflator module to avoid accidental deployment and possible personal injury.

1. Never carry the inflator module by the wires or connector on the underside of the module.

2. When carrying a live inflator module, hold securely with both hands, and ensure that the bag and trim cover are pointed away.

3. Place the inflator module on a bench or other surface with the bag and trim cover facing up.

4. With the inflator module on the bench, never place anything on or close to the module which may be thrown in the event of an accidental deployment.

DISARMING

1. Before servicing the vehicle, refer to the precautions in the beginning of this section.

2. Align the steering wheel so the vehicle wheels are pointing in the straight-ahead position.

3. Turn the ignition switch to the **LOCK** position.

4. Remove the SIR or AIR BAG fuse from the fuse block.

5. Remove the Connector Position Assurance (CPA) device, then disengage the yellow 2-way SIR wiring harness connector at the base of the steering column.

ARMING

✱✱ CAUTION

After the repairs, enable the system as follows:

1. Turn the ignition switch to the **LOCK** position.

2. Engage the yellow 2-way connector at the base of the steering column, then install the CPA device.

3. Reinstall the SIR or AIR BAG fuse.

4. Turn the ignition switch to the **RUN** position.

5. Verify the SIR indicator light flashes 7–9 times, if not, inspect the system for malfunction.

Rack and Pinion Steering Gear

REMOVAL & INSTALLATION

1.9L Engine

1. Before servicing the vehicle, refer to the precautions in the beginning of this section.

2. Remove or disconnect the following:

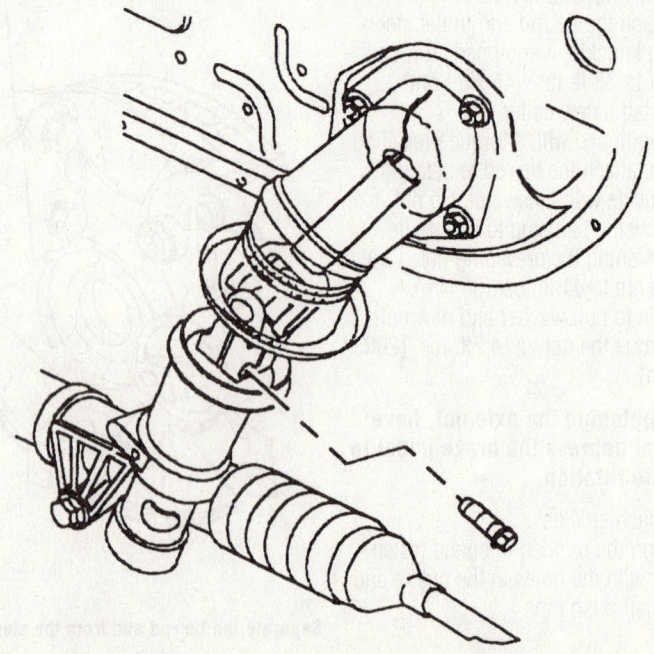

The pinch bolt is located under the intermediate shaft cover—1.9L engine

79222Z834

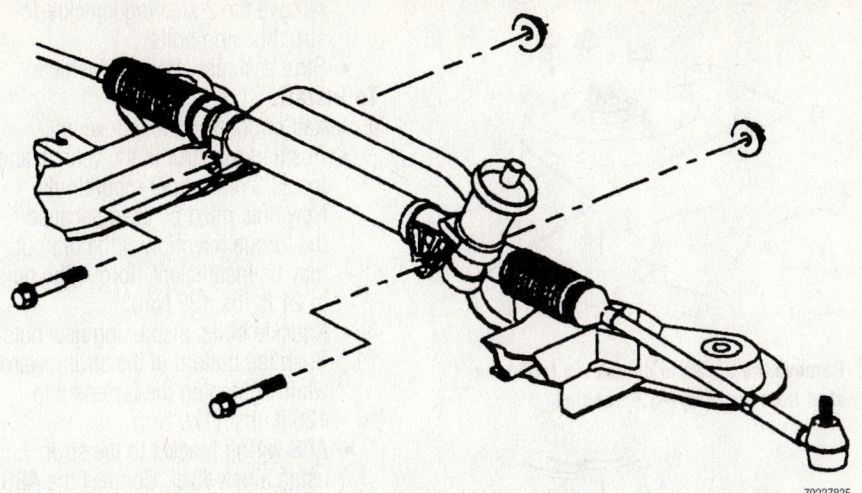

79222Z835

Remove the steering gear-to-cradle fasteners, then remove the gear through the left fender-well—1.9L engine

- Negative battery cable
- Both front wheels
- Tie rod end cotter pins and discard them
- Tie rod end from the steering knuckle
- Left side splash shield
- Loosen the intermediate shaft cover from the steering gear and move it aside
- Pinch bolt
- Steering gear to cradle fasteners
- Steering gear through the left fender well

3. On vehicles with power steering, place a suitable container under the steering assembly. Disconnect the pressure and return lines at the steering gear and allow the system to drain.

To install:

4. Install or connect the following:
- Steering gear
- Steering gear to cradle. Torque the new nuts to 37 ft. lbs. (50 Nm).
- Intermediate shaft to the steering gear. Torque the pinch bolt to 35 ft. lbs. (47 Nm).
- Left side splash shield
- Tie rod ends to the steering knuckle. Torque the castle nuts to 33 ft. lbs. (45 Nm).
- New cotter pins to the castle nuts
- Front wheels
- Negative battery cable

5. Check the alignment and adjust as necessary.

6. On vehicles with power steering, bleed the power steering system.

2.2L and 3.0L Engines

1. Before servicing the vehicle, refer to the precautions in the beginning of this section.

2. Remove or disconnect the following:
- Negative battery cable
- Both front wheels
- Intermediate shaft to steering gear pinch bolt and disconnect the shaft from the steering gear
- Rear exhaust manifold pipe heat shield, for 3.0L engine
- Rear transmission mount through bolt and transmission mount to frame bolt
- Power steering pump pressure and return hoses and allow them to drain
- Right front lower splash shield
- Exhaust manifold pipe, on 2.2L engine with manual transmission and all 3.0L engine
- Remaining rear transmission mount to frame bolts
- Tie rod end torque prevailing nuts and discard them
- Separate the tie rod ends from the steering knuckles
- Steering gear to frame bolts
- Steering gear heat shield, on 2.2L engine with automatic transmission
- Stabilizer bar links from the strut
- Front suspension support assemblies
- Loosen the remaining frame to body fasteners until there is clearance to remove the steering gear

- Steering gear through the left side wheel opening

To install:

3. One at a time, remove the frame bolts and replace the cage nuts. Torque retention of the old fasteners may not be sufficient.

4. Install or connect the following:
- Steering gear through the left wheel opening
- Raise the frame assembly to the undercarriage. When properly aligned, torque the fasteners to 66 ft. lbs. (90 Nm) plus a 46–60 degree turn
- Suspension supports with new bolts. Torque the bolts to 66 ft. lbs. (90 Nm) plus a 45–60 degree turn
- Steering gear to the frame with new bolts. Torque the bolts to 35 ft. lbs. (45 Nm) plus 45–60 degrees
- Steering gear heat shield, on 2.2L engine with an automatic transmission. Torque the bolts to 35 inch lbs. (4 Nm).
- Tie rod ends to the steering knuckle. When properly seated, torque the fastener to 33 ft. lbs. (45 Nm).
- New tie rod end nut. Torque the nut to 44 ft. lbs. (60 Nm).
- Stabilizer bar links to the strut. Torque the links to 48 ft. lbs. (65 Nm).
- Rear transmission to frame bolts. Torque the bolts to 44 ft. lbs. (60 Nm).
- Power steering pressure and return lines. Torque the fasteners to 20 ft. lbs. (27 Nm).
- Exhaust manifold pipe, on all 3.0L and 2.2L engines with a manual transmission. Torque the nuts to 22 ft. lbs. (30 Nm).
- Exhaust manifold pipe. Torque the bolts to 15 ft. lbs. (20 Nm).
- Front wheels
- Rear transmission mount to frame bolt. Torque the bolt to 66 ft. lbs. (90 Nm).
- Exhaust manifold pipe heat shield, on 3.0L engine. Torque the bolts to 71 inch lbs. (8 Nm).
- Intermediate shaft to the steering gear. Torque the new pinch bolt to 21 ft. lbs. (28 Nm).
- Negative battery cable

5. Check the alignment and adjust if necessary.

6. Bleed the power steering system.

POWER STEERING SYSTEM BLEEDING

1. Fill the P/S fluid reservoir.
2. Raise the front of the vehicle just sufficiently so that the drive wheels are off the ground, then safely support the vehicle.
3. Bleed the system by turning the wheels from side-to-side without hitting the stops. It may take several cycles to bleed the system.

➡**Maintain the reservoir at the FULL mark during this procedure.**

4. Lower the vehicle.
5. Start the engine and, with the transmission in **P** (automatic transmission) or **N** (manual transmission), check the fluid level with the engine idling. If necessary, add fluid to bring the level to the FULL mark.
6. Road test the vehicle and check for proper operation. Recheck the fluid level and make sure it is at or slightly above the FULL mark after the system has stabilized at normal operating temperature.

Strut

REMOVAL & INSTALLATION

Front

1.9L ENGINE

1. Before servicing the vehicle, refer to the precautions in the beginning of this section.
2. If equipped with an Anti-lock Brake System (ABS), disconnect the negative battery cable, then raise and support the vehicle safely. Be sure the vehicle is at a height where underhood access is still possible.
3. Remove or disconnect the following:
   - Front wheel
   - Unplug and disconnect the Anti-lock Brake System (ABS) wire from the strut wiring bracket. Note the wiring position for assembly purposes, then place the ABS wiring out of the way to prevent damage. If the strut is being replaced, drill the rivet head retaining the ABS wiring bracket to the strut and remove the bracket
   - Loosen the 2 steering knuckle-to-strut housing bolts, but do not remove them at this time. For reassembly purposes, matchmark the strut position to the steering knuckle
   - 3 upper strut-to-body nuts and discard them
   - Place a rag over the CV-joint seal to protect it from damage, then

Remove the 3 nuts to detach the top of the strut from the body—1.9L engine

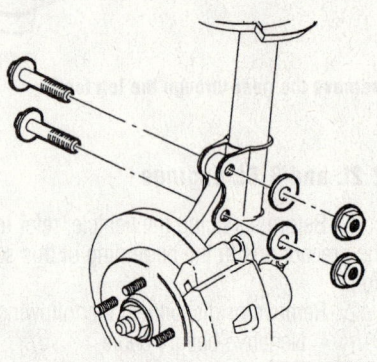

Matchmark, then remove the 2 bolts that secure the strut to the knuckle assembly—1.9L engine

remove the 2 steering knuckle-to-strut housing bolts
   - Strut assembly from the vehicle

To install:

4. Install or connect the following:
   - Position the strut in the vehicle and install 3 new upper mount nuts. New nuts must be used because the torque retention of the old nut may be insufficient. Torque the nuts to 21 ft. lbs. (29 Nm).
   - Knuckle bolts, also using new nuts. Push the bottom of the strut inward while tightening the fasteners to 126 ft. lbs. (170 Nm)
   - ABS wiring bracket to the strut using a new rivet. Connect the ABS wiring to the bracket and install the wiring to the speed sensor connector. Be sure the wiring is positioned as noted during removal
   - Wheel assembly, remove the supports and lower the vehicle.
   - Negative battery cable

5. Check and adjust the alignment if necessary.

2.2L AND 3.0L ENGINES

1. Before servicing the vehicle, refer to the precautions in the beginning of this section.

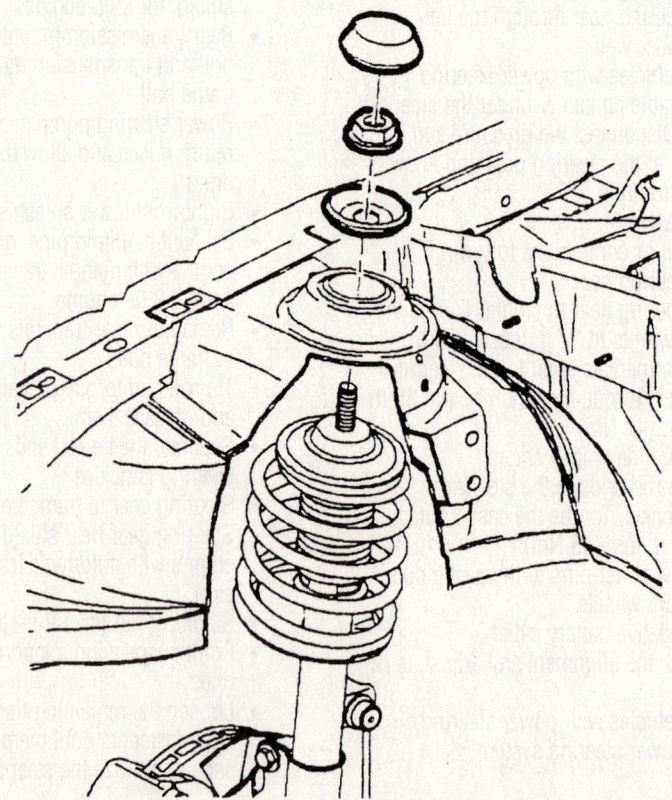

Remove the strut to body attaching nut—2.2L and 3.0L engines

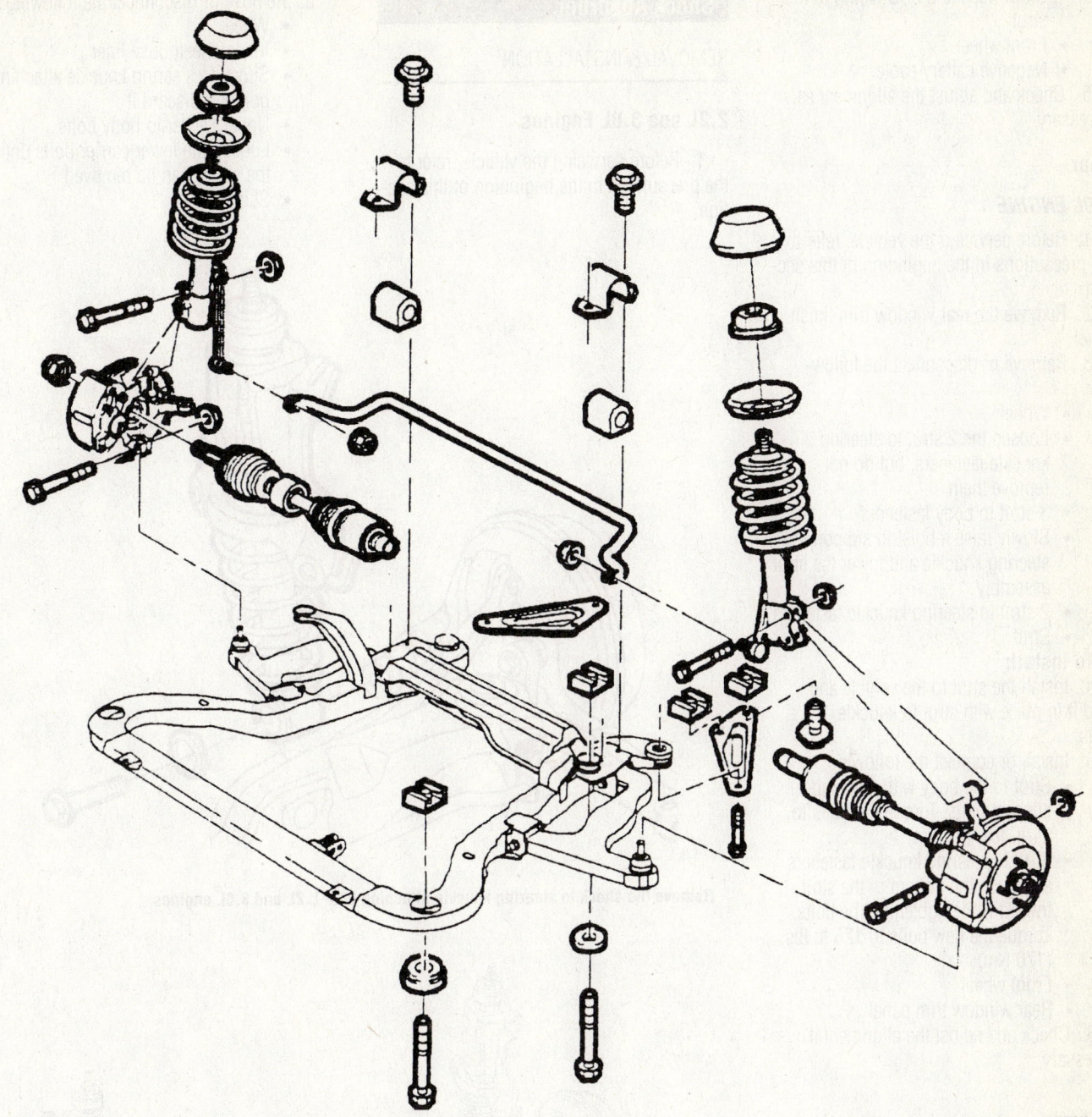

9306ZG68

Exploded view of the front suspension—2.2L and 3.0L engines

2. If equipped with an Anti-lock Brake System (ABS), disconnect the negative battery cable, then raise and support the vehicle safely. Be sure the vehicle is at a height where underhood access is still possible.

3. Remove or disconnect the following:
- Front wheel
- Brake hose and ABS harness from the strut assembly
- Loosen the steering knuckle to strut fasteners, but do not remove them

- Stabilizer bar link to the strut assembly attaching nut and move it toward the rear of the vehicle
- Strut to body attaching nuts
- Place a rag over the CV-joint seal to protect it from damage, then remove the 2 steering knuckle-to-strut housing bolts
- Steering knuckle to strut fasteners
- Strut assembly from the vehicle

To install:

4. Install or connect the following:
- Strut to the body. Torque the new attaching nut to 40 ft. lbs. (55 Nm).
- Strut to the steering knuckle. Torque the new fasteners to 37 ft. lbs. (50 Nm) then an additional 66 ft. lbs. (90 Nm) plus a 45 degree turn
- Stabilizer bar link to the strut. Torque the fastener to 50 ft. lbs. (65 Nm).

- Brake hose and ABS wiring to the strut
- Front wheel
- Negative battery cable

5. Check and adjust the alignment as necessary.

Rear

1.9L ENGINE

1. Before servicing the vehicle, refer to the precautions in the beginning of this section.

2. Remove the rear window trim finish panel.

3. Remove or disconnect the following:

- Wheel
- Loosen the 2 strut to steering knuckle fasteners, but do not remove them
- 3 strut to body fasteners
- Slowly raise a hoist to support the steering knuckle and lower the strut assembly
- 2 strut to steering knuckle fasteners
- Strut

To install:

4. Install the strut to the vehicle and hold it in place with strut to knuckle bolts.

5. Install or connect the following:

- Strut to the body with new upper support bolts. Torque the bolts to 21 ft. lbs. (29 Nm).
- Strut to steering knuckle fasteners and push the bottom of the strut inward while tightening the bolts. Torque the new bolts to 126 ft. lbs. (170 Nm).
- Front wheel
- Rear window trim panel

6. Check and adjust the alignment if necessary.

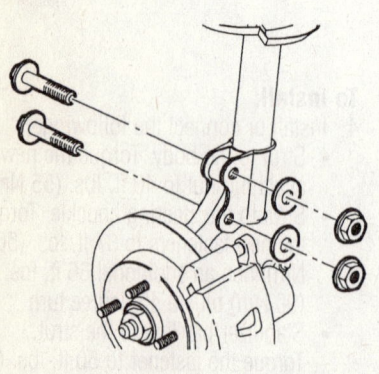

Remove the two strut to steering knuckle fasteners—1.9L engine

7922Z837

Shock Absorber

REMOVAL & INSTALLATION

2.2L and 3.0L Engines

1. Before servicing the vehicle, refer to the precautions in the beginning of this section.

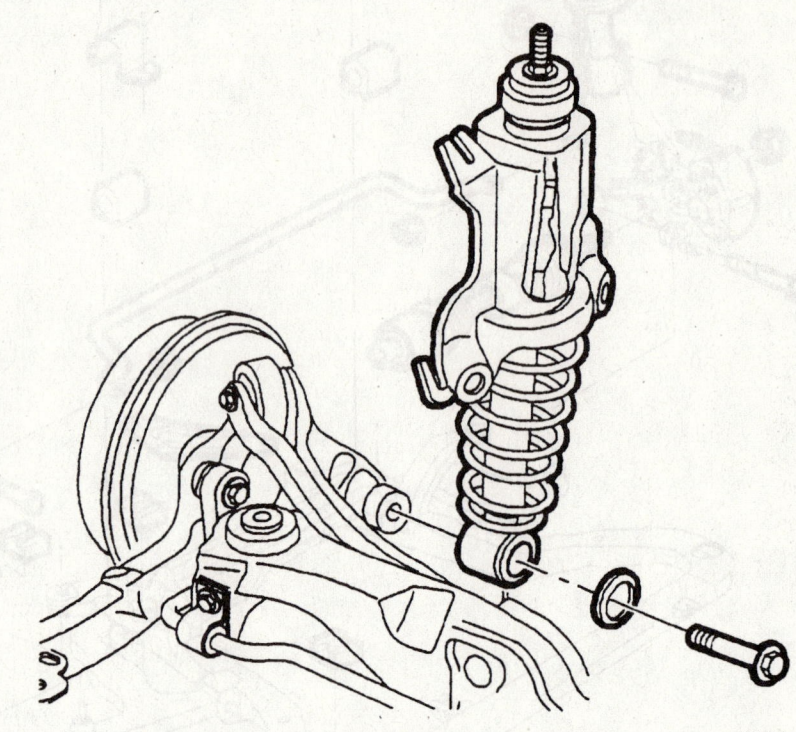

Remove the shock to steering knuckle attaching bolt—2.2L and 3.0L engines

9306ZG69

2. Remove or disconnect the following:

- Wheel
- Inner wheelhouse liner
- Shock to steering knuckle attaching bolt and discard it
- Upper carrier to body bolts
- Loosen the lower carrier bolts until the shock can be removed
- Shock

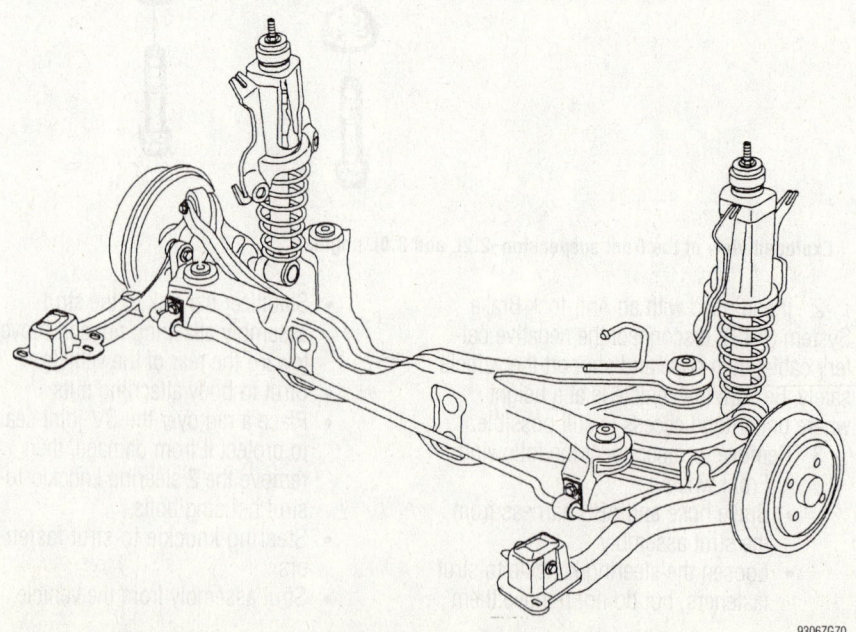

Exploded view of the rear suspension—2.2L and 3.0L engine

9306ZG70

To install:

3. Install or connect the following:
- Carrier to body. Torque the bolts to 40 ft. lbs. (55 Nm).
- Carrier to steering knuckle with a new bolt. Torque the bolt to 110 ft. lbs. (150 Nm) plus 30 degrees
- Inner wheelhouse liner
- Wheel

Coil Spring

REMOVAL & INSTALLATION

Front

1.9L ENGINE

1. Before servicing the vehicle, refer to the precautions in the beginning of this section.
2. Remove or disconnect the following:
- Strut from the vehicle
- Mount the strut in a bench vise, then attach a spring compressor/holding fixture; be sure that the strut component is firmly secured
- Compress the spring sufficiently to completely unload the upper strut mount
- Shaft nut while holding the strut

stationary with a Torx® head socket wrench
- Upper spring support and inspect the rubber for cracks or deterioration
- Spring from the strut and inspect the spring for damage
- Dust shield assembly and inspect for cracks or deterioration
- Strut from the vise or applicable holding fixture and retract the strut shaft, checking for smooth, even resistance

3. If replacing the coil spring, carefully release the spring compressor.

To install:

4. Secure the strut in the bench vise or applicable holding fixture.
5. Extend the strut shaft to the limit of its travel.
6. Install or connect the following:
- Dust shield assembly onto the strut, then install the spring with the compressor tool installed
- Spring isolator and the strut mount to the top of the assembly
- Guide the strut shaft through the upper strut mount assembly. Compress the coil until the washer and shaft nut can be installed to the end of the shaft, but do not over-compress and damage the spring

- Tighten the shaft to the nut using a Torx® head socket wrench and a torque wrench, while holding the nut steady with an open end wrench. Tighten the fastener to 37 ft. lbs. (50 Nm).
- Release the spring compressor tool and remove the strut from the fixture
- Strut assembly in the vehicle.

2.2L AND 3.0L ENGINES

1. Before servicing the vehicle, refer to the precautions in the beginning of this section.
2. Remove or disconnect the following:
- Strut from the vehicle
- Place the strut into a spring compressor. Fasten the assembly with a strut to steering knuckle bolt through the lower mounting hole
- Compress the spring enough to completely unload the upper strut mount
- Strut shaft nut while holding the shaft stationary with a TORX® socket
- Release the spring compressor and tilt the strut outward
- Upper strut mount assembly
- Spring

To install:

3. Install or connect the following:
- Strut into spring compressor
- Extend the strut shaft to its full travel
- Hollow bumper onto the strut
- Spring to the strut and make certain that it is properly positioned in the seat and isolator
- Upper spring seat and strut mount
- Compress the spring while guiding the strut shaft through the upper strut mount assembly. Do not over compress the spring
- Torque the strut shaft nut to 40 ft. lbs. (55 Nm).

4. Release the spring compressor tool
5. Strut to the vehicle

Rear

1.9L ENGINE

1. Before servicing the vehicle, refer to the precautions in the beginning of this section.
2. Remove or disconnect the following:
- Strut assembly from the vehicle
- Mount the strut in a bench vise,

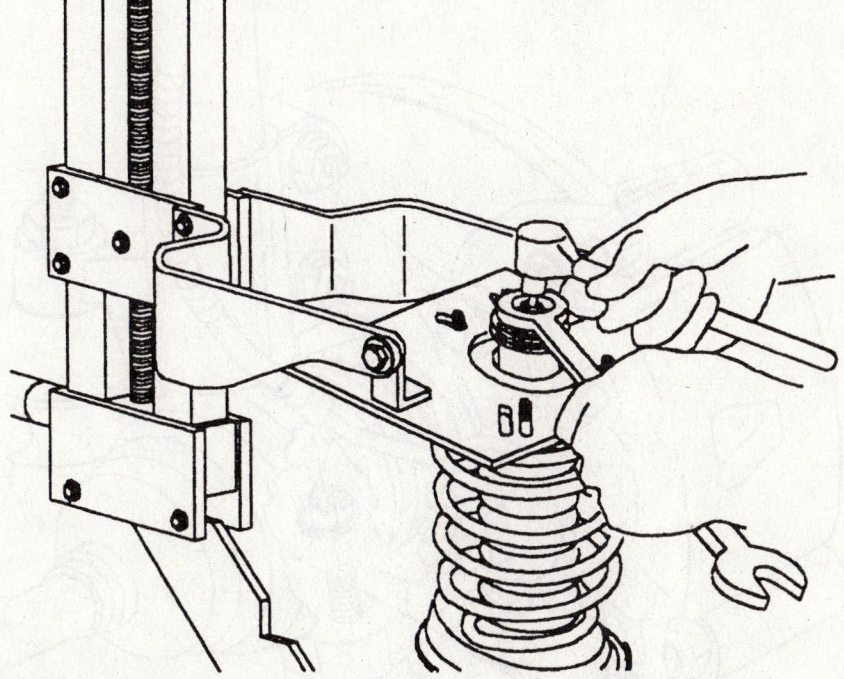

Remove the strut shaft nut while the coil spring is compressed to unload the upper strut mount–1.9L engines

7922Z838

Turn to Section 5 for brake system applications

then attach a suitable spring compressor/holding fixture; be sure that the strut component is firmly secured

- Compress the spring sufficiently to completely unload the upper strut mount
- Strut shaft nut while holding the strut stationary with a Torx® head socket wrench
- Upper spring support and inspect the rubber for cracks or deterioration
- Spring from the strut and inspect the spring for damage
- Dust shield assembly and inspect for cracks or deterioration
- Strut from the vise or applicable holding fixture and retract the strut shaft, checking for smooth, even resistance

3. If replacing the coil spring, carefully release the spring compressor.

To assemble:

4. Secure the strut in the bench vise, or applicable holding fixture.

5. Extend the strut shaft to the limit of its travel.

6. Install or connect the following:
- Dust shield assembly onto the strut, then install the spring with the compressor tool installed
- Spring isolator and the strut mount to the top of the assembly
- Guide the strut shaft through the upper strut mount assembly. Compress the coil until the washer and shaft nut can be installed to the end of the shaft, but do not over-compress and damage the spring
- Tighten the shaft to the nut using a Torx® head socket wrench and a torque wrench, while holding the nut steady with an open-end wrench. Tighten the fastener to 37 ft. lbs. (50 Nm).
- Release the spring compressor tool and remove the strut from the fixture
- Strut to the vehicle

2.2L AND 3.0L ENGINES

1. Before servicing the vehicle, refer to the precautions in the beginning of this section.

2. Remove or disconnect the following:
- Shock absorber assembly from the vehicle
- Mount the carrier assembly Spring Compressor SA9155S, in a holding fixture
- Mount the shock assembly to the

spring compressor using an adapter, SA9155–3

- Compress the spring enough to unload the upper spring supports
- Shock absorber shaft nut while holding the shaft securely with a TORX® socket
- Release the spring compressor and remove the carrier assembly
- Rear suspension support and inspect the inner and outer bumpers for cracks or deterioration, replace if necessary
- Rear spring upper insulator
- Extend and retract the shock absorber and check for smooth resistance

To install:

3. Install or connect the following:
- Shock into a spring compressor
- Extend the shock to its full limit of travel
- Inner and outer bumpers and make certain that the springs are properly positioned in their support seats
- Compress the spring while guiding the shock absorber shaft through the upper mount until the washer and nut can be installed. Torque the shaft nut to 15 ft. lbs. (20 Nm) while holding the shaft nut with a TORX® socket.

- Release the compressor tool and remove the carrier from the compressor
- Shock absorber to the vehicle

Lower Control Arm

REMOVAL & INSTALLATION

Front

1.9L ENGINE

1. Before servicing the vehicle, refer to the precautions in the beginning of this section.

2. Remove or disconnect the following:
- Wheel
- Lower control arm ball stud cotter pin and discard the pin
- Loosen the castle nut until it is level with the top of the ball stud

➡ **Use caution not do damage the Anti-lock Braking System (ABS) speed sensor ring. If the ring is damaged a malfunction of the ABS system is possible.**

3. Separate the lower control arm from the steering knuckle, using a Lower Control Arm Ball Stud Separator tool SA9132S

4. Remove or disconnect the following:

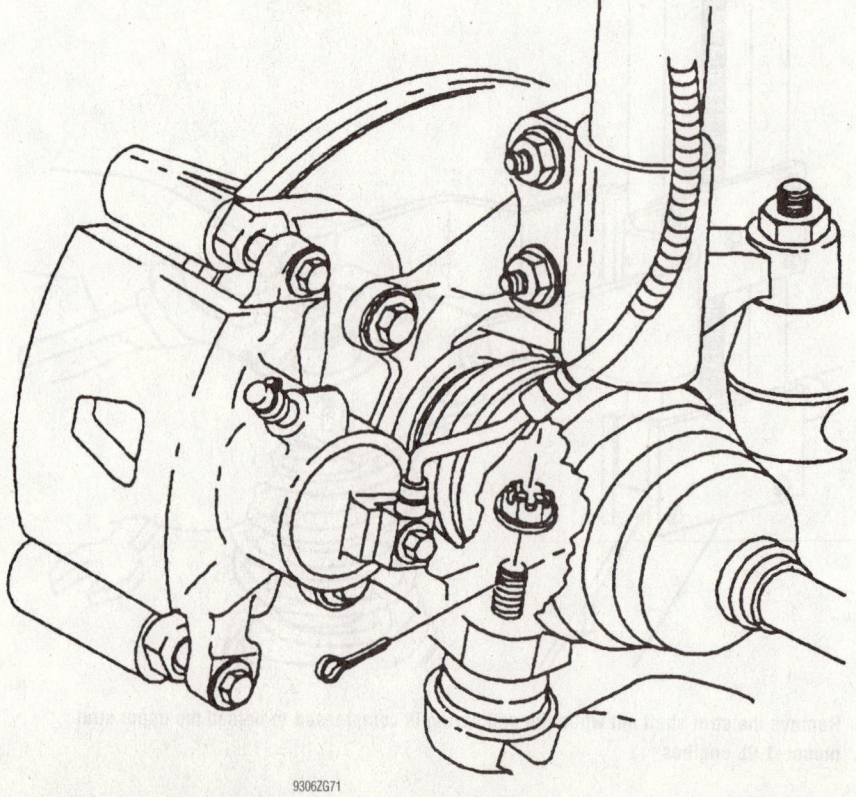

9306ZG71

Connect the ball stud to the steering knuckle–1.9L engines

- Lower control arm castle nut
- Front inner fender splash shield and remove the push pins
- Front section of the shield first on the left hand side and the rear section first on the right side of the vehicle
- Lower control arm to cradle fasteners
- front stabilizer bar nut at the lower control arm
- Lower control arm

To install:

5. Install or connect the following:
- Control arm to the front stabilizer bar
- Position the end of the control arm into the cradle. Torque the bolt to 92 ft. lbs. (125 Nm) and the nut to 74 ft. lbs. (100 Nm).
- Control arm to front stabilizer bar nut. Torque the nut to 106 ft. lbs. (144 Nm).
- Ball stud to the steering knuckle. Torque the castle nut to 55 ft. lbs. (75 Nm) and install a new cotter pin
- Rear section of the shield first on the left side and the front section first on the right side of the vehicle
- Inner fender splash shield
- Align the molded in fasteners with the cradle holes and push them straight in
- Wheel

6. Check and adjust the alignment if necessary.

2.2L AND 3.0L ENGINES

1. Before servicing the vehicle, refer to the precautions in the beginning of this section.

2. Remove or disconnect the following:
- Wheel
- Ball stud bolt

➡**Use caution not do damage the Antilock Braking System (ABS) speed sensor ring. If the ring is damaged a malfunction of the ABS system is possible.**

- Separate the ball stud from the steering knuckle by using a pry bar
- Lower control arm to frame bolts
- Lower control arm

To install:

3. Install or connect the following:
- Control arm to the frame. Torque the new bolts to 65 ft. lbs. (90 Nm) plus 75 degrees
- Ball stud to steering knuckle.

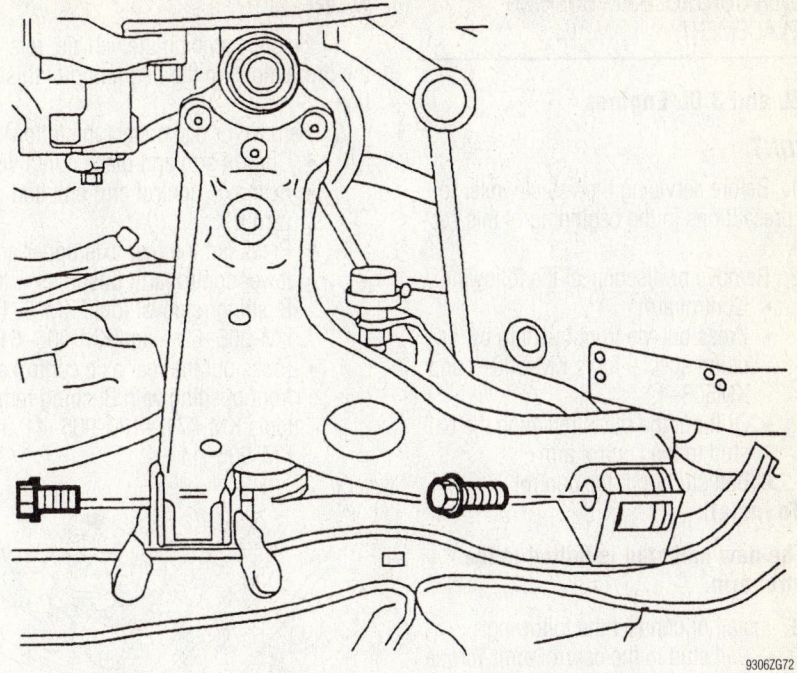

Remove the lower control arm to frame bolts–2.2L and 3.0L engines

9306ZG72

Torque the bolt to 75 ft. lbs. (100 Nm).
- Wheel
- Check and adjust the alignment, if necessary.

Rear

2.2L AND 3.0L ENGINES

1. Before servicing the vehicle, refer to the precautions in the beginning of this section.

2. Remove or disconnect the following:
- Rear wheel
- Rear brake hose and bracket from the control arm
- Caliper, if equipped
- Brake drum/rotor
- Antilock Braking System (ABS) sensor harness, if equipped
- Hub
- Parking brake cable and support
- Separate the backing plate from the control arm
- Shock absorber to control arm bolt
- Rear stabilizer bar link to rear control arm bolt
- Loosen the rear suspension upper and lower control arm to rear axle fasteners
- Rear axle to control arm and discard the bolts
- Rear upper and lower suspensions control arm bolts and discard them

- Rear control arm

To install:

3. Install or connect the following:
- Control arm and install new rear axle control arm bolts. Do not tighten them at this time
- Upper and lower rear suspension control arm bolts
- Torque the rear axle control arm bolts and the upper and lower rear suspension bolts to 65 ft. lbs. (90 Nm) plus 30 degrees
- Shock absorber to rear axle control arm. Torque the new bolt to 110 ft. lbs. (150 Nm) plus 30 degrees
- Stabilizer bar link to the control arm. Torque the bolt 41 ft. lbs. (55 Nm).
- Backing plate and hub assembly. Torque the bolts to 37 ft. lbs. (50 Nm) plus 30 degrees
- Rear drum/disc. Torque the bolts to 35 inch lbs. (4 Nm).
- Rear brake caliper. Torque the bolts to 59 ft. lbs. (80 Nm), if equipped
- Parking brake cable and support bracket. Torque the bolts to 71 inch lbs. (8 Nm).
- Brake line bracket to the control arm. Torque the bolts to 71 inch lbs. (8 Nm).
- Rear wheel

4. Check and adjust the alignment, as needed.

LOWER CONTROL ARM BUSHING REPLACEMENT

2.2L and 3.0L Engines

FRONT

1. Before servicing the vehicle, refer to the precautions in the beginning of this section.

2. Remove or disconnect the following:
   - Control arm
   - Press out the front bushing by using special tools KM-508-3 and KM508-1
   - Drill out the rivets retaining the ball stud to the control arm
   - Ball stud from the control

To install:

➡ **The new ball stud is bolted to the control arm.**

3. Install or connect the following:
   - Ball stud to the control arm. Torque the new bolts to 25 ft. lbs. (35 Nm).
   - Press in the new control arm bushing using special tools KM508-1, KM508-2 and KM508-3
   - Control arm to the frame. Torque the new bolts to 65 ft. lbs. (90 Nm) plus 75 degrees
   - Ball stud to the steering knuckle. Torque the bolts to 75 ft. lbs. (100 Nm).

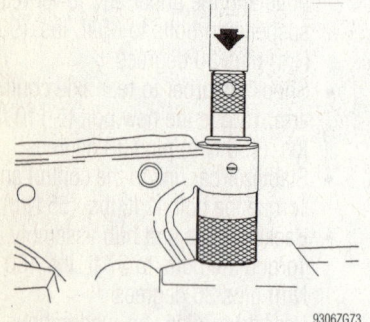

Press out the control arm bushing

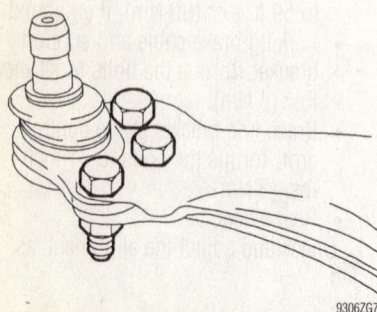

The new ball stud is bolted into the control arm—2.2L and 3.0L engines

REAR

1. Before servicing the vehicle, refer to the precautions in the beginning of this section.

2. Remove or disconnect the following:
   - Control arm and place it in a vise
   - Rear axle control arm bolt and discard it
   - Press out the rear axle upper and lower control arm bushings with Bushing removal tools KM-671—KM-906-62—and KM-906-61
   - Press out the rear axle control arm front bushing with Bushing removal tools KM-671—KM-906-41 and KM-906-44

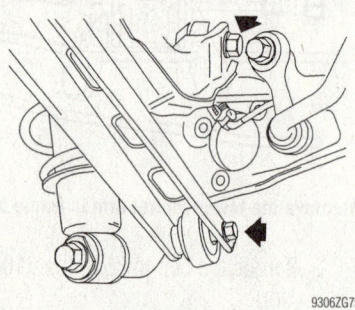

Remove the rear axle control arm upper and lower bushings

To install:

3. Install or connect the following:
   - Press in the new rear axle front control arm bushing using special tools KM-671, KM-906-42 and KM-906-43
   - Press in the rear axle upper and lower control arm bushings with Bushing Removal tools KM-671, KM-906-64 and KM-906-631
   - Rear axle control arm bracket. Torque the new bolt to 65 ft. lbs. (90 Nm) plus 60 degrees

Wheel Bearings

ADJUSTMENT

The wheel bearing are sealed at the factory and do not require any adjustment or maintenance.

REMOVAL & INSTALLATION

Front

1.9L ENGINE

1. Before servicing the vehicle, refer to the precautions in the beginning of this section.

2. If equipped with an Antilock Braking System (ABS), disconnect the negative battery cable.

3. Loosen the front halfshaft nut, while an assistant depresses the brake pedal, then raise and support the vehicle safely.

4. Remove or disconnect the following:
   - Wheel
   - Brake caliper mounting bracket bolts and suspend the assembly from the strut spring with wire
   - Loosen the strut-to-knuckle bolts, but do not remove at this time
   - Rotor, axle nut and washer
   - Cotter pin from the lower control arm ball joint. Back the ball joint nut until the top of the nut is even with the top of the threads
   - Separate the lower control arm from the steering knuckle, then remove the nut. Do not use a wedge tool or seal damage may occur

➡ **The outer CV-joint for vehicles equipped with ABS contains a speed sensor ring. Use of an incorrect tool to separate the control arm from the knuckle may result in damage and loss of the ABS system.**

   - Tie rod cotter pin and castle nut, then separate the tie rod end from the knuckle
   - ABS wheel speed sensor electrical connector
   - Suspend the halfshaft from the body with wire, then remove the 2 knuckle-to-strut fasteners and remove the knuckle/hub assembly from the vehicle. If difficulty is encountered, position a block of wood on the end of the halfshaft and tap on the wood with a hammer to free the hub assembly

5. Disassemble the knuckle hub assembly as follows:
   a. If equipped, remove the ABS wheel speed sensor from the knuckle.

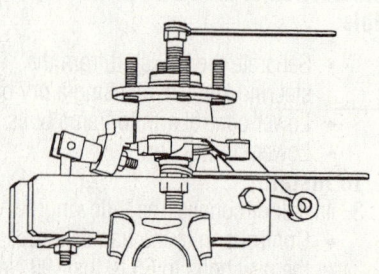

Tighten the hub driver screw to remove the hub while the assembly is held firmly in a vise—1.9L engine

➡**Any time the hub or bearing is separated from the steering knuckle, a new bearing must be used upon assembly.**

6. Install Wheel Bearing Removing tools SA9159S, to the knuckle and secure the assembly in a vise.

7. Hold the hub driver with a wrench and tighten the hub driver screw to remove the hub. If the inner bearing race is pulled out with the hub, remove the race with a bearing race remover.

8. Remove the assembly from the vise and separate the wheel hub removal tool from the knuckle.

9. Remove the bearing retainer snapring.

10. Position the knuckle in a shop press on a knuckle support tube and press the bearing from the knuckle with a small driver.

To install:

11. If necessary, assemble the knuckle hub assembly as follows:

a. Use a large driver and press in the new bearing until seated.

b. Use the small driver and the knuckle support tube to press in the hub

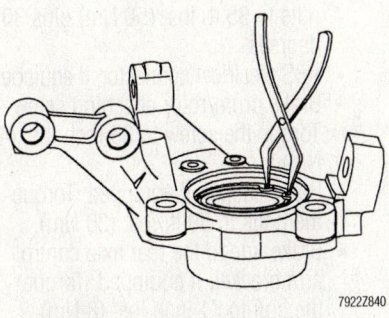

Remove the bearing retainer snapring before pressing out the bearing—1.9L engine

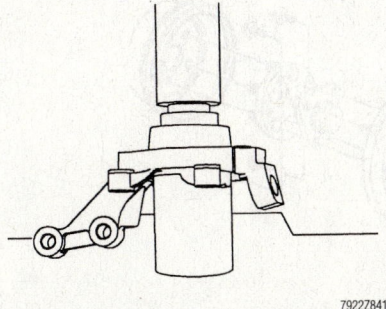

Carefully press the bearing out of the knuckle after removing the snapring—1.9L engine

assembly. The small driver must be used to support the bearing inner race with its small (pilot) side facing towards the press and away from the bearing.

c. Install the bearing retainer snapring.

12. Install the ABS wheel speed sensor into the knuckle. Torque the fastener to 72 inch lbs. (8 Nm), if equipped.

➡**Service knuckles may not have holes for brake dust shield mounting. The dust shield is no longer required and does not have to be reinstalled. Also, should the shield become damaged, it may be removed; there is no need to repair or replace it. But, should a shield be removed and discarded, the shield should also be removed from the opposite side to maintain balance/symmetry.**

13. Thoroughly clean and lubricate the ball joint stud threads of the lower control arm and tie rod end. Install the knuckle/hub assembly onto the axle shaft. Then, install the washer with a new nut, but do not tighten the nut at this time.

14. Install or connect the following:

• Lower control arm ball stud through the knuckle bore and install the nut, but do not tighten at this time
• Steering knuckle-to-strut fasteners, but do not tighten at this time
• Tie rod end and nut, then torque the nut to 33 ft. lbs. (45 Nm) and install a new cotter pin. If necessary, tighten the nut additionally, do not back off to insert the cotter pin
• Push inward on the bottom of the strut and torque the knuckle fasteners to 126 ft. lbs. (170 Nm).
• Torque the lower control arm ball stud nut to 55 ft. lbs. (75 Nm), tighten additionally, if necessary, and install a new cotter pin
• Rotor onto the hub, then install the caliper mount bracket onto the knuckle. Tighten the mount bracket assembly bolts to 81 ft. lbs. (110 Nm).
• While an assistant depresses the brake pedal, tighten the halfshaft nut to 103 ft. lbs. (140 Nm).
• Wheel assembly and lower the vehicle
• Negative battery cable

15. Check and adjust the alignment, if necessary.

2.2L AND 3.0L ENGINES

1. Before servicing the vehicle, refer to the precautions in the beginning of this section.

2. If equipped with an Antilock Braking System (ABS), disconnect the negative battery cable.

3. Loosen the front halfshaft nut, while an assistant depresses the brake pedal, then raise and support the vehicle safely.

4. Remove or disconnect the following:

• Wheel
• Brake caliper mounting bracket bolts and suspend the assembly from the strut spring with wire
• Brake rotor and dust shield
• ABS sensor and bracket, if equipped
• Loosen the strut-to-knuckle bolts, but do not remove at this time
• Axle to hub nut and discard it
• Tie rod end nut and discard it

5. If difficulty is encountered, position a block of wood on the end of the halfshaft and tap on the wood with a hammer to free the hub assembly.

• Steering knuckle/hub assembly

6. To remove the wheel bearing proceed, as follows:

a. Install Wheel Bearing Removing tools SA9159S, to the knuckle and secure the assembly in a vise.

b. Hold the hub driver with a wrench and tighten the hub driver screw to remove the hub. If the inner bearing race is pulled out with the hub, remove the race with a bearing race remover.

c. Remove the assembly from the vise and separate the wheel hub removal tool from the knuckle.

d. Remove the bearing retainer snapring.

e. Position the knuckle in a shop

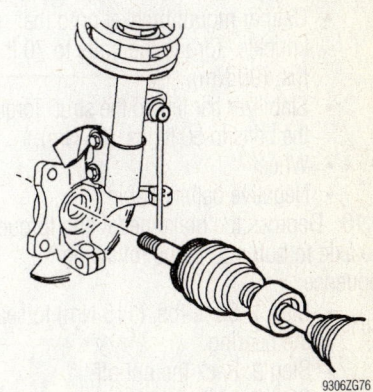

Separate the axle from the wheel hub—2.2L and 3.0L engines

press on a knuckle support tube and press the bearing from the knuckle with a small driver.

To install:

7. If necessary, assemble the knuckle hub assembly, as follows:

   a. Use a suitable large driver and press in the new bearing until seated.

   b. Use the small driver and the knuckle support tube to press in the hub assembly. The small driver must be used to support the bearing inner race with its small (pilot) side facing towards the press and away from the bearing.

   c. Install the bearing retainer snap ring.

8. Thoroughly clean and lubricate the ball joint stud threads of the lower control arm and tie rod end.

9. Install or connect the following:

- Knuckle/hub assembly onto the axle shaft. Then, install the washer with a new nut, but do not tighten the nut at this time
- Lower control arm ball stud through the knuckle bore and install the nut, but do not tighten at this time
- Steering knuckle-to-strut fasteners. Torque the fasteners to 40 ft. lbs. (50 Nm); then, to 65 ft. lbs. (90 Nm) plus 45 degrees
- Torque the ball stud fastener to 75 ft. lbs. (100 Nm).
- Tie rod end into the steering knuckle using a Linkage Installer tool J44015. Torque the fastener to 35 ft. lbs. (45 Nm).
- ABS sensor and mounting bracket, if equipped. Torque the bolts to 71 inch lbs. (8 Nm).
- Dust shield. Torque the bolts to 35 in lbs. (4 Nm).
- Rotor and screw. Torque the screw to 27 inch lbs. (3.5 Nm).
- Caliper mount bracket onto the knuckle. Torque the bolts to 70 ft. lbs. (90 Nm).
- Stabilizer bar link to the strut. Torque the bolts to 50 ft. lbs. (65 Nm).
- Wheel
- Negative battery cable

10. Depress the brake pedal and torque the axle to hub nut, in the following sequence:

- Step 1: 85 ft. lbs. (115 Nm) to seat the bearing.
- Step 2: Back the nut off
- Step 3: 15 ft. lbs. (20 Nm).
- Step 4: Turn the nut an additional 90 degrees, using a torque angle gauge

11. Install the cotter pin.

12. Check and adjust the alignment

Rear

1.9L ENGINE

Unlike the front wheel bearings, which may be removed from the hub for replacement, the rear wheel hub and bearing assembly is not serviceable. If damaged or worn, the hub and bearing assembly must be replaced as a unit.

1. Before servicing the vehicle, refer to the precautions in the beginning of this section.

2. Remove or disconnect the following:

- Negative battery cable, if equipped with an Antilock Braking System (ABS)
- Rear wheel
- ABS speed sensor connector, if equipped
- Caliper assembly-to-knuckle mounting bolts and support it with a wire from the strut, then remove the rotor, if equipped with disc brakes
- Brake drum, if equipped with drum brakes
- 4 hub/bearing-to-knuckle bolts, then remove the assembly from the vehicle

To install:

3. Install or connect the following:

- Brake backing plate, hub/bearing assembly and retaining bolts. Torque the bolts to 63 ft. lbs. (85 Nm).
- Brake drum or rotor and caliper assembly. Torque the caliper retaining bolts to 63 ft. lbs. (85 Nm), if equipped
- ABS speed sensor connector, if equipped
- Brake drum, if equipped
- Brake rotor, if equipped

- Caliper to the steering knuckle, if equipped. Torque the bolts to 63 ft. lbs. (85 Nm).
- Rear wheel
- Negative battery cable

2.2L AND 3.0L ENGINES

1. Before servicing the vehicle, refer to the precautions in the beginning of this section.

2. Remove or disconnect the following:

- Negative battery cable, if equipped with an Antilock Braking System (ABS)
- Rear wheel
- Brake line to rear axle control arm attaching clip, if equipped with rear disc brakes
- Caliper to steering knuckle bolts and move the caliper aside, if equipped with rear disc brakes
- Brake drum/rotor
- ABS electrical connector, if equipped
- Hub to control arm nuts and discard them
- Hub

To install:

3. Install or connect the following:

- Hub to control arm. Torque the new nuts to 35 ft. lbs. (50 Nm) plus 30 degrees
- ABS electrical connector, if equipped
- Brake drum/rotor attaching screw. Torque the screw to 35 inch lbs. (4 Nm).
- Brake caliper, if equipped. Torque the bolts to 59 ft. lbs. (80 Nm).
- Brake line to the rear axle control arm bracket, if equipped. Torque the bolt to 71 inch lbs. (8 Nm).
- Rear wheel
- Negative battery cable

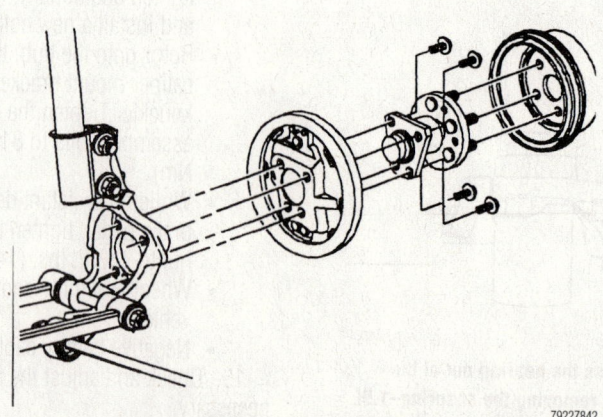

Exploded view of the rear hub/bearing assembly—drum brake set-up shown—1.9L engine

79227842

GLOSSARY

ABS: Anti-lock braking system. An electro-mechanical braking system which is designed to minimize or prevent wheel lock-up during braking.

ABSOLUTE PRESSURE: Atmospheric (barometric) pressure plus the pressure gauge reading.

ACCELERATOR PUMP: A small pump located in the carburetor that feeds fuel into the air/fuel mixture during acceleration.

ACCUMULATOR: A device that controls shift quality by cushioning the shock of hydraulic oil pressure being applied to a clutch or band.

ACTUATING MECHANISM: The mechanical output devices of a hydraulic system, for example, clutch pistons and band servos.

ACTUATOR: The output component of a hydraulic or electronic system.

ADVANCE: Setting the ignition timing so that spark occurs earlier before the piston reaches top dead center (TDC).

ADAPTIVE MEMORY (ADAPTIVE STRATEGY): The learning ability of the TCM or PCM to redefine its decision-making process to provide optimum shift quality.

AFTER TOP DEAD CENTER (ATDC): The point after the piston reaches the top of its travel on the compression stroke.

AIR BAG: Device on the inside of the car designed to inflate on impact of crash, protecting the occupants of the car.

AIR CHARGE TEMPERATURE (ACT) SENSOR: The temperature of the airflow into the engine is measured by an ACT sensor, usually located in the lower intake manifold or air cleaner. ALDL (assembly line diagnostic link): Electrical connector for scanning ECM/PCM/TCM input and output devices.

AIR CLEANER: An assembly consisting of a housing, filter and any connecting ductwork. The filter element is made up of a porous paper, sometimes with a wire mesh screening, and is designed to prevent airborne particles from entering the engine through the carburetor or throttle body.

AIR INJECTION: One method of reducing harmful exhaust emissions by injecting air into each of the exhaust ports of an engine. The fresh air entering the hot exhaust manifold causes any remaining fuel to be burned before it can exit the tailpipe.

AIR PUMP: An emission control device that supplies fresh air to the exhaust manifold to aid in more completely burning exhaust gases.

AIR/FUEL RATIO: The ratio of air-to-gasoline by weight in the fuel mixture drawn into the engine.

ALIGNMENT RACK: A special drive-on vehicle lift apparatus/measuring device used to adjust a vehicle's toe, caster and camber angles.

ALL WHEEL DRIVE: Term used to describe a full time four wheel drive system or any other vehicle drive system that continuously delivers power to all four wheels. This system is found primarily on station wagon vehicles and SUVs not utilized for significant off road use.

ALTERNATING CURRENT (AC): Electric current that flows first in one direction, then in the opposite direction, continually reversing flow.

ALTERNATOR: A device which produces AC (alternating current) which is converted to DC (direct current) to charge the car battery.

AMMETER: An instrument, calibrated in amperes, used to measure the flow of an electrical current in a circuit. Ammeters are always connected in series with the circuit being tested.

AMPERAGE: The total amount of current (amperes) flowing in a circuit.

AMPLIFIER: A device used in an electrical circuit to increase the voltage of an output signal.

AMP/HR. RATING (BATTERY): Measurement of the ability of a battery to deliver a stated amount of current for a stated period of time. The higher the amp/hr. rating, the better the battery.

AMPERE: The rate of flow of electrical current present when one volt of electrical pressure is applied against one ohm of electrical resistance.

ANALOG COMPUTER: Any microprocessor that uses similar (analogous) electrical signals to make its calculations.

ANODIZED: A special coating applied to the surface of aluminum valves for extended service life.

ANTIFREEZE: A substance (ethylene or propylene glycol) added to the coolant to prevent freezing in cold weather.

ANTI-FOAM AGENTS: Minimize fluid foaming from the whipping action encountered in the converter and planetary action.

ANTI-WEAR AGENTS: Zinc agents that control wear on the gears, bushings, and thrust washers.

ANTI-LOCK BRAKING SYSTEM: A supplementary system to the base hydraulic system that prevents sustained lock-up of the wheels during braking as well as automatically controlling wheel slip.

ANTI-ROLL BAR: See stabilizer bar.

ARC: A flow of electricity through the air between two electrodes or contact points that produces a spark.

ARMATURE: A laminated, soft iron core wrapped by a wire that converts electrical energy to mechanical energy as in a motor or relay. When rotated in a magnetic field, it changes mechanical energy into electrical energy as in a generator.

ATDC: After Top Dead Center.

ATF: Automatic transmission fluid.

ATMOSPHERIC PRESSURE: The pressure on the Earth's surface caused by the weight of the air in the atmosphere. At sea level, this pressure is 14.7 psi at 32°F (101 kPa at 0°C).

ATOMIZATION: The breaking down of a liquid into a fine mist that can be suspended in air.

AUXILIARY ADD-ON COOLER: A supplemental transmission fluid cooling device that is installed in series with the heat exchanger (cooler), located inside the radiator, to provide additional support to cool the hot fluid leaving the torque converter.

AUXILIARY PRESSURE: An added fluid pressure that is introduced into a regulator or balanced valve system to control valve movement. The auxiliary pressure itself can be either a fixed or a variable value. (See balanced valve; regulator valve.)

AWD: All wheel drive.

AXIAL FORCE: A side or end thrust force acting in or along the same plane as the power flow.

AXIAL PLAY: Movement parallel to a shaft or bearing bore.

AXLE CAPACITY: The maximum load-carrying capacity of the axle itself, as specified by the manufacturer. This is usually a higher number than the GAWR.

AXLE RATIO: This is a number (3.07:1, 4.56:1, for example) expressing the ratio between driveshaft revolutions and wheel revolutions. A low numerical ratio allows the engine to work easier because it doesn't have to turn as fast. A high numerical ratio means that the engine has to turn more rpm's to move the wheels through the same number of turns.

BACKFIRE: The sudden combustion of gases in the intake or exhaust system that results in a loud explosion.

BACKLASH: The clearance or play between two parts, such as meshed gears.

BACKPRESSURE: Restrictions in the exhaust system that slow the exit of exhaust gases from the combustion chamber.

BAKELITE®: A heat resistant, plastic insulator material commonly used in printed circuit boards and transistorized components.

BALANCED VALVE: A valve that is positioned by opposing auxiliary hydraulic pressures and/or spring force. Examples include mainline regulator, throttle, and governor valves. (See regulator valve.)

BAND: A flexible ring of steel with an inner lining of friction material. When tightened around the outside of a drum, a planetary member is held stationary to the transmission/transaxle case.

BALL BEARING: A bearing made up of hardened inner and outer races between which hardened steel balls roll.

BALL JOINT: A ball and matching socket connecting suspension components (steering knuckle to lower control arms). It permits rotating movement in any direction between the components that are joined.

BARO (BAROMETRIC PRESSURE SENSOR): Measures the change in the intake manifold pressure caused by changes in altitude.

BAROMETRIC MANIFOLD ABSOLUTE PRESSURE (BMAP) SENSOR: Operates similarly to a conventional MAP sensor; reads intake manifold pressure and is also responsible for determining altitude and barometric pressure prior to engine operation.

BAROMETRIC PRESSURE: (See atmospheric pressure.)

BALLAST RESISTOR: A resistor in the primary ignition circuit that lowers voltage after the engine is started to reduce wear on ignition components.

BATTERY: A direct current electrical storage unit, consisting of the basic active materials of lead and sulfuric acid, which converts chemical energy into electrical energy. Used to provide current for the operation of the starter as well as other equipment, such as the radio, lighting, etc.

BEAD: The portion of a tire that holds it on the rim.

BEARING: A friction reducing, supportive device usually located between a stationary part and a moving part.

BEFORE TOP DEAD CENTER (BTDC): The point just before the piston reaches the top of its travel on the compression stroke.

BELTED TIRE: Tire construction similar to bias-ply tires, but using two or more layers of reinforced belts between body plies and the tread.

BEZEL: Piece of metal surrounding radio, headlights, gauges or similar components; sometimes used to hold the glass face of a gauge in the dash.

BIAS-PLY TIRE: Tire construction, using body ply reinforcing cords which run at alternating angles to the center line of the tread.

BI-METAL TEMPERATURE SENSOR: Any sensor or switch made of two dissimilar types of metal that bend when heated or cooled due to the different expansion rates of the alloys. These types of sensors usually function as an on/off switch.

BLOCK: See Engine Block.

BLOW-BY: Combustion gases, composed of water vapor and unburned fuel, that leak past the piston rings into the crankcase during normal engine operation. These gases are removed by the PCV system to prevent the buildup of harmful acids in the crankcase.

BOOK TIME: See Labor Time.

BOOK VALUE: The average value of a car, widely used to determine trade-in and resale value.

BOOST VALVE: Used at the base of the regulator valve to increase mainline pressure.

BORE: Diameter of a cylinder.

BRAKE CALIPER: The housing that fits over the brake disc. The caliper holds the brake pads, which are pressed against the discs by the caliper pistons when the brake pedal is depressed.

BRAKE HORSEPOWER(BHP): The actual horsepower available at the engine flywheel as measured by a dynamometer.

BRAKE FADE: Loss of braking power, usually caused by excessive heat after repeated brake applications.

BRAKE HORSEPOWER: Usable horsepower of an engine measured at the crankshaft.

BRAKE PAD: A brake shoe and lining assembly used with disc brakes.

BRAKE PROPORTIONING VALVE: A valve on the master cylinder which restricts hydraulic brake pressure to the wheels to a specified amount, preventing wheel lock-up.

BREAKAWAY: Often used by Chrysler to identify first-gear operation in D and 2 ranges. In these ranges, first-gear operation depends on a one-way roller clutch that holds on acceleration and releases (breaks away) on deceleration, resulting in a freewheeling coast-down condition.

BRAKE SHOE: The backing for the brake lining. The term is, however, usually applied to the assembly of the brake backing and lining.

BREAKER POINTS: A set of points inside the distributor, operated by a cam, which make and break the ignition circuit.

BRINNELLING: A wear pattern identified by a series of indentations at regular intervals. This condition is caused by a lack of lube, overload situations, and/or vibrations.

BTDC: Before Top Dead Center.

BUMP: Sudden and forceful apply of a clutch or band.

BUSHING: A liner, usually removable, for a bearing; an anti-friction liner used in place of a bearing.

CALIFORNIA ENGINE: An engine certified by the EPA for use in California only; conforms to more stringent emission regulations than Federal engine.

CALIPER: A hydraulically activated device in a disc brake system,

which is mounted straddling the brake rotor (disc). The caliper contains at least one piston and two brake pads. Hydraulic pressure on the piston(s) forces the pads against the rotor.

CAPACITY: The quantity of electricity that can be delivered from a unit, as from a battery in ampere-hours, or output, as from a generator.

CAMBER: One of the factors of wheel alignment. Viewed from the front of the car, it is the inward or outward tilt of the wheel. The top of the tire will lean outward (positive camber) or inward (negative camber).

CAMSHAFT: A shaft in the engine on which are the lobes (cams) which operate the valves. The camshaft is driven by the crankshaft, via a belt, chain or gears, at one half the crankshaft speed.

CANCER: Rust on a car body.

CAPACITOR: A device which stores an electrical charge.

CARBON MONOXIDE (CO): A colorless, odorless gas given off as a normal byproduct of combustion. It is poisonous and extremely dangerous in confined areas, building up slowly to toxic levels without warning if adequate ventilation is not available.

CARBURETOR: A device, usually mounted on the intake manifold of an engine, which mixes the air and fuel in the proper proportion to allow even combustion.

CASTER: The forward or rearward tilt of an imaginary line drawn through the upper ball joint and the center of the wheel. Viewed from the sides, positive caster (forward tilt) lends directional stability, while negative caster (rearward tilt) produces instability.

CATALYTIC CONVERTER: A device installed in the exhaust system, like a muffler, that converts harmful byproducts of combustion into carbon dioxide and water vapor by means of a heat-producing chemical reaction.

CENTRIFUGAL ADVANCE: A mechanical method of advancing the spark timing by using flyweights in the distributor that react to centrifugal force generated by the distributor shaft rotation.

CENTRIFUGAL FORCE: The outward pull of a revolving object, away from the center of revolution. Centrifugal force increases with the speed of rotation.

CETANE RATING: A measure of the ignition value of diesel fuel. The higher the cetane rating, the better the fuel. Diesel fuel cetane rating is roughly comparable to gasoline octane rating.

CHECK VALVE: Any one-way valve installed to permit the flow of air, fuel or vacuum in one direction only.

CHOKE: The valve/plate that restricts the amount of air entering an engine on the induction stroke, thereby enriching the air/fuel ratio.

CHUGGLE: Bucking or jerking condition that may be engine related and may be most noticeable when converter clutch is engaged; similar to the feel of towing a trailer.

CIRCLIP: A split steel snapring that fits into a groove to hold various parts in place.

CIRCUIT BREAKER: A switch which protects an electrical circuit from overload by opening the circuit when the current flow exceeds a pre-determined level. Some circuit breakers must be reset manually, while most reset automatically.

CIRCUIT: Any unbroken path through which an electrical current can flow. Also used to describe fuel flow in some instances.

CIRCUIT, BYPASS: Another circuit in parallel with the major circuit through which power is diverted.

CIRCUIT, CLOSED: An electrical circuit in which there is no interruption of current flow.

CIRCUIT, GROUND: The non-insulated portion of a complete circuit used as a common potential point. In automotive circuits, the ground is composed of metal parts, such as the engine, body sheet metal, and frame and is usually a negative potential.

CIRCUIT, HOT: That portion of a circuit not at ground potential. The hot circuit is usually insulated and is connected to the positive side of the battery.

CIRCUIT, OPEN: A break or lack of contact in an electrical circuit, either intentional (switch) or unintentional (bad connection or broken wire).

CIRCUIT, PARALLEL: A circuit having two or more paths for current flow with common positive and negative tie points. The same voltage is applied to each load device or parallel branch.

CIRCUIT, SERIES: An electrical system in which separate parts are connected end to end, using one wire, to form a single path for current to flow.

CIRCUIT, SHORT: A circuit that is accidentally completed in an electrical path for which it was not intended.

CLAMPING (ISOLATION) DIODES: Diodes positioned in a circuit to prevent self-induction from damaging electronic components.

CLEARCOAT: A transparent layer which, when sprayed over a vehicle's paint job, adds gloss and depth as well as an additional protective coating to the finish.

CLUTCH: Part of the power train used to connect/disconnect power to the rear wheels.

CLUTCH, FLUID: The same as a fluid coupling. A fluid clutch or coupling performs the same function as a friction clutch by utilizing fluid friction and inertia as opposed to solid friction used by a friction clutch. (See fluid coupling.)

CLUTCH, FRICTION: A coupling device that provides a means of smooth and positive engagement and disengagement of engine torque to the vehicle powertrain. Transmission of power through the clutch is accomplished by bringing one or more rotating drive members into contact with complementing driven members.

COAST: Vehicle deceleration caused by engine braking conditions.

COEFFICIENT OF FRICTION: The amount of surface tension between two contacting surfaces; identified by a scientifically calculated number.

COIL: Part of the ignition system that boosts the relatively low voltage supplied by the car's electrical system to the high voltage required to fire the spark plugs.

COMBINATION MANIFOLD: An assembly which includes both the intake and exhaust manifolds in one casting.

COMBINATION VALVE: A device used in some fuel systems that routes fuel vapors to a charcoal storage canister instead of venting them into the atmo-sphere. The valve relieves fuel tank pressure and allows fresh air into the tank as the fuel level drops to prevent a vapor lock situation.

COMBUSTION CHAMBER: The part of the engine in the cylinder head where combustion takes place.

COMPOUND GEAR: A gear consisting of two or more simple gears with a common shaft.

COMPOUND PLANETARY: A gearset that has more than the three elements found in a simple gearset and is constructed by combining members of two planetary gearsets to create additional gear ratio possibilities.

COMPRESSION CHECK: A test involving removing each spark plug and inserting a gauge. When the engine is cranked, the gauge will record a pressure reading in the individual cylinder. General operating condition can be determined from a compression check.

COMPRESSION RATIO: The ratio of the volume between the piston and cylinder head when the piston is at the bottom of its stroke (bottom dead center) and when the piston is at the top of its stroke (top dead center).

COMPUTER: An electronic control module that correlates input data according to prearranged engineered instructions; used for the management of an actuator system or systems.

CONDENSER: 1. An electrical device which acts to store an electrical charge, preventing voltage surges. 2. A radiator-like device in the air conditioning system in which refrigerant gas condenses into a liquid, giving off heat.

CONDUCTOR: Any material through which an electrical current can be transmitted easily.

CONNECTING ROD: The connecting link between the crankshaft and piston.

CONSTANT VELOCITY JOINT: Type of universal joint in a halfshaft assembly in which the output shaft turns at a constant angular velocity without variation, provided that the speed of the input shaft is constant.

CONTINUITY: Continuous or complete circuit. Can be checked with an ohmmeter.

CONTROL ARM: The upper or lower suspension components which are mounted on the frame and support the ball joints and steering knuckles.

CONVENTIONAL IGNITION: Ignition system which uses breaker points.

CONVERTER: (See torque converter.)

CONVERTER LOCKUP: The switching from hydrodynamic to direct mechanical drive, usually through the application of a friction element called the converter clutch.

COOLANT: Mixture of water and anti-freeze circulated through the engine to carry off heat produced by the engine.

CORROSION INHIBITOR: An inhibitor in ATF that prevents corrosion of bushings, thrust washers, and oil cooler brazed joints.

COUNTERSHAFT: An intermediate shaft which is rotated by a mainshaft and transmits, in turn, that rotation to a working part.

COUPLING PHASE: Occurs when the torque converter is operating at its greatest hydraulic efficiency. The speed differential between the impeller and the turbine is at its minimum. At this point, the stator freewheels, and there is no torque multiplication.

CRANKCASE: The lower part of an engine in which the crankshaft and related parts operate.

CRANKSHAFT: Engine component (connected to pistons by connecting rods) which converts the reciprocating (up and down) motion of pistons to rotary motion used to turn the driveshaft.

CURB WEIGHT: The weight of a vehicle without passengers or payload, but including all fluids (oil, gas, coolant, etc.) and other equipment specified as standard.

CURRENT: The flow (or rate) of electrons moving through a circuit. Current is measured in amperes (amp).

CURRENT FLOW CONVENTIONAL: Current flows through a circuit from the positive terminal of the source to the negative terminal (plus to minus).

CURRENT FLOW, ELECTRON: Current or electrons flow from the negative terminal of the source, through the circuit, to the positive terminal (minus to plus).

CV-JOINT: Constant velocity joint.

CYCLIC VIBRATIONS: The off-center movement of a rotating object that is affected by its initial balance, speed of rotation, and working angles.

CYLINDER BLOCK: See engine block.

CYLINDER HEAD: The detachable portion of the engine, usually fastened to the top of the cylinder block and containing all or most of the combustion chambers. On overhead valve engines, it contains the valves and their operating parts. On overhead cam engines, it contains the camshaft as well.

CYLINDER: In an engine, the round hole in the engine block in which the piston(s) ride.

DATA LINK CONNECTOR (DLC): Current acronym/term applied to the federally mandated, diagnostic junction connector that is used to monitor ECM/PC/TCM inputs, processing strategies, and outputs including diagnostic trouble codes (DTCs).

DEAD CENTER: The extreme top or bottom of the piston stroke.

DECELERATION BUMP: When referring to a torque converter clutch in the applied position, a sudden release of the accelerator pedal causes a forceful reversal of power through the drivetrain (engine braking), just prior to the apply plate actually being released.

DELAYED (LATE OR EXTENDED): Condition where shift is expected but does not occur for a period of time, for example, where clutch or band engagement does not occur as quickly as expected during part throttle or wide open throttle apply of accelerator or when manually downshifting to a lower range.

DETENT: A spring-loaded plunger, pin, ball, or pawl used as a holding device on a ratchet wheel or shaft. In automatic transmissions, a detent mechanism is used for locking the manual valve in place.

DETENT DOWNSHIFT: (See kickdown.)

DETERGENT: An additive in engine oil to improve its operating characteristics.

DETONATION: An unwanted explosion of the air/fuel mixture in the combustion chamber caused by excess heat and compression, advanced timing, or an overly lean mixture. Also referred to as "ping".

DEXRON®: A brand of automatic transmission fluid.

DIAGNOSTIC TROUBLE CODES (DTCs): A digital display from the control module memory that identifies the input, processor, or output device circuit that is related to the powertrain emission/driveability malfunction detected. Diagnostic trouble codes can be read by the MIL to flash any codes or by using a handheld scanner.

DIAPHRAGM: A thin, flexible wall separating two cavities, such as in a vacuum advance unit.

DIESELING: The engine continues to run after the car is shut off; caused by fuel continuing to be burned in the combustion chamber.

DIFFERENTIAL: A geared assembly which allows the transmission of motion between drive axles, giving one axle the ability to rotate faster than the other, as in cornering.

DIFFERENTIAL AREAS: When opposing faces of a spool valve are acted upon by the same pressure but their areas differ in size, the face with the larger area produces the differential force and valve movement. (See spool valve.)

DIFFERENTIAL FORCE: (See differential areas.) digital readout: A display of numbers or a combination of numbers and letters.

DIGITAL VOLT OHMMETER: An electronic diagnostic tool used to measure voltage, ohms and amps as well as several other functions, with the readings displayed on a digital screen in tenths, hundredths and thousandths.

DIODE: An electrical device that will allow current to flow in one direction only.

DIRECT CURRENT (DC): Electrical current that flows in one direction only.

DIRECT DRIVE: The gear ratio is 1:1, with no change occurring in the torque and speed input/output relationship.

DISC BRAKE: A hydraulic braking assembly consisting of a brake disc, or rotor, mounted on an axle shaft, and a caliper assembly containing, usually two brake pads which are activated by hydraulic pressure. The pads are forced against the sides of the disc, creating friction which slows the vehicle.

DISPERSANTS: Suspend dirt and prevent sludge buildup. double bump (double feel): Two sudden and forceful applies of a clutch or band.

DISPLACEMENT: The total volume of air that is displaced by all pistons as the engine turns through one complete revolution.

DISTRIBUTOR: A mechanically driven device on an engine which is responsible for electrically firing the spark plug at a pre-determined point of the piston stroke.

DOHC: Double overhead camshaft.

DOUBLE OVERHEAD CAMSHAFT: The engine utilizes two camshafts mounted in one cylinder head. One camshaft operates the exhaust valves, while the other operates the intake valves.

DOWEL PIN: A pin, inserted in mating holes in two different parts allowing those parts to maintain a fixed relationship.

DRIVELINE: The drive connection between the transmission and the drive wheels.

DRIVE TRAIN: The components that transmit the flow of power from the engine to the wheels. The components include the clutch, transmission, driveshafts (or axle shafts in front wheel drive), U-joints and differential.

DRUM BRAKE: A braking system which consists of two brake shoes and one or two wheel cylinders, mounted on a fixed backing plate, and a brake drum, mounted on an axle, which revolves around the assembly.

DRY CHARGED BATTERY: Battery to which electrolyte is added when the battery is placed in service.

DVOM: Digital volt ohmmeter

DWELL: The rate, measured in degrees of shaft rotation, at which an electrical circuit cycles on and off.

DYNAMIC: A sealing application in which there is rotating or reciprocating motion between the parts.

EARLY: Condition where shift occurs before vehicle has reached proper speed, which tends to labor engine after upshift.

EBCM: See Electronic Control Unit (ECU).

ECM: See Electronic Control Unit (ECU).

ECU: Electronic control unit.

ELECTRODE: Conductor (positive or negative) of electric current.

ELECTROLYSIS: A surface etching or bonding of current conducting transmission/transaxle components that may occur when grounding straps are missing or in poor condition.

ELECTROLYTE: A solution of water and sulfuric acid used to activate the battery. Electrolyte is extremely corrosive.

ELECTROMAGNET: A coil that produces a magnetic field when current flows through its windings.

ELECTROMAGNETIC INDUCTION: A method to create (generate) current flow through the use of magnetism.

ELECTROMAGNETISM: The effects surrounding the relationship between electricity and magnetism.

ELECTROMOTIVE FORCE (EMF): The force or pressure (voltage) that causes current movement in an electrical circuit.

ELECTRONIC CONTROL UNIT: A digital computer that controls engine (and sometimes transmission, brake or other vehicle system) functions based on data received from various sensors. Examples used by some manufacturers include Electronic Brake Control Module (EBCM), Engine Control Module (ECM), Powertrain Control Module (PCM) or Vehicle Control Module (VCM).

ELECTRONIC IGNITION: A system in which the timing and firing of the spark plugs is controlled by an electronic control unit, usually called a module. These systems have no points or condenser.

ELECTRONIC PRESSURE CONTROL (EPC) SOLENOID: A specially designed solenoid containing a spool valve and spring assembly to control fluid mainline pressure. A variable current flow, controlled by the ECM/PCM, varies the internal force of the solenoid on the spool valve and resulting mainline pressure. (See variable force solenoid.)

ELECTRONICS: Miniaturized electrical circuits utilizing semiconductors, solid-state devices, and printed circuits. Electronic circuits utilize small amounts of power.

ELECTRONIFICATION: The application of electronic circuitry to a mechanical device. Regarding automatic transmissions, electrification is incorporated into converter clutch lockup, shift scheduling, and line pressure control systems.

ELECTROSTATIC DISCHARGE (ESD): An unwanted, high-voltage electrical current released by an individual who has taken on a static charge of electricity. Electronic components can be easily damaged by ESD.

ELEMENT: A device within a hydrodynamic drive unit designed with a set of blades to direct fluid flow.

ENAMEL: Type of paint that dries to a smooth, glossy finish.

END BUMP (END FEEL OR SLIP BUMP): Firmer feel at end of shift when compared with feel at start of shift.

END-PLAY: The clearance/gap between two components that allows for expansion of the parts as they warm up, to prevent binding and to allow space for lubrication.

ENERGY: The ability or capacity to do work.

ENGINE: The primary motor or power apparatus of a vehicle, which converts liquid or gas fuel into mechanical energy.

ENGINE BLOCK: The basic engine casting containing the cylinders, the crankshaft main bearings, as well as machined surfaces for the mounting of other components such as the cylinder head, oil pan, transmission, etc..

ENGINE BRAKING: Use of engine to slow vehicle by manually downshifting during zero-throttle coast down.

ENGINE CONTROL MODULE (ECM): Manages the engine and incorporates output control over the torque converter clutch solenoid. (Note: Current designation for the ECM in late model vehicles is PCM.)

ENGINE COOLANT TEMPERATURE (ECT) SENSOR: Prevents converter clutch engagement with a cold engine; also used for shift timing and shift quality.

EP LUBRICANT: EP (extreme pressure) lubricants are specially formulated for use with gears involving heavy loads (transmissions, differentials, etc.).

ETHYL: A substance added to gasoline to improve its resistance to knock, by slowing down the rate of combustion.

ETHYLENE GLYCOL: The base substance of antifreeze.

EXHAUST MANIFOLD: A set of cast passages or pipes which conduct exhaust gases from the engine.

FAIL-SAFE (BACKUP) CONTROL: A substitute value used by the PCM/TCM to replace a faulty signal from an input sensor. The temporary value allows the vehicle to continue to be operated.

FAST IDLE: The speed of the engine when the choke is on. Fast idle speeds engine warm-up.

FEDERAL ENGINE: An engine certified by the EPA for use in any of the 49 states (except California).

FEEDBACK: A circuit malfunction whereby current can find another path to feed load devices.

FEELER GAUGE: A blade, usually metal, of precisely predetermined thickness, used to measure the clearance between two parts.

FILAMENT: The part of a bulb that glows; the filament creates high resistance to current flow and actually glows from the resulting heat.

FINAL DRIVE: An essential part of the axle drive assembly where final gear reduction takes place in the powertrain. In RWD applications and north-south FWD applications, it must also change the power flow direction to the axle shaft by ninety degrees. (Also see axle ratio).

FIRING ORDER: The order in which combustion occurs in the cylinders of an engine. Also the order in which spark is distributed to the plugs by the distributor.

FIRM: A noticeable quick apply of a clutch or band that is considered normal with medium to heavy throttle shift; should not be confused with harsh or rough.

FLAME FRONT: The term used to describe certain aspects of the fuel explosion in the cylinders. The flame front should move in a controlled pattern across the cylinder, rather than simply exploding immediately.

FLARE (SLIPPING): A quick increase in engine rpm accompanied by momentary loss of torque; generally occurs during shift.

FLAT ENGINE: Engine design in which the pistons are horizontally opposed. Porsche, Subaru and some old VW are common examples of flat engines.

FLAT RATE: A dealership term referring to the amount of money paid to a technician for a repair or diagnostic service based on that particular service versus dealership's labor time (NOT based on the actual time the technician spent on the job).

FLAT SPOT: A point during acceleration when the engine seems to lose power for an instant.

FLOODING: The presence of too much fuel in the intake manifold and combustion chamber which prevents the air/fuel mixture from firing, thereby causing a no-start situation.

FLUID: A fluid can be either liquid or gas. In hydraulics, a liquid is used for transmitting force or motion.

FLUID COUPLING: The simplest form of hydrodynamic drive, the fluid coupling consists of two look-alike members with straight radial varies referred to as the impeller (pump) and the turbine. input torque is always equal to the output torque.

FLUID DRIVE: Either a fluid coupling or a fluid torque converter. (See hydrodynamic drive units.)

FLUID TORQUE CONVERTER: A hydrodynamic drive that has the ability to act both as a torque multiplier and fluid coupling. (See hydrodynamic drive units; torque converter.)

FLUID VISCOSITY: The resistance of a liquid to flow. A cold fluid (oil) has greater viscosity and flows more slowly than a hot fluid (oil).

FLYWHEEL: A heavy disc of metal attached to the rear of the crankshaft. It smoothes the firing impulses of the engine and keeps the crankshaft turning during periods when no firing takes place. The starter also engages the flywheel to start the engine.

FOOT POUND (ft. lbs. or sometimes, ft. lb.): The amount of energy or work needed to raise an item weighing one pound, a distance of one foot.

FREEZE PLUG: A plug in the engine block which will be pushed out if the coolant freezes. Sometimes called expansion plugs, they protect the block from cracking should the coolant freeze.

FRICTION: The resistance that occurs between contacting surfaces. This relationship is expressed by a ratio called the coefficient of friction (CL).

FRICTION, COEFFICIENT OF: The amount of surface tension between two contacting surfaces; expressed by a scientifically calculated number.

FRONT END ALIGNMENT: A service to set caster, camber and toe-in to the correct specifications. This will ensure that the car steers and handles properly and that the tires wear properly.

FRICTION MODIFIER: Changes the coefficient of friction of the fluid between the mating steel and composition clutch/band surfaces during the engagement process and allows for a certain amount of intentional slipping for a good "shift-feel." full throttle detent downshift: A quick apply of accelerator pedal to its full travel, forcing a downshift.

FRONTAL AREA: The total frontal area of a vehicle exposed to air flow.

FUEL FILTER: A component of the fuel system containing a porous paper element used to prevent any impurities from entering the engine through the fuel system. It usually takes the form of a canister-like housing, mounted in-line with the fuel hose, located anywhere on a vehicle between the fuel tank and engine.

FUEL INJECTION: A system replacing the carburetor that sprays fuel into the cylinder through nozzles. The amount of fuel can be more precisely controlled with fuel injection.

FULL FLOATING AXLE: An axle in which the axle housing extends through the wheel giving bearing support on the outside of the housing. The front axle of a four-wheel drive vehicle is usually a full floating axle, as are the rear axles of many larger (1 ton and over) pick-ups and vans.

FULL-TIME FOUR-WHEEL DRIVE: A four-wheel drive system that continuously delivers power to all four wheels. A differential between the front and rear driveshafts permits variations in axle speeds to control gear wind-up without damage.

FUSE: A protective device in a circuit which prevents circuit overload by breaking the circuit when a specific amperage is present. The device is constructed around a strip or wire of a lower amperage rating than the circuit it is designed to protect. When an amperage higher than that stamped on the fuse is present in the circuit, the strip or wire melts, opening the circuit.

FUSIBLE LINK: A piece of wire in a wiring harness that performs the same job as a fuse. If overloaded, the fusible link will melt and interrupt the circuit.

FWD: Front wheel drive.

GAWR: (Gross axle weight rating) the total maximum weight an axle is designed to carry.

GCW: (Gross combined weight) total combined weight of a tow vehicle and trailer.

GARAGE SHIFT: initial engagement feel of transmission, neutral to reverse or neutral to a forward drive.

GARAGE SHIFT FEEL: A quick check of the engagement quality and responsiveness of reverse and forward gears. This test is done with the vehicle stationary.

GEAR: A toothed mechanical device that acts as a rotating lever to transmit power or turning effort from one shaft to another. (See gear ratio.)

GEAR RATIO: A ratio expressing the number of turns a smaller gear will make to turn a larger gear through one revolution. The ratio is found by dividing the number of teeth on the smaller gear into the number of teeth on the larger gear.

GEARBOX: Transmission

GEAR REDUCTION: Torque is multiplied and speed decreased by the factor of the gear ratio. For example, a 3:1 gear ratio changes an input torque of 180 ft. lbs. and an input speed of 2700 rpm to 540 Ft. lbs. and 900 rpm, respectively. (No account is taken of frictional losses, which are always present.)

GEARTRAIN: A succession of intermeshing gears that form an assembly and provide for one or more torque changes as the power input is transmitted to the power output.

GEL COAT: A thin coat of plastic resin covering fiberglass body panels.

GENERATOR: A device which produces direct current (DC) necessary to charge the battery.

GOVERNOR: A device that senses vehicle speed and generates a hydraulic oil pressure. As vehicle speed increases, governor oil pressure rises.

GROUND CIRCUIT: (See circuit, ground.)

GROUND SIDE SWITCHING: The electrical/electronic circuit control switch is located after the circuit load.

GVWR: (Gross vehicle weight rating) total maximum weight a vehicle is designed to carry including the weight of the vehicle, passengers, equipment, gas, oil, etc.

HALOGEN: A special type of lamp known for its quality of brilliant white light. Originally used for fog lights and driving lights.

HARD CODES: DTCs that are present at the time of testing; also called continuous or current codes.

HARSH(ROUGH): An apply of a clutch or band that is more noticeable than a firm one; considered undesirable at any throttle position.

HEADER TANK: An expansion tank for the radiator coolant. It can be located remotely or built into the radiator.

HEAT RANGE: A term used to describe the ability of a spark plug to carry away heat. Plugs with longer nosed insulators take longer to carry heat off effectively.

HEAT RISER: A flapper in the exhaust manifold that is closed when the engine is cold, causing hot exhaust gases to heat the intake manifold providing better cold engine operation. A thermostatic spring opens the flapper when the engine warms up.

HEAVY THROTTLE: Approximately three-fourths of accelerator pedal travel.

HEMI: A name given an engine using hemispherical combustion chambers.

HERTZ (HZ): The international unit of frequency equal to one cycle per second (10,000 Hertz equals 10,000 cycles per second).

HIGH-IMPEDANCE DVOM (DIGITAL VOLT-OHMMETER): This styled device provides a built-in resistance value and is capable of limiting circuit current flow to safe milliamp levels.

HIGH RESISTANCE: Often refers to a circuit where there is an excessive amount of opposition to normal current flow.

HORSEPOWER: A measurement of the amount of work; one horsepower is the amount of work necessary to lift 33,000 lbs. one foot in one minute. Brake horsepower (bhp) is the horsepower delivered by an engine on a dynamometer. Net horsepower is the power remaining (measured at the flywheel of the engine) that can be used to turn the wheels after power is consumed through friction and running the engine accessories (water pump, alternator, air pump, fan etc.)

HOT CIRCUIT: (See circuit, hot; hot lead.) hot lead: A wire or conductor in the power side of the circuit. (See circuit, hot.)

HOT SIDE SWITCHING: The electrical/electronic circuit control switch is located before the circuit load.

HUB: The center part of a wheel or gear.

HUNTING (BUSYNESS): Repeating quick series of up-shifts and downshifts that causes noticeable change in engine rpm, for example, as in a 4-3-4 shift pattern.

HYDRAULICS: The use of liquid under pressure to transfer force of motion.

HYDROCARBON (HC): Any chemical compound made up of hydrogen and carbon. A major pollutant formed by the engine as a by-product of combustion.

HYDRODYNAMIC DRIVE UNITS: Devices that transmit power solely by the action of a kinetic fluid flow in a closed recirculating path. An impeller energizes the fluid and discharges the high-speed jet stream into the turbine for power output.

HYDROMETER: An instrument used to measure the specific gravity of a solution.

HYDROPLANING: A phenomenon of driving when water builds up under the tire tread, causing it to lose contact with the road. Slowing down will usually restore normal tire contact with the road.

HYPOID GEARSET: The drive pinion gear may be placed below or above the centerline of the driven gear; often used as a final drive gearset.

IDLE MIXTURE: The mixture of air and fuel (usually about 14:1) being fed to the cylinders. The idle mixture screw(s) are sometimes adjusted as part of a tune-up.

IDLER ARM: Component of the steering linkage which is a geometric duplicate of the steering gear arm. It supports the right side of the center steering link.

IMPELLER: Often called a pump, the impeller is the power input (drive) member of a hydrodynamic drive. As part of the torque converter cover, it acts as a centrifugal pump and puts the fluid in motion.

INCH POUND (inch lbs.; sometimes in. lb. or in. lbs.): One twelfth of a foot pound.

INDUCTANCE: The force that produces voltage when a conductor is passed through a magnetic field.

INDUCTION: A means of transferring electrical energy in the form of a magnetic field. Principle used in the ignition coil to increase voltage.

INITIAL FEEL: A distinct firmer feel at start of shift when compared with feel at finish of shift.

INJECTOR: A device which receives metered fuel under relatively low pressure and is activated to inject the fuel into the engine under relatively high pressure at a predetermined time.

INPUT: In an automatic transmission, the source of power from the engine is absorbed by the torque converter, which provides the power input into the transmission. The turbine drives the input(turbine)shaft.

INPUT SHAFT: The shaft to which torque is applied, usually carrying the driving gear or gears.

INTAKE MANIFOLD: A casting of passages or pipes used to conduct air or a fuel/air mixture to the cylinders.

INTERNAL GEAR: The ring-like outer gear of a planetary gearset with the gear teeth cut on the inside of the ring to provide a mesh with the planet pinions.

ISOLATION (CLAMPING) DIODES: Diodes positioned in a circuit to prevent self-induction from damaging electronic components.

IX ROTARY GEAR PUMP: Contains two rotating members, one shaped with internal gear teeth and the other with external gear teeth. As the gears separate, the fluid fills the gaps between gear teeth, is pulled across a crescent-shaped divider, and then is forced to flow through the outlet as the gears mesh.

IX ROTARY LOBE PUMP: Sometimes referred to as a gerotor type pump. Two rotating members, one shaped with internal lobes and the other with external lobes, separate and then mesh to cause fluid to flow.

JOURNAL: The bearing surface within which a shaft operates.

JUMPER CABLES: Two heavy duty wires with large alligator clips used to provide power from a charged battery to a discharged battery mounted in a vehicle.

JUMPSTART: Utilizing the sufficiently charged battery of one vehicle to start the engine of another vehicle with a discharged battery by the use of jumper cables.

KEY: A small block usually fitted in a notch between a shaft and a hub to prevent slippage of the two parts.

KICKDOWN: Detent downshift system; either linkage, cable, or electrically controlled.

KILO: A prefix used in the metric system to indicate one thousand.

KNOCK: Noise which results from the spontaneous ignition of a portion of the air-fuel mixture in the engine cylinder caused by overly advanced ignition timing or use of incorrectly low octane fuel for that engine.

KNOCK SENSOR: An input device that responds to spark knock, caused by over advanced ignition timing.

LABOR TIME: A specific amount of time required to perform a certain repair or diagnostic service as defined by a vehicle or after-market manufacturer .

LACQUER: A quick-drying automotive paint.

LATE: Shift that occurs when engine is at higher than normal rpm for given amount of throttle.

LIGHT-EMITTING DIODE (LED): A semiconductor diode that emits light as electrical current flows through it; used in some electronic display devices to emit a red or other color light.

LIGHT THROTTLE: Approximately one-fourth of accelerator pedal travel.

LIMITED SLIP: A type of differential which transfers driving force to the wheel with the best traction.

LIMP-IN MODE: Electrical shutdown of the transmission/ transaxle output solenoids, allowing only forward and reverse gears that are hydraulically energized by the manual valve. This permits the vehicle to be driven to a service facility for repair.

LIP SEAL: Molded synthetic rubber seal designed with an outer sealing edge (lip) that points into the fluid containing area to be sealed. This type of seal is used where rotational and axial forces are present.

LITHIUM-BASE GREASE: Chassis and wheel bearing grease using lithium as a base. Not compatible with sodium-base grease.

LOAD DEVICE: A circuit's resistance that converts the electrical energy into light, sound, heat, or mechanical movement.

LOAD RANGE: Indicates the number of plies at which a tire is rated. Load range B equals four-ply rating; C equals six-ply rating; and, D equals an eight-ply rating.

LOAD TORQUE: The amount of output torque needed from the transmission/transaxle to overcome the vehicle load.

LOCKING HUBS: Accessories used on part-time four-wheel drive systems that allow the front wheels to be disengaged from the drive train when four-wheel drive is not being used. When four-wheel drive is desired, the hubs are engaged, locking the wheels to the drive train.

LOCKUP CONVERTER: A torque converter that operates hydraulically and mechanically. When an internal apply plate (lockup plate) clamps to the torque converter cover, hydraulic slippage is eliminated.

LOCK RING: See Circlip or Snapring

MAGNET: Any body with the property of attracting iron or steel.

MAGNETIC FIELD: The area surrounding the poles of a magnet that is affected by its attraction or repulsion forces.

MAIN LINE PRESSURE: Often called control pressure or line pressure, it refers to the pressure of the oil leaving the pump and is controlled by the pressure regulator valve.

MALFUNCTION INDICATOR LAMP (MIL): Previously known as a check engine light, the dash-mounted MIL illuminates and signals the driver that an emission or driveability problem with the powertrain has been detected by the ECM/PCM. When this occurs, at least one diagnostic trouble code (DTC) has been stored into the control module memory.

MANIFOLD ABSOLUTE PRESSURE (MAP) SENSOR: Reads the amount of air pressure (vacuum) in the engine's intake manifold system; its signal is used to analyze engine load conditions.

MANIFOLD VACUUM: Low pressure in an engine intake manifold formed just below the throttle plates. Manifold vacuum is highest at idle and drops under acceleration.

MANIFOLD: A casting of passages or set of pipes which connect the cylinders to an inlet or outlet source.

MANUAL LEVER POSITION SWITCH (MLPS): A mechanical switching unit that is typically mounted externally to the transmission/transaxle to inform the PCM/ECM which gear range the driver has selected.

MANUAL VALVE: Located inside the transmission/transaxle, it is directly connected to the driver's shift lever. The position of the manual valve determines which hydraulic circuits will be charged with oil pressure and the operating mode of the transmission.

MANUAL VALVE LEVER POSITION SENSOR (MVLPS): The input from this device tells the TCM what gear range was selected.

MASS AIR FLOW (MAF) SENSOR: Measures the airflow into the engine.

MASTER CYLINDER: The primary fluid pressurizing device in a hydraulic system. In automotive use, it is found in brake and hydraulic clutch systems and is pedal activated, either directly or, in a power brake system, through the power booster.

MacPherson STRUT: A suspension component combining a shock absorber and spring in one unit.

MEDIUM THROTTLE: Approximately one-half of accelerator pedal travel.

MEGA: A metric prefix indicating one million.

MEMBER: An independent component of a hydrodynamic unit such as an impeller, a stator, or a turbine. It may have one or more elements.

MERCON: A fluid developed by Ford Motor Company in 1988. It contains a friction modifier and closely resembles operating characteristics of Dexron.

METAL SEALING RINGS: Made from cast iron or aluminum, their primary application is with dynamic components involving pressure sealing circuits of rotating members. These rings are designed with either butt or hook lock end joints.

METER (ANALOG): A linear-style meter representing data as lengths; a needle-style instrument interfacing with logical numerical increments. This style of electrical meter uses relatively low impedance internal resistance and cannot be used for testing electronic circuitry.

METER(DIGITAL): Uses numbers as a direct readout to show values. Most meters of this style use high impedance internal resistance and must be used for testing low current electronic circuitry.

MICRO: A metric prefix indicating one-millionth (0.000001).

MILLI: A metric prefix indicating one-thousandth (0.001).

MINIMUM THROTTLE: The least amount of throttle opening required for upshift; normally close to zero throttle.

MISFIRE: Condition occurring when the fuel mixture in a cylinder fails to ignite, causing the engine to run roughly.

MODULE: Electronic control unit, amplifier or igniter of solid state or integrated design which controls the current flow in the ignition primary circuit based on input from the pick-up coil. When the module opens the primary circuit, high secondary voltage is induced in the coil.

MODULATED: In an electronic-hydraulic converter clutch system (or shift valve system), the term modulated refers to the pulsing of a solenoid, at a variable rate. This action controls the buildup of oil pressure in the hydraulic circuit to allow a controlled amount of clutch slippage.

MODULATED CONVERTER CLUTCH CONTROL (MCCC): A pulse width duty cycle valve that controls the converter lockup apply pressure and maximizes smoother transitions between lock and unlock conditions.

MODULATOR PRESSURE (THROTTLE PRESSURE): A hydraulic signal oil pressure relating to the amount of engine load, based on either the amount of throttle plate opening or engine vacuum.

MODULATOR VALVE: A regulator valve that is controlled by engine vacuum, providing a hydraulic pressure that varies in relation to engine torque. The hydraulic torque signal functions to delay the shift pattern and provide a line pressure boost. (See throttle valve.)

MOTOR: An electromagnetic device used to convert electrical energy into mechanical energy.

MULTIPLE-DISC CLUTCH: A grouping of steel and friction lined plates that, when compressed together by hydraulic pressure acting upon a piston, lock or unlock a planetary member.

MULTI-WEIGHT: Type of oil that provides adequate lubrication at both high and low temperatures.

needed to move one amp through a resistance of one ohm.

MUSHY: Same as soft; slow and drawn out clutch apply with very little shift feel.

MUTUAL INDUCTION: The generation of current from one wire circuit to another by movement of the magnetic field surrounding a current-carrying circuit as its ampere flow increases or decreases.

NEEDLE BEARING: A bearing which consists of a number (usually a large number) of long, thin rollers.

NITROGEN OXIDE (NOx): One of the three basic pollutants found in the exhaust emission of an internal combustion engine. The amount of NOx usually varies in an inverse proportion to the amount of HC and CO.

NONPOSITIVE SEALING: A sealing method that allows some minor leakage, which normally assists in lubrication.

O2 SENSOR: Located in the engine's exhaust system, it is an input device to the ECM/PCM for managing the fuel delivery and ignition system. A scanner can be used to observe the fluctuating voltage readings produced by an O2 sensor as the oxygen content of the exhaust is analyzed.

O-RING SEAL: Molded synthetic rubber seal designed with a circular cross-section. This type of seal is used primarily in static applications.

OBD II (ON-BOARD DIAGNOSTICS, SECOND GENERATION): Refers to the federal law mandating tighter control of 1996 and newer vehicle emissions, active monitoring of related devices, and standardization of terminology, data link connectors, and other technician concerns.

OCTANE RATING: A number, indicating the quality of gasoline based on its ability to resist knock. The higher the number, the better the quality. Higher compression engines require higher octane gas.

OEM: Original Equipment Manufactured. OEM equipment is that furnished standard by the manufacturer.

OFFSET: The distance between the vertical center of the wheel and the mounting surface at the lugs. Offset is positive if the center is outside the lug circle; negative offset puts the center line inside the lug circle.

OHM'S LAW: A law of electricity that states the relationship between voltage, current, and resistance. Volts = amperes x ohms

OHM: The unit used to measure the resistance of conductor-to-electrical flow. One ohm is the amount of resistance that limits current flow to one ampere in a circuit with one volt of pressure.

OHMMETER: An instrument used for measuring the resistance, in ohms, in an electrical circuit.

ONE-WAY CLUTCH: A mechanical clutch of roller or sprag design that resists torque or transmits power in one direction only. It is used to either hold or drive a planetary member.

ONE-WAY ROLLER CLUTCH: A mechanical device that transmits or holds torque in one direction only.

OPENCIRCUIT: A break or lack of contact in an electrical circuit, either intentional (switch) or unintentional (bad connection or broken wire).

ORIFICE: Located in hydraulic oil circuits, it acts as a restriction. It slows down fluid flow to either create back pressure or delay pressure buildup downstream.

OSCILLOSCOPE: A piece of test equipment that shows electric impulses as a pattern on a screen. Engine performance can be analyzed by interpreting these patterns.

OUTPUT SHAFT: The shaft which transmits torque from a device, such as a transmission.

OUTPUT SPEED SENSOR (OSS): Identifies transmission/transaxle output shaft speed for shift timing and may be used to calculate TCC slip; often functions as the VSS (vehicle speed sensor).

OVERDRIVE: (1.) A device attached to or incorporated in a transmission/transaxle that allows the engine to turn less than one full revolution for every complete revolution of the wheels. The net effect is to reduce engine rpm, thereby using less fuel. A typical overdrive gear ratio would be .87:1, instead of the normal 1:1 in high gear. (2.) A gear assembly which produces more shaft revolutions than that transmitted to it.

OVERDRIVE PLANETARY GEARSET: A single planetary gearset designed to provide a direct drive and overdrive ratio. When coupled to a three-speed transmission/transaxle configuration, a four-speed/overdrive unit is present.

OVERHEAD CAMSHAFT (OHC): An engine configuration in which the camshaft is mounted on top of the cylinder head and operates the valve either directly or by means of rocker arms.

OVERHEAD VALVE (OHV): An engine configuration in which all of the valves are located in the cylinder head and the camshaft is located in the cylinder block. The camshaft operates the valves via lifters and pushrods.

OVERRUNCLUTCH: Another name for a one-way mechanical clutch. Applies to both roller and sprag designs.

OVERSTEER: The tendency of some vehicles, when steering into a turn, to over-respond or steer more than required, which could result in excessive slip of the rear wheels. Opposite of under-steer.

OXIDATION STABILIZERS: Absorb and dissipate heat. Automatic transmission fluid has high resistance to varnish and sludge buildup that occurs from excessive heat that is generated primarily in the torque converter. Local temperatures as high as 6000F (3150C) can occur at the clutch plates during engagement, and this heat must be absorbed and dissipated. If the fluid cannot withstand the heat, it burns or oxidizes, resulting in an almost immediate destruction of friction materials, clogged filter screen and hydraulic passages, and sticky valves.

OXIDES OF NITROGEN: See nitrogen oxide (NOx).

OXYGEN SENSOR: Used with a feedback system to sense the presence of oxygen in the exhaust gas and signal the computer which can use the voltage signal to determine engine operating efficiency and adjust the air/fuel ratio.

PARALLEL CIRCUIT: (See circuit, parallel.)

PARTS WASHER: A basin or tub, usually with a built-in pump mechanism and hose used for circulating chemical solvent for the purpose of cleaning greasy, oily and dirty components.

PART-TIME FOUR WHEEL DRIVE: A system that is normally in the two wheel drive mode and only runs in four-wheel drive when the system is manually engaged because more traction is desired. Two or four wheel drive is normally selected by a lever to engage the front axle, but if locking hubs are used, these must also be manually engaged in the Lock position. Otherwise, the front axle will not drive the front wheels.

PASSIVE RESTRAINT: Safety systems such as air bags or automatic seat belts which operate with no action required on the part of the driver or passenger. Mandated by Federal regulations on all vehicles sold in the U.S. after 1990.

PAYLOAD: The weight the vehicle is capable of carrying in addition to its own weight. Payload includes weight of the driver, passengers and cargo, but not coolant, fuel, lubricant, spare tire, etc.

PCM: Powertrain control module.

PCV VALVE: A valve usually located in the rocker cover that vents crankcase vapors back into the engine to be reburned.

PERCOLATION: A condition in which the fuel actually "boils," due to excessive heat. Percolation prevents proper atomization of the fuel causing rough running.

PICK-UP COIL: The coil in which voltage is induced in an electronic ignition.

PINION GEAR: The smallest gear in a drive gear assembly. piston: A disc or cup that fits in a cylinder bore and is free to move. In hydraulics, it provides the means of converting hydraulic pressure into a usable force. Examples of piston applications are found in servo, clutch, and accumulator units.

PING: A metallic rattling sound produced by the engine during acceleration. It is usually due to incorrect ignition timing or a poor grade of gasoline.

PINION: The smaller of two gears. The rear axle pinion drives the ring gear which transmits motion to the axle shafts.

PISTON RING: An open-ended ring which fits into a groove on the outer diameter of the piston. Its chief function is to form a seal between the piston and cylinder wall. Most automotive pistons have three rings: two for compression sealing; one for oil sealing.

PITMAN ARM: A lever which transmits steering force from the steering gear to the steering linkage.

PLANET CARRIER: A basic member of a planetary gear assembly that carries the pinion gears.

PLANET PINIONS: Gears housed in a planet carrier that are in constant mesh with the sun gear and internal gear. Because they have their own independent rotating centers, the pinions are capable of rotating around the sun gear or the inside of the internal gear.

PLANETARY GEAR RATIO: The reduction or overdrive ratio developed by a planetary gearset.

PLANETARY GEARSET: In its simplest form, it is made up of a basic assembly group containing a sun gear, internal gear, and planet carrier. The gears are always in constant mesh and offer a wide range of gear ratio possibilities.

PLANETARY GEARSET (COMPOUND): Two planetary gearsets combined together.

PLANETARY GEARSET (SIMPLE): An assembly of gears in constant mesh consisting of a sun gear, several pinion gears mounted in a carrier, and a ring gear. It provides gear ratio and direction changes, in addition to a direct drive and a neutral.

PLY RATING: A. rating given a tire which indicates strength (but not necessarily actual plies). A two-ply/four-ply rating has only two plies, but the strength of a four-ply tire.

POLARITY: Indication (positive or negative) of the two poles of a battery.

PORT: An opening for fluid intake or exhaust.

POSITIVE SEALING: A sealing method that completely prevents leakage.

POTENTIAL: Electrical force measured in volts; sometimes used interchangeably with voltage.

POWER: The ability to do work per unit of time, as expressed in horsepower; one horsepower equals 33,000 ft. lbs. of work per minute, or 550 ft. lbs. of work per second.

POWER FLOW: The systematic flow or transmission of power through the gears, from the input shaft to the output shaft.

POWER-TO-WEIGHT RATIO: Ratio of horsepower to weight of car.

POWERTRAIN: See Drivetrain.

POWERTRAIN CONTROL MODULE(PCM): Current designation for the engine control module (ECM). In many cases, late model vehicle control units manage the engine as well as the transmission. In other settings, the PCM controls the engine and is interfaced with a TCM to control transmission functions.

Ppm: Parts per million; unit used to measure exhaust emissions.

PREIGNITION: Early ignition of fuel in the cylinder, sometimes due to glowing carbon deposits in the combustion chamber. Preignition can be damaging since combustion takes place prematurely.

PRELOAD: A predetermined load placed on a bearing during assembly or by adjustment.

PRESS FIT: The mating of two parts under pressure, due to the inner diameter of one being smaller than the outer diameter of the other, or vice versa; an interference fit.

PRESSURE: The amount of force exerted upon a surface area.

PRESSURE CONTROL SOLENOID (PCS): An output device that provides a boost oil pressure to the mainline regulator valve to control line pressure. Its operation is determined by the amount of current sent from the PCM.

PRESSURE GAUGE: An instrument used for measuring the fluid pressure in a hydraulic circuit.

PRESSURE REGULATOR VALVE: In automatic transmissions, its purpose is to regulate the pressure of the pump output and supply the basic fluid pressure necessary to operate the transmission. The regulated fluid pressure may be referred to as mainline pressure, line pressure, or control pressure.

PRESSURE SWITCH ASSEMBLY (PSA): Mounted inside the transmission, it is a grouping of oil pressure switches that inputs to the PCM when certain hydraulic passages are charged with oil pressure.

PRESSURE PLATE: A spring-loaded plate (part of the clutch) that transmits power to the driven (friction) plate when the clutch is engaged.

PRIMARY CIRCUIT: The low voltage side of the ignition system which consists of the ignition switch, ballast resistor or resistance wire, bypass, coil, electronic control unit and pick-up coil as well as the connecting wires and harnesses.

PROFILE: Term used for tire measurement (tire series), which is the ratio of tire height to tread width.

PROM (PROGRAMMABLE READ-ONLY MEMORY): The heart of the computer that compares input data and makes the engineered program or strategy decisions about when to trigger the appropriate output based on stored computer instructions.

Pulse generator: A two-wire pickup sensor used to produce a fluctuating electrical signal. This changing signal is read by the controller to determine the speed of the object and can be used to measure transmission/transaxle input speed, output speed, and vehicle speed.

PSI: Pounds per square inch; a measurement of pressure.

PULSE WIDTH DUTY CYCLE SOLENOID (PULSE WIDTH MODULATED SOLENOID): A computer-controlled solenoid that turns on and off at a variable rate producing a modulated oil pressure; often referred to as a pulse width modulated (PWM) solenoid. Employed in many electronic automatic transmissions and transaxles, these solenoids are used to manage shift control and converter clutch hydraulic circuits.

PUSHROD: A steel rod between the hydraulic valve lifter and the valve rocker arm in overhead valve (OHV) engines.

PUMP: A mechanical device designed to create fluid flow and pressure buildup in a hydraulic system.

QUARTER PANEL: General term used to refer to a rear fender. Quarter panel is the area from the rear door opening to the tail light area and from rear wheel well to the base of the trunk and roof-line.

RACE: The surface on the inner or outer ring of a bearing on which the balls, needles or rollers move.

RACK AND PINION: A type of automotive steering system using a pinion gear attached to the end of the steering shaft. The pinion meshes with a long rack attached to the steering linkage.

RADIAL TIRE: Tire design which uses body cords running at right angles to the center line of the tire. Two or more belts are used to give tread strength. Radials can be identified by their characteristic sidewall bulge.

RADIATOR: Part of the cooling system for a water-cooled engine, mounted in the front of the vehicle and connected to the engine with rubber hoses. Through the radiator, excess combustion heat is dissipated into the atmosphere through forced convection using a water and glycol based mixture that circulates through, and cools, the engine.

RANGE REFERENCE AND CLUTCH/BAND APPLY CHART: A guide that shows the application of clutches and bands for each gear, within the selector range positions. These charts are extremely useful for understanding how the unit operates and for diagnosing malfunctions.

RAVIGNEAUX GEARSET: A compound planetary gearset that features matched dual planetary pinions (sets of two) mounted in a single planet carrier. Two sun gears and one ring mesh with the carrier pinions.

REACTION MEMBER: The stationary planetary member, in a planetary gearset, that is grounded to the transmission/transaxle case through the use of friction and wedging devices known as bands, disc clutches, and one-way clutches.

REACTION PRESSURE: The fluid pressure that moves a spool valve against an opposing force or forces; the area on which the opposing force acts. The opposing force can be a spring or a combination of spring force and auxiliary hydraulic force.

REACTOR, TORQUE CONVERTER: The reaction member of a fluid torque converter, more commonly called a stator. (See stator.)

REAR MAIN OIL SEAL: A synthetic or rope-type seal that prevents oil from leaking out of the engine past the rear main crankshaft bearing.

RECIRCULATING BALL: Type of steering system in which recirculating steel balls occupy the area between the nut and worm wheel, causing a reduction in friction.

RECTIFIER: A device (used primarily in alternators) that permits electrical current to flow in one direction only.

REDUCTION: (See gear reduction.) regulator valve: A valve that changes the pressure of the oil in a hydraulic circuit as the oil passes through the valve by bleeding off (or exhausting) some of the volume of oil supplied to the valve.

REFRIGERANT 12 (R-12) or 134 (R-134): The generic name of the refrigerant used in automotive air conditioning systems.

REGULATOR: A device which maintains the amperage and/or voltage levels of a circuit at predetermined values.

RELAY: A switch which automatically opens and/or closes a circuit.

RELAY VALVE: A valve that directs flow and pressure. Relay valves simply connect or disconnect interrelated passages without restricting the fluid flow or changing the pressure.

RELIEF VALVE: A spring-loaded, pressure-operated valve that limits oil pressure buildup in a hydraulic circuit to a predetermined maximum value.

RELUCTOR: A wheel that rotates inside the distributor and triggers the release of voltage in an electronic ignition.

RESERVOIR: The storage area for fluid in a hydraulic system; often called a sump.

RESIN: A liquid plastic used in body work.

RESIDUAL MAGNETISM: The magnetic strength stored in a material after a magnetizing field has been removed.

RESISTANCE: The opposition to the flow of current through a circuit or electrical device, and is measured in ohms. Resistance is equal to the voltage divided by the amperage.

RESISTOR SPARK PLUG: A spark plug using a resistor to shorten the spark duration. This suppresses radio interference and lengthens plug life.

RESISTOR: A device, usually made of wire, which offers a preset amount of resistance in an electrical circuit.

RESULTANT FORCE: The single effective directional thrust of the fluid force on the turbine produced by the vortex and rotary forces acting in different planes.

RETARD: Set the ignition timing so that spark occurs later (fewer degrees before TDC).

RHEOSTAT: A device for regulating a current by means of a variable resistance.

RING GEAR: The name given to a ring-shaped gear attached to a differential case, or affixed to a flywheel or as part of a planetary gear set.

ROADLOAD: grade.

ROCKER ARM: A lever which rotates around a shaft pushing down (opening) the valve with an end when the other end is pushed up by the pushrod. Spring pressure will later close the valve.

ROCKER PANEL: The body panel below the doors between the wheel opening.

ROLLER BEARING: A bearing made up of hardened inner and outer races between which hardened steel rollers move.

ROLLER CLUTCH: A type of one-way clutch design using rollers and springs mounted within an inner and outer cam race assembly.

ROTARY FLOW: The path of the fluid trapped between the blades of the members as they revolve with the rotation of the torque converter cover (rotational inertia).

ROTOR: (1.) The disc-shaped part of a disc brake assembly, upon which the brake pads bear; also called, brake disc. (2.) The device mounted atop the distributor shaft, which passes current to the distributor cap tower contacts.

ROTARY ENGINE: See Wankel engine.

RPM: Revolutions per minute (usually indicates engine speed).

RTV: A gasket making compound that cures as it is exposed to the atmosphere. It is used between surfaces that are not perfectly machined to one another, leaving a slight gap that the RTV fills and in which it hardens. The letters RTV represent room temperature vulcanizing.

RUN-ON: Condition when the engine continues to run, even when the key is turned off. See dieseling.

SEALED BEAM: A automotive headlight. The lens, reflector and filament from a single unit.

SEATBELT INTERLOCK: A system whereby the car cannot be started unless the seatbelt is buckled.

SECONDARY CIRCUIT: The high voltage side of the ignition system, usually above 20,000 volts. The secondary includes the ignition coil, coil wire, distributor cap and rotor, spark plug wires and spark plugs.

SELF-INDUCTION: The generation of voltage in a current-carrying wire by changing the amount of current flowing within that wire.

SEMI-CONDUCTOR: A material (silicon or germanium) that is neither a good conductor nor an insulator; used in diodes and transistors.

SEMI-FLOATING AXLE: In this design, a wheel is attached to the axle shaft, which takes both drive and cornering loads. Almost all solid axle passenger cars and light trucks use this design.

SENDING UNIT: A mechanical, electrical, hydraulic or electromagnetic device which transmits information to a gauge.

SENSOR: Any device designed to measure engine operating conditions or ambient pressures and temperatures. Usually electronic in nature and designed to send a voltage signal to an on-board computer, some sensors may operate as a simple on/off switch or they may provide a variable voltage signal (like a potentiometer) as conditions or measured parameters change.

SERIES CIRCUIT: (See circuit, series.)

SERPENTINE BELT: An accessory drive belt, with small multiple v-ribs, routed around most or all of the engine-powered accessories such as the alternator and power steering pump. Usually both the front and the back side of the belt comes into contact with various pulleys.

SERVO: In an automatic transmission, it is a piston in a cylinder assembly that converts hydraulic pressure into mechanical force and movement; used for the application of the bands and clutches.

SHIFT BUSYNESS: When referring to a torque converter clutch, it is the frequent apply and release of the clutch plate due to uncommon driving conditions.

SHIFT VALVE: Classified as a relay valve, it triggers the automatic shift in response to a governor and a throttle signal by directing fluid to the appropriate band and clutch apply combination to cause the shift to occur.

SHIM: Spacers of precise, predetermined thickness used between parts to establish a proper working relationship.

SHIMMY: Vibration (sometimes violent) in the front end caused by misaligned front end, out of balance tires or worn suspension components.

SHORT CIRCUIT: An electrical malfunction where current takes the path of least resistance to ground (usually through damaged insulation). Current flow is excessive from low resistance resulting in a blown fuse.

SHUDDER: Repeated jerking or stick-slip sensation, similar to chuggle but more severe and rapid in nature, that may be most noticeable during certain ranges of vehicle speed; also used to define condition after converter clutch engagement.

SIMPSON GEARSET: A compound planetary gear train that integrates two simple planetary gearsets referred to as the front planetary and the rear planetary.

SINGLE OVERHEAD CAMSHAFT: See overhead camshaft.

SKIDPLATE: A metal plate attached to the underside of the body to protect the fuel tank, transfer case or other vulnerable parts from damage.

SLAVE CYLINDER: In automotive use, a device in the hydraulic clutch system which is activated by hydraulic force, disengaging the clutch.

SLIPPING: Noticeable increase in engine rpm without vehicle speed increase; usually occurs during or after initial clutch or band engagement.

SLUDGE: Thick, black deposits in engine formed from dirt, oil, water, etc. It is usually formed in engines when oil changes are neglected.

SNAP RING: A circular retaining clip used inside or outside a shaft or part to secure a shaft, such as a floating wrist pin.

SOFT: Slow, almost unnoticeable clutch apply with very little shift feel.

SOFTCODES: DTCs that have been set into the PCM memory but are not present at the time of testing; often referred to as history or intermittent codes.

SOHC: Single overhead camshaft.

SOLENOID: An electrically operated, magnetic switching device.

SPALLING: A wear pattern identified by metal chips flaking off the hardened surface. This condition is caused by foreign particles, overloading situations, and/or normal wear.

SPARK PLUG: A device screwed into the combustion chamber of a spark ignition engine. The basic construction is a conductive core inside of a ceramic insulator, mounted in an outer conductive base. An electrical charge from the spark plug wire travels along the conductive core and jumps a preset air gap to a grounding point or points at the end of the conductive base. The resultant spark ignites the fuel/air mixture in the combustion chamber.

SPECIFIC GRAVITY (BATTERY): The relative weight of liquid (battery electrolyte) as compared to the weight of an equal volume of water.

SPLINES: Ridges machined or cast onto the outer diameter of a shaft or inner diameter of a bore to enable parts to mate without rotation.

SPLIT TORQUE DRIVE: In a torque converter, it refers to parallel paths of torque transmission, one of which is mechanical and the other hydraulic.

SPONGY PEDAL: A soft or spongy feeling when the brake pedal is depressed. It is usually due to air in the brake lines.

SPOOLVALVE: A precision-machined, cylindrically shaped valve made up of lands and grooves. Depending on its position in the valve bore, various interconnecting hydraulic circuit passages are either opened or closed.

SPRAG CLUTCH: A type of one-way clutch design using cams or contoured-shaped sprags between inner and outer races. (See one-way clutch.)

SPRUNG WEIGHT: The weight of a car supported by the springs.

SQUARE-CUT SEAL: Molded synthetic rubber seal designed with a square- or rectangular-shaped cross-section. This type of seal is used for both dynamic and static applications.

SRS: Supplemental restraint system

STABILIZER (SWAY) BAR: A bar linking both sides of the suspension. It resists sway on turns by taking some of added load from one wheel and putting it on the other.

STAGE: The number of turbine sets separated by a stator. A turbine set may be made up of one or more turbine members. A three-element converter is classified as a single stage.

STALL: In fluid drive transmission/transaxle applications, stall refers to engine rpm with the transmission/transaxle engaged and the vehicle stationary; throttle valve can be in any position between closed and wide open.

STALL SPEED: In fluid drive transmission/transaxle applications, stall speed refers to the maximum engine rpm with the transmission/transaxle engaged and vehicle stationary, when the throttle valve is wide open. (See stall; stall test.)

STALL TEST: A procedure recommended by many manufacturers to help determine the integrity of an engine, the torque converter stator, and certain clutch and band combinations. With the shift lever in each of the forward and reverse positions and with the brakes firmly applied, the accelerator pedal is momentarily pressed to the wide open throttle (WOT) position. The engine rpm reading at full throttle can provide clues for diagnosing the condition of the items listed above.

STALL TORQUE: The maximum design or engineered torque ratio of a fluid torque converter, produced under stall speed conditions. (See stall speed.)

STARTER: A high-torque electric motor used for the purpose of starting the engine, typically through a high ratio geared drive connected to the flywheel ring gear.

STATIC: A sealing application in which the parts being sealed do not move in relation to each other.

STATOR (REACTOR): The reaction member of a fluid torque converter that changes the direction of the fluid as it leaves the turbine to enter the impeller vanes. During the torque multiplication phase, this action assists the impeller's rotary force and results in an increase in torque.

STEERING GEOMETRY: Combination of various angles of suspension components (caster, camber, toe-in); roughly equivalent to front end alignment.

STRAIGHT WEIGHT: Term designating motor oil as suitable for use within a narrow range of temperatures. Outside the narrow temperature range its flow characteristics will not adequately lubricate.

STROKE: The distance the piston travels from bottom dead center to top dead center.

SUBSTITUTION: Replacing one part suspected of a defect with a like part of known quality.

SUMP: The storage vessel or reservoir that provides a ready source of fluid to the pump. In an automatic transmission, the sump is the oil pan. All fluid eventually returns to the sump for recycling into the hydraulic system.

SUN GEAR: In a planetary gearset, it is the center gear that meshes with a cluster of planet pinions.

SUPERCHARGER: An air pump driven mechanically by the engine through belts, chains, shafts or gears from the crankshaft. Two general types of supercharger are the positive displacement and centrifugal type, which pump air in direct relationship to the speed of the engine.

SUPPLEMENTAL RESTRAINT SYSTEM: See air bag.

SURGE: Repeating engine-related feeling of acceleration and deceleration that is less intense than chuggle.

SWITCH: A device used to open, close, or redirect the current in an electrical circuit.

SYNCHROMESH: A manual transmission/transaxle that is equipped with devices (synchronizers) that match the gear speeds so that the transmission/transaxle can be downshifted without clashing gears.

SYNTHETIC OIL: Non-petroleum based oil.

TACHOMETER: A device used to measure the rotary speed of an engine, shaft, gear, etc., usually in rotations per minute.

TDC: Top dead center. The exact top of the piston's stroke.

TEFLON SEALING RINGS: Teflon is a soft, durable, plastic-like material that is resistant to heat and provides excellent sealing. These rings are designed with either scarf-cut joints or as one-piece rings. Teflon sealing rings have replaced many metal ring applications.

TERMINAL: A device attached to the end of a wire or cable to make an electrical connection.

TEST LIGHT, CIRCUIT-POWERED: Uses available circuit voltage to test circuit continuity.

TEST LIGHT, SELF-POWERED: Uses its own battery source to test circuit continuity.

THERMISTOR: A special resistor used to measure fluid temperature; it decreases its resistance with increases in temperature.

THERMOSTAT: A valve, located in the cooling system of an engine, which is closed when cold and opens gradually in response to engine heating, controlling the temperature of the coolant and rate of coolant flow.

THERMOSTATIC ELEMENT: A heat-sensitive, spring-type device that controls a drain port from the upper sump area to the lower sump. When the transaxle fluid reaches operating temperature, the port is closed and the upper sump fills, thus reducing the fluid level in the lower sump.

THROTTLE POSITION (TP) SENSOR: Reads the degree of throttle opening; its signal is used to analyze engine load conditions. The ECM/PCM decides to apply the TCC, or to disengage it for coast or load conditions that need a converter torque boost.

THROTTLE PRESSURE/MODULATOR PRESSURE: A hydraulic signal oil pressure relating to the amount of engine load, based on either the amount of throttle plate opening or engine vacuum.

THROTTLE VALVE: A regulating or balanced valve that is controlled mechanically by throttle linkage or engine vacuum. It sends a hydraulic signal to the shift valve body to control shift timing and shift quality. (See balanced valve; modulator valve.)

THROW-OUT BEARING: As the clutch pedal is depressed, the throwout bearing moves against the spring fingers of the pressure plate, forcing the pressure plate to disengage from the driven disc.

TIE ROD: A rod connecting the steering arms. Tie rods have threaded ends that are used to adjust toe-in.

TIE-UP: Condition where two opposing clutches are attempting to apply at same time, causing engine to labor with noticeable loss of engine rpm.

TIMING BELT: A square-toothed, reinforced rubber belt that is driven by the crankshaft and operates the camshaft.

TIMING CHAIN: A roller chain that is driven by the crankshaft and operates the camshaft.

TIRE ROTATION: Moving the tires from one position to another to make the tires wear evenly.

TOE-IN (OUT): A term comparing the extreme front and rear of the front tires. Closer together at the front is toe-in; farther apart at the front is toe-out.

TOP DEAD CENTER (TDC): The point at which the piston reaches the top of its travel on the compression stroke.

TORQUE: Measurement of turning or twisting force, expressed as foot-pounds or inch-pounds.

TORQUE CONVERTER: A turbine used to transmit power from a driving member to a driven member via hydraulic action, providing changes in drive ratio and torque. In automotive use, it links the driveplate at the rear of the engine to the automatic transmission.

TORQUE CONVERTER CLUTCH: The apply plate (lockup plate) assembly used for mechanical power flow through the converter.

TORQUE PHASE: Sometimes referred to as slip phase or stall phase, torque multiplication occurs when the turbine is turning at a slower speed than the impeller, and the stator is reactionary (stationary). This sequence generates a boost in output torque.

TORQUE RATING (STALL TORQUE): The maximum torque multiplication that occurs during stall conditions, with the engine at wide open throttle (WOT) and zero turbine speed.

TORQUE RATIO: An expression of the gear ratio factor on torque effect. A 3:1 gear ratio or 3:1 torque ratio increases the torque input by the ratio factor of 3. Input torque (100 ft. lbs.)x 3 = output torque (300 ft. lbs.)

TRACTION: The amount of usable tractive effort before the drive wheels slip on the road contact surface.

TORSION BAR SUSPENSION: Long rods of spring steel which take the place of springs. One end of the bar is anchored and the other arm (attached to the suspension) is free to twist. The bars' resistance to twisting causes springing action.

TRACK: Distance between the centers of the tires where they contact the ground.

TRACTION CONTROL: A control system that prevents the spinning of a vehicle's drive wheels when excess power is applied.

TRACTIVE EFFORT: The amount of force available to the drive wheels, to move the vehicle.

TRANSAXLE: A single housing containing the transmission and differential. Transaxles are usually found on front engine/front wheel drive or rear engine/rear wheel drive cars.

TRANSDUCER: A device that changes energy from one form to another. For example, a transducer in a microphone changes sound energy to electrical energy. In automotive air-conditioning controls used in automatic temperature systems, a transducer changes an electrical signal to a vacuum signal, which operates mechanical doors.

TRANSMISSION: A powertrain component designed to modify torque and speed developed by the engine; also provides direct drive, reverse, and neutral.

TRANSMISSION CONTROL MODULE (TCM): Manages transmission functions. These vary according to the manufacturer's product design but may include converter clutch operation, electronic shift scheduling, and mainline pressure.

TRANSMISSION FLUID TEMPERATURE (TFT) SENSOR: Originally called a transmission oil temperature (TOT) sensor, this input device to the ECM/PCM senses the fluid temperature and provides a resistance value. It operates on the thermistor principle.

TRANSMISSION INPUT SPEED (TIS) SENSOR: Measures turbine shaft (input shaft) rpm's and compares to engine rpm's to determine torque converter slip. When compared to the transmission output speed sensor or VSS, gear ratio and clutch engagement timing can be determined.

TRANSMISSION OIL TEMPERATURE (TOT) SENSOR: (See transmission fluid temperature (TFT) sensor.)

TRANSMISSION RANGE SELECTOR (TRS) SWITCH: Tells the module which gear shift position the driver has chosen. turbine: The output (driven) member of a fluid coupling or fluid torque converter. It is splined to the input (turbine) shaft of the transmission.

TRANSFER CASE: A gearbox driven from the transmission that delivers power to both front and rear driveshafts in a four-wheel drive system. Transfer cases usually have a high and low range set of gears, used depending on how much pulling power is needed.

TRANSISTOR: A semi-conductor component which can be actuated by a small voltage to perform an electrical switching function.

TREAD WEAR INDICATOR: Bars molded into the tire at right angles to the tread that appear as horizontal bars when 1/16in. of tread remains.

TREAD WEAR PATTERN: The pattern of wear on tires which can be "read" to diagnose problems in the front suspension.

TUNE-UP: A regular maintenance function, usually associated with the replacement and adjustment of parts and components in the electrical and fuel systems of a vehicle for the purpose of attaining optimum performance.

TURBOCHARGER: An exhaust driven pump which compresses intake air and forces it into the combustion chambers at higher than atmospheric pressures. The increased air pressure allows more fuel to be burned and results in increased horsepower being produced.

TURBULENCE: The interference of molecules of a fluid (or vapor) with each other in a fluid flow.

TYPE F: Transmission fluid developed and used by Ford Motor Company up to 1982. This fluid type provides a high coefficient of friction.

TYPE 7176: The preferred choice of transmission fluid for Chrysler automatic transmissions and transaxles. Developed in 1986, it closely resembles Dexron and Mercon. Type 7176 is the recommended service fill fluid for all Chrysler products utilizing a lockup torque converter dating back to 1978.

U-JOINT (UNIVERSAL JOINT): A flexible coupling in the drive train that allows the driveshafts or axle shafts to operate at different angles and still transmit rotary power.

UNDERSTEER: The tendency of a car to continue straight ahead while negotiating a turn.

UNIT BODY: Design in which the car body acts as the frame.

UNLEADED FUEL: Fuel which contains no lead (a common gasoline additive). The presence of lead in fuel will destroy the functioning elements of a catalytic converter, making it useless.

UNSPRUNG WEIGHT: The weight of car components not supported by the springs (wheels, tires, brakes, rear axle, control arms, etc.).

UPSHIFT: A shift that results in a decrease in torque ratio and an increase in speed.

VACUUM: A negative pressure; any pressure less than atmospheric pressure.

VACUUM ADVANCE: A device which advances the ignition timing in response to increased engine vacuum.

VACUUM GAUGE: An instrument used for measuring the existing vacuum in a vacuum circuit or chamber. The unit of measure is inches (of mercury in a barometer).

VACUUM MODULATOR: Generates a hydraulic oil pressure in response to the amount of engine vacuum.

VALVES: Devices that can open or close fluid passages in a hydraulic system and are used for directing fluid flow and controlling pressure.

VALVE BODY ASSEMBLY: The main hydraulic control assembly of the transmission/transaxle that contains numerous valves, check balls, and other components to control the distribution of pressurized oil throughout the transmission.

VALVE CLEARANCE: The measured gap between the end of the valve stem and the rocker arm, cam lobe or follower that activates the valve.

VALVE GUIDES: The guide through which the stem of the valve passes. The guide is designed to keep the valve in proper alignment.

VALVE LASH (clearance): The operating clearance in the valve train.

VALVE TRAIN: The system that operates intake and exhaust valves, consisting of camshaft, valves and springs, lifters, pushrods and rocker arms.

VAPOR LOCK: Boiling of the fuel in the fuel lines due to excess heat. This will interfere with the flow of fuel in the lines and can completely stop the flow. Vapor lock normally only occurs in hot weather.

VARIABLE DISPLACEMENT (VARIABLE CAPACITY) VANE PUMP: Slipper-type vanes, mounted in a revolving rotor and contained within the bore of a movable slide, capture and then force fluid to flow. Movement of the slide to various positions changes the size of the vane chambers and the amount of fluid flow. Note: GM refers to this pump design as variable displacement, and Ford terms it variable capacity.

VARIABLE FORCE SOLENOID (VFS): Commonly referred to as the electronic pressure control (EPC) solenoid, it replaces the cable/linkage style of TV system control and is integrated with a spool valve and spring assembly to control pressure. A variable computer-controlled current flow varies the internal force of the solenoid on the spool valve and resulting control pressure.

VARIABLE ORIFICE THERMAL VALVE: Temperature-sensitive hydraulic oil control device that adjusts the size of a circuit path opening. By altering the size of the opening, the oil flow rate is adapted for cold to hot oil viscosity changes.

VARNISH: Term applied to the residue formed when gasoline gets old and stale.

VCM: See Electronic Control Unit (ECU).

VEHICLE SPEED SENSOR (VSS): Provides an electrical signal to the computer module, measuring vehicle speed, and affects the torque converter clutch engagement and release.

VESPEL SEALING RINGS: Hard plastic material that produces excellent sealing in dynamic settings. These rings are found in late versions of the 4T60 and in all 4T60-E and 4T80-E transaxles.

VISCOSITY: The ability of a fluid to flow. The lower the viscosity rating, the easier the fluid will flow. 10 weight motor oil will flow much easier than 40 weight motor oil.

VISCOSITY INDEX IMPROVERS: Keeps the viscosity nearly constant with changes in temperature. This is especially important at low temperatures, when the oil needs to be thin to aid in shifting and for cold-weather starting. Yet it must not be so thin that at high temperatures it will cause excessive hydraulic leakage so that pumps are unable to maintain the proper pressures.

VISCOUS CLUTCH: A specially designed torque converter clutch apply plate that, through the use of a silicon fluid, clamps smoothly and absorbs torsional vibrations.

VOLT: Unit used to measure the force or pressure of electricity. It is defined as the pressure

VOLTAGE: The electrical pressure that causes current to flow. Voltage is measured in volts (V).

VOLTAGE, APPLIED: The actual voltage read at a given point in a circuit. It equals the available voltage of the power supply minus the losses in the circuit up to that point.

VOLTAGE DROP: The voltage lost or used in a circuit by normal loads such as a motor or lamp or by abnormal loads such as a poor (high-resistance) lead or terminal connection.

VOLTAGE REGULATOR: A device that controls the current output of the alternator or generator.

VOLTMETER: An instrument used for measuring electrical force in units called volts. Voltmeters are always connected parallel with the circuit being tested.

VORTEX FLOW: The crosswise or circulatory flow of oil between the blades of the members caused by the centrifugal pumping action of the impeller.

WANKEL ENGINE: An engine which uses no pistons. In place of pistons, triangular-shaped rotors revolve in specially shaped housings.

WATER PUMP: A belt driven component of the cooling system that mounts on the engine, circulating the coolant under pressure.

WATT: The unit for measuring electrical power. One watt is the product of one ampere and one volt (watts equals amps times volts). Wattage is the horsepower of electricity (746 watts equal one horsepower).

WHEEL ALIGNMENT: Inclusive term to describe the front end geometry (caster, camber, toe-in/out).

WHEEL CYLINDER: Found in the automotive drum brake assembly, it is a device, actuated by hydraulic pressure, which, through internal pistons, pushes the brake shoes outward against the drums.

WHEEL WEIGHT: Small weights attached to the wheel to balance the wheel and tire assembly. Out-of-balance tires quickly wear out and also give erratic handling when installed on the front.

WHEELBASE: Distance between the center of front wheels and the center of rear wheels.

WIDE OPEN THROTTLE (WOT): Full travel of accelerator pedal.

WORK: The force exerted to move a mass or object. Work involves motion; if a force is exerted and no motion takes place, no work is done. Work per unit of time is called power. Work = force x distance = ft. lbs. 33,000 ft. lbs. in one minute = 1 horsepower

ZERO-THROTTLE COAST DOWN: A full release of accelerator pedal while vehicle is in motion and in drive range.

Commonly Used Abbreviations

2

2WD	Two Wheel Drive

4

4WD	Four Wheel Drive

A

A/C	Air Conditioning
ABDC	After Bottom Dead Center
ABS	Anti-lock Brakes
AC	Alternating Current
ACL	Air cleaner
ACT	Air Charge Temperature
AIR	Secondary Air Injection
ALCL	Assembly Line Communications Link
ALDL	Assembly Line Diagnostic Link
AT	Automatic Transaxle/Transmission
ATDC	After Top Dead Center
ATF	Automatic Transmission Fluid
ATS	Air Temperature Sensor
AWD	All Wheel Drive

B

BAP	Barometric Absolute Pressure
BARO	Barometric Pressure
BBDC	Before Bottom Dead Center
BCM	Body Control Module
BDC	Bottom Dead Center
BPT	Backpressure Transducer
BTDC	Before Top Dead Center
BVSV	Bimetallic Vacuum Switching Valve

C

CAC	Charge Air Cooler
CARB	California Air Resources Board
CAT	Catalytic Converter
CCC	Computer Command Control
CCCC	Computer Controlled Catalytic Converter
CCCI	Computer Controlled Coil Ignition
CCD	Computer Controlled Dwell
CDI	Capacitor Discharge Ignition
CEC	Computerized Engine Control
CFI	Continuous Fuel Injection
CIS	Continuous Injection System
CIS-E	Continuous Injection System - Electronic
CKP	Crankshaft Position
CL	Closed Loop
CMP	Camshaft Position
CPP	Clutch Pedal Position
CTOX	Continuous Trap Oxidizer System
CTP	Closed Throttle Position
CVC	Constant Vacuum Control
CYL	Cylinder

D

DBC	Dual Bed Catalyst
DC	Direct Current
DFI	Direct Fuel Injection
DIS	Distributorless Ignition System
DLC	Data Link Connector
DMM	Digital Multimeter
DOHC	Double Overhead Camshaft
DRB	Diagnostic Readout Box
DTC	Diagnostic Trouble Code
DTM	Diagnostic Test Mode
DVOM	Digital Volt/Ohmmeter

E

EBCM	Electronic Brake Control Module
ECM	Engine Control Module
ECT	Engine Coolant Temperature
ECU	Engine Control Unit or Electronic Control Unit
EDIS	Electronic Distributorless Ignition System
EEC	Electronic Engine Control
EEPROM	Electrically Erasable Programmable Read Only Memory
EFE	Early Fuel Evaporation
EGR	Exhaust Gas Recirculation
EGRT	Exhaust Gas Recirculation Temperature
EGRVC	EGR Valve Control
EPROM	Erasable Programmable Read Only Memory
EVAP	Evaporative Emissions
EVP	EGR Valve Position

F

FBC	Feedback Carburetor
FEEPROM	Flash Electrically Erasable Programmable Read Only Memory
FF	Flexible Fuel
FI	Fuel Injection
FT	Fuel Trim
FWD	Front Wheel Drive

G

GND	Ground

H

HAC	High Altitude Compensation
HEGO	Heated Exhaust Gas Oxygen sensor
HEI	High Energy Ignition
HO2 Sensor	Heated Oxygen Sensor

I

IAC	Idle Air Control
IAT	Intake Air Temperature
ICM	Ignition Control Module
IFI	Indirect Fuel Injection
IFS	Inertia Fuel Shutoff
ISC	Idle Speed Control
IVSV	Idle Vacuum Switching Valve

Commonly Used Abbreviations

K

KOEO	Key On, Engine Off
KOER	Key ON, Engine Running
KS	Knock Sensor

M

MAF	Mass Air Flow
MAP	Manifold Absolute Pressure
MAT	Manifold Air Temperature
MC	Mixture Control
MDP	Manifold Differential Pressure
MFI	Multiport Fuel Injection
MIL	Malfunction Indicator Lamp or Maintenance
MST	Manifold Surface Temperature
MVZ	Manifold Vacuum Zone

N

NVRAM	Nonvolatile Random Access Memory

O

O2 Sensor	Oxygen Sensor
OBD	On-Board Diagnostic
OC	Oxidation Catalyst
OHC	Overhead Camshaft
OL	Open Loop

P

P/S	Power Steering
PAIR	Pulsed Secondary Air Injection
PCM	Powertrain Control Module
PCS	Purge Control Solenoid
PCV	Positive Crankcase Ventilation
PIP	Profile Ignition Pick-up
PNP	Park/Neutral Position
PROM	Programmable Read Only Memory
PSP	Power Steering Pressure
PTO	Power Take-Off
PTOX	Periodic Trap Oxidizer System

R

RABS	Rear Anti-lock Brake System
RAM	Random Access Memory
ROM	Read Only Memory
RPM	Revolutions Per Minute
RWAL	Rear Wheel Anti-lock Brakes
RWD	Rear Wheel Drive

S

SBC	Single Bed Converter
SBEC	Single Board Engine Controller
SC	Supercharger
SCB	Supercharger Bypass
SFI	Sequential Multiport Fuel Injection
SIR	Supplemental Inflatable Restraint
SOHC	Single Overhead Camshaft
SPL	Smoke Puff Limiter
SPOUT	Spark Output
SRI	Service Reminder Indicator
SRS	Supplemental Restraint System
SRT	System Readiness Test
SSI	Solid State Ignition
ST	Scan Tool
STO	Self-Test Output

T

TAC	Thermostatic Air Clearner
TBI	Throttle Body Fuel Injection
TC	Turbocharger
TCC	Torque Converter Clutch
TCM	Transmission Control Module
TDC	Top Dead Center
TFI	Thick Film Ignition
TP	Throttle Position
TR Sensor	Transaxle/Transmission Range Sensor
TVV	Thermal Vacuum Valve
TWC	Three-way Catalytic Converter

V

VAF	Volume Air Flow, or Vane Air Flow
VAPS	Variable Assist Power Steering
VRV	Vacuum Regulator Valve
VSS	Vehicle Speed Sensor
VSV	Vacuum Switching Valve

W

WOT	Wide Open Throttle
WU-TWC	Warm Up Three-way Catalytic Converter

ENGLISH TO METRIC CONVERSION: TORQUE

To convert foot-pounds (ft. lbs.) to Newton-meters (Nm), multiply the number of ft. lbs. by 1.36
To convert Newton-meters (Nm) to foot-pounds (ft. lbs.), multiply the number of Nm by 0.7376

ft. lbs.	Nm	ft. lbs.	Nm	ft. lbs.	Nm	ft. lbs.	Nm
0.1	0.1	34	46.2	76	103.4	118	160.5
0.2	0.3	35	47.6	77	104.7	119	161.8
0.3	0.4	36	49.0	78	106.1	120	163.2
0.4	0.5	37	50.3	79	107.4	121	164.6
0.5	0.7	38	51.7	80	108.8	122	165.9
0.6	0.8	39	53.0	81	110.2	123	167.3
0.7	1.0	40	54.4	82	111.5	124	168.6
0.8	1.1	41	55.8	83	112.9	125	170.0
0.9	1.2	42	57.1	84	114.2	126	171.4
1	1.4	43	58.5	85	115.6	127	172.7
2	2.7	44	59.8	86	117.0	128	174.1
3	4.1	45	61.2	87	118.3	129	175.4
4	5.4	46	62.6	88	119.7	130	176.8
5	6.8	47	63.9	89	121.0	131	178.2
6	8.2	48	65.3	90	122.4	132	179.5
7	9.5	49	66.6	91	123.8	133	180.9
8	10.9	50	68.0	92	125.1	134	182.2
9	12.2	51	69.4	93	126.5	135	183.6
10	13.6	52	70.7	94	127.8	136	185.0
11	15.0	53	72.1	95	129.2	137	186.3
12	16.3	54	73.4	96	130.6	138	187.7
13	17.7	55	74.8	97	131.9	139	189.0
14	19.0	56	76.2	98	133.3	140	190.4
15	20.4	57	77.5	99	134.6	141	191.8
16	21.8	58	78.9	100	136.0	142	193.1
17	23.1	59	80.2	101	137.4	143	194.5
18	24.5	60	81.6	102	138.7	144	195.8
19	25.8	61	83.0	103	140.1	145	197.2
20	27.2	62	84.3	104	141.4	146	198.6
21	28.6	63	85.7	105	142.8	147	199.9
22	29.9	64	87.0	106	144.2	148	201.3
23	31.3	65	88.4	107	145.5	149	202.6
24	32.6	66	89.8	108	146.9	150	204.0
25	34.0	67	91.1	109	148.2	151	205.4
26	35.4	68	92.5	110	149.6	152	206.7
27	36.7	69	93.8	111	151.0	153	208.1
28	38.1	70	95.2	112	152.3	154	209.4
29	39.4	71	96.6	113	153.7	155	210.8
30	40.8	72	97.9	114	155.0	156	212.2
31	42.2	73	99.3	115	156.4	157	213.5
32	43.5	74	100.6	116	157.8	158	214.9
33	44.9	75	102.0	117	159.1	159	216.2

METRIC TO ENGLISH CONVERSION: TORQUE

To convert foot-pounds (ft. lbs.) to Newton-meters (Nm), multiply the number of ft. lbs. by 1.36
To convert Newton-meters (Nm) to foot-pounds (ft. lbs.), multiply the number of Nm by 0.7376

Nm	ft. lbs.	Nm	ft. lbs.	Nm	ft. lbs.	Nm	ft. lbs.	Nm	ft. lbs.
0.1	0.1	34	25.0	76	55.9	118	86.8	160	117.6
0.2	0.1	35	25.7	77	56.6	119	87.5	161	118.4
0.3	0.2	36	26.5	78	57.4	120	88.2	162	119.1
0.4	0.3	37	27.2	79	58.1	121	89.0	163	119.9
0.5	0.4	38	27.9	80	58.8	122	89.7	164	120.6
0.6	0.4	39	28.7	81	59.6	123	90.4	165	121.3
0.7	0.5	40	29.4	82	60.3	124	91.2	166	122.1
0.8	0.6	41	30.1	83	61.0	125	91.9	167	122.8
0.9	0.7	42	30.9	84	61.8	126	92.6	168	123.5
1	0.7	43	31.6	85	62.5	127	93.4	169	124.3
2	1.5	44	32.4	86	63.2	128	94.1	170	125.0
3	2.2	45	33.1	87	64.0	129	94.9	171	125.7
4	2.9	46	33.8	88	64.7	130	95.6	172	126.5
5	3.7	47	34.6	89	65.4	131	96.3	173	127.2
6	4.4	48	35.3	90	66.2	132	97.1	174	127.9
7	5.1	49	36.0	91	66.9	133	97.8	175	128.7
8	5.9	50	36.8	92	67.6	134	98.5	176	129.4
9	6.6	51	37.5	93	68.4	135	99.3	177	130.1
10	7.4	52	38.2	94	69.1	136	100.0	178	130.9
11	8.1	53	39.0	95	69.9	137	100.7	179	131.6
12	8.8	54	39.7	96	70.6	138	101.5	180	132.4
13	9.6	55	40.4	97	71.3	139	102.2	181	133.1
14	10.3	56	41.2	98	72.1	140	102.9	182	133.8
15	11.0	57	41.9	99	72.8	141	103.7	183	134.6
16	11.8	58	42.6	100	73.5	142	104.4	184	135.3
17	12.5	59	43.4	101	74.3	143	105.1	185	136.0
18	13.2	60	44.1	102	75.0	144	105.9	186	136.8
19	14.0	61	44.9	103	75.7	145	106.6	187	137.5
20	14.7	62	45.6	104	76.5	146	107.4	188	138.2
21	15.4	63	46.3	105	77.2	147	108.1	189	139.0
22	16.2	64	47.1	106	77.9	148	108.8	190	139.7
23	16.9	65	47.8	107	78.7	149	109.6	191	140.4
24	17.6	66	48.5	108	79.4	150	110.3	192	141.2
25	18.4	67	49.3	109	80.1	151	111.0	193	141.9
26	19.1	68	50.0	110	80.9	152	111.8	194	142.6
27	19.9	69	50.7	111	81.6	153	112.5	195	143.4
28	20.6	70	51.5	112	82.4	154	113.2	196	144.1
29	21.3	71	52.2	113	83.1	155	114.0	197	144.9
30	22.1	72	52.9	114	83.8	156	114.7	198	145.6
31	22.8	73	53.7	115	84.6	157	115.4	199	146.3
32	23.5	74	54.4	116	85.3	158	116.2	200	147.1
33	24.3	75	55.1	117	86.0	159	116.9	201	147.8

ENGLISH/METRIC CONVERSION: TEMPERATURE

To convert Fahrenheit (F°) to Celsius (C°), take F° temperature and subtract 32, multiply the result by 5 and divide the result by 9

To convert Celsius (C°) to Fahrenheit (F°), take C° temperature and multiply it by 9, divide the result by 5 and add 32

F°	C°	F°	C°	C°	F°	C°	F°
-40	-40.0	150	65.6	-38	-36.4	46	114.8
-35	-37.2	155	68.3	-36	-32.8	48	118.4
-30	-34.4	160	71.1	-34	-29.2	50	122
-25	-31.7	165	73.9	-32	-25.6	52	125.6
-20	-28.9	170	76.7	-30	-22	54	129.2
-15	-26.1	175	79.4	-28	-18.4	56	132.8
-10	-23.3	180	82.2	-26	-14.8	58	136.4
-5	-20.6	185	85.0	-24	-11.2	60	140
0	-17.8	190	87.8	-22	-7.6	62	143.6
1	-17.2	195	90.6	-20	-4	64	147.2
2	-16.7	200	93.3	-18	-0.4	66	150.8
3	-16.1	205	96.1	-16	3.2	68	154.4
4	-15.6	210	98.9	-14	6.8	70	158
5	-15.0	212	100.0	-12	10.4	72	161.6
10	-12.2	215	101.7	-10	14	74	165.2
15	-9.4	220	104.4	-8	17.6	76	168.8
20	-6.7	225	107.2	-6	21.2	78	172.4
25	-3.9	230	110.0	-4	24.8	80	176
30	-1.1	235	112.8	-2	28.4	82	179.6
35	1.7	240	115.6	0	32	84	183.2
40	4.4	245	118.3	2	35.6	86	186.8
45	7.2	250	121.1	4	39.2	88	190.4
50	10.0	255	123.9	6	42.8	90	194
55	12.8	260	126.7	8	46.4	92	197.6
60	15.6	265	129.4	10	50	94	201.2
65	18.3	270	132.2	12	53.6	96	204.8
70	21.1	275	135.0	14	57.2	98	208.4
75	23.9	280	137.8	16	60.8	100	212
80	26.7	285	140.6	18	64.4	102	215.6
85	29.4	290	143.3	20	68	104	219.2
90	32.2	295	146.1	22	71.6	106	222.8
95	35.0	300	148.9	24	75.2	108	226.4
100	37.8	305	151.7	26	78.8	110	230
105	40.6	310	154.4	28	82.4	112	233.6
110	43.3	315	157.2	30	86	114	237.2
115	46.1	320	160.0	32	89.6	116	240.8
120	48.9	325	162.8	34	93.2	118	244.4
125	51.7	330	165.6	36	96.8	120	248
130	54.4	335	168.3	38	100.4	122	251.6
135	57.2	340	171.1	40	104	124	255.2
140	60.0	345	173.9	42	107.6	126	258.8
145	62.8	350	176.7	44	111.2	128	262.4

LENGTH CONVERSION

To convert inches (in.) to millimeters (mm), multiply the number of inches by 25.4

To convert millimeters (mm) to inches (in.), multiply the number of millimeters by 0.04

Inches	Millimeters	Inches	Millimeters	Inches	Millimeters	Inches	Millimeters
0.0001	0.00254	0.005	0.1270	0.09	2.286	4	101.6
0.0002	0.00508	0.006	0.1524	0.1	2.54	5	127.0
0.0003	0.00762	0.007	0.1778	0.2	5.08	6	152.4
0.0004	0.01016	0.008	0.2032	0.3	7.62	7	177.8
0.0005	0.01270	0.009	0.2286	0.4	10.16	8	203.2
0.0006	0.01524	0.01	0.254	0.5	12.70	9	228.6
0.0007	0.01778	0.02	0.508	0.6	15.24	10	254.0
0.0008	0.02032	0.03	0.762	0.7	17.78	11	279.4
0.0009	0.02286	0.04	1.016	0.8	20.32	12	304.8
0.001	0.0254	0.05	1.270	0.9	22.86	13	330.2
0.002	0.0508	0.06	1.524	1	25.4	14	355.6
0.003	0.0762	0.07	1.778	2	50.8	15	381.0
0.004	0.1016	0.08	2.032	3	76.2	16	406.4

ENGLISH/METRIC CONVERSION: LENGTH

To convert inches (in.) to millimeters (mm), multiply the number of inches by 25.4

To convert millimeters (mm) to inches (in.), multiply the number of millimeters by 0.04

Inches Fraction	Inches Decimal	Millimeters Decimal	Inches Fraction	Inches Decimal	Millimeters Decimal	Inches Fraction	Inches Decimal	Millimeters Decimal
1/64	0.016	0.397	11/32	0.344	8.731	11/16	0.688	17.463
1/32	0.031	0.794	23/64	0.359	9.128	45/64	0.703	17.859
3/64	0.047	1.191	3/8	0.375	9.525	23/32	0.719	18.256
1/16	0.063	1.588	25/64	0.391	9.922	47/64	0.734	18.653
5/64	0.078	1.984	13/32	0.406	10.319	3/4	0.750	19.050
3/32	0.094	2.381	27/64	0.422	10.716	49/64	0.766	19.447
7/64	0.109	2.778	7/16	0.438	11.113	25/32	0.781	19.844
1/8	0.125	3.175	29/64	0.453	11.509	51/64	0.797	20.241
9/64	0.141	3.572	15/32	0.469	11.906	13/16	0.813	20.638
5/32	0.156	3.969	31/64	0.484	12.303	53/64	0.828	21.034
11/64	0.172	4.366	1/2	0.500	12.700	27/32	0.844	21.431
3/16	0.188	4.763	33/64	0.516	13.097	55/64	0.859	21.828
13/64	0.203	5.159	17/32	0.531	13.494	7/8	0.875	22.225
7/32	0.219	5.556	35/64	0.547	13.891	57/64	0.891	22.622
15/64	0.234	5.953	9/16	0.563	14.288	29/32	0.906	23.019
1/4	0.250	6.350	37/64	0.578	14.684	59/64	0.922	23.416
17/64	0.266	6.747	19/32	0.594	15.081	15/16	0.938	23.813
9/32	0.281	7.144	39/64	0.609	15.478	61/64	0.953	24.209
19/64	0.297	7.541	5/8	0.625	15.875	31/32	0.969	24.606
5/16	0.313	7.938	41/64	0.641	16.272	63/64	0.984	25.003
21/64	0.328	8.334	21/32	0.656	16.669	1/1	1.000	25.400
			43/64	0.672	17.066			